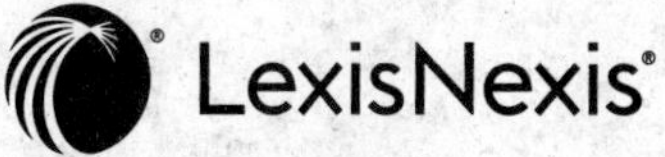
LexisNexis®

IMMIGRATION LAW HANDBOOK

2025 EDITION

Includes enactments of the 118th Congress through P.L. 119-5 and the Code of Federal Regulations with the exception of the amendments appearing at 90 FR 18927, May 5, 2025.

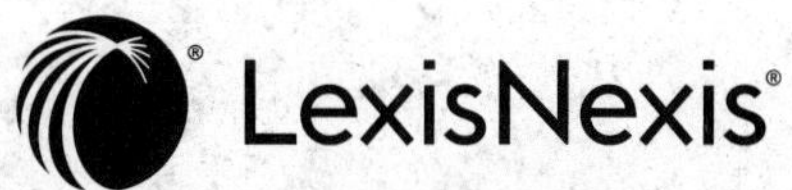

QUESTIONS ABOUT THIS PUBLICATION?

For CUSTOMER SERVICE ASSISTANCE concerning replacement pages, shipments, billing, reprint permission, or other matters,

please contact Customer Support at our self-service portal
available 24/7 at *supportcenter.lexisnexis.com/print*
or call us at 800-833-9844

For EDITORIAL content questions concerning this publication,

email: *llp.clp@lexisnexis.com*

For information on other LEXISNEXIS MATTHEW BENDER publications,

please call us at 877-394-8826
or visit our online bookstore at *www.lexisnexis.com/bookstore*

ISBN: 978-1-6633-9098-1

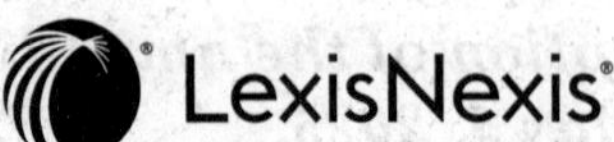

Matthew Bender & Company, Inc.
Editorial Offices
9443 Springboro Pike
Miamisburg, OH 45342
800-833-9844

www.lexisnexis.com

(Pub. 69130)

FOREWORD

The material presented herewith in convenient form is LexisNexis' ***Immigration Law Handbook***, as currently amended to include changes to the United States Code through P.L. 119-5 and the Code of Federal Regulations with the exception of the amendments appearing at 90 FR 18927, May 5, 2025. All changes to these rules and laws have been incorporated into the text. History notes are included, and editorial comments, references to USCS and CFR sources, and suggested corrections to the source material are indicated in brackets for the convenience of the user. Also included are Legislative Highlights that summarize changes to the topics of immigration and human trafficking in updated United States Code sections.

We are committed to providing attorneys and law enforcement professionals with the most comprehensive, current and useful publications possible. If you have comments and suggestions please write to Immigration Law Handbook Editor, LexisNexis, 9443 Springboro Pike, Miamisburg, OH 45342; call us toll-free at 1-800-833-9844; visit our website at http://www.lexisnexis.com; or E mail us at llp.clp@lexisnexis.com. By providing us with your informed comments, you will be assured of having available a working tool which increases in value each year.

Visit the LexisNexis internet home page at http://www.lexisnexis.com for an online bookstore, technical support, customer service, and other company information.

June 2025

TRANSITION TO DEPARTMENT OF HOMELAND SECURITY

On November 25, 2002, the President signed into law the Homeland Security Act of 2002, which created the new Department of Homeland Security (DHS). Pursuant to the provisions of the Act, DHS came into existence on January 24, 2003. As provided by the Act and by the Department of Homeland Security Reorganization Plan of November 25, 2002, the functions of the Immigration and Naturalization Service (INS), and all authorities with respect to those functions, transferred to DHS on March 1, 2003; the INS was abolished on that date. The transition and saving provisions of the Act provide that references relating to the INS in statutes, regulations, directives, or delegations of authority shall be deemed to refer to the appropriate official or component of the Department of Homeland Security.

TABLE OF CONTENTS

TABLE OF CONTENTS

Code of Federal Regulations

Federal Rules

2024 Legislative Changes to the IMMIGRATION LAW HANDBOOK

UNITED STATES CODE

U.S.C.S. TITLE 5

Section	*Change*	*Public Law*	*Eff. Date*
552a	Amended	118-104	10/02/2024

U.S.C.S. TITLE 18

Section	*Change*	*Public Law*	*Eff. Date*
201	Amended	118-78	07/30/2024

U.S.C.S. TITLE 21

Section	*Change*	*Public Law*	*Eff. Date*
802	Amended	118-189	12/23/2024

CODE OF FEDERAL REGULATIONS

C.F.R. TITLE 8

Section	*Change*	*FR Page*	*Date*
103.6	(g) and (h) revised	535, 556	01/06/2025
103.7	(d)(1) removed; (d)(7)(vii) and (16) added; (d)(13) revised	22607, 22628	04/02/2024
106.1	Correction: (f)(2) revised	20101	03/21/2024
106.2	Correction: (a)(3)(xi) and (44)(iv)(E) added; (a)(4)(ii), (c)(4), (5)(i), (ii), and (6) amended; (a)(46) introductory text and (c)(11) revised	20101	03/21/2024
106.3	Correction: (a)(3)(iii), (b)(3)(vi), and (8)(i) amended; (b)(1)(vii) added	20101	03/21/2024
106.3	(a)(3)(ii)(A) revised	5519, 5519	01/17/2025
204.2	Correction: (a)(1)(iii) amended; interim	4587, 4588	01/15/2025
208.13	(g) added; interim	81156	10/07/2024
208.13	(g) revised; (h) added	81156, 81284	10/07/2024
208.13	Regulation at 85 FR 84193 eff. date delayed to 12-31-25	105386	12/27/2024
208.16	Regulation at 85 FR 84193 eff. date delayed to 12-31-25	105386	12/27/2024
208.30	(e)(2) amended; (e)(5) revised; eff. 1-17-25	103370, 103413	12/18/2024
208.30	Regulation at 85 FR 84194 eff. date delayedto 12-31-25	105386	12/27/2024
208.31	(c) and (g) revised; eff. 1-17-25	103370	12/18/2024
208.35	(Subpart D) Added; interim	81156	10/07/2024
208.35	(a)(2)(i)(C) and section amended; (b)(2)(i) revised	81156, 81284	10/07/2024

C.F.R. TITLE 8 *(Continued)*

Section	*Change*	*FR Page*	*Date*
212.2	Correction: (f) amended; (i)(2) revised	65165, 65165	08/09/2024
212.16	Revised	34864, 34930	04/30/2024
212.19	(b)(1), (c)(1), (e), (h)(1), and (j) revised	6194, 6396	01/31/2024
212.19	(a)(5)(i), (ii), (b)(2)(ii)(B)(1), (2), (c)(2)(ii)(B)(1), and (3) revised	60298, 60301	07/25/2024
214.1-214.15	Designated as Subpart A; heading added	34864, 34931	04/30/2024
214.1	(c)(5) redesignated as (c)(7); new (c)(5) and (6) added; (c)(1), (4), and new (7) revised; eff. 1-17-25	103054, 103195	12/18/2024
214.2	Correction: (w)(5) amended	20101	03/21/2024
214.2	(m)(l)(i)(B) and (r) Table 2 amended; (f)(6)(iii)(B) and (m)(9)(vi) revised; (f)(9)(ii)(F)(2) removed	22903, 22912	04/03/2024
214.2	Redesignated	34864, 34931	04/30/2024
214.2	(h) Table 3 amended; (h)(6)(xv) and (32) added; eff. through 12-2-27	95626, 95681	12/02/2024
214.2	(f)(5)(vi)(A), (h)(2)(i)(E), (F), (4)(i)(B), (iii) heading, (A), (iv) introductory text, (8)(iii)(F)(2)(iv), (4), (9)(i), (11)(ii), (14), (19)(iii)(B)(4), (C), (iv), (l)(14)(i), (o)(11), and (p)(13) revised; (h)(2)(i)(B) removed; (h)(4)(ii) and (11)(iii)(A)(6) amended; (h)(4)(iii)(F), (iv)(C), (9)(ii)(D), (iii)(E), (11)(iii)(A)(7), and (33) added; eff. 1-17-25	103054, 103196	12/18/2024
214.2	(h)(2)(i)(I) redesignated as (h)(2)(i)(J); new (h)(2)(i)(I), (5)(viii)(D), (10)(iv), (11)(iv), (16)(iii), and (30) added; (h)(2)(i)(D), (ii), (iii), (5)(viii)(B), (C), (ix), (xi), (6)(i), (vii), (13)(i), (iv), (v), (16)(ii), and (20) revised; (h)(5)(i)(F), (iii)(B), and (xii) removed; eff. 1-17-25	103202, 103327	12/18/2024
214.14	Revised	34864, 34931	04/30/2024
214.200-214.216	(Subpart C) Added	34864, 34931	04/30/2024
214.204	Correction: (c)(2) amended	68081	08/23/2024
214.205	Correction: (a) and (f) amended	68081	08/23/2024
214.205	Correction: (a)(1) through (3) added	2921	01/14/2024
214.211	Correction: (e)(2)(i) amended	68081	08/23/2024
217.2	Amended	78783, 78785	09/26/2024
217.2	Amended	105391, 105392	12/27/2024
235.6	Regulation at 85 FR 84196 eff. date delayed to 12-31-25	105386	12/27/2024
235.7	Heading revised; (a)(1)(ii) through (iv) redesignated as (a)(1)(iii) through (v); new (a)(1)(ii) added	22607, 22628	04/02/2024
235.12	(a), (c), (d)(2), (3), (e)(1), (g), (h), (j) heading, (2) introductory text, (4), and (k) revised; (l) removed	22607, 22628	04/02/2024
235.14	Added	22607, 22629	04/02/2024
235.15	Added; interim	48710, 48770	06/07/2024
235.15	Amended	81156, 81285	10/07/2024
245.23	Revised	34864, 34941	04/30/2024
258.4	Added	23501, 23503	04/04/2024
264.1	(a) table and (b) table amended; interim	11793, 11800	03/12/2025
270.3	(b)(1)(ii)(A) through (D) revised	1, 9	01/02/2025
274a.2	(b)(1)(vii) amended; eff. 1-13-25	101208, 101267	12/13/2024

2024 Legislative Changes to the IMMIGRATION LAW HANDBOOK
(Continued)

C.F.R. TITLE 8 *(Continued)*

Section	*Change*	*FR Page*	*Date*
274a.8	(b) revised	1, 9	01/02/2025
274a.10	(b)(1)(ii)(A) through (C) and (2) introductory text revised	53849, 53859	06/28/2024
274a.10	(b)(1)(ii)(A) through (C) revised; (b)(2) introductory text amended	1, 9	01/02/2025
274a.12	(b)(35) added; eff. through 12-2-27	95626, 95683	12/02/2025
274a.12	(b)(21) revised; eff. 1-17-25	103202, 103334	12/18/2025
274a.13	(d)(5) heading revised; eff. through 10-15-25	24628, 24676	04/08/2024
274a.13	(d)(6) added; eff. through 9-30-25	24628, 24676	04/08/2024
274a.13	(d)(1) introductory text, (1)(i), and (3) revised; (d)(5) and (6) removed; eff. 1-13-25	101208, 101267	12/13/2025
280.53	(b)(1) through (15) revised	1, 10	01/02/2025
1001.1	(gg) and (hh) added	46742, 46787	05/29/2024
1003.0	(b)(2)(ii) revised	46742, 46787	05/29/2024
1003.1	(a)(1) and (4) amended	46742, 46787	05/29/2024
1003.1	(a)(2)(i)(E), (c), (d)(1) introductory text, (ii), (3)(iii), (iv), (6)(ii), (iii), (v), (7), (e) introductory text, (1) through (3), (4)(i) introductory text, (ii), (7), (8) introductory text, (i) through (iii), (v), and (f) revised; (d)(3)(v) and (k) removed; (l) and (m) added	15525, 15408	04/14/2025
1003.2	Nomenclature change; (a), (b)(1), (c)(3)(iii), (iv), (f), (g)(3), and (i) revised; (c)(2) amended; (c)(3)(v) through (vii) removed; (c)(4) added	46742, 46790	05/29/2024
1003.3	(c)(1) and (2) revised	46742, 46791	05/29/2024
1003.5	Revised	46742, 46791	05/29/2024
1003.7	Amended	46742, 46791	05/29/2024
1003.9	(b)(5) revised	46742, 46792	05/29/2024
1003.10	(b) amended	46742, 46792	05/29/2024
1003.18	Heading revised; (a) heading, (b) heading, (c), and (d) added	46742, 46792	05/29/2024
1003.23	Heading, (b)(1), and (4)(iii)(B) amended; (a), (b)(1)(iii) through (v), (2), (3), (4)(i), and (ii) revised; (b)(4)(v) and (vi) removed	46742, 46793	05/29/2024
1003.42	Nomenclature change; (a), (d), and (e) revised; (b), (c), and (f) through (i) amended; interim	105392, 105401	12/27/2024
1003.42	Regulation at 85 FR 84196 eff. date delayed to 12-31-25	105386	12/27/2024
1003.55	(Subpart D) Added	46742, 46794	05/29/2024
1208.13	(g) added; interim	48710, 48769	06/07/2024
1208.13	(g) revised; (h) added	81156, 81285	10/07/2024
1208.13	Regulation at 85 FR 84196 eff. date delayed to 12-31-25	105386	12/27/2024
1208.16	Regulation at 85 FR 84197 eff. date delayed to 12-31-25	105386	12/27/2024
1208.30	Regulation at 85 FR 84197 eff. date delayed to 12-31-25	105386	12/27/2024
1208.31	Nomenclature change; heading and (g) introductory text revised; (b) through (d) removed; interim	105392, 105402	12/27/2024
1208.33	(a)(3)(i)(C) amended	81156, 81285	10/07/2024

2024 Legislative Changes to the IMMIGRATION LAW HANDBOOK
(Continued)

C.F.R. TITLE 8 *(Continued)*

Section	*Change*	*FR Page*	*Date*
1208.33	Nomenclature change; (a)(2)(i) and (3)(i)(C) amended; (b)(1), (2)(i), and (ii) revised; interim	105392, 105402	12/27/2024
1208.35	(Subpart D) Added; interim	48710, 48771	06/07/2024
1208.35	(a)(2)(i)(C) and section amended; (b)(2)(iii) revised	81156, 81285	10/07/2024
1208.35	(a)(2)(i)(C) amended; interim	105392, 105403	12/27/2024
1235.6	Regulation at 85 FR 84198 eff. date delayed to 12-31-25	05386	12/27/2024
1239.2	(b) added; (f) removed	46742, 46794	05/29/2024
1240.26	Nomenclature change; (b)(3)(i) introductory text, (A), (c) (4), (ii), and (i) amended; (k)(1), (2) introductory text, (3) introductory text, (4), and (l) revised	46742, 46795	05/29/2024

C.F.R. TITLE 22

Section	*Change*	*FR Page*	*Date*
40.21	(a)(5) revised	67857, 67859	08/22/2024
40.22	(c) revised	67857, 67859	08/22/2024
42.11	Correction: Table 1 amended	60565, 60566	07/26/2024
42.11	Table 1 amended	99076, 99078	12/10/2024
42.34	Revised	99076, 99079	12/10/2024
50.40	(f) added	41308, 41310	05/13/2024
50.52	(Subpart D) Added	41308, 41310	05/13/2024
51.20-51.29	(Subpart B) Added	41311	05/13/2024
51.28	(a)(3)(i), (4)(i), and (ii) revised	60566, 60568	07/26/2024

FEDERAL RULES OF EVIDENCE

Rule	*Change*	*Eff. Date*
107	Added	12/01/2024
613	Amended	12/01/2024
801	Amended	12/01/2024
804	Amended	12/01/2024
1006	Amended	12/01/2024

IMMIGRATION LAW HIGHLIGHTS
OF THE SECOND SESSION OF THE 118th CONGRESS

RECORDS

5 U.S.C.S. § 552a

No agency shall disclose any record which is contained in a system of records by any means of communication to any person, or to another agency, except pursuant to a written request by, or with the prior written consent of, the individual to whom the record pertains, unless disclosure of the record would be, along with other agencies, to the Director of the Congressional Budget Office, or any authorized representative of the Director, in the course of performance of the duties of the Congressional Budget Office.

IMMIGRATION LAW
CLASSIFICATIONS AND CHARTS

GLOSSARY OF ABBREVIATIONS USED IN THESE CHARTS

AmCon	American Consulate	**INA**	Immigration and Nationality Act of 1952, as amended [8 U.S.C. 1101 et seq.]
AmEmb	American Embassy	**IPPCTP**	Irish Peace Process Cultural and Training Program
BCC	Border Crossing Card/Laser Visa	**IIRAIRA**	Illegal Immigration Reform And Immigrant Responsibility Act
C.F.R.	Code of Federal Regulations	**IV**	Immigrant Visa
COS	Change of Status	**LPR**	Lawful Permanent Resident
D/C	Duration of Course		NAFTA repealed
D/S	Duration of Status	**NIV**	Nonimmigrant Visa
DOD	Department of Defense	**NTE**	Not to Exceed
DOL	Department of Labor	**OJT**	On-the-Job Training
DOS	Department of State	**OLP**	Outlying Possessions
DSO	Designated School Official	**PP**	Passport
EOS	Extension of Stay	**POE**	Port-of-Entry
ETA-750	Labor Certification	**USC**	United States Citizen
EVP	Exchange Visitor Program	**U.S.C.**	United States Code
EVSL	Exchange Visitor Skills List	**USMCA**	United States-Mexico-Canada Agreement
IAFIS	Integrated Automatic Fingerprint Identification System	**VWP**	Visa Waiver Program
IMMACT 90	Immigration Act of 1990	WHTI	Western Hemisphere Travel Initiative

IMMIGRATION LAW
CLASSIFICATIONS AND CHARTS
NONIMMIGRANT CLASSIFICATIONS

Note: *No nonimmigrant visa shall be issued to any alien from a country that is a state sponsor of international terrorism unless the Secretary of State determines that such an alien does not pose a threat to the safety or national security of the US.*

Classification	***Sym***	***Max Adm***	***Remarks***
Ambassador, Public Minister, Career Diplomat, Consular Officer, Immediate Family (See 22 C.F.R. 41.21 for definition of "immediate family"). Career courier must be regularly and professionally employed as a courier and must be a national of country represented.	A-1	D/S	Inadmissible for INA § 212(a)(3)(A), (B), (C) only.* No foreign residence requirement. Passport valid only to date of admission.
Other Foreign Govt. Official or Employee coming to the U.S. or Immediate Family. Includes technical and support staff of A-1, and courier NOT regularly employed as a courier BUT who has official position with gov't to which he owes allegiance	A-2	D/S	Inadmissible for INA § 212(a)(3)(A) (B),(C) only.* May include alien military personnel on temporary assignment in U.S. and not traveling on NATO orders. Passport valid only to date of admission. No foreign residence required.

**Except those provisions relating to reasonable requirements of passports and visas as a means of identifica-tion and documentation necessary to establish these qualifications.*

Classification	Sym	Max Adm	Remarks
Attendant, Servant or Personal Employee of A-1 or A-2 or Immediate Family	A-3	3 years	Inadmissible on all grounds. Normal PP & NIV requirements apply. No foreign residence required.
Temporary Visitor for BUSINESS: Business as defined in INA § 101(a)(15)(B) refers to conventions, conferences, consultations and other legitimate activities of a commercial or professional nature. It does not include labor for hire or local employment. Reference 8 C.F.R. 214.2(b) and 9 FAM 41.31	B-1	1 year	Must show that they have foreign residence they do not intend to abandon. Acting courier (need not be national or employed by gov't represented). Admitted for time necessary to complete business. Includes "deadheading crewmen." Includes honorarium.* Admit minimum 6 months to avoid needless extensions UNLESS • Passport validity • Supervisor concurrence

** May accept honorarium payment and incidental expenses for normal activity lasting no more than 9 days. May not accept payment on expenses from more than 5 institutions in previous 6 months. INA § 212(g), 8 USC § 1182(g)*

Classification	Sym	Max Adm	Remarks
Temporary Visitor for PLEASURE: The term pleasure as used in INA 101(a)(15)(B), refers to legitimate activities of a recreational character, including tourism, amusement, visits with friends or relatives, rest, medical treatment and activities of a fraternal, social or service nature.	B-2	1 year	Proof of an unrelinquished foreign residence. Prospective students. Minimum period of admission is 6 months UNLESS • Passport validity • Supervisor concurrence
Alien in Transit (direct and continuous travel through the United States).	C-1	29 days	No EOS or change of status. Normal PP and NIV requirements. Sufficient funds, ability to effect transit and enter foreign country. Includes "deadheading crew."
Alien in Transit to U.N. Headquarters District under Sec. 11. (3), (4) or (5) of the HQ Agreement.	C-2	D/S at United Nations	Inadmissible only under INA § 212(a)(3)(A), (B), (C) and INA § 212(a)(7)(B). Travel limited to a 25-mile radius of Columbus Circle, New York, NY. Passport only needs to be valid on day of application for admission.

Classification	*Sym*	*Max Adm*	*Remarks*
Foreign Government Official, Immediate Family, Attendant, Servant or Personal Employee of official, In Transit through the U.S.	C-3	29 days	Inadmissible only under INA § 212(a)(3)(A), (B), (C) and § 212(a)(7)(B). No EOS. Passport valid for at least 30 days from date of admission.
Commonwealth of the Northern Mariana Islands Transitional Worker	CW-1	NTE 5 years	No EOS/COS/AOS. Normal PP and NIV requirements. Must be working for CNMI employer.
Dependant of CW-1 worker	CW-2	NTE 5 years	No EOS/COS/AOS. Normal PP and NIV requirements. Must be working for CNMI employer.
The term "crewman" as defined in § 101(a)(15)(D)(i) means a person serving in any capacity on board a vessel or aircraft. Crewmen arriving on vessels must depart as crewmembers on the same vessel as arrival. Crewmen arriving on an aircraft must depart as crewmembers on the same transportation line. Longshore work CANNOT be performed EXCEPT when it involves: 1) Safety; 2) Prevailing practices; 3) Reciprocity with other countries. ** A crewman's landing permit*	D-1	29 days	Issue I-95 (unless they have I-184*). Not to be admitted when strike or lockout is in effect, EXCEPT where alien: 1) Was employed w/employer at least 1 year; 2) Served at least one in each of the 3 previous 12 months; 3) Shall continue to serve. When a strike or lockout rule is set aside, exception to rule must be stated on manifest; same must be done when alien will engage in longshore work. No EOS. No Change of Status (COS), No Extension of Status (EOS), No Adjustment of Status. (8 C.F.R. 214.1(c)(3) and 8 C.F.R. 248.2(a)(2)).
Crewmen departing on vessel other than one of arrival or other means of transportation. Crewmen departing on different airline than one of arrival or other means of transportation. No extension of stay or change of status for Ds. A vessel master may request to have their vessel and assigned crewmembers remain beyond 29 days on a form I-253. Each crewmember will then be granted voluntary departure in lieu of formal removal and have their Form I-95 endorsed for up to 120 days (See § 240B(a)(2) INA)	D-2	29 days	Used when crewmen are changing employer, signing off, or being discharged. Issued I-95. Requires an approved Form I-408. Aliens arriving as crewmen of vessels may present a seaman's book in lieu of a passport.

Interpretive notes regarding "D" classification may be found at 9 FAM 41.41.

To qualify for "D" status, crewmen arriving aboard vessels from a foreign place must depart the U.S. within 29 days of initial arrival. In order to effect a departure in terms of the INA and State Department regulations, a vessel must sail from the U.S. and call upon a foreign port or place; travel to international waters or cruises to nowhere do not satisfy the foreign departure requirement. This provision does not apply to fishing vessels in Guam that sail to international waters. Pursuant to P.L. 99-505, such a vessel is considered to have departed the United States.

Classification	*Sym*	*Max Adm*	*Remarks*
Treaty Trader, Spouse or Child(ren). Taiwan government employees issued E-1 visas endorsed "CCNAA" (Coordination Council for Northern American Affairs) and Visas endorsed "TECRO" as of 1995 are to be admitted for duration of status (D/S).** Taiwan PP valid only to date of admission. All E-1s require NIV. **[9 FAM 41.51, Exhibit 1.]* ***[9 FAM 41.22, PN.1, PN1.1, PN2]*	E-1	2 years	**Must be a national of a treaty* country.** Involved in trade and services and/or trade and technology. Can't be manual, unskilled labor. **Usually executive or manager**. EOS in increments of not more than 2 years. Spouse and child status depends on principal alien (nationality is not material.) Spouse can work; needs employment authorized" endorsement or other work permit. Effective 1/1/04 citizens of Chile and Singapore eligible. Normal PP requirements apply.
Treaty Investor, Spouse or Child(ren). To develop and direct the activities of a bona fide enterprise in which he has invested substantial amount of capital. All E-2s require NIV. Requires PP unless exempt. **[9 FAM 41.51, Exhibit 1.]*	E-2	2 years	**Must be a national of a treaty* country.** Can't use the investment to immigrate, or as a marginal enterprise solely to earn a living. EOS in increments of not more than 2 years. Spouse can work; needs "employment authorized" endorsement or other work permit. Effective 1/1/04 citizens of Chile & Singapore eligible.
Commonwealth of the Northern Mariana Islands Investor, Spouse or Child(ren)	E-2C	NTE 5 years	Must have been long-term investor in the CNMI prior to transition and maintained investment after transition U.S. Immigration Law. (See 74 F.R. 61517)
Unless otherwise provided for in this chapter, an alien shall not be admitted in E classification for a period of time extending more than 6 months beyond the expiration date of the alien's passport.			8 CFR 214.2(19)(iii) *Applies to E-1, E-2, and E-3.*
Nationals of Australia, who are professionals coming to the U.S. to perform services in a "specialty occupation."	E-3	2 years	All E-3's require a NIV. Normal PP requirements apply. Classification includes spouse and child (nationality is not material).
Spouse or child of E-3	E-3D		Spouse may apply for work authorization.
Returning National of Australia who are professionals coming to the U.S. to perform services in a specialty occupation to uninterrupted employ-ment.	E-3R		
Academic Student NOTE: Prohibited from attending public elementary school (K-8), publicly funded adult education program, or public secondary school unless attending less than 12 months and reimbursing school full, unsubsidized per capita cost. Attendance in one of these areas renders or forms the basis to render an alien inadmissible in accordance with § 212(a)(6)(G) INA.	F-1	D/S	1. Must be in possession of a SEVIS-generated Form I-20AB. 2. Must maintain a "full course of study." [8 C.F.R. 214.2(f)(6)]. 3. Proof of unrelinquished residence is required. 4. A student making initial entry may be admitted 30 days prior to start date listed on SEVIS I-20AB. There is no restriction on a returning student. 5. ALL initial entry foreign students issued a SEVIS-generated form on or after 9/1/04 are required to pay a SEVIS fee. 6. Requires passport and visa unless exempt. Passport must be valid for at least 6 months on date of entry.

Classification	*Sym*	*Max Adm*	*Remarks*
			Payment of SEVIS fee is demonstrated on Form I797 or internet receipt
Spouse or child of F-1 student. **Dependents of F-1 Border Commuter Students are NOT eligible for F-2 status.*	F-2*	D/S	1. Must be in possession of a separate SEVIS Form I-20AB identified by "Dependent Copy." 2. Status derived from F-1 prin-cipal alien. 3. May engage in study that is avocational or recreational. 4. F-2 spouse may not engage in full-time study. 5. F-2 child may only engage in full-time study in elementary or secondary school (K-12). 6. Proof of an unrelinquished residence is re-quired. 7. Employment is not authorized. 8. Requires passport and visa, unless exempt. Normal PP/ NIV requirements apply.
Border Commuter Students (Citizen of Canada or Mexico) There is no derivative classification for the spouse and/or dependents of a F-3 Border Commuter Student.	F-3*	Admitted for a fixed admission period for each semester, quarter, or term [8 C.F.R. 214.2(f) (18)(iii)]	1. Must be in possession of a new SEVIS-generated Form I-20AB for each new semester or term. 2. Must be enrolled in a full course of study, albe-it on a part-timo basis [8 C.F.R. 214.2(f)(18)(ii)]. 3. Enrolled in an approved school within 75 miles of a U.S. land border. 4. Must maintain actual residence in country of nationality and seek admission to the U.S. at a land border port of entry. 5. Employment not authorized except for curric-ular practical training or post-completion prac-tical training. 6. Requires passport and visa unless exempt. Normal passport and visa requirements apply.
(Citizen of Canada or Mexico)	G-1	D/S	Inadmissible for INA § 212(a)(3)(A), (B), (C) only.* Foreign government recognized de jure by U.S. and member of international organization [8 C.F.R. 316.20(c)]. Passport valid only to date of application for admission. No proof of foreign residence. **Except those provisions relating to reasonable requirements of passports and visas as a means of identification and documentation necessary to establish these qualifications.*
	G-2	D/S	Same as above.
There is no derivative classification for the spouse and/or dependents of a F-3 Border Commuter Student.	G-3	D/S	Same as above.
	G-4	D/S	Same as above. Alien on the payroll of a designated internation-al organization.

* INA § 101(a)(15)(F)(iii) distinguishes this class from a full-time academic student

Classification	*Sym*	*Max Adm*	*Remarks*
	F-3*	Admitted for a fixed admission period for each semester, quarter, or term [8 C.F.R. 214.2(f)(18)(iii)]	*1. Must be in possession of a new SEVIS-generated Form I-20AB for each new semester or term.*
2. Must be enrolled in a full course of study, albeit on a part-time basis. [8 C.F.R. 214.2(f)(18)(ii)].	H-1B	3 years	Approved I-129 petition required for all H-1Bs. Labor condition application (LCA) required for all except DOD workers. After FY 2003, cap 65,000 (excluding DOD); DOD limited to 100 per year. No foreign residence requirement. Validity of petition plus 10 days before and after validity period.
	H-1B	DOD 5 years	
	H-1B	3 years	Maximum period of admission is 3 years plus 1 year extension not to exceed 7 years or 10 years for DOD workers.
3. Enrolled in an approved school within 75 miles of a U.S. land border.	H-1B1	1 year	Must be a citizen of Chile or Singa-pore. No petition required. Numerical limits apply. Normal PP/NIV require-ments apply. No limits on Extensions
4. Must maintain actual residence in country of nationality and seek admission to the U.S. at a land border port of entry.	H-lC	3 years	Approved I-129 required filed with Vermont Service Center regardless of place of employment. LCA required. Proof of unrelinquished residence not required.
5. Employment not authorized except for curricular practical training or post-completion practical training.	H-2A	1 year	Foreign residence requirement. Validity of petition plus one week before and not to exceed 30 days after the validity of the petition. Approved I-129 and Labor Certification required. No annual numerical limits, Maximum unin-terrupted period of 3 years (8 C.F.R. 214.2(viii)(B)).
6. Requires passport and visa unless exempt. Normal passport and visa requirements apply.	H-2B	1 year	Requires approved I-129, Labor Certification. Annual numerical limits of 66,000*. Foreign residence requirement. Validity of petition plus 10 days before and after validity period.

H-2B Special Situation allows the filing of a Form I-129 Petition without a Labor Certification at a NY, ME or VT port of entry only for musicians working in the U.S. for no more than 30 days within 50 miles of the Canadian Border.

**Guam and Commonwealth of the Northern Mariana Islands (CNMI) are statutorily exempt numerical limita-tions from November 28, 2009, until December 31, 2014. See PL 110-229 for more information*

Returning H-2B Workers Must be returning H-2B to qualify for this classification	H-2R	1 year	Applicant must have an approved I-129 Petition containing a certification from the employer that the applicant is a returning worker. Will not count against current FY annual limit.

Classification	*Sym*	*Max Adm*	*Remarks*
Nationals of the following countries are eligible to participate in the H-2A and H-2B nonimmigrant worker programs: Argentina, Australia, Austria, Barbados, Belize, Brazil, Bulgaria, Canada, Chile, Costa Rica, Croatia, Dominican Republic, Ecuador, El Salvador, Estonia, Ethiopia, Fiji, Grenada, Guatemala, Haiti, Honduras, Hungary, Iceland, Ireland, Israel, Italy, Jamaica, Japan, Kiribati, Latvia, Lithuania, Macedonia, Mexico, Moldova, Montenegro, Nauru, The Netherlands, Nicaragua, New Zealand, Norway, Panama, Papua, New Guinea, Peru The Philippines, Poland, Romania, Samoa, Serbia, Slovakia, Slovenia, Solomon Islands, South Africa, South Korea, Spain, Switzerland, Thai-land, Tonga, Turkey, Tuvalu, Ukraine, United Kingdom, Uruguay, Vanuatu.			
Trainee receiving training in any field of endeavor such as: Agriculture, Commerce, Communication, Finance, Government, Transportation and the Professions. Training can not be graduate medical or educational training	H-3	Up to 2 years	Requires approved I-129. Proposed training not available in alien's country. Cannot displace U.S. workers. Training useful in pursuing career outside U.S. No labor certification, no numerical limits. Validity of petition plus 10 days before and after validity period.
Special Education participants must be coming to participate in a program which provides for practical training & experience in the education of children w/ physical, mental or emo-tional disabilities.	H-3	Up to 18 months	Not to exceed 50 per fiscal year. No labor certification.
Spouse or Child of Alien classified H-1B, H-1B1, H-1C, H2A/B, or H-3	H-4	Same as Principal	Must accompany or follow to join principal alien. Status depends on principal.
Foreign Media Representative Classification also includes spouse and child. Status depends on principal alien. Principal "I" status is reciprocity-based. Employees of independent production companies also qualify. *[9 FAM 41.52 N2.2]*	I	D/S	Camera crews producing films for commercial entertainment or advertising must qualify as Os or Ps. Principal cannot change employment w/o CIS approval. Dependents may attend school w/o change of status but may not work. No proof of unrelinquished foreign residence. Normal PP and NIV requirements, unless exempt.
Exchange Visitor Educational, cultural, and scientific exchanges. Exchange visitors from the People's Republic of China and former Soviet bloc countries may have their J-1 visas noted "CHINEX" or "SILEX." This notation must be placed in block 26 on reverse of Form I-94. An exchange alien ***may*** (exceptions apply) be subject to the two year home-country physical presence requirement [INA § 212(e)]. The list of governmentally financed programs and the "Skills List" needed to make this determination are contained in Appendix 15-1 IFM. Exchange Visitors Skills List *[9 FAM 41.62 Exhibit II]* An initial exchange visitor may be admitted for a period up to 30 days before the report date or start of approved program	J-1	D/S	All Js must be in possession of an original SEVIS-generated Form DS-2019 endorsed by the program sponsor in BLUE ink. All initial entry foreign students issued a SEVIS-generated form on or after 9/1/04 are required to pay a SEVIS fee. New requirements go into effect on July 19, 2007. The trainee program in both the speciality and non-speciality categories have been replaced with a new intern category (22 CFR 62.22). Any Form DS-2019 issued on or after July 19, 2007 must include completing new form DS-7002 to potential trainees or interns. Exchange participants making an initial entry may be admitted up to 30 days prior to the report date or start date of the approved program listed on SEVIS-generated Form DS-2019. There are no restrictions on how early a returning exchange participant may enter the U.S. Requires proof of unrelinquished foreign residence. Normal PP and NIV requirements, unless exempt.

Classification	Sym	Max Adm	Remarks
Spouse or Child of J-1 Exchange Visitor	J-2	D/S	Spouse and minor children must indi-vidually present an original SEVIS-generated DS-2019. May apply to CIS for employment. Employment will not be authorized if needed to support the J-1 principal alien and must be to support the fam-ily's customary recreational, cultural activities, and related travel (See 8 C.F.R. 214.2(j)(1)(v)). Requires proof of unrelinquished foreign residence. Normal PP and NIV requirements, unless exempt. May study in the U.S. without being required to apply for a student (F-1) visa or change to F-1 status..
Fiancé or fiancée of USC (United States Citizen) All Ks require NIV. Require PP unless exempt.	K-1	90 days	Must be eligible for IV w/ petition filed on I-129F, valid 4 months; pass medical exam, and marry USC within 90 days of entry. Employment authorized. No EOS. May adjust to LPR under INA § 245.
Child of K-1 Fiancé(e) of USC All Ks require NIV. Require PP unless exempt.	K-2	90 days	Must meet definition of "Child" and must be listed on I-129F. No EOS. Admissible up to 1 year after entry of K-1.
Spouse of USC* Require PP unless exempt. All Ks require NIV. There is no requirement to cancel other NIVs in alien's passport (See 22 C.F.R. 41.122(h))	K-3	2 years	Valid marriage w/ USC who filed I-130 that is pending. Employment may be authorized. (National Field Processing Center, Lee's Summit, Missouri adjudicates all I-129Fs for K-3 visas.) No change of status available
** Defer if initial 2 year period of admission is expired and only admit up to expiration.*			
Child of K-3 All Ks require NIV. Require PP unless exempt.	K-4	Shorter of 2 years or until 21st birthday	Must be unmarried child (under 21) of K-3, accompanying or following to join K-3; does not require separate I-129F or I-130.
Intracompany Transferee (Executive, Managerial) **or** Bringing specialized knowledge about some aspect of the company's operation **One year if coming to open a new office.*	L-1A L-1B	3 years* 3 years*	Must have worked for the same, subsidiary, or affiliate company for at least 1 continuous year ("L-1 Reform Act of 2004" will require new L-1 blanket petition applicants to meet 1 year requirement) within the preceding 3 years in managerial capacity or involving specialized knowledge. Beneficiary of approved I-129. No foreign residence required. No numerical limits. Canadian citizens may apply at a class "A" port on Canadian/U.S. Border or preflight inspection in Canada under NAFTA.

Classification	Sym	Max Adm	Remarks
Spouse or child of Transferee L-1 Intracompany	L-2	Same as principal	Must accompany or follow to join prin-cipal alien. Status depends on principal. Spouse needs "employment author-ized" endorsement or other work permit; may attend school without changing status. Spouse needs a valid EAD prior to working in the U.S. (8 C.F.R. 214.2(l)(7)(ii)). Minor children may not be employed.
Vocational or Other Nonacademic Student Students making initial entry may be admitted up to 30 days before the report or start up date listed on SEVIS Form I-20MN. There are no restrictions on returning students.	M-1	D/C + 30 days NTE 1 year	Must be in possession of a SEVIS-generated Form I-20MN. Foreign students issued a SEVIS-generated Form on or after 9/1/04 are required to pay a SEVIS fee. May only work during practical training. Requires proof of foreign residence. Requires PP and NIV unless exempt.
Border Commuter Student (Citizen of Canada or Mexico) All initial entry foreign students issued a SEVIS-generated form after 9/1/04 are required to pay a SEVIS fee.	M-1	D/C NTE 1 year Additional 30 day period of stay does not apply. [8 C.F.R. 214.2(m)(19)(iii)]	Must be in possession of a new SEVIS-generated Form I-20MN for each new semester or term. Enrolled in a full course of study, albeit on a part-time basis in an approved school within 75 miles of a U.S. land border. Must maintain actual residence in student's country of nationality. Requires PP and NIV unless exempt.
Spouse or child of M-1 Student **Dependents of M-1 Border Commuter Students are NOT eligible for M-2 status.*	M-2*	D/C + 30 days NTE 1 year	Must be in possession of a separate SEVIS Form I-20MN for each dependent issued in own name as identified by "Dependent Copy" over the bar code. Status derived from principal M-1 alien. M-2 spouse may not engage in full-time study. M-2 child may study full-time at an elementary or secondary school (K-12). M-2 spouse and child may engage in study that is avocational or recreational. Employment not authorized. Proof of foreign residence is required. Requires PP and NIV unless exempt.
NATO Nonimmigrants Principal Permanent Representatives of Member State to NATO, Official Staff, and Immediate Family	NATO-1	D/S	Normally exempt inspection. [8 C.F.R. 235.1(c)]*
Other Representatives of Member State to NATO and Immediate Family. NATO Military and Dependents.	NATO-2	D/S	Normally exempt inspection. [8 C.F.R. 235.1(c)]*
Official Clerical Staff of NATO Representative and Member of Immediate Family	NATO-3	D/S	Normally exempt inspection. [8 C.F.R. 235.1(c)]*
Official of NATO (other than NATO-1) or Immediate Family	NATO-4	D/S	Normally exempt inspection. [8 C.F.R. 235.1(c)]*

Classification	*Sym*	*Max Adm*	*Remarks*
Expert, other than NATO-4, employed in Missions and their Dependents	NATO-5	D/S	Normally exempt inspection. [8 C.F.R. 235.1(c)]*
Civilian employees of NATO Military and their Dependents	NATO-6	D/S	Needs PP and NIV. PP needs to be valid at entry only.
Attendant, Servant, Personal Employer of NATO-1 through NATO-6 or Immediate Family	NATO-7	3 years	Needs PP & NIV. Name of Employer in Data Block 26 on reverse of Form I-94.

**8 C.F.R. 235.1(c) also provides that any alien member of a force of a NATO country may, upon request, be inspected and his or her entry as an alien be recorded. NATO military stationed in the U.S. for a significant period of time (over six months) have a Form I-94, for "quality of life" reasons, such as to secure a social security number or a state-issued driver's license. To ensure that these persons routinely receive a Form I-94 at the time of inspection, the Department of State has recommended that NATO military personnel entering the U.S. for a significant period of time be issued a visa at a U.S. Embassy or Consulate.*

NATO Countries

Albania	Denmark	Iceland	North Macedonia	Slovenia
Belgium	Estonia	Italy	Norway	Spain
Bulgaria	France	Latvia	Poland	Turkey
Canada	Germany	Lithuania	Portugal	United Kingdom of Great Britain & No. Ireland
Croatia	Greece	Luxembourg	Romania	United States
Czech Rep	Hungary	Netherlands	Slovakia	*Updated March 2022*

Parent of Alien classed SK3	N-8	3 years or to 21st birthday of child, which ever is less.	Special Immigrant under INA § 101(a)(27)(I)(i) or (L). Only if while alien is a child. EOS, 3 year increments. Work authorized.
Child of N8 or of SK1, SK2, or SK4	N-9	If child of N-8, admit to same date as N-8. If child of SK, admit to lesser of 3 years or 21st birth-day.	A special immigrant under this section is either an unmarried son or daughter of a G-1 with 7 years of physical pres-ence or a NATO-6 non-immigrant.
Alien of Extraordinary Ability in the Sciences, Education, Business, or Athletics; or have extraordinary ability in the Arts or extraordinary achievements in the motion picture or television industry. Extraordinary—sustained national or international acclaim or a record of such achievement in television or film and coming to work in the area of that achievement.	O-1	3 years	Normal PP/NIV requirements. Must be approved to work a specific event or performance. Extension up to 1 year to complete or continue same event. Consultation required for O-1 & O-2. Validity of petition plus 10 days be-fore and after validity period. Ap-proved I-129 petition. No foreign residence requirement. Must use a U.S. Agency or Agent subject to service of process IAW § 274A INA

Classification	*Sym*	*Max Adm*	*Remarks*
Accompanying alien who is coming solely to assist in the artistic or athletic performance by an O-1 (Must be an integral part of the actual performance or events, possess critical skills and experience with the O-1 and have foreign residence and no plans to abandon it.)	O-2	Same as O-1	Normal PP/NIV requirements. Must possess critical skills and experience specific to principal's needs. Must have a working relationship with O-1 for at least 1 year. O-2 **may precede O-1 principal**. (This is the only NI Classification that can precede the principal). Validity of petition plus 10 days before and after petition period.
Spouse or Child of O-1 or O-2	O-3	Same as O-1 and O-2	Status depends on principal. Foreign residence requirement. May not work, but may attend school without changing status. Validity of petition plus 10 days before and after petition period.
Internationally Recognized Athlete or Member of Internationally Recognized Entertainment Group or Essential support personnel. All Ps require consultation with labor organization	P-1	5 years individual athlete 1 year team or group	Athletes may come as an individual or as part of a group or team. Entertainers MUST come as part of a group. 75% of group must have been together 1 year or more. EOS in increments of up to 1 year. Must have foreign residence does not intend to abandon. Validity of petition plus 10 days before and after validity period.
Artist or Entertainer in Reciprocal Exchange Program	P-2	1 year	Consultation required. EOS in increments of up to 1 year. Relates to both individuals and groups. Includes "Essential support personnel." Validity of petition plus 10 days before and after validity period.
Artist or Entertainer coming to perform, teach, or coach in a Culturally Unique Program. Relates to individuals and members of a group. Culturally Unique—a style of artistic expression, methodology, or medium which is unique to a particular country, nation, class, ethnicity, religion, tribe, or other group of persons	P-3	1 year	EOS in increments of up to 1 year. Consultation required. Includes "essential support personnel." Validity of petition plus 10 days before and after validity period.
Spouses or Child(ren) of P-1, P-2, P-3 Athlete, Artist or Entertainer	P-4	Same as Principal	Status depends on principal. May NOT work but may attend school without changing status.
International Cultural Exchange Program Participant	Q-1	15 months	The Exchange Program MUST: (1) Share culture of alien's country w/ American public. (2) Take place where public is exposed to culture as part of a structured program. (3) Cultural visitor's employment may not be independent of exchange program. No provision for spouse or children. Must remain outside U.S. for 1 yr after expiration of status. Max. initial period, 15 months.

Classification	*Sym*	*Max Adm*	*Remarks*
Irish Peace Process Cultural and Training Program (IPPCTP) Principal	Q-2	24 months*	Alien coming to U.S. to gain or upgrade skills through training and temporary employment opportunities and to experience living in a diverse and peaceful environment. Participants and dependents that remain outside the U.S. in excess of 3 consecutive months will be required to reapply to the program and be in possession of a new Q-2 or Q-3 NIV and a Certification Letter issued by the DOS Program Manager. Must remain outside U.S. 2 years after expiration of status.
Spouse and Minor Children of Q-2 only. **Effective 10/01/2008 this program is repealed.**	Q-3		

**In December 2004, Congress amended and extended the program (P.L. 108-449). Some major changes were introduced, including reducing the Q-2 period of admission from 36 to 24 months.*

Classification	*Sym*	*Max Adm*	*Remarks*
Religious Worker Alien who for at least the 2 years immediately preceding the time of application for admission has been a member of a religious denomination having a bona fide non-profit religious organization in the United States. An "R" who has spent 5 years in U.S. must exit U.S. and stay out for 1 year before eligible for readmission.	R-1	Up to 30* months	Must be coming solely to carry on vocation of minister; or to work for the religious organization at its request in a professional capacity or a religious vocation or occupation. Petition required for . . . entry and extensions (I-129). EOS 30 months with a maximum of 5 years with extensions No petition required for initial entry but one is required for extensions (I-129). EOS: 2 years with max of 5 years in U.S. Proof of unrelinquished foreign residence not required. Must remain outside U.S. for 1 year after expiration of status. Max initial period of admission 30 months

** Does not apply to commuter R-1s who demonstrate they do not reside in the US or seasonal or intermittent or was aggregate of less than 6 months. Clear and convincing evidence must be provided with petition. FR Vol. 73 No. 229 November 26, 2008*

Classification	*Sym*	*Max Adm*	*Remarks*
Spouse or child of R-1 Religious Worker	R-2	Up to 30 months	Status depends on principal. May NOT work, but may attend school without changing status. Proof of unrelinquished foreign residence not required.
Alien Witness or Informant, supplying critical, reliable information concerning a criminal organization or enterprise, whose presence in the U.S. is required for the successful investigation or prosecution of the criminal organization. All grounds of inadmissibility may be waived EXCEPT INA § 212(a)(3)(E). (OSI may waive this provision.) Limit of 200 visas.	S-5	3 years	I-854 must be submitted in his or her behalf. Must report his or her whereabouts/activities to the Attorney General on a quarterly basis. Must not be convicted of any criminal offense punishable by more than one year in prison and must waive their right to contest deportation proceedings, except for applying for withholding of deportation. Change of status prohibited under INA § 248. No EOS.
Alien Witness or Informant, supplying critical, reliable information about terrorist organization, enterprise, or operation, who will be placed in danger as a result of supplying that information; and is eligible to receive a reward under separate U.S. State Department legislation.	S-6	3 years	Requires I-854. Other remarks same as S-5. No EOS.

Classification	*Sym*	*Max Adm*	*Remarks*
Qualified Family Members of S-5 or S-6 Witness or Informant. This includes the spouse, married & unmarried sons & daughters, & parents.	S-7	3 years	Same as S-5, S-6. 101(A)(15)(S) qualified family members may accompany or follow to join.
NAFTA Professional Canadian/Mexican citizen seeking entry to engage in business activities at a professional level. [8 C.F.R. 214.6(c); Appendix 1603.D.1 to Annex 1603 of the NAFTA.] Temporary entry, as defined in Chapter 16 of the NAFTA, Article 1608, is "entry into the territory of a party by a business person of another party without the intent to establish permanent residence". The doctrine of dual intent does not apply to TNs	TN	3 years* (eff. 10/16/08)	Canadian citizens can present documentation at any Class "A" POE, a U.S. airport handling international flights or PFI Airport. Mexican citizens require PP and NIV. Effective 1/1/04 Mexicans do not require an approved I-129 or LCA. Numerical limits do not apply. E/S and COS for both filed with NSC.
Spouse or child of TN NAFTA Professional	TD	3 years* (eff. 10/16/08)	Documentation as required. Status depends on principal.
**The period of admission depends on the documentation submitted in the form of an employment offer and the anticipated length of employment.*			
Victim of Severe Form of Trafficking in Persons (See 8 C.F.R. 214.11) TVP Act of 2000 [22 U.S.C. 7102]	T-1*	3 years	• Is physically present in U.S. territories and possessions or at a POE. • Has complied with reasonable request in investigation and prosecution OR is < 18 years old and would suffer hardship and severe harm if removed from U.S.
Spouse of T-1 Victim	T-2		All requests for T-1 status submitted to VSC on a Form I-914 petition. USCIS may waive any fees.
Child of T-1 Victim	T-3		Requires an alien's physical presence in the U.S. as a condition of eligibility. May request a closure or stop of removal proceeding if deportable or removable
Parent of T-1 Victim, if T-1 is a child under 21 yrs. old.	T-4		Same as above.
Sibling of T-1 Victim	T-5		
** T-1 may not exceed 5000 in any fiscal year*			
Victim of Criminal Activity As defined in 8 C.F.R. 214.14 May apply for status from inside or outside the U.S.	U-1	Validity of approved form I-918 petition Cannot exceed 4 years No Fee	Suffered abuse as result of criminal activity violating laws of or occurring in U.S., territories, or possessions; status may be granted if aid in investigation certified by government official; Attorney General may convert to permanent resident status on humanitarian grounds. Not to exceed 10,000 in any Fiscal Year
Spouse of U-1 Victim	U-2	same as U-1	Accompanying or following to join U-1

IMMIGRATION LAW
CLASSIFICATIONS AND CHARTS

Classification	*Sym*	*Max Adm*	*Remarks*
Child of U-1 Victim	U-3	same as U-1	Accompanying or following to join U-1
Parent of U-1 Victim	U-4	same as U-1	Principal petitioner is less than 21 years of age.
Unmarried siblings under 18 years of age	U-5	same as U-1	Principal petitioner is less than 21 years of age.
Spouse of Legal Permanent Resident Alien* (See 8 C.F.R. 214.15) Exempt 212(a)(9)(B)(i)(I) & (II) if seeking admission All Vs require NIV. Petition must be filed and pending prior to December 31, 2000	V-1	2 years	Travel Abroad: An alien who applies for and obtains V nonimmigrant status in the United States will be issued Form I-797. Form I-797 does not serve as a travel document. If such an alien departs the United States, he or she must obtain a V visa from a consular office abroad in order to be readmitted to the U.S as a V nonimmigrant. This visa requirement, however, does not apply if the alien traveled to contiguous territory or adjacent islands, possesses another valid visa, and is eligible for automatic revalidation. EAD required.

**Readmission: If the alien had a current priority date and filed an I-485 before departing the U.S., admit for 2 years. If the alien had a current priority date and did not file an I-485 before departing the U.S., admit for 6 months. If the alien did not have a current priority and was therefore unable to file an I-485, admit for 2 years. See 8 C.F.R. 214.15 (g)(4)(i).*

Child of Legal Permanent Resident Alien (Beneficiary of an approved petition in his/her own name) All Vs require NIV.	V-2	Admit for 2 years or 45 days after the child's 21st birthday, whichever comes first	Not dependent on parent's status. Must meet definition of "child" for initial status. Status holders 21 years of age or older will not "age out."
Child of V-1 or V-2 Derivative child of his/her parent's petition All Vs require NIV.	V-3	Admit for 2 years or 45 days after the child's 21st birthday, whichever comes first	Same as above. Dependent on parent's status.
Visitor for BUSINESS admitted under Visa Waiver Program (VWP). "Deadheading crew" and crew members with letters indicating they are joining a vessel docked in U.S. may be admitted in this class.	WB	90 days	(*See* VISA WAIVER PROGRAM (VWP) provisions [8 C.F.R. 217] below.)
Visitor for PLEASURE (Tourist) admitted under Visa Waiver Program (VWP). Aliens in transit through the U.S. may be admitted in this class.	WT	90 days	

Classification	*Sym*	*Max Adm*	*Remarks*

Visa Waiver Program [8 C.F.R. 217.2, 212.1, 22 C.F.R. 41.2]

- Relates to visitors for business (WB) and for pleasure (WT). (See previous page.)
- Each applicant must possess a valid, unexpired passport from a VWP designated country and must present a completed, signed Form I-94W. [8 C.F.R. 217.2(b)]*
- Applicants must be admitted for 90 days or less in either WB or WT category on FORM I-94W.
- Applicants may enter at all Classification "A" ports-of-entry (POEs).*
- Applicants arriving by air or sea must arrive on a carrier that is signatory to the VWP. (See list of signatory carriers on pages 48 to 63.)
- Applicants arriving by air or sea must possess a ticket, valid for at least one year, to any foreign place/port other than contiguous territory or an adjacent island unless they permanently reside there. (See next page for Adjacent Islands.)
- Applicants arriving at land border POEs are required to prove economic solvency and a foreign residence to which they intend to return; (round trip transportation ticket is not required).
- Aliens in transit are eligible under VWP if they meet all other program requirements.
- Aliens that were previously removed from the U.S. as deportable aliens are ineligible.
- Must not fall under any inadmissibility provision, or appear in any "lookout" database.
- Aliens who had previously violated the terms of admission under the VWP or the predecador VWPP are ineligible.
- An alien refused admission under the VWP on or after October 30, 2000 must apply for a visa.
- Alien must obtain an approved Electronic System for Travel Authorization (ESTA) prior to travel to the U.S. However, not required for arrivals by land.
- U.S. Military dependants who arrive on U.S. military or DOD contracted commercial aircraft may be admitted under the VWP.

** Completed and signed I-94W not used in air and land environments when applicant has a valid ESTA.*
POEs for aliens arriving by land or sea are classified by types of aliens that can be inspected: "A," ALL aliens; "B," Border Crossers or those that need no documents; or "C," aliens entering as Crewmen aboard vessels.* ***[8 C.F.R. 100.4(c)(2)]

Visa Waiver Program Designated Countries [8 C.F.R. 217.2; 22 C.F.R. 41.2(*l*)]

Andorra	Denmark	Iceland	Luxembourg	Poland	Slovenia
Australia	Estonia	Ireland	Malta	Portugal	Spain
Austria	Finland	Italy	Monaco	Republic of Korea	Sweden
Belgium	France	Japan	The Netherlands	San Marino	Switzerland
Brunei	Germany	Latvia	New Zealand	Singapore	Taiwan
Chile	Greece	Liechtenstein	Norway	Slovak Republic	U.K.**
Czech Republic	Hungary	Lithuania			

***(British citizens only with the unrestricted right of permanent abode in England, Scotland, Wales, Northern Ireland, the Channel Islands and the Isle of Man).*

Machine readable passport requirement of all individuals (including infants).

The term "adjacent island" means Anguilla, Antigua, Aruba, Bahamas, Barbados, Barbuda, Bermuda, Bonaire, British Virgin Islands, Cayman Islands, Cuba, Curacao, Dominica, the Dominican Republic, Grenada, Guadeloupe, Haiti, Jamaica, Marie-Galante, Martinique, Miquelon, Montserrat, Saba, Saint-Barthelemy, Saint Christopher, Saint Eustatius, Saint Kitts-Nevis, Saint Lucia, Saint Maarten, Saint Martin, Saint Pierre, Saint Vincent and Grenadines, Trinidad and Tobago, Turks and Caicos Islands, and other British, French, and Netherlands territory or possession bordering on the Caribbean Sea.

On 6/26/05, all participants required to have machine readable passports. On 10/26/05, all participating VWP countries to produce passport with digital picture, and on 10/26/06, integrated circuit chip or e-passport.

NATIONALITY CHARTS

Birth Abroad in Wedlock: Chart #1

PERIOD Step 1:	PARENTS Step 2:	USC PARENT Step 3:	CHILD Step 4:
Period in which child was born	**Citizenship of the parents at time of child's birth**	**Determine if residence or physical presence requirement was met prior to the birth of the child. If yes, the child was a USC at birth.**	**Determine if child has lost U.S. citizenship. The child lost on the date it became impossible to meet the retention requirements.**
Prior to 5/24/34	Either parent a USC*	U.S. citizen resided in the U.S.	NONE
On or after 5/24/34 and prior to 1/13/41	Both parents USCs	One parent resided in the U.S.	NONE
	One USC parent and one alien	USC parent resided in the U.S.	**5 years residence in the U.S. or OLP between ages 13 and 21 (must start before age 16) **OR**
On or after 1/13/41 and prior to 12/24/52	One USC parent and one alien	USC parent resided in the U.S. or OLP for 10 years, at least 5 of which were after age 16. **Note 3** *Special Provisions* for honorable service in U.S. Armed Forces: Between 12/7/41 and noon on 12/31/46, 10 years residence, at least 5 of which were after age 12. **Note 3** Between noon on 12/31/46 and 12/24/52, 10 years physical presence, at least 5 of which were after age 14. **Note 4**	**5 years continuous physical presence in U.S. between ages of 14 and 28 (must start after age 14 and before age 23), OR **2 years continuous physical presence in U.S. between ages of 14 and 28 (must start before age 26), OR **NONE, if at time of child's birth, USC parent was employed by the U.S. Government or any organization specified under 201(g) of the 1940 Act; ***HOWEVER***, does not apply if parent used a special provision. **Notes 1, 2, 6**
On/after 12/24/52 and prior to 11/14/86	Both parents USCs	One had resided in the U.S. or OLP	NONE
	Both parents USCs	One had resided in U.S. or OLP	NONE
	One USC parent and one alien	USC parent physically present in U.S. or OLP 10 years, at least 5 after age 14. **Note 5**	NONE
On/after 11/14/86	Both parents USCs	One had resided in the U.S. or OLP	NONE
	One USC parent and one alien	USC physically present in U.S. or OLP 5 years, at least 2 after the age of 14. Note 5	NONE

IMMIGRATION LAW
CLASSIFICATIONS AND CHARTS

NOTES:

1. Absence of less than 12 months in the aggregate during the 5-year period did not break continuity of residence or physical presence; absences of less than 60 days in the 2-year period in the aggregate will not break continuity of physical presence [i.e., "stop-time rule"]. Absences abroad in the U.S. Armed Forces after a person had begun to comply with the period required by INA § 301(b) for retention are regarded as constructive physical presence. [*See* 7 Foreign Affairs Manual 1133.5-4].

2. A child is not required to meet the retention requirements if, prior to his 18th birthday, the child began to reside permanently in the U.S. and the alien parent naturalized. [Public Law 92-584 of October 27, 1972].

3. Includes periods abroad of honorable service in U.S. Armed Forces. Absences abroad due to employment or schooling also counted if the person maintained a place of general abode in the U.S. [See, 7 Foreign Affairs Manual 1133.3-2].

4. Pursuant to the Act of March 16, 1956 (70 Stat. 50) [See, 7 Foreign Affairs Manual 1134.4]. Honorable service in U.S. Armed Forces counted as constructive physical presence.

5. Includes periods abroad of honorable service in U.S. Armed Forces and employment by the U.S. Government or an international organization [or the dependent unmarried son or daughter member of the household of such employee].

6. Public Law 95-432 of October 10, 1978 repealed retention requirements prospectively only. Anyone born on or after 10/10/52 (i.e., not age 26 on 10/10/78) no longer had retention requirements.

* USC mother added due to Immigration and Nationality Technical Corrections Act of 1994 (INTCA).

** Retention requirements were repealed effective 10/10/78; INTCA made non-retroactive restoration of citizenship available by taking an oath of allegiance.

IMMIGRATION LAW
CLASSIFICATIONS AND CHARTS

Children Born Abroad Out of Wedlock: Chart #2

Birth date of child	**To U.S. Citizen Mother**
Prior to 5/24/34	Mother had resided in the U.S. or an OLP at any time prior to the child's birth (retroactive grant by § 205 of the 1940 Act—effective 1/13/1941. A child did ***not*** acquire U.S. citizenship retroactively under § 205 of the 1940 Act if the facts reveal that its alien father legitimated the child prior to 1/13/1941 <u>and</u> such legitimation occurred before the child's 21st birthday.
On/after 5/24/34 & prior to 12/24/52	Mother had resided in the U.S. or OLP at any time prior to the child's birth.
On/after 12/24/52	Mother had one year of continuous physical presence in the U.S. or OLP at any time prior to child's birth.
	To U.S. Citizen Mother AND U.S. Citizen Father 1. USC mother unable to transmit. (Check above section first). 2. USC father legitimates (refer to time periods below for appropriate statute). 3a. One parent had resided in U.S. prior to child's birth (prior to 1/13/41). 3b. One parent had resided in U.S. or OLP prior to child's birth (after 1/13/41)
Birth date of child	**To U.S. Citizen Father and Alien Mother – Child Legitimated**
Prior to 5/24/34	1. Child legitimated at any time after birth under laws of father's domicile. 2. USC father had resided in U.S. prior to child's birth.
On/after 5/24/34 & prior to 1/13/41	1. Child legitimated at any time under laws of father's domicile. 2. USC father had resided in U.S. prior to child's birth. 3. Child met retention requirements—see historical period 2 of CHART 1.
On/after 1/13/41 & prior to 12/24/52	1. Child legitimated before age 21 under laws of father's domicile or by paternity established by court adjudication. 2. USC father, prior to child's birth, had met the required residence—see historical period 3 of CHART 1. 3. Child met retention requirements—see historical period 3 of CHART 1.
On/after 12/24/52 & prior to 11/14/86	1. Child legitimated before age 21 under laws of father's or child's domicile. 2. Child legitimated PRIOR to 11/14/86. 3. Child must be unmarried. 4. USC father, prior to child's birth, physically present in U.S. or OLP 10 years, at least 5 after age 14*. (A child born on/after 11/14/68 can opt to follow rules in historical period 5.)
Relationship Established	**To U.S. Citizen Father and Alien Mother – Child Legitimated or Acknowledged**
On/after 11/14/86	1. Child legitimated OR acknowledged before age 18: Legitimated under law of child's residence or domicile, <u>OR</u> Paternity acknowledged in writing under oath, <u>OR</u> Paternity established by court adjudication. 2. Blood relationship established between father and child by clear and convincing evidence. 3. Father (unless deceased) has agreed in writing under oath to provide financial support until child reaches age 18. 4. Child must be unmarried. 5. USC father, prior to child's birth, physically present in U.S. or OLP 5 years, at least 2 after age 14*. These provisions also apply to persons who were under 18 as of 11/14/86. Those between ages 15 and 18 on 11/14/ 86 could elect to have the legitimation rule in effect prior to the 1986 amendment apply to them.

* Periods of honorable service in the U.S. Armed Forces, employment with U.S. government, or employment with an international organization [or an unmarried son or daughter member of the household of such employee] are included [i.e., as constructive physical presence].

Derivative Citizenship of Children: Chart #3

A child may derive U.S. citizenship during the below listed historical periods if such child was under the statutory age AND:

1. the child was lawfully admitted [including adjustment of status] for permanent residence AND
2. the parent(s) naturalized. It does not matter in which order the actions occurred.

Period in which last action took place	**Child became a LPR before the statutory age of:**	**Naturalization of parent(s) prior to the statutory age of the child**	**Remarks**
Prior to 5/24/34	21 Years	Either parent	NONE
On/after 5/24/34 & prior to 1/13/41	21 Years	Either parent	U.S. citizenship effective 5 years from date child became a LPR.** Illegitimate child could only derive from the mother.
		Both parents*	NONE
On/after 1/13/41 & prior to 12/24/52	18 Years	Both parents*	Child born out of wedlock was not eligible at this time. *Child not eligible derived on 12/24/52 if under the age of 16, remained an LPR and the mother was still a USC.*
On/after12/24/52 & prior to 10/5/78	18 Years	Both parents*	Child unmarried
On/after 10/5/78 & prior to 2/27/01	18 Years	Both parents*	Adopted child now included and can derive up to age 18 provided the adoption occurred prior to age 16. Child must be residing in the U.S. at the time of the adoptive parents' naturalization, in the custody of the adoptive parents and pursuant to lawful admission. Child unmarried
On/after 2/27/01	18 years	One USC parent by naturalization or birth.	Child is residing in the U.S. pursuant to a lawful admission for permanent residence in the legal and physical custody of the USC parent. Adopted child of a USC must meet the adopted child requirements of § 101(b)(1) INA. Any other child*** must meet definition in § 101(c)(1) INA.

* The definition of both parents includes:

a. The surviving parent should one die, **OR**
b. The naturalized parent having legal custody where there has been a divorce or after 1/13/41 a legal separation, OR
c. The alien parent who naturalizes when the other parent is *already* a USC, **OR**
d. The mother of a child born out of wedlock, as long as the child had not been legitimated. Exceptions: child born on/after 1/13/41 and prior to 12/24/52 AND on/after 2/27/01.

** Child relieved of the remainder of the 5-year wait if the naturalized parent comes to meet definition of "both parents."

*** Any child not adopted must meet the definition in § 101(c)(1) INA as used in title III:
The term "child" means an unmarried person under twenty-one years of age and includes a child legitimated under the law of the child's residence or domicile, or under the law of the father's residence or domicile, whether in the United States or elsewhere, and, except as otherwise provided in sections 320 and 321 of title III, a child adopted in the United States, if such legitimation or adoption takes place before the child reaches the age of 16 years (except to the extent that the child is described in subparagraph (E)(ii) or (F)(ii) of subsection (b)(1), and the child is in the legal custody of the legitimating or adopting parent or parents at the time of such legitimation or adoption.

Effective September 26, 2003 a child born out of wedlock who has not been legitimated may derive citizenship automatically under INA § 320 through the naturalization of the child's mother.

Children's Citizenship Through Application Guidelines for § 322 Adjudications: Chart #4

On or after 11/2/02, a U.S. citizen parent may apply for naturalization on behalf of a child born **outside** of the U.S. If the citizen parent has died during the preceding 5 years, a citizen grandparent or citizen legal guardian may apply. [CCA 2000, P.L. 106-395, as amended by the 21st Century Department of Justice Appropriations Act, P.L. 107-273]
The child must be residing **outside** the U.S. in the legal and physical custody of the U.S. citizen parent. If the citizen parent is deceased, the child does not have to be residing in the legal and physical custody of the grandparent or legal guardian applicant. However, the child must be residing outside the U.S. in the legal and physical custody of an individual who does not object to the application.
The child is **temporarily** present in the U.S. pursuant to a lawful admission, and is maintaining such lawful status. Both the child and the USC applicant must appear at an interview.
The adjudication and the taking of the oath, unless waived because the child is unable to understand its meaning by reason of mental incapacity or young age, **must** be completed before the child's 18th birthday.

CHILD	CITIZEN PARENT	CITIZEN APPLICANT
The N-600K, Application for Citizenship and Issu-ance of Certificate under §322, may be filed from abroad.	**One** citizen parent can file the applica-tion. Parent's requirements are identi-cal for natural or adopted child.	If the citizen parent has died during the preced-ing 5 years, a USC grandparent (a U.S. citizen parent of the U.S. citizen parent), or USC legal guardian may file the application.

Natural Child	Adopted Child	CITIZEN PARENT	CITIZEN APPLICANT
Must meet definition of child in 101(c)(1) INA [See 8 C.F.R. 322.1] This means a biological legitimate child, or a child who was legiti-mized, while in the legal custody of the legitimiz-ing parens(s) prior to reaching the 16th birthday.	Must meet the require-ments of adopted child in 101(b)(1) INA, having com-plied with the two years of legal custody and two years of joint residence. An orphan who does not meet 101(b)(1)(E) INA requirements must have an approved Form I-600, Petition to Classify Orphan as an Immediate Relative or be eligible to have an I-130 approved un-der §101(b)(1)(E)	At time of adjudication, must have been physi-cally present in the U.S. for pe-riods totaling 5 years, at least 2 of these years must be after the parent's 14th birthday. **OR** A child may benefit from their U.S. citizen grandpar-ent* (living or deceased) so long as the grandparent met the physical presence requirement at the time of death.	At time of death, the USC parent must have been physically present in the U.S. for periods totaling 5 years, at least 2 of these years must be after the par-ent's 14th birthday. **OR** A child may benefit from their U.S. citizen grandpar-ent* (living or deceased) so long as the grandparent met the physical presence requirement at the time of death.

** If filed within 5 years of the USC parents death*
See USCIS Press Release at http://www.uscis.gov/files/pressrelease/PolMemo94Pub.pdf accessed on November 10, 2010

IMMIGRATION LAW AND NATIONALITY ACT OF 1952

U.S. CODE CONVERSION TABLE

For reader convenience, this chart illustrates where sections of the Immigration and Nationality Act of 1952 have been codified in the U.S. Code.

Immigration and Nationality Act of 1952 Section	*U.S. Code Section*
Title I — GENERAL PROVISIONS	
§ 101	8 U.S.C. § 1101
§ 102	8 U.S.C. § 1102
§ 103	8 U.S.C. § 1103
§ 104	8 U.S.C. § 1104
§ 105	8 U.S.C. § 1105
§ 106	8 U.S.C. § 1105a

Title II—IMMIGRATION	
Chapter 1 — Selection System	
§ 201	8 U.S.C. § 1151
§ 202	8 U.S.C. § 1152
§ 203	8 U.S.C. § 1153
§ 204	8 U.S.C. § 1154
§ 205	8 U.S.C. § 1155
§ 206	8 U.S.C. § 1156
§ 207	8 U.S.C. § 1157
§ 208	8 U.S.C. § 1158
§ 209	8 U.S.C. § 1159
§ 210	8 U.S.C. § 1160
§ 210A	8 U.S.C. § 1161 [Repealed]
Chapter 2 — Qualifications for Aliens; Travel Control of Citizens and Aliens	
§ 211	8 U.S.C. § 1181
§ 212	8 U.S.C. § 1182
§ 213	8 U.S.C. § 1183
§ 213A	8 U.S.C. § 1183a
§ 214	8 U.S.C. § 1184
§ 215	8 U.S.C. § 1185
§ 216	8 U.S.C. § 1186a
§ 216A	8 U.S.C. § 1186b
§ 217	8 U.S.C. § 1187
§ 218	8 U.S.C. § 1188
§ 219	8 U.S.C. § 1189
Chapter 3 — Issuance of Entry Documents	
§ 221	8 U.S.C. § 1201
§ 222	8 U.S.C. § 1202
§ 223	8 U.S.C. § 1203
§ 224	8 U.S.C. § 1204

U.S. CODE CONVERSION TABLE

Immigration and Nationality Act of 1952 Section	*U.S. Code Section*
Chapter 4 — Inspection, Apprehension, Examination, Exclusion, and Removal	
§ 231	8 U.S.C. § 1221
§ 232	8 U.S.C. § 1222
§ 233	8 U.S.C. § 1223
§ 234	8 U.S.C. § 1224
§ 235	8 U.S.C. § 1225
§ 235A	8 U.S.C. § 1225a
§ 236	8 U.S.C. § 1226
§ 236A	8 U.S.C. § 1226a
§ 237	8 U.S.C. § 1227
§ 238	8 U.S.C. § 1228
§ 239	8 U.S.C. § 1229
§ 240	8 U.S.C. § 1229a
§ 240A	8 U.S.C. § 1229b
§ 240B	8 U.S.C. § 1229c
§ 240C	8 U.S.C. § 1230
§ 241	8 U.S.C. § 1231
§ 242	8 U.S.C. § 1252
§ 242A	8 U.S.C. § 1252a [Transferred]
§ 242B	8 U.S.C. § 1252b [Repealed]
§ 243	8 U.S.C. § 1253
§ 244	8 U.S.C. § 1254a
Chapter 5 — Adjustment and Change of Status	
§ 245	8 U.S.C. § 1255
§ 245A	8 U.S.C. § 1255a
§ 246	8 U.S.C. § 1256
§ 247	8 U.S.C. § 1257
§ 248	8 U.S.C. § 1258
§ 249	8 U.S.C. § 1259
§ 250	8 U.S.C. § 1260
Chapter 6 — Special Provisions Relating to Alien Crewmen	
§ 251	8 U.S.C. § 1281
§ 252	8 U.S.C. § 1282
§ 253	8 U.S.C. § 1283
§ 254	8 U.S.C. § 1284
§ 255	8 U.S.C. § 1285
§ 256	8 U.S.C. § 1286
§ 257	8 U.S.C. § 1287
§ 258	8 U.S.C. § 1288
Chapter 7 — Registration of Aliens	
§ 261	8 U.S.C. § 1301
§ 262	8 U.S.C. § 1302

U.S. CODE CONVERSION TABLE

Immigration and Nationality Act of 1952 Section	*U.S. Code Section*
§ 263	8 U.S.C. § 1303
§ 264	8 U.S.C. § 1304
§ 265	8 U.S.C. § 1305
§ 266	8 U.S.C. § 1306
Chapter 8 — General Penalty Provisions	
§ 271	8 U.S.C. § 1321
§ 272	8 U.S.C. § 1322
§ 273	8 U.S.C. § 1323
§ 274	8 U.S.C. § 1324
§ 274A	8 U.S.C. § 1324a
§ 274B	8 U.S.C. § 1324b
§ 274C	8 U.S.C. § 1324c
§ 274D	8 U.S.C. § 1324d
§ 275	8 U.S.C. § 1325
§ 276	8 U.S.C. § 1326
§ 277	8 U.S.C. § 1327
§ 278	8 U.S.C. § 1328
§ 279	8 U.S.C. § 1329
§ 280	8 U.S.C. § 1330
Chapter 9—Miscellaneous	
§ 282	8 U.S.C. § 1352
§ 283	8 U.S.C. § 1353
§ 284	8 U.S.C. § 1354
§ 285	8 U.S.C. § 1355
§ 286	8 U.S.C. § 1356
§ 287	8 U.S.C. § 1357
§ 288	8 U.S.C. § 1358
§ 289	8 U.S.C. § 1359
§ 290	8 U.S.C. § 1360
§ 291	8 U.S.C. § 1361
§ 292	8 U.S.C. § 1362
§ 293	8 U.S.C. § 1363
§ 294	8 U.S.C. § 1363a
§ 295	8 U.S.C. § 1363b [Repealed]

Title III **Chapter 1 — Nationality At Birth and Collective Naturalization**	
§ 301	8 U.S.C. § 1401
§ 302	8 U.S.C. § 1402
§ 303	8 U.S.C. § 1403
§ 304	8 U.S.C. § 1404
§ 305	8 U.S.C. § 1405
§ 306	8 U.S.C. § 1406
§ 307	8 U.S.C. § 1407
§ 308	8 U.S.C. § 1408

Immigration and Nationality Act of 1952 Section	*U.S. Code Section*
§ 309	8 U.S.C. § 1409
Chapter 2 — Nationality through Naturalization	
§ 310	8 U.S.C. § 1421
§ 311	8 U.S.C. § 1422
§ 312	8 U.S.C. § 1423
§ 313	8 U.S.C. § 1424
§ 314	8 U.S.C. § 1425
§ 315	8 U.S.C. § 1426
§ 316	8 U.S.C. § 1427
§ 317	8 U.S.C. § 1428
§ 318	8 U.S.C. § 1429
§ 319	8 U.S.C. § 1430
§ 320	8 U.S.C. § 1431
§ 321	8 U.S.C. § 1432 [Repealed]
§ 322	8 U.S.C. § 1433
§ 323	8 U.S.C. § 1434
§ 324	8 U.S.C. § 1435
§ 325	8 U.S.C. § 1436
§ 326	8 U.S.C. § 1437
§ 327	8 U.S.C. § 1438
§ 328	8 U.S.C. § 1439
§ 329	8 U.S.C. § 1440
§ 329-A	8 U.S.C. § 1440-1
§ 330	8 U.S.C. § 1441
§ 331	8 U.S.C. § 1442
§ 332	8 U.S.C. § 1443
§ 333	8 U.S.C. § 1444
§ 334	8 U.S.C. § 1445
§ 335	8 U.S.C. § 1446
§ 336	8 U.S.C. § 1447
§ 337	8 U.S.C. § 1448
§ 338	8 U.S.C. § 1449
§ 339	8 U.S.C. § 1450
§ 340	8 U.S.C. § 1451
§ 341	8 U.S.C. § 1452
§ 342	8 U.S.C. § 1453
§ 343	8 U.S.C. § 1454
§ 344	8 U.S.C. § 1455
§ 345	8 U.S.C. § 1456 [Repealed]
§ 346	8 U.S.C. § 1457
§ 347	8 U.S.C. § 1458
§ 348	8 U.S.C. § 1459
Chapter 3 — Loss of Nationality	
§ 349	8 U.S.C. § 1481
§ 350	8 U.S.C. § 1482 [Repealed]

U.S. CODE CONVERSION TABLE

Immigration and Nationality Act of 1952 Section	*U.S. Code Section*
§ 351	8 U.S.C. § 1483
§§ 352 to 355	8 U.S.C. § § 1484—1487 [Repealed]
§ 356	8 U.S.C. § 1488
§ 357	8 U.S.C. § 1489
Chapter 4 — Miscellaneous	
§ 358	8 U.S.C. § 1501
§ 359	8 U.S.C. § 1502
§ 360	8 U.S.C. § 1503
§ 361	8 U.S.C. § 1504

Title IV — MISCELLANEOUS AND REFUGEE ASSISTANCE	
Chapter 1 — Miscellaneous	
§ 404	8 U.S.C. § 1101, note
§ 405	8 U.S.C. § 1101, note
§ 406	8 U.S.C. § 1101, note
§ 407	8 U.S.C. § 1101, note
Chapter 2 — Refugee Assistance	
§ 411	8 U.S.C. § 1521
§ 412	8 U.S.C. § 1522
§ 413	8 U.S.C. § 1523
§ 414	8 U.S.C. § 1524

TITLE V — ALIEN TERRORIST REMOVAL PROCEDURES	
§ 501	8 U.S.C. § 1531
§ 502	8 U.S.C. § 1532
§ 503	8 U.S.C. § 1533
§ 504	8 U.S.C. § 1534
§ 505	8 U.S.C. § 1535
§ 506	8 U.S.C. § 1536
§ 507	8 U.S.C. § 1537

Citations to Public Laws affecting or amending the Immigration And Nationality Act of 1952

Pub. L. 117-360.........."Energy Security and Lightering Independence Act of 2022"

Pub. l. 117-263.........."James M. Inhofe National Defense Authorization Act for Fiscal Year 2023"

Pub. L. 117-103.........."Consolidated Appropriations Act, 2022"

Pub. L. 116-113.........."United States-Mexico-Canada Agreement Implementation Act"

Pub. L. 115-425.........."Frederick Douglass Trafficking Victims Prevention and Protection Reauthorization Act of 2018"

Pub. L. 115-393.........."Trafficking Victims Protection Act of 2017"

Pub. L. 114-125.........."Trade Facilitation and Trade Enforcement Act of 2015"

Pub. L. 111-287.........."International Adoption Simplification Act"

Pub. L. 111-198.........."Homebuyer Assistance and Improvement Act of 2010"

Pub. L. 111-145.........."United States Capitol Police Administrative Technical Corrections Act of 2009"

Pub. L. 111-122 ....Human Rights Enforcement Act of 2009

Pub. L. 111-117 ....Consolidated Appropriations Act, 2010

Pub. L. 111-9 ....To extend certain immigration programs

Pub. L. 110-457 ....William Wilberforce Trafficking Victims Protection Reauthorization Act of 2008

Pub. L. 110-391 ....Special Immigrant Nonminister Religious Worker Program Act

Pub. L. 110-382 ....Military Personnel Citizenship Processing Act

Pub. L. 110-362 ....To extend for 5 years the program relating to waiver of the foreign country residence requirement with respect to international medical graduates, and for other purposes

Pub. L. 110-340 ....Child Soldiers Accountability Act of 2008

Pub. L. 110-293 ....Tom Lantos and Henry J. Hyde United States Global Leadership Against HIV/AIDS, Tuberculosis, and Malaria Reauthorization Act of 2008

Pub. L. 110-246 ....Food, Conservation, and Energy Act of 2008

Pub. L. 110-234 ....Food, Conservation, and Energy Act of 2008

Pub. L. 110-229 ....Consolidated Natural Resources Act of 2008

Pub. L. 110-53 ....Implementing Recommendations of the 9/11 Commission Act of 2007

Pub. L. 110-36 ....A bill to increase the number of Iraqi and Afghani translators and interpreters who may be admitted to the United States as special immigrants, and for other purposes

Pub. L. 110-28 ...........U.S. Troop Readiness, Veterans' Care, Katrina Recovery, and Iraq Accountability Appropriations Act, 2007

Pub. L. 109-477.........Physicians for Underserved Areas Act

Pub. L. 109-472.........Department of State Authorities Act of 2006

Pub. L. 109-463.........Creating Opportunities for Minor League Professionals, Entertainers, and Teams through Legal Entry Act of 2006

Pub. L. 109-423.........Nursing Relief for Disadvantaged Areas Reauthorization Act of 2005

Pub. L. 109-367.........Secure Fence Act of 2006

Pub. L. 109-364.........John Warner National Defense Authorization Act for Fiscal Year 2007

Pub. L. 109-271 ....Technical Corrections to the Violence Against Women and Department of Justice Reauthorization Act of 2005

Pub. L. 109-270 ....Carl D. Perkins Career and Technical Education Improvement Act of 2006

Pub. L. 109-248.........Adam Walsh Child Protection and Safety Act of 2006

Pub. L. 109-163 ....National Defense Authorization Act for Fiscal Year 2006

Citations to Public Laws

Pub. L. 109-162 .... Violence Against Women and Department of Justice Reauthorization Act of 2005

Pub. L. 109-97 .... Agriculture, Rural Development, Food and Drug Administration, and Related Agencies Appropriations Act, 2006

Pub. L. 109-90 .... Department of Homeland Security Appropriations Act, 2006

Pub. L. 109-13 .... REAL ID ACT OF 2005

Pub. L. 108-458 .... Intelligence Reform and Terrorism Prevention Act of 2004

Pub. L. 108-449 .... To amend and extend the Irish Peace Process Cultural and Training Program Act of 1998

Pub. L. 108-447 .... Consolidated Appropriations Act, 2005 (Includes L-1 Visa and H-1B Visa Reform Act, and the H-1B Visa Reform Act of 2004)

Pub. L. 108-441 .... To improve access to physicians in medically underserved areas

Pub. L. 108-390 .... To improve the process for verifying an individual's eligibility for employment

Pub. L. 108-199 .... Consolidated Appropriations Act, 2004

Pub. L. 108-193 .... Trafficking Victims Protection Reauthorization Act of 2003

Pub. L. 108-177 .... Intelligence Authorization Act for Fiscal Year 2004

Pub. L. 108-156 .... Basic Pilot Program Extension and Expansion Act of 2003

Pub. L. 108-136 .... National Defense Authorization Act for Fiscal Year 2004

Pub. L. 108-99 .... Extension of the Special Immigrant Religious Worker Program

Pub. L. 108-90 .... Department of Homeland Security Appropriations Act, 2004

Pub. L. 108-78 .... United States-Singapore Free Trade Agreement Implementation Act

Pub. L. 108-77 .... United States-Chile Free Trade Agreement Implementation Act

Pub. L. 108-7 .... Consolidated Appropriations Resolution, 2003

Pub. L. 107-296 .... Homeland Security Act of 2002

Pub. L. 107-274 .... Border Commuter Student Act of 2002

Pub. L. 107-273 .... 21st Century Department of Justice Appropriations Authorization Act

Pub. L. 107-258 .... Persian Gulf War POW/MIA Accountability Act of 2002

Pub. L. 107-234 .... Extension of Irish Peace Process Cultural and Training Program

Pub. L. 107-208 .... Child Status Protection Act

Pub. L. 107-206 .... 2002 Supplemental Appropriations Act for Further Recovery From and Response To Terrorist Attacks on the United States

Pub. L. 107-173 .... Enhanced Security and Visa Entry Reform Act of 2002

Pub. L. 107-150 .... Family Sponsor Immigration Act of 2002

Pub. L. 107-128 .... Extend Pilot Program for Employment Eligibility Verification

Pub. L. 107-125 .... Provide Work Authorization for Nonimmigrant Spouses of Intracompany Transferees

Pub. L. 107-124 .... Provide Work Authorization for Nonimmigrant Spouses of Treaty Traders and Treaty Investors

Pub. L. 107-108 .... Intelligence Authorization Act for Fiscal Year 2002

Pub. L. 107-77 .... Departments of Commerce, Justice, and State, the Judiciary, and Related Agencies Appropriations Act, 2002

Pub. L. 107-56 .... Uniting and Strengthening America by Providing Appropriate Tools Required to Intercept and Obstruct Terrorism (USA PATRIOT ACT) Act of 2001

Pub. L. 107-45 .... To Provide Permanent Authority for the Admission of "S" Visa Nonimmigrants

Pub. L. 107-43 .... United States-Jordan Free Trade Area Implementation Act

Citations to Public Laws

Pub. L. 106-570.........Assistance for International Malaria Control Act

Pub. L. 106-554.........Consolidated Appropriations Act of 2001

Pub. L. 106-553.........Making Appropriations for the Government of the District of Columbia and Other Activities Chargeable in Whole or in Part Against the Revenues of Said District of Columbia for the Fiscal Year Ending September 30, 2001 and for Other Purposes

Pub. L. 106-536.........Special Immigrant Status for Certain United States International Broadcasting Employees

Pub. L. 106-484.........Bring Them Home Alive Act of 2000

Pub. L. 106-451.........Wartime Violation of Italian Americans Civil Liberties Act

Pub. L. 106-448.........Waiver of Oath of Renunciation and Allegiance for Naturalization of Aliens having Certain Disabilities Act of 2000

Pub. L. 106-429.........Making appropriations for foreign operations, export financing, and related programs for the fiscal year ending September 30, 2001, and for other purposes

Pub. L. 106-415.........Extension of Hmong Veterans' Naturalization Act of 2000

Pub. L. 106-409.........Religious Workers Act of 2000

Pub. L. 106-406.........International Patient Act of 2000

Pub. L. 106-396.........Visa Waiver Permanent Program Act

Pub. L. 106-395.........Child Citizenship Act of 2000

Pub. L. 106-386.........Victims of Trafficking and Violence Protection Act of 2000

Pub. L. 106-378.........Adjustment of Status of Certain Syrian Nationals

Pub. L. 106-313.........American Competitiveness in the Twenty-first Century Act of 2000

Pub. L. 106-311.........Fee Increase for the Employees of H-1B Non-immigrant Workers Act of 2000

Pub. L. 106-279.........Intercountry Adoption Act of 2000

Pub. L. 106-246.........Aiding Colombian Terrorists

Pub. L. 106-215.........Immigration and Naturalization Service Data Management Improvement Act of 2000

Pub. L. 106-207.........Hmong Veteran's Naturalization Act of 2000

Pub. L. 106-185.........Civil Asset Forfeiture Reform Act of 2000

Pub. L. 106-139.........Adopted alien who is less than 18 years of age may be considered a child if adopted with or after a sibling who is considered a child under the Act

Pub. L. 106-120.........Intelligence Authorization Act for Fiscal Year 2000

Pub. L. 106-113.........Consolidated appropriations for the fiscal year ending September 30, 2000, and for other purposes

Pub. L. 106-104.........To extend the "S" nonimmigrant visa category for two additional years, and to authorize appropriations for the refugee assistance program

Pub. L. 106-95...........Nursing Relief for Disadvantaged Areas Act of 1999

Pub. L. 106-78...........Making appropriations for Agriculture, Rural Development, Food and Drug Administration, and Related Agencies programs for the fiscal year ending September 30, 2000, and for other purposes

Pub. L. 105-360.........Extension into Fiscal Year 1999 of Visa Processing Period for Diversity Applicants Whose Visa Processing was Suspended During Fiscal Year 1998 Due to Embassy Bombings

Pub. L. 105-332.........Carl D. Perkins Vocational and Applied Technology Education Amendments of 1998

Pub. L. 105-320.........Torture Victims Relief Act of 1998

Pub. L. 105-319.........Irish Peace Process Cultural and Training Act of 1998

Pub. L. 105-306.........Noncitizen Benefit Clarification and Other Technical Amendments Act of 1998

Citations to Public Laws

Pub. L. 105-292 .... International Religious Freedom Act of 1998

Pub. L. 105-277 .... Omnibus Consolidated Appropriations

Pub. L. 105-259 .... Extension of Date of Development of Automated Entry-Exit Control System

Pub. L. 105-173 .... Immigration and Nationality — Visa Waiver Pilot Program — Data Regarding Nonimmigrant Overstay Rates

Pub. L. 105-141 .... To establish a program in local prisons to identify, prior to arraignment, criminal aliens and aliens who are unlawfully present in the United States, and for other purposes

Pub. L. 105-139 .... Technical corrections to the Nicaraguan Adjustment and Central American Relief Act

Pub. L. 105-119 .... Departments of Commerce, Justice, and State, the Judiciary, and Related Agencies Appropriations Act, 1998

Pub. L. 105-100 .... Nicaraguan Adjustment and Central American Relief Act

Pub. L. 105-85 .... National Defense Authorization Act, 1998

Pub. L. 105-78 .... Departments of Labor, Health and Human Services, and Education Appropriations Act, 1998

Pub. L. 105-73 .... To amend the Immigration and Nationality Act to exempt internationally adopted children 10 years of age or younger from the immunization requirement in section 212(a)(1)(A)(ii) of such Act

Pub. L. 105-65 .... Departments of Veterans Affairs and Housing and Urban Development, and Independent Agencies Appropriations Act, 1998

Pub. L. 105-54 .... Extension of deadlines for religious workers and for paperwork changes in employer sanctions; and to require the Secretary of State to waive or reduce fee for charitable service workers.

Pub. L. 105-46 .... Continuing Appropriations, 1998

Pub. L. 105-38 .... Amend the Immigration and Nationality Technical Corrections Act of 1994 (Pub. L. 103-416)

Pub. L. 104-302 .... Extend the authorized period of stay within the United States for certain nurses

Pub. L. 104-208 .... Illegal Immigration Reform and Immigrant Responsibility Act of 1996

Pub. L. 104-132 .... Antiterrorism and Effective Death Penalty Act of 1996

Pub. L. 104-114 .... To seek international sanctions against the Castro government in Cuba, to plan for support of a transition government leading to a democratically elected government in Cuba, and for other purposes

Pub. L. 104-51 .... Immigration and Nationality Act; Amendment

Pub. L. 103-416 .... Immigration and Nationality Technical Corrections Act of 1994

Pub. L. 103-415 .... Technical and Conforming Amendments

Pub. L. 103-236 .... To authorize appropriations for the Department of State, the United States Information Agency, and related agencies, and for other purposes

Pub. L. 102-395 .... The Judiciary Appropriations Act, 1993

Pub. L. 102-232 .... Miscellaneous and Technical Immigration and Naturalization Amendments of 1991

Pub. L. 101-649 .... Immigration Act of 1990

Pub. L. 100-102 .... In part, as amended by Pub. L. 101-167, Pub. L. 101-513 and Pub. L. 101-649 AMERASIAN IMMIGRATION

Pub. L. 99-603 .... Immigration Reform and Control Act of 1986

IMMIGRATION AND NATIONALITY ACT OF 1952, AS AMENDED

(Complete Act)

TITLE I—GENERAL PROVISIONS

TITLE II—IMMIGRATION

Chapter 1—Selection System

Chapter 2—Qualifications for Admission of Aliens; Travel Control of Citizens and Aliens

Chapter 3—Issuance of Entry Documents

Chapter 4—Inspection, Apprehension, Examination, Exclusion, and Removal

Chapter 5—Adjustment and Change of Status

Chapter 6—Special Provisions Relating to Alien Crewmen

Chapter 7—Registration of Aliens

261. Alien seeking entry; contents.
262. Registration of aliens.
263. Registration of special groups.
264. Forms for registration and fingerprinting.
265. Notices of change of address.
266. Penalties.

Chapter 8—General Penalty Provisions

271. Prevention of unauthorized landing of aliens.
272. Bringing in aliens subject to denial of admission on a health-related ground; persons liable; clearance papers; exceptions; "person" defined.
273. Unlawful bringing of aliens into United States.
274. Bringing in and harboring certain aliens.
274A. Unlawful employment of aliens.
274B. Unfair immigration-related employment practices.
274C. Penalties for document fraud.
274D. Civil penalties for failure to depart.
275. Improper entry by alien.
276. Reentry of removed aliens.
277. Aiding or assisting certain aliens to enter.
278. Importation of alien for immoral purpose.
279. Jurisdiction of district courts.
280. Collection of penalties and expenses.

Chapter 9—Miscellaneous

281. Nonimmigrant visa fees.
282. Printing of reentry permits and blank forms of manifests and crew lists; sale to public.
283. Travel expenses and expense of transporting remains of officers and employees dying outside of United States.
284. Applicability to members of the armed forces.
285. Disposal of privileges at immigrant stations; rentals; retail sale; disposition of receipts.
286. Disposition of moneys collected under the provisions of this title.
287. Powers of immigration officers and employees.
288. Local jurisdiction over immigrant stations.
289. Application to American Indians born in Canada.
290. Establishment of central file; information from other departments and agencies.
291. Burden of proof upon alien.
292. Right to counsel.
293. Deposit of and interest on cash received to secure immigration bonds.
294. Undercover investigation authority.
295. [Repealed].

TITLE III

Chapter 1—Nationality at Birth and Collective Naturalization

301. Nationals and citizens of the United States at birth.
302. Persons born in Puerto Rico on or after April 11, 1899.
303. Persons born in the Canal Zone or Republic of Panama on or after February 26, 1904.
304. Persons born in Alaska on or after March 30, 1867.
305. Persons born in Hawaii.
306. Persons living in and born in the Virgin Islands.
307. Persons living in and born in Guam.
308. Nationals but not citizens of the United States at birth.
309. Children born out of wedlock.

Chapter 2—Nationality Through Naturalization

310. Naturalization authority.
311. Eligibility for naturalization.
312. Requirements as to understanding the English language, history, principles and form of government of the United States.
313. Prohibition upon the naturalization of persons opposed to government or law, or who favor totalitarian forms of government.
314. Ineligibility to naturalization of deserters from the armed forces.
315. Citizenship denied alien relieved of service in armed forces because of alienage.
316. Requirements of naturalization.
317. Temporary absence of persons performing religious duties.
318. Prerequisite to naturalization; burden of proof.
319. Married persons and employees of certain nonprofit organizations.
320. Children born outside the United States and residing permanently in the United States; conditions under which citizenship automatically acquired.
321. [Repealed].
322. Children born and residing outside the United States; conditions for acquiring certificate of citizenship.
323. [Repealed].
324. Former citizens of United States regaining citizenship.
325. Nationals but not citizens; residence within outlying possessions.
326. Resident Philippine citizens excepted from certain requirements.
327. Former citizens losing citizenship by entering the armed forces of foreign countries during World War II.
328. Naturalization through service in the armed forces.
329. Naturalization through active-duty service in the armed forces during World War I, World War II, Korean hostilities, Vietnam hostilities, or other periods of military hostilities.
329A. Posthumous citizenship through death while on active-duty service in the armed forces during World War I, World War II, the Korean hostilities, the Vietnam hostilities, or in other periods of military hostilities.
330. Constructive residence through service on certain United States vessels.
331. Alien enemies.
332. Administration.
333. Photographs; number.
334. Application for naturalization; declaration of intention.
335. Investigation of applicants; examination of applications.
336. Hearings on denials of applications for naturalization.
337. Oath of renunciation and allegiance.
338. Certificate of naturalization; contents.
339. Functions and duties of clerks and records of declarations of intention and applications for naturalization.
340. Revocation of naturalization.

TITLE I—GENERAL PROVISIONS

§ 101. [8 U.S.C. § 1101] Definitions.

(a) As used in this Act—

(1) The term "administrator" means the official designated by the Secretary of State pursuant to section 104(b) of this Act [8 USCS § 1104(b)].

(2) The term "advocates" includes, but is not limited to, advises, recommends, furthers by overt act, and admits belief in.

(3) The term "alien" means any person not a citizen or national of the United States.

(4) The term "application for admission" has reference to the application for admission into the United States and not to the application for the issuance of an immigrant or nonimmigrant visa.

(5) The term "Attorney General" means the Attorney General of the United States.

(6) The term "border crossing identification card" means a document of identity bearing that designation issued to an alien who is lawfully admitted for permanent residence, or to an alien who is a resident in foreign contiguous territory, by a consular officer or an immigration officer for the purpose of crossing over the borders between the United States and foreign contiguous territory in accordance with such conditions for its issuance and use as may be prescribed by regulations. Such regulations shall provide that (A) each such document include a biometric identifier (such as the fingerprint or handprint of the alien) that is machine readable and (B) an alien presenting a border crossing identification card is not permitted to cross over the border into the United States unless the biometric identifier contained on the card matches the appropriate biometric characteristic of the alien.

(7) The term "clerk of court" means a clerk of a naturalization court.

(8) The terms "Commissioner" and "Deputy Commissioner" mean the Commissioner of Immigration and Naturalization and a Deputy Commissioner of Immigration and Naturalization, respectively.

(9) The term "consular officer" means any consular, diplomatic, or other officer or employee of the United States designated under regulations prescribed under authority contained in this Act, for the purpose of issuing immigrant or nonimmigrant visas or, when used in title III [8 USCS §§ 1401 et seq.], for the purpose of adjudicating nationality.

(10) The term "crewman" means a person serving in any capacity on board a vessel or aircraft.

(11) The term "diplomatic visa" means a nonimmigrant visa bearing that title and issued to a nonimmigrant in accordance with such regulations as the Secretary of State may prescribe.

(12) The term "doctrine" includes, but is not limited to, policies, practices, purposes, aims, or procedures.

(13) (A) The terms "admission" and "admitted" mean, with respect to an alien, the lawful entry of the alien into the United States after inspection and authorization by an immigration officer.

(B) An alien who is paroled under section 212(d)(5) [8 USCS § 1182(d)(5)] or permitted to land temporarily as an alien crewman shall not be considered to have been admitted.

(C) An alien lawfully admitted for permanent residence in the United States shall not be regarded as seeking an admission into the United States for purposes of the immigration laws unless the alien—

(i) has abandoned or relinquished that status,

(ii) has been absent from the United States for a continuous period in excess of 180 days,

(iii) has engaged in illegal activity after having departed the United States,

(iv) has departed from the United States while under legal process seeking removal of the alien from the United States, including removal proceedings under this Act and extradition proceedings,

(v) has committed an offense identified in section 212(a)(2) [8 USCS § 1182(a)(2)], unless since such offense the alien has been granted relief under section 212(h) or 240A(a) [8 USCS § 1182(h) or 1229b(a)], or

(vi) is attempting to enter at a time or place other than as designated by immigration officers or has not been admitted to the United States after inspection and authorization by an immigration officer.

(14) The term "foreign state" includes outlying possessions of a foreign state, but self-governing dominions or territories under mandate or trusteeship shall be regarded as separate foreign states.

(15) The term "immigrant" means every alien except an alien who is within one of the following classes of nonimmigrant aliens—

(A) (i) an ambassador, public minister, or career diplomatic or an ambassador, public minister, or career diplomatic or consular officer who has been accredited by a foreign government recognized de jure by the United States and who is accepted by the President or by the Secretary of State, and the members of the alien's immediate family;

(ii) upon a basis of reciprocity, other officials and employees who have been accredited by a foreign government recognized de jure by the United States, who are accepted by the Secretary of State, and the members of their immediate families; and

(iii) upon a basis of reciprocity, attendants, servants, personal employees, and members of their immediate families, of the officials and employees who have a nonimmigrant status under (i) and (ii) above;

(B) an alien (other than one coming for the purpose of study or of performing skilled or unskilled labor or as a representative of foreign press, radio, film, or other foreign information media coming to engage in such vocation) having a residence in a foreign country which he has no intention of abandoning and who is visiting the United States temporarily for business or temporarily for pleasure;

(C) (i) an alien in immediate and continuous transit through the United States, for a period not to exceed 29 days;

(ii) an alien who qualifies as a person entitled to pass in transit to and from the United Nations Headquarters District (as defined in section 209A(e) of the State Department Basic Authorities Act of 1956 (22 U.S.C. 4309a(e))) and foreign countries, under the provisions of paragraphs (3), (4), and (5) of section 11 of the Agreement regarding the Headquarters of the United Nations, done at Lake Success June 26, 1947 (61 Stat. 758); or

(iii) an alien passing in transit through the United States to board a vessel on which the alien will perform, or to disembark from a vessel on which the alien performed, ship-to-ship liquid cargo transfer operations to or from another vessel engaged in foreign trade, for a period not to exceed 180 days;

(D) (i) an alien crewman serving in good faith as such in a capacity required for normal operation and service on board a vessel, as defined in section 258(a) [8 USCS § 1288(a)] (other than a fishing vessel having its home port or an operating base in the United States), or aircraft, who intends to land temporarily and solely in pursuit of his calling as a crewman and to depart from the United States with the vessel or aircraft on which he arrived or some other vessel or aircraft;

(ii) an alien crewman serving in good faith as such in any capacity required for normal operations and service aboard a fishing vessel having its home port or an operating base in the United States who intends to land temporarily in Guam or the Commonwealth of the Northern Mariana Islands and solely in pursuit of his calling as a crewman and to depart from Guam or the Commonwealth of the Northern Mariana Island with the vessel on which he arrived; or

(iii) an alien crewman performing ship-to-ship liquid cargo transfer operations to or from another vessel engaged in foreign trade, who intends to land temporarily solely in pursuit of the alien's responsibilities as a crewman and to depart from the United States on the vessel on which the alien arrived or on another vessel or aircraft, for a period not to exceed 180 days;

(E) an alien entitled to enter the United States under and in pursuance of the provisions of a treaty of commerce and navigation between the United States and the foreign state of which the alien is a national (or, in the case of an alien who acquired the relevant nationality through a financial investment and who has not previously been granted status under this subparagraph, the foreign state of which the alien is a national and in which the alien has been domiciled for a continuous period of not less than 3 years at any point before applying for a nonimmigrant visa under this subparagraph), and the spouse and children of any such alien if accompanying or following to join such alien: (i) solely to carry on substantial trade, including trade in services or trade in technology, principally between the United States and the foreign state of which the alien is a national; (ii) solely to develop and direct the operations of an enterprise in which the alien has invested, or of an enterprise in which the alien is actively in the process of investing, a substantial amount of capital; or (iii) solely to perform services in a specialty occupation in the United States if the alien is a national of the Commonwealth of Australia and with respect to whom the Secretary of Labor determines and certifies to the Secretary of Homeland Security and the Secretary of State that the intending employer has filed with the Secretary of Labor an attestation under section 212(t)(1) [8 USCS § 1182(t)(1)];

(F) (i) an alien having a residence in a foreign country which he has no intention of abandoning, who is a bona fide student qualified to pursue a full course of study and who seeks to enter the United States temporarily and solely for the purpose of pursuing such a course of study consistent with section 214*(l)* at an established college, university, seminary, conservatory, academic high school, elementary school, or other academic institution or in an accredited language training program in the United States, particularly designated by him and approved by the Attorney General after consultation with the Secretary of Education, which institution or place of study shall have agreed to report to the Attorney General the termination of attendance of each nonimmigrant student, and if any such institution of learning or place of study fails to make reports promptly the approval shall be withdrawn, (ii) the alien spouse and minor children of any alien described in clause (i) if accompanying or following to join such an alien, and (iii) an alien who is a national of Canada or Mexico, who maintains actual residence and place of abode in the country of nationality, who is described in clause (i) except that the alien's qualifications for and actual course of study may be full or part-time, and who commutes to the United States institution or place of study from Canada or Mexico;

(G) (i) a designated principal resident representative of a foreign government recognized de jure by the United States, which foreign government is a member of an international organization entitled to enjoy privileges, exemptions, and immunities as an international organization under the International Organizations Immunities Act (59 Stat. 669), accredited resident members of the staff of such representatives, and members of his or their immediate family;

(ii) other accredited representatives of such a foreign government to such international organizations, and the members of their immediate families;

(iii) an alien able to qualify under (i) or (ii) above except for the fact that the government of which such alien is an accredited representative is not recognized de jure by the United States, or that the government of which he is an accredited representative is not a member of such international organization, and the members of his immediate family;

(iv) officers, or employees of such international organizations, and the members of their immediate families;

(v) attendants, servants, and personal employees of any such representative, officer, or employee, and the members of the immediate families of such attendants, servants, and personal employees;

(H) [Caution: For expiration of amendments made to this subparagraph by Act Nov. 12, 1999, P. L. 106-95, see § 2(e) of such Act, which appears as 8 USCS § 1182 note.] an alien (i)(a) [Deleted] (b) subject to section 212(j)(2) [8 USCS § 1182(j)(2)] who is coming temporarily to the United States to perform services (other than services described in subclause (a) during the period in which such subclause applies and other than services described in subclause (ii)(a) or in subparagraph (O) or (P)) in a specialty occupation described in section 214(i)(1) [8 USCS § 1184(i)(1)] or as a fashion model, who meets the requirements for the occupation specified in section 214(i)(2) [8 USCS § 1184(i)(2)] or, in the case of a fashion model, is of distinguished merit and ability, and with respect to whom the Secretary of Labor determines and certifies to the Attorney General that the intending employer has filed with the Secretary an application under section 212(n)(1) [8 USCS § 1182(n)(1)], or (b1) who is entitled to enter the United States under and in pursuance of the provisions of an agreement listed in section 214(g)(8)(A) [8 USCS § 1184(g)(8)(A)], who is engaged in a specialty occupation described in section 214(i)(3) [8 USCS § 1184(i)(3)], and with respect to whom the Secretary of Labor determines and certifies to the Secretary of Homeland Security and the Secretary of State that the intending employer has filed with the Secretary of Labor an attestation under section 212(t)(1) [8 USCS § 1182(t)(1)], or (c) who is coming temporarily to the United States to perform services as a registered nurse, who meets the qualifications described in section 212(m)(1) [8 USCS § 1182(m)(1)], and with respect to whom the Secretary of Labor determines and certifies to the Attorney General that an unexpired attestation is on file and in effect under section 212(m)(2) [8 USCS § 1182(m)(2)] for the facility (as defined in section 212(m)(6)) [8 USCS § 1182(m)(6)]) for which the alien will perform the services; or (ii)(a) having a residence in a foreign country which he has no intention of abandoning who is coming temporarily to the United States to perform agricultural labor or services, as defined by the Secretary of Labor in regulations and including agricultural labor defined in section 3121(g) of the Internal Revenue Code of 1986 [26 USCS § 3121(g)], agriculture as defined in section 3(f) of the Fair Labor Standards Act of 1938 (29

U.S.C. 203(f)), and the pressing of apples for cider on a farm, of a temporary or seasonal nature, or (b) having a residence in a foreign country which he has no intention of abandoning who is coming temporarily to the United States to perform other temporary service or labor if unemployed persons capable of performing such service or labor cannot be found in this country, but this clause shall not apply to graduates of medical schools coming to the United States to perform services as members of the medical profession; or (iii) having a residence in a foreign country which he has no intention of abandoning who is coming temporarily to the United States as a trainee, other than to receive graduate medical education or training; and the alien spouse and minor children of any such alien specified in this paragraph if accompanying him or following to join him, in a training program that is not designed primarily to provide productive employment;

(I) upon a basis of reciprocity, an alien who is a bona fide representative of foreign press, radio, film, or other foreign information media, who seeks to enter the United States solely to engage in such vocation, and the spouse and children of such a representative, if accompanying or following to join him;

(J) an alien having a residence in a foreign country which he has no intention of abandoning who is a bona fide student, scholar, trainee, teacher, professor, research assistant, specialist, or leader in a field of specialized knowledge or skill, or other person of similar description, who is coming temporarily to the United States as a participant in a program designated by the Director of the United States Information Agency, for the purpose of teaching, instructing or lecturing, studying, observing, conducting research, consulting, demonstrating special skills, or receiving training and who, if he is coming to the United States to participate in a program under which he will receive graduate medical education or training, also meets the requirements of section 212(j) [8 USCS § 1182(j)], and the alien spouse and minor children of any such alien if accompanying him or following to join him;

(K) subject to subsections (d) and (p) of section 214 [8 USCS § 1184], an alien who—

(i) is the fiancée or fiancé of a citizen of the United States (other than a citizen described in section 204(a)(1)(A)(viii)(I) [8 USCS § 1154(a)(1)(A)(viii)(I)]) and who seeks to enter the United States solely to conclude a valid marriage with the petitioner within ninety days after admission;

(ii) has concluded a valid marriage with a citizen of the United States (other than a citizen described in section 204(a)(1)(A)(viii)(I) [8 USCS § 1154(a)(1)(A)(viii)(I)]) who is the petitioner, is the beneficiary of a petition to accord a status under section 201(b)(2)(A)(i) [8 USCS § 1151(b)(2)(A)(i)] that was filed under section 204 [8 USCS § 1154] by the petitioner, and seeks to enter the United States to await the approval of such petition and the availability to the alien of an immigrant visa; or

(iii) is the minor child of an alien described in clause (i) or (ii) and is accompanying, or following to join, the alien;

(L) subject to section 214(c)(2) [8 USCS § 1184(c)(2)], an alien who, within 3 years preceding the time of his application for admission into the United States, has been employed continuously for one year by a firm or corporation or other legal entity or an affiliate or subsidiary thereof and who seeks to enter the United States temporarily in order to continue to render his services to the same employer or a subsidiary or affiliate thereof in a capacity that is managerial, executive, or involves specialized knowledge, and the alien spouse and minor children of any such alien if accompanying him or following to join him;

(M) (i) an alien having a residence in a foreign country which he has no intention of abandoning who seeks to enter the United States temporarily and solely for the purpose of pursuing a full course of study at an established vocational or other recognized nonacademic institution (other than in a language training program) in the United States particularly designated by him and approved by the Attorney General, after consultation with the Secretary of Education, which institution shall have agreed to report to the Attorney General the termination of attendance of each nonimmigrant nonacademic student and if any such institution fails to make reports promptly the approval shall be withdrawn, (ii) the alien spouse and minor children of any alien described in clause (i) if accompanying or following to join such an alien, and (iii) an alien who is a national of Canada or Mexico, who maintains actual residence and place of abode in the country of nationality, who is described in clause (i) except that the alien's course of study may be full or part-time, and who commutes to the United States institution or place of study from Canada or Mexico;

(N) (i) the parent of an alien accorded the status of special immigrant under paragraph (27)(I)(i) (or under analogous authority under paragraph (27)(L)), but only if and while the alien is a child, or

(ii) a child of such parent or of an alien accorded the status of a special immigrant under clause (ii), (iii), or (iv) of paragraph (27)(I) (or under analogous authority under paragraph (27)(L));

(O) an alien who—

(i) has extraordinary ability in the sciences, arts, education, business, or athletics which has been demonstrated by sustained national or international acclaim or, with regard to motion picture and television productions a demonstrated record of extraordinary achievement, and whose achievements have been recognized in the field through extensive documentation, and seeks to enter the United States to continue work in the area of extraordinary ability;

(ii) (I) seeks to enter the United States temporarily and solely for the purpose of accompanying and assisting in the artistic or athletic performance by an alien who is admitted under clause (i) for a specific event or events,

(II) is an integral part of such actual performance,

(III) (a) has critical skills and experience with such alien which are not of a general nature and which cannot be performed by other individuals, or (b) in the case of a motion picture or television production, has skills and experience with such alien which are not of a general nature and which are critical either based on a pre-existing longstanding working relationship or, with respect to the specific production, because significant production (including pre- and post-production work) will take place both inside and outside the United States and the continuing participation of the alien is essential to the successful completion of the production, and

(IV) has a foreign residence which the alien has no intention of abandoning; or

(iii) is the alien spouse or child of an alien described in clause (i) or (ii) and is accompanying, or following to join, the alien;

(P) an alien having a foreign residence which the alien has no intention of abandoning who—

(i) (a) is described in section 214(c)(4)(A) [8 USCS § 1184(c)(4)(A)] (relating to athletes), or (b) is described in section 214(c)(4)(B) [8 USCS § 1184(c)(4)(B)] (relating to entertainment groups);

(ii) (I) performs as an artist or entertainer, individually or as part of a group, or is an integral part of the performance of such a group, and

(II) seeks to enter the United States temporarily and solely for the purpose of performing as such an artist or entertainer or with such a group under a reciprocal exchange program which is between an organization or organizations in the United States and an organization or organizations in one or more foreign states and which provides for the temporary exchange of artists and entertainers, or groups of artists and entertainers;

(iii) (I) performs as an artist or entertainer, individually or as part of a group, or is an integral part of the performance of such a group, and

(II) seeks to enter the United States temporarily and solely to perform, teach, or coach as such an artist or entertainer or with such a group under a commercial or noncommercial program that is culturally unique; or

(iv) is the spouse or child of an alien described in clause (i), (ii), or (iii) and is accompanying, or following to join, the alien;

(Q) an alien having a residence in a foreign country which he has no intention of abandoning who is coming temporarily (for a period not to exceed 15 months) to the United States as a participant in an international cultural exchange program approved by the Secretary of Homeland Security for the purpose of providing practical training, employment, and the sharing of the history, culture, and traditions of the country of the alien's nationality and who will be employed under the same wages and working conditions as domestic workers;

(R) an alien, and the spouse and children of the alien if accompanying or following to join the alien, who—

(i) for the 2 years immediately preceding the time of application for admission, has been a member of a religious denomination having a bona fide nonprofit, religious organization in the United States; and

(ii) seeks to enter the United States for a period not to exceed 5 years to perform the work described in subclause (I), (II), or (III) of paragraph (27)(C)(ii);

(S) subject to section 214(k) [8 USCS § 1184(k)], an alien—

(i) who the Attorney General determines—

(I) is in possession of critical reliable information concerning a criminal organization or enterprise;

(II) is willing to supply or has supplied such information to Federal or State law enforcement authorities or a Federal or State court; and

(III) whose presence in the United States the Attorney General determines is essential to the success of an authorized criminal investigation or the successful prosecution of an individual involved in the criminal organization or enterprise; or

(ii) who the Secretary of State and the Attorney General jointly determine—

(I) is in possession of critical reliable information concerning a terrorist organization, enterprise, or operation;

(II) is willing to supply or has supplied such information to Federal law enforcement authorities or a Federal court;

(III) will be or has been placed in danger as a result of providing such information; and

(IV) is eligible to receive a reward under section 36(a) of the State Department Basic Authorities Act of 1956 [22 USCS § 2708(a)],

and, if the Attorney General (or with respect to clause (ii), the Secretary of State and the Attorney General jointly) considers it to be appropriate, the spouse, married and unmarried sons and daughters, and parents of an alien described in clause (i) or (ii) if accompanying, or following to join, the alien;

(T) (i) subject to section 214(o) [8 USCS § 1184(o)], an alien who the Secretary of Homeland Security, or in the case of subclause (III)(aa) the Secretary of Homeland Security, in consultation with the Attorney General, determines—

(I) is or has been a victim of a severe form of trafficking in persons, as defined in section 103 of the Trafficking Victims Protection Act of 2000 [22 USCS § 7102];

(II) is physically present in the United States, American Samoa, or the Commonwealth of the Northern Mariana Islands, or at a port of entry thereto, on account of such trafficking, including physical presence on account of the alien having been allowed entry into the United States for participation in investigative or judicial processes associated with an act or a perpetrator of trafficking;

(III) (aa) has complied with any reasonable request for assistance in the Federal, State, or local investigation or prosecution of acts of trafficking or the investigation of crime where acts of trafficking are at least one central reason for the commission of that crime;

(bb) in consultation with the Attorney General, as appropriate, is unable to cooperate with a request described in item (aa) due to physical or psychological trauma; or

(cc) has not attained 18 years of age; and

(IV) [the alien] would suffer extreme hardship involving unusual and severe harm upon removal; and

(ii) if accompanying, or following to join, the alien described in clause (i)—

(I) in the case of an alien described in clause (i) who is under 21 years of age, the spouse, children, unmarried siblings under 18 years of age on the date on which such alien applied for status under such clause, and parents of such alien;

(II) in the case of an alien described in clause (i) who is 21 years of age or older, the spouse and children of such alien; or

(III) any parent or unmarried sibling under 18 years of age, or any adult or minor children of a derivative beneficiary of the alien, as of an alien described in subclause (I) or (II) who the Secretary of Homeland Security, in consultation with the law enforcement officer investigating a severe form of trafficking, determines faces a present danger of retaliation as a result of the alien's escape from the severe form of trafficking or cooperation with law enforcement.

(U) (i) subject to section 214(p) [8 USCS § 1184(p)], an alien who files a petition for status under this subparagraph, if the Secretary of Homeland Security determines that—

(I) the alien has suffered substantial physical or mental abuse as a result of having been a victim of criminal activity described in clause (iii);

(II) the alien (or in the case of an alien child under the age of 16, the parent, guardian, or next friend of the alien) possesses information concerning criminal activity described in clause (iii);

(III) the alien (or in the case of an alien child under the age of 16, the parent, guardian, or next friend of the alien) has been helpful, is being helpful, or is likely to be helpful to a Federal, State, or local law enforcement official, to a Federal, State, or local prosecutor, to a Federal or State judge, to the Service, or to other Federal, State, or local authorities investigating or prosecuting criminal activity described in clause (iii); and

(IV) the criminal activity described in clause (iii) violated the laws of the United States or occurred in the United States (including in Indian country and military installations) or the territories and possessions of the United States;

(ii) if accompanying, or following to join, the alien described in clause (i)—

(I) in the case of an alien described in clause (i) who is under 21 years of age, the spouse, children, unmarried siblings under 18 years of age on the date on which such alien applied for status under such clause, and parents of such alien; or

(II) in the case of an alien described in clause (i) who is 21 years of age or older, the spouse and children of such alien; and

(iii) the criminal activity referred to in this clause is that involving one or more of the following or any similar activity in violation of Federal, State, or local criminal law: rape; torture; trafficking; incest; domestic violence; sexual assault; abusive sexual contact; prostitution; sexual exploitation; stalking; female genital mutilation; being held hostage; peonage; involuntary servitude; slave trade; kidnapping; abduction; unlawful criminal restraint; false imprisonment; blackmail; extortion; manslaughter; murder; felonious assault; witness tampering; obstruction of justice; perjury; fraud in foreign labor contracting (as defined in section 1351 of title 18, United States Code); or attempt, conspiracy, or solicitation to commit any of the above mentioned crimes; or

(V) subject to section 214(q) [8 USCS § 1184(q)], an alien who is the beneficiary (including a child of the principal alien, if eligible to receive a visa under section 203(d) [8 USCS § 1153(d)]) of a petition to accord a status under section 203(a)(2)(A) [8 USCS § 1153(a)(2)(A)] that was filed with the Attorney General under section 204 [8 USCS § 1154] on or before the date of the enactment of the Legal Immigration Family Equity Act [enacted Dec. 21, 2000], if—

(i) such petition has been pending for 3 years or more; or

(ii) such petition has been approved, 3 years or more have elapsed since such filing date, and—

(I) an immigrant visa is not immediately available to the alien because of a waiting list of applicants for visas under section 203(a)(2)(A) [8 USCS § 1153(a)(2)(A)]; or

(II) the alien's application for an immigrant visa, or the alien's application for adjustment of status under section 245 [8 USCS § 1255], pursuant to the approval of such petition, remains pending.

(16) The term "immigrant visa" means an immigrant visa required by this Act and properly issued by a consular officer at his office outside of the United States to an eligible immigrant under the provisions of this Act.

(17) The term "immigration laws" includes this Act and all laws, conventions, and treaties of the United States relating to the immigration, exclusion, deportation, expulsion, or removal of aliens.

(18) The term "immigration officer" means any employee or class of employees of the Service or of the United States designated by the Attorney General, individually or by regulation, to perform the functions of an immigration officer specified by this Act or any section thereof.

(19) The term "ineligible to citizenship," when used in reference to any individual, means, notwithstanding the provisions of any treaty relating to military service, an individual who is, or was at any time, permanently debarred from becoming a citizen of the United States under section 3(a) of the Selective Training and Service Act of 1940, as amended (54 Stat. 885; 55 Stat. 844), or under section 4(a) of the Selective Service Act of 1948, as amended (62 Stat. 605; 65 Stat. 76) [section 4(a) of the Military Selective Service Act, 50 USCS § 3803(a)], or under any section of this Act, or any other Act, or under any law amendatory of, supplementary to, or in substitution for, any of such sections or Acts.

(20) The term "lawfully admitted for permanent residence" means the status of having been lawfully accorded the privilege of residing permanently in the United States as an immigrant in accordance with the immigration laws, such status not having changed.

(21) The term "national" means a person owing permanent allegiance to a state.

(22) The term "national of the United States" means (A) a citizen of the United States, or (B) a person who, though not a citizen of the United States, owes permanent allegiance to the United States.

(23) The term "naturalization" means the conferring of nationality of a state upon a person after birth, by any means whatsoever.

(24) [Repealed]

(25) The term "noncombatant service" shall not include service in which the individual is not subject to military discipline, court martial, or does not wear the uniform of any branch of the armed forces.

(26) The term "nonimmigrant visa" means a visa properly issued to an alien as an eligible nonimmigrant by a competent officer as provided in this Act.

(27) The term "special immigrant" means—

(A) an immigrant, lawfully admitted for permanent residence, who is returning from a temporary visit abroad;

(B) an immigrant who was a citizen of the United States and may, under section 324(a) or 327 of title III [8 USCS §§ 1435(a) or 1438], apply for reacquisition of citizenship;

(C) an immigrant, and the immigrant's spouse and children if accompanying or following to join the immigrant, who—

(i) for at least 2 years immediately preceding the time of application for admission, has been a member of a religious denomination having a bona fide nonprofit, religious organization in the United States;

(ii) seeks to enter the United States—

(I) solely for the purpose of carrying on the vocation of a minister of that religious denomination,

(II) before September 30, 2015, in order to work for the organization at the request of the organization in a professional capacity in a religious vocation or occupation, or

(III) before September 30, 2015, in order to work for the organization (or for a bona fide organization which is affiliated with the religious denomination and is exempt from taxation as an organization described in section 501(c)(3) of the Internal Revenue Code of 1986 [26 USCS § 501(c)(3)]) at the request of the organization in a religious vocation or occupation; and

(iii) has been carrying on such vocation, professional work, or other work continuously for at least the 2-year period described in clause (i);

(D) an immigrant who—

(i) is an employee, or an honorably retired former employee, of the United States Government abroad, or of the American Institute in Taiwan, and who has performed faithful service for a total of fifteen years, or more, and his accompanying spouse and children: Provided, That the principal officer of a Foreign Service establishment (or, in the case of the American Institute in Taiwan, the Director thereof), in his discretion, shall have recommended the granting of special immigrant status to such alien in exceptional circumstances and the Secretary of State approves such recommendation and finds that it is in the national interest to grant such status; or

(ii) is the surviving spouse or child of an employee of the United States Government abroad: Provided, That the employee performed faithful service for a total of not less than 15 years or was killed in the line of duty;

(E) an immigrant, and his accompanying spouse and children, who is or has been an employee of the Panama Canal Company or Canal Zone Government before the date on which the Panama Canal Treaty of 1977 (as described in section 3(a)(1) of the Panama Canal Act of 1979 [22 USCS § 3602(a)(1)]) enters into force, who was resident in the Canal Zone on the effective date of the exchange of instruments of ratification of such Treaty, and who has performed faithful service as such an employee for one year or more;

(F) an immigrant, and his accompanying spouse and children, who is a Panamanian national and (i) who, before the date on which such Panama Canal Treaty of 1977 enters into force, has been honorably retired from United States Government employment in the Canal Zone with a total of 15 years or more of faithful service, or (ii) who, on the date on which such Treaty enters into force, has been employed by the United States Government in the Canal Zone with a total of 15 years or more of faithful service and who subsequently is honorably retired from such employment or continues to be employed by the United States Government in an area of the former Canal Zone;

(G) an immigrant, and his accompanying spouse and children, who was an employee of the Panama Canal Company or Canal Zone Government on the effective date of the exchange of instruments of ratification of such Panama Canal Treaty of 1977, who has performed faithful service for five years or more as such an employee, and whose personal safety, or the personal safety of whose spouse or children, as a direct result of such Treaty, is reasonably placed in danger because of the special nature of any of that employment;

(H) an immigrant, and his accompanying spouse and children, who—

(i) has graduated from a medical school or has qualified to practice medicine in a foreign state,

(ii) was fully and permanently licensed to practice medicine in a State on January 9, 1978, and was practicing medicine in a State on that date,

(iii) entered the United States as a nonimmigrant under subsection (a)(15)(H) or (a)(15)(J) before January 10, 1978, and

(iv) has been continuously present in the United States in the practice or study of medicine since the date of such entry;

(I) (i) an immigrant who is the unmarried son or daughter of an officer or employee, or of a former officer or employee, of an international organization described in paragraph (15)(G)(i), and who (I) while maintaining the status of a nonimmigrant under paragraph (15)(G)(iv) or paragraph (15)(N), has resided and been physically present in the United States for periods totaling at least one-half of the seven years before the date of application for a visa or for adjustment of status to a status under this subparagraph and for a period or periods aggregating at least seven years between the ages of five and 21 years, and (II) applies for a visa or adjustment of status under this subparagraph no later than his twenty-fifth birthday or six months after the date of enactment of the Immigration Technical Corrections Act of 1988 [enacted Oct. 24, 1988], whichever is later;

(ii) an immigrant who is the surviving spouse of a deceased officer or employee of such an international organization, and who (I) while maintaining the status of a nonimmigrant under paragraph (15)(G)(iv) or paragraph (15)(N), has resided and been physically present in the United States for periods totaling at least one-half of the seven years before the date of application for a visa or for adjustment of status to a status under this subparagraph and for a period or periods aggregating at least 15 years before the date of the death of such officer or employee, and (II) files a petition for status under this subparagraph no later than six months after the date of such death or six months after the date of enactment of the Immigration Technical Corrections Act of 1988 [enacted Oct. 24, 1988], whichever is later;

(iii) an immigrant who is a retired officer or employee of such an international organization, and who (I) while maintaining the status of a nonimmigrant under paragraph (15)(G)(iv), has resided and been physically present in the United States for periods totaling at least one-half of the seven years before the date of application for a visa or for adjustment of status to a status under this subparagraph and for a period or periods aggregating at least 15 years before the date of the officer or employee's retirement from any such international organization, and (II) files a petition for status under this subparagraph no later than six months after the date of such retirement or six months after the date of enactment of the Immigration and Nationality Technical Corrections Act of 1994 [enacted Oct. 25, 1994], whichever is later; or

(iv) an immigrant who is the spouse of a retired officer or employee accorded the status of special immigrant under clause (iii), accompanying or following to join such retired officer or employee as a member of his immediate family;

(J) an immigrant who is present in the United States—

(i) who has been declared dependent on a juvenile court located in the United States or whom such a court has legally committed to, or placed under the custody of, an agency or department of a State, or an individual or entity appointed by a State or juvenile court located in the United States, and whose reunification with 1 or both of the immigrant's parents is not viable due to abuse, neglect, abandonment, or a similar basis found under State law;

(ii) for whom it has been determined in administrative or judicial proceedings that it would not be in the alien's best interest to be returned to the alien's or parent's previous country of nationality or country of last habitual residence; and

(iii) in whose case the Secretary of Homeland Security consents to the grant of special immigrant juvenile status, except that—

(I) no juvenile court has jurisdiction to determine the custody status or placement of an alien in the custody of the Secretary of Health and Human Services unless the Secretary of Health and Human Services specifically consents to such jurisdiction; and

(II) no natural parent or prior adoptive parent of any alien provided special immigrant status under this subparagraph shall thereafter, by virtue of such parentage, be accorded any right, privilege, or status under this Act;

(K) an immigrant who has served honorably on active duty in the Armed Forces of the United States after October 15, 1978, and after original lawful enlistment outside the United States (under a treaty or agreement in effect on the date of the enactment of this subparagraph) for a period or periods aggregating—

(i) 12 years and who, if separated from such service, was never separated except under honorable conditions, or

(ii) 6 years, in the case of an immigrant who is on active duty at the time of seeking special immigrant status under this subparagraph and who has reenlisted to incur a total active duty service obligation of at least 12 years,

and the spouse or child of any such immigrant if accompanying or following to join the immigrant, but only if the executive department under which the immigrant serves or served recommends the granting of special immigrant status to the immigrant;

(L) an immigrant who would be described in clause (i), (ii), (iii), or (iv) of subparagraph (I) if any reference in such a clause—

(i) to an international organization described in paragraph (15)(G)(i) were treated as a reference to the North Atlantic Treaty Organization (NATO);

(ii) to a nonimmigrant under paragraph (15)(G)(iv) were treated as a reference to a nonimmigrant classifiable under NATO-6 (as a member of a civilian component accompanying a force entering in accordance with the provisions of the NATO Status-of-Forces Agreement, a member of a civilian component attached to or employed by an Allied Headquarters under the "Protocol on the Status of International Military Headquarters" set up pursuant to the North Atlantic Treaty, or as a dependent); and

(iii) to the Immigration Technical Corrections Act of 1988 or to the Immigration and Nationality Technical Corrections Act of 1994 were a reference to the American Competitiveness and Workforce Improvement Act of 1998[; or]

(M) subject to the numerical limitations of section 203(b)(4) [8 USCS § 1153(b)(4)], an immigrant who seeks to enter the United States to work as a broadcaster in the United States for the International Broadcasting Bureau of the Broadcasting Board of Governors [United States Agency for Global Media], or for a grantee of the Broadcasting Board of Governors [United States Agency for Global Media], and the immigrant's accompanying spouse and children.

(28) The term "organization" means, but is not limited to, an organization, corporation, company, partnership, association, trust, foundation or fund; and includes a group of persons, whether or not incorporated, permanently or temporarily associated together with joint action on any subject or subjects.

(29) The term "outlying possessions of the United States" means American Samoa and Swains Island.

(30) The term "passport" means any travel document issued by competent authority showing the bearer's origin, identity, and nationality if any, which is valid for the admission of the bearer into a foreign country.

(31) The term "permanent" means a relationship of continuing or lasting nature, as distinguished from temporary, but a relationship may be permanent even though it is one that may be dissolved eventually at the instance either of the United States or of the individual, in accordance with law.

(32) The term "profession" shall include but not be limited to architects, engineers, lawyers, physicians, surgeons, and teachers in elementary or secondary schools, colleges, academies, or seminaries.

(33) The term "residence" means the place of general abode; the place of general abode of a person means his principal, actual dwelling place in fact, without regard to intent.

(34) The term "Service" means the Immigration and Naturalization Service of the Department of Justice.

(35) The term [terms] "spouse," "wife," or "husband" do not include a spouse, wife, or husband by reason of any marriage ceremony where the contracting parties thereto are not physically present in the presence of each other, unless the marriage shall have been consummated.

(36) The term "State" includes the District of Columbia, Puerto Rico, Guam, the Virgin Islands of the United States, and the Commonwealth of the Northern Mariana Islands.

(37) The term "totalitarian party" means an organization which advocates the establishment in the United States of a totalitarian dictatorship or totalitarianism. The terms "totalitarian dictatorship" and "totalitarianism" mean and refer to systems of government not representative in fact, characterized by (A) the existence of a single political party, organized on a dictatorial basis, with so close an identity between such party and its policies and the governmental policies of the country in which it exists, that the party and the government constitute an indistinguishable unit, and (B) the forcible suppression of opposition to such party.

(38) The term "United States," except as otherwise specifically herein provided, when used in a geographical sense, means the continental United States, Alaska, Hawaii, Puerto Rico, Guam, the Virgin Islands of the United States, and the Commonwealth of the Northern Mariana Islands.

(39) The term "unmarried," when used in reference to any individual as of any time, means an individual who at such time is not married, whether or not previously married.

(40) The term "world communism" means a revolutionary movement, the purpose of which is to establish eventually a Communist totalitarian dictatorship in any or all the countries of the world through the medium of an internationally coordinated Communist political movement.

(41) The term "graduates of a medical school" means aliens who have graduated from a medical school or who have qualified to practice medicine in a foreign state, other than such aliens who are of national or international renown in the field of medicine.

(42) The term "refugee" means (A) any person who is outside any country of such person's nationality or, in the case of a person having no nationality, is outside any country in which such person last habitually resided, and who is unable or unwilling to return to, and is unable or unwilling to avail himself or herself of the protection of, that country because of persecution or a well-founded fear of persecution on account of race, religion, nationality, membership in a particular social group, or political opinion, or (B) in such special circumstances as the President after appropriate consultation (as defined in section 207(e) of this Act [8 USCS § 1157(e)]) may specify, any person who is within the country of such person's nationality or, in the case of a person having no nationality, within the country in which such person is habitually residing, and who is persecuted or who has a well-founded fear of persecution on account of race, religion, nationality, membership in a particular social group, or political opinion. The term "refugee" does not include any person who ordered, incited, assisted, or otherwise participated in the persecution of any person on account of race, religion, nationality, membership in a particular social group, or political opinion. For purposes of determinations under this Act, a person who has been forced to abort a pregnancy or to undergo involuntary sterilization, or who has been persecuted for failure or refusal to undergo such a procedure or for other resistance to a coercive population control program, shall be deemed to have been persecuted on account of political opinion, and a person who has a well founded fear that he or she will be forced to undergo such a procedure or subject to persecution for such failure, refusal, or resistance shall be deemed to have a well founded fear of persecution on account of political opinion.

(43) The term "aggravated felony" means—

(A) murder, rape, or sexual abuse of a minor;

(B) illicit trafficking in a controlled substance (as defined in section 102 of the Controlled Substances Act [21 USCS § 802]), including a drug trafficking crime (as defined in section 924(c) of title 18, United States Code);

(C) illicit trafficking in firearms or destructive devices (as defined in section 921 of title 18, United States Code) or in explosive materials (as defined in section 841(c) of that title [18 USCS § 841(c)]);

(D) an offense described in section 1956 of title 18, United States Code (relating to laundering of monetary instruments) or section 1957 of that title [18 USCS §

1957] (relating to engaging in monetary transactions in property derived from specific unlawful activity) if the amount of the funds exceeded $10,000;

(E) an offense described in—

(i) section 842(h) or (i) of title 18, United States Code, or section 844(d), (e), (f), (g), (h), or (i) of that title [18 USCS § 844(d), (e), (f), (g), (h), or (i)] (relating to explosive materials offenses);

(ii) section 922(g)(1), (2), (3), (4), or (5), (j), (n), (o), (p), or (r) or 924(b) or (h) of title 18, United States Code (relating to firearms offenses); or

(iii) section 5861 of the Internal Revenue Code of 1986[26 USCS § 5861] (relating to firearms offenses);

(F) a crime of violence (as defined in section 16 of title 18, United States Code, but not including a purely political offense) for which the term of imprisonment [is] at least one year;

(G) a theft offense (including receipt of stolen property) or burglary offense for which the term of imprisonment [is] at least one year;

(H) an offense described in section 875, 876, 877, or 1202 of title 18, United States Code (relating to the demand for or receipt of ransom);

(I) an offense described in section 2251, 2251A, or 2252 of title 18, United States Code (relating to child pornography);

(J) an offense described in section 1962 of title 18, United States Code (relating to racketeer influenced corrupt organizations), or an offense described in section 1084 (if it is a second or subsequent offense) or 1955 of that title (relating to gambling offenses) [18 USCS § 1084 or 1955], for which a sentence of one year imprisonment or more may be imposed;

(K) an offense that—

(i) relates to the owning, controlling, managing, or supervising of a prostitution business;

(ii) is described in section 2421, 2422, or 2423 of title 18, United States Code (relating to transportation for the purpose of prostitution) if committed for commercial advantage; or

(iii) is described in any of sections 1581–1585 or 1588–1591 of title 18, United States Code (relating to peonage, slavery, involuntary servitude, and trafficking in persons);

(L) an offense described in—

(i) section 793 (relating to gathering or transmitting national defense information), 798 (relating to disclosure of classified information), 2153 (relating to sabotage) or 2381 or 2382 (relating to treason) of title 18, United States Code;

(ii) section 601 of the National Security Act of 1947 [50 USCS §3121] (relating to protecting the identity of undercover intelligence agents);

(iii) section 601 of the National Security Act of 1947 [50 USCS §3121] (relating to protecting the identity of undercover agents);

(M) an offense that—

(i) involves fraud or deceit in which the loss to the victim or victims exceeds $10,000; or

(ii) is described in section 7201 of the Internal Revenue Code of 1986 [26 USCS § 7201] (relating to tax evasion) in which the revenue loss to the Government exceeds $10,000;

(N) an offense described in paragraph (1)(A) or (2) of section 274(a) [8 USCS § 1324(a)(1)(A) or (2)] (relating to alien smuggling), except in the case of a first offense for which the alien has affirmatively shown that the alien committed the offense for the purpose of assisting, abetting, or aiding only the alien's spouse, child, or parent (and no other individual) to violate a provision of this Act[;]

(O) an offense described in section 275(a) or 276 [8 USCS § 1325(a) or 1326] committed by an alien who was previously deported on the basis of a conviction for an offense described in another subparagraph of this paragraph;

(P) an offense (i) which either is falsely making, forging, counterfeiting, mutilating, or altering a passport or instrument in violation of section 1543 of title 18, United States Code, or is described in section 1546(a) of such title [18 USCS § 1546(a)] (relating to document fraud) and (ii) for which the term of imprisonment is at least 12 months, except in the case of a first offense for which the alien has affirmatively shown that the alien committed the offense for the purpose of assisting, abetting, or aiding only the alien's spouse, child, or parent (and no other individual) to violate a provision of this Act;

(Q) an offense relating to a failure to appear by a defendant for service of sentence if the underlying offense is punishable by imprisonment for a term of 5 years or more;

(R) an offense relating to commercial bribery, counterfeiting, forgery, or trafficking in vehicles the identification numbers of which have been altered for which the term of imprisonment is at least one year;

(S) an offense relating to obstruction of justice, perjury or subornation of perjury, or bribery of a witness, for which the term of imprisonment is at least one year;

(T) an offense relating to a failure to appear before a court pursuant to a court order to answer to or dispose of a charge of a felony for which a sentence of 2 years' imprisonment or more may be imposed; and

(U) an attempt or conspiracy to commit an offense described in this paragraph.

The term applies to an offense described in this paragraph whether in violation of Federal or State law and applies to such an offense in violation of the law of a foreign country for which the term of imprisonment was completed within the previous 15 years. Notwithstanding any other provision of law (including any effective date), the term applies regardless of whether the conviction was entered before, on, or after the date of enactment of this paragraph.

(44) (A) The term "managerial capacity" means an assignment within an organization in which the employee primarily—

(i) manages the organization, or a department, subdivision, function, or component of the organization;

(ii) supervises and controls the work of other supervisory, professional, or managerial employees, or manages an essential function within the organization, or a department or subdivision of the organization;

(iii) if another employee or other employees are directly supervised, has the authority to hire and fire or recommend those as well as other personnel actions (such as promotion and leave authorization) or, if no other employee is directly supervised, functions at a senior level within the organizational hierarchy or with respect to the function managed; and

(iv) exercises discretion over the day-to-day operations of the activity or function for which the employee has authority.

A first-line supervisor is not considered to be acting in a managerial capacity merely by virtue of the supervisor's supervisory duties unless the employees supervised are professional.

(B) The term "executive capacity" means an assignment within an organization in which the employee primarily—

(i) directs the management of the organization or a major component or function of the organization;

(ii) establishes the goals and policies of the organization, component, or function;

(iii) exercises wide latitude in discretionary decision-making; and

(iv) receives only general supervision or direction from higher level executives, the board of directors, or stockholders of the organization.

(C) If staffing levels are used as a factor in determining whether an individual is acting in a managerial or executive capacity, the Attorney General shall take into account the reasonable needs of the organization, component, or function in light of the overall purpose and stage of development of the organization, component, or function. An individual shall not be considered to be acting in a managerial or executive capacity (as previously defined) merely on the basis of the number of employees that the individual supervises or has supervised or directs or has directed.

(45) The term "substantial" means, for purposes of paragraph (15)(E) with reference to trade or capital, such an amount of trade or capital as is established by the Secretary of State, after consultation with appropriate agencies of Government.

(46) The term "extraordinary ability" means, for purposes of section 101(a)(15)(O)(i) [8 USCS § 1101(a)(15)(O)(i)], in the case of the arts, distinction.

(47) (A) The term "order of deportation" means the order of the special inquiry officer, or other such administrative officer to whom the Attorney General has delegated the responsibility for determining whether an alien is deportable, concluding that the alien is deportable or ordering deportation.

(B) The order described under subparagraph (A) shall become final upon the earlier of—

(i) a determination by the Board of Immigration Appeals affirming such order; or

(ii) the expiration of the period in which the alien is permitted to seek review of such order by the Board of Immigration Appeals.

(48) (A) The term "conviction" means, with respect to an alien, a formal judgment of guilt of the alien entered by a court or, if adjudication of guilt has been withheld, where—

(i) a judge or jury has found the alien guilty or the alien has entered a plea of guilty or nolo contendere or has admitted sufficient facts to warrant a finding of guilt, and

(ii) the judge has ordered some form of punishment, penalty, or restraint on the alien's liberty to be imposed.

(B) Any reference to a term of imprisonment or a sentence with respect to an offense is deemed to include the period of incarceration or confinement ordered by a court of law regardless of any suspension of the imposition or execution of that imprisonment or sentence in whole or in part.

(49) The term "stowaway" means any alien who obtains transportation without the consent of the owner, charterer, master or person in command of any vessel or aircraft through concealment aboard such vessel or aircraft. A passenger who boards with a valid ticket is not to be considered a stowaway.

(50) The term "intended spouse" means any alien who meets the criteria set forth in section 204(a)(1)(A)(iii)(II)(aa)(BB), 204(a)(1)(B)(ii)(II)(aa)(BB), or 240A(b)(2)(A)(i)(III) [8 USCS § 1154(a)(1)(A)(iii)(II)(aa)(BB), 1154(a)(1)(B)(ii)(II)(aa)(BB), or 1229b(b)(2)(A)(i)(III)].

(51) The term "VAWA self-petitioner" means an alien, or a child of the alien, who qualifies for relief under—

(A) clause (iii), (iv), or (vii) of section 204(a)(1)(A) [8 USCS § 1154(a)(1)(A)];

(B) clause (ii) or (iii) of section 204(a)(1)(B) [8 USCS § 1154(a)(1)(B)];

(C) section 216(c)(4)(C) [8 USCS § 1186(c)(4)(C)];

(D) the first section of Public Law 89-732 (8 U.S.C. 1255 note) (commonly known as the Cuban Adjustment Act) as a child or spouse who has been battered or subjected to extreme cruelty;

(E) section 902(d)(1)(B) of the Haitian Refugee Immigration Fairness Act of 1998 (8 U.S.C. 1255 note);

(F) section 202(d)(1) of the Nicaraguan Adjustment and Central American Relief Act [8 USCS § 1255 note]; or

(G) section 309 of the Illegal Immigration Reform and Immigrant Responsibility Act of 1996 (division C of Public Law 104-208) [note to this section].

(52) The term "accredited language training program" means a language training program that is accredited by an accrediting agency recognized by the Secretary of Education.

(b) As used in titles I and II [8 USCS §§ 1101 et seq., 1151 et seq.]—

(1) The term "child" means an unmarried person under twenty-one years of age who is—

(A) a child born in wedlock;

(B) a stepchild, whether or not born out of wedlock, provided the child had not reached the age of eighteen years at the time the marriage creating the status of stepchild occurred;

(C) a child legitimated under the law of the child's residence or domicile, or under the law of the father's residence or domicile, whether in or outside the United States, if such legitimation takes place before the child reaches the age of eighteen years and the child is in the legal custody of the legitimating parent or parents at the time of such legitimation;

(D) a child born out of wedlock, by, through whom, or on whose behalf a status, privilege, or benefit is sought by virtue of the relationship of the child to its natural mother or to its natural father if the father has or had a bona fide parent-child relationship with the person;

(E) (i) a child adopted while under the age of sixteen years if the child has been in the legal custody of, and has resided with, the adopting parent or parents for at least two years or if the child has been battered or subject to extreme cruelty by the adopting parent or by a family member of the adopting parent residing in the same household: Provided, That no natural parent of any such adopted child shall thereafter, by virtue of such parentage, be accorded any right, privilege, or status under this Act; or

(ii) subject to the same proviso as in clause (i), a child who: (I) is a natural sibling of a child described in clause (i) or subparagraph (F)(i); (II) was adopted by the adoptive parent or parents of the sibling described in such clause or subparagraph; and (III) is otherwise described in clause (i), except that the child was adopted while under the age of 18 years;

(F) (i) a child, under the age of sixteen at the time a petition is filed in his behalf to accord a classification as an immediate relative under section 201(b) [8 USCS § 1151(b)], who is an orphan because of the death or disappearance of, abandonment or desertion by, or separation or loss from, both parents, or for whom the sole or surviving parent is incapable of providing the proper care and has in writing irrevocably released the child for emigration and adoption; who has been adopted abroad by a United States citizen and spouse jointly, or by an unmarried United States citizen who is at least 25 years of age, at least 1 of whom personally saw and observed the child before or during the adoption proceedings; or who is coming to the United States for adoption by a United States citizen and spouse jointly, or by an unmarried United States citizen at least twenty-five years of age, who have or has complied with the preadoption requirements, if any, of the child's proposed residence: Provided, That the Attorney General is satisfied that proper care will be furnished the child if admitted to the United States: Provided further, That no natural parent or prior adoptive parent of any such child shall thereafter, by virtue of such parentage, be accorded any right, privilege, or status under this Act; or

(ii) subject to the same provisos as in clause (i), a child who: (I) is a natural sibling of a child described in clause (i) or subparagraph (E)(i); (II) has been adopted abroad, or is coming to the United States for adoption, by the adoptive parent (or prospective adoptive parent) or parents of the sibling described in such clause or subparagraph; and (III) is otherwise described in clause (i), except that the child is under the age of 18 at the time a petition is filed in his or her behalf to accord a classification as an immediate relative under section 201(b) [8 USCS § 1151(b)]; or

(G) (i) a child, younger than 16 years of age at the time a petition is filed on the child's behalf to accord a classification as an immediate relative under section 201(b) [8 USCS § 1151(b)], who has been adopted in a foreign state that is a party to the Convention on Protection of Children and Co-operation in Respect of Intercountry Adoption, done at The Hague on May 29, 1993, or who is emigrating from such a foreign state to be adopted in the United States by a United States citizen and spouse jointly or by an unmarried United States citizen who is at least 25 years of age, Provided, That—

(I) the Secretary of Homeland Security is satisfied that proper care will be furnished the child if admitted to the United States;

(II) the child's natural parents (or parent, in the case of a child who has one sole or surviving parent because of the death or disappearance of, abandonment or desertion by, the other parent), or other persons or institutions that retain legal custody of the child, have freely given their written irrevocable consent to the termination of their legal relationship with the child, and to the child's emigration and adoption;

(III) in the case of a child having two living natural parents, the natural parents are incapable of providing proper care for the child;

(IV) the Secretary of Homeland Security is satisfied that the purpose of the adoption is to form a bona fide parent-child relationship, and the parent-child relationship of the child and the natural parents has been terminated (and in carrying out both obligations under this subclause the Secretary of Homeland Security may consider whether there is a petition pending to confer immigrant status on one or both of such natural parents); and

(V) in the case of a child who has not been adopted—

(aa) the competent authority of the foreign state has approved the child's emigration to the United States for the purpose of adoption by the prospective adoptive parent or parents; and

(bb) the prospective adoptive parent or parents has or have complied with any pre-adoption requirements of the child's proposed residence; and

(ii) except that no natural parent or prior adoptive parent of any such child shall thereafter, by virtue of such parentage, be accorded any right, privilege, or status under this chapter; or

(iii) subject to the same provisos as in clauses (i) and (ii), a child who—

(I) is a natural sibling of a child described in clause (i), subparagraph (E)(i), or subparagraph (F)(i);

(II) was adopted abroad, or is coming to the United States for adoption, by the adoptive parent (or prospective adoptive parent) or parents of the sibling described in clause (i), subparagraph (E)(i), or subparagraph (F)(i); and

(III) is otherwise described in clause (i), except that the child is younger than 18 years of age at the time a petition is filed on his or her behalf for classification as an immediate relative under section 201(b) [8 USCS § 1151(b)].

(2) The terms "parent," "father," or "mother" mean a parent, father, or mother only where the relationship exists by reason of any of the circumstances set forth in (1) above, except that, for purposes of paragraph (1)(F) (other than the second proviso therein) and paragraph (1)(G)(i) in the case of a child born out of wedlock described in paragraph (1)(D) (and not described in paragraph (1)(C)), the term "parent" does not include the natural father of the child if the father has disappeared or abandoned or deserted the child or if the father has in writing irrevocably released the child for emigration and adoption.

(3) The term "person" means an individual or an organization.

(4) The term "immigration judge" means an attorney whom the Attorney General appoints as an administrative judge within the Executive Office for Immigration Review, qualified to conduct specified classes of proceedings, including a hearing under section 240 [8 USCS § 1229a]. An immigration judge shall be subject to such supervision and shall perform such duties as the Attorney General shall prescribe, but shall not be employed by the Immigration and Naturalization Service.

(5) The term "adjacent islands" includes Saint Pierre, Miquelon, Cuba, the Dominican Republic, Haiti, Bermuda, the Bahamas, Barbados, Jamaica, the Windward and Leeward Islands, Trinidad, Martinique, and other British, French, and Netherlands territory or possessions in or bordering on the Caribbean Sea.

(c) As used in title III [8 USCS §§ 1401 et seq.]—

(1) The term "child" means an unmarried person under twenty-one years of age and includes a child legitimated under the law of the child's residence or domicile, or under the law of the father's residence or domicile, whether in the United States or elsewhere, and, except as otherwise provided in sections 320 and 321 of title III [8 USCS §§ 1431, 1432], a child adopted in the United States, if such legitimation or adoption takes place before the child reaches the age of 16 years (except to the extent that the child is described in subparagraph (E)(ii) or (F)(ii) of subsection (b)(1)), and the child is in the legal custody of the legitimating or adopting parent or parents at the time of such legitimation or adoption.

(2) The terms "parent," "father," and "mother" include in the case of a posthumous child a deceased parent, father, and mother.

(d) [Repealed]

(e) For the purposes of this Act—

(1) The giving, loaning, or promising of support or of money or any other thing of value to be used for advocating any doctrine shall constitute the advocating of such doctrine; but nothing in this paragraph shall be construed as an exclusive definition of advocating.

(2) The giving, loaning, or promising of support or of money or any other thing of value for any purpose to any organization shall be presumed to constitute affiliation therewith; but nothing in this paragraph shall be construed as an exclusive definition of affiliation.

(3) Advocating the economic, international, and governmental doctrines of world communism means advocating the establishment of a totalitarian Communist dictatorship in any or all of the countries of the world through the medium of an internationally coordinated Communist movement.

(f) For the purposes of this Act—

No person shall be regarded as, or found to be, a person of good moral character who, during the period for which good moral character is required to be established, is, or was—

(1) a habitual drunkard;

(2) [Repealed]

(3) a member of one or more of the classes of persons, whether inadmissible or not, described in paragraphs (2)(D), (6)(E), and (10)(A) of section 212(a) of this Act [8 USCS § 1182(a)]; or subparagraphs (A) and (B) of section 212(a)(2) [8 USCS § 1182(a)(2)] and subparagraph (C) thereof [of such section] (except as such paragraph relates to a single offense of simple possession of 30 grams or less of marihuana), if the offense described therein, for which such person was convicted or of which he admits the commission, was committed during such period;

(4) one whose income is derived principally from illegal gambling activities;

(5) one who has been convicted of two or more gambling offenses committed during such period;

(6) one who has given false testimony for the purpose of obtaining any benefits under this Act;

(7) one who during such period has been confined, as a result of conviction, to a penal institution for an aggregate period of one hundred and eighty days or more, regardless of whether the offense, or offenses, for which he has been confined were committed within or without such period;

(8) one who at any time has been convicted of an aggravated felony (as defined in subsection (a)(43)); or

(9) one who at any time has engaged in conduct described in section 212(a)(3)(E) [8 USCS § 1182(a)(3)(E)] (relating to assistance in Nazi persecution, participation in genocide, or commission of acts of torture or extrajudicial killings) or 212(a)(2)(G) [8 USCS § 1182(a)(2)(G)] (relating to severe violations of religious freedom).

The fact that any person is not within any of the foregoing classes shall not preclude a finding that for other reasons such person is or was not of good moral character. In the case of an alien who makes a false statement or claim of citizenship, or who registers to vote or votes in a Federal, State, or local election (including an initiative, recall, or referendum) in violation of a lawful restriction of such registration or voting to citizens, if each natural parent of the alien (or, in the case of an adopted alien, each adoptive parent of the alien) is or was a citizen (whether by birth or naturalization), the alien permanently resided in the United States prior to attaining the age of 16, and the alien reasonably believed at the time of such statement, claim, or violation that he or she was a citizen, no finding that the alien is, or was, not of good moral character may be made based on it.

(g) For the purposes of this Act any alien ordered deported or removed (whether before or after the enactment of this Act [enacted June 27, 1952]) who has left the United States, shall be considered to have been deported or removed in pursuance of law, irrespective of the source from which the expenses of his transportation were defrayed or of the place to which he departed.

(h) For purposes of section 212(a)(2)(E) [8 USCS § 1182(a)(2)(E)], the term "serious criminal offense" means—

(1) any felony;

(2) any crime of violence, as defined in section 16 of title 18 of the United States Code; or

(3) any crime of reckless driving or of driving while intoxicated or under the influence of alcohol or of prohibited substances if such crime involves personal injury to another.

(i) With respect to each nonimmigrant alien described in subsection (a)(15)(T)(i)—

(1) the Secretary of Homeland Security, the Attorney General, and other Government officials, where appropriate, shall provide the alien with a referral to a nongovernmental organization that would advise the alien regarding the alien's options while in the United States and the resources available to the alien; and

(2) the Secretary of Homeland Security shall, during the period the alien is in lawful temporary resident status under that subsection, grant the alien authorization to engage in employment in the United States and provide the alien with an "employment authorized" endorsement or other appropriate work permit.

HISTORY: (June 27, 1952, ch 477, Title I, § 101, 66 Stat. 166; Sept. 11, 1957, P. L. 85-316, §§ 1, 2, 71 Stat. 639; July 7, 1958, P. L. 85-508, § 22, 72 Stat. 351; March 18, 1959, P. L. 86-3, § 20(a), 73 Stat. 13; Sept. 21, 1961, P. L. 87-256, § 109(a), (b), 75 Stat. 534; Sept. 26, 1961, P. L. 87-301, §§ 1, 2, 7, 75 Stat. 650, 653; Oct. 3, 1965, P. L. 89-236, §§ 8, 24, 79 Stat. 916, 922; Nov. 2, 1966, P. L. 89-710, 80 Stat. 1104; April 7, 1970, P. L. 91-225, § 1, 84 Stat. 116; Dec. 16, 1975, P. L. 94-155, 89 Stat. 824; Oct. 12, 1976, P. L. 94-484, Title VI, § 601(b), (e), 90 Stat. 2301, 2302; Oct. 20, 1976, P. L. 94-571, § 7(a), 90 Stat. 2706; Oct. 12, 1976, P. L. 94-484, Title VI, § 602(c), as added Aug. 1, 1977, P. L. 95-83, Title III, § 307(q)(3), 91 Stat. 395; Aug. 17, 1977, P. L. 95-105, Title I, § 109(b)(3), 91 Stat 847; Sept. 27, 1979, P. L. 96-70, Title III, Ch 1, § 3201(a), 93 Stat. 496; March 17, 1980, P. L. 96-212, Title II, § 201(a), 94 Stat. 102; Dec. 29, 1981, P. L. 97-116, §§ 2, 5(d)(1), 18(a), 95 Stat. 1611, 1614, 1619; Oct. 30, 1984, Priv. L. 98-47, § 3, 98 Stat. 3435; Oct. 21, 1986, P. L. 99-505, § 1, 100 Stat. 1806; Nov. 6, 1986, P. L. 99-603, Title III, Part A, § 301(a), Part B, §§ 312, 315(a), 100 Stat. 3411, 3434, 3439; Nov. 14, 1986, P. L. 99-653, §§ 2, 3, 100 Stat. 3655; Oct. 1, 1988, P. L. 100-459, Title II, § 210(a), 102 Stat. 2203; Oct. 24, 1988, P. L. 100-525, §§ 2(o)(1), 8(b), 9(a), 102 Stat. 2613, 2617, 2619; Nov. 18, 1988, P. L. 100-690, Title VII, Subtitle J, § 7342, 102 Stat. 4469; Nov. 21, 1989, P. L. 101-162, Title VI, § 611(a), 103 Stat. 1038; Dec. 18, 1989, P. L. 101-238, § 3(a), 103 Stat. 2100; Feb. 16, 1990, P. L. 101-246, Title I, Part C, § 131(b), 104 Stat. 31; Nov. 29, 1990, P. L. 101-649, Title I, Subtitle B, Part 2, § 123, Subtitle D, §§ 151(a), 153(a), Subtitle E, § 161(f)(2)(A), Title II, Subtitle A, §§ 203(c), 204(a), (c), 205(c)(1), (d), (e), 206(c), 207(a), 208, 209, Title IV, § 407(a)(2), Title V, Subtitle A, §§ 501(a), 509(a), Title VI, § 603(a)(1), 104 Stat. 4995, 5004, 5005, 5012, 5018, 5019, 5020, 5023, 5026, 5027, 5040, 5048, 5051, 5082; Oct. 1, 1991, P. L. 102-110, § 2(a), 105 Stat. 555; Dec. 12, 1991, P. L. 102-232, Title II, §§ 203(a), 205(a)–(c), 206(b), (c)(1), (d), 207(b), 302(e)(8)(A), 303(a)(5)(A), (7)(A), 305(m)(1), 306(a)(1), 309(b)(1), 105 Stat. 1737, 1740, 1741, 1746, 1747, 1748, 1750, 1751, 1758; April 30, 1994, P. L. 103-236, Title I, Part C, § 162(h)(1), 108 Stat. 407; Sept. 13, 1994, P. L. 103-322, Title XIII, § 130003(a), 108 Stat. 2024; Oct. 5, 1994, P. L. 103-337, Div C, Title XXXVI, § 3605, 108 Stat. 3113; Oct. 25, 1994, P. L. 103-416, Title II, §§ 201, 202, 214, 219(a), 222(a), 108 Stat. 4310, 4311, 4314, 4316, 4320; Nov. 15, 1995, P. L. 104-51, § 1, 109 Stat. 467; April 24, 1996, P. L. 104-132, Title IV, Subtitle D, § 440(b), (e), 110 Stat. 1277; Sept. 30, 1996, P. L. 104-208, Div C, Title I, Subtitle A, § 104(a), Title III, Subtitle A, §§ 301(a), 308(d)(3)(A), (4)(A), (e)(3), (f)(1)(A), (B), Subtitle B, §§ 321(a), (b), 322(a)(1), (2)(A), Subtitle E, § 361(a), Subtitle F, § 371(a), Title VI, Subtitle A, § 601(a), Subtitle B, § 625(a)(2), Subtitle E, § 671(a)(3)(B), (b)(5), (e)(2), 110 Stat. 3009-555, 3009-575, 3009-617, 3009-620, 3009-621, 3009-627, 3009-629, 3009-644, 3009-645, 3009-689, 3009-700, 3009-721, 3009-722, 3009-723; Oct. 6, 1997, P. L. 105-54, § 1(a), 111 Stat. 1175; Nov. 26, 1997, P. L. 105-119, Title I, § 113, 111 Stat. 2460; Oct. 21, 1998, P. L. 105-277, Div C, Title IV, § 421, Div G, Title XXII, Ch 2, § 2222(e), 112 Stat. 2681-657, 2681-819; Oct. 30, 1998, P. L. 105-319, § 2(b), (d)(2), 112 Stat. 3014, 3015; Nov. 12, 1999, P. L. 106-95, § 2(a), (c), 113 Stat. 1312, 1316; Dec. 7, 1999, P. L. 106-139, § 1(a), (b)(1), 113 Stat. 1696; Oct. 6, 2000, P. L. 106-279, Title III, § 302(a), (c), 114 Stat. 838, 839; Oct. 28, 2000, P. L. 106-386, Div A, § 107(e)(1), (4), Div B, Title V, §§ 1503(a), 1513(b), 114 Stat. 1477, 1479, 1518, 1534; Oct. 30, 2000, P. L. 106-395, Title II, § 201(a)(1), 114 Stat. 1633; Nov. 1, 2000, P. L. 106-409, § 2(a), 114 Stat. 1787; Nov. 22, 2000, P. L. 106-536, § 1(a), 114 Stat. 2560; Dec. 21, 2000, P. L. 106-553, § 1(a)(2), 114 Stat. 2762; Jan. 16, 2002, P. L. 107-125, § 2(b), 115 Stat. 2403; Oct. 4, 2002, P. L. 107-234, § 1(4), 116 Stat. 1481; Nov. 2, 2002, P. L. 107-274, § 2(a), (b), 116 Stat. 1923; Sept. 3, 2003, P. L. 108-77, Title IV, § 402(a)(1), 117 Stat. 939; Oct. 15, 2003, P. L. 108-99, § 1, 117 Stat. 1176; Dec. 19, 2003, P. L. 108-193, §§ 4(b)(1), (5), 8(a)(1), 117 Stat. 2878, 2879, 2886; Dec. 10, 2004, P. L. 108-449, § 1(a)(2)(B), (3)(A), (b)(1), 118 Stat. 3469, 3470; Dec. 17, 2004, P. L. 108-458, Title V, Subtitle E, § 5504, 118 Stat. 3741; May 11, 2005, P. L. 109-13, Div B, Title V, § 501(a), 119 Stat. 321; Oct. 18, 2005, P. L. 109-90, Title V, § 536, 119 Stat. 2087; Jan. 5, 2006, P. L. 109-162, Title VIII, Subtitle A, §§ 801, 805(d), Subtitle B, § 811, Subtitle C, § 822(c)(1), 119 Stat. 3053, 3056, 3057, 3063; July 27, 2006, P. L. 109-248, Title IV, § 402(b), 120 Stat. 623; May 8, 2008, P. L. 110-229, Title VII, Subtitle A, § 702(j)(1)–(3), 122 Stat. 866; Oct. 10, 2008, P. L. 110-391, § 2(a), 122 Stat. 4193; Dec. 23, 2008, P. L. 110-457, Title II, Subtitle A, § 201(a), Subtitle D, § 235(d)(1), 122 Stat. 5052, 5079; March 20, 2009, P. L. 111-9, § 1, 123 Stat. 989; Oct. 28, 2009, P. L. 111-83, Title V, § 568(a)(1), 123 Stat. 2186; Nov. 30, 2010, P. L. 111-287, § 3, 124 Stat. 3058; Dec. 14, 2010, P. L. 111-306, § 1(a), 124 Stat. 3280; Sept. 28, 2012, P. L. 112-176, § 3, 126 Stat. 1325; March 7, 2013, P. L. 113-4, Title VIII, § 801, Title XII, Subtitle B, Part II, §§ 1221, 1222, 127 Stat. 110, 144; Jan. 17, 2014, P. L. 113-76, Div K, Title VII, § 7083, 128 Stat. 567; July 30, 2021, P.L. 117-31, Title IV, § 403(a), 135 Stat. 318; Dec. 23, 2022, P.L. 117-263, Div E, Title LIX, Subtitle A, § 5902(b), 136 Stat. 3440; Jan. 5, 2023, P.L. 117-360, § 2, 136 Stat. 6292.)

§ 102. [8 U.S.C. § 1102] Diplomatic and semidiplomatic immunities.

Except as otherwise provided in this Act, for so long as they continue in the nonimmigrant classes enumerated in this section, the provisions of this Act relating to ineligibility to receive visas and the removal of aliens shall not be construed to apply to nonimmigrants—

(1) within the class described in paragraph (15)(A)(i) of section 101(a) [8 USCS § 1101(a)(15)(A)(i)], except those provisions relating to reasonable requirements of passports and visas as a means of identification and documentation necessary to establish their qualifications under such paragraph (15)(A)(i) [8 USCS § 1101(a)(15)(A)(i)], and, under such rules and regulations as the President may deem to be necessary, the provisions of subparagraphs (A) through (C) of section 212(a)(3) [8 USCS § 1182(a)(3)(A)–(C)];

(2) within the class described in paragraph (15)(G)(i) of section 101(a) [8 USCS § 1101(a)(15)(G)(i)], except those provisions relating to reasonable requirements of passports and visas as a means of identification and documentation necessary to establish their qualifications under such paragraph (15)(G)(i) [8 USCS § 1101(a)(15)(G)(i)], and the provisions of subparagraphs (A) through (C) of section 212(a)(3) [8 USCS § 1182(a)(3)(A)–(C)]; and

(3) within the classes described in paragraphs (15)(A)(ii), (15)(G)(ii), (15)(G)(iii), or (15)(G)(iv) of section 101(a) [8 USCS § 1101(a)(15)(A)(ii), (15)(G)(ii), (15)(G)(iii), or (15)(G)(iv)], except those provisions relating to reasonable requirements of passports and visas as a means of identification and documentation necessary to establish their qualifications under such paragraphs, and the provisions of subparagraphs (A) through (C) of section 212(a)(3) [8 USCS § 1182(a)(3)(A)–(C)].

HISTORY: (June 27, 1952, ch 477, Title I, § 102, 66 Stat. 173; Oct. 24, 1988, P. L. 100-525, § 9(b), 102 Stat. 2619; Nov. 29, 1990, P. L. 101-649, Title VI, § 603(a)(2), 104 Stat. 5082; Dec. 12, 1991, P. L. 102-232, Title III, § 307(i), 105 Stat. 1756; Sept. 30, 1996, P. L. 104-208, Div C, Title III, Subtitle A, § 308(d)(4)(B), 110 Stat. 3009-617.)

§ 103. [8 U.S.C. § 1103] Powers and duties of the Secretary, the Under Secretary, and the Attorney General.

(a) Secretary of Homeland Security.

(1) The Secretary of Homeland Security shall be charged with the administration and enforcement of this Act and all other laws relating to the immigration and naturalization of aliens, except insofar as this Act or such laws relate to the powers, functions, and duties conferred upon the President, Attorney General, the Secretary of State, the officers of the Department of State, or diplomatic or consular officers: Provided, however, That determination and ruling by the Attorney General with respect to all questions of law shall be controlling.

(2) He shall have control, direction, and supervision of all employees and of all the files and records of the Service.

(3) He shall establish such regulations; prescribe such forms of bond, reports, entries, and other papers; issue such instructions; and perform such other acts as he deems necessary for carrying out his authority under the provisions of this Act.

(4) He may require or authorize any employee of the Service or the Department of Justice to perform or exercise any of the powers, privileges, or duties conferred or imposed by this Act or regulations issued thereunder upon any other employee of the Service.

(5) He shall have the power and duty to control and guard the boundaries and borders of the United States against the illegal entry of aliens and shall, in his discretion, appoint for that purpose such number of employees of the Service as to him shall appear necessary and proper.

(6) He is authorized to confer or impose upon any employee of the United States, with the consent of the head of the Department or other independent establishment under whose jurisdiction the employee is serving, any of the powers, privileges, or duties conferred or imposed by this Act or regulations issued thereunder upon officers or employees of the Service.

(7) He may, with the concurrence of the Secretary of State, establish offices of the Service in foreign countries; and, after consultation with the Secretary of State, he may, whenever in his judgment such action may be necessary to accomplish the purposes of this Act, detail employees of the Service for duty in foreign countries.

(8) After consultation with the Secretary of State, the Attorney General may authorize officers of a foreign country to be stationed at preclearance facilities in the United States for the purpose of ensuring that persons traveling from or through the United States to that foreign country comply with that country's immigration and related laws.

(9) Those officers may exercise such authority and perform such duties as United States immigration officers are authorized to exercise and perform in that foreign country under reciprocal agreement, and they shall enjoy such reasonable privileges and immunities necessary for the performance of their duties as the government of their country extends to United States immigration officers.

(10) In the event the Attorney General determines that an actual or imminent mass influx of aliens arriving off the coast of the United States, or near a land border, presents urgent circumstances requiring an immediate Federal response, the Attorney General may authorize any State or local law enforcement officer, with the consent of the head of the department, agency, or establishment under whose jurisdiction the individual is serving, to perform or exercise any of the powers, privileges, or duties conferred or imposed by this Act or regulations issued thereunder upon officers or employees of the Service.

(11) The Attorney General, in support of persons in administrative detention in non-Federal institutions, is authorized—

(A) to make payments from funds appropriated for the administration and enforcement of the laws relating to immigration, naturalization, and alien registration for necessary clothing, medical care, necessary guard hire, and the housing, care, and security of persons detained by the Service pursuant to Federal law under an agreement with a State or political subdivision of a State; and

(B) to enter into a cooperative agreement with any State, territory, or political subdivision thereof, for the necessary construction, physical renovation, acquisition of equipment, supplies or materials required to establish acceptable conditions of confinement and detention services in any State or unit of local government which agrees to provide guaranteed bed space for persons detained by the Service.

(b) Land acquisition authority.

(1) The Attorney General may contract for or buy any interest in land, including temporary use rights, adjacent to or in the vicinity of an international land border when the Attorney General deems the land essential to control and guard the boundaries and borders of the United States against any violation of this Act.

(2) The Attorney General may contract for or buy any interest in land identified pursuant to paragraph (1) as soon as the lawful owner of that interest fixes a price for it and the Attorney General considers that price to be reasonable.

(3) When the Attorney General and the lawful owner of an interest identified pursuant to paragraph (1) are unable to agree upon a reasonable price, the Attorney General may commence condemnation proceedings pursuant to the Act of August 1, 1888 (Chapter 728; 25 Stat. 357) [40 USCS § 3113].

(4) The Attorney General may accept for the United States a gift of any interest in land identified pursuant to paragraph (1).

(c) Commissioner; appointment. The Commissioner shall be a citizen of the United States and shall be appointed by the President, by and with the advice and consent of the Senate. He shall be charged with any and all responsibilities and authority in the administration of the Service and of this Act which are conferred upon the Attorney General as may be delegated to him by the Attorney General or which may be prescribed by the Attorney General. The Commissioner may enter into cooperative agreements with State and local law enforcement agencies for the purpose of assisting in the enforcement of the immigration laws.

(d) Statistical information system.

(1) The Commissioner, in consultation with interested academicians, government agencies, and other parties, shall provide for a system for collection and dissemination, to Congress and the public, of information (not in individually identifiable form) useful in evaluating the social, economic, environmental, and demographic impact of immigration laws.

(2) Such information shall include information on the alien population in the United States, on the rates of naturalization and emigration of resident aliens, on aliens who have been admitted, paroled, or granted asylum, on nonimmigrants in the United States (by occupation, basis for admission, and duration of stay), on aliens who have not been admitted or have been removed from the United States, on the number of applications filed and granted for cancellation of removal, and on the number of aliens estimated to be present unlawfully in the United States in each fiscal year.

(3) Such system shall provide for the collection and dissemination of such information not less often than annually.

(e) Annual report.

(1) The Commissioner shall submit to Congress annually a report which contains a summary of the information collected under subsection (d) and an analysis of trends in immigration and naturalization.

(2) Each annual report shall include information on the number, and rate of denial administratively, of applications for naturalization, for each district office of the Service and by national origin group.

(f) Minimum number of agents in States. The Attorney General shall allocate to each State not fewer than 10 full-time active duty agents of the Immigration and Naturalization Service to carry out the functions of the Service, in order to ensure the effective enforcement of this Act.

(g) Attorney General.

(1) In general. The Attorney General shall have such authorities and functions under this Act and all other laws relating to the immigration and naturalization of aliens as were exercised by the Executive Office for Immigration Review, or by the Attorney General with respect to the Executive Office for Immigration Review, on the day before the effective date of the Immigration Reform, Accountability and Security Enhancement Act of 2002.

(2) Powers. The Attorney General shall establish such regulations, prescribe such forms of bond, reports, entries, and other papers, issue such instructions, review such administrative determinations in immigration proceedings, delegate such authority, and perform such other acts as the Attorney General determines to be necessary for carrying out this section.

HISTORY: (June 27, 1952, ch 477, Title I, § 103, 66 Stat. 173; Oct. 24, 1988, P. L. 100-525, § 9(c), 102 Stat. 2619; Nov. 29, 1990, P. L. 101-649, Title I, Subtitle C, § 142, 104 Stat. 5004; Sept. 30, 1996, P. L. 104-208, Div C, Title I, Subtitle A, § 102(d), Subtitle B, § 125, Subtitle C, § 134(a), Title III, Subtitle A, § 308(d)(4)(C), (e)(4), Subtitle F, §§ 372, 373, 110 Stat. 3009-555, 3009-562, 3009-564, 3009-618, 3009-620, 3009-646; Nov. 25, 2002, P. L. 107-296, Title XI, Subtitle A, § 1102, 116 Stat. 2273; Feb. 20, 2003, P. L. 108-7, Div L, § 105(a)(1), (2), 117 Stat. 531; Dec. 17, 2004, P. L. 108-458, Title V, Subtitle E, § 5505(a), 118 Stat. 3741; Dec. 22, 2009, P. L. 111-122, § 2(a), 123 Stat. 3480.)

§ 104. [8 U.S.C. § 1104] Secretary of State.

(a) Powers and duties. The Secretary of State shall be charged with the administration and the enforcement of the provisions of this Act and all other immigration and nationality laws relating to (1) the powers, duties and functions of diplomatic and consular officers of the United States, except those powers, duties and functions conferred upon the consular officers relating to the granting or refusal of visas; (2) the powers, duties and functions of the Administrator; and (3) the determination of nationality of a person not in the United States. He shall establish such regulations; prescribe such forms of reports, entries and other papers; issue such instructions; and perform such other acts as he deems necessary for carrying out such provisions. He is authorized to confer or impose upon any employee of tAdmission, admitted and entryhe United States, with the consent of the head of the department or independent establishment under whose jurisdiction the employee is serving, any of the powers, functions, or duties conferred or imposed by this Act or regulations issued thereunder upon officers or employees of the Department of State or of the American Foreign Service.

(b) Designation and duties of Administrator. The Secretary of State shall designate an Administrator who shall be a citizen of the United States, qualified by experience. The Administrator shall maintain close liaison with the appropriate committees of Congress in order that they may be advised regarding the administration of this Act by consular officers. The Administrator shall be charged with any and all responsibility and authority in the administration of this Act which are conferred on the Secretary of State as may be delegated to the Administrator by the Secretary of State or which may be prescribed by the Secretary of State, and shall perform such other duties as the Secretary of State may prescribe.

(c) Passport Office, Visa Office, and other offices; directors. Within the Department of State there shall be a Passport Office, a Visa Office, and such other offices as the Secretary of State may deem to be appropriate, each office to be headed by a director. The Directors of the Passport Office and the Visa Office shall be experienced in the administration of the nationality and immigration laws.

(d) Transfer of duties. The functions heretofore performed by the Passport Division and the Visa Division of the Department of State shall hereafter be performed by the Passport Office and the Visa Office, respectively.

(e) General Counsel of Visa Office; appointment and duties. There shall be a General Counsel of the Visa Office, who shall be appointed by the Secretary of State and who shall serve under the general direction of the Legal Adviser of the Department of State. The General Counsel shall have authority to maintain liaison with the appropriate officers of the Service with a view to securing uniform interpretations of the provisions of this Act.

HISTORY: (June 27, 1952, ch 477, Title I, § 104, 66 Stat. 174; June 28, 1962, P. L. 87-510, § 4(a)(2), 76 Stat. 123; Aug. 14, 1964, P. L. 88-426, Title III, § 305(43), 78 Stat. 428; Aug. 17, 1977, P. L. 95-105, Title I, § 109(b)(1), 91 Stat 847; Oct. 24, 1988, P. L. 100-525, § 9(d), 102 Stat. 2620; April 30, 1994, P. L. 103-236, Title I, Part C, § 162(h)(2), 108 Stat. 407.)

§ 105. [8 U.S.C. § 1105] Liaison with internal security officers; data exchange.

(a) In general. The Commissioner and the Administrator shall have authority to maintain direct and continuous liaison with the Directors of the Federal Bureau of Investigation and the Central Intelligence Agency and with other internal security officers of the Government for the purpose of obtaining and exchanging information for use in enforcing the provisions of this Act in the interest of the internal and border security of the United States. The Commissioner and the Administrator shall maintain direct and continuous liaison with each other with a view to a coordinated, uniform, and efficient administration of this Act, and all other immigration and nationality laws.

(b) Access to National Crime Information Center files.

(1) The Attorney General and the Director of the Federal Bureau of Investigation shall provide the Department of State and the Service access to the criminal history record information contained in the National Crime Information Center's Interstate Identification Index (NCIC-III), Wanted Persons File, and to any other files maintained by the National Crime Information Center that may be mutually agreed upon by the Attorney General and the agency receiving the access, for the purpose of determining whether or not a visa applicant or applicant for admission has a criminal history record indexed in any such file.

(2) Such access shall be provided by means of extracts of the records for placement in the automated visa lookout or other appropriate database, and shall be provided without any fee or charge.

(3) The Federal Bureau of Investigation shall provide periodic updates of the extracts at intervals mutually agreed upon with the agency receiving the access. Upon receipt of such updated extracts, the receiving agency shall make corresponding updates to its database and destroy previously provided extracts.

(4) Access to an extract does not entitle the Department of State to obtain the full content of the corresponding automated criminal history record. To obtain the full content of a criminal history record, the Department of State shall submit the applicant's fingerprints and any appropriate fingerprint processing fee authorized by law to the Criminal Justice Information Services Division of the Federal Bureau of Investigation.

(c) Reconsideration upon development of more cost effective means of sharing information. The provision of the extracts described in subsection (b) may be reconsidered by the Attorney General and the receiving agency upon the development and deployment of a more cost-effective and efficient means of sharing the information.

(d) Regulations. For purposes of administering this section, the Department of State shall, prior to receiving access to NCIC data but not later than 4 months after the date of enactment of this subsection [enacted Oct. 26, 2001], promulgate final regulations—

(1) to implement procedures for the taking of fingerprints; and

(2) to establish the conditions for the use of the information received from the Federal Bureau of Investigation, in order—

(A) to limit the redissemination of such information;

(B) to ensure that such information is used solely to determine whether or not to issue a visa to an alien or to admit an alien to the United States;

(C) to ensure the security, confidentiality, and destruction of such information; and

(D) to protect any privacy rights of individuals who are subjects of such information.

HISTORY: (June 27, 1952, ch 477, Title I, § 105, 66 Stat. 175; Aug. 17, 1977, P. L. 95-105, Title I, § 109(b)(2), 91 Stat 847; April 30, 1994, P. L. 103-236, Title I, Part C, § 162(h)(3),

108 Stat. 408; Oct. 26, 2001, P. L. 107-56, Title IV, Subtitle A, § 403(a), 115 Stat. 343.)

§ 106. [8 U.S.C. § 1105a] Employment authorization for battered spouses of certain nonimmigrants.

(a) In general. In the case of an alien spouse admitted under subparagraph (A), (E)(iii), (G), or (H) of section 101(a)(15) [8 USCS § 1101(a)(15)] who is accompanying or following to join a principal alien admitted under subparagraph (A), (E)(iii), (G), or (H) of such section, respectively, the Secretary of Homeland Security may authorize the alien spouse to engage in employment in the United States and provide the spouse with an 'employment authorized' endorsement or other appropriate work permit if the alien spouse demonstrates that during the marriage the alien spouse or a child of the alien spouse has been battered or has been the subject of extreme cruelty perpetrated by the spouse of the alien spouse. Requests for relief under this section shall be handled under the procedures that apply to aliens seeking relief under section 204(a)(1)(A)(iii) [8 USCS § 1154(a)(1)(A)(iii)].

(b) Construction. The grant of employment authorization pursuant to this section shall not confer upon the alien any other form of relief.

HISTORY: (June 27, 1952, ch 477, Title I, § 106, as added Jan. 5, 2006, P. L. 109-162, Title VIII, Subtitle B, § 814(c), 119 Stat. 3059.)

TITLE II—IMMIGRATION

Chapter 1—Selection System

§ 201. [8 U.S.C. § 1151] Worldwide level of immigration.

(a) In general. Exclusive of aliens described in subsection (b), aliens born in a foreign state or dependent area who may be issued immigrant visas or who may otherwise acquire the status of an alien lawfully admitted to the United States for permanent residence are limited to—

(1) family-sponsored immigrants described in section 203(a) [8 USCS § 1153(a)] (or who are admitted under section 211(a) [8 USCS § 1181(a)] on the basis of a prior issuance of a visa to their accompanying parent under section 203(a) [8 USCS § 1153(a)]) in a number not to exceed in any fiscal year the number specified in subsection (c) for that year, and not to exceed in any of the first 3 quarters of any year 27 percent of the worldwide level under such subsection for all of such fiscal year;

(2) employment-based immigrants described in section 203(b) [8 USCS § 1153(b)] (or who are admitted under section 211(a) [8 USCS § 1181(a)] on the basis of a prior issuance of a visa to their accompanying parent under section 203(b) [8 USCS § 1153(b)]), in a number not to exceed in any fiscal year the number specified in subsection (d) for that year, and not to exceed in any of the first 3 quarters of any fiscal year 27 percent of the worldwide level under such subsection for all of such fiscal year; and

(3) for fiscal years beginning with fiscal year 1995, diversity immigrants described in section 203(c) [8 USCS § 1153(c)] (or who are admitted under section 211(a) [8 USCS § 1181(a)] on the basis of a prior issuance of a visa to their accompanying parent under section 203(c) [8 USCS § 1153(c)]) in a number not to exceed in any fiscal year the number specified in subsection (e) for that year, and not to exceed in any of the first 3 quarters of any fiscal year 27 percent of the worldwide level under such subsection for all of such fiscal year.

(b) Aliens not subject to direct numerical limitations. Aliens described in this subsection, who are not subject to the worldwide levels or numerical limitations of subsection (a), are as follows:

(1) (A) Special immigrants described in subparagraph (A) or (B) of section 101(a)(27) [8 USCS § 1101(a)(27)(A) or (B)].

(B) Aliens who are admitted under section 207 [8 USCS § 1157] or whose status is adjusted under section 209 [8 USCS § 1159].

(C) Aliens whose status is adjusted to permanent residence under section 210 or 245A [8 USCS § 1160 or 1255a].

(D) Aliens whose removal is canceled under section 240A(a) [8 USCS § 1229b(a)].

(E) Aliens provided permanent resident status under section 249 [8 USCS § 1259].

(2) (A) (i) Immediate relatives. For purposes of this subsection, the term "immediate relatives" means the children, spouses, and parents of a citizen of the United States, except that, in the case of parents, such citizens shall be at least 21 years of age. In the case of an alien who was the spouse of a citizen of the United States and was not legally separated from the citizen at the time of the citizen's death, the alien (and each child of the alien) shall be considered, for purposes of this subsection, to remain an immediate relative after the date of the citizen's death but only if the spouse files a petition under section 204(a)(1)(A)(ii) [8 USCS § 1154(a)(1)(A)(ii)] within 2 years after such date and only until the date the spouse remarries. For purposes of this clause, an alien who has filed a petition under clause (iii) or (iv) of section 204(a)(1)(A) of this Act [8 USCS § 1154(a)(1)(A)] remains an immediate relative in the event that the United States citizen spouse or parent loses United States citizenship on account of the abuse.

(ii) Aliens admitted under section 211(a) [8 USCS § 1181(a)] on the basis of a prior issuance of a visa to their accompanying parent who is such an immediate relative.

(B) Aliens born to an alien lawfully admitted for permanent residence during a temporary visit abroad.

(c) Worldwide level of family-sponsored immigrants.

(1) (A) The worldwide level of family-sponsored immigrants under this subsection for a fiscal year is, subject to subparagraph (B), equal to—

(i) 480,000, minus

(ii) the sum of the number computed under paragraph (2) and the number computed under paragraph (4), plus

(iii) the number (if any) computed under paragraph (3).

(B) (i) For each of fiscal years 1992, 1993, and 1994, 465,000 shall be substituted for 480,000 in subparagraph (A)(i).

(ii) In no case shall the number computed under subparagraph (A) be less than 226,000.

(2) The number computed under this paragraph for a fiscal year is the sum of the number of aliens described in subparagraphs (A) and (B) of subsection (b)(2) who were issued immigrant visas or who otherwise acquired the status of aliens lawfully admitted to the United States for permanent residence in the previous fiscal year.

(3) (A) The number computed under this paragraph for fiscal year 1992 is zero.

(B) The number computed under this paragraph for fiscal year 1993 is the difference (if any) between the worldwide level established under paragraph (1) for the previous fiscal year and the number of visas issued under section 203(a) [8 USCS § 1153(a)] during that fiscal year.

(C) The number computed under this paragraph for a subsequent fiscal year is the difference (if any) between the maximum number of visas which may be issued under section 203(b) [8 USCS § 1153(b)] (relating to employment-based immigrants) during the previous fiscal year and the number of visas issued under that section during that year.

(4) The number computed under this paragraph for a fiscal year (beginning with fiscal year 1999) is the number of aliens who were paroled into the United States under section 212(d)(5) [8 USCS § 1182(d)(5)] in the second preceding fiscal year—

(A) who did not depart from the United States (without advance parole) within 365 days; and

(B) who (i) did not acquire the status of aliens lawfully admitted to the United States for permanent residence in the two preceding fiscal years, or (ii) acquired such status in such years under a provision of law (other than section 201(b) [subsec. (b) of this section]) which exempts such adjustment from the numerical limitation on the worldwide level of immigration under this section.

(5) If any alien described in paragraph (4) (other than an alien described in paragraph (4)(B)(ii)) is subsequently admitted as an alien lawfully admitted for permanent residence, such alien shall not again be considered for purposes of paragraph (1).

(d) Worldwide level of employment-based immigrants.

(1) The worldwide level of employment-based immigrants under this subsection for a fiscal year is equal to—

(A) 140,000, plus

(B) the number computed under paragraph (2).

(2) (A) The number computed under this paragraph for fiscal year 1992 is zero.

(B) The number computed under this paragraph for fiscal year 1993 is the difference (if any) between the worldwide level established under paragraph (1) for the previous fiscal year and the number of visas issued under section 203(b) [8 USCS § 1153(b)] during that fiscal year.

(C) The number computed under this paragraph for a subsequent fiscal year is the difference (if any) between the maximum number of visas which may be issued under section 203(a) [8 USCS § 1153(a)] (relating to family-sponsored immigrants) during the previous fiscal year and the number of visas issued under that section during that year.

(e) Worldwide level of diversity immigrants. The worldwide level of diversity immigrants is equal to 55,000 for each fiscal year.

(f) Rules for determining whether certain aliens are immediate relatives.

(1) Age on petition filing date. Except as provided in paragraphs (2) and (3), for purposes of subsection (b)(2)(A)(i), a determination of whether an alien satisfies the age requirement in the matter preceding subparagraph (A) of section 101(b)(1) [8 USCS § 1101(b)(1)] shall be made using the age of the alien on the date on which the petition is filed with the Attorney General under section 204 [8 USCS § 1154] to classify the alien as an immediate relative under subsection (b)(2)(A)(i).

(2) Age on parent's naturalization date. In the case of a petition under section 204 [8 USCS § 1154] initially filed for an alien child's classification as a family-sponsored immigrant under section 203(a)(2)(A) [8 USCS § 1153(a)(2)(A)], based on the child's parent being lawfully admitted for permanent residence, if the petition is later converted, due to the naturalization of the parent, to a petition to classify the alien as an immediate relative under subsection (b)(2)(A)(i), the determination described in paragraph (1) shall be made using the age of the alien on the date of the parent's naturalization.

(3) Age on marriage termination date. In the case of a petition under section 204 [8 USCS § 1154] initially filed for an alien's classification as a family-sponsored immigrant under section 203(a)(3) [8 USCS § 1153(a)(3)], based on the alien's being a married son or daughter of a citizen, if the petition is later converted, due to the legal termination of the alien's marriage, to a petition to classify the alien as an immediate relative under subsection (b)(2)(A)(i) or as an unmarried son or daughter of a citizen under section 203(a)(1) [8 USCS § 1153(a)(1)], the determination described in paragraph (1) shall be made using the age of the alien on the date of the termination of the marriage.

(4) Application to self-petitions. Paragraphs (1) through (3) shall apply to self-petitioners and derivatives of self-petitioners.

HISTORY: (June 27, 1952, ch 477, Title II, Ch 1, § 201, 66 Stat. 175; Oct. 3, 1965, P. L. 89-236, § 1, 79 Stat. 911; Oct. 20, 1976, P. L. 94-571, § 2, 90 Stat. 2703; Oct. 5, 1978, P. L. 95-412, § 1, 92 Stat. 907; March 17, 1980, P. L. 96-212, Title II, § 203(a), 94 Stat. 106; Dec. 29, 1981, P. L. 97-116, § 20, 95 Stat. 1621; Nov. 29, 1990, P. L. 101-649, Title I, Subtitle A, § 101(a), 104 Stat. 4980; Dec. 12, 1991, P. L. 102-232, Title III,

§ 302(a)(1), 105 Stat. 1742; Sept. 13, 1994, P. L. 103-322, Title IV, Subtitle G, § 40701(b)(2), 108 Stat. 1954; Oct. 25, 1994, P. L. 103-416, Title II, § 219(b)(1), 108 Stat. 4316; Sept. 30, 1996, P. L. 104-208, Div C, Title III, Subtitle A, § 308(e)(5), (g)(8)(A)(i), Title VI, Subtitle A, § 603, Subtitle E, § 671(d)(1)(A),110 Stat. 3009-620, 3009-624, 3009-690, 3009-723; Oct. 28, 2000, P. L. 106-386, Div B, Title V, § 1507(a)(3), 114 Stat. 1530; Aug. 6, 2002, P. L. 107-208, § 2, 116 Stat. 927; Jan. 5, 2006, P. L. 109-162, Title VIII, Subtitle A, § 805(b)(1), 119 Stat. 3056; Oct. 28, 2009, P. L. 111-83, Title V, § 568(c)(1), 123 Stat. 2186.)

§ 202. [8 U.S.C. § 1152] Numerical limitations on individual foreign states.

(a) Per country level.

(1) Nondiscrimination.

(A) Except as specifically provided in paragraph (2) and in sections 101(a)(27), 201(b)(2)(A)(i), and 203 [8 USCS §§ 1101(a)(27), 1151(b)(2)(A)(i), 1153], no person shall receive any preference or priority or be discriminated against in the issuance of an immigrant visa because of the person's race, sex, nationality, place of birth, or place of residence.

(B) Nothing in this paragraph shall be construed to limit the authority of the Secretary of State to determine the procedures for the processing of immigrant visa applications or the locations where such applications will be processed.

(2) Per country level for family-sponsored and employment-based immigrants. Subject to paragraphs (3), (4), and (5), the total number of immigrant visas made available to natives of any single foreign state or dependent area under subsections (a) and (b) of section 203 [8 USCS § 1153] in any fiscal year may not exceed 7 percent (in the case of a single foreign state) or 2 percent (in the case of a dependent area) of the total number of such visas made available under such subsections in that fiscal year.

(3) Exception if additional visas available. If because of the application of paragraph (2) with respect to one or more foreign states or dependent areas, the total number of visas available under both subsections (a) and (b) of section 203 [8 USCS § 1153(a), (b)] for a calendar quarter exceeds the number of qualified immigrants who otherwise may be issued such a visa, paragraph (2) shall not apply to visas made available to such states or areas during the remainder of such calendar quarter.

(4) Special rules for spouses and children of lawful permanent resident aliens.

(A) 75 percent of 2nd preference set-aside for spouses and children not subject to per country limitation.

(i) In general. Of the visa numbers made available under section 203(a) [8 USCS § 1153(a)] to immigrants described in section 203(a)(2)(A) [8 USCS § 1152(a)(2)(A)] in any fiscal year, 75 percent of the 2-A floor (as defined in clause (ii)) shall be issued without regard to the numerical limitation under paragraph (2).

(ii) 2-A floor defined. In this paragraph, the term "2-A floor" means, for a fiscal year, 77 percent of the total number of visas made available under section 203(a) [8 USCS § 1153(a)] to immigrants described in section 203(a)(2) [8 USCS § 1153(a)(2)] in the fiscal year.

(B) Treatment of remaining 25 percent for countries subject to subsection (e).

(i) In general. Of the visa numbers made available under section 203(a) [8 USCS § 1153(a)] to immigrants described in section 203(a)(2)(A) [8 USCS § 1153(a)(2)(A)] in any fiscal year, the remaining 25 percent of the 2-A floor shall be available in the case of a state or area that is subject to subsection (e) only to the extent that the total number of visas issued into accordance with subparagraph (A) to natives of the foreign state or area is less than the subsection (e) ceiling (as defined in clause (ii)).

(ii) Subsection (e) ceiling defined. In clause (i), the term "subsection (e) ceiling" means, for a foreign state or dependent area, 77 percent of the maximum number of visas that may be made available under section 203(a) [8 USCS § 1153(a)] to immigrants who are natives of the state or area under section 203(a)(2) [8 USCS § 1153(a)(2)] consistent with subsection (e).

(C) Treatment of unmarried sons and daughters in countries subject to subsection (e). In the case of a foreign state or dependent area to which subsection (e) applies, the number of immigrant visas that may be made available to natives of the state or area under section 203(a)(2)(B) [8 USCS § 1153(a)(2)(B)] may not exceed—

(i) 23 percent of the maximum number of visas that may be made available under section 203(a) [8 USCS § 1153(a)] to immigrants of the state or area described in section 203(a)(2) [8 USCS § 1153(a)(2)] consistent with subsection (e), or

(ii) the number (if any) by which the maximum number of visas that may be made available under section 203(a) [8 USCS § 1153(a)] to immigrants of the state or area described in section 203(a)(2) [8 USCS § 1153(a)(2)] consistent with subsection (e) exceeds the number of visas issued under section 203(a)(2)(A) [8 USCS § 1153(a)(2)(A)], whichever is greater.

(D) Limiting pass down for certain countries subject to subsection (e). In the case of a foreign state or dependent area to which subsection (e) applies, if the total number of visas issued under section 203(a)(2) [8 USCS § 1153(a)(2)] exceeds the maximum number of visas that may be made available to immigrants of the state or area under section 203(a)(2) [8 USCS § 1153(a)(2)] consistent with subsection (e) (determined without regard to this paragraph), in applying paragraphs (3) and (4) of section 203(a) [8 USCS § 1153(a)(3), (4)] under subsection (e)(2) all visas shall be deemed to have been required for the classes specified in paragraphs (1) and (2) of such section.

(5) Rules for employment-based immigrants.

(A) Employment-based immigrants not subject to per country limitation if additional visas available. If the total number of visas available under paragraph (1), (2), (3), (4), or (5) of section 203(b) [8 USCS § 1153(b)] for a calendar quarter exceeds the number of qualified immigrants who may otherwise be issued such visas, the visas made available under that paragraph shall be issued without regard to the numerical limitation under paragraph (2) of this subsection during the remainder of the calendar quarter.

(B) Limiting fall across for certain countries subject to subsection (e). In the case of a foreign state or dependent area to which subsection (e) applies, if the total number of visas issued under section 203(b) [8 USCS § 1153(b)] exceeds the maximum number of visas that may be made available to immigrants of the state or area under section 203(b) [8 USCS § 1153(b)] consistent with subsection (e) (determined without regard to this paragraph), in applying subsection (e) all visas shall be deemed to have been required for the classes of aliens specified in section 203(b) [8 USCS § 1153(b)].

(b) Rules for chargeability. Each independent country, self-governing dominion, mandated territory, and territory under the international trusteeship system of the United Nations, other than the United States and its outlying possessions, shall be treated as a separate foreign state for the purposes of a numerical level established under subsection (a)(2) when approved by the Secretary of State. All other inhabited lands shall be attributed to a foreign state specified by the Secretary of State. For the purposes of this Act the foreign state to which an immigrant is chargeable shall be determined by birth within such foreign state except that (1) an alien child, when accompanied by or following to join his alien parent or parents, may be charged to the foreign state of either parent if such parent has received or would be qualified for an immigrant visa, if necessary to prevent the separation of the child from the parent or parents, and if immigration charged to the foreign state to which such parent has been or would be chargeable has not reached a numerical level established under subsection (a)(2) for that fiscal year; (2) if an alien is chargeable to a different foreign state from that of his spouse, the foreign state to which such alien is chargeable may, if necessary to prevent the separation of husband and wife, be determined by the foreign state of the spouse he is accompanying or following to join, if such spouse has received or would be qualified for an immigrant visa and if immigration charged to the foreign state to which such spouse has been or would be chargeable has not reached a numerical level established under subsection (a)(2) for that fiscal year; (3) an alien born in the United States shall be considered as having been born in the country of which he is a citizen or subject, or, if he is not a citizen or subject of any country, in the last foreign country in which he had his residence as determined by the consular officer; (4) an alien born within any foreign state in which neither of his parents was born and in which neither of his parents had a residence at the time of such alien's birth may be charged to the foreign state of either parent.

(c) Chargeability for dependent areas. Any immigrant born in a colony or other component or dependent area of a foreign state overseas from the foreign state, other than an alien described in section 201(b) [8 USCS § 1151(b)], shall be chargeable for the purpose of the limitation set forth in section 202(a) [8 USCS § 1152(a)], to the foreign state.

(d) Changes in territory. In the case of any change in the territorial limits of foreign states, the Secretary of State shall, upon recognition of such change, issue appropriate instructions to all diplomatic and consular offices.

(e) Special rules for countries at ceiling. If it is determined that the total number of immigrant visas made available under subsections (a) and (b) of section 203 [8 USCS § 1153] to natives of any single foreign state or dependent area will exceed the numerical limitation specified in subsection (a)(2) in any fiscal year, in determining the allotment of immigrant visa numbers to natives under subsections (a) and (b) of section 203 [8 USCS § 1153], visa numbers with respect to natives of that state or area shall be allocated (to the extent practicable and otherwise consistent with this section and section 203 [8 USCS § 1153]) in a manner so that—

(1) the ratio of the visa numbers made available under section 203(a) [8 USCS § 1153(a)]) to the visa numbers made available under section 203(b) [8 USCS § 1153(b)] is equal to the ratio of the worldwide level of immigration under section 201(c) [8 USCS § 1151(c)] to such level under section 201(d) [8 USCS § 1151(d)];

(2) except as provided in subsection (a)(4), the proportion of the visa numbers made available under each of paragraphs (1) through (4) of section 203(a) [8 USCS § 1153(a)] is equal to the ratio of the total number of visas made available under the respective paragraph to the total number of visas made available under section 203(a) [8 USCS § 1153(a)], and

(3) except as provided in subsection (a)(5), the proportion of the visa numbers made available under each of paragraphs (1) through (5) of section 203(b) [8 USCS § 1153(b)] is equal to the ratio of the total number of visas made available under the respective paragraph to the total number of visas made available under section 203(b) [8 USCS § 1153(b)].

Nothing in this subsection shall be construed as limiting the number of visas that may be issued to natives of a foreign state or dependent area under section 203(a) or 203(b) [8 USCS § 1153(a) or (b)] if there is insufficient demand for visas for such natives under section 203(b) or 203(a) [8 USCS § 1153(b) or (a)], respectively, or as limiting the number of visas that may be issued under section 203(a)(2)(A) [8 USCS § 1153(a)(2)(A)] pursuant to subsection (a)(4)(A).

HISTORY: (June 27, 1952, ch 477, Title II, Ch 1, § 202, 66 Stat. 176; Sept. 26, 1961, P.L. 87-301, § 9, 75 Stat. 654; Oct. 3, 1965, P.L. 89-236, § 2, 79 Stat. 911; Oct. 20, 1976, P.L. 94-571, § 3, 90 Stat. 2703; Oct. 5, 1978, P.L. 95-412, § 2, 92 Stat. 907; March 17, 1980, P.L. 96-212, Title II, § 203(b), 94 Stat. 107; Dec. 29, 1981, P.L. 97-116, §§ 18(c), 20(b), 95 Stat. 1620, 1622; Nov. 6, 1986, P.L. 99-603, Title III, Part B, § 311(a), 100 Stat. 3434; Nov. 14, 1986, P.L. 99-653, § 4, 100 Stat. 3655; Nov. 14, 1986, P.L. 99-653, § 4, 100 Stat. 3655 (as amended Oct. 24, 1988, P.L. 100-525, § 8(c), 102 Stat. 2617); Oct. 24, 1988, P.L. 100-525, § 9(f), 102 Stat. 2620; Nov. 29, 1990, P.L. 101-649, Title I, Subtitle A, § 102, 104 Stat. 4982; Dec. 12, 1991, P.L. 102-232, Title III, § 302(a)(3), 105 Stat. 1742; Sept. 30, 1996, P.L. 104-208, Div C, Title VI, Subtitle C, § 633, 110 Stat. 3009-701.); as amended Oct. 17, 2000, P.L. 106-313, Title I, § 104(a), (b), 114 Stat. 1252.)

§ 203. [8 U.S.C. § 1153] Allocation of immigrant visas.

(a) Preference allocation for family-sponsored immigrants. Aliens subject to the worldwide level specified in section 201(c) [8 USCS § 1151(c)] for family-sponsored immigrants shall be allotted visas as follows:

(1) Unmarried sons and daughters of citizens. Qualified immigrants who are the unmarried sons or daughters of citizens of the United States shall be allocated visas in a number not to exceed 23,400, plus any visas not required for the class specified in paragraph (4).

(2) Spouses and unmarried sons and unmarried daughters of permanent resident aliens. Qualified immigrants—

(A) who are the spouses or children of an alien lawfully admitted for permanent residence, or

(B) who are the unmarried sons or unmarried daughters (but are not the children) of an alien lawfully admitted for permanent residence,

shall be allocated visas in a number not to exceed 114,200, plus the number (if any) by which such worldwide level exceeds 226,000, plus any visas not required for the class specified in paragraph (1); except that not less than 77 percent of such visa numbers shall be allocated to aliens described in subparagraph (A).

(3) Married sons and married daughters of citizens. Qualified immigrants who are the married sons or married daughters of citizens of the United States shall be allocated visas in a number not to exceed 23,400, plus any visas not required for the classes specified in paragraphs (1) and (2).

(4) Brothers and sisters of citizens. Qualified immigrants who are the brothers or sisters of citizens of the United States, if such citizens are at least 21 years of age, shall be allocated visas in a number not to exceed 65,000, plus any visas not required for the classes specified in paragraphs (1) through (3).

(b) Preference allocation for employment-based immigrants. Aliens subject to the worldwide level specified in section 201(d) [8 USCS § 1151(d)] for employment-based immigrants in a fiscal year shall be allotted visas as follows:

(1) Priority workers. Visas shall first be made available in a number not to exceed 28.6 percent of such worldwide level, plus any visas not required for the classes specified in paragraphs (4) and (5), to qualified immigrants who are aliens described in any of the following subparagraphs (A) through (C):

(A) Aliens with extraordinary ability. An alien is described in this subparagraph if—

(i) the alien has extraordinary ability in the sciences, arts, education, business, or athletics which has been demonstrated by sustained national or international acclaim and whose achievements have been recognized in the field through extensive documentation,

(ii) the alien seeks to enter the United States to continue work in the area of extraordinary ability, and

(iii) the alien's entry into the United States will substantially benefit prospectively the United States.

(B) Outstanding professors and researchers. An alien is described in this subparagraph if—

(i) the alien is recognized internationally as outstanding in a specific academic area,

(ii) the alien has at least 3 years of experience in teaching or research in the academic area, and

(iii) the alien seeks to enter the United States—

(I) for a tenured position (or tenure-track position) within a university or institution of higher education to teach in the academic area,

(II) for a comparable position with a university or institution of higher education to conduct research in the area, or

(III) for a comparable position to conduct research in the area with a department, division, or institute of a private employer, if the department, division, or institute employs at least 3 persons full-time in research activities and has achieved documented accomplishments in an academic field.

(C) Certain multinational executives and managers. An alien is described in this subparagraph if the alien, in the 3 years preceding the time of the alien's application for classification and admission into the United States under this subparagraph, has been employed for at least 1 year by a firm or corporation or other legal entity or an affiliate or subsidiary thereof and the alien seeks to enter the United States in order to continue to render services to the same employer or to a subsidiary or affiliate thereof in a capacity that is managerial or executive.

(2) Aliens who are members of the professions holding advanced degrees or aliens of exceptional ability.

(A) In general. Visas shall be made available, in a number not to exceed 28.6 percent of such worldwide level plus any visas not required for the classes specified in paragraph (1), to qualified immigrants who are members of the professions holding advanced degrees or their equivalent or who because of their exceptional ability in the sciences, arts, or business, will substantially benefit prospectively the national economy, cultural or educational interests, or welfare of the United States, and whose services in the sciences, arts, professions, or business are sought by an employer in the United States.

(B) (i) Subject to clause (ii), the Attorney General may, when the Attorney General deems it to be in the national interest, waive the requirements of subparagraph (A) that an alien's services in the sciences, arts, professions, or business be sought by an employer in the United States.

(ii) (I) The Attorney General shall grant a national interest waiver pursuant to clause (i) on behalf of any alien physician with respect to whom a petition for preference classification has been filed under subparagraph (A) if—

(aa) the alien physician agrees to work full time as a physician in an area or areas designated by the Secretary of Health and Human Services as having a shortage of health care professionals or at a health care facility under the jurisdiction of the Secretary of Veterans Affairs; and

(bb) a Federal agency or a department of public health in any State has previously determined that the alien physician's work in such an area or at such facility was in the public interest.

(II) No permanent resident visa may be issued to an alien physician described in subclause (I) by the Secretary of State under section 204(b) [8 USCS § 1154(b)], and the Attorney General may not adjust the status of such an alien physician from that of a nonimmigrant alien to that of a permanent resident alien under section 245 [8 USCS § 1255], until such time as the alien has worked full time as a physician for an aggregate of 5 years (not including the time served in the status of an alien described in section 101(a)(15)(J) [8 USCS § 1101(a)(15)(J)]), in an area or areas designated by the Secretary of Health and Human Services as having a shortage of health care professionals or at a health care facility under the jurisdiction of the Secretary of Veterans Affairs.

(III) Nothing in this subparagraph may be construed to prevent the filing of a petition with the Attorney General for classification under section 204(a) [8 USCS § 1154(a)], or the filing of an application for adjustment of status under section 245 [8 USCS § 1255], by an alien physician described in subclause (I) prior to the date by which such alien physician has completed the service described in subclause (II).

(IV) The requirements of this subsection do not affect waivers on behalf of alien physicians approved under section 203(b)(2)(B) [subsec. (b)(2)(B) of this section] before the enactment date of this subsection. In the case of a physician for whom an application for a waiver was filed under section 203(b)(2)(B) [subsec. (b)(2)(B) of this section] prior to November 1, 1998, the Attorney General shall grant a national interest waiver pursuant to section 203(b)(2)(B) [subsec. (b)(2)(B) of this section] except that the alien is required to have worked full time as a physician for an aggregate of 3 years (not including time served in the status of an alien described in section 101(a)(15)(J) [8 USCS § 1101(a)(15)(J)]) before a visa can be issued to the alien under section 204(b) [8 USCS § 1154(b)] or the status of the alien is adjusted to permanent resident under section 245 [8 USCS § 1255].

(C) Determination of exceptional ability. In determining under subparagraph (A) whether an immigrant has exceptional ability, the possession of a degree, diploma, certificate, or similar award from a college, university, school, or other institution of learning or a license to practice or certification for a particular profession or occupation shall not by itself be considered sufficient evidence of such exceptional ability.

(3) Skilled workers, professionals, and other workers.

(A) In general. Visas shall be made available, in a number not to exceed 28.6 percent of such worldwide level, plus any visas not required for the classes specified in paragraphs (1) and (2), to the following classes of aliens who are not described in paragraph (2):

(i) Skilled workers. Qualified immigrants who are capable, at the time of petitioning for classification under this paragraph, of performing skilled labor (requiring at least 2 years training or experience), not of a temporary or seasonal nature, for which qualified workers are not available in the United States.

(ii) Professionals. Qualified immigrants who hold baccalaureate degrees and who are members of the professions.

(iii) Other workers. Other qualified immigrants who are capable at the time of petitioning for classification under this paragraph, of performing unskilled labor, not of a temporary or seasonal nature, for which qualified workers are not available in the United States.

(B) Limitation on other workers. Not more than 10,000 of the visas made available under this paragraph in any fiscal year may be available for qualified immigrants described in subparagraph (A)(iii).

(C) Labor certification required. An immigrant visa may not be issued to an immigrant under subparagraph (A) until the consular officer is in receipt of a determination made by the Secretary of Labor pursuant to the provisions of section 212(a)(5)(A) [8 USCS § 1182(a)(5)(A)].

(4) Certain special immigrants. Visas shall be made available, in a number not to exceed 7.1 percent of such worldwide level, to qualified special immigrants described in section 101(a)(27) [8 USCS § 1101(a)(27)] (other than those described in subparagraph (A) or (B) thereof), of which not more than 5,000 may be made available in any fiscal year to special immigrants described in subclause (II) or (III) of section 101(a)(27)(C)(ii) [8 USCS § 1101(a)(27)(C)(ii)(II) or (III)], and not more than 100 may be made available in any fiscal year to special immigrants, excluding spouses and children, who are described in section 101(a)(27)(M) [8 USCS § 1101(a)(27)(M)].

(5) Employment creation.

(A) In general. Visas shall be made available, in a number not to exceed 7.1 percent of such worldwide level to qualified immigrants seeking to enter the United States for the purpose of engaging in a new commercial enterprise (including a limited partnership)—

(i) in which such alien has invested (after the date of the enactment of the Immigration Act of 1990 [enacted Nov. 29, 1990]) or, is actively in the process of investing, capital in an amount not less than the amount specified in subparagraph (C) and which is expected to remain invested for not less than 2 years; and

(ii) which will benefit the United States economy by creating full-time employment for not fewer than 10 United States citizens, United States nationals, or aliens lawfully admitted for permanent residence or other immigrants lawfully authorized to be employed in the United States (other than the immigrant and the immigrant's spouse, sons, or daughters).

(B) Designations and reserved visas.

(i) Reserved visas.

(I) In general. Of the visas made available under this paragraph in each fiscal year—

(aa) 20 percent shall be reserved for qualified immigrants who invest in a rural area;

(bb) 10 percent shall be reserved for qualified immigrants who invest in an area designated by the Secretary of Homeland Security under clause (ii) as a high unemployment area; and

(cc) 2 percent shall be reserved for qualified immigrants who invest in infrastructure projects.

(II) Unused visas.

(aa) Carryover. At the end of each fiscal year, any unused visas reserved for qualified immigrants investing in each of the categories described in items (aa) through (cc) of subclause (I) shall remain available within the same category for the immediately succeeding fiscal year.

(bb) General availability. Visas described in items (aa) through (cc) of subclause (I) that are not issued by the end of the succeeding fiscal year referred to in item (aa) shall be made available to qualified immigrants described under subparagraph (A).

(ii) Designation of high unemployment area.

(I) In general. The Secretary of Homeland Security, or a designee of the Secretary who is an employee of the Department of Homeland Security, may designate, as a high unemployment area, a census tract, or contiguous census tracts, in which—

(aa) the new commercial enterprise is principally doing business; and

(bb) the weighted average of the unemployment rate for the census tracts, based on the labor force employment measure for each applicable census tract and any adjacent tract included under subclause (III), is not less than 150 percent of the national average unemployment rate.

(II) Prohibition on designation by any other official. A targeted employment area may not be designated as a high unemployment area by—

(aa) a Federal official other than the Secretary of Homeland Security or a designee of the Secretary; or

(bb) any official of a State or local government.

(III) Inclusion. In making a designation under subclause (I), the Secretary of Homeland Security may include a census tract directly adjacent to a census tract or contiguous census tracts described in that subclause.

(IV) Duration.

(aa) In general. A designation under this clause shall be in effect for the 2-year period beginning on—

(AA) the date on which an application under subparagraph (F) is filed; or

(BB) in the case of an alien who is not subject to subparagraph (F), at the time of investment.

(bb) Renewal. A designation under this clause may be renewed for 1 or more additional 2-year periods if the applicable area continues to meet the criteria described in subclause (I).

(V) Additional investment not required. An immigrant investor who has invested the amount of capital required by subparagraph (C) in a targeted employment area designated as a high unemployment area during the period in which the area is so designated shall not be required to increase the amount of investment due to the expiration of the designation.

(iii) Infrastructure projects.

(I) In general. The Secretary of Homeland Security shall determine whether a specific capital investment project meets the definition of "infrastructure project" set forth in subparagraph (D)(iv).

(II) Prohibition on designation by any other official. A determination under subclause (I) may not be made by—

(aa) a Federal official other than the Secretary of Homeland Security or a designee of the Secretary; or

(bb) any official of a State or local government.

(C) Amount of capital required.

(i) In general. Except as otherwise provided in this subparagraph, the amount of capital required under subparagraph (A) shall be $1,050,000.

(ii) Adjustment for targeted employment areas and infrastructure projects. The amount of capital required under subparagraph (A) for an investment in a targeted employment area or in an infrastructure project shall be $800,000.

(iii) Automatic adjustment in minimum investment amount.

(I) In general. Beginning on January 1, 2027, and every 5 years thereafter, the amount in clause (i) shall automatically adjust for petitions filed on or after the effective date of each adjustment, based on the cumulative annual percentage change in the unadjusted consumer price index for all urban consumers (all items; U.S. city average) reported by the Bureau of Labor Statistics between January 1, 2022, and the date of adjustment. The qualifying investment amounts shall be rounded down to the nearest $50,000. The Secretary of Homeland Security shall update such amounts by publication of a technical amendment in the Federal Register.

(II) Beginning on January 1, 2027, and every 5 years thereafter, the amount in clause (ii) shall automatically adjust for petitions filed on or after the effective date of each adjustment, to be equal to 75 percent of the standard investment amount under subclause (I).

(iv) Adjustment for high employment areas. In the case of an investment made in a part of a metropolitan statistical area that at the time of the investment—

(I) is not a targeted employment area, and

(II) is an area with an unemployment rate significantly below the national average unemployment rate,

the Secretary of Homeland Security may specify an amount of capital required under subparagraph (A) that is greater than (but not greater than 3 times) the amount specified in clause (i), as adjusted under clause (iii).

(D) Definitions. In this paragraph:

(i) Affiliated job-creating entity. The term "affiliated job-creating entity" means any job-creating entity that is controlled, managed, or owned by any of the people involved with the regional center or new commercial enterprise under section 203(b)(5)(H)(v) [8 USCS § 1153(b)(5)(H)(v)].

(ii) Capital. The term "capital"—

(I) means cash and all real, personal, or mixed tangible assets owned and controlled by the alien investor, or held in trust for the benefit of the alien and to which the alien has unrestricted access;

(II) shall be valued at fair market value in United States dollars, in accordance with Generally Accepted Accounting Principles or other standard accounting practice adopted by the Securities and Exchange Commission, at the time it is invested under this paragraph;

(III) does not include—

(aa) assets directly or indirectly acquired by unlawful means, including any cash proceeds of indebtedness secured by such assets;

(bb) capital invested in exchange for a note, bond, convertible debt, obligation, or any other debt arrangement between the alien investor and the new commercial enterprise;

(cc) capital invested with a guaranteed rate of return on the amount invested by the alien investor; or

(dd) except as provided in subclause (IV), capital invested that is subject to any agreement between the alien investor and the new commercial enterprise that provides the investor with a contractual right to repayment, such as a mandatory redemption at a certain time or upon the occurrence of a certain event, or a put or sell-back option held by the alien investor, even if such contractual right is contingent on the success of the new commercial enterprise, such as having sufficient available cash flow; and

(IV) includes capital invested that—

(aa) is subject to a buy back option that may be exercised solely at the discretion of the new commercial enterprise; and

(bb) results in the alien investor withdrawing his or her petition unless the alien investor has fulfilled his or her sustainment period and other requirements under this paragraph.

(iii) Certifier. The term "certifier" means a person in a position of substantive authority for the management or operations of a regional center, new commercial enterprise, affiliated job-creating entity, or issuer of securities, such as a principal executive officer or principal financial officer, with knowledge of such entities' policies and procedures related to compliance with the requirements under this paragraph.

(iv) Infrastructure project. The term "infrastructure project" means a capital investment project in a filed or approved business plan, which is administered by a governmental entity (such as a Federal, State, or local agency or authority) that is the job-creating entity contracting with a regional center or new commercial enterprise to receive capital investment under the regional center program described in subparagraph (E) from alien investors or the new commercial enterprise as financing for maintaining, improving, or constructing a public works project.

(v) Job-creating entity. The term "job-creating entity" means any organization formed in the United States for the ongoing conduct of lawful business, including sole proprietorship, partnership (whether limited or general), corporation, limited liability company, business trust, or other entity, which may be publicly or privately owned, including an entity consisting of a holding company and its wholly owned subsidiaries or affiliates (provided that each subsidiary or affiliate is engaged in an activity formed for the ongoing conduct of a lawful business) that receives, or is established to receive, capital investment from alien investors or a new commercial enterprise under the regional center program described in this subparagraph and which is responsible for creating jobs to satisfy the requirement under subparagraph (A)(ii).

(vi) New commercial enterprise. The term "new commercial enterprise" means any for-profit organization formed in the United States for the ongoing conduct of lawful business, including sole proprietorship, partnership (whether limited or general), holding company and its wholly owned subsidiaries (provided that each subsidiary is engaged in a for-profit activity formed for the ongoing conduct of a lawful business), joint venture, corporation, business trust, limited liability company, or other entity (which may be publicly or privately owned) that receives, or is established to receive, capital investment from investors under this paragraph.

(vii) Rural area. The term "rural area" means any area other than an area within a metropolitan statistical area (as designated by the Director of the Office of Management and Budget) or within the outer boundary of any city or town having a population of 20,000 or more (based on the most recent decennial census of the United States).

(viii) Targeted employment area. The term "targeted employment area" means, at the time of investment, a rural area or an area designated by the Secretary of Homeland Security under subparagraph (B)(ii) as a high unemployment area.

(E) Regional center program.

(i) In general. Visas under this subparagraph shall be made available through September 30, 2027, to qualified immigrants (and the eligible spouses and children of such immigrants) pooling their investments with 1 or more qualified immigrants participating in a program implementing this paragraph that involves a regional center in the United States, which has been designated by the Secretary of Homeland Security on the basis of a proposal for the promotion of economic growth, including prospective job creation and increased domestic capital investment.

(ii) Processing. In processing petitions under section 204(a)(1)(H) for classification under this paragraph, the Secretary of Homeland Security—

(I) shall prioritize the processing and adjudication of petitions for rural areas;

(II) may process petitions in a manner and order established by the Secretary; and

(III) shall deem such petitions to include records previously filed with the Secretary pursuant to subparagraph (F) if the alien petitioner certifies that such records are incorporated by reference into the alien's petition.

(iii) Establishment of a regional center. A regional center shall operate within a defined, contiguous, and limited geographic area, which shall be described in the proposal and be consistent with the purpose of concentrating pooled investment within such area. The proposal to establish a regional center shall demonstrate that the pooled investment will have a substantive economic impact on such geographic area, and shall include—

(I) reasonable predictions, supported by economically and statistically valid and transparent forecasting tools, concerning the amount of investment that will be pooled, the kinds of commercial enterprises that will receive such investments, details of the jobs that will be created directly or indirectly as a result of such investments, and other positive economic effects such investments will have;

(II) a description of the policies and procedures in place reasonably designed to monitor new commercial enterprises and any associated job-creating entity to seek to ensure compliance with—

(aa) all applicable laws, regulations, and Executive orders of the United States, including immigration laws, criminal laws, and securities laws; and

(bb) all securities laws of each State in which securities offerings will be conducted, investment advice will be rendered, or the offerors or offerees reside;

(III) attestations and information confirming that all persons involved with the regional center meet the requirements under clauses (i) and (ii) of subparagraph (H);

(IV) a description of the policies and procedures in place that are reasonably designed to ensure program compliance; and

(V) the identities of all natural persons involved in the regional center, as described in subparagraph (H)(v).

(iv) Indirect job creation.

(I) In general. The Secretary of Homeland Security shall permit aliens seeking admission under this subparagraph to satisfy only up to 90 percent of the requirement under subparagraph (A)(ii) with jobs that are estimated to be created indirectly through investment under this paragraph in accordance with this subparagraph. An employee of the new commercial enterprise or job-creating entity may be considered to hold a job that has been directly created.

(II) Construction activity lasting less than 2 years. If the jobs estimated to be created are created by construction activity lasting less than 2 years, the Secretary shall permit aliens seeking admission under this subparagraph to satisfy only up to 75 percent of the requirement under subparagraph (A)(ii) with jobs that are estimated to be created indirectly through investment under this paragraph in accordance with this subparagraph.

(v) Compliance.

(I) In general. In determining compliance with subparagraph (A)(ii), the Secretary of Homeland Security shall permit aliens seeking admission under this subparagraph to rely on economically and statistically valid methodologies for determining the number of jobs created by the program, including—

(aa) jobs estimated to have been created directly, which may be verified using such methodologies; and

(bb) consistent with this subparagraph, jobs estimated to have been directly or indirectly created through capital expenditures, revenues generated from increased exports, improved regional productivity, job creation, and increased domestic capital investment resulting from the program.

(II) Job and investment requirements.

(aa) Relocated jobs. In determining compliance with the job creation requirement under subparagraph (A)(ii), the Secretary of Homeland Security may include jobs estimated to be created under a methodology that attributes jobs to prospective tenants occupying commercial real estate created or improved by capital investments if the number of such jobs estimated to be created has been determined by an economically and statistically valid methodology and such jobs are not existing jobs that have been relocated.

(bb) Publicly available bonds. The Secretary of Homeland Security shall prescribe regulations to ensure that alien investor capital may not be utilized, by a new commercial enterprise or otherwise, to purchase municipal bonds or any other bonds, if such bonds are available to the general public, either as part of a primary offering or from a secondary market.

(cc) Construction activity jobs. If the number of direct jobs estimated to be created has been determined by an economically and statistically valid methodology, and such direct jobs are created by construction activity lasting less than 2 years, the number of such jobs that may be considered direct jobs for purposes of clause (iv) shall be calculated by multiplying the total number of such jobs estimated to be created by the fraction of the 2-year period that the construction activity lasts.

(vi) Amendments. The Secretary of Homeland Security shall—

(I) require a regional center—

(aa) to notify the Secretary, not later than 120 days before the implementation of significant proposed changes to its organizational structure, ownership, or administration, including the sale of such center, or other arrangements which would result in individuals not previously subject to the requirements under subparagraph (H) becoming involved with the regional center; or

(bb) if exigent circumstances are present, to provide the notice described in item (aa) to the Secretary not later than 5 business days after a change described in such item; and

(II) adjudicate business plans under subparagraph (F) and petitions under section 204(a)(1)(H) [8 USCS § 1154(a)(1)(H)] during any notice period as long as the amendment to the business or petition does not negatively impact program eligibility.

(vii) Record keeping and audits.

(I) Record keeping. Each regional center shall make and preserve, during the 5-year period beginning on the last day of the Federal fiscal year in which any transactions occurred, books, ledgers, records, and other documentation from the regional center, new commercial enterprise, or job-creating entity used to support—

(aa) any claims, evidence, or certifications contained in the regional center's annual statements under subparagraph (G); and (bb) associated petitions by aliens seeking classification under this section or removal of conditions under section 216A [8 USCS § 1186b].

(II) Audits. The Secretary shall audit each regional center not less frequently than once every 5 years. Each such audit shall include a review of any documentation required to be maintained under subclause (I) for the preceding 5 years and a review of the flow of alien investor capital into any capital investment project. To the extent multiple regional centers are located at a single site, the Secretary may audit multiple regional centers in a single site visit.

(III) Termination. The Secretary shall terminate the designation of a regional center that fails to consent to an audit under subclause (II) or deliberately attempts to impede such an audit.

(F) Business plans for regional center investments.

(i) Application for approval of an investment in a commercial enterprise. A regional center shall file an application with the Secretary of Homeland Security for each particular investment offering through an associated new commercial enterprise before any alien files a petition for classification under this paragraph by reason of investment in that offering. The application shall include—

(I) a comprehensive business plan for a specific capital investment project;

(II) a credible economic analysis regarding estimated job creation that is based upon economically and statistically valid and transparent methodologies;

(III) any documents filed with the Securities and Exchange Commission under the Securities Act of 1933 (15 U.S.C. 77a et seq.) or with the securities regulator of any State, as required by law;

(IV) any investment and offering documents, including subscription, investment, partnership, and operating agreements, private placement memoranda, term sheets, biographies of management, officers, directors, and any person with similar responsibilities, the description of the business plan to be provided to potential alien investors, and marketing materials used, or drafts prepared for use, in connection with the offering, which shall contain references, as appropriate, to—

(aa) all material investment risks associated with the new commercial enterprise and the job-creating entity;

(bb) any conflicts of interest that currently exist or may arise among the regional center, the new commercial enterprise, the job-creating entity, or the principals, attorneys, or individuals responsible for recruitment or promotion of such entities;

(cc) any pending material litigation or bankruptcy, or material adverse judgments or bankruptcy orders issued during the most recent 10-year period, in the United States or in another country, affecting the regional center, the new commercial enterprise, any associated job-creating entity, or any other enterprise in which any principal of any of the aforementioned entities held majority ownership at the time; and

(dd) (AA) any fees, ongoing interest, or other compensation paid, or to be paid by the regional center, the new commercial enterprise, or any issuer of securities intended to be offered to alien investors, to agents, finders, or broker dealers involved in the offering of securities to alien investors in connection with the investment;

(BB) a description of the services performed, or that will be performed, by such person to entitle the person to such fees, interest, or compensation; and

(CC) the name and contact information of any such person, if known at the time of filing;

(V) a description of the policies and procedures, such as those related to internal and external due diligence, reasonably designed to cause the regional center and any issuer of securities intended to be offered to alien investors in connection with the relevant capital investment project, to comply, as applicable, with the securities laws of the United States and the laws of the applicable States in connection with the offer, purchase, or sale of its securities; and

(VI) a certification from the regional center, and any issuer of securities intended to be offered to alien investors in connection with the relevant capital investment project, that their respective agents and employees, and any parties associated with the regional center and such issuer of securities affiliated with the regional center are in compliance with the securities laws of the United States and the laws of the applicable States in connection with the offer, purchase, or sale of its securities, to the best of the certifier's knowledge, after a due diligence investigation.

(ii) Effect of approval of a business plan for an investment in a regional center's commercial enterprise. The approval of an application under this subparagraph, including an approval before the date of the enactment of this subparagraph, shall be binding for purposes of the adjudication of subsequent petitions seeking classification under this paragraph by immigrants investing in the same offering described in such application, and of petitions by the same immigrants filed under section 216A [8 USCS § 1186b] unless—

(I) the applicant engaged in fraud, misrepresentation, or criminal misuse;

(II) such approval would threaten public safety or national security;

(III) there has been a material change that affects eligibility;

(IV) the discovery of other evidence affecting program eligibility was not disclosed by the applicant during the adjudication process; or

(V) the previous adjudication involved a material mistake of law or fact.

(iii) Amendments.

(I) Approval. The Secretary of Homeland Security may establish procedures by which a regional center may seek approval of an amendment to an approved application under this subparagraph that reflects changes specified by the Secretary to any information, documents, or other aspects of the investment offering described in such approved application not later than 30 days after any such changes.

(II) Incorporation. Upon the approval of a timely filed amendment to an approved application, any changes reflected in such amendment may be incorporated into and considered in determining program eligibility through adjudication of—

(aa) pending petitions from immigrants investing in the offering described in the approved application who are seeking classification under this paragraph; and

(bb) petitions by immigrants described in item (aa) that are filed under section 216A [8 USCS § 1186b].

(iv) Site visits. The Secretary of Homeland Security shall—

(I) perform site visits to regional centers not earlier than 24 hours after providing notice of such site visit; and

(II) perform at least 1 site visit to, as applicable, each new commercial enterprise or job-creating entity, or the business locations where any jobs that are claimed as being created.

(v) Parameters for capital redeployment.

(I)In general. The Secretary of Homeland Security shall prescribe regulations, in accordance with subchapter II of chapter 5 and chapter 7 of title 5, United States Code [5 USCS §§ 551 et seq. and 701 et seq.] (commonly known as the "Administrative Procedure Act"), that allow a new commercial enterprise to redeploy investment funds anywhere within the United States or its territories for the purpose of maintaining the investors' capital at risk if—

(aa) the new commercial enterprise has executed the business plan for a capital investment project in good faith without a material change;

(bb) the new commercial enterprise has created a sufficient number of new full time positions to satisfy the job creation requirements of the program for all investors in the new commercial enterprise, either directly or indirectly, as evidenced by the methodologies set forth in this Act;

(cc) the job creating entity has repaid the capital initially deployed in conformity with the initial investment contemplated by the business plan; and

(dd) the capital, after repayment by the job creating entity, remains at risk and it is not redeployed in passive investments, such as stocks or bonds.

(II)Termination. The Secretary of Homeland Security shall terminate the designation of a regional center if the Secretary determines that a new commercial enterprise has violated any of the requirements under subclause (I) in the redeployment of funds invested in such regional center.

(G) Regional center annual statements.

(i) In general. Each regional center designated under subparagraph (E) shall submit an annual statement, in a manner prescribed by the Secretary of Homeland Security. Each such statement shall include—

(I) a certification stating that, to the best of the certifier's knowledge, after a due diligence investigation, the regional center is in compliance with clauses (i) and (ii) of subparagraph (H);

(II) a certification described in subparagraph (I)(ii)(II);

(III) a certification stating that, to the best of the certifier's knowledge, after a due diligence investigation, the regional center is in compliance with subparagraph (K)(iii);

(IV) a description of any pending material litigation or bankruptcy proceedings, or material litigation or bankruptcy proceedings resolved during the preceding fiscal year, involving the regional center, the new commercial enterprise, or any affiliated job-creating entity;

(V) an accounting of all individual alien investor capital invested in the regional center, new commercial enterprise, and job-creating entity;

(VI) for each new commercial enterprise associated with the regional center—

(aa) an accounting of the aggregate capital invested in the new commercial enterprise and any job-creating entity by alien investors under this paragraph for each capital investment project being undertaken by the new commercial enterprise;

(bb) a description of how the capital described in item (aa) is being used to execute each capital investment project in the filed business plan or plans;

(cc) evidence that 100 percent of the capital described in item (aa) has been committed to each capital investment project;

(dd) detailed evidence of the progress made toward the completion of each capital investment project;

(ee) an accounting of the aggregate direct jobs created or preserved;

(ff) to the best of the regional center's knowledge, for all fees, including administrative fees, loan monitoring fees, loan management fees, commissions and similar transaction-based compensation, collected from alien investors by the regional center, the new commercial enterprise, any affiliated job-creating entity, any affiliated issuer of securities intended to be offered to alien investors, or any promoter, finder, broker-dealer, or other entity engaged by any of the aforementioned entities to locate individual investors—

(AA) a description of all fees collected;

(BB) an accounting of the entities that received such fees; and

(CC) the purpose for which such fees were collected;

(gg) any documentation referred to in subparagraph (F)(i)(IV) if there has been a material change during the preceding fiscal year; and

(hh) a certification by the regional center that the information provided under items (aa) through (gg) is accurate, to the best of the certifier's knowledge, after a due diligence investigation; and

(VII) a description of the regional center's policies and procedures that are designed to enable the regional center to comply with applicable Federal labor laws.

(ii) Amendment of annual statements. The Secretary of Homeland Security—

(I) shall require the regional center to amend or supplement an annual statement required under clause (i) if the Secretary determines that such statement is deficient; and

(II) may require the regional center to amend or supplement such annual statement if the Director determines that such an amendment or supplement is appropriate.

(iii) Sanctions.

(I) Effect of violation. The Director shall sanction any regional center entity in accordance with subclause (II) if the regional center fails to submit an annual statement or if the Director determines that the regional center—

(aa) knowingly submitted or caused to be submitted a statement, certification, or any information submitted pursuant to this subparagraph that contained an untrue statement of material fact; or

(bb) is conducting itself in a manner inconsistent with its designation under subparagraph (E), including any willful, undisclosed, and material deviation by new commercial enterprises from any filed business plan for such new commercial enterprises.

(II) Authorized sanctions. The Director shall establish a graduated set of sanctions based on the severity of the violations referred to in subclause (I), including—

(aa) fines equal to not more than 10 percent of the total capital invested by alien investors in the regional center's new commercial enterprises or job-creating entities directly involved in such violations, the payment of which shall not in any circumstance utilize any of such alien investors' capital investments, and which shall be deposited into the EB-5 Integrity Fund established under subparagraph (J);

(bb) temporary suspension from participation in the program described in subparagraph (E), which may be lifted by the Director if the individual or entity cures the alleged violation after being provided such an opportunity by the Director;

(cc) permanent bar from participation in the program described in subparagraph (E) for 1 or more individuals or business entities associated with the regional center, new commercial enterprise, or job-creating entity; and

(dd) termination of regional center designation.

(iv) Availability of annual statements to investors. Not later than 30 days after a request from an alien investor, a regional center shall make available to such alien investor a copy of the filed annual statement and any amendments filed to such statement, which shall be redacted to exclude any information unrelated to such alien investor or the new commercial enterprise or job creating entity into which the alien investor invested.

(H) Bona fides of persons involved with regional center program.

(i) In general. The Secretary of Homeland Security may not permit any person to be involved with any regional center, new commercial enterprise, or job-creating entity if—

(I) the person has been found to have committed—

(aa) a criminal or civil offense involving fraud or deceit within the previous 10 years;

(bb) a civil offense involving fraud or deceit that resulted in a liability in excess of $1,000,000; or

(cc) a crime for which the person was convicted and sentenced to a term of imprisonment of more than 1 year;

(II) the person is subject to a final order, for the duration of any penalty imposed by such order, of a State securities commission (or an agency or officer of a State performing similar functions), a State authority that supervises or examines banks, savings associations, or credit unions, a State insurance commission (or an agency or officer of a State performing similar functions), an appropriate Federal banking agency, the Commodity Futures Trading Commission, the Securities and Exchange Commission, a financial self-regulatory organization recognized by the Securities and Exchange Commission, or the National Credit Union Administration, which is based on a violation of any law or regulation that—

(aa) prohibits fraudulent, manipulative, or deceptive conduct; or

(bb) bars the person from—

(AA) association with an entity regulated by such commission, authority, agency, or officer;

(BB) appearing before such commission, authority, agency, or officer;

(CC) engaging in the business of securities, insurance, or banking; or

(DD) engaging in savings association or credit union activities;

(III) the Secretary determines that the person is engaged in, has ever been engaged in, or seeks to engage in—

(aa) any illicit trafficking in any controlled substance or in any listed chemical (as defined in section 102 of the Controlled Substances Act [21 USCS § 802]);

(bb) any activity relating to espionage, sabotage, or theft of intellectual property;

(cc) any activity related to money laundering (as described in section 1956 or 1957 of title 18, United States Code [18 USCS § 1956 or 1957]);

(dd) any terrorist activity (as defined in section 212(a)(3)(B) [8 USCS § 1182(a)(3)(B)]);

(ee) any activity constituting or facilitating human trafficking or a human rights offense;

(ff) any activity described in section 212(a)(3)(E) [8 USCS § 1182(a)(3)(E)]; or

(gg) the violation of any statute, regulation, or Executive order regarding foreign financial transactions or foreign asset control; or

(IV) the person—

(aa) is, or during the preceding 10 years has been, included on the Department of Justice's List of Currently Disciplined Practitioners; or

(bb) during the preceding 10 years, has received a reprimand or has otherwise been publicly disciplined for conduct related to fraud or deceit by a State bar association of which the person is or was a member.

(ii) Foreign involvement in regional center program.

(I) Lawful status required. A person may not be involved with a regional center unless the person—

(aa) is a national of the United States or an individual who has been lawfully admitted for permanent residence (as such terms are defined in paragraphs (20) and (22) of section 101(a) [8 USCS § 1101(a)]); and

(bb) is not the subject of rescission or removal proceedings.

(II) Foreign governments. No agency, official, or other similar entity or representative of a foreign government entity may provide capital to, or be directly or indirectly involved with the ownership or administration of, a regional center, a new commercial enterprise, or a job-creating entity, except that a foreign or domestic investment fund or other investment vehicle that is wholly or partially owned, directly or indirectly, by a bona fide foreign sovereign wealth fund or a foreign state-owned enterprise otherwise permitted to do business in the United States may be involved with the ownership, but not the administration, of a job-creating entity that is not an affiliated job-creating entity.

(III) Rulemaking. Not later than 270 days after the date of the enactment of the EB-5 Reform and Integrity Act of 2022 [enacted March 15, 2022], the Secretary shall issue regulations implementing subparagraphs (I) and (II).

(iii)Information required. The Secretary of Homeland Security—

(I) shall require such attestations and information, including the submission of fingerprints or other biometrics to the Federal Bureau of Investigation with respect to a regional center, a new commercial enterprise, and any affiliated job creating entity, and persons involved with such entities (as described in clause (v)), as may be necessary to determine whether such entities are in compliance with clauses (i) and (ii);

(II) shall perform such criminal record checks and other background and database checks with respect to a regional center, a new commercial enterprise, and any affiliated job-creating entity, and persons involved with such entities (as described in clause (v)), as may be necessary to determine whether such entities are in compliance with clauses (i) and (ii); and

(III) may, at the Secretary's discretion, require the information described to in subclause (I) and may perform the checks described in subclause (II) with respect to any job creating entity and persons involved with such entity if there is a reasonable basis to believe such entity or person is not in compliance with clauses (i) and (ii).

(iv) Termination.

(I)In general. The Secretary of Homeland Security may suspend or terminate the designation of any regional center, or the participation under the program of any new commercial enterprise or job-creating entity under this paragraph if the Secretary determines that such entity—

(aa) knowingly involved a person with such entity in violation of clause (i) or (ii) by failing, within 14 days of acquiring such knowledge—

(AA) to take commercially reasonable efforts to discontinue the prohibited person's involvement; or

(BB) to provide notice to the Secretary;

(bb) failed to provide an attestation or information requested by the Secretary under clause (iii)(I); or

(cc) knowingly provided any false attestation or information under clause (iii)(I).

(II) Limitation. The Secretary's authorized sanctions under subclause (I) shall be limited to entities that have engaged in any activity described in subclause (I).

(III) Information.

(aa) Notification. The Secretary, after performing the criminal record checks and other background checks described in clause (iii), shall notify a regional center, new commercial enterprise, or job-creating entity whether any person involved with such entities is not in compliance with clause (i) or (ii), unless the information that provides the basis for the determination is classified or disclosure is otherwise prohibited under law.

(bb) Effect of failure to respond. If the regional center, new commercial enterprise, or job-creating entity fails to discontinue the prohibited person's involvement with the regional center, new commercial enterprise, or job-creating entity, as applicable, within 30 days after receiving such notification, such entity shall be deemed to have knowledge under subclause (I)(aa) that the involvement of such person with the entity is in violation of clause (i) or (ii).

(v) Persons involved with a regional center, new commercial enterprise, or job-creating entity. For the purposes of this paragraph, unless otherwise determined by the Secretary of Homeland Security, a person is involved with a regional center, a new commercial enterprise, any affiliated job-creating entity, as applicable, if the person is, directly or indirectly, in a position of substantive authority to make operational or managerial decisions over pooling, securitization, investment, release, acceptance, or control or use of any funding that was procured under the program described in subparagraph (E). An individual may be in a position of substantive authority if the person serves as a principal, a representative, an administrator, an owner, an officer, a board member, a manager, an executive, a general partner, a fiduciary, an agent, or in a similar position at the regional center, new commercial enterprise, or job-creating entity, respectively.

(I) Compliance with securities laws.

(i) Jurisdiction.

(I) In general. The United States has jurisdiction, including subject matter jurisdiction, over the purchase or sale of any security offered or sold, or any investment advice provided, by any regional center or any party associated with a regional center for purposes of the securities laws.

(II) Compliance with regulations. For purposes of section 5 of the Securities Act of 1933 (15 U.S.C. 77e), a regional center or any party associated with a regional center is not precluded from offering or selling a security pursuant to Regulation S (17 C. F. R. 230.901 et seq.) to the extent that such offering or selling otherwise complies with that regulation.

(III) Savings provision. Subclause (I) is not intended to modify any existing rules or regulations of the Securities and Exchange Commission related to the application of section 15(a) of the Securities and Exchange Act of 1934 (15 U.S.C. 78o(a)) to foreign brokers or dealers.

(ii) Regional center certifications required.

(I) Initial certification. The Secretary of Homeland Security may not approve an application for regional center designation or regional center amendment unless the regional center certifies that, to the best of the certifier's knowledge, after a due diligence investigation, the regional center is in compliance with and has policies and procedures, including those related to internal and external due diligence, reasonably designed to confirm, as applicable, that all parties associated with the regional center are and will remain in compliance with the securities laws of the United States and of any State in which—

(aa) the offer, purchase, or sale of securities was conducted;

(bb) the issuer of securities was located; or

(cc) the investment advice was provided by the regional center or parties associated with the regional center.

(II) Reissue. A regional center shall annually reissue a certification described in subclause (I), in accordance with subparagraph (G), to certify compliance with clause (iii) by stating that—

(aa) the certification is made by a certifier;

(bb) to the best of the certifier's knowledge, after a due diligence investigation, all such offers, purchases, and sales of securities or the provision of investment advice complied with the securities laws of the United States and the securities laws of any State in which—

(AA) the offer, purchase, or sale of securities was conducted;

(BB) the issuer of securities was located; or

(CC) the investment advice was provided; and

(cc) records, data, and information related to such offers, purchases, and sales have been maintained.

(III) Effect of noncompliance. If a regional center, through its due diligence, discovered during the previous fiscal year that the regional center or any party associated with the regional center was not in compliance with the securities laws of the United States or the securities laws of any State in which the securities activities were conducted by any party associated with the regional center, the certifier shall—

(aa) describe the activities that led to noncompliance;

(bb) describe the actions taken to remedy the noncompliance; and

(cc) certify that the regional center and all parties associated with the regional center are currently in compliance, to the best of the certifier's knowledge, after a due diligence investigation.

(iii) Oversight required. Each regional center shall—

(I) use commercially reasonable efforts to monitor and supervise compliance with the securities laws in relations to all offers, purchases, and sales of, and investment advice relating to, securities made by parties associated with the regional center;

(II) maintain records, data, and information relating to all such offers, purchases, sales, and investment advice during the 5-year period beginning on the date of their creation; and

(III) make the records, data, and information described in subclause (II) available to the Secretary or to the Securities and Exchange Commission upon request.

(iv) Suspension or termination. In addition to any other authority provided to the Secretary under this paragraph, the Secretary, in the Secretary's discretion, may suspend or terminate the designation of any regional center or impose other sanctions against the regional center if the regional center, or any parties associated with the regional center that the regional center knew or reasonably should have known—

(I) are permanently or temporarily enjoined by order, judgment, or decree of any court of competent jurisdiction in connection with the offer, purchase, or sale of a security or the provision of investment advice;

(II) are subject to any final order of the Securities and Exchange Commission or a State securities regulator that—

(aa) bars such person from association with an entity regulated by the Securities and Exchange Commission or a State securities regulator; or

(bb) constitutes a final order based on a finding of an intentional violation or a violation related to fraud or deceit in connection with the offer, purchase, or sale of, or investment advice relating to, a security; or

(III) submitted, or caused to be submitted, a certification described in clause (ii) that contained an untrue statement of a material fact or omitted to state a material fact necessary in order to make the statements made, in light of the circumstances under which they were made, not misleading.

(v) Defined term. In this subparagraph, the term "parties associated with a regional center" means—

(I) the regional center;

(II) any new commercial enterprise or affiliated job-creating entity or issuer of securities associated with the regional center;

(III) the regional center's and new commercial enterprise's owners, officers, directors, managers, partners, agents, employees, promoters and attorneys, or similar position, as determined by the Secretary; and

(IV) any person under the control of the regional center, new commercial enterprise, or issuer of securities associated with the regional center who is responsible for the marketing, offering, or sale of any security offered in connection with the capital investment project.

(vi) Savings provision. Nothing in this subparagraph may be construed to impair or limit the authority of the Securities and Exchange Commission under the Federal securities laws or any State securities regulator under State securities laws.

(J) EB-5 Integrity Fund.

(i) Establishment. There is established in the United States Treasury a special fund, which shall be known as the "EB-5 Integrity Fund" (referred to in this subparagraph as the "Fund"). Amounts deposited into the Fund shall be available to the Secretary of Homeland Security until expended for the purposes set forth in clause (iii).

(ii) Fees.

(I)Annual fee. On October 1, 2022, and each October 1 thereafter, the Secretary of Homeland Security shall collect for the Fund an annual fee—

(aa) except as provided in item (bb), of $20,000 from each regional center designated under subparagraph (E); and

(bb) of $10,000 from each such regional center with 20 or fewer total investors in the preceding fiscal year in its new commercial enterprises.

(II) Petition fee. Beginning on October 1, 2022, the Secretary shall collect a fee of $1,000 for the Fund with each petition filed under section 204(a)(1)(H) [8 USCS § 1154(a)(1)(H)] for classification under subparagraph (E). The fee under this subclause is in addition to the fee that the Secretary is authorized to establish and collect for each petition to recover the costs of adjudication and naturalization services under section 286(m) [8 USCS § 1356(m)].

(III) Increases. The Secretary may increase the amounts under this clause by prescribing such regulations as may be necessary to ensure that amounts in the Fund are sufficient to carry out the purposes set forth in clause (iii).

(iii) Permissible uses of fund. The Secretary shall—

(I) use not less than 1/3 of the amounts deposited into the Fund for investigations based outside of the United States, including—

(aa) monitoring and investigating program-related events and promotional activities; and

(bb) ensuring an alien investor's compliance with subparagraph (L); and

(II) use amounts deposited into the Fund—

(aa) to detect and investigate fraud or other crimes;

(bb) to determine whether regional centers, new commercial enterprises, job-creating entities, and alien investors (and their alien spouses and alien children) comply with the immigration laws;

(cc) to conduct audits and site visits; and

(dd) as the Secretary determines to be necessary, including monitoring compliance with the requirements under section 107 of the EB-5 Reform and Integrity Act of 2022 [8 USCS § 1153a].

(iv) Failure to pay fee. The Secretary of Homeland Security shall—

(I) impose a reasonable penalty, which shall be deposited into the Fund, if any regional center does not pay the fee required under clause (ii) within 30 days after the date on which such fee is due; and

(II) terminate the designation of any regional center that does not pay the fee required under clause (ii) within 90 days after the date on which such fee is due.

(v) Report. The Secretary shall submit an annual report to the Committee on the Judiciary of the Senate and the Committee on the Judiciary of the House of Representatives that describes how amounts in the Fund were expended during the previous fiscal year.

(K) Direct and third-party promoters.

(i) Rules and standards. Direct and third-party promoters (including migration agents) of a regional center, any new commercial enterprise, an affiliated job-creating entity, or an issuer of securities intended to be offered to alien investors in connection with a particular capital investment project shall comply with the rules and standards prescribed by the Secretary of Homeland Security and any applicable Federal or State securities laws, to oversee promotion of any offering of securities related to the EB-5 Program, including—

(I) registration with U.S. Citizenship and Immigration Services, which—

(aa) includes identifying and contact information for such promoter and confirmation of the existence of the written agreement required under clause (iii); and

(bb) may be made publicly available at the discretion of the Secretary;

(II) certification by each promoter that such promoter is not ineligible under subparagraph (H)(i);

(III) guidelines for accurately representing the visa process to foreign investors; and

(IV) guidelines describing permissible fee arrangements under applicable securities and immigration laws.

(ii) Effect of violation. If the Secretary determines that a direct or third-party promoter has violated clause (i), the Secretary shall suspend or permanently bar such individual from participation in the program described in subparagraph (E).

(iii) Compliance. Each regional center, new commercial enterprise, and affiliated job-creating entity shall maintain a written agreement between or among such entities and each direct or third-party promoter operating on behalf of such entities that outlines the rules and standards prescribed under clause (i).

(iv) Disclosure. Each petition filed under section 204(a)(1)(H) [8 USCS § 1154(a)(1)(H)] shall include a disclosure, signed by the investor, that reflects all fees, ongoing interest, and other compensation paid to any person that the regional center or new commercial enterprise knows has received, or will receive, in connection with the investment, including compensation to agents, finders, or broker dealers involved in the offering, to the extent not already specifically identified in the business plan filed under subparagraph (F).

(L) Source of funds.

(i) In general. An alien investor shall demonstrate that the capital required under subparagraph (A) and any funds used to pay administrative costs and fees associated with the alien's investment were obtained from a lawful source and through lawful means.

(ii) Required information. The Secretary of Homeland Security shall require that an alien investor's petition under this paragraph contain, as applicable—

(I) business and tax records, or similar records, including—

(aa) foreign business registration records;

(bb) corporate or partnership tax returns (or tax returns of any other entity in any form filed in any country or subdivision of such country), and personal tax returns, including income, franchise, property (whether real, personal, or intangible), or any other tax returns of any kind, filed during the past 7 years (or another period to be determined by the Secretary to ensure that the investment is obtained from a lawful source of funds) with any taxing jurisdiction within or outside the United States by or on behalf of the alien investor; and

(cc) any other evidence identifying any other source of capital or administrative fees;

(II) evidence related to monetary judgments against the alien investor, including certified copies of any judgments, and evidence of all pending governmental civil or criminal actions, governmental administrative proceedings, and any private civil actions (pending or otherwise) involving possible monetary judgments against the alien investor from any court within or outside the United States; and

(III) the identity of all persons who transfer into the United States, on behalf of the investor, any funds that are used to meet the capital requirement under subparagraph (A).

(iii) Gift and loan restrictions.

(I) In general. Gifted and borrowed funds may not be counted toward the minimum capital investment requirement under subparagraph (C) unless such funds—

(aa) were gifted or loaned to the alien investor in good faith; and

(bb) were not gifted or loaned to circumvent any limitations imposed on permissible sources of capital under this subparagraph, including but not limitod to proceeds from illegal activity.

(II) Records requirement. If funds invested under subparagraph (A) are gifted or loaned to the alien investor, the Secretary shall require that the alien investor's petition under this paragraph includes the records described in subclauses (I) and (II) of clause (ii) from the donor or, if other than a bank, the lender.

(M) Treatment of good faith investors following program noncompliance.

(i) Termination or debarment of EB-5 entity. Except as provided in clause (vi), upon the termination or debarment, as applicable, from the program under this paragraph of a regional center, a new commercial enterprise, or a job-creating entity—

(I) an otherwise qualified petition under section 204(a)(1)(H) [8 USCS § 1154(a)(1)(H)] or the conditional permanent residence of an alien who has been admitted to the United States pursuant to section 216A(a)(1) [8 USCS § 1186b(a)(1)] based on an investment in a terminated regional center, new commercial enterprise, or job-creating entity shall remain valid or continue to be authorized, as applicable, consistent with this subparagraph; and

(II) the Secretary of Homeland Security shall notify the alien beneficiaries of such petitions of such termination or debarment.

(ii)New regional center or investment. The petition under section 204(a)(1)(H) [8 USCS § 1154(a)(1)(H)] of an alien described in clause (i) and the conditional permanent resident status of an alien described in clause (i) shall be terminated 180 days after notification of the termination from the program under this paragraph of a regional center, a new commercial enterprise, or a job creating entity (but not sooner than 180 days after the date of the enactment of the EB-5 Reform and Integrity Act of 2022 [enacted March 15, 2022]) unless—

(I) in the case of the termination of a regional center—

(aa) the new commercial enterprise associates with an approved regional center, regardless of the approved geographical boundaries of such regional center's designation; or

(bb) such alien makes a qualifying investment in another new commercial enterprise; or

(II) in the case of the debarment of a new commercial enterprise or job-creating entity, such alien—

(aa) associates with a new commercial enterprise in good standing; and

(bb) invests additional investment capital solely to the extent necessary to satisfy remaining job creation requirements under subparagraph (A)(ii).

(iii) Amendments.

(I) Filing requirement. The Secretary shall permit a petition described in clause (i)(I) to be amended to allow such petition to meet the applicable eligibility requirements under clause (ii), or to notify the Secretary that a pending or approved petition continues to meet the eligibility requirements described in clause (ii) notwithstanding termination or debarment described in clause (i) if such amendment is filed not later than 180 days after the Secretary provides notification of termination or debarment of a regional center, a new commercial enterprise, or a job-creating entity, as applicable.

(II) Determination of eligibility. For purposes of determining eligibility under subclause (I)—

(aa) the Secretary shall permit amendments to the business plan, without such facts underlying the amendment being deemed a material change; and

(bb) may deem any funds obtained or recovered by an alien investor, directly or indirectly, from claims against third parties, including insurance proceeds, or any additional investment capital provided by the alien, to be such alien's investment capital for the purposes of subparagraph (A) if such investment otherwise complies with the requirements under this paragraph and section 216A [8 USCS § 1186b].

(iv) Removal of conditions. Aliens described in subclauses (I)(bb) and (II) of clause (ii) shall be eligible to have their conditions removed pursuant to section 216A [8 USCS § 1186b] beginning on the date that is 2 years after the date of the subsequent investment.

(v) Remedies. For petitions approved under clause (ii), including following an amendment filed under clause (iii), the Secretary—

(I) shall retain the immigrant visa priority date related to the original petition and prevent age-out of derivative beneficiaries; and

(II) may hold such petition in abeyance and extend any applicable deadlines under this paragraph.

(vi) Exception. If the Secretary has reason to believe that an alien was a knowing participant in the conduct that led to the termination of a regional center, new commercial enterprise, or job-creating entity described in clause (i)—

(I) the alien shall not be accorded any benefit under this subparagraph; and

(II) the Secretary shall—

(aa) notify the alien of such belief; and

(bb) subject to section 216A(b)(2) [8 USCS § 1186b(b)(2)], shall deny or initiate proceedings to revoke the approval of such alien's petition, application, or benefit (and that of any spouse or child, if applicable) described in this paragraph.

(N) Threats to the national interest.

(i) Denial or revocation. The Secretary of Homeland Security shall deny or revoke the approval of a petition, application, or benefit described in this paragraph, including the documents described in clause (ii), if the Secretary determines, in the Secretary's discretion, that the approval of such petition, application, or benefit is contrary to the national interest of the United States for reasons relating to threats to public safety or national security.

(ii)Documents. The documents described in this clause are—

(I) a certification, designation, or amendment to the designation of a regional center;

(II) a petition seeking classification of an alien as an alien investor under this paragraph;

(III) a petition to remove conditions under section 216A [8 USCS § 1186b];

(IV) an application for approval of a business plan in a new commercial enterprise under subparagraph (F); or

(V) a document evidencing conditional permanent resident status that was issued to an alien pursuant to section 216A [8 USCS § 1186b].

(iii) Debarment. If a regional center, new commercial enterprise, or job-creating entity has its designation or participation in the program under this paragraph terminated for reasons relating to public safety or national security, any person associated with such regional center, new commercial enterprise, or job-creating entity, including an alien investor, shall be permanently barred from future participation in the program under this paragraph if the Secretary of Homeland Security, in the Secretary's discretion, determines, by a preponderance of the evidence, that such person was a knowing participant in the conduct that led to the termination.

(iv) Notice. If the Secretary of Homeland Security determines that the approval of a petition, application, or benefit described in this paragraph should be denied or revoked pursuant to clause (i), the Secretary shall—

(I) notify the relevant individual, regional center, or commercial entity of such determination;

(II) deny or revoke such petition, application, or benefit or terminate the permanent resident status of the alien (and the alien spouse and alien children of such immigrant), as of the date of such determination; and

(III) provide any United States-owned regional center, new commercial enterprise, or job creating entity an explanation for such determination unless the relevant information is classified or disclosure is otherwise prohibited under law.

(v) Judicial review. Notwithstanding any other provision of law (statutory or nonstatutory), including section 2241 of title 28, United States Code, or any other habeas corpus provision, and sections 1361 and 1651 of such title [28 USCS §§ 1361 and 1651], no court shall have jurisdiction to review a denial or revocation under this subparagraph. Nothing in this clause may be construed as precluding review of constitutional claims or questions of law raised upon a petition for review filed with an appropriate court of appeals in accordance with section 242 [8 USCS § 1252].

(O) Fraud, misrepresentation, and criminal misuse.

(i) Denial or revocation. Subject to subparagraph (M), the Secretary of Homeland Security shall deny or revoke the approval of a petition, application, or benefit described in this paragraph, including the documents described in subparagraph (N)(ii), if the Secretary determines, in the Secretary's discretion, that such petition, application, or benefit was predicated on or involved fraud, deceit, intentional material misrepresentation, or criminal misuse.

(ii) Debarment. If a regional center, new commercial enterprise, or job-creating entity has its designation or participation in the program under this paragraph terminated for reasons relating to fraud, intentional material misrepresentation, or criminal misuse, any person associated with such regional center, new commercial enterprise, or job-creating entity, including an alien investor, shall be permanently barred from future participation in the program if the Secretary determines, in the Secretary's discretion, by a preponderance of the evidence, that such person was a knowing participant in the conduct that led to the termination.

(iii) Notice. If the Secretary determines that the approval of a petition, application, or benefit described in this paragraph should be denied or revoked pursuant to clause (i), the Secretary shall—

(I) notify the relevant individual, regional center, or commercial entity of such determination; and

(II) deny or revoke such petition, application, or benefit or terminate the permanent resident status of the alien (and the alien spouse and alien children of such immigrant), in accordance with clause (i), as of the date of such determination.

(P) Administrative appellate review.

(i) In general. The Director of U.S. Citizenship and Immigration Services shall provide an opportunity for an administrative appellate review by the Administrative Appeals Office of U.S. Citizenship and Immigration Services of any determination made under this paragraph, including—

(I) an application for regional center designation or regional center amendment;

(II) an application for approval of a business plan filed under subparagraph (F);

(III) a petition by an alien investor for status as an immigrant under this paragraph;

(IV) the termination or suspension of any benefit accorded under this paragraph; and

(V) any sanction imposed by the Secretary under this paragraph.

(ii) Judicial review. Subject to subparagraph (N)(v) and section 242(a)(2) [8 USCS § 1252(a)(2)], and notwithstanding any other provision of law (statutory or nonstatutory), including section 2241 of title 28, United States Code, or any other habeas corpus provision, and sections 1361 and 1651 of such title [28 USCS §§ 1361 and 1651], no court shall have jurisdiction to review a determination under this paragraph until the regional center, its associated entities, or the alien investor has exhausted all administrative appeals.

(Q) Fund administration.

(i) In general. Each new commercial enterprise shall deposit and maintain the capital investment of each alien investor in a separate account, including amounts held in escrow.

(ii) Use of funds. Amounts in a separate account may only—

(I) be transferred to another separate account or a job creating entity;

(II) otherwise be deployed into the capital investment project for which the funds were intended; or

(III) be transferred to the alien investor who contributed the funds as a refund of that investor's capital investment, if otherwise permitted under this paragraph.

(iii) Deployment of funds into an affiliated job-creating entity. If amounts are transferred to an affiliated job-creating entity pursuant to clause (ii)(I)—

(I) the affiliated job-creating entity shall maintain such amounts in a separate account until they are deployed into the capital investment project for which they were intended; and

(II) not later than 30 days after such amounts are deployed pursuant to subclause (I), the affiliated job-creating entity shall provide written notice to the fund administrator retained pursuant to clause (iv) that a construction consultant or other individual authorized by the Secretary has verified that such amounts have been deployed into the project.

(iv)Fund administrator. Except as provided in clause (v), the new commercial enterprise shall retain a fund administrator to fulfill the requirements under this subparagraph. The fund administrator—

(I) shall be independent of, and not directly related to, the new commercial enterprise, the regional center associated with the new commercial enterprise, the job creating entity, or any of the principals or managers of such entities;

(II) shall be licensed, active, and in good standing as—

(aa) a certified public accountant;

(bb) an attorney;

(cc) a broker-dealer or investment adviser registered with the Securities and Exchange Commission; or

(dd) an individual or company that otherwise meets such requirements as may be established by the Secretary;

(III) shall monitor and track any transfer of amounts from the separate account;

(IV) shall serve as a cosignatory on all separate accounts;

(V) before any transfer of amounts from a separate account, shall—

(aa) verify that the transfer complies with all governing documents, including organizational, operational, and investment documents; and

(bb) approve such transfer with a written or electronic signature;

(VI) shall periodically provide each alien investor with information about the activity of the account in which the investor's capital investment is held, including—

(aa) the name and location of the bank or financial institution at which the account is maintained;

(bb) the history of the account; and

(cc) any additional information required by the Secretary; and

(VII) shall make and preserve, during the 5-year period beginning on the last day of the Federal fiscal year in which any transactions occurred, books, ledgers, records, and other documentation necessary to comply with this clause, which shall be provided to the Secretary upon request.

(v) Waiver.

(I) Waiver permitted. The Secretary of Homeland Security, after consultation with the Securities and Exchange Commission, may waive the requirements under clause (iv) for any new commercial enterprise or affiliated job-creating entity that is controlled by or under common control of an investment adviser or broker-dealer that is registered with the Securities and Exchange Commission if the Secretary, in the Secretary's discretion, determines that the Securities and Exchange Commission provides comparable protections and transparency for alien investors as the protections and transparency provided under clause (iv).

(II) Waiver required. The Secretary of Homeland Security shall waive the requirements under clause (iv) for any new commercial enterprise that commissions an annual independent financial audit of such new commercial enterprise or job creating entity conducted in accordance with Generally Accepted Auditing Standards, which audit shall be provided to the Secretary and all investors in the new commercial enterprise.

(vi) Defined term. In this subparagraph, the term "separate account" means an account that—

(I) is maintained in the United States by a new commercial enterprise or job creating entity at a federally regulated bank or at another financial institution (as defined in section 20 of title 18, United States Code [18 USCS § 20]) in the United States;

(II) is insured; and

(III) contains only the pooled investment funds of alien investors in a new commercial enterprise with respect to a single capital investment project.

(R) Required checks. Any petition filed by an alien under section 204(a)(1)(H) [8 USCS § 1154(a)(1)(H)] may not be approved under this paragraph unless the Secretary of Homeland Security has searched for the alien and any associated employer of such alien on the

Specially Designated Nationals List of the Department of the Treasury Office of Foreign Assets Control.

(S) Protection from expired legislation. Notwithstanding the expiration of legislation authorizing the regional center program under subparagraph (E), the Secretary of Homeland Security—

(i) shall continue processing petitions under sections 204(a)(1)(H) and 216A [8 USCS §§ 1154(a)(1)(H) and 1186b] based on an investment in a new commercial enterprise associated with a regional center that were filed on or before September 30, 2026;

(ii) may not deny a petition described in clause (i) based on the expiration of such legislation; and

(iii) may not suspend or terminate the allocation of visas to the beneficiaries of approved petitions described in clause (i).

(6) Special rules for "K" special immigrants.

(A) Not counted against numerical limitation in year involved. Subject to subparagraph (B), the number of immigrant visas made available to special immigrants under section 101(a)(27)(K) [8 USCS § 1101(a)(27)(K)] in a fiscal year shall not be subject to the numerical limitations of this subsection or of section 202(a) [8 USCS § 1152(a)].

(B) Counted against numerical limitations in following year.

(i) Reduction in employment-based immigrant classifications. The number of visas made available in any fiscal year under paragraphs (1), (2), and (3) shall each be reduced by 1/3 of the number of visas made available in the previous fiscal year to special immigrants described in section 101(a)(27)(K) [8 USCS § 1101(a)(27)(K)].

(ii) Reduction in per country level. The number of visas made available in each fiscal year to natives of a foreign state under section 202(a) [8 USCS § 1152(a)] shall be reduced by the number of visas made available in the previous fiscal year to special immigrants described in section 101(a)(27)(K) [8 USCS § 1101(a)(27)(K)] who are natives of the foreign state.

(iii) Reduction in employment-based immigrant classifications within per country ceiling. In the case of a foreign state subject to section 202(e) [8 USCS § 1152(e)] in a fiscal year (and in the previous fiscal year), the number of visas made available and allocated to each of paragraphs (1) through (3) of this subsection in the fiscal year shall be reduced by 1/3 of the number of visas made available in the previous fiscal year to special immigrants described in section 101(a)(27)(K) [8 USCS § 1101(a)(27)(K))] who are natives of the foreign state.

(c) Diversity immigrants.

(1) In general. Except as provided in paragraph (2), aliens subject to the worldwide level specified in section 201(e) [8 USCS § 1151(e)] for diversity immigrants shall be allotted visas each fiscal year as follows:

(A) Determination of preference immigration. The Attorney General shall determine for the most recent previous 5-fiscal-year period for which data are available, the total number of aliens who are natives of each foreign state and who (i) were admitted or otherwise provided lawful permanent resident status (other than under this subsection) and (ii) were subject to the numerical limitations of section 201(a) [8 USCS § 1151(a)] (other than paragraph (3) thereof) or who were admitted or otherwise provided lawful permanent resident status as an immediate relative or other alien described in section 201(b)(2) [8 USCS § 1151(b)(2)].

(B) Identification of high-admission and low-admission regions and high-admission and low-admission states. The Attorney General—

(i) shall identify—

(I) each region (each in this paragraph referred to as a "high-admission region") for which the total of the numbers determined under subparagraph (A) for states in the region is greater than 1/6 of the total of all such numbers, and

(II) each other region (each in this paragraph referred to as a "low-admission region"); and

(ii) shall identify—

(I) each foreign state for which the number determined under subparagraph (A) is greater than 50,000 (each such state in this paragraph referred to as a "high-admission state"), and

(II) each other foreign state (each such state in this paragraph referred to as a "low-admission state").

(C) Determination of percentage of worldwide immigration attributable to high-admission regions. The Attorney General shall determine the percentage of the total of the numbers determined under subparagraph (A) that are numbers for foreign states in high-admission regions.

(D) Determination of regional populations excluding high-admission states and ratios of populations of regions within low-admission regions and high-admission regions. The Attorney General shall determine—

(i) based on available estimates for each region, the total population of each region not including the population of any high-admission state;

(ii) for each low-admission region, the ratio of the population of the region determined under clause (i) to the total of the populations determined under such clause for all the low-admission regions; and

(iii) for each high-admission region, the ratio of the population of the region determined under clause (i) to the total of the populations determined under such clause for all the high-admission regions.

(E) Distribution of visas.

(i) No visas for natives of high-admission states. The percentage of visas made available under this paragraph to natives of a high-admission state is 0.

(ii) For low-admission states in low-admission regions. Subject to clauses (iv) and (v), the percentage of visas made available under this paragraph to natives (other than natives of a high-admission state) in a low-admission region is the product of—

(I) the percentage determined under subparagraph (C), and

(II) the population ratio for that region determined under subparagraph (D)(ii).

(iii) For low-admission states in high-admission regions. Subject to clauses (iv) and (v), the percentage of visas made available under this paragraph to natives (other than natives of a high-admission state) in a high-admission region is the product of—

(I) 100 percent minus the percentage determined under subparagraph (C), and

(II) the population ratio for that region determined under subparagraph (D)(iii).

(iv) Redistribution of unused visa numbers. If the Secretary of State estimates that the number of immigrant visas to be issued to natives in any region for a fiscal year under this paragraph is less than the number of immigrant visas made available to such natives under this paragraph for the fiscal year, subject to clause (v), the excess visa numbers shall be made available to natives (other than natives of a high-admission state) of the other regions in proportion to the percentages otherwise specified in clauses (ii) and (iii).

(v) Limitation on visas for natives of a single foreign state. The percentage of visas made available under this paragraph to natives of any single foreign state for any fiscal year shall not exceed 7 percent.

(F) "Region" defined. Only for purposes of administering the diversity program under this subsection, Northern Ireland shall be treated as a separate foreign state, each colony or other component or dependent area of a foreign state overseas from the foreign state shall be treated as part of the foreign state, and the areas described in each of the following clauses shall be considered to be a separate region:

(i) Africa.

(ii) Asia.

(iii) Europe.

(iv) North America (other than Mexico).

(v) Oceania.

(vi) South America, Mexico, Central America, and the Caribbean.

(2) Requirement of education or work experience. An alien is not eligible for a visa under this subsection unless the alien—

(A) has at least a high school education or its equivalent, or

(B) has, within 5 years of the date of application for a visa under this subsection, at least 2 years of work experience in an occupation which requires at least 2 years of training or experience.

(3) Maintenance of information. The Secretary of State shall maintain information on the age, occupation, education level, and other relevant characteristics of immigrants issued visas under this subsection.

(d) Treatment of family members. A spouse or child as defined in subparagraph (A), (B), (C), (D), or (E) of section 101(b)(1) [8 USCS § 1101(b)(1)(A), (B), (C), (D), or (E)] shall, if not otherwise entitled to an immigrant status and the immediate issuance of a visa under subsection (a), (b), or (c), be entitled to the same status, and the same order of consideration provided in the respective subsection, if accompanying or following to join, the spouse or parent.

(e) Order of consideration.

(1) Immigrant visas made available under subsection (a) or (b) shall be issued to eligible immigrants in the order in which a petition in behalf of each such immigrant is filed with the Attorney General (or in the case of special immigrants under section 101(a)(27)(D) [8 USCS § 1101(a)(27)(D)], with the Secretary of State) as provided in section 204(a) [8 USCS § 1154(a)].

(2) Immigrant visa numbers made available under subsection (c) (relating to diversity immigrants) shall be issued to eligible qualified immigrants strictly in a random order established by the Secretary of State for the fiscal year involved.

(3) Waiting lists of applicants for visas under this section shall be maintained in accordance with regulations prescribed by the Secretary of State.

(f) Authorization for issuance. In the case of any alien claiming in his application for an immigrant visa to be described in section 201(b)(2) [8 USCS § 1151(b)(2)] or in subsection (a), (b), or (c) of this section, the consular officer shall not grant such status until he has been authorized to do so as provided by section 204 [8 USCS § 1154].

(g) Lists. For purposes of carrying out the Secretary's responsibilities in the orderly administration of this section, the Secretary of State may make reasonable estimates of the anticipated numbers of visas to be issued during any quarter of any fiscal year within each of the categories under subsections (a), (b), and (c) and to rely upon such estimates in authorizing the issuance of visas. The Secretary of State shall terminate the registration of any alien who fails to apply for an immigrant visa within one year following notification to the alien of the availability of such visa, but the Secretary shall reinstate the registration of any such alien who establishes within 2 years following the date of notification of the availability of such visa that such failure to apply was due to circumstances beyond the alien's control.

(h) Rules for determining whether certain aliens are children.

(1) In general. For purposes of subsections (a)(2)(A) and (d), a determination of whether an alien satisfies the age requirement in the matter preceding subparagraph (A) of section 101(b)(1) [8 USCS § 1101(b)(1)] shall be made using—

(A) the age of the alien on the date on which an immigrant visa number becomes available for such alien (or, in the case of subsection (d), the date on which an immigrant visa number became available for the alien's parent), but only if the alien has sought to acquire the status of an alien lawfully admitted for permanent residence within one year of such availability; reduced by

(B) the number of days in the period during which the applicable petition described in paragraph (2) was pending.

(2) Petitions described. The petition described in this paragraph is—

(A) with respect to a relationship described in subsection (a)(2)(A), a petition filed under section 204 [8 USCS § 1154] for classification of an alien child under subsection (a)(2)(A); or

(B) with respect to an alien child who is a derivative beneficiary under subsection (d), a petition filed under section 204 [8 USCS § 1154] for classification of the alien's parent under subsection (a), (b), or (c).

(3) Retention of priority date. If the age of an alien is determined under paragraph (1) to be 21 years of age or older for the purposes of subsections (a)(2)(A) and (d), the alien's petition shall automatically be converted to the appropriate category and the alien shall retain the original priority date issued upon receipt of the original petition.

(4) Application to self-petitions. Paragraphs (1) through (3) shall apply to self-petitioners and derivatives of self-petitioners.

(5) Age determination for children of alien investors. An alien who has reached 21 years of age and has been admitted under subsection (d) as a lawful permanent resident on a conditional basis as the child of an alien lawfully admitted for permanent residence under subsection (b)(5), whose lawful permanent resident status on a conditional basis is terminated under section 216A [8 USCS § 1186b] or subsection (b)(5)(M), shall continue to be considered a child of the principal alien for the purpose of a subsequent immigrant petition by such alien under subsection (b)(5) if the alien remains unmarried and the subsequent petition is filed by the principal alien not later than 1 year after the termination of conditional lawful permanent resident status. No alien shall be considered a child under this paragraph with respect to more than 1 petition filed after the alien reaches 21 years of age.

HISTORY: (JJune 27, 1952, ch 477, Title II, Ch 1, § 203, 66 Stat. 178; Sept. 11, 1957, P. L. 85-316, § 3, 71 Stat. 639; Sept. 22, 1959, P. L. 86-363, §§ 1–3, 73 Stat. 644; Oct. 3, 1965, P. L. 89-236, § 3, 79 Stat. 912; Oct. 20, 1976, P. L. 94-571, § 4, 90 Stat. 2705; Oct. 5, 1978, P. L. 95-412, §§ 1, 3, 92 Stat. 907, 917; Oct. 5, 1978, P. L. 95-417, § 1, 92 Stat. 917; March 17, 1980, P. L. 96-212, Title II, § 203(c), (i), 94 Stat. 107, 108; Nov. 29, 1990, P. L. 101-649, Title I, Subtitle B, Part 1, § 111, Part 2, § 121(a), Part 3, § 131, Subtitle E, § 162(a)(1),Title VI, § 603(a)(3), 104 Stat. 4986, 4987, 4997, 5009, 5082; Oct. 1, 1991, P. L. 102-110, § 2(b), 105 Stat. 555; Dec. 12, 1991, P. L. 102-232, Title III, § 302(b)(2), (e)(3), 105 Stat. 1743, 1745; Oct. 25, 1994, P. L. 103-416, Title II, §§ 212(b), 219(c), 108 Stat. 4314, 4316; Nov. 12, 1999, P. L. 106-95, § 5, 113 Stat. 1318; Nov. 29, 1999, P. L. 106-113, Div B, § 1000(a)(1), 113 Stat. 1535; Nov. 22, 2000, P. L. 106-536, § 1(b)(1), 114 Stat. 2560; Aug. 6, 2002, P. L. 107-208, § 3, 116 Stat. 928; Nov. 2, 2002, P. L. 107-273, Div C, Title I, Subtitle B, Ch. 2, §§ 11035, 11036(a), 116 Stat. 1846; Jan. 5, 2006, P. L. 109-162, Title VIII, Subtitle A, § 805(b)(2), 119 Stat. 3056; Mar. 15, 2022, P.L. 117-103, Div BB, §§ 102(a), (b), 103(b)(1), (c)(1), 108, 136 Stat. 1070, 1074, 1075, 1100, 1109.)

§ 204. [8 U.S.C. § 1154] Procedure for granting immigrant status.

(a) Petitioning procedure.

(1) (A) (i) Except as provided in clause (viii), any citizen of the United States claiming that an alien is entitled to classification by reason of a relationship described in paragraph (1), (3), or (4) of section 203(a) [8 USCS § 1153(a)] or to an immediate relative status under section 201(b)(2)(A)(i) [8 USCS § 1151(b)(2)(A)(i)] may file a petition with the Attorney General for such classification.

(ii) An alien spouse described in the second sentence of section 201(b)(2)(A)(i) [8 USCS § 1151(b)(2)(A)(i)] also may file a petition with the Attorney General under this subparagraph for classification of the alien (and the alien's children) under such section.

(iii) (I) An alien who is described in subclause (II) may file a petition with the Attorney General under this clause for classification of the alien (and any child of the alien) if the alien demonstrates to the Attorney General that—

(aa) the marriage or the intent to marry the United States citizen was entered into in good faith by the alien; and

(bb) during the marriage or relationship intended by the alien to be legally a marriage, the alien or a child of the alien has been battered or has been the subject of extreme cruelty perpetrated by the alien's spouse or intended spouse.

(II) For purposes of subclause (I), an alien described in this subclause is an alien—

(aa) (AA) who is the spouse of a citizen of the United States;

(BB) who believed that he or she had married a citizen of the United States and with whom a marriage ceremony was actually performed and who otherwise meets any applicable requirements under this Act to establish the existence of and bona fides of a marriage, but whose marriage is not legitimate solely because of the bigamy of such citizen of the United States; or

(CC) who was a bona fide spouse of a United States citizen within the past 2 years and—

(aaa) whose spouse died within the past 2 years;

(bbb) whose spouse lost or renounced citizenship status within the past 2 years related to an incident of domestic violence; or

(ccc) who demonstrates a connection between the legal termination of the marriage within the past 2 years and battering or extreme cruelty by the United States citizen spouse;

(bb) who is a person of good moral character;

(cc) who is eligible to be classified as an immediate relative under section 201(b)(2)(A)(i) [8 USCS § 1151(b)(2)(A)(i)] or who would have been so classified but for the bigamy of the citizen of the United States that the alien intended to marry; and

(dd) who has resided with the alien's spouse or intended spouse.

(iv) An alien who is the child of a citizen of the United States, or who was a child of a United States citizen parent who within the past 2 years lost or renounced citizenship status related to an incident of domestic violence, and who is a person of good moral character, who is eligible to be classified as an immediate relative under section 201(b)(2)(A)(i) [8 USCS § 1151(b)(2)(A)(i)], and who resides, or has resided in the past, with the citizen parent may file a petition with the Attorney General under this subparagraph for classification of the alien (and any child of the alien) under such section if the alien demonstrates to the Attorney General that the alien has been battered by or has been the subject of extreme cruelty perpetrated by the alien's citizen parent. For purposes of this clause, residence includes any period of visitation.

(v) An alien who—

(I) is the spouse, intended spouse, or child living abroad of a citizen who—

(aa) is an employee of the United States Government;

(bb) is a member of the uniformed services (as defined in section 101(a) of title 10, United States Code); or

(cc) has subjected the alien or the alien's child to battery or extreme cruelty in the United States; and

(II) is eligible to file a petition under clause (iii) or (iv),

shall file such petition with the Attorney General under the procedures that apply to self-petitioners under clause (iii) or (iv), as applicable.

(vi) For the purposes of any petition filed under clause (iii) or (iv), the denaturalization, loss or renunciation of citizenship, death of the abuser, divorce, or changes to the abuser's citizenship status after filing of the petition shall not adversely affect the approval of the petition, and for approved petitions shall not preclude the classification of the eligible self-petitioning spouse or child as an immediate relative or affect the alien's ability to adjust status under subsections (a) and (c) of section 245 [8 USCS § 1255] or obtain status as a lawful permanent resident based on the approved self-petition under such clauses.

(vii) An alien may file a petition with the Secretary of Homeland Security under this subparagraph for classification of the alien under section 201(b)(2)(A)(i) [8 USCS § 1151(b)(2)(A)(i)] if the alien—

(I) is the parent of a citizen of the United States or was a parent of a citizen of the United States who, within the past 2 years, lost or renounced citizenship status related to an incident of domestic violence or died;

(II) is a person of good moral character;

(III) is eligible to be classified as an immediate relative under section 201(b)(2)(A)(i) [8 USCS § 1151(b)(2)(A)(i)];

(IV) resides, or has resided, with the citizen daughter or son; and

(V) demonstrates that the alien has been battered or subject to extreme cruelty by the citizen daughter or son.

(viii) (I) Clause (i) shall not apply to a citizen of the United States who has been convicted of a specified offense against a minor, unless the Secretary of Homeland Security, in the Secretary's sole and unreviewable discretion, determines that the citizen poses no risk to the alien with respect to whom a petition described in clause (i) is filed.

(II) For purposes of subclause (I), the term "specified offense against a minor" is defined as in section 111 of the Adam Walsh Child Protection and Safety Act of 2006 [34 USCS § 20911].

(B) (i) (I) Except as provided in subclause (II), any alien lawfully admitted for permanent residence claiming that an alien is entitled to a classification by reason of the relationship described in section 203(a)(2) [8 USCS § 1153(a)(2)] may file a petition with the Attorney General for such classification.

[(II)](I) Subclause (I) shall not apply in the case of an alien lawfully admitted for permanent residence who has been convicted of a specified offense against a minor (as defined in subparagraph (A)(viii)(II)), unless the Secretary of Homeland Security, in the Secretary's sole and unreviewable discretion, determines that such person poses no risk to the alien with respect to whom a petition described in subclause (I) is filed.

(ii) (I) An alien who is described in subclause (II) may file a petition with the Attorney General under this clause for classification of the alien (and any child of the alien) if such a child has not been classified under clause (iii) of section 203(a)(2)(A) [8 USCS § 1153(a)(2)(A)] and if the alien demonstrates to the Attorney General that—

(aa) the marriage or the intent to marry the lawful permanent resident was entered into in good faith by the alien; and

(bb) during the marriage or relationship intended by the alien to be legally a marriage, the alien or a child of the alien has been battered or has been the subject of extreme cruelty perpetrated by the alien's spouse or intended spouse.

(II) For purposes of subclause (I), an alien described in this paragraph is an alien—

(aa) (AA) who is the spouse of a lawful permanent resident of the United States; or

(BB) who believed that he or she had married a lawful permanent resident of the United States and with whom a marriage ceremony was actually performed and who otherwise meets any applicable requirements under this Act to establish the existence of and bona fides of a marriage, but whose marriage is not legitimate solely because of the bigamy of such lawful permanent resident of the United States; or

(CC) who was a bona fide spouse of a lawful permanent resident within the past 2 years and—

(aaa) whose spouse lost status within the past 2 years due to an incident of domestic violence; or

(bbb) who demonstrates a connection between the legal termination of the marriage within the past 2 years and battering or extreme cruelty by the lawful permanent resident spouse;

(bb) who is a person of good moral character;

(cc) who is eligible to be classified as a spouse of an alien lawfully admitted for permanent residence under section 203(a)(2)(A) [8 USCS § 1153(a)(2)(A)] or who would have been so classified but for the bigamy of the lawful permanent resident of the United States that the alien intended to marry; and

(dd) who has resided with the alien's spouse or intended spouse.

(iii) An alien who is the child of an alien lawfully admitted for permanent residence, or who was the child of a lawful permanent resident who within the past 2 years lost lawful permanent resident status due to an incident of domestic violence, and who is a person of good moral character, who is eligible for classification under section 203(a)(2)(A) [8 USCS § 1153(a)(2)(A)], and who resides, or has resided in the past, with the alien's permanent resident alien parent may file a petition with the Attorney General under this subparagraph for classification of the alien (and any child of the alien) under such section if the alien demonstrates to the Attorney General that the alien has been battered by or has been the subject of extreme cruelty perpetrated by the alien's permanent resident parent.

(iv) An alien who—

(I) is the spouse, intended spouse, or child living abroad of a lawful permanent resident who—

(aa) is an employee of the United States Government;

(bb) is a member of the uniformed services (as defined in section 101(a) of title 10, United States Code); or

(cc) has subjected the alien or the alien's child to battery or extreme cruelty in the United States; and

(II) is eligible to file a petition under clause (ii) or (iii),

shall file such petition with the Attorney General under the procedures that apply to self-petitioners under clause (ii) or (iii), as applicable.

(v) (I) For the purposes of any petition filed or approved under clause (ii) or (iii), divorce, or the loss of lawful permanent resident status by a spouse or parent after the filing of a petition under that clause shall not adversely affect approval of the petition, and, for an approved petition, shall not affect the alien's ability to adjust status under subsections (a) and (c) of section 245 [8 USCS § 1255] or obtain status as a lawful permanent resident based on an approved self-petition under clause (ii) or (iii).

(II) Upon the lawful permanent resident spouse or parent becoming or establishing the existence of United States citizenship through naturalization, acquisition of citizenship, or other means, any petition filed with the Immigration and Naturalization Service and pending or approved under clause (ii) or (iii) on behalf of an alien who has been battered or subjected to extreme cruelty shall be deemed reclassified as a petition filed under subparagraph (A) even if the acquisition of citizenship occurs after divorce or termination of parental rights.

(C) Notwithstanding section 101(f) [8 USCS § 1101(f)], an act or conviction that is waivable with respect to the petitioner for purposes of a determination of the petitioner's admissibility under section 212(a) [8 USCS § 1182(a)] or deportability under section 237(a) [8 USCS § 1227(a)] shall not bar the Attorney General from finding the petitioner to be of good moral character under subparagraph (A)(iii), (A)(iv), (B)(ii), or (B)(iii) if the Attorney General finds that the act or conviction was connected to the alien's having been battered or subjected to extreme cruelty.

(D) (i) (I) Any child who attains 21 years of age who has filed a petition under clause (iv) of section 204(a)(1)(A) or section 204(a)(1)(B)(iii) [subsec. (a)(1)(A) or (a)(1)(B)(iii) of this section] that was filed or approved before the date on which the child attained 21 years of age shall be considered (if the child has not been admitted or approved for lawful permanent residence by the date the child attained 21 years of age) a petitioner for preference status under paragraph (1), (2), or (3) of section 203(a) [8 USCS § 1153(a)], whichever paragraph is applicable, with the same priority date assigned to the self-petition filed under clause (iv) of section 204(a)(1)(A) or section 204(a)(1)(B)(iii) [subsec. (a)(1)(A) or (a)(1)(B)(iii) of this section]. No new petition shall be required to be filed.

(II) Any individual described in subclause (I) is eligible for deferred action and work authorization.

(III) Any derivative child who attains 21 years of age who is included in a petition described in clause (ii) that was filed or approved before the date on which the child attained 21 years of age shall be considered (if the child has not been admitted or approved for lawful permanent residence by the date the child attained 21 years of age) a VAWA self-petitioner with the same priority date as that assigned to the petitioner in any petition described in clause (ii). No new petition shall be required to be filed.

(IV) Any individual described in subclause (III) and any derivative child of a petition described in clause (ii) is eligible for deferred action and work authorization.

(ii) The petition referred to in clause (i)(III) is a petition filed by an alien under subparagraph (A)(iii), (A)(iv), (B)(ii) or (B)(iii) in which the child is included as a derivative beneficiary.

(iii) Nothing in the amendments made by the Child Status Protection Act shall be construed to limit or deny any right or benefit provided under this subparagraph.

(iv) Any alien who benefits from this subparagraph may adjust status in accordance with subsections (a) and (c) of section 245 [8 USCS § 1255] as an alien having an approved petition for classification under subparagraph (A)(iii), (A)(iv), (B)(ii), or (B)(iii).

(v) For purposes of this paragraph, an individual who is not less than 21 years of age, who qualified to file a petition under subparagraph (A)(iv) or (B)(iii) as of the day before the date on which the individual attained 21 years of age, and who did not file such a petition before such day, shall be treated as having filed a petition under such subparagraph as of such day if a petition is filed for the status described in such subparagraph before the individual attains 25 years of age and the individual shows that the abuse was at least one central reason for the filing delay. Clauses (i) through (iv) of this subparagraph shall apply to an individual described in this clause in the same manner as an individual filing a petition under subparagraph (A)(iv) or (B)(iii).

(E) Any alien desiring to be classified under section 203(b)(1)(A) [8 USCS § 1153(b)(1)(A)], or any person on behalf of such an alien, may file a petition with the Attorney General for such classification.

(F) Any employer desiring and intending to employ within the United States an alien entitled to classification under section 203(b)(1)(B), 203(b)(1)(C), 203(b)(2), or 203(b)(3) [8 USCS § 1153(b)(1)(B), (C), (2), or (3)] may file a petition with the Attorney General for such classification.

(G) (i) Any alien (other than a special immigrant under section 101(a)(27)(D) [8 USCS § 1101(a)(27)(D)] desiring to be classified under section 203(b)(4) [8 USCS § 1153(b)(4)], or any person on behalf of such an alien, may file a petition with the Attorney General for such classification.

(ii) Aliens claiming status as a special immigrant under section 101(a)(27)(D) [8 USCS § 1101(a)(27)(D)] may file a petition only with the Secretary of State and only after notification by the Secretary that such status has been recommended and approved pursuant to such section.

(H) (i) Any alien seeking classification under section 203(b)(5) [8 USCS § 1153(b)(5)] may file a petition for such classification with the Secretary of Homeland Security. An alien seeking to pool his or her investment with 1 or more additional aliens seeking classification under section 203(b)(5) [8 USCS § 1153(b)(5)] shall file for such classification in accordance with section 203(b)(5)(E) [8 USCS § 1153(b)(5)(E)], or before the date of the enactment of the EB-5 Reform and Integrity Act of 2022 [enacted March 15, 2022], in accordance with section 203(b)(5) [8 USCS § 1153(b)(5)]. An alien petitioning for classification under section 203(b)(5)(E) [8 USCS § 1153(b)(5)(E)] may file a petition with the Secretary after a regional center has filed an application for approval of an investment under section 203(b)(5)(F) [8 USCS § 1153(b)(5)(F)].

(ii) A petitioner described in clause (i) shall establish eligibility at the time he or she files a petition for classification under section 203(b)(5) [8 USCS § 1153(b)(5)]. A petitioner who was eligible for such classification at the time of such filing shall be deemed eligible for such classification at the time such petition is adjudicated, subject to the approval of the petitioner's associated application under section 203(b)(5)(F) [8 USCS § 1153(b)(5)(F)], if applicable.

(I) (i) Any alien desiring to be provided an immigrant visa under section 203(c) [8 USCS § 1153(c)] may file a petition at the place and time determined by the Secretary of State by regulation. Only one such petition may be filed by an alien with respect to any petitioning period established. If more than one petition is submitted all such petitions submitted for such period by the alien shall be voided.

(ii) (I) The Secretary of State shall designate a period for the filing of petitions with respect to visas which may be issued under section 203(c) [8 USCS § 1153(c)] for the fiscal year beginning after the end of the period.

(II) Aliens who qualify, through random selection, for a visa under section 203(c) [8 USCS § 1153(c)] shall remain eligible to receive such visa only through the end of the specific fiscal year for which they were selected.

(III) The Secretary of State shall prescribe such regulations as may be necessary to carry out this clause.

(iii) A petition under this subparagraph shall be in such form as the Secretary of State may by regulation prescribe and shall contain such information and be supported by such documentary evidence as the Secretary of State may require.

(J) In acting on petitions filed under clause (iii) or (iv) of subparagraph (A) or clause (ii) or (iii) of subparagraph (B), or in making determinations under subparagraphs (C) and (D), the Attorney General shall consider any credible evidence relevant to the petition. The determination of what evidence is credible and the weight to be given that evidence shall be within the sole discretion of the Attorney General.

(K) Upon the approval of a petition as a VAWA self-petitioner, the alien—

(i) is eligible for work authorization; and

(ii) may be provided an "employment authorized" endorsement or appropriate work permit incidental to such approval.

(L) Notwithstanding the previous provisions of this paragraph, an individual who was a VAWA petitioner or who had the status of a nonimmigrant under subparagraph (T) or (U) of section 101(a)(15) [8 USCS § 1101(a)(15)] may not file a petition for classification under this section or section 214 [8 USCS § 1184] to classify any person who committed the battery or extreme cruelty or trafficking against the individual (or the individual's child) which established the individual's (or individual's child [child's]) eligibility as a VAWA petitioner or for such nonimmigrant status.

(2) (A) The Attorney General may not approve a spousal second preference petition for the classification of the spouse of an alien if the alien, by virtue of a prior marriage, has been accorded the status of an alien lawfully admitted for permanent residence as the spouse of a citizen of the United States or as the spouse of an alien lawfully admitted for permanent residence, unless—

(i) a period of 5 years has elapsed after the date the alien acquired the status of an alien lawfully admitted for permanent residence, or

(ii) the alien establishes to the satisfaction of the Attorney General by clear and convincing evidence that the prior marriage (on the basis of which the alien obtained the status of an alien lawfully admitted for permanent residence) was not entered into for the purpose of evading any provision of the immigration laws.

In this subparagraph, the term "spousal second preference petition" refers to a petition, seeking preference status under section 203(a)(2) [8 USCS § 1153(a)(2)], for an alien as a spouse of an alien lawfully admitted for permanent residence.

(B) Subparagraph (A) shall not apply to a petition filed for the classification of the spouse of an alien if the prior marriage of the alien was terminated by the death of his or her spouse.

(b) Investigation; consultation; approval; authorization to grant preference status. After an investigation of the facts in each case, and after consultation with the Secretary of Labor with respect to petitions to accord a status under section 203(b)(2) or 203(b)(3) [8 USCS § 1153(b)(2) or (3)], the Attorney General shall, if he determines that the facts stated in the petition are true and that the alien in behalf of whom the petition is made is an immediate relative specified in section 201(b) [8 USCS § 1151(b)] or is eligible for preference under subsection (a) or (b) of section 203 [8 USCS § 1153], approve the petition and forward one copy thereof to the Department of State. The Secretary of State shall then authorize the consular officer concerned to grant the preference status.

(c) Limitation on orphan petitions approved for a single petitioner; prohibition against approval in cases of marriages entered into in order to evade immigration laws; restriction on future entry of aliens involved with marriage fraud. Notwithstanding the provisions of subsection (b) no petition shall be approved if (1) the alien has previously been accorded, or has sought to be accorded, an immediate relative or preference status as the spouse of a citizen of the United States or the spouse of an alien lawfully admitted for permanent residence, by reason of a marriage determined by the Attorney General to have been entered into for the purpose of evading the immigration laws, or (2) the Attorney General has determined that the alien has attempted or conspired to enter into a marriage for the purpose of evading the immigration laws.

(d) Recommendation of valid home-study.

(1) Notwithstanding the provisions of subsections (a) and (b) no petition may be approved on behalf of a child defined in subparagraph (F) or (G) of section 101(b)(1) [8 USCS § 1101(b)(1)] unless a valid home-study has been favorably recommended by an agency of the State of the child's proposed residence, or by an agency authorized by that State to conduct such a study, or, in the case of a child adopted abroad, by an appropriate public or private adoption agency which is licensed in the United States.

(2) Notwithstanding the provisions of subsections (a) and (b), no petition may be approved on behalf of a child defined in section 101(b)(1)(G) [8 USCS § 1101(b)(1)(G)] unless the Secretary of State has certified that the central authority of the child's country of origin has notified the United States central authority under the convention referred to in such section 101(b)(1)(G) [8 USCS § 1101(b)(1)(G)] that a United States citizen habitually resident in the United States has effected final adoption of the child, or has been granted custody of the child for the purpose of emigration and adoption, in accordance with such convention and the Intercountry Adoption Act of 2000.

(e) Subsequent finding of non-entitlement to preference classification. Nothing in this section shall be construed to entitle an immigrant, in behalf of whom a petition under this section is approved, to be admitted [to] the United States as an immigrant under subsection (a), (b), or (c) of section 203 [8 USCS § 1153] or as an immediate relative under section 201(b) [8 USCS § 1151(b)] if upon his arrival at a port of entry in the United States he is found not to be entitled to such classification.

(f) Preferential treatment for children fathered by United States citizens and born in Korea, Vietnam, Laos, Kampuchea, or Thailand after 1950 and before Oct. 22, 1982.

(1) Any alien claiming to be an alien described in paragraph (2)(A) of this subsection (or any person on behalf of such an alien) may file a petition with the Attorney General for classification under section 201(b), 203(a)(1), or 203(a)(3) [8 USCS § 1151(b), 1153(a)(1), or (3)], as appropriate. After an investigation of the facts of each case the Attorney General shall, if the conditions described in paragraph (2) are met, approve the petition and forward one copy to the Secretary of State.

(2) The Attorney General may approve a petition for an alien under paragraph (1) if—

(A) he has reason to believe that the alien was born in Korea, Vietnam, Laos, Kampuchea, or Thailand after 1950 and before the date of the enactment of this subsection [enacted Oct. 22, 1982], and was fathered by a United States citizen;

(B) he has received an acceptable guarantee of legal custody and financial responsibility described in paragraph (4); and

(C) in the case of an alien under eighteen years of age, (i) the alien's placement with a sponsor in the United States has been arranged by an appropriate public, private, or State child welfare agency licensed in the United States and actively involved in the intercountry placement of children and (ii) the alien's mother or guardian has in writing irrevocably released the alien for emigration.

(3) In considering petitions filed under paragraph (1), the Attorney General shall—

(A) consult with appropriate governmental officials and officials of private voluntary organizations in the country of the alien's birth in order to make the determinations described in subparagraphs (A) and (C) (ii) of paragraph 2[(2)]; and

(B) consider the physical appearance of the alien and any evidence provided by the petitioner, including birth and baptismal certificates, local civil records, photographs of, and letters or proof of financial support from, a putative father who is a citizen of the United States, and the testimony of witnesses, to the extent it is relevant or probative.

(4) (A) A guarantee of legal custody and financial responsibility for an alien described in paragraph (2) must—

(i) be signed in the presence of an immigration officer or consular officer by an individual (hereinafter in this paragraph referred to as the "sponsor") who is twenty-one years of age or older, is of good moral character, and is a citizen of the United States or alien lawfully admitted for permanent residence, and

(ii) provide that the sponsor agrees (I) in the case of an alien under eighteen years of age, to assume legal custody for the alien after the alien's departure to the United States and until the alien becomes eighteen years of age, in accordance with the laws of the State where the alien and the sponsor will reside, and (II) to furnish, during the five-year period beginning on the date of the alien's acquiring the status of an alien lawfully admitted for permanent residence, or during the period beginning on the date of the alien's acquiring the status of an alien lawfully admitted for permanent residence and ending on the date on which the alien becomes twenty-one years of age, whichever period is longer, such financial support as is necessary to maintain the family in the United States of which the alien is a member at a level equal to at least 125 per centum of the current official poverty line (as established by the Director of the Office of Management and Budget, under section 673(2) of the Omnibus Budget Reconciliation Act of 1981 [42 USCS § 9902(2)] and as revised by the Secretary of Health and Human Services under the second and third sentences of such section) for a family of the same size as the size of the alien's family.

(B) A guarantee of legal custody and financial responsibility described in subparagraph (A) may be enforced with respect to an alien against his sponsor in a civil suit brought by the Attorney General in the United States district court for the district in which the sponsor resides, except that a sponsor or his estate shall not be liable under such a guarantee if the sponsor dies or is adjudicated a bankrupt under title 11, United States Code [11 USCS §§ 101 et seq.].

(g) Restriction on petitions based on marriages entered while in exclusion or deportation proceedings. Notwithstanding subsection (a), except as provided in section 245(e)(3) [8 USCS § 1255(e)(3)], a petition may not be approved to grant an alien immediate relative status or preference status by reason of a marriage which was entered into during the period described in section 245(e)(2) [8 USCS § 1255(e)(2)], until the alien has resided outside the United States for a 2-year period beginning after the date of the marriage.

(h) Survival of rights to petition. The legal termination of a marriage may not be the sole basis for revocation under section 205 [8 USCS § 1155] of a petition filed under subsection (a)(1)(A)(iii) or a petition filed under subsection (a)(1)(B)(ii) pursuant to conditions described in subsection (a)(1)(A)(iii)(I). Remarriage of an alien whose petition was approved under section 204(a)(1)(B)(ii) or 204(a)(1)(A)(iii) [subsec. (a)(1)(B)(ii) or (a)(1)(A)(iii) of this section] or marriage of an alien described in clause (iv) or (vi) of section 204(a)(1)(A) or in section 204(a)(1)(B)(iii) [subsec. (a)(1)(A) or (a)(1)(B)(iii) of this section] shall not be the basis for revocation of a petition approval under section 205 [8 USCS § 1155].

(i) Professional athletes.

(1) In general. A petition under subsection (a)(4)(D) [(a)(1)(D)] for classification of a professional athlete shall remain valid for the athlete after the athlete changes employers, if the new employer is a team in the same sport as the team which was the employer who filed the petition.

(2) Definition. For purposes of paragraph (1), the term "professional athlete" means an individual who is employed as an athlete by—

(A) a team that is a member of an association of 6 or more professional sports teams whose total combined revenues exceed $10,000,000 per year, if the association governs the conduct of its members and regulates the contests and exhibitions in which its member teams regularly engage; or

(B) any minor league team that is affiliated with such an association.

(j) Job flexibility for long delayed applicants for adjustment of status to permanent residence. A petition under subsection (a)(1)(D) for an individual whose application for adjustment of status pursuant to section 245 [8 USCS § 1255] has been filed and remained unadjudicated for 180 days or more shall remain valid with respect to a new job if the individual changes jobs or employers if the new job is in the same or a similar occupational classification as the job for which the petition was filed.

(k) Procedures for unmarried sons and daughters of citizens.

(1) In general. Except as provided in paragraph (2), in the case of a petition under this section initially filed for an alien unmarried son or daughter's classification as a family-sponsored immigrant under section 203(a)(2)(B) [8 USCS § 1153(a)(2)(B)], based on a parent of the son or daughter being an alien lawfully admitted for permanent residence, if such parent subsequently becomes a naturalized citizen of the United States, such petition shall be converted to a petition to classify the unmarried son or daughter as a family-sponsored immigrant under section 203(a)(1) [8 USCS § 1153(a)(1)].

(2) Exception. Paragraph (1) does not apply if the son or daughter files with the Attorney General a written statement that he or she elects not to have such conversion occur (or if it has occurred, to have such conversion revoked). Where such an election has been made, any determination with respect to the son or daughter's eligibility for admission as a family-sponsored immigrant shall be made as if such naturalization had not taken place.

(3) Priority date. Regardless of whether a petition is converted under this subsection or not, if an unmarried son or daughter described in this subsection was assigned a priority date with respect to such petition before such naturalization, he or she may maintain that priority date.

(4) Clarification. This subsection shall apply to a petition if it is properly filed, regardless of whether it was approved or not before such naturalization.

(l) Surviving relative consideration for certain petitions and applications.

(1) In general. An alien described in paragraph (2) who resided in the United States at the time of the death of the qualifying relative and who continues to reside in the United States shall have such petition described in paragraph (2), or an application for adjustment of status to that of a person admitted for lawful permanent residence based upon the family relationship described in paragraph (2), and any related applications, adjudicated notwithstanding the death of the qualifying relative, unless the Secretary of Homeland Security determines, in the unreviewable discretion of the Secretary, that approval would not be in the public interest.

(2) Alien described. An alien described in this paragraph is an alien who, immediately prior to the death of his or her qualifying relative, was—

(A) the beneficiary of a pending or approved petition for classification as an immediate relative (as described in section 201(b)(2)(A)(i) [8 USCS § 1151(b)(2)(A)(i)]);

(B) the beneficiary of a pending or approved petition for classification under section 203(a) or (d) [8 USCS § 1153(a) or (d)];

(C) a derivative beneficiary of a pending or approved petition for classification under section 203(b)

[8 USCS § 1153(b)] (as described in section 203(d) [8 USCS § 1153(d)]);

(D) the beneficiary of a pending or approved refugee/asylee relative petition under section 207 or 208 [8 USCS § 1157 or 1158];

(E) an alien admitted in "T" nonimmigrant status as described in section 101(a)(15)(T)(ii) [8 USCS § 1101(a)(15)(T)(ii)] or in "U" nonimmigrant status as described in section 101(a)(15)(U)(ii) [8 USCS § 1101(a)(15)(U)(ii)];

(F) a child of an alien who filed a pending or approved petition for classification or application for adjustment of status or other benefit specified in section 101(a)(51) [8 USCS § 1101(a)(51)] as a VAWA self-petitioner; or

(G) an asylee (as described in section 208(b)(3) [8 USCS § 1158(b)(3)]).

HISTORY: (June 27, 1952, ch 477, Title II, Ch 1, § 204, 66 Stat. 179; Oct. 24, 1962, P. L. 87-885, § 3, 76 Stat. 1427; Oct. 3, 1965, P. L. 89-236, § 4, 79 Stat. 915; Oct. 20, 1976, P. L. 94-571, § 7(b), 90 Stat. 2706; Oct. 5, 1978, P. L. 95-417, §§ 2, 3, 92 Stat. 917; Oct. 19, 1980, P. L. 96-470, Title II, § 207, 94 Stat. 2245; Dec. 29, 1981, P. L. 97-116, §§ 3, 18(d), 95 Stat. 1611, 1620; Oct. 22, 1982, P. L. 97-359, § 1, 96 Stat. 1716; Nov. 10, 1986, P. L. 99-639, §§ 2(c), 4(a), 5(b), 100 Stat. 3541, 3543; Oct. 24, 1988, P. L. 100-525, § 9(q), 102 Stat. 2620; Nov. 29, 1990, P. L. 101-649, Title I, Subtitle E, § 162(b), Title VII, § 702(b), 104 Stat. 5010, 5086; Dec. 12, 1991, P. L. 102-232, Title III, §§ 302(e)(4), (5), 308(b), 309(b)(5), 105 Stat. 1745, 1746, 1757, 1758; Sept. 13, 1994, P. L. 103-322, Title IV, Subtitle G, § 40701(a), (b)(1), (c), 108 Stat. 1953, 1954; Oct. 25, 1994, P. L. 103-416, Title II, § 219(b)(2), 108 Stat. 4316; Sept. 30, 1996, P. L. 104-208, Div C, Title III, Subtitle A, § 308(e)(1)(A), (f)(2)(A), Title VI, Subtitle B, § 624(b), 110 Stat. 3009-619, 3009-621, 3009-699; Oct. 6, 2000, P. L. 106-279, Title III, § 302(b), 114 Stat. 839; Oct. 17, 2000, P. L. 106-313, Title I, § 106(c)(1), 114 Stat. 1254; Oct. 28, 2000, P. L. 106-386, Div B, Title V, §§ 1503(b)–(d), 1507(a)(1), (2), (b), 114 Stat. 1518, 1529, 1530; Aug. 6, 2002, P. L. 107-208, §§ 6, 7, 116 Stat. 929; Jan. 5, 2006, P. L. 109-162, Title VIII, Subtitle A, §§ 805(a), (c), 814(b), (e), 816, 119 Stat. 3056, 3059, 3060; July 27, 2006, P. L. 109-248, Title IV, § 402(a), 120 Stat. 622; Aug. 12, 2006, P. L. 109-271, § 6(a), 120 Stat. 762; Oct. 28, 2009, P. L. 111-83, Title V, § 568(d)(1), 123 Stat. 2187; March 7, 2013, P. L. 113-4, Title VIII, § 803, 127 Stat. 111; March 26, 2013, P. L. 113-6, Div D, Title V, § 563, 127 Stat. 380; Mar. 15, 2022, P.L. 117-103, Div BB, § 105(a), 136 Stat. 1103.)

OTHER PROVISIONS:

Effective date of March 26, 2013 amendment. Act March 26, 2013, P. L. 113-6, Div D, Title V, § 563, 127 Stat. 380, provides that the addition of subsec. (a)(1)(I)(iv) by such Act is effective during the period beginning on October 1, 2013, and ending on September 30, 2014.

§ 205. [8 U.S.C. § 1155] Revocation of approval of petitions; notice of revocation; effective date.

The Secretary of Homeland Security may, at any time, for what he deems to be good and sufficient cause, revoke the approval of any petition approved by him under section 204 [8 USCS § 1154]. Such revocation shall be effective as of the date of approval of any such petition.

HISTORY: (June 27, 1952, ch 477, Title II, Ch 1, § 205, 66 Stat. 180; Sept. 22, 1959, P. L. 86-363, § 5(a), (b), 73 Stat. 644; Sept. 26, 1961, P. L. 87-301, §§ 3, 10, 75 Stat. 650, 654; Oct. 3, 1965, P. L. 89-236, § 5, 79 Stat. 916; Sept. 30, 1996, P. L. 104-208, Div C, Title III, Subtitle A, § 308(g)(3)(A), 110 Stat. 3009-622; Dec. 17, 2004, P. L. 108-458, Title V, Subtitle C, § 5304(c), 118 Stat. 3736.)

§ 206. [8 U.S.C. § 1156] Unused immigrant visas.

If an immigrant having an immigrant visa is denied admission to the United States and removed, or does not apply for admission before the expiration of the validity of his visa, or if an alien having an immigrant visa issued to him as a preference immigrant is found not to be a preference immigrant, an immigrant visa or a preference immigrant visa, as the case may be, may be issued in lieu thereof to another qualified alien.

HISTORY: (June 27, 1952, ch 477, Title II, Ch 1, § 206, 66 Stat. 181; Oct. 3, 1965, P. L. 89-236, § 6, 79 Stat. 916; Sept. 30, 1996, P. L. 104-208, Div C, Title III, Subtitle A, § 308(d)(4)(D), 110 Stat. 3009-618.)

§ 207. [8 U.S.C. § 1157] Annual admission of refugees and admission of emergency situation refugees.

(a) Maximum number of admissions; increases for humanitarian concerns; allocations.

(1) Except as provided in subsection (b), the number of refugees who may be admitted under this section in fiscal year 1980, 1981, or 1982, may not exceed fifty thousand unless the President determines, before the beginning of the fiscal year and after appropriate consultation (as defined in subsection (e)), that admission of a specific number of refugees in excess of such number is justified by humanitarian concerns or is otherwise in the national interest.

(2) Except as provided in subsection (b), the number of refugees who may be admitted under this section in any fiscal year after fiscal year 1982 shall be such number as the President determines, before the beginning of the fiscal year and after appropriate consultation, is justified by humanitarian concerns or is otherwise in the national interest.

(3) Admissions under this subsection shall be allocated among refugees of special humanitarian concern to the United States in accordance with a determination made by the President after appropriate consultation.

(4) In the determination made under this subsection for each fiscal year (beginning with fiscal year 1992), the President shall enumerate, with the respective number of refugees so determined, the number of aliens who were granted asylum in the previous year.

(b) Determinations by President respecting number of admissions for humanitarian concerns. If the President determines, after appropriate consultation, that (1) an unforeseen emergency refugee situation exists, (2) the admission of certain refugees in response to the emergency refugee situation is justified by grave humanitarian concerns or is otherwise in the national interest, and (3) the admission to the United States of these refugees cannot be accomplished under subsection (a), the President may fix a number of refugees to be admitted to the United States during the succeeding period (not to exceed twelve months) in response to the emergency refugee situation and such admissions shall be allocated among refugees of special humanitarian concern to the United States in accordance with a determination made by the President after the appropriate consultation provided under this subsection.

(c) Admission by Attorney General of refugees; criteria; admission status of spouse or child; applicability of other statutory requirements; termination of refugee status of alien, spouse or child.

(1) Subject to the numerical limitations established pursuant to subsections (a) and (b), the Attorney General may, in the Attorney General's discretion and pursuant to such regulations as the Attorney General may prescribe, admit any refugee who is not firmly resettled in any foreign country, is determined to be of special humanitarian concern to the United States, and is admissible (except as otherwise provided under paragraph (3)) as an immigrant under this Act.

(2) (A) A spouse or child (as defined in section 101(b)(1)(A), (B), (C), (D), or (E)) [8 USCS § 1101(b)(1), (A), (B), (C), (D) or (E)] of any refugee who qualifies for admission under paragraph (1) shall, if not otherwise entitled to admission under paragraph (1) and if not a person described in the second sentence of section 101(a)(42) [8 USCS § 1101(a)(42)], be entitled to the same admission status as such refugee if accompanying, or following to join, such refugee and if the spouse or child is admissible (except as otherwise provided under paragraph (3)) as an immigrant under this Act. Upon the spouse's or child's admission to the United States, such admission shall be charged against the numerical limitation established in accordance with the appropriate subsection under which the refugee's admission is charged.

(B) An unmarried alien who seeks to accompany, or follow to join, a parent granted admission as a refugee under this subsection, and who was under 21 years of age on the date on which such parent applied for refugee status under this section, shall continue to be classified as a child for purposes of this paragraph, if the alien attained 21 years of age after such application was filed but while it was pending.

(3) The provisions of paragraphs (4), (5), and (7)(A) of section 212(a) [8 USCS § 1182(a)(4), (5), and (7)(A)] shall not be applicable to any alien seeking admission to the United States under this subsection, and the Attorney General may waive any other provision of such section (other than paragraph (2)(C) or subparagraph (A), (B), (C), or (E) of paragraph (3)) with respect to such an alien for humanitarian purposes, to assure family unity, or when it is otherwise in the public interest. Any such waiver by the Attorney General shall be in writing and shall be granted only on an individual basis following an investigation. The Attorney General shall provide for the annual reporting to Congress of the number of waivers granted under this paragraph in the previous fiscal year and a summary of the reasons for granting such waivers.

(4) The refugee status of any alien (and of the spouse or child of the alien) may be terminated by the Attorney General pursuant to such regulations as the Attorney General may prescribe if the Attorney General determines that the alien was not in fact a refugee within the meaning of section 101(a)(42) [8 USCS § 1101(a)(42)] at the time of the alien's admission.

(d) Oversight reporting and consultation requirements.

(1) Before the start of each fiscal year the President shall report to the Committees on the Judiciary of the House of Representatives and of the Senate regarding the foreseeable number of refugees who will be in need of resettlement during the fiscal year and the anticipated allocation of refugee admissions during the fiscal year. The President shall provide for periodic discussions between designated representatives of the President and members of such committees regarding changes in the worldwide refugee situation, the progress of refugee admissions, and the possible need for adjustments in the allocation of admissions among refugees.

(2) As soon as possible after representatives of the President initiate appropriate consultation with respect to the number of refugee admissions under subsection (a) or with respect to the admission of refugees in response to an emergency refugee situation under subsection (b), the Committees on the Judiciary of the House of Representatives and of the Senate shall cause to have printed in the Congressional Record of the substance of such consultation.

(3) (A) After the President initiates appropriate consultation prior to making a determination under subsection (a), a hearing to review the proposed determination shall be held unless public disclosure of the details of the proposal would jeopardize the lives or safety of individuals.

(B) After the President initiates appropriate consultation prior to making a determination, under subsection (b), that the number of refugee admissions should be increased because of an unforeseen emergency refugee situation, to the extent that time and the nature of the emergency refugee situation permit, a hearing to review the proposal to increase refugee admissions shall be held unless public disclosure of the details of the proposal would jeopardize the lives or safety of individuals.

(e) "Appropriate consultation" defined. For purposes of this section, the term "appropriate consultation" means, with respect to the admission of refugees and allocation of refugee admissions, discussions in person by designated Cabinet-level representatives of the President with members of the Committees on the Judiciary of the Senate and of the House of Representatives to review the refugee situation or emergency refugee situation, to project the extent of possible participation of the United States therein, to discuss the reasons for believing that the proposed admission of refugees is justified by humanitarian concerns or grave humanitarian concerns or is otherwise in the national interest, and to provide such members with the following information:

(1) A description of the nature of the refugee situation.

(2) A description of the number and allocation of the refugees to be admitted and an analysis of conditions within the countries from which they came.

(3) A description of the proposed plans for their movement and resettlement and the estimated cost of their movement and resettlement.

(4) An analysis of the anticipated social, economic, and demographic impact of their admission to the United States.

(5) A description of the extent to which other countries will admit and assist in the resettlement of such refugees.

(6) An analysis of the impact of the participation of the United States in the resettlement of such refugee on the foreign policy interests of the United States.

(7) Such additional information as may be appropriate or requested by such members.

To the extent possible, information described in this subsection shall be provided at least two weeks in advance of discussions in person by designated representatives of the President with such members.

(f) Training.

(1) The Attorney General, in consultation with the Secretary of State, shall provide all United States officials adjudicating refugee cases under this section with the same training as that provided to officers adjudicating asylum cases under section 208 [8 USCS § 1158].

(2) Such training shall include country-specific conditions, instruction on the internationally recognized right to freedom of religion, instruction on methods of religious persecution practiced in foreign countries, and applicable distinctions within a country between the nature of and treatment of various religious practices and believers.

HISTORY: (June 27, 1952, ch 477, Title II, Ch. 1, § 207, as added March 17, 1980, P. L. 96-212, Title II, § 201(b), 94 Stat. 103; Oct. 24, 1988, P. L. 100-525, § 9(h), 102 Stat. 2620; Nov. 29, 1990, P. L. 101-649, Title I, Subtitle A, § 104(b), Title VI, § 603(a)(4), 104 Stat. 4985, 5082; Dec. 12, 1991, P. L. 102-232, Title III, § 307(l)(1), 105 Stat. 1756; Sept. 30, 1996, P. L. 104-208, Div C, Title VI, Subtitle A, § 601(b), 110 Stat. 3009-689; Oct. 27, 1998, P. L. 105-292, Title VI, § 602(a), 112 Stat. 2812; Aug. 6, 2002, P. L. 107-208, § 5, 116 Stat. 929; May 11, 2005, P. L. 109-13, Div B, Title I, § 101(g)(2), 119 Stat. 305.)

§ 208. [8 U.S.C. § 1158] Asylum.

(a) Authority to apply for asylum.

(1) In general. Any alien who is physically present in the United States or who arrives in the United States (whether or not at a designated port of arrival and including an alien who is brought to the United States after having been interdicted in international or United States waters), irrespective of such alien's status, may apply for asylum in accordance with this section or, where applicable, section 235(b) [8 USCS § 1225(b)].

(2) Exceptions.

(A) Safe third country. Paragraph (1) shall not apply to an alien if the Attorney General determines that the alien may be removed, pursuant to a bilateral or multilateral agreement, to a country (other than the country of the alien's nationality or, in the case of an alien having no nationality, the country of the alien's last habitual residence) in which the alien's life or freedom would not be threatened on account of race, religion, nationality, membership in a particular social group, or political opinion, and where the alien would have access to a full and fair procedure for determining a claim to asylum or equivalent temporary protection, unless the Attorney General finds that it is in the public interest for the alien to receive asylum in the United States.

(B) Time limit. Subject to subparagraph (D), paragraph (1) shall not apply to an alien unless the alien demonstrates by clear and convincing evidence that the application has been filed within 1 year after the date of the alien's arrival in the United States.

(C) Previous asylum applications. Subject to subparagraph (D), paragraph (1) shall not apply to an alien if the alien has previously applied for asylum and had such application denied.

(D) Changed circumstances. An application for asylum of an alien may be considered, notwithstanding subparagraphs (B) and (C), if the alien demonstrates to the satisfaction of the Attorney General either the existence of changed circumstances which materially affect the applicant's eligibility for asylum or extraordinary circumstances relating to the delay in filing an application within the period specified in subparagraph (B).

(E) Applicability. Subparagraphs (A) and (B) shall not apply to an unaccompanied alien child (as defined in section 462(g) of the Homeland Security Act of 2002 (6 U.S.C. 279(g))).

(3) Limitation on judicial review. No court shall have jurisdiction to review any determination of the Attorney General under paragraph (2).

(b) Conditions for granting asylum.

(1) In general.

(A) Eligibility. The Secretary of Homeland Security or the Attorney General may grant asylum to an alien who has applied for asylum in accordance with the requirements and procedures established by the Secretary of Homeland Security or the Attorney General under this section if the Secretary of Homeland Security or the Attorney General determines that such alien is a refugee within the meaning of section 101(a)(42)(A) [8 USCS § 1101(a)(42)(A)].

(B) Burden of proof.

(i) In general. The burden of proof is on the applicant to establish that the applicant is a refugee, within the meaning of section 101(a)(42)(A) [8 USCS § 1101(a)(42)(A)]. To establish that the applicant is a refugee within the meaning of such section, the applicant must establish that race, religion, nationality, membership in a particular social group, or political opinion was or will be at least one central reason for persecuting the applicant.

(ii) Sustaining burden. The testimony of the applicant may be sufficient to sustain the applicant's burden without corroboration, but only if the applicant satisfies the trier of fact that the applicant's testimony is credible, is persuasive, and refers to specific facts sufficient to demonstrate that the applicant is a refugee. In determining whether the applicant has met the applicant's burden, the trier of fact may weigh the credible testimony along with other evidence of record.

Where the trier of fact determines that the applicant should provide evidence that corroborates otherwise credible testimony, such evidence must be provided unless the applicant does not have the evidence and cannot reasonably obtain the evidence.

(iii) Credibility determination. Considering the totality of the circumstances, and all relevant factors, a trier of fact may base a credibility determination on the demeanor, candor, or responsiveness of the applicant or witness, the inherent plausibility of the applicant's or witness's account, the consistency between the applicant's or witness's written and oral statements (whenever made and whether or not under oath, and considering the circumstances under which the statements were made), the internal consistency of each such statement, the consistency of such statements with other evidence of record (including the reports of the Department of State on country conditions), and any inaccuracies or falsehoods in such statements, without regard to whether an inconsistency, inaccuracy, or falsehood goes to the heart of the applicant's claim, or any other relevant factor. There is no presumption of credibility, however, if no adverse credibility determination is explicitly made, the applicant or witness shall have a rebuttable presumption of credibility on appeal.

(2) Exceptions.

(A) In general. Paragraph (1) shall not apply to an alien if the Attorney General determines that—

(i) the alien ordered, incited, assisted, or otherwise participated in the persecution of any person on account of race, religion, nationality, membership in a particular social group, or political opinion;

(ii) the alien, having been convicted by a final judgment of a particularly serious crime, constitutes a danger to the community of the United States;

(iii) there are serious reasons for believing that the alien has committed a serious nonpolitical crime outside the United States prior to the arrival of the alien in the United States;

(iv) there are reasonable grounds for regarding the alien as a danger to the security of the United States;

(v) the alien is described in subclause (I), (II), (III), (IV), or (VI) of section 212(a)(3)(B)(i) [8 USCS § 1182(a)(3)(B)(i)] or section 237(a)(4)(B) [8 USCS § 1227(a)(4)(B)] (relating to terrorist activity), unless, in the case only of an alien described in subclause (IV) of section 212(a)(3)(B)(i) [8 USCS § 1182(a)(3)(B)(i)], the Attorney General determines, in the Attorney General's discretion, that there are not reasonable grounds for regarding the alien as a danger to the security of the United States; or

(vi) the alien was firmly resettled in another country prior to arriving in the United States.

(B) Special rules.

(i) Conviction of aggravated felony. For purposes of clause (ii) of subparagraph (A), an alien who has been convicted of an aggravated felony shall be considered to have been convicted of a particularly serious crime.

(ii) Offenses. The Attorney General may designate by regulation offenses that will be considered to be a crime described in clause (ii) or (iii) of subparagraph (A).

(C) Additional limitations. The Attorney General may by regulation establish additional limitations and conditions, consistent with this section, under which an alien shall be ineligible for asylum under paragraph (1).

(D) No judicial review. There shall be no judicial review of a determination of the Attorney General under subparagraph (A)(v).

(3) Treatment of spouse and children.

(A) In general. A spouse or child (as defined in section 101(b)(1)(A), (B), (C), (D), or (E) [8 USCS § 1101(b)(1)(A), (B), (C), (D), or (E)]) of an alien who is granted asylum under this subsection may, if not otherwise eligible for asylum under this section, be granted the same status as the alien if accompanying, or following to join, such alien.

(B) Continued classification of certain aliens as children. An unmarried alien who seeks to accompany, or follow to join, a parent granted asylum under this subsection, and who was under 21 years of age on the date on which such parent applied for asylum under this section, shall continue to be classified as a child for purposes of this paragraph and section 209(b)(3) [8 USCS § 1159(b)(3)], if the alien attained 21 years of age after such application was filed but while it was pending.

(C) Initial jurisdiction. An asylum officer (as defined in section 235(b)(1)(E) [8 USCS § 1225(b)(1)(E)]) shall have initial jurisdiction over any asylum application filed by an unaccompanied alien child (as defined in section 462(g) of the Homeland Security Act of 2002 (6 U.S.C. 279(g))), regardless of whether filed in accordance with this section or section 235(b) [8 USCS § 1225(b)].

(c) Asylum status.

(1) In general. In the case of an alien granted asylum under subsection (b), the Attorney General—

(A) shall not remove or return the alien to the alien's country of nationality or, in the case of a person having no nationality, the country of the alien's last habitual residence;

(B) shall authorize the alien to engage in employment in the United States and provide the alien with appropriate endorsement of that authorization; and

(C) may allow the alien to travel abroad with the prior consent of the Attorney General.

(2) Termination of asylum. Asylum granted under subsection (b) does not convey a right to remain permanently in the United States, and may be terminated if the Attorney General determines that—

(A) the alien no longer meets the conditions described in subsection (b)(1) owing to a fundamental change in circumstances;

(B) the alien meets a condition described in subsection (b)(2);

(C) the alien may be removed, pursuant to a bilateral or multilateral agreement, to a country (other than the country of the alien's nationality or, in the case of an alien having no nationality, the country of the alien's last habitual residence) in which the alien's life or freedom would not be threatened on account of race, religion, nationality, membership in a particular social group, or political opinion, and where the alien is eligible to receive asylum or equivalent temporary protection;

(D) the alien has voluntarily availed himself or herself of the protection of the alien's country of nationality or, in the case of an alien having no nationality, the alien's country of last habitual residence, by returning to such country with permanent resident status or the reasonable possibility of obtaining such status with the same rights and obligations pertaining to other permanent residents of that country; or

(E) the alien has acquired a new nationality and enjoys the protection of the country of his or her new nationality.

(3) Removal when asylum is terminated. An alien described in paragraph (2) is subject to any applicable grounds of inadmissibility or deportability under section [sections] 212(a) and 237(a) [8 USCS §§ 1182(a), 1227(a)], and the alien's removal or return shall be directed by the Attorney General in accordance with sections 240 and 241 [8 USCS §§ 1229a, 1231].

(d) Asylum procedure.

(1) Applications. The Attorney General shall establish a procedure for the consideration of asylum applications filed under subsection (a). The Attorney General may require applicants to submit fingerprints and a photograph at such time and in such manner to be determined by regulation by the Attorney General.

(2) Employment. An applicant for asylum is not entitled to employment authorization, but such authorization may be provided under regulation by the Attorney General. An applicant who is not otherwise eligible for employment authorization shall not be granted such authorization prior to 180 days after the date of filing of the application for asylum.

(3) Fees. The Attorney General may impose fees for the consideration of an application for asylum, for employment authorization under this section, and for adjustment of status under section 209(b) [8 USCS § 1159(b)]. Such fees shall not exceed the Attorney General's costs in adjudicating the applications. The Attorney General may provide for the assessment and payment of such fees over a period of time or by installments. Nothing in this paragraph shall be construed to require the Attorney General to charge fees for adjudication services provided to asylum applicants, or to limit the authority of the Attorney General to set adjudication and naturalization fees in accordance with section 286(m) [8 USCS § 1356(m)].

(4) Notice of privilege of counsel and consequences of frivolous application. At the time of filing an application for asylum, the Attorney General shall—

(A) advise the alien of the privilege of being represented by counsel and of the consequences, under paragraph (6), of knowingly filing a frivolous application for asylum; and

(B) provide the alien a list of persons (updated not less often than quarterly) who have indicated their availability to represent aliens in asylum proceedings on a pro bono basis.

(5) Consideration of asylum applications.

(A) Procedures. The procedure established under paragraph (1) shall provide that—

(i) asylum cannot be granted until the identity of the applicant has been checked against all appropriate records or databases maintained by the Attorney General and by the Secretary of State, including the Automated Visa Lookout System, to determine any grounds on which the alien may be inadmissible to or deportable from the United States, or ineligible to apply for or be granted asylum;

(ii) in the absence of exceptional circumstances, the initial interview or hearing on the asylum application shall commence not later than 45 days after the date an application is filed;

(iii) in the absence of exceptional circumstances, final administrative adjudication of the asylum application, not including administrative appeal, shall be completed within 180 days after the date an application is filed;

(iv) any administrative appeal shall be filed within 30 days of a decision granting or denying asylum, or within 30 days of the completion of removal proceedings before an immigration judge under section 240 [8 USCS § 1229a], whichever is later; and

(v) in the case of an applicant for asylum who fails without prior authorization or in the absence of exceptional circumstances to appear for an interview or hearing, including a hearing under section 240 [8 USCS § 1229a], the application may be dismissed or the applicant may be otherwise sanctioned for such failure.

(B) Additional regulatory conditions. The Attorney General may provide by regulation for any other conditions or limitations on the consideration of an application for asylum not inconsistent with this Act.

(6) Frivolous applications. If the Attorney General determines that an alien has knowingly made a frivolous application for asylum and the alien has received the notice under paragraph (4)(A), the alien shall be permanently ineligible for any benefits under this Act, effective as of the date of a final determination on such application.

(7) No private right of action. Nothing in this subsection shall be construed to create any substantive or procedural right or benefit that is legally enforceable by any party against the United States or its agencies or officers or any other person.

(e) Commonwealth of the Northern Mariana Islands. The provisions of this section and section 209(b) [8 USCS § 1159(b)] shall apply to persons physically present in the Commonwealth of the Northern Mariana Islands or arriving in the Commonwealth (whether or not at a designated port of arrival and including persons who are brought to the Commonwealth after having been interdicted in international or United States waters) only on or after January 1, 2014.

HISTORY: (June 27, 1952, ch 477, Title II, Ch 1, § 208, as added March 17, 1980, P.L. 96-212, Title II, § 201(b), 94 Stat. 105; Nov. 29, 1990, P. L. 101-649, Title V, Subtitle A, § 515(a)(1), 104 Stat. 5053; Sept. 13, 1994, P. L. 103-322, Title XIII, § 130005(b), 108 Stat. 2028; April 24, 1996, P. L. 104-132, Title IV, Subtitle C, § 421(a), 110 Stat. 1270; Sept. 30, 1996, P. L.

104-208, Div C, Title VI, Subtitle A, § 604(a), 110 Stat. 3009-690; Oct. 26, 2001, P. L. 107-56, Title IV, Subtitle B, § 411(b)(2), 115 Stat. 348; Aug. 6, 2002, P. L. 107-208, § 4, 116 Stat. 928; May 11, 2005, P. L. 109-13, Div B, Title I, § 101(a), (b), 119 Stat. 302; May 8, 2008, P. L. 110-229, Title VII, Subtitle A, § 702(j)(4), 122 Stat. 866; Dec. 23, 2008, P. L. 110-457, Title II, Subtitle D, § 235(d)(7), 122 Stat. 5080.)

§ 209. [8 U.S.C. § 1159] Adjustment of status of refugees.

(a) Inspection and examination by Department of Homeland Security.

(1) Any alien who has been admitted to the United States under section 207 [8 USCS § 1157]—

(A) whose admission has not been terminated by the Secretary of Homeland Security or the Attorney General pursuant to such regulations as the Secretary of Homeland Security or the Attorney General may prescribe,

(B) who has been physically present in the United States for at least one year, and

(C) who has not acquired permanent resident status,

shall, at the end of such year period, return or be returned to the custody of the Department of Homeland Security for inspection and examination for admission to the United States as an immigrant in accordance with the provisions of sections 235, 240, and 241 [8 USCS §§ 1225, 1229a, and 1231].

(2) Any alien who is found upon inspection and examination by an immigration officer pursuant to paragraph (1) or after a hearing before an immigration judge to be admissible (except as otherwise provided under subsection (c)) as an immigrant under this Act at the time of the alien's inspection and examination shall, notwithstanding any numerical limitation specified in this Act, be regarded as lawfully admitted to the United States for permanent residence as of the date of such alien's arrival into the United States.

(b) Requirements for adjustment. The Secretary of Homeland Security or the Attorney General, in the Secretary's or the Attorney General's discretion and under such regulations as the Secretary or the Attorney General may prescribe, may adjust to the status of an alien lawfully admitted for permanent residence the status of any alien granted asylum who—

(1) applies for such adjustment,

(2) has been physically present in the United States for at least one year after being granted asylum,

(3) continues to be a refugee within the meaning of section 101(a)(42)(A) [8 USCS § 1101(a)(42)(A)] or a spouse or child of such a refugee,

(4) is not firmly resettled in any foreign country, and

(5) is admissible (except as otherwise provided under subsection (c)) as an immigrant under this Act at the time of examination for adjustment of such alien.

Upon approval of an application under this subsection, the Secretary of Homeland Security or the Attorney General shall establish a record of the alien's admission for lawful permanent residence as of the date one year before the date of the approval of the application.

(c) Coordination with8 USCS § 1182. The provisions of paragraphs (4), (5), and (7)(A) of section 212(a) [8 USCS § 1182(a)] shall not be applicable to any alien seeking adjustment of status under this section, and the Secretary of Homeland Security or the Attorney General may waive any other provision of such section (other than paragraph (2)(C) or subparagraph (A), (B), (C), or (F) of paragraph (3)) with respect to such an alien for humanitarian purposes, to assure family unity, or when it is otherwise in the public interest.

HISTORY: (June 27, 1952, ch 477, Title II, Ch 1, § 209, as added March 17, 1980, P. L. 96-212, Title II, § 201(b), 94 Stat. 105; Nov. 29, 1990, P. L. 101-649, Title I, Subtitle A, § 104(a)(1), Title VI, § 603(a)(4), 104 Stat. 4985, 5082; Dec. 12, 1991, P. L. 102-232, Title III, § 307(l)(1), 105 Stat. 1756; Sept. 30, 1996, P. L. 104-208, Div C, Title III, Subtitle A, § 308(g)(3)(A), (4)(A), Subtitle F, § 371(b)(2), 110 Stat. 3009-622, 3009-645; May 11, 2005, P. L. 109-13, Div B, Title I, § 101(g)(1), 119 Stat. 305.)

§ 210. [8 U.S.C. § 1160] Special agricultural workers.

(a) Lawful residence.

(1) In general. The Attorney General shall adjust the status of an alien to that of an alien lawfully admitted for temporary residence if the Attorney General determines that the alien meets the following requirements:

(A) Application period. The alien must apply for such adjustment during the 18-month period beginning on the first day of the seventh month that begins after the date of enactment of this section [enacted Nov. 6, 1986].

(B) Performance of seasonal agricultural services and residence in the United States. The alien must establish that he has—

(i) resided in the United States, and

(ii) performed seasonal agricultural services in the United States for at least 90 man-days,

during the 12-month period ending on May 1, 1986. For purposes of the previous sentence, performance of seasonal agricultural services in the United States for more than one employer on any one day shall be counted as performance of services for only 1 man-day.

(C) Admissible as immigrant. The alien must establish that he is admissible to the United States as an immigrant, except as otherwise provided under subsection (c)(2).

(2) Adjustment to permanent residence. The Attorney General shall adjust the status of any alien provided lawful temporary resident status under paragraph (1) to that of an alien lawfully admitted for permanent residence on the following date:

(A) Group 1. Subject to the numerical limitation established under subparagraph (C), in the case of an alien who has established, at the time of application for temporary residence under paragraph (1), that the alien performed seasonal agricultural services in the United States for at least 90 man-days during each of the 12-month periods ending on May 1, 1984, 1985, and 1986, the adjustment shall occur on the first day after the end of the one-year period that begins on the later of (I) the date the alien was granted such temporary resident status, or (II) the day after the last day of the application period described in paragraph (1)(A).

(B) Group 2. In the case of aliens to which subparagraph (A) does not apply, the adjustment shall occur on the day after the last day of the two-year period that begins on the later of (I) the date the alien was granted such temporary resident status, or (II) the day after the last day of the application period described in paragraph (1)(A).

(C) Numerical limitation. Subparagraph (A) shall not apply to more than 350,000 aliens. If more than 350,000 aliens meet the requirements of such subparagraph, such subparagraph shall apply to the 350,000 aliens whose applications for adjustment were first filed under paragraph (1) and subparagraph (B) shall apply to the remaining aliens.

(3) Termination of temporary residence.

(A) During the period of temporary resident status granted an alien under paragraph (1), the Attorney General may terminate such status only upon a determination under this Act that the alien is deportable.

(B) Before any alien becomes eligible for adjustment of status under paragraph (2), the Attorney General may deny adjustment to permanent status and provide for termination of the temporary resident status granted such alien under paragraph (1) if—

(i) the Attorney General finds by a preponderance of the evidence that the adjustment to temporary resident status was the result of fraud or willful misrepresentation as set out in section 212(a)(6)(C)(xi) [8 USCS § 1182(a)(6)(C)(i)], or

(ii) the alien commits an act that (I) makes the alien inadmissible to the United States as an immigrant, except as provided under subsection (c)(2), or (II) is convicted of a felony or 3 or more misdemeanors committed in the United States.

(4) Authorized travel and employment during temporary residence. During the period an alien is in lawful temporary resident status granted under this subsection, the alien has the right to travel abroad (including commutation from a residence abroad) and shall be granted authorization to engage in employment in the United States and shall be provided an "employment authorized" endorsement or other appropriate work permit, in the same manner as for aliens lawfully admitted for permanent residence.

(5) In general. Except as otherwise provided in this subsection, an alien who acquires the status of an alien lawfully admitted for temporary residence under paragraph (1), such status not having changed, is considered to be an alien lawfully admitted for permanent residence (as described in section 101(a)(20) [8 USCS § 1101(a)(20)]), other than under any provision of the immigration laws.

(b) Applications for adjustment of status.

(1) To whom may be made.

(A) Within the United States. The Attorney General shall provide that applications for adjustment of status under subsection (a) may be filed—

(i) with the Attorney General, or

(ii) with a designated entity (designated under paragraph (2)), but only if the applicant consents to the forwarding of the application to the Attorney General.

(B) Outside the United States. The Attorney General, in cooperation with the Secretary of State, shall provide a procedure whereby an alien may apply for adjustment of status under subsection (a)(1) at an appropriate consular office outside the United States. If the alien otherwise qualifies for such adjustment, the Attorney General shall provide such documentation of authorization to enter the United States and to have the alien's status adjusted upon entry as may be necessary to carry out the provisions of this section.

(2) Designation of entities to receive applications. For purposes of receiving applications under this section, the Attorney General—

(A) shall designate qualified voluntary organizations and other qualified State, local, community, farm labor organizations, and associations of agricultural employers, and

(B) may designate such other persons as the Attorney General determines are qualified and have substantial experience, demonstrated competence, and traditional long-term involvement in the preparation and submittal of applications for adjustment of status under section 209 or 245 [8 USCS § 1159 or 1255], Public Law 89-732 [8 USCS § 1255 note], or Public Law 95-145.

(3) Proof of eligibility.

(A) In general. An alien may establish that he meets the requirement of subsection (a)(1)(B)(ii) through government employment records, records supplied by employers or collective bargaining organizations, and such other reliable documentation as the alien may provide. The Attorney General shall establish special procedures to credit properly work in cases in which an alien was employed under an assumed name.

(B) Documentation of work history.

(i) An alien applying for adjustment of status under subsection (a)(1) has the burden of proving by a preponderance of the evidence that the alien has worked the requisite number of man-days (as required under subsection (a)(1)(B)(ii)).

(ii) If an employer or farm labor contractor employing such an alien has kept proper and adequate records respecting such employment, the alien's burden of proof under clause (i) may be met by securing timely production of those records under regulations to be promulgated by the Attorney General.

(iii) An alien can meet such burden of proof if the alien establishes that the alien has in fact performed the work described in subsection (a)(1)(B)(ii) by producing sufficient evidence to show the extent of that employment as a matter of just and reasonable inference. In such a case, the burden then shifts to the Attorney General to disprove the alien's evidence with a showing which negates the reasonableness of the inference to be drawn from the evidence.

(4) Treatment of applications by designated entities. Each designated entity must agree to forward to the Attorney General applications filed with it in accordance with paragraph (1)(A)(ii) but not to forward

to the Attorney General applications filed with it unless the applicant has consented to such forwarding. No such entity may make a determination required by this section to be made by the Attorney General.

(5) Limitation on access to information. Files and records prepared for purposes of this section by designated entities operating under this section are confidential and the Attorney General and the Service shall not have access to such files or records relating to an alien without the consent of the alien, except as allowed by a court order issued pursuant to paragraph (6) of this subsection.

(6) Confidentiality of information.

(A) In general. Except as provided in this paragraph, neither the Attorney General, nor any other official or employee of the Department of Justice, or bureau or agency thereof, may—

(i) use the information furnished by the applicant pursuant to an application filed under this section for any purpose other than to make a determination on the application, including a determination under subsection (a)(3)(B), or for enforcement of paragraph (7);

(ii) make any publication whereby the information furnished by any particular individual can be identified; or

(iii) permit anyone other than the sworn officers and employees of the Department or bureau or agency or, with respect to applications filed with a designated entity, that designated entity, to examine individual applications.

(B) Required disclosures. The Attorney General shall provide information furnished under this section, and any other information derived from such furnished information, to a duly recognized law enforcement entity in connection with a criminal investigation or prosecution, when such information is requested in writing by such entity, or to an official coroner for purposes of affirmatively identifying a deceased individual (whether or not such individual is deceased as a result of a crime).

(C) Construction.

(i) In general. Nothing in this paragraph shall be construed to limit the use, or release, for immigration enforcement purposes or law enforcement purposes of information contained in files or records of the Service pertaining to an application filed under this section, other than information furnished by an applicant pursuant to the application, or any other information derived from the application, that is not available from any other source.

(ii) Criminal convictions. Information concerning whether the applicant has at any time been convicted of a crime may be used or released for immigration enforcement or law enforcement purposes.

(D) Crime. Whoever knowingly uses, publishes, or permits information to be examined in violation of this paragraph shall be fined not more than $10,000.

(7) Penalties for false statements in applications.

(A) Criminal penalty. Whoever—

(i) files an application for adjustment of status under this section and knowingly and willfully falsifies, conceals, or covers up a material fact or makes any false, fictitious, or fraudulent statements or representations, or makes or uses any false writing or document knowing the same to contain any false, fictitious, or fraudulent statement or entry, or

(ii) creates or supplies a false writing or document for use in making such an application,

shall be fined in accordance with title 18, United States Code, or imprisoned not more than five years, or both.

(B) Exclusion. An alien who is convicted of a crime under subparagraph (A) shall be considered to be inadmissible to the United States on the ground described in section 212(a)(6)(C)(i) [8 USCS § 1182(a)(6)(C)(i)].

(c) Waiver of numerical limitations and certain grounds for exclusion.

(1) Numerical limitations do not apply. The numerical limitations of sections 201 and 202 [8 USCS §§ 1151, 1152] shall not apply to the adjustment of aliens to lawful permanent resident status under this section.

(2) Waiver of grounds for exclusion. In the determination of an alien's admissibility under subsection (a)(1)(C)—

(A) Grounds of exclusion not applicable. The provisions of paragraphs (5) and (7)(A) of section 212(a) [8 USCS § 1182(a)(5) and (7)(A)] shall not apply.

(B) Waiver of other grounds.

(i) In general. Except as provided in clause (ii), the Attorney General may waive any other provision of section 212(a) [8 USCS § 1182(a)] in the case of individual aliens for humanitarian purposes, to assure family unity, or when it is otherwise in the public interest.

(ii) Grounds that may not be waived. The following provisions of section 212(a) [8 USCS § 1182(a)] may not be waived by the Attorney General under clause (i):

(I) Paragraphs (2)(A) and (2)(B) (relating to criminals).

(II) Paragraph (4) (relating to aliens likely to become public charges).

(III) Paragraph (2)(C) (relating to drug offenses), except for so much of such paragraph as relates to a single offense of simple possession of 30 grams or less of marihuana.

(IV) Paragraph (3) (relating to security and related grounds), other than subparagraph (B) thereof.

(C) Special rule for determination of public charge. An alien is not ineligible for adjustment of status under this section due to being inadmissible under section 212(a)(4) [8 USCS § 1182(a)(4)] if the alien demonstrates a history of employment in the United States evidencing self-support without reliance on public cash assistance.

(d) Temporary stay of exclusion or deportation and work authorization for certain applicants.

(1) Before application period. The Attorney General shall provide that in the case of an alien who is apprehended before the beginning of the application period described in subsection (a)(1) and who can establish a nonfrivolous case of eligibility to have his status adjusted under subsection (a) (but for the fact that he may not apply for such adjustment until the beginning of such period), until the alien has had the opportunity during the first 30 days of the application period

to complete the filing of an application for adjustment, the alien—

(A) may not be excluded or deported, and

(B) shall be granted authorization to engage in employment in the United States and be provided an "employment authorized" endorsement or other appropriate work permit.

(2) During application period. The Attorney General shall provide that in the case of an alien who presents a nonfrivolous application for adjustment of status under subsection (a) during the application period, and until a final determination on the application has been made in accordance with this section, the alien—

(A) may not be excluded or deported, and

(B) shall be granted authorization to engage in employment in the United States and be provided an "employment authorized" endorsement or other appropriate work permit.

(3) Use of application fees to offset program costs. No application fees collected by the Service pursuant to this subsection may be used by the Service to offset the costs of the special agricultural worker legalization program until the Service implements the program consistent with the statutory mandate as follows:

(A) During the application period described in subsection (a)(1)(A) the Service the INS may grant temporary admission to the United States, work authorization, and provide an "employment authorized" endorsement or other appropriate work permit to any alien who presents a preliminary application for adjustment of status under subsection (a) at a designated port of entry on the southern land border. An alien who does not enter through a port of entry is subject to deportation and removal as otherwise provided in this Act.

(B) During the application period described in subsection (a)(1)(A) any alien who has filed an application for adjustment of status within the United States as provided in subsection (b)(1)(A) pursuant to the provision of 8 CFR section 210.1(j) is subject to paragraph (2) of this subsection.

(C) A preliminary application is defined as a fully completed and signed application with fee and photographs which contains specific information concerning the performance of qualifying employment in the United States and the documentary evidence which the applicant intends to submit as proof of such employment. The applicant must be otherwise admissible to the United States and must establish to the satisfaction of the examining officer during an interview that his or her claim to eligibility for special agriculture worker status is credible.

(e) Administrative and judicial review.

(1) Administrative and judicial review. There shall be no administrative or judicial review of a determination respecting an application for adjustment of status under this section except in accordance with this subsection.

(2) Administrative review.

(A) Single level of administrative appellate review. The Attorney General shall establish an appellate authority to provide for a single level of administrative appellate review of such a determination.

(B) Standard for review. Such administrative appellate review shall be based solely upon the administrative record established at the time of the determination on the application and upon such additional or newly discovered evidence as may not have been available at the time of the determination.

(3) Judicial review.

(A) Limitation to review of exclusion or deportation. There shall be judicial review of such a denial only in the judicial review of an order of exclusion or deportation under section 106 [former 8 USCS § 1105a] (as in effect before October 1, 1996).

(B) Standard for judicial review. Such judicial review shall be based solely upon the administrative record established at the time of the review by the appellate authority and the findings of fact and determinations contained in such record shall be conclusive unless the applicant can establish abuse of discretion or that the findings are directly contrary to clear and convincing facts contained in the record considered as a whole.

(f) Temporary disqualification of newly legalized aliens from receiving aid to families with dependent children. During the five-year period beginning on the date an alien was granted lawful temporary resident status under subsection (a), and notwithstanding any other provision of law, the alien is not eligible for assistance under a State program funded under part A of title IV of the Social Security Act [42 USCS §§ 601 et seq.]. Notwithstanding the previous sentence, in the case of an alien who would be eligible for assistance under a State program funded under part A of title IV of the Social Security Act [42 USCS §§ 601 et seq.] but for the previous sentence, the provisions of paragraph (3) of section 245A(h) [8 USCS § 1255a(h)] shall apply in the same manner as they apply with respect to paragraph (1) of such section and, for this purpose, any reference in section 245A(h)(3) [8 USCS § 1255a(h)] to paragraph (1) is deemed a reference to the previous sentence.

(g) Treatment of special agricultural workers. For all purposes (subject to subsections (a)(5) and (f)) an alien whose status is adjusted under this section to that of an alien lawfully admitted for permanent residence, such status not having changed, shall be considered to be an alien lawfully admitted for permanent residence (within the meaning of section 101(a)(20) [8 USCS § 1101(a)(20)]).

(h) "Seasonal agricultural services" defined. In this section, the term "seasonal agricultural services" means the performance of field work related to planting, cultural practices, cultivating, growing and harvesting of fruits and vegetables of every kind and other perishable commodities, as defined in regulations by the Secretary of Agriculture.

HISTORY: (June 27, 1952, ch 477, Title II, Ch 1, § 210, as added Nov. 6, 1986, P. L. 99-603, Title III, Part A, § 302(a)(1), 100 Stat. 3417; Dec. 22, 1987, P. L. 100-202, § 101(a) [Title II, § 211], 101 Stat. 1329-18; Oct. 24, 1988, P. L. 100-525, § 2(m), 102 Stat. 2613; Dec. 18, 1989, P. L. 101-238, § 4, 103 Stat.

2103; Nov. 29, 1990, P. L. 101-649, Title VI, § 603(a)(5), 104 Stat. 5082; Dec. 12, 1991, P. L. 102-232, Title III, §§ 307(j), 309(b)(6), 105 Stat. 1756, 1758; Oct. 25, 1994, P. L. 103-416, Title II, § 219(d), (z)(7), 108 Stat. 4316, 4318; April 24, 1996, P. L. 104-132, Title IV, Subtitle D, § 431(b), 110 Stat. 1273; Aug. 22, 1996, P. L. 104-193, Title I, § 110(s)(1), 110 Stat. 2175; Sept. 30, 1996, P. L. 104-208, Div C, Title III, Subtitle A, § 308(g)(2)(B), Subtitle F, § 384(d)(1), Title VI, Subtitle B, § 623(b), 110 Stat. 3009-622, 3009-653, 3009-697.)

§ 210A. [8 U.S.C. § 1161] [Repealed].

HISTORY: This section (Act June 27, 1952, ch 477, Title II, Ch 1, § 210A, as added Nov. 6, 1986, P.L. 99-603, Title III, Part A, § 303(a), 100 Stat. 3422; Oct. 24, 1988, P.L. 100-525, § 2(n)(1), 102 Stat. 2613; Nov. 29, 1990, P.L. 101-649, Title VI, § 603(a)(6), (b)(1), 104 Stat. 5083, 5085; Dec. 12, 1991, P.L. 102-232, Title III, § 307(*l*)(2) 105 Stat. 1756) was repealed by Oct. 25, 1994, P.L. 103-416, Title II, § 219(ee)(1), 108 Stat. 4319 (effective on enactment, as provided by § 219(ee)(3) of such Act, as added Act Sept. 30, 1996, P.L. 104-208, Div C, Title VI, Subtitle E, § 671(b)(10), 110 Stat. 3009-722). It provided for determination of agricultural labor shortages and admission of additional special agricultural workers.

Chapter 2—Qualifications for Aliens; Travel Control of Citizens and Aliens

§ 211. [8 U.S.C. § 1181] Admission of immigrants into the United States.

(a) Documents required; admission under quotas before June 30, 1968. Except as provided in subsection (b) and subsection (c) no immigrant shall be admitted into the United States unless at the time of application for admission he (1) has a valid unexpired immigrant visa or was born subsequent to the issuance of such visa of the accompanying parent, and (2) presents a valid unexpired passport or other suitable travel document, or document of identity and nationality, if such document is required under the regulations issued by the Attorney General. With respect to immigrants to be admitted under quotas of quota areas prior to June 30, 1968, no immigrant visa shall be deemed valid unless the immigrant is properly chargeable to the quota area under the quota of which the visa is issued.

(b) Readmission without required documents; Attorney General's discretion. Notwithstanding the provisions of section 212(a)(7)(A) of this Act [8 USCS § 1182(a)(7)(A)] in such cases or in such classes of cases and under such conditions as may be by regulations prescribed, returning resident immigrants, defined in section 101(a)(27)(A) [8 USCS § 1101(a)(27)(A)], who are otherwise admissible may be readmitted to the United States by the Attorney General in his discretion without being required to obtain a passport, immigrant visa, reentry permit or other documentation.

(c) Nonapplicability to aliens admitted as refugees. The provisions of subsection (a) shall not apply to an alien whom the Attorney General admits to the United States under section 207 [8 USCS § 1157].

HISTORY: (June 27, 1952, ch 477, Title II, Ch 2, § 211, 66 Stat. 181; Oct. 3, 1965, P. L. 89-236, § 9, 79 Stat. 917; Oct. 20, 1976, P. L. 94-571, § 7(c), 90 Stat. 2706; March 17, 1980, P.L. 96-212, Title II, § 202, 94 Stat. 106; Nov. 29, 1990, P. L. 101-649, Title VI, § 603(a)(7), 104 Stat. 5083.)

§ 212. [8 U.S.C. § 1182] Inadmissible aliens.

(a) Classes of aliens ineligible for visas or admission. Except as otherwise provided in this Act, aliens who are inadmissible under the following paragraphs are ineligible to receive visas and ineligible to be admitted to the United States:

(1) Health-related grounds.

(A) In general. Any alien—

(i) who is determined (in accordance with regulations prescribed by the Secretary of Health and Human Services) to have a communicable disease of public health significance; [,]

(ii) except as provided in subparagraph (C), who seeks admission as an immigrant, or who seeks adjustment of status to the status of an alien lawfully admitted for permanent residence, and who has failed to present documentation of having received vaccination against vaccine-preventable diseases, which shall include at least the following diseases: mumps, measles, rubella, polio, tetanus and diphtheria toxoids, pertussis, influenza type B and hepatitis B, and any other vaccinations against vaccine-preventable diseases recommended by the Advisory Committee for Immunization Practices,

(iii) who is determined (in accordance with regulations prescribed by the Secretary of Health and Human Services in consultation with the Attorney General)—

(I) to have a physical or mental disorder and behavior associated with the disorder that may pose, or has posed, a threat to the property, safety, or welfare of the alien or others, or

(II) to have had a physical or mental disorder and a history of behavior associated with the disorder, which behavior has posed a threat to the property, safety, or welfare of the alien or others and which behavior is likely to recur or to lead to other harmful behavior, or

(iv) who is determined (in accordance with regulations prescribed by the Secretary of Health and Human Services) to be a drug abuser or addict,

is inadmissible.

(B) Waiver authorized. For provision authorizing waiver of certain clauses of subparagraph (A), see subsection (g).

(C) Exception from immunization requirement for adopted children 10 years of age or younger. Clause (ii) of subparagraph (A) shall not apply to a child who—

(i) is 10 years of age or younger,

(ii) is described in subparagraph (F) or (G) of section 101(b)(1) [8 USCS § 1101(b)(1)], and

(iii) is seeking an immigrant visa as an immediate relative under section 201(b) [8 USCS § 1151(b)],

if, prior to the admission of the child, an adoptive parent or prospective adoptive parent of the child, who has sponsored the child for admission as an immediate relative, has executed an affidavit stating that the parent is aware of the provisions of subparagraph (A) (ii) and will ensure that, within 30 days of the child's admission, or at the earliest time that is medically appropriate, the child will receive the vaccinations identified in such subparagraph.

(2) Criminal and related grounds.

(A) Conviction of certain crimes.

(i) In general. Except as provided in clause (ii), any alien convicted of, or who admits having committed or who admits committing acts which constitute the essential elements of—

(I) a crime involving moral turpitude (other than a purely political offense) or an attempt or conspiracy to commit such a crime, or

(II) a violation of (or a conspiracy or attempt to violate) any law or regulation of a State, the United States, or a foreign country relating to a controlled substance (as defined in section 102 of the Controlled Substances Act (21 U.S.C. 802)),

is inadmissible.

(ii) Exception. Clause (i)(I) shall not apply to an alien who committed only one crime if—

(I) the crime was committed when the alien was under 18 years of age, and the crime was committed (and the alien released from any confinement to a prison or correctional institution imposed for the crime) more than 5 years before the date of application for a visa or other documentation and the date of application for admission to the United States, or

(II) the maximum penalty possible for the crime of which the alien was convicted (or which the alien admits having committed or of which the acts that the alien admits having committed constituted the essential elements) did not exceed imprisonment for one year and, if the alien was convicted of such crime, the alien was not sentenced to a term of imprisonment in excess of 6 months (regardless of the extent to which the sentence was ultimately executed).

(B) Multiple criminal convictions. Any alien convicted of 2 or more offenses (other than purely political offenses), regardless of whether the conviction was in a single trial or whether the offenses arose from a single scheme of misconduct and regardless of whether the offenses involved moral turpitude, for which the aggregate sentences to confinement were 5 years or more is inadmissible.

(C) Controlled substance traffickers. Any alien who the consular officer or the Attorney General knows or has reason to believe—

(i) is or has been an illicit trafficker in any controlled substance or in any listed chemical (as defined in section 102 of the Controlled Substances Act (21 U.S.C. 802)), or is or has been a knowing aider, abettor, assister, conspirator, or colluder with others in the illicit trafficking in any such controlled or listed substance or chemical, or endeavored to do so; or

(ii) is the spouse, son, or daughter of an alien inadmissible under clause (i), has, within the previous 5 years, obtained any financial or other benefit from the illicit activity of that alien, and knew or reasonably should have known that the financial or other benefit was the product of such illicit activity,

is inadmissible.

(D) Prostitution and commercialized vice. Any alien who—

(i) is coming to the United States solely, principally, or incidentally to engage in prostitution, or has engaged in prostitution within 10 years of the date of application for a visa, admission, or adjustment of status,

(ii) directly or indirectly procures or attempts to procure, or (within 10 years of the date of application for a visa, admission, or adjustment of status) procured or attempted to procure or to import, prostitutes or persons for the purpose of prostitution, or receives or (within such 10-year period) received, in whole or in part, the proceeds of prostitution, or

(iii) is coming to the United States to engage in any other unlawful commercialized vice, whether or not related to prostitution,

is inadmissible.

(E) Certain aliens involved in serious criminal activity who have asserted immunity from prosecution. Any alien—

(i) who has committed in the United States at any time a serious criminal offense (as defined in section 101(h) [8 USCS § 1101(h)]).

(ii) for whom immunity from criminal jurisdiction was exercised with respect to that offense,

(iii) who as a consequence of the offense and exercise of immunity has departed from the United States, and

(iv) who has not subsequently submitted fully to the jurisdiction of the court in the United States having jurisdiction with respect to that offense,

is inadmissible.

(F) Waiver authorized. For provision authorizing waiver of certain subparagraphs of this paragraph, see subsection (h).

(G) Foreign government officials who have committed particularly severe violations of religious freedom. Any alien who, while serving as a foreign government official, was responsible for or directly carried out, at any time, particularly severe violations of religious freedom, as defined in section 3 of the International Religious Freedom Act of 1998 (22 U.S.C. 6402), is inadmissible.

(H) Significant traffickers in persons.

(i) In general. Any alien who commits or conspires to commit human trafficking offenses in the United States or outside the United States, or who the consular officer, the Secretary of Homeland Security, the Secretary of State, or the Attorney General knows or has reason to believe is or has been a knowing aider, abettor, assister, conspirator, or colluder with such a trafficker in severe forms of trafficking in persons, as defined in the section 103 of such Act [22 USCS § 7102], is inadmissible.

(ii) Beneficiaries of trafficking. Except as provided in clause (iii), any alien who the consular officer or the Attorney General knows or has reason to believe is the spouse, son, or daughter of an alien inadmissible under clause (i), has, within the previous 5 years, obtained any financial or other benefit from the illicit activity of that alien, and knew or reasonably should have known that the financial or other benefit was the product of such illicit activity, is inadmissible.

(iii) Exception for certain sons and daughters. Clause (ii) shall not apply to a son or daughter who was a child at the time he or she received the benefit described in such clause.

(I) Money laundering. Any alien—

(i) who a consular officer or the Attorney General knows, or has reason to believe, has engaged, is engaging, or seeks to enter the United States to engage, in an offense which is described in section 1956 or 1957 of title 18, United States Code (relating to laundering of monetary instruments); or

(ii) who a consular officer or the Attorney General knows is, or has been, a knowing aider, abettor, assister, conspirator, or colluder with others in an offense which is described in such section;

is inadmissible.

(3) Security and related grounds.

(A) In general. Any alien who a consular officer or the Attorney General knows, or has reasonable ground to believe, seeks to enter the United States to engage solely, principally, or incidentally in—

(i) any activity (I) to violate any law of the United States relating to espionage or sabotage or (II) to violate or evade any law prohibiting the export from the United States of goods, technology, or sensitive information,

(ii) any other unlawful activity, or

(iii) any activity a purpose of which is the opposition to, or the control or overthrow of, the Government of the United States by force, violence, or other unlawful means,

is inadmissible.

(B) Terrorist activities.

(i) In general. Any alien who—

(I) has engaged in a terrorist activity;

(II) a consular officer, the Attorney General, or the Secretary of Homeland Security knows, or has reasonable ground to believe, is engaged in or is likely to engage after entry in any terrorist activity (as defined in clause (iv));

(III) has, under circumstances indicating an intention to cause death or serious bodily harm, incited terrorist activity;

(IV) is a representative (as defined in clause (v)) of—

(aa) a terrorist organization (as defined in clause (vi)); or

(bb) a political, social, or other group that endorses or espouses terrorist activity;

(V) is a member of a terrorist organization described in subclause (I) or (II) of clause (vi);

(VI) is a member of a terrorist organization described in clause (vi)(III), unless the alien can demonstrate by clear and convincing evidence that the alien did not know, and should not reasonably have known, that the organization was a terrorist organization;

(VII) endorses or espouses terrorist activity or persuades others to endorse or espouse terrorist activity or support a terrorist organization;

(VIII) has received military-type training (as defined in section 2339D(c)(1) of title 18, United States Code [18 USCS § 2339D(c)(1)]) from or on behalf of any organization that, at the time the training was received, was a terrorist organization (as defined in clause (vi)); or

(IX) is the spouse or child of an alien who is inadmissible under this subparagraph, if the activity causing the alien to be found inadmissible occurred within the last 5 years,

is inadmissible. An alien who is an officer, official, representative, or spokesman of the Palestine Liberation Organization is considered, for purposes of this Act, to be engaged in a terrorist activity.

(ii) Exception. Subclause (IX) of clause (i) does not apply to a spouse or child—

(I) who did not know or should not reasonably have known of the activity causing the alien to be found inadmissible under this section; or

(II) whom the consular officer or Attorney General has reasonable grounds to believe has renounced the activity causing the alien to be found inadmissible under this section.

(iii) "Terrorist activity" defined. As used in this Act, the term "terrorist activity" means any activity which is unlawful under the laws of the place where it is committed (or which, if it had been committed in the United States, would be unlawful under the laws of the United States or any State) and which involves any of the following:

(I) The highjacking or sabotage of any conveyance (including an aircraft, vessel, or vehicle).

(II) The seizing or detaining, and threatening to kill, injure, or continue to detain, another individual in order to compel a third person (including a governmental organization) to do or abstain from doing any act as an explicit or implicit condition for the release of the individual seized or detained.

(III) A violent attack upon an internationally protected person (as defined in section 1116(b)(4) of title 18, United States Code) or upon the liberty of such a person.

(IV) An assassination.

(V) The use of any—

(a) biological agent, chemical agent, or nuclear weapon or device, or

(b) explosive, firearm, or other weapon or dangerous device (other than for mere personal monetary gain),

with intent to endanger, directly or indirectly, the safety of one or more individuals or to cause substantial damage to property.

(VI) A threat, attempt, or conspiracy to do any of the foregoing.

(iv) "Engage in terrorist activity" defined. As used in this Act, the term "engage in terrorist activity" means, in an individual capacity or as a member of an organization—

(I) to commit or to incite to commit, under circumstances indicating an intention to cause death or serious bodily injury, a terrorist activity;

(II) to prepare or plan a terrorist activity;

(III) to gather information on potential targets for terrorist activity;

(IV) to solicit funds or other things of value for—

(aa) a terrorist activity;

(bb) a terrorist organization described in clause (vi)(I) or (vi)(II); or

(cc) a terrorist organization described in clause (vi)(III), unless the solicitor can demonstrate by clear and convincing evidence that he did not know, and should not reasonably have known, that the organization was a terrorist organization;

(V) to solicit any individual—

(aa) to engage in conduct otherwise described in this subsection;

(bb) for membership in a terrorist organization described in clause (vi)(I) or (vi)(II); or

(cc) for membership in a terrorist organization described in clause (vi)(III) unless the solicitor can demonstrate by clear and convincing evidence that he did not know, and should not reasonably have known, that the organization was a terrorist organization; or

(VI) to commit an act that the actor knows, or reasonably should know, affords material support, including a safe house, transportation, communications, funds, transfer of funds or other material financial benefit, false documentation or identification, weapons (including chemical, biological, or radiological weapons), explosives, or training—

(aa) for the commission of a terrorist activity;

(bb) to any individual who the actor knows, or reasonably should know, has committed or plans to commit a terrorist activity;

(cc) to a terrorist organization described in subclause (I) or (II) of clause (vi) or to any member of such an organization; or

(dd) to a terrorist organization described in clause (vi)(III), or to any member of such an organization, unless the actor can demonstrate by clear and convincing evidence that the actor did not know, and should not reasonably have known, that the organization was a terrorist organization.

(v) "Representative" defined. As used in this paragraph, the term "representative" includes an officer, official, or spokesman of an organization, and any person who directs, counsels, commands, or induces an organization or its members to engage in terrorist activity.

(vi) "Terrorist organization" defined. As used in this section, the term "terrorist organization" means an organization—

(I) designated under section 219 [8 USCS § 1189];

(II) otherwise designated, upon publication in the Federal Register, by the Secretary of State in consultation with or upon the request of the Attorney General or the Secretary of Homeland Security, as a terrorist organization, after finding that the organization engages in the activities described in subclauses (I) through (VI) of clause (iv); or

(III) that is a group of two or more individuals, whether organized or not, which engages in, or has a subgroup which engages in, the activities described in subclauses (I) through (VI) of clause (iv).

(C) Foreign policy.

(i) In general. An alien whose entry or proposed activities in the United States the Secretary of State has reasonable ground to believe would have potentially serious adverse foreign policy consequences for the United States is inadmissible.

(ii) Exception for officials. An alien who is an official of a foreign government or a purported government, or who is a candidate for election to a foreign government office during the period immediately preceding the election for that office, shall not be excludable or subject to restrictions or conditions on entry into the United States under clause (i) solely because of the alien's past, current, or expected beliefs, statements, or associations, if such beliefs, statements, or associations would be lawful within the United States.

(iii) Exception for other aliens. An alien, not described in clause (ii), shall not be excludable or subject to restrictions or conditions on entry into the United States under clause (i) because of the alien's past, current, or expected beliefs, statements, or associations, if such beliefs, statements, or associations would be lawful within the United States, unless the Secretary of State personally determines that the alien's admission would compromise a compelling United States foreign policy interest.

(iv) Notification of determinations. If a determination is made under clause (iii) with respect to an alien, the Secretary of State must notify on a timely basis the chairmen of the Committees on the Judiciary and Foreign Affairs of the House of Representatives and of the Committees on the Judiciary and Foreign Relations of the Senate of the identity of the alien and the reasons for the determination.

(D) Immigrant membership in totalitarian party.

(i) In general. Any immigrant who is or has been a member of or affiliated with the Communist or any other totalitarian party (or subdivision or affiliate thereof), domestic or foreign, is inadmissible.

(ii) Exception for involuntary membership. Clause (i) shall not a alien because of membership or affiliation if the alien establishes to the satisfaction of the consular officer when applying for a visa (or to the satisfaction of the Attorney General when applying for admission) that the membership or affiliation is or was involuntary, or is or was solely when under 16 years of age, by operation of law, or for purposes of obtaining employment, food rations, or other essentials of living and whether necessary for such purposes.

(iii) Exception for past membership. Clause (i) shall not apply to an alien because of membership or affiliation if the alien establishes to the satisfaction of the consular officer when applying for a visa (or to the satisfaction of the Attorney General when applying for admission) that—

(I) the membership or affiliation terminated at least—

(a) 2 years before the date of such application, or

(b) 5 years before the date of such application, in the case of an alien whose membership or affiliation was with the party controlling the government of a foreign state that is a totalitarian dictatorship as of such date, and

(II) the alien is not a threat to the security of the United States.

(iv) Exception for close family members. The Attorney General may, in the Attorney General's discretion, waive the application of clause (i) in the case of an immigrant who is the parent, spouse, son, daughter, brother, or sister of a citizen of the United States or a spouse, son, or daughter of an alien lawfully admitted for permanent residence for humanitarian purposes, to assure family unity, or when it is otherwise in the public interest if the immigrant is not a threat to the security of the United States.

(E) Participants in Nazi persecution, genocide, or the commission of any act of torture or extrajudicial killing.

(i) Participation in Nazi persecutions. Any alien who, during the period beginning on March 23, 1933, and ending on May 8, 1945, under the direction of, or in association with—

(I) the Nazi government of Germany,

(II) any government in any area occupied by the military forces of the Nazi government of Germany,

(III) any government established with the assistance or cooperation of the Nazi government of Germany, or

(IV) any government which was an ally of the Nazi government of Germany,

ordered, incited, assisted, or otherwise participated in the persecution of any person because of race, religion, national origin, or political opinion is inadmissible.

(ii) Participation in genocide. Any alien who ordered, incited, assisted, or otherwise participated in genocide, as defined in section 1091(a) of title 18, United States Code, is inadmissible.

(iii) Commission of acts of torture or extrajudicial killings. Any alien who, outside the United States, has committed, ordered, incited, assisted, or otherwise participated in the commission of—

(I) any act of torture, as defined in section 2340 of title 18, United States Code; or

(II) under color of law of any foreign nation, any extrajudicial killing, as defined in section 3(a) of the Torture Victim Protection Act of 1991 (28 U.S.C. 1350 note),

is inadmissible.

(F) Association with terrorist organizations. Any alien who the Secretary of State, after consultation with the Attorney General, or the Attorney General, after consultation with the Secretary of State, determines has been associated with a terrorist organization and intends while in the United States to engage solely, principally, or incidentally in activities that could endanger the welfare, safety, or security of the United States is inadmissible.

(G) Recruitment or use of child soldiers. Any alien who has engaged in the recruitment or use of child soldiers in violation of section 2442 of title 18, United States Code, is inadmissible.

(4) Public charge.

(A) In general. Any alien who, in the opinion of the consular officer at the time of application for a visa, or in the opinion of the Attorney General at the time of application for admission or adjustment of status, is likely at any time to become a public charge is inadmissible.

(B) Factors to be taken into account.

(i) In determining whether an alien is inadmissible under this paragraph, the consular officer or the Attorney General shall at a minimum consider the alien's—

(I) age;

(II) health;

(III) family status;

(IV) assets, resources, and financial status; and

(V) education and skills.

(ii) In addition to the factors under clause (i), the consular officer or the Attorney General may also consider any affidavit of support under section 213A [8 USCS § 1183a] for purposes of exclusion under this paragraph.

(C) Family-sponsored immigrants. Any alien who seeks admission or adjustment of status under a visa number issued under section 201(b)(2) or 203(a) [8 USCS § 1151(b)(2) or 1153(a)] is inadmissible under this paragraph unless—

(i) the alien has obtained—

(I) status as a spouse or a child of a United States citizen pursuant to clause (ii), (iii), or (iv) of section 204(a)(1)(A) [8 USCS § 1154(a)(1)(A)(ii), (iii), or (iv)];

(II) classification pursuant to clause (ii) or (iii) of section 204(a)(1)(B) [8 USCS § 1154(a)(1)(B)]; or

(III) classification or status as a VAWA self-petitioner; or

(ii) the person petitioning for the alien's admission (and any additional sponsor required under section 213A(f) [8 USCS § 1183a(f)] or any alternative sponsor permitted under paragraph (5)(B) of such section) has executed an affidavit of support described in section 213A [8 USCS § 1183a] with respect to such alien.

(D) Certain employment-based immigrants. Any alien who seeks admission or adjustment of status under a visa number issued under section 203(b) [8 USCS § 1153(b)] by virtue of a classification petition filed by a relative of the alien (or by an entity in which such relative has a significant ownership interest) is inadmissible under this paragraph unless such relative has executed an affidavit of support described in section 213A [8 USCS § 1183a] with respect to such alien.

(E) Special rule for qualified alien victims. Subparagraphs (A), (B), and (C) shall not apply to an alien who—

(i) is a VAWA self-petitioner;

(ii) is an applicant for, or is granted, nonimmigrant status under section 101(a)(15)(U) [8 USCS § 1101(a)(15)(U)]; or

(iii) is a qualified alien described in section 431(c) of the Personal Responsibility and Work Opportunity Reconciliation Act of 1996 (8 U.S.C. 1641(c)).

(5) Labor certification and qualifications for certain immigrants.

(A) Labor certification.

(i) In general. Any alien who seeks to enter the United States for the purpose of performing skilled or unskilled labor is inadmissible, unless the Secretary of Labor has determined and certified to the Secretary of State and the Attorney General that—

(I) there are not sufficient workers who are able, willing, qualified (or equally qualified in the case of an alien described in clause (ii)) and available at the time of application for a visa and admission to the United States and at the place where the alien is to perform such skilled or unskilled labor, and

(II) the employment of such alien will not adversely affect the wages and working conditions of workers in the United States similarly employed.

(ii) Certain aliens subject to special rule. For purposes of clause (i)(I), an alien described in this clause is an alien who—

(I) is a member of the teaching profession, or

(II) has exceptional ability in the sciences or the arts.

(iii) Professional athletes.

(I) In general. A certification made under clause (i) with respect to a professional athlete shall remain valid with respect to the athlete after the athlete changes employer, if the new employer is a team in the same sport as the team which employed the athlete when the athlete first applied for the certification.

(II) Definition. For purposes of subclause (I), the term "professional athlete" means an individual who is employed as an athlete by—

(aa) a team that is a member of an association of 6 or more professional sports teams whose total combined revenues exceed $10,000,000 per year, if the association governs the conduct of its members and regulates the contests and exhibitions in which its member teams regularly engage; or

(bb) any minor league team that is affiliated with such an association.

(iv) Long delayed adjustment applicants. A certification made under clause (i) with respect to an individual whose petition is covered by section 204(j) [8 USCS § 1154(j)] shall remain valid with respect to a new job accepted by the individual after the individual changes jobs or employers if the new job is in the same or a similar occupational classification as the job for which the certification was issued.

(B) Unqualified physicians. An alien who is a graduate of a medical school not accredited by a body or bodies approved for the purpose by the Secretary of Education (regardless of whether such school of medicine is in the United States) and who is coming to the United States principally to perform services as a member of the medical profession is inadmissible, unless the alien (i) has passed parts I and II of the National Board of Medical Examiners Examination (or an equivalent examination as determined by the Secretary of Health and Human Services) and (ii) is competent in oral and written English. For purposes of the previous sentence, an alien who is a graduate of a medical school shall be considered to have passed parts I and II of the National Board of Medical Examiners if the alien was fully and permanently licensed to practice medicine in a State on January 9, 1978, and was practicing medicine in a State on that date.

(C) Uncertified foreign health-care workers. Subject to subsection (r), any alien who seeks to enter the United States for the purpose of performing labor as a health-care worker, other than a physician, is inadmissible unless the alien presents to the consular officer, or, in the case of an adjustment of status, the Attorney General, a certificate from the Commission on Graduates of Foreign Nursing Schools, or a certificate from an equivalent independent credentialing organization approved by the Attorney General in consultation with the Secretary of Health and Human Services, verifying that—

(i) the alien's education, training, license, and experience—

(I) meet all applicable statutory and regulatory requirements for entry into the United States under the classification specified in the application;

(II) are comparable with that required for an American health-care worker of the same type; and

(III) are authentic and, in the case of a license, unencumbered;

(ii) the alien has the level of competence in oral and written English considered by the Secretary of Health and Human Services, in consultation with the Secretary of Education, to be appropriate for health care work of the kind in which the alien will be engaged, as shown by an appropriate score on one or more nationally recognized, commercially available, standardized assessments of the applicant's ability to speak and write; and

(iii) if a majority of States licensing the profession in which the alien intends to work recognize a test predicting the success on the profession's licensing or certification examination, the alien has passed such a test or has passed such an examination.

For purposes of clause (ii), determination of the standardized tests required and of the minimum scores that are appropriate are within the sole discretion of the Secretary of Health and Human Services and are not subject to further administrative or judicial review.

(D) Application of grounds. The grounds for inadmissibility of aliens under subparagraphs (A) and (B) shall apply to immigrants seeking admission or adjustment of status under paragraph (2) or (3) of section 203(b) [8 USCS § 1153(b)(2) or (3)].

(6) Illegal entrants and immigration violators.

(A) Aliens present without admission or parole.

(i) In general. An alien present in the United States without being admitted or paroled, or who arrives in the United States at any time or place other than as designated by the Attorney General, is inadmissible.

(ii) Exception for certain battered women and children. Clause (i) shall not apply to an alien who demonstrates that—

(I) the alien is a VAWA self-petitioner;

(II) (a) the alien has been battered or subjected to extreme cruelty by a spouse or parent, or by a member of the spouse's or parent's family residing in the same household as the alien and the spouse or parent consented or acquiesced to such battery or cruelty, or (b) the alien's child has been battered or subjected to extreme cruelty by a spouse or parent of the alien (without the active participation of the alien in the battery or cruelty) or by a member of the spouse's or parent's family residing in the same household as the alien when the spouse or parent consented to or acquiesced in such battery or cruelty and the alien did not actively participate in such battery or cruelty, and

(III) there was a substantial connection between the battery or cruelty described in subclause (I) or (II) and the alien's unlawful entry into the United States.

(B) Failure to attend removal proceeding. Any alien who without reasonable cause fails or refuses to attend or remain in attendance at a proceeding to determine the alien's inadmissibility or deportability and who seeks admission to the United States within 5 years of such alien's subsequent departure or removal is inadmissible.

(C) Misrepresentation.

(i) In general. Any alien who, by fraud or willfully misrepresenting a material fact, seeks to procure (or has sought to procure or has procured) a visa, other documentation, or admission into the United States or other benefit provided under this Act is inadmissible.

(ii) Falsely claiming citizenship.

(I) In general. Any alien who falsely represents, or has falsely represented, himself or herself to be a citizen of the United States for any purpose or benefit under this Act (including section 274A [8 USCS § 1324a]) or any other Federal or State law is inadmissible.

(II) Exception. In the case of an alien making a representation described in subclause (I), if each natural parent of the alien (or, in the case of an adopted alien, each adoptive parent of the alien) is or was a citizen (whether by birth or naturalization), the alien permanently resided in the United States prior to attaining the age of 16, and the alien reasonably believed at the time of making such representation that he or she was a citizen, the alien shall not be considered to be inadmissible under any provision of this subsection based on such representation.

(iii) Waiver authorized. For provision authorizing waiver of clause (i), see subsection (i).

(D) Stowaways. Any alien who is a stowaway is inadmissible.

(E) Smugglers.

(i) In general. Any alien who at any time knowingly has encouraged, induced, assisted, abetted, or aided any other alien to enter or to try to enter the United States in violation of law is inadmissible.

(ii) Special rule in the case of family reunification. Clause (i) shall not apply in the case of alien who is an eligible immigrant (as defined in section 301(b)(1) of the Immigration Act of 1990 [8 USCS § 1255a note]), was physically present in the United States on May 5, 1988, and is seeking admission as an immediate relative or under section 203(a)(2) [8 USCS § 1153(a)(2)] (including under section 112 of the Immigration Act of 1990 [8 USCS § 1153 note]) or benefits under section 301(a) of the Immigration Act of 1990 [8 USCS § 1255a note] if the alien, before May 5, 1988, has encouraged, induced, assisted, abetted, or aided only the alien's spouse, parent, son, or daughter (and no other individual) to enter the United States in violation of law.

(iii) Waiver authorized. For provision authorizing waiver of clause (i), see subsection (d)(11).

(F) Subject of civil penalty.

(i) In general. An alien who is the subject of a final order for violation of section 274C [8 USCS § 1324c] is inadmissible.

(ii) Waiver authorized. For provision authorizing waiver of clause (i), see subsection (d)(12).

(G) Student visa abusers. An alien who obtains the status of a nonimmigrant under section 101(a)(15)(F)(i) [8 USCS § 1101(a)(15)(F)(i)] and who violates a term or condition of such status under section 214(*l*) is inadmissible until the alien has been outside the United States for a continuous period of 5 years after the date of the violation.

(7) Documentation requirements.

(A) Immigrants.

(i) In general. Except as otherwise specifically provided in this Act, any immigrant at the time of application for admission—

(I) who is not in possession of a valid unexpired immigrant visa, reentry permit, border crossing identification card, or other valid entry document required by this Act, and a valid unexpired passport, or other suitable travel document, or document of identity and nationality if such document is required under the regulations issued by the Attorney General under section 211(a) [8 USCS § 1181(a)], or

(II) whose visa has been issued without compliance with the provisions of section 203 [8 USCS § 1183],

is inadmissible.

(ii) Waiver authorized. For provision authorizing waiver of clause (i), see subsection (k).

(B) Nonimmigrants.

(i) In general. Any nonimmigrant who—

(I) is not in possession of a passport valid for a minimum of six months from the date of the expiration of the initial period of the alien's admission or contemplated initial period of stay authorizing the alien to return to the country from which the alien came or to proceed to and enter some other country during such period, or

(II) is not in possession of a valid nonimmigrant visa or border crossing identification card at the time of application for admission,

is inadmissible.

(ii) General waiver authorized. For provision authorizing waiver of clause (i), see subsection (d)(4).

(iii) Guam and Northern Mariana Islands visa waiver. For provision authorizing waiver of clause (i) in the case of visitors to Guam or the Commonwealth of the Northern Mariana Islands, see subsection (*l*).

(iv) Visa waiver program. For authority to waive the requirement of clause (i) under a program, see section 217 [8 USCS § 1187].

(8) Ineligible for citizenship.

(A) In general. Any immigrant who is permanently ineligible to citizenship is inadmissible.

(B) Draft evaders. Any person who has departed from or who has remained outside the United States to avoid or evade training or service in the armed forces in time of war or a period declared by the President to be a national emergency is inadmissible, except that this subparagraph shall not apply to an alien who at the time of such departure was a nonimmigrant and who is seeking to reenter the United States as a nonimmigrant.

(9) Aliens previously removed.

(A) Certain aliens previously removed.

(i) Arriving aliens. Any alien who has been ordered removed under section 235(b)(1) [8 USCS § 1225(b)(1)] or at the end of proceedings under section 240 [8 USCS § 1229a] initiated upon the alien's arrival in the United States and who again seeks admission within 5 years of the date of such removal (or within 20 years in the case of a second or subsequent removal or at any time in the case of an alien convicted of an aggravated felony) is inadmissible.

(ii) Other aliens. Any alien not described in clause (i) who—

(I) has been ordered removed under section 240 [8 USCS § 1229a] or any other provision of law, or

(II) departed the United States while an order of removal was outstanding,

and who seeks admission within 10 years of the date of such alien's departure or removal (or within 20 years of such date in the case of a second or subsequent removal or at any time in the case of an alien convicted of an aggravated felony) is inadmissible.

(iii) Exception. Clauses (i) and (ii) shall not apply to an alien seeking admission within a period if, prior to the date of the alien's reembarkation at a place outside the United States or attempt to be admitted from foreign contiguous territory, the Attorney General has consented to the alien's reapplying for admission.

(B) Aliens unlawfully present.

(i) In general. Any alien (other than an alien lawfully admitted for permanent residence) who—

(I) was unlawfully present in the United States for a period of more than 180 days but less than 1 year, voluntarily departed the United States (whether or not pursuant to section 244(e) [section 240B]) prior to the commencement of proceedings under section 235(b)(1) [8 USCS § 1225(b)(1)] or section 240 [8 USCS § 1229a], and again seeks admission within 3 years of the date of such alien's departure or removal, or

(II) has been unlawfully present in the United States for one year or more, and who again seeks admission within 10 years of the date of such alien's departure or removal from the United States,

is inadmissible.

(ii) Construction of unlawful presence. For purposes of this paragraph, an alien is deemed to be unlawfully present in the United States if the alien is present in the United States after the expiration of the period of stay authorized by the Attorney General or is present in the United States without being admitted or paroled.

(iii) Exceptions.

(I) Minors. No period of time in which an alien is under 18 years of age shall be taken into account in determining the period of unlawful presence in the United States under clause (i).

(II) Asylees. No period of time in which an alien has a bona fide application for asylum pending under section 208 [8 USCS § 1158] shall be taken into account in determining the period of unlawful presence in the United States under clause (i) unless the alien during such period was employed without authorization in the United States.

(III) Family unity. No period of time in which the alien is a beneficiary of family unity protection pursuant to section 301 of the Immigration Act of 1990 [8 USCS § 1255a note] shall be taken into account in determining the period of unlawful presence in the United States under clause (i).

(IV) Battered women and children. Clause (i) shall not apply to an alien who would be described in paragraph (6)(A)(ii) if "violation of the terms of the alien's nonimmigrant visa" were substituted for "unlawful entry into the United States" in subclause (III) of that paragraph.

(V) Victims of a severe form of trafficking in persons. Clause (i) shall not apply to an alien who demonstrates that the severe form of trafficking (as that term is defined in section 103 of the Trafficking Victims Protection Act of 2000 (22 U.S.C. 7102)) was at least one central reason for the alien's unlawful presence in the United States.

(iv) Tolling for good cause. In the case of an alien who—

(I) has been lawfully admitted or paroled into the United States,

(II) has filed a nonfrivolous application for a change or extension of status before the date of expiration of the period of stay authorized by the Attorney General, and

(III) has not been employed without authorization in the United States before or during the pendency of such application,

the calculation of the period of time specified in clause (i)(I) shall be tolled during the pendency of such application, but not to exceed 120 days.

(v) Waiver. The Attorney General has sole discretion to waive clause (i) in the case of an immigrant who is the spouse or son or daughter of a United States citizen or of an alien lawfully admitted for permanent residence, if it is established to the satisfaction of the Attorney General that the refusal of admission to such immigrant alien would result in extreme hardship to the citizen or lawfully resident spouse or parent of such alien. No court shall have jurisdiction to review a decision or action by the Attorney General regarding a waiver under this clause.

(C) Aliens unlawfully present after previous immigration violations.

(i) In general. Any alien who—

(I) has been unlawfully present in the United States for an aggregate period of more than 1 year, or

(II) has been ordered removed under section 235(b)(1) [8 USCS § 1225(b)(1)], section 240 [8 USCS § 1229a], or any other provision of law,

and who enters or attempts to reenter the United States without being admitted is inadmissible.

(ii) Exception. Clause (i) shall not apply to an alien seeking admission more than 10 years after the date of the alien's last departure from the United States if, prior to the alien's reembarkation at a place outside the United States or attempt to be readmitted from a foreign contiguous territory, the Secretary of Homeland Security has consented to the alien's reapplying for admission.

(iii) Waiver. The Secretary of Homeland Security may waive the application of clause (i) in the case of an alien who is a VAWA self-petitioner if there is a connection between—

(I) the alien's battering or subjection to extreme cruelty; and

(II) the alien's removal, departure from the United States, reentry or reentries into the United States; or attempted reentry into the United States.

(10) Miscellaneous.

(A) Practicing polygamists. Any immigrant who is coming to the United States to practice polygamy is inadmissible.

(B) Guardian required to accompany helpless alien. Any alien—

(i) who is accompanying another alien who is inadmissible and who is certified to be helpless from sickness, mental or physical disability, or infancy pursuant to section 232(c) [8 USCS § 1222(c)], and

(ii) whose protection or guardianship is determined to be required by the alien described in clause (i),

is inadmissible.

(C) International child abduction.

(i) In general. Except as provided in clause (ii), any alien who, after entry of an order by a court in the United States granting custody to a person of a United States citizen child who detains or retains the child, or withholds custody of the child, outside the United States from the person granted custody by that order, is inadmissible until the child is surrendered to the person granted custody by that order.

(ii) Aliens supporting abductors and relatives of abductors. Any alien who—

(I) is known by the Secretary of State to have intentionally assisted an alien in the conduct described in clause (i),

(II) is known by the Secretary of State to be intentionally providing material support or safe haven to an alien described in clause (i), or

(III) is a spouse (other than the spouse who is the parent of the abducted child), child (other than the abducted child), parent, sibling, or agent of an alien described in clause (i), if such person has been designated by the Secretary of State at the Secretary's sole and unreviewable discretion, is inadmissible until the child described in clause (i) is surrendered to the person granted custody by the order described in that clause, and such person and child are permitted to return to the United States or such person's place of residence.

(iii) Exceptions. Clauses (i) and (ii) shall not apply—

(I) to a government official of the United States who is acting within the scope of his or her official duties;

(II) to a government official of any foreign government if the official has been designated by the Secretary of State at the Secretary's sole and unreviewable discretion; or

(III) so long as the child is located in a foreign state that is a party to the Convention on the Civil Aspects of International Child Abduction, done at The Hague on October 25, 1980.

(D) Unlawful voters.

(i) In general. Any alien who has voted in violation of any Federal, State, or local constitutional provision, statute, ordinance, or regulation is inadmissible.

(ii) Exception. In the case of an alien who voted in a Federal, State, or local election (including an initiative, recall, or referendum) in violation of a lawful restriction of voting to citizens, if each natural parent of the alien (or, in the case of an adopted alien, each adoptive parent of the alien) is or was a citizen (whether by birth or naturalization), the alien permanently resided in the United States prior to attaining the age of 16, and the alien reasonably believed at the time of such violation that he or she was a citizen, the alien shall not be considered to be inadmissible under any provision of this subsection based on such violation.

(E) Former citizens who renounced citizenship to avoid taxation. Any alien who is a former citizen of the United States who officially renounces United States citizenship and who is determined by the Attorney General to have renounced United States citizenship for the purpose of avoiding taxation by the United States is inadmissible.

(b) Notices of denials.

(1) Subject to paragraphs (2) and (3), if an alien's application for a visa, for admission to the United States, or for adjustment of status is denied by an immigration or consular officer because the officer determines the alien to be inadmissible under subsection (a), the officer shall provide the alien with a timely written notice that—

(A) states the determination, and

(B) lists the specific provision or provisions of law under which the alien is inadmissible or [ineligible for] adjustment of status.

(2) The Secretary of State may waive the requirements of paragraph (1) with respect to a particular alien or any class or classes of inadmissible aliens.

(3) Paragraph (1) does not apply to any alien inadmissible under paragraph (2) or (3) of subsection (a).

(c) [Repealed]

(d) Temporary admission of nonimmigrants.

(1) The Attorney General shall determine whether a ground for inadmissibility exists with respect to a nonimmigrant described in section 101(a)(15)(S) [8 USCS § 1101(a)(15)(S)]. The Attorney General, in the Attorney General's discretion, may waive the application of subsection (a) (other than paragraph (3)(E)) in the case of a nonimmigrant described in section 101(a)(15)(S) [8 USCS § 1101(a)(15)(S)], if the Attorney General considers it to be in the national interest to do so. Nothing in this section shall be regarded as prohibiting the Immigration and Naturalization Service from instituting removal proceedings against an alien admitted as a nonimmigrant under section 101(a)(15)(S) [8 USCS § 1101(a)(15)(S)] for conduct committed after the alien's admission into the United States, or for conduct or a condition that was not disclosed to the Attorney General prior to the alien's admission as a nonimmigrant under section 101(a)(15)(S) [8 USCS § 1101(a)(15)(S)].

(2) [Repealed]

(3) (A) Except as provided in this subsection, an alien (i) who is applying for a nonimmigrant visa and is known or believed by the consular officer to be ineligible for such visa under subsection (a) (other than paragraphs (3)(A)(i)(I), (3)(A)(ii), (3)(A)(iii), (3)(C), and clauses (i) and (ii) of paragraph (3)(E) of such subsection), may, after approval by the Attorney General of a recommendation by the Secretary of State or by the consular officer that the alien be admitted temporarily despite his inadmissibility, be granted such a visa and may be admitted into the United States temporarily as a nonimmigrant in the discretion of the Attorney General, or (ii) who is inadmissible under subsection (a) (other than paragraphs (3)(A)(i)(I), (3)(A)(ii), (3)(A)(iii), (3)(C), and clauses (i) and (ii) of paragraph (3)(E) of such subsection), but who is in possession of appropriate documents or is granted a waiver thereof and is seeking admission, may be admitted into the United States temporarily as a nonimmigrant in the discretion of the Attorney General. The Attorney General shall prescribe conditions, including exaction of such bonds as may be necessary, to control and regulate the admission and return of inadmissible aliens applying for temporary admission under this paragraph.

(B) (i) The Secretary of State, after consultation with the Attorney General and the Secretary of Homeland Security, or the Secretary of Homeland Security, after consultation with the Secretary of State and the Attorney General, may determine in such Secretary's sole unreviewable discretion that subsection (a)(3)(B) shall not apply with respect to an alien within the scope of that subsection or that subsection (a)(3)(B)(vi)(III) shall not apply to a group within the scope of that subsection, except that no such waiver may be extended to an alien who is within the scope of subsection (a)(3)(B)(i)(II), no such waiver may be extended to an alien who is a member or representative of, has voluntarily and knowingly engaged in or endorsed or espoused or persuaded others to endorse or espouse or support terrorist activity on behalf of, or has voluntarily and knowingly received military-type training from a terrorist organization that is described in subclause (I) or (II) of subsection (a)(3)(B)(vi), and no such waiver may be extended to a group that has engaged [in] terrorist activity against the United States or another democratic country or that has purposefully engaged in a pattern or practice of terrorist activity that is directed at civilians. Such a determination shall neither prejudice the ability of the United States Government to commence criminal or civil proceedings involving a beneficiary of such a determination or any other person, nor create any substantive or procedural right or benefit for a beneficiary of such a determination or any other person. Notwithstanding any other provision of law (statutory or nonstatutory), including section 2241 of title 28, or any other habeas corpus provision, and sections 1361 and 1651 of such title [28 USCS §§ 1361 and 1651], no court shall have jurisdiction to review such a determination or revocation except in a proceeding for review of a final order of removal pursuant to section 1252 of this title [8 USCS § 1252], and review shall be limited to the extent provided in section 1252(a)(2)(D) [8 USCS § 1252(a)(2)(D)]. The Secretary of State may not exercise the discretion provided in this clause with respect to an alien at any time during which the alien is the subject of pending removal proceedings under section 1229a of this title [8 USCS § 1229a].

(ii) Not later than 90 days after the end of each fiscal year, the Secretary of State and the Secretary of Homeland Security shall each provide to the Committees on the Judiciary of the House of Representatives and of the Senate, the Committee on International Relations of the House of Representatives, the Committee on Foreign Relations of the Senate, and the Committee on Homeland Security of the House of Representatives a report on the aliens to whom such Secretary has applied clause (i). Within one week of applying clause (i) to a group, the Secretary of State or the Secretary of Homeland Security shall provide a report to such Committees.

(4) Either or both of the requirements of paragraph (7)(B)(i) of subsection (a) may be waived by the Attorney General and the Secretary of State acting jointly (A) on the basis of unforeseen emergency in individual cases, or (B) on the basis of reciprocity with respect to nationals of foreign contiguous territory or of adjacent islands and residents thereof having a common nationality with such nationals, or (C) in the case of aliens proceeding in immediate and continuous transit through the United States under contracts authorized in section 238(c) [233(c)] [8 USCS § 1223(c)].

(5) (A) The Attorney General may except as provided in subparagraph (B) or in section 214(f) [8 USCS § 1184(f)], in his discretion parole into the United States temporarily under such conditions as he may prescribe only on a case-by-case basis for urgent humanitarian reasons or significant public benefit any alien applying for admission to the United States, but such parole of such alien shall not be regarded as an admission of the alien and when the purposes of such parole shall, in the opinion of the Attorney General, have been served the alien shall forthwith return or be returned to the custody from which he was paroled and thereafter his case shall continue to be dealt with in the same manner as that of any other applicant for admission to the United States.

(B) The Attorney General may not parole into the United States an alien who is a refugee unless the Attorney General determines that compelling reasons in the public interest with respect to that particular alien require that the alien be paroled into the United States rather than be admitted as a refugee under section 207 [8 USCS § 1157].

(6) [Repealed]

(7) The provisions of subsection (a) (other than paragraph (7)) shall be applicable to any alien who shall leave Guam, the Commonwealth of the Northern Mariana Islands, Puerto Rico, or the Virgin Islands of the United States, and who seeks to enter the continental United States or any other place under the jurisdiction of the United States. The Attorney General shall by regulations provide a method and procedure for the temporary admission to the United States of the aliens described in this proviso. Any alien described in

this paragraph, who is denied admission to the United States, shall be immediately removed in the manner provided by section 241(c) of this Act [8 USCS § 1231(c)].

(8) Upon a basis of reciprocity accredited officials of foreign governments, their immediate families, attendants, servants, and personal employees may be admitted in immediate and continuous transit through the United States without regard to the provisions of this section except paragraphs (3)(A), (3)(B), (3)(C), and (7)(B) of subsection (a) of this section.

(9), (10) [Repealed]

(11) The Attorney General may, in his discretion for humanitarian purposes, to assure family unity, or when it is otherwise in the public interest, waive application of clause (i) of subsection (a)(6)(E) in the case of any alien lawfully admitted for permanent residence who temporarily proceeded abroad voluntarily and not under an order of removal, and who is otherwise admissible to the United States as a returning resident under section 211(b) [8 USCS § 1181(b)] and in the case of an alien seeking admission or adjustment of status as an immediate relative or immigrant under section 203(a) [8 USCS § 1153(a)] (other than paragraph (4) thereof), if the alien has encouraged, induced, assisted, abetted, or aided only an individual who at the time of such action was the alien's spouse, parent, son, or daughter (and no other individual) to enter the United States in violation of law.

(12) The Attorney General may, in the discretion of the Attorney General for humanitarian purposes or to assure family unity, waive application of clause (i) of subsection (a)(6)(F)—

(A) in the case of an alien lawfully admitted for permanent residence who temporarily proceeded abroad voluntarily and not under an order of deportation or removal and who is otherwise admissible to the United States as a returning resident under section 211(b) [8 USCS § 1181(b)], and

(B) in the case of an alien seeking admission or adjustment of status under section 201(b)(2)(A) [8 USCS § 1151(b)(2)(A)] or under section 203(a) [8 USCS § 1153(a)],

if no previous civil money penalty was imposed against the alien under section 274C [8 USCS § 1324c] and the offense was committed solely to assist, aid, or support the alien's spouse or child (and not another individual). No court shall have jurisdiction to review a decision of the Attorney General to grant or deny a waiver under this paragraph.

(13) (A) The Secretary of Homeland Security shall determine whether a ground for inadmissibility exists with respect to a nonimmigrant described in section 101(a)(15)(T) [8 USCS § 1101(a)(15)(T)], except that the ground for inadmissibility described in subsection (a)(4) shall not apply with respect to such a nonimmigrant.

(B) In addition to any other waiver that may be available under this section, in the case of a nonimmigrant described in section 101(a)(15)(T) [8 USCS § 1101(a)(15)(T)], if the Secretary of Homeland Security considers it to be in the national interest to do so, the Secretary of Homeland Security, in the Attorney General's [Secretary's] discretion, may waive the application of—

(i) subsection (a)(1); and

(ii) any other provision of subsection (a) (excluding paragraphs (3), (4), (10)(C), and (10[)](E)) if the activities rendering the alien inadmissible under the provision were caused by, or were incident to, the victimization described in section 101(a)(15)(T)(i)(I) [8 USCS § 1101(a)(15)(T)(i)(I)].

(14) The Secretary of Homeland Security shall determine whether a ground of inadmissibility exists with respect to a nonimmigrant described in section 101(a)(15)(U) [8 USCS § 1101(a)(15)(U)]. The Secretary of Homeland Security, in the Attorney General's [Secretary's] discretion, may waive the application of subsection (a) (other than paragraph (3)(E)) in the case of a nonimmigrant described in section 101(a)(15)(U) [8 USCS § 1101(a)(15)(U)], if the Secretary of Homeland Security considers it to be in the public or national interest to do so.

(e) Educational visitor status; foreign residence requirement; waiver. No person admitted under section 101(a)(15)(J) [8 USCS § 1101(a)(15)(J)] or acquiring such status after admission (i) whose participation in the program for which he came to the United States was financed in whole or in part, directly or indirectly, by an agency of the Government of the United States or by the government of the country of his nationality or his last residence, (ii) who at the time of admission or acquisition of status under section 101(a)(15)(J) [8 USCS § 1101(a)(15)(J)] was a national or resident of a country which the Director of the United States Information Agency, pursuant to regulations prescribed by him, had designated as clearly requiring the services of persons specialized knowledge or skill in which the alien was engaged, or (iii) who came to the United States or acquired such status in order to receive graduate medical education or training, shall be eligible to apply for an immigrant visa, or for permanent residence, or for a nonimmigrant visa under section 101(a)(15)(H) or section 101(a)(15)(L) [8 USCS § 1101(a)(15)(H) or (L)] until it is established that such person has resided and been physically present in the country of his nationality or his last residence for an aggregate of at least two years following departure from the United States: Provided, That upon the favorable recommendation of the Director, pursuant to the request of an interested United States Government agency (or, in the case of an alien described in clause (iii), pursuant to the request of a State Department of Public Health, or its equivalent), or of the Commissioner of Immigration and Naturalization after he has determined that the departure from the United States would impose exceptional hardship upon the alien's spouse or child (if such spouse or child is a citizen of the United States or a lawfully resident alien), or that the alien cannot return to the country of his nationality or last residence because he would be subject to persecution on account of race, religion, or political opinion, the Attorney General may waive the requirement of such two-year foreign residence abroad in the case of any alien whose admission to the United States is found by the Attorney General to be in the public interest except that in the case of a waiver requested by a State Department of Public Health, or its equivalent, or in the case of a waiver requested by an interested United States Government agency on behalf of an alien described in clause (iii), the waiver shall be subject to the requirements of section 214*(l)* [8 USCS § 1184*(l)*]: And provided further, That, except in the case of an alien described in clause (iii), the Attorney General may, upon the favorable recommendation of the Director waive such two-year foreign residence requirement in any case in which the foreign country of the alien's nationality or last residence has furnished the Director a statement in writing that it has no objection to such waiver in the case of such alien.

(f) Suspension of entry or imposition of restrictions by President. Whenever the President finds that the entry of any aliens or of any class of aliens into the United States would be detrimental to the interests of the United States, he may by proclamation, and for such period as he shall deem necessary, suspend the entry of all aliens or any class of aliens as immigrants or nonimmigrants, or impose on the entry of aliens any restrictions he may deem to be appropriate. Whenever the Attorney General finds that a commercial airline has failed to comply with regulations of the Attorney General relating to requirements of airlines for the detection of fraudulent documents used by passengers traveling to the United States (including the training of personnel in such detection), the Attorney General may suspend the entry of some or all aliens transported to the United States by such airline.

(g) Bond and conditions for admission of alien inadmissible on health-related grounds. The Attorney General may waive the application of—

(1) subsection (a)(1)(A)(i) in the case of any alien who—

(A) is the spouse or the unmarried son or daughter, or the minor unmarried lawfully adopted child, of a United States citizen, or of an alien lawfully admitted for permanent residence, or of an alien who has been issued an immigrant visa,

(B) has a son or daughter who is a United States citizen, or an alien lawfully admitted for permanent residence, or an alien who has been issued an immigrant visa; or

(C) is a VAWA self-petitioner,

in accordance with such terms, conditions, and controls, if any, including the giving of bond, as the Attorney General, in the discretion of the Attorney General after consultation with the Secretary of Health and Human Services, may by regulation prescribe;

(2) subsection (a)(1)(A)(ii) in the case of any alien—

(A) who receives vaccination against the vaccine-preventable disease or diseases for which the alien has failed to present documentation of previous vaccination,

(B) for whom a civil surgeon, medical officer, or panel physician (as those terms are defined by section 34.2 of title 42 of the Code of Federal Regulations) certifies, according to such regulations as the Secretary of Health and Human Services may prescribe, that such vaccination would not be medically appropriate, or

(C) under such circumstances as the Attorney General provides by regulation, with respect to whom the requirement of such a vaccination would be contrary to the alien's religious beliefs or moral convictions; or

(3) subsection (a)(1)(A)(iii) in the case of any alien, in accordance with such terms, conditions, and controls, if any, including the giving of bond, as the Attorney General, in the discretion of the Attorney General after consultation with the Secretary of Health and Human Services, may by regulation prescribe.

(h) Waiver of subsec. (a)(2)(A)(i)(I), (II), (B), (D), and (E). The Attorney General may, in his discretion, waive the application of subparagraphs (A)(i)(I), (B), (D), and (E) of subsection (a)(2) and subparagraph (A)(i)(II) of such subsection insofar as it relates to a single offense of simple possession of 30 grams or less of marijuana if—

(1) (A) in the case of any immigrant it is established to the satisfaction of the Attorney General that—

(i) the alien is inadmissible only under subparagraph (D)(i) or (D)(ii) of such subsection or the activities for which the alien is inadmissible occurred more than 15 years before the date of the alien's application for a visa, admission, or adjustment of status, and

(ii) the admission to the United States of such alien would not be contrary to the national welfare, safety, or security of the United States,

(iii) the alien has been rehabilitated; or

(B) in the case of an immigrant who is the spouse, parent, son, or daughter of a citizen of the United States or an alien lawfully admitted for permanent residence if it is established to the satisfaction of the Attorney General that the alien's denial of admission would result in extreme hardship to the United States citizen or lawfully resident spouse, parent, son, or daughter of such alien; or

(C) the alien is a VAWA self-petitioner; and

(2) the Attorney General, in his discretion, and pursuant to such terms, conditions and procedures as he may by regulations prescribe, has consented to the alien's applying or reapplying for a visa, for admission to the United States, or adjustment of status.

No waiver shall be provided under this subsection in the case of an alien who has been convicted of (or who has admitted committing acts that constitute) murder or criminal acts involving torture, or an attempt or conspiracy to commit murder or a criminal act involving torture. No waiver shall be granted under this subsection in the case of an alien who has previously been admitted to the United States as an alien lawfully admitted for permanent residence if either since the date of such admission the alien has been convicted of an aggravated felony or the alien has not lawfully resided continuously in the United States for a period of not less than 7 years immediately preceding the date of initiation of proceedings to remove the alien from the United States. No court shall have jurisdiction to review a decision of the Attorney General to grant or deny a waiver under this subsection.

(i) Admission of immigrant inadmissible for fraud or willful misrepresentation of material fact.

(1) The Attorney General may, in the discretion of the Attorney General, waive the application of clause (i) of subsection (a)(6)(C) in the case of an immigrant who is the spouse, son, or daughter of a United States citizen or of an alien lawfully admitted for permanent residence if it is established to the satisfaction of the Attorney General that the refusal of admission to the United States of such immigrant alien would result in extreme hardship to the citizen or lawfully resident spouse or parent of such an alien or, in the case of a VAWA self-petitioner, the alien demonstrates extreme hardship to the alien or the alien's United States citizen, lawful permanent resident, or qualified alien parent or child.

(2) No court shall have jurisdiction to review a decision or action of the Attorney General regarding a waiver under paragraph (1).

(j) Limitation on immigration of foreign medical graduates.

(1) The additional requirements referred to in section 101(a)(15)(J) [8 USCS § 1101(a)(15)(J)] for an alien who is coming to the United States under a program under which he will receive graduate medical education or training are as follows:

(A) A school of medicine or of one of the other health professions, which is accredited by a body or bodies approved for the purpose by the Secretary of Education, has agreed in writing to provide the graduate medical education or training under the program for which the alien is coming to the United States or to assume responsibility for arranging for the provision thereof by an appropriate public or nonprofit private institution or agency, except that, in the case of such an agreement by a school of medicine, any one or more of its affiliated hospitals which are to participate in the provision of the graduate medical education or training must join in the agreement.

(B) Before making such agreement, the accredited school has been satisfied that the alien (i) is a graduate of a school of medicine which is accredited by a body or bodies approved for the purpose by the Secretary of Education (regardless of whether such school of medicine is in the United States); or (ii)(I) has passed parts I and II of the National Board of Medical Examiners Examination (or an equivalent examination as determined by the Secretary of Health and Human Services), (II) has competency in oral and written English, (III) will be able to adapt to the educational and cultural environment in which he will be receiving his education or training, and (IV) has adequate prior education and training to participate satisfactorily in the program for which he is coming to the United States. For the purposes of this subparagraph, an alien who is a graduate of a medical school shall be considered to have passed parts I and II of the National Board of Medical Examiners examination if the alien was fully and permanently licensed to practice medicine in a State on January 9, 1978, and was practicing medicine in a State on that date.

(C) The alien has made a commitment to return to the country of his nationality or last residence upon completion of the education or training for which he is coming to the United States, and the government of the country of his nationality or last residence has provided a written assurance, satisfactory to the Secretary of Health and Human Services, that there is a need in that country for persons with the skills the alien will acquire in such education or training.

(D) The duration of the alien's participation in the program of graduate medical education or training for which the alien is coming to the United States is limited to the time typically required to complete such program, as determined by the Director of the United States Information Agency at the time of the alien's admission into the United States, based on criteria which are established in coordination with the Secretary of Health and Human Services and which take into consideration the published requirements of the medical specialty board which administers such education or training program; except that—

(i) such duration is further limited to seven years unless the alien has demonstrated to the satisfaction of the Director that the country to which the alien will return at the end of such specialty education or training has an exceptional need for an individual trained in such specialty, and

(ii) the alien may, once and not later than two years after the date the alien is admitted to the United States as an exchange visitor or acquires exchange visitor status, change the alien's designated program of graduate medical education or training if the Director approves the change and if a commitment and written assurance with respect to the alien's new program have been provided in accordance with subparagraph (C).

(E) The alien furnishes the Attorney General each year with an affidavit (in such form as the Attorney General shall prescribe) that attests that the alien (i) is in good standing in the program of graduate medical education or training in which the alien is participating, and (ii) will return to the country of his nationality or last residence upon completion of the education or training for which he came to the United States.

(2) An alien who is a graduate of a medical school and who is coming to the United States to perform services as a member of the medical profession may not be admitted as a nonimmigrant under section 101(a)(15)(H)(i)(b) [8 USCS § 1101(a)(15)(H)(i)(b)] unless—

(A) the alien is coming pursuant to an invitation from a public or nonprofit private educational or research institution or agency in the United States to teach or conduct research, or both, at or for such institution or agency, or

(B) (i) the alien has passed the Federation licensing examination (administered by the Federation of State Medical Boards of the United States) or an equivalent examination as determined by the Secretary of Health and Human Services, and

(ii) (I) has competency in oral and written English or (II) is a graduate of a school of medicine which is accredited by a body or bodies approved for the purpose by the Secretary of Education (regardless of whether such school of medicine is in the United States).

(k) Attorney General's discretion to admit otherwise inadmissible aliens who possess immigrant visas. Any alien, inadmissible from the United States under paragraph (5)(A) or (7)(A)(i) of subsection (a), who is in possession of an immigrant visa may, if otherwise admissible, be admitted in the discretion of the Attorney General if the Attorney General is satisfied that inadmissibility was not known to, and could not have been ascertained by the exercise of reasonable diligence by, the immigrant before the time of departure of the vessel or aircraft from the last port outside the United States and outside foreign contiguous territory or, in the case of an immigrant coming from foreign contiguous territory, before the time of the immigrant's application for admission.

(l) Guam and Northern Mariana Islands visa waiver program.

(1) In general. The requirement of subsection (a)(7)(B)(i) may be waived by the Secretary of Homeland Security, in the case of an alien applying for admission as a nonimmigrant visitor for business or pleasure and solely for entry into and stay in Guam or the Commonwealth of the Northern Mariana Islands for a period not to exceed 45 days, if the Secretary of Homeland Security, after consultation with the Secretary of the Interior, the Secretary of State, the Governor of Guam and the Governor of the Commonwealth of the Northern Mariana Islands, determines that—

(A) an adequate arrival and departure control system has been developed in Guam and the Commonwealth of the Northern Mariana Islands; and

(B) such a waiver does not represent a threat to the welfare, safety, or security of the United States or its territories and commonwealths.

(2) Alien waiver of rights. An alien may not be provided a waiver under this subsection unless the alien has waived any right—

(A) to review or appeal under this Act [8 USCS §§ 1101 et seq.] an immigration officer's determination as to the admissibility of the alien at the port of entry into Guam or the Commonwealth of the Northern Mariana Islands; or

(B) to contest, other than on the basis of an application for withholding of removal under section 241(b)(3) of this Act [8 USCS § 1231(b)(3)] or under the Convention Against Torture, or an application for asylum if permitted under section 208 [8 USCS § 1158], any action for removal of the alien.

(3) Regulations. All necessary regulations to implement this subsection shall be promulgated by the Secretary of Homeland Security, in consultation with the Secretary of the Interior and the Secretary of State, on or before the 180th day after the date of enactment of the Consolidated Natural Resources Act of 2008 [enacted May 8, 2008]. The promulgation of such regulations shall be considered a foreign affairs function for purposes of section 553(a) of title 5, United States Code [5 USCS § 553(a)]. At a minimum, such regulations should include, but not necessarily be limited to—

(A) a listing of all countries whose nationals may obtain the waiver also provided by this subsection, except that such regulations shall provide for a listing of any country from which the Commonwealth has received a significant economic benefit from the number of visitors for pleasure within the one-year period preceding the date of enactment of the Consolidated Natural Resources Act of 2008 [enacted May 8, 2008], unless the Secretary of Homeland Security determines that such country's inclusion on such list would represent a threat to the welfare, safety, or security of the United States or its territories; and

(B) any bonding requirements for nationals of some or all of those countries who may present an increased risk of overstays or other potential problems, if different from such requirements otherwise provided by law for nonimmigrant visitors.

(4) Factors. In determining whether to grant or continue providing the waiver under this subsection to nationals of any country, the Secretary of Homeland Security, in consultation with the Secretary of the Interior and the Secretary of State, shall consider all factors that the Secretary deems relevant, including electronic travel authorizations, procedures for reporting lost and stolen passports, repatriation of aliens, rates of refusal for nonimmigrant visitor visas, overstays, exit systems, and information exchange.

(5) Suspension. The Secretary of Homeland Security shall monitor the admission of nonimmigrant visitors to Guam and the Commonwealth of the Northern Mariana Islands under this subsection. If the Secretary determines that such admissions have resulted in an unacceptable number of visitors from a country remaining unlawfully in Guam or the Commonwealth of the Northern Mariana Islands, unlawfully obtaining entry to other parts of the United States, or seeking withholding of removal or asylum, or that visitors from a country pose a risk to law enforcement or security interests of Guam or the Commonwealth of the Northern Mariana Islands or of the United States (including the interest in the enforcement of the immigration laws of the United States), the Secretary shall suspend the admission of nationals of such country under this subsection. The Secretary of Homeland Security may in the Secretary's discretion suspend the Guam and Northern Mariana Islands visa waiver program at any time, on a country-by-country basis, for other good cause.

(6) Addition of countries. The Governor of Guam and the Governor of the Commonwealth of the Northern Mariana Islands may request the Secretary of the Interior and the Secretary of Homeland Security to add a particular country to the list of countries whose nationals may obtain the waiver provided by this subsection, and the Secretary of Homeland Security may grant such request after consultation with the Secretary of the Interior and the Secretary of State, and may promulgate regulations with respect to the inclusion of that country and any special requirements the Secretary of Homeland Security, in the Secretary's sole discretion, may impose prior to allowing nationals of that country to obtain the waiver provided by this subsection.

(m) Requirements for admission of nonimmigrant nurses.

(1) The qualifications referred to in section 101(a)(15)(H)(i)(c) [8 USCS § 1101(a)(15)(H)(i)(c)], with respect to an alien who is coming to the United States to perform nursing services for a facility, are that the alien—

(A) has obtained a full and unrestricted license to practice professional nursing in the country where the alien obtained nursing education or has received nursing education in the United States;

(B) has passed an appropriate examination (recognized in regulations promulgated in consultation with the Secretary of Health and Human Services) or has a full and unrestricted license under State law to practice professional nursing in the State of intended employment; and

(C) is fully qualified and eligible under the laws (including such temporary or interim licensing requirements which authorize the nurse to be employed) governing the place of intended employment to engage in the practice of professional nursing as a registered nurse immediately upon admission to the United States and is authorized under such laws to be employed by the facility.

(2) (A) The attestation referred to in section 101(a)(15)(H)(i)(c) [8 USCS § 1101(a)(15)(H)(i)(c)], with respect to a facility for which an alien will perform services, is an attestation as to the following:

(i) The facility meets all the requirements of paragraph (6).

(ii) The employment of the alien will not adversely affect the wages and working conditions of registered nurses similarly employed.

(iii) The alien employed by the facility will be paid the wage rate for registered nurses similarly employed by the facility.

(iv) The facility has taken and is taking timely and significant steps designed to recruit and retain sufficient registered nurses who are United States citizens or immigrants who are authorized to perform nursing services, in order to remove as quickly as reasonably possible the dependence of the facility on nonimmigrant registered nurses.

(v) There is not a strike or lockout in the course of a labor dispute, the facility did not lay off and will not lay off a registered nurse employed by the facility within the period beginning 90 days before and ending 90 days after the date of filing of any visa petition, and the employment of such an alien is not intended or designed to influence an election for a bargaining representative for registered nurses of the facility.

(vi) At the time of the filing of the petition for registered nurses under section 101(a)(15)(H)(i)(c) [8 USCS § 1101(a)(15)(H)(i)(c)], notice of the filing has been provided by the facility to the bargaining representative of the registered nurses at the facility or, where there is no such bargaining representative, notice of the filing has been provided to the registered nurses employed at the facility through posting in conspicuous locations.

(vii) The facility will not, at any time, employ a number of aliens issued visas or otherwise provided nonimmigrant status under section 101(a)(15)(H)(i)(c) [8 USCS § 1101(a)(15)(H)(i)(c)] that exceeds 33 percent of the total number of registered nurses employed by the facility.

(viii) The facility will not, with respect to any alien issued a visa or otherwise provided nonimmigrant status under section 101(a)(15)(H)(i)(c) [8 USCS § 1101(a)(15)(H)(i)(c)]—

(I) authorize the alien to perform nursing services at any worksite other than a worksite controlled by the facility; or

(II) transfer the place of employment of the alien from one worksite to another.

Nothing in clause (iv) shall be construed as requiring a facility to have taken significant steps described in such clause before the date of the enactment of the Nursing Relief for Disadvantaged Areas Act of 1999 [enacted Nov. 12, 1999]. A copy of the attestation shall be provided, within 30 days of the date of filing, to registered nurses employed at the facility on the date of filing.

(B) For purposes of subparagraph (A)(iv), each of the following shall be considered a significant step reasonably designed to recruit and retain registered nurses:

(i) Operating a training program for registered nurses at the facility or financing (or providing participation in) a training program for registered nurses elsewhere.

(ii) Providing career development programs and other methods of facilitating health care workers to become registered nurses.

(iii) Paying registered nurses wages at a rate higher than currently being paid to registered nurses similarly employed in the geographic area.

(iv) Providing reasonable opportunities for meaningful salary advancement by registered nurses.

The steps described in this subparagraph shall not be considered to be an exclusive list of the significant steps that may be taken to meet the conditions of subparagraph (A)(iv). Nothing in this subparagraph shall require a facility to take more than one step if the facility can demonstrate that taking a second step is not reasonable.

(C) Subject to subparagraph (E), an attestation under subparagraph (A)—

(i) shall expire on the date that is the later of—

(I) the end of the one-year period beginning on the date of its filing with the Secretary of Labor; or

(II) the end of the period of admission under section 101(a)(15)(H)(i)(c) [8 USCS § 1101(a)(15)(H)(i)(c)] of the last alien with respect to whose admission it was applied (in accordance with clause (ii)); and

(ii) shall apply to petitions filed during the one-year period beginning on the date of its filing with the Secretary of Labor if the facility states in each such petition that it continues to comply with the conditions in the attestation.

(D) A facility may meet the requirements under this paragraph with respect to more than one registered nurse in a single petition.

(E) (i) The Secretary of Labor shall compile and make available for public examination in a timely manner in Washington, D.C., a list identifying facilities which have filed petitions for nonimmigrants under section 101(a)(15)(H)(i)(c) [8 USCS § 1101(a)(15)(H)(i)(c)] and, for each such facility, a copy of the facility's attestation under subparagraph (A) (and accompanying documentation) and each such petition filed by the facility.

(ii) The Secretary of Labor shall establish a process, including reasonable time limits, for the receipt, investigation, and disposition of complaints respecting a facility's failure to meet conditions attested to or a facility's misrepresentation of a material fact in an attestation. Complaints may be filed by any aggrieved person or organization (including bargaining representatives, associations deemed appropriate by the Secretary, and other aggrieved parties as determined under regulations of the Secretary). The Secretary shall conduct an investigation under this clause if there is reasonable cause to believe that a facility fails to meet conditions attested to. Subject to the time limits established under this clause, this subparagraph shall apply regardless of whether an attestation is expired or unexpired at the time a complaint is filed.

(iii) Under such process, the Secretary shall provide, within 180 days after the date such a complaint is filed, for a determination as to whether or not a basis exists to make a finding described in clause (iv). If the Secretary determines that such a basis exists, the Secretary shall provide for notice of such determination to the interested parties and an opportunity for a hearing on the complaint within 60 days of the date of the determination.

(iv) If the Secretary of Labor finds, after notice and opportunity for a hearing, that a facility (for which an attestation is made) has failed to meet a condition attested to or that there was a misrepresentation of material fact in the attestation, the Secretary shall notify the Attorney General of such finding and may, in addition, impose such other administrative remedies (including civil monetary penalties in an amount not to exceed $1,000 per nurse per violation, with the total penalty not to exceed $10,000 per violation) as the Secretary determines to be appropriate. Upon receipt of such notice, the Attorney General shall not approve petitions filed with respect to a facility during a period of at least one year for nurses to be employed by the facility.

(v) In addition to the sanctions provided for under clause (iv), if the Secretary of Labor finds, after notice and an opportunity for a hearing, that a facility has violated the condition attested to under subparagraph (A)(iii) (relating to payment of registered nurses at the prevailing wage rate), the Secretary shall order the facility to provide for payment of such amounts of back pay as may be required to comply with such condition.

(F) (i) The Secretary of Labor shall impose on a facility filing an attestation under subparagraph (A) a filing fee, in an amount prescribed by the Secretary based on the costs of carrying out the Secretary's duties under this subsection, but not exceeding $250.

(ii) Fees collected under this subparagraph shall be deposited in a fund established for this purpose in the Treasury of the United States.

(iii) The collected fees in the fund shall be available to the Secretary of Labor, to the extent and in such amounts as may be provided in appropriations Acts, to cover the costs described in clause (i), in addition to any other funds that are available to the Secretary to cover such costs.

(3) The period of admission of an alien under section 101(a)(15)(H)(i)(c) [8 USCS § 1101(a)(15)(H)(i)(c)] shall be 3 years.

(4) The total number of nonimmigrant visas issued pursuant to petitions granted under section 101(a)(15)(H)(i)(c) [8 USCS § 1101(a)(15)(H)(i)(c)] in each fiscal year shall not exceed 500. The number of such visas issued for employment in each State in each fiscal year shall not exceed the following:

(A) For States with populations of less than 9,000,000, based upon the 1990 decennial census of population, 25 visas.

(B) For States with populations of 9,000,000 or more, based upon the 1990 decennial census of population, 50 visas.

(C) If the total number of visas available under this paragraph for a fiscal year quarter exceeds the number of qualified nonimmigrants who may be issued such visas during those quarters, the visas made available under this paragraph shall be issued without regard to the numerical limitation under subparagraph (A) or (B) of this paragraph during the last fiscal year quarter.

(5) A facility that has filed a petition under section 101(a)(15)(H)(i)(c) [8 USCS § 1101(a)(15)(H)(i)(c)] to employ a nonimmigrant to perform nursing services for the facility—

(A) shall provide the nonimmigrant a wage rate and working conditions commensurate with those of nurses similarly employed by the facility;

(B) shall require the nonimmigrant to work hours commensurate with those of nurses similarly employed by the facility; and

(C) shall not interfere with the right of the nonimmigrant to join or organize a union.

(6) For purposes of this subsection and section 101(a)(15)(H)(i)(c) [8 USCS § 1101(a)(15)(H)(i)(c)], the term "facility" means a subsection (d) hospital (as defined in section 1886(d)(1)(B) of the Social Security Act (42 U.S.C. 1395ww(d)(1)(B))) that meets the following requirements:

(A) As of March 31, 1997, the hospital was located in a health professional shortage area (as defined in section 332 of the Public Health Service Act (42 U.S.C. 254e)).

(B) Based on its settled cost report filed under title XVIII of the Social Security Act [42 USCS §§ 1395 et seq.] for its cost reporting period beginning during fiscal year 1994—

(i) the hospital has not less than 190 licensed acute care beds;

(ii) the number of the hospital's inpatient days for such period which were made up of patients who (for such days) were entitled to benefits under part A of such title [42 USCS §§ 1395c et seq.] is not less than

35 percent of the total number of such hospital's acute care inpatient days for such period; and

(iii) the number of the hospital's inpatient days for such period which were made up of patients who (for such days) were eligible for medical assistance under a State plan approved under title XIX of the Social Security Act [42 USCS §§ 1396 et seq.], is not less than 28 percent of the total number of such hospital's acute care inpatient days for such period.

(7) For purposes of paragraph (2)(A)(v), the term "lay off", with respect to a worker—

(A) means to cause the worker's loss of employment, other than through a discharge for inadequate performance, violation of workplace rules, cause, voluntary departure, voluntary retirement, or the expiration of a grant or contract; but

(B) does not include any situation in which the worker is offered, as an alternative to such loss of employment, a similar employment opportunity with the same employer at equivalent or higher compensation and benefits than the position from which the employee was discharged, regardless of whether or not the employee accepts the offer.

Nothing in this paragraph is intended to limit an employee's or an employer's rights under a collective bargaining agreement or other employment contract.

(n) Labor condition application.

(1) No alien may be admitted or provided status as an H-1B nonimmigrant in an occupational classification unless the employer has filed with the Secretary of Labor an application stating the following:

(A) The employer—

(i) is offering and will offer during the period of authorized employment to aliens admitted or provided status as an H-1B non-immigrant wages that are at least—

(I) the actual wage level paid by the employer to all other individuals with similar experience and qualifications for the specific employment in question, or

(II) the prevailing wage level for the occupational classification in the area of employment,

whichever is greater, based on the best information available as of the time of filing the application, and

(ii) will provide working conditions for such a nonimmigrant that will not adversely affect the working conditions of workers similarly employed.

(B) There is not a strike or lockout in the course of a labor dispute in the occupational classification at the place of employment.

(C) The employer, at the time of filing the application—

(i) has provided notice of the filing under this paragraph to the bargaining representative (if any) of the employer's employees in the occupational classification and area for which aliens are sought, or

(ii) if there is no such bargaining representative, has provided notice of filing in the occupational classification through such methods as physical posting in conspicuous locations at the place of employment or electronic notification to employees in the occupational classification for which H-1B nonimmigrants are sought.

(D) The application shall contain a specification of the number of workers sought, the occupational classification in which the workers will be employed, and wage rate and conditions under which they will be employed.

(E) (i) In the case of an application described in clause (ii), the employer did not displace and will not displace a United States worker (as defined in paragraph (4)) employed by the employer within the period beginning 90 days before and ending 90 days after the date of filing of any visa petition supported by the application.

(ii) An application described in this clause is an application filed on or after the date final regulations are first promulgated to carry out this subparagraph, [and before] by an H-1B-dependent employer (as defined in paragraph (3)) or by an employer that has been found, on or after the date of the enactment of the American Competitiveness and Workforce Improvement Act of 1998 [enacted Oct. 21, 1998], under paragraph (2)(C) or (5) to have committed a willful failure or misrepresentation during the 5-year period preceding the filing of the application. An application is not described in this clause if the only H-1B nonimmigrants sought in the application are exempt H-1B nonimmigrants.

(F) In the case of an application described in subparagraph (E)(ii), the employer will not place the nonimmigrant with another employer (regardless of whether or not such other employer is an H-1B-dependent employer) where—

(i) the nonimmigrant performs duties in whole or in part at one or more worksites owned, operated, or controlled by such other employer; and

(ii) there are indicia of an employment relationship between the nonimmigrant and such other employer;

unless the employer has inquired of the other employer as to whether, and has no knowledge that, within the period beginning 90 days before and ending 90 days after the date of the placement of the nonimmigrant with the other employer, the other employer has displaced or intends to displace a United States worker employed by the other employer.

(G) (i) In the case of an application described in subparagraph (E)(ii), subject to clause (ii), the employer, prior to filing the application—

(I) has taken good faith steps to recruit, in the United States using procedures that meet industry-wide standards and offering compensation that is at least as great as that required to be offered to H-1B nonimmigrants under subparagraph (A), United States workers for the job for which the nonimmigrant or nonimmigrants is or are sought; and

(II) has offered the job to any United States worker who applies and is equally or better qualified for the job for which the nonimmigrant or nonimmigrants is or are sought.

(ii) The conditions described in clause (i) shall not apply to an application filed with respect to the employment of an H-1B nonimmigrant who is described in subparagraph (A), (B), or (C) of section 203(b)(1) [8 USCS § 1153(b)(1)].

The employer shall make available for public examination, within one working day after the date on which an application under this paragraph is filed, at the employer's principal place of business or worksite, a copy of each such application (and such accompanying documents as are necessary). The Secretary shall compile, on a current basis, a list (by employer and by occupational classification) of the applications filed under this subsection. Such list shall include the wage rate, number of aliens sought, period of intended employment, and date of need. The Secretary shall make such list available for public examination in Washington, D.C. The Secretary of Labor shall review such an application only for completeness and obvious inaccuracies. Unless the Secretary finds that the application is incomplete or obviously inaccurate, the Secretary shall provide the certification described in section 101(a)(15)(H)(i)(b) [8 USCS § 1101(a)(15)(H)(i)(b)] within 7 days of the date of the filing of the application. The application form shall include a clear statement explaining the liability under subparagraph (F) of a placing employer if the other employer described in such subparagraph displaces a United States worker as described in such subparagraph. Nothing in subparagraph (G) shall be construed to prohibit an employer from using legitimate selection criteria relevant to the job that are normal or customary to the type of job involved, so long as such criteria are not applied in a discriminatory manner.

(2) (A) Subject to paragraph (5)(A), the Secretary shall establish a process for the receipt, investigation, and disposition of complaints respecting a petitioner's failure to meet a condition specified in an application submitted under paragraph (1) or a petitioner's misrepresentation of material facts in such an application. Complaints may be filed by any aggrieved person or organization (including bargaining representatives). No investigation or hearing shall be conducted on a complaint concerning such a failure or misrepresentation unless the complaint was filed not later than 12 months after the date of the failure or misrepresentation, respectively. The Secretary shall conduct an investigation under this paragraph if there is reasonable cause to believe that such a failure or misrepresentation has occurred.

(B) Under such process, the Secretary shall provide, within 30 days after the date such a complaint is filed, for a determination as to whether or not a reasonable basis exists to make a finding described in subparagraph (C). If the Secretary determines that such a reasonable basis exists, the Secretary shall provide for notice of such determination to the interested parties and an opportunity for a hearing on the complaint, in accordance with section 556 of title 5, United States Code, within 60 days after the date of the determination. If such a hearing is requested, the Secretary shall make a finding concerning the matter by not later than 60 days after the date of the hearing. In the case of similar complaints respecting the same applicant, the Secretary may consolidate the hearings under this subparagraph on such complaints.

(C) (i) If the Secretary finds, after notice and opportunity for a hearing, a failure to meet a condition of paragraph (1)(B), (1)(E), or (1)(F), a substantial failure to meet a condition of paragraph (1)(C), (1)(D), or (1)(G)(i)(I), or a misrepresentation of material fact in an application—

(I) the Secretary shall notify the Attorney General of such finding and may, in addition, impose such other administrative remedies (including civil monetary penalties in an amount not to exceed $1,000 per violation) as the Secretary determines to be appropriate; and

(II) the Attorney General shall not approve petitions filed with respect to that employer under section 204 or 214(c) [8 USCS § 1154 or 1184(c)] during a period of at least 1 year for aliens to be employed by the employer.

(ii) If the Secretary finds, after notice and opportunity for a hearing, a willful failure to meet a condition of paragraph (1), a willful misrepresentation of material fact in an application, or a violation of clause (iv)—

(I) the Secretary shall notify the Attorney General of such finding and may, in addition, impose such other administrative remedies (including civil monetary penalties in an amount not to exceed $5,000 per violation) as the Secretary determines to be appropriate; and

(II) the Attorney General shall not approve petitions filed with respect to that employer under section 204 or 214(c) [8 USCS § 1154 or 1184(c)] during a period of at least 2 years for aliens to be employed by the employer.

(iii) If the Secretary finds, after notice and opportunity for a hearing, a willful failure to meet a condition of paragraph (1) or a willful misrepresentation of material fact in an application, in the course of which failure or misrepresentation the employer displaced a United States worker employed by the employer within the period beginning 90 days before and ending 90 days after the date of filing of any visa petition supported by the application—

(I) the Secretary shall notify the Attorney General of such finding and may, in addition, impose such other administrative remedies (including civil monetary penalties in an amount not to exceed $35,000 per violation) as the Secretary determines to be appropriate; and

(II) the Attorney General shall not approve petitions filed with respect to that employer under section 204 or 214(c) [8 USCS § 1154 or 1184(c)] during a period of at least 3 years for aliens to be employed by the employer.

(iv) It is a violation of this clause for an employer who has filed an application under this subsection to intimidate, threaten, restrain, coerce, blacklist, discharge, or in any other manner discriminate against an employee (which term, for purposes of this clause, includes a former employee and an applicant for employment) because the employee has disclosed information to the employer, or to any other person, that the employee reasonably believes evidences a violation of this subsection, or any rule or regulation pertaining to this subsection, or because the employee cooperates or seeks to cooperate in an investigation or other proceeding concerning the employer's compliance with the requirements of this subsection or any rule or regulation pertaining to this subsection.

(v) The Secretary of Labor and the Attorney General shall devise a process under which an H-1B nonimmigrant who files a complaint regarding a violation of clause (iv) and is otherwise eligible to remain and work in the United States may be allowed to seek other appropriate employment in the United States for a period not to exceed the maximum period of stay authorized for such nonimmigrant classification.

(vi) (I) It is a violation of this clause for an employer who has filed an application under this subsection to require an H-1B nonimmigrant to pay a penalty for ceasing employment with the employer prior to a date agreed to by the nonimmigrant and the employer. The Secretary shall determine whether a required payment is a penalty (and not liquidated damages) pursuant to relevant State law.

(II) It is a violation of this clause for an employer who has filed an application under this subsection to require an alien who is the subject of a petition filed under section 214(c)(1) [8 USCS § 1184(c)(1)], for which a fee is imposed under section 214(c)(9) [8 USCS § 1184(c)(9)], to reimburse, or otherwise compensate, the employer for part or all of the cost of such fee. It is a violation of this clause for such an employer otherwise to accept such reimbursement or compensation from such an alien.

(III) If the Secretary finds, after notice and opportunity for a hearing, that an employer has committed a violation of this clause, the Secretary may impose a civil monetary penalty of $1,000 for each such violation and issue an administrative order requiring the return to the nonimmigrant of any amount paid in violation of this clause, or, if the nonimmigrant cannot be located, requiring payment of any such amount to the general fund of the Treasury.

(vii) (I) It is a failure to meet a condition of paragraph (1)(A) for an employer, who has filed an application under this subsection and who places an H-1B nonimmigrant designated as a full-time employee on the petition filed under section 214(c)(1) [8 USCS § 1184(c)(1)] by the employer with respect to the nonimmigrant, after the nonimmigrant has entered into employment with the employer, in nonproductive status due to a decision by the employer (based on factors such as lack of work), or due to the nonimmigrant's lack of a permit or license, to fail to pay the nonimmigrant full-time wages in accordance with paragraph (1)(A) for all such nonproductive time.

(II) It is a failure to meet a condition of paragraph (1)(A) for an employer, who has filed an application under this subsection and who places an H-1B nonimmigrant designated as a part-time employee on the petition filed under section 214(c)(1) [8 USCS § 1184(c)(1)] by the employer with respect to the nonimmigrant, after the nonimmigrant has entered into employment with the employer, in nonproductive status under circumstances described in subclause (I), to fail to pay such a nonimmigrant for such hours as are designated on such petition consistent with the rate of pay identified on such petition.

(III) In the case of an H-1B nonimmigrant who has not yet entered into employment with an employer who has had approved an application under this subsection, and a petition under section 214(c)(1) [8 USCS § 1184(c)(1)], with respect to the nonimmigrant, the provisions of subclauses (I) and (II) shall apply to the employer beginning 30 days after the date the nonimmigrant first is admitted into the United States pursuant to the petition, or 60 days after the date the nonimmigrant becomes eligible to work for the employer (in the case of a nonimmigrant who is present in the United States on the date of the approval of the petition).

(IV) This clause does not apply to a failure to pay wages to an H-1B nonimmigrant for nonproductive time due to non-work-related factors, such as the voluntary request of the nonimmigrant for an absence or circumstances rendering the nonimmigrant unable to work.

(V) This clause shall not be construed as prohibiting an employer that is a school or other educational institution from applying to an H-1B nonimmigrant an established salary practice of the employer, under which the employer pays to H-1B nonimmigrants and United States workers in the same occupational classification an annual salary in disbursements over fewer than 12 months, if—

(aa) the nonimmigrant agrees to the compressed annual salary payments prior to the commencement of the employment; and

(bb) the application of the salary practice to the nonimmigrant does not otherwise cause the nonimmigrant to violate any condition of the nonimmigrant's authorization under this Act to remain in the United States.

(VI) This clause shall not be construed as superseding clause (viii).

(viii) It is a failure to meet a condition of paragraph (1)(A) for an employer who has filed an application under this subsection to fail to offer to an H-1B nonimmigrant, during the nonimmigrant's period of authorized employment, benefits and eligibility for benefits (including the opportunity to participate in health, life, disability, and other insurance plans; the opportunity to participate in retirement and savings plans; and cash bonuses and noncash compensation, such as stock options (whether or not based on performance)) on the same basis, and in accordance with the same criteria, as the employer offers to United States workers.

(D) If the Secretary finds, after notice and opportunity for a hearing, that an employer has not paid wages at the wage level specified under the application and required under paragraph (1), the Secretary shall order the employer to provide for parent of such amounts of back pay as may be required to comply with the requirements of paragraph (1), whether or not a penalty under subparagraph (C) has been imposed.

(E) If an H-1B-dependent employer places a nonexempt H-1B nonimmigrant with another employer as provided under paragraph (1)(F) and the other employer has displaced or displaces a United States worker employed by such other employer during the period described in such paragraph, such displacement shall be considered for purposes of this paragraph a failure, by the placing employer, to meet a condition specified in an application submitted under paragraph (1); except that the Attorney General may impose a sanction described in subclause (II) of subparagraph (C)(i), (C)(ii), or (C)(iii) only if the Secretary of Labor found that such placing employer—

(i) knew or had reason to know of such displacement at the time of the placement of the nonimmigrant with the other employer; or

(ii) has been subject to a sanction under this subparagraph based upon a previous placement of an H-1B nonimmigrant with the same other employer.

(F) The Secretary may, on a case-by-case basis, subject an employer to random investigations for a period of up to 5 years, beginning on the date (on or after the date of the enactment of the American Competitiveness and Workforce Improvement Act of 1998 [enacted Oct. 21, 1998]) on which the employer is found by the Secretary to have committed a willful failure to meet a condition of paragraph (1) (or has been found under paragraph (5) to have committed a willful failure to meet the condition of paragraph (1)(G)(i)(II)) or to have made a willful misrepresentation of material fact in an application. The preceding sentence shall apply to an employer regardless of whether or not the employer is an H-1B-dependent employer. The authority of the Secretary under this subparagraph shall not be construed to be subject to, or limited by, the requirements of subparagraph (A).

(G) (i) The Secretary of Labor may initiate an investigation of any employer that employs nonimmigrants described in section 101(a)(15)(H)(i)(b) [8 USCS § 1101(a)(15)(H)(i)(b)] if the Secretary of Labor has reasonable cause to believe that the employer is not in compliance with this subsection. In the case of an investigation under this clause, the Secretary of Labor (or the acting Secretary in the case of the absence of [or] disability of the Secretary of Labor) shall personally certify that reasonable cause exists and shall approve commencement of the investigation. The investigation may be initiated for reasons other than completeness and obvious inaccuracies by the employer in complying with this subsection.

(ii) If the Secretary of Labor receives specific credible information from a source who is likely to have knowledge of an employer's practices or employment conditions, or an employer's compliance with the employer's labor condition application under paragraph (1), and whose identity is known to the Secretary of Labor, and such information provides reasonable cause to believe that the employer has committed a willful failure to meet a condition of paragraph (1)(A), (1)(B), (1)(C), (1)(E), (1)(F), or (1)(G)(i)(I), has engaged in a pattern or practice of failures to meet such a condition, or has committed a substantial failure to meet such a condition that affects multiple employees, the Secretary of Labor may conduct an investigation into the alleged failure or failures. The Secretary of Labor may withhold the identity of the source from the employer, and the source's identity shall not be subject to disclosure under section 552 of title 5, United States Code.

(iii) The Secretary of Labor shall establish a procedure for any person desiring to provide to the Secretary of Labor information described in clause (ii) that may be used, in whole or in part, as the basis for the commencement of an investigation described in such clause, to provide the information in writing on a form developed and provided by the Secretary of Labor and completed by or on behalf of the person. The person may not be an officer or employee of the Department of Labor, unless the information satisfies the requirement of clause (iv)(II) (although an officer or employee of the Department of Labor may complete the form on behalf of the person).

(iv) Any investigation initiated or approved by the Secretary of Labor under clause (ii) shall be based on information that satisfies the requirements of such clause and that—

(I) originates from a source other than an officer or employee of the Department of Labor; or

(II) was lawfully obtained by the Secretary of Labor in the course of lawfully conducting another Department of Labor investigation under this Act of [or] any other Act.

(v) The receipt by the Secretary of Labor of information submitted by an employer to the Attorney General or the Secretary of Labor for purposes of securing the employment of a nonimmigrant described in section 101(a)(15)(H)(i)(b) [8 USCS § 1101(a)(15)(H)(i)(b)] shall not be considered a receipt of information for purposes of clause (ii).

(vi) No investigation described in clause (ii) (or hearing described in clause (viii) based on such investigation) may be conducted with respect to information about a failure to meet a condition described in clause (ii), unless the Secretary of Labor receives the information not later than 12 months after the date of the alleged failure.

(vii) The Secretary of Labor shall provide notice to an employer with respect to whom there is reasonable cause to initiate an investigation described in clauses [clause] (i) or (ii), prior to the commencement of an investigation under such clauses, of the intent to conduct an investigation. The notice shall be provided in such a manner, and shall contain sufficient detail, to permit the employer to respond to the allegations before an investigation is commenced. The Secretary of Labor is not required to comply with this clause if the Secretary of Labor determines that to do so would interfere with an effort by the Secretary of Labor to secure compliance by the employer with the requirements of this subsection. There shall be no judicial review of a determination by the Secretary of Labor under this clause.

(viii) An investigation under clauses [clause] (i) or (ii) may be conducted for a period of up to 60 days. If the Secretary of Labor determines after such an investigation that a reasonable basis exists to make a finding that the employer has committed a willful failure to meet a condition of paragraph (1)(A), (1)(B), (1)(C), (1)(E), (1)(F), or (1)(G)(i)(I), has engaged in a pattern or practice of failures to meet such a condition, or has committed a substantial failure to meet such a condition that affects multiple employees, the Secretary of Labor shall provide for notice of such determination to the interested parties and an opportunity for a hearing in accordance with section 556 of title 5, United States Code, within 120 days after the date of the determination. If such a hearing is requested, the Secretary of Labor shall make a finding concerning the matter by not later than 120 days after the date of the hearing.

(H) (i) Except as provided in clauses (ii) and (iii), a person or entity is considered to have complied with the requirements of this subsection, notwithstanding a technical or procedural failure to meet such requirements, if there was a good faith attempt to comply with the requirements.

(ii) Clause (i) shall not apply if—

(I) the Department of Labor (or another enforcement agency) has explained to the person or entity the basis for the failure;

(II) the person or entity has been provided a period of not less than 10 business days (beginning after the date of the explanation) within which to correct the failure; and

(III) the person or entity has not corrected the failure voluntarily within such period.

(iii) A person or entity that, in the course of an investigation, is found to have violated the prevailing wage requirements set forth in paragraph (1)(A), shall not be assessed fines or other penalties for such violation if the person or entity can establish that the manner in which the prevailing wage was calculated was consistent with recognized industry standards and practices.

(iv) Clauses (i) and (iii) shall not apply to a person or entity that has engaged in or is engaging in a pattern or practice of willful violations of this subsection.

(I) Nothing in this subsection shall be construed as superseding or preempting any other enforcement-related authority under this Act (such as the authorities under section 274B [8 USCS § 1324b]), or any other Act.

(3) (A) For purposes of this subsection, the term "H-1B-dependent employer" means an employer that—

(i) (I) has 25 or fewer full-time equivalent employees who are employed in the United States; and (II) employs more than 7 H-1B nonimmigrants;

(ii) (I) has at least 26 but not more than 50 full-time equivalent employees who are employed in the United States; and (II) employs more than 12 H-1B nonimmigrants; or

(iii) (I) has at least 51 full-time equivalent employees who are employed in the United States; and (II) employs H-1B nonimmigrants in a number that is equal to at least 15 percent of the number of such full-time equivalent employees.

(B) For purposes of this subsection—

(i) the term "exempt H-1B nonimmigrant" means an H-1B nonimmigrant who—

(I) receives wages (including cash bonuses and similar compensation) at an annual rate equal to at least $60,000; or

(II) has attained a master"s or higher degree (or its equivalent) in a specialty related to the intended employment; and

(ii) the term "nonexempt H-1B nonimmigrant" means an H-1B nonimmigrant who is not an exempt H-1B nonimmigrant.

(C) For purposes of subparagraph (A)—

(i) in computing the number of full-time equivalent employees and the number of H-1B nonimmigrants, exempt H-1B nonimmigrants shall not be taken into account during the longer of—

(I) the 6-month period beginning on the date of the enactment of the American Competitiveness and Workforce Improvement Act of 1998 [enacted Oct. 21, 1998]; or

(II) the period beginning on the date of the enactment of the American Competitiveness and Workforce Improvement Act of 1998 [enacted Oct. 21, 1998] and ending on the date final regulations are issued to carry out this paragraph; and

(ii) any group treated as a single employer under subsection (b), (c), (m), or (o) of section 414 of the Internal Revenue Code of 1986 [26 USCS § 414] shall be treated as a single employer.

(4) For purposes of this subsection:

(A) The term "area of employment" means the area within normal commuting distance of the worksite or physical location where the work of the H-1B nonimmigrant is or will be performed. If such worksite or location is within a Metropolitan Statistical Area, any place within such area is deemed to be within the area of employment.

(B) In the case of an application with respect to one or more H-1B nonimmigrants by an employer, the employer is considered to "displace" a United States worker from a job if the employer lays off the worker from a job that is essentially the equivalent of the job for which the nonimmigrant or nonimmigrants is or are sought. A job shall not be considered to be essentially equivalent of another job unless it involves essentially the same responsibilities, was held by a United States worker with substantially equivalent qualifications and experience, and is located in the same area of employment as the other job.

(C) The term "H-1B nonimmigrant" means an alien admitted or provided status as a nonimmigrant described in section 101(a)(15)(H)(i)(B) [8 USCS § 1101(a)(15)(H)(i)(B)].

(D) (i) The term "lays off", with respect to a worker—

(I) means to cause the worker's loss of employment, other than through a discharge for inadequate performance, violation of workplace rules, cause, voluntary departure, voluntary retirement, or the expiration of a grant or contract (other than a temporary employment contract entered into in order to evade a condition described in subparagraph (E) or (F) of paragraph (1)); but

(II) does not include any situation in which the worker is offered, as an alternative to such loss of employment, a similar employment opportunity with the same employer (or, in the case of a placement of a worker with another employer under paragraph (1)(F), with either employer described in such paragraph) at equivalent or higher compensation and benefits than the position from which the employee was discharged, regardless of whether or not the employee accepts the offer.

(ii) Nothing in this subparagraph is intended to limit an employee's rights under a collective bargaining agreement or other employment contract.

(E) The term "United States worker" means an employee who—

(i) is a citizen or national of the United States; or

(ii) is an alien who is lawfully admitted for permanent residence, is admitted as a refugee under section 207 [8 USCS § 1157], is granted asylum under section 208 [8 USCS § 1158], or is an immigrant otherwise authorized, by this Act or by the Attorney General, to be employed.

(5) (A) This paragraph shall apply instead of subparagraphs (A) through (E) of paragraph (2) in the case of a violation described in subparagraph (B), but shall not be construed to limit or affect the authority of the Secretary or the Attorney General with respect to any other violation.

(B) The Attorney General shall establish a process for the receipt, initial review, and disposition in accordance with this paragraph of complaints respecting an employer's failure to meet the condition of paragraph (1)(G)(i)(II) or a petitioner's misrepresentation of material facts with respect to such condition. Complaints may be filed by an aggrieved individual who has submitted a resume or otherwise applied in a reasonable manner for the job that is the subject of the condition. No proceeding shall be conducted under this paragraph on a complaint concerning such a failure or misrepresentation unless the Attorney General determines that the complaint was filed not later than 12 months after the date of the failure or misrepresentation, respectively.

(C) If the Attorney General finds that a complaint has been filed in accordance with subparagraph (B) and there is reasonable cause to believe that such a failure or misrepresentation described in such complaint has occurred, the Attorney General shall initiate binding arbitration proceedings by requesting the Federal Mediation and Conciliation Service to appoint an arbitrator from the roster of arbitrators maintained by such Service. The procedure and rules of such Service shall be applicable to the selection of such arbitrator and to such arbitration proceedings. The Attorney General shall pay the fee and expenses of the arbitrator.

(D) (i) The arbitrator shall make findings respecting whether a failure or misrepresentation described in subparagraph (B) occurred. If the arbitrator concludes that failure or misrepresentation was willful, the arbitrator shall make a finding to that effect. The arbitrator may not find such a failure or misrepresentation (or that such a failure or misrepresentation was willful) unless the complainant demonstrates such a failure or misrepresentation (or its willful character) by clear and convincing evidence. The arbitrator shall transmit the findings in the form of a written opinion to the parties to the arbitration and the Attorney General. Such findings shall be final and conclusive, and, except as provided in this subparagraph, no official or court of the United States shall have power or jurisdiction to review any such findings.

(ii) The Attorney General may review and reverse or modify the findings of an arbitrator only on the same bases as an award of an arbitrator may be vacated or modified under section 10 or 11 of title 9, United States Code.

(iii) With respect to the findings of an arbitrator, a court may review only the actions of the Attorney General under clause (ii) and may set aside such actions only on the grounds described in subparagraph (A), (B), or (C) of section 706(a)(2) of title 5, United States Code. Notwithstanding any other provision of law, such judicial review may only be brought in an appropriate United States court of appeals.

(E) If the Attorney General receives a finding of an arbitrator under this paragraph that an employer has failed to meet the condition of paragraph (1)(G)(i)(II) or has misrepresented a material fact with respect to such condition, unless the Attorney General reverses or modifies the finding under subparagraph (D)(ii)—

(i) the Attorney General may impose administrative remedies (including civil monetary penalties in an amount not to exceed $1,000 per violation or $5,000 per violation in the case of a willful failure or misrepresentation) as the Attorney General determines to be appropriate; and

(ii) the Attorney General is authorized to not approve petitions filed, with respect to that employer and for aliens to be employed by the employer, under section 204 or 214(c) [8 USCS § 1154 or 1184(c)]—

(I) during a period of not more than 1 year; or

(II) in the case of a willful failure or willful misrepresentation, during a period of not more than 2 years.

(F) The Attorney General shall not delegate, to any other employee or official of the Department of Justice, any function of the Attorney General under this paragraph, until 60 days after the Attorney General has submitted a plan for such delegation to the Committees on the Judiciary of the United States House of Representatives and the Senate.

(o) [Terminated]

(p) Computation of prevailing wage level.

(1) In computing the prevailing wage level for an occupational classification in an area of employment for purposes of subsections (a)(5)(A), (n)(1)(A)(i)(II), and (t)(1)(A)(i)(II) in the case of an employee of—

(A) an institution of higher education (as defined in section 101(a) of the Higher Education Act of 1965 [20 USCS § 1001(a)]), or a related or affiliated nonprofit entity; or

(B) a nonprofit research organization or a Governmental research organization,

the prevailing wage level shall only take into account employees at such institutions and organizations in the area of employment.

(2) With respect to a professional athlete (as defined in subsection (a)(5)(A)(iii)(II)) when the job opportunity is covered by professional sports league rules or regulations, the wage set forth in those rules or regu-

lations shall be considered as not adversely affecting the wages of United States workers similarly employed and be considered the prevailing wage.

(3) The prevailing wage required to be paid pursuant to subsections (a)(5)(A), (n)(1)(A)(i)(II), and (t)(1)(A)(i)(II) shall be 100 percent of the wage determined pursuant to those sections.

(4) Where the Secretary of Labor uses, or makes available to employers, a governmental survey to determine the prevailing wage, such survey shall provide at least 4 levels of wages commensurate with experience, education, and the level of supervision. Where an existing government survey has only 2 levels, 2 intermediate levels may be created by dividing by 3, the difference between the 2 levels offered, adding the quotient thus obtained to the first level and subtracting that quotient from the second level.

(q) Academic honoraria. Any alien admitted under section 101(a)(15)(B) [8 USCS § 1101(a)(15)(B)] may accept an honorarium payment and associated incidental expenses for a usual academic activity or activities (lasting not longer than 9 days at any single institution), as defined by the Attorney General in consultation with the Secretary of Education, if such payment is offered by an institution or organization described in subsection (p)(1) and is made for services conducted for the benefit of that institution or entity and if the alien has not accepted such payment or expenses from more than 5 institutions or organizations in the previous 6-month period.

(r) Exception for certain alien nurses.Subsection (a)(5)(C) shall not apply to an alien who seeks to enter the United States for the purpose of performing labor as a nurse who presents to the consular officer (or in the case of an adjustment of status, the Attorney General) a certified statement from the Commission on Graduates of Foreign Nursing Schools (or an equivalent independent credentialing organization approved for the certification of nurses under subsection (a)(5)(C) by the Attorney General in consultation with the Secretary of Health and Human Services) that—

(1) the alien has a valid and unrestricted license as a nurse in a State where the alien intends to be employed and such State verifies that the foreign licenses of alien nurses are authentic and unencumbered;

(2) the alien has passed the National Council Licensure Examination (NCLEX);

(3) the alien is a graduate of a nursing program—

(A) in which the language of instruction was English;

(B) located in a country—

(i) designated by such commission not later than 30 days after the date of the enactment of the Nursing Relief for Disadvantaged Areas Act of 1999 [enacted Nov. 12, 1999], based on such commission's assessment that the quality of nursing education in that country, and the English language proficiency of those who complete such programs in that country, justify the country's designation; or

(ii) designated on the basis of such an assessment by unanimous agreement of such commission and any equivalent credentialing organizations which have been approved under subsection (a)(5)(C) for the certification of nurses under this subsection; and

(C) (i) which was in operation on or before the date of the enactment of the Nursing Relief for Disadvantaged Areas Act of 1999 [enacted Nov. 12, 1999]; or

(ii) has been approved by unanimous agreement of such commission and any equivalent credentialing organizations which have been approved under subsection (a)(5)(C) for the certification of nurses under this subsection.

(s) Consideration of benefits received as battered alien in determination of inadmissibility as likely to become public charge. In determining whether an alien described in subsection (a)(4)(C)(i) is inadmissible under subsection (a)(4) or ineligible to receive an immigrant visa or otherwise to adjust to the status of permanent resident by reason of subsection (a)(4), the consular officer or the Attorney General shall not consider any benefits the alien may have received that were authorized under section 501 of the Illegal Immigration Reform and Immigrant Responsibility Act of 1996 (8 U.S.C. 1641(c)).

(t) Nonimmigrant professionals; labor attestations.

(1) No alien may be admitted or provided status as a nonimmigrant under section 101(a)(15)(H)(i)(b1) [8 USCS § 1101(a)(15)(H)(i)(b1)] or section 101(a)(15)(E)(iii) [8 USCS § 1101(a)(15)(E)(iii)] in an occupational classification unless the employer has filed with the Secretary of Labor an attestation stating the following:

(A) The employer—

(i) is offering and will offer during the period of authorized employment to aliens admitted or provided status under section 101(a)(15)(H)(i)(b1) [8 USCS § 1101(a)(15)(H)(i)(b1)] or section 101(a)(15)(E)(iii) [8 USCS § 1101(a)(15)(E)(iii)] wages that are at least—

(I) the actual wage level paid by the employer to all other individuals with similar experience and qualifications for the specific employment in question; or

(II) the prevailing wage level for the occupational classification in the area of employment,

whichever is greater, based on the best information available as of the time of filing the attestation; and

(ii) will provide working conditions for such a nonimmigrant that will not adversely affect the working conditions of workers similarly employed.

(B) There is not a strike or lockout in the course of a labor dispute in the occupational classification at the place of employment.

(C) The employer, at the time of filing the attestation—

(i) has provided notice of the filing under this paragraph to the bargaining representative (if any) of the employer's employees in the occupational classification and area for which aliens are sought; or

(ii) if there is no such bargaining representative, has provided notice of filing in the occupational classification through such methods as physical posting in conspicuous locations at the place of employment or electronic notification to employees in the occupational classification for which nonimmigrants under section 101(a)(15)(H)(i)(b1) [8 USCS § 1101(a)(15)(H)(i)(b1)] or section 101(a)(15)(E)(iii) [8 USCS § 1101(a)(15)(E)(iii)] are sought.

(D) A specification of the number of workers sought, the occupational classification in which the workers will be employed, and wage rate and conditions under which they will be employed.

(2) (A) The employer shall make available for public examination, within one working day after the date on which an attestation under this subsection is filed, at the employer's principal place of business or worksite, a copy of each such attestation (and such accompanying documents as are necessary).

(B) (i) The Secretary of Labor shall compile, on a current basis, a list (by employer and by occupational classification) of the attestations filed under this subsection. Such list shall include, with respect to each attestation, the wage rate, number of aliens sought, period of intended employment, and date of need.

(ii) The Secretary of Labor shall make such list available for public examination in Washington, D.C.

(C) The Secretary of Labor shall review an attestation filed under this subsection only for completeness and obvious inaccuracies. Unless the Secretary of Labor finds that an attestation is incomplete or obviously inaccurate, the Secretary of Labor shall provide the certification described in section 101(a)(15)(H)(i)(b1) [8 USCS § 1101(a)(15)(H)(i)(b1)] or section 101(a)(15)(E)(iii) [8 USCS § 1101(a)(15)(E)(iii)] within 7 days of the date of the filing of the attestation.

(3) (A) The Secretary of Labor shall establish a process for the receipt, investigation, and disposition of complaints respecting the failure of an employer to meet a condition specified in an attestation submitted under this subsection or misrepresentation by the employer of material facts in such an attestation. Complaints may be filed by any aggrieved person or organization (including bargaining representatives). No investigation or hearing shall be conducted on a complaint concerning such a failure or misrepresentation unless the complaint was filed not later than 12 months after the date of the failure or misrepresentation, respectively. The Secretary of Labor shall conduct an investigation under this paragraph if there is reasonable cause to believe that such a failure or misrepresentation has occurred.

(B) Under the process described in subparagraph (A), the Secretary of Labor shall provide, within 30 days after the date a complaint is filed, for a determination as to whether or not a reasonable basis exists to make a finding described in subparagraph (C). If the Secretary of Labor determines that such a reasonable basis exists, the Secretary of Labor shall provide for notice of such determination to the interested parties and an opportunity for a hearing on the complaint, in accordance with section 556 of title 5, United States Code, within 60 days after the date of the determination. If such a hearing is requested, the Secretary of Labor shall make a finding concerning the matter by not later than 60 days after the date of the hearing. In the case of similar complaints respecting the same applicant, the Secretary of Labor may consolidate the hearings under this subparagraph on such complaints.

(C) (i) If the Secretary of Labor finds, after notice and opportunity for a hearing, a failure to meet a condition of paragraph (1)(B), a substantial failure to meet a condition of paragraph (1)(C) or (1)(D), or a misrepresentation of material fact in an attestation—

(I) the Secretary of Labor shall notify the Secretary of State and the Secretary of Homeland Security of such finding and may, in addition, impose such other administrative remedies (including civil monetary penalties in an amount not to exceed $1,000 per violation) as the Secretary of Labor determines to be appropriate; and

(II) the Secretary of State or the Secretary of Homeland Security, as appropriate, shall not approve petitions or applications filed with respect to that employer under section 204, 214(c), 101(a)(15)(H)(i)(b1), or 101(a)(15)(E)(iii) [8 USCS § 1154, 1184(c), 1101(a)(15)(H)(i)(b1), or 1101(a)(15)(E)(iii)] during a period of at least 1 year for aliens to be employed by the employer.

(ii) If the Secretary of Labor finds, after notice and opportunity for a hearing, a willful failure to meet a condition of paragraph (1), a willful misrepresentation of material fact in an attestation, or a violation of clause (iv)—

(I) the Secretary of Labor shall notify the Secretary of State and the Secretary of Homeland Security of such finding and may, in addition, impose such other administrative remedies (including civil monetary penalties in an amount not to exceed $5,000 per violation) as the Secretary of Labor determines to be appropriate; and

(II) the Secretary of State or the Secretary of Homeland Security, as appropriate, shall not approve petitions or applications filed with respect to that employer under section 204, 214(c), 101(a)(15)(H)(i)(b1), or 101(a)(15)(E)(iii) [8 USCS § 1154, 1184(c), 1101(a)(15)(H)(i)(b1), or 1101(a)(15)(E)(iii)] during a period of at least 2 years for aliens to be employed by the employer.

(iii) If the Secretary of Labor finds, after notice and opportunity for a hearing, a willful failure to meet a condition of paragraph (1) or a willful misrepresentation of material fact in an attestation, in the course of which failure or misrepresentation the employer displaced a United States worker employed by the employer within the period beginning 90 days before and ending 90 days after the date of filing of any visa petition or application supported by the attestation—

(I) the Secretary of Labor shall notify the Secretary of State and the Secretary of Homeland Security of such finding and may, in addition, impose such other administrative remedies (including civil monetary penalties in an amount not to exceed $35,000 per violation) as the Secretary of Labor determines to be appropriate; and

(II) the Secretary of State or the Secretary of Homeland Security, as appropriate, shall not approve petitions or applications filed with respect to that employer under section 204, 214(c), 101(a)(15)(H)(i)(b1), or 101(a)(15)(E)(iii) [8 USCS § 1154, 1184(c), 1101(a)(15)(H)(i)(b1), or 1101(a)(15)(E)(iii)] during a period of at least 3 years for aliens to be employed by the employer.

(iv) It is a violation of this clause for an employer who has filed an attestation under this subsection to intimidate, threaten, restrain, coerce, blacklist, discharge, or in any other manner discriminate against an employee (which term, for purposes of this clause, includes a former employee and an applicant for employment) because the employee has disclosed information to the employer, or to any other person, that the employee reasonably believes evidences a violation of this subsection, or any rule or regulation pertaining to this subsection, or because the employee cooperates or seeks to cooperate in an investigation or other proceeding concerning the employer's compliance with the requirements of this subsection or any rule or regulation pertaining to this subsection.

(v) The Secretary of Labor and the Secretary of Homeland Security shall devise a process under which a nonimmigrant under section 101(a)(15)(H)(i)(b1) [8 USCS § 1101(a)(15)(H)(i)(b1)] or section 101(a)(15)(E)(iii) [8 USCS § 1101(a)(15)(E)(iii)] who files a complaint regarding a violation of clause (iv) and is otherwise eligible to remain and work in the United States may be allowed to seek other appropriate employment in the United States for a period not to exceed the maximum period of stay authorized for such nonimmigrant classification.

(vi) (I) It is a violation of this clause for an employer who has filed an attestation under this subsection to require a nonimmigrant under section 101(a)(15)(II)(i)(b1) [8 USCS § 1101(a)(15)(H)(i)(b1)] or section 101(a)(15)(E)(iii) [8 USCS § 1101(a)(15)(E)(iii)] to pay a penalty for ceasing employment with the employer prior to a date agreed to by the nonimmigrant and the employer. The Secretary of Labor shall determine whether a required payment is a penalty (and not liquidated damages) pursuant to relevant State law.

(II) If the Secretary of Labor finds, after notice and opportunity for a hearing, that an employer has committed a violation of this clause, the Secretary of Labor may impose a civil monetary penalty of $1,000 for each such violation and issue an administrative order requiring the return to the nonimmigrant of any amount paid in violation of this clause, or, if the nonimmigrant cannot be located, requiring payment of any such amount to the general fund of the Treasury.

(vii) (I) It is a failure to meet a condition of paragraph (1)(A) for an employer who has filed an attestation under this subsection and who places a nonimmigrant under section 101(a)(15)(H)(i)(b1) [8 USCS § 1101(a)(15)(H)(i)(b1)] or section 101(a)(15)(E)(iii) [8 USCS § 1101(a)(15)(E)(iii)] designated as a full-time employee in the attestation, after the nonimmigrant has entered into employment with the employer, in nonproductive status due to a decision by the employer (based on factors such as lack of work), or due to the nonimmigrant's lack of a permit or license, to fail to pay the nonimmigrant full-time wages in accordance with paragraph (1)(A) for all such nonproductive time.

(II) It is a failure to meet a condition of paragraph (1)(A) for an employer who has filed an attestation under this subsection and who places a nonimmigrant under section 101(a)(15)(H)(i)(b1) [8 USCS § 1101(a)(15)(H)(i)(b1)] or section 101(a)(15)(E)(iii) [8 USCS § 1101(a)(15)(E)(iii)] designated as a part-time employee in the attestation, after the nonimmigrant has entered into employment with the employer, in nonproductive status under circumstances described in subclause (I), to fail to pay such a nonimmigrant for such hours as are designated on the attestation consistent with the rate of pay identified on the attestation.

(III) In the case of a nonimmigrant under section 101(a)(15)(H)(i)(b1) [8 USCS § 1101(a)(15)(H)(i)(b1)] or section 101(a)(15)(E)(iii) [8 USCS § 1101(a)(15)(E)(iii)] who has not yet entered into employment with an employer who has had approved an attestation under this subsection with respect to the nonimmigrant, the provisions of subclauses (I) and (II) shall apply to the employer beginning 30 days after the date the nonimmigrant first is admitted into the United States, or 60 days after the date the nonimmigrant becomes eligible to work for the employer in the case of a nonimmigrant who is present in the United States on the date of the approval of the attestation filed with the Secretary of Labor.

(IV) This clause does not apply to a failure to pay wages to a nonimmigrant under section 101(a)(15)(H)(i)(b1) [8 USCS § 1101(a)(15)(H)(i)(b1)] or section 101(a)(15)(E)(iii) [8 USCS § 1101(a)(15)(E)(iii)] for nonproductive time due to non-work-related factors, such as the voluntary request of the nonimmigrant for an absence or circumstances rendering the nonimmigrant unable to work.

(V) This clause shall not be construed as prohibiting an employer that is a school or other educational institution from applying to a nonimmigrant under section 101(a)(15)(H)(i)(b1) [8 USCS § 1101(a)(15)(H)(i)(b1)] or section 101(a)(15)(E)(iii) [8 USCS § 1101(a)(15)(E)(iii)] an established salary practice of the employer, under which the employer pays to nonimmigrants under section 101(a)(15)(H)(i)(b1) [8 USCS § 1101(a)(15)(H)(i)(b1)] or section 101(a)(15)(E)(iii) [8 USCS § 1101(a)(15)(E)(iii)] and United States workers in the same occupational classification an annual salary in disbursements over fewer than 12 months, if—

(aa) the nonimmigrant agrees to the compressed annual salary payments prior to the commencement of the employment; and

(bb) the application of the salary practice to the nonimmigrant does not otherwise cause the nonimmigrant to violate any condition of the nonimmigrant's authorization under this Act to remain in the United States.

(VI) This clause shall not be construed as superseding clause (viii).

(viii) It is a failure to meet a condition of paragraph (1)(A) for an employer who has filed an attestation under this subsection to fail to offer to a nonimmigrant under section 101(a)(15)(H)(i)(b1) [8 USCS § 1101(a)(15)(H)(i)(b1)] or section 101(a)(15)(E)(iii) [8 USCS § 1101(a)(15)(E)(iii)], during the nonimmigrant's period of authorized employment, benefits and eligibility for benefits (including the opportunity to participate in health, life, disability, and other insurance plans; the opportunity to participate in retirement and savings plans; and cash bonuses and non-cash compensation, such as stock options (whether or not based on performance)) on the same basis, and in accordance with the same criteria, as the employer offers to United States workers.

(D) If the Secretary of Labor finds, after notice and opportunity for a hearing, that an employer has not paid wages at the wage level specified in the attestation and required under paragraph (1), the Secretary of Labor shall order the employer to provide for payment of such amounts of back pay as may be required to comply with the requirements of paragraph (1), whether or not a penalty under subparagraph (C) has been imposed.

(E) The Secretary of Labor may, on a case-by-case basis, subject an employer to random investigations for a period of up to 5 years, beginning on the date on which the employer is found by the Secretary of Labor to have committed a willful failure to meet a condition of paragraph (1) or to have made a willful misrepresentation of material fact in an attestation. The authority of the Secretary of Labor under this subparagraph shall not be construed to be subject to, or limited by, the requirements of subparagraph (A).

(F) Nothing in this subsection shall be construed as superseding or preempting any other enforcement-related authority under this Act (such as the authorities under section 274B [8 USCS § 1324b]), or any other Act.

(4) For purposes of this subsection:

(A) The term "area of employment" means the area within normal commuting distance of the worksite or physical location where the work of the nonimmigrant under section 101(a)(15)(H)(i)(b1) [8 USCS § 1101(a)(15)(H)(i)(b1)] or section 101(a)(15)(E)(iii) [8 USCS § 1101(a)(15)(E)(iii)] is or will be performed. If such worksite or location is within a Metropolitan Statistical Area, any place within such area is deemed to be within the area of employment.

(B) In the case of an attestation with respect to one or more nonimmigrants under section 101(a)(15)(H)(i)(b1) [8 USCS § 1101(a)(15)(H)(i)(b1)] or section 101(a)(15)(E)(iii) [8 USCS § 1101(a)(15)(E)(iii)] by an employer, the employer is considered to "displace" a United States worker from a job if the employer lays off the worker from a job that is essentially the equivalent of the job for which the nonimmigrant or nonimmigrants is or are sought. A job shall not be considered to be essentially equivalent of another job unless it involves essentially the same responsibilities, was held by a United States worker with substantially equivalent qualifications and experience, and is located in the same area of employment as the other job.

(C) (i) The term "lays off", with respect to a worker—

(I) means to cause the worker's loss of employment, other than through a discharge for inadequate performance, violation of workplace rules, cause, voluntary departure, voluntary retirement, or the expiration of a grant or contract; but

(II) does not include any situation in which the worker is offered, as an alternative to such loss of employment, a similar employment opportunity with the same employer at equivalent or higher compensation and benefits than the position from which the employee was discharged, regardless of whether or not the employee accepts the offer.

(ii) Nothing in this subparagraph is intended to limit an employee's rights under a collective bargaining agreement or other employment contract.

(D) The term "United States worker" means an employee who—

(i) is a citizen or national of the United States; or

(ii) is an alien who is lawfully admitted for permanent residence, is admitted as a refugee under section 207 of this title [8 USCS § 1157], is granted asylum under section 208 [8 USCS § 1158], or is an immigrant otherwise authorized, by this Act or by the Secretary of Homeland Security, to be employed.

[(u)] (t) Foreign residence requirement.

(1) Except as provided in paragraph (2), no person admitted under section 101(a)(15)(Q)(ii)(I) [8 USCS § 1101(a)(15)(Q)(ii)(I)], or acquiring such status after admission, shall be eligible to apply for nonimmigrant status, an immigrant visa, or permanent residence under this Act until it is established that such person has resided and been physically present in the person's country of nationality or last residence for an aggregate of at least 2 years following departure from the United States.

(2) The Secretary of Homeland Security may waive the requirement of such 2-year foreign residence abroad if the Secretary determines that—

(A) departure from the United States would impose exceptional hardship upon the alien's spouse or child (if such spouse or child is a citizen of the United States or an alien lawfully admitted for permanent residence); or

(B) the admission of the alien is in the public interest or the national interest of the United States.

HISTORY: (June 27, 1952, ch 477, Title II, Ch 2, § 212, 66 Stat. 182; July 18, 1956, ch 629, Title III, § 301(a), 70 Stat. 575; July 7, 1958, P. L. 85-508, § 23, 72 Stat. 351; March 18, 1959, P. L. 86-3, § 20(b), 73 Stat. 13; July 14, 1960, P. L. 86-648, § 8, 74 Stat. 505; Sept. 21, 1961, P. L. 87-256, § 109(c), 75 Stat. 535; Sept. 26, 1961, P. L. 87-301, §§ 11–15, 75 Stat. 654; Oct. 3, 1965, P. L. 89-236, §§ 10, 15, 79 Stat. 917, 919; April 7, 1970, P. L. 91-225, § 2, 84 Stat. 116; Oct. 12, 1976, P. L. 94-484, Title VI, § 601(a), (c), (d), 90 Stat. 2300, 2301; Oct. 20, 1976, P. L. 94-571, §§ 5, 7(d), 90 Stat. 2705, 2706; Aug. 1, 1977, P. L. 95-83, Title III, 307(q)(1), (2), 91 Stat. 394; Oct. 30, 1978, P. L. 95-549, Title I, §§ 101, 102, 92 Stat. 2065; Sept. 27, 1979, P. L. 96-70, Title III, Ch 2, § 3201(b), 93 Stat. 497; March 17, 1980, P. L. 96-212, Title II, § 203(d), (f), 94 Stat. 107; Dec. 17, 1980, P. L. 96-538, Title IV, § 404, 94 Stat. 3192; Dec. 29, 1981, P. L. 97-116, §§ 4, 5(a), (b), 18(e), 95 Stat. 1611, 1612, 1620; Oct. 5, 1984, P. L. 98-454, Title VI, § 602 [(a)], 98 Stat. 1737; Aug. 27, 1986, P. L. 99-396, § 14(a), 100 Stat. 842; Oct. 27, 1986, P. L. 99-570, Title I, Subtitle M, § 1751(a), 100 Stat. 3207-47; Nov. 10, 1986, P. L. 99-639, § 6(a), 100 Stat. 3543; Nov. 14, 1986, P. L. 99-653, § 7(a), 100 Stat. 3657; Oct. 12, 1984, P. L. 98-473, Title II, Ch II, § 220(a)(9), 98 Stat. 2027; Aug. 27, 1986, P. L. 99-396, § 14(a); Nov. 14, 1986, P. L. 99-653, § 7(d)(2); Dec. 22, 1987, P. L. 100-204, Title VIII, § 806(c), 101 Stat. 1399; Oct. 24, 1988, P. L. 100-525, §§ 3(1)(A), 7(c), 8(f)(2), 9(i), 102 Stat. 1614, 2614, 2616, 2617, 2620.; Nov. 18,

1988, P. L. 100-690, Title VII, Subtitle J, § 7349(a), 102 Stat. 4473; Dec. 18, 1989, P. L. 101-238, § 3(b), 103 Stat. 2100; Feb. 16, 1990, P. L. 101-246, Title I, Part C, § 131(a), (c), 104 Stat. 31; Nov. 29, 1990, P. L. 101-649, Title I, Subtitle E, § 162(e)(1), (f)(2)(B), Title II, Subtitle A, § 202(b), Subtitle B, § 205(c)(3), Title V, Subtitle A, §§ 511(a), 514(a), Title VI, §§ 601(a), (b), (d), 603(a)(19), 104 Stat. 5011, 5012, 5014, 5020, 5052, 5053, 5067, 5075, 5084.; Dec. 12, 1991, P. L. 102-232, Title III, §§ 302(e)(6), (9), 303(a)(5)(B), (6), (7)(B), 306(a)(10), (12), 307(a)–(g), 105 Stat. 1746, 1747, 1751, 1753.; June 10, 1993, P. L. 103-43, Title XX, § 2007(a), 107 Stat. 210; Aug. 26, 1994, P. L. 103-317, Title V, § 506(a), 108 Stat. 1765; Sept. 13, 1994, P. L. 103-322, Title XIII, § 130003(b)(1), 108 Stat. 2024; Oct. 25, 1994, P. L. 103-416, Title II, §§ 203(a), 219(e), (z)(1), (5), 220(a), 108 Stat. 4311, 4316, 4318, 4319.; April 24, 1996, P. L. 104-132, Title IV, Subtitle B, §§ 411, 412, Subtitle C, § 440(d), 110 Stat. 1268, 1269, 1277; Sept. 30, 1996, P. L. 104-208, Div C, Title I, Subtitle B, § 124(b)(1), Title III, Subtitle A, §§ 301(b)(1), (c)(1), 304(b), 305(c), 306(d), 308(c)(2)(B), (d)(1), (e)(1)(B), (C), (2)(A), (6), (f)(1)(C)–(F), (3)(A), (g)(4)(B), (10)(A), (H), Subtitle B, § 322(a)(2)(B), Subtitle C, §§ 341(a), (b), 342(a), 343, 344(a), 345(a), 346(a), 347(a), 348(a), 349, 351(a), 352(a), 355, Title V, Subtitle B, § 531(a), Title VI, Subtitle A, § 602(a), Subtitle B, §§ 622(b), 624(a), Subtitle E, § 671(e)(3), 110 Stat. 3009-562, 3009-575, 3009-578, 3009-597, 3009-607, 3009-612, 3009-616, 3009-619, 3009-620, 3009-621, 3009-622, 3009-625, 3009-629, 3009-635, 3009-636, 3009-637, 3009-638, 3009-639, 3009-640, 3009-641, 3009-644, 3009-674, 3009-689, 3009-695, 3009-698, 3009-723; Nov. 12, 1997, P. L. 105-73, § 1, 111 Stat. 1459; Oct. 21, 1998, P. L. 105-277, Div C, Title IV, Subtitle A, §§ 412(a)–(c), 413(a)–(e)(1), (f), 415(a), Subtitle C, § 431(a), Div G, Subdiv B, Title XXII, Ch 2, § 2226(a), 112 Stat. 2681-642, 2681-645, 2681-651, 2681-654, 2681-658, 2681-820; Oct. 27, 1998, P. L. 105-292, Title VI, § 604(a), 112 Stat. 2814; Nov. 12, 1999, P. L. 106-95, §§ 2(b), 4(a), 113 Stat. 1312, 1317; Dec. 3, 1999, P. L. 106-120, Title VIII, § 809, 113 Stat. 1632; Oct. 17, 2000, P. L. 106-313, Title I, §§ 106(c)(2), 107(a), 114 Stat. 1254, 1255; Oct. 28, 2000, P. L. 106-386, Div A, §§ 107(e)(3), 111(d), Div B, Title V, §§ 1505(a), (c)(1), (d)–(f), 1513(e), 114 Stat. 1478, 1485, 1525, 1526, 1536.; Oct. 30, 2000, P. L. 106-395, Title II, § 201(b)(1), (2), 114 Stat. 1633; Oct. 30, 2000, P. L. 106-396, Title I, § 101(b)(1), 114 Stat. 1638; Oct. 26, 2001, P. L. 107-56, Title IV, Subtitle B, § 411(a), Title X, § 1006(a), 115 Stat. 345, 394; March 13, 2002, P. L. 107-150, § 2(a)(2), 116 Stat. 74; Nov. 2, 2002, P. L. 107-273, Div C, Title I, Subtitle A, § 11018(c), 116 Stat. 1825; Sept. 3, 2003, P. L. 108-77, Title IV, § 402(b), (c), 117 Stat. 940; Dec. 19, 2003, P. L. 108-193, §§ 4(b)(4), 8(a)(2), 117 Stat. 2879, 2886; Dec. 8, 2004, P. L. 108-447, Div J, Title IV, Subtitle B, §§ 422(a), 423, 424(a)(1), (b), 118 Stat. 3353, 3355; Dec. 10, 2004, P. L. 108-449, § 1(b)(2), 118 Stat. 3470; Dec. 17, 2004, P. L. 108-458, Title V, Subtitle E, §§ 5501(a), 5502(a), 5503, 118 Stat. 3740, 3741; May 11, 2005, P. L. 109-13, Div B, Title I, §§ 103(a)–(c), 104, Title V, § 501(d), 119 Stat. 306, 309, 322; Jan. 5, 2006, P. L. 109-162, Title VIII, Subtitle A, § 802, 119 Stat. 3054; Aug. 12, 2006, P. L. 109-271, § 6(b), 120 Stat. 762; Dec. 26, 2007, P. L. 110-161, Div J, Title VI, § 691(a), (c), 121 Stat. 2364, 2365; May 8, 2008, P. L. 110-229, Title VII, Subtitle A, § 702(b)(2), (3), (d), 122 Stat. 860, 862; July 30, 2008, P. L. 110-293, Title III, Subtitle A, § 305, 122 Stat. 2963; Oct. 3, 2008, P. L. 110-340, § 2(b), 122 Stat. 3736; Dec. 23, 2008, P. L. 110-457, Title II, Subtitle C, § 222(f)(1), Subtitle D, § 234, 122 Stat. 5071, 5074; Dec. 22, 2009, P. L. 111-122, § 3(b), 123 Stat. 3481; Nov. 30, 2010, P. L. 111-287, § 2, 124 Stat. 3058; March 7, 2013, P. L. 113-4, Title VIII, § 804, 127 Stat. 111.)

OTHER PROVISIONS:

Applicability of Nov. 12, 1999 amendments to 8 USCS §§ 1101(a)(15)(H)(i) and 1182(m). Act Nov. 12, 1999, P.L. 106-95, § 2(e), 113 Stat. 1317; Dec. 20, 2006, P.L. 109-423, § 2(2), 120 Stat. 2900, provides: "The amendments made by this section [amending 8 USCS §§ 1101(a)(15)(H)(i) and 1182(m)] shall apply to classification petitions filed for nonimmigrant status only during the period--

"(1) beginning on the date that interim or final regulations are first promulgated under subsection (d) [note to this section]; and

"(2) ending on the date that is 3 years after the date of the enactment of the Nursing Relief for Disadvantaged Areas Reauthorization Act of 2005 [enacted Dec. 20, 2006].".

§ 213. [8 U.S.C. § 1183] Admission of certain aliens on giving bond or undertaking; return upon permanent departure.

An alien inadmissible under paragraph (4) of section 212(a) [8 USCS § 1182(a)(4)] may, if otherwise admissible, be admitted in the discretion of the Attorney General (subject to the affidavit of support requirement and attribution of sponsor's income and resources under section 213A [8 USCS § 1183a]) upon the giving of a suitable and proper bond or undertaking approved by the Attorney General, in such amount and containing such conditions as he may prescribe, to the United States, and to all States, territories, counties, towns, municipalities, and districts thereof holding the United States and all States, territories, counties, towns, municipalities, and districts thereof harmless against such alien becoming a public charge. Such bond or undertaking shall terminate upon the permanent departure from the United States, the naturalization, or the death of such alien, and any sums or other security held to secure performance thereof, except to the extent forfeited for violation of the terms thereof, shall be returned to the person by whom furnished, or to his legal representatives. Suit may be brought thereon in the name and by the proper law officers of the United States for the use of the United States, or of any State, territory, district, county, town, or municipality in which such alien becomes a public charge, irrespective of whether a demand for payment of public expenses has been made.

HISTORY: (June 27, 1952, ch 477, Title II, Ch 2, § 213, 66 Stat. 188; July 10, 1970, P. L. 91-313, § 1, 84 Stat. 413; Nov. 29, 1990, P. L. 101-649, Title VI, § 603(a)(8), 104 Stat. 5083; Sept. 30, 1996, P. L. 104-208, Div C, Title III, Subtitle A, § 308(d)(3)(A), Title V, Subtitle D, § 564(f), 110 Stat. 3009-617, 3009-684.)

§ 213A. [8 U.S.C. § 1183a] Requirements for sponsor's affidavit of support.

(a) Enforceability.

(1) Terms of affidavit. No affidavit of support may be accepted by the Attorney General or by any consular officer to establish that an alien is not excludable as a public charge under section 212(a)(4) [8 USCS § 1182(a)(4)] unless such affidavit is executed by a sponsor of the alien as a contract—

(A) in which the sponsor agrees to provide support to maintain the sponsored alien at an annual income that is not less than 125 percent of the Federal poverty line during the period in which the affidavit is enforceable;

(B) that is legally enforceable against the sponsor by the sponsored alien, the Federal Government, any

State (or any political subdivision of such State), or by any other entity that provides any means-tested public benefit (as defined in subsection (e)), consistent with the provisions of this section; and

(C) in which the sponsor agrees to submit to the jurisdiction of any Federal or State court for the purpose of actions brought under subsection (b)(2).

(2) Period of enforceability. An affidavit of support shall be enforceable with respect to benefits provided for an alien before the date the alien is naturalized as a citizen of the United States, or, if earlier, the termination date provided under paragraph (3).

(3) Termination of period of enforceability upon completion of required period of employment, etc.

(A) In general. An affidavit of support is not enforceable after such time as the alien (i) has worked 40 qualifying quarters of coverage as defined under title II of the Social Security Act [42 USCS §§ 401 et seq.] or can be credited with such qualifying quarters as provided under subparagraph (B), and (ii) in the case of any such qualifying quarter creditable for any period beginning after December 31, 1996, did not receive any Federal means-tested public benefit (as provided under section 403 of the Personal Responsibility and Work Opportunity Reconciliation Act of 1996 [8 USCS § 1613]) during any such period.

(B) Qualifying quarters. For purposes of this section, in determining the number of qualifying quarters of coverage under title II of the Social Security Act [42 USCS §§ 401 et seq.] an alien shall be credited with—

(i) all of the qualifying quarters of coverage as defined under title II of the Social Security Act [42 USCS §§ 401 et seq.] worked by a parent of such alien while the alien was under age 18, and

(ii) all of the qualifying quarters worked by a spouse of such alien during their marriage and the alien remains married to such spouse or such spouse is deceased.

No such qualifying quarter of coverage that is creditable under title II of the Social Security Act [42 USCS §§ 401 et seq.] for any period beginning after December 31, 1996, may be credited to an alien under clause (i) or (ii) if the parent or spouse (as the case may be) of such alien received any Federal means-tested public benefit (as provided under section 403 of the Personal Responsibility and Work Opportunity Reconciliation Act of 1996 [8 USCS § 1613]) during the period for which such qualifying quarter of coverage is so credited.

(C) Provision of information to save system. The Attorney General shall ensure that appropriate information regarding the application of this paragraph is provided to the system for alien verification of eligibility (SAVE) described in section 1137(d)(3) of the Social Security Act [42 USCS § 1320b-7(d)(3)].

(b) Reimbursement of Government expenses.

(1) Request for reimbursement.

(A) Requirement. Upon notification that a sponsored alien has received any means-tested public benefit, the appropriate nongovernmental entity which provided such benefit or the appropriate entity of the Federal Government, a State, or any political subdivision of a State shall request reimbursement by the sponsor in an amount which is equal to the unreimbursed costs of such benefit.

(B) Regulations. The Attorney General, in consultation with the heads of other appropriate Federal agencies, shall prescribe such regulations as may be necessary to carry out subparagraph (A).

(2) Actions to compel reimbursement.

(A) In case of nonresponse. If within 45 days after a request for reimbursement under paragraph (1)(A), the appropriate entity has not received a response from the sponsor indicating a willingness to commence payment an action may be brought against the sponsor pursuant to the affidavit of support.

(B) In case of failure to pay. If the sponsor fails to abide by the repayment terms established by the appropriate entity, the entity may bring an action against the sponsor pursuant to the affidavit of support.

(C) Limitation on actions. No cause of action may be brought under this paragraph later than 10 years after the date on which the sponsored alien last received any means-tested public benefit to which the affidavit of support applies.

(3) Use of collection agencies. If the appropriate entity under paragraph (1)(A) requests reimbursement from the sponsor or brings an action against the sponsor pursuant to the affidavit of support, the appropriate entity may appoint or hire an individual or other person to act on behalf of such entity acting under the authority of law for purposes of collecting any amounts owed.

(c) Remedies. Remedies available to enforce an affidavit of support under this section include any or all of the remedies described in section 3201, 3203, 3204, or 3205 of title 28, United States Code, as well as an order for specific performance and payment of legal fees and other costs of collection, and include corresponding remedies available under Statelaw. A Federal agency may seek to collect amounts owed under this section in accordance with the provisions of subchapter II of chapter 37 of title 31, United States Code [31 USCS §§ 3711 et seq.].

(d) Notification of change of address.

(1) General requirement. The sponsor shall notify the Attorney General and the State in which the sponsored alien is currently a resident within 30 days of any change of address of the sponsor during the period in which an affidavit of support is enforceable.

(2) Penalty. Any person subject to the requirement of paragraph (1) who fails to satisfy such requirement shall, after notice and opportunity to be heard, be subject to a civil penalty of—

(A) not less than $250 or more than $2,000, or

(B) if such failure occurs with knowledge that the sponsored alien has received any means-tested public benefits (other than benefits described in section 401(b), 403(c)(2), or 411(b) of the Personal Responsibility and Work Opportunity Reconciliation Act of 1996 [8 USCS § 1611(b), 1613(c)(2), or 1621(b)]) not less than $2,000 or more than $5,000.

The Attorney General shall enforce this paragraph under appropriate regulations.

(e) Jurisdiction. An action to enforce an affidavit of support executed under subsection (a) may be brought against the sponsor in any appropriate court—

(1) by a sponsored alien, with respect to financial support; or

(2) by the appropriate entity of the Federal Government, a State or any political subdivision of a State, or by any other nongovernmental entity under subsection (b)(2), with respect to reimbursement.

(f) Sponsor defined.

(1) In general. For purposes of this section the term "sponsor" in relation to a sponsored alien means an individual who executes an affidavit of support with respect to the sponsored alien and who—

(A) is a citizen or national of the United States or an alien who is lawfully admitted to the United States for permanent residence;

(B) is at least 18 years of age;

(C) is domiciled in any of the several States of the United States, the District of Columbia, or any territory or possession of the United States;

(D) is petitioning for the admission of the alien under section 204 [8 USCS § 1154]; and

(E) demonstrates (as provided in paragraph (6)) the means to maintain an annual income equal to at least 125 percent of the Federal poverty line.

(2) Income requirement case. Such term also includes an individual who does not meet the requirement of paragraph (1)(E) but accepts joint and several liability together with an individual under paragraph (5)(A).

(3) Active duty armed services case. Such term also includes an individual who does not meet the requirement of paragraph (1)(E) but is on active duty (other than active duty for training) in the Armed Forces of the United States, is petitioning for the admission of the alien under section 204 [8 USCS § 1154] as the spouse or child of the individual, and demonstrates (as provided in paragraph (6)) the means to maintain an annual income equal to at least 100 percent of the Federal poverty line.

(4) Certain employment-based immigrants case. Such term also includes an individual—

(A) who does not meet the requirement of paragraph (1)(D), but is the relative of the sponsored alien who filed a classification petition for the sponsored alien as an employment-based immigrant under section 203(b) [8 USCS § 1153(b)] or who has a significant ownership interest in the entity that filed such a petition; and

(B) (i) who demonstrates (as provided under paragraph (6)) the means to maintain an annual income equal to at least 125 percent of the Federal poverty line, or

(ii) does not meet the requirement of paragraph (1)(E) but accepts joint and several liability together with an individual under paragraph (5)(A).

(5) Non-petitioning cases. Such term also includes an individual who does not meet the requirement of paragraph (1)(D) but who—

(A) accepts joint and several liability with a petitioning sponsor under paragraph (2) or relative of an employment-based immigrant under paragraph (4) and who demonstrates (as provided under paragraph (6)) the means to maintain an annual income equal to at least 125 percent of the Federal poverty line; or

(B) is a spouse, parent, mother-in-law, father-in-law, sibling, child (if at least 18 years of age), son, daughter, son-in-law, daughter-in-law, sister-in-law, brother-in-law, grandparent, or grandchild of a sponsored alien or a legal guardian of a sponsored alien, meets the requirements of paragraph (1) (other than subparagraph (D)), and executes an affidavit of support with respect to such alien in a case in which—

(i) the individual petitioning under section 204 of this Act [8 USCS § 1154] for the classification of such alien died after the approval of such petition, and the Secretary of Homeland Security has determined for humanitarian reasons that revocation of such petition under section 205 [8 USCS § 1155] would be inappropriate; or

(ii) the alien's petition is being adjudicated pursuant to section 204*(l)* [8 USCS § 1154*(l)*] (surviving relative consideration).

(6) Demonstration of means to maintain income.

(A) In general.

(i) Method of demonstration. For purposes of this section, a demonstration of the means to maintain income shall include provision of a certified copy of the individual's Federal income tax return for the individual's 3 most recent taxable years and a written statement, executed under oath or as permitted under penalty of perjury under section 1746 of title 28, United States Code, that the copies are certified copies of such returns.

(ii) Flexibility. For purposes of this section, aliens may demonstrate the means to maintain income through demonstration of significant assets of the sponsored alien or of the sponsor, if such assets are available for the support of the sponsored alien.

(iii) Percent of poverty. For purposes of this section, a reference to an annual income equal to at least a particular percentage of the Federal poverty line means an annual income equal to at least such percentage of the Federal poverty line for a family unit of a size equal to the number of members of the sponsor's household (including family and non-family dependents) plus the total number of other dependents and aliens sponsored by that sponsor.

(B) Limitation. The Secretary of State, or the Attorney General in the case of adjustment of status, may provide that the demonstration under subparagraph (A) applies only to the most recent taxable year.

(g) [Not enacted]

(h) "Federal poverty line" defined. For purposes of this section, the term "Federal poverty line" means the level of income equal to the official poverty line (as defined by the Director of the Office of Management and Budget, as revised annually by the Secretary of Health and Human Services, in accordance with section 673(2) of the Omnibus Budget Reconciliation Act of 1981 (42 U.S.C. 9902)) that is applicable to a family of the size involved.

(i) Sponsor's social security account number required to be provided.

(1) An affidavit of support shall include the social security account number of each sponsor.

(2) The Attorney General shall develop an automated system to maintain the social security account number data provided under paragraph (1).

(3) The Attorney General shall submit an annual report to the Committees on the Judiciary of the House of Representatives and the Senate setting forth—

(A) for the most recent fiscal year for which data are available the number of sponsors under this section and the number of sponsors in compliance with the financial obligations of this section; and

(B) a comparison of such numbers with the numbers of such sponsors for the preceding fiscal year.

HISTORY: (June 27, 1952, ch 477, Title II, Ch 2, § 213A, as added Aug. 22, 1996, P. L. 104-193, Title IV, Subtitle C, § 423(a), 110 Stat. 2271; Sept. 30, 1996, P. L. 104-208, Div C, Title V, Subtitle C, § 551(a), 110 Stat. 3009-675; March 13, 2002, P. L. 107-150, § 2(a)(1), (3), 116 Stat. 74, 75; Oct. 28, 2009, P. L. 111-83, Title V, § 568(e), 123 Stat. 2187.)

§ 214. [8 U.S.C. § 1184] Admission of nonimmigrants.

(a) Regulations.

(1) The admission to the United States of any alien as a nonimmigrant shall be for such time and under such conditions as the Attorney General may by regulations prescribe, including when he deems necessary the giving of a bond with sufficient surety in such sum and containing such conditions as the Attorney General shall prescribe, to insure that at the expiration of such time or upon failure to maintain the status under which he was admitted, or to maintain any status subsequently acquired under section 248 [8 USCS § 1258], such alien will depart from the United States. No alien admitted to Guam or the Commonwealth of the Northern Mariana Islands without a visa pursuant to section 212*(l)* [8 USCS § 1182*(l)*] may be authorized to enter or stay in the United States other than in Guam or the Commonwealth of the Northern Mariana Islands or to remain in Guam or the Commonwealth of the Northern Mariana Islands for a period exceeding 45 days from date of admission to Guam or the Commonwealth of the Northern Mariana Islands. No alien admitted to the United States without a visa pursuant to section 217 [8 USCS § 1187] may be authorized to remain in the United States as a nonimmigrant visitor for a period exceeding 90 days from the date of admission.

(2) (A) The period of authorized status as a nonimmigrant described in section 101(a)(15)(O) [8 USCS § 1101(a)(15)(O)] shall be for such period as the Attorney General may specify in order to provide for the event (or events) for which the nonimmigrant is admitted.

(B) The period of authorized status as a nonimmigrant described in section 101(a)(15)(P) [8 USCS § 1101(a)(15)(P)] shall be for such period as the Attorney General may specify in order to provide for the competition, event, or performance for which the nonimmigrant is admitted. In the case of nonimmigrants admitted as individual athletes under section 101(a)(15)(P) [8 USCS § 1101(a)(15)(P)], the period of authorized status may be for an initial period (not to exceed 5 years) during which the nonimmigrant will perform as an athlete and such period may be extended by the Attorney General for an additional period of up to 5 years.

(b) Presumption of status; written waiver. Every alien (other than a nonimmigrant described in subparagraph (L) or (V) of section 101(a)(15) [8 USCS § 1101(a)(15)], and other than a nonimmigrant described in any provision of section 101(a)(15)(H)(i) [8 USCS § 1101(a)(15)(H)(i)] except subclause (b1) of such section) shall be presumed to be an immigrant until he establishes to the satisfaction of the consular officer, at the time of application for a visa, and the immigration officers, at the time of application for admission, that he is entitled to a nonimmigrant status under section 101(a)(15) [8 USCS § 1101(a)(15)]. An alien who is an officer or employee of any foreign government or of any international organization entitled to enjoy privileges, exemptions, and immunities under the International Organizations Immunities Act, or an alien who is the attendant, servant, employee, or member of the immediate family of any such alien shall not be entitled to apply for or receive an immigrant visa, or to enter the United States as an immigrant unless he executes a written waiver in the same form and substance as is prescribed by section 247(b) [8 USCS § 1257(b)].

(c) Petition of importing employer.

(1) The question of importing any alien as a nonimmigrant under subparagraph (H), (L), (O), or (P)(i) of section 101(a)(15) [8 USCS § 1101(a)(15)] (excluding nonimmigrants under section 101(a)(15)(H)(i)(b1) [8 USCS § 1101(a)(15)(H)(i)(b1)]) in any specific case or specific cases shall be determined by the Attorney General, after consultation with appropriate agencies of the Government, upon petition of the importing employer. Such petition shall be made and approved before the visa is granted. The petition shall be in such form and contain such information as the Attorney General shall prescribe. The approval of such a petition shall not, of itself, be construed as establishing that the alien is a nonimmigrant. For purposes of this subsection with respect to nonimmigrants described in section 101(a)(15)(H)(ii)(a) [8 USCS § 1101(a)(15)(H)(ii)(a)], the term "appropriate agencies of Government" means the Department of Labor and includes the Department of Agriculture. The provisions of section 218 [8 USCS § 1188] shall apply to the question of importing any alien as a nonimmigrant under section 101(a)(15)(H)(ii)(a) [8 USCS § 1101(a)(15)(H)(ii)(a)].

(2) (A) The Attorney General shall provide for a procedure under which an importing employer which meets requirements established by the Attorney General may file a blanket petition to import aliens as nonimmigrants described in section 101(a)(15)(L) [8 USCS § 1101(a)(15)(L)] instead of filing individual petitions under paragraph (1) to import such aliens. Such procedure shall permit the expedited processing of visas for admission of aliens covered under such a petition.

(B) For purposes of section 101(a)(15)(L) [8 USCS § 1101(a)(15)(L)], an alien is considered to be serving in a capacity involving specialized knowledge with respect to a company if the alien has a special knowledge of the company product and its application in international markets or has an advanced level of knowledge of processes and procedures of the company.

(C) The Attorney General shall provide a process for reviewing and acting upon petitions under this subsection with respect to nonimmigrants described in section 101(a)(15)(L) [8 USCS § 1101(a)(15)(L)] within 30 days after the date a completed petition has been filed.

(D) The period of authorized admission for—

(i) a nonimmigrant admitted to render services in a managerial or executive capacity under section 101(a)(15)(L) [8 USCS § 1101(a)(15)(L)] shall not exceed 7 years, or

(ii) a nonimmigrant admitted to render services in a capacity that involves specialized knowledge under section 101(a)(15)(L) [8 USCS § 1101(a)(15)(L)] shall not exceed 5 years.

(E) In the case of an alien spouse admitted under section 101(a)(15)(L) [8 USCS § 1101(a)(15)(L)], who is accompanying or following to join a principal alien admitted under such section, the Attorney General shall authorize the alien spouse to engage in employment in the United States and provide the spouse with an "employment authorized" endorsement or other appropriate work permit.

(F) An alien who will serve in a capacity involving specialized knowledge with respect to an employer for purposes of section 101(a)(15)(L) [8 USCS § 1101(a)(15)(L)] and will be stationed primarily at the worksite of an employer other than the petitioning employer or its affiliate, subsidiary, or parent shall not be eligible for classification under section 101(a)(15)(L) [8 USCS § 1101(a)(15)(L)] if—

(i) the alien will be controlled and supervised principally by such unaffiliated employer; or

(ii) the placement of the alien at the worksite of the unaffiliated employer is essentially an arrangement to provide labor for hire for the unaffiliated employer, rather than a placement in connection with the provision of a product or service for which specialized knowledge specific to the petitioning employer is necessary.

(3) The Attorney General shall approve a petition—

(A) with respect to a nonimmigrant described in section 101(a)(15)(O)(i) [8 USCS § 1101(a)(15)(O)(i)] only after consultation in accordance with paragraph (6) or, with respect to aliens seeking entry for a motion picture or television production, after consultation with the appropriate union representing the alien's occupational peers and a management organization in the area of the alien's ability, or

(B) with respect to a nonimmigrant described in section 101(a)(15)(O)(ii) [8 USCS § 1101(a)(15)(O)(ii)] after consultation in accordance with paragraph (6) or, in the case of such an alien seeking entry for a motion picture or television production, after consultation with such a labor organization and a management organization in the area of the alien's ability.

In the case of an alien seeking entry for a motion picture or television production, (i) any opinion under the previous sentence shall only be advisory, (ii) any such opinion that recommends denial must be in writing, (iii) in making the decision the Attorney General shall consider the exigencies and scheduling of the production, and (iv) the Attorney General shall append to the decision any such opinion. The Attorney General shall provide by regulation for the waiver of the consultation requirement under subparagraph (A) in the case of aliens who have been admitted as nonimmigrants under section 101(a)(15)(O)(i) [8 USCS § 1101(a)(15)(O)(i)] because of extraordinary ability in the arts and who seek readmission to perform similar services within 2 years after the date of a consultation under such subparagraph. Not later than 5 days after the date such a waiver is provided, the Attorney General shall forward a copy of the petition and all supporting documentation to the national office of an appropriate labor organization.

(4) (A) For purposes of section 101(a)(15)(P)(i)(a) [8 USCS § 1101(a)(15)(P)(i)(a)], an alien is described in this subparagraph if the alien—

(i) (I) performs as an athlete, individually or as part of a group or team, at an internationally recognized level of performance;

(II) is a professional athlete, as defined in section 204(i)(2) [8 USCS § 1154(i)(2)];

(III) performs as an athlete, or as a coach, as part of a team or franchise that is located in the United States and a member of a foreign league or association of 15 or more amateur sports teams, if—

(aa) the foreign league or association is the highest level of amateur performance of that sport in the relevant foreign country;

(bb) participation in such league or association renders players ineligible, whether on a temporary or permanent basis, to earn a scholarship in, or participate in, that sport at a college or university in the United States under the rules of the National Collegiate Athletic Association; and

(cc) a significant number of the individuals who play in such league or association are drafted by a major sports league or a minor league affiliate of such a sports league; or

(IV) is a professional athlete or amateur athlete who performs individually or as part of a group in a theatrical ice skating production; and

(ii) seeks to enter the United States temporarily and solely for the purpose of performing—

(I) as such an athlete with respect to a specific athletic competition; or

(II) in the case of an individual described in clause (i)(IV), in a specific theatrical ice skating production or tour.

(B) (i) For purposes of section 101(a)(15)(P)(i)(b) [8 USCS § 1101(a)(15)(P)(i)(b)], an alien is described in this subparagraph if the alien—

(I) performs with or is an integral and essential part of the performance of an entertainment group that has (except as provided in clause (ii)) been recognized internationally as being outstanding in the discipline for a sustained and substantial period of time,

(II) in the case of a performer or entertainer, except as provided in clause (iii), has had a sustained and substantial relationship with that group (ordinarily for at least one year) and provides functions integral to the performance of the group, and

(III) seeks to enter the United States temporarily and solely for the purpose of performing as such a performer or entertainer or as an integral and essential part of a performance.

(ii) In the case of an entertainment group that is recognized nationally as being outstanding in its discipline for a sustained and substantial period of time, the Attorney General may, in consideration of special circumstances, waive the international recognition requirement of clause (i)(I).

(iii) (I) The one-year relationship requirement of clause (i)(II) shall not apply to 25 percent of the performers and entertainers in a group.

(II) The Attorney General may waive such one-year relationship requirement for an alien who because of illness or unanticipated and exigent circumstances replaces an essential member of the group and for an alien who augments the group by performing a critical role.

(iv) The requirements of subclauses (I) and (II) of clause (i) shall not apply to alien circus personnel who perform as part of a circus or circus group or who constitute an integral and essential part of the performance of such circus or circus group, but only if such personnel are entering the United States to join a circus that has been recognized nationally as outstanding for a sustained and substantial period of time or as part of such a circus.

(C) A person may petition the Attorney General for classification of an alien as a nonimmigrant under section 101(a)(15)(P) [8 USCS § 1101(a)(15)(P)].

(D) The Attorney General shall approve petitions under this subsection with respect to nonimmigrants described in clause (i) or (iii) of section 101(a)(15)(P) [8 USCS § 1101(a)(15)(P)(i) or (iii)] only after consultation in accordance with paragraph (6).

(E) The Attorney General shall approve petitions under this subsection for nonimmigrants described in section 101(a)(15)(P)(ii) [8 USCS § 1101(a)(15)(P)(ii)] only after consultation with labor organizations representing artists and entertainers in the United States.

(F) (i) No nonimmigrant visa under section 101(a)(15)(P)(i)(a) [8 USCS § 1101(a)(15)(P)(i)(a)] shall be issued to any alien who is a national of a country that is a state sponsor of international terrorism unless the Secretary of State determines, in consultation with the Secretary of Homeland Security and the heads of other appropriate United States agencies, that such alien does not pose a threat to the safety, national security, or national interest of the United States. In making a determination under this subparagraph, the Secretary of State shall apply standards developed by the Secretary of State, in consultation with the Secretary of Homeland Security and the heads of other appropriate United States agencies, that are applicable to the nationals of such states.

(ii) In this subparagraph, the term "state sponsor of international terrorism" means any country the government of which has been determined by the Secretary of State under any of the laws specified in clause (iii) to have repeatedly provided support for acts of international terrorism.

(iii) The laws specified in this clause are the following:

(I) Section 6(j)(1)(A) of the Export Administration Act of 1979 (50 U.S.C. App. 2405(j)(1)(A) [former 50 USCS § 4605(j)(1)(A)]) (or successor statute).

(II) Section 40(d) of the Arms Export Control Act (22 U.S.C. 2780(d)).

(III) Section 620A(a) of the Foreign Assistance Act of 1961 (22 U.S.C. 2371(a)).

(G) The Secretary of Homeland Security shall permit a petition under this subsection to seek classification of more than 1 alien as a nonimmigrant under section 101(a)(15)(P)(i)(a) [8 USCS § 1101(a)(15)(P)(i)(a)].

(H) The Secretary of Homeland Security shall permit an athlete, or the employer of an athlete, to seek admission to the United States for such athlete under a provision of this Act other than section 101(a)(15)(P)(i) [8 USCS § 1101(a)(15)(P)(i)] if the athlete is eligible under such other provision.

(5) (A) In the case of an alien who is provided nonimmigrant status under section 101(a)(15)(H)(i)(b) or 101(a)(15)(H)(ii)(b) [8 USCS § 1101(a)(15)(H)(i)(b) or (ii)(b)] and who is dismissed from employment by the employer before the end of the period of authorized admission, the employer shall be liable for the reasonable costs of return transportation of the alien abroad.

(B) In the case of an alien who is admitted to the United States in nonimmigrant status under section 101(a)(15)(O) or 101(a)(15)(P) [8 USCS § 1101(a)(15)(O) or (P)] and whose employment terminates for reasons other than voluntary resignation, the employer whose offer of employment formed the basis of such nonimmigrant status and the petitioner are jointly and severally liable for the reasonable cost of return transportation of the alien abroad. The petitioner shall provide assurance satisfactory to the Attorney General that the reasonable cost of that transportation will be provided.

(6) (A) (i) To meet the consultation requirement of paragraph (3)(A) in the case of a petition for a nonimmigrant described in section 101(a)(15)(O)(i) [8 USCS § 1101(a)(15)(O)(i)] (other than with respect to aliens seeking entry for a motion picture or television production), the petitioner shall submit with the petition an advisory opinion from a peer group (or other person or persons of its choosing, which may include a labor organization) with expertise in the specific field involved.

(ii) To meet the consultation requirement of paragraph (3)(B) in the case of a petition for a nonimmigrant described in section 101(a)(15)(O)(ii) [8 USCS § 1101(a)(15)(O)(ii)] (other than with respect to aliens seeking entry for a motion picture or television production), the petitioner shall submit with the petition an advisory opinion from a labor organization with expertise in the skill area involved.

(iii) To meet the consultation requirement of paragraph (4)(D) in the case of a petition for a nonimmigrant described in section 101(a)(15)(P)(i) or 101(a)(15)(P)(iii) [8 USCS § 1101(a)(15)(P)(i) or (iii)], the petitioner shall submit with the petition an advisory opinion from a labor organization with expertise in the specific field of athletics or entertainment involved.

(B) To meet the consultation requirements of subparagraph (A), unless the petitioner submits with the petition an advisory opinion from an appropriate labor organization, the Attorney General shall forward a copy of the petition and all supporting documentation to the national office of an appropriate labor organization within 5 days of the date of receipt of the petition. If there is a collective bargaining representative of an employer's employees in the occupational classification for which the alien is being sought, that representative shall be the appropriate labor organization.

(C) In those cases in which a petitioner described in subparagraph (A) establishes that an appropriate peer group (including a labor organization) does not exist, the Attorney General shall adjudicate the petition without requiring an advisory opinion.

(D) Any person or organization receiving a copy of a petition described in subparagraph (A) and supporting documents shall have no more than 15 days following the date of receipt of such documents within which to submit a written advisory opinion or comment or to provide a letter of no objection. Once the 15-day period has expired and the petitioner has had an opportunity, where appropriate, to supply rebuttal evidence, the Attorney General shall adjudicate such petition in no more than 14 days. The Attorney General may shorten any specified time period for emergency reasons if no unreasonable burden would be thus imposed on any participant in the process.

(E) (i) The Attorney General shall establish by regulation expedited consultation procedures in the case of nonimmigrant artists or entertainers described in section 101(a)(15)(O) or 101(a)(15)(P) [8 USCS § 1101(a)(15)(O) or (P)] to accommodate the exigencies and scheduling of a given production or event.

(ii) The Attorney General shall establish by regulation expedited consultation procedures in the case of nonimmigrant athletes described in section 101(a)(15)(O)(i) or 101(a)(15)(P)(i) [8 USCS § 1101(a)(15)(O)(i) or (P)(i)] in the case of emergency circumstances (including trades during a season).

(F) No consultation required under this subsection by the Attorney General with a nongovernmental entity shall be construed as permitting the Attorney General to delegate any authority under this subsection to such an entity. The Attorney General shall give such weight to advisory opinions provided under this section as the Attorney General determines, in his sole discretion, to be appropriate.

(7) If a petition is filed and denied under this subsection, the Attorney General shall notify the petitioner of the determination and the reasons for the denial and of the process by which the petitioner may appeal the determination.

(8) The Attorney General shall submit annually to the Committees on the Judiciary of the House of Representatives and of the Senate a report describing, with respect to petitions under each subcategory of subparagraphs (H), (O), (P), and (Q) of section 101(a)(15) [8 USCS § 1101(a)(15)(H),(O), (P), (Q)] the following:

(A) The number of such petitions which have been filed.

(B) The number of such petitions which have been approved and the number of workers (by occupation) included in such approved petitions.

(C) The number of such petitions which have been denied and the number of workers (by occupation) requested in such denied petitions.

(D) The number of such petitions which have been withdrawn.

(E) The number of such petitions which are awaiting final action.

(9) (A) The Attorney General shall impose a fee on an employer (excluding any employer that is a primary or secondary education institution, an institution of higher education, as defined in section 101(a) of the Higher Education Act of 1965 (20 U.S.C. 1001(a))), a nonprofit entity related to or affiliated with any such institution, a nonprofit entity which engages in established curriculum-related clinical training of students registered at any such institution, a nonprofit research organization, or a governmental research organization) filing [before] a petition under paragraph (1)—

(i) initially to grant an alien nonimmigrant status described in section 101(a)(15)(H)(i)(b) [8 USCS § 1101(a)(15)(H)(i)(b)];

(ii) to extend the stay of an alien having such status (unless the employer previously has obtained an extension for such alien); or

(iii) to obtain authorization for an alien having such status to change employers.

(B) The amount of the fee shall be $1,500 for each such petition except that the fee shall be half the amount for each such petition by any employer with not more than 25 full-time equivalent employees who are employed in the United States (determined by including any affiliate or subsidiary of such employer).

(C) Fees collected under this paragraph shall be deposited in the Treasury in accordance with section 286(s) [8 USCS § 1356(s)].

(10) An amended H-1B petition shall not be required where the petitioning employer is involved in a corporate restructuring, including but not limited to a merger, acquisition, or consolidation, where a new corporate entity succeeds to the interests and obligations of the original petitioning employer and where the terms and conditions of employment remain the same but for the identity of the petitioner.

(11) (A) Subject to subparagraph (B), the Secretary of Homeland Security or the Secretary of State, as appropriate, shall impose a fee on an employer who has filed an attestation described in section 212(t) [8 USCS § 1182(t)]—

(i) in order that an alien may be initially granted nonimmigrant status described in section 101(a)(15)(H)(i)(b1) [8 USCS § 1101(a)(15)(H)(i)(b1)]; or

(ii) in order to satisfy the requirement of the second sentence of subsection (g)(8)(C) for an alien having such status to obtain certain extensions of stay.

(B) The amount of the fee shall be the same as the amount imposed by the Secretary of Homeland Security under paragraph (9), except that if such paragraph does not authorize such Secretary to impose any fee, no fee shall be imposed under this paragraph.

(C) Fees collected under this paragraph shall be deposited in the Treasury in accordance with section 286(s) [8 USCS § 1356(s)].

(12) (A) In addition to any other fees authorized by law, the Secretary of Homeland Security shall impose a fraud prevention and detection fee on an employer filing a petition under paragraph (1)—

(i) initially to grant an alien nonimmigrant status described in subparagraph (H)(i)(b) or (L) of section 101(a)(15) [8 USCS § 1101(a)(15)]; or

(ii) to obtain authorization for an alien having such status to change employers.

(B) In addition to any other fees authorized by law, the Secretary of State shall impose a fraud prevention and detection fee on an alien filing an application abroad for a visa authorizing admission to the United States as a nonimmigrant described in section 101(a)(15)(L) [8 USCS § 1101(a)(15)(L)], if the alien is covered under a blanket petition described in paragraph (2)(A).

(C) The amount of the fee imposed under subparagraph (A) or (B) shall be $500.

(D) The fee imposed under subparagraph (A) or (B) shall only apply to principal aliens and not to the spouses or children who are accompanying or following to join such principal aliens.

(E) Fees collected under this paragraph shall be deposited in the Treasury in accordance with section 286(v) [8 USCS § 1356(v)].

(13) (A) In addition to any other fees authorized by law, the Secretary of Homeland Security shall impose a fraud prevention and detection fee on an employer filing a petition under paragraph (1) for nonimmigrant workers described in section 101(a)(15)(H)(ii)(b) [8 USCS § 1101(a)(15)(H)(ii)(b)].

(B) The amount of the fee imposed under subparagraph (A) shall be $150.

(14) (A) If the Secretary of Homeland Security finds, after notice and an opportunity for a hearing, a substantial failure to meet any of the conditions of the petition to admit or otherwise provide status to a nonimmigrant worker under section 101(a)(15)(H)(ii)(b) [8 USCS § 1101(a)(15)(H)(ii)(b)] or a willful misrepresentation of a material fact in such petition—

(i) the Secretary of Homeland Security may, in addition to any other remedy authorized by law, impose such administrative remedies (including civil monetary penalties in an amount not to exceed $10,000 per violation) as the Secretary of Homeland Security determines to be appropriate; and

(ii) the Secretary of Homeland Security may deny petitions filed with respect to that employer under section 204 [8 USCS § 1154] or paragraph (1) of this subsection during a period of at least 1 year but not more than 5 years for aliens to be employed by the employer.

(B) The Secretary of Homeland Security may delegate to the Secretary of Labor, with the agreement of the Secretary of Labor, any of the authority given to the Secretary of Homeland Security under subparagraph (A)(i).

(C) In determining the level of penalties to be assessed under subparagraph (A), the highest penalties shall be reserved for willful failures to meet any of the conditions of the petition that involve harm to United States workers.

(D) In this paragraph, the term 'substantial failure' means the willful failure to comply with the requirements of this section that constitutes a significant deviation from the terms and conditions of a petition.

(d) Issuance of visa to fiancée or fiancé of citizen.

(1) A visa shall not be issued under the provisions of section 101(a)(15)(K)(i) [8 USCS § 1101(a)(15)(K)(i)] until the consular officer has received a petition filed in the United States by the fiancée or fiancé of the applying alien and approved by the Secretary of Homeland Security. The petition shall be in such form and contain such information as the Secretary of Homeland Security shall, by regulation, prescribe. Such information shall include information on any criminal convictions of the petitioner for any specified crime described in paragraph (3)(B) and information on any permanent protection or restraining order issued against the petitioner related to any specified crime described in paragraph (3)(B)(i). It shall be approved only after satisfactory evidence is submitted by the petitioner to establish that the parties have previously met in person within 2 years before the date of filing the petition, have a bona fide intention to marry, and are legally able and actually willing to conclude a valid marriage in the United States within a period of ninety days after the alien's arrival, except that the Secretary of Homeland Security in his discretion may waive the requirement that the parties have previously met in person. In the event the marriage with the petitioner does not occur within three months after the admission of the said alien and minor children, they shall be required to depart from the United States and upon failure to do so shall be removed in accordance with sections 240 and 241 [8 USCS §§ 1229a, 1231].

(2) (A) Subject to subparagraphs (B) and (C), the Secretary of Homeland Security may not approve a petition under paragraph (1) unless the Secretary has verified that—

(i) the petitioner has not, previous to the pending petition, petitioned under paragraph (1) with respect to two or more applying aliens; and

(ii) if the petitioner has had such a petition previously approved, 2 years have elapsed since the filing of such previously approved petition.

(B) The Secretary of Homeland Security may, in the Secretary's discretion, waive the limitations in subparagraph (A) if justification exists for such a waiver. Except in extraordinary circumstances and subject to subparagraph (C), such a waiver shall not be granted if the petitioner has a record of violent criminal offenses against a person or persons.

(C) (i) The Secretary of Homeland Security is not limited by the criminal court record and shall grant a waiver of the condition described in the second sentence of subparagraph (B) in the case of a petitioner described in clause (ii).

(ii) A petitioner described in this clause is a petitioner who has been battered or subjected to extreme cruelty and who is or was not the primary perpetrator of violence in the relationship upon a determination that—

(I) the petitioner was acting in self-defense;

(II) the petitioner was found to have violated a protection order intended to protect the petitioner; or

(III) the petitioner committed, was arrested for, was convicted of, or pled guilty to committing a crime that did not result in serious bodily injury and where there was a connection between the crime and the petitioner's having been battered or subjected to extreme cruelty.

(iii) In acting on applications under this subparagraph, the Secretary of Homeland Security shall consider any credible evidence relevant to the application. The determination of what evidence is credible and the weight to be given that evidence shall be within the sole discretion of the Secretary.

(3) In this subsection:

(A) The terms "domestic violence", "sexual assault", "child abuse and neglect", "dating violence", "elder abuse", and "stalking" have the meaning given such terms in section 3 of the Violence Against Women and Department of Justice Reauthorization Act of 2005.

(B) The term "specified crime" means the following:

(i) Domestic violence, sexual assault, child abuse and neglect, dating violence, elder abuse, stalking, or an attempt to commit any such crime.

(ii) Homicide, murder, manslaughter, rape, abusive sexual contact, sexual exploitation, incest, torture, trafficking, peonage, holding hostage, involuntary servitude, slave trade, kidnapping, abduction, unlawful criminal restraint, false imprisonment, or an attempt to commit any of the crimes described in this clause.

(iii) At least three convictions for crimes relating to a controlled substance or alcohol not arising from a single act.

(e) Nonimmigrant professionals and annual numerical limit.

(1) An alien who is a citizen of Canada or Mexico, and the spouse and children of any such alien if accompanying or following to join such alien, who seeks to enter the United States under and pursuant to the provisions of Section D of Annex 16-A of the USMCA (as defined in section 3 of the United States-Mexico-Canada Agreement Implementation Act [19 USCS § 4502]) to engage in business activities at a professional level as provided for in such Annex, may be admitted for such purpose under regulations of the Attorney General promulgated after consultation with the Secretaries of State and Labor. For purposes of this Act, including the issuance of entry documents and the application of subsection (b), such alien shall be treated as if seeking classification, or classifiable, as a nonimmigrant under section 101(a)(15) [8 USCS § 1101(a)(15)]. For purposes of this paragraph, the term "citizen of Mexico" means "citizen" as defined in article 16.1 of the USMCA.

(2) In the case of an alien spouse admitted under section 101(a)(15)(E) [8 USCS § 1101(a)(15)(E)], who is accompanying or following to join a principal alien admitted under such section, the Attorney General shall authorize the alien spouse to engage in employment in the United States and provide the spouse with an "employment authorized" endorsement or other appropriate work permit.

(f) Denial of crewmember status in the case of certain labor disputes.

(1) Except as provided in paragraph (3), no alien shall be entitled to nonimmigrant status described in section 101(a)(15)(D) [8 USCS § 1101(a)(15)(D)] if the alien intends to land for the purpose of performing service on board a vessel of the United States (as defined in section 2101(46) of title 46, United States Code) or on an aircraft of an air carrier (as defined in section 40102(a)(2) of title 49, United States Code) during a labor dispute where there is a strike or lockout in the bargaining unit of the employer in which the alien intends to perform such service.

(2) An alien described in paragraph (1)—

(A) may not be paroled into the United States pursuant to section 212(d)(5) [8 USCS § 1182(d)(5)] unless the Attorney General determines that the parole of such alien is necessary to protect the national security of the United States; and

(B) shall be considered not to be a bona fide crewman for purposes of section 252(b) [8 USCS § 1282(b)].

(3) Paragraph (1) shall not apply to an alien if the air carrier or owner or operator of such vessel that employs the alien provides documentation that satisfies the Attorney General that the alien—

(A) has been an employee of such employer for a period of not less than 1 year preceding the date that a strike or lawful lockout commenced;

(B) has served as a qualified crewman for such employer at least once in each of 3 months during the 12-month period preceding such date; and

(C) shall continue to provide the same services that such alien provided as such a crewman.

(g) Temporary workers and trainees; limitation of numbers.

(1) The total number of aliens who may be issued visas or otherwise provided nonimmigrant status during any fiscal year (beginning with fiscal year 1992)—

(A) under section 101(a)(15)(H)(i)(b) [8 USCS § 1101(a)(15)(H)(i)(b)], may not exceed—

(i) 65,000 in each fiscal year before fiscal year 1999;

(ii) 115,000 in fiscal year 1999;

(iii) 115,000 in fiscal year 2000;

(iv) 195,000 in fiscal year 2001;

(v) 195,000 in fiscal year 2002;

(vi) 195,000 in fiscal year 2003; and

(vii) 65,000 in each succeeding fiscal year; or

(B) under section 101(a)(15)(H)(ii)(b) [8 USCS § 1101(a)(15)(H)(ii)(b)] may not exceed 66,000.

(2) The numerical limitations of paragraph (1) shall only apply to principal aliens and not to the spouses or children of such aliens.

(3) Aliens who are subject to the numerical limitations of paragraph (1) shall be issued visas (or otherwise provided nonimmigrant status) in the order in which petitions are filed for such visas or status. If an alien who was issued a visa or otherwise provided nonimmigrant status and counted against the numerical limitations of paragraph (1) is found to have been issued such visa or otherwise provided such status by fraud or willfully misrepresenting a material fact and such visa or nonimmigrant status is revoked, then one number shall be restored to the total number of aliens who may be issued visas or otherwise provided such status under the numerical limitations of paragraph (1) in the fiscal year in which the petition is revoked, regardless of the fiscal year in which the petition was approved.

(4) In the case of a nonimmigrant described in section 101(a)(15)(H)(i)(b) [8 USCS § 1101(a)(15)(H)(i)(b)], the period of authorized admission as such a nonimmigrant may not exceed 6 years.

(5) The numerical limitations contained in paragraph (1)(A) shall not apply to any nonimmigrant alien issued a visa or otherwise provided status under section 101(a)(15)(H)(i)(b) [8 USCS § 1101(a)(15)(H)(i)(b)] who—

(A) is employed (or has received an offer of employment) at an institution of higher education (as defined in section 101(a) of the Higher Education Act of 1965 (20 U.S.C. 1001(a))), or a related or affiliated nonprofit entity;

(B) is employed (or has received an offer of employment) at a nonprofit research organization or a governmental research organization; or

(C) has earned a master's or higher degree from a United States institution of higher education (as defined in section 101(a) of the Higher Education Act of 1965 (20 U.S.C. 1001(a)), until the number of aliens who are exempted from such numerical limitation during such year exceeds 20,000.

(6) Any alien who ceases to be employed by an employer described in paragraph (5)(A) shall, if employed as a nonimmigrant alien described in section 101(a)(15)(H)(i)(b) [8 USCS § 1101(a)(15)(H)(i)(b)], who has not previously been counted toward the numerical limitations contained in paragraph (1)(A), be counted toward those limitations the first time the alien is employed by an employer other than one described in paragraph (5).

(7) Any alien who has already been counted, within the 6 years prior to the approval of a petition described in subsection (c), toward the numerical limitations of paragraph (1)(A) shall not again be counted toward those limitations unless the alien would be eligible for a full 6 years of authorized admission at the time the petition is filed. Where multiple petitions are approved for 1 alien, that alien shall be counted only once.

(8) (A) The agreements referred to in section 101(a)(15)(H)(i)(b1)) [8 USCS § 1101(a)(15)(H)(i)(b1)] are—

(i) the United States-Chile Free Trade Agreement; and

(ii) the United States-Singapore Free Trade Agreement.

(B) (i) The Secretary of Homeland Security shall establish annual numerical limitations on approvals of initial applications by aliens for admission under section 101(a)(15)(H)(i)(b1) [8 USCS § 1101(a)(15)(H)(i)(b1)].

(ii) The annual numerical limitations described in clause (i) shall not exceed—

(I) 1,400 for nationals of Chile (as defined in article 14.9 of the United States-Chile Free Trade Agreement) for any fiscal year; and

(II) 5,400 for nationals of Singapore (as defined in Annex 1A of the United States-Singapore Free Trade Agreement) for any fiscal year.

(iii) The annual numerical limitations described in clause (i) shall only apply to principal aliens and not to the spouses or children of such aliens.

(iv) The annual numerical limitation described in paragraph (1)(A) is reduced by the amount of the annual numerical limitations established under clause (i). However, if a numerical limitation established under clause (i) has not been exhausted at the end of a given fiscal year, the Secretary of Homeland Security shall adjust upwards the numerical limitation in paragraph (1)(A) for that fiscal year by the amount remaining in the numerical limitation under clause (i). Visas under section 101(a)(15)(H)(i)(b) [8 USCS § 1101(a)(15)(H)(i)(b)] may be issued pursuant to such adjustment within the first 45 days of the next fiscal year to aliens who had applied for such visas during the fiscal year for which the adjustment was made.

(C) The period of authorized admission as a nonimmigrant under section 101(a)(15)(H)(i)(b1) [8 USCS § 1101(a)(15)(H)(i)(b1)] shall be 1 year, and may be extended, but only in 1-year increments. After every second extension, the next following extension shall not be granted unless the Secretary of Labor had determined and certified to the Secretary of Homeland Security and the Secretary of State that the intending employer has filed with the Secretary of Labor an attestation under section 212(t)(1) [8 USCS § 1182(t)(1)] for the purpose of permitting the nonimmigrant to obtain such extension.

(D) The numerical limitation described in paragraph (1)(A) for a fiscal year shall be reduced by one for each alien granted an extension under subparagraph (C) during such year who has obtained 5 or more consecutive prior extensions.

(9) (A) Subject to subparagraphs (B) and (C), an alien who has already been counted toward the numerical limitation of paragraph (1)(B) during fiscal year 2013, 2014, or 2015 shall not again be counted toward such limitation during fiscal year 2016. Such an alien shall be considered a returning worker.

(B) A petition to admit or otherwise provide status under section 101(a)(15)(H)(ii)(b) [8 USCS § 1101(a)(15)(H)(ii)(b)] shall include, with respect to a returning worker—

(i) all information and evidence that the Secretary of Homeland Security determines is required to support a petition for status under section 101(a)(15)(H)(ii)(b) [8 USCS § 1101(a)(15)(H)(ii)(b)];

(ii) the full name of the alien; and

(iii) a certification to the Department of Homeland Security that the alien is a returning worker.

(C) An H-2B visa or grant of nonimmigrant status for a returning worker shall be approved only if the alien is confirmed to be a returning worker by—

(i) the Department of State; or

(ii) if the alien is visa exempt or seeking to change to status under section 101(a)(15)(H)(ii)(b) [8 USCS § 1101(a)(15)(H)(ii)(b)], the Department of Homeland Security.

(10) The numerical limitations of paragraph (1)(B) shall be allocated for a fiscal year so that the total number of aliens subject to such numerical limits who enter the United States pursuant to a visa or are accorded nonimmigrant status under section 101(a)(15)(H)(ii)(b) [8 USCS § 1101(a)(15)(H)(ii)(b)] during the first 6 months of such fiscal year is not more than 33,000.

(11) (A) The Secretary of State may not approve a number of initial applications submitted for aliens described in section 101(a)(15)(E)(iii) [8 USCS § 1101(a)(15)(E)(iii)] that is more than the applicable numerical limitation set out in this paragraph.

(B) The applicable numerical limitation referred to in subparagraph (A) is 10,500 for each fiscal year.

(C) The applicable numerical limitation referred to in subparagraph (A) shall only apply to principal aliens and not to the spouses or children of such aliens.

(h) Intention to abandon foreign residence. The fact that an alien is the beneficiary of an application for a preference status filed under section 204 [8 USCS § 1154] or has otherwise sought permanent residence in the United States shall not constitute evidence of an intention to abandon a foreign residence for purposes of obtaining a visa as a nonimmigrant described in subparagraph (H)(i)(b) or (c), (L), or (V) of section 101(a)(15) [8 USCS § 1101(a)(15)] or otherwise obtaining or maintaining the status of a nonimmigrant described in such subparagraph, if the alien had obtained a change of status under section 248 [8 USCS § 1258] to a classification as such a nonimmigrant before the alien's most recent departure from the United States.

(i) "Specialty occupation" defined.

(1) Except as provided in paragraph (3), for purposes of section 101(a)(15)(H)(i)(b) [8 USCS § 1101(a)(15)(H)(i)(b)], section 101(a)(15)(E)(iii) [8 USCS § 1101(a)(15)(E)(iii)], and paragraph (2), the term "specialty occupation" means an occupation that requires—

(A) theoretical and practical application of a body of highly specialized knowledge, and

(B) attainment of a bachelor's or higher degree in the specific specialty (or its equivalent) as a minimum for entry into the occupation in the United States.

(2) For purposes of section 101(a)(15)(H)(i)(b) [8 USCS § 1101(a)(15)(H)(i)(b)], the requirements of this paragraph, with respect to a specialty occupation, are—

(A) full state licensure to practice in the occupation, if such licensure is required to practice in the occupation,

(B) completion of the degree described in paragraph (1)(B) for the occupation, or

(C) (i) experience in the specialty equivalent to the completion of such degree, and

(ii) recognition of expertise in the specialty through progressively responsible positions relating to the specialty.

(3) For purposes of section 101(a)(15)(H)(i)(b1) [8 USCS § 1101(a)(15)(H)(i)(b1)], the term "specialty occupation" means an occupation that requires—

(A) theoretical and practical application of a body of specialized knowledge; and

(B) attainment of a bachelor's or higher degree in the specific specialty (or its equivalent) as a minimum for entry into the occupation in the United States.

(j) Labor disputes.

(1) Notwithstanding any other provision of this Act, an alien who is a citizen of Canada or Mexico who seeks to enter the United States under and pursuant to the provisions of Section B, Section C, or Section D of Annex 16-A of the USMCA (as defined in section 3 of the United States-Mexico-Canada Agreement Implementation Act [19 USCS § 4502]), shall not be classified as a nonimmigrant under such provisions if there is in progress a strike or lockout in the course of a labor dispute in the occupational classification at the place or intended place of employment, unless such alien establishes, pursuant to regulations promulgated by the Attorney General, that the alien's entry will not affect adversely the settlement of the strike or lockout or the employment of any person who is involved in the strike or lockout. Notice of a determination under this paragraph shall be given as may be required by paragraph 3 of article 16.4 of the USMCA. For purposes of this paragraph, the term "citizen of Mexico" means "citizen" as defined in article 16.1 of the USMCA.

(2) Notwithstanding any other provision of this Act except section 212(t)(1) [8 USCS § 1182(t)(1)], and subject to regulations promulgated by the Secretary of Homeland Security, an alien who seeks to enter the United States under and pursuant to the provisions of an agreement listed in subsection (g)(8)(A), and the spouse and children of such an alien if accompanying or following to join the alien, may be denied admission as a nonimmigrant under subparagraph (E), (L), or (H)(i)(b1) of section 101(a)(15) [8 USCS § 1101(a)(15)] if there is in progress a labor dispute in the occupational classification at the place or intended place of employment, unless such alien establishes, pursuant to regulations promulgated by the Secretary of Homeland Security after consultation with the Secretary of Labor, that the alien's entry will not affect adversely the settlement of the labor dispute or the employment of any person who is involved in the labor dispute. Notice of a determination under this paragraph shall be given as may be required by such agreement.

(k) Numerical limitations; period of admission; conditions for admission and stay; annual report.

(1) The number of aliens who may be provided a visa as nonimmigrants under section 101(a)(15)(S)(i) [8 USCS § 1101(a)(15)(S)(i)] in any fiscal year may not exceed 200. The number of aliens who may be provided

a visa as nonimmigrants under section 101(a)(15)(S)(ii) [8 USCS § 1101(a)(15)(S)(ii)] in any fiscal year may not exceed 50.

(2) The period of admission of an alien as such a nonimmigrant may not exceed 3 years. Such period may not be extended by the Attorney General.

(3) As a condition for the admission, and continued stay in lawful status, of such a nonimmigrant, the nonimmigrant—

(A) shall report not less often than quarterly to the Attorney General such information concerning the alien's whereabouts and activities as the Attorney General may require;

(B) may not be convicted of any criminal offense punishable by a term of imprisonment of 1 year or more after the date of such admission;

(C) must have executed a form that waives the nonimmigrant's right to contest, other than on the basis of an application for withholding of removal, any action for deportation of the alien instituted before the alien obtains lawful permanent resident status; and

(D) shall abide by any other condition, limitation, or restriction imposed by the Attorney General.

(4) The Attorney General shall submit a report annually to the Committee on the Judiciary of the House of Representatives and the Committee on the Judiciary of the Senate concerning—

(A) the number of such nonimmigrants admitted;

(B) the number of successful criminal prosecutions or investigations resulting from cooperation of such aliens;

(C) the number of terrorist acts prevented or frustrated resulting from cooperation of such aliens;

(D) the number of such nonimmigrants whose admission or cooperation has not resulted in successful criminal prosecution or investigation or the prevention or frustration of a terrorist act; and

(E) the number of such nonimmigrants who have failed to report quarterly (as required under paragraph (3)) or who have been convicted of crimes in the United States after the date of their admission as such a nonimmigrant.

(l) Restrictions on waiver.

(1) In the case of a request by an interested State agency, or by an interested Federal agency, for a waiver of the 2-year foreign residence requirement under section 212(e) [8 USCS § 1182(e)] on behalf of an alien described in clause (iii) of such section, the Attorney General shall not grant such waiver unless—

(A) in the case of an alien who is otherwise contractually obligated to return to a foreign country, the government of such country furnishes the Director of the United States Information Agency with a statement in writing that it has no objection to such waiver;

(B) in the case of a request by an interested State agency, the grant of such waiver would not cause the number of waivers allotted for that State for that fiscal year to exceed 30;

(C) in the case of a request by an interested Federal agency or by an interested State agency—

(i) the alien demonstrates a bona fide offer of full-time employment at a health facility or health care organization, which employment has been determined by the Attorney General to be in the public interest; and

(ii) the alien agrees to begin employment with the health facility or health care organization within 90 days of receiving such waiver, and agrees to continue to work for a total of not less than 3 years (unless the Attorney General determines that extenuating circumstances exist, such as closure of the facility or hardship to the alien, which would justify a lesser period of employment at such health facility or health care organization, in which case the alien must demonstrate another bona fide offer of employment at a health facility or health care organization for the remainder of such 3-year period); and

(D) in the case of a request by an interested Federal agency (other than a request by an interested Federal agency to employ the alien full-time in medical research or training) or by an interested State agency, the alien agrees to practice primary care or specialty medicine in accordance with paragraph (2) for a total of not less than 3 years only in the geographic area or areas which are designated by the Secretary of Health and Human Services as having a shortage of health care professionals, except that—

(i) in the case of a request by the Department of Veterans Affairs, the alien shall not be required to practice medicine in a geographic area designated by the Secretary;

(ii) in the case of a request by an interested State agency, the head of such State agency determines that the alien is to practice medicine under such agreement in a facility that serves patients who reside in one or more geographic areas so designated by the Secretary of Health and Human Services (without regard to whether such facility is located within such a designated geographic area), and the grant of such waiver would not cause the number of the waivers granted on behalf of aliens for such State for a fiscal year (within the limitation in subparagraph (B)) in accordance with the conditions of this clause to exceed 10; and

(iii) in the case of a request by an interested Federal agency or by an interested State agency for a waiver for an alien who agrees to practice specialty medicine in a facility located in a geographic area so designated by the Secretary of Health and Human Services, the request shall demonstrate, based on criteria established by such agency, that there is a shortage of health care professionals able to provide services in the appropriate medical specialty to the patients who will be served by the alien.

(2) (A) Notwithstanding section 248(a)(2) [8 USCS § 1258(a)(2)], the Attorney General may change the status of an alien who qualifies under this subsection and section 212(e) [8 USCS § 1182(e)] to that of an alien described in section 101(a)(15)(H)(i)(b) [8 USCS § 1101(a)(15)(H)(i)(b)]. The numerical limitations contained in subsection (g)(1)(A) shall not apply to any alien whose status is changed under the preceding sentence, if the alien obtained a waiver of the 2-year foreign residence requirement upon a request by an interested Federal agency or an interested State agency.

(B) No person who has obtained a change of status under subparagraph (A) and who has failed to fulfill the terms of the contract with the health facility or health care organization named in the waiver application shall be eligible to apply for an immigrant visa, for permanent residence, or for any other change of nonimmigrant status, until it is established that such person has resided and been physically present in the country of his nationality or his last residence for an aggregate of at least 2 years following departure from the United States.

(3) Notwithstanding any other provision of this subsection, the 2-year foreign residence requirement under section 212(e) [8 USCS § 1182(e)] shall apply with respect to an alien described in clause (iii) of such section, who has not otherwise been accorded status under section 101(a)(27)(H) [8 USCS § 1101(a)(27)(H)], if—

(A) at any time the alien ceases to comply with any agreement entered into under subparagraph (C) or (D) of paragraph (1); or

(B) the alien's employment ceases to benefit the public interest at any time during the 3-year period described in paragraph (1)(C).

(m) Nonimmigrant elementary and secondary school students.

(1) An alien may not be accorded status as a nonimmigrant under clause (i) or (iii) of section 101(a)(15)(F) [8 USCS § 1101(a)(15)(F)] in order to pursue a course of study—

(A) at a public elementary school or in a publicly funded adult education program; or

(B) at a public secondary school unless—

(i) the aggregate period of such status at such a school does not exceed 12 months with respect to any alien, and

(ii) the alien demonstrates that the alien has reimbursed the local educational agency that administers the school for the full, unsubsidized per capita cost of providing education at such school for the period of the alien's attendance.

(2) An alien who obtains the status of a nonimmigrant under clause (i) or (iii) of section 101(a)(15)(F) [8 USCS § 1101(a)(15)(F)] in order to pursue a course of study at a private elementary or secondary school or in a language training program that is not publicly funded shall be considered to have violated such status, and the alien's visa under section 101(a)(15)(F) [8 USCS § 1101(a)(15)(F)] shall be void, if the alien terminates or abandons such course of study at such a school and undertakes a course of study at a public elementary school, in a publicly funded adult education program, in a publicly funded adult education language training program, or at a public secondary school (unless the requirements of paragraph (1)(B) are met).

(n) Increased portability of H-1B status.

(1) A nonimmigrant alien described in paragraph (2) who was previously issued a visa or otherwise provided nonimmigrant status under section 101(a)(15)(H)(i)(b) [8 USCS § 1101(a)(15)(H)(i)(b)] is authorized to accept new employment upon the filing by the prospective employer of a new petition on behalf of such nonimmigrant as provided under subsection (a). Employment authorization shall continue for such alien until the new petition is adjudicated. If the new petition is denied, such authorization shall cease.

(2) A nonimmigrant alien described in this paragraph is a nonimmigrant alien—

(A) who has been lawfully admitted into the United States;

(B) on whose behalf an employer has filed a nonfrivolous petition for new employment before the date of expiration of the period of stay authorized by the Attorney General; and

(C) who, subsequent to such lawful admission, has not been employed without authorization in the United States before the filing of such petition.

(o) Nonimmigrants guilty of trafficking in persons.

(1) No alien shall be eligible for admission to the United States under section 101(a)(15)(T) [8 USCS § 1101(a)(15)(T)] if there is substantial reason to believe that the alien has committed an act of a severe form of trafficking in persons (as defined in section 103 of the Trafficking Victims Protection Act of 2000 [22 USCS § 7102]).

(2) The total number of aliens who may be issued visas or otherwise provided nonimmigrant status during any fiscal year under section 101(a)(15)(T) [8 USCS § 1101(a)(15)(T)] may not exceed 5,000.

(3) The numerical limitation of paragraph (2) shall only apply to principal aliens and not to the spouses, sons, daughters, siblings, or parents of such aliens.

(4) An unmarried alien who seeks to accompany, or follow to join, a parent granted status under section 101(a)(15)(T)(i) [8 USCS § 1101(a)(15)(T)(i)], and who was under 21 years of age on the date on which such parent applied for such status, shall continue to be classified as a child for purposes of section 101(a)(15)(T)(ii) [8 USCS § 1101(a)(15)(T)(ii)], if the alien attains 21 years of age after such parent's application was filed but while it was pending.

(5) An alien described in clause (i) of section 101(a)(15)(T) [8 USCS § 1101(a)(15)(T)] shall continue to be treated as an alien described in clause (ii)(I) of such section if the alien attains 21 years of age after the alien's application for status under such clause (i) is filed but while it is pending.

(6) In making a determination under section 101(a)(15)(T)(i)(III)(aa) [8 USCS § 1101(a)(15)(T)(i)(III)(aa)] with respect to an alien, statements from State and local law enforcement officials that the alien has complied with any reasonable request for assistance in the investigation or prosecution of crimes such as kidnapping, rape, slavery, or other forced labor offenses, where severe forms of trafficking in persons (as defined in section 103 of the Trafficking Victims Protection Act of 2000 [22 USCS § 7102]) appear to have been involved, shall be considered.

(7) (A) Except as provided in subparagraph (B), an alien who is issued a visa or otherwise provided nonimmigrant status under section 101(a)(15)(T) [8 USCS § 1101(a)(15)(T)] may be granted such status for a period of not more than 4 years.

(B) An alien who is issued a visa or otherwise provided nonimmigrant status under section 101(a)(15)(T) [8 USCS § 1101(a)(15)(T)] may extend the period of such status beyond the period described in subparagraph (A) if—

(i) a Federal, State, or local law enforcement official, prosecutor, judge, or other authority investigating or prosecuting activity relating to human trafficking or certifies that the presence of the alien in the United States is necessary to assist in the investigation or prosecution of such activity;

(ii) the alien is eligible for relief under section 245*(l)* [8 USCS § 1255*(l)*] and is unable to obtain such relief because regulations have not been issued to implement such section; or

(iii) the Secretary of Homeland Security determines that an extension of the period of such nonimmigrant status is warranted due to exceptional circumstances.

(C) Nonimmigrant status under section 101(a)(15)(T) [8 USCS § 1101(a)(15)(T)] shall be extended during the pendency of an application for adjustment of status under section 245*(l)* [8 USCS § 1255*(l)*].

(p) Requirements applicable to8 USCS § 1101(a)(15)(U) visas.

(1) Petitioning procedures for section 101(a)(15)(U) [8 USCS § 1101(a)(15)(U)] visas. The petition filed by an alien under section 101(a)(15)(U)(i) [8 USCS § 1101(a)(15)(U)(i)] shall contain a certification from a Federal, State, or local law enforcement official, prosecutor, judge, or other Federal, State, or local authority investigating criminal activity described in section 101(a)(15)(U)(iii) [8 USCS § 1101(a)(15)(U)(iii)]. This certification may also be provided by an official of the Service whose ability to provide such certification is not limited to information concerning immigration violations. This certification shall state that the alien "has been helpful, is being helpful, or is likely to be helpful" in the investigation or prosecution of criminal activity described in section 101(a)(15)(U)(iii) [8 USCS § 1101(a)(15)(U)(iii)].

(2) Numerical limitations.

(A) The number of aliens who may be issued visas or otherwise provided status as nonimmigrants under section 101(a)(15)(U) [8 USCS § 1101(a)(15)(U)] in any fiscal year shall not exceed 10,000.

(B) The numerical limitations in subparagraph (A) shall only apply to principal aliens described in section 101(a)(15)(U)(i) [8 USCS § 1101(a)(15)(U)(i)], and not to spouses, children, or, in the case of alien children, the alien parents of such children.

(3) Duties of the Attorney General with respect to "U" visa nonimmigrants. With respect to nonimmigrant aliens described in subsection (a)(15)(U)—

(A) the Attorney General and other government officials, where appropriate, shall provide those aliens with referrals to nongovernmental organizations to advise the aliens regarding their options while in the United States and the resources available to them; and

(B) the Attorney General shall, during the period those aliens are in lawful temporary resident status under that subsection, provide the aliens with employment authorization.

(4) Credible evidence considered. In acting on any petition filed under this subsection, the consular officer or the Attorney General, as appropriate, shall consider any credible evidence relevant to the petition.

(5) Nonexclusive relief. Nothing in this subsection limits the ability of aliens who qualify for status under section 101(a)(15)(U) [8 USCS § 1101(a)(15)(U)] to seek any other immigration benefit or status for which the alien may be eligible.

(6) Duration of status. The authorized period of status of an alien as a nonimmigrant under section 101(a)(15)(U) [8 USCS § 1101(a)(15)(U)] shall be for a period of not more than 4 years, but shall be extended upon certification from a Federal, State, or local law enforcement official, prosecutor, judge, or other Federal, State, or local authority investigating or prosecuting criminal activity described in section 101(a)(15)(U)(iii) [8 USCS § 1101(a)(15)(U)(iii)] that the alien's presence in the United States is required to assist in the investigation or prosecution of such criminal activity. The Secretary of Homeland Security may extend, beyond the 4-year period authorized under this section, the authorized period of status of an alien as a nonimmigrant under section 101(a)(15)(U) [8 USCS § 1101(a)(15)(U)] if the Secretary determines that an extension of such period is warranted due to exceptional circumstances. Such alien's nonimmigrant status shall be extended beyond the 4-year period authorized under this section if the alien is eligible for relief under section 245(m) [8 USCS § 1255(m)] and is unable to obtain such relief because regulations have not been issued to implement such section and shall be extended during the pendency of an application for adjustment of status under section 245(m) [8 USCS § 1255(m)]. The Secretary may grant work authorization to any alien who has a pending, bona fide application for nonimmigrant status under section 101(a)(15)(U) [8 USCS § 1101(a)(15)(U)].

(7) Age determinations.

(A) Children. An unmarried alien who seeks to accompany, or follow to join, a parent granted status under section 101(a)(15)(U)(i) [8 USCS § 1101(a)(15)(U)(i)], and who was under 21 years of age on the date on which such parent petitioned for such status, shall continue to be classified as a child for purposes of section 101(a)(15)(U)(ii) [8 USCS § 1101(a)(15)(U)(ii)], if the alien attains 21 years of age after such parent's petition was filed but while it was pending.

(B) Principal aliens. An alien described in clause (i) of section 101(a)(15)(U) [8 USCS § 1101(a)(15)(U)] shall continue to be treated as an alien described in clause (ii)(I) of such section if the alien attains 21 years of age after the alien's application for status under such clause (i) is filed but while it is pending.

(q) Employment of nonimmigrants described in8 USCS § 1101(a)(15)(V).

(1) In the case of a nonimmigrant described in section 101(a)(15)(V) [8 USCS § 1101(a)(15)(V)]—

(A) the Attorney General shall authorize the alien to engage in employment in the United States during the period of authorized admission and shall provide the alien with an "employment authorized" endorsement or other appropriate document signifying authorization of employment; and

(B) the period of authorized admission as such a nonimmigrant shall terminate 30 days after the date on which any of the following is denied:

(i) The petition filed under section 204 [8 USCS § 1154] to accord the alien a status under section 203(a)(2)(A) [8 USCS § 1153(a)(2)(A)] (or, in the case of a child granted nonimmigrant status based on eligibility to receive a visa under section 203(d) [8 USCS § 1153(d)], the petition filed to accord the child's parent a status under section 203(a)(2)(A) [8 USCS § 1153(a)(2)(A)]).

(ii) The alien's application for an immigrant visa pursuant to the approval of such petition.

(iii) The alien's application for adjustment of status under section 245 [8 USCS § 1255] pursuant to the approval of such petition.

(2) In determining whether an alien is eligible to be admitted to the United States as a nonimmigrant under section 101(a)(15)(V) [8 USCS § 1101(a)(15)(V)], the grounds for inadmissibility specified in section 212(a)(9)(B) [8 USCS § 1182(a)(9)(B)] shall not apply.

(3) The status of an alien physically present in the United States may be adjusted by the Attorney General, in the discretion of the Attorney General and under such regulations as the Attorney General may prescribe, to that of a nonimmigrant under section 101(a)(15)(V) [8 USCS § 1101(a)(15)(V)], if the alien—

(A) applies for such adjustment;

(B) satisfies the requirements of such section; and

(C) is eligible to be admitted to the United States, except in determining such admissibility, the grounds for inadmissibility specified in paragraphs (6)(A), (7), and (9)(B) of section 212(a) [8 USCS § 1182(a)] shall not apply.

(r) Visas of nonimmigrants described in8 USCS § 1101(a)(15)(K)(ii).

(1) A visa shall not be issued under the provisions of section 101(a)(15)(K)(ii) [8 USCS § 1101(a)(15)(K)(ii)] until the consular officer has received a petition filed in the United States by the spouse of the applying alien and approved by the Attorney General. The petition shall be in such form and contain such information as the Attorney General shall, by regulation, prescribe. Such information shall include information on any criminal convictions of the petitioner for any specified crime described in paragraph (5)(B) and information on any permanent protection or restraining order issued against the petitioner related to any specified crime described in subsection [paragraph] (5)(B)(i).

(2) In the case of an alien seeking admission under section 101(a)(15)(K)(ii) [8 USCS § 1101(a)(15)(K)(ii)] who concluded a marriage with a citizen of the United States outside the United States, the alien shall be considered inadmissible under section 212(a)(7)(B) [8 USCS § 1182(a)(7)(B)] if the alien is not at the time of application for admission in possession of a valid nonimmigrant visa issued by a consular officer in the foreign state in which the marriage was concluded.

(3) In the case of a nonimmigrant described in section 101(a)(15)(K)(ii) [8 USCS § 1101(a)(15)(K)(ii)], and any child of such a nonimmigrant who was admitted as accompanying, or following to join, such a nonimmigrant, the period of authorized admission shall terminate 30 days after the date on which any of the following is denied:

(A) The petition filed under section 204 [8 USCS § 1154] to accord the principal alien status under section 201(b)(2)(A)(i) [8 USCS § 1151(b)(2)(A)(i)].

(B) The principal alien's application for an immigrant visa pursuant to the approval of such petition.

(C) The principal alien's application for adjustment of status under section 245 [8 USCS § 1255] pursuant to the approval of such petition.

(4) (A) The Secretary of Homeland Security shall create a database for the purpose of tracking multiple visa petitions filed for fiancé(e)s and spouses under clauses (i) and (ii) of section 101(a)(15)(K) [8 USCS § 1101(a)(15)(K)]. Upon approval of a second visa petition under section 101(a)(15)(K) [8 USCS § 1101(a)(15)(K)] for a fiancé(e) or spouse filed by the same United States citizen petitioner, the petitioner shall be notified by the Secretary that information concerning the petitioner has been entered into the multiple visa petition tracking database. All subsequent fiancé(e)s or spouse nonimmigrant visa petitions filed by that petitioner under such section shall be entered in the database.

(B) (i) Once a petitioner has had two fiancé(e) or spousal petitions approved under clause (i) or (ii) of section 101(a)(15)(K) [8 USCS § 1101(a)(15)(K)], if a subsequent petition is filed under such section less than 10 years after the date the first visa petition was filed under such section, the Secretary of Homeland Security shall notify both the petitioner and beneficiary of any such subsequent petition about the number of previously approved fiancé(e) or spousal petitions listed in the database.

(ii) To notify the beneficiary as required by clause (i), the Secretary of Homeland Security shall provide such notice to the Secretary of State for inclusion in the mailing to the beneficiary described in section 833(a)(5)(A)(i) of the International Marriage Broker Regulation Act of 2005 (8 U.S.C. 1375a(a)(5)(A)(i)).

(5) In this subsection:

(A) The terms "domestic violence", "sexual assault", "child abuse and neglect", "dating violence", 'elder abuse", and "stalking" have the meaning given such terms in section 3 of the Violence Against Women and Department of Justice Reauthorization Act of 2005.

(B) The term "specified crime" means the following:

(i) Domestic violence, sexual assault, child abuse and neglect, dating violence, elder abuse, stalking, or an attempt to commit any such crime.

(ii) Homicide, murder, manslaughter, rape, abusive sexual contact, sexual exploitation, incest, torture, trafficking, peonage, holding hostage, involuntary servitude, slave trade, kidnapping, abduction, unlawful criminal restraint, false imprisonment, or an attempt to commit any of the crimes described in this clause.

(iii) At least three convictions for crimes relating to a controlled substance or alcohol not arising from a single act.

HISTORY: (June 27, 1952, ch 477, Title II, Ch 2, § 214, 66 Stat. 189; April 7, 1970, P. L. 91-225, § 3, 84 Stat. 117; Oct. 5, 1984, P. L. 98-454, Title VI, § 602(b), 98 Stat. 1737; Nov. 6, 1986, P. L. 99-603, Title III, Part A, § 301(b), Part B, § 313(b), 100 Stat. 3411, 3438; Nov. 10, 1986, P. L. 99-639, § 3(a), (c), 100 Stat. 3542; Sept. 28, 1988, P. L. 100-449, Title III, § 307(b), 102 Stat. 1877; Oct. 24, 1988, P. L. 100-525, § 2(l)(1), 102 Stat. 2612; Nov. 29, 1990, P. L. 101-649, Title II, Subtitle A, §§ 202(a), 205(a), (b), (c)(2), 206(b), 207(b), 104 Stat. 5014, 5019, 5023, 5025; Dec. 12, 1991, P. L. 102-232, Title II, §§ 202(a), 203(b), 204, 205(d),(e), 206(a), (c)(2), 207(a)–(c)(1), Title III, § 303(a)(10)–(12), 105 Stat. 1737, 1738, 1740, 1741; Jan. 29, 2020, P.L. 116-113, Title III, Subtitle B, § 311(b), (c) [Dec. 8, 1993, P. L. 103-182, Title III, Subtitle D, § 341(b), (c), 107 Stat. 2116]; Sept. 13, 1994, P. L. 103-322, Title XIII, § 130003(b)(2), 108 Stat. 2025; Oct. 25, 1994, P. L. 103-416, Title II, § 220(b), 108 Stat. 4319; Sept. 30, 1996, P. L. 104-208, Div C, Title III, Subtitle A, § 308(e)(1)(D), (2)(B), (f)(1)(G), (H), (3)(B), (g)(5)(A)(i), (7)(A), Title VI, Subtitle B, §§ 621, 622(c), 625(a)(1), Subtitle E, § 671(a)(3)(A), (e)(4)(A), 110 Stat. 3009-619, 3009-620, 3009-621, 3009-623, 3009-695, 3009-699, 3009-721, 3009-723; Oct. 27, 1997, P. L. 105-65, Title I, § 108, 111 Stat. 1350; Oct. 21, 1998, P. L. 105-277, Div C, Title IV, Subtitle A, §§ 411(a), 414(a), 112 Stat. 2681-642, 2681-651; Nov. 13, 1999, P. L. 106-104, § 2, 113 Stat. 1483; Oct. 17, 2000, P. L. 106-311, § 1, 114 Stat. 1247; Oct. 17, 2000, P. L. 106-313, Title I, §§ 102(a), 103, 105(a), 108, 114 Stat. 1251–1253, 1255; Oct. 28, 2000, P. L. 106-386, Div A, § 107(e)(2), Div B, Title V, § 1513(c), 114 Stat. 1478, 1535; P. L. 106-396, Title IV, § 401, 114 Stat. 1647; Dec. 21, 2000, P. L. 106-553, § 1(a)(2), 114 Stat. 2762; Oct. 1, 2001, P. L. 107-45, § 1, 115 Stat. 258; Jan. 16, 2002, P. L. 107-124, 115 Stat. 2402; Jan. 16, 2002, P. L. 107-125, §§ 1, 2(a), 115 Stat. 2403; Nov. 2, 2002, P. L. 107-273, Div C, Title I, Subtitle A, § 11018(a), 116 Stat. 1825; Nov. 2, 2002, P. L. 107-274, § 2(c), 116 Stat. 1923; Sept. 3, 2003, P. L. 108-77, Title IV, §§ 402(a)(2), (d)(1), 403, 404, 117 Stat. 940, 946; Sept. 3, 2003, P. L. 108-78, Title IV, § 402, 117 Stat. 970; Dec. 19, 2003, P. L. 108-193, §§ 4(b)(2), 8(a)(3), 117 Stat. 2878, 2886; Dec. 3, 2004, P. L. 108-441, § 1(b)–(d), 118 Stat. 2630; Dec. 8, 2004, P. L. 108-447, Div J, Title IV, Subtitle A, §§ 412(a), 413(a), Subtitle B, §§ 422(b), 425(a), 426(a), 118 Stat. 3351, 3352, 3353, 3356, 3357; May 11, 2005, P. L. 109-13, Div B, Title IV, §§ 402(a), 403(a), 404(a), 405, Title V, § 501(b), (c), 119 Stat. 318, 319, 320, 321; Jan. 5, 2006, P. L. 109-162, Title VIII, Subtitle C, § 821(a), (b), (c)(2), Subtitle D, § 832(a)(1), (2), 119 Stat. 3062, 3066; Oct. 17, 2006, P. L. 109-364, Div A, Title X, Subtitle H, § 1074(a), 120 Stat. 2403; Dec. 22, 2006, P. L. 109-463, § 2, 120 Stat. 3477; May 8, 2008, P. L. 110-229, Title VII, Subtitle A, § 702(b)(1), 122 Stat. 860; Oct. 8, 2008, P. L. 110-362, § 2, 122 Stat. 4013; Dec. 23, 2008, P. L. 110-457, Title II, Subtitle A, § 201(b), (c), 122 Stat. 5053; March 7, 2013, P. L. 113-4, Title VIII, §§ 805(a), 807(a), 127 Stat. 111, 112; Dec. 18, 2015, P. L. 114-113, Div F, Title V, § 565, 129 Stat. 2523; Jan. 29, 2020, P.L. 116-113, Title V, § 503(b)(1)–(3), (c), 134 Stat. 71.)

§ 215. [8 U.S.C. § 1185] Travel control of citizens and aliens.

(a) Restrictions and prohibitions. Unless otherwise ordered by the President, it shall be unlawful—

(1) for any alien to depart from or enter or attempt to depart from or enter the United States except under such reasonable rules, regulations, and orders, and subject to such limitations and exceptions as the President may prescribe;

(2) for any person to transport or attempt to transport from or into the United States another person with knowledge or reasonable cause to believe that the departure or entry of such other person is forbidden by this section;

(3) for any person knowingly to make any false statement in an application for permission to depart from or enter the United States with intent to induce or secure the granting of such permission either for himself or for another;

(4) for any person knowingly to furnish or attempt to furnish or assist in furnishing to another a permit or evidence of permission to depart or enter not issued and designed for such other person's use;

(5) for any person knowingly to use or attempt to use any permit or evidence of permission to depart or enter not issued and designed for his use;

(6) for any person to forge, counterfeit, mutilate, or alter, or cause or procure to be forged, counterfeited, mutilated, or altered, any permit or evidence of permission to depart from or enter the United States;

(7) for any person knowingly to use or attempt to use or furnish to another for use any false, forged, counterfeited, mutilated, or altered permit, or evidence of permission, or any permit or evidence of permission which, though originally valid, has become or been made void or invalid.

(b) Citizens. Except as otherwise provided by the President and subject to such limitations and exceptions as the President may authorize and prescribe, it shall be unlawful for any citizen of the United States to depart from or enter, or attempt to depart from or enter, the United States unless he bears a valid United States passport.

(c) Definitions. The term "United States" as used in this section includes the Canal Zone, and all territory and waters, continental or insular, subject to the jurisdiction of the United States. The term "person" as used in this section shall be deemed to mean any individual, partnership, association, company, or other incorporated body of individuals, or corporation, or body politic.

(d) Nonadmission of certain aliens. Nothing in this section shall be construed to entitle an alien to whom a permit to enter the United States has been issued to enter the United States, if, upon arrival in the United States, he is found to be inadmissible under any of the provisions of this Act, or any other law, relating to the entry of aliens into the United States.

(e) Revocation of proclamation as affecting penalties. The revocation of any rule, regulation, or order issued in pursuance of this section shall not prevent prosecution for any offense committed, or the imposition of any penalties or forfeitures, liability for which was incurred under this section prior to the revocation of such rule, regulation, or order.

(f) Permits to enter. Passports, visas, reentry permits, and other documents required for entry under this Act may be considered as permits to enter for the purposes of this section.

HISTORY: (June 27, 1952, ch 477, Title II, Ch 2, § 215, 66 Stat. 190; Oct. 7, 1978, P. L. 95-426, Title VII, § 707(a)–(d), 92 Stat. 993; Oct. 25, 1994, P. L. 103-416, Title II, § 204(a), 108 Stat. 4311.)

§ 216. [8 U.S.C. § 1186a] Conditional permanent resident status for certain alien spouses and sons and daughters.

(a) In general.

(1) Conditional basis for status. Notwithstanding any other provision of this Act, an alien spouse (as defined in subsection (h)(1)) and an alien son or daughter (as defined in subsection (h)(2)) shall be considered, at the time of obtaining the status of an alien lawfully admitted for permanent residence, to have obtained such status on a conditional basis subject to the provisions of this section.

(2) Notice of requirements.

(A) At time of obtaining permanent residence. At the time an alien spouse or alien son or daughter obtains permanent resident status on a conditional basis under paragraph (1), the Secretary of Homeland Security shall provide for notice to such a spouse, son, or daughter respecting the provisions of this section and the requirements of subsection (c)(1) to have the conditional basis of such status removed.

(B) At time of required petition. In addition, the Secretary of Homeland Security shall attempt to provide notice to such a spouse, son, or daughter, at or about the beginning of the 90-day period described in subsection (d)(2)(A), of the requirements of subsections [subsection] (c)(1).

(C) Effect of failure to provide notice. The failure of the Secretary of Homeland Security to provide a notice under this paragraph shall not affect the enforcement of the provisions of this section with respect to such a spouse, son, or daughter.

(b) Termination of status if finding that qualifying marriage improper.

(1) In general. In the case of an alien with permanent resident status on a conditional basis under subsection (a), if the Secretary of Homeland Security determines, before the second anniversary of the alien's obtaining the status of lawful admission for permanent residence, that—

(A) the qualifying marriage—

(i) was entered into for the purpose of procuring an alien's admission as an immigrant, or

(ii) has been judicially annulled or terminated, other than through the death of a spouse; or

(B) a fee or other consideration was given (other than a fee or other consideration to an attorney for assistance in preparation of a lawful petition) for the filing of a petition under section 204(a) [8 USCS § 1154(a)] or subsection (d) or (p) of section 214 [8 USCS § 1184] with respect to the alien;

the Secretary of Homeland Security shall so notify the parties involved and, subject to paragraph (2), shall terminate the permanent resident status of the alien (or aliens) involved as of the date of the determination.

(2) Hearing in removal proceeding. Any alien whose permanent resident status is terminated under paragraph (1) may request a review of such determination in a proceeding to remove the alien. In such proceeding, the burden of proof shall be on the Secretary of Homeland Security to establish, by a preponderance of the evidence, that a condition described in paragraph (1) is met.

(c) Requirements of timely petition and interview for removal of condition.

(1) In general. In order for the conditional basis established under subsection (a) for an alien spouse or an alien son or daughter to be removed—

(A) the alien spouse and the petitioning spouse (if not deceased) jointly must submit to the Secretary of Homeland Security, during the period described in subsection (d)(2), a petition which requests the removal of such conditional basis and which states, under penalty of perjury, the facts and information described in subsection (d)(1), and

(B) in accordance with subsection (d)(3), the alien spouse and the petitioning spouse (if not deceased) must appear for a personal interview before an officer or employee of the Department of Homeland Security respecting the facts and information described in subsection (d)(1).

(2) Termination of permanent resident status for failure to file petition or have personal interview.

(A) In general. In the case of an alien with permanent resident status on a conditional basis under subsection (a), if—

(i) no petition is filed with respect to the alien in accordance with the provisions of paragraph (1)(A), or

(ii) unless there is good cause shown, the alien spouse and petitioning spouse fail to appear at the interview described in paragraph (1)(B),

the Secretary of Homeland Security shall terminate the permanent resident status of the alien as of the second anniversary of the alien's lawful admission for permanent residence.

(B) Hearing in removal proceeding. In any removal proceeding with respect to an alien whose permanent resident status is terminated under subparagraph (A), the burden of proof shall be on the alien to establish compliance with the conditions of paragraphs (1)(A) and (1)(B).

(3) Determination after petition and interview.

(A) In general. If—

(i) a petition is filed in accordance with the provisions of paragraph (1)(A), and

(ii) the alien spouse and petitioning spouse appear at the interview described in paragraph (1)(B),

the Secretary of Homeland Security shall make a determination, within 90 days of the date of the interview, as to whether the facts and information described in subsection (d)(1) and alleged in the petition are true with respect to the qualifying marriage.

(B) Removal of conditional basis if favorable determination. If the Secretary of Homeland Security determines that such facts and information are true, the Secretary of Homeland Security shall so notify the parties involved and shall remove the conditional basis of the parties effective as of the second anniversary of the alien's obtaining the status of lawful admission for permanent residence.

(C) Termination if adverse determination. If the Secretary of Homeland Security determines that such facts and information are not true, the Secretary of

Homeland Security shall so notify the parties involved and, subject to subparagraph (D), shall terminate the permanent resident status of an alien spouse or an alien son or daughter as of the date of the determination.

(D) Hearing in removal proceeding. Any alien whose permanent resident status is terminated under subparagraph (C) may request a review of such determination in a proceeding to remove the alien. In such proceeding, the burden of proof shall be on the Secretary of Homeland Security to establish, by a preponderance of the evidence, that the facts and information described in subsection (d)(1) and alleged in the petition are not true with respect to the qualifying marriage.

(4) Hardship waiver. The Secretary of Homeland Security, in the Secretary's discretion, may remove the conditional basis of the permanent resident status for an alien who fails to meet the requirements of paragraph (1) if the alien demonstrates that —

(A) extreme hardship would result if such alien is removed;

(B) the qualifying marriage was entered into in good faith by the alien spouse, but the qualifying marriage has been terminated (other than through the death of the spouse) and the alien was not at fault in failing to meet the requirements of paragraph (1); or

(C) the qualifying marriage was entered into in good faith by the alien spouse and during the marriage the alien spouse or child was battered by or was the subject of extreme cruelty perpetrated by his or her spouse or citizen or permanent resident parent and the alien was not at fault in failing to meet the requirements of paragraph (1); or

(D) the alien meets the requirements under section 204(a)(1)(A)(iii)(II)(aa)(BB) [8 USCS § 1154(a)(1)(A)(iii)(II)(aa)(BB)] and following the marriage ceremony was battered by or subject to extreme cruelty perpetrated by the alien's intended spouse and was not at fault in failing to meet the requirements of paragraph (1).

In determining extreme hardship, the Secretary of Homeland Security shall consider circumstances occurring only during the period that the alien was admitted for permanent residence on a conditional basis. In acting on applications under this paragraph, the Secretary shall consider any credible evidence relevant to the application. The determination of what evidence is credible and the weight to be given that evidence shall be within the sole discretion of the Secretary. The Secretary shall, by regulation, establish measures to protect the confidentiality of information concerning any abused alien spouse or child, including information regarding the whereabouts of such spouse or child.

(d) Details of petition and interview.

(1) Contents of petition. Each petition under subsection (c)(1)(A) shall contain the following facts and information:

(A) Statement of proper marriage and petitioning process. The facts are that—

(i) the qualifying marriage—

(I) was entered into in accordance with the laws of the place where the marriage took place,

(II) has not been judicially annulled or terminated, other than through the death of a spouse, and

(III) was not entered into for the purpose of procuring an alien's admission as an immigrant; and

(ii) no fee or other consideration was given (other than a fee or other consideration to an attorney for assistance in preparation of a lawful petition) for the filing of a petition under section 204(a) [8 USCS § 1154(a)] or subsection (d) or (p) of section 214 [8 USCS § 1184] with respect to the alien spouse or alien son or daughter.

(B) Statement of additional information. The information is a statement of—

(i) the actual residence of each party to the qualifying marriage since the date the alien spouse obtained permanent resident status on a conditional basis under subsection (a), and

(ii) the place of employment (if any) of each such party since such date, and the name of the employer of such party.

(2) Period for filing petition.

(A) 90-day period before second anniversary. Except as provided in subparagraph (B), the petition under subsection (c)(1)(A) must be filed during the 90-day period before the second anniversary of the alien's obtaining the status of lawful admission for permanent residence.

(B) Date petitions for good cause. Such a petition may be considered if filed after such date, but only if the alien establishes to the satisfaction of the Secretary of Homeland Security good cause and extenuating circumstances for failure to file the petition during the period described in subparagraph (A).

(C) Filing of petitions during removal. In the case of an alien who is the subject of removal hearings as a result of failure to file a petition on a timely basis in accordance with subparagraph (A), the Secretary of Homeland Security may stay such removal proceedings against an alien pending the filing of the petition under subparagraph (B).

(3) Personal interview. The interview under subsection (c)(1)(B) shall be conducted within 90 days after the date of submitting a petition under subsection (c)(1)(A) and at a local office of the Department of Homeland Security, designated by the Secretary of Homeland Security, which is convenient to the parties involved. The Secretary of Homeland Security, in the Secretary's discretion, may waive the deadline for such an interview or the requirement for such an interview in such cases as may be appropriate.

(e) Treatment of period for purposes of naturalization. For purposes of title III, in the case of an alien who is in the United States as a lawful permanent resident on a conditional basis under this section, the alien shall be considered to have been admitted as an alien lawfully admitted for permanent residence and to be in the United States as an alien lawfully admitted to the United States for permanent residence.

(f) Treatment of certain waivers. In the case of an alien who has permanent residence status on a conditional basis under this section, if, in order to obtain such status, the alien obtained a waiver under subsection (h) or (i) of section 212 [8 USCS § 1182(h) or (i)] of certain grounds of inadmissibility, such waiver terminates upon the termination of such permanent residence status under this section.

(g) Service in Armed Forces.

(1) Filing petition. The 90-day period described in subsection (d)(2)(A) shall be tolled during any period of time in which the alien spouse or petitioning spouse is a member of the Armed Forces of the United States and serving abroad in an active-duty status in the Armed Forces, except that, at the option of the petitioners, the petition may be filed during such active-duty service at any time after the commencement of such 90-day period.

(2) Personal interview. The 90-day period described in the first sentence of subsection (d)(3) shall be tolled during any period of time in which the alien spouse or petitioning spouse is a member of the Armed Forces of the United States and serving abroad in an active-duty status in the Armed Forces, except that nothing in this paragraph shall be construed to prohibit the Secretary of Homeland Security from waiving the requirement for an interview under subsection (c)(1)(B) pursuant to the Secretary's authority under the second sentence of subsection (d)(3).

(h) Definitions. In this section:

(1) The term "alien spouse" means an alien who obtains the status of an alien lawfully admitted for permanent residence (whether on a conditional basis or otherwise)—

(A) as an immediate relative (described in section 201(b) [8 USCS § 1151(b)]) as the spouse of a citizen of the United States,

(B) under section 214(d) [8 USCS § 1184(d)] as the fiancee or fiance of a citizen of the United States, or

(C) under section 203(a)(2) [8 USCS § 1153(a)(2)] as the spouse of an alien lawfully admitted for permanent residence, residence,

by virtue of a marriage which was entered into less than 24 months before the date the alien obtains such status by virtue of such marriage, but does not include such an alien who only obtains such status as a result of section 203(d) [8 USCS § 1153(d)].

(2) The term "alien son or daughter" means an alien who obtains the status of an alien lawfully admitted for permanent residence (whether on a conditional basis or otherwise) by virtue of being the son or daughter of an individual through a qualifying marriage.

(3) The term "qualifying marriage" means the marriage described to in paragraph (1).

(4) The term "petitioning spouse" means the spouse of a qualifying marriage, other than the alien.

HISTORY: (June 27, 1952, ch 477, Title II, Ch 2, § 216, as added Nov. 10, 1986, P. L. 99-639, § 2(a), 100 Stat. 3537; Oct. 24, 1988, P. L. 100-525, § 7(a), 102 Stat. 2616; Nov. 29, 1990, P. L. 101-649, Title VII, § 701(a), 104 Stat. 5085; Dec. 12, 1991, P. L. 102-232, Title III, § 302(e)(8)(B), 105 Stat. 1746; Sept. 13, 1994, P. L. 103-322, Title IV, Subtitle G, § 40702(a), 108 Stat. 1955; Sept. 30, 1996, P. L. 104-208, Div C, Title III, Subtitle A, § 308(d)(4)(E), (e)(7), (f)(1)(I), (J), 110 Stat. 3009-618, 3009-620, 3009-621; Dec. 21, 2000, P. L. 106-553, § 1(a)(2), 114 Stat. 2762; Nov. 23, 2011, P. L. 112-58, § 1, 125 Stat. 747; March 7, 2013, P. L. 113-4, Title VIII, § 806, 127 Stat. 112.)

§ 216A. [8 U.S.C. § 1186b] Conditional permanent resident status for certain alien entrepreneurs, spouses, and children [Effective until March 15, 2024].

(a) In general.

(1) Conditional basis for status. An alien investor, alien spouse, and alien child shall be considered, at the time of obtaining status as an alien lawfully admitted for permanent residence, to have obtained such status on a conditional basis subject to the provisions of this section.

(2) Notice of requirements.

(A) At time of obtaining permanent residence. At the time an alien investor, alien spouse, or alien child obtains permanent resident status on a conditional basis under paragraph (1), the Secretary of Homeland Security shall provide for notice to such an investor, spouse, or child respecting the provisions of this section and the requirements of subsection (c)(1) to have the conditional basis of such status removed.

(B) At time of required petition. In addition, the Secretary of Homeland Security shall attempt to provide notice to such an investor, spouse, or child, at or about the beginning of the 90-day period described in subsection (d)(2)(A), of the requirements of subsection (c)(1).

(C) Effect of failure to provide notice. The failure of the Secretary of Homeland Security to provide a notice under this paragraph shall not affect the enforcement of the provisions of this section with respect to such an investor, spouse, or child.

(b) Termination of status if finding that qualifying investment improper.

(1) In general. In the case of an alien investor with permanent resident status on a conditional basis under subsection (a), if the Secretary of Homeland Security determines, before the second anniversary of the alien's obtaining the status of lawful admission for permanent residence, that—

(A) the investment in the commercial enterprise was intended solely as a means of evading the immigration laws of the United States,

(B) the alien did not invest the requisite capital; or

(C) the alien was otherwise not conforming to the requirements of section 203(b)(5) [8 USCS § 1153(b)(5)],

then the Secretary of Homeland Security shall so notify the alien involved and, subject to paragraph (2), shall terminate the permanent resident status of the alien (and the alien spouse and alien child) involved as of the date of the determination.

(2) Hearing in removal proceeding. Any alien whose permanent resident status is terminated under paragraph (1) may request a review of such determination in a proceeding to remove the alien. In such proceeding, the burden of proof shall be on the Secretary of Homeland Security to establish, by a preponderance of the evidence, that a condition described in paragraph (1) is met.

(c) Requirements for removal of condition.

(1) In general. Except as provided in paragraph (3)(D), in order for the conditional basis established un-

der subsection (a) for an alien investor, alien spouse, or alien child to be removed—

(A) the alien investor shall submit to the Secretary of Homeland Security, during the period described in subsection (d)(2), a petition which requests the removal of such conditional basis and which states, under penalty of perjury, the facts and information described in subsection (d)(1);

(B) in accordance with subsection (d)(3), the alien investor shall appear for a personal interview before an officer or employee of the Department of Homeland Security respecting the facts and information described in subsection (d)(1); and

(2) Termination of permanent resident status for failure to file petition or have personal interview.

(A) In general. In the case of an alien with permanent resident status on a conditional basis under subsection (a), if—

(i) no petition is filed with respect to the alien in accordance with the provisions of paragraph (1)(A), or

(ii) unless there is good cause shown, the alien investor fails to appear at the interview described in paragraph (1)(B) (if required under subsection (d)(3)),

the Secretary of Homeland Security shall terminate the permanent resident status of the alien (and the alien's spouse and children if it was obtained on a conditional basis under this section or section 216 [8 USCS § 1186a]) as of the second anniversary of the alien's lawful admission for permanent residence.

(B) Hearing in removal proceeding. In any removal proceeding with respect to an alien whose permanent resident status is terminated under subparagraph (A), the burden of proof shall be on the alien to establish compliance with the conditions of paragraphs (1)(A) and (1)(B).

(3) Determination after petition and interview.

(A) In general. If—

(i) a petition is filed in accordance with the provisions of paragraph (1)(A), and

(ii) the alien investor appears at any interview described in paragraph (1)(B),

the Secretary of Homeland Security shall make a determination, within 90 days of the date of such filing or interview (whichever is later), as to whether the facts and information described in subsection (d)(1) and alleged in the petition are true with respect to the qualifying commercial enterprise.

(B) Removal or extension of conditional basis.

(i) In general. Except as provided in clause (ii), if the Secretary determines that the facts and information contained in a petition submitted under paragraph (1)(A) are true, including demonstrating that the alien complied with subsection (d)(1)(B)(i), the Secretary shall—

(I) notify the alien involved of such determination; and

(II) remove the conditional basis of the alien's status effective as of the second anniversary of the alien's lawful admission for permanent residence.

(ii) Exception. If the petition demonstrates that the facts and information are true and that the alien is in compliance with subsection (d)(1)(B)(ii)—

(I) the Secretary, in the Secretary's discretion, may provide a 1-year extension of the alien's conditional status; and

(II) (aa) if the alien files a petition not later than 30 days after the third anniversary of the alien's lawful admission for permanent residence demonstrating that the alien complied with subsection (d)(1)(B)(i), the Secretary shall remove the conditional basis of the alien's status effective as of such third anniversary; or

(bb) if the alien does not file the petition described in item (aa), the conditional status shall terminate at the end of such additional year.

(C) Termination if adverse determination. If the Secretary of Homeland Security determines that such facts and information are not true, the Secretary of Homeland Security shall so notify the alien involved and, subject to subparagraph (D), shall terminate the permanent resident status of an alien investor, alien spouse, or alien child as of the date of the determination.

(D) Hearing in removal proceeding. Any alien whose permanent resident status is terminated under subparagraph (C) may request a review of such determination in a proceeding to remove the alien. In such proceeding, the burden of proof shall be on the Secretary of Homeland Security to establish, by a preponderance of the evidence, that the facts and information described in subsection (d)(1) and alleged in the petition are not true with respect to the qualifying commercial enterprise.

(d) Details of petition and interview.

(1) Contents of petition. Each petition under subsection (c)(1)(A) shall contain facts and information demonstrating that the alien—

(A) invested the requisite capital;

(B) (i) created the employment required under section 203(b)(5)(A)(ii) [8 USCS § 1153(b)(5)(A)(ii)]; or

(ii) is actively in the process of creating the employment required under section 203(b)(5)(A)(ii) [8 USCS § 1153(b)(5)(A)(ii)] and will create such employment before the third anniversary of the alien's lawful admission for permanent residence, provided that such alien's capital will remain invested during such time; and

(C) is otherwise conforming to the requirements of section 203(b)(5) [8 USCS § 1153(b)(5)].

(2) Period for filing petition.

(A) Ninety-day period before second anniversary.

(i) In general. Except as provided in clause (ii) and subparagraph (B), a petition under subsection (c)(1)(A) shall be filed during the 90-day period immediately preceding the second anniversary of the alien investor's lawful admission for permanent residence.

(ii) Exception. Aliens described in subclauses (I)(bb) and (II) of section 203(b)(5)(M)(ii) [8 USCS § 1153(b)(5)(M)(ii)] shall file a petition under subsection (c)(1)(A) during the 90-day period before the second anniversary of the subsequent investment.

(B) Date petitions for good cause. Such a petition may be considered if filed after such date, but only if the alien establishes to the satisfaction of the Secretary of Homeland Security good cause and extenuating circumstances for failure to file the petition during the period described in subparagraph (A).

(C) Filing of petitions during deportation. In the case of an alien who is the subject of removal hearings as a result of failure to file a petition on a timely basis in accordance with subparagraph (A), the Attorney General may stay such removal proceedings against an alien pending the filing of the petition under subparagraph (B).

(3) Personal interview.

(A) In general. The interview under subsection (c)(1)(B) shall be conducted within 90 days after the date of submitting a petition under subsection (c)(1)(A) and at a local office of the Department of Homeland Security, designated by the Secretary of Homeland Security, which is convenient to the parties involved.

(B) Waiver. The Secretary of Homeland Security, in the Secretary's discretion, may waive the deadline for an interview under subsection (c)(1)(B) or the requirement for such an interview according to criteria developed by U.S. Citizenship and Immigration Services, in consultation with its Fraud Detection and National Security Directorate and U.S. Immigration and Customs Enforcement, provided that such criteria do not include a reduction of case processing times or the allocation of adjudicatory resources. A waiver may not be granted under this subparagraph if the alien to be interviewed—

(i) invested in a regional center, new commercial enterprise, or job-creating entity that was sanctioned under section 203(b)(5) [8 USCS § 1153(b)(5)]; or

(ii) is in a class of aliens determined by the Secretary to be threats to public safety or national security.

(e) Treatment of period for purposes of naturalization. For purposes of title III, in the case of an alien who is in the United States as a lawful permanent resident on a conditional basis under this section, the alien shall be considered to have been admitted as an alien lawfully admitted for permanent residence and to be in the United States as an alien lawfully admitted to the United States for permanent residence.

(f) Definitions. In this section:

(1) The term "alien investor" means an alien who obtains the status of an alien lawfully admitted for permanent residence (whether on a conditional basis or otherwise) under section 203(b)(5) [8 USCS § 1153(b)(5)].

(2) The term "alien spouse" and the term "alien child" mean an alien who obtains the status of an alien lawfully admitted for permanent residence (whether on a conditional basis or otherwise) by virtue of being the spouse or child, respectively, of an alien investor.

(3) The term "commercial enterprise" includes any entity formed for the purpose of doing for profit business.

HISTORY: (June 27, 1952, ch 466, Title II, Ch 2, § 216A, as added Nov. 29, 1990, P. L. 101-649, Title I, Subtitle B, Part 2, § 121(b)(1), 104 Stat. 4990; Dec. 12, 1991, P. L. 102-232, Title III, ' 302(b)(3), 105 Stat. 1743; Sept. 30, 1996, P. L. 104-208, Div C, Title III, Subtitle A, § 308(e)(8), 110 Stat. 3009-620; Nov. 2, 2002, P. L. 107-273, Div C, Title I, Subtitle B, Ch. 2, § 11036(b), 116 Stat. 1847; Mar. 15, 2022, P.L. 117-103, Div BB, § 104(a)(1)–(5)(B)(iii), (C)–(7), 136 Stat. 1100—1102.)

§ 216A. [8 U.S.C. § 1186b] Conditional permanent resident status for certain alien entrepreneurs, spouses, and children [Effective March 15, 2024].

(a) In general.

(1) Conditional basis for status. An alien investor, alien spouse, and alien child shall be considered, at the time of obtaining status as an alien lawfully admitted for permanent residence, to have obtained such status on a conditional basis subject to the provisions of this section.

(2) Notice of requirements.

(A) At time of obtaining permanent residence. At the time an alien investor, alien spouse, or alien child obtains permanent resident status on a conditional basis under paragraph (1), the Secretary of Homeland Security shall provide for notice to such an investor, spouse, or child respecting the provisions of this section and the requirements of subsection (c)(1) to have the conditional basis of such status removed.

(B) At time of required petition. In addition, the Secretary of Homeland Security shall attempt to provide notice to such an investor, spouse, or child, at or about the beginning of the 90-day period described in subsection (d)(2)(A), of the requirements of subsection (c)(1).

(C) Effect of failure to provide notice. The failure of the Secretary of Homeland Security to provide a notice under this paragraph shall not affect the enforcement of the provisions of this section with respect to such an investor, spouse, or child.

(b) Termination of status if finding that qualifying investment improper.

(1) In general. In the case of an alien investor with permanent resident status on a conditional basis under subsection (a), if the Secretary of Homeland Security determines, before the second anniversary of the alien's obtaining the status of lawful admission for permanent residence, that—

(A) the investment in the commercial enterprise was intended solely as a means of evading the immigration laws of the United States,

(B) the alien did not invest the requisite capital; or

(C) the alien was otherwise not conforming to the requirements of section 203(b)(5) [8 USCS § 1153(b)(5)],

then the Secretary of Homeland Security shall so notify the alien involved and, subject to paragraph (2), shall terminate the permanent resident status of the alien (and the alien spouse and alien child) involved as of the date of the determination.

(2) Hearing in removal proceeding. Any alien whose permanent resident status is terminated under paragraph (1) may request a review of such determination in a proceeding to remove the alien. In such proceeding, the burden of proof shall be on the Secretary of Homeland Security to establish, by a preponderance of the evidence, that a condition described in paragraph (1) is met.

(c) Requirements for removal of condition.

(1) In general. Except as provided in paragraph (3)(D), in order for the conditional basis established under subsection (a) for an alien investor, alien spouse, or alien child to be removed—

(A) the alien investor shall submit to the Secretary of Homeland Security, during the period described in subsection (d)(2), a petition which requests the removal of such conditional basis and which states, under penalty of perjury, the facts and information described in subsection (d)(1);

(B) in accordance with subsection (d)(3), the alien investor shall appear for a personal interview before an officer or employee of the Department of Homeland Security respecting the facts and information described in subsection (d)(1); and

(C) the Secretary shall have performed a site visit to the relevant corporate office or business location described in section 203(b)(5)(F)(iv) [8 USCS § 1153(b)(5)(F)(iv)].

(2) Termination of permanent resident status for failure to file petition or have personal interview.

(A) In general. In the case of an alien with permanent resident status on a conditional basis under subsection (a), if—

(i) no petition is filed with respect to the alien in accordance with the provisions of paragraph (1)(A), or

(ii) unless there is good cause shown, the alien investor fails to appear at the interview described in paragraph (1)(B) (if required under subsection (d)(3)),

the Secretary of Homeland Security shall terminate the permanent resident status of the alien (and the alien's spouse and children if it was obtained on a conditional basis under this section or section 216 [8 USCS § 1186a]) as of the second anniversary of the alien's lawful admission for permanent residence.

(B) Hearing in removal proceeding. In any removal proceeding with respect to an alien whose permanent resident status is terminated under subparagraph (A), the burden of proof shall be on the alien to establish compliance with the conditions of paragraphs (1)(A) and (1)(B).

(3) Determination after petition and interview.

(A) In general. If—

(i) a petition is filed in accordance with the provisions of paragraph (1)(A), and

(ii) the alien investor appears at any interview described in paragraph (1)(B),

the Secretary of Homeland Security shall make a determination, within 90 days of the date of such filing or interview (whichever is later), as to whether the facts and information described in subsection (d)(1) and alleged in the petition are true with respect to the qualifying commercial enterprise.

(B) Removal or extension of conditional basis.

(i) In general. Except as provided in clause (ii), if the Secretary determines that the facts and information contained in a petition submitted under paragraph (1)(A) are true, including demonstrating that the alien complied with subsection (d)(1)(B)(i), the Secretary shall—

(I) notify the alien involved of such determination; and

(II) remove the conditional basis of the alien's status effective as of the second anniversary of the alien's lawful admission for permanent residence.

(ii) Exception. If the petition demonstrates that the facts and information are true and that the alien is in compliance with subsection (d)(1)(B)(ii)—

(I) the Secretary, in the Secretary's discretion, may provide a 1-year extension of the alien's conditional status; and

(II) (aa) if the alien files a petition not later than 30 days after the third anniversary of the alien's lawful admission for permanent residence demonstrating that the alien complied with subsection (d)(1)(B)(i), the Secretary shall remove the conditional basis of the alien's status effective as of such third anniversary; or

(bb) if the alien does not file the petition described in item (aa), the conditional status shall terminate at the end of such additional year.

(C) Termination if adverse determination. If the Secretary of Homeland Security determines that such facts and information are not true, the Secretary of Homeland Security shall so notify the alien involved and, subject to subparagraph (D), shall terminate the permanent resident status of an alien investor, alien spouse, or alien child as of the date of the determination.

(D) Hearing in removal proceeding. Any alien whose permanent resident status is terminated under subparagraph (C) may request a review of such determination in a proceeding to remove the alien. In such proceeding, the burden of proof shall be on the Secretary of Homeland Security to establish, by a preponderance of the evidence, that the facts and information described in subsection (d)(1) and alleged in the petition are not true with respect to the qualifying commercial enterprise.

(d) Details of petition and interview.

(1) Contents of petition. Each petition under subsection (c)(1)(A) shall contain facts and information demonstrating that the alien—

(A) invested the requisite capital;

(B) (i) created the employment required under section 203(b)(5)(A)(ii) [8 USCS § 1153(b)(5)(A)(ii)]; or

(ii) is actively in the process of creating the employment required under section 203(b)(5)(A)(ii) [8 USCS § 1153(b)(5)(A)(ii)] and will create such employment before the third anniversary of the alien's lawful admission for permanent residence, provided that such alien's capital will remain invested during such time; and

(C) is otherwise conforming to the requirements of section 203(b)(5) [8 USCS § 1153(b)(5)].

(2) Period for filing petition.

(A) Ninety-day period before second anniversary.

(i) In general. Except as provided in clause (ii) and subparagraph (B), a petition under subsection (c)(1)(A) shall be filed during the 90-day period immediately preceding the second anniversary of the alien investor's lawful admission for permanent residence.

(ii) Exception. Aliens described in subclauses (I)(bb) and (II) of section 203(b)(5)(M)(ii) [8 USCS § 1153(b)(5)(M)(ii)] shall file a petition under subsection (c)(1)(A) during the 90-day period before the second anniversary of the subsequent investment.

(B) Date petitions for good cause. Such a petition may be considered if filed after such date, but only if the alien establishes to the satisfaction of the Secretary of Homeland Security good cause and extenuating circumstances for failure to file the petition during the period described in subparagraph (A).

(C) Filing of petitions during deportation. In the case of an alien who is the subject of removal hearings as a result of failure to file a petition on a timely basis in accordance with subparagraph (A), the Attorney General may stay such removal proceedings against an alien pending the filing of the petition under subparagraph (B).

(3) Personal interview.

(A) In general. The interview under subsection (c)(1)(B) shall be conducted within 90 days after the date of submitting a petition under subsection (c)(1)(A) and at a local office of the Department of Homeland Security, designated by the Secretary of Homeland Security, which is convenient to the parties involved.

(B) Waiver. The Secretary of Homeland Security, in the Secretary's discretion, may waive the deadline for an interview under subsection (c)(1)(B) or the requirement for such an interview according to criteria developed by U.S. Citizenship and Immigration Services, in consultation with its Fraud Detection and National Security Directorate and U.S. Immigration and Customs Enforcement, provided that such criteria do not include a reduction of case processing times or the allocation of adjudicatory resources. A waiver may not be granted under this subparagraph if the alien to be interviewed—

(i) invested in a regional center, new commercial enterprise, or job-creating entity that was sanctioned under section 203(b)(5) [8 USCS § 1153(b)(5)]; or

(ii) is in a class of aliens determined by the Secretary to be threats to public safety or national security.

(e) Treatment of period for purposes of naturalization. For purposes of title III, in the case of an alien who is in the United States as a lawful permanent resident on a conditional basis under this section, the alien shall be considered to have been admitted as an alien lawfully admitted for permanent residence and to be in the United States as an alien lawfully admitted to the United States for permanent residence.

(f) Definitions. In this section:

(1) The term "alien investor" means an alien who obtains the status of an alien lawfully admitted for permanent residence (whether on a conditional basis or otherwise) under section 203(b)(5) [8 USCS § 1153(b)(5)].

(2) The term "alien spouse" and the term "alien child" mean an alien who obtains the status of an alien lawfully admitted for permanent residence (whether on a conditional basis or otherwise) by virtue of being the spouse or child, respectively, of an alien investor.

(3) The term "commercial enterprise" includes any entity formed for the purpose of doing for profit business.

HISTORY: (June 27, 1952, ch 466, Title II, Ch 2, § 216A, as added Nov. 29, 1990, P. L. 101-649, Title I, Subtitle B, Part 2, § 121(b)(1), 104 Stat. 4990; Dec. 12, 1991, P. L. 102-232, Title III, ' 302(b)(3), 105 Stat. 1743; Sept. 30, 1996, P. L. 104-208, Div C, Title III, Subtitle A, § 308(e)(8), 110 Stat. 3009-620; Nov. 2, 2002, P. L. 107-273, Div C, Title I, Subtitle B, Ch. 2, § 11036(b), 116 Stat. 1847; Mar. 15, 2022, P.L. 117-103, Div BB, § 104(a)(1)–(5)(B)(iii), (C)–(7), 136 Stat. 1100—1102; Mar. 15, 2022, P.L. 117-103, Div BB, § 104(a), 136 Stat. 1100.)

§ 217. [8 U.S.C. § 1187] Visa waiver program for certain visitors.

(a) Establishment of program. The Secretary of Homeland Security and the Secretary of State are authorized to establish a program (hereinafter in this section referred to as the "program") under which the requirement of paragraph (7)(B)(i)(II) of section 212(a) [8 USCS § 1182(a)(7)(B)(i)(II)] may be waived by the Secretary of Homeland Security, in consultation with the Secretary of State and in accordance with this section, in the case of an alien who meets the following requirements:

(1) Seeking entry as tourist for 90 days or less. The alien is applying for admission during the program as a nonimmigrant visitor (described in section 101(a)(15)(B) [8 USCS § 1101(a)(15)(B)]) for a period not exceeding 90 days.

(2) National of program country. The alien is a national of, and presents a passport issued by, a country which—

(A) extends (or agrees to extend), either on its own or in conjunction with one or more other countries that are described in subparagraph (B) and that have established with it a common area for immigration admissions, reciprocal privileges to citizens and nationals of the United States, and

(B) is designated as a [pilot] program country under subsection (c).

(3) Passport requirements. The alien, at the time of application for admission, is in possession of a valid unexpired passport that satisfies the following:

(A) Machine readable. The passport is a machine-readable passport that is tamper-resistant, incorporates document authentication identifiers, and otherwise satisfies the internationally accepted standard for machine readability.

(B) Electronic. Beginning on April 1, 2016, the passport is an electronic passport that is fraud-resistant, contains relevant biographic and biometric information (as determined by the Secretary of Homeland Security), and otherwise satisfies internationally accepted standards for electronic passports.

(4) Executes immigration forms. The alien before the time of such admission completes such immigration form as the Secretary of Homeland Security shall establish.

(5) Entry into the United States. If arriving by sea or air, the alien arrives at the port of entry into the United States on a carrier, including any carrier conducting operations under part 135 of title 14, Code

of Federal Regulations, or a noncommercial aircraft that is owned or operated by a domestic corporation conducting operations under part 91 of title 14, Code of Federal Regulations[,] which has entered into an agreement with the Secretary of Homeland Security pursuant to subsection (e). The Secretary of Homeland Security is authorized to require a carrier conducting operations under part 135 of title 14, Code of Federal Regulations, or a domestic corporation conducting operations under part 91 of that title, to give suitable and proper bond, in such reasonable amount and containing such conditions as the Secretary of Homeland Security may deem sufficient to ensure compliance with the indemnification requirements of this section, as a term of such an agreement.

(6) Not a safety threat. The alien has been determined not to represent a threat to the welfare, health, safety, or security of the United States.

(7) No previous violation. If the alien previously was admitted without a visa under this section, the alien must not have failed to comply with the conditions of any previous admission as such a nonimmigrant.

(8) Round-trip ticket. The alien is in possession of a round-trip transportation ticket (unless this requirement is waived by the Secretary of Homeland Security under regulations or the alien is arriving at the port of entry on an aircraft operated under part 135 of title 14, Code of Federal Regulations, or a noncommercial aircraft that is owned or operated by a domestic corporation conducting operations under part 91 of title 14, Code of Federal Regulations).

(9) Automated system check. The identity of the alien has been checked using an automated electronic database containing information about the inadmissibility of aliens to uncover any grounds on which the alien may be inadmissible to the United States, and no such ground has been found.

(10) Electronic transmission of identification information. Operators of aircraft under part 135 of title 14, Code of Federal Regulations, or operators of noncommercial aircraft that are owned or operated by a domestic corporation conducting operations under part 91 of title 14, Code of Federal Regulations, carrying any alien passenger who will apply for admission under this section shall furnish such information as the Secretary of Homeland Security by regulation shall prescribe as necessary for the identification of any alien passenger being transported and for the enforcement of the immigration laws. Such information shall be electronically transmitted not less than one hour prior to arrival at the port of entry for purposes of checking for inadmissibility using the automated electronic database.

(11) Eligibility determination under the electronic system for travel authorization. Beginning on the date on which the electronic system for travel authorization developed under subsection (h)(3) is fully operational, each alien traveling under the program shall, before applying for admission to the United States, electronically provide to the system biographical information and such other information as the Secretary of Homeland Security shall determine necessary to determine the eligibility of, and whether there exists a law enforcement or security risk in permitting, the alien to travel to the United States. Upon review of such biographical information, the Secretary of Homeland Security shall determine whether the alien is eligible to travel to the United States under the program.

(12) Not present In Iraq, Syria, or any other country or area of concern.

(A) In general. Except as provided in subparagraphs (B) and (C)—

(i) the alien has not been present, at any time on or after March 1, 2011—

(I) in Iraq or Syria;

(II) in a country that is designated by the Secretary of State under section 6(j) of the Export Administration Act of 1979 (50 U.S.C. 2405) [former 50 USCS § 4605(j)] (as continued in effect under the International Emergency Economic Powers Act (50 U.S.C. 1701 et seq.)), section 40 of the Arms Export Control Act (22 U.S.C. 2780), section 620A of the Foreign Assistance Act of 1961 (22 U.S.C. 2371), or any other provision of law, as a country, the government of which has repeatedly provided support of acts of international terrorism; or

(III) in any other country or area of concern designated by the Secretary of Homeland Security under subparagraph (D); and

(ii) regardless of whether the alien is a national of a program country, the alien is not a national of—

(I) Iraq or Syria;

(II) a country that is designated, at the time the alien applies for admission, by the Secretary of State under section 6(j) of the Export Administration Act of 1979 (50 U.S.C. 2405) [former 50 USCS § 4605(j)] (as continued in effect under the International Emergency Economic Powers Act (50 U.S.C. 1701 et seq.)), section 40 of the Arms Export Control Act (22 U.S.C. 2780), section 620A of the Foreign Assistance Act of 1961 (22 U.S.C. 2371), or any other provision of law, as a country, the government of which has repeatedly provided support of acts of international terrorism; or

(III) any other country that is designated, at the time the alien applies for admission, by the Secretary of Homeland Security under subparagraph (D).

(B) Certain military personnel and government employees. Subparagraph (A)(i) shall not apply in the case of an alien if the Secretary of Homeland Security determines that the alien was present—

(i) in order to perform military service in the armed forces of a program country; or

(ii) in order to carry out official duties as a full time employee of the government of a program country.

(C) Waiver. The Secretary of Homeland Security may waive the application of subparagraph (A) to an alien if the Secretary determines that such a waiver is in the law enforcement or national security interests of the United States.

(D) Countries or areas of concern.

(i) In general. Not later than 60 days after the date of the enactment of this paragraph [enacted Dec. 18, 2015], the Secretary of Homeland Security, in consultation with the Secretary of State and the Director of National Intelligence, shall determine whether the requirement under subparagraph (A) shall apply to any other country or area.

(ii) Criteria. In making a determination under clause (i), the Secretary shall consider—

(I) whether the presence of an alien in the country or area increases the likelihood that the alien is a credible threat to the national security of the United States;

(II) whether a foreign terrorist organization has a significant presence in the country or area; and

(III) whether the country or area is a safe haven for terrorists.

(iii) Annual review. The Secretary shall conduct a review, on an annual basis, of any determination made under clause (i).

(E) Report. Beginning not later than one year after the date of the enactment of this paragraph [enacted Dec. 18, 2015], and annually thereafter, the Secretary of Homeland Security shall submit to the Committee on Homeland Security, the Committee on Foreign Affairs, the Permanent Select Committee on Intelligence, and the Committee on the Judiciary of the House of Representatives, and the Committee on Homeland Security and Governmental Affairs, the Committee on Foreign Relations, the Select Committee on Intelligence, and the Committee on the Judiciary of the Senate a report on each instance in which the Secretary exercised the waiver authority under subparagraph (C) during the previous year.

(b) Waiver of rights. An alien may not be provided a waiver under the program unless the alien has waived any right—

(1) to review or appeal under this Act of an immigration officer's determination as to the admissibility of the alien at the port of entry into the United States, or

(2) to contest, other than on the basis of an application for asylum, any action for removal of the alien.

(c) Designation of program countries.

(1) In general. The Secretary of Homeland Security, in consultation with the Secretary of State, "may designate" any country as a program country if it meets the requirements of paragraph (2).

(2) Qualifications. Except as provided in subsection (f), a country may not be designated as a program country unless the following requirements are met:

(A) Low nonimmigrant visa refusal rate. Either—

(i) the average number of refusals of nonimmigrant visitor visas for nationals of that country during—

(I) the two previous full fiscal years was less than 2.0 percent of the total number of nonimmigrant visitor visas for nationals of that country which were granted or refused during those years; and

(II) either of such two previous full fiscal years was less than 2.5 percent of the total number of nonimmigrant visitor visas for nationals of that country which were granted or refused during that year; or

(ii) such refusal rate for nationals of that country during the previous full fiscal year was less than 3.0 percent.

(B) Passport program.

(i) Issuance of passports. The government of the country certifies that it issues to its citizens passports described in subparagraph (A) of subsection (a)(3), and on or after April 1, 2016, passports described in subparagraph (B) of subsection (a)(3).

(ii) Validation of passports. Not later than October 1, 2016, the government of the country certifies that it has in place mechanisms to validate passports described in subparagraphs (A) and (B) of subsection (a)(3) at each key port of entry into that country. This requirement shall not apply to travel between countries which fall within the Schengen Zone.

(C) Law enforcement and security interests. The Secretary of Homeland Security, in consultation with the Secretary of State—

(i) evaluates the effect that the country's designation would have on the law enforcement and security interests of the United States (including the interest in enforcement of the immigration laws of the United States and the existence and effectiveness of its agreements and procedures for extraditing to the United States individuals, including its own nationals, who commit crimes that violate United States law);

(ii) determines that such interests would not be compromised by the designation of the country; and

(iii) submits a written report to the Committee on the Judiciary, the Committee on Foreign Affairs, and the Committee on Homeland Security of the House of Representatives and the Committee on the Judiciary and the Committee on Foreign Relations of the Senate regarding the country's qualification for designation that includes an explanation of such determination.

(D) Reporting lost and stolen passports. The government of the country enters into an agreement with the United States to report, or make available through Interpol or other means as designated by the Secretary of Homeland Security, to the United States Government information about the theft or loss of passports not later than 24 hours after becoming aware of the theft or loss and in a manner specified in the agreement.

(E) Repatriation of aliens. The government of the country accepts for repatriation any citizen, former citizen, or national of the country against whom a final executable order of removal is issued not later than three weeks after the issuance of the final order of removal. Nothing in this subparagraph creates any duty for the United States or any right for any alien with respect to removal or release. Nothing in this subparagraph gives rise to any cause of action or claim under this paragraph or any other law against any official of the United States or of any State to compel the release, removal, or consideration for release or removal of any alien.

(F) Passenger information exchange. The government of the country enters into an agreement with the United States to share information regarding whether citizens and nationals of that country traveling to the United States represent a threat to the security or welfare of the United States or its citizens, and fully implements such agreement.

(G) Interpol screening. Not later than 270 days after the date of the enactment of this subparagraph [enacted Dec. 18, 2015], except in the case of a country in which there is not an international airport, the government of the country certifies to the Secretary of Homeland Security that, to the maximum extent allowed under the laws of the country, it is screening, for unlawful activity, each person who is not a citizen or national of that country who is admitted to or departs that country, by using relevant databases and notices maintained by Interpol, or other means designated by the Secretary of Homeland Security. This requirement shall not apply to travel between countries which fall within the Schengen Zone.

(3) Continuing and subsequent qualifications. For each fiscal year after the initial period—

(A) Continuing qualification. In the case of a country which was a program country in the previous fiscal year, a country may not be designated as a program country unless the sum of—

(i) the total of the number of nationals of that country who were denied admission at the time of arrival or withdrew their application for admission during such previous fiscal year as a nonimmigrant visitor, and

(ii) the total number of nationals of that country who were admitted as nonimmigrant visitors during such previous fiscal year and who violated the terms of such admission,

was less than 2 percent of the total number of nationals of that country who applied for admission as nonimmigrant visitors during such previous fiscal year.

(B) New countries. In the case of another country, the country may not be designated as a program country unless the following requirements are met:

(i) Low nonimmigrant visa refusal rate in previous 2-year period. The average number of refusals of nonimmigrant visitor visas for nationals of that country during the two previous full fiscal years was less than 2 percent of the total number of nonimmigrant visitor visas for nationals of that country which were granted or refused during those years.

(ii) Low nonimmigrant visa refusal rate in each of the 2 previous years. The average number of refusals of nonimmigrant visitor visas for nationals of that country during either of such two previous full fiscal years was less than 2.5 percent of the total number of nonimmigrant visitor visas for nationals of that country which were granted or refused during that year.

(4) Initial period. For purposes of paragraphs (2) and (3), the term "initial period" means the period beginning at the end of the 30-day period described in subsection (b)(1) and ending on the last day of the first fiscal year which begins after such 30-day period.

(5) Written reports on continuing qualification; designation terminations.

(A) Periodic evaluations.

(i) In general. The Secretary of Homeland Security, in consultation with the Secretary of State, periodically (but not less than once every 2 years)—

(I) shall evaluate the effect of each program country's continued designation on the law enforcement and security interests of the United States (including the interest in enforcement of the immigration laws of the United States and the existence and effectiveness of its agreements and procedures for extraditing to the United States individuals, including its own nationals, who commit crimes that violate United States law);

(II) shall determine, based upon the evaluation in subclause (I), whether any such designation ought to be continued or terminated under subsection (d);

(III) shall submit a written report to the Committee on the Judiciary, the Committee on Foreign Affairs, the Permanent Select Committee on Intelligence, and the Committee on Homeland Security, of the House of Representatives and the Committee on the Judiciary, the Committee on Foreign Relations, the Select Committee on Intelligence, and the Committee on Homeland Security and Governmental Affairs of the Senate regarding the continuation or termination of the country's designation that includes an explanation of such determination and the effects described in subclause (I); and

(IV) shall submit to Congress a report regarding the implementation of the electronic system for travel authorization under subsection (h)(3) and the participation of new countries in the program through a waiver under paragraph (8); and

(V) shall submit to the committees described in subclause (III), a report that includes an assessment of the threat to the national security of the United States of the designation of each country designated as a program country, including the compliance of the government of each such country with the requirements under subparagraphs (D) and (F) of paragraph (2), as well as each such government's capacity to comply with such requirements.

(ii) Effective date. A termination of the designation of a country under this subparagraph shall take effect on the date determined by the Secretary of Homeland Security, in consultation with the Secretary of State.

(iii) Redesignation. In the case of a termination under this subparagraph, the Secretary of Homeland Security shall redesignate the country as a program country, without regard to subsection (f) or paragraph (2) or (3), when the Secretary of Homeland Security, in consultation with the Secretary of State, determines that all causes of the termination have been eliminated.

(B) Emergency termination.

(i) In general. In the case of a program country in which an emergency occurs that the Secretary of Homeland Security, in consultation with the Secretary of State, determines threatens the law enforcement or security interests of the United States (including the interest in enforcement of the immigration laws of the United States), the Secretary of Homeland Security shall immediately terminate the designation of the country as a program country.

(ii) Definition. For purposes of clause (i), the term "emergency" means—

(I) the overthrow of a democratically elected government;

(II) war (including undeclared war, civil war, or other military activity) on the territory of the program country;

(III) a severe breakdown in law and order affecting a significant portion of the program country's territory;

(IV) a severe economic collapse in the program country; or

(V) any other extraordinary event in the program country that threatens the law enforcement or security interests of the United States (including the interest in enforcement of the immigration laws of the United States) and where the country's participation in the program could contribute to that threat.

(iii) Redesignation. The Secretary of Homeland Security may redesignate the country as a program country, without regard to subsection (f) or paragraph (2) or (3), when the Secretary of Homeland Security, in consultation with the Secretary of State, determines that—

(I) at least 6 months have elapsed since the effective date of the termination;

(II) the emergency that caused the termination has ended; and

(III) the average number of refusals of nonimmigrant visitor visas for nationals of that country during the period of termination under this subparagraph was less than 3.0 percent of the total number of nonimmigrant visitor visas for nationals of that country which were granted or refused during such period.

(iv) Program suspension authority. The Director of National Intelligence shall immediately inform the Secretary of Homeland Security of any current and credible threat which poses an imminent danger to the United States or its citizens and originates from a country participating in the visa waiver program. Upon receiving such notification, the Secretary, in consultation with the Secretary of State—

(I) may suspend a country from the visa waiver program without prior notice;

(II) shall notify any country suspended under subclause (I) and, to the extent practicable without disclosing sensitive intelligence sources and methods, provide justification for the suspension; and

(III) shall restore the suspended country's participation in the visa waiver program upon a determination that the threat no longer poses an imminent danger to the United States or its citizens.

(C) Treatment of nationals after termination. For purposes of this paragraph—

(i) nationals of a country whose designation is terminated under subparagraph (A) or (B) shall remain eligible for a waiver under subsection (a) until the effective date of such termination; and

(ii) a waiver under this section that is provided to such a national for a period described in subsection (a)(1) shall not, by such termination, be deemed to have been rescinded or otherwise rendered invalid, if the waiver is granted prior to such termination.

(6) Computation of visa refusal rates. For purposes of determining the eligibility of a country to be designated as a program country, the calculation of visa refusal rates shall not include any visa refusals which incorporate any procedures based on, or are otherwise based on, race, sex, or disability, unless otherwise specifically authorized by law or regulation. No court shall have jurisdiction under this paragraph to review any visa refusal, the denial of admission to the United States of any alien by the Secretary of Homeland Security, the Secretary's computation of the visa refusal rate, or the designation or nondesignation of any country.

(7) Visa waiver information.

(A) In general. In refusing the application of nationals of a program country for United States visas, or the applications of nationals of a country seeking entry into the visa waiver program, a consular officer shall not knowingly or intentionally classify the refusal of the visa under a category that is not included in the calculation of the visa refusal rate only so that the percentage of that country's visa refusals is less than the percentage limitation applicable to qualification for participation in the visa waiver program.

(B) Reporting requirement. On May 1 of each year, for each country under consideration for inclusion in the visa waiver program, the Secretary of State shall provide to the appropriate congressional committees—

(i) the total number of nationals of that country that applied for United States visas in that country during the previous calendar year;

(ii) the total number of such nationals who received United States visas during the previous calendar year;

(iii) the total number of such nationals who were refused United States visas during the previous calendar year;

(iv) the total number of such nationals who were refused United States visas during the previous calendar year under each provision of this Act under which the visas were refused; and

(v) the number of such nationals that were refused under section 214(b) [8 USCS § 1184(b)] as a percentage of the visas that were issued to such nationals.

(C) Certification. Not later than May 1 of each year, the United States chief of mission, acting or permanent, to each country under consideration for inclusion in the visa waiver program shall certify to the appropriate congressional committees that the information described in subparagraph (B) is accurate and provide a copy of that certification to those committees.

(D) Consideration of countries in the visa waiver program. Upon notification to the Secretary of Homeland Security that a country is under consideration for inclusion in the visa waiver program, the Secretary of State shall provide all of the information described in subparagraph (B) to the Secretary of Homeland Security.

(E) Definition. In this paragraph, the term "appropriate congressional committees" means the Committee on the Judiciary and the Committee on Foreign Relations of the Senate and the Committee on the Judiciary and the Committee on International Relations of the House of Representatives.

(8) Nonimmigrant visa refusal rate flexibility.

(A) Certification.

(i) In general. On the date on which an air exit system is in place that can verify the departure of not less than 97 percent of foreign nationals who exit through airports of the United States and the electronic system for travel authorization required under subsection (h)(3) is fully operational, the Secretary of Homeland Security shall certify to Congress that such air exit system and electronic system for travel authorization are in place.

(ii) Notification to Congress. The Secretary shall notify Congress in writing of the date on which the air exit system under clause (i) fully satisfies the biometric requirements specified in subsection (i).

(iii) Temporary suspension of waiver authority. Notwithstanding any certification made under clause (i), if the Secretary has not notified Congress in accordance with clause (ii) by June 30, 2009, the Secretary's waiver authority under subparagraph (B) shall be suspended beginning on July 1, 2009, until such time as the Secretary makes such notification.

(iv) Rule of construction. Nothing in this paragraph shall be construed as in any way abrogating the reporting requirements under subsection (i)(3).

(B) Waiver. After certification by the Secretary under subparagraph (A), the Secretary, in consultation with the Secretary of State, may waive the application of paragraph (2)(A) for a country if—

(i) the country meets all security requirements of this section;

(ii) the Secretary of Homeland Security determines that the totality of the country's security risk mitigation measures provide assurance that the country's participation in the program would not compromise the law enforcement, security interests, or enforcement of the immigration laws of the United States;

(iii) there has been a sustained reduction in the rate of refusals for nonimmigrant visas for nationals of the country and conditions exist to continue such reduction;

(iv) the country cooperated with the Government of the United States on counterterrorism initiatives, information sharing, and preventing terrorist travel before the date of its designation as a program country, and the Secretary of Homeland Security and the Secretary of State determine that such cooperation will continue; and

(v) (I) the rate of refusals for nonimmigrant visitor visas for nationals of the country during the previous full fiscal year was not more than ten percent; or

(II) the visa overstay rate for the country for the previous full fiscal year does not exceed the maximum visa overstay rate, once such rate is established under subparagraph (C).

(C) Maximum visa overstay rate.

(i) Requirement to establish. After certification by the Secretary under subparagraph (A), the Secretary and the Secretary of State jointly shall use information from the air exit system referred to in such subparagraph to establish a maximum visa overstay rate for countries participating in the program pursuant to a waiver under subparagraph (B). The Secretary of Homeland Security shall certify to Congress that such rate would not compromise the law enforcement, security interests, or enforcement of the immigration laws of the United States.

(ii) Visa overstay rate defined. In this paragraph the term "visa overstay rate" means, with respect to a country, the ratio of—

(I) the total number of nationals of that country who were admitted to the United States on the basis of a nonimmigrant visa whose periods of authorized stays ended during a fiscal year but who remained unlawfully in the United States beyond such periods; to

(II) the total number of nationals of that country who were admitted to the United States on the basis of a nonimmigrant visa during that fiscal year.

(iii) Report and publication. The Secretary of Homeland Security shall on the same date submit to Congress and publish in the Federal Register information relating to the maximum visa overstay rate established under clause (i). Not later than 60 days after such date, the Secretary shall issue a final maximum visa overstay rate above which a country may not participate in the program.

(9) Discretionary security-related considerations. In determining whether to waive the application of paragraph (2)(A) for a country, pursuant to paragraph (8), the Secretary of Homeland Security, in consultation with the Secretary of State, shall take into consideration other factors affecting the security of the United States, including—

(A) airport security standards in the country;

(B) whether the country assists in the operation of an effective air marshal program;

(C) the standards of passports and travel documents issued by the country; and

(D) other security-related factors, including the country's cooperation with the United States' initiatives toward combating terrorism and the country's cooperation with the United States intelligence community in sharing information regarding terrorist threats.

(10) Technical assistance. The Secretary of Homeland Security, in consultation with the Secretary of State, shall provide technical assistance to program countries to assist those countries in meeting the requirements under this section. The Secretary of Homeland Security shall ensure that the program office within the Department of Homeland Security is adequately staffed and has resources to be able to provide such technical assistance, in addition to its duties to effectively monitor compliance of the countries participating in the program with all the requirements of the program.

(11) Independent review.

(A) In general. Prior to the admission of a new country into the program under this section, and in conjunction with the periodic evaluations required under subsection (c)(5)(A), the Director of National Intelligence shall conduct an independent intelligence assessment of a nominated country and member of the program.

(B) Reporting requirement. The Director shall provide to the Secretary of Homeland Security, the

Secretary of State, and the Attorney General the independent intelligence assessment required under subparagraph (A).

(C) Contents. The independent intelligence assessment conducted by the Director shall include—

(i) a review of all current, credible terrorist threats of the subject country;

(ii) an evaluation of the subject country's counterterrorism efforts;

(iii) an evaluation as to the extent of the country's sharing of information beneficial to suppressing terrorist movements, financing, or actions;

(iv) an assessment of the risks associated with including the subject country in the program; and

(v) recommendations to mitigate the risks identified in clause (iv).

(12) Designation of high risk program countries.

(A) In general. The Secretary of Homeland Security, in consultation with the Director of National Intelligence and the Secretary of State, shall evaluate program countries on an annual basis based on the criteria described in subparagraph (B) and shall identify any program country, the admission of nationals from which under the visa waiver program under this section, the Secretary determines presents a high risk to the national security of the United States.

(B) Criteria. In evaluating program countries under subparagraph (A), the Secretary of Homeland Security, in consultation with the Director of National Intelligence and the Secretary of State, shall consider the following criteria:

(i) The number of nationals of the country determined to be ineligible to travel to the United States under the program during the previous year.

(ii) The number of nationals of the country who were identified in United States Government databases related to the identities of known or suspected terrorists during the previous year.

(iii) The estimated number of nationals of the country who have traveled to Iraq or Syria at any time on or after March 1, 2011 to engage in terrorism.

(iv) The capacity of the country to combat passport fraud.

(v) The level of cooperation of the country with the counter-terrorism efforts of the United States.

(vi) The adequacy of the border and immigration control of the country.

(vii) Any other criteria the Secretary of Homeland Security determines to be appropriate.

(C) Suspension of designation. The Secretary of Homeland Security, in consultation with the Secretary of State, may suspend the designation of a program country based on a determination that the country presents a high risk to the national security of the United States under subparagraph (A) until such time as the Secretary determines that the country no longer presents such a risk.

(D) Report. Not later than 60 days after the date of the enactment of this paragraph [enacted Dec. 18, 2015], and annually thereafter, the Secretary of Homeland Security, in consultation with the Director of National Intelligence and the Secretary of State, shall submit to the Committee on Homeland Security, the Committee on Foreign Affairs, the Permanent Select Committee on Intelligence, and the Committee on the Judiciary of the House of Representatives, and the Committee on Homeland Security and Governmental Affairs, the Committee on Foreign Relations, the Select Committee on Intelligence, and the Committee on the Judiciary of the Senate a report, which includes an evaluation and threat assessment of each country determined to present a high risk to the national security of the United States under subparagraph (A).

(d) Authority. Notwithstanding any other provision of this section, the Secretary of Homeland Security, in consultation with the Secretary of State, may for any reason (including national security) refrain from waiving the visa requirement in respect to nationals of any country which may otherwise qualify for designation or may, at any time, rescind any waiver or designation previously granted under this section. The Secretary of Homeland Security may not waive any eligibility requirement under this section unless the Secretary notifies, with respect to the House of Representatives, the Committee on Homeland Security, the Committee on the Judiciary, the Committee on Foreign Affairs, and the Committee on Appropriations, and with respect to the Senate, the Committee on Homeland Security and Governmental Affairs, the Committee on the Judiciary, the Committee on Foreign Relations, and the Committee on Appropriations not later than 30 days before the effective date of such waiver.

(e) Carrier agreements.

(1) In general. The agreement referred to in subsection (a)(4) is an agreement between a carrier (including any carrier conducting operations under part 135 of title 14, Code of Federal Regulations) or a domestic corporation conducting operations under part 91 of that title and the Secretary of Homeland Security under which the carrier (including any carrier conducting operations under part 135 of title 14, Code of Federal Regulations) or a domestic corporation conducting operations under part 91 of that title agrees, in consideration of the waiver of the visa requirement with respect to a nonimmigrant visitor under the program—

(A) to indemnify the United States against any costs for the transportation of the alien from the United States if the visitor is refused admission to the United States or remains in the United States unlawfully after the 90-day period described in subsection (a)(1)(A),

(B) to submit daily to immigration officers any immigration forms received with respect to nonimmigrant visitors provided a waiver under the program,

(C) to be subject to the imposition of fines resulting from the transporting into the United States of a national of a designated country without a passport pursuant to regulations promulgated by the Secretary of Homeland Security, and

(D) to collect, provide, and share passenger data as required under subsection (h)(1)(B).

(2) Termination of agreements. The Secretary of Homeland Security may terminate an agreement under paragraph (1) with five days' notice to the carrier (including any carrier conducting operations under

part 135 of title 14, Code of Federal Regulations) or a domestic corporation conducting operations under part 91 of that title for the failure by a carrier (including any carrier conducting operations under part 135 of title 14, Code of Federal Regulations) or a domestic corporation conducting operations under part 91 of that title to meet the terms of such agreement.

(3) Business aircraft requirements.

(A) In general. For purposes of this section, a domestic corporation conducting operations under part 91 of title 14, Code of Federal Regulations[,] that owns or operates a noncommercial aircraft is a corporation that is organized under the laws of any of the States of the United States or the District of Columbia and is accredited by or a member of a national organization that sets business aviation standards. The Secretary of Homeland Security shall prescribe by regulation the provision of such information as the Secretary of Homeland Security deems necessary to identify the domestic corporation, its officers, employees, shareholders, its place of business, and its business activities.

(B) Collections. In addition to any other fee authorized by law, the Secretary of Homeland Security is authorized to charge and collect, on a periodic basis, an amount from each domestic corporation conducting operations under part 91 of title 14, Code of Federal Regulations, for nonimmigrant visa waiver admissions on noncommercial aircraft owned or operated by such domestic corporation equal to the total amount of fees assessed for issuance of nonimmigrant visa waiver arrival/departure forms at land border ports of entry. All fees collected under this paragraph shall be deposited into the Immigration User Fee Account established under section 286(h) [8 USCS § 1356(h)].

(f) Duration and termination of designation.

(1) In general.

(A) Determination and notification of disqualification rate. Upon determination by the Secretary of Homeland Security that a program country's disqualification rate is 2 percent or more, the Secretary of Homeland Security shall notify the Secretary of State.

(B) Probationary status. If the program country's disqualification rate is greater than 2 percent but less than 3.5 percent, the Secretary of Homeland Security shall place the program country in probationary status for a period not to exceed 2 full fiscal years following the year in which the determination under subparagraph (A) is made.

(C) Termination of designation. Subject to paragraph (3), if the program country's disqualification rate is 3.5 percent or more, the Secretary of Homeland Security shall terminate the country's designation as a program country effective at the beginning of the second fiscal year following the fiscal year in which the determination under subparagraph (A) is made.

(2) Termination of probationary status.

(A) In general. If the Secretary of Homeland Security determines at the end of the probationary period described in paragraph (1)(B) that the program country placed in probationary status under such paragraph has failed to develop a machine-readable passport program as required by section [subsection] (c)(2) (C), or has a disqualification rate of 2 percent or more, the Secretary of Homeland Security shall terminate the designation of the country as a program country. If the Secretary of Homeland Security determines that the program country has developed a machine-readable passport program and has a disqualification rate of less than 2 percent, the Secretary of Homeland Security shall redesignate the country as a program country.

(B) Effective date. A termination of the designation of a country under subparagraph (A) shall take effect on the first day of the first fiscal year following the fiscal year in which the determination under such subparagraph is made. Until such date, nationals of the country shall remain eligible for a waiver under subsection (a).

(3) Nonapplicability of certain provisions. Paragraph (1)(C) shall not apply unless the total number of nationals of a program country described in paragraph (4)(A) exceeds 100.

(4) Definition. For purposes of this subsection, the term "disqualification rate" means the percentage which—

(A) the total number of nationals of the program country who were—

(i) denied admission at the time of arrival or withdrew their application for admission during the most recent fiscal year for which data are available; and

(ii) admitted as nonimmigrant visitors during such fiscal year and who violated the terms of such admission; bears to

(B) the total number of nationals of such country who applied for admission as nonimmigrant visitors during such fiscal year.

(5) Failure to report passport thefts. If the Secretary of Homeland Security and the Secretary of State jointly determine that the program country is not reporting the theft or loss of passports, as required by subsection (c)(2)(D), Secretary of Homeland Security shall terminate the designation of the country as a program country.

(6) Failure to share information.

(A) In general. If the Secretary of Homeland Security and the Secretary of State jointly determine that the program country is not sharing information, as required by subsection (c)(2)(F), the Secretary of Homeland Security shall terminate the designation of the country as a program country.

(B) Redesignation. In the case of a termination under this paragraph, the Secretary of Homeland Security shall redesignate the country as a program country, without regard to paragraph (2) or (3) of subsection (c) or paragraphs (1) through (4), when the Secretary of Homeland Security, in consultation with the Secretary of State, determines that the country is sharing information, as required by subsection (c)(2)(F).

(7) Failure to screen.

(A) In general. Beginning on the date that is 270 days after the date of the enactment of this paragraph [enacted Dec. 18, 2015], if the Secretary of Homeland Security and the Secretary of State jointly determine that the program country is not conducting the screening required by subsection (c)(2)(G), the Secretary of Homeland Security shall terminate the designation of the country as a program country.

(B) Redesignation. In the case of a termination under this paragraph, the Secretary of Homeland Security shall redesignate the country as a program country, without regard to paragraph (2) or (3) of subsection (c) or paragraphs (1) through (4), when the Secretary of Homeland Security, in consultation with the Secretary of State, determines that the country is conducting the screening required by subsection (c)(2)(G).

(g) Visa application sole method to dispute denial of waiver based on a ground of inadmissibility. In the case of an alien denied a waiver under the program by reason of a ground of inadmissibility described in section 212(a) [8 USCS § 1182(a)] that is discovered at the time of the alien's application for the waiver or through the use of an automated electronic database required under subsection (a)(9), the alien may apply for a visa at an appropriate consular office outside the United States. There shall be no other means of administrative or judicial review of such a denial, and no court or person otherwise shall have jurisdiction to consider any claim attacking the validity of such a denial.

(h) Use of information technology systems.

(1) Automated entry-exit control system.

(A) System. Not later than October 1, 2001, the Secretary of Homeland Security shall develop and implement a fully automated entry and exit control system that will collect a record of arrival and departure for every alien who arrives and departs by sea or air at a port of entry into the United States and is provided a waiver under the program.

(B) Requirements. The system under subparagraph (A) shall satisfy the following requirements:

(i) Data collection by carriers. Not later than October 1, 2001, the records of arrival and departure described in subparagraph (A) shall be based, to the maximum extent practicable, on passenger data collected and electronically transmitted to the automated entry and exit control system by each carrier that has an agreement under subsection (a)(4).

(ii) Data provision by carriers. Not later than October 1, 2002, no waiver may be provided under this section to an alien arriving by sea or air at a port of entry into the United States on a carrier unless the carrier is electronically transmitting to the automated entry and exit control system passenger data determined by the Secretary of Homeland Security to be sufficient to permit the Secretary of Homeland Security to carry out this paragraph.

(iii) Calculation. The system shall contain sufficient data to permit the Secretary of Homeland Security to calculate, for each program country and each fiscal year, the portion of nationals of that country who are described in subparagraph (A) and for whom no record of departure exists, expressed as a percentage of the total number of such nationals who are so described.

(C) Reporting.

(i) Percentage of nationals lacking departure record. As part of the annual report required to be submitted under section 110(e)(1) of the Illegal Immigration Reform and Immigrant Responsibility Act of 1996 [8 USCS § 1365a(e)(1)], the Secretary of Homeland Security shall include a section containing the calculation described in subparagraph (B)(iii) for each program country for the previous fiscal year, together with an analysis of that information.

(ii) System effectiveness. Not later than December 31, 2004, the Secretary of Homeland Security shall submit a written report to the Committee on the Judiciary of the United States House of Representatives and of the Senate containing the following:

(I) The conclusions of the Secretary of Homeland Security regarding the effectiveness of the automated entry and exit control system to be developed and implemented under this paragraph.

(II) The recommendations of the Secretary of Homeland Security regarding the use of the calculation described in subparagraph (B)(iii) as a basis for evaluating whether to terminate or continue the designation of a country as a program country.

The report required by this clause may be combined with the annual report required to be submitted on that date under section 110(e)(1) of the Illegal Immigration Reform and Immigrant Responsibility Act of 1996 [8 USCS § 1365a(e)(1)].

(2) Automated data sharing system.

(A) System. The Secretary of Homeland Security and the Secretary of State shall develop and implement an automated data sharing system that will permit them to share data in electronic form from their respective records systems regarding the admissibility of aliens who are nationals of a program country.

(B) Requirements. The system under subparagraph (A) shall satisfy the following requirements:

(i) Supplying information to immigration officers conducting inspections at ports of entry. Not later than October 1, 2002, the system shall enable immigration officers conducting inspections at ports of entry under section 235 [8 USCS § 1225] to obtain from the system, with respect to aliens seeking a waiver under the program—

(I) any photograph of the alien that may be contained in the records of the Department of State or the Service; and

(II) information on whether the alien has ever been determined to be ineligible to receive a visa or ineligible to be admitted to the United States.

(ii) Supplying photographs of inadmissible aliens. The system shall permit the Secretary of Homeland Security electronically to obtain any photograph contained in the records of the Secretary of State pertaining to an alien who is a national of a program country and has been determined to be ineligible to receive a visa.

(iii) Maintaining records on applications for admission. The system shall maintain, for a minimum of 10 years, information about each application for admission made by an alien seeking a waiver under the program, including the following:

(I) The name or Service identification number of each immigration officer conducting the inspection of the alien at the port of entry.

(II) Any information described in clause (i) that is obtained from the system by any such officer.

(III) The results of the application.

(3) Electronic system for travel authorization.

(A) System. The Secretary of Homeland Security, in consultation with the Secretary of State, shall develop and implement a fully automated electronic system for travel authorization (referred to in this paragraph as the "System") to collect such biographical and other information as the Secretary of Homeland Security determines necessary to determine, in advance of travel, the eligibility of, and whether there exists a law enforcement or security risk in permitting, the [an] alien to travel to the United States.

(B) Fees.

(i) In general. No later than 6 months after the date of enactment of the Travel Promotion Act of 2009 [enacted March 4, 2010], the Secretary of Homeland Security shall establish a fee for the use of the System and begin assessment and collection of that fee. The initial fee shall be the sum of—

(I) $17 per travel authorization; and

(II) an amount that will at least ensure recovery of the full costs of providing and administering the System, as determined by the Secretary.

(ii) Disposition of amounts collected. Amounts collected under clause (i)(I) shall be credited to the Travel Promotion Fund established by subsection (d) of the Travel Promotion Act of 2009 (22 U.S.C. 2131(d)). Amounts collected under clause (i)(II) shall be transferred to the general fund of the Treasury and made available to pay the costs incurred to administer the System.

(iii) Sunset of Travel Promotion Fund fee. The Secretary may not collect the fee authorized by clause (i)(I) for fiscal years beginning after October 31, 2028.

(C) Validity.

(i) Period. The Secretary of Homeland Security, in consultation with the Secretary of State, shall prescribe regulations that provide for a period, not to exceed three years, during which a determination of eligibility to travel under the program will be valid. Notwithstanding any other provision under this section, the Secretary of Homeland Security may revoke any such determination or shorten the period of eligibility under any such determination at any time and for any reason.

(ii) Limitation. A determination by the Secretary of Homeland Security that an alien is eligible to travel to the United States under the program is not a determination that the alien is admissible to the United States.

(iii) Not a determination of visa eligibility. A determination by the Secretary of Homeland Security that an alien who applied for authorization to travel to the United States through the System is not eligible to travel under the program is not a determination of eligibility for a visa to travel to the United States and shall not preclude the alien from applying for a visa.

(iv) Judicial review. Notwithstanding any other provision of law, no court shall have jurisdiction to review an eligibility determination under the System.

(D) Fraud detection. The Secretary of Homeland Security shall research opportunities to incorporate into the System technology that will detect and prevent fraud and deception in the System.

(E) Additional and previous countries of citizenship. The Secretary of Homeland Security shall collect from an applicant for admission pursuant to this section information on any additional or previous countries of citizenship of that applicant. The Secretary shall take any information so collected into account when making determinations as to the eligibility of the alien for admission pursuant to this section.

(F) Report on certain limitations on travel. Not later than 30 days after the date of the enactment of this subparagraph [enacted Dec. 18, 2015] and annually thereafter, the Secretary of Homeland Security, in consultation with the Secretary of State, shall submit to the Committee on Homeland Security, the Committee on the Judiciary, and the Committee on Foreign Affairs of the House of Representatives, and the Committee on Homeland Security and Governmental Affairs, the Committee on the Judiciary, and the Committee on Foreign Relations of the Senate a report on the number of individuals who were denied eligibility to travel under the program, or whose eligibility for such travel was revoked during the previous year, and the number of such individuals determined, in accordance with subsection (a)(6), to represent a threat to the national security of the United States, and shall include the country or countries of citizenship of each such individual.

(i) Exit system.

(1) In general. Not later than one year after the date of the enactment of this subsection [enacted Aug. 3, 2007], the Secretary of Homeland Security shall establish an exit system that records the departure on a flight leaving the United States of every alien participating in the visa waiver program established under this section.

(2) System requirements. The system established under paragraph (1) shall—

(A) match biometric information of the alien against relevant watch lists and immigration information; and

(B) compare such biometric information against manifest information collected by air carriers on passengers departing the United States to confirm such aliens have departed the United States.

(3) Report. Not later than 180 days after the date of the enactment of this subsection [enacted Aug. 3, 2007], the Secretary shall submit to Congress a report that describes—

(A) the progress made in developing and deploying the exit system established under this subsection; and

(B) the procedures by which the Secretary shall improve the method of calculating the rates of nonimmigrants who overstay their authorized period of stay in the United States.

HISTORY: June 27, 1952, ch 466, Title II, Ch 2, § 217, as added Nov. 6, 1986, P. L. 99-603, Title III, Part B, § 313(a), 100 Stat. 3435; Oct. 24, 1988, P. L. 100-525, § 2(p)(1), (2), 102 Stat. 2613; Nov. 29, 1990, P. L. 101-649, Title II, Subtitle A, § 201(a), 104 Stat. 5012; Dec. 12, 1991, P. L. 102-232, Title III, §§ 303(a)(1), (2), 307(l)(3), 105 Stat. 1746, 1756; Oct. 25, 1994, P. L. 103-415, § 1(m), 108 Stat. 4301; Oct. 25, 1994, P. L. 103-416, Title II, §§ 210, 211, 108 Stat. 4312, 4313; Sept. 30, 1996, P. L. 104-208, Div C, Title III, Subtitle A, § 308(d)(4)(F), (e)(9), Title VI, Subtitle C, § 635(a), (b), (c)(1), (3), 110 Stat. 3009-618, 3009-620, 3009-702, 3009-703; Nov. 26, 1997, P. L. 105-119, Title I, § 125, 111 Stat. 2471; April 27, 1998, P. L. 105-173, §§ 1, 3, 112 Stat. 56; Oct. 30, 2000, P. L. 106-396, Title I, § 101(a), Title II, §§ 201–207, Title IV, § 403(a)–(d), 114 Stat. 1637, 1638, 1647; Oct. 26, 2001, P. L. 107-56, Title IV, Subtitle B, § 417(c), (d), 115 Stat. 355; May 14, 2002, P. L. 107-173, Title III, § 307(a), 116 Stat. 556; Aug. 3, 2007, P. L. 110-53, Title VII, Subtitle B, § 711(c), (d)(1), 121 Stat. 339; March 4, 2010, P. L. 111-145, § 9(h) [9(e)], 124 Stat. 62; July 2, 2010, P. L. 111-198, § 5(a), 124 Stat. 1357; Dec. 16, 2014, P. L. 113-235, Div B, Title VII, §§ 605(b), 606(1), 128 Stat. 2219; Dec. 18, 2015, P. L. 114-113, Div O, Title II, §§ 202(a), (b), 203–205(a), (b), 206, 207(a), (b), 209, 129 Stat. 2989, 2993, 2995; Feb. 9, 2018, P. L. 115-123, Div C, Title II, § 30203(a), 132 Stat. 126; Dec. 20, 2019, P.L. 116-94, Div I, Title VIII, § 806, 133 Stat. 3029; Mar. 15, 2022, P.L. 117-103, Div EE, § 101, 136 Stat. 1111.

§ 218. [8 U.S.C. § 1188] Admission of temporary H-2A workers.

(a) Conditions for approval of H-2A petitions.

(1) A petition to import an alien as an H-2A worker (as defined in subsection (i)(2)) may not be approved by the Attorney General unless the petitioner has applied to the Secretary of Labor for a certification that—

(A) there are not sufficient workers who are able, willing, and qualified, and who will be available at the time and place needed, to perform the labor or services involved in the petition, and

(B) the employment of the alien in such labor or services will not adversely affect the wages and working conditions of workers in the United States similarly employed.

(2) The Secretary of Labor may require by regulation, as a condition of issuing the certification, the payment of a fee to recover the reasonable costs of processing applications for certification.

(b) Conditions for denial of labor certification. The Secretary of Labor may not issue a certification under subsection (a) with respect to an employer if the conditions described in that subsection are not met or if any of the following conditions are met:

(1) There is a strike or lockout in the course of a labor dispute which, under the regulations, precludes such certification.

(2) (A) The employer during the previous two-year period employed H-2A workers and the Secretary of Labor has determined, after notice and opportunity for a hearing, that the employer at any time during that period substantially violated a material term or condition of the labor certification with respect to the employment of domestic or nonimmigrant workers.

(B) No employer may be denied certification under subparagraph (A) for more than three years for any violation described in such subparagraph.

(3) The employer has not provided the Secretary with satisfactory assurances that if the employment for which the certification is sought is not covered by State workers' compensation law, the employer will provide, at no cost to the worker, insurance covering injury and disease arising out of and in the course of the worker's employment which will provide benefits at least equal to those provided under the State workers' compensation law for comparable employment.

(4) The Secretary determines that the employer has not made positive recruitment efforts within a multi-state region of traditional or expected labor supply where the Secretary finds that there are a significant number of qualified United States workers who, if recruited, would be willing to make themselves available for work at the time and place needed. Positive recruitment under this paragraph is in addition to, and shall be conducted within the same time period as, the circulation through the interstate employment service system of the employer's job offer. The obligation to engage in positive recruitment under this paragraph shall terminate on the date the H-2A workers depart for the employer's place of employment.

(c) Special rules for consideration of applications. The following rules shall apply in the case of the filing and consideration of an application for a labor certification under this section:

(1) Deadline for filing applications. The Secretary of Labor may not require that the application be filed more than 45 days before the first date the employer requires the labor or services of the H-2A worker.

(2) Notice within seven days of deficiencies.

(A) The employer shall be notified in writing within seven days of the date of filing if the application does not meet the standards (other than that described in subsection (a)(1)(A)) for approval.

(B) If the application does not meet such standards, the notice shall include the reasons therefor and the Secretary shall provide an opportunity for the prompt resubmission of a modified application.

(3) Issuance of certification.

(A) The Secretary of Labor shall make, not later than 30 days before the date such labor or services are first required to be performed, the certification described in subsection (a)(1) if—

(i) the employer has complied with the criteria for certification (including criteria for the recruitment of eligible individuals as prescribed by the Secretary), and

(ii) the employer does not actually have, or has not been provided with referrals of, qualified eligible individuals who have indicated their availability to perform such labor or services on the terms and conditions of a job offer which meets the requirements of the Secretary.

In considering the question of whether a specific qualification is appropriate in a job offer, the Secretary shall apply the normal and accepted qualifications required by non-H-2A-employers in the same or comparable occupations and crops.

(B) (i) For a period of 3 years subsequent to the effective date of this section, labor certifications shall remain effective only if, from the time the foreign worker departs for the employer's place of employment, the employer will provide employment to any qualified United States worker who applies to the employer until 50 percent of the period of the work contract, under which the foreign worker who is in the job was hired, has elapsed. In addition, the employer will offer to provide benefits, wages and working conditions required pursuant to this section and regulations.

(ii) The requirement of clause (i) shall not apply to any employer who—

(I) did not, during any calendar quarter during the preceding calendar year, use more than 500 man-days of agricultural labor, as defined in section 3(u) of the Fair Labor Standards Act of 1938 (29 U.S.C. 203(u)),

(II) is not a member of an association which has petitioned for certification under this section for its members, and

(III) has not otherwise associated with other employers who are petitioning for temporary foreign workers under this section.

(iii) Six months before the end of the 3-year period described in clause (i), the Secretary of Labor shall consider the findings of the report mandated by section 403(a)(4)(D) of the Immigration Reform and Control Act of 1986 [note to this section] as well as other relevant materials, including evidence of benefits to United States workers and costs to employers, addressing the advisability of continuing a policy which requires an employer, as a condition for certification under this section, to continue to accept qualified, eligible United States workers for employment after the date the H-2A workers depart for work with the employer. The Secretary's review of such findings and materials shall lead to the issuance of findings in furtherance of the Congressional policy that aliens not be admitted under this section unless there are not sufficient workers in the United States who are able, willing, and qualified to perform the labor or service needed and that the employment of the aliens in such labor or services will not adversely affect the wages and working conditions of workers in the United States similarly employed. In the absence of the enactment of Federal legislation prior to three months before the end of the 3-year period described in clause (i) which addresses the subject matter of this subparagraph, the Secretary shall immediately publish the findings required by this clause, and shall promulgate, on an interim or final basis, regulations based on his findings which shall be effective no later than three years from the effective date of this section.

(iv) In complying with clause (i) of this subparagraph, an association shall be allowed to refer or transfer workers among its members: Provided, That for purposes of this section an association acting as an agent for its members shall not be considered a joint employer merely because of such referral or transfer.

(v) United States workers referred or transferred pursuant to clause (iv) of this subparagraph shall not be treated disparately.

(vi) An employer shall not be liable for payments under section 655.202(b)(6) of title 20, Code of Federal Regulations (or any successor regulation) with respect to an H-2A worker who is displaced due to compliance with the requirement of this subparagraph, if the Secretary of Labor certifies that the H-2A worker was displaced because of the employer's compliance with clause (i) of this subparagraph.

(vii) (I) No person or entity shall willfully and knowingly withhold domestic workers prior to the arrival of H-2A workers in order to force the hiring of domestic workers under clause (i).

(II) Upon the receipt of a complaint by an employer that a violation of subclause (I) has occurred the Secretary shall immediately investigate. He shall within 36 hours of the receipt of the complaint issue findings concerning the alleged violation. Where the Secretary finds that a violation has occurred, he shall immediately suspend the application of clause (i) of this subparagraph with respect to that certification for that date of need.

(4) Housing. Employers shall furnish housing in accordance with regulations. The employer shall be permitted at the employer's option to provide housing meeting applicable Federal standards for temporary labor camps or to secure housing which meets the local standards for rental and/or public accommodations or other substantially similar class of habitation: Provided, That in the absence of applicable local standards, State standards for rental and/or public accommodations or other substantially similar class of habitation shall be met: Provided further, That in the absence of applicable local or State standards, Federal temporary labor camp standards shall apply: Provided further, That the Secretary of Labor shall issue regulations which address the specific requirements of housing for employees principally engaged in the range production of livestock: Provided further, That when it is the prevailing practice in the area and occupation of intended employment to provide family housing, family housing shall be provided to workers with families who request it: And provided further, That nothing in this paragraph shall require an employer to provide or secure housing for workers who are not entitled to it under the temporary labor certification regulations in effect on June 1, 1986. The determination as to whether the housing furnished by an employer for an H-2A worker meets the requirements imposed by this paragraph must be made prior to the date specified in paragraph (3)(A) by which the Secretary of Labor is required to make a certification described in subsection (a)(1) with respect to a petition for the importation of such worker.

(d) Roles of agricultural associations.

(1) Permitting filing by agricultural associations. A petition to import an alien as a temporary agricultural worker, and an application for a labor certification with respect to such a worker, may be filed by an association of agricultural producers which use agricultural services.

(2) Treatment of associations acting as employers. If an association is a joint or sole employer of temporary agricultural workers, the certifications granted under this section to the association may be used for the certified job opportunities of any of its producer members and such workers may be transferred among its producer members to perform agricultural services of a temporary or seasonal nature for which the certifications were granted.

(3) Treatment of violations.

(A) Member's violation does not necessarily disqualify association or other members. If an individual producer member of a joint employer association is determined to have committed an act that under subsection (b)(2) results in the denial of certification with respect to the member, the denial shall apply only to that member of the association unless the Secretary determines that the association or other member participated in, had knowledge of, or reason to know of, the violation.

(B) Association's violation does not necessarily disqualify members.

(i) If an association representing agricultural producers as a joint employer is determined to have committed an act that under subsection (b)(2) results in the denial of certification with respect to the association, the denial shall apply only to the association and does not apply to any individual producer member of the association unless the Secretary determines that the member participated in, had knowledge of, or reason to know of, the violation.

(ii) If an association of agricultural producers certified as a sole employer is determined to have committed an act that under subsection (b)(2) results in the denial of certification with respect to the association, no individual producer member of such association may be the beneficiary of the services of temporary alien agricultural workers admitted under this section in the commodity and occupation in which such aliens were employed by the association which was denied certification during the period such denial is in force, unless such producer member employs such aliens in the commodity and occupation in question directly or through an association which is a joint employer of such workers with the producer member.

(e) Expedited administrative appeals of certain determinations.

(1) Regulations shall provide for an expedited procedure for the review of a denial of certification under subsection (a)(1) or a revocation of such a certification or, at the applicant's request, for a de novo administrative hearing respecting the denial or revocation.

(2) The Secretary of Labor shall expeditiously, but in no case later than 72 hours after the time a new determination is requested, make a new determination on the request for certification in the case of an H-2A worker if able, willing, and qualified eligible individuals are not actually available at the time such labor or services are required and a certification was denied in whole or in part because of the availability of qualified workers. If the employer asserts that any eligible individual who has been referred is not able, willing, or qualified, the burden of proof is on the employer to establish that the individual referred is not able, willing, or qualified because of employment-related reasons.

(f) Violators disqualified for 5 years. An alien may not be admitted to the United States as a temporary agricultural worker if the alien was admitted to the United States as such a worker within the previous five-year period and the alien during that period violated a term or condition of such previous admission.

(g) Authorizations of appropriations.

(1) There are authorized to be appropriated for each fiscal year, beginning with fiscal year 1987, $10,000,000 for the purposes—

(A) of recruiting domestic workers for temporary labor and services which might otherwise be performed by nonimmigrants described in section 101(a)(15)(H)(ii)(a) [8 USCS § 1101(a)(15)(H)(ii)(a)], and

(B) of monitoring terms and conditions under which such nonimmigrants (and domestic workers employed by the same employers) are employed in the United States.

(2) The Secretary of Labor is authorized to take such actions, including imposing appropriate penalties and seeking appropriate injunctive relief and specific performance of contractual obligations, as may be necessary to assure employer compliance with terms and conditions of employment under this section.

(3) There are authorized to be appropriated for each fiscal year, beginning with fiscal year 1987, such sums as may be necessary for the purpose of enabling the Secretary of Labor to make determinations and certifications under this section and under section 212(a)(5)(A)(i) [8 USCS § 1182(a)(5)(A)(i)].

(4) There are authorized to be appropriated for each fiscal year, beginning with fiscal year 1987, such sums as may be necessary for the purposes of enabling the Secretary of Agriculture to carry out the Secretary's duties and responsibilities under this section.

(h) Miscellaneous provisions.

(1) The Attorney General shall provide for such endorsement of entry and exit documents of nonimmigrants described in section 101(a)(15)(H)(ii) [8 USCS § 1101(a)(15)(H)(ii)] as may be necessary to carry out this section and to provide notice for purposes of section 274A [8 USCS § 1324a].

(2) The provisions of subsections (a) and (c) of section 214 [8 USCS § 1184(a), (c)] and the provisions of this section preempt any State or local law regulating admissibility of nonimmigrant workers.

(i) Definitions. For purposes of this section:

(1) The term "eligible individual" means, with respect to employment, an individual who is not an unauthorized alien (as defined in section 274A(h)(3) [8 USCS § 1324a(h)](3)) with respect to that employment.

(2) The term "H-2A worker" means a nonimmigrant described in section 101(a)(15)(H)(ii)(a) [8 USCS § 1101(a)(15)(H)(ii)(a)].

HISTORY: (June 27, 1952, ch 477, Title II, Ch 2, § 218 [216], as added Nov. 6, 1986, P. L. 99-603, Title III, Part A, § 301(c), 100 Stat. 3411; Oct. 24, 1988, P. L. 100-525, § 2(l)(2), (3), 102 Stat. 2612; Dec. 12, 1991, P. L. 102-232, Title III, §§ 307(l)(4), 309(b)(8), 105 Stat. 1756, 1759; Oct. 25, 1994, P. L.

103-416, Title II, § 219(z)(8), 108 Stat. 4318; Oct. 22, 1999, P. L. 106-78, Title VII, § 748, 113 Stat. 1167; Dec. 21, 2000, P. L. 106-554, § 1(a)(1), 114 Stat. 2763.)

§ 219. [8 U.S.C. § 1189] Designation of foreign terrorist organizations.

(a) Designation.

(1) In general. The Secretary is authorized to designate an organization as a foreign terrorist organization in accordance with this subsection if the Secretary finds that—

(A) the organization is a foreign organization;

(B) the organization engages in terrorist activity (as defined in section 212(a)(3)(B) [8 USCS § 1182(a)(3)(B)][)] or terrorism (as defined in section 140(d)(2) of the Foreign Relations Authorization Act, Fiscal Years 1988 and 1989 (22 U.S.C. 2656f(d)(2)), or retains the capability and intent to engage in terrorist activity or terrorism[)]; and

(C) the terrorist activity or terrorism of the organization threatens the security of United States nationals or the national security of the United States.

(2) Procedure.

(A) Notice.

(i) To congressional leaders. Seven days before making a designation under this subsection, the Secretary shall, by classified communication, notify the Speaker and Minority Leader of the House of Representatives, the President pro tempore, Majority Leader, and Minority Leader of the Senate, and the members of the relevant committees of the House of Representatives and the Senate, in writing, of the intent to designate an organization under this subsection, together with the findings made under paragraph (1) with respect to that organization, and the factual basis therefor.

(ii) Publication in Federal Register. The Secretary shall publish the designation in the Federal Register seven days after providing the notification under clause (i).

(B) Effect of designation.

(i) For purposes of section 2339B of title 18, United States Code, a designation under this subsection shall take effect upon publication under subparagraph (A)(ii).

(ii) Any designation under this subsection shall cease to have effect upon an Act of Congress disapproving such designation.

(C) Freezing of assets. Upon notification under paragraph (2)(A)(i), the Secretary of the Treasury may require United States financial institutions possessing or controlling any assets of any foreign organization included in the notification to block all financial transactions involving those assets until further directive from either the Secretary of the Treasury, Act of Congress, or order of court.

(3) Record.

(A) In general. In making a designation under this subsection, the Secretary shall create an administrative record.

(B) Classified information. The Secretary may consider classified information in making a designation under this subsection. Classified information shall not be subject to disclosure for such time as it remains classified, except that such information may be disclosed to a court ex parte and in camera for purposes of judicial review under subsection (c).

(4) Period of designation.

(A) In general. A designation under this subsection shall be effective for all purposes until revoked under paragraph (5) or (6) or set aside pursuant to subsection (c).

(B) Review of designation upon petition.

(i) In general. The Secretary shall review the designation of a foreign terrorist organization under the procedures set forth in clauses (iii) and (iv) if the designated organization files a petition for revocation within the petition period described in clause (ii).

(ii) Petition period. For purposes of clause (i)—

(I) if the designated organization has not previously filed a petition for revocation under this subparagraph, the petition period begins 2 years after the date on which the designation was made; or

(II) if the designated organization has previously filed a petition for revocation under this subparagraph, the petition period begins 2 years after the date of the determination made under clause (iv) on that petition.

(iii) Procedures. Any foreign terrorist organization that submits a petition for revocation under this subparagraph must provide evidence in that petition that the relevant circumstances described in paragraph (1) are sufficiently different from the circumstances that were the basis for the designation such that a revocation with respect to the organization is warranted.

(iv) Determination.

(I) In general. Not later than 180 days after receiving a petition for revocation submitted under this subparagraph, the Secretary shall make a determination as to such revocation.

(II) Classified information. The Secretary may consider classified information in making a determination in response to a petition for revocation. Classified information shall not be subject to disclosure for such time as it remains classified, except that such information may be disclosed to a court ex parte and in camera for purposes of judicial review under subsection (c).

(III) Publication of determination. A determination made by the Secretary under this clause shall be published in the Federal Register.

(IV) Procedures. Any revocation by the Secretary shall be made in accordance with paragraph (6).

(C) Other review of designation.

(i) In general. If in a 5-year period no review has taken place under subparagraph (B), the Secretary shall review the designation of the foreign terrorist organization in order to determine whether such designation should be revoked pursuant to paragraph (6).

(ii) Procedures. If a review does not take place pursuant to subparagraph (B) in response to a petition for revocation that is filed in accordance with that subparagraph, then the review shall be conducted pursuant to procedures established by the Secretary. The results of such review and the applicable procedures shall not be reviewable in any court.

(iii) Publication of results of review. The Secretary shall publish any determination made pursuant to this subparagraph in the Federal Register.

(5) Revocation by Act of Congress. The Congress, by an Act of Congress, may block or revoke a designation made under paragraph (1).

(6) Revocation based on change in circumstances.

(A) In general. The Secretary may revoke a designation made under paragraph (1) at any time, and shall revoke a designation upon completion of a review conducted pursuant to subparagraphs (B) and (C) of paragraph (4) if the Secretary finds that—

(i) the circumstances that were the basis for the designation have changed in such a manner as to warrant revocation; or

(ii) the national security of the United States warrants a revocation.

(B) Procedure. The procedural requirements of paragraphs (2) and (3) shall apply to a revocation under this paragraph. Any revocation shall take effect on the date specified in the revocation or upon publication in the Federal Register if no effective date is specified.

(7) Effect of revocation. The revocation of a designation under paragraph (5) or (6) shall not affect any action or proceeding based on conduct committed prior to the effective date of such revocation.

(8) Use of designation in trial or hearing. If a designation under this subsection has become effective under paragraph (2)(B) a defendant in a criminal action or an alien in a removal proceeding shall not be permitted to raise any question concerning the validity of the issuance of such designation as a defense or an objection at any trial or hearing.

(b) Amendments to a designation.

(1) In general. The Secretary may amend a designation under this subsection if the Secretary finds that the organization has changed its name, adopted a new alias, dissolved and then reconstituted itself under a different name or names, or merged with another organization.

(2) Procedure. Amendments made to a designation in accordance with paragraph (1) shall be effective upon publication in the Federal Register. Subparagraphs (B) and (C) of subsection (a)(2) shall apply to an amended designation upon such publication. Paragraphs (2)(A)(i), (4), (5), (6), (7), and (8) of subsection (a) shall also apply to an amended designation.

(3) Administrative record. The administrative record shall be corrected to include the amendments as well as any additional relevant information that supports those amendments.

(4) Classified information. The Secretary may consider classified information in amending a designation in accordance with this subsection. Classified information shall not be subject to disclosure for such time as it remains classified, except that such information may be disclosed to a court ex parte and in camera for purposes of judicial review under subsection (c).

(c) Judicial review of designation.

(1) In general. Not later than 30 days after publication in the Federal Register of a designation, an amended designation, or a determination in response to a petition for revocation, the designated organization may seek judicial review in the United States Court of Appeals for the District of Columbia Circuit.

(2) Basis of review. Review under this subsection shall be based solely upon the administrative record, except that the Government may submit, for ex parte and in camera review, classified information used in making the designation, amended designation, or determination in response to a petition for revocation.

(3) Scope of review. The Court shall hold unlawful and set aside a designation, amended designation, or determination in response to a petition for revocation the court finds to be—

(A) arbitrary, capricious, an abuse of discretion, or otherwise not in accordance with law;

(B) contrary to constitutional right, power, privilege, or immunity;

(C) in excess of statutory jurisdiction, authority, or limitation, or short of statutory right;

(D) lacking substantial support in the administrative record taken as a whole or in classified information submitted to the court under paragraph (2),[;] or

(E) not in accord with the procedures required by law.

(4) Judicial review invoked. The pendency of an action for judicial review of a designation, amended designation, or determination in response to a petition for revocation shall not affect the application of this section, unless the court issues a final order setting aside the designation, amended designation, or determination in response to a petition for revocation.

(d) Definitions. As used in this section—

(1) the term "classified information" has the meaning given that term in section 1(a) of the Classified Information Procedures Act (18 U.S.C. App.);

(2) the term "national security" means the national defense, foreign relations, or economic interests of the United States;

(3) the term "relevant committees" means the Committees on the Judiciary, Intelligence, and Foreign Relations of the Senate and the Committees on the Judiciary, Intelligence, and International Relations of the House of Representatives; and

(4) the term "Secretary" means the Secretary of State, in consultation with the Secretary of the Treasury and the Attorney General.

HISTORY: (June 27, 1952, ch 477, Title II, Ch 2, § 219, as added April 24, 1996, P. L. 104-132, Title III, Subtitle A, § 302(a), 110 Stat. 1248; Sept. 30, 1996, P. L. 104-208, Div C, Title III, Subtitle D, § 356, Title VI, Subtitle E, § 671(c)(1), 110 Stat. 3009-644, 3009-722; Oct. 26, 2001, P. L. 107-56, Title IV, Subtitle B, § 411(c), 115 Stat. 349; Dec. 17, 2004, P. L. 108-458, Title VII, Subtitle A, § 7119(a)–(c), 118 Stat. 3801.)

Chapter 3—Issuance of Entry Documents

§ 221. [8 U.S.C. § 1201] Issuance of visas.

(a) Immigrants; nonimmigrants.

(1) Under the conditions hereinafter prescribed and subject to the limitations prescribed in this Act or regulations issued thereunder, a consular officer may issue (A) to an immigrant who has made proper application therefor, an immigrant visa which shall

consist of the application provided for in section 222 [8 USCS § 1202], visaed by such consular officer, and shall specify the foreign state, if any, to which the immigrant is charged, the immigrant's particular status under such foreign state, the preference, immediate relative, or special immigrant classification to which the alien is charged, the date on which the validity of the visa shall expire, and such additional information as may be required; and (B) to a nonimmigrant who has made proper application therefor, a nonimmigrant visa, which shall specify the classification under section 101(a)(15) [8 USCS § 1101(a)(15)] of the nonimmigrant, the period during which the nonimmigrant visa shall be valid, and such additional information as may be required.

(2) The Secretary of State shall provide to the Service an electronic version of the visa file of each alien who has been issued a visa to ensure that the data in that visa file is available to immigration inspectors at the United States ports of entry before the arrival of the alien at such a port of entry.

(b) Registration; photographs; waiver of requirement. Each alien who applies for a visa shall be registered in connection with his application, and shall furnish copies of his photograph signed by him for such use as may be by regulations required. The requirements of this subsection may be waived in the discretion of the Secretary of State in the case of any alien who is within that class of nonimmigrants enumerated in sections 101(a)(15)(A), and 101(a)(15)(G) [8 USCS § 1101(a)(15)(A) and (G)], or in the case of any alien who is granted a diplomatic visa on a diplomatic passport or on the equivalent thereof.

(c) Period of validity; renewal or replacement.

(1) Immigrant visas. An immigrant visa shall be valid for such period, not exceeding six months, as shall be by regulations prescribed, except that any visa issued to a child lawfully adopted by a United States citizen and spouse while such citizen is serving abroad in the United States Armed Forces, or is employed abroad by the United States Government, or is temporarily abroad on business, shall be valid until such time, for a period not to exceed three years, as the adoptive citizen parent returns to the United States in due course of his service, employment, or business.

(2) Nonimmigrant visas. A nonimmigrant visa shall be valid for such periods as shall be by regulations prescribed. In prescribing the period of validity of a nonimmigrant visa in the case of nationals of any foreign country who are eligible for such visas, the Secretary of State shall, insofar as practicable, accord to such nationals the same treatment upon a reciprocal basis as such foreign country accords to nationals of the United States who are within a similar class; except that in the case of aliens who are nationals of a foreign country and who either are granted refugee status and firmly resettled in another foreign country or are granted permanent residence and residing in another foreign country, the Secretary of State may prescribe the period of validity of such a visa based upon the treatment granted by that other foreign country to alien refugees and permanent residents, respectively, in the United States.

(3) Visa replacement. An immigrant visa may be replaced under the original number during the fiscal year in which the original visa was issued for an immigrant who establishes to the satisfaction of the consular officer that the immigrant—

(A) was unable to use the original immigrant visa during the period of its validity because of reasons beyond his control and for which he was not responsible;

(B) is found by a consular officer to be eligible for an immigrant visa; and

(C) pays again the statutory fees for an application and an immigrant visa.

(4) Fee waiver. If an immigrant visa was issued, on or after March 27, 2013, for a child who has been lawfully adopted, or who is coming to the United States to be adopted, by a United States citizen, any statutory immigrant visa fees relating to a renewal or replacement of such visa may be waived or, if already paid, may be refunded upon request, subject to such criteria as the Secretary of State may prescribe, if—

(A) the immigrant child was unable to use the original immigrant visa during the period of its validity as a direct result of extraordinary circumstances, including the denial of an exit permit; and

(B) if such inability was attributable to factors beyond the control of the adopting parent or parents and of the immigrant.

(d) Physical examination. Prior to the issuance of an immigrant visa to any alien, the consular officer shall require such alien to submit to a physical and mental examination in accordance with such regulations as may be prescribed. Prior to the issuance of a nonimmigrant visa to any alien, the consular officer may require such alien to submit to a physical or mental examination, or both, if in his opinion such examination is necessary to ascertain whether such alien is eligible to receive a visa.

(e) Surrender of visa. Each immigrant shall surrender his immigrant visa to the immigration officer at the port of entry, who shall endorse on the visa the date and the port of arrival, the identity of the vessel or other means of transportation by which the immigrant arrived, and such other endorsements as may be by regulations required.

(f) Surrender of documents. Each nonimmigrant shall present or surrender to the immigration officer at the port of entry such documents as may be by regulation required. In the case of an alien crewman not in possession of any individual documents other than a passport and until such time as it becomes practicable to issue individual documents, such alien crewman may be admitted, subject to the provisions of this title, if his name appears in the crew list of the vessel or aircraft on which he arrives and the crew list is visaed by a consular officer, but the consular officer shall have the right to deny admission to any alien crewman from the crew list visa.

(g) Non-issuance of visas or other documents. No visa or other documentation shall be issued to an alien if (1) it appears to the consular officer, from statements in the application, or in the papers submitted therewith, that such alien is ineligible to receive a visa or such other documentation under section 212 [8 USCS § 1182], or any other provision of law, (2) the application fails to comply with the provisions of this Act, or the regulations issued thereunder, or (3) the consular officer knows or has reason to believe that such alien is ineligible to receive a visa or such other documentation under section 212 [8 USCS § 1182], or any other provision of law: Provided, That a visa or other documentation may be issued to an alien who is within the purview of section 212(a)(4) [8 USCS § 1182(a)(4)], if such alien is otherwise entitled to receive a visa or other documentation, upon receipt of notice by the consular officer from the Attorney General of the giving of a bond or undertaking providing indemnity as in the case of aliens admitted under section 213 [8 USCS § 1183]; Provided further, That a visa may be issued to an alien defined in section 101(a)(15)(B) or (F) [8 USCS § 1101(a)(15)(B) or (F)], if such alien is otherwise entitled to receive a visa, upon receipt of a notice by the consular officer from the Attorney General of the giving of a bond with sufficient surety in such sum and containing such conditions as the consular officer shall prescribe, to insure that at the expiration of the time for which such alien has been admitted by the Attorney General, as provided in section 214(a) [8 USCS § 1184(a)], or upon failure to maintain the status under which he was admitted, or to maintain any status subsequently acquired under section 248 of the Act [8 USCS § 1258], such alien will depart from the United States.

(h) Nonadmission upon arrival. Nothing in this Act shall be construed to entitle any alien, to whom a visa or other documentation has been issued, to be admitted [to] the United States, if, upon arrival at a port of entry in the United States, he is found to be inadmissible under this Act, or any other provision of law. The substance of this subsection shall appear upon every visa application.

(i) Revocation of visas or documents. After the issuance of a visa or other documentation to any alien, the consular officer or the Secretary of State may at any time, in his discretion, revoke such visa or other documentation. Notice of such revocation shall be communicated to the Attorney General, and such revocation shall invalidate the visa or other documentation from the date of issuance: Provided, That carriers or transportation companies, and masters, commanding officers, agents, owners, charterers, or consignees, shall not be penalized under section 273(b) [8 USCS § 1323(b)] for action taken in reliance on such visas or other documentation, unless they received due notice of such revocation prior to the alien's embarkation. There shall be no means of judicial review (including review pursuant to section 2241 of title 28, United States Code, or any other habeas corpus provision, and sections 1361 and 1651 of such title) of a revocation under this subsection, except in the context of a removal proceeding if such revocation provides the sole ground for removal under section 237(a)(1)(B) [8 USCS § 1227(a)(1)(B)].

HISTORY: (June 27, 1952, ch 477, Title II, Ch 3, § 221, 66 Stat. 191; Sept. 26, 1961, P. L. 87-301, § 4, 75 Stat. 651; Oct. 3, 1965, P. L. 89-236, §§ 11(a), (b), 17, 79 Stat. 918, 919; Dec. 29, 1981, P. L. 97-116, § 18(f), 95 Stat. 1620; Nov. 14, 1986, P. L. 99-653, § 5(a)-(c), 100 Stat. 3656; Nov. 14, 1986, P. L. 99-652, § 5(1)–(3) [(a)–(c)], 100 Stat. 3656; Oct. 24, 1988, P. L. 100-525, § 8(d)(1), 102 Stat. 2617; Nov. 29, 1990, P. L. 101-649, Title VI, § 603(a)(9), 104 Stat. 5083; Dec. 12, 1991, P. L. 102-232, Title III, § 302(e)(8)(C), 105 Stat. 1746; Sept. 30, 1996, P. L. 104-208, Div C, Title III, Subtitle A, § 308(d)(4)(G), (f)(2)(B), Title VI, Subtitle C, § 631, 110 Stat. 3009-618, 3009-621, 3009-700; May 14, 2002, P. L. 107-173, Title III, § 301, 116 Stat. 552; Dec. 17, 2004, P. L. 108-458, Title V, Subtitle C, § 5304(a), 118 Stat. 3736; Oct. 16, 2015, P. L. 114-70, § 2, 129 Stat. 561.)

§ 222. [8 U.S.C. § 1202] Application for visas.

(a) Immigrant visas. Every alien applying for an immigrant visa and for alien registration shall make application therefor in such form and manner and at such place as shall be by regulations prescribed. In the application the alien shall state his full and true name, and any other name which he has used or by which he has been known; age and sex; the date and place of his birth; and such additional information necessary to the identification of the applicant and the enforcement of the immigration and nationality laws as may be by regulations prescribed.

(b) Other documentary evidence for immigrant visa. Every alien applying for an immigrant visa shall present a valid unexpired passport or other suitable travel document, or document of identity and nationality, if such document is required under the regulations issued by the Secretary of State. The immigrant shall furnish to the consular officer with his application a copy of a certification by the appropriate police authorities stating what their records show concerning the immigrant; a certified copy of any existing prison record, military record, and record of his birth; and a certified copy of all other records or documents concerning him or his case which may be required by the consular officer. The copy of each document so furnished shall be permanently attached to the application and become a part thereof. In the event that the immigrant establishes to the satisfaction of the consular officer that any document or record required by this subsection is unobtainable, the consular officer may permit the immigrant to submit in lieu of such document or record other satisfactory evidence of the fact to which such document or record would, if obtainable, pertain. All immigrant visa applications shall be reviewed and adjudicated by a consular officer.

(c) Nonimmigrant visas; nonimmigrant registration; form, manner and contents of application. Every alien applying for a nonimmigrant visa and for alien registration shall make application therefor in such form and manner as shall be by regulations prescribed. In the application the alien shall state his full and true name, the date and place of birth, his nationality, the purpose and length of his intended stay in the United States; his marital status; and such additional information necessary to the identification of the applicant, the determination of his eligibility for a nonimmigrant visa, and the enforcement of the immigration and nationality laws as may be by regulations prescribed. The alien shall provide complete and accurate information in response to any request for information contained in the application. At the discretion of the Secretary of State, application forms for the various classes of nonimmigrant admissions described in section 101(a)(15) [8 USCS § 1101(a)(15)] may vary according to the class of visa being requested.

(d) Other documentary evidence for nonimmigrant visa. Every alien applying for a nonimmigrant visa and alien registration shall furnish to the consular officer, with his application, a certified copy of such documents pertaining to him as may be by regulations required. All nonimmigrant visa applications shall be reviewed and adjudicated by a consular officer.

(e) Signing and verification of application. Except as may be otherwise prescribed by regulations, each application for an immigrant visa shall be signed by the applicant in the presence of the consular officer, and verified by the oath of the applicant administered by the consular officer. The application for an immigrant visa, when visaed by the consular officer, shall become the immigrant visa. The application for a nonimmigrant visa or other documentation as a nonimmigrant shall be disposed of as may be by regulations prescribed. The issuance of a nonimmigrant visa shall, except as may be otherwise by regulations prescribed, be evidenced by a stamp[, or other] placed in the alien's passport.

(f) Confidential nature of records. The records of the Department of State and of diplomatic and consular offices of the United States pertaining to the issuance or refusal of visas or permits to enter the United States shall be considered confidential and shall be used only for the formulation, amendment, administration, or enforcement of the immigration, nationality, and other laws of the United States, except that—

(1) in the discretion of the Secretary of State certified copies of such records may be made available to a court which certifies that the information contained in such records is needed by the court in the interest of the ends of justice in a case pending before the court. [; and]

(2) the Secretary of State, in the Secretary's discretion and on the basis of reciprocity, may provide to a foreign government information in the Department of State's computerized visa lookout database and, when necessary and appropriate, other records covered by this section related to information in the database—

(A) with regard to individual aliens, at any time on a case-by-case basis for the purpose of preventing, investigating, or punishing acts that would constitute a crime in the United States, including, but not limited to, terrorism or trafficking in controlled substances, persons, or illicit weapons; or

(B) with regard to any or all aliens in the database, pursuant to such conditions as the Secretary of State shall establish in an agreement with the foreign government in which that government agrees to use such information and records for the purposes described in subparagraph (A) or to deny visas to persons who would be inadmissible to the United States.

(g) Nonimmigrant visa void at conclusion of authorized period of stay.

(1) In the case of an alien who has been admitted on the basis of a nonimmigrant visa and remained in the United States beyond the period of stay authorized by the Attorney General, such visa shall be void beginning after the conclusion of such period of stay.

(2) An alien described in paragraph (1) shall be ineligible to be readmitted to the United States as a nonimmigrant, except—

(A) on the basis of a visa (other than the visa described in paragraph (1)) issued in a consular office located in the country of the alien's nationality (or, if there is no office in such country, in such other consular office as the Secretary of State shall specify); or

(B) where extraordinary circumstances are found by the Secretary of State to exist.

(h) In person interview with consular officer. Notwithstanding any other provision of this Act, the Secretary of State shall require every alien applying for a nonimmigrant visa—

(1) who is at least 14 years of age and not more than 79 years of age to submit to an in person interview with a consular officer unless the requirement for such interview is waived—

(A) by a consular official and such alien is—

(i) within that class of nonimmigrants enumerated in subparagraph (A) or (G) of section 101(a)(15) [8 USCS § 1101(a)(15)];

(ii) within the NATO visa category;

(iii) within that class of nonimmigrants enumerated in section 101(a)(15)(C)(iii) [8 USCS § 1101(a)(15)(C)(iii)] (referred to as the "C-3 visa" category); or

(iv) granted a diplomatic or official visa on a diplomatic or official passport or on the equivalent thereof;

(B) by a consular official and such alien is applying for a visa—

(i) not more than 12 months after the date on which such alien's prior visa expired;

(ii) for the visa classification for which such prior visa was issued;

(iii) from the consular post located in the country of such alien's usual residence, unless otherwise prescribed in regulations that require an applicant to apply for a visa in the country of which such applicant is a national; and

(iv) the consular officer has no indication that such alien has not complied with the immigration laws and regulations of the United States; or

(C) by the Secretary of State if the Secretary determines that such waiver is—

(i) in the national interest of the United States; or

(ii) necessary as a result of unusual or emergent circumstances; and

(2) notwithstanding paragraph (1), to submit to an in person interview with a consular officer if such alien—

(A) is not a national or resident of the country in which such alien is applying for a visa;

(B) was previously refused a visa, unless such refusal was overcome or a waiver of ineligibility has been obtained;

(C) is listed in the Consular Lookout and Support System (or successor system at the Department of State);

(D) is a national of a country officially designated by the Secretary of State as a state sponsor of terrorism, except such nationals who possess nationalities of countries that are not designated as state sponsors of terrorism;

(E) requires a security advisory opinion or other Department of State clearance, unless such alien is—

(i) within that class of nonimmigrants enumerated in subparagraph (A) or (G) of section 101(a)(15) [8 USCS § 1101(a)(15)];

(ii) within the NATO visa category;

(iii) within that class of nonimmigrants enumerated in section 101(a)(15)(C)(iii) [8 USCS § 1101(a)(15)(C)] (referred to as the "C-3 visa" category); or

(iv) an alien who qualifies for a diplomatic or official visa, or its equivalent; or

(F) is identified as a member of a group or sector that the Secretary of State determines—

(i) poses a substantial risk of submitting inaccurate information in order to obtain a visa;

(ii) has historically had visa applications denied at a rate that is higher than the average rate of such denials; or

(iii) poses a security threat to the United States.

HISTORY: (June 27, 1952, ch 477, Title II, Ch 3, § 222, 66 Stat. 193; Sept. 26, 1961, P. L. 87-301, § 6, 75 Stat. 653; Oct. 3, 1965, P. L. 89-236. § 11(c), 79 Stat. 918; Nov. 14, 1986, P. L. 99-653, § 6, 100 Stat. 3656; Nov. 14, 1986, P. L. 99-653, § 6, 100 Stat. 3656; Oct. 24, 1988, P. L. 100-525, §§ 8(e), 9(j) 102 Stat. 2617, 2620; Oct. 25, 1994, P. L. 103-416, Title II, § 205(a), 108 Stat. 4311; Sept. 30, 1996, P. L. 104-208, Div C, Title VI, Subtitle C, §§ 632(a), 634, 110 Stat. 3009-701; Oct. 26, 2001, P. L. 107-56, Title IV, Subtitle B, § 413, 115 Stat. 353; Dec. 17, 2004, P. L. 108-458, Title V, Subtitle C, §§ 5301, 5302, Title VII, Subtitle B, § 7203(b), 118 Stat. 3735, 3814.)

§ 223. [8 U.S.C. § 1203] Reentry permit.

(a) Application; contents. (1) Any alien lawfully admitted for permanent residence, or (2) any alien lawfully admitted to the United States pursuant to clause 6 of section 3 of the Immigration Act of 1924, between July 1, 1924, and July 5, 1932, both dates inclusive, who intends to depart temporarily from the United States may make application to the Attorney General for a permit to reenter the United States, stating the length of his intended absence or absences, and the reasons therefor. Such applications shall be made under oath, and shall be in such form, contain such information, and be accompanied by such photographs of the applicant as may be by regulations prescribed.

(b) Issuance of permit; nonrenewability. If the Attorney General finds (1) that the applicant under subsection (a)(1) has been lawfully admitted to the United States for permanent residence, or that the applicant under subsection (a)(2) has since admission maintained the status required of him at the time of his admission and such applicant desires to visit abroad and to return to the United States to resume the status existing at the time of his departure for such visit, (2) that the application is made in good faith, and (3) that the alien's proposed departure from the United States would not be contrary to the interests of the United States, the Attorney General may, in his discretion, issue the permit, which shall be valid for not more than two years from the date of issuance and shall not be renewable. The permit shall be in such form as shall be by regulations prescribed for the complete identification of the alien.

(c) Multiple reentries. During the period of validity, such permit may be used by the alien in making one or more applications for reentry into the United States.

(d) Presented and surrendered. Upon the return of the alien to the United States the permit shall be presented to the immigration officer at the port of entry, and upon the expiration of its validity, the permit shall be surrendered to the Service.

(e) Permit in lieu of visa. A permit issued under this section in the possession of the person to whom issued, shall be accepted in lieu of any visa which otherwise would be required from such person under this Act. Otherwise a permit issued under this section shall have no effect under the immigration laws except to show that the alien to whom it was issued is returning from a temporary visit abroad; but nothing in this section shall be construed as making such permit the exclusive means of establishing that the alien is so returning.

HISTORY: (June 27, 1952, ch 477, Title II, Ch 3, § 223, 66 Stat. 194; Dec. 29, 1981, P. L. 97-116, § 6, 95 Stat. 1615.)

§ 224. [8 U.S.C. § 1204] Immediate relative and special immigrant visas.

A consular officer may, subject to the limitations provided in section 221 [8 USCS § 1201], issue an immigrant visa to a special immigrant or immediate relative as such upon satisfactory proof, under regulations prescribed under this Act, that the applicant is entitled to special immigrant or immediate relative status.

HISTORY: (June 27, 1952, ch 477, Title II, Ch 3, § 224, 66 Stat. 195; Oct. 3, 1965, P. L. 89-236, §§ 11(d), 79 Stat. 918.)

Chapter 4—Inspection, Apprehension, Examination, Exclusion, and Removal

§ 231. [8 U.S.C. § 1221] Lists of alien and citizen passengers arriving and departing.

(a) Arrival manifests. For each commercial vessel or aircraft transporting any person to any seaport or airport of the United States from any place outside the United States, it shall be the duty of an appropriate official specified in subsection (d) to provide to any United States border officer (as defined in subsection (i)) at that port manifest information about each passenger, crew member, and other occupant transported on such vessel or aircraft prior to arrival at that port.

(b) Departure manifests. For each commercial vessel or aircraft taking passengers on board at any seaport or airport of the United States, who are destined to any place outside the United States, it shall be the duty of an appropriate official specified in subsection (d) to provide any United States border officer (as defined in subsection (i)) before departure from such port manifest information about each passenger, crew member, and other occupant to be transported.

(c) Contents of manifest. The information to be provided with respect to each person listed on a manifest required to be provided under subsection (a) or (b) shall include—

(1) complete name;

(2) date of birth;

(3) citizenship;

(4) sex;

(5) passport number and country of issuance;

(6) country of residence;

(7) United States visa number, date, and place of issuance, where applicable;

(8) alien registration number, where applicable;

(9) United States address while in the United States; and

(10) such other information the Attorney General, in consultation with the Secretary of State, and the Secretary of Treasury determines as being necessary for the identification of the persons transported and for the enforcement of the immigration laws and to protect safety and national security.

(d) Appropriate officials specified. An appropriate official specified in this subsection is the master or commanding officer, or authorized agent, owner, or consignee, of the commercial vessel or aircraft concerned.

(e) Deadline for requirement of electronic transmission of manifest information. Not later than January 1, 2003, manifest information required to be provided under subsection (a) or (b) shall be transmitted electronically by the appropriate official specified in subsection (d) to an immigration officer.

(f) Prohibition. No operator of any private or public carrier that is under a duty to provide manifest information under this section shall be granted clearance papers until the appropriate official specified in subsection (d) has complied with the requirements of this subsection, except that, in the case of commercial vessels or aircraft that the Attorney General determines are making regular trips to the United States, the Attorney General may, when expedient, arrange for the provision of manifest information of persons departing the United States at a later date.

(g) Penalties against noncomplying shipments, aircraft, or carriers [Caution: For inflation-adjusted civil monetary penalties, see8 CFR 280.53.]. If it shall appear to the satisfaction of the Attorney General that an appropriate official specified in subsection (d), any public or private carrier, or the agent of any transportation line, as the case may be, has refused or failed to provide manifest information required by subsection (a) or (b), or that the manifest information provided is not accurate and full based on information provided to the carrier, such official, carrier, or agent, as the case may be, shall pay to the Commissioner the sum of $1,000 for each person with respect to whom such accurate and full manifest information is not provided, or with respect to whom the manifest information is not prepared as prescribed by this section or by regulations issued pursuant thereto. No commercial vessel or aircraft shall be granted clearance pending determination of the question of the liability to the payment of such penalty, or while it remains unpaid, and no such penalty shall be remitted or refunded, except that clearance may be granted prior to the determination of such question upon the deposit with the Commissioner of a bond or undertaking approved by the Attorney General or a sum sufficient to cover such penalty.

(h) Waiver. The Attorney General may waive the requirements of subsection (a) or (b) upon such circumstances and conditions as the Attorney General may by regulation prescribe.

(i) United States border officer defined. In this section, the term "United States border officer" means, with respect to a particular port of entry into the United States, any United States official who is performing duties at that port of entry.

(j) Record of citizens and resident aliens leaving permanently for foreign countries. The Attorney General may authorize immigration officers to record the following information regarding every resident person leaving the United States by way of the Canadian or Mexican borders for permanent residence in a foreign country: Names, age, and sex; whether married or single; calling or occupation; whether able to read or write; nationality; country of birth; country of which citizen or subject; race; last permanent residence in the United States; intended future permanent residence; and time and port of last arrival in the United States; and if a United States citizen or national, the facts on which claim to that status is based

HISTORY: (June 27, 1952, ch 477, Title II, Ch 4, § 231, 66 Stat. 195; Dec. 29, 1981, P. L. 97-116, § 18(g), 95 Stat. 1620; Nov. 29, 1990, P. L. 101-649, Title V, Subtitle D, § 543(a)(1), 104 Stat. 5057; Dec. 12, 1991, P. L. 102-232, Title III, § 306(c)(4)(A), 105 Stat. 1752; Nov. 28, 2001, P. L. 107-77, Title I, § 115, 115 Stat. 768; May 14, 2002, P. L. 107-173, Title IV, § 402(a), 116 Stat. 557.)

§ 232. [8 U.S.C. § 1222] Detention of aliens for physical and mental examination.

(a) Detention of aliens. For the purpose of determining whether aliens (including alien crewmen) arriving at ports of the United States belong to any of the classes inadmissible under this Act, by reason of being afflicted with any of the diseases or mental or physical defects or disabilities set forth in section 212(a) [8 USCS § 1182(a)], or whenever the Attorney General has received information showing that any aliens are coming from a country or have embarked at a place where any of such diseases are prevalent or epidemic, such aliens shall be detained for a sufficient time to enable the immigration officers and medical officers to subject such aliens to observation and an examination sufficient to determine whether or not they belong to inadmissible classes.

(b) Physical and mental examination. The physical and mental examination of arriving aliens (including alien crewmen) shall be made by medical officers of the United States Public Health Service, who shall conduct all medical examinations and shall certify, for the information of the immigration officers and the immigration judges, any physical and mental defect or disease observed by such medical officers in any such alien. If medical officers of the United States Public Health Service are not available, civil surgeons of not less than four years' professional experience may be employed for such service upon such terms as may be prescribed by the Attorney General. Aliens (including alien crewmen) arriving at ports of the United States shall be examined by at least one such medical officer or civil surgeon under such administrative regulations as the Attorney General may prescribe, and under medical regulations prepared by the Secretary of Health and Human Services. Medical officers of the United States Public Health Service who have had special training in the diagnosis of insanity and mental defects shall be detailed for duty or employed at such ports of entry as the Attorney General may designate, and such medical officers shall be provided with suitable facilities for the detention and examination of all arriving aliens who it is suspected may be inadmissible under paragraph (1) of section 212(a) [8 USCS § 1182(a)(1)], and the services of interpreters shall be provided for such examination. Any alien certified under paragraph (1) of section 212(a) [8 USCS § 1182(a)(1)] may appeal to a board of medical officers of the United States Public Health Service, which shall be convened by the Secretary of Health and Human Services, and any such alien may introduce before such board one expert medical witness at his own cost and expense.

(c) Certification of certain helpless aliens. If an examining medical officer determines that an alien arriving in the United States is inadmissible, is helpless from sickness, mental or physical disability, or infancy, and is accompanied by another alien whose protection or guardianship may be required, the officer may certify such fact for purposes of applying section 212(a)(10)(B) [8 USCS § 1182(a)(1)(B)] with respect to the other alien.

HISTORY: (June 27, 1952, ch 477, Title II, Ch 4, § 232, 66 Stat. 196; Oct. 18, 1986, P. L. 99-500, Title I, § 101(b) [Title II, § 206(a)] 100 Stat. 1738-56; Oct. 30, 1986, P. L. 99-591, Title I, § 101(b) [Title II, § 206(a)], 100 Stat. 3341-56; Oct. 24, 1988, P. L. 100-525, § 4(b)(1), (2), (d), 102 Stat. 2615; Sept. 30, 1996, P. L. 104-208, Div C, Title III, Subtitle A, §§ 308(b)(2), (3), (c)(2)(A), (d)(3)(A), (4)(H), 110 Stat. 3009-615, 3009-616, 3009-617, 3009-618.)

§ 233. [8 U.S.C. § 1223] Entry through or from foreign territory and adjacent islands.

(a) Necessity of transportation contract. The Attorney General shall have power to enter into contracts with transportation lines for the inspection and admission of aliens coming to the United States from foreign territory or from adjacent islands. No such transportation line shall be allowed to land any such alien in the United States until and unless it has entered into any such contracts which may be required by the Attorney General.

(b) Landing stations. Every transportation line engaged in carrying alien passengers for hire to the United States from foreign territory or from adjacent islands shall provide and maintain at its expense suitable landing stations, approved by the Attorney General, conveniently located at the point or points of entry. No such transportation line shall be allowed to land any alien passengers in the United States, until such landing stations are provided, and unless such stations are thereafter maintained to the satisfaction of the Attorney General.

(c) Landing agreements. The Attorney General shall have power to enter into contracts including bonding agreements with transportation lines to guarantee the passage through the United States in immediate and continuous transit of aliens destined to foreign countries. Notwithstanding any other provision of this Act, such aliens may not have their classification changed under section 248 [8 USCS § 1258].

(d) Definitions. As used in this section the terms "transportation line" and "transportation company" include, but are not limited to, the owner, charterer, consignee, or authorized agent operating any vessel or aircraft or railroad train bringing aliens to the United States, to foreign territory, or to adjacent islands.

HISTORY: (June 27, 1952, ch 477, Title II, Ch 4, § 233 [238], 66 Stat. 202; Nov. 14, 1986, P. L. 99-653, § 7(b), 100 Stat. 3657; Sept. 30, 1996, P. L. 104-208, Div C, Title III, Subtitle A, § 308(b)(4), (f)(4), Subtitle E, § 362, 110 Stat. 3009-615, 3009-622, 3009-645.)

§ 234. [8 U.S.C. § 1224] Designation of ports of entry for aliens arriving by aircraft.

The Attorney General is authorized (1) by regulation to designate as ports of entry for aliens arriving by aircraft any of the ports of entry for civil aircraft designated as such in accordance with law; (2) by regulation to provide such reasonable requirements for aircraft in civil air navigation with respect to giving notice of intention to land in advance of landing, or notice of landing, as shall be deemed necessary for purposes of administration and enforcement of this Act; and (3) by regulation to provide for the application to civil air navigation of the provisions of this Act where not expressly so provided in this Act to such extent and upon such conditions as he deems necessary. Any person who violates any regulation made under this section shall be subject to a civil penalty of $2,000 which may be remitted or mitigated by the Attorney General in accordance with such proceedings as the Attorney General shall by regulation prescribe. In case the violation is by the owner or person in command of the aircraft, the penalty shall be a lien upon the aircraft, and such aircraft may be libeled therefor in the appropriate United States court. The determination by the Attorney General and remission or mitigation of the civil penalty shall be final. In case the violation is by the owner or person in command of the aircraft, the penalty shall be a lien upon the aircraft and may be collected by proceedings in rem which shall conform as nearly as may be to civil suits in admiralty. The Supreme Court of the United States, and under its direction other courts of the United States, are authorized to prescribe rules regulating such proceedings against aircraft in any particular not otherwise provided by law. Any aircraft made subject to a lien by this section may be summarily seized by, and placed in the custody of such persons as the Attorney General may by regulation prescribe. The aircraft may be released from such custody upon deposit of such amount not exceeding $2,000 as the Attorney General may prescribe, or of a bond in such sum and with such sureties as the Attorney General may prescribe, conditioned upon the payment of the penalty which may be finally determined by the Attorney General.

HISTORY: (June 27, 1952, ch 477, Title II, Ch 4, § 234 [239], 66 Stat. 203; Nov. 29, 1990, P. L. 101-649, Title V, Subtitle D, § 543(a)(3), 104 Stat. 5058; Dec. 12, 1991, P. L. 102-232, Title III, § 306(c)(2), 105 Stat. 1752; Sept. 30, 1996, P. L. 104-208, Div C, Title III, Subtitle A, § 304(a)(1), 110 Stat. 3009-587.)

§ 235. [8 U.S.C. § 1225] Inspection by immigration officers; expedited removal of inadmissible arriving aliens; referral for hearing.

(a) Inspection.

(1) Aliens treated as applicants for admission. An alien present in the United States who has not been admitted or who arrives in the United States (whether or not at a designated port of arrival and including an alien who is brought to the United States after having been interdicted in international or United States waters) shall be deemed for purposes of this Act an applicant for admission.

(2) Stowaways. An arriving alien who is a stowaway is not eligible to apply for admission or to be admitted and shall be ordered removed upon inspection by an immigration officer. Upon such inspection if the alien indicates an intention to apply for asylum under section 208 [8 USCS § 1158] or a fear of persecution, the officer shall refer the alien for an interview under subsection (b)(1)(B). A stowaway may apply for asylum only if the stowaway is found to have a credible fear of persecution under subsection (b)(1)(B). In no case may a stowaway be considered an applicant for admission or eligible for a hearing under section 240 [8 USCS § 1229a].

(3) Inspection. All aliens (including alien crewmen) who are applicants for admission or otherwise seeking admission or readmission to or transit through the United States shall be inspected by immigration officers.

(4) Withdrawal of application for admission. An alien applying for admission may, in the discretion of the Attorney General and at any time, be permitted to withdraw the application for admission and depart immediately from the United States.

(5) Statements. An applicant for admission may be required to state under oath any information sought by an immigration officer regarding the purposes and intentions of the applicant in seeking admission to the United States, including the applicant's intended length of stay and whether the applicant intends to remain permanently or become a United States citizen, and whether the applicant is inadmissible.

(b) Inspection of applicants for admission.

(1) Inspection of aliens arriving in the United States and certain other aliens who have not been admitted or paroled.

(A) Screening.

(i) In general. If an immigration officer determines that an alien (other than an alien described in subparagraph (F)) who is arriving in the United States or is described in clause (iii) is inadmissible under section 212(a)(6)(C) or 212(a)(7) [8 USCS § 1182(a)(6)(C) or 1182(a)(7)], the officer shall order the alien removed from the United States without further hearing or review unless the alien indicates either an intention to apply for asylum under section 208 [8 USCS § 1158] or a fear of persecution.

(ii) Claims for asylum. If an immigration officer determines that an alien (other than an alien described in subparagraph (F)) who is arriving in the United States or is described in clause (iii) is inadmissible under section 212(a)(6)(C) or 212(a)(7) [8 USCS § 1182(a)(6)(C) or 1182(a)(7)] and the alien indicates either an intention to apply for asylum under section 208 [8 USCS § 1158] or a fear of persecution, the officer shall refer the alien for an interview by an asylum officer under subparagraph (B).

(iii) Application to certain other aliens.

(I) In general. The Attorney General may apply clauses (i) and (ii) of this subparagraph to any or all aliens described in subclause (II) as designated by the Attorney General. Such designation shall be in the sole and unreviewable discretion of the Attorney General and may be modified at any time.

(II) Aliens described. An alien described in this clause is an alien who is not described in subparagraph (F), who has not been admitted or paroled into the United States, and who has not affirmatively shown, to the satisfaction of an immigration officer, that alien has been physically present in the United States continuously for the 2-year period immediately prior to the date of the determination of inadmissibility under this subparagraph.

(B) Asylum interviews.

(i) Conduct by asylum officers. An asylum officer shall conduct interviews of aliens referred under subparagraph (A)(ii), either at a port of entry or at such other place designated by the Attorney General.

(ii) Referral of certain aliens. If the officer determines at the time of the interview that an alien has a credible fear of persecution (within the meaning of clause (v)), the alien shall be detained for further consideration of the application for asylum.

(iii) Removal without further review if no credible fear of persecution.

(I) In general. Subject to subclause (III), if the officer determines that an alien does not have a credible fear of persecution, the officer shall order the alien removed from the United States without further hearing or review.

(II) Record of determination. The officer shall prepare a written record of a determination under subclause (I). Such record shall include a summary of the material facts as stated by the applicant, such additional facts (if any) relied upon by the officer, and the officer's analysis of why, in the light of such facts, the alien has not established a credible fear of persecution. A copy of the officer's interview notes shall be attached to the written summary.

(III) Review of determination. The Attorney General shall provide by regulation and upon the alien's request for prompt review by an immigration judge of a determination under subclause (I) that the alien does not have a credible fear of persecution. Such review shall include an opportunity for the alien to be heard and questioned by the immigration judge, either in person or by telephonic or video connection. Review shall be concluded as expeditiously as possible, to the maximum extent practicable within 24 hours, but in no case later than 7 days after the date of the determination under subclause (I).

(IV) Mandatory detention. Any alien subject to the procedures under this clause shall be detained pending a final determination of credible fear of persecution and, if found not to have such a fear, until removed.

(iv) Information about interviews. The Attorney General shall provide information concerning the asylum interview described in this subparagraph to aliens who may be eligible. An alien who is eligible for such interview may consult with a person or persons of the alien's choosing prior to the interview or any review thereof, according to regulations prescribed by the Attorney General. Such consultation shall be at no expense to the Government and shall not unreasonably delay the process.

(v) Credible fear of persecution defined. For purposes of this subparagraph, the term "credible fear of persecution" means that there is a significant possibility, taking into account the credibility of the statements made by the alien in support of the alien's claim and such other facts as are known to the officer, that the alien could establish eligibility for asylum under section 208 [8 USCS § 1158].

(C) Limitation on administrative review. Except as provided in subparagraph (B)(iii)(III), a removal order entered in accordance with subparagraph (A)(i) or (B)(iii)(I) is not subject to administrative appeal, except that the Attorney General shall provide by regulation for prompt review of such an order under subparagraph (A)(i) against an alien who claims under oath, or as permitted under penalty of perjury under section 1746 of title 28, United States Code, after having been warned of the penalties for falsely making such claim under such conditions, to have been lawfully admitted for permanent residence, to have been admitted as a refugee under section 207 [8 USCS § 1157], or to have been granted asylum under section 208 [8 USCS § 1158].

(D) Limit on collateral attacks. In any action brought against an alien under section 275(a) or section 276 [8 USCS § 1325(a) or 1326], the court shall not have jurisdiction to hear any claim attacking the validity of an order of removal entered under subparagraph (A)(i) or (B)(iii).

(E) Asylum officer defined. As used in this paragraph, the term "asylum officer" means an immigration officer who—

(i) has had professional training in country conditions, asylum law, and interview techniques comparable to that provided to full-time adjudicators of applications under section 208 [8 USCS § 1158], and

(ii) is supervised by an officer who meets the condition described in clause (i) and has had substantial experience adjudicating asylum applications.

(F) Exception. Subparagraph (A) shall not apply to an alien who is a native or citizen of a country in the Western Hemisphere with whose government the United States does not have full diplomatic relations and who arrives by aircraft at a port of entry.

(G) Commonwealth of the Northern Mariana Islands. Nothing in this subsection shall be construed to authorize or require any person described in section 208(e) [8 USCS § 1158(e)] to be permitted to apply for asylum under section 208 [8 USCS § 1158] at any time before January 1, 2014.

(2) Inspection of other aliens.

(A) In general. Subject to subparagraphs (B) and (C), in the case of an alien who is an applicant for admission, if the examining immigration officer determines that an alien seeking admission is not clearly and beyond a doubt entitled to be admitted, the alien shall be detained for a proceeding under section 240 [8 USCS § 1229a].

(B) Exception. Subparagraph (A) shall not apply to an alien—

(i) who is a crewman,

(ii) to whom paragraph (1) applies, or

(iii) who is a stowaway.

(C) Treatment of aliens arriving from contiguous territory. In the case of an alien described in subparagraph (A) who is arriving on land (whether or not at a designated port of arrival) from a foreign territory contiguous to the United States, the Attorney General may return the alien to that territory pending a proceeding under section 240 [8 USCS § 1229a].

(3) Challenge of decision. The decision of the examining immigration officer, if favorable to the admission of any alien, shall be subject to challenge by any other immigration officer and such challenge shall operate to take the alien whose privilege to be admitted is so challenged, before an immigration judge for a proceeding under section 240 [8 USCS § 1229a].

(c) Removal of aliens inadmissible on security and related grounds.

(1) Removal without further hearing. If an immigration officer or an immigration judge suspects that an arriving alien may be inadmissible under subparagraph (A) (other than clause (ii)), (B), or (C) of section 212(a)(3) [8 USCS § 1182(a)(3)], the officer or judge shall—

(A) order the alien removed, subject to review under paragraph (2);

(B) report the order of removal to the Attorney General; and

(C) not conduct any further inquiry or hearing until ordered by the Attorney General.

(2) Review of order.

(A) The Attorney General shall review orders issued under paragraph (1).

(B) If the Attorney General—

(i) is satisfied on the basis of confidential information that the alien is inadmissible under subparagraph

(A) (other than clause (ii)), (B), or (C) of section 212(a)(3) [8 USCS § 1182(a)(3)], and

(ii) after consulting with appropriate security agencies of the United States Government, concludes that disclosure of the information would be prejudicial to the public interest, safety, or security,the Attorney General may order the alien removed without further inquiry or hearing by an immigration judge.

(C) If the Attorney General does not order the removal of the alien under subparagraph (B), the Attorney General shall specify the further inquiry or hearing that shall be conducted in the case.

(3) Submission of statement and information. The alien or the alien's representative may submit a written statement and additional information for consideration by the Attorney General.

(d) Authority relating to inspections.

(1) Authority to search conveyances. Immigration officers are authorized to board and search any vessel, aircraft, railway car, or other conveyance or vehicle in which they believe aliens are being brought into the United States.

(2) Authority to order detention and delivery of arriving aliens. Immigration officers are authorized to order an owner, agent, master, commanding officer, person in charge, purser, or consignee of a vessel or aircraft bringing an alien (except an alien crewmember) to the United States—

(A) to detain the alien on the vessel or at the airport of arrival, and

(B) to deliver the alien to an immigration officer for inspection or to a medical officer for examination.

(3) Administration of oath and consideration of evidence. The Attorney General and any immigration officer shall have power to administer oaths and to take and consider evidence of or from any person touching the privilege of any alien or person he believes or suspects to be an alien to enter, reenter, transit through, or reside in the United States or concerning any matter which is material and relevant to the enforcement of this Act and the administration of the Service.

(4) Subpoena authority.

(A) The Attorney General and any immigration officer shall have power to require by subpoena the attendance and testimony of witnesses before immigration officers and the production of books, papers, and documents relating to the privilege of any person to enter, reenter, reside in, or pass through the United States or concerning any matter which is material and relevant to the enforcement of this Act and the administration of the Service, and to that end may invoke the aid of any court of the United States.

(B) Any United States district court within the jurisdiction of which investigations or inquiries are being conducted by an immigration officer may, in the event of neglect or refusal to respond to a subpoena issued under this paragraph or refusal to testify before an immigration officer, issue an order requiring such persons to appear before an immigration officer, produce books, papers, and documents if demanded, and testify, and any failure to obey such order of the court may be punished by the court as a contempt thereof.

HISTORY: (June 27, 1952, ch 477, Title II, Ch 4, § 235, 66 Stat. 198; Nov. 29, 1990, P. L. 101-649, Title VI, § 603(a)(11), 104 Stat. 5083; April 24, 1996, P. L. 104-132, Title IV, Subtitle C, §§ 422(a), 423(b), 110 Stat. 1270, 1272; Sept. 30, 1996, P. L. 104-208, Div C, Title III, Subtitle A, §§ 302(a), 308(d)(5), Subtitle F, § 371(b)(4), 110 Stat. 3009-579, 3009-619, 3009-645; May 8, 2008, P. L. 110-229, Title VII, Subtitle A, § 702(j)(5), 122 Stat. 867.)

§ 235A. [8 U.S.C. § 1225a] Preinspection at foreign airports.

(a) Establishment of preinspection stations.

(1) New stations. Subject to paragraph (5), not later than October 31, 1998, the Attorney General, in consultation with the Secretary of State, shall establish and maintain preinspection stations in at least 5 of the foreign airports that are among the 10 foreign airports which the Attorney General identifies as serving as last points of departure for the greatest numbers of inadmissible alien passengers who arrive from abroad by air at ports of entry within the United States. Such preinspection stations shall be in addition to any preinspection stations established prior to the date of the enactment of such Act.

(2) Report. Not later than October 31, 1998, the Attorney General shall report to the Committees on the Judiciary of the House of Representatives and of the Senate on the implementation of paragraph (1).

(3) Data collection. Not later than November 1, 1997, and each subsequent November 1, the Attorney General shall compile data identifying—

(A) the foreign airports which served as last points of departure for aliens who arrived by air at United States ports of entry without valid documentation during the preceding fiscal years;

(B) the number and nationality of such aliens arriving from each such foreign airport; and

(C) the primary routes such aliens followed from their country of origin to the United States.

(4) Subject to paragraph (5), not later than January 1, 2008, the Secretary of Homeland Security, in consultation with the Secretary of State, shall establish preinspection stations in at least 25 additional foreign airports, which the Secretary of Homeland Security, in consultation with the Secretary of State, determines, based on the data compiled under paragraph (3) and such other information as may be available, would most effectively facilitate the travel of admissible aliens and reduce the number of inadmissible aliens, especially aliens who are potential terrorists, who arrive from abroad by air at points of entry within the United States. Such preinspection stations shall be in addition to those established before September 30, 1996, or pursuant to paragraph (1).

(5) Conditions. Prior to the establishment of a preinspection station, the Attorney General, in consultation with the Secretary of State, shall ensure that—

(A) employees of the United States stationed at the preinspection station and their accompanying family members will receive appropriate protection;

(B) such employees and their families will not be subject to unreasonable risks to their welfare and safety; and

(C) the country in which the preinspection station is to be established maintains practices and procedures with respect to asylum seekers and refugees in accordance with the Convention Relating to the Status of Refugees (done at Geneva, July 28, 1951), or the Protocol Relating to the Status of Refugees (done at New York, January 31, 1967), or that an alien in the country otherwise has recourse to avenues of protection from return topersecution.

(b) Establishment of carrier consultant program and immigration security initiative. The Secretary of Homeland Security shall assign additional immigration officers to assist air carriers in the detection of fraudulent documents at foreign airports which, based on the records maintained pursuant to subsection (a)(3), served as a point of departure for a significant number of arrivals at United States ports of entry without valid documentation, but where no preinspection station exists. Beginning not later than December 31, 2006, the number of airports selected for an assignment under this subsection shall be at least 50.

HISTORY: (June 27, 1952, ch 477, § 235A, as added Sept. 30, 1996, P. L. 104-208, Div C, Title I, Subtitle B, § 123(a), 110 Stat. 3009-560; Dec. 17, 2004, P. L. 108-458, Title VII, Subtitle B, §§ 7206(a), 7210(d)(1), 118 Stat. 3817, 3825.)

§ 236. [8 U.S.C. § 1226] Apprehension and detention of aliens.

(a) Arrest, detention, and release. On a warrant issued by the Attorney General, an alien may be arrested and detained pending a decision on whether the alien is to be removed from the United States. Except as provided in subsection (c) and pending such decision, the Attorney General—

(1) may continue to detain the arrested alien; and

(2) may release the alien on—

(A) bond of at least $1,500 with security approved by, and containing conditions prescribed by, the Attorney General; or

(B) conditional parole; but

(3) may not provide the alien with work authorization (including an "employment authorized" endorsement or other appropriate work permit), unless the alien is lawfully admitted for permanent residence or otherwise would (without regard to removal proceedings) be provided such authorization.

(b) Revocation of bond or parole. The Attorney General at any time may revoke a bond or parole authorized under subsection (a), rearrest the alien under the original warrant, and detain the alien.

(c) Detention of criminal aliens.

(1) Custody. The Attorney General shall take into custody any alien who—

(A) is inadmissible by reason of having committed any offense covered in section 212(a)(2) [8 USCS § 1182(a)(2)],

(B) is deportable by reason of having committed any offense covered in section 237(a)(2)(A)(ii), (A)(iii), (B), (C), or (D) [8 USCS § 1227(a)(2)(A)(ii), (A)(iii), (B), (C), or (D)],

(C) is deportable under section 237(a)(2)(A)(i) [8 USCS § 1227(a)(2)(A)(i)] on the basis of an offense for which the alien has been sentence [sentenced] to a term of imprisonment of at least 1 year, or

(D) is inadmissible under section 212(a)(3)(B) [8 USCS § 1182(a)(3)(B)] or deportable under section 237(a)(4)(B) [8 USCS § 1227(a)(4)(B)],

when the alien is released, without regard to whether the alien is released on parole, supervised release, or probation, and without regard to whether the alien may be arrested or imprisoned again for the same offense.

(2) Release. The Attorney General may release an alien described in paragraph (1) only if the Attorney General decides pursuant to section 3521 of title 18, United States Code, that release of the alien from custody is necessary to provide protection to a witness, a potential witness, a person cooperating with an investigation into major criminal activity, or an immediate family member or close associate of a witness, potential witness, or person cooperating with such an investigation, and the alien satisfies the Attorney General that the alien will not pose a danger to the safety of other persons or of property and is likely to appear for any scheduled proceeding. A decision relating to such release shall take place in accordance with a procedure that considers the severity of the offense committed by the alien.

(d) Identification of criminal aliens.

(1) The Attorney General shall devise and implement a system—

(A) to make available, daily (on a 24-hour basis), to Federal, State, and local authorities the investigative resources of the Service to determine whether individuals arrested by such authorities for aggravated felonies are aliens;

(B) to designate and train officers and employees of the Service to serve as a liaison to Federal, State, and local law enforcement and correctional agencies and courts with respect to the arrest, conviction, and release of any alien charged with an aggravated felony; and

(C) which uses computer resources to maintain a current record of aliens who have been convicted of an aggravated felony, and indicates those who have been removed.

(2) The record under paragraph (1)(C) shall be made available—

(A) to inspectors at ports of entry and to border patrol agents at sector headquarters for purposes of immediate identification of any alien who was previously ordered removed and is seeking to reenter the United States, and

(B) to officials of the Department of State for use in its automated visa lookout system.

(3) Upon the request of the governor or chief executive officer of any State, the Service shall provide assistance to State courts in the identification of aliens unlawfully present in the United States pending criminal prosecution.

(e) Judicial review. The Attorney General's discretionary judgment regarding the application of this section shall not be subject to review. No court may set aside any action or decision by the Attorney General under this section regarding the detention or release of any alien or the grant, revocation, or denial of bond or parole.

HISTORY: (June 27, 1952, ch 477, Title II, Ch 4, § 236, 66 Stat. 200; Nov. 29, 1990, P. L. 101-649, Title V, Subtitle A, § 504(c), Title VI, § 603(a)(12), 104 Stat. 5050, 5083; Dec. 12, 1991, P. L. 102-232, Title III, § 306(a)(5), 105 Stat. 1751; Sept. 30, 1996, P. L. 104-208, Div C, Title III, Subtitle A, § 303(a), Subtitle F, § 371(b)(5), 110 Stat. 3009-585, 3009-645.)

§ 236A. [8 U.S.C. § 1226a] Mandatory detention of suspected terrorists; habeas corpus; judicial review.

(a) Detention of terrorist aliens.

(1) Custody. The Attorney General shall take into custody any alien who is certified under paragraph (3).

(2) Release. Except as provided in paragraphs (5) and (6), the Attorney General shall maintain custody of such an alien until the alien is removed from the United States. Except as provided in paragraph (6), such custody shall be maintained irrespective of any relief from removal for which the alien may be eligible, or any relief from removal granted the alien, until the Attorney General determines that the alien is no longer an alien who may be certified under paragraph (3). If the alien is finally determined not to be removable, detention pursuant to this subsection shall terminate.

(3) Certification. The Attorney General may certify an alien under this paragraph if the Attorney General has reasonable grounds to believe that the alien—

(A) is described in section 212(a)(3)(A)(i), 212(a)(3)(A)(iii), 212(a)(3)(B), 237(a)(4)(A)(i), 237(a)(4)(A)(iii), or 237(a)(4)(B) [8 USCS § 1182(a)(3)(A)(i), 1182(a)(3)(A)(iii), 1182(a)(3)(B), 1227(a)(4)(A)(i), 1227(a)(4)(A)(iii), or 1227(a)(4)(B)]; or

(B) is engaged in any other activity that endangers the national security of the United States.

(4) Nondelegation. The Attorney General may delegate the authority provided under paragraph (3) only to the Deputy Attorney General. The Deputy Attorney General may not delegate such authority.

(5) Commencement of proceedings. The Attorney General shall place an alien detained under paragraph (1) in removal proceedings, or shall charge the alien with a criminal offense, not later than 7 days after the commencement of such detention. If the requirement of the preceding sentence is not satisfied, the Attorney General shall release the alien.

(6) Limitation on indefinite detention. An alien detained solely under paragraph (1) who has not been removed under section 241(a)(1)(A) [8 USCS § 1231(a)(1)(A)], and whose removal is unlikely in the reasonably foreseeable future, may be detained for additional periods of up to six months only if the release of the alien will threaten the national security of the United States or the safety of the community or any person.

(7) Review of certification. The Attorney General shall review the certification made under paragraph (3) every 6 months. If the Attorney General determines, in the Attorney General's discretion, that the certification should be revoked, the alien may be released on such conditions as the Attorney General deems appropriate, unless such release is otherwise prohibited by law. The alien may request each 6 months in writing that the Attorney General reconsider the certification and may submit documents or other evidence in support of that request.

(b) Habeas corpus and judicial review.

(1) In general. Judicial review of any action or decision relating to this section (including judicial review of the merits of a determination made under subsection (a)(3) or (a)(6)) is available exclusively in habeas corpus proceedings consistent with this subsection. Except as provided in the preceding sentence, no court shall have jurisdiction to review, by habeas corpus petition or otherwise, any such action or decision.

(2) Application.

(A) In general. Notwithstanding any other provision of law, including section 2241(a) of title 28, United States Code, habeas corpus proceedings described in paragraph (1) may be initiated only by an application filed with—

(i) the Supreme Court;

(ii) any justice of the Supreme Court;

(iii) any circuit judge of the United States Court of Appeals for the District of Columbia Circuit; or

(iv) any district court otherwise having jurisdiction to entertain it.

(B) Application transfer. Section 2241(b) of title 28, United States Code, shall apply to an application for a writ of habeas corpus described in subparagraph (A).

(3) Appeals. Notwithstanding any other provision of law, including section 2253 of title 28, in habeas corpus proceedings described in paragraph (1) before a circuit or district judge, the final order shall be subject to review, on appeal, by the United States Court of Appeals for the District of Columbia Circuit. There shall be no right of appeal in such proceedings to any other circuit court of appeals.

(4) Rule of decision. The law applied by the Supreme Court and the United States Court of Appeals for the District of Columbia Circuit shall be regarded as the rule of decision in habeas corpus proceedings described in paragraph (1).

(c) Statutory construction. The provisions of this section shall not be applicable to any other provision of this Act.

HISTORY: (June 27, 1952, ch 477, Title II, Ch 4, § 236A, as added Oct. 26, 2001, P. L. 107-56, Title IV, Subtitle B, § 412(a), 115 Stat. 350.)

§ 237. [8 U.S.C. § 1227] Deportable aliens.

(a) Classes of deportable aliens. Any alien (including an alien crewman) in and admitted to the United States shall, upon the order of the Attorney General, be removed if the alien is within one or more of the following classes of deportable aliens:

(1) Inadmissible at time of entry or of adjustment of status or violates status.

(A) Inadmissible aliens. Any alien who at the time of entry or adjustment of status was within one or more of the classes of aliens inadmissible by the law existing at such time is deportable.

(B) Present in violation of law. Any alien who is present in the United States in violation of this Act or any other law of the United States, or whose nonimmigrant visa (or other documentation authorizing admission into the United States as a nonimmigrant) has been revoked under section 221(i) [8 USCS § 1201(i)], is deportable.

(C) Violated nonimmigrant status or condition of entry.

(i) Nonimmigrant status violators. Any alien who was admitted as a nonimmigrant and who has failed to maintain the nonimmigrant status in which the alien was admitted or to which it was changed under section 248 [8 USCS § 1258], or to comply with the conditions of any such status, is deportable.

(ii) Violators of conditions of entry. Any alien whom the Secretary of Health and Human Services certifies has failed to comply with terms, conditions, and controls that were imposed under section 212(g) [8 USCS § 1182(g)] is deportable.

(D) Termination of conditional permanent residence.

(i) In general. Any alien with permanent resident status on a conditional basis under section 216 [8 USCS § 1186a] (relating to conditional permanent resident status for certain alien spouses and sons and daughters) or under section 216A [8 USCS § 1186b] (relating to conditional permanent resident status for certain alien entrepreneurs, spouses, and children) who has had such status terminated under such respective section is deportable.

(ii) Exception Clause (i) shall not apply in the cases described in section 216(c)(4) [8 USCS § 1186a(c)(4)] (relating to certain hardship waivers).

(E) Smuggling.

(i) In general. Any alien who (prior to the date of entry, at the time of any entry, or within 5 years of the date of any entry) knowingly has encouraged, induced, assisted, abetted, or aided any other alien to enter or to try to enter the United States in violation of law is deportable.

(ii) Special rule in the case of family reunification. Clause (i) shall not apply in the case of alien who is an eligible immigrant (as defined in section 301(b)(1) of the Immigration Act of 1990 [8 USCS § 1255a note]), was physically present in the United States on May 5, 1988, and is seeking admission as an immediate relative or under section 203(a)(2) [8 USCS § 1153(a)(2)] (including under section 112 of the Immigration Act of 1990 [8 USCS § 1153 note]) or benefits under section 301(a) of the Immigration Act of 1990 [8 USCS § 1255a note] if the alien, before May 5, 1988, has encouraged, induced, assisted, abetted, or aided only the alien's spouse, parent, son, or daughter (and no other individual) to enter the United States in violation of law.

(iii) Waiver authorized. The Attorney General may, in his discretion for humanitarian purposes, to assure family unity, or when it is otherwise in the public interest, waive application of clause (i) in the case of any alien lawfully admitted for permanent residence if the alien has encouraged, induced, assisted, abetted, or aided only an individual who at the time of the offense was the alien's spouse, parent, son, or daughter (and no other individual) to enter the United States in violation of law.

(F) [Deleted]

(G) Marriage fraud. An alien shall be considered to be deportable as having procured a visa or other documentation by fraud (within the meaning of section 212(a)(6)(C)(i)) [8 USCS § 1182(a)(6)(C)(i)] and to be in the United States in violation of this Act (within the meaning of subparagraph (B)) if—

(i) the alien obtains any admission into the United States with an immigrant visa or other documentation procured on the basis of a marriage entered into less than 2 years prior to such admission of the alien and which, within 2 years subsequent to any admission of the alien in the United States, shall be judicially annulled or terminated, unless the alien establishes to the satisfaction of the Attorney General that such marriage was not contracted for the purpose of evading any provisions of the immigration laws, or

(ii) it appears to the satisfaction of the Attorney General that the alien has failed or refused to fulfill the alien's marital agreement which in the opinion of the Attorney General was made for the purpose of procuring the alien's admission as an immigrant.

(H) Waiver authorized for certain misrepresentations. The provisions of this paragraph relating to the removal of aliens within the United States on the ground that they were inadmissible at the time of admission as aliens described in section 212(a)(6)(C)(i) [8 USCS § 1182(i)], whether willful or innocent, may, in the discretion of the Attorney General, be waived for any alien (other than an alien described in paragraph (4)(D)) who—

(i) (I) is the spouse, parent, son, or daughter of a citizen of the United States or of an alien lawfully admitted to the United States for permanent residence; and

(II) was in possession of an immigrant visa or equivalent document and was otherwise admissible to the United States at the time of such admission except for those grounds of inadmissibility specified under paragraphs (5)(A) and (7)(A) of section 212(a) [8 USCS § 1182(a)] which were a direct result of that fraud or misrepresentation.

(ii) is a VAWA self-petitioner.

A waiver of removal for fraud or misrepresentation granted under this subparagraph shall also operate to waive removal based on the grounds of inadmissibility directly resulting from such fraud or misrepresentation.

(2) Criminal offenses.

(A) General crimes.

(i) Crimes of moral turpitude. Any alien who—

(I) is convicted of a crime involving moral turpitude committed within five years (or 10 years in the case of an alien provided lawful permanent resident status under section 245(j) [8 USCS § 1255(j)]) after the date of admission, and

(II) is convicted of a crime for which a sentence of one year or longer may be imposed,

is deportable.

(ii) Multiple criminal convictions. Any alien who at any time after admission is convicted of two or more crimes involving moral turpitude, not arising out of a single scheme of criminal misconduct, regardless of whether confined therefor and regardless of whether the convictions were in a single trial, is deportable.

(iii) Aggravated felony. Any alien who is convicted of an aggravated felony at any time after admission is deportable.

(iv) High speed flight. Any alien who is convicted of a violation of section 758 of title 18, United States Code (relating to high speed flight from an immigration checkpoint), is deportable.

(v) Failure to register as a sex offender. Any alien who is convicted under section 2250 of title 18, United States Code [18 USCS § 2250], is deportable.

(vi) Waiver authorized. Clauses (i), (ii), (iii), and (iv) shall not apply in the case of an alien with respect to a criminal conviction if the alien subsequent to the criminal conviction has been granted a full and unconditional pardon by the President of the United States or by the Governor of any of the several States.

(B) Controlled substances.

(i) Conviction. Any alien who at any time after admission has been convicted of a violation of (or a conspiracy or attempt to violate) any law or regulation of a State, the United States, or a foreign country relating to a controlled substance (as defined in section 102 of the Controlled Substances Act (21 U.S.C. 802)), other than a single offense involving possession for one's own use of 30 grams or less of marijuana, is deportable.

(ii) Drug abusers and addicts. Any alien who is, or at any time after admission has been, a drug abuser or addict is deportable.

(C) Certain firearm offenses. Any alien who at any time after admission is convicted under any law of purchasing, selling, offering for sale, exchanging, using, owning, possessing, or carrying, or of attempting or conspiring to purchase, sell, offer for sale, exchange, use, own, possess, or carry, any weapon, part, or accessory which is a firearm or destructive device (as defined in section 921(a) of title 18, United States Code) in violation of any law is deportable.

(D) Miscellaneous crimes. Any alien who at any time has been convicted (the judgment on such conviction becoming final) of, or has been so convicted of a conspiracy or attempt to violate—

(i) any offense under chapter 37 [18 USCS §§ 791 et seq.] (relating to espionage), chapter 105 [18 USCS §§ 2151 et seq.] (relating to sabotage), or chapter 115 [18 USCS §§ 2381 et seq.] (relating to treason and sedition) of title 18, United States Code, for which a term of imprisonment of five or more years may be imposed;

(ii) any offense under section 871 or 960 of title 18, United States Code;

(iii) a violation of any provision of the Military Selective Service Act (50 U.S.C. App. 451 et seq. [50 USCS §§ 3801 et seq.]) or the Trading With the Enemy Act (50 U.S.C. App. 1 et seq. [50 USCS §§ 4301 et seq.]); or

(iv) a violation of section 215 or 278 of this Act [8 USCS § 1185 or 1328], is deportable.

(E) Crimes of domestic violence, stalking, or violation of protection order, crimes against children [and].

(i) Domestic violence, stalking, and child abuse. Any alien who at any time after admission is convicted of a crime of domestic violence, a crime of stalking, or a crime of child abuse, child neglect, or child abandonment is deportable. For purposes of this clause, the term "crime of domestic violence" means any crime of violence (as defined in section 16 of title 18, United States Code) against a person committed by a current or former spouse of the person, by an individual with whom the person shares a child in common, by an individual who is cohabiting with or has cohabited with the person as a spouse, by an individual similarly situated to a spouse of the person under the domestic or family violence laws of the jurisdiction where the offense occurs, or by any other individual against a person who is protected from that individual's acts under the domestic or family violence laws of the United States or any State, Indian tribal government, or unit of local government.

(ii) Violators of protection orders. Any alien who at any time after admission is enjoined under a protection order issued by a court and whom the court determines has engaged in conduct that violates the portion of a protection order that involves protection against credible threats of violence, repeated harassment, or bodily injury to the person or persons for whom the protection order was issued is deportable. For purposes of this clause, the term "protection order" means any injunction issued for the purpose of preventing violent or threatening acts of domestic violence, including temporary or final orders issued by civil or criminal courts (other than support or child custody orders or provisions) whether obtained by filing an independent action or as a pendente lite order in another proceeding.

(F) Trafficking. Any alien described in section 212(a)(2)(H) [8 USCS § 1182(a)(2)(H)] is deportable.

(3) Failure to register and falsification of documents.

(A) Change of address. An alien who has failed to comply with the provisions of section 265 [8 USCS § 1305] is deportable, unless the alien establishes to the satisfaction of the Attorney General that such failure was reasonably excusable or was not willful.

(B) Failure to register or falsification of documents. Any alien who at any time has been convicted—

(i) under section 266(c) of this Act [8 USCS § 1306(c)] or under section 36(c) of the Alien Registration Act, 1940,

(ii) of a violation of, or an attempt or a conspiracy to violate, any provision of the Foreign Agents Registration Act of 1938 (22 U.S.C. 611 et seq.), or

(iii) of a violation of, or an attempt or a conspiracy to violate, section 1546 of title 18, United States Code (relating to fraud and misuse of visas, permits, and other entry documents),

is deportable.

(C) Document fraud.

(i) In general. An alien who is the subject of a final order for violation of section 274C [8 USCS § 1324c] is deportable.

(ii) Waiver authorized. The Attorney General may waive clause (i) in the case of an alien lawfully admitted for permanent residence if no previous civil money penalty was imposed against the alien under section 274C [8 USCS § 1324c] and the offense was incurred solely to assist, aid, or support the alien's spouse or child (and no other individual). No court shall have jurisdiction to review a decision of the Attorney General to grant or deny a waiver under this clause.

(D) Falsely claiming citizenship.

(i) In general. Any alien who falsely represents, or has falsely represented, himself to be a citizen of the United States for any purpose or benefit under this Act (including section 274A [8 USCS § 1324a]) or any Federal or State law is deportable.

(ii) Exception. In the case of an alien making a representation described in clause (i), if each natural parent of the alien (or, in the case of an adopted alien, each adoptive parent of the alien) is or was a citizen (whether by birth or naturalization), the alien permanently resided in the United States prior to attaining the age of 16, and the alien reasonably believed at the time of making such representation that he or she was a citizen, the alien shall not be considered to be deportable under any provision of this subsection based on such representation.

(4) Security and related grounds.

(A) In general. Any alien who has engaged, is engaged, or at any time after admission engages in—

(i) any activity to violate any law of the United States relating to espionage or sabotage or to violate or evade any law prohibiting the export from the United States of goods, technology, or sensitive information,

(ii) any other criminal activity which endangers public safety or national security, or

(iii) any activity a purpose of which is the opposition to, or the control or overthrow of, the Government of the United States by force, violence, or other unlawful means,

is deportable.

(B) Terrorist activities. Any alien who is described in subparagraph (B) or (F) of section 212(a)(3) [8 USCS § 1182(a)(3)] is deportable.

(C) Foreign policy.

(i) In general. An alien whose presence or activities in the United States the Secretary of State has reasonable ground to believe would have potentially serious adverse foreign policy consequences for the United States is deportable.

(ii) Exceptions. The exceptions described in clauses (ii) and (iii) of section 212(a)(3)(C) [8 USCS § 1182(a)(3)(C)] shall apply to deportability under clause (i) in the same manner as they apply to inadmissibility under section 212 (a)(3)(C)(i) [8 USCS § 1182(a)(3)(C) (i)].

(D) Participated in Nazi persecution, genocide, or the commission of any act of torture or extrajudicial killing. Any alien described in clause (i), (ii), or (iii) or section 212 (a)(3)(E) [8 USCS § 1182(a)(3)(E)] is deportable.

(E) Participated in the commission of severe violations of religious freedom. Any alien described in section 212(a)(2)(G) [8 USCS § 1182(a)(2)(G)] is deportable.

(F) Recruitment or use of child soldiers. Any alien who has engaged in the recruitment or use of child soldiers in violation of section 2442 of title 18, United States Code, is deportable.

(5) Public charge. Any alien who, within five years after the date of entry, has become a public charge from causes not affirmatively shown to have arisen since entry is deportable.

(6) Unlawful voters.

(A) In general. Any alien who has voted in violation of any Federal, State, or local constitutional provision, statute, ordinance, or regulation is deportable.

(B) Exception. In the case of an alien who voted in a Federal, State, or local election (including an initiative, recall, or referendum) in violation of a lawful restriction of voting to citizens, if each natural parent of the alien (or, in the case of an adopted alien, each adoptive parent of the alien) is or was a citizen (whether by birth or naturalization), the alien permanently resided in the United States prior to attaining the age of 16, and the alien reasonably believed at the time of such violation that he or she was a citizen, the alien shall not be considered to be deportable under any provision of this subsection based on such violation.

(7) Waiver for victims of domestic violence.

(A) In general. The Attorney General is not limited by the criminal court record and may waive the application of paragraph (2)(E)(i) (with respect to crimes of domestic violence and crimes of stalking) and (ii) in the case of an alien who has been battered or subjected to extreme cruelty and who is not and was not the primary perpetrator of violence in the relationship—

[(i)] upon a determination that—

(I) the alien was acting is [in] self-defense;

(II) the alien was found to have violated a protection order intended to protect the alien; or

(III) the alien committed, was arrested for, was convicted of, or pled guilty to committing a crime—

(aa) that did not result in serious bodily injury; and

(bb) where there was a connection between the crime and the alien's having been battered or subjected to extreme cruelty.

(B) Credible evidence considered. In acting on applications under this paragraph, the Attorney General shall consider any credible evidence relevant to the application. The determination of what evidence is credible and the weight to be given that evidence shall be within the sole discretion of the Attorney General.

(b) Deportation of certain nonimmigrants. An alien, admitted as a nonimmigrant under the provisions of either section 101(a)(15)(A)(i) or 101(a)(15)(G)(i) [8 USCS § 1101(a)(15)(A)(i) or (a)(15)(G)(i)], and who fails to maintain a status under either of those provisions, shall not be required to depart from the United States without the approval of the Secretary of State, unless such alien is subject to deportation under paragraph (4) of subsection (a).

(c) Waiver of grounds for deportation. Paragraphs (1)(A), (1)(B), (1)(C), (1)(D), and (3)(A) of subsection (a) (other than so much of paragraph (1) as relates to a ground of inadmissibility described in paragraph (2) or (3) of section 212 (a) [8 USCS § 1182(a)(2) or (3)] shall not apply to a special immigrant described in section 101(a)(27)(J) [8 USCS § 1101(a)(27)(J)] based upon circumstances that existed before the date the alien was provided such special immigrant status.

(d) Administrative stay.

(1) If the Secretary of Homeland Security determines that an application for nonimmigrant status under subparagraph (T) or (U) of section 101(a)(15) [8 USCS § 1101(a)(15)] filed for an alien in the United States sets forth a prima facie case for approval, the Secretary may grant the alien an administrative stay of a final order of removal under section 241(c)(2) [8 USCS § 1231(c)(2)] until—

(A) the application for nonimmigrant status under such subparagraph (T) or (U) is approved; or

(B) there is a final administrative denial of the application for such nonimmigrant status after the exhaustion of administrative appeals.

(2) The denial of a request for an administrative stay of removal under this subsection shall not preclude the alien from applying for a stay of removal, deferred action, or a continuance or abeyance of removal proceedings under any other provision of the immigration laws of the United States.

(3) During any period in which the administrative stay of removal is in effect, the alien shall not be removed.

(4) Nothing in this subsection may be construed to limit the authority of the Secretary of Homeland Security or the Attorney General to grant a stay of removal or deportation in any case not described in this subsection.

HISTORY: (June 27, 1952, ch 477, Title II, Ch 5, § 237 [241], 66 Stat. 204; July 18, 1956, ch 629, Title III, § 301(b), (c), 70 Stat. 575; July 14, 1960, P. L. 86-648, § 9, 74 Stat. 505; Sept. 26, 1961, P. L. 87-301, § 16, 75 Stat. 655; Oct. 3, 1965, P. L. 89-236, § 11(e), 79 Stat. 918; Oct. 20, 1976, P. L. 94-571, § 7(e), 90 Stat. 2706; Oct. 30, 1978, P. L. 95-549, Title I, § 103, 92 Stat. 2065; Dec. 29, 1981, P. L. 97-116, § 8, 95 Stat. 1616; Oct. 27, 1986, P. L. 99-570, Title I, Subtitle M, § 1751(b), 100 Stat. 3207-47; Nov. 6, 1986, P. L. 99-603, Title III, Part A, § 303(b), 100 Stat. 3431; Nov. 10, 1986, P. L. 99-639, § 2(b), 100 Stat. 3541; Nov. 14, 1986, P. L. 99-653, § 7(c) in part, 100 Stat. 3657; Oct. 24, 1988, P. L. 100-525, §§ 2(n)(2), 9(m), 102 Stat. 2613, 2620; Nov. 18, 1988, P. L. 100-690, Title VII, Subtitle J, §§ 7344(a)(2), 7348(a), 102 Stat. 4471, 4473; Nov. 29, 1990, P. L. 101-649, Title I, Subtitle D, § 153 (b) Title V, Subtitle A, §§ 505(a), 508(a), Subtitle D, § 544(b), Title V, § 602(a), (b), 104 Stat. 5006, 5050, 5051, 5061, 5077, 5081; Dec. 12, 1991, P. L. 102-232, Title III, §§ 302(d)(3), 307(h), (k), 105 Stat. 1745, 1755, 1756; Sept. 13, 1994, P. L. 103-322, Title XIII, § 130003(d), 108 Stat. 2026; Oct. 25, 1994, P. L. 103-416, Title II, §§ 203(b), 219(g), 108 Stat. 4311, 4317; April 24, 1996, P. L. 104-132, Title IV, Subtitle B, § 414(a), Subtitle C, § 435(a), 110 Stat. 1270, 1275; Sept. 30, 1996, P. L. 104-208, Div C, Title I, Subtitle A, § 108(c), Title III, Subtitle A, §§ 301(d), 305(a)(2), 308(d)(2), (3)(A), (e)(1)(E), (2)(C), (f)(1)(L)–(N), (5), Subtitle C, §§ 344(b), 345(b), 347(b), 350(a), 351(b), Title VI, Subtitle E, § 671(a)(4)(B), (d)(1)(C), 110 Stat. 3009-558, 3009-579, 3009-598, 3009-617, 3009-619, 3009-620, 3009-621, 3009-637, 3009-638, 309-639, 3009-640, 3009-721, 3009-723; Oct. 28, 2000, P. L. 106-386, Div B, Title V, § 1505(b)(1), (c)(2), 114 Stat. 1525, 1526; Oct. 30, 2000, P. L. 106-395, Title II, § 201(c)(1), (2), 114 Stat. 1634; Oct. 26, 2001, P. L. 107-56, Title IV, Subtitle B, § 411(b)(1), 115 Stat. 348; Dec. 17, 2004, P. L. 108-458, Title V, Subtitle C, § 5304(b), Subtitle D, § 5402, Subtitle E, §§ 5501(b), 5502(b), 118 Stat. 3736, 3737, 3740, 3741; May 11, 2005, P. L. 109-13, Div B, Title I, § 105(a)(1), (b), 119 Stat. 309, 310; July 27, 2006, P. L. 109-248, Title IV, § 401, 120 Stat. 622; Aug. 12, 2006, P. L. 109-271, § 6(c), 120 Stat. 763; Oct. 3, 2008, P. L. 110-340, § 2(c), 122 Stat. 3736; Dec. 23, 2008, P. L. 110-457, Title II, Subtitle A, § 204, Subtitle C, § 222(f)(2), 122 Stat. 5060, 5071.)

§ 238. [8 U.S.C. § 1228] Expedited removal of aliens convicted of committing aggravated felonies.

(a) Removal of criminal aliens.

(1) In general. The Attorney General shall provide for the availability of special removal proceedings at certain Federal, State, and local correctional facilities for aliens convicted of any criminal offense covered in section 241 [237] (a)(2)(A)(iii), (B), (C), or (D) [8 USCS § 1227(a)(2)(iii), (B), (C), or (D)], or any offense covered by section 237(a)(2)(A)(ii) [8 USCS § 1227(a)(2)(A)(ii)] for which both predicate offenses are, without regard to the date of their commission, otherwise covered by section 237(a)(2)(A)(i) [8 USCS § 1227(a)(2)(A)(i)]. Such proceedings shall be conducted in conformity with section 240 [8 USCS § 1229a] (except as otherwise provided in this section), and in a manner which eliminates the need for additional detention at any processing center of the Service and in a manner which assures expeditious removal following the end of the alien's incarceration for the underlying sentence. Nothing in this section shall be construed to create any substantive or procedural right or benefit that is legally enforceable by any party against the United States or its agencies or officers or any other person.

(2) Implementation. With respect to an alien convicted of an aggravated felony who is taken into custody by the Attorney General pursuant to section 236(c) [8 USCS § 1226(c)], the Attorney General shall, to the maximum extent practicable, detain any such felon at a facility at which other such aliens are detained. In the selection of such facility, the Attorney General shall make reasonable efforts to ensure that the alien's access to counsel and right to counsel under section 292 [8 USCS § 1362] are not impaired.

(3) Expedited proceedings.

(A) Notwithstanding any other provision of law, the Attorney General shall provide for the initiation and, to the extent possible, the completion of removal proceedings, and any administrative appeals thereof, in the case of any alien convicted of an aggravated felony before the alien's release from incarceration for the underlying aggravated felony.

(B) Nothing in this section shall be construed as requiring the Attorney General to effect the removal of any alien sentenced to actual incarceration, before release from the penitentiary or correctional institution where such alien is confined.

(4) Review.

(A) The Attorney General shall review and evaluate removal proceedings conducted under this section.

(B) The Comptroller General shall monitor, review, and evaluate removal proceedings conducted under this section. Within 18 months after the effective date of this section, the Comptroller General shall submit a report to such Committees concerning the extent to which removal proceedings conducted under this section may adversely affect the ability of such aliens to contest removal effectively.

(b) Removal of aliens who are not permanent residents.

(1) The Attorney General may, in the case of an alien described in paragraph (2), determine the deportability of such alien under section 237(a)(2)(A)(iii) [8 USCS § 1227(a)(2)(A)(iii)] (relating to conviction of an aggravated felony) and issue an order of removal pursuant to the procedures set forth in this subsection or section 240 [8 USCS § 1229a].

(2) An alien is described in this paragraph if the alien—

(A) was not lawfully admitted for permanent residence at the time at which proceedings under this section commenced; or

(B) had permanent resident status on a conditional basis (as described in section 216 [8 USCS § 1186a]) at the time that proceedings under this section commenced.

(3) The Attorney General may not execute any order described in paragraph (1) until 14 calendar days have passed from the date that such order was issued, unless waived by the alien, in order that the alien has an opportunity to apply for judicial review under section 242 [8 USCS § 1252].

(4) Proceedings before the Attorney General under this subsection shall be in accordance with such regulations as the Attorney General shall prescribe. The Attorney General shall provide that—

(A) the alien is given reasonable notice of the charges and of the opportunity described in subparagraph (C);

(B) the alien shall have the privilege of being represented (at no expense to the government) by such counsel, authorized to practice in such proceedings, as the alien shall choose;

(C) the alien has a reasonable opportunity to inspect the evidence and rebut the charges;

(D) a determination is made for the record that the individual upon whom the notice for the proceeding under this section is served (either in person or by mail) is, in fact, the alien named in such notice;

(E) a record is maintained for judicial review; and

(F) the final order of removal is not adjudicated by the same person who issues the charges.

(5) No alien described in this section shall be eligible for any relief from removal that the Attorney General may grant in the Attorney General's discretion.

(c) Presumption of deportability. An alien convicted of an aggravated felony shall be conclusively presumed to be deportable from the United States.

[(d)](c) Judicial removal.

(1) Authority. Notwithstanding any other provision of this Act, a United States district court shall have jurisdiction to enter a judicial order of removal at the time of sentencing against an alien who is deportable, if such an order has been requested by the United States Attorney with the concurrence of the Commissioner and if the court chooses to exercise such jurisdiction.

(2) Procedure.

(A) The United States Attorney shall file with the United States district court, and serve upon the defendant and the Service, prior to commencement of the trial or entry of a guilty plea a notice of intent to request judicial removal.

(B) Notwithstanding section 242B, the United States Attorney, with the concurrence of the Commissioner, shall file at least 30 days prior to the date set for sentencing a charge containing factual allegations regarding the alienage of the defendant and identifying the crime or crimes which make the defendant deportable under section 241 [237] (a)(2)(A) [8 USCS § 1227(a)(2)(A)].

(C) If the court determines that the defendant has presented substantial evidence to establish prima facie eligibility for relief from removal under this Act, the Commissioner shall provide the court with a recommendation and report regarding the alien's eligibility for relief. The court shall either grant or deny the relief sought.

(D) (i) The alien shall have a reasonable opportunity to examine the evidence against him or her, to present evidence on his or her own behalf, and to cross-examine witnesses presented by the Government.

(ii) The court, for the purposes of determining whether to enter an order described in paragraph (1), shall only consider evidence that would be admissible in proceedings conducted pursuant to section 240 [8 USCS § 1229a].

(iii) Nothing in this subsection shall limit the information a court of the United States may receive or consider for the purposes of imposing an appropriate sentence.

(iv) The court may order the alien removed if the Attorney General demonstrates that the alien is deportable under this Act.

(3) Notice, appeal, and execution of judicial order of removal.

(A) (i) A judicial order of removal or denial of such order may be appealed by either party to the court of appeals for the circuit in which the district court is located.

(ii) Except as provided in clause (iii), such appeal shall be considered consistent with the requirements described in section 242 [8 USCS § 1252].

(iii) Upon execution by the defendant of a valid waiver of the right to appeal the conviction on which the order of removal is based, the expiration of the period described in section 242(b)(1) [8 USCS § 1252(b)(1)], or the final dismissal of an appeal from such conviction, the order of removal shall become final and shall be executed at the end of the prison term in accordance with the terms of the order. If the conviction is reversed on direct appeal, the order entered pursuant to this section shall be void.

(B) As soon as is practicable after entry of a judicial order of removal, the Commissioner shall provide the defendant with written notice of the order of removal, which shall designate the defendant's country of choice for removal and any alternate country pursuant to section 243(a).

(4) Denial of judicial order. Denial of a request for a judicial order of removal shall not preclude the Attorney General from initiating removal proceedings pursuant to section 240 [8 USCS § 1229a] upon the same ground of deportability or upon any other ground of deportability provided under section 241 [237] (a) [8 USCS § 1227(a)].

(5) Stipulated judicial order of removal. The United States Attorney, with the concurrence of the Commissioner, may, pursuant to Federal Rule of Criminal Procedure 11 [USCS, Court Rules, FRCrP 11], enter into a plea agreement which calls for the alien, who is deportable under this Act, to waive the right to notice and a hearing under this section, and stipulate to the entry of a judicial order of removal from the United States as a condition of the plea agreement or as a condition of probation or supervised release, or both. The United States district court, in both felony and misdemeanor cases, and a United States magistrate judge in misdemeanor cases, may accept such a stipulation and shall have jurisdiction to enter a judicial order of removal pursuant to the terms of such stipulation.

HISTORY: (June 27, 1952, ch 477, Title II, Ch 5, § 238 [242A], as added Nov. 18, 1988, P. L. 100-690, Title VII, Subtitle J, § 7347(a), 102 Stat. 4471; Nov. 29, 1990, P. L. 101-649, Title V, Subtitle A, § 506(a), 104 Stat. 5050; Dec. 12, 1991, P. L. 102-232, Title III, § 309(b)(10), 105 Stat. 1759; Sept. 13, 1994, P. L. 103-322, Title XIII, § 130004(a), (c), 108 Stat. 2026, 2027; Oct. 25, 1994, P. L. 103-416, Title II, §§ 223(a), 224(a), 108 Stat. 4322; April 24, 1996, P. L. 104-132, Title IV, Subtitle D, §§ 440(g), 442(a), (c), 110 Stat. 1278, 1279, 1280; Sept. 30, 1996, P. L. 104-208, Div C, Title III, Subtitle A, §§ 304(c)(1), 306(d), 308(b)(5), (c)(1), (4)(A), (e)(1)(F), (2)(D), (10), (g)(2)(A), (C), (5)(A)(ii), (C), (D), (10)(H), Subtitle F, § 374(a), Title VI, Subtitle E, § 671(b)(13), (c)(5), (6), 110 Stat. 3009-597, 3009-612, 3009-615, 3009-619, 3009-620, 3009-622, 3009-625, 3009-647, 3009-722, 3009-723.)

§ 239. [8 U.S.C. § 1229] Initiation of removal proceedings.

(a) Notice to appear.

(1) In general. In removal proceedings under section 240 [8 USCS § 1229a], written notice (in this section referred to as a "notice to appear") shall be given in person to the alien (or, if personal service is not practicable, through service by mail to the alien or to the alien's counsel of record, if any) specifying the following:

(A) The nature of the proceedings against the alien.

(B) The legal authority under which the proceedings are conducted.

(C) The acts or conduct alleged to be in violation of law.

(D) The charges against the alien and the statutory provisions alleged to have been violated.

(E) The alien may be represented by counsel and the alien will be provided (i) a period of time to secure counsel under subsection (b)(1) and (ii) a current list of counsel prepared under subsection (b)(2).

(F) (i) The requirement that the alien must immediately provide (or have provided) the Attorney General with a written record of an address and telephone number (if any) at which the alien may be contacted respecting proceedings under section 240 [8 USCS § 1229a].

(ii) The requirement that the alien must provide the Attorney General immediately with a written record of any change of the alien's address or telephone number.

(iii) The consequences under section 240(b)(5) [8 USCS § 1229a(b)(5)] of failure to provide address and telephone information pursuant to this subparagraph.

(G) (i) The time and place at which the proceedings will be held.

(ii) The consequences under section 240(b)(5) [8 USCS § 1229a(b)(5)] of the failure, except under exceptional circumstances, to appear at such proceedings.

(2) Notice of change in time or place of proceedings.

(A) In general. In removal proceedings under section 240 [8 USCS § 1229a], in the case of any change or postponement in the time and place of such proceedings, subject to subparagraph (B) a written notice shall be given in person to the alien (or, if personal service is not practicable, through service by mail to the alien or to the alien's counsel of record, if any) specifying—

(i) the new time or place of the proceedings, and

(ii) the consequences under section 240(b)(5) [8 USCS § 1229a(b)(5)] of failing, except under exceptional circumstances, to attend such proceedings.

(B) Exception. In the case of an alien not in detention, a written notice shall not be required under this paragraph if the alien has failed to provide the address required under paragraph (1)(F).

(3) Central address files. The Attorney General shall create a system to record and preserve on a timely basis notices of addresses and telephone numbers (and changes) provided under paragraph (1)(F).

(b) Securing of counsel.

(1) In general. In order that an alien be permitted the opportunity to secure counsel before the first hearing date in proceedings under section 240 [8 USCS § 1229a], the hearing date shall not be scheduled earlier than 10 days after the service of the notice to appear, unless the alien requests in writing an earlier hearing date.

(2) Current lists of counsel. The Attorney General shall provide for lists (updated not less often than quarterly) of persons who have indicated their availability to represent pro bono aliens in proceedings under section 240 [8 USCS § 1229a]. Such lists shall be provided under subsection (a)(1)(E) and otherwise made generally available.

(3) Rule of construction. Nothing in this subsection may be construed to prevent the Attorney General from proceeding against an alien pursuant to section 240 [8 USCS § 1229a] if the time period described in paragraph (1) has elapsed and the alien has failed to secure counsel.

(c) Service by mail. Service by mail under this section shall be sufficient if there is proof of attempted delivery to the last address provided by the alien in accordance with subsection (a)(1)(F).

(d) Prompt initiation of removal.

(1) In the case of an alien who is convicted of an offense which makes the alien deportable, the Attorney

General shall begin any removal proceeding as expeditiously as possible after the date of the conviction.

(2) Nothing in this subsection shall be construed to create any substantive or procedural right or benefit that is legally enforceable by any party against the United States or its agencies or officers or any other person.

(e) Certification of compliance with restrictions on disclosure.

(1) In general. In cases where an enforcement action leading to a removal proceeding was taken against an alien at any of the locations specified in paragraph (2), the Notice to Appear shall include a statement that the provisions of section 384 of the Illegal Immigration Reform and Immigrant Responsibility Act of 1996 (8 U.S.C. 1367) have been complied with.

(2) Locations. The locations specified in this paragraph are as follows:

(A) At a domestic violence shelter, a rape crisis center, supervised visitation center, family justice center, a victim services, or victim services provider, or a community-based organization.

(B) At a courthouse (or in connection with that appearance of the alien at a courthouse) if the alien is appearing in connection with a protection order case, child custody case, or other civil or criminal case relating to domestic violence, sexual assault, trafficking, or stalking in which the alien has been battered or subject to extreme cruelty or if the alien is described in subparagraph (T) or (U) of section 101(a)(15) [8 USCS § 1101(a)(15)].

HISTORY: (June 27, 1952, ch 477, Title II, Ch 4, § 239, as added Sept. 30, 1996, P. L. 104-208, Div C, Title III, Subtitle A, § 304(a)(3), 110 Stat. 3009-587; Jan. 5, 2006, P. L. 109-162, Title VIII, Subtitle C, § 825(c)(1), 119 Stat. 3065; Aug. 12, 2006, P. L. 109-271, § 6(d), 120 Stat. 763.)

§ 240. [8 U.S.C. § 1229a] Removal proceedings.

(a) Proceeding.

(1) In general. An immigration judge shall conduct proceedings for deciding the inadmissibility or deportability of an alien.

(2) Charges. An alien placed in proceedings under this section may be charged with any applicable ground of inadmissibility under section 212(a) [8 USCS § 1182(a)] or any applicable ground of deportability under section 237(a) [8 USCS § 1227(a)].

(3) Exclusive procedures. Unless otherwise specified in this Act, a proceeding under this section shall be the sole and exclusive procedure for determining whether an alien may be admitted to the United States or, if the alien has been so admitted, removed from the United States. Nothing in this section shall affect proceedings conducted pursuant to section 238 [8 USCS § 1228].

(b) Conduct of proceeding.

(1) Authority of immigration judge. The immigration judge shall administer oaths, receive evidence, and interrogate, examine, and cross-examine the alien and any witnesses. The immigration judge may issue subpoenas for the attendance of witnesses and presentation of evidence. The immigration judge shall have authority (under regulations prescribed by the Attorney General) to sanction by civil money penalty any action (or inaction) in contempt of the judge's proper exercise of authority under this Act.

(2) Form of proceeding.

(A) In general. The proceeding may take place—

(i) in person,

(ii) where agreed to by the parties, in the absence of the alien,

(iii) through video conference, or

(iv) subject to subparagraph (B), through telephone conference.

(B) Consent required in certain cases. An evidentiary hearing on the merits may only be conducted through a telephone conference with the consent of the alien involved after the alien has been advised of the right to proceed in person or through video conference.

(3) Presence of alien. If it is impracticable by reason of an alien's mental incompetency for the alien to be present at the proceeding, the Attorney General shall prescribe safeguards to protect the rights and privileges of the alien.

(4) Aliens rights in proceeding. In proceedings under this section, under regulations of the Attorney General—

(A) the alien shall have the privilege of being represented, at no expense to the Government, by counsel of the alien's choosing who is authorized to practice in such proceedings,

(B) the alien shall have a reasonable opportunity to examine the evidence against the alien, to present evidence on the alien's own behalf, and to cross-examine witnesses presented by the Government but these rights shall not entitle the alien to examine such national security information as the Government may proffer in opposition to the alien's admission to the United States or to an application by the alien for discretionary relief under this Act, and

(C) a complete record shall be kept of all testimony and evidence produced at the proceeding.

(5) Consequences of failure to appear.

(A) In general. Any alien who, after written notice required under paragraph (1) or (2) of section 239(a) [8 USCS § 1229(a)] has been provided to the alien or the alien's counsel of record, does not attend a proceeding under this section, shall be ordered removed in absentia if the Service establishes by clear, unequivocal, and convincing evidence that the written notice was so provided and that the alien is removable (as defined in subsection (e)(2)). The written notice by the Attorney General shall be considered sufficient for purposes of this subparagraph if provided at the most recent address provided under section 239(a)(1)(F) [8 USCS § 1229(a)(1)(F)].

(B) No notice if failure to provide address information. No written notice shall be required under subparagraph (A) if the alien has failed to provide the address required under section 239(a)(1)(F) [8 USCS § 1229(a)(1)(F)].

(C) Rescission of order. Such an order may be rescinded only—

(i) upon a motion to reopen filed within 180 days after the date of the order of removal if the alien demonstrates that the failure to appear was because of exceptional circumstances (as defined in subsection (e)(1)), or

(ii) upon a motion to reopen filed at any time if the alien demonstrates that the alien did not receive notice in accordance with paragraph (1) or (2) of section 239(a) [8 USCS § 1229(a)] or the alien demonstrates that the alien was in Federal or State custody and the failure to appear was through no fault of the alien.

The filing of the motion to reopen described in clause (i) or (ii) shall stay the removal of the alien pending disposition of the motion by the immigration judge.

(D) Effect on judicial review. Any petition for review under section 242 [8 USCS § 1252] of an order entered in absentia under this paragraph shall (except in cases described in section 242(b)(5) [8 USCS § 1252(b)(5)]) be confined to (i) the validity of the notice provided to the alien, (ii) the reasons for the alien's not attending the proceeding, and (iii) whether or not the alien is removable.

(E) Additional application to certain aliens in contiguous territory. The preceding provisions of this paragraph shall apply to all aliens placed in proceedings under this section, including any alien who remains in a contiguous foreign territory pursuant to section 235(b)(2)(C) [8 USCS § 1225(b)(2)(C)].

(6) Treatment of frivolous behavior. The Attorney General shall, by regulation—

(A) define in a proceeding before an immigration judge or before an appellate administrative body under this title, frivolous behavior for which attorneys may be sanctioned,

(B) specify the circumstances under which an administrative appeal of a decision or ruling will be considered frivolous and will be summarily dismissed, and

(C) impose appropriate sanctions (which may include suspension and disbarment) in the case of frivolous behavior.

Nothing in this paragraph shall be construed as limiting the authority of the Attorney General to take actions with respect to inappropriate behavior.

(7) Limitation on discretionary relief for failure to appear. Any alien against whom a final order of removal is entered in absentia under this subsection and who, at the time of the notice described in paragraph (1) or (2) of section 239(a) [8 USCS § 1229(a)], was provided oral notice, either in the alien's native language or in another language the alien understands, of the time and place of the proceedings and of the consequences under this paragraph of failing, other than because of exceptional circumstances (as defined in subsection (e)(1)) to attend a proceeding under this section, shall not be eligible for relief under section 240A, 240B, 245, 248, or 249 [8 USCS § 1229b, 1229c, 1255, 1258, or 1259] for a period of 10 years after the date of the entry of the final order of removal.

(c) Decision and burden of proof.

(1) Decision.

(A) In general. At the conclusion of the proceeding the immigration judge shall decide whether an alien is removable from the United States. The determination of the immigration judge shall be based only on the evidence produced at the hearing.

(B) Certain medical decisions. If a medical officer or civil surgeon or board of medical officers has certified under section 232(b) [8 USCS § 1222(b)] that an alien has a disease, illness, or addiction which would make the alien inadmissible under paragraph (1) of section 212(a) [8 USCS § 1182(a)], the decision of the immigration judge shall be based solely upon such certification.

(2) Burden on alien. In the proceeding the alien has the burden of establishing—

(A) if the alien is an applicant for admission, that the alien is clearly and beyond doubt entitled to be admitted and is not inadmissible under section 212 [8 USCS § 1182]; or

(B) by clear and convincing evidence, that the alien is lawfully present in the United States pursuant to a prior admission.

In meeting the burden of proof under subparagraph (B), the alien shall have access to the alien's visa or other entry document, if any, and any other records and documents, not considered by the Attorney General to be confidential, pertaining to the alien's admission or presence in the United States.

(3) Burden on service in cases of deportable aliens.

(A) In general. In the proceeding the Service has the burden of establishing by clear and convincing evidence that, in the case of an alien who has been admitted to the United States, the alien is deportable. No decision on deportability shall be valid unless it is based upon reasonable, substantial, and probative evidence.

(B) Proof of convictions. In any proceeding under this Act, any of the following documents or records (or a certified copy of such an official document or record) shall constitute proof of a criminal conviction:

(i) An official record of judgment and conviction.

(ii) An official record of plea, verdict, and sentence.

(iii) A docket entry from court records that indicates the existence of the conviction.

(iv) Official minutes of a court proceeding or a transcript of a court hearing in which the court takes notice of the existence of the conviction.

(v) An abstract of a record of conviction prepared by the court in which the conviction was entered, or by a State official associated with the State's repository of criminal justice records, that indicates the charge or section of law violated, the disposition of the case, the existence and date of conviction, and the sentence.

(vi) Any document or record prepared by, or under the direction of, the court in which the conviction was entered that indicates the existence of a conviction.

(vii) Any document or record attesting to the conviction that is maintained by an official of a State or Federal penal institution, which is the basis for that institution's authority to assume custody of the individual named in the record.

(C) Electronic records. In any proceeding under this Act, any record of conviction or abstract that has been submitted by electronic means to the Service from a State or court shall be admissible as evidence to prove a criminal conviction if it is—

(i) certified by a State official associated with the State's repository of criminal justice records as an official record from its repository or by a court official from the court in which the conviction was entered as an official record from its repository, and

(ii) certified in writing by a Service official as having been received electronically from the State's record repository or the court's record repository.

A certification under clause (i) may be by means of a computer-generated signature and statement of authenticity.

(4) Applications for relief from removal.

(A) In general. An alien applying for relief or protection from removal has the burden of proof to establish that the alien—

(i) satisfies the applicable eligibility requirements; and

(ii) with respect to any form of relief that is granted in the exercise of discretion, that the alien merits a favorable exercise of discretion.

(B) Sustaining burden. The applicant must comply with the applicable requirements to submit information or documentation in support of the applicant's application for relief or protection as provided by law or by regulation or in the instructions for the application form. In evaluating the testimony of the applicant or other witness in support of the application, the immigration judge will determine whether or not the testimony is credible, is persuasive, and refers to specific facts sufficient to demonstrate that the applicant has satisfied the applicant's burden of proof. In determining whether the applicant has met such burden, the immigration judge shall weigh the credible testimony along with other evidence of record. Where the immigration judge determines that the applicant should provide evidence which corroborates otherwise credible testimony, such evidence must be provided unless the applicant demonstrates that the applicant does not have the evidence and cannot reasonably obtain the evidence.

(C) Credibility determination. Considering the totality of the circumstances, and all relevant factors, the immigration judge may base a credibility determination on the demeanor, candor, or responsiveness of the applicant or witness, the inherent plausibility of the applicant's or witness's account, the consistency between the applicant's or witness's written and oral statements (whenever made and whether or not under oath, and considering the circumstances under which the statements were made), the internal consistency of each such statement, the consistency of such statements with other evidence of record (including the reports of the Department of State on country conditions), and any inaccuracies or falsehoods in such statements, without regard to whether an inconsistency, inaccuracy, or falsehood goes to the heart of the applicant's claim, or any other relevant factor. There is no presumption of credibility, however, if no adverse credibility determination is explicitly made, the applicant or witness shall have a rebuttable presumption of credibility on appeal.

(5) Notice. If the immigration judge decides that the alien is removable and orders the alien to be removed, the judge shall inform the alien of the right to appeal that decision and of the consequences for failure to depart under the order of removal, including civil and criminal penalties.

(6) Motions to reconsider.

(A) In general. The alien may file one motion to reconsider a decision that the alien is removable from the United States.

(B) Deadline. The motion must be filed within 30 days of the date of entry of a final administrative order of removal.

(C) Contents. The motion shall specify the errors of law or fact in the previous order and shall be supported by pertinent authority.

(7) Motions to reopen.

(A) In general. An alien may file one motion to reopen proceedings under this section, except that this limitation shall not apply so as to prevent the filing of one motion to reopen described in subparagraph (C) (iv).

(B) Contents. The motion to reopen shall state the new facts that will be proven at a hearing to be held if the motion is granted, and shall be supported by affidavits or other evidentiary material.

(C) Deadline.

(i) In general. Except as provided in this subparagraph, the motion to reopen shall be filed within 90 days of the date of entry of a final administrative order of removal.

(ii) Asylum. There is no time limit on the filing of a motion to reopen if the basis of the motion is to apply for relief under sections [section] 208 or 241(b)(3) [8 USCS § 1158 or 1251(b)(3)] and is based on changed country conditions arising in the country of nationality or the country to which removal has been ordered, if such evidence is material and was not available and would not have been discovered or presented at the previous proceeding.

(iii) Failure to appear. The filing of a motion to reopen an order entered pursuant to subsection (b)(5) is subject to the deadline specified in subparagraph (C) of such subsection.

(iv) Special rule for battered spouses, children, and parents. Any limitation under this section on the deadlines for filing such motions shall not apply—

(I) if the basis for the motion is to apply for relief under clause (iii) or (iv) of section 204(a)(1)(A) [8 USCS § 1154(a)(1)(A)], clause (ii) or (iii) of section 204(a)(1)(B) [8 USCS § 1154(a)(1)(B)],[,] section 240A(b) [8 USCS § 1229b(b)], or section 244(a)(3) (as in effect on March 31, 1997) [former 8 USCS § 1254(a)(3)];

(II) if the motion is accompanied by a cancellation of removal application to be filed with the Attorney General or by a copy of the self-petition that has been or will be filed with the Immigration and Naturalization Service upon the granting of the motion to reopen;

(III) if the motion to reopen is filed within 1 year of the entry of the final order of removal, except that the Attorney General may, in the Attorney General's discretion, waive this time limitation in the case of an alien who demonstrates extraordinary circumstances or extreme hardship to the alien's child; and

(IV) if the alien is physically present in the United States at the time of filing the motion.

The filing of a motion to reopen under this clause shall only stay the removal of a qualified alien (as defined in section 431(c)(1)(B) of the Personal Responsibility and Work Opportunity Reconciliation Act of 1996 (8 U.S.C. 1641(c)(1)(B))[)] pending the final disposition of the motion, including exhaustion of all appeals if the motion establishes that the alien is a qualified alien.

(d) Stipulated removal. The Attorney General shall provide by regulation for the entry by an immigration judge of an order of removal stipulated to by the alien (or the alien's representative) and the Service. A stipulated order shall constitute a conclusive determination of the alien's removability from the United States.

(e) Definitions. In this section and section 240A [8 USCS § 1229b]:

(1) Exceptional circumstances. The term "exceptional circumstances"' refers to exceptional circumstances (such as battery or extreme cruelty to the alien or any child or parent of the alien, serious illness of the alien, or serious illness or death of the spouse, child, or parent of the alien, but not including less compelling circumstances) beyond the control of the alien.

(2) Removable. The term "removable" means—

(A) in the case of an alien not admitted to the United States, that the alien is inadmissible under section 212 [8 USCS § 1182], or

(B) in the case of an alien admitted to the United States, that the alien is deportable under section 237 [8 USCS § 1227].

HISTORY: (June 27, 1952, ch 477, Title II, Ch 4, § 240, as added Sept. 30, 1996, P. L. 104-208, Div C, Title III, Subtitle A, § 304(a)(3), 110 Stat. 3009-589; Oct. 28, 2000, P. L. 106-386, Div B, Title V, § 1506(c)(1)(A), 114 Stat. 1528; May 11, 2005, P. L. 109-13, Div B, Title I, § 101(d), 119 Stat. 304; Jan. 5, 2006, P. L. 109-162, Title VIII, Subtitle B, § 813(a)(1), Subtitle C, § 825(a), 119 Stat. 3057, 3063.)

§ 240A. [8 U.S.C. § 1229b] Cancellation of removal; adjustment of status.

(a) Cancellation of removal for certain permanent residents. The Attorney General may cancel removal in the case of an alien who is inadmissible or deportable from the United States if the alien—

(1) has been an alien lawfully admitted for permanent residence for not less than 5 years,

(2) has resided in the United States continuously for 7 years after having been admitted in any status, and

(3) has not been convicted of any aggravated felony.

(b) Cancellation of removal and adjustment of status for certain nonpermanent residents.

(1) In general. The Attorney General may cancel removal of, and adjust to the status of an alien lawfully admitted for permanent residence, an alien who is inadmissible or deportable from the United States if the alien—

(A) has been physically present in the United States for a continuous period of not less than 10 years immediately preceding the date of such application;

(B) has been a person of good moral character during such period;

(C) has not been convicted of an offense under section 212(a)(2), 237(a)(2), or 237(a)(3) [8 USCS § 1182(a)(2), 1227(a)(2), or 1227(a)(3)], subject to paragraph (5); and

(D) establishes that removal would result in exceptional and extremely unusual hardship to the alien's spouse, parent, or child, who is a citizen of the United States or an alien lawfully admitted for permanent residence.

(2) Special rule for battered spouse or child.

(A) Authority. The Attorney General may cancel removal of, and adjust to the status of an alien lawfully admitted for permanent residence, an alien who is inadmissible or deportable from the United States if the alien demonstrates that—

(i) (I) the alien has been battered or subjected to extreme cruelty by a spouse or parent who is or was a United States citizen (or is the parent of a child of a United States citizen and the child has been battered or subjected to extreme cruelty by such citizen parent);

(II) the alien has been battered or subjected to extreme cruelty by a spouse or parent who is or was a lawful permanent resident (or is the parent of a child of an alien who is or was a lawful permanent resident and the child has been battered or subjected to extreme cruelty by such permanent resident parent); or

(III) the alien has been battered or subjected to extreme cruelty by a United States citizen or lawful permanent resident whom the alien intended to marry, but whose marriage is not legitimate because of that United States citizen's or lawful permanent resident's bigamy;

(ii) the alien has been physically present in the United States for a continuous period of not less than 3 years immediately preceding the date of such application, and the issuance of a charging document for removal proceedings shall not toll the 3-year period of continuous physical presence in the United States;

(iii) the alien has been a person of good moral character during such period, subject to the provisions of subparagraph (C);

(iv) the alien is not inadmissible under paragraph (2) or (3) of section 212(a) [8 USCS § 1182(a)], is not deportable under paragraphs (1)(G) or (2) through (4) of section 237(a) [8 USCS § 1227(a)], subject to paragraph (5), and has not been convicted of an aggravated felony; and

(v) the removal would result in extreme hardship to the alien, the alien's child, or the alien's parent.

(B) Physical presence. Notwithstanding subsection (d)(2), for purposes of subparagraph (A)(ii) or for purposes of section 244(a)(3) [former 8 USCS § 1254(a)(3)] (as in effect before the title III-A effective date in section 309 of the Illegal Immigration Reform and Immigrant Responsibility Act of 1996 [8 USCS § 1101 note]), an alien shall not be considered to have failed to maintain continuous physical presence by reason of an absence if the alien demonstrates a connection between the absence and the battering or extreme cruelty perpetrated against the alien. No absence or portion of an absence connected to the battering or extreme cruelty shall count toward the 90-day or 180-day limits established in subsection (d)(2). If any absence or aggregate absences exceed 180 days, the absences or portions of the absences will not be considered to break the period of continuous presence. Any such period of time excluded from the 180-day limit shall be excluded in computing the time during which the alien has been physically present for purposes of the 3-year requirement set forth in this subparagraph, subparagraph (A)(ii), and section 244(a)(3) [former 8 USCS § 1254(a)(3)] (as in effect before the title III-A effective date in section 309 of the Illegal Immigration Reform and Immigrant Responsibility Act of 1996 [8 USCS § 1101 note]).

(C) Good moral character. Notwithstanding section 101(f) [8 USCS § 1101(f)], an act or conviction that does not bar the Attorney General from granting relief under this paragraph by reason of subparagraph (A)(iv) shall not bar the Attorney General from finding the alien to be of good moral character under subparagraph (A)(iii) or section 244(a)(3) [former 8 USCS § 1254(a)(3)] (as in effect before the title III-A effective date in section 309 of the Illegal Immigration Reform and Immigrant Responsibility Act of 1996 [8 USCS § 1101 note]), if the Attorney General finds that the act or conviction was connected to the alien's having been battered or subjected to extreme cruelty and determines that a waiver is otherwise warranted.

(D) Credible evidence considered. In acting on applications under this paragraph, the Attorney General shall consider any credible evidence relevant to the application. The determination of what evidence is credible and the weight to be given that evidence shall be within the sole discretion of the Attorney General.

(3) Recordation of date. With respect to aliens who the Attorney General adjusts to the status of an alien lawfully admitted for permanent residence under paragraph (1) or (2), the Attorney General shall record the alien's lawful admission for permanent residence as of the date of the Attorney General's cancellation of removal under paragraph (1) or (2).

(4) Children of battered aliens and parents of battered alien children.

(A) In general. The Attorney General shall grant parole under section 212(d)(5) [8 USCS § 1182(d)(5)] to any alien who is a—

(i) child of an alien granted relief under section 240A(b)(2) [subsec. (b)(2) of this section] or 244(a)(3) [former 8 USCS § 1254(a)(3)] (as in effect before the title III-A effective date in section 309 of the Illegal Immigration Reform and Immigrant Responsibility Act of 1996 [8 USCS § 1101 note]); or

(ii) parent of a child alien granted relief under section 240A(b)(2) [subsec. (b)(2) of this section] or 244(a)(3) [former 8 USCS § 1254(a)(3)] (as in effect before the title III-A effective date in section 309 of the Illegal Immigration Reform and Immigrant Responsibility Act of 1996 [8 USCS § 1101 note]).

(B) Duration of parole. The grant of parole shall extend from the time of the grant of relief under section 240A(b)(2) [subsec. (b)(2) of this section] or section 244(a)(3) [former 8 USCS § 1254(a)(3)] (as in effect before the title III-A effective date in section 309 of the Illegal Immigration Reform and Immigrant Responsibility Act of 1996 [8 USCS § 1101 note]) to the time the application for adjustment of status filed by aliens covered under this paragraph has been finally adjudicated. Applications for adjustment of status filed by aliens covered under this paragraph shall be treated as if they were VAWA self-petitioners. Failure by the alien granted relief under section 240A(b)(2) [subsec. (b)(2) of this section] or section 244(a)(3) [former 8 USCS § 1254(a)(3)] (as in effect before the title III-A effective date in section 309 of the Illegal Immigration Reform and Immigrant Responsibility Act of 1996 [8 USCS § 1101 note]) to exercise due diligence in filing a visa petition on behalf of an alien described in clause (i) or (ii) may result in revocation of parole.

(5) Application of domestic violence waiver authority. The authority provided under section 237(a)(7) [8 USCS § 1227(a)(7)] may apply under paragraphs (1)(B), (1)(C), and (2)(A)(iv) in a cancellation of removal and adjustment of status proceeding.

(6) Relatives of trafficking victims.

(A) In general. Upon written request by a law enforcement official, the Secretary of Homeland Security may parole under section 212(d)(5) [8 USCS § 1182(d)(5)] any alien who is a relative of an alien granted continued presence under section 107(c)(3)(A) of the Trafficking Victims Protection Act (22 U.S.C. 7105(c)(3)(A)), if the relative—

(i) was, on the date on which law enforcement applied for such continued presence—

(I) in the case of an alien granted continued presence who is under 21 years of age, the spouse, child, parent, or unmarried sibling under 18 years of age, of the alien; or

(II) in the case of an alien granted continued presence who is 21 years of age or older, the spouse or child of the alien; or

(ii) is a parent or sibling of the alien who the requesting law enforcement official, in consultation with the Secretary of Homeland Security, as appropriate, determines to be in present danger of retaliation as a result of the alien's escape from the severe form of trafficking or cooperation with law enforcement, irrespective of age.

(B) Duration of parole.

(i) In general. The Secretary may extend the parole granted under subparagraph (A) until the final adjudication of the application filed by the principal alien under section 101(a)(15)(T)(ii) [8 USCS § 1101(a)(15)(T)(ii)].

(ii) Other limits on duration. If an application described in clause (i) is not filed, the parole granted under subparagraph (A) may extend until the later of—

(I) the date on which the principal alien's authority to remain in the United States under section 107(c)(3)(A) of the Trafficking Victims Protection Act (22 U.S.C. 7105(c)(3)(A)) is terminated; or

(II) the date on which a civil action filed by the principal alien under section 1595 of title 18, United States Code, is concluded.

(iii) Due diligence. Failure by the principal alien to exercise due diligence in filing a visa petition on behalf of an alien described in clause (i) or (ii) of subparagraph (A), or in pursuing the civil action described in clause (ii)(II) (as determined by the Secretary of Homeland Security in consultation with the Attorney General), may result in revocation of parole.

(C) Other limitations. A relative may not be granted parole under this paragraph if—

(i) the Secretary of Homeland Security or the Attorney General has reason to believe that the relative was knowingly complicit in the trafficking of an alien permitted to remain in the United States under section 107(c)(3)(A) of the Trafficking Victims Protection Act (22 U.S.C. 7105(c)(3)(A)); or

(ii) the relative is an alien described in paragraph (2) or (3) of section 212(a) [8 USCS § 1182(a)] or paragraph (2) or (4) of section 237(a) [8 USCS § 1227(a)].

(c) Aliens ineligible for relief. The provisions of subsections (a) and (b)(1) shall not apply to any of the following aliens:

(1) An alien who entered the United States as a crewman subsequent to June 30, 1964.

(2) An alien who was admitted to the United States as a nonimmigrant exchange alien as defined in section 101(a)(15)(J) [8 USCS § 1101(a)(15)(J)], or has acquired the status of such a nonimmigrant exchange alien after admission, in order to receive graduate medical education or training, regardless of whether or not the alien is subject to or has fulfilled the two-year foreign residence requirement of section 212(e) [8 USCS § 1182(e)].

(3) An alien who—

(A) was admitted to the United States as a nonimmigrant exchange alien as defined in section 101(a)(15)(J) [8 USCS § 1101(a)(15)(J)] or has acquired the status of such a nonimmigrant exchange alien after admission other than to receive graduate medical education or training,

(B) is subject to the two-year foreign residence requirement of section 212(e) [8 USCS § 1182(e)], and

(C) has not fulfilled that requirement or received a waiver thereof.

(4) An alien who is inadmissible under section 212(a)(3) [8 USCS § 1182(a)(3)] or deportable under section 237(a)(4) [8 USCS § 1227(a)(4)].

(5) An alien who is described in section 241(b)(3)(B)(i) [8 USCS § 1251(b)(3)(B)(i)].

(6) An alien whose removal has previously been cancelled under this section or whose deportation was suspended under section 244(a) [former 8 USCS § 1254(a)] or who has been granted relief under section 212(c) [former 8 USCS § 1182(c)], as such sections were in effect before the date of the enactment of the Illegal Immigration Reform and Immigrant Responsibility Act of 1996 [enacted Sept. 30, 1996].

(d) Special rules relating to continuous residence or physical presence.

(1) Termination of continuous period. For purposes of this section, any period of continuous residence or continuous physical presence in the United States shall be deemed to end (A) except in the case of an alien who applies for cancellation of removal under subsection (b)(2), when the alien is served a notice to appear under section 239(a) [8 USCS § 1229(a)], or (B) when the alien has committed an offense referred to in section 212(a)(2) [8 USCS § 1182(a)(2)] that renders the alien inadmissible to the United States under section 212(a)(2) [8 USCS § 1182(a)(2)] or removable from the United States under section 237(a)(2) or 237(a)(4) [8 USCS § 1227(a)(2) or 1227(a)(4)], whichever is earliest.

(2) Treatment of certain breaks in presence. An alien shall be considered to have failed to maintain continuous physical presence in the United States under subsections (b)(1) and (b)(2) if the alien has departed from the United States for any period in excess of 90 days or for any periods in the aggregate exceeding 180 days.

(3) Continuity not required because of honorable service in armed forces and presence upon entry into service. The requirements of continuous residence or continuous physical presence in the United States under subsections (a) and (b) shall not apply to an alien who—

(A) has served for a minimum period of 24 months in an active-duty status in the Armed Forces of the United States and, if separated from such service, was separated under honorable conditions, and

(B) at the time of the alien's enlistment or induction was in the United States.

(e) Annual limitation.

(1) Aggregate limitation. Subject to paragraphs (2) and (3), the Attorney General may not cancel the removal and adjust the status under this section, nor suspend the deportation and adjust the status under section 244(a) [former 8 USCS § 1254(a)] (as in effect before the enactment of the Illegal Immigration Reform and Immigrant Responsibility Act of 1996 [enacted Sept. 30, 1996]), of a total of more than 4,000 aliens in any fiscal year. The previous sentence shall apply regardless of when an alien applied for such cancellation and adjustment, or such suspension and adjustment, and whether such an alien had previously applied for suspension of deportation under such section 244(a) [8 USCS § 1254(a)]. The numerical limitation under this paragraph shall apply to the aggregate number of decisions in any fiscal year to cancel the removal (and adjust the status) of an alien, or suspend the deportation (and adjust the status) of an alien, under this section or such section 244(a) [8 USCS § 1254(a)].

(2) Fiscal year 1997. For fiscal year 1997, paragraph (1) shall only apply to decisions to cancel the removal of an alien, or suspend the deportation of an alien, made after April 1, 1997. Notwithstanding any other provision of law, the Attorney General may cancel the removal or suspend the deportation, in addition to the normal allotment for fiscal year 1998, of a number of aliens equal to 4,000 less the number of such cancellations of removal and suspensions of deportation granted in fiscal year 1997 after April 1, 1997.

(3) Exception for certain aliens. Paragraph (1) shall not apply to the following:

(A) Aliens described in section 309(c)(5)(C)(i) of the Illegal Immigration Reform and Immigrant Responsibility Act of 1996 [8 USCS § 1101 note] (as amended by the Nicaraguan Adjustment and Central American Relief Act).

(B) Aliens in deportation proceedings prior to April 1, 1997, who applied for suspension of deportation under section 244(a)(3) [former 8 USCS § 1254(a)(3)] (as in effect before the date of the enactment of the Illegal Immigration Reform and Immigrant Responsibility Act of 1996 [enacted Sept. 30, 1996]).

HISTORY: (June 27, 1952, ch 477, Title II, Ch 4, § 240A, as added Sept. 30, 1996, P. L. 104-208, Div C, Title III, Subtitle A, § 304(a)(3), 110 Stat. 3009-594; Nov. 19, 1997, P. L. 105-100, Title II, § 204(a)–(c), 111 Stat. 2200; Oct. 28, 2000, P. L. 106-386, Div B, Title V, §§ 1504(a), (b), 1505(b)(2), 1506(b)(1), 114 Stat. 1522, 1525, 1527; Jan. 5, 2006, P. L. 109-162, Title VIII, Subtitle B, § 813(c), Subtitle C, § 822(a), (b), 119 Stat. 3058, 3062; Aug. 12, 2006, P. L. 109-271, § 6(e), 120 Stat. 763; Dec. 23, 2008, P. L. 110-457, Title II, Subtitle A, § 205(b), 122 Stat. 5062.)

§ 240B. [8 U.S.C. § 1229c] Voluntary departure.

(a) Certain conditions.

(1) In general. The Attorney General may permit an alien voluntarily to depart the United States at the alien's own expense under this subsection, in lieu of being subject to proceedings under section 240 [8 USCS § 1229a] or prior to the completion of such proceedings, if the alien is not deportable under section 237(a)(2)(A)(iii) or section 237(a)(4)(B) [8 USCS § 1227(a)(2)(A)(iii) or 1227(a)(4)(B)].

(2) Period.

(A) In general. Subject to subparagraph (B), permission to depart voluntarily under this subsection shall not be valid for a period exceeding 120 days.

(B) Three-year pilot program waiver. During the period October 1, 2000, through September 30, 2003, and subject to subparagraphs (C) and (D)(ii), the Attorney General may, in the discretion of the Attorney General for humanitarian purposes, waive application of subparagraph (A) in the case of an alien—

(i) who was admitted to the United States as a nonimmigrant visitor (described in section 101(a)(15)(B) [8 USCS § 1101(a)(15)(B)]) under the provisions of the visa waiver pilot program established pursuant to section 217 [8 USCS § 1187], seeks the waiver for the purpose of continuing to receive medical treatment in the United States from a physician associated with a health care facility, and submits to the Attorney General—

(I) a detailed diagnosis statement from the physician, which includes the treatment being sought and the expected time period the alien will be required to remain in the United States;

(II) a statement from the health care facility containing an assurance that the alien's treatment is not being paid through any Federal or State public health assistance, that the alien's account has no outstanding balance, and that such facility will notify the Service when the alien is released or treatment is terminated; and

(III) evidence of financial ability to support the alien's day-to-day expenses while in the United States (including the expenses of any family member described in clause (ii)) and evidence that any such alien or family member is not receiving any form of public assistance; or

(ii) who—

(I) is a spouse, parent, brother, sister, son, daughter, or other family member of a principal alien described in clause (i); and

(II) entered the United States accompanying, and with the same status as, such principal alien.

(C) Waiver limitations.

(i) Waivers under subparagraph (B) may be granted only upon a request submitted by a Service district office to Service headquarters.

(ii) Not more than 300 waivers may be granted for any fiscal year for a principal alien under subparagraph (B)(i).

(iii) (I) Except as provided in subclause (II), in the case of each principal alien described in subparagraph (B)(i) not more than one adult may be granted a waiver under subparagraph (B)(ii).

(II) Not more than two adults may be granted a waiver under subparagraph (B)(ii) in a case in which—

(aa) the principal alien described in subparagraph (B)(i) is a dependent under the age of 18; or

(bb) one such adult is age 55 or older or is physically handicapped.

(D) Report to Congress; suspension of waiver authority.

(i) Not later than March 30 of each year, the Commissioner shall submit to the Congress an annual report regarding all waivers granted under subparagraph (B) during the preceding fiscal year.

(ii) Notwithstanding any other provision of law, the authority of the Attorney General under subparagraph (B) shall be suspended during any period in which an annual report under clause (i) is past due and has not been submitted.

(3) Bond. The Attorney General may require an alien permitted to depart voluntarily under this subsection to post a voluntary departure bond, to be surrendered upon proof that the alien has departed the United States within the time specified.

(4) Treatment of aliens arriving in the United States. In the case of an alien who is arriving in the United States and with respect to whom proceedings under section 240 [8 USCS § 1229a] are (or would otherwise be) initiated at the time of such alien's arrival, paragraph (1) shall not apply. Nothing in this paragraph shall be construed as preventing such an alien from withdrawing the application for admission in accordance with section 235(a)(4) [8 USCS § 1225(a)(4)].

(b) At conclusion of proceedings.

(1) In general. The Attorney General may permit an alien voluntarily to depart the United States at the alien's own expense if, at the conclusion of a proceeding under section 240 [8 USCS § 1229a], the immigration judge enters an order granting voluntary departure in lieu of removal and finds that—

(A) the alien has been physically present in the United States for a period of at least one year immediately preceding the date the notice to appear was served under section 239(a) [8 USCS § 1229(a)];

(B) the alien is, and has been, a person of good moral character for at least 5 years immediately preceding the alien's application for voluntary departure;

(C) the alien is not deportable under section 237(a)(2)(A)(iii) or section 237(a)(4) [8 USCS § 1227(a)(2)(A)(iii) or 1227(a)(4)]; and

(D) the alien has established by clear and convincing evidence that the alien has the means to depart the United States and intends to do so.

(2) Period. Permission to depart voluntarily under this subsection shall not be valid for a period exceeding 60 days.

(3) Bond. An alien permitted to depart voluntarily under this subsection shall be required to post a voluntary departure bond, in an amount necessary to ensure that the alien will depart, to be surrendered upon proof that the alien has departed the United States within the time specified.

(c) Aliens not eligible. The Attorney General shall not permit an alien to depart voluntarily under this section if the alien was previously permitted to so depart after having been found inadmissible under section 212(a)(6)(A) [8 USCS § 1182(a)(6)(A)].

(d) Civil penalty for failure to depart.

(1) In general. Subject to paragraph (2), if an alien is permitted to depart voluntarily under this section and voluntarily fails to depart the United States within the time period specified, the alien—

(A) shall be subject to a civil penalty of not less than $1,000 and not more than $5,000; and

(B) shall be ineligible, for a period of 10 years, to receive any further relief under this section and sections 240A, 245, 248, and 249 [8 USCS §§ 1229b, 1255, 1258, and 1259].

(2) Application of VAWA protections. The restrictions on relief under paragraph (1) shall not apply to relief under section 240A or 245 [8 USCS § 1229b or 1255] on the basis of a petition filed by a VAWA self-petitioner, or a petition filed under section 240A(b)(2) [8 USCS § 1229b(b)(2)], or under section 244(a)(3) [former 8 USCS § 1254(a)(3)] (as in effect prior to March 31, 1997), if the extreme cruelty or battery was at least one central reason for the alien's overstaying the grant of voluntary departure.

(3) Notice of penalties. The order permitting an alien to depart voluntarily shall inform the alien of the penalties under this subsection.

(e) Additional conditions. The Attorney General may by regulation limit eligibility for voluntary departure under this section for any class or classes of aliens. No court may review any regulation issued under this subsection.

(f) Judicial review. No court shall have jurisdiction over an appeal from denial of a request for an order of voluntary departure under subsection (b), nor shall any court order a stay of an alien's removal pending consideration of any claim with respect to voluntary departure.

HISTORY: (JJune 27, 1952, ch 477, Title II, Ch 4, § 240B, as added Sept. 30, 1996, P. L. 104-208, Div C, Title III, Subtitle A, § 304(a)(3), 110 Stat. 3009-596; Nov. 1, 2000, P. L. 106-406, § 2, 114 Stat. 1755; Jan. 5, 2006, P. L. 109-162, Title VIII, Subtitle B, § 812, 119 Stat. 3057.)

§ 240C. [8 U.S.C. § 1230] Records of admission.

(a) The Attorney General shall cause to be filed, as a record of admission of each immigrant, the immigrant visa required by section 221(e) [8 USCS § 1201(e)] to be surrendered at the port of entry by the arriving alien to an immigration officer.

(b) The Attorney General shall cause to be filed such record of the admission into the United States of each immigrant admitted under section 211(b) [8 USCS § 1181(b)] and of each nonimmigrant as the Attorney General deems necessary for the enforcement of the immigration laws.

HISTORY: (June 27, 1952, ch 477, Title II, Ch 4, § 240C [240], 66 Stat. 204; Sept. 30, 1996, P. L. 104-208, Div C, Title III, Subtitle A, §§ 304(a)(2), 308(f)(1)(K), 110 Stat. 3009-587, 3009-621.)

§ 241. [8 U.S.C. § 1231] Detention and removal of aliens ordered removed.

(a) Detention, release, and removal of aliens ordered removed.

(1) Removal period.

(A) In general. Except as otherwise provided in this section, when an alien is ordered removed, the Attorney General shall remove the alien from the United States within a period of 90 days (in this section referred to as the "removal period").

(B) Beginning of period. The removal period begins on the latest of the following:

(i) The date the order of removal becomes administratively final.

(ii) If the removal order is judicially reviewed and if a court orders a stay of the removal of the alien, the date of the court's final order.

(iii) If the alien is detained or confined (except under an immigration process), the date the alien is released from detention or confinement.

(C) Suspension of period. The removal period shall be extended beyond a period of 90 days and the alien may remain in detention during such extended period if the alien fails or refuses to make timely application in good faith for travel or other documents necessary to the alien's departure or conspires or acts to prevent the alien's removal subject to an order of removal.

(2) Detention. During the removal period, the Attorney General shall detain the alien. Under no circumstance during the removal period shall the Attorney General release an alien who has been found inadmissible under section 212(a)(2) or 212(a)(3)(B) [8 USCS § 1182(a)(2) or (a)(3)(B)] or deportable under section 237(a)(2) or 237(a)(4)(B) [8 USCS § 1227(a)(2) or (a)(4)(B)].

(3) Supervision after 90-day period. If the alien does not leave or is not removed within the removal period, the alien, pending removal, shall be subject to supervision under regulations prescribed by the Attorney General. The regulations shall include provisions requiring the alien—

(A) to appear before an immigration officer periodically for identification;

(B) to submit, if necessary, to a medical and psychiatric examination at the expense of the United States Government;

(C) to give information under oath about the alien's nationality, circumstances, habits, associations, and activities, and other information the Attorney General considers appropriate; and

(D) to obey reasonable written restrictions on the alien's conduct or activities that the Attorney General prescribes for the alien.

(4) Aliens imprisoned, arrested, or on parole, supervised release, or probation.

(A) In general. Except as provided in section 343(a) of the Public Health Service Act (42 U.S.C. 259(a)) and paragraph (2) [subparagraph (B)], the Attorney General may not remove an alien who is sentenced to imprisonment until the alien is released from imprisonment. Parole, supervised release, probation, or possibility of arrest or further imprisonment is not a reason to defer removal.

(B) Exception for removal of nonviolent offenders prior to completion of sentence of imprisonment. The Attorney General is authorized to remove an alien in accordance with applicable procedures under this Act before the alien has completed a sentence of imprisonment—

(i) in the case of an alien in the custody of the Attorney General, if the Attorney General determines that (I) the alien is confined pursuant to a final conviction for a nonviolent offense (other than an offense related to smuggling or harboring of aliens or an offense described in section 101(a)(43)(B), (C), (E), (I), or (L) [8 USCS § 1101(a)(43)(B), (C), (E), (I), or (L)] [)] and (II) the removal of the alien is appropriate and in the best interest of the United States; or

(ii) in the case of an alien in the custody of a State (or a political subdivision of a State), if the chief State official exercising authority with respect to the incarceration of the alien determines that (I) the alien is confined pursuant to a final conviction for a nonviolent offense (other than an offense described in section 101(a)(43)(C) or (E) [8 USCS § 1101(a)(43)(C)]), (II) the removal is appropriate and in the best interest of the State, and (III) submits a written request to the Attorney General that such alien be so removed.

(C) Notice. Any alien removed pursuant to this paragraph shall be notified of the penalties under the laws of the United States relating to the reentry of deported aliens, particularly the expanded penalties for aliens removed under subparagraph (B).

(D) No private right. No cause or claim may be asserted under this paragraph against any official of the United States or of any State to compel the release, removal, or consideration for release or removal of any alien.

(5) Reinstatement of removal orders against aliens illegally reentering. If the Attorney General finds that an alien has reentered the United States illegally after having been removed or having departed voluntarily, under an order of removal, the prior order of removal is reinstated from its original date and is not subject to being reopened or reviewed, the alien is not eligible and may not apply for any relief under this Act, and the alien shall be removed under the prior order at any time after the reentry.

(6) Inadmissible or criminal aliens. An alien ordered removed who is inadmissible under section 212 [8 USCS § 1182], removable under section 237(a)(1)(C), 237(a)(2), or 237(a)(4) [8 USCS § 1227(a)(1)(C), (a)(2), or (a)(4)] or who has been determined by the Attorney General to be a risk to the community or unlikely to comply with the order of removal, may be detained beyond the removal period and, if released, shall be subject to the terms of supervision in paragraph (3).

(7) Employment authorization. No alien ordered removed shall be eligible to receive authorization to be employed in the United States unless the Attorney General makes a specific finding that—

(A) the alien cannot be removed due to the refusal of all countries designated by the alien or under this section to receive the alien, or

(B) the removal of the alien is otherwise impracticable or contrary to the public interest.

(b) Countries to which aliens may be removed.

(1) Aliens arriving at the United States. Subject to paragraph (3)—

(A) In general. Except as provided by subparagraphs (B) and (C), an alien who arrives at the United States and with respect to whom proceedings under section 240 [8 USCS § 1229a] were initiated at the time of such alien's arrival shall be removed to the country in which the alien boarded the vessel or aircraft on which the alien arrived in the United States.

(B) Travel from contiguous territory. If the alien boarded the vessel or aircraft on which the alien arrived in the United States in a foreign territory contiguous to the United States, an island adjacent to the United States, or an island adjacent to a foreign territory contiguous to the United States, and the alien is not a native, citizen, subject, or national of, or does not reside in, the territory or island, removal shall be to the country in which the alien boarded the vessel that transported the alien to the territory or island.

(C) Alternative countries. If the government of the country designated in subparagraph (A) or (B) is unwilling to accept the alien into that country's territory, removal shall be to any of the following countries, as directed by the Attorney General:

(i) The country of which the alien is a citizen, subject, or national.

(ii) The country in which the alien was born.

(iii) The country in which the alien has a residence.

(iv) A country with a government that will accept the alien into the country's territory if removal to each country described in a previous clause of this subparagraph is impracticable, inadvisable, or impossible.

(2) Other aliens. Subject to paragraph (3)—

(A) Selection of country by alien. Except as otherwise provided in this paragraph—

(i) any alien not described in paragraph (1) who has been ordered removed may designate one country to which the alien wants to be removed, and

(ii) the Attorney General shall remove the alien to the country the alien so designates.

(B) Limitation on designation. An alien may designate under subparagraph (A)(i) a foreign territory contiguous to the United States, an adjacent island, or an island adjacent to a foreign territory contiguous to the United States as the place to which the alien is to be removed only if the alien is a native, citizen, subject, or national of, or has resided in, that designated territory or island.

(C) Disregarding designation. The Attorney General may disregard a designation under subparagraph (A)(i) if—

(i) the alien fails to designate a country promptly;

(ii) the government of the country does not inform the Attorney General finally, within 30 days after the date the Attorney General first inquires, whether the government will accept the alien into the country;

(iii) the government of the country is not willing to accept the alien into the country; or

(iv) the Attorney General decides that removing the alien to the country is prejudicial to the United States.

(D) Alternative country. If an alien is not removed to a country designated under subparagraph (A)(i), the Attorney General shall remove the alien to a country of which the alien is a subject, national, or citizen unless the government of the country—

(i) does not inform the Attorney General or the alien finally, within 30 days after the date the Attorney General first inquires or within another period of time the Attorney General decides is reasonable, whether the government will accept the alien into the country; or

(ii) is not willing to accept the alien into the country.

(E) Additional removal countries. If an alien is not removed to a country under the previous subparagraphs of this paragraph, the Attorney General shall remove the alien to any of the following countries:

(i) The country from which the alien was admitted to the United States.

(ii) The country in which is located the foreign port from which the alien left for the United States or for a foreign territory contiguous to the United States.

(iii) A country in which the alien resided before the alien entered the country from which the alien entered the United States.

(iv) The country in which the alien was born.

(v) The country that had sovereignty over the alien's birthplace when the alien was born.

(vi) The country in which the alien's birthplace is located when the alien is ordered removed.

(vii) If impracticable, inadvisable, or impossible to remove the alien to each country described in a previous clause of this subparagraph, another country whose government will accept the alien into that country.

(F) Removal country when United States is at war. When the United States is at war and the Attorney General decides that it is impracticable, inadvisable, inconvenient, or impossible to remove an alien under this subsection because of the war, the Attorney General may remove the alien—

(i) to the country that is host to a government in exile of the country of which the alien is a citizen or subject if the government of the host country will permit the alien's entry; or

(ii) if the recognized government of the country of which the alien is a citizen or subject is not in exile, to a country, or a political or territorial subdivision of a country, that is very near the country of which the alien is a citizen or subject, or, with the consent of the government of the country of which the alien is a citizen or subject, to another country.

(3) Restriction on removal to a country where alien's life or freedom would be threatened.

(A) In general. Notwithstanding paragraphs (1) and (2), the Attorney General may not remove an alien to a country if the Attorney General decides that the alien's life or freedom would be threatened in that country because of the alien's race, religion, nationality, membership in a particular social group, or political opinion.

(B) Exception. Subparagraph (A) does not apply to an alien deportable under section 237(a)(4)(D) [8 USCS § 1227(a)(4)(D)] or if the Attorney General decides that—

(i) the alien ordered, incited, assisted, or otherwise participated in the persecution of an individual because of the individual's race, religion, nationality, membership in a particular social group, or political opinion;

(ii) the alien, having been convicted by a final judgment of a particularly serious crime is a danger to the community of the United States;

(iii) there are serious reasons to believe that the alien committed a serious nonpolitical crime outside the United States before the alien arrived in the United States; or

(iv) there are reasonable grounds to believe that the alien is a danger to the security of the United States.

For purposes of clause (ii), an alien who has been convicted of an aggravated felony (or felonies) for which the alien has been sentenced to an aggregate term of imprisonment of at least 5 years shall be considered to have committed a particularly serious crime. The previous sentence shall not preclude the Attorney General from determining that, notwithstanding the length of sentence imposed, an alien has been convicted of a particularly serious crime. For purposes of clause (iv), an alien who is described in section 237(a)(4)(B) [8 USCS § 1227(a)(4)(B)] shall be considered to be an alien with respect to whom there are reasonable grounds for regarding as a danger to the security of the United States.

(C) Sustaining burden of proof; credibility determinations. In determining whether an alien has demonstrated that the alien's life or freedom would be threatened for a reason described in subparagraph (A), the trier of fact shall determine whether the alien has sustained the alien's burden of proof, and shall make credibility determinations, in the manner described in clauses (ii) and (iii) of section 208(b)(1)(B) [8 USCS § 1158(b)(1)(B)].

(c) Removal of aliens arriving at port of entry.

(1) Vessels and aircraft. An alien arriving at a port of entry of the United States who is ordered removed

either without a hearing under section 235(b)(1) or 235(c) [8 USCS § 1225(b)(1) or (c)] or pursuant to proceedings under section 240 [8 USCS § 1229a] initiated at the time of such alien's arrival shall be removed immediately on a vessel or aircraft owned by the owner of the vessel or aircraft on which the alien arrived in the United States, unless—

(A) it is impracticable to remove the alien on one of those vessels or aircraft within a reasonable time, or

(B) the alien is a stowaway—

(i) who has been ordered removed in accordance with section 235(a)(1) [8 USCS § 1225(a)(1)],

(ii) who has requested asylum, and

(iii) whose application has not been adjudicated or whose asylum application has been denied but who has not exhausted all appeal rights.

(2) Stay of removal.

(A) In general. The Attorney General may stay the removal of an alien under this subsection if the Attorney General decides that—

(i) immediate removal is not practicable or proper; or

(ii) the alien is needed to testify in the prosecution of a person for a violation of a law of the United States or of any State.

(B) Payment of detention costs. During the period an alien is detained because of a stay of removal under subparagraph (A)(ii), the Attorney General may pay from the appropriation "Immigration and Naturalization Service—Salaries and Expenses"—

(i) the cost of maintenance of the alien; and

(ii) a witness fee of $1 a day.

(C) Release during stay. The Attorney General may release an alien whose removal is stayed under subparagraph (A)(ii) on—

(i) the alien's filing a bond of at least $500 with security approved by the Attorney General;

(ii) condition that the alien appear when required as a witness and for removal; and

(iii) other conditions the Attorney General may prescribe.

(3) Costs of detention and maintenance pending removal.

(A) In general. Except as provided in subparagraph (B) and subsection (d) [(e)], an owner of a vessel or aircraft bringing an alien to the United States shall pay the costs of detaining and maintaining the alien—

(i) while the alien is detained under subsection (d) (1), and

(ii) in the case of an alien who is a stowaway, while the alien is being detained pursuant to—

(I) subsection (d)(2)(A) or (d)(2)(B)(i),

(II) subsection (d)(2)(B)(ii) or (iii) for the period of time reasonably necessary for the owner to arrange for repatriation or removal of the stowaway, including obtaining necessary travel documents, but not to extend beyond the date on which it is ascertained that such travel documents cannot be obtained from the country to which the stowaway is to be returned, or

(III) section 235(b)(1)(B)(ii) [8 USCS § 1225(b)(1)(B)(ii)], for a period not to exceed 15 days (excluding Saturdays, Sundays, and holidays) commencing on the first such day which begins on the earlier of 72 hours after the time of the initial presentation of the stowaway for inspection or at the time the stowaway is determined to have a credible fear of persecution.

(B) Nonapplication. Subparagraph (A) shall not apply if—

(i) the alien is a crewmember;

(ii) the alien has an immigrant visa;

(iii) the alien has a nonimmigrant visa or other documentation authorizing the alien to apply for temporary admission to the United States and applies for admission not later than 120 days after the date the visa or documentation was issued;

(iv) the alien has a reentry permit and applies for admission not later than 120 days after the date of the alien's last inspection and admission;

(v) (I) the alien has a nonimmigrant visa or other documentation authorizing the alien to apply for temporary admission to the United States or a reentry permit;

(II) the alien applies for admission more than 120 days after the date the visa or documentation was issued or after the date of the last inspection and admission under the reentry permit; and

(III) the owner of the vessel or aircraft satisfies the Attorney General that the existence of the condition relating to inadmissibility could not have been discovered by exercising reasonable care before the alien boarded the vessel or aircraft; or

(vi) the individual claims to be a national of the United States and has a United States passport.

(d) Requirements of persons providing transportation.

(1) Removal at time of arrival. An owner, agent, master, commanding officer, person in charge, purser, or consignee of a vessel or aircraft bringing an alien (except an alien crewmember) to the United States shall—

(A) receive an alien back on the vessel or aircraft or another vessel or aircraft owned or operated by the same interests if the alien is ordered removed under this part; and

(B) take the alien to the foreign country to which the alien is ordered removed.

(2) Alien stowaways. An owner, agent, master, commanding officer, charterer, or consignee of a vessel or aircraft arriving in the United States with an alien stowaway—

(A) shall detain the alien on board the vessel or aircraft, or at such place as the Attorney General shall designate, until completion of the inspection of the alien by an immigration officer;

(B) may not permit the stowaway to land in the United States, except pursuant to regulations of the Attorney General temporarily—

(i) for medical treatment,

(ii) for detention of the stowaway by the Attorney General, or

(iii) for departure or removal of the stowaway; and

(C) if ordered by an immigration officer, shall remove the stowaway on the vessel or aircraft or on another vessel or aircraft.

The Attorney General shall grant a timely request to remove the stowaway under subparagraph (C) on a vessel or aircraft other than that on which the stowaway arrived if the requester has obtained any travel documents necessary for departure or repatriation of the stowaway and removal of the stowaway will not be unreasonably delayed.

(3) Removal upon order. An owner, agent, master, commanding officer, person in charge, purser, or consignee of a vessel, aircraft, or other transportation line shall comply with an order of the Attorney General to take on board, guard safely, and transport to the destination specified any alien ordered to be removed under this Act.

(e) Payment of expenses of removal.

(1) Costs of removal at time of arrival. In the case of an alien who is a stowaway or who is ordered removed either without a hearing under section 235(a)(1) [235(b)(1)] or 235(c) [8 USCS § 1225(b)(1) or (c)] or pursuant to proceedings under section 240 [8 USCS § 1229a] initiated at the time of such alien's arrival, the owner of the vessel or aircraft (if any) on which the alien arrived in the United States shall pay the transportation cost of removing the alien. If removal is on a vessel or aircraft not owned by the owner of the vessel or aircraft on which the alien arrived in the United States, the Attorney General may—

(A) pay the cost from the appropriation "Immigration and Naturalization Service—Salaries and Expenses"; and

(B) recover the amount of the cost in a civil action from the owner, agent, or consignee of the vessel or aircraft (if any) on which the alien arrived in the United States.

(2) Costs of removal to port of removal for aliens admitted or permitted to land. In the case of an alien who has been admitted or permitted to land and is ordered removed, the cost (if any) of removal of the alien to the port of removal shall be at the expense of the appropriation for the enforcement of this Act.

(3) Costs of removal from port of removal for aliens admitted or permitted to land.

(A) Through appropriation. Except as provided in subparagraph (B), in the case of an alien who has been admitted or permitted to land and is ordered removed, the cost (if any) of removal of the alien from the port of removal shall be at the expense of the appropriation for the enforcement of this Act.

(B) Through owner.

(i) In general. In the case of an alien described in clause (ii), the cost of removal of the alien from the port of removal may be charged to any owner of the vessel, aircraft, or other transportation line by which the alien came to the United States.

(ii) Aliens described. An alien described in this clause is an alien who—

(I) is admitted to the United States (other than lawfully admitted for permanent residence) and is ordered removed within 5 years of the date of admission based on a ground that existed before or at the time of admission, or

(II) is an alien crewman permitted to land temporarily under section 252 [8 USCS § 1282] and is ordered removed within 5 years of the date of landing.

(C) Costs of removal of certain aliens granted voluntary departure. In the case of an alien who has been granted voluntary departure under section 240B [8 USCS § 1229c] and who is financially unable to depart at the alien's own expense and whose removal the Attorney General deems to be in the best interest of the United States, the expense of such removal may be paid from the appropriation for the enforcement of this Act.

(f) Aliens requiring personal care during removal.

(1) In general. If the Attorney General believes that an alien being removed requires personal care because of the alien's mental or physical condition, the Attorney General may employ a suitable person for that purpose who shall accompany and care for the alien until the alien arrives at the final destination.

(2) Costs. The costs of providing the service described in paragraph (1) shall be defrayed in the same manner as the expense of removing the accompanied alien is defrayed under this section.

(g) Places of detention.

(1) In general. The Attorney General shall arrange for appropriate places of detention for aliens detained pending removal or a decision on removal. When United States Government facilities are unavailable or facilities adapted or suitably located for detention are unavailable for rental, the Attorney General may expend from the appropriation "Immigration and Naturalization Service—Salaries and Expenses", without regard to section 3709 of the Revised Statutes (41 U.S.C. 5) [41 USCS § 6101], amounts necessary to acquire land and to acquire, build, remodel, repair, and operate facilities (including living quarters for immigration officers if not otherwise available) necessary for detention.

(2) Detention facilities of the immigration and naturalization service. Prior to initiating any project for the construction of any new detention facility for the Service, the Commissioner shall consider the availability for purchase or lease of any existing prison, jail, detention center, or other comparable facility suitable for such use.

(h) Statutory construction. Nothing in this section shall be construed to create any substantive or procedural right or benefit that is legally enforceable by any party against the United States or its agencies or officers or any other person.

(i) Incarceration.

(1) If the chief executive officer of a State (or, if appropriate, a political subdivision of the State) exercising authority with respect to the incarceration of an undocumented criminal alien submits a written request to the Attorney General, the Attorney General shall, as determined by the Attorney General—

(A) enter into a contractual arrangement which provides for compensation to the State or a political subdivision of the State, as may be appropriate, with respect to the incarceration of the undocumented criminal alien; or

(B) take the undocumented criminal alien into the custody of the Federal Government and incarcerate the alien.

(2) Compensation under paragraph (1)(A) shall be the average cost of incarceration of a prisoner in the relevant State as determined by the Attorney General.

(3) For purposes of this subsection, the term "undocumented criminal alien" means an alien who—

(A) has been convicted of a felony or two or more misdemeanors; and

(B) (i) entered the United States without inspection or at any time or place other than as designated by the Attorney General;

(ii) was the subject of exclusion or deportation proceedings at the time he or she was taken into custody by the State or a political subdivision of the State; or

(iii) was admitted as a nonimmigrant and at the time he or she was taken into custody by the State or a political subdivision of the State has failed to maintain the nonimmigrant status in which the alien was admitted or to which it was changed under section 248 [8 USCS § 1258], or to comply with the conditions of any such status.

(4) (A) In carrying out paragraph (1), the Attorney General shall give priority to the Federal incarceration of undocumented criminal aliens who have committed aggravated felonies.

(B) The Attorney General shall ensure that undocumented criminal aliens incarcerated in Federal facilities pursuant to this subsection are held in facilities which provide a level of security appropriate to the crimes for which they were convicted.

(5) There are authorized to be appropriated to carry out this subsection—

(A) $750,000,000 for fiscal year 2006;

(B) $850,000,000 for fiscal year 2007; and

(C) $950,000,000 for each of the fiscal years 2008 through 2011.

(6) Amounts appropriated pursuant to the authorization of appropriations in paragraph (5) that are distributed to a State or political subdivision of a State, including a municipality, may be used only for correctional purposes.

HISTORY: (June 27, 1952, ch 477, Title II, Ch. 4, § 241, as added Sept. 30, 1996, P. L. 104-208, Div C, Title III, Subtitle A, §§ 305(a)(3), 306(a)(1), Subtitle B, § 328(a)(1), 110 Stat. 3009-598, 3009-607, 3009-630; Nov. 2, 2002, P. L. 107-273, Div C, Title I, Subtitle A, § 11014, 116 Stat. 1824; May 11, 2005, P. L. 109-13, Div B, Title I, § 101(c), 119 Stat. 303; Jan. 5, 2006, P. L. 109-162, Title XI, Subtitle C, § 1196(a), (b), 119 Stat. 3130.)

§ 242. [8 U.S.C. § 1252] Judicial review of orders of removal.

(a) Applicable provisions.

(1) General orders of removal. Judicial review of a final order of removal (other than an order of removal without a hearing pursuant to section 235(b)(1) [8 USCS § 1225(b)(1)]) is governed only by chapter 158 of title 28 of the United States Code [28 USCS §§ 2341 et seq.], except as provided in subsection (b) and except that the court may not order the taking of additional evidence under section 2347(c) of such title.

(2) Matters not subject to judicial review.

(A) Review relating to section 235(b)(1). Notwithstanding any other provision of law (statutory or nonstatutory), including section 2241 of title 28, United States Code [28 USCS § 2241], or any other habeas corpus provision, and sections 1361 and 1651 of such title [28 USCS §§ 1361 and 1651], no court shall have jurisdiction to review—

(i) except as provided in subsection (e), any individual determination or to entertain any other cause or claim arising from or relating to the implementation or operation of an order of removal pursuant to section 235(b)(1) [8 USCS § 1225(b)(1)],

(ii) except as provided in subsection (e), a decision by the Attorney General to invoke the provisions of such section,

(iii) the application of such section to individual aliens, including the determination made under section 235(b)(1)(B) [8 USCS § 1225(b)(1)(B)], or

(iv) except as provided in subsection (e), procedures and policies adopted by the Attorney General to implement the provisions of section 235(b)(1) [8 USCS § 1225(b)(1)].

(B) Denials of discretionary relief. Notwithstanding any other provision of law (statutory or nonstatutory), including section 2241 of title 28, United States Code [28 USCS § 2241], or any other habeas corpus provision, and sections 1361 and 1651 of such title [28 USCS §§ 1361 and 1651], and except as provided in subparagraph (D), and regardless of whether the judgment, decision, or action is made in removal proceedings, no court shall have jurisdiction to review—

(i) any judgment regarding the granting of relief under section 212(h), 212(i), 240A, 240B, or 245 [8 USCS § 1182(h), 1182(i), 1229b, 1229c, or 1255], or

(ii) any other decision or action of the Attorney General or the Secretary of Homeland Security the authority for which is specified under this title [8 USCS §§ 1151 et seq.] to be in the discretion of the Attorney General or the Secretary of Homeland Security, other than the granting of relief under section 208(a) [8 USCS § 1158(a)].

(C) Orders against criminal aliens. Notwithstanding any other provision of law (statutory or nonstatutory), including section 2241 of title 28, United States Code [28 USCS § 2241], or any other habeas corpus provision, and sections 1361 and 1651 of such title [28 USCS §§ 1361 and 1651], and except as provided in subparagraph (D), no court shall have jurisdiction to review any final order of removal against an alien who is removable by reason of having committed a criminal offense covered in section 212(a)(2) or 237(a)(2)(A)(iii), (B), (C), or (D) [8 USCS § 1182(a)(2) or 1227(a)(2)(A)(iii), (B), (C), or (D)], or any offense covered by section 237(a)(2)(A)(ii) [8 USCS § 1227(a)(2)(A)(ii)] for which both predicate offenses are, without regard to their date of commission, otherwise covered by section 237(a)(2)(A)(i) [8 USCS § 1227(a)(2)(A)(i)].

(D) Judicial review of certain legal claims. Nothing in subparagraph (B) or (C), or in any other provision of this Act (other than this section) which limits or eliminates judicial review, shall be construed as precluding review of constitutional claims or questions of law raised upon a petition for review filed with an appropriate court of appeals in accordance with this section.

(3) Treatment of certain decisions. No alien shall have a right to appeal from a decision of an immigration judge which is based solely on a certification described in section 240(c)(1)(B) [8 USCS § 1229a(c)(1)(B)].

(4) Claims under the United Nations Convention. Notwithstanding any other provision of law (statutory or nonstatutory), including section 2241 of title 28, United States Code [28 USCS § 2241], or any other habeas corpus provision, and sections 1361 and 1651 of such title [28 USCS §§ 1361 and 1651], a petition for review filed with an appropriate court of appeals in accordance with this section shall be the sole and exclusive means for judicial review of any cause or claim under the United Nations Convention Against Torture and Other Forms of Cruel, Inhuman, or Degrading Treatment or Punishment, except as provided in subsection (e).

(5) Exclusive means of review. Notwithstanding any other provision of law (statutory or nonstatutory), including section 2241 of title 28, United States Code [28 USCS § 2241], or any other habeas corpus provision, and sections 1361 and 1651 of such title [28 USCS §§ 1361 and 1651], a petition for review filed with an appropriate court of appeals in accordance with this section shall be the sole and exclusive means for judicial review of an order of removal entered or issued under any provision of this Act, except as provided in subsection (e). For purposes of this Act, in every provision that limits or eliminates judicial review or jurisdiction to review, the terms "judicial review" and "jurisdiction to review" include habeas corpus review pursuant to section 2241 of title 28, United States Code [28 USCS § 2241], or any other habeas corpus provision, sections 1361 and 1651 of such title [28 USCS §§ 1361 and 1651], and review pursuant to any other provision of law (statutory or nonstatutory).

(b) Requirements for review of orders of removal. With respect to review of an order of removal under subsection (a)(1), the following requirements apply:

(1) Deadline. The petition for review must be filed not later than 30 days after the date of the final order of removal.

(2) Venue and forms. The petition for review shall be filed with the court of appeals for the judicial circuit in which the immigration judge completed the proceedings. The record and briefs do not have to be printed. The court of appeals shall review the proceeding on a typewritten record and on typewritten briefs.

(3) Service.

(A) In general. The respondent is the Attorney General. The petition shall be served on the Attorney General and on the officer or employee of the Service in charge of the Service district in which the final order of removal under section 240 [8 USCS § 1229a] was entered.

(B) Stay of order. Service of the petition on the officer or employee does not stay the removal of an alien pending the court's decision on the petition, unless the court orders otherwise.

(C) Alien's brief. The alien shall serve and file a brief in connection with a petition for judicial review not later than 40 days after the date on which the administrative record is available, and may serve and file a reply brief not later than 14 days after service of the brief of the Attorney General, and the court may not extend these deadlines except upon motion for good cause shown. If an alien fails to file a brief within the time provided in this paragraph, the court shall dismiss the appeal unless a manifest injustice would result.

(4) Scope and standard for review. Except as provided in paragraph (5)(B)—

(A) the court of appeals shall decide the petition only on the administrative record on which the order of removal is based,

(B) the administrative findings of fact are conclusive unless any reasonable adjudicator would be compelled to conclude to the contrary,

(C) a decision that an alien is not eligible for admission to the United States is conclusive unless manifestly contrary to law, and

(D) the Attorney General's discretionary judgment whether to grant relief under section 208(a) [8 USCS § 1158(a)] shall be conclusive unless manifestly contrary to the law and an abuse of discretion.

No court shall reverse a determination made by a trier of fact with respect to the availability of corroborating evidence, as described in section 208(b)(1)(B), 240(c)(4)(B), or 241(b)(3)(C) [8 USCS § 1158(b)(1)(B), 1229a(c)(4)(B), or 1231(b)(3)(C)], unless the court finds, pursuant to section 242(b)(4)(B) [subsec. (b)(4)(B) of this section], that a reasonable trier of fact is compelled to conclude that such corroborating evidence is unavailable.

(5) Treatment of nationality claims.

(A) Court determination if no issue of fact. If the petitioner claims to be a national of the United States and the court of appeals finds from the pleadings and affidavits that no genuine issue of material fact about the petitioner's nationality is presented, the court shall decide the nationality claim.

(B) Transfer if issue of fact. If the petitioner claims to be a national of the United States and the court of appeals finds that a genuine issue of material fact about the petitioner's nationality is presented, the court shall transfer the proceeding to the district court of the United States for the judicial district in which the petitioner resides for a new hearing on the nationality claim and a decision on that claim as if an action had been brought in the district court under section 2201 of title 28, United States Code.

(C) Limitation on determination. The petitioner may have such nationality claim decided only as provided in this paragraph.

(6) Consolidation with review of motions to reopen or reconsider. When a petitioner seeks review of an order under this section, any review sought of a motion to reopen or reconsider the order shall be consolidated with the review of the order.

(7) Challenge to validity of orders in certain criminal proceedings.

(A) In general. If the validity of an order of removal has not been judicially decided, a defendant in a criminal proceeding charged with violating section 243(a) [8 USCS § 1253(a)] may challenge the validity of the order in the criminal proceeding only by filing a separate motion before trial. The district court, without a jury, shall decide the motion before trial.

(B) Claims of United States nationality. If the defendant claims in the motion to be a national of the United States and the district court finds that—

(i) no genuine issue of material fact about the defendant's nationality is presented, the court shall decide the motion only on the administrative record on which the removal order is based and the administrative findings of fact are conclusive if supported by reasonable, substantial, and probative evidence on the record considered as a whole; or

(ii) a genuine issue of material fact about the defendant's nationality is presented, the court shall hold a new hearing on the nationality claim and decide that claim as if an action had been brought under section 2201 of title 28, United States Code.

The defendant may have such nationality claim decided only as provided in this subparagraph.

(C) Consequence of invalidation. If the district court rules that the removal order is invalid, the court shall dismiss the indictment for violation of section 243(a) [8 USCS § 1253(a)]. The United States Government may appeal the dismissal to the court of appeals for the appropriate circuit within 30 days after the date of the dismissal.

(D) Limitation on filing petitions for review. The defendant in a criminal proceeding under section 243(a) [8 USCS § 1253(a)] may not file a petition for review under subsection (a) during the criminal proceeding.

(8) Construction. This subsection—

(A) does not prevent the Attorney General, after a final order of removal has been issued, from detaining the alien under section 241(a) [8 USCS § 1231(a)];

(B) does not relieve the alien from complying with section 241(a)(4) [8 USCS § 1231(a)(4)] and section 243(g); and

(C) does not require the Attorney General to defer removal of the alien.

(9) Consolidation of questions for judicial review. Judicial review of all questions of law and fact, including interpretation and application of constitutional and statutory provisions, arising from any action taken or proceeding brought to remove an alien from the United States under this title [8 USCS §§ 1151 et seq.] shall be available only in judicial review of a final order under this section. Except as otherwise provided in this section, no court shall have jurisdiction, by habeas corpus under section 2241 of title 28, United States Code [28 USCS § 2241], or any other habeas corpus provision, by section 1361 or 1651 of such title [28 USCS § 1361 or 1651], or by any other provision of law (statutory or nonstatutory), to review such an order or such questions of law or fact.

(c) Requirements for petition. A petition for review or habeas corpus of an order of removal—

(1) shall attach a copy of such order, and

(2) shall state whether a court has upheld the validity of the order, and, if so, shall state the name of the court, the date of the court's ruling, and the kind of proceeding.

(d) Review of final orders. A court may review a final order of removal only if—

(1) the alien has exhausted all administrative remedies available to the alien as of right, and

(2) another court has not decided the validity of the order, unless the reviewing court finds that the petition presents grounds that could not have been presented in the prior judicial proceeding or that the remedy provided by the prior proceeding was inadequate or ineffective to test the validity of the order.

(e) Judicial review of orders under section 235(b)(1).

(1) Limitations on relief. Without regard to the nature of the action or claim and without regard to the identity of the party or parties bringing the action, no court may—

(A) enter declaratory, injunctive, or other equitable relief in any action pertaining to an order to exclude an alien in accordance with section 235(b)(1) [8 USCS § 1225(b)(1)] except as specifically authorized in a subsequent paragraph of this subsection, or

(B) certify a class under Rule 23 of the Federal Rules of Civil Procedure in any action for which judicial review is authorized under a subsequent paragraph of this subsection.

(2) Habeas corpus proceedings. Judicial review of any determination made under section 235(b)(1) [8 USCS § 1225(b)(1)] is available in habeas corpus proceedings, but shall be limited to determinations of—

(A) whether the petitioner is an alien,

(B) whether the petitioner was ordered removed under such section, and

(C) whether the petitioner can prove by a preponderance of the evidence that the petitioner is an alien lawfully admitted for permanent residence, has been admitted as a refugee under section 207 [8 USCS § 1157], or has been granted asylum under section 208 [8 USCS § 1158], such status not having been terminated, and is entitled to such further inquiry as prescribed by the Attorney General pursuant to section 235(b)(1)(C) [8 USCS § 1225(b)(1)(C)].

(3) Challenges on validity of the system.

(A) In general. Judicial review of determinations under section 235(b) [8 USCS § 1225(b)] and its implementation is available in an action instituted in the United States District Court for the District of Columbia, but shall be limited to determinations of—

(i) whether such section, or any regulation issued to implement such section, is constitutional; or

(ii) whether such a regulation, or a written policy directive, written policy guideline, or written procedure issued by or under the authority of the Attorney General to implement such section, is not consistent with applicable provisions of this title or is otherwise in violation of law.

(B) Deadlines for bringing actions. Any action instituted under this paragraph must be filed no later than 60 days after the date the challenged section, regulation, directive, guideline, or procedure described in clause (i) or (ii) of subparagraph (A) is first implemented.

(C) Notice of appeal. A notice of appeal of an order issued by the District Court under this paragraph may be filed not later than 30 days after the date of issuance of such order.

(D) Expeditious consideration of cases. It shall be the duty of the District Court, the Court of Appeals, and the Supreme Court of the United States to advance on the docket and to expedite to the greatest possible extent the disposition of any case considered under this paragraph.

(4) Decision. In any case where the court determines that the petitioner—

(A) is an alien who was not ordered removed under section 235(b)(1) [8 USCS § 1225(b)(1)], or

(B) has demonstrated by a preponderance of the evidence that the alien is an alien lawfully admitted for permanent residence, has been admitted as a refugee under section 207 [8 USCS § 1157], or has been granted asylum under section 208 [8 USCS § 1158], the court may order no remedy or relief other than to require that the petitioner be provided a hearing in accordance with section 240 [8 USCS § 1229a]. Any alien who is provided a hearing under section 240 [8 USCS § 1229a] pursuant to this paragraph may thereafter obtain judicial review of any resulting final order of removal pursuant to subsection (a)(1).

(5) Scope of inquiry. In determining whether an alien has been ordered removed under section 235(b)(1) [8 USCS § 1225(b)(1)], the court's inquiry shall be limited to whether such an order in fact was issued and whether it relates to the petitioner. There shall be no review of whether the alien is actually inadmissible or entitled to any relief from removal.

(f) Limit on injunctive relief.

(1) In general. Regardless of the nature of the action or claim or of the identity of the party or parties bringing the action, no court (other than the Supreme Court) shall have jurisdiction or authority to enjoin or restrain the operation of the provisions of chapter 4 of title II [8 USCS §§ 1221 et seq.], as amended by the Illegal Immigration Reform and Immigrant Responsibility Act of 1996, other than with respect to the application of such provisions to an individual alien against whom proceedings under such chapter have been initiated.

(2) Particular cases. Notwithstanding any other provision of law, no court shall enjoin the removal of any alien pursuant to a final order under this section unless the alien shows by clear and convincing evidence that the entry or execution of such order is prohibited as a matter of law.

(g) Exclusive jurisdiction. Except as provided in this section and notwithstanding any other provision of law (statutory or nonstatutory), including section 2241 of title 28, United States Code [28 USCS § 2241], or any other habeas corpus provision, and sections 1361 and 1651 of such title [28 USCS §§ 1361 and 1651], no court shall have jurisdiction to hear any cause or claim by or on behalf of any alien arising from the decision or action by the Attorney General to commence proceedings, adjudicate cases, or execute removal orders against any alien under this Act.

HISTORY: (June 27, 1952, ch 477, Title II, Ch 5, § 242, 66 Stat. 208; Sept. 3, 1954, ch 1263, § 17, 68 Stat. 1232; Dec. 29, 1981, P. L. 97-116, § 18(h)(1), 95 Stat. 1620; Nov. 6, 1986, P. L. 99-603, Title VII, § 701, 100 Stat. 3445; Oct. 12, 1984, P. L. 98-473, Title II, Ch II, § 220(b), 98 Stat. 2029; Oct. 24, 1988, P. L. 100-525, § 9(n), 102 Stat. 2620; Nov. 18, 1988, P. L. 100-690, Title VII, Subtitle J, § 7343(a), 102 Stat. 4470; Nov. 29, 1990, P. L. 101-649, Title V, Subtitle A, § 504(a), Subtitle D, § 545(e), Title VI, § 603(b)(2), 104 Stat. 5049, 5066, 5085; Dec. 12, 1991, P. L. 102-232, Title III, §§ 306(a)(4), (c)(7), 307(m)(2), 309(b)(9), 105 Stat. 1751, 1753, 1757, 1759; Sept. 13, 1994, P. L. 103-322, Title II, Subtitle C, § 20301(a), Title XIII, § 130001(a), 108 Stat. 1823, 2023; Oct. 25, 1994, P. L. 103-416, Title II, §§ 219(h), 224(b), 108 Stat. 4317, 4324; April 24, 1996, P. L. 104-132, Title IV, Subtitle D, §§ 436(a), (b)(1), 438, 440(c), (h), 110 Stat. 1275, 1277, 1279; Sept. 30, 1996, P. L. 104-208, Div C, Title III, Subtitle A, §§ 306(a)(1), (2), (d), 308(g)(10)(H), Subtitle F, § 371(b)(6), 110 Stat. 3009-607, 3009-612, 3009-625, 3009-645; May 11, 2005, P. L. 109-13, Div B, Title I, §§ 101(e), (f), 106(a), 119 Stat. 305, 310.)

§ 242A. [8 U.S.C. § 1252a] [Transferred].

HISTORY: This section, enacted as § 242A of Act June 27, 1952, ch 477, was redesignated § 238 of such Act by Act Sept. 30, 1996, P.L. 104-208, Div C, Title III, Subtitle A, § 308(b)(5), 110 Stat. 3009-615, and was transferred by the compilers of the United States Code to 8 USCS § 1228.

§ 242B. [8 U.S.C. § 1252b] [Repealed].

HISTORY: This section (Act June 27, 1952, ch 477, Title II, Ch 5, § 242B, as added Nov. 29, 1990, P.L. 101-649, Title V, Subtitle D, § 545(a), 104 Stat. 5061; Dec. 12, 1991, P.L. 102-232, Title III, § 306(c)(6), 105 Stat. 1753; Oct. 25, 1994, P.L. 103-416, Title II, § 219(i), 108 Stat. 4317; Sept. 30, 1996, P.L. 104-208, Div C, Title III, Subtitle F, § 371(b)(7), 110 Stat. 3009-645) was repealed by Act Sept. 30, 1996, P.L. 104-208, Div C, Title III, Subtitle A, § 308(b)(6), 110 Stat. 3009-615 (effective as provided by § 309(a) of such Act, which appears as 8 USCS § 1101 note). It provided for deportation procedures.

§ 243. [8 U.S.C. § 1253] Penalties related to removal.

(a) Penalty for failure to depart.

(1) In general. Any alien against whom a final order of removal is outstanding by reason of being a member of any of the classes described in section 237(a) [8 USCS § 1227(a)], who—

(A) willfully fails or refuses to depart from the United States within a period of 90 days from the date of the final order of removal under administrative processes, or if judicial review is had, then from the date of the final order of the court,

(B) willfully fails or refuses to make timely application in good faith for travel or other documents necessary to the alien's departure,

(C) connives or conspires, or takes any other action, designed to prevent or hamper or with the purpose of preventing or hampering the alien's departure pursuant to such, or

(D) willfully fails or refuses to present himself or herself for removal at the time and place required by the Attorney General pursuant to such order,

shall be fined under title 18, United States Code, or imprisoned not more than four years (or 10 years if the alien is a member of any of the classes described in paragraph (1)(E), (2), (3), or (4) of section 237(a) [8 USCS § 1227(a)]), or both.

(2) Exception. It is not a violation of paragraph (1) to take any proper steps for the purpose of securing cancellation of or exemption from such order of removal or for the purpose of securing the alien's release from incarceration or custody.

(3) Suspension. The court may for good cause suspend the sentence of an alien under this subsection and order the alien's release under such conditions as the court may prescribe. In determining whether good cause has been shown to justify releasing the alien, the court shall take into account such factors as—

(A) the age, health, and period of detention of the alien;

(B) the effect of the alien's release upon the national security and public peace or safety;

(C) the likelihood of the alien's resuming or following a course of conduct which made or would make the alien deportable;

(D) the character of the efforts made by such alien himself and by representatives of the country or countries to which the alien's removal is directed to expedite the alien's departure from the United States;

(E) the reason for the inability of the Government of the United States to secure passports, other travel documents, or removal facilities from the country or countries to which the alien has been ordered removed; and

(F) the eligibility of the alien for discretionary relief under the immigration laws.

(b) Willful failure to comply with terms of release under supervision. An alien who shall willfully fail to comply with regulations or requirements issued pursuant to section 241(a)(3) [8 USCS § 1231(a)(3)] or knowingly give false information in response to an inquiry under such section shall be fined not more than $1,000 or imprisoned for not more than one year, or both.

(c) Penalties relating to vessels and aircraft.

(1) Civil penalties.

(A) Failure to carry out certain orders. If the Attorney General is satisfied that a person has violated subsection (d) or (e) of section 241 [8 USCS § 1231], the person shall pay to the Commissioner the sum of $2,000 for each violation.

(B) Failure to remove alien stowaways. If the Attorney General is satisfied that a person has failed to remove an alien stowaway as required under section 241(d)(2) [8 USCS § 1231(d)(2)], the person shall pay to the Commissioner the sum of $5,000 for each alien stowaway not removed.

(C) No compromise. The Attorney General may not compromise the amount of such penalty under this paragraph.

(2) Clearing vessels and aircraft.

(A) Clearance before decision on liability. A vessel or aircraft may be granted clearance before a decision on liability is made under paragraph (1) only if a bond approved by the Attorney General or an amount sufficient to pay the civil penalty is deposited with the Commissioner.

(B) Prohibition on clearance while penalty unpaid. A vessel or aircraft may not be granted clearance if a civil penalty imposed under paragraph (1) is not paid.

(d) Discontinuing granting visas to nationals of country denying or delaying accepting alien. On being notified by the Attorney General that the government of a foreign country denies or unreasonably delays accepting an alien who is a citizen, subject, national, or resident of that country after the Attorney General asks whether the government will accept the alien under this section, the Secretary of State shall order consular officers in that foreign country to discontinue granting immigrant visas or nonimmigrant visas, or both, to citizens, subjects, nationals, and residents of that country until the Attorney General notifies the Secretary that the country has accepted the alien.

HISTORY: (June 27, 1952, ch 477, Title II, Ch 5, § 243, 66 Stat. 212; Oct. 3, 1965, P. L. 89-236, § 11(f), 79 Stat. 918; Oct. 30, 1978, P. L. 95-549, Title I, § 104, 92 Stat. 2066; March 17, 1980, P. L. 96-212, Title II, § 203(e), 94 Stat. 107; Dec. 29, 1981, P. L. 97-116, § 18(i), 95 Stat. 1620; Nov. 29, 1990, P. L. 101-649, Title V, Subtitle A, § 515(a)(2), Title VI, § 603(b)(3), 104 Stat. 5053, 5085; April 24, 1996, P. L. 104-132, Title IV, Subtitle B, § 413(a), (f), 110 Stat. 1269; Sept. 30, 1996, P. L. 104-208, Div C, Title III, Subtitle A, § 307(a), 110 Stat. 3009-612.)

§ 244. [8 U.S.C. § 1254a] Temporary protected status.

(a) Granting of status.

(1) In general. In the case of an alien who is a national of a foreign state designated under subsection (b) (or in the case of an alien having no nationality, is a person who last habitually resided in such designated state) and who meets the requirements of subsection (c), the Attorney General, in accordance with this section—

(A) may grant the alien temporary protected status in the United States and shall not remove the alien from the United States during the period in which such status is in effect, and

(B) shall authorize the alien to engage in employment in the United States and provide the alien with an "employment authorized" endorsement or other appropriate work permit.

(2) Duration of work authorization. Work authorization provided under this section shall be effective throughout the period the alien is in temporary protected status under this section.

(3) Notice.

(A) Upon the granting of temporary protected status under this section, the Attorney General shall provide the alien with information concerning such status under this section.

(B) If, at the time of initiation of a removal proceeding against an alien, the foreign state (of which the alien is a national) is designated under subsection (b), the Attorney General shall promptly notify the alien of the temporary protected status that may be available under this section.

(C) If, at the time of designation of a foreign state under subsection (b), an alien (who is a national of such state) is in a removal proceeding under this title, the Attorney General shall promptly notify the alien of the temporary protected status that may be available under this section.

(D) Notices under this paragraph shall be provided in a form and language that the alien can understand.

(4) Temporary treatment for eligible aliens.

(A) In the case of an alien who can establish a prima facie case of eligibility for benefits under paragraph (1), but for the fact that the period of registration under subsection (c)(1)(A)(iv) has not begun, until the alien has had a reasonable opportunity to register during the first 30 days of such period, the Attorney General shall provide for the benefits of paragraph (1).

(B) In the case of an alien who establishes a prima facie case of eligibility for benefits under paragraph (1), until a final determination with respect to the alien's eligibility for such benefits under paragraph (1) has been made, the alien shall be provided such benefits.

(5) Clarification. Nothing in this section shall be construed as authorizing the Attorney General to deny temporary protected status to an alien based on the alien's immigration status or to require any alien, as a condition of being granted such status, either to relinquish nonimmigrant or other status the alien may have or to execute any waiver of other rights under this Act. The granting of temporary protected status under this section shall not be considered to be inconsistent with the granting of nonimmigrant status under this Act.

(b) Designations.

(1) In general. The Attorney General, after consultation with appropriate agencies of the Government, may designate any foreign state (or any part of such foreign state) under this subsection only if—

(A) the Attorney General finds that there is an ongoing armed conflict within the state and, due to such conflict, requiring the return of aliens who are nationals of that state to that state (or to the part of the state) would pose a serious threat to their personal safety;

(B) the Attorney General finds that—

(i) there has been an earthquake, flood, drought, epidemic, or other environmental disaster in the state resulting in a substantial, but temporary, disruption of living conditions in the area affected,

(ii) the foreign state is unable, temporarily, to handle adequately the return to the state of aliens who are nationals of the state, and

(iii) the foreign state officially has requested designation under this subparagraph; or

(C) the Attorney General finds that there exist extraordinary and temporary conditions in the foreign state that prevent aliens who are nationals of the state from returning to the state in safety, unless the Attorney General finds that permitting the aliens to remain temporarily in the United States is contrary to the national interest of the United States.

A designation of a foreign state (or part of such foreign state) under this paragraph shall not become effective unless notice of the designation (including a statement of the findings under this paragraph and the effective date of the designation) is published in the Federal Register. In such notice, the Attorney General shall also state an estimate of the number of nationals of the foreign state designated who are (or within the effective period of the designation are likely to become) eligible for temporary protected status under this section and their immigration status in the United States.

(2) Effective period of designation for foreign states. The designation of a foreign state (or part of such foreign state) under paragraph (1) shall—

(A) take effect upon the date of publication of the designation under such paragraph, or such later date as the Attorney General may specify in the notice published under such paragraph, and

(B) shall remain in effect until the effective date of the termination of the designation under paragraph (3)(B).

For purposes of this section, the initial period of designation of a foreign state (or part thereof) under paragraph (1) is the period, specified by the Attorney General, of not less than 6 months and not more than 18 months.

(3) Periodic review, terminations, and extensions of designations.

(A) Periodic review. At least 60 days before end of the initial period of designation, and any extended period of designation, of a foreign state (or part thereof) under this section the Attorney General, after consultation with appropriate agencies of the Government, shall review the conditions in the foreign state (or part of such foreign state) for which a designation is in effect under this subsection and shall determine whether the conditions for such designation under this subsection continue to be met. The Attorney General shall provide on a timely basis for the publication of notice of each such determination (including the basis for the determination, and, in the case of an affirmative determination, the period of extension of designation under subparagraph (C)) in the Federal Register.

(B) Termination of designation. If the Attorney General determines under subparagraph (A) that a foreign state (or part of such foreign state) no longer continues to meet the conditions for designation under paragraph (1), the Attorney General shall terminate the designation by publishing notice in the Federal Register of the determination under this subparagraph (including the basis for the determination). Such termination is effective in accordance with subsection (d)(3), but shall not be effective earlier than 60 days after the date the notice is published or, if later, the expiration of the most recent previous extension under subparagraph (C).

(C) Extension of designation. If the Attorney General does not determine under subparagraph (A) that a foreign state (or part of such foreign state) no longer meets the conditions for designation under paragraph (1), the period of designation of the foreign state is extended for an additional period of 6 months (or, in the discretion of the Attorney General, a period of 12 or 18 months).

(4) Information concerning protected status at time of designations. At the time of a designation of a foreign state under this subsection, the Attorney General shall make available information respecting the temporary protected status made available to aliens who are nationals of such designated foreign state.

(5) Review.

(A) Designations. There is no judicial review of any determination of the Attorney General with respect to the designation, or termination or extension of a designation, of a foreign state under this subsection.

(B) Application to individuals. The Attorney General shall establish an administrative procedure for the review of the denial of benefits to aliens under this subsection. Such procedure shall not prevent an alien from asserting protection under this section in removal proceedings if the alien demonstrates that the alien is a national of a state designated under paragraph (1).

(c) Aliens eligible for temporary protected status.

(1) In general.

(A) Nationals of designated foreign states. Subject to paragraph (3), an alien, who is a national of a state designated under subsection (b)(1) or in the case of an alien having no nationality, is a person who last habitually resided in such designated state), meets the requirements of this paragraph only if—

(i) the alien has been continuously physically present in the United States since the effective date of the most recent designation of that state;

(ii) the alien has continuously resided in the United States since such date as the Attorney General may designate;

(iii) the alien is admissible as an immigrant, except as otherwise provided under paragraph (2)(A), and is not ineligible for temporary protected status under paragraph (2)(B); and

(iv) to the extent and in a manner which the Attorney General establishes, the alien registers for the temporary protected status under this section during a registration period of not less than 180 days.

(B) Registration fee. The Attorney General may require payment of a reasonable fee as a condition of registering an alien under subparagraph (A)(iv) (including providing an alien with an "employment authorized" endorsement or other appropriate work permit under this section). The amount of any such fee shall not exceed $50. In the case of aliens registered pursuant to a designation under this section made after July 17, 1991, the Attorney General may impose a separate, additional fee for providing an alien with documentation of work authorization. Notwithstanding section 3302 of title 31, United States Code, all fees collected under this subparagraph shall be credited to the appropriation to be used in carrying out this section.

(2) Eligibility standards.

(A) Waiver of certain grounds for inadmissibility. In the determination of an alien's admissibility for purposes of subparagraph (A)(iii) of paragraph (1)—

(i) the provisions of paragraphs (5) and (7)(A) of section 212(a) [8 USCS § 1182(a)(5), (7)(A)] shall not apply;

(ii) except as provided in clause (iii), the Attorney General may waive any other provision of section 212(a) [8 USCS § 1182(a)] in the case of individual aliens for humanitarian purposes, to assure family unity, or when it is otherwise in the public interest; but

(iii) the Attorney General may not waive—

(I) paragraphs (2)(A) and (2)(B) (relating to criminals) of such section,

(II) paragraph (2)(C) of such section (relating to drug offenses), except for so much of such paragraph as relates to a single offense of simple possession of 30 grams or less of marijuana, or

(III) paragraphs (3)(A), (3)(B), (3)(C), and (3)(E) of such section (relating to national security and participation in the Nazi persecutions or those who have engaged in genocide).

(B) Aliens ineligible. An alien shall not be eligible for temporary protected status under this section if the Attorney General finds that—

(i) the alien has been convicted of any felony or 2 or more misdemeanors committed in the United States, or

(ii) the alien is described in section 208(b)(2)(A) [8 USCS § 1158(b)(2)(A)].

(3) Withdrawal of temporary protected status. The Attorney General shall withdraw temporary protected status granted to an alien under this section if—

(A) the Attorney General finds that the alien was not in fact eligible for such status under this section,

(B) except as provided in paragraph (4) and permitted in subsection (f)(3), the alien has not remained continuously physically present in the United States from the date the alien first was granted temporary protected status under this section, or

(C) the alien fails, without good cause, to register with the Attorney General annually, at the end of each 12-month period after the granting of such status, in a form and manner specified by the Attorney General.

(4) Treatment of brief, casual, and innocent departures and certain other absences.

(A) For purposes of paragraphs (1)(A)(i) and (3)(B), an alien shall not be considered to have failed to maintain continuous physical presence in the United States by virtue of brief, casual, and innocent absences from the United States, without regard to whether such absences were authorized by the Attorney General.

(B) For purposes of paragraph (1)(A)(ii), an alien shall not be considered to have failed to maintain continuous residence in the United States by reason of a brief, casual, and innocent absence described in subparagraph (A) or due merely to a brief temporary trip abroad required by emergency or extenuating circumstances outside the control of the alien.

(5) Construction. Nothing in this section shall be construed as authorizing an alien to apply for admission to, or to be admitted to, the United States in order to apply for temporary protected status under this section.

(6) Confidentiality of information. The Attorney General shall establish procedures to protect the confidentiality of information provided by aliens under this section.

(d) Documentation.

(1) Initial issuance. Upon the granting of temporary protected status to an alien under this section, the Attorney General shall provide for the issuance of such temporary documentation and authorization as may be necessary to carry out the purposes of this section.

(2) Period of validity. Subject to paragraph (3), such documentation shall be valid during the initial period of designation of the foreign state (or part thereof) involved and any extension of such period. The Attorney General may stagger the periods of validity of the documentation and authorization in order to provide for an orderly renewal of such documentation and authorization and for an orderly transition (under paragraph (3)) upon the termination of a designation of a foreign state (or any part of such foreign state).

(3) Effective date of terminations. If the Attorney General terminates the designation of a foreign state (or part of such foreign state) under subsection (b)(3)(B), such termination shall only apply to documentation and authorization issued or renewed after the effective date of the publication of notice of the determination under that subsection (or, at the Attorney General's option, after such period after the effective date of the determination as the Attorney General determines to be appropriate in order to provide for an orderly transition).

(4) Detention of the alien. An alien provided temporary protected status under this section shall not be detained by the Attorney General on the basis of the alien's immigration status in the United States.

(e) Relation of period of temporary protected status to cancellation of removal. With respect to an alien granted temporary protected status under this section, the period of such status shall not be counted as a period of physical presence in the United States for purposes of section 240A(a) [8 USCS § 1229b(a)] unless the Attorney General determines that extreme hardship exists. Such period shall not cause a break in the continuity of residence of the period before and after such period for purposes of such section.

(f) Benefits and status during period of temporary protected status. During a period in which an alien is granted temporary protected status under this section—

(1) the alien shall not be considered to be permanently residing in the United States under color of law;

(2) the alien may be deemed ineligible for public assistance by a State (as defined in section 101(a)(36) [8 USCS § 1101(a)(36)]) or any political subdivision thereof which furnishes such assistance;

(3) the alien may travel abroad with the prior consent of the Attorney General; and

(4) for purposes of adjustment of status under section 245 [8 USCS § 1255] and change of status under section 248 [8 USCS § 1258], the alien shall be considered as being in, and maintaining, lawful status as a nonimmigrant.

(g) Exclusive remedy. Except as otherwise specifically provided, this section shall constitute the exclusive authority of the Attorney General under law to permit aliens who are or may become otherwise deportable or have been paroled into the United States to remain in the United States temporarily because of their particular nationality or region of foreign state of nationality.

(h) Limitation on consideration in the Senate of legislation adjusting status.

(1) In general. Except as provided in paragraph (2), it shall not be in order in the Senate to consider any bill, resolution, or amendment that—

(A) provides for adjustment to lawful temporary or permanent resident alien status for any alien receiving temporary protected status under this section, or

(B) has the effect of amending this subsection or limiting the application of this subsection.

(2) Supermajority required. Paragraph (1) may be waived or suspended in the Senate only by the affirmative vote of three-fifths of the Members duly chosen and sworn. An affirmative vote of three-fifths of the Members of the Senate duly chosen and sworn shall be required in the Senate to sustain an appeal of the ruling of the Chair on a point of order raised under paragraph (1).

(3) Rules. Paragraphs (1) and (2) are enacted—

(A) as an exercise of the rulemaking power of the Senate and as such they are deemed a part of the rules of the Senate, but applicable only with respect to the matters described in paragraph (1) and supersede other rules of the Senate only to the extent that such paragraphs are inconsistent therewith; and

(B) with full recognition of the constitutional right of the Senate to change such rules at any time, in the same manner as in the case of any other rule of the Senate.

(i) Annual report and review.

(1) Annual report. Not later than March 1 of each year (beginning with 1992), the Attorney General, after consultation with the appropriate agencies of the Government, shall submit a report to the Committees on the Judiciary of the House of Representatives and of the Senate on the operation of this section during the previous year. Each report shall include—

(A) a listing of the foreign states or parts thereof designated under this section;

(B) the number of nationals of each such state who have been granted temporary protected status under this section and their immigration status before being granted such status, and

(C) an explanation of the reasons why foreign states or parts thereof were designated under subsection (b)(1) and, with respect to foreign states or parts thereof previously designated, why the designation was terminated or extended under subsection (b)(3).

(2) Committee report. No later than 180 days after the date of receipt of such a report, the Committee on the Judiciary of each House of Congress shall report to its respective House such oversight findings and legislation as it deems appropriate.

HISTORY: (June 27, 1952, ch 477, Title II, § 244 [244A], as added Nov. 29, 1990, P. L. 101-649, Title III, § 302(a), Title VI, § 603(a)(24), 104 Stat. 5030, 5084; Dec. 12, 1991, P. L. 102-232, Title III, §§ 304(b), 307(l)(5), 105 Stat. 1749, 1756; Oct.

25, 1994, P. L. 103-416, Title II, § 219(j), (z)(2), 108 Stat. 4317, 4318; Sept. 30, 1996, P. L. 104-208, Div C, Title III, Subtitle A, §§ 308(b)(7), (e)(1)(G), (11), (g)(7)(E)(i), (8)(A)(i), 110 Stat. 3009-615, 3009-619, 3009-620, 3009-624.)

Chapter 5—Adjustment and Change of Status

§ 245. [8 U.S.C. § 1255] Adjustment of status of nonimmigrant to that of person admitted for permanent residence.

(a) Status as person admitted for permanent residence on application and eligibility for immigrant visa. The status of an alien who was inspected and admitted or paroled into the United States or the status of any other alien having an approved petition for classification as a VAWA self-petitioner may be adjusted by the Attorney General, in his discretion and under such regulations as he may prescribe, to that of an alien lawfully admitted for permanent residence if (1) the alien makes an application for such adjustment, (2) the alien is eligible to receive an immigrant visa and is admissible to the United States for permanent residence, and (3) an immigrant visa is immediately available to him at the time his application is filed.

(b) Record of lawful admission for permanent residence; reduction of preference visas. Upon the approval of an application for adjustment made under subsection (a), the Attorney General shall record the alien's lawful admission for permanent residence as of the date the order of the Attorney General approving the application for the adjustment of status is made, and the Secretary of State shall reduce by one the number of the preference visas authorized to be issued under sections 202 and 203 [8 USCS §§ 1152, 1153] within the class to which the alien is chargeable for the fiscal year then current.

(c) Alien crewmen, aliens continuing or accepting unauthorized employment, and aliens admitted in transit without a visa. Other than an alien having an approved petition for classification as a VAWA self-petitioner, subsection (a) shall not be applicable to (1) an alien crewman; (2) subject to subsection (k), an alien (other than an immediate relative as defined in section 201(b) [8 USCS § 1151(b)] or a special immigrant described in section 101(a)(27)(H), (I), (J), or (K) [8 USCS § 1101(a)(27)(H), (I), (J), or (K)]) who hereafter continues in or accepts unauthorized employment prior to filing an application for adjustment of status or who is in unlawful immigration status on the date of filing the application for adjustment of status or who has failed (other than through no fault of his own or for technical reasons) to maintain continuously a lawful status since entry into the United States; (3) any alien admitted in transit without visa under section 212(d)(4)(C) [8 USCS § 1182(d)(4)(C)]; (4) an alien (other than an immediate relative as defined in section 201(b) [8 USCS § 1151(b)]) who was admitted as a nonimmigrant visitor without a visa under section 212(*l*) or section 217 [8 USCS § 1182(*l*) or 1187]; (5) an alien who was admitted as a nonimmigrant described in section 101(a)(15)(S) [8 USCS § 1101(a)(15)(S)], [;] (6) an alien who is deportable under section 237(a)(4)(B) [8 USCS § 1227(a)(4)(B)]; (7) any alien who seeks adjustment of status to that of an immigrant under section 203(b) [8 USCS § 1153(b)] and is not in a lawful nonimmigrant status; or (8) any alien who was employed while the alien was an unauthorized alien, as defined in section 274A(h)(3) [8 USCS § 1324a(h)(3)], or who has otherwise violated the terms of a nonimmigrant visa.

(d) Alien admitted for permanent residence on conditional basis; fiancee or fiance of citizen. The Attorney General may not adjust, under subsection (a), the status of an alien lawfully admitted to the United States for permanent residence on a conditional basis under section 216 [8 USCS § 1186a]. The Attorney General may not adjust, under subsection (a), the status of a nonimmigrant alien described in section 101(a)(15)(K) [8 USCS § 1101(a)(15)(K)] except to that of an alien lawfully admitted to the United States on a conditional basis under section 216 [8 USCS § 1186a] as a result of the marriage of the nonimmigrant (or, in the case of a minor child, the parent) to the citizen who filed the petition to accord that alien's nonimmigrant status under section 101(a)(15)(K) [8 USCS § 1101(a)(15)(K)].

(e) Restriction on adjustment of status based upon marriages entered while in admissibility or deportation proceedings; bona fide marriage exception.

(1) Except as provided in paragraph (3), an alien who is seeking to receive an immigrant visa on the basis of a marriage which was entered into during the period described in paragraph (2) may not have the alien's status adjusted under subsection (a).

(2) The period described in this paragraph is the period during which administrative or judicial proceedings are pending regarding the alien's right to be admitted or remain in the United States.

(3) Paragraph (1) and section 204(g) [8 USCS § 1154(g)] shall not apply with respect to a marriage if the alien establishes by clear and convincing evidence to the satisfaction of the Attorney General that the marriage was entered into in good faith and in accordance with the laws of the place where the marriage took place and the marriage was not entered into for the purpose of procuring the alien's admission as an immigrant and no fee or other consideration was given (other than a fee or other consideration to an attorney for assistance in preparation of a lawful petition) for the filing of a petition under section 204(a) [8 USCS § 1154(a)] or subsection (d) or (p) of section 214 [8 USCS § 1184] with respect to the alien spouse or alien son or daughter. In accordance with regulations, there shall be only one level of administrative appellate review for each alien under the previous sentence.

(f) Limitation on adjustment of status. The Attorney General may not adjust, under subsection (a), the status of an alien lawfully admitted to the United States for permanent residence on a conditional basis under section 216A [8 USCS § 1186b].

(g) Special immigrants. In applying this section to a special immigrant described in section 101(a)(27)(K) [8 USCS § 1101(a)(27)(K)], such an immigrant shall be deemed, for purposes of subsection (a), to have been paroled into the United States.

(h) Application with respect to special immigrants. In applying this section to a special immigrant described in section 101(a)(27)(J) [8 USCS § 1101(a)(27)(J)]—

(1) such an immigrant shall be deemed, for purposes of subsection (a), to have been paroled into the United States; and

(2) in determining the alien's admissibility as an immigrant—

(A) paragraphs (4), (5)(A), (6)(A), (6)(C), (6)(D), (7)(A), and (9)(B) of section 212(a) [8 USCS § 1182(a)] shall not apply; and

(B) the Attorney General may waive other paragraphs of section 212(a) [8 USCS § 1182(a)] (other than paragraphs (2)(A), (2)(B), (2)(C) (except for so much of such paragraph as related to a single offense of simple possession of 30 grams or less of marijuana), (3)(A), (3)(B), (3)(C), and (3)(E)) in the case of individual aliens for humanitarian purposes, family unity, or when it is otherwise in the public interest.

The relationship between an alien and the alien's natural parents or prior adoptive parents shall not be considered a factor in making a waiver under paragraph (2)(B). Nothing in this subsection or section 101(a)(27)(J) [8 USCS § 1101(a)(27)(J)] shall be construed as authorizing an alien to apply for admission or be admitted to the United States in order to obtain special immigrant status described in such section.

(i) Adjustment in status of certain aliens physically present in the United States.

(1) Notwithstanding the provisions of subsections (a) and (c) of this section, an alien physically present in the United States—

(A) who—

(i) entered the United States without inspection; or

(ii) is within one of the classes enumerated in subsection (c) of this section;

(B) who is the beneficiary (including a spouse or child of the principal alien, if eligible to receive a visa under section 203(d) [8 USC § 1153(d)]) of—

(i) a petition for classification under section 204 [8 USC § 1154] that was filed with the Attorney General on or before April 30, 2001; or

(ii) an application for a labor certification under section 212(a)(5)(A) [8 USC § 1182(a)(5)(A)] that was filed pursuant to the regulations of the Secretary of Labor on or before such date; and

(C) who, in the case of a beneficiary of a petition for classification, or an application for labor certification, described in subparagraph (B) that was filed after January 14, 1998, is physically present in the United States on the date of the enactment of the LIFE Act Amendments of 2000 [enacted Dec. 21, 2000];

may apply to the Attorney General for the adjustment of his or her status to that of an alien lawfully admitted for permanent residence. The Attorney General may accept such application only if the alien remits with such application a sum equalling $1,000 as of the date of receipt of the application, but such sum shall not be required from a child under the age of seventeen, or an alien who is the spouse or unmarried child of an individual who obtained temporary or permanent resident status under section 210 or 245A of the Immigration and Nationality Act [8 USCS § 1160 or 1255a] or section 202 of the Immigration Reform and Control Act of 1986 [8 USCS § 1255a note] at any date, who—

(i) as of May 5, 1988, was the unmarried child or spouse of the individual who obtained temporary or permanent resident status under section 210 or 245A of the Immigration and Nationality Act [8 USCS § 1160 or 1255a] or section 202 of the Immigration Reform and Control Act of 1986 [8 USCS § 1255a note];

(ii) entered the United States before May 5, 1988, resided in the United States on May 5, 1988, and is not a lawful permanent resident; and

(iii) applied for benefits under section 301(a) of the Immigration Act of 1990 [8 USCS § 1255a note]. The sum specified herein shall be in addition to the fee normally required for the processing of an application under this section.

(2) Upon receipt of such an application and the sum hereby required, the Attorney General may adjust the status of the alien to that of an alien lawfully admitted for permanent residence if—

(A) the alien is eligible to receive an immigrant visa and is admissible to the United States for permanent residence; and

(B) an immigrant visa is immediately available to the alien at the time the application is filed.

(3) (A) The portion of each application fee (not to exceed $200) that the Attorney General determines is required to process an application under this section and is remitted to the Attorney General pursuant to paragraphs (1) and (2) of this subsection shall be disposed of by the Attorney General as provided in subsections (m), (n), and (o) of section 286 [8 USCS § 1356].

(B) Any remaining portion of such fees remitted under such paragraphs shall be deposited by the Attorney General into the Breached Bond/Detention Fund established under section 286(r) [8 USCS § 1356(r)], except that in the case of fees attributable to applications for a beneficiary with respect to whom a petition for classification, or an application for labor certification, described in paragraph (1)(B) was filed after January 14, 1998, one-half of such remaining portion shall be deposited by the Attorney General into the Immigration Examinations Fee Account established under section 286(m) [8 USCS § 1356(m)].

(j) Adjustment to permanent resident status.

(1) If, in the opinion of the Attorney General—

(A) a nonimmigrant admitted into the United States under section 101(a)(15)(S)(i) [8 USCS § 1101(a)(15)(S)(i)] has supplied information described in subclause (I) of such section; and

(B) the provision of such information has substantially contributed to the success of an authorized criminal investigation or the prosecution of an individual described in subclause (III) of that section,

the Attorney General may adjust the status of the alien (and the spouse, married and unmarried sons and daughters, and parents of the alien if admitted under that section) to that of an alien lawfully admitted for permanent residence if the alien is not described in section 212(a)(3)(E) [8 USCS § 1182(a)(3)(E)].

(2) If, in the sole discretion of the Attorney General—

(A) a nonimmigrant admitted into the United States under section 101(a)(15)(S)(ii) [8 USCS § 1101(a)(15)(S)(ii)] has supplied information described in subclause (I) of such section, and

(B) the provision of such information has substantially contributed to—

(i) the prevention or frustration of an act of terrorism against a United States person or United States property, or

(ii) the success of an authorized criminal investigation of, or the prosecution of, an individual involved in such an act of terrorism, and

(C) the nonimmigrant has received a reward under section 36(a) of the State Department Basic Authorities Act of 1956 [22 USCS § 2708(a)],

the Attorney General may adjust the status of the alien (and the spouse, married and unmarried sons and daughters, and parents of the alien if admitted under such section) to that of an alien lawfully admitted for permanent residence if the alien is not described in section 212(a)(3)(E) [8 USCS § 1182(a)(3)(E)].

(3) Upon the approval of adjustment of status under paragraph (1) or (2), the Attorney General shall record the alien's lawful admission for permanent residence as of the date of such approval and the Secretary of State shall reduce by one the number of visas authorized to be issued under sections 201(d) and 203(b)(4) [8 USCS §§ 1151(d) and 1153(b)(4)] for the fiscal year then current.

(k) Inapplicability of certain provisions for certain employment-based immigrants. An alien who is eligible to receive an immigrant visa under paragraph (1), (2), (3), or (5) of section 203(b) [8 USCS § 1153(b)(1), (2), (3), or (5)] (or, in the case of an alien who is an immigrant described in section 101(a)(27)(C) [8 USCS § 1101(a)(27)(C)], under section 203(b)(4) [8 USCS § 1153(b)(4)]) may adjust status pursuant to subsection (a) and notwithstanding subsection (c)(2), (c)(7), and (c)(8), if—

(1) the alien, on the date of filing an application for adjustment of status, is present in the United States pursuant to a lawful admission;

(2) the alien, subsequent to such lawful admission has not, for an aggregate period exceeding 180 days—

(A) failed to maintain, continuously, a lawful status;

(B) engaged in unauthorized employment; or

(C) otherwise violated the terms and conditions of the alien's admission.

(l) Adjustment of status for victims of trafficking.

(1) If, in the opinion of the Secretary of Homeland Security, or in the case of subparagraph (C)(i), in the opinion of the Secretary of Homeland Security, in consultation with the Attorney General, as appropriate[,] a nonimmigrant admitted into the United States under section 101(a)(15)(T)(i) [8 USCS § 1101(a)(15)(T)(i)]—

(A) has been physically present in the United States for a continuous period of at least 3 years since the date of admission as a nonimmigrant under section 101(a)(15)(T)(i) [8 USCS § 1101(a)(15)(T)(i)], or has been physically present in the United States for a continuous period during the investigation or prosecution of acts of trafficking and that, in the opinion of the Attorney General, the investigation or prosecution is complete, whichever period of time is less;

(B) subject to paragraph (6), has, throughout such period, been a person of good moral character; and

(C) (i) has, during such period, complied with any reasonable request for assistance in the investigation or prosecution of acts of trafficking;

(ii) the alien would suffer extreme hardship involving unusual and severe harm upon removal from the United States; or

(iii) was younger than 18 years of age at the time of the victimization qualifying the alien for relief under section 101(a)(15)(T) [8 USCS § 1101(a)(15)(T)]. [,]

the Secretary of Homeland Security may adjust the status of the alien (and any person admitted under section 101(a)(15)(T)(ii) [8 USCS § 1101(a)(15)(T)(ii)] as the spouse, parent, sibling, or child of the alien) to that of an alien lawfully admitted for permanent residence.

(2) Paragraph (1) shall not apply to an alien admitted under section 101(a)(15)(T) [8 USCS § 1101(a)(15)(T)] who is inadmissible to the United States by reason of a ground that has not been waived under section 212 [8 USCS § 1182], except that, if the Secretary of Homeland Security considers it to be in the national interest to do so, the Secretary of Homeland Security, in the Attorney General's [Secretary's] discretion, may waive the application of—

(A) paragraphs (1) and (4) of section 212(a) [8 USCS § 1182(a)]; and

(B) any other provision of such section (excluding paragraphs (3), (10)(C), and (10[)](E)), if the activities rendering the alien inadmissible under the provision were caused by, or were incident to, the victimization described in section 101(a)(15)(T)(i)(I) [8 USCS § 1101(a)(15)(T)(i)(I)].

(3) An alien shall be considered to have failed to maintain continuous physical presence in the United States under paragraph (1)(A) if the alien has departed from the United States for any period in excess of 90 days or for any periods in the aggregate exceeding 180 days, unless—

(A) the absence was necessary to assist in the investigation or prosecution described in paragraph (1)(A); or

(B) an official involved in the investigation or prosecution certifies that the absence was otherwise justified.

(4) (A) The total number of aliens whose status may be adjusted under paragraph (1) during any fiscal year may not exceed 5,000.

(B) The numerical limitation of subparagraph (A) shall only apply to principal aliens and not to the spouses, sons, daughters, siblings, or parents of such aliens.

(5) Upon the approval of adjustment of status under paragraph (1), the Secretary of Homeland Security shall record the alien's lawful admission for permanent residence as of the date of such approval.

(6) For purposes of paragraph (1)(B), the Secretary of Homeland Security may waive consideration of a disqualification from good moral character with respect to an alien if the disqualification was caused by, or incident to, the trafficking described in section 101(a)(15)(T)(i)(I) [8 USCS § 1101(a)(15)(T)(i)(I)].

(7) The Secretary of Homeland Security shall permit aliens to apply for a waiver of any fees associated with filing an application for relief through final adjudication of the adjustment of status for a VAWA self-petitioner and for relief under sections 101(a)(15)(T), 101(a)(15)(U), 106, 240A(b)(2), and 244(a)(3) (as in effect on March 31, 1997) [8 USCS §§ 1101(a)(5)(T), 1101(a)(15)(U), 1229b(b)(2), and former 8 USCS § 1254(a)(3)].

(m) Adjustment of status for victims of crimes against women.

(1) The Secretary of Homeland Security may adjust the status of an alien admitted into the United States (or otherwise provided nonimmigrant status) under section 101(a)(15)(U) [8 USCS § 1101(a)(15)(U)] to that of an alien lawfully admitted for permanent residence if the alien is not described in section 212(a)(3)(E) [8 USCS § 1182(a)(3)(E)], unless the Secretary determines based on affirmative evidence that the alien unreasonably refused to provide assistance in a criminal investigation or prosecution, if—

(A) the alien has been physically present in the United States for a continuous period of at least 3 years since the date of admission as a nonimmigrant under clause (i) or (ii) of section 101(a)(15)(U) [8 USCS § 1101(a)(15)(U)]; and

(B) in the opinion of the Secretary of Homeland Security, the alien's continued presence in the United States is justified on humanitarian grounds, to ensure family unity, or is otherwise in the public interest.

(2) An alien shall be considered to have failed to maintain continuous physical presence in the United States under paragraph (1)(A) if the alien has departed from the United States for any period in excess of 90 days or for any periods in the aggregate exceeding 180 days unless the absence is in order to assist in the investigation or prosecution or unless an official involved in the investigation or prosecution certifies that the absence was otherwise justified.

(3) Upon approval of adjustment of status under paragraph (1) of an alien described in section 101(a)(15)(U)(i) [8 USCS § 1101(a)(15)(U)(i)] the Secretary of Homeland Security may adjust the status of or issue an immigrant visa to a spouse, a child, or, in the case of an alien child, a parent who did not receive a nonimmigrant visa under section 101(a)(15)(U)(ii) [8 USCS § 1101(a)(15)(U)(ii)] if the Secretary considers the grant of such status or visa necessary to avoid extreme hardship.

(4) Upon the approval of adjustment of status under paragraph (1) or (3), the Secretary of Homeland Security shall record the alien's lawful admission for permanent residence as of the date of such approval.

(5) (A) The Secretary of Homeland Security shall consult with the Attorney General, as appropriate, in making a determination under paragraph (1) whether affirmative evidence demonstrates that the alien unreasonably refused to provide assistance to a Federal law enforcement official, Federal prosecutor, Federal judge, or other Federal authority investigating or prosecuting criminal activity described in section 101(a)(15)(U)(iii) [8 USCS § 1101(a)(15)(U)(iii)].

(B) Nothing in paragraph (1)(B) may be construed to prevent the Secretary from consulting with the Attorney General in making a determination whether affirmative evidence demonstrates that the alien unreasonably refused to provide assistance to a State or local law enforcement official, State or local prosecutor, State or local judge, or other State or local authority investigating or prosecuting criminal activity described in section 101(a)(15)(U)(iii) [8 USCS § 1101(a)(15)(U)(iii)].

(n) If the approval of a petition for classification under section 203(b)(5) [8 USCS § 1153(b)(5)] would make a visa immediately available to the alien beneficiary, the alien beneficiary's application for adjustment of status under this section shall be considered to be properly filed whether the application is submitted concurrently with, or subsequent to, the visa petition.

HISTORY: (June 27, 1952, ch 477, Title II, subch 5, § 245, 66 Stat. 217; Aug. 21, 1958, P. L. 85-700, § 1, 72 Stat. 699; July 14, 1960, P. L. 86-648, § 10, 74 Stat. 505; Oct. 3, 1965, P. L. 89-236, § 13, 79 Stat. 918; Oct. 20, 1976, P. L. 94-571, § 6, 90 Stat. 2705; Dec. 29, 1981, P. L. 97-116, § 5(d)(2), 95 Stat. 1614; Nov. 6, 1986, P. L. 99-603, Title I, Part B, § 117, Title III, Part B, § 313(c), 100 Stat. 3384, 3438; Nov. 10, 1986, P. L. 99-639, §§ 2(e), 3(b), 5(a), 100 Stat. 3542, 3543; Nov. 6, 1986, P. L. 99-603, Title III, Part B, § 313(c); Nov. 10, 1986, P. L. 99-639, § 3(b), 100 Stat. 3542; Oct. 24, 1988, P. L. 100-525, §§ 2(f)(1), (p)(3), 7(b), 102 Stat. 2611, 2613, 2616; Nov. 29, 1990, P. L. 101-649, Title I, Subtitle B, Part 2, § 121(b)(4), Subtitle E, § 162(e)(3), Title VII, § 702(a), 104 Stat. 4994, 5011, 5086; Oct. 1, 1991, P. L. 102-110, § 2(c), 105 Stat. 556; Dec. 12, 1991, P. L. 102-232, Title III, §§ 302(d)(2), (e)(7), 308(a), 105 Stat. 1744, 1746, 1747; Aug. 26, 1994, P. L. 103-317, Title V, § 506(b), 108 Stat. 1765; Sept. 13, 1994, P. L. 103-322, Title XIII, § 130002(c), 108 Stat. 2025; Oct. 25, 1994, P. L. 103-416, Title II, § 219(k), 108 Stat. 4317; April 24, 1996, P. L. 104-132, Title IV, Subtitle B, § 413(d), 110 Stat. 1269; Sept. 30, 1996, P. L. 104-208, Div C, Title III, Subtitle A, § 308(f)(1)(O), (2)(C), (g)(10)(B), Subtitle F, §§ 375, 376(a), Title VI, Subtitle E, § 671(a)(4)(A), (5), 110 Stat. 3009-621, 3009-625, 3009-648, 3009-721; Nov. 26, 1997, P. L. 105-119, Title I, §§ 110(3), 111(a), (c), 111 Stat. 2458; Oct. 28, 2000, P. L. 106-386, Div A, § 107(f), Div B, Title V, §§ 1506(a)(1), 1513(f), 114 Stat. 1479, 1527, 1536; Dec. 21, 2000, P. L. 106-553, § 1(a)(2), 114 Stat. 2762; Dec. 21, 2000, P. L. 106-554, § 1(a)(4), 114 Stat. 2763; Dec. 19, 2003, P. L. 108-193, §§ 4(b)(3), 8(a)(4), 117 Stat. 2879, 2886; Jan. 5, 2006, P. L. 109-162, Title VIII, Subtitle A, § 803, 119 Stat. 3054; Aug. 12, 2006, P. L. 109-271, § 6(f), 120 Stat. 763; Dec. 23, 2008, P. L. 110-457, Title II, Subtitle A, § 201(d), (e), Subtitle D, § 235(d)(3), 122 Stat. 5053, 5080; Mar. 15, 2022, P.L. 117-103, Div BB, § 102(d), 136 Stat. 1075.)

§ 245A. [8 U.S.C. § 1255a] Adjustment of status of certain entrants before Jan. 1, 1982, to that of person admitted for lawful residence. [Caution: See prospective amendment note below.]

(a) Temporary resident status. The Attorney General shall adjust the status of an alien to that of an alien lawfully admitted for temporary residence if the alien meets the following requirements:

(1) Timely applications.

(A) During application period. Except as provided in subparagraph (B), the alien must apply for such adjustment during the 12-month period beginning on a date (not later than 180 days after the date of enactment of this section [enacted Nov. 6, 1986]) designated by the Attorney General.

(B) Application within 30 days of show-cause order. An alien who, at any time during the first 11 months of the 12-month period described in subparagraph (A), is the subject of an order to show cause issued under section 242 [8 USCS § 1252] (as in effect before October 1, 1996), must make application under this section not later than the end of the 30-day period beginning either on the first day of such 12-month period or on the date of the issuance of such order, whichever day is later.

(C) Information included in application. Each application under this subsection shall contain such information as the Attorney General may require, including information on living relatives of the applicant with respect to whom a petition for preference or other status may be filed by the applicant at any later date under section 204(a) [8 USCS § 1154(a)].

(2) Continuous unlawful residence since 1982.

(A) In general. The alien must establish that he entered the United States before January 1, 1982, and that he has resided continuously in the United States in an unlawful status since such date and through the date the application is filed under this subsection.

(B) Nonimmigrants. In the case of an alien who entered the United States as a nonimmigrant before January 1, 1982, the alien must establish that the alien's period of authorized stay as a nonimmigrant expired before such date through the passage of time or the alien's unlawful status was known to the Government as of such date.

(C) Exchange visitors. If the alien was at any time a nonimmigrant exchange alien (as defined in section 101(a)(15)(J) [8 USCS § 1101(a)(15)(J)]), the alien must establish that the alien was not subject to the two-year foreign residence requirement of section 212(e) [8 USCS § 1182(e)] or has fulfilled that requirement or received a waiver thereof.

(3) Continuous physical presence since enactment.

(A) In general. The alien must establish that the alien has been continuously physically present in the United States since the date of the enactment of this section [enacted Nov. 6, 1986].

(B) Treatment of brief, casual, and innocent absences. An alien shall not be considered to have failed to maintain continuous physical presence in the United States for purposes of subparagraph (A) by virtue of brief, casual, and innocent absences from the United States.

(C) Admissions. Nothing in this section shall be construed as authorizing an alien to apply for admission to, or to be admitted to, the United States in order to apply for adjustment of status under this subsection.

(4) Admissible as immigrant. The alien must establish that he—

(A) is admissible to the United States as an immigrant, except as otherwise provided under subsection (d)(2),

(B) has not been convicted of any felony or of three or more misdemeanors committed in the United States,

(C) has not assisted in the persecution of any person or persons on account of race, religion, nationality, membership in a particular social group, or political opinion, and

(D) is registered or registering under the Military Selective Service Act [50 USCS §§ 3801 et seq.], if the alien is required to be so registered under that Act.

For purposes of this subsection, an alien in the status of a Cuban and Haitian entrant described in paragraph (1) or (2)(A) of section 501(e) of Public Law 96-422 [8 USCS § 1522 note] shall be considered to have entered the United States and to be in an unlawful status in the United States.

(b) Subsequent adjustment to permanent residence and nature of temporary resident status.

(1) Adjustment to permanent residence. The Attorney General shall adjust the status of any alien provided lawful temporary resident status under subsection (a) to that of an alien lawfully admitted for permanent residence if the alien meets the following requirements:

(A) Timely application after one year's residence. The alien must apply for such adjustment during the 2-year period beginning with the nineteenth month that begins after the date the alien was granted such temporary resident status.

(B) Continuous residence.

(i) In general. The alien must establish that he has continuously resided in the United States since the date the alien was granted such temporary resident status.

(ii) Treatment of certain absences. An alien shall not be considered to have lost the continuous residence referred to in clause (i) by reason of an absence from the United States permitted under paragraph (3)(A).

(C) Admissible as immigrant. The alien must establish that he—

(i) is admissible to the United States as an immigrant, except as otherwise provided under subsection (d)(2), and

(ii) has not been convicted of any felony or three or more misdemeanors committed in the United States.

(D) Basic citizenship skills.

(i) In general. The alien must demonstrate that he either—

(I) meets the requirements of section 312(a) [8 USCS § 1423(a)] (relating to minimal understanding of ordinary English and a knowledge and understanding of the history and government of the United States), or

(II) is satisfactorily pursuing a course of study (recognized by the Attorney General) to achieve such an understanding of English and such a knowledge and understanding of the history and government of the United States.

(ii) Exception for elderly or developmentally disabled individuals. The Attorney General may, in his discretion, waive all or part of the requirements of clause (i) in the case of an alien who is 65 years of age or older or who is developmentally disabled.

(iii) Relation to naturalization examination. In accordance with regulations of the Attorney General, an alien who has demonstrated under clause (i)(I) that the alien meets the requirements of section 312(a) [8 USCS § 1423(a)] may be considered to have satisfied the requirements of that section for purposes of becoming naturalized as a citizen of the United States under title III [8 USCS §§ 1401 et seq.].

(2) Termination of temporary residence. The Attorney General shall provide for termination of temporary resident status granted an alien under subsection (a)–

(A) if it appears to the Attorney General that the alien was in fact not eligible for such status;

(B) if the alien commits an act that (i) makes the alien inadmissible to the United States as an immigrant, except as otherwise provided under subsection (d)(2), or (ii) is convicted of any felony or three or more misdemeanors committed in the United States; or

(C) at the end of the 43rd month beginning after the date the alien is granted such status, unless the alien has filed an application for adjustment of such status pursuant to paragraph (1) and such application has not been denied.

(3) Authorized travel and employment during temporary residence. During the period an alien is in lawful temporary resident status granted under subsection (a)—

(A) Authorization of travel abroad. The Attorney General shall, in accordance with regulations, permit the alien to return to the United States after such brief and casual trips abroad as reflect an intention on the part of the alien to adjust to lawful permanent resident status under paragraph (1) and after brief temporary trips abroad occasioned by a family obligation involving an occurrence such as the illness or death of a close relative or other family need.

(B) Authorization of employment. The Attorney General shall grant the alien authorization to engage in employment in the United States and provide to that alien an "employment authorized" endorsement or other appropriate work permit.

(c) Applications for adjustment of status.

(1) To whom may be made. The Attorney General shall provide that the applications for adjustment of status under subsection (a) may be filed—

(A) with the Attorney General, or

(B) with a qualified designated entity, but only if the applicant consents to the forwarding of the application to the Attorney General.

As used in this section, the term "qualified designated entity" means an organization or person designated under paragraph (2).

(2) Designation of qualified entities to receive applications. For purposes of assisting in the program of legalization provided under this section, the Attorney General—

(A) shall designate qualified voluntary organizations and other qualified State, local, and community organizations, and

(B) may designate such other persons as the Attorney General determines are qualified and have substantial experience, demonstrated competence, and traditional long-term involvement in the preparation and submittal of applications for adjustment of status under section 209 or 245 [8 USCS § 1159 or 1255], Public Law 89-732, or Public Law 95-145 [8 USCS § 1255 notes].

(3) Treatment of applications by designated entities. Each qualified designated entity must agree to forward to the Attorney General applications filed with it in accordance with paragraph (1)(B) but not to forward to the Attorney General applications filed with it unless the applicant has consented to such forwarding. No such entity may make a determination required by this section to be made by the Attorney General.

(4) Limitation on access to information. Files and records of qualified designated entities relating to an alien's seeking assistance or information with respect to filing an application under this section are confidential and the Attorney General and the Service shall not have access to such files or records relating to an alien without the consent of the alien.

(5) Confidentiality of information.

(A) In general. Except as provided in this paragraph, neither the Attorney General, nor any other official or employee of the Department of Justice, or bureau or agency thereof, may—

(i) use the information furnished by the applicant pursuant to an application filed under this section for any purpose other than to make a determination on the application, for enforcement of paragraph (6), or for the preparation of reports to Congress under section 404 of the Immigration Reform and Control Act of 1986 [note to this section];

(ii) make any publication whereby the information furnished by any particular applicant can be identified; or

(iii) permit anyone other than the sworn officers and employees of the Department or bureau or agency or, with respect to applications filed with a designated entity, that designated entity, to examine individual applications.

(B) Required disclosures. The Attorney General shall provide the information furnished under this section, and any other information derived from such furnished information, to a duly recognized law enforcement entity in connection with a criminal investigation or prosecution, when such information is requested in writing by such entity, or to an official coroner for purposes of affirmatively identifying a deceased individual (whether or not such individual is deceased as a result of a crime).

(C) Authorized disclosures. The Attorney General may provide, in the Attorney General's discretion, for the furnishing of information furnished under this section in the same manner and circumstances as census information may be disclosed by the Secretary of Commerce under section 8 of title 13, United States Code.

(D) Construction.

(i) In general. Nothing in this paragraph shall be construed to limit the use, or release, for immigration enforcement purposes or law enforcement purposes of information contained in files or records of the Service pertaining to an application filed under this section, other than information furnished by an applicant pursuant to the application, or any other information derived from the application, that is not available from any other source.

(ii) Criminal convictions. Information concerning whether the applicant has at any time been convicted of a crime may be used or released for immigration enforcement or law enforcement purposes.

(E) Crime. Whoever knowingly uses, publishes, or permits information to be examined in violation of this paragraph shall be fined not more than $10,000.

(6) Penalties for false statements in applications. Whoever files an application for adjustment of status under this section and knowingly and willfully falsifies, misrepresents, conceals, or covers up a material fact or makes any false, fictitious, or fraudulent statements or representations, or makes or uses any false writing or document knowing the same to contain any false, fictitious, or fraudulent statement or entry, shall be fined in accordance with title 18, United States Code [18 USCS §§ 1 et seq.], or imprisoned not more than five years, or both.

(7) Application fees.

(A) Fee schedule. The Attorney General shall provide for a schedule of fees to be charged for the filing of applications for adjustment under subsection (a) or (b)(1). The Attorney General shall provide for an additional fee for filing an application for adjustment under subsection (b)(1) after the end of the first year of the 2-year period described in subsection (b)(1)(A).

(B) Use of fees. The Attorney General shall deposit payments received under this paragraph in a separate account and amounts in such account shall be available, without fiscal year limitation, to cover administrative and other expenses incurred in connection with the review of applications filed under this section.

(C) Immigration-related unfair employment practices. Not to exceed $3,000,000 of the unobligated balances remaining in the account established in subparagraph (B) shall be available in fiscal year 1992 and each fiscal year thereafter for grants, contracts, and cooperative agreements to community-based organizations for outreach programs, to be administered by the Office of Special Counsel for Immigration-Related Unfair Employment Practices: Provided, That such amounts shall be in addition to any funds appropriated to the Office of Special Counsel for such purposes: Provided further, That none of the funds made available by this section shall be used by the Office of Special Counsel to establish regional offices.

(d) Waiver of numerical limitations and certain grounds for exclusion.

(1) Numerical limitations do not apply. The numerical limitations of sections 201 and 202 [8 USCS §§ 1151, 1152] shall not apply to the adjustment of aliens to lawful permanent resident status under this section.

(2) Waiver of grounds for exclusion. In the determination of an alien's admissibility under subsections (a)(4)(A), (b)(1)(C)(i), and (b)(2)(B)—

(A) Grounds of exclusion not applicable. The provisions of paragraphs (5) and (7)(A) of section 212(a) [8 USCS § 1182(a)(5) and (7)(A)] shall not apply.

(B) Waiver of other grounds.

(i) In general. Except as provided in clause (ii), the Attorney General may waive any other provision of section 212(a) [8 USCS § 1182(a)] in the case of individual aliens for humanitarian purposes, to assure family unity, or when it is otherwise in the public interest.

(ii) Grounds that may not be waived. The following provisions of section 212(a) [8 USCS § 1182(a)] may not be waived by the Attorney General under clause (i):

(I) Paragraphs (2)(A) and (2)(B) (relating to criminals).

(II) Paragraph (2)(C) (relating to drug offenses), except for so much of such paragraph as relates to a single offense of simple possession of 30 grams or less of marijuana.

(III) Paragraph (3) (relating to security and related grounds).

(IV) Paragraph (4) (relating to aliens likely to become public charges) insofar as it relates to an application for adjustment to permanent residence.

Subclause (IV) (prohibiting the waiver of section 212(a)(4) [8 USCS § 1182(a)(4)]) shall not apply to an alien who is or was an aged, blind, or disabled individual (as defined in section 1614(a)(1) of the Social Security Act [42 USCS § 1382c(a)(1)]).

(iii) Special rule for determination of public charge. An alien is not ineligible for adjustment of status under this section due to being inadmissible under section 212(a)(4) [8 USCS § 1182(a)(4)] if the alien demonstrates a history of employment in the United States evidencing self-support without receipt of public cash assistance.

(C) Medical examination. The alien shall be required, at the alien's expense, to undergo such a medical examination (including a determination of immunization status) as is appropriate and conforms to generally accepted professional standards of medical practice.

(e) Temporary stay of deportation and work authorization for certain applicants.

(1) Before application period. The Attorney General shall provide that in the case of an alien who is apprehended before the beginning of the application period described in subsection (a)(1)(A) and who can establish a prima facie case of eligibility to have his status adjusted under subsection (a) (but for the fact that he may not apply for such adjustment until the beginning of such period), until the alien has had the opportunity during the first 30 days of the application period to complete the filing of an application for adjustment, the alien—

(A) may not be deported, and

(B) shall be granted authorization to engage in employment in the United States and be provided an "employment authorized" endorsement or other appropriate work permit.

(2) During application period. The Attorney General shall provide that in the case of an alien who presents a prima facie application for adjustment of status

under subsection (a) during the application period, and until a final determination on the application has been made in accordance with this section, the alien—

(A) may not be deported, and

(B) shall be granted authorization to engage in employment in the United States and be provided an "employment authorized" endorsement or other appropriate work permit.

(f) Administrative and judicial review.

(1) Administrative and judicial review. There shall be no administrative or judicial review of a determination respecting an application for adjustment of status under this section except in accordance with this subsection.

(2) No review for late filings. No denial of adjustment of status under this section based on a late filing of an application for such adjustment may be reviewed by a court of the United States or of any State or reviewed in any administrative proceeding of the United States Government.

(3) Administrative review.

(A) Single level of administrative appellate review. The Attorney General shall establish an appellate authority to provide for a single level of administrative appellate review of a determination described in paragraph (1).

(B) Standard for review. Such administrative appellate review shall be based solely upon the administrative record established at the time of the determination on the application and upon such additional or newly discovered evidence as may not have been available at the time of the determination.

(4) Judicial review.

(A) Limitation to review of deportation. There shall be judicial review of such a denial only in the judicial review of an order of deportation under section 106 [former 8 USCS § 1105a] (as in effect before October 1, 1996).

(B) Standard for judicial review. Such judicial review shall be based solely upon the administrative record established at the time of the review by the appellate authority and the findings of fact and determinations contained in such record shall be conclusive unless the applicant can establish abuse of discretion or that the findings are directly contrary to clear and convincing facts contained in the record considered as a whole.

(C) Jurisdiction of courts. Notwithstanding any other provision of law, no court shall have jurisdiction of any cause of action or claim by or on behalf of any person asserting an interest under this section unless such person in fact filed an application under this section within the period specified by subsection (a)(1), or attempted to file a complete application and application fee with an authorized legalization officer of the Service but had the application and fee refused by that officer.

(g) Implementation of section.

(1) Regulations. The Attorney General, after consultation with the Committees on the Judiciary of the House of Representatives and of the Senate, shall prescribe—

(A) regulations establishing a definition of the term "resided continuously", as used in this section, and the evidence needed to establish that an alien has resided continuously in the United States for purposes of this section, and

(B) such other regulations as may be necessary to carry out this section.

(2) Considerations. In prescribing regulations described in paragraph (1)(A)—

(A) Periods of continuous residence. The Attorney General shall specify individual periods, and aggregate periods, of absence from the United States which will be considered to break a period of continuous residence in the United States and shall take into account absences due merely to brief and casual trips abroad.

(B) Absences caused by deportation or advanced parole. The Attorney General shall provide that—

(i) an alien shall not be considered to have resided continuously in the United States, if, during any period for which continuous residence is required, the alien was outside the United States as a result of a departure under an order of deportation, and

(ii) any period of time during which an alien is outside the United States pursuant to the advance parole procedures of the Service shall not be considered as part of the period of time during which an alien is outside the United States for purposes of this section.

(C) Waivers of certain absences. The Attorney General may provide for a waiver, in the discretion of the Attorney General, of the periods specified under subparagraph (A) in the case of an absence from the United States due merely to a brief temporary trip abroad required by emergency or extenuating circumstances outside the control of the alien.

(D) Use of certain documentation. The Attorney General shall require that—

(i) continuous residence and physical presence in the United States must be established through documents, together with independent corroboration of the information contained in such documents, and

(ii) the documents provided under clause (i) be employment-related if employment-related documents with respect to the alien are available to the applicant.

(3) Interim final regulations. Regulations prescribed under this section may be prescribed to take effect on an interim final basis if the Attorney General determines that this is necessary in order to implement this section in a timely manner.

(h) Temporary disqualification of newly legalized aliens from receiving certain public welfare assistance.

(1) In general. During the five-year period beginning on the date an alien was granted lawful temporary resident status under subsection (a), and notwithstanding any other provision of law—

(A) except as provided in paragraphs (2) and (3), the alien is not eligible for—

(i) any program of financial assistance furnished under Federal law (whether through grant, loan, guarantee, or otherwise) on the basis of financial need, as such programs are identified by the Attorney General in consultation with other appropriate heads of the various departments and agencies of Government (but in any event including the State program of assistance under part A of title IV of the Social Security Act) [42 USCS §§ 601 et seq.],

(ii) medical assistance under a State plan approved under title XIX of the Social Security Act [42 USCS §§ 1396 et seq.], and

(iii) assistance under the Food and Nutrition Act of 2008 [7 USCS §§ 2011 et seq.]; and

(B) a State or political subdivision therein may, to the extent consistent with subparagraph (A) and paragraphs (2) and (3), provide that the alien is not eligible for the programs of financial assistance or for medical assistance described in subparagraph (A)(ii) furnished under the law of that State or political subdivision.

Unless otherwise specifically provided by this section or other law, an alien in temporary lawful residence status granted under subsection (a) shall not be considered (for purposes of any law of a State or political subdivision providing for a program of financial assistance) to be permanently residing in the United States under color of law.

(2) Exceptions. Paragraph (1) shall not apply—

(A) to a Cuban and Haitian entrant (as defined in paragraph (1) or (2)(A) of section 501(e) of Public Law 96-422 [8 USCS § 1522 note], as in effect on April 1, 1983), or

(B) in the case of assistance (other than assistance under a State program funded under part A of title IV of the Social Security Act [42 USCS §§ 601 et seq.]) which is furnished to an alien who is an aged, blind, or disabled individual (as defined in section 1614(a)(1) of the Social Security Act [42 USCS § 1382c(a)(1)]).

(3) Restricted medicaid benefits.

(A) Clarification of entitlement. Subject to the restrictions under subparagraph (B), for the purpose of providing aliens with eligibility to receive medical assistance—

(i) paragraph (1) shall not apply,

(ii) aliens who would be eligible for medical assistance but for the provisions of paragraph (1) shall be deemed, for purposes of title XIX of the Social Security Act [42 USCS §§ 1396 et seq.], to be so eligible, and

(iii) aliens lawfully admitted for temporary residence under this section, such status not having changed, shall be considered to be permanently residing in the United States under color of law.

(B) Restriction of benefits.

(i) Limitation to emergency services and services for pregnant women. Notwithstanding any provision of title XIX of the Social Security Act [42 USCS §§ 1396 et seq.] (including subparagraphs (B) and (C) of section 1902(a)(10) of such Act [42 USCS § 1396a(a)(10)(B), (C)], aliens who, but for subparagraph (A), would be ineligible for medical assistance under paragraph (1), are only eligible for such assistance with respect to—

(I) emergency services (as defined for purposes of section 1916(a)(2)(D) of the Social Security Act [42 USCS § 1396o(a)(2)(D)]), and

(II) services described in section 1916(a)(2)(B) of such Act [42 USCS § 1396o(a)(2)(B)] (relating to service for pregnant women).

(ii) No restriction for exempt aliens and children. The restrictions of clause (i) shall not apply to aliens who are described in paragraph (2) or who are under 18 years of age.

(C) Definition of medical assistance. In this paragraph, the term "medical assistance" refers to medical assistance under a State plan approved under title XIX of the Social Security Act [42 USCS §§ 1396 et seq.].

(4) Treatment of certain programs. Assistance furnished under any of the following provisions of law shall not be construed to be financial assistance described in paragraph (1)(A)(i):

(A) The Richard B. Russell National School Lunch Act [42 USCS §§ 1751 et seq.].

(B) The Child Nutrition Act of 1966 [42 USCS §§ 1771 et seq.].

(C) The [The] Carl D. Perkins Career and Technical Education Act of 2006 [20 USCS §§ 2301 et seq.].

(D) Title I of the Elementary and Secondary Education Act of 1965 [20 USCS §§ 6301 et seq.].

(E) The Headstart-Follow Through Act [former 42 USCS §§ 9861 et seq.].

(F) Title I of the Workforce Innovation and Opportunity Act [29 USCS § 3111 et seq.].

(G) Title IV of the Higher Education Act of 1965.

(H) The Public Health Service Act [42 USCS §§ 201 et seq.].

(I) Titles V, XVI, and XX, and parts B, D, and E of title IV, of the Social Security Act [42 USCS §§ 701 et seq., 1381 et seq., and 1379 et seq., and 620 et seq., 651 et seq., 671 et seq.] (and titles I, X, XIV, and XVI of such Act [42 USCS §§ 301 et seq., 1201 et seq, 1351 et seq., 1381 et seq.] as in effect without regard to the amendment made by section 301 of the Social Security Amendments of 1972 [amending 42 USCS §§ 1381 et seq.]).

(5) Adjustment not affecting Fascell-Stone benefits. For the purpose of section 501 of the Refugee Education Assistance Act of 1980 (Public Law 96-122), assistance shall be continued under such section with respect to an alien without regard to the alien's adjustment of status under this section.

(i) Dissemination of information on legalization program. Beginning not later than the date designated by the Attorney General under subsection (a)(1)(A), the Attorney General, in cooperation with qualified designated entities, shall broadly disseminate information respecting the benefits which aliens may receive under this section and the requirements to obtain such benefits

HISTORY: (June 27, 1952, ch 477, Title II, Ch 5, § 245A, as added Nov. 6, 1986, P. L. 99-603, Title II, § 201(a)(1), 100 Stat. 3394; Oct. 24, 1988, P. L. 100-525, § 2(h)(1), 102 Stat. 2611; Nov. 29, 1990, P. L. 101-649, Title VI, § 603(a)(13), Title VII, § 703,104 Stat. 5083, 5086; Oct. 28, 1991, P. L. 102-140, Title I, 105 Stat. 785; Dec. 12, 1991, P. L. 102-232, Title III, § 307l(6), 105 Stat. 1756; Oct. 20, 1994, P. L. 103-382, Title III, Part I, § 394(g), 108 Stat. 4028; Oct. 25, 1994, P. L. 103-416, Title I, § 108(b), Title II, § 219(l)(1), 108 Stat. 4310, 4317; April 24, 1996, P. L. 104-132, Title IV, Subtitle D, § 431(a), 110 Stat. 1273; Aug. 22, 1996, P. L. 104-193, Title I, § 110(s)(2), 110 Stat. 2175; Sept. 30, 1996, P. L. 104-208, Div C, Title III, Subtitle A, § 308(g)(2)(B), (5)(A)(iii), Subtitle F, §§ 377(a), 384(d)(1), Title

VI, Subtitle B, § 623(a), 110 Stat. 3009-622, 3009-623, 3009-649, 3009-653, 3009-696; Oct. 21, 1998, P. L. 105-277, Div A, § 101(f) [Title VIII, Subtitle IV, § 405(d)(4), (f)(4)], 112 Stat. 2681-419, 2681-430; Oct. 31, 1998, P. L. 105-332, § 3(a), 112 Stat. 3125; Oct. 22, 1999, P. L. 106-78, Title VII, § 752(b)(5), 113 Stat. 1169; Aug. 12, 2006, P. L. 109-270, § 2(a), 120 Stat. 746; May 22, 2008, P. L. 110-234, Title IV, Subtitle A, Part I, § 4002(b)(1)(B), (2)(J), 122 Stat. 1096, 1097; June 18, 2008, P. L. 110-246, § 4(a), Title IV, Subtitle A, Part I, § 4002(b)(1)(B), (2)(J), 122 Stat. 1664, 1857, 1858; July 22, 2014, P. L. 113-128, Title V, Subtitle B, § 512(q), 128 Stat. 1712.)

PROSPECTIVE AMENDMENT:

Amendment of subsec. (h)(4)(F), effective July 1, 2015. Act July 22, 2014, P.L. 113-128, Title V, Subtitle B, § 512(q), 128 Stat. 1712 (effective 7/1/2015, as provided by § 506(a) of such Act, which appears as 29 USCS § 3101 note) provides that subsec. (h)(4)(F) of this section is amended by striking "Title I of the Workforce Investment Act of 1998" and inserting "Title I of the Workforce Innovation and Opportunity Act [29 USCS § 3111 et seq.]".

§ 246. [8 U.S.C. § 1256] Rescission of adjustment of status; report to Congress; effect upon naturalized citizen.

(a) If, at any time within five years after the status of a person has been otherwise adjusted under the provisions of section 245 or 249 of this Act [8 USCS § 1255 or 1259] or any other provision of law to that of an alien lawfully admitted for permanent residence, it shall appear to the satisfaction of the Attorney General that the person was not in fact eligible for such adjustment of status, the Attorney General shall rescind the action taken granting an adjustment of status to such person and cancelling removal in the case of such person if that occurred and the person shall thereupon be subject to all provisions of this Act to the same extent as if the adjustment of status had not been made. Nothing in this subsection shall require the Attorney General to rescind the alien's status prior to commencement of procedures to remove the alien under section 240 [8 USCS § 1229a], and an order of removal issued by an immigration judge shall be sufficient to rescind the alien's status.

(b) Any person who has become a naturalized citizen of the United States upon the basis of a record of a lawful admission for permanent residence, created as a result of an adjustment of status for which such person was not in fact eligible, and which is subsequently rescinded under subsection (a) of this section, shall be subject to the provisions of section 340 of this Act [8 USCS § 1451] as a person whose naturalization was procured by concealment of a material fact or by willful misrepresentation.

HISTORY: (June 27, 1952, ch 477, Title II, Ch 5, § 246, 66 Stat. 217; Oct. 25, 1994, P. L. 103-416, Title II, § 219(m), 108 Stat. 4317; Sept. 30, 1996, P. L. 104-208, Div C, Title III, Subtitle A, § 308(e)(1)(H), Subtitle F, § 378(a), 110 Stat. 3009-619, 3009-649.)

§ 247. [8 U.S.C. § 1257] Adjustment of status of certain resident aliens to nonimmigrant status; exceptions.

(a) The status of an alien lawfully admitted for permanent residence shall be adjusted by the Attorney General, under such regulations as he may prescribe, to that of a nonimmigrant under paragraph (15)(A), (15)(E), or (15)(G) of section 101(a) [8 USCS § 1101(a)(15)(A), (E), or (G)], if such alien had at the time of admission or subsequently acquires an occupational status which would, if he were seeking admission to the United States, entitle him to a nonimmigrant status under such sections [paragraphs]. As of the date of the Attorney General's order making such adjustment of status, the Attorney General shall cancel the record of the alien's admission for permanent residence, and the immigrant status of such alien shall thereby be terminated.

(b) The adjustment of status required by subsection (a) shall not be applicable in the case of any alien who requests that he be permitted to retain his status as an immigrant and who, in such form as the Attorney General may require, executes and files with the Attorney General a written waiver of all rights, privileges, exemptions, and immunities under any law or any executive order which would otherwise accrue to him because of the acquisition of an occupational status entitling him to a nonimmigrant status under paragraphs (15)(A), (15)(E), or (15)(G) of section 101(a) [8 USCS § 1101(a)(15)(A), (E), or (G)].

HISTORY: (June 27, 1952, ch 477, Title II, Ch 5, § 247, 66 Stat. 218; Sept. 30, 1996, P. L. 104-208, Div C, Title III, Subtitle A, § 308(f)(1)(P), 110 Stat. 3009-621.)

§ 248. [8 U.S.C. § 1258] Change of nonimmigrant classification.

(a) The Secretary of Homeland Security may, under such conditions as he may prescribe, authorize a change from any nonimmigrant classification to any other nonimmigrant classification in the case of any alien lawfully admitted to the United States as a nonimmigrant who is continuing to maintain that status and who is not inadmissible under section 212(a)(9)(B)(i) [8 USCS § 1182(a)(9)(B)(i)] (or whose inadmissibility under such section is waived under section 212(a)(9)(B)(v) [8 USCS § 1182(a)(9)(B)(v)]), except (subject to subsection (b)) in the case of—

(1) an alien classified as a nonimmigrant under subparagraph (C), (D), (K), or (S) of section 101(a)(15) [8 USCS § 1101(a)(15)(C), (D), (K), or (S)],

(2) an alien classified as a nonimmigrant under subparagraph (J) of section 101(a)(15) [8 USCS § 1101(a)(15)(J)] who came to the United States or acquired such classification in order to receive graduate medical education or training,

(3) an alien (other than an alien described in paragraph (2)) classified as a nonimmigrant under subparagraph (J) of section 101(a)(15) [8 USCS § 1101(a)(15)(J)] who is subject to the two-year foreign residence requirement of section 212(e) [8 USCS § 1182(e)] and has not received a waiver thereof, unless such alien applies to have the alien's classification changed from classification under subparagraph (J) of section 101(a)(15) [8 USCS § 1101(a)(15)(J)] to a classification under subparagraph (A) or (G) of such section [8 USCS § 1101(a)(15)(A) or (G)], and

(4) an alien admitted as a nonimmigrant visitor without a visa under section 212*(l)* or section 217 [8 USCS § 1182*(l)* or 1187].

(b) The exceptions specified in paragraphs (1) through (4) of subsection (a) shall not apply to a change of nonimmigrant classification to that of a nonimmigrant under subparagraph (T) or (U) of section 101(a)(15) [8 USCS § 1101(a)(15)].

HISTORY: (June 27, 1952, ch 477, Title II, Ch 5, § 248, 66 Stat. 218; Sept. 21, 1961, P. L. 87-256, § 109(d), 75 Stat. 535; Dec. 29, 1981, P. L. 97-116, § 10, 95 Stat. 1617; Nov. 6, 1986, P. L. 99-603, Title III, Part B, § 313(d), 100 Stat. 3439; Sept. 13, 1994, P. L. 103-322, Title XIII, § 130003(b)(3), 108 Stat. 2025; Sept. 30, 1996, P. L. 104-208, Div C, Title III, Subtitle A, § 301(b)(2), Title VI, Subtitle E, § 671(a)(2), 110 Stat. 3009-578, 3009-721; Jan. 5, 2006, P. L. 109-162, Title VIII, Subtitle C, § 821(c)(1), 119 Stat. 3062.)

§ 249. [8 U.S.C. § 1259] Record of admission for permanent residence in the case of certain aliens who entered the United States prior to January 1, 1972.

A record of lawful admission for permanent residence may, in the discretion of the Attorney General and under such regulations as he may prescribe, be made in the case of any alien, as of the date of the approval of his application or, if entry occurred prior to July 1, 1924, as of the date of such entry, if no such record is otherwise available and such alien shall satisfy the Attorney General that he is not inadmissible under section 212(a)(3)(E) [8 USCS § 1182(a)(3)(E)] or under section 212(a) [8 USCS § 1182(a)] insofar as it relates to criminals, procurers and other immoral persons, subversives, violators of the narcotic laws or smugglers of aliens, and he establishes that he—

(a) entered the United States prior to January 1, 1972;

(b) has had his residence in the United States continuously since such entry;

(c) is a person of good moral character; and

(d) is not ineligible to citizenship and is not deportable under section 237(a)(4)(B) [8 USCS § 1227(a)(4)(B)].

HISTORY: (June 27, 1952, ch 477, Title II, Ch 5, § 249, 66 Stat. 219; Aug. 8, 1958, P. L. 85-616, 72 Stat. 546; Oct. 3, 1965, P. L. 89-236, § 19, 79 Stat. 920; Nov. 6, 1986, P. L. 99-603, Title II, § 203(a), (b), 100 Stat. 3405; Nov. 6, 1986, P. L. 99-603, Title II, § 3405; Oct. 24, 1988, P. L. 100-525, § 2(j), 102 Stat. 2612; Nov. 29, 1990, P. L. 101-649, Title VI, § 603(a)(14), 104 Stat. 5083; April 24, 1996, P. L. 104-132, Title IV, Subtitle B, § 413(e), 110 Stat. 1269; Sept. 30, 1996, P. L. 104-208, Div C, Title III, Subtitle A, § 308(g)(10)(C), 110 Stat. 3009-625.)

§ 250. [8 U.S.C. § 1260] Removal of aliens falling into distress.

The Attorney General may remove from the United States any alien who falls into distress or who needs public aid from causes arising subsequent to his entry, and is desirous of being so removed, to the native country of such alien, or to the country from which he came, or to the country of which he is a citizen or subject, or to any other country to which he wishes to go and which will receive him, at the expense of the appropriation for the enforcement of this Act. Any alien so removed shall be ineligible to apply for or receive a visa or other documentation for readmission, or to apply for admission to the United States except with the prior approval of the Attorney General.

HISTORY: (June 27, 1952, ch 477, Title II, Ch 5, § 250, 66 Stat. 219.)

Chapter 6—Special Provisions Relating to Alien Crewmen

§ 251. [8 U.S.C. § 1281] Alien crewmen.

(a) Arrival; submission of list; exceptions. Upon arrival of any vessel or aircraft in the United States from any place outside the United States it shall be the duty of the owner, agent, consignee, master, or commanding officer thereof to deliver to an immigration officer at the port of arrival (1) a complete, true, and correct list containing the names of all aliens employed on such vessel or aircraft, the positions they respectively hold in the crew of the vessel or aircraft, when and where they were respectively shipped or engaged, and those to be paid off or discharged in the port of arrival; or (2) in the discretion of the Attorney General, such a list containing so much of such information, or such additional or supplemental information, as the Attorney General shall by regulations prescribe. In the case of a vessel engaged solely in traffic on the Great Lakes, Saint Lawrence River, and connecting waterways, such lists shall be furnished at such times as the Attorney General may require.

(b) Reports of illegal landings. It shall be the duty of any owner, agent, consignee, master, or commanding officer of any vessel or aircraft to report to an immigration officer, in writing, as soon as discovered, all cases in which any alien crewman has illegally landed in the United States from the vessel or aircraft, together with a description of such alien and any information likely to lead to his apprehension.

(c) Departure; submission of list; exceptions. Before the departure of any vessel or aircraft from any port in the United States, it shall be the duty of the owner, agent, consignee, master, or commanding officer thereof, to deliver to an immigration officer at that port (1) a list containing the names of all alien employees who were not employed thereon at the time of the arrival at that port but who will leave such port thereon at the time of the departure of such vessel or aircraft and the names of those, if any, who have been paid off or discharged, and of those, if any, who have deserted or landed at that port, or (2) in the discretion of the Attorney General, such a list containing so much of such information, or such additional or supplemental information, as the Attorney General shall by regulations prescribe. In the case of a vessel engaged solely in traffic on the Great Lakes, Saint Lawrence River, and connecting waterways, such lists shall be furnished at such times as the Attorney General may require.

(d) Violations [Caution: For inflation-adjusted civil monetary penalties, see8 CFR 280.53(c).]. In case any owner, agent, consignee, master, or commanding officer shall fail to deliver complete, true, and correct lists or reports of aliens, or to report cases of desertion or landing, as required by subsections (a), (b), and (c), such owner, agent, consignee, master, or commanding officer, shall, if required by the Attorney General, pay to the Commissioner the sum of $200 for each alien concerning whom such lists are not delivered or such reports are not made as required in the preceding subsections. In the case that any owner, agent, consignee, master, or commanding officer of a vessel shall secure services of an alien crewman described in section 101(a)(15)(D)(i) [8 USCS § 1101(a)(15)(D)(i)] to perform longshore work not included in the normal operation and service on board the vessel under section 258 [8 USCS § 1288], the owner, agent, consignee, master, or commanding officer shall pay to the Commissioner the sum of $5,000, and such fine shall be a lien against the vessel. No such vessel or aircraft shall be granted clearance from any port at which it arrives pending the determination of the question of the liability to the payment of such fine, and if such fine is imposed, while it remains unpaid. No such fine shall be remitted or refunded. Clearance may be granted prior to the determination of such question upon deposit of a bond or a sum sufficient to cover such fine.

(e) Regulations. The Attorney General is authorized to prescribe by regulations the circumstances under which a vessel or aircraft shall be deemed to be arriving in, or departing from the United States or any port thereof within the meaning of any provision of this chapter [8 USCS §§ 1281 et seq.].

HISTORY: (June 27, 1952, ch 477, Title II, Ch 6, § 251, 66 Stat. 219; Nov. 29, 1990, P. L. 101-649, Title II, Subtitle A, § 203(b), 104 Stat. 5018; Dec. 12, 1991, P. L. 102-232, Title III, § 303(a)(3), 105 Stat. 1746.)

§ 252. [8 U.S.C. § 1282] Conditional permits to land temporarily.

(a) Period of time. No alien crewman shall be permitted to land temporarily in the United States except as provided in this section, section 212(d)(3), section 212(d)(5), and section 253 [8 USCS §§ 1182(d)(3), (5), and 1283]. If an immigration officer finds upon examination that an alien crewman is a nonimmigrant under paragraph (15)(D) of section 101(a) [8 USCS § 1101(a)(15)(D)] and is otherwise admissible and has agreed to accept such permit, he may, in his discretion, grant the crewman a conditional permit to land temporarily pursuant to regulations prescribed by the Attorney General, subject to revocation in subsequent proceedings as provided in subsection (b), and for a period of time, in any event, not to exceed—

(1) the period of time (not exceeding twenty-nine days) during which the vessel or aircraft on which he arrived remains in port, if the immigration officer is satisfied that the crewman intends to depart on the vessel or aircraft on which he arrived;

(2) twenty-nine days, if the immigration officer is satisfied that the crewman intends to depart, within the period for which he is permitted to land, on a vessel or aircraft other than the one on which he arrived; or

(3) 180 days, if the immigration officer determines that the crewman—

(A) intends to depart, within the period for which the crewman is permitted to land, on the same vessel or on a vessel or aircraft other than the vessel on which the crewman arrived; and

(B) will perform ship-to-ship liquid cargo transfer operations to or from any other vessel engaged in foreign trade during such period.

(b) Revocation; expenses of detention. Pursuant to regulations prescribed by the Attorney General, any immigration officer may, in his discretion, if he determines that an alien is not a bona fide crewman, or does not intend to depart on the vessel or aircraft which brought him, revoke the conditional permit to land which was granted such crewman under the provisions of subsection (a)(1), take such crewman into custody, and require the master or commanding officer of the vessel or aircraft on which the crewman arrived to receive and detain him on board such vessel or aircraft, if practicable, and such crewman shall be removed from the United States at the expense of the transportation line which brought him to the United States. Until such alien is so removed, any expenses of his detention shall be borne by such transportation company. Nothing in this section shall be construed to require the procedure prescribed in section 240 of this Act [8 USCS § 1229a] to cases falling within the provisions of this subsection.

(c) Penalties. Any alien crewman who willfully remains in the United States in excess of the number of days allowed in any conditional permit issued under subsection (a) shall be fined under title 18, United States Code, or imprisoned not more than 6 months, or both.

HISTORY: (June 27, 1952, ch 477, Title II, Ch 6, § 252, 66 Stat. 220; Nov. 29, 1990, P. L. 101-649, Title V, Subtitle D, § 543(b)(1), 104 Stat. 5059; Dec. 12, 1991, P. L. 102-232, Title III, § 306(c)(2), 105 Stat. 1752; Sept. 30, 1996, P. L. 104-208, Div C, Title III, Subtitle A, § 308(e)(2)(E), (g)(5)(A)(i), 110 Stat. 3009-620, 3009-623; Jan. 5, 2023, P.L. 117-360, § 3, 136 Stat. 6293.)

§ 253. [8 U.S.C. § 1283] Hospital treatment of alien crewman afflicted with certain diseases.

An alien crewman, including an alien crewman ineligible for a conditional permit to land under section 252(a) [8 USCS § 1282(a)], who is found on arrival in a port of the United States to be afflicted with any of the disabilities or diseases mentioned in section 255 [8 USCS § 1285], shall be placed in a hospital designated by the immigration officer in charge at the port of arrival and treated, all expenses connected therewith, including burial in the event of death, to be borne by the owner, agent, consignee, commanding officer, or master of the vessel or aircraft, and not to be deducted from the crewman's wages. No such vessel or aircraft shall be granted clearance until such expenses are paid, or their payment appropriately guaranteed, and the collector of customs is so notified by the immigration officer in charge. An alien crewman suspected of being afflicted with any such disability or disease may be removed from the vessel or aircraft on which he arrived to an immigration station, or other appropriate place, for such observation as will enable the examining surgeons to determine definitely whether or not he is so afflicted, all expenses connected therewith to be borne in the manner hereinbefore prescribed. In cases in which it appears to the satisfaction of the immigration officer in charge that it will not be possible within a reasonable time to effect a cure, the return of the alien crewman shall be enforced on, or at the expense of, the transportation line on which he came, upon such conditions as the Attorney General shall prescribe, to insure that the alien shall be properly cared for and protected, and that the spread of contagion shall be guarded against.

HISTORY: (June 27, 1952, ch 477, Title II, Ch 6, § 253, 66 Stat. 221.)

§ 254. [8 U.S.C. § 1284] Control of alien crewmen.

(a) Penalties for failure [Caution: For inflation-adjusted civil monetary penalties, see8 CFR 280.53(c).]. The owner, agent, consignee, charterer, master, or commanding officer of any vessel or aircraft arriving in the United States from any place outside thereof who fails (1) to detain on board the vessel, or in the case of an aircraft to detain at a place specified by an immigration officer at the expense of the airline, any alien crewman employed thereon until an immigration officer has completely inspected such alien crewman, including a physical examination by the medical examiner, or (2) to detain any alien crewman on board the vessel, or in the case of an aircraft at a place specified by an immigration officer at the expense of the airline, after such inspection unless a conditional permit to land temporarily has been granted such alien crewman under section 252 [8 USCS § 1282] or unless an alien crewman has been permitted to land temporarily under section 212(d)(5) or 253 [8 USCS § 1182(d)(5) or 1283] for medical or hospital treatment, or (3) to remove such alien crewman if required to do so by an immigration officer, whether such removal requirement is imposed before or after the crewman is permitted to land temporarily under section 212(d)(5), 252, or 253 [8 USCS § 1182(d)(5), 1282, or 1283], shall pay to the Commissioner the sum of $3,000 for each alien crewman in respect of whom any such failure occurs. No such vessel or aircraft shall be granted clearance pending the determination of the liability to the payment of such fine, or while the fine remains unpaid, except that clearance may be granted prior to the determination of such question upon the deposit of a sum sufficient to cover such fine, or of a bond with sufficient surety to secure the payment thereof approved by the Commissioner. The Attorney General may, upon application in writing therefor, mitigate such penalty to not less than $500 for each alien crewman in respect of whom such failure occurs, upon such terms as he shall think proper.

(b) Prima facie evidence against transportation line. Except as may be otherwise prescribed by regulations issued by the Attorney General, proof that an alien crewman did not appear upon the outgoing manifest of the vessel or aircraft on which he arrived in the United States from any place outside thereof, or that he was reported by the master or commanding officer of such vessel or aircraft as a deserter, shall be prima facie evidence of a failure to detain or remove such alien crewman.

(c) Removal on other than arriving vessel or aircraft; expenses. If the Attorney General finds that removal of an alien crewman under this section on the vessel or aircraft on which he arrived is impracticable or impossible, or would cause undue hardship to such alien crewman, he may cause the alien crewman to be removed from the port of arrival or any other port on another vessel or aircraft of the same transportation line, unless the Attorney General finds this to be impracticable. All expenses incurred in connection with such removal, including expenses incurred in transferring an alien crewman from one place in the United States to another under such conditions and safeguards as the Attorney General shall impose, shall be paid by the owner or owners of the vessel or aircraft on which the alien arrived in the United States. The vessel or aircraft on which the alien arrived shall not be granted clearance until such expenses have been paid or their payment guaranteed to the satisfaction of the Attorney General. An alien crewman who is transferred within the United States in accordance with this subsection shall not be regarded as having been landed in the United States.

HISTORY: (June 27, 1952, ch 477, Title II, Ch 6, § 254, 66 Stat. 221; Nov. 29, 1990, P. L. 101-649, Title V, Subtitle D, § 543(a)(4), 104 Stat. 5058; Dec. 12, 1991, P. L. 102-232, Title III, § 306(c)(4)(C), 105 Stat. 1752; Sept. 30, 1996, P. L. 104-208, Div C, Title III, Subtitle A, § 308(e)(1)(I), (2)(F), (12), 110 Stat. 3009-619, 3009-620.)

§ 255. [8 U.S.C. § 1285] Employment on passenger vessels of aliens afflicted with certain disabilities.

It shall be unlawful for any vessel or aircraft carrying passengers between a port of the United States and a port outside thereof to have employed on board upon arrival in the United States any alien afflicted with feeblemindedness, insanity, epilepsy, tuberculosis in any form, leprosy, or any dangerous contagious disease. If it appears to the satisfaction of the Attorney General, from an examination made by a medical officer of the United States Public Health Service, and is so certified by such officer, that any such alien was so afflicted at the time he was shipped or engaged and taken on board such vessel or aircraft and that the existence of such affliction might have been detected by means of a competent medical examination at such time, the owner, commanding officer, agent, consignee, or master thereof shall pay for each alien so afflicted to the Commissioner the sum of $1,000. No vessel or aircraft shall be granted clearance pending the determination of the question of the liability to the payment of such sums, or while such sums remain unpaid, except that clearance may be granted prior to the determination of such question upon the deposit of an amount sufficient to cover such sums or of a bond approved by the Commissioner with sufficient surety to secure the payment thereof. Any such fine may, in the discretion of the Attorney General, be mitigated or remitted.

HISTORY: (June 27, 1952, ch 477, Title II, Ch 6, § 255, 66 Stat. 222; Nov. 29, 1990, P.L. 101-649, Title V, Subtitle D, § 543(a)(5), 104 Stat. 5058.)

§ 256. [8 U.S.C. § 1286] Discharge of alien crewmen; penalties.

It shall be unlawful for any person, including the owner, agent, consignee, charterer, master, or commanding officer of any vessel or aircraft, to pay off or discharge any alien crewman, except an alien lawfully admitted for permanent residence, employed on board a vessel or aircraft arriving in the United States without first having obtained the consent of the Attorney General. If it shall appear to the satisfaction of the Attorney General that any alien crewman has been paid off or discharged in the United States in violation of the provisions of this section, such owner, agent, consignee, charterer, master, commanding officer, or other person, shall pay to the Commissioner the sum of $3,000 for each such violation. No vessel or aircraft shall be granted clearance pending the determination of the question of the liability to the payment of such sums, or while such sums remain unpaid, except that clearance may be granted prior to the determination of such question upon the deposit of an amount sufficient to cover such sums, or of a bond approved by the Commissioner with sufficient surety to secure the payment thereof. Such fine may, in the discretion of the Attorney General, be mitigated to not less than $1,500 for each violation, upon such terms as he shall think proper.

HISTORY: (June 27, 1952, ch 477, Title II, Ch 6, § 256, 66 Stat. 223; Nov. 29, 1990, P. L. 101-649, Title V, Subtitle D, § 543(a)(6), 104 Stat. 5058.)

§ 257. [8 U.S.C. § 1287] Alien crewmen brought into the United States with intent to evade immigration laws; penalties.

Any person, including the owner, agent, consignee, master, or commanding officer of any vessel or aircraft arriving in the United States from any place outside thereof, who shall knowingly sign on the vessel's articles, or bring to the United States as one of the crew of such vessel or aircraft, any alien, with intent to permit or assist such alien to enter or land in the United States in violation of law, or who shall falsely and knowingly represent to a consular officer at the time of application for visa, or to the immigration officer at the port of arrival in the United States, that such alien is a bona fide member of the crew employed in any capacity regularly required for normal operation and services aboard such vessel or aircraft, shall be liable to a penalty not exceeding $10,000 for each such violation, for which sum such vessel or aircraft shall be liable and may be seized and proceeded against by way of libel in any district court of the United States having jurisdiction of the offense.

HISTORY: (June 27, 1952, ch 477, Title II, Ch 6, § 257, 66 Stat. 223; Nov. 29, 1990, P. L. 101-649, Title V, Subtitle D, § 543(a)(7), 104 Stat. 5058.)

§ 258. [8 U.S.C. § 1288] Limitations on performance of longshore work by alien crewmen.

(a) In general. For purposes of section 101(a)(15)(D)(i) [8 USCS § 1101(a)(15)(D)(i)], the term "normal operation and service on board a vessel" does not include any activity that is longshore work (as defined in subsection (b)), except as provided under subsection (c), (d), or (e).

(b) "Longshore work" defined.

(1) In general. In this section, except as provided in paragraph (2), the term "longshore work" means any activity relating to the loading or unloading of cargo, the operation of cargo-related equipment (whether or not integral to the vessel), and the handling of mooring lines on the dock when the vessel is made fast or let go, in the United States or the coastal waters thereof.

(2) Exception for safety and environmental protection. The term "longshore work" does not include the loading or unloading of any cargo for which the Secretary of Transportation has, under the authority contained in chapter 37 of title 46, United States Code [46 USCS §§ 3701 et seq.] (relating to Carriage of Liquid Bulk Dangerous Cargoes), section 311 of the Federal Water Pollution Control Act [33 USCS § 1321], section 4106 of the Oil Pollution Act of 1990, or section 5103(b), 5104, 5106, 5107, or 5110 of title 49, United States Code prescribed regulations which govern—

(A) the handling or stowage of such cargo,

(B) the manning of vessels and the duties, qualifications, and training of the officers and crew of vessels carrying such cargo, and

(C) the reduction or elimination of discharge during ballasting, tank cleaning, handling of such cargo.

(3) Construction. Nothing in this section shall be construed as broadening, limiting, or otherwise modifying the meaning or scope of longshore work for purposes of any other law, collective bargaining agreement, or international agreement.

(c) Prevailing practice exception.

(1) Subsection (a) shall not apply to a particular activity of longshore work in and about a local port if—

(A) (i) there is in effect in the local port one or more collective bargaining agreements each covering at least 30 percent of the number of individuals employed in performing longshore work and (ii) each such agreement (covering such percentage of longshore workers) permits the activity to be performed by alien crewmen under the terms of such agreement; or

(B) there is no collective bargaining agreement in effect in the local port covering at least 30 percent of the number of individuals employed in performing longshore work, and an employer of alien crewmen (or the employer's designated agent or representative) has filed with the Secretary of Labor at least 14 days before the date of performance of the activity (or later, if necessary due to an unanticipated emergency, but not later than the date of performance of the activity) an attestation setting-forth facts and evidence to show that—

(i) the performance of the activity by alien crewmen is permitted under the prevailing practice of the particular port as of the date of filing of the attestation and that the use of alien crewmen for such activity—

(I) is not during a strike or lockout in the course of a labor dispute, and

(II) is not intended or designed to influence an election of a bargaining representative for workers in the local port; and

(ii) notice of the attestation has been provided by the owner, agent, consignee, master, or commanding officer to the bargaining representative of longshore workers in the local port, or, where there is no such bargaining representative, notice of the attestation has been provided to longshore workers employed at the local port.

In applying subparagraph (B) in the case of a particular activity of longshore work consisting of the use of an automated self-unloading conveyor belt or vacuum-actuated system on a vessel, the attestation shall be required to be filed only if the Secretary of Labor finds, based on a preponderance of the evidence which may be submitted by any interested party, that the performance of such particular activity is not described in clause (i) of such subparagraph.

(2) Subject to paragraph (4), an attestation under paragraph (1) shall—

(A) expire at the end of the 1-year period beginning on the date of its filing with the Secretary of Labor, and

(B) apply to aliens arriving in the United States during such 1-year period if the owner, agent, consignee, master, or commanding officer states in each list under section 251 [8 USCS § 1281] that it continues to comply with the conditions in the attestation.

(3) An owner, agent, consignee, master, or commanding officer may meet the requirements under this subsection with respect to more than one alien crewman in a single list.

(4) (A) The Secretary of Labor shall compile and make available for public examination in a timely manner in Washington, D.C., a list identifying owners, agents, consignees, masters, or commanding officers which have filed lists for nonimmigrants described in section 101(a)(15)(D)(i) [8 USCS § 1101(a)(15)(D)(i)] with respect to whom an attestation under paragraph (1) or subsection (d)(1) is made and, for each such entity, a copy of the entity's attestation under paragraph (1) or subsection (d)(1) (and accompanying documentation) and each such list filed by the entity.

(B) (i) The Secretary of Labor shall establish a process for the receipt, investigation, and disposition of complaints respecting an entity's failure to meet conditions attested to, an entity's misrepresentation of a material fact in an attestation, or, in the case described in the last sentence of paragraph (1), whether the performance of the particular activity is or is not described in paragraph (1)(B)(i).

(ii) Complaints may be filed by any aggrieved person or organization (including bargaining representatives, associations deemed appropriate by the Secretary, and other aggrieved parties as determined under regulations of the Secretary).

(iii) The Secretary shall promptly conduct an investigation under this subparagraph if there is reasonable cause to believe that an entity fails to meet conditions attested to, an entity has misrepresented a material fact in the attestation, or, in the case described in the last sentence of paragraph (1), the performance of the particular activity is not described in paragraph (1)(B)(i).

(C) (i) If the Secretary determines that reasonable cause exists to conduct an investigation with respect to an attestation, a complaining party may request that the activities attested to by the employer cease during the hearing process described in subparagraph (D). If such a request is made, the attesting employer shall be issued notice of such request and shall respond within 14 days to the notice. If the Secretary makes an initial determination that the complaining party's position is supported by a preponderance of the evidence submitted, the Secretary shall require immediately that the employer cease and desist from such activities until completion of the process described in subparagraph (D).

(ii) If the Secretary determines that reasonable cause exists to conduct an investigation with respect to a matter under the last sentence of paragraph (1), a complaining party may request that the activities of the employer cease during the hearing process described in subparagraph (D) unless the employer files with the Secretary of Labor an attestation under paragraph (1). If such a request is made, the employer shall be issued notice of such request and shall respond within 14 days to the notice. If the Secretary makes an initial determination that the complaining party's position is supported by a preponderance of the evidence submitted, the Secretary shall require immediately that the employer cease and desist from such activities until completion of the process described in subparagraph (D) unless the employer files with the Secretary of Labor an attestation under paragraph (1).

(D) Under the process established under subparagraph (B), the Secretary shall provide, within 180 days after the date a complaint is filed (or later for good cause shown), for a determination as to whether or not a basis exists to make a finding described in subparagraph (E). The Secretary shall provide notice of such determination to the interested parties and an opportunity for a hearing on the complaint within 60 days of the date of the determination.

(E) (i) If the Secretary of Labor finds, after notice and opportunity for a hearing, that an entity has failed to meet a condition attested to or has made a misrepresentation of material fact in the attestation, the Secretary shall notify the Attorney General of such finding and may, in addition, impose such other administrative remedies (including civil monetary penalties in an amount not to exceed $5,000 for each alien crewman performing unauthorized longshore work) as the Secretary determines to be appropriate. Upon receipt of such notice, the Attorney General shall not permit the vessels owned or chartered by such entity to enter any port of the United States during a period of up to 1 year.

(ii) If the Secretary of Labor finds, after notice and opportunity for a hearing, that, in the case described in the last sentence of paragraph (1), the performance of the particular activity is not described in subparagraph (B)(i), the Secretary shall notify the Attorney General of such finding and, thereafter, the attestation described in paragraph (1) shall be required of the employer for the performance of the particular activity.

(F) A finding by the Secretary of Labor under this paragraph that the performance of an activity by alien crewmen is not permitted under the prevailing practice of a local port shall preclude for one year the filing of a subsequent attestation concerning such activity in the port under paragraph (1).

(5) Except as provided in paragraph (5) of subsection (d), this subsection shall not apply to longshore work performed in the State of Alaska.

(d) State of Alaska exception.

(1) Subsection (a) shall not apply to a particular activity of longshore work at a particular location in the State of Alaska if an employer of alien crewmen has filed an attestation with the Secretary of Labor at least 30 days before the date of the first performance of the activity (or anytime up to 24 hours before the first performance of the activity, upon a showing that the employer could not have reasonably anticipated the need to file an attestation for that location at that time) setting forth facts and evidence to show that—

(A) the employer will make a bona fide request for United States longshore workers who are qualified and available in sufficient numbers to perform the activity at the particular time and location from the parties to whom notice has been provided under clauses (ii) and (iii) of subparagraph (D), except that—

(i) wherever two or more contract stevedoring companies have signed a joint collective bargaining agreement with a single labor organization described in subparagraph (D)(i), the employer may request longshore workers from only one of such contract stevedoring companies, and

(ii) a request for longshore workers to an operator of a private dock may be made only for longshore work to be performed at that dock and only if the operator meets the requirements of section 32 of the Longshoremen's and Harbor Workers' Compensation Act [33 USCS § 932];

(B) the employer will employ all those United States longshore workers made available in response to the request made pursuant to subparagraph (A) who are qualified and available in sufficient numbers and who are needed to perform the longshore activity at the particular time and location;

(C) the use of alien crewmembers for such activity is not intended or designed to influence an election of a bargaining representative for workers in the State of Alaska; and

(D) notice of the attestation has been provided by the employer to—

(i) labor organizations which have been recognized as exclusive bargaining representatives of United States longshore workers within the meaning of the National Labor Relations Act [29 USCS §§ 151 et seq.] and which make available or intend to make available workers to the particular location where the longshore work is to be performed,

(ii) contract stevedoring companies which employ or intend to employ United States longshore workers at that location, and

(iii) operators of private docks at which the employer will use longshore workers.

(2) (A) An employer filing an attestation under paragraph (1) who seeks to use alien crewmen to perform longshore work shall be responsible while the attestation is valid to make bona fide requests for United States longshore workers under paragraph (1)(A) and to employ United States longshore workers, as provided in paragraph (1)(B), before using alien crewmen to perform the activity or activities specified in the attestation, except that an employer shall not be required to request longshore workers from a party if that party has notified the employer in writing that it does not intend to make available United States longshore workers to the location at which the longshore work is to be performed.

(B) If a party that has provided such notice subsequently notifies the employer in writing that it is prepared to make available United States longshore workers who are qualified and available in sufficient numbers to perform the longshore activity to the location at which the longshore work is to be performed, then the employer's obligations to that party under subparagraphs (A) and (B) of paragraph (1) shall begin 60 days following the issuance of such notice.

(3) (A) In no case shall an employer filing an attestation be required—

(i) to hire less than a full work unit of United States longshore workers needed to perform the longshore activity;

(ii) to provide overnight accommodations for the longshore workers while employed; or

(iii) to provide transportation to the place of work, except where—

(I) surface transportation is available;

(II) such transportation may be safely accomplished;

(III) travel time to the vessel does not exceed one-half hour each way; and

(IV) travel distance to the vessel from the point of embarkation does not exceed 5 miles.

(B) In the cases of Wide Bay, Alaska, and Klawock/Craig, Alaska, the travel times and travel distances specified in subclauses (III) and (IV) of subparagraph (A)(iii) shall be extended to 45 minutes and 7 ½ miles, respectively, unless the party responding to the request for longshore workers agrees to the lesser time and distance limitations specified in those subclauses.

(4) Subject to subparagraphs (A) through (D) of subsection (c)(4), attestations filed under paragraph (1) of this subsection shall—

(A) expire at the end of the 1-year period beginning on the date the employer anticipates the longshore work to begin, as specified in the attestation filed with the Secretary of Labor, and

(B) apply to aliens arriving in the United States during such 1-year period if the owner, agent, consignee, master, or commanding officer states in each list under section 251 [8 USCS § 1281] that it continues to comply with the conditions in the attestation.

(5) (A) Except as otherwise provided by subparagraph (B), subsection (c)(3) and subparagraphs (A) through (E) of subsection (c)(4) shall apply to attestations filed under this subsection.

(B) The use of alien crewmen to perform longshore work in Alaska consisting of the use of an automated self-unloading conveyor belt or vacuum-actuated system on a vessel shall be governed by the provisions of subsection (c).

(6) For purposes of this subsection—

(A) the term "contract stevedoring companies" means those stevedoring companies licensed to do business in the State of Alaska that meet the requirements of section 32 of the Longshoremen's and Harbor Workers' Compensation Act (33 U.S.C. 932);

(B) the term "employer" includes any agent or representative designated by the employer; and

(C) the terms "qualified" and "available in sufficient numbers" shall be defined by reference to industry standards in the State of Alaska, including safety considerations.

(e) Reciprocity exception.

(1) In general. Subject to the determination of the Secretary of State pursuant to paragraph (2), the Attorney General shall permit an alien crewman to perform an activity constituting longshore work if—

(A) the vessel is registered in a country that by law, regulation, or in practice does not prohibit such activity by crewmembers aboard United States vessels; and

(B) nationals of a country (or countries) which by law, regulation, or in practice does not prohibit such activity by crewmembers aboard United States vessels hold a majority of the ownership interest in the vessel.

(2) Establishment of list. The Secretary of State shall, in accordance with section 553 of title 5, United States Code, compile and annually maintain a list, of longshore work by particular activity, of countries where performance of such a particular activity by crewmembers aboard United States vessels is prohibited by law, regulation, or in practice in the country. By not later than 90 days after the date of the enactment of this section [enacted Nov. 29, 1990], the Secretary shall publish a notice of proposed rulemaking to establish such list. The Secretary shall first establish such list by not later than 180 days after the date of the enactment of this section [enacted Nov. 29, 1990].

(3) "In practice" defined. For purposes of this subsection, the term "in practice" refers to an activity normally performed in such country during the one-year period preceding the arrival of such vessel into the United or coastal waters thereof.

HISTORY: (June 27, 1952, ch 477, Title II, Ch 6, § 258, as added Nov. 29, 1990, P. L. 101-649, Title II, Subtitle A, § 203(a)(1), 104 Stat. 5015; Dec. 12, 1991, P. L. 102-232, Title III, § 303(a)(4), 105 Stat. 1747; Dec. 17, 1993, P. L. 103-198, § 8(a), (b), 107 Stat. 2313; Dec. 20, 1993, P. L. 103-206, Title III, § 323(a), (b), 107 Stat. 2428; Oct. 25, 1994, P. L. 103-416, Title II, § 219(f), (gg), 108 Stat. 4317, 4319; Sept. 30, 1996, P. L. 104-208, Div C, Title VI, Subtitle E, § 671(e)(4)(B), 110 Stat. 3009-723.)

Chapter 7—Registration of Aliens

§ 261. [8 U.S.C. § 1301] Alien seeking entry; contents.

No visa shall be issued to any alien seeking to enter the United States until such alien has been registered in accordance with section 221(b) [8 USCS § 1201(b)].

HISTORY: (June 27, 1952, ch 477, Title II, Ch 7, § 261, 66 Stat. 223; Nov. 14, 1986, P. L. 99-653, § 8, 100 Stat. 3657; Oct. 24, 1988, P. L. 100-525, § 8(g), 102 Stat. 2617).)

§ 262. [8 U.S.C. § 1302] Registration of aliens.

(a) It shall be the duty of every alien now [June 27, 1952] or hereafter in the United States, who (1) is fourteen years of age or older, (2) has not been registered and fingerprinted under section 221(b) of this Act [8 USCS § 1201(b)] or section 30 or 31 of the Alien Registration Act, 1940, and (3) remains in the United States for thirty days or longer, to apply for registration and to be fingerprinted before the expiration of such thirty days.

(b) It shall be the duty of every parent or legal guardian of any alien now or hereafter in the United States, who (1) is less than fourteen years of age, (2) has not been registered under section 221(b) of this Act [8 USCS § 1201(b)] or section 30 or 31 of the Alien Registration Act, 1940, and (3) remains in the United States for thirty days or longer, to apply for the registration of such alien before the expiration of such thirty days. Whenever any alien attains his fourteenth birthday in the United States he shall, within thirty days thereafter, apply in person for registration and to be fingerprinted.

(c) The Attorney General may, in his discretion and on the basis of reciprocity pursuant to such regulations as he may prescribe, waive the requirement of fingerprinting specified in subsections (a) and (b) in the case of any nonimmigrant.

HISTORY: (June 27, 1952, ch 477, Title II, Ch 7, § 262, 66 Stat. 224; Nov. 14, 1986, P. L. 99-653, § 9, 100 Stat. 3657; Oct. 24, 1988, P. L. 100-525, § 8(h), 102 Stat. 261; Oct. 25, 1994, P. L. 103-416, Title II, § 219(n), 108 Stat. 4317.)

§ 263. [8 U.S.C. § 1303] Registration of special groups.

(a) Notwithstanding the provisions of sections 261 and 262 [8 USCS §§ 1301, 1302], the Attorney General is authorized to prescribe special regulations and forms for the registration and fingerprinting of (1) alien crewman, (2) holders of border-crossing identification cards, (3) aliens confined in institutions within the United States, (4) aliens under order of removal, (5) aliens who are or have been on criminal probation or criminal parole within the United States, and (6) aliens of any other class not lawfully admitted to the United States for permanent residence.

(b) The provisions of section 262 [8 USCS § 1302] and of this section shall not be applicable to any alien who is in the United States as a nonimmigrant under section 101(a)(15)(A) or 101(a)(15)(G) [8 USCS § 1101(a)(15)(A) or (G)] until the alien ceases to be entitled to such a nonimmigrant status.

HISTORY: (June 27, 1952, ch 477, Title II, Ch 7, § 263, 66 Stat. 224; Sept. 30, 1996, P. L. 104-208, Div C, Title III, Subtitle A, § 308(e)(1)(J), Subtitle B, § 323, 110 Stat. 3009-619, 3009-629.)

§ 264. [8 U.S.C. § 1304] Forms for registration and fingerprinting.

(a) Preparation; contents. The Attorney General and the Secretary of State jointly are authorized and directed to prepare forms for the registration of aliens under section 261 of this title [8 USCS § 1301], and the Attorney General is authorized and directed to prepare forms for the registration and fingerprinting of aliens under section 262 of this title [8 USCS § 1302]. Such forms shall contain inquiries with respect to (1) the date and place of entry of the alien into the United States; (2) activities in which he has been and intends to be engaged; (3) the length of time he expects to remain in the United States; (4) the police and criminal record, if any, of such alien; and (5) such additional matters as may be prescribed.

(b) Confidential nature. All registration and fingerprint records made under the provisions of this title shall be confidential, and shall be made available only (1) pursuant to section 287(f)(2) [8 USCS § 1357(f)(2)], and (2) to such persons or agencies as may be designated by the Attorney General.

(c) Information under oath. Every person required to apply for the registration of himself or another under this title shall submit under oath the information required for such registration. Any person authorized under regulations issued by the Attorney General to register aliens under this title shall be authorized to administer oaths for such purpose.

(d) Certificate of alien registration or alien receipt card. Every alien in the United States who has been registered and fingerprinted under the provisions of the Alien Registration Act, 1940, or under the provisions of this Act shall be issued a certificate of alien registration or an alien registration receipt card in such form and manner and at such time as shall be prescribed under regulations issued by the Attorney General.

(e) Personal possession of registration or receipt card; penalties. Every alien, eighteen years of age and over, shall at all times carry with him and have in his personal possession any certificate of alien registration or alien registration receipt card issued to him pursuant to subsection (d). Any alien who fails to comply with the provisions of this subsection shall be guilty of a misdemeanor and shall upon conviction for each offense be fined not to exceed $100 or be imprisoned not more than thirty days, or both.

(f) Inclusion of alien's social security account number. Notwithstanding any other provision of law, the Attorney General is authorized to require any alien to provide the alien's social security account number for purposes of inclusion in any record of the alien maintained by the Attorney General or the Service.

HISTORY: (June 27, 1952, ch 477, Title II, Ch 7, § 264, 66 Stat. 224; Nov. 14, 1986, P. L. 99-653, § 10, 100 Stat. 3657; Nov. 14, 1986, P. L. 99-653, § 10, 100 Stat. 3657; Oct. 24, 1988, P. L. 100-525, § 8(i), 102 Stat. 2517; Nov. 29, 1990, P. L. 101-649, Title V, Subtitle A, § 503(b)(2), 104 Stat. 5049; Sept. 30, 1996, P. L. 104-208, Div C, Title IV, Subtitle B, § 415, 110 Stat. 3009-669.)

§ 265. [8 U.S.C. § 1305] Notices of change of address.

(a) Notification of change. Each alien required to be registered under this title who is within the United States shall notify the Attorney General in writing of each change of address and new address within ten days from the date of such change and furnish with such notice such additional information as the Attorney General may require by regulation.

(b) Current address of natives of any one or more foreign states. The Attorney General may in his discretion, upon ten days notice, require the natives of any one or more foreign states, or any class or group thereof, who are within the United States and who are required to be registered under this title, to notify the Attorney General of their current addresses and furnish such additional information as the Attorney General may require.

(c) Notice to parent or legal guardian. In the case of an alien for whom a parent or legal guardian is required to apply for registration, the notice required by this section shall be given to such parent or legal guardian.

HISTORY: (June 27, 1952, ch 477, Title II, Ch 7, § 265, 66 Stat. 225; Dec. 29, 1981, P. L. 97-116, § 11, 95 Stat. 1617; Oct. 24, 1988, P. L. 100-525, § 9(o), 102 Stat. 2620.)

§ 266. [8 U.S.C. § 1306] Penalties.

(a) Willful failure to register. Any alien required to apply for registration and to be fingerprinted in the United States who willfully fails or refuses to make such application or to be fingerprinted, and any parent or legal guardian required to apply for the registration of any alien who willfully fails or refuses to file application for the registration of such alien shall be guilty of a misdemeanor and shall, upon conviction thereof, be fined not to exceed $1,000 or be imprisoned not more than six months, or both.

(b) Failure to notify change of address. Any alien or any parent or legal guardian in the United States of any alien who fails to give written notice to the Attorney General, as required by section 265 of this title [8 USCS § 1305], shall be guilty of a misdemeanor and shall, upon conviction thereof, be fined not to exceed $200 or be imprisoned not more than thirty days, or both. Irrespective of whether an alien is convicted and punished as herein provided, any alien who fails to give written notice to the Attorney General, as required by section 265 [8 USCS § 1305], shall be taken into custody and removed in the manner provided by chapter 4 of this title [8 USCS §§ 1221 et seq.], unless such alien establishes to the satisfaction of the Attorney General that such failure was reasonably excusable or was not willful.

(c) Fraudulent statements. Any alien or any parent or legal guardian of any alien, who files an application for registration containing statements known by him to be false, or who procures or attempts to procure registration of himself or another person through fraud, shall be guilty of a misdemeanor and shall, upon conviction thereof, be fined not to exceed $1,000, or be imprisoned not more than six months, or both; and any alien so convicted shall, upon the warrant of the Attorney General, be taken into custody and be removed in the manner provided in chapter 4 of this title [8 USCS §§ 1221 et seq.].

(d) Counterfeiting. Any person who with unlawful intent photographs, prints, or in any other manner makes, or executes, any engraving, photograph, print, or impression in the likeness of any certificate of alien registration or an alien registration receipt card or any colorable imitation thereof, except when and as authorized under such rules and regulations as may be prescribed by the Attorney General, shall upon conviction be fined not to exceed $5,000 or be imprisoned not more than five years, or both.

HISTORY: (June 27, 1952, ch 477, Title II, Ch 7, § 266, 66 Stat. 225; Sept. 30, 1996, P. L. 104-208, Div C, Title III, Subtitle A, § 308(e)(2)(G), (g)(9)(A), 110 Stat. 3009-620, 3009-624.)

Chapter 8—General Penalty Provisions

§ 271. [8 U.S.C. § 1321] Prevention of unauthorized landing of aliens.

(a) Failure to report; penalties [Caution: For inflation-adjusted civil monetary penalties, see8 CFR 280.53(c).]. It shall be the duty of every person, including the owners, masters, officers, and agents of vessels, aircraft, transportation lines, or international bridges or toll roads, other than transportation lines which may enter into a contract as provided in section 238 [233] [8 USCS § 1223], bringing an alien to, or providing a means for an alien to come to, the United States (including an alien crewman whose case is not covered by section 254(a) [8 USCS § 1284(a)]) to prevent the landing of such alien in the United States at a port of entry other than as designated by the Attorney General or at any time or place other than as designated by the immigration officers. Any such person, owner, master, officer, or agent who fails to comply with the foregoing requirements shall be liable to a penalty to be imposed by the Attorney General of $3,000 for each such violation, which may, in the discretion of the Attorney General, be remitted or mitigated by him in accordance with such proceedings as he shall by regulation prescribe. Such penalty shall be a lien upon the vessel or aircraft whose owner, master, officer, or agent violates the provisions of this section, and such vessel or aircraft may be libeled therefor in the appropriate United States court.

(b) Prima facie evidence. Proof that the alien failed to present himself at the time and place designated by the immigration officers shall be prima facie evidence that such alien has landed in the United States at a time or place other than as designated by the immigration officers.

(c) Liability of owners and operators of international bridges and toll roads.

(1) Any owner or operator of a railroad line, international Any owner or operator of a railroad line, international bridge, or toll road who establishes to the satisfaction of the Attorney General that the person has acted diligently and reasonably to fulfill the duty imposed by subsection (a) shall not be liable for the penalty described in such subsection, notwithstanding the failure of the person to prevent the unauthorized landing of any alien.

(2) (A) At the request of any person described in paragraph (1), At the request of any person described in paragraph (1), the Attorney General shall inspect any facility established, or any method utilized, at a point of entry into the United States by such person for the purpose of complying with subsection (a). The Attorney General shall approve any such facility or method (for such period of time as the Attorney General may prescribe) which the Attorney General determines is satisfactory for such purpose.

(B) Proof that any person described in paragraph (1) has diligently maintained any facility, or utilized any method, which has been approved by the Attorney General under subparagraph (A) (within the period for which the approval is effective) shall be prima facie evidence that such person acted diligently and reasonably to fulfill the duty imposed by subsection (a) (within the meaning of paragraph (1) of this subsection).

HISTORY: (June 27, 1952, ch 477, Title II, subch 8, § 271, 66 Stat. 226; Nov. 6, 1986, P. L. 99-603, Title I, Part B, § 114, 100 Stat. 3383; Nov. 29, 1990, P. L. 101-649, Title V, Subtitle D, § 543(a)(8), 104 Stat. 5058.)

§ 272. [8 U.S.C. § 1322] Bringing in aliens subject to denial of admission on a health-related ground; persons liable; clearance papers; exceptions; "person" defined.

(a) [Caution: For inflation-adjusted civil monetary penalties, see 8 CFR 280.53(c).] Any person who shall bring to the United States an alien (other than an alien crewman) who is inadmissible under section 212(a)(1) [8 USCS § 1182(a)(1)] shall pay Commissioner for each and every alien so afflicted the sum of $3,000 unless (1) the alien was in possession of a valid, unexpired immigrant visa, or (2) the alien was allowed to land in the United States, or (3) the alien was in possession of a valid unexpired nonimmigrant visa or other document authorizing such alien to apply for temporary admission to the United States or an unexpired reentry permit issued to him, and (A) such application was made within one hundred and twenty days of the date of issuance of the visa or other document, or in the case of an alien in possession of a reentry permit, within one hundred and twenty days of the date on which the alien was last examined and admitted by the Service, or (B) in the event the application was made later than one hundred and twenty days of the date of issuance of the visa or other document or such examination and admission, if such person establishes to the satisfaction of the Attorney General that the existence of the condition causing inadmissibility could not have been detected by the exercise of due diligence prior to the alien's embarkation.

(b) No vessel or aircraft shall be granted clearance papers pending determination of the question of liability to the payment of any fine under this section, or while the fines remain unpaid, nor shall such fines be remitted or refunded; but clearance may be granted prior to the determination of such question upon the deposit of a sum sufficient to cover such fines or of a bond with sufficient surety to secure the payment thereof, approved by the Commissioner.

(c) Nothing contained in this section shall be construed to subject transportation companies to a fine for bringing to ports of entry in the United States aliens who are entitled by law to exemption from the provisions of section 212(a) [8 USCS § 1182(a)].

(d) As used in this section, the term "person" means the owner, master, agent, commanding officer, charterer, or consignee of any vessel or aircraft.

HISTORY: (JJune 27, 1952, ch 477, Title 11, Ch 8, § 272, 66 Stat. 226; Oct. 3, 1965, P. L. 89-236, § 18, 79 Stat. 920; Nov. 29, 1990, P. L. 101-649, Title V, Subtitle D, § 543(a)(9), Title VI, § 603(a)(15), 104 Stat. 5058, 5083; Dec. 12, 1991, P. L. 102-232, Title III, § 307(l)(7), 105 Stat. 1757; Oct. 25, 1994, P. L. 103-416, Title II, § 219(o), 108 Stat. 4317; Sept. 30, 1996, P. L. 104-208, Div C, Title III, Subtitle A, § 308(d)(3)(A), (4)(I)(i), 110 Stat. 3009-617, 3009-618.)

§ 273. [8 U.S.C. § 1323] Unlawful bringing of aliens into United States.

(a) Persons liable.

(1) It shall be unlawful for any person, including any transportation company, or the owner, master, commanding officer, agent, charterer, or consignee of any vessel or aircraft, to bring to the United States from any place outside thereof (other than from foreign contiguous territory) any alien who does not have a valid passport and an unexpired visa, if a visa was required under this Act or regulations issued thereunder.

(2) It is unlawful for an owner, agent, master, commanding officer, person in charge, purser, or consignee of a vessel or aircraft who is bringing an alien (except an alien crewmember) to the United States to take any consideration to be kept or returned contingent on whether an alien is admitted to, or ordered removed from, the United States.

(b) Evidence [Caution: For inflation-adjusted civil monetary penalties, see8 CFR 280.53(c).]. If it appears to the satisfaction of the Attorney General that any alien has been so brought, such person, or transportation company, or the master, commanding officer, agent, owner, charterer, or consignee of any such vessel or aircraft, shall pay to the Commissioner a fine of $3,000 for each alien so brought and, except in the case of any such alien who is admitted, or permitted to land temporarily, in addition, an amount equal to that paid by such alien for his transportation from the initial point of departure, indicated in his ticket, to the port of arrival, such latter fine to be delivered by the Commissioner to the alien on whose account the assessment is made. No vessel or aircraft shall be granted clearance pending the determination of the liability to the payment of such fine or while such fine remains unpaid, except that clearance may be granted prior to the determination of such question upon the deposit of an amount sufficient to cover such fine, or of a bond with sufficient surety to secure the payment thereof approved by the Commissioner.

(c) Remission or refund. Except as provided in subsection (e), such fine shall not be remitted or refunded, unless it appears to the satisfaction of the Attorney General that such person, and the owner, master, commanding officer, agent, charterer, and consignee of the vessel or aircraft, prior to the departure of the vessel or aircraft from the last port outside the United States, did not know, and could not have ascertained, by the exercise of reasonable diligence, that the individual transported was an alien and that a valid passport or visa was required.

(d) [Repealed]

(e) Reduction, refund, or waiver. A fine under this section may be reduced, refunded, or waived under such regulations as the Attorney General shall prescribe in cases in which—

(1) the carrier demonstrates that it had screened all passengers on the vessel or aircraft in accordance with procedures prescribed by the Attorney General, or

(2) circumstances exist that the Attorney General determines would justify such reduction, refund, or waiver.

HISTORY: (June 27, 1952, ch 477, Title II, Ch 8, § 273, 66 Stat. 227; Nov. 29, 1990, P. L. 101-649, Title II, Subtitle A, § 201(b), Title V, Subtitle D, § 543(a)(10), 104 Stat. 5014, 5058; Dec. 12, 1991, P. L. 102-232, Title III, § 306(c)(4)(B), 105 Stat. 1752; Oct. 25, 1994, P. L. 103-416, Title II, §§ 209(a), 216, 219(p), 108 Stat. 4312, 4315, 4317; Sept. 30, 1996, P. L. 104-208, Div C, Title III, Subtitle A, § 308(c)(3), (e)(13), Subtitle F, § 371(b)(8), Title VI, Subtitle E, § 671(b)(6), (7), 110 Stat. 3009-616, 3009-620, 3009-645, 3009-722.)

§ 274. [8 U.S.C. § 1324] Bringing in and harboring certain aliens.

(a) Criminal penalties.

(1) (A) Any person who—

(i) knowing that a person is an alien, brings to or attempts to bring to the United States in any manner whatsoever such person at a place other than a designated port of entry or place other than as designated by the Commissioner, regardless of whether such alien has received prior official authorization to come to, enter, or reside in the United States and regardless of any future official action which may be taken with respect to such alien;

(ii) knowing or in reckless disregard of the fact that an alien has come to, entered, or remains in the United States in violation of law, transports, or moves or attempts to transport or move such alien within the United States by means of transportation or otherwise, in furtherance of such violation of law;

(iii) knowing or in reckless disregard of the fact that an alien has come to, entered, or remains in the United States in violation of law, conceals, harbors, or shields from detection, or attempts to conceal, harbor, or shield from detection, such alien in any place, including any building or any means of transportation;

(iv) encourages or induces an alien to come to, enter, or reside in the United States, knowing or in reckless disregard of the fact that such coming to, entry, or residence is or will be in violation of law; or

(v) (I) engages in any conspiracy to commit any of the preceding acts, or

(II) aids or abets the commission of any of the preceding acts,

shall be punished as provided in subparagraph (B).

(B) A person who violates subparagraph (A) shall, for each alien in respect to whom such a violation occurs—

(i) in the case of a violation of subparagraph (A)(i) or (v)(I) or in the case of a violation of subparagraph (A)(ii), (iii), or (iv) in which the offense was done for the purpose of commercial advantage or private financial gain, be fined under title 18, United States Code, imprisoned not more than 10 years, or both;

(ii) in the case of a violation of subparagraph (A) (ii), (iii), (iv), or (v)(II), be fined under title 18, United States Code, imprisoned not more than 5 years, or both;

(iii) in the case of a violation of subparagraph (A) (i), (ii), (iii), (iv), or (v) during and in relation to which the person causes serious bodily injury (as defined in section 1365 of title 18, United States Code) to, or places in jeopardy the life of, any person, be fined under title 18, United States Code, imprisoned not more than 20 years, or both; and

(iv) in the case of a violation of subparagraph (A) (i), (ii), (iii), (iv), or (v) resulting in the death of any person, be punished by death or imprisoned for any term of years or for life, fined under title 18, United States Code, or both.

(C) It is not a violation of clauses [clause] (ii) or (iii) of subparagraph (A), or of clause (iv) of subparagraph (A) except where a person encourages or induces an alien to come to or enter the United States, for a religious denomination having a bona fide nonprofit, religious organization in the United States, or the agents or officers of such denomination or organization, to encourage, invite, call, allow, or enable an alien who is present in the United States to perform the vocation of a minister or missionary for the denomination or organization in the United States as a volunteer who is not compensated as an employee, notwithstanding the provision of room, board, travel, medical assistance, and other basic living expenses, provided the minister or missionary has been a member of the denomination for at least one year.

(2) Any person who, knowing or in reckless disregard of the fact that an alien has not received prior official authorization to come to, enter, or reside in the United States, brings to or attempts to bring to the United States in any manner whatsoever, such alien, regardless of any official action which may later be taken with respect to such alien shall, for each alien in respect to whom a violation of this paragraph occurs—

(A) be fined in accordance with title 18, United States Code, or imprisoned not more than 1 year, or both; or

(B) in the case of—

(i) an offense committed with the intent or with reason to believe that the alien unlawfully brought into the United States will commit an offense against the United States or any State punishable by imprisonment for more than 1 year,

(ii) an offense done for the purpose of commercial advantage or private financial gain, or

(iii) an offense in which the alien is not upon arrival immediately brought and presented to an appropriate immigration officer at a designated port of entry,

be fined under title 18, United States Code, and shall be imprisoned, in the case of a first or second violation of subparagraph (B)(iii), not more than 10 years, in the case of a first or second violation of subparagraph (B)(i) or (B)(ii), not less than 3 nor more than 10 years, and for any other violation, not less than 5 nor more than 15 years.

(3) (A) Any person who, during any 12-month period, knowingly hires for employment at least 10 individuals with actual knowledge that the individuals are aliens described in subparagraph (B) shall be fined under title 18, United States Code, or imprisoned for not more than 5 years, or both.

(B) An alien described in this subparagraph is an alien who—

(i) is an unauthorized alien (as defined in section 274A(h)(3) [8 USCS § 1324a(h)(3)]), and

(ii) has been brought into the United States in violation of this subsection.

(4) In the case of a person who has brought aliens into the United States in violation of this subsection, the sentence otherwise provided for may be increased by up to 10 years if—

(A) the offense was part of an ongoing commercial organization or enterprise;

(B) aliens were transported in groups of 10 or more; and

(C) (i) aliens were transported in a manner that endangered their lives; or

(ii) the aliens presented a life-threatening health risk to people in the United States.

(b) Seizure and forfeiture.

(1) In general. Any conveyance, including any vessel, vehicle, or aircraft, that has been or is being used in the commission of a violation of subsection (a), the gross proceeds of such violation, and any property traceable to such conveyance or proceeds, shall be seized and subject to forfeiture.

(2) Applicable procedures. Seizures and forfeitures under this subsection shall be governed by the provisions of chapter 46 of title 18, United States Code [18 USCS §§ 981 et seq.], relating to civil forfeitures, including section 981(d) of such title, except that such duties as are imposed upon the Secretary of the Treasury under the customs laws described in that section shall be performed by such officers, agents, and other persons as may be designated for that purpose by the Attorney General.

(3) Prima facie evidence in determinations of violations. In determining whether a violation of subsection (a) has occurred, any of the following shall be prima facie evidence that an alien involved in the alleged violation had not received prior official authorization to come to, enter, or reside in the United States or that

such alien had come to, entered, or remained in the United States in violation of law:

(A) Records of any judicial or administrative proceeding in which that alien's status was an issue and in which it was determined that the alien had not received prior official authorization to come to, enter, or reside in the United States or that such alien had come to, entered, or remained in the United States in violation of law.

(B) Official records of the Service or of the Department of State showing that the alien had not received prior official authorization to come to, enter, or reside in the United States or that such alien had come to, entered, or remained in the United States in violation of law.

(C) Testimony, by an immigration officer having personal knowledge of the facts concerning that alien's status, that the alien had not received prior official authorization to come to, enter, or reside in the United States or that such alien had come to, entered, or remained in the United States in violation of law.

(c) Authority to arrest. No officer or person shall have authority to make any arrest for a violation of any provision of this section except officers and employees of the Service designated by the Attorney General, either individually or as a member of a class, and all other officers whose duty it is to enforce criminal laws.

(d) Admissibility of videotaped witness testimony. Notwithstanding any provision of the Federal Rules of Evidence, the videotaped (or otherwise audiovisually preserved) deposition of a witness to a violation of subsection (a) who has been deported or otherwise expelled from the United States, or is otherwise unable to testify, may be admitted into evidence in an action brought for that violation if the witness was available for cross examination and the deposition otherwise complies with the Federal Rules of Evidence.

(e) Outreach program. The Secretary of Homeland Security, in consultation with the Attorney General and the Secretary of State, as appropriate, shall develop and implement an outreach program to educate the public in the United States and abroad about the penalties for bringing in and harboring aliens in violation of this section.

HISTORY: (June 27, 1952, ch 477, Title II, Ch 8, § 274, 66 Stat. 228; Nov. 2, 1978, P. L. 95-582, § 2, 92 Stat. 2479; Dec. 29, 1981, P. L. 97-116, § 12, 985 Stat. 1617; Nov. 6, 1986, P. L. 99-603, Title I, Part B, § 112, 100 Stat. 3381; Oct. 24, 1988, P. L. 100-525, § 2(d)(1), 102 Stat. 2610; Sept. 13, 1994, P. L. 103-322, Title VI, § 60024, 108 Stat. 1981; Sept. 30, 1996, P. L. 104-208, Div C, Title II, Subtitle A, § 203(a)–(d), Subtitle B, § 219, Title VI, Subtitle E, § 671(a)(1), 110 Stat. 3009-565, 3009-574, 3009-721; April 25, 2000, P. L. 106-185, § 18(a), 114 Stat. 222; Dec. 17, 2004, P. L. 108-458, Title V, Subtitle D, § 5401, 118 Stat. 3737; Nov. 10, 2005, P. L. 109-97, Title VII, § 796, 119 Stat. 2165.)

§ 274A. [8 U.S.C. § 1324a] Unlawful employment of aliens.

(a) Making employment of unauthorized aliens unlawful.

(1) In general. It is unlawful for a person or other entity—

(A) to hire, or to recruit or refer for a fee, for employment in the United States an alien knowing the alien is an unauthorized alien (as defined in subsection (h)(3)) with respect to such employment, or

(B) (i) to hire for employment in the United States an individual without complying with the requirements of subsection (b) or (ii) if the person or entity is an agricultural association, agricultural employer, or farm labor contractor (as defined in section 3 of the Migrant and Seasonal Agricultural Worker Protection Act [29 USCS § 1802], to hire, or to recruit or refer for a fee, for employment in the United States an individual without complying with the requirements of subsection (b).

(2) Continuing employment. It is unlawful for a person or other entity, after hiring an alien for employment in accordance with paragraph (1), to continue to employ the alien in the United States knowing the alien is (or has become) an unauthorized alien with respect to such employment.

(3) Defense. A person or entity that establishes that it has complied in good faith with the requirements of subsection (b) with respect to the hiring, recruiting, or referral for employment of an alien in the United States has established an affirmative defense that the person or entity has not violated paragraph (1)(A) with respect to such hiring, recruiting, or referral.

(4) Use of labor through contract. For purposes of this section, a person or other entity who uses a contract, subcontract, or exchange, entered into, renegotiated, or extended after the date of the enactment of this section, to obtain the labor of an alien in the United States knowing that the alien is an unauthorized alien (as defined in subsection (h)(3)) with respect to performing such labor, shall be considered to have hired the alien for employment in the United States in violation of paragraph (1)(A).

(5) Use of State employment agency documentation. For purposes of paragraphs (1)(B) and (3), a person or entity shall be deemed to have complied with the requirements of subsection (b) with respect to the hiring of an individual who was referred for such employment by a State employment agency (as defined by the Attorney General), if the person or entity has and retains (for the period and in the manner described in subsection (b)(3)) appropriate documentation of such referral by that agency, which documentation certifies that the agency has complied with the procedures specified in subsection (b) with respect to the individual's referral.

(6) Treatment of documentation for certain employees.

(A) In general. For purposes of this section, if—

(i) an individual is a member of a collective-bargaining unit and is employed, under a collective bargaining agreement entered into between one or more employee organizations and an association of two or more employers, by an employer that is a member of such association, and

(ii) within the period specified in subparagraph (B), another employer that is a member of the association (or an agent of such association on behalf of the employer) has complied with the requirements of subsection (b) with respect to the employment of the individual,

the subsequent employer shall be deemed to have complied with the requirements of subsection (b) with respect to the hiring of the employee and shall not be liable for civil penalties described in subsection (e)(5).

(B) Period. The period described in this subparagraph is 3 years, or, if less, the period of time that the individual is authorized to be employed in the United States.

(C) Liability.

(i) In general. If any employer that is a member of an association hires for employment in the United States an individual and relies upon the provisions of subparagraph (A) to comply with the requirements of subsection (b) and the individual is an alien not authorized to work in the United States, then for the purposes of paragraph (1)(A), subject to clause (ii), the employer shall be presumed to have known at the time of hiring or afterward that the individual was an alien not authorized to work in the United States.

(ii) Rebuttal of presumption. The presumption established by clause (i) may be rebutted by the employer only through the presentation of clear and convincing evidence that the employer did not know (and could not reasonably have known) that the individual at the time of hiring or afterward was an alien not authorized to work in the United States.

(iii) Exception. Clause (i) shall not apply in any prosecution under subsection (f)(1).

(7) Application to Federal Government. For purposes of this section, the term "entity" includes an entity in any branch of the Federal Government.

(b) Employment verification system. The requirements referred to in paragraphs (1)(B) and (3) of subsection (a) are, in the case of a person or other entity hiring, recruiting, or referring an individual for employment in the United States, the requirements specified in the following three paragraphs:

(1) Attestation after examination of documentation.

(A) In general. The person or entity must attest, under penalty of perjury and on a form designated or established by the Attorney General by regulation, that it has verified that the individual is not an unauthorized alien by examining—

(i) a document described in subparagraph (B), or

(ii) a document described in subparagraph (C) and a document described in subparagraph (D).

Such attestation may be manifested by either a hand-written or an electronic signature. A person or entity has complied with the requirement of this paragraph with respect to examination of a document if the document reasonably appears on its face to be genuine. If an individual provides a document or combination of documents that reasonably appears on its face to be genuine and that is sufficient to meet the requirements of the first sentence of this paragraph, nothing in this paragraph shall be construed as requiring the person or entity to solicit the production of any other document or as requiring the individual to produce such another document.

(B) Documents establishing both employment authorization and identity. A document described in this subparagraph is an individual's—

(i) United States passport; [or]

(ii) resident alien card, alien registration card, or other document designated by the Attorney General, if the document—

(I) contains a photograph of the individual and such other personal identifying information relating to the individual as the Attorney General finds, by regulation, sufficient for purposes of this subsection,

(II) is evidence of authorization of employment in the United States, and

(III) contains security features to make it resistant to tampering, counterfeiting, and fraudulent use.

(C) Documents evidencing employment authorization. A document described in this subparagraph is an individual's—

(i) social security account number card (other than such a card which specifies on the face that the issuance of the card does not authorize employment in the United States); or

(ii) other documentation evidencing authorization of employment in the United States which the Attorney General finds, by regulation, to be acceptable for purposes of this section.

(D) Documents establishing identity of individual. A document described in this subparagraph is an individual's—

(i) driver's license or similar document issued for the purpose of identification by a State, if it contains a photograph of the individual or such other personal identifying information relating to the individual as the Attorney General finds, by regulation, sufficient for purposes of this section; or

(ii) in the case of individuals under 16 years of age or in a State which does not provide for issuance of an identification document (other than a driver's license) referred to in clause (i), documentation of personal identity of such other type as the Attorney General finds, by regulation, provides a reliable means of identification.

(E) Authority to prohibit use of certain documents. If the Attorney General finds, by regulation, that any document described in subparagraph (B), (C), or (D) as establishing employment authorization or identity does not reliably establish such authorization or identity or is being used fraudulently to an unacceptable degree, the Attorney General may prohibit or place conditions on its use for purposes of this subsection.

(2) Individual attestation of employment authorization. The individual must attest, under penalty of perjury on the form designated or established for purposes of paragraph (1), that the individual is a citizen or national of the United States, an alien lawfully admitted for permanent residence, or an alien who is authorized under this Act or by the Attorney General to be hired, recruited, or referred for such employment. Such attestation may be manifested by either a hand-written or an electronic signature.

(3) Retention of verification form. After completion of such form in accordance with paragraphs (1) and (2),

the person or entity must retain a paper, microfiche, microfilm, or electronic version of the form and make it available for inspection by officers of the Service, the Special Counsel for Immigration-Related Unfair Employment Practices or the Department of Labor during a period beginning on the date of the hiring, recruiting, or referral of the individual and ending—

(A) in the case of the recruiting or referral for a fee (without hiring) of an individual, three years after the date of the recruiting or referral, and

(B) in the case of the hiring of an individual—

(i) three years after the date of such hiring, or

(ii) one year after the date the individual's employment is terminated,

whichever is later.

(4) Copying of documentation permitted. Notwithstanding any other provision of law, the person or entity may copy a document presented by an individual pursuant to this subsection and may retain the copy, but only (except as otherwise permitted under law) for the purpose of complying with the requirements of this subsection.

(5) Limitation on use of attestation form. A form designated or established by the Attorney General under this subsection and any information contained in or appended to such form, may not be used for purposes other than for enforcement of this Act and sections 1001, 1028, 1546, and 1621 of title 18, United States Code.

(6) Good faith compliance.

(A) In general. Except as provided in subparagraphs (B) and (C), a person or entity is considered to have complied with a requirement of this subsection notwithstanding a technical or procedural failure to meet such requirement if there was a good faith attempt to comply with the requirement.

(B) Exception if failure to correct after notice. Subparagraph (A) shall not apply if—

(i) the Service (or another enforcement agency) has explained to the person or entity the basis for the failure,

(ii) the person or entity has been provided a period of not less than 10 business days (beginning after the date of the explanation) within which to correct the failure, and

(iii) the person or entity has not corrected the failure voluntarily within such period.

(C) Exception for pattern or practice violators. Subparagraph (A) shall not apply to a person or entity that has or is engaging in a pattern or practice of violations of subsection (a)(1)(A) or (a)(2).

(c) No authorization of national identification cards. Nothing in this section shall be construed to authorize, directly or indirectly, the issuance or use of national identification cards or the establishment of a national identification card.

(d) Evaluation and changes in employment verification system.

(1) Presidential monitoring and improvements in system.

(A) Monitoring. The President shall provide for the monitoring and evaluation of the degree to which the employment verification system established under subsection (b) provides a secure system to determine employment eligibility in the United States and shall examine the suitability of existing Federal and State identification systems for use for this purpose.

(B) Improvements to establish secure system. To the extent that the system established under subsection (b) is found not to be a secure system to determine employment eligibility in the United States, the President shall, subject to paragraph (3) and taking into account the results of any demonstration projects conducted under paragraph (4), implement such changes in (including additions to) the requirements of subsection (b) as may be necessary to establish a secure system to determine employment eligibility in the United States. Such changes in the system may be implemented only if the changes conform to the requirements of paragraph (2).

(2) Restrictions on changes in system. Any change the President proposes to implement under paragraph (1) in the verification system must be designed in a manner so the verification system, as so changed, meets the following requirements:

(A) Reliable determination of identity. The system must be capable of reliably determining whether—

(i) a person with the identity claimed by an employee or prospective employee is eligible to work, and

(ii) the employee or prospective employee is claiming the identity of another individual.

(B) using of counterfeit-resistant documents. If the system requires that a document be presented to or examined by an employer, the document must be in a form which is resistant to counterfeiting and tampering.

(C) Limited use of system. Any personal information utilized by the system may not be made available to Government agencies, employers, and other persons except to the extent necessary to verify that an individual is not an unauthorized alien.

(D) Privacy of information. The system must protect the privacy and security of personal information and identifiers utilized in the system.

(E) Limited denial of verification. A verification that an employee or prospective employee is eligible to be employed in the United States may not be withheld or revoked under the system for any reason other than that the employee or prospective employee is an unauthorized alien.

(F) Limited use for law enforcement purposes. The system may not be used for law enforcement purposes, other than for enforcement of this Act or sections 1001, 1028, 1546, and 1621 of title 18, United States Code.

(G) Restriction on use of new documents. If the system requires individuals to present a new card or other document (designed specifically for use for this purpose) at the time of hiring, recruitment, or referral, then such document may not be required to be presented for any purpose other than under this Act (or enforcement of sections 1001, 1028, 1546, and 1621 of title 18, United States Code) nor to be carried on one's person.

(3) Notice to Congress before implementing changes.

(A) In general. The President may not implement any change under paragraph (1) unless at least—

(i) 60 days,

(ii) one year, in the case of a major change described in subparagraph (D)(iii), or

(iii) two years, in the case of a major change described in clause (i) or (ii) of subparagraph (D),

before the date of implementation of the change, the President has prepared and transmitted to the Committee on the Judiciary of the House of Representatives and to the Committee on the Judiciary of the Senate a written report setting forth the proposed change. If the President proposes to make any change regarding social security account number cards, the President shall transmit to the Committee on Ways and Means of the House of Representatives and to the Committee on Finance of the Senate a written report setting forth the proposed change. The President promptly shall cause to have printed in the Federal Register the substance of any major change (described in subparagraph (D)) proposed and reported to Congress.

(B) Contents of report. In any report under subparagraph (A) the President shall include recommendations for the establishment of civil and criminal sanctions for unauthorized use or disclosure of the information or identifiers contained in such system.

(C) Congressional review of major changes.

(i) Hearings and review. The Committees on the Judiciary of the House of Representatives and of the Senate shall cause to have printed in the Congressional Record the substance of any major change described in subparagraph (D), shall hold hearings respecting the feasibility and desirability of implementing such a change, and, within the two year period before implementation, shall report to their respective Houses findings on whether or not such a change should be implemented.

(ii) Congressional action. No major change may be implemented unless the Congress specifically provides, in an appropriations or other Act, for funds for implementation of the change.

(D) Major changes requiring two years notice and Congressional review. As used in this paragraph, the term "major change" means a change which would—

(i) require an individual to present a new card or other document (designed specifically for use for this purpose) at the time of hiring, recruitment, or referral,

(ii) provide for a telephone verification system under which an employer, recruiter, or referrer must transmit to a Federal official information concerning the immigration status of prospective employees and the official transmits to the person, and the person must record, a verification code, or

(iii) require any change in any card used for accounting purposes under the Social Security Act [42 USCS §§ 301 et seq.], including any change requiring that the only social security account number cards which may be presented in order to comply with subsection (b)(1)(C)(i) are such cards as are in a counterfeit-resistant form consistent with the second sentence of section 205(c)(2)(D) of the Social Security Act [42 USCS § 405(c)(2)(D)].

(E) General revenue funding of Social Security card changes. Any costs incurred in developing and implementing any change described in subparagraph (D)(iii) for purposes of this subsection shall not be paid for out of any trust fund established under the Social Security Act [42 USCS §§ 301 et seq.].

(4) Demonstration projects.

(A) Authority. The President may undertake demonstration projects (consistent with paragraph (2)) of different changes in the requirements of subsection (b). No such project may extend over a period of longer than five years.

(B) Reports on projects. The President shall report to the Congress on the results of demonstration projects conducted under this paragraph.

(e) Compliance [Caution: For inflation-adjusted civil monetary penalties, see8 CFR 274a.10.].

(1) Complaints and investigations. The Attorney General shall establish procedures—

(A) for individuals and entities to file written, signed complaints respecting potential violations of subsection (a) or (g)(1),

(B) for the investigation of those complaints which, on their face, have a substantial probability of validity,

(C) for the investigation of such other violations of subsection (a) or (g)(1) as the Attorney General determines to be appropriate, and

(D) for the designation in the Service of a unit which has, as its primary duty, the prosecution of cases of violations of subsection (a) or (g)(1) under this subsection.

(2) Authority in investigations. In conducting investigations and hearings under this subsection—

(A) immigration officers and administrative law judges shall have reasonable access to examine evidence of any person or entity being investigated,

(B) administrative law judges may, if necessary, compel by subpoena the attendance of witnesses and the production of evidence at any designated place or hearing, and

(C) immigration officers designated by the Commissioner may compel by subpoena the attendance of witnesses and the production of evidence at any designated place prior to the filing of a complaint in a case under paragraph (2).

In case of contumacy or refusal to obey a subpoena lawfully issued under this paragraph and upon application of the Attorney General, an appropriate district court of the United States may issue an order requiring compliance with such subpoena and any failure to obey such order may be punished by such court as a contempt thereof.

(3) Hearing.

(A) In general. Before imposing an order described in paragraph (4), (5), or (6) against a person or entity under this subsection for a violation of subsection (a), the Attorney General shall provide the person or entity with notice and, upon request made within a reasonable time (of not less than 30 days, as established by the Attorney General) of the date of the notice, a hearing respecting the violation.

(B) Conduct of hearing. Any hearing so requested shall be conducted before an administrative law judge. The hearing shall be conducted in accordance with the requirements of section 554 of title 5, United States Code. The hearing shall be held at the nearest practicable place to the place where the person or entity resides or of the place where the alleged violation occurred. If no hearing is so requested, the Attorney General's imposition of the order shall constitute a final and unappealable order.

(C) Issuance of orders. If the administrative law judge determines, upon the preponderance of the evidence received, that a person or entity named in the complaint has violated subsection (a), the administrative law judge shall state his findings of fact and issue and cause to be served on such person or entity an order described in paragraph (4), (5), or (6).

(4) Cease and desist order with civil money penalty for hiring, recruiting, and referral violations. With respect to a violation of subsection (a)(1)(A) or (a)(2), the order under this subsection—

(A) shall require the person or entity to cease and desist from such violations and to pay a civil penalty in an amount of—

(i) not less than $250 and not more than $2,000 for each unauthorized alien with respect to whom a violation of either such subsection occurred,

(ii) not less than $2,000 and not more than $5,000 for each such alien in the case of a person or entity previously subject to one order under this paragraph, or

(iii) not less than $3,000 and not more than $10,000 for each such alien in the case of a person or entity previously subject to more than one order under this paragraph; and

(B) may require the person or entity—

(i) to comply with the requirements of subsection (b) (or subsection (d) if applicable) with respect to individuals hired (or recruited or referred for employment for a fee) during a period of up to three years, and

(ii) to take such other remedial action as is appropriate.

In applying this subsection in the case of a person or entity composed of distinct, physically separate subdivisions each of which provides separately for the hiring, recruiting, or referring for employment, without reference to the practices of, and not under the control of or common control with, another subdivision, each such subdivision shall be considered a separate person or entity.

(5) Order for civil money penalty for paperwork violations. With respect to a violation of subsection (a)(1)(B), the order under this subsection shall require the person or entity to pay a civil penalty in an amount of not less than $100 and not more than $1,000 for each individual with respect to whom such violation occurred. In determining the amount of the penalty, due consideration shall be given to the size of the business of the employer being charged, the good faith of the employer, the seriousness of the violation, whether or not the individual was an unauthorized alien, and the history of previous violations.

(6) Order for prohibited indemnity bonds. With respect to a violation of subsection (g)(1), the order under this subsection may provide for the remedy described in subsection (g)(2).

(7) Administrative appellate review. The decision and order of an administrative law judge shall become the final agency decision and order of the Attorney General unless either (A) within 30 days, an official delegated by regulation to exercise review authority over the decision and order modifies or vacates the decision and order, or (B) within 30 days of the date of such a modification or vacation (or within 60 days of the date of decision and order of an administrative law judge if not so modified or vacated) the decision and order is referred to the Attorney General pursuant to regulations, in which case the decision and order of the Attorney General shall become the final agency decision and order under this subsection. The Attorney General may not delegate the Attorney General's authority under this paragraph to any entity which has review authority over immigration-related matters.

(8) Judicial review. A person or entity adversely affected by a final order respecting an assessment may, within 45 days after the date the final order is issued, file a petition in the Court of Appeals for the appropriate circuit for review of the order.

(9) Enforcement of orders. If a person or entity fails to comply with a final order issued under this subsection against the person or entity, the Attorney General shall file a suit to seek compliance with the order in any appropriate district court of the United States. In any such suit, the validity and appropriateness of the final order shall not be subject to review.

(f) Criminal penalties and injunctions for pattern or practice violations.

(1) Criminal penalty. Any person or entity which engages in a pattern or practice of violations of subsection (a)(1)(A) or (a)(2) shall be fined not more than $3,000 for each unauthorized alien with respect to whom such a violation occurs, imprisoned for not more than six months for the entire pattern or practice, or both, notwithstanding the provisions of any other Federal law relating to fine levels.

(2) Enjoining of pattern or practice violations. Whenever the Attorney General has reasonable cause to believe that a person or entity is engaged in a pattern or practice of employment, recruitment, or referral in violation of paragraph (1)(A) or (2) of subsection (a), the Attorney General may bring a civil action in the appropriate district court of the United States requesting such relief, including a permanent or temporary injunction, restraining order, or other order against the person or entity, as the Attorney General deems necessary.

(g) Prohibition of indemnity bonds.

(1) Prohibition. It is unlawful for a person or other entity, in the hiring, recruiting, or referring for employment of any individual, to require the individual to post a bond or security, to pay or agree to pay an amount, or otherwise to provide a financial guarantee

or indemnity, against any potential liability arising under this section relating to such hiring, recruiting, or referring of the individual.

(2) Civil penalty. Any person or entity which is determined, after notice and opportunity for an administrative hearing under subsection (e), to have violated paragraph (1) shall be subject to a civil penalty of $1,000 for each violation and to an administrative order requiring the return of any amounts received in violation of such paragraph to the employee or, if the employee cannot be located, to the general fund of the Treasury.

(h) Miscellaneous provisions.

(1) Documentation. In providing documentation or endorsement of authorization of aliens (other than aliens lawfully admitted for permanent residence) authorized to be employed in the United States, the Attorney General shall provide that any limitations with respect to the period or type of employment or employer shall be conspicuously stated on the documentation or endorsement.

(2) Preemption. The provisions of this section preempt any State or local law imposing civil or criminal sanctions (other than through licensing and similar laws) upon those who employ, or recruit or refer for a fee for employment, unauthorized aliens.

(3) Definition of unauthorized alien. As used in this section, the term "unauthorized alien" means, with respect to the employment of an alien at a particular time, that the alien is not at that time either (A) an alien lawfully admitted for permanent residence, or (B) authorized to be so employed by this Act or by the Attorney General.

HISTORY: (June 27, 1952, ch 477, Title II, Ch 8, § 274A, as added Nov. 6, 1986, P. L. 99-603, Title I, Part A, § 101(a)(1), 100 Stat. 3360; Oct. 24, 1988, P. L. 100-525, § 2(a)(1), 102 Stat. 2609; Nov. 29, 1990, P. L. 101-649, Title V, Subtitle B, § 521(a), Subtitle C, § 538(a), 104 Stat. 5053, 5056; Dec. 12, 1991, P. L. 102-232, Title III, §§ 306(b)(2), 309(b)(11), 105 Stat. 1752, 1759; Oct. 25, 1994, P. L. 103-416, Title II, §§ 213, 219(z)(4), 108 Stat. 4314, 4318; Sept. 30, 1996, P. L. 104-208, Div C, Title III, Subtitle F, § 379(a), Title IV, Subtitle B, §§ 411(a), 412(a)–(d), 416, 110 Stat. 3009-649, 3009-666, 3009-669; Oct. 30, 2004, P. L. 108-390, § 1(a), 118 Stat. 2242.)

§ 274B. [8 U.S.C. § 1324b] Unfair immigration-related employment practices.

(a) Prohibition of discrimination based on national origin or citizenship status.

(1) General rule. It is an unfair immigration-related employment practice for a person or other entity to discriminate against any individual (other than an unauthorized alien, as defined in section 274A(h)(3) [8 USCS § 1324a(h)(3)]) with respect to the hiring, or recruitment or referral for a fee, of the individual for employment or the discharging of the individual from employment-

(A) because of such individual's national origin, or

(B) in the case of a protected individual (as defined in paragraph (3)), because of such individual's citizenship status.

(2) Exceptions. Paragraph (1) shall not apply to—

(A) a person or other entity that employs three or fewer employees,

(B) a person's or entity's discrimination because of an individual's national origin if the discrimination with respect to that person or entity and that individual is covered under section 703 of the Civil Rights Act of 1964 [42 USCS § 2000e-2], or

(C) discrimination because of citizenship status which is otherwise required in order to comply with law, regulation, or executive order, or required by Federal, State, or local government contract, or which the Attorney General determines to be essential for an employer to do business with an agency or department of the Federal, State, or local government.

(3) Definition of protected individual. As used in paragraph (1), the term "protected individual" means an individual who—

(A) is a citizen or national of the United States, or

(B) is an alien who is lawfully admitted for permanent residence, is granted the status of an alien lawfully admitted for temporary residence under section 210(a) or 245A(a)(1) [8 USCS § 1160(a) or 1255a(a)(1)], is admitted as a refugee under section 207 [8 USCS § 1157], or is granted asylum under section 208 [8 USCS § 1158]; but does not include (i) an alien who fails to apply for naturalization within six months of the date the alien first becomes eligible (by virtue of period of lawful permanent residence) to apply for naturalization or, if later, within six months after the date of the enactment of this section and (ii) an alien who has applied on a timely basis, but has not been naturalized as a citizen within 2 years after the date of the application, unless the alien can establish that the alien is actively pursuing naturalization, except that time consumed in the Service's processing the application shall not be counted toward the 2-year period.

(4) Additional exception providing right to prefer equally qualified citizens. Notwithstanding any other provision of this section, it is not an unfair immigration-related employment practice for a person or other entity to prefer to hire, recruit, or refer an individual who is a citizen or national of the United States over another individual who is an alien if the two individuals are equally qualified.

(5) Prohibition of intimidation or retaliation. It is also an unfair immigration-related employment practice for a person or other entity to intimidate, threaten, coerce, or retaliate against any individual for the purpose of interfering with any right or privilege secured under this section or because the individual intends to file or has filed a charge or a complaint, testified, assisted, or participated in an manner in an investigation, proceeding, or hearing under section. An individual so intimidated, threatened, coerced, or retaliated against shall be considered, for purposes of subsections (d) and (g), to have been discriminated against.

(6) Treatment of certain documentary practices as employment practices. A person's or other entity's request, for purposes of satisfying the requirements of section 274A(b) [8 USCS § 1324a(b)], for more or different documents than are required under such section or refusing to honor documents tendered that on their

face reasonably appear to be genuine shall be treated as an unfair immigration-related employment practice if made for the purpose or with the intent of discriminating against an individual in violation of paragraph (1).

(b) Charges of violations.

(1) In general. Except as provided in paragraph (2), any person alleging that the person is adversely affected directly by an unfair immigration-related employment practice (or a person on that person's behalf) or an officer of the Service alleging that an unfair immigration-related employment practice has occurred or is occurring may file a charge respecting such practice or violation with the Special Counsel (appointed under subsection (c)). Charges shall be in writing under oath or affirmation and shall contain such information as the Attorney General requires. The Special Counsel by certified mail shall serve a notice of the charge (including the date, place, and circumstances of the alleged unfair immigration-related employment practice) on the person or entity involved within 10 days.

(2) No overlap with EEOC complaints. No charge may be filed respecting an unfair immigration-related employment practice described in subsection (a)(1)(A) if a charge with respect to that practice based on the same set of facts has been filed with the Equal Employment Opportunity Commission under title VII of the Civil Rights Act of 1964 [42 USCS §§ 2000e et seq.], unless the charge is dismissed as being outside the scope of such title [42 USCS §§ 2000e et seq.]. No charge respecting an employment practice may be filed with the Equal Employment Opportunity Commission under such title [42 USCS §§ 2000e et seq.] if a charge with respect to such practice based on the same set of facts has been filed under this subsection, unless the charge is dismissed under this section as being outside the scope of this section.

(c) Special Counsel.

(1) Appointment. The President shall appoint, by and with the advice and consent of the Senate, a Special Counsel for Immigration-Related Unfair Employment Practices (hereinafter in this section referred to as the "Special Counsel") within the Department of Justice to serve for a term of four years. In the case of a vacancy in the office of the Special Counsel the President may designate the officer or employee who shall act as Special Counsel during such vacancy.

(2) Duties. The Special Counsel shall be responsible for investigation of charges and issuance of complaints under this section and in respect of the prosecution of all such complaints before administrative law judges and the exercise of certain functions under subsection (j)(1).

(3) Compensation. The Special Counsel is entitled to receive compensation at a rate not to exceed the rate now or hereafter provided for grade GS-17 of the General Schedule, under section 5332 of title 5, United States Code [5 USCS § 5332].

(4) Regional offices. The Special Counsel, in accordance with regulations of the Attorney General, shall establish such regional offices as may be necessary to carry out his duties.

(d) Investigation of charges.

(1) By special counsel. The Special Counsel shall investigate each charge received and, within 120 days of the date of the receipt of the charge, determine whether or not there is reasonable cause to believe that the charge is true and whether or not to bring a complaint with respect to the charge before an administrative law judge. The Special Counsel may, on his own initiative, conduct investigations respecting unfair immigration-related employment practices and, based on such an investigation and subject to paragraph (3), file a complaint before such a judge.

(2) Private actions. If the Special Counsel, after receiving such a charge respecting an unfair immigration-related employment practice which alleges knowing and intentional discriminatory activity or a pattern or practice of discriminatory activity, has not filed a complaint before an administrative law judge with respect to such charge within such 120-day period, the Special Counsel shall notify the person making the charge of the determination not to file such a complaint during such period and the person making the charge may (subject to paragraph (3)) file a complaint directly before such a judge within 90 days after the date of receipt of the notice. The Special Counsel's failure to file such a complaint within such 120-day period shall not affect the right of the Special Counsel to investigate the charge or to bring a complaint before an administrative law judge during such 90-day period.

(3) Time limitations on complaints. No complaint may be filed respecting any unfair immigration-related employment practice occurring more than 180 days prior to the date of the filing of the charge with the Special Counsel. This subparagraph shall not prevent the subsequent amending of a charge or complaint under subsection (e)(1).

(e) Hearings.

(1) Notice. Whenever a complaint is made that a person or entity has engaged in or is engaging in any such unfair immigration-related employment practice, an administrative law judge shall have power to issue and cause to be served upon such person or entity a copy of the complaint and a notice of hearing before the judge at a place therein fixed, not less than five days after the serving of the complaint. Any such complaint may be amended by the judge conducting the hearing, upon the motion of the party filing the complaint,in the judge's discretion at any time prior to the issuance of an order based thereon. The person or entity so complained of shall have the right to file an answer to the original or amended complaint and to appear in person or otherwise and give testimony at the place and time fixed in the complaint.

(2) Judges hearing cases. Hearings on complaints under this subsection shall be considered before administrative law judges who are specially designated by the Attorney General as having special training respecting employment discrimination and, to the extent practicable, before such judges who only consider cases under this section.

(3) Complainant as party. Any person filing a charge with the Special Counsel respecting an un-

fair immigration-related employment practice shall be considered a party to any complaint before an administrative law judge respecting such practice and any subsequent appeal respecting that complaint. In the discretion of the judge conducting the hearing, any other person may be allowed to intervene in the proceeding and to present testimony.

(f) Testimony and authority of hearing officers.

(1) Testimony. The testimony taken by the administrative law judge shall be reduced to writing. Thereafter, the judge, in his discretion, upon notice may provide for the taking of further testimony or hear argument.

(2) Authority of administrative law judges. In conducting investigations and hearings under this subsection and in accordance with regulations of the Attorney General, the Special Counsel and administrative law judges shall have reasonable access to examine evidence of any person or entity being investigated. The administrative law judges by subpoena may compel the attendance of witnesses and the production of evidence at any designated place or hearing. In case of contumacy or refusal to obey a subpoena lawfully issued under this paragraph and upon application of the administrative law judge, an appropriate district court of the United States may issue an order requiring compliance with such subpoena and any failure to obey such order may be punished by such court as a contempt thereof.

(g) Determinations.

(1) Order. The administrative law judge shall issue and cause to be served on the parties to the proceeding an order, which shall be final unless appealed as provided under subsection (i).

(2) Orders finding violations.

(A) In general. If, upon the preponderance of the evidence, an administrative law judge determines that any person or entity named in the complaint has engaged in or is engaging in any such unfair immigration-related employment practice, then the judge shall state his findings of fact and shall issue and cause to be served on such person or entity an order which requires such person or entity to cease and desist from such unfair immigration-related employment practice.

(B) Contents of order. Such an order also may require the person or entity —

(i) to comply with the requirements of section 274A(b) [8 USCS § 1324a(b)] with respect to individuals hired (or recruited or referred for employment for a fee) during a period of up to three years;

(ii) to retain for the period referred to in clause (i) and only for purposes consistent with section 274A(b)(5) [8 USCS § 1324a(b)(5)], the name and address of each individual who applies, in person or in writing, for hiring for an existing position, or for recruiting or referring for a fee, for employment in the United States;

(iii) to hire individuals directly and adversely affected, with or without back pay;

(iv) (I) except as provided in subclauses (II) through (I) through (IV), to pay a civil penalty of not less than $250 and not more than $2,000 for each individual discriminated against,

(II) except as provided in subclauses (III) and (IV), in the case of a person or entity previously subject to a single order under this paragraph, to pay a civil penalty of not less than $2,000 and not more than $5,000 for each individual discriminated against,

(III) except as provided in subclause (IV), in the case of a person or entity previously subject to more than one order under this paragraph, to pay a civil penalty of not less than $3,000 and not more than $10,000 for each individual discriminated against, and

(IV) in the case of an unfair immigration-related employment practice described in subsection (a)(6), to pay a civil penalty of not less than $100 and not more than $1,000 for each individual discriminated against;

(v) to post notices to employees about their rights under this section and employers' obligations under section 274A [8 USCS § 1324a];

(vi) to educate all personnel involved in hiring and complying with this section or section 274A [8 USCS § 1324a] about the requirements of this section or such section;

(vii) to remove (in an appropriate case) a false performance review or false warning from an employees personnel file; and

(viii) to lift (in an appropriate case) any restrictions on any employee's assignments, work shifts, or movements.

(C) Limitation on back pay remedy. In providing a remedy under subparagraph (B)(iii), back pay liability shall not accrue from a date more than two years prior to the date of the filing of a charge with the Special Counsel. Interim earnings or amounts earnable with reasonable diligence by the individual or individuals discriminated against shall operate to reduce the back pay otherwise allowable under such subparagraph. No order shall require the hiring of an individual as an employee or the payment to an individual of any back pay, if the individual was refused employment for any reason other than discrimination on account of national origin or citizenship status.

(D) Treatment of distinct entities. In applying this subsection in the case of a person or entity composed of distinct, physically separate subdivisions each of which provides separately for the hiring, recruiting, or referring for employment, without reference to the practices of, and not under the control of or common control with, another subdivision, each such subdivision shall be considered a separate person or entity.

(3) Orders not finding violations. If upon the preponderance of the evidence an administrative law judge determines that the person or entity named in the complaint has not engaged and is not engaging in any such unfair immigration-related employment practice, then the judge shall state his findings of fact and shall issue an order dismissing the complaint.

(h) Awarding of attorney's fees. In any complaint respecting an unfair immigration-related employment practice, an administrative law judge, in the judge's discretion, may allow a prevailing party, other than the United States, a reasonable attorney's fee, if the losing party's argument is without reasonable foundation in law and fact.

(i) Review of final orders.

(1) In general. Not later than 60 days after the entry of such final order, any person aggrieved by such final order may seek a review of such order in the United States court of appeals for the circuit in which the violation is alleged to have occurred or in which the employer resides or transacts business.

(2) Further review. Upon the filing of the record with the court, the jurisdiction of the court shall be exclusive and its judgment shall be final, except that the same shall be subject to review by the Supreme Court of the United States upon writ of certiorari or certification as provided in section 1254 of title 28, United States Code [28 USCS § 1254].

(j) Court enforcement of administrative orders.

(1) In general. If an order of the agency is not appealed under subsection (i)(1), the Special Counsel (or, if the Special Counsel fails to act, the person filing the charge) may petition the United States district court for the district in which a violation of the order is alleged to have occurred, or in which the respondent resides or transacts business, for the enforcement of the order of the administrative law judge, by filing in such court a written petition praying that such order be enforced.

(2) Court enforcement order. Upon the filing of such petition, the court shall have jurisdiction to make and enter a decree enforcing the order of the administrative law judge. In such a proceeding, the order of the administrative law judge shall not be subject to review.

(3) Enforcement decree in original review. If, upon appeal of an order under subsection (i)(1), the United States court of appeals does not reverse such order, such court shall have the jurisdiction to make and enter a decree enforcing the order of the administrative law judge.

(4) Awarding of attorney's fees. In any judicial proceeding under subsection (i) or this subsection, the court, in its discretion, may allow a prevailing party, other than the United States, a reasonable attorney's fee a part of costs but only if the losing party's argument is without reasonable foundation in law and fact.

(k) Termination dates.

(1) This section shall not apply to discrimination in hiring, recruiting, referring, or discharging of individuals occurring after the date of any termination of the provisions of section 274A [8 USCS § 1324a], under subsection *(l)* of that section.

(2) The provisions of this section shall terminate 30 calendar days after receipt of the last report required to be transmitted under section 274A(j) if—

(A) the Comptroller General determines, and so reports in such report that—

(i) no significant discrimination has resulted, against citizens or national of the United States or against any eligible workers seeking employment, from the implementation of section 274A [8 USCS § 1324a], or

(ii) such section has created an unreasonable burden on employers hiring such workers; and

(B) there has been enacted, within such period of 30 calendar days, a joint resolution stating in substance that the Congress approves the findings of the Comptroller General contained in such report.

The provisions of subsections (m) and (n) of section 274A [8 USCS § 1324a] shall apply to any joint resolution under subparagraph (B) in the same manner as they apply to a joint resolution under subsection *(l)* of such section.

(l) Dissemination of information concerning anti-discrimination provisions.

(1) Not later than 3 months after the date of the enactment of this subsection [enacted Nov. 29, 1990], the Special Counsel, in cooperation with the chairman of the Equal Employment Opportunity Commission, the Secretary of Labor, and the Administrator of the Small Business Administration, shall conduct a campaign to disseminate information respecting the rights and remedies prescribed under this section and under title VII of the Civil Rights Act of 1964 [42 USCS §§ 2000e et seq.] in connection with unfair immigration-related employment practices. Such campaign shall be aimed at increasing the knowledge of employers, employees, and the general public concerning employer and employee rights, responsibilities, and remedies under this section and such title [42 USCS §§ 2000e et seq.].

(2) In order to carry out the campaign under this subsection, the Special Counsel—

(A) may, to the extent deemed appropriate and subject to the availability of appropriations, contract with public and private organizations for outreach activities under the campaign, and

(B) shall consult with the Secretary of Labor, the chairman of the Equal Employment Opportunity Commission, and the heads of such other agencies as may be appropriate.

(3) There are authorized to be appropriated to carry out this subsection $10,000,000 for each fiscal year (beginning with fiscal year 1991).

HISTORY: (June 27, 1952, ch 477, Title II, Ch 8, § 274B, as added Nov. 6, 1986, P. L. 99-603, Title I, Part A, § 102(a), 100 Stat. 3374; Oct. 24, 1988, P. L. 100-525, § 2(b), 102 Stat. 2610; Nov. 29, 1990, P. L. 101-649, Title V, Subtitle C, §§ 531, 532(a), 533(a), 534(a), 535(a), 536(a), 537(a), 539(a), 104 Stat. 5054-5056; Dec. 12, 1991, P. L. 102-232, Title III, § 306(b)(1), (2), (c)(1), 105 Stat. 1752; Oct. 25, 1994, P. L. 103-416, Title II, § 219(q), 108 Stat. 4317; Sept. 30, 1996, P. L. 104-208, Div C, Title IV, Subtitle C, § 421(a), Title VI, Subtitle E, § 671(d)(1)(B), 110 Stat. 3009-670, 3990-723.)

§ 274C. [8 U.S.C. § 1324c] Penalties for document fraud.

(a) Activities prohibited. It is unlawful for any person or entity knowingly—

(1) to forge, counterfeit, alter, or falsely make any document for the purpose of satisfying a requirement of this Act or to obtain a benefit under this Act,

(2) to use, attempt to use, possess, obtain, accept, or receive or to provide any forged, counterfeit, altered, or falsely made document in order to satisfy any requirement of this Act or to obtain a benefit under this Act,

(3) to use or attempt to use or to provide or attempt to provide any document lawfully issued to or with respect to a person other than the possessor (including a deceased individual) for the purpose of satisfying a

requirement of this Act or obtaining a benefit under this Act,

(4) to accept or receive or to provide any document lawfully issued to or with respect to a person other than the possessor (including a deceased individual) for the purpose of complying with section 274A(b) [8 USCS § 1324a(b)] or obtaining a benefit under this Act, or

(5) to prepare, file, or assist another in preparing or filing, any application for benefits under this Act, or any document required under this Act, or any document submitted in connection with such application or document, with knowledge or in reckless disregard of the fact that such application or document was falsely made or, in whole or in part, does not relate to the person on whose behalf it was or is being submitted, or

(6) (A) to present before boarding a common carrier for the purpose of coming to the United States a document which relates to the alien's eligibility to enter the United States, and (B) to fail to present such document to an immigration officer upon arrival at a United States port of entry.

(b) Exception. This section does not prohibit any lawfully authorized investigative, protective, or intelligence activity of a law enforcement agency of the United States, a State, or a subdivision of a State, or of an intelligence agency of the United States, or any activity authorized under chapter 224 of title 18, United States Code [18 USCS §§ 3521 et seq.].

(c) Construction. Nothing in this section shall be construed to diminish or qualify any of the penalties available for activities by this section but proscribed as well in title 18, United States Code.

(d) Enforcement.

(1) Authority in investigations. In conducting investigations and hearings under this subsection—

(A) immigration officers and administrative law judges shall have reasonable access to examine evidence of any person or entity being investigated,

(B) administrative law judges, may, if necessary, compel by subpoena the attendance of witnesses and the production of evidence at any designated place or hearing, and

(C) immigration officers designated by the Commissioner may compel by subpoena the attendance of witnesses and the production of evidence at any designated place prior to the filing of a complaint in a case under paragraph (2).

In case of contumacy or refusal to obey a subpoena lawfully issued under this paragraph and upon application of the Attorney General, an appropriate district court of the United States may issue an order requiring compliance with such subpoena and any failure to obey such order may be punished by such court as a contempt thereof.

(2) Hearing.

(A) In general. Before imposing an order described in paragraph (3) against a person or entity under this subsection for a violation of subsection (a), the Attorney General shall provide the person or entity with notice and, upon request made within a reasonable time (of not less than 30 days, as established by the Attorney General) of the date of the notice, a hearing respecting the violation.

(B) Conduct of hearing. Any hearing so requested shall be conducted before an administrative law judge. The hearing shall be conducted in accordance with the requirements of section 554 of title 5, United States Code. The hearing shall be held at the nearest practicable place to the place where the person or entity resides or of the place where the alleged violation occurred. If no hearing is so requested, the Attorney General's imposition of the order shall constitute a final and unappealable order.

(C) Issuance of orders. If the administrative law judge determines, upon the preponderance of the evidence received, that a person or entity has violated subsection (a), the administrative law judge shall state his findings of fact and issue and cause to be served on such person or entity an order described in paragraph (3).

(3) Cease and desist order with civil money penalty [Caution: For inflation-adjusted civil monetary penalties, see 8 CFR 270.3(b)(1)(ii).]. With respect to a violation of subsection (a), the order under this subsection shall require the person or entity to cease and desist from such violations and to pay a civil penalty in an amount of—

(A) not less than $250 and not more than $2,000 for each document that is the subject of a violation under subsection (a), or

(B) in the case of a person or entity previously subject to an order under this paragraph, not less than $2,000 and not more than $5,000 for each document that is the subject of a violation under subsection (a).

In applying this subsection in the case of a person or entity composed of distinct, physically separate subdivisions each of which provides separately for the hiring, recruiting, or referring for employment, without reference to the practices of, and not under the control of or common control with, another subdivision, each such subdivision shall be considered a separate person or entity.

(4) Administrative appellate review. The decision and order of an administrative law judge shall become the final agency decision and order of the Attorney General unless either (A) within 30 days, an official delegated by regulation to exercise review authority over the decision and order modifies or vacates the decision and order, or (B) within 30 days of the date of such a modification or vacation (or within 60 days of the date of decision and order of an administrative law judge if not so modified or vacated) the decision and order is referred to the Attorney General pursuant to regulations, in which case the decision and order of the Attorney General shall become the final agency decision and order under this subsection.

(5) Judicial review. A person or entity adversely affected by a final order under this section may, within 45 days after the date the final order is issued, file a petition in the Court of Appeals for the appropriate circuit for review of the order.

(6) Enforcement of orders. If a person or entity fails to comply with a final order issued under this section

against the person or entity, the Attorney General shall file a suit to seek compliance with the order in any appropriate district court of the United States. In any such suit, the validity and appropriateness of the final order shall not be subject to review.

(7) Waiver by Attorney General. The Attorney General may waive the penalties imposed by this section with respect to an alien who knowingly violates subsection (a)(6) if the alien is granted asylum under section 208 [8 USCS § 1158] or withholding of removal under section 241(b)(3) [8 USCS § 1251(b)(3)].

(e) Criminal penalties for failure to disclose role as document preparer.

(1) Whoever, in any matter within the jurisdiction of the Service, knowingly and willfully fails to disclose, conceals, or covers up the fact that they have, on behalf of any person and for a fee or other remuneration, prepared or assisted in preparing an application which was falsely made (as defined in subsection (f)) for immigration benefits, shall be fined in accordance with title 18, United States Code, imprisoned for not more than 5 years, or both, and prohibited from preparing or assisting in preparing, whether or not for a fee or other remuneration, any other such application.

(2) Whoever, having been convicted of a violation of paragraph (1), knowingly and willfully prepares or assists in preparing an application for immigration benefits pursuant to this Act, or the regulations promulgated thereunder, whether or not for a fee or other remuneration and regardless of whether in any matter within the jurisdiction of the Service, shall be fined in accordance with title 18, United States Code, imprisoned for not more than 15 years, or both, and prohibited from preparing or assisting in preparing any other such application.

(f) Falsely make. For purposes of this section, the term "falsely make" means to prepare or provide an application or document, with knowledge or in reckless disregard of the fact that the application or document contains a false, fictitious, or fraudulent statement or material representation, or has no basis in law or fact, or otherwise fails to state a fact which is material to the purpose for which it was submitted.

HISTORY: (June 27, 1952, ch 477, Title II, Ch 8, § 274C, as added Nov. 29, 1990, P. L. 101-649, Title V, Subtitle D, § 544(a), 104 Stat. 5059; Dec. 12, 1991, P. L. 102-232, Title III, § 306(c)(5)(A), 105 Stat. 1752; Oct. 25, 1994, P. L. 103-416, Title II, § 219(r), 108 Stat. 4317; Sept. 30, 1996, P. L. 104-208, Div C, Title II, Subtitle B, § 212(a)–(d), 213, 220, Title III, Subtitle A, § 308(g)(10)(D), Subtitle F, § 379(a), 110 Stat. 3009-570, 3009-571, 3009-575, 3009-625, 3009-650.)

§ 274D. [8 U.S.C. § 1324d] Civil penalties for failure to depart.

(a) In general. Any alien subject to a final order of removal who—

(1) willfully fails or refuses to—

(A) depart from the United States pursuant to the order,

(B) make timely application in good faith for travel or other documents necessary for departure, or

(C) present for removal at the time and place required by the Attorney General; or

(2) conspires to or takes any action designed to prevent or hamper the alien's departure pursuant to the order,

shall pay a civil penalty of not more than $500 to the Commissioner for each day the alien is in violation of this section.

(b) Construction. Nothing in this section shall be construed to diminish or qualify any penalties to which an alien may be subject for activities proscribed by section 243(a) [8 USCS § 1253(a)] or any other section of this Act.

HISTORY: (June 27, 1952, ch 477, Title II, Ch 8, § 274D, as added Sept. 30, 1996, P. L. 104-208, Div C, Title III, Subtitle F, § 380(a), 110 Stat. 3009-650.)

§ 275. [8 U.S.C. § 1325] Improper entry by alien.

(a) Improper time or place; avoidance of examination or inspection; misrepresentation and concealment of facts. Any alien who (1) enters or attempts to enter the United States at any time or place other than as designated by immigration officers, or (2) eludes examination or inspection by immigration officers, or (3) attempts to enter or obtains entry to the United States by a willfully false or misleading representation or the willful concealment of a material fact, shall, for the first commission of any such offense, be fined under title 18, United States Code, or imprisoned not more than 6 months, or both, and, for a subsequent commission of any such offense, be fined under title 18, United States Code, or imprisoned not more than 2 years, or both.

(b) Improper time or place; civil penalties. Any alien who is apprehended while entering (or attempting to enter) the United States at a time or place other than as designated by immigration officers shall be subject to a civil penalty of—

(1) at least $50 and not more than $250 for each such entry (or attempted entry); or

(2) twice the amount specified in paragraph (1) in the case of an alien who has been previously subject to a civil penalty under this subsection.

Civil penalties under this subsection are in addition to, and not in lieu of, any criminal or other civil penalties that may be imposed.

(c) Marriage fraud. Any individual who knowingly enters into a marriage for the purpose of evading any provision of the immigration laws shall be imprisoned for not more than 5 years, or fined not more than $250,000, or both.

(d) Immigration-related entrepreneurship fraud. Any individual who knowingly establishes a commercial enterprise for the purpose of evading any provision of the immigration laws shall be imprisoned for not more than 5 years, fined in accordance with title 18, United States Code, or both.

HISTORY: (June 27, 1952, ch 477, Title II, Ch 8, § 275, 66 Stat. 229; Nov. 10, 1986, P. L. 99-639, § 2(d), 100 Stat. 3542; Nov. 29, 1990, P. L. 101-649, Title I, Subtitle B, Part 2, § 121(b)(3), Title V, Subtitle D, § 543(b)(2), 104 Stat. 4994, 5059; Dec. 12, 1991, P. L. 102-232, Title III, § 306(c)(3), 105 Stat. 1752; Sept. 30, 1996, P. L. 104-208, Div C, Title I, Subtitle A, § 105(a), 110 Stat. 3009-556.)

§ 276. [8 U.S.C. § 1326] Reentry of removed aliens.

(a) In general. Subject to subsection (b), any alien who—

(1) has been denied admission, excluded, deported, or removed or has departed the United States while an order of exclusion, deportation, or removal is outstanding, and thereafter

(2) enters, attempts to enter, or is at any time found in, the United States, unless (A) prior to his reembarkation at a place outside the United States or his application for admission from foreign contiguous territory, the Attorney General has expressly consented to such alien's reapplying for admission; or (B) with respect to an alien previously denied admission and removed, unless such alien shall establish that he was not required to obtain such advance consent under this or any prior Act,

shall be fined under title 18, United States Code, or imprisoned not more than 2 years or both.

(b) Criminal penalties for reentry of certain removed aliens. Notwithstanding subsection (a), in the case of any alien described in such subsection—

(1) whose removal was subsequent to a conviction for commission of three or more misdemeanors involving drugs, crimes against the person, or both, or a felony (other than an aggravated felony), such alien shall be fined under title 18, United States Code, imprisoned not more than 10 years, or both;

(2) whose removal was subsequent to a conviction for commission of an aggravated felony, such alien shall be fined under such title, imprisoned not more than 20 years, or both;

(3) who has been excluded from the United States pursuant to section 235(c) [8 USCS § 1225(c)] because the alien was excludable under section 212(a)(3)(B) [8 USCS § 1182(a)(3)(B)] or who has been removed from the United States pursuant to the provisions of title V [8 USCS §§ 1531 et seq.], and who thereafter, without the permission of the Attorney General, enters the United States, or attempts to do so, shall be fined under title 18, United States Code, and imprisoned for a period of 10 years, which sentence shall not run concurrently with any other sentence.[;] or

(4) who was removed from the United States pursuant to section 241(a)(4)(B) [8 USCS § 1231(a)(4)(B)] who thereafter, without the permission of the Attorney General, enters, attempts to enter, or is at any time found in, the United States (unless the Attorney General has expressly consented to such alien's reentry) shall be fined under title 18, United States Code, imprisoned for not more than 10 years, or both.

For the purposes of this subsection, the term "removal" includes any agreement in which an alien stipulates to removal during (or not during) a criminal trial under either Federal or State law.

(c) Reentry of alien deported prior to completion of term of imprisonment. Any alien deported pursuant to section 242(h)(2) [8 USCS § 1252(h)(2)] who enters, attempts to enter, or is at any time found in, the United States (unless the Attorney General has expressly consented to such alien's reentry) shall be incarcerated for the remainder of the sentence of imprisonment which was pending at the time of deportation without any reduction for parole or supervised release. Such alien shall be subject to such other penalties relating to the reentry of deported aliens as may be available under this section or any other provision of law.

(d) Limitation on collateral attack on underlying deportation order. In a criminal proceeding under this section, an alien may not challenge the validity of the deportation order described in subsection (a)(1) or subsection (b) unless the alien demonstrates that—

(1) the alien exhausted any administrative remedies that may have been available to seek relief against the order;

(2) the deportation proceedings at which the order was issued improperly deprived the alien of the opportunity for judicial review; and

(3) the entry of the order was fundamentally unfair.

HISTORY: (June 27, 1952, ch 477, Title II, Ch 8, § 276, 66 Stat. 229; Nov. 18, 1988, P. L. 100-690, Title VII, Subtitle J, § 7345(a), 102 Stat. 4471; Nov. 29, 1990, P. L. 101-649, Title V, Subtitle D, § 543(b)(3), 104 Stat. 5059; Sept. 13, 1994, P. L. 103-322, Title XIII, § 130001(b), 108 Stat. 2023; April 24, 1996, P. L. 104-132, Title IV, Subtitle A, § 401(c), Subtitle C, §§ 438(b), 441(a), 110 Stat. 1267, 1276, 1279; Sept. 30, 1996, P. L. 104-208, Div C, Title III, Subtitle A, §§ 305(b), 308(d)(4)(J), (e)(1)(K), (14)(A), Subtitle B, § 324(a), (b), 110 Stat. 3009-606, 3009-618, 3009-619, 3009-620, 3009-629.)

§ 277. [8 U.S.C. § 1327] Aiding or assisting certain aliens to enter.

Any person who knowingly aids or assists any alien inadmissible under section 212(a)(2) [8 USCS § 1182(a)(2)] (insofar as an alien inadmissible under such section has been convicted of an aggravated felony) or 212(a)(3) [8 USCS § 1182(a)(3)] (other than subparagraph (E) thereof) to enter the United States, or who connives or conspires with any person or persons to allow, procure, or permit any such alien to enter the United States, shall be fined under title 18, United States Code, or imprisoned not more than 10 years, or both.

HISTORY: (June 27, 1952, ch 477, Title II, Ch 8, § 277, 66 Stat. 229; Nov. 18, 1988, P. L. 100-690, Title VII, Subtitle J, § 7346(a), (c)(1), 102 Stat. 4471; Nov. 29, 1990, P. L. 101-649, Title V, Subtitle D, § 543(b)(4), Title VI, § 603(a)(16), 104 Stat. 5059, 5084; Sept. 30, 1996, P. L. 104-208, Div C, Title III, Subtitle A, § 308(d)(3)(A), 110 Stat. 3009-617.)

§ 278. [8 U.S.C. § 1328] Importation of alien for immoral purpose.

The importation into the United States of any alien for the purpose of prostitution, or for any other immoral purpose, is hereby forbidden. Whoever shall, directly or indirectly, import, or attempt to import into the United States any alien for the purpose of prostitution or for any other immoral purpose, or shall hold or attempt to hold any alien for any such purpose in pursuance of such illegal importation, or shall keep, maintain, control, support, employ, or harbor in any house or other place, for the purpose of prostitution or for any other immoral purpose, any alien, in pursuance of such illegal importation, shall be fined under title 18, United States Code, or imprisoned not more than 10 years, or both. The trial and punishment of offenses under this section may be in any district to or into which such alien is brought in pursuance of importation by the person or persons accused, or in any district in which a violation of any of the provisions of this section occurs. In all prosecutions under this section, the testimony of a husband or wife shall be admissible and competent evidence against each other.

HISTORY: (June 27, 1952, ch 477, Title II, Ch 8, § 278, 66 Stat. 230; Nov. 29, 1990, P. L. 101-649, Title V, Subtitle D, § 543(b)(5), 104 Stat. 5059.)

§ 279. [8 U.S.C. § 1329] Jurisdiction of district courts.

The district courts of the United States shall have jurisdiction of all causes, civil and criminal, brought by the United States that arise under the provisions of this title. It shall be the duty of the United States attorney of the proper district to prosecute every such suit when brought by the United States. Notwithstanding any other law, such prosecutions or suits may be instituted at any place in the United States at which the violation may occur or at which the person charged with a violation under section 275 or 276 [8 USCS § 1325 or 1326] may be apprehended. No suit or proceeding for a violation of any of the provisions of this title shall be settled, compromised, or discontinued without the consent of the court in which it is pending and any such settlement, compromise, or discontinuance shall be entered of record with the reasons therefor. Nothing in this section shall be construed as providing jurisdiction for suits against the United States or its agencies or officers.

HISTORY: (June 27, 1952, ch 477, Title II, Ch 8, § 279, 66 Stat. 230; Sept. 30, 1996, P. L. 104-208, Div C, Title III, Subtitle F, § 381(a), 110 Stat. 3009-650.)

§ 280. [8 U.S.C. § 1330] Collection of penalties and expenses.

(a) Notwithstanding any other provisions of this title, the withholding or denial of clearance of or a lien upon any vessel or aircraft provided for in section 231, 234, 243(c)(2), 251, 253, 254, 255, 256, 271, 272, or 273 of this title [8 USCS § 1221, 1224, 1253(c)(2), 1281, 1283, 1284, 1285, 1286, 1321, 1322, or 1323] shall not be regarded as the sole and exclusive means or remedy for the enforcement of payments of any fine, penalty or expenses imposed or incurred under such sections, but, in the discretion of the Attorney General, the amount thereof may be recovered by civil suit, in the name of the United States, from any person made liable under any of such sections.

(b) (1) There is established in the general fund of the Treasury a separate account which shall be known as the "Immigration Enforcement Account". Notwithstanding any other section of this title, there shall be deposited as offsetting receipts into the Immigration Enforcement Account amounts described in paragraph (2) to remain available until expended.

(2) The amounts described in this paragraph are the following:

(A) The increase in penalties collected resulting from the amendments made by sections 203(b) and 543(a) of the Immigration Act of 1990.

(B) Civil penalties collected under sections 240B(d), 274C, 274D, and 275(b) [8 USCS §§ 1229c(d), 1324c, 1324d, and 1325(b)].

(3) (A) The Secretary of the Treasury shall refund out of the Immigration Enforcement Account to any appropriation the amount paid out of such appropriation for expenses incurred by the Attorney General for activities that enhance enforcement of provisions of this title. Such activities include—

(i) the identification, investigation, apprehension, detention, and removal of criminal aliens;

(ii) the maintenance and updating of a system to identify and track criminal aliens, deportable aliens, inadmissible aliens, and aliens illegally entering the United States; and

(iii) for the repair, maintenance, or construction on the United States border, in areas experiencing high levels of apprehensions of illegal aliens, of structures to deter illegal entry into the United States.

(B) The amounts which are required to be refunded under subparagraph (A) shall be refunded at least quarterly on the basis of estimates made by the Attorney General of the expenses referred to in subparagraph (A). Proper adjustments shall be made in the amounts subsequently refunded under subparagraph (A) to the extent prior estimates were in excess of, or less than, the amount required to be refunded under subparagraph (A).

(C) The amounts required to be refunded from the Immigration Enforcement Account for fiscal year 1996 and thereafter shall be refunded in accordance with estimates made in the budget request of the Attorney General for those fiscal years. Any proposed changes in the amounts designated in such budget requests shall only be made after notification to the Committees on Appropriations of the House of Representatives and the Senate in accordance with section 605 of Public Law 104-134 [unclassified].

(D) The Attorney General shall prepare and submit annually to the Congress statements of financial condition of the Immigration Enforcement Account, including beginning account balance, revenues, withdrawals, and ending account balance and projection for the ensuing fiscal year.

HISTORY: (June 27, 1952, ch 477, Title II, Ch 8, § 280, 66 Stat. 230; Nov. 29, 1990, P. L. 101-649, Title V, Subtitle D, § 542(a), 104 Stat. 5057; Oct. 25, 1994, P. L. 103-416, Title II, § 219(s), 108 Stat. 4317; Sept. 30, 1996, P. L. 104-208, Div C, Title III, Subtitle A, § 308(g)(4)(C), Subtitle F, § 382(a), 110 Stat. 3009-623, 3009-651.)

Chapter 9—Miscellaneous

§ 281. [8 U.S.C. § 1351] Nonimmigrant visa fees.

The fees for the furnishing and verification of applications for visas by nonimmigrants of each foreign country and for the issuance of visas to nonimmigrants of each foreign country shall be prescribed by the Secretary of State, if practicable, in amounts corresponding to the total of all visa, entry, residence, or other similar fees, taxes, or charges assessed or levied against nationals of the United States by the foreign countries of which such nonimmigrants are nationals or stateless residents: Provided, That nonimmigrant visas issued to aliens coming to the United States in transit to and from the headquarters district of the United Nations in accordance with the provisions of the Headquarters Agreement shall be gratis. Subject to such criteria as the Secretary of State may prescribe, including the duration of stay of the alien and the financial burden upon the charitable organization, the Secretary of State shall waive or reduce the fee for application and issuance of a nonimmigrant visa for any alien coming to the United States primarily for, or in activities related to, a charitable purpose involving health or nursing care, the provision of food or housing, job training, or any other similar direct service or assistance to poor or otherwise needy individuals in the United States.

HISTORY: (June 27, 1952, ch 477, Title II, Ch 9, § 281, 66 Stat. 230; Oct. 3, 1965, P. L. 89-236, § 14, 79 Stat. 919; Oct. 21, 1968, P. L. 90-609, § 1, 82 Stat. 1199; Oct. 6, 1997, P. L. 105-54, § 2(a), 111 Stat. 1175.)

§ 282. [8 U.S.C. § 1352] Printing of reentry permits and blank forms of manifests and crew lists; sale to public.

(a) Reentry permits issued under section 223 [8 USCS § 1203] shall be printed on distinctive safety paper and shall be prepared and issued under regulations prescribed by the Attorney General.

(b) The Public Printer [Director of the Government Publishing Office] is authorized to print for sale to the public by the Superintendent of Documents, upon prepayment, copies of blank forms of manifests and crew lists and such other forms as may be prescribed and authorized by the Attorney General to be sold pursuant to the provisions of this title.

HISTORY: (June 27, 1952, ch 477, Title II, Ch 9, § 283, 66 Stat. 231; Oct. 24, 1988, P.L. 100-525, § 9(p), 102 Stat. 2621.)

§ 283. [8 U.S.C. § 1353] Travel expenses and expense of transporting remains of officers and employees dying outside of United States.

When officers, inspectors, or other employees of the Service are ordered to perform duties in a foreign country, or are transferred from one station to another, in the United States or in a foreign country, or while performing duties in any foreign country become eligible for voluntary retirement and return to the United States, they shall be allowed their traveling expenses in accordance with such regulations as the Attorney General may deem advisable, and they may also be allowed, within the discretion and under written orders of the Attorney General, the expenses incurred for the transfer of their wives and dependent children, their household effects and other personal property, including the expenses for packing, crating, freight, unpacking, temporary storage, and drayage thereof in accordance with subchapter II of chapter 57 of title 5, United States Code [5 USCS §§ 5721 et seq.]. The expense of transporting the remains of such officers, inspectors, or other employees who die while in, or in transit to, a foreign country in the discharge of their official duties to their former homes in this country for interment, and the ordinary and necessary expenses of such interment and of preparation for shipment, are authorized to be paid on the written order of the Attorney General.

HISTORY: (June 27, 1952, ch 477, Title II, Ch 9, § 283, 66 Stat. 231; Oct. 24, 1988, P.L. 100-525, § 9(p), 102 Stat. 2621.)

§ 284. [8 U.S.C. § 1354] Applicability to members of the armed forces.

(a) Nothing contained in this title shall be construed so as to limit, restrict, deny, or affect the coming into or departure from the United States of an alien member of the Armed Forces of the United States who is in the uniform of, or who bears documents identifying him as a member of, such Armed Forces, and who is coming to or departing from the United States under official orders or permit of such Armed Forces: Provided, That nothing contained in this section shall be construed to give to or confer upon any such alien any other privileges, rights, benefits, exemptions, or immunities under this Act, which are not otherwise specifically granted by this Act.

(b) If a person lawfully admitted for permanent residence is the spouse or child of a member of the Armed Forces of the United States, is authorized to accompany the member and reside abroad with the member pursuant to the member's official orders, and is so accompanying and residing with the member (in marital union if a spouse), then the residence and physical presence of the person abroad shall not be treated as—

(1) an abandonment or relinquishment of lawful permanent resident status for purposes of clause (i) of section 101(a)(13)(C) [8 USCS § 1101(a)(13)(C)]; or

(2) an absence from the United States for purposes of clause (ii) of such section.

HISTORY: (June 27, 1952, ch 477, Title II, Ch 9, § 284, 66 Stat. 232; Jan. 28, 2008, P.L. 110-181, Div A, Title VI, Subtitle G, § 673, 122 Stat. 185.)

§ 285. [8 U.S.C. § 1355] Disposal of privileges at immigrant stations; rentals; retail sale; disposition of receipts.

(a) Subject to such conditions and limitations as the Attorney General shall prescribe, all exclusive privileges of exchanging money, transporting passengers or baggage, keeping eating houses, or other like privileges in connection with any United States immigrant station, shall be disposed of to the lowest responsible and capable bidder (other than an alien) in accordance with the provisions of section 3709 of the Revised Statutes, as amended (41 U. S. C. 5) [41 USCS § 6101], and for the use of Government property in connection with the exercise of such exclusive privileges a reasonable rental may be charged. The feeding of aliens, or the furnishing of any other necessary service in connection with any United States immigrant station, may be performed by the Service without regard to the foregoing provisions of this subsection if the Attorney General shall find that it would be advantageous to the Government in terms of economy and efficiency. No intoxicating liquors shall be sold at any immigrant station.

(b) Such articles determined by the Attorney General to be necessary to the health and welfare of aliens detained at any immigrant station, when not otherwise readily procurable by such aliens, may be sold at reasonable prices to such aliens through Government canteens operated by the Service, under such conditions and limitations as the Attorney General shall prescribe.

(c) All rentals or other receipts accruing from the disposal of privileges, and all moneys arising from the sale of articles through Service-operated canteens, authorized by this section, shall be covered into the Treasury to the credit of the appropriation for the enforcement of this title.

HISTORY: (June 27, 1952, ch 477, Title II, Ch 9, § 285, 66 Stat. 232.)

§ 286. [8 U.S.C. § 1356] Disposition of moneys collected under the provisions of this title.

(a) Detention, transportation, hospitalization, and all other expenses of detained aliens; expenses of landing stations. All moneys paid into the Treasury to reimburse the Service for detention, transportation, hospitalization, and all other expenses of detained aliens paid from the appropriation for the enforcement of this Act, and all moneys paid into the Treasury to reimburse the Service for expenses of landing stations referred to in section 238(b) [233(b)] [8 USCS § 1223(b)] paid by the Service from the appropriation for the enforcement of this Act, shall be credited to the appropriation for the enforcement of this Act for the fiscal year in which the expenses were incurred.

(b) Purchase of evidence. Moneys expended from appropriations for the Service for the purchase of evidence and subsequently recovered shall be reimbursed to the current appropriation for the Service.

(c) Fees and administrative fines and penalties; exception. Except as otherwise provided in subsection (a) and subsection (b), or in any other provision of this title, all moneys received in payment of fees and administrative fines and penalties under this title shall be covered into the Treasury as miscellaneous receipts: Provided, however, That all fees received from applicants residing in the Virgin Islands of the United States, and in Guam, required to be paid under section 281 [8 USCS § 1351], shall be paid over to the Treasury of the Virgin Islands and to the Treasury of Guam, respectively.

(d) Schedule of fees. In addition to any other fee authorized by law, the Attorney General shall charge and collect $7 per individual for the immigration inspection of each passenger arriving at a port of entry in the United States, or for the preinspection of a passenger in a place outside of the United States prior to such arrival, aboard a commercial aircraft or commercial vessel.

(e) Limitations on fees.

(1) Except as provided in paragraph (3), no fee shall be charged under subsection (d) for immigration inspection or preinspection provided in connection with the arrival of any passenger, other than aircraft passengers, whose journey originated in the following:

(A) Canada,

(B) Mexico,

(C) a State, territory or possession of the United States, or

(D) any adjacent island (within the meaning of section 101(b)(5) [8 USCS § 1101(b)(5)]).

(2) No fee may be charged under subsection (d) with respect to the arrival of any passenger—

(A) who is in transit to a destination outside the United States, and

(B) for whom immigration inspection services are not provided.

(3) The Attorney General shall charge and collect $3 per individual for the immigration inspection or pre-inspection of each commercial vessel passenger whose journey originated in the United States or in any place set forth in paragraph (1): Provided, That this requirement shall not apply to immigration inspection at designated ports of entry of passengers arriving by ferry, or by Great Lakes vessels on the Great Lakes and connecting waterways when operating on a regular schedule. For the purposes of this paragraph, the term "ferry" means a vessel, in other than ocean or coastwise service, having provisions only for deck passengers and/or vehicles, operating on a short run on a frequent schedule between two points over the most direct water route, and offering a public service of a type normally attributed to a bridge or tunnel.

(f) Collection.

(1) Each person that issues a document or ticket to an individual for transportation by a commercial vessel or commercial aircraft into the United States shall—

(A) collect from that individual the fee charged under subsection (d) at the time the document or ticket is issued; and

(B) identify on that document or ticket the fee charged under subsection (d) as a Federal inspection fee.

(2) If—

(A) a document or ticket for transportation of a passenger into the United States is issued in a foreign country; and

(B) the fee charged under subsection (d) is not collected at the time such document or ticket is issued;

the person providing transportation to such passenger shall collect such fee at the time such passenger departs from the United States and shall provide such passenger a receipt for the payment of such fee.

(3) The person who collects fees under paragraph (1) or (2) shall remit those fees to the Attorney General at any time before the date that is thirty-one days after the close of the calendar quarter in which the fees are collected, except the fourth quarter payment for fees collected from airline passengers shall be made on the date that is ten days before the end of the fiscal year, and the first quarter payment shall include any collections made in the preceding quarter that were not remitted with the previous payment. Regulations issued by the Attorney General under this subsection with respect to the collection of the fees charged under subsection (d) and the remittance of such fees to the Treasury of the United States shall be consistent with the regulations issued by the Secretary of the Treasury for the collection and remittance of the taxes imposed by subchapter C of chapter 33 of the Internal Revenue Code of 1986 [26 USCS §§ 4261 et seq.], but only to the extent the regulations issued with respect to such taxes do not conflict with the provisions of this section.

(g) Provision of immigration inspection and preinspection services. Notwithstanding the Act of March 2, 1931, 46 Stat. 1467 (8 U.S.C. 1353b), or any other provision of law, the immigration services required to be provided to passengers upon arrival in the United States on scheduled airline flights shall be adequately provided when needed and at no cost (other than the fees imposed under subsection (d)) to airlines and airline passengers at:

(1) immigration serviced airports, and

(2) places located outside of the United States at which an immigration officer is stationed for the purpose of providing such immigration services.

(h) Disposition of receipts.

(1) (A) There is established in the general fund of the Treasury a separate account which shall be known as the "Immigration User Fee Account". Notwithstanding any other section of this title, there shall be deposited as offsetting receipts into the Immigration User Fee Account all fees collected under subsection (d) of this section, to remain available until expended. At the end of each 2-year period, beginning with the creation of this account, the Attorney General, following a public rulemaking with opportunity for notice and comment, shall submit a report to the Congress concerning the status of the account, including any balances therein, and recommend any adjustment in the prescribed fee that may be required to ensure that the receipts collected from the fee charged for the succeeding two years equal, as closely as possible, the cost of providing these services.

(B) Notwithstanding any other provisions of law, all civil fines or penalties collected pursuant to sections 243(c), 271, and 273 of this title [8 USCS §§ 1253(c), 1321, 1323] and all liquidated damages and expenses collected pursuant to this Act shall be deposited in the Immigration User Fee Account.

(2) (A) The Secretary of the Treasury shall refund out of the Immigration User Fee Account to any appropriation the amount paid out of such appropriation for expenses incurred by the Attorney General in providing immigration inspection and preinspection services for commercial aircraft or vessels and in—

(i) providing overtime immigration inspection services for commercial aircraft or vessels;

(ii) administration of debt recovery, including the establishment and operation of a national collections office;

(iii) expansion, operation and maintenance of information systems for nonimmigrant control and debt collection;

(iv) detection of fraudulent documents used by passengers traveling to the United States, including training of, and technical assistance to, commercial airline personnel regarding such detection;

(v) providing detention and removal services for inadmissible aliens arriving on commercial aircraft and vessels and for any alien who is inadmissible under section 212(a) [8 USCS § 1182(a)] who has attempted illegal entry into the United States through avoidance of immigration inspection at air or sea ports-of-entry; and

(vi) providing removal and asylum proceedings at air or sea ports-of-entry for inadmissible aliens arriving on commercial aircraft and vessels including immigration removal proceedings resulting from presentation of fraudulent documents and failure to present documentation and for any alien who is inadmissible under section 212(a) [8 USCS § 1182(a)] who has attempted illegal entry into the United States through avoidance of immigration inspection at air or sea ports-of-entry.

The Attorney General shall provide for expenditures for training and assistance described in clause (iv) in an amount, for any fiscal year, not less than 5 percent of the total of the expenses incurred that are described in the previous sentence.

(B) The amounts which are required to be refunded under subparagraph (A) shall be refunded at least quarterly on the basis of estimates made by the Attorney General of the expenses referred to in subparagraph (A). Proper adjustments shall be made in the amounts subsequently refunded under subparagraph (A) to the extent prior estimates were in excess of, or less than, the amount required to be refunded under subparagraph (A).

(i) Reimbursement. Notwithstanding any other provision of law, the Attorney General is authorized to receive reimbursement from the owner, operator, or agent of a private or commercial aircraft, train, or vessel, or from any airport, rail line, or seaport authority for expenses incurred by the Attorney General in providing immigration inspection services which are rendered at the request of such person or authority (including the salary and expenses of individuals employed by the Attorney General to provide such immigration inspection services). Reimbursements under this subsection may be collected in advance of the provision of such immigration inspection services. Notwithstanding subsection (h)(1)(B), and only to the extent provided in appropriations Acts, any amounts collected under this subsection shall be credited as offsetting collections to the currently applicable appropriation, account, or fund of U.S. Customs and Border Protection, remain available until expended, and be available for the purposes for which such appropriation, account, or fund is authorized to be used.

(j) Regulations. The Attorney General may prescribe such rules and regulations as may be necessary to carry out the provisions of this section.

(k) Advisory committee. In accordance with the provisions of chapter 10 of title 5, United States Code [5 USCS §§ 1001 et seq.], the Attorney General shall establish an advisory committee, whose membership shall consist of representatives from the airline and other transportation industries who may be subject to any fee or charge authorized by law or proposed by the Immigration and Naturalization Service for the purpose of covering expenses incurred by the Immigration and Naturalization Service. The advisory committee shall meet on a periodic basis and shall advise the Attorney General on issues related to the performance of the inspectional services of the Immigration and Naturalization Service. This advice shall include, but not be limited to, such issues as the time periods during which such services should be performed, the proper number and deployment of inspection officers, the level of fees, and the appropriateness of any proposed fee. The Attorney General shall give substantial consideration to the views of the advisory committee in the exercise of his duties.

(l) Report to Congress. In addition to the reporting requirements established pursuant to subsection (h), the Attorney General shall prepare and submit annually to the Congress, not later than March 31st of each year, a statement of the financial condition of the "Immigration User Fee Account" including beginning account balance, revenues, withdrawals and their purpose, ending balance, projections for the ensuing fiscal year and a full and complete workload analysis showing on a port by port basis the current and projected need for inspectors. The statement shall indicate the success rate of the Immigration and Naturalization

Service in meeting the forty-five minute inspection standard and shall provide detailed statistics regarding the number of passengers inspected within the standard, progress that is being made to expand the utilization of United States citizen by-pass, the number of passengers for whom the standard is not met and the length of their delay, locational breakdown of these statistics and the steps being taken to correct any nonconformity.

(m) Immigration Examinations Fee Account. Notwithstanding any other provisions of law, all adjudication fees as are designated by the Attorney General in regulations shall be deposited as offsetting receipts into a separate account entitled "Immigration Examinations Fee Account" in the Treasury of the United States, whether collected directly by the Attorney General or through clerks of courts: Provided, however, That all fees received by the Attorney General from applicants residing in the Virgin Islands of the United States, and in Guam, under this subsection shall be paid over to the treasury of the Virgin Islands and to the treasury of Guam: Provided further, That fees for providing adjudication and naturalization services may be set at a level that will ensure recovery of the full costs of providing all such services, including the costs of similar services provided without charge to asylum applicants or other immigrants. Such fees may also be set at a level that will recover any additional costs associated with the administration of the fees collected.

(n) Reimbursement of administrative expenses; transfer of deposits to General Fund of United States Treasury. All deposits into the "Immigration Examinations Fee Account" shall remain available until expended to the Attorney General to reimburse any appropriation the amount paid out of such appropriation for expenses in providing immigration adjudication and naturalization services and the collection, safeguarding and accounting for fees deposited in and funds reimbursed from the "Immigration Examinations Fee Account".

(o) Annual financial reports to Congress. The Attorney General shall prepare and submit annually to Congress statements of financial condition of the "Immigration Examinations Fee Account", including beginning account balance, revenues, withdrawals, and ending account balance and projections for the ensuing fiscal year.

(p) Additional effective dates. The provisions set forth in subsections (m), (n), and (o) of this section apply to adjudication and naturalization services performed and to related fees collected on or after October 1, 1988.

(q) Land Border Inspection Fee Account.

(1) (A) (i) Notwithstanding any other provision of law, the Attorney General is authorized to establish, by regulation, not more than 96 projects under which a fee may be charged and collected for inspection services provided at one or more land border points of entry. Such projects may include the establishment of commuter lanes to be made available to qualified United States citizens and aliens, as determined by the Attorney General.

(ii) This subparagraph shall take effect, with respect to any project described in clause (1) [(i)] that was not authorized to be commenced before the date of the enactment of the Illegal Immigration Reform and Immigrant Responsibility Act of 1996 [enacted Sept. 30, 1996], 30 days after submission of a written plan by the Attorney General detailing the proposed implementation of such project.

(iii) The Attorney General shall prepare and submit on a quarterly basis a status report on each land border inspection project implemented under this subparagraph.

(B) The Attorney General, in consultation with the Secretary of the Treasury, may conduct pilot projects to demonstrate the use of designated ports of entry after working hours through the use of card reading machines or other appropriate technology.

(2) All of the fees collected under this subsection, including receipts for services performed in processing forms I-94, I-94W, and I-68, and other similar applications processed at land border ports of entry, shall be deposited as offsetting receipts in a separate account within the general fund of the Treasury of the United States, to remain available until expended. Such account shall be known as the Land Border Inspection Fee Account.

(3) (A) The Secretary of the Treasury shall refund, at least on a quarterly basis amounts to any appropriations for expenses incurred in providing inspection services at land border points of entry. Such expenses shall include—

(i) the providing of overtime inspection services;

(ii) the expansion, operation and maintenance of information systems for nonimmigrant control;

(iii) the hire of additional permanent and temporary inspectors;

(iv) the minor construction costs associated with the addition of new traffic lanes (with the concurrence of the General Services Administration);

(v) the detection of fraudulent documents used by passengers travelling to the United States;

(vi) providing for the administration of said account.

(B) The amounts required to be refunded from the Land Border Inspection Fee Account for fiscal years 1992 and thereafter shall be refunded in accordance with estimates made in the budget request of the Attorney General for those fiscal years: Provided, That any proposed changes in the amounts designated in said budget requests shall only be made after notification to the Committees on Appropriations of the House of Representatives and the Senate in accordance with section 606 of Public Law 101-162 [unclassified].

(4) The Attorney General will prepare and submit annually to the Congress statements of financial condition of the Land Border Immigration Fee Account, including beginning account balance, revenues, withdrawals, and ending account balance and projection for the ensuing fiscal year.

(r) Breached Bond/Detention Fund.

(1) Notwithstanding any other provision of law, there is established in the general fund of the Treasury a separate account which shall be known as the Breached Bond/Detention Fund (in this subsection referred to as the "Fund").

(2) There shall be deposited as offsetting receipts into the Fund all breached cash and surety bonds, in excess of $8,000,000, posted under this Act which are recovered by the Department of Justice, and amount [amounts] described in section 245(i)(3)(b) [245(i)(3)(B)] [8 USCS § 1255(i)(3)(B)].

(3) Such amounts as are deposited into the Fund shall remain available until expended and shall be refunded out of the Fund by the Secretary of the Treasury, at least on a quarterly basis, to the Attorney General for the following purposes—

(i) for expenses incurred in the collection of breached bonds, and

(ii) for expenses associated with the detention of illegal aliens.

(4) The amounts required to be refunded from the Fund for fiscal year 1998 and thereafter shall be refunded in accordance with estimates made in the budget request of the President for those fiscal years. Any proposed changes in the amounts designated in such budget requests shall only be made after Congressional reprogramming notification in accordance with the reprogramming guidelines for the applicable fiscal year.

(5) The Attorney General shall prepare and submit annually to the Congress, statements of financial condition of the Fund, including the beginning balance, receipts, refunds to appropriations, transfers to the general fund, and the ending balance.

(6) For fiscal year 1993 only, the Attorney General may transfer up to $1,000,000 from the Immigration User Fee Account to the Fund for initial expenses necessary to enhance collection efforts: Provided, That any such transfers shall be refunded from the Fund back to the Immigration User Fee Account by December 31, 1993.

(s) H-1B Nonimmigrant Petitioner Account.

(1) In general. There is established in the general fund of the Treasury a separate account, which shall be known as the "H-1B Nonimmigrant Petitioner Account". Notwithstanding any other section of this title, there shall be deposited as offsetting receipts into the account all fees collected under paragraphs (9) and (11) of section 214(c) [8 USCS § 1184(c)].

(2) Use of fees for job training. 50 percent of amounts deposited into the H-1B Nonimmigrant Petitioner Account shall remain available to the Secretary of Labor until expended for demonstration programs and projects described in section 414(c) of the American Competitiveness and Workforce Improvement Act of 1998 [29 USCS § 2916a].

(3) Use of fees for low-income scholarship program. 30 percent of the amounts deposited into the H-1B Nonimmigrant Petitioner Account shall remain available to the Director of the National Science Foundation until expended for scholarships described in section 414(d) of the American Competitiveness and Workforce Improvement Act of 1998 [42 USCS § 1869c] for low-income students enrolled in a program of study leading to a degree in mathematics, engineering, or computer science.

(4) National Science Foundation competitive grant program for K-12 math, science and technology education.

(A) In general. 10 percent of the amounts deposited into the H-1B Nonimmigrant Petitioner Account shall remain available to the Director of the National Science Foundation until expended to carry out a direct or matching grant program to support private-public partnerships in K-12 education.

(B) Types of programs covered. The Director shall award grants to such programs, including those which support the development and implementation of standards-based instructional materials models and related student assessments that enable K-12 students to acquire an understanding of science, mathematics, and technology, as well as to develop critical thinking skills; provide systemic improvement in training K-12 teachers and education for students in science, mathematics, and technology; support the professional development of K-12 math and science teachers in the use of technology in the classroom; stimulate system-wide K-12 reform of science, mathematics, and technology in rural, economically disadvantaged regions of the United States; provide externships and other opportunities for students to increase their appreciation and understanding of science, mathematics, engineering, and technology (including summer institutes sponsored by an institution of higher education for students in grades 7-12 that provide instruction in such fields); involve partnerships of industry, educational institutions, and community organizations to address the educational needs of disadvantaged communities; provide college preparatory support to expose and prepare students for careers in science, mathematics, engineering, and technology; and provide for carrying out systemic reform activities under section 3(a)(1) of the National Science Foundation Act of 1950 (42 U.S.C. 1862(a)(1)).

(5) Use of fees for duties relating to petitions. 5 percent of the amounts deposited into the H-1B Nonimmigrant Petitioner Account shall remain available to the Secretary of Homeland Security until expended to carry out duties under paragraphs (1) and (9) of section 214(c) [8 USCS § 1184(c)] related to petitions made for nonimmigrants described in section 101(a)(15)(H)(i)(b) [8 USCS § 1101(a)(15)(H)(i)(b)], under paragraph (1) (C) or (D) of section 204 [204(a)] [8 USCS § 1154(a)] related to petitions for immigrants described in section 203(b) [8 USCS § 1153(b)].

(6) Use of fees for application processing and enforcement. For fiscal year 1999, 5 percent [4 percent] of the amounts deposited into the H-1B Nonimmigrant Petitioner Account shall remain available to the Secretary of Labor until expended for decreasing the processing time for applications under section 212(n)(1) [8 USCS § 1182(n)(1)] and for carrying out section 212(n)(2) [8 USCS § 1182(n)(2)]. Beginning with fiscal year 2000, 5 percent of the amounts deposited into the

H-1B Nonimmigrant Petitioner Account shall remain available to the Secretary of Labor until expended for decreasing the processing time for applications under section 212(n)(1) [8 USCS § 1182(n)(1)] and section 212(a)(5)(A) [8 USCS § 1182(a)(5)(A)].

(t) Genealogy Fee.

(1) There is hereby established the Genealogy Fee for providing genealogy research and information services. This fee shall be deposited as offsetting collections into the Examinations Fee Account. Fees for such research and information services may be set at a level that will ensure the recovery of the full costs of providing all such services.

(2) The Attorney General will prepare and submit annually to Congress statements of the financial condition of the Genealogy Fee.

(3) Any officer or employee of the Immigration and Naturalization Service shall collect fees prescribed under regulation before disseminating any requested genealogical information.

(u) Premium fee for certain immigration benefit types.

(1) In general. The Secretary of Homeland Security is authorized to establish and collect a premium fee for the immigration benefit types described in paragraph (2). Such fee shall be paid in addition to any other fees authorized by law, deposited as offsetting receipts in the Immigration Examinations Fee Account established under subsection (m), and used for the purposes described in paragraph (4).

(2) Immigration benefit types. Subject to reasonable conditions or limitations, the Secretary shall establish a premium fee under paragraph (1) in connection with—

(A) employment-based nonimmigrant petitions and associated applications for dependents of the beneficiaries of such petitions;

(B) employment-based immigrant petitions filed by or on behalf of aliens described in paragraph (1), (2), or (3) of section 203(b) [8 USCS § 1153(b)];

(C) applications to change or extend nonimmigrant status;

(D) applications for employment authorization; and

(E) any other immigration benefit type that the Secretary deems appropriate for premium processing.

(3) Amount of fee.

(A) In general. Subject to subparagraph (C), with respect to an immigration benefit type designated for premium processing by the Secretary on or before August 1, 2020, the premium fee shall be $2,500, except that the premium fee for a petition for classification of a nonimmigrant described in subparagraph (H)(ii)(b) or (R) of section 101(a)(15) [8 USCS § 1101(a)(15)] shall be $1,500.

(B) Other immigration benefit types. With respect to an immigration benefit type designated for premium processing but not described in subparagraph (A), the initial premium fee shall be established by regulation, which shall include a detailed methodology supporting the proposed premium fee amount.

(C) Biennial adjustment. The Secretary may adjust a premium fee under subparagraph (A) or (B) on a biennial basis by the percentage (if any) by which the Consumer Price Index for All Urban Consumers for the month of June preceding the date on which such adjustment takes effect exceeds the Consumer Price Index for All Urban Consumers for the same month of the second preceding calendar year. The provisions of section 553 of title 5, United States Code, shall not apply to an adjustment authorized under this subparagraph.

(4) Use of fee. Fees collected under this subsection may only be used by U.S. Citizenship and Immigration Services to—

(A) provide the services described in paragraph (5) to premium processing requestors;

(B) make infrastructure improvements in adjudications processes and the provision of information and services to immigration and naturalization benefit requestors;

(C) respond to adjudication demands, including by reducing the number of pending immigration and naturalization benefit requests; and

(D) otherwise offset the cost of providing adjudication and naturalization services.

(5) Premium processing services. The Secretary—

(A) may suspend the availability of premium processing for designated immigration benefit requests only if circumstances prevent the completion of processing of a significant number of such requests within the required period; and

(B) shall ensure that premium processing requestors have direct and reliable access to current case status information as well as the ability to communicate with the premium processing units at each service center or office that provides premium processing services.

(v) Fraud Prevention and Detection Account.

(1) In general. There is established in the general fund of the Treasury a separate account, which shall be known as the "Fraud Prevention and Detection Account". Notwithstanding any other provision of law, there shall be deposited as offsetting receipts into the account all fees collected under paragraph (12) or (13) of section 214(c) [8 USCS § 1184(c)].

(2) Use of fees to combat fraud.

(A) Secretary of State. One-third of the amounts deposited into the Fraud Prevention and Detection Account shall remain available to the Secretary of State until expended for programs and activities at United States embassies and consulates abroad—

(i) to increase the number [of] diplomatic security personnel assigned exclusively or primarily to the function of preventing and detecting fraud by applicants for visas described in subparagraph (H)(i), (H)(ii), or (L) of section 101(a)(15) [8 USCS § 1101(a)(15)];

(ii) otherwise to prevent and detect visa fraud, including primarily fraud by applicants for visas described in subparagraph (H)(i), (H)(ii), or (L) of section 101(a)(15) [8 USCS § 1101(a)(15)], in cooperation with the Secretary of Homeland Security or pursuant to the terms of a memorandum of understanding or other agreement between the Secretary of State and the Secretary of Homeland Security; and

(iii) upon request by the Secretary of Homeland Security, to assist such Secretary in carrying out the fraud prevention and detection programs and activities described in subparagraph (B).

(B) Secretary of Homeland Security. One-third of the amounts deposited into the Fraud Prevention and Detection Account shall remain available to the Secretary of Homeland Security until expended for programs and activities to prevent and detect immigration benefit fraud, including fraud with respect to petitions filed under paragraph (1) or (2)(A) of section 214(c) [8 USCS § 1184(c)] to grant an alien nonimmigrant status described in subparagraph (H) or (L) of section 101(a)(15) [8 USCS § 1101(a)(15)].

(C) Secretary of Labor. One-third of the amounts deposited into the Fraud Prevention and Detection Account shall remain available to the Secretary of Labor until expended for wage and hour enforcement programs and activities otherwise authorized to be conducted by the Secretary of Labor that focus on industries likely to employ nonimmigrants, including enforcement programs and activities described in section 212(n) [8 USCS § 1182(n)] and enforcement programs and activities related to section 214(c)(14)(A)(i) [8 USCS § 1184(c)(14)(A)(i)].

(D) Consultation. The Secretary of State, the Secretary of Homeland Security, and the Secretary of Labor shall consult one another with respect to the use of the funds in the Fraud Prevention and Detection Account or for programs and activities to prevent and detect fraud with respect to petitions under paragraph (1) or (2)(A) of section 214(c) [8 USCS § 1184(c)] to grant an alien nonimmigrant status described in section 101(a)(15)(H)(ii) [8 USCS § 1101(a)(15)(H)(ii)].

HISTORY: (June 27, 1952, ch 477, Title II, Ch 9, § 286, 66 Stat. 232; Dec. 29, 1981, P. L. 97-116, § 13, 95 Stat. 1618; Oct. 18, 1986, P. L. 99-500; Title I, § 101(b) [Title II, § 205(a)], 100 Stat. 3341-53; Oct. 30, 1986, P. L. 100-591, § 101(b) [Title II, § 205(a), 100 Stat. 3341-53 (as amended Oct. 24, 1988, P. L. 100-525, § 4(a)(2)(A), 102 Stat. 2615); Nov. 14, 1986, P. L. 99-653, § 7(d)(1) (as added Oct. 24, 1988, P. L. 100-525, § 8(f), 102 Stat. 2617); July 11, 1987, P. L. 100-71, Title I, ch I, 101 Stat. 394; Oct. 1, 1988, P. L. 100-459, Title II, § 209(a), 102 Stat. 2203; Oct. 24, 1988, P. L. 100-525, § 4(a)(1), 102 Stat. 2614; Nov. 21, 1989, P. L. 101-162, Title II, 103 Stat. 1000; Nov. 5, 1990, P. L. 101-515, Title II, § 210(a), (d), 104 Stat. 2120, 2121; Dec. 12, 1991, P. L. 102-232, Title III, § 309(a)(1)(A)(i), (B), (2), (b)(12), 105 Stat. 1757, 1758, 1759; Oct. 6, 1992, P. L. 102-395, Title I, § 112, 106 Stat. 1843; Oct. 27, 1993, P. L. 103-121, Title I, 107 Stat. 1161; Oct. 25, 1994, P. L. 103-416, Title II, § 219(t), 108 Stat. 4317; Sept. 30, 1996, P. L. 104-208, Div C, Title I, Subtitle B, § 122(a), 124(a)(1), Title III, Subtitle A, § 308(d)(3)(A), (4)(K), (e)(1)(L), Subtitle F, §§ 376(b), 382(b), Title VI, Subtitle E, § 671(b)(11), (e)(5), (6), 110 Stat. 3009-560, 3009-562, 3009-617, 3009-618, 3009-619, 3009-648, 3009-651, 3009-722, 3009-723; Nov. 26, 1997, P. L. 105-119, Title I, § 110(1), (2), 111 Stat. 2458; Oct. 21, 1998, P. L. 105-277, Div A, § 101(b) [Title I, § 114], Div C, Title IV, § 414(b), 112 Stat. 2681-68, 2681-652; Nov. 29, 1999, P. L. 106-113, Div B, § 1000(a)(1), 113 Stat. 1535; Oct. 17, 2000, P. L. 106-313, Title I, §§ 110(a), 113, 114 Stat. 1255, 1261; Dec. 21, 2000, P. L. 106-553, § 1(a)(2), 114 Stat. 2762; Dec. 21, 2000, P. L. 106-554, § 1(a)(1), 114 Stat. 2763; Nov. 28, 2001, P. L. 107-77, Title I, §§ 109, 110, 115 Stat. 765; May 14, 2002, P. L. 107-173, Title IV, § 403(a), 116 Stat. 559; Aug. 2, 2002, P. L. 107-206, Title I, Ch. 2, § 202, 116 Stat. 832; Nov. 2, 2002, P. L. 107-273, Div C, Title I, Subtitle A, § 11016(2), 116 Stat. 1824; Nov. 25, 2002, P. L. 107-296, Title IV, Subtitle E, § 457, 116 Stat. 2201; Feb. 20, 2003, P. L. 108-7, Div B, Title I, § 108, Div L, § 107, 117 Stat. 67, 532; Sept. 3, 2003, P. L. 108-77, Title IV, § 402(d)(2), 117 Stat. 946; Dec. 8, 2004, P. L. 108-447, Div J, Title IV, Subtitle B, §§ 426(b), 427, 118 Stat. 3357, 3358; May 11, 2005, P. L. 109-13, Div A, Title VI, § 6046, Div B, Title IV, § 403(b), 119 Stat. 295, 319; Jan. 11, 2007, P. L. 109-472, § 2, 120 Stat. 3554; Dec. 16, 2009, P. L. 111-117, Div D, Title V, § 524(a), 123 Stat. 3283; Feb. 24, 2016, P. L. 114-125, Title VIII, Subtitle B, § 818(a), 130 Stat. 222; Oct. 5, 2018, P.L. 115-254, Div B, Title V, § 573, 132 Stat. 3389; Oct. 1, 2020, P.L. 116-159, Div D, Title I, § 4102(a), 134 Stat. 738; Dec. 27, 2022, P.L. 117-286, § 4(a)(44), 136 Stat. 4310.)

§ 287. [8 U.S.C. § 1357] Powers of immigration officers and employees.

(a) Powers without warrant. Any officer or employee of the Service authorized under regulations prescribed by the Attorney General shall have power without warrant—

(1) to interrogate any alien or person believed to be an alien as to his right to be or to remain in the United States;

(2) to arrest any alien who in his presence or view is entering or attempting to enter the United States in violation of any law or regulation made in pursuance of law regulating the admission, exclusion, expulsion, or removal of aliens, or to arrest any alien in the United States, if he has reason to believe that the alien so arrested is in the United States in violation of any such law or regulation and is likely to escape before a warrant can be obtained for his arrest, but the alien arrested shall be taken without unnecessary delay for examination before an officer of the Service having authority to examine aliens as to their right to enter or remain in the United States;

(3) within a reasonable distance from any external boundary of the United States, to board and search for aliens any vessel within the territorial waters of the United States and any railway car, aircraft, conveyance, or vehicle, and within a distance of twenty-five miles from any such external boundary to have access to private lands, but not dwellings, for the purpose of patrolling the border to prevent the illegal entry of aliens into the United States;

(4) to make arrests for felonies which have been committed and which are cognizable under any law of the United States regulating the admission, exclusion, expulsion, or removal of aliens, if he has reason to believe that the person so arrested is guilty of such felony and if there is likelihood of the person escaping before a warrant can be obtained for his arrest, but the person arrested shall be taken without unnecessary delay before the nearest available officer empowered to commit persons charged with offenses against the laws of the United States; and

(5) to make arrests—

(A) for any offense against the United States, if the offense is committed in the officer's or employee's presence, or

(B) for any felony cognizable under the laws of the United States, if the officer or employee has reasonable grounds to believe that the person to be arrested has committed or is committing such felony,

if the officer or employee is performing duties relating to the enforcement of the immigration laws at the time of the arrest and if there is a likelihood of the person escaping before a warrant can be obtained for his arrest.

Under regulations prescribed by the Attorney General, an officer or employee of the Service may carry a firearm and may execute and serve any order, warrant, subpoena, summons, or other process issued under the authority of the United States. The authority to make arrests under paragraph (5)(B) shall only be effective on and after the date on which the Attorney General publishes final regulations which (i) prescribe the categories of officers and employees of the Service who may use force (including deadly force) and the circumstances under which such force may be used, (ii) establish standards with respect to enforcement activities of the Service, (iii) require that any officer or employee of the Service is not authorized to make arrests under paragraph (5)(B) unless the officer or employee has received certification as having completed a training program which covers such arrests and standards described in clause (ii), and (iv) establish an expedited, internal review process for violations of such standards, which process is consistent with standard agency procedure regarding confidentiality of matters related to internal investigations.

(b) Administration of oath; taking of evidence. Any officer or employee of the Service designated by the Attorney General, whether individually or as one of a class, shall have power and authority to administer oaths and to take and consider evidence concerning the privilege of any person to enter, reenter, pass through, or reside in the United States, or concerning any matter which is material or relevant to the enforcement of this Act and the administration of the Service; and any person to whom such oath has been administered (or who has executed an unsworn declaration, certificate, verification, or statement under penalty of perjury as permitted under section 1746 of title 28, United States Code), under the provisions of this Act, who shall knowingly or willfully give false evidence or swear (or subscribe under penalty of perjury as permitted under section 1746 of title 28, United States Code) to any false statement concerning any matter referred to in this subsection shall be guilty of perjury and shall be punished as provided by section 1621, title 18, United States Code.

(c) Search without warrant. Any officer or employee of the Service authorized and designated under regulations prescribed by the Attorney General, whether individually or as one of a class, shall have power to conduct a search, without warrant, of the person, and of the personal effects in the possession of any person seeking admission to the United States, concerning whom such officer or employee may have reasonable cause to suspect that grounds exist for denial of admission to the United States under this Act which would be disclosed by such search.

(d) Detainer of aliens for violation of controlled substances laws. In the case of an alien who is arrested by a Federal, State, or local law enforcement official for a violation of any law relating to controlled substances, if the official (or another official)—

(1) has reason to believe that the alien may not have been lawfully admitted to the United States or otherwise is not lawfully present in the United States,

(2) expeditiously informs an appropriate officer or employee of the Service authorized and designated by the Attorney General of the arrest and of facts concerning the status of the alien, and

(3) requests the Service to determine promptly whether or not to issue a detainer to detain the alien,

the officer or employee of the Service shall promptly determine whether or not to issue such a detainer. If such a detainer is issued and the alien is not otherwise detained by Federal, State, or local officials, the Attorney General shall effectively and expeditiously take custody of the alien.

(e) Restriction on warrantless entry in case of outdoor agricultural operations. Notwithstanding any other provision of this section other than paragraph (3) of subsection (a), an officer or employee of the Service may not enter without the consent of the owner (or agent thereof) or a properly executed warrant onto the premises of a farm or other outdoor agricultural operation for the purpose of interrogating a person believed to be an alien as to the person's right to be or to remain in the United States.

(f) Fingerprinting and photographing of certain aliens.

(1) Under regulations of the Attorney General, the Commissioner shall provide for the fingerprinting and photographing of each alien 14 years of age or older against whom a proceeding is commenced under section 240 [8 USCS § 1229a].

(2) Such fingerprints and photographs shall be made available to Federal, State, and local law enforcement agencies, upon request.

(g) Performance of immigration officer functions by State officers and employees.

(1) Notwithstanding section 1342 of title 31, United States Code, the Attorney General may enter into a written agreement with a State, or any political subdivision of a State, pursuant to which an officer or employee of the State or subdivision, who is determined by the Attorney General to be qualified to perform a function of an immigration officer in relation to the investigation, apprehension, or detention of aliens in the United States (including the transportation of such aliens across State lines to detention centers), may carry out such function at the expense of the State or political subdivision and to the extent consistent with State and local law.

(2) An agreement under this subsection shall require that an officer or employee of a State or political subdivision of a State performing a function under the agreement shall have knowledge of, and adhere to, Federal law relating to the function, and shall contain a written certification that the officers or employees performing the function under the agreement have re-

ceived adequate training regarding the enforcement of relevant Federal immigration laws.

(3) In performing a function under this subsection, an officer or employee of a State or political subdivision of a State shall be subject to the direction and supervision of the Attorney General.

(4) In performing a function under this subsection, an officer or employee of a State or political subdivision of a State may use Federal property or facilities, as provided in a written agreement between the Attorney General and the State or subdivision.

(5) With respect to each officer or employee of a State or political subdivision who is authorized to perform a function under this subsection, the specific powers and duties that may be, or are required to be, exercised or performed by the individual, the duration of the authority of the individual, and the position of the agency of the Attorney General who is required to supervise and direct the individual, shall be set forth in a written agreement between the Attorney General and the State or political subdivision.

(6) The Attorney General may not accept a service under this subsection if the service will be used to displace any Federal employee.

(7) Except as provided in paragraph (8), an officer or employee of a State or political subdivision of a State performing functions under this subsection shall not be treated as a Federal employee for any purpose other than for purposes of chapter 81 of title 5, United States Code [5 USCS §§ 8101 et seq.] (relating to compensation for injury), and sections 2671 through 2680 of title 28, United States Code (relating to tort claims).

(8) An officer or employee of a State or political subdivision of a State acting under color of authority under this subsection, or any agreement entered into under this subsection, shall be considered to be acting under color of Federal authority for purposes of determining the liability, and immunity from suit, of the officer or employee in a civil action brought under Federal or State law.

(9) Nothing in this subsection shall be construed to require any State or political subdivision of a State to enter into an agreement with the Attorney General under this subsection.

(10) Nothing in this subsection shall be construed to require an agreement under this subsection in order for any officer or employee of a State or political subdivision of a State—

(A) to communicate with the Attorney General regarding the immigration status of any individual, including reporting knowledge that a particular alien is not lawfully present in the United States; or

(B) otherwise to cooperate with the Attorney General in the identification, apprehension, detention, or removal of aliens not lawfully present in the United States.

(h) Protecting abused juveniles. An alien described in section 101(a)(27)(J) of the Immigration and Nationality Act [8 USCS § 1101(a)(27)(J)] who has been battered, abused, neglected, or abandoned, shall not be compelled to contact the alleged abuser (or family member of the alleged abuser) at any stage of applying for special immigrant juvenile status, including after a request for the consent of the Secretary of Homeland Security under section 101(a)(27)(J)(iii)(I) of such Act [8 USCS § 1101(a)(27)(J)(iii)(I)].

HISTORY: (June 27, 1952, ch 477, Title II, Ch 9, § 287, 66 Stat. 233; Oct. 18, 1976, P. L. 94-550, § 7, 90 Stat. 2535; Oct. 27, 1986, P. L. 99-570, Title I, Subtitle M, § 1751(d), 100 Stat. 3207-47; Nov. 6, 1986, P. L. 99-603, Title I, Part B, § 116, 100 Stat. 3384; Oct. 24, 1988, P. L. 100-525, §§ 2(e), 5, 102 Stat. 2610, 2615; Nov. 29, 1990, P. L. 101-649, Title V, Subtitle A, § 503(a), (b)(1), 104 Stat. 5048, 5049; Dec. 12, 1991, P. L. 102-232, Title III, § 306(a)(3), 105 Stat. 1751; Sept. 30, 1996, P. L. 104-208, Div C, Title I, Subtitle C, § 133, Title III, Subtitle A, § 308(d)(4)(L), (e)(1)(M), (g)(5)(A)(i), 110 Stat. 3009-563, 3009-618, 3009-619, 3009-623; Jan. 5, 2006, P. L. 109-162, Title VIII, Subtitle C, § 826, 119 Stat. 3065; Aug. 12, 2006, P. L. 109-271, § 6(g), 120 Stat. 763.)

§ 288. [8 U.S.C. § 1358] Local jurisdiction over immigrant stations.

The officers in charge of the various immigrant stations shall admit therein the proper State and local officers charged with the enforcement of the laws of the State or Territory of the United States in which any such immigrant station is located in order that such State and local officers may preserve the peace and make arrests for crimes under the laws of the States and Territories. For the purpose of this section the jurisdiction of such State and local officers and of the State and local courts shall extend over such immigrant stations.

HISTORY: (June 27, 1952, ch 477, Title II, Ch 9, § 288, 66 Stat. 234.)

§ 289. [8 U.S.C. § 1359] Application to American Indians born in Canada.

Nothing in this title shall be construed to affect the right of American Indians born in Canada to pass the borders of the United States, but such right shall extend only to persons who possess at least 50 per centum of blood of the American Indian race.

HISTORY: (June 27, 1952, ch 477, Title II, Ch 9, § 289, 66 Stat. 234.)

§ 290. [8 U.S.C. § 1360] Establishment of central file; information from other departments and agencies.

(a) Establishment of central file. There shall be established in the office of the Commissioner, for the use of the security and enforcement agencies of the Government of the United States, a central index, which shall contain the names of all aliens heretofore admitted or denied admission to the United States, insofar as such information is available from the existing records of the Service, and the names of all aliens hereafter admitted or denied admission to the United States, the names of their sponsors of record, if any, and such other relevant information as the Attorney General shall require as an aid to the proper enforcement of this Act.

(b) Information from other departments and agencies. Any information in any records kept by any department or agency of the Government as to the identity and location of aliens in the United States shall be made available to the Service upon request made by the Attorney General to the head of any such department or agency.

(c) Reports on social security account numbers and earnings of aliens not authorized to work.

(1) Not later than 3 months after the end of each fiscal year (beginning with fiscal year 1996), the Commissioner of Social Security shall report to the Committees on the Judiciary of the House of Representatives and the Senate on the aggregate quantity of social security account numbers issued to aliens not authorized to be employed, with respect to which, in such fiscal year, earnings were reported to the Social Security Administration.

(2) If earnings are reported on or after January 1, 1997, to the Social Security Administration on a social security account number issued to an alien not authorized to work in the United States, the Commissioner of Social Security shall provide the Attorney General with information regarding the name and address of the alien, the name and address of the person reporting the earnings, and the amount of the earnings. The information shall be provided in an electronic form agreed upon by the Commissioner and the Attorney General.

(d) Certification of search of Service records. A written certification signed by the Attorney General or by any officer of the Service designated by the Attorney General to make such certification, that after diligent search no record or entry of a specified nature is found to exist in the records of the Service, shall be admissible as evidence in any proceeding as evidence that the records of the Service contain no such record or entry, and shall have the same effect as the testimony of a witness given in open court.

HISTORY: (June 27, 1952, ch 477, Title II, Ch 9, § 290, 66 Stat. 234; Oct. 24, 1988, P. L. 100-525, § 9(q), 102 Stat. 2621; Sept. 30, 1996, P. L. 104-208, Div C, Title III, Subtitle A, § 308(d)(4)(M), Title IV, Subtitle B, § 414(a), 110 Stat. 3009-618, 3009-669.)

§ 291. [8 U.S.C. § 1361] Burden of proof upon alien.

Whenever any person makes application for a visa or any other document required for entry, or makes application for admission, or otherwise attempts to enter the United States, the burden of proof shall be upon such person to establish that he is eligible to receive such visa or such document, or is not inadmissible under any provision of this Act, and, if an alien, that he is entitled to the nonimmigrant, immigrant, special immigrant, immediate relative, or refugee status claimed, as the case may be. If such person fails to establish to the satisfaction of the consular officer that he is eligible to receive a visa or other document required for entry, no visa or other document required for entry shall be issued to such person, nor shall such person be admitted to the United States unless he establishes to the satisfaction of the Attorney General that he is not inadmissible under any provision of this Act. In any removal proceeding under chapter 4 [8 USCS §§ 1221 et seq.] against any person, the burden of proof shall be upon such person to show the time, place, and manner of his entry into the United States, but in presenting such proof he shall be entitled to the production of his visa or other entry document, if any, and of any other documents and records, not considered by the Attorney General to be confidential, pertaining to such entry in the custody of the Service. If such burden of proof is not sustained, such person shall be presumed to be in the United States in violation of law.

HISTORY: (June 27, 1952, ch 477, Title II, Ch 9, § 291, 66 Stat. 234; Dec. 29, 1981, P. L. 97-116, § 18(k)(1), 95 Stat. 1620; Sept. 30, 1996, P. L. 104-208, Div C, Title III, Subtitle A, § 308(d)(4)(N), (e)(1)(N), (g)(9)(A), 110 Stat. 3009-618, 3009-619, 3009-624.)

§ 292. [8 U.S.C. § 1362] Right to counsel.

In any removal proceedings before an immigration judge and in any appeal proceedings before the Attorney General from any such removal proceedings, the person concerned shall have the privilege of being represented (at no expense to the Government) by such counsel, authorized to practice in such proceedings, as he shall choose.

HISTORY: (June 27, 1952, ch 477, Title II, Ch 9, § 292, 66 Stat. 235; Sept. 30, 1996, P.L. 104-208, Div C, Title III, Subtitle A, § 308(d)(4)(O), Subtitle F, § 371(b)(9), 110 Stat. 3009-619, 3009-645.)

§ 293. [8 U.S.C. § 1363] Deposit of and interest on cash received to secure immigration bonds.

(a) Cash received by the Attorney General as security o(a) Cash received by the Attorney General as security on an immigration bond shall be deposited in the Treasury of the United States in trust for the obligor on the bond, and shall bear interest payable at a rate determined by the Secretary of the Treasury, except that in no case shall the interest rate exceed 3 per centum per annum. Such interest shall accrue from date of deposit occurring after April 27, 1966, to and including date of withdrawal or date of breach of the immigration bond, whichever occurs first: Provided, That cash received by the Attorney General as security on an immigration bond, and deposited by him in the postal savings system prior to discontinuance of the system, shall accrue interest as provided in this section from the date such cash ceased to accrue interest under the system. Appropriations to the Treasury Department for interest on uninvested funds shall be available for payment of said interest.

(b) The interest accruing on cash received by the Attorney General as security on an immigration bond shall be subject to the same disposition as prescribed for the principal cash, except that interest accruing to the date of breach of the immigration bond shall be paid to the obligor on the bond.

HISTORY: (June 27, 1952, ch 477, Title II, Ch 9, § 293, as added July 10, 1970, P. L. 91-313, § 2, 84 Stat. 413.)

§ 294. [8 U.S.C. § 1363a] Undercover investigation authority.

(a) In general. With respect to any undercover investigative operation of the Service which is necessary for the detection and prosecution of crimes against the United States—

(1) sums appropriated for the Service may be used for leasing space within the United States and the territories and possessions of the United States without regard to the following provisions of law:

(A) section 3679(a) of the Revised Statutes (31 U.S.C. 1341),

(B) section 3732(a) of the Revised Statutes (41 U.S.C. 11(a)) [41 USCS § 6301],

(C) section 305 of the Act of June 30, 1949 (63 Stat. 396; 41 U.S.C. 255) [41 USCS §§ 4501 et seq.],

(D) the third undesignated paragraph under the heading "Miscellaneous" of the Act of March 3, 1877 (19 Stat. 370; 40 U.S.C. 34) [40 USCS § 8141],

(E) section 3648 of the Revised Statutes (31 U.S.C. 3324),

(F) section 3741 of the Revised Statutes (41 U.S.C. 22) [41 USCS § 6306], and

(G) subsections (a) and (c) of section 304 of the Federal Property and Administrative Services Act of 1949 (63 Stat. 395; 41 U.S.C. 254 (a) and (c)) [41 USCS § 3901];

(2) sums appropriated for the Service may be used to establish or to acquire proprietary corporations or business entities as part of an undercover operation, and to operate such corporations or business entities on a commercial basis, without regard to the provisions of section 304 of the Government Corporation Control Act (31 U.S.C. 9102);

(3) sums appropriated for the Service, and the proceeds from the undercover operation, may be deposited in banks or other financial institutions without regard to the provisions of section 648 of title 18, United States Code, and of section 3639 of the Revised Statutes (31 U.S.C. 3302); and

(4) the proceeds from the undercover operation may be used to offset necessary and reasonable expenses incurred in such operation without regard to the provisions of section 3617 of the Revised Statutes (31 U.S.C. 3302).

The authority set forth in this subsection may be exercised only upon written certification of the Commissioner, in consultation with the Deputy Attorney General, that any action authorized by paragraph (1), (2), (3), or (4) is necessary for the conduct of the undercover operation.

(b) Disposition of proceeds no longer required. As soon as practicable after the proceeds from an undercover investigative operation, carried out under paragraphs (3) and (4) of subsection (a), are no longer necessary for the conduct of the operation, the proceeds or the balance of the proceeds remaining at the time shall be deposited into the Treasury of the United States as miscellaneous receipts.

(c) Disposition of certain corporations and business entities. If a corporation or business entity established or acquired as part of an undercover operation under paragraph (2) of subsection (a) with a net value of over $50,000 is to be liquidated, sold, or otherwise disposed of, the Service, as much in advance as the Commissioner or Commissioner's designee determines practicable, shall report the circumstances to the Attorney General, the Director of the Office of Management and Budget, and the Comptroller General. The proceeds of the liquidation, sale, or other disposition, after obligations are met, shall be deposited in the Treasury of the United States as miscellaneous receipts.

(d) Financial audits. The Service shall conduct detailed financial audits of closed undercover operations on a quarterly basis and shall report the results of the audits in writing to the Deputy Attorney General.

HISTORY: (June 27, 1952, ch 477, Title II, Ch 9, § 294, as added Sept. 30, 1996, P. L. 104-208, Div C, Title II, Subtitle A, § 205(a), 110 Stat. 3009-567.)

§ 295. [8 U.S.C. § 1363b] [Repealed].

HISTORY: This section (Act June 27, 1952, ch 477, Title II, Ch 9, § 295, as added Sept. 30, 1996, P.L. 104-208, Div C, Title VI, Subtitle B, § 626(a), 110 Stat. 3009-700) was repealed by Act Oct. 21, 1998, P.L. 105-277, Div A, § 101(b) [Title I, § 109(b)], 112 Stat. 2681-67. It provided for transportation of remains of immigration officers and border patrol agents killed in the line of duty.

TITLE III

Chapter 1—Nationality At Birth and Collective Naturalization

§ 301. [8 U.S.C. § 1401] Nationals and citizens of the United States at birth.

The following shall be nationals and citizens of the United States at birth:

(a) a person born in the United States, and subject to the jurisdiction thereof;

(b) a person born in the United States to a member of an Indian, Eskimo, Aleutian, or other aboriginal tribe: Provided, That the granting of citizenship under this subsection shall not in any manner impair or otherwise affect the right of such person to tribal or other property;

(c) a person born outside of the United States and its outlying possessions of parents both of whom are citizens of the United States and one of whom has had a residence in the United States or one of its outlying possessions, prior to the birth of such person;

(d) a person born outside of the United States and its outlying possessions of parents one of whom is a citizen of the United States who has been physically present in the United States or one of its outlying possessions for a continuous period of one year prior to the birth of such person, and the other of whom is a national, but not a citizen of the United States;

(e) a person born in an outlying possession of the United States of parents one of whom is a citizen of the United States who has been physically present in the United States or one of its outlying possessions for a continuous period of one year at any time prior to the birth of such person;

(f) a person of unknown parentage found in the United States while under the age of five years, until shown, prior to his attaining the age of twenty-one years, not to have been born in the United States;

(g) a person born outside the geographical limits of the United States and its outlying possessions of parents one of whom is an alien, and the other a citizen of the United States who, prior to the birth of such person, was physically present in the United States or its outlying possessions for a period or periods totaling not less than five years, at least two of which were after attaining the age of fourteen years: Provided, That any periods of honorable service in the Armed Forces of the United States, or periods of employment with the United States Government or with an international organization as that term is defined in section 1 of the International Organizations Immunities Act (59 Stat. 669; 22 U.S.C. 288) [22 USCS § 288] by such citizen parent, or any periods during which such citizen parent is physically present abroad as the dependent unmarried son or daughter and a member of the household of a person (A) honorably serving with the Armed Forces of the United States, or (B) employed by the United States Government or an international organization as defined in section 1 of the International Organizations Immunities Act [22 USCS § 288], may be included in order to satisfy the physical-presence requirement of this paragraph. This proviso shall be applicable to persons born on or after December 24, 1952, to the same extent as if it had become effective in its present form on that date; and

(h) a person born before noon (Eastern Standard Time) May 24, 1934, outside the limits and jurisdiction of the United States of an alien father and a mother who is a citizen of the United States who, prior to the birth of such person, had resided in the United States.

HISTORY: (June 27, 1952, ch 477, Title III, Ch 1, § 301, 66 Stat. 235; Nov. 6, 1966, P. L. 89-770, 80 Stat. 1322; Oct. 27, 1972, P. L. 92-584, §§ 1, 3, 86 Stat. 1289; Oct. 10, 1978, P. L. 95-432, §§ 1, 3, 92 Stat. 1046; Nov. 14, 1986, P. L. 99-653, § 12, 100 Stat. 3657; Oct. 25, 1994, P. L. 103-416, Title I, § 101(a), 108 Stat. 4306.)

§ 302. [8 U.S.C. § 1402] Persons born in Puerto Rico on or after April 11, 1899.

All persons born in Puerto Rico on or after April 11, 1899, and prior to January 13, 1941, subject to the jurisdiction of the United States, residing on January 13, 1941, in Puerto Rico or other territory over which the United States exercises rights of sovereignty and not citizens of the United States under any other Act, are hereby declared to be citizens of the United States as of January 13, 1941. All persons born in Puerto Rico on or after January 13, 1941, and subject to the jurisdiction of the United States, are citizens of the United States at birth.

HISTORY: (June 27, 1952, ch 477, Title III, Ch 1, § 302, 66 Stat. 236.)

§ 303. [8 U.S.C. § 1403] Persons born in the Canal Zone or Republic of Panama on or after February 26, 1904.

(a) Any person born in the Canal Zone on or after February 26, 1904, and whether before or after the effective date of this Act, whose father or mother or both at the time of the birth of such person was or is a citizen of the United States, is declared to be a citizen of the United States.

(b) Any person born in the Republic of Panama on or after February 26, 1904, and whether before or after the effective date of this Act, whose father or mother or both at the time of the birth of such person was or is a citizen of the United States employed by the Government of the United States or by the Panama Railroad Company, or its successor in title, is declared to be a citizen of the United States.

HISTORY: (June 27, 1952, ch 477, Title III, Ch 1, § 303, 66 Stat. 236.)

§ 304. [8 U.S.C. § 1404] Persons born in Alaska on or after March 30, 1867.

A person born in Alaska on or after March 30, 1867, except a noncitizen Indian, is a citizen of the United States at birth. A noncitizen Indian born in Alaska on or after March 30, 1867, and prior to June 2, 1924, is declared to be a citizen of the United States as of June 2, 1924. An Indian born in Alaska on or after June 2, 1924, is a citizen of the United States at birth.

HISTORY: (June 27, 1952, ch 477, Title III, Ch 1, § 304, 66 Stat. 237.)

§ 305. [8 U.S.C. § 1405] Persons born in Hawaii.

A person born in Hawaii on or after August 12, 1898, and before April 30, 1900, is declared to be a citizen of the United States as of April 30, 1900. A person born in Hawaii on or after April 30, 1900, is a citizen of the United States at birth. A person who was a citizen of the Republic of Hawaii on August 12, 1898, is declared to be a citizen of the United States as of April 30, 1900.

HISTORY: (June 27, 1952, ch 477, Title III, Ch 1, § 305, 66 Stat. 237.)

§ 306. [8 U.S.C. § 1406] Persons living in and born in the Virgin Islands.

(a) The following persons and their children born subsequent to January 17, 1917, and prior to February 25, 1927, are declared to be citizens of the United States as of February 25, 1927:

(1) All former Danish citizens who, on January 17, 1917, resided in the Virgin Islands of the United States, and were residing in those islands or in the United States or Puerto Rico on February 25, 1927, and who did not make the declaration required to preserve their Danish citizenship by article 6 of the treaty entered into on August 4, 1916, between the United States and Denmark, or who, having made such a declaration have heretofore renounced or may hereafter renounce it by a declaration before a court of record;

(2) All natives of the Virgin Islands of the United States who, on January 17, 1917, resided in those islands, and were residing in those islands or in the United States or Puerto Rico on February 25, 1927, and who were not on February 25, 1927, citizens or subjects of any foreign country;

(3) All natives of the Virgin Islands of the United States who, on January 17, 1917, resided in the United States, and were residing in those islands on February 25, 1927, and who were not on February 25, 1927, citizens or subjects of any foreign country; and

(4) All natives of the Virgin Islands of the United States who, on June 28, 1932, were residing is continental United States, the Virgin Islands of the United States, Puerto Rico, the Canal Zone, or any other insular possession or territory of the United States, and who, on June 28, 1932, were not citizens or subjects of any foreign country, regardless of their place of residence on January 17, 1917.

(b) All persons born in the Virgin Islands of the United States on or after January 17, 1917, and prior to February 25, 1927, and subject to the jurisdiction of the United States are declared to be citizens of the United States as of February 25, 1927; and all persons born in those islands on or after February 25, 1927, and subject to the jurisdiction of the United States, are declared to be citizens of the United States at birth.

HISTORY: (June 27, 1952, ch 477, Title III, Ch 1, § 306, 66 Stat. 237.)

§ 307. [8 U.S.C. § 1407] Persons living in and born in Guam.

(a) The following persons, and their children born after April 11, 1899, are declared to be citizens of the United States as of August 1, 1950, if they were residing on August 1, 1950, on the island of Guam or other territory over which the United States exercises rights of sovereignty:

(1) All inhabitants of the island of Guam on April 11, 1899, including those temporarily absent from the island on that date, who were Spanish subjects, who after that date continued to reside in Guam or other territory over which the United States exercises sovereignty, and who have taken no affirmative steps to preserve or acquire foreign nationality; and

(2) All persons born in the island of Guam who resided in Guam on April 11, 1899, including those temporarily absent from the island on that date, who after that date continued to reside in Guam or other territory over which the United States exercises sovereignty, and who have taken no affirmative steps to preserve or acquire foreign nationality.

(b) All persons born in the island of Guam on or after April 11, 1899 (whether before or after August 1, 1950) subject to the jurisdiction of the United States, are hereby declared to be citizens of the United States: Provided, That in the case of any person born before August 1, 1950, he has taken no affirmative steps to preserve or acquire foreign nationality.

(c) Any person hereinbefore described who is a citizen or national of a country other than the United States and desires to retain his present political status shall have made, prior to August 1, 1952, a declaration under oath of such desire, said declaration to be in form and executed in the manner prescribed by regulations. From and after the making of such a declaration any such person shall be held not to be a national of the United States by virtue of this Act.

HISTORY: (June 27, 1952, ch 477, Title III, Ch 1, § 307, 66 Stat. 237.)

§ 308. [8 U.S.C. § 1408] Nationals but not citizens of the United States at birth.

Unless otherwise provided in section 301 of this title [8 USCS § 1401], the following shall be nationals, but not citizens, of the United States at birth:

(1) A person born in an outlying possession of the United States on or after the date of formal acquisition of such possession;

(2) A person born outside the United States and its outlying possessions of parents both of whom are nationals, but not citizens, of the United States, and have had a residence in the United States, or one of its outlying possessions prior to the birth of such person;

(3) A person of unknown parentage found in an outlying possession of the United States while under the age of five years, until shown, prior to his attaining the age of twenty-one years, not to have been born in such outlying possession; and

(4) A person born outside the United States and its outlying possessions of parents one of whom is an alien, and the other a national, but not a citizen, of the United States who, prior to the birth of such person, was physically present in the United States or its outlying possessions for a period or periods totaling not less than seven years in any continuous period of ten years—

(A) during which the national parent was not outside the United States or its outlying possessions for a continuous period of more than one year, and

(B) at least five years of which were after attaining the age of fourteen years.

The proviso of section 301(g) [8 USCS § 1401(g)] shall apply to the national parent under this paragraph in the same manner as it applies to the citizen parent under that section.

HISTORY: (June 27, 1952, ch 477, Title III, Ch 1, § 308, 66 Stat. 238; Aug. 27, 1986, P.L. 99-396, § 15(a), 100 Stat. 842; Aug. 27, 1986, P.L. 99-396, § 15(a), 100 Stat. 842; Oct. 24, 1988, P.L. 100-525, § 3(2), 102 Stat. 2614.)

§ 309. [8 U.S.C. § 1409] Children born out of wedlock.

(a) The provisions of paragraphs (c), (d), (e), and (g) of section 301 [8 USCS § 1401(c)–(e), (g)], and of paragraph (2) of section 308 [8 USCS § 1408(2)], shall apply as of the date of birth to a person born out of wedlock if—

(1) a blood relationship between the person and the father is established by clear and convincing evidence,

(2) the father had the nationality of the United States at the time of the person's birth,

(3) the father (unless deceased) has agreed in writing to provide financial support for the person until the person reaches the age of 18 years, and

(4) while the person is under the age of 18 years—

(A) the person is legitimated under the law of the person's residence or domicile,

(B) the father acknowledges paternity of the person in writing under oath, or

(C) the paternity of the person is established by adjudication of a competent court.

(b) Except as otherwise provided in section 405 [8 USCS § 1101 note], the provisions of section 301(g) [8 USCS § 1401(g)] shall apply to a child born out of wedlock on or after January 13, 1941, and before December 24, 1952, as of the date of birth, if the paternity of such child is established at any time while such child is under the age of twenty-one years by legitimation.

(c) Notwithstanding the provision of subsection (a) of this section, a person born, after December 23, 1952, outside the United States and out of wedlock shall be held to have acquired at birth the nationality status of his mother, if the mother had the nationality of the United States at the time of such person's birth, and if the mother had previously been physically present in the United States or one of its outlying possessions for a continuous period of one year.

HISTORY: (June 27, 1952, ch 477, Title III, Ch 1, § 309, 66 Stat. 238; Dec. 29, 1981, P. L. 97-116, § 18 (l), 95 Stat. 1620; Nov. 14, 1986, P. L. 99-653, § 13, 100 Stat. 3657; Nov. 14, 1986, P. L. 99-653, § 13, 100 Stat. 3657 (as amended Oct. 24, 1988, P. L. 100-525, § 8(k), 102 Stat. 2617); Oct. 24, 1988, P. L. 100-525, § 9(r), 102 Stat. 2621.)(Act June 27, 1952, ch 477, Title III, Ch 1, § 309, 66 Stat. 238; Dec. 29, 1981, P. L. 97-116, § 18 (l), 95 Stat. 1620; Nov. 14, 1986, P. L. 99-653, § 13, 100 Stat. 3657; Nov. 14, 1986, P. L. 99-653, § 13, 100 Stat. 3657 (as amended Oct. 24, 1988, P. L. 100-525, § 8(k), 102 Stat. 2617); Oct. 24, 1988, P. L. 100-525, § 9(r), 102 Stat. 2621.)

Chapter 2—Nationality through Naturalization

§ 310. [8 U.S.C. § 1421] Naturalization authority.

(a) Authority in Attorney General. The sole authority to naturalize persons as citizens of the United States is conferred upon the Attorney General.

(b) Court authority to administer oaths.

(1) Jurisdiction. Subject to section 337(c) [8 USCS § 1448(c)]—

(A) General jurisdiction. Except as provided in subparagraph (B), each applicant for naturalization may choose to have the oath of allegiance under section 337(a) [8 USCS § 1448(a)] administered by the Attorney General or by an eligible court described in paragraph (5). Each such eligible court shall have authority to administer such oath of allegiance to persons residing within the jurisdiction of the court.

(B) Exclusive authority. An eligible court described in paragraph (5) that wishes to have exclusive authority to administer the oath of allegiance under section 337(a) [8 USCS § 1448(a)] to persons residing within the jurisdiction of the court during the period described in paragraph (3)(A)(i) shall notify the Attorney General of such wish and, subject to this subsection, shall have such exclusive authority with respect to such persons during such period.

(2) Information.

(A) General information. In the case of a court exercising authority under paragraph (1), in accordance with procedures established by the Attorney General—

(i) the applicant for naturalization shall notify the Attorney General of the intent to be naturalized before the court, and

(ii) the Attorney General—

(I) shall forward to the court (not later than 10 days after the date of approval of an application for naturalization in the case of a court which has provided notice under paragraph (1)(B)) such information as may be necessary to administer the oath of allegiance under section 337(a) [8 USCS § 1448(a)], and

(II) shall promptly forward to the court a certificate of naturalization (prepared by the Attorney General).

(B) Assignment of individuals in the case of exclusive authority. If an eligible court has provided notice under paragraph (1)(B), the Attorney General shall inform each person (residing within the jurisdiction of the court), at the time of the approval of the person's application for naturalization, of—

(i) the court's exclusive authority to administer the oath of allegiance under section 337(a) [8 USCS § 1448(a)] to such a person during the period specified in paragraph (3)(A)(i), and

(ii) the date or dates (if any) under paragraph (3)(B) on which the court has scheduled oath administration ceremonies.

If more than one eligible court in an area has provided notice under paragraph (1)(B), the Attorney General shall permit the person, at the time of the approval, to choose the court to which the information will be forwarded for administration of the oath of allegiance under this section.

(3) Scope of exclusive authority.

(A) Limited period and advance notice required. The exclusive authority of a court to administer the oath of allegiance under paragraph (1)(B) shall apply with respect to a person—

(i) only during the 45-day period beginning on the date on which the Attorney General certifies to the court that an applicant is eligible for naturalization, and

(ii) only if the court has notified the Attorney General, prior to the date of certification of eligibility, of the day or days (during such 45-day period) on which the court has scheduled oath administration ceremonies.

(B) Authority of Attorney General. Subject to subparagraph (C), the Attorney General shall not administer the oath of allegiance to a person under subsection (a) during the period in which exclusive authority to administer the oath of allegiance may be exercised by an eligible court under this subsection with respect to that person.

(C) Waiver of exclusive authority. Notwithstanding the previous provisions of this paragraph, a court may waive exclusive authority to administer the oath of allegiance under section 337(a) [8 USCS § 1448(a)] to a person under this subsection if the Attorney General has not provided the court with the certification described in subparagraph (A)(i) within a reasonable time before the date scheduled by the court for oath administration ceremonies. Upon notification of a court's waiver of jurisdiction, the Attorney General shall promptly notify the applicant.

(4) Issuance of certificates. The Attorney General shall provide for the issuance of certificates of natu-

ralization at the time of administration of the oath of allegiance.

(5) Eligible courts. For purposes of this section, the term "eligible court" means—

(A) a district court of the United States in any State, or

(B) any court of record in any State having a seal, a clerk, and jurisdiction in actions in law or equity, or law and equity, in which the amount in controversy is unlimited.

(c) Judicial review. A person whose application for naturalization under this title is denied, after a hearing before an immigration officer under section 336(a) [8 USCS § 1447(a)], may seek review of such denial before the United States district court or the district in which such person resides in accordance with chapter 7 of title 5, United States Code [5 USCS §§ 701 et seq.]. Such review shall be de novo, and the court shall make its own findings of fact and conclusions of law and shall, at the request of the petitioner, conduct a hearing de novo on the application.

(d) Sole procedure. A person may only be naturalized as a citizen of the United States in the manner and under the conditions prescribed in this title and not otherwise.

HISTORY: (June 27, 1952, ch 477, Title III, Ch 2, § 310, 66 Stat. 239; July 7, 1958, P. L. 85-508, § 25, 72 Stat. 351; March 18, 1959, P. L. 86-3, § 20(c), 73 Stat. 13; Sept. 26, 1961, P. L. 87-301, § 17, 75 Stat. 656; Oct. 24, 1988, P. L. 100-525, § 9(s), 102 Stat. 2621; Nov. 29, 1990, P. L. 101-649, Title IV, § 401(a), 104 Stat. 5038; Dec. 12, 1991, P. L. 102-232, Title I, § 102(a), Title III, § 305(a), 105 Stat. 1734, 1749; Oct. 25, 1994, P. L. 103-416, Title II, § 219(u), 108 Stat. 4318.)

§ 311. [8 U.S.C. § 1422] Eligibility for naturalization.

The right of a person to become a naturalized citizen of the United States shall not be denied or abridged because of race or sex or because such person is married.

HISTORY: (June 27, 1952, ch 477, Title III, Ch 2, § 311, 66 Stat. 239; Oct. 24, 1988, P.L. 100-525, § 9(t), 102 Stat. 2621.)

§ 312. [8 U.S.C. § 1423] Requirements as to understanding the English language, history, principles and form of government of the United States.

(a) No person except as otherwise provided in this title shall hereafter be naturalized as a citizen of the United States upon his own application who cannot demonstrate—

(1) an understanding of the English language, including an ability to read, write, and speak words in ordinary usage in the English language: Provided, That the requirements of this paragraph relating to ability to read and write shall be met if the applicant can read or write simple words and phrases to the end that a reasonable test of his literacy shall be made and that no extraordinary or unreasonable condition shall be imposed upon the applicant; and

(2) a knowledge and understanding of the fundamentals of the history, and of the principles and form of government, of the United States.

(b) (1) The requirements of subsection (a) shall not apply to any person who is unable because of physical or developmental disability or mental impairment to comply therewith.

(2) The requirement of subsection (a)(1) shall not apply to any person who, on the date of the filing of the person's application for naturalization as provided in section 334 [8 USCS § 1445], either—

(A) is over fifty years of age and has been living in the United States for periods totaling at least twenty years subsequent to a lawful admission for permanent residence, or

(B) is over fifty-five years of age and has been living in the United States for periods totaling at least fifteen years subsequent to a lawful admission for permanent residence.

(3) The Attorney General, pursuant to regulations, shall provide for special consideration, as determined by the Attorney General, concerning the requirement of subsection (a)(2) with respect to any person who, on the date of the filing of the person's application for naturalization as provided in section 334 [8 USCS § 1445], is over sixty-five years of age and has been living in the United States for periods totaling at least twenty years subsequent to a lawful admission for permanent residence.

HISTORY: (June 27, 1952, ch 477, Title III, Ch 2, § 312, 66 Stat. 239; Nov. 2, 1978, P. L. 95-579, § 3, 92 Stat. 2474; Nov. 29, 1990, P. L. 101-649, Title IV, § 403, 104 Stat. 5039; Dec. 12, 1991, P. L. 102-232, Title, § 305(m)(2), 105 Stat. 1750; Oct. 25, 1994, P. L. 103-416, Title I, § 108(a), 108 Stat. 4309.)

§ 313. [8 U.S.C. § 1424] Prohibition upon the naturalization of persons opposed to government or law, or who favor totalitarian forms of government.

(a) Notwithstanding the provisions of section 405(b) [8 USCS § 1101 note], no person shall hereafter be naturalized as a citizen of the United States—

(1) who advocates or teaches, or who is a member of or affiliated with any organization that advocates or teaches, opposition to all organized government; or

(2) who is a member of or affiliated with (A) the Communist Party of the United States; (B) any other totalitarian party of the United States; (C) the Communist Political Association; (D) the Communist or other totalitarian party of any state of the United States, of any foreign state, or of any political or geographical subdivision of any foreign state; (E) any section, subsidiary, branch, affiliate, or subdivision of any such association or party; or (F) the direct predecessors or successors of any such association or party, regardless of what name such group or organization may have used, may now bear, or may hereafter adopt, unless such alien establishes that he did not have knowledge or reason to believe at the time he became a member of or affiliated with such an organization (and did not thereafter and prior to the date upon which such organization was so registered or so required to be registered have such knowledge or reason to believe) that such organization was a Communist-front organization; or

(3) who, although not within any of the other provisions of this section, advocates the economic, international, and governmental doctrines of world communism or the establishment in the United States of a totalitarian dictatorship, or who is a member of or affiliated with any organization that advocates the economic, international, and governmental doctrines of world communism or the establishment in the United States of a totalitarian dictatorship, either through its own utterances or through any written or printed publications issued or published by or with the permission or consent of or under authority of such organization or paid for by the funds of such organization; or

(4) who advocates or teaches or who is a member of or affiliated with any organization that advocates or teaches (A) the overthrow by force or violence or other unconstitutional means of the Government of the United States or of all forms of law; or (B) the duty, necessity, or propriety of the unlawful assaulting or killing of any officer or officers (either of specific individuals or of officers generally) of the Government of the United States or of any other organized government because of his or their official character; or (C) the unlawful damage, injury, or destruction of property; or (D) sabotage; or

(5) who writes or publishes or causes to be written or published, or who knowingly circulates, distributes, prints, or displays, or knowingly causes to be circulated, distributed, printed, published, or displayed, or who knowingly has in his possession for the purpose of circulation, publication, distribution, or display, any written or printed matter, advocating or teaching opposition to all organized government, or advocating (A) the overthrow by force, violence, or other unconstitutional means of the Government of the United States or of all forms of law; or (B) the duty, necessity, or propriety of the unlawful assaulting or killing of any officer or officers (either of specific individuals or of officers generally) of the Government of the United States or of any other organized government, because of his or their official character; or (C) the unlawful damage, injury, or destruction of property; or (D) sabotage; or (E) the economic, international, and governmental doctrines of world communism or the establishment in the United States of a totalitarian dictatorship; or

(6) who is a member of or affiliated with any organization that writes, circulates, distributes, prints, publishes, or displays, or causes to be written, circulated, distributed, printed, published, or displayed, or that has in its possession for the purpose of circulation, distribution, publication, issue, or display, any written or printed matter of the character described in subparagraph (5).

(b) The provisions of this section or of any other section of this Act shall not be construed as declaring that any of the organizations referred to in this section or in any other section of this Act do not advocate the overthrow of the Government of the United States by force, violence, or other unconstitutional means.

(c) The provisions of this section shall be applicable to any applicant for naturalization who at any time within a period of ten years immediately preceding the filing of the application for naturalization or after such filing and before taking the final oath of citizenship is, or has been found to be within any of the classes enumerated within this section, notwithstanding that at the time the application is filed he may not be included within such classes.

(d) Any person who is within any of the classes described in subsection (a) solely because of past membership in, or past affiliation with, a party or organization may be naturalized without regard to the provisions of subsection (c) if such person establishes that such membership or affiliation is or was involuntary, or occurred and terminated prior to the attainment by such alien of the age of sixteen years, or that such membership or affiliation is or was by operation of law, or was for purposes of obtaining employment, food rations, or other essentials of living and where necessary for such purposes.

(e) A person may be naturalized under this title [8 USCS §§ 1401 et seq.] without regard to the prohibitions in subsections (a)(2) and (c) of this section if the person—

(1) is otherwise eligible for naturalization;

(2) is within the class described in subsection (a)(2) solely because of past membership in, or past affiliation with, a party or organization described in that subsection;

(3) does not fall within any other of the classes described in that subsection; and

(4) is determined by the Director of Central Intelligence, in consultation with the Secretary of Defense when Department of Defense activities are relevant to the determination, and with the concurrence of the Attorney General and the Secretary of Homeland Security, to have made a contribution to the national security or to the national intelligence mission of the United States.

HISTORY: (June 27, 1952, ch 477, Title III, Ch 2, § 313, 66 Stat. 240; Oct. 24, 1988, P. L. 100-525, § 9(u), 102 Stat. 2621; Nov. 29, 1990, P. L. 101-649, Title IV, § 407(c)(1), 104 Stat. 5041; Dec. 12, 1991, P. L. 102-232, Title III, § 309(b)(13), 105 Stat. 1759; Oct. 25, 1994, P. L. 103-416, Title II, § 219(v), 108 Stat. 4318; Dec. 3, 1999, P. L. 106-120, Title III, § 306, 113 Stat. 1612; Dec. 13, 2003, P. L. 108-177, Title III, Subtitle E, § 373, 117 Stat. 2628.)

§ 314. [8 U.S.C. § 1425] Ineligibility to naturalization of deserters from the armed forces.

A person who, at any time during which the United States has been or shall be at war, deserted or shall desert the military, air, or naval forces of the United States, or who, having been duly enrolled, departed, or shall depart from the jurisdiction of the district in which enrolled, or who, whether or not having been duly enrolled, went or shall go beyond the limits of the United States, with intent to avoid any draft into the military, air, or naval service, lawfully ordered, shall, upon conviction thereof by a court martial or a court of competent jurisdiction, be permanently ineligible to become a citizen of the United States; and such deserters and evaders shall be forever incapable of holding any office of trust or of profit under the United States, or of exercising any rights of citizens thereof.

HISTORY: (June 27, 1952, ch 477, Title III, Ch 2, § 314, 66 Stat. 241.)

§ 315. [8 U.S.C. § 1426] Citizenship denied alien relieved of service in armed forces because of alienage.

(a) Permanent ineligibility. Notwithstanding the provisions of section 405(b) [8 USCS § 1101 note] but subject to subsection (c), any alien who applies or has applied for exemption or discharge from training or service in the Armed Forces or in the National Security Training Corps of the United States on the ground that he is an alien, and is or was relieved or discharged from such training or service on such ground, shall be permanently ineligible to become a citizen of the United States.

(b) Conclusiveness of records. The records of the Selective Service System or of the Department of Defense shall be conclusive as to whether an alien was relieved or discharged from such liability for training or service because he was an alien.

(c) Service in armed forces of foreign country. An alien shall not be ineligible for citizenship under this section or otherwise because of an exemption from training or service in the Armed Forces of the United States pursuant to the exercise of rights under a treaty, if before the time of the exercise of such rights the alien served in the Armed Forces of a foreign country of which the alien was a national.

HISTORY: (June 27, 1952, ch 477, Title III, Ch 2, § 315, 66 Stat. 242; Oct. 24, 1988, P. L. 100-525, § 9(v), 102 Stat. 2621; Nov. 29, 1990, P. L. 101-649, Title IV, § 404, 104 Stat. 5039.)

§ 316. [8 U.S.C. § 1427] Requirements of naturalization.

(a) Residence. No person, except as otherwise provided in this title, shall be naturalized unless such applicant, (1) immediately preceding the date of filing his application for naturalization has resided continuously, after being lawfully admitted for permanent residence, within the United States for at least five years and during the five years immediately preceding the date of filing his application has been physically present therein for periods totaling at least half of that time[,] and who has resided within the State or within the district of the Service in the United States in which the applicant filed the application for at least three months, (2) has resided continuously within the United States from the date of the application up to the time of admission to citizenship, and (3) during all the periods referred to in this subsection has been and still is a person of good moral character, attached to the principles of the Constitution of the United States, and well disposed to the good order and happiness of the United States.

(b) Absences. Absence from the United States of more than six months but less than one year during the period for which continuous residence is required for admission to citizenship, immediately preceding the date of filing the application for naturalization, or during the period between the date of filing the application and the date of any hearing under section 336(a) [8 USCS § 1447(a)], shall break the continuity of such residence, unless the applicant shall establish to the satisfaction of the Attorney General that he did not in fact abandon his residence in the United States during such period.

Absence from the United States for a continuous period of one year or more during the period for which continuous residence is required for admission to citizenship (whether preceding or subsequent to the filing of the application for naturalization) shall break the continuity of such residence, except that in the case of a person who has been physically present and residing in the United States, after being lawfully admitted for permanent residence, for an uninterrupted period of at least one year, and who thereafter is employed by or under contract with the Government of the United States or an American institution of research recognized as such by the Attorney General, or is employed by an American firm or corporation engaged in whole or in part in the development of foreign trade and commerce of the United States, or a subsidiary thereof more than 50 per centum of whose stock is owned by an American firm or corporation, or is employed by a public international organization of which the United States is a member by treaty or statute and by which the alien was not employed until after being lawfully admitted for permanent residence, no period of absence from the United States shall break the continuity of residence if—

(1) prior to the beginning of such period of employment (whether such period begins before or after his departure from the United States), but prior to the expiration of one year of continuous absence from the United States, the person has established to the satisfaction of the Attorney General that his absence from the United States for such period is to be on behalf of such Government, or for the purpose of carrying on scientific research on behalf of such institution, or to be engaged in the development of such foreign trade and commerce or whose residence abroad is necessary to the protection of the property rights in such countries of such firm or corporation, or to be employed by a public international organization of which the United States is a member by treaty or statute and by which the alien was not employed until after being lawfully admitted for permanent residence; and

(2) such person proves to the satisfaction of the court that his absence from the United States for such period has been for such purpose.

The spouse and dependent unmarried sons and daughters who are members of the household of a person who qualifies for the benefits of this subsection shall also be entitled to such benefits during the period for which they were residing abroad as dependent members of the household of the person.

(c) Physical presence. The granting of the benefits of subsection (b) of this section shall not relieve the applicant from the requirement of physical presence within the United States for the period specified in subsection (a) of this section, except in the case of those persons who are employed by, or under contract with, the Government of the United States. In the case of a person employed by or under contract with Central Intelligence Agency, the requirement in subsection (b) of an uninterrupted period of at least one year of physical presence in the United States may be complied with by such person at any time prior to filing an application for naturalization.

(d) Moral character. No finding by the Attorney General that the applicant is not deportable shall be accepted as conclusive evidence of good moral character.

(e) Determination. In determining whether the applicant has sustained the burden of establishing good moral character and the other qualifications for citizenship specified in subsection (a) of this section, the Attorney General shall not be limited to the applicant's conduct during the five years preceding the filing of the petition, but may take into consideration as a basis for such determination the applicant's conduct and acts at any time prior to that period.

(f) Persons making extraordinary contributions to national security.

(1) Whenever the Director of Central Intelligence, the Attorney General and the Commissioner of Immigration determine that an applicant otherwise eligible for naturalization has made an extraordinary contribution to the national security of the United States or to the conduct of United States intelligence activities, the applicant may be naturalized without regard to the residence and physical presence requirements of this section, or to the prohibitions of section 313 of this Act [8 USCS § 1424], and no residence within a particular State or district of the Service in the United States shall be required: Provided, That the applicant has continuously resided in the United States for at least one year prior to naturalization: Provided further, That the provisions of this subsection shall not apply to any alien described in clauses (i) through (v) of section 208(b)(2)(A) of this Act [8 USCS § 1158(b)(2)(A)].

(2) An applicant for naturalization under this subsection may be administered the oath of allegiance under section 337(a) [8 USCS § 1448(a)] by any district court of the United States, without regard to the residence of the applicant. Proceedings under this subsection shall be conducted in a manner consistent with the protection of intelligence sources, methods and activities.

(3) The number of aliens naturalized pursuant to this subsection in any fiscal year shall not exceed five. The Director of Central Intelligence shall inform the Select Committee on Intelligence and the Committee on the Judiciary of the Senate and the Permanent Select Committee on Intelligence and the Committee on the Judiciary of the House of Representatives within a reasonable time prior to the filing of each petition under the provisions of this subsection.

HISTORY: (June 27, 1952, ch 477, Title III, Ch 2, § 316, 66 Stat. 242; Dec. 29, 1981, P. L. 97-116, § 14, 95 Stat. 1619; Dec. 4, 1985, P. L. 99-169, Title VI, § 601, 99 Stat. 1007; Nov. 29, 1990, P. L. 101-649, Title IV, §§ 402, 407(c)(2), (d)(1), (e)(1), 104 Stat. 5038, 5041, 5046; Sept. 30, 1996, P. L. 104-208, Div C, Title III, Subtitle A, § 308(g)(7)(F), 110 Stat. 3009-624; Dec. 30, 2005, P. L. 109-149, Title V, § 518, 119 Stat. 2882.)

§ 317. [8 U.S.C. § 1428] Temporary absence of persons performing religious duties.

Any person who is authorized to perform the ministerial or priestly functions of a religious denomination having a bona fide organization within the United States, or any person who is engaged solely by a religious denomination or by an interdenominational mission organization having a bona fide organization within the United States as a missionary, brother, nun, or sister, who (1) has been lawfully admitted to the United States for permanent residence, (2) has at any time thereafter and before filing an application for naturalization been physically present and residing within the United States for an uninterrupted period of at least one year, and (3) has heretofore been or may hereafter be absent temporarily from the United States in connection with or for the purpose of performing the ministerial or priestly functions of such religious denomination, or serving as a missionary, brother, nun, or sister, shall be considered as being physically present and residing in the United States for the purpose of naturalization within the meaning of section 316(a) [8 USCS § 1427(a)], notwithstanding any such absence from the United States, if he shall in all other respects comply with the requirements of the naturalization law. Such person shall prove to the satisfaction of the Attorney General that his absence from the United States has been solely for the purpose of performing the ministerial or priestly functions of such religious denomination, or of serving as a missionary, brother, nun, or sister.

HISTORY: (June 27, 1952, ch 477, Title III, Ch 2, § 317, 66 Stat. 243; Nov. 29, 1990, P. L. 101-649, Title IV, § 407(c)(3), (d)(2), 104 Stat. 5041.)

§ 318. [8 U.S.C. § 1429] Prerequisite to naturalization; burden of proof.

Except as otherwise provided in this title, no person shall be naturalized unless he has been lawfully admitted to the United States for permanent residence in accordance with all applicable provisions of this Act. The burden of proof shall be upon such person to show that he entered the United States lawfully, and the time, place, and manner of such entry into the United States, but in presenting such proof he shall be entitled to the production of his immigrant visa, if any, or of other entry document, if any, and of any other documents and records, not considered by the Attorney General to be confidential, pertaining to such entry, in the custody of the Service. Notwithstanding the provisions of section 405(b) [8 USCS § 1101 note], and except as provided in sections 328 and 329 [8 USCS §§ 1439 and 1440] no person shall be naturalized against whom there is outstanding a final finding of deportability pursuant to a warrant of arrest issued under the provisions of this or any other Act; and no application for naturalization shall be considered by the Attorney General court if there is pending against the applicant a removal proceeding pursuant to a warrant of arrest issued under the provisions of this or any other Act: Provided, That the findings of the Attorney General in terminating removal proceedings or in canceling the removal of an alien pursuant to the provisions of this Act, shall not be deemed binding in any way upon the Attorney General with respect to the question of whether such person has established his eligibility for naturalization as required by this title.

HISTORY: (June 27, 1952, ch 477, Title III, Ch 2, § 318, 66 Stat. 244; Oct. 24, 1968, P. L. 90-633, § 4, 82 Stat. 1344; Nov. 29, 1990, P. L. 101-649, Title IV, § 407(c)(4), (d)(3), 104 Stat. 5041; Sept. 30, 1996, P. L. 104-208, Div C, Title III, Subtitle A, § 308(e)(1)(O), (15), 110 Stat. 3009-619, 3009-620.)

§ 319. [8 U.S.C. § 1430] Married persons and employees of certain nonprofit organizations.

(a) Any person whose spouse is a citizen of the United States, or any person who obtained status as a lawful permanent resident by reason of his or her status as a spouse or child of a United States citizen who battered him or her or subjected him or her to extreme cruelty, may be naturalized upon compliance with all the requirements of this title except the provisions of paragraph (1) of section 316(a) [8 USCS § 1427(a)(1)] if such person immediately preceding the date of filing his application for naturalization has resided continuously, after being lawfully admitted for permanent residence, within the United States for at least three years, and during the three years immediately preceding the date of filing his application has been living in marital union with the citizen spouse (except in the case of a person who has been battered or subjected to extreme cruelty by a United States citizen spouse or parent), who has been a United States citizen during all of such period, and has been physically present in the United States for periods totaling at least half of that time and has resided within the State or the district of the Service in the United States in which the applicant filed his application for at least three months.

(b) Any person, (1) whose spouse is (A) a citizen of the United States, (B) in the employment of the Government of the United States, or of an American institution of research recognized as such by the Attorney General, or of an American firm or corporation engaged in whole or in part in the development of foreign trade and commerce of the United States, or a subsidiary thereof, or of a public international organization in which the United States participates by treaty or statute, or is authorized to perform the ministerial or priestly functions of a religious denomination having a bona fide organization within the United States, or is engaged solely as a missionary by a religious denomination or by an interdenominational mission organization having a bona fide organization within the United States, and (C) regularly stationed abroad in such employment, and (2) who is in the United States at the time of naturalization, and (3) who declares before the Attorney General in good faith an intention to take up residence within the United States immediately upon the termination of such employment abroad of the citizen spouse, may be naturalized upon compliance with all the requirements of the naturalization laws, except that no prior residence or specified period of physical presence within the United States or within a State or a district of the Service in the United States or proof thereof shall be required.

(c) Any person who (1) is employed by a bona fide United States incorporated nonprofit organization which is principally engaged in conducting abroad through communications media the dissemination of information which significantly promotes United States interests abroad and which is recognized as such by the Attorney General, and (2) has been so employed continuously for a period of not less than five years after a lawful admission for permanent residence, and (3) who files his application for naturalization while so employed or within six months following the termination thereof, and (4) who is in the United States at the time of naturalization, and (5) who declares before the Attorney General in good faith an intention to take up residence within the United States immediately upon termination of such employment, may be naturalized upon compliance with all the requirements of this title except that no prior residence or specified period of physical presence within the United States or any State or district of the Service in the United States, or proof thereof, shall be required.

(d) Any person who is the surviving spouse, child, or parent of a United States citizen, whose citizen spouse, parent, or child dies during a period of honorable service in an active duty status in the Armed Forces of the United States and who, in the case of a surviving spouse, was living in marital union with the citizen spouse at the time of his death, may be naturalized upon compliance with all the requirements of this title except that no prior residence or specified physical presence within the United States, or within a State or a district of the Service in the United States shall be required. For purposes of this subsection, the terms "United States citizen" and "citizen spouse" include a person granted posthumous citizenship under section 329A [8 USCS § 1440-1].

(e) (1) In the case of a person lawfully admitted for permanent residence in the United States who is the spouse of a member of the Armed Forces of the United States, is authorized to accompany such member and reside abroad with the member pursuant to the member's official orders, and is so accompanying and residing with the member in marital union, such residence and physical presence abroad shall be treated, for purposes of subsection (a) and section 316(a) [8 USCS § 1427(a)], as residence and physical presence in—

(A) the United States; and

(B) any State or district of the Department of Homeland Security in the United States.

(2) Notwithstanding any other provision of law, a spouse described in paragraph (1) shall be eligible for naturalization proceedings overseas pursuant to section 1701(d) of the National Defense Authorization Act for Fiscal Year 2004 (Public Law 108-136; 8 U.S.C. 1443a).

HISTORY: (June 27, 1952, ch 477, Title III, Ch 2, § 319, 66 Stat. 244; Aug. 20, 1958, P.L. 85-697, § 2, 72 Stat. 687; Dec. 18, 1967, P.L. 90-215, § 1(a), 81 Stat. 661; June 29, 1968, P.L. 90-369, 82 Stat. 279; Nov. 29, 1990, P.L. 101-649, Title IV, §§ 407(b)(1), (c)(5), (d)(4), 104 Stat. 5040, 5041; Oct. 28, 2000,

P.L. 106-386, Div B, Title V, § 1503(e), 114 Stat. 1522; Nov. 24, 2003, P.L. 108-136, Div A, Title XVII, § 1703(f)(1), (h), 117 Stat. 1695, 1696; Jan. 28, 2008, P.L. 110-181, Div A, Title VI, Subtitle G, § 674(a), 122 Stat. 185.)

§ 320. [8 U.S.C. § 1431] Children born outside the United States and lawfully admitted for permanent residence; conditions under which citizenship automatically acquired.

(a) A child born outside of the United States automatically becomes a citizen of the United States when all of the following conditions have been fulfilled:

(1) At least one parent of the child is a citizen of the United States, whether by birth or naturalization.

(2) The child is under the age of eighteen years.

(3) The child is residing in the United States in the legal and physical custody of the citizen parent pursuant to a lawful admission for permanent residence.

(b) Subsection (a) shall apply to a child adopted by a United States citizen parent if the child satisfies the requirements applicable to adopted children under section 101(b)(1) [8 USCS § 1101(b)(1)].

(c) Subsection (a)(3) is deemed satisfied in the case of a child who is lawfully admitted for permanent residence in the United States if—

(1) the child is residing in the legal and physical custody of a citizen parent who is—

(A) stationed and residing abroad as an employee of the Government of the United States; or

(B) residing abroad in marital union with an employee of the Government of the United States who is stationed abroad; or

(2) the child is—

(A) residing in the legal and physical custody of a citizen parent who is—

(i) stationed and residing abroad as a member of the Armed Forces of the United States; or

(ii) authorized to accompany and reside abroad with a member of the Armed Forces of the United States pursuant to the member's official orders, and is so accompanying and residing abroad with the member in marital union; and

(B) authorized to accompany such member and reside abroad with the member pursuant to the member's official orders, and is so accompanying and residing with the member.

(d) A Certificate of Citizenship or other Federal document issued or requested to be amended under this section shall reflect the child's name and date of birth as indicated on a State court order, birth certificate, certificate of foreign birth, certificate of birth abroad, or similar State vital records document issued by the child's State of residence in the United States after the child has been adopted or readopted in that State.

HISTORY: (June 27, 1952, ch 477, Title III, Ch 2, § 319, 66 Stat. 244; Aug. 20, 1958, P. L. 85-697, § 2, 72 Stat. 687; Dec. 18, 1967, P. L. 90-215, § 1(a), 81 Stat. 661; June 29, 1968, P. L. 90-369, 82 Stat. 279; Nov. 29, 1990, P. L. 101-649, Title IV, §§ 407(b)(1), (c)(5), (d)(4), 104 Stat. 5040, 5041; Oct. 28, 2000, P. L. 106-386, Div B, Title V, § 1503(e), 114 Stat. 1522; Nov. 24, 2003, P. L. 108-136, Div A, Title XVII, § 1703(f)(1), (h), 117 Stat. 1695, 1696; Jan. 28, 2008, P. L. 110-181, Div A, Title VI, Subtitle G, § 674(a), 122 Stat. 185.)

§ 321. [8 U.S.C. § 1432] [Repealed].

HISTORY: This section (Act June 27, 1952, ch 477, Title III, Ch 2, § 321, 66 Stat. 245; Oct. 5, 1978, P.L. 95-417, § 5, 92 Stat. 918; Dec. 29, 1981, P.L. 97-116, § 18(m), 95 Stat. 1620; Nov. 14, 1986, P.L. 99-653, § 15, 100 Stat. 3658; Nov. 14, 1986, P.L. 99-653, § 15, 100 Stat. 3658; Oct. 24, 1988, P.L. 100-525, § 8(*l*), 102 Stat. 2618) was repealed by Act Oct. 30, 2000, P.L. 106-395, Title I, § 103(a), 114 Stat. 1631 (effective 120 days after enactment, as provided by § 104 of such Act, which appears as 8 USCS § 1431 note). It related to conditions for automatic citizenship for children born outside of the United States of alien parents.

§ 322. [8 U.S.C. § 1433] Children born and residing outside the United States; conditions for acquiring certificate of citizenship.

(a) Application by citizen parents; requirements. A parent who is a citizen of the United States (or, if the citizen parent has died during the preceding 5 years, a citizen grandparent or citizen legal guardian) may apply for naturalization on behalf of a child born outside of the United States who has not acquired citizenship automatically under section 320 [8 USCS § 1431]. The Attorney General shall issue a certificate of citizenship to such applicant upon proof, to the satisfaction of the Attorney General, that the following conditions have been fulfilled:

(1) At least one parent is (or, at the time of his or her death, was) a citizen of the United States, whether by birth or naturalization.

(2) The United States citizen parent—

(A) has (or, at the time of his or her death, had) been physically present in the United States or its outlying possessions for a period or periods totaling not less than five years, at least two of which were after attaining the age of fourteen years; or

(B) has (or, at the time of his or her death, had) a citizen parent who has been physically present in the United States or its outlying possessions for a period or periods totaling not less than five years, at least two of which were after attaining the age of fourteen years.

(3) The child is under the age of eighteen years.

(4) The child is residing outside of the United States in the legal and physical custody of the applicant (or, if the citizen parent is deceased, an individual who does not object to the application).

(5) The child is temporarily present in the United States pursuant to a lawful admission, and is maintaining such lawful status.

(b) Attainment of citizenship status; receipt of certificate. Upon approval of the application (which may be filed from abroad) and, except as provided in the last sentence of section 337(a) [8 USCS § 1448(a)], upon taking and subscribing before an officer of the Service within the United States to the oath of allegiance required by this Act of an applicant for naturalization, the child shall become a citizen of the United States and shall be furnished by the Attorney General with a certificate of citizenship.

(c) Adopted children. Subsections (a) and (b) shall apply to a child adopted by a United States citizen parent if the child satisfies the requirements applicable to adopted children under section 101(b)(1) [8 USCS § 1101(b)(1)].

(d) Overseas naturalization for military children. In the case of a child of a member of the Armed Forces of the United States who is authorized to accompany such member and reside abroad with the member pursuant to the member's official orders, and is so accompanying and residing with the member—

(1) any period of time during which the member of the Armed Forces is residing abroad pursuant to official orders shall be treated, for purposes of subsection (a)(2)(A), as physical presence in the United States;

(2) subsection (a)(5) shall not apply; and

(3) the oath of allegiance described in subsection (b) may be subscribed to abroad pursuant to section 1701(d) of the National Defense Authorization Act for Fiscal Year 2004 (Public Law 108-136; 8 U.S.C. 1443a).

HISTORY: (June 27, 1952, ch 477, Title III, Ch 2, § 322, 66 Stat. 246; Oct. 5, 1978, P. L. 95-417, § 6, 92 Stat. 918; Dec. 29, 1981, P. L. 97-116, § 18(m), (n), 95 Stat. 1620, 1621; Nov. 14, 1986, P. L. 99-653, § 16, 100 Stat. 3658; Oct. 24, 1988, P. L. 100-525, § 8(l), 102 Stat. 2618; Nov. 29, 1990, P. L. 101-649, Title IV, § 407(b)(2), (c)(6), (d)(5), 104 Stat. 5040; Dec. 12, 1991, P. L. 102-232, Title III, § 305(m)(3), 105 Stat. 1750; Oct. 25, 1994, P. L. 103-416, Title I, § 102(a), 108 Stat. 4306; Dec. 7, 1999, P. L. 106-139, § 1(b)(2), 113 Stat. 1697; Oct. 30, 2000, P. L. 106-395, Title I, § 102(a), 114 Stat. 1632; Nov. 2, 2002, P. L. 107-273, Div C, Title I, Subtitle A, § 11030B, 116 Stat. 1837; Jan. 28, 2008, P. L. 110-181, Div A, Title VI, Subtitle G, § 674(b), 122 Stat. 186.

§ 323. [8 U.S.C. § 1434] [Repealed].

HISTORY: This section (Act June 27, 1952, ch 477, Title III, subch 2, § 323, 66 Stat. 246; Sept. 11, 1957, P.L. 85-316, § 11, 71 Stat. 642, Aug. 20, 1958, P.L. 85-697, § 1, 72 Stat. 687) was repealed by Act Oct. 5, 1978, P.L. 95-417, § 7, 92 Stat. 918. It provided for citizenship of children adopted by citizens.

§ 324. [8 U.S.C. § 1435] Former citizens of United States regaining citizenship.

(a) Requirements. Any person formerly a citizen of the United States who (1) prior to September 22, 1922, lost United States citizenship by marriage to an alien, or by the loss of United States citizenship of such person's spouse, or (2) on or after September 22, 1922, lost United States citizenship by marriage to an alien ineligible to citizenship, may if no other nationality was acquired by an affirmative act of such person other than by marriage be naturalized upon compliance with all requirements of this title, except—

(1) no period of residence or specified period of physical presence within the United States or within the State or district of the Service in the United States where the application is filed shall be required; and

(2) the application need not set forth that it is the intention of the applicant to reside permanently within the United States.

Such person, or any person who was naturalized in accordance with the provisions of section 317(a) of the Nationality Act of 1940, shall have, from and after her naturalization, the status of a native-born or naturalized citizen of the United States, whichever status existed in the case of such person prior to the loss of citizenship: Provided, That nothing contained herein or in any other provision of law shall be construed as conferring United States citizenship retroactively upon such person, or upon any person who was naturalized in accordance with the provisions of section 317(a) of the Nationality Act of 1940, during any period in which such person was not a citizen.

(b) Additional requirements. No person who is otherwise eligible for naturalization in accordance with the provisions of subsection (a) of this section shall be naturalized unless such person shall establish to the satisfaction of the Attorney General that she has been a person of good moral character, attached to the principles of the Constitution of the United States, and well disposed to the good order and happiness of the United States for a period of not less than five years immediately preceding the date of filing an application for naturalization and up to the time of admission to citizenship, and, unless she has resided continuously in the United States since the date of her marriage, has been lawfully admitted for permanent residence prior to filing her petition for naturalization.

(c) Oath of allegiance.

(1) A woman who was a citizen of the United States at birth and (A) who has or is believed to have lost her United States citizenship solely by reason of her marriage prior to September 22, 1922, to an alien, or by her marriage on or after such date to an alien ineligible to citizenship, (B) whose marriage to such alien shall have terminated subsequent to January 12, 1941, and (C) who has not acquired by an affirmative act other than by marriage any other nationality, shall, from and after taking the oath of allegiance required by section 337 of this title [8 USCS § 1448], be a citizen of the United States and have the status of a citizen of the United States by birth, without filing an application for naturalization, and notwithstanding any of the other provisions of this title except the provisions of section 313 [8 USCS § 1424]: Provided, That nothing contained herein or in any other provision of law shall be construed as conferring United States citizenship retroactively upon such person, or upon any person who was naturalized in accordance with the provisions of section 317(b) of the Nationality Act of 1940, during any period in which such person was not a citizen.

(2) Such oath of allegiance may be taken abroad before a diplomatic or consular officer of the United States, or in the United States before the Attorney General or the judge or clerk of a court described in section 310(b) [8 USCS § 1421(b)].

(3) Such oath of allegiance shall be entered in the records of the appropriate embassy, legation, consulate, court, or the Attorney General, and upon demand, a certified copy of the proceedings, including a copy of the oath administered, under the seal of the embassy, legation, consulate, court, or the Attorney General, shall be delivered to such woman at a cost not exceeding $5, which certified copy shall be evidence of the facts stated therein before any court of record or judicial tribunal and in any department or agency of the Government of the United States.

(d) Persons losing citizenship for failure to meet physical presence retention requirement.

(1) A person who was a citizen of the United States at birth and lost such citizenship for failure to meet the physical presence retention requirements under section 301(b) [8 USCS § 1401(b)] (as in effect before October 10, 1978), shall, from and after taking the oath of allegiance required by section 337 [8 USCS § 1448] be a citizen of the United States and have the status of a citizen of the United States by birth, without filing an application for naturalization, and notwithstanding any of the other provisions of this title except the provisions of section 313 [8 USCS § 1424]. Nothing in this subsection or any other provision of law shall be construed as conferring United States citizenship retroactively upon such person during any period in which such person was not a citizen.

(2) The provisions of paragraphs (2) and (3) of subsection (c) shall apply to a person regaining citizenship under paragraph (1) in the same manner as they apply under subsection (c)(1).

HISTORY: (June 27, 1952, ch 477, Title III, Ch 2, § 324, 66 Stat. 246; Oct. 24, 1988, P. L. 100-525, § 9(x), 102 Stat. 2621; Nov. 29, 1990, P. L. 101-649, Title IV, § 407(b)(3), (c)(7), (d)(6), 104 Stat. 5040; Oct. 25, 1994, P. L. 103-416, Title I, § 103(a), 108 Stat. 4307.)

§ 325. [8 U.S.C. § 1436] Nationals but not citizens; residence within outlying possessions.

A person not a citizen who owes permanent allegiance to the United States, and who is otherwise qualified, may, if he becomes a resident of any State, be naturalized upon compliance with the applicable requirements of this title, except that in applications for naturalization filed under the provisions of this section residence and physical presence within the United States within the meaning of this title shall include residence and physical presence within any of the outlying possessions of the United States.

HISTORY: (June 27, 1952, ch 477, Title III, Ch 2, § 325, 66 Stat. 248; Nov. 29, 1990, P.L. 101-649, Title IV, § 407(c)(8), 104 Stat. 5041.)

§ 326. [8 U.S.C. § 1437] Resident Philippine citizens excepted from certain requirements.

Any person who (1) was a citizen of the Commonwealth of the Philippines on July 2, 1946, (2) entered the United States prior to May 1, 1934, and (3) has, since such entry, resided continuously in the United States shall be regarded as having been lawfully admitted to the United States for permanent residence for the purpose of applying for naturalization under this title.

HISTORY: (June 27, 1952, ch 477, Title III, Ch 2, § 326, 66 Stat. 248; Nov. 29, 1990, P.L. 101-649, Title IV, § 407(c)(9), 104 Stat. 5041.)

§ 327. [8 U.S.C. § 1438] Former citizens losing citizenship by entering the armed forces of foreign countries during World War II.

(a) Requirements; oath; certified copies of oath. Any person who, (1) during World War II and while a citizen of the United States, served in the military, air, or naval forces of any country at war with a country with which the United States was at war after December 7, 1941, and before September 2, 1945, and (2) has lost United States citizenship by reason of entering or serving in such forces, or taking an oath or obligation for the purpose of entering such forces, may, upon compliance with all the provisions of title III of this Act, except section 316(a) [8 USCS § 1427(a)], and except as otherwise provided in subsection (b), be naturalized by taking before the Attorney General or before a court described in section 310(b) [8 USCS § 1421(b)] the oath required by section 337 of this title [8 USCS § 1448]. Certified copies of such oath shall be sent by such court to the Department of State and to the Department of Justice and by the Attorney General to the Secretary of State.

(b) Exceptions. No person shall be naturalized under subsection (a) of this section unless he—

(1) is, and has been for a period of at least five years immediately preceding taking the oath required in subsection (a), a person of good moral character, attached to the principles of the Constitution of the United States and well disposed to the good order and happiness of the United States; and

(2) has been lawfully admitted to the United States for permanent residence and intends to reside permanently in the United States.

(c) Status. Any person naturalized in accordance with the provisions of this section, or any person who was naturalized in accordance with the provisions of section 323 of the Nationality Act of 1940, shall have, from and after such naturalization, the status of a native-born or naturalized, citizen of the United States, whichever status existed in the case of such person prior to the loss of citizenship: Provided, That nothing contained herein, or in any other provision of law, shall be construed as conferring United States citizenship retroactively upon any such person during any period in which such person was not a citizen.

(d) Span of World War II. For the purpose of this section, World War II shall be deemed to have begun on September 1, 1939, and to have terminated on September 2, 1945.

(e) Inapplicability to certain persons. This section shall not apply to any person who during World War II served in the armed forces of a country while such country was at war with the United States.

HISTORY: (June 27, 1952, ch 477, Title III, Ch 2, § 327, 66 Stat. 248; Nov. 29, 1990, P. L. 101-649, Title IV, § 407(d)(7), 104 Stat. 5042.)

§ 328. [8 U.S.C. § 1439] Naturalization through service in the armed forces.

(a) Requirements. A person who has served honorably at any time in the armed forces of the United States for a period or periods aggregating one year, and who, if separated from such service, was never separated except under honorable conditions, may be naturalized without having resided, continuously immediately preceding the date of filing such person's application, in the United States for at least five years, and in the State or district of the Service in the United States in which the application for naturalization is filed for at least three months, and without having been physically present in the United States for any specified period, if such petition is filed while the applicant is still in the service or within six months after the termination of such service.

(b) Exceptions. A person filing an applicant under subsection (a) of this section shall comply in all other respects with the requirements of this title, except that—

(1) no residence within a State or district of the Service in the United States shall be required;

(2) notwithstanding section 318 [8 USCS § 1429] insofar as it relates to deportability, such applicant may be naturalized immediately if the applicant be then actually in the Armed Forces of the United States, and if prior to the filing of the applicant shall have appeared before and been examined by a representative of the Service;

(3) the applicant shall furnish to the Secretary of Homeland Security, prior to any hearing upon his application, a certified statement from the proper executive department for each period of his service upon which he relies for the benefits of this section, clearly showing that such service was honorable and that no discharges from service, including periods of service not relied upon by him for the benefits of this section, were other than honorable (the certificate or certificates herein provided for shall be conclusive evidence of such service and discharge); and

(4) notwithstanding any other provision of law, no fee shall be charged or collected from the applicant for filing the application, or for the issuance of a certificate of naturalization upon being granted citizenship, and no clerk of any State court shall charge or collect any fee for such services unless the laws of the State require such charge to be made, in which case nothing more than the portion of the fee required to be paid to the State shall be charged or collected.

(c) Periods when not in service. In the case such applicant's service was not continuous, the applicant's residence in the United States and State or district of the Service in the United States, good moral character, attachment to the principles of the Constitution of the United States, and favorable disposition toward the good order and happiness of the United States, during any period within five years immediately preceding the date of filing such petition between the periods of applicant's service in the Armed Forces, shall be alleged in the application filed under the provisions of subsection (a) of this section, and proved at any hearing thereon. Such allegation and proof shall also be made as to any period between the termination of petitioner's service and the filing of the application for naturalization.

(d) Residence requirements. The applicant shall comply with the requirements of section 316(a) of this title [8 USCS § 1427(a)], if the termination of such service has been more than six months preceding the date of filing the application for naturalization, except that such service within five years immediately preceding the date of filing such application shall be considered as residence and physical presence within the United States.

(e) Moral character.Any such period or periods of service under honorable conditions, and good moral character, attachment to the principles of the Constitution of the United States, and favorable disposition toward the good order and happiness of the United States, during such service, shall be proved by duly authenticated copies of the records of the executive departments having custody of the records of such service, and such authenticated copies of records shall be accepted in lieu of compliance with the provisions of section 316(a) [8 USCS § 1427(a)].

(f) Revocation. Citizenship granted pursuant to this section may be revoked in accordance with section 340 [8 USCS § 1451] if the person is separated from the Armed Forces under other than honorable conditions before the person has served honorably for a period or periods aggregating five years. Such ground for revocation shall be in addition to any other provided by law, including the grounds described in section 340 [8 USCS § 1451]. The fact that the naturalized person was separated from the service under other than honorable conditions shall be proved by a duly authenticated certification from the executive department under which the person was serving at the time of separation. Any period or periods of service shall be proved by duly authenticated copies of the records of the executive departments having custody of the records of such service.

(g), (h) Repealed]

HISTORY: (June 27, 1952, ch 477, Title III, Ch 2, § 328, 66 Stat. 249; Oct. 24, 1968, P. L. 90-633, § 5, 82 Stat. 1344; Dec. 29, 1981, P. L. 97-116, § 15(e), 95 Stat. 1619; Nov. 29, 1990, P. L. 101-649, Title IV, § 407(b)(4), (c)(10), (d)(8), 104 Stat. 5040; Dec. 12, 1991, P. L. 102-232, Title III, § 305(c), 105 Stat. 1750; Nov. 24, 2003, P. L. 108-136, Div A, Title XVII, § 1701(a), (b)(1), (c)(1)(A), (f), 117 Stat. 1691, 1692; Oct. 9, 2008, P. L. 110-382, §§ 3(a), 4, 122 Stat. 4088, 4089.)

§ 329. [8 U.S.C. § 1440.] Naturalization through active-duty service in the armed forces during World War I, World War II, Korean hostilities, Vietnam hostilities, or other periods of military hostilities.

(a) Requirements. Any person who, while an alien or a noncitizen national of the United States, has served honorably as a member of the Selected Reserve of the Ready Reserve or in an active-duty status in the military, air, or naval forces of the United States during either World War I or during a period beginning September 1, 1939, and ending December 31, 1946, or during a period beginning June 25, 1950, and ending July 1, 1955, or during a period beginning February 28, 1961, and ending on a date designated by the President by Executive order as of the date of termination of the Vietnam hostilities, or thereafter during any other period which the President by Executive order shall designate as a period in which Armed Forces of the United States are or were engaged in military operations involving armed conflict with a hostile foreign force, and who, if separated from such service, was separated under honorable conditions, may be naturalized as provided in this section if (1) at the time of enlistment, reenlistment, extension of enlistment, or induction such person shall have been in the United States, the Canal Zone, American Samoa, or Swains Island, or on board a public vessel owned or operated by the United States for noncommercial service, whether or not he has been lawfully admitted to the United States for permanent residence, or (2) at any time subsequent to enlistment or induction such person shall have been lawfully admitted to the United States for permanent residence. The executive department under which such person served shall determine whether persons have served honorably in an active-duty status, and whether separation from such service was under honorable conditions: Provided, however, That no person who is or has been separated from such service on account of alienage, or who was a conscientious objector who performed no military, air, or naval duty whatever or refused to wear the uniform, shall be regarded as having served honorably or having been separated under honorable conditions for the purposes of this section. No period of service in the Armed Forces shall be made the basis of an application for naturalization under this section if the applicant has previously been naturalized on the basis of the same period of service.

(b) Exceptions. A person filing an application under subsection (a) of this section shall comply in all other respects with the requirements of this title, except that—

(1) he may be naturalized regardless of age, and notwithstanding the provisions of section 318 [8 USCS § 1429] as they relate to deportability and the provisions of section 331 [8 USCS § 1442];

(2) no period of residence or specified period of physical presence within the United States or any State or district of the Service in the United States shall be required;

(3) service in the military, air, or naval forces of the United States shall be proved by a duly authenticated certification from the executive department under which the applicant served or is serving, which shall state whether the applicant served honorably in active duty status during either World War I or during a period beginning September 1, 1939, and ending December 31, 1946 or during a period beginning June 25, 1950, and ending July 1, 1955, or during a period beginning February 28, 1961, and ending on a date designated by the President by Executive order as the date of termination of the Vietnam hostilities, or thereafter during any other period which the President by Executive order shall designate as a period in which Armed Forces of the United States are or were engaged in military operations involving armed conflict with a hostile foreign force, and was separated from such service under honorable conditions; and

(4) notwithstanding any other provision of law, no fee shall be charged or collected from the applicant for filing a petition for naturalization or for the issuance of a certificate of naturalization upon citizenship being granted to the applicant, and no clerk of any State court shall charge or collect any fee for such services unless the laws of the State require such charge to be made, in which case nothing more than the portion of the fee required to be paid to the State shall be charged or collected.

(c) Revocation. Citizenship granted pursuant to this section may be revoked in accordance with section 340 [8 USCS § 1451] if the person is separated from the Armed Forces under other than honorable conditions before the person has served honorably for a period or periods aggregating five years. Such ground for revocation shall be in addition to any other provided by law, including the grounds described in section 340 [8 USCS § 1451]. The fact that the naturalized person was separated from the service under other than honorable conditions shall be proved by a duly authenticated certification from the executive department under which the person was serving at the time of separation. Any period or periods of service shall be proved by duly authenticated copies of the records of the executive departments having custody of the records of such service.

HISTORY: (June 27, 1952, ch 477, Title III, Ch 2, § 329, 66 Stat. 250; Sept. 26, 1961, P. L. 87-301, § 8, 75 Stat. 654; Oct. 24, 1968, P. L. 90-633, §§ 1, 2, 6, 82 Stat. 1343, 1344; Dec. 29, 1981, P. L. 97-116, § 15(a), 95 Stat. 1619; Oct. 24, 1988, P. L. 100-525, § 9(y), 102 Stat. 2621; Nov. 29, 1990, P. L. 101-649, Title IV, § 407(b)(5), (c)(11), 104 Stat. 5040, 5041; Dec. 12, 1991, P. L. 102-232, Title III, § 305(b), 105 Stat. 1749; Nov. 18, 1997, P. L. 105-85, Div A, Title X, Subtitle G, § 1080(a), 111 Stat. 1916; Nov. 24, 2003, P. L. 108-136, Div A, Title XVII, §§ 1701(b)(2), (c)(1)(B), 1702, 117 Stat. 1691, 1692, 1693.)

§ 329A. [8 U.S.C. § 1440-1] Posthumous citizenship through death while on active-duty service in the armed forces during World War I, World War II, the Korean hostilities, the Vietnam hostilities, or in other periods of military hostilities.

(a) Permitting granting of posthumous citizenship. Notwithstanding any other provision of this title, the Secretary of Homeland Security shall provide, in accordance with this section, for the granting of posthumous citizenship at the time of death to a person described in subsection (b) if the Secretary of Homeland Security approves an application for that posthumous citizenship under subsection (c).

(b) Noncitizens eligible for posthumous citizenship. A person referred to in subsection (a) is a person who, while an alien or a noncitizen national of the United States—

(1) served honorably in an active-duty status in the military, air, or naval forces of the United States during any period described in the first sentence of section 329(a) [8 USCS § 1440(a)],

(2) died as a result of injury or disease incurred in or aggravated by that service, and

(3) satisfied the requirements of clause (1) or (2) of the first sentence of section 329(a) [8 USCS § 1440(a)].

The executive department under which the person so served shall determine whether the person satisfied the requirements of paragraphs (1) and (2).

(c) Requests for posthumous citizenship.

(1) In general. A request for the granting of posthumous citizenship to a person described in subsection (b) may be filed on behalf of that person—

(A) upon locating the next-of-kin, and if so requested by the next-of-kin, by the Secretary of Defense or the Secretary's designee with the Bureau of Citizenship and Immigration Services in the Department of Homeland Security immediately upon the death of that person; or

(B) by the next-of-kin.

(2) Approval. The Director of the Bureau of Citizenship and Immigration Services shall approve a request for posthumous citizenship filed by the next-of-kin in accordance with paragraph (1)(B) if—

(A) the request is filed not later than 2 years after—

(i) the date of enactment of this section; or

(ii) the date of the person's death;

whichever date is later;

(B) the request is accompanied by a duly authenticated certificate from the executive department under which the person served which states that the person satisfied the requirements of paragraphs (1) and (2) of subsection (b); and

(C) the Director finds that the person satisfied the requirement of subsection (b)(3).

(d) Documentation of posthumous citizenship. If the Director of the Bureau of Citizenship and Immigration Services approves the request referred to in subsection (c), the Director shall send to the next-of-kin of the person who is granted citizenship, a suitable document which states that the United States considers the person to have been a citizen of the United States at the time of the person's death.

HISTORY: (June 27, 1952, ch 477, § 329A, as added March 6, 1990, P. L. 101-249, § 2(a), 104 Stat. 94; Nov. 2, 2002, P. L. 107-273, Div C, Title I, Subtitle A, § 11030(b), 116 Stat. 1836; Nov. 24, 2003, P. L. 108-136, Div A, Title XVII, §§ 17032(g), 1704, 117 Stat. 1695, 1696.)

§ 330. [8 U.S.C. § 1441] Constructive residence through service on certain United States vessels.

Any periods of time during all of which a person who was previously lawfully admitted for permanent residence has served honorably or with good conduct, in any capacity other than as a member of the Armed Forces of the United States, (A) on board a vessel operated by the United States, or an agency thereof, the full legal and equitable title to which is in the United States; or (B) on board a vessel whose home port is in the United States, and (i) which is registered under the laws of the United States, or (ii) the full legal and equitable title to which is in a citizen of the United States, or a corporation organized under the laws of any of the several States of the United States, shall be deemed residence and physical presence within the United States within the meaning of section 316(a) of this title [8 USCS § 1427(a)], if such service occurred within five years immediately preceding the date such person shall file an application for naturalization. Service on vessels described in clause (A) of this section shall be proved by duly authenticated copies of the records of the executive departments or agency having custody of the records of such service. Service on vessels described in clause (B) of this subsection may be proved by certificates from the masters of such vessels.

HISTORY: (June 27, 1952, ch 477, Title III, Ch 2, § 330, 66 Stat. 251; Oct. 24, 1988, P. L. 100-525, § 9(z), 102 Stat. 2621; Nov. 29, 1990, P. L. 101-649, Title IV, § 407(c)(12), 104 Stat. 5041; Dec. 12, 1991, P. L. 102-232, Title III, § 305(m)(5), 105 Stat. 1750.)

§ 331. [8 U.S.C. § 1442] Alien enemies.

(a) Naturalization under specified conditions. An alien who is a native, citizen, subject, or denizen of any country, state, or sovereignty with which the United States is at war may, after his loyalty has been fully established upon investigation by the Attorney General, be naturalized as a citizen of the United States if such alien's application for naturalization shall be pending at the beginning of the state of war and the applicant is otherwise entitled to admission to citizenship.

(b) Procedure. An alien embraced within this section shall not have his application for naturalization considered or heard except after 90 days' notice to the Attorney General to be considered at the examination or hearing, and the Attorney General's objection to such consideration shall cause the application to be continued from time to time for so long as the Attorney General may require.

(c) Exceptions from classification. The Attorney General may, in his discretion, upon investigation fully establishing the loyalty of any alien enemy who did not have an application for naturalization pending at the beginning of the state of war, except such alien enemy from the classification of alien enemy for the purposes of this title, and thereupon such alien shall have the privilege of filing an application for naturalization.

(d) Effect of cessation of hostilities. An alien who is a native, citizen, subject, or denizen of any country, state, or sovereignty with which the United States is at war shall cease to be an alien enemy within the meaning of this section upon the determination by proclamation of the President, or by concurrent resolution of the Congress, that hostilities between the United States and such country, state, or sovereignty have ended.

(e) Apprehension and removal. Nothing contained herein shall be taken or construed to interfere with or prevent the apprehension and removal, consistent with law, of any alien enemy at any time prior to the actual naturalization of such alien.

HISTORY: (June 27, 1952, ch 477, Title III, Ch 2, § 331, 66 Stat. 252; Nov. 29, 1990, P. L. 101-649, Title IV, § 407(c)(13), (d)(9), (e)(2), 104 Stat. 5041, 5042, 5046.)

§ 332. [8 U.S.C. § 1443.] Administration.

(a) Rules and regulations governing examination of applicants. The Attorney General shall make such rules and regulations as may be necessary to carry into effect the provisions of this chapter and is authorized to prescribe the scope and nature of the examination of applicants for naturalization as to their admissibility to citizenship. Such examination shall be limited to inquiry concerning the applicant's residence, physical presence in the United States, good moral character, understanding of and attachment to the fundamental principles of the Constitution of the United States, ability to read, write, and speak English, and other qualifications to become a naturalized citizen as required by law, and shall be uniform throughout the United States.

(b) Instruction in citizenship. The Attorney General is authorized to promote instruction and training in citizenship responsibilities of applicants for naturalization including the sending of names of candidates for naturalization to the public schools, preparing and distributing citizenship textbooks to such candidates as are receiving instruction in preparation for citizenship within or under the supervision of the public schools, preparing and distributing monthly an immigration and naturalization bulletin and securing the aid of and cooperating with official State and national organizations, including those concerned with vocational education.

(c) Prescription of forms. The Attorney General shall prescribe and furnish such forms as may be required to give effect to the provisions of this chapter, and only such forms as may be so provided shall be legal. All certificates of naturalization and of citizenship shall be printed on safety paper and shall be consecutively numbered in separate series.

(d) Administration of oaths and depositions. Employees of the Service may be designated by the Attorney General to administer oaths and to take depositions without charge in matters relating to the administration of the naturalization and citizenship laws. In cases where there is a likelihood of unusual delay or of hardship, the Attorney General may, in his discretion, authorize such depositions to be taken before a postmaster without charge, or before a notary public or other person authorized to administer oaths for general purposes.

(e) Issuance of certificate of naturalization or citizenship. A certificate of naturalization or of citizenship issued by the Attorney General under the authority of this title shall have the same effect in all courts, tribunals, and public offices of the United States, at home and abroad, of the District of Columbia, and of each State, Territory, and outlying possession of the United States, as a certificate of naturalization or of citizenship issued by a court having naturalization jurisdiction.

(f) Copies of records. Certifications and certified copies of all papers, documents, certificates, and records required or authorized to be issued, used, filed, recorded, or kept under any and all provisions of this Act shall be admitted in evidence equally with the originals in any and all cases and proceedings under this Act and in all cases and proceedings in which the originals thereof might be admissible as evidence.

(g) Furnished quarters for photographic studios. The officers in charge of property owned or leased by the Government are authorized, upon the recommendation of the Attorney General, to provide quarters, without payment of rent, in any building occupied by the Service, for a photographic studio, operated by welfare organizations without profit and solely for the benefit of persons seeking to comply with requirements under the immigration and nationality laws. Such studio shall be under the supervision of the Attorney General.

(h) Public education regarding naturalization benefits. In order to promote the opportunities and responsibilities of United States citizenship, the Attorney General shall broadly distribute information concerning the benefits which persons may receive under this title and the requirements to obtain such benefits. In carrying out this subsection, the Attorney General shall seek the assistance of appropriate community groups, private voluntary agencies, and other relevant organizations. There are authorized to be appropriated (for each fiscal year beginning with fiscal year 1991) such sums as may be necessary to carry out this subsection.

HISTORY: (June 27, 1952, ch 477, Title III, Ch 2, § 332, 66 Stat. 252; Nov. 29, 1990, P. L. 101-649, Title IV, §§ 406, 407(d)(10), 104 Stat. 5040, 5042; Dec. 12, 1991, P. L. 102-232, Title III, § 305(m)(6), 105 Stat. 1750.)

§ 333. [8 U.S.C. § 1444] Photographs; number.

(a) Three identical photographs of the applicant shall be signed by and furnished by each applicant for naturalization or citizenship. One of such photographs shall be affixed by the Attorney General to the original certificate of naturalization issued to the naturalized citizen and one to the duplicate certificate of naturalization required to be forwarded to the Service.

(b) Three identical photographs of the applicant shall be furnished by each applicant for—

(1) a record of lawful admission for permanent residence to be made under section 249 [8 USCS § 1259];

(2) a certificate of derivative citizenship;

(3) a certificate of naturalization or of citizenship;

(4) a special certificate of naturalization;

(5) a certificate of naturalization or of citizenship, in lieu of one lost, mutilated, or destroyed;

(6) a new certificate of citizenship in the new name of any naturalized citizen who, subsequent to naturalization, has had his name changed by order of a court of competent jurisdiction or by marriage; and

(7) a declaration of intention.

One such photograph shall be affixed to each such certificate issued by the Attorney General and one shall be affixed to the copy of such certificate retained by the Service.

HISTORY: (June 27, 1952, ch 477, Title III, Ch 2, § 333, 66 Stat. 253; Nov. 29, 1990, P. L. 101-649, Title IV, § 407(c)(14), (d)(11), 104 Stat. 5041, 5042; Oct. 25, 1994, P. L. 103-416, Title II, § 219(w), 108 Stat. 4318.)

§ 334. [8 U.S.C. § 1445.] Application for naturalization; declaration of intention.

(a) Evidence and form. An applicant for naturalization shall make and file with the Attorney General a sworn application in writing, signed by the applicant in the applicant's own handwriting if physically able to write, which application shall be on a form prescribed by the Attorney General and shall include averments of all facts which in the opinion of the Attorney General may be material to the applicant's naturalization, and required to be proved under this title. In the case of an applicant subject to a requirement of continuous residence under section 316(a) or 319(a) [8 USCS § 1427(a) or 1430(a)], the application for naturalization may be filed up to 3 months before the date the applicant would first otherwise meet such continuous residence requirement.

(b) Who may file. No person shall file a valid application for naturalization unless he shall have attained the age of eighteen years. An application for naturalization by an alien shall contain an averment of lawful admission for permanent residence.

(c) Holding of hearings. Hearings under section 336(a) [8 USCS § 1447(a)] on applications for naturalization shall be held at regular intervals specified by the Attorney General.

(d) Filing of application. Except as provided in subsection (e), an application for naturalization shall be filed in the office of the Attorney General.

(e) Substitute filing place and administering oath other than before Attorney General. A person may file an application for naturalization other than in the office of the Attorney General, and an oath of allegiance administered other than in a public ceremony before the Attorney General or a court, if the Attorney General determines that the person has an illness or other disability which—

(1) is of a permanent nature and is sufficiently serious to prevent the person's personal appearance, or

(2) is of a nature which so incapacitates the person as to prevent him from personally appearing.

(f) Declaration of intention. An alien over 18 years of age who is residing in the United States pursuant to a lawful admission for permanent residence may file with the Attorney General a declaration of intention to become a citizen of the United States. Such a declaration shall be filed in duplicate and in a form prescribed by the Attorney General and shall be accompanied by an application prescribed and approved by the Attorney General. Nothing in this subsection shall be construed as requiring any such alien to make and file a declaration of intention as a condition precedent to filing a petition for naturalization nor shall any such declaration of intention be regarded as conferring or having conferred upon any such alien United States citizenship or nationality or the right to United States citizenship or nationality, nor shall such declaration be regarded as evidence of such alien's lawful admission for permanent residence in any proceeding, action, or matter arising under this or any other Act.

HISTORY: (June 27, 1952, ch 477, Title III, Ch 2, § 334, 66 Stat. 254; Dec. 29, 1981, P. L. 97-116, § 15(b), 95 Stat. 1619; Nov. 29, 1990, P. L. 101-649, Title IV, §§ 401(b), 407(c)(15), (d)(12), 104 Stat. 5038, 5041, 5042; Dec. 12, 1991, P. L. 102-232, Title III, § 305(d), (e), (m)(7), 105 Stat. 1750.)

§ 335. [8 U.S.C. § 1446] Investigation of applicants; examination of applications.

(a) Waiver. Before a person may be naturalized, an employee of the Service, or of the United States designated by the Attorney General, shall conduct a personal investigation of the person applying for naturalization in the vicinity or vicinities in which such person has maintained his actual place of abode and in the vicinity or vicinities in which such person has been employed or has engaged in business or work for at least five years immediately preceding the filing of his application for naturalization. The Attorney General may, in his discretion, waive a personal investigation in an individual case or in such case or classes of cases as may be designated by him.

(b) Conduct of examinations; authority of designees; record. The Attorney General shall designate employees of the Service to conduct examinations upon petitions for naturalization. For such purposes any such employee so designated is hereby authorized to take testimony concerning any matter touching or in any way affecting the admissibility of any applicant for naturalization, to administer oaths, including the oath of the applicant for naturalization, and to require by subpena the attendance and testimony of witnesses, including applicant, before such employee so designated and the production of relevant books, papers, and documents, and to that end may invoke the aid of any district court of the United States; and any such court may, in the event of neglect or refusal to respond to a subpena issued by any such employee so designated or refusal to testify before such employee so designated issue an order requiring such person to answer before such employee so designated, produce relevant books, papers, and documents if demanded, and testify; and any failure to obey such order of the court may be punished by the court as a contempt thereof. The record of the examination authorized by this subsection shall be admissible as evidence in any hearing conducted by an immigration officer under section 336(a) [8 USCS § 1447(a)]. Any such employee shall, at the examination, inform the petitioner of the remedies available to the petitioner under section 336 [8 USCS § 1447].

(c) Transmittal of record of examination. The record of the examination upon any application for naturalization may, in the discretion of the Attorney General, be transmitted to the Attorney General and the determination with respect thereto of the employee designated to conduct such examination shall when made also be transmitted to the Attorney General.

(d) Determination to grant or deny application. The employee designated to conduct any such examination shall make a determination as to whether the application should be granted or denied, with reasons therefor.

(e) Withdrawal of application. After an application for naturalization has been filed with the Attorney General, the applicant shall not be permitted to withdraw his application, except with the consent of the Attorney General. In cases where the Attorney General does not consent to the withdrawal of the application, the application shall be determined on its merits and a final order determination made accordingly. In cases where the applicant fails to prosecute his application, the application shall be decided on the merits unless the Attorney General dismisses it for lack of prosecution.

(f) Transfer of application. An applicant for naturalization who moves from the district of the Service in the United States in which the application is pending may, at any time thereafter, request the Service to transfer the application to any district of the Service in the United States which may act on the application. The transfer shall not be made without the consent of the Attorney General. In the case of such a transfer, the proceedings on the application shall continue as though the application had originally been filed in the district of the Service to which the application is transferred.

HISTORY: (June 27, 1952, ch 477, Title III, Ch 2, § 335, 66 Stat. 255; Dec. 29, 1981, P. L. 97-116, § 15(c), 95 Stat. 1619; Oct. 24, 1988, P. L. 100-525, § 9(aa), (bb), 102 Stat. 2621; Nov. 29, 1990, P. L. 101-649, Title IV, §§ 401(c), 407(c)(16), (d)(13), 104 Stat. 5038, 5041, 5043; Dec. 12, 1991, P. L. 102-232, Title III, § 305(f), 105 Stat. 1750.)

§ 336. [8 U.S.C. § 1447] Hearings on denials of applications for naturalization.

(a) Request for hearing before immigration officer. If, after an examination under section 335 [8 USCS § 1446], an application for naturalization is denied, the applicant may request a hearing before an immigration officer.

(b) Request for hearing before district court. If there is a failure to make a determination under section 335 [8 USCS § 1446] before the end of the 120-day period after the date on which the examination is conducted under such section, the applicant may apply to the United States district court for the district in which the applicant resides for a hearing on the matter. Such court has jurisdiction over the matter and may either determine the matter or remand the matter, with appropriate instructions, to the Service to determine the matter.

(c) Appearance of Attorney General. The Attorney General shall have the right to appear before any immigration officer in any naturalization proceedings for the purpose of cross-examining the applicant and the witnesses produced in support of the petition concerning any matter touching or in any way affecting the applicant's right to admission to citizenship, and shall have the right to call witnesses, including the applicant, produce evidence, and be heard in opposition to, or in favor of, the granting of any application in naturalization proceedings.

(d) Subpena of witnesses. The immigration officer shall, if the applicant requests it at the time of filing the request for hearing, issue a subpena for the witnesses named by such petitioner to appear upon the day set for the hearing, but in case such witnesses cannot be produced upon the hearing other witnesses may be summoned upon notice to the Attorney General, in such manner and at such time as the Attorney General may by regulation prescribe. Such subpenas may be enforced in the same manner as subpenas under section 335(b) [8 USCS § 1446(b)] may be enforced.

(e) Change of name. It shall be lawful at the time and as a part of the administration by a court of the oath of allegiance under section 337(a) [8 USCS § 1448(a)], for the court, in its discretion, upon the bona fide prayer of the applicant included in an appropriate petition to the court, to make a decree changing the name of said person, and the certificate of naturalization shall be issued in accordance therewith.

HISTORY: (June 27, 1952, ch 477, Title III, Ch 2, § 336, 66 Stat. 257; Dec. 5, 1969, P. L. 91-136, 83 Stat. 283; Dec. 29, 1981, P. L. 97-116, § 15(d), 95 Stat. 1619; Oct. 24, 1988, P. L. 100-525, § 9(cc), 102 Stat. 2621; Nov. 29, 1990, P. L. 101-649, Title IV, § 407(c)(17), (d)(14), 104 Stat. 5041, 5044; Dec. 12, 1991, P. L. 102-232, Title III, § 305(g), (h), 105 Stat. 1750.)

§ 337. [8 U.S.C. § 1448] Oath of renunciation and allegiance.

(a) Public ceremony. A person who has applied for naturalization shall, in order to be and before being admitted to citizenship, take in a public ceremony before the Attorney General or a court with jurisdiction under section 310(b) [8 USCS § 1421(b)] an oath (1) to support the Constitution of the United States; (2) to renounce and abjure absolutely and entirely all allegiance and fidelity to any foreign prince, potentate, state, or sovereignty of whom or which the applicant was before a subject or citizen; (3) to support and defend the Constitution and the laws of the United States against all enemies, foreign and domestic; (4) to bear true faith and allegiance to the same; and (5) (A) to bear arms on behalf of the United States when required by the law, or (B) to perform noncombatant service in the Armed Forces of the United States when required by the law, or (C) to perform work of national importance under civilian direction when required by the law. Any such person shall be required to take an oath containing the substance of clauses (1) through (5) of the preceding sentence, except that a person who shows by clear and convincing evidence to the satisfaction of the Attorney General that he is opposed to the bearing of arms in the Armed Forces of the United States by reason of religious training and belief shall be required to take an oath containing the substance of clauses (1) through (4) and clauses (5)(B) and (5)(C), and a person who shows by clear and convincing evidence to the satisfaction of the Attorney General that he is opposed to any type of service in the Armed Forces of the United States by reason of religious training and belief shall be required to take an oath containing the substance of clauses (1) through (4) and clause (5)(C). The term "religious training and belief" as used in this section shall mean an individual's belief in a relation to a Supreme Being involving duties superior to those arising from any human relation, but does not include essentially political, sociological, or philosophical views or a merely personal moral code. In the case of the naturalization of a child under the provisions of section 322 of this title [8 USCS § 1433] the Attorney General may waive the taking of the oath if in the opinion of the Attorney General the child is unable to understand its meaning. The Attorney General may waive the taking of the oath by a person if in the opinion of the Attorney General the person is unable to understand, or to communicate an understanding of, its meaning because of a physical or developmental disability or mental impairment. If the Attorney General waives the taking of the oath by a person under the preceding sentence, the person shall be considered to have met the requirements of section 316(a)(3) [8 USCS

§ 1427(a)(3)] with respect to attachment to the principles of the Constitution and well disposition to the good order and happiness of the United States.

(b) Hereditary titles or orders of nobility. In case the person applying for naturalization has borne any hereditary title, or has been of any of the orders of nobility in any foreign state, the petitioner shall in addition to complying with the requirements of subsection (a) of this section, make under oath in the same public ceremony in which the oath of allegiance is administered, an express renunciation of such title or order of nobility, and such renunciation shall be recorded as a part of such proceedings.

(c) Expedited judicial oath administration ceremony. Notwithstanding section 310(b) [8 USCS § 1421(b)], an individual may be granted an expedited judicial oath administration ceremony or administrative naturalization by the Attorney General upon demonstrating sufficient cause. In determining whether to grant an expedited judicial oath administration ceremony, a court shall consider special circumstances (such as serious illness of the applicant or a member of the applicant's immediate family, permanent disability sufficiently incapacitating as to prevent the applicant's personal appearance at the scheduled ceremony, developmental disability or advanced age, or exigent circumstances relating to travel or employment). If an expedited judicial oath administration ceremony is impracticable, the court shall refer such individual to the Attorney General who may provide for immediate administrative naturalization.

(d) Rules and regulations. The Attorney General shall prescribe rules and procedures to ensure that the ceremonies conducted by the Attorney General for the administration of oaths of allegiance under this section are public, conducted frequently and at regular intervals, and are in keeping with the dignity of the occasion.

HISTORY: (June 27, 1952, ch 477, Title III, Ch 2, § 337, 66 Stat. 258; Dec. 29, 1981, P. L. 97-116, § 18(o), 95 Stat. 1621; Nov. 29, 1990, P. L. 101-649, Title IV, § 407(c)(18), (d)(15), 104 Stat. 5041, 5044; Dec. 12, 1991, P. L. 102-232, Title I, §§ 102(b)(2), 305(i), 105 Stat. 1736, 1750; Nov. 6, 2000, P. L. 106-448, § 1, 114 Stat. 1939.)

§ 338. [8 U.S.C. § 1449] Certificate of naturalization; contents.

A person admitted to citizenship in conformity with the provisions of this title shall be entitled upon such admission to receive from the Attorney General a certificate of naturalization, which shall contain substantially the following information: Number of application for naturalization; number of certificate of naturalization; date of naturalization; name, signature, place of residence, autographed photograph, and personal description of the naturalized person, including age, sex, marital status, and country of former nationality; location of the district office of the Service in which the application was filed and the title, authority, and location of the official or court administering the oath of allegiance; statement that the Attorney General having found that the petitioner had complied in all respects with all of the applicable provisions of the naturalization laws of the United States, and was entitled to be admitted a citizen of the United States of America, thereupon ordered that the applicant be admitted as a citizen of the United States of America; attestation of an immigration officer; and the seal of the Department of Justice.

HISTORY: (June 27, 1952, ch 477, Title III, Ch 2, § 338, 66 Stat. 259; Nov. 29, 1990, P.L. 101-649, Title IV, § 407(c)(19), (d)(16), 104 Stat. 5041, 5045; Dec. 12, 1991, P.L. 102-232, Title III, § 305(j), 105 Stat. 1750; Oct. 25, 1994, P.L. 103-416, Title 1, § 104(a), Title II, § 219(z)(3), 108 Stat. 4308, 4318.)

§ 339. [8 U.S.C. § 1450] Functions and duties of clerks and records of declarations of intention and applications for naturalization.

(a) The clerk of each court that administers oaths of allegiance under section 337 [8 USCS § 1448] shall—

(1) deliver to each person administered the oath of allegiance by the court pursuant to section 337(a) [8 USCS § 1448(a)] the certificate of naturalization prepared by the Attorney General pursuant to section 310(b)(2)(A)(ii) [8 USCS § 1421(b)(2)(A)(ii)] ,

(2) forward to the Attorney General a list of applicants actually taking the oath at each scheduled ceremony and information concerning each person to whom such an oath is administered by the court, within 30 days after the close of the month in which the oath was administered,

(3) forward to the Attorney General certified copies of such other proceedings and orders instituted in or issued out of the court affecting or relating to the naturalization of persons as may be required from time to time by the Attorney General; and

(4) be responsible for all blank certificates of naturalization received by them from time to time from the Attorney General and shall account to the Attorney General for them whenever required to do so.

No certificate of naturalization received by any clerk of court which may be defaced or injured in such manner as to prevent its use as herein provided shall in any case be destroyed, but such certificates shall be returned to the Attorney General.

(b) Each district office of the Service in the United States shall maintain, in chronological order, indexed, and consecutively numbered, as part of its permanent records, all declarations of intention and applications for naturalization filed with the office.

HISTORY: (June 27, 1952, ch 477, Title III, Ch 2, § 339, 66 Stat. 259; Nov. 29, 1990, P.L. 101-649, Title IV, § 407(d)(17), 104 Stat. 5045; Dec. 12, 1991, P.L. 102-232, Title I, § 102(b)(1), 105 Stat. 1735.)

§ 340. [8 U.S.C. § 1451] Revocation of naturalization.

(a) Concealment of material evidence; refusal to testify. It shall be the duty of the United States attorneys for the respective districts, upon affidavit showing good cause therefor, to institute proceedings in any district court of the United States in the judicial district in which the naturalized citizen may reside at the time of bringing suit, for the purpose of revoking and setting aside the order admitting such person to citizenship and canceling the certificate of naturalization on the ground that such order and certificate of naturalization were illegally procured or were procured by concealment of a material fact or by willful misrepresentation, and such revocation and setting aside of the order admitting such person to citizenship and such canceling of certificate of naturalization shall be effective as of the original date of the order and certificate, respectively: Provided, That refusal on the part of a naturalized citizen within a period of ten years following his naturalization to testify as a witness in any proceeding before a congressional committee concerning his subversive activities, in a case where such person has been convicted of contempt for such refusal, shall be held to constitute a ground for revocation of such person's naturalization under this subsection as having been procured by concealment of a material fact or by willful misrepresentation. If the naturalized citizen does not reside in any judicial district in the United States at the time of bringing such suit, the proceedings may be instituted in the United States District Court for the District of Columbia or in the United States district court in the judicial district in which such person last had his residence.

(b) Notice to party. The party to whom was granted the naturalization alleged to have been illegally procured or procured by concealment of a material fact or by willful misrepresentation shall, in any such proceedings under subsection (a) of this section, have sixty days' personal notice, unless waived by such party, in which to make answer to the petition of the United States; and if such naturalized person be absent from the United States or from the judicial district in which such person last had his residence, such notice shall be given either by personal service upon him or by publication in the manner provided for the service of summons by publication or upon absentees by the laws of the State or the place where such suit is brought.

(c) Membership in certain organizations; prima facie evidence. If a person who shall have been naturalized after December 24, 1952 shall within five years next following such naturalization become a member of or affiliated with any organization, membership in or affiliation with which at the time of naturalization would have precluded such person from naturalization under the provisions of section 313 [8 USCS § 1424], it shall be considered prima facie evidence that such person was not attached to the principles of the Constitution of the United States and was not well disposed to the good order and happiness of the United States at the time of naturalization, and, in the absence of countervailing evidence, it shall be sufficient in the proper proceeding to authorize the revocation and setting aside of the order admitting such person to citizenship and the cancellation of the certificate of naturalization as having been obtained by concealment of a material fact or by willful misrepresentation, and such revocation and setting aside of the order admitting such person to citizenship and such canceling of certificate of naturalization shall be effective as of the original date of the order and certificate, respectively.

(d) Applicability to citizenship through naturalization of parent or spouse. Any person who claims United States citizenship through the naturalization of a parent or spouse in whose case there is a revocation and setting aside of the order admitting such parent or spouse to citizenship under the provisions of subsection (a) of this section on the ground that the order and certificate of naturalization were procured by concealment of a material fact or by willful misrepresentation shall be deemed to have lost and to lose his citizenship and any right or privilege of citizenship which he may have, now has, or may hereafter acquire under and by virtue of such naturalization of such parent or spouse, regardless of whether such person is residing within or without the United States at the time of the revocation and setting aside of the order admitting such parent or spouse to citizenship. Any person who claims United States citizenship through the naturalization of a parent or spouse in whose case there is a revocation and setting aside of the order admitting such parent or spouse to citizenship and the cancellation of the certificate of naturalization under the provisions of subsection (c) of this section, or under the provisions of section 329(c) of this title [8 USCS § 1440(c)] on any ground other than that the order and certificate of naturalization were procured by concealment of a material fact or by willful misrepresentation, shall be deemed to have lost and to lose his citizenship and any right or privilege of citizenship which would have been enjoyed by such person had there not been a revocation and setting aside of the order admitting such parent or spouse to citizenship and the cancellation of the certificate of naturalization, unless such person is residing in the United States at the time of the revocation and setting aside of the order admitting such parent or spouse to citizenship and the cancellation of the certificate of naturalization.

(e) Citizenship unlawfully procured. When a person shall be convicted under section 1425 of title 18 of the United States Code of knowingly procuring naturalization in violation of law, the court in which such conviction is had shall thereupon revoke, set aside, and declare void the final order admitting such person to citizenship, and shall declare the certificate of naturalization of such person to be canceled. Jurisdiction is hereby conferred on the courts having jurisdiction of the trial of such offense to make such adjudication.

(f) Cancellation of certificate of naturalization. Whenever an order admitting an alien to citizenship shall be revoked and set aside or a certificate of naturalization shall be canceled, or both, as provided in this section, the court in which such judgment or decree is rendered shall make an order canceling such certificate and shall send a certified copy of such order to the Attorney General. The clerk of court shall transmit a copy of such order and judgment to the Attorney General. A person holding a certificate of naturalization or citizenship which has been canceled as provided by this section shall upon notice by the court by which the decree of cancellation was made, or by the Attorney General, surrender the same to the Attorney General.

(g) Applicability to certificates of naturalization and citizenship. The provisions of this section shall apply not only to any naturalization granted and to certificates of naturalization and citizenship issued under the provisions of this title, but to any naturalization heretofore granted by any court, and to all certificates of naturalization and citizenship which may have been issued heretofore by any court or by the Commissioner based upon naturalization granted by any court, or by a designated representative of the Commissioner under the provisions of section 702 of the Nationality Act of 1940, as amended, or by such designated representative under any other act.

(h) Power to correct, reopen, alter, modify or vacate order. Nothing contained in this section shall be regarded as limiting, denying, or restricting the power of the Attorney General to correct, reopen, alter, modify, or vacate an order naturalizing the person.

HISTORY: (June 27, 1952, ch 477, Title III, Ch 2, § 340, 66 Stat. 260; Sept. 3, 1954, ch 1263, § 18, 68 Stat. 1232; Sept. 26, 1961, P. L. 87-301, § 18, 75 Stat. 656; Nov. 14, 1986, P. L. 99-653, § 17, 100 Stat. 3658; Oct. 24, 1988, P. L. 100-525, § 9(dd), 102 Stat. 2621; Nov. 29, 1990, P. L. 101-649, Title IV, § 407(d)(18), 104 Stat. 5046; Dec. 12, 1991, P. L. 102-232, Title III, § 305(k), 105 Stat. 1750; Oct. 25, 1994, P. L. 103-416, Title I, § 104(b), (c), 108 Stat. 4308.)

§ 341. [8 U.S.C. § 1452] Certificates of citizenship or U.S. non-citizen national status; procedure.

(a) Application to Attorney General for certificate of citizenship; proof; oath of allegiance. A person who claims to have derived United States citizenship through the naturalization of a parent or through the naturalization or citizenship of a husband, or who is a citizen of the United States by virtue of the provisions of section 1993 of the United States Revised Statutes, or of section 1993 of the United States Revised Statutes, as amended by section 1 of the Act of May 24, 1934 (48 Stat. 797), or who is a citizen of the United States by virtue of the provisions of subsection (c), (d), (e), (g), or (i) of section 201 of the Nationality Act of 1940, as amended (54 Stat. 1138; 8 U.S.C. 601), or of the Act of May 7, 1934 (48 Stat. 667), or of paragraph (c), (d), (e), or (g) of section 301 of this title [8 USCS § 1401(c), (d), (e), or (g)], or under the provisions of the Act of August 4, 1937 (50 Stat. 558), or under the provisions of section 203 or 205 of the Nationality Act of 1940 (54 Stat. 1139; 8 U. S. C. 603, 605), or under the provisions of section 303 of this title [8 USCS § 1403], may apply to the Attorney General for a certificate of citizenship. Upon proof to the satisfaction of the Attorney General that the applicant is a citizen, and that the applicant's alleged citizenship was derived as claimed, or acquired, as the case may be, and upon taking and subscribing before a member of the Service within the United States to the oath of allegiance required by this Act of an applicant for naturalization, such individual shall be furnished by the Attorney General with a certificate of citizenship, but only if such individual is at the time within the United States.

(b) Application to Secretary of State for certificate of non-citizen national status; proof; oath of allegiance. A person who claims to be a national, but not a citizen, of the United States may apply to the Secretary of State for a certificate of non-citizen national status. Upon—

(1) proof to the satisfaction of the Secretary of State that the applicant is a national, but not a citizen, of the United States, and

(2) in the case of such a person born outside of the United States or its outlying possessions, taking and subscribing, before an immigration officer within the United States or its outlying possessions, to the oath of allegiance required by this Act of a petitioner for naturalization,

the individual shall be furnished by the Secretary of State with a certificate of non-citizen national status, but only if the individual is at the time within the United States or its outlying possessions

HISTORY: (June 27, 1952, ch 477, Title III, Ch 2, § 341, 66 Stat. 263; Dec. 29, 1981, P. L. 97-116, § 18(p), 95 Stat. 1621; Aug. 27, 1986, P. L. 99-396, § 16(a), 100 Stat. 843; Nov. 14, 1986, P. L. 99-653, § 22, 100 Stat. 3658; Oct. 24, 1988, P. L. 100-525, § 8(q), 102 Stat. 2618; Dec. 12, 1991, P. L. 102-232, Title III, § 305(m)(8), 105 Stat. 1750; Oct. 25, 1994, P. L. 103-416, Title I, § 102(b), 108 Stat. 4307.)

§ 342. [8 U.S.C. § 1453] Cancellation of certificates issued by the Attorney General, the Commissioner or a Deputy Commissioner; action not to affect citizenship status.

The Attorney General is authorized to cancel any certificate of citizenship, certificate of naturalization, copy of a declaration of intention, or other certificate, document or record heretofore issued or made by the Commissioner or a Deputy Commissioner or hereafter made by the Attorney General if it shall appear to the Attorney General's satisfaction that such document or record was illegally or fraudulently obtained from, or was created through illegality or by fraud practiced upon, him or the Commissioner or a Deputy Commissioner; but the person for or to whom such document or record has been issued or made shall be given at such person's last-known place of address written notice of the intention to cancel such document or record with the reasons therefor and shall be given at least sixty days in which to show cause why such document or record should not be canceled. The cancellation under this section of any document purporting to show the citizenship status of the person to whom it was issued shall affect only the document and not the citizenship status of the person in whose name the document was issued.

HISTORY: (June 27, 1952, ch 477, Title III, Ch 2, § 342, 66 Stat. 263.)

§ 343. [8 U.S.C. § 1454] Documents and copies issued by Attorney General.

(a) If any certificate of naturalization or citizenship issued to any citizen or any declaration of intention furnished to any declarant is lost, mutilated, or destroyed, the citizen or declarant may make application to the Attorney General for a new certificate or declaration. If the Attorney General finds that the certificate or declaration is lost, mutilated, or destroyed, he shall issue to the applicant a new certificate or declaration. If the certificate or declaration has been mutilated, it shall be surrendered to the Attorney General before the applicant may receive such new certificate or declaration.

If the certification or declaration has been lost, the applicant or any other person who shall have, or may come into possession of it is hereby required to surrender it to the Attorney General.

(b) The Attorney General shall issue for any naturalized citizen, on such citizen's application therefor, a special certificate of naturalization for use by such citizen only for the purpose of obtaining recognition as a citizen of the United States by a foreign state. Such certificate when issued shall be furnished to the Secretary of State for transmission to the proper authority in such foreign state.

(c) If the name of any naturalized citizen has, subsequent to naturalization, been changed by order of any court of competent jurisdiction, or by marriage, the citizen may make application for a new certificate of naturalization in the new name of such citizen. If the Attorney General finds the name of the applicant to have been changed as claimed, the Attorney General shall issue to the applicant a new certificate and shall notify the naturalization court of such action.

(d) The Attorney General is authorized to make and issue certifications of any part of the naturalization records of any court, or of any certificate of naturalization or citizenship, for use in complying with any statute, State or Federal, or in any judicial proceeding. No such certification shall be made by any clerk of court except upon order of the court.

HISTORY: (June 27, 1952, ch 477, Title III, Ch 2, § 343, 66 Stat. 263; Oct. 24, 1988, P. L. 100-235, § 9(ee), 102 Stat. 2621.)

§ 344. [8 U.S.C. § 1455] Fiscal provisions.

(a) The Attorney General shall charge, collect, and account for fees prescribed by the Attorney General pursuant to section 9701 of title 31, United States Code for the following:

(1) Making, filing, and docketing an application for naturalization, including the hearing on such application, if such hearing be held, and a certificate of naturalization, if the issuance of such certificate is authorized by the Attorney General.

(2) Receiving and filing a declaration of intention, and issuing a duplicate thereof.

(b) Notwithstanding the provisions of this Act or any other law, no fee shall be charged or collected for an application for declaration of intention or a certificate of naturalization in lieu of a declaration or a certificate alleged to have been lost, mutilated, or destroyed, submitted by a person who was a member of the military or naval forces of the United States at any time after April 20, 1898, and before July 5, 1902; or at any time after April 5, 1917, and before November 12, 1918; or who served on the Mexican border as a member of the Regular Army or National Guard between June 1916 and April 1917; or who has served or hereafter serves in the military, air, or naval forces of the United States after September 16, 1940, and who was not at any time during such period or thereafter separated from such forces under other than honorable conditions, who was not a conscientious objector who performed no military duty whatever or refused to wear the uniform, or who was not at any time during such period or thereafter discharged from such military, air, or naval forces on account of alienage.

(c) Except as provided by section 286(q)(2) [8 USCS § 1356(q)(2)] or any other law, all fees collected by the Attorney General shall be deposited by the Attorney General in the Treasury of the United States except that all fees collected or paid over on or after October 1, 1988, shall be deposited in the Immigration Examinations Fee Account established under section 286(m) [8 USCS § 1356(m)]: Provided, however, That all fees received by the Attorney General from applicants residing in the Virgin Islands of the United States, and in Guam, under this title, shall be paid over to the treasury of the Virgin Islands and to the treasury of Guam, respectively.

(d) During the time when the United States is at war the Attorney General may not charge or collect a naturalization fee from an alien in the military, air, or naval service of the United States for filing an application for naturalization or issuing a certificate of naturalization upon admission to citizenship.

(e) In addition to the other fees required by this title, the applicant for naturalization shall, upon the filing of a petition for naturalization, deposit with and pay to the Attorney General a sum of money sufficient to cover the expense of subpenaing and paying the legal fees of any witnesses for whom such applicant may request a subpena, and upon the final discharge of such witnesses, they shall receive, if they demand the same from the Attorney General, the customary and usual witness fees from the moneys which the applicant shall have paid to the Attorney General for such purpose, and the residue, if any, shall be returned by the Attorney General to the applicant.

(f) (1) The Attorney General shall pay over to courts administering oaths of allegiance to persons under this title a specified percentage of all fees described in subsection (a)(1) collected by the Attorney General with respect to persons administered the oath of allegiance by the respective courts. The Attorney General, annually and in consultation with the courts, shall determine the specified percentage based on the proportion, of the total costs incurred by the Service and courts for essential services directly related to the naturalization process, which are incurred by courts.

(2) The Attorney General shall provide on an annual basis to the Committees on the Judiciary of the House of Representatives and of the Senate a detailed report on the use of the fees described in paragraph (1) and shall consult with such Committees before increasing such fees.

HISTORY: (June 27, 1952, ch 477, Title III, Ch 2, § 344, 66 Stat. 264; July 7, 1958, P. L. 85-508, § 26, 72 Stat. 351; Oct. 21, 1968, P. L. 90-609, § 3, 82 Stat. 1200; Dec. 29, 1981, P. L. 97-116, § 16, 95 Stat. 1619; Oct. 1, 1988, P. L. 100-459, Title II, § 209(b), 102 Stat. 2203; Oct. 24, 1988, P. L. 100-525, § 9(ff), 102 Stat. 2621; Nov. 29, 1990, P. L. 101-649, Title IV, § 407(c)(20), (d)(19), 104 Stat. 5041, 5046; Dec. 12, 1991, P. L. 102-232, Title , §§ 102(b)(3), 305(l), 309(a)(1)(A)((ii), (b)(14), 105 Stat. 1736, 1750, 1758, 1759; Nov. 2, 2002, P. L. 107-273, Div C, Title I, Subtitle A, § 11016(1), 116 Stat. 1824.)

§ 345. [8 U.S.C. § 1456] [Repealed].

HISTORY: This section (Act June 27, 1952, ch 477, Title III, Ch 2, § 345, 66 Stat. 266) was repealed by Act Sept. 2, 1960, P.L. 86-682, § 12(c), 74 Stat. 728, effective Sept. 1, 1960, as provided by § 11. Similar provisions were reenacted as 39 USCS § 3202. This section related to free transmittal of official mail in naturalization matters.

§ 346. [8 U.S.C. § 1457] Publication and distribution of citizenship textbooks; use of naturalization fees.

Authorization is hereby granted for the publication and distribution of the citizenship textbook described in subsection (b) of section 332 [8 USCS § 1443(b)] and for the reimbursement of the appropriation of the Department of Justice upon the records of the Treasury Department from the naturalization fees deposited in the Treasury through the Service for the cost of such publication and distribution, such reimbursement to be made upon statements by the Attorney General of books so published and distributed.

HISTORY: (June 27, 1952, ch 477, Title III, Ch 2, § 346, 66 Stat. 266.)

§ 347. [8 U.S.C. § 1458] Compilation of naturalization statistics and payment for equipment.

The Attorney General is authorized and directed to prepare from the records in the custody of the Service a report upon those heretofore seeking citizenship to show by nationalities their relation to the numbers of aliens annually arriving and to the prevailing census populations of the foreign-born, their economic, vocational, and other classification, in statistical form, with analytical comment thereon, and to prepare such report annually hereafter. Payment for the equipment used in preparing such compilation shall be made from the appropriation for the enforcement of this Act by the Service.

HISTORY: (June 27, 1952, ch 477, Title III, Ch 2, § 347, 66 Stat. 266.)

§ 348. [8 U.S.C. § 1459]. [Repealed].

HISTORY: This section (Act June 27, 1952, ch 477, Title III, Ch 2, § 348, 66 Stat. 267; Oct. 24, 1988, P.L. 100-525, § 9(gg), 102 Stat. 2622) was repealed by Act Nov. 29, 1990, P.L. 101-649, Title IV, § 407(d)(20), 104 Stat. 5046, effective on enactment and as provided by § 408 of such Act, which appears as 8 USCS § 1421 note. This section provided for admissibility in evidence of statements voluntarily made to officers or employees in the course of their official duties; failure of clerk of court to duty; and penalties.

Chapter 3—Loss of Nationality

§ 349. [8 U.S.C. § 1481] Loss of nationality by native-born or naturalized citizen; voluntary action; burden of proof; presumptions.

(a) A person who is a national of the United States whether by birth or naturalization, shall lose his nationality by voluntarily performing any of the following acts with the intention of relinquishing United States nationality—

(1) obtaining naturalization in a foreign state upon his own application or upon an application filed by a duly authorized agent, after having attained the age of eighteen years; or

(2) taking an oath or making an affirmation or other formal declaration of allegiance to a foreign state or a political subdivision thereof, after having attained the age of eighteen years; or

(3) entering, or serving in, the armed forces of a foreign state if (A) such armed forces are engaged in hostilities against the United States, or (B) such persons serve as a commissioned or noncommissioned officer; or

(4) (A) accepting, serving in, or performing the duties of any office, post, or employment under the government of a foreign state or a political subdivision thereof, after attaining the age of eighteen years if he has or acquires the nationality of such foreign state; or (B) accepting, serving in, or performing the duties of any office, post, or employment under the government of a foreign state or a political subdivision thereof, after attaining the age of eighteen years for which office, post, or employment an oath, affirmation, or declaration of allegiance is required; or

(5) making a formal renunciation of nationality before a diplomatic or consular officer of the United States in a foreign state, in such form as may be prescribed by the Secretary of State; or

(6) making in the United States a formal written renunciation of nationality in such form as may be prescribed by, and before such officer as may be designated by, the Attorney General, whenever the United States shall be in a state of war and the Attorney General shall approve such renunciation as not contrary to the interests of national defense; or

(7) committing any act of treason against, or attempting by force to overthrow, or bearing arms against, the United States, violating or conspiring to violate any of the provisions of section 2383 of title 18, United States Code, or willfully performing any act in violation of section 2385 of title 18, United States Code, or violating section 2384 of said title by engaging in a conspiracy to overthrow, put down, or to destroy by force the Government of the United States, or to levy war against them, if and when he is convicted thereof by a court martial or by a court of competent jurisdiction.

(b) Whenever the loss of United States nationality is put in issue in any action or proceeding commenced on or after the enactment of this subsection [enacted Sept. 26, 1961] under, or by virtue of, the provisions of this or any other Act, the burden shall be upon the person or party claiming that such loss occurred, to establish such claim by a preponderance of the evidence. Any person who commits or performs, or who has committed or performed, any act of expatriation under the provisions of this or any other Act shall be presumed to have done so voluntarily, but such presumption may be rebutted upon a showing, by a preponderance of the evidence, that the act or acts committed or performed were not done voluntarily.

HISTORY: (June 27, 1952, ch 477, Title III, Ch 3, § 349, 66 Stat. 267; Sept. 3, 1954, ch 1256, § 2, 68 Stat. 1146; Sept. 26, 1961, P. L. 87-301, § 19, 75 Stat. 656; Sept. 14, 1976, P. L.

94-412, Title V, § 501(a), 90 Stat. 1258; Oct. 10, 1978, P. L. 95-432, §§ 2 in part, 4, 92 Stat. 1046; Dec. 29, 1981, P. L. 97-116, § 18(k)(2), (g), 95 Stat. 1620, 1621; Nov. 14, 1986, P. L. 99-653, §§ 18, 19, 100 Stat. 3658; Oct. 24, 1988, P. L. 100-525, §§ 8(m), (n), 9(hh), 102 Stat. 2618, 2622.)

§ 350. [8 U.S.C. § 1482] [Repealed].

HISTORY: This section (Act June 27, 1952, ch 477, Title III, Ch 3, § 350, 66 Stat. 269) was repealed by Act Oct 10, 1978, P.L. 95-432, § 1 in part, 92 Stat. 1046, effective Oct. 10, 1978, as provided in part by § 1 of such Act, which appears as 8 USCS § 1101 note. It related to dual nationals and divestiture of their nationality.

§ 351. [8 U.S.C. § 1483] Restrictions on loss of nationality.

(a) Except as provided in paragraphs (6) and (7) of section 349(a) of this title [8 USCS § 1481(a)(6) and (7)], no national of the United States can lose United States nationality under this Act while within the United States or any of its outlying possessions, but loss of nationality shall result from the performance within the United States or any of its outlying possessions of any of the acts or the fulfillment of any of the conditions specified in this chapter if and when the national thereafter takes up a residence outside the United States and its outlying possessions.

(b) A national who within six months after attaining the age of eighteen years asserts his claim to United States nationality, in such manner as the Secretary of State shall by regulation prescribe, shall not be deemed to have lost United States nationality by the commission, prior to his eighteenth birthday, of any of the acts specified in paragraphs (3), and (5) of section 349(a) of this title.

HISTORY: (June 27, 1952, ch 477, Title III, Ch 3, § 351, 66 Stat. 269; Dec. 29, 1981, P. L. 97-116, § 18(r), 95 Stat. 1621; Nov. 14, 1986, P. L. 99-653, § 20, 100 Stat. 3658; Oct. 24, 1988, P. L. 100-525, § 8(o), 102 Stat. 2618; Oct. 25, 1994, P. L. 103-416, Title I, § 105(a), 108 Stat. 4308; Sept. 30, 1996, P. L. 104-208, Div C, Title VI, Subtitle E, § 671(b)(3), 110 Stat. 3009-721.)

§§ 352 to 355. [8 U.S.C. § § 1484—1487] [Repealed].

HISTORY: These sections (§§ 1484-1487-Act June 27, 1952, ch 477, Title III, Ch 3, §§ 352-355, 66 Stat. 269-272; Aug. 4, 1959, P.L. 86-129, §§ 1-3, 73 Stat. 274; Sept. 26, 1961, P.L. 87-301, § 20, 75 Stat. 656) were repealed by Act Oct. 10, 1978, P.L. 95-432, § 2 in part, 92 Stat. 1046. Section 1484 provided for the loss of nationality by a naturalized national; § 1485 provided for exceptions as to certain nationals; § 1486 provided an exception concerning residence abroad as to certain nationals; and § 1487 provided for loss of American nationality through a parent's expatriation under former 8 USCS § 1482 or 1484 not to be effective until such person attained the age of 25 years.

§ 356. [8 U.S.C. § 1488] Nationality lost solely from performance of acts or fulfillment of conditions.

The loss of nationality, under this chapter shall result solely from the performance by a national of the acts or fulfillment of the conditions specified in this chapter.

HISTORY: (June 27, 1952, ch 477, Title III, Ch 3, § 356, 66 Stat. 272.)

§ 357. [8 U.S.C. § 1489] Application of treaties; exceptions.

Nothing in this title shall be applied in contravention of the provisions of any treaty or convention to which the United States is a party and which has been ratified by the Senate before December 25, 1952: Provided, however, That no woman who was a national of the United States shall be deemed to have lost her nationality solely by reason of her marriage to an alien on or after September 22, 1922, or to an alien racially ineligible to citizenship on or after March 3, 1931, or, in the case of a woman who was a United States citizen at birth, through residence abroad following such marriage, notwithstanding the provisions of any existing treaty or convention.

HISTORY: (June 27, 1952, ch 477, Title III, Ch 3, § 357, 66 Stat. 272; Oct. 24, 1988, P. L. 100-525, § 9(ii), 102 Stat. 2622.)

Chapter 4—Miscellaneous

§ 358. [8 U.S.C. § 1501] Certificate of diplomatic or consular officer of the United States as to loss of American nationality.

Whenever a diplomatic or consular officer of the United States has reason to believe that a person while in a foreign state has lost his United States nationality under any provision of chapter 3 of this title, or under any provision of chapter IV of the Nationality Act of 1940, as amended, he shall certify the facts upon which such belief is based to the Department of State, in writing, under regulations prescribed by the Secretary of State. If the report of the diplomatic or consular officer is approved by the Secretary of State, a copy of the certificate shall be forwarded to the Attorney General, for his information, and the diplomatic or consular office in which the report was made shall be directed to forward a copy of the certificate to the person to whom it relates. Approval by the Secretary of State of a certificate under this section shall constitute a final administrative determination of loss of United States nationality under this Act, subject to such procedures for administrative appeal as the Secretary may prescribe by regulation, and also shall constitute a denial of a right or privilege of United States nationality for purposes of section 360 [8 USCS § 1503].

HISTORY: (June 27, 1952, ch 477, Title III, Ch 4, § 358, 66 Stat. 272; Oct. 25, 1994, P.L. 103-416, Title I, § 106, 108 Stat. 4309.)

§ 359. [8 U.S.C. § 1502] Certificate of nationality issued by Secretary of State for a naturalized citizen of the United States for use in proceedings of a foreign state.

The Secretary of State is hereby authorized to issue, in his discretion and in accordance with rules and regulations prescribed by him, a certificate of nationality for any person not a naturalized citizen of the United States who presents satisfactory evidence that he is an American national and that such certificate is needed for use in judicial or administrative proceedings in a foreign state. Such certificate shall be solely for use in the case for which it was issued and shall be transmitted by the Secretary of State through appropriate official channels to the judicial or administrative officers of the foreign state in which it is to be used.

HISTORY: (June 27, 1952, ch 477, Title III, Ch 4, § 359, 66 Stat. 273.)

§ 360. [8 U.S.C. § 1503] Denial of rights and privileges as national.

(a) Proceedings for declaration of United States nationality. If any person who is within the United States claims a right or privilege as a national of the United States and is denied such right or privilege by any department or independent agency, or official thereof, upon the ground that he is not a national of the United States, such person may institute an action under the provisions of section 2201 of title 28, United States Code, against the head of such department or independent agency for a judgment declaring him to be a national of the United States, except that no such action may be instituted in any case if the issue of such person's status as a national of the United States (1) arose by reason of, or in connection with any removal proceeding under the provisions of this or any other act, or (2) is in issue in any such removal proceeding. An action under this subsection may be instituted only within five years after the final administrative denial of such right or privilege and shall be filed in the district court of the United States for the district in which such person resides or claims a residence, and jurisdiction over such officials in such cases is hereby conferred upon those courts.

(b) Application for certificate of identity; appeal. If any person who is not within the United States claims a right or privilege as a national of the United States and is denied such right or privilege by any department or independent agency, or official thereof, upon the ground that he is not a national of the United States, such person may make application to a diplomatic or consular officer of the United States in the foreign country in which he is residing for a certificate of identity for the purpose of traveling to a port of entry in the United States and applying for admission. Upon proof to the satisfaction of such diplomatic or consular officer that such application is made in good faith and has a substantial basis, he shall issue to such person a certificate of identity. From any denial of an application for such certificate the applicant shall be entitled to an appeal to the Secretary of State, who, if he approves the denial, shall state in writing his reasons for his decision. The Secretary of State shall prescribe rules and regulations for the issuance of certificates of identity as above provided. The provisions of this subsection shall be applicable only to a person who at some time prior to his application for the certificate of identity has been physically present in the United States, or to a person under sixteen years of age who was born abroad of a United States citizen parent.

(c) Application for admission to United States under certificate of identity; revision of determination. A person who has been issued a certificate of identity under the provisions of subsection (b), and while in possession thereof, may apply for admission to the United States at any port of entry, and shall be subject to all the provisions of this Act relating to the conduct of proceedings involving aliens seeking admission to the United States. A final determination by the Attorney General that any such person is not entitled to admission to the United States shall be subject to review by any court of competent jurisdiction in habeas corpus proceedings and not otherwise. Any person described in this section who is finally denied admission to the United States shall be subject to all the provisions of this Act relating to aliens seeking admission to the United States.

HISTORY: (June 27, 1952, ch 477, Title III, Ch 4, § 360, 66 Stat. 273; Sept. 30, 1996, P. L. 104-208, Div C, Title III, Subtitle A, § 308(d)(4)(P), 110 Stat. 3009-619.)

§ 361. [8 U.S.C. § 1504] Cancellation of United States passports and Consular Reports of Birth.

(a) The Secretary of State is authorized to cancel any United States passport or Consular Report of Birth, or certified copy thereof, if it appears that such document was illegally, fraudulently, or erroneously obtained from, or was created through illegality or fraud practiced upon, the Secretary. The person for or to whom such document has been issued or made shall be given, at such person's last known address, written notice of the cancellation of such document, together with the procedures for seeking a prompt post-cancellation hearing. The cancellation under this section of any document purporting to show the citizenship status of the person to whom it was issued shall affect only the document and not the citizenship status of the person in whose name the document was issued.

(b) For purposes of this section, the term "Consular Report of Birth" refers to the report, designated as a "Report of Birth Abroad of a Citizen of the United States", issued by a consular officer to document a citizen born abroad.

HISTORY: (June 27, 1952, ch 477, Title III, Ch 4, § 361, as added Oct. 25, 1994, P. L. 103-416, Title I, § 107(a), 108 Stat. 4309.)

TITLE IV—MISCELLANEOUS AND REFUGEE ASSISTANCE

Chapter 1—Miscellaneous

§ 404. [8 U.S.C. § 1101, note] Authorization of appropriations.

(a) There are authorized to be appropriated such sums as may be necessary to carry out the provisions of this Act (other than chapter 2 of title IV [8 USCS §§ 1521 et seq.]).

(b) (1) There are authorized to be appropriated (for fiscal year 1991 and any subsequent fiscal year) to an immigration emergency fund, to be established in the Treasury, an amount sufficient to provide for a balance of $35,000,000 in such fund, to be used to carry out paragraph (2) and to provide for an increase in border patrol or other enforcement activities of the Service and for reimbursement of State and localities in providing assistance as requested by the Attorney General in meeting an immigration emergency, except that no amounts may be withdrawn from such fund with respect to an emergency unless the President has determined that the immigration emergency exists and has certified such fact to the Judiciary Committees of the House of Representatives and of the Senate.

(2) (A) Funds which are authorized to be appropriated by paragraph (1), subject to the dollar limitation contained in subparagraph (B), shall be available, by application for the reimbursement of States and localities providing assistance as required by the Attorney General, to States and localities whenever—

(i) a district director of the Service certifies to the Commissioner that the number of asylum applications filed in the respective district during a calendar quarter exceeds by at least 1,000 the number of such applications filed in that district during the preceding calendar quarter,

(ii) the lives, property, safety, or welfare of the residents of a State or locality are endangered, or

(iii) in any other circumstances as determined by the Attorney General.

In applying clause (i), the providing of parole at a point of entry in a district shall be deemed to constitute an application for asylum in the district.

(B) Not more than $20,000,000 shall be made available for all localities under this paragraph.

(C) For purposes of subparagraph (A), the requirement of paragraph (1) that an immigration emergency be determined shall not apply.

(D) A decision with respect to an application for reimbursement under subparagraph (A) shall be made by the Attorney General within 15 days after the date of receipt of the application.

HISTORY: Act June 27, 1952, ch 477, § 404, 66 Stat. 280, as amended Dec. 29, 1981, P. L. 97-116, § 18(s), 95 Stat. 1621 (effective on enactment on 12/29/81, as provided by § 21(a) of such Act, which appears as a note to this section); Nov. 6, 1986, P. L. 99-603, Title I, Part B, § 113, 100 Stat. 3383; Nov. 29, 1990, P. L. 101-649, Title VII, § 705(a), 104 Stat. 5087, applicable as provided by § 705(b) of such Act, which appears as a note to this section; Dec. 12, 1991, P. L. 102-232, Title III, § 308(d), 105 Stat. 1757 (effective as if included in Act Nov. 29, 1990, as provided by § 310(1) of Act Dec. 12, 1991, which appears as 8 USCS § 1101 note).

§ 405. [8 U.S.C. § 1101, note] Saving clause.

(a) Nothing contained in this Act [8 USCS §§ 1101 et seq. generally; for full classification, consult USCS Tables volumes], unless otherwise specifically provided therein, shall be construed to affect the validity of any declaration of intention, petition for naturalization, certificate of naturalization, certificate of citizenship, warrant of arrest, order or warrant of deportation, order of exclusion, or other document or proceeding which shall be valid at the time this Act [8 USCS §§ 1101 et seq. generally; for full classification, consult USCS Tables volumes] shall take effect; or to affect any prosecution, suit, action, or proceedings, civil or criminal, brought, or any status, condition, right in process of acquisition, act, thing, liability, obligation, or matter, civil or criminal, done or existing, at the time this Act [8 USCS §§ 1101 et seq. generally; for full classification, consult USCS Tables volumes] shall take effect; but as to all such prosecutions, suits, actions, proceedings, statutes, conditions, rights, acts, things, liabilities, obligations, or matters the statutes or parts of statutes repealed by this Act [8 USCS §§ 1101 et seq. generally; for full classification, consult USCS Tables volumes] are, unless otherwise specifically provided therein, hereby continued in force and effect. When an immigrant, in possession of an unexpired immigrant visa issued prior to the effective date of this Act [8 USCS §§ 1101 et seq. generally; for full classification, consult USCS Tables volumes], makes application for admission, his admissibility shall be determined under the provisions of law in effect on the date of the issuance of such visa. An application for suspension of deportation under section 19 of the Immigration Act of 1917, as amended [former 8 USCS § 155], or for adjustment of status under section 4 of the Displaced Persons Act of 1948, as amended [former 50 USCS appx. § 1953], which is pending on the date of enactment of this Act [enacted June 27, 1952], shall be regarded as a proceeding within the meaning of this subsection.

(b) Except as otherwise specifically provided in title III, any petition for naturalization heretofore filed which may be pending at the time this Act [8 USCS §§ 1101 et seq. generally; for full classification, consult USCS Tables volumes] shall take effect shall be heard and determined in accordance with the requirements of law in effect when such petition was filed.

(c) Except as otherwise specifically provided in this Act [8 USCS §§ 1101 et seq. generally; for full classification, consult USCS Tables volumes] the repeal of any statute by this Act [8 USCS §§ 1101 et seq. generally; for full classification, consult USCS Tables volumes] shall not terminate nationality heretofore lawfully acquired nor restore nationality heretofore lost under any law of the United States or any treaty to which the United States may have been a party.

(d) Except as otherwise specifically provided in this Act [8 USCS §§ 1101 et seq. generally; for full classification, consult USCS Table volumes], or any amendment thereto, fees, charges and prices for purposes specified in title V of the Independent Offices Appropriation Act, 1952 (Public Law 137, Eighty-second Congress, approved August 31, 1951), may be fixed and established in the manner and by the head of any Federal Agency as specified in that Act.

(e) This Act shall not be construed to repeal, alter, or amend section 231(a) of the Act of April 30, 1946 (60 Stat. 148; 22 U. S. C. 1281(a)) [22 USCS § 1281(a)], the Act of June 20, 1949 (Public Law 110, section 8, Eighty-first Congress, first session; 63 Stat. 208) [50 USCS § 403h], the Act of June 5, 1950 (Public Law 535, Eighty-first Congress, second session) [former 22 USCS §§ 1501 et seq.], nor title V of the Agricultural Act of 1949, as amended (Public Law 78, Eighty-second Congress, first session).

HISTORY: Act June 27, 1952, ch 477, Title IV, § 405, 66 Stat. 166, provides.

§ 406. [8 U.S.C. § 1101, note] Separability.

If any particular provision of this Act [8 USCS §§ 1101 et seq. generally; for full classification, consult USCS Tables volumes], or the application thereof to any person or circumstance, is held invalid, the remainder of the Act and the application of such provision to other persons or circumstances shall not be affected thereby.

HISTORY: Act June 27, 1952, ch 477, Title IV, § 406, 66 Stat. 166.

§ 407. [8 U.S.C. § 1101, note] Effective date.

Except as provided in subsection (k) of section 401 [former 8 USCS § 1106(k)], this Act [8 USCS §§ 1101 et seq. generally; for full classification, consult USCS Tables volumes] shall take effect at 12:01 ante meridian United States Eastern Standard Time on the one hundred eightieth day immediately following the date of its enactment [enacted June 27, 1952].

HISTORY: Act June 27, 1952, ch 477, Title IV, § 407, 66 Stat. 281.

Chapter 2—Refugee Assistance

§ 411. [8 U.S.C. § 1521] Office of Refugee Resettlement; establishment; appointment of Director; functions.

(a) There is established, within the Department of Health and Human Services, an office to be known as the Office of Refugee Resettlement (hereinafter in this chapter referred to as the "Office"). The head of the Office shall be a Director (hereinafter in this chapter referred to as the "Director"), to be appointed by the Secretary of Health and Human Services (hereinafter in this chapter referred to as the "Secretary").

(b) The function of the Office and its Director is to fund and administer (directly or through arrangements with other Federal agencies), in consultation with the Secretary of State, programs of the Federal Government under this chapter.

HISTORY: (June 27, 1952, ch 477, Title IV, Ch 2, § 411, as added March 17, 1980, P.L. 96-212, Title III, § 311(a)(2), 94 Stat. 111; April 30, 1994, P. L. 103-236, Title I, Part C, § 162(n)(1), 108 Stat. 409.)

§ 412. [8 U.S.C. § 1522] Authorization for programs for domestic resettlement of and assistance to refugees.

(a) Conditions and considerations.

(1) (A) In providing assistance under this section, the Director shall, to the extent of available appropriations, (i) make available sufficient resources for employment training and placement in order to achieve economic self-sufficiency among refugees as quickly as possible, (ii) provide refugees with the opportunity to acquire sufficient English language training to enable them to become effectively resettled as quickly as possible, (iii) insure that cash assistance is made available to refugees in such a manner as not to discourage their economic self-sufficiency, in accordance with subsection (e)(2), and (iv) insure that women have the same opportunities as men to participate in training and instruction.

(B) It is the intent of Congress that in providing refugee assistance under this section—

(i) employable refugees should be placed on jobs as soon as possible after their arrival in the United States;

(ii) social service funds should be focused on employment-related services, English-as-a-second-language training (in nonwork hours where possible), and case-management services; and

(iii) local voluntary agency activities should be conducted in close cooperation and advance consultation with State and local governments.

(2) (A) The Director and the Federal agency administering subsection (b)(1) shall consult regularly (not less often than quarterly) with State and local governments and private nonprofit voluntary agencies concerning the sponsorship process and the intended distribution of refugees among the States and localities before their placement in those States and localities.

(B) The Director shall develop and implement, in consultation with representatives of voluntary agencies and State and local governments, policies and strategies for the placement and resettlement of refugees within the United States.

(C) Such policies and strategies, to the extent practicable and except under such unusual circumstances as the Director may recognize, shall—

(i) insure that a refugee is not initially placed or resettled in an area highly impacted (as determined under regulations prescribed by the Director after consultation with such agencies and governments) by the presence of refugees or comparable populations unless the refugee has a spouse, parent, sibling, son, or daughter residing in that area,

(ii) provide for a mechanism whereby representatives of local affiliates of voluntary agencies regularly (not less often than quarterly) meet with representatives of State and local governments to plan and coordinate in advance of their arrival the appropriate placement of refugees among the various States and localities, and

(iii) take into account—

(I) the proportion of refugees and comparable entrants in the population in the area,

(II) the availability of employment opportunities, affordable housing, and public and private resources (including educational, health care, and mental health services) for refugees in the area,

(III) the likelihood of refugees placed in the area becoming self-sufficient and free from long-term dependence on public assistance, and

(IV) the secondary migration of refugees to and from the area that is likely to occur.

(D) With respect to the location of placement of refugees within a State, the Federal agency administering subsection (b)(1) shall, consistent with such policies and strategies and to the maximum extent possible, take into account recommendations of the State.

(3) In the provision of domestic assistance under this section, the Director shall make a periodic assessment, based on refugee population and other relevant factors, of the relative needs of refugees for assistance

and services under this chapter and the resources available to meet such needs. The Director shall compile and maintain data on secondary migration of refugees within the United States and, by State of residence and nationality, on the proportion of refugees receiving cash or medical assistance described in subsection (e). In allocating resources, the Director shall avoid duplication of services and provide for maximum coordination between agencies providing related services.

(4) (A) No grant or contract may be awarded under this section unless an appropriate proposal and application (including a description of the agency's ability to perform the services specified in the proposal) are submitted to, and approved by, the appropriate administering official. Grants and contracts under this section shall be made to those agencies which the appropriate administering official determines can best perform the services. Payments may be made for activities authorized under this chapter in advance or by way of reimbursement. In carrying out this section, the Director, the Secretary of State, and any such other appropriate administering official are authorized—

(i) to make loans, and

(ii) to accept and use money, funds, property, and services of any kind made available by gift, devise, bequest, grant, or otherwise for the purpose of carrying out this section.

(B) No funds may be made available under this chapter (other than under subsection (b)(1)) to States or political subdivisions in the form of block grants, per capita grants, or similar consolidated grants or contracts. Such funds shall be made available under separate grants or contracts—

(i) for medical screening and initial medical treatment under subsection (b)(5),

(ii) for services for refugees under subsection (c)(1),

(iii) for targeted assistance project grants under subsection (c)(2), and

(iv) for assistance for refugee children under subsection (d)(2).

(C) The Director may not delegate to a State or political subdivision his authority to review or approve grants or contracts under this chapter or the terms under which such grants or contracts are made.

(5) Assistance and services funded under this section shall be provided to refugees without regard to race, religion, nationality, sex, or political opinion.

(6) As a condition for receiving assistance under this section, a State must—

(A) submit to the Director a plan which provides—

(i) a description of how the State intends to encourage effective refugee resettlement and to promote economic self-sufficiency as quickly as possible,

(ii) a description of how the State will insure that language training and employment services are made available to refugees receiving cash assistance,

(iii) for the designation of an individual, employed by the State, who will be responsible for insuring coordination of public and private resources in refugee resettlement,

(iv) for the care and supervision of and legal responsibility for unaccompanied refugee children in the State, and

(v) for the identification of refugees who at the time of resettlement in the State are determined to have medical conditions requiring, or medical histories indicating a need for, treatment or observation and such monitoring of such treatment or observation as may be necessary;

(B) meet standards, goals, and priorities, developed by the Director, which assure the effective resettlement of refugees and which promote their economic self-sufficiency as quickly as possible and the efficient provision of services; and

(C) submit to the Director, within a reasonable period of time after the end of each fiscal year, a report on the uses of funds provided under this chapter which the State is responsible for administering.

(7) The Secretary, together with the Secretary of State with respect to assistance provided by the Secretary of State under subsection (b), shall develop a system of monitoring the assistance provided under this section. This system shall include—

(A) evaluations of the effectiveness of the programs funded under this section and the performance of States, grantees, and contractors;

(B) financial auditing and other appropriate monitoring to detect any fraud, abuse, or mismanagement in the operation of such programs; and

(C) data collection on the services provided and the results achieved.

(8) The Attorney General shall provide the Director with information supplied by refugees in conjunction with their applications to the Attorney General for adjustment of status, and the Director shall compile, summarize, and evaluate such information.

(9) The Secretary, the Secretary of Education, the Attorney General, and the Secretary of State may issue such regulations as each deems appropriate to carry out this chapter.

(10) For purposes of this chapter, the term "refugee" includes any alien described in section 207(c)(2) [8 USCS § 1157(c)(2)].

(b) Program of initial resettlement.

(1) (A) For—

(i) fiscal years 1980 and 1981, the Secretary of State is authorized, and

(ii) fiscal year 1982 and succeeding fiscal years, the Director (except as provided in subparagraph (B)) is authorized,

to make grants to, and contracts with, public or private nonprofit agencies for initial resettlement (including initial reception and placement with sponsors) of refugees in the United States. Grants to, or contracts with, private nonprofit voluntary agencies under this paragraph shall be made consistent with the objectives of this chapter, taking into account the different resettlement approaches and practices of such agencies. Resettlement assistance under this paragraph shall be provided in coordination with the Director's provision of other assistance under this chapter. Funds provided to agencies under such grants and contracts may only be obligated or expended during the fiscal year in which they are provided (or the subsequent fiscal year or such subsequent fiscal period as the Federal contracting agency may approve) to carry out the purposes of this subsection.

(B) If the President determines that the Director should not administer the program under this paragraph, the authority of the Director under the first sentence of subparagraph (A) shall be exercised by such officer as the President shall from time to time specify.

(2) The Director is authorized to develop programs for such orientation, instruction in English, and job training for refugees, and such other education and training of refugees, as facilitates their resettlement in the United States. The Director is authorized to implement such programs, in accordance with the provisions of this section, with respect to refugees in the United States. The Secretary of State is authorized to implement such programs with respect to refugees awaiting entry into the United States.

(3) The Secretary is authorized to make arrangements (including cooperative arrangements with other Federal agencies) for the temporary care of refugees in the United States in emergency circumstances, including the establishment of processing centers, if necessary, without regard to such provisions of law (other than the Renegotiation Act of 1951 and section 414(b) of this chapter [8 USCS § 1524(b)]) regulating the making, performance, amendment, or modification of contracts and the expenditure of funds of the United States Government as the Secretary may specify.

(4) The Secretary shall—

(A) assure that an adequate number of trained staff are available at the location at which the refugees enter the United States to assure that all necessary medical records are available and in proper order;

(B) provide for the identification of refugees who have been determined to have medical conditions affecting the public health and requiring treatment;

(C) assure that State or local health officials at the resettlement destination within the United States of each refugee are promptly notified of the refugee's arrival and provided with all applicable medical records; and

(D) provide for such monitoring of refugees identified under subparagraph (B) as will insure that they receive appropriate and timely treatment.

The Secretary shall develop and implement methods for monitoring and assessing the quality of medical screening and related health services provided to refugees awaiting resettlement in the United States.

(5) The Director is authorized to make grants to, and enter into contracts with, State and local health agencies for payments to meet their costs of providing medical screening and initial medical treatment to refugees.

(6) The Comptroller General shall directly conduct an annual financial audit of funds expended under each grant or contract made under paragraph (1) for fiscal year 1986 and for fiscal year 1987.

(7) Each grant or contract with an agency under paragraph (1) shall require the agency to do the following:

(A) To provide quarterly performance and financial status reports to the Federal agency administering paragraph (1).

(B) (i) To provide, directly or through its local affiliate, not To provide, directly or through its local affiliate, notice to the appropriate county or other local welfare office at the time that the agency becomes aware that a refugee is offered employment and to provide notice to the refugee that such notice has been provided, and

(ii) upon request of such a welfare office to which a refugee has applied for cash assistance, to furnish that office with documentation respecting any cash or other resources provided directly by the agency to the refugee under this subsection.

(C) To assure that refugees, known to the agency as having been identified pursuant to paragraph (4)(B) as having medical conditions affecting the public health and requiring treatment, report to the appropriate county or other health agency upon their resettlement in an area.

(D) To fulfill its responsibility to provide for the basic needs (including food, clothing, shelter, and transportation for job interviews and training) of each refugee resettled and to develop and implement a resettlement plan including the early employment of each refugee resettled and to monitor the implementation of such plan.

(E) To transmit to the Federal agency administering paragraph (1) an annual report describing the following:

(i) The number of refugees placed (by county of placement) and the expenditures made in the year under the grant or contract, including the proportion of such expenditures used for administrative purposes and for provision of services.

(ii) The proportion of refugees placed by the agency in the previous year who are receiving cash or medical assistance described in subsection (e).

(iii) The efforts made by the agency to monitor placement of the refugees and the activities of local affiliates of the agency.

(iv) The extent to which the agency has coordinated its activities with local social service providers in a manner which avoids duplication of activities and has provided notices to local welfare offices and the reporting of medical conditions of certain aliens to local health departments in accordance with subparagraphs (B)(i) and (C).

(v) Such other information as the agency administering paragraph (1) deems to be appropriate in monitoring the effectiveness of agencies in carrying out their functions under such grants and contracts.

The agency administering paragraph (1) shall promptly forward a copy of each annual report transmitted under subparagraph (E) to the Committees on the Judiciary of the House of Representatives and of the Senate.

(8) The Federal agency administering paragraph (1) shall establish criteria for the performance of agencies under grants and contracts under that paragraph, and shall include criteria relating to an agency's—

(A) efforts to reduce welfare dependency among refugees resettled by that agency,

(B) collection of travel loans made to refugees resettled by that agency for travel to the United States,

(C) arranging for effective local sponsorship and other nonpublic assistance for refugees resettled by that agency,

(D) cooperation with refugee mutual assistance associations, local social service providers, health agencies, and welfare offices,

(E) compliance with the guidelines established by the Director for the placement and resettlement of refugees within the United States, and

(F) compliance with other requirements contained in the grant or contract, including the reporting and other requirements under subsection (b)(7).

The Federal administering agency shall use the criteria in the process of awarding or renewing grants and contracts under paragraph (1).

(c) Project grants and controls for services for refugees.

(1) (A) The Director is authorized to make grants to, and enter into contracts with, public or private nonprofit agencies for projects specifically designated—

(i) to assist refugees in obtaining the skills which are necessary for economic self-sufficiency, including projects for job training, employment services, day care, professional refresher training, and other recertification services;

(ii) to provide training in English where necessary (regardless of whether the refugees are employed or receiving cash or other assistance); and

(iii) to provide where specific needs have been shown and recognized by the Director, health (including mental health) services, social services, educational and other services.

(B) The funds available for a fiscal year for grants and contracts under subparagraph (A) shall be allocated among the States based on the total number of refugees (including children and adults) who arrived in the United States not more than 36 months before the beginning of such fiscal year and who are actually residing in each State (taking into account secondary migration) as of the beginning of the fiscal year.

(C) Any limitation which the Director establishes on the proportion of funds allocated to a State under this paragraph that the State may use for services other than those described in subsection (a)(1)(B)(ii) shall not apply if the Director receives a plan (established by or in consultation with local governments) and determines that the plan provides for the maximum appropriate provision of employment-related services for, and the maximum placement of, employable refugees consistent with performance standards established under section 106 of the Job Training Partnership Act [former 29 USCS § 1516].

(2) (A) The Director is authorized to make grants to States for The Director is authorized to make grants to States for assistance to counties and similar areas in the States where, because of factors such as unusually large refugee populations (including secondary migration), high refugee concentrations, and high use of public assistance by refugees, there exists and can be demonstrated a specific need for supplementation of available resources for services to refugees.

(B) Grants shall be made available under this paragraph—

(i) primarily for the purpose of facilitating refugee employment and achievement of self-sufficiency,

(ii) in a manner that does not supplant other refugee program funds and that assures that not less than 95 percent of the amount of the grant award is made available to the county or other local entity.

(d) Assistance for refugee children.

(1) The Secretary of Education is authorized to make grants, and enter into contracts, for payments for projects to provide special educational services (including English language training) to refugee children in elementary and secondary schools were a demonstrated need has been shown.

(2) (A) The Director is authorized to provide assistance, reimbursement to States, and grants to and contracts with public and private nonprofit agencies, for the provision of child welfare services, including foster care maintenance payments and services and health care, furnished to any refugee child (except as provided in subparagraph (B)) during the thirty-six month period beginning with the first month in which such refugee child is in the United States.

(B) (i) In the case of a refugee child who is unaccompanied by a parent or other close adult relative (as defined by the Director), the services described in subparagraph (A) may be furnished until the month after the child attains eighteen years of age (or such higher age as the State's child welfare services plan under part B of title IV of the Social Security Act [42 USCS §§ 620 et seq.] prescribes for the availability of such services to any other child in that State).

(ii) The Director shall attempt to arrange for the placement under the laws of the States of such unaccompanied refugee children, who have been accepted for admission to the United States, before (or as soon as possible after) their arrival in the United States. During any interim period which such a child is in the United States or in transit to the United States but before the child is so placed, the Director shall assume legal responsibility (including financial responsibility) for the child, if necessary, and is authorized to make necessary decisions to provide for the child's immediate care.

(iii) In carrying out the Director's responsibilities under clause (ii), the Director is authorized to enter into contracts with appropriate public or private nonprofit agencies under such conditions as the Director determines to be appropriate.

(iv) The Director shall prepare and maintain a list of (I) all such unaccompanied children who have entered the United States after April 1, 1975, (II) the names and last known residences of their parents (if living) at the time of arrival, and (III) the children's location, status, and progress.

(e) Cash assistance and medical assistance to refugees.

(1) The Director is authorized to provide assistance, reimbursement to States, and grants to, and contracts with, public or private nonprofit agencies for 100 per centum of the cash assistance and medical assistance provided to any refugee during the thirty-six month period beginning with the first month in which such refugee has entered the United States and for the identifiable and reasonable administrative costs of providing this assistance.

(2) (A) Cash assistance provided under this subsection to an employable refugee is conditioned, except for good cause shown—

(i) on the refugee's registration with an appropriate agency providing employment services described in subsection (c)(1)(A)(i), or, if there is no such agency available, with an appropriate State or local employment service;

(ii) on the refugee's participation in any available and appropriate social service or targeted assistance program (funded under subsection (c)) providing job or language training in the area in which the refugee resides; and

(iii) on the refugee's acceptance of appropriate offers of employment.

(B) Cash assistance shall not be made available to refugees who are full-time students in institutions of higher education (as defined by the Director after consultation with the Secretary of Education).

(C) In the case of a refugee who—

(i) refuses an offer of employment which has been determined to be appropriate either by the agency responsible for the initial resettlement of the refugee under subsection (b) or by the appropriate State or local employment service,

(ii) refuses to go to a job interview which has been arranged through such agency or service, or

(iii) refuses to participate in a social service or targeted assistance program referred to in subparagraph (A)(ii) which such agency or service determines to be available and appropriate,

cash assistance to the refugee shall be terminated (after opportunity for an administrative hearing) for a period of three months (for the first such refusal) or for a period of six months (for any subsequent refusal).

(3) The Director shall develop plans to provide English training and other appropriate services and training to refugees receiving cash assistance.

(4) If a refugee is eligible for aid or assistance under a State program funded under part A of title IV or under title XIX [42 USCS §§ 601 et seq. or 1396 et seq.] of the Social Security Act, or for supplemental security income benefits (including State supplementary payments) under the program established under title XVI of that Act [42 USCS §§ 1381 et seq.], funds authorized under this subsection shall only be used for the non-Federal share of such aid or assistance, or for such supplementary payments, with respect to cash and medical assistance provided with respect to such refugee under this paragraph.

(5) The Director is authorized to allow for the provision of medical assistance under paragraph (1) to any refugee, during the one-year period after entry, who does not qualify for assistance under a State plan approved under title XIX of the Social Security Act [42 USCS §§ 1396 et seq.] on account of any resources or income requirement of such plan, but only if the Director determines that—

(A) this will (i) encourage economic self-sufficiency, or (ii) avoid a significant burden on State and local governments; and

(B) the refugee meets such alternative financial resources and income requirements as the Director shall establish.

(6) As a condition for receiving assistance, reimbursement, or a contract under this subsection and notwithstanding any other provision of law, a State or agency must provide assurances that whenever a refugee applies for cash or medical assistance for which assistance or reimbursement is provided under this subsection, the State or agency must notify promptly the agency (or local affiliate) which provided for the initial resettlement of the refugee under subsection (b) of the fact that the refugee has so applied.

(7) (A) The Secretary shall develop and implement alternative projects for refugees who have been in the United States less than thirty-six months, under which refugees are provided interim support, medical services, support services, and case management, as needed, in a manner that encourages self-sufficiency, reduces welfare dependency, and fosters greater coordination among the resettlement agencies and service providers. The Secretary may permit alternative projects to cover specific groups of refugees who have been in the United States 36 months or longer if the Secretary determines that refugees in the group have been significantly and disproportionately dependent on welfare and need the services provided under the project in order to become self-sufficient and that their coverage under the projects would be cost-effective.

(B) Refugees covered under such alternative projects shall be precluded from receiving cash or medical assistance under any other paragraph of this subsection or under title XIX or part A of title IV of the Social Security Act [42 USCS §§ 1396 et seq. or 601 et seq.]

(C) The Secretary shall report to Congress not later than October 31, 1985, on the results of these projects and on any recommendations respecting changes in the refugee assistance program under this section to take into account such results.

(D) To the extent that the use of such funds is consistent with the purposes of such provisions, funds appropriated under section 414(a) of this Act [8 USCS § 1524(a)], part A of title IV of the Social Security Act, or title XIX of such Act [42 USCS §§ 601 et seq. or 1396 et seq.], may be used for the purpose of implementing and evaluating alternative projects under this paragraph.

(8) In its provision of assistance to refugees, a State or political subdivision shall consider the recommen-

dations of, and assistance provided by, agencies with grants or contracts under subsection (b)(1).

(f) Assistance to States and counties for incarceration of certain Cuban nationals; priority for removal and return to Cuba.

(1) The Attorney General shall pay compensation to States and to counties for costs incurred by the States and counties to confine in prisons, during the fiscal year for which such payment is made, nationals of Cuba who—

(A) were paroled into the United States in 1980 by the Attorney General,

(B) after such parole committed any violation of State or county law for which a term of imprisonment was imposed, and

(C) at the time of such parole and such violation were not aliens lawfully admitted to the United States—

(i) for permanent residence, or

(ii) under the terms of an immigrant or a nonimmigrant visa issued,

under this Act [8 USCS §§ 1521 et seq.].

(2) For a State or county to be eligible to receive compensation under this subsection, the chief executive officer of the State or county shall submit to the Attorney General, in accordance with rules to be issued by the Attorney General, an application containing—

(A) the number and names of the Cuban nationals with respect to whom the State or county is entitled to such compensation, and

(B) such other information as the Attorney General may require.

(3) For a fiscal year the Attorney General shall pay the costs described in paragraph (1) to each State and county determined by the Attorney General to be eligible under paragraph (2); except that if the amounts appropriated for the fiscal year to carry out this subsection are insufficient to cover all such payments, each of such payments shall be ratably reduced so that the total of such payments equals the amounts so appropriated.

(4) The authority of the Attorney General to pay compensation under this subsection shall be effective for any fiscal year only to the extent and in such amounts as may be provided in advance in appropriation Acts.

(5) It shall be the policy of the United States Government that the President, in consultation with the Attorney General and all other appropriate Federal officials and all appropriate State and county officials referred to in paragraph (2), shall place top priority on seeking the expeditious removal from this country and the return to Cuba of Cuban nationals described in paragraph (1) by any reasonable and responsible means, and to this end the Attorney General may use the funds authorized to carry out this subsection to conduct such policy.

HISTORY: (June 27, 1952, ch 477, Title IV, Ch 2, § 412, as added March 17, 1980, P.L. 96-212, Title III, Part B, § 311(a)(2), 94 Stat. 111; Oct. 25, 1982, P. L. 97-363, §§ 3(a), 4–6, 96 Stat. 1734–1736; Nov. 22, 1983, P. L. 98-164, Title X, § 1011(b), 97 Stat. 1061; Oct. 12, 1984, P. L. 98-473, Title I, § 101(d) in part, 98 Stat. 1877; Nov. 6, 1986, P. L. 99-605, §§ 3-5(c), 6(a), (b), (d), 8, 9(a), (b), 10, 12, 13, 100 Stat. 3449, 3453-3455; Oct. 24, 1988, P. L. 100-525, § 6(b), 102 Stat. 2616; April 30, 1994, P. L. 103-236, Title I, Part C, § 162(n)(2), 108 Stat. 409; Oct. 25, 1994, P. L. 103-416, Title II, § 219(x), 108 Stat. 4318; Aug. 22, 1996, P. L. 104-193, Title I, § 110(s)(3), 110 Stat. 2175; Sept. 30, 1996, P. L. 104-208, Div C, Title VI, Subtitle E, § 671(e)(7), 110 Stat. 3009-723.)

§ 413. [8 U.S.C. § 1523] Congressional reports.

(a) The Secretary shall submit a report on activities under this chapter to the Committees on the Judiciary of the House of Representatives and of the Senate not later than the January 31 following the end of each fiscal year, beginning with fiscal year 1980.

(b) Each such report shall contain—

(1) an updated profile of the employment and labor force statistics for refugees who have entered the United States within the five-fiscal-year period immediately preceding the fiscal year within which the report is to be made and for refugees who entered earlier and who have shown themselves to be significantly and disproportionately dependent on welfare, as well as a description of the extent to which refugees received the forms of assistance or services under this chapter during that period;

(2) a description of the geographic location of refugees;

(3) a summary of the results of the monitoring and evaluation conducted under section 412(a)(7) [8 USCS § 1522(a)(7)] during the period for which the report is submitted;

(4) a description of (A) the activities, expenditures, and policies of the Office under this chapter and of the activities of States, voluntary agencies, and sponsors, and (B) the Director's plans for improvement of refugee resettlement;

(5) evaluations of the extent to which (A) the services provided under this chapter are assisting refugees in achieving economic self-sufficiency, achieving ability in English, and achieving employment commensurate with their skills and abilities, and (B) any fraud, abuse, or mismanagement has been reported in the provisions of services or assistance;

(6) a description of any assistance provided by the Director pursuant to section 412(e)(5) [8 USCS § 1522(e)(5)];

(7) a summary of the location and status of unaccompanied refugee children admitted to the United States; and

(8) a summary of the information compiled and evaluation made under section 412(a)(8) [8 USCS § 1522(a)(8)].

HISTORY: (June 27, 1952, ch 477, Title IV, Ch 2, § 413, as added March 17, 1980, P. L. 96-212, Title III, Part B, § 311(a)(2), 94 Stat. 115; Oct. 25, 1982, P. L. 97-363, §§ 3(b), 7, 96 Stat. 1734, 1737; Nov. 6, 1986, P. L. 99-605, § 11, 100 Stat. 3455; Oct. 24, 1988, P. L. 100-525, § 9(jj), 102 Stat. 2622; April 30, 1994, P. L. 103-236, Title I, Part C, § 162(n)(3), 108 Stat. 409.)

§ 414. [8 U.S.C. § 1524] Authorization of appropriations.

(a) There are authorized to be appropriated for each of fiscal years 2000 through 2002 such sums as may be necessary to carry out this chapter.

(b) The authority to enter into contracts under this chapter shall be effective for any fiscal year only to such extent or in such amounts as are provided in advance in appropriation Acts.

HISTORY: (June 27, 1952, ch 477, Title IV, Ch 2, § 414, as added March 17, 1980, P.L. 96-212, Title III, Part B, § 311(a)(2), 94 Stat. 116; Oct. 25, 1982, P. L. 97-363, § 2, 96 Stat. 1734; Nov. 6, 1986, P. L. 99-605, § 2, 100 Stat. 3449; Oct. 24, 1988, P. L. 100-525, § 6(a), 102 Stat. 2616; Oct. 1, 1991, P. L. 102-110, § 5, 105 Stat. 558; June 8, 1993, P. L. 103-37, § 1, 107 Stat. 107; Oct. 25, 1994, P. L. 103-416, Title II, § 208, 108 Stat. 4312; Nov. 13, 1997, P. L. 105-78, Title VI, § 604(a), 111 Stat. 1521.; Dec. 2, 1997, P. L. 105-136, § 1(a), 111 Stat. 2639; Nov. 13, 1999, P. L. 106-104, § 3, 113 Stat. 1483.)

TITLE V—ALIEN TERRORIST REMOVAL PROCEDURES

§ 501. [8 U.S.C. § 1531] Definitions.

As used in this title [8 USCS §§ 1531 et seq.]—

(1) the term "alien terrorist" means any alien described in section 241(a)(4)(B) [237(a)(4)(B)] [8 USCS § 1227(a)(4)(B)];

(2) the term "classified information" has the same meaning as in section 1(a) of the Classified Information Procedures Act (18 U.S.C. App.);

(3) the term "national security" has the same meaning as in section 1(b) of the Classified Information Procedures Act (18 U.S.C. App.);

(4) the term "removal court" means the court described in section 502 [8 USCS § 1532];

(5) the term "removal hearing" means the hearing described in section 504 [8 USCS § 1534];

(6) the term "removal proceeding" means a proceeding under this title [8 USCS §§ 1531 et seq.]; and

(7) the term "special attorney" means an attorney who is on the panel established under section 502(e) [8 USCS § 1532(e)].

HISTORY: (June 27, 1952, ch 477, Title V, § 501, as added April 24, 1996, P. L. 104-132, Title IV, Subtitle A, § 401(a), 110 Stat. 1259; Sept. 30, 1996, P. L. 104-208, Div C, Title III, Subtitle D, § 354(a)(5), 110 Stat. 3009-643.)

§ 502. [8 U.S.C. § 1532] Establishment of removal court.

(a) Designation of judges. The Chief Justice of the United States shall publicly designate 5 district court judges from 5 of the United States judicial circuits who shall constitute a court that shall have jurisdiction to conduct all removal proceedings. The Chief Justice may, in the Chief Justice's discretion, designate the same judges under this section as are designated pursuant to section 103(a) of the Foreign Intelligence Surveillance Act of 1978 (50 U.S.C. 1803(a)).

(b) Terms. Each judge designated under subsection (a) shall serve for a term of 5 years and shall be eligible for redesignation, except that of the members first designated—

(1) 1 member shall serve for a term of 1 year;

(2) 1 member shall serve for a term of 2 years;

(3) 1 member shall serve for a term of 3 years; and

(4) 1 member shall serve for a term of 4 years.

(c) Chief judge.

(1) Designation. The Chief Justice shall publicly designate one of the judges of the removal court to be the chief judge of the removal court.

(2) Responsibilities. The chief judge shall—

(A) promulgate rules to facilitate the functioning of the removal court; and

(B) assign the consideration of cases to the various judges on the removal court.

(d) Expeditious and confidential nature of proceedings. The provisions of section 103(c) of the Foreign Intelligence Surveillance Act of 1978 (50 U.S.C. 1803(c)) shall apply to removal proceedings in the same manner as they apply to proceedings under that Act.

(e) Establishment of panel of special attorneys. The removal court shall provide for the designation of a panel of attorneys each of whom—

(1) has a security clearance which affords the attorney access to classified information, and

(2) has agreed to represent permanent resident aliens with respect to classified information under section 504(e)(3) [8 USCS § 1534(e)(3)] in accordance with (and subject to the penalties under) this title [8 USCS §§ 1531 et seq.].

HISTORY: (June 27, 1952, ch 477, Title V, § 502, as added April 24, 1996, P. L. 104-132, Title IV, Subtitle A, § 401(a), 110 Stat. 1259; Sept. 30, 1996, P. L. 104-208, Div C, Title III, Subtitle D, § 354(a)(4), 110 Stat. 3009-643.)

§ 503. [8 U.S.C. § 1533] Removal court procedure.

(a) Application.

(1) In general. In any case in which the Attorney General has classified information that an alien is an alien terrorist, the Attorney General may seek removal of the alien under this title [8 USCS §§ 1531 et seq.] by filing an application with the removal court that contains—

(A) the identity of the attorney in the Department of Justice making the application;

(B) a certification by the Attorney General or the Deputy Attorney General that the application satisfies the criteria and requirements of this section;

(C) the identity of the alien for whom authorization for the removal proceeding is sought; and

(D) a statement of the facts and circumstances relied on by the Department of Justice to establish probable cause that—

(i) the alien is an alien terrorist;

(ii) the alien is physically present in the United States; and

(iii) with respect to such alien, removal under title II would pose a risk to the national security of the United States.

(2) Filing. An application under this section shall be submitted ex parte and in camera, and shall be filed under seal with the removal court.

(b) Right to dismiss. The Attorney General may dismiss a removal action under this title [8 USCS §§ 1531 et seq.] at any stage of the proceeding.

(c) Consideration of application.

(1) Basis for decision. In determining whether to grant an application under this section, a single judge of the removal court may consider, ex parte and in camera, in addition to the information contained in the application—

(A) other information, including classified information, presented under oath or affirmation; and

(B) testimony received in any hearing on the application, of which a verbatim record shall be kept.

(2) Approval of order. The judge shall issue an order granting the application, if the judge finds that there is probable cause to believe that—

(A) the alien who is the subject of the application has been correctly identified and is an alien terrorist present in the United States; and

(B) removal under title II [8 USCS §§ 1151 et seq.] would pose a risk to the national security of the United States.

(3) Denial of order. If the judge denies the order requested in the application, the judge shall prepare a written statement of the reasons for the denial, taking all necessary precautions not to disclose any classified information contained in the Government's application.

(d) Exclusive provisions. If an order is issued under this section granting an application, the rights of the alien regarding removal and expulsion shall be governed solely by this title [8 USCS §§ 1531 et seq.], and except as they are specifically referenced in this title [8 USCS §§ 1531 et seq.], no other provisions of this Act shall be applicable.

HISTORY: (June 27, 1952, ch 477, Title V, § 503, as added April 24, 1996, P. L. 104-132, Title IV, Subtitle A, § 401(a), 110 Stat. 1259.)

§ 504. [8 U.S.C. § 1534] Removal hearing.

(a) In general.

(1) Expeditious hearing. In any case in which an application for an order is approved under section 503(c)(2) [8 USCS § 1533(c)(2)], a removal hearing shall be conducted under this section as expeditiously as practicable for the purpose of determining whether the alien to whom the order pertains should be removed from the United States on the grounds that the alien is an alien terrorist.

(2) Public hearing. The removal hearing shall be open to the public.

(b) Notice. An alien who is the subject of a removal hearing under this title [8 USCS §§ 1531 et seq.] shall be given reasonable notice of—

(1) the nature of the charges against the alien, including a general account of the basis for the charges; and

(2) the time and place at which the hearing will be held.

(c) Rights in hearing.

(1) Right of counsel. The alien shall have a right to be present at such hearing and to be represented by counsel. Any alien financially unable to obtain counsel shall be entitled to have counsel assigned to represent the alien. Such counsel shall be appointed by the judge pursuant to the plan for furnishing representation for any person financially unable to obtain adequate representation for the district in which the hearing is conducted, as provided for in section 3006A of title 18, United States Code. All provisions of that section shall apply and, for purposes of determining the maximum amount of compensation, the matter shall be treated as if a felony was charged.

(2) Introduction of evidence. Subject to the limitations in subsection (e), the alien shall have a reasonable opportunity to introduce evidence on the alien's own behalf.

(3) Examination of witnesses. Subject to the limitations in subsection (e), the alien shall have a reasonable opportunity to examine the evidence against the alien and to cross-examine any witness.

(4) Record. A verbatim record of the proceedings and of all testimony and evidence offered or produced at such a hearing shall be kept.

(5) Removal decision based on evidence at hearing. The decision of the judge regarding removal shall be based only on that evidence introduced at the removal hearing.

(d) Subpoenas.

(1) Request. At any time prior to the conclusion of the removal hearing, either the alien or the Department of Justice may request the judge to issue a subpoena for the presence of a named witness (which subpoena may also command the person to whom it is directed to produce books, papers, documents, or other objects designated therein) upon a satisfactory showing that the presence of the witness is necessary for the determination of any material matter. Such a request may be made ex parte except that the judge shall inform the Department of Justice of any request for a subpoena by the alien for a witness or material if compliance with such a subpoena would reveal classified evidence or the source of that evidence. The Department of Justice shall be given a reasonable opportunity to oppose the issuance of such a subpoena.

(2) Payment for attendance. If an application for a subpoena by the alien also makes a showing that the alien is financially unable to pay for the attendance of a witness so requested, the court may order the costs incurred by the process and the fees of the witness so subpoenaed to be paid from funds appropriated for the enforcement of title II [8 USCS §§ 1151 et seq.].

(3) Nationwide service. A subpoena under this subsection may be served anywhere in the United States.

(4) Witness fees. A witness subpoenaed under this subsection shall receive the same fees and expenses as a witness subpoenaed in connection with a civil proceeding in a court of the United States.

(5) No access to classified information. Nothing in this subsection is intended to allow an alien to have access to classified information.

(e) Discovery.

(1) In general. For purposes of this title [8 USCS §§ 1531 et seq.]—

(A) the Government is authorized to use in a removal proceedings [proceeding] the fruits of electronic surveillance and unconsented physical searches authorized under the Foreign Intelligence Surveillance Act of 1978 (50 U.S.C. 1801 et seq.) without regard to subsections (c), (e), (f), (g), and (h) of section 106 of that Act [50 USCS § 1806(c), (e), (f), (g), and (h)] and discovery of information derived pursuant to such Act, or otherwise collected for national security purposes, shall not be authorized if disclosure would present a risk to the national security of the United States;

(B) an alien subject to removal under this title [8 USCS §§ 1531 et seq.] shall not be entitled to suppress evidence that the alien alleges was unlawfully obtained; and

(C) section 3504 of title 18, United States Code, and section 1806(c) of title 50, United States Code, shall not apply if the Attorney General determines that public disclosure would pose a risk to the national security of the United States because it would disclose classified information or otherwise threaten the integrity of a pending investigation.

(2) Protective orders. Nothing in this title [8 USCS §§ 1531 et seq.] shall prevent the United States from seeking protective orders and from asserting privileges ordinarily available to the United States to protect against the disclosure of classified information, including the invocation of the military and State secrets privileges.

(3) Treatment of classified information.

(A) Use. The judge shall examine, ex parte and in camera, any evidence for which the Attorney General determines that public disclosure would pose a risk to the national security of the United States or to the security of any individual because it would disclose classified information and neither the alien nor the public shall be informed of such evidence or its sources other than through reference to the summary provided pursuant to this paragraph. Notwithstanding the previous sentence, the Department of Justice may, in its discretion and, in the case of classified information, after coordination with the originating agency, elect to introduce such evidence in open session.

(B) Submission. With respect to such information, the Government shall submit to the removal court an unclassified summary of the specific evidence that does not pose that risk.

(C) Approval. Not later than 15 days after submission, the judge shall approve the summary if the judge finds that it is sufficient to enable the alien to prepare a defense. The Government shall deliver to the alien a copy of the unclassified summary approved under this subparagraph.

(D) Disapproval.

(i) In general. If an unclassified summary is not approved by the removal court under subparagraph (C), the Government shall be afforded 15 days to correct the deficiencies identified by the court and submit a revised unclassified summary.

(ii) Revised summary. If the revised unclassified summary is not approved by the court within 15 days of its submission pursuant to subparagraph (C), the removal hearing shall be terminated unless the judge makes the findings under clause (iii).

(iii) Findings. The findings described in this clause are, with respect to an alien, that—

(I) the continued presence of the alien in the United States would likely cause serious and irreparable harm to the national security or death or serious bodily injury to any person, and

(II) the provision of the summary would likely cause serious and irreparable harm to the national security or death or serious bodily injury to any person.

(E) Continuation of hearing without summary. If a judge makes the findings described in subparagraph (D)(iii)—

(i) if the alien involved is an alien lawfully admitted for permanent residence, the procedures described in subparagraph (F) shall apply; and

(ii) in all cases the special removal hearing shall continue, the Department of Justice shall cause to be delivered to the alien a statement that no summary is possible, and the classified information submitted in camera and ex parte may be used pursuant to this paragraph.

(F) Special procedures for access and challenges to classified information by special attorneys in case of lawful permanent aliens.

(i) In general. The procedures described in this subparagraph are that the judge (under rules of the removal court) shall designate a special attorney to assist the alien—

(I) by reviewing in camera the classified information on behalf of the alien, and

(II) by challenging through an in camera proceeding the veracity of the evidence contained in the classified information.

(ii) Restrictions on disclosure. A special attorney receiving classified information under clause (i)—

(I) shall not disclose the information to the alien or to any other attorney representing the alien, and

(II) who discloses such information in violation of subclause (I) shall be subject to a fine under title 18, United States Code, imprisoned for not less than 10 years nor more than 25 years, or both.

(f) Arguments. Following the receipt of evidence, the Government and the alien shall be given fair opportunity to present argument as to whether the evidence is sufficient to justify the removal of the alien. The Government shall open the argument. The alien shall be permitted to reply. The Government shall then be permitted to reply in rebuttal. The judge may allow any part of the argument that refers to evidence received in camera and ex parte to be heard in camera and ex parte.

(g) Burden of proof. In the hearing, it is the Government's burden to prove, by the preponderance of the evidence, that the alien is subject to removal because the alien is an alien terrorist.

(h) Rules of Evidence. The Federal Rules of Evidence shall not apply in a removal hearing.

(i) Determination of deportation. If the judge, after considering the evidence on the record as a whole, finds that the Government has met its burden, the judge shall order the alien removed and detained pending removal from the United States. If the alien was released pending the removal hearing, the judge shall order the Attorney General to take the alien into custody.

(j) Written order. At the time of issuing a decision as to whether the alien shall be removed, the judge shall prepare a written order containing a statement of facts found and conclusions of law. Any portion of the order that would reveal the substance or source of information received in camera and ex parte pursuant to subsection (e) shall not be made available to the alien or the public.

(k) No right to ancillary relief. At no time shall the judge consider or provide for relief from removal based on—

(1) asylum under section 208 [8 USCS § 1158];

(2) [by] withholding of removal under section 241(b)(3) [8 USCS § 1251(b)(3)];

(3) suspension of deportation under cancellation of removal under section 240A [8 USCS § 1229b];

(4) voluntary departure under section 244(e);

(5) adjustment of status under section 245 [8 USCS § 1255]; or

(6) registry under section 249 [8 USCS § 1259].

(l) Report on terrorist removal proceedings. Not later than 3 months from the date of the enactment of this subsection [enacted Dec. 28, 2001], the Attorney General shall submit to Congress a report concerning the effect and efficacy of alien terrorist removal proceedings, including the reasons why proceedings pursuant to this section have not been used by the Attorney General in the past and the effect on the use of these proceedings after the enactment of the USA PATRIOT Act of 2001 (Public Law 107-56).

HISTORY: (June 27, 1952, ch 477, Title V, § 504, as added April 24, 1996, P. L. 104-132, Title IV, Subtitle A, § 401(a), 110 Stat. 1260; Sept. 30, 1996, P. L. 104-208, Div C, Title III, Subtitle A, § 308(g)(7)(B), (8)(B), Subtitle D, §§ 354(a)(1), (2), (b), 357, 110 Stat. 3009-623, 3009-624, 3009-641, 3009-643, 3009-644; Dec. 28, 2001, P. L. 107-108, Title III, § 313, 115 Stat. 1401.)

§ 505. [8 U.S.C. § 1535] Appeals.

(a) Appeal of denial of application for removal proceedings.

(1) In general. The Attorney General may seek a review of the denial of an order sought in an application filed pursuant to section 503 [8 USCS § 1533]. The appeal shall be filed in the United States Court of Appeals for the District of Columbia Circuit by notice of appeal filed not later than 20 days after the date of such denial.

(2) Record on appeal. The entire record of the proceeding shall be transmitted to the Court of Appeals under seal, and the Court of Appeals shall hear the matter ex parte.

(3) Standard of review. The Court of Appeals shall—

(A) review questions of law de novo; and

(B) set aside a finding of fact only if such finding was clearly erroneous.

(b) Appeal of determination regarding summary of classified information.

(1) In general. The United States may take an interlocutory appeal to the United States Court of Appeals for the District of Columbia Circuit of—

(A) any determination by the judge pursuant to section 504(e)(3) [8 USCS § 1534(e)(3)]; or

(B) the refusal of the court to make the findings permitted by section 504(e)(3) [8 USCS § 1534(e)(3)].

(2) Record. In any interlocutory appeal taken pursuant to this subsection, the entire record, including any proposed order of the judge, any classified information and the summary of evidence, shall be transmitted to the Court of Appeals. The classified information shall be transmitted under seal. A verbatim record of such appeal shall be kept under seal in the event of any other judicial review.

(c) Appeal of decision in hearing.

(1) In general. Subject to paragraph (2), the decision of the judge after a removal hearing may be appealed by either the alien or the Attorney General to the United States Court of Appeals for the District of Columbia Circuit by notice of appeal filed not later than 20 days after the date on which the order is issued. The order shall not be enforced during the pendency of an appeal under this subsection.

(2) Automatic appeals in cases of permanent resident aliens in which no summary provided.

(A) In general. Unless the alien waives the right to a review under this paragraph, in any case involving an alien lawfully admitted for permanent residence who is denied a written summary of classified information under section 504(e)(3) [8 USCS § 1534(e)(3)] and with respect to which the procedures described in section 504(e)(3)(F) [8 USCS § 1534(e)(3)(F)] apply, any order issued by the judge shall be reviewed by the Court of Appeals for the District of Columbia Circuit.

(B) Use of special attorney. With respect to any issue relating to classified information that arises in such review, the alien shall be represented only by the special attorney designated under section 504(e)(3)(F)(i) [8 USCS § 1534(e)(3)(F)(i)] on behalf of the alien.

(3) Transmittal of record. In an appeal or review to the Court of Appeals pursuant to this subsection—

(A) the entire record shall be transmitted to the Court of Appeals; and

(B) information received in camera and ex parte, and any portion of the order that would reveal the substance or source of such information, shall be transmitted under seal.

(4) Expedited appellate proceeding. In an appeal or review to the Court of Appeals under this subsection—

(A) the appeal or review shall be heard as expeditiously as practicable and the court may dispense with full briefing and hear the matter solely on the record of the judge of the removal court and on such briefs or motions as the court may require to be filed by the parties;

(B) the Court of Appeals shall issue an opinion not later than 60 days after the date of the issuance of the final order of the district court;

(C) the court shall review all questions of law de novo; and

(D) a finding of fact shall be accorded deference by the reviewing court and shall not be set aside unless such finding was clearly erroneous, except that in the case of a review under paragraph (2) in which an alien lawfully admitted for permanent residence was denied a written summary of classified information under section 504(c)(3) [section 504(e)(3)] [8 USCS § 1534(e)(3)], the Court of Appeals shall review questions of fact de novo.

(d) Certiorari. Following a decision by the Court of Appeals pursuant to subsection (c), the alien or the Attorney General may petition the Supreme Court for a writ of certiorari. In any such case, any information transmitted to the Court of Appeals under seal shall, if such information is also submitted to the Supreme Court, be transmitted under seal. Any order of removal shall not be stayed pending disposition of a writ of certiorari, except as provided by the Court of Appeals or a Justice of the Supreme Court.

(e) Appeal of detention order.

(1) In general. Sections 3145 through 3148 of title 18, United States Code, pertaining to review and appeal of a release or detention order, penalties for failure to appear, penalties for an offense committed while on release, and sanctions for violation of a release condition shall apply to an alien to whom section 507(b)(1) [8 USCS § 1537(b)(1)] applies. In applying the previous sentence—

(A) for purposes of section 3145 of such title an appeal shall be taken to the United States Court of Appeals for the District of Columbia Circuit; and

(B) for purposes of section 3146 of such title the alien shall be considered released in connection with a charge of an offense punishable by life imprisonment.

(2) No review of continued detention. The determinations and actions of the Attorney General pursuant to section 507(b)(2)(C) [8 USCS § 1537(b)(2)(C)] shall not be subject to judicial review, including application for a writ of habeas corpus, except for a claim by the alien that continued detention violates the alien's rights under the Constitution. Jurisdiction over any such challenge shall lie exclusively in the United States Court of Appeals for the District of Columbia Circuit.

HISTORY: (June 27, 1952, ch 477, Title V, § 505, as added April 24, 1996, P. L. 104-132, Title IV, Subtitle A, § 401(a), 110 Stat. 1263; Sept. 30, 1996, P. L. 104-208, Div C, Title III, Subtitle D, § 354(a)(3), 110 Stat. 3009-642.)

§ 506. [8 U.S.C. § 1536] Custody and release pending removal hearing.

(a) Upon filing application.

(1) In general. Subject to paragraphs (2) and (3), the Attorney General may—

(A) take into custody any alien with respect to whom an application under section 503 [8 USCS § 1533] has been filed; and

(B) retain such an alien in custody in accordance with the procedures authorized by this title [8 USCS §§ 1531 et seq.].

(2) Special rules for permanent resident aliens.

(A) Release hearing. An alien lawfully admitted for permanent residence shall be entitled to a release hearing before the judge assigned to hear the removal hearing. Such an alien shall be detained pending the removal hearing, unless the alien demonstrates to the court that the alien—

(i) is a person lawfully admitted for permanent residence in the United States;

(ii) if released upon such terms and conditions as the court may prescribe (including the posting of any monetary amount), is not likely to flee; and

(iii) will not endanger national security, or the safety of any person or the community, if released.

(B) Information considered. The judge may consider classified information submitted in camera and ex parte in making a determination whether to release an alien pending the removal hearing.

(3) Release if order denied and no review sought.

(A) In general. Subject to subparagraph (B), if a judge of the removal court denies the order sought in an application filed pursuant to section 503 [8 USCS § 1533], and the Attorney General does not seek review of such denial, the alien shall be released from custody.

(B) Application of regular procedures. Subparagraph (A) shall not prevent the arrest and detention of the alien pursuant to title II.

(b) Conditional release if order denied and review sought.

(1) In general. If a judge of the removal court denies the order sought in an application filed pursuant to section 503 [8 USCS § 1533] and the Attorney General seeks review of such denial, the judge shall release the alien from custody subject to the least restrictive condition, or combination of conditions, of release described in section 3142(b) and clauses (i) through (xiv) of section 3142(c)(1)(B) of title 18, United States Code, that—

(A) will reasonably assure the appearance of the alien at any future proceeding pursuant to this title [8 USCS §§ 1531 et seq.]; and

(B) will not endanger the safety of any other person or the community.

(2) No release for certain aliens. If the judge finds no such condition or combination of conditions, as described in paragraph (1), the alien shall remain in custody until the completion of any appeal authorized by this title [8 USCS §§ 1531 et seq.]

HISTORY: (June 27, 1952, ch 477, Title V, § 506, as added April 24, 1996, P. L. 104-132, Title IV, Subtitle A, § 401(a), 110 Stat. 1265.)

§ 507. [8 U.S.C. § 1537] Custody and release after removal hearing.

(a) Release.

(1) In general. Subject to paragraph (2), if the judge decides that an alien should not be removed, the alien shall be released from custody.

(2) Custody pending appeal. If the Attorney General takes an appeal from such decision, the alien shall remain in custody, subject to the provisions of section 3142 of title 18, United States Code.

(b) Custody and removal.

(1) Custody. If the judge decides that an alien shall be removed, the alien shall be detained pending the outcome of any appeal. After the conclusion of any judicial review thereof which affirms the removal order,

the Attorney General shall retain the alien in custody and remove the alien to a country specified under paragraph (2).

(2) Removal.

(A) In general. The removal of an alien shall be to any country which the alien shall designate if such designation does not, in the judgment of the Attorney General, in consultation with the Secretary of State, impair the obligation of the United States under any treaty (including a treaty pertaining to extradition) or otherwise adversely affect the foreign policy of the United States.

(B) Alternate countries. If the alien refuses to designate a country to which the alien wishes to be removed or if the Attorney General, in consultation with the Secretary of State, determines that removal of the alien to the country so designated would impair a treaty obligation or adversely affect United States foreign policy, the Attorney General shall cause the alien to be removed to any country willing to receive such alien.

(C) Continued detention. If no country is willing to receive such an alien, the Attorney General may, notwithstanding any other provision of law, retain the alien in custody. The Attorney General, in coordination with the Secretary of State, shall make periodic efforts to reach agreement with other countries to accept such an alien and at least every 6 months shall provide to the attorney representing the alien at the removal hearing a written report on the Attorney General's efforts. Any alien in custody pursuant to this subparagraph shall be released from custody solely at the discretion of the Attorney General and subject to such conditions as the Attorney General shall deem appropriate.

(D) Fingerprinting. Before an alien is removed from the United States pursuant to this subsection, or pursuant to an order of removal because such alien is inadmissible under section 212(a)(3)(B) [8 USCS § 1182(a)(3)(B)], the alien shall be photographed and fingerprinted, and shall be advised of the provisions of section 276(b) [8 USCS § 1326(b)].

(c) Continued detention pending trial.

(1) Delay in removal. The Attorney General may hold in abeyance the removal of an alien who has been ordered removed, pursuant to this title [8 USCS §§ 1531 et seq.], to allow the trial of such alien on any Federal or State criminal charge and the service of any sentence of confinement resulting from such a trial.

(2) Maintenance of custody. Pending the commencement of any service of a sentence of confinement by an alien described in paragraph (1), such an alien shall remain in the custody of the Attorney General, unless the Attorney General determines that temporary release of the alien to the custody of State authorities for confinement in a State facility is appropriate and would not endanger national security or public safety.

(3) Subsequent removal. Following the completion of a sentence of confinement by an alien described in paragraph (1), or following the completion of State criminal proceedings which do not result in a sentence of confinement of an alien released to the custody of State authorities pursuant to paragraph (2), such an alien shall be returned to the custody of the Attorney General who shall proceed to the removal of the alien under this title [8 USCS §§ 1531 et seq.].

(d) Application of certain provisions relating to escape of prisoners. For purposes of sections 751 and 752 of title 18, United States Code, an alien in the custody of the Attorney General pursuant to this title [8 USCS §§ 1531 et seq.] shall be subject to the penalties provided by those sections in relation to a person committed to the custody of the Attorney General by virtue of an arrest on a charge of a felony.

(e) Rights of aliens in custody.

(1) Family and attorney visits. An alien in the custody of the Attorney General pursuant to this title [8 USCS §§ 1531 et seq.] shall be given reasonable opportunity, as determined by the Attorney General, to communicate with and receive visits from members of the alien's family, and to contact, retain, and communicate with an attorney.

(2) Diplomatic contact. An alien in the custody of the Attorney General pursuant to this title [8 USCS §§ 1531 et seq.] shall have the right to contact an appropriate diplomatic or consular official of the alien's country of citizenship or nationality or of any country providing representation services therefore. The Attorney General shall notify the appropriate embassy, mission, or consular office of the alien's detention.

HISTORY: (June 27, 1952, ch 477, Title V, § 507, as added April 24, 1996, P. L. 104-132, Title IV, Subtitle A, § 401(a), 110 Stat. 1266; Sept. 30, 1996, P. L. 104-208, Div C, Title III, Subtitle A, § 308(d)(4)(Q), 110 Stat. 3009-619.)

APPENDICES TO THE IMMIGRATION AND NATIONALITY ACT OF 1952

(Editorially created)

Appendix A. — NACARA (As amended)
Appendix B. — HRIFA (As amended)
Appendix C. — LIFE Act (As amended)
Appendix D. — LIFE Act Amendments of 2000
Appendix E. — Freestanding transitional, effective dates, savings, monitoring and interagency communication provisions of IIRIRA (As amended)
Appendix F. — Freestanding provisions in the Victims of Trafficking and Violence Protection Act of 2000
Appendix G. — Freestanding provisions for identity confirmation technology, records access, and immigration benefits for victims of terrorism in the USA PATRIOT Act (As amended)
Appendix H. — Enhanced Border Security and Visa Entry Reform Act of 2002
Appendix I. — Immigration Benefits, 21st Century Department of Justice Appropriations Authorization Act
Appendix J. — Pilot Immigration Program [P.L. 102-395].
Appendix K. — Extension of Posthumous Benefits to Surviving Spouses, Children, and Parents [P.L. 108-236, §§ 1703(a) to (e)]

****

APPENDIX A — NACARA (AS AMENDED)[1]

Title II of Public Law 105-100

§ 201. Short title Appendix A, § 201

This title may be cited as the "Nicaraguan Adjustment and Central American Relief Act".

§ 202. Adjustment of status of certain Nicaraguans and Cubans Appendix A, § 202

(a) Adjustment of status.

(1) In general. The status of any alien described in subsection (b) shall be adjusted by the Attorney General to that of an alien lawfully admitted for permanent residence, if the alien

(A) applies for such adjustment before April 1, 2000; and

(B) is otherwise admissible to the United States for permanent residence, except in determining such admissibility the grounds for inadmissibility specified in paragraphs (4), (5), (6)(A), (7)(A), and (9)(B) of section 212(a) of the Immigration and Nationality Act shall not apply.

(2)[2] Rules in applying certain provisions. In the case of an alien described in subsection (b) or (d) who is applying for adjustment of status under this section

(A) the provisions of section 241(a)(5) of the Immigration and Nationality Act shall not apply; and

(B) the Attorney General may grant the alien a waiver of the grounds of inadmissibility under subparagraphs (A) and (C) of section 212(a)(9) of such Act. In granting waivers under subparagraph (B), the Attorney General shall use standards used in granting consent under subparagraphs (A)(iii) and (C)(ii) of such section 212(a)(9).

(3) Relationship of application to certain orders. An alien present in the United States who has been ordered excluded, deported, removed, or ordered to depart voluntarily from the United States under any provision of the Immigration and Nationality Act may, notwithstanding such order, apply for adjustment of status under paragraph (1). Such an alien may not be required, as a condition of submitting or granting such application, to file a separate motion to reopen, reconsider, or vacate such order. If the Attorney General grants the application, the Attorney General shall cancel the order. If the Attorney General renders a final administrative decision to deny the application, the order shall be effective and enforceable to the same extent as if the application had not been made.

(b) Aliens eligible for adjustment of status.

(1) In general. The benefits provided by subsection (a) shall apply to any alien who is a national of Nicaragua or Cuba and who has been physically present in the United States for a continuous period, beginning not later than December 1, 1995, and ending not earlier than the date the application for adjustment under such subsection is filed, except an alien shall not be considered to have failed to maintain continuous physical presence by reason of an absence, or absences, from the United States for any periods in the aggregate not exceeding 180 days.

(2) Proof of commencement of continuous presence. For purposes of establishing that the period of continuous physical presence referred to in paragraph (1) commenced not later than December 1, 1995, an alien—

(A) shall demonstrate that the alien, prior to December 1,

(i) applied to the Attorney General for asylum;

(ii) was issued an order to show cause under section 242 or 242B of the Immigration and Nationality Act (as in effect prior to April 1, 1997);

(iii) was placed in exclusion proceedings under section 236 of such Act (as so in effect);

(iv) applied for adjustment of status under section 245 of such Act;

(v) applied to the Attorney General for employment authorization;

(vi) performed service, or engaged in a trade or business, within the United States which is evidenced by records maintained by the Commissioner of Social Security; or

(vii) applied for any other benefit under the Immigration and Nationality Act by means of an application establishing the alien's presence in the United States prior to December 1, 1995; or

(B) shall make such other demonstration of physical presence as the Attorney General may provide for by regulation.

(c) Stay of removal; work authorization.

(1) In general. The Attorney General shall provide by regulation for an alien subject to a final order of deportation or removal to seek a stay of such order based on the filing of an application under subsection (a).

(2) During certain proceedings. Notwithstanding any provision of the Immigration and Nationality Act, the Attorney General shall not order any alien to be removed from the United States, if the alien is in exclusion, deportation, or removal proceedings under any provision of such Act and has applied for adjustment of status under subsection (a), except where the Attorney General has rendered a final administrative determination to deny the application.

(3) Work authorization. The Attorney General may authorize an alien who has applied for adjustment of status under subsection (a) to engage in employment in the United States during the pendency of such application and may provide the alien with an "employment authorized" endorsement or other appropriate document signifying authorization of employment, except that if such application is pending for a period exceeding 180 days, and has not been denied, the Attorney General shall authorize such employment.

(d) Adjustment of status for spouses and children.

(1) In general. The status of an alien shall be adjusted by the Attorney General to that of an alien lawfully admitted for permanent residence, if—

1. Shown as amended by H.R. 1565, P.L. 105-139, 111 Stat. 2644 (1997), eff. as if included in NACARA).

2. Added by § 1505 of LIFE Act Amendments of 2000, enacted by reference in P.L. 106-554, 114 Stat. 2763A-326 (December 21, 2000).

(A) the alien is a national of Nicaragua or Cuba;

(B)[3] the alien—

(i) is the spouse, child, or unmarried son or daughter of an alien whose status is adjusted to that of an alien lawfully admitted for permanent residence under subsection (a), except that in the case of such an unmarried son or daughter, the son or daughter shall be required to establish that the son or daughter has been physically present in the United States for a continuous period beginning not later than December 1, 1995, and ending not earlier than the date on which the application for adjustment under this subsection is filed; or

(ii) was, at the time at which an alien filed for adjustment under subsection (a), the spouse or child of an alien whose status is adjusted to that of an alien lawfully admitted for permanent residence under subsection (a), and the spouse, child, or child of the spouse has been battered or subjected to extreme cruelty by the alien that filed for adjustment under sub-section (a);

(C) the alien applies for such adjustment and is physically present in the United States on the date the application is filed;

(D) the alien is otherwise admissible to the United States for permanent residence, except in determining such admissibility the grounds for inadmissibility specified in paragraphs

(4), (5), (6)(A), (7)(A), and (9)(B) of section 212(a) of the Immigration and Nationality Act shall not apply; and

(E) applies for such adjustment before April 1, 2000.

(2) Proof of continuous presence. For purposes of establishing the period of continuous physical presence referred to in paragraph (1)(B), an alien—

(A) shall demonstrate that such period commenced not later than December 1, 1995, in a manner consistent with subsection (b)(2); and

(B) shall not be considered to have failed to maintain continuous physical presence by reason of an absence, or absences, from the United States for any period in the aggregate not exceeding 180 days.

(3)[4] Procedure. In acting on an application under this section with respect to a spouse or child who has been battered or subjected to extreme cruelty, the Attorney General shall apply section 204(a)(1)(H).

(e) Availability of administrative review. The Attorney General shall provide to applicants for adjustment of status under subsection (a) the same right to, and procedures for, administrative review as are provided to—

(1) applicants for adjustment of status under section 245 of the Immigration and Nationality Act; or

(2) aliens subject to removal proceedings under section 240 of such Act.

(f) Limitation on judicial review. A determination by the Attorney General as to whether the status of any alien should be adjusted under this section is final and shall not be subject to review by any court.

(g) No offset in number of visas available. When an alien is granted the status of having been lawfully admitted for permanent residence pursuant to this section, the Secretary of State shall not be required to reduce the number of immigrant visas authorized to be issued under any provision of the Immigration and Nationality Act.

(h) Application of Immigration and Nationality Act provisions. Except as otherwise specifically provided in this section, the definitions contained in the Immigration and Nationality Act shall apply in the administration of this section. Nothing contained in this section shall be held to repeal, amend, alter, modify, affect, or restrict the powers, duties, functions, or authority of the Attorney General in the administration and enforcement of such Act or any other law relating to immigration, nationality, or naturalization. The fact that an alien may be eligible to be granted the status of having been lawfully admitted for permanent residence under this section shall not preclude the alien from seeking such status under any other provision of law for which the alien may be eligible.

§ 203. Modification of certain transition rules Appendix A, § 203

(a) Transitional rules with regard to suspension of deportation.

(1) In general. Section 309(c)(5) of the Illegal Immigration Reform and Immigrant Responsibility Act of 1996 (P.L. 104-208; division C; 110 Stat. 3009-627) is amended to read as follows:

"(5) Transitional rules with regard to suspension of deportation.

"(A) In general. Subject to subparagraphs (B) and (C), paragraphs (1) and (2) of section 240A(d) of the Immigration and Nationality Act (relating to continuous residence or physical presence) shall apply to orders to show cause (including those referred to in section 242B(a)(1) of the Immigration and Nationality Act, as in effect before the title III-A effective date), issued before, on, or after the date of the enactment of this Act.

"(B) Exception for certain orders. In any case in which the Attorney General elects to terminate and reinitiate proceedings in accordance with paragraph (3) of this subsection, paragraphs (1) and (2) of section 240A(d) of the Immigration and Nationality Act shall not apply to an order to show cause issued before April 1, 1997.

"(C) Special rule for certain aliens granted temporary protection from deportation.

"(i) In general. For purposes of calculating the period of continuous physical presence under section 244(a) of the Immigration and Nationality Act (as in effect before the title III-A effective date) or section 240A of such Act (as in effect after the title III-A effective date), subparagraph (A) and paragraphs (1) and (2) of section 240A(d) of the Immigration and Nationality Act shall not apply in the case of an alien, regardless of whether the alien is in exclusion or deportation proceedings before the title III-A effective date, who has not been con-

3. Amended by § 1510(a) of BIWPA, P.L. 106-386, 114 Stat. 1464 (October 28, 2000), eff. as if included in the enactment of IIRIRA.

4. Added by section 1510(a) of BIWPA, P.L. 106-386, 114 Stat. 1464(October 28, 2000).

victed at any time of an aggravated felony (as defined in section 101(a) of the Immigration and Nationality Act) and

"(I) was not apprehended after December 19, 1990, at the time of entry, and is

"(aa) a Salvadoran national who first entered the United States on or before September 19, 1990, and who registered for benefits pursuant to the settlement agreement in American Baptist Churches, et al. v. Thornburgh (ABC), 760 F. Supp. 796(N. D. Cal. 1991) on or before October 31, 1991, or applied for temporary protected status on or before October 31, 1991; or

"(bb) a Guatemalan national who first entered the United States on or before October 1, 1990, and who registered for benefits pursuant to such settlement agreement on or before December 31, 1991;

"(II) is a Guatemalan or Salvadoran national who filed an application for asylum with the Immigration and Naturalization Service on or before April 1, 1990;

"(III) is the spouse or child (as defined in section 101(b)(1) of the Immigration and Nationality Act) of an individual, at the time a decision is rendered to suspend the deportation, or cancel the removal, of such individual, if the individual has been determined to be described in this clause (excluding this subclause and subclause (IV));

"(IV) is the unmarried son or daughter of an alien parent, at the time a decision is rendered to suspend the deportation, or cancel the removal, of such alien parent, if

"(aa) the alien parent has been determined to be described in this clause (excluding this subclause and subclause (III)); and

"(bb) in the case of a son or daughter who is 21 years of age or older at the time such decision is rendered, the son or daughter entered the United States on or before October 1, 1990; or

"(V) is an alien who entered the United States on or before December 31, 1990, who filed an application for asylum on or before December 31, 1991, and who, at the time of filing such application, was a national of the Soviet Union, Russia, any republic of the former Soviet Union, Latvia, Estonia, Lithuania, Poland, Czechoslovakia, Romania, Hungary, Bulgaria, Albania, East Germany, Yugoslavia, or any state of the former Yugoslavia.

"(VI)[5] is an alien who was issued an order to show cause or was in deportation proceedings before April 1, 1997, and who applied for suspension of deportation under section 244(a)(3) of the Immigration and Nationality Act (as in effect before the date of the enactment of this Act); or

"(VII)[6] (aa) was the spouse or child of an alien described in subclause (I), (II), or (V)

"(AA) at the time at which a decision is rendered to suspend the deportation or cancel the removal of the alien;

"(BB) at the time at which the alien filed an application for suspension of deportation or cancellation of removal; or

"(CC) at the time at which the alien registered for benefits under the settlement agreement in American Baptist Churches, et. al. v. Thornburgh (ABC), applied for temporary protected status, or applied for asylum; and

"(bb) the spouse, child, or child of the spouse has been battered or subjected to extreme cruelty by the alien described in subclause (I), (II), or (V).

"(ii) Limitation on judicial review. A determination by the Attorney General as to whether an alien satisfies the requirements of this clause (i) is final and shall not be subject to review by any court. Nothing in the preceding sentence shall be construed as limiting the application of section 242(a)(2)(B) of the Immigration and Nationality Act (as in effect after the title III-A effective date) to other eligibility determinations pertaining to discretionary relief under this Act.

"(iii)[7] Consideration of petitions. In acting on a petition filed under subclause (VII) of clause (i) the provisions set forth in section 204(a)(1)(H) shall apply.

"(iv)[8] Residence with spouse or parent not required. For purposes of the application of clause (i)(VII), a spouse or child shall not be required to demonstrate that he or she is residing with the spouse or parent in the United States.".

(2) Conforming amendment. Subsection (c) of section 309 of the Illegal Immigration Reform and Immigrant Responsibility Act of 1996 (P.L. 104-208; division C; 110 Stat. 3009-625) is amended by striking the subsection designation and the subsection heading and inserting the following:

"(c) Transition for certain aliens.".

(b) Special rule for cancellation of removal. Section 309 of the Illegal Immigration Reform and Immigrant Responsibility Act of 1996 (P.L. 104-208; 110 Stat. 3009-625) is amended by adding at the end the following:

"(f) Special rule for cancellation of removal.

"(1) In general. Subject to the provisions of the Immigration and Nationality Act (as in effect after the title III-A effective date), other than subsections (b)(1), (d)(1), and (e) of section 240A of such Act (but including section 242(a)(2)(B) of such Act), the Attorney General may, under section 240A of such Act, cancel removal of, and adjust to the status of an alien lawfully admitted for permanent residence, an alien who is inadmissible or deportable from the United States, if the alien applies for such relief, the alien is described in subsection (c)(5)(C)(i) of this section, and

"(A) the alien

"(i) is not inadmissible or deportable under paragraph (2) or (3) of section 212(a) or paragraph (2), (3), or (4) of section 237(a) of the Immigration and Nationality

5. Added by § 1506(b) of BIWPA, P.L. 106-386, 114 Stat. 1464 (October 28, 2000), eff. as if included in the enactment of NACARA.

6. Id. by § 1510(b), eff. as if included in the enactment of NACARA.

7. Id.

8. Id.

Act and is not an alien described in section 241(b)(3)(B)(i) of such Act;

"(ii) has been physically present in the United States for a continuous period of not less than 7 years immediately preceding the date of such application;

"(iii) has been a person of good moral character during such period; and

"(iv) establishes that removal would result in extreme hardship to the alien or to the alien's spouse, parent, or child, who is a citizen of the United States or an alien lawfully admitted for permanent residence; or

"(B) the alien

"(i) is inadmissible or deportable under section 212(a)(2), 237(a)(2) (other than 237(a)(2)(A)(iii)), or 237(a)(3) of the Immigration and Nationality Act;

"(ii) is not an alien described in section 241(b)(3)(B)(i) or 101(a)(43) of such Act;

"(iii) has been physically present in the United States for a continuous period of not less than 10 years immediately following the commission of an act, or the assumption of a status, constituting a ground for removal;

"(iv) has been a person of good moral character during such period; and

"(v) establishes that removal would result in exceptional and extremely unusual hardship to the alien or to the alien's spouse, parent, or child, who is a citizen of the United States or an alien lawfully admitted for permanent residence.

"(2) Treatment of certain breaks in presence. Section 240A(d)(2) shall apply for purposes of calculating any period of continuous physical presence under this subsection, except that the reference to subsection (b)(1) in such section shall be considered to be a reference to paragraph (1) of this section.".

(c) Motions to reopen deportation or removal proceedings. Section 309 of the Illegal Immigration Reform and Immigrant Responsibility Act of 1996 (P.L. 104-208; 110 Stat. 3009-625), as amended by subsection (b), is further amended by adding at the end the following:

"(g) Motions to reopen deportation or removal proceedings. Notwithstanding any limitation imposed by law on motions to reopen removal or deportation proceedings (except limitations premised on an alien's conviction of an aggravated felony (as defined in section 101(a) of the Immigration and Nationality Act)), any alien who has become eligible for cancellation of removal or suspension of deportation as a result of the amendments made by section 203 of the Nicaraguan Adjustment and Central American Relief Act may file one motion to reopen removal or deportation proceedings to apply for cancellation of removal or suspension of deportation. The Attorney General shall designate a specific time period in which all such motions to reopen are required to be filed. The period shall begin not later than 60 days after the date of the enactment of the Nicaraguan Adjustment and Central American Relief Act and shall extend for a period not to exceed 240 days.".

(d) Temporary reduction in diversity visas.

(1) Beginning in fiscal year 1999, subject to paragraph (2), the number of visas otherwise available for a fiscal year under section 201(e) of the Immigration and Nationality Act shall be reduced by 5,000 from the number of visas otherwise available under that section for such fiscal year.

(2) In no case shall the reduction under paragraph (1) for a fiscal year exceed the amount by which—

(A) one-half of the total number of individuals described in subclauses (I), (II), (III), and (IV) of section 309(c)(5)(C)(i) of the Illegal Immigration Reform and Immigrant Responsibility Act of 1996 who have adjusted their status to that of aliens lawfully admitted for permanent residence under the Nicaraguan Adjustment and Central American Relief Act as of the end of the previous fiscal year; exceeds

(B) the total of the reductions in available visas under this subsection for all previous fiscal years.

(e) Temporary reduction in other workers' visas.

(1) Beginning in the fiscal year following the fiscal year in which a visa has been made available under section 203(b)(3)(A)(iii) of the Immigration and Nationality Act for all aliens who are the beneficiary of a petition approved under section 204 of such Act as of the date of the enactment of this Act for classification under section 203(b)(3)(A)(iii) of such Act, subject to paragraph (2), visas available under section 203(b)(3)(A)(iii) of that Act shall be reduced by 5,000 from the number of visas otherwise available under that section for such fiscal year.

(2) In no case shall the reduction under paragraph (1) for a fiscal year exceed the amount by which—

(A) the number computed under subsection (d)(2)(A); exceeds

(B) the total of the reductions in available visas under this subsection for all previous fiscal years.

(f) Effective date. The amendments made by this section to the Illegal Immigration Reform and Immigrant Responsibility Act of 1996 shall take effect as if included in the enactment of such Act.

§ 204. Limitation on cancellations of removal and suspensions of deportation Appendix A, § 204

(a) Annual limitation. Section 240A(e) of the Immigration and Nationality Act (8 U.S.C. 1229b (e)) is amended to read as follows:

"(e) Annual limitation.

"(1) Aggregate limitation. Subject to paragraphs (2) and (3), the Attorney General may not cancel the removal and adjust the status under this section, nor suspend the deportation and adjust the status under section 244(a) (as in effect before the enactment of the Illegal Immigration Reform and Immigrant Responsibility Act of 1996), of a total of more than 4,000 aliens in any fiscal year. The previous sentence shall apply regardless of when an alien applied for such cancellation and adjustment, or such suspension and adjustment, and whether such an alien had previously applied for suspension of deportation under such section 244(a). The numerical limitation under this paragraph shall apply to the aggregate number of decisions in any fiscal year to cancel the removal (and adjust the status) of an alien, or suspend the deportation (and adjust the status) of an alien, under this section or such section 244(a).

"(2) Fiscal year 1997. For fiscal year 1997, paragraph (1) shall only apply to decisions to cancel the removal of an alien, or suspend the deportation of an alien, made after April 1, 1997. Notwithstanding any other provision of law, the Attorney General may cancel the removal or suspend the deportation, in addition to the normal allotment for fiscal year 1998, of a number of aliens equal to 4,000 less the number of such cancellations of removal and suspensions of deportation granted in fiscal year 1997 after April 1, 1997.

"(3) Exception for certain aliens. Paragraph (1) shall not apply to the following:

"(A) Aliens described in section 309(c)(5)(C)(i) of the Illegal Immigration Reform and Immigrant Responsibility Act of 1996 (as amended by the Nicaraguan Adjustment and Central American Relief Act).

"(B) Aliens in deportation proceedings prior to April 1, 1997, who applied for suspension of deportation under section 244(a)(3) (as in effect before the date of the enactment of the Illegal Immigration Reform and Immigrant Responsibility Act of 1996).".

(b) Cancellation of removal and adjustment of status for certain nonpermanent residents. Section 240A(b) of the Immigration and Nationality Act (8 U.S.C. 1229b (b)) is amended in each of paragraphs (1) and (2) by striking "may cancel removal in the case of an alien" and inserting "may cancel removal of, and adjust to the status of an alien lawfully admitted for permanent residence, an alien".

(c) Recordation of date. Section 240A(b)(3) of the Immigration and Nationality Act (8 U.S.C. 1229b (b)(3)) is amended to read as follows:

"(3) Recordation of date. With respect to aliens who the Attorney General adjusts to the status of an alien lawfully admitted for permanent residence under paragraph (1) or (2), the Attorney General shall record the alien's lawful admission for permanent residence as of the date of the Attorney General's cancellation of removal under paragraph (1) or (2).".

(d) April 1 effective date for aggregate limitation. Section 309(c)(7) of the Illegal Immigration Reform and

Immigrant Responsibility Act of 1996 (P.L. 104-208; division C; 110 Stat. 3009-627) is amended to read as follows:

"(7) Limitation on suspension of deportation. After April 1, 1997, the Attorney General may not suspend the deportation and adjust the status under section 244 of the Immigration and Nationality Act (as in effect before the title III-A effective date) of any alien in any fiscal year, except in accordance with section 240A(e) of such Act. The previous sentence shall apply regardless of when an alien applied for such suspension and adjustment.".

(e) Effective date. The amendments made by this section shall take effect as if included in the enactment of the Illegal Immigration Reform and Immigrant Responsibility Act of 1996 (P.L. 104-208; 110 Stat. 3009-546).

****

APPENDIX B — HRIFA (AS AMENDED)[9]

Haitian Refugee Immigration Fairness Act Of 1998

Title IX of Section 101(h) of Division A of P.L. 105-277; 112 Stat. 2681-538 (October 21, 1998) Treasury and General Government Appropriations Act, 1999

§ 901. Short title Appendix B, § 901

This title may be cited as the "Haitian Refugee Immigration Fairness Act of 1998".

§ 902. Adjustment of status of certain Haitian nationals Appendix B, § 902

(a) Adjustment of status:

(1) In general: The status of any alien described in subsection (b) shall be adjusted by the Attorney General to that of an alien lawfully admitted for permanent residence, if the alien

(A) applies for such adjustment before April 1, 2000; and

(B) is otherwise admissible to the United States for permanent residence, except that, in determining such admissibility, the grounds for inadmissibility specified in paragraphs (4), (5), (6)(A), (7)(A), and (9)(B) of section 212(a) of the Immigration and Nationality Act shall not apply.

(2)[10] Inapplicability of certain provisions. In the case of an alien described in subsection (b) or (d) who is applying for adjustment of status under this section

(A) the provisions of section 241(a)(5) of the Immigration and Nationality Act shall not apply; and

(B) the Attorney General may grant the alien a waiver of the grounds of inadmissibility under subparagraphs (A) and

(C) of section 212(a)(9) of such Act.

In granting waivers under subparagraph (B), the Attorney General shall use standards used in granting consent under subparagraphs (A)(iii) and (C)(ii) of such section 212(a)(9).

(3) Relationship of application to certain orders: An alien present in the United States who has been ordered excluded, deported, removed, or ordered to depart voluntarily from the United States under any provision of the Immigration and Nationality Act may, notwithstanding such order, apply for adjustment of status under paragraph (1). Such an alien may not be required, as a condition on submitting or granting

9. As amended by BIWPA, P.L. 106-386, 114 Stat. 1464 (October reference in Pub. L. No. 106-554, 114 Stat. 2763A-326 (December 21, 28, 2000) and by the LIFE Act Amendments of 2000, enacted by 2000).

10. Added by § 1502(b) of the LIFE Act Amendments.

such application, to file a separate motion to reopen, reconsider, or vacate such order. If the Attorney General grants the application, the Attorney General shall cancel the order. If the Attorney General makes a final decision to deny the application, the order shall be effective and enforceable to the same extent as if the application had not been made.

(b) Aliens eligible for adjustment of status: The benefits provided by subsection (a) shall apply to any alien who is a national of Haiti who

(1) was present in the United States on December 31, 1995, who

(A) filed for asylum before December 31, 1995,

(B) was paroled into the United States prior to December 31, 1995, after having been identified as having a credible fear of persecution, or paroled for emergent reasons or reasons deemed strictly in the public interest, or

(C) was a child (as defined in the text above subparagraph

(A) of section 101(b)(1) of the Immigration and Nationality Act (8 U.S.C. 1101(b)(1)) at the time of arrival in the United States and on December 31, 1995, and who

(i) arrived in the United States without parents in the United States and has remained without parents in the United States since such arrival,

(ii) became orphaned subsequent to arrival in the United States, or

(iii) was abandoned by parents or guardians prior to April 1, 1998 and has remained abandoned since such abandonment; and

(2) has been physically present in the United States for a continuous period beginning not later than December 31, 1995, and ending not earlier than the date the application for such adjustment is filed, except that an alien shall not be considered to have failed to maintain continuous physical presence by reason of an absence, or absences, from the United States for any period or periods amounting in the aggregate to not more than 180 days.

(c) Stay of removal:

(1) In general: The Attorney General shall provide by regulation for an alien who is subject to a final order of deportation or removal or exclusion to seek a stay of such order based on the filing of an application under subsection (a).

(2) During certain proceedings. Notwithstanding any provision of the Immigration and Nationality Act, the Attorney General shall not order any alien to be removed from the United States, if the alien is in exclusion, deportation, or removal proceedings under any provision of such Act and has applied for adjustment of status under subsection (a), except where the Attorney General has made a final determination to deny the application.

(3) Work authorization. The Attorney General may authorize an alien who has applied for adjustment of status under subsection (a) to engage in employment in the United States during the pendency of such application and may provide the alien with an 'employment authorized' endorsement or other appropriate document signifying authorization of employment, except that if such application is pending for a period exceeding 180 days, and has not been denied, the Attorney General shall authorize such employment.

(d) Adjustment of status for spouses and children.

(1) In general. The status of an alien shall be adjusted by the Attorney General to that of an alien lawfully admitted for permanent residence, if—

(A) the alien is a national of Haiti;

(B)[11](i) the alien is the spouse, child, or unmarried son or daughter of an alien whose status is adjusted to that of an alien lawfully admitted for permanent residence under subsection (a), except that, in the case of such an unmarried son or daughter, the son or daughter shall be required to establish that the son or daughter has been physically present in the United States for a continuous period beginning not later than December 1, 1995, and ending not earlier than the date on which the application for such adjustment is filed;

(ii) at the time of filing of the application for adjustment under subsection (a), the alien is the spouse or child of an alien whose status is adjusted to that of an alien lawfully admitted for permanent residence under subsection (a) and the spouse, child, or child of the spouse has been battered or subjected to extreme cruelty by the individual described in subsection (a); and

(iii) in acting on applications under this section with respect to spouses or children who have been battered or subjected to extreme cruelty, the Attorney General shall apply the provisions of section 204(a)(1)(H).

(C) the alien applies for such adjustment and is physically present in the United States on the date the application is filed; and

(D) the alien is otherwise admissible to the United States for permanent residence, except that, in determining such admissibility, the grounds for inadmissibility specified in paragraphs (4), (5), (6)(A), (7)(A), and (9)(B) of section 212(a) of the Immigration and Nationality Act shall not apply.

(2) Proof of continuous presence. For purposes of establishing the period of continuous physical presence referred to in paragraph (1)(B), an alien shall not be considered to have failed to maintain continuous physical presence by reason of an absence, or absences, from the United States for any period or periods amounting in the aggregate to not more than 180 days.

(e) Availability of administrative review. The Attorney General shall provide to applicants for adjustment of status under subsection (a) the same right to, and procedures for, administrative review as are provided to—

(1) applicants for adjustment of status under section 245 of the Immigration and Nationality Act; or

(2) aliens subject to removal proceedings under section 240 of such Act.

---

11. Amended by § 1511 of BIWPA, P.L. 106-386, 114 Stat. 1464 (October 28, 2000), eff. as if included in the Haitian Refugee Immigration Fairness Act of 1998, div. A, § 101(h) of P.L. 105-277, 112 Stat. 2681 (October 21, 1998).

(f) Limitation on judicial review. A determination by the Attorney General as to whether the status of any alien should be adjusted under this section is final and shall not be subject to review by any court.

(g) No offset in number of visas available. When an alien is granted the status of having been lawfully admitted for permanent resident pursuant to this section, the Secretary of State shall not be required to reduce the number of immigrant visas authorized to be issued under any provision of the Immigration and Nationality Act.

(h) Application of Immigration and Nationality Act provisions: Except as otherwise specifically provided in this title, the definitions contained in the Immigration and Nationality Act shall apply in the administration of this section. Nothing contained in this title shall be held to repeal, amend, alter, modify, effect, or restrict the powers, duties, functions, or authority of the Attorney General in the administration and enforcement of such Act or any other law relating to immigration, nationality, or naturalization. The fact that an alien may be eligible to be granted the status of having been lawfully admitted for permanent residence under this section shall not preclude the alien from seeking such status under any other provision of law for which the alien may be eligible.

(i) Adjustment of status has no effect on eligibility for welfare and public benefits: No alien whose status has been adjusted in accordance with this section and who was not a qualified alien on the date of enactment of this Act may, solely on the basis of such adjusted status, be considered to be a qualified alien under section 431(b) of the Personal Responsibility and Work Opportunity Reconciliation Act of 1996 (8 U.S.C. 1641(b)), as amended by section 5302 of the Balanced Budget Act of 1997 (P.L. 105-33; 111 Stat. 598), for purposes of determining the alien's eligibility for supplemental security income benefits under title XVI of the Social Security Act (42 U.S.C. 1381 et seq.) or medical assistance under title XIX of such Act (42 U.S.C. 1396 et seq.).

(j) Period of applicability: Subsection (i) shall not apply after October 1, 2003.

(k)[12] [Report.] Not later than 6 months after the date of the enactment of this Act, and every 6 months thereafter (until all applications for adjustment of status under this section have been finally adjudicated), the Comptroller General of the United States shall submit to the Committees on the Judiciary and the Committees on Appropriations of the United States House of Representatives and the United States Senate report containing the following:

(1) (A) The number of aliens who applied for adjustment of status under subsection (a), including a breakdown specifying the number of such applicants who are described in subparagraph (A), (B), or (C) of subsection (b)(1), respectively.

(B) the number of aliens described in subparagraph (A) whose status was adjusted under this section, including breakdown described in the subparagraph.

12. Heading editorially supplied.

(2) (A) The number of aliens who applied for adjustment of status under subsection (d), including a breakdown specifying the number of such applicants who are sponsors, children, or unmarried sons or daughters described in such subsection, respectively.

(B) The number of aliens described in subparagraph (A) whose status was adjusted under this section, including breakdown described in the subparagraph. Appendix B, § 903

§ 903. Collection of data on detained asylum seekers

(a) In general: The Attorney General shall regularly collect data on a nation-wide basis with respect to asylum seekers in detention in the United States, including the following information:

(1) The number of detainees.

(2) An identification of the countries of origin of the detainees.

(3) The percentage of each gender within the total number of detainees.

(4) The number of detainees listed by each year of age of the detainees.

(5) The location of each detainee by detention facility.

(6) With respect to each facility where detainees are held, whether the facility is also used to detain criminals and whether any of the detainees are held in the same cells as criminals.

(7) The number and frequency of the transfers of detainees between detention facilities.

(8) The average length of detention and the number of detainees by category of the length of detention.

(9) The rate of release from detention of detainees for each district of the Immigration and Naturalization Service.

(10) A description of the disposition of cases.

(b) Annual reports: Beginning October 1, 1999, and not later than October 1 of each year thereafter, the Attorney General shall submit to the Committee on the Judiciary of each House of Congress a report setting forth the data collected under subsection (a) for the fiscal year ending September 30 of that year.

(c) Availability to public: Copies of the data collected under subsection (a) shall be made available to members of the public upon request pursuant to such

§ 904. Collection of data on other detained aliens Appendix B, § 904

(a) In general: The Attorney General shall regularly collect data on a nationwide basis on aliens being detained in the United States by the Immigration and Naturalization Service other than the aliens described in section 903, including the following information:

(1) The number of detainees who are criminal aliens and the number of detainees who are noncriminal aliens who are not seeking asylum.

(2) An identification of the ages, gender, and countries of origin of detainees within each category described in paragraph (1).

(3) The types of facilities, whether facilities of the Immigration and Naturalization Service or other Fed-

eral, State, or local facilities, in which each of the categories of detainees described in paragraph (1) are held.

(b) Length of detention, transfers, and dispositions:

a With respect to detainees who are criminal aliens and detainees who are noncriminal aliens who are not seeking asylum, the Attorney General shall also collect data concerning—

(1) the number and frequency of transfers between detention facilities for each category of detainee;

(2) the average length of detention of each category of detainee;

(3) for each category of detainee, the number of detainees who have been detained for the same length of time, in a 3-month increments;

(4) for each category of detainee, the rate of release from detention for each district of the Immigration and Naturalization Service; and

(5) for each category of detainee, the disposition of detention, including whether detention ended due to deportation, release on parole, or any other release.

(c) Criminal aliens: With respect to criminal aliens, the a Attorney General shall also collect data concerning

(1) the number of criminal aliens apprehended under the immigration laws and not detained by the Attorney General; and

(2) a list of crimes committed by criminal aliens after the decision was made not to detain them, to the extent this information can be derived by cross-checking the list of criminal aliens not detained with other databases accessible to the Attorney General.

(d) Annual reports: Beginning on October 1, 1999, and not later than October 1 of each year thereafter, the Attorney General shall submit to the Committee on the Judiciary of each House of Congress a report setting forth the data collected under subsections (a), (b), and (c) for the fiscal year ending September 30 of that year.

(e) Availability to public: Copies of the data collected under subsections (a), (b), and (c) shall be made available to members of the public upon request pursuant to such regulations as the Attorney General shall prescribe.

****

APPENDIX C — LIFE ACT (AS AMENDED)[13]

Title XI of H.R. 5548, enacted by reference in Pub. L. No. 106-553, 114 Stat. 2762A-142 (December 21, 2000)

Title XI — Encouraging Immigrant Family Reunification

13. As amended by the LIFE Act Amendments of 2000, enacted by reference in Pub. L. 106-554, 114 Stat. 2763A-324 (December 21, 2000). (Free-standing portions of the LIFE Act Amendments of 2000 are shown in Appendix D of this publication).

§ 1101. Short title Appendix C, § 1101

This title may be cited as

(1) the "Legal Immigration Family Equity Act"; or

(2) the "LIFE Act". Appendix C, § 1102

§ 1102. Nonimmigrant status for spouses and children of permanent residents awaiting the availability of an immigrant visa; provisions affecting subsequent adjustment of status for such nonimmigrants

(a) In general. Section 101(a)(15) of the Immigration and Nationality Act (8 U.S.C. 1101(a)(15)) is amended

(1) in subparagraph (T), by striking "or" at the end;

(2) in subparagraph (U), by striking the period at the end and inserting "; or"; and

(3) by adding at the end the following:

"(V) subject to section 214(o), an alien who is the beneficiary (including a child of the principal alien, if eligible to receive a visa under section 203(d)) of a petition to accord a status under section 203(a)(2)(A) that was filed with the Attorney General under section 204 on or before the date of the enactment of the Legal Immigration Family Equity Act, if—

"(i) such petition has been pending for 3 years or more; or

"(ii) such petition has been approved, 3 years or more have elapsed since such filing date, and

"(I) an immigrant visa is not immediately available to the alien because of a waiting list of applicants for visas under section 203(a)(2)(A); or

"(II) the alien's application for an immigrant visa, or the alien's application for adjustment of status under section 245, pursuant to the approval of such petition, remains pending."

(b) Provisions affecting nonimmigrant status. Section 214 of the Immigration and Nationality Act (8 U.S.C. 1184) is amended by adding at the end the following:

"(o)(1) In the case of a nonimmigrant described in section 101(a)(15)(V)

"(A) the Attorney General shall authorize the alien to engage in employment in the United States during the period of authorized admission and shall provide the alien with an 'employment authorized' endorsement or other appropriate document signifying authorization of employment; and

"(B) the period of authorized admission as such a nonimmigrant shall terminate 30 days after the date on which any of the following is denied:

"(i) The petition filed under section 204 to accord the alien a status under section 203(a)(2)(A) (or, in the case of a child granted nonimmigrant status based on eligibility to receive a visa under section 203(d), the petition filed to accord the child's parent a status under section 203(a)(2)(A)).

"(ii) The alien's application for an immigrant visa pursuant to the approval of such petition.

"(iii) The alien's application for adjustment of status under section 245 pursuant to the approval of such petition.

"(2) In determining whether an alien is eligible to be admitted to the United States as a nonimmigrant under section 101(a)(15)(V), the grounds for inadmissibility specified in section 212(a)(9)(B) shall not apply.

"(3) The status of an alien physically present in the United States may be adjusted by the Attorney General, in the discretion of the Attorney General and under such regulations as the Attorney General may prescribe, to that of a nonimmigrant under section 101(a)(15)(V), if the alien

"(A) applies for such adjustment;

"(B) satisfies the requirements of such section; and

"(C) is eligible to be admitted to the United States, except in determining such admissibility, the grounds for inadmissibility specified in paragraphs (6)(A), (7), and (9)(B) of section 212(a) shall not apply.".

(c)[14] Provisions affecting permanent resident status. Section 245 of the Immigration and Nationality Act (8 U.S.C. 1255) is amended by adding at the end the following:

(m) ***

(d) Conforming amendments

(1) Admission of nonimmigrants. Section 214 of the Immigration and Nationality Act (8 U.S.C. 1184) is amended, in each of subsections (b) and (h), by striking "(H)(i) or *(l)*" and inserting "(H)(i), *(l)*, or (V)".

(2) Adjustment of status—Section 245 of the Immigration and Nationality Act (8 U.S.C. 1255) is amended

(A) in each of subsections (d) and (f), by striking "under subsection (a)," each place such term appears and inserting "under subsection (a) or (m),"; and

(B) in subsection (e)(1), by striking "subsection (a)." and inserting "subsection (a) or (m).".

(e) Effective date. The amendments made by this section shall take effect on the date of the enactment of this Act and shall apply to an alien who is the beneficiary of a classification petition filed under section 204 of the Immigration and Nationality Act on or before the date of the enactment of this Act.

§ 1103. Nonimmigrant status for spouses and children of citizens awaiting the availability of an immigrant visa Appendix C, § 1103

(a) In general. Section 101(a)(15)(K) of the Immigration and Nationality Act (8 U.S.C. 1101(a)(15)(K)) is amended to read as follows:

"(K) subject to subsections (d) and (p) of section 214, an alien who

"(i) is the fiancée or fiancé of a citizen of the United States and who seeks to enter the United States solely to conclude a valid marriage with the petitioner within ninety days after admission;

"(ii) has concluded a valid marriage with a citizen of the United States who is the petitioner, is the beneficiary of a petition to accord a status under section 201(b)(2)(A)(i) that was filed under section 204 by the petitioner, and seeks to enter the United States to await the approval of such petition and the availability to the alien of an immigrant visa; or

"(iii) is the minor child of an alien described in clause (i) or (ii) and is accompanying, or following to join, the alien;".

(b) Provisions affecting nonimmigrant status. Section 214 of the Immigration and Nationality Act (8 U.S.C. 1184), as amended by section 2 of this Act, is further amended by adding at the end the following:

"(p) (1) A visa shall not be issued under the provisions of section 101(a)(15)(K)(ii) until the consular officer has received a petition filed in the United States by the spouse of the applying alien and approved by the Attorney General. The petition shall be in such form and contain such information as the Attorney General shall, by regulation, prescribe.

"(2) In the case of an alien seeking admission under section 101(a)(15)(K)(ii) who concluded a marriage with a citizen of the United States outside the United States, the alien shall be considered inadmissible under section 212(a)(7)(B) if the alien is not at the time of application for admission in possession of a valid nonimmigrant visa issued by a consular officer in the foreign state in which the marriage was concluded.

"(3) In the case of a nonimmigrant described in section 101(a)(15)(K)(ii), and any child of such a nonimmigrant who was admitted as accompanying, or following to join, such a nonimmigrant, the period of authorized admission shall terminate 30 days after the date on which any of the following is denied:[15]

"(A) The petition filed under section 204 to accord the principal alien status under section 201(b)(2)(A)(i).

"(B) The principal alien's application for an immigrant visa pursuant to the approval of such petition.

"(C) The principal alien's application for adjustment of status under section 245 pursuant to the approval of such petition.".

(c) Conforming amendments

(1) Admission of nonimmigrants. Section 214(d) of the Immigration and Nationality Act (8 U.S.C. 1184(d)) is amended bystriking"101(a)(15)(K)"andinserting"101(a)(15)(K)(i)".

(2) Conditional permanent resident status. Section 216 of the Immigration and Nationality Act (8 U.S.C. 1186a) is amended, in each of subsections (b)(1)(B) and (d)(1)(A)(ii), by striking "214(d)" and inserting "subsection (d) or (p) of section 214".

(3) Adjustment of status. Section 245 of the Immigration and Nationality Act (8 U.S.C. 1255) is amended—

(A) in subsection (d), by striking "(relating to an alien fiancée or fiancé or the minor child of such alien)"; and

(B) in subsection (e)(3), by striking "214(d)" and inserting "subsection (d) or (p) of section 214".

(d) Effective date. The amendments made by this section shall take effect on the date of the enactment of this Act and shall apply to an alien who is the beneficiary of a classification petition filed under section 204

14. This amendment, which was intended to create a new 245(m) was repealed before it was enacted by § 1502(b) of the LIFE Act Amendments of 2000, enacted by reference in P.L. 106-554, 114 Stat. 2763A-324 (December 21, 2000).

15. Sic. Nonconforming punctuation using a colon and periods in following three subparagraphs are errors in original (should be dash and semicolons respectively).

of the Immigration and Nationality Act before, on, or after the date of the enactment of this Act.

§ 1104. Adjustment of status of certain class action participants who entered before January 11 1982, to that of person admitted for lawful residence Appendix C, § 1104

(a) In general. In the case of an eligible alien described in subsection (b), the provisions of section 245A of the Immigration and Nationality Act (8 U.S.C. 1255a), as modified by subsection (c), shall apply to the alien.

(b) Eligible aliens described. An alien is an eligible alien described in this subsection if, before October 1, 2000, the alien filed with the Attorney General a written claim for class membership, with or without a filing fee, pursuant to a court order issued in the case of—

(1) Catholic Social Services, Inc. v. Meese, vacated sub nom. Renov. Catholic Social Services, Inc., 509 U.S. 43 (1993);

(2) League of United Latin American Citizens v. INS, vacated sub nom. Reno v. Catholic Social Services, Inc., 509 U.S. 43 (1993) and

(3) Zambrano v. INS, vacated sub nom. Immigration and Naturalization Service v. Zambrano, 509 U.S. 918 (1993).[16]

(c) Modifications to provisions governing adjustment of status. The modifications to section 245A of the Immigration and Nationality Act that apply to an eligible alien described in subsection (b) of this section are the following:

(1) Temporary resident status. Subsection (a) of such section 245A shall not apply.

(2) Adjustment to permanent resident status. In lieu of paragraphs (1) and (2) of subsection (b) of such section 245A, the Attorney General shall be required to adjust the status of an eligible alien described in subsection (b) of this section to that of an alien lawfully admitted for permanent residence if the alien meets the following requirements:

(A) Application period. The alien must file with the Attorney General an application for such adjustment during the 12-month period beginning on the date on which the Attorney General issues final regulations to implement this section.

(B) Continuous unlawful residence

(i) In general. The alien must establish that the alien entered the United States before January 11 1982, and that he or she has resided continuously in the United States in an unlawful status since such date and through May 41 1988. In determining whether an alien maintained continuous unlawful residence in the United States for purposes of this subparagraph, the regulations prescribed by the Attorney General under section 245A(g) of the Immigration and Nationality Act that were most recently in effect before the date of the enactment of this Act shall apply.

16. Added by § 1503 of LIFE Act Amendments of 2000, enacted by reference in P.L. 106-554, 114 Stat. 2763A-324 (December 21, 2000).

(ii) Nonimmigrants. In the case of an alien who entered the United States as a nonimmigrant before January 11 1982, the alien must establish that the alien's period of authorized stay as a nonimmigrant expired before such date through the passage of time or the alien's unlawful status was known to the Government as of such date.

(iii) Exchange visitors. If the alien was at any time a nonimmigrant exchange alien (as defined in section 101(a)(15)(J) of the Immigration and Nationality Act (8 U.S.C. 1101(a)(15)(J)), the alien must establish that the alien was not subject to the two-year foreign residence requirement of section 212(e) of such Act or has fulfilled that requirement or received a waiver thereof.

(iv) Cuban and Haitian entrants. For purposes of this section, an alien in the status of a Cuban and Haitian entrant described in paragraph (1) or (2)(A) of section 501(e) of P.L. 96-422 shall be considered to have entered the United States and to be in an unlawful status in the United States.

(C) Continuous physical presence

(i) In general. The alien must establish that the alien was continuously physically present in the United States during the period beginning on November 61 1986, and ending on May 41 1988, except that—

(I) an alien shall not be considered to have failed to maintain continuous physical presence in the United States for purposes of this subparagraph by virtue of brief, casual, and innocent absences from the United States; and

(II) brief, casual, and innocent absences from the United States shall not be limited to absences with advance parole.

(ii) Admissions. Nothing in this section shall be construed as authorizing an alien to apply for admission to, or to be admitted to, the United States in order to apply for adjustment of status under this section or section 245A of the Immigration and Nationality Act.

(D) Admissible as immigrant. The alien must establish that the alien—

(i) is admissible to the United States as an immigrant, except as otherwise provided under section 245A(d)(2) of the Immigration and Nationality Act;

(ii) has not been convicted of any felony or of three or more misdemeanors committed in the United States;

(iii) has not assisted in the persecution of any person or persons on account of race, religion, nationality, membership in a particular social group, or political opinion; and

(iv) is registered or registering under the Military Selective Service Act, if the alien is required to be so registered under that Act.

(E) Basic citizenship skills

(i) In general. The alien must demonstrate that the alien either—

(I) meets the requirements of section 312(a) of the Immigration and Nationality Act (8 U.S.C. 1423(a)) (relating to minimal understanding of ordinary English and a knowledge and understanding of the history and government of the United States); or

(II) is satisfactorily pursuing a course of study (recognized by the Attorney General) to achieve such an understanding of English and such a knowledge and understanding of the history and government of the United States.

(ii) Exception for elderly or developmentally disabled individual. The Attorney General may, in the discretion of the Attorney General, waive all or part of the requirements of clause (i) in the case of an alien who is 65 years of age or older or who is developmentally disabled.

(iii) Relation to naturalization examination. In accordance with regulations of the Attorney General, an alien who has demonstrated under clause (i)(I) that the alien meets the requirements of section 312(a) of the Immigration and Nationality Act may be considered to have satisfied the requirements of that section for purposes of becoming naturalized as a citizen of the United States under title III of such Act.

(3) Temporary stay of removal, authorized travel, and employment during pendency of application. In lieu of subsections (b)(3) and (e)(2) of such section 245A, the Attorney General shall provide that, in the case of an eligible alien described in subsection (b) of this section who presents a prima facie application for adjustment of status to that of an alien lawfully admitted for permanent residence under such section 245A during the application period described in paragraph (2)(A), until a final determination on the application has been made

(A) the alien may not be deported or removed from the United States;

(B) the Attorney General shall, in accordance with regulations, permit the alien to return to the United States after such brief and casual trips abroad as reflect an intention on the part of the alien to adjust to lawful permanent resident status and after brief temporary trips abroad occasioned by a family obligation involving an occurrence such as the illness or death of a close relative or other family need; and

(C) the Attorney General shall grant the alien authorization to engage in employment in the United States and provide to that alien an "employment authorized" endorsement or other appropriate work permit.

(4) Applications. Paragraphs (1) through (4) of subsection (c) of such section 245A shall not apply.

(5) Confidentiality of information. Subsection (c)(5) of such section 245A shall apply to information furnished by an eligible alien described in subsection (b) pursuant to any application filed under such section 245A or this section, except that the Attorney General (and other officials and employees of the Department of Justice and any bureau or agency thereof) may use such information for purposes of rescinding, pursuant to section 246(a) of the Immigration and Nationality Act (8 U.S.C. 1256(a)), any adjustment of status obtained by the alien.

(6) Use of fees for immigration—related unfair employment practices. Notwithstanding subsection (c)(7)(C) of such section 245A, no application fee paid to the Attorney General pursuant to this section by an eligible alien described in subsection (b) of this section shall be available in any fiscal year for the purpose described in such subsection (c)(7)(C).

(7) Temporary stay of removal and work authorization for certain applicants before application period. In lieu of subsection (e)(1) of such section 245A, the Attorney General shall provide that in the case of an eligible alien described in subsection (b) of this section who is apprehended before the beginning of the application period described in paragraph (2)(A) and who can establish a prima facie case of eligibility to have his status adjusted under such section 245A pursuant to this section (but for the fact that he may not apply for such adjustment until the beginning of such period), until the alien has had the opportunity during the first 30 days of the application period to complete the filing of an application for adjustment, the alien

(A) may not be deported or removed from the United States; and

(B) shall be granted authorization to engage in employment in the United States and be provided an "employment authorized" endorsement or other appropriate work permit.

(8) Jurisdiction of courts. Effective as of November 61 1986, subsection (f)(4)(C) of such section 245A shall not apply to an eligible alien described in subsection (b) of this section.

(9) Public welfare assistance. Subsection (h) of such section 245A shall not apply.

(10)[17] Conforming application of consent provision. In addition to the waivers provided in subsection (d)(2) of such section 245A of the Immigration and Nationality Act, the Attorney General may grant the alien a waiver of the grounds of inadmissibility under subparagraphs (A) and (C) of section 212(a)(9) of such Act (8 U.S.C. 1182(a)(9)). In granting such waivers, the Attorney General shall use standards used in granting consent under subparagraphs (A)(iii) and (C)(ii) of such section.

(d) Applications from abroad. The Attorney General shall establish a process under which an alien who has become eligible to apply for adjustment of status to that of an alien lawfully admitted for permanent residence as a result of the enactment of this section and who is not physically present in the United States may apply for such adjustment from abroad.

(e) Deadline for regulations. The Attorney General shall issue regulations to implement this section not later than 120 days after the date of the enactment of this Act.

(f) Administrative and judicial review. The provisions of subparagraphs (A) and (B) of section 245A(f)(4) of the Immigration and Nationality Act (8 U.S.C. 1255a (f)(4)) shall apply to administrative or judicial review of a determination under this section or of a determination respecting an application for adjustment of status under section 245A of the Immigration and Nationality Act filed pursuant to this section.

17. Added by § 1503(b) of LIFE Act Amendments of 2000, en- acted by reference in Pub. L. 106-554, 114 Stat. 2763A-324 (December 21, 2000).

(g)[18] In applicability of removal order reinstatement. Section 241(a)(5) of the Immigration and Nationality Act shall not apply with respect to an alien who is applying for adjustment of status under this section.

(h)[19] Definition. For purposes of this section, the term "such section 245A" means section 245A of the Immigration and Nationality Act (8 U.S.C. 1255a).

****

APPENDIX D — LIFE ACT AMENDMENTS OF 2000[20]

Title XV of HR 5666, enacted by reference in P.L.106-554, 114 Stat. 2763A-324(December 21, 2000)

§ 1501. Short title Appendix D, § 1501

This title may be cited as the "LIFE Act Amendments of 2000".

***

§ 1504. Application of family unity provisions to spouses and unmarried children of certain LIFE Act beneficiaries Appendix D, § 1504

(a) Immigration benefits. Except as provided in subsection (d), in the case of an eligible spouse or child (as described in subsection (b)), the Attorney General

(1) shall not remove the alien on a ground specified in paragraph (1)(A), (1)(B), (1)(C), or (3)(A) of section 237(a) of the Immigration and Nationality Act (8 U.S.C. 1227(a)), other than so much of paragraph (1)(A) of such section as relates to a ground of inadmissibility described in paragraph (2) or (3) of section 212(a) of such Act (8 U.S.C. 1182(a)); and

(2) shall authorize the alien to engage in employment in the United States during the period of time in which protection is provided under paragraph (1) and shall provide the alien with an "employment authorized" endorsement or other appropriate document signifying authorization of employment.

(b) Eligible spouses and children. For purposes of this section, the term "eligible spouse or child" means an alien who is the spouse or unmarried child of an alien described in section 1104(b) of the Legal Immigration Family Equity Act if the spouse or child

(1) entered the United States before December 11 1988; and

(2) resided in the United States on such date.

(c) Process for relief for eligible spouses and children outside the United States. If an alien has obtained lawful permanent resident status under section 1104 of the Legal Immigration Family Equity Act and the alien has an eligible spouse or child who is no longer physically present in the United States, the Attorney General shall establish a process under which the eligible spouse or child may be paroled into the United States in order to obtain the benefits of subsection (a) unless the Attorney General finds that the spouse or child would be inadmissible or deportable on any ground, other than a ground for which the alien would not be subject to removal under subsection (a)(1). An alien so paroled shall not be treated as paroled into the United States for purposes of section 201(c)(4) of the Immigration and Nationality Act (8 U.S.C. 1151(c)(4)).

(d) Exception. An alien is not eligible for the benefits of this section if the Attorney General finds that—

(1) the alien has been convicted of a felony or three or more misdemeanors in the United States; or

(2) the alien is described in section 241(b)(3)(B) of the Immigration and Nationality Act (8 U.S.C. 1231(b)(3)(B)).

(e) Application of definitions. Except as otherwise specifically provided in this section, the definitions contained in the Immigration and Nationality Act shall apply in the administration of this section.

§ 1505. Miscellaneous amendments to various adjustment and relief acts Appendix D, § 1505

(a) Nicaraguan Adjustment and Central American Relief Act.

(1) In general. Section 202(a) of the Nicaraguan Adjustment and Central American Relief Act is amended

***

(2) Permitting motion to reopen. Not withstanding any time and number limitations imposed by law on motions to reopen exclusion, removal, or deportation proceedings (except limitations premised on an alien's conviction of an aggravated felony (as defined by section 101(a) of the Immigration and Nationality Act)), a national of Cuba or Nicaragua who has become eligible for adjustment of status under the Nicaraguan Adjustment and Central American Relief Act as a result of the amendments made by paragraph (1), may file one motion to reopen exclusion, deportation, or removal proceedings to apply for such adjustment under that Act. The scope of any proceeding reopened on this basis shall be limited to a determination of the alien's eligibility for adjustment of status under that Act. All such motions shall be filed within 180 days of the date of the enactment of this Act.

(b) Haitian Refugee Immigration Fairness Act of 1998.

(1) Inapplicability of certain provisions. Section 902(a) of the Haitian Refugee Immigration Fairness Act of 1998 is amended

***

(2) Permitting motion to reopen. Not withstanding any time and number limitations imposed by law on motions to reopen exclusion, removal, or deportation proceedings (except limitations premised on an alien's conviction of an aggravated felony (as defined by section 101(a) of the Immigration and Nationality Act)),

18. Id.
19. Redesignated by P.L. 106-554, 114 Stat. 2763A-324 (December 21, 2000).
20. Only the free-standing provisions of the LIFE Act Amendments of 2000 are shown here since the amendments to the INA and other provisions of law are incorporated therein.

a national of Haiti who has become eligible for adjustment of status under the Haitian Refugee Immigration Fairness Act of 1998 as a result of the amendments made by paragraph (1), may file one motion to reopen exclusion, deportation, or removal proceedings to apply for such adjustment under that Act. The scope of any proceeding reopened on this basis shall be limited to a determination of the alien's eligibility for adjustment of status under that Act. All such motions shall be filed within 180 days of the date of the enactment of this Act.

***

§ 1506. Effective date Appendix D, § 1506

This title shall take effect as if included in the enactment of the Legal Immigration Family Equity Act.

****

APPENDIX E — IIRIRA

Illegal Immigration Reform and Immigrant Responsibility Act of 1996

Sections 308 (excerpt), 309; Title IV, Subtitle A: Sections 401 through 405, 641 and 642 of P.L. 104-208, 110 Stat. 3009-546 (Sept. 30, 1996) (As amended)[21]

Free-standing Transitional, Effective Dates, Savings, Monitoring, Pilot Program, and Interagency Communication Provisions of IIRIRA

§ 308. * Appendix E, § 308**

(g) Conforming references to reorganized sections.

(1) References to sections 232, 234, 238, 239, 240, 241, 242A, and 244A. Any reference in law in effect on the day before the date of the enactment of this Act to section 232, 234, 238, 239, 240, 241, 242A, or 244A of the Immigration and Nationality Act (or a subdivision of such section) is deemed, as of the title III-A effective date, to refer to section 232(a), 232(b), 233, 234, 234A, 237, 238, or 244 of such Act (or the corresponding subdivision of such section), as redesignated by this subtitle. Any reference in law to section 241(or a subdivision of such section) of the Immigration and Nationality Act in an amendment made by a subsequent subtitle of this title is deemed a reference (as of the title III-A effective date) to section 237(or the corresponding subdivision of such section), as redesignated by this subtitle.

***

21. See footnotes citing relevant amendments at affected sections.

§ 309[22]. Effective dates; transition Appendix E, § 309

(a) In general. Except as provided in this section and sections 303(b)(2), 306(c), 308(d)(2)(D), or 308(d)(5) of this division, this subtitle and the amendments made by this subtitle shall take effect on the first day of the first month beginning more than 180 days after the date of the enactment of this Act (in this title referred to as the "title III-A effective date").

(b) Promulgation of regulations. The Attorney General shall first promulgate regulations to carry out this subtitle by not later than 30 days before the title III-A effective date.

(c)[23] Transition for certain aliens.

(1) General rule that new rules do not apply. Subject to the succeeding provisions of this subsection, in the case of an alien who is in exclusion or deportation proceedings as of the title III-A effective date—

(A) the amendments made by this subtitle shall not apply, and

(B) the proceedings (including judicial review thereof) shall continue to be conducted without regard to such amendments.

(2) Attorney General option to elect to apply new procedures. In a case described in paragraph (1) in which an evidentiary hearing under section 236 or 242 and 242B of the Immigration and Nationality Act has not commenced as of the title III-A effective date, the Attorney General may elect to proceed under chapter 4 of title II of such Act (as amended by this subtitle). The Attorney General shall provide notice of such election to the alien involved not later than 30 days before the date any evidentiary hearing is commenced. If the Attorney General makes such election, the notice of hearing provided to the alien under section 235 or 242(a) of such Act shall be valid as if provided under section 239 of such Act (as amended by this subtitle) to confer jurisdiction on the immigration judge.

(3) Attorney General option to terminate and reinitiate proceedings. In the case described in paragraph (1), the Attorney General may elect to terminate proceedings in which there has not been a final administrative decision and to reinitiate proceedings under chapter 4 of title II the Immigration and Nationality Act (as amended by this subtitle). Any determination in the terminated proceeding shall not be binding in the reinitiated proceeding.

(4) Transitional changes in judicial review. In the case described in paragraph (1) in which a final order

22. As amended by P.L. 105-100, 111 Stat. 2193 (November 19, 1997), District of Columbia Appropriations, FY 1998, (Containing the Nicaraguan and Central American Relief Act of 1997 [NACARA]); VTVPA is the Victims of Trafficking and Violence Protection Act of 2000 (includes the Battered Immigrant Women Protection Act of 2000 [BIWPA]) P.L. 106-386, 114 Stat. 1464 (October 28, 2000) and LIFE, enacted by reference in P.L. 106-553, 114 Stat. 2762A-142 (December 21, 2000) (as amended by the LIFE Act Amendments of 2000, enacted by reference in P.L. 106-554, 114 Stat. 2763A-324 (December 21, 2000)).

23. Id.

of exclusion or deportation is entered more than 30 days after the date of the enactment of this Act, notwithstanding any provision of section 106 of the Immigration and Nationality Act (as in effect as of the date of the enactment of this Act) to the contrary—

(A) in the case of judicial review of a final order of exclusion, subsection (b) of such section shall not apply and the action for judicial review shall be governed by the provisions of subsections (a) and (c) of such in the same manner as they apply to judicial review of orders of deportation;

(B) a court may not order the taking of additional evidence under section 2347(c) of title 28, United States Code;

(C) the petition for judicial review must be filed not later than 30 days after the date of the final order of exclusion or deportation;

(D) the petition for review shall be filed with the court of appeals for the judicial circuit in which the administrative proceedings before the special inquiry officer or immigration judge were completed;

(E) there shall be no appeal of any discretionary decision under section 212(c), 212(h), 212(i), 244, or 245 of the Immigration and Nationality Act (as in effect as of the date of the enactment of this Act);

(F) service of the petition for review shall not stay the deportation of an alien pending the court's decision on the petition, unless the court orders otherwise; and

(G) there shall be no appeal permitted in the case of an alien who is inadmissible or deportable by reason of having committed a criminal offense covered in section 212(a)(2) or section 241(a)(2)(A)(iii), (B), (C), or (D) of the Immigration and Nationality Act (as in effect as of the date of the enactment of this Act), or any offense covered by section 241(a)(2)(A)(ii) of such Act (as in effect on such date) for which both predicate offenses are, without regard to their date of commission, otherwise covered by section 241(a)(2)(A)(i) of such Act (as so in effect).

(5) Transitional rules with regard to suspension of deportation.

(A) In general. Subject to subparagraphs (B) and (C), paragraphs (1) and (2) of section 240A(d) of the Immigration and Nationality Act (relating to continuous residence or physical presence) shall apply to orders to show cause (including those referred to in section 242B(a)(1) of the Immigration and Nationality Act, as in effect before the title III-A effective date), issued before, on, or after the date of the enactment of this Act.

(B) Exception for certain orders. In any case in which the Attorney General elects to terminate and reinitiate proceedings in accordance with paragraph (3) of this subsection, paragraphs (1) and (2) of section 240A(d) of the Immigration and Nationality Act shall not apply to an order to show cause issued before April 1, 1997.

(C) Special rule for certain aliens granted temporary protection from deportation and for battered spouses and children.

(i) In general. For purposes of calculating the period of continuous physical presence under section 244(a) of the Immigration and Nationality Act (as in effect before the title III-A effective date) or section 240A of such Act (as in effect after the title III-A effective date), subparagraph (A) and paragraphs (1) and (2) of section 240A(d) of the Immigration and Nationality Act shall not apply in the case of an alien, regardless of whether the alien is in exclusion or deportation proceedings before the title III-A effective date, who has not been convicted at any time of an aggravated felony (as defined in section 101(a) of the Immigration and Nationality Act) and—

(I) was not apprehended after December 19, 1990, at the time of entry, and is—

(aa) a Salvadoran national who first entered the United States on or before September 19, 1990, and who registered for benefits pursuant to the settlement agreement in American Baptist Churches, et al. v. Thornburgh (ABC), 760 F. Supp. 796 (N. D. Cal. 1991) on or before October 31, 1991, or applied for temporary protected status on or before October 31, 1991; or

(bb) a Guatemalan national who first entered the United States on or before October 1, 1990, and who registered for benefits pursuant to such settlement agreement on or before December 31, 1991;

(II) is a Guatemalan or Salvadoran national who filed an application for asylum with the Immigration and Naturalization Service on or before April 1, 1990;

(III) is the spouse or child (as defined in section 101(b)(1) of the Immigration and Nationality Act) of an individual, at the time a decision is rendered to suspend the deportation, or cancel the removal, of such individual, if the individual has been determined to be described in this clause (excluding this subclause and subclause (IV));

(IV) is the unmarried son or daughter of an alien parent, at the time a decision is rendered to suspend the deportation, or cancel the removal, of such alien parent, if—

(aa) the alien parent has been determined to be described in this clause (excluding this subclause and subclause (III)); and

(bb) in the case of a son or daughter who is 21 years of age or older at the time such decision is rendered, the son or daughter entered the United States on or before October 1, 1990;

(V) is an alien who entered the United States on or before December 31, 1990, who filed an application for asylum on or before December 31, 1991, and who, at the time of filing such application, was a national of the Soviet Union, Russia, any republic of the former Soviet Union, Latvia, Estonia, Lithuania, Poland, Czechoslovakia, Romania, Hungary, Bulgaria, Albania, East Germany, Yugoslavia, or any state of the former Yugoslavia; or

(VI)[24] is an alien who was issued an order to show cause or was in deportation proceedings before April 1, 1997, and who applied for suspension of deportation under section 244(a)(3) of the Immigration and

24. Added by § 1506(b)(3)(B) of BIWPA, P.L. 106-386, 114 Stat. 1528 (October 28, 2000). Effective as if included in the enactment of IIRIRA.

Nationality Act (as in effect before the date of the enactment of this Act); or

(VII)[25](aa) was the spouse or child of an alien described in subclause (I), (II), or (V)(AA) at the time at which a decision is rendered to suspend the deportation or cancel the removal of the alien;

(BB) at the time at which the alien filed an application for suspension of deportation or cancellation of removal; or

(CC) at the time at which the alien registered for benefits under the settlement agreement in American Baptist Churches, et. al. v. Thornburgh (ABC), applied for temporary protected status, or applied for asylum; and

(bb) the spouse, child, or child of the spouse has been battered or subjected to extreme cruelty by the alien described in subclause (I), (II), or (V).

(ii) Limitation on judicial review. A determination by the Attorney General as to whether an alien satisfies the requirements of this clause (i) is final and shall not be subject to review by any court. Nothing in the preceding sentence shall be construed as limiting the application of section 242(a)(2)(B) of the Immigration and Nationality Act (as in effect after the title III-A effective date) to other eligibility determinations pertaining to discretionary relief under this Act.

(iii)[26] Consideration of petitions. In acting on a petition filed under subclause (VII) of clause (i) the provisions set forth in section 204(a)(1)(H) shall apply.

(iv)[27] Residence with spouse or parent not required. For purposes of the application of clause (i)(VII), a spouse or child shall not be required to demonstrate that he or she is residing with the spouse or parent in the United States.

(6) Transition for certain family unity aliens. The Attorney General may waive the application of section 212(a)(9) of the Immigration and Nationality Act, as inserted by section 301(b)(1) of this division, in the case of an alien who is provided benefits under the provisions of section 301 of the Immigration Act of 1990 (relating to family unity).

(7) Limitation on suspension of deportation. The Attorney General may not suspend the deportation and adjust the status under section 244 of the Immigration and Nationality Act of more than 4,000 aliens in any fiscal year (beginning after the date of the enactment of this Act). The previous sentence shall apply regardless of when an alien applied for such suspension and adjustment.

(d) Transitional references. For purposes of carrying out the Immigration and Nationality Act, as amended by this subtitle—

(1) any reference in section 212(a)(1)(A) of such Act to the term "inadmissible" is deemed to include a reference to the term "excludable", and

(2) any reference in law to an order of removal shall be deemed to include a reference to an order of exclusion and deportation or an order of deportation.

(e) Transition. No period of time before the date of the enactment of this Act shall be included in the period of 1 year described in section 212(a)(6)(B)(i) of the Immigration and Nationality Act (as amended by section 301(c) of this division).

(f) Special rule for cancellation of removal.

(1) In general. Subject to the provisions of the Immigration and Nationality Act (as in effect after the title III-A effective date), other than subsections (b)(1), (d)(1), and (e) of section 240A of such Act (but including section 242(a)(2)(B) of such Act), the Attorney General may, under section 240A of such Act, cancel removal of, and adjust to the status of an alien lawfully admitted for permanent residence, an alien who is inadmissible or deportable from the United States, if the alien applies for such relief, the alien is described in subsection (c)(5)(C)(i) of this section, and

(A) the alien—

(i) is not inadmissible or deportable under paragraph (2) or (3) of section 212(a) or paragraph (2), (3), or (4) of section 237(a) of the Immigration and Nationality Act and is not an alien described in section 241(b)(3)(B)(i) of such Act;

(ii) has been physically present in the United States for a continuous period of not less than 7 years immediately preceding the date of such application;

(iii) has been a person of good moral character during such period; and

(iv) establishes that removal would result in extreme hardship to the alien or to the alien's spouse, parent, or child, who is a citizen of the United States or an alien lawfully admitted for permanent residence; or

(B) the alien—

(i) is inadmissible or deportable under section 212(a)(2), 237(a)(2) (other than 237(a)(2)(A)(iii)), or 237(a)(3) of the Immigration and Nationality Act;

(ii) is not an alien described in section 241(b)(3)(B)(i) or 101(a)(43) of such Act;

(iii) has been physically present in the United States for a continuous period of not less than 10 years immediately following the commission of an act, or the assumption of a status, constituting a ground for removal;

(iv) has been a person of good moral character during such period; and

(v) establishes that removal would result in exceptional and extremely unusual hardship to the alien or to the alien's spouse, parent, or child, who is a citizen of the United States or an alien lawfully admitted for permanent residence.

(2) Treatment of certain breaks in presence. Section 240A(d)(2) shall apply for purposes of calculating any period of continuous physical presence under this subsection, except that the reference to subsection (b)(1) in such section shall be considered to be a reference to paragraph (1) of this section.

(g) Motions to reopen deportation or removal proceedings. Notwithstanding any limitation imposed by law on motions to reopen removal or deportation

25. Added by § 1510(b) of BIWPA, P.L. 106-386, 114 Stat. 1531(October 28, 2000).

26. Id.

27. Id.

proceedings (except limitations premised on an alien's conviction of an aggravated felony (as defined in section 101(a) of the Immigration and Nationality Act)), any alien who has become eligible for cancellation of removal or suspension of deportation as a result of the amendments made by section 203 of the Nicaraguan Adjustment and Central American Relief Act may file one motion to reopen removal or deportation proceedings to apply for cancellation of removal or suspension of deportation. The Attorney General shall designate a specific time period in which all such motions to reopen are required to be filed. The period shall begin not later than 60 days after the date of the enactment of the Nicaraguan Adjustment and Central American Relief Act and shall extend for a period not to exceed 240 days.

(h)[28] Relief and motions to reopen.

(1) Relief. An alien described in subsection (c)(5)(C)(i) who is otherwise eligible for—

(A) suspension of deportation pursuant to section 244(a) of the Immigration and Nationality Act, as in effect before the title III-A effective date; or

(B) cancellation of removal, pursuant to section 240A(b) of the Immigration and Nationality Act and subsection (f) of this section;

shall not be barred from applying for such relief by operation of section 241(a)(5) of the Immigration and National Act, as in effect after the title III-A effective date.

(2) Additional motion to reopen permitted. Notwithstanding any limitation imposed by law on motions to reopen removal or deportation proceedings (except limitations premised on an alien's conviction of an aggravated felony (as defined by section 101(a) of the Immigration and Nationality Act)), any alien who is described in subsection (c)(5)(C)(i) and who has become eligible for cancellation of removal or suspension of deportation as a result of the enactment of paragraph (1) may file one motion to reopen removal or deportation proceedings in order to apply for cancellation of removal or suspension of deportation. The scope of any proceeding reopened on this basis shall be limited to a determination of the alien's eligibility for cancellation of removal or suspension of deportation. The Attorney General shall designate a specific time period in which all such motions to reopen are required to be filed. The period shall begin not later than 60 days after the date of the enactment of this subsection and shall extend for a period not to exceed 240 days.

(3) Construction. Nothing in this subsection shall preclude an alien from filing a motion to reopen pursuant to section 240(b)(5)(C)(ii) of the Immigration and Nationality Act, or section 242B(c)(3)(B) of such Act (as in effect before the title III-A effective date).

***

28. Added by § 1505 of the LIFE Act Amendments of 2000, enacted by reference in P.L. 106-554, 114 Stat. 2763A-327 (December 21, 2000), eff. as if included in the LIFE Act.

Title IV — Enforcement of Restrictions against Employment[29]

Subtitle A — Pilot Programs for Employment Eligibility Confirmation

§ 401.[30] Establishment of programs Appendix E, § 401

(a) In general. The Secretary of Homeland Security shall conduct 3 pilot programs of employment eligibility confirmation under this subtitle.

(b) Implementation deadline; termination. The Secretary of Homeland Security shall implement the pilot programs in a manner that permits persons and other entities to have elections under section 402 of this division made and in effect no later than 1 year after the date of the enactment of this Act [enacted Sept. 30, 1996]. Unless the Congress otherwise provides, the Secretary of Homeland Security shall terminate a pilot program at the end of the 11-year period[31] beginning on the first day the pilot program is in effect.

(c) Scope of operation of pilot programs. The Secretary of Homeland Security shall provide for the operation—

(1)[32] of the basic pilot program (described in section 403(a) of this division) in, at a minimum, 5 of the 7 States with the highest estimated population of aliens who are not lawfully present in the United States, and the Secretary of Homeland Security shall expand the operation of the program to all 50 States not later than December 1, 2004;

(2) of the citizen attestation pilot program (described in section 403(b) of this division) in at least 5 States (or, if fewer, all of the States) that meet the condition described in section 403(b)(2)(A) of this division; and

(3) of the machine-readable-document pilot program (described in section 403(c) of this division) in at least 5 States (or, if fewer, all of the States) that meet the condition described in section 403(c)(2) of this division.

(d) References in subtitle. In this subtitle—

(1) Pilot program references. The terms "program" or "pilot program" refer to any of the 3 pilot programs provided for under this subtitle.

29. Amended by P.L. 108-156, § 3(d), 117 Stat. 1945 (December 3, 2003) to replace "Attorney General" with "Secretary of Homeland Security" each place it appears.

30. As amended by P.L. 107-128, § 2, 115 Stat. 2407 (January 16, 2002).

31. Changed from "6-year period" by P.L. 108-156, § 2, 117 Stat. 1944 (December 3, 2003)

32. Amended by P.L. 108-156, § 3(a), 117 Stat. 1944 (December 3, 2003)

(2) Confirmation system. The term "confirmation system" means the confirmation system established under section 404 of this division.

(3) References to section 274A. Any reference in this subtitle to section 274A (or a subdivision of such section) is deemed a reference to such section (or subdivision thereof) of the Immigration and Nationality Act.

(4) I-9 or similar form. The term "I-9 or similar form" means the form used for purposes of section 274A(b)(1)(A) or such other form as the Secretary of Homeland Security determines to be appropriate.

(5) Limited application to recruiters and referrers. Any reference to recruitment or referral (or a recruiter or referrer) in relation to employment is deemed a reference only to such recruitment or referral (or recruiter or referrer) that is subject to section 274A(a)(1)(B)(ii).

(6) United States citizenship. The term "United States citizenship" includes United States nationality.

(7) State. The term "State" has the meaning given such term in section 101(a)(36) of the Immigration and Nationality Act.

§ 402.[33] Voluntary election to participate in a pilot program Appendix E, § 402

(a) Voluntary election. Subject to subsection (c)(3)(B), any person or other entity that conducts any hiring (or recruitment or referral) in a State in which a pilot program is operating may elect to participate in that pilot program. Except as specifically provided in subsection (e), the Secretary of Homeland Security may not require any person or other entity to participate in a pilot program.

(b) Benefit of rebuttable presumption.

(1) In general. If a person or other entity is participating in a pilot program and obtains confirmation of identity and employment eligibility in compliance with the terms and conditions of the program with respect to the hiring (or recruitment or referral) of an individual for employment in the United States, the person or entity has established a rebuttable presumption that the person or entity has not violated section 274A(a)(1)(A) with respect to such hiring (or such recruitment or referral).

(2) Construction. Paragraph (1) shall not be construed as preventing a person or other entity that has an election in effect under subsection (a) from establishing an affirmative defense under section 274A(a)(3) if the person or entity complies with the requirements of section 274A(a)(1)(B) but fails to obtain confirmation under paragraph (1).

(c)[34] General terms of elections.

(1) In general. An election under subsection (a) shall be in such form and manner, under such terms and conditions, and shall take effect, as the Secretary of Homeland Security shall specify. The Secretary of Homeland Security may not impose any fee as a condition of making an election or participating in a pilot program.

(2) Scope of election.

(A) In general. Subject to paragraph (3), any electing person or other entity may provide that the election under subsection (a) shall apply (during the period in which the election is in effect)—

(i) to all its hiring (and all recruitment or referral) in the State (or States) in which the pilot program is operating, or

(ii) to its hiring (or recruitment or referral) in one or more pilot program States or one or more places of hiring (or recruitment or referral, as the case may be) in the pilot program States.

(B)[35] Application of programs in non-pilot program states. In addition, the Secretary of Homeland Security may permit a person or entity electing the citizen attestation pilot program (described in 403(b) of this division) or the machine-readable-document pilot program (described in section 403(c) of this division) to provide that the election applies to its hiring (or recruitment or referral) in one or more States or places of hiring (or recruitment or referral) in which the pilot program is not otherwise operating but only if such States meet the requirements of 403(b)(2)(A) and 403(c)(2) of this division, respectively.

(3)[36] Termination of elections. The Secretary of Homeland Security may terminate an election by a person or other entity under this section because the person or entity has substantially failed to comply with its obligations under the pilot program. A person or other entity may terminate an election in such form and manner as the Secretary of Homeland Security shall specify.

(d) Consultation, education, and publicity.

(1) Consultation. The Secretary of Homeland Security shall closely consult with representatives of employers (and recruiters and referrers) in the development and implementation of the pilot programs, including the education of employers (and recruiters and referrers) about such programs.

(2) Publicity. The Secretary of Homeland Security shall widely publicize the election process and pilot programs, including the voluntary nature of the pilot programs and the advantages to employers (and recruiters and referrers) of making an election under this section.

(3) Assistance through district offices. The Secretary of Homeland Security shall designate one or more individuals in each District office of the Immigration and Naturalization Service for a Service District in which a pilot program is being implemented—

(A) to inform persons and other entities that seek information about pilot programs of the voluntary nature of such programs, and

33. Amended by P.L. 108-156, § 3(c), (d), 117 Stat. 1944, 1945 (December 3, 2003).

34. Amended by P.L. 108-156, § 3(c)(1) to (3), (d), 117 Stat. 1944, 1945 (December 3, 2003).

35. Amended by P.L. 108-156, § 3(c)(1), 117 Stat. 1944 (December 3, 2003).

36. Former paragraph (3) deleted and former paragraph (4) redesignated as (3) by P.L. 108-156, § 3(c)(2), (3), 117 Stat. 1944, 1945 (December 3, 2003).

(B) to assist persons and other entities in electing and participating in any pilot programs in effect in the District, in complying with the requirements of section 274A, and in facilitating confirmation of the identity and employment eligibility of individuals consistent with such section.

(e) Select entities required to participate in a pilot program.

(1) Federal government.

(A) Executive departments.

(i) In general. Each Department of the Federal Government shall elect to participate in a pilot program and shall comply with the terms and conditions of such an election

(ii) Election. Subject to clause (iii), the Secretary of each such Department—

(I) shall elect the pilot program (or programs) in which the Department shall participate, and

(II) may limit the election to hiring occurring in certain States (or geographic areas) covered by the program (or programs) and in specified divisions within the Department, so long as all hiring by such divisions and in such locations is covered.

(iii) Role of Secretary of Homeland Security. The Secretary of Homeland Security shall assist and coordinate elections under this subparagraph in such manner as assures that—

(I) a significant portion of the total hiring within each Department within States covered by a pilot program is covered under such a program, and

(II) there is significant participation by the Federal Executive branch in each of the pilot programs.

(B) Legislative branch. Each Member of Congress, each officer of Congress, and the head of each agency of the legislative branch, that conducts hiring in a State in which a pilot program is operating shall elect to participate in a pilot program, may specify which pilot program or programs (if there is more than one) in which the Member, officer, or agency will participate, and shall comply with the terms and conditions of such an election.

(2) Application to certain violators. An order under section 274A(e)(4) or section 274B(g) of the Immigration and Nationality Act may require the subject of the order to participate in, and comply with the terms of, a pilot program with respect to the subject's hiring (or recruitment or referral) of individuals in a State covered by such a program.

(3) Consequence of failure to participate. If a person or other entity is required under this subsection to participate in a pilot program and fails to comply with the requirements of such program with respect to an individual—

(A) such failure shall be treated as a violation of section 274A(a)(1)(B) with respect to that individual, and

(B) a rebuttable presumption is created that the person or entity has violated section 274A(a)(1)(A).

Subparagraph (B) shall not apply in any prosecution under section 274A(f)(1).

(f) Construction. This subtitle shall not affect the authority of the Secretary of Homeland Security under any other law (including section 274A(d)(4)) to conduct demonstration projects in relation to section 274A.

§ 403. Procedures for participants in pilot programs Appendix E, § 403

(a) Basic pilot program. A person or other entity that elects to participate in the basic pilot program described in this subsection agrees to conform to the following procedures in the case of the hiring (or recruitment or referral) for employment in the United States of each individual covered by the election:

(1) Provision of additional information. The person or entity shall obtain from the individual (and the individual shall provide) and shall record on the I-9 or similar form—

(A) the individual's social security account number, if the individual has been issued such a number, and

(B) if the individual does not attest to United States citizenship under section 274A(b)(2), such identification or authorization number established by the Immigration and Naturalization Service for the alien as the Secretary of Homeland Security shall specify, and shall retain the original form and make it available for inspection for the period and in the manner required of I-9 forms under section 274A(b)(3).

(2) Presentation of documentation.

(A) In general. The person or other entity, and the individual whose identity and employment eligibility are being confirmed, shall, subject to subparagraph (B), fulfill the requirements of section 274A(b) with the following modifications:

(i) A document referred to in section 274A(b)(1)(B)(ii) (as redesignated by section 412(a) of this division) must be designated by the Secretary of Homeland Security as suitable for the purpose of identification in a pilot program.

(ii) A document referred to in section 274A(b)(1)(D) must contain a photograph of the individual.

(iii) The person or other entity has complied with the requirements of section 274A(b)(1) with respect to examination of a document if the document reasonably appears on its face to be genuine and it reasonably appears to pertain to the individual whose identity and work eligibility is being confirmed.

(B) Limitation of requirement to examine documentation. If the Secretary of Homeland Security finds that a pilot program would reliably determine with respect to an individual whether—

(i) the person with the identity claimed by the individual is authorized to work in the United States, and

(ii) the individual is claiming the identity of another person, if a person or entity could fulfill the requirement to examine documentation contained in subparagraph (A) of section 274A(b)(1) by examining a document specified in either subparagraph (B) or (D) of such section, the Secretary of Homeland Security may provide that, for purposes of such requirement, only such a document need be examined. In such case, any reference in section 274A(b)(1)(A) to a verification that an individual is not an unauthorized alien shall be deemed to be a verification of the individual's identity.

(3) Seeking confirmation.

(A) In general. The person or other entity shall make an inquiry, as provided in section 404(a)(1) of this division, using the confirmation system to seek confirmation of the identity and employment eligibility of an individual, by not later than the end of 3 working days (as specified by the Secretary of Homeland Security) after the date of the hiring (or recruitment or referral, as the case may be).

(B) Extension of time period. If the person or other entity in good faith attempts to make an inquiry during such 3 working days and the confirmation system has registered that not all inquiries were received during such time, the person or entity can make an inquiry in the first subsequent working day in which the confirmation system registers that it has received all inquiries. If the confirmation system cannot receive inquiries at all times during a day, the person or entity merely has to assert that the entity attempted to make the inquiry on that day for the previous sentence to apply to such an inquiry, and does not have to provide any additional proof concerning such inquiry.

(4) Confirmation or nonconfirmation.

(A) Confirmation upon initial inquiry. If the person or other entity receives an appropriate confirmation of an individual's identity and work eligibility under the confirmation system within the time period specified under section 404(b) of this division, the person or entity shall record on the I-9 or similar form an appropriate code that is provided under the system and that indicates a final confirmation of such identity and work eligibility of the individual.

(B) Nonconfirmation upon initial inquiry and secondary verification.

(i) Nonconfirmation. If the person or other entity receives a tentative nonconfirmation of an individual's identity or work eligibility under the confirmation system within the time period specified under 404(b) of this division, the person or entity shall so inform the individual for whom the confirmation is sought.

(ii) No contest. If the individual does not contest the non-confirmation within the time period specified in section 404(c) of this division, the nonconfirmation shall be considered final. The person or entity shall then record on the I-9 or similar form an appropriate code which has been provided under the system to indicate a tentative nonconfirmation.

(iii) Contest. If the individual does contest the nonconfirmation, the individual shall utilize the process for secondary verification provided under section 404(c) of this division. The nonconfirmation will remain tentative until a final confirmation or nonconfirmation is provided by the confirmation system within the time period specified in such section. In no case shall an employer terminate employment of an individual because of a failure of the individual to have identity and work eligibility confirmed under this section until a nonconfirmation becomes final. Nothing in this clause shall apply to a termination of employment for any reason other than because of such a failure.

(iv) Recording of conclusion on form. If a final confirmation or nonconfirmation is provided by the confirmation system under section 404(c) of this division regarding an individual, the person or entity shall record on the I-9 or similar form an appropriate code that is provided under the system and that indicates a confirmation or nonconfirmation of identity and work eligibility of the individual.

(C) Consequences of nonconfirmation.

(i) Termination or notification of continued employment. If the person or other entity has received a final nonconfirmation regarding an individual under subparagraph (B), the person or entity may terminate employment (or recruitment or referral) of the individual. If the person or entity does not terminate employment (or recruitment or referral) of the individual, the person or entity shall notify the Secretary of Homeland Security of such fact through the confirmation system or in such other manner as the Secretary of Homeland Security may specify.

(ii) Failure to notify. If the person or entity fails to provide notice with respect to an individual as required under clause (i), the failure is deemed to constitute a violation of section 274A(a)(1)(B) with respect to that individual and the applicable civil monetary penalty under section 274A(e)(5)shall be (notwithstanding the amounts specified in such section) no less than $500 and no more than $1,000 for each individual with respect to whom such violation occurred.

(iii) Continued employment after final nonconfirmation. If the person or other entity continues to employ (or to recruit or refer) an individual after receiving final nonconfirmation, a rebuttable presumption is created that the person or entity has violated section 274A(a)(1)(A). The previous sentence shall not apply in any prosecution under section 274A(f)(1).

(b) Citizen attestation pilot program.

(1) In general. Except as provided in paragraphs (3) through (5), the procedures applicable under the citizen attestation pilot program under this subsection shall be the same procedures as those under the basic pilot program under subsection (a).

(2) Restrictions.

(A) State document requirement to participate in pilot program. The Secretary of Homeland Security may not provide for the operation of the citizen attestation pilot program in a State unless each driver's license or similar identification document described in section 274A(b)(1)(D)(i) issued by the State—

(i) contains a photograph of the individual involved, and

(ii) has been determined by the Secretary of Homeland Security to have security features, and to have been issued through application and issuance procedures, which make such document sufficiently resistant to counterfeiting, tampering, and fraudulent use that it is a reliable means of identification for purposes of this section.

(B) Authorization to limit employer participation. The Secretary of Homeland Security may restrict the number of persons or other entities that may elect to participate in the citizen attestation pilot program under this subsection as the Secretary of Homeland Security determines to be necessary to produce a representative sample of employers and to reduce the potential impact of fraud.

(3) No confirmation required for certain individuals attesting to U.S. citizenship. In the case of a person or other entity hiring (or recruiting or referring) an individual under the citizen attestation pilot program, if the individual attests to United States citizenship (under penalty of perjury on an I-9 or similar form which form states on its face the criminal and other penalties provided under law for a false representation of United States citizenship)—

(A) the person or entity may fulfill the requirement to examine documentation contained in subparagraph (A) of section 274A(b)(1) by examining a document specified in either subparagraph (B)(i) or (D) of such section; and

(B) the person or other entity is not required to comply with respect to such individual with the procedures described in paragraphs (3) and (4) of subsection (a), but only if the person or entity retains the form and makes it available for inspection in the same manner as in the case of an I-9 form under section 274A(b)(3).

(4) Waiver of document presentation requirement in certain cases.

(A) In general. In the case of a person or entity that elects, in a manner specified by the Secretary of Homeland Security consistent with subparagraph (B), to participate in the pilot program under this paragraph, if an individual being hired (or recruited or referred) attests (in the manner described in paragraph (3)) to United States citizenship and the person or entity retains the form on which the attestation is made and makes it available for inspection in the same manner as in the case of an I-9 form under section 274A(b)(3), the person or entity is not required to comply with the procedures described in section 274A(b).

(B) Restriction. The Secretary of Homeland Security shall restrict the election under this paragraph to no more than 1,000 employers and, to the extent practicable, shall select among employers seeking to make such election in a manner that provides for such an election by a representative sample of employers.

(5) Nonreviewable determinations. The determinations of the Secretary of Homeland Security under paragraphs

(2) and (4) are within the discretion of the Secretary of Homeland Security and are not subject to judicial or administrative review.

(c) Machine-readable-document pilot program.

(1) In general. Except as provided in paragraph (3), the procedures applicable under the machine-readable-document pilot program under this subsection shall be the same procedures as those under the basic pilot program under subsection (a).

(2) State document requirement to participate in pilot program. The Secretary of Homeland Security may not provide for the operation of the machine-readable-document pilot program in a State unless driver's licenses and similar identification documents described in section 274A(b)(1)(D)(i) issued by the State include a machine-readable social security account number.

(3) Use of machine-readable documents. If the individual whose identity and employment eligibility must be confirmed presents to the person or entity hiring (or recruiting or referring) the individual a license or other document described in paragraph (2) that includes a machine-readable social security account number, the person or entity must make an inquiry through the confirmation system by using a machine-readable feature of such document. If the individual does not attest to United States citizenship under section 274A(b)(2), the individual's identification or authorization number described in subsection (a)(1)(B) shall be provided as part of the inquiry.

(d) Protection from liability for actions taken on the basis of information provided by the confirmation system. No person or entity participating in a pilot program shall be civilly or criminally liable under any law for any action taken in good faith reliance on information provided through the confirmation system.

§ 404. Employment eligibility confirmation system Appendix E, § 404

(a) In general. The Secretary of Homeland Security shall establish a pilot program confirmation system through which the Secretary of Homeland Security (or a designee of the Secretary of Homeland Security, which may be a nongovernmental entity)—

(1) responds to inquiries made by electing persons and other entities (including those made by the transmittal of data from machine-readable documents under the machine-readable pilot program) at any time through a toll-free telephone line or other toll-free electronic media concerning an individual's identity and whether the individual is authorized to be employed, and

(2) maintains records of the inquiries that were made, of confirmations provided (or not provided), and of the codes provided to inquirers as evidence of their compliance with their obligations under the pilot programs.

To the extent practicable, the Secretary of Homeland Security shall seek to establish such a system using one or more nongovernmental entities.

(b) Initial response. The confirmation system shall provide confirmation or a tentative nonconfirmation of an individual's identity and employment eligibility within 3 working days of the initial inquiry. If providing confirmation or tentative nonconfirmation, the confirmation system shall provide an appropriate code indicating such confirmation or such nonconfirmation.

(c) Secondary verification process in case of tentative nonconfirmation. In cases of tentative nonconfirmation, the Secretary of Homeland Security shall specify, in consultation with the Commissioner of Social Security and the Commissioner of the Immigration and Naturalization Service, an available secondary verification process to confirm the validity of information provided and to provide a final confirmation or nonconfirmation within 10 working days after the date of the tentative nonconfirmation. When final confirmation or nonconfirmation is provided, the confirmation system shall provide an appropriate code indicating such confirmation or nonconfirmation.

(d) Design and operation of system. The confirmation system shall be designed and operated—

(1) to maximize its reliability and ease of use by persons and other entities making elections under section 402(a) of this division consistent with insulating and protecting the privacy and security of the underlying information;

(2) to respond to all inquiries made by such persons and entities on whether individuals are authorized to be employed and to register all times when such inquiries are not received;

(3) with appropriate administrative, technical, and physical safeguards to prevent unauthorized disclosure of personal information; and

(4) to have reasonable safeguards against the system's resulting in unlawful discriminatory practices based on national origin or citizenship status, including—

(A) the selective or unauthorized use of the system to verify eligibility;

(B) the use of the system prior to an offer of employment; or

(C) the exclusion of certain individuals from consideration for employment as a result of a perceived likelihood that additional verification will be required, beyond what is required for most job applicants.

(e) Responsibilities of the Commissioner of Social Security. As part of the confirmation system, the Commissioner of Social Security, in consultation with the entity responsible for administration of the system, shall establish a reliable, secure method, which, within the time periods specified under subsections (b) and (c), compares the name and social security account number provided in an inquiry against such information maintained by the Commissioner in order to confirm (or not confirm) the validity of the information provided regarding an individual whose identity and employment eligibility must be confirmed, the correspondence of the name and number, and whether the individual has presented a social security account number that is not valid for employment. The Commissioner shall not disclose or release social security information (other than such confirmation or nonconfirmation).

(f) Responsibilities of the Commissioner of the Immigration and Naturalization Service. As part of the confirmation system, the Commissioner of the Immigration and Naturalization Service, in consultation with the entity responsible for administration of the system, shall establish a reliable, secure method, which, within the time periods specified under subsections (b) and (c), compares the name and alien identification or authorization number described in section 403(a)(1)(B) of this division which are provided in an inquiry against such information maintained by the Commissioner in order to confirm (or not confirm) the validity of the information provided, the correspondence of the name and number, and whether the alien is authorized to be employed in the United States.

(g) Updating information. The Commissioners of Social Security and the Immigration and Naturalization Service shall update their information in a manner that promotes the maximum accuracy and shall provide a process for the prompt correction of erroneous information, including instances in which it is brought to their attention in the secondary verification process described in subsection (c).

(h) Limitation on use of the confirmation system and any related systems.

(1) In general. Notwithstanding any other provision of law, nothing in this subtitle shall be construed to permit or allow any department, bureau, or other agency of the United States Government to utilize any information, data base, or other records assembled under this subtitle for any other purpose other than as provided for under a pilot program.

(2) No national identification card. Nothing in this subtitle shall be construed to authorize, directly or indirectly, the issuance or use of national identification cards or the establishment of a national identification card.

§ 405.[37] Reports Appendix E, § 405

(a) In general. The Secretary of Homeland Security shall submit to the Committees on the Judiciary of the House of Representatives and of the Senate reports on the pilot programs within 3 months after the end of the third and fourth years in which the programs are in effect. Such reports shall—

(1) assess the degree of fraudulent attesting of United States citizenship,

(2) include recommendations on whether or not the pilot programs should be continued or modified, and

(3) assess the benefits of the pilot programs to employers and the degree to which they assist in the enforcement of section 274A.

(b) Report on expansion. Not later than June 1, 2004, the Secretary of Homeland Security shall submit to the Committees on the Judiciary of the House of Representatives and the Senate a report—

(1) evaluating whether the problems identified by the report submitted under subsection (a) have been substantially resolved; and

(2) describing what actions the Secretary of Homeland Security shall take before undertaking the expansion of the basic pilot program to all 50 States in accordance with section 401(c)(1), in order to resolve any outstanding problems raised in the report filed under subsection (a). Appendix E, § 641

37. Amended by P.L. 108-156, § 3(b), (d), 117 Stat. 1944 (December 3, 2003).

§ 641.[38], [39] [8 U.S.C. 1372] Program to collect information relating to non-immigrant foreign students and other exchange program participants

(a) In general.

(1) Program. The Attorney General, in consultation with the Secretary of State and the Secretary of Education, shall develop and conduct a program to collect from approved institutions of higher education, other approved educational institutions, and designated exchange visitor programs in the United States the information described in subsection (c) with respect to aliens who—

(A) have the status, or are applying for the status, of nonimmigrants under subparagraph (F), (J), or (M) of section 101(a)(15) of the Immigration and Nationality Act; and (B) are nationals of the countries designated under subsection (b).

(2) Deadline. The program shall commence not later than January 1, 1998.

(3)[40] Aliens for whom a visa is required. The Attorney General, in consultation with the Secretary of State, shall establish an electronic means to monitor and verify

(A) the issuance of documentation of acceptance of a foreign student by an approved institution of higher education or other approved educational institution, or of an exchange visitor program participant by a designated exchange visitor program;

(B) the transmittal of the documentation referred to in subparagraph (A) to the Department of State for use by the Bureau of Consular Affairs;

(C) the issuance of a visa to a foreign student or an exchange visitor program participant;

(D) the admission into the United States of the foreign student or exchange visitor program participant;

(E) the notification to an approved institution of higher education, other approved educational institution, or exchange visitor program sponsor that the foreign student or exchange visitor participant has been admitted into the United States;

(F) the registration and enrollment of that foreign student in such approved institution of higher education or other approved educational institution, or the participation of that exchange visitor in such designated exchange visitor program, as the case may be; and

(G) any other relevant act by the foreign student or exchange visitor program participant, including a changing of school or designated exchange visitor program and any termination of studies or participation in a designated exchange visitor program.

(4)[41] Reporting requirements. Not later than 30 days after the deadline for registering for classes for an academic term of an approved institution of higher education or other approved educational institution for which documentation is issued for an alien as described in paragraph (3)(A), or the scheduled commencement of participation by an alien in a designated exchange visitor program, as the case may be, the institution or program, respectively, shall report to the Immigration and Naturalization Service any failure of the alien to enroll or to commence participation.

(b) Covered countries. The Attorney General, in consultation with the Secretary of State, shall designate countries for purposes of subsection (a)(1)(B). The Attorney General shall initially designate not less than 5 countries and may designate additional countries at any time while the program is being conducted.

(d) Authorization of appropriations. There is authorized to be appropriated to the Department of Justice $36,800,000 for the period beginning on the date of enactment of this Act [USA Patriot Act, enacted October 26, 2001] and ending on January 1, 2003, to fully implement and expand prior to January 1, 2003, the program established by section 641(a) of the Illegal Immigration Reform and Immigrant Responsibility Act of 1996 (8 U.S.C. 1372(a))."

(c) Information to be collected.

(1)[42] Ingeneral. The information for collection under subsection (a) with respect to an alien consists of—

(A) the identity and current address in the United States of the alien;

(B) the nonimmigrant classification of the alien and the date on which a visa under the classification was issued or extended or the date on which a change to such classification was approved by the Attorney General;

(C) in the case of a student at an approved institution of higher education, or other approved educational institution,[43] the current academic status of the alien, including whether the alien is maintaining status as a full-time student or, in the case of a participant in a designated exchange visitor program, whether the alien is satisfying the terms and conditions of such program;

(D) in the case of a student at an approved institution of higher education, or other approved educational

38. As amended by P.L. 106-396, title IV, §§ 404—406, 114 Stat. 1649 (October 30, 2000); P.L. 106-553, § 1(a)(2), 114 Stat. 2762 (December 21, 2000); P.L. 107-56, title IV, subtitle B, § 416(c), 115 Stat. 354 (October 26, 2001).

39. Section 416 of the USA PATRIOT Act, P.L. 107-56, 115 Stat. 354 (October 26, 2001) further provides the following, which applies equally but is not codified as part of the Immigration and Nationality Act: "(a) Full implementation and expansion of foreign student visa monitoring program required. The Attorney General, in consultation with the Secretary of State, shall fully implement and expand the program established by section 641(a) of the Illegal Immigration Reform and Immigrant Responsibility Act of 1996 (8 U.S.C. 1372(a)). (b) Integration with port of entry information. For each alien with respect to whom information is collected under section 641 of the Illegal Immigration Reform and Immigrant Responsibility Act of 1996 (8 U.S.C. 1372), the Attorney General, in consultation with the Secretary of State, shall include information on the date of entry and port of entry. * * *

40. Added by § 501(a)(1) of P.L. 107-173, 116 Stat. 560 (May 14, 2002).

41. Id.

42. Amended by § 501(a)(2) of P.L. 107-173, 116 Stat. 561 (May 14, 2002).

43. Sic. Probably should delete second comma.

institution,[44] any disciplinary action taken by the institution against the alien as a result of the alien's being convicted of a crime or, in the case of a participant in a designated exchange visitor program, any change in the alien's participation as a result of the alien's being convicted of a crime; and

(E) the date of entry and port of entry;

(F) the date of the alien's enrollment in an approved institution of higher education, other approved educational institution, or designated exchange visitor program in the United States;

(G) the degree program, if applicable, and field of study; and

(H) the date of the alien's termination of enrollment and the reason for such termination (including graduation, disciplinary action or other dismissal, and failure to re-enroll).

(2) FERPA. The Family Educational Rights and Privacy Act of 1974 shall not apply to aliens described in subsection (a) to the extent that the Attorney General determines necessary to carry out the program under subsection (a).

(3) Electronic collection. The information described in paragraph (1) shall be collected electronically, where practicable.

(4) Computer software.

(A) Collecting institutions. To the extent practicable, the Attorney General shall design the program in a manner that permits approved institutions of higher education, other approved educational institutions, and designated exchange visitor programs to use existing software for the collection, storage, and data processing of information described in paragraph (1).

(B) Attorney general. To the extent practicable, the Attorney General shall use or enhance existing software for the collection, storage, and data processing of information described in paragraph (1).

(5)[45] Reporting requirements. The Attorney General shall prescribe by regulation reporting requirements by taking into account the curriculum calendar of the approved institution of higher education, other approved educational institution, or exchange visitor program.

(d) Participation by institutions of higher education and exchange visitor programs.

(1) Condition. The information described in subsection

(c) shall be provided by institutions of higher education, other approved educational institutions, or exchange visitor programs as a condition of—

(A) in the case of an approved institution of higher education, or other approved educational institution,[46] the continued approval of the institution under subparagraph (F) or (M) of section 101(a)(15) of the Immigration and Nationality Act [1101]; and

(B) in the case of an approved institution of higher education or a designated exchange visitor program, the granting of authority to issue documents to an alien demonstrating the alien's eligibility for a visa under subparagraph (F), (J), or (M) of section 101(a)(15) of such Act.

(2) Effect of failure to provide information. If an approved institution of higher education, other approved educational institution, or a designated exchange visitor program fails to provide the specified information, such approvals and such issuance of visas shall be revoked or denied.

(e)[47] Funding.

(1) In general. Beginning on April 1, 1997, the Attorney General shall impose on, and collect from, each alien described in paragraph (3), with respect to whom the institution or program is required by subsection (a) to collect information, a fee established by the Attorney General under paragraph (4) at a time prior to the alien being classified under subparagraph (F), (J), or (M) of section 101(a)(15) of the Immigration and Nationality Act [1101].

(2) Remittance. The fees collected under paragraph (1) shall be remitted by the alien pursuant to a schedule established by the Attorney General for immediate deposit and availability as described under section 286(m) of the Immigration and Nationality Act [1356].

(3) Aliens described. An alien referred to in paragraph

(1) is an alien who seeks nonimmigrant status under subparagraph (F), (J), or (M) of section 101(a)(15) of the Immigration and Nationality Act [1101] (other than a nonimmigrant under section 101(a)(15)(J) of such Act who seeks to come to the United States as a participant in a program sponsored by the Federal Government).

(4) Amount and use of fees.

(A)[48] Establishment of amount. The Attorney General shall establish the amount of the fee to be imposed on, and collected from, an alien under paragraph (1). Except as provided in subsection (g)(2), the fee imposed on any individual may not exceed $100, except that in the case of an alien admitted under section 101(a)(15)(J) of the Immigration and Nationality Act [1101] as an au pair, camp counselor, or participant in a summer work travel program, the fee shall not exceed $40.[49] The amount of the fee shall be based on the Attorney General's estimate of the cost per alien of conducting the information collection program described in this section.

(A)[50] stablishment of amount. The Attorney General shall establish the amount of the fee to be imposed on, and collected from, an alien under paragraph (1).

44. Sic. Probably should delete second comma.

45. Added by § 501(a)(3) of P.L. 107-173, 116 Stat. 561 (May 14, 2002).

46. Sic. Probably should delete second comma.

47. P.L. 107-56, § 416(c)(3), 115 Stat. 354 (October 26, 2001) purports to amend paragraphs (1) and (2) of this subsection by inserting ", other approved educational institution," after "higher education" each place it occurs. Because of prior amendments, these amendments could not be executed.

48. As amended by P.L. 106-396, 114 Stat. 1649 (October 30, 2000); see other subparagraph (A) below.

49. Id.

50. As amended by P.L. 106-553, 114 Stat. 2762 (December 21, 2000); see other subparagraph (A) above.

Except as provided in subsection (g)(2), the fee imposed on any individual may not exceed $100, except that in the case of an alien admitted under section 101(a)(15)(J) of the Immigration and Nationality Act [1101] as an au pair, camp counselor, or participant in a summer work travel program, the fee shall not exceed $35.[51] The amount of the fee shall be based on the Attorney General's estimate of the cost per alien of conducting the information collection program described in this section.

(B) Use. Fees collected under paragraph (1) shall be deposited as offsetting receipts into the Immigration Examinations Fee Account (established under section 286(m) of the Immigration and Nationality Act [1356]) and shall remain available until expended for the Attorney General to reimburse any appropriation the amount paid out of which is for expenses in carrying out this section. Such expenses include, but are not necessarily limited to, those incurred by the Secretary of State in connection with the program under subsection (a).

(5) Proof of payment. The alien shall present proof of payment of the fee before the granting of—

(A) a visa under section 222 of the Immigration and Nationality Act [1202] or, in the case of an alien who is exempt from the visa requirement described in section 212(d)(4) of the Immigration and Nationality Act [1182], admission to the United States; or

(B) change of nonimmigrant classification under section 248 of the Immigration and Nationality Act [1258] to a classification described in paragraph (3).

(6) Implementation. The provisions of section 553 of title 5, United States Code (relating to rule-making) shall not apply to the extent the Attorney General determines necessary to ensure the expeditious, initial implementation of this section.

(f) Joint report. Not later than 4 years after the commencement of the program established under subsection (a), the Attorney General, the Secretary of State, and the Secretary of Education shall jointly submit to the Committees on the Judiciary of the Senate and the House of Representatives a report on the operations of the program and the feasibility of expanding the program to cover the nationals of all countries.

(g) Worldwide applicability of the program.

(1) Expansion of program. Not later than 12 months after the submission of the report required by subsection (f), the Attorney General, in consultation with the Secretary of State and the Secretary of Education, shall commence expansion of the program to cover the nationals of all countries.

(2) Revision of fee. After the program has been expanded, as provided in paragraph (1), the Attorney General may, on a periodic basis, revise the amount of the fee imposed and collected under subsection (e) in order to take into account changes in the cost of carrying out the program.

(h) Definitions. As used in this section:

(1) Approved institution of higher education. The term "approved institution of higher education" means a college or university approved by the Attorney General, in consultation with the Secretary of Education, under subparagraph (F), (J), or (M) of section 101(a)(15) of the Immigration and Nationality Act [1101].

(2) Designated exchange visitor program. The term "designated exchange visitor program" means a program that has been—

(A) designated by the Secretary of State for purposes of section 101(a)(15)(J) of the Immigration and Nationality Act [1101]; and

(B) selected by the Attorney General for purposes of the program under this section.

(3) Other approved educational institution. The term "other approved educational institution" includes any air flight school, language training school, or vocational school, approved by the Attorney General, in consultation with the Secretary of Education and the Secretary of State, under subparagraph (F), (J), or (M) of section 101(a)(15) of the Immigration and Nationality Act [1101].

51. Id.

§ 642.[52] [8 U.S.C. 1373] Communication between government agencies and the Immigration and Naturalization Service Appendix E, § 642

(a) In general. Notwithstanding any other provision of Federal, State, or local law, a Federal, State, or local government entity or official may not prohibit, or in any way restrict, any government entity or official from sending to, or receiving from, the Immigration and Naturalization Service information regarding the citizenship or immigration status, lawful or unlawful, of any individual.

(b) Additional authority of government entities. Notwithstanding any other provision of Federal, State, or local law, no person or agency may prohibit, or in any way restrict, a Federal, State, or local government entity from doing any of the following with respect to information regarding the immigration status, lawful or unlawful, of any individual:

(1) Sending such information to, or requesting or receiving such information from, the Immigration and Naturalization Service.

(2) Maintaining such information.

(3) Exchanging such information with any other Federal, State, or local government entity.

(c) Obligation to respond to inquiries. The Immigration and Naturalization Service shall respond to an inquiry by a Federal, State, or local government agency, seeking to verify or ascertain the citizenship or immigration status of any individual within the jurisdiction of the agency for any purpose authorized by law, by providing the requested verification or status information.

****

52. Added by IIRIRA, P.L. 104-208, div. C, title VI, subtitle D, 110 Stat. 3009-707 (Sept. 30, 1996). Free-standing provisions of this section apply equally but are not codified as part of the Immigration and Nationality Act.

APPENDIX F — VTVPA VICTIMS OF TRAFFICKING AND VIOLENCE PROTECTIONACT OF 2000

P.L. 106-386, 114 Stat. 1464 (October 28, 2000)

§ 1506. Restoring immigration protections under the Violence Against Women Act of 1994. Appendix F, § 1506

***

(c) Eliminating time limitations on motions to reopen removal and deportation proceedings for victims of domestic violence.

(1) Removal proceedings. (Amendments incorporated.)

***

(2) Deportation proceedings.

(A) In general. Notwithstanding any limitation imposed by law on motions to reopen or rescind deportation proceedings under the Immigration and Nationality Act (as in effect before the title III-A effective date in section 309 of the Illegal Immigration Reform and Immigrant Responsibility Act of 1996 (8 U.S.C. 1101 note)), there is no time limit on the filing of a motion to reopen such proceedings, and the deadline specified in section 242B(c)(3) of the Immigration and Nationality Act (as so in effect) (8 U.S.C. 1252b(c)(3)) does not apply—

(i) if the basis of the motion is to apply for relief under clause (iii) or (iv) of section 204(a)(1)(A) of the Immigration and Nationality Act (8 U.S.C. 1154(a)(1)(A)), clause (ii) or

(ii) of section 204(a)(1)(B) of such Act (8 U.S.C. 1154(a)(1)(B)), or section 244(a)(3) of such Act (as so in effect) (8 U.S.C. 1254(a)(3)); and

(iii) if the motion is accompanied by a suspension of deportation application to be filed with the Attorney General or by a copy of the self-petition that will be filed with the Immigration and Naturalization Service upon the granting of the motion to reopen.

(B) Applicability. Subparagraph (A) shall apply to motions filed by aliens who—

(i) are, or were, in deportation proceedings under the Immigration and Nationality Act (as in effect before the title III-A effective date in section 309 of the Illegal Immigration Reform and Immigrant Responsibility Act of 1996 (8 U.S.C. 1101 note)); and

(ii) have become eligible to apply for relief under clause

(iii) or (iv) of section 204(a)(1)(A) of the Immigration and Nationality Act (8 U.S.C. 1154(a)(1)(A)), clause (ii) or (iii) of section 204(a)(1)(B) of such Act (8 U.S.C. 1154(a)(1)(B)), or section 244(a)(3) of such Act (as in effect before the title III-A effective date in section 309 of the Illegal Immigration Reform and Immigrant Responsibility Act of 1996 (8 U.S.C. 1101 note)) as a result of the amendments made by—

(I) subtitle G of title IV of the Violent Crime Control and Law Enforcement Act of 1994 (P.L. 103-322; 108 Stat. 1953 et seq.); or

(II) this title.

****

APPENDIX G — USA PATRIOT ACT

P.L. 107-56, title IV, subtitles A (excerpts) and C (October 26, 2001)(As amended)

Free-standing provisions for identity confirmation technology, records access, and immigration benefits for victims of terrorism

***

§ 403. Access by the Department of State and the INS to certain identifying information in the criminal history records of visa applicants and applicants for admission to the United States Appendix G, § 403

***

(c)[53] [8 U.S.C. 1379] Technology standard to confirm identity

(1)[54] In general. The Attorney General and the Secretary of State jointly, through the National Institute of Standards and Technology (NIST), and in consultation with the Secretary of the Treasury and other Federal law enforcement and intelligence agencies the Attorney General or Secretary of State deems appropriate and in consultation with Congress, shall within 15 months after the date of the enactment of this section, develop and certify a technology standard, including appropriate biometric identifier standards, that can be used to verify the identity of persons applying for a United States visa or such persons seeking to enter the United States pursuant to a visa for the purposes of conducting background checks, confirming identity, and ensuring that a person has not received a visa under a different name or such person seeking to enter the United States pursuant to a visa.

(2)[55] Interoperable. The technology standard developed pursuant to paragraph (1), shall be the technological basis for a cross-agency, cross-platform electronic system that is a cost-effective, efficient, fully interoperable means to share law enforcement and intelligence information necessary to confirm the identity of such persons applying for a United States visa or such person seeking to enter the United States pursuant to a visa.

---

53. Added by P.L. 107-56, 115 Stat. 344 (October 26, 2001).
54. Amended by P.L. 107-173, §§ 201(c)(5)(A) and 202(a)(4)(B)(i), 116 Stat. 548, 549 (May 14, 2002).
55. Amended by P.L. 107-173, § 202(a)(4)(B)(ii), 116 Stat. 549 (May 14, 2002).

(3) Accessible. The electronic system described in paragraph (2), once implemented, shall be readily and easily accessible to—

(A) all consular officers responsible for the issuance of visas;

(B) all Federal inspection agents at all United States border inspection points; and

(C) all law enforcement and intelligence officers as determined by regulation to be responsible for investigation or identification of aliens admitted to the United States pursuant to a visa.

(4)[56] Report. Not later than one year after the date of the enactment of this Act [enacted October 26, 2001], and every 2 years thereafter, the Attorney General and the Secretary of State shall jointly, in consultation with the Secretary of Treasury, report to Congress describing the development, implementation, efficacy, and privacy implications of the technology standard and electronic database system described in this subsection.

(5) Funding. There is authorized to be appropriated to the Secretary of State, the Attorney General, and the Director of the National Institute of Standards and Technology such sums as may be necessary to carry out the provisions of this subsection.

(d)[57] [8 U.S.C. 1105 note] Statutory construction Nothing in this section, or in any other law, shall be construed to limit the authority of the Attorney General or the Director of the Federal Bureau of Investigation to provide access to the criminal history record information contained in the National Crime Information Center's (NCIC) Interstate Identification Index (NCIC-III), or to any other information maintained by the NCIC, to any Federal agency or officer authorized to enforce or administer the immigration laws of the United States, for the purpose of such enforcement or administration, upon terms that are consistent with the National Crime Prevention and Privacy Compact Act of 1998 (subtitle A of title II of P.L. 105-251; 42 U.S.C. 14611-16) and section 552a of title 5, United States Code.

***

§ 405.[58] [8 U.S.C. 1379 note]. Report on the integrated automated fingerprint identification system for ports of entry and overseas consular posts Appendix G, § 405

(a) In general. The Attorney General, in consultation with the appropriate heads of other Federal agencies, including the Secretary of State, Secretary of the Treasury, and the Secretary of Transportation, shall report to Congress on the feasibility of enhancing the Integrated Automated Fingerprint Identification System (IAFIS) of the Federal Bureau of Investigation and other identification systems in order to better identify a person who holds a foreign passport or a visa and may be wanted in connection with a criminal investigation in the United States or abroad, before the issuance of a visa to that person or the entry or exit from the United States by that person.

(b) Authorization of appropriations. There is authorized to be appropriated not less than $2,000,000 to carry out this section.

***

Subtitle C — Preservation of Immigration Benefits for Victims of Terrorism

P.L. 107-56, §§ 421—428, 115 Stat. 356 to 363 (October 26, 2001)

§ 421. Special immigrant status Appendix G, § 421

(a) In general. For purposes of the Immigration and Nationality Act (8 U.S.C. 1101 et seq.), the Attorney General may provide an alien described in subsection (b) with the status of a special immigrant under section 101(a)(27) of such Act (8 U.S.C. 1101(a)(27)), if the alien—

(1) files with the Attorney General a petition under section 204 of such Act (8 U.S.C. 1154) for classification under section 203(b)(4) of such Act (8 U.S.C. 1153(b)(4)); and

(2) is otherwise eligible to receive an immigrant visa and is otherwise admissible to the United States for permanent residence, except in determining such admissibility, the grounds for inadmissibility specified in section 212(a)(4) of such Act (8 U.S.C. 1182(a)(4)) shall not apply.

(b) Aliens described.

(1) Principal aliens. An alien is described in this subsection if—

(A) the alien was the beneficiary of—

(i) a petition that was filed with the Attorney General on or before September 11, 2001—

(I) under section 204 of the Immigration and Nationality Act (8 U.S.C. 1154) to classify the alien as a family-sponsored immigrant under section 203(a) of such Act (8 U.S.C. 1153(a)) or as an employment-based immigrant under section 203(b) of such Act (8 U.S.C. 1153(b)); or

(II) under section 214(d) (8 U.S.C. 1184(d)) of such Act to authorize the issuance of a nonimmigrant visa to the alien under section 101(a)(15)(K) of such Act (8 U.S.C. 1101(a)(15)(K)); or

(ii) an application for labor certification under section 212(a)(5)(A) of such Act (8 U.S.C. 1182(a)(5)(A)) that was filed under regulations of the Secretary of Labor on or before such date; and

(B) such petition or application was revoked or terminated (or otherwise rendered null), either before or after its approval, due to a specified terrorist activity that directly resulted in—

(i) the death or disability of the petitioner, applicant, or alien beneficiary; or

56. Amended by P.L. 107-173, § 201(c)(5)(B), 116 Stat. 548 (May 14, 2002).

57. Added by P.L. 107-56, 115 Stat. 345 (October 26, 2001).

58. Id.

(ii) loss of employment due to physical damage to, or destruction of, the business of the petitioner or applicant.

(2) Spouses and children.

(A) In general. An alien is described in this subsection if—

(i) the alien was, on September 10, 2001, the spouse or child of a principal alien described in paragraph (1); and

(ii) the alien—

(I) is accompanying such principal alien; or

(II) is following to join such principal alien not later than September 11, 2003.

(B) Construction. For purposes of construing the terms "accompanying" and "following to join" in subparagraph (A)(ii), any death of a principal alien that is described in paragraph (1)(B)(i) shall be disregarded.

(3) Grandparents of orphans. An alien is described in this subsection if the alien is a grandparent of a child, both of whose parents died as a direct result of a specified terrorist activity, if either of such deceased parents was, on September 10, 2001, a citizen or national of the United States or an alien lawfully admitted for permanent residence in the United States.

(c) Priority date. Immigrant visas made available under this section shall be issued to aliens in the order in which a petition on behalf of each such alien is filed with the Attorney General under subsection (a)(1), except that if an alien was assigned a priority date with respect to a petition described in subsection (b)(1)(A)(i), the alien may maintain that priority date.

(d) Numerical limitations. For purposes of the application of sections 201 through 203 of the Immigration and Nationality Act (8 U.S.C. 1151—1153) in any fiscal year, aliens eligible to be provided status under this section shall be treated as special immigrants described in section 101(a)(27) of such Act (8 U.S.C. 1101(a)(27)) who are not described in subparagraph (A), (B), (C), or (K) of such section.

§ 422. Extension of filing or reentry deadlines Appendix G, § 422

(a) Automatic extension of nonimmigrant status.

(1) In general. Notwithstanding section 214 of the Immigration and Nationality Act (8 U.S.C. 1184), in the case of an alien described in paragraph (2) who was lawfully present in the United States as a nonimmigrant on September 10, 2001, the alien may remain lawfully in the United States in the same nonimmigrant status until the later of—

(A) the date such lawful nonimmigrant status otherwise would have terminated if this subsection had not been enacted; or

(B) 1 year after the death or onset of disability described in paragraph (2).

(2) Aliens described.

(A) Principal aliens. An alien is described in this paragraph if the alien was disabled as a direct result of a specified terrorist activity.

(B) Spouses and children. An alien is described in this paragraph if the alien was, on September 10, 2001, the spouse or child of—

(i) a principal alien described in subparagraph (A); or

(ii) an alien who died as a direct result of a specified terrorist activity.

(3) Authorized employment. During the period in which a principal alien or alien spouse is in lawful nonimmigrant status under paragraph (1), the alien shall be provided an "employment authorized" endorsement or other appropriate document signifying authorization of employment not later than 30 days after the alien requests such authorization.

(b) New deadlines for extension or change of nonimmigrant status.

(1) Filing delays. In the case of an alien who was lawfully present in the United States as a nonimmigrant on September 10, 2001, if the alien was prevented from filing a timely application for an extension or change of nonimmigrant status as a direct result of a specified terrorist activity, the alien's application shall be considered timely filed if it is filed not later than 60 days after it otherwise would have been due.

(2) Departure delays. In the case of an alien who was lawfully present in the United States as a nonimmigrant on September 10, 2001, if the alien is unable timely to depart the United States as a direct result of a specified terrorist activity, the alien shall not be considered to have been unlawfully present in the United States during the period beginning on September 11, 2001, and ending on the date of the alien's departure, if such departure occurs on or before November 11, 2001.

(3) Special rule for aliens unable to return from abroad.

(A) Principal aliens. In the case of an alien who was in a lawful nonimmigrant status on September 10, 2001, but who was not present in the United States on such date, if the alien was prevented from returning to the United States in order to file a timely application for an extension of nonimmigrant status as a direct result of a specified terrorist activity—

(i) the alien's application shall be considered timely filed if it is filed not later than 60 days after it otherwise would have been due; and

(ii) the alien's lawful nonimmigrant status shall be considered to continue until the later of—

(I) the date such status otherwise would have terminated if this subparagraph had not been enacted; or

(II) the date that is 60 days after the date on which the application described in clause (i) otherwise would have been due.

(B) Spouses and children. In the case of an alien who is the spouse or child of a principal alien described in subparagraph (A), if the spouse or child was in a lawful nonimmigrant status on September 10, 2001, the spouse or child may remain lawfully in the United States in the same nonimmigrant status until the later of—

(i) the date such lawful nonimmigrant status otherwise would have terminated if this subparagraph had not been enacted; or

(ii) the date that is 60 days after the date on which the application described in subparagraph

(A) otherwise would have been due.

(4) Circumstances preventing timely action.

(A) Filing delays. For purposes of paragraph (1), circumstances preventing an alien from timely acting are—

(i) office closures;

(ii) mail or courier service cessations or delays; and

(iii) other closures, cessations, or delays affecting case processing or travel necessary to satisfy legal requirements.

(B) Departure and return delays. For purposes of paragraphs (2) and (3), circumstances preventing an alien from timely acting are—

(i) office closures;

(ii) airline flight cessations or delays; and

(iii) other closures, cessations, or delays affecting case processing or travel necessary to satisfy legal requirements.

(c) Diversity immigrants.

(1) Waiver of fiscal year limitation. Notwithstanding section 203(e)(2) of the Immigration and Nationality Act (8 U.S.C. 1153(e)(2)), an immigrant visa number issued to an alien under section 203(c) of such Act for fiscal year 2001 may be used by the alien during the period beginning on October 1, 2001, and ending on April 1, 2002, if the alien establishes that the alien was prevented from using it during fiscal year 2001 as a direct result of a specified terrorist activity.

(2) Worldwide level. In the case of an alien entering the United States as a lawful permanent resident, or adjusting to that status, under paragraph (1) or (3), the alien shall be counted as a diversity immigrant for fiscal year 2001 for purposes of section 201(e) of the Immigration and Nationality Act (8 U.S.C. 1151(e)), unless the worldwide level under such section for such year has been exceeded, in which case the alien shall be counted as a diversity immigrant for fiscal year 2002.

(3) Treatment of family members of certain aliens. In the case of a principal alien issued an immigrant visa number under section 203(c) of the Immigration and Nationality Act (8 U.S.C. 1153(c)) for fiscal year 2001, if such principal alien died as a direct result of a specified terrorist activity, the aliens who were, on September 10, 2001, the spouse and children of such principal alien shall, until June 30, 2002, if not otherwise entitled to an immigrant status and the immediate issuance of a visa under subsection (a), (b), or (c) of section 203 of such Act, be entitled to the same status, and the same order of consideration, that would have been provided to such alien spouse or child under section 203(d) of such Act as if the principal alien were not deceased and as if the spouse or child's visa application had been adjudicated by September 30, 2001.

(4) Circumstances preventing timely action. For purposes of paragraph (1), circumstances preventing an alien from using an immigrant visa number during fiscal year 2001 are—

(A) office closures;

(B) mail or courier service cessations or delays;

(C) airline flight cessations or delays; and

(D) other closures, cessations, or delays affecting case processing or travel necessary to satisfy legal requirements.

(d) Extension of expiration of immigrant visas.

(1) In general. Notwithstanding the limitations under section 221(c) of the Immigration and Nationality Act (8 U.S.C. 1201(c)), in the case of any immigrant visa issued to an alien that expires or expired before December 31, 2001, if the alien was unable to effect entry into the United States as a direct result of a specified terrorist activity, then the period of validity of the visa is extended until December 31, 2001, unless a longer period of validity is otherwise provided under this subtitle.

(2) Circumstances preventing entry. For purposes of this subsection, circumstances preventing an alien from effecting entry into the United States are—

(A) office closures;

(B) airline flight cessations or delays; and

(C) other closures, cessations, or delays affecting case processing or travel necessary to satisfy legal requirements.

(e) Grants of parole extended.

(1) In general. In the case of any parole granted by the Attorney General under section 212(d)(5) of the Immigration and Nationality Act (8 U.S.C. 1182(d)(5)) that expires on a date on or after September 11, 2001, if the alien beneficiary of the parole was unable to return to the United States prior to the expiration date as a direct result of a specified terrorist activity, the parole is deemed extended for an additional 90 days.

(2) Circumstances preventing return. For purposes of this subsection, circumstances preventing an alien from timely returning to the United States are—

(A) office closures;

(B) airline flight cessations or delays; and

(C) other closures, cessations, or delays affecting case processing or travel necessary to satisfy legal requirements.

(f) Voluntary departure. Notwithstanding section 240B of the Immigration and Nationality Act (8 U.S.C. 1229c), if a period for voluntary departure under such section expired during the period beginning on September 11, 2001, and ending on October 11, 2001, such voluntary departure period is deemed extended for an additional 30 days.

§ 423. Humanitarian relief for certain surviving spouses and children Appendix G, § 423

(a) Treatment as immediate relatives.

(1) Spouses. Notwithstanding the second sentence of section 201(b)(2)(A)(i) of the Immigrationand Nationality Act (8 U.S.C. 1151(b)(2)(A)(i)), in the case of an alien who was the spouse of a citizen of the United States at the time of the citizen's death and was not legally separated from the citizen at the time of the citizen's death, if the citizen died as a direct result of a specified terrorist activity, the alien (and each child of the alien) shall be considered, for purposes of section 201(b) of such Act, to remain an immediate relative after the date of the citizen's death, but only if the alien files a petition under section 204(a)(1)(A)(ii) of

such Act within 2 years after such date and only until the date the alien remarries. For purposes of such section 204(a)(1)(A)(ii), an alien granted relief under the preceding sentence shall be considered an alien spouse described in the second sentence of section 201(b)(2)(A)(i) of such Act.

(2) Children.

(A) In general. In the case of an alien who was the child of a citizen of the United States at the time of the citizen's death, if the citizen died as a direct result of a specified terrorist activity, the alien shall be considered, for purposes of section 201(b) of the Immigration and Nationality Act (8 U.S.C. 1151(b)), to remain an immediate relative after the date of the citizen's death (regardless of changes in age or marital status thereafter), but only if the alien files a petition under subparagraph (B) within 2 years after such date.

(B) Petitions. An alien described in subparagraph (A) may file a petition with the Attorney General for classification of the alien under section 201(b)(2)(A)(i) of the Immigration and Nationality Act (8 U.S.C. 1151(b)(2)(A)(i)). For purposes of such Act, such a petition shall be considered a petition filed under section 204(a)(1)(A) of such Act (8 U.S.C. 1154(a)(1)(A)).

(b) Spouses, children, unmarried sons and daughters of lawful permanent resident aliens.

(1) In general. Any spouse, child, or unmarried son or daughter of an alien described in paragraph (3) who is included in a petition for classification as a family-sponsored immigrant under section 203(a)(2) of the Immigration and Nationality Act (8 U.S.C. 1153(a)(2)) that was filed by such alien before September 11, 2001, shall be considered (if the spouse, child, son, or daughter has not been admitted or approved for lawful permanent residence by such date) a valid petitioner for preference status under such section with the same priority date as that assigned prior to the death described in paragraph (3)(A). No new petition shall be required to be filed. Such spouse, child, son, or daughter may be eligible for deferred action and work authorization.

(2) Self-petitions. Any spouse, child, or unmarried son or daughter of an alien described in paragraph (3) who is not a beneficiary of a petition for classification as a family-sponsored immigrant under section 203(a)(2) of the Immigration and Nationality Act may file a petition for such classification with the Attorney General, if the spouse, child, son, or daughter was present in the United States on September 11, 2001.

Such spouse, child, son, or daughter may be eligible for deferred action and work authorization.

(3) Aliens described. An alien is described in this paragraph if the alien—

(A) died as a direct result of a specified terrorist activity; and

(B) on the day of such death, was lawfully admitted for permanent residence in the United States.

(c) Applications for adjustment of status by surviving spouses and children of employment-based immigrants.

(1) In general. Any alien who was, on September 10, 2001, the spouse or child of an alien described in paragraph (2), and who applied for adjustment of status prior to the death described in paragraph (2)(A), may have such application adjudicated as if such death had not occurred.

(2) Aliens described. An alien is described in this paragraph if the alien—

(A) died as a direct result of a specified terrorist activity; and

(B) on the day before such death, was—

(i) an alien lawfully admitted for permanent residence in the United States by reason of having been allotted a visa under section 203(b) of the Immigration and Nationality Act (8 U.S.C. 1153(b)); or

(ii) an applicant for adjustment of status to that of an alien described in clause (i), and admissible to the United States for permanent residence.

(d) Waiver of public charge grounds. In determining the admissibility of any alien accorded an immigration benefit under this section, the grounds for inadmissibility specified in section 212(a)(4) of the Immigration and Nationality Act (8 U.S.C. 1182(a)(4)) shall not apply.

§ 424. "Age-out" protection for children Appendix G, § 424

For purposes of the administration of the Immigration and Nationality Act (8 U.S.C. 1101 et seq.), in the case of an alien—

(1) whose 21st birthday occurs in September 2001, and who is the beneficiary of a petition or application filed under such Act on or before September 11, 2001, the alien shall be considered to be a child for 90 days after the alien's 21st birthday for purposes of adjudicating such petition or application; and

(2) whose 21st birthday occurs after September 2001, and who is the beneficiary of a petition or application filed under such Act on or before September 11, 2001, the alien shall be considered to be a child for 45 days after the alien's 21st birthday for purposes of adjudicating such petition or application.

§ 425. Temporary administrative relief Appendix G, § 425

The Attorney General, for humanitarian purposes or to ensure family unity, may provide temporary administrative relief to any alien who—

(1) was lawfully present in the United States on September 10, 2001;

(2) was on such date the spouse, parent, or child of an individual who died or was disabled as a direct result of a specified terrorist activity; and

(3) is not otherwise entitled to relief under any other provision of this subtitle.

§ 426. Evidence of death, disability, or loss of employment Appendix G, § 426

(a) In general. The Attorney General shall establish appropriate standards for evidence demonstrating, for purposes of this subtitle, that any of the following occurred as a direct result of a specified terrorist activity:

(1) Death.

(2) Disability.

(3) Loss of employment due to physical damage to, or destruction of, a business.

(b) Waiver of regulations. The Attorney General shall carry out subsection (a) as expeditiously as possible. The Attorney General is not required to promulgate regulations prior to implementing this subtitle.

§ 427. No benefits to terrorists or family members of terrorists Appendix G, § 427

Notwithstanding any other provision of this subtitle, nothing in this subtitle shall be construed to provide any benefit or relief to—

(1) any individual culpable for a specified terrorist activity; or

(2) any family member of any individual described in paragraph (1).

§ 428. Definitions Appendix G, § 428

(a) Application of Immigration and Nationality Act provisions. Except as otherwise specifically provided in this subtitle, the definitions used in the Immigration and Nationality Act [8 USCU 1101 et seq.] (excluding the definitions applicable exclusively to title III of such Act) shall apply in the administration of this subtitle.

(b) Specified terrorist activity. For purposes of this subtitle, the term "specified terrorist activity" means any terrorist activity conducted against the Government or the people of the United States on September 11, 2001.

****

APPENDIX H — ENHANCED BORDER SECURITY AND VISA ENTRY REFORM ACT OF 2002

P.L. 107-173, 116 Stat. 543 (May 14, 2002) and Related Amendments

§ 2.[59], [60] [8 U.S.C. 1701] Definitions Appendix H, § 2

In this Act:

(1) Alien. The term "alien" has the meaning given the term in section 101(a)(3) of the Immigration and Nationality Act.

(2) Appropriate committees of Congress. The term "appropriate committees of Congress" means the following:

(A) The Committee on the Judiciary, the Select Committee on Intelligence, and the Committee on Foreign Relations of the Senate.

(B) The Committee on the Judiciary, the Permanent Select Committee on Intelligence, and the Committee on International Relations of the House of Representatives.

(3) Chimera system. The term "Chimera system" means the interoperable electronic data system required to be developed and implemented by § 202(a)(2).

(4) Federal law enforcement agencies. The term "Federal law enforcement agencies" means the following:

(A) The United States Secret Service.

(B) The Drug Enforcement Administration.

(C) The Federal Bureau of Investigation.

(D) The Immigration and Naturalization Service.

(E) The United States Marshall Service.

(F) The Naval Criminal Investigative Service.

(G)[61] The Coast Guard.

(H) The Diplomatic Security Service.

(I) The United States Postal Inspection Service.

(J) The Bureau of Alcohol, Tobacco, Firearms, and Explosives, Department of Justice.

(K) The United States Customs Service.

(l) The National Park Service.

(5) Intelligence community. The term "intelligence community" has the meaning given that termin section 3(4)of the National Security Act of 1947 (50 U.S.C. 401a(4)).

(6) President. The term "President" means the President of the United States, acting through the Assistant to the President for Homeland Security, in coordination with the Secretary of State, the Commissioner of Immigration and Naturalization, the Attorney General, the Director of Central Intelligence, the Director of the Federal Bureau of Investigation, the Secretary of Transportation, the Commissioner of Customs, and the Secretary of the Treasury.

(7) USA PATRIOT Act. The term "USA PATRIOT Act" means the Uniting and Strengthening America by Providing Appropriate Tools Required to Intercept and Obstruct Terrorism (USA PATRIOT ACT) Act of 2001 (P.L. 107-56).

Title I — Funding

§ 101.[62] [8 U.S.C. 1711] Authorization of appropriations for hiring and training government personnel Appendix H, § 101

(a) Additional personnel.

(1) INS inspectors. Subject to the availability of appropriations, during each of the fiscal years 2003 through 2006, the Attorney General shall increase the number of inspectors and associated support staff in the Immigration and Naturalization Service by the equivalent of at least 200 full-time employees over the number of inspectors and associated support staff in the Immigration and Naturalization Service authorized by the USA PATRIOT Act.

59. Added by P.L. 107-173, § 2, 116 Stat. 544 (May 14, 2002), as amended by P.L. 107-296, § 1112(c), 116 Stat. 2276 (November 25, 2002).

60. See P.L. 108-458, § 5201, 118 Stat. 3733 (December 17, 2004) for provisions regarding submission (not later than June 17, 2004) to the President and congressional committees by the Secretary of Homeland Security of a comprehensive plan for the systematic surveillance of the southwest border of the United States by remotely piloted aircraft.

61. Amended by P.L. 108-293, § 619, 118 Stat. 1062 (August 9, 2004).

62. Added by P.L. 107-173, § 101, 116 Stat. 545 (May 14, 2002).

(2) INS investigative personnel. Subject to the availability of appropriations, during each of the fiscal years 2003 through 2006, the Attorney General shall increase the number of investigative and associated support staff of the Immigration and Naturalization Service by the equivalent of at least 200 full-time employees over the number of investigators and associated support staff in the Immigration and Naturalization Service authorized by the USA PATRIOT Act.

(3) Authorization of appropriations. There are authorized to be appropriated such sums as may be necessary to carry out this subsection, including such sums as may be necessary to provide facilities, attorney personnel and support staff, and other resources needed to support the increased number of inspectors, investigative staff, and associated support staff.

(b) Authorization of appropriations for INS staffing.

(1) In general. There are authorized to be appropriated for the Department of Justice such sums as may be necessary to provide an increase in the annual rate of basic pay effective October 1, 2002—

(A) for all journeyman Border Patrol agents and inspectors who have completed at least one year's service and are receiving an annual rate of basic pay for positions at GS-9 of the General Schedule under section 5332 of title 5, United States Code, from the annual rate of basic pay payable for positions at GS-9 of the General Schedule under such section 5332, to an annual rate of basic pay payable for positions at GS-11 of the General Schedule under such section 5332;

(B) for inspections assistants, from the annual rate of basic pay payable for positions at GS-5 of the General Schedule under section 5332 of title 5, United States Code, to an annual rate of basic pay payable for positions at GS-7 of the General Schedule under such section 5332; and

(C) for the support staff associated with the personnel described in subparagraphs (A) and (B), at the appropriate GS level of the General Schedule under such section 5332.

(c) Authorization of appropriations for training. There are authorized to be appropriated such sums as may be necessary—

(1) to appropriately train Immigration and Naturalization Service personnel on an ongoing basis—

(A) to ensure that their proficiency levels are acceptable to protect the borders of the United States; and

(B) otherwise to enforce and administer the laws within their jurisdiction;

(2) to provide adequate continuing cross-training to agencies staffing the United States border and ports of entry to effectively and correctly apply applicable United States laws;

(3) to fully train immigration officers to use the appropriate lookout databases and to monitor passenger traffic patterns; and

(4) to expand the Carrier Consultant Program described in section 235(b) of the Immigration and Nationality Act (8 U.S.C. 1225A(b)).

(d) Authorization of appropriations for consular functions.

(1) Responsibilities. The Secretary of State shall—

(A) implement enhanced security measures for the review of visa applicants;

(B) staff the facilities and programs associated with the activities described in subparagraph (A); and

(C) provide ongoing training for consular officers and diplomatic security agents.

(2) Authorization of appropriations. There are authorized to be appropriated for the Department of State such sums as may be necessary to carry out paragraph (1).

§ 102.[63], [64] [8 U.S.C. 1712] Authorization of appropriations for improvements in technology and infrastructure

(a) Funding of technology. Appendix H, § 102

(1) Authorization of appropriations. In addition to funds otherwise available for such purpose, there are authorized to be appropriated $150,000,000 to the Immigration and Naturalization Service for purposes of—

(A) making improvements in technology (including infrastructure support, computer security, and information technology development) for improving border security;

(B) expanding, utilizing, and improving technology to improve border security; and

(C) facilitating the flow of commerce and persons at ports of entry, including improving and expanding programs for preenrollment and preclearance.

(2) Waiver of fees. Federal agencies involved in border security may waive all or part of enrollment fees for technology-based programs to encourage participation by United States citizens and aliens in such programs. Any agency that waives any part of any such fee may establish its fees for other services at a level that will ensure the recovery from other users of the amounts waived.

(3) Offset of increases in fees. The Attorney General may, to the extent reasonable, increase land border fees for the issuance of arrival-departure documents to offset technology costs.

(b) Improvement and expansion of INS, State Department, and customs facilities. There are authorized to be appropriated to the Immigration and Naturalization Service and the Department of State such sums as may be necessary to improve and expand facilities for use by the personnel of those agencies.

63. Added by P.L. 107-173, § 102, 116 Stat. 546 (May 14, 2002).
64. See Title V, Border Protection, Immigration, and Visa Matters, Subtitle A, Advanced Technology Northern Border Security Pilot Program, §§ 5101 through 5105 of P.L. 108-458, 118 Stat. 3732, 3733 (December 17, 2004) for provisions regarding establishment of a pilot program to test advanced technologies for improved border security between ports of entry along the northern border of the United States.

§ 103.[65] [8 U.S.C. 1713] Machine-readable visa fees Appendix H, § 103

(a) (Omitted.)

(b) Fee amount. The machine-readable visa fee charged by the Department of State shall be the higher of $65 or the cost of the machine-readable visa service, as determined by the Secretary of State after conducting a study of the cost of such service.

(c) Surcharge. The Department of State is authorized to charge a surcharge of $10, in addition to the machine-readable visa fee, for issuing a machine-readable visa in a nonmachine-readable passport.

(d) Availability of collected fees. Notwithstanding any other provision of law, amounts collected as fees described in this section shall be credited as an offsetting collection to any appropriation for the Department of State to recover costs of providing consular services. Amounts so credited shall be available, until expended, for the same purposes as the appropriation to which credited.

[8 U.S.C. § 1714].[66] Surcharges for consular services in support of enhanced border security

Beginning in fiscal year 2005 and thereafter, the Secretary of State is authorized to charge surcharges related to consular services in support of enhanced border security that are in addition to the passport and immigrant visa fees in effect on January 1, 2004: Provided, That funds collected pursuant to this authority shall be credited to this account, and shall be available until expended for the purposes of such account: Provided further, That such surcharges shall be $12 on passport fees, and $45 on immigrant visa fees.

Title II — Interagency Information Sharing

§ 201.[67] [8 U.S.C. 1721] Interim measures for access to and coordination of law enforcement and other information Appendix H, § 201

(a) Interim directive. Until the plan required by subsection (c) is implemented, Federal law enforcement agencies and the intelligence community shall, to the maximum extent practicable, share any information with the Department of State and the Immigration and Naturalization Service relevant to the admissibility and deportability of aliens, consistent with the plan described in subsection (c).

(b) Report identifying law enforcement and intelligence information.

(1) In general. Not later than 120 days after the date of enactment of this Act, the President shall submit to the appropriate committees of Congress a report identifying Federal law enforcement and the intelligence community information needed by the Department of State to screen visa applicants, or by the Immigration and Naturalization Service to screen applicants for admission to the United States, and to identify those aliens inadmissible or deportable under the Immigration and Nationality Act.

(2) (Omitted.)

(c) Coordination plan.

(1) Requirement for plan. Not later than one year after the date of enactment of the USA PATRIOT Act, the President shall develop and implement a plan based on the findings of the report under subsection (b) that requires Federal law enforcement agencies and the intelligence community to provide to the Department of State and the Immigration and Naturalization Service all information identified in that report as expeditiously as practicable.

(2) Consultation requirement. In the preparation and implementation of the plan under this subsection, the President shall consult with the appropriate committees of Congress.

(3) Protections regarding information and uses thereof. The plan under this subsection shall establish conditions for using the information described in subsection (b) received by the Department of State and Immigration and Naturalization Service—

(A) to limit the redissemination of such information;

(B) to ensure that such information is used solely to determine whether to issue a visa to an alien or to determine the admissibility or deportability of an alien to the United States, except as otherwise authorized under Federal law;

(C) to ensure the accuracy, security, and confidentiality of such information;

(D) to protect any privacy rights of individuals who are subjects of such information;

(E) to provide data integrity through the timely removal and destruction of obsolete or erroneous names and information; and

(F)[68] in a manner that protects the sources and methods used to acquire intelligence information as required by section 103(c)(7)of the National Security Act of 1947 (50 U.S.C. 4033(c)(7)).

(4) Criminal penalties for misuse of information. Any person who obtains information under this subsection without authorization or exceeding authorized access (as defined in section 1030(e) of title 18, United States Code), and who uses such information in the manner described in any of the paragraphs (1) through (7) of section 1030(a) of such title, or attempts to use such information in such manner, shall be subject to the same penalties as are applicable under section 1030(c) of such title for violation of that paragraph.

(5) (Omitted.)

§ 202.[69] [8 U.S.C. 1722] Interoperable law enforcement and intelligence data system with name-matching capacity and training Appendix H, § 202

(a) Interoperable law enforcement and intelligence electronic data system.

65. Added by P.L. 107-173, § 103, 116 Stat. 547 (May 14, 2002).

66. Added by P.L. 108-447, div. B, title IV, 118 Stat. 2896 (December 8, 2004).

67. Added by P.L. 107-173, § 201, 116 Stat. 547 (May 14, 2002).

68. Amended by P.L. 108-177, Title III, § 377(f), 117 Stat. 2631, (December 13, 2003.).

69. Added by P.L. 107-173, § 202, 116 Stat. 548 (May 14, 2002).

(1) Requirement for integrated immigration and naturalization data system. The Immigration and Naturalization Service shall fully integrate all databases and data systems maintained by the Service that process or contain information on aliens. The fully integrated data system shall be an interoperable component of the electronic data system described in paragraph (2).

(2) Requirement for interoperable data system. Upon the date of commencement of implementation of the plan required by § 201(c), the President shall develop and implement an interoperable electronic data system to provide current and immediate access to information in databases of Federal law enforcement agencies and the intelligence community that is relevant to determine whether to issue a visa or to determine the admissibility or deportability of an alien (also known as the "Chimera system").

(3) Consultation requirement. In the development and implementation of the data system under this subsection, the President shall consult with the Director of the National Institute of Standards and Technology (NIST) and any such other agency as may be deemed appropriate.

(4) Technology standard.

(A) In general. The data system developed and implemented under this subsection, and the databases referred to in paragraph (2), shall utilize the technology standard established pursuant to section 403(c) of the USA PATRIOT Act, as amended by § 201(c)(5) and subparagraph (B).

(B) (Omitted.)

(5) Access to information in data system. Subject to paragraph (6), information in the data system under this subsection shall be readily and easily accessible—

(A) to any consular officer responsible for the issuance of visas;

(B) to any Federal official responsible for determining an alien's admissibility to or deportability from the United States; and

(C) to any Federal law enforcement or intelligence officer determined by regulation to be responsible for the investigation or identification of aliens.

(6) Limitation on access. The President shall, in accordance with applicable Federal laws, establish procedures to restrict access to intelligence information in the data system under this subsection, and the databases referred to in paragraph (2), under circumstances in which such information is not to be disclosed directly to Government officials under paragraph (5).

(b) Name-search capacity and support.

(1) In general. The interoperable electronic data system required by subsection (a) shall—

(A) have the capacity to compensate for disparate name formats among the different data bases referred to in subsection (a);

(B) be searchable on a linguistically sensitive basis;

(C) provide adequate user support;

(D) to the extent practicable, utilize commercially available technology; and

(E) be adjusted and improved, based upon experience with the databases and improvements in the underlying technologies and sciences, on a continuing basis.

(2) Linguistically sensitive searches.

(A) In general. To satisfy the requirement of paragraph (1)(B), the interoperable electronic database shall be searchable based on linguistically sensitive algorithms that—

(i) account for variations in name formats and transliterations, including varied spellings and varied separation or combination of name elements, within a particular language; and

(ii) incorporate advanced linguistic, mathematical, statistical, and anthropological research and methods.

(B) Languages required.

(i) Priority languages. Linguistically sensitive algorithms shall be developed and implemented for no fewer than 4 languages designated as high priorities by the Secretary of State, after consultation with the Attorney General and the Director of Central Intelligence.

(ii) Implementation schedule. Of the 4 linguistically sensitive algorithms required to be developed and implemented under clause (i)—

(I) the highest priority language algorithms shall be implemented within 18 months after the date of enactment of this Act; and

(II) an additional language algorithm shall be implemented each succeeding year for the next three years.

(3) Adequate user support. The Secretary of State and the Attorney General shall jointly prescribe procedures to ensure that consular and immigration officers can, as required, obtain assistance in resolving identity and other questions that may arise about the names of aliens seeking visas or admission to the United States that may be subject to variations in format, transliteration, or other similar phenomenon.

(4) Interim reports. Six months after the date of enactment of this Act, the President shall submit a report to the appropriate committees of Congress on the progress in implementing each requirement of this section.

(5) Reports by intelligence agencies.

(A) Current standards. Not later than 60 days after the date of enactment of this Act, the Director of Central Intelligence shall complete the survey and issue the report previously required by section 309(a) of the Intelligence Authorization Act for Fiscal Year 1998 (50 U.S.C. 403-3 note).

(B) Guidelines. Not later than 120 days after the date of enactment of this Act, the Director of Central Intelligence shall issue the guidelines and submit the copy of those guidelines previously required by section 309(b) of the Intelligence Authorization Act for Fiscal Year 1998 (50 U.S.C. 403-3 note).

(6) Authorization of appropriations. There are authorized to be appropriated such sums as are necessary to carry out the provisions of this subsection.

§ 203.[70] [8 U.S.C. 1723] Commission on interoperable data sharing Appendix H, § 203

(a) Establishment. Not later than one year after the date of enactment of the USA PATRIOT Act, the President shall establish a Commission on Interoperable Data Sharing (in this section referred to as the "Commission"). The purposes of the Commission shall be to—

(1) monitor the protections described in § 201(c)(3);

(2) provide oversight of the interoperable electronic data system described in § 202; and

(3) report to Congress annually on the Commission's findings and recommendations.

(b) Composition. The Commission shall consist of nine members, who shall be appointed by the President, as follows:

(1) One member, who shall serve as Chair of the Commission.

(2) Eight members, who shall be appointed from a list of nominees jointly provided by the Speaker of the House of Representatives, the Minority Leader of the House of Representatives, the Majority Leader of the Senate, and the Minority Leader of the Senate.

(c) Considerations. The Commission shall consider recommendations regarding the following issues:

(1) Adequate protection of privacy concerns inherent in the design, implementation, or operation of the interoperable electronic data system.

(2) Timely adoption of security innovations, consistent with generally accepted security standards, to protect the integrity and confidentiality of information to prevent the risks of accidental or unauthorized loss, access, destruction, use modification, or disclosure of information.

(3) The adequacy of mechanisms to permit the timely correction of errors in data maintained by the interoperable data system.

(4) Other protections against unauthorized use of data to guard against the misuse of the interoperable data system or the data maintained by the system, including recommendations for modifications to existing laws and regulations to sanction misuse of the system.

(d) Authorization of appropriations. There are authorized to be appropriated to the Commission such sums as may be necessary to carry out this section.

§ 204.[71] [8 U.S.C. 1724] Personnel management authorities for positions involved in the development and implementation of the interoperable electronic data system ("Chimera system") Appendix H, § 204

(a) In general. Notwithstanding any other provision of law relating to position classification or employee pay or performance, the Attorney General may hire and fix the compensation of necessary scientific, technical, engineering, and other analytical personnel for the purpose of the development and implementation of the interoperable electronic data system described in section § 202(a)(2) (also known as the "Chimera system").

(b) Limitation on rate of pay. Except as otherwise provided by law, no employee compensated under subsection (a) may be paid at a rate in excess of the rate payable for a position at level III of the Executive Schedule.

(c) Limitation on total calendar year payments. Total payments to employees under any system established under this section shall be subject to the limitation on payments to employees under section 5307 of title 5, United States Code.

(d) Operating plan. Not later than 90 days after the date of enactment of this Act, the Attorney General shall submit to the Committee on Appropriations, the Committee on the Judiciary, the Select Committee on Intelligence, and the Committee on Foreign Relations of the Senate and the Committee on Appropriations, the Committee on the Judiciary, the Permanent Select Committee on Intelligence, and the Committee on International Relations of the House of Representatives an operating plan—

(1) describing the Attorney General's intended use of the authority under this section; and

(2) identifying any provisions of title 5, United States Code, being waived for purposes of the development and implementation of the Chimera system.

(e) Termination date. The authority of this section shall terminate upon the implementation of the Chimera system.

Title III — Visa Issuance

§ 302.[72] [8 U.S.C. 1731] Implementation of an integrated entry and exit data system Appendix H, § 302

(a) Development of system. In developing the integrated entry and exit data system for the ports of entry, as required by the Immigration and Naturalization Service Data Management Improvement Act of 2000 (P.L. 106-215), the Attorney General and the Secretary of State shall—

(1) implement, fund, and use a technology standard under section 403(c) of the USA PATRIOT Act (as amended by §§ 201(c)(5) and 202(a)(4)(B)) at United States ports of entry and at consular posts abroad;

(2) establish a database containing the arrival and departure data from machine-readable visas, passports, and other travel and entry documents possessed by aliens; and

(3) make interoperable all security databases relevant to making determinations of admissibility under section 212 of the Immigration and Nationality Act.

(b) Implementation. In implementing the provisions of subsection (a), the Immigration and Naturalization Service and the Department of State shall—

(1) utilize technologies that facilitate the lawful and efficient cross-border movement of commerce and

70. Added by § 203 of P.L. 107-173, 116 Stat. 551 (May 14, 2002).

71. Added by § 204 of P.L. 107-173, 116 Stat. 551 (May 14, 2002).

72. Added by § 302 of P.L. 107-173, 116 Stat. 552 (May 14, 2002).

persons without compromising the safety and security of the United States; and

(2) consider implementing the North American National Security Program described in § 401.

§ 303.[73] [8 U.S.C. 1732] Machine-readable, tamper-resistant entry and exit documents

(a) Report. Appendix H, § 303

(1) In general. Not later than 180 days after the date of enactment of this Act, the Attorney General, the Secretary of State, and the National Institute of Standards and Technology (NIST), acting jointly, shall submit to the appropriate committees of Congress a comprehensive report assessing the actions that will be necessary, and the considerations to be taken into account, to achieve fully, not later than October 26, 2004—

(A) implementation of the requirements of subsections (b) and (c); and

(B) deployment of the equipment and software to allow biometric comparison and authentication of the documents described in subsections (b) and (c).

(2) Estimates. In addition to the assessment required by paragraph (1), the report required by that paragraph shall include an estimate of the costs to be incurred, and the personnel, man-hours, and other support required, by the Department of Justice, the Department of State, and NIST to achieve the objectives of subparagraphs (A) and (B) of paragraph (1).

(b) Requirements.

(1) In general. Not later than October 26, 2004, the Attorney General and the Secretary of State shall issue to aliens only machine-readable, tamper-resistant visas and other travel and entry documents that use biometric identifiers. The Attorney General and the Secretary of State shall jointly establish document authentication standards and biometric identifiers standards to be employed on such visas and other travel and entry documents from among those biometric identifiers recognized by domestic and international standards organizations.

(2) Readers and scanners at ports of entry.

(A) In general. Not later than October 26, 2005, the Attorney General, in consultation with the Secretary of State, shall install at all ports of entry of the United States equipment and software to allow biometric comparison and authentication of all United States visas and other travel and entry documents issued to aliens, and passports issued pursuant to subsection (c)(1).

(B) Use of readers and scanners. The Attorney General, in consultation with the Secretary of State, shall utilize biometric data readers and scanners that—

(i) domestic and international standards organizations determine to be highly accurate when used to verify identity;

(ii) can read the biometric identifiers utilized under subsections (b)(1) and (c)(1); and

(iii) can authenticate the document presented to verify identity.

(3) Use of technology standard. The systems employed to implement paragraphs (1) and (2) shall utilize the technology standard established pursuant to section 403(c) of the USA PATRIOT Act, as amended by §§ 201(c)(5) and 202(a)(4)(B).

(c) Technology standard for visa waiver participants.

(1) Certification requirement. Not later than October 26, 2005, the government of each country that is designated to participate in the visa waiver program established under section 217 of the Immigration and Nationality Act shall certify, as a condition for designation or continuation of that designation, that it has a program to issue to its nationals machine-readable passports that are tamper-resistant and incorporate biometric and document authentication identifiers that comply with applicable biometric and document identifying standards established by the International Civil Aviation Organization. This paragraph shall not be construed to rescind the requirement of section 217(a)(3) of the Immigration and Nationality Act.

(2) Use of technology standard. On and after October 26, 2005, any alien applying for admission under the visa waiver program under section 217 of the Immigration and Nationality Act shall present a passport that meets the requirements of paragraph (1) unless the alien's passport was issued prior to that date.

(d) Authorization of appropriations. There are authorized to be appropriated such sums as may be necessary to carry out this section, including reimbursement to international and domestic standards organizations.

§ 304.[74] [8 U.S.C. 1733] Terrorist lookout committees Appendix H, § 304

(a) Establishment. The Secretary of State shall require a terrorist lookout committee to be maintained within each United States mission to a foreign country.

(b) Purpose. The purpose of each committee established under subsection (a) shall be—

(1) to utilize the cooperative resources of all elements of the United States mission in the country in which the consular post is located to identify known or potential terrorists and to develop information on those individuals;

(2) to ensure that such information is routinely and consistently brought to the attention of appropriate United States officials for use in administering the immigration laws of the United States; and

(3) to ensure that the names of known and suspected terrorists are entered into the appropriate lookout databases.

(c) Composition; chair. The Secretary shall establish rules governing the composition of such committees.

(d) Meetings. Each committee established under subsection (a) shall meet at least monthly to share in-

73. Added by § 303 of P.L. 107-173, 116 Stat. 553 (May 14, 2002); amended at (b)(2)(A) by P.L. 108-299, § 1, 118 Stat. 1100 (August 9, 2004).

74. Added by P.L. 107-173, § 304, 116 Stat. 554 (May 14, 2002).

formation pertaining to the committee's purpose as described in subsection (b)(2).

(e) Periodic reports to the Secretary of State. Each committee established under subsection (a) shall submit monthly reports to the Secretary of State describing the committee's activities, whether or not information on known or suspected terrorists was developed during the month.

(f) Reports to Congress. The Secretary of State shall submit a report on a quarterly basis to the appropriate committees of Congress on the status of the committees established under subsection (a).

(g) Authorization of appropriations. There are authorized to be appropriated such sums as may be necessary to implement this section.

§ 305.[75] [8 U.S.C. 1734] Improved training for consular officers Appendix H, § 305

(a)[76] Training. The Secretary of State shall require that all consular officers responsible for adjudicating visa applications, before undertaking to perform consular responsibilities, receive specialized training in the effective screening of visa applicants who pose a potential threat to the safety or security of the United States. Such officers shall be specially and extensively trained in the identification of aliens inadmissible under section 212(a)(3)(A) and (B) of the Immigration and Nationality Act, interagency and international intelligence sharing regarding terrorists and terrorism, and cultural-sensitivity toward visa applicants. In accordance with section 7201(d) of the 9/11 Commission Implementation Act of 2004 [P.L. 108-458, §§ 7001 et seq.], and as part of the consular training provided to such officers by the Secretary of State, such officers shall also receive training in detecting fraudulent documents and general document forensics and shall be required as part of such training to work with immigration officers conducting inspections of applicants for admission into the United States at ports of entry.

(b) Use of foreign intelligence information. As an on going component of the training required in subsection (a), the Secretary of State shall coordinate with the Assistant to the President for Homeland Security, Federal law enforcement agencies, and the intelligence community to compile and disseminate to the Bureau of Consular Affairs reports, bulletins, updates, and other current unclassified information relevant to terrorists and terrorism and to screening visa applicants who pose a potential threat to the safety or security of the United States.

(c)[77] [Repealed]

75. Added by P.L. 107-173, § 305, 116 Stat. 555 (May 14, 2002).

76. As amended by P.L. 108-458, § 7203(c), 118 Stat. 3814 (December 17, 2004).

77. Repealed by P.L. 114-113, Div. O, Title II, 202(c), 129 Stat. 2989 (December 18, 2015)

§ 306.[78] [8 U.S.C. 1735] Restriction on issuance of visas to nonimmigrants from countries that are state sponsors of international terrorism Appendix H, § 306

(a) In general. No nonimmigrant visa under section 101(a)(15) of the Immigration and Nationality Act shall be issued to any alien from a country that is a state sponsor of international terrorism unless the Secretary of State determines, in consultation with the Attorney General and the heads of other appropriate United States agencies, that such alien does not pose a threat to the safety or national security of the United States. In making a determination under this subsection, the Secretary of State shall apply standards developed by the Secretary of State, in consultation with the Attorney General and the heads of other appropriate United States agencies, that are applicable to the nationals of such states.

(b) State sponsor of international terrorism defined.

(1) In general. In this section, the term "state sponsor of international terrorism" means any country the government of which has been determined by the Secretary of State under any of the laws specified in paragraph (2) to have repeatedly provided support for acts of international terrorism.

(2) Laws under which determinations were made. The laws specified in this paragraph are the following:

(A) Section 6(j)(1)(A) of the Export Administration Act of 1979 (or successor statute).

(B) Section 40(d) of the Arms Export Control Act.

(C) Section 620A(a) of the Foreign Assistance Act of 1961.

§ 307. Designation of program countries under the visa waiver program. Appendix H, § 307

***

(b)[79] [8 U.S.C. 1736] Check of lookout databases. Prior to the admission of an alien under the visa waiver program established under section 217 of the Immigration and Nationality Act, the Immigration and Naturalization Service shall determine that the applicant for admission does not appear in any of the appropriate lookout databases available to immigration inspectors at the time the alien seeks admission to the United States.

§ 308.[80] [8 U.S.C. 1737] Tracking system for stolen passports Appendix H, § 308

(a) Entering stolen passport identification numbers in the interoperable data system.

(1) In general. Beginning with implementation under section 202 of the law enforcement and intelligence data system, not later than 72 hours after receiving notification of the loss or theft of a United States or for-

78. Added by P.L. 107-173, § 306, 116 Stat. 555 (May 14, 2002).

79. Added by P.L. 107-173, § 307(b), 116 Stat. 556 (May 14, 2002).

80. Added by P.L. 107-173, § 308, 116 Stat. 556 (May 14, 2002).

eign passport, the Attorney General and the Secretary of State, as appropriate, shall enter into such system the corresponding identification number for the lost or stolen passport.

(2) Entry of information on previously lost or stolen passports. To the extent practicable, the Attorney General, in consultation with the Secretary of State, shall enter into such system the corresponding identification numbers for the United States and foreign passports lost or stolen prior to the implementation of such system.

(b) Transition period. Until such time as the law enforcement and intelligence data system described in section 202 is fully implemented, the Attorney General shall enter the data described in subsection (a) into an existing data system being used to determine the admissibility or deportability of aliens.

§ 309.[81] [8 U.S.C. 1738] Identification documents for certain newly admitted aliens Appendix H, § 309

Not later than 180 days after the date of enactment of this Act, the Attorney General shall ensure that, immediately upon the arrival in the United States of an individual admitted under section 207 of the Immigration and Nationality Act (8 U.S.C. 1157), or immediately upon an alien being granted asylum under section 208 of such Act (8 U.S.C. 1158), the alien will be issued an employment authorization document. Such document shall, at a minimum, contain the fingerprint and photograph of such alien.

Title IV — Inspection and Admission of Aliens

§ 401.[82] [8 U.S.C. 1751] Study of the feasibility of a North American national security program Appendix H, § 401

(a) In general. The President shall conduct a study of the feasibility of establishing a North American National Security Program to enhance the mutual security and safety of the United States, Canada, and Mexico.

(b) Study elements. In conducting the study required by subsection (a), the President shall consider the following:

(1) Preclearance. The feasibility of establishing a program enabling foreign national travelers to the United States to submit voluntarily to a preclearance procedure established by the Department of State and the Immigration and Naturalization Service to determine whether such travelers are admissible to the United States under section 212 of the Immigration and Nationality Act. Consideration shall be given to the feasibility of expanding the preclearance program to include the preclearance both of foreign nationals traveling to Canada and foreign nationals traveling to Mexico.

(2) Preinspection. The feasibility of expanding preinspection facilities at foreign airports as described in section 235A of the Immigration and Nationality Act. Consideration shall be given to the feasibility of expanding preinspections to foreign nationals on air flights destined for Canada and Mexico, and the cross training and funding of inspectors from Canada and Mexico.

(3) Conditions. A determination of the measures necessary to ensure that the conditions required by section 235A(a)(5) of the Immigration and Nationality Act are satisfied, including consultation with experts recognized for their expertise regarding the conditions required by that section.

(c) Report. Not later than 1 year after the date of enactment of this Act, the President shall submit to the appropriate committees of Congress a report setting forth the findings of the study conducted under subsection (a).

(d) Authorization of appropriations. There are authorized to be appropriated such sums as may be necessary to carry out this section.

§ 403. Time period for inspections. Appendix H, § 403

***

(b)[83] [8 U.S.C. 1752] Staffing levels at ports of entry The Immigration and Naturalization Service shall staff ports of entry at such levels that would be adequate to meet traffic flow and inspection time objectives efficiently without compromising the safety and security of the United States. Estimated staffing levels under workforce models for the Immigration and Naturalization Service shall be based on the goal of providing immigration services described in section 286(g) of such Act within 45 minutes of a passenger's presentation for inspection.

§ 404.[84] [8 U.S.C. 1753] Joint United States-Canada projects for alternative inspections services Appendix H, § 404

(a) In general. United States border inspections agencies, including the Immigration and Naturalization Service, acting jointly and under an agreement of cooperation with the Government of Canada, may conduct joint United States-Canada inspections projects on the international border between the two countries. Each such project may provide alternative inspections services and shall undertake to harmonize the criteria for inspections applied by the two countries in implementing those projects.

(b) Annual report. The Attorney General and the Secretary of the Treasury shall prepare and submit annually to Congress a report on the joint United States-Canada inspections projects conducted under subsection (a).

(c) Exemption from Administrative Procedure Act and Paperwork Reduction Act. Subchapter II of chapter 5 of title 5, United States Code (commonly referred

81. Added by P.L. 107-173, § 309, 116 Stat. 556 (May 14, 2002).
82. Added by P.L. 107-173, § 401, 116 Stat. 557 (May 14, 2002).
83. Added by P.L. 107-173, § 403(b), 116 Stat. 559 (May 14, 2002).
84. Added by P.L. 107-173, § 404, 116 Stat. 560 (May14, 2002).

to as the "Administrative Procedure Act") and chapter 35 of title 44, United States Code (commonly referred to as the "Paperwork Reduction Act") shall not apply to fee setting for services and other administrative requirements relating to projects described in subsection (a), except that fees and forms established for such projects shall be published as a notice in the Federal Register.

Title V — Foreign Students and Exchange Visitors

§ 501.[85] [8 U.S.C. 1761] Foreign student monitoring program Appendix H, § 501

(a) (Omitted.)

(b) Information required of the visa applicant. Prior to the issuance of a visa under subparagraph (F), subparagraph (M), or, with respect to an alien seeking to attend an approved institution of higher education, subparagraph (J) of section 101(a)(15) of the Immigration and Nationality Act, each alien applying for such visa shall provide to a consular officer the following information:

(1) The alien's address in the country of origin.

(2) The names and addresses of the alien's spouse, children, parents, and siblings.

(3) The names of contacts of the alien in the alien's country of residence who could verify information about the alien.

(4) Previous work history, if any, including the names and addresses of employers.

(c) Transitional program.

(1) In general. Not later than 120 days after the date of enactment of this Act and until such time as the system described in section 641 of the Illegal Immigration Reform and Immigrant Responsibility Act (as amended by subsection (a)) is fully implemented, the following requirements shall apply:

(A) Restrictions on issuance of visas. A visa may not be issued to an alien under subparagraph (F), subparagraph (M), or, with respect to an alien seeking to attend an approved institution of higher education, subparagraph (J) of section 101(a)(15) of the Immigration and Nationality Act, unless—

(i) the Department of State has received from an approved institution of higher education or other approved educational institution electronic evidence of documentation of the alien's acceptance at that institution; and

(ii) the consular officer has adequately reviewed the applicant's visa record.

(B) Notification upon visa issuance. Upon the issuance of a visa under section 101(a)(15)(F) or (M) of the Immigration and Nationality Act to an alien, the Secretary of State shall transmit to the Immigration and Naturalization Service a notification of the issuance of that visa.

(C) Notification upon admission of alien. The Immigration and Naturalization Service shall notify the approved institution of higher education or other approved educational institution that an alien accepted for such institution or program has been admitted to the United States.

(D) Notification of failure of enrollment. Not later than 30 days after the deadline for registering for classes for an academic term, the approved institution of higher education or other approved educational institution shall inform the Immigration and Naturalization Service through data-sharing arrangements of any failure of any alien described in subparagraph (C) to enroll or to commence participation.

(2) Requirement to submit list of approved institutions. Not later than 30 days after the date of enactment of this Act, the Attorney General shall provide the Secretary of State with a list of all approved institutions of higher education and other approved educational institutions that are authorized to receive nonimmigrants under section 101(a)(15)(F) or (M) of the Immigration and Nationality Act.

(3) Authorization of appropriations. There are authorized to be appropriated such sums as may be necessary to carry out this subsection.

§ 502.[86] [8 U.S.C. 1762] Review of institutions and other entities authorized to enroll or sponsor certain non-immigrants Appendix H, § 502

(a) Periodic review of compliance. Not later than two years after the date of enactment of this Act, and every two years thereafter, the Commissioner of Immigration and Naturalization, in consultation with the Secretary of Education, shall conduct a review of the institutions certified to receive nonimmigrants under section 101(a)(15)(F), (M), or (J) of the Immigration and Nationality Act. Each review shall determine whether the institutions are in compliance with—

(1) recordkeeping and reporting requirements to receive nonimmigrants under section 101(a)(15)(F), (M), or (J) of that Act; and

(2) recordkeeping and reporting requirements under section 641 of the Illegal Immigration Reform and Immigrant Responsibility Act of 1996.

(b) Periodic review of sponsors of exchange visitors.

(1) Requirement for reviews. Not later than two years after the date of enactment of this Act, and every two years thereafter, the Secretary of State shall conduct a review of the entities designated to sponsor exchange visitor program participants under section 101(a)(15)(J) of the Immigration and Nationality Act.

(2) Determinations. On the basis of reviews of entities under paragraph (1), the Secretary shall determine whether the entities are in compliance with—

(A) recordkeeping and reporting requirements to receive nonimmigrant exchange visitor program participants under section 101(a)(15)(J) of the Immigration and Nationality Act; and

(B) recordkeeping and reporting requirements under section 641 of the Illegal Immigration Reform and Immigrant Responsibility Act of 1996 (8 U.S.C. 1372).

(c) Effect of material failure to comply. Material failure of an institution or other entity to comply with

85. Added by P.L. 107-173, § 501, 116 Stat. 560 (May 14, 2002).

86. Added by P.L. 107-173, § 502, 116 Stat. 563 (May 14, 2002).

the recordkeeping and reporting requirements to receive nonimmigrant students or exchange visitor program participants under section 101(a)(15)(F), (M), or (J) of the Immigration and Nationality Act, or section 641 of the Illegal Immigration Reform and Immigrant Responsibility Act of 1996 (8 U.S.C. 1372), shall result in the suspension for at least one year or termination, at the election of the Commissioner of Immigration and Naturalization, of the institution's approval to receive such students, or result in the suspension for at least one year or termination, at the election of the Secretary of State, of the other entity's designation to sponsor exchange visitor program participants, as the case may be.

Title VI — Miscellaneous Provisions

§ 602.[87] [8 U.S.C. 1771] General Accounting Office study

(a) Requirement for study..

(1) In general. The Comptroller General of the United States shall conduct a study to determine the feasibility and utility of implementing a requirement that each nonimmigrant alien in the United States submit to the Commissioner of Immigration and Naturalization each year a current address and, where applicable, the name and address of an employer.

(2) Nonimmigrant alien defined. In paragraph (1), the term "nonimmigrant alien" means an alien described in section 101(a)(15) of the Immigration and Nationality Act.

(b) Report. Not later than 1 year after the date of enactment of this Act, the Comptroller General shall submit to Congress a report on the results of the study under subsection (a). The report shall include the Comptroller General's findings, together with any recommendations that the Comptroller General considers appropriate.

§ 603.[88] [8 U.S.C. 1772] International cooperation Appendix H, § 603

(a) International electronic data system. The Secretary of State and the Commissioner of Immigration and Naturalization, in consultation with the Assistant to the President for Homeland Security, shall jointly conduct a study of the alternative approaches (including the costs of, and procedures necessary for, each alternative approach) for encouraging or requiring Canada, Mexico, and countries treated as visa waiver program countries under section 217 of the Immigration and Nationality Act to develop an intergovernmental network of interoperable electronic data systems that—

(1) facilitates real-time access to that country's law enforcement and intelligence information that is needed by the Department of State and the Immigration and Naturalization Service to screen visa applicants and applicants for admission into the United States to identify aliens who are inadmissible or deportable under the Immigration and Nationality Act;

(2) is interoperable with the electronic data system implemented under section 202; and

(3) performs in accordance with implementation of the technology standard referred to in section 202(a).

(b) Report. Not later than 1 year after the date of enactment of this Act, the Secretary of State and the Attorney General shall submit to the appropriate committees of Congress a report setting forth the findings of the study conducted under subsection (a).

§ 604.[89] [8 U.S.C. 1773] Statutory construction Appendix H, § 604

Nothing in this Act shall be construed to impose requirements that are inconsistent with the North American Free Trade Agreement or to require additional documents for aliens for whom documentary requirements are waived under section 212(d)(4)(B) of the Immigration and Nationality Act (8 U.S.C. 1182(d)(4)(B)).

§ 605.[90] [8 U.S.C. 1774] Annual report on aliens who fail to appear after release on own recognizance Appendix H, § 605

(a) Requirement for report. Not later than January 15 of each year, the Attorney General shall submit to the appropriate committees of Congress a report on the total number of aliens who, during the preceding year, failed to attend a removal proceeding after having been arrested outside a port of entry, served a notice to appear under section 239(a)(1) of the Immigration and Nationality Act (8 U.S.C. 1229(a)(1)), and released on the alien's own recognizance. The report shall also take into account the number of cases in which there were defects in notices of hearing or the service of notices of hearing, together with a description and analysis of the effects, if any, that the defects had on the attendance of aliens at the proceedings.

(b) Initial report. Notwithstanding the time for submission of the annual report provided in subsection (a), the report for 2001 shall be submitted not later than 6 months after the date of enactment of this Act.

§ 606.[91] [8 U.S.C. 1775] Retention of nonimmigrant visa applications by the Department of State Appendix H, § 606

The Department of State shall retain, for a period of seven years from the date of application, every application for a nonimmigrant visa under section 101(a)(15) of the Immigration and Nationality Act (8 U.S.C. 1101(a)(15)) in a form that will be admissible in the courts of the United States or in administrative proceedings, including removal proceedings under such Act, without regard to whether the application was approved or denied.

87. Added by P.L. 107-173, § 602, 116 Stat. 564 (May 14, 2002).
88. Added by P.L. 107-173, § 603, 116 Stat. 564 (May 14, 2002).
89. Added by P.L. 107-173, § 604, 116 Stat. 565 (May 14, 2002).
90. Added by P.L. 107-173, § 605, 116 Stat. 565 (May 14, 2002).
91. Added by P.L. 107-173, § 606, 116 Stat. 565 (May 14, 2002).

§ 607.[92], [93] [8 U.S.C. 1776] Training program Appendix H, § 607

(1) Review, evaluation, and revision of existing training programs. The Secretary of Homeland Security shall—

(A) review and evaluate the training regarding travel and identity documents, and techniques, patterns, and trends associated with terrorist travel that is provided to personnel of the Department of Homeland Security;

(B) in coordination with the Secretary of State, review and evaluate the training described in subparagraph (A) that is provided to relevant personnel of the Department of State; and

(C) in coordination with the Secretary of State, develop and implement an initial training and periodic retraining program—

(i) to teach border, immigration, and consular officials (who inspect or review travel or identity documents as part of their official duties) how to effectively detect, intercept, and disrupt terrorist travel; and

(ii) to ensure that the officials described in clause (i) regularly receive the most current information on such matters and are periodically retrained on the matters described in paragraph (2).

(2) Required topics of revised programs. The training program developed under paragraph (1)(C) shall include training in—

(A) methods for identifying fraudulent and genuine travel documents;

(B) methods for detecting terrorist indicators on travel documents and other relevant identity documents;

(C) recognition of travel patterns, tactics, and behaviors exhibited by terrorists;

(Deffective utilization of information contained in databases and data systems available to the Department of Homeland Security; and

(E) other topics determined to be appropriate by the Secretary of Homeland Security, in consultation with the Secretary of State or the Director of National Intelligence.

(3) Implementation.

(A) Department of Homeland Security.

(i) In general. The Secretary of Homeland Security shall provide all border and immigration officials who inspect or review travel or identity documents as part of their official duties with the training described in paragraph (1)(C).

(ii) Report to Congress. Not later than 12 months after the date of enactment of this Act, and annually thereafter for a period of 3 years, the Secretary of Homeland Security shall submit a report to Congress that—

(I) describes the number of border and immigration officials who inspect or review identity documents as part of their official duties, and the proportion of whom have received the revised training program described in paragraph (1)(C)(i);

(II) explains the reasons, if any, for not completing the requisite training described in paragraph (1)(C)(i);

(III) provides a timetable for completion of the training described in paragraph (1)(C)(i) for those who have not received such training; and

(IV) describes the status of periodic retraining of appropriate personnel described in paragraph (1)(C)(ii).

(B) Department of State.

(i) In general. The Secretary of State shall provide all consular officers who inspect or review travel or identity documents as part of their official duties with the training described in paragraph (1)(C).

(ii) Report to Congress. Not later than 12 months after the date of enactment of this Act [enacted December 17, 2004], and annually thereafter for a period of 3 years, the Secretary of State shall submit a report to Congress that—

(I) describes the number of consular officers who inspect or review travel or identity documents as part of their official duties, and the proportion of whom have received the revised training program described in paragraph (1)(C)(i);

(II) explains the reasons, if any, for not completing the requisite training described in paragraph (1)(C)(i);

(III) provides a timetable for completion of the training described in paragraph (1)(C)(i) for those who have not received such training; and

(IV) describes the status of periodic retraining of appropriate personnel described in paragraph (1)(C)(ii).

(4) Assistance to others. The Secretary of Homeland Security may assist States, Indian tribes, local governments, and private organizations to establish training programs related to terrorist travel intelligence.

(5) Authorization of appropriations. There are authorized to be appropriated such sums as may be necessary for each of the fiscal years 2005 through 2009 to carry out the provisions of this subsection.

§ 608.[94] [8 U.S.C. 1777] Establishment of Human Smuggling and Trafficking Center.

(a) Establishment. There is established a Human Smuggling and Trafficking Center (referred to in this section as the "Center"). Appendix H, § 608

(b) Operation. The Secretary of State, the Secretary of Homeland Security, and the Attorney General shall operate the Center in accordance with the Memorandum of Understanding entitled, "Human Smuggling and Trafficking Center (HSTC), Charter".

(c) Functions. In addition to such other responsibilities as the President may assign, the Center shall—

92. Added by P.L. 108-458, § 7201(d), 118 Stat. 3811 (December 17, 2004).

93. See § 7201(a) of P.L. 108-458, 118 Stat. 3808 (December 17, 2004) for congressional findings regarding counterterrorist travel intelligence.

94. Added by P.L. 108-458, § 7202, 118 Stat. 3813 (December 17, 2004); Amended by P. L. 110-53, Title VII, Subtitle C, § 721(a)-(c), 121 Stat. 346 (August 3, 2007).

(1) serve as the focal point for interagency efforts to integrate and disseminate intelligence and information related to terrorist travel;

(2) serve as a clearinghouse with respect to all relevant information from all Federal Government agencies in support of the United States strategy to prevent separate, but related, issues of clandestine terrorist travel and facilitation of migrant smuggling and trafficking of persons;

(3) ensure cooperation among all relevant policy, law enforcement, diplomatic, and intelligence agencies of the Federal Government to improve effectiveness and to convert all information available to the Federal Government relating to clandestine terrorist travel and facilitation, migrant smuggling, and trafficking of persons into tactical, operational, and strategic intelligence that can be used to combat such illegal activities; and

(4) prepare and submit to Congress, on an annual basis, a strategic assessment regarding vulnerabilities in the United States and foreign travel system that may be exploited by international terrorists, human smugglers and traffickers, and their facilitators.

(d) Director. The Secretary of Homeland Security shall nominate an official of the Government of the United States to serve as the Director of the Center, in accordance with the requirements of the memorandum of understanding entitled the "Human Smuggling and Trafficking Center (HSTC) Charter".

(e) Staffing of the Center.

(1) In general. The Secretary of Homeland Security, in cooperation with heads of other relevant agencies and departments, shall ensure that the Center is staffed with not fewer than 40 full-time equivalent positions, including, as appropriate, detailees from the following:

(A) Agencies and offices within the Department of Homeland Security, including the following:

(i) The Office of Intelligence and Analysis.

(ii) The Transportation Security Administration.

(iii) United States Citizenship and Immigration Services.

(iv) United States Customs and Border Protection.

(v) The United States Coast Guard.

(vi) United States Immigration and Customs Enforcement.

(B) Other departments, agencies, or entities, including the following:

(i) The Central Intelligence Agency.

(ii) The Department of Defense.

(iii) The Department of the Treasury.

(iv) The National Counterterrorism Center.

(v) The National Security Agency.

(vi) The Department of Justice.

(vii) The Department of State.

(viii) Any other relevant agency or department.

(2) Expertise of detailees. The Secretary of Homeland Security, in cooperation with the head of each agency, department, or other entity referred to in paragraph (1), shall ensure that the detailees provided to the Center under such paragraph include an adequate number of personnel who are—

(A) intelligence analysts or special agents with demonstrated experience related to human smuggling, trafficking in persons, or terrorist travel; and

(B) personnel with experience in the areas of—

(i) consular affairs;

(ii) counterterrorism;

(iii) criminal law enforcement;

(iv) intelligence analysis;

(v) prevention and detection of document fraud;

(vi) border inspection;

(vii) immigration enforcement; or

(viii) human trafficking and combating severe forms of trafficking in persons.

(3) Enhanced personnel management.

(A) Incentives for service in certain positions.

(i) In general. The Secretary of Homeland Security, and the heads of other relevant agencies, shall prescribe regulations or promulgate personnel policies to provide incentives for service on the staff of the Center, particularly for serving terms of at least two years duration.

(ii) Forms of incentives. Incentives under clause (i) may include financial incentives, bonuses, and such other awards and incentives as the Secretary and the heads of other relevant agencies, consider appropriate.

(B) Enhanced promotion for service at the center. Notwithstanding any other provision of law, the Secretary of Homeland Security, and the heads of other relevant agencies, shall ensure that personnel who are assigned or detailed to service at the Center shall be considered for promotion at rates equivalent to or better than similarly situated personnel of such agencies who are not so assigned or detailed, except that this subparagraph shall not apply in the case of personnel who are subject to the provisions of the Foreign Service Act of 1980.

(f) Administrative support and funding. The Secretary of Homeland Security shall provide to the Center the administrative support and funding required for its maintenance, including funding for personnel, leasing of office space, supplies, equipment, technology, training, and travel expenses necessary for the Center to carry out its functions.

(g) Report.

(1) Initial report. Not later than 180 days after December 17, 2004, the President shall transmit to Congress a report regarding the implementation of this section, including a description of the staffing and resource needs of the Center.

(2) Follow-up report. Not later than 180 days after the date of the enactment of the Implementing Recommendations of the 9/11 Commission Act of 2007 [enacted August 3, 2007], the President shall transmit to Congress a report regarding the operation of the Center and the activities carried out by the Center, including a description of—

(A) the roles and responsibilities of each agency or department that is participating in the Center;

(B) the mechanisms used to share information among each such agency or department;

(C) the personnel provided to the Center by each such agency or department;

(D) the type of information and reports being disseminated by the Center;

(E) any efforts by the Center to create a centralized Federal Government database to store information related to unlawful travel of foreign nationals, including a description of any such database and of the manner in which information utilized in such a database would be collected, stored, and shared;

(F) how each agency and department shall utilize its resources to ensure that the Center uses intelligence to focus and drive its efforts;

(G) efforts to consolidate networked systems for the Center;

(H) the mechanisms for the sharing of homeland security information from the Center to the Office of Intelligence and Analysis, including how such sharing shall be consistent with section 1016(b) [6 U.S.C. § 485(b)];

(I) the ability of participating personnel in the Center to freely access necessary databases and share information regarding issues related to human smuggling, trafficking in persons, and terrorist travel;

(J) how the assignment of personnel to the Center is incorporated into the civil service career path of such personnel; and

(K) cooperation and coordination efforts, including any memorandums of understanding, among participating agencies and departments regarding issues related to human smuggling, trafficking in persons, and terrorist travel.

(h) Relationship to the NCTC. As part of its mission to combat terrorist travel, the Center shall work to support the efforts of the National Counterterrorism Center.

(i) Coordination with the Office of Intelligence and Analysis. The Office of Intelligence and Analysis, in coordination with the Center, shall submit to relevant State, local, and tribal law enforcement agencies periodic reports regarding terrorist threats related to human smuggling, human trafficking, and terrorist travel.

****

APPENDIX I — IMMIGRATION BENEFITS, 21ST CENTURYDEPARTMENT OF JUSTICE APPROPRIATIONS AUTHORIZATION ACT

Chapter 1 of P.L. 107-273, div. C, title I, subtitle B, 116 Stat. 1837 (November 2, 2002)[95]

§ 11031. Removal of conditional basis of permanent resident status for certain alien entrepreneurs, spouses, and children Appendix I, § 11031

(a) In general. In lieu of the provisions of section 216A(c)(3) of the Immigration and Nationality Act, subsection (c) shall apply in the case of an eligible alien described in subsection (b)(1).

(b) Eligible aliens described.

(1) In general. An alien is an eligible alien described in this subsection if the alien—

(A) filed, under section 204(a)(1)(H) of the Immigration and Nationality Act (or any predecessor provision), a petition to accord the alien a status under section 203(b)(5) of such Act that was approved by the Attorney General after January 1, 1995, and before August 31, 1998;

(B) pursuant to such approval, obtained the status of an alien entrepreneur with permanent resident status on a conditional basis described in section 216A of such Act; and

(C) timely filed, in accordance with section 216A(c)(1)(A) of such Act and before the date of the enactment of this Act [enacted November 2, 2002], a petition requesting the removal of such conditional basis.

(2) Reopening petitions previously denied.

(A) In general. In the case of a petition described in paragraph (1)(C) that was denied under section 216A(c)(3)(C) of the Immigration and Nationality Act before the date of the enactment of this Act, upon a motion to reopen such petition filed by the eligible alien not later than 60 days after such date, the Attorney General shall make determinations on such petition pursuant to subsection (c).

(B) Petitioners abroad. In the case of such an eligible alien who is no longer physically present in the United States, the Attorney General shall establish a process under which the alien may be paroled into the United States if necessary in order to obtain the determinations under subsection (c), unless the Attorney General finds that—

(i) the alien is inadmissible or deportable on any ground; or

(ii) the petition described in paragraph (1)(C) was denied on the ground that it contains a material misrepresentation in the facts and information described in section 216A(d)(1) of the Immigration and Nationality Act and alleged in the petition with respect to a commercial enterprise.

(C) Deportation or removal proceedings. In the case of such an eligible alien who was placed in deportation or removal proceedings by reason of the denial of the petition described in paragraph (1)(C), a motion to reopen filed under subparagraph (A) shall be treated as a motion to reopen such proceedings. The Attorney General shall grant such motion notwithstanding any time and number limitations imposed by law on motions to reopen such proceedings, except that the scope of any proceeding reopened on this basis shall be limited to whether any order of deportation or removal should be vacated, and the alien granted the status of an alien lawfully admitted for permanent residence (unconditionally or on a conditional basis), by reason of the determinations made under subsection (c). An alien who is inadmissible or deportable on any ground shall not be granted such status, except that this prohibition shall not apply to an alien who has been paroled into the United States under subparagraph (B).

95. The following free-standing provisions, §§ 11031 to 11034 of P.L. 107-273, are classified as notes to § 1186b of title 8, United Statues Code, which corresponds to § 216A of the INA.

(c) Determinations on petitions.

(1) Initial determination.

(A) In general. With respect to each eligible alien described in subsection (b)(1), the Attorney General shall make a determination, not later than 180 days after the date of the enactment of this Act [enacted November 2, 2002], whether—

(i) the petition described in subsection (b)(1)(C) contains any material misrepresentation in the facts and information described in section 216A(d)(1) of the Immigration and Nationality Act and alleged in the petition with respect to a commercial enterprise (regardless of whether such enterprise is a limited partnership and regardless of whether the alien entered the enterprise after its formation);

(ii) subject to subparagraphs (B) and (C), such enterprise created full-time jobs for not fewer than 10 United States citizens or aliens lawfully admitted for permanent residence or other immigrants lawfully authorized to be employed in the United States (other than the eligible alien and the alien's spouse, sons, or daughters), and those jobs exist or existed on any of the dates described in subparagraph (D); and

(iii) on any of the dates described in subparagraph (D), the alien is in substantial compliance with the capital investment requirement described in section 216A(d)(1)(B) of the Immigration and Nationality Act.

(B) Investment under pilot immigration program. For purposes of subparagraph (A)(ii), an investment that satisfies the requirements of section 610(c) of the Departments of Commerce, Justice, and State, the Judiciary, and Related Agencies Appropriations Act, 1993 [P.L. 102-395] (8 U.S.C. 1153 note), as in effect on the date of the enactment of this Act [enacted November 2, 2002], shall be deemed to satisfy the requirements of such subparagraph.

(C) Exception for troubled businesses. In the case of an eligible alien who has made a capital investment in a troubled business (as defined in 8 CFR 204.6(e), as in effect on the date of the enactment of this Act [enacted November 2, 2002]), in lieu of the determination under subparagraph (A)(ii), the Attorney General shall determine whether the number of employees of the business, as measured on any of the dates described in subparagraph (D), is at no less than the pre-investment level.

(D) Dates. The dates described in this subparagraph are the following:

(i) The date on which the petition described in subsection (b)(1)(C) is filed.

(ii) 6 months after the date described in clause (I).

(iii) The date on which the determination under subparagraph (A) or (C) is made.

(E) Removal of conditional basis if favorable determination. If the Attorney General renders an affirmative determination with respect to clauses (ii) and (iii) of subparagraph (A), and if the Attorney General renders a negative determination with respect to clause (i) of such subparagraph, the Attorney General shall so notify the alien involved and shall remove the conditional basis of the alien's status (and that of the alien's spouse and children if it was obtained under section 216A of the Immigration and Nationality Act (8 U.S.C. 1186b)) effective as of the second anniversary of the alien's lawful admission for permanent residence.

(D) Dates. The dates described in this subparagraph are the following:

(i) The date on which the petition described in subsection (b)(1)(C) is filed.

(ii) 6 months after the date described in clause (I).

(iii) The date on which the determination under subparagraph (A) or (C) is made.

(E) Removal of conditional basis if favorable determination. If the Attorney General renders an affirmative determination with respect to clauses (ii) and (iii) of subparagraph (A), and if the Attorney General renders a negative determination with respect to clause (i) of such subparagraph, the Attorney General shall so notify the alien involved and shall remove the conditional basis of the alien's status (and that of the alien's spouse and children if it was obtained under section 216A of the Immigration and Nationality Act effective as of the second anniversary of the alien's lawful admission for permanent residence.

(F) Requirements relating to adverse determinations.

(i) Notice. If the Attorney General renders an adverse determination with respect to clause (i), (ii), or (iii) of subparagraph (A), the Attorney General shall so notify the alien involved. The notice shall be in writing and shall state the factual basis for any adverse determination. The Attorney General shall provide the alien with an opportunity to submit evidence to rebut any adverse determination. If the Attorney General reverses all adverse determinations pursuant to such rebuttal, the Attorney General shall so notify the alien involved and shall remove the conditional basis of the alien's status (and that of the alien's spouse and children if it was obtained under section 216A of the Immigration and Nationality Act effective as of the second anniversary of the alien's lawful admission for permanent residence.

(ii) Continuation of conditional basis if certain adverse determinations. If the Attorney General renders an adverse determination with respect to clause (ii) or (iii) of subparagraph (A), and the eligible alien's rebuttal does not cause the Attorney General to reverse such determination, the Attorney General shall continue the conditional basis of the alien's permanent resident status (and that of the alien's spouse and children if it was obtained under section 216A of the Immigration and Nationality Act for a 2-year period.

(iii) Termination if adverse determination. If the Attorney General renders an adverse determination with respect to subparagraph (A)(i), and the eligible alien's rebuttal does not cause the Attorney General to reverse such determination, the Attorney General shall so notify the alien involved and, subject to subsection (d), shall terminate the permanent resident status of the alien (and that of the alien's spouse and children if it was obtained on a conditional basis under section 216A of the Immigration and Nationality Act.

(iv) Administrative and judicial review. An alien may seek administrative review of an adverse determination made under subparagraph (A) by filing a petition for such review with the Board of Immigration Appeals. If the Board of Immigration Appeals denies the petition, the alien may seek judicial review. The procedures for judicial review under this clause shall be the same as the procedures for judicial review of a final order of removal under section 242(a)(1) of the Immigration and Nationality Act (8 U.S.C. 1252(a)(1)). During the period in which an administrative or judicial appeal under this clause is pending, the Attorney General shall continue the conditional basis of the alien's permanent resident status (and that of the alien's spouse and children if it was obtained under section 216A of the Immigration and Nationality Act.

(2) Second determination.

(A) Authorization to consider investments in other commercial enterprises. In determining under this paragraph whether to remove a conditional basis continued under paragraph (1)(F)(ii) with respect to an alien, the Attorney General shall consider any capital investment made by the alien in a commercial enterprise (regardless of whether such enterprise is a limited partnership and regardless of whether the alien entered the enterprise after its formation), in the United States, regardless of whether that investment was made before or after the determinations under paragraph (1) and regardless of whether the commercial enterprise is the same as that considered in the determinations under such paragraph, if facts and information with respect to the investment and the enterprise are included in the petition submitted under subparagraph (B).

(B) Petition. In order for a conditional basis continued under paragraph (1)(F)(ii) for an eligible alien (and the alien's spouse and children) to be removed, the alien must submit to the Attorney General, during the period described in subparagraph (C), a petition which requests the removal of such conditional basis and which states, under penalty of perjury, the facts and information described in subparagraphs (A) and (B) of section 216A(d)(1) of the Immigration and Nationality Act with respect to any commercial enterprise (regardless of whether such enterprise is a limited partnership and regardless of whether the alien entered the enterprise after its formation) which the alien desires to have considered under this paragraph, regardless of whether such enterprise was created before or after the determinations made under paragraph (1).

(C) Period for filing petition.

(i) 90-day period before second anniversary. Except as provided in clause (ii), the petition under subparagraph (B) must be filed during the 90-day period before the second anniversary of the continuation, under paragraph (1)(F)(ii), of the conditional basis of the alien's lawful admission for permanent residence.

(ii) Date petitions for good cause. Such a petition may be considered if filed after such date, but only if the alien establishes to the satisfaction of the Attorney General good cause and extenuating circumstances for failure to file the petition during the period described in clause (i).

(D) Termination of permanent resident status for failure to file petition.

(i) In general. In the case of an alien with permanent resident status on a conditional basis under paragraph (1)(F)(ii), if no petition is filed with respect to the alien in accordance with subparagraph (B), the Attorney General shall terminate the permanent resident status of the alien (and the alien's spouse and children if it was obtained on a conditional basis under section 216A of the Immigration and Nationality Act as of the second anniversary of the continuation, under paragraph (1)(F)(ii), of the conditional basis of the alien's lawful admission for permanent residence.

(ii) Hearing in removal proceeding. In any removal proceeding with respect to an alien whose permanent resident status is terminated under clause (i), the burden of proof shall be on the alien to establish compliance with subparagraph (B).

(E) Determinations after petition. If a petition is filed by an eligible alien in accordance with subparagraph (B), the Attorney General shall make a determination, within 90 days of the date of such filing, whether—

(i) the petition contains any material misrepresentation in the facts and information alleged in the petition with respect to the commercial enterprises included in such petition;

(ii) all such enterprises, considered together, created full-time jobs for not fewer than 10 United States citizens or aliens lawfully admitted for permanent residence or other immigrants lawfully authorized to be employed in the United States (other than the eligible alien and the alien's spouse, sons, or daughters), and those jobs exist on the date on which the determination is made, except that—

(I) this clause shall apply only if the Attorney General made an adverse determination with respect to the eligible alien under paragraph (1)(A)(ii);

(II) the provisions of subparagraphs (B) and (C) of paragraph (1) shall apply to a determination under this clause in the same manner as they apply to a determination under paragraph (1)(A)(ii); and

(III) if the Attorney General determined under paragraph (1)(A)(ii) that any jobs satisfying the requirement of such paragraph were created, the number of those jobs shall be subtracted from the number of jobs otherwise needed to satisfy the requirement of this clause; and

(iii) considering all such enterprises together, on the date on which the determination is made, the eligible alien is in substantial compliance with the capital investment requirement described in section 216A(d)(1)(B) of the Immigration and Nationality Act, except that—

(I) this clause shall apply only if the Attorney General made an adverse determination with respect to the eligible alien under paragraph (1)(A)(iii); and

(II) if the Attorney General determined under paragraph (1)(A)(iii) that any capital amount was invested that could be credited towards compliance with the capital investment requirement described in section 216A(d)(1)(B) of the Immigration and Nationality Act, such amount shall be subtracted from the amount of capital otherwise needed to satisfy the requirement of this clause.

(F) Removal of conditional basis if favorable determination. If the Attorney General renders an affirmative determination with respect to clauses (ii) and (iii) of subparagraph (E), and if the Attorney General renders a negative determination with respect to clause (i) of such subparagraph, the Attorney General shall so notify the alien involved and shall remove the conditional basis of the alien's status (and that of the alien's spouse and children if it was obtained under section 216A of the Immigration and Nationality Act effective as of the second anniversary of the continuation, under paragraph (1)(F)(ii), of the conditional basis of the alien's lawful admission for permanent residence.

(G) Requirements relating to adverse determinations.

(i) Notice. If the Attorney General renders an adverse determination under subparagraph (E), the Attorney General shall so notify the alien involved. The notice shall be in writing and shall state the factual basis for any adverse determination. The Attorney General shall provide the alien with an opportunity to submit evidence to rebut any adverse determination. If the Attorney General reverses all adverse determinations pursuant to such rebuttal, the Attorney General shall so notify the alien involved and shall remove the conditional basis of the alien's status (and that of the alien's spouse and children if it was obtained under section 216A of the Immigration and Nationality Act effective as of the second anniversary of the continuation, under paragraph (1)(F)(ii), of the conditional basis of the alien's lawful admission for permanent residence.

(ii) Termination if adverse determination. If the eligible alien's rebuttal does not cause the Attorney General to reverse each adverse determination under subparagraph (E), the Attorney General shall so notify the alien involved and, subject to subsection (d), shall terminate the permanent resident status of the alien (and that of the alien's spouse and children if it was obtained on a conditional basis under section 216A of the Immigration and Nationality Act.

(d) Hearing in removal proceeding. Any alien whose permanent resident status is terminated under paragraph (1)(F)(iii) or (2)(G)(ii) of subsection (c) may request a review of such determination in a proceeding to remove the alien. In such proceeding, the burden of proof shall be on the Attorney General.

(e) Clarification with respect to children. In the case of an alien who obtained the status of an alien lawfully admitted for permanent residence on a conditional basis before the date of the enactment of this Act [enacted November 2, 2002] by virtue of being the child of an eligible alien described in subsection (b)(1), the alien shall be considered to be a child for purposes of this section regardless of any change in age or marital status after obtaining such status.

(f) Definition of full-time. For purposes of this section, the term "full-time" means a position that requires at least 35 hours of service per week at any time, regardless of who fills the position.

§ 11032. Conditional permanent resident status for certain alien entrepreneurs, spouses, and children Appendix I, § 11032

(a) In general. With respect to each eligible alien described in subsection (b), the Attorney General or the Secretary of State shall approve the application described in subsection (b)(2) and grant the alien (and any spouse or child of the alien, if the spouse or child is eligible to receive a visa under section 203(d) of the Immigration and Nationality Act the status of an alien lawfully admitted for permanent residence on a conditional basis under section 216A of such Act Such application shall be approved not later than 180 days after the date of the enactment of this Act [enacted November 2, 2002].

(b) Eligible aliens described. An alien is an eligible alien described in this subsection if the alien—

(1) filed, under section 204(a)(1)(H) of the Immigration and Nationality Act (or any predecessor provision), a petition to accord the alien a status under section 203(b)(5) of such Act that was approved by the Attorney General after January 1, 1995, and before August 31, 1998;

(2) pursuant to such approval, timely filed before the date of the enactment of this Act [enacted November 2, 2002] an application for adjustment of status under section 245 of such Act or an application for an immigrant visa under section 203(b)(5) of such Act; and

(3) is not inadmissible or deportable on any ground

(c) Treatment of certain applications.

(1) Revocation of approval of petitions. If the Attorney General revoked the approval of a petition described in subsection (b)(1), such revocation shall be disregarded for purposes of this section if it was based on a determination that the alien failed to satisfy section 203(b)(5)(A)(ii) of the Immigration and Nationality Act.

(2) Applications no longer pending.

(A) In general. If an application described in subsection (b)(2) is not pending on the date of the enactment of this Act [enacted November 2, 2002], the Attorney General shall disregard the circumstances leading to such lack of pendency and treat it as reopened, if such lack of pendency is due to a determination that the alien—

(i) failed to satisfy section 203(b)(5)(A)(ii) of the Immigration and Nationality Act; or

(ii) departed the United States without advance parole.

(B) Applicants abroad. In the case of an eligible alien who filed an application for adjustment of status described in subsection (b)(2), but who is no longer physically present in the United States, the Attorney General shall establish a process under which the alien may be paroled into the United States if necessary in order to obtain adjustment of status under this section.

(d) Recordation of date; reduction of numbers. Upon the approval of an application under subsection (a), the Attorney General shall record the alien's lawful admission for permanent residence on a conditional basis as of the date of such approval and the Secretary of State shall reduce by one the number of visas authorized to be issued under sections 201(d) and 203(b)(5) of the Immigration and Nationality Act for the fiscal year then current.

(e) Removal of conditional basis.

(1) Petition. In order for a conditional basis established under this section for an alien (and the alien's spouse and children) to be removed, the alien must satisfy the requirements of section 216A(c)(1) of the Immigration and Nationality Act, including the submission of a petition in accordance with subparagraph (A) of such section. Such petition may include the facts and information described in subparagraphs (A) and (B) of section 216A(d)(1) of the Immigration and Nationality Act with respect to any commercial enterprise (regardless of whether such enterprise is a limited partnership and regardless of whether the alien entered the enterprise after its formation) in the United States in which the alien has made a capital investment at any time.

(2) Determination. In carrying out section 216A(c)(3) of the Immigration and Nationality Act with respect to an alien described in paragraph (1), the Attorney General, in lieu of the determination described in such section 216A(c)(3), shall make a determination, within 90 days of the date of such filing, whether—

(A) the petition described in paragraph (1) contains any material misrepresentation in the facts and information alleged in the petition with respect to the commercial enterprises included in the petition;

(B) subject to subparagraphs (B) and (C) of section 11031(c)(1), all such enterprises, considered together, created full-time jobs for not fewer than 10 United States citizens or aliens lawfully admitted for permanent residence or other immigrants lawfully authorized to be employed in the United States (other than the alien and the alien's spouse, sons, or daughters), and those jobs exist or existed on either of the dates described in paragraph (3); and

(C) considering the alien's investments in such enterprises on either of the dates described in paragraph (3), or on both such dates, the alien is or was in substantial compliance with the capital investment requirement described in section 216A(d)(1)(B) of the Immigration and Nationality Act.

(3) Dates. The dates described in this paragraph are the following:

(A) The date on which the application described in subsection (b)(2) was filed.

(B) The date on which the determination under paragraph

(2) is made.

(f) Clarification with respect to children. In the case of an alien who was a child on the date on which the application described in subsection (b)(2) was filed, the alien shall be considered to be a child for purposes of this section regardless of any change in age or marital status after such date.

§ 11033. Regulations Appendix I, § 11033

The Immigration and Naturalization Service shall promulgate regulations to implement this chapter not later than 120 days after the date of enactment of this Act [enacted November 2, 2002]. Until such regulations are promulgated, the Attorney General shall not deny a petition filed or pending under section 216A(c)(1)(A) of the Immigration and Nationality Act that relates to an eligible alien described in section 11031, or on an application filed or pending under section 245 of such Act that relates to an eligible alien described in section 11032. Until such regulations are promulgated, the Attorney General shall not initiate or proceed with removal proceedings under section 240 of the Immigration and Nationality Act that relate to an eligible alien described in section 11031 or 11032.

§ 11034. Definitions Appendix I, § 11034

Except as otherwise provided, the terms used in this chapter shall have the meaning given such terms in section 101(b) of the Immigration and Nationality Act (8 U.S.C. 1101(b)).

****

APPENDIX J— PILOT IMMIGRATION PROGRAM

Departments of Commerce, Justice, and State, the Judiciary, and Related Agencies Appropriations Act, 1993 P.L. 102-395, title VI, § 610, 106 Stat. 1874 (October 6, 1992), (As amended.)[96,97]

§ 610. Pilot Immigration Program Appendix J, § 610

(a) Of the visas otherwise available under section 203(b)(5) of the Immigration and Nationality Act, the Secretary of State, together with the Attorney General, shall set aside visas for a pilot program to implement the provisions of such section. Such pilot program shall involve a regional center in the United States, designated by the Secretary of Homeland Security on the basis of a general proposal, for the promotion of

96. Amended by P.L. 105-119, title I, § 116(a), 111 Stat. 2467 (November 26, 1997); P.L. 106-396, § 402, 114 Stat. 1647 (October 30, 2000); P.L. 107-273, div. C, title I, subtitle B, chapter 2, § 11037; 116 Stat. 1847 (November 2, 2002); and the Basic Pilot Program Extension and Expansion Act of 2003, P.L. 108-156, § 4, 117 Stat. 1945 (December 3, 2003).

97. P.L. 107-273, div. C, title I, subtitle B, chapter 2, § 11037, provided that the amendment to § 610(a) apply to the following:
(1) any proposal for a regional center pending before the Secretary of Homeland Security (whether for an initial decision or on appeal) on or after the date of the enactment of this Act [November 2, 2002]; and
(2) any of the following petitions, if filed on or after the date of the enactment of this Act:
(A) A petition under section 204(a)(1)(H) of the Immigration and Nationality Act (or any predecessor provision) (or any predecessor provision), with respect to status under section 203(b)(5) of such Act.
(B) A petition under section 216A(c)(1)(A) of such Act to remove the conditional basis of an alien's permanent resident status.

economic growth, including increased export sales, improved regional productivity, job creation, or increased domestic capital investment. A regional center shall have jurisdiction over a limited geographic area, which shall be described in the proposal and consistent with the purpose of concentrating pooled investment in defined economic zones. The establishment of a regional center may be based on general predictions, contained in the proposal, concerning the kinds of commercial enterprises that will receive capital from aliens, the jobs that will be created directly or indirectly as a result of such capital investments, and the other positive economic effects such capital investments will have.

(b) For purposes of the pilot program established in subsection (a), beginning on October 1, 1992, but no later than October 1, 1993, the Secretary of State, together with the Attorney General, shall set aside 3,000 visas annually for 15 years to include such aliens as are eligible for admission under section 203(b)(5) of the Immigration and Nationality Act and this section, as well as spouses or children which are eligible, under the terms of the Immigration and Nationality Act, to accompany or follow to join such aliens.

(c) In determining compliance with section 203(b)(5)(A)(iii) of the Immigration and Nationality Act, and notwithstanding the requirements of 8 CFR 204.6, the Secretary of Homeland Security shall permit aliens admitted under the pilot program described in this section to establish reasonable methodologies for determining the number of jobs created by the pilot program, including such jobs which are estimated to have been created indirectly through revenues generated from increased exports, improved regional productivity, job creation, or increased domestic capital investment resulting from the pilot program.

(d) In processing petitions under section 204(a)(1)(H) of the Immigration and Nationality Act for classification under section 203(b)(5) of such Act, the Secretary of Homeland Security may give priority to petitions filed by aliens seeking admission under the pilot program described in this section.

Notwithstanding section 203(e) of such Act, immigrant visas made available under such section 203(b)(5) may be issued to such aliens in an order that takes into account any priority accorded under the preceding sentence.

****

APPENDIX K — EXTENSION OF POSTHUMOUS BENEFITS TO SURVIVING SPOUSES, CHILDREN, AND PARENTS

P. L. 108-136, § 1703(a) — (e), 117 Stat. 1693 to 1695 (November 24, 2003) eff. September 1, 2001

§ 1703. Extension of posthumous benefits to surviving spouses, children, and parents Appendix K, § 1703

(a) Treatment as immediate relatives.

(1) Spouses. Notwithstanding the second sentence of section 201(b)(2)(A)(i) of the Immigration and Nationality Act, in the case of an alien who was the spouse of a citizen of the United States at the time of the citizen's death and was not legally separated from the citizen at the time of the citizen's death, if the citizen served honorably in an active duty status in the military, air, or naval forces of the United States and died as a result of injury or disease incurred in or aggravated by combat, the alien (and each child of the alien) shall be considered, for purposes of section 201(b) of such Act, to remain an immediate relative after the date of the citizen's death, but only if the alien files a petition under section 204(a)(1)(A)(ii) of such Act within 2 years after such date and only until the date the alien remarries. For purposes of such section 204(a)(1)(A)(ii), an alien granted relief under the preceding sentence shall be considered an alien spouse described in the second sentence of section 201(b)(2)(A)(i) of such Act.

(2) Children.

(A) In general. In the case of an alien who was the child of a citizen of the United States at the time of the citizen's death, if the citizen served honorably in an active duty status in the military, air, or naval forces of the United States and died as a result of injury or disease incurred in or aggravated by combat, the alien shall be considered, for purposes of section 201(b) of the Immigration and Nationality Act, to remain an immediate relative after the date of the citizen's death (regardless of changes in age or marital status thereafter), but only if the alien files a petition under subparagraph (B) within 2 years after such date.

(B) Petitions. An alien described in subparagraph (A) may file a petition with the Secretary of Homeland Security for classification of the alien under section 201(b)(2)(A)(i) of the Immigration and Nationality Act. For purposes of such Act, such a petition shall be considered a petition filed under section 204(a)(1)(A) of such Act.

(3) Parents.

(A) In general. In the case of an alien who was the parent of a citizen of the United States at the time of the citizen's death, if the citizen served honorably in an active duty status in the military, air, or naval forces of the United States and died as a result of injury or disease incurred in or aggravated by combat, the alien shall be considered, for purposes of section 201(b) of the Immigration and Nationality Act, to remain an immediate relative after the date of the citizen's death (regardless of changes in age or marital status thereafter), but only if the alien files a petition under subparagraph (B) within 2 years after such date.

(B) Petitions. An alien described in subparagraph (A) may file a petition with the Secretary of Homeland Security for classification of the alien under section 201(b)(2)(A)(i) of the Immigration and Nationality Act. For purposes of such Act, such a petition shall be considered a petition filed under section 204(a)(1)(A) of such Act.

(C) Exception. Not withstanding section 201(b)(2)(A)(i) of the Immigration and Nationality Act, for purposes of this paragraph, a citizen described in subparagraph (A) does not have to be 21 years of age for a parent to benefit under this paragraph.

(b) Applications for adjustment of status by surviving spouses, children, and parents.

(1) In general. Notwithstanding subsections (a) and (c) of section 245 of the Immigration and Nationality Act, any alien who was the spouse, child, or parent of an alien described in paragraph (2), and who applied for adjustment of status prior to the death described in paragraph (2)(B), may have such application adjudicated as if such death had not occurred.

(2) Alien described. An alien is described in this paragraph if the alien—

(A) served honorably in an active duty status in the military, air, or naval forces of the United States;

(B) died as a result of injury or disease incurred in or aggravated by combat; and

(C) was granted posthumous citizenship under section 329A of the Immigration and Nationality Act.

(c) Spouses and children of lawful permanent resident aliens.

(1) Treatment as immediate relatives.

(A) In general. A spouse or child of an alien described in paragraph (3) who is included in a petition for classification as a family-sponsored immigrant under section 203(a)(2) of the Immigration and Nationality Act that was filed by such alien, shall be considered (if the spouse or child has not been admitted or approved for lawful permanent residence by such date) a valid petitioner for immediate relative status under section 201(b)(2)(A)(i) of the Immigration and Nationality Act. Such spouse or child shall be eligible for deferred action, advance parole, and work authorization.

(B) Petitions. An alien spouse or child described in subparagraph (A) may file a petition with the Secretary of Homeland Security for classification of the alien under section 201(b)(2)(A)(i) of the Immigration and Nationality Act. For purposes of such Act, such a petition shall be considered a petition filed under section 204(a)(1)(A) of such Act.

(2) Self-petitions. Any spouse or child of an alien described in paragraph (3) who is not a beneficiary of a petition for classification as a family-sponsored immigrant may file a petition for such classification under section 201(b)(2)(A)(i) of the Immigration and Nationality Act with the Secretary of Homeland Security, but only if the spouse or child files a petition within 2 years after such date. Such spouse or child shall be eligible for deferred action, advance parole, and work authorization.

(3) Alien described. An alien is described in this paragraph if the alien—

(A) served honorably in an active duty status in the military, air, or naval forces of the United States;

(B) died as a result of injury or disease incurred in or aggravated by combat; and

(C) was granted posthumous citizenship under section 329A of the Immigration and Nationality Act.

(d) Parents of lawful permanent resident aliens.

(1) Self-petitions. Any parent of an alien described in paragraph (2) may file a petition for classification under section 201(b)(2)(A)(i) of the Immigration and Nationality Act, but only if the parent files a petition within 2 years after such date. For purposes of such Act, such petition shall be considered a petition filed under section 204(a)(1)(A) of such Act. Such parent shall be eligible for deferred action, advance parole, and work authorization.

(2) Alien described. An alien is described in this paragraph if the alien—

(A) served honorably in an active duty status in the military, air, or naval forces of the United States;

(B) died as a result of injury or disease incurred in or aggravated by combat; and

(C) was granted posthumous citizenship under section 329A of the Immigration and Nationality Act.

(e) Waiver of ground for inadmissibility. In determining the admissibility of any alien accorded an immigration benefit under this section for purposes of the Immigration and Nationality Act, the ground for inadmissibility specified in section 212(a)(4) of such Act shall not apply.

UNITED STATES CODE

TITLE 5. GOVERNMENT ORGANIZATION AND EMPLOYEES

PART I. THE AGENCIES GENERALLY

CHAPTER 5. ADMINISTRATIVE PROCEDURE

SUBCHAPTER II. ADMINISTRATIVE PROCEDURE

SUBCHAPTER II. ADMINISTRATIVE PROCEDURE

§ 552a. Records maintained on individuals

(a) Definitions. For purposes of this section—

(1) the term "agency" means agency as defined in section 552[(f)](e) of this title [5 USCS § 552(f)];

(2) the term "individual" means a citizen of the United States or an alien lawfully admitted for permanent residence;

(3) the term "maintain" includes maintain, collect, use, or disseminate;

(4) the term "record" means any item, collection, or grouping of information about an individual that is maintained by an agency, including, but not limited to, his education, financial transactions, medical history, and criminal or employment history and that contains his name, or the identifying number, symbol, or other identifying particular assigned to the individual, such as a finger or voice print or a photograph;

(5) the term "system of records" means a group of any records under the control of any agency from which information is retrieved by the name of the individual or by some identifying number, symbol, or other identifying particular assigned to the individual;

(6) the term "statistical record" means a record in a system of records maintained for statistical research or reporting purposes only and not used in whole or in part in making any determination about an identifiable individual, except as provided by section 8 of title 13 [13 USCS § 8];

(7) the term "routine use" means, with respect to the disclosure of a record, the use of such record for a purpose which is compatible with the purpose for which it was collected; and

(8) the term "matching program"—

(A) means any computerized comparison of—

(i) two or more automated systems of records or a system of records with non-Federal records for the purpose of—

(I) establishing or verifying the eligibility of, or continuing compliance with statutory and regulatory requirements by, applicants for, recipients or beneficiaries of, participants in, or providers of services with respect to, cash or in-kind assistance or payments under Federal benefit programs, or

(II) recouping payments or delinquent debts under such Federal benefit programs, or

(ii) two or more automated Federal personnel or payroll systems of records or a system of Federal personnel or payroll records with non-Federal records,

(B) but does not include—

(i) matches performed to produce aggregate statistical data without any personal identifiers;

(ii) matches performed to support any research or statistical project, the specific data of which may not be used to make decisions concerning the rights, benefits, or privileges of specific individuals;

(iii) matches performed, by an agency (or component thereof) which performs as its principal function any activity pertaining to the enforcement of criminal laws, subsequent to the initiation of a specific criminal or civil law enforcement investigation of a named person or persons for the purpose of gathering evidence against such person or persons;

(iv) matches of tax information (I) pursuant to section 6103(d) of the Internal Revenue Code of 1986 [26 USCS § 6103(d)], (II) for purposes of tax administration as defined in section 6103(b)(4) of such Code [26 USCS § 6103(b)(4)], (III) for the purpose of intercepting a tax refund due an individual under authority granted by section 404(e), 464, or 1137 of the Social Security Act [42 USCS § 604(e), 664, or 1320b-7]; or (IV) for the purpose of intercepting a tax refund due an individual under any other tax refund intercept program authorized by statute which has been determined by the Director of the Office of Management and Budget to contain verification, notice, and hearing requirements that are substantially similar to the procedures in section 1137 of the Social Security Act [42 USCS § 1320b-7];

(v) matches—

(I) using records predominantly relating to Federal personnel, that are performed for routine administrative purposes (subject to guidance provided by the Director of the Office of Management and Budget pursuant to subsection (v)); or

(II) conducted by an agency using only records from systems of records maintained by that agency;

if the purpose of the match is not to take any adverse financial, personnel, disciplinary, or other adverse action against Federal personnel;

(vi) matches performed for foreign counterintelligence purposes or to produce background checks for security clearances of Federal personnel or Federal contractor personnel;

(vii) matches performed incident to a levy described in section 6103(k)(8) of the Internal Revenue Code of 1986 [26 USCS § 6103(k)(8)];

(viii) matches performed pursuant to section 202(x)(3) or 1611(e)(1) of the Social Security Act (42 U.S.C. 402(x)(3), 1382(e)(1));

(ix) matches performed by the Secretary of Health and Human Services or the Inspector General of the Department of Health and Human Services with respect to potential fraud, waste, and abuse, including matches of a system of records with non-Federal records; or

(x) matches performed pursuant to section 3(d)(4) of the Achieving a Better Life Experience Act of 2014;

(9) the term "recipient agency" means any agency, or contractor thereof, receiving records contained in a system of records from a source agency for use in a matching program;

(10) the term "non-Federal agency" means any State or local government, or agency thereof, which receives records contained in a system of records from a source agency for use in a matching program;

(11) the term "source agency" means any agency which discloses records contained in a system of records to be used in a matching program, or any State or local government, or agency thereof, which discloses records to be used in a matching program;

(12) the term "Federal benefit program" means any program administered or funded by the Federal Government, or by any agent or State on behalf of the Federal Government, providing cash or in-kind assistance in the form of payments, grants, loans, or loan guarantees to individuals; and

(13) the term "Federal personnel" means officers and employees of the Government of the United States, members of the uniformed services (including members of the Reserve Components), individuals entitled to receive immediate or deferred retirement benefits under any retirement program of the Government of the United States (including survivor benefits).

(b) Conditions of disclosure. No agency shall disclose any record which is contained in a system of records by any means of communication to any person, or to another agency, except pursuant to a written request by, or with the prior written consent of, the individual to whom the record pertains, unless disclosure of the record would be—

(1) to those officers and employees of the agency which maintains the record who have a need for the record in the performance of their duties;

(2) required under section 552 of this title [5 USCS § 552];

(3) for a routine use as defined in subsection (a)(7) of this section and described under subsection (e)(4)(D) of this section;

(4) to the Bureau of the Census for purposes of planning or carrying out a census or survey or related activity pursuant to the provisions of title 13;

(5) to a recipient who has provided the agency with advance adequate written assurance that the record will be used solely as a statistical research or reporting record, and the record is to be transferred in a form that is not individually identifiable;

(6) to the National Archives and Records Administration as a record which has sufficient historical or other value to warrant its continued preservation by the United States Government, or for evaluation by the Archivist of the United States or the designee of the Archivist to determine whether the record has such value;

(7) to another agency or to an instrumentality of any governmental jurisdiction within or under the control of the United States for a civil or criminal law enforcement activity if the activity is authorized by law, and if the head of the agency or instrumentality has made a written request to the agency which maintains the record specifying the particular portion desired and the law enforcement activity for which the record is sought;

(8) to a person pursuant to a showing of compelling circumstances affecting the health or safety of an individual if upon such disclosure notification is transmitted to the last known address of such individual;

(9) to either House of Congress, or, to the extent of matter within its jurisdiction, any committee or subcommittee thereof, any joint committee of Congress or subcommittee of any such joint committee;

(10) to the Comptroller General, or any of his authorized representatives, in the course of the performance of the duties of the General Accounting Office [Government Accountability Office];

(11) to the Director of the Congressional Budget Office, or any authorized representative of the Director, in the course of performance of the duties of the Congressional Budget Office;

(12) pursuant to the order of a court of competent jurisdiction; or

(13) to a consumer reporting agency in accordance with section 3711(e) of title 31 [31 USCS § 3711(e)].

(c) Accounting of certain disclosures. Each agency, with respect to each system of records under its control, shall—

(1) except for disclosures made under subsections (b)(1) or (b)(2) of this section, keep an accurate accounting of—

(A) the date, nature, and purpose of each disclosure of a record to any person or to another agency made under subsection (b) of this section; and

(B) the name and address of the person or agency to whom the disclosure is made;

(2) retain the accounting made under paragraph (1) of this subsection for at least five years or the life of the record, whichever is longer, after the disclosure for which the accounting is made;

(3) except for disclosures made under subsection (b)(7) of this section, make the accounting made under paragraph (1) of this subsection available to the individual named in the record at his request; and

(4) inform any person or other agency about any correction or notation of dispute made by the agency in accordance with subsection (d) of this section of any record that has been disclosed to the person or agency if an accounting of the disclosure was made.

(d) Access to records. Each agency that maintains a system of records shall—

(1) upon request by any individual to gain access to his record or to any information pertaining to him which is contained in the system, permit him and upon his request, a person of his own choosing to accompany him, to review the record and have a copy made of all or any portion thereof in a form comprehensible to him,

except that the agency may require the individual to furnish a written statement authorizing discussion of that individual's record in the accompanying person's presence;

(2) permit the individual to request amendment of a record pertaining to him and—

(A) not later than 10 days (excluding Saturdays, Sundays, and legal public holidays) after the date of receipt of such request, acknowledge in writing such receipt; and

(B) promptly, either—

(i) make any correction of any portion thereof which the individual believes is not accurate, relevant, timely, or complete; or

(ii) inform the individual of its refusal to amend the record in accordance with his request, the reason for the refusal, the procedures established by the agency for the individual to request a review of that refusal by the head of the agency or an officer designated by the head of the agency, and the name and business address of that official;

(3) permit the individual who disagrees with the refusal of the agency to amend his record to request a review of such refusal, and not later than 30 days (excluding Saturdays, Sundays, and legal public holidays) from the date on which the individual requests such review, complete such review and make a final determination unless, for good cause shown, the head of the agency extends such 30-day period; and if, after his review, the reviewing official also refuses to amend the record in accordance with the request, permit the individual to file with the agency a concise statement setting forth the reasons for his disagreement with the refusal of the agency, and notify the individual of the provisions for judicial review of the reviewing official's determination under subsection (g)(1)(A) of this section;

(4) in any disclosure, containing information about which the individual has filed a statement of disagreement, occurring after the filing of the statement under paragraph (3) of this subsection, clearly note any portion of the record which is disputed and provide copies of the statement and, if the agency deems it appropriate, copies of a concise statement of the reasons of the agency for not making the amendments requested, to persons or other agencies to whom the disputed record has been disclosed; and

(5) nothing in this section shall allow an individual access to any information compiled in reasonable anticipation of a civil action or proceeding.

(e) Agency requirements. Each agency that maintains a system of records shall—

(1) maintain in its records only such information about an individual as is relevant and necessary to accomplish a purpose of the agency required to be accomplished by statute or by executive order of the President;

(2) collect information to the greatest extent practicable directly from the subject individual when the information may result in adverse determinations about an individual's rights, benefits, and privileges under Federal programs;

(3) inform each individual whom it asks to supply information, on the form which it uses to collect the information or on a separate form that can be retained by the individual—

(A) the authority (whether granted by statute, or by executive order of the President) which authorizes the solicitation of the information and whether disclosure of such information is mandatory or voluntary;

(B) the principal purpose or purposes for which the information is intended to be used;

(C) the routine uses which may be made of the information, as published pursuant to paragraph (4)(D) of this subsection; and

(D) the effects on him, if any, of not providing all or any party of the requested information;

(4) subject to the provisions of paragraph (11) of this subsection, publish in the Federal Register upon establishment or revision a notice of the existence and character of the system of records, which notice shall include—

(A) the name and location of the system;

(B) the categories of individuals on whom records are maintained in the system;

(C) the categories of records maintained in the system;

(D) each routine use of the records contained in the system, including the categories of users and the purpose of such use;

(E) the policies and practices of the agency regarding storage, retrievability, access controls, retention, and disposal of the records;

(F) the title and business address of the agency official who is responsible for the system of records;

(G) the agency procedures whereby an individual can be notified at his request if the system of records contains a record pertaining to him;

(H) the agency procedures whereby an individual can be notified at his request how he can gain access to any record pertaining to him contained in the system of records, and how he can contest its content; and

(I) the categories of sources or records in the system;

(5) maintain all records which are used by the agency in making any determination about any individual with such accuracy, relevance, timeliness, and completeness as is reasonably necessary to assure fairness to the individual in the determination;

(6) prior to disseminating any record about an individual to any person other than an agency, unless the dissemination is made pursuant to subsection (b)(2) of this section, make reasonable efforts to assure that such records are accurate, complete, timely, and relevant for agency purposes;

(7) maintain no record describing how any individual exercises rights guaranteed by the First Amendment unless expressly authorized by statute or by the individual about whom the record is maintained or unless pertinent to and within the scope of an authorized law enforcement activity;

(8) make reasonable efforts to serve notice on an individual when any record on such individual is made available to any person under compulsory legal process when such process becomes a matter of public record;

(9) establish rules of conduct for persons involved in the design, development, operation, or maintenance of any system of records, or in maintaining any record, and instruct each such person with respect to such rules and the requirements of this section, including any other rules and procedures adopted pursuant to this section and the penalties for noncompliance;

(10) establish appropriate administrative, technical, and physical safeguards to insure the security and confidentiality of records and to protect against any anticipated threats or hazards to their security or integrity which could result in substantial harm, embarrassment, inconvenience, or unfairness to any individual on whom information is maintained;

(11) at least 30 days prior to publication of information under paragraph (4)(D) of this subsection, publish in the Federal Register notice of any new use or intended use of the information in the system, and provide an opportunity for interested persons to submit written data, views, or arguments to the agency; and

(12) [Caution: For effective date, see 1988 Amendment note] if such agency is a recipient agency or a source agency in a matching program with a non-Federal agency, with respect to any establishment or revision of a matching program, at least 30 days prior to conducting such program, publish in the Federal Register notice of such establishment or revision.

(f) Agency rules. In order to carry out the provisions of this section, each agency that maintains a system of records shall promulgate rules, in accordance with the requirements (including general notice) of section 553 of this title [5 USCS § 553], which shall—

(1) establish procedures whereby an individual can be notified in response to his request if any system of records named by the individual contains a record pertaining to him;

(2) define reasonable times, places, and requirements for identifying an individual who requests his record or information pertaining to him before the agency shall make the record or information available to the individual;

(3) establish procedures for the disclosure to an individual upon his request of his record or information pertaining to him, including special procedure, if deemed necessary, for the disclosure to an individual of medical records, including psychological records, pertaining to him;

(4) establish procedures for reviewing a request from an individual concerning the amendment of any record or information pertaining to the individual, for making a determination on the request, for an appeal within the agency of an initial adverse agency determination, and for whatever additional means may be necessary for each individual to be able to exercise fully his rights under this section; and

(5) establish fees to be charged, if any, to any individual for making copies of his record, excluding the cost of any search for and review of the record.

The Office of the Federal Register shall biennially compile and publish the rules promulgated under this subsection and agency notices published under subsection (e)(4) of this section in a form available to the public at low cost.

(g) Civil remedies.

(1) Whenever any agency—

(A) makes a determination under subsection (d)(3) of this section not to amend an individual's record in accordance with his request, or fails to make such review in conformity with that subsection;

(B) refuses to comply with an individual request under subsection (d)(1) of this section;

(C) fails to maintain any record concerning any individual with such accuracy, relevance, timeliness, and completeness as is necessary to assure fairness in any determination relating to the qualifications, character, rights, or opportunities of, or benefits to the individual that may be made on the basis of such record, and consequently a determination is made which is adverse to the individual; or

(D) fails to comply with any other provision of this section, or any rule promulgated thereunder, in such a way as to have an adverse effect on an individual,

the individual may bring a civil action against the agency, and the district courts of the United States shall have jurisdiction in the matters under the provisions of this subsection.

(2)(A) In any suit brought under the provisions of subsection (g)(1)(A) of this section, the court may order the agency to amend the individual's record in accordance with his request or in such other way as the court may direct. In such a case the court shall determine the matter de novo.

(B) The court may assess against the United States reasonable attorney fees and other litigation costs reasonably incurred in any case under this paragraph in which the complainant has substantially prevailed.

(3)(A) In any suit brought under the provisions of subsection (g)(1)(B) of this section, the court may enjoin the agency from withholding the records and order the production to the complainant of any agency records improperly withheld from him. In such a case the court shall determine the matter de novo, and may examine the contents of any agency records in camera to determine whether the records or any portion thereof may be withheld under any of the exemptions set forth in subsection (k) of this section, and the burden is on the agency to sustain its action.

(B) The court may assess against the United States reasonable attorney fees and other litigation costs reasonably incurred in any case under this paragraph in which the complainant has substantially prevailed.

(4) In any suit brought under the provisions of subsection (g)(1)(C) or (D) of this section in which the court determines that the agency acted in a manner which was intentional or willful, the United States shall be liable to the individual in an amount equal to the sum of—

(A) actual damages sustained by the individual as a result of the refusal or failure, but in no case shall a person entitled to recovery receive less than the sum of $1,000; and

(B) the costs of the action together with reasonable attorney fees as determined by the court.

(5) An action to enforce any liability created under this section may be brought in the district court of the United States in the district in which the complainant resides, or has his principal place of business, or in which the agency records are situated, or in the District of Columbia, without regard to the amount in controversy, within two years from the date on which the cause of action arises, except that where an agency has materially and willfully misrepresented any information required under this section to be disclosed to an individual and the information so misrepresented is material to establishment of the liability of the agency to the individual under this section, the action may be brought at any time within two years after discovery by the individual of the misrepresentation. Nothing in this section shall be construed to authorize any civil action by reason of any injury sustained as the result of a disclosure of a record prior to September 27, 1975.

(h) Rights of legal guardians. For the purposes of this section, the parent of any minor, or the legal guardian of any individual who has been declared to be incompetent due to physical or mental incapacity or age by a court of competent jurisdiction, may act on behalf of the individual.

(i) Criminal penalties.

(1) Any officer or employee of an agency, who by virtue of his employment or official position, has possession of, or access to, agency records which contain individually identifiable information the disclosure of which is prohibited by this section or by rules or regulations established thereunder, and who knowing that disclosure of the specific material is so prohibited, willfully discloses the material in any manner to any person or agency not entitled to receive it, shall be guilty of a misdemeanor and fined not more than $5,000.

(2) Any officer or employee of any agency who willfully maintains a system of records without meeting the notice requirements of subsection (e)(4) of this section shall be guilty of a misdemeanor and fined not more than $5,000.

(3) Any person who knowingly and willfully requests or obtains any record concerning an individual from an agency under false pretenses shall be guilty of a misdemeanor and fined not more than $5,000.

(j) General exemptions. The head of any agency may promulgate rules, in accordance with the requirements (including general notice) of sections 553(b)(1), (2), and (3), (c), and (e) of this title [5 USCS § 553], to exempt any system of records within the agency from any part of this section except subsections (b), (c)(1) and (2), (e)(4)(A) through (F), (e)(6), (7), (9), (10), and (11), and (i) if the system of records is—

(1) maintained by the Central Intelligence Agency; or

(2) maintained by an agency or component thereof which performs as its principal function any activity pertaining to the enforcement of criminal laws, including police efforts to prevent, control, or reduce crime or to apprehend criminals, and the activities of prosecutors, courts, correctional, probation, pardon, or parole authorities, and which consists of (A) information compiled for the purpose of identifying individual criminal offenders and alleged offenders and consisting only of identifying data and notations of arrests, the nature and disposition of criminal charges, sentencing, confinement, release, and parole and probation status; (B) information compiled for the purpose of a criminal investigation, including reports of informants and investigators, and associated with an identifiable individual; or (C) reports identifiable to an individual compiled at any stage of the process of enforcement of the criminal laws from arrest or indictment through release from supervision.

At the time rules are adopted under this subsection, the agency shall include in the statement required under section 553(c) of this title [5 USCS § 553(c)], the reasons why the system of records is to be exempted from a provision of this section.

(k) Specific exemptions. The head of any agency may promulgate rules, in accordance with the requirements (including general notice) of sections 553(b)(1), (2), and (3), (c), and (e) of this title [5 USCS § 553], to exempt any system of records within the agency from subsections (c)(3), (d), (e)(1), (e)(4)(G), (H), and (I) and (f) of this section if the system of records is—

(1) subject to provisions of section 552(b)(1) of this title [5 USCS § 552(b)(1)];

(2) investigatory material compiled for law enforcement purposes, other than material within the scope of subsection (j)(2) of this section: *Provided, however,* That if any individual is denied any right, privilege, or benefit that he would otherwise be entitled by Federal law, or for which he would otherwise be eligible, as a result of the maintenance of such material, such material shall be provided to such individual, except to the extent that the disclosure of such material would reveal the identity of a source who furnished information to the Government under an express promise that the identity of the source would be held in confidence, or, prior to the effective date of this section, under an implied promise that the identity of the source would be held in confidence;

(3) maintained in connection with providing protective services to the President of the United States or other individuals pursuant to section 3056 of title 18;

(4) required by statute to be maintained and used solely as statistical records;

(5) investigatory material compiled solely for the purpose of determining suitability, eligibility, or qualifications for Federal civilian employment, military service, Federal contracts, or access to classified information, but only to the extent that the disclosure of such material would reveal the identity of a source who furnished information to the Government under an express promise that the identity of the source would be held in confidence, or, prior to the effective date of this section, under an implied promise that the identity of the source would be held in confidence;

(6) testing or examination material used solely to determine individual qualifications for appointment or promotion in the Federal service the disclosure of which would compromise the objectivity or fairness of the testing or examination process; or

(7) evaluation material used to determine potential for promotion in the armed services, but only to the extent that the disclosure of such material would reveal the identity of a source who furnished information to the Government under an express promise that the identity of the source would be held in confidence, or, prior to the effective date of this section, under an implied promise that the identity of the source would be held in confidence.

At the time rules are adopted under this subsection, the agency shall include in the statement required under section 553(c) of this title [5 USCS § 553(c)], the reasons why the system of records is to be exempted from a provision of this section.

(l) Archival records.

(1) Each agency record which is accepted by the Archivist of the United States for storage, processing, and servicing in accordance with section 3103 of title 44 [44 USCS § 3103] shall, for the purposes of this section, be considered to be maintained by the agency which deposited the record and shall be subject to the provisions of this section. The Archivist of the United States shall not disclose the record except to the agency which maintains the record, or under rules established by that agency which are not inconsistent with the provisions of this section.

(2) Each agency record pertaining to an identifiable individual which was transferred to the National Archives of the United States as a record which has sufficient historical or other value to warrant its continued preservation by the United States Government, prior to the effective date of this section, shall, for the purposes of this section, be considered to be maintained by the National Archives and shall not be subject to the provisions of this section, except that a statement generally describing such records (modeled after the requirements relating to records subject to subsections (e)(4)(A) through (G) of this section) shall be published in the Federal Register.

(3) Each agency record pertaining to an identifiable individual which is transferred to the National Archives of the United States as a record which has sufficient historical or other value to warrant its continued preservation by the United States Government, on or after the effective date of this section [effective 270 days following Dec. 31, 1974], shall, for the purposes of this section, be considered to be maintained by the National Archives and shall be exempt from the requirements of this section except subsections (e)(4)(A) through (G) and (e)(9) of this section.

(m) Government contractors.

(1) When an agency provides by a contract for the operation by or on behalf of the agency of a system of records to accomplish an agency function, the agency shall, consistent with its authority, cause the requirements of this section to be applied to such system. For purposes of subsection (i) of this section any such contractor and any employee of such contractor, if such contract is agreed to on or after the effective date of this section, shall be considered to be an employee of an agency.

(2) A consumer reporting agency to which a record is disclosed under section 3711(e) of title 31 [31 USCS § 3711(e)] shall not be considered a contractor for the purposes of this section.

(n) Mailing lists. An individual's name and address may not be sold or rented by an agency unless such action is specifically authorized by law. This provision shall not be construed to require the withholding of names and addresses otherwise permitted to be made public.

(o) Matching agreements.

(1) No record which is contained in a system of records may be disclosed to a recipient agency or non-Federal agency for use in a computer matching program except pursuant to a written agreement between the source agency and the recipient agency or non-Federal agency specifying—

(A) the purpose and legal authority for conducting the program;

(B) the justification for the program and the anticipated results, including a specific estimate of any savings;

(C) a description of the records that will be matched, including each data element that will be used, the approximate number of records that will be matched, and the projected starting and completion dates of the matching program;

(D) procedures for providing individualized notice at the time of application, and notice periodically thereafter as directed by the Data Integrity Board of such agency (subject to guidance provided by the Director of the Office of Management and Budget pursuant to subsection (v)), to—

(i) applicants for and recipients of financial assistance or payments under Federal benefit programs, and

(ii) applicants for and holders of positions as Federal personnel, that any information provided by such applicants, recipients, holders and individuals may be subject to verification through matching programs;

(E) procedures for verifying information produced in such matching program as required by subsection (p);

(F) procedures for the retention and timely destruction of identifiable records created by a recipient agency or non-Federal agency in such matching program;

(G) procedures for ensuring the administrative, technical, and physical security of the records matched and the results of such programs;

(H) prohibitions on duplication and redisclosure of records provided by the source agency within or outside the recipient agency or the non-Federal agency, except where required by law or essential to the conduct of the matching program;

(I) procedures governing the use by a recipient agency or non-Federal agency of records provided in a matching program by a source agency, including procedures governing return of the records to the source agency or destruction of records used in such program;

(J) information on assessments that have been made on the accuracy of the records that will be used in such matching program; and

(K) that the Comptroller General may have access to all records of a recipient agency or a non-Federal agency that the Comptroller General deems necessary in order to monitor or verify compliance with the agreement.

(2)(A) A copy of each agreement entered into pursuant to paragraph (1) shall—

(i) be transmitted to the Committee on Governmental Affairs of the Senate and the Committee on Government Operations of the House of Representatives; and

(ii) be available upon request to the public.

(B) No such agreement shall be effective until 30 days after the date on which such a copy is transmitted pursuant to subparagraph (A)(i).

(C) Such an agreement shall remain in effect only for such period, not to exceed 18 months, as the Data Integrity Board of the agency determines is appropriate in light of the purposes, and length of time necessary for the conduct, of the matching program.

(D) Within 3 months prior to the expiration of such an agreement pursuant to subparagraph (C), the Data Integrity Board of the agency may, without additional review, renew the matching agreement for a current, ongoing matching program for not more than one additional year if—

(i) such program will be conducted without any change; and

(ii) each party to the agreement certifies to the Board in writing that the program has been conducted in compliance with the agreement.

(p) Verification and opportunity to contest findings.

(1) In order to protect any individual whose records are used in a matching program, no recipient agency, non-Federal agency, or source agency may suspend, terminate, reduce, or make a final denial of any financial assistance or payment under a Federal benefit program to such individual, or take other adverse action against such individual, as a result of information produced by such matching program, until—

(A)(i) the agency has independently verified the information; or

(ii) the Date Integrity Board of the agency, or in the case of a non-Federal agency the Data Integrity Board of the source agency, determines in accordance with guidance issued by the Director of the Office of Management and Budget that—

(I) the information is limited to identification and amount of benefits paid by the source agency under a Federal benefit program; and

(II) there is a high degree of confidence that the information provided to the recipient agency is accurate;

(B) the individual receives a notice from the agency containing a statement of its findings and informing the individual of the opportunity to contest such findings; and

(C)(i) the expiration of any time period established for the program by statute or regulation for the individual to respond to that notice; or

(ii) in the case of a program for which no such period is established, the end of the 30-day period beginning on the date on which notice under subparagraph (B) is mailed or otherwise provided to the individual.

(2) Independent verification referred to in paragraph (1) requires investigation and confirmation of specific information relating to an individual that is used as a basis for an adverse action against the individual, including where applicable investigation and confirmation of—

(A) the amount of any asset or income involved;

(B) whether such individual actually has or had access to such asset or income for such individual's own use; and

(C) the period or periods when the individual actually had such asset or income.

(3) Notwithstanding paragraph (1), an agency may take any appropriate action otherwise prohibited by such paragraph if the agency determines that the public health or public safety may be adversely affected or significantly threatened during any notice period required by such paragraph.

(q) Sanctions.

(1) Notwithstanding any other provision of law, no source agency may disclose any record which is contained in a system of records to a recipient agency or non-Federal agency for a matching program if such source agency has reason to believe that the requirements of subsection (p), or any matching agreement entered into pursuant to subsection (o), or both, are not being met by such recipient agency.

(2) No source agency may renew a matching agreement unless—

(A) the recipient agency or non-Federal agency has certified that it has complied with the provisions of that agreement; and

(B) the source agency has no reason to believe that the certification is inaccurate.

(r) Report on new systems and matching programs. Each agency that proposes to establish or make a significant change in a system of records or a matching program shall provide adequate advance notice of any such proposal (in duplicate) to the Committee on Government Operations of the House of Representatives, the Committee on Governmental Affairs of the Senate, and the Office of Management and Budget in order to permit an evaluation of the probable or potential effect of such proposal on the privacy or other rights of individuals.

(s) Biennial report. The President shall biennally submit to the Speaker of the House of Representatives and the President pro tempore of the Senate a report—

(1) describing the actions of the Director of the Office of Management and Budget pursuant to section 6 of the Privacy Act of 1974 during the preceding 2 years;

(2) describing the exercise of individual rights of access and amendment under this section during such years;

(3) identifying changes in or additions to systems of records;

(4) containing such other information concerning administration of this section as may be necessary or useful to the Congress in reviewing the effectiveness of this section in carrying out the purposes of the Privacy Act of 1974 [note to this section].

(t) Effect of other laws.

(1) No agency shall rely on any exemption contained in section 552 of this title [5 USCS § 552] to withhold from an individual any record which is otherwise accessible to such individual under the provisions of this section.

(2) No agency shall rely on any exemption in this section to withhold from an individual any record which is otherwise accessible to such individual under the provisions of section 552 of this title [5 USCS § 552].

(u) Data Integrity Boards.

(1) Every agency conducting or participating in a matching program shall establish a Data Integrity Board to oversee and coordinate among the various components of such agency the agency's implementation of this section.

(2) Each Data Integrity Board shall consist of senior officials designated by the head of the agency, and shall include any senior official designated by the head of the agency as responsible for implementation of this section, and the inspector general of the agency, if any. The inspector general shall not serve as chairman of the Data Integrity Board.

(3) Each Data Integrity Board—

(A) shall review, approve, and maintain all written agreements for receipt or disclosure of agency records for matching programs to ensure compliance with subsection (o), and all relevant statutes, regulations, and guidelines;

(B) shall review all matching programs in which the agency has participated during the year, either as a source agency or recipient agency, determine compliance with applicable laws, regulations, guidelines, and agency agreements, and assess the costs and benefits of such programs;

(C) shall review all recurring matching programs in which the agency has participated during the year, either as a source agency or recipient agency, for continued justification for such disclosures;

(D) shall compile an annual report, which shall be submitted to the head of the agency and the Office of Management and Budget and made available to the public on request, describing the matching activities of the agency, including—

(i) matching programs in which the agency has participated as a source agency or recipient agency;

(ii) matching agreements proposed under subsection (o) that were disapproved by the Board;

(iii) any changes in membership or structure of the Board in the preceding year;

(iv) the reasons for any waiver of the requirement in paragraph (4) of this section for completion and submission of a cost-benefit analysis prior to the approval of a matching program;

(v) any violations of matching agreements that have been alleged or identified and any corrective action taken; and

(vi) any other information required by the Director of the Office of Management and Budget to be included in such report;

(E) shall serve as a clearinghouse for receiving and providing information on the accuracy, completeness, and reliability of records used in matching programs;

(F) shall provide interpretation and guidance to agency components and personnel on the requirements of this section for matching programs;

(G) shall review agency recordkeeping and disposal policies and practices for matching programs to assure compliance with this section; and

(H) may review and report on any agency matching activities that are not matching programs.

(4)(A) Except as provided in subparagraphs (B) and (C), a Data Integrity Board shall not approve any written agreement for a matching program unless the agency has completed and submitted to such Board a cost-benefit analysis of the proposed program and such analysis demonstrates that the program is likely to be cost effective.

(B) The Board may waive the requirements of subparagraph (A) of this paragraph if it determines in writing, in accordance with guidelines prescribed by the Director of the Office of Management and Budget, that a cost-benefit analysis is not required.

(C) A cost-benefit analysis shall not be required under subparagraph (A) prior to the initial approval of a written agreement for a matching program that is specifically required by statute. Any subsequent written agreement for such a program shall not be approved by the Data Integrity Board unless the agency has submitted a cost-benefit analysis of the program as conducted under the preceding approval of such agreement.

(5)(A) If a matching agreement is disapproved by a Data Integrity Board, any party to such agreement may appeal the disapproval to the Director of the Office of Management and Budget. Timely notice of the filing of such an appeal shall be provided by the Director of the Office of Management and Budget to the Committee on Governmental Affairs of the Senate and the Committee on Government Operations of the House of Representatives.

(B) The Director of the Office of Management and Budget may approve a matching agreement notwithstanding the disapproval of a Data Integrity Board if the Director determines that—

(i) the matching program will be consistent with all applicable legal, regulatory, and policy requirements;

(ii) there is adequate evidence that the matching agreement will be cost-effective; and

(iii) the matching program is in the public interest.

(C) The decision of the Director to approve a matching agreement shall not take effect until 30 days after it is reported to committees described in subparagraph (A).

(D) If the Data Integrity Board and the Director of the Office of Management and Budget disapprove a matching program proposed by the inspector general of an agency, the inspector general may report the disapproval to the head of the agency and to the Congress.

(6) In the reports required by paragraph (3)(D), agency matching activities that are not matching programs may be reported on an aggregate basis, if and to the extent necessary to protect ongoing law enforcement or counterintelligence investigations.

(v) Office of Management and Budget responsi-

bilities. The Director of the Office of Management and Budget shall—

(1) develop and, after notice and opportunity for public comment, prescribe guidelines and regulations for the use of agencies in implementing the provisions of this section; and

(2) provide continuing assistance to and oversight of the implementation of this section by agencies.

(w) Applicability to Bureau of Consumer Financial Protection. Except as provided in the Consumer Financial Protection Act of 2010, this section shall apply with respect to the Bureau of Consumer Financial Protection.

(Added Dec. 31, 1974, P. L. 93-579, § 3, 88 Stat. 1897; Dec. 31, 1975, P. L. 94-183, § 2(2), 89 Stat 1057; Oct. 25, 1982, P. L. 97-365, § 2, 96 Stat. 1749; Dec. 21, 1982, P. L. 97-375, Title II, § 201(a), (b), 96 Stat. 1821; Jan. 12, 1983, P. L. 97-452, § 2(a)(1), 96 Stat. 2478; Oct. 15, 1984, P. L. 98-477, § 2(c), 98 Stat. 2211; Oct. 19, 1984, P. L. 98-497, Title I, § 107(g), 98 Stat. 2292; Oct. 18, 1988, P. L. 100-503, §§ 2-5, 6(a), 7, 8, 102 Stat. 2507–2514; Nov. 5, 1990, P. L. 101-508, Title VII, Subtitle C, § 7201(b)(1), 104 Stat. 1388-334; Aug. 10, 1993, P. L. 103-66, Title XIII, Ch 2, Subch A, Part V, § 13581(c), 107 Stat. 611; Aug. 22, 1996, P. L. 104-193, Title I, § 110(w), 110 Stat. 2175; Oct. 2, 1996, P. L. 104-226, § 1(b)(3), 110 Stat. 3033; Oct. 19, 1996, P. L. 104-316, Title I, § 115(g)(2)(B), 110 Stat. 3835; Aug. 5, 1997, P. L. 105-34, Title IX, Subtitle C, § 1026(b)(2), 111 Stat. 925; Nov. 10, 1998, P. L. 105-362, Title XIII, § 1301(d), 112 Stat. 3293; Dec. 17, 1999, P. L. 106-170, Title IV, § 402(a)(2), 113 Stat. 1908; March 23, 2010, P. L. 111-148, Title VI, Subtitle E, § 6402(b)(2), 124 Stat. 756; July 21, 2010, P. L. 111-203, Title X, Subtitle H, § 1082, 124 Stat. 2080; Dec. 19, 2014, P. L. 113-295, Div B, Title I, § 102(d), 128 Stat. 4062; Oct. 2, 2024, P.L. 118-104, § 2, 138 Stat. 1586.)

HISTORY; ANCILLARY LAWS AND DIRECTIVES

Amendment Notes

1988.

Act Oct. 18, 1988, in subsec. (f), in the concluding matter, substituted "biennially" for "annually"; substituted subsec. (o) (designated in the directory language as subsec. (r), such being effective as provided by § 10 of the Act, which appears as a note to this section), for one which read: "(o) Report on new systems. Each agency shall provide adequate advance notice to Congress and the Office of Management and Budget of any proposal to establish or alter any system of records in order to permit an evaluation of the probable or potential effect of such proposal on the privacy and other personal or property rights of individuals or the disclosure of information relating to such individuals, and its effect on the preservation of the constitutional principles of federalism and separation of powers."; in subsec. (p) (designated in the directory language as subsec. (s), such being effective as provided by § 10 of the Act, which appears as a note to this section), in the heading, substituted "Biennial" for "Annual", in the introductory matter, substituted "biennially submit" for "annually submit", in para. (1), substituted "preceding 2 years" for "preceding year", and in para. (2), substituted "such years" for "such year".

Such Act further (effective as provided by § 10 of such Act, which appears as a note to this section), in subsec. (a), in para. (6), deleted "and" following the concluding semicolon, in para. (7), substituted a period for the concluding semicolon, and added paras. (8)–(13).

Such Act further (effective as above), in subsec. (e), in para. (10), deleted "and" following "maintained;", in para. (11), substituted "; and" for the concluding period, and added para. (12).

Such Act further (effective as above) redesignated former subsecs. (o), (p), and (q) as subsecs. (r), (s), and (t), respectively, and added new subsecs. (o), (p), and (q); and added subsec. (v).

TITLE 8.
ALIENS AND NATIONALITY

(Complete Title)

CHAPTER 12.
IMMIGRATION AND NATIONALITY

GENERAL PROVISIONS

§ 1101. Definitions

(a) As used in this Act—

(1) The term "administrator" means the official designated by the Secretary of State pursuant to section 104(b) of this Act [8 USCS § 1104(b)].

(2) The term "advocates" includes, but is not limited to, advises, recommends, furthers by overt act, and admits belief in.

(3) The term "alien" means any person not a citizen or national of the United States.

(4) The term "application for admission" has reference to the application for admission into the United States and not to the application for the issuance of an immigrant or nonimmigrant visa.

(5) The term "Attorney General" means the Attorney General of the United States.

(6) The term "border crossing identification card" means a document of identity bearing that designation issued to an alien who is lawfully admitted for permanent residence, or to an alien who is a resident in foreign contiguous territory, by a consular officer or an immigration officer for the purpose of crossing over the borders between the United States and foreign contiguous territory in accordance with such conditions for its issuance and use as may be prescribed by regulations. Such regulations shall provide that (A) each such document include a biometric identifier (such as the fingerprint or handprint of the alien) that is machine readable and (B) an alien presenting a border crossing identification card is not permitted to cross over the border into the United States unless the biometric identifier contained on the card matches the appropriate biometric characteristic of the alien.

(7) The term "clerk of court" means a clerk of a naturalization court.

(8) The terms "Commissioner" and "Deputy Commissioner" mean the Commissioner of Immigration and Naturalization and a Deputy Commissioner of Immigration and Naturalization, respectively.

(9) The term "consular officer" means any consular, diplomatic, or other officer or employee of the United States designated under regulations prescribed under authority contained in this Act, for the purpose of issuing immigrant or nonimmigrant visas or, when used in title III [8 USCS §§ 1401 et seq.], for the purpose of adjudicating nationality.

(10) The term "crewman" means a person serving in any capacity on board a vessel or aircraft.

(11) The term "diplomatic visa" means a nonimmigrant visa bearing that title and issued to a nonimmigrant in accordance with such regulations as the Secretary of State may prescribe.

(12) The term "doctrine" includes, but is not limited to, policies, practices, purposes, aims, or procedures.

(13)(A) The terms "admission" and "admitted" mean, with respect to an alien, the lawful entry of the alien into the United States after inspection and authorization by an immigration officer.

(B) An alien who is paroled under section 212(d)(5) [8 USCS § 1182(d)(5)] or permitted to land temporarily as an alien crewman shall not be considered to have been admitted.

(C) An alien lawfully admitted for permanent residence in the United States shall not be regarded as seeking an admission into the United States for purposes of the immigration laws unless the alien—

(i) has abandoned or relinquished that status,

(ii) has been absent from the United States for a continuous period in excess of 180 days,

(iii) has engaged in illegal activity after having departed the United States,

(iv) has departed from the United States while under legal process seeking removal of the alien from the United States, including removal proceedings under this Act and extradition proceedings,

(v) has committed an offense identified in section 212(a)(2) [8 USCS § 1182(a)(2)], unless since such offense the alien has been granted relief under section 212(h) or 240A(a) [8 USCS § 1182(h) or 1229b(a)], or

(vi) is attempting to enter at a time or place other than as designated by immigration officers or has not been admitted to the United States after inspection and authorization by an immigration officer.

(14) The term "foreign state" includes outlying possessions of a foreign state, but self-governing dominions or territories under mandate or trusteeship shall be regarded as separate foreign states.

(15) The term "immigrant" means every alien except an alien who is within one of the following classes of nonimmigrant aliens—

(A)(i) an ambassador, public minister, or career diplomatic or consular officer who has been accredited by a foreign government recognized de jure by the United States and who is accepted by the President or by the Secretary of State, and the members of the alien's immediate family;

(ii) upon a basis of reciprocity, other officials and employees who have been accredited by a foreign government recognized de jure by the United States, who are accepted by the Secretary of State, and the members of their immediate families; and

(iii) upon a basis of reciprocity, attendants, servants, personal employees, and members of their immediate families, of the officials and employees who have a nonimmigrant status under (i) and (ii) above;

(B) an alien (other than one coming for the purpose of study or of performing skilled or unskilled labor or as a representative of foreign press, radio, film, or other foreign information media coming to engage in such vocation) having a residence in a foreign country which he has no intention of abandoning and who is visiting the United States temporarily for business or temporarily for pleasure;

(C)(i) an alien in immediate and continuous transit through the United States, for a period not to exceed 29 days;

(ii) an alien who qualifies as a person entitled to pass in transit to and from the United Nations Headquarters District (as defined in section 209A(e) of the State Department Basic Authorities Act of 1956 (22 U.S.C. 4309a(e))) and foreign countries, under the provisions of paragraphs (3), (4), and (5) of section 11 of the Agreement regarding the Headquarters of the United Nations, done at Lake Success June 26, 1947 (61 Stat. 758); or

(iii) an alien passing in transit through the United States to board a vessel on which the alien will perform, or to disembark from a vessel on which the alien performed, ship-to-ship liquid cargo transfer operations to or from another vessel engaged in foreign trade, for a period not to exceed 180 days;

(D)(i) an alien crewman serving in good faith as such in a capacity required for normal operation and service on board a vessel, as defined in section 258(a) [8 USCS § 1288(a)] (other than a fishing vessel having its home port or an operating base in the United States), or aircraft, who intends to land temporarily and solely in pursuit of his calling as a crewman and to depart from the United States with the vessel or aircraft on which he arrived or some other vessel or aircraft;

(ii) an alien crewman serving in good faith as such in any capacity required for normal operations and service aboard a fishing vessel having its home port or an operating base in the United States who intends to land temporarily in Guam or the Commonwealth of the Northern Mariana Islands and solely in pursuit of his calling as a crewman and to depart from Guam or the Commonwealth of the Northern Mariana Island with the vessel on which he arrived; or

(iii) an alien crewman performing ship-to-ship liquid cargo transfer operations to or from another vessel engaged in foreign trade, who intends to land temporarily solely in pursuit of the alien's responsibilities as a crewman and to depart from the United States on the vessel on which the alien arrived or on another vessel or aircraft, for a period not to exceed 180 days;

(E) an alien entitled to enter the United States under and in pursuance of the provisions of a treaty of commerce and navigation between the United States and the foreign state of which the alien is a national (or, in the case of an alien who acquired the relevant nationality through a financial investment and who has not previously been granted status under this subparagraph, the foreign state of which the alien is a national and in which the alien has been domiciled for a continuous period of not less than 3 years at any point before applying for a nonimmigrant visa under this subparagraph), and the spouse and children of any such alien if accompanying or following to join such alien: (i) solely to carry on substantial trade, including trade in services or trade in technology, principally between the United States and the foreign state of which the alien is a national; (ii) solely to develop and direct the operations of an enterprise in which the alien has invested, or of an enterprise in which the alien is actively in the process of investing, a substantial amount of capital; or (iii) solely to perform services in a specialty occupation in the United States if the alien is a national of the Commonwealth of Australia and with respect to whom the Secretary of Labor determines and certifies to the Secretary of Homeland Security and the Secretary of State that the intending employer has filed with the Secretary of Labor an attestation under section 212(t)(1) [8 USCS § 1182(t)(1)];

(F) (i) an alien having a residence in a foreign country which he has no intention of abandoning, who is a bona fide student qualified to pursue a full course of study and who seeks to enter the United States temporarily and solely for the purpose of pursuing such a course of study consistent with section 214(l) at an established college, university, seminary, conservatory, academic high school, elementary school, or other academic institution or in an accredited language training program in the United States, particularly designated by him and approved by the Attorney General after consultation with the Secretary of Education, which institution or place of study shall have agreed to report to the Attorney General the termination of attendance of each nonimmigrant student, and if any such institution of learning or place of study fails to make reports promptly the approval shall be withdrawn, (ii) the alien spouse and minor children of any alien described in clause (i) if accompanying or following to join such an alien, and (iii) an alien who is a national of Canada or Mexico, who maintains actual residence and place of abode in the country of nationality, who is described in clause (i) except that the alien's qualifications for and actual course of study may be full or part-time, and who commutes to the United States institution or place of study from Canada or Mexico;

(G)(i) a designated principal resident representative of a foreign government recognized de jure by the United States, which foreign government is a member of an international organization entitled to enjoy privileges, exemptions, and immunities as an international organization under the International Organizations

Immunities Act (59 Stat. 669), accredited resident members of the staff of such representatives, and members of his or their immediate family;

(ii) other accredited representatives of such a foreign government to such international organizations, and the members of their immediate families;

(iii) an alien able to qualify under (i) or (ii) above except for the fact that the government of which such alien is an accredited representative is not recognized de jure by the United States, or that the government of which he is an accredited representative is not a member of such international organization, and the members of his immediate family;

(iv) officers, or employees of such international organizations, and the members of their immediate families;

(v) attendants, servants, and personal employees of any such representative, officer, or employee, and the members of the immediate families of such attendants, servants, and personal employees;

(H) **[Caution: For expiration of amendments made to this subparagraph by Act Nov. 12, 1999, P. L. 106-95, see § 2(e) of such Act, which appears as 8 USCS § 1182 note.]** an alien (i)(a) [Deleted] (b) subject to section 212(j)(2) [8 USCS § 1182(j)(2)] who is coming temporarily to the United States to perform services (other than services described in subclause (a) during the period in which such subclause applies and other than services described in subclause (ii)(a) or in subparagraph (O) or (P)) in a specialty occupation described in section 214(i)(1) [8 USCS § 1184(i)(1)] or as a fashion model, who meets the requirements for the occupation specified in section 214(i)(2) [8 USCS § 1184(i)(2)] or, in the case of a fashion model, is of distinguished merit and ability, and with respect to whom the Secretary of Labor determines and certifies to the Attorney General that the intending employer has filed with the Secretary an application under section 212(n)(1) [8 USCS § 1182(n)(1)], or (b1) who is entitled to enter the United States under and in pursuance of the provisions of an agreement listed in section 214(g)(8)(A) [8 USCS § 1184(g)(8)(A)], who is engaged in a specialty occupation described in section 214(i)(3) [8 USCS § 1184(i)(3)], and with respect to whom the Secretary of Labor determines and certifies to the Secretary of Homeland Security and the Secretary of State that the intending employer has filed with the Secretary of Labor an attestation under section 212(t)(1) [8 USCS § 1182(t)(1)], or (c) who is coming temporarily to the United States to perform services as a registered nurse, who meets the qualifications described in section 212(m)(1) [8 USCS § 1182(m)(1)], and with respect to whom the Secretary of Labor determines and certifies to the Attorney General that an unexpired attestation is on file and in effect under section 212(m)(2) [8 USCS § 1182(m)(2)] for the facility (as defined in section 212(m)(6)) [8 USCS § 1182(m)(6)]) for which the alien will perform the services; or (ii)(a) having a residence in a foreign country which he has no intention of abandoning who is coming temporarily to the United States to perform agricultural labor or services, as defined by the Secretary of Labor in regulations and including agricultural labor defined in section 3121(g) of the Internal Revenue Code of 1986 [26 USCS § 3121(g)], agriculture as defined in section 3(f) of the Fair Labor Standards Act of 1938 (29 U.S.C. 203(f)), and the pressing of apples for cider on a farm, of a temporary or seasonal nature, or (b) having a residence in a foreign country which he has no intention of abandoning who is coming temporarily to the United States to perform other temporary service or labor if unemployed persons capable of performing such service or labor cannot be found in this country, but this clause shall not apply to graduates of medical schools coming to the United States to perform services as members of the medical profession; or (iii) having a residence in a foreign country which he has no intention of abandoning who is coming temporarily to the United States as a trainee, other than to receive graduate medical education or training, in a training program that is not designed primarily to provide productive employment; and the alien spouse and minor children of any such alien specified in this paragraph if accompanying him or following to join him;

(I) upon a basis of reciprocity, an alien who is a bona fide representative of foreign press, radio, film, or other foreign information media, who seeks to enter the United States solely to engage in such vocation, and the spouse and children of such a representative, if accompanying or following to join him;

(J) an alien having a residence in a foreign country which he has no intention of abandoning who is a bona fide student, scholar, trainee, teacher, professor, research assistant, specialist, or leader in a field of specialized knowledge or skill, or other person of similar description, who is coming temporarily to the United States as a participant in a program designated by the Director of the United States Information Agency, for the purpose of teaching, instructing or lecturing, studying, observing, conducting research, consulting, demonstrating special skills, or receiving training and who, if he is coming to the United States to participate in a program under which he will receive graduate medical education or training, also meets the requirements of section 212(j) [8 USCS § 1182(j)], and the alien spouse and minor children of any such alien if accompanying him or following to join him;

(K) subject to subsections (d) and (p) of section 214 [8 USCS § 1184], an alien who—

(i) is the fiancée or fiancé of a citizen of the United States (other than a citizen described in section 204(a)(1)(A)(viii)(I) [8 USCS § 1154(a)(1)(A)(viii)(I)]) and who seeks to enter the United States solely to conclude a valid marriage with the petitioner within ninety days after admission;

(ii) has concluded a valid marriage with a citizen of the United States (other than a citizen described in section 204(a)(1)(A)(viii)(I) [8 USCS § 1154(a)(1)(A)(viii)(I)]) who is the petitioner, is the beneficiary of a petition to accord a status under section 201(b)(2)(A)(i) [8 USCS § 1151(b)(2)(A)(i)] that was filed under section 204 [8 USCS § 1154] by the petitioner, and seeks to enter the United States to await the approval of such petition and the availability to the alien of an immigrant visa; or

(iii) is the minor child of an alien described in clause (i) or (ii) and is accompanying, or following to join, the alien;

(L) subject to section 214(c)(2) [8 USCS § 1184(c)(2)], an alien who, within 3 years preceding the time of his application for admission into the United States, has been employed continuously for one year by a firm or corporation or other legal entity or an affiliate or subsidiary thereof and who seeks to enter the United States temporarily in order to continue to render his services to the same employer or a subsidiary or affiliate thereof in a capacity that is managerial, executive, or involves specialized knowledge, and the alien spouse and minor children of any such alien if accompanying him or following to join him;

(M) (i) an alien having a residence in a foreign country which he has no intention of abandoning who seeks to enter the United States temporarily and solely for the purpose of pursuing a full course of study at an established vocational or other recognized nonacademic institution (other than in a language training program) in the United States particularly designated by him and approved by the Attorney General, after consultation with the Secretary of Education, which institution shall have agreed to report to the Attorney General the termination of attendance of each nonimmigrant nonacademic student and if any such institution fails to make reports promptly the approval shall be withdrawn, (ii) the alien spouse and minor children of any alien described in clause (i) if accompanying or following to join such an alien, and (iii) an alien who is a national of Canada or Mexico, who maintains actual residence and place of abode in the country of nationality, who is described in clause (i) except that the alien's course of study may be full or part-time, and who commutes to the United States institution or place of study from Canada or Mexico;

(N)(i) the parent of an alien accorded the status of special immigrant under paragraph (27)(I)(i) (or under analogous authority under paragraph (27)(L)), but only if and while the alien is a child, or

(ii) a child of such parent or of an alien accorded the status of a special immigrant under clause (ii), (iii), or (iv) of paragraph (27)(I) (or under analogous authority under paragraph (27)(L));

(O) an alien who—

(i) has extraordinary ability in the sciences, arts, education, business, or athletics which has been demonstrated by sustained national or international acclaim or, with regard to motion picture and television productions a demonstrated record of extraordinary achievement, and whose achievements have been recognized in the field through extensive documentation, and seeks to enter the United States to continue work in the area of extraordinary ability;

(ii)(I) seeks to enter the United States temporarily and solely for the purpose of accompanying and assisting in the artistic or athletic performance by an alien who is admitted under clause (i) for a specific event or events,

(II) is an integral part of such actual performance,

(III) (a) has critical skills and experience with such alien which are not of a general nature and which cannot be performed by other individuals, or (b) in the case of a motion picture or television production, has skills and experience with such alien which are not of a general nature and which are critical either based on a pre-existing longstanding working relationship or, with respect to the specific production, because significant production (including pre- and post-production work) will take place both inside and outside the United States and the continuing participation of the alien is essential to the successful completion of the production, and

(IV) has a foreign residence which the alien has no intention of abandoning; or

(iii) is the alien spouse or child of an alien described in clause (i) or (ii) and is accompanying, or following to join, the alien;

(P) an alien having a foreign residence which the alien has no intention of abandoning who—

(i) (a) is described in section 214(c)(4)(A) [8 USCS § 1184(c)(4)(A)] (relating to athletes), or (b) is described in section 214(c)(4)(B) [8 USCS § 1184(c)(4)(B)] (relating to entertainment groups);

(ii)(I) performs as an artist or entertainer, individually or as part of a group, or is an integral part of the performance of such a group, and

(II) seeks to enter the United States temporarily and solely for the purpose of performing as such an artist or entertainer or with such a group under a reciprocal exchange program which is between an organization or organizations in the United States and an organization or organizations in one or more foreign states and which provides for the temporary exchange of artists and entertainers, or groups of artists and entertainers;

(iii)(I) performs as an artist or entertainer, individually or as part of a group, or is an integral part of the performance of such a group, and

(II) seeks to enter the United States temporarily and solely to perform, teach, or coach as such an artist or entertainer or with such a group under a commercial or noncommercial program that is culturally unique; or

(iv) is the spouse or child of an alien described in clause (i), (ii), or (iii) and is accompanying, or following to join, the alien;

(Q) an alien having a residence in a foreign country which he has no intention of abandoning who is coming temporarily (for a period not to exceed 15 months) to the United States as a participant in an international cultural exchange program approved by the Secretary of Homeland Security for the purpose of providing practical training, employment, and the sharing of the history, culture, and traditions of the country of the alien's nationality and who will be employed under the same wages and working conditions as domestic workers;

(R) an alien, and the spouse and children of the alien if accompanying or following to join the alien, who—

(i) for the 2 years immediately preceding the time of application for admission, has been a member of a religious denomination having a bona fide nonprofit, religious organization in the United States; and

(ii) seeks to enter the United States for a period not to exceed 5 years to perform the work described in subclause (I), (II), or (III) of paragraph (27)(C)(ii);

(S) subject to section 214(k) [8 USCS § 1184(k)], an alien—

(i) who the Attorney General determines—

(I) is in possession of critical reliable information concerning a criminal organization or enterprise;

(II) is willing to supply or has supplied such information to Federal or State law enforcement authorities or a Federal or State court; and

(III) whose presence in the United States the Attorney General determines is essential to the success of an authorized criminal investigation or the successful prosecution of an individual involved in the criminal organization or enterprise; or

(ii) who the Secretary of State and the Attorney General jointly determine—

(I) is in possession of critical reliable information concerning a terrorist organization, enterprise, or operation;

(II) is willing to supply or has supplied such information to Federal law enforcement authorities or a Federal court;

(III) will be or has been placed in danger as a result of providing such information; and

(IV) is eligible to receive a reward under section 36(a) of the State Department Basic Authorities Act of 1956 [22 USCS § 2708(a)],

and, if the Attorney General (or with respect to clause (ii), the Secretary of State and the Attorney General jointly) considers it to be appropriate, the spouse, married and unmarried sons and daughters, and parents of an alien described in clause (i) or (ii) if accompanying, or following to join, the alien;

(T)(i) subject to section 214(o) [8 USCS § 1184(o)], an alien who the Secretary of Homeland Security, or in the case of subclause (III)(aa) the Secretary of Homeland Security, in consultation with the Attorney General, determines—

(I) is or has been a victim of a severe form of trafficking in persons, as defined in section 103 of the Trafficking Victims Protection Act of 2000 [22 USCS § 7102];

(II) is physically present in the United States, American Samoa, or the Commonwealth of the Northern Mariana Islands, or at a port of entry thereto, on account of such trafficking, including physical presence on account of the alien having been allowed entry into the United States for participation in investigative or judicial processes associated with an act or a perpetrator of trafficking;

(III)(aa) has complied with any reasonable request for assistance in the Federal, State, or local investigation or prosecution of acts of trafficking or the investigation of crime where acts of trafficking are at least one central reason for the commission of that crime;

(bb) in consultation with the Attorney General, as appropriate, is unable to cooperate with a request described in item (aa) due to physical or psychological trauma; or

(cc) has not attained 18 years of age; and

(IV) [the alien] would suffer extreme hardship involving unusual and severe harm upon removal; and

(ii) if accompanying, or following to join, the alien described in clause (i)—

(I) in the case of an alien described in clause (i) who is under 21 years of age, the spouse, children, unmarried siblings under 18 years of age on the date on which such alien applied for status under such clause, and parents of such alien;

(II) in the case of an alien described in clause (i) who is 21 years of age or older, the spouse and children of such alien; or

(III) any parent or unmarried sibling under 18 years of age, or any adult or minor children of a derivative beneficiary of the alien, as of an alien described in subclause (I) or (II) who the Secretary of Homeland Security, in consultation with the law enforcement officer investigating a severe form of trafficking, determines faces a present danger of retaliation as a result of the alien's escape from the severe form of trafficking or cooperation with law enforcement.

(U)(i) subject to section 214(p) [8 USCS § 1184(p)], an alien who files a petition for status under this subparagraph, if the Secretary of Homeland Security determines that—

(I) the alien has suffered substantial physical or mental abuse as a result of having been a victim of criminal activity described in clause (iii);

(II) the alien (or in the case of an alien child under the age of 16, the parent, guardian, or next friend of the alien) possesses information concerning criminal activity described in clause (iii);

(III) the alien (or in the case of an alien child under the age of 16, the parent, guardian, or next friend of the alien) has been helpful, is being helpful, or is likely to be helpful to a Federal, State, or local law enforcement official, to a Federal, State, or local prosecutor, to a Federal or State judge, to the Service, or to other Federal, State, or local authorities investigating or prosecuting criminal activity described in clause (iii); and

(IV) the criminal activity described in clause (iii) violated the laws of the United States or occurred in the United States (including in Indian country and military installations) or the territories and possessions of the United States;

(ii) if accompanying, or following to join, the alien described in clause (i)—

(I) in the case of an alien described in clause (i) who is under 21 years of age, the spouse, children, unmarried siblings under 18 years of age on the date on which such alien applied for status under such clause, and parents of such alien; or

(II) in the case of an alien described in clause (i) who is 21 years of age or older, the spouse and children of such alien; and

(iii) the criminal activity referred to in this clause is that involving one or more of the following or any similar activity in violation of Federal, State, or local criminal law: rape; torture; trafficking; incest; domestic violence; sexual assault; abusive sexual contact; prostitution; sexual exploitation; stalking; female genital mutilation; being held hostage; peonage; involuntary servitude; slave trade; kidnapping; abduction; unlawful criminal restraint; false imprisonment; blackmail; extortion; manslaughter; murder; felonious assault; witness tampering; obstruction of justice; perjury; fraud in foreign labor contracting (as defined in section 1351 of title 18, United States Code); or attempt, conspiracy, or solicitation to commit any of the above mentioned crimes; or

(V) subject to section 214(q) [8 USCS § 1184(q)], an alien who is the beneficiary (including a child of the principal alien, if eligible to receive a visa under section 203(d) [8 USCS § 1153(d)]) of a petition to accord a status under section 203(a)(2)(A) [8 USCS § 1153(a)(2)(A)] that was filed with the Attorney General under section 204 [8 USCS § 1154] on or before the date of the enactment of the Legal Immigration Family Equity Act [enacted Dec. 21, 2000], if—

(i) such petition has been pending for 3 years or more; or

(ii) such petition has been approved, 3 years or more have elapsed since such filing date, and—

(I) an immigrant visa is not immediately available to the alien because of a waiting list of applicants for visas under section 203(a)(2)(A) [8 USCS § 1153(a)(2)(A)]; or

(II) the alien's application for an immigrant visa, or the alien's application for adjustment of status under section 245 [8 USCS § 1255], pursuant to the approval of such petition, remains pending.

(16) The term "immigrant visa" means an immigrant visa required by this Act and properly issued by a consular officer at his office outside of the United States to an eligible immigrant under the provisions of this Act.

(17) The term "immigration laws" includes this Act and all laws, conventions, and treaties of the United States relating to the immigration, exclusion, deportation, expulsion, or removal of aliens.

(18) The term "immigration officer" means any employee or class of employees of the Service or of the United States designated by the Attorney General, individually or by regulation, to perform the functions of an immigration officer specified by this Act or any section thereof.

(19) The term "ineligible to citizenship," when used in reference to any individual, means, notwithstanding the provisions of any treaty relating to military service, an individual who is, or was at any time, permanently debarred from becoming a citizen of the United States under section 3(a) of the Selective Training and Service Act of 1940, as amended (54 Stat. 885; 55 Stat. 844), or under section 4(a) of the Selective Service Act of 1948, as amended (62 Stat. 605; 65 Stat. 76) [section 4(a) of the Military Selective Service Act, 50 USCS § 3803(a)], or under any section of this Act, or any other Act, or under any law amendatory of, supplementary to, or in substitution for, any of such sections or Acts.

(20) The term "lawfully admitted for permanent residence" means the status of having been lawfully accorded the privilege of residing permanently in the United States as an immigrant in accordance with the immigration laws, such status not having changed.

(21) The term "national" means a person owing permanent allegiance to a state.

(22) The term "national of the United States" means (A) a citizen of the United States, or (B) a person who, though not a citizen of the United States, owes permanent allegiance to the United States.

(23) The term "naturalization" means the conferring of nationality of a state upon a person after birth, by any means whatsoever.

(24) [Repealed]

(25) The term "noncombatant service" shall not include service in which the individual is not subject to military discipline, court martial, or does not wear the uniform of any branch of the armed forces.

(26) The term "nonimmigrant visa" means a visa properly issued to an alien as an eligible nonimmigrant by a competent officer as provided in this Act.

(27) The term "special immigrant" means—

(A) an immigrant, lawfully admitted for permanent residence, who is returning from a temporary visit abroad;

(B) an immigrant who was a citizen of the United States and may, under section 324(a) or 327 of title III [8 USCS §§ 1435(a) or 1438], apply for reacquisition of citizenship;

(C) an immigrant, and the immigrant's spouse and children if accompanying or following to join the immigrant, who—

(i) for at least 2 years immediately preceding the time of application for admission, has been a member of a religious denomination having a bona fide nonprofit, religious organization in the United States;

(ii) seeks to enter the United States—

(I) solely for the purpose of carrying on the vocation of a minister of that religious denomination,

(II) before September 30, 2015, in order to work for the organization at the request of the organization in a professional capacity in a religious vocation or occupation, or

(III) before September 30, 2015, in order to work for the organization (or for a bona fide organization which is affiliated with the religious denomination and is exempt from taxation as an organization described in section 501(c)(3) of the Internal Revenue Code of 1986 [26 USCS § 501(c)(3)]) at the request of the organization in a religious vocation or occupation; and

(iii) has been carrying on such vocation, professional work, or other work continuously for at least the 2-year period described in clause (i);

(D) an immigrant who—

(i) is an employee, or an honorably retired former employee, of the United States Government abroad, or of the American Institute in Taiwan, and who has performed faithful service for a total of fifteen years, or more, and his accompanying spouse and children: *Provided,* That the principal officer of a Foreign Service establishment (or, in the case of the American Institute in Taiwan, the Director thereof), in his discretion, shall have recommended the granting of special immigrant status to such alien in exceptional circumstances and the Secretary of State approves such recommendation and finds that it is in the national interest to grant such status; or

(ii) is the surviving spouse or child of an employee of the United States Government abroad: *Provided,* That the employee performed faithful service for a total of not less than 15 years or was killed in the line of duty;

(E) an immigrant, and his accompanying spouse and children, who is or has been an employee of the Panama Canal Company or Canal Zone Government before the date on which the Panama Canal Treaty of 1977 (as described in section 3(a)(1) of the Panama Canal Act of 1979 [22 USCS § 3602(a)(1)]) enters into force, who was resident in the Canal Zone on the effective date of the exchange of instruments of ratification of such Treaty, and who has performed faithful service as such an employee for one year or more;

(F) an immigrant, and his accompanying spouse and children, who is a Panamanian national and (i) who, before the date on which such Panama Canal Treaty of 1977 enters into force, has been honorably retired from United States Government employment in the Canal Zone with a total of 15 years or more of faithful service, or (ii) who, on the date on which such Treaty enters into force, has been employed by the United States Government in the Canal Zone with a total of 15 years or more of faithful service and who subsequently is honorably retired from such employment or continues to be employed by the United States Government in an area of the former Canal Zone;

(G) an immigrant, and his accompanying spouse and children, who was an employee of the Panama Canal Company or Canal Zone Government on the effective date of the exchange of instruments of ratification of such Panama Canal Treaty of 1977, who has performed faithful service for five years or more as such an employee, and whose personal safety, or the personal safety of whose spouse or children, as a direct result of such Treaty, is reasonably placed in danger because of the special nature of any of that employment;

(H) an immigrant, and his accompanying spouse and children, who—

(i) has graduated from a medical school or has qualified to practice medicine in a foreign state,

(ii) was fully and permanently licensed to practice medicine in a State on January 9, 1978, and was practicing medicine in a State on that date,

(iii) entered the United States as a nonimmigrant under subsection (a)(15)(H) or (a)(15)(J) before January 10, 1978, and

(iv) has been continuously present in the United States in the practice or study of medicine since the date of such entry;

(I)(i) an immigrant who is the unmarried son or daughter of an officer or employee, or of a former officer or employee, of an international organization described in paragraph (15)(G)(i), and who (I) while maintaining the status of a nonimmigrant under paragraph (15)(G)(iv) or paragraph (15)(N), has resided and been physically present in the United States for periods totaling at least one-half of the seven years before the date of application for a visa or for adjustment of status to a status under this subparagraph and for a period or periods aggregating at least seven years between the ages of five and 21 years, and (II) applies for a visa or adjustment of status under this subparagraph no later than his twenty-fifth birthday or six months after the date of enactment of the Immigration Technical Corrections Act of 1988 [enacted Oct. 24, 1988], whichever is later;

(ii) an immigrant who is the surviving spouse of a deceased officer or employee of such an international organization, and who (I) while maintaining the status of a nonimmigrant under paragraph (15)(G)(iv) or paragraph (15)(N), has resided and been physically present in the United States for periods totaling at least one-half of the seven years before the date of application for a visa or for adjustment of status to a status under this subparagraph and for a period or periods aggregating at least 15 years before the date of the death of such officer or employee, and (II) files a petition for status under this subparagraph no later than six months after the date of such death or six months after the date of enactment of the Immigration Technical Corrections Act of 1988 [enacted Oct. 24, 1988], whichever is later;

(iii) an immigrant who is a retired officer or employee of such an international organization, and who (I) while maintaining the status of a nonimmigrant under paragraph (15)(G)(iv), has resided and been physically present in the United States for periods totaling at least one-half of the seven years before the date of application for a visa or for adjustment of status to a status under this subparagraph and for a period or periods aggregating at least 15 years before the date of the officer or employee's retirement from any such international organization, and (II) files a petition for status under this subparagraph no later than six months after the date of such retirement or six months after the date of enactment of the Immigration and Nationality Technical Corrections Act of 1994 [enacted Oct. 25, 1994], whichever is later; or

(iv) an immigrant who is the spouse of a retired officer or employee accorded the status of special immigrant under clause (iii), accompanying or following to join such retired officer or employee as a member of his immediate family;

(J) an immigrant who is present in the United States—

(i) who has been declared dependent on a juvenile court located in the United States or whom such a court has legally committed to, or placed under the custody of, an agency or department of a State, or an individual or entity appointed by a State or juvenile court located in the United States, and whose reunification with 1 or both of the immigrant's parents is not viable due to abuse, neglect, abandonment, or a similar basis found under State law;

(ii) for whom it has been determined in administrative or judicial proceedings that it would not be in the alien's best interest to be returned to the alien's or parent's previous country of nationality or country of last habitual residence; and

(iii) in whose case the Secretary of Homeland Security consents to the grant of special immigrant juvenile status, except that—

(I) no juvenile court has jurisdiction to determine the custody status or placement of an alien in the custody of the Secretary of Health and Human Services unless the Secretary of Health and Human Services specifically consents to such jurisdiction; and

(II) no natural parent or prior adoptive parent of any alien provided special immigrant status under this subparagraph shall thereafter, by virtue of such parentage, be accorded any right, privilege, or status under this Act;

(K) an immigrant who has served honorably on active duty in the Armed Forces of the United States after October 15, 1978, and after original lawful enlistment outside the United States (under a treaty or agreement in effect on the date of the enactment of this subparagraph) for a period or periods aggregating—

(i) 12 years and who, if separated from such service, was never separated except under honorable conditions, or

(ii) 6 years, in the case of an immigrant who is on active duty at the time of seeking special immigrant status under this subparagraph and who has reenlisted to incur a total active duty service obligation of at least 12 years,

and the spouse or child of any such immigrant if accompanying or following to join the immigrant, but only if the executive department under which the immigrant serves or served recommends the granting of special immigrant status to the immigrant;

(L) an immigrant who would be described in clause (i), (ii), (iii), or (iv) of subparagraph (I) if any reference in such a clause—

(i) to an international organization described in paragraph (15)(G)(i) were treated as a reference to the North Atlantic Treaty Organization (NATO);

(ii) to a nonimmigrant under paragraph (15)(G)(iv) were treated as a reference to a nonimmigrant classifiable under NATO-6 (as a member of a civilian component accompanying a force entering in accordance with the provisions of the NATO Status-of-Forces Agreement, a member of a civilian component attached to or employed by an Allied Headquarters under the "Protocol on the Status of International Military Headquarters" set up pursuant to the North Atlantic Treaty, or as a dependent); and

(iii) to the Immigration Technical Corrections Act of 1988 or to the Immigration and Nationality Technical Corrections Act of 1994 were a reference to the American Competitiveness and Workforce Improvement Act of 1998[; or]

(M) subject to the numerical limitations of section 203(b)(4) [8 USCS § 1153(b)(4)], an immigrant who seeks to enter the United States to work as a broadcaster in the United States for the International Broadcasting Bureau of the Broadcasting Board of Governors [United States Agency for Global Media], or for a grantee of the Broadcasting Board of Governors [United States Agency for Global Media], and the immigrant's accompanying spouse and children.

(28) The term "organization" means, but is not limited to, an organization, corporation, company, partnership, association, trust, foundation or fund; and includes a group of persons, whether or not incorporated, permanently or temporarily associated together with joint action on any subject or subjects.

(29) The term "outlying possessions of the United States" means American Samoa and Swains Island.

(30) The term "passport" means any travel document issued by competent authority showing the bearer's origin, identity, and nationality if any, which is valid for the admission of the bearer into a foreign country.

(31) The term "permanent" means a relationship of continuing or lasting nature, as distinguished from temporary, but a relationship may be permanent even though it is one that may be dissolved eventually at the instance either of the United States or of the individual, in accordance with law.

(32) The term "profession" shall include but not be limited to architects, engineers, lawyers, physicians, surgeons, and teachers in elementary or secondary schools, colleges, academies, or seminaries.

(33) The term "residence" means the place of general abode; the place of general abode of a person means his principal, actual dwelling place in fact, without regard to intent.

(34) The term "Service" means the Immigration and Naturalization Service of the Department of Justice.

(35) The term [terms] "spouse," "wife," or "husband" do not include a spouse, wife, or husband by reason of any marriage ceremony where the contracting parties thereto are not physically present in the presence of each other, unless the marriage shall have been consummated.

(36) The term "State" includes the District of Columbia, Puerto Rico, Guam, the Virgin Islands of the United States, and the Commonwealth of the Northern Mariana Islands.

(37) The term "totalitarian party" means an organization which advocates the establishment in the United States of a totalitarian dictatorship or totalitarianism. The terms "totalitarian dictatorship" and "totalitarianism" mean and refer to systems of government not representative in fact, characterized by (A) the existence of a single political party, organized on a dictatorial basis, with so close an identity between such party and its policies and the governmental policies of the country in which it exists, that the party and the government constitute an indistinguishable unit, and (B) the forcible suppression of opposition to such party.

(38) The term "United States," except as otherwise specifically herein provided, when used in a geographical sense, means the continental United States, Alaska, Hawaii, Puerto Rico, Guam, the Virgin Islands of the United States, and the Commonwealth of the Northern Mariana Islands.

(39) The term "unmarried," when used in reference to any individual as of any time, means an individual who at such time is not married, whether or not previously married.

(40) The term "world communism" means a revolutionary movement, the purpose of which is to establish

eventually a Communist totalitarian dictatorship in any or all the countries of the world through the medium of an internationally coordinated Communist political movement.

(41) The term "graduates of a medical school" means aliens who have graduated from a medical school or who have qualified to practice medicine in a foreign state, other than such aliens who are of national or international renown in the field of medicine.

(42) The term "refugee" means (A) any person who is outside any country of such person's nationality or, in the case of a person having no nationality, is outside any country in which such person last habitually resided, and who is unable or unwilling to return to, and is unable or unwilling to avail himself or herself of the protection of, that country because of persecution or a well-founded fear of persecution on account of race, religion, nationality, membership in a particular social group, or political opinion, or (B) in such special circumstances as the President after appropriate consultation (as defined in section 207(e) of this Act [8 USCS § 1157(e)]) may specify, any person who is within the country of such person's nationality or, in the case of a person having no nationality, within the country in which such person is habitually residing, and who is persecuted or who has a well-founded fear of persecution on account of race, religion, nationality, membership in a particular social group, or political opinion. The term "refugee" does not include any person who ordered, incited, assisted, or otherwise participated in the persecution of any person on account of race, religion, nationality, membership in a particular social group, or political opinion. For purposes of determinations under this Act, a person who has been forced to abort a pregnancy or to undergo involuntary sterilization, or who has been persecuted for failure or refusal to undergo such a procedure or for other resistance to a coercive population control program, shall be deemed to have been persecuted on account of political opinion, and a person who has a well founded fear that he or she will be forced to undergo such a procedure or subject to persecution for such failure, refusal, or resistance shall be deemed to have a well founded fear of persecution on account of political opinion.

(43) The term "aggravated felony" means—

(A) murder, rape, or sexual abuse of a minor;

(B) illicit trafficking in a controlled substance (as defined in section 102 of the Controlled Substances Act [21 USCS § 802]), including a drug trafficking crime (as defined in section 924(c) of title 18, United States Code);

(C) illicit trafficking in firearms or destructive devices (as defined in section 921 of title 18, United States Code) or in explosive materials (as defined in section 841(c) of that title [18 USCS § 841(c)]);

(D) an offense described in section 1956 of title 18, United States Code (relating to laundering of monetary instruments) or section 1957 of that title [18 USCS § 1957] (relating to engaging in monetary transactions in property derived from specific unlawful activity) if the amount of the funds exceeded $10,000;

(E) an offense described in—

(i) section 842(h) or (i) of title 18, United States Code, or section 844(d), (e), (f), (g), (h), or (i) of that title [18 USCS § 844(d), (e), (f), (g), (h), or (i)] (relating to explosive materials offenses);

(ii) section 922(g)(1), (2), (3), (4), or (5), (j), (n), (o), (p), or (r) or 924(b) or (h) of title 18, United States Code (relating to firearms offenses); or

(iii) section 5861 of the Internal Revenue Code of 1986 [26 USCS § 5861] (relating to firearms offenses);

(F) a crime of violence (as defined in section 16 of title 18, United States Code, but not including a purely political offense) for which the term of imprisonment [is] at least one year;

(G) a theft offense (including receipt of stolen property) or burglary offense for which the term of imprisonment [is] at least one year;

(H) an offense described in section 875, 876, 877, or 1202 of title 18, United States Code (relating to the demand for or receipt of ransom);

(I) an offense described in section 2251, 2251A, or 2252 of title 18, United States Code (relating to child pornography);

(J) an offense described in section 1962 of title 18, United States Code (relating to racketeer influenced corrupt organizations), or an offense described in section 1084 (if it is a second or subsequent offense) or 1955 of that title (relating to gambling offenses) [18 USCS § 1084 or 1955], for which a sentence of one year imprisonment or more may be imposed;

(K) an offense that—

(i) relates to the owning, controlling, managing, or supervising of a prostitution business;

(ii) is described in section 2421, 2422, or 2423 of title 18, United States Code (relating to transportation for the purpose of prostitution) if committed for commercial advantage; or

(iii) is described in any of sections 1581–1585 or 1588–1591 of title 18, United States Code (relating to peonage, slavery, involuntary servitude, and trafficking in persons);

(L) an offense described in—

(i) section 793 (relating to gathering or transmitting national defense information), 798 (relating to disclosure of classified information), 2153 (relating to sabotage) or 2381 or 2382 (relating to treason) of title 18, United States Code;

(ii) section 601 of the National Security Act of 1947 [50 USCS § 3121] (relating to protecting the identity of undercover intelligence agents);

(iii) section 601 of the National Security Act of 1947 [50 USCS § 3121] (relating to protecting the identity of undercover agents);

(M) an offense that—

(i) involves fraud or deceit in which the loss to the victim or victims exceeds $10,000; or

(ii) is described in section 7201 of the Internal Revenue Code of 1986 [26 USCS § 7201] (relating to tax evasion) in which the revenue loss to the Government exceeds $10,000;

(N) an offense described in paragraph (1)(A) or (2) of section 274(a) [8 USCS § 1324(a)(1)(A) or (2)] (relating to alien smuggling), except in the case of a first offense for which the alien has affirmatively shown that the alien committed the offense for the purpose of assisting, abetting, or aiding only the alien's spouse, child, or parent (and no other individual) to violate a provision of this Act[;]

(O) an offense described in section 275(a) or 276 [8 USCS § 1325(a) or 1326] committed by an alien who was previously deported on the basis of a conviction for an offense described in another subparagraph of this paragraph;

(P) an offense (i) which either is falsely making, forging, counterfeiting, mutilating, or altering a passport or instrument in violation of section 1543 of title 18, United States Code, or is described in section 1546(a) of such title [18 USCS § 1546(a)] (relating to document fraud) and (ii) for which the term of imprisonment is at least 12 months, except in the case of a first offense for which the alien has affirmatively shown that the alien committed the offense for the purpose of assisting, abetting, or aiding only the alien's spouse, child, or parent (and no other individual) to violate a provision of this Act;

(Q) an offense relating to a failure to appear by a defendant for service of sentence if the underlying offense is punishable by imprisonment for a term of 5 years or more;

(R) an offense relating to commercial bribery, counterfeiting, forgery, or trafficking in vehicles the identification numbers of which have been altered for which the term of imprisonment is at least one year;

(S) an offense relating to obstruction of justice, perjury or subornation of perjury, or bribery of a witness, for which the term of imprisonment is at least one year;

(T) an offense relating to a failure to appear before a court pursuant to a court order to answer to or dispose of a charge of a felony for which a sentence of 2 years' imprisonment or more may be imposed; and

(U) an attempt or conspiracy to commit an offense described in this paragraph.

The term applies to an offense described in this paragraph whether in violation of Federal or State law and applies to such an offense in violation of the law of a foreign country for which the term of imprisonment was completed within the previous 15 years. Notwithstanding any other provision of law (including any effective date), the term applies regardless of whether the conviction was entered before, on, or after the date of enactment of this paragraph.

(44)(A) The term "managerial capacity" means an assignment within an organization in which the employee primarily—

(i) manages the organization, or a department, subdivision, function, or component of the organization;

(ii) supervises and controls the work of other supervisory, professional, or managerial employees, or manages an essential function within the organization, or a department or subdivision of the organization;

(iii) if another employee or other employees are directly supervised, has the authority to hire and fire or recommend those as well as other personnel actions (such as promotion and leave authorization) or, if no other employee is directly supervised, functions at a senior level within the organizational hierarchy or with respect to the function managed; and

(iv) exercises discretion over the day-to-day operations of the activity or function for which the employee has authority.

A first-line supervisor is not considered to be acting in a managerial capacity merely by virtue of the supervisor's supervisory duties unless the employees supervised are professional.

(B) The term "executive capacity" means an assignment within an organization in which the employee primarily—

(i) directs the management of the organization or a major component or function of the organization;

(ii) establishes the goals and policies of the organization, component, or function;

(iii) exercises wide latitude in discretionary decision-making; and

(iv) receives only general supervision or direction from higher level executives, the board of directors, or stockholders of the organization.

(C) If staffing levels are used as a factor in determining whether an individual is acting in a managerial or executive capacity, the Attorney General shall take into account the reasonable needs of the organization, component, or function in light of the overall purpose and stage of development of the organization, component, or function. An individual shall not be considered to be acting in a managerial or executive capacity (as previously defined) merely on the basis of the number of employees that the individual supervises or has supervised or directs or has directed.

(45) The term "substantial" means, for purposes of paragraph (15)(E) with reference to trade or capital, such an amount of trade or capital as is established by the Secretary of State, after consultation with appropriate agencies of Government.

(46) The term "extraordinary ability" means, for purposes of section 101(a)(15)(O)(i) [8 USCS § 1101(a)(15)(O)(i)], in the case of the arts, distinction.

(47)(A) The term "order of deportation" means the order of the special inquiry officer, or other such administrative officer to whom the Attorney General has delegated the responsibility for determining whether an alien is deportable, concluding that the alien is deportable or ordering deportation.

(B) The order described under subparagraph (A) shall become final upon the earlier of—

(i) a determination by the Board of Immigration Appeals affirming such order; or

(ii) the expiration of the period in which the alien is permitted to seek review of such order by the Board of Immigration Appeals.

(48)(A) The term "conviction" means, with respect to an alien, a formal judgment of guilt of the alien entered by a court or, if adjudication of guilt has been withheld, where—

(i) a judge or jury has found the alien guilty or the alien has entered a plea of guilty or nolo contendere or has admitted sufficient facts to warrant a finding of guilt, and

(ii) the judge has ordered some form of punishment, penalty, or restraint on the alien's liberty to be imposed.

(B) Any reference to a term of imprisonment or a sentence with respect to an offense is deemed to include the period of incarceration or confinement ordered by a court of law regardless of any suspension of the imposition or execution of that imprisonment or sentence in whole or in part.

(49) The term "stowaway" means any alien who obtains transportation without the consent of the owner, charterer, master or person in command of any vessel or aircraft through concealment aboard such vessel or aircraft. A passenger who boards with a valid ticket is not to be considered a stowaway.

(50) The term "intended spouse" means any alien who meets the criteria set forth in section 204(a)(1)(A)(iii)(II)(aa)(BB), 204(a)(1)(B)(ii)(II)(aa)(BB), or 240A(b)(2)(A)(i)(III) [8 USCS § 1154(a)(1)(A)(iii)(II)(aa)(BB), 1154(a)(1)(B)(ii)(II)(aa)(BB), or 1229b(b)(2)(A)(i)(III)].

(51) The term "VAWA self-petitioner" means an alien, or a child of the alien, who qualifies for relief under—

(A) clause (iii), (iv), or (vii) of section 204(a)(1)(A) [8 USCS § 1154(a)(1)(A)];

(B) clause (ii) or (iii) of section 204(a)(1)(B) [8 USCS § 1154(a)(1)(B)];

(C) section 216(c)(4)(C) [8 USCS § 1186(c)(4)(C)];

(D) the first section of Public Law 89-732 (8 U.S.C. 1255 note) (commonly known as the Cuban Adjustment Act) as a child or spouse who has been battered or subjected to extreme cruelty;

(E) section 902(d)(1)(B) of the Haitian Refugee Immigration Fairness Act of 1998 (8 U.S.C. 1255 note);

(F) section 202(d)(1) of the Nicaraguan Adjustment and Central American Relief Act [8 USCS § 1255 note]; or

(G) section 309 of the Illegal Immigration Reform and Immigrant Responsibility Act of 1996 (division C of Public Law 104-208) [note to this section].

(52) The term "accredited language training program" means a language training program that is accredited by an accrediting agency recognized by the Secretary of Education.

(b) As used in titles I and II [8 USCS §§ 1101 et seq., 1151 et seq.]—

(1) The term "child" means an unmarried person under twenty-one years of age who is—

(A) a child born in wedlock;

(B) a stepchild, whether or not born out of wedlock, provided the child had not reached the age of eighteen years at the time the marriage creating the status of stepchild occurred;

(C) a child legitimated under the law of the child's residence or domicile, or under the law of the father's residence or domicile, whether in or outside the United States, if such legitimation takes place before the child reaches the age of eighteen years and the child is in the legal custody of the legitimating parent or parents at the time of such legitimation;

(D) a child born out of wedlock, by, through whom, or on whose behalf a status, privilege, or benefit is sought by virtue of the relationship of the child to its natural mother or to its natural father if the father has or had a bona fide parent-child relationship with the person;

(E)(i) a child adopted while under the age of sixteen years if the child has been in the legal custody of, and has resided with, the adopting parent or parents for at least two years or if the child has been battered or subject to extreme cruelty by the adopting parent or by a family member of the adopting parent residing in the same household: *Provided,* That no natural parent of any such adopted child shall thereafter, by virtue of such parentage, be accorded any right, privilege, or status under this Act; or

(ii) subject to the same proviso as in clause (i), a child who: (I) is a natural sibling of a child described in clause (i) or subparagraph (F)(i); (II) was adopted by the adoptive parent or parents of the sibling described in such clause or subparagraph; and (III) is otherwise described in clause (i), except that the child was adopted while under the age of 18 years;

(F)(i) a child, under the age of sixteen at the time a petition is filed in his behalf to accord a classification as an immediate relative under section 201(b) [8 USCS § 1151(b)], who is an orphan because of the death or disappearance of, abandonment or desertion by, or separation or loss from, both parents, or for whom the sole or surviving parent is incapable of providing the proper care and has in writing irrevocably released the child for emigration and adoption; who has been adopted abroad by a United States citizen and spouse jointly, or by an unmarried United States citizen who is at least 25 years of age, at least 1 of whom personally saw and observed the child before or during the adoption proceedings; or who is coming to the United States for adoption by a United States citizen and spouse jointly, or by an unmarried United States citizen at least twenty-five years of age, who have or has complied with the preadoption requirements, if any, of the child's proposed residence: *Provided,* That the Attorney General is satisfied that proper care will be furnished the child if admitted to the United States: *Provided further,* That no natural parent or prior adoptive parent of any such child shall thereafter, by virtue of such parentage, be accorded any right, privilege, or status under this Act; or

(ii) subject to the same provisos as in clause (i), a child who: (I) is a natural sibling of a child described in clause (i) or subparagraph (E)(i); (II) has been adopted abroad, or is coming to the United States for adoption, by the adoptive parent (or prospective adoptive parent) or parents of the sibling described in such clause or subparagraph; and (III) is otherwise described in clause (i), except that the child is under the age of 18 at the time a petition is filed in his or her behalf to accord a classification as an immediate relative under section 201(b) [8 USCS § 1151(b)]; or

(G)(i) a child, younger than 16 years of age at the time a petition is filed on the child's behalf to accord a classification as an immediate relative under section 201(b) [8 USCS § 1151(b)], who has been adopted in a foreign state that is a party to the Convention on Protection of Children and Co-operation in Respect of Intercountry Adoption, done at The Hague on May 29,

1993, or who is emigrating from such a foreign state to be adopted in the United States by a United States citizen and spouse jointly or by an unmarried United States citizen who is at least 25 years of age, *Provided,* That—

(I) the Secretary of Homeland Security is satisfied that proper care will be furnished the child if admitted to the United States;

(II) the child's natural parents (or parent, in the case of a child who has one sole or surviving parent because of the death or disappearance of, abandonment or desertion by, the other parent), or other persons or institutions that retain legal custody of the child, have freely given their written irrevocable consent to the termination of their legal relationship with the child, and to the child's emigration and adoption;

(III) in the case of a child having two living natural parents, the natural parents are incapable of providing proper care for the child;

(IV) the Secretary of Homeland Security is satisfied that the purpose of the adoption is to form a bona fide parent-child relationship, and the parent-child relationship of the child and the natural parents has been terminated (and in carrying out both obligations under this subclause the Secretary of Homeland Security may consider whether there is a petition pending to confer immigrant status on one or both of such natural parents); and

(V) in the case of a child who has not been adopted—

(aa) the competent authority of the foreign state has approved the child's emigration to the United States for the purpose of adoption by the prospective adoptive parent or parents; and

(bb) the prospective adoptive parent or parents has or have complied with any pre-adoption requirements of the child's proposed residence; and

(ii) except that no natural parent or prior adoptive parent of any such child shall thereafter, by virtue of such parentage, be accorded any right, privilege, or status under this chapter; or

(iii) subject to the same provisos as in clauses (i) and (ii), a child who—

(I) is a natural sibling of a child described in clause (i), subparagraph (E)(i), or subparagraph (F)(i);

(II) was adopted abroad, or is coming to the United States for adoption, by the adoptive parent (or prospective adoptive parent) or parents of the sibling described in clause (i), subparagraph (E)(i), or subparagraph (F)(i); and

(III) is otherwise described in clause (i), except that the child is younger than 18 years of age at the time a petition is filed on his or her behalf for classification as an immediate relative under section 201(b) [8 USCS § 1151(b)].

(2) The terms "parent," "father," or "mother" mean a parent, father, or mother only where the relationship exists by reason of any of the circumstances set forth in (1) above, except that, for purposes of paragraph (1)(F) (other than the second proviso therein) and paragraph (1)(G)(i) in the case of a child born out of wedlock described in paragraph (1)(D) (and not described in paragraph (1)(C)), the term "parent" does not include the natural father of the child if the father has disappeared or abandoned or deserted the child or if the father has in writing irrevocably released the child for emigration and adoption.

(3) The term "person" means an individual or an organization.

(4) The term "immigration judge" means an attorney whom the Attorney General appoints as an administrative judge within the Executive Office for Immigration Review, qualified to conduct specified classes of proceedings, including a hearing under section 240 [8 USCS § 1229a]. An immigration judge shall be subject to such supervision and shall perform such duties as the Attorney General shall prescribe, but shall not be employed by the Immigration and Naturalization Service.

(5) The term "adjacent islands" includes Saint Pierre, Miquelon, Cuba, the Dominican Republic, Haiti, Bermuda, the Bahamas, Barbados, Jamaica, the Windward and Leeward Islands, Trinidad, Martinique, and other British, French, and Netherlands territory or possessions in or bordering on the Caribbean Sea.

(c) As used in title III [8 USCS §§ 1401 et seq.]—

(1) The term "child" means an unmarried person under twenty-one years of age and includes a child legitimated under the law of the child's residence or domicile, or under the law of the father's residence or domicile, whether in the United States or elsewhere, and, except as otherwise provided in sections 320 and 321 of title III [8 USCS §§ 1431, 1432], a child adopted in the United States, if such legitimation or adoption takes place before the child reaches the age of 16 years (except to the extent that the child is described in subparagraph (E)(ii) or (F)(ii) of subsection (b)(1)), and the child is in the legal custody of the legitimating or adopting parent or parents at the time of such legitimation or adoption.

(2) The terms "parent," "father," and "mother" include in the case of a posthumous child a deceased parent, father, and mother.

(d) [Repealed]

(e) For the purposes of this Act—

(1) The giving, loaning, or promising of support or of money or any other thing of value to be used for advocating any doctrine shall constitute the advocating of such doctrine; but nothing in this paragraph shall be construed as an exclusive definition of advocating.

(2) The giving, loaning, or promising of support or of money or any other thing of value for any purpose to any organization shall be presumed to constitute affiliation therewith; but nothing in this paragraph shall be construed as an exclusive definition of affiliation.

(3) Advocating the economic, international, and governmental doctrines of world communism means advocating the establishment of a totalitarian Communist dictatorship in any or all of the countries of the world through the medium of an internationally coordinated Communist movement.

(f) For the purposes of this Act—

No person shall be regarded as, or found to be, a person of good moral character who, during the period for which good moral character is required to be established, is, or was—

(1) a habitual drunkard;

(2) [Repealed]

(3) a member of one or more of the classes of persons, whether inadmissible or not, described in paragraphs (2)(D), (6)(E), and (10)(A) of section 212(a) of this Act [8 USCS § 1182(a)]; or subparagraphs (A) and (B) of section 212(a)(2) [8 USCS § 1182(a)(2)] and subparagraph (C) thereof [of such section] (except as such paragraph relates to a single offense of simple possession of 30 grams or less of marihuana), if the offense described therein, for which such person was convicted or of which he admits the commission, was committed during such period;

(4) one whose income is derived principally from illegal gambling activities;

(5) one who has been convicted of two or more gambling offenses committed during such period;

(6) one who has given false testimony for the purpose of obtaining any benefits under this Act;

(7) one who during such period has been confined, as a result of conviction, to a penal institution for an aggregate period of one hundred and eighty days or more, regardless of whether the offense, or offenses, for which he has been confined were committed within or without such period;

(8) one who at any time has been convicted of an aggravated felony (as defined in subsection (a)(43)); or

(9) one who at any time has engaged in conduct described in section 212(a)(3)(E) [8 USCS § 1182(a)(3)(E)] (relating to assistance in Nazi persecution, participation in genocide, or commission of acts of torture or extrajudicial killings) or 212(a)(2)(G) [8 USCS § 1182(a)(2)(G)] (relating to severe violations of religious freedom).

The fact that any person is not within any of the foregoing classes shall not preclude a finding that for other reasons such person is or was not of good moral character. In the case of an alien who makes a false statement or claim of citizenship, or who registers to vote or votes in a Federal, State, or local election (including an initiative, recall, or referendum) in violation of a lawful restriction of such registration or voting to citizens, if each natural parent of the alien (or, in the case of an adopted alien, each adoptive parent of the alien) is or was a citizen (whether by birth or naturalization), the alien permanently resided in the United States prior to attaining the age of 16, and the alien reasonably believed at the time of such statement, claim, or violation that he or she was a citizen, no finding that the alien is, or was, not of good moral character may be made based on it.

(g) For the purposes of this Act any alien ordered deported or removed (whether before or after the enactment of this Act [enacted June 27, 1952]) who has left the United States, shall be considered to have been deported or removed in pursuance of law, irrespective of the source from which the expenses of his transportation were defrayed or of the place to which he departed.

(h) For purposes of section 212(a)(2)(E) [8 USCS § 1182(a)(2)(E)], the term "serious criminal offense" means—

(1) any felony;

(2) any crime of violence, as defined in section 16 of title 18 of the United States Code; or

(3) any crime of reckless driving or of driving while intoxicated or under the influence of alcohol or of prohibited substances if such crime involves personal injury to another.

(i) With respect to each nonimmigrant alien described in subsection (a)(15)(T)(i)—

(1) the Secretary of Homeland Security, the Attorney General, and other Government officials, where appropriate, shall provide the alien with a referral to a nongovernmental organization that would advise the alien regarding the alien's options while in the United States and the resources available to the alien; and

(2) the Secretary of Homeland Security shall, during the period the alien is in lawful temporary resident status under that subsection, grant the alien authorization to engage in employment in the United States and provide the alien with an "employment authorized" endorsement or other appropriate work permit.

(June 27, 1952, ch 477, Title I, § 101, 66 Stat. 166; Sept. 11, 1957, P. L. 85-316, §§ 1, 2, 71 Stat. 639; July 7, 1958, P. L. 85-508, § 22, 72 Stat. 351; March 18, 1959, P. L. 86-3, § 20(a), 73 Stat. 13; Sept. 21, 1961, P. L. 87-256, § 109(a), (b), 75 Stat. 534; Sept. 26, 1961, P. L. 87-301, §§ 1, 2, 7, 75 Stat. 650, 653; Oct. 3, 1965, P. L. 89-236, §§ 8, 24, 79 Stat. 916, 922; Nov. 2, 1966, P. L. 89-710, 80 Stat. 1104; April 7, 1970, P. L. 91-225, § 1, 84 Stat. 116; Dec. 16, 1975, P. L. 94-155, 89 Stat. 824; Oct. 12, 1976, P. L. 94-484, Title VI, § 601(b), (e), 90 Stat. 2301, 2302; Oct. 20, 1976, P. L. 94-571, § 7(a), 90 Stat. 2706; Oct. 12, 1976, P. L. 94-484, Title VI, § 602(c), as added Aug. 1, 1977, P. L. 95-83, Title III, § 307(q)(3), 91 Stat. 395; Aug. 17, 1977, P. L. 95-105, Title I, § 109(b)(3), 91 Stat 847; Sept. 27, 1979, P. L. 96-70, Title III, Ch 1, § 3201(a), 93 Stat. 496; March 17, 1980, P. L. 96-212, Title II, § 201(a), 94 Stat. 102; Dec. 29, 1981, P. L. 97-116, §§ 2, 5(d)(1), 18(a), 95 Stat. 1611, 1614, 1619; Oct. 30, 1984, Priv. L. 98-47, § 3, 98 Stat. 3435; Oct. 21, 1986, P. L. 99-505, § 1, 100 Stat. 1806; Nov. 6, 1986, P. L. 99-603, Title III, Part A, § 301(a), Part B, §§ 312, 315(a), 100 Stat. 3411, 3434, 3439; Nov. 14, 1986, P. L. 99-653, §§ 2, 3, 100 Stat. 3655; Oct. 1, 1988, P. L. 100-459, Title II, § 210(a), 102 Stat. 2203; Oct. 24, 1988, P. L. 100-525, §§ 2(o)(1), 8(b), 9(a), 102 Stat. 2613, 2617, 2619; Nov. 18, 1988, P. L. 100-690, Title VII, Subtitle J, § 7342, 102 Stat. 4469; Nov. 21, 1989, P. L. 101-162, Title VI, § 611(a), 103 Stat. 1038; Dec. 18, 1989, P. L. 101-238, § 3(a), 103 Stat. 2100; Feb. 16, 1990, P. L. 101-246, Title I, Part C, § 131(b), 104 Stat. 31; Nov. 29, 1990, P. L. 101-649, Title I, Subtitle B, Part 2, § 123, Subtitle D, §§ 151(a), 153(a), Subtitle E, § 161(f)(2)(A), Title II, Subtitle A, §§ 203(c), 204(a), (c), 205(c)(1), (d), (e), 206(c), 207(a), 208, 209, Title IV, § 407(a)(2), Title V, Subtitle A, §§ 501(a), 509(a), Title VI, § 603(a)(1), 104 Stat. 4995, 5004, 5005, 5012, 5018, 5019, 5020, 5023, 5026, 5027, 5040, 5048, 5051, 5082; Oct. 1, 1991, P. L. 102-110, § 2(a), 105 Stat. 555; Dec. 12, 1991, P. L. 102-232, Title II, §§ 203(a), 205(a)–(c), 206(b), (c)(1), (d), 207(b), 302(e)(8)(A), 303(a)(5)(A), (7)(A), 305(m)(1), 306(a)(1), 309(b)(1), 105 Stat. 1737, 1740, 1741, 1746, 1747, 1748, 1750, 1751, 1758; April 30, 1994, P. L. 103-236, Title I, Part C, § 162(h)(1), 108 Stat. 407; Sept. 13, 1994, P. L. 103-322, Title XIII, § 130003(a), 108 Stat. 2024; Oct. 5, 1994, P. L. 103-337, Div C, Title XXXVI, § 3605, 108 Stat. 3113; Oct. 25, 1994, P. L. 103-416, Title II, §§ 201, 202, 214, 219(a), 222(a), 108 Stat. 4310, 4311, 4314, 4316, 4320; Nov. 15, 1995, P. L. 104-51, § 1, 109 Stat. 467; April 24, 1996, P. L. 104-132, Title IV, Subtitle D, § 440(b), (e), 110 Stat. 1277; Sept. 30, 1996, P. L. 104-208, Div C, Title I, Subtitle A, § 104(a), Title III, Subtitle A, §§ 301(a), 308(d)(3)(A), (4)(A), (e)(3), (f)(1)(A),

(B), Subtitle B, §§ 321(a), (b), 322(a)(1), (2)(A), Subtitle E, § 361(a), Subtitle F, § 371(a), Title VI, Subtitle A, § 601(a), Subtitle B, § 625(a)(2), Subtitle E, § 671(a)(3)(B), (b)(5), (e)(2), 110 Stat. 3009-555, 3009-575, 3009-617, 3009-620, 3009-621, 3009-627, 3009-629, 3009-644, 3009-645, 3009-689, 3009-700, 3009-721, 3009-722, 3009-723; Oct. 6, 1997, P. L. 105-54, § 1(a), 111 Stat. 1175; Nov. 26, 1997, P. L. 105-119, Title I, § 113, 111 Stat. 2460; Oct. 21, 1998, P. L. 105-277, Div C, Title IV, § 421, Div G, Title XXII, Ch 2, § 2222(e), 112 Stat. 2681-657, 2681-819; Oct. 30, 1998, P. L. 105-319, § 2(b), (d)(2), 112 Stat. 3014, 3015; Nov. 12, 1999, P. L. 106-95, § 2(a), (c), 113 Stat. 1312, 1316; Dec. 7, 1999, P. L. 106-139, § 1(a), (b)(1), 113 Stat. 1696; Oct. 6, 2000, P. L. 106-279, Title III, § 302(a), (c), 114 Stat. 838, 839; Oct. 28, 2000, P. L. 106-386, Div A, § 107(e)(1), (4), Div B, Title V, §§ 1503(a), 1513(b), 114 Stat. 1477, 1479, 1518, 1534; Oct. 30, 2000, P. L. 106-395, Title II, § 201(a)(1), 114 Stat. 1633; Nov. 1, 2000, P. L. 106-409, § 2(a), 114 Stat. 1787; Nov. 22, 2000, P. L. 106-536, § 1(a), 114 Stat. 2560; Dec. 21, 2000, P. L. 106-553, § 1(a)(2), 114 Stat. 2762; Jan. 16, 2002, P. L. 107-125, § 2(b), 115 Stat. 2403; Oct. 4, 2002, P. L. 107-234, § 1(4), 116 Stat. 1481; Nov. 2, 2002, P. L. 107-274, § 2(a), (b), 116 Stat. 1923; Sept. 3, 2003, P. L. 108-77, Title IV, § 402(a)(1), 117 Stat. 939; Oct. 15, 2003, P. L. 108-99, § 1, 117 Stat. 1176; Dec. 19, 2003, P. L. 108-193, §§ 4(b)(1), (5), 8(a)(1), 117 Stat. 2878, 2879, 2886; Dec. 10, 2004, P. L. 108-449, § 1(a)(2)(B), (3)(A), (b)(1), 118 Stat. 3469, 3470; Dec. 17, 2004, P. L. 108-458, Title V, Subtitle E, § 5504, 118 Stat. 3741; May 11, 2005, P. L. 109-13, Div B, Title V, § 501(a), 119 Stat. 321; Oct. 18, 2005, P. L. 109-90, Title V, § 536, 119 Stat. 2087; Jan. 5, 2006, P. L. 109-162, Title VIII, Subtitle A, §§ 801, 805(d), Subtitle B, § 811, Subtitle C, § 822(c)(1), 119 Stat. 3053, 3056, 3057, 3063; July 27, 2006, P. L. 109-248, Title IV, § 402(b), 120 Stat. 623; May 8, 2008, P. L. 110-229, Title VII, Subtitle A, § 702(j)(1)–(3), 122 Stat. 866; Oct. 10, 2008, P. L. 110-391, § 2(a), 122 Stat. 4193; Dec. 23, 2008, P. L. 110-457, Title II, Subtitle A, § 201(a), Subtitle D, § 235(d)(1), 122 Stat. 5052, 5079; March 20, 2009, P. L. 111-9, § 1, 123 Stat. 989; Oct. 28, 2009, P. L. 111-83, Title V, § 568(a)(1), 123 Stat. 2186; Nov. 30, 2010, P. L. 111-287, § 3, 124 Stat. 3058; Dec. 14, 2010, P. L. 111-306, § 1(a), 124 Stat. 3280; Sept. 28, 2012, P. L. 112-176, § 3, 126 Stat. 1325; March 7, 2013, P. L. 113-4, Title VIII, § 801, Title XII, Subtitle B, Part II, §§ 1221, 1222, 127 Stat. 110, 144; Jan. 17, 2014, P. L. 113-76, Div K, Title VII, § 7083, 128 Stat. 567; July 30, 2021, P.L. 117-31, Title IV, § 403(a), 135 Stat. 318; Dec. 23, 2022, P.L. 117-263, Div E, Title LIX, Subtitle A, § 5902(b), 136 Stat. 3440; Jan. 5, 2023, P.L. 117-360, § 2, 136 Stat. 6292.)

§ 1102. Diplomatic and semidiplomatic immunities

Except as otherwise provided in this Act, for so long as they continue in the nonimmigrant classes enumerated in this section, the provisions of this Act relating to ineligibility to receive visas and the removal of aliens shall not be construed to apply to nonimmigrants—

(1) within the class described in paragraph (15)(A)(i) of section 101(a) [8 USCS § 1101(a)(15)(A)(i)], except those provisions relating to reasonable requirements of passports and visas as a means of identification and documentation necessary to establish their qualifications under such paragraph (15)(A)(i) [8 USCS § 1101(a)(15)(A)(i)], and, under such rules and regulations as the President may deem to be necessary, the provisions of subparagraphs (A) through (C) of section 212(a)(3) [8 USCS § 1182(a)(3)(A)–(C)];

(2) within the class described in paragraph (15)(G)(i) of section 101(a) [8 USCS § 1101(a)(15)(G)(i)], except those provisions relating to reasonable requirements of passports and visas as a means of identification and documentation necessary to establish their qualifications under such paragraph (15)(G)(i) [8 USCS § 1101(a)(15)(G)(i)], and the provisions of subparagraphs (A) through (C) of section 212(a)(3) [8 USCS § 1182(a)(3)(A)–(C)]; and

(3) within the classes described in paragraphs (15)(A)(ii), (15)(G)(ii), (15)(G)(iii), or (15)(G)(iv) of section 101(a) [8 USCS § 1101(a)(15)(A)(ii), (15)(G)(ii), (15)(G)(iii), or (15)(G)(iv)], except those provisions relating to reasonable requirements of passports and visas as a means of identification and documentation necessary to establish their qualifications under such paragraphs, and the provisions of subparagraphs (A) through (C) of section 212(a)(3) [8 USCS § 1182(a)(3)(A)–(C)].

(June 27, 1952, ch 477, Title I, § 102, 66 Stat. 173; Oct. 24, 1988, P. L. 100-525, § 9(b), 102 Stat. 2619; Nov. 29, 1990, P. L. 101-649, Title VI, § 603(a)(2), 104 Stat. 5082; Dec. 12, 1991, P. L. 102-232, Title III, § 307(i), 105 Stat. 1756; Sept. 30, 1996, P. L. 104-208, Div C, Title III, Subtitle A, § 308(d)(4)(B), 110 Stat. 3009-617.)

§ 1103. Powers and duties of the Secretary, the Under Secretary, and the Attorney General

(a) Secretary of Homeland Security.

(1) The Secretary of Homeland Security shall be charged with the administration and enforcement of this Act and all other laws relating to the immigration and naturalization of aliens, except insofar as this Act or such laws relate to the powers, functions, and duties conferred upon the President, Attorney General, the Secretary of State, the officers of the Department of State, or diplomatic or consular officers: *Provided, however,* That determination and ruling by the Attorney General with respect to all questions of law shall be controlling.

(2) He shall have control, direction, and supervision of all employees and of all the files and records of the Service.

(3) He shall establish such regulations; prescribe such forms of bond, reports, entries, and other papers; issue such instructions; and perform such other acts as he deems necessary for carrying out his authority under the provisions of this Act.

(4) He may require or authorize any employee of the Service or the Department of Justice to perform or exercise any of the powers, privileges, or duties conferred or imposed by this Act or regulations issued thereunder upon any other employee of the Service.

(5) He shall have the power and duty to control and guard the boundaries and borders of the United States against the illegal entry of aliens and shall, in his discretion, appoint for that purpose such number of employees of the Service as to him shall appear necessary and proper.

(6) He is authorized to confer or impose upon any employee of the United States, with the consent of the head of the Department or other independent establishment under whose jurisdiction the employee is serving, any of the powers, privileges, or duties conferred or

imposed by this Act or regulations issued thereunder upon officers or employees of the Service.

(7) He may, with the concurrence of the Secretary of State, establish offices of the Service in foreign countries; and, after consultation with the Secretary of State, he may, whenever in his judgment such action may be necessary to accomplish the purposes of this Act, detail employees of the Service for duty in foreign countries.

(8) After consultation with the Secretary of State, the Attorney General may authorize officers of a foreign country to be stationed at preclearance facilities in the United States for the purpose of ensuring that persons traveling from or through the United States to that foreign country comply with that country's immigration and related laws.

(9) Those officers may exercise such authority and perform such duties as United States immigration officers are authorized to exercise and perform in that foreign country under reciprocal agreement, and they shall enjoy such reasonable privileges and immunities necessary for the performance of their duties as the government of their country extends to United States immigration officers.

(10) In the event the Attorney General determines that an actual or imminent mass influx of aliens arriving off the coast of the United States, or near a land border, presents urgent circumstances requiring an immediate Federal response, the Attorney General may authorize any State or local law enforcement officer, with the consent of the head of the department, agency, or establishment under whose jurisdiction the individual is serving, to perform or exercise any of the powers, privileges, or duties conferred or imposed by this Act or regulations issued thereunder upon officers or employees of the Service.

(11) The Attorney General, in support of persons in administrative detention in non-Federal institutions, is authorized—

(A) to make payments from funds appropriated for the administration and enforcement of the laws relating to immigration, naturalization, and alien registration for necessary clothing, medical care, necessary guard hire, and the housing, care, and security of persons detained by the Service pursuant to Federal law under an agreement with a State or political subdivision of a State; and

(B) to enter into a cooperative agreement with any State, territory, or political subdivision thereof, for the necessary construction, physical renovation, acquisition of equipment, supplies or materials required to establish acceptable conditions of confinement and detention services in any State or unit of local government which agrees to provide guaranteed bed space for persons detained by the Service.

(b) Land acquisition authority.

(1) The Attorney General may contract for or buy any interest in land, including temporary use rights, adjacent to or in the vicinity of an international land border when the Attorney General deems the land essential to control and guard the boundaries and borders of the United States against any violation of this Act.

(2) The Attorney General may contract for or buy any interest in land identified pursuant to paragraph (1) as soon as the lawful owner of that interest fixes a price for it and the Attorney General considers that price to be reasonable.

(3) When the Attorney General and the lawful owner of an interest identified pursuant to paragraph (1) are unable to agree upon a reasonable price, the Attorney General may commence condemnation proceedings pursuant to the Act of August 1, 1888 (Chapter 728; 25 Stat. 357) [40 USCS § 3113].

(4) The Attorney General may accept for the United States a gift of any interest in land identified pursuant to paragraph (1).

(c) Commissioner; appointment. The Commissioner shall be a citizen of the United States and shall be appointed by the President, by and with the advice and consent of the Senate. He shall be charged with any and all responsibilities and authority in the administration of the Service and of this Act which are conferred upon the Attorney General as may be delegated to him by the Attorney General or which may be prescribed by the Attorney General. The Commissioner may enter into cooperative agreements with State and local law enforcement agencies for the purpose of assisting in the enforcement of the immigration laws.

(d) Statistical information system.

(1) The Commissioner, in consultation with interested academicians, government agencies, and other parties, shall provide for a system for collection and dissemination, to Congress and the public, of information (not in individually identifiable form) useful in evaluating the social, economic, environmental, and demographic impact of immigration laws.

(2) Such information shall include information on the alien population in the United States, on the rates of naturalization and emigration of resident aliens, on aliens who have been admitted, paroled, or granted asylum, on nonimmigrants in the United States (by occupation, basis for admission, and duration of stay), on aliens who have not been admitted or have been removed from the United States, on the number of applications filed and granted for cancellation of removal, and on the number of aliens estimated to be present unlawfully in the United States in each fiscal year.

(3) Such system shall provide for the collection and dissemination of such information not less often than annually.

(e) Annual report.

(1) The Commissioner shall submit to Congress annually a report which contains a summary of the information collected under subsection (d) and an analysis of trends in immigration and naturalization.

(2) Each annual report shall include information on the number, and rate of denial administratively, of applications for naturalization, for each district office of the Service and by national origin group.

(f) Minimum number of agents in States. The Attorney General shall allocate to each State not fewer than 10 full-time active duty agents of the Immigration and Naturalization Service to carry out the functions of the Service, in order to ensure the effective enforcement of this Act.

(g) Attorney General.

(1) In general. The Attorney General shall have such authorities and functions under this Act and all other laws relating to the immigration and naturalization of aliens as were exercised by the Executive Office for Immigration Review, or by the Attorney General with respect to the Executive Office for Immigration Review, on the day before the effective date of the Immigration Reform, Accountability and Security Enhancement Act of 2002.

(2) Powers. The Attorney General shall establish such regulations, prescribe such forms of bond, reports, entries, and other papers, issue such instructions, review such administrative determinations in immigration proceedings, delegate such authority, and perform such other acts as the Attorney General determines to be necessary for carrying out this section.

(June 27, 1952, ch 477, Title I, § 103, 66 Stat. 173; Oct. 24, 1988, P. L. 100-525, § 9(c), 102 Stat. 2619; Nov. 29, 1990, P. L. 101-649, Title I, Subtitle C, § 142, 104 Stat. 5004; Sept. 30, 1996, P. L. 104-208, Div C, Title I, Subtitle A, § 102(d), Subtitle B, § 125, Subtitle C, § 134(a), Title III, Subtitle A, § 308(d)(4)(C), (e)(4), Subtitle F, §§ 372, 373, 110 Stat. 3009-555, 3009-562, 3009-564, 3009-618, 3009-620, 3009-646; Nov. 25, 2002, P. L. 107-296, Title XI, Subtitle A, § 1102, 116 Stat. 2273; Feb. 20, 2003, P. L. 108-7, Div L, § 105(a)(1), (2), 117 Stat. 531; Dec. 17, 2004, P. L. 108-458, Title V, Subtitle E, § 5505(a), 118 Stat. 3741; Dec. 22, 2009, P. L. 111-122, § 2(a), 123 Stat. 3480.)

§ 1104. Powers and duties of Secretary of State

(a) Powers and duties. The Secretary of State shall be charged with the administration and the enforcement of the provisions of this Act and all other immigration and nationality laws relating to (1) the powers, duties and functions of diplomatic and consular officers of the United States, except those powers, duties and functions conferred upon the consular officers relating to the granting or refusal of visas; (2) the powers, duties and functions of the Administrator; and (3) the determination of nationality of a person not in the United States. He shall establish such regulations; prescribe such forms of reports, entries and other papers; issue such instructions; and perform such other acts as he deems necessary for carrying out such provisions. He is authorized to confer or impose upon any employee of the United States, with the consent of the head of the department or independent establishment under whose jurisdiction the employee is serving, any of the powers, functions, or duties conferred or imposed by this Act or regulations issued thereunder upon officers or employees of the Department of State or of the American Foreign Service.

(b) Designation and duties of Administrator. The Secretary of State shall designate an Administrator who shall be a citizen of the United States, qualified by experience. The Administrator shall maintain close liaison with the appropriate committees of Congress in order that they may be advised regarding the administration of this Act by consular officers. The Administrator shall be charged with any and all responsibility and authority in the administration of this Act which are conferred on the Secretary of State as may be delegated to the Administrator by the Secretary of State or which may be prescribed by the Secretary of State, and shall perform such other duties as the Secretary of State may prescribe.

(c) Passport Office, Visa Office, and other offices; directors. Within the Department of State there shall be a Passport Office, a Visa Office, and such other offices as the Secretary of State may deem to be appropriate, each office to be headed by a director. The Directors of the Passport Office and the Visa Office shall be experienced in the administration of the nationality and immigration laws.

(d) Transfer of duties. The functions heretofore performed by the Passport Division and the Visa Division of the Department of State shall hereafter be performed by the Passport Office and the Visa Office, respectively.

(e) General Counsel of Visa Office; appointment and duties. There shall be a General Counsel of the Visa Office, who shall be appointed by the Secretary of State and who shall serve under the general direction of the Legal Adviser of the Department of State. The General Counsel shall have authority to maintain liaison with the appropriate officers of the Service with a view to securing uniform interpretations of the provisions of this Act.

(June 27, 1952, ch 477, Title I, § 104, 66 Stat. 174; June 28, 1962, P. L. 87-510, § 4(a)(2), 76 Stat. 123; Aug. 14, 1964, P. L. 88-426, Title III, § 305(43), 78 Stat. 428; Aug. 17, 1977, P. L. 95-105, Title I, § 109(b)(1), 91 Stat 847; Oct. 24, 1988, P. L. 100-525, § 9(d), 102 Stat. 2620; April 30, 1994, P. L. 103-236, Title I, Part C, § 162(h)(2), 108 Stat. 407.)

§ 1105. Liaison with internal security officers; data exchange

(a) In general. The Commissioner and the Administrator shall have authority to maintain direct and continuous liaison with the Directors of the Federal Bureau of Investigation and the Central Intelligence Agency and with other internal security officers of the Government for the purpose of obtaining and exchanging information for use in enforcing the provisions of this Act in the interest of the internal and border security of the United States. The Commissioner and the Administrator shall maintain direct and continuous liaison with each other with a view to a coordinated, uniform, and efficient administration of this Act, and all other immigration and nationality laws.

(b) Access to National Crime Information Center files.

(1) The Attorney General and the Director of the Federal Bureau of Investigation shall provide the Department of State and the Service access to the criminal history record information contained in the National Crime Information Center's Interstate Identification Index (NCIC-III), Wanted Persons File, and to any other files maintained by the National Crime Information Center that may be mutually agreed upon by the Attorney General and the agency receiving the access, for the purpose of determining whether or not a visa

applicant or applicant for admission has a criminal history record indexed in any such file.

(2) Such access shall be provided by means of extracts of the records for placement in the automated visa lookout or other appropriate database, and shall be provided without any fee or charge.

(3) The Federal Bureau of Investigation shall provide periodic updates of the extracts at intervals mutually agreed upon with the agency receiving the access. Upon receipt of such updated extracts, the receiving agency shall make corresponding updates to its database and destroy previously provided extracts.

(4) Access to an extract does not entitle the Department of State to obtain the full content of the corresponding automated criminal history record. To obtain the full content of a criminal history record, the Department of State shall submit the applicant's fingerprints and any appropriate fingerprint processing fee authorized by law to the Criminal Justice Information Services Division of the Federal Bureau of Investigation.

(c) Reconsideration upon development of more cost effective means of sharing information. The provision of the extracts described in subsection (b) may be reconsidered by the Attorney General and the receiving agency upon the development and deployment of a more cost-effective and efficient means of sharing the information.

(d) Regulations. For purposes of administering this section, the Department of State shall, prior to receiving access to NCIC data but not later than 4 months after the date of enactment of this subsection [enacted Oct. 26, 2001], promulgate final regulations—

(1) to implement procedures for the taking of fingerprints; and

(2) to establish the conditions for the use of the information received from the Federal Bureau of Investigation, in order—

(A) to limit the redissemination of such information;

(B) to ensure that such information is used solely to determine whether or not to issue a visa to an alien or to admit an alien to the United States;

(C) to ensure the security, confidentiality, and destruction of such information; and

(D) to protect any privacy rights of individuals who are subjects of such information.

(June 27, 1952, ch 477, Title I, § 105, 66 Stat. 175; Aug. 17, 1977, P. L. 95-105, Title I, § 109(b)(2), 91 Stat 847; April 30, 1994, P. L. 103-236, Title I, Part C, § 162(h)(3), 108 Stat. 408; Oct. 26, 2001, P. L. 107-56, Title IV, Subtitle A, § 403(a), 115 Stat. 343.)

§ 1105a. Employment authorization for battered spouses of certain nonimmigrants

(a) In general. In the case of an alien spouse admitted under subparagraph (A), (E)(iii), (G), or (H) of section 101(a)(15) [8 USCS § 1101(a)(15)] who is accompanying or following to join a principal alien admitted under subparagraph (A), (E)(iii), (G), or (H) of such section, respectively, the Secretary of Homeland Security may authorize the alien spouse to engage in employment in the United States and provide the spouse with an 'employment authorized' endorsement or other appropriate work permit if the alien spouse demonstrates that during the marriage the alien spouse or a child of the alien spouse has been battered or has been the subject of extreme cruelty perpetrated by the spouse of the alien spouse. Requests for relief under this section shall be handled under the procedures that apply to aliens seeking relief under section 204(a)(1)(A)(iii) [8 USCS § 1154(a)(1)(A)(iii)].

(b) Construction. The grant of employment authorization pursuant to this section shall not confer upon the alien any other form of relief.

(June 27, 1952, ch 477, Title I, § 106, as added Jan. 5, 2006, P. L. 109-162, Title VIII, Subtitle B, § 814(c), 119 Stat. 3059.)

§ 1106. [Repealed]

§ 1107. Additional report

At the beginning and midpoint of each fiscal year, the Secretary of Homeland Security shall submit to the Committees on the Judiciary of the House of Representatives and the Senate, a written report providing a description of internal affairs operations at U.S. Citizenship and Immigration Services, including the general state of such operations and a detailed description of investigations that are being conducted (or that were conducted during the previous six months) and the resources devoted to such investigations. The first such report shall be submitted not later than April 1, 2006.

(March 9, 2006, P. L. 109-177, Title I, § 109(c), 120 Stat. 205.)

IMMIGRATION

SELECTION SYSTEM

Section

ADMISSION QUALIFICATIONS FOR ALIENS; TRAVEL CONTROL OF CITIZENS AND ALIENS

Section
1183a. Requirements for sponsor's affidavit of support
1184. Admission of nonimmigrants
1184a. Philippine Traders as nonimmigrants
1185. Travel control of citizens and aliens
1186. [Transferred]
1186a. Conditional permanent resident status for certain alien spouses and sons and daughters
1186b. Conditional permanent resident status for certain alien entrepreneurs, spouses, and children
1187. Visa waiver program for certain visitors
1187a. Provision of assistance to non-program countries
1188. Admission of temporary H-2A workers
1189. Designation of foreign terrorist organizations

ISSUANCE OF ENTRY DOCUMENTS

1201. Issuance of visas
1201a. [Repealed]
1202. Application for visas
1203. Reentry permit
1204. Immediate relative and special immigrant visas
1205. [Repealed]

INSPECTION, APPREHENSION, EXAMINATION, EXCLUSION, AND REMOVAL

1221. Lists of alien and citizen passengers arriving and departing
1222. Detention of aliens for physical and mental examination
1223. Entry through or from foreign territory and adjacent islands
1224. Designation of ports of entry for aliens arriving by aircraft
1225. Inspection by immigration officers; expedited removal of inadmissible arriving aliens; referral for hearing
1225a. Preinspection at foreign airports
1226. Apprehension and detention of aliens
1226a. Mandatory detention of suspected terrorists; habeas corpus; judicial review
1227. Deportable aliens
1228. Expedited removal of aliens convicted of committing aggravated felonies
1229. Initiation of removal proceedings
1229a. Removal proceedings
1229b. Cancellation of removal; adjustment of status
1229c. Voluntary departure
1230. Records of admission
1231. Detention and removal of aliens ordered removed
1232. Enhancing efforts to combat the trafficking of children

ADJUSTMENT AND CHANGE OF STATUS

1251. [Transferred]
1251a. [Repealed]
1252. Judicial review of orders of removal
1252a. [Transferred]
1252b. [Repealed]
1252c. Authorizing state and local law enforcement officials to arrest and detain certain illegal aliens
1253. Penalties related to removal
1254. [Repealed]
1254a. Temporary protected status
1254b. Collection of fees under temporary protected status program
1255. Adjustment of status of nonimmigrant to that of person admitted for permanent residence
1255a. Adjustment of status of certain entrants before Jan. 1, 1982, to that of person admitted for lawful residence

Section
1255b. Adjustment of status of certain nonimmigrants to that of persons admitted for permanent residence
1256. Rescission of adjustment of status; report to Congress; effect upon naturalized citizen
1257. Adjustment of status of certain resident aliens to nonimmigrant status; exceptions
1258. Change of nonimmigrant classification
1259. Record of admission for permanent residence in the case of certain aliens who entered the United States prior to January 1, 1972
1260. Removal of aliens falling into distress

SPECIAL PROVISIONS RELATING TO ALIEN CREWMEN

1281. Alien crewmen
1282. Conditional permits to land temporarily
1283. Hospital treatment of alien crewman afflicted with certain diseases
1284. Control of alien crewmen
1285. Employment on passenger vessels of aliens afflicted with certain disabilities
1286. Discharge of alien crewmen; penalties
1287. Alien crewmen brought into the United States with intent to evade immigration laws; penalties
1288. Limitations on performance of longshore work by alien crewmen

REGISTRATION OF ALIENS

1301. Alien seeking entry; contents
1302. Registration of aliens
1303. Registration of special groups
1304. Forms for registration and fingerprinting
1305. Notices of change of address
1306. Penalties

GENERAL PENALTY PROVISIONS

1321. Prevention of unauthorized landing of aliens
1322. Bringing in aliens subject to denial of admission on a health-related ground; persons liable; clearance papers; exceptions; "person" defined
1323. Unlawful bringing of aliens into United States
1324. Bringing in and harboring certain aliens
1324a. Unlawful employment of aliens
1324b. Unfair immigration-related employment practices
1324c. Penalties for document fraud
1324d. Civil penalties for failure to depart
1325. Improper entry by alien
1326. Reentry of removed aliens
1327. Aiding or assisting certain aliens to enter
1328. Importation of alien for immoral purpose
1329. Jurisdiction of district courts
1330. Collection of penalties and expenses

MISCELLANEOUS

1351. Nonimmigrant visa fees
1352. Printing of reentry permits and blank forms of manifests and crew lists; sale to public
1353. Travel expenses and expense of transporting remains of officers and employees dying outside of United States
1353a. Officers and employees; overtime services; extra compensation; length of working day
1353b. Extra compensation; payment
1353c. Immigration officials; service in foreign contiguous territory
1353d. Disposition of money received as extra compensation
1354. Applicability to members of the armed forces

SELECTION SYSTEM

§ 1151. Worldwide level of immigration

(a) In general. Exclusive of aliens described in subsection (b), aliens born in a foreign state or dependent area who may be issued immigrant visas or who may otherwise acquire the status of an alien lawfully admitted to the United States for permanent residence are limited to—

(1) family-sponsored immigrants described in section 203(a) [8 USCS § 1153(a)] (or who are admitted under section 211(a) [8 USCS § 1181(a)] on the basis of a prior issuance of a visa to their accompanying parent under section 203(a) [8 USCS § 1153(a)]) in a number not to exceed in any fiscal year the number specified in subsection (c) for that year, and not to exceed in any of the first 3 quarters of any fiscal year 27 percent of the worldwide level under such subsection for all of such fiscal year;

(2) employment-based immigrants described in section 203(b) [8 USCS § 1153(b)] (or who are admitted under section 211(a) [8 USCS § 1181(a)] on the basis of a prior issuance of a visa to their accompanying parent under section 203(b) [8 USCS § 1153(b)]), in a number not to exceed in any fiscal year the number specified in subsection (d) for that year, and not to exceed in any of the first 3 quarters of any fiscal year 27 percent of the worldwide level under such subsection for all of such fiscal year; and

(3) for fiscal years beginning with fiscal year 1995, diversity immigrants described in section 203(c) [8 USCS § 1153(c)] (or who are admitted under section 211(a) [8 USCS § 1181(a)] on the basis of a prior issuance of a visa to their accompanying parent under section 203(c) [8 USCS § 1153(c)]) in a number not to exceed in any fiscal year the number specified in subsection (e) for that year, and not to exceed in any of the first 3 quarters of any fiscal year 27 percent of the worldwide level under such subsection for all of such fiscal year.

(b) Aliens not subject to direct numerical limitations. Aliens described in this subsection, who are not subject to the worldwide levels or numerical limitations of subsection (a), are as follows:

(1)(A) Special immigrants described in subparagraph (A) or (B) of section 101(a)(27) [8 USCS § 1101(a)(27)(A) or (B)].

(B) Aliens who are admitted under section 207 [8 USCS § 1157] or whose status is adjusted under section 209 [8 USCS § 1159].

(C) Aliens whose status is adjusted to permanent residence under section 210 or 245A [8 USCS § 1160 or 1255a].

(D) Aliens whose removal is canceled under section 240A(a) [8 USCS § 1229b(a)].

(E) Aliens provided permanent resident status under section 249 [8 USCS § 1259].

(2)(A)(i) Immediate relatives. For purposes of this subsection, the term "immediate relatives" means the children, spouses, and parents of a citizen of the United States, except that, in the case of parents, such citizens shall be at least 21 years of age. In the case of an alien who was the spouse of a citizen of the United States and was not legally separated from the citizen at the time of the citizen's death, the alien (and each child of the alien) shall be considered, for purposes of this subsection, to remain an immediate relative after the date of the citizen's death but only if the spouse files a petition under section 204(a)(1)(A)(ii) [8 USCS § 1154(a)(1)(A)(ii)] within 2 years after such date and only until the date the spouse remarries. For purposes of this clause, an alien who has filed a petition under clause (iii) or (iv) of section 204(a)(1)(A) of this Act [8

USCS § 1154(a)(1)(A)] remains an immediate relative in the event that the United States citizen spouse or parent loses United States citizenship on account of the abuse.

(ii) Aliens admitted under section 211(a) [8 USCS § 1181(a)] on the basis of a prior issuance of a visa to their accompanying parent who is such an immediate relative.

(B) Aliens born to an alien lawfully admitted for permanent residence during a temporary visit abroad.

(c) Worldwide level of family-sponsored immigrants.

(1)(A) The worldwide level of family-sponsored immigrants under this subsection for a fiscal year is, subject to subparagraph (B), equal to—

(i) 480,000, minus

(ii) the sum of the number computed under paragraph (2) and the number computed under paragraph (4), plus

(iii) the number (if any) computed under paragraph (3).

(B)(i) For each of fiscal years 1992, 1993, and 1994, 465,000 shall be substituted for 480,000 in subparagraph (A)(i).

(ii) In no case shall the number computed under subparagraph (A) be less than 226,000.

(2) The number computed under this paragraph for a fiscal year is the sum of the number of aliens described in subparagraphs (A) and (B) of subsection (b)(2) who were issued immigrant visas or who otherwise acquired the status of aliens lawfully admitted to the United States for permanent residence in the previous fiscal year.

(3)(A) The number computed under this paragraph for fiscal year 1992 is zero.

(B) The number computed under this paragraph for fiscal year 1993 is the difference (if any) between the worldwide level established under paragraph (1) for the previous fiscal year and the number of visas issued under section 203(a) [8 USCS § 1153(a)] during that fiscal year.

(C) The number computed under this paragraph for a subsequent fiscal year is the difference (if any) between the maximum number of visas which may be issued under section 203(b) [8 USCS § 1153(b)] (relating to employment-based immigrants) during the previous fiscal year and the number of visas issued under that section during that year.

(4) The number computed under this paragraph for a fiscal year (beginning with fiscal year 1999) is the number of aliens who were paroled into the United States under section 212(d)(5) [8 USCS § 1182(d)(5)] in the second preceding fiscal year—

(A) who did not depart from the United States (without advance parole) within 365 days; and

(B) who (i) did not acquire the status of aliens lawfully admitted to the United States for permanent residence in the two preceding fiscal years, or (ii) acquired such status in such years under a provision of law (other than section 201(b) [subsec. (b) of this section]) which exempts such adjustment from the numerical limitation on the worldwide level of immigration under this section.

(5) If any alien described in paragraph (4) (other than an alien described in paragraph (4)(B)(ii)) is subsequently admitted as an alien lawfully admitted for permanent residence, such alien shall not again be considered for purposes of paragraph (1).

(d) Worldwide level of employment-based immigrants.

(1) The worldwide level of employment-based immigrants under this subsection for a fiscal year is equal to—

(A) 140,000, plus

(B) the number computed under paragraph (2).

(2)(A) The number computed under this paragraph for fiscal year 1992 is zero.

(B) The number computed under this paragraph for fiscal year 1993 is the difference (if any) between the worldwide level established under paragraph (1) for the previous fiscal year and the number of visas issued under section 203(b) [8 USCS § 1153(b)] during that fiscal year.

(C) The number computed under this paragraph for a subsequent fiscal year is the difference (if any) between the maximum number of visas which may be issued under section 203(a) [8 USCS § 1153(a)] (relating to family-sponsored immigrants) during the previous fiscal year and the number of visas issued under that section during that year.

(e) Worldwide level of diversity immigrants. The worldwide level of diversity immigrants is equal to 55,000 for each fiscal year.

(f) Rules for determining whether certain aliens are immediate relatives.

(1) Age on petition filing date. Except as provided in paragraphs (2) and (3), for purposes of subsection (b)(2)(A)(i), a determination of whether an alien satisfies the age requirement in the matter preceding subparagraph (A) of section 101(b)(1) [8 USCS § 1101(b)(1)] shall be made using the age of the alien on the date on which the petition is filed with the Attorney General under section 204 [8 USCS § 1154] to classify the alien as an immediate relative under subsection (b)(2)(A)(i).

(2) Age on parent's naturalization date. In the case of a petition under section 204 [8 USCS § 1154] initially filed for an alien child's classification as a family-sponsored immigrant under section 203(a)(2)(A) [8 USCS § 1153(a)(2)(A)], based on the child's parent being lawfully admitted for permanent residence, if the petition is later converted, due to the naturalization of the parent, to a petition to classify the alien as an immediate relative under subsection (b)(2)(A)(i), the determination described in paragraph (1) shall be made using the age of the alien on the date of the parent's naturalization.

(3) Age on marriage termination date. In the case of a petition under section 204 [8 USCS § 1154] initially filed for an alien's classification as a family-sponsored immigrant under section 203(a)(3) [8 USCS § 1153(a)(3)], based on the alien's being a married son or daughter of a citizen, if the petition is later converted, due to the legal termination of the alien's marriage, to

a petition to classify the alien as an immediate relative under subsection (b)(2)(A)(i) or as an unmarried son or daughter of a citizen under section 203(a)(1) [8 USCS § 1153(a)(1)], the determination described in paragraph (1) shall be made using the age of the alien on the date of the termination of the marriage.

(4) Application to self-petitions. Paragraphs (1) through (3) shall apply to self-petitioners and derivatives of self-petitioners.

(June 27, 1952, ch 477, Title II, Ch 1, § 201, 66 Stat. 175; Oct. 3, 1965, P. L. 89-236, § 1, 79 Stat. 911; Oct. 20, 1976, P. L. 94-571, § 2, 90 Stat. 2703; Oct. 5, 1978, P. L. 95-412, § 1, 92 Stat. 907; March 17, 1980, P. L. 96-212, Title II, § 203(a), 94 Stat. 106; Dec. 29, 1981, P. L. 97-116, § 20, 95 Stat. 1621; Nov. 29, 1990, P. L. 101-649, Title I, Subtitle A, § 101(a), 104 Stat. 4980; Dec. 12, 1991, P. L. 102-232, Title III, § 302(a)(1), 105 Stat. 1742; Sept. 13, 1994, P. L. 103-322, Title IV, Subtitle G, § 40701(b)(2), 108 Stat. 1954; Oct. 25, 1994, P. L. 103-416, Title II, § 219(b)(1), 108 Stat. 4316; Sept. 30, 1996, P. L. 104-208, Div C, Title III, Subtitle A, § 308(e)(5), (g)(8)(A)(i), Title VI, Subtitle A, § 603, Subtitle E, § 671(d)(1)(A),110 Stat. 3009-620, 3009-624, 3009-690, 3009-723; Oct. 28, 2000, P. L. 106-386, Div B, Title V, § 1507(a)(3), 114 Stat. 1530; Aug. 6, 2002, P. L. 107-208, § 2, 116 Stat. 927; Jan. 5, 2006, P. L. 109-162, Title VIII, Subtitle A, § 805(b)(1), 119 Stat. 3056; Oct. 28, 2009, P. L. 111-83, Title V, § 568(c)(1), 123 Stat. 2186.)

§ 1151a. [Repealed]

§ 1152. Numerical limitations on individual foreign states

(a) Per country level.

(1) Nondiscrimination.

(A) Except as specifically provided in paragraph (2) and in sections 101(a)(27), 201(b)(2)(A)(i), and 203 [8 USCS §§ 1101(a)(27), 1151(b)(2)(A)(i), 1153], no person shall receive any preference or priority or be discriminated against in the issuance of an immigrant visa because of the person's race, sex, nationality, place of birth, or place of residence.

(B) Nothing in this paragraph shall be construed to limit the authority of the Secretary of State to determine the procedures for the processing of immigrant visa applications or the locations where such applications will be processed.

(2) Per country level for family-sponsored and employment-based immigrants. Subject to paragraphs (3), (4), and (5), the total number of immigrant visas made available to natives of any single foreign state or dependent area under subsections (a) and (b) of section 203 [8 USCS § 1153] in any fiscal year may not exceed 7 percent (in the case of a single foreign state) or 2 percent (in the case of a dependent area) of the total number of such visas made available under such subsections in that fiscal year.

(3) Exception if additional visas available. If because of the application of paragraph (2) with respect to one or more foreign states or dependent areas, the total number of visas available under both subsections (a) and (b) of section 203 [8 USCS § 1153(a), (b)] for a calendar quarter exceeds the number of qualified immigrants who otherwise may be issued such a visa, paragraph (2) shall not apply to visas made available to such states or areas during the remainder of such calendar quarter.

(4) Special rules for spouses and children of lawful permanent resident aliens.

(A) 75 percent of 2nd preference set-aside for spouses and children not subject to per country limitation.

(i) In general. Of the visa numbers made available under section 203(a) [8 USCS § 1153(a)] to immigrants described in section 203(a)(2)(A) [8 USCS § 1153(a)(2)(A)] in any fiscal year, 75 percent of the 2-A floor (as defined in clause (ii)) shall be issued without regard to the numerical limitation under paragraph (2).

(ii) 2-A floor defined. In this paragraph, the term "2-A floor" means, for a fiscal year, 77 percent of the total number of visas made available under section 203(a) [8 USCS § 1153(a)] to immigrants described in section 203(a)(2) [8 USCS § 1153(a)(2)] in the fiscal year.

(B) Treatment of remaining 25 percent for countries subject to subsection (e).

(i) In general. Of the visa numbers made available under section 203(a) [8 USCS § 1153(a)] to immigrants described in section 203(a)(2)(A) [8 USCS § 1153(a)(2)(A)] in any fiscal year, the remaining 25 percent of the 2-A floor shall be available in the case of a state or area that is subject to subsection (e) only to the extent that the total number of visas issued into accordance with subparagraph (A) to natives of the foreign state or area is less than the subsection (e) ceiling (as defined in clause (ii)).

(ii) Subsection (e) ceiling defined. In clause (i), the term "subsection (e) ceiling" means, for a foreign state or dependent area, 77 percent of the maximum number of visas that may be made available under section 203(a) [8 USCS § 1153(a)] to immigrants who are natives of the state or area under section 203(a)(2) [8 USCS § 1153(a)(2)] consistent with subsection (e).

(C) Treatment of unmarried sons and daughters in countries subject to subsection (e). In the case of a foreign state or dependent area to which subsection (e) applies, the number of immigrant visas that may be made available to natives of the state or area under section 203(a)(2)(B) [8 USCS § 1153(a)(2)(B)] may not exceed—

(i) 23 percent of the maximum number of visas that may be made available under section 203(a) [8 USCS § 1153(a)] to immigrants of the state or area described in section 203(a)(2) [8 USCS § 1153(a)(2)] consistent with subsection (e), or

(ii) the number (if any) by which the maximum number of visas that may be made available under section 203(a) [8 USCS § 1153(a)] to immigrants of the state or area described in section 203(a)(2) [8 USCS § 1153(a)(2)] consistent with subsection (e) exceeds the number of visas issued under section 203(a)(2)(A) [8 USCS § 1153(a)(2)(A)],

whichever is greater.

(D) Limiting pass down for certain countries subject to subsection (e). In the case of a foreign state or dependent area to which subsection (e) applies, if the total number of visas issued under section 203(a)(2) [8 USCS § 1153(a)(2)] exceeds the maximum number of visas that may be made available to immigrants of the state or area under section 203(a)(2) [8 USCS § 1153(a)(2)] consistent with subsection (e) (determined without regard to this paragraph), in applying paragraphs (3) and (4) of section 203(a) [8 USCS § 1153(a)(3), (4)] under subsection (e)(2) all visas shall be deemed to have been required for the classes specified in paragraphs (1) and (2) of such section.

(5) Rules for employment-based immigrants.

(A) Employment-based immigrants not subject to per country limitation if additional visas available. If the total number of visas available under paragraph (1), (2), (3), (4), or (5) of section 203(b) [8 USCS § 1153(b)] for a calendar quarter exceeds the number of qualified immigrants who may otherwise be issued such visas, the visas made available under that paragraph shall be issued without regard to the numerical limitation under paragraph (2) of this subsection during the remainder of the calendar quarter.

(B) Limiting fall across for certain countries subject to subsection (e). In the case of a foreign state or dependent area to which subsection (e) applies, if the total number of visas issued under section 203(b) [8 USCS § 1153(b)] exceeds the maximum number of visas that may be made available to immigrants of the state or area under section 203(b) [8 USCS § 1153(b)] consistent with subsection (e) (determined without regard to this paragraph), in applying subsection (e) all visas shall be deemed to have been required for the classes of aliens specified in section 203(b) [8 USCS § 1153(b)].

(b) Rules for chargeability. Each independent country, self-governing dominion, mandated territory, and territory under the international trusteeship system of the United Nations, other than the United States and its outlying possessions, shall be treated as a separate foreign state for the purposes of a numerical level established under subsection (a)(2) when approved by the Secretary of State. All other inhabited lands shall be attributed to a foreign state specified by the Secretary of State. For the purposes of this Act the foreign state to which an immigrant is chargeable shall be determined by birth within such foreign state except that (1) an alien child, when accompanied by or following to join his alien parent or parents, may be charged to the foreign state of either parent if such parent has received or would be qualified for an immigrant visa, if necessary to prevent the separation of the child from the parent or parents, and if immigration charged to the foreign state to which such parent has been or would be chargeable has not reached a numerical level established under subsection (a)(2) for that fiscal year; (2) if an alien is chargeable to a different foreign state from that of his spouse, the foreign state to which such alien is chargeable may, if necessary to prevent the separation of husband and wife, be determined by the foreign state of the spouse he is accompanying or following to join, if such spouse has received or would be qualified for an immigrant visa and if immigration charged to the foreign state to which such spouse has been or would be chargeable has not reached a numerical level established under subsection (a)(2) for that fiscal year; (3) an alien born in the United States shall be considered as having been born in the country of which he is a citizen or subject, or, if he is not a citizen or subject of any country, in the last foreign country in which he had his residence as determined by the consular officer; (4) an alien born within any foreign state in which neither of his parents was born and in which neither of his parents had a residence at the time of such alien's birth may be charged to the foreign state of either parent.

(c) Chargeability for dependent areas. Any immigrant born in a colony or other component or dependent area of a foreign state overseas from the foreign state, other than an alien described in section 201(b) [8 USCS § 1151(b)], shall be chargeable for the purpose of the limitation set forth in section 202(a) [8 USCS § 1152(a)], to the foreign state.

(d) Changes in territory. In the case of any change in the territorial limits of foreign states, the Secretary of State shall, upon recognition of such change, issue appropriate instructions to all diplomatic and consular offices.

(e) Special rules for countries at ceiling. If it is determined that the total number of immigrant visas made available under subsections (a) and (b) of section 203 [8 USCS § 1153] to natives of any single foreign state or dependent area will exceed the numerical limitation specified in subsection (a)(2) in any fiscal year, in determining the allotment of immigrant visa numbers to natives under subsections (a) and (b) of section 203 [8 USCS § 1153], visa numbers with respect to natives of that state or area shall be allocated (to the extent practicable and otherwise consistent with this section and section 203 [8 USCS § 1153]) in a manner so that—

(1) the ratio of the visa numbers made available under section 203(a) [8 USCS § 1153(a)]) to the visa numbers made available under section 203(b) [8 USCS § 1153(b)] is equal to the ratio of the worldwide level of immigration under section 201(c) [8 USCS § 1151(c)] to such level under section 201(d) [8 USCS § 1151(d)];

(2) except as provided in subsection (a)(4), the proportion of the visa numbers made available under each of paragraphs (1) through (4) of section 203(a) [8 USCS § 1153(a)] is equal to the ratio of the total number of visas made available under the respective paragraph to the total number of visas made available under section 203(a) [8 USCS § 1153(a)], and

(3) except as provided in subsection (a)(5), the proportion of the visa numbers made available under each of paragraphs (1) through (5) of section 203(b) [8 USCS § 1153(b)] is equal to the ratio of the total number of visas made available under the respective paragraph to the total number of visas made available under section 203(b) [8 USCS § 1153(b)].

Nothing in this subsection shall be construed as limiting the number of visas that may be issued to natives of a foreign state or dependent area under section 203(a) or 203(b) [8 USCS § 1153(a) or (b)] if there is insufficient demand for visas for such natives under section 203(b) or 203(a) [8 USCS § 1153(b) or (a)], respectively, or as limiting the number of visas that may, be issued under section 203(a)(2)(A) [8 USCS § 1153(a)(2)(A)] pursuant to subsection (a)(4)(A).

(June 27, 1952, ch 477, Title II, Ch 1, § 202, 66 Stat. 176; Sept. 26, 1961, P. L. 87-301, § 9, 75 Stat. 654; Oct. 3, 1965, P. L. 89-236, § 2, 79 Stat. 911; Oct. 20, 1976, P. L. 94-571, § 3, 90 Stat. 2703; Oct. 5, 1978, P. L. 95-412, § 2, 92 Stat. 907; March 17, 1980, P. L. 96-212, Title II, § 203(b), 94 Stat. 107; Dec. 29, 1981, P. L. 97-116, §§ 18(c), 20(b), 95 Stat. 1620, 1622; Nov. 6, 1986, P. L. 99-603, Title III, Part B, § 311(a), 100 Stat. 3434; Nov. 14, 1986, P. L. 99-653, § 4, 100 Stat. 3655; Nov. 14, 1986, P. L. 99-653, § 4, 100 Stat. 3655 (as amended Oct. 24, 1988, P. L. 100-525, § 8(c), 102 Stat. 2617); Oct. 24, 1988, P. L. 100-525, § 9(f), 102 Stat. 2620; Nov. 29, 1990, P. L. 101-649, Title I, Subtitle A, § 102, 104 Stat. 4982; Dec. 12, 1991, P. L. 102-232, Title III, § 302(a)(3), 105 Stat. 1742; Sept. 30, 1996, P. L. 104-208, Div C, Title VI, Subtitle C, § 633, 110 Stat. 3009-701; Oct. 17, 2000, P. L. 106-313, Title I, § 104(a), (b), 114 Stat. 1252.)

§ 1153. Allocation of immigrant visas

(a) Preference allocation for family-sponsored immigrants. Aliens subject to the worldwide level specified in section 201(c) [8 USCS § 1151(c)] for family-sponsored immigrants shall be allotted visas as follows:

(1) Unmarried sons and daughters of citizens. Qualified immigrants who are the unmarried sons or daughters of citizens of the United States shall be allocated visas in a number not to exceed 23,400, plus any visas not required for the class specified in paragraph (4).

(2) Spouses and unmarried sons and unmarried daughters of permanent resident aliens. Qualified immigrants—

(A) who are the spouses or children of an alien lawfully admitted for permanent residence, or

(B) who are the unmarried sons or unmarried daughters (but are not the children) of an alien lawfully admitted for permanent residence,

shall be allocated visas in a number not to exceed 114,200, plus the number (if any) by which such worldwide level exceeds 226,000, plus any visas not required for the class specified in paragraph (1); except that not less than 77 percent of such visa numbers shall be allocated to aliens described in subparagraph (A).

(3) Married sons and married daughters of citizens. Qualified immigrants who are the married sons or married daughters of citizens of the United States shall be allocated visas in a number not to exceed 23,400, plus any visas not required for the classes specified in paragraphs (1) and (2).

(4) Brothers and sisters of citizens. Qualified immigrants who are the brothers or sisters of citizens of the United States, if such citizens are at least 21 years of age, shall be allocated visas in a number not to exceed 65,000, plus any visas not required for the classes specified in paragraphs (1) through (3).

(b) Preference allocation for employment-based immigrants. Aliens subject to the worldwide level specified in section 201(d) [8 USCS § 1151(d)] for employment-based immigrants in a fiscal year shall be allotted visas as follows:

(1) Priority workers. Visas shall first be made available in a number not to exceed 28.6 percent of such worldwide level, plus any visas not required for the classes specified in paragraphs (4) and (5), to qualified immigrants who are aliens described in any of the following subparagraphs (A) through (C):

(A) Aliens with extraordinary ability. An alien is described in this subparagraph if—

(i) the alien has extraordinary ability in the sciences, arts, education, business, or athletics which has been demonstrated by sustained national or international acclaim and whose achievements have been recognized in the field through extensive documentation,

(ii) the alien seeks to enter the United States to continue work in the area of extraordinary ability, and

(iii) the alien's entry into the United States will substantially benefit prospectively the United States.

(B) Outstanding professors and researchers. An alien is described in this subparagraph if—

(i) the alien is recognized internationally as outstanding in a specific academic area,

(ii) the alien has at least 3 years of experience in teaching or research in the academic area, and

(iii) the alien seeks to enter the United States—

(I) for a tenured position (or tenure-track position) within a university or institution of higher education to teach in the academic area,

(II) for a comparable position with a university or institution of higher education to conduct research in the area, or

(III) for a comparable position to conduct research in the area with a department, division, or institute of a private employer, if the department, division, or institute employs at least 3 persons full-time in research activities and has achieved documented accomplishments in an academic field.

(C) Certain multinational executives and managers. An alien is described in this subparagraph if the alien, in the 3 years preceding the time of the alien's application for classification and admission into the United States under this subparagraph, has been employed for at least 1 year by a firm or corporation or other legal entity or an affiliate or subsidiary thereof and the alien seeks to enter the United States in order to continue to render services to the same employer or to a subsidiary or affiliate thereof in a capacity that is managerial or executive.

(2) Aliens who are members of the professions holding advanced degrees or aliens of exceptional ability.

(A) In general. Visas shall be made available, in a number not to exceed 28.6 percent of such worldwide level plus any visas not required for the classes specified in paragraph (1), to qualified immigrants who are members of the professions holding advanced degrees or their equivalent or who because of their exceptional ability in the sciences, arts, or business, will substantially benefit prospectively the national economy, cultural or educational interests, or welfare of the United States, and whose services in the sciences, arts, professions, or business are sought by an employer in the United States.

(B) Waiver of job offer.

(i) National interest waiver. Subject to clause (ii), the Attorney General may, when the Attorney General deems it to be in the national interest, waive the requirements of subparagraph (A) that an alien's services in the sciences, arts, professions, or business be sought by an employer in the United States.

(ii) Physicians working in shortage areas or veterans facilities.

(I) In general. The Attorney General shall grant a national interest waiver pursuant to clause (i) on behalf of any alien physician with respect to whom a petition for preference classification has been filed under subparagraph (A) if—

(aa) the alien physician agrees to work full time as a physician in an area or areas designated by the Secretary of Health and Human Services as having a shortage of health care professionals or at a health care facility under the jurisdiction of the Secretary of Veterans Affairs; and

(bb) a Federal agency or a department of public health in any State has previously determined that the alien physician's work in such an area or at such facility was in the public interest.

(II) Prohibition. No permanent resident visa may be issued to an alien physician described in subclause (I) by the Secretary of State under section 204(b) [8 USCS § 1154(b)], and the Attorney General may not adjust the status of such an alien physician from that of a nonimmigrant alien to that of a permanent resident alien under section 245 [8 USCS § 1255], until such time as the alien has worked full time as a physician for an aggregate of 5 years (not including the time served in the status of an alien described in section 101(a)(15)(J) [8 USCS § 1101(a)(15)(J)]), in an area or areas designated by the Secretary of Health and Human Services as having a shortage of health care professionals or at a health care facility under the jurisdiction of the Secretary of Veterans Affairs.

(III) Statutory construction. Nothing in this subparagraph may be construed to prevent the filing of a petition with the Attorney General for classification under section 204(a) [8 USCS § 1154(a)], or the filing of an application for adjustment of status under section 245 [8 USCS § 1255], by an alien physician described in subclause (I) prior to the date by which such alien physician has completed the service described in subclause (II).

(IV) Effective date. The requirements of this subsection do not affect waivers on behalf of alien physicians approved under section 203(b)(2)(B) [subsec. (b)(2)(B) of this section] before the enactment date of this subsection. In the case of a physician for whom an application for a waiver was filed under section 203(b)(2)(B) [subsec. (b)(2)(B) of this section] prior to November 1, 1998, the Attorney General shall grant a national interest waiver pursuant to section 203(b)(2)(B) [subsec. (b)(2)(B) of this section] except that the alien is required to have worked full time as a physician for an aggregate of 3 years (not including time served in the status of an alien described in section 101(a)(15)(J) [8 USCS § 1101(a)(15)(J)]) before a visa can be issued to the alien under section 204(b) [8 USCS § 1154(b)] or the status of the alien is adjusted to permanent resident under section 245 [8 USCS § 1255].

(C) Determination of exceptional ability. In determining under subparagraph (A) whether an immigrant has exceptional ability, the possession of a degree, diploma, certificate, or similar award from a college, university, school, or other institution of learning or a license to practice or certification for a particular profession or occupation shall not by itself be considered sufficient evidence of such exceptional ability.

(3) Skilled workers, professionals, and other workers.

(A) In general. Visas shall be made available, in a number not to exceed 28.6 percent of such worldwide level, plus any visas not required for the classes specified in paragraphs (1) and (2), to the following classes of aliens who are not described in paragraph (2):

(i) Skilled workers. Qualified immigrants who are capable, at the time of petitioning for classification under this paragraph, of performing skilled labor (requiring at least 2 years training or experience), not of a temporary or seasonal nature, for which qualified workers are not available in the United States.

(ii) Professionals. Qualified immigrants who hold baccalaureate degrees and who are members of the professions.

(iii) Other workers. Other qualified immigrants who are capable at the time of petitioning for classification under this paragraph, of performing unskilled labor, not of a temporary or seasonal nature, for which qualified workers are not available in the United States.

(B) Limitation on other workers. Not more than 10,000 of the visas made available under this paragraph in any fiscal year may be available for qualified immigrants described in subparagraph (A)(iii).

(C) Labor certification required. An immigrant visa may not be issued to an immigrant under subparagraph (A) until the consular officer is in receipt of a determination made by the Secretary of Labor pursuant to the provisions of section 212(a)(5)(A) [8 USCS § 1182(a)(5)(A)].

(4) Certain special immigrants. Visas shall be made available, in a number not to exceed 7.1 percent of such worldwide level, to qualified special immigrants described in section 101(a)(27) [8 USCS § 1101(a)(27)] (other than those described in subparagraph (A) or (B) thereof), of which not more than 5,000 may be made available in any fiscal year to special immigrants described in subclause (II) or (III) of section 101(a)(27)(C)(ii) [8 USCS § 1101(a)(27)(C)(ii)(II) or (III)], and not more than 100 may be made available in any fiscal year to special immigrants, excluding spouses and children, who are described in section 101(a)(27)(M) [8 USCS § 1101(a)(27)(M)].

(5) Employment creation.

(A) In general. Visas shall be made available, in a number not to exceed 7.1 percent of such worldwide level to qualified immigrants seeking to enter the United States for the purpose of engaging in a new commercial enterprise (including a limited partnership)—

(i) in which such alien has invested (after the date of the enactment of the Immigration Act of 1990 [enacted Nov. 29, 1990]) or, is actively in the process of investing, capital in an amount not less than the amount specified in subparagraph (C) and which is expected to remain invested for not less than 2 years; and

(ii) which will benefit the United States economy by creating full-time employment for not fewer than 10 United States citizens, United States nationals, or aliens lawfully admitted for permanent residence or other immigrants lawfully authorized to be employed in the United States (other than the immigrant and the immigrant's spouse, sons, or daughters).

(B) Designations and reserved visas.

(i) Reserved visas.

(I) In general. Of the visas made available under this paragraph in each fiscal year—

(aa) 20 percent shall be reserved for qualified immigrants who invest in a rural area;

(bb) 10 percent shall be reserved for qualified immigrants who invest in an area designated by the Secretary of Homeland Security under clause (ii) as a high unemployment area; and

(cc) 2 percent shall be reserved for qualified immigrants who invest in infrastructure projects.

(II) Unused visas.

(aa) Carryover. At the end of each fiscal year, any unused visas reserved for qualified immigrants investing in each of the categories described in items (aa) through (cc) of subclause (I) shall remain available within the same category for the immediately succeeding fiscal year.

(bb) General availability. Visas described in items (aa) through (cc) of subclause (I) that are not issued by the end of the succeeding fiscal year referred to in item (aa) shall be made available to qualified immigrants described under subparagraph (A).

(ii) Designation of high unemployment area.

(I) In general. The Secretary of Homeland Security, or a designee of the Secretary who is an employee of the Department of Homeland Security, may designate, as a high unemployment area, a census tract, or contiguous census tracts, in which—

(aa) the new commercial enterprise is principally doing business; and

(bb) the weighted average of the unemployment rate for the census tracts, based on the labor force employment measure for each applicable census tract and any adjacent tract included under subclause (III), is not less than 150 percent of the national average unemployment rate.

(II) Prohibition on designation by any other official. A targeted employment area may not be designated as a high unemployment area by—

(aa) a Federal official other than the Secretary of Homeland Security or a designee of the Secretary; or

(bb) any official of a State or local government.

(III) Inclusion. In making a designation under subclause (I), the Secretary of Homeland Security may include a census tract directly adjacent to a census tract or contiguous census tracts described in that subclause.

(IV) Duration.

(aa) In general. A designation under this clause shall be in effect for the 2-year period beginning on—

(AA) the date on which an application under subparagraph (F) is filed; or

(BB) in the case of an alien who is not subject to subparagraph (F), at the time of investment.

(bb) Renewal. A designation under this clause may be renewed for 1 or more additional 2-year periods if the applicable area continues to meet the criteria described in subclause (I).

(V) Additional investment not required. An immigrant investor who has invested the amount of capital required by subparagraph (C) in a targeted employment area designated as a high unemployment area during the period in which the area is so designated shall not be required to increase the amount of investment due to the expiration of the designation.

(iii) Infrastructure projects.

(I) In general. The Secretary of Homeland Security shall determine whether a specific capital investment project meets the definition of "infrastructure project" set forth in subparagraph (D)(iv).

(II) Prohibition on designation by any other official. A determination under subclause (I) may not be made by—

(aa) a Federal official other than the Secretary of Homeland Security or a designee of the Secretary; or

(bb) any official of a State or local government.

(C) Amount of capital required.

(i) In general. Except as otherwise provided in this subparagraph, the amount of capital required under subparagraph (A) shall be $1,050,000.

(ii) Adjustment for targeted employment areas and infrastructure projects. The amount of capital required under subparagraph (A) for an investment in a targeted employment area or in an infrastructure project shall be $800,000.

(iii) Automatic adjustment in minimum investment amount.

(I) In general. Beginning on January 1, 2027, and every 5 years thereafter, the amount in clause (i) shall automatically adjust for petitions filed on or after the effective date of each adjustment, based on the cumulative annual percentage change in the unadjusted consumer price index for all urban consumers (all items; U.S. city average) reported by the Bureau of Labor Statistics between January 1, 2022, and the date of adjustment. The qualifying investment amounts shall be rounded down to the nearest $50,000. The Secretary of Homeland Security shall update such amounts by publication of a technical amendment in the Federal Register.

(II) Beginning on January 1, 2027, and every 5 years thereafter, the amount in clause (ii) shall automatically adjust for petitions filed on or after the effective date of each adjustment, to be equal to 75 percent of the standard investment amount under subclause (I).

(iv) Adjustment for high employment areas. In the case of an investment made in a part of a metropolitan statistical area that at the time of the investment—

(I) is not a targeted employment area, and

(II) is an area with an unemployment rate significantly below the national average unemployment rate, the Secretary of Homeland Security may specify an amount of capital required under subparagraph (A) that is greater than (but not greater than 3 times) the amount specified in clause (i), as adjusted under clause (iii).

(D) Definitions. In this paragraph:

(i) Affiliated job-creating entity. The term "affiliated job-creating entity" means any job-creating entity that is controlled, managed, or owned by any of the people involved with the regional center or new commercial enterprise under section 203(b)(5)(H)(v) [8 USCS § 1153(b)(5)(H)(v)].

(ii) Capital. The term "capital"—

(I) means cash and all real, personal, or mixed tangible assets owned and controlled by the alien investor, or held in trust for the benefit of the alien and to which the alien has unrestricted access;

(II) shall be valued at fair market value in United States dollars, in accordance with Generally Accepted Accounting Principles or other standard accounting practice adopted by the Securities and Exchange Commission, at the time it is invested under this paragraph;

(III) does not include—

(aa) assets directly or indirectly acquired by unlawful means, including any cash proceeds of indebtedness secured by such assets;

(bb) capital invested in exchange for a note, bond, convertible debt, obligation, or any other debt arrangement between the alien investor and the new commercial enterprise;

(cc) capital invested with a guaranteed rate of return on the amount invested by the alien investor; or

(dd) except as provided in subclause (IV), capital invested that is subject to any agreement between the alien investor and the new commercial enterprise that provides the investor with a contractual right to repayment, such as a mandatory redemption at a certain time or upon the occurrence of a certain event, or a put or sell-back option held by the alien investor, even if such contractual right is contingent on the success of the new commercial enterprise, such as having sufficient available cash flow; and

(IV) includes capital invested that—

(aa) is subject to a buy back option that may be exercised solely at the discretion of the new commercial enterprise; and

(bb) results in the alien investor withdrawing his or her petition unless the alien investor has fulfilled his or her sustainment period and other requirements under this paragraph.

(iii) Certifier. The term "certifier" means a person in a position of substantive authority for the management or operations of a regional center, new commercial enterprise, affiliated job-creating entity, or issuer of securities, such as a principal executive officer or principal financial officer, with knowledge of such entities' policies and procedures related to compliance with the requirements under this paragraph.

(iv) Infrastructure project. The term "infrastructure project" means a capital investment project in a filed or approved business plan, which is administered by a governmental entity (such as a Federal, State, or local agency or authority) that is the job-creating entity contracting with a regional center or new commercial enterprise to receive capital investment under the regional center program described in subparagraph (E) from alien investors or the new commercial enterprise as financing for maintaining, improving, or constructing a public works project.

(v) Job-creating entity. The term "job-creating entity" means any organization formed in the United States for the ongoing conduct of lawful business, including sole proprietorship, partnership (whether limited or general), corporation, limited liability company, business trust, or other entity, which may be publicly or privately owned, including an entity consisting of a holding company and its wholly owned subsidiaries or affiliates (provided that each subsidiary or affiliate is engaged in an activity formed for the ongoing conduct of a lawful business) that receives, or is established to receive, capital investment from alien investors or a new commercial enterprise under the regional center program described in this subparagraph and which is responsible for creating jobs to satisfy the requirement under subparagraph (A)(ii).

(vi) New commercial enterprise. The term "new commercial enterprise" means any for-profit organization formed in the United States for the ongoing conduct of lawful business, including sole proprietorship, partnership (whether limited or general), holding company and its wholly owned subsidiaries (provided that each subsidiary is engaged in a for-profit activity formed for the ongoing conduct of a lawful business), joint venture, corporation, business trust, limited liability company, or other entity (which may be publicly or privately owned) that receives, or is established to receive, capital investment from investors under this paragraph.

(vii) Rural area. The term "rural area" means any area other than an area within a metropolitan statistical area (as designated by the Director of the Office of Management and Budget) or within the outer boundary of any city or town having a population of 20,000 or more (based on the most recent decennial census of the United States).

(viii) Targeted employment area. The term "targeted employment area" means, at the time of investment, a rural area or an area designated by the Secretary of Homeland Security under subparagraph (B)(ii) as a high unemployment area.

(E) Regional center program.

(i) In general. Visas under this subparagraph shall be made available through September 30, 2027, to qualified immigrants (and the eligible spouses and children of such immigrants) pooling their investments with 1 or more qualified immigrants participating in a program implementing this paragraph that involves a regional center in the United States, which has been designated by the Secretary of Homeland Security on the basis of a proposal for the promotion of economic growth, including prospective job creation and increased domestic capital investment.

(ii) Processing. In processing petitions under section 204(a)(1)(H) for classification under this paragraph, the Secretary of Homeland Security—

(I) shall prioritize the processing and adjudication of petitions for rural areas;

(II) may process petitions in a manner and order established by the Secretary; and

(III) shall deem such petitions to include records previously filed with the Secretary pursuant to subparagraph (F) if the alien petitioner certifies that such records are incorporated by reference into the alien's petition.

(iii) Establishment of a regional center. A regional center shall operate within a defined, contiguous, and limited geographic area, which shall be described in the proposal and be consistent with the purpose of concentrating pooled investment within such area. The proposal to establish a regional center shall demonstrate that the pooled investment will have a substantive economic impact on such geographic area, and shall include—

(I) reasonable predictions, supported by economically and statistically valid and transparent forecasting tools, concerning the amount of investment that will be pooled, the kinds of commercial enterprises that will receive such investments, details of the jobs that will be created directly or indirectly as a result of such investments, and other positive economic effects such investments will have;

(II) a description of the policies and procedures in place reasonably designed to monitor new commercial enterprises and any associated job-creating entity to seek to ensure compliance with—

(aa) all applicable laws, regulations, and Executive orders of the United States, including immigration laws, criminal laws, and securities laws; and

(bb) all securities laws of each State in which securities offerings will be conducted, investment advice will be rendered, or the offerors or offerees reside;

(III) attestations and information confirming that all persons involved with the regional center meet the requirements under clauses (i) and (ii) of subparagraph (H);

(IV) a description of the policies and procedures in place that are reasonably designed to ensure program compliance; and

(V) the identities of all natural persons involved in the regional center, as described in subparagraph (H)(v).

(iv) Indirect job creation.

(I) In general. The Secretary of Homeland Security shall permit aliens seeking admission under this subparagraph to satisfy only up to 90 percent of the requirement under subparagraph (A)(ii) with jobs that are estimated to be created indirectly through investment under this paragraph in accordance with this subparagraph. An employee of the new commercial enterprise or job-creating entity may be considered to hold a job that has been directly created.

(II) Construction activity lasting less than 2 years. If the jobs estimated to be created are created by construction activity lasting less than 2 years, the Secretary shall permit aliens seeking admission under this subparagraph to satisfy only up to 75 percent of the requirement under subparagraph (A)(ii) with jobs that are estimated to be created indirectly through investment under this paragraph in accordance with this subparagraph.

(v) Compliance.

(I) In general. In determining compliance with subparagraph (A)(ii), the Secretary of Homeland Security shall permit aliens seeking admission under this subparagraph to rely on economically and statistically valid methodologies for determining the number of jobs created by the program, including—

(aa) jobs estimated to have been created directly, which may be verified using such methodologies; and

(bb) consistent with this subparagraph, jobs estimated to have been directly or indirectly created through capital expenditures, revenues generated from increased exports, improved regional productivity, job creation, and increased domestic capital investment resulting from the program.

(II) Job and investment requirements.

(aa) Relocated jobs. In determining compliance with the job creation requirement under subparagraph (A)(ii), the Secretary of Homeland Security may include jobs estimated to be created under a methodology that attributes jobs to prospective tenants occupying commercial real estate created or improved by capital investments if the number of such jobs estimated to be created has been determined by an economically and statistically valid methodology and such jobs are not existing jobs that have been relocated.

(bb) Publicly available bonds. The Secretary of Homeland Security shall prescribe regulations to ensure that alien investor capital may not be utilized, by a new commercial enterprise or otherwise, to purchase municipal bonds or any other bonds, if such bonds are available to the general public, either as part of a primary offering or from a secondary market.

(cc) Construction activity jobs. If the number of direct jobs estimated to be created has been determined by an economically and statistically valid methodology, and such direct jobs are created by construction activity lasting less than 2 years, the number of such jobs that may be considered direct jobs for purposes of clause (iv) shall be calculated by multiplying the total number of such jobs estimated to be created by the fraction of the 2-year period that the construction activity lasts.

(vi) Amendments. The Secretary of Homeland Security shall—

(I) require a regional center—

(aa) to notify the Secretary, not later than 120 days before the implementation of significant proposed changes to its organizational structure, ownership, or administration, including the sale of such center, or other arrangements which would result in individuals not previously subject to the requirements under subparagraph (H) becoming involved with the regional center; or

(bb) if exigent circumstances are present, to provide the notice described in item (aa) to the Secretary not later than 5 business days after a change described in such item; and

(II) adjudicate business plans under subparagraph (F) and petitions under section 204(a)(1)(H) [8 USCS §

1154(a)(1)(H)] during any notice period as long as the amendment to the business or petition does not negatively impact program eligibility.

(vii) Record keeping and audits.

(I) Record keeping. Each regional center shall make and preserve, during the 5-year period beginning on the last day of the Federal fiscal year in which any transactions occurred, books, ledgers, records, and other documentation from the regional center, new commercial enterprise, or job-creating entity used to support—

(aa) any claims, evidence, or certifications contained in the regional center's annual statements under subparagraph (G); and

(bb) associated petitions by aliens seeking classification under this section or removal of conditions under section 216A [8 USCS § 1186b].

(II) Audits. The Secretary shall audit each regional center not less frequently than once every 5 years. Each such audit shall include a review of any documentation required to be maintained under subclause (I) for the preceding 5 years and a review of the flow of alien investor capital into any capital investment project. To the extent multiple regional centers are located at a single site, the Secretary may audit multiple regional centers in a single site visit.

(III) Termination. The Secretary shall terminate the designation of a regional center that fails to consent to an audit under subclause (II) or deliberately attempts to impede such an audit.

(F) Business plans for regional center investments.

(i) Application for approval of an investment in a commercial enterprise. A regional center shall file an application with the Secretary of Homeland Security for each particular investment offering through an associated new commercial enterprise before any alien files a petition for classification under this paragraph by reason of investment in that offering. The application shall include—

(I) a comprehensive business plan for a specific capital investment project;

(II) a credible economic analysis regarding estimated job creation that is based upon economically and statistically valid and transparent methodologies;

(III) any documents filed with the Securities and Exchange Commission under the Securities Act of 1933 (15 U.S.C. 77a et seq.) or with the securities regulator of any State, as required by law;

(IV) any investment and offering documents, including subscription, investment, partnership, and operating agreements, private placement memoranda, term sheets, biographies of management, officers, directors, and any person with similar responsibilities, the description of the business plan to be provided to potential alien investors, and marketing materials used, or drafts prepared for use, in connection with the offering, which shall contain references, as appropriate, to—

(aa) all material investment risks associated with the new commercial enterprise and the job-creating entity;

(bb) any conflicts of interest that currently exist or may arise among the regional center, the new commercial enterprise, the job-creating entity, or the principals, attorneys, or individuals responsible for recruitment or promotion of such entities;

(cc) any pending material litigation or bankruptcy, or material adverse judgments or bankruptcy orders issued during the most recent 10-year period, in the United States or in another country, affecting the regional center, the new commercial enterprise, any associated job-creating entity, or any other enterprise in which any principal of any of the aforementioned entities held majority ownership at the time; and

(dd)(AA) any fees, ongoing interest, or other compensation paid, or to be paid by the regional center, the new commercial enterprise, or any issuer of securities intended to be offered to alien investors, to agents, finders, or broker dealers involved in the offering of securities to alien investors in connection with the investment;

(BB) a description of the services performed, or that will be performed, by such person to entitle the person to such fees, interest, or compensation; and

(CC) the name and contact information of any such person, if known at the time of filing;

(V) a description of the policies and procedures, such as those related to internal and external due diligence, reasonably designed to cause the regional center and any issuer of securities intended to be offered to alien investors in connection with the relevant capital investment project, to comply, as applicable, with the securities laws of the United States and the laws of the applicable States in connection with the offer, purchase, or sale of its securities; and

(VI) a certification from the regional center, and any issuer of securities intended to be offered to alien investors in connection with the relevant capital investment project, that their respective agents and employees, and any parties associated with the regional center and such issuer of securities affiliated with the regional center are in compliance with the securities laws of the United States and the laws of the applicable States in connection with the offer, purchase, or sale of its securities, to the best of the certifier's knowledge, after a due diligence investigation.

(ii) Effect of approval of a business plan for an investment in a regional center's commercial enterprise. The approval of an application under this subparagraph, including an approval before the date of the enactment of this subparagraph, shall be binding for purposes of the adjudication of subsequent petitions seeking classification under this paragraph by immigrants investing in the same offering described in such application, and of petitions by the same immigrants filed under section 216A [8 USCS § 1186b] unless—

(I) the applicant engaged in fraud, misrepresentation, or criminal misuse;

(II) such approval would threaten public safety or national security;

(III) there has been a material change that affects eligibility;

(IV) the discovery of other evidence affecting program eligibility was not disclosed by the applicant during the adjudication process; or

(V) the previous adjudication involved a material mistake of law or fact.

(iii) Amendments.

(I) Approval. The Secretary of Homeland Security may establish procedures by which a regional center may seek approval of an amendment to an approved application under this subparagraph that reflects changes specified by the Secretary to any information, documents, or other aspects of the investment offering described in such approved application not later than 30 days after any such changes.

(II) Incorporation. Upon the approval of a timely filed amendment to an approved application, any changes reflected in such amendment may be incorporated into and considered in determining program eligibility through adjudication of—

(aa) pending petitions from immigrants investing in the offering described in the approved application who are seeking classification under this paragraph; and

(bb) petitions by immigrants described in item (aa) that are filed under section 216A [8 USCS § 1186b].

(iv) Site visits. The Secretary of Homeland Security shall—

(I) perform site visits to regional centers not earlier than 24 hours after providing notice of such site visit; and

(II) perform at least 1 site visit to, as applicable, each new commercial enterprise or job-creating entity, or the business locations where any jobs that are claimed as being created.

(v) Parameters for capital redeployment.

(I) In general. The Secretary of Homeland Security shall prescribe regulations, in accordance with subchapter II of chapter 5 and chapter 7 of title 5, United States Code [5 USCS §§ 551 et seq. and 701 et seq.] (commonly known as the "Administrative Procedure Act"), that allow a new commercial enterprise to redeploy investment funds anywhere within the United States or its territories for the purpose of maintaining the investors' capital at risk if—

(aa) the new commercial enterprise has executed the business plan for a capital investment project in good faith without a material change;

(bb) the new commercial enterprise has created a sufficient number of new full time positions to satisfy the job creation requirements of the program for all investors in the new commercial enterprise, either directly or indirectly, as evidenced by the methodologies set forth in this Act;

(cc) the job creating entity has repaid the capital initially deployed in conformity with the initial investment contemplated by the business plan; and

(dd) the capital, after repayment by the job creating entity, remains at risk and it is not redeployed in passive investments, such as stocks or bonds.

(II) Termination. The Secretary of Homeland Security shall terminate the designation of a regional center if the Secretary determines that a new commercial enterprise has violated any of the requirements under subclause (I) in the redeployment of funds invested in such regional center.

(G) Regional center annual statements.

(i) In general. Each regional center designated under subparagraph (E) shall submit an annual statement, in a manner prescribed by the Secretary of Homeland Security. Each such statement shall include—

(I) a certification stating that, to the best of the certifier's knowledge, after a due diligence investigation, the regional center is in compliance with clauses (i) and (ii) of subparagraph (H);

(II) a certification described in subparagraph (I)(ii)(II);

(III) a certification stating that, to the best of the certifier's knowledge, after a due diligence investigation, the regional center is in compliance with subparagraph (K)(iii);

(IV) a description of any pending material litigation or bankruptcy proceedings, or material litigation or bankruptcy proceedings resolved during the preceding fiscal year, involving the regional center, the new commercial enterprise, or any affiliated job-creating entity;

(V) an accounting of all individual alien investor capital invested in the regional center, new commercial enterprise, and job-creating entity;

(VI) for each new commercial enterprise associated with the regional center—

(aa) an accounting of the aggregate capital invested in the new commercial enterprise and any job-creating entity by alien investors under this paragraph for each capital investment project being undertaken by the new commercial enterprise;

(bb) a description of how the capital described in item (aa) is being used to execute each capital investment project in the filed business plan or plans;

(cc) evidence that 100 percent of the capital described in item (aa) has been committed to each capital investment project;

(dd) detailed evidence of the progress made toward the completion of each capital investment project;

(ee) an accounting of the aggregate direct jobs created or preserved;

(ff) to the best of the regional center's knowledge, for all fees, including administrative fees, loan monitoring fees, loan management fees, commissions and similar transaction-based compensation, collected from alien investors by the regional center, the new commercial enterprise, any affiliated job-creating entity, any affiliated issuer of securities intended to be offered to alien investors, or any promoter, finder, broker-dealer, or other entity engaged by any of the aforementioned entities to locate individual investors—

(AA) a description of all fees collected;

(BB) an accounting of the entities that received such fees; and

(CC) the purpose for which such fees were collected;

(gg) any documentation referred to in subparagraph (F)(i)(IV) if there has been a material change during the preceding fiscal year; and

(hh) a certification by the regional center that the information provided under items (aa) through (gg) is accurate, to the best of the certifier's knowledge, after a due diligence investigation; and

(VII) a description of the regional center's policies and procedures that are designed to enable the regional center to comply with applicable Federal labor laws.

(ii) Amendment of annual statements. The Secretary of Homeland Security—

(I) shall require the regional center to amend or supplement an annual statement required under clause (i) if the Secretary determines that such statement is deficient; and

(II) may require the regional center to amend or supplement such annual statement if the Director determines that such an amendment or supplement is appropriate.

(iii) Sanctions.

(I) Effect of violation. The Director shall sanction any regional center entity in accordance with subclause (II) if the regional center fails to submit an annual statement or if the Director determines that the regional center—

(aa) knowingly submitted or caused to be submitted a statement, certification, or any information submitted pursuant to this subparagraph that contained an untrue statement of material fact; or

(bb) is conducting itself in a manner inconsistent with its designation under subparagraph (E), including any willful, undisclosed, and material deviation by new commercial enterprises from any filed business plan for such new commercial enterprises.

(II) Authorized sanctions. The Director shall establish a graduated set of sanctions based on the severity of the violations referred to in subclause (I), including—

(aa) fines equal to not more than 10 percent of the total capital invested by alien investors in the regional center's new commercial enterprises or job-creating entities directly involved in such violations, the payment of which shall not in any circumstance utilize any of such alien investors' capital investments, and which shall be deposited into the EB-5 Integrity Fund established under subparagraph (J);

(bb) temporary suspension from participation in the program described in subparagraph (E), which may be lifted by the Director if the individual or entity cures the alleged violation after being provided such an opportunity by the Director;

(cc) permanent bar from participation in the program described in subparagraph (E) for 1 or more individuals or business entities associated with the regional center, new commercial enterprise, or job-creating entity; and

(dd) termination of regional center designation.

(iv) Availability of annual statements to investors. Not later than 30 days after a request from an alien investor, a regional center shall make available to such alien investor a copy of the filed annual statement and any amendments filed to such statement, which shall be redacted to exclude any information unrelated to such alien investor or the new commercial enterprise or job creating entity into which the alien investor invested.

(H) Bona fides of persons involved with regional center program.

(i) In general. The Secretary of Homeland Security may not permit any person to be involved with any regional center, new commercial enterprise, or job-creating entity if—

(I) the person has been found to have committed—

(aa) a criminal or civil offense involving fraud or deceit within the previous 10 years;

(bb) a civil offense involving fraud or deceit that resulted in a liability in excess of $1,000,000; or

(cc) a crime for which the person was convicted and sentenced to a term of imprisonment of more than 1 year;

(II) the person is subject to a final order, for the duration of any penalty imposed by such order, of a State securities commission (or an agency or officer of a State performing similar functions), a State authority that supervises or examines banks, savings associations, or credit unions, a State insurance commission (or an agency or officer of a State performing similar functions), an appropriate Federal banking agency, the Commodity Futures Trading Commission, the Securities and Exchange Commission, a financial self-regulatory organization recognized by the Securities and Exchange Commission, or the National Credit Union Administration, which is based on a violation of any law or regulation that—

(aa) prohibits fraudulent, manipulative, or deceptive conduct; or

(bb) bars the person from—

(AA) association with an entity regulated by such commission, authority, agency, or officer;

(BB) appearing before such commission, authority, agency, or officer;

(CC) engaging in the business of securities, insurance, or banking; or

(DD) engaging in savings association or credit union activities;

(III) the Secretary determines that the person is engaged in, has ever been engaged in, or seeks to engage in—

(aa) any illicit trafficking in any controlled substance or in any listed chemical (as defined in section 102 of the Controlled Substances Act [21 USCS § 802]);

(bb) any activity relating to espionage, sabotage, or theft of intellectual property;

(cc) any activity related to money laundering (as described in section 1956 or 1957 of title 18, United States Code [18 USCS § 1956 or 1957]);

(dd) any terrorist activity (as defined in section 212(a)(3)(B) [8 USCS § 1182(a)(3)(B)]);

(ee) any activity constituting or facilitating human trafficking or a human rights offense;

(ff) any activity described in section 212(a)(3)(E) [8 USCS § 1182(a)(3)(E)]; or

(gg) the violation of any statute, regulation, or Executive order regarding foreign financial transactions or foreign asset control; or

(IV) the person—

(aa) is, or during the preceding 10 years has been, included on the Department of Justice's List of Currently Disciplined Practitioners; or

(bb) during the preceding 10 years, has received a reprimand or has otherwise been publicly disciplined for conduct related to fraud or deceit by a State bar association of which the person is or was a member.

(ii) Foreign involvement in regional center program.

(I) Lawful status required. A person may not be involved with a regional center unless the person—

(aa) is a national of the United States or an individual who has been lawfully admitted for permanent residence (as such terms are defined in paragraphs (20) and (22) of section 101(a) [8 USCS § 1101(a)]); and

(bb) is not the subject of rescission or removal proceedings.

(II) Foreign governments. No agency, official, or other similar entity or representative of a foreign government entity may provide capital to, or be directly or indirectly involved with the ownership or administration of, a regional center, a new commercial enterprise, or a job-creating entity, except that a foreign or domestic investment fund or other investment vehicle that is wholly or partially owned, directly or indirectly, by a bona fide foreign sovereign wealth fund or a foreign state-owned enterprise otherwise permitted to do business in the United States may be involved with the ownership, but not the administration, of a job-creating entity that is not an affiliated job-creating entity.

(III) Rulemaking. Not later than 270 days after the date of the enactment of the EB-5 Reform and Integrity Act of 2022 [enacted March 15, 2022], the Secretary shall issue regulations implementing subparagraphs (I) and (II).

(iii) Information required. The Secretary of Homeland Security—

(I) shall require such attestations and information, including the submission of fingerprints or other biometrics to the Federal Bureau of Investigation with respect to a regional center, a new commercial enterprise, and any affiliated job creating entity, and persons involved with such entities (as described in clause (v)), as may be necessary to determine whether such entities are in compliance with clauses (i) and (ii);

(II) shall perform such criminal record checks and other background and database checks with respect to a regional center, a new commercial enterprise, and any affiliated job-creating entity, and persons involved with such entities (as described in clause (v)), as may be necessary to determine whether such entities are in compliance with clauses (i) and (ii); and

(III) may, at the Secretary's discretion, require the information described to in subclause (I) and may perform the checks described in subclause (II) with respect to any job creating entity and persons involved with such entity if there is a reasonable basis to believe such entity or person is not in compliance with clauses (i) and (ii).

(iv) Termination.

(I) In general. The Secretary of Homeland Security may suspend or terminate the designation of any regional center, or the participation under the program of any new commercial enterprise or job-creating entity under this paragraph if the Secretary determines that such entity—

(aa) knowingly involved a person with such entity in violation of clause (i) or (ii) by failing, within 14 days of acquiring such knowledge—

(AA) to take commercially reasonable efforts to discontinue the prohibited person's involvement; or

(BB) to provide notice to the Secretary;

(bb) failed to provide an attestation or information requested by the Secretary under clause (iii)(I); or

(cc) knowingly provided any false attestation or information under clause (iii)(I).

(II) Limitation. The Secretary's authorized sanctions under subclause (I) shall be limited to entities that have engaged in any activity described in subclause (I).

(III) Information.

(aa) Notification. The Secretary, after performing the criminal record checks and other background checks described in clause (iii), shall notify a regional center, new commercial enterprise, or job-creating entity whether any person involved with such entities is not in compliance with clause (i) or (ii), unless the information that provides the basis for the determination is classified or disclosure is otherwise prohibited under law.

(bb) Effect of failure to respond. If the regional center, new commercial enterprise, or job-creating entity fails to discontinue the prohibited person's involvement with the regional center, new commercial enterprise, or job-creating entity, as applicable, within 30 days after receiving such notification, such entity shall be deemed to have knowledge under subclause (I)(aa) that the involvement of such person with the entity is in violation of clause (i) or (ii).

(v) Persons involved with a regional center, new commercial enterprise, or job-creating entity. For the purposes of this paragraph, unless otherwise determined by the Secretary of Homeland Security, a person is involved with a regional center, a new commercial enterprise, any affiliated job-creating entity, as applicable, if the person is, directly or indirectly, in a position of substantive authority to make operational or managerial decisions over pooling, securitization, investment, release, acceptance, or control or use of any funding that was procured under the program described in subparagraph (E). An individual may be in a position of substantive authority if the person serves as a principal, a representative, an administrator, an owner, an officer, a board member, a manager, an executive, a general partner, a fiduciary, an agent, or in a similar position at the regional center, new commercial enterprise, or job-creating entity, respectively.

(I) Compliance with securities laws.

(i) Jurisdiction.

(I) In general. The United States has jurisdiction, including subject matter jurisdiction, over the purchase or sale of any security offered or sold, or any investment advice provided, by any regional center or any party associated with a regional center for purposes of the securities laws.

(II) Compliance with regulations. For purposes of section 5 of the Securities Act of 1933 (15 U.S.C. 77e), a regional center or any party associated with a regional center is not precluded from offering or selling a security pursuant to Regulation S (17 C.F.R. 230.901 et seq.) to the extent that such offering or selling otherwise complies with that regulation.

(III) Savings provision. Subclause (I) is not intended to modify any existing rules or regulations of the Securities and Exchange Commission related to the application of section 15(a) of the Securities and Exchange Act of 1934 (15 U.S.C. 78o(a)) to foreign brokers or dealers.

(ii) Regional center certifications required.

(I) Initial certification. The Secretary of Homeland Security may not approve an application for regional center designation or regional center amendment unless the regional center certifies that, to the best of the certifier's knowledge, after a due diligence investigation, the regional center is in compliance with and has policies and procedures, including those related to internal and external due diligence, reasonably designed to confirm, as applicable, that all parties associated with the regional center are and will remain in compliance with the securities laws of the United States and of any State in which—

(aa) the offer, purchase, or sale of securities was conducted;

(bb) the issuer of securities was located; or

(cc) the investment advice was provided by the regional center or parties associated with the regional center.

(II) Reissue. A regional center shall annually reissue a certification described in subclause (I), in accordance with subparagraph (G), to certify compliance with clause (iii) by stating that—

(aa) the certification is made by a certifier;

(bb) to the best of the certifier's knowledge, after a due diligence investigation, all such offers, purchases, and sales of securities or the provision of investment advice complied with the securities laws of the United States and the securities laws of any State in which—

(AA) the offer, purchase, or sale of securities was conducted;

(BB) the issuer of securities was located; or

(CC) the investment advice was provided; and

(cc) records, data, and information related to such offers, purchases, and sales have been maintained.

(III) Effect of noncompliance. If a regional center, through its due diligence, discovered during the previous fiscal year that the regional center or any party associated with the regional center was not in compliance with the securities laws of the United States or the securities laws of any State in which the securities activities were conducted by any party associated with the regional center, the certifier shall—

(aa) describe the activities that led to noncompliance;

(bb) describe the actions taken to remedy the noncompliance; and

(cc) certify that the regional center and all parties associated with the regional center are currently in compliance, to the best of the certifier's knowledge, after a due diligence investigation.

(iii) Oversight required. Each regional center shall—

(I) use commercially reasonable efforts to monitor and supervise compliance with the securities laws in relations to all offers, purchases, and sales of, and investment advice relating to, securities made by parties associated with the regional center;

(II) maintain records, data, and information relating to all such offers, purchases, sales, and investment advice during the 5-year period beginning on the date of their creation; and

(III) make the records, data, and information described in subclause (II) available to the Secretary or to the Securities and Exchange Commission upon request.

(iv) Suspension or termination. In addition to any other authority provided to the Secretary under this paragraph, the Secretary, in the Secretary's discretion, may suspend or terminate the designation of any regional center or impose other sanctions against the regional center if the regional center, or any parties associated with the regional center that the regional center knew or reasonably should have known—

(I) are permanently or temporarily enjoined by order, judgment, or decree of any court of competent jurisdiction in connection with the offer, purchase, or sale of a security or the provision of investment advice;

(II) are subject to any final order of the Securities and Exchange Commission or a State securities regulator that—

(aa) bars such person from association with an entity regulated by the Securities and Exchange Commission or a State securities regulator; or

(bb) constitutes a final order based on a finding of an intentional violation or a violation related to fraud or deceit in connection with the offer, purchase, or sale of, or investment advice relating to, a security; or

(III) submitted, or caused to be submitted, a certification described in clause (ii) that contained an untrue statement of a material fact or omitted to state a material fact necessary in order to make the statements made, in light of the circumstances under which they were made, not misleading.

(v) Defined term. In this subparagraph, the term "parties associated with a regional center" means—

(I) the regional center;

(II) any new commercial enterprise or affiliated job-creating entity or issuer of securities associated with the regional center;

(III) the regional center's and new commercial enterprise's owners, officers, directors, managers, partners, agents, employees, promoters and attorneys, or similar position, as determined by the Secretary; and

(IV) any person under the control of the regional center, new commercial enterprise, or issuer of securities associated with the regional center who is responsible for the marketing, offering, or sale of any security offered in connection with the capital investment project.

(vi) Savings provision. Nothing in this subparagraph may be construed to impair or limit the authority of the Securities and Exchange Commission under the Federal securities laws or any State securities regulator under State securities laws.

(J) EB-5 Integrity Fund.

(i) Establishment. There is established in the United States Treasury a special fund, which shall be known as the "EB-5 Integrity Fund" (referred to in this subparagraph as the "Fund"). Amounts deposited into the Fund shall be available to the Secretary of Homeland Security until expended for the purposes set forth in clause (iii).

(ii) Fees.

(I) Annual fee. On October 1, 2022, and each October 1 thereafter, the Secretary of Homeland Security shall collect for the Fund an annual fee—

(aa) except as provided in item (bb), of $20,000 from each regional center designated under subparagraph (E); and

(bb) of $10,000 from each such regional center with 20 or fewer total investors in the preceding fiscal year in its new commercial enterprises.

(II) Petition fee. Beginning on October 1, 2022, the Secretary shall collect a fee of $1,000 for the Fund with each petition filed under section 204(a)(1)(H) [8 USCS § 1154(a)(1)(H)] for classification under subparagraph (E). The fee under this subclause is in addition to the fee that the Secretary is authorized to establish and collect for each petition to recover the costs of adjudication and naturalization services under section 286(m) [8 USCS § 1356(m)].

(III) Increases. The Secretary may increase the amounts under this clause by prescribing such regulations as may be necessary to ensure that amounts in the Fund are sufficient to carry out the purposes set forth in clause (iii).

(iii) Permissible uses of fund. The Secretary shall—

(I) use not less than $^1/_3$ of the amounts deposited into the Fund for investigations based outside of the United States, including—

(aa) monitoring and investigating program-related events and promotional activities; and

(bb) ensuring an alien investor's compliance with subparagraph (L); and

(II) use amounts deposited into the Fund—

(aa) to detect and investigate fraud or other crimes;

(bb) to determine whether regional centers, new commercial enterprises, job-creating entities, and alien investors (and their alien spouses and alien children) comply with the immigration laws;

(cc) to conduct audits and site visits; and

(dd) as the Secretary determines to be necessary, including monitoring compliance with the requirements under section 107 of the EB-5 Reform and Integrity Act of 2022 [8 USCS § 1153a].

(iv) Failure to pay fee. The Secretary of Homeland Security shall—

(I) impose a reasonable penalty, which shall be deposited into the Fund, if any regional center does not pay the fee required under clause (ii) within 30 days after the date on which such fee is due; and

(II) terminate the designation of any regional center that does not pay the fee required under clause (ii) within 90 days after the date on which such fee is due.

(v) Report. The Secretary shall submit an annual report to the Committee on the Judiciary of the Senate and the Committee on the Judiciary of the House of Representatives that describes how amounts in the Fund were expended during the previous fiscal year.

(K) Direct and third-party promoters.

(i) Rules and standards. Direct and third-party promoters (including migration agents) of a regional center, any new commercial enterprise, an affiliated job-creating entity, or an issuer of securities intended to be offered to alien investors in connection with a particular capital investment project shall comply with the rules and standards prescribed by the Secretary of Homeland Security and any applicable Federal or State securities laws, to oversee promotion of any offering of securities related to the EB-5 Program, including—

(I) registration with U.S. Citizenship and Immigration Services, which—

(aa) includes identifying and contact information for such promoter and confirmation of the existence of the written agreement required under clause (iii); and

(bb) may be made publicly available at the discretion of the Secretary;

(II) certification by each promoter that such promoter is not ineligible under subparagraph (H)(i);

(III) guidelines for accurately representing the visa process to foreign investors; and

(IV) guidelines describing permissible fee arrangements under applicable securities and immigration laws.

(ii) Effect of violation. If the Secretary determines that a direct or third-party promoter has violated clause (i), the Secretary shall suspend or permanently bar such individual from participation in the program described in subparagraph (E).

(iii) Compliance. Each regional center, new commercial enterprise, and affiliated job-creating entity shall maintain a written agreement between or among such entities and each direct or third-party promoter operating on behalf of such entities that outlines the rules and standards prescribed under clause (i).

(iv) Disclosure. Each petition filed under section 204(a)(1)(H) [8 USCS § 1154(a)(1)(H)] shall include a disclosure, signed by the investor, that reflects all fees, ongoing interest, and other compensation paid to any person that the regional center or new commercial enterprise knows has received, or will receive, in connection with the investment, including compensation to agents, finders, or broker dealers involved in the offering, to the extent not already specifically identified in the business plan filed under subparagraph (F).

(L) Source of funds.

(i) In general. An alien investor shall demonstrate that the capital required under subparagraph (A) and any funds used to pay administrative costs and fees associated with the alien's investment were obtained from a lawful source and through lawful means.

(ii) Required information. The Secretary of Homeland Security shall require that an alien investor's petition under this paragraph contain, as applicable—

(I) business and tax records, or similar records, including—

(aa) foreign business registration records;

(bb) corporate or partnership tax returns (or tax returns of any other entity in any form filed in any country or subdivision of such country), and personal tax returns, including income, franchise, property (whether real, personal, or intangible), or any other tax returns of any kind, filed during the past 7 years (or another period to be determined by the Secretary to ensure that the investment is obtained from a lawful source of funds) with any taxing jurisdiction within or outside the United States by or on behalf of the alien investor; and

(cc) any other evidence identifying any other source of capital or administrative fees;

(II) evidence related to monetary judgments against the alien investor, including certified copies of any judgments, and evidence of all pending governmental civil or criminal actions, governmental administrative proceedings, and any private civil actions (pending or otherwise) involving possible monetary judgments against the alien investor from any court within or outside the United States; and

(III) the identity of all persons who transfer into the United States, on behalf of the investor, any funds that are used to meet the capital requirement under subparagraph (A).

(iii) Gift and loan restrictions.

(I) In general. Gifted and borrowed funds may not be counted toward the minimum capital investment requirement under subparagraph (C) unless such funds—

(aa) were gifted or loaned to the alien investor in good faith; and

(bb) were not gifted or loaned to circumvent any limitations imposed on permissible sources of capital under this subparagraph, including but not limited to proceeds from illegal activity.

(II) Records requirement. If funds invested under subparagraph (A) are gifted or loaned to the alien investor, the Secretary shall require that the alien investor's petition under this paragraph includes the records described in subclauses (I) and (II) of clause (ii) from the donor or, if other than a bank, the lender.

(M) Treatment of good faith investors following program noncompliance.

(i) Termination or debarment of EB-5 entity. Except as provided in clause (vi), upon the termination or debarment, as applicable, from the program under this paragraph of a regional center, a new commercial enterprise, or a job-creating entity—

(I) an otherwise qualified petition under section 204(a)(1)(H) [8 USCS § 1154(a)(1)(H)] or the conditional permanent residence of an alien who has been admitted to the United States pursuant to section 216A(a)(1) [8 USCS § 1186b(a)(1)] based on an investment in a terminated regional center, new commercial enterprise, or job-creating entity shall remain valid or continue to be authorized, as applicable, consistent with this subparagraph; and

(II) the Secretary of Homeland Security shall notify the alien beneficiaries of such petitions of such termination or debarment.

(ii) New regional center or investment. The petition under section 204(a)(1)(H) [8 USCS § 1154(a)(1)(H)] of an alien described in clause (i) and the conditional permanent resident status of an alien described in clause (i) shall be terminated 180 days after notification of the termination from the program under this paragraph of a regional center, a new commercial enterprise, or a job creating entity (but not sooner than 180 days after the date of the enactment of the EB-5 Reform and Integrity Act of 2022 [enacted March 15, 2022]) unless—

(I) in the case of the termination of a regional center—

(aa) the new commercial enterprise associates with an approved regional center, regardless of the approved geographical boundaries of such regional center's designation; or

(bb) such alien makes a qualifying investment in another new commercial enterprise; or

(II) in the case of the debarment of a new commercial enterprise or job-creating entity, such alien—

(aa) associates with a new commercial enterprise in good standing; and

(bb) invests additional investment capital solely to the extent necessary to satisfy remaining job creation requirements under subparagraph (A)(ii).

(iii) Amendments.

(I) Filing requirement. The Secretary shall permit a petition described in clause (i)(I) to be amended to allow such petition to meet the applicable eligibility requirements under clause (ii), or to notify the Secretary that a pending or approved petition continues to meet the eligibility requirements described in clause (ii) notwithstanding termination or debarment described in clause (i) if such amendment is filed not later than 180 days after the Secretary provides notification of termination or debarment of a regional center, a new commercial enterprise, or a job-creating entity, as applicable.

(II) Determination of eligibility. For purposes of determining eligibility under subclause (I)—

(aa) the Secretary shall permit amendments to the business plan, without such facts underlying the amendment being deemed a material change; and

(bb) may deem any funds obtained or recovered by an alien investor, directly or indirectly, from claims against third parties, including insurance proceeds, or any additional investment capital provided by the alien, to be such alien's investment capital for the purposes of subparagraph (A) if such investment otherwise complies with the requirements under this paragraph and section 216A [8 USCS § 1186b].

(iv) Removal of conditions. Aliens described in subclauses (I)(bb) and (II) of clause (ii) shall be eligible to have their conditions removed pursuant to section 216A [8 USCS § 1186b] beginning on the date that is 2 years after the date of the subsequent investment.

(v) Remedies. For petitions approved under clause (ii), including following an amendment filed under clause (iii), the Secretary—

(I) shall retain the immigrant visa priority date related to the original petition and prevent age-out of derivative beneficiaries; and

(II) may hold such petition in abeyance and extend any applicable deadlines under this paragraph.

(vi) Exception. If the Secretary has reason to believe that an alien was a knowing participant in the conduct that led to the termination of a regional center, new commercial enterprise, or job-creating entity described in clause (i)—

(I) the alien shall not be accorded any benefit under this subparagraph; and

(II) the Secretary shall—

(aa) notify the alien of such belief; and

(bb) subject to section 216A(b)(2) [8 USCS § 1186b(b)(2)], shall deny or initiate proceedings to revoke the approval of such alien's petition, application, or benefit (and that of any spouse or child, if applicable) described in this paragraph.

(N) Threats to the national interest.

(i) Denial or revocation. The Secretary of Homeland Security shall deny or revoke the approval of a petition, application, or benefit described in this paragraph, including the documents described in clause (ii), if the Secretary determines, in the Secretary's discretion, that the approval of such petition, application, or benefit is contrary to the national interest of the United States for reasons relating to threats to public safety or national security.

(ii) Documents. The documents described in this clause are—

(I) a certification, designation, or amendment to the designation of a regional center;

(II) a petition seeking classification of an alien as an alien investor under this paragraph;

(III) a petition to remove conditions under section 216A [8 USCS § 1186b];

(IV) an application for approval of a business plan in a new commercial enterprise under subparagraph (F); or

(V) a document evidencing conditional permanent resident status that was issued to an alien pursuant to section 216A [8 USCS § 1186b].

(iii) Debarment. If a regional center, new commercial enterprise, or job-creating entity has its designation or participation in the program under this paragraph terminated for reasons relating to public safety or national security, any person associated with such regional center, new commercial enterprise, or job-creating entity, including an alien investor, shall be permanently barred from future participation in the program under this paragraph if the Secretary of Homeland Security, in the Secretary's discretion, determines, by a preponderance of the evidence, that such person was a knowing participant in the conduct that led to the termination.

(iv) Notice. If the Secretary of Homeland Security determines that the approval of a petition, application, or benefit described in this paragraph should be denied or revoked pursuant to clause (i), the Secretary shall—

(I) notify the relevant individual, regional center, or commercial entity of such determination;

(II) deny or revoke such petition, application, or benefit or terminate the permanent resident status of the alien (and the alien spouse and alien children of such immigrant), as of the date of such determination; and

(III) provide any United States-owned regional center, new commercial enterprise, or job creating entity an explanation for such determination unless the relevant information is classified or disclosure is otherwise prohibited under law.

(v) Judicial review. Notwithstanding any other provision of law (statutory or nonstatutory), including section 2241 of title 28, United States Code, or any other habeas corpus provision, and sections 1361 and 1651 of such title [28 USCS §§ 1361 and 1651], no court shall have jurisdiction to review a denial or revocation under this subparagraph. Nothing in this clause may be construed as precluding review of constitutional claims or questions of law raised upon a petition for review filed with an appropriate court of appeals in accordance with section 242 [8 USCS § 1252].

(O) Fraud, misrepresentation, and criminal misuse.

(i) Denial or revocation. Subject to subparagraph (M), the Secretary of Homeland Security shall deny or revoke the approval of a petition, application, or benefit described in this paragraph, including the documents described in subparagraph (N)(ii), if the Secretary determines, in the Secretary's discretion, that such petition, application, or benefit was predicated on or involved fraud, deceit, intentional material misrepresentation, or criminal misuse.

(ii) Debarment. If a regional center, new commercial enterprise, or job-creating entity has its designation or participation in the program under this paragraph terminated for reasons relating to fraud, intentional material misrepresentation, or criminal misuse, any person associated with such regional center, new commercial enterprise, or job-creating entity, including an alien investor, shall be permanently barred from future participation in the program if the Secretary determines, in the Secretary's discretion, by a preponderance of the evidence, that such person was a knowing participant in the conduct that led to the termination.

(iii) Notice. If the Secretary determines that the approval of a petition, application, or benefit described in this paragraph should be denied or revoked pursuant to clause (i), the Secretary shall—

(I) notify the relevant individual, regional center, or commercial entity of such determination; and

(II) deny or revoke such petition, application, or benefit or terminate the permanent resident status of the alien (and the alien spouse and alien children of such immigrant), in accordance with clause (i), as of the date of such determination.

(P) Administrative appellate review.

(i) In general. The Director of U.S. Citizenship and Immigration Services shall provide an opportunity for an administrative appellate review by the Administrative Appeals Office of U.S. Citizenship and Immigration Services of any determination made under this paragraph, including—

(I) an application for regional center designation or regional center amendment;

(II) an application for approval of a business plan filed under subparagraph (F);

(III) a petition by an alien investor for status as an immigrant under this paragraph;

(IV) the termination or suspension of any benefit accorded under this paragraph; and

(V) any sanction imposed by the Secretary under this paragraph.

(ii) Judicial review. Subject to subparagraph (N)(v) and section 242(a)(2) [8 USCS § 1252(a)(2)], and notwithstanding any other provision of law (statutory or nonstatutory), including section 2241 of title 28, United States Code, or any other habeas corpus provision, and sections 1361 and 1651 of such title [28 USCS §§ 1361 and 1651], no court shall have jurisdiction to review a determination under this paragraph until the regional center, its associated entities, or the alien investor has exhausted all administrative appeals.

(Q) Fund administration.

(i) In general. Each new commercial enterprise shall deposit and maintain the capital investment of each alien investor in a separate account, including amounts held in escrow.

(ii) Use of funds. Amounts in a separate account may only—

(I) be transferred to another separate account or a job creating entity;

(II) otherwise be deployed into the capital investment project for which the funds were intended; or

(III) be transferred to the alien investor who contributed the funds as a refund of that investor's capital investment, if otherwise permitted under this paragraph.

(iii) Deployment of funds into an affiliated job-creating entity. If amounts are transferred to an affiliated job-creating entity pursuant to clause (ii)(I)—

(I) the affiliated job-creating entity shall maintain such amounts in a separate account until they are deployed into the capital investment project for which they were intended; and

(II) not later than 30 days after such amounts are deployed pursuant to subclause (I), the affiliated job-creating entity shall provide written notice to the fund administrator retained pursuant to clause (iv) that a construction consultant or other individual authorized by the Secretary has verified that such amounts have been deployed into the project.

(iv) Fund administrator. Except as provided in clause (v), the new commercial enterprise shall retain a fund administrator to fulfill the requirements under this subparagraph. The fund administrator—

(I) shall be independent of, and not directly related to, the new commercial enterprise, the regional center associated with the new commercial enterprise, the job creating entity, or any of the principals or managers of such entities;

(II) shall be licensed, active, and in good standing as—

(aa) a certified public accountant;

(bb) an attorney;

(cc) a broker-dealer or investment adviser registered with the Securities and Exchange Commission; or

(dd) an individual or company that otherwise meets such requirements as may be established by the Secretary;

(III) shall monitor and track any transfer of amounts from the separate account;

(IV) shall serve as a cosignatory on all separate accounts;

(V) before any transfer of amounts from a separate account, shall—

(aa) verify that the transfer complies with all governing documents, including organizational, operational, and investment documents; and

(bb) approve such transfer with a written or electronic signature;

(VI) shall periodically provide each alien investor with information about the activity of the account in which the investor's capital investment is held, including—

(aa) the name and location of the bank or financial institution at which the account is maintained;

(bb) the history of the account; and

(cc) any additional information required by the Secretary; and

(VII) shall make and preserve, during the 5-year period beginning on the last day of the Federal fiscal year in which any transactions occurred, books, ledgers, records, and other documentation necessary to comply with this clause, which shall be provided to the Secretary upon request.

(v) Waiver.

(I) Waiver permitted. The Secretary of Homeland Security, after consultation with the Securities and Exchange Commission, may waive the requirements under clause (iv) for any new commercial enterprise or affiliated job-creating entity that is controlled by or under common control of an investment adviser or broker-dealer that is registered with the Securities and Exchange Commission if the Secretary, in the Secretary's discretion, determines that the Securities and Exchange Commission provides comparable protections and transparency for alien investors as the protections and transparency provided under clause (iv).

(II) Waiver required. The Secretary of Homeland Security shall waive the requirements under clause (iv) for any new commercial enterprise that commissions an annual independent financial audit of such new commercial enterprise or job creating entity conducted in accordance with Generally Accepted Auditing Standards, which audit shall be provided to the Secretary and all investors in the new commercial enterprise.

(vi) Defined term. In this subparagraph, the term "separate account" means an account that—

(I) is maintained in the United States by a new commercial enterprise or job creating entity at a federally regulated bank or at another financial institution (as defined in section 20 of title 18, United States Code [18 USCS § 20]) in the United States;

(II) is insured; and

(III) contains only the pooled investment funds of alien investors in a new commercial enterprise with respect to a single capital investment project.

(R) Required checks. Any petition filed by an alien under section 204(a)(1)(H) [8 USCS § 1154(a)(1)(H)] may not be approved under this paragraph unless the Secretary of Homeland Security has searched for the alien and any associated employer of such alien on the

Specially Designated Nationals List of the Department of the Treasury Office of Foreign Assets Control.

(S) Protection from expired legislation. Notwithstanding the expiration of legislation authorizing the regional center program under subparagraph (E), the Secretary of Homeland Security—

(i) shall continue processing petitions under sections 204(a)(1)(H) and 216A [8 USCS §§ 1154(a)(1)(H) and 1186b] based on an investment in a new commercial enterprise associated with a regional center that were filed on or before September 30, 2026;

(ii) may not deny a petition described in clause (i) based on the expiration of such legislation; and

(iii) may not suspend or terminate the allocation of visas to the beneficiaries of approved petitions described in clause (i).

(6) Special rules for "K" special immigrants.

(A) Not counted against numerical limitation in year involved. Subject to subparagraph (B), the number of immigrant visas made available to special immigrants under section 101(a)(27)(K) [8 USCS § 1101(a)(27)(K)] in a fiscal year shall not be subject to the numerical limitations of this subsection or of section 202(a) [8 USCS § 1152(a)].

(B) Counted against numerical limitations in following year.

(i) Reduction in employment-based immigrant classifications. The number of visas made available in any fiscal year under paragraphs (1), (2), and (3) shall each be reduced by $^1/_3$ of the number of visas made available in the previous fiscal year to special immigrants described in section 101(a)(27)(K) [8 USCS § 1101(a)(27)(K)].

(ii) Reduction in per country level. The number of visas made available in each fiscal year to natives of a foreign state under section 202(a) [8 USCS § 1152(a)] shall be reduced by the number of visas made available in the previous fiscal year to special immigrants described in section 101(a)(27)(K) [8 USCS § 1101(a)(27)(K)] who are natives of the foreign state.

(iii) Reduction in employment-based immigrant classifications within per country ceiling. In the case of a foreign state subject to section 202(e) [8 USCS § 1152(e)] in a fiscal year (and in the previous fiscal year), the number of visas made available and allocated to each of paragraphs (1) through (3) of this subsection in the fiscal year shall be reduced by $^1/_3$ of the number of visas made available in the previous fiscal year to special immigrants described in section 101(a)(27)(K) [8 USCS § 1101(a)(27)(K))] who are natives of the foreign state.

(c) Diversity immigrants.

(1) In general. Except as provided in paragraph (2), aliens subject to the worldwide level specified in section 201(e) [8 USCS § 1151(e)] for diversity immigrants shall be allotted visas each fiscal year as follows:

(A) Determination of preference immigration. The Attorney General shall determine for the most recent previous 5-fiscal-year period for which data are available, the total number of aliens who are natives of each foreign state and who (i) were admitted or otherwise provided lawful permanent resident status (other than under this subsection) and (ii) were subject to the numerical limitations of section 201(a) [8 USCS § 1151(a)] (other than paragraph (3) thereof) or who were admitted or otherwise provided lawful permanent resident status as an immediate relative or other alien described in section 201(b)(2) [8 USCS § 1151(b)(2)].

(B) Identification of high-admission and low-admission regions and high-admission and low-admission states. The Attorney General—

(i) shall identify—

(I) each region (each in this paragraph referred to as a "high-admission region") for which the total of the numbers determined under subparagraph (A) for states in the region is greater than $^1/_6$ of the total of all such numbers, and

(II) each other region (each in this paragraph referred to as a "low-admission region"); and

(ii) shall identify—

(I) each foreign state for which the number determined under subparagraph (A) is greater than 50,000 (each such state in this paragraph referred to as a "high-admission state"), and

(II) each other foreign state (each such state in this paragraph referred to as a "low-admission state").

(C) Determination of percentage of worldwide immigration attributable to high-admission regions. The Attorney General shall determine the percentage of the total of the numbers determined under subparagraph (A) that are numbers for foreign states in high-admission regions.

(D) Determination of regional populations excluding high-admission states and ratios of populations of regions within low-admission regions and high-admission regions. The Attorney General shall determine—

(i) based on available estimates for each region, the total population of each region not including the population of any high-admission state;

(ii) for each low-admission region, the ratio of the population of the region determined under clause (i) to the total of the populations determined under such clause for all the low-admission regions; and

(iii) for each high-admission region, the ratio of the population of the region determined under clause (i) to the total of the populations determined under such clause for all the high-admission regions.

(E) Distribution of visas.

(i) No visas for natives of high-admission states. The percentage of visas made available under this paragraph to natives of a high-admission state is 0.

(ii) For low-admission states in low-admission regions. Subject to clauses (iv) and (v), the percentage of visas made available under this paragraph to natives (other than natives of a high-admission state) in a low-admission region is the product of—

(I) the percentage determined under subparagraph (C), and

(II) the population ratio for that region determined under subparagraph (D)(ii).

(iii) For low-admission states in high-admission regions. Subject to clauses (iv) and (v), the percentage of visas made available under this paragraph to natives (other than natives of a high-admission state) in a high-admission region is the product of—

(I) 100 percent minus the percentage determined under subparagraph (C), and

(II) the population ratio for that region determined under subparagraph (D)(iii).

(iv) Redistribution of unused visa numbers. If the Secretary of State estimates that the number of immigrant visas to be issued to natives in any region for a fiscal year under this paragraph is less than the number of immigrant visas made available to such natives under this paragraph for the fiscal year, subject to clause (v), the excess visa numbers shall be made available to natives (other than natives of a high-admission state) of the other regions in proportion to the percentages otherwise specified in clauses (ii) and (iii).

(v) Limitation on visas for natives of a single foreign state. The percentage of visas made available under this paragraph to natives of any single foreign state for any fiscal year shall not exceed 7 percent.

(F) "Region" defined. Only for purposes of administering the diversity program under this subsection, Northern Ireland shall be treated as a separate foreign state, each colony or other component or dependent area of a foreign state overseas from the foreign state shall be treated as part of the foreign state, and the areas described in each of the following clauses shall be considered to be a separate region:

(i) Africa.

(ii) Asia.

(iii) Europe.

(iv) North America (other than Mexico).

(v) Oceania.

(vi) South America, Mexico, Central America, and the Caribbean.

(2) Requirement of education or work experience. An alien is not eligible for a visa under this subsection unless the alien—

(A) has at least a high school education or its equivalent, or

(B) has, within 5 years of the date of application for a visa under this subsection, at least 2 years of work experience in an occupation which requires at least 2 years of training or experience.

(3) Maintenance of information. The Secretary of State shall maintain information on the age, occupation, education level, and other relevant characteristics of immigrants issued visas under this subsection.

(d) Treatment of family members. A spouse or child as defined in subparagraph (A), (B), (C), (D), or (E) of section 101(b)(1) [8 USCS § 1101(b)(1)(A), (B), (C), (D), or (E)] shall, if not otherwise entitled to an immigrant status and the immediate issuance of a visa under subsection (a), (b), or (c), be entitled to the same status, and the same order of consideration provided in the respective subsection, if accompanying or following to join, the spouse or parent.

(e) Order of consideration.

(1) Immigrant visas made available under subsection (a) or (b) shall be issued to eligible immigrants in the order in which a petition in behalf of each such immigrant is filed with the Attorney General (or in the case of special immigrants under section 101(a)(27)(D) [8 USCS § 1101(a)(27)(D)], with the Secretary of State) as provided in section 204(a) [8 USCS § 1154(a)].

(2) Immigrant visa numbers made available under subsection (c) (relating to diversity immigrants) shall be issued to eligible qualified immigrants strictly in a random order established by the Secretary of State for the fiscal year involved.

(3) Waiting lists of applicants for visas under this section shall be maintained in accordance with regulations prescribed by the Secretary of State.

(f) Authorization for issuance. In the case of any alien claiming in his application for an immigrant visa to be described in section 201(b)(2) [8 USCS § 1151(b)(2)] or in subsection (a), (b), or (c) of this section, the consular officer shall not grant such status until he has been authorized to do so as provided by section 204 [8 USCS § 1154].

(g) Lists. For purposes of carrying out the Secretary's responsibilities in the orderly administration of this section, the Secretary of State may make reasonable estimates of the anticipated numbers of visas to be issued during any quarter of any fiscal year within each of the categories under subsections (a), (b), and (c) and to rely upon such estimates in authorizing the issuance of visas. The Secretary of State shall terminate the registration of any alien who fails to apply for an immigrant visa within one year following notification to the alien of the availability of such visa, but the Secretary shall reinstate the registration of any such alien who establishes within 2 years following the date of notification of the availability of such visa that such failure to apply was due to circumstances beyond the alien's control.

(h) Rules for determining whether certain aliens are children.

(1) In general. For purposes of subsections (a)(2)(A) and (d), a determination of whether an alien satisfies the age requirement in the matter preceding subparagraph (A) of section 101(b)(1) [8 USCS § 1101(b)(1)] shall be made using—

(A) the age of the alien on the date on which an immigrant visa number becomes available for such alien (or, in the case of subsection (d), the date on which an immigrant visa number became available for the alien's parent), but only if the alien has sought to acquire the status of an alien lawfully admitted for permanent residence within one year of such availability; reduced by

(B) the number of days in the period during which the applicable petition described in paragraph (2) was pending.

(2) Petitions described. The petition described in this paragraph is—

(A) with respect to a relationship described in subsection (a)(2)(A), a petition filed under section 204 [8 USCS § 1154] for classification of an alien child under subsection (a)(2)(A); or

(B) with respect to an alien child who is a derivative beneficiary under subsection (d), a petition filed under section 204 [8 USCS § 1154] for classification of the alien's parent under subsection (a), (b), or (c).

(3) Retention of priority date. If the age of an alien is determined under paragraph (1) to be 21 years of age or older for the purposes of subsections (a)(2)(A) and (d), the alien's petition shall automatically be converted to the appropriate category and the alien shall retain the original priority date issued upon receipt of the original petition.

(4) Application to self-petitions. Paragraphs (1) through (3) shall apply to self-petitioners and derivatives of self-petitioners.

(5) Age determination for children of alien investors. An alien who has reached 21 years of age and has been admitted under subsection (d) as a lawful permanent resident on a conditional basis as the child of an alien lawfully admitted for permanent residence under subsection (b)(5), whose lawful permanent resident status on a conditional basis is terminated under section 216A [8 USCS § 1186b] or subsection (b)(5)(M), shall continue to be considered a child of the principal alien for the purpose of a subsequent immigrant petition by such alien under subsection (b)(5) if the alien remains unmarried and the subsequent petition is filed by the principal alien not later than 1 year after the termination of conditional lawful permanent resident status. No alien shall be considered a child under this paragraph with respect to more than 1 petition filed after the alien reaches 21 years of age.

(June 27, 1952, ch 477, Title II, Ch 1, § 203, 66 Stat. 178; Sept. 11, 1957, P. L. 85-316, § 3, 71 Stat. 639; Sept. 22, 1959, P. L. 86-363, §§ 1–3, 73 Stat. 644; Oct. 3, 1965, P. L. 89-236, § 3, 79 Stat. 912; Oct. 20, 1976, P. L. 94-571, § 4, 90 Stat. 2705; Oct. 5, 1978, P. L. 95-412, §§ 1, 3, 92 Stat. 907, 917; Oct. 5, 1978, P. L. 95-417, § 1, 92 Stat. 917; March 17, 1980, P. L. 96-212, Title II, § 203(c), (i), 94 Stat. 107, 108; Nov. 29, 1990, P. L. 101-649, Title I, Subtitle B, Part 1, § 111, Part 2, § 121(a), Part 3, § 131, Subtitle E, § 162(a)(1),Title VI, § 603(a)(3), 104 Stat. 4986, 4987, 4997, 5009, 5082; Oct. 1, 1991, P. L. 102-110, § 2(b), 105 Stat. 555; Dec. 12, 1991, P. L. 102-232, Title III, § 302(b)(2), (e)(3), 105 Stat. 1743, 1745; Oct. 25, 1994, P. L. 103-416, Title II, §§ 212(b), 219(c), 108 Stat. 4314, 4316; Nov. 12, 1999, P. L. 106-95, § 5, 113 Stat. 1318; Nov. 29, 1999, P. L. 106-113, Div B, § 1000(a)(1), 113 Stat. 1535; Nov. 22, 2000, P. L. 106-536, § 1(b)(1), 114 Stat. 2560; Aug. 6, 2002, P. L. 107-208, § 3, 116 Stat. 928; Nov. 2, 2002, P. L. 107-273, Div C, Title I, Subtitle B, Ch. 2, §§ 11035, 11036(a), 116 Stat. 1846; Jan. 5, 2006, P. L. 109-162, Title VIII, Subtitle A, § 805(b)(2), 119 Stat. 3056; Mar. 15, 2022, P.L. 117-103, Div BB, §§ 102(a), (b), 103(b)(1), (c)(1), 108, 136 Stat. 1070, 1074, 1075, 1100, 1109.)

§ 1153a. Transparency

(a) In general. Employees of the Department of Homeland Security, including the Secretary of Homeland Security, the Secretary's counselors, the Assistant Secretary for the Private Sector, the Director of U.S. Citizenship and Immigration Services, counselors to such Director, and the Chief of the Immigrant Investor Programs Office (or any successor to such Office) at U.S. Citizenship and Immigration Services, shall act impartially and may not give preferential treatment to any entity, organization, or individual in connection with any aspect of the immigrant visa program described in section 203(b)(5) of the Immigration and Nationality Act (8 U.S.C. 1153(b)(5)).

(b) Improper activities. Activities that constitute preferential treatment under subsection (a) shall include—

(1) working on, or in any way attempting to influence, in a manner not available to or accorded to all other petitioners, applicants, and seekers of benefits under the immigrant visa program referred to in subsection (a), the standard processing of an application, petition, or benefit for—

(A) a regional center;

(B) a new commercial enterprise;

(C) a job-creating entity; or

(D) any person or entity associated with such regional center, new commercial enterprise, or job-creating entity; and

(2) meeting or communicating with persons associated with the entities listed in paragraph (1), at the request of such persons, in a manner not available to or accorded to all other petitioners, applicants, and seekers of benefits under such immigrant visa program.

(c) Reporting of communications.

(1) Written communication. Employees of the Department of Homeland Security, including the officials listed in subsection (a), shall include, in the record of proceeding for a case under section 203(b)(5) of the Immigration and Nationality Act (8 U.S.C. 1153(b)(5)), actual or electronic copies of all case-specific written communication, including emails from government and private accounts, with non-Department persons or entities advocating for regional center applications or individual petitions under such section that are pending on or after the date of the enactment of this Act [enacted March 15, 2022] (other than routine communications with other agencies of the Federal Government regarding the case, including communications involving background checks and litigation defense).

(2) Oral communication. If substantive oral communication, including telephonic communication, virtual communication, or in-person meetings, takes place between officials of the Department of Homeland Security and non-Department persons or entities advocating for regional center applications or individual petitions under section 203(b)(5) of such Act [8 USCS § 1153(b)(5)] that are pending on or after the date of the enactment of this Act [enacted March 15, 2022] (except communications exempted under paragraph (1))—

(A) the conversation shall be recorded; or

(B) detailed minutes of the session shall be taken and included in the record of proceeding.

(3) Notification.

(A) In general. If the Secretary, in the course of written or oral communication described in this subsection, receives evidence about a specific case from anyone other than an affected party or his or her representative (excluding Federal Government or law enforcement sources), such information may not be made part of the record of proceeding and may not be considered in adjudicative proceedings unless—

(i) the affected party has been given notice of such evidence; and

(ii) if such evidence is derogatory, the affected party has been given an opportunity to respond to the evidence.

(B) Information from law enforcement, intelligence agencies, or confidential sources.

(i) Law enforcement or intelligence agencies. Evidence received from law enforcement or intelligence agencies may not be made part of the record of proceeding without the consent of the relevant agency or law enforcement entity.

(ii) Whistleblowers, confidential sources, or intelligence agencies. Evidence received from whistleblowers, other confidential sources, or the intelligence community that is included in the record of proceeding and considered in adjudicative proceedings shall be handled in a manner that does not reveal the identity of the whistleblower or confidential source, or reveal classified information.

(d) Consideration of evidence.

(1) In general. No case-specific communication with persons or entities that are not part of the Department of Homeland Security may be considered in the adjudication of an application or petition under section 203(b)(5) of the Immigration and Nationality Act (8 U.S.C. 1153(b)(5)) unless the communication is included in the record of proceeding of the case.

(2) Waiver. The Secretary of Homeland Security may waive the requirement under paragraph (1) only in the interests of national security or for investigative or law enforcement purposes.

(e) Channels of communication.

(1) Email address or equivalent. The Director of U.S. Citizenship and Immigration Services shall maintain an email account (or equivalent means of communication) for persons or entities—

(A) with inquiries regarding specific petitions or applications under the immigrant visa program described in section 203(b)(5) of the Immigration and Nationality Act (8 U.S.C. 1153(b)(5)); or

(B) seeking information that is not case-specific about the immigrant visa program described in such section 203(b)(5) [8 USCS § 1153(b)(5)].

(2) Communication only through appropriate channels or offices.

(A) Announcement of appropriate channels of communication. Not later than 40 days after the date of the enactment of this Act [enacted March 15, 2022], the Director of U.S. Citizenship and Immigration Services shall announce that the only channels or offices by which industry stakeholders, petitioners, applicants, and seekers of benefits under the immigrant visa program described in section 203(b)(5) of the Immigration and Nationality Act (8 U.S.C. 1153(b)(5)) may communicate with the Department of Homeland Security regarding specific cases under such section (except for communication made by applicants and petitioners pursuant to regular adjudicatory procedures), or information that is not case-specific about the visa program applicable to certain cases under such section, are through—

(i) the email address or equivalent channel described in paragraph (1);

(ii) the National Customer Service Center, or any successor to such Center; or

(iii) the Office of Public Engagement, Immigrant Investor Program Office, including the Stakeholder Engagement Branch, or any successors to those Offices or that Branch.

(B) Direction of incoming communications.

(i) In general. Employees of the Department of Homeland Security shall direct communications described in subparagraph (A) to the channels of communication or offices listed in clauses (i) through (iii) of subparagraph (A).

(ii) Rule of construction. Nothing in this subparagraph may be construed to prevent—

(I) any person from communicating with the Ombudsman of U.S. Citizenship and Immigration Services regarding the immigrant investor program under section 203(b)(5) of the Immigration and Nationality Act (8 U.S.C. 1153(b)(5)); or

(II) the Ombudsman from resolving problems regarding such immigrant investor program pursuant to the authority granted under section 452 of the Homeland Security Act of 2002 (6 U.S.C. 272).

(C) Log.

(i) In general. The Director of U.S. Citizenship and Immigration Services shall maintain a written or electronic log of—

(I) all communications described in subparagraph (A) and communications from Members of Congress, which shall reference the date, time, and subject of the communication, and the identity of the Department official, if any, to whom the inquiry was forwarded;

(II) with respect to written communications described in subsection (c)(1), the date on which the communication was received, the identities of the sender and addressee, and the subject of the communication; and

(III) with respect to oral communications described in subsection (c)(2), the date on which the communication occurred, the participants in the conversation or meeting, and the subject of the communication.

(ii) Transparency. The log of communications described in clause (i) shall be made publicly available in accordance with section 552 of title 5, United States Code (commonly known as the "Freedom of Information Act").

(3) Publication of information. Not later than 30 days after a person or entity inquiring about a specific case or generally about the immigrant visa program described in section 203(b)(5) of the Immigration and Nationality Act (8 U.S.C. 1153(b)(5)) receives, as a result of a communication with an official of the Department of Homeland Security, generally applicable information that is not case-specific about program requirements or administration that has not been made publicly available by the Department, the Director of U.S. Citizenship and Immigration Services shall publish such information on the U.S. Citizenship and Immigration Services website as an update to the relevant Frequently Asked Questions page or by some other comparable mechanism.

(f) Penalty.

(1) In general. Any person who intentionally violates the prohibition on preferential treatment under this section or intentionally violates the reporting requirements under subsection (c) shall be disciplined in accordance with paragraph (2).

(2) Sanctions. Not later than 90 days after the date of the enactment of this Act [enacted March 15, 2022], the Secretary of Homeland Security shall establish a graduated set of sanctions based on the severity of the violation referred to in paragraph (1), which may include, in addition to any criminal or civil penalties that may be imposed, written reprimand, suspension, demotion, or removal.

(g) Rule of construction regarding classified information. Nothing in this section may be construed to modify any law, regulation, or policy regarding the handling or disclosure of classified information.

(h) Rule of construction regarding private right of action. Nothing in this section may be construed to create or authorize a private right of action to challenge a decision of an employee of the Department of Homeland Security.

(i) Effective date. This section, and the amendments made by this section, shall take effect on the date of the enactment of this Act [enacted March 15, 2022].

(March 15, 2022, P.L. 117-103, Div BB, § 107, 136 Stat. 1105.)

§ 1154. Procedure for granting immigrant status

(a) Petitioning procedure.

(1)(A)(i) Except as provided in clause (viii), any citizen of the United States claiming that an alien is entitled to classification by reason of a relationship described in paragraph (1), (3), or (4) of section 203(a) [8 USCS § 1153(a)] or to an immediate relative status under section 201(b)(2)(A)(i) [8 USCS § 1151(b)(2)(A)(i)] may file a petition with the Attorney General for such classification.

(ii) An alien spouse described in the second sentence of section 201(b)(2)(A)(i) [8 USCS § 1151(b)(2)(A)(i)] also may file a petition with the Attorney General under this subparagraph for classification of the alien (and the alien's children) under such section.

(iii)(I) An alien who is described in subclause (II) may file a petition with the Attorney General under this clause for classification of the alien (and any child of the alien) if the alien demonstrates to the Attorney General that—

(aa) the marriage or the intent to marry the United States citizen was entered into in good faith by the alien; and

(bb) during the marriage or relationship intended by the alien to be legally a marriage, the alien or a child of the alien has been battered or has been the subject of extreme cruelty perpetrated by the alien's spouse or intended spouse.

(II) For purposes of subclause (I), an alien described in this subclause is an alien—

(aa)(AA) who is the spouse of a citizen of the United States;

(BB) who believed that he or she had married a citizen of the United States and with whom a marriage ceremony was actually performed and who otherwise meets any applicable requirements under this Act to establish the existence of and bona fides of a marriage, but whose marriage is not legitimate solely because of the bigamy of such citizen of the United States; or

(CC) who was a bona fide spouse of a United States citizen within the past 2 years and—

(aaa) whose spouse died within the past 2 years;

(bbb) whose spouse lost or renounced citizenship status within the past 2 years related to an incident of domestic violence; or

(ccc) who demonstrates a connection between the legal termination of the marriage within the past 2 years and battering or extreme cruelty by the United States citizen spouse;

(bb) who is a person of good moral character;

(cc) who is eligible to be classified as an immediate relative under section 201(b)(2)(A)(i) [8 USCS § 1151(b)(2)(A)(i)] or who would have been so classified but for the bigamy of the citizen of the United States that the alien intended to marry; and

(dd) who has resided with the alien's spouse or intended spouse.

(iv) An alien who is the child of a citizen of the United States, or who was a child of a United States citizen parent who within the past 2 years lost or renounced citizenship status related to an incident of domestic violence, and who is a person of good moral character, who is eligible to be classified as an immediate relative under section 201(b)(2)(A)(i) [8 USCS § 1151(b)(2)(A)(i)], and who resides, or has resided in the past, with the citizen parent may file a petition with the Attorney General under this subparagraph for classification of the alien (and any child of the alien) under such section if the alien demonstrates to the Attorney General that the alien has been battered by or has been the subject of extreme cruelty perpetrated by the alien's citizen parent. For purposes of this clause, residence includes any period of visitation.

(v) An alien who—

(I) is the spouse, intended spouse, or child living abroad of a citizen who—

(aa) is an employee of the United States Government;

(bb) is a member of the uniformed services (as defined in section 101(a) of title 10, United States Code); or

(cc) has subjected the alien or the alien's child to battery or extreme cruelty in the United States; and

(II) is eligible to file a petition under clause (iii) or (iv),

shall file such petition with the Attorney General under the procedures that apply to self-petitioners under clause (iii) or (iv), as applicable.

(vi) For the purposes of any petition filed under clause (iii) or (iv), the denaturalization, loss or renunciation of citizenship, death of the abuser, divorce, or changes to the abuser's citizenship status after filing of the petition shall not adversely affect the approval of the petition, and for approved petitions shall not preclude the classification of the eligible self-petitioning spouse or child as an immediate relative or affect the alien's ability to adjust status under subsections (a) and

(c) of section 245 [8 USCS § 1255] or obtain status as a lawful permanent resident based on the approved self-petition under such clauses.

(vii) An alien may file a petition with the Secretary of Homeland Security under this subparagraph for classification of the alien under section 201(b)(2)(A)(i) [8 USCS § 1151(b)(2)(A)(i)] if the alien—

(I) is the parent of a citizen of the United States or was a parent of a citizen of the United States who, within the past 2 years, lost or renounced citizenship status related to an incident of domestic violence or died;

(II) is a person of good moral character;

(III) is eligible to be classified as an immediate relative under section 201(b)(2)(A)(i) [8 USCS § 1151(b)(2)(A)(i)];

(IV) resides, or has resided, with the citizen daughter or son; and

(V) demonstrates that the alien has been battered or subject to extreme cruelty by the citizen daughter or son.

(viii)(I) Clause (i) shall not apply to a citizen of the United States who has been convicted of a specified offense against a minor, unless the Secretary of Homeland Security, in the Secretary's sole and unreviewable discretion, determines that the citizen poses no risk to the alien with respect to whom a petition described in clause (i) is filed.

(II) For purposes of subclause (I), the term "specified offense against a minor" is defined as in section 111 of the Adam Walsh Child Protection and Safety Act of 2006 [34 USCS § 20911].

(B)(i)(I) Except as provided in subclause (II), any alien lawfully admitted for permanent residence claiming that an alien is entitled to a classification by reason of the relationship described in section 203(a)(2) [8 USCS § 1153(a)(2)] may file a petition with the Attorney General for such classification.

[(II)](I) Subclause (I) shall not apply in the case of an alien lawfully admitted for permanent residence who has been convicted of a specified offense against a minor (as defined in subparagraph (A)(viii)(II)), unless the Secretary of Homeland Security, in the Secretary's sole and unreviewable discretion, determines that such person poses no risk to the alien with respect to whom a petition described in subclause (I) is filed.

(ii)(I) An alien who is described in subclause (II) may file a petition with the Attorney General under this clause for classification of the alien (and any child of the alien) if such a child has not been classified under clause (iii) of section 203(a)(2)(A) [8 USCS § 1153(a)(2)(A)] and if the alien demonstrates to the Attorney General that—

(aa) the marriage or the intent to marry the lawful permanent resident was entered into in good faith by the alien; and

(bb) during the marriage or relationship intended by the alien to be legally a marriage, the alien or a child of the alien has been battered or has been the subject of extreme cruelty perpetrated by the alien's spouse or intended spouse.

(II) For purposes of subclause (I), an alien described in this paragraph is an alien—

(aa)(AA) who is the spouse of a lawful permanent resident of the United States; or

(BB) who believed that he or she had married a lawful permanent resident of the United States and with whom a marriage ceremony was actually performed and who otherwise meets any applicable requirements under this Act to establish the existence of and bona fides of a marriage, but whose marriage is not legitimate solely because of the bigamy of such lawful permanent resident of the United States; or

(CC) who was a bona fide spouse of a lawful permanent resident within the past 2 years and—

(aaa) whose spouse lost status within the past 2 years due to an incident of domestic violence; or

(bbb) who demonstrates a connection between the legal termination of the marriage within the past 2 years and battering or extreme cruelty by the lawful permanent resident spouse;

(bb) who is a person of good moral character;

(cc) who is eligible to be classified as a spouse of an alien lawfully admitted for permanent residence under section 203(a)(2)(A) [8 USCS § 1153(a)(2)(A)] or who would have been so classified but for the bigamy of the lawful permanent resident of the United States that the alien intended to marry; and

(dd) who has resided with the alien's spouse or intended spouse.

(iii) An alien who is the child of an alien lawfully admitted for permanent residence, or who was the child of a lawful permanent resident who within the past 2 years lost lawful permanent resident status due to an incident of domestic violence, and who is a person of good moral character, who is eligible for classification under section 203(a)(2)(A) [8 USCS § 1153(a)(2)(A)], and who resides, or has resided in the past, with the alien's permanent resident alien parent may file a petition with the Attorney General under this subparagraph for classification of the alien (and any child of the alien) under such section if the alien demonstrates to the Attorney General that the alien has been battered by or has been the subject of extreme cruelty perpetrated by the alien's permanent resident parent.

(iv) An alien who—

(I) is the spouse, intended spouse, or child living abroad of a lawful permanent resident who—

(aa) is an employee of the United States Government;

(bb) is a member of the uniformed services (as defined in section 101(a) of title 10, United States Code); or

(cc) has subjected the alien or the alien's child to battery or extreme cruelty in the United States; and

(II) is eligible to file a petition under clause (ii) or (iii),

shall file such petition with the Attorney General under the procedures that apply to self-petitioners under clause (ii) or (iii), as applicable.

(v)(I) For the purposes of any petition filed or approved under clause (ii) or (iii), divorce, or the loss of lawful permanent resident status by a spouse or parent after the filing of a petition under that clause shall not adversely affect approval of the petition, and, for an approved petition, shall not affect the alien's ability to adjust status under subsections (a) and (c) of section 245 [8 USCS § 1255] or obtain status as a lawful permanent resident based on an approved self-petition under clause (ii) or (iii).

(II) Upon the lawful permanent resident spouse or parent becoming or establishing the existence of United States citizenship through naturalization, acquisition of citizenship, or other means, any petition filed with the Immigration and Naturalization Service and pending or approved under clause (ii) or (iii) on behalf of an alien who has been battered or subjected to extreme cruelty shall be deemed reclassified as a petition filed under subparagraph (A) even if the acquisition of citizenship occurs after divorce or termination of parental rights.

(C) Notwithstanding section 101(f) [8 USCS § 1101(f)], an act or conviction that is waivable with respect to the petitioner for purposes of a determination of the petitioner's admissibility under section 212(a) [8 USCS § 1182(a)] or deportability under section 237(a) [8 USCS § 1227(a)] shall not bar the Attorney General from finding the petitioner to be of good moral character under subparagraph (A)(iii), (A)(iv), (B)(ii), or (B)(iii) if the Attorney General finds that the act or conviction was connected to the alien's having been battered or subjected to extreme cruelty.

(D)(i)(I) Any child who attains 21 years of age who has filed a petition under clause (iv) of section 204(a)(1)(A) or section 204(a)(1)(B)(iii) [subsec. (a)(1)(A) or (a)(1)(B)(iii) of this section] that was filed or approved before the date on which the child attained 21 years of age shall be considered (if the child has not been admitted or approved for lawful permanent residence by the date the child attained 21 years of age) a petitioner for preference status under paragraph (1), (2), or (3) of section 203(a) [8 USCS § 1153(a)], whichever paragraph is applicable, with the same priority date assigned to the self-petition filed under clause (iv) of section 204(a)(1)(A) or section 204(a)(1)(B)(iii) [subsec. (a)(1)(A) or (a)(1)(B)(iii) of this section]. No new petition shall be required to be filed.

(II) Any individual described in subclause (I) is eligible for deferred action and work authorization.

(III) Any derivative child who attains 21 years of age who is included in a petition described in clause (ii) that was filed or approved before the date on which the child attained 21 years of age shall be considered (if the child has not been admitted or approved for lawful permanent residence by the date the child attained 21 years of age) a VAWA self-petitioner with the same priority date as that assigned to the petitioner in any petition described in clause (ii). No new petition shall be required to be filed.

(IV) Any individual described in subclause (III) and any derivative child of a petition described in clause (ii) is eligible for deferred action and work authorization.

(ii) The petition referred to in clause (i)(III) is a petition filed by an alien under subparagraph (A)(iii), (A)(iv), (B)(ii) or (B)(iii) in which the child is included as a derivative beneficiary.

(iii) Nothing in the amendments made by the Child Status Protection Act shall be construed to limit or deny any right or benefit provided under this subparagraph.

(iv) Any alien who benefits from this subparagraph may adjust status in accordance with subsections (a) and (c) of section 245 [8 USCS § 1255] as an alien having an approved petition for classification under subparagraph (A)(iii), (A)(iv), (B)(ii), or (B)(iii).

(v) For purposes of this paragraph, an individual who is not less than 21 years of age, who qualified to file a petition under subparagraph (A)(iv) or (B)(iii) as of the day before the date on which the individual attained 21 years of age, and who did not file such a petition before such day, shall be treated as having filed a petition under such subparagraph as of such day if a petition is filed for the status described in such subparagraph before the individual attains 25 years of age and the individual shows that the abuse was at least one central reason for the filing delay. Clauses (i) through (iv) of this subparagraph shall apply to an individual described in this clause in the same manner as an individual filing a petition under subparagraph (A)(iv) or (B)(iii).

(E) Any alien desiring to be classified under section 203(b)(1)(A) [8 USCS § 1153(b)(1)(A)], or any person on behalf of such an alien, may file a petition with the Attorney General for such classification.

(F) Any employer desiring and intending to employ within the United States an alien entitled to classification under section 203(b)(1)(B), 203(b)(1)(C), 203(b)(2), or 203(b)(3) [8 USCS § 1153(b)(1)(B), (C), (2), or (3)] may file a petition with the Attorney General for such classification.

(G)(i) Any alien (other than a special immigrant under section 101(a)(27)(D) [8 USCS § 1101(a)(27)(D)] desiring to be classified under section 203(b)(4) [8 USCS § 1153(b)(4)], or any person on behalf of such an alien, may file a petition with the Attorney General for such classification.

(ii) Aliens claiming status as a special immigrant under section 101(a)(27)(D) [8 USCS § 1101(a)(27)(D)] may file a petition only with the Secretary of State and only after notification by the Secretary that such status has been recommended and approved pursuant to such section.

(H)(i) Any alien seeking classification under section 203(b)(5) [8 USCS § 1153(b)(5)] may file a petition for such classification with the Secretary of Homeland Security. An alien seeking to pool his or her investment with 1 or more additional aliens seeking classification under section 203(b)(5) [8 USCS § 1153(b)(5)] shall file for such classification in accordance with section 203(b)(5)(E) [8 USCS § 1153(b)(5)(E)], or before the date of the enactment of the EB-5 Reform and Integrity Act of 2022 [enacted March 15, 2022], in accordance with section 203(b)(5) [8 USCS § 1153(b)(5)]. An alien petitioning for classification under section 203(b)(5)(E) [8 USCS § 1153(b)(5)(E)] may file a petition with the Secretary after a regional center has filed an application for approval of an investment under section 203(b)(5)(F) [8 USCS § 1153(b)(5)(F)].

(ii) A petitioner described in clause (i) shall establish eligibility at the time he or she files a petition for classification under section 203(b)(5) [8 USCS § 1153(b)(5)]. A petitioner who was eligible for such classification at the time of such filing shall be deemed eligible for such classification at the time such petition is adjudicated, subject to the approval of the petitioner's associated application under section 203(b)(5)(F) [8 USCS § 1153(b)(5)(F)], if applicable.

(I)(i) Any alien desiring to be provided an immigrant visa under section 203(c) [8 USCS § 1153(c)] may file a petition at the place and time determined by the Secretary of State by regulation. Only one such petition may be filed by an alien with respect to any petitioning period established. If more than one petition is submitted all such petitions submitted for such period by the alien shall be voided.

(ii)(I) The Secretary of State shall designate a period for the filing of petitions with respect to visas which may be issued under section 203(c) [8 USCS § 1153(c)] for the fiscal year beginning after the end of the period.

(II) Aliens who qualify, through random selection, for a visa under section 203(c) [8 USCS § 1153(c)] shall remain eligible to receive such visa only through the end of the specific fiscal year for which they were selected.

(III) The Secretary of State shall prescribe such regulations as may be necessary to carry out this clause.

(iii) A petition under this subparagraph shall be in such form as the Secretary of State may by regulation prescribe and shall contain such information and be supported by such documentary evidence as the Secretary of State may require.

(J) In acting on petitions filed under clause (iii) or (iv) of subparagraph (A) or clause (ii) or (iii) of subparagraph (B), or in making determinations under subparagraphs (C) and (D), the Attorney General shall consider any credible evidence relevant to the petition. The determination of what evidence is credible and the weight to be given that evidence shall be within the sole discretion of the Attorney General.

(K) Upon the approval of a petition as a VAWA self-petitioner, the alien—

(i) is eligible for work authorization; and

(ii) may be provided an "employment authorized" endorsement or appropriate work permit incidental to such approval.

(L) Notwithstanding the previous provisions of this paragraph, an individual who was a VAWA petitioner or who had the status of a nonimmigrant under subparagraph (T) or (U) of section 101(a)(15) [8 USCS § 1101(a)(15)] may not file a petition for classification under this section or section 214 [8 USCS § 1184] to classify any person who committed the battery or extreme cruelty or trafficking against the individual (or the individual's child) which established the individual's (or individual's child [child's]) eligibility as a VAWA petitioner or for such nonimmigrant status.

(2)(A) The Attorney General may not approve a spousal second preference petition for the classification of the spouse of an alien if the alien, by virtue of a prior marriage, has been accorded the status of an alien lawfully admitted for permanent residence as the spouse of a citizen of the United States or as the spouse of an alien lawfully admitted for permanent residence, unless—

(i) a period of 5 years has elapsed after the date the alien acquired the status of an alien lawfully admitted for permanent residence, or

(ii) the alien establishes to the satisfaction of the Attorney General by clear and convincing evidence that the prior marriage (on the basis of which the alien obtained the status of an alien lawfully admitted for permanent residence) was not entered into for the purpose of evading any provision of the immigration laws.

In this subparagraph, the term "spousal second preference petition" refers to a petition, seeking preference status under section 203(a)(2) [8 USCS § 1153(a)(2)], for an alien as a spouse of an alien lawfully admitted for permanent residence.

(B) Subparagraph (A) shall not apply to a petition filed for the classification of the spouse of an alien if the prior marriage of the alien was terminated by the death of his or her spouse.

(b) Investigation; consultation; approval; authorization to grant preference status. After an investigation of the facts in each case, and after consultation with the Secretary of Labor with respect to petitions to accord a status under section 203(b)(2) or 203(b)(3) [8 USCS § 1153(b)(2) or (3)], the Attorney General shall, if he determines that the facts stated in the petition are true and that the alien in behalf of whom the petition is made is an immediate relative specified in section 201(b) [8 USCS § 1151(b)] or is eligible for preference under subsection (a) or (b) of section 203 [8 USCS § 1153], approve the petition and forward one copy thereof to the Department of State. The Secretary of State shall then authorize the consular officer concerned to grant the preference status.

(c) Limitation on orphan petitions approved for a single petitioner; prohibition against approval in cases of marriages entered into in order to evade immigration laws; restriction on future entry of aliens involved with marriage fraud. Notwithstanding the provisions of subsection (b) no petition shall be approved if (1) the alien has previously been accorded, or has sought to be accorded, an immediate relative or preference status as the spouse of a citizen of the United States or the spouse of an alien lawfully admitted for permanent residence, by reason of a marriage determined by the Attorney General to have been entered into for the purpose of evading the immigration laws, or (2) the Attorney General has determined that the alien has attempted or conspired to enter into a marriage for the purpose of evading the immigration laws.

(d) Recommendation of valid home-study.

(1) Notwithstanding the provisions of subsections (a) and (b) no petition may be approved on behalf of a child

defined in subparagraph (F) or (G) of section 101(b)(1) [8 USCS § 1101(b)(1)] unless a valid home-study has been favorably recommended by an agency of the State of the child's proposed residence, or by an agency authorized by that State to conduct such a study, or, in the case of a child adopted abroad, by an appropriate public or private adoption agency which is licensed in the United States.

(2) Notwithstanding the provisions of subsections (a) and (b), no petition may be approved on behalf of a child defined in section 101(b)(1)(G) [8 USCS § 1101(b)(1)(G)] unless the Secretary of State has certified that the central authority of the child's country of origin has notified the United States central authority under the convention referred to in such section 101(b)(1)(G) [8 USCS § 1101(b)(1)(G)] that a United States citizen habitually resident in the United States has effected final adoption of the child, or has been granted custody of the child for the purpose of emigration and adoption, in accordance with such convention and the Intercountry Adoption Act of 2000.

(e) Subsequent finding of non-entitlement to preference classification. Nothing in this section shall be construed to entitle an immigrant, in behalf of whom a petition under this section is approved, to be admitted [to] the United States as an immigrant under subsection (a), (b), or (c) of section 203 [8 USCS § 1153] or as an immediate relative under section 201(b) [8 USCS § 1151(b)] if upon his arrival at a port of entry in the United States he is found not to be entitled to such classification.

(f) Preferential treatment for children fathered by United States citizens and born in Korea, Vietnam, Laos, Kampuchea, or Thailand after 1950 and before Oct. 22, 1982.

(1) Any alien claiming to be an alien described in paragraph (2)(A) of this subsection (or any person on behalf of such an alien) may file a petition with the Attorney General for classification under section 201(b), 203(a)(1), or 203(a)(3) [8 USCS § 1151(b), 1153(a)(1), or (3)], as appropriate. After an investigation of the facts of each case the Attorney General shall, if the conditions described in paragraph (2) are met, approve the petition and forward one copy to the Secretary of State.

(2) The Attorney General may approve a petition for an alien under paragraph (1) if—

(A) he has reason to believe that the alien was born in Korea, Vietnam, Laos, Kampuchea, or Thailand after 1950 and before the date of the enactment of this subsection [enacted Oct. 22, 1982], and was fathered by a United States citizen;

(B) he has received an acceptable guarantee of legal custody and financial responsibility described in paragraph (4); and

(C) in the case of an alien under eighteen years of age, (i) the alien's placement with a sponsor in the United States has been arranged by an appropriate public, private, or State child welfare agency licensed in the United States and actively involved in the intercountry placement of children and (ii) the alien's mother or guardian has in writing irrevocably released the alien for emigration.

(3) In considering petitions filed under paragraph (1), the Attorney General shall—

(A) consult with appropriate governmental officials and officials of private voluntary organizations in the country of the alien's birth in order to make the determinations described in subparagraphs (A) and (C)(ii) of paragraph 2[(2)]; and

(B) consider the physical appearance of the alien and any evidence provided by the petitioner, including birth and baptismal certificates, local civil records, photographs of, and letters or proof of financial support from, a putative father who is a citizen of the United States, and the testimony of witnesses, to the extent it is relevant or probative.

(4)(A) A guarantee of legal custody and financial responsibility for an alien described in paragraph (2) must—

(i) be signed in the presence of an immigration officer or consular officer by an individual (hereinafter in this paragraph referred to as the "sponsor") who is twenty-one years of age or older, is of good moral character, and is a citizen of the United States or alien lawfully admitted for permanent residence, and

(ii) provide that the sponsor agrees (I) in the case of an alien under eighteen years of age, to assume legal custody for the alien after the alien's departure to the United States and until the alien becomes eighteen years of age, in accordance with the laws of the State where the alien and the sponsor will reside, and (II) to furnish, during the five-year period beginning on the date of the alien's acquiring the status of an alien lawfully admitted for permanent residence, or during the period beginning on the date of the alien's acquiring the status of an alien lawfully admitted for permanent residence and ending on the date on which the alien becomes twenty-one years of age, whichever period is longer, such financial support as is necessary to maintain the family in the United States of which the alien is a member at a level equal to at least 125 per centum of the current official poverty line (as established by the Director of the Office of Management and Budget, under section 673(2) of the Omnibus Budget Reconciliation Act of 1981 [42 USCS § 9902(2)] and as revised by the Secretary of Health and Human Services under the second and third sentences of such section) for a family of the same size as the size of the alien's family.

(B) A guarantee of legal custody and financial responsibility described in subparagraph (A) may be enforced with respect to an alien against his sponsor in a civil suit brought by the Attorney General in the United States district court for the district in which the sponsor resides, except that a sponsor or his estate shall not be liable under such a guarantee if the sponsor dies or is adjudicated a bankrupt under title 11, United States Code [11 USCS §§ 101 et seq.].

(g) Restriction on petitions based on marriages entered while in exclusion or deportation proceedings. Notwithstanding subsection (a), except as provided in section 245(e)(3) [8 USCS § 1255(e)(3)], a petition may not be approved to grant an alien immediate relative status or preference status by reason of a marriage which was entered into during the period described in section 245(e)(2) [8 USCS § 1255(e)(2)], until the alien has resided outside the United States for a 2-year period beginning after the date of the marriage.

(h) Survival of rights to petition. The legal termination of a marriage may not be the sole basis for revocation under section 205 [8 USCS § 1155] of a petition filed under subsection (a)(1)(A)(iii) or a petition filed under subsection (a)(1)(B)(ii) pursuant to conditions described in subsection (a)(1)(A)(iii)(I). Remarriage of an alien whose petition was approved under section 204(a)(1)(B)(ii) or 204(a)(1)(A)(iii) [subsec. (a)(1)(B)(ii) or (a)(1)(A)(iii) of this section] or marriage of an alien described in clause (iv) or (vi) of section 204(a)(1)(A) or in section 204(a)(1)(B)(iii) [subsec. (a)(1)(A) or (a)(1)(B)(iii) of this section] shall not be the basis for revocation of a petition approval under section 205 [8 USCS § 1155].

(i) Professional athletes.

(1) In general. A petition under subsection (a)(4)(D) [(a)(1)(D)] for classification of a professional athlete shall remain valid for the athlete after the athlete changes employers, if the new employer is a team in the same sport as the team which was the employer who filed the petition.

(2) Definition. For purposes of paragraph (1), the term "professional athlete" means an individual who is employed as an athlete by—

(A) a team that is a member of an association of 6 or more professional sports teams whose total combined revenues exceed $10,000,000 per year, if the association governs the conduct of its members and regulates the contests and exhibitions in which its member teams regularly engage; or

(B) any minor league team that is affiliated with such an association.

(j) Job flexibility for long delayed applicants for adjustment of status to permanent residence. A petition under subsection (a)(1)(D) for an individual whose application for adjustment of status pursuant to section 245 [8 USCS § 1255] has been filed and remained unadjudicated for 180 days or more shall remain valid with respect to a new job if the individual changes jobs or employers if the new job is in the same or a similar occupational classification as the job for which the petition was filed.

(k) Procedures for unmarried sons and daughters of citizens.

(1) In general. Except as provided in paragraph (2), in the case of a petition under this section initially filed for an alien unmarried son or daughter's classification as a family-sponsored immigrant under section 203(a)(2)(B) [8 USCS § 1153(a)(2)(B)], based on a parent of the son or daughter being an alien lawfully admitted for permanent residence, if such parent subsequently becomes a naturalized citizen of the United States, such petition shall be converted to a petition to classify the unmarried son or daughter as a family-sponsored immigrant under section 203(a)(1) [8 USCS § 1153(a)(1)].

(2) Exception. Paragraph (1) does not apply if the son or daughter files with the Attorney General a written statement that he or she elects not to have such conversion occur (or if it has occurred, to have such conversion revoked). Where such an election has been made, any determination with respect to the son or daughter's eligibility for admission as a family-sponsored immigrant shall be made as if such naturalization had not taken place.

(3) Priority date. Regardless of whether a petition is converted under this subsection or not, if an unmarried son or daughter described in this subsection was assigned a priority date with respect to such petition before such naturalization, he or she may maintain that priority date.

(4) Clarification. This subsection shall apply to a petition if it is properly filed, regardless of whether it was approved or not before such naturalization.

(l) Surviving relative consideration for certain petitions and applications.

(1) In general. An alien described in paragraph (2) who resided in the United States at the time of the death of the qualifying relative and who continues to reside in the United States shall have such petition described in paragraph (2), or an application for adjustment of status to that of a person admitted for lawful permanent residence based upon the family relationship described in paragraph (2), and any related applications, adjudicated notwithstanding the death of the qualifying relative, unless the Secretary of Homeland Security determines, in the unreviewable discretion of the Secretary, that approval would not be in the public interest.

(2) Alien described. An alien described in this paragraph is an alien who, immediately prior to the death of his or her qualifying relative, was—

(A) the beneficiary of a pending or approved petition for classification as an immediate relative (as described in section 201(b)(2)(A)(i) [8 USCS § 1151(b)(2)(A)(i)]);

(B) the beneficiary of a pending or approved petition for classification under section 203(a) or (d) [8 USCS § 1153(a) or (d)];

(C) a derivative beneficiary of a pending or approved petition for classification under section 203(b) [8 USCS § 1153(b)] (as described in section 203(d) [8 USCS § 1153(d)]);

(D) the beneficiary of a pending or approved refugee/asylee relative petition under section 207 or 208 [8 USCS § 1157 or 1158];

(E) an alien admitted in "T" nonimmigrant status as described in section 101(a)(15)(T)(ii) [8 USCS § 1101(a)(15)(T)(ii)] or in "U" nonimmigrant status as described in section 101(a)(15)(U)(ii) [8 USCS § 1101(a)(15)(U)(ii)];

(F) a child of an alien who filed a pending or approved petition for classification or application for adjustment of status or other benefit specified in section 101(a)(51) [8 USCS § 1101(a)(51)] as a VAWA self-petitioner; or

(G) an asylee (as described in section 208(b)(3) [8 USCS § 1158(b)(3)]).

(June 27, 1952, ch 477, Title II, Ch 1, § 204, 66 Stat. 179; Oct. 24, 1962, P. L. 87-885, § 3, 76 Stat. 1427; Oct. 3, 1965, P. L. 89-236, § 4, 79 Stat. 915; Oct. 20, 1976, P. L. 94-571, § 7(b), 90 Stat. 2706; Oct. 5, 1978, P. L. 95-417, §§ 2, 3, 92 Stat. 917; Oct. 19, 1980, P. L. 96-470, Title II, § 207, 94 Stat. 2245; Dec. 29, 1981, P. L. 97-116, §§ 3, 18(d), 95 Stat. 1611, 1620; Oct. 22, 1982, P. L. 97-359, § 1, 96 Stat. 1716; Nov. 10, 1986, P. L. 99-639, §§ 2(c), 4(a), 5(b), 100 Stat. 3541, 3543; Oct. 24, 1988, P. L. 100-525, § 9(q), 102 Stat. 2620; Nov. 29, 1990, P. L. 101-649, Title I, Subtitle E, § 162(b), Title VII, § 702(b), 104 Stat. 5010, 5086; Dec. 12, 1991, P. L. 102-232, Title III, §§ 302(e)(4), (5), 308(b), 309(b)(5), 105 Stat. 1745, 1746, 1757, 1758; Sept. 13, 1994, P. L. 103-322, Title IV, Subtitle G, § 40701(a), (b)(1), (c), 108 Stat. 1953, 1954; Oct. 25, 1994, P. L. 103-416, Title II, § 219(b)(2), 108 Stat. 4316; Sept. 30, 1996, P. L. 104-208, Div C, Title III, Subtitle A, § 308(e)(1)(A), (f)(2)(A), Title VI, Subtitle B, § 624(b), 110 Stat. 3009-619, 3009-621, 3009-699; Oct. 6, 2000, P. L. 106-279, Title III, § 302(b), 114 Stat. 839; Oct. 17, 2000, P. L. 106-313, Title I, § 106(c)(1), 114 Stat. 1254; Oct. 28, 2000, P. L. 106-386, Div B, Title V, §§ 1503(b)–(d), 1507(a)(1), (2), (b), 114 Stat. 1518, 1529, 1530; Aug. 6, 2002, P. L. 107-208, §§ 6, 7, 116 Stat. 929; Jan. 5, 2006, P. L. 109-162, Title VIII, Subtitle A, §§ 805(a), (c), 814(b), (e), 816, 119 Stat. 3056, 3059, 3060; July 27, 2006, P. L. 109-248, Title IV, § 402(a), 120 Stat. 622; Aug. 12, 2006, P. L. 109-271, § 6(a), 120 Stat. 762; Oct. 28, 2009, P. L. 111-83, Title V, § 568(d)(1), 123 Stat. 2187; March 7, 2013, P. L. 113-4, Title VIII, § 803, 127 Stat. 111; March 26, 2013, P. L. 113-6, Div D, Title V, § 563, 127 Stat. 380; Mar. 15, 2022, P.L. 117-103, Div BB, § 105(a), 136 Stat. 1103.)

§ 1155. Revocation of approval of petitions; effective date

The Secretary of Homeland Security may, at any time, for what he deems to be good and sufficient cause, revoke the approval of any petition approved by him under section 204 [8 USCS § 1154]. Such revocation shall be effective as of the date of approval of any such petition.

(June 27, 1952, ch 477, Title II, Ch 1, § 205, 66 Stat. 180; Sept. 22, 1959, P. L. 86-363, § 5(a), (b), 73 Stat. 644; Sept. 26, 1961, P. L. 87-301, §§ 3, 10, 75 Stat. 650, 654; Oct. 3, 1965, P. L. 89-236, § 5, 79 Stat. 916; Sept. 30, 1996, P. L. 104-208, Div C, Title III, Subtitle A, § 308(g)(3)(A), 110 Stat. 3009-622; Dec. 17, 2004, P. L. 108-458, Title V, Subtitle C, § 5304(c), 118 Stat. 3736.)

§ 1156. Unused immigrant visas

If an immigrant having an immigrant visa is denied admission to the United States and removed, or does not apply for admission before the expiration of the validity of his visa, or if an alien having an immigrant visa issued to him as a preference immigrant is found not to be a preference immigrant, an immigrant visa or a preference immigrant visa, as the case may be, may be issued in lieu thereof to another qualified alien.

(June 27, 1952, ch 477, Title II, Ch 1, § 206, 66 Stat. 181; Oct. 3, 1965, P. L. 89-236, § 6, 79 Stat. 916; Sept. 30, 1996, P. L. 104-208, Div C, Title III, Subtitle A, § 308(d)(4)(D), 110 Stat. 3009-618.)

§ 1157. Annual admission of refugees and admission of emergency situation refugees

(a) Maximum number of admissions; increases for humanitarian concerns; allocations.

(1) Except as provided in subsection (b), the number of refugees who may be admitted under this section in fiscal year 1980, 1981, or 1982, may not exceed fifty thousand unless the President determines, before the beginning of the fiscal year and after appropriate consultation (as defined in subsection (e)), that admission of a specific number of refugees in excess of such number is justified by humanitarian concerns or is otherwise in the national interest.

(2) Except as provided in subsection (b), the number of refugees who may be admitted under this section in any fiscal year after fiscal year 1982 shall be such number as the President determines, before the beginning of the fiscal year and after appropriate consultation, is justified by humanitarian concerns or is otherwise in the national interest.

(3) Admissions under this subsection shall be allocated among refugees of special humanitarian concern to the United States in accordance with a determination made by the President after appropriate consultation.

(4) In the determination made under this subsection for each fiscal year (beginning with fiscal year 1992), the President shall enumerate, with the respective number of refugees so determined, the number of aliens who were granted asylum in the previous year.

(b) Determinations by President respecting number of admissions for humanitarian concerns. If the President determines, after appropriate consultation, that (1) an unforeseen emergency refugee situation exists, (2) the admission of certain refugees in response to the emergency refugee situation is justified by grave humanitarian concerns or is otherwise in the national interest, and (3) the admission to the United States of these refugees cannot be accomplished under subsection (a), the President may fix a number of refugees to be admitted to the United States during the succeeding period (not to exceed twelve months) in response to the emergency refugee situation and such admissions shall be allocated among refugees of special humanitarian concern to the United States in accordance with a determination made by the President after the appropriate consultation provided under this subsection.

(c) Admission by Attorney General of refugees; criteria; admission status of spouse or child; applicability of other statutory requirements; termination of refugee status of alien, spouse or child.

(1) Subject to the numerical limitations established pursuant to subsections (a) and (b), the Attorney General may, in the Attorney General's discretion and pursuant to such regulations as the Attorney General may prescribe, admit any refugee who is not firmly resettled in any foreign country, is determined to be of special humanitarian concern to the United States, and is admissible (except as otherwise provided under paragraph (3)) as an immigrant under this Act.

(2)(A) A spouse or child (as defined in section 101(b)(1)(A), (B), (C), (D), or (E)) [8 USCS § 1101(b)(1), (A), (B), (C), (D) or (E)] of any refugee who qualifies for admission under paragraph (1) shall, if not otherwise entitled to admission under paragraph (1) and if not a person described in the second sentence of section 101(a)(42) [8 USCS § 1101(a)(42)], be entitled to the same admission status as such refugee if accompanying, or following to join, such refugee and if the spouse or child is admissible (except as otherwise provided under paragraph (3)) as an immigrant under this Act. Upon the spouse's or child's admission to the United States, such admission shall be charged against the numerical limitation established in accordance with the appropriate subsection under which the refugee's admission is charged.

(B) An unmarried alien who seeks to accompany, or follow to join, a parent granted admission as a refugee under this subsection, and who was under 21 years of age on the date on which such parent applied for refugee status under this section, shall continue to be classified as a child for purposes of this paragraph, if the alien attained 21 years of age after such application was filed but while it was pending.

(3) The provisions of paragraphs (4), (5), and (7)(A) of section 212(a) [8 USCS § 1182(a)(4), (5), and (7)(A)] shall not be applicable to any alien seeking admission to the United States under this subsection, and the Attorney General may waive any other provision of such section (other than paragraph (2)(C) or subparagraph (A), (B), (C), or (E) of paragraph (3)) with respect to such an alien for humanitarian purposes, to assure family unity, or when it is otherwise in the public interest. Any such waiver by the Attorney General shall be in writing and shall be granted only on an individual basis following an investigation. The Attorney General shall provide for the annual reporting to Congress of the number of waivers granted under this paragraph in the previous fiscal year and a summary of the reasons for granting such waivers.

(4) The refugee status of any alien (and of the spouse or child of the alien) may be terminated by the Attorney General pursuant to such regulations as the Attorney General may prescribe if the Attorney General determines that the alien was not in fact a refugee within the meaning of section 101(a)(42) [8 USCS § 1101(a)(42)] at the time of the alien's admission.

(d) Oversight reporting and consultation requirements.

(1) Before the start of each fiscal year the President shall report to the Committees on the Judiciary of the House of Representatives and of the Senate regarding the foreseeable number of refugees who will be in need of resettlement during the fiscal year and the anticipated allocation of refugee admissions during the fiscal year. The President shall provide for periodic discussions between designated representatives of the President and members of such committees regarding changes in the worldwide refugee situation, the progress of refugee admissions, and the possible need for adjustments in the allocation of admissions among refugees.

(2) As soon as possible after representatives of the President initiate appropriate consultation with respect to the number of refugee admissions under subsection (a) or with respect to the admission of refugees in response to an emergency refugee situation under subsection (b), the Committees on the Judiciary of the House of Representatives and of the Senate shall cause to have printed in the Congressional Record of the substance of such consultation.

(3)(A) After the President initiates appropriate consultation prior to making a determination under subsection (a), a hearing to review the proposed determination shall be held unless public disclosure of the details of the proposal would jeopardize the lives or safety of individuals.

(B) After the President initiates appropriate consultation prior to making a determination, under subsection (b), that the number of refugee admissions should be increased because of an unforeseen emergency refugee situation, to the extent that time and the nature of the emergency refugee situation permit, a hearing to review the proposal to increase refugee admissions shall be held unless public disclosure of the details of the proposal would jeopardize the lives or safety of individuals.

(e) "Appropriate consultation" defined. For purposes of this section, the term "appropriate consultation" means, with respect to the admission of refugees and allocation of refugee admissions, discussions in person by designated Cabinet-level representatives of the President with members of the Committees on the Judiciary of the Senate and of the House of Representatives to review the refugee situation or emergency refugee situation, to project the extent of possible participation of the United States therein, to discuss the reasons for believing that the proposed admission of refugees is justified by humanitarian concerns or grave humanitarian concerns or is otherwise in the national interest, and to provide such members with the following information:

(1) A description of the nature of the refugee situation.

(2) A description of the number and allocation of the refugees to be admitted and an analysis of conditions within the countries from which they came.

(3) A description of the proposed plans for their movement and resettlement and the estimated cost of their movement and resettlement.

(4) An analysis of the anticipated social, economic, and demographic impact of their admission to the United States.

(5) A description of the extent to which other countries will admit and assist in the resettlement of such refugees.

(6) An analysis of the impact of the participation of the United States in the resettlement of such refugees on the foreign policy interests of the United States.

(7) Such additional information as may be appropriate or requested by such members.

To the extent possible, information described in this subsection shall be provided at least two weeks in advance of discussions in person by designated representatives of the President with such members.

(f) Training.

(1) The Attorney General, in consultation with the Secretary of State, shall provide all United States

officials adjudicating refugee cases under this section with the same training as that provided to officers adjudicating asylum cases under section 208 [8 USCS § 1158].

(2) Such training shall include country-specific conditions, instruction on the internationally recognized right to freedom of religion, instruction on methods of religious persecution practiced in foreign countries, and applicable distinctions within a country between the nature of and treatment of various religious practices and believers.

(June 27, 1952, ch 477, Title II, Ch. 1, § 207, as added March 17, 1980, P. L. 96-212, Title II, § 201(b), 94 Stat. 103; Oct. 24, 1988, P. L. 100-525, § 9(h), 102 Stat. 2620; Nov. 29, 1990, P. L. 101-649, Title I, Subtitle A, § 104(b), Title VI, § 603(a)(4), 104 Stat. 4985, 5082; Dec. 12, 1991, P. L. 102-232, Title III, § 307(l)(1), 105 Stat. 1756; Sept. 30, 1996, P. L. 104-208, Div C, Title VI, Subtitle A, § 601(b), 110 Stat. 3009-689; Oct. 27, 1998, P. L. 105-292, Title VI, § 602(a), 112 Stat. 2812; Aug. 6, 2002, P. L. 107-208, § 5, 116 Stat. 929; May 11, 2005, P. L. 109-13, Div B, Title I, § 101(g)(2), 119 Stat. 305.)

§ 1158. Asylum

(a) Authority to apply for asylum.

(1) In general. Any alien who is physically present in the United States or who arrives in the United States (whether or not at a designated port of arrival and including an alien who is brought to the United States after having been interdicted in international or United States waters), irrespective of such alien's status, may apply for asylum in accordance with this section or, where applicable, section 235(b) [8 USCS § 1225(b)].

(2) Exceptions.

(A) Safe third country. Paragraph (1) shall not apply to an alien if the Attorney General determines that the alien may be removed, pursuant to a bilateral or multilateral agreement, to a country (other than the country of the alien's nationality or, in the case of an alien having no nationality, the country of the alien's last habitual residence) in which the alien's life or freedom would not be threatened on account of race, religion, nationality, membership in a particular social group, or political opinion, and where the alien would have access to a full and fair procedure for determining a claim to asylum or equivalent temporary protection, unless the Attorney General finds that it is in the public interest for the alien to receive asylum in the United States.

(B) Time limit. Subject to subparagraph (D), paragraph (1) shall not apply to an alien unless the alien demonstrates by clear and convincing evidence that the application has been filed within 1 year after the date of the alien's arrival in the United States.

(C) Previous asylum applications. Subject to subparagraph (D), paragraph (1) shall not apply to an alien if the alien has previously applied for asylum and had such application denied.

(D) Changed circumstances. An application for asylum of an alien may be considered, notwithstanding subparagraphs (B) and (C), if the alien demonstrates to the satisfaction of the Attorney General either the existence of changed circumstances which materially affect the applicant's eligibility for asylum or extraordinary circumstances relating to the delay in filing an application within the period specified in subparagraph (B).

(E) Applicability. Subparagraphs (A) and (B) shall not apply to an unaccompanied alien child (as defined in section 462(g) of the Homeland Security Act of 2002 (6 U.S.C. 279(g))).

(3) Limitation on judicial review. No court shall have jurisdiction to review any determination of the Attorney General under paragraph (2).

(b) Conditions for granting asylum.

(1) In general.

(A) Eligibility. The Secretary of Homeland Security or the Attorney General may grant asylum to an alien who has applied for asylum in accordance with the requirements and procedures established by the Secretary of Homeland Security or the Attorney General under this section if the Secretary of Homeland Security or the Attorney General determines that such alien is a refugee within the meaning of section 101(a)(42)(A) [8 USCS § 1101(a)(42)(A)].

(B) Burden of proof.

(i) In general. The burden of proof is on the applicant to establish that the applicant is a refugee, within the meaning of section 101(a)(42)(A) [8 USCS § 1101(a)(42)(A)]. To establish that the applicant is a refugee within the meaning of such section, the applicant must establish that race, religion, nationality, membership in a particular social group, or political opinion was or will be at least one central reason for persecuting the applicant.

(ii) Sustaining burden. The testimony of the applicant may be sufficient to sustain the applicant's burden without corroboration, but only if the applicant satisfies the trier of fact that the applicant's testimony is credible, is persuasive, and refers to specific facts sufficient to demonstrate that the applicant is a refugee. In determining whether the applicant has met the applicant's burden, the trier of fact may weigh the credible testimony along with other evidence of record. Where the trier of fact determines that the applicant should provide evidence that corroborates otherwise credible testimony, such evidence must be provided unless the applicant does not have the evidence and cannot reasonably obtain the evidence.

(iii) Credibility determination. Considering the totality of the circumstances, and all relevant factors, a trier of fact may base a credibility determination on the demeanor, candor, or responsiveness of the applicant or witness, the inherent plausibility of the applicant's or witness's account, the consistency between the applicant's or witness's written and oral statements (whenever made and whether or not under oath, and considering the circumstances under which the statements were made), the internal consistency of each such statement, the consistency of such statements with other evidence of record (including the reports of the Department of State on country conditions), and any inaccuracies or falsehoods in such statements, without regard to whether an inconsistency, inaccuracy, or falsehood goes to the heart of the applicant's claim, or any other relevant factor. There is no presumption of credibility, however, if no adverse credibility determination is explicitly made, the applicant or witness shall have a rebuttable presumption of credibility on appeal.

(2) Exceptions.

(A) In general. Paragraph (1) shall not apply to an alien if the Attorney General determines that—

(i) the alien ordered, incited, assisted, or otherwise participated in the persecution of any person on account of race, religion, nationality, membership in a particular social group, or political opinion;

(ii) the alien, having been convicted by a final judgment of a particularly serious crime, constitutes a danger to the community of the United States;

(iii) there are serious reasons for believing that the alien has committed a serious nonpolitical crime outside the United States prior to the arrival of the alien in the United States;

(iv) there are reasonable grounds for regarding the alien as a danger to the security of the United States;

(v) the alien is described in subclause (I), (II), (III), (IV), or (VI) of section 212(a)(3)(B)(i) [8 USCS § 1182(a)(3)(B)(i)] or section 237(a)(4)(B) [8 USCS § 1227(a)(4)(B)] (relating to terrorist activity), unless, in the case only of an alien described in subclause (IV) of section 212(a)(3)(B)(i) [8 USCS § 1182(a)(3)(B)(i)], the Attorney General determines, in the Attorney General's discretion, that there are not reasonable grounds for regarding the alien as a danger to the security of the United States; or

(vi) the alien was firmly resettled in another country prior to arriving in the United States.

(B) Special rules.

(i) Conviction of aggravated felony. For purposes of clause (ii) of subparagraph (A), an alien who has been convicted of an aggravated felony shall be considered to have been convicted of a particularly serious crime.

(ii) Offenses. The Attorney General may designate by regulation offenses that will be considered to be a crime described in clause (ii) or (iii) of subparagraph (A).

(C) Additional limitations. The Attorney General may by regulation establish additional limitations and conditions, consistent with this section, under which an alien shall be ineligible for asylum under paragraph (1).

(D) No judicial review. There shall be no judicial review of a determination of the Attorney General under subparagraph (A)(v).

(3) Treatment of spouse and children.

(A) In general. A spouse or child (as defined in section 101(b)(1)(A), (B), (C), (D), or (E) [8 USCS § 1101(b)(1)(A), (B), (C), (D), or (E)]) of an alien who is granted asylum under this subsection may, if not otherwise eligible for asylum under this section, be granted the same status as the alien if accompanying, or following to join, such alien.

(B) Continued classification of certain aliens as children. An unmarried alien who seeks to accompany, or follow to join, a parent granted asylum under this subsection, and who was under 21 years of age on the date on which such parent applied for asylum under this section, shall continue to be classified as a child for purposes of this paragraph and section 209(b)(3) [8 USCS § 1159(b)(3)], if the alien attained 21 years of age after such application was filed but while it was pending.

(C) Initial jurisdiction. An asylum officer (as defined in section 235(b)(1)(E) [8 USCS § 1225(b)(1)(E)]) shall have initial jurisdiction over any asylum application filed by an unaccompanied alien child (as defined in section 462(g) of the Homeland Security Act of 2002 (6 U.S.C. 279(g))), regardless of whether filed in accordance with this section or section 235(b) [8 USCS § 1225(b)].

(c) Asylum status.

(1) In general. In the case of an alien granted asylum under subsection (b), the Attorney General—

(A) shall not remove or return the alien to the alien's country of nationality or, in the case of a person having no nationality, the country of the alien's last habitual residence;

(B) shall authorize the alien to engage in employment in the United States and provide the alien with appropriate endorsement of that authorization; and

(C) may allow the alien to travel abroad with the prior consent of the Attorney General.

(2) Termination of asylum. Asylum granted under subsection (b) does not convey a right to remain permanently in the United States, and may be terminated if the Attorney General determines that—

(A) the alien no longer meets the conditions described in subsection (b)(1) owing to a fundamental change in circumstances;

(B) the alien meets a condition described in subsection (b)(2);

(C) the alien may be removed, pursuant to a bilateral or multilateral agreement, to a country (other than the country of the alien's nationality or, in the case of an alien having no nationality, the country of the alien's last habitual residence) in which the alien's life or freedom would not be threatened on account of race, religion, nationality, membership in a particular social group, or political opinion, and where the alien is eligible to receive asylum or equivalent temporary protection;

(D) the alien has voluntarily availed himself or herself of the protection of the alien's country of nationality or, in the case of an alien having no nationality, the alien's country of last habitual residence, by returning to such country with permanent resident status or the reasonable possibility of obtaining such status with the same rights and obligations pertaining to other permanent residents of that country; or

(E) the alien has acquired a new nationality and enjoys the protection of the country of his or her new nationality.

(3) Removal when asylum is terminated. An alien described in paragraph (2) is subject to any applicable grounds of inadmissibility or deportability under section [sections] 212(a) and 237(a) [8 USCS §§ 1182(a), 1227(a)], and the alien's removal or return shall be directed by the Attorney General in accordance with sections 240 and 241 [8 USCS §§ 1229a, 1231].

(d) Asylum procedure.

(1) Applications. The Attorney General shall establish a procedure for the consideration of asylum appli-

cations filed under subsection (a). The Attorney General may require applicants to submit fingerprints and a photograph at such time and in such manner to be determined by regulation by the Attorney General.

(2) Employment. An applicant for asylum is not entitled to employment authorization, but such authorization may be provided under regulation by the Attorney General. An applicant who is not otherwise eligible for employment authorization shall not be granted such authorization prior to 180 days after the date of filing of the application for asylum.

(3) Fees. The Attorney General may impose fees for the consideration of an application for asylum, for employment authorization under this section, and for adjustment of status under section 209(b) [8 USCS § 1159(b)]. Such fees shall not exceed the Attorney General's costs in adjudicating the applications. The Attorney General may provide for the assessment and payment of such fees over a period of time or by installments. Nothing in this paragraph shall be construed to require the Attorney General to charge fees for adjudication services provided to asylum applicants, or to limit the authority of the Attorney General to set adjudication and naturalization fees in accordance with section 286(m) [8 USCS § 1356(m)].

(4) Notice of privilege of counsel and consequences of frivolous application. At the time of filing an application for asylum, the Attorney General shall—

(A) advise the alien of the privilege of being represented by counsel and of the consequences, under paragraph (6), of knowingly filing a frivolous application for asylum; and

(B) provide the alien a list of persons (updated not less often than quarterly) who have indicated their availability to represent aliens in asylum proceedings on a pro bono basis.

(5) Consideration of asylum applications.

(A) Procedures. The procedure established under paragraph (1) shall provide that—

(i) asylum cannot be granted until the identity of the applicant has been checked against all appropriate records or databases maintained by the Attorney General and by the Secretary of State, including the Automated Visa Lookout System, to determine any grounds on which the alien may be inadmissible to or deportable from the United States, or ineligible to apply for or be granted asylum;

(ii) in the absence of exceptional circumstances, the initial interview or hearing on the asylum application shall commence not later than 45 days after the date an application is filed;

(iii) in the absence of exceptional circumstances, final administrative adjudication of the asylum application, not including administrative appeal, shall be completed within 180 days after the date an application is filed;

(iv) any administrative appeal shall be filed within 30 days of a decision granting or denying asylum, or within 30 days of the completion of removal proceedings before an immigration judge under section 240 [8 USCS § 1229a], whichever is later; and

(v) in the case of an applicant for asylum who fails without prior authorization or in the absence of exceptional circumstances to appear for an interview or hearing, including a hearing under section 240 [8 USCS § 1229a], the application may be dismissed or the applicant may be otherwise sanctioned for such failure.

(B) Additional regulatory conditions. The Attorney General may provide by regulation for any other conditions or limitations on the consideration of an application for asylum not inconsistent with this Act.

(6) Frivolous applications. If the Attorney General determines that an alien has knowingly made a frivolous application for asylum and the alien has received the notice under paragraph (4)(A), the alien shall be permanently ineligible for any benefits under this Act, effective as of the date of a final determination on such application.

(7) No private right of action. Nothing in this subsection shall be construed to create any substantive or procedural right or benefit that is legally enforceable by any party against the United States or its agencies or officers or any other person.

(e) Commonwealth of the Northern Mariana Islands. The provisions of this section and section 209(b) [8 USCS § 1159(b)] shall apply to persons physically present in the Commonwealth of the Northern Mariana Islands or arriving in the Commonwealth (whether or not at a designated port of arrival and including persons who are brought to the Commonwealth after having been interdicted in international or United States waters) only on or after January 1, 2014.

(June 27, 1952, ch 477, Title II, Ch 1, § 208, as added March 17, 1980, P.L. 96-212, Title II, § 201(b), 94 Stat. 105; Nov. 29, 1990, P. L. 101-649, Title V, Subtitle A, § 515(a)(1), 104 Stat. 5053; Sept. 13, 1994, P. L. 103-322, Title XIII, § 130005(b), 108 Stat. 2028; April 24, 1996, P. L. 104-132, Title IV, Subtitle C, § 421(a), 110 Stat. 1270; Sept. 30, 1996, P. L. 104-208, Div C, Title VI, Subtitle A, § 604(a), 110 Stat. 3009-690; Oct. 26, 2001, P. L. 107-56, Title IV, Subtitle B, § 411(b)(2), 115 Stat. 348; Aug. 6, 2002, P. L. 107-208, § 4, 116 Stat. 928; May 11, 2005, P. L. 109-13, Div B, Title I, § 101(a), (b), 119 Stat. 302; May 8, 2008, P. L. 110-229, Title VII, Subtitle A, § 702(j)(4), 122 Stat. 866; Dec. 23, 2008, P. L. 110-457, Title II, Subtitle D, § 235(d)(7), 122 Stat. 5080.)

§ 1159. Adjustment of status of refugees

(a) Inspection and examination by Department of Homeland Security.

(1) Any alien who has been admitted to the United States under section 207 [8 USCS § 1157]—

(A) whose admission has not been terminated by the Secretary of Homeland Security or the Attorney General pursuant to such regulations as the Secretary of Homeland Security or the Attorney General may prescribe,

(B) who has been physically present in the United States for at least one year, and

(C) who has not acquired permanent resident status, shall, at the end of such year period, return or be returned to the custody of the Department of Homeland Security for inspection and examination for admission to the United States as an immigrant in accordance with the provisions of sections 235, 240, and 241 [8 USCS §§ 1225, 1229a, and 1231].

(2) Any alien who is found upon inspection and examination by an immigration officer pursuant to paragraph (1) or after a hearing before an immigration judge to be admissible (except as otherwise provided under subsection (c)) as an immigrant under this Act at the time of the alien's inspection and examination shall, notwithstanding any numerical limitation specified in this Act, be regarded as lawfully admitted to the United States for permanent residence as of the date of such alien's arrival into the United States.

(b) Requirements for adjustment. The Secretary of Homeland Security or the Attorney General, in the Secretary's or the Attorney General's discretion and under such regulations as the Secretary or the Attorney General may prescribe, may adjust to the status of an alien lawfully admitted for permanent residence the status of any alien granted asylum who—

(1) applies for such adjustment,

(2) has been physically present in the United States for at least one year after being granted asylum,

(3) continues to be a refugee within the meaning of section 101(a)(42)(A) [8 USCS § 1101(a)(42)(A)] or a spouse or child of such a refugee,

(4) is not firmly resettled in any foreign country, and

(5) is admissible (except as otherwise provided under subsection (c)) as an immigrant under this Act at the time of examination for adjustment of such alien.

Upon approval of an application under this subsection, the Secretary of Homeland Security or the Attorney General shall establish a record of the alien's admission for lawful permanent residence as of the date one year before the date of the approval of the application.

(c) Coordination with 8 USCS § 1182. The provisions of paragraphs (4), (5), and (7)(A) of section 212(a) [8 USCS § 1182(a)] shall not be applicable to any alien seeking adjustment of status under this section, and the Secretary of Homeland Security or the Attorney General may waive any other provision of such section (other than paragraph (2)(C) or subparagraph (A), (B), (C), or (E) of paragraph (3)) with respect to such an alien for humanitarian purposes, to assure family unity, or when it is otherwise in the public interest.

(June 27, 1952, ch 477, Title II, Ch 1, § 209, as added March 17, 1980, P. L. 96-212, Title II, § 201(b), 94 Stat. 105; Nov. 29, 1990, P. L. 101-649, Title I, Subtitle A, § 104(a)(1), Title VI, § 603(a)(4), 104 Stat. 4985, 5082; Dec. 12, 1991, P. L. 102-232, Title III, § 307(l)(1), 105 Stat. 1756; Sept. 30, 1996, P. L. 104-208, Div C, Title III, Subtitle A, § 308(g)(3)(A), (4)(A), Subtitle F, § 371(b)(2), 110 Stat. 3009-622, 3009-645; May 11, 2005, P. L. 109-13, Div B, Title I, § 101(g)(1), 119 Stat. 305.)

§ 1160. Special agricultural workers

(a) Lawful residence.

(1) In general. The Attorney General shall adjust the status of an alien to that of an alien lawfully admitted for temporary residence if the Attorney General determines that the alien meets the following requirements:

(A) Application period. The alien must apply for such adjustment during the 18-month period beginning on the first day of the seventh month that begins after the date of enactment of this section [enacted Nov. 6, 1986].

(B) Performance of seasonal agricultural services and residence in the United States. The alien must establish that he has—

(i) resided in the United States, and

(ii) performed seasonal agricultural services in the United States for at least 90 man-days,

during the 12-month period ending on May 1, 1986. For purposes of the previous sentence, performance of seasonal agricultural services in the United States for more than one employer on any one day shall be counted as performance of services for only 1 man-day.

(C) Admissible as immigrant. The alien must establish that he is admissible to the United States as an immigrant, except as otherwise provided under subsection (c)(2).

(2) Adjustment to permanent residence. The Attorney General shall adjust the status of any alien provided lawful temporary resident status under paragraph (1) to that of an alien lawfully admitted for permanent residence on the following date:

(A) Group 1. Subject to the numerical limitation established under subparagraph (C), in the case of an alien who has established, at the time of application for temporary residence under paragraph (1), that the alien performed seasonal agricultural services in the United States for at least 90 man-days during each of the 12-month periods ending on May 1, 1984, 1985, and 1986, the adjustment shall occur on the first day after the end of the one-year period that begins on the later of (I) the date the alien was granted such temporary resident status, or (II) the day after the last day of the application period described in paragraph (1)(A).

(B) Group 2. In the case of aliens to which subparagraph (A) does not apply, the adjustment shall occur on the day after the last day of the two-year period that begins on the later of (I) the date the alien was granted such temporary resident status, or (II) the day after the last day of the application period described in paragraph (1)(A).

(C) Numerical limitation. Subparagraph (A) shall not apply to more than 350,000 aliens. If more than 350,000 aliens meet the requirements of such subparagraph, such subparagraph shall apply to the 350,000 aliens whose applications for adjustment were first filed under paragraph (1) and subparagraph (B) shall apply to the remaining aliens.

(3) Termination of temporary residence.

(A) During the period of temporary resident status granted an alien under paragraph (1), the Attorney General may terminate such status only upon a determination under this Act that the alien is deportable.

(B) Before any alien becomes eligible for adjustment of status under paragraph (2), the Attorney General may deny adjustment to permanent status and provide for termination of the temporary resident status granted such alien under paragraph (1) if—

(i) the Attorney General finds by a preponderance of the evidence that the adjustment to temporary resident status was the result of fraud or willful misrepresentation as set out in section 212(a)(6)(C)(xi) [8 USCS § 1182(a)(6)(C)(i)], or

(ii) the alien commits an act that (I) makes the alien inadmissible to the United States as an immigrant, except as provided under subsection (c)(2), or (II) is convicted of a felony or 3 or more misdemeanors committed in the United States.

(4) Authorized travel and employment during temporary residence. During the period an alien is in lawful temporary resident status granted under this subsection, the alien has the right to travel abroad (including commutation from a residence abroad) and shall be granted authorization to engage in employment in the United States and shall be provided an "employment authorized" endorsement or other appropriate work permit, in the same manner as for aliens lawfully admitted for permanent residence.

(5) In general. Except as otherwise provided in this subsection, an alien who acquires the status of an alien lawfully admitted for temporary residence under paragraph (1), such status not having changed, is considered to be an alien lawfully admitted for permanent residence (as described in section 101(a)(20) [8 USCS § 1101(a)(20)]), other than under any provision of the immigration laws.

(b) Applications for adjustment of status.

(1) To whom may be made.

(A) Within the United States. The Attorney General shall provide that applications for adjustment of status under subsection (a) may be filed—

(i) with the Attorney General, or

(ii) with a designated entity (designated under paragraph (2)), but only if the applicant consents to the forwarding of the application to the Attorney General.

(B) Outside the United States. The Attorney General, in cooperation with the Secretary of State, shall provide a procedure whereby an alien may apply for adjustment of status under subsection (a)(1) at an appropriate consular office outside the United States. If the alien otherwise qualifies for such adjustment, the Attorney General shall provide such documentation of authorization to enter the United States and to have the alien's status adjusted upon entry as may be necessary to carry out the provisions of this section.

(2) Designation of entities to receive applications. For purposes of receiving applications under this section, the Attorney General—

(A) shall designate qualified voluntary organizations and other qualified State, local, community, farm labor organizations, and associations of agricultural employers, and

(B) may designate such other persons as the Attorney General determines are qualified and have substantial experience, demonstrated competence, and traditional long-term involvement in the preparation and submittal of applications for adjustment of status under section 209 or 245 [8 USCS § 1159 or 1255], Public Law 89-732 [8 USCS § 1255 note], or Public Law 95-145.

(3) Proof of eligibility.

(A) In general. An alien may establish that he meets the requirement of subsection (a)(1)(B)(ii) through government employment records, records supplied by employers or collective bargaining organizations, and such other reliable documentation as the alien may provide. The Attorney General shall establish special procedures to credit properly work in cases in which an alien was employed under an assumed name.

(B) Documentation of work history.

(i) An alien applying for adjustment of status under subsection (a)(1) has the burden of proving by a preponderance of the evidence that the alien has worked the requisite number of man-days (as required under subsection (a)(1)(B)(ii)).

(ii) If an employer or farm labor contractor employing such an alien has kept proper and adequate records respecting such employment, the alien's burden of proof under clause (i) may be met by securing timely production of those records under regulations to be promulgated by the Attorney General.

(iii) An alien can meet such burden of proof if the alien establishes that the alien has in fact performed the work described in subsection (a)(1)(B)(ii) by producing sufficient evidence to show the extent of that employment as a matter of just and reasonable inference. In such a case, the burden then shifts to the Attorney General to disprove the alien's evidence with a showing which negates the reasonableness of the inference to be drawn from the evidence.

(4) Treatment of applications by designated entities. Each designated entity must agree to forward to the Attorney General applications filed with it in accordance with paragraph (1)(A)(ii) but not to forward to the Attorney General applications filed with it unless the applicant has consented to such forwarding. No such entity may make a determination required by this section to be made by the Attorney General.

(5) Limitation on access to information. Files and records prepared for purposes of this section by designated entities operating under this section are confidential and the Attorney General and the Service shall not have access to such files or records relating to an alien without the consent of the alien, except as allowed by a court order issued pursuant to paragraph (6) of this subsection.

(6) Confidentiality of information.

(A) In general. Except as provided in this paragraph, neither the Attorney General, nor any otherofficial or employee of the Department of Justice, or bureau or agency thereof, may—

(i) use the information furnished by the applicant pursuant to an application filed under this section for any purpose other than to make a determination on the application, including a determination under subsection (a)(3)(B), or for enforcement of paragraph (7);

(ii) make any publication whereby the information furnished by any particular individual can be identified; or

(iii) permit anyone other than the sworn officers and employees of the Department or bureau or agency or, with respect to applications filed with a designated entity, that designated entity, to examine individual applications.

(B) Required disclosures. The Attorney General shall provide information furnished under this section, and any other information derived from such furnished information, to a duly recognized law enforcement entity in connection with a criminal investigation or prosecution, when such information is requested in writing by such entity, or to an official coroner for purposes of affirmatively identifying a deceased individual (whether or not such individual is deceased as a result of a crime).

(C) Construction.

(i) In general. Nothing in this paragraph shall be construed to limit the use, or release, for immigration enforcement purposes or law enforcement purposes of information contained in files or records of the Service pertaining to an application filed under this section, other than information furnished by an applicant pursuant to the application, or any other information derived from the application, that is not available from any other source.

(ii) Criminal convictions. Information concerning whether the applicant has at any time been convicted of a crime may be used or released for immigration enforcement or law enforcement purposes.

(D) Crime. Whoever knowingly uses, publishes, or permits information to be examined in violation of this paragraph shall be fined not more than $10,000.

(7) Penalties for false statements in applications.

(A) Criminal penalty. Whoever—

(i) files an application for adjustment of status under this section and knowingly and willfully falsifies, conceals, or covers up a material fact or makes any false, fictitious, or fraudulent statements or representations, or makes or uses any false writing or document knowing the same to contain any false, fictitious, or fraudulent statement or entry, or

(ii) creates or supplies a false writing or document for use in making such an application,

shall be fined in accordance with title 18, United States Code, or imprisoned not more than five years, or both.

(B) Exclusion. An alien who is convicted of a crime under subparagraph (A) shall be considered to be inadmissible to the United States on the ground described in section 212(a)(6)(C)(i) [8 USCS § 1182(a)(6)(C)(i)].

(c) Waiver of numerical limitations and certain grounds for exclusion.

(1) Numerical limitations do not apply. The numerical limitations of sections 201 and 202 [8 USCS §§ 1151, 1152] shall not apply to the adjustment of aliens to lawful permanent resident status under this section.

(2) Waiver of grounds for exclusion. In the determination of an alien's admissibility under subsection (a)(1)(C)—

(A) Grounds of exclusion not applicable. The provisions of paragraphs (5) and (7)(A) of section 212(a) [8 USCS § 1182(a)(5) and (7)(A)] shall not apply.

(B) Waiver of other grounds.

(i) In general. Except as provided in clause (ii), the Attorney General may waive any other provision of section 212(a) [8 USCS § 1182(a)] in the case of individual aliens for humanitarian purposes, to assure family unity, or when it is otherwise in the public interest.

(ii) Grounds that may not be waived. The following provisions of section 212(a) [8 USCS § 1182(a)] may not be waived by the Attorney General under clause (i):

(I) Paragraphs (2)(A) and (2)(B) (relating to criminals).

(II) Paragraph (4) (relating to aliens likely to become public charges).

(III) Paragraph (2)(C) (relating to drug offenses), except for so much of such paragraph as relates to a single offense of simple possession of 30 grams or less of marihuana.

(IV) Paragraph (3) (relating to security and related grounds), other than subparagraph (B) thereof.

(C) Special rule for determination of public charge. An alien is not ineligible for adjustment of status under this section due to being inadmissible under section 212(a)(4) [8 USCS § 1182(a)(4)] if the alien demonstrates a history of employment in the United States evidencing self-support without reliance on public cash assistance.

(d) Temporary stay of exclusion or deportation and work authorization for certain applicants.

(1) Before application period. The Attorney General shall provide that in the case of an alien who is apprehended before the beginning of the application period described in subsection (a)(1) and who can establish a nonfrivolous case of eligibility to have his status adjusted under subsection (a) (but for the fact that he may not apply for such adjustment until the beginning of such period), until the alien has had the opportunity during the first 30 days of the application period to complete the filing of an application for adjustment, the alien—

(A) may not be excluded or deported, and

(B) shall be granted authorization to engage in employment in the United States and be provided an "employment authorized" endorsement or other appropriate work permit.

(2) During application period. The Attorney General shall provide that in the case of an alien who presents a nonfrivolous application for adjustment of status under subsection (a) during the application period, and until a final determination on the application has been made in accordance with this section, the alien—

(A) may not be excluded or deported, and

(B) shall be granted authorization to engage in employment in the United States and be provided an "employment authorized" endorsement or other appropriate work permit.

(3) Use of application fees to offset program costs. No application fees collected by the Service pursuant to this subsection may be used by the Service to offset the costs of the special agricultural worker legalization program until the Service implements the program consistent with the statutory mandate as follows:

(A) During the application period described in subsection (a)(1)(A) the Service the INS may grant temporary admission to the United States, work authorization, and provide an "employment authorized" endorsement or other appropriate work permit to any alien who presents a preliminary application for adjustment of status under subsection (a) at a designated port of entry on the southern land border. An alien who does not enter through a port of entry is subject to deportation and removal as otherwise provided in this Act.

(B) During the application period described in subsection (a)(1)(A) any alien who has filed an application for adjustment of status within the United States as provided in subsection (b)(1)(A) pursuant to the provision of 8 CFR section 210.1(j) is subject to paragraph (2) of this subsection.

(C) A preliminary application is defined as a fully completed and signed application with fee and photographs which contains specific information concerning the performance of qualifying employment in the United States and the documentary evidence which the applicant intends to submit as proof of such employment. The applicant must be otherwise admissible to the United States and must establish to the satisfaction of the examining officer during an interview that his or her claim to eligibility for special agriculture worker status is credible.

(e) Administrative and judicial review.

(1) Administrative and judicial review. There shall be no administrative or judicial review of a determination respecting an application for adjustment of status under this section except in accordance with this subsection.

(2) Administrative review.

(A) Single level of administrative appellate review. The Attorney General shall establish an appellate authority to provide for a single level of administrative appellate review of such a determination.

(B) Standard for review. Such administrative appellate review shall be based solely upon the administrative record established at the time of the determination on the application and upon such additional or newly discovered evidence as may not have been available at the time of the determination.

(3) Judicial review.

(A) Limitation to review of exclusion or deportation. There shall be judicial review of such a denial only in the judicial review of an order of exclusion or deportation under section 106 [former 8 USCS § 1105a] (as in effect before October 1, 1996).

(B) Standard for judicial review. Such judicial review shall be based solely upon the administrative record established at the time of the review by the appellate authority and the findings of fact and determinations contained in such record shall be conclusive unless the applicant can establish abuse of discretion or that the findings are directly contrary to clear and convincing facts contained in the record considered as a whole.

(f) Temporary disqualification of newly legalized aliens from receiving aid to families with dependent children. During the five-year period beginning on the date an alien was granted lawful temporary resident status under subsection (a), and notwithstanding any other provision of law, the alien is not eligible for assistance under a State program funded under part A of title IV of the Social Security Act [42 USCS §§ 601 et seq.]. Notwithstanding the previous sentence, in the case of an alien who would be eligible for assistance under a State program funded under part A of title IV of the Social Security Act [42 USCS §§ 601 et seq.] but for the previous sentence, the provisions of paragraph (3) of section 245A(h) [8 USCS § 1255a(h)] shall apply in the same manner as they apply with respect to paragraph (1) of such section and, for this purpose, any reference in section 245A(h)(3) [8 USCS § 1255a(h)] to paragraph (1) is deemed a reference to the previous sentence.

(g) Treatment of special agricultural workers. For all purposes (subject to subsections (a)(5) and (f)) an alien whose status is adjusted under this section to that of an alien lawfully admitted for permanent residence, such status not having changed, shall be considered to be an alien lawfully admitted for permanent residence (within the meaning of section 101(a)(20) [8 USCS § 1101(a)(20)]).

(h) "Seasonal agricultural services" defined. In this section, the term "seasonal agricultural services" means the performance of field work related to planting, cultural practices, cultivating, growing and harvesting of fruits and vegetables of every kind and other perishable commodities, as defined in regulations by the Secretary of Agriculture.

(June 27, 1952, ch 477, Title II, Ch 1, § 210, as added Nov. 6, 1986, P. L. 99-603, Title III, Part A, § 302(a)(1), 100 Stat. 3417; Dec. 22, 1987, P. L. 100-202, § 101(a) [Title II, § 211], 101 Stat. 1329-18; Oct. 24, 1988, P. L. 100-525, § 2(m), 102 Stat. 2613; Dec. 18, 1989, P. L. 101-238, § 4, 103 Stat. 2103; Nov. 29, 1990, P. L. 101-649, Title VI, § 603(a)(5), 104 Stat. 5082; Dec. 12, 1991, P. L. 102-232, Title III, §§ 307(j), 309(b)(6), 105 Stat. 1756, 1758; Oct. 25, 1994, P. L. 103-416, Title II, § 219(d), (z)(7), 108 Stat. 4316, 4318; April 24, 1996, P. L. 104-132, Title IV, Subtitle D, § 431(b), 110 Stat. 1273; Aug. 22, 1996, P. L. 104-193, Title I, § 110(s)(1), 110 Stat. 2175; Sept. 30, 1996, P. L. 104-208, Div C, Title III, Subtitle A, § 308(g)(2)(B), Subtitle F, § 384(d)(1), Title VI, Subtitle B, § 623(b), 110 Stat. 3009-622, 3009-653, 3009-697.)

§ 1161. [Repealed]

ADMISSION QUALIFICATIONS FOR ALIENS; TRAVEL CONTROL OF CITIZENS AND ALIENS

§ 1181. Admission of immigrants into the United States

(a) Documents required; admission under quotas before June 30, 1968. Except as provided in subsection (b) and subsection (c) no immigrant shall be admitted into the United States unless at the time of application for admission he (1) has a valid unexpired immigrant visa or was born subsequent to the issuance of such visa of the accompanying parent, and (2) presents a valid unexpired passport or other suitable travel document, or document of identity and nationality, if such document is required under the regulations issued by the Attorney General. With respect to immigrants to be admitted under quotas of quota areas prior to June 30, 1968, no immigrant visa shall be deemed valid unless the immigrant is properly chargeable to the quota area under the quota of which the visa is issued.

(b) Readmission without required documents; Attorney General's discretion. Notwithstanding the provisions of section 212(a)(7)(A) of this Act [8 USCS § 1182(a)(7)(A)] in such cases or in such classes of cases and under such conditions as may be by regulations prescribed, returning resident immigrants, defined in section 101(a)(27)(A) [8 USCS § 1101(a)(27)(A)], who are otherwise admissible may be readmitted to the United States by the Attorney General in his discretion without being required to obtain a passport, immigrant visa, reentry permit or other documentation.

(c) Nonapplicability to aliens admitted as refugees. The provisions of subsection (a) shall not apply to an alien whom the Attorney General admits to the United States under section 207 [8 USCS § 1157].

(June 27, 1952, ch 477, Title II, Ch 2, § 211, 66 Stat. 181; Oct. 3, 1965, P. L. 89-236, § 9, 79 Stat. 917; Oct. 20, 1976, P. L. 94-571, § 7(c), 90 Stat. 2706; March 17, 1980, P.L. 96-212, Title II, § 202, 94 Stat. 106; Nov. 29, 1990, P. L. 101-649, Title VI, § 603(a)(7), 104 Stat. 5083.)

§ 1182. Inadmissible aliens

(a) Classes of aliens ineligible for visas or admission. Except as otherwise provided in this Act, aliens who are inadmissible under the following paragraphs are ineligible to receive visas and ineligible to be admitted to the United States:

(1) Health-related grounds.

(A) In general. Any alien

(i) who is determined (in accordance with regulations prescribed by the Secretary of Health and Human Services) to have a communicable disease of public health significance; [,]

(ii) except as provided in subparagraph (C), who seeks admission as an immigrant, or who seeks adjustment of status to the status of an alien lawfully admitted for permanent residence, and who has failed to present documentation of having received vaccination against vaccine-preventable diseases, which shall include at least the following diseases: mumps, measles, rubella, polio, tetanus and diphtheria toxoids, pertussis, influenza type B and hepatitis B, and any other vaccinations against vaccine-preventable diseases recommended by the Advisory Committee for Immunization Practices,

(iii) who is determined (in accordance with regulations prescribed by the Secretary of Health and Human Services in consultation with the Attorney General)

(I) to have a physical or mental disorder and behavior associated with the disorder that may pose, or has posed, a threat to the property, safety, or welfare of the alien or others, or

(II) to have had a physical or mental disorder and a history of behavior associated with the disorder, which behavior has posed a threat to the property, safety, or welfare of the alien or others and which behavior is likely to recur or to lead to other harmful behavior, or

(iv) who is determined (in accordance with regulations prescribed by the Secretary of Health and Human Services) to be a drug abuser or addict,

is inadmissible.

(B) Waiver authorized. For provision authorizing waiver of certain clauses of subparagraph (A), see subsection (g).

(C) Exception from immunization requirement for adopted children 10 years of age or younger. Clause (ii) of subparagraph (A) shall not apply to a child who

(i) is 10 years of age or younger,

(ii) is described in subparagraph (F) or (G) of section 101(b)(1) [8 USCS § 1101(b)(1)], and

(iii) is seeking an immigrant visa as an immediate relative under section 201(b) [8 USCS § 1151(b)],

if, prior to the admission of the child, an adoptive parent or prospective adoptive parent of the child, who has sponsored the child for admission as an immediate relative, has executed an affidavit stating that the parent is aware of the provisions of subparagraph (A)(ii) and will ensure that, within 30 days of the child's admission, or at the earliest time that is medically appropriate, the child will receive the vaccinations identified in such subparagraph.

(2) Criminal and related grounds.

(A) Conviction of certain crimes.

(i) In general. Except as provided in clause (ii), any alien convicted of, or who admits having committed or who admits committing acts which constitute the essential elements of

(I) a crime involving moral turpitude (other than a purely political offense) or an attempt or conspiracy to commit such a crime, or

(II) a violation of (or a conspiracy or attempt to violate) any law or regulation of a State, the United States, or a foreign country relating to a controlled substance (as defined in section 102 of the Controlled Substances Act (21 U.S.C. 802)),

is inadmissible.

(ii) Exception. Clause (i)(I) shall not apply to an alien who committed only one crime if

(I) the crime was committed when the alien was under 18 years of age, and the crime was committed (and the alien released from any confinement to a prison or correctional institution imposed for the crime) more than 5 years before the date of application for a visa or other documentation and the date of application for admission to the United States, or

(II) the maximum penalty possible for the crime of which the alien was convicted (or which the alien admits having committed or of which the acts that the alien admits having committed constituted the essential elements) did not exceed imprisonment for one year and, if the alien was convicted of such crime, the alien was not sentenced to a term of imprisonment in excess of 6 months (regardless of the extent to which the sentence was ultimately executed).

(B) Multiple criminal convictions. Any alien convicted of 2 or more offenses (other than purely political offenses), regardless of whether the conviction was in a single trial or whether the offenses arose from a single scheme of misconduct and regardless of whether the offenses involved moral turpitude, for which the aggregate sentences to confinement were 5 years or more is inadmissible.

(C) Controlled substance traffickers. Any alien who the consular officer or the Attorney General knows or has reason to believe

(i) is or has been an illicit trafficker in any controlled substance or in any listed chemical (as defined in section 102 of the Controlled Substances Act (21 U.S.C. 802)), or is or has been a knowing aider, abettor, assister, conspirator, or colluder with others in the illicit trafficking in any such controlled or listed substance or chemical, or endeavored to do so; or

(ii) is the spouse, son, or daughter of an alien inadmissible under clause (i), has, within the previous 5 years, obtained any financial or other benefit from the illicit activity of that alien, and knew or reasonably should have known that the financial or other benefit was the product of such illicit activity,

is inadmissible.

(D) Prostitution and commercialized vice. Any alien who

(i) is coming to the United States solely, principally, or incidentally to engage in prostitution, or has engaged in prostitution within 10 years of the date of application for a visa, admission, or adjustment of status,

(ii) directly or indirectly procures or attempts to procure, or (within 10 years of the date of application for a visa, admission, or adjustment of status) procured or attempted to procure or to import, prostitutes or persons for the purpose of prostitution, or receives or (within such 10-year period) received, in whole or in part, the proceeds of prostitution, or

(iii) is coming to the United States to engage in any other unlawful commercialized vice, whether or not related to prostitution,

is inadmissible.

(E) Certain aliens involved in serious criminal activity who have asserted immunity from prosecution. Any alien

(i) who has committed in the United States at any time a serious criminal offense (as defined in section 101(h) [8 USCS § 1101(h)]),

(ii) for whom immunity from criminal jurisdiction was exercised with respect to that offense,

(iii) who as a consequence of the offense and exercise of immunity has departed from the United States, and

(iv) who has not subsequently submitted fully to the jurisdiction of the court in the United States having jurisdiction with respect to that offense,

is inadmissible.

(F) Waiver authorized. For provision authorizing waiver of certain subparagraphs of this paragraph, see subsection (h).

(G) Foreign government officials who have committed particularly severe violations of religious freedom. Any alien who, while serving as a foreign government official, was responsible for or directly carried out, at any time, particularly severe violations of religious freedom, as defined in section 3 of the International Religious Freedom Act of 1998 (22 U.S.C. 6402), is inadmissible.

(H) Significant traffickers in persons.

(i) In general. Any alien who commits or conspires to commit human trafficking offenses in the United States or outside the United States, or who the consular officer, the Secretary of Homeland Security, the Secretary of State, or the Attorney General knows or has reason to believe is or has been a knowing aider, abettor, assister, conspirator, or colluder with such a trafficker in severe forms of trafficking in persons, as defined in the section 103 of such Act [22 USCS § 7102], is inadmissible.

(ii) Beneficiaries of trafficking. Except as provided in clause (iii), any alien who the consular officer or the Attorney General knows or has reason to believe is the spouse, son, or daughter of an alien inadmissible under clause (i), has, within the previous 5 years, obtained any financial or other benefit from the illicit activity of that alien, and knew or reasonably should have known that the financial or other benefit was the product of such illicit activity, is inadmissible.

(iii) Exception for certain sons and daughters. Clause (ii) shall not apply to a son or daughter who was a child at the time he or she received the benefit described in such clause.

(I) Money laundering. Any alien

(i) who a consular officer or the Attorney General knows, or has reason to believe, has engaged, is engaging, or seeks to enter the United States to engage, in an offense which is described in section 1956 or 1957 of title 18, United States Code (relating to laundering of monetary instruments); or

(ii) who a consular officer or the Attorney General knows is, or has been, a knowing aider, abettor, assister, conspirator, or colluder with others in an offense which is described in such section;

is inadmissible.

(3) Security and related grounds.

(A) In general. Any alien who a consular officer or the Attorney General knows, or has reasonable ground to believe, seeks to enter the United States to engage solely, principally, or incidentally in

(i) any activity (I) to violate any law of the United States relating to espionage or sabotage or (II) to violate or evade any law prohibiting the export from the United States of goods, technology, or sensitive information,

(ii) any other unlawful activity, or

(iii) any activity a purpose of which is the opposition to, or the control or overthrow of, the Government of the United States by force, violence, or other unlawful means,

is inadmissible.

(B) Terrorist activities.

(i) In general. Any alien who

(I) has engaged in a terrorist activity;

(II) a consular officer, the Attorney General, or the Secretary of Homeland Security knows, or has reasonable ground to believe, is engaged in or is likely to engage after entry in any terrorist activity (as defined in clause (iv));

(III) has, under circumstances indicating an intention to cause death or serious bodily harm, incited terrorist activity;

(IV) is a representative (as defined in clause (v)) of

(aa) a terrorist organization (as defined in clause (vi)); or

(bb) a political, social, or other group that endorses or espouses terrorist activity;

(V) is a member of a terrorist organization described in subclause (I) or (II) of clause (vi);

(VI) is a member of a terrorist organization described in clause (vi)(III), unless the alien can demonstrate by clear and convincing evidence that the alien did not know, and should not reasonably have known, that the organization was a terrorist organization;

(VII) endorses or espouses terrorist activity or persuades others to endorse or espouse terrorist activity or support a terrorist organization;

(VIII) has received military-type training (as defined in section 2339D(c)(1) of title 18, United States Code [18 USCS § 2339D(c)(1)]) from or on behalf of any organization that, at the time the training was received, was a terrorist organization (as defined in clause (vi)); or

(IX) is the spouse or child of an alien who is inadmissible under this subparagraph, if the activity causing the alien to be found inadmissible occurred within the last 5 years,

is inadmissible. An alien who is an officer, official, representative, or spokesman of the Palestine Liberation Organization is considered, for purposes of this Act, to be engaged in a terrorist activity.

(ii) Exception. Subclause (IX) of clause (i) does not apply to a spouse or child

(I) who did not know or should not reasonably have known of the activity causing the alien to be found inadmissible under this section; or

(II) whom the consular officer or Attorney General has reasonable grounds to believe has renounced the activity causing the alien to be found inadmissible under this section.

(iii) "Terrorist activity" defined. As used in this Act, the term "terrorist activity" means any activity which is unlawful under the laws of the place where it is committed (or which, if it had been committed in the United States, would be unlawful under the laws of the United States or any State) and which involves any of the following:

(I) The highjacking or sabotage of any conveyance (including an aircraft, vessel, or vehicle).

(II) The seizing or detaining, and threatening to kill, injure, or continue to detain, another individual in order to compel a third person (including a governmental organization) to do or abstain from doing any act as an explicit or implicit condition for the release of the individual seized or detained.

(III) A violent attack upon an internationally protected person (as defined in section 1116(b)(4) of title 18, United States Code) or upon the liberty of such a person.

(IV) An assassination.

(V) The use of any

(a) biological agent, chemical agent, or nuclear weapon or device, or

(b) explosive, firearm, or other weapon or dangerous device (other than for mere personal monetary gain), with intent to endanger, directly or indirectly, the safety of one or more individuals or to cause substantial damage to property.

(VI) A threat, attempt, or conspiracy to do any of the foregoing.

(iv) "Engage in terrorist activity" defined. As used in this Act, the term "engage in terrorist activity" means, in an individual capacity or as a member of an organization

(I) to commit or to incite to commit, under circumstances indicating an intention to cause death or serious bodily injury, a terrorist activity;

(II) to prepare or plan a terrorist activity;

(III) to gather information on potential targets for terrorist activity;

(IV) to solicit funds or other things of value for

(aa) a terrorist activity;

(bb) a terrorist organization described in clause (vi)(I) or (vi)(II); or

(cc) a terrorist organization described in clause (vi)(III), unless the solicitor can demonstrate by clear and convincing evidence that he did not know, and should not reasonably have known, that the organization was a terrorist organization;

(V) to solicit any individual

(aa) to engage in conduct otherwise described in this subsection;

(bb) for membership in a terrorist organization described in clause (vi)(I) or (vi)(II); or

(cc) for membership in a terrorist organization described in clause (vi)(III) unless the solicitor can demonstrate by clear and convincing evidence that he did not know, and should not reasonably have known, that the organization was a terrorist organization; or

(VI) to commit an act that the actor knows, or reasonably should know, affords material support, including a safe house, transportation, communications, funds, transfer of funds or other material financial benefit, false documentation or identification, weapons (including chemical, biological, or radiological weapons), explosives, or training

(aa) for the commission of a terrorist activity;

(bb) to any individual who the actor knows, or reasonably should know, has committed or plans to commit a terrorist activity;

(cc) to a terrorist organization described in subclause (I) or (II) of clause (vi) or to any member of such an organization; or

(dd) to a terrorist organization described in clause (vi)(III), or to any member of such an organization, unless the actor can demonstrate by clear and convincing evidence that the actor did not know, and should not reasonably have known, that the organization was a terrorist organization.

(v) "Representative" defined. As used in this paragraph, the term "representative" includes an officer, official, or spokesman of an organization, and any person who directs, counsels, commands, or induces an organization or its members to engage in terrorist activity.

(vi) "Terrorist organization" defined. As used in this section, the term "terrorist organization" means an organization

(I) designated under section 219 [8 USCS § 1189];

(II) otherwise designated, upon publication in the Federal Register, by the Secretary of State in consultation with or upon the request of the Attorney General or the Secretary of Homeland Security, as a terrorist organization, after finding that the organization engages in the activities described in subclauses (I) through (VI) of clause (iv); or

(III) that is a group of two or more individuals, whether organized or not, which engages in, or has a subgroup which engages in, the activities described in subclauses (I) through (VI) of clause (iv).

(C) Foreign policy.

(i) In general. An alien whose entry or proposed activities in the United States the Secretary of State has reasonable ground to believe would have potentially serious adverse foreign policy consequences for the United States is inadmissible.

(ii) Exception for officials. An alien who is an official of a foreign government or a purported government, or who is a candidate for election to a foreign government office during the period immediately preceding the election for that office, shall not be excludable or subject to restrictions or conditions on entry into the United States under clause (i) solely because of the alien's past, current, or expected beliefs, statements, or associations, if such beliefs, statements, or associations would be lawful within the United States.

(iii) Exception for other aliens. An alien, not described in clause (ii), shall not be excludable or subject to restrictions or conditions on entry into the United States under clause (i) because of the alien's past, current, or expected beliefs, statements, or associations, if such beliefs, statements, or associations would be lawful within the United States, unless the Secretary of State personally determines that the alien's admission would compromise a compelling United States foreign policy interest.

(iv) Notification of determinations. If a determination is made under clause (iii) with respect to an alien, the Secretary of State must notify on a timely basis the chairmen of the Committees on the Judiciary and Foreign Affairs of the House of Representatives and of the Committees on the Judiciary and Foreign Relations of the Senate of the identity of the alien and the reasons for the determination.

(D) Immigrant membership in totalitarian party.

(i) In general. Any immigrant who is or has been a member of or affiliated with the Communist or any other totalitarian party (or subdivision or affiliate thereof), domestic or foreign, is inadmissible.

(ii) Exception for involuntary membership. Clause (i) shall not apply to an alien because of membership or affiliation if the alien establishes to the satisfaction of the consular officer when applying for a visa (or to the satisfaction of the Attorney General when applying for admission) that the membership or affiliation is or was involuntary, or is or was solely when under 16 years of age, by operation of law, or for purposes of obtaining employment, food rations, or other essentials of living and whether necessary for such purposes.

(iii) Exception for past membership. Clause (i) shall not apply to an alien because of membership or affiliation if the alien establishes to the satisfaction of the consular officer when applying for a visa (or to the satisfaction of the Attorney General when applying for admission) that

(I) the membership or affiliation terminated at least

(a) 2 years before the date of such application, or

(b) 5 years before the date of such application, in the case of an alien whose membership or affiliation was with the party controlling the government of a foreign state that is a totalitarian dictatorship as of such date, and

(II) the alien is not a threat to the security of the United States.

(iv) Exception for close family members. The Attorney General may, in the Attorney General's discretion, waive the application of clause (i) in the case of an immigrant who is the parent, spouse, son, daughter, brother, or sister of a citizen of the United States or a spouse, son, or daughter of an alien lawfully admitted for permanent residence for humanitarian purposes, to assure family unity, or when it is otherwise in the public interest if the immigrant is not a threat to the security of the United States.

(E) Participants in Nazi persecution, genocide, or the commission of any act of torture or extrajudicial killing.

(i) Participation in Nazi persecutions. Any alien who, during the period beginning on March 23, 1933, and ending on May 8, 1945, under the direction of, or in association with

(I) the Nazi government of Germany,

(II) any government in any area occupied by the military forces of the Nazi government of Germany,

(III) any government established with the assistance or cooperation of the Nazi government of Germany, or

(IV) any government which was an ally of the Nazi government of Germany,

ordered, incited, assisted, or otherwise participated in the persecution of any person because of race, religion, national origin, or political opinion is inadmissible.

(ii) Participation in genocide. Any alien who ordered, incited, assisted, or otherwise participated in genocide, as defined in section 1091(a) of title 18, United States Code, is inadmissible.

(iii) Commission of acts of torture or extrajudicial killings. Any alien who, outside the United States, has committed, ordered, incited, assisted, or otherwise participated in the commission of

(I) any act of torture, as defined in section 2340 of title 18, United States Code; or

(II) under color of law of any foreign nation, any extrajudicial killing, as defined in section 3(a) of the Torture Victim Protection Act of 1991 (28 U.S.C. 1350 note),

is inadmissible.

(F) Association with terrorist organizations. Any alien who the Secretary of State, after consultation with the Attorney General, or the Attorney General, after consultation with the Secretary of State, determines has been associated with a terrorist organization and intends while in the United States to engage solely, principally, or incidentally in activities that could endanger the welfare, safety, or security of the United States is inadmissible.

(G) Recruitment or use of child soldiers. Any alien who has engaged in the recruitment or use of child soldiers in violation of section 2442 of title 18, United States Code, is inadmissible.

(4) Public charge.

(A) In general. Any alien who, in the opinion of the consular officer at the time of application for a visa, or in the opinion of the Attorney General at the time of application for admission or adjustment of status, is likely at any time to become a public charge is inadmissible.

(B) Factors to be taken into account.

(i) In determining whether an alien is inadmissible under this paragraph, the consular officer or the Attorney General shall at a minimum consider the alien's

(I) age;

(II) health;

(III) family status;

(IV) assets, resources, and financial status; and

(V) education and skills.

(ii) In addition to the factors under clause (i), the consular officer or the Attorney General may also consider any affidavit of support under section 213A [8 USCS § 1183a] for purposes of exclusion under this paragraph.

(C) Family-sponsored immigrants. Any alien who seeks admission or adjustment of status under a visa number issued under section 201(b)(2) or 203(a) [8 USCS § 1151(b)(2) or 1153(a)] is inadmissible under this paragraph unless

(i) the alien has obtained

(I) status as a spouse or a child of a United States citizen pursuant to clause (ii), (iii), or (iv) of section 204(a)(1)(A) [8 USCS § 1154(a)(1)(A)(ii), (iii), or (iv)];

(II) classification pursuant to clause (ii) or (iii) of section 204(a)(1)(B) [8 USCS § 1154(a)(1)(B)]; or

(III) classification or status as a VAWA self-petitioner; or

(ii) the person petitioning for the alien's admission (and any additional sponsor required under section 213A(f) [8 USCS § 1183a(f)] or any alternative sponsor permitted under paragraph (5)(B) of such section) has executed an affidavit of support described in section 213A [8 USCS § 1183a] with respect to such alien.

(D) Certain employment-based immigrants. Any alien who seeks admission or adjustment of status under a visa number issued under section 203(b) [8 USCS § 1153(b)] by virtue of a classification petition filed by a relative of the alien (or by an entity in which such relative has a significant ownership interest) is inadmissible under this paragraph unless such relative has executed an affidavit of support described in section 213A [8 USCS § 1183a] with respect to such alien.

(E) Special rule for qualified alien victims. Subparagraphs (A), (B), and (C) shall not apply to an alien who

(i) is a VAWA self-petitioner;

(ii) is an applicant for, or is granted, nonimmigrant status under section 101(a)(15)(U) [8 USCS § 1101(a)(15)(U)]; or

(iii) is a qualified alien described in section 431(c) of the Personal Responsibility and Work Opportunity Reconciliation Act of 1996 (8 U.S.C. 1641(c)).

(5) Labor certification and qualifications for certain immigrants.

(A) Labor certification.

(i) In general. Any alien who seeks to enter the United States for the purpose of performing skilled or unskilled labor is inadmissible, unless the Secretary of Labor has determined and certified to the Secretary of State and the Attorney General that

(I) there are not sufficient workers who are able, willing, qualified (or equally qualified in the case of an alien described in clause (ii)) and available at the time of application for a visa and admission to the United States and at the place where the alien is to perform such skilled or unskilled labor, and

(II) the employment of such alien will not adversely affect the wages and working conditions of workers in the United States similarly employed.

(ii) Certain aliens subject to special rule. For purposes of clause (i)(I), an alien described in this clause is an alien who

(I) is a member of the teaching profession, or

(II) has exceptional ability in the sciences or the arts.

(iii) Professional athletes.

(I) In general. A certification made under clause (i) with respect to a professional athlete shall remain valid with respect to the athlete after the athlete changes employer, if the new employer is a team in the same sport as the team which employed the athlete when the athlete first applied for the certification.

(II) Definition. For purposes of subclause (I), the term "professional athlete" means an individual who is employed as an athlete by

(aa) a team that is a member of an association of 6 or more professional sports teams whose total combined revenues exceed $10,000,000 per year, if the association governs the conduct of its members and regulates the contests and exhibitions in which its member teams regularly engage; or

(bb) any minor league team that is affiliated with such an association.

(iv) Long delayed adjustment applicants. A certification made under clause (i) with respect to an individual whose petition is covered by section 204(j) [8 USCS § 1154(j)] shall remain valid with respect to a new job accepted by the individual after the individual changes jobs or employers if the new job is in the same or a similar occupational classification as the job for which the certification was issued.

(B) Unqualified physicians. An alien who is a graduate of a medical school not accredited by a body or bodies approved for the purpose by the Secretary of Education (regardless of whether such school of medicine is in the United States) and who is coming to the United States principally to perform services as a member of the medical profession is inadmissible, unless the alien (i) has passed parts I and II of the National Board of Medical Examiners Examination (or an equivalent examination as determined by the Secretary of Health and Human Services) and (ii) is competent in oral and written English. For purposes of the previous sentence, an alien who is a graduate of a medical school shall be considered to have passed parts I and II of the National Board of Medical Examiners if the alien was fully and permanently licensed to practice medicine in a State on January 9, 1978, and was practicing medicine in a State on that date.

(C) Uncertified foreign health-care workers. Subject to subsection (r), any alien who seeks to enter the United States for the purpose of performing labor as a health-care worker, other than a physician, is inadmissible unless the alien presents to the consular officer, or, in the case of an adjustment of status, the Attorney General, a certificate from the Commission on Graduates of Foreign Nursing Schools, or a certificate from an equivalent independent credentialing organization approved by the Attorney General in consultation with the Secretary of Health and Human Services, verifying that

(i) the alien's education, training, license, and experience

(I) meet all applicable statutory and regulatory requirements for entry into the United States under the classification specified in the application;

(II) are comparable with that required for an American health-care worker of the same type; and

(III) are authentic and, in the case of a license, unencumbered;

(ii) the alien has the level of competence in oral and written English considered by the Secretary of Health and Human Services, in consultation with the Secretary of Education, to be appropriate for health care work of the kind in which the alien will be engaged, as shown by an appropriate score on one or more nationally recognized, commercially available, standardized assessments of the applicant's ability to speak and write; and

(iii) if a majority of States licensing the profession in which the alien intends to work recognize a test predicting the success on the profession's licensing or certification examination, the alien has passed such a test or has passed such an examination.

For purposes of clause (ii), determination of the standardized tests required and of the minimum scores that are appropriate are within the sole discretion of the Secretary of Health and Human Services and are not subject to further administrative or judicial review.

(D) Application of grounds. The grounds for inadmissibility of aliens under subparagraphs (A) and (B) shall apply to immigrants seeking admission or adjustment of status under paragraph (2) or (3) of section 203(b) [8 USCS § 1153(b)(2) or (3)].

(6) Illegal entrants and immigration violators.

(A) Aliens present without admission or parole.

(i) In general. An alien present in the United States without being admitted or paroled, or who arrives in the United States at any time or place other than as designated by the Attorney General, is inadmissible.

(ii) Exception for certain battered women and children. Clause (i) shall not apply to an alien who demonstrates that

(I) the alien is a VAWA self-petitioner;

(II) (a) the alien has been battered or subjected to extreme cruelty by a spouse or parent, or by a member of the spouse's or parent's family residing in the same household as the alien and the spouse or parent consented or acquiesced to such battery or cruelty, or (b) the alien's child has been battered or subjected to extreme cruelty by a spouse or parent of the alien (without the active participation of the alien in the battery or cruelty) or by a member of the spouse's or parent's family residing in the same household as the alien when the spouse or parent consented to or acquiesced in such battery or cruelty and the alien did not actively participate in such battery or cruelty, and

(III) there was a substantial connection between the battery or cruelty described in subclause (I) or (II) and the alien's unlawful entry into the United States.

(B) Failure to attend removal proceeding. Any alien who without reasonable cause fails or refuses to attend or remain in attendance at a proceeding to determine the alien's inadmissibility or deportability and who seeks admission to the United States within 5 years of such alien's subsequent departure or removal is inadmissible.

(C) Misrepresentation.

(i) In general. Any alien who, by fraud or willfully misrepresenting a material fact, seeks to procure (or has sought to procure or has procured) a visa, other documentation, or admission into the United States or other benefit provided under this Act is inadmissible.

(ii) Falsely claiming citizenship.

(I) In general. Any alien who falsely represents, or has falsely represented, himself or herself to be a citizen of the United States for any purpose or benefit under this Act (including section 274A [8 USCS § 1324a]) or any other Federal or State law is inadmissible.

(II) Exception. In the case of an alien making a representation described in subclause (I), if each natural parent of the alien (or, in the case of an adopted alien, each adoptive parent of the alien) is or was a citizen (whether by birth or naturalization), the alien permanently resided in the United States prior to attaining the age of 16, and the alien reasonably believed at the time of making such representation that he or she was a citizen, the alien shall not be considered to be inadmissible under any provision of this subsection based on such representation.

(iii) Waiver authorized. For provision authorizing waiver of clause (i), see subsection (i).

(D) Stowaways. Any alien who is a stowaway is inadmissible.

(E) Smugglers.

(i) In general. Any alien who at any time knowingly has encouraged, induced, assisted, abetted, or aided any other alien to enter or to try to enter the United States in violation of law is inadmissible.

(ii) Special rule in the case of family reunification. Clause (i) shall not apply in the case of alien who is an eligible immigrant (as defined in section 301(b)(1) of the Immigration Act of 1990 [8 USCS § 1255a note]), was physically present in the United States on May 5, 1988, and is seeking admission as an immediate relative or under section 203(a)(2) [8 USCS § 1153(a)(2)] (including under section 112 of the Immigration Act of 1990 [8 USCS § 1153 note]) or benefits under section 301(a) of the Immigration Act of 1990 [8 USCS § 1255a note] if the alien, before May 5, 1988, has encouraged, induced, assisted, abetted, or aided only the alien's spouse, parent, son, or daughter (and no other individual) to enter the United States in violation of law.

(iii) Waiver authorized. For provision authorizing waiver of clause (i), see subsection (d)(11).

(F) Subject of civil penalty.

(i) In general. An alien who is the subject of a final order for violation of section 274C [8 USCS § 1324c] is inadmissible.

(ii) Waiver authorized. For provision authorizing waiver of clause (i), see subsection (d)(12).

(G) Student visa abusers. An alien who obtains the status of a nonimmigrant under section 101(a)(15)(F)(i) [8 USCS § 1101(a)(15)(F)(i)] and who violates a term or condition of such status under section 214(l) is inadmissible until the alien has been outside the United States for a continuous period of 5 years after the date of the violation.

(7) Documentation requirements.

(A) Immigrants.

(i) In general. Except as otherwise specifically provided in this Act, any immigrant at the time of application for admission

(I) who is not in possession of a valid unexpired immigrant visa, reentry permit, border crossing identification card, or other valid entry document required by this Act, and a valid unexpired passport, or other suitable travel document, or document of identity and nationality if such document is required under the regulations issued by the Attorney General under section 211(a) [8 USCS § 1181(a)], or

(II) whose visa has been issued without compliance with the provisions of section 203 [8 USCS § 1183],

is inadmissible.

(ii) Waiver authorized. For provision authorizing waiver of clause (i), see subsection (k).

(B) Nonimmigrants.

(i) In general. Any nonimmigrant who

(I) is not in possession of a passport valid for a minimum of six months from the date of the expiration of the initial period of the alien's admission or contemplated initial period of stay authorizing the alien to return to the country from which the alien came or to proceed to and enter some other country during such period, or

(II) is not in possession of a valid nonimmigrant visa or border crossing identification card at the time of application for admission,

is inadmissible.

(ii) General waiver authorized. For provision authorizing waiver of clause (i), see subsection (d)(4).

(iii) Guam and Northern Mariana Islands visa waiver. For provision authorizing waiver of clause (i) in the case of visitors to Guam or the Commonwealth of the Northern Mariana Islands, see subsection (l).

(iv) Visa waiver program. For authority to waive the requirement of clause (i) under a program, see section 217 [8 USCS § 1187].

(8) Ineligible for citizenship.

(A) In general. Any immigrant who is permanently ineligible to citizenship is inadmissible.

(B) Draft evaders. Any person who has departed from or who has remained outside the United States to avoid or evade training or service in the armed forces in time of war or a period declared by the President to be a national emergency is inadmissible, except that this subparagraph shall not apply to an alien who at the time of such departure was a nonimmigrant and who is seeking to reenter the United States as a nonimmigrant.

(9) Aliens previously removed.

(A) Certain aliens previously removed.

(i) Arriving aliens. Any alien who has been ordered removed under section 235(b)(1) [8 USCS § 1225(b)(1)] or at the end of proceedings under section 240 [8 USCS § 1229a] initiated upon the alien's arrival in the United States and who again seeks admission within 5 years of the date of such removal (or within 20 years in the case of a second or subsequent removal or at any time in the case of an alien convicted of an aggravated felony) is inadmissible.

(ii) Other aliens. Any alien not described in clause (i) who

(I) has been ordered removed under section 240 [8 USCS § 1229a] or any other provision of law, or

(II) departed the United States while an order of removal was outstanding,

and who seeks admission within 10 years of the date of such alien's departure or removal (or within 20 years of such date in the case of a second or subsequent removal or at any time in the case of an alien convicted of an aggravated felony) is inadmissible.

(iii) Exception. Clauses (i) and (ii) shall not apply to an alien seeking admission within a period if, prior to the date of the alien's reembarkation at a place outside the United States or attempt to be admitted from foreign contiguous territory, the Attorney General has consented to the alien's reapplying for admission.

(B) Aliens unlawfully present.

(i) In general. Any alien (other than an alien lawfully admitted for permanent residence) who

(I) was unlawfully present in the United States for a period of more than 180 days but less than 1 year, voluntarily departed the United States (whether or not pursuant to section 244(e) [section 240B]) prior to the commencement of proceedings under section 235(b)(1) [8 USCS § 1225(b)(1)] or section 240 [8 USCS § 1229a], and again seeks admission within 3 years of the date of such alien's departure or removal, or

(II) has been unlawfully present in the United States for one year or more, and who again seeks admission within 10 years of the date of such alien's departure or removal from the United States,

is inadmissible.

(ii) Construction of unlawful presence. For purposes of this paragraph, an alien is deemed to be unlawfully present in the United States if the alien is present in the United States after the expiration of the period of stay authorized by the Attorney General or is present in the United States without being admitted or paroled.

(iii) Exceptions.

(I) Minors. No period of time in which an alien is under 18 years of age shall be taken into account in determining the period of unlawful presence in the United States under clause (i).

(II) Asylees. No period of time in which an alien has a bona fide application for asylum pending under section 208 [8 USCS § 1158] shall be taken into account in determining the period of unlawful presence in the United States under clause (i) unless the alien during such period was employed without authorization in the United States.

(III) Family unity. No period of time in which the alien is a beneficiary of family unity protection pursuant to section 301 of the Immigration Act of 1990 [8 USCS § 1255a note] shall be taken into account in determining the period of unlawful presence in the United States under clause (i).

(IV) Battered women and children. Clause (i) shall not apply to an alien who would be described in paragraph (6)(A)(ii) if "violation of the terms of the alien's nonimmigrant visa" were substituted for "unlawful entry into the United States" in subclause (III) of that paragraph.

(V) Victims of a severe form of trafficking in persons. Clause (i) shall not apply to an alien who demonstrates that the severe form of trafficking (as that term is defined in section 103 of the Trafficking Victims Protection Act of 2000 (22 U.S.C. 7102)) was at least one central reason for the alien's unlawful presence in the United States.

(iv) Tolling for good cause. In the case of an alien who

(I) has been lawfully admitted or paroled into the United States,

(II) has filed a nonfrivolous application for a change or extension of status before the date of expiration of the period of stay authorized by the Attorney General, and

(III) has not been employed without authorization in the United States before or during the pendency of such application,

the calculation of the period of time specified in clause (i)(I) shall be tolled during the pendency of such application, but not to exceed 120 days.

(v) Waiver. The Attorney General has sole discretion to waive clause (i) in the case of an immigrant who is the spouse or son or daughter of a United States citizen or of an alien lawfully admitted for permanent residence, if it is established to the satisfaction of the Attorney General that the refusal of admission to such immigrant alien would result in extreme hardship to the citizen or lawfully resident spouse or parent of such alien. No court shall have jurisdiction to review a decision or action by the Attorney General regarding a waiver under this clause.

(C) Aliens unlawfully present after previous immigration violations.

(i) In general. Any alien who

(I) has been unlawfully present in the United States for an aggregate period of more than 1 year, or

(II) has been ordered removed under section 235(b)(1) [8 USCS § 1225(b)(1)], section 240 [8 USCS § 1229a], or any other provision of law,

and who enters or attempts to reenter the United States without being admitted is inadmissible.

(ii) Exception. Clause (i) shall not apply to an alien seeking admission more than 10 years after the date of the alien's last departure from the United States if, prior to the alien's reembarkation at a place outside the United States or attempt to be readmitted from a foreign contiguous territory, the Secretary of Homeland Security has consented to the alien's reapplying for admission.

(iii) Waiver. The Secretary of Homeland Security may waive the application of clause (i) in the case of an alien who is a VAWA self-petitioner if there is a connection between

(I) the alien's battering or subjection to extreme cruelty; and

(II) the alien's removal, departure from the United States, reentry or reentries into the United States; or attempted reentry into the United States.

(10) Miscellaneous.

(A) Practicing polygamists. Any immigrant who is coming to the United States to practice polygamy is inadmissible.

(B) Guardian required to accompany helpless alien. Any alien

(i) who is accompanying another alien who is inadmissible and who is certified to be helpless from sickness, mental or physical disability, or infancy pursuant to section 232(c) [8 USCS § 1222(c)], and

(ii) whose protection or guardianship is determined to be required by the alien described in clause (i),

is inadmissible.

(C) International child abduction.

(i) In general. Except as provided in clause (ii), any alien who, after entry of an order by a court in the United States granting custody to a person of a United States citizen child who detains or retains the child, or withholds custody of the child, outside the United States from the person granted custody by that order, is inadmissible until the child is surrendered to the person granted custody by that order.

(ii) Aliens supporting abductors and relatives of abductors. Any alien who

(I) is known by the Secretary of State to have intentionally assisted an alien in the conduct described in clause (i),

(II) is known by the Secretary of State to be intentionally providing material support or safe haven to an alien described in clause (i), or

(III) is a spouse (other than the spouse who is the parent of the abducted child), child (other than the abducted child), parent, sibling, or agent of an alien described in clause (i), if such person has been designated by the Secretary of State at the Secretary's sole and unreviewable discretion, is inadmissible until the child described in clause (i) is surrendered to the person granted custody by the order described in that clause, and such person and child are permitted to return to the United States or such person's place of residence.

(iii) Exceptions. Clauses (i) and (ii) shall not apply

(I) to a government official of the United States who is acting within the scope of his or her official duties;

(II) to a government official of any foreign government if the official has been designated by the Secretary of State at the Secretary's sole and unreviewable discretion; or

(III) so long as the child is located in a foreign state that is a party to the Convention on the Civil Aspects of International Child Abduction, done at The Hague on October 25, 1980.

(D) Unlawful voters.

(i) In general. Any alien who has voted in violation of any Federal, State, or local constitutional provision, statute, ordinance, or regulation is inadmissible.

(ii) Exception. In the case of an alien who voted in a Federal, State, or local election (including an initiative, recall, or referendum) in violation of a lawful restriction of voting to citizens, if each natural parent of the alien (or, in the case of an adopted alien, each adoptive parent of the alien) is or was a citizen (whether by birth or naturalization), the alien permanently resided in the United States prior to attaining the age of 16, and the alien reasonably believed at the time of such violation that he or she was a citizen, the alien shall not be considered to be inadmissible under any provision of this subsection based on such violation.

(E) Former citizens who renounced citizenship to avoid taxation. Any alien who is a former citizen of the United States who officially renounces United States citizenship and who is determined by the Attorney General to have renounced United States citizenship for the purpose of avoiding taxation by the United States is inadmissible.

(b) Notices of denials.

(1) Subject to paragraphs (2) and (3), if an alien's application for a visa, for admission to the United States, or for adjustment of status is denied by an immigration or consular officer because the officer determines the alien to be inadmissible under subsection (a), the officer shall provide the alien with a timely written notice that

(A) states the determination, and

(B) lists the specific provision or provisions of law under which the alien is inadmissible or [ineligible for] adjustment of status.

(2) The Secretary of State may waive the requirements of paragraph (1) with respect to a particular alien or any class or classes of inadmissible aliens.

(3) Paragraph (1) does not apply to any alien inadmissible under paragraph (2) or (3) of subsection (a).

(c) [Repealed]

(d) Temporary admission of nonimmigrants.

(1) The Attorney General shall determine whether a ground for inadmissibility exists with respect to a nonimmigrant described in section 101(a)(15)(S) [8 USCS § 1101(a)(15)(S)]. The Attorney General, in the Attorney General's discretion, may waive the application of subsection (a) (other than paragraph (3)(E)) in the case of a nonimmigrant described in section 101(a)(15)(S) [8 USCS § 1101(a)(15)(S)], if the Attorney General considers it to be in the national interest to do so. Nothing in this section shall be regarded as prohibiting the Immigration and Naturalization Service from instituting removal proceedings against an alien admitted as a nonimmigrant under section 101(a)(15)(S) [8 USCS § 1101(a)(15)(S)] for conduct committed after the alien's admission into the United States, or for conduct or a condition that was not disclosed to the Attorney General prior to the alien's admission as a nonimmigrant under section 101(a)(15)(S) [8 USCS § 1101(a)(15)(S)].

(2) [Repealed]

(3)(A) Except as provided in this subsection, an alien (i) who is applying for a nonimmigrant visa and is known or believed by the consular officer to be ineligible for such visa under subsection (a) (other than paragraphs (3)(A)(i)(I), (3)(A)(ii), (3)(A)(iii), (3)(C), and clauses (i) and (ii) of paragraph (3)(E) of such subsection), may, after approval by the Attorney General of a recommendation by the Secretary of State or by the consular officer that the alien be admitted temporarily despite his inadmissibility, be granted such a visa and may be admitted into the United States temporarily as a nonimmigrant in the discretion of the Attorney General, or (ii) who is inadmissible under subsection (a) (other than paragraphs (3)(A)(i)(I), (3)(A)(ii), (3)(A)(iii), (3)(C), and clauses (i) and (ii) of paragraph (3)(E) of such subsection), but who is in possession of appropriate documents or is granted a waiver thereof and is seeking admission, may be admitted into the United States temporarily as a nonimmigrant in the discretion of the Attorney General. The Attorney General shall prescribe conditions, including exaction of such bonds as may be necessary, to control and regulate the admission and return of inadmissible aliens applying for temporary admission under this paragraph.

(B)(i) The Secretary of State, after consultation with the Attorney General and the Secretary of Homeland Security, or the Secretary of Homeland Security, after consultation with the Secretary of State and the Attorney General, may determine in such Secretary's sole unreviewable discretion that subsection (a)(3)(B) shall not apply with respect to an alien within the scope of that subsection or that subsection (a)(3)(B)(vi)(III) shall not apply to a group within the scope of that subsection, except that no such waiver may be extended to an alien who is within the scope of subsection (a)(3)(B)(i)(II), no such waiver may be extended to an alien who is a member or representative of, has voluntarily and knowingly engaged in or endorsed or espoused or persuaded others to endorse or espouse or support terrorist activity on behalf of, or has voluntarily and knowingly received military-type training from a terrorist organization that is described in subclause (I) or (II) of subsection (a)(3)(B)(vi), and no such waiver may be extended to a group that has engaged [in] terrorist activity against the United States or another democratic country or that has purposefully engaged in a pattern or practice of terrorist activity that is directed at civilians. Such a determination shall neither prejudice the ability of the United States Government to commence criminal or civil proceedings involving a beneficiary of such a determination or any other person, nor create any substantive or procedural right or benefit for a beneficiary of such a determination or any other person. Notwithstanding any other provision of law (statutory or nonstatutory), including section 2241 of title 28, or any other habeas corpus provision, and sections 1361 and 1651 of such title [28 USCS §§ 1361 and 1651], no court shall have jurisdiction to review such a determination or revocation except in a proceeding for review of a final order of removal pursuant to section 1252 of this title [8 USCS § 1252], and review shall be limited to the extent provided in section 1252(a)(2)(D) [8 USCS § 1252(a)(2)(D)]. The Secretary of State may not exercise the discretion provided in this clause with respect to an alien at any time during which the alien is the subject of pending removal proceedings under section 1229a of this title [8 USCS § 1229a].

(ii) Not later than 90 days after the end of each fiscal year, the Secretary of State and the Secretary of Homeland Security shall each provide to the Committees on the Judiciary of the House of Representatives and of the Senate, the Committee on International Relations of the House of Representatives, the Committee on Foreign Relations of the Senate, and the Committee on Homeland Security of the House of Representatives a report on the aliens to whom such Secretary has applied clause (i). Within one week of applying clause (i) to a group, the Secretary of State or the Secretary of Homeland Security shall provide a report to such Committees.

(4) Either or both of the requirements of paragraph (7)(B)(i) of subsection (a) may be waived by the Attorney General and the Secretary of State acting jointly (A) on the basis of unforeseen emergency in individual cases, or (B) on the basis of reciprocity with respect to nationals of foreign contiguous territory or of adjacent islands and residents thereof having a common nationality with such nationals, or (C) in the case of aliens proceeding in immediate and continuous transit through the United States under contracts authorized in section 238(c) [233(c)] [8 USCS § 1223(c)].

(5)(A) The Secretary of Homeland Security may except as provided in subparagraph (B) or in section 214(f) [8 USCS § 1184(f)], in his discretion parole into the United States temporarily under such conditions as he may prescribe only on a case-by-case basis for urgent humanitarian reasons or significant public benefit any alien applying for admission to the United States, but such parole of such alien shall not be regarded as an admission of the alien and when the purposes of such parole shall, in the opinion of the Secretary of Homeland Security, have been served the alien shall forthwith return or be returned to the custody from which he was paroled and thereafter his case shall continue to be dealt with in the same manner as that of any other applicant for admission to the United States.

(B) The Secretary of Homeland Security may not parole into the United States an alien who is a refugee unless the Secretary of Homeland Security determines that compelling reasons in the public interest with respect to that particular alien require that the alien be paroled into the United States rather than be admitted as a refugee under section 207 [8 USCS § 1157].

(C) The attorney general of a State, or other authorized State officer, alleging a violation of the limitation under subparagraph (A) that parole solely be granted on a case-by-case basis and solely for urgent humanitarian reasons or a significant public benefit, that harms such State or its residents shall have standing to bring an action against the Secretary of Homeland Security on behalf of such State or the residents of such State in an appropriate district court of the United States to obtain appropriate injunctive relief. The court shall advance on the docket and expedite the disposition of a civil action filed under this subparagraph to the greatest extent practicable. For purposes of this subparagraph, a State or its residents shall be considered to have been harmed if the State or its residents experience harm, including financial harm in excess of $100.

(6) [Repealed]

(7) The provisions of subsection (a) (other than paragraph (7)) shall be applicable to any alien who shall leave Guam, the Commonwealth of the Northern Mariana Islands, Puerto Rico, or the Virgin Islands of the United States, and who seeks to enter the continental United States or any other place under the jurisdiction of the United States. The Attorney General shall by regulations provide a method and procedure for the temporary admission to the United States of the aliens described in this proviso. Any alien described in this paragraph, who is denied admission to the United States, shall be immediately removed in the manner provided by section 241(c) of this Act [8 USCS § 1231(c)].

(8) Upon a basis of reciprocity accredited officials of foreign governments, their immediate families, attendants, servants, and personal employees may be admitted in immediate and continuous transit through the United States without regard to the provisions of this section except paragraphs (3)(A), (3)(B), (3)(C), and (7)(B) of subsection (a) of this section.

(9), (10) [Repealed]

(11) The Attorney General may, in his discretion for humanitarian purposes, to assure family unity, or when it is otherwise in the public interest, waive application of clause (i) of subsection (a)(6)(E) in the case of any alien lawfully admitted for permanent residence who temporarily proceeded abroad voluntarily and not under an order of removal, and who is otherwise admissible to the United States as a returning resident under section 211(b) [8 USCS § 1181(b)] and in the case of an alien seeking admission or adjustment of status as an immediate relative or immigrant under section 203(a) [8 USCS § 1153(a)] (other than paragraph (4) thereof), if the alien has encouraged, induced, assisted, abetted, or aided only an individual who at the time of such action was the alien's spouse, parent, son, or daughter (and no other individual) to enter the United States in violation of law.

(12) The Attorney General may, in the discretion of the Attorney General for humanitarian purposes or to assure family unity, waive application of clause (i) of subsection (a)(6)(F)

(A) in the case of an alien lawfully admitted for permanent residence who temporarily proceeded abroad voluntarily and not under an order of deportation or removal and who is otherwise admissible to the United States as a returning resident under section 211(b) [8 USCS § 1181(b)], and

(B) in the case of an alien seeking admission or adjustment of status under section 201(b)(2)(A) [8 USCS § 1151(b)(2)(A)] or under section 203(a) [8 USCS § 1153(a)],

if no previous civil money penalty was imposed against the alien under section 274C [8 USCS § 1324c] and the offense was committed solely to assist, aid, or support the alien's spouse or child (and not another individual). No court shall have jurisdiction to review a decision of the Attorney General to grant or deny a waiver under this paragraph.

(13)(A) The Secretary of Homeland Security shall determine whether a ground for inadmissibility exists with respect to a nonimmigrant described in section 101(a)(15)(T) [8 USCS § 1101(a)(15)(T)], except that the ground for inadmissibility described in subsection (a)(4) shall not apply with respect to such a nonimmigrant.

(B) In addition to any other waiver that may be available under this section, in the case of a nonimmigrant described in section 101(a)(15)(T) [8 USCS § 1101(a)(15)(T)], if the Secretary of Homeland Security considers it to be in the national interest to do so, the Secretary of Homeland Security, in the Attorney General's [Secretary's] discretion, may waive the application of

(i) subsection (a)(1); and

(ii) any other provision of subsection (a) (excluding paragraphs (3), (4), (10)(C), and (10[)](E)) if the activities rendering the alien inadmissible under the provision were caused by, or were incident to, the victimization described in section 101(a)(15)(T)(i)(I) [8 USCS § 1101(a)(15)(T)(i)(I)].

(14) The Secretary of Homeland Security shall determine whether a ground of inadmissibility exists with respect to a nonimmigrant described in section 101(a)(15)(U) [8 USCS § 1101(a)(15)(U)]. The Secretary of Homeland Security, in the Attorney General's [Secretary's] discretion, may waive the application of subsection (a) (other than paragraph (3)(E)) in the case of a nonimmigrant described in section 101(a)(15)(U) [8 USCS § 1101(a)(15)(U)], if the Secretary of Homeland Security considers it to be in the public or national interest to do so.

(e) Educational visitor status; foreign residence requirement; waiver. No person admitted under section 101(a)(15)(J) [8 USCS § 1101(a)(15)(J)] or acquiring such status after admission (i) whose participation in the program for which he came to the United States was financed in whole or in part, directly or indirectly, by an agency of the Government of the United States or by the government of the country of his nationality or his last residence, (ii) who at the time of admission or acquisition of status under section 101(a)(15)(J) [8 USCS § 1101(a)(15)(J)] was a national or resident of a country which the Director of the United States Information Agency, pursuant to regulations prescribed by him, had designated as clearly requiring the services of persons engaged in the field of specialized knowledge or skill in which the alien was engaged, or (iii) who came to the United States or acquired such status in order to receive graduate medical education or training, shall be eligible to apply for an immigrant visa, or for permanent residence, or for a nonimmigrant visa under section 101(a)(15)(H) or section 101(a)(15)(L) [8 USCS § 1101(a)(15)(H) or (L)] until it is established that such person has resided and been physically present in the country of his nationality or his last residence for an aggregate of at least two years following departure from the United States: *Provided,* That upon the favorable recommendation of the Director, pursuant to the request of an interested United States Government agency (or, in the case of an alien described in clause (iii), pursuant to the request of a State Department of Public Health, or its equivalent), or of the Commissioner of Immigration and Naturalization after he has determined that the departure from the United States would impose exceptional hardship upon the alien's spouse or child (if such spouse or child is a citizen of the United States or a lawfully resident alien), or that the alien cannot return to the country of his nationality or last residence because he would be subject to persecution on account of race, religion, or political opinion, the Attorney General may waive the requirement of such two-year foreign residence abroad in the case of any alien whose admission to the United States is found by the Attorney General to be in the public interest except that in the case of a waiver requested by a State Department of Public Health, or its equivalent, or in the case of a waiver requested by an interested United States Government agency on behalf of an alien described in clause (iii), the waiver shall be subject to the requirements of section 214(l) [8 USCS § 1184(l)]: *And provided further,* That, except in the case of an alien described in clause (iii), the Attorney General may, upon the favorable recommendation of the Director waive such two-year foreign residence requirement in any case in which the foreign country of the alien's nationality or last residence has furnished the Director a statement in writing that it has no objection to such waiver in the case of such alien.

(f) Suspension of entry or imposition of restrictions by President. Whenever the President finds that the entry of any aliens or of any class of aliens into the United States would be detrimental to the interests of the United States, he may by proclamation, and for such period as he shall deem necessary, suspend the entry of all aliens or any class of aliens as immigrants or nonimmigrants, or impose on the entry of aliens any restrictions he may deem to be appropriate. Whenever the Attorney General finds that a commercial airline has failed to comply with regulations of the Attorney General relating to requirements of airlines for the detection of fraudulent documents used by passengers traveling to the United States (including the training of personnel in such detection), the Attorney General may suspend the entry of some or all aliens transported to the United States by such airline.

(g) Bond and conditions for admission of alien inadmissible on health-related grounds. The Attorney General may waive the application of

(1) subsection (a)(1)(A)(i) in the case of any alien who

(A) is the spouse or the unmarried son or daughter, or the minor unmarried lawfully adopted child, of a United States citizen, or of an alien lawfully admitted for permanent residence, or of an alien who has been issued an immigrant visa,

(B) has a son or daughter who is a United States citizen, or an alien lawfully admitted for permanent residence, or an alien who has been issued an immigrant visa; or

(C) is a VAWA self-petitioner,

in accordance with such terms, conditions, and controls, if any, including the giving of bond, as the Attorney General, in the discretion of the Attorney General after consultation with the Secretary of Health and Human Services, may by regulation prescribe;

(2) subsection (a)(1)(A)(ii) in the case of any alien

(A) who receives vaccination against the vaccine-preventable disease or diseases for which the alien has failed to present documentation of previous vaccination,

(B) for whom a civil surgeon, medical officer, or panel physician (as those terms are defined by section 34.2 of title 42 of the Code of Federal Regulations) certifies, according to such regulations as the Secretary of Health and Human Services may prescribe, that such vaccination would not be medically appropriate, or

(C) under such circumstances as the Attorney General provides by regulation, with respect to whom the requirement of such a vaccination would be contrary to the alien's religious beliefs or moral convictions; or

(3) subsection (a)(1)(A)(iii) in the case of any alien, in accordance with such terms, conditions, and controls, if any, including the giving of bond, as the Attorney General, in the discretion of the Attorney General after consultation with the Secretary of Health and Human Services, may by regulation prescribe.

(h) Waiver of subsec. (a)(2)(A)(i)(I), (II), (B), (D), and (E). The Attorney General may, in his discretion, waive the application of subparagraphs (A)(i)(I), (B), (D), and (E) of subsection (a)(2) and subparagraph (A)(i)(II) of such subsection insofar as it relates to a single offense of simple possession of 30 grams or less of marijuana if

(1)(A) in the case of any immigrant it is established to the satisfaction of the Attorney General that

(i) the alien is inadmissible only under subparagraph (D)(i) or (D)(ii) of such subsection or the activities for which the alien is inadmissible occurred more than 15 years before the date of the alien's application for a visa, admission, or adjustment of status, and

(ii) the admission to the United States of such alien would not be contrary to the national welfare, safety, or security of the United States,

(iii) the alien has been rehabilitated; or

(B) in the case of an immigrant who is the spouse, parent, son, or daughter of a citizen of the United States or an alien lawfully admitted for permanent residence if it is established to the satisfaction of the Attorney General that the alien's denial of admission would result in extreme hardship to the United States citizen or lawfully resident spouse, parent, son, or daughter of such alien; or

(C) the alien is a VAWA self-petitioner; and

(2) the Attorney General, in his discretion, and pursuant to such terms, conditions and procedures as he may by regulations prescribe, has consented to the alien's applying or reapplying for a visa, for admission to the United States, or adjustment of status.

No waiver shall be provided under this subsection in the case of an alien who has been convicted of (or who has admitted committing acts that constitute) murder or criminal acts involving torture, or an attempt or conspiracy to commit murder or a criminal act involving torture. No waiver shall be granted under this subsection in the case of an alien who has previously been admitted to the United States as an alien lawfully admitted for permanent residence if either since the date of such admission the alien has been convicted of an aggravated felony or the alien has not lawfully resided continuously in the United States for a period of not less than 7 years immediately preceding the date of initiation of proceedings to remove the alien from the United States. No court shall have jurisdiction to review a decision of the Attorney General to grant or deny a waiver under this subsection.

(i) Admission of immigrant inadmissible for fraud or willful misrepresentation of material fact.

(1) The Attorney General may, in the discretion of the Attorney General, waive the application of clause (i) of subsection (a)(6)(C) in the case of an immigrant who is the spouse, son, or daughter of a United States citizen or of an alien lawfully admitted for permanent residence if it is established to the satisfaction of the Attorney General that the refusal of admission to the United States of such immigrant alien would result in extreme hardship to the citizen or lawfully resident spouse or parent of such an alien or, in the case of a VAWA self-petitioner, the alien demonstrates extreme hardship to the alien or the alien's United States citizen, lawful permanent resident, or qualified alien parent or child.

(2) No court shall have jurisdiction to review a decision or action of the Attorney General regarding a waiver under paragraph (1).

(j) Limitation on immigration of foreign medical graduates.

(1) The additional requirements referred to in section 101(a)(15)(J) [8 USCS § 1101(a)(15)(J)] for an alien who is coming to the United States under a program under which he will receive graduate medical education or training are as follows:

(A) A school of medicine or of one of the other health professions, which is accredited by a body or bodies approved for the purpose by the Secretary of Education, has agreed in writing to provide the graduate medical education or training under the program for which the alien is coming to the United States or to assume responsibility for arranging for the provision thereof by an appropriate public or nonprofit private institution or agency, except that, in the case of such an agreement by a school of medicine, any one or more of its affiliated hospitals which are to participate in the provision of the graduate medical education or training must join in the agreement.

(B) Before making such agreement, the accredited school has been satisfied that the alien (i) is a graduate of a school of medicine which is accredited by a body or bodies approved for the purpose by the Secretary of Education (regardless of whether such school of medicine is in the United States); or (ii)(I) has passed parts I and II of the National Board of Medical Examiners Examination (or an equivalent examination as determined by the Secretary of Health and Human Services), (II) has competency in oral and written English, (III) will be able to adapt to the educational and cultural environment in which he will be receiving his education or training, and (IV) has adequate prior education and training to participate satisfactorily in the program for which he is coming to the United States. For the purposes of this subparagraph, an alien who is a graduate of a medical school shall be considered to have passed parts I and II of the National Board of Medical Examiners examination if the alien was fully and permanently licensed to practice medicine in a State on January 9, 1978, and was practicing medicine in a State on that date.

(C) The alien has made a commitment to return to the country of his nationality or last residence upon completion of the education or training for which he is coming to the United States, and the government of the country of his nationality or last residence has provided a written assurance, satisfactory to the Secretary of Health and Human Services, that there is a need in that country for persons with the skills the alien will acquire in such education or training.

(D) The duration of the alien's participation in the program of graduate medical education or training for which the alien is coming to the United States is limited to the time typically required to complete such program, as determined by the Director of the United States Information Agency at the time of the alien's admission into the United States, based on criteria which are established in coordination with the Secretary of Health and Human Services and which take into consideration the published requirements of the medical specialty board which administers such education or training program; except that

(i) such duration is further limited to seven years unless the alien has demonstrated to the satisfaction of the Director that the country to which the alien will return at the end of such specialty education or training has an exceptional need for an individual trained in such specialty, and

(ii) the alien may, once and not later than two years after the date the alien is admitted to the United States as an exchange visitor or acquires exchange visitor status, change the alien's designated program of graduate medical education or training if the Director approves the change and if a commitment and written assurance with respect to the alien's new program have been provided in accordance with subparagraph (C).

(E) The alien furnishes the Attorney General each year with an affidavit (in such form as the Attorney General shall prescribe) that attests that the alien (i) is in good standing in the program of graduate medical education or training in which the alien is participating, and (ii) will return to the country of his nationality or last residence upon completion of the education or training for which he came to the United States.

(2) An alien who is a graduate of a medical school and who is coming to the United States to perform services as a member of the medical profession may not be admitted as a nonimmigrant under section 101(a)(15)(H)(i)(b) [8 USCS § 1101(a)(15)(H)(i)(b)] unless

(A) the alien is coming pursuant to an invitation from a public or nonprofit private educational or research institution or agency in the United States to teach or conduct research, or both, at or for such institution or agency, or

(B)(i) the alien has passed the Federation licensing examination (administered by the Federation of State Medical Boards of the United States) or an equivalent examination as determined by the Secretary of Health and Human Services, and

(ii) (I) has competency in oral and written English or (II) is a graduate of a school of medicine which is accredited by a body or bodies approved for the purpose by the Secretary of Education (regardless of whether such school of medicine is in the United States).

(k) Attorney General's discretion to admit otherwise inadmissible aliens who possess immigrant visas. Any alien, inadmissible from the United States under paragraph (5)(A) or (7)(A)(i) of subsection (a), who is in possession of an immigrant visa may, if otherwise admissible, be admitted in the discretion of the Attorney General if the Attorney General is satisfied that inadmissibility was not known to, and could not have been ascertained by the exercise of reasonable diligence by, the immigrant before the time of departure of the vessel or aircraft from the last port outside the United States and outside foreign contiguous territory or, in the case of an immigrant coming from foreign contiguous territory, before the time of the immigrant's application for admission.

(l) Guam and Northern Mariana Islands visa waiver program.

(1) In general. The requirement of subsection (a)(7)(B)(i) may be waived by the Secretary of Homeland Security, in the case of an alien applying for admission as a nonimmigrant visitor for business or pleasure and solely for entry into and stay in Guam or the Commonwealth of the Northern Mariana Islands for a period not to exceed 45 days, if the Secretary of Homeland Security, after consultation with the Secretary of the Interior, the Secretary of State, the Governor of Guam and the Governor of the Commonwealth of the Northern Mariana Islands, determines that

(A) an adequate arrival and departure control system has been developed in Guam and the Commonwealth of the Northern Mariana Islands; and

(B) such a waiver does not represent a threat to the welfare, safety, or security of the United States or its territories and commonwealths.

(2) Alien waiver of rights. An alien may not be provided a waiver under this subsection unless the alien has waived any right

(A) to review or appeal under this Act [8 USCS §§ 1101 et seq.] an immigration officer's determination as to the admissibility of the alien at the port of entry into Guam or the Commonwealth of the Northern Mariana Islands; or

(B) to contest, other than on the basis of an application for withholding of removal under section 241(b)(3) of this Act [8 USCS § 1231(b)(3)] or under the Convention Against Torture, or an application for asylum if permitted under section 208 [8 USCS § 1158], any action for removal of the alien.

(3) Regulations. All necessary regulations to implement this subsection shall be promulgated by the Secretary of Homeland Security, in consultation with the Secretary of the Interior and the Secretary of State, on or before the 180th day after the date of enactment of the Consolidated Natural Resources Act of 2008 [enacted May 8, 2008]. The promulgation of such regulations shall be considered a foreign affairs function for purposes of section 553(a) of title 5, United States Code [5 USCS § 553(a)]. At a minimum, such regulations should include, but not necessarily be limited to

(A) a listing of all countries whose nationals may obtain the waiver also provided by this subsection, except that such regulations shall provide for a listing of any country from which the Commonwealth has received a significant economic benefit from the number of visitors for pleasure within the one-year period preceding the date of enactment of the Consolidated Natural Resources Act of 2008 [enacted May 8, 2008], unless the Secretary of Homeland Security determines that such country's inclusion on such list would represent a threat to the welfare, safety, or security of the United States or its territories; and

(B) any bonding requirements for nationals of some or all of those countries who may present an increased risk of overstays or other potential problems, if different from such requirements otherwise provided by law for nonimmigrant visitors.

(4) Factors. In determining whether to grant or continue providing the waiver under this subsection to nationals of any country, the Secretary of Homeland Security, in consultation with the Secretary of the Interior and the Secretary of State, shall consider all factors that the Secretary deems relevant, including electronic travel authorizations, procedures for reporting lost and stolen passports, repatriation of aliens, rates of refusal for nonimmigrant visitor visas, overstays, exit systems, and information exchange.

(5) Suspension. The Secretary of Homeland Security shall monitor the admission of nonimmigrant visitors to Guam and the Commonwealth of the Northern Mariana Islands under this subsection. If the Secretary determines that such admissions have resulted in an unacceptable number of visitors from a country remaining unlawfully in Guam or the Commonwealth of the Northern Mariana Islands, unlawfully obtaining entry to other parts of the United States, or seeking withholding of removal or asylum, or that visitors from a country pose a risk to law enforcement or security interests of Guam or the Commonwealth of the Northern Mariana Islands or of the United States (including the interest in the enforcement of the immigration laws of the United States), the Secretary shall suspend the admission of nationals of such country under this subsection. The Secretary of Homeland Security may in the Secretary's discretion suspend the Guam and Northern Mariana Islands visa waiver program at any time, on a country-by-country basis, for other good cause.

(6) Addition of countries. The Governor of Guam and the Governor of the Commonwealth of the Northern Mariana Islands may request the Secretary of the Interior and the Secretary of Homeland Security to add a particular country to the list of countries whose nationals may obtain the waiver provided by this subsection, and the Secretary of Homeland Security may grant such request after consultation with the Secretary of the Interior and the Secretary of State, and may promulgate regulations with respect to the inclusion of that country and any special requirements the Secretary of Homeland Security, in the Secretary's sole discretion, may impose prior to allowing nationals of that country to obtain the waiver provided by this subsection.

(m) Requirements for admission of nonimmigrant nurses.

(1) The qualifications referred to in section 101(a)(15)(H)(i)(c) [8 USCS § 1101(a)(15)(H)(i)(c)], with respect to an alien who is coming to the United States to perform nursing services for a facility, are that the alien

(A) has obtained a full and unrestricted license to practice professional nursing in the country where the alien obtained nursing education or has received nursing education in the United States;

(B) has passed an appropriate examination (recognized in regulations promulgated in consultation with the Secretary of Health and Human Services) or has a full and unrestricted license under State law to practice professional nursing in the State of intended employment; and

(C) is fully qualified and eligible under the laws (including such temporary or interim licensing requirements which authorize the nurse to be employed) governing the place of intended employment to engage in the practice of professional nursing as a registered nurse immediately upon admission to the United States and is authorized under such laws to be employed by the facility.

(2)(A) The attestation referred to in section 101(a)(15)(H)(i)(c) [8 USCS § 1101(a)(15)(H)(i)(c)], with respect to a facility for which an alien will perform services, is an attestation as to the following:

(i) The facility meets all the requirements of paragraph (6).

(ii) The employment of the alien will not adversely affect the wages and working conditions of registered nurses similarly employed.

(iii) The alien employed by the facility will be paid the wage rate for registered nurses similarly employed by the facility.

(iv) The facility has taken and is taking timely and significant steps designed to recruit and retain sufficient registered nurses who are United States citizens or immigrants who are authorized to perform nursing services, in order to remove as quickly as reasonably possible the dependence of the facility on nonimmigrant registered nurses.

(v) There is not a strike or lockout in the course of a labor dispute, the facility did not lay off and will not lay off a registered nurse employed by the facility within the period beginning 90 days before and ending 90 days after the date of filing of any visa petition, and the employment of such an alien is not intended or designed to influence an election for a bargaining representative for registered nurses of the facility.

(vi) At the time of the filing of the petition for registered nurses under section 101(a)(15)(H)(i)(c) [8 USCS § 1101(a)(15)(H)(i)(c)], notice of the filing has been provided by the facility to the bargaining representative of the registered nurses at the facility or, where there is no such bargaining representative, notice of the filing has been provided to the registered nurses employed at the facility through posting in conspicuous locations.

(vii) The facility will not, at any time, employ a number of aliens issued visas or otherwise provided nonimmigrant status under section 101(a)(15)(H)(i)(c) [8 USCS § 1101(a)(15)(H)(i)(c)] that exceeds 33 percent of the total number of registered nurses employed by the facility.

(viii) The facility will not, with respect to any alien issued a visa or otherwise provided nonimmigrant status under section 101(a)(15)(H)(i)(c) [8 USCS § 1101(a)(15)(H)(i)(c)]

(I) authorize the alien to perform nursing services at any worksite other than a worksite controlled by the facility; or

(II) transfer the place of employment of the alien from one worksite to another.

Nothing in clause (iv) shall be construed as requiring a facility to have taken significant steps described in such clause before the date of the enactment of the Nursing Relief for Disadvantaged Areas Act of 1999 [enacted Nov. 12, 1999]. A copy of the attestation shall be provided, within 30 days of the date of filing, to registered nurses employed at the facility on the date of filing.

(B) For purposes of subparagraph (A)(iv), each of the following shall be considered a significant step reasonably designed to recruit and retain registered nurses:

(i) Operating a training program for registered nurses at the facility or financing (or providing participation in) a training program for registered nurses elsewhere.

(ii) Providing career development programs and other methods of facilitating health care workers to become registered nurses.

(iii) Paying registered nurses wages at a rate higher than currently being paid to registered nurses similarly employed in the geographic area.

(iv) Providing reasonable opportunities for meaningful salary advancement by registered nurses.

The steps described in this subparagraph shall not be considered to be an exclusive list of the significant steps that may be taken to meet the conditions of subparagraph (A)(iv). Nothing in this subparagraph shall require a facility to take more than one step if the facility can demonstrate that taking a second step is not reasonable.

(C) Subject to subparagraph (E), an attestation under subparagraph (A)

(i) shall expire on the date that is the later of

(I) the end of the one-year period beginning on the date of its filing with the Secretary of Labor; or

(II) the end of the period of admission under section 101(a)(15)(H)(i)(c) [8 USCS § 1101(a)(15)(H)(i)(c)] of the last alien with respect to whose admission it was applied (in accordance with clause (ii)); and

(ii) shall apply to petitions filed during the one-year period beginning on the date of its filing with the Secretary of Labor if the facility states in each such petition that it continues to comply with the conditions in the attestation.

(D) A facility may meet the requirements under this paragraph with respect to more than one registered nurse in a single petition.

(E)(i) The Secretary of Labor shall compile and make available for public examination in a timely manner in Washington, D.C., a list identifying facilities which have filed petitions for nonimmigrants under section 101(a)(15)(H)(i)(c) [8 USCS § 1101(a)(15)(H)(i)(c)] and, for each such facility, a copy of the facility's attestation under subparagraph (A) (and accompanying documentation) and each such petition filed by the facility.

(ii) The Secretary of Labor shall establish a process, including reasonable time limits, for the receipt, investigation, and disposition of complaints respecting a facility's failure to meet conditions attested to or a facility's misrepresentation of a material fact in an attestation. Complaints may be filed by any aggrieved person or organization (including bargaining representatives, associations deemed appropriate by the Secretary, and other aggrieved parties as determined under regulations of the Secretary). The Secretary shall conduct an investigation under this clause if there is reasonable cause to believe that a facility fails to meet conditions attested to. Subject to the time limits established under this clause, this subparagraph shall apply regardless of whether an attestation is expired or unexpired at the time a complaint is filed.

(iii) Under such process, the Secretary shall provide, within 180 days after the date such a complaint is filed, for a determination as to whether or not a basis exists to make a finding described in clause (iv). If the Secretary determines that such a basis exists, the Secretary shall provide for notice of such determination to the interested parties and an opportunity for a hearing on the complaint within 60 days of the date of the determination.

(iv) If the Secretary of Labor finds, after notice and opportunity for a hearing, that a facility (for which an attestation is made) has failed to meet a condition attested to or that there was a misrepresentation of material fact in the attestation, the Secretary shall notify the Attorney General of such finding and may, in addition, impose such other administrative remedies (including civil monetary penalties in an amount not to exceed $1,000 per nurse per violation, with the total penalty not to exceed $10,000 per violation) as the Secretary determines to be appropriate. Upon receipt of such notice, the Attorney General shall not approve petitions filed with respect to a facility during a period of at least one year for nurses to be employed by the facility.

(v) In addition to the sanctions provided for under clause (iv), if the Secretary of Labor finds, after notice and an opportunity for a hearing, that a facility has violated the condition attested to under subparagraph (A)(iii) (relating to payment of registered nurses at the prevailing wage rate), the Secretary shall order the facility to provide for payment of such amounts of back pay as may be required to comply with such condition.

(F)(i) The Secretary of Labor shall impose on a facility filing an attestation under subparagraph (A) a filing fee, in an amount prescribed by the Secretary based on the costs of carrying out the Secretary's duties under this subsection, but not exceeding $250.

(ii) Fees collected under this subparagraph shall be deposited in a fund established for this purpose in the Treasury of the United States.

(iii) The collected fees in the fund shall be available to the Secretary of Labor, to the extent and in such amounts as may be provided in appropriations Acts, to cover the costs described in clause (i), in addition to any other funds that are available to the Secretary to cover such costs.

(3) The period of admission of an alien under section 101(a)(15)(H)(i)(c) [8 USCS § 1101(a)(15)(H)(i)(c)] shall be 3 years.

(4) The total number of nonimmigrant visas issued pursuant to petitions granted under section 101(a)(15)(H)(i)(c) [8 USCS § 1101(a)(15)(H)(i)(c)] in each fiscal year shall not exceed 500. The number of such visas issued for employment in each State in each fiscal year shall not exceed the following:

(A) For States with populations of less than 9,000,000, based upon the 1990 decennial census of population, 25 visas.

(B) For States with populations of 9,000,000 or more, based upon the 1990 decennial census of population, 50 visas.

(C) If the total number of visas available under this paragraph for a fiscal year quarter exceeds the number of qualified nonimmigrants who may be issued such visas during those quarters, the visas made available under this paragraph shall be issued without regard to the numerical limitation under subparagraph (A) or (B) of this paragraph during the last fiscal year quarter.

(5) A facility that has filed a petition under section 101(a)(15)(H)(i)(c) [8 USCS § 1101(a)(15)(H)(i)(c)] to employ a nonimmigrant to perform nursing services for the facility

(A) shall provide the nonimmigrant a wage rate and working conditions commensurate with those of nurses similarly employed by the facility;

(B) shall require the nonimmigrant to work hours commensurate with those of nurses similarly employed by the facility; and

(C) shall not interfere with the right of the nonimmigrant to join or organize a union.

(6) For purposes of this subsection and section 101(a)(15)(H)(i)(c) [8 USCS § 1101(a)(15)(H)(i)(c)], the term "facility" means a subsection (d) hospital (as defined in section 1886(d)(1)(B) of the Social Security Act (42 U.S.C. 1395ww(d)(1)(B))) that meets the following requirements:

(A) As of March 31, 1997, the hospital was located in a health professional shortage area (as defined in section 332 of the Public Health Service Act (42 U.S.C. 254e)).

(B) Based on its settled cost report filed under title XVIII of the Social Security Act [42 USCS §§ 1395 et seq.] for its cost reporting period beginning during fiscal year 1994

(i) the hospital has not less than 190 licensed acute care beds;

(ii) the number of the hospital's inpatient days for such period which were made up of patients who (for such days) were entitled to benefits under part A of such title [42 USCS §§ 1395c et seq.] is not less than 35 percent of the total number of such hospital's acute care inpatient days for such period; and

(iii) the number of the hospital's inpatient days for such period which were made up of patients who (for such days) were eligible for medical assistance under a State plan approved under title XIX of the Social Security Act [42 USCS §§ 1396 et seq.], is not less than 28 percent of the total number of such hospital's acute care inpatient days for such period.

(7) For purposes of paragraph (2)(A)(v), the term "lay off", with respect to a worker

(A) means to cause the worker's loss of employment, other than through a discharge for inadequate performance, violation of workplace rules, cause, voluntary departure, voluntary retirement, or the expiration of a grant or contract; but

(B) does not include any situation in which the worker is offered, as an alternative to such loss of employment, a similar employment opportunity with the same employer at equivalent or higher compensation and benefits than the position from which the employee was discharged, regardless of whether or not the employee accepts the offer.

Nothing in this paragraph is intended to limit an employee's or an employer's rights under a collective bargaining agreement or other employment contract.

(n) Labor condition application.

(1) No alien may be admitted or provided status as an H-1B nonimmigrant in an occupational classification unless the employer has filed with the Secretary of Labor an application stating the following:

(A) The employer

(i) is offering and will offer during the period of authorized employment to aliens admitted or provided status as an H-1B non-immigrant wages that are at least

(I) the actual wage level paid by the employer to all other individuals with similar experience and qualifications for the specific employment in question, or

(II) the prevailing wage level for the occupational classification in the area of employment,
whichever is greater, based on the best information available as of the time of filing the application, and

(ii) will provide working conditions for such a nonimmigrant that will not adversely affect the working conditions of workers similarly employed.

(B) There is not a strike or lockout in the course of a labor dispute in the occupational classification at the place of employment.

(C) The employer, at the time of filing the application

(i) has provided notice of the filing under this paragraph to the bargaining representative (if any) of the employer's employees in the occupational classification and area for which aliens are sought, or

(ii) if there is no such bargaining representative, has provided notice of filing in the occupational classification through such methods as physical posting in conspicuous locations at the place of employment or electronic notification to employees in the occupational classification for which H-1B nonimmigrants are sought.

(D) The application shall contain a specification of the number of workers sought, the occupational classification in which the workers will be employed, and wage rate and conditions under which they will be employed.

(E)(i) In the case of an application described in clause (ii), the employer did not displace and will not displace a United States worker (as defined in paragraph (4)) employed by the employer within the period beginning 90 days before and ending 90 days after the date of filing of any visa petition supported by the application.

(ii) An application described in this clause is an application filed on or after the date final regulations are first promulgated to carry out this subparagraph, [and before] by an H-1B-dependent employer (as defined in paragraph (3)) or by an employer that has been found, on or after the date of the enactment of the American Competitiveness and Workforce Improvement Act of 1998 [enacted Oct. 21, 1998], under paragraph (2)(C) or (5) to have committed a willful failure or misrepresentation during the 5-year period preceding the filing of the application. An application is not described in this clause if the only H-1B nonimmigrants sought in the application are exempt H-1B nonimmigrants.

(F) In the case of an application described in subparagraph (E)(ii), the employer will not place the nonimmigrant with another employer (regardless of whether or not such other employer is an H-1B-dependent employer) where

(i) the nonimmigrant performs duties in whole or in part at one or more worksites owned, operated, or controlled by such other employer; and

(ii) there are indicia of an employment relationship between the nonimmigrant and such other employer;
unless the employer has inquired of the other employer as to whether, and has no knowledge that, within the period beginning 90 days before and ending 90 days after the date of the placement of the nonimmigrant with the other employer, the other employer has displaced or intends to displace a United States worker employed by the other employer.

(G)(i) In the case of an application described in subparagraph (E)(ii), subject to clause (ii), the employer, prior to filing the application

(I) has taken good faith steps to recruit, in the United States using procedures that meet industry-wide standards and offering compensation that is at least as great as that required to be offered to H-1B nonimmigrants under subparagraph (A), United States workers for the job for which the nonimmigrant or nonimmigrants is or are sought; and

(II) has offered the job to any United States worker who applies and is equally or better qualified for the job for which the nonimmigrant or nonimmigrants is or are sought.

(ii) The conditions described in clause (i) shall not apply to an application filed with respect to the employment of an H-1B nonimmigrant who is described in subparagraph (A), (B), or (C) of section 203(b)(1) [8 USCS § 1153(b)(1)].
The employer shall make available for public examination, within one working day after the date on which an application under this paragraph is filed, at the employer's principal place of business or worksite, a copy of each such application (and such accompanying documents as are necessary). The Secretary shall compile, on a current basis, a list (by employer and by occupational classification) of the applications filed under this subsection. Such list shall include the wage rate, number of aliens sought, period of intended employment, and date of need. The Secretary shall make such list available for public examination in Washington, D.C. The Secretary of Labor shall review such an application only for completeness and obvious inaccuracies. Unless the Secretary finds that the application is incomplete or obviously inaccurate, the Secretary shall provide the certification described in section 101(a)(15)(H)(i)(b) [8 USCS § 1101(a)(15)(H)(i)(b)] within 7 days of the date of the filing of the application. The application form shall include a clear statement explaining the liability under subparagraph (F) of a placing employer if the other employer described in such subparagraph displaces a United States worker as described in such subparagraph. Nothing in subparagraph (G) shall be construed to prohibit an employer from using legitimate selection criteria relevant to the job that are normal or customary to the type of job involved, so long as such criteria are not applied in a discriminatory manner.

(2)(A) Subject to paragraph (5)(A), the Secretary shall establish a process for the receipt, investigation, and disposition of complaints respecting a petitioner's failure to meet a condition specified in an application submitted under paragraph (1) or a petitioner's misrepresentation of material facts in such an application. Complaints may be filed by any aggrieved person or organization (including bargaining representatives). No investigation or hearing shall be conducted on a complaint concerning such a failure or misrepresentation unless the complaint was filed not later than 12 months after the date of the failure or misrepresentation, respectively. The Secretary shall conduct an investigation under this paragraph if there is reasonable cause to believe that such a failure or misrepresentation has occurred.

(B) Under such process, the Secretary shall provide, within 30 days after the date such a complaint is filed, for a determination as to whether or not a reasonable basis exists to make a finding described in subparagraph (C). If the Secretary determines that such a reasonable basis exists, the Secretary shall provide for notice of such determination to the interested parties and an opportunity for a hearing on the complaint, in accordance with section 556 of title 5, United States Code, within 60 days after the date of the determination. If such a hearing is requested, the Secretary shall make a finding concerning the matter by not later than 60 days after the date of the hearing. In the case of similar complaints respecting the same applicant, the Secretary may consolidate the hearings under this subparagraph on such complaints.

(C)(i) If the Secretary finds, after notice and opportunity for a hearing, a failure to meet a condition of paragraph (1)(B), (1)(E), or (1)(F), a substantial failure to meet a condition of paragraph (1)(C), (1)(D), or (1)(G)(i)(I), or a misrepresentation of material fact in an application

(I) the Secretary shall notify the Attorney General of such finding and may, in addition, impose such other administrative remedies (including civil monetary penalties in an amount not to exceed $1,000 per violation) as the Secretary determines to be appropriate; and

(II) the Attorney General shall not approve petitions filed with respect to that employer under section 204 or 214(c) [8 USCS § 1154 or 1184(c)] during a period of at least 1 year for aliens to be employed by the employer.

(ii) If the Secretary finds, after notice and opportunity for a hearing, a willful failure to meet a condition of paragraph (1), a willful misrepresentation of material fact in an application, or a violation of clause (iv)

(I) the Secretary shall notify the Attorney General of such finding and may, in addition, impose such other administrative remedies (including civil monetary penalties in an amount not to exceed $5,000 per violation) as the Secretary determines to be appropriate; and

(II) the Attorney General shall not approve petitions filed with respect to that employer under section 204 or 214(c) [8 USCS § 1154 or 1184(c)] during a period of at least 2 years for aliens to be employed by the employer.

(iii) If the Secretary finds, after notice and opportunity for a hearing, a willful failure to meet a condition of paragraph (1) or a willful misrepresentation of material fact in an application, in the course of which failure or misrepresentation the employer displaced a United States worker employed by the employer within the period beginning 90 days before and ending 90 days after the date of filing of any visa petition supported by the application

(I) the Secretary shall notify the Attorney General of such finding and may, in addition, impose such other administrative remedies (including civil monetary penalties in an amount not to exceed $35,000 per violation) as the Secretary determines to be appropriate; and

(II) the Attorney General shall not approve petitions filed with respect to that employer under section 204 or 214(c) [8 USCS § 1154 or 1184(c)] during a period of at least 3 years for aliens to be employed by the employer.

(iv) It is a violation of this clause for an employer who has filed an application under this subsection to intimidate, threaten, restrain, coerce, blacklist, discharge, or in any other manner discriminate against an employee (which term, for purposes of this clause, includes a former employee and an applicant for employment) because the employee has disclosed information to the employer, or to any other person, that the employee reasonably believes evidences a violation of this subsection, or any rule or regulation pertaining to this subsection, or because the employee cooperates or seeks to cooperate in an investigation or other proceeding concerning the employer's compliance with the requirements of this subsection or any rule or regulation pertaining to this subsection.

(v) The Secretary of Labor and the Attorney General shall devise a process under which an H-1B nonimmigrant who files a complaint regarding a violation of clause (iv) and is otherwise eligible to remain and work in the United States may be allowed to seek other appropriate employment in the United States for a period not to exceed the maximum period of stay authorized for such nonimmigrant classification.

(vi)(I) It is a violation of this clause for an employer who has filed an application under this subsection to require an H-1B nonimmigrant to pay a penalty for ceasing employment with the employer prior to a date agreed to by the nonimmigrant and the employer. The Secretary shall determine whether a required payment is a penalty (and not liquidated damages) pursuant to relevant State law.

(II) It is a violation of this clause for an employer who has filed an application under this subsection to require an alien who is the subject of a petition filed under section 214(c)(1) [8 USCS § 1184(c)(1)], for which a fee is imposed under section 214(c)(9) [8 USCS § 1184(c)(9)], to reimburse, or otherwise compensate, the employer for part or all of the cost of such fee. It is a violation of this clause for such an employer otherwise to accept such reimbursement or compensation from such an alien.

(III) If the Secretary finds, after notice and opportunity for a hearing, that an employer has committed a violation of this clause, the Secretary may impose a civil monetary penalty of $1,000 for each such violation and issue an administrative order requiring the return to the nonimmigrant of any amount paid in violation of this clause, or, if the nonimmigrant cannot be located, requiring payment of any such amount to the general fund of the Treasury.

(vii)(I) It is a failure to meet a condition of paragraph (1)(A) for an employer, who has filed an application under this subsection and who places an H-1B nonimmigrant designated as a full-time employee on the petition filed under section 214(c)(1) [8 USCS § 1184(c)(1)] by the employer with respect to the nonimmigrant, after the nonimmigrant has entered into employment with the employer, in nonproductive status due to a decision by the employer (based on factors such as lack of work), or due to the nonimmigrant's lack of a permit or license, to fail to pay the nonimmigrant full-time wages in accordance with paragraph (1)(A) for all such nonproductive time.

(II) It is a failure to meet a condition of paragraph (1)(A) for an employer, who has filed an application under this subsection and who places an H-1B nonimmigrant designated as a part-time employee on the petition filed under section 214(c)(1) [8 USCS § 1184(c)(1)] by the employer with respect to the nonimmigrant, after the nonimmigrant has entered into employment with the employer, in nonproductive status under circumstances described in subclause (I), to fail to pay such a nonimmigrant for such hours as are designated on such petition consistent with the rate of pay identified on such petition.

(III) In the case of an H-1B nonimmigrant who has not yet entered into employment with an employer who has had approved an application under this subsection, and a petition under section 214(c)(1) [8 USCS § 1184(c)(1)], with respect to the nonimmigrant, the provisions of subclauses (I) and (II) shall apply to the employer beginning 30 days after the date the nonimmigrant first is admitted into the United States pursuant to the petition, or 60 days after the date the nonimmigrant becomes eligible to work for the employer (in the case of a nonimmigrant who is present in the United States on the date of the approval of the petition).

(IV) This clause does not apply to a failure to pay wages to an H-1B nonimmigrant for nonproductive time due to non-work-related factors, such as the voluntary request of the nonimmigrant for an absence or circumstances rendering the nonimmigrant unable to work.

(V) This clause shall not be construed as prohibiting an employer that is a school or other educational institution from applying to an H-1B nonimmigrant an established salary practice of the employer, under which the employer pays to H-1B nonimmigrants and United States workers in the same occupational classification an annual salary in disbursements over fewer than 12 months, if

(aa) the nonimmigrant agrees to the compressed annual salary payments prior to the commencement of the employment; and

(bb) the application of the salary practice to the nonimmigrant does not otherwise cause the nonimmigrant to violate any condition of the nonimmigrant's authorization under this Act to remain in the United States.

(VI) This clause shall not be construed as superseding clause (viii).

(viii) It is a failure to meet a condition of paragraph (1)(A) for an employer who has filed an application under this subsection to fail to offer to an H-1B nonimmigrant, during the nonimmigrant's period of authorized employment, benefits and eligibility for benefits (including the opportunity to participate in health, life, disability, and other insurance plans; the opportunity to participate in retirement and savings plans; and cash bonuses and noncash compensation, such as stock options (whether or not based on performance)) on the same basis, and in accordance with the same criteria, as the employer offers to United States workers.

(D) If the Secretary finds, after notice and opportunity for a hearing, that an employer has not paid wages at the wage level specified under the application and required under paragraph (1), the Secretary shall order the employer to provide for parent of such amounts of back pay as may be required to comply with the requirements of paragraph (1), whether or not a penalty under subparagraph (C) has been imposed.

(E) If an H-1B-dependent employer places a nonexempt H-1B nonimmigrant with another employer as provided under paragraph (1)(F) and the other employer has displaced or displaces a United States worker employed by such other employer during the period described in such paragraph, such displacement shall be considered for purposes of this paragraph a failure, by the placing employer, to meet a condition specified in an application submitted under paragraph (1); except that the Attorney General may impose a sanction described in subclause (II) of subparagraph (C)(i), (C)(ii), or (C)(iii) only if the Secretary of Labor found that such placing employer

(i) knew or had reason to know of such displacement at the time of the placement of the nonimmigrant with the other employer; or

(ii) has been subject to a sanction under this subparagraph based upon a previous placement of an H-1B nonimmigrant with the same other employer.

(F) The Secretary may, on a case-by-case basis, subject an employer to random investigations for a period of up to 5 years, beginning on the date (on or after the date of the enactment of the American Competitiveness and Workforce Improvement Act of 1998 [enacted Oct. 21, 1998]) on which the employer is found by the Secretary to have committed a willful failure to meet a condition of paragraph (1) (or has been found under paragraph (5) to have committed a willful failure to meet the condition of paragraph (1)(G)(i)(II)) or to have made a willful misrepresentation of material fact in an application. The preceding sentence shall apply to an employer regardless of whether or not the employer is an H-1B-dependent employer. The authority of the Secretary under this subparagraph shall not be construed to be subject to, or limited by, the requirements of subparagraph (A).

(G)(i) The Secretary of Labor may initiate an investigation of any employer that employs nonimmigrants described in section 101(a)(15)(H)(i)(b) [8 USCS § 1101(a)(15)(H)(i)(b)] if the Secretary of Labor has reasonable cause to believe that the employer is not in compliance with this subsection. In the case of an investigation under this clause, the Secretary of Labor (or the acting Secretary in the case of the absence of [or] disability of the Secretary of Labor) shall personally certify that reasonable cause exists and shall approve commencement of the investigation. The investigation may be initiated for reasons other than completeness and obvious inaccuracies by the employer in complying with this subsection.

(ii) If the Secretary of Labor receives specific credible information from a source who is likely to have knowledge of an employer's practices or employment conditions, or an employer's compliance with the employer's labor condition application under paragraph (1), and whose identity is known to the Secretary of Labor, and such information provides reasonable cause to believe that the employer has committed a willful failure to meet a condition of paragraph (1)(A), (1)(B), (1)(C), (1)(E), (1)(F), or (1)(G)(i)(I), has engaged in a pattern or practice of failures to meet such a condition, or has committed a substantial failure to meet such a condition that affects multiple employees, the Secretary of Labor may conduct an investigation into the alleged failure or failures. The Secretary of Labor may withhold the identity of the source from the employer, and the source's identity shall not be subject to disclosure under section 552 of title 5, United States Code.

(iii) The Secretary of Labor shall establish a procedure for any person desiring to provide to the Secretary of Labor information described in clause (ii) that may be used, in whole or in part, as the basis for the commencement of an investigation described in such clause, to provide the information in writing on a form developed and provided by the Secretary of Labor and completed by or on behalf of the person. The person may not be an officer or employee of the Department of Labor, unless the information satisfies the requirement of clause (iv)(II) (although an officer or employee of the Department of Labor may complete the form on behalf of the person).

(iv) Any investigation initiated or approved by the Secretary of Labor under clause (ii) shall be based on information that satisfies the requirements of such clause and that

(I) originates from a source other than an officer or employee of the Department of Labor; or

(II) was lawfully obtained by the Secretary of Labor in the course of lawfully conducting another Department of Labor investigation under this Act of [or] any other Act.

(v) The receipt by the Secretary of Labor of information submitted by an employer to the Attorney General or the Secretary of Labor for purposes of securing the employment of a nonimmigrant described in section 101(a)(15)(H)(i)(b) [8 USCS § 1101(a)(15)(H)(i)(b)] shall not be considered a receipt of information for purposes of clause (ii).

(vi) No investigation described in clause (ii) (or hearing described in clause (viii) based on such investigation) may be conducted with respect to information about a failure to meet a condition described in clause (ii), unless the Secretary of Labor receives the information not later than 12 months after the date of the alleged failure.

(vii) The Secretary of Labor shall provide notice to an employer with respect to whom there is reasonable cause to initiate an investigation described in clauses [clause] (i) or (ii), prior to the commencement of an investigation under such clauses, of the intent to conduct an investigation. The notice shall be provided in such a manner, and shall contain sufficient detail, to permit the employer to respond to the allegations before an investigation is commenced. The Secretary of Labor is not required to comply with this clause if the Secretary of Labor determines that to do so would interfere with an effort by the Secretary of Labor to secure compliance by the employer with the requirements of this subsection. There shall be no judicial review of a determination by the Secretary of Labor under this clause.

(viii) An investigation under clauses [clause] (i) or (ii) may be conducted for a period of up to 60 days. If the Secretary of Labor determines after such an investigation that a reasonable basis exists to make a finding that the employer has committed a willful failure to meet a condition of paragraph (1)(A), (1)(B), (1)(C), (1)(E), (1)(F), or (1)(G)(i)(I), has engaged in a pattern or practice of failures to meet such a condition, or has committed a substantial failure to meet such a condition that affects multiple employees, the Secretary of Labor shall provide for notice of such determination to the interested parties and an opportunity for a hearing in accordance with section 556 of title 5, United States Code, within 120 days after the date of the determination. If such a hearing is requested, the Secretary of Labor shall make a finding concerning the matter by not later than 120 days after the date of the hearing.

(H)(i) Except as provided in clauses (ii) and (iii), a person or entity is considered to have complied with the requirements of this subsection, notwithstanding a technical or procedural failure to meet such requirements, if there was a good faith attempt to comply with the requirements.

(ii) Clause (i) shall not apply if

(I) the Department of Labor (or another enforcement agency) has explained to the person or entity the basis for the failure;

(II) the person or entity has been provided a period of not less than 10 business days (beginning after the date of the explanation) within which to correct the failure; and

(III) the person or entity has not corrected the failure voluntarily within such period.

(iii) A person or entity that, in the course of an investigation, is found to have violated the prevailing wage requirements set forth in paragraph (1)(A), shall not be assessed fines or other penalties for such violation if the person or entity can establish that the manner in which the prevailing wage was calculated was consistent with recognized industry standards and practices.

(iv) Clauses (i) and (iii) shall not apply to a person or entity that has engaged in or is engaging in a pattern or practice of willful violations of this subsection.

(I) Nothing in this subsection shall be construed as superseding or preempting any other enforcement-related authority under this Act (such as the authorities under section 274B [8 USCS § 1324b]), or any other Act.

(3)(A) For purposes of this subsection, the term "H-1B-dependent employer" means an employer that

(i) (I) has 25 or fewer full-time equivalent employees who are employed in the United States; and (II) employs more than 7 H-1B nonimmigrants;

(ii) (I) has at least 26 but not more than 50 full-time equivalent employees who are employed in the United States; and (II) employs more than 12 H-1B nonimmigrants; or

(iii) (I) has at least 51 full-time equivalent employees who are employed in the United States; and (II) employs H-1B nonimmigrants in a number that is equal to at least 15 percent of the number of such full-time equivalent employees.

(B) For purposes of this subsection

(i) the term "exempt H-1B nonimmigrant" means an H-1B nonimmigrant who

(I) receives wages (including cash bonuses and similar compensation) at an annual rate equal to at least $60,000; or

(II) has attained a master's or higher degree (or its equivalent) in a specialty related to the intended employment; and

(ii) the term "nonexempt H-1B nonimmigrant" means an H-1B nonimmigrant who is not an exempt H-1B nonimmigrant.

(C) For purposes of subparagraph (A)

(i) in computing the number of full-time equivalent employees and the number of H-1B nonimmigrants, exempt H-1B nonimmigrants shall not be taken into account during the longer of

(I) the 6-month period beginning on the date of the enactment of the American Competitiveness and Workforce Improvement Act of 1998 [enacted Oct. 21, 1998]; or

(II) the period beginning on the date of the enactment of the American Competitiveness and Workforce Improvement Act of 1998 [enacted Oct. 21, 1998] and ending on the date final regulations are issued to carry out this paragraph; and

(ii) any group treated as a single employer under subsection (b), (c), (m), or (o) of section 414 of the Internal Revenue Code of 1986 [26 USCS § 414] shall be treated as a single employer.

(4) For purposes of this subsection:

(A) The term "area of employment" means the area within normal commuting distance of the worksite or physical location where the work of the H-1B nonimmigrant is or will be performed. If such worksite or location is within a Metropolitan Statistical Area, any place within such area is deemed to be within the area of employment.

(B) In the case of an application with respect to one or more H-1B nonimmigrants by an employer, the employer is considered to "displace" a United States worker from a job if the employer lays off the worker from a job that is essentially the equivalent of the job for which the nonimmigrant or nonimmigrants is or are sought. A job shall not be considered to be essentially equivalent of another job unless it involves essentially the same responsibilities, was held by a United States worker with substantially equivalent qualifications and experience, and is located in the same area of employment as the other job.

(C) The term "H-1B nonimmigrant" means an alien admitted or provided status as a nonimmigrant described in section 101(a)(15)(H)(i)(B) [8 USCS § 1101(a)(15)(H)(i)(B)].

(D)(i) The term "lays off", with respect to a worker

(I) means to cause the worker's loss of employment, other than through a discharge for inadequate performance, violation of workplace rules, cause, voluntary departure, voluntary retirement, or the expiration of a grant or contract (other than a temporary employment contract entered into in order to evade a condition described in subparagraph (E) or (F) of paragraph (1)); but

(II) does not include any situation in which the worker is offered, as an alternative to such loss of employment, a similar employment opportunity with the same employer (or, in the case of a placement of a worker with another employer under paragraph (1)(F), with either employer described in such paragraph) at equivalent or higher compensation and benefits than the position from which the employee was discharged, regardless of whether or not the employee accepts the offer.

(ii) Nothing in this subparagraph is intended to limit an employee's rights under a collective bargaining agreement or other employment contract.

(E) The term "United States worker" means an employee who

(i) is a citizen or national of the United States; or

(ii) is an alien who is lawfully admitted for permanent residence, is admitted as a refugee under section 207 [8 USCS § 1157], is granted asylum under section 208 [8 USCS § 1158], or is an immigrant otherwise authorized, by this Act or by the Attorney General, to be employed.

(5)(A) This paragraph shall apply instead of subparagraphs (A) through (E) of paragraph (2) in the case of a violation described in subparagraph (B), but shall not be construed to limit or affect the authority of the Secretary or the Attorney General with respect to any other violation.

(B) The Attorney General shall establish a process for the receipt, initial review, and disposition in accordance with this paragraph of complaints respecting an employer's failure to meet the condition of paragraph (1)(G)(i)(II) or a petitioner's misrepresentation of material facts with respect to such condition. Complaints may be filed by an aggrieved individual who has submitted a resume or otherwise applied in a reasonable manner for the job that is the subject of the condition. No proceeding shall be conducted under this paragraph on a complaint concerning such a failure or misrepresentation unless the Attorney General determines that the complaint was filed not later than 12 months after the date of the failure or misrepresentation, respectively.

(C) If the Attorney General finds that a complaint has been filed in accordance with subparagraph (B) and there is reasonable cause to believe that such a failure or misrepresentation described in such complaint has occurred, the Attorney General shall initiate binding arbitration proceedings by requesting the Federal Mediation and Conciliation Service to appoint an arbitrator from the roster of arbitrators maintained by such

Service. The procedure and rules of such Service shall be applicable to the selection of such arbitrator and to such arbitration proceedings. The Attorney General shall pay the fee and expenses of the arbitrator.

(D)(i) The arbitrator shall make findings respecting whether a failure or misrepresentation described in subparagraph (B) occurred. If the arbitrator concludes that failure or misrepresentation was willful, the arbitrator shall make a finding to that effect. The arbitrator may not find such a failure or misrepresentation (or that such a failure or misrepresentation was willful) unless the complainant demonstrates such a failure or misrepresentation (or its willful character) by clear and convincing evidence. The arbitrator shall transmit the findings in the form of a written opinion to the parties to the arbitration and the Attorney General. Such findings shall be final and conclusive, and, except as provided in this subparagraph, no official or court of the United States shall have power or jurisdiction to review any such findings.

(ii) The Attorney General may review and reverse or modify the findings of an arbitrator only on the same bases as an award of an arbitrator may be vacated or modified under section 10 or 11 of title 9, United States Code.

(iii) With respect to the findings of an arbitrator, a court may review only the actions of the Attorney General under clause (ii) and may set aside such actions only on the grounds described in subparagraph (A), (B), or (C) of section 706(a)(2) of title 5, United States Code. Notwithstanding any other provision of law, such judicial review may only be brought in an appropriate United States court of appeals.

(E) If the Attorney General receives a finding of an arbitrator under this paragraph that an employer has failed to meet the condition of paragraph (1)(G)(i)(II) or has misrepresented a material fact with respect to such condition, unless the Attorney General reverses or modifies the finding under subparagraph (D)(ii)

(i) the Attorney General may impose administrative remedies (including civil monetary penalties in an amount not to exceed $1,000 per violation or $5,000 per violation in the case of a willful failure or misrepresentation) as the Attorney General determines to be appropriate; and

(ii) the Attorney General is authorized to not approve petitions filed, with respect to that employer and for aliens to be employed by the employer, under section 204 or 214(c) [8 USCS § 1154 or 1184(c)]

(I) during a period of not more than 1 year; or

(II) in the case of a willful failure or willful misrepresentation, during a period of not more than 2 years.

(F) The Attorney General shall not delegate, to any other employee or official of the Department of Justice, any function of the Attorney General under this paragraph, until 60 days after the Attorney General has submitted a plan for such delegation to the Committees on the Judiciary of the United States House of Representatives and the Senate.

(o) [Terminated]

(p) Computation of prevailing wage level.

(1) In computing the prevailing wage level for an occupational classification in an area of employment for purposes of subsections (a)(5)(A), (n)(1)(A)(i)(II), and (t)(1)(A)(i)(II) in the case of an employee of

(A) an institution of higher education (as defined in section 101(a) of the Higher Education Act of 1965 [20 USCS § 1001(a)]), or a related or affiliated nonprofit entity; or

(B) a nonprofit research organization or a Governmental research organization,

the prevailing wage level shall only take into account employees at such institutions and organizations in the area of employment.

(2) With respect to a professional athlete (as defined in subsection (a)(5)(A)(iii)(II)) when the job opportunity is covered by professional sports league rules or regulations, the wage set forth in those rules or regulations shall be considered as not adversely affecting the wages of United States workers similarly employed and be considered the prevailing wage.

(3) The prevailing wage required to be paid pursuant to subsections (a)(5)(A), (n)(1)(A)(i)(II), and (t)(1)(A)(i)(II) shall be 100 percent of the wage determined pursuant to those sections.

(4) Where the Secretary of Labor uses, or makes available to employers, a governmental survey to determine the prevailing wage, such survey shall provide at least 4 levels of wages commensurate with experience, education, and the level of supervision. Where an existing government survey has only 2 levels, 2 intermediate levels may be created by dividing by 3, the difference between the 2 levels offered, adding the quotient thus obtained to the first level and subtracting that quotient from the second level.

(q) Academic honoraria. Any alien admitted under section 101(a)(15)(B) [8 USCS § 1101(a)(15)(B)] may accept an honorarium payment and associated incidental expenses for a usual academic activity or activities (lasting not longer than 9 days at any single institution), as defined by the Attorney General in consultation with the Secretary of Education, if such payment is offered by an institution or organization described in subsection (p)(1) and is made for services conducted for the benefit of that institution or entity and if the alien has not accepted such payment or expenses from more than 5 institutions or organizations in the previous 6-month period.

(r) Exception for certain alien nurses. Subsection (a)(5)(C) shall not apply to an alien who seeks to enter the United States for the purpose of performing labor as a nurse who presents to the consular officer (or in the case of an adjustment of status, the Attorney General) a certified statement from the Commission on Graduates of Foreign Nursing Schools (or an equivalent independent credentialing organization approved for the certification of nurses under subsection (a)(5)(C) by the Attorney General in consultation with the Secretary of Health and Human Services) that

(1) the alien has a valid and unrestricted license as a nurse in a State where the alien intends to be employed and such State verifies that the foreign licenses of alien nurses are authentic and unencumbered;

(2) the alien has passed the National Council Licensure Examination (NCLEX);

(3) the alien is a graduate of a nursing program

(A) in which the language of instruction was English;

(B) located in a country

(i) designated by such commission not later than 30 days after the date of the enactment of the Nursing Relief for Disadvantaged Areas Act of 1999 [enacted Nov. 12, 1999], based on such commission's assessment that the quality of nursing education in that country, and the English language proficiency of those who complete such programs in that country, justify the country's designation; or

(ii) designated on the basis of such an assessment by unanimous agreement of such commission and any equivalent credentialing organizations which have been approved under subsection (a)(5)(C) for the certification of nurses under this subsection; and

(C)(i) which was in operation on or before the date of the enactment of the Nursing Relief for Disadvantaged Areas Act of 1999 [enacted Nov. 12, 1999]; or

(ii) has been approved by unanimous agreement of such commission and any equivalent credentialing organizations which have been approved under subsection (a)(5)(C) for the certification of nurses under this subsection.

(s) Consideration of benefits received as battered alien in determination of inadmissibility as likely to become public charge. In determining whether an alien described in subsection (a)(4)(C)(i) is inadmissible under subsection (a)(4) or ineligible to receive an immigrant visa or otherwise to adjust to the status of permanent resident by reason of subsection (a)(4), the consular officer or the Attorney General shall not consider any benefits the alien may have received that were authorized under section 501 of the Illegal Immigration Reform and Immigrant Responsibility Act of 1996 (8 U.S.C. 1641(c)).

(t) Nonimmigrant professionals; labor attestations.

(1) No alien may be admitted or provided status as a nonimmigrant under section 101(a)(15)(H)(i)(b1) [8 USCS § 1101(a)(15)(H)(i)(b1)] or section 101(a)(15)(E)(iii) [8 USCS § 1101(a)(15)(E)(iii)] in an occupational classification unless the employer has filed with the Secretary of Labor an attestation stating the following:

(A) The employer

(i) is offering and will offer during the period of authorized employment to aliens admitted or provided status under section 101(a)(15)(H)(i)(b1) [8 USCS § 1101(a)(15)(H)(i)(b1)] or section 101(a)(15)(E)(iii) [8 USCS § 1101(a)(15)(E)(iii)] wages that are at least

(I) the actual wage level paid by the employer to all other individuals with similar experience and qualifications for the specific employment in question; or

(II) the prevailing wage level for the occupational classification in the area of employment,

whichever is greater, based on the best information available as of the time of filing the attestation; and

(ii) will provide working conditions for such a nonimmigrant that will not adversely affect the working conditions of workers similarly employed.

(B) There is not a strike or lockout in the course of a labor dispute in the occupational classification at the place of employment.

(C) The employer, at the time of filing the attestation

(i) has provided notice of the filing under this paragraph to the bargaining representative (if any) of the employer's employees in the occupational classification and area for which aliens are sought; or

(ii) if there is no such bargaining representative, has provided notice of filing in the occupational classification through such methods as physical posting in conspicuous locations at the place of employment or electronic notification to employees in the occupational classification for which nonimmigrants under section 101(a)(15)(H)(i)(b1) [8 USCS § 1101(a)(15)(H)(i)(b1)] or section 101(a)(15)(E)(iii) [8 USCS § 1101(a)(15)(E)(iii)] are sought.

(D) A specification of the number of workers sought, the occupational classification in which the workers will be employed, and wage rate and conditions under which they will be employed.

(2)(A) The employer shall make available for public examination, within one working day after the date on which an attestation under this subsection is filed, at the employer's principal place of business or worksite, a copy of each such attestation (and such accompanying documents as are necessary).

(B)(i) The Secretary of Labor shall compile, on a current basis, a list (by employer and by occupational classification) of the attestations filed under this subsection. Such list shall include, with respect to each attestation, the wage rate, number of aliens sought, period of intended employment, and date of need.

(ii) The Secretary of Labor shall make such list available for public examination in Washington, D.C.

(C) The Secretary of Labor shall review an attestation filed under this subsection only for completeness and obvious inaccuracies. Unless the Secretary of Labor finds that an attestation is incomplete or obviously inaccurate, the Secretary of Labor shall provide the certification described in section 101(a)(15)(H)(i)(b1) [8 USCS § 1101(a)(15)(H)(i)(b1)] or section 101(a)(15)(E)(iii) [8 USCS § 1101(a)(15)(E)(iii)] within 7 days of the date of the filing of the attestation.

(3)(A) The Secretary of Labor shall establish a process for the receipt, investigation, and disposition of complaints respecting the failure of an employer to meet a condition specified in an attestation submitted under this subsection or misrepresentation by the employer of material facts in such an attestation. Complaints may be filed by any aggrieved person or organization (including bargaining representatives). No investigation or hearing shall be conducted on a complaint concerning such a failure or misrepresentation unless the complaint was filed not later than 12 months after the date of the failure or misrepresentation, respectively. The Secretary of Labor shall conduct an investigation under this paragraph if there is reasonable cause to believe that such a failure or misrepresentation has occurred.

(B) Under the process described in subparagraph (A), the Secretary of Labor shall provide, within 30 days after the date a complaint is filed, for a determination as to whether or not a reasonable basis exists to make a finding described in subparagraph (C). If the Secretary of Labor determines that such a reasonable basis exists, the Secretary of Labor shall provide for notice of such determination to the interested parties and an opportunity for a hearing on the complaint, in accordance with section 556 of title 5, United States Code, within 60 days after the date of the determination. If such a hearing is requested, the Secretary of Labor shall make a finding concerning the matter by not later than 60 days after the date of the hearing. In the case of similar complaints respecting the same applicant, the Secretary of Labor may consolidate the hearings under this subparagraph on such complaints.

(C)(i) If the Secretary of Labor finds, after notice and opportunity for a hearing, a failure to meet a condition of paragraph (1)(B), a substantial failure to meet a condition of paragraph (1)(C) or (1)(D), or a misrepresentation of material fact in an attestation

(I) the Secretary of Labor shall notify the Secretary of State and the Secretary of Homeland Security of such finding and may, in addition, impose such other administrative remedies (including civil monetary penalties in an amount not to exceed $1,000 per violation) as the Secretary of Labor determines to be appropriate; and

(II) the Secretary of State or the Secretary of Homeland Security, as appropriate, shall not approve petitions or applications filed with respect to that employer under section 204, 214(c), 101(a)(15)(H)(i)(b1), or 101(a)(15)(E)(iii) [8 USCS § 1154, 1184(c), 1101(a)(15)(H)(i)(b1), or 1101(a)(15)(E)(iii)] during a period of at least 1 year for aliens to be employed by the employer.

(ii) If the Secretary of Labor finds, after notice and opportunity for a hearing, a willful failure to meet a condition of paragraph (1), a willful misrepresentation of material fact in an attestation, or a violation of clause (iv)

(I) the Secretary of Labor shall notify the Secretary of State and the Secretary of Homeland Security of such finding and may, in addition, impose such other administrative remedies (including civil monetary penalties in an amount not to exceed $5,000 per violation) as the Secretary of Labor determines to be appropriate; and

(II) the Secretary of State or the Secretary of Homeland Security, as appropriate, shall not approve petitions or applications filed with respect to that employer under section 204, 214(c), 101(a)(15)(H)(i)(b1), or 101(a)(15)(E)(iii) [8 USCS § 1154, 1184(c), 1101(a)(15)(H)(i)(b1), or 1101(a)(15)(E)(iii)] during a period of at least 2 years for aliens to be employed by the employer.

(iii) If the Secretary of Labor finds, after notice and opportunity for a hearing, a willful failure to meet a condition of paragraph (1) or a willful misrepresentation of material fact in an attestation, in the course of which failure or misrepresentation the employer displaced a United States worker employed by the employer within the period beginning 90 days before and ending 90 days after the date of filing of any visa petition or application supported by the attestation

(I) the Secretary of Labor shall notify the Secretary of State and the Secretary of Homeland Security of such finding and may, in addition, impose such other administrative remedies (including civil monetary penalties in an amount not to exceed $35,000 per violation) as the Secretary of Labor determines to be appropriate; and

(II) the Secretary of State or the Secretary of Homeland Security, as appropriate, shall not approve petitions or applications filed with respect to that employer under section 204, 214(c), 101(a)(15)(H)(i)(b1), or 101(a)(15)(E)(iii) [8 USCS § 1154, 1184(c), 1101(a)(15)(H)(i)(b1), or 1101(a)(15)(E)(iii)] during a period of at least 3 years for aliens to be employed by the employer.

(iv) It is a violation of this clause for an employer who has filed an attestation under this subsection to intimidate, threaten, restrain, coerce, blacklist, discharge, or in any other manner discriminate against an employee (which term, for purposes of this clause, includes a former employee and an applicant for employment) because the employee has disclosed information to the employer, or to any other person, that the employee reasonably believes evidences a violation of this subsection, or any rule or regulation pertaining to this subsection, or because the employee cooperates or seeks to cooperate in an investigation or other proceeding concerning the employer's compliance with the requirements of this subsection or any rule or regulation pertaining to this subsection.

(v) The Secretary of Labor and the Secretary of Homeland Security shall devise a process under which a nonimmigrant under section 101(a)(15)(H)(i)(b1) [8 USCS § 1101(a)(15)(H)(i)(b1)] or section 101(a)(15)(E)(iii) [8 USCS § 1101(a)(15)(E)(iii)] who files a complaint regarding a violation of clause (iv) and is otherwise eligible to remain and work in the United States may be allowed to seek other appropriate employment in the United States for a period not to exceed the maximum period of stay authorized for such nonimmigrant classification.

(vi)(I) It is a violation of this clause for an employer who has filed an attestation under this subsection to require a nonimmigrant under section 101(a)(15)(H)(i)(b1) [8 USCS § 1101(a)(15)(H)(i)(b1)] or section 101(a)(15)(E)(iii) [8 USCS § 1101(a)(15)(E)(iii)] to pay a penalty for ceasing employment with the employer prior to a date agreed to by the nonimmigrant and the employer. The Secretary of Labor shall determine whether a required payment is a penalty (and not liquidated damages) pursuant to relevant State law.

(II) If the Secretary of Labor finds, after notice and opportunity for a hearing, that an employer has committed a violation of this clause, the Secretary of Labor may impose a civil monetary penalty of $1,000 for each such violation and issue an administrative order requiring the return to the nonimmigrant of any amount paid in violation of this clause, or, if the nonimmigrant cannot be located, requiring payment of any such amount to the general fund of the Treasury.

(vii)(I) It is a failure to meet a condition of paragraph (1)(A) for an employer who has filed an attestation under this subsection and who places a nonimmigrant under section 101(a)(15)(H)(i)(b1) [8 USCS § 1101(a)(15)(H)(i)(b1)] or section 101(a)(15)(E)(iii) [8 USCS § 1101(a)(15)(E)(iii)] designated as a full-time employee in the attestation, after the nonimmigrant has entered into employment with the employer, in nonproductive status due to a decision by the employer (based on factors such as lack of work), or due to the nonimmigrant's lack of a permit or license, to fail to pay the nonimmigrant full-time wages in accordance with paragraph (1)(A) for all such nonproductive time.

(II) It is a failure to meet a condition of paragraph (1)(A) for an employer who has filed an attestation under this subsection and who places a nonimmigrant under section 101(a)(15)(H)(i)(b1) [8 USCS § 1101(a)(15)(H)(i)(b1)] or section 101(a)(15)(E)(iii) [8 USCS § 1101(a)(15)(E)(iii)] designated as a part-time employee in the attestation, after the nonimmigrant has entered into employment with the employer, in nonproductive status under circumstances described in subclause (I), to fail to pay such a nonimmigrant for such hours as are designated on the attestation consistent with the rate of pay identified on the attestation.

(III) In the case of a nonimmigrant under section 101(a)(15)(H)(i)(b1) [8 USCS § 1101(a)(15)(H)(i)(b1)] or section 101(a)(15)(E)(iii) [8 USCS § 1101(a)(15)(E)(iii)] who has not yet entered into employment with an employer who has had approved an attestation under this subsection with respect to the nonimmigrant, the provisions of subclauses (I) and (II) shall apply to the employer beginning 30 days after the date the nonimmigrant first is admitted into the United States, or 60 days after the date the nonimmigrant becomes eligible to work for the employer in the case of a nonimmigrant who is present in the United States on the date of the approval of the attestation filed with the Secretary of Labor.

(IV) This clause does not apply to a failure to pay wages to a nonimmigrant under section 101(a)(15)(H)(i)(b1) [8 USCS § 1101(a)(15)(H)(i)(b1)] or section 101(a)(15)(E)(iii) [8 USCS § 1101(a)(15)(E)(iii)] for nonproductive time due to non-work-related factors, such as the voluntary request of the nonimmigrant for an absence or circumstances rendering the nonimmigrant unable to work.

(V) This clause shall not be construed as prohibiting an employer that is a school or other educational institution from applying to a nonimmigrant under section 101(a)(15)(H)(i)(b1) [8 USCS § 1101(a)(15)(H)(i)(b1)] or section 101(a)(15)(E)(iii) [8 USCS § 1101(a)(15)(E)(iii)] an established salary practice of the employer, under which the employer pays to nonimmigrants under section 101(a)(15)(H)(i)(b1) [8 USCS § 1101(a)(15)(H)(i)(b1)] or section 101(a)(15)(E)(iii) [8 USCS § 1101(a)(15)(E)(iii)] and United States workers in the same occupational classification an annual salary in disbursements over fewer than 12 months, if

(aa) the nonimmigrant agrees to the compressed annual salary payments prior to the commencement of the employment; and

(bb) the application of the salary practice to the nonimmigrant does not otherwise cause the nonimmigrant to violate any condition of the nonimmigrant's authorization under this Act to remain in the United States.

(VI) This clause shall not be construed as superseding clause (viii).

(viii) It is a failure to meet a condition of paragraph (1)(A) for an employer who has filed an attestation under this subsection to fail to offer to a nonimmigrant under section 101(a)(15)(H)(i)(b1) [8 USCS § 1101(a)(15)(H)(i)(b1)] or section 101(a)(15)(E)(iii) [8 USCS § 1101(a)(15)(E)(iii)], during the nonimmigrant's period of authorized employment, benefits and eligibility for benefits (including the opportunity to participate in health, life, disability, and other insurance plans; the opportunity to participate in retirement and savings plans; and cash bonuses and non-cash compensation, such as stock options (whether or not based on performance)) on the same basis, and in accordance with the same criteria, as the employer offers to United States workers.

(D) If the Secretary of Labor finds, after notice and opportunity for a hearing, that an employer has not paid wages at the wage level specified in the attestation and required under paragraph (1), the Secretary of Labor shall order the employer to provide for payment of such amounts of back pay as may be required to comply with the requirements of paragraph (1), whether or not a penalty under subparagraph (C) has been imposed.

(E) The Secretary of Labor may, on a case-by-case basis, subject an employer to random investigations for a period of up to 5 years, beginning on the date on which the employer is found by the Secretary of Labor to have committed a willful failure to meet a condition of paragraph (1) or to have made a willful misrepresentation of material fact in an attestation. The authority of the Secretary of Labor under this subparagraph shall not be construed to be subject to, or limited by, the requirements of subparagraph (A).

(F) Nothing in this subsection shall be construed as superseding or preempting any other enforcement-related authority under this Act (such as the authorities under section 274B [8 USCS § 1324b]), or any other Act.

(4) For purposes of this subsection:

(A) The term "area of employment" means the area within normal commuting distance of the worksite or physical location where the work of the nonimmigrant under section 101(a)(15)(H)(i)(b1) [8 USCS § 1101(a)(15)(H)(i)(b1)] or section 101(a)(15)(E)(iii) [8 USCS § 1101(a)(15)(E)(iii)] is or will be performed. If such worksite or location is within a Metropolitan Statistical Area, any place within such area is deemed to be within the area of employment.

(B) In the case of an attestation with respect to one or more nonimmigrants under section 101(a)(15)(H)(i)(b1) [8 USCS § 1101(a)(15)(H)(i)(b1)] or section 101(a)(15)(E)(iii) [8 USCS § 1101(a)(15)(E)(iii)] by an employer, the employer is considered to "displace" a United States worker from a job if the employer lays off the worker from a job that is essentially the equivalent of the job for which the nonimmigrant or nonimmigrants is or are sought. A job shall not be considered to be essentially equivalent of another job unless it involves essentially the same responsibilities, was held by a United States worker with substantially equivalent qualifications and experience, and is located in the same area of employment as the other job.

(C)(i) The term "lays off", with respect to a worker

(I) means to cause the worker's loss of employment, other than through a discharge for inadequate performance, violation of workplace rules, cause, voluntary departure, voluntary retirement, or the expiration of a grant or contract; but

(II) does not include any situation in which the worker is offered, as an alternative to such loss of employment, a similar employment opportunity with the same employer at equivalent or higher compensation and benefits than the position from which the employee was discharged, regardless of whether or not the employee accepts the offer.

(ii) Nothing in this subparagraph is intended to limit an employee's rights under a collective bargaining agreement or other employment contract.

(D) The term "United States worker" means an employee who

(i) is a citizen or national of the United States; or

(ii) is an alien who is lawfully admitted for permanent residence, is admitted as a refugee under section 207 of this title [8 USCS § 1157], is granted asylum under section 208 [8 USCS § 1158], or is an immigrant otherwise authorized, by this Act or by the Secretary of Homeland Security, to be employed.

[(u)](t) Foreign residence requirement.

(1) Except as provided in paragraph (2), no person admitted under section 101(a)(15)(Q)(ii)(I) [8 USCS § 1101(a)(15)(Q)(ii)(I)], or acquiring such status after admission, shall be eligible to apply for nonimmigrant status, an immigrant visa, or permanent residence under this Act until it is established that such person has resided and been physically present in the person's country of nationality or last residence for an aggregate of at least 2 years following departure from the United States.

(2) The Secretary of Homeland Security may waive the requirement of such 2-year foreign residence abroad if the Secretary determines that

(A) departure from the United States would impose exceptional hardship upon the alien's spouse or child (if such spouse or child is a citizen of the United States or an alien lawfully admitted for permanent residence); or

(B) the admission of the alien is in the public interest or the national interest of the United States.

(June 27, 1952, ch 477, Title II, Ch 2, § 212, 66 Stat. 182; July 18, 1956, ch 629, Title III, § 301(a), 70 Stat. 575; July 7, 1958, P. L. 85-508, § 23, 72 Stat. 351; March 18, 1959, P. L. 86-3, § 20(b), 73 Stat. 13; July 14, 1960, P. L. 86-648, § 8, 74 Stat. 505; Sept. 21, 1961, P. L. 87-256, § 109(c), 75 Stat. 535; Sept. 26, 1961, P. L. 87-301, §§ 11–15, 75 Stat. 654; Oct. 3, 1965, P. L. 89-236, §§ 10, 15, 79 Stat. 917, 919; April 7, 1970, P. L. 91-225, § 2, 84 Stat. 116; Oct. 12, 1976, P. L. 94-484, Title VI, § 601(a), (c), (d), 90 Stat. 2300, 2301; Oct. 20, 1976, P. L. 94-571, §§ 5, 7(d), 90 Stat. 2705, 2706; Aug. 1, 1977, P. L. 95-83, Title III, 307(q)(1), (2), 91 Stat. 394; Oct. 30, 1978, P. L. 95-549, Title I, §§ 101, 102, 92 Stat. 2065; Sept. 27, 1979, P. L. 96-70, Title III, Ch 2, § 3201(b), 93 Stat. 497; March 17, 1980, P. L. 96-212, Title II, § 203(d), (f), 94 Stat. 107; Dec. 17, 1980, P. L. 96-538, Title IV, § 404, 94 Stat. 3192; Dec. 29, 1981, P. L. 97-116, §§ 4, 5(a), (b), 18(e), 95 Stat. 1611, 1612, 1620; Oct. 5, 1984, P. L. 98-454, Title VI, § 602 [(a)], 98 Stat. 1737; Aug. 27, 1986, P. L. 99-396, § 14(a), 100 Stat. 842; Oct. 27, 1986, P. L. 99-570, Title I, Subtitle M, § 1751(a), 100 Stat. 3207-47; Nov. 10, 1986, P. L. 99-639, § 6(a), 100 Stat. 3543; Nov. 14, 1986, P. L. 99-653, § 7(a), 100 Stat. 3657; Oct. 12, 1984, P. L. 98-473, Title II, Ch II, § 220(a)(9), 98 Stat. 2027; Aug. 27, 1986, P. L. 99-396, § 14(a); Nov. 14, 1986, P. L. 99-653, § 7(d)(2); Dec. 22, 1987, P. L. 100-204, Title VIII, § 806(c), 101 Stat. 1399; Oct. 24, 1988, P. L. 100-525, §§ 3(1)(A), 7(c), 8(f)(2), 9(i), 102 Stat. 1614, 2614, 2616, 2617, 2620.; Nov. 18, 1988, P. L. 100-690, Title VII, Subtitle J, § 7349(a), 102 Stat. 4473; Dec. 18, 1989, P. L. 101-238, § 3(b), 103 Stat. 2100; Feb. 16, 1990, P. L. 101-246, Title I, Part C, § 131(a), (c), 104 Stat. 31; Nov. 29, 1990, P. L. 101-649, Title I, Subtitle E, § 162(e)(1), (f)(2)(B), Title II, Subtitle A, § 202(b), Subtitle B, § 205(c)(3), Title V, Subtitle A, §§ 511(a), 514(a), Title VI, §§ 601(a), (b), (d), 603(a)(19), 104 Stat. 5011, 5012, 5014, 5020, 5052, 5053, 5067, 5075, 5084.; Dec. 12, 1991, P. L. 102-232, Title III, §§ 302(e)(6), (9), 303(a)(5)(B), (6), (7)(B), 306(a)(10), (12), 307(a)–(g), 105 Stat. 1746, 1747, 1751, 1753.; June 10, 1993, P. L. 103-43, Title XX, § 2007(a), 107 Stat. 210; Aug. 26, 1994, P. L. 103-317, Title V, § 506(a), 108 Stat. 1765; Sept. 13, 1994, P. L. 103-322, Title XIII, § 130003(b)(1), 108 Stat. 2024; Oct. 25, 1994, P. L. 103-416, Title II, §§ 203(a), 219(e), (z)(1), (5), 220(a), 108 Stat. 4311, 4316, 4318, 4319.; April 24, 1996, P. L. 104-132, Title IV, Subtitle B, §§ 411, 412, Subtitle C, § 440(d), 110 Stat. 1268, 1269, 1277; Sept. 30, 1996, P. L. 104-208, Div C, Title I, Subtitle B, § 124(b)(1), Title III, Subtitle A, §§ 301(b)(1), (c)(1), 304(b), 305(c), 306(d), 308(c)(2)(B), (d)(1), (e)(1)(B), (C), (2)(A), (6), (f)(1)(C)–(F), (3)(A), (g)(4)(B), (10)(A), (H), Subtitle B, § 322(a)(2)(B), Subtitle C, §§ 341(a), (b), 342(a), 343, 344(a), 345(a), 346(a), 347(a), 348(a), 349, 351(a), 352(a), 355, Title V, Subtitle B, § 531(a), Title VI, Subtitle A, § 602(a), Subtitle B, §§ 622(b), 624(a), Subtitle E, § 671(e)(3), 110 Stat. 3009-562, 3009-575, 3009-578, 3009-597, 3009-607, 3009-612, 3009-616, 3009-619, 3009-620, 3009-621, 3009-622, 3009-625, 3009-629, 3009-635, 3009-636, 3009-637, 3009-638, 3009-639, 3009-640, 3009-641, 3009-644, 3009-674, 3009-689, 3009-695, 3009-698, 3009-723; Nov. 12, 1997, P. L. 105-73, § 1, 111 Stat. 1459; Oct. 21, 1998, P. L. 105-277, Div C, Title IV, Subtitle A, §§ 412(a)–(c), 413(a)–(e)(1), (f), 415(a), Subtitle C, § 431(a), Div G, Subdiv B, Title XXII, Ch 2, § 2226(a), 112 Stat. 2681-642, 2681-645, 2681-651, 2681-654, 2681-658, 2681-820; Oct. 27, 1998, P. L. 105-292, Title VI, § 604(a), 112 Stat. 2814; Nov. 12, 1999, P. L. 106-95, §§ 2(b), 4(a), 113 Stat. 1312, 1317; Dec. 3, 1999, P. L. 106-120, Title VIII, § 809, 113 Stat. 1632; Oct. 17, 2000, P. L. 106-313, Title I, §§ 106(c)(2), 107(a), 114 Stat. 1254, 1255; Oct. 28, 2000, P. L. 106-386, Div A, §§ 107(e)(3), 111(d), Div B, Title V, §§ 1505(a), (c)(1), (d)–(f), 1513(e), 114 Stat. 1478, 1485, 1525, 1526, 1536.; Oct. 30, 2000, P. L. 106-395, Title II, § 201(b)(1), (2), 114 Stat. 1633; Oct. 30, 2000, P. L. 106-396, Title I, § 101(b)(1), 114 Stat. 1638; Oct. 26, 2001, P. L. 107-56, Title IV, Subtitle B, § 411(a), Title X, § 1006(a), 115 Stat. 345, 394; March 13, 2002, P. L. 107-150, § 2(a)(2), 116 Stat. 74; Nov. 2, 2002, P. L. 107-273, Div C, Title I, Subtitle A, § 11018(c), 116 Stat. 1825; Sept. 3, 2003, P. L. 108-77, Title IV, § 402(b), (c), 117 Stat. 940; Dec. 19, 2003, P. L. 108-193, §§ 4(b)(4), 8(a)(2), 117 Stat. 2879, 2886; Dec. 8, 2004, P. L. 108-447, Div J, Title IV, Subtitle B, §§ 422(a), 423, 424(a)(1), (b), 118 Stat. 3353, 3355; Dec. 10, 2004, P. L. 108-449, § 1(b)(2), 118 Stat. 3470; Dec. 17, 2004, P. L. 108-458, Title V, Subtitle E, §§ 5501(a), 5502(a), 5503, 118 Stat. 3740, 3741; May 11, 2005, P. L. 109-13, Div B, Title I, §§ 103(a)–(c), 104, Title V, § 501(d), 119 Stat. 306, 309, 322; Jan. 5, 2006, P. L. 109-162, Title VIII, Subtitle A, § 802, 119 Stat. 3054; Aug. 12, 2006, P. L. 109-271, § 6(b), 120 Stat. 762; Dec. 26, 2007, P. L. 110-161, Div J, Title VI, § 691(a), (c),

121 Stat. 2364, 2365; May 8, 2008, P. L. 110-229, Title VII, Subtitle A, § 702(b)(2), (3), (d), 122 Stat. 860, 862; July 30, 2008, P. L. 110-293, Title III, Subtitle A, § 305, 122 Stat. 2963; Oct. 3, 2008, P. L. 110-340, § 2(b), 122 Stat. 3736; Dec. 23, 2008, P. L. 110-457, Title II, Subtitle C, § 222(f)(1), Subtitle D, § 234, 122 Stat. 5071, 5074; Dec. 22, 2009, P. L. 111-122, § 3(b), 123 Stat. 3481; Nov. 30, 2010, P. L. 111-287, § 2, 124 Stat. 3058; March 7, 2013, P. L. 113-4, Title VIII, § 804, 127 Stat. 111; Jan. 29, 2025, P.L. 119-1, § 3(d), 139 Stat. 4.)

§§ 1182a–1182c. [Repealed]

§ 1182d. Denial of visas to confiscators of American property

(a) Denial of visas. Except as otherwise provided in section 401 of the Cuban Liberty and Democratic Solidarity (LIBERTAD) Act of 1996 (Public Law 104-114) [22 USCS § 6091], and subject to subsection (b), the Secretary of State may deny the issuance of a visa to any alien who—

(1) through the abuse of position, including a governmental or political party position, converts or has converted for personal gain real property that has been confiscated or expropriated, a claim to which is owned by a national of the United States, or who is complicit in such a conversion; or

(2) induces any of the actions or omissions described in paragraph (1) by any person.

(b) Exceptions. Subsection (a) shall not apply to—

(1) any country established by international mandate through the United Nations; or

(2) any territory recognized by the United States Government to be in dispute.

(c) Reporting requirement. Not later than 6 months after the date of enactment of this Act [enacted Oct. 21, 1998], and every 12 months thereafter, the Secretary of State shall submit to the Speaker of the House of Representatives and to the chairman of the Committee on Foreign Relations of the Senate a report, including—

(1) a list of aliens who have been denied a visa under this subsection; and

(2) a list of aliens who could have been denied a visa under subsection (a) but were issued a visa and an explanation as to why each such visa was issued.

(Oct. 21, 1998, P. L. 105-277, Div G, Subdiv B, Title XXII, Ch 2, § 2225, 112 Stat. 2681-819.)

§ 1182e. Denial of entry into United States of foreign nationals engaged in establishment or enforcement of forced abortion or sterilization policy

(a) Denial of entry. Notwithstanding any other provision of law, the Secretary of State may not issue any visa to, and the Attorney General may not admit to the United States, any foreign national whom the Secretary finds, based on credible and specific information, to have been directly involved in the establishment or enforcement of population control policies forcing a woman to undergo an abortion against her free choice or forcing a man or woman to undergo sterilization against his or her free choice, unless the Secretary has substantial grounds for believing that the foreign national has discontinued his or her involvement with, and support for, such policies.

(b) Exceptions. The prohibitions in subsection (a) shall not apply in the case of a foreign national who is a head of state, head of government, or cabinet level minister.

(c) Waiver. The Secretary of State may waive the prohibitions in subsection (a) with respect to a foreign national if the Secretary—

(1) determines that it is important to the national interest of the United States to do so; and

(2) provides written notification to the appropriate congressional committees containing a justification for the waiver.

(Nov. 29, 1999, P. L. 106-113, Div B, § 1000(a)(7), 113 Stat. 1536.)

§ 1182f. Denial of entry into United States of Chinese and other nationals engaged in coerced organ or bodily tissue transplantation

(a) Denial of entry. Notwithstanding any other provision of law and except as provided in subsection (b), the Secretary shall direct consular officers not to issue a visa to any person whom the Secretary finds, based on credible and specific information, to have been directly involved with the coercive transplantation of human organs or bodily tissue, unless the Secretary has substantial grounds for believing that the foreign national has discontinued his or her involvement with, and support for, such practices.

(b) Exception. The prohibitions in subsection (a) do not apply to an applicant who is a head of state, head of government, or cabinet-level minister.

(c) Waiver. The Secretary may waive the prohibitions in subsection (a) with respect to a foreign national if the Secretary—

(1) determines that it is important to the national interest of the United States to do so; and

(2) not later than 30 days after the issuance of a visa, provides written notification to the appropriate congressional committees containing a justification for the waiver.

(Sept. 30, 2002, P. L. 107-228, Div A, Subtitle C, § 232, 116 Stat. 1372.)

§ 1183. Admission of aliens on giving bond or undertaking; return upon permanent departure

An alien inadmissible under paragraph (4) of section 212(a) [8 USCS § 1182(a)(4)] may, if otherwise admissible, be admitted in the discretion of the Attorney General (subject to the affidavit of support requirement and attribution of sponsor's income and resources under section 213A [8 USCS § 1183a]) upon the giving of a suitable and proper bond or undertaking approved by the Attorney General, in such amount and containing such conditions as he may prescribe, to the United States, and to all States, territories, counties, towns, municipalities, and districts thereof holding the United States and all States, territories, counties, towns, municipalities, and districts thereof harmless against such alien becoming a public charge. Such bond or undertaking shall terminate upon the permanent departure from the United States, the naturalization, or the death of such alien, and any sums or other security held to secure performance thereof, except to the extent forfeited for violation of the terms thereof, shall be returned to the person by whom furnished, or to his legal representatives. Suit may be brought thereon in the name and by the proper law officers of the United States for the use of the United States, or of any State, territory, district, county, town, or municipality in which such alien becomes a public charge, irrespective of whether a demand for payment of public expenses has been made.

(June 27, 1952, ch 477, Title II, Ch 2, § 213, 66 Stat. 188; July 10, 1970, P. L. 91-313, § 1, 84 Stat. 413; Nov. 29, 1990, P. L. 101-649, Title VI, § 603(a)(8), 104 Stat. 5083; Sept. 30, 1996, P. L. 104-208, Div C, Title III, Subtitle A, § 308(d)(3)(A), Title V, Subtitle D, § 564(f), 110 Stat. 3009-617, 3009-684.)

§ 1183a. Requirements for sponsor's affidavit of support

(a) Enforceability.

(1) Terms of affidavit. No affidavit of support may be accepted by the Attorney General or by any consular officer to establish that an alien is not excludable as a public charge under section 212(a)(4) [8 USCS § 1182(a)(4)] unless such affidavit is executed by a sponsor of the alien as a contract—

(A) in which the sponsor agrees to provide support to maintain the sponsored alien at an annual income that is not less than 125 percent of the Federal poverty line during the period in which the affidavit is enforceable;

(B) that is legally enforceable against the sponsor by the sponsored alien, the Federal Government, any State (or any political subdivision of such State), or by any other entity that provides any means-tested public benefit (as defined in subsection (e)), consistent with the provisions of this section; and

(C) in which the sponsor agrees to submit to the jurisdiction of any Federal or State court for the purpose of actions brought under subsection (b)(2).

(2) Period of enforceability. An affidavit of support shall be enforceable with respect to benefits provided for an alien before the date the alien is naturalized as a citizen of the United States, or, if earlier, the termination date provided under paragraph (3).

(3) Termination of period of enforceability upon completion of required period of employment, etc.

(A) In general. An affidavit of support is not enforceable after such time as the alien (i) has worked 40 qualifying quarters of coverage as defined under title II of the Social Security Act [42 USCS §§ 401 et seq.] or can be credited with such qualifying quarters as provided under subparagraph (B), and (ii) in the case of any such qualifying quarter creditable for any period beginning after December 31, 1996, did not receive any Federal means-tested public benefit (as provided under section 403 of the Personal Responsibility and Work Opportunity Reconciliation Act of 1996 [8 USCS § 1613]) during any such period.

(B) Qualifying quarters. For purposes of this section, in determining the number of qualifying quarters of coverage under title II of the Social Security Act [42 USCS §§ 401 et seq.] an alien shall be credited with—

(i) all of the qualifying quarters of coverage as defined under title II of the Social Security Act [42 USCS §§ 401 et seq.] worked by a parent of such alien while the alien was under age 18, and

(ii) all of the qualifying quarters worked by a spouse of such alien during their marriage and the alien remains married to such spouse or such spouse is deceased.

No such qualifying quarter of coverage that is creditable under title II of the Social Security Act [42 USCS §§ 401 et seq.] for any period beginning after December 31, 1996, may be credited to an alien under clause (i) or (ii) if the parent or spouse (as the case may be) of such alien received any Federal means-tested public benefit (as provided under section 403 of the Personal Responsibility and Work Opportunity Reconciliation Act of 1996 [8 USCS § 1613]) during the period for which such qualifying quarter of coverage is so credited.

(C) Provision of information to save system. The Attorney General shall ensure that appropriate information regarding the application of this paragraph is provided to the system for alien verification of eligibility (SAVE) described in section 1137(d)(3) of the Social Security Act [42 USCS § 1320b-7(d)(3)].

(b) Reimbursement of Government expenses.

(1) Request for reimbursement.

(A) Requirement. Upon notification that a sponsored alien has received any means-tested public benefit, the appropriate nongovernmental entity which provided such benefit or the appropriate entity of the Federal Government, a State, or any political subdivision of a State shall request reimbursement by the sponsor in an amount which is equal to the unreimbursed costs of such benefit.

(B) Regulations. The Attorney General, in consultation with the heads of other appropriate Federal agencies, shall prescribe such regulations as may be necessary to carry out subparagraph (A).

(2) Actions to compel reimbursement.

(A) In case of nonresponse. If within 45 days after a request for reimbursement under paragraph (1)(A), the appropriate entity has not received a response from the sponsor indicating a willingness to commence payment an action may be brought against the sponsor pursuant to the affidavit of support.

(B) In case of failure to pay. If the sponsor fails to abide by the repayment terms established by the appropriate entity, the entity may bring an action against the sponsor pursuant to the affidavit of support.

(C) Limitation on actions. No cause of action may be brought under this paragraph later than 10 years after the date on which the sponsored alien last received any means-tested public benefit to which the affidavit of support applies.

(3) Use of collection agencies. If the appropriate entity under paragraph (1)(A) requests reimbursement from the sponsor or brings an action against the sponsor pursuant to the affidavit of support, the appropriate entity may appoint or hire an individual or other person

to act on behalf of such entity acting under the authority of law for purposes of collecting any amounts owed.

(c) Remedies. Remedies available to enforce an affidavit of support under this section include any or all of the remedies described in section 3201, 3203, 3204, or 3205 of title 28, United States Code, as well as an order for specific performance and payment of legal fees and other costs of collection, and include corresponding remedies available under State law. A Federal agency may seek to collect amounts owed under this section in accordance with the provisions of subchapter II of chapter 37 of title 31, United States Code [31 USCS §§ 3711 et seq.].

(d) Notification of change of address.

(1) General requirement. The sponsor shall notify the Attorney General and the State in which the sponsored alien is currently a resident within 30 days of any change of address of the sponsor during the period in which an affidavit of support is enforceable.

(2) Penalty. Any person subject to the requirement of paragraph (1) who fails to satisfy such requirement shall, after notice and opportunity to be heard, be subject to a civil penalty of—

(A) not less than $250 or more than $2,000, or

(B) if such failure occurs with knowledge that the sponsored alien has received any means-tested public benefits (other than benefits described in section 401(b), 403(c)(2), or 411(b) of the Personal Responsibility and Work Opportunity Reconciliation Act of 1996 [8 USCS § 1611(b), 1613(c)(2), or 1621(b)]) not less than $2,000 or more than $5,000.

The Attorney General shall enforce this paragraph under appropriate regulations.

(e) Jurisdiction. An action to enforce an affidavit of support executed under subsection (a) may be brought against the sponsor in any appropriate court—

(1) by a sponsored alien, with respect to financial support; or

(2) by the appropriate entity of the Federal Government, a State or any political subdivision of a State, or by any other nongovernmental entity under subsection (b)(2), with respect to reimbursement.

(f) Sponsor defined.

(1) In general. For purposes of this section the term "sponsor" in relation to a sponsored alien means an individual who executes an affidavit of support with respect to the sponsored alien and who—

(A) is a citizen or national of the United States or an alien who is lawfully admitted to the United States for permanent residence;

(B) is at least 18 years of age;

(C) is domiciled in any of the several States of the United States, the District of Columbia, or any territory or possession of the United States;

(D) is petitioning for the admission of the alien under section 204 [8 USCS § 1154]; and

(E) demonstrates (as provided in paragraph (6)) the means to maintain an annual income equal to at least 125 percent of the Federal poverty line.

(2) Income requirement case. Such term also includes an individual who does not meet the requirement of paragraph (1)(E) but accepts joint and several liability together with an individual under paragraph (5)(A).

(3) Active duty armed services case. Such term also includes an individual who does not meet the requirement of paragraph (1)(E) but is on active duty (other than active duty for training) in the Armed Forces of the United States, is petitioning for the admission of the alien under section 204 [8 USCS § 1154] as the spouse or child of the individual, and demonstrates (as provided in paragraph (6)) the means to maintain an annual income equal to at least 100 percent of the Federal poverty line.

(4) Certain employment-based immigrants case. Such term also includes an individual—

(A) who does not meet the requirement of paragraph (1)(D), but is the relative of the sponsored alien who filed a classification petition for the sponsored alien as an employment-based immigrant under section 203(b) [8 USCS § 1153(b)] or who has a significant ownership interest in the entity that filed such a petition; and

(B)(i) who demonstrates (as provided under paragraph (6)) the means to maintain an annual income equal to at least 125 percent of the Federal poverty line, or

(ii) does not meet the requirement of paragraph (1)(E) but accepts joint and several liability together with an individual under paragraph (5)(A).

(5) Non-petitioning cases. Such term also includes an individual who does not meet the requirement of paragraph (1)(D) but who—

(A) accepts joint and several liability with a petitioning sponsor under paragraph (2) or relative of an employment-based immigrant under paragraph (4) and who demonstrates (as provided under paragraph (6)) the means to maintain an annual income equal to at least 125 percent of the Federal poverty line; or

(B) is a spouse, parent, mother-in-law, father-in-law, sibling, child (if at least 18 years of age), son, daughter, son-in-law, daughter-in-law, sister-in-law, brother-in-law, grandparent, or grandchild of a sponsored alien or a legal guardian of a sponsored alien, meets the requirements of paragraph (1) (other than subparagraph (D)), and executes an affidavit of support with respect to such alien in a case in which—

(i) the individual petitioning under section 204 of this Act [8 USCS § 1154] for the classification of such alien died after the approval of such petition, and the Secretary of Homeland Security has determined for humanitarian reasons that revocation of such petition under section 205 [8 USCS § 1155] would be inappropriate; or

(ii) the alien's petition is being adjudicated pursuant to section 204(l) [8 USCS § 1154(l)] (surviving relative consideration).

(6) Demonstration of means to maintain income.

(A) In general.

(i) Method of demonstration. For purposes of this section, a demonstration of the means to maintain income shall include provision of a certified copy of the individual's Federal income tax return for the individual's 3 most recent taxable years and a written statement, executed under oath or as permitted under penalty of perjury under section 1746 of title 28, United States Code, that the copies are certified copies of such returns.

(ii) Flexibility. For purposes of this section, aliens may demonstrate the means to maintain income through demonstration of significant assets of the sponsored alien or of the sponsor, if such assets are available for the support of the sponsored alien.

(iii) Percent of poverty. For purposes of this section, a reference to an annual income equal to at least a particular percentage of the Federal poverty line means an annual income equal to at least such percentage of the Federal poverty line for a family unit of a size equal to the number of members of the sponsor's household (including family and non-family dependents) plus the total number of other dependents and aliens sponsored by that sponsor.

(B) Limitation. The Secretary of State, or the Attorney General in the case of adjustment of status, may provide that the demonstration under subparagraph (A) applies only to the most recent taxable year.

(g) [Not enacted]

(h) "Federal poverty line" defined. For purposes of this section, the term "Federal poverty line" means the level of income equal to the official poverty line (as defined by the Director of the Office of Management and Budget, as revised annually by the Secretary of Health and Human Services, in accordance with section 673(2) of the Omnibus Budget Reconciliation Act of 1981 (42 U.S.C. 9902)) that is applicable to a family of the size involved.

(i) Sponsor's social security account number required to be provided.

(1) An affidavit of support shall include the social security account number of each sponsor.

(2) The Attorney General shall develop an automated system to maintain the social security account number data provided under paragraph (1).

(3) The Attorney General shall submit an annual report to the Committees on the Judiciary of the House of Representatives and the Senate setting forth—

(A) for the most recent fiscal year for which data are available the number of sponsors under this section and the number of sponsors in compliance with the financial obligations of this section; and

(B) a comparison of such numbers with the numbers of such sponsors for the preceding fiscal year.

(June 27, 1952, ch 477, Title II, Ch 2, § 213A, as added Aug. 22, 1996, P. L. 104-193, Title IV, Subtitle C, § 423(a), 110 Stat. 2271; Sept. 30, 1996, P. L. 104-208, Div C, Title V, Subtitle C, § 551(a), 110 Stat. 3009-675; March 13, 2002, P. L. 107-150, § 2(a)(1), (3), 116 Stat. 74, 75; Oct. 28, 2009, P. L. 111-83, Title V, § 568(e), 123 Stat. 2187.)

§ 1184. Admission of nonimmigrants

(a) Regulations.

(1) The admission to the United States of any alien as a nonimmigrant shall be for such time and under such conditions as the Attorney General may by regulations prescribe, including when he deems necessary the giving of a bond with sufficient surety in such sum and containing such conditions as the Attorney General shall prescribe, to insure that at the expiration of such time or upon failure to maintain the status under which he was admitted, or to maintain any status subsequently acquired under section 248 [8 USCS § 1258], such alien will depart from the United States. No alien admitted to Guam or the Commonwealth of the Northern Mariana Islands without a visa pursuant to section 212(l) [8 USCS § 1182(l)] may be authorized to enter or stay in the United States other than in Guam or the Commonwealth of the Northern Mariana Islands or to remain in Guam or the Commonwealth of the Northern Mariana Islands for a period exceeding 45 days from date of admission to Guam or the Commonwealth of the Northern Mariana Islands. No alien admitted to the United States without a visa pursuant to section 217 [8 USCS § 1187] may be authorized to remain in the United States as a nonimmigrant visitor for a period exceeding 90 days from the date of admission.

(2)(A) The period of authorized status as a nonimmigrant described in section 101(a)(15)(O) [8 USCS § 1101(a)(15)(O)] shall be for such period as the Attorney General may specify in order to provide for the event (or events) for which the nonimmigrant is admitted.

(B) The period of authorized status as a nonimmigrant described in section 101(a)(15)(P) [8 USCS § 1101(a)(15)(P)] shall be for such period as the Attorney General may specify in order to provide for the competition, event, or performance for which the nonimmigrant is admitted. In the case of nonimmigrants admitted as individual athletes under section 101(a)(15)(P) [8 USCS § 1101(a)(15)(P)], the period of authorized status may be for an initial period (not to exceed 5 years) during which the nonimmigrant will perform as an athlete and such period may be extended by the Attorney General for an additional period of up to 5 years.

(b) Presumption of status; written waiver. Every alien (other than a nonimmigrant described in subparagraph (L) or (V) of section 101(a)(15) [8 USCS § 1101(a)(15)], and other than a nonimmigrant described in any provision of section 101(a)(15)(H)(i) [8 USCS § 1101(a)(15)(H)(i)] except subclause (b1) of such section) shall be presumed to be an immigrant until he establishes to the satisfaction of the consular officer, at the time of application for a visa, and the immigration officers, at the time of application for admission, that he is entitled to a nonimmigrant status under section 101(a)(15) [8 USCS § 1101(a)(15)]. An alien who is an officer or employee of any foreign government or of any international organization entitled to enjoy privileges, exemptions, and immunities under the International Organizations Immunities Act, or an alien who is the attendant, servant, employee, or member of the immediate family of any such alien shall not be entitled to apply for or receive an immigrant visa, or to enter the United States as an immigrant unless he executes a written waiver in the same form and substance as is prescribed by section 247(b) [8 USCS § 1257(b)].

(c) Petition of importing employer.

(1) The question of importing any alien as a nonimmigrant under subparagraph (H), (L), (O), or (P)(i) of section 101(a)(15) [8 USCS § 1101(a)(15)] (excluding nonimmigrants under section 101(a)(15)(H)(i)(b1) [8

USCS § 1101(a)(15)(H)(i)(b1)]) in any specific case or specific cases shall be determined by the Attorney General, after consultation with appropriate agencies of the Government, upon petition of the importing employer. Such petition shall be made and approved before the visa is granted. The petition shall be in such form and contain such information as the Attorney General shall prescribe. The approval of such a petition shall not, of itself, be construed as establishing that the alien is a nonimmigrant. For purposes of this subsection with respect to nonimmigrants described in section 101(a)(15)(H)(ii)(a) [8 USCS § 1101(a)(15)(H)(ii)(a)], the term "appropriate agencies of Government" means the Department of Labor and includes the Department of Agriculture. The provisions of section 218 [8 USCS § 1188] shall apply to the question of importing any alien as a nonimmigrant under section 101(a)(15)(H)(ii)(a) [8 USCS § 1101(a)(15)(H)(ii)(a)].

(2)(A) The Attorney General shall provide for a procedure under which an importing employer which meets requirements established by the Attorney General may file a blanket petition to import aliens as nonimmigrants described in section 101(a)(15)(L) [8 USCS § 1101(a)(15)(L)] instead of filing individual petitions under paragraph (1) to import such aliens. Such procedure shall permit the expedited processing of visas for admission of aliens covered under such a petition.

(B) For purposes of section 101(a)(15)(L) [8 USCS § 1101(a)(15)(L)], an alien is considered to be serving in a capacity involving specialized knowledge with respect to a company if the alien has a special knowledge of the company product and its application in international markets or has an advanced level of knowledge of processes and procedures of the company.

(C) The Attorney General shall provide a process for reviewing and acting upon petitions under this subsection with respect to nonimmigrants described in section 101(a)(15)(L) [8 USCS § 1101(a)(15)(L)] within 30 days after the date a completed petition has been filed.

(D) The period of authorized admission for—

(i) a nonimmigrant admitted to render services in a managerial or executive capacity under section 101(a)(15)(L) [8 USCS § 1101(a)(15)(L)] shall not exceed 7 years, or

(ii) a nonimmigrant admitted to render services in a capacity that involves specialized knowledge under section 101(a)(15)(L) [8 USCS § 1101(a)(15)(L)] shall not exceed 5 years.

(E) In the case of an alien spouse admitted under section 101(a)(15)(L) [8 USCS § 1101(a)(15)(L)], who is accompanying or following to join a principal alien admitted under such section, the Attorney General shall authorize the alien spouse to engage in employment in the United States and provide the spouse with an "employment authorized" endorsement or other appropriate work permit.

(F) An alien who will serve in a capacity involving specialized knowledge with respect to an employer for purposes of section 101(a)(15)(L) [8 USCS § 1101(a)(15)(L)] and will be stationed primarily at the worksite of an employer other than the petitioning employer or its affiliate, subsidiary, or parent shall not be eligible for classification under section 101(a)(15)(L) [8 USCS § 1101(a)(15)(L)] if—

(i) the alien will be controlled and supervised principally by such unaffiliated employer; or

(ii) the placement of the alien at the worksite of the unaffiliated employer is essentially an arrangement to provide labor for hire for the unaffiliated employer, rather than a placement in connection with the provision of a product or service for which specialized knowledge specific to the petitioning employer is necessary.

(3) The Attorney General shall approve a petition—

(A) with respect to a nonimmigrant described in section 101(a)(15)(O)(i) [8 USCS § 1101(a)(15)(O)(i)] only after consultation in accordance with paragraph (6) or, with respect to aliens seeking entry for a motion picture or television production, after consultation with the appropriate union representing the alien's occupational peers and a management organization in the area of the alien's ability, or

(B) with respect to a nonimmigrant described in section 101(a)(15)(O)(ii) [8 USCS § 1101(a)(15)(O)(ii)] after consultation in accordance with paragraph (6) or, in the case of such an alien seeking entry for a motion picture or television production, after consultation with such a labor organization and a management organization in the area of the alien's ability.

In the case of an alien seeking entry for a motion picture or television production, (i) any opinion under the previous sentence shall only be advisory, (ii) any such opinion that recommends denial must be in writing, (iii) in making the decision the Attorney General shall consider the exigencies and scheduling of the production, and (iv) the Attorney General shall append to the decision any such opinion. The Attorney General shall provide by regulation for the waiver of the consultation requirement under subparagraph (A) in the case of aliens who have been admitted as nonimmigrants under section 101(a)(15)(O)(i) [8 USCS § 1101(a)(15)(O)(i)] because of extraordinary ability in the arts and who seek readmission to perform similar services within 2 years after the date of a consultation under such subparagraph. Not later than 5 days after the date such a waiver is provided, the Attorney General shall forward a copy of the petition and all supporting documentation to the national office of an appropriate labor organization.

(4)(A) For purposes of section 101(a)(15)(P)(i)(a) [8 USCS § 1101(a)(15)(P)(i)(a)], an alien is described in this subparagraph if the alien—

(i)(I) performs as an athlete, individually or as part of a group or team, at an internationally recognized level of performance;

(II) is a professional athlete, as defined in section 204(i)(2) [8 USCS § 1154(i)(2)];

(III) performs as an athlete, or as a coach, as part of a team or franchise that is located in the United States and a member of a foreign league or association of 15 or more amateur sports teams, if—

(aa) the foreign league or association is the highest level of amateur performance of that sport in the relevant foreign country;

(bb) participation in such league or association renders players ineligible, whether on a temporary or permanent basis, to earn a scholarship in, or participate in, that sport at a college or university in the United States under the rules of the National Collegiate Athletic Association; and

(cc) a significant number of the individuals who play in such league or association are drafted by a major sports league or a minor league affiliate of such a sports league; or

(IV) is a professional athlete or amateur athlete who performs individually or as part of a group in a theatrical ice skating production; and

(ii) seeks to enter the United States temporarily and solely for the purpose of performing—

(I) as such an athlete with respect to a specific athletic competition; or

(II) in the case of an individual described in clause (i)(IV), in a specific theatrical ice skating production or tour.

(B)(i) For purposes of section 101(a)(15)(P)(i)(b) [8 USCS § 1101(a)(15)(P)(i)(b)], an alien is described in this subparagraph if the alien—

(I) performs with or is an integral and essential part of the performance of an entertainment group that has (except as provided in clause (ii)) been recognized internationally as being outstanding in the discipline for a sustained and substantial period of time,

(II) in the case of a performer or entertainer, except as provided in clause (iii), has had a sustained and substantial relationship with that group (ordinarily for at least one year) and provides functions integral to the performance of the group, and

(III) seeks to enter the United States temporarily and solely for the purpose of performing as such a performer or entertainer or as an integral and essential part of a performance.

(ii) In the case of an entertainment group that is recognized nationally as being outstanding in its discipline for a sustained and substantial period of time, the Attorney General may, in consideration of special circumstances, waive the international recognition requirement of clause (i)(I).

(iii)(I) The one-year relationship requirement of clause (i)(II) shall not apply to 25 percent of the performers and entertainers in a group.

(II) The Attorney General may waive such one-year relationship requirement for an alien who because of illness or unanticipated and exigent circumstances replaces an essential member of the group and for an alien who augments the group by performing a critical role.

(iv) The requirements of subclauses (I) and (II) of clause (i) shall not apply to alien circus personnel who perform as part of a circus or circus group or who constitute an integral and essential part of the performance of such circus or circus group, but only if such personnel are entering the United States to join a circus that has been recognized nationally as outstanding for a sustained and substantial period of time or as part of such a circus.

(C) A person may petition the Attorney General for classification of an alien as a nonimmigrant under section 101(a)(15)(P) [8 USCS § 1101(a)(15)(P)].

(D) The Attorney General shall approve petitions under this subsection with respect to nonimmigrants described in clause (i) or (iii) of section 101(a)(15)(P) [8 USCS § 1101(a)(15)(P)(i) or (iii)] only after consultation in accordance with paragraph (6).

(E) The Attorney General shall approve petitions under this subsection for nonimmigrants described in section 101(a)(15)(P)(ii) [8 USCS § 1101(a)(15)(P)(ii)] only after consultation with labor organizations representing artists and entertainers in the United States.

(F)(i) No nonimmigrant visa under section 101(a)(15)(P)(i)(a) [8 USCS § 1101(a)(15)(P)(i)(a)] shall be issued to any alien who is a national of a country that is a state sponsor of international terrorism unless the Secretary of State determines, in consultation with the Secretary of Homeland Security and the heads of other appropriate United States agencies, that such alien does not pose a threat to the safety, national security, or national interest of the United States. In making a determination under this subparagraph, the Secretary of State shall apply standards developed by the Secretary of State, in consultation with the Secretary of Homeland Security and the heads of other appropriate United States agencies, that are applicable to the nationals of such states.

(ii) In this subparagraph, the term "state sponsor of international terrorism" means any country the government of which has been determined by the Secretary of State under any of the laws specified in clause (iii) to have repeatedly provided support for acts of international terrorism.

(iii) The laws specified in this clause are the following:

(I) Section 6(j)(1)(A) of the Export Administration Act of 1979 (50 U.S.C. App. 2405(j)(1)(A) [former 50 USCS § 4605(j)(1)(A)]) (or successor statute).

(II) Section 40(d) of the Arms Export Control Act (22 U.S.C. 2780(d)).

(III) Section 620A(a) of the Foreign Assistance Act of 1961 (22 U.S.C. 2371(a)).

(G) The Secretary of Homeland Security shall permit a petition under this subsection to seek classification of more than 1 alien as a nonimmigrant under section 101(a)(15)(P)(i)(a) [8 USCS § 1101(a)(15)(P)(i)(a)].

(H) The Secretary of Homeland Security shall permit an athlete, or the employer of an athlete, to seek admission to the United States for such athlete under a provision of this Act other than section 101(a)(15)(P)(i) [8 USCS § 1101(a)(15)(P)(i)] if the athlete is eligible under such other provision.

(5)(A) In the case of an alien who is provided nonimmigrant status under section 101(a)(15)(H)(i)(b) or 101(a)(15)(H)(ii)(b) [8 USCS § 1101(a)(15)(H)(i)(b) or (ii)(b)] and who is dismissed from employment by the employer before the end of the period of authorized admission, the employer shall be liable for the reasonable costs of return transportation of the alien abroad.

(B) In the case of an alien who is admitted to the United States in nonimmigrant status under section

101(a)(15)(O) or 101(a)(15)(P) [8 USCS § 1101(a)(15)(O) or (P)] and whose employment terminates for reasons other than voluntary resignation, the employer whose offer of employment formed the basis of such nonimmigrant status and the petitioner are jointly and severally liable for the reasonable cost of return transportation of the alien abroad. The petitioner shall provide assurance satisfactory to the Attorney General that the reasonable cost of that transportation will be provided.

(6)(A)(i) To meet the consultation requirement of paragraph (3)(A) in the case of a petition for a nonimmigrant described in section 101(a)(15)(O)(i) [8 USCS § 1101(a)(15)(O)(i)] (other than with respect to aliens seeking entry for a motion picture or television production), the petitioner shall submit with the petition an advisory opinion from a peer group (or other person or persons of its choosing, which may include a labor organization) with expertise in the specific field involved.

(ii) To meet the consultation requirement of paragraph (3)(B) in the case of a petition for a nonimmigrant described in section 101(a)(15)(O)(ii) [8 USCS § 1101(a)(15)(O)(ii)] (other than with respect to aliens seeking entry for a motion picture or television production), the petitioner shall submit with the petition an advisory opinion from a labor organization with expertise in the skill area involved.

(iii) To meet the consultation requirement of paragraph (4)(D) in the case of a petition for a nonimmigrant described in section 101(a)(15)(P)(i) or 101(a)(15)(P)(iii) [8 USCS § 1101(a)(15)(P)(i) or (iii)], the petitioner shall submit with the petition an advisory opinion from a labor organization with expertise in the specific field of athletics or entertainment involved.

(B) To meet the consultation requirements of subparagraph (A), unless the petitioner submits with the petition an advisory opinion from an appropriate labor organization, the Attorney General shall forward a copy of the petition and all supporting documentation to the national office of an appropriate labor organization within 5 days of the date of receipt of the petition. If there is a collective bargaining representative of an employer's employees in the occupational classification for which the alien is being sought, that representative shall be the appropriate labor organization.

(C) In those cases in which a petitioner described in subparagraph (A) establishes that an appropriate peer group (including a labor organization) does not exist, the Attorney General shall adjudicate the petition without requiring an advisory opinion.

(D) Any person or organization receiving a copy of a petition described in subparagraph (A) and supporting documents shall have no more than 15 days following the date of receipt of such documents within which to submit a written advisory opinion or comment or to provide a letter of no objection. Once the 15-day period has expired and the petitioner has had an opportunity, where appropriate, to supply rebuttal evidence, the Attorney General shall adjudicate such petition in no more than 14 days. The Attorney General may shorten any specified time period for emergency reasons if no unreasonable burden would be thus imposed on any participant in the process.

(E)(i) The Attorney General shall establish by regulation expedited consultation procedures in the case of nonimmigrant artists or entertainers described in section 101(a)(15)(O) or 101(a)(15)(P) [8 USCS § 1101(a)(15)(O) or (P)] to accommodate the exigencies and scheduling of a given production or event.

(ii) The Attorney General shall establish by regulation expedited consultation procedures in the case of nonimmigrant athletes described in section 101(a)(15)(O)(i) or 101(a)(15)(P)(i) [8 USCS § 1101(a)(15)(O)(i) or (P)(i)] in the case of emergency circumstances (including trades during a season).

(F) No consultation required under this subsection by the Attorney General with a nongovernmental entity shall be construed as permitting the Attorney General to delegate any authority under this subsection to such an entity. The Attorney General shall give such weight to advisory opinions provided under this section as the Attorney General determines, in his sole discretion, to be appropriate.

(7) If a petition is filed and denied under this subsection, the Attorney General shall notify the petitioner of the determination and the reasons for the denial and of the process by which the petitioner may appeal the determination.

(8) The Attorney General shall submit annually to the Committees on the Judiciary of the House of Representatives and of the Senate a report describing, with respect to petitions under each subcategory of subparagraphs (H), (O), (P), and (Q) of section 101(a)(15) [8 USCS § 1101(a)(15)(H),(O), (P), (Q)] the following:

(A) The number of such petitions which have been filed.

(B) The number of such petitions which have been approved and the number of workers (by occupation) included in such approved petitions.

(C) The number of such petitions which have been denied and the number of workers (by occupation) requested in such denied petitions.

(D) The number of such petitions which have been withdrawn.

(E) The number of such petitions which are awaiting final action.

(9)(A) The Attorney General shall impose a fee on an employer (excluding any employer that is a primary or secondary education institution, an institution of higher education, as defined in section 101(a) of the Higher Education Act of 1965 (20 U.S.C. 1001(a))), a nonprofit entity related to or affiliated with any such institution, a nonprofit entity which engages in established curriculum-related clinical training of students registered at any such institution, a nonprofit research organization, or a governmental research organization) filing [before] a petition under paragraph (1)—

(i) initially to grant an alien nonimmigrant status described in section 101(a)(15)(H)(i)(b) [8 USCS § 1101(a)(15)(H)(i)(b)];

(ii) to extend the stay of an alien having such status (unless the employer previously has obtained an extension for such alien); or

(iii) to obtain authorization for an alien having such status to change employers.

(B) The amount of the fee shall be $1,500 for each such petition except that the fee shall be half the amount for each such petition by any employer with not more than 25 full-time equivalent employees who are employed in the United States (determined by including any affiliate or subsidiary of such employer).

(C) Fees collected under this paragraph shall be deposited in the Treasury in accordance with section 286(s) [8 USCS § 1356(s)].

(10) An amended H-1B petition shall not be required where the petitioning employer is involved in a corporate restructuring, including but not limited to a merger, acquisition, or consolidation, where a new corporate entity succeeds to the interests and obligations of the original petitioning employer and where the terms and conditions of employment remain the same but for the identity of the petitioner.

(11)(A) Subject to subparagraph (B), the Secretary of Homeland Security or the Secretary of State, as appropriate, shall impose a fee on an employer who has filed an attestation described in section 212(t) [8 USCS § 1182(t)]—

(i) in order that an alien may be initially granted nonimmigrant status described in section 101(a)(15)(H)(i)(b1) [8 USCS § 1101(a)(15)(H)(i)(b1)]; or

(ii) in order to satisfy the requirement of the second sentence of subsection (g)(8)(C) for an alien having such status to obtain certain extensions of stay.

(B) The amount of the fee shall be the same as the amount imposed by the Secretary of Homeland Security under paragraph (9), except that if such paragraph does not authorize such Secretary to impose any fee, no fee shall be imposed under this paragraph.

(C) Fees collected under this paragraph shall be deposited in the Treasury in accordance with section 286(s) [8 USCS § 1356(s)].

(12)(A) In addition to any other fees authorized by law, the Secretary of Homeland Security shall impose a fraud prevention and detection fee on an employer filing a petition under paragraph (1)—

(i) initially to grant an alien nonimmigrant status described in subparagraph (H)(i)(b) or (L) of section 101(a)(15) [8 USCS § 1101(a)(15)]; or

(ii) to obtain authorization for an alien having such status to change employers.

(B) In addition to any other fees authorized by law, the Secretary of State shall impose a fraud prevention and detection fee on an alien filing an application abroad for a visa authorizing admission to the United States as a nonimmigrant described in section 101(a)(15)(L) [8 USCS § 1101(a)(15)(L)], if the alien is covered under a blanket petition described in paragraph (2)(A).

(C) The amount of the fee imposed under subparagraph (A) or (B) shall be $500.

(D) The fee imposed under subparagraph (A) or (B) shall only apply to principal aliens and not to the spouses or children who are accompanying or following to join such principal aliens.

(E) Fees collected under this paragraph shall be deposited in the Treasury in accordance with section 286(v) [8 USCS § 1356(v)].

(13)(A) In addition to any other fees authorized by law, the Secretary of Homeland Security shall impose a fraud prevention and detection fee on an employer filing a petition under paragraph (1) for nonimmigrant workers described in section 101(a)(15)(H)(ii)(b) [8 USCS § 1101(a)(15)(H)(ii)(b)].

(B) The amount of the fee imposed under subparagraph (A) shall be $150.

(14)(A) If the Secretary of Homeland Security finds, after notice and an opportunity for a hearing, a substantial failure to meet any of the conditions of the petition to admit or otherwise provide status to a nonimmigrant worker under section 101(a)(15)(H)(ii)(b) [8 USCS § 1101(a)(15)(H)(ii)(b)] or a willful misrepresentation of a material fact in such petition—

(i) the Secretary of Homeland Security may, in addition to any other remedy authorized by law, impose such administrative remedies (including civil monetary penalties in an amount not to exceed $10,000 per violation) as the Secretary of Homeland Security determines to be appropriate; and

(ii) the Secretary of Homeland Security may deny petitions filed with respect to that employer under section 204 [8 USCS § 1154] or paragraph (1) of this subsection during a period of at least 1 year but not more than 5 years for aliens to be employed by the employer.

(B) The Secretary of Homeland Security may delegate to the Secretary of Labor, with the agreement of the Secretary of Labor, any of the authority given to the Secretary of Homeland Security under subparagraph (A)(i).

(C) In determining the level of penalties to be assessed under subparagraph (A), the highest penalties shall be reserved for willful failures to meet any of the conditions of the petition that involve harm to United States workers.

(D) In this paragraph, the term 'substantial failure' means the willful failure to comply with the requirements of this section that constitutes a significant deviation from the terms and conditions of a petition.

(d) Issuance of visa to fiancée or fiancé of citizen.

(1) A visa shall not be issued under the provisions of section 101(a)(15)(K)(i) [8 USCS § 1101(a)(15)(K)(i)] until the consular officer has received a petition filed in the United States by the fiancée or fiancé of the applying alien and approved by the Secretary of Homeland Security. The petition shall be in such form and contain such information as the Secretary of Homeland Security shall, by regulation, prescribe. Such information shall include information on any criminal convictions of the petitioner for any specified crime described in paragraph (3)(B) and information on any permanent protection or restraining order issued against the petitioner related to any specified crime described in paragraph (3)(B)(i). It shall be approved only after satisfactory evidence is submitted by the petitioner to establish

that the parties have previously met in person within 2 years before the date of filing the petition, have a bona fide intention to marry, and are legally able and actually willing to conclude a valid marriage in the United States within a period of ninety days after the alien's arrival, except that the Secretary of Homeland Security in his discretion may waive the requirement that the parties have previously met in person. In the event the marriage with the petitioner does not occur within three months after the admission of the said alien and minor children, they shall be required to depart from the United States and upon failure to do so shall be removed in accordance with sections 240 and 241 [8 USCS §§ 1229a, 1231].

(2)(A) Subject to subparagraphs (B) and (C), the Secretary of Homeland Security may not approve a petition under paragraph (1) unless the Secretary has verified that—

(i) the petitioner has not, previous to the pending petition, petitioned under paragraph (1) with respect to two or more applying aliens; and

(ii) if the petitioner has had such a petition previously approved, 2 years have elapsed since the filing of such previously approved petition.

(B) The Secretary of Homeland Security may, in the Secretary's discretion, waive the limitations in subparagraph (A) if justification exists for such a waiver. Except in extraordinary circumstances and subject to subparagraph (C), such a waiver shall not be granted if the petitioner has a record of violent criminal offenses against a person or persons.

(C)(i) The Secretary of Homeland Security is not limited by the criminal court record and shall grant a waiver of the condition described in the second sentence of subparagraph (B) in the case of a petitioner described in clause (ii).

(ii) A petitioner described in this clause is a petitioner who has been battered or subjected to extreme cruelty and who is or was not the primary perpetrator of violence in the relationship upon a determination that—

(I) the petitioner was acting in self-defense;

(II) the petitioner was found to have violated a protection order intended to protect the petitioner; or

(III) the petitioner committed, was arrested for, was convicted of, or pled guilty to committing a crime that did not result in serious bodily injury and where there was a connection between the crime and the petitioner's having been battered or subjected to extreme cruelty.

(iii) In acting on applications under this subparagraph, the Secretary of Homeland Security shall consider any credible evidence relevant to the application. The determination of what evidence is credible and the weight to be given that evidence shall be within the sole discretion of the Secretary.

(3) In this subsection:

(A) The terms "domestic violence", "sexual assault", "child abuse and neglect", "dating violence", "elder abuse", and "stalking" have the meaning given such terms in section 3 of the Violence Against Women and Department of Justice Reauthorization Act of 2005.

(B) The term "specified crime" means the following:

(i) Domestic violence, sexual assault, child abuse and neglect, dating violence, elder abuse, stalking, or an attempt to commit any such crime.

(ii) Homicide, murder, manslaughter, rape, abusive sexual contact, sexual exploitation, incest, torture, trafficking, peonage, holding hostage, involuntary servitude, slave trade, kidnapping, abduction, unlawful criminal restraint, false imprisonment, or an attempt to commit any of the crimes described in this clause.

(iii) At least three convictions for crimes relating to a controlled substance or alcohol not arising from a single act.

(e) Nonimmigrant professionals and annual numerical limit.

(1) An alien who is a citizen of Canada or Mexico, and the spouse and children of any such alien if accompanying or following to join such alien, who seeks to enter the United States under and pursuant to the provisions of Section D of Annex 16-A of the USMCA (as defined in section 3 of the United States-Mexico-Canada Agreement Implementation Act [19 USCS § 4502]) to engage in business activities at a professional level as provided for in such Annex, may be admitted for such purpose under regulations of the Attorney General promulgated after consultation with the Secretaries of State and Labor. For purposes of this Act, including the issuance of entry documents and the application of subsection (b), such alien shall be treated as if seeking classification, or classifiable, as a nonimmigrant under section 101(a)(15) [8 USCS § 1101(a)(15)]. For purposes of this paragraph, the term "citizen of Mexico" means "citizen" as defined in article 16.1 of the USMCA.

(2) In the case of an alien spouse admitted under section 101(a)(15)(E) [8 USCS § 1101(a)(15)(E)], who is accompanying or following to join a principal alien admitted under such section, the Attorney General shall authorize the alien spouse to engage in employment in the United States and provide the spouse with an "employment authorized" endorsement or other appropriate work permit.

(f) Denial of crewmember status in the case of certain labor disputes.

(1) Except as provided in paragraph (3), no alien shall be entitled to nonimmigrant status described in section 101(a)(15)(D) [8 USCS § 1101(a)(15)(D)] if the alien intends to land for the purpose of performing service on board a vessel of the United States (as defined in section 2101(46) of title 46, United States Code) or on an aircraft of an air carrier (as defined in section 40102(a)(2) of title 49, United States Code) during a labor dispute where there is a strike or lockout in the bargaining unit of the employer in which the alien intends to perform such service.

(2) An alien described in paragraph (1)—

(A) may not be paroled into the United States pursuant to section 212(d)(5) [8 USCS § 1182(d)(5)] unless the Attorney General determines that the parole of such alien is necessary to protect the national security of the United States; and

(B) shall be considered not to be a bona fide crewman for purposes of section 252(b) [8 USCS § 1282(b)].

(3) Paragraph (1) shall not apply to an alien if the air carrier or owner or operator of such vessel that employs the alien provides documentation that satisfies the Attorney General that the alien—

(A) has been an employee of such employer for a period of not less than 1 year preceding the date that a strike or lawful lockout commenced;

(B) has served as a qualified crewman for such employer at least once in each of 3 months during the 12-month period preceding such date; and

(C) shall continue to provide the same services that such alien provided as such a crewman.

(g) Temporary workers and trainees; limitation of numbers.

(1) The total number of aliens who may be issued visas or otherwise provided nonimmigrant status during any fiscal year (beginning with fiscal year 1992)—

(A) under section 101(a)(15)(H)(i)(b) [8 USCS § 1101(a)(15)(H)(i)(b)], may not exceed—

(i) 65,000 in each fiscal year before fiscal year 1999;

(ii) 115,000 in fiscal year 1999;

(iii) 115,000 in fiscal year 2000;

(iv) 195,000 in fiscal year 2001;

(v) 195,000 in fiscal year 2002;

(vi) 195,000 in fiscal year 2003; and

(vii) 65,000 in each succeeding fiscal year; or

(B) under section 101(a)(15)(H)(ii)(b) [8 USCS § 1101(a)(15)(H)(ii)(b)] may not exceed 66,000.

(2) The numerical limitations of paragraph (1) shall only apply to principal aliens and not to the spouses or children of such aliens.

(3) Aliens who are subject to the numerical limitations of paragraph (1) shall be issued visas (or otherwise provided nonimmigrant status) in the order in which petitions are filed for such visas or status. If an alien who was issued a visa or otherwise provided nonimmigrant status and counted against the numerical limitations of paragraph (1) is found to have been issued such visa or otherwise provided such status by fraud or willfully misrepresenting a material fact and such visa or nonimmigrant status is revoked, then one number shall be restored to the total number of aliens who may be issued visas or otherwise provided such status under the numerical limitations of paragraph (1) in the fiscal year in which the petition is revoked, regardless of the fiscal year in which the petition was approved.

(4) In the case of a nonimmigrant described in section 101(a)(15)(H)(i)(b) [8 USCS § 1101(a)(15)(H)(i)(b)], the period of authorized admission as such a nonimmigrant may not exceed 6 years.

(5) The numerical limitations contained in paragraph (1)(A) shall not apply to any nonimmigrant alien issued a visa or otherwise provided status under section 101(a)(15)(H)(i)(b) [8 USCS § 1101(a)(15)(H)(i)(b)] who—

(A) is employed (or has received an offer of employment) at an institution of higher education (as defined in section 101(a) of the Higher Education Act of 1965 (20 U.S.C. 1001(a))), or a related or affiliated nonprofit entity;

(B) is employed (or has received an offer of employment) at a nonprofit research organization or a governmental research organization; or

(C) has earned a master's or higher degree from a United States institution of higher education (as defined in section 101(a) of the Higher Education Act of 1965 (20 U.S.C. 1001(a)), until the number of aliens who are exempted from such numerical limitation during such year exceeds 20,000.

(6) Any alien who ceases to be employed by an employer described in paragraph (5)(A) shall, if employed as a nonimmigrant alien described in section 101(a)(15)(H)(i)(b) [8 USCS § 1101(a)(15)(H)(i)(b)], who has not previously been counted toward the numerical limitations contained in paragraph (1)(A), be counted toward those limitations the first time the alien is employed by an employer other than one described in paragraph (5).

(7) Any alien who has already been counted, within the 6 years prior to the approval of a petition described in subsection (c), toward the numerical limitations of paragraph (1)(A) shall not again be counted toward those limitations unless the alien would be eligible for a full 6 years of authorized admission at the time the petition is filed. Where multiple petitions are approved for 1 alien, that alien shall be counted only once.

(8)(A) The agreements referred to in section 101(a)(15)(H)(i)(b1)) [8 USCS § 1101(a)(15)(H)(i)(b1)] are—

(i) the United States-Chile Free Trade Agreement; and

(ii) the United States-Singapore Free Trade Agreement.

(B)(i) The Secretary of Homeland Security shall establish annual numerical limitations on approvals of initial applications by aliens for admission under section 101(a)(15)(H)(i)(b1) [8 USCS § 1101(a)(15)(H)(i)(b1)].

(ii) The annual numerical limitations described in clause (i) shall not exceed—

(I) 1,400 for nationals of Chile (as defined in article 14.9 of the United States-Chile Free Trade Agreement) for any fiscal year; and

(II) 5,400 for nationals of Singapore (as defined in Annex 1A of the United States-Singapore Free Trade Agreement) for any fiscal year.

(iii) The annual numerical limitations described in clause (i) shall only apply to principal aliens and not to the spouses or children of such aliens.

(iv) The annual numerical limitation described in paragraph (1)(A) is reduced by the amount of the annual numerical limitations established under clause (i). However, if a numerical limitation established under clause (i) has not been exhausted at the end of a given fiscal year, the Secretary of Homeland Security shall adjust upwards the numerical limitation in paragraph (1)(A) for that fiscal year by the amount remaining in the numerical limitation under clause (i). Visas under section 101(a)(15)(H)(i)(b) [8 USCS § 1101(a)(15)(H)(i)(b)] may be issued pursuant to such adjustment within the first 45 days of the next fiscal year to aliens who had applied for such visas during the fiscal year for which the adjustment was made.

(C) The period of authorized admission as a nonimmigrant under section 101(a)(15)(H)(i)(b1) [8 USCS § 1101(a)(15)(H)(i)(b1)] shall be 1 year, and may be extended, but only in 1-year increments. After every second extension, the next following extension shall not be granted unless the Secretary of Labor had determined and certified to the Secretary of Homeland Security and the Secretary of State that the intending employer has filed with the Secretary of Labor an attestation under section 212(t)(1) [8 USCS § 1182(t)(1)] for the purpose of permitting the nonimmigrant to obtain such extension.

(D) The numerical limitation described in paragraph (1)(A) for a fiscal year shall be reduced by one for each alien granted an extension under subparagraph (C) during such year who has obtained 5 or more consecutive prior extensions.

(9)(A) Subject to subparagraphs (B) and (C), an alien who has already been counted toward the numerical limitation of paragraph (1)(B) during fiscal year 2013, 2014, or 2015 shall not again be counted toward such limitation during fiscal year 2016. Such an alien shall be considered a returning worker.

(B) A petition to admit or otherwise provide status under section 101(a)(15)(H)(ii)(b) [8 USCS § 1101(a)(15)(H)(ii)(b)] shall include, with respect to a returning worker—

(i) all information and evidence that the Secretary of Homeland Security determines is required to support a petition for status under section 101(a)(15)(H)(ii)(b) [8 USCS § 1101(a)(15)(H)(ii)(b)];

(ii) the full name of the alien; and

(iii) a certification to the Department of Homeland Security that the alien is a returning worker.

(C) An H-2B visa or grant of nonimmigrant status for a returning worker shall be approved only if the alien is confirmed to be a returning worker by—

(i) the Department of State; or

(ii) if the alien is visa exempt or seeking to change to status under section 101(a)(15)(H)(ii)(b) [8 USCS § 1101(a)(15)(H)(ii)(b)], the Department of Homeland Security.

(10) The numerical limitations of paragraph (1)(B) shall be allocated for a fiscal year so that the total number of aliens subject to such numerical limits who enter the United States pursuant to a visa or are accorded nonimmigrant status under section 101(a)(15)(H)(ii)(b) [8 USCS § 1101(a)(15)(H)(ii)(b)] during the first 6 months of such fiscal year is not more than 33,000.

(11)(A) The Secretary of State may not approve a number of initial applications submitted for aliens described in section 101(a)(15)(E)(iii) [8 USCS § 1101(a)(15)(E)(iii)] that is more than the applicable numerical limitation set out in this paragraph.

(B) The applicable numerical limitation referred to in subparagraph (A) is 10,500 for each fiscal year.

(C) The applicable numerical limitation referred to in subparagraph (A) shall only apply to principal aliens and not to the spouses or children of such aliens.

(h) Intention to abandon foreign residence. The fact that an alien is the beneficiary of an application for a preference status filed under section 204 [8 USCS § 1154] or has otherwise sought permanent residence in the United States shall not constitute evidence of an intention to abandon a foreign residence for purposes of obtaining a visa as a nonimmigrant described in subparagraph (H)(i)(b) or (c), (L), or (V) of section 101(a)(15) [8 USCS § 1101(a)(15)] or otherwise obtaining or maintaining the status of a nonimmigrant described in such subparagraph, if the alien had obtained a change of status under section 248 [8 USCS § 1258] to a classification as such a nonimmigrant before the alien's most recent departure from the United States.

(i) "Specialty occupation" defined.

(1) Except as provided in paragraph (3), for purposes of section 101(a)(15)(H)(i)(b) [8 USCS § 1101(a)(15)(H)(i)(b)], section 101(a)(15)(E)(iii) [8 USCS § 1101(a)(15)(E)(iii)], and paragraph (2), the term "specialty occupation" means an occupation that requires—

(A) theoretical and practical application of a body of highly specialized knowledge, and

(B) attainment of a bachelor's or higher degree in the specific specialty (or its equivalent) as a minimum for entry into the occupation in the United States.

(2) For purposes of section 101(a)(15)(H)(i)(b) [8 USCS § 1101(a)(15)(H)(i)(b)], the requirements of this paragraph, with respect to a specialty occupation, are—

(A) full state licensure to practice in the occupation, if such licensure is required to practice in the occupation,

(B) completion of the degree described in paragraph (1)(B) for the occupation, or

(C)(i) experience in the specialty equivalent to the completion of such degree, and

(ii) recognition of expertise in the specialty through progressively responsible positions relating to the specialty.

(3) For purposes of section 101(a)(15)(H)(i)(b1) [8 USCS § 1101(a)(15)(H)(i)(b1)], the term "specialty occupation" means an occupation that requires—

(A) theoretical and practical application of a body of specialized knowledge; and

(B) attainment of a bachelor's or higher degree in the specific specialty (or its equivalent) as a minimum for entry into the occupation in the United States.

(j) Labor disputes.

(1) Notwithstanding any other provision of this Act, an alien who is a citizen of Canada or Mexico who seeks to enter the United States under and pursuant to the provisions of Section B, Section C, or Section D of Annex 16-A of the USMCA (as defined in section 3 of the United States-Mexico-Canada Agreement Implementation Act [19 USCS § 4502]), shall not be classified as a nonimmigrant under such provisions if there is in progress a strike or lockout in the course of a labor dispute in the occupational classification at the place or intended place of employment, unless such alien establishes, pursuant to regulations promulgated by the Attorney General, that the alien's entry will not affect adversely the settlement of the strike or lockout or the employment of any person who is involved in the strike

or lockout. Notice of a determination under this paragraph shall be given as may be required by paragraph 3 of article 16.4 of the USMCA. For purposes of this paragraph, the term "citizen of Mexico" means "citizen" as defined in article 16.1 of the USMCA.

(2) Notwithstanding any other provision of this Act except section 212(t)(1) [8 USCS § 1182(t)(1)], and subject to regulations promulgated by the Secretary of Homeland Security, an alien who seeks to enter the United States under and pursuant to the provisions of an agreement listed in subsection (g)(8)(A), and the spouse and children of such an alien if accompanying or following to join the alien, may be denied admission as a nonimmigrant under subparagraph (E), (L), or (H)(i)(b1) of section 101(a)(15) [8 USCS § 1101(a)(15)] if there is in progress a labor dispute in the occupational classification at the place or intended place of employment, unless such alien establishes, pursuant to regulations promulgated by the Secretary of Homeland Security after consultation with the Secretary of Labor, that the alien's entry will not affect adversely the settlement of the labor dispute or the employment of any person who is involved in the labor dispute. Notice of a determination under this paragraph shall be given as may be required by such agreement.

(k) Numerical limitations; period of admission; conditions for admission and stay; annual report.

(1) The number of aliens who may be provided a visa as nonimmigrants under section 101(a)(15)(S)(i) [8 USCS § 1101(a)(15)(S)(i)] in any fiscal year may not exceed 200. The number of aliens who may be provided a visa as nonimmigrants under section 101(a)(15)(S)(ii) [8 USCS § 1101(a)(15)(S)(ii)] in any fiscal year may not exceed 50.

(2) The period of admission of an alien as such a nonimmigrant may not exceed 3 years. Such period may not be extended by the Attorney General.

(3) As a condition for the admission, and continued stay in lawful status, of such a nonimmigrant, the nonimmigrant—

(A) shall report not less often than quarterly to the Attorney General such information concerning the alien's whereabouts and activities as the Attorney General may require;

(B) may not be convicted of any criminal offense punishable by a term of imprisonment of 1 year or more after the date of such admission;

(C) must have executed a form that waives the nonimmigrant's right to contest, other than on the basis of an application for withholding of removal, any action for deportation of the alien instituted before the alien obtains lawful permanent resident status; and

(D) shall abide by any other condition, limitation, or restriction imposed by the Attorney General.

(4) The Attorney General shall submit a report annually to the Committee on the Judiciary of the House of Representatives and the Committee on the Judiciary of the Senate concerning—

(A) the number of such nonimmigrants admitted;

(B) the number of successful criminal prosecutions or investigations resulting from cooperation of such aliens;

(C) the number of terrorist acts prevented or frustrated resulting from cooperation of such aliens;

(D) the number of such nonimmigrants whose admission or cooperation has not resulted in successful criminal prosecution or investigation or the prevention or frustration of a terrorist act; and

(E) the number of such nonimmigrants who have failed to report quarterly (as required under paragraph (3)) or who have been convicted of crimes in the United States after the date of their admission as such a nonimmigrant.

(l) Restrictions on waiver.

(1) In the case of a request by an interested State agency, or by an interested Federal agency, for a waiver of the 2-year foreign residence requirement under section 212(e) [8 USCS § 1182(e)] on behalf of an alien described in clause (iii) of such section, the Attorney General shall not grant such waiver unless—

(A) in the case of an alien who is otherwise contractually obligated to return to a foreign country, the government of such country furnishes the Director of the United States Information Agency with a statement in writing that it has no objection to such waiver;

(B) in the case of a request by an interested State agency, the grant of such waiver would not cause the number of waivers allotted for that State for that fiscal year to exceed 30;

(C) in the case of a request by an interested Federal agency or by an interested State agency—

(i) the alien demonstrates a bona fide offer of full-time employment at a health facility or health care organization, which employment has been determined by the Attorney General to be in the public interest; and

(ii) the alien agrees to begin employment with the health facility or health care organization within 90 days of receiving such waiver, and agrees to continue to work for a total of not less than 3 years (unless the Attorney General determines that extenuating circumstances exist, such as closure of the facility or hardship to the alien, which would justify a lesser period of employment at such health facility or health care organization, in which case the alien must demonstrate another bona fide offer of employment at a health facility or health care organization for the remainder of such 3-year period); and

(D) in the case of a request by an interested Federal agency (other than a request by an interested Federal agency to employ the alien full-time in medical research or training) or by an interested State agency, the alien agrees to practice primary care or specialty medicine in accordance with paragraph (2) for a total of not less than 3 years only in the geographic area or areas which are designated by the Secretary of Health and Human Services as having a shortage of health care professionals, except that—

(i) in the case of a request by the Department of Veterans Affairs, the alien shall not be required to practice medicine in a geographic area designated by the Secretary;

(ii) in the case of a request by an interested State agency, the head of such State agency determines that the alien is to practice medicine under such agreement in a facility that serves patients who reside in one or more geographic areas so designated by the Secretary of Health and Human Services (without regard to whether such facility is located within such a designated geographic area), and the grant of such waiver would not cause the number of the waivers granted on behalf of aliens for such State for a fiscal year (within the limitation in subparagraph (B)) in accordance with the conditions of this clause to exceed 10; and

(iii) in the case of a request by an interested Federal agency or by an interested State agency for a waiver for an alien who agrees to practice specialty medicine in a facility located in a geographic area so designated by the Secretary of Health and Human Services, the request shall demonstrate, based on criteria established by such agency, that there is a shortage of health care professionals able to provide services in the appropriate medical specialty to the patients who will be served by the alien.

(2)(A) Notwithstanding section 248(a)(2) [8 USCS § 1258(a)(2)], the Attorney General may change the status of an alien who qualifies under this subsection and section 212(e) [8 USCS § 1182(e)] to that of an alien described in section 101(a)(15)(H)(i)(b) [8 USCS § 1101(a)(15)(H)(i)(b)]. The numerical limitations contained in subsection (g)(1)(A) shall not apply to any alien whose status is changed under the preceding sentence, if the alien obtained a waiver of the 2-year foreign residence requirement upon a request by an interested Federal agency or an interested State agency.

(B) No person who has obtained a change of status under subparagraph (A) and who has failed to fulfill the terms of the contract with the health facility or health care organization named in the waiver application shall be eligible to apply for an immigrant visa, for permanent residence, or for any other change of nonimmigrant status, until it is established that such person has resided and been physically present in the country of his nationality or his last residence for an aggregate of at least 2 years following departure from the United States.

(3) Notwithstanding any other provision of this subsection, the 2-year foreign residence requirement under section 212(e) [8 USCS § 1182(e)] shall apply with respect to an alien described in clause (iii) of such section, who has not otherwise been accorded status under section 101(a)(27)(H) [8 USCS § 1101(a)(27)(H)], if—

(A) at any time the alien ceases to comply with any agreement entered into under subparagraph (C) or (D) of paragraph (1); or

(B) the alien's employment ceases to benefit the public interest at any time during the 3-year period described in paragraph (1)(C).

(m) Nonimmigrant elementary and secondary school students.

(1) An alien may not be accorded status as a nonimmigrant under clause (i) or (iii) of section 101(a)(15)(F) [8 USCS § 1101(a)(15)(F)] in order to pursue a course of study—

(A) at a public elementary school or in a publicly funded adult education program; or

(B) at a public secondary school unless—

(i) the aggregate period of such status at such a school does not exceed 12 months with respect to any alien, and

(ii) the alien demonstrates that the alien has reimbursed the local educational agency that administers the school for the full, unsubsidized per capita cost of providing education at such school for the period of the alien's attendance.

(2) An alien who obtains the status of a nonimmigrant under clause (i) or (iii) of section 101(a)(15)(F) [8 USCS § 1101(a)(15)(F)] in order to pursue a course of study at a private elementary or secondary school or in a language training program that is not publicly funded shall be considered to have violated such status, and the alien's visa under section 101(a)(15)(F) [8 USCS § 1101(a)(15)(F)] shall be void, if the alien terminates or abandons such course of study at such a school and undertakes a course of study at a public elementary school, in a publicly funded adult education program, in a publicly funded adult education language training program, or at a public secondary school (unless the requirements of paragraph (1)(B) are met).

(n) Increased portability of H-1B status.

(1) A nonimmigrant alien described in paragraph (2) who was previously issued a visa or otherwise provided nonimmigrant status under section 101(a)(15)(H)(i)(b) [8 USCS § 1101(a)(15)(H)(i)(b)] is authorized to accept new employment upon the filing by the prospective employer of a new petition on behalf of such nonimmigrant as provided under subsection (a). Employment authorization shall continue for such alien until the new petition is adjudicated. If the new petition is denied, such authorization shall cease.

(2) A nonimmigrant alien described in this paragraph is a nonimmigrant alien—

(A) who has been lawfully admitted into the United States;

(B) on whose behalf an employer has filed a nonfrivolous petition for new employment before the date of expiration of the period of stay authorized by the Attorney General; and

(C) who, subsequent to such lawful admission, has not been employed without authorization in the United States before the filing of such petition.

(o) Nonimmigrants guilty of trafficking in persons.

(1) No alien shall be eligible for admission to the United States under section 101(a)(15)(T) [8 USCS § 1101(a)(15)(T)] if there is substantial reason to believe that the alien has committed an act of a severe form of trafficking in persons (as defined in section 103 of the Trafficking Victims Protection Act of 2000 [22 USCS § 7102]).

(2) The total number of aliens who may be issued visas or otherwise provided nonimmigrant status during any fiscal year under section 101(a)(15)(T) [8 USCS § 1101(a)(15)(T)] may not exceed 5,000.

(3) The numerical limitation of paragraph (2) shall only apply to principal aliens and not to the spouses, sons, daughters, siblings, or parents of such aliens.

(4) An unmarried alien who seeks to accompany, or follow to join, a parent granted status under section 101(a)(15)(T)(i) [8 USCS § 1101(a)(15)(T)(i)], and who was under 21 years of age on the date on which such parent applied for such status, shall continue to be classified as a child for purposes of section 101(a)(15)(T)(ii) [8 USCS § 1101(a)(15)(T)(ii)], if the alien attains 21 years of age after such parent's application was filed but while it was pending.

(5) An alien described in clause (i) of section 101(a)(15)(T) [8 USCS § 1101(a)(15)(T)] shall continue to be treated as an alien described in clause (ii)(I) of such section if the alien attains 21 years of age after the alien's application for status under such clause (i) is filed but while it is pending.

(6) In making a determination under section 101(a)(15)(T)(i)(III)(aa) [8 USCS § 1101(a)(15)(T)(i)(III)(aa)] with respect to an alien, statements from State and local law enforcement officials that the alien has complied with any reasonable request for assistance in the investigation or prosecution of crimes such as kidnapping, rape, slavery, or other forced labor offenses, where severe forms of trafficking in persons (as defined in section 103 of the Trafficking Victims Protection Act of 2000 [22 USCS § 7102]) appear to have been involved, shall be considered.

(7)(A) Except as provided in subparagraph (B), an alien who is issued a visa or otherwise provided nonimmigrant status under section 101(a)(15)(T) [8 USCS § 1101(a)(15)(T)] may be granted such status for a period of not more than 4 years.

(B) An alien who is issued a visa or otherwise provided nonimmigrant status under section 101(a)(15)(T) [8 USCS § 1101(a)(15)(T)] may extend the period of such status beyond the period described in subparagraph (A) if—

(i) a Federal, State, or local law enforcement official, prosecutor, judge, or other authority investigating or prosecuting activity relating to human trafficking or certifies that the presence of the alien in the United States is necessary to assist in the investigation or prosecution of such activity;

(ii) the alien is eligible for relief under section 245(l) [8 USCS § 1255(l)] and is unable to obtain such relief because regulations have not been issued to implement such section; or

(iii) the Secretary of Homeland Security determines that an extension of the period of such nonimmigrant status is warranted due to exceptional circumstances.

(C) Nonimmigrant status under section 101(a)(15)(T) [8 USCS § 1101(a)(15)(T)] shall be extended during the pendency of an application for adjustment of status under section 245(l) [8 USCS § 1255(l)].

(p) Requirements applicable to 8 USCS § 1101(a)(15)(U) visas.

(1) Petitioning procedures for section 101(a)(15)(U) [8 USCS § 1101(a)(15)(U)] visas. The petition filed by an alien under section 101(a)(15)(U)(i) [8 USCS § 1101(a)(15)(U)(i)] shall contain a certification from a Federal, State, or local law enforcement official, prosecutor, judge, or other Federal, State, or local authority investigating criminal activity described in section 101(a)(15)(U)(iii) [8 USCS § 1101(a)(15)(U)(iii)]. This certification may also be provided by an official of the Service whose ability to provide such certification is not limited to information concerning immigration violations. This certification shall state that the alien "has been helpful, is being helpful, or is likely to be helpful" in the investigation or prosecution of criminal activity described in section 101(a)(15)(U)(iii) [8 USCS § 1101(a)(15)(U)(iii)].

(2) Numerical limitations.

(A) The number of aliens who may be issued visas or otherwise provided status as nonimmigrants under section 101(a)(15)(U) [8 USCS § 1101(a)(15)(U)] in any fiscal year shall not exceed 10,000.

(B) The numerical limitations in subparagraph (A) shall only apply to principal aliens described in section 101(a)(15)(U)(i) [8 USCS § 1101(a)(15)(U)(i)], and not to spouses, children, or, in the case of alien children, the alien parents of such children.

(3) Duties of the Attorney General with respect to "U" visa nonimmigrants. With respect to nonimmigrant aliens described in subsection (a)(15)(U)—

(A) the Attorney General and other government officials, where appropriate, shall provide those aliens with referrals to nongovernmental organizations to advise the aliens regarding their options while in the United States and the resources available to them; and

(B) the Attorney General shall, during the period those aliens are in lawful temporary resident status under that subsection, provide the aliens with employment authorization.

(4) Credible evidence considered. In acting on any petition filed under this subsection, the consular officer or the Attorney General, as appropriate, shall consider any credible evidence relevant to the petition.

(5) Nonexclusive relief. Nothing in this subsection limits the ability of aliens who qualify for status under section 101(a)(15)(U) [8 USCS § 1101(a)(15)(U)] to seek any other immigration benefit or status for which the alien may be eligible.

(6) Duration of status. The authorized period of status of an alien as a nonimmigrant under section 101(a)(15)(U) [8 USCS § 1101(a)(15)(U)] shall be for a period of not more than 4 years, but shall be extended upon certification from a Federal, State, or local law enforcement official, prosecutor, judge, or other Federal, State, or local authority investigating or prosecuting criminal activity described in section 101(a)(15)(U)(iii) [8 USCS § 1101(a)(15)(U)(iii)] that the alien's presence in the United States is required to assist in the investigation or prosecution of such criminal activity. The Secretary of Homeland Security may extend, beyond the 4-year period authorized under this section, the authorized period of status of an alien as a nonimmigrant under section 101(a)(15)(U) [8 USCS § 1101(a)(15)(U)] if the Secretary determines that an extension of such period is warranted due to exceptional circumstances. Such alien's nonimmigrant status shall be extended beyond the 4-year period authorized under this section if the alien is eligible for relief under

section 245(m) [8 USCS § 1255(m)] and is unable to obtain such relief because regulations have not been issued to implement such section and shall be extended during the pendency of an application for adjustment of status under section 245(m) [8 USCS § 1255(m)]. The Secretary may grant work authorization to any alien who has a pending, bona fide application for nonimmigrant status under section 101(a)(15)(U) [8 USCS § 1101(a)(15)(U)].

(7) Age determinations.

(A) Children. An unmarried alien who seeks to accompany, or follow to join, a parent granted status under section 101(a)(15)(U)(i) [8 USCS § 1101(a)(15)(U)(i)], and who was under 21 years of age on the date on which such parent petitioned for such status, shall continue to be classified as a child for purposes of section 101(a)(15)(U)(ii) [8 USCS § 1101(a)(15)(U)(ii)], if the alien attains 21 years of age after such parent's petition was filed but while it was pending.

(B) Principal aliens. An alien described in clause (i) of section 101(a)(15)(U) [8 USCS § 1101(a)(15)(U)] shall continue to be treated as an alien described in clause (ii)(I) of such section if the alien attains 21 years of age after the alien's application for status under such clause (i) is filed but while it is pending.

(q) Employment of nonimmigrants described in 8 USCS § 1101(a)(15)(V).

(1) In the case of a nonimmigrant described in section 101(a)(15)(V) [8 USCS § 1101(a)(15)(V)]—

(A) the Attorney General shall authorize the alien to engage in employment in the United States during the period of authorized admission and shall provide the alien with an "employment authorized" endorsement or other appropriate document signifying authorization of employment; and

(B) the period of authorized admission as such a nonimmigrant shall terminate 30 days after the date on which any of the following is denied:

(i) The petition filed under section 204 [8 USCS § 1154] to accord the alien a status under section 203(a)(2)(A) [8 USCS § 1153(a)(2)(A)] (or, in the case of a child granted nonimmigrant status based on eligibility to receive a visa under section 203(d) [8 USCS § 1153(d)], the petition filed to accord the child's parent a status under section 203(a)(2)(A) [8 USCS § 1153(a)(2)(A)]).

(ii) The alien's application for an immigrant visa pursuant to the approval of such petition.

(iii) The alien's application for adjustment of status under section 245 [8 USCS § 1255] pursuant to the approval of such petition.

(2) In determining whether an alien is eligible to be admitted to the United States as a nonimmigrant under section 101(a)(15)(V) [8 USCS § 1101(a)(15)(V)], the grounds for inadmissibility specified in section 212(a)(9)(B) [8 USCS § 1182(a)(9)(B)] shall not apply.

(3) The status of an alien physically present in the United States may be adjusted by the Attorney General, in the discretion of the Attorney General and under such regulations as the Attorney General may prescribe, to that of a nonimmigrant under section 101(a)(15)(V) [8 USCS § 1101(a)(15)(V)], if the alien—

(A) applies for such adjustment;

(B) satisfies the requirements of such section; and

(C) is eligible to be admitted to the United States, except in determining such admissibility, the grounds for inadmissibility specified in paragraphs (6)(A), (7), and (9)(B) of section 212(a) [8 USCS § 1182(a)] shall not apply.

(r) Visas of nonimmigrants described in 8 USCS § 1101(a)(15)(K)(ii).

(1) A visa shall not be issued under the provisions of section 101(a)(15)(K)(ii) [8 USCS § 1101(a)(15)(K)(ii)] until the consular officer has received a petition filed in the United States by the spouse of the applying alien and approved by the Attorney General. The petition shall be in such form and contain such information as the Attorney General shall, by regulation, prescribe. Such information shall include information on any criminal convictions of the petitioner for any specified crime described in paragraph (5)(B) and information on any permanent protection or restraining order issued against the petitioner related to any specified crime described in subsection [paragraph] (5)(B)(i).

(2) In the case of an alien seeking admission under section 101(a)(15)(K)(ii) [8 USCS § 1101(a)(15)(K)(ii)] who concluded a marriage with a citizen of the United States outside the United States, the alien shall be considered inadmissible under section 212(a)(7)(B) [8 USCS § 1182(a)(7)(B)] if the alien is not at the time of application for admission in possession of a valid nonimmigrant visa issued by a consular officer in the foreign state in which the marriage was concluded.

(3) In the case of a nonimmigrant described in section 101(a)(15)(K)(ii) [8 USCS § 1101(a)(15)(K)(ii)], and any child of such a nonimmigrant who was admitted as accompanying, or following to join, such a nonimmigrant, the period of authorized admission shall terminate 30 days after the date on which any of the following is denied:

(A) The petition filed under section 204 [8 USCS § 1154] to accord the principal alien status under section 201(b)(2)(A)(i) [8 USCS § 1151(b)(2)(A)(i)].

(B) The principal alien's application for an immigrant visa pursuant to the approval of such petition.

(C) The principal alien's application for adjustment of status under section 245 [8 USCS § 1255] pursuant to the approval of such petition.

(4)(A) The Secretary of Homeland Security shall create a database for the purpose of tracking multiple visa petitions filed for fiancé(e)s and spouses under clauses (i) and (ii) of section 101(a)(15)(K) [8 USCS § 1101(a)(15)(K)]. Upon approval of a second visa petition under section 101(a)(15)(K) [8 USCS § 1101(a)(15)(K)] for a fiancé(e) or spouse filed by the same United States citizen petitioner, the petitioner shall be notified by the Secretary that information concerning the petitioner has been entered into the multiple visa petition tracking database. All subsequent fiancé(e)s or spouse nonimmigrant visa petitions filed by that petitioner under such section shall be entered in the database.

(B)(i) Once a petitioner has had two fiancé(e) or spousal petitions approved under clause (i) or (ii) of section 101(a)(15)(K) [8 USCS § 1101(a)(15)(K)], if a subsequent petition is filed under such section less than 10 years after the date the first visa petition was filed under such section, the Secretary of Homeland Security shall notify both the petitioner and beneficiary of any such subsequent petition about the number of previously approved fiancé(e) or spousal petitions listed in the database.

(ii) To notify the beneficiary as required by clause (i), the Secretary of Homeland Security shall provide such notice to the Secretary of State for inclusion in the mailing to the beneficiary described in section 833(a)(5)(A)(i) of the International Marriage Broker Regulation Act of 2005 (8 U.S.C. 1375a(a)(5)(A)(i)).

(5) In this subsection:

(A) The terms "domestic violence", "sexual assault", "child abuse and neglect", "dating violence", 'elder abuse", and "stalking" have the meaning given such terms in section 3 of the Violence Against Women and Department of Justice Reauthorization Act of 2005.

(B) The term "specified crime" means the following:

(i) Domestic violence, sexual assault, child abuse and neglect, dating violence, elder abuse, stalking, or an attempt to commit any such crime.

(ii) Homicide, murder, manslaughter, rape, abusive sexual contact, sexual exploitation, incest, torture, trafficking, peonage, holding hostage, involuntary servitude, slave trade, kidnapping, abduction, unlawful criminal restraint, false imprisonment, or an attempt to commit any of the crimes described in this clause.

(iii) At least three convictions for crimes relating to a controlled substance or alcohol not arising from a single act.

(June 27, 1952, ch 477, Title II, Ch 2, § 214, 66 Stat. 189; April 7, 1970, P. L. 91-225, § 3, 84 Stat. 117; Oct. 5, 1984, P. L. 98-454, Title VI, § 602(b), 98 Stat. 1737; Nov. 6, 1986, P. L. 99-603, Title III, Part A, § 301(b), Part B, § 313(b), 100 Stat. 3411, 3438; Nov. 10, 1986, P. L. 99-639, § 3(a), (c), 100 Stat. 3542; Sept. 28, 1988, P. L. 100-449, Title III, § 307(b), 102 Stat. 1877; Oct. 24, 1988, P. L. 100-525, § 2(l)(1), 102 Stat. 2612; Nov. 29, 1990, P. L. 101-649, Title II, Subtitle A, §§ 202(a), 205(a), (b), (c)(2), 206(b), 207(b), 104 Stat. 5014, 5019, 5023, 5025; Dec. 12, 1991, P. L. 102-232, Title II, §§ 202(a), 203(b), 204, 205(d),(e), 206(a), (c)(2), 207(a)–(c)(1), Title III, § 303(a)(10)–(12), 105 Stat. 1737, 1738, 1740, 1741; Jan. 29, 2020, P.L. 116-113, Title III, Subtitle B, § 311(b), (c) [Dec. 8, 1993, P. L. 103-182, Title III, Subtitle D, § 341(b), (c), 107 Stat. 2116]; Sept. 13, 1994, P. L. 103-322, Title XIII, § 130003(b)(2), 108 Stat. 2025; Oct. 25, 1994, P. L. 103-416, Title II, § 220(b), 108 Stat. 4319; Sept. 30, 1996, P. L. 104-208, Div C, Title III, Subtitle A, § 308(e)(1)(D), (2)(B), (f)(1)(G), (H), (3)(B), (g)(5)(A)(i), (7)(A), Title VI, Subtitle B, §§ 621, 622(c), 625(a)(1), Subtitle E, § 671(a)(3)(A), (e)(4)(A), 110 Stat. 3009-619, 3009-620, 3009-621, 3009-623, 3009-695, 3009-699, 3009-721, 3009-723; Oct. 27, 1997, P. L. 105-65, Title I, § 108, 111 Stat. 1350; Oct. 21, 1998, P. L. 105-277, Div C, Title IV, Subtitle A, §§ 411(a), 414(a), 112 Stat. 2681-642, 2681-651; Nov. 13, 1999, P. L. 106-104, § 2, 113 Stat. 1483; Oct. 17, 2000, P. L. 106-311, § 1, 114 Stat. 1247; Oct. 17, 2000, P. L. 106-313, Title I, §§ 102(a), 103, 105(a), 108, 114 Stat. 1251–1253, 1255; Oct. 28, 2000, P. L. 106-386, Div A, § 107(e)(2), Div B, Title V, § 1513(c), 114 Stat. 1478, 1535; P. L. 106-396, Title IV, § 401, 114 Stat. 1647; Dec. 21, 2000, P. L. 106-553, § 1(a)(2), 114 Stat. 2762; Oct. 1, 2001, P. L. 107-45, § 1, 115 Stat. 258; Jan. 16, 2002, P. L. 107-124, 115 Stat. 2402; Jan. 16, 2002, P. L. 107-125, §§ 1, 2(a), 115 Stat. 2403; Nov. 2, 2002, P. L. 107-273, Div C, Title I, Subtitle A, § 11018(a), 116 Stat. 1825; Nov. 2, 2002, P. L. 107-274, § 2(c), 116 Stat. 1923; Sept. 3, 2003, P. L. 108-77, Title IV, §§ 402(a)(2), (d)(1), 403, 404, 117 Stat. 940, 946; Sept. 3, 2003, P. L. 108-78, Title IV, § 402, 117 Stat. 970; Dec. 19, 2003, P. L. 108-193, §§ 4(b)(2), 8(a)(3), 117 Stat. 2878, 2886; Dec. 3, 2004, P. L. 108-441, § 1(b)–(d), 118 Stat. 2630; Dec. 8, 2004, P. L. 108-447, Div J, Title IV, Subtitle A, §§ 412(a), 413(a), Subtitle B, §§ 422(b), 425(a), 426(a), 118 Stat. 3351, 3352, 3353, 3356, 3357; May 11, 2005, P. L. 109-13, Div B, Title IV, §§ 402(a), 403(a), 404(a), 405, Title V, § 501(b), (c), 119 Stat. 318, 319, 320, 321; Jan. 5, 2006, P. L. 109-162, Title VIII, Subtitle C, § 821(a), (b), (c)(2), Subtitle D, § 832(a)(1), (2), 119 Stat. 3062, 3066; Oct. 17, 2006, P. L. 109-364, Div A, Title X, Subtitle H, § 1074(a), 120 Stat. 2403; Dec. 22, 2006, P. L. 109-463, § 2, 120 Stat. 3477; May 8, 2008, P. L. 110-229, Title VII, Subtitle A, § 702(b)(1), 122 Stat. 860; Oct. 8, 2008, P. L. 110-362, § 2, 122 Stat. 4013; Dec. 23, 2008, P. L. 110-457, Title II, Subtitle A, § 201(b), (c), 122 Stat. 5053; March 7, 2013, P. L. 113-4, Title VIII, §§ 805(a), 807(a), 127 Stat. 111, 112; Dec. 18, 2015, P. L. 114-113, Div F, Title V, § 565, 129 Stat. 2523; Jan. 29, 2020, P.L. 116-113, Title V, § 503(b)(1)–(3), (c), 134 Stat. 71.)

§ 1184a. Philippine Traders as nonimmigrants

Upon a basis of reciprocity secured by agreement entered into by the President of the United States and the President of the Philippines, a national of the Philippines, and the spouse and children of any such national if accompanying or following to join him, may, if otherwise eligible for a visa and if otherwise admissible into the United States under the Immigration and Nationality Act (66 Stat. 163), be considered to be classifiable as a nonimmigrant under section 101(a)(15)(E) of said Act [8 USCS § 1101(a)(15)(E)] if entering solely for the purposes specified in subsection (i) or (ii) of said section.

(June 18, 1954, ch 323, 68 Stat. 264.)

§ 1185. Travel control of citizens and aliens

(a) Restrictions and prohibitions. Unless otherwise ordered by the President, it shall be unlawful—

(1) for any alien to depart from or enter or attempt to depart from or enter the United States except under such reasonable rules, regulations, and orders, and subject to such limitations and exceptions as the President may prescribe;

(2) for any person to transport or attempt to transport from or into the United States another person with knowledge or reasonable cause to believe that the departure or entry of such other person is forbidden by this section;

(3) for any person knowingly to make any false statement in an application for permission to depart from or enter the United States with intent to induce or secure the granting of such permission either for himself or for another;

(4) for any person knowingly to furnish or attempt to furnish or assist in furnishing to another a permit or evidence of permission to depart or enter not issued and designed for such other person's use;

(5) for any person knowingly to use or attempt to use any permit or evidence of permission to depart or enter not issued and designed for his use;

(6) for any person to forge, counterfeit, mutilate, or alter, or cause or procure to be forged, counterfeited, mutilated, or altered, any permit or evidence of permission to depart from or enter the United States;

(7) for any person knowingly to use or attempt to use or furnish to another for use any false, forged, counterfeited, mutilated, or altered permit, or evidence of permission, or any permit or evidence of permission which, though originally valid, has become or been made void or invalid.

(b) Citizens. Except as otherwise provided by the President and subject to such limitations and exceptions as the President may authorize and prescribe, it shall be unlawful for any citizen of the United States to depart from or enter, or attempt to depart from or enter, the United States unless he bears a valid United States passport.

(c) Definitions. The term "United States" as used in this section includes the Canal Zone, and all territory and waters, continental or insular, subject to the jurisdiction of the United States. The term "person" as used in this section shall be deemed to mean any individual, partnership, association, company, or other incorporated body of individuals, or corporation, or body politic.

(d) Nonadmission of certain aliens. Nothing in this section shall be construed to entitle an alien to whom a permit to enter the United States has been issued to enter the United States, if, upon arrival in the United States, he is found to be inadmissible under any of the provisions of this Act, or any other law, relating to the entry of aliens into the United States.

(e) Revocation of proclamation as affecting penalties. The revocation of any rule, regulation, or order issued in pursuance of this section shall not prevent prosecution for any offense committed, or the imposition of any penalties or forfeitures, liability for which was incurred under this section prior to the revocation of such rule, regulation, or order.

(f) Permits to enter. Passports, visas, reentry permits, and other documents required for entry under this Act may be considered as permits to enter for the purposes of this section.

(June 27, 1952, ch 477, Title II, Ch 2, § 215, 66 Stat. 190; Oct. 7, 1978, P. L. 95-426, Title VII, § 707(a)–(d), 92 Stat. 993; Oct. 25, 1994, P. L. 103-416, Title II, § 204(a), 108 Stat. 4311.)

§ 1186. [Transferred]

§ 1186a. Conditional permanent resident status for certain alien spouses and sons and daughters

(a) In general.

(1) Conditional basis for status. Notwithstanding any other provision of this Act, an alien spouse (as defined in subsection (h)(1)) and an alien son or daughter (as defined in subsection (h)(2)) shall be considered, at the time of obtaining the status of an alien lawfully admitted for permanent residence, to have obtained such status on a conditional basis subject to the provisions of this section.

(2) Notice of requirements.

(A) At time of obtaining permanent residence. At the time an alien spouse or alien son or daughter obtains permanent resident status on a conditional basis under paragraph (1), the Secretary of Homeland Security shall provide for notice to such a spouse, son, or daughter respecting the provisions of this section and the requirements of subsection (c)(1) to have the conditional basis of such status removed.

(B) At time of required petition. In addition, the Secretary of Homeland Security shall attempt to provide notice to such a spouse, son, or daughter, at or about the beginning of the 90-day period described in subsection (d)(2)(A), of the requirements of subsections [subsection] (c)(1).

(C) Effect of failure to provide notice. The failure of the Secretary of Homeland Security to provide a notice under this paragraph shall not affect the enforcement of the provisions of this section with respect to such a spouse, son, or daughter.

(b) Termination of status if finding that qualifying marriage improper.

(1) In general. In the case of an alien with permanent resident status on a conditional basis under subsection (a), if the Secretary of Homeland Security determines, before the second anniversary of the alien's obtaining the status of lawful admission for permanent residence, that—

(A) the qualifying marriage—

(i) was entered into for the purpose of procuring an alien's admission as an immigrant, or

(ii) has been judicially annulled or terminated, other than through the death of a spouse; or

(B) a fee or other consideration was given (other than a fee or other consideration to an attorney for assistance in preparation of a lawful petition) for the filing of a petition under section 204(a) [8 USCS § 1154(a)] or subsection (d) or (p) of section 214 [8 USCS § 1184] with respect to the alien;

the Secretary of Homeland Security shall so notify the parties involved and, subject to paragraph (2), shall terminate the permanent resident status of the alien (or aliens) involved as of the date of the determination.

(2) Hearing in removal proceeding. Any alien whose permanent resident status is terminated under paragraph (1) may request a review of such determination in a proceeding to remove the alien. In such proceeding, the burden of proof shall be on the Secretary of Homeland Security to establish, by a preponderance of the evidence, that a condition described in paragraph (1) is met.

(c) Requirements of timely petition and interview for removal of condition.

(1) In general. In order for the conditional basis established under subsection (a) for an alien spouse or an alien son or daughter to be removed—

(A) the alien spouse and the petitioning spouse (if not deceased) jointly must submit to the Secretary of Homeland Security, during the period described in subsection (d)(2), a petition which requests the removal of such conditional basis and which states, under penalty of perjury, the facts and information described in subsection (d)(1), and

(B) in accordance with subsection (d)(3), the alien spouse and the petitioning spouse (if not deceased) must appear for a personal interview before an officer or employee of the Department of Homeland Security respecting the facts and information described in subsection (d)(1).

(2) Termination of permanent resident status for failure to file petition or have personal interview.

(A) In general. In the case of an alien with permanent resident status on a conditional basis under subsection (a), if—

(i) no petition is filed with respect to the alien in accordance with the provisions of paragraph (1)(A), or

(ii) unless there is good cause shown, the alien spouse and petitioning spouse fail to appear at the interview described in paragraph (1)(B),

the Secretary of Homeland Security shall terminate the permanent resident status of the alien as of the second anniversary of the alien's lawful admission for permanent residence.

(B) Hearing in removal proceeding. In any removal proceeding with respect to an alien whose permanent resident status is terminated under subparagraph (A), the burden of proof shall be on the alien to establish compliance with the conditions of paragraphs (1)(A) and (1)(B).

(3) Determination after petition and interview.

(A) In general. If—

(i) a petition is filed in accordance with the provisions of paragraph (1)(A), and

(ii) the alien spouse and petitioning spouse appear at the interview described in paragraph (1)(B),

the Secretary of Homeland Security shall make a determination, within 90 days of the date of the interview, as to whether the facts and information described in subsection (d)(1) and alleged in the petition are true with respect to the qualifying marriage.

(B) Removal of conditional basis if favorable determination. If the Secretary of Homeland Security determines that such facts and information are true, the Secretary of Homeland Security shall so notify the parties involved and shall remove the conditional basis of the parties effective as of the second anniversary of the alien's obtaining the status of lawful admission for permanent residence.

(C) Termination if adverse determination. If the Secretary of Homeland Security determines that such facts and information are not true, the Secretary of Homeland Security shall so notify the parties involved and, subject to subparagraph (D), shall terminate the permanent resident status of an alien spouse or an alien son or daughter as of the date of the determination.

(D) Hearing in removal proceeding. Any alien whose permanent resident status is terminated under subparagraph (C) may request a review of such determination in a proceeding to remove the alien. In such proceeding, the burden of proof shall be on the Secretary of Homeland Security to establish, by a preponderance of the evidence, that the facts and information described in subsection (d)(1) and alleged in the petition are not true with respect to the qualifying marriage.

(4) Hardship waiver. The Secretary of Homeland Security, in the Secretary's discretion, may remove the conditional basis of the permanent resident status for an alien who fails to meet the requirements of paragraph (1) if the alien demonstrates that —

(A) extreme hardship would result if such alien is removed;

(B) the qualifying marriage was entered into in good faith by the alien spouse, but the qualifying marriage has been terminated (other than through the death of the spouse) and the alien was not at fault in failing to meet the requirements of paragraph (1); or

(C) the qualifying marriage was entered into in good faith by the alien spouse and during the marriage the alien spouse or child was battered by or was the subject of extreme cruelty perpetrated by his or her spouse or citizen or permanent resident parent and the alien was not at fault in failing to meet the requirements of paragraph (1); or

(D) the alien meets the requirements under section 204(a)(1)(A)(iii)(II)(aa)(BB) [8 USCS § 1154(a)(1)(A)(iii)(II)(aa)(BB)] and following the marriage ceremony was battered by or subject to extreme cruelty perpetrated by the alien's intended spouse and was not at fault in failing to meet the requirements of paragraph (1).

In determining extreme hardship, the Secretary of Homeland Security shall consider circumstances occurring only during the period that the alien was admitted for permanent residence on a conditional basis. In acting on applications under this paragraph, the Secretary shall consider any credible evidence relevant to the application. The determination of what evidence is credible and the weight to be given that evidence shall be within the sole discretion of the Secretary. The Secretary shall, by regulation, establish measures to protect the confidentiality of information concerning any abused alien spouse or child, including information regarding the whereabouts of such spouse or child.

(d) Details of petition and interview.

(1) Contents of petition. Each petition under subsection (c)(1)(A) shall contain the following facts and information:

(A) Statement of proper marriage and petitioning process. The facts are that—

(i) the qualifying marriage—

(I) was entered into in accordance with the laws of the place where the marriage took place,

(II) has not been judicially annulled or terminated, other than through the death of a spouse, and

(III) was not entered into for the purpose of procuring an alien's admission as an immigrant; and

(ii) no fee or other consideration was given (other than a fee or other consideration to an attorney for assistance in preparation of a lawful petition) for the filing of a petition under section 204(a) [8 USCS § 1154(a)] or subsection (d) or (p) of section 214 [8 USCS § 1184] with respect to the alien spouse or alien son or daughter.

(B) Statement of additional information. The information is a statement of—

(i) the actual residence of each party to the qualifying marriage since the date the alien spouse obtained permanent resident status on a conditional basis under subsection (a), and

(ii) the place of employment (if any) of each such party since such date, and the name of the employer of such party.

(2) Period for filing petition.

(A) 90-day period before second anniversary. Except as provided in subparagraph (B), the petition under subsection (c)(1)(A) must be filed during the 90-day period before the second anniversary of the alien's obtaining the status of lawful admission for permanent residence.

(B) Date petitions for good cause. Such a petition may be considered if filed after such date, but only if the alien establishes to the satisfaction of the Secretary of Homeland Security good cause and extenuating circumstances for failure to file the petition during the period described in subparagraph (A).

(C) Filing of petitions during removal. In the case of an alien who is the subject of removal hearings as a result of failure to file a petition on a timely basis in accordance with subparagraph (A), the Secretary of Homeland Security may stay such removal proceedings against an alien pending the filing of the petition under subparagraph (B).

(3) Personal interview. The interview under subsection (c)(1)(B) shall be conducted within 90 days after the date of submitting a petition under subsection (c)(1)(A) and at a local office of the Department of Homeland Security, designated by the Secretary of Homeland Security, which is convenient to the parties involved. The Secretary of Homeland Security, in the Secretary's discretion, may waive the deadline for such an interview or the requirement for such an interview in such cases as may be appropriate.

(e) Treatment of period for purposes of naturalization. For purposes of title III, in the case of an alien who is in the United States as a lawful permanent resident on a conditional basis under this section, the alien shall be considered to have been admitted as an alien lawfully admitted for permanent residence and to be in the United States as an alien lawfully admitted to the United States for permanent residence.

(f) Treatment of certain waivers. In the case of an alien who has permanent residence status on a conditional basis under this section, if, in order to obtain such status, the alien obtained a waiver under subsection (h) or (i) of section 212 [8 USCS § 1182(h) or (i)] of certain grounds of inadmissibility, such waiver terminates upon the termination of such permanent residence status under this section.

(g) Service in Armed Forces.

(1) Filing petition. The 90-day period described in subsection (d)(2)(A) shall be tolled during any period of time in which the alien spouse or petitioning spouse is a member of the Armed Forces of the United States and serving abroad in an active-duty status in the Armed Forces, except that, at the option of the petitioners, the petition may be filed during such active-duty service at any time after the commencement of such 90-day period.

(2) Personal interview. The 90-day period described in the first sentence of subsection (d)(3) shall be tolled during any period of time in which the alien spouse or petitioning spouse is a member of the Armed Forces of the United States and serving abroad in an active-duty status in the Armed Forces, except that nothing in this paragraph shall be construed to prohibit the Secretary of Homeland Security from waiving the requirement for an interview under subsection (c)(1)(B) pursuant to the Secretary's authority under the second sentence of subsection (d)(3).

(h) Definitions. In this section:

(1) The term "alien spouse" means an alien who obtains the status of an alien lawfully admitted for permanent residence (whether on a conditional basis or otherwise)—

(A) as an immediate relative (described in section 201(b) [8 USCS § 1151(b)]) as the spouse of a citizen of the United States,

(B) under section 214(d) [8 USCS § 1184(d)] as the fiancee or fiance of a citizen of the United States, or

(C) under section 203(a)(2) [8 USCS § 1153(a)(2)] as the spouse of an alien lawfully admitted for permanent residence, residence,

by virtue of a marriage which was entered into less than 24 months before the date the alien obtains such status by virtue of such marriage, but does not include such an alien who only obtains such status as a result of section 203(d) [8 USCS § 1153(d)].

(2) The term "alien son or daughter" means an alien who obtains the status of an alien lawfully admitted for permanent residence (whether on a conditional basis or otherwise) by virtue of being the son or daughter of an individual through a qualifying marriage.

(3) The term "qualifying marriage" means the marriage described to in paragraph (1).

(4) The term "petitioning spouse" means the spouse of a qualifying marriage, other than the alien.

(June 27, 1952, ch 477, Title II, Ch 2, § 216, as added Nov. 10, 1986, P. L. 99-639, § 2(a), 100 Stat. 3537; Oct. 24, 1988, P. L. 100-525, § 7(a), 102 Stat. 2616; Nov. 29, 1990, P. L. 101-649, Title VII, § 701(a), 104 Stat. 5085; Dec. 12, 1991, P. L. 102-232, Title III, § 302(e)(8)(B), 105 Stat. 1746; Sept. 13, 1994, P. L. 103-322, Title IV, Subtitle G, § 40702(a), 108 Stat. 1955; Sept. 30, 1996, P. L. 104-208, Div C, Title III, Subtitle A, § 308(d)(4)(E), (e)(7), (f)(1)(I), (J), 110 Stat. 3009-618, 3009-620, 3009-621; Dec. 21, 2000, P. L. 106-553, § 1(a)(2), 114 Stat. 2762; Nov. 23, 2011, P. L. 112-58, § 1, 125 Stat. 747; March 7, 2013, P. L. 113-4, Title VIII, § 806, 127 Stat. 112.)

§ 1186b. Conditional permanent resident status for certain alien entrepreneurs, spouses, and children

(a) In general.

(1) Conditional basis for status. An alien investor, alien spouse, and alien child shall be considered, at the time of obtaining status as an alien lawfully admitted for permanent residence, to have obtained such status on a conditional basis subject to the provisions of this section.

(2) Notice of requirements.

(A) At time of obtaining permanent residence. At the time an alien investor, alien spouse, or alien child obtains permanent resident status on a conditional basis under paragraph (1), the Secretary of Homeland Security shall provide for notice to such an investor, spouse, or child respecting the provisions of this section and the requirements of subsection (c)(1) to have the conditional basis of such status removed.

(B) At time of required petition. In addition, the Secretary of Homeland Security shall attempt to provide notice to such an investor, spouse, or child, at or about the beginning of the 90-day period described in subsection (d)(2)(A), of the requirements of subsection (c)(1).

(C) Effect of failure to provide notice. The failure of the Secretary of Homeland Security to provide a notice under this paragraph shall not affect the enforcement of the provisions of this section with respect to such an investor, spouse, or child.

(b) Termination of status if finding that qualifying investment improper.

(1) In general. In the case of an alien investor with permanent resident status on a conditional basis under subsection (a), if the Secretary of Homeland Security determines, before the second anniversary of the alien's obtaining the status of lawful admission for permanent residence, that—

(A) the investment in the commercial enterprise was intended solely as a means of evading the immigration laws of the United States,

(B) the alien did not invest the requisite capital; or

(C) the alien was otherwise not conforming to the requirements of section 203(b)(5) [8 USCS § 1153(b)(5)],

then the Secretary of Homeland Security shall so notify the alien involved and, subject to paragraph (2), shall terminate the permanent resident status of the alien (and the alien spouse and alien child) involved as of the date of the determination.

(2) Hearing in removal proceeding. Any alien whose permanent resident status is terminated under paragraph (1) may request a review of such determination in a proceeding to remove the alien. In such proceeding, the burden of proof shall be on the Secretary of Homeland Security to establish, by a preponderance of the evidence, that a condition described in paragraph (1) is met.

(c) Requirements for removal of condition.

(1) In general. Except as provided in paragraph (3)(D), in order for the conditional basis established under subsection (a) for an alien investor, alien spouse, or alien child to be removed—

(A) the alien investor shall submit to the Secretary of Homeland Security, during the period described in subsection (d)(2), a petition which requests the removal of such conditional basis and which states, under penalty of perjury, the facts and information described in subsection (d)(1);

(B) in accordance with subsection (d)(3), the alien investor shall appear for a personal interview before an officer or employee of the Department of Homeland Security respecting the facts and information described in subsection (d)(1); and

(C) the Secretary shall have performed a site visit to the relevant corporate office or business location described in section 203(b)(5)(F)(iv) [8 USCS § 1153(b)(5)(F)(iv)].

(2) Termination of permanent resident status for failure to file petition or have personal interview.

(A) In general. In the case of an alien with permanent resident status on a conditional basis under subsection (a), if—

(i) no petition is filed with respect to the alien in accordance with the provisions of paragraph (1)(A), or

(ii) unless there is good cause shown, the alien investor fails to appear at the interview described in paragraph (1)(B) (if required under subsection (d)(3)),

the Secretary of Homeland Security shall terminate the permanent resident status of the alien (and the alien's spouse and children if it was obtained on a conditional basis under this section or section 216 [8 USCS § 1186a]) as of the second anniversary of the alien's lawful admission for permanent residence.

(B) Hearing in removal proceeding. In any removal proceeding with respect to an alien whose permanent resident status is terminated under subparagraph (A), the burden of proof shall be on the alien to establish compliance with the conditions of paragraphs (1)(A) and (1)(B).

(3) Determination after petition and interview.

(A) In general. If—

(i) a petition is filed in accordance with the provisions of paragraph (1)(A), and

(ii) the alien investor appears at any interview described in paragraph (1)(B),

the Secretary of Homeland Security shall make a determination, within 90 days of the date of such filing or interview (whichever is later), as to whether the facts and information described in subsection (d)(1) and alleged in the petition are true with respect to the qualifying commercial enterprise.

(B) Removal or extension of conditional basis.

(i) In general. Except as provided in clause (ii), if the Secretary determines that the facts and information contained in a petition submitted under paragraph (1)(A) are true, including demonstrating that the alien complied with subsection (d)(1)(B)(i), the Secretary shall—

(I) notify the alien involved of such determination; and

(II) remove the conditional basis of the alien's status effective as of the second anniversary of the alien's lawful admission for permanent residence.

(ii) Exception. If the petition demonstrates that the facts and information are true and that the alien is in compliance with subsection (d)(1)(B)(ii)—

(I) the Secretary, in the Secretary's discretion, may provide a 1-year extension of the alien's conditional status; and

(II)(aa) if the alien files a petition not later than 30 days after the third anniversary of the alien's lawful admission for permanent residence demonstrating that the alien complied with subsection (d)(1)(B)(i), the Secretary shall remove the conditional basis of the alien's status effective as of such third anniversary; or (bb) if the alien does not file the petition described in item (aa), the conditional status shall terminate at the end of such additional year.

(C) Termination if adverse determination. If the Secretary of Homeland Security determines that such facts and information are not true, the Secretary of Homeland Security shall so notify the alien involved and, subject to subparagraph (D), shall terminate the permanent resident status of an alien investor, alien spouse, or alien child as of the date of the determination.

(D) Hearing in removal proceeding. Any alien whose permanent resident status is terminated under subparagraph (C) may request a review of such determination in a proceeding to remove the alien. In such proceeding, the burden of proof shall be on the Secretary of Homeland Security to establish, by a preponderance of the evidence, that the facts and information described in subsection (d)(1) and alleged in the petition are not true with respect to the qualifying commercial enterprise.

(d) Details of petition and interview.

(1) Contents of petition. Each petition under subsection (c)(1)(A) shall contain facts and information demonstrating that the alien—

(A) invested the requisite capital;

(B)(i) created the employment required under section 203(b)(5)(A)(ii) [8 USCS § 1153(b)(5)(A)(ii)]; or

(ii) is actively in the process of creating the employment required under section 203(b)(5)(A)(ii) [8 USCS § 1153(b)(5)(A)(ii)] and will create such employment before the third anniversary of the alien's lawful admission for permanent residence, provided that such alien's capital will remain invested during such time; and

(C) is otherwise conforming to the requirements of section 203(b)(5) [8 USCS § 1153(b)(5)].

(2) Period for filing petition.

(A) Ninety-day period before second anniversary.

(i) In general. Except as provided in clause (ii) and subparagraph (B), a petition under subsection (c)(1)(A) shall be filed during the 90-day period immediately preceding the second anniversary of the alien investor's lawful admission for permanent residence.

(ii) Exception. Aliens described in subclauses (I)(bb) and (II) of section 203(b)(5)(M)(ii) [8 USCS § 1153(b)(5)(M)(ii)] shall file a petition under subsection (c)(1)(A) during the 90-day period before the second anniversary of the subsequent investment.

(B) Date petitions for good cause. Such a petition may be considered if filed after such date, but only if the alien establishes to the satisfaction of the Secretary of Homeland Security good cause and extenuating circumstances for failure to file the petition during the period described in subparagraph (A).

(C) Filing of petitions during deportation. In the case of an alien who is the subject of removal hearings as a result of failure to file a petition on a timely basis in accordance with subparagraph (A), the Attorney General may stay such removal proceedings against an alien pending the filing of the petition under subparagraph (B).

(3) Personal interview.

(A) In general. The interview under subsection (c)(1)(B) shall be conducted within 90 days after the date of submitting a petition under subsection (c)(1)(A) and at a local office of the Department of Homeland Security, designated by the Secretary of Homeland Security, which is convenient to the parties involved.

(B) Waiver. The Secretary of Homeland Security, in the Secretary's discretion, may waive the deadline for an interview under subsection (c)(1)(B) or the requirement for such an interview according to criteria developed by U.S. Citizenship and Immigration Services, in consultation with its Fraud Detection and National Security Directorate and U.S. Immigration and Customs Enforcement, provided that such criteria do not include a reduction of case processing times or the allocation of adjudicatory resources. A waiver may not be granted under this subparagraph if the alien to be interviewed—

(i) invested in a regional center, new commercial enterprise, or job-creating entity that was sanctioned under section 203(b)(5) [8 USCS § 1153(b)(5)]; or

(ii) is in a class of aliens determined by the Secretary to be threats to public safety or national security.

(e) Treatment of period for purposes of naturalization. For purposes of title III, in the case of an alien who is in the United States as a lawful permanent resident on a conditional basis under this section, the alien shall be considered to have been admitted as an alien lawfully admitted for permanent residence and to be in the United States as an alien lawfully admitted to the United States for permanent residence.

(f) Definitions. In this section:

(1) The term "alien investor" means an alien who obtains the status of an alien lawfully admitted for permanent residence (whether on a conditional basis or otherwise) under section 203(b)(5) [8 USCS § 1153(b)(5)].

(2) The term "alien spouse" and the term "alien child" mean an alien who obtains the status of an alien lawfully admitted for permanent residence (whether on a conditional basis or otherwise) by virtue of being the spouse or child, respectively, of an alien investor.

(3) The term "commercial enterprise" includes any entity formed for the purpose of doing for profit business.

(June 27, 1952, ch 466, Title II, Ch 2, § 216A, as added Nov. 29, 1990, P. L. 101-649, Title I, Subtitle B, Part 2, § 121(b)(1), 104 Stat. 4990; Dec. 12, 1991, P. L. 102-232, Title III, § 302(b)(3), 105 Stat. 1743; Sept. 30, 1996, P. L. 104-208, Div C, Title III, Subtitle A, § 308(e)(8), 110 Stat. 3009-620; Nov. 2, 2002, P. L. 107-273, Div C, Title I, Subtitle B, Ch. 2, § 11036(b), 116 Stat. 1847; Mar. 15, 2022, P.L. 117-103, Div BB, § 104(a), 136 Stat. 1100.)

§ 1187. Visa waiver program for certain visitors

(a) Establishment of program. The Secretary of Homeland Security and the Secretary of State are authorized to establish a program (hereinafter in this section referred to as the "program") under which the requirement of paragraph (7)(B)(i)(II) of section 212(a) [8 USCS § 1182(a)(7)(B)(i)(II)] may be waived by the

Secretary of Homeland Security, in consultation with the Secretary of State and in accordance with this section, in the case of an alien who meets the following requirements:

(1) Seeking entry as tourist for 90 days or less. The alien is applying for admission during the program as a nonimmigrant visitor (described in section 101(a)(15)(B) [8 USCS § 1101(a)(15)(B)]) for a period not exceeding 90 days.

(2) National of program country. The alien is a national of, and presents a passport issued by, a country which—

(A) extends (or agrees to extend), either on its own or in conjunction with one or more other countries that are described in subparagraph (B) and that have established with it a common area for immigration admissions, reciprocal privileges to citizens and nationals of the United States, and

(B) is designated as a [pilot] program country under subsection (c).

(3) Passport requirements. The alien, at the time of application for admission, is in possession of a valid unexpired passport that satisfies the following:

(A) Machine readable. The passport is a machine-readable passport that is tamper-resistant, incorporates document authentication identifiers, and otherwise satisfies the internationally accepted standard for machine readability.

(B) Electronic. Beginning on April 1, 2016, the passport is an electronic passport that is fraud-resistant, contains relevant biographic and biometric information (as determined by the Secretary of Homeland Security), and otherwise satisfies internationally accepted standards for electronic passports.

(4) Executes immigration forms. The alien before the time of such admission completes such immigration form as the Secretary of Homeland Security shall establish.

(5) Entry into the United States. If arriving by sea or air, the alien arrives at the port of entry into the United States on a carrier, including any carrier conducting operations under part 135 of title 14, Code of Federal Regulations, or a noncommercial aircraft that is owned or operated by a domestic corporation conducting operations under part 91 of title 14, Code of Federal Regulations[,] which has entered into an agreement with the Secretary of Homeland Security pursuant to subsection (e). The Secretary of Homeland Security is authorized to require a carrier conducting operations under part 135 of title 14, Code of Federal Regulations, or a domestic corporation conducting operations under part 91 of that title, to give suitable and proper bond, in such reasonable amount and containing such conditions as the Secretary of Homeland Security may deem sufficient to ensure compliance with the indemnification requirements of this section, as a term of such an agreement.

(6) Not a safety threat. The alien has been determined not to represent a threat to the welfare, health, safety, or security of the United States.

(7) No previous violation. If the alien previously was admitted without a visa under this section, the alien must not have failed to comply with the conditions of any previous admission as such a nonimmigrant.

(8) Round-trip ticket. The alien is in possession of a round-trip transportation ticket (unless this requirement is waived by the Secretary of Homeland Security under regulations or the alien is arriving at the port of entry on an aircraft operated under part 135 of title 14, Code of Federal Regulations, or a noncommercial aircraft that is owned or operated by a domestic corporation conducting operations under part 91 of title 14, Code of Federal Regulations).

(9) Automated system check. The identity of the alien has been checked using an automated electronic database containing information about the inadmissibility of aliens to uncover any grounds on which the alien may be inadmissible to the United States, and no such ground has been found.

(10) Electronic transmission of identification information. Operators of aircraft under part 135 of title 14, Code of Federal Regulations, or operators of noncommercial aircraft that are owned or operated by a domestic corporation conducting operations under part 91 of title 14, Code of Federal Regulations, carrying any alien passenger who will apply for admission under this section shall furnish such information as the Secretary of Homeland Security by regulation shall prescribe as necessary for the identification of any alien passenger being transported and for the enforcement of the immigration laws. Such information shall be electronically transmitted not less than one hour prior to arrival at the port of entry for purposes of checking for inadmissibility using the automated electronic database.

(11) Eligibility determination under the electronic system for travel authorization. Beginning on the date on which the electronic system for travel authorization developed under subsection (h)(3) is fully operational, each alien traveling under the program shall, before applying for admission to the United States, electronically provide to the system biographical information and such other information as the Secretary of Homeland Security shall determine necessary to determine the eligibility of, and whether there exists a law enforcement or security risk in permitting, the alien to travel to the United States. Upon review of such biographical information, the Secretary of Homeland Security shall determine whether the alien is eligible to travel to the United States under the program.

(12) Not present In Iraq, Syria, or any other country or area of concern.

(A) In general. Except as provided in subparagraphs (B) and (C)—

(i) the alien has not been present, at any time on or after March 1, 2011—

(I) in Iraq or Syria;

(II) in a country that is designated by the Secretary of State under section 6(j) of the Export Administration Act of 1979 (50 U.S.C. 2405) [former 50 USCS § 4605(j)] (as continued in effect under the International Emergency Economic Powers Act (50 U.S.C. 1701 et seq.)), section 40 of the Arms Export Control Act (22 U.S.C. 2780), section 620A of the Foreign Assistance Act of 1961 (22 U.S.C. 2371), or any other provision of law, as a country, the government of which has repeatedly provided support of acts of international terrorism; or

(III) in any other country or area of concern designated by the Secretary of Homeland Security under subparagraph (D); and

(ii) regardless of whether the alien is a national of a program country, the alien is not a national of—

(I) Iraq or Syria;

(II) a country that is designated, at the time the alien applies for admission, by the Secretary of State under section 6(j) of the Export Administration Act of 1979 (50 U.S.C. 2405) [former 50 USCS § 4605(j)] (as continued in effect under the International Emergency Economic Powers Act (50 U.S.C. 1701 et seq.)), section 40 of the Arms Export Control Act (22 U.S.C. 2780), section 620A of the Foreign Assistance Act of 1961 (22 U.S.C. 2371), or any other provision of law, as a country, the government of which has repeatedly provided support of acts of international terrorism; or

(III) any other country that is designated, at the time the alien applies for admission, by the Secretary of Homeland Security under subparagraph (D).

(B) Certain military personnel and government employees. Subparagraph (A)(i) shall not apply in the case of an alien if the Secretary of Homeland Security determines that the alien was present—

(i) in order to perform military service in the armed forces of a program country; or

(ii) in order to carry out official duties as a full time employee of the government of a program country.

(C) Waiver. The Secretary of Homeland Security may waive the application of subparagraph (A) to an alien if the Secretary determines that such a waiver is in the law enforcement or national security interests of the United States.

(D) Countries or areas of concern.

(i) In general. Not later than 60 days after the date of the enactment of this paragraph [enacted Dec. 18, 2015], the Secretary of Homeland Security, in consultation with the Secretary of State and the Director of National Intelligence, shall determine whether the requirement under subparagraph (A) shall apply to any other country or area.

(ii) Criteria. In making a determination under clause (i), the Secretary shall consider—

(I) whether the presence of an alien in the country or area increases the likelihood that the alien is a credible threat to the national security of the United States;

(II) whether a foreign terrorist organization has a significant presence in the country or area; and

(III) whether the country or area is a safe haven for terrorists.

(iii) Annual review. The Secretary shall conduct a review, on an annual basis, of any determination made under clause (i).

(E) Report. Beginning not later than one year after the date of the enactment of this paragraph [enacted Dec. 18, 2015], and annually thereafter, the Secretary of Homeland Security shall submit to the Committee on Homeland Security, the Committee on Foreign Affairs, the Permanent Select Committee on Intelligence, and the Committee on the Judiciary of the House of Representatives, and the Committee on Homeland Security and Governmental Affairs, the Committee on Foreign Relations, the Select Committee on Intelligence, and the Committee on the Judiciary of the Senate a report on each instance in which the Secretary exercised the waiver authority under subparagraph (C) during the previous year.

(b) Waiver of rights. An alien may not be provided a waiver under the program unless the alien has waived any right—

(1) to review or appeal under this Act of an immigration officer's determination as to the admissibility of the alien at the port of entry into the United States, or

(2) to contest, other than on the basis of an application for asylum, any action for removal of the alien.

(c) Designation of program countries.

(1) In general. The Secretary of Homeland Security, in consultation with the Secretary of State, "may designate" any country as a program country if it meets the requirements of paragraph (2).

(2) Qualifications. Except as provided in subsection (f), a country may not be designated as a program country unless the following requirements are met:

(A) Low nonimmigrant visa refusal rate. Either—

(i) the average number of refusals of nonimmigrant visitor visas for nationals of that country during—

(I) the two previous full fiscal years was less than 2.0 percent of the total number of nonimmigrant visitor visas for nationals of that country which were granted or refused during those years; and

(II) either of such two previous full fiscal years was less than 2.5 percent of the total number of nonimmigrant visitor visas for nationals of that country which were granted or refused during that year; or

(ii) such refusal rate for nationals of that country during the previous full fiscal year was less than 3.0 percent.

(B) Passport program.

(i) Issuance of passports. The government of the country certifies that it issues to its citizens passports described in subparagraph (A) of subsection (a)(3), and on or after April 1, 2016, passports described in subparagraph (B) of subsection (a)(3).

(ii) Validation of passports. Not later than October 1, 2016, the government of the country certifies that it has in place mechanisms to validate passports described in subparagraphs (A) and (B) of subsection (a)(3) at each key port of entry into that country. This requirement shall not apply to travel between countries which fall within the Schengen Zone.

(C) Law enforcement and security interests. The Secretary of Homeland Security, in consultation with the Secretary of State—

(i) evaluates the effect that the country's designation would have on the law enforcement and security interests of the United States (including the interest in enforcement of the immigration laws of the United States and the existence and effectiveness of its agreements and procedures for extraditing to the United States individuals, including its own nationals, who commit crimes that violate United States law);

(ii) determines that such interests would not be compromised by the designation of the country; and

(iii) submits a written report to the Committee on the Judiciary, the Committee on Foreign Affairs, and the Committee on Homeland Security of the House of Representatives and the Committee on the Judiciary and the Committee on Foreign Relations of the Senate regarding the country's qualification for designation that includes an explanation of such determination.

(D) Reporting lost and stolen passports. The government of the country enters into an agreement with the United States to report, or make available through Interpol or other means as designated by the Secretary of Homeland Security, to the United States Government information about the theft or loss of passports not later than 24 hours after becoming aware of the theft or loss and in a manner specified in the agreement.

(E) Repatriation of aliens. The government of the country accepts for repatriation any citizen, former citizen, or national of the country against whom a final executable order of removal is issued not later than three weeks after the issuance of the final order of removal. Nothing in this subparagraph creates any duty for the United States or any right for any alien with respect to removal or release. Nothing in this subparagraph gives rise to any cause of action or claim under this paragraph or any other law against any official of the United States or of any State to compel the release, removal, or consideration for release or removal of any alien.

(F) Passenger information exchange. The government of the country enters into an agreement with the United States to share information regarding whether citizens and nationals of that country traveling to the United States represent a threat to the security or welfare of the United States or its citizens, and fully implements such agreement.

(G) Interpol screening. Not later than 270 days after the date of the enactment of this subparagraph [enacted Dec. 18, 2015], except in the case of a country in which there is not an international airport, the government of the country certifies to the Secretary of Homeland Security that, to the maximum extent allowed under the laws of the country, it is screening, for unlawful activity, each person who is not a citizen or national of that country who is admitted to or departs that country, by using relevant databases and notices maintained by Interpol, or other means designated by the Secretary of Homeland Security. This requirement shall not apply to travel between countries which fall within the Schengen Zone.

(3) Continuing and subsequent qualifications. For each fiscal year after the initial period—

(A) Continuing qualification. In the case of a country which was a program country in the previous fiscal year, a country may not be designated as a program country unless the sum of—

(i) the total of the number of nationals of that country who were denied admission at the time of arrival or withdrew their application for admission during such previous fiscal year as a nonimmigrant visitor, and

(ii) the total number of nationals of that country who were admitted as nonimmigrant visitors during such previous fiscal year and who violated the terms of such admission,

was less than 2 percent of the total number of nationals of that country who applied for admission as nonimmigrant visitors during such previous fiscal year.

(B) New countries. In the case of another country, the country may not be designated as a program country unless the following requirements are met:

(i) Low nonimmigrant visa refusal rate in previous 2-year period. The average number of refusals of nonimmigrant visitor visas for nationals of that country during the two previous full fiscal years was less than 2 percent of the total number of nonimmigrant visitor visas for nationals of that country which were granted or refused during those years.

(ii) Low nonimmigrant visa refusal rate in each of the 2 previous years. The average number of refusals of nonimmigrant visitor visas for nationals of that country during either of such two previous full fiscal years was less than 2.5 percent of the total number of nonimmigrant visitor visas for nationals of that country which were granted or refused during that year.

(4) Initial period. For purposes of paragraphs (2) and (3), the term "initial period" means the period beginning at the end of the 30-day period described in subsection (b)(1) and ending on the last day of the first fiscal year which begins after such 30-day period.

(5) Written reports on continuing qualification; designation terminations.

(A) Periodic evaluations.

(i) In general. The Secretary of Homeland Security, in consultation with the Secretary of State, periodically (but not less than once every 2 years)—

(I) shall evaluate the effect of each program country's continued designation on the law enforcement and security interests of the United States (including the interest in enforcement of the immigration laws of the United States and the existence and effectiveness of its agreements and procedures for extraditing to the United States individuals, including its own nationals, who commit crimes that violate United States law);

(II) shall determine, based upon the evaluation in subclause (I), whether any such designation ought to be continued or terminated under subsection (d);

(III) shall submit a written report to the Committee on the Judiciary, the Committee on Foreign Affairs, the Permanent Select Committee on Intelligence, and the Committee on Homeland Security, of the House of Representatives and the Committee on the Judiciary, the Committee on Foreign Relations, the Select Committee on Intelligence, and the Committee on Homeland Security and Governmental Affairs of the Senate regarding the continuation or termination of the country's designation that includes an explanation of such determination and the effects described in subclause (I); and

(IV) shall submit to Congress a report regarding the implementation of the electronic system for travel authorization under subsection (h)(3) and the participation of new countries in the program through a waiver under paragraph (8); and

(V) shall submit to the committees described in subclause (III), a report that includes an assessment of the threat to the national security of the United States of the designation of each country designated as a program country, including the compliance of the government of each such country with the requirements under subparagraphs (D) and (F) of paragraph (2), as well as each such government's capacity to comply with such requirements.

(ii) Effective date. A termination of the designation of a country under this subparagraph shall take effect on the date determined by the Secretary of Homeland Security, in consultation with the Secretary of State.

(iii) Redesignation. In the case of a termination under this subparagraph, the Secretary of Homeland Security shall redesignate the country as a program country, without regard to subsection (f) or paragraph (2) or (3), when the Secretary of Homeland Security, in consultation with the Secretary of State, determines that all causes of the termination have been eliminated.

(B) Emergency termination.

(i) In general. In the case of a program country in which an emergency occurs that the Secretary of Homeland Security, in consultation with the Secretary of State, determines threatens the law enforcement or security interests of the United States (including the interest in enforcement of the immigration laws of the United States), the Secretary of Homeland Security shall immediately terminate the designation of the country as a program country.

(ii) Definition. For purposes of clause (i), the term "emergency" means—

(I) the overthrow of a democratically elected government;

(II) war (including undeclared war, civil war, or other military activity) on the territory of the program country;

(III) a severe breakdown in law and order affecting a significant portion of the program country's territory;

(IV) a severe economic collapse in the program country; or

(V) any other extraordinary event in the program country that threatens the law enforcement or security interests of the United States (including the interest in enforcement of the immigration laws of the United States) and where the country's participation in the program could contribute to that threat.

(iii) Redesignation. The Secretary of Homeland Security may redesignate the country as a program country, without regard to subsection (f) or paragraph (2) or (3), when the Secretary of Homeland Security, in consultation with the Secretary of State, determines that—

(I) at least 6 months have elapsed since the effective date of the termination;

(II) the emergency that caused the termination has ended; and

(III) the average number of refusals of nonimmigrant visitor visas for nationals of that country during the period of termination under this subparagraph was less than 3.0 percent of the total number of nonimmigrant visitor visas for nationals of that country which were granted or refused during such period.

(iv) Program suspension authority. The Director of National Intelligence shall immediately inform the Secretary of Homeland Security of any current and credible threat which poses an imminent danger to the United States or its citizens and originates from a country participating in the visa waiver program. Upon receiving such notification, the Secretary, in consultation with the Secretary of State—

(I) may suspend a country from the visa waiver program without prior notice;

(II) shall notify any country suspended under subclause (I) and, to the extent practicable without disclosing sensitive intelligence sources and methods, provide justification for the suspension; and

(III) shall restore the suspended country's participation in the visa waiver program upon a determination that the threat no longer poses an imminent danger to the United States or its citizens.

(C) Treatment of nationals after termination. For purposes of this paragraph—

(i) nationals of a country whose designation is terminated under subparagraph (A) or (B) shall remain eligible for a waiver under subsection (a) until the effective date of such termination; and

(ii) a waiver under this section that is provided to such a national for a period described in subsection (a)(1) shall not, by such termination, be deemed to have been rescinded or otherwise rendered invalid, if the waiver is granted prior to such termination.

(6) Computation of visa refusal rates. For purposes of determining the eligibility of a country to be designated as a program country, the calculation of visa refusal rates shall not include any visa refusals which incorporate any procedures based on, or are otherwise based on, race, sex, or disability, unless otherwise specifically authorized by law or regulation. No court shall have jurisdiction under this paragraph to review any visa refusal, the denial of admission to the United States of any alien by the Secretary of Homeland Security, the Secretary's computation of the visa refusal rate, or the designation or nondesignation of any country.

(7) Visa waiver information.

(A) In general. In refusing the application of nationals of a program country for United States visas, or the applications of nationals of a country seeking entry into the visa waiver program, a consular officer shall not knowingly or intentionally classify the refusal of the visa under a category that is not included in the calculation of the visa refusal rate only so that the percentage of that country's visa refusals is less than the percentage limitation applicable to qualification for participation in the visa waiver program.

(B) Reporting requirement. On May 1 of each year, for each country under consideration for inclusion in the visa waiver program, the Secretary of State shall provide to the appropriate congressional committees—

(i) the total number of nationals of that country that applied for United States visas in that country during the previous calendar year;

(ii) the total number of such nationals who received United States visas during the previous calendar year;

(iii) the total number of such nationals who were refused United States visas during the previous calendar year;

(iv) the total number of such nationals who were refused United States visas during the previous calendar year under each provision of this Act under which the visas were refused; and

(v) the number of such nationals that were refused under section 214(b) [8 USCS § 1184(b)] as a percentage of the visas that were issued to such nationals.

(C) Certification. Not later than May 1 of each year, the United States chief of mission, acting or permanent, to each country under consideration for inclusion in the visa waiver program shall certify to the appropriate congressional committees that the information described in subparagraph (B) is accurate and provide a copy of that certification to those committees.

(D) Consideration of countries in the visa waiver program. Upon notification to the Secretary of Homeland Security that a country is under consideration for inclusion in the visa waiver program, the Secretary of State shall provide all of the information described in subparagraph (B) to the Secretary of Homeland Security.

(E) Definition. In this paragraph, the term "appropriate congressional committees" means the Committee on the Judiciary and the Committee on Foreign Relations of the Senate and the Committee on the Judiciary and the Committee on International Relations of the House of Representatives.

(8) Nonimmigrant visa refusal rate flexibility.

(A) Certification.

(i) In general. On the date on which an air exit system is in place that can verify the departure of not less than 97 percent of foreign nationals who exit through airports of the United States and the electronic system for travel authorization required under subsection (h)(3) is fully operational, the Secretary of Homeland Security shall certify to Congress that such air exit system and electronic system for travel authorization are in place.

(ii) Notification to Congress. The Secretary shall notify Congress in writing of the date on which the air exit system under clause (i) fully satisfies the biometric requirements specified in subsection (i).

(iii) Temporary suspension of waiver authority. Notwithstanding any certification made under clause (i), if the Secretary has not notified Congress in accordance with clause (ii) by June 30, 2009, the Secretary's waiver authority under subparagraph (B) shall be suspended beginning on July 1, 2009, until such time as the Secretary makes such notification.

(iv) Rule of construction. Nothing in this paragraph shall be construed as in any way abrogating the reporting requirements under subsection (i)(3).

(B) Waiver. After certification by the Secretary under subparagraph (A), the Secretary, in consultation with the Secretary of State, may waive the application of paragraph (2)(A) for a country if—

(i) the country meets all security requirements of this section;

(ii) the Secretary of Homeland Security determines that the totality of the country's security risk mitigation measures provide assurance that the country's participation in the program would not compromise the law enforcement, security interests, or enforcement of the immigration laws of the United States;

(iii) there has been a sustained reduction in the rate of refusals for nonimmigrant visas for nationals of the country and conditions exist to continue such reduction;

(iv) the country cooperated with the Government of the United States on counterterrorism initiatives, information sharing, and preventing terrorist travel before the date of its designation as a program country, and the Secretary of Homeland Security and the Secretary of State determine that such cooperation will continue; and

(v)(I) the rate of refusals for nonimmigrant visitor visas for nationals of the country during the previous full fiscal year was not more than ten percent; or

(II) the visa overstay rate for the country for the previous full fiscal year does not exceed the maximum visa overstay rate, once such rate is established under subparagraph (C).

(C) Maximum visa overstay rate.

(i) Requirement to establish. After certification by the Secretary under subparagraph (A), the Secretary and the Secretary of State jointly shall use information from the air exit system referred to in such subparagraph to establish a maximum visa overstay rate for countries participating in the program pursuant to a waiver under subparagraph (B). The Secretary of Homeland Security shall certify to Congress that such rate would not compromise the law enforcement, security interests, or enforcement of the immigration laws of the United States.

(ii) Visa overstay rate defined. In this paragraph the term "visa overstay rate" means, with respect to a country, the ratio of—

(I) the total number of nationals of that country who were admitted to the United States on the basis of a nonimmigrant visa whose periods of authorized stays ended during a fiscal year but who remained unlawfully in the United States beyond such periods; to

(II) the total number of nationals of that country who were admitted to the United States on the basis of a nonimmigrant visa during that fiscal year.

(iii) Report and publication. The Secretary of Homeland Security shall on the same date submit to Congress and publish in the Federal Register information relating to the maximum visa overstay rate established under clause (i). Not later than 60 days after such date, the Secretary shall issue a final maximum visa overstay rate above which a country may not participate in the program.

(9) Discretionary security-related considerations. In determining whether to waive the application of paragraph (2)(A) for a country, pursuant to paragraph (8), the Secretary of Homeland Security, in consultation with the Secretary of State, shall take into consider-

ation other factors affecting the security of the United States, including—

(A) airport security standards in the country;

(B) whether the country assists in the operation of an effective air marshal program;

(C) the standards of passports and travel documents issued by the country; and

(D) other security-related factors, including the country's cooperation with the United States' initiatives toward combating terrorism and the country's cooperation with the United States intelligence community in sharing information regarding terrorist threats.

(10) Technical assistance. The Secretary of Homeland Security, in consultation with the Secretary of State, shall provide technical assistance to program countries to assist those countries in meeting the requirements under this section. The Secretary of Homeland Security shall ensure that the program office within the Department of Homeland Security is adequately staffed and has resources to be able to provide such technical assistance, in addition to its duties to effectively monitor compliance of the countries participating in the program with all the requirements of the program.

(11) Independent review.

(A) In general. Prior to the admission of a new country into the program under this section, and in conjunction with the periodic evaluations required under subsection (c)(5)(A), the Director of National Intelligence shall conduct an independent intelligence assessment of a nominated country and member of the program.

(B) Reporting requirement. The Director shall provide to the Secretary of Homeland Security, the Secretary of State, and the Attorney General the independent intelligence assessment required under subparagraph (A).

(C) Contents. The independent intelligence assessment conducted by the Director shall include—

(i) a review of all current, credible terrorist threats of the subject country;

(ii) an evaluation of the subject country's counterterrorism efforts;

(iii) an evaluation as to the extent of the country's sharing of information beneficial to suppressing terrorist movements, financing, or actions;

(iv) an assessment of the risks associated with including the subject country in the program; and

(v) recommendations to mitigate the risks identified in clause (iv).

(12) Designation of high risk program countries.

(A) In general. The Secretary of Homeland Security, in consultation with the Director of National Intelligence and the Secretary of State, shall evaluate program countries on an annual basis based on the criteria described in subparagraph (B) and shall identify any program country, the admission of nationals from which under the visa waiver program under this section, the Secretary determines presents a high risk to the national security of the United States.

(B) Criteria. In evaluating program countries under subparagraph (A), the Secretary of Homeland Security, in consultation with the Director of National Intelligence and the Secretary of State, shall consider the following criteria:

(i) The number of nationals of the country determined to be ineligible to travel to the United States under the program during the previous year.

(ii) The number of nationals of the country who were identified in United States Government databases related to the identities of known or suspected terrorists during the previous year.

(iii) The estimated number of nationals of the country who have traveled to Iraq or Syria at any time on or after March 1, 2011 to engage in terrorism.

(iv) The capacity of the country to combat passport fraud.

(v) The level of cooperation of the country with the counter-terrorism efforts of the United States.

(vi) The adequacy of the border and immigration control of the country.

(vii) Any other criteria the Secretary of Homeland Security determines to be appropriate.

(C) Suspension of designation. The Secretary of Homeland Security, in consultation with the Secretary of State, may suspend the designation of a program country based on a determination that the country presents a high risk to the national security of the United States under subparagraph (A) until such time as the Secretary determines that the country no longer presents such a risk.

(D) Report. Not later than 60 days after the date of the enactment of this paragraph [enacted Dec. 18, 2015], and annually thereafter, the Secretary of Homeland Security, in consultation with the Director of National Intelligence and the Secretary of State, shall submit to the Committee on Homeland Security, the Committee on Foreign Affairs, the Permanent Select Committee on Intelligence, and the Committee on the Judiciary of the House of Representatives, and the Committee on Homeland Security and Governmental Affairs, the Committee on Foreign Relations, the Select Committee on Intelligence, and the Committee on the Judiciary of the Senate a report, which includes an evaluation and threat assessment of each country determined to present a high risk to the national security of the United States under subparagraph (A).

(d) Authority. Notwithstanding any other provision of this section, the Secretary of Homeland Security, in consultation with the Secretary of State, may for any reason (including national security) refrain from waiving the visa requirement in respect to nationals of any country which may otherwise qualify for designation or may, at any time, rescind any waiver or designation previously granted under this section. The Secretary of Homeland Security may not waive any eligibility requirement under this section unless the Secretary notifies, with respect to the House of Representatives, the Committee on Homeland Security, the Committee on the Judiciary, the Committee on Foreign Affairs, and the Committee on Appropriations, and with respect to the Senate, the Committee on Homeland Security and Governmental Affairs, the Committee on the Judiciary, the Committee on Foreign Relations, and the Committee on Appropriations not later than 30 days before the effective date of such waiver.

(e) Carrier agreements.

(1) In general. The agreement referred to in subsection (a)(4) is an agreement between a carrier (including any carrier conducting operations under part 135 of title 14, Code of Federal Regulations) or a domestic corporation conducting operations under part 91 of that title and the Secretary of Homeland Security under which the carrier (including any carrier conducting operations under part 135 of title 14, Code of Federal Regulations) or a domestic corporation conducting operations under part 91 of that title agrees, in consideration of the waiver of the visa requirement with respect to a nonimmigrant visitor under the program—

(A) to indemnify the United States against any costs for the transportation of the alien from the United States if the visitor is refused admission to the United States or remains in the United States unlawfully after the 90-day period described in subsection (a)(1)(A),

(B) to submit daily to immigration officers any immigration forms received with respect to nonimmigrant visitors provided a waiver under the program,

(C) to be subject to the imposition of fines resulting from the transporting into the United States of a national of a designated country without a passport pursuant to regulations promulgated by the Secretary of Homeland Security, and

(D) to collect, provide, and share passenger data as required under subsection (h)(1)(B).

(2) Termination of agreements. The Secretary of Homeland Security may terminate an agreement under paragraph (1) with five days' notice to the carrier (including any carrier conducting operations under part 135 of title 14, Code of Federal Regulations) or a domestic corporation conducting operations under part 91 of that title for the failure by a carrier (including any carrier conducting operations under part 135 of title 14, Code of Federal Regulations) or a domestic corporation conducting operations under part 91 of that title to meet the terms of such agreement.

(3) Business aircraft requirements.

(A) In general. For purposes of this section, a domestic corporation conducting operations under part 91 of title 14, Code of Federal Regulations[,] that owns or operates a noncommercial aircraft is a corporation that is organized under the laws of any of the States of the United States or the District of Columbia and is accredited by or a member of a national organization that sets business aviation standards. The Secretary of Homeland Security shall prescribe by regulation the provision of such information as the Secretary of Homeland Security deems necessary to identify the domestic corporation, its officers, employees, shareholders, its place of business, and its business activities.

(B) Collections. In addition to any other fee authorized by law, the Secretary of Homeland Security is authorized to charge and collect, on a periodic basis, an amount from each domestic corporation conducting operations under part 91 of title 14, Code of Federal Regulations, for nonimmigrant visa waiver admissions on noncommercial aircraft owned or operated by such domestic corporation equal to the total amount of fees assessed for issuance of nonimmigrant visa waiver arrival/departure forms at land border ports of entry. All fees collected under this paragraph shall be deposited into the Immigration User Fee Account established under section 286(h) [8 USCS § 1356(h)].

(f) Duration and termination of designation.

(1) In general.

(A) Determination and notification of disqualification rate. Upon determination by the Secretary of Homeland Security that a program country's disqualification rate is 2 percent or more, the Secretary of Homeland Security shall notify the Secretary of State.

(B) Probationary status. If the program country's disqualification rate is greater than 2 percent but less than 3.5 percent, the Secretary of Homeland Security shall place the program country in probationary status for a period not to exceed 2 full fiscal years following the year in which the determination under subparagraph (A) is made.

(C) Termination of designation. Subject to paragraph (3), if the program country's disqualification rate is 3.5 percent or more, the Secretary of Homeland Security shall terminate the country's designation as a program country effective at the beginning of the second fiscal year following the fiscal year in which the determination under subparagraph (A) is made.

(2) Termination of probationary status.

(A) In general. If the Secretary of Homeland Security determines at the end of the probationary period described in paragraph (1)(B) that the program country placed in probationary status under such paragraph has failed to develop a machine-readable passport program as required by section [subsection] (c)(2)(C), or has a disqualification rate of 2 percent or more, the Secretary of Homeland Security shall terminate the designation of the country as a program country. If the Secretary of Homeland Security determines that the program country has developed a machine-readable passport program and has a disqualification rate of less than 2 percent, the Secretary of Homeland Security shall redesignate the country as a program country.

(B) Effective date. A termination of the designation of a country under subparagraph (A) shall take effect on the first day of the first fiscal year following the fiscal year in which the determination under such subparagraph is made. Until such date, nationals of the country shall remain eligible for a waiver under subsection (a).

(3) Nonapplicability of certain provisions. Paragraph (1)(C) shall not apply unless the total number of nationals of a program country described in paragraph (4)(A) exceeds 100.

(4) Definition. For purposes of this subsection, the term "disqualification rate" means the percentage which—

(A) the total number of nationals of the program country who were—

(i) denied admission at the time of arrival or withdrew their application for admission during the most recent fiscal year for which data are available; and

(ii) admitted as nonimmigrant visitors during such fiscal year and who violated the terms of such admission; bears to

(B) the total number of nationals of such country who applied for admission as nonimmigrant visitors during such fiscal year.

(5) Failure to report passport thefts. If the Secretary of Homeland Security and the Secretary of State jointly determine that the program country is not reporting the theft or loss of passports, as required by subsection (c)(2)(D), Secretary of Homeland Security shall terminate the designation of the country as a program country.

(6) Failure to share information.

(A) In general. If the Secretary of Homeland Security and the Secretary of State jointly determine that the program country is not sharing information, as required by subsection (c)(2)(F), the Secretary of Homeland Security shall terminate the designation of the country as a program country.

(B) Redesignation. In the case of a termination under this paragraph, the Secretary of Homeland Security shall redesignate the country as a program country, without regard to paragraph (2) or (3) of subsection (c) or paragraphs (1) through (4), when the Secretary of Homeland Security, in consultation with the Secretary of State, determines that the country is sharing information, as required by subsection (c)(2)(F).

(7) Failure to screen.

(A) In general. Beginning on the date that is 270 days after the date of the enactment of this paragraph [enacted Dec. 18, 2015], if the Secretary of Homeland Security and the Secretary of State jointly determine that the program country is not conducting the screening required by subsection (c)(2)(G), the Secretary of Homeland Security shall terminate the designation of the country as a program country.

(B) Redesignation. In the case of a termination under this paragraph, the Secretary of Homeland Security shall redesignate the country as a program country, without regard to paragraph (2) or (3) of subsection (c) or paragraphs (1) through (4), when the Secretary of Homeland Security, in consultation with the Secretary of State, determines that the country is conducting the screening required by subsection (c)(2)(G).

(g) Visa application sole method to dispute denial of waiver based on a ground of inadmissibility. In the case of an alien denied a waiver under the program by reason of a ground of inadmissibility described in section 212(a) [8 USCS § 1182(a)] that is discovered at the time of the alien's application for the waiver or through the use of an automated electronic database required under subsection (a)(9), the alien may apply for a visa at an appropriate consular office outside the United States. There shall be no other means of administrative or judicial review of such a denial, and no court or person otherwise shall have jurisdiction to consider any claim attacking the validity of such a denial.

(h) Use of information technology systems.

(1) Automated entry-exit control system.

(A) System. Not later than October 1, 2001, the Secretary of Homeland Security shall develop and implement a fully automated entry and exit control system that will collect a record of arrival and departure for every alien who arrives and departs by sea or air at a port of entry into the United States and is provided a waiver under the program.

(B) Requirements. The system under subparagraph (A) shall satisfy the following requirements:

(i) Data collection by carriers. Not later than October 1, 2001, the records of arrival and departure described in subparagraph (A) shall be based, to the maximum extent practicable, on passenger data collected and electronically transmitted to the automated entry and exit control system by each carrier that has an agreement under subsection (a)(4).

(ii) Data provision by carriers. Not later than October 1, 2002, no waiver may be provided under this section to an alien arriving by sea or air at a port of entry into the United States on a carrier unless the carrier is electronically transmitting to the automated entry and exit control system passenger data determined by the Secretary of Homeland Security to be sufficient to permit the Secretary of Homeland Security to carry out this paragraph.

(iii) Calculation. The system shall contain sufficient data to permit the Secretary of Homeland Security to calculate, for each program country and each fiscal year, the portion of nationals of that country who are described in subparagraph (A) and for whom no record of departure exists, expressed as a percentage of the total number of such nationals who are so described.

(C) Reporting.

(i) Percentage of nationals lacking departure record. As part of the annual report required to be submitted under section 110(e)(1) of the Illegal Immigration Reform and Immigrant Responsibility Act of 1996 [8 USCS § 1365a(e)(1)], the Secretary of Homeland Security shall include a section containing the calculation described in subparagraph (B)(iii) for each program country for the previous fiscal year, together with an analysis of that information.

(ii) System effectiveness. Not later than December 31, 2004, the Secretary of Homeland Security shall submit a written report to the Committee on the Judiciary of the United States House of Representatives and of the Senate containing the following:

(I) The conclusions of the Secretary of Homeland Security regarding the effectiveness of the automated entry and exit control system to be developed and implemented under this paragraph.

(II) The recommendations of the Secretary of Homeland Security regarding the use of the calculation described in subparagraph (B)(iii) as a basis for evaluating whether to terminate or continue the designation of a country as a program country.

The report required by this clause may be combined with the annual report required to be submitted on that date under section 110(e)(1) of the Illegal Immigration Reform and Immigrant Responsibility Act of 1996 [8 USCS § 1365a(e)(1)].

(2) Automated data sharing system.

(A) System. The Secretary of Homeland Security and the Secretary of State shall develop and implement an automated data sharing system that will permit them to share data in electronic form from their respective records systems regarding the admissibility of aliens who are nationals of a program country.

(B) Requirements. The system under subparagraph (A) shall satisfy the following requirements:

(i) Supplying information to immigration officers conducting inspections at ports of entry. Not later than October 1, 2002, the system shall enable immigration officers conducting inspections at ports of entry under section 235 [8 USCS § 1225] to obtain from the system, with respect to aliens seeking a waiver under the program—

(I) any photograph of the alien that may be contained in the records of the Department of State or the Service; and

(II) information on whether the alien has ever been determined to be ineligible to receive a visa or ineligible to be admitted to the United States.

(ii) Supplying photographs of inadmissible aliens. The system shall permit the Secretary of Homeland Security electronically to obtain any photograph contained in the records of the Secretary of State pertaining to an alien who is a national of a program country and has been determined to be ineligible to receive a visa.

(iii) Maintaining records on applications for admission. The system shall maintain, for a minimum of 10 years, information about each application for admission made by an alien seeking a waiver under the program, including the following:

(I) The name or Service identification number of each immigration officer conducting the inspection of the alien at the port of entry.

(II) Any information described in clause (i) that is obtained from the system by any such officer.

(III) The results of the application.

(3) Electronic system for travel authorization.

(A) System. The Secretary of Homeland Security, in consultation with the Secretary of State, shall develop and implement a fully automated electronic system for travel authorization (referred to in this paragraph as the "System") to collect such biographical and other information as the Secretary of Homeland Security determines necessary to determine, in advance of travel, the eligibility of, and whether there exists a law enforcement or security risk in permitting, the [an] alien to travel to the United States.

(B) Fees.

(i) In general. No later than 6 months after the date of enactment of the Travel Promotion Act of 2009 [enacted March 4, 2010], the Secretary of Homeland Security shall establish a fee for the use of the System and begin assessment and collection of that fee. The initial fee shall be the sum of—

(I) $17 per travel authorization; and

(II) an amount that will at least ensure recovery of the full costs of providing and administering the System, as determined by the Secretary.

(ii) Disposition of amounts collected. Amounts collected under clause (i)(I) shall be credited to the Travel Promotion Fund established by subsection (d) of the Travel Promotion Act of 2009 (22 U.S.C. 2131(d)). Amounts collected under clause (i)(II) shall be transferred to the general fund of the Treasury and made available to pay the costs incurred to administer the System.

(iii) Sunset of Travel Promotion Fund fee. The Secretary may not collect the fee authorized by clause (i)(I) for fiscal years beginning after October 31, 2028.

(C) Validity.

(i) Period. The Secretary of Homeland Security, in consultation with the Secretary of State, shall prescribe regulations that provide for a period, not to exceed three years, during which a determination of eligibility to travel under the program will be valid. Notwithstanding any other provision under this section, the Secretary of Homeland Security may revoke any such determination or shorten the period of eligibility under any such determination at any time and for any reason.

(ii) Limitation. A determination by the Secretary of Homeland Security that an alien is eligible to travel to the United States under the program is not a determination that the alien is admissible to the United States.

(iii) Not a determination of visa eligibility. A determination by the Secretary of Homeland Security that an alien who applied for authorization to travel to the United States through the System is not eligible to travel under the program is not a determination of eligibility for a visa to travel to the United States and shall not preclude the alien from applying for a visa.

(iv) Judicial review. Notwithstanding any other provision of law, no court shall have jurisdiction to review an eligibility determination under the System.

(D) Fraud detection. The Secretary of Homeland Security shall research opportunities to incorporate into the System technology that will detect and prevent fraud and deception in the System.

(E) Additional and previous countries of citizenship. The Secretary of Homeland Security shall collect from an applicant for admission pursuant to this section information on any additional or previous countries of citizenship of that applicant. The Secretary shall take any information so collected into account when making determinations as to the eligibility of the alien for admission pursuant to this section.

(F) Report on certain limitations on travel. Not later than 30 days after the date of the enactment of this subparagraph [enacted Dec. 18, 2015] and annually thereafter, the Secretary of Homeland Security, in consultation with the Secretary of State, shall submit to the Committee on Homeland Security, the Committee on the Judiciary, and the Committee on Foreign Affairs of the House of Representatives, and the Committee on Homeland Security and Governmental Affairs, the Committee on the Judiciary, and the Committee on Foreign Relations of the Senate a report on the number of individuals who were denied eligibility to travel under the program, or whose eligibility for such travel was revoked during the previous year, and the number of such individuals determined, in accordance with subsection (a)(6), to represent a threat to the national security of the United States, and shall include the country or countries of citizenship of each such individual.

(i) Exit system.

(1) In general. Not later than one year after the date of the enactment of this subsection [enacted Aug. 3, 2007], the Secretary of Homeland Security shall establish an exit system that records the departure on a flight leaving the United States of every alien participating in the visa waiver program established under this section.

(2) System requirements. The system established under paragraph (1) shall—

(A) match biometric information of the alien against relevant watch lists and immigration information; and

(B) compare such biometric information against manifest information collected by air carriers on passengers departing the United States to confirm such aliens have departed the United States.

(3) Report. Not later than 180 days after the date of the enactment of this subsection [enacted Aug. 3, 2007], the Secretary shall submit to Congress a report that describes—

(A) the progress made in developing and deploying the exit system established under this subsection; and

(B) the procedures by which the Secretary shall improve the method of calculating the rates of nonimmigrants who overstay their authorized period of stay in the United States.

(June 27, 1952, ch 466, Title II, Ch 2, § 217, as added Nov. 6, 1986, P. L. 99-603, Title III, Part B, § 313(a), 100 Stat. 3435; Oct. 24, 1988, P. L. 100-525, § 2(p)(1), (2), 102 Stat. 2613; Nov. 29, 1990, P. L. 101-649, Title II, Subtitle A, § 201(a), 104 Stat. 5012; Dec. 12, 1991, P. L. 102-232, Title III, §§ 303(a)(1), (2), 307(l)(3), 105 Stat. 1746, 1756; Oct. 25, 1994, P. L. 103-415, § 1(m), 108 Stat. 4301; Oct. 25, 1994, P. L. 103-416, Title II, §§ 210, 211, 108 Stat. 4312, 4313; Sept. 30, 1996, P. L. 104-208, Div C, Title III, Subtitle A, § 308(d)(4)(F), (e)(9), Title VI, Subtitle C, § 635(a), (b), (c)(1), (3), 110 Stat. 3009-618, 3009-620, 3009-702, 3009-703; Nov. 26, 1997, P. L. 105-119, Title I, § 125, 111 Stat. 2471; April 27, 1998, P. L. 105-173, §§ 1, 3, 112 Stat. 56; Oct. 30, 2000, P. L. 106-396, Title I, § 101(a), Title II, §§ 201–207, Title IV, § 403(a)–(d), 114 Stat. 1637, 1638, 1647; Oct. 26, 2001, P. L. 107-56, Title IV, Subtitle B, § 417(c), (d), 115 Stat. 355; May 14, 2002, P. L. 107-173, Title III, § 307(a), 116 Stat. 556; Aug. 3, 2007, P. L. 110-53, Title VII, Subtitle B, § 711(c), (d)(1), 121 Stat. 339; March 4, 2010, P. L. 111-145, § 9(h) [9(e)], 124 Stat. 62; July 2, 2010, P. L. 111-198, § 5(a), 124 Stat. 1357; Dec. 16, 2014, P. L. 113-235, Div B, Title VII, §§ 605(b), 606(1), 128 Stat. 2219; Dec. 18, 2015, P. L. 114-113, Div O, Title II, §§ 202(a), (b), 203–205(a), (b), 206, 207(a), (b), 209, 129 Stat. 2989, 2993, 2995; Feb. 9, 2018, P. L. 115-123, Div C, Title II, § 30203(a), 132 Stat. 126; Dec. 20, 2019, P.L. 116-94, Div I, Title VIII, § 806, 133 Stat. 3029; Mar. 15, 2022, P.L. 117-103, Div EE, § 101, 136 Stat. 1111.)

§ 1187a. Provision of assistance to non-program countries

The Secretary of Homeland Security, in consultation with the Secretary of State, shall provide assistance in a risk-based manner to countries that do not participate in the visa waiver program under section 217 of the Immigration and Nationality Act (8 U.S.C. 1187) to assist those countries in—

(1) submitting to Interpol information about the theft or loss of passports of citizens or nationals of such a country; and

(2) issuing, and validating at the ports of entry of such a country, electronic passports that are fraud-resistant, contain relevant biographic and biometric information (as determined by the Secretary of Homeland Security), and otherwise satisfy internationally accepted standards for electronic passports.

(Dec. 18, 2015, P. L. 114-113, Div O, Title II, § 208, 129 Stat. 2995.)

§ 1188. Admission of temporary H-2A workers

(a) Conditions for approval of H-2A petitions.

(1) A petition to import an alien as an H-2A worker (as defined in subsection (i)(2)) may not be approved by the Attorney General unless the petitioner has applied to the Secretary of Labor for a certification that—

(A) there are not sufficient workers who are able, willing, and qualified, and who will be available at the time and place needed, to perform the labor or services involved in the petition, and

(B) the employment of the alien in such labor or services will not adversely affect the wages and working conditions of workers in the United States similarly employed.

(2) The Secretary of Labor may require by regulation, as a condition of issuing the certification, the payment of a fee to recover the reasonable costs of processing applications for certification.

(b) Conditions for denial of labor certification. The Secretary of Labor may not issue a certification under subsection (a) with respect to an employer if the conditions described in that subsection are not met or if any of the following conditions are met:

(1) There is a strike or lockout in the course of a labor dispute which, under the regulations, precludes such certification.

(2)(A) The employer during the previous two-year period employed H-2A workers and the Secretary of Labor has determined, after notice and opportunity for a hearing, that the employer at any time during that period substantially violated a material term or condition of the labor certification with respect to the employment of domestic or nonimmigrant workers.

(B) No employer may be denied certification under subparagraph (A) for more than three years for any violation described in such subparagraph.

(3) The employer has not provided the Secretary with satisfactory assurances that if the employment for which the certification is sought is not covered by State workers' compensation law, the employer will provide, at no cost to the worker, insurance covering injury and disease arising out of and in the course of the worker's employment which will provide benefits at least equal to those provided under the State workers' compensation law for comparable employment.

(4) The Secretary determines that the employer has not made positive recruitment efforts within a multi-state region of traditional or expected labor supply where the Secretary finds that there are a significant number of qualified United States workers who, if recruited, would be willing to make themselves available for work at the time and place needed. Positive recruitment under this paragraph is in addition to, and

shall be conducted within the same time period as, the circulation through the interstate employment service system of the employer's job offer. The obligation to engage in positive recruitment under this paragraph shall terminate on the date the H-2A workers depart for the employer's place of employment.

(c) Special rules for consideration of applications. The following rules shall apply in the case of the filing and consideration of an application for a labor certification under this section:

(1) Deadline for filing applications. The Secretary of Labor may not require that the application be filed more than 45 days before the first date the employer requires the labor or services of the H-2A worker.

(2) Notice within seven days of deficiencies.

(A) The employer shall be notified in writing within seven days of the date of filing if the application does not meet the standards (other than that described in subsection (a)(1)(A)) for approval.

(B) If the application does not meet such standards, the notice shall include the reasons therefor and the Secretary shall provide an opportunity for the prompt resubmission of a modified application.

(3) Issuance of certification.

(A) The Secretary of Labor shall make, not later than 30 days before the date such labor or services are first required to be performed, the certification described in subsection (a)(1) if—

(i) the employer has complied with the criteria for certification (including criteria for the recruitment of eligible individuals as prescribed by the Secretary), and

(ii) the employer does not actually have, or has not been provided with referrals of, qualified eligible individuals who have indicated their availability to perform such labor or services on the terms and conditions of a job offer which meets the requirements of the Secretary. In considering the question of whether a specific qualification is appropriate in a job offer, the Secretary shall apply the normal and accepted qualifications required by non-H-2A-employers in the same or comparable occupations and crops.

(B)(i) For a period of 3 years subsequent to the effective date of this section, labor certifications shall remain effective only if, from the time the foreign worker departs for the employer's place of employment, the employer will provide employment to any qualified United States worker who applies to the employer until 50 percent of the period of the work contract, under which the foreign worker who is in the job was hired, has elapsed. In addition, the employer will offer to provide benefits, wages and working conditions required pursuant to this section and regulations.

(ii) The requirement of clause (i) shall not apply to any employer who—

(I) did not, during any calendar quarter during the preceding calendar year, use more than 500 man-days of agricultural labor, as defined in section 3(u) of the Fair Labor Standards Act of 1938 (29 U.S.C. 203(u)),

(II) is not a member of an association which has petitioned for certification under this section for its members, and

(III) has not otherwise associated with other employers who are petitioning for temporary foreign workers under this section.

(iii) Six months before the end of the 3-year period described in clause (i), the Secretary of Labor shall consider the findings of the report mandated by section 403(a)(4)(D) of the Immigration Reform and Control Act of 1986 [note to this section] as well as other relevant materials, including evidence of benefits to United States workers and costs to employers, addressing the advisability of continuing a policy which requires an employer, as a condition for certification under this section, to continue to accept qualified, eligible United States workers for employment after the date the H-2A workers depart for work with the employer. The Secretary's review of such findings and materials shall lead to the issuance of findings in furtherance of the Congressional policy that aliens not be admitted under this section unless there are not sufficient workers in the United States who are able, willing, and qualified to perform the labor or service needed and that the employment of the aliens in such labor or services will not adversely affect the wages and working conditions of workers in the United States similarly employed. In the absence of the enactment of Federal legislation prior to three months before the end of the 3-year period described in clause (i) which addresses the subject matter of this subparagraph, the Secretary shall immediately publish the findings required by this clause, and shall promulgate, on an interim or final basis, regulations based on his findings which shall be effective no later than three years from the effective date of this section.

(iv) In complying with clause (i) of this subparagraph, an association shall be allowed to refer or transfer workers among its members: *Provided,* That for purposes of this section an association acting as an agent for its members shall not be considered a joint employer merely because of such referral or transfer.

(v) United States workers referred or transferred pursuant to clause (iv) of this subparagraph shall not be treated disparately.

(vi) An employer shall not be liable for payments under section 655.202(b)(6) of title 20, Code of Federal Regulations (or any successor regulation) with respect to an H-2A worker who is displaced due to compliance with the requirement of this subparagraph, if the Secretary of Labor certifies that the H-2A worker was displaced because of the employer's compliance with clause (i) of this subparagraph.

(vii)(I) No person or entity shall willfully and knowingly withhold domestic workers prior to the arrival of H-2A workers in order to force the hiring of domestic workers under clause (i).

(II) Upon the receipt of a complaint by an employer that a violation of subclause (I) has occurred the Secretary shall immediately investigate. He shall within 36 hours of the receipt of the complaint issue findings concerning the alleged violation. Where the Secretary finds that a violation has occurred, he shall immediately suspend the application of clause (i) of this subparagraph with respect to that certification for that date of need.

(4) Housing. Employers shall furnish housing in accordance with regulations. The employer shall be permitted at the employer's option to provide housing meeting applicable Federal standards for temporary labor camps or to secure housing which meets the local standards for rental and/or public accommodations or other substantially similar class of habitation: *Provided,* That in the absence of applicable local standards, State standards for rental and/or public accommodations or other substantially similar class of habitation shall be met: *Provided further,* That in the absence of applicable local or State standards, Federal temporary labor camp standards shall apply: *Provided further,* That the Secretary of Labor shall issue regulations which address the specific requirements of housing for employees principally engaged in the range production of livestock: *Provided further,* That when it is the prevailing practice in the area and occupation of intended employment to provide family housing, family housing shall be provided to workers with families who request it: *And provided further,* That nothing in this paragraph shall require an employer to provide or secure housing for workers who are not entitled to it under the temporary labor certification regulations in effect on June 1, 1986. The determination as to whether the housing furnished by an employer for an H-2A worker meets the requirements imposed by this paragraph must be made prior to the date specified in paragraph (3)(A) by which the Secretary of Labor is required to make a certification described in subsection (a)(1) with respect to a petition for the importation of such worker.

(d) Roles of agricultural associations.

(1) Permitting filing by agricultural associations. A petition to import an alien as a temporary agricultural worker, and an application for a labor certification with respect to such a worker, may be filed by an association of agricultural producers which use agricultural services.

(2) Treatment of associations acting as employers. If an association is a joint or sole employer of temporary agricultural workers, the certifications granted under this section to the association may be used for the certified job opportunities of any of its producer members and such workers may be transferred among its producer members to perform agricultural services of a temporary or seasonal nature for which the certifications were granted.

(3) Treatment of violations.

(A) Member's violation does not necessarily disqualify association or other members. If an individual producer member of a joint employer association is determined to have committed an act that under subsection (b)(2) results in the denial of certification with respect to the member, the denial shall apply only to that member of the association unless the Secretary determines that the association or other member participated in, had knowledge of, or reason to know of, the violation.

(B) Association's violation does not necessarily disqualify members.

(i) If an association representing agricultural producers as a joint employer is determined to have committed an act that under subsection (b)(2) results in the denial of certification with respect to the association, the denial shall apply only to the association and does not apply to any individual producer member of the association unless the Secretary determines that the member participated in, had knowledge of, or reason to know of, the violation.

(ii) If an association of agricultural producers certified as a sole employer is determined to have committed an act that under subsection (b)(2) results in the denial of certification with respect to the association, no individual producer member of such association may be the beneficiary of the services of temporary alien agricultural workers admitted under this section in the commodity and occupation in which such aliens were employed by the association which was denied certification during the period such denial is in force, unless such producer member employs such aliens in the commodity and occupation in question directly or through an association which is a joint employer of such workers with the producer member.

(e) Expedited administrative appeals of certain determinations.

(1) Regulations shall provide for an expedited procedure for the review of a denial of certification under subsection (a)(1) or a revocation of such a certification or, at the applicant's request, for a de novo administrative hearing respecting the denial or revocation.

(2) The Secretary of Labor shall expeditiously, but in no case later than 72 hours after the time a new determination is requested, make a new determination on the request for certification in the case of an H-2A worker if able, willing, and qualified eligible individuals are not actually available at the time such labor or services are required and a certification was denied in whole or in part because of the availability of qualified workers. If the employer asserts that any eligible individual who has been referred is not able, willing, or qualified, the burden of proof is on the employer to establish that the individual referred is not able, willing, or qualified because of employment-related reasons.

(f) Violators disqualified for 5 years. An alien may not be admitted to the United States as a temporary agricultural worker if the alien was admitted to the United States as such a worker within the previous five-year period and the alien during that period violated a term or condition of such previous admission.

(g) Authorizations of appropriations.

(1) There are authorized to be appropriated for each fiscal year, beginning with fiscal year 1987, $10,000,000 for the purposes—

(A) of recruiting domestic workers for temporary labor and services which might otherwise be performed by nonimmigrants described in section 101(a)(15)(H)(ii)(a) [8 USCS § 1101(a)(15)(H)(ii)(a)], and

(B) of monitoring terms and conditions under which such nonimmigrants (and domestic workers employed by the same employers) are employed in the United States.

(2) The Secretary of Labor is authorized to take such actions, including imposing appropriate penalties and seeking appropriate injunctive relief and specific performance of contractual obligations, as may be necessary to assure employer compliance with terms and conditions of employment under this section.

(3) There are authorized to be appropriated for each fiscal year, beginning with fiscal year 1987, such sums as may be necessary for the purpose of enabling the Secretary of Labor to make determinations and certifications under this section and under section 212(a)(5)(A)(i) [8 USCS § 1182(a)(5)(A)(i)].

(4) There are authorized to be appropriated for each fiscal year, beginning with fiscal year 1987, such sums as may be necessary for the purposes of enabling the Secretary of Agriculture to carry out the Secretary's duties and responsibilities under this section.

(h) Miscellaneous provisions.

(1) The Attorney General shall provide for such endorsement of entry and exit documents of nonimmigrants described in section 101(a)(15)(H)(ii) [8 USCS § 1101(a)(15)(H)(ii)] as may be necessary to carry out this section and to provide notice for purposes of section 274A [8 USCS § 1324a].

(2) The provisions of subsections (a) and (c) of section 214 [8 USCS § 1184(a), (c)] and the provisions of this section preempt any State or local law regulating admissibility of nonimmigrant workers.

(i) Definitions. For purposes of this section:

(1) The term "eligible individual" means, with respect to employment, an individual who is not an unauthorized alien (as defined in section 274A(h)(3) [8 USCS § 1324a(h)](3)) with respect to that employment.

(2) The term "H-2A worker" means a nonimmigrant described in section 101(a)(15)(H)(ii)(a) [8 USCS § 1101(a)(15)(H)(ii)(a)].

(June 27, 1952, ch 477, Title II, Ch 2, § 218 [216], as added Nov. 6, 1986, P. L. 99-603, Title III, Part A, § 301(c), 100 Stat. 3411; Oct. 24, 1988, P. L. 100-525, § 2(l)(2), (3), 102 Stat. 2612; Dec. 12, 1991, P. L. 102-232, Title III, §§ 307(l)(4), 309(b)(8), 105 Stat. 1756, 1759; Oct. 25, 1994, P. L. 103-416, Title II, § 219(z)(8), 108 Stat. 4318; Oct. 22, 1999, P. L. 106-78, Title VII, § 748, 113 Stat. 1167; Dec. 21, 2000, P. L. 106-554, § 1(a)(1) [Title V, § 105] 114 Stat. 2763, 2763A-11.)

§ 1189. Designation of foreign terrorist organizations

(a) Designation.

(1) In general. The Secretary is authorized to designate an organization as a foreign terrorist organization in accordance with this subsection if the Secretary finds that—

(A) the organization is a foreign organization;

(B) the organization engages in terrorist activity (as defined in section 212(a)(3)(B) [8 USCS § 1182(a)(3)(B)][)] or terrorism (as defined in section 140(d)(2) of the Foreign Relations Authorization Act, Fiscal Years 1988 and 1989 (22 U.S.C. 2656f(d)(2)), or retains the capability and intent to engage in terrorist activity or terrorism[)]; and

(C) the terrorist activity or terrorism of the organization threatens the security of United States nationals or the national security of the United States.

(2) Procedure.

(A) Notice.

(i) To congressional leaders. Seven days before making a designation under this subsection, the Secretary shall, by classified communication, notify the Speaker and Minority Leader of the House of Representatives, the President pro tempore, Majority Leader, and Minority Leader of the Senate, and the members of the relevant committees of the House of Representatives and the Senate, in writing, of the intent to designate an organization under this subsection, together with the findings made under paragraph (1) with respect to that organization, and the factual basis therefor.

(ii) Publication in Federal Register. The Secretary shall publish the designation in the Federal Register seven days after providing the notification under clause (i).

(B) Effect of designation.

(i) For purposes of section 2339B of title 18, United States Code, a designation under this subsection shall take effect upon publication under subparagraph (A)(ii).

(ii) Any designation under this subsection shall cease to have effect upon an Act of Congress disapproving such designation.

(C) Freezing of assets. Upon notification under paragraph (2)(A)(i), the Secretary of the Treasury may require United States financial institutions possessing or controlling any assets of any foreign organization included in the notification to block all financial transactions involving those assets until further directive from either the Secretary of the Treasury, Act of Congress, or order of court.

(3) Record.

(A) In general. In making a designation under this subsection, the Secretary shall create an administrative record.

(B) Classified information. The Secretary may consider classified information in making a designation under this subsection. Classified information shall not be subject to disclosure for such time as it remains classified, except that such information may be disclosed to a court ex parte and in camera for purposes of judicial review under subsection (c).

(4) Period of designation.

(A) In general. A designation under this subsection shall be effective for all purposes until revoked under paragraph (5) or (6) or set aside pursuant to subsection (c).

(B) Review of designation upon petition.

(i) In general. The Secretary shall review the designation of a foreign terrorist organization under the procedures set forth in clauses (iii) and (iv) if the designated organization files a petition for revocation within the petition period described in clause (ii).

(ii) Petition period. For purposes of clause (i)—

(I) if the designated organization has not previously filed a petition for revocation under this subparagraph, the petition period begins 2 years after the date on which the designation was made; or

(II) if the designated organization has previously filed a petition for revocation under this subparagraph, the petition period begins 2 years after the date of the determination made under clause (iv) on that petition.

(iii) Procedures. Any foreign terrorist organization that submits a petition for revocation under this subparagraph must provide evidence in that petition that the relevant circumstances described in paragraph (1) are sufficiently different from the circumstances that were the basis for the designation such that a revocation with respect to the organization is warranted.

(iv) Determination.

(I) In general. Not later than 180 days after receiving a petition for revocation submitted under this subparagraph, the Secretary shall make a determination as to such revocation.

(II) Classified information. The Secretary may consider classified information in making a determination in response to a petition for revocation. Classified information shall not be subject to disclosure for such time as it remains classified, except that such information may be disclosed to a court ex parte and in camera for purposes of judicial review under subsection (c).

(III) Publication of determination. A determination made by the Secretary under this clause shall be published in the Federal Register.

(IV) Procedures. Any revocation by the Secretary shall be made in accordance with paragraph (6).

(C) Other review of designation.

(i) In general. If in a 5-year period no review has taken place under subparagraph (B), the Secretary shall review the designation of the foreign terrorist organization in order to determine whether such designation should be revoked pursuant to paragraph (6).

(ii) Procedures. If a review does not take place pursuant to subparagraph (B) in response to a petition for revocation that is filed in accordance with that subparagraph, then the review shall be conducted pursuant to procedures established by the Secretary. The results of such review and the applicable procedures shall not be reviewable in any court.

(iii) Publication of results of review. The Secretary shall publish any determination made pursuant to this subparagraph in the Federal Register.

(5) Revocation by Act of Congress. The Congress, by an Act of Congress, may block or revoke a designation made under paragraph (1).

(6) Revocation based on change in circumstances.

(A) In general. The Secretary may revoke a designation made under paragraph (1) at any time, and shall revoke a designation upon completion of a review conducted pursuant to subparagraphs (B) and (C) of paragraph (4) if the Secretary finds that—

(i) the circumstances that were the basis for the designation have changed in such a manner as to warrant revocation; or

(ii) the national security of the United States warrants a revocation.

(B) Procedure. The procedural requirements of paragraphs (2) and (3) shall apply to a revocation under this paragraph. Any revocation shall take effect on the date specified in the revocation or upon publication in the Federal Register if no effective date is specified.

(7) Effect of revocation. The revocation of a designation under paragraph (5) or (6) shall not affect any action or proceeding based on conduct committed prior to the effective date of such revocation.

(8) Use of designation in trial or hearing. If a designation under this subsection has become effective under paragraph (2)(B) a defendant in a criminal action or an alien in a removal proceeding shall not be permitted to raise any question concerning the validity of the issuance of such designation as a defense or an objection at any trial or hearing.

(b) Amendments to a designation.

(1) In general. The Secretary may amend a designation under this subsection if the Secretary finds that the organization has changed its name, adopted a new alias, dissolved and then reconstituted itself under a different name or names, or merged with another organization.

(2) Procedure. Amendments made to a designation in accordance with paragraph (1) shall be effective upon publication in the Federal Register. Subparagraphs (B) and (C) of subsection (a)(2) shall apply to an amended designation upon such publication. Paragraphs (2)(A)(i), (4), (5), (6), (7), and (8) of subsection (a) shall also apply to an amended designation.

(3) Administrative record. The administrative record shall be corrected to include the amendments as well as any additional relevant information that supports those amendments.

(4) Classified information. The Secretary may consider classified information in amending a designation in accordance with this subsection. Classified information shall not be subject to disclosure for such time as it remains classified, except that such information may be disclosed to a court ex parte and in camera for purposes of judicial review under subsection (c).

(c) Judicial review of designation.

(1) In general. Not later than 30 days after publication in the Federal Register of a designation, an amended designation, or a determination in response to a petition for revocation, the designated organization may seek judicial review in the United States Court of Appeals for the District of Columbia Circuit.

(2) Basis of review. Review under this subsection shall be based solely upon the administrative record, except that the Government may submit, for ex parte and in camera review, classified information used in making the designation, amended designation, or determination in response to a petition for revocation.

(3) Scope of review. The Court shall hold unlawful and set aside a designation, amended designation, or determination in response to a petition for revocation the court finds to be—

(A) arbitrary, capricious, an abuse of discretion, or otherwise not in accordance with law;

(B) contrary to constitutional right, power, privilege, or immunity;

(C) in excess of statutory jurisdiction, authority, or limitation, or short of statutory right;

(D) lacking substantial support in the administrative record taken as a whole or in classified information submitted to the court under paragraph (2),[;] or

(E) not in accord with the procedures required by law.

(4) Judicial review invoked. The pendency of an action for judicial review of a designation, amended designation, or determination in response to a petition for revocation shall not affect the application of this section, unless the court issues a final order setting aside the designation, amended designation, or determination in response to a petition for revocation.

(d) Definitions. As used in this section—

(1) the term "classified information" has the meaning given that term in section 1(a) of the Classified Information Procedures Act (18 U.S.C. App.);

(2) the term "national security" means the national defense, foreign relations, or economic interests of the United States;

(3) the term "relevant committees" means the Committees on the Judiciary, Intelligence, and Foreign Relations of the Senate and the Committees on the Judiciary, Intelligence, and International Relations of the House of Representatives; and

(4) the term "Secretary" means the Secretary of State, in consultation with the Secretary of the Treasury and the Attorney General.

(June 27, 1952, ch 477, Title II, Ch 2, § 219, as added April 24, 1996, P. L. 104-132, Title III, Subtitle A, § 302(a), 110 Stat. 1248; Sept. 30, 1996, P. L. 104-208, Div C, Title III, Subtitle D, § 356, Title VI, Subtitle E, § 671(c)(1), 110 Stat. 3009-644, 3009-722; Oct. 26, 2001, P. L. 107-56, Title IV, Subtitle B, § 411(c), 115 Stat. 349; Dec. 17, 2004, P. L. 108-458, Title VII, Subtitle A, § 7119(a)–(c), 118 Stat. 3801.)

ISSUANCE OF ENTRY DOCUMENTS

§ 1201. Issuance of visas

(a) Immigrants; nonimmigrants.

(1) Under the conditions hereinafter prescribed and subject to the limitations prescribed in this Act or regulations issued thereunder, a consular officer may issue (A) to an immigrant who has made proper application therefor, an immigrant visa which shall consist of the application provided for in section 222 [8 USCS § 1202], visaed by such consular officer, and shall specify the foreign state, if any, to which the immigrant is charged, the immigrant's particular status under such foreign state, the preference, immediate relative, or special immigrant classification to which the alien is charged, the date on which the validity of the visa shall expire, and such additional information as may be required; and (B) to a nonimmigrant who has made proper application therefor, a nonimmigrant visa, which shall specify the classification under section 101(a)(15) [8 USCS § 1101(a)(15)] of the nonimmigrant, the period during which the nonimmigrant visa shall be valid, and such additional information as may be required.

(2) The Secretary of State shall provide to the Service an electronic version of the visa file of each alien who has been issued a visa to ensure that the data in that visa file is available to immigration inspectors at the United States ports of entry before the arrival of the alien at such a port of entry.

(b) Registration; photographs; waiver of requirement. Each alien who applies for a visa shall be registered in connection with his application, and shall furnish copies of his photograph signed by him for such use as may be by regulations required. The requirements of this subsection may be waived in the discretion of the Secretary of State in the case of any alien who is within that class of nonimmigrants enumerated in sections 101(a)(15)(A), and 101(a)(15)(G) [8 USCS § 1101(a)(15)(A) and (G)], or in the case of any alien who is granted a diplomatic visa on a diplomatic passport or on the equivalent thereof.

(c) Period of validity; renewal or replacement.

(1) Immigrant visas. An immigrant visa shall be valid for such period, not exceeding six months, as shall be by regulations prescribed, except that any visa issued to a child lawfully adopted by a United States citizen and spouse while such citizen is serving abroad in the United States Armed Forces, or is employed abroad by the United States Government, or is temporarily abroad on business, shall be valid until such time, for a period not to exceed three years, as the adoptive citizen parent returns to the United States in due course of his service, employment, or business.

(2) Nonimmigrant visas. A nonimmigrant visa shall be valid for such periods as shall be by regulations prescribed. In prescribing the period of validity of a nonimmigrant visa in the case of nationals of any foreign country who are eligible for such visas, the Secretary of State shall, insofar as practicable, accord to such nationals the same treatment upon a reciprocal basis as such foreign country accords to nationals of the United States who are within a similar class; except that in the case of aliens who are nationals of a foreign country and who either are granted refugee status and firmly resettled in another foreign country or are granted permanent residence and residing in another foreign country, the Secretary of State may prescribe the period of validity of such a visa based upon the treatment granted by that other foreign country to alien refugees and permanent residents, respectively, in the United States.

(3) Visa replacement. An immigrant visa may be replaced under the original number during the fiscal year in which the original visa was issued for an immigrant who establishes to the satisfaction of the consular officer that the immigrant—

(A) was unable to use the original immigrant visa during the period of its validity because of reasons beyond his control and for which he was not responsible;

(B) is found by a consular officer to be eligible for an immigrant visa; and

(C) pays again the statutory fees for an application and an immigrant visa.

(4) Fee waiver. If an immigrant visa was issued, on or after March 27, 2013, for a child who has been lawfully adopted, or who is coming to the United States to be adopted, by a United States citizen, any statutory immigrant visa fees relating to a renewal or replacement of such visa may be waived or, if already paid, may be refunded upon request, subject to such criteria as the Secretary of State may prescribe, if—

(A) the immigrant child was unable to use the original immigrant visa during the period of its validity as a direct result of extraordinary circumstances, including the denial of an exit permit; and

(B) if such inability was attributable to factors beyond the control of the adopting parent or parents and of the immigrant.

(d) Physical examination. Prior to the issuance of an immigrant visa to any alien, the consular officer shall require such alien to submit to a physical and mental examination in accordance with such regulations as may be prescribed. Prior to the issuance of a nonimmigrant visa to any alien, the consular officer may require such alien to submit to a physical or mental examination, or both, if in his opinion such examination is necessary to ascertain whether such alien is eligible to receive a visa.

(e) Surrender of visa. Each immigrant shall surrender his immigrant visa to the immigration officer at the port of entry, who shall endorse on the visa the date and the port of arrival, the identity of the vessel or other means of transportation by which the immigrant arrived, and such other endorsements as may be by regulations required.

(f) Surrender of documents. Each nonimmigrant shall present or surrender to the immigration officer at the port of entry such documents as may be by regulation required. In the case of an alien crewman not in possession of any individual documents other than a passport and until such time as it becomes practicable to issue individual documents, such alien crewman may be admitted, subject to the provisions of this title, if his name appears in the crew list of the vessel or aircraft on which he arrives and the crew list is visaed by a consular officer, but the consular officer shall have the right to deny admission to any alien crewman from the crew list visa.

(g) Non-issuance of visas or other documents. No visa or other documentation shall be issued to an alien if (1) it appears to the consular officer, from statements in the application, or in the papers submitted therewith, that such alien is ineligible to receive a visa or such other documentation under section 212 [8 USCS § 1182], or any other provision of law, (2) the application fails to comply with the provisions of this Act, or the regulations issued thereunder, or (3) the consular officer knows or has reason to believe that such alien is ineligible to receive a visa or such other documentation under section 212 [8 USCS § 1182], or any other provision of law: *Provided,* That a visa or other documentation may be issued to an alien who is within the purview of section 212(a)(4) [8 USCS § 1182(a)(4)], if such alien is otherwise entitled to receive a visa or other documentation, upon receipt of notice by the consular officer from the Attorney General of the giving of a bond or undertaking providing indemnity as in the case of aliens admitted under section 213 [8 USCS § 1183]; *Provided further,* That a visa may be issued to an alien defined in section 101(a)(15)(B) or (F) [8 USCS § 1101(a)(15)(B) or (F)], if such alien is otherwise entitled to receive a visa, upon receipt of a notice by the consular officer from the Attorney General of the giving of a bond with sufficient surety in such sum and containing such conditions as the consular officer shall prescribe, to insure that at the expiration of the time for which such alien has been admitted by the Attorney General, as provided in section 214(a) [8 USCS § 1184(a)], or upon failure to maintain the status under which he was admitted, or to maintain any status subsequently acquired under section 248 of the Act [8 USCS § 1258], such alien will depart from the United States.

(h) Nonadmission upon arrival. Nothing in this Act shall be construed to entitle any alien, to whom a visa or other documentation has been issued, to be admitted [to] the United States, if, upon arrival at a port of entry in the United States, he is found to be inadmissible under this Act, or any other provision of law. The substance of this subsection shall appear upon every visa application.

(i) Revocation of visas or documents. After the issuance of a visa or other documentation to any alien, the consular officer or the Secretary of State may at any time, in his discretion, revoke such visa or other documentation. Notice of such revocation shall be communicated to the Attorney General, and such revocation shall invalidate the visa or other documentation from the date of issuance: *Provided,* That carriers or transportation companies, and masters, commanding officers, agents, owners, charterers, or consignees, shall not be penalized under section 273(b) [8 USCS § 1323(b)] for action taken in reliance on such visas or other documentation, unless they received due notice of such revocation prior to the alien's embarkation. There shall be no means of judicial review (including review pursuant to section 2241 of title 28, United States Code, or any other habeas corpus provision, and sections 1361 and 1651 of such title) of a revocation under this subsection, except in the context of a removal proceeding if such revocation provides the sole ground for removal under section 237(a)(1)(B) [8 USCS § 1227(a)(1)(B)].

(June 27, 1952, ch 477, Title II, Ch 3, § 221, 66 Stat. 191; Sept. 26, 1961, P. L. 87-301, § 4, 75 Stat. 651; Oct. 3, 1965, P. L. 89-236, §§ 11(a), (b), 17, 79 Stat. 918, 919; Dec. 29, 1981, P. L. 97-116, § 18(f), 95 Stat. 1620; Nov. 14, 1986, P. L. 99-653, § 5(a)-(c), 100 Stat. 3656; Nov. 14, 1986, P. L. 99-652, § 5(1)–(3) [(a)–(c)], 100 Stat. 3656; Oct. 24, 1988, P. L. 100-525, § 8(d)(1), 102 Stat. 2617; Nov. 29, 1990, P. L. 101-649, Title VI, § 603(a)(9), 104 Stat. 5083; Dec. 12, 1991, P. L. 102-232, Title III, § 302(e)(8)(C), 105 Stat. 1746; Sept. 30, 1996, P. L. 104-208, Div C, Title III, Subtitle A, § 308(d)(4)(G), (f)(2)(B), Title VI, Subtitle C, § 631, 110 Stat. 3009-618, 3009-621, 3009-700; May 14, 2002, P. L. 107-173, Title III, § 301, 116 Stat. 552; Dec. 17, 2004, P. L. 108-458, Title V, Subtitle C, § 5304(a), 118 Stat. 3736; Oct. 16, 2015, P. L. 114-70, § 2, 129 Stat. 561.)

§ 1201a. [Repealed]

§ 1202. Application for visas

(a) Immigrant visas. Every alien applying for an immigrant visa and for alien registration shall make application therefor in such form and manner and at such place as shall be by regulations prescribed. In the application the alien shall state his full and true name, and any other name which he has used or by which he has been known; age and sex; the date and place of his birth; and such additional information necessary to the identification of the applicant and the enforcement of the immigration and nationality laws as may be by regulations prescribed.

(b) Other documentary evidence for immigrant visa. Every alien applying for an immigrant visa shall present a valid unexpired passport or other suitable travel document, or document of identity and nationality, if such document is required under the regulations issued by the Secretary of State. The immigrant shall furnish to the consular officer with his application a copy of a certification by the appropriate police authorities stating what their records show concerning the immigrant; a certified copy of any existing prison record, military record, and record of his birth; and a certified copy of all other records or documents concerning him or his case which may be required by the consular officer. The copy of each document so furnished shall be permanently attached to the application and become a part thereof. In the event that the immigrant establishes to the satisfaction of the consular officer that any document or record required by this subsection is unobtainable, the consular officer may permit the immigrant to submit in lieu of such document or record other satisfactory evidence of the fact to which such document or record would, if obtainable, pertain. All immigrant visa applications shall be reviewed and adjudicated by a consular officer.

(c) Nonimmigrant visas; nonimmigrant registration; form, manner and contents of application. Every alien applying for a nonimmigrant visa and for alien registration shall make application therefor in such form and manner as shall be by regulations prescribed. In the application the alien shall state his full and true name, the date and place of birth, his nationality, the purpose and length of his intended stay in the United States; his marital status; and such additional information necessary to the identification of the applicant, the determination of his eligibility for a nonimmigrant visa, and the enforcement of the immigration and nationality laws as may be by regulations prescribed. The alien shall provide complete and accurate information in response to any request for information contained in the application. At the discretion of the Secretary of State, application forms for the various classes of nonimmigrant admissions described in section 101(a)(15) [8 USCS § 1101(a)(15)] may vary according to the class of visa being requested.

(d) Other documentary evidence for nonimmigrant visa. Every alien applying for a nonimmigrant visa and alien registration shall furnish to the consular officer, with his application, a certified copy of such documents pertaining to him as may be by regulations required. All nonimmigrant visa applications shall be reviewed and adjudicated by a consular officer.

(e) Signing and verification of application. Except as may be otherwise prescribed by regulations, each application for an immigrant visa shall be signed by the applicant in the presence of the consular officer, and verified by the oath of the applicant administered by the consular officer. The application for an immigrant visa, when visaed by the consular officer, shall become the immigrant visa. The application for a nonimmigrant visa or other documentation as a nonimmigrant shall be disposed of as may be by regulations prescribed. The issuance of a nonimmigrant visa shall, except as may be otherwise by regulations prescribed, be evidenced by a stamp[, or other] placed in the alien's passport.

(f) Confidential nature of records. The records of the Department of State and of diplomatic and consular offices of the United States pertaining to the issuance or refusal of visas or permits to enter the United States shall be considered confidential and shall be used only for the formulation, amendment, administration, or enforcement of the immigration, nationality, and other laws of the United States, except that—

(1) in the discretion of the Secretary of State certified copies of such records may be made available to a court which certifies that the information contained in such records is needed by the court in the interest of the ends of justice in a case pending before the court. [; and]

(2) the Secretary of State, in the Secretary's discretion and on the basis of reciprocity, may provide to a foreign government information in the Department of State's computerized visa lookout database and, when necessary and appropriate, other records covered by this section related to information in the database—

(A) with regard to individual aliens, at any time on a case-by-case basis for the purpose of preventing, investigating, or punishing acts that would constitute a crime in the United States, including, but not limited to, terrorism or trafficking in controlled substances, persons, or illicit weapons; or

(B) with regard to any or all aliens in the database, pursuant to such conditions as the Secretary of State shall establish in an agreement with the foreign government in which that government agrees to use such information and records for the purposes described in subparagraph (A) or to deny visas to persons who would be inadmissible to the United States.

(g) Nonimmigrant visa void at conclusion of authorized period of stay.

(1) In the case of an alien who has been admitted on the basis of a nonimmigrant visa and remained in the United States beyond the period of stay authorized by the Attorney General, such visa shall be void beginning after the conclusion of such period of stay.

(2) An alien described in paragraph (1) shall be ineligible to be readmitted to the United States as a nonimmigrant, except—

(A) on the basis of a visa (other than the visa described in paragraph (1)) issued in a consular office located in the country of the alien's nationality (or, if there is no office in such country, in such other consular office as the Secretary of State shall specify); or

(B) where extraordinary circumstances are found by the Secretary of State to exist.

(h) In person interview with consular officer. Notwithstanding any other provision of this Act, the Secretary of State shall require every alien applying for a nonimmigrant visa—

(1) who is at least 14 years of age and not more than 79 years of age to submit to an in person interview with a consular officer unless the requirement for such interview is waived—

(A) by a consular official and such alien is—

(i) within that class of nonimmigrants enumerated in subparagraph (A) or (G) of section 101(a)(15) [8 USCS § 1101(a)(15)];

(ii) within the NATO visa category;

(iii) within that class of nonimmigrants enumerated in section 101(a)(15)(C)(iii) [8 USCS § 1101(a)(15)(C)(iii)] (referred to as the "C-3 visa" category); or

(iv) granted a diplomatic or official visa on a diplomatic or official passport or on the equivalent thereof;

(B) by a consular official and such alien is applying for a visa—

(i) not more than 12 months after the date on which such alien's prior visa expired;

(ii) for the visa classification for which such prior visa was issued;

(iii) from the consular post located in the country of such alien's usual residence, unless otherwise prescribed in regulations that require an applicant to apply for a visa in the country of which such applicant is a national; and

(iv) the consular officer has no indication that such alien has not complied with the immigration laws and regulations of the United States; or

(C) by the Secretary of State if the Secretary determines that such waiver is—

(i) in the national interest of the United States; or

(ii) necessary as a result of unusual or emergent circumstances; and

(2) notwithstanding paragraph (1), to submit to an in person interview with a consular officer if such alien—

(A) is not a national or resident of the country in which such alien is applying for a visa;

(B) was previously refused a visa, unless such refusal was overcome or a waiver of ineligibility has been obtained;

(C) is listed in the Consular Lookout and Support System (or successor system at the Department of State);

(D) is a national of a country officially designated by the Secretary of State as a state sponsor of terrorism, except such nationals who possess nationalities of countries that are not designated as state sponsors of terrorism;

(E) requires a security advisory opinion or other Department of State clearance, unless such alien is—

(i) within that class of nonimmigrants enumerated in subparagraph (A) or (G) of section 101(a)(15) [8 USCS § 1101(a)(15)];

(ii) within the NATO visa category;

(iii) within that class of nonimmigrants enumerated in section 101(a)(15)(C)(iii) [8 USCS § 1101(a)(15)(C)] (referred to as the "C-3 visa" category); or

(iv) an alien who qualifies for a diplomatic or official visa, or its equivalent; or

(F) is identified as a member of a group or sector that the Secretary of State determines—

(i) poses a substantial risk of submitting inaccurate information in order to obtain a visa;

(ii) has historically had visa applications denied at a rate that is higher than the average rate of such denials; or

(iii) poses a security threat to the United States.

(June 27, 1952, ch 477, Title II, Ch 3, § 222, 66 Stat. 193; Sept. 26, 1961, P. L. 87-301, § 6, 75 Stat. 653; Oct. 3, 1965, P. L. 89-236. § 11(c), 79 Stat. 918; Nov. 14, 1986, P. L. 99-653, § 6, 100 Stat. 3656; Nov. 14, 1986, P. L. 99-653, § 6, 100 Stat. 3656; Oct. 24, 1988, P. L. 100-525, §§ 8(e), 9(j) 102 Stat. 2617, 2620; Oct. 25, 1994, P. L. 103-416, Title II, § 205(a), 108 Stat. 4311; Sept. 30, 1996, P. L. 104-208, Div C, Title VI, Subtitle C, §§ 632(a), 634, 110 Stat. 3009-701; Oct. 26, 2001, P. L. 107-56, Title IV, Subtitle B, § 413, 115 Stat. 353; Dec. 17, 2004, P. L. 108-458, Title V, Subtitle C, §§ 5301, 5302, Title VII, Subtitle B, § 7203(b), 118 Stat. 3735, 3814.)

§ 1203. Reentry permit

(a) Application; contents. (1) Any alien lawfully admitted for permanent residence, or (2) any alien lawfully admitted to the United States pursuant to clause 6 of section 3 of the Immigration Act of 1924, between July 1, 1924, and July 5, 1932, both dates inclusive, who intends to depart temporarily from the United States may make application to the Attorney General for a permit to reenter the United States, stating the length of his intended absence or absences, and the reasons therefor. Such applications shall be made under oath, and shall be in such form, contain such information, and be accompanied by such photographs of the applicant as may be by regulations prescribed.

(b) Issuance of permit; nonrenewability. If the Attorney General finds (1) that the applicant under subsection (a)(1) has been lawfully admitted to the United States for permanent residence, or that the applicant under subsection (a)(2) has since admission maintained the status required of him at the time of his admission and such applicant desires to visit abroad and to return to the United States to resume the status existing at the time of his departure for such visit, (2) that the application is made in good faith, and (3) that the alien's proposed departure from the United States would not be contrary to the interests of the United States, the Attorney General may, in his discretion, issue the permit, which shall be valid for not more than two years from the date of issuance and shall not be renewable. The permit shall be in such form as shall be by regulations prescribed for the complete identification of the alien.

(c) Multiple reentries. During the period of validity, such permit may be used by the alien in making one or more applications for reentry into the United States.

(d) Presented and surrendered. Upon the return of the alien to the United States the permit shall be presented to the immigration officer at the port of entry, and upon the expiration of its validity, the permit shall be surrendered to the Service.

(e) Permit in lieu of visa. A permit issued under this section in the possession of the person to whom issued, shall be accepted in lieu of any visa which otherwise would be required from such person under this Act. Otherwise a permit issued under this section shall have no effect under the immigration laws except to show that the alien to whom it was issued is returning from a temporary visit abroad; but nothing in this section shall be construed as making such permit the exclusive means of establishing that the alien is so returning.

(June 27, 1952, ch 477, Title II, Ch 3, § 223, 66 Stat. 194; Dec. 29, 1981, P. L. 97-116, § 6, 95 Stat. 1615.)

§ 1204. Immediate relative and special immigrant visas

A consular officer may, subject to the limitations provided in section 221 [8 USCS § 1201], issue an immigrant visa to a special immigrant or immediate relative as such upon satisfactory proof, under regulations prescribed under this Act, that the applicant is entitled to special immigrant or immediate relative status.

(June 27, 1952, ch 477, Title II, Ch 3, § 224, 66 Stat. 195; Oct. 3, 1965, P. L. 89-236, §§ 11(d), 79 Stat. 918.)

§ 1205. [Repealed]

INSPECTION, APPREHENSION, EXAMINATION, EXCLUSION, AND REMOVAL

§ 1221. Lists of alien and citizen passengers arriving and departing

(a) Arrival manifests. For each commercial vessel or aircraft transporting any person to any seaport or airport of the United States from any place outside the United States, it shall be the duty of an appropriate official specified in subsection (d) to provide to any United States border officer (as defined in subsection (i)) at that port manifest information about each passenger, crew member, and other occupant transported on such vessel or aircraft prior to arrival at that port.

(b) Departure manifests. For each commercial vessel or aircraft taking passengers on board at any seaport or airport of the United States, who are destined to any place outside the United States, it shall be the duty of an appropriate official specified in subsection (d) to provide any United States border officer (as defined in subsection (i)) before departure from such port manifest information about each passenger, crew member, and other occupant to be transported.

(c) Contents of manifest. The information to be provided with respect to each person listed on a manifest required to be provided under subsection (a) or (b) shall include—

(1) complete name;

(2) date of birth;

(3) citizenship;

(4) sex;

(5) passport number and country of issuance;

(6) country of residence;

(7) United States visa number, date, and place of issuance, where applicable;

(8) alien registration number, where applicable;

(9) United States address while in the United States; and

(10) such other information the Attorney General, in consultation with the Secretary of State, and the Secretary of Treasury determines as being necessary for the identification of the persons transported and for the enforcement of the immigration laws and to protect safety and national security.

(d) Appropriate officials specified. An appropriate official specified in this subsection is the master or commanding officer, or authorized agent, owner, or consignee, of the commercial vessel or aircraft concerned.

(e) Deadline for requirement of electronic transmission of manifest information. Not later than January 1, 2003, manifest information required to be provided under subsection (a) or (b) shall be transmitted electronically by the appropriate official specified in subsection (d) to an immigration officer.

(f) Prohibition. No operator of any private or public carrier that is under a duty to provide manifest information under this section shall be granted clearance papers until the appropriate official specified in subsection (d) has complied with the requirements of this subsection, except that, in the case of commercial vessels or aircraft that the Attorney General determines are making regular trips to the United States, the Attorney General may, when expedient, arrange for the provision of manifest information of persons departing the United States at a later date.

(g) Penalties against noncomplying shipments, aircraft, or carriers [Caution: For inflation-adjusted civil monetary penalties, see 8 CFR 280.53.]. If it shall appear to the satisfaction of the Attorney General that an appropriate official specified in subsection (d), any public or private carrier, or the agent of any transportation line, as the case may be, has refused or failed to provide manifest information required by subsection (a) or (b), or that the manifest information provided is not accurate and full based on information provided to the carrier, such official, carrier, or agent, as the case may be, shall pay to the Commissioner the sum of $1,000 for each person with respect to whom such accurate and full manifest information is not provided, or with respect to whom the manifest information is not prepared as prescribed by this section or by regulations issued pursuant thereto. No commercial vessel or aircraft shall be granted clearance pending determination of the question of the liability to the payment of such penalty, or while it remains unpaid, and no such penalty shall be remitted or refunded, except that clearance may be granted prior to the determination of such question upon the deposit with the Commissioner of a bond or undertaking approved by the Attorney General or a sum sufficient to cover such penalty.

(h) Waiver. The Attorney General may waive the requirements of subsection (a) or (b) upon such circumstances and conditions as the Attorney General may by regulation prescribe.

(i) United States border officer defined. In this section, the term "United States border officer" means, with respect to a particular port of entry into the United States, any United States official who is performing duties at that port of entry.

(j) Record of citizens and resident aliens leaving permanently for foreign countries. The Attorney General may authorize immigration officers to record the following information regarding every resident person leaving the United States by way of the Canadian or Mexican borders for permanent residence in a foreign country: Names, age, and sex; whether married or single; calling or occupation; whether able to read or write; nationality; country of birth; country of which citizen or subject; race; last permanent residence in the United States; intended future permanent residence; and time and port of last arrival in the United States; and if a United States citizen or national, the facts on which claim to that status is based.

(June 27, 1952, ch 477, Title II, Ch 4, § 231, 66 Stat. 195; Dec. 29, 1981, P. L. 97-116, § 18(g), 95 Stat. 1620; Nov. 29, 1990, P. L. 101-649, Title V, Subtitle D, § 543(a)(1), 104 Stat. 5057; Dec. 12, 1991, P. L. 102-232, Title III, § 306(c)(4)(A), 105 Stat. 1752; Nov. 28, 2001, P. L. 107-77, Title I, § 115, 115 Stat. 768; May 14, 2002, P. L. 107-173, Title IV, § 402(a), 116 Stat. 557.)

§ 1222. Detention of aliens for physical and mental examination

(a) Detention of aliens. For the purpose of determining whether aliens (including alien crewmen) arriving at ports of the United States belong to any of the classes inadmissible under this Act, by reason of being afflicted with any of the diseases or mental or physical defects or disabilities set forth in section 212(a) [8 USCS § 1182(a)], or whenever the Attorney General has received information showing that any aliens are coming from a country or have embarked at a place where any of such diseases are prevalent or epidemic, such aliens shall be detained for a sufficient time to enable the immigration officers and medical officers to subject such aliens to observation and an examination sufficient to determine whether or not they belong to inadmissible classes.

(b) Physical and mental examination. The physical and mental examination of arriving aliens (including alien crewmen) shall be made by medical officers of the United States Public Health Service, who shall conduct all medical examinations and shall certify, for the information of the immigration officers and the immigration judges, any physical and mental defect or disease observed by such medical officers in any such alien. If medical officers of the United States Public Health Service are not available, civil surgeons of not less than four years' professional experience may be employed for such service upon such terms as may be prescribed by the Attorney General. Aliens (including alien crewmen) arriving at ports of the United States shall be examined by at least one such medical officer or civil surgeon under such administrative regulations as the Attorney General may prescribe, and under medical regulations prepared by the Secretary of Health and Human Services. Medical officers of the United States Public Health Service who have had special training in the diagnosis of insanity and mental defects shall be detailed for duty or employed at such ports of entry as the Attorney General may designate, and such medical officers shall be provided with suitable facilities for the detention and examination of all arriving aliens who it is suspected may be inadmissible under paragraph (1) of section 212(a) [8 USCS § 1182(a)(1)], and the services of interpreters shall be provided for such examination. Any alien certified under paragraph (1) of section 212(a) [8 USCS § 1182(a)(1)] may appeal to a board of medical officers of the United States Public Health Service, which shall be convened by the Secretary of Health and Human Services, and any such alien may introduce before such board one expert medical witness at his own cost and expense.

(c) Certification of certain helpless aliens. If an examining medical officer determines that an alien arriving in the United States is inadmissible, is helpless from sickness, mental or physical disability, or infancy, and is accompanied by another alien whose protection or guardianship may be required, the officer may certify such fact for purposes of applying section 212(a)(10)(B) [8 USCS § 1182(a)(1)(B)] with respect to the other alien.

(June 27, 1952, ch 477, Title II, Ch 4, § 232, 66 Stat. 196; Oct. 18, 1986, P. L. 99-500, Title I, § 101(b) [Title II, § 206(a)] 100 Stat. 1738-56; Oct. 30, 1986, P. L. 99-591, Title I, § 101(b) [Title II, § 206(a)], 100 Stat. 3341-56; Oct. 24, 1988, P. L. 100-525, § 4(b)(1), (2), (d), 102 Stat. 2615; Sept. 30, 1996, P. L. 104-208, Div C, Title III, Subtitle A, §§ 308(b)(2), (3), (c)(2)(A), (d)(3)(A), (4)(H), 110 Stat. 3009-615, 3009-616, 3009-617, 3009-618.)

§ 1223. Entry through or from foreign territory and adjacent islands

(a) Necessity of transportation contract. The Attorney General shall have power to enter into contracts with transportation lines for the inspection and admission of aliens coming to the United States from foreign territory or from adjacent islands. No such transportation line shall be allowed to land any such alien in the United States until and unless it has entered into any such contracts which may be required by the Attorney General.

(b) Landing stations. Every transportation line engaged in carrying alien passengers for hire to the United States from foreign territory or from adjacent islands shall provide and maintain at its expense suitable landing stations, approved by the Attorney General, conveniently located at the point or points of entry. No such transportation line shall be allowed to land any alien passengers in the United States, until such landing stations are provided, and unless such stations are thereafter maintained to the satisfaction of the Attorney General.

(c) Landing agreements. The Attorney General shall have power to enter into contracts including bonding agreements with transportation lines to guarantee the passage through the United States in immediate and continuous transit of aliens destined to foreign countries. Notwithstanding any other provision of this Act, such aliens may not have their classification changed under section 248 [8 USCS § 1258].

(d) Definitions. As used in this section the terms "transportation line" and "transportation company" include, but are not limited to, the owner, charterer, consignee, or authorized agent operating any vessel or aircraft or railroad train bringing aliens to the United States, to foreign territory, or to adjacent islands.

(June 27, 1952, ch 477, Title II, Ch 4, § 233 [238], 66 Stat. 202; Nov. 14, 1986, P. L. 99-653, § 7(b), 100 Stat. 3657; Sept. 30, 1996, P. L. 104-208, Div C, Title III, Subtitle A, § 308(b)(4), (f)(4), Subtitle E, § 362, 110 Stat. 3009-615, 3009-622, 3009-645.)

§ 1224. Designation of ports of entry for aliens arriving by aircraft [Caution: For inflation-adjusted civil monetary penalties, see 8 CFR 280.53(c).]

The Attorney General is authorized (1) by regulation to designate as ports of entry for aliens arriving by aircraft any of the ports of entry for civil aircraft designated as such in accordance with law; (2) by regulation to provide such reasonable requirements for aircraft in civil air navigation with respect to giving notice of intention to land in advance of landing, or notice of landing, as shall be deemed necessary for purposes of administration and enforcement of this Act; and (3) by regulation to provide for the application to civil air navigation of the provisions of this Act where not expressly so provided in this Act to such extent and upon such conditions as he deems necessary. Any person who violates any regulation made under this section shall be subject to a civil penalty of $2,000 which may be remitted or mitigated by the Attorney General in accordance with such proceedings as the Attorney General shall by regulation prescribe. In case the violation is by the owner or person in command of the aircraft, the penalty shall be a lien upon the aircraft, and such aircraft may be libeled therefor in the appropriate United States court. The determination by the Attorney General and remission or mitigation of the civil penalty shall be final. In case the violation is by the owner or person in command of the aircraft, the penalty shall be a lien upon the aircraft and may be collected by proceedings in rem which shall conform as nearly as may be to civil suits in admiralty. The Supreme Court of the United States, and under its direction other courts of the United States, are authorized to prescribe rules regulating such proceedings against aircraft in any particular not otherwise provided by law. Any aircraft made subject to a lien by this section may be summarily seized by, and placed in the custody of such persons as the Attorney General may by regulation prescribe. The aircraft may be released from such custody upon deposit of such amount not exceeding $2,000 as the Attorney General may prescribe, or of a bond in such sum and with such sureties as the Attorney General may prescribe, conditioned upon the payment of the penalty which may be finally determined by the Attorney General.

(June 27, 1952, ch 477, Title II, Ch 4, § 234 [239], 66 Stat. 203; Nov. 29, 1990, P. L. 101-649, Title V, Subtitle D, § 543(a)(3), 104 Stat. 5058; Dec. 12, 1991, P. L. 102-232, Title III, § 306(c)(2), 105 Stat. 1752; Sept. 30, 1996, P. L. 104-208, Div C, Title III, Subtitle A, § 304(a)(1), 110 Stat. 3009-587.)

§ 1225. Inspection by immigration officers; expedited removal of inadmissible arriving aliens; referral for hearing

(a) Inspection.

(1) Aliens treated as applicants for admission. An alien present in the United States who has not been admitted or who arrives in the United States (whether or not at a designated port of arrival and including an alien who is brought to the United States after having been interdicted in international or United States waters) shall be deemed for purposes of this Act an applicant for admission.

(2) Stowaways. An arriving alien who is a stowaway is not eligible to apply for admission or to be admitted and shall be ordered removed upon inspection by an immigration officer. Upon such inspection if the alien indicates an intention to apply for asylum under section 208 [8 USCS § 1158] or a fear of persecution, the officer shall refer the alien for an interview under subsection (b)(1)(B). A stowaway may apply for asylum only if the stowaway is found to have a credible fear of persecution under subsection (b)(1)(B). In no case may a stowaway be considered an applicant for admission or eligible for a hearing under section 240 [8 USCS § 1229a].

(3) Inspection. All aliens (including alien crewmen) who are applicants for admission or otherwise seeking admission or readmission to or transit through the United States shall be inspected by immigration officers.

(4) Withdrawal of application for admission. An alien applying for admission may, in the discretion of the Attorney General and at any time, be permitted to withdraw the application for admission and depart immediately from the United States.

(5) Statements. An applicant for admission may be required to state under oath any information sought by an immigration officer regarding the purposes and intentions of the applicant in seeking admission to the United States, including the applicant's intended length of stay and whether the applicant intends to remain permanently or become a United States citizen, and whether the applicant is inadmissible.

(b) Inspection of applicants for admission.

(1) Inspection of aliens arriving in the United States and certain other aliens who have not been admitted or paroled.

(A) Screening.

(i) In general. If an immigration officer determines that an alien (other than an alien described in subparagraph (F)) who is arriving in the United States or is described in clause (iii) is inadmissible under section 212(a)(6)(C) or 212(a)(7) [8 USCS § 1182(a)(6)(C) or 1182(a)(7)], the officer shall order the alien removed from the United States without further hearing or review unless the alien indicates either an intention to apply for asylum under section 208 [8 USCS § 1158] or a fear of persecution.

(ii) Claims for asylum. If an immigration officer determines that an alien (other than an alien described in subparagraph (F)) who is arriving in the United States or is described in clause (iii) is inadmissible under section 212(a)(6)(C) or 212(a)(7) [8 USCS § 1182(a)(6)(C) or 1182(a)(7)] and the alien indicates either an intention to apply for asylum under section 208 [8 USCS § 1158] or a fear of persecution, the officer shall refer the alien for an interview by an asylum officer under subparagraph (B).

(iii) Application to certain other aliens.

(I) In general. The Attorney General may apply clauses (i) and (ii) of this subparagraph to any or all aliens described in subclause (II) as designated by the Attorney General. Such designation shall be in the sole and unreviewable discretion of the Attorney General and may be modified at any time.

(II) Aliens described. An alien described in this clause is an alien who is not described in subparagraph (F), who has not been admitted or paroled into the United States, and who has not affirmatively shown, to the satisfaction of an immigration officer, that the alien has been physically present in the United States continuously for the 2-year period immediately prior to the date of the determination of inadmissibility under this subparagraph.

(B) Asylum interviews.

(i) Conduct by asylum officers. An asylum officer shall conduct interviews of aliens referred under subparagraph (A)(ii), either at a port of entry or at such other place designated by the Attorney General.

(ii) Referral of certain aliens. If the officer determines at the time of the interview that an alien has a credible fear of persecution (within the meaning of clause (v)), the alien shall be detained for further consideration of the application for asylum.

(iii) Removal without further review if no credible fear of persecution.

(I) In general. Subject to subclause (III), if the officer determines that an alien does not have a credible fear of persecution, the officer shall order the alien removed from the United States without further hearing or review.

(II) Record of determination. The officer shall prepare a written record of a determination under subclause (I). Such record shall include a summary of the material facts as stated by the applicant, such additional facts (if any) relied upon by the officer, and the officer's analysis of why, in the light of such facts, the alien has not established a credible fear of persecution. A copy of the officer's interview notes shall be attached to the written summary.

(III) Review of determination. The Attorney General shall provide by regulation and upon the alien's request for prompt review by an immigration judge of a determination under subclause (I) that the alien does not have a credible fear of persecution. Such review shall include an opportunity for the alien to be heard and questioned by the immigration judge, either in person or by telephonic or video connection. Review shall be concluded as expeditiously as possible, to the maximum extent practicable within 24 hours, but in no case later than 7 days after the date of the determination under subclause (I).

(IV) Mandatory detention. Any alien subject to the procedures under this clause shall be detained pending a final determination of credible fear of persecution and, if found not to have such a fear, until removed.

(iv) Information about interviews. The Attorney General shall provide information concerning the asylum interview described in this subparagraph to aliens who may be eligible. An alien who is eligible for such interview may consult with a person or persons of the alien's choosing prior to the interview or any review thereof, according to regulations prescribed by the Attorney General. Such consultation shall be at no expense to the Government and shall not unreasonably delay the process.

(v) Credible fear of persecution defined. For purposes of this subparagraph, the term "credible fear of persecution" means that there is a significant possibility, taking into account the credibility of the statements made by the alien in support of the alien's claim and such other facts as are known to the officer, that the alien could establish eligibility for asylum under section 208 [8 USCS § 1158].

(C) Limitation on administrative review. Except as provided in subparagraph (B)(iii)(III), a removal order entered in accordance with subparagraph (A)(i) or (B)(iii)(I) is not subject to administrative appeal, except that the Attorney General shall provide by regulation for prompt review of such an order under subparagraph (A)(i) against an alien who claims under oath, or as permitted under penalty of perjury under section 1746 of title 28, United States Code, after having been warned of the penalties for falsely making such claim under such conditions, to have been lawfully admitted for permanent residence, to have been admitted as a refugee under section 207 [8 USCS § 1157], or to have been granted asylum under section 208 [8 USCS § 1158].

(D) Limit on collateral attacks. In any action brought against an alien under section 275(a) or section 276 [8 USCS § 1325(a) or 1326], the court shall not have jurisdiction to hear any claim attacking the validity of an order of removal entered under subparagraph (A)(i) or (B)(iii).

(E) Asylum officer defined. As used in this paragraph, the term "asylum officer" means an immigration officer who—

(i) has had professional training in country conditions, asylum law, and interview techniques comparable to that provided to full-time adjudicators of applications under section 208 [8 USCS § 1158], and

(ii) is supervised by an officer who meets the condition described in clause (i) and has had substantial experience adjudicating asylum applications.

(F) Exception. Subparagraph (A) shall not apply to an alien who is a native or citizen of a country in the Western Hemisphere with whose government the United States does not have full diplomatic relations and who arrives by aircraft at a port of entry.

(G) Commonwealth of the Northern Mariana Islands. Nothing in this subsection shall be construed to authorize or require any person described in section 208(e) [8 USCS § 1158(e)] to be permitted to apply for asylum under section 208 [8 USCS § 1158] at any time before January 1, 2014.

(2) Inspection of other aliens.

(A) In general. Subject to subparagraphs (B) and (C), in the case of an alien who is an applicant for admission, if the examining immigration officer determines that an alien seeking admission is not clearly and beyond a doubt entitled to be admitted, the alien shall be detained for a proceeding under section 240 [8 USCS § 1229a].

(B) Exception. Subparagraph (A) shall not apply to an alien—

(i) who is a crewman,

(ii) to whom paragraph (1) applies, or

(iii) who is a stowaway.

(C) Treatment of aliens arriving from contiguous territory. In the case of an alien described in subparagraph (A) who is arriving on land (whether or not at a designated port of arrival) from a foreign territory contiguous to the United States, the Attorney General may return the alien to that territory pending a proceeding under section 240 [8 USCS § 1229a].

(3) Enforcement by attorney general of a state. The attorney general of a State, or other authorized State officer, alleging a violation of the detention and removal requirements under paragraph (1) or (2) that harms such State or its residents shall have standing to bring an action against the Secretary of Homeland Security on behalf of such State or the residents of such State in an appropriate district court of the United States to obtain appropriate injunctive relief. The court shall advance on the docket and expedite the disposition of a civil action filed under this paragraph to the greatest extent practicable. For purposes of this paragraph, a State or its residents shall be considered to have been harmed if the State or its residents experience harm, including financial harm in excess of $100.

(4) Challenge of decision. The decision of the examining immigration officer, if favorable to the admission of any alien, shall be subject to challenge by any other immigration officer and such challenge shall operate to take the alien whose privilege to be admitted is so challenged, before an immigration judge for a proceeding under section 240 [8 USCS § 1229a].

(c) Removal of aliens inadmissible on security and related grounds.

(1) Removal without further hearing. If an immigration officer or an immigration judge suspects that an arriving alien may be inadmissible under subparagraph (A) (other than clause (ii)), (B), or (C) of section 212(a)(3) [8 USCS § 1182(a)(3)], the officer or judge shall—

(A) order the alien removed, subject to review under paragraph (2);

(B) report the order of removal to the Attorney General; and

(C) not conduct any further inquiry or hearing until ordered by the Attorney General.

(2) Review of order.

(A) The Attorney General shall review orders issued under paragraph (1).

(B) If the Attorney General—

(i) is satisfied on the basis of confidential information that the alien is inadmissible under subparagraph (A) (other than clause (ii)), (B), or (C) of section 212(a)(3) [8 USCS § 1182(a)(3)], and

(ii) after consulting with appropriate security agencies of the United States Government, concludes that disclosure of the information would be prejudicial to the public interest, safety, or security,the Attorney General may order the alien removed without further inquiry or hearing by an immigration judge.

(C) If the Attorney General does not order the removal of the alien under subparagraph (B), the Attorney General shall specify the further inquiry or hearing that shall be conducted in the case.

(3) Submission of statement and information. The alien or the alien's representative may submit a written statement and additional information for consideration by the Attorney General.

(d) Authority relating to inspections.

(1) Authority to search conveyances. Immigration officers are authorized to board and search any vessel, aircraft, railway car, or other conveyance or vehicle in which they believe aliens are being brought into the United States.

(2) Authority to order detention and delivery of arriving aliens. Immigration officers are authorized to order an owner, agent, master, commanding officer, person in charge, purser, or consignee of a vessel or aircraft bringing an alien (except an alien crewmember) to the United States—

(A) to detain the alien on the vessel or at the airport of arrival, and

(B) to deliver the alien to an immigration officer for inspection or to a medical officer for examination.

(3) Administration of oath and consideration of evidence. The Attorney General and any immigration officer shall have power to administer oaths and to take and consider evidence of or from any person touching the privilege of any alien or person he believes or suspects to be an alien to enter, reenter, transit through, or reside in the United States or concerning any matter which is material and relevant to the enforcement of this Act and the administration of the Service.

(4) Subpoena authority.

(A) The Attorney General and any immigration officer shall have power to require by subpoena the attendance and testimony of witnesses before immigration officers and the production of books, papers, and documents relating to the privilege of any person to enter, reenter, reside in, or pass through the United States or concerning any matter which is material and relevant to the enforcement of this Act and the administration of the Service, and to that end may invoke the aid of any court of the United States.

(B) Any United States district court within the jurisdiction of which investigations or inquiries are being conducted by an immigration officer may, in the event of neglect or refusal to respond to a subpoena issued under this paragraph or refusal to testify before an immigration officer, issue an order requiring such persons to appear before an immigration officer, produce books, papers, and documents if demanded, and testify, and any failure to obey such order of the court may be punished by the court as a contempt thereof.

(June 27, 1952, ch 477, Title II, Ch 4, § 235, 66 Stat. 198; Nov. 29, 1990, P. L. 101-649, Title VI, § 603(a)(11), 104 Stat. 5083; April 24, 1996, P. L. 104-132, Title IV, Subtitle C, §§ 422(a), 423(b), 110 Stat. 1270, 1272; Sept. 30, 1996, P. L. 104-208, Div C, Title III, Subtitle A, §§ 302(a), 308(d)(5), Subtitle F, § 371(b)(4), 110 Stat. 3009-579, 3009-619, 3009-645; May 8, 2008, P. L. 110-229, Title VII, Subtitle A, § 702(j)(5), 122 Stat. 867; Jan. 29, 2025, P.L. 119-1, § 3(a), 139 Stat. 3.)

§ 1225a. Preinspection at foreign airports

(a) Establishment of preinspection stations.

(1) New stations. Subject to paragraph (5), not later than October 31, 1998, the Attorney General, in consultation with the Secretary of State, shall establish and maintain preinspection stations in at least 5 of the foreign airports that are among the 10 foreign airports which the Attorney General identifies as serving as last points of departure for the greatest numbers of inadmissible alien passengers who arrive from abroad by air at ports of entry within the United States. Such preinspection stations shall be in addition to any preinspection stations established prior to the date of the enactment of such Act.

(2) Report. Not later than October 31, 1998, the Attorney General shall report to the Committees on the Judiciary of the House of Representatives and of the Senate on the implementation of paragraph (1).

(3) Data collection. Not later than November 1, 1997, and each subsequent November 1, the Attorney General shall compile data identifying—

(A) the foreign airports which served as last points of departure for aliens who arrived by air at United States ports of entry without valid documentation during the preceding fiscal years;

(B) the number and nationality of such aliens arriving from each such foreign airport; and

(C) the primary routes such aliens followed from their country of origin to the United States.

(4) Subject to paragraph (5), not later than January 1, 2008, the Secretary of Homeland Security, in consultation with the Secretary of State, shall establish preinspection stations in at least 25 additional foreign airports, which the Secretary of Homeland Security, in consultation with the Secretary of State, determines, based on the data compiled under paragraph (3) and such other information as may be available, would most effectively facilitate the travel of admissible aliens and reduce the number of inadmissible aliens, especially aliens who are potential terrorists, who arrive from abroad by air at points of entry within the United States. Such preinspection stations shall be in addition to those established before September 30, 1996, or pursuant to paragraph (1).

(5) Conditions. Prior to the establishment of a preinspection station, the Attorney General, in consultation with the Secretary of State, shall ensure that—

(A) employees of the United States stationed at the preinspection station and their accompanying family members will receive appropriate protection;

(B) such employees and their families will not be subject to unreasonable risks to their welfare and safety; and

(C) the country in which the preinspection station is to be established maintains practices and procedures with respect to asylum seekers and refugees in accordance with the Convention Relating to the Status of Refugees (done at Geneva, July 28, 1951), or the Protocol Relating to the Status of Refugees (done at New York, January 31, 1967), or that an alien in the country otherwise has recourse to avenues of protection from return to persecution.

(b) Establishment of carrier consultant program and immigration security initiative. The Secretary of Homeland Security shall assign additional immigration officers to assist air carriers in the detection of fraudulent documents at foreign airports which, based on the records maintained pursuant to subsection (a)(3), served as a point of departure for a significant number of arrivals at United States ports of entry without valid documentation, but where no preinspection station exists. Beginning not later than December 31, 2006, the number of airports selected for an assignment under this subsection shall be at least 50.

(June 27, 1952, ch 477, § 235A, as added Sept. 30, 1996, P. L. 104-208, Div C, Title I, Subtitle B, § 123(a), 110 Stat. 3009-560; Dec. 17, 2004, P. L. 108-458, Title VII, Subtitle B, §§ 7206(a), 7210(d)(1), 118 Stat. 3817, 3825.)

§ 1226. Apprehension and detention of aliens

(a) Arrest, detention, and release. On a warrant issued by the Attorney General, an alien may be arrested and detained pending a decision on whether the alien is to be removed from the United States. Except as provided in subsection (c) and pending such decision, the Attorney General—

(1) may continue to detain the arrested alien; and

(2) may release the alien on—

(A) bond of at least $1,500 with security approved by, and containing conditions prescribed by, the Attorney General; or

(B) conditional parole; but

(3) may not provide the alien with work authorization (including an "employment authorized" endorsement or other appropriate work permit), unless the alien is lawfully admitted for permanent residence or otherwise would (without regard to removal proceedings) be provided such authorization.

(b) Revocation of bond or parole. The Attorney General at any time may revoke a bond or parole authorized under subsection (a), rearrest the alien under the original warrant, and detain the alien.

(c) Detention of criminal aliens.

(1) Custody. The Attorney General shall take into custody any alien who—

(A) is inadmissible by reason of having committed any offense covered in section 212(a)(2) [8 USCS § 1182(a)(2)],

(B) is deportable by reason of having committed any offense covered in section 237(a)(2)(A)(ii), (A)(iii), (B), (C), or (D) [8 USCS § 1227(a)(2)(A)(ii), (A)(iii), (B), (C), or (D)],

(C) is deportable under section 237(a)(2)(A)(i) [8 USCS § 1227(a)(2)(A)(i)] on the basis of an offense for which the alien has been sentence [sentenced] to a term of imprisonment of at least 1 year,

(D) is inadmissible under section 212(a)(3)(B) [8 USCS § 1182(a)(3)(B)] or deportable under section 237(a)(4)(B) [8 USCS § 1227(a)(4)(B)], or

(E)(i) is inadmissible under paragraph (6)(A), (6)(C), or (7) of section 1182(a) of this title [8 USCS § 1182(a)]; and

(ii) is charged with, is arrested for, is convicted of, admits having committed, or admits committing acts which constitute the essential elements of any burglary, theft, larceny, shoplifting, or assault of a law enforcement officer offense, or any crime that results in death or serious bodily injury to another person,

when the alien is released, without regard to whether the alien is released on parole, supervised release, or probation, and without regard to whether the alien may be arrested or imprisoned again for the same offense.

(2) Definition. For purposes of paragraph (1)(E), the terms "burglary", "theft", "larceny", "shoplifting", "assault of a law enforcement officer", and "serious bodily injury" have the meanings given such terms in the jurisdiction in which the acts occurred.

(3) Detainer. The Secretary of Homeland Security shall issue a detainer for an alien described in paragraph (1)(E) and, if the alien is not otherwise detained by Federal, State, or local officials, shall effectively and expeditiously take custody of the alien.

(4) Release. The Attorney General may release an alien described in paragraph (1) only if the Attorney General decides pursuant to section 3521 of title 18, United States Code, that release of the alien from custody is necessary to provide protection to a witness, a potential witness, a person cooperating with an investigation into major criminal activity, or an immediate family member or close associate of a witness, potential witness, or person cooperating with such an investigation, and the alien satisfies the Attorney General that the alien will not pose a danger to the safety of other persons or of property and is likely to appear for any scheduled proceeding. A decision relating to such release shall take place in accordance with a procedure that considers the severity of the offense committed by the alien.

(d) Identification of criminal aliens.

(1) The Attorney General shall devise and implement a system—

(A) to make available, daily (on a 24-hour basis), to Federal, State, and local authorities the investigative resources of the Service to determine whether individuals arrested by such authorities for aggravated felonies are aliens;

(B) to designate and train officers and employees of the Service to serve as a liaison to Federal, State, and local law enforcement and correctional agencies and courts with respect to the arrest, conviction, and release of any alien charged with an aggravated felony; and

(C) which uses computer resources to maintain a current record of aliens who have been convicted of an aggravated felony, and indicates those who have been removed.

(2) The record under paragraph (1)(C) shall be made available—

(A) to inspectors at ports of entry and to border patrol agents at sector headquarters for purposes of immediate identification of any alien who was previously ordered removed and is seeking to reenter the United States, and

(B) to officials of the Department of State for use in its automated visa lookout system.

(3) Upon the request of the governor or chief executive officer of any State, the Service shall provide assistance to State courts in the identification of aliens unlawfully present in the United States pending criminal prosecution.

(e) Judicial review. The Attorney General's discretionary judgment regarding the application of this section shall not be subject to review. No court may set aside any action or decision by the Attorney General under this section regarding the detention of any alien or the revocation or denial of bond or parole.

(f) Enforcement by attorney general of a state. The attorney general of a State, or other authorized State officer, alleging an action or decision by the Attorney General or Secretary of Homeland Security under this section to release any alien or grant bond or parole to any alien that harms such State or its residents shall have standing to bring an action against the Attorney General or Secretary of Homeland Security on behalf of such State or the residents of such State in an appropriate district court of the United States to obtain appropriate injunctive relief. The court shall advance on the docket and expedite the disposition of a civil action filed under this subsection to the greatest extent practicable. For purposes of this subsection, a State or its residents shall be considered to have been harmed if the State or its residents experience harm, including financial harm in excess of $100.".

(June 27, 1952, ch 477, Title II, Ch 4, § 236, 66 Stat. 200; Nov. 29, 1990, P. L. 101-649, Title V, Subtitle A, § 504(c), Title VI, § 603(a)(12), 104 Stat. 5050, 5083; Dec. 12, 1991, P. L. 102-232, Title III, § 306(a)(5), 105 Stat. 1751; Sept. 30, 1996, P. L. 104-208, Div C, Title III, Subtitle A, § 303(a), Subtitle F, § 371(b)(5), 110 Stat. 3009-585, 3009-645; Jan. 29, 2025, P.L. 119-1, §§ 2, 3(b), 139 Stat. 3, 4.)

§ 1226a. Mandatory detention of suspected terrorists; habeas corpus; judicial review

(a) Detention of terrorist aliens.

(1) Custody. The Attorney General shall take into custody any alien who is certified under paragraph (3).

(2) Release. Except as provided in paragraphs (5) and (6), the Attorney General shall maintain custody of such an alien until the alien is removed from the United States. Except as provided in paragraph (6), such custody shall be maintained irrespective of any relief from removal for which the alien may be eligible, or any relief from removal granted the alien, until the Attorney General determines that the alien is no longer an alien who may be certified under paragraph (3). If the alien is finally determined not to be removable, detention pursuant to this subsection shall terminate.

(3) Certification. The Attorney General may certify an alien under this paragraph if the Attorney General has reasonable grounds to believe that the alien—

(A) is described in section 212(a)(3)(A)(i), 212(a)(3)(A)(iii), 212(a)(3)(B), 237(a)(4)(A)(i), 237(a)(4)(A)(iii), or 237(a)(4)(B) [8 USCS § 1182(a)(3)(A)(i), 1182(a)(3)(A)(iii), 1182(a)(3)(B), 1227(a)(4)(A)(i), 1227(a)(4)(A)(iii), or 1227(a)(4)(B)]; or

(B) is engaged in any other activity that endangers the national security of the United States.

(4) Nondelegation. The Attorney General may delegate the authority provided under paragraph (3) only to the Deputy Attorney General. The Deputy Attorney General may not delegate such authority.

(5) Commencement of proceedings. The Attorney General shall place an alien detained under paragraph (1) in removal proceedings, or shall charge the alien with a criminal offense, not later than 7 days after the commencement of such detention. If the requirement of the preceding sentence is not satisfied, the Attorney General shall release the alien.

(6) Limitation on indefinite detention. An alien detained solely under paragraph (1) who has not been removed under section 241(a)(1)(A) [8 USCS § 1231(a)(1)(A)], and whose removal is unlikely in the reasonably foreseeable future, may be detained for additional periods of up to six months only if the release of the alien will threaten the national security of the United States or the safety of the community or any person.

(7) Review of certification. The Attorney General shall review the certification made under paragraph (3) every 6 months. If the Attorney General determines, in the Attorney General's discretion, that the certification should be revoked, the alien may be released on such conditions as the Attorney General deems appropriate, unless such release is otherwise prohibited by law. The alien may request each 6 months in writing that the Attorney General reconsider the certification and may submit documents or other evidence in support of that request.

(b) Habeas corpus and judicial review.

(1) In general. Judicial review of any action or decision relating to this section (including judicial review of the merits of a determination made under subsection (a)(3) or (a)(6)) is available exclusively in habeas corpus proceedings consistent with this subsection. Except as provided in the preceding sentence, no court shall have jurisdiction to review, by habeas corpus petition or otherwise, any such action or decision.

(2) Application.

(A) In general. Notwithstanding any other provision of law, including section 2241(a) of title 28, United States Code, habeas corpus proceedings described in paragraph (1) may be initiated only by an application filed with—

(i) the Supreme Court;

(ii) any justice of the Supreme Court;

(iii) any circuit judge of the United States Court of Appeals for the District of Columbia Circuit; or

(iv) any district court otherwise having jurisdiction to entertain it.

(B) Application transfer. Section 2241(b) of title 28, United States Code, shall apply to an application for a writ of habeas corpus described in subparagraph (A).

(3) Appeals. Notwithstanding any other provision of law, including section 2253 of title 28, in habeas corpus proceedings described in paragraph (1) before a circuit or district judge, the final order shall be subject to review, on appeal, by the United States Court of Appeals for the District of Columbia Circuit. There shall be no right of appeal in such proceedings to any other circuit court of appeals.

(4) Rule of decision. The law applied by the Supreme Court and the United States Court of Appeals for the District of Columbia Circuit shall be regarded as the rule of decision in habeas corpus proceedings described in paragraph (1).

(c) Statutory construction. The provisions of this section shall not be applicable to any other provision of this Act.

(June 27, 1952, ch 477, Title II, Ch 4, § 236A, as added Oct. 26, 2001, P. L. 107-56, Title IV, Subtitle B, § 412(a), 115 Stat. 350.)

§ 1227. Deportable aliens

(a) Classes of deportable aliens. Any alien (including an alien crewman) in and admitted to the United States shall, upon the order of the Attorney General, be removed if the alien is within one or more of the following classes of deportable aliens:

(1) Inadmissible at time of entry or of adjustment of status or violates status.

(A) Inadmissible aliens. Any alien who at the time of entry or adjustment of status was within one or more of the classes of aliens inadmissible by the law existing at such time is deportable.

(B) Present in violation of law. Any alien who is present in the United States in violation of this Act or any other law of the United States, or whose nonimmigrant visa (or other documentation authorizing admission into the United States as a nonimmigrant) has been revoked under section 221(i) [8 USCS § 1201(i)], is deportable.

(C) Violated nonimmigrant status or condition of entry.

(i) Nonimmigrant status violators. Any alien who was admitted as a nonimmigrant and who has failed to maintain the nonimmigrant status in which the alien was admitted or to which it was changed under section 248 [8 USCS § 1258], or to comply with the conditions of any such status, is deportable.

(ii) Violators of conditions of entry. Any alien whom the Secretary of Health and Human Services certifies has failed to comply with terms, conditions, and controls that were imposed under section 212(g) [8 USCS § 1182(g)] is deportable.

(D) Termination of conditional permanent residence.

(i) In general. Any alien with permanent resident status on a conditional basis under section 216 [8 USCS § 1186a] (relating to conditional permanent resident status for certain alien spouses and sons and daughters) or under section 216A [8 USCS § 1186b] (relating to conditional permanent resident status for certain alien entrepreneurs, spouses, and children) who has had such status terminated under such respective section is deportable.

(ii) Exception Clause (i) shall not apply in the cases described in section 216(c)(4) [8 USCS § 1186a(c)(4)] (relating to certain hardship waivers).

(E) Smuggling.

(i) In general. Any alien who (prior to the date of entry, at the time of any entry, or within 5 years of the date of any entry) knowingly has encouraged, induced, assisted, abetted, or aided any other alien to enter or to try to enter the United States in violation of law is deportable.

(ii) Special rule in the case of family reunification. Clause (i) shall not apply in the case of alien who is an eligible immigrant (as defined in section 301(b)(1) of the Immigration Act of 1990 [8 USCS § 1255a note]), was physically present in the United States on May 5, 1988, and is seeking admission as an immediate relative or under section 203(a)(2) [8 USCS § 1153(a)(2)] (including under section 112 of the Immigration Act of 1990 [8 USCS § 1153 note]) or benefits under section 301(a) of the Immigration Act of 1990 [8 USCS § 1255a note] if the alien, before May 5, 1988, has encouraged, induced, assisted, abetted, or aided only the alien's spouse, parent, son, or daughter (and no other individual) to enter the United States in violation of law.

(iii) Waiver authorized. The Attorney General may, in his discretion for humanitarian purposes, to assure family unity, or when it is otherwise in the public interest, waive application of clause (i) in the case of any alien lawfully admitted for permanent residence if the alien has encouraged, induced, assisted, abetted, or aided only an individual who at the time of the offense was the alien's spouse, parent, son, or daughter (and no other individual) to enter the United States in violation of law.

(F) [Deleted]

(G) Marriage fraud. An alien shall be considered to be deportable as having procured a visa or other documentation by fraud (within the meaning of section 212(a)(6)(C)(i)) [8 USCS § 1182(a)(6)(C)(i)] and to be in the United States in violation of this Act (within the meaning of subparagraph (B)) if—

(i) the alien obtains any admission into the United States with an immigrant visa or other documentation procured on the basis of a marriage entered into less than 2 years prior to such admission of the alien and which, within 2 years subsequent to any admission of the alien in the United States, shall be judicially annulled or terminated, unless the alien establishes to the satisfaction of the Attorney General that such marriage was not contracted for the purpose of evading any provisions of the immigration laws, or

(ii) it appears to the satisfaction of the Attorney General that the alien has failed or refused to fulfill the alien's marital agreement which in the opinion of the Attorney General was made for the purpose of procuring the alien's admission as an immigrant.

(H) Waiver authorized for certain misrepresentations. The provisions of this paragraph relating to the removal of aliens within the United States on the ground that they were inadmissible at the time of admission as aliens described in section 212(a)(6)(C)(i) [8 USCS § 1182(i)], whether willful or innocent, may, in the discretion of the Attorney General, be waived for any alien (other than an alien described in paragraph (4)(D)) who—

(i)(I) is the spouse, parent, son, or daughter of a citizen of the United States or of an alien lawfully admitted to the United States for permanent residence; and

(II) was in possession of an immigrant visa or equivalent document and was otherwise admissible to the United States at the time of such admission except for those grounds of inadmissibility specified under paragraphs (5)(A) and (7)(A) of section 212(a) [8 USCS § 1182(a)] which were a direct result of that fraud or misrepresentation.

(ii) is a VAWA self-petitioner.

A waiver of removal for fraud or misrepresentation granted under this subparagraph shall also operate to waive removal based on the grounds of inadmissibility directly resulting from such fraud or misrepresentation.

(2) Criminal offenses.

(A) General crimes.

(i) Crimes of moral turpitude. Any alien who—

(I) is convicted of a crime involving moral turpitude committed within five years (or 10 years in the case of an alien provided lawful permanent resident status under section 245(j) [8 USCS § 1255(j)]) after the date of admission, and

(II) is convicted of a crime for which a sentence of one year or longer may be imposed,

is deportable.

(ii) Multiple criminal convictions. Any alien who at any time after admission is convicted of two or more crimes involving moral turpitude, not arising out of a single scheme of criminal misconduct, regardless of whether confined therefor and regardless of whether the convictions were in a single trial, is deportable.

(iii) Aggravated felony. Any alien who is convicted of an aggravated felony at any time after admission is deportable.

(iv) High speed flight. Any alien who is convicted of a violation of section 758 of title 18, United States Code (relating to high speed flight from an immigration checkpoint), is deportable.

(v) Failure to register as a sex offender. Any alien who is convicted under section 2250 of title 18, United States Code [18 USCS § 2250], is deportable.

(vi) Waiver authorized. Clauses (i), (ii), (iii), and (iv) shall not apply in the case of an alien with respect to a criminal conviction if the alien subsequent to the criminal conviction has been granted a full and unconditional pardon by the President of the United States or by the Governor of any of the several States.

(B) Controlled substances.

(i) Conviction. Any alien who at any time after admission has been convicted of a violation of (or a conspiracy or attempt to violate) any law or regulation of a State, the United States, or a foreign country relating to a controlled substance (as defined in section 102 of the Controlled Substances Act (21 U.S.C. 802)), other than a single offense involving possession for one's own use of 30 grams or less of marijuana, is deportable.

(ii) Drug abusers and addicts. Any alien who is, or at any time after admission has been, a drug abuser or addict is deportable.

(C) Certain firearm offenses. Any alien who at any time after admission is convicted under any law of purchasing, selling, offering for sale, exchanging, using, owning, possessing, or carrying, or of attempting or conspiring to purchase, sell, offer for sale, exchange, use, own, possess, or carry, any weapon, part, or accessory which is a firearm or destructive device (as defined in section 921(a) of title 18, United States Code) in violation of any law is deportable.

(D) Miscellaneous crimes. Any alien who at any time has been convicted (the judgment on such conviction becoming final) of, or has been so convicted of a conspiracy or attempt to violate—

(i) any offense under chapter 37 [18 USCS §§ 791 et seq.] (relating to espionage), chapter 105 [18 USCS §§ 2151 et seq.] (relating to sabotage), or chapter 115 [18 USCS §§ 2381 et seq.] (relating to treason and sedition) of title 18, United States Code, for which a term of imprisonment of five or more years may be imposed;

(ii) any offense under section 871 or 960 of title 18, United States Code;

(iii) a violation of any provision of the Military Selective Service Act (50 U.S.C. App. 451 et seq. [50 USCS §§ 3801 et seq.]) or the Trading With the Enemy Act (50 U.S.C. App. 1 et seq. [50 USCS §§ 4301 et seq.]); or

(iv) a violation of section 215 or 278 of this Act [8 USCS § 1185 or 1328], is deportable.

(E) Crimes of domestic violence, stalking, or violation of protection order, crimes against children [and].

(i) Domestic violence, stalking, and child abuse. Any alien who at any time after admission is convicted of a crime of domestic violence, a crime of stalking, or a crime of child abuse, child neglect, or child abandonment is deportable. For purposes of this clause, the term "crime of domestic violence" means any crime of violence (as defined in section 16 of title 18, United States Code) against a person committed by a current or former spouse of the person, by an individual with whom the person shares a child in common, by an individual who is cohabiting with or has cohabited with the person as a spouse, by an individual similarly situated to a spouse of the person under the domestic or family violence laws of the jurisdiction where the offense occurs, or by any other individual against a person who is protected from that individual's acts under the domestic or family violence laws of the United States or any State, Indian tribal government, or unit of local government.

(ii) Violators of protection orders. Any alien who at any time after admission is enjoined under a protection order issued by a court and whom the court determines has engaged in conduct that violates the portion of a protection order that involves protection against credible threats of violence, repeated harassment, or bodily injury to the person or persons for whom the protection order was issued is deportable. For purposes of this clause, the term "protection order" means any injunction issued for the purpose of preventing violent or threatening acts of domestic violence, including temporary or final orders issued by civil or criminal courts (other than support or child custody orders or provisions) whether obtained by filing an independent action or as a pendente lite order in another proceeding.

(F) Trafficking. Any alien described in section 212(a)(2)(H) [8 USCS § 1182(a)(2)(H)] is deportable.

(3) Failure to register and falsification of documents.

(A) Change of address. An alien who has failed to comply with the provisions of section 265 [8 USCS § 1305] is deportable, unless the alien establishes to the satisfaction of the Attorney General that such failure was reasonably excusable or was not willful.

(B) Failure to register or falsification of documents. Any alien who at any time has been convicted—

(i) under section 266(c) of this Act [8 USCS § 1306(c)] or under section 36(c) of the Alien Registration Act, 1940,

(ii) of a violation of, or an attempt or a conspiracy to violate, any provision of the Foreign Agents Registration Act of 1938 (22 U.S.C. 611 et seq.), or

(iii) of a violation of, or an attempt or a conspiracy to violate, section 1546 of title 18, United States Code (relating to fraud and misuse of visas, permits, and other entry documents),

is deportable.

(C) Document fraud.

(i) In general. An alien who is the subject of a final order for violation of section 274C [8 USCS § 1324c] is deportable.

(ii) Waiver authorized. The Attorney General may waive clause (i) in the case of an alien lawfully admitted for permanent residence if no previous civil money penalty was imposed against the alien under section 274C [8 USCS § 1324c] and the offense was incurred solely to assist, aid, or support the alien's spouse or child (and no other individual). No court shall have jurisdiction to review a decision of the Attorney General to grant or deny a waiver under this clause.

(D) Falsely claiming citizenship.

(i) In general. Any alien who falsely represents, or has falsely represented, himself to be a citizen of the United States for any purpose or benefit under this Act (including section 274A [8 USCS § 1324a]) or any Federal or State law is deportable.

(ii) Exception. In the case of an alien making a representation described in clause (i), if each natural parent of the alien (or, in the case of an adopted alien, each adoptive parent of the alien) is or was a citizen (whether by birth or naturalization), the alien permanently resided in the United States prior to attaining the age of 16, and the alien reasonably believed at the time of making such representation that he or she was a citizen, the alien shall not be considered to be deportable under any provision of this subsection based on such representation.

(4) Security and related grounds.

(A) In general. Any alien who has engaged, is engaged, or at any time after admission engages in—

(i) any activity to violate any law of the United States relating to espionage or sabotage or to violate or evade any law prohibiting the export from the United States of goods, technology, or sensitive information,

(ii) any other criminal activity which endangers public safety or national security, or

(iii) any activity a purpose of which is the opposition to, or the control or overthrow of, the Government of the United States by force, violence, or other unlawful means,

is deportable.

(B) Terrorist activities. Any alien who is described in subparagraph (B) or (F) of section 212(a)(3) [8 USCS § 1182(a)(3)] is deportable.

(C) Foreign policy.

(i) In general. An alien whose presence or activities in the United States the Secretary of State has reasonable ground to believe would have potentially serious adverse foreign policy consequences for the United States is deportable.

(ii) Exceptions. The exceptions described in clauses (ii) and (iii) of section 212(a)(3)(C) [8 USCS § 1182(a)(3)(C)] shall apply to deportability under clause (i) in the same manner as they apply to inadmissibility under section 212 (a)(3)(C)(i) [8 USCS § 1182(a)(3)(C)(i)].

(D) Participated in Nazi persecution, genocide, or the commission of any act of torture or extrajudicial killing. Any alien described in clause (i), (ii), or (iii) or section 212 (a)(3)(E) [8 USCS § 1182(a)(3)(E)] is deportable.

(E) Participated in the commission of severe violations of religious freedom. Any alien described in section 212(a)(2)(G) [8 USCS § 1182(a)(2)(G)] is deportable.

(F) Recruitment or use of child soldiers. Any alien who has engaged in the recruitment or use of child soldiers in violation of section 2442 of title 18, United States Code, is deportable.

(5) Public charge. Any alien who, within five years after the date of entry, has become a public charge from causes not affirmatively shown to have arisen since entry is deportable.

(6) Unlawful voters.

(A) In general. Any alien who has voted in violation of any Federal, State, or local constitutional provision, statute, ordinance, or regulation is deportable.

(B) Exception. In the case of an alien who voted in a Federal, State, or local election (including an initiative, recall, or referendum) in violation of a lawful restriction of voting to citizens, if each natural parent of the alien (or, in the case of an adopted alien, each adoptive parent of the alien) is or was a citizen (whether by birth or naturalization), the alien permanently resided in the United States prior to attaining the age of 16, and the alien reasonably believed at the time of such violation that he or she was a citizen, the alien shall not be considered to be deportable under any provision of this subsection based on such violation.

(7) Waiver for victims of domestic violence.

(A) In general. The Attorney General is not limited by the criminal court record and may waive the application of paragraph (2)(E)(i) (with respect to crimes of domestic violence and crimes of stalking) and (ii) in the case of an alien who has been battered or subjected to extreme cruelty and who is not and was not the primary perpetrator of violence in the relationship—

[(i)] upon a determination that—

(I) the alien was acting is [in] self-defense;

(II) the alien was found to have violated a protection order intended to protect the alien; or

(III) the alien committed, was arrested for, was convicted of, or pled guilty to committing a crime—

(aa) that did not result in serious bodily injury; and

(bb) where there was a connection between the crime and the alien's having been battered or subjected to extreme cruelty.

(B) Credible evidence considered. In acting on applications under this paragraph, the Attorney General shall consider any credible evidence relevant to the application. The determination of what evidence is credible and the weight to be given that evidence shall be within the sole discretion of the Attorney General.

(b) Deportation of certain nonimmigrants. An alien, admitted as a nonimmigrant under the provisions of either section 101(a)(15)(A)(i) or 101(a)(15)(G)(i) [8 USCS § 1101(a)(15)(A)(i) or (a)(15)(G)(i)], and who fails to maintain a status under either of those provisions, shall not be required to depart from the United States without the approval of the Secretary of State, unless such alien is subject to deportation under paragraph (4) of subsection (a).

(c) Waiver of grounds for deportation. Paragraphs (1)(A), (1)(B), (1)(C), (1)(D), and (3)(A) of subsection (a) (other than so much of paragraph (1) as relates to a ground of inadmissibility described in paragraph (2) or (3) of section 212 (a) [8 USCS § 1182(a)(2) or (3)] shall not apply to a special immigrant described in section 101(a)(27)(J) [8 USCS § 1101(a)(27)(J)] based upon circumstances that existed before the date the alien was provided such special immigrant status.

(d) Administrative stay.

(1) If the Secretary of Homeland Security determines that an application for nonimmigrant status under subparagraph (T) or (U) of section 101(a)(15) [8 USCS § 1101(a)(15)] filed for an alien in the United States sets forth a prima facie case for approval, the Secretary may grant the alien an administrative stay of a final order of removal under section 241(c)(2) [8 USCS § 1231(c)(2)] until—

(A) the application for nonimmigrant status under such subparagraph (T) or (U) is approved; or

(B) there is a final administrative denial of the application for such nonimmigrant status after the exhaustion of administrative appeals.

(2) The denial of a request for an administrative stay of removal under this subsection shall not preclude the alien from applying for a stay of removal, deferred action, or a continuance or abeyance of removal proceedings under any other provision of the immigration laws of the United States.

(3) During any period in which the administrative stay of removal is in effect, the alien shall not be removed.

(4) Nothing in this subsection may be construed to limit the authority of the Secretary of Homeland Security or the Attorney General to grant a stay of removal or deportation in any case not described in this subsection.

(June 27, 1952, ch 477, Title II, Ch 5, § 237 [241], 66 Stat. 204; July 18, 1956, ch 629, Title III, § 301(b), (c), 70 Stat. 575; July 14, 1960, P. L. 86-648, § 9, 74 Stat. 505; Sept. 26, 1961, P. L. 87-301, § 16, 75 Stat. 655; Oct. 3, 1965, P. L. 89-236, § 11(e), 79 Stat. 918; Oct. 20, 1976, P. L. 94-571, § 7(e), 90 Stat. 2706; Oct. 30, 1978, P. L. 95-549, Title I, § 103, 92 Stat. 2065; Dec. 29, 1981, P. L. 97-116, § 8, 95 Stat. 1616; Oct. 27, 1986, P. L. 99-570, Title I, Subtitle M, § 1751(b), 100 Stat. 3207-47; Nov. 6, 1986, P. L. 99-603, Title III, Part A, § 303(b), 100 Stat. 3431; Nov. 10, 1986, P. L. 99-639, § 2(b), 100 Stat. 3541; Nov. 14, 1986, P. L. 99-653, § 7(c) in part, 100 Stat. 3657; Oct. 24, 1988, P. L. 100-525, §§ 2(n)(2), 9(m), 102 Stat. 2613, 2620; Nov. 18, 1988, P. L. 100-690, Title VII, Subtitle J, §§ 7344(a)(2), 7348(a), 102 Stat. 4471, 4473; Nov. 29, 1990, P. L. 101-649, Title I, Subtitle D, § 153 (b) Title V, Subtitle A, §§ 505(a), 508(a), Subtitle D, § 544(b), Title V, § 602(a), (b), 104 Stat. 5006, 5050, 5051, 5061, 5077, 5081; Dec. 12, 1991, P. L. 102-232, Title III, §§ 302(d)(3), 307(h), (k), 105 Stat. 1745, 1755, 1756; Sept. 13, 1994, P. L. 103-322, Title XIII, § 130003(d), 108 Stat. 2026; Oct. 25, 1994, P. L. 103-416, Title II, §§ 203(b), 219(g), 108 Stat. 4311, 4317; April 24, 1996, P. L. 104-132, Title IV, Subtitle B, § 414(a), Subtitle C, § 435(a), 110 Stat. 1270, 1275; Sept. 30, 1996, P. L. 104-208, Div C, Title I, Subtitle A, § 108(c), Title III, Subtitle A, §§ 301(d), 305(a)(2), 308(d)(2), (3)(A), (e)(1)(E), (2)(C), (f)(1)(L)–(N), (5), Subtitle C, §§ 344(b), 345(b), 347(b), 350(a), 351(b), Title VI, Subtitle E, § 671(a)(4)(B), (d)(1)(C), 110 Stat. 3009-558, 3009-579, 3009-598, 3009-617, 3009-619, 3009-620, 3009-621, 3009-637, 3009-638, 309-639, 3009-640, 3009-721, 3009-723; Oct. 28, 2000, P. L. 106-386, Div B, Title V, § 1505(b)(1), (c)(2), 114 Stat. 1525, 1526; Oct. 30, 2000, P. L. 106-395, Title II, § 201(c)(1), (2), 114 Stat. 1634; Oct. 26, 2001, P. L. 107-56, Title IV, Subtitle B, § 411(b)(1), 115 Stat. 348; Dec. 17, 2004, P. L. 108-458, Title V, Subtitle C, § 5304(b), Subtitle D, § 5402, Subtitle E, §§ 5501(b), 5502(b), 118 Stat. 3736, 3737, 3740, 3741; May 11, 2005, P. L. 109-13, Div B, Title I, § 105(a)(1), (b), 119 Stat. 309, 310; July 27, 2006, P. L. 109-248, Title IV, § 401, 120 Stat. 622; Aug. 12, 2006, P. L. 109-271, § 6(c), 120 Stat. 763; Oct. 3, 2008, P. L. 110-340, § 2(c), 122 Stat. 3736; Dec. 23, 2008, P. L. 110-457, Title II, Subtitle A, § 204, Subtitle C, § 222(f)(2), 122 Stat. 5060, 5071.)

§ 1228. Expedited removal of aliens convicted of committing aggravated felonies

(a) Removal of criminal aliens.

(1) In general. The Attorney General shall provide for the availability of special removal proceedings at certain Federal, State, and local correctional facilities for aliens convicted of any criminal offense covered in section 241 [237] (a)(2)(A)(iii), (B), (C), or (D) [8 USCS § 1227(a)(2)(iii), (B), (C), or (D)], or any offense covered by section 237(a)(2)(A)(ii) [8 USCS § 1227(a)(2)(A)(ii)] for which both predicate offenses are, without regard to the date of their commission, otherwise covered by section 237(a)(2)(A)(i) [8 USCS § 1227(a)(2)(A)(i)]. Such proceedings shall be conducted in conformity with section 240 [8 USCS § 1229a] (except as otherwise provided in this section), and in a manner which eliminates the need for additional detention at any processing center of the Service and in a manner which assures expeditious removal following the end of the alien's incarceration for the underlying sentence. Nothing in this section shall be construed to create any substantive or procedural right or benefit that is legally enforceable by any party against the United States or its agencies or officers or any other person.

(2) Implementation. With respect to an alien convicted of an aggravated felony who is taken into custody by the Attorney General pursuant to section 236(c) [8 USCS § 1226(c)], the Attorney General shall, to the maximum extent practicable, detain any such felon at a facility at which other such aliens are detained. In the selection of such facility, the Attorney General shall make reasonable efforts to ensure that the alien's access to counsel and right to counsel under section 292 [8 USCS § 1362] are not impaired.

(3) Expedited proceedings.

(A) Notwithstanding any other provision of law, the Attorney General shall provide for the initiation and, to the extent possible, the completion of removal proceedings, and any administrative appeals thereof, in the case of any alien convicted of an aggravated felony before the alien's release from incarceration for the underlying aggravated felony.

(B) Nothing in this section shall be construed as requiring the Attorney General to effect the removal of any alien sentenced to actual incarceration, before release from the penitentiary or correctional institution where such alien is confined.

(4) Review.

(A) The Attorney General shall review and evaluate removal proceedings conducted under this section.

(B) The Comptroller General shall monitor, review, and evaluate removal proceedings conducted under this section. Within 18 months after the effective date of this section, the Comptroller General shall submit a report to such Committees concerning the extent to which removal proceedings conducted under this section may adversely affect the ability of such aliens to contest removal effectively.

(b) Removal of aliens who are not permanent residents.

(1) The Attorney General may, in the case of an alien described in paragraph (2), determine the deportability of such alien under section 237(a)(2)(A)(iii) [8 USCS § 1227(a)(2)(A)(iii)] (relating to conviction of an aggravated felony) and issue an order of removal pursuant to the procedures set forth in this subsection or section 240 [8 USCS § 1229a].

(2) An alien is described in this paragraph if the alien—

(A) was not lawfully admitted for permanent residence at the time at which proceedings under this section commenced; or

(B) had permanent resident status on a conditional basis (as described in section 216 [8 USCS § 1186a]) at the time that proceedings under this section commenced.

(3) The Attorney General may not execute any order described in paragraph (1) until 14 calendar days have passed from the date that such order was issued, unless waived by the alien, in order that the alien has an opportunity to apply for judicial review under section 242 [8 USCS § 1252].

(4) Proceedings before the Attorney General under this subsection shall be in accordance with such regulations as the Attorney General shall prescribe. The Attorney General shall provide that—

(A) the alien is given reasonable notice of the charges and of the opportunity described in subparagraph (C);

(B) the alien shall have the privilege of being represented (at no expense to the government) by such counsel, authorized to practice in such proceedings, as the alien shall choose;

(C) the alien has a reasonable opportunity to inspect the evidence and rebut the charges;

(D) a determination is made for the record that the individual upon whom the notice for the proceeding under this section is served (either in person or by mail) is, in fact, the alien named in such notice;

(E) a record is maintained for judicial review; and

(F) the final order of removal is not adjudicated by the same person who issues the charges.

(5) No alien described in this section shall be eligible for any relief from removal that the Attorney General may grant in the Attorney General's discretion.

(c) Presumption of deportability. An alien convicted of an aggravated felony shall be conclusively presumed to be deportable from the United States.

[(d)](c) Judicial removal.

(1) Authority. Notwithstanding any other provision of this Act, a United States district court shall have jurisdiction to enter a judicial order of removal at the time of sentencing against an alien who is deportable, if such an order has been requested by the United States Attorney with the concurrence of the Commissioner and if the court chooses to exercise such jurisdiction.

(2) Procedure.

(A) The United States Attorney shall file with the United States district court, and serve upon the defendant and the Service, prior to commencement of the trial or entry of a guilty plea a notice of intent to request judicial removal.

(B) Notwithstanding section 242B, the United States Attorney, with the concurrence of the Commissioner, shall file at least 30 days prior to the date set for sentencing a charge containing factual allegations regarding the alienage of the defendant and identifying the crime or crimes which make the defendant deportable under section 241 [237] (a)(2)(A) [8 USCS § 1227(a)(2)(A)].

(C) If the court determines that the defendant has presented substantial evidence to establish prima facie eligibility for relief from removal under this Act, the Commissioner shall provide the court with a recommendation and report regarding the alien's eligibility for relief. The court shall either grant or deny the relief sought.

(D)(i) The alien shall have a reasonable opportunity to examine the evidence against him or her, to present evidence on his or her own behalf, and to cross-examine witnesses presented by the Government.

(ii) The court, for the purposes of determining whether to enter an order described in paragraph (1), shall only consider evidence that would be admissible in proceedings conducted pursuant to section 240 [8 USCS § 1229a].

(iii) Nothing in this subsection shall limit the information a court of the United States may receive or consider for the purposes of imposing an appropriate sentence.

(iv) The court may order the alien removed if the Attorney General demonstrates that the alien is deportable under this Act.

(3) Notice, appeal, and execution of judicial order of removal.

(A)(i) A judicial order of removal or denial of such order may be appealed by either party to the court of appeals for the circuit in which the district court is located.

(ii) Except as provided in clause (iii), such appeal shall be considered consistent with the requirements described in section 242 [8 USCS § 1252].

(iii) Upon execution by the defendant of a valid waiver of the right to appeal the conviction on which the order of removal is based, the expiration of the period described in section 242(b)(1) [8 USCS § 1252(b)(1)], or the final dismissal of an appeal from such conviction, the order of removal shall become final and shall be executed at the end of the prison term in accordance with the terms of the order. If the conviction is reversed on direct appeal, the order entered pursuant to this section shall be void.

(B) As soon as is practicable after entry of a judicial order of removal, the Commissioner shall provide the defendant with written notice of the order of removal, which shall designate the defendant's country of choice for removal and any alternate country pursuant to section 243(a).

(4) Denial of judicial order. Denial of a request for a judicial order of removal shall not preclude the Attorney General from initiating removal proceedings pursuant to section 240 [8 USCS § 1229a] upon the same ground of deportability or upon any other ground of deportability provided under section 241 [237] (a) [8 USCS § 1227(a)].

(5) Stipulated judicial order of removal. The United States Attorney, with the concurrence of the Commissioner, may, pursuant to Federal Rule of Criminal Procedure 11 [USCS, Court Rules, FRCrP 11], enter into a plea agreement which calls for the alien, who is deportable under this Act, to waive the right to notice and a hearing under this section, and stipulate to the entry of a judicial order of removal from the United States as a condition of the plea agreement or as a

condition of probation or supervised release, or both. The United States district court, in both felony and misdemeanor cases, and a United States magistrate judge in misdemeanor cases, may accept such a stipulation and shall have jurisdiction to enter a judicial order of removal pursuant to the terms of such stipulation.

(June 27, 1952, ch 477, Title II, Ch 5, § 238 [242A], as added Nov. 18, 1988, P. L. 100-690, Title VII, Subtitle J, § 7347(a), 102 Stat. 4471; Nov. 29, 1990, P. L. 101-649, Title V, Subtitle A, § 506(a), 104 Stat. 5050; Dec. 12, 1991, P. L. 102-232, Title III, § 309(b)(10), 105 Stat. 1759; Sept. 13, 1994, P. L. 103-322, Title XIII, § 130004(a), (c), 108 Stat. 2026, 2027; Oct. 25, 1994, P. L. 103-416, Title II, §§ 223(a), 224(a), 108 Stat. 4322; April 24, 1996, P. L. 104-132, Title IV, Subtitle D, §§ 440(g), 442(a), (c), 110 Stat. 1278, 1279, 1280; Sept. 30, 1996, P. L. 104-208, Div C, Title III, Subtitle A, §§ 304(c)(1), 306(d), 308(b)(5), (c)(1), (4)(A), (e)(1)(F), (2)(D), (10), (g)(2)(A), (C), (5)(A)(ii), (C), (D), (10)(H), Subtitle F, § 374(a), Title VI, Subtitle E, § 671(b)(13), (c)(5), (6), 110 Stat. 3009-597, 3009-612, 3009-615, 3009-616, 3009-619, 3009-620, 3009-622, 3009-623, 3009-625, 3009-647, 3009-722, 3009-723.)

§ 1229. Initiation of removal proceedings

(a) Notice to appear.

(1) In general. In removal proceedings under section 240 [8 USCS § 1229a], written notice (in this section referred to as a "notice to appear") shall be given in person to the alien (or, if personal service is not practicable, through service by mail to the alien or to the alien's counsel of record, if any) specifying the following:

USCS—T.8 § 1229

(A) The nature of the proceedings against the alien.

(B) The legal authority under which the proceedings are conducted.

(C) The acts or conduct alleged to be in violation of law.

(D) The charges against the alien and the statutory provisions alleged to have been violated.

(E) The alien may be represented by counsel and the alien will be provided (i) a period of time to secure counsel under subsection (b)(1) and (ii) a current list of counsel prepared under subsection (b)(2).

(F)(i) The requirement that the alien must immediately provide (or have provided) the Attorney General with a written record of an address and telephone number (if any) at which the alien may be contacted respecting proceedings under section 240 [8 USCS § 1229a].

(ii) The requirement that the alien must provide the Attorney General immediately with a written record of any change of the alien's address or telephone number.

(iii) The consequences under section 240(b)(5) [8 USCS § 1229a(b)(5)] of failure to provide address and telephone information pursuant to this subparagraph.

(G)(i) The time and place at which the proceedings will be held.

(ii) The consequences under section 240(b)(5) [8 USCS § 1229a(b)(5)] of the failure, except under exceptional circumstances, to appear at such proceedings.

(2) Notice of change in time or place of proceedings.

(A) In general. In removal proceedings under section 240 [8 USCS § 1229a], in the case of any change or postponement in the time and place of such proceedings, subject to subparagraph (B) a written notice shall be given in person to the alien (or, if personal service is not practicable, through service by mail to the alien or to the alien's counsel of record, if any) specifying—

(i) the new time or place of the proceedings, and

(ii) the consequences under section 240(b)(5) [8 USCS § 1229a(b)(5)] of failing, except under exceptional circumstances, to attend such proceedings.

(B) Exception. In the case of an alien not in detention, a written notice shall not be required under this paragraph if the alien has failed to provide the address required under paragraph (1)(F).

(3) Central address files. The Attorney General shall create a system to record and preserve on a timely basis notices of addresses and telephone numbers (and changes) provided under paragraph (1)(F).

(b) Securing of counsel.

(1) In general. In order that an alien be permitted the opportunity to secure counsel before the first hearing date in proceedings under section 240 [8 USCS § 1229a], the hearing date shall not be scheduled earlier than 10 days after the service of the notice to appear, unless the alien requests in writing an earlier hearing date.

(2) Current lists of counsel. The Attorney General shall provide for lists (updated not less often than quarterly) of persons who have indicated their availability to represent pro bono aliens in proceedings under section 240 [8 USCS § 1229a]. Such lists shall be provided under subsection (a)(1)(E) and otherwise made generally available.

(3) Rule of construction. Nothing in this subsection may be construed to prevent the Attorney General from proceeding against an alien pursuant to section 240 [8 USCS § 1229a] if the time period described in paragraph (1) has elapsed and the alien has failed to secure counsel.

(c) Service by mail. Service by mail under this section shall be sufficient if there is proof of attempted delivery to the last address provided by the alien in accordance with subsection (a)(1)(F).

(d) Prompt initiation of removal.

(1) In the case of an alien who is convicted of an offense which makes the alien deportable, the Attorney General shall begin any removal proceeding as expeditiously as possible after the date of the conviction.

(2) Nothing in this subsection shall be construed to create any substantive or procedural right or benefit that is legally enforceable by any party against the United States or its agencies or officers or any other person.

(e) Certification of compliance with restrictions on disclosure.

(1) In general. In cases where an enforcement action leading to a removal proceeding was taken against an alien at any of the locations specified in paragraph (2), the Notice to Appear shall include a statement that the provisions of section 384 of the Illegal Immigration Reform and Immigrant Responsibility Act of 1996 (8 U.S.C. 1367) have been complied with.

(2) Locations. The locations specified in this paragraph are as follows:

(A) At a domestic violence shelter, a rape crisis center, supervised visitation center, family justice center, a victim services, or victim services provider, or a community-based organization.

(B) At a courthouse (or in connection with that appearance of the alien at a courthouse) if the alien is appearing in connection with a protection order case, child custody case, or other civil or criminal case relating to domestic violence, sexual assault, trafficking, or stalking in which the alien has been battered or subject to extreme cruelty or if the alien is described in subparagraph (T) or (U) of section 101(a)(15) [8 USCS § 1101(a)(15)].

(June 27, 1952, ch 477, Title II, Ch 4, § 239, as added Sept. 30, 1996, P. L. 104-208, Div C, Title III, Subtitle A, § 304(a)(3), 110 Stat. 3009-587; Jan. 5, 2006, P. L. 109-162, Title VIII, Subtitle C, § 825(c)(1), 119 Stat. 3065; Aug. 12, 2006, P. L. 109-271, § 6(d), 120 Stat. 763.)

§ 1229a. Removal proceedings

(a) Proceeding.

(1) In general. An immigration judge shall conduct proceedings for deciding the inadmissibility or deportability of an alien.

(2) Charges. An alien placed in proceedings under this section may be charged with any applicable ground of inadmissibility under section 212(a) [8 USCS § 1182(a)] or any applicable ground of deportability under section 237(a) [8 USCS § 1227(a)].

(3) Exclusive procedures. Unless otherwise specified in this Act, a proceeding under this section shall be the sole and exclusive procedure for determining whether an alien may be admitted to the United States or, if the alien has been so admitted, removed from the United States. Nothing in this section shall affect proceedings conducted pursuant to section 238 [8 USCS § 1228].

(b) Conduct of proceeding.

(1) Authority of immigration judge. The immigration judge shall administer oaths, receive evidence, and interrogate, examine, and cross-examine the alien and any witnesses. The immigration judge may issue subpoenas for the attendance of witnesses and presentation of evidence. The immigration judge shall have authority (under regulations prescribed by the Attorney General) to sanction by civil money penalty any action (or inaction) in contempt of the judge's proper exercise of authority under this Act.

(2) Form of proceeding.

(A) In general. The proceeding may take place—

(i) in person,

(ii) where agreed to by the parties, in the absence of the alien,

(iii) through video conference, or

(iv) subject to subparagraph (B), through telephone conference.

(B) Consent required in certain cases. An evidentiary hearing on the merits may only be conducted through a telephone conference with the consent of the alien involved after the alien has been advised of the right to proceed in person or through video conference.

(3) Presence of alien. If it is impracticable by reason of an alien's mental incompetency for the alien to be present at the proceeding, the Attorney General shall prescribe safeguards to protect the rights and privileges of the alien.

(4) Aliens rights in proceeding. In proceedings under this section, under regulations of the Attorney General—

(A) the alien shall have the privilege of being represented, at no expense to the Government, by counsel of the alien's choosing who is authorized to practice in such proceedings,

(B) the alien shall have a reasonable opportunity to examine the evidence against the alien, to present evidence on the alien's own behalf, and to cross-examine witnesses presented by the Government but these rights shall not entitle the alien to examine such national security information as the Government may proffer in opposition to the alien's admission to the United States or to an application by the alien for discretionary relief under this Act, and

(C) a complete record shall be kept of all testimony and evidence produced at the proceeding.

(5) Consequences of failure to appear.

(A) In general. Any alien who, after written notice required under paragraph (1) or (2) of section 239(a) [8 USCS § 1229(a)] has been provided to the alien or the alien's counsel of record, does not attend a proceeding under this section, shall be ordered removed in absentia if the Service establishes by clear, unequivocal, and convincing evidence that the written notice was so provided and that the alien is removable (as defined in subsection (e)(2)). The written notice by the Attorney General shall be considered sufficient for purposes of this subparagraph if provided at the most recent address provided under section 239(a)(1)(F) [8 USCS § 1229(a)(1)(F)].

(B) No notice if failure to provide address information. No written notice shall be required under subparagraph (A) if the alien has failed to provide the address required under section 239(a)(1)(F) [8 USCS § 1229(a)(1)(F)].

(C) Rescission of order. Such an order may be rescinded only—

(i) upon a motion to reopen filed within 180 days after the date of the order of removal if the alien demonstrates that the failure to appear was because of exceptional circumstances (as defined in subsection (e)(1)), or

(ii) upon a motion to reopen filed at any time if the alien demonstrates that the alien did not receive notice in accordance with paragraph (1) or (2) of section 239(a) [8 USCS § 1229(a)] or the alien demonstrates that the alien was in Federal or State custody and the failure to appear was through no fault of the alien.

The filing of the motion to reopen described in clause (i) or (ii) shall stay the removal of the alien pending disposition of the motion by the immigration judge.

(D) Effect on judicial review. Any petition for review under section 242 [8 USCS § 1252] of an order entered in absentia under this paragraph shall (except in cases described in section 242(b)(5) [8 USCS § 1252(b)(5)]) be confined to (i) the validity of the notice provided to the alien, (ii) the reasons for the alien's not attending the proceeding, and (iii) whether or not the alien is removable.

(E) Additional application to certain aliens in contiguous territory. The preceding provisions of this paragraph shall apply to all aliens placed in proceedings under this section, including any alien who remains in a contiguous foreign territory pursuant to section 235(b)(2)(C) [8 USCS § 1225(b)(2)(C)].

(6) Treatment of frivolous behavior. The Attorney General shall, by regulation—

(A) define in a proceeding before an immigration judge or before an appellate administrative body under this title, frivolous behavior for which attorneys may be sanctioned,

(B) specify the circumstances under which an administrative appeal of a decision or ruling will be considered frivolous and will be summarily dismissed, and

(C) impose appropriate sanctions (which may include suspension and disbarment) in the case of frivolous behavior.

Nothing in this paragraph shall be construed as limiting the authority of the Attorney General to take actions with respect to inappropriate behavior.

(7) Limitation on discretionary relief for failure to appear. Any alien against whom a final order of removal is entered in absentia under this subsection and who, at the time of the notice described in paragraph (1) or (2) of section 239(a) [8 USCS § 1229(a)], was provided oral notice, either in the alien's native language or in another language the alien understands, of the time and place of the proceedings and of the consequences under this paragraph of failing, other than because of exceptional circumstances (as defined in subsection (e)(1)) to attend a proceeding under this section, shall not be eligible for relief under section 240A, 240B, 245, 248, or 249 [8 USCS § 1229b, 1229c, 1255, 1258, or 1259] for a period of 10 years after the date of the entry of the final order of removal.

(c) Decision and burden of proof.

(1) Decision.

(A) In general. At the conclusion of the proceeding the immigration judge shall decide whether an alien is removable from the United States. The determination of the immigration judge shall be based only on the evidence produced at the hearing.

(B) Certain medical decisions. If a medical officer or civil surgeon or board of medical officers has certified under section 232(b) [8 USCS § 1222(b)] that an alien has a disease, illness, or addiction which would make the alien inadmissible under paragraph (1) of section 212(a) [8 USCS § 1182(a)], the decision of the immigration judge shall be based solely upon such certification.

(2) Burden on alien. In the proceeding the alien has the burden of establishing—

(A) if the alien is an applicant for admission, that the alien is clearly and beyond doubt entitled to be admitted and is not inadmissible under section 212 [8 USCS § 1182]; or

(B) by clear and convincing evidence, that the alien is lawfully present in the United States pursuant to a prior admission.

In meeting the burden of proof under subparagraph (B), the alien shall have access to the alien's visa or other entry document, if any, and any other records and documents, not considered by the Attorney General to be confidential, pertaining to the alien's admission or presence in the United States.

(3) Burden on service in cases of deportable aliens.

(A) In general. In the proceeding the Service has the burden of establishing by clear and convincing evidence that, in the case of an alien who has been admitted to the United States, the alien is deportable. No decision on deportability shall be valid unless it is based upon reasonable, substantial, and probative evidence.

(B) Proof of convictions. In any proceeding under this Act, any of the following documents or records (or a certified copy of such an official document or record) shall constitute proof of a criminal conviction:

(i) An official record of judgment and conviction.

(ii) An official record of plea, verdict, and sentence.

(iii) A docket entry from court records that indicates the existence of the conviction.

(iv) Official minutes of a court proceeding or a transcript of a court hearing in which the court takes notice of the existence of the conviction.

(v) An abstract of a record of conviction prepared by the court in which the conviction was entered, or by a State official associated with the State's repository of criminal justice records, that indicates the charge or section of law violated, the disposition of the case, the existence and date of conviction, and the sentence.

(vi) Any document or record prepared by, or under the direction of, the court in which the conviction was entered that indicates the existence of a conviction.

(vii) Any document or record attesting to the conviction that is maintained by an official of a State or Federal penal institution, which is the basis for that institution's authority to assume custody of the individual named in the record.

(C) Electronic records. In any proceeding under this Act, any record of conviction or abstract that has been submitted by electronic means to the Service from a State or court shall be admissible as evidence to prove a criminal conviction if it is—

(i) certified by a State official associated with the State's repository of criminal justice records as an official record from its repository or by a court official from the court in which the conviction was entered as an official record from its repository, and

(ii) certified in writing by a Service official as having been received electronically from the State's record repository or the court's record repository.

A certification under clause (i) may be by means of a computer-generated signature and statement of authenticity.

(4) Applications for relief from removal.

(A) In general. An alien applying for relief or protection from removal has the burden of proof to establish that the alien—

(i) satisfies the applicable eligibility requirements; and

(ii) with respect to any form of relief that is granted in the exercise of discretion, that the alien merits a favorable exercise of discretion.

(B) Sustaining burden. The applicant must comply with the applicable requirements to submit information or documentation in support of the applicant's application for relief or protection as provided by law or by regulation or in the instructions for the application form. In evaluating the testimony of the applicant or other witness in support of the application, the immigration judge will determine whether or not the testimony is credible, is persuasive, and refers to specific facts sufficient to demonstrate that the applicant has satisfied the applicant's burden of proof. In determining whether the applicant has met such burden, the immigration judge shall weigh the credible testimony along with other evidence of record. Where the immigration judge determines that the applicant should provide evidence which corroborates otherwise credible testimony, such evidence must be provided unless the applicant demonstrates that the applicant does not have the evidence and cannot reasonably obtain the evidence.

(C) Credibility determination. Considering the totality of the circumstances, and all relevant factors, the immigration judge may base a credibility determination on the demeanor, candor, or responsiveness of the applicant or witness, the inherent plausibility of the applicant's or witness's account, the consistency between the applicant's or witness's written and oral statements (whenever made and whether or not under oath, and considering the circumstances under which the statements were made), the internal consistency of each such statement, the consistency of such statements with other evidence of record (including the reports of the Department of State on country conditions), and any inaccuracies or falsehoods in such statements, without regard to whether an inconsistency, inaccuracy, or falsehood goes to the heart of the applicant's claim, or any other relevant factor. There is no presumption of credibility, however, if no adverse credibility determination is explicitly made, the applicant or witness shall have a rebuttable presumption of credibility on appeal.

(5) Notice. If the immigration judge decides that the alien is removable and orders the alien to be removed, the judge shall inform the alien of the right to appeal that decision and of the consequences for failure to depart under the order of removal, including civil and criminal penalties.

(6) Motions to reconsider.

(A) In general. The alien may file one motion to reconsider a decision that the alien is removable from the United States.

(B) Deadline. The motion must be filed within 30 days of the date of entry of a final administrative order of removal.

(C) Contents. The motion shall specify the errors of law or fact in the previous order and shall be supported by pertinent authority.

(7) Motions to reopen.

(A) In general. An alien may file one motion to reopen proceedings under this section, except that this limitation shall not apply so as to prevent the filing of one motion to reopen described in subparagraph (C)(iv).

(B) Contents. The motion to reopen shall state the new facts that will be proven at a hearing to be held if the motion is granted, and shall be supported by affidavits or other evidentiary material.

(C) Deadline.

(i) In general. Except as provided in this subparagraph, the motion to reopen shall be filed within 90 days of the date of entry of a final administrative order of removal.

(ii) Asylum. There is no time limit on the filing of a motion to reopen if the basis of the motion is to apply for relief under sections [section] 208 or 241(b)(3) [8 USCS § 1158 or 1251(b)(3)] and is based on changed country conditions arising in the country of nationality or the country to which removal has been ordered, if such evidence is material and was not available and would not have been discovered or presented at the previous proceeding.

(iii) Failure to appear. The filing of a motion to reopen an order entered pursuant to subsection (b)(5) is subject to the deadline specified in subparagraph (C) of such subsection.

(iv) Special rule for battered spouses, children, and parents. Any limitation under this section on the deadlines for filing such motions shall not apply—

(I) if the basis for the motion is to apply for relief under clause (iii) or (iv) of section 204(a)(1)(A) [8 USCS § 1154(a)(1)(A)], clause (ii) or (iii) of section 204(a)(1)(B) [8 USCS § 1154(a)(1)(B)],[,] section 240A(b) [8 USCS § 1229b(b)], or section 244(a)(3) (as in effect on March 31, 1997) [former 8 USCS § 1254(a)(3)];

(II) if the motion is accompanied by a cancellation of removal application to be filed with the Attorney General or by a copy of the self-petition that has been or will be filed with the Immigration and Naturalization Service upon the granting of the motion to reopen;

(III) if the motion to reopen is filed within 1 year of the entry of the final order of removal, except that the Attorney General may, in the Attorney General's discretion, waive this time limitation in the case of an alien who demonstrates extraordinary circumstances or extreme hardship to the alien's child; and

(IV) if the alien is physically present in the United States at the time of filing the motion.

The filing of a motion to reopen under this clause shall only stay the removal of a qualified alien (as defined in section 431(c)(1)(B) of the Personal Responsibility and Work Opportunity Reconciliation Act of 1996 (8 U.S.C. 1641(c)(1)(B))[)] pending the final disposition of the motion, including exhaustion of all appeals if the motion establishes that the alien is a qualified alien.

(d) Stipulated removal. The Attorney General shall provide by regulation for the entry by an immigration judge of an order of removal stipulated to by the alien (or the alien's representative) and the Service. A stipulated order shall constitute a conclusive determination of the alien's removability from the United States.

(e) Definitions. In this section and section 240A [8 USCS § 1229b]:

(1) Exceptional circumstances. The term "exceptional circumstances"' refers to exceptional circum-

stances (such as battery or extreme cruelty to the alien or any child or parent of the alien, serious illness of the alien, or serious illness or death of the spouse, child, or parent of the alien, but not including less compelling circumstances) beyond the control of the alien.

(2) Removable. The term "removable" means—

(A) in the case of an alien not admitted to the United States, that the alien is inadmissible under section 212 [8 USCS § 1182], or

(B) in the case of an alien admitted to the United States, that the alien is deportable under section 237 [8 USCS § 1227].

(June 27, 1952, ch 477, Title II, Ch 4, § 240, as added Sept. 30, 1996, P. L. 104-208, Div C, Title III, Subtitle A, § 304(a)(3), 110 Stat. 3009-589; Oct. 28, 2000, P. L. 106-386, Div B, Title V, § 1506(c)(1)(A), 114 Stat. 1528; May 11, 2005, P. L. 109-13, Div B, Title I, § 101(d), 119 Stat. 304; Jan. 5, 2006, P. L. 109-162, Title VIII, Subtitle B, § 813(a)(1), Subtitle C, § 825(a), 119 Stat. 3057, 3063.)

§ 1229b. Cancellation of removal; adjustment of status

(a) Cancellation of removal for certain permanent residents. The Attorney General may cancel removal in the case of an alien who is inadmissible or deportable from the United States if the alien—

(1) has been an alien lawfully admitted for permanent residence for not less than 5 years,

(2) has resided in the United States continuously for 7 years after having been admitted in any status, and

(3) has not been convicted of any aggravated felony.

(b) Cancellation of removal and adjustment of status for certain nonpermanent residents.

(1) In general. The Attorney General may cancel removal of, and adjust to the status of an alien lawfully admitted for permanent residence, an alien who is inadmissible or deportable from the United States if the alien—

(A) has been physically present in the United States for a continuous period of not less than 10 years immediately preceding the date of such application;

(B) has been a person of good moral character during such period;

(C) has not been convicted of an offense under section 212(a)(2), 237(a)(2), or 237(a)(3) [8 USCS § 1182(a)(2), 1227(a)(2), or 1227(a)(3)], subject to paragraph (5); and

(D) establishes that removal would result in exceptional and extremely unusual hardship to the alien's spouse, parent, or child, who is a citizen of the United States or an alien lawfully admitted for permanent residence.

(2) Special rule for battered spouse or child.

(A) Authority. The Attorney General may cancel removal of, and adjust to the status of an alien lawfully admitted for permanent residence, an alien who is inadmissible or deportable from the United States if the alien demonstrates that—

(i)(I) the alien has been battered or subjected to extreme cruelty by a spouse or parent who is or was a United States citizen (or is the parent of a child of a United States citizen and the child has been battered or subjected to extreme cruelty by such citizen parent);

(II) the alien has been battered or subjected to extreme cruelty by a spouse or parent who is or was a lawful permanent resident (or is the parent of a child of an alien who is or was a lawful permanent resident and the child has been battered or subjected to extreme cruelty by such permanent resident parent); or

(III) the alien has been battered or subjected to extreme cruelty by a United States citizen or lawful permanent resident whom the alien intended to marry, but whose marriage is not legitimate because of that United States citizen's or lawful permanent resident's bigamy;

(ii) the alien has been physically present in the United States for a continuous period of not less than 3 years immediately preceding the date of such application, and the issuance of a charging document for removal proceedings shall not toll the 3-year period of continuous physical presence in the United States;

(iii) the alien has been a person of good moral character during such period, subject to the provisions of subparagraph (C);

(iv) the alien is not inadmissible under paragraph (2) or (3) of section 212(a) [8 USCS § 1182(a)], is not deportable under paragraphs (1)(G) or (2) through (4) of section 237(a) [8 USCS § 1227(a)], subject to paragraph (5), and has not been convicted of an aggravated felony; and

(v) the removal would result in extreme hardship to the alien, the alien's child, or the alien's parent.

(B) Physical presence. Notwithstanding subsection (d)(2), for purposes of subparagraph (A)(ii) or for purposes of section 244(a)(3) [former 8 USCS § 1254(a)(3)] (as in effect before the title III-A effective date in section 309 of the Illegal Immigration Reform and Immigrant Responsibility Act of 1996 [8 USCS § 1101 note]), an alien shall not be considered to have failed to maintain continuous physical presence by reason of an absence if the alien demonstrates a connection between the absence and the battering or extreme cruelty perpetrated against the alien. No absence or portion of an absence connected to the battering or extreme cruelty shall count toward the 90-day or 180-day limits established in subsection (d)(2). If any absence or aggregate absences exceed 180 days, the absences or portions of the absences will not be considered to break the period of continuous presence. Any such period of time excluded from the 180-day limit shall be excluded in computing the time during which the alien has been physically present for purposes of the 3-year requirement set forth in this subparagraph, subparagraph (A)(ii), and section 244(a)(3) [former 8 USCS § 1254(a)(3)] (as in effect before the title III-A effective date in section 309 of the Illegal Immigration Reform and Immigrant Responsibility Act of 1996 [8 USCS § 1101 note]).

(C) Good moral character. Notwithstanding section 101(f) [8 USCS § 1101(f)], an act or conviction that does not bar the Attorney General from granting relief under this paragraph by reason of subparagraph (A)(iv) shall not bar the Attorney General from finding the alien to be of good moral character under subparagraph (A)(iii) or section 244(a)(3) [former 8 USCS § 1254(a)(3)] (as in effect before the title III-A effective date in section 309 of the Illegal Immigration Reform and Immigrant Responsibility Act of 1996 [8 USCS § 1101 note]), if the Attorney General finds that the act or conviction was connected to the alien's having been battered or subjected to extreme cruelty and determines that a waiver is otherwise warranted.

(D) Credible evidence considered. In acting on applications under this paragraph, the Attorney General shall consider any credible evidence relevant to the application. The determination of what evidence is credible and the weight to be given that evidence shall be within the sole discretion of the Attorney General.

(3) Recordation of date. With respect to aliens who the Attorney General adjusts to the status of an alien lawfully admitted for permanent residence under paragraph (1) or (2), the Attorney General shall record the alien's lawful admission for permanent residence as of the date of the Attorney General's cancellation of removal under paragraph (1) or (2).

(4) Children of battered aliens and parents of battered alien children.

(A) In general. The Attorney General shall grant parole under section 212(d)(5) [8 USCS § 1182(d)(5)] to any alien who is a—

(i) child of an alien granted relief under section 240A(b)(2) [subsec. (b)(2) of this section] or 244(a)(3) [former 8 USCS § 1254(a)(3)] (as in effect before the title III-A effective date in section 309 of the Illegal Immigration Reform and Immigrant Responsibility Act of 1996 [8 USCS § 1101 note]); or

(ii) parent of a child alien granted relief under section 240A(b)(2) [subsec. (b)(2) of this section] or 244(a)(3) [former 8 USCS § 1254(a)(3)] (as in effect before the title III-A effective date in section 309 of the Illegal Immigration Reform and Immigrant Responsibility Act of 1996 [8 USCS § 1101 note]).

(B) Duration of parole. The grant of parole shall extend from the time of the grant of relief under section 240A(b)(2) [subsec. (b)(2) of this section] or section 244(a)(3) [former 8 USCS § 1254(a)(3)] (as in effect before the title III-A effective date in section 309 of the Illegal Immigration Reform and Immigrant Responsibility Act of 1996 [8 USCS § 1101 note]) to the time the application for adjustment of status filed by aliens covered under this paragraph has been finally adjudicated. Applications for adjustment of status filed by aliens covered under this paragraph shall be treated as if the applicants were VAWA self-petitioners. Failure by the alien granted relief under section 240A(b)(2) [subsec. (b)(2) of this section] or section 244(a)(3) [former 8 USCS § 1254(a)(3)] (as in effect before the title III-A effective date in section 309 of the Illegal Immigration Reform and Immigrant Responsibility Act of 1996 [8 USCS § 1101 note]) to exercise due diligence in filing a visa petition on behalf of an alien described in clause (i) or (ii) may result in revocation of parole.

(5) Application of domestic violence waiver authority. The authority provided under section 237(a)(7) [8 USCS § 1227(a)(7)] may apply under paragraphs (1)(B), (1)(C), and (2)(A)(iv) in a cancellation of removal and adjustment of status proceeding.

(6) Relatives of trafficking victims.

(A) In general. Upon written request by a law enforcement official, the Secretary of Homeland Security may parole under section 212(d)(5) [8 USCS § 1182(d)(5)] any alien who is a relative of an alien granted continued presence under section 107(c)(3)(A) of the Trafficking Victims Protection Act (22 U.S.C. 7105(c)(3)(A)), if the relative—

(i) was, on the date on which law enforcement applied for such continued presence—

(I) in the case of an alien granted continued presence who is under 21 years of age, the spouse, child, parent, or unmarried sibling under 18 years of age, of the alien; or

(II) in the case of an alien granted continued presence who is 21 years of age or older, the spouse or child of the alien; or

(ii) is a parent or sibling of the alien who the requesting law enforcement official, in consultation with the Secretary of Homeland Security, as appropriate, determines to be in present danger of retaliation as a result of the alien's escape from the severe form of trafficking or cooperation with law enforcement, irrespective of age.

(B) Duration of parole.

(i) In general. The Secretary may extend the parole granted under subparagraph (A) until the final adjudication of the application filed by the principal alien under section 101(a)(15)(T)(ii) [8 USCS § 1101(a)(15)(T)(ii)].

(ii) Other limits on duration. If an application described in clause (i) is not filed, the parole granted under subparagraph (A) may extend until the later of—

(I) the date on which the principal alien's authority to remain in the United States under section 107(c)(3)(A) of the Trafficking Victims Protection Act (22 U.S.C. 7105(c)(3)(A)) is terminated; or

(II) the date on which a civil action filed by the principal alien under section 1595 of title 18, United States Code, is concluded.

(iii) Due diligence. Failure by the principal alien to exercise due diligence in filing a visa petition on behalf of an alien described in clause (i) or (ii) of subparagraph (A), or in pursuing the civil action described in clause (ii)(II) (as determined by the Secretary of Homeland Security in consultation with the Attorney General), may result in revocation of parole.

(C) Other limitations. A relative may not be granted parole under this paragraph if—

(i) the Secretary of Homeland Security or the Attorney General has reason to believe that the relative was knowingly complicit in the trafficking of an alien permitted to remain in the United States under section 107(c)(3)(A) of the Trafficking Victims Protection Act (22 U.S.C. 7105(c)(3)(A)); or

(ii) the relative is an alien described in paragraph (2) or (3) of section 212(a) [8 USCS § 1182(a)] or paragraph (2) or (4) of section 237(a) [8 USCS § 1227(a)].

(c) Aliens ineligible for relief. The provisions of subsections (a) and (b)(1) shall not apply to any of the following aliens:

(1) An alien who entered the United States as a crewman subsequent to June 30, 1964.

(2) An alien who was admitted to the United States as a nonimmigrant exchange alien as defined in section 101(a)(15)(J) [8 USCS § 1101(a)(15)(J)], or has acquired the status of such a nonimmigrant exchange alien after admission, in order to receive graduate medical education or training, regardless of whether or not the alien is subject to or has fulfilled the two-year foreign residence requirement of section 212(e) [8 USCS § 1182(e)].

(3) An alien who—

(A) was admitted to the United States as a nonimmigrant exchange alien as defined in section 101(a)(15)(J) [8 USCS § 1101(a)(15)(J)] or has acquired the status of such a nonimmigrant exchange alien after admission other than to receive graduate medical education or training,

(B) is subject to the two-year foreign residence requirement of section 212(e) [8 USCS § 1182(e)], and

(C) has not fulfilled that requirement or received a waiver thereof.

(4) An alien who is inadmissible under section 212(a)(3) [8 USCS § 1182(a)(3)] or deportable under section 237(a)(4) [8 USCS § 1227(a)(4)].

(5) An alien who is described in section 241(b)(3)(B)(i) [8 USCS § 1251(b)(3)(B)(i)].

(6) An alien whose removal has previously been cancelled under this section or whose deportation was suspended under section 244(a) [former 8 USCS § 1254(a)] or who has been granted relief under section 212(c) [former 8 USCS § 1182(c)], as such sections were in effect before the date of the enactment of the Illegal Immigration Reform and Immigrant Responsibility Act of 1996 [enacted Sept. 30, 1996].

(d) Special rules relating to continuous residence or physical presence.

(1) Termination of continuous period. For purposes of this section, any period of continuous residence or continuous physical presence in the United States shall be deemed to end (A) except in the case of an alien who applies for cancellation of removal under subsection (b)(2), when the alien is served a notice to appear under section 239(a) [8 USCS § 1229(a)], or (B) when the alien has committed an offense referred to in section 212(a)(2) [8 USCS § 1182(a)(2)] that renders the alien inadmissible to the United States under section 212(a)(2) [8 USCS § 1182(a)(2)] or removable from the United States under section 237(a)(2) or 237(a)(4) [8 USCS § 1227(a)(2) or 1227(a)(4)], whichever is earliest.

(2) Treatment of certain breaks in presence. An alien shall be considered to have failed to maintain continuous physical presence in the United States under subsections (b)(1) and (b)(2) if the alien has departed from the United States for any period in excess of 90 days or for any periods in the aggregate exceeding 180 days.

(3) Continuity not required because of honorable service in armed forces and presence upon entry into service. The requirements of continuous residence or continuous physical presence in the United States under subsections (a) and (b) shall not apply to an alien who—

(A) has served for a minimum period of 24 months in an active-duty status in the Armed Forces of the United States and, if separated from such service, was separated under honorable conditions, and

(B) at the time of the alien's enlistment or induction was in the United States.

(e) Annual limitation.

(1) Aggregate limitation. Subject to paragraphs (2) and (3), the Attorney General may not cancel the removal and adjust the status under this section, nor suspend the deportation and adjust the status under section 244(a) [former 8 USCS § 1254(a)] (as in effect before the enactment of the Illegal Immigration Reform and Immigrant Responsibility Act of 1996 [enacted Sept. 30, 1996]), of a total of more than 4,000 aliens in any fiscal year. The previous sentence shall apply regardless of when an alien applied for such cancellation and adjustment, or such suspension and adjustment, and whether such an alien had previously applied for suspension of deportation under such section 244(a) [8 USCS § 1254(a)]. The numerical limitation under this paragraph shall apply to the aggregate number of decisions in any fiscal year to cancel the removal (and adjust the status) of an alien, or suspend the deportation (and adjust the status) of an alien, under this section or such section 244(a) [8 USCS § 1254(a)].

(2) Fiscal year 1997. For fiscal year 1997, paragraph (1) shall only apply to decisions to cancel the removal of an alien, or suspend the deportation of an alien, made after April 1, 1997. Notwithstanding any other provision of law, the Attorney General may cancel the removal or suspend the deportation, in addition to the normal allotment for fiscal year 1998, of a number of aliens equal to 4,000 less the number of such cancellations of removal and suspensions of deportation granted in fiscal year 1997 after April 1, 1997.

(3) Exception for certain aliens. Paragraph (1) shall not apply to the following:

(A) Aliens described in section 309(c)(5)(C)(i) of the Illegal Immigration Reform and Immigrant Responsibility Act of 1996 [8 USCS § 1101 note] (as amended by the Nicaraguan Adjustment and Central American Relief Act).

(B) Aliens in deportation proceedings prior to April 1, 1997, who applied for suspension of deportation under section 244(a)(3) [former 8 USCS § 1254(a)(3)] (as in effect before the date of the enactment of the Illegal Immigration Reform and Immigrant Responsibility Act of 1996 [enacted Sept. 30, 1996]).

(June 27, 1952, ch 477, Title II, Ch 4, § 240A, as added Sept. 30, 1996, P. L. 104-208, Div C, Title III, Subtitle A, § 304(a)(3), 110 Stat. 3009-594; Nov. 19, 1997, P. L. 105-100, Title II, § 204(a)–(c), 111 Stat. 2200; Oct. 28, 2000, P. L. 106-386, Div B, Title V, §§ 1504(a), (b), 1505(b)(2), 1506(b)(1), 114 Stat. 1522, 1525, 1527; Jan. 5, 2006, P. L. 109-162, Title VIII, Subtitle B, § 813(c), Subtitle C, § 822(a), (b), 119 Stat. 3058, 3062; Aug. 12, 2006, P. L. 109-271, § 6(e), 120 Stat. 763; Dec. 23, 2008, P. L. 110-457, Title II, Subtitle A, § 205(b), 122 Stat. 5062.)

§ 1229c. Voluntary departure

(a) Certain conditions.

(1) In general. The Attorney General may permit an alien voluntarily to depart the United States at the alien's own expense under this subsection, in lieu of being subject to proceedings under section 240 [8 USCS § 1229a] or prior to the completion of such proceedings, if the alien is not deportable under section 237(a)(2)(A)(iii) or section 237(a)(4)(B) [8 USCS § 1227(a)(2)(A)(iii) or 1227(a)(4)(B)].

(2) Period.

(A) In general. Subject to subparagraph (B), permission to depart voluntarily under this subsection shall not be valid for a period exceeding 120 days.

(B) Three-year pilot program waiver. During the period October 1, 2000, through September 30, 2003, and subject to subparagraphs (C) and (D)(ii), the Attorney General may, in the discretion of the Attorney General for humanitarian purposes, waive application of subparagraph (A) in the case of an alien—

(i) who was admitted to the United States as a nonimmigrant visitor (described in section 101(a)(15)(B) [8 USCS § 1101(a)(15)(B)]) under the provisions of the visa waiver pilot program established pursuant to section 217 [8 USCS § 1187], seeks the waiver for the purpose of continuing to receive medical treatment in the United States from a physician associated with a health care facility, and submits to the Attorney General—

(I) a detailed diagnosis statement from the physician, which includes the treatment being sought and the expected time period the alien will be required to remain in the United States;

(II) a statement from the health care facility containing an assurance that the alien's treatment is not being paid through any Federal or State public health assistance, that the alien's account has no outstanding balance, and that such facility will notify the Service when the alien is released or treatment is terminated; and

(III) evidence of financial ability to support the alien's day-to-day expenses while in the United States (including the expenses of any family member described in clause (ii)) and evidence that any such alien or family member is not receiving any form of public assistance; or

(ii) who—

(I) is a spouse, parent, brother, sister, son, daughter, or other family member of a principal alien described in clause (i); and

(II) entered the United States accompanying, and with the same status as, such principal alien.

(C) Waiver limitations.

(i) Waivers under subparagraph (B) may be granted only upon a request submitted by a Service district office to Service headquarters.

(ii) Not more than 300 waivers may be granted for any fiscal year for a principal alien under subparagraph (B)(i).

(iii)(I) Except as provided in subclause (II), in the case of each principal alien described in subparagraph (B)(i) not more than one adult may be granted a waiver under subparagraph (B)(ii).

(II) Not more than two adults may be granted a waiver under subparagraph (B)(ii) in a case in which—

(aa) the principal alien described in subparagraph (B)(i) is a dependent under the age of 18; or

(bb) one such adult is age 55 or older or is physically handicapped.

(D) Report to Congress; suspension of waiver authority.

(i) Not later than March 30 of each year, the Commissioner shall submit to the Congress an annual report regarding all waivers granted under subparagraph (B) during the preceding fiscal year.

(ii) Notwithstanding any other provision of law, the authority of the Attorney General under subparagraph (B) shall be suspended during any period in which an annual report under clause (i) is past due and has not been submitted.

(3) Bond. The Attorney General may require an alien permitted to depart voluntarily under this subsection to post a voluntary departure bond, to be surrendered upon proof that the alien has departed the United States within the time specified.

(4) Treatment of aliens arriving in the United States. In the case of an alien who is arriving in the United States and with respect to whom proceedings under section 240 [8 USCS § 1229a] are (or would otherwise be) initiated at the time of such alien's arrival, paragraph (1) shall not apply. Nothing in this paragraph shall be construed as preventing such an alien from withdrawing the application for admission in accordance with section 235(a)(4) [8 USCS § 1225(a)(4)].

(b) At conclusion of proceedings.

(1) In general. The Attorney General may permit an alien voluntarily to depart the United States at the alien's own expense if, at the conclusion of a proceeding under section 240 [8 USCS § 1229a], the immigration judge enters an order granting voluntary departure in lieu of removal and finds that—

(A) the alien has been physically present in the United States for a period of at least one year immediately preceding the date the notice to appear was served under section 239(a) [8 USCS § 1229(a)];

(B) the alien is, and has been, a person of good moral character for at least 5 years immediately preceding the alien's application for voluntary departure;

(C) the alien is not deportable under section 237(a)(2)(A)(iii) or section 237(a)(4) [8 USCS § 1227(a)(2)(A)(iii) or 1227(a)(4)]; and

(D) the alien has established by clear and convincing evidence that the alien has the means to depart the United States and intends to do so.

(2) Period. Permission to depart voluntarily under this subsection shall not be valid for a period exceeding 60 days.

(3) Bond. An alien permitted to depart voluntarily under this subsection shall be required to post a voluntary departure bond, in an amount necessary to ensure that the alien will depart, to be surrendered upon proof that the alien has departed the United States within the time specified.

(c) Aliens not eligible. The Attorney General shall not permit an alien to depart voluntarily under this section if the alien was previously permitted to so depart after having been found inadmissible under section 212(a)(6)(A) [8 USCS § 1182(a)(6)(A)].

(d) Civil penalty for failure to depart.

(1) In general. Subject to paragraph (2), if an alien is permitted to depart voluntarily under this section and voluntarily fails to depart the United States within the time period specified, the alien—

(A) shall be subject to a civil penalty of not less than $1,000 and not more than $5,000; and

(B) shall be ineligible, for a period of 10 years, to receive any further relief under this section and sections 240A, 245, 248, and 249 [8 USCS §§ 1229b, 1255, 1258, and 1259].

(2) Application of VAWA protections. The restrictions on relief under paragraph (1) shall not apply to relief under section 240A or 245 [8 USCS § 1229b or 1255] on the basis of a petition filed by a VAWA self-petitioner, or a petition filed under section 240A(b)(2) [8 USCS § 1229b(b)(2)], or under section 244(a)(3) [former 8 USCS § 1254(a)(3)] (as in effect prior to March 31, 1997), if the extreme cruelty or battery was at least one central reason for the alien's overstaying the grant of voluntary departure.

(3) Notice of penalties. The order permitting an alien to depart voluntarily shall inform the alien of the penalties under this subsection.

(e) Additional conditions. The Attorney General may by regulation limit eligibility for voluntary departure under this section for any class or classes of aliens. No court may review any regulation issued under this subsection.

(f) Judicial review. No court shall have jurisdiction over an appeal from denial of a request for an order of voluntary departure under subsection (b), nor shall any court order a stay of an alien's removal pending consideration of any claim with respect to voluntary departure.

(June 27, 1952, ch 477, Title II, Ch 4, § 240B, as added Sept. 30, 1996, P. L. 104-208, Div C, Title III, Subtitle A, § 304(a)(3), 110 Stat. 3009-596; Nov. 1, 2000, P. L. 106-406, § 2, 114 Stat. 1755; Jan. 5, 2006, P. L. 109-162, Title VIII, Subtitle B, § 812, 119 Stat. 3057.)

§ 1230. Records of admission

(a) The Attorney General shall cause to be filed, as a record of admission of each immigrant, the immigrant visa required by section 221(e) [8 USCS § 1201(e)] to be surrendered at the port of entry by the arriving alien to an immigration officer.

(b) The Attorney General shall cause to be filed such record of the admission into the United States of each immigrant admitted under section 211(b) [8 USCS § 1181(b)] and of each nonimmigrant as the Attorney General deems necessary for the enforcement of the immigration laws.

(June 27, 1952, ch 477, Title II, Ch 4, § 240C [240], 66 Stat. 204; Sept. 30, 1996, P. L. 104-208, Div C, Title III, Subtitle A, §§ 304(a)(2), 308(f)(1)(K), 110 Stat. 3009-587, 3009-621.)

§ 1231. Detention and removal of aliens ordered removed

(a) Detention, release, and removal of aliens ordered removed.

(1) Removal period.

(A) In general. Except as otherwise provided in this section, when an alien is ordered removed, the Attorney General shall remove the alien from the United States within a period of 90 days (in this section referred to as the "removal period").

(B) Beginning of period. The removal period begins on the latest of the following:

(i) The date the order of removal becomes administratively final.

(ii) If the removal order is judicially reviewed and if a court orders a stay of the removal of the alien, the date of the court's final order.

(iii) If the alien is detained or confined (except under an immigration process), the date the alien is released from detention or confinement.

(C) Suspension of period. The removal period shall be extended beyond a period of 90 days and the alien may remain in detention during such extended period if the alien fails or refuses to make timely application in good faith for travel or other documents necessary to the alien's departure or conspires or acts to prevent the alien's removal subject to an order of removal.

(2) Detention.

(A) In general. During the removal period, the Attorney General shall detain the alien. Under no circumstance during the removal period shall the Attorney General release an alien who has been found inadmissible under section 212(a)(2) or 212(a)(3)(B) [8 USCS § 1182(a)(2) or (a)(3)(B)] or deportable under section 237(a)(2) or 237(a)(4)(B) [8 USCS § 1227(a)(2) or (a)(4)(B)].

(B) Enforcement by attorney general of a state. The attorney general of a State, or other authorized State officer, alleging a violation of the detention requirement under subparagraph (A) that harms such State or its residents shall have standing to bring an action against the Secretary of Homeland Security on behalf of such State or the residents of such State in an appropriate district court of the United States to obtain appropriate injunctive relief. The court shall advance on the docket and expedite the disposition of a civil action filed under this subparagraph to the greatest extent practicable. For purposes of this subparagraph, a State or its residents shall be considered to have been harmed if the State or its residents experience harm, including financial harm in excess of $100.

(3) Supervision after 90-day period. If the alien does not leave or is not removed within the removal period, the alien, pending removal, shall be subject to supervision under regulations prescribed by the Attorney General. The regulations shall include provisions requiring the alien—

(A) to appear before an immigration officer periodically for identification;

(B) to submit, if necessary, to a medical and psychiatric examination at the expense of the United States Government;

(C) to give information under oath about the alien's nationality, circumstances, habits, associations, and activities, and other information the Attorney General considers appropriate; and

(D) to obey reasonable written restrictions on the alien's conduct or activities that the Attorney General prescribes for the alien.

(4) Aliens imprisoned, arrested, or on parole, supervised release, or probation.

(A) In general. Except as provided in section 343(a) of the Public Health Service Act (42 U.S.C. 259(a)) and paragraph (2) [subparagraph (B)], the Attorney General may not remove an alien who is sentenced to imprisonment until the alien is released from imprisonment. Parole, supervised release, probation, or possibility of arrest or further imprisonment is not a reason to defer removal.

(B) Exception for removal of nonviolent offenders prior to completion of sentence of imprisonment. The Attorney General is authorized to remove an alien in accordance with applicable procedures under this Act before the alien has completed a sentence of imprisonment—

(i) in the case of an alien in the custody of the Attorney General, if the Attorney General determines that (I) the alien is confined pursuant to a final conviction for a nonviolent offense (other than an offense related to smuggling or harboring of aliens or an offense described in section 101(a)(43)(B), (C), (E), (I), or (L) [8 USCS § 1101(a)(43)(B), (C), (E), (I), or (L)] [)] and (II) the removal of the alien is appropriate and in the best interest of the United States; or

(ii) in the case of an alien in the custody of a State (or a political subdivision of a State), if the chief State official exercising authority with respect to the incarceration of the alien determines that (I) the alien is confined pursuant to a final conviction for a nonviolent offense (other than an offense described in section 101(a)(43)(C) or (E) [8 USCS § 1101(a)(43)(C)]), (II) the removal is appropriate and in the best interest of the State, and (III) submits a written request to the Attorney General that such alien be so removed.

(C) Notice. Any alien removed pursuant to this paragraph shall be notified of the penalties under the laws of the United States relating to the reentry of deported aliens, particularly the expanded penalties for aliens removed under subparagraph (B).

(D) No private right. No cause or claim may be asserted under this paragraph against any official of the United States or of any State to compel the release, removal, or consideration for release or removal of any alien.

(5) Reinstatement of removal orders against aliens illegally reentering. If the Attorney General finds that an alien has reentered the United States illegally after having been removed or having departed voluntarily, under an order of removal, the prior order of removal is reinstated from its original date and is not subject to being reopened or reviewed, the alien is not eligible and may not apply for any relief under this Act, and the alien shall be removed under the prior order at any time after the reentry.

(6) Inadmissible or criminal aliens. An alien ordered removed who is inadmissible under section 212 [8 USCS § 1182], removable under section 237(a)(1)(C), 237(a)(2), or 237(a)(4) [8 USCS § 1227(a)(1)(C), (a)(2), or (a)(4)] or who has been determined by the Attorney General to be a risk to the community or unlikely to comply with the order of removal, may be detained beyond the removal period and, if released, shall be subject to the terms of supervision in paragraph (3).

(7) Employment authorization. No alien ordered removed shall be eligible to receive authorization to be employed in the United States unless the Attorney General makes a specific finding that—

(A) the alien cannot be removed due to the refusal of all countries designated by the alien or under this section to receive the alien, or

(B) the removal of the alien is otherwise impracticable or contrary to the public interest.

(b) Countries to which aliens may be removed.

(1) Aliens arriving at the United States. Subject to paragraph (3)—

(A) In general. Except as provided by subparagraphs (B) and (C), an alien who arrives at the United States and with respect to whom proceedings under section 240 [8 USCS § 1229a] were initiated at the time of such alien's arrival shall be removed to the country in which the alien boarded the vessel or aircraft on which the alien arrived in the United States.

(B) Travel from contiguous territory. If the alien boarded the vessel or aircraft on which the alien arrived in the United States in a foreign territory contiguous to the United States, an island adjacent to the United States, or an island adjacent to a foreign territory contiguous to the United States, and the alien is not a native, citizen, subject, or national of, or does not reside in, the territory or island, removal shall be to the country in which the alien boarded the vessel that transported the alien to the territory or island.

(C) Alternative countries. If the government of the country designated in subparagraph (A) or (B) is unwilling to accept the alien into that country's territory, removal shall be to any of the following countries, as directed by the Attorney General:

(i) The country of which the alien is a citizen, subject, or national.

(ii) The country in which the alien was born.

(iii) The country in which the alien has a residence.

(iv) A country with a government that will accept the alien into the country's territory if removal to each country described in a previous clause of this subparagraph is impracticable, inadvisable, or impossible.

(2) Other aliens. Subject to paragraph (3)—

(A) Selection of country by alien. Except as otherwise provided in this paragraph—

(i) any alien not described in paragraph (1) who has been ordered removed may designate one country to which the alien wants to be removed, and

(ii) the Attorney General shall remove the alien to the country the alien so designates.

(B) Limitation on designation. An alien may designate under subparagraph (A)(i) a foreign territory contiguous to the United States, an adjacent island, or an island adjacent to a foreign territory contiguous to the United States as the place to which the alien is to be removed only if the alien is a native, citizen, subject, or national of, or has resided in, that designated territory or island.

(C) Disregarding designation. The Attorney General may disregard a designation under subparagraph (A)(i) if—

(i) the alien fails to designate a country promptly;

(ii) the government of the country does not inform the Attorney General finally, within 30 days after the date the Attorney General first inquires, whether the government will accept the alien into the country;

(iii) the government of the country is not willing to accept the alien into the country; or

(iv) the Attorney General decides that removing the alien to the country is prejudicial to the United States.

(D) Alternative country. If an alien is not removed to a country designated under subparagraph (A)(i), the Attorney General shall remove the alien to a country of which the alien is a subject, national, or citizen unless the government of the country—

(i) does not inform the Attorney General or the alien finally, within 30 days after the date the Attorney General first inquires or within another period of time the Attorney General decides is reasonable, whether the government will accept the alien into the country; or

(ii) is not willing to accept the alien into the country.

(E) Additional removal countries. If an alien is not removed to a country under the previous subparagraphs of this paragraph, the Attorney General shall remove the alien to any of the following countries:

(i) The country from which the alien was admitted to the United States.

(ii) The country in which is located the foreign port from which the alien left for the United States or for a foreign territory contiguous to the United States.

(iii) A country in which the alien resided before the alien entered the country from which the alien entered the United States.

(iv) The country in which the alien was born.

(v) The country that had sovereignty over the alien's birthplace when the alien was born.

(vi) The country in which the alien's birthplace is located when the alien is ordered removed.

(vii) If impracticable, inadvisable, or impossible to remove the alien to each country described in a previous clause of this subparagraph, another country whose government will accept the alien into that country.

(F) Removal country when United States is at war. When the United States is at war and the Attorney General decides that it is impracticable, inadvisable, inconvenient, or impossible to remove an alien under this subsection because of the war, the Attorney General may remove the alien—

(i) to the country that is host to a government in exile of the country of which the alien is a citizen or subject if the government of the host country will permit the alien's entry; or

(ii) if the recognized government of the country of which the alien is a citizen or subject is not in exile, to a country, or a political or territorial subdivision of a country, that is very near the country of which the alien is a citizen or subject, or, with the consent of the government of the country of which the alien is a citizen or subject, to another country.

(3) Restriction on removal to a country where alien's life or freedom would be threatened.

(A) In general. Notwithstanding paragraphs (1) and (2), the Attorney General may not remove an alien to a country if the Attorney General decides that the alien's life or freedom would be threatened in that country because of the alien's race, religion, nationality, membership in a particular social group, or political opinion.

(B) Exception. Subparagraph (A) does not apply to an alien deportable under section 237(a)(4)(D) [8 USCS § 1227(a)(4)(D)] or if the Attorney General decides that—

(i) the alien ordered, incited, assisted, or otherwise participated in the persecution of an individual because of the individual's race, religion, nationality, membership in a particular social group, or political opinion;

(ii) the alien, having been convicted by a final judgment of a particularly serious crime is a danger to the community of the United States;

(iii) there are serious reasons to believe that the alien committed a serious nonpolitical crime outside the United States before the alien arrived in the United States; or

(iv) there are reasonable grounds to believe that the alien is a danger to the security of the United States. For purposes of clause (ii), an alien who has been convicted of an aggravated felony (or felonies) for which the alien has been sentenced to an aggregate term of imprisonment of at least 5 years shall be considered to have committed a particularly serious crime. The previous sentence shall not preclude the Attorney General from determining that, notwithstanding the length of sentence imposed, an alien has been convicted of a particularly serious crime. For purposes of clause (iv), an alien who is described in section 237(a)(4)(B) [8 USCS § 1227(a)(4)(B)] shall be considered to be an alien with respect to whom there are reasonable grounds for regarding as a danger to the security of the United States.

(C) Sustaining burden of proof; credibility determinations. In determining whether an alien has demonstrated that the alien's life or freedom would be threatened for a reason described in subparagraph (A), the trier of fact shall determine whether the alien has sustained the alien's burden of proof, and shall make credibility determinations, in the manner described in clauses (ii) and (iii) of section 208(b)(1)(B) [8 USCS § 1158(b)(1)(B)].

(c) Removal of aliens arriving at port of entry.

(1) Vessels and aircraft. An alien arriving at a port of entry of the United States who is ordered removed either without a hearing under section 235(b)(1) or 235(c) [8 USCS § 1225(b)(1) or (c)] or pursuant to proceedings under section 240 [8 USCS § 1229a] initiated at the time of such alien's arrival shall be removed immediately on a vessel or aircraft owned by the owner of the vessel or aircraft on which the alien arrived in the United States, unless—

(A) it is impracticable to remove the alien on one of those vessels or aircraft within a reasonable time, or

(B) the alien is a stowaway—

(i) who has been ordered removed in accordance with section 235(a)(1) [8 USCS § 1225(a)(1)],

(ii) who has requested asylum, and

(iii) whose application has not been adjudicated or whose asylum application has been denied but who has not exhausted all appeal rights.

(2) Stay of removal.

(A) In general. The Attorney General may stay the removal of an alien under this subsection if the Attorney General decides that—

(i) immediate removal is not practicable or proper; or

(ii) the alien is needed to testify in the prosecution of a person for a violation of a law of the United States or of any State.

(B) Payment of detention costs. During the period an alien is detained because of a stay of removal under subparagraph (A)(ii), the Attorney General may pay from the appropriation "Immigration and Naturalization Service—Salaries and Expenses"—

(i) the cost of maintenance of the alien; and

(ii) a witness fee of $1 a day.

(C) Release during stay. The Attorney General may release an alien whose removal is stayed under subparagraph (A)(ii) on—

(i) the alien's filing a bond of at least $500 with security approved by the Attorney General;

(ii) condition that the alien appear when required as a witness and for removal; and

(iii) other conditions the Attorney General may prescribe.

(3) Costs of detention and maintenance pending removal.

(A) In general. Except as provided in subparagraph (B) and subsection (d) [(e)], an owner of a vessel or aircraft bringing an alien to the United States shall pay the costs of detaining and maintaining the alien—

(i) while the alien is detained under subsection (d)(1), and

(ii) in the case of an alien who is a stowaway, while the alien is being detained pursuant to—

(I) subsection (d)(2)(A) or (d)(2)(B)(i),

(II) subsection (d)(2)(B)(ii) or (iii) for the period of time reasonably necessary for the owner to arrange for repatriation or removal of the stowaway, including obtaining necessary travel documents, but not to extend beyond the date on which it is ascertained that such travel documents cannot be obtained from the country to which the stowaway is to be returned, or

(III) section 235(b)(1)(B)(ii) [8 USCS § 1225(b)(1)(B)(ii)], for a period not to exceed 15 days (excluding Saturdays, Sundays, and holidays) commencing on the first such day which begins on the earlier of 72 hours after the time of the initial presentation of the stowaway for inspection or at the time the stowaway is determined to have a credible fear of persecution.

(B) Nonapplication. Subparagraph (A) shall not apply if—

(i) the alien is a crewmember;

(ii) the alien has an immigrant visa;

(iii) the alien has a nonimmigrant visa or other documentation authorizing the alien to apply for temporary admission to the United States and applies for admission not later than 120 days after the date the visa or documentation was issued;

(iv) the alien has a reentry permit and applies for admission not later than 120 days after the date of the alien's last inspection and admission;

(v)(I) the alien has a nonimmigrant visa or other documentation authorizing the alien to apply for temporary admission to the United States or a reentry permit;

(II) the alien applies for admission more than 120 days after the date the visa or documentation was issued or after the date of the last inspection and admission under the reentry permit; and

(III) the owner of the vessel or aircraft satisfies the Attorney General that the existence of the condition relating to inadmissibility could not have been discovered by exercising reasonable care before the alien boarded the vessel or aircraft; or

(vi) the individual claims to be a national of the United States and has a United States passport.

(d) Requirements of persons providing transportation.

(1) Removal at time of arrival. An owner, agent, master, commanding officer, person in charge, purser, or consignee of a vessel or aircraft bringing an alien (except an alien crewmember) to the United States shall—

(A) receive an alien back on the vessel or aircraft or another vessel or aircraft owned or operated by the same interests if the alien is ordered removed under this part; and

(B) take the alien to the foreign country to which the alien is ordered removed.

(2) Alien stowaways. An owner, agent, master, commanding officer, charterer, or consignee of a vessel or aircraft arriving in the United States with an alien stowaway—

(A) shall detain the alien on board the vessel or aircraft, or at such place as the Attorney General shall designate, until completion of the inspection of the alien by an immigration officer;

(B) may not permit the stowaway to land in the United States, except pursuant to regulations of the Attorney General temporarily—

(i) for medical treatment,

(ii) for detention of the stowaway by the Attorney General, or

(iii) for departure or removal of the stowaway; and

(C) if ordered by an immigration officer, shall remove the stowaway on the vessel or aircraft or on another vessel or aircraft.

The Attorney General shall grant a timely request to remove the stowaway under subparagraph (C) on a vessel or aircraft other than that on which the stowaway arrived if the requester has obtained any travel documents necessary for departure or repatriation of the stowaway and removal of the stowaway will not be unreasonably delayed.

(3) Removal upon order. An owner, agent, master, commanding officer, person in charge, purser, or consignee of a vessel, aircraft, or other transportation line shall comply with an order of the Attorney General to take on board, guard safely, and transport to the destination specified any alien ordered to be removed under this Act.

(e) Payment of expenses of removal.

(1) Costs of removal at time of arrival. In the case of an alien who is a stowaway or who is ordered removed either without a hearing under section 235(a)(1) [235(b)(1)] or 235(c) [8 USCS § 1225(b)(1) or (c)] or pursuant to proceedings under section 240 [8 USCS § 1229a] initiated at the time of such alien's arrival, the owner of the vessel or aircraft (if any) on which the alien arrived in the United States shall pay the transportation cost of removing the alien. If removal is on a vessel or aircraft not owned by the owner of the vessel or aircraft on which the alien arrived in the United States, the Attorney General may—

(A) pay the cost from the appropriation "Immigration and Naturalization Service—Salaries and Expenses"; and

(B) recover the amount of the cost in a civil action from the owner, agent, or consignee of the vessel or aircraft (if any) on which the alien arrived in the United States.

(2) Costs of removal to port of removal for aliens admitted or permitted to land. In the case of an alien who has been admitted or permitted to land and is ordered removed, the cost (if any) of removal of the alien to the port of removal shall be at the expense of the appropriation for the enforcement of this Act.

(3) Costs of removal from port of removal for aliens admitted or permitted to land.

(A) Through appropriation. Except as provided in subparagraph (B), in the case of an alien who has been admitted or permitted to land and is ordered removed, the cost (if any) of removal of the alien from the port of removal shall be at the expense of the appropriation for the enforcement of this Act.

(B) Through owner.

(i) In general. In the case of an alien described in clause (ii), the cost of removal of the alien from the port of removal may be charged to any owner of the vessel, aircraft, or other transportation line by which the alien came to the United States.

(ii) Aliens described. An alien described in this clause is an alien who—

(I) is admitted to the United States (other than lawfully admitted for permanent residence) and is ordered removed within 5 years of the date of admission based on a ground that existed before or at the time of admission, or

(II) is an alien crewman permitted to land temporarily under section 252 [8 USCS § 1282] and is ordered removed within 5 years of the date of landing.

(C) Costs of removal of certain aliens granted voluntary departure. In the case of an alien who has been granted voluntary departure under section 240B [8 USCS § 1229c] and who is financially unable to depart at the alien's own expense and whose removal the Attorney General deems to be in the best interest of the United States, the expense of such removal may be paid from the appropriation for the enforcement of this Act.

(f) Aliens requiring personal care during removal.

(1) In general. If the Attorney General believes that an alien being removed requires personal care because of the alien's mental or physical condition, the Attorney General may employ a suitable person for that purpose who shall accompany and care for the alien until the alien arrives at the final destination.

(2) Costs. The costs of providing the service described in paragraph (1) shall be defrayed in the same manner as the expense of removing the accompanied alien is defrayed under this section.

(g) Places of detention.

(1) In general. The Attorney General shall arrange for appropriate places of detention for aliens detained pending removal or a decision on removal. When United States Government facilities are unavailable or facilities adapted or suitably located for detention are unavailable for rental, the Attorney General may expend from the appropriation "Immigration and Naturalization Service—Salaries and Expenses", without regard to section 3709 of the Revised Statutes (41 U.S.C. 5) [41 USCS § 6101], amounts necessary to acquire land and to acquire, build, remodel, repair, and operate facilities (including living quarters for immigration officers if not otherwise available) necessary for detention.

(2) Detention facilities of the immigration and naturalization service. Prior to initiating any project for the construction of any new detention facility for the Service, the Commissioner shall consider the availability for purchase or lease of any existing prison, jail, detention center, or other comparable facility suitable for such use.

(h) Statutory construction. Nothing in this section shall be construed to create any substantive or procedural right or benefit that is legally enforceable by any party against the United States or its agencies or officers or any other person.

(i) Incarceration.

(1) If the chief executive officer of a State (or, if appropriate, a political subdivision of the State) exercising authority with respect to the incarceration of an undocumented criminal alien submits a written request to the Attorney General, the Attorney General shall, as determined by the Attorney General—

(A) enter into a contractual arrangement which provides for compensation to the State or a political subdivision of the State, as may be appropriate, with respect to the incarceration of the undocumented criminal alien; or

(B) take the undocumented criminal alien into the custody of the Federal Government and incarcerate the alien.

(2) Compensation under paragraph (1)(A) shall be the average cost of incarceration of a prisoner in the relevant State as determined by the Attorney General.

(3) For purposes of this subsection, the term "undocumented criminal alien" means an alien who—

(A) has been convicted of a felony or two or more misdemeanors; and

(B)(i) entered the United States without inspection or at any time or place other than as designated by the Attorney General;

(ii) was the subject of exclusion or deportation proceedings at the time he or she was taken into custody by the State or a political subdivision of the State; or

(iii) was admitted as a nonimmigrant and at the time he or she was taken into custody by the State or a political subdivision of the State has failed to maintain the nonimmigrant status in which the alien was admitted or to which it was changed under section 248 [8 USCS § 1258], or to comply with the conditions of any such status.

(4)(A) In carrying out paragraph (1), the Attorney General shall give priority to the Federal incarceration of undocumented criminal aliens who have committed aggravated felonies.

(B) The Attorney General shall ensure that undocumented criminal aliens incarcerated in Federal facilities pursuant to this subsection are held in facilities which provide a level of security appropriate to the crimes for which they were convicted.

(5) There are authorized to be appropriated to carry out this subsection—

(A) $750,000,000 for fiscal year 2006;

(B) $850,000,000 for fiscal year 2007; and

(C) $950,000,000 for each of the fiscal years 2008 through 2011.

(6) Amounts appropriated pursuant to the authorization of appropriations in paragraph (5) that are distributed to a State or political subdivision of a State, including a municipality, may be used only for correctional purposes.

(June 27, 1952, ch 477, Title II, Ch. 4, § 241, as added Sept. 30, 1996, P. L. 104-208, Div C, Title III, Subtitle A, §§ 305(a)(3), 306(a)(1), Subtitle B, § 328(a)(1), 110 Stat. 3009-598, 3009-607, 3009-630; Nov. 2, 2002, P. L. 107-273, Div C, Title I, Subtitle A, § 11014, 116 Stat. 1824; May 11, 2005, P. L. 109-13, Div B, Title I, § 101(c), 119 Stat. 303; Jan. 5, 2006, P. L. 109-162, Title XI, Subtitle C, § 1196(a), (b), 119 Stat. 3130; Jan. 29, 2025, P.L. 119-1, § 3(e), 139 Stat. 5.)

§ 1232. Enhancing efforts to combat the trafficking of children

(a) Combating child trafficking at the border and ports of entry of the United States.

(1) Policies and procedures. In order to enhance the efforts of the United States to prevent trafficking in persons, the Secretary of Homeland Security, in conjunction with the Secretary of State, the Attorney General, and the Secretary of Health and Human Services, shall develop policies and procedures to ensure that unaccompanied alien children in the United States are safely repatriated to their country of nationality or of last habitual residence.

(2) Special rules for children from contiguous countries.

(A) Determinations. Any unaccompanied alien child who is a national or habitual resident of a country that is contiguous with the United States shall be treated in accordance with subparagraph (B), if the Secretary of Homeland Security determines, on a case-by-case basis, that—

(i) such child has not been a victim of a severe form of trafficking in persons, and there is no credible evidence that such child is at risk of being trafficked upon return to the child's country of nationality or of last habitual residence;

(ii) such child does not have a fear of returning to the child's country of nationality or of last habitual residence owing to a credible fear of persecution; and

(iii) the child is able to make an independent decision to withdraw the child's application for admission to the United States.

(B) Return. An immigration officer who finds an unaccompanied alien child described in subparagraph (A) at a land border or port of entry of the United States and determines that such child is inadmissible under the Immigration and Nationality Act (8 U.S.C. 1101 et seq.) may—

(i) permit such child to withdraw the child's application for admission pursuant to section 235(a)(4) of the Immigration and Nationality Act (8 U.S.C. 1225(a)(4)); and

(ii) return such child to the child's country of nationality or country of last habitual residence.

(C) Contiguous country agreements. The Secretary of State shall negotiate agreements between the United States and countries contiguous to the United States with respect to the repatriation of children. Such agreements shall be designed to protect children from severe forms of trafficking in persons, and shall, at a minimum, provide that—

(i) no child shall be returned to the child's country of nationality or of last habitual residence unless returned to appropriate employees or officials, including child welfare officials where available, of the accepting country's government;

(ii) no child shall be returned to the child's country of nationality or of last habitual residence outside of reasonable business hours; and

(iii) border personnel of the countries that are parties to such agreements are trained in the terms of such agreements.

(3) Rule for other children. The custody of unaccompanied alien children not described in paragraph (2)(A) who are apprehended at the border of the United States or at a United States port of entry shall be treated in accordance with subsection (b).

(4) Screening. Within 48 hours of the apprehension of a child who is believed to be described in paragraph (2)(A), but in any event prior to returning such child to the child's country of nationality or of last habitual residence, the child shall be screened to determine whether the child meets the criteria listed in paragraph (2)(A). If the child does not meet such criteria, or if no determination can be made within 48 hours of apprehension, the child shall immediately be transferred to the Secretary of Health and Human Services and treated in accordance with subsection (b). Nothing in this paragraph may be construed to preclude an earlier transfer of the child.

(5) Ensuring the safe repatriation of children.

(A) Repatriation pilot program. To protect children from trafficking and exploitation, the Secretary of State shall create a pilot program, in conjunction with the Secretary of Health and Human Services and the Secretary of Homeland Security, nongovernmental organizations, and other national and international agencies and experts, to develop and implement best practices to ensure the safe and sustainable repatriation and reintegration of unaccompanied alien children into their country of nationality or of last habitual residence, including placement with their families, legal guardians, or other sponsoring agencies.

(B) Assessment of country conditions. The Secretary of Homeland Security shall consult the Department of State's Country Reports on Human Rights Practices and the Trafficking in Persons Report in assessing whether to repatriate an unaccompanied alien child to a particular country.

(C) Report on repatriation of unaccompanied alien children. Not later than 18 months after the date of the enactment of this Act, and annually thereafter, the Secretary of State and the Secretary of Health and Human Services, with assistance from the Secretary of Homeland Security, shall submit a report to the Committee on the Judiciary of the Senate and the Committee on the Judiciary of the House of Representatives on efforts to improve repatriation programs for unaccompanied alien children. Such report shall include—

(i) the number of unaccompanied alien children ordered removed and the number of such children actually removed from the United States;

(ii) a statement of the nationalities, ages, and gender of such children;

(iii) a description of the policies and procedures used to effect the removal of such children from the United States and the steps taken to ensure that such children were safely and humanely repatriated to their country of nationality or of last habitual residence, including a description of the repatriation pilot program created pursuant to subparagraph (A);

(iv) a description of the type of immigration relief sought and denied to such children;

(v) any information gathered in assessments of country and local conditions pursuant to paragraph (2); and

(vi) statistical information and other data on unaccompanied alien children as provided for in section 462(b)(1)(J) of the Homeland Security Act of 2002 (6 U.S.C. 279(b)(1)(J)).

(D) Placement in removal proceedings. Any unaccompanied alien child sought to be removed by the Department of Homeland Security, except for an unaccompanied alien child from a contiguous country subject to exceptions under subsection (a)(2), shall be—

(i) placed in removal proceedings under section 240 of the Immigration and Nationality Act (8 U.S.C. 1229a);

(ii) eligible for relief under section 240B of such Act (8 U.S.C. 1229c) at no cost to the child; and

(iii) provided access to counsel in accordance with subsection (c)(5).

(b) Combating child trafficking and exploitation in the United States.

(1) Care and custody of unaccompanied alien children. Consistent with section 462 of the Homeland Security Act of 2002 (6 U.S.C. 279), and except as otherwise provided under subsection (a), the care and custody of all unaccompanied alien children, including responsibility for their detention, where appropriate, shall be the responsibility of the Secretary of Health and Human Services.

(2) Notification. Each department or agency of the Federal Government shall notify the Department of Health and Human services [Services] within 48 hours upon—

(A) the apprehension or discovery of an unaccompanied alien child; or

(B) any claim or suspicion that an alien in the custody of such department or agency is under 18 years of age.

(3) Transfers of unaccompanied alien children. Except in the case of exceptional circumstances, any department or agency of the Federal Government that has an unaccompanied alien child in custody shall transfer the custody of such child to the Secretary of Health and Human Services not later than 72 hours after determining that such child is an unaccompanied alien child.

(4) Age determinations. The Secretary of Health and Human Services, in consultation with the Secretary of Homeland Security, shall develop procedures to make a prompt determination of the age of an alien, which shall be used by the Secretary of Homeland Security and the Secretary of Health and Human Services for children in their respective custody. At a minimum, these procedures shall take into account multiple forms of evidence, including the non-exclusive use of radiographs, to determine the age of the unaccompanied alien.

(c) Providing safe and secure placements for children.

(1) Policies and programs. The Secretary of Health and Human Services, Secretary of Homeland Security, Attorney General, and Secretary of State shall establish policies and programs to ensure that unaccompanied alien children in the United States are protected from traffickers and other persons seeking to victimize or otherwise engage such children in criminal, harmful, or exploitative activity, including policies and programs reflecting best practices in witness security programs.

(2) Safe and secure placements.

(A) Minors in Department of Health and Human Services custody. Subject to section 462(b)(2) of the Homeland Security Act of 2002 (6 U.S.C. 279(b)(2)), an unaccompanied alien child in the custody of the Secretary of Health and Human Services shall be promptly placed in the least restrictive setting that is in the best interest of the child. In making such placements, the Secretary may consider danger to self, danger to the community, and risk of flight. Placement of child trafficking victims may include placement in an Unaccompanied Refugee Minor program, pursuant to section 412(d) of the Immigration and Nationality Act (8 U.S.C.

1522(d)), if a suitable family member is not available to provide care. A child shall not be placed in a secure facility absent a determination that the child poses a danger to self or others or has been charged with having committed a criminal offense. The placement of a child in a secure facility shall be reviewed, at a minimum, on a monthly basis, in accordance with procedures prescribed by the Secretary, to determine if such placement remains warranted.

(B) Aliens transferred from Department of Health and Human Services to Department of Homeland Security custody. If a minor described in subparagraph (A) reaches 18 years of age and is transferred to the custody of the Secretary of Homeland Security, the Secretary shall consider placement in the least restrictive setting available after taking into account the alien's danger to self, danger to the community, and risk of flight. Such aliens shall be eligible to participate in alternative to detention programs, utilizing a continuum of alternatives based on the alien's need for supervision, which may include placement of the alien with an individual or an organizational sponsor, or in a supervised group home.

(3) Safety and suitability assessments.

(A) In general. Subject to the requirements of subparagraph (B), an unaccompanied alien child may not be placed with a person or entity unless the Secretary of Health and Human Services makes a determination that the proposed custodian is capable of providing for the child's physical and mental well-being. Such determination shall, at a minimum, include verification of the custodian's identity and relationship to the child, if any, as well as an independent finding that the individual has not engaged in any activity that would indicate a potential risk to the child.

(B) Home studies. Before placing the child with an individual, the Secretary of Health and Human Services shall determine whether a home study is first necessary. A home study shall be conducted for a child who is a victim of a severe form of trafficking in persons, a special needs child with a disability (as defined in section 3 of the Americans with Disabilities Act of 1990 (42 U.S.C. 12102(2))), a child who has been a victim of physical or sexual abuse under circumstances that indicate that the child's health or welfare has been significantly harmed or threatened, or a child whose proposed sponsor clearly presents a risk of abuse, maltreatment, exploitation, or trafficking to the child based on all available objective evidence. The Secretary of Health and Human Services shall conduct follow-up services, during the pendency of removal proceedings, on children for whom a home study was conducted and is authorized to conduct follow-up services in cases involving children with mental health or other needs who could benefit from ongoing assistance from a social welfare agency.

(C) Access to information. Not later than 2 weeks after receiving a request from the Secretary of Health and Human Services, the Secretary of Homeland Security shall provide information necessary to conduct suitability assessments from appropriate Federal, State, and local law enforcement and immigration databases.

(4) Legal orientation presentations. The Secretary of Health and Human Services shall cooperate with the Executive Office for Immigration Review to ensure that custodians receive legal orientation presentations provided through the Legal Orientation Program administered by the Executive Office for Immigration Review. At a minimum, such presentations shall address the custodian's responsibility to attempt to ensure the child's appearance at all immigration proceedings and to protect the child from mistreatment, exploitation, and trafficking.

(5) Access to counsel. The Secretary of Health and Human Services shall ensure, to the greatest extent practicable and consistent with section 292 of the Immigration and Nationality Act (8 U.S.C. 1362), that all unaccompanied alien children who are or have been in the custody of the Secretary or the Secretary of Homeland Security, and who are not described in subsection (a)(2)(A), have counsel to represent them in legal proceedings or matters and protect them from mistreatment, exploitation, and trafficking. To the greatest extent practicable, the Secretary of Health and Human Services shall make every effort to utilize the services of pro bono counsel who agree to provide representation to such children without charge.

(6) Child advocates.

(A) In general. The Secretary of Health and Human Services is authorized to appoint independent child advocates for child trafficking victims and other vulnerable unaccompanied alien children. A child advocate shall be provided access to materials necessary to effectively advocate for the best interest of the child. The child advocate shall not be compelled to testify or provide evidence in any proceeding concerning any information or opinion received from the child in the course of serving as a child advocate. The child advocate shall be presumed to be acting in good faith and be immune from civil liability for lawful conduct of duties as described in this provision.

(B) Appointment of child advocates.

(i) Initial sites. Not later than 2 years after the date of the enactment of the Violence Against Women Reauthorization Act of 2013 [enacted March 7, 2013], the Secretary of Health and Human Services shall appoint child advocates at 3 new immigration detention sites to provide independent child advocates for trafficking victims and vulnerable unaccompanied alien children.

(ii) Additional sites. Not later than 3 years after the date of the enactment of the Violence Against Women Reauthorization Act of 2013 [enacted March 7, 2013], the Secretary shall appoint child advocates at not more than 3 additional immigration detention sites.

(iii) Selection of sites. Sites at which child advocate programs will be established under this subparagraph shall be located at immigration detention sites at which more than 50 children are held in immigration custody, and shall be selected sequentially, with priority given to locations with—

(I) the largest number of unaccompanied alien children; and

(II) the most vulnerable populations of unaccompanied children.

(C) Restrictions.

(i) Administrative expenses. A child advocate program may not use more that 10 percent of the Federal funds received under this section for administrative expenses.

(ii) Nonexclusivity. Nothing in this section may be construed to restrict the ability of a child advocate program under this section to apply for or obtain funding from any other source to carry out the programs described in this section.

(iii) Contribution of funds. A child advocate program selected under this section shall contribute non-Federal funds, either directly or through in-kind contributions, to the costs of the child advocate program in an amount that is not less than 25 percent of the total amount of Federal funds received by the child advocate program under this section. In-kind contributions may not exceed 40 percent of the matching requirement under this clause.

(D) Annual report to Congress. Not later than 1 year after the date of the enactment of the Violence Against Women Reauthorization Act of 2013 [enacted March 7, 2013], and annually thereafter, the Secretary of Health and Human Services shall submit a report describing the activities undertaken by the Secretary to authorize the appointment of independent Child Advocates for trafficking victims and vulnerable unaccompanied alien children to the Committee on the Judiciary of the Senate and the Committee on the Judiciary of the House of Representatives.

(E) Assessment of Child Advocate Program.

(i) In general. As soon as practicable after the date of the enactment of the Violence Against Women Reauthorization Act of 2013 [enacted March 7, 2013], the Comptroller General of the United States shall conduct a study regarding the effectiveness of the Child Advocate Program operated by the Secretary of Health and Human Services.

(ii) Matters to be studied. In the study required under clause (i), the Comptroller General shall— collect information and analyze the following:

(I) analyze the effectiveness of existing child advocate programs in improving outcomes for trafficking victims and other vulnerable unaccompanied alien children;

(II) evaluate the implementation of child advocate programs in new sites pursuant to subparagraph (B);

(III) evaluate the extent to which eligible trafficking victims and other vulnerable unaccompanied children are receiving child advocate services and assess the possible budgetary implications of increased participation in the program;

(IV) evaluate the barriers to improving outcomes for trafficking victims and other vulnerable unaccompanied children; and

(V) make recommendations on statutory changes to improve the Child Advocate Program in relation to the matters analyzed under subclauses (I) through (IV).

(iii) GAO report. Not later than 3 years after the date of the enactment of this Act [enacted March 7, 2013], the Comptroller General of the United States shall submit the results of the study required under this subparagraph to—

(I) the Committee on the Judiciary of the Senate;

(II) the Committee on Health, Education, Labor, and Pensions of the Senate;

(III) the Committee on the Judiciary of the House of Representatives; and

(IV) the Committee on Education and the Workforce of the House of Representatives.

(F) Authorization of appropriations. There are authorized to be appropriated to the Secretary of Health and Human Services to carry out this subsection—

(i) $ 1,000,000 for each of the fiscal years 2014 and 2015; and

(ii) $ 2,000,000 for each of the fiscal years 2018 through 2021.

(d) Permanent protection for certain at-risk children.

(1) [Omitted]

(2) Expeditious adjudication. All applications for special immigrant status under section 101(a)(27)(J) of the Immigration and Nationality Act (8 U.S.C. 1101(a)(27)(J)) shall be adjudicated by the Secretary of Homeland Security not later than 180 days after the date on which the application is filed.

(3) [Omitted]

(4) Eligibility for assistance.

(A) In general. A child who has been granted special immigrant status under section 101(a)(27)(J) of the Immigration and Nationality Act (8 U.S.C. 1101(a)(27)(J)) and who was in the custody of the Secretary of Health and Human Services at the time a dependency order was granted for such child, was receiving services pursuant to section 501(a) of the Refugee Education Assistance Act of 1980 (8 U.S.C. 1522 note) at the time such dependency order was granted, or has been granted status under section 101(a)(15)(U) of the Immigration and Nationality Act (8 U.S.C. 1101(a)(15)(U)),[,] shall be eligible for placement and services under section 412(d) of the Immigration and Nationality Act (8 U.S.C. 1522(d)) until the earlier of—

(i) the date on which the child reaches the age designated in section 412(d)(2)(B) of the Immigration and Nationality Act (8 U.S.C. 1522(d)(2)(B)); or

(ii) the date on which the child is placed in a permanent adoptive home.

(B) State reimbursement. Subject to the availability of appropriations, if State foster care funds are expended on behalf of a child who is not described in subparagraph (A) and has been granted special immigrant status under section 101(a)(27)(J) of the Immigration and Nationality Act (8 U.S.C. 1101(a)(27)(J)), or status under section 101(a)(15)(U) of the Immigration and Nationality Act (8 U.S.C. 1101(a)(15)(U)),[,] the Federal Government shall reimburse the State in which the child resides for such expenditures by the State.

(5) State courts acting in loco parentis. A department or agency of a State, or an individual or entity appointed by a State court or juvenile court located in the

United States, acting in loco parentis, shall not be considered a legal guardian for purposes of this section or section 462 of the Homeland Security Act of 2002 (6 U.S.C. 279).

(6) Transition rule. Notwithstanding any other provision of law, an alien described in section 101(a)(27)(J) of the Immigration and Nationality Act (8 U.S.C. 1101(a)(27)(J)), as amended by paragraph (1), may not be denied special immigrant status under such section after the date of the enactment of this Act based on age if the alien was a child on the date on which the alien applied for such status.

(7) [Omitted]

(8) Specialized needs of unaccompanied alien children. Applications for asylum and other forms of relief from removal in which an unaccompanied alien child is the principal applicant shall be governed by regulations which take into account the specialized needs of unaccompanied alien children and which address both procedural and substantive aspects of handling unaccompanied alien children's cases.

(e) Training. The Secretary of State, the Secretary of Homeland Security, the Secretary of Health and Human Services, and the Attorney General shall provide specialized training to all Federal personnel, and upon request, state [State] and local personnel, who have substantive contact with unaccompanied alien children. Such personnel shall be trained to work with unaccompanied alien children, including identifying children who are victims of severe forms of trafficking in persons, and children for whom asylum or special immigrant relief may be appropriate, including children described in subsection (a)(2).

(f) [Omitted]

(g) Definition of unaccompanied alien child. For purposes of this section, the term "unaccompanied alien child" has the meaning given such term in section 462(g) of the Homeland Security Act of 2002 (6 U.S.C. 279(g)).

(h) Effective date. This section—

(1) shall take effect on the date that is 90 days after the date of the enactment of this Act [enacted Dec. 23, 2008]; and

(2) shall also apply to all aliens in the United States in pending proceedings before the Department of Homeland Security or the Executive Office for Immigration Review, or related administrative or Federal appeals, on the date of the enactment of this Act [enacted Dec. 23, 2008].

(i) Grants and contracts. The Secretary of Health and Human Services may award grants to, and enter into contracts with, voluntary agencies to carry out this section and section 462 of the Homeland Security Act of 2002 (6 U.S.C. 279).

(Dec. 23, 2008, P. L. 110-457, Title II, Subtitle D, § 235, 122 Stat. 5074; March 7, 2013, P. L. 113-4, Title XII, Subtitle D, §§ 1261–1263, 127 Stat. 156; Dec. 21, 2018, P.L. 115-393, Title III, § 301(d), 132 Stat. 5272.)

ADJUSTMENT AND CHANGE OF STATUS

§ 1251. [Transferred]

§ 1251a. [Repealed]

§ 1252. Judicial review of orders of removal

(a) Applicable provisions.

(1) General orders of removal. Judicial review of a final order of removal (other than an order of removal without a hearing pursuant to section 235(b)(1) [8 USCS § 1225(b)(1)]) is governed only by chapter 158 of title 28 of the United States Code [28 USCS §§ 2341 et seq.], except as provided in subsection (b) and except that the court may not order the taking of additional evidence under section 2347(c) of such title.

(2) Matters not subject to judicial review.

(A) Review relating to section 235(b)(1). Notwithstanding any other provision of law (statutory or nonstatutory), including section 2241 of title 28, United States Code [28 USCS § 2241], or any other habeas corpus provision, and sections 1361 and 1651 of such title [28 USCS §§ 1361 and 1651], no court shall have jurisdiction to review—

(i) except as provided in subsection (e), any individual determination or to entertain any other cause or claim arising from or relating to the implementation or operation of an order of removal pursuant to section 235(b)(1) [8 USCS § 1225(b)(1)],

(ii) except as provided in subsection (e), a decision by the Attorney General to invoke the provisions of such section,

(iii) the application of such section to individual aliens, including the determination made under section 235(b)(1)(B) [8 USCS § 1225(b)(1)(B)], or

(iv) except as provided in subsection (e), procedures and policies adopted by the Attorney General to implement the provisions of section 235(b)(1) [8 USCS § 1225(b)(1)].

(B) Denials of discretionary relief. Notwithstanding any other provision of law (statutory or nonstatutory), including section 2241 of title 28, United States Code [28 USCS § 2241], or any other habeas corpus provision, and sections 1361 and 1651 of such title [28 USCS §§ 1361 and 1651], and except as provided in subparagraph (D), and regardless of whether the judgment, decision, or action is made in removal proceedings, no court shall have jurisdiction to review—

(i) any judgment regarding the granting of relief under section 212(h), 212(i), 240A, 240B, or 245 [8 USCS § 1182(h), 1182(i), 1229b, 1229c, or 1255], or

(ii) any other decision or action of the Attorney General or the Secretary of Homeland Security the authority for which is specified under this title [8 USCS §§ 1151 et seq.] to be in the discretion of the Attorney General or the Secretary of Homeland Security, other than the granting of relief under section 208(a) [8 USCS § 1158(a)].

(C) Orders against criminal aliens. Notwithstanding any other provision of law (statutory or nonstatutory), including section 2241 of title 28, United States Code [28 USCS § 2241], or any other habeas corpus provision, and sections 1361 and 1651 of such title [28 USCS §§ 1361 and 1651], and except as provided in subparagraph (D), no court shall have jurisdiction to review any final order of removal against an alien who is removable by reason of having committed a criminal offense covered in section 212(a)(2) or 237(a)(2)(A)(iii), (B), (C), or (D) [8 USCS § 1182(a)(2) or 1227(a)(2)(A)(iii), (B), (C), or (D)], or any offense covered by section 237(a)(2)(A)(ii) [8 USCS § 1227(a)(2)(A)(ii)] for which both predicate offenses are, without regard to their date of commission, otherwise covered by section 237(a)(2)(A)(i) [8 USCS § 1227(a)(2)(A)(i)].

(D) Judicial review of certain legal claims. Nothing in subparagraph (B) or (C), or in any other provision of this Act (other than this section) which limits or eliminates judicial review, shall be construed as precluding review of constitutional claims or questions of law raised upon a petition for review filed with an appropriate court of appeals in accordance with this section.

(3) Treatment of certain decisions. No alien shall have a right to appeal from a decision of an immigration judge which is based solely on a certification described in section 240(c)(1)(B) [8 USCS § 1229a(c)(1)(B)].

(4) Claims under the United Nations Convention. Notwithstanding any other provision of law (statutory or nonstatutory), including section 2241 of title 28, United States Code [28 USCS § 2241], or any other habeas corpus provision, and sections 1361 and 1651 of such title [28 USCS §§ 1361 and 1651], a petition for review filed with an appropriate court of appeals in accordance with this section shall be the sole and exclusive means for judicial review of any cause or claim under the United Nations Convention Against Torture and Other Forms of Cruel, Inhuman, or Degrading Treatment or Punishment, except as provided in subsection (e).

(5) Exclusive means of review. Notwithstanding any other provision of law (statutory or nonstatutory), including section 2241 of title 28, United States Code [28 USCS § 2241], or any other habeas corpus provision, and sections 1361 and 1651 of such title [28 USCS §§ 1361 and 1651], a petition for review filed with an appropriate court of appeals in accordance with this section shall be the sole and exclusive means for judicial review of an order of removal entered or issued under any provision of this Act, except as provided in subsection (e). For purposes of this Act, in every provision that limits or eliminates judicial review or jurisdiction to review, the terms "judicial review" and "jurisdiction to review" include habeas corpus review pursuant to section 2241 of title 28, United States Code [28 USCS § 2241], or any other habeas corpus provision, sections 1361 and 1651 of such title [28 USCS §§ 1361 and 1651], and review pursuant to any other provision of law (statutory or nonstatutory).

(b) Requirements for review of orders of removal. With respect to review of an order of removal under subsection (a)(1), the following requirements apply:

(1) Deadline. The petition for review must be filed not later than 30 days after the date of the final order of removal.

(2) Venue and forms. The petition for review shall be filed with the court of appeals for the judicial circuit in which the immigration judge completed the proceedings. The record and briefs do not have to be printed. The court of appeals shall review the proceeding on a typewritten record and on typewritten briefs.

(3) Service.

(A) In general. The respondent is the Attorney General. The petition shall be served on the Attorney General and on the officer or employee of the Service in charge of the Service district in which the final order of removal under section 240 [8 USCS § 1229a] was entered.

(B) Stay of order. Service of the petition on the officer or employee does not stay the removal of an alien pending the court's decision on the petition, unless the court orders otherwise.

(C) Alien's brief. The alien shall serve and file a brief in connection with a petition for judicial review not later than 40 days after the date on which the administrative record is available, and may serve and file a reply brief not later than 14 days after service of the brief of the Attorney General, and the court may not extend these deadlines except upon motion for good cause shown. If an alien fails to file a brief within the time provided in this paragraph, the court shall dismiss the appeal unless a manifest injustice would result.

(4) Scope and standard for review. Except as provided in paragraph (5)(B)—

(A) the court of appeals shall decide the petition only on the administrative record on which the order of removal is based,

(B) the administrative findings of fact are conclusive unless any reasonable adjudicator would be compelled to conclude to the contrary,

(C) a decision that an alien is not eligible for admission to the United States is conclusive unless manifestly contrary to law, and

(D) the Attorney General's discretionary judgment whether to grant relief under section 208(a) [8 USCS § 1158(a)] shall be conclusive unless manifestly contrary to the law and an abuse of discretion.

No court shall reverse a determination made by a trier of fact with respect to the availability of corroborating evidence, as described in section 208(b)(1)(B), 240(c)(4)(B), or 241(b)(3)(C) [8 USCS § 1158(b)(1)(B), 1229a(c)(4)(B), or 1231(b)(3)(C)], unless the court finds, pursuant to section 242(b)(4)(B) [subsec. (b)(4)(B) of this section], that a reasonable trier of fact is compelled to conclude that such corroborating evidence is unavailable.

(5) Treatment of nationality claims.

(A) Court determination if no issue of fact. If the petitioner claims to be a national of the United States and the court of appeals finds from the pleadings and affidavits that no genuine issue of material fact about the petitioner's nationality is presented, the court shall decide the nationality claim.

(B) Transfer if issue of fact. If the petitioner claims to be a national of the United States and the court of appeals finds that a genuine issue of material fact about the petitioner's nationality is presented, the court shall transfer the proceeding to the district court of the United States for the judicial district in which the petitioner resides for a new hearing on the nationality claim and a decision on that claim as if an action had been brought in the district court under section 2201 of title 28, United States Code.

(C) Limitation on determination. The petitioner may have such nationality claim decided only as provided in this paragraph.

(6) Consolidation with review of motions to reopen or reconsider. When a petitioner seeks review of an order under this section, any review sought of a motion to reopen or reconsider the order shall be consolidated with the review of the order.

(7) Challenge to validity of orders in certain criminal proceedings.

(A) In general. If the validity of an order of removal has not been judicially decided, a defendant in a criminal proceeding charged with violating section 243(a) [8 USCS § 1253(a)] may challenge the validity of the order in the criminal proceeding only by filing a separate motion before trial. The district court, without a jury, shall decide the motion before trial.

(B) Claims of United States nationality. If the defendant claims in the motion to be a national of the United States and the district court finds that—

(i) no genuine issue of material fact about the defendant's nationality is presented, the court shall decide the motion only on the administrative record on which the removal order is based and the administrative findings of fact are conclusive if supported by reasonable, substantial, and probative evidence on the record considered as a whole; or

(ii) a genuine issue of material fact about the defendant's nationality is presented, the court shall hold a new hearing on the nationality claim and decide that claim as if an action had been brought under section 2201 of title 28, United States Code.

The defendant may have such nationality claim decided only as provided in this subparagraph.

(C) Consequence of invalidation. If the district court rules that the removal order is invalid, the court shall dismiss the indictment for violation of section 243(a) [8 USCS § 1253(a)]. The United States Government may appeal the dismissal to the court of appeals for the appropriate circuit within 30 days after the date of the dismissal.

(D) Limitation on filing petitions for review. The defendant in a criminal proceeding under section 243(a) [8 USCS § 1253(a)] may not file a petition for review under subsection (a) during the criminal proceeding.

(8) Construction. This subsection—

(A) does not prevent the Attorney General, after a final order of removal has been issued, from detaining the alien under section 241(a) [8 USCS § 1231(a)];

(B) does not relieve the alien from complying with section 241(a)(4) [8 USCS § 1231(a)(4)] and section 243(g); and

(C) does not require the Attorney General to defer removal of the alien.

(9) Consolidation of questions for judicial review. Judicial review of all questions of law and fact, including interpretation and application of constitutional and statutory provisions, arising from any action taken or proceeding brought to remove an alien from the United States under this title [8 USCS §§ 1151 et seq.] shall be available only in judicial review of a final order under this section. Except as otherwise provided in this section, no court shall have jurisdiction, by habeas corpus under section 2241 of title 28, United States Code [28 USCS § 2241], or any other habeas corpus provision, by section 1361 or 1651 of such title [28 USCS § 1361 or 1651], or by any other provision of law (statutory or nonstatutory), to review such an order or such questions of law or fact.

(c) Requirements for petition. A petition for review or habeas corpus of an order of removal—

(1) shall attach a copy of such order, and

(2) shall state whether a court has upheld the validity of the order, and, if so, shall state the name of the court, the date of the court's ruling, and the kind of proceeding.

(d) Review of final orders. A court may review a final order of removal only if—

(1) the alien has exhausted all administrative remedies available to the alien as of right, and

(2) another court has not decided the validity of the order, unless the reviewing court finds that the petition presents grounds that could not have been presented in the prior judicial proceeding or that the remedy provided by the prior proceeding was inadequate or ineffective to test the validity of the order.

(e) Judicial review of orders under section 235(b)(1).

(1) Limitations on relief. Without regard to the nature of the action or claim and without regard to the identity of the party or parties bringing the action, no court may—

(A) enter declaratory, injunctive, or other equitable relief in any action pertaining to an order to exclude an alien in accordance with section 235(b)(1) [8 USCS § 1225(b)(1)] except as specifically authorized in a subsequent paragraph of this subsection, or

(B) certify a class under Rule 23 of the Federal Rules of Civil Procedure in any action for which judicial review is authorized under a subsequent paragraph of this subsection.

(2) Habeas corpus proceedings. Judicial review of any determination made under section 235(b)(1) [8 USCS § 1225(b)(1)] is available in habeas corpus proceedings, but shall be limited to determinations of—

(A) whether the petitioner is an alien,

(B) whether the petitioner was ordered removed under such section, and

(C) whether the petitioner can prove by a preponderance of the evidence that the petitioner is an alien lawfully admitted for permanent residence, has been admitted as a refugee under section 207 [8 USCS § 1157], or has been granted asylum under section 208 [8 USCS § 1158], such status not having been terminated, and is entitled to such further inquiry as prescribed by the Attorney General pursuant to section 235(b)(1)(C) [8 USCS § 1225(b)(1)(C)].

(3) Challenges on validity of the system.

(A) In general. Judicial review of determinations under section 235(b) [8 USCS § 1225(b)] and its implementation is available in an action instituted in the

United States District Court for the District of Columbia, but shall be limited to determinations of—

(i) whether such section, or any regulation issued to implement such section, is constitutional; or

(ii) whether such a regulation, or a written policy directive, written policy guideline, or written procedure issued by or under the authority of the Attorney General to implement such section, is not consistent with applicable provisions of this title or is otherwise in violation of law.

(B) Deadlines for bringing actions. Any action instituted under this paragraph must be filed no later than 60 days after the date the challenged section, regulation, directive, guideline, or procedure described in clause (i) or (ii) of subparagraph (A) is first implemented.

(C) Notice of appeal. A notice of appeal of an order issued by the District Court under this paragraph may be filed not later than 30 days after the date of issuance of such order.

(D) Expeditious consideration of cases. It shall be the duty of the District Court, the Court of Appeals, and the Supreme Court of the United States to advance on the docket and to expedite to the greatest possible extent the disposition of any case considered under this paragraph.

(4) Decision. In any case where the court determines that the petitioner—

(A) is an alien who was not ordered removed under section 235(b)(1) [8 USCS § 1225(b)(1)], or

(B) has demonstrated by a preponderance of the evidence that the alien is an alien lawfully admitted for permanent residence, has been admitted as a refugee under section 207 [8 USCS § 1157], or has been granted asylum under section 208 [8 USCS § 1158], the court may order no remedy or relief other than to require that the petitioner be provided a hearing in accordance with section 240 [8 USCS § 1229a]. Any alien who is provided a hearing under section 240 [8 USCS § 1229a] pursuant to this paragraph may thereafter obtain judicial review of any resulting final order of removal pursuant to subsection (a)(1).

(5) Scope of inquiry. In determining whether an alien has been ordered removed under section 235(b)(1) [8 USCS § 1225(b)(1)], the court's inquiry shall be limited to whether such an order in fact was issued and whether it relates to the petitioner. There shall be no review of whether the alien is actually inadmissible or entitled to any relief from removal.

(f) Limit on injunctive relief.

(1) In general. Regardless of the nature of the action or claim or of the identity of the party or parties bringing the action, no court (other than the Supreme Court) shall have jurisdiction or authority to enjoin or restrain the operation of the provisions of chapter 4 of title II [8 USCS §§ 1221 et seq.], as amended by the Illegal Immigration Reform and Immigrant Responsibility Act of 1996, other than with respect to the application of such provisions to an individual alien against whom proceedings under such chapter have been initiated.

(2) Particular cases. Notwithstanding any other provision of law, no court shall enjoin the removal of any alien pursuant to a final order under this section unless the alien shows by clear and convincing evidence that the entry or execution of such order is prohibited as a matter of law.

(3) Certain actions. Paragraph (1) shall not apply to an action brought pursuant to section 235(b)(3) [8 USCS § 1225(b)(3)], subsections (e) or (f) of section 236 [8 USCS § 1226], or section 241(a)(2)(B) [8 USCS § 1231(a)(2)(B)].

(g) Exclusive jurisdiction. Except as provided in this section and notwithstanding any other provision of law (statutory or nonstatutory), including section 2241 of title 28, United States Code [28 USCS § 2241], or any other habeas corpus provision, and sections 1361 and 1651 of such title [28 USCS §§ 1361 and 1651], no court shall have jurisdiction to hear any cause or claim by or on behalf of any alien arising from the decision or action by the Attorney General to commence proceedings, adjudicate cases, or execute removal orders against any alien under this Act.

(June 27, 1952, ch 477, Title II, Ch 5, § 242, 66 Stat. 208; Sept. 3, 1954, ch 1263, § 17, 68 Stat. 1232; Dec. 29, 1981, P. L. 97-116, § 18(h)(1), 95 Stat. 1620; Nov. 6, 1986, P. L. 99-603, Title VII, § 701, 100 Stat. 3445; Oct. 12, 1984, P. L. 98-473, Title II, Ch II, § 220(b), 98 Stat. 2029; Oct. 24, 1988, P. L. 100-525, § 9(n), 102 Stat. 2620; Nov. 18, 1988, P. L. 100-690, Title VII, Subtitle J, § 7343(a), 102 Stat. 4470; Nov. 29, 1990, P. L. 101-649, Title V, Subtitle A, § 504(a), Subtitle D, § 545(e), Title VI, § 603(b)(2), 104 Stat. 5049, 5066, 5085; Dec. 12, 1991, P. L. 102-232, Title III, §§ 306(a)(4), (c)(7), 307(m)(2), 309(b)(9), 105 Stat. 1751, 1753, 1757, 1759; Sept. 13, 1994, P. L. 103-322, Title II, Subtitle C, § 20301(a), Title XIII, § 130001(a), 108 Stat. 1823, 2023; Oct. 25, 1994, P. L. 103-416, Title II, §§ 219(h), 224(b), 108 Stat. 4317, 4324; April 24, 1996, P. L. 104-132, Title IV, Subtitle D, §§ 436(a), (b)(1), 438, 440(c), (h), 110 Stat. 1275, 1277, 1279; Sept. 30, 1996, P. L. 104-208, Div C, Title III, Subtitle A, §§ 306(a)(1), (2), (d), 308(g)(10)(H), Subtitle F, § 371(b)(6), 110 Stat. 3009-607, 3009-612, 3009-625, 3009-645; May 11, 2005, P. L. 109-13, Div B, Title I, §§ 101(e), (f), 106(a), 119 Stat. 305, 310; Jan. 29, 2025, P.L. 119-1, § 3(f), 139 Stat. 5.)

§ 1252a. [Transferred]

§ 1252b. [Repealed]

§ 1252c. Authorizing state and local law enforcement officials to arrest and detain certain illegal aliens

(a) In general. Notwithstanding any other provision of law, to the extent permitted by relevant State and local law, State and local law enforcement officials are authorized to arrest and detain an individual who—

(1) is an alien illegally present in the United States; and

(2) has previously been convicted of a felony in the United States and deported or left the United States after such conviction,

but only after the State or local law enforcement officials obtain appropriate confirmation from the Immigration and Naturalization Service of the status of such individual and only for such period of time as may be required for the Service to take the individual into Federal custody for purposes of deporting or removing the alien from the United States.

(b) Cooperation. The Attorney General shall cooperate with the States to assure that information in the control of the Attorney General, including information in the National Crime Information Center, that would assist State and local law enforcement officials in carrying out duties under subsection (a) is made available to such officials.

(April 24, 1996, P. L. 104-132, Title IV, Subtitle D, § 439, 110 Stat. 1276.)

§ 1253. Penalties related to removal

(a) Penalty for failure to depart.

(1) In general. Any alien against whom a final order of removal is outstanding by reason of being a member of any of the classes described in section 237(a) [8 USCS § 1227(a)], who—

(A) willfully fails or refuses to depart from the United States within a period of 90 days from the date of the final order of removal under administrative processes, or if judicial review is had, then from the date of the final order of the court,

(B) willfully fails or refuses to make timely application in good faith for travel or other documents necessary to the alien's departure,

(C) connives or conspires, or takes any other action, designed to prevent or hamper or with the purpose of preventing or hampering the alien's departure pursuant to such, or

(D) willfully fails or refuses to present himself or herself for removal at the time and place required by the Attorney General pursuant to such order,

shall be fined under title 18, United States Code, or imprisoned not more than four years (or 10 years if the alien is a member of any of the classes described in paragraph (1)(E), (2), (3), or (4) of section 237(a) [8 USCS § 1227(a)]), or both.

(2) Exception. It is not a violation of paragraph (1) to take any proper steps for the purpose of securing cancellation of or exemption from such order of removal or for the purpose of securing the alien's release from incarceration or custody.

(3) Suspension. The court may for good cause suspend the sentence of an alien under this subsection and order the alien's release under such conditions as the court may prescribe. In determining whether good cause has been shown to justify releasing the alien, the court shall take into account such factors as—

(A) the age, health, and period of detention of the alien;

(B) the effect of the alien's release upon the national security and public peace or safety;

(C) the likelihood of the alien's resuming or following a course of conduct which made or would make the alien deportable;

(D) the character of the efforts made by such alien himself and by representatives of the country or countries to which the alien's removal is directed to expedite the alien's departure from the United States;

(E) the reason for the inability of the Government of the United States to secure passports, other travel documents, or removal facilities from the country or countries to which the alien has been ordered removed; and

(F) the eligibility of the alien for discretionary relief under the immigration laws.

(b) Willful failure to comply with terms of release under supervision. An alien who shall willfully fail to comply with regulations or requirements issued pursuant to section 241(a)(3) [8 USCS § 1231(a)(3)] or knowingly give false information in response to an inquiry under such section shall be fined not more than $1,000 or imprisoned for not more than one year, or both.

(c) Penalties relating to vessels and aircraft.

(1) Civil penalties.

(A) Failure to carry out certain orders. If the Attorney General is satisfied that a person has violated subsection (d) or (e) of section 241 [8 USCS § 1231], the person shall pay to the Commissioner the sum of $2,000 for each violation.

(B) Failure to remove alien stowaways. If the Attorney General is satisfied that a person has failed to remove an alien stowaway as required under section 241(d)(2) [8 USCS § 1231(d)(2)], the person shall pay to the Commissioner the sum of $5,000 for each alien stowaway not removed.

(C) No compromise. The Attorney General may not compromise the amount of such penalty under this paragraph.

(2) Clearing vessels and aircraft.

(A) Clearance before decision on liability. A vessel or aircraft may be granted clearance before a decision on liability is made under paragraph (1) only if a bond approved by the Attorney General or an amount sufficient to pay the civil penalty is deposited with the Commissioner.

(B) Prohibition on clearance while penalty unpaid. A vessel or aircraft may not be granted clearance if a civil penalty imposed under paragraph (1) is not paid.

(d) Discontinuing granting visas to nationals of country denying or delaying accepting alien. On being notified by the Attorney General that the government of a foreign country denies or unreasonably delays accepting an alien who is a citizen, subject, national, or resident of that country after the Attorney General asks whether the government will accept the alien under this section, the Secretary of State shall order consular officers in that foreign country to discontinue granting immigrant visas or nonimmigrant visas, or both, to citizens, subjects, nationals, and residents of that country until the Attorney General notifies the Secretary that the country has accepted the alien.

(e) Enforcement by attorney general of a State. The attorney general of a State, or other authorized State officer, alleging a violation of the requirement to discontinue granting visas to citizens, subjects, nationals, and residents as described in subsection (d) that harms such State or its residents shall have standing to bring an action against the Secretary of State on behalf of such State or the residents of such State in an appropriate district court of the United States to obtain appropriate injunctive relief. The court shall advance on the docket and expedite the disposition of a civil action filed under this subsection to the greatest extent practicable. For purposes of this subsection, a State or its residents shall be considered to have been harmed if the State or its residents experience harm, including financial harm in excess of $100.

(June 27, 1952, ch 477, Title II, Ch 5, § 243, 66 Stat. 212; Oct. 3, 1965, P. L. 89-236, § 11(f), 79 Stat. 918; Oct. 30, 1978, P. L. 95-549, Title I, § 104, 92 Stat. 2066; March 17, 1980, P. L. 96-212, Title II, § 203(e), 94 Stat. 107; Dec. 29, 1981, P. L. 97-116, § 18(i), 95 Stat. 1620; Nov. 29, 1990, P. L. 101-649, Title V, Subtitle A, § 515(a)(2), Title VI, § 603(b)(3), 104 Stat. 5053, 5085; April 24, 1996, P. L. 104-132, Title IV, Subtitle B, § 413(a), (f), 110 Stat. 1269; Sept. 30, 1996, P. L. 104-208, Div C, Title III, Subtitle A, § 307(a), 110 Stat. 3009-612; Jan. 29, 2025, P.L. 119-1, § 3(c), 139 Stat. 4.)

§ 1254. [Repealed]

§ 1254a. Temporary protected status

(a) Granting of status.

(1) In general. In the case of an alien who is a national of a foreign state designated under subsection (b) (or in the case of an alien having no nationality, is a person who last habitually resided in such designated state) and who meets the requirements of subsection (c), the Attorney General, in accordance with this section—

(A) may grant the alien temporary protected status in the United States and shall not remove the alien from the United States during the period in which such status is in effect, and

(B) shall authorize the alien to engage in employment in the United States and provide the alien with an "employment authorized" endorsement or other appropriate work permit.

(2) Duration of work authorization. Work authorization provided under this section shall be effective throughout the period the alien is in temporary protected status under this section.

(3) Notice.

(A) Upon the granting of temporary protected status under this section, the Attorney General shall provide the alien with information concerning such status under this section.

(B) If, at the time of initiation of a removal proceeding against an alien, the foreign state (of which the alien is a national) is designated under subsection (b), the Attorney General shall promptly notify the alien of the temporary protected status that may be available under this section.

(C) If, at the time of designation of a foreign state under subsection (b), an alien (who is a national of such state) is in a removal proceeding under this title, the Attorney General shall promptly notify the alien of the temporary protected status that may be available under this section.

(D) Notices under this paragraph shall be provided in a form and language that the alien can understand.

(4) Temporary treatment for eligible aliens.

(A) In the case of an alien who can establish a prima facie case of eligibility for benefits under paragraph (1), but for the fact that the period of registration under subsection (c)(1)(A)(iv) has not begun, until the alien has had a reasonable opportunity to register during the first 30 days of such period, the Attorney General shall provide for the benefits of paragraph (1).

(B) In the case of an alien who establishes a prima facie case of eligibility for benefits under paragraph (1), until a final determination with respect to the alien's eligibility for such benefits under paragraph (1) has been made, the alien shall be provided such benefits.

(5) Clarification. Nothing in this section shall be construed as authorizing the Attorney General to deny temporary protected status to an alien based on the alien's immigration status or to require any alien, as a condition of being granted such status, either to relinquish nonimmigrant or other status the alien may have or to execute any waiver of other rights under this Act. The granting of temporary protected status under this section shall not be considered to be inconsistent with the granting of nonimmigrant status under this Act.

(b) Designations.

(1) In general. The Attorney General, after consultation with appropriate agencies of the Government, may designate any foreign state (or any part of such foreign state) under this subsection only if—

(A) the Attorney General finds that there is an ongoing armed conflict within the state and, due to such conflict, requiring the return of aliens who are nationals of that state to that state (or to the part of the state) would pose a serious threat to their personal safety;

(B) the Attorney General finds that—

(i) there has been an earthquake, flood, drought, epidemic, or other environmental disaster in the state resulting in a substantial, but temporary, disruption of living conditions in the area affected,

(ii) the foreign state is unable, temporarily, to handle adequately the return to the state of aliens who are nationals of the state, and

(iii) the foreign state officially has requested designation under this subparagraph; or

(C) the Attorney General finds that there exist extraordinary and temporary conditions in the foreign state that prevent aliens who are nationals of the state from returning to the state in safety, unless the Attorney General finds that permitting the aliens to remain temporarily in the United States is contrary to the national interest of the United States.

A designation of a foreign state (or part of such foreign state) under this paragraph shall not become effective unless notice of the designation (including a statement of the findings under this paragraph and the effective date of the designation) is published in the Federal Register. In such notice, the Attorney General shall also state an estimate of the number of nationals of the foreign state designated who are (or within the effective period of the designation are likely to become) eligible for temporary protected status under this section and their immigration status in the United States.

(2) Effective period of designation for foreign states. The designation of a foreign state (or part of such foreign state) under paragraph (1) shall—

(A) take effect upon the date of publication of the designation under such paragraph, or such later date as the Attorney General may specify in the notice published under such paragraph, and

(B) shall remain in effect until the effective date of the termination of the designation under paragraph (3)(B).

For purposes of this section, the initial period of designation of a foreign state (or part thereof) under paragraph (1) is the period, specified by the Attorney General, of not less than 6 months and not more than 18 months.

(3) Periodic review, terminations, and extensions of designations.

(A) Periodic review. At least 60 days before end of the initial period of designation, and any extended period of designation, of a foreign state (or part thereof) under this section the Attorney General, after consultation with appropriate agencies of the Government, shall review the conditions in the foreign state (or part of such foreign state) for which a designation is in effect under this subsection and shall determine whether the conditions for such designation under this subsection continue to be met. The Attorney General shall provide on a timely basis for the publication of notice of each such determination (including the basis for the determination, and, in the case of an affirmative determination, the period of extension of designation under subparagraph (C)) in the Federal Register.

(B) Termination of designation. If the Attorney General determines under subparagraph (A) that a foreign state (or part of such foreign state) no longer continues to meet the conditions for designation under paragraph (1), the Attorney General shall terminate the designation by publishing notice in the Federal Register of the determination under this subparagraph (including the basis for the determination). Such termination is effective in accordance with subsection (d)(3), but shall not be effective earlier than 60 days after the date the notice is published or, if later, the expiration of the most recent previous extension under subparagraph (C).

(C) Extension of designation. If the Attorney General does not determine under subparagraph (A) that a foreign state (or part of such foreign state) no longer meets the conditions for designation under paragraph (1), the period of designation of the foreign state is extended for an additional period of 6 months (or, in the discretion of the Attorney General, a period of 12 or 18 months).

(4) Information concerning protected status at time of designations. At the time of a designation of a foreign state under this subsection, the Attorney General shall make available information respecting the temporary protected status made available to aliens who are nationals of such designated foreign state.

(5) Review.

(A) Designations. There is no judicial review of any determination of the Attorney General with respect to the designation, or termination or extension of a designation, of a foreign state under this subsection.

(B) Application to individuals. The Attorney General shall establish an administrative procedure for the review of the denial of benefits to aliens under this subsection. Such procedure shall not prevent an alien from asserting protection under this section in removal proceedings if the alien demonstrates that the alien is a national of a state designated under paragraph (1).

(c) Aliens eligible for temporary protected status.

(1) In general.

(A) Nationals of designated foreign states. Subject to paragraph (3), an alien, who is a national of a state designated under subsection (b)(1) or in the case of an alien having no nationality, is a person who last habitually resided in such designated state), meets the requirements of this paragraph only if—

(i) the alien has been continuously physically present in the United States since the effective date of the most recent designation of that state;

(ii) the alien has continuously resided in the United States since such date as the Attorney General may designate;

(iii) the alien is admissible as an immigrant, except as otherwise provided under paragraph (2)(A), and is not ineligible for temporary protected status under paragraph (2)(B); and

(iv) to the extent and in a manner which the Attorney General establishes, the alien registers for the temporary protected status under this section during a registration period of not less than 180 days.

(B) Registration fee. The Attorney General may require payment of a reasonable fee as a condition of registering an alien under subparagraph (A)(iv) (including providing an alien with an "employment authorized" endorsement or other appropriate work permit under this section). The amount of any such fee shall not exceed $50. In the case of aliens registered pursuant to a designation under this section made after July 17, 1991, the Attorney General may impose a separate, additional fee for providing an alien with documentation of work authorization. Notwithstanding section 3302 of title 31, United States Code, all fees collected under this subparagraph shall be credited to the appropriation to be used in carrying out this section.

(2) Eligibility standards.

(A) Waiver of certain grounds for inadmissibility. In the determination of an alien's admissibility for purposes of subparagraph (A)(iii) of paragraph (1)—

(i) the provisions of paragraphs (5) and (7)(A) of section 212(a) [8 USCS § 1182(a)(5), (7)(A)] shall not apply;

(ii) except as provided in clause (iii), the Attorney General may waive any other provision of section 212(a) [8 USCS § 1182(a)] in the case of individual aliens for humanitarian purposes, to assure family unity, or when it is otherwise in the public interest; but

(iii) the Attorney General may not waive—

(I) paragraphs (2)(A) and (2)(B) (relating to criminals) of such section,

(II) paragraph (2)(C) of such section (relating to drug offenses), except for so much of such paragraph as relates to a single offense of simple possession of 30 grams or less of marijuana, or

(III) paragraphs (3)(A), (3)(B), (3)(C), and (3)(E) of such section (relating to national security and participation in the Nazi persecutions or those who have engaged in genocide).

(B) Aliens ineligible. An alien shall not be eligible for temporary protected status under this section if the Attorney General finds that—

(i) the alien has been convicted of any felony or 2 or more misdemeanors committed in the United States, or

(ii) the alien is described in section 208(b)(2)(A) [8 USCS § 1158(b)(2)(A)].

(3) Withdrawal of temporary protected status. The Attorney General shall withdraw temporary protected status granted to an alien under this section if—

(A) the Attorney General finds that the alien was not in fact eligible for such status under this section,

(B) except as provided in paragraph (4) and permitted in subsection (f)(3), the alien has not remained continuously physically present in the United States from the date the alien first was granted temporary protected status under this section, or

(C) the alien fails, without good cause, to register with the Attorney General annually, at the end of each 12-month period after the granting of such status, in a form and manner specified by the Attorney General.

(4) Treatment of brief, casual, and innocent departures and certain other absences.

(A) For purposes of paragraphs (1)(A)(i) and (3)(B), an alien shall not be considered to have failed to maintain continuous physical presence in the United States by virtue of brief, casual, and innocent absences from the United States, without regard to whether such absences were authorized by the Attorney General.

(B) For purposes of paragraph (1)(A)(ii), an alien shall not be considered to have failed to maintain continuous residence in the United States by reason of a brief, casual, and innocent absence described in subparagraph (A) or due merely to a brief temporary trip abroad required by emergency or extenuating circumstances outside the control of the alien.

(5) Construction. Nothing in this section shall be construed as authorizing an alien to apply for admission to, or to be admitted to, the United States in order to apply for temporary protected status under this section.

(6) Confidentiality of information. The Attorney General shall establish procedures to protect the confidentiality of information provided by aliens under this section.

(d) Documentation.

(1) Initial issuance. Upon the granting of temporary protected status to an alien under this section, the Attorney General shall provide for the issuance of such temporary documentation and authorization as may be necessary to carry out the purposes of this section.

(2) Period of validity. Subject to paragraph (3), such documentation shall be valid during the initial period of designation of the foreign state (or part thereof) involved and any extension of such period. The Attorney General may stagger the periods of validity of the documentation and authorization in order to provide for an orderly renewal of such documentation and authorization and for an orderly transition (under paragraph (3)) upon the termination of a designation of a foreign state (or any part of such foreign state).

(3) Effective date of terminations. If the Attorney General terminates the designation of a foreign state (or part of such foreign state) under subsection (b)(3)(B), such termination shall only apply to documentation and authorization issued or renewed after the effective date of the publication of notice of the determination under that subsection (or, at the Attorney General's option, after such period after the effective date of the determination as the Attorney General determines to be appropriate in order to provide for an orderly transition).

(4) Detention of the alien. An alien provided temporary protected status under this section shall not be detained by the Attorney General on the basis of the alien's immigration status in the United States.

(e) Relation of period of temporary protected status to cancellation of removal. With respect to an alien granted temporary protected status under this section, the period of such status shall not be counted as a period of physical presence in the United States for purposes of section 240A(a) [8 USCS § 1229b(a)] unless the Attorney General determines that extreme hardship exists. Such period shall not cause a break in the continuity of residence of the period before and after such period for purposes of such section.

(f) Benefits and status during period of temporary protected status. During a period in which an alien is granted temporary protected status under this section—

(1) the alien shall not be considered to be permanently residing in the United States under color of law;

(2) the alien may be deemed ineligible for public assistance by a State (as defined in section 101(a)(36) [8 USCS § 1101(a)(36)]) or any political subdivision thereof which furnishes such assistance;

(3) the alien may travel abroad with the prior consent of the Attorney General; and

(4) for purposes of adjustment of status under section 245 [8 USCS § 1255] and change of status under section 248 [8 USCS § 1258], the alien shall be considered as being in, and maintaining, lawful status as a nonimmigrant.

(g) Exclusive remedy. Except as otherwise specifically provided, this section shall constitute the exclusive authority of the Attorney General under law to permit aliens who are or may become otherwise deportable or have been paroled into the United States to remain in the United States temporarily because of their particular nationality or region of foreign state of nationality.

(h) Limitation on consideration in the Senate of legislation adjusting status.

(1) In general. Except as provided in paragraph (2), it shall not be in order in the Senate to consider any bill, resolution, or amendment that—

(A) provides for adjustment to lawful temporary or permanent resident alien status for any alien receiving temporary protected status under this section, or

(B) has the effect of amending this subsection or limiting the application of this subsection.

(2) Supermajority required. Paragraph (1) may be waived or suspended in the Senate only by the affirmative vote of three-fifths of the Members duly chosen and sworn. An affirmative vote of three-fifths of the Members of the Senate duly chosen and sworn shall be required in the Senate to sustain an appeal of the ruling of the Chair on a point of order raised under paragraph (1).

(3) Rules. Paragraphs (1) and (2) are enacted—

(A) as an exercise of the rulemaking power of the Senate and as such they are deemed a part of the rules of the Senate, but applicable only with respect to the matters described in paragraph (1) and supersede other rules of the Senate only to the extent that such paragraphs are inconsistent therewith; and

(B) with full recognition of the constitutional right of the Senate to change such rules at any time, in the same manner as in the case of any other rule of the Senate.

(i) Annual report and review.

(1) Annual report. Not later than March 1 of each year (beginning with 1992), the Attorney General, after consultation with the appropriate agencies of the Government, shall submit a report to the Committees on the Judiciary of the House of Representatives and of the Senate on the operation of this section during the previous year. Each report shall include—

(A) a listing of the foreign states or parts thereof designated under this section,

(B) the number of nationals of each such state who have been granted temporary protected status under this section and their immigration status before being granted such status, and

(C) an explanation of the reasons why foreign states or parts thereof were designated under subsection (b)(1) and, with respect to foreign states or parts thereof previously designated, why the designation was terminated or extended under subsection (b)(3).

(2) Committee report. No later than 180 days after the date of receipt of such a report, the Committee on the Judiciary of each House of Congress shall report to its respective House such oversight findings and legislation as it deems appropriate.

(June 27, 1952, ch 477, Title II, § 244 [244A], as added Nov. 29, 1990, P. L. 101-649, Title III, § 302(a), Title VI, § 603(a)(24), 104 Stat. 5030, 5084; Dec. 12, 1991, P. L. 102-232, Title III, §§ 304(b), 307(l)(5), 105 Stat. 1749, 1756; Oct. 25, 1994, P. L. 103-416, Title II, § 219(j), (z)(2), 108 Stat. 4317, 4318; Sept. 30, 1996, P. L. 104-208, Div C, Title III, Subtitle A, §§ 308(b)(7), (e)(1)(G), (11), (g)(7)(E)(i), (8)(A)(i), 110 Stat. 3009-615, 3009-619, 3009-620, 3009-624.)

§ 1254b. Collection of fees under temporary protected status program

(a) In addition to collection of registration fees described in section 244(c)(1)(B) of the Immigration and Nationality Act (8 U.S.C. 1254a(c)(1)(B)), fees for fingerprinting services, biometric services, and other necessary services may be collected when administering the program described in section 244 of such Act.

(b) Subsection (a) shall be construed to apply for fiscal year 1998 and each fiscal year thereafter.

(Oct. 28, 2009, P. L. 111-83, Title V, § 549, 123 Stat. 2177.)

§ 1255. Adjustment of status of nonimmigrant to that of person admitted for permanent residence

(a) Status as person admitted for permanent residence on application and eligibility for immigrant visa. The status of an alien who was inspected and admitted or paroled into the United States or the status of any other alien having an approved petition for classification as a VAWA self-petitioner may be adjusted by the Attorney General, in his discretion and under such regulations as he may prescribe, to that of an alien lawfully admitted for permanent residence if (1) the alien makes an application for such adjustment, (2) the alien is eligible to receive an immigrant visa and is admissible to the United States for permanent residence, and (3) an immigrant visa is immediately available to him at the time his application is filed.

(b) Record of lawful admission for permanent residence; reduction of preference visas. Upon the approval of an application for adjustment made under subsection (a), the Attorney General shall record the alien's lawful admission for permanent residence as of the date the order of the Attorney General approving the application for the adjustment of status is made, and the Secretary of State shall reduce by one the number of the preference visas authorized to be issued under sections 202 and 203 [8 USCS §§ 1152, 1153] within the class to which the alien is chargeable for the fiscal year then current.

(c) Alien crewmen, aliens continuing or accepting unauthorized employment, and aliens admitted in transit without a visa. Other than an alien having an approved petition for classification as a VAWA self-petitioner, subsection (a) shall not be applicable to (1) an alien crewman; (2) subject to subsection (k), an alien (other than an immediate relative as defined in section 201(b) [8 USCS § 1151(b)] or a special immigrant described in section 101(a)(27)(H), (I), (J), or (K) [8 USCS § 1101(a)(27)(H), (I), (J), or (K)]) who hereafter continues in or accepts unauthorized employment prior to filing an application for adjustment of status or who is in unlawful immigration status on the date of filing the application for adjustment of status or who has failed (other than through no fault of his own or for technical reasons) to maintain continuously a lawful status since entry into the United States; (3) any alien admitted in transit without visa under section 212(d)(4)(C) [8 USCS § 1182(d)(4)(C)]; (4) an alien (other than an immediate relative as defined in section 201(b) [8 USCS § 1151(b)]) who was admitted as a nonimmigrant visitor without a visa under section 212(l) or section 217 [8 USCS § 1182(l) or 1187]; (5) an alien who was admitted as a nonimmigrant described in section 101(a)(15)(S) [8 USCS § 1101(a)(15)(S)], [;] (6) an alien who is deportable under section 237(a)(4)(B) [8 USCS § 1227(a)(4)(B)]; (7) any alien who seeks adjustment of status to that of an immigrant under section 203(b) [8 USCS § 1153(b)] and is not in a lawful nonimmigrant status; or (8) any alien who was employed while the alien was an unauthorized alien, as defined in section 274A(h)(3) [8 USCS § 1324a(h)(3)], or who has otherwise violated the terms of a nonimmigrant visa.

(d) Alien admitted for permanent residence on conditional basis; fiancee or fiance of citizen. The Attorney General may not adjust, under subsection (a), the status of an alien lawfully admitted to the United States for permanent residence on a conditional basis under section 216 [8 USCS § 1186a]. The Attorney General may not adjust, under subsection (a), the status of a nonimmigrant alien described in section 101(a)(15)(K) [8 USCS § 1101(a)(15)(K)] except to that of an alien lawfully admitted to the United States on a conditional basis under section 216 [8 USCS § 1186a] as a result of the marriage of the nonimmigrant (or, in the case of a minor child, the parent) to the citizen who filed the petition to accord that alien's nonimmigrant status under section 101(a)(15)(K) [8 USCS § 1101(a)(15)(K)].

(e) Restriction on adjustment of status based upon marriages entered while in admissibility or deportation proceedings; bona fide marriage exception.

(1) Except as provided in paragraph (3), an alien who is seeking to receive an immigrant visa on the basis of a marriage which was entered into during the period described in paragraph (2) may not have the alien's status adjusted under subsection (a).

(2) The period described in this paragraph is the period during which administrative or judicial proceedings are pending regarding the alien's right to be admitted or remain in the United States.

(3) Paragraph (1) and section 204(g) [8 USCS § 1154(g)] shall not apply with respect to a marriage if the alien establishes by clear and convincing evidence to the satisfaction of the Attorney General that the marriage was entered into in good faith and in accordance with the laws of the place where the marriage took place and the marriage was not entered into for the purpose of procuring the alien's admission as an immigrant and no fee or other consideration was given (other than a fee or other consideration to an attorney for assistance in preparation of a lawful petition) for the filing of a petition under section 204(a) [8 USCS § 1154(a)] or subsection (d) or (p) of section 214 [8 USCS § 1184] with respect to the alien spouse or alien son or daughter. In accordance with regulations, there shall be only one level of administrative appellate review for each alien under the previous sentence.

(f) Limitation on adjustment of status. The Attorney General may not adjust, under subsection (a), the status of an alien lawfully admitted to the United States for permanent residence on a conditional basis under section 216A [8 USCS § 1186b].

(g) Special immigrants. In applying this section to a special immigrant described in section 101(a)(27)(K) [8 USCS § 1101(a)(27)(K)], such an immigrant shall be deemed, for purposes of subsection (a), to have been paroled into the United States.

(h) Application with respect to special immigrants. In applying this section to a special immigrant described in section 101(a)(27)(J) [8 USCS § 1101(a)(27)(J)]—

(1) such an immigrant shall be deemed, for purposes of subsection (a), to have been paroled into the United States; and

(2) in determining the alien's admissibility as an immigrant—

(A) paragraphs (4), (5)(A), (6)(A), (6)(C), (6)(D), (7)(A), and (9)(B) of section 212(a) [8 USCS § 1182(a)] shall not apply; and

(B) the Attorney General may waive other paragraphs of section 212(a) [8 USCS § 1182(a)] (other than paragraphs (2)(A), (2)(B), (2)(C) (except for so much of such paragraph as related to a single offense of simple possession of 30 grams or less of marijuana), (3)(A), (3)(B), (3)(C), and (3)(E)) in the case of individual aliens for humanitarian purposes, family unity, or when it is otherwise in the public interest.

The relationship between an alien and the alien's natural parents or prior adoptive parents shall not be considered a factor in making a waiver under paragraph (2)(B). Nothing in this subsection or section 101(a)(27)(J) [8 USCS § 1101(a)(27)(J)] shall be construed as authorizing an alien to apply for admission or be admitted to the United States in order to obtain special immigrant status described in such section.

(i) Adjustment in status of certain aliens physically present in the United States.

(1) Notwithstanding the provisions of subsections (a) and (c) of this section, an alien physically present in the United States—

(A) who—

(i) entered the United States without inspection; or

(ii) is within one of the classes enumerated in subsection (c) of this section;

(B) who is the beneficiary (including a spouse or child of the principal alien, if eligible to receive a visa under section 203(d) [8 USC § 1153(d)]) of—

(i) a petition for classification under section 204 [8 USC § 1154] that was filed with the Attorney General on or before April 30, 2001; or

(ii) an application for a labor certification under section 212(a)(5)(A) [8 USC § 1182(a)(5)(A)] that was filed pursuant to the regulations of the Secretary of Labor on or before such date; and

(C) who, in the case of a beneficiary of a petition for classification, or an application for labor certification, described in subparagraph (B) that was filed after January 14, 1998, is physically present in the United States on the date of the enactment of the LIFE Act Amendments of 2000 [enacted Dec. 21, 2000];

may apply to the Attorney General for the adjustment of his or her status to that of an alien lawfully admitted for permanent residence. The Attorney General may accept such application only if the alien remits with such application a sum equalling $1,000 as of the date of receipt of the application, but such sum shall not be required from a child under the age of seventeen, or an alien who is the spouse or unmarried child of an individual who obtained temporary or permanent resident status under section 210 or 245A of the Immigration and Nationality Act [8 USCS § 1160 or 1255a] or section 202 of the Immigration Reform and Control Act of 1986 [8 USCS § 1255a note] at any date, who—

(i) as of May 5, 1988, was the unmarried child or spouse of the individual who obtained temporary or permanent resident status under section 210 or 245A of the Immigration and Nationality Act [8 USCS § 1160 or 1255a] or section 202 of the Immigration Reform and Control Act of 1986 [8 USCS § 1255a note];

(ii) entered the United States before May 5, 1988, resided in the United States on May 5, 1988, and is not a lawful permanent resident; and

(iii) applied for benefits under section 301(a) of the Immigration Act of 1990 [8 USCS § 1255a note]. The sum specified herein shall be in addition to the fee normally required for the processing of an application under this section.

(2) Upon receipt of such an application and the sum hereby required, the Attorney General may adjust the status of the alien to that of an alien lawfully admitted for permanent residence if—

(A) the alien is eligible to receive an immigrant visa and is admissible to the United States for permanent residence; and

(B) an immigrant visa is immediately available to the alien at the time the application is filed.

(3)(A) The portion of each application fee (not to exceed $200) that the Attorney General determines is required to process an application under this section and is remitted to the Attorney General pursuant to paragraphs (1) and (2) of this subsection shall be disposed of by the Attorney General as provided in subsections (m), (n), and (o) of section 286 [8 USCS § 1356].

(B) Any remaining portion of such fees remitted under such paragraphs shall be deposited by the Attorney General into the Breached Bond/Detention Fund established under section 286(r) [8 USCS § 1356(r)], except that in the case of fees attributable to applications for a beneficiary with respect to whom a petition for classification, or an application for labor certification, described in paragraph (1)(B) was filed after January 14, 1998, one-half of such remaining portion shall be deposited by the Attorney General into the Immigration Examinations Fee Account established under section 286(m) [8 USCS § 1356(m)].

(j) Adjustment to permanent resident status.

(1) If, in the opinion of the Attorney General—

(A) a nonimmigrant admitted into the United States under section 101(a)(15)(S)(i) [8 USCS § 1101(a)(15)(S)(i)] has supplied information described in subclause (I) of such section; and

(B) the provision of such information has substantially contributed to the success of an authorized criminal investigation or the prosecution of an individual described in subclause (III) of that section,

the Attorney General may adjust the status of the alien (and the spouse, married and unmarried sons and daughters, and parents of the alien if admitted under that section) to that of an alien lawfully admitted for permanent residence if the alien is not described in section 212(a)(3)(E) [8 USCS § 1182(a)(3)(E)].

(2) If, in the sole discretion of the Attorney General—

(A) a nonimmigrant admitted into the United States under section 101(a)(15)(S)(ii) [8 USCS § 1101(a)(15)(S)(ii)] has supplied information described in subclause (I) of such section, and

(B) the provision of such information has substantially contributed to—

(i) the prevention or frustration of an act of terrorism against a United States person or United States property, or

(ii) the success of an authorized criminal investigation of, or the prosecution of, an individual involved in such an act of terrorism, and

(C) the nonimmigrant has received a reward under section 36(a) of the State Department Basic Authorities Act of 1956 [22 USCS § 2708(a)],

the Attorney General may adjust the status of the alien (and the spouse, married and unmarried sons and daughters, and parents of the alien if admitted under such section) to that of an alien lawfully admitted for permanent residence if the alien is not described in section 212(a)(3)(E) [8 USCS § 1182(a)(3)(E)].

(3) Upon the approval of adjustment of status under paragraph (1) or (2), the Attorney General shall record the alien's lawful admission for permanent residence as of the date of such approval and the Secretary of State shall reduce by one the number of visas authorized to be issued under sections 201(d) and 203(b)(4) [8 USCS §§ 1151(d) and 1153(b)(4)] for the fiscal year then current.

(k) Inapplicability of certain provisions for certain employment-based immigrants. An alien who is eligible to receive an immigrant visa under paragraph (1), (2), (3), or (5) of section 203(b) [8 USCS § 1153(b)(1), (2), (3), or (5)] (or, in the case of an alien who is an immigrant described in section 101(a)(27)(C) [8 USCS § 1101(a)(27)(C)], under section 203(b)(4) [8 USCS § 1153(b)(4)]) may adjust status pursuant to subsection (a) and notwithstanding subsection (c)(2), (c)(7), and (c)(8), if—

(1) the alien, on the date of filing an application for adjustment of status, is present in the United States pursuant to a lawful admission;

(2) the alien, subsequent to such lawful admission has not, for an aggregate period exceeding 180 days—

(A) failed to maintain, continuously, a lawful status;

(B) engaged in unauthorized employment; or

(C) otherwise violated the terms and conditions of the alien's admission.

(l) Adjustment of status for victims of trafficking.

(1) If, in the opinion of the Secretary of Homeland Security, or in the case of subparagraph (C)(i), in the opinion of the Secretary of Homeland Security, in consultation with the Attorney General, as appropriate[,] a nonimmigrant admitted into the United States under section 101(a)(15)(T)(i) [8 USCS § 1101(a)(15)(T)(i)]—

(A) has been physically present in the United States for a continuous period of at least 3 years since the date of admission as a nonimmigrant under section 101(a)(15)(T)(i) [8 USCS § 1101(a)(15)(T)(i)], or has been physically present in the United States for a continuous period during the investigation or prosecution of acts of trafficking and that, in the opinion of the

Attorney General, the investigation or prosecution is complete, whichever period of time is less;

(B) subject to paragraph (6), has, throughout such period, been a person of good moral character; and

(C)(i) has, during such period, complied with any reasonable request for assistance in the investigation or prosecution of acts of trafficking;

(ii) the alien would suffer extreme hardship involving unusual and severe harm upon removal from the United States; or

(iii) was younger than 18 years of age at the time of the victimization qualifying the alien for relief under section 101(a)(15)(T) [8 USCS § 1101(a)(15)(T)]. [,]

the Secretary of Homeland Security may adjust the status of the alien (and any person admitted under section 101(a)(15)(T)(ii) [8 USCS § 1101(a)(15)(T)(ii)] as the spouse, parent, sibling, or child of the alien) to that of an alien lawfully admitted for permanent residence.

(2) Paragraph (1) shall not apply to an alien admitted under section 101(a)(15)(T) [8 USCS § 1101(a)(15)(T)] who is inadmissible to the United States by reason of a ground that has not been waived under section 212 [8 USCS § 1182], except that, if the Secretary of Homeland Security considers it to be in the national interest to do so, the Secretary of Homeland Security, in the Attorney General's [Secretary's] discretion, may waive the application of—

(A) paragraphs (1) and (4) of section 212(a) [8 USCS § 1182(a)]; and

(B) any other provision of such section (excluding paragraphs (3), (10)(C), and (10[)](E)), if the activities rendering the alien inadmissible under the provision were caused by, or were incident to, the victimization described in section 101(a)(15)(T)(i)(I) [8 USCS § 1101(a)(15)(T)(i)(I)].

(3) An alien shall be considered to have failed to maintain continuous physical presence in the United States under paragraph (1)(A) if the alien has departed from the United States for any period in excess of 90 days or for any periods in the aggregate exceeding 180 days, unless—

(A) the absence was necessary to assist in the investigation or prosecution described in paragraph (1)(A); or

(B) an official involved in the investigation or prosecution certifies that the absence was otherwise justified.

(4)(A) The total number of aliens whose status may be adjusted under paragraph (1) during any fiscal year may not exceed 5,000.

(B) The numerical limitation of subparagraph (A) shall only apply to principal aliens and not to the spouses, sons, daughters, siblings, or parents of such aliens.

(5) Upon the approval of adjustment of status under paragraph (1), the Secretary of Homeland Security shall record the alien's lawful admission for permanent residence as of the date of such approval.

(6) For purposes of paragraph (1)(B), the Secretary of Homeland Security may waive consideration of a disqualification from good moral character with respect to an alien if the disqualification was caused by, or incident to, the trafficking described in section 101(a)(15)(T)(i)(I) [8 USCS § 1101(a)(15)(T)(i)(I)].

(7) The Secretary of Homeland Security shall permit aliens to apply for a waiver of any fees associated with filing an application for relief through final adjudication of the adjustment of status for a VAWA self-petitioner and for relief under sections 101(a)(15)(T), 101(a)(15)(U), 106, 240A(b)(2), and 244(a)(3) (as in effect on March 31, 1997) [8 USCS §§ 1101(a)(5)(T), 1101(a)(15)(U), 1229b(b)(2), and former 8 USCS § 1254(a)(3)].

(m) Adjustment of status for victims of crimes against women.

(1) The Secretary of Homeland Security may adjust the status of an alien admitted into the United States (or otherwise provided nonimmigrant status) under section 101(a)(15)(U) [8 USCS § 1101(a)(15)(U)] to that of an alien lawfully admitted for permanent residence if the alien is not described in section 212(a)(3)(E) [8 USCS § 1182(a)(3)(E)], unless the Secretary determines based on affirmative evidence that the alien unreasonably refused to provide assistance in a criminal investigation or prosecution, if—

(A) the alien has been physically present in the United States for a continuous period of at least 3 years since the date of admission as a nonimmigrant under clause (i) or (ii) of section 101(a)(15)(U) [8 USCS § 1101(a)(15)(U)]; and

(B) in the opinion of the Secretary of Homeland Security, the alien's continued presence in the United States is justified on humanitarian grounds, to ensure family unity, or is otherwise in the public interest.

(2) An alien shall be considered to have failed to maintain continuous physical presence in the United States under paragraph (1)(A) if the alien has departed from the United States for any period in excess of 90 days or for any periods in the aggregate exceeding 180 days unless the absence is in order to assist in the investigation or prosecution or unless an official involved in the investigation or prosecution certifies that the absence was otherwise justified.

(3) Upon approval of adjustment of status under paragraph (1) of an alien described in section 101(a)(15)(U)(i) [8 USCS § 1101(a)(15)(U)(i)] the Secretary of Homeland Security may adjust the status of or issue an immigrant visa to a spouse, a child, or, in the case of an alien child, a parent who did not receive a nonimmigrant visa under section 101(a)(15)(U)(ii) [8 USCS § 1101(a)(15)(U)(ii)] if the Secretary considers the grant of such status or visa necessary to avoid extreme hardship.

(4) Upon the approval of adjustment of status under paragraph (1) or (3), the Secretary of Homeland Security shall record the alien's lawful admission for permanent residence as of the date of such approval.

(5)(A) The Secretary of Homeland Security shall consult with the Attorney General, as appropriate, in making a determination under paragraph (1) whether affirmative evidence demonstrates that the alien unreasonably refused to provide assistance to a Federal law enforcement official, Federal prosecutor, Federal judge, or other Federal authority investigating or prosecuting criminal activity described in section 101(a)(15)(U)(iii) [8 USCS § 1101(a)(15)(U)(iii)].

(B) Nothing in paragraph (1)(B) may be construed to prevent the Secretary from consulting with the Attorney General in making a determination whether affirmative evidence demonstrates that the alien unreasonably refused to provide assistance to a State or local law enforcement official, State or local prosecutor, State or local judge, or other State or local authority investigating or prosecuting criminal activity described in section 101(a)(15)(U)(iii) [8 USCS § 1101(a)(15)(U)(iii)].

(n) If the approval of a petition for classification under section 203(b)(5) [8 USCS § 1153(b)(5)] would make a visa immediately available to the alien beneficiary, the alien beneficiary's application for adjustment of status under this section shall be considered to be properly filed whether the application is submitted concurrently with, or subsequent to, the visa petition.

(June 27, 1952, ch 477, Title II, subch 5, § 245, 66 Stat. 217; Aug. 21, 1958, P. L. 85-700, § 1, 72 Stat. 699; July 14, 1960, P. L. 86-648, § 10, 74 Stat. 505; Oct. 3, 1965, P. L. 89-236, § 13, 79 Stat. 918; Oct. 20, 1976, P. L. 94-571, § 6, 90 Stat. 2705; Dec. 29, 1981, P. L. 97-116, § 5(d)(2), 95 Stat. 1614; Nov. 6, 1986, P. L. 99-603, Title I, Part B, § 117, Title III, Part B, § 313(c), 100 Stat. 3384, 3438; Nov. 10, 1986, P. L. 99-639, §§ 2(e), 3(b), 5(a), 100 Stat. 3542, 3543; Nov. 6, 1986, P. L. 99-603, Title III, Part B, § 313(c); Nov. 10, 1986, P. L. 99-639, § 3(b), 100 Stat. 3542; Oct. 24, 1988, P. L. 100-525, §§ 2(f)(1), (p)(3), 7(b), 102 Stat. 2611, 2613, 2616; Nov. 29, 1990, P. L. 101-649, Title I, Subtitle B, Part 2, § 121(b)(4), Subtitle E, § 162(e)(3), Title VII, § 702(a), 104 Stat. 4994, 5011, 5086; Oct. 1, 1991, P. L. 102-110, § 2(c), 105 Stat. 556; Dec. 12, 1991, P. L. 102-232, Title III, §§ 302(d)(2), (e)(7), 308(a), 105 Stat. 1744, 1746, 1747; Aug. 26, 1994, P. L. 103-317, Title V, § 506(b), 108 Stat. 1765; Sept. 13, 1994, P. L. 103-322, Title XIII, § 130002(c), 108 Stat. 2025; Oct. 25, 1994, P. L. 103-416, Title II, § 219(k), 108 Stat. 4317; April 24, 1996, P. L. 104-132, Title IV, Subtitle B, § 413(d), 110 Stat. 1269; Sept. 30, 1996, P. L. 104-208, Div C, Title III, Subtitle A, § 308(f)(1)(O), (2)(C), (g)(10)(B), Subtitle F, §§ 375, 376(a), Title VI, Subtitle E, § 671(a)(4)(A), (5), 110 Stat. 3009-621, 3009-625, 3009-648, 3009-721; Nov. 26, 1997, P. L. 105-119, Title I, §§ 110(3), 111(a), (c), 111 Stat. 2458; Oct. 28, 2000, P. L. 106-386, Div A, § 107(f), Div B, Title V, §§ 1506(a)(1), 1513(f), 114 Stat. 1479, 1527, 1536; Dec. 21, 2000, P. L. 106-553, § 1(a)(2), 114 Stat. 2762; Dec. 21, 2000, P. L. 106-554, § 1(a)(4), 114 Stat. 2763; Dec. 19, 2003, P. L. 108-193, §§ 4(b)(3), 8(a)(4), 117 Stat. 2879, 2886; Jan. 5, 2006, P. L. 109-162, Title VIII, Subtitle A, § 803, 119 Stat. 3054; Aug. 12, 2006, P. L. 109-271, § 6(f), 120 Stat. 763; Dec. 23, 2008, P. L. 110-457, Title II, Subtitle A, § 201(d), (e), Subtitle D, § 235(d)(3), 122 Stat. 5053, 5080; Mar. 15, 2022, P.L. 117-103, Div BB, § 102(d), 136 Stat. 1075.)

§ 1255a. Adjustment of status of certain entrants before Jan. 1, 1982, to that of person admitted for lawful residence

(a) Temporary resident status. The Attorney General shall adjust the status of an alien to that of an alien lawfully admitted for temporary residence if the alien meets the following requirements:

(1) Timely applications.

(A) During application period. Except as provided in subparagraph (B), the alien must apply for such adjustment during the 12-month period beginning on a date (not later than 180 days after the date of enactment of this section [enacted Nov. 6, 1986]) designated by the Attorney General.

(B) Application within 30 days of show-cause order. An alien who, at any time during the first 11 months of the 12-month period described in subparagraph (A), is the subject of an order to show cause issued under section 242 [8 USCS § 1252] (as in effect before October 1, 1996), must make application under this section not later than the end of the 30-day period beginning either on the first day of such 12-month period or on the date of the issuance of such order, whichever day is later.

(C) Information included in application. Each application under this subsection shall contain such information as the Attorney General may require, including information on living relatives of the applicant with respect to whom a petition for preference or other status may be filed by the applicant at any later date under section 204(a) [8 USCS § 1154(a)].

(2) Continuous unlawful residence since 1982.

(A) In general. The alien must establish that he entered the United States before January 1, 1982, and that he has resided continuously in the United States in an unlawful status since such date and through the date the application is filed under this subsection.

(B) Nonimmigrants. In the case of an alien who entered the United States as a nonimmigrant before January 1, 1982, the alien must establish that the alien's period of authorized stay as a nonimmigrant expired before such date through the passage of time or the alien's unlawful status was known to the Government as of such date.

(C) Exchange visitors. If the alien was at any time a nonimmigrant exchange alien (as defined in section 101(a)(15)(J) [8 USCS § 1101(a)(15)(J)]), the alien must establish that the alien was not subject to the two-year foreign residence requirement of section 212(e) [8 USCS § 1182(e)] or has fulfilled that requirement or received a waiver thereof.

(3) Continuous physical presence since enactment.

(A) In general. The alien must establish that the alien has been continuously physically present in the United States since the date of the enactment of this section [enacted Nov. 6, 1986].

(B) Treatment of brief, casual, and innocent absences. An alien shall not be considered to have failed to maintain continuous physical presence in the United States for purposes of subparagraph (A) by virtue of brief, casual, and innocent absences from the United States.

(C) Admissions. Nothing in this section shall be construed as authorizing an alien to apply for admission to, or to be admitted to, the United States in order to apply for adjustment of status under this subsection.

(4) Admissible as immigrant. The alien must establish that he—

(A) is admissible to the United States as an immigrant, except as otherwise provided under subsection (d)(2),

(B) has not been convicted of any felony or of three or more misdemeanors committed in the United States,

(C) has not assisted in the persecution of any person or persons on account of race, religion, nationality, membership in a particular social group, or political opinion, and

(D) is registered or registering under the Military Selective Service Act [50 USCS §§ 3801 et seq.], if the alien is required to be so registered under that Act.

For purposes of this subsection, an alien in the status of a Cuban and Haitian entrant described in paragraph (1) or (2)(A) of section 501(e) of Public Law 96-422 [8 USCS § 1522 note] shall be considered to have entered the United States and to be in an unlawful status in the United States.

(b) Subsequent adjustment to permanent residence and nature of temporary resident status.

(1) Adjustment to permanent residence. The Attorney General shall adjust the status of any alien provided lawful temporary resident status under subsection (a) to that of an alien lawfully admitted for permanent residence if the alien meets the following requirements:

(A) Timely application after one year's residence. The alien must apply for such adjustment during the 2-year period beginning with the nineteenth month that begins after the date the alien was granted such temporary resident status.

(B) Continuous residence.

(i) In general. The alien must establish that he has continuously resided in the United States since the date the alien was granted such temporary resident status.

(ii) Treatment of certain absences. An alien shall not be considered to have lost the continuous residence referred to in clause (i) by reason of an absence from the United States permitted under paragraph (3)(A).

(C) Admissible as immigrant. The alien must establish that he—

(i) is admissible to the United States as an immigrant, except as otherwise provided under subsection (d)(2), and

(ii) has not been convicted of any felony or three or more misdemeanors committed in the United States.

(D) Basic citizenship skills.

(i) In general. The alien must demonstrate that he either—

(I) meets the requirements of section 312(a) [8 USCS § 1423(a)] (relating to minimal understanding of ordinary English and a knowledge and understanding of the history and government of the United States), or

(II) is satisfactorily pursuing a course of study (recognized by the Attorney General) to achieve such an understanding of English and such a knowledge and understanding of the history and government of the United States.

(ii) Exception for elderly or developmentally disabled individuals. The Attorney General may, in his discretion, waive all or part of the requirements of clause (i) in the case of an alien who is 65 years of age or older or who is developmentally disabled.

(iii) Relation to naturalization examination. In accordance with regulations of the Attorney General, an alien who has demonstrated under clause (i)(I) that the alien meets the requirements of section 312(a) [8 USCS § 1423(a)] may be considered to have satisfied the requirements of that section for purposes of becoming naturalized as a citizen of the United States under title III [8 USCS §§ 1401 et seq.].

(2) Termination of temporary residence. The Attorney General shall provide for termination of temporary resident status granted an alien under subsection (a)–

(A) if it appears to the Attorney General that the alien was in fact not eligible for such status;

(B) if the alien commits an act that (i) makes the alien inadmissible to the United States as an immigrant, except as otherwise provided under subsection (d)(2), or (ii) is convicted of any felony or three or more misdemeanors committed in the United States; or

(C) at the end of the 43rd month beginning after the date the alien is granted such status, unless the alien has filed an application for adjustment of such status pursuant to paragraph (1) and such application has not been denied.

(3) Authorized travel and employment during temporary residence. During the period an alien is in lawful temporary resident status granted under subsection (a)—

(A) Authorization of travel abroad. The Attorney General shall, in accordance with regulations, permit the alien to return to the United States after such brief and casual trips abroad as reflect an intention on the part of the alien to adjust to lawful permanent resident status under paragraph (1) and after brief temporary trips abroad occasioned by a family obligation involving an occurrence such as the illness or death of a close relative or other family need.

(B) Authorization of employment. The Attorney General shall grant the alien authorization to engage in employment in the United States and provide to that alien an "employment authorized" endorsement or other appropriate work permit.

(c) Applications for adjustment of status.

(1) To whom may be made. The Attorney General shall provide that the applications for adjustment of status under subsection (a) may be filed—

(A) with the Attorney General, or

(B) with a qualified designated entity, but only if the applicant consents to the forwarding of the application to the Attorney General.

As used in this section, the term "qualified designated entity" means an organization or person designated under paragraph (2).

(2) Designation of qualified entities to receive applications. For purposes of assisting in the program of legalization provided under this section, the Attorney General—

(A) shall designate qualified voluntary organizations and other qualified State, local, and community organizations, and

(B) may designate such other persons as the Attorney General determines are qualified and have substantial experience, demonstrated competence, and traditional long-term involvement in the preparation and submittal of applications for adjustment of status under section 209 or 245 [8 USCS § 1159 or 1255], Public Law 89-732, or Public Law 95-145 [8 USCS § 1255 notes].

(3) Treatment of applications by designated entities. Each qualified designated entity must agree to forward to the Attorney General applications filed with it in accordance with paragraph (1)(B) but not to forward to the Attorney General applications filed with it unless the applicant has consented to such forwarding. No such entity may make a determination required by this section to be made by the Attorney General.

(4) Limitation on access to information. Files and records of qualified designated entities relating to an alien's seeking assistance or information with respect to filing an application under this section are confidential and the Attorney General and the Service shall not have access to such files or records relating to an alien without the consent of the alien.

(5) Confidentiality of information.

(A) In general. Except as provided in this paragraph, neither the Attorney General, nor any other official or employee of the Department of Justice, or bureau or agency thereof, may—

(i) use the information furnished by the applicant pursuant to an application filed under this section for any purpose other than to make a determination on the application, for enforcement of paragraph (6), or for the preparation of reports to Congress under section 404 of the Immigration Reform and Control Act of 1986 [note to this section];

(ii) make any publication whereby the information furnished by any particular applicant can be identified; or

(iii) permit anyone other than the sworn officers and employees of the Department or bureau or agency or, with respect to applications filed with a designated entity, that designated entity, to examine individual applications.

(B) Required disclosures. The Attorney General shall provide the information furnished under this section, and any other information derived from such furnished information, to a duly recognized law enforcement entity in connection with a criminal investigation or prosecution, when such information is requested in writing by such entity, or to an official coroner for purposes of affirmatively identifying a deceased individual (whether or not such individual is deceased as a result of a crime).

(C) Authorized disclosures. The Attorney General may provide, in the Attorney General's discretion, for the furnishing of information furnished under this section in the same manner and circumstances as census information may be disclosed by the Secretary of Commerce under section 8 of title 13, United States Code.

(D) Construction.

(i) In general. Nothing in this paragraph shall be construed to limit the use, or release, for immigration enforcement purposes or law enforcement purposes of information contained in files or records of the Service pertaining to an application filed under this section, other than information furnished by an applicant pursuant to the application, or any other information derived from the application, that is not available from any other source.

(ii) Criminal convictions. Information concerning whether the applicant has at any time been convicted of a crime may be used or released for immigration enforcement or law enforcement purposes.

(E) Crime. Whoever knowingly uses, publishes, or permits information to be examined in violation of this paragraph shall be fined not more than $10,000.

(6) Penalties for false statements in applications. Whoever files an application for adjustment of status under this section and knowingly and willfully falsifies, misrepresents, conceals, or covers up a material fact or makes any false, fictitious, or fraudulent statements or representations, or makes or uses any false writing or document knowing the same to contain any false, fictitious, or fraudulent statement or entry, shall be fined in accordance with title 18, United States Code [18 USCS §§ 1 et seq.], or imprisoned not more than five years, or both.

(7) Application fees.

(A) Fee schedule. The Attorney General shall provide for a schedule of fees to be charged for the filing of applications for adjustment under subsection (a) or (b)(1). The Attorney General shall provide for an additional fee for filing an application for adjustment under subsection (b)(1) after the end of the first year of the 2-year period described in subsection (b)(1)(A).

(B) Use of fees. The Attorney General shall deposit payments received under this paragraph in a separate account and amounts in such account shall be available, without fiscal year limitation, to cover administrative and other expenses incurred in connection with the review of applications filed under this section.

(C) Immigration-related unfair employment practices. Not to exceed $3,000,000 of the unobligated balances remaining in the account established in subparagraph (B) shall be available in fiscal year 1992 and each fiscal year thereafter for grants, contracts, and cooperative agreements to community-based organizations for outreach programs, to be administered by the Office of Special Counsel for Immigration-Related Unfair Employment Practices: *Provided,* That such amounts shall be in addition to any funds appropriated to the Office of Special Counsel for such purposes: *Provided further,* That none of the funds made available by this section shall be used by the Office of Special Counsel to establish regional offices.

(d) Waiver of numerical limitations and certain grounds for exclusion.

(1) Numerical limitations do not apply. The numerical limitations of sections 201 and 202 [8 USCS §§ 1151, 1152] shall not apply to the adjustment of aliens to lawful permanent resident status under this section.

(2) Waiver of grounds for exclusion. In the determination of an alien's admissibility under subsections (a)(4)(A), (b)(1)(C)(i), and (b)(2)(B)—

(A) Grounds of exclusion not applicable. The provisions of paragraphs (5) and (7)(A) of section 212(a) [8 USCS § 1182(a)(5) and (7)(A)] shall not apply.

(B) Waiver of other grounds.

(i) In general. Except as provided in clause (ii), the Attorney General may waive any other provision of section 212(a) [8 USCS § 1182(a)] in the case of individual aliens for humanitarian purposes, to assure family unity, or when it is otherwise in the public interest.

(ii) Grounds that may not be waived. The following provisions of section 212(a) [8 USCS § 1182(a)] may not be waived by the Attorney General under clause (i):

(I) Paragraphs (2)(A) and (2)(B) (relating to criminals).

(II) Paragraph (2)(C) (relating to drug offenses), except for so much of such paragraph as relates to a single offense of simple possession of 30 grams or less of marijuana.

(III) Paragraph (3) (relating to security and related grounds).

(IV) Paragraph (4) (relating to aliens likely to become public charges) insofar as it relates to an application for adjustment to permanent residence.

Subclause (IV) (prohibiting the waiver of section 212(a)(4) [8 USCS § 1182(a)(4)]) shall not apply to an alien who is or was an aged, blind, or disabled individual (as defined in section 1614(a)(1) of the Social Security Act [42 USCS § 1382c(a)(1)]).

(iii) Special rule for determination of public charge. An alien is not ineligible for adjustment of status under this section due to being inadmissible under section 212(a)(4) [8 USCS § 1182(a)(4)] if the alien demonstrates a history of employment in the United States evidencing self-support without receipt of public cash assistance.

(C) Medical examination. The alien shall be required, at the alien's expense, to undergo such a medical examination (including a determination of immunization status) as is appropriate and conforms to generally accepted professional standards of medical practice.

(e) Temporary stay of deportation and work authorization for certain applicants.

(1) Before application period. The Attorney General shall provide that in the case of an alien who is apprehended before the beginning of the application period described in subsection (a)(1)(A) and who can establish a prima facie case of eligibility to have his status adjusted under subsection (a) (but for the fact that he may not apply for such adjustment until the beginning of such period), until the alien has had the opportunity during the first 30 days of the application period to complete the filing of an application for adjustment, the alien—

(A) may not be deported, and

(B) shall be granted authorization to engage in employment in the United States and be provided an "employment authorized" endorsement or other appropriate work permit.

(2) During application period. The Attorney General shall provide that in the case of an alien who presents a prima facie application for adjustment of status under subsection (a) during the application period, and until a final determination on the application has been made in accordance with this section, the alien—

(A) may not be deported, and

(B) shall be granted authorization to engage in employment in the United States and be provided an "employment authorized" endorsement or other appropriate work permit.

(f) Administrative and judicial review.

(1) Administrative and judicial review. There shall be no administrative or judicial review of a determination respecting an application for adjustment of status under this section except in accordance with this subsection.

(2) No review for late filings. No denial of adjustment of status under this section based on a late filing of an application for such adjustment may be reviewed by a court of the United States or of any State or reviewed in any administrative proceeding of the United States Government.

(3) Administrative review.

(A) Single level of administrative appellate review. The Attorney General shall establish an appellate authority to provide for a single level of administrative appellate review of a determination described in paragraph (1).

(B) Standard for review. Such administrative appellate review shall be based solely upon the administrative record established at the time of the determination on the application and upon such additional or newly discovered evidence as may not have been available at the time of the determination.

(4) Judicial review.

(A) Limitation to review of deportation. There shall be judicial review of such a denial only in the judicial review of an order of deportation under section 106 [former 8 USCS § 1105a] (as in effect before October 1, 1996).

(B) Standard for judicial review. Such judicial review shall be based solely upon the administrative record established at the time of the review by the appellate authority and the findings of fact and determinations contained in such record shall be conclusive unless the applicant can establish abuse of discretion or that the findings are directly contrary to clear and convincing facts contained in the record considered as a whole.

(C) Jurisdiction of courts. Notwithstanding any other provision of law, no court shall have jurisdiction of any cause of action or claim by or on behalf of any person asserting an interest under this section unless such person in fact filed an application under this section within the period specified by subsection (a)(1), or attempted to file a complete application and application fee with an authorized legalization officer of the Service but had the application and fee refused by that officer.

(g) Implementation of section.

(1) Regulations. The Attorney General, after consultation with the Committees on the Judiciary of the House of Representatives and of the Senate, shall prescribe—

(A) regulations establishing a definition of the term "resided continuously", as used in this section, and the evidence needed to establish that an alien has resided continuously in the United States for purposes of this section, and

(B) such other regulations as may be necessary to carry out this section.

(2) Considerations. In prescribing regulations described in paragraph (1)(A)—

(A) Periods of continuous residence. The Attorney General shall specify individual periods, and aggregate periods, of absence from the United States which will be considered to break a period of continuous residence in the United States and shall take into account absences due merely to brief and casual trips abroad.

(B) Absences caused by deportation or advanced parole. The Attorney General shall provide that—

(i) an alien shall not be considered to have resided continuously in the United States, if, during any period for which continuous residence is required, the alien was outside the United States as a result of a departure under an order of deportation, and

(ii) any period of time during which an alien is outside the United States pursuant to the advance parole procedures of the Service shall not be considered as part of the period of time during which an alien is outside the United States for purposes of this section.

(C) Waivers of certain absences. The Attorney General may provide for a waiver, in the discretion of the Attorney General, of the periods specified under subparagraph (A) in the case of an absence from the United States due merely to a brief temporary trip abroad required by emergency or extenuating circumstances outside the control of the alien.

(D) Use of certain documentation. The Attorney General shall require that—

(i) continuous residence and physical presence in the United States must be established through documents, together with independent corroboration of the information contained in such documents, and

(ii) the documents provided under clause (i) be employment-related if employment-related documents with respect to the alien are available to the applicant.

(3) Interim final regulations. Regulations prescribed under this section may be prescribed to take effect on an interim final basis if the Attorney General determines that this is necessary in order to implement this section in a timely manner.

(h) Temporary disqualification of newly legalized aliens from receiving certain public welfare assistance.

(1) In general. During the five-year period beginning on the date an alien was granted lawful temporary resident status under subsection (a), and notwithstanding any other provision of law—

(A) except as provided in paragraphs (2) and (3), the alien is not eligible for—

(i) any program of financial assistance furnished under Federal law (whether through grant, loan, guarantee, or otherwise) on the basis of financial need, as such programs are identified by the Attorney General in consultation with other appropriate heads of the various departments and agencies of Government (but in any event including the State program of assistance under part A of title IV of the Social Security Act) [42 USCS §§ 601 et seq.],

(ii) medical assistance under a State plan approved under title XIX of the Social Security Act [42 USCS §§ 1396 et seq.], and

(iii) assistance under the Food and Nutrition Act of 2008 [7 USCS §§ 2011 et seq.]; and

(B) a State or political subdivision therein may, to the extent consistent with subparagraph (A) and paragraphs (2) and (3), provide that the alien is not eligible for the programs of financial assistance or for medical assistance described in subparagraph (A)(ii) furnished under the law of that State or political subdivision.

Unless otherwise specifically provided by this section or other law, an alien in temporary lawful residence status granted under subsection (a) shall not be considered (for purposes of any law of a State or political subdivision providing for a program of financial assistance) to be permanently residing in the United States under color of law.

(2) Exceptions. Paragraph (1) shall not apply—

(A) to a Cuban and Haitian entrant (as defined in paragraph (1) or (2)(A) of section 501(e) of Public Law 96-422 [8 USCS § 1522 note], as in effect on April 1, 1983), or

(B) in the case of assistance (other than assistance under a State program funded under part A of title IV of the Social Security Act [42 USCS §§ 601 et seq.]) which is furnished to an alien who is an aged, blind, or disabled individual (as defined in section 1614(a)(1) of the Social Security Act [42 USCS § 1382c(a)(1)]).

(3) Restricted medicaid benefits.

(A) Clarification of entitlement. Subject to the restrictions under subparagraph (B), for the purpose of providing aliens with eligibility to receive medical assistance—

(i) paragraph (1) shall not apply,

(ii) aliens who would be eligible for medical assistance but for the provisions of paragraph (1) shall be deemed, for purposes of title XIX of the Social Security Act [42 USCS §§ 1396 et seq.], to be so eligible, and

(iii) aliens lawfully admitted for temporary residence under this section, such status not having changed, shall be considered to be permanently residing in the United States under color of law.

(B) Restriction of benefits.

(i) Limitation to emergency services and services for pregnant women. Notwithstanding any provision of title XIX of the Social Security Act [42 USCS §§ 1396 et seq.] (including subparagraphs (B) and (C) of section 1902(a)(10) of such Act [42 USCS § 1396a(a)(10)(B), (C)], aliens who, but for subparagraph (A), would be ineligible for medical assistance under paragraph (1), are only eligible for such assistance with respect to—

(I) emergency services (as defined for purposes of section 1916(a)(2)(D) of the Social Security Act [42 USCS § 1396o(a)(2)(D)]), and

(II) services described in section 1916(a)(2)(B) of such Act [42 USCS § 1396o(a)(2)(B)] (relating to service for pregnant women).

(ii) No restriction for exempt aliens and children. The restrictions of clause (i) shall not apply to aliens who are described in paragraph (2) or who are under 18 years of age.

(C) Definition of medical assistance. In this paragraph, the term "medical assistance" refers to medical assistance under a State plan approved under title XIX of the Social Security Act [42 USCS §§ 1396 et seq.].

(4) Treatment of certain programs. Assistance furnished under any of the following provisions of law shall not be construed to be financial assistance described in paragraph (1)(A)(i):

(A) The Richard B. Russell National School Lunch Act [42 USCS §§ 1751 et seq.].

(B) The Child Nutrition Act of 1966 [42 USCS §§ 1771 et seq.].

(C) The [The] Carl D. Perkins Career and Technical Education Act of 2006 [20 USCS §§ 2301 et seq.].

(D) Title I of the Elementary and Secondary Education Act of 1965 [20 USCS §§ 6301 et seq.].

(E) The Headstart-Follow Through Act [former 42 USCS §§ 9861 et seq.].

(F) Title I of the Workforce Innovation and Opportunity Act [29 USCS § 3111 et seq.].

(G) Title IV of the Higher Education Act of 1965.

(H) The Public Health Service Act [42 USCS §§ 201 et seq.].

(I) Titles V, XVI, and XX, and parts B, D, and E of title IV, of the Social Security Act [42 USCS §§ 701 et seq., 1381 et seq., and 1379 et seq., and 620 et seq., 651 et seq., 671 et seq.] (and titles I, X, XIV, and XVI of such Act [42 USCS §§ 301 et seq., 1201 et seq, 1351 et seq., 1381 et seq.] as in effect without regard to the amendment made by section 301 of the Social Security Amendments of 1972 [amending 42 USCS §§ 1381 et seq.]).

(5) Adjustment not affecting Fascell-Stone benefits. For the purpose of section 501 of the Refugee Education Assistance Act of 1980 (Public Law 96-122), assistance shall be continued under such section with respect to an alien without regard to the alien's adjustment of status under this section.

(i) Dissemination of information on legalization program. Beginning not later than the date designated by the Attorney General under subsection (a)(1)(A), the Attorney General, in cooperation with qualified designated entities, shall broadly disseminate information respecting the benefits which aliens may receive under this section and the requirements to obtain such benefits.

(June 27, 1952, ch 477, Title II, Ch 5, § 245A, as added Nov. 6, 1986, P. L. 99-603, Title II, § 201(a)(1), 100 Stat. 3394; Oct. 24, 1988, P. L. 100-525, § 2(h)(1), 102 Stat. 2611; Nov. 29, 1990, P. L. 101-649, Title VI, § 603(a)(13), Title VII, § 703,104 Stat. 5083, 5086; Oct. 28, 1991, P. L. 102-140, Title I, 105 Stat. 785; Dec. 12, 1991, P. L. 102-232, Title III, § 307l(6), 105 Stat. 1756; Oct. 20, 1994, P. L. 103-382, Title III, Part I, § 394(g), 108 Stat. 4028; Oct. 25, 1994, P. L. 103-416, Title I, § 108(b), Title II, § 219(l)(1), 108 Stat. 4310, 4317; April 24, 1996, P. L. 104-132, Title IV, Subtitle D, § 431(a), 110 Stat. 1273; Aug. 22, 1996, P. L. 104-193, Title I, § 110(s)(2), 110 Stat. 2175; Sept. 30, 1996, P. L. 104-208, Div C, Title III, Subtitle A, § 308(g)(2)(B), (5)(A)(iii), Subtitle F, §§ 377(a), 384(d)(1), Title VI, Subtitle B, § 623(a), 110 Stat. 3009-622, 3009-623, 3009-649, 3009-653, 3009-696; Oct. 21, 1998, P. L. 105-277, Div A, § 101(f) [Title VIII, Subtitle IV, § 405(d)(4), (f)(4)], 112 Stat. 2681-419, 2681-430; Oct. 31, 1998, P. L. 105-332, § 3(a), 112 Stat. 3125; Oct. 22, 1999, P. L. 106-78, Title VII, § 752(b)(5), 113 Stat. 1169; Aug. 12, 2006, P. L. 109-270, § 2(a), 120 Stat. 746; May 22, 2008, P. L. 110-234, Title IV, Subtitle A, Part I, § 4002(b)(1)(B), (2)(J), 122 Stat. 1096, 1097; June 18, 2008, P. L. 110-246, § 4(a), Title IV, Subtitle A, Part I, § 4002(b)(1)(B), (2)(J), 122 Stat. 1664, 1857, 1858; July 22, 2014, P. L. 113-128, Title V, Subtitle B, § 512(q), 128 Stat. 1712.)

§ 1255b. Adjustment of status of certain nonimmigrants to that of persons admitted for permanent residence

Notwithstanding any other provision of law—

(a) Application. Any alien admitted to the United States as a nonimmigrant under the provisions of either section 101(a)(15)(A)(i) or (ii) or 101(a)(15)(G)(i) or (ii) of the Immigration and Nationality Act [8 USCS § 1101(a)(15)(A)(i) or (ii) or (G)(i) or (ii)], who has failed to maintain a status under any of those provisions, may apply to the Attorney General for adjustment of his status to that of an alien lawfully admitted for permanent residence.

(b) Record of admission. If, after consultation with the Secretary of State, it shall appear to the satisfaction of the Attorney General that the alien has shown compelling reasons demonstrating both that the alien is unable to return to the country represented by the government which accredited the alien or the member of the alien's immediate family and that adjustment of the alien's status to that of an alien lawfully admitted for permanent residence would be in the national interest, that the alien is a person of good moral character, that he is admissible for permanent residence under the Immigration and Nationality Act, and that such action would not be contrary to the national welfare, safety, or security, the Attorney General, in his discretion, may record the alien's lawful admission for permanent residence as of the date the order of the Attorney General approving the application for adjustment of status is made.

(c) Report to the Congress; resolution not favoring adjustment of status; reduction of quota. A complete and detailed statement of the facts and pertinent provisions of law in the case shall be reported to the Congress with the reasons for such adjustment of status. Such reports shall be submitted on the first day of each calendar month in which Congress is in session. The Secretary of State shall, if the alien was classifiable as a quota immigrant at the time of his entry, reduce by one the quota of the quota area to which the alien is chargeable under section 202 of the Immigration and Nationality Act [8 USCS § 1152] for the fiscal year then current or the next following year in which a quota is available. No quota shall be so reduced by more than 50 per centum in any fiscal year.

(d) Limitations. The number of aliens who may be granted the status of aliens lawfully admitted for permanent residence in any fiscal year, pursuant to this section, shall not exceed fifty.

(Sept. 11, 1957, P. L. 85-316, § 13, 71 Stat. 642; Dec. 29, 1981, P. L. 97-116, § 17, 95 Stat. 1619; Oct. 24, 1988, P. L. 100-525, § 9(kk), 102 Stat. 2622; Oct. 25, 1994, P. L. 103-416, Title II, § 207, 108 Stat. 4312; Sept. 30, 1996, P. L. 104-208, Div C, Title VI, Subtitle E, § 671(b)(4), 110 Stat. 3009-721.)

§ 1256. Rescission of adjustment of status; report to Congress; effect upon naturalized citizen

(a) If, at any time within five years after the status of a person has been otherwise adjusted under the provisions of section 245 or 249 of this Act [8 USCS § 1255 or 1259] or any other provision of law to that of an alien lawfully admitted for permanent residence, it shall appear to the satisfaction of the Attorney General that the person was not in fact eligible for such adjustment of status, the Attorney General shall rescind the action taken granting an adjustment of status to such person and cancelling removal in the case of such person if that occurred and the person shall thereupon be subject to all provisions of this Act to the same extent as if the adjustment of status had not been made. Nothing in this subsection shall require the Attorney General to rescind the alien's status prior to commencement of procedures to remove the alien under section 240 [8 USCS § 1229a], and an order of removal issued by an immigration judge shall be sufficient to rescind the alien's status.

(b) Any person who has become a naturalized citizen of the United States upon the basis of a record of a lawful admission for permanent residence, created as a result of an adjustment of status for which such person was not in fact eligible, and which is subsequently rescinded under subsection (a) of this section, shall be subject to the provisions of section 340 of this Act [8 USCS § 1451] as a person whose naturalization was procured by concealment of a material fact or by willful misrepresentation.

(June 27, 1952, ch 477, Title II, Ch 5, § 246, 66 Stat. 217; Oct. 25, 1994, P. L. 103-416, Title II, § 219(m), 108 Stat. 4317; Sept. 30, 1996, P. L. 104-208, Div C, Title III, Subtitle A, § 308(e)(1)(H), Subtitle F, § 378(a), 110 Stat. 3009-619, 3009-649.)

§ 1257. Adjustment of status of certain resident aliens to nonimmigrant status; exceptions

(a) The status of an alien lawfully admitted for permanent residence shall be adjusted by the Attorney General, under such regulations as he may prescribe, to that of a nonimmigrant under paragraph (15)(A), (15)(E), or (15)(G) of section 101(a) [8 USCS § 1101(a)(15)(A), (E), or (G)], if such alien had at the time of admission or subsequently acquires an occupational status which would, if he were seeking admission to the United States, entitle him to a nonimmigrant status under such sections [paragraphs]. As of the date of the Attorney General's order making such adjustment of status, the Attorney General shall cancel the record of the alien's admission for permanent residence, and the immigrant status of such alien shall thereby be terminated.

(b) The adjustment of status required by subsection (a) shall not be applicable in the case of any alien who requests that he be permitted to retain his status as an immigrant and who, in such form as the Attorney General may require, executes and files with the Attorney General a written waiver of all rights, privileges, exemptions, and immunities under any law or any executive order which would otherwise accrue to him because of the acquisition of an occupational status entitling him to a nonimmigrant status under paragraphs (15)(A), (15)(E), or (15)(G) of section 101(a) [8 USCS § 1101(a)(15)(A), (E), or (G)].

(June 27, 1952, ch 477, Title II, Ch 5, § 247, 66 Stat. 218; Sept. 30, 1996, P. L. 104-208, Div C, Title III, Subtitle A, § 308(f)(1)(P), 110 Stat. 3009-621.)

§ 1258. Change of nonimmigrant classification

(a) The Secretary of Homeland Security may, under such conditions as he may prescribe, authorize a change from any nonimmigrant classification to any other nonimmigrant classification in the case of any alien lawfully admitted to the United States as a nonimmigrant who is continuing to maintain that status and who is not inadmissible under section 212(a)(9)(B)(i) [8 USCS § 1182(a)(9)(B)(i)] (or whose inadmissibility under such section is waived under section 212(a)(9)(B)(v) [8 USCS § 1182(a)(9)(B)(v)]), except (subject to subsection (b)) in the case of—

(1) an alien classified as a nonimmigrant under subparagraph (C), (D), (K), or (S) of section 101(a)(15) [8 USCS § 1101(a)(15)(C), (D), (K), or (S)],

(2) an alien classified as a nonimmigrant under subparagraph (J) of section 101(a)(15) [8 USCS § 1101(a)(15)(J)] who came to the United States or acquired such classification in order to receive graduate medical education or training,

(3) an alien (other than an alien described in paragraph (2)) classified as a nonimmigrant under subparagraph (J) of section 101(a)(15) [8 USCS § 1101(a)(15)(J)] who is subject to the two-year foreign residence requirement of section 212(e) [8 USCS § 1182(e)] and has not received a waiver thereof, unless such alien applies to have the alien's classification changed from classification under subparagraph (J) of section 101(a)(15) [8 USCS § 1101(a)(15)(J)] to a classification under subparagraph (A) or (G) of such section [8 USCS § 1101(a)(15)(A) or (G)], and

(4) an alien admitted as a nonimmigrant visitor without a visa under section 212(l) or section 217 [8 USCS § 1182(l) or 1187].

(b) The exceptions specified in paragraphs (1) through (4) of subsection (a) shall not apply to a change of nonimmigrant classification to that of a nonimmigrant under subparagraph (T) or (U) of section 101(a)(15) [8 USCS § 1101(a)(15)].

(June 27, 1952, ch 477, Title II, Ch 5, § 248, 66 Stat. 218; Sept. 21, 1961, P. L. 87-256, § 109(d), 75 Stat. 535; Dec. 29, 1981, P. L. 97-116, § 10, 95 Stat. 1617; Nov. 6, 1986, P. L. 99-603, Title III, Part B, § 313(d), 100 Stat. 3439; Sept. 13, 1994, P. L. 103-322, Title XIII, § 130003(b)(3), 108 Stat. 2025; Sept. 30, 1996, P. L. 104-208, Div C, Title III, Subtitle A, § 301(b)(2), Title VI, Subtitle E, § 671(a)(2), 110 Stat. 3009-578, 3009-721; Jan. 5, 2006, P. L. 109-162, Title VIII, Subtitle C, § 821(c)(1), 119 Stat. 3062.)

§ 1259. Record of admission for permanent residence in the case of certain aliens who entered the United States prior to January 1, 1972

A record of lawful admission for permanent residence may, in the discretion of the Attorney General and under such regulations as he may prescribe, be made in the case of any alien, as of the date of the approval of his application or, if entry occurred prior to July 1, 1924, as of the date of such entry, if no such record is otherwise available and such alien shall satisfy the Attorney General that he is not inadmissible under section 212(a)(3)(E) [8 USCS § 1182(a)(3)(E)] or under section 212(a) [8 USCS § 1182(a)] insofar as it relates to criminals, procurers and other immoral persons, subversives, violators of the narcotic laws or smugglers of aliens, and he establishes that he—

(a) entered the United States prior to January 1, 1972;

(b) has had his residence in the United States continuously since such entry;

(c) is a person of good moral character; and

(d) is not ineligible to citizenship and is not deportable under section 237(a)(4)(B) [8 USCS § 1227(a)(4)(B)].

(June 27, 1952, ch 477, Title II, Ch 5, § 249, 66 Stat. 219; Aug. 8, 1958, P. L. 85-616, 72 Stat. 546; Oct. 3, 1965, P. L. 89-236, § 19, 79 Stat. 920; Nov. 6, 1986, P. L. 99-603, Title II, § 203(a), (b), 100 Stat. 3405; Nov. 6, 1986, P. L. 99-603, Title II, § 3405; Oct. 24, 1988, P. L. 100-525, § 2(j), 102 Stat. 2612; Nov. 29, 1990, P. L. 101-649, Title VI, § 603(a)(14), 104 Stat. 5083; April 24, 1996, P. L. 104-132, Title IV, Subtitle B, § 413(e), 110 Stat. 1269; Sept. 30, 1996, P. L. 104-208, Div C, Title III, Subtitle A, § 308(g)(10)(C), 110 Stat. 3009-625.)

§ 1260. Removal of aliens falling into distress

The Attorney General may remove from the United States any alien who falls into distress or who needs public aid from causes arising subsequent to his entry, and is desirous of being so removed, to the native country of such alien, or to the country from which he came, or to the country of which he is a citizen or subject, or to any other country to which he wishes to go and which will receive him, at the expense of the appropriation for the enforcement of this Act. Any alien so removed shall be ineligible to apply for or receive a visa or other documentation for readmission, or to apply for admission to the United States except with the prior approval of the Attorney General.

(June 27, 1952, ch 477, Title II, Ch 5, § 250, 66 Stat. 219.)

SPECIAL PROVISIONS RELATING TO ALIEN CREWMEN

§ 1281. Alien crewmen

(a) Arrival; submission of list; exceptions. Upon arrival of any vessel or aircraft in the United States from any place outside the United States it shall be the duty of the owner, agent, consignee, master, or commanding officer thereof to deliver to an immigration officer at the port of arrival (1) a complete, true, and correct list containing the names of all aliens employed on such vessel or aircraft, the positions they respectively hold in the crew of the vessel or aircraft, when and where they were respectively shipped or engaged, and those to be paid off or discharged in the port of arrival; or (2) in the discretion of the Attorney General, such a list containing so much of such information, or such additional or supplemental information, as the Attorney General shall by regulations prescribe. In the case of a vessel engaged solely in traffic on the Great Lakes, Saint Lawrence River, and connecting waterways, such lists shall be furnished at such times as the Attorney General may require.

(b) Reports of illegal landings. It shall be the duty of any owner, agent, consignee, master, or commanding officer of any vessel or aircraft to report to an immigration officer, in writing, as soon as discovered, all cases in which any alien crewman has illegally landed in the United States from the vessel or aircraft, together with a description of such alien and any information likely to lead to his apprehension.

(c) Departure; submission of list; exceptions. Before the departure of any vessel or aircraft from any port in the United States, it shall be the duty of the owner, agent, consignee, master, or commanding officer thereof, to deliver to an immigration officer at that port (1) a list containing the names of all alien employees who were not employed thereon at the time of the arrival at that port but who will leave such port thereon at the time of the departure of such vessel or aircraft and the names of those, if any, who have been paid off or discharged, and of those, if any, who have deserted or landed at that port, or (2) in the discretion of the Attorney General, such a list containing so much of such information, or such additional or supplemental information, as the Attorney General shall by regulations prescribe. In the case of a vessel engaged solely in traffic on the Great Lakes, Saint Lawrence River, and connecting waterways, such lists shall be furnished at such times as the Attorney General may require.

(d) Violations [Caution: For inflation-adjusted civil monetary penalties, see 8 CFR 280.53(c).]. In case any owner, agent, consignee, master, or commanding officer shall fail to deliver complete, true, and correct lists or reports of aliens, or to report cases of desertion or landing, as required by subsections (a), (b), and (c), such owner, agent, consignee, master, or commanding officer, shall, if required by the Attorney General, pay to the Commissioner the sum of $200 for each alien concerning whom such lists are not delivered or such reports are not made as required in the preceding subsections. In the case that any owner, agent, consignee, master, or commanding officer of a vessel shall secure services of an alien crewman described in section 101(a)(15)(D)(i) [8 USCS § 1101(a)(15)(D)(i)] to perform longshore work not included in the normal operation and service on board the vessel under section 258 [8 USCS § 1288], the owner, agent, consignee, master, or commanding officer shall pay to the Commissioner the sum of $5,000, and such fine shall be a lien against the vessel. No such vessel or aircraft shall be granted clearance from any port at which it arrives pending the determination of the question of the liability to the payment of such fine, and if such fine is imposed, while it remains unpaid. No such fine shall be remitted or refunded. Clearance may be granted prior to the determination of such question upon deposit of a bond or a sum sufficient to cover such fine.

(e) Regulations. The Attorney General is authorized to prescribe by regulations the circumstances under which a vessel or aircraft shall be deemed to be arriving in, or departing from the United States or any port thereof within the meaning of any provision of this chapter [8 USCS §§ 1281 et seq.].

(June 27, 1952, ch 477, Title II, Ch 6, § 251, 66 Stat. 219; Nov. 29, 1990, P. L. 101-649, Title II, Subtitle A, § 203(b), 104 Stat. 5018; Dec. 12, 1991, P. L. 102-232, Title III, § 303(a)(3), 105 Stat. 1746.)

§ 1282. Conditional permits to land temporarily

(a) Period of time. No alien crewman shall be permitted to land temporarily in the United States except as provided in this section, section 212(d)(3), section 212(d)(5), and section 253 [8 USCS §§ 1182(d)(3), (5), and 1283]. If an immigration officer finds upon examination that an alien crewman is a nonimmigrant under paragraph (15)(D) of section 101(a) [8 USCS § 1101(a)(15)(D)] and is otherwise admissible and has agreed to accept such permit, he may, in his discretion, grant the crewman a conditional permit to land temporarily pursuant to regulations prescribed by the Attorney General, subject to revocation in subsequent proceedings as provided in subsection (b), and for a period of time, in any event, not to exceed—

(1) the period of time (not exceeding twenty-nine days) during which the vessel or aircraft on which he arrived remains in port, if the immigration officer is satisfied that the crewman intends to depart on the vessel or aircraft on which he arrived;

(2) twenty-nine days, if the immigration officer is satisfied that the crewman intends to depart, within the period for which he is permitted to land, on a vessel or aircraft other than the one on which he arrived; or

(3) 180 days, if the immigration officer determines that the crewman—

(A) intends to depart, within the period for which the crewman is permitted to land, on the same vessel or on a vessel or aircraft other than the vessel on which the crewman arrived; and

(B) will perform ship-to-ship liquid cargo transfer operations to or from any other vessel engaged in foreign trade during such period.

(b) Revocation; expenses of detention. Pursuant to regulations prescribed by the Attorney General, any immigration officer may, in his discretion, if he determines that an alien is not a bona fide crewman, or does not intend to depart on the vessel or aircraft which brought him, revoke the conditional permit to land which was granted such crewman under the provisions of subsection (a)(1), take such crewman into custody, and require the master or commanding officer of the vessel or aircraft on which the crewman arrived to receive and detain him on board such vessel or aircraft, if practicable, and such crewman shall be removed from the United States at the expense of the transportation line which brought him to the United States. Until such alien is so removed, any expenses of his detention shall be borne by such transportation company. Nothing in this section shall be construed to require the procedure prescribed in section 240 of this Act [8 USCS § 1229a] to cases falling within the provisions of this subsection.

(c) Penalties. Any alien crewman who willfully remains in the United States in excess of the number of days allowed in any conditional permit issued under subsection (a) shall be fined under title 18, United States Code, or imprisoned not more than 6 months, or both.

(June 27, 1952, ch 477, Title II, Ch 6, § 252, 66 Stat. 220; Nov. 29, 1990, P. L. 101-649, Title V, Subtitle D, § 543(b)(1), 104 Stat. 5059; Dec. 12, 1991, P. L. 102-232, Title III, § 306(c)(2), 105 Stat. 1752; Sept. 30, 1996, P. L. 104-208, Div C, Title III, Subtitle A, § 308(e)(2)(E), (g)(5)(A)(i), 110 Stat. 3009-620, 3009-623; Jan. 5, 2023, P.L. 117-360, § 3, 136 Stat. 6293.)

§ 1283. Hospital treatment of alien crewman afflicted with certain diseases

An alien crewman, including an alien crewman ineligible for a conditional permit to land under section 252(a) [8 USCS § 1282(a)], who is found on arrival in a port of the United States to be afflicted with any of the disabilities or diseases mentioned in section 255 [8 USCS § 1285], shall be placed in a hospital designated by the immigration officer in charge at the port of arrival and treated, all expenses connected therewith, including burial in the event of death, to be borne by the owner, agent, consignee, commanding officer, or master of the vessel or aircraft, and not to be deducted from the crewman's wages. No such vessel or aircraft shall be granted clearance until such expenses are paid, or their payment appropriately guaranteed, and the collector of customs is so notified by the immigration officer in charge. An alien crewman suspected of being afflicted with any such disability or disease may be removed from the vessel or aircraft on which he arrived to an immigration station, or other appropriate place, for such observation as will enable the examining surgeons to determine definitely whether or not he is so afflicted, all expenses connected therewith to be borne in the manner hereinbefore prescribed. In cases in which it appears to the satisfaction of the immigration officer in charge that it will not be possible within a reasonable time to effect a cure, the return of the alien crewman shall be enforced on, or at the expense of, the transportation line on which he came, upon such conditions as the Attorney General shall prescribe, to insure that the alien shall be properly cared for and protected, and that the spread of contagion shall be guarded against.

(June 27, 1952, ch 477, Title II, Ch 6, § 253, 66 Stat. 221.)

§ 1284. Control of alien crewmen

(a) Penalties for failure [Caution: For inflation-adjusted civil monetary penalties, see 8 CFR 280.53(c).]. The owner, agent, consignee, charterer, master, or commanding officer of any vessel or aircraft arriving in the United States from any place outside thereof who fails (1) to detain on board the vessel, or in the case of an aircraft to detain at a place specified by an immigration officer at the expense of the airline, any alien crewman employed thereon until an immigration officer has completely inspected such alien crewman, including a physical examination by the medical examiner, or (2) to detain any alien crewman on board the vessel, or in the case of an aircraft at a place specified by an immigration officer at the expense of the airline, after such inspection unless a conditional permit to land temporarily has been granted such alien crewman under section 252 [8 USCS § 1282] or unless an alien crewman has been permitted to land temporarily under section 212(d)(5) or 253 [8 USCS § 1182(d)(5) or 1283] for medical or hospital treatment, or (3) to remove such alien crewman if required to do so by an immigration officer, whether such removal requirement is imposed before or after the crewman is permitted to land temporarily under section 212(d)(5), 252, or 253 [8 USCS § 1182(d)(5), 1282, or 1283], shall pay to the Commissioner the sum of $3,000 for each alien crewman in respect of whom any such failure occurs. No such vessel or aircraft shall be granted clearance pending the determination of the liability to the payment of such fine, or while the fine remains unpaid, except that clearance may be granted prior to the determination of such question upon the deposit of a sum sufficient to cover such fine, or of a bond with sufficient surety to secure the payment thereof approved by the Commissioner. The Attorney General may, upon application in writing therefor, mitigate such penalty to not less than $500 for each alien crewman in respect of whom such failure occurs, upon such terms as he shall think proper.

(b) Prima facie evidence against transportation line. Except as may be otherwise prescribed by regulations issued by the Attorney General, proof that an alien crewman did not appear upon the outgoing manifest of the vessel or aircraft on which he arrived in the United States from any place outside thereof, or that he was reported by the master or commanding officer of such vessel or aircraft as a deserter, shall be prima facie evidence of a failure to detain or remove such alien crewman.

(c) Removal on other than arriving vessel or aircraft; expenses. If the Attorney General finds that removal of an alien crewman under this section on the vessel or aircraft on which he arrived is impracticable or impossible, or would cause undue hardship to such alien crewman, he may cause the alien crewman to be removed from the port of arrival or any other port on another vessel or aircraft of the same transportation line, unless the Attorney General finds this to be impracticable. All expenses incurred in connection with such removal, including expenses incurred in transferring an alien crewman from one place in the United States to another under such conditions and safeguards as the Attorney General shall impose, shall be paid by the owner or owners of the vessel or aircraft on which the alien arrived in the United States. The vessel or aircraft on which the alien arrived shall not be granted clearance until such expenses have been paid or their payment guaranteed to the satisfaction of the Attorney General. An alien crewman who is transferred within the United States in accordance with this subsection shall not be regarded as having been landed in the United States.

(June 27, 1952, ch 477, Title II, Ch 6, § 254, 66 Stat. 221; Nov. 29, 1990, P. L. 101-649, Title V, Subtitle D, § 543(a)(4), 104 Stat. 5058; Dec. 12, 1991, P. L. 102-232, Title III, § 306(c)(4)(C), 105 Stat. 1752; Sept. 30, 1996, P. L. 104-208, Div C, Title III, Subtitle A, § 308(e)(1)(I), (2)(F), (12), 110 Stat. 3009-619, 3009-620.)

§ 1285. Employment on passenger vessels of aliens afflicted with certain disabilities [Caution: For inflation-adjusted civil monetary penalties, see 8 CFR 280.53(c).]

It shall be unlawful for any vessel or aircraft carrying passengers between a port of the United States and a port outside thereof to have employed on board upon arrival in the United States any alien afflicted with feeblemindedness, insanity, epilepsy, tuberculosis in any form, leprosy, or any dangerous contagious disease. If it appears to the satisfaction of the Attorney General, from an examination made by a medical officer of the United States Public Health Service, and is so certified by such officer, that any such alien was so afflicted at the time he was shipped or engaged and taken on board such vessel or aircraft and that the existence of such affliction might have been detected by means of a competent medical examination at such time, the owner, commanding officer, agent, consignee, or master thereof shall pay for each alien so afflicted to the Commissioner the sum of $1,000. No vessel or aircraft shall be granted clearance pending the determination of the question of the liability to the payment of such sums, or while such sums remain unpaid, except that clearance may be granted prior to the determination of such question upon the deposit of an amount sufficient to cover such sums or of a bond approved by the Commissioner with sufficient surety to secure the payment thereof. Any such fine may, in the discretion of the Attorney General, be mitigated or remitted.

(June 27, 1952, ch 477, Title II, Ch 6, § 255, 66 Stat. 222; Nov. 29, 1990, P. L. 101-649, Title V, Subtitle D, § 543(a)(5), 104 Stat. 5058.)

§ 1286. Discharge of alien crewmen; penalties [Caution: For inflation-adjusted civil monetary penalties, see 8 CFR 280.53(c).]

It shall be unlawful for any person, including the owner, agent, consignee, charterer, master, or commanding officer of any vessel or aircraft, to pay off or discharge any alien crewman, except an alien lawfully admitted for permanent residence, employed on board a vessel or aircraft arriving in the United States without first having obtained the consent of the Attorney General. If it shall appear to the satisfaction of the Attorney General that any alien crewman has been paid off or discharged in the United States in violation of the provisions of this section, such owner, agent, consignee, charterer, master, commanding officer, or other person, shall pay to the Commissioner the sum of $3,000 for each such violation. No vessel or aircraft shall be granted clearance pending the determination of the question of the liability to the payment of such sums, or while such sums remain unpaid, except that clearance may be granted prior to the determination of such question upon the deposit of an amount sufficient to cover such sums, or of a bond approved by the Commissioner with sufficient surety to secure the payment thereof. Such fine may, in the discretion of the Attorney General, be mitigated to not less than $1,500 for each violation, upon such terms as he shall think proper.

(June 27, 1952, ch 477, Title II, Ch 6, § 256, 66 Stat. 223; Nov. 29, 1990, P. L. 101-649, Title V, Subtitle D, § 543(a)(6), 104 Stat. 5058.)

§ 1287. Alien crewmen brought into the United States with intent to evade immigration laws; penalties [Caution: For inflation-adjusted civil monetary penalties, see 8 CFR 280.53(c).]

Any person, including the owner, agent, consignee, master, or commanding officer of any vessel or aircraft arriving in the United States from any place outside thereof, who shall knowingly sign on the vessel's articles, or bring to the United States as one of the crew of such vessel or aircraft, any alien, with intent to permit or assist such alien to enter or land in the United States in violation of law, or who shall falsely and knowingly represent to a consular officer at the time of application for visa, or to the immigration officer at the port of arrival in the United States, that such alien is a bona fide member of the crew employed in any capacity regularly required for normal operation and services aboard such vessel or aircraft, shall be liable to a penalty not exceeding $10,000 for each such violation, for which sum such vessel or aircraft shall be liable and may be seized and proceeded against by way of libel in any district court of the United States having jurisdiction of the offense.

(June 27, 1952, ch 477, Title II, Ch 6, § 257, 66 Stat. 223; Nov. 29, 1990, P. L. 101-649, Title V, Subtitle D, § 543(a)(7), 104 Stat. 5058.)

§ 1288. Limitations on performance of longshore work by alien crewmen

(a) In general. For purposes of section 101(a)(15)(D)(i) [8 USCS § 1101(a)(15)(D)(i)], the term "normal operation and service on board a vessel" does not include any activity that is longshore work (as defined in subsection (b)), except as provided under subsection (c), (d), or (e).

(b) "Longshore work" defined.

(1) In general. In this section, except as provided in paragraph (2), the term "longshore work" means any activity relating to the loading or unloading of cargo, the operation of cargo-related equipment (whether or not integral to the vessel), and the handling of mooring lines on the dock when the vessel is made fast or let go, in the United States or the coastal waters thereof.

(2) Exception for safety and environmental protection. The term "longshore work" does not include the loading or unloading of any cargo for which the Secretary of Transportation has, under the authority contained in chapter 37 of title 46, United States Code [46 USCS §§ 3701 et seq.] (relating to Carriage of Liquid Bulk Dangerous Cargoes), section 311 of the Federal Water Pollution Control Act [33 USCS § 1321], section 4106 of the Oil Pollution Act of 1990, or section 5103(b), 5104, 5106, 5107, or 5110 of title 49, United States Code prescribed regulations which govern—

(A) the handling or stowage of such cargo,

(B) the manning of vessels and the duties, qualifications, and training of the officers and crew of vessels carrying such cargo, and

(C) the reduction or elimination of discharge during ballasting, tank cleaning, handling of such cargo.

(3) Construction. Nothing in this section shall be construed as broadening, limiting, or otherwise modifying the meaning or scope of longshore work for purposes of any other law, collective bargaining agreement, or international agreement.

(c) Prevailing practice exception.

(1) Subsection (a) shall not apply to a particular activity of longshore work in and about a local port if—

(A) (i) there is in effect in the local port one or more collective bargaining agreements each covering at least 30 percent of the number of individuals employed in performing longshore work and (ii) each such agreement (covering such percentage of longshore workers) permits the activity to be performed by alien crewmen under the terms of such agreement; or

(B) there is no collective bargaining agreement in effect in the local port covering at least 30 percent of the number of individuals employed in performing longshore work, and an employer of alien crewmen (or the employer's designated agent or representative) has filed with the Secretary of Labor at least 14 days before the date of performance of the activity (or later, if necessary due to an unanticipated emergency, but not later than the date of performance of the activity) an attestation setting-forth facts and evidence to show that—

(i) the performance of the activity by alien crewmen is permitted under the prevailing practice of the particular port as of the date of filing of the attestation and that the use of alien crewmen for such activity—

(I) is not during a strike or lockout in the course of a labor dispute, and

(II) is not intended or designed to influence an election of a bargaining representative for workers in the local port; and

(ii) notice of the attestation has been provided by the owner, agent, consignee, master, or commanding officer to the bargaining representative of longshore workers in the local port, or, where there is no such bargaining representative, notice of the attestation has been provided to longshore workers employed at the local port.

In applying subparagraph (B) in the case of a particular activity of longshore work consisting of the use of an automated self-unloading conveyor belt or vacuum-actuated system on a vessel, the attestation shall be required to be filed only if the Secretary of Labor finds, based on a preponderance of the evidence which may be submitted by any interested party, that the performance of such particular activity is not described in clause (i) of such subparagraph.

(2) Subject to paragraph (4), an attestation under paragraph (1) shall—

(A) expire at the end of the 1-year period beginning on the date of its filing with the Secretary of Labor, and

(B) apply to aliens arriving in the United States during such 1-year period if the owner, agent, consignee, master, or commanding officer states in each list under section 251 [8 USCS § 1281] that it continues to comply with the conditions in the attestation.

USCS—T.8 § 1288

(3) An owner, agent, consignee, master, or commanding officer may meet the requirements under this subsection with respect to more than one alien crewman in a single list.

(4)(A) The Secretary of Labor shall compile and make available for public examination in a timely manner in Washington, D.C., a list identifying owners, agents, consignees, masters, or commanding officers which have filed lists for nonimmigrants described in section 101(a)(15)(D)(i) [8 USCS § 1101(a)(15)(D)(i)] with respect to whom an attestation under paragraph (1) or subsection (d)(1) is made and, for each such entity, a copy of the entity's attestation under paragraph (1) or subsection (d)(1) (and accompanying documentation) and each such list filed by the entity.

(B)(i) The Secretary of Labor shall establish a process for the receipt, investigation, and disposition of complaints respecting an entity's failure to meet conditions attested to, an entity's misrepresentation of a material fact in an attestation, or, in the case described in the last sentence of paragraph (1), whether the performance of the particular activity is or is not described in paragraph (1)(B)(i).

(ii) Complaints may be filed by any aggrieved person or organization (including bargaining representatives, associations deemed appropriate by the Secretary, and other aggrieved parties as determined under regulations of the Secretary).

(iii) The Secretary shall promptly conduct an investigation under this subparagraph if there is reasonable cause to believe that an entity fails to meet conditions attested to, an entity has misrepresented a material fact in the attestation, or, in the case described in the last sentence of paragraph (1), the performance of the particular activity is not described in paragraph (1)(B)(i).

(C)(i) If the Secretary determines that reasonable cause exists to conduct an investigation with respect to an attestation, a complaining party may request that the activities attested to by the employer cease during the hearing process described in subparagraph (D). If such a request is made, the attesting employer shall be issued notice of such request and shall respond within 14 days to the notice. If the Secretary makes an initial determination that the complaining party's position is supported by a preponderance of the evidence submitted, the Secretary shall require immediately that the employer cease and desist from such activities until completion of the process described in subparagraph (D).

(ii) If the Secretary determines that reasonable cause exists to conduct an investigation with respect to a matter under the last sentence of paragraph (1), a complaining party may request that the activities of the employer cease during the hearing process described in subparagraph (D) unless the employer files with the Secretary of Labor an attestation under paragraph (1). If such a request is made, the employer shall be issued notice of such request and shall respond within 14 days to the notice. If the Secretary makes an initial determination that the complaining party's position is supported by a preponderance of the evidence submitted, the Secretary shall require immediately that the employer cease and desist from such activities until completion of the process described in subparagraph (D) unless the employer files with the Secretary of Labor an attestation under paragraph (1).

(D) Under the process established under subparagraph (B), the Secretary shall provide, within 180 days after the date a complaint is filed (or later for good cause shown), for a determination as to whether or not a basis exists to make a finding described in subparagraph (E). The Secretary shall provide notice of such determination to the interested parties and an opportunity for a hearing on the complaint within 60 days of the date of the determination.

(E)(i) If the Secretary of Labor finds, after notice and opportunity for a hearing, that an entity has failed to meet a condition attested to or has made a misrepresentation of material fact in the attestation, the Secretary shall notify the Attorney General of such finding and may, in addition, impose such other administrative remedies (including civil monetary penalties in an amount not to exceed $5,000 for each alien crewman performing unauthorized longshore work) as the Secretary determines to be appropriate. Upon receipt of such notice, the Attorney General shall not permit the vessels owned or chartered by such entity to enter any port of the United States during a period of up to 1 year.

(ii) If the Secretary of Labor finds, after notice and opportunity for a hearing, that, in the case described in the last sentence of paragraph (1), the performance of the particular activity is not described in subparagraph (B)(i), the Secretary shall notify the Attorney General of such finding and, thereafter, the attestation described in paragraph (1) shall be required of the employer for the performance of the particular activity.

(F) A finding by the Secretary of Labor under this paragraph that the performance of an activity by alien crewmen is not permitted under the prevailing practice of a local port shall preclude for one year the filing of a subsequent attestation concerning such activity in the port under paragraph (1).

(5) Except as provided in paragraph (5) of subsection (d), this subsection shall not apply to longshore work performed in the State of Alaska.

(d) State of Alaska exception.

(1) Subsection (a) shall not apply to a particular activity of longshore work at a particular location in the State of Alaska if an employer of alien crewmen has filed an attestation with the Secretary of Labor at least 30 days before the date of the first performance of the activity (or anytime up to 24 hours before the first performance of the activity, upon a showing that the employer could not have reasonably anticipated the need to file an attestation for that location at that time) setting forth facts and evidence to show that—

(A) the employer will make a bona fide request for United States longshore workers who are qualified and available in sufficient numbers to perform the activity at the particular time and location from the parties to whom notice has been provided under clauses (ii) and (iii) of subparagraph (D), except that—

(i) wherever two or more contract stevedoring companies have signed a joint collective bargaining agreement with a single labor organization described in subparagraph (D)(i), the employer may request longshore workers from only one of such contract stevedoring companies, and

(ii) a request for longshore workers to an operator of a private dock may be made only for longshore work to be performed at that dock and only if the operator meets the requirements of section 32 of the Longshoremen's and Harbor Workers' Compensation Act [33 USCS § 932];

(B) the employer will employ all those United States longshore workers made available in response to the request made pursuant to subparagraph (A) who are qualified and available in sufficient numbers and who are needed to perform the longshore activity at the particular time and location;

(C) the use of alien crewmembers for such activity is not intended or designed to influence an election of a bargaining representative for workers in the State of Alaska; and

(D) notice of the attestation has been provided by the employer to—

(i) labor organizations which have been recognized as exclusive bargaining representatives of United States longshore workers within the meaning of the National Labor Relations Act [29 USCS §§ 151 et seq.] and which make available or intend to make available workers to the particular location where the longshore work is to be performed,

(ii) contract stevedoring companies which employ or intend to employ United States longshore workers at that location, and

(iii) operators of private docks at which the employer will use longshore workers.

(2)(A) An employer filing an attestation under paragraph (1) who seeks to use alien crewmen to perform longshore work shall be responsible while the attestation is valid to make bona fide requests for United States longshore workers under paragraph (1)(A) and to employ United States longshore workers, as provided in paragraph (1)(B), before using alien crewmen to perform the activity or activities specified in the attestation, except that an employer shall not be required to request longshore workers from a party if that party has notified the employer in writing that it does not intend to make available United States longshore workers to the location at which the longshore work is to be performed.

(B) If a party that has provided such notice subsequently notifies the employer in writing that it is prepared to make available United States longshore workers who are qualified and available in sufficient numbers to perform the longshore activity to the location at which the longshore work is to be performed, then the employer's obligations to that party under subparagraphs (A) and (B) of paragraph (1) shall begin 60 days following the issuance of such notice.

(3)(A) In no case shall an employer filing an attestation be required—

(i) to hire less than a full work unit of United States longshore workers needed to perform the longshore activity;

(ii) to provide overnight accommodations for the longshore workers while employed; or

(iii) to provide transportation to the place of work, except where—

(I) surface transportation is available;

(II) such transportation may be safely accomplished;

(III) travel time to the vessel does not exceed one-half hour each way; and

(IV) travel distance to the vessel from the point of embarkation does not exceed 5 miles.

(B) In the cases of Wide Bay, Alaska, and Klawock/Craig, Alaska, the travel times and travel distances specified in subclauses (III) and (IV) of subparagraph (A)(iii) shall be extended to 45 minutes and 7 ½ miles, respectively, unless the party responding to the request for longshore workers agrees to the lesser time and distance limitations specified in those subclauses.

(4) Subject to subparagraphs (A) through (D) of subsection (c)(4), attestations filed under paragraph (1) of this subsection shall—

(A) expire at the end of the 1-year period beginning on the date the employer anticipates the longshore work to begin, as specified in the attestation filed with the Secretary of Labor, and

(B) apply to aliens arriving in the United States during such 1-year period if the owner, agent, consignee, master, or commanding officer states in each list under section 251 [8 USCS § 1281] that it continues to comply with the conditions in the attestation.

(5)(A) Except as otherwise provided by subparagraph (B), subsection (c)(3) and subparagraphs (A) through (E) of subsection (c)(4) shall apply to attestations filed under this subsection.

(B) The use of alien crewmen to perform longshore work in Alaska consisting of the use of an automated self-unloading conveyor belt or vacuum-actuated system on a vessel shall be governed by the provisions of subsection (c).

(6) For purposes of this subsection—

(A) the term "contract stevedoring companies" means those stevedoring companies licensed to do business in the State of Alaska that meet the requirements of section 32 of the Longshoremen's and Harbor Workers' Compensation Act (33 U.S.C. 932);

(B) the term "employer" includes any agent or representative designated by the employer; and

(C) the terms "qualified" and "available in sufficient numbers" shall be defined by reference to industry standards in the State of Alaska, including safety considerations.

(e) Reciprocity exception.

(1) In general. Subject to the determination of the Secretary of State pursuant to paragraph (2), the Attorney General shall permit an alien crewman to perform an activity constituting longshore work if—

(A) the vessel is registered in a country that by law, regulation, or in practice does not prohibit such activity by crewmembers aboard United States vessels; and

(B) nationals of a country (or countries) which by law, regulation, or in practice does not prohibit such activity by crewmembers aboard United States vessels hold a majority of the ownership interest in the vessel.

(2) Establishment of list. The Secretary of State shall, in accordance with section 553 of title 5, United States Code, compile and annually maintain a list, of longshore work by particular activity, of countries where performance of such a particular activity by crewmembers aboard United States vessels is prohibited by law, regulation, or in practice in the country. By not later than 90 days after the date of the enactment of this section [enacted Nov. 29, 1990], the Secretary shall publish a notice of proposed rulemaking to establish such list. The Secretary shall first establish such list by not later than 180 days after the date of the enactment of this section [enacted Nov. 29, 1990].

(3) "In practice" defined. For purposes of this subsection, the term "in practice" refers to an activity normally performed in such country during the one-year period preceding the arrival of such vessel into the United or coastal waters thereof.

(June 27, 1952, ch 477, Title II, Ch 6, § 258, as added Nov. 29, 1990, P. L. 101-649, Title II, Subtitle A, § 203(a)(1), 104 Stat. 5015; Dec. 12, 1991, P. L. 102-232, Title III, § 303(a)(4), 105 Stat. 1747; Dec. 17, 1993, P. L. 103-198, § 8(a), (b), 107 Stat. 2313; Dec. 20, 1993, P. L. 103-206, Title III, § 323(a), (b), 107 Stat. 2428; Oct. 25, 1994, P. L. 103-416, Title II, § 219(f), (gg), 108 Stat. 4317, 4319; Sept. 30, 1996, P. L. 104-208, Div C, Title VI, Subtitle E, § 671(e)(4)(B), 110 Stat. 3009-723.)

REGISTRATION OF ALIENS

§ 1301. Alien seeking entry; contents

No visa shall be issued to any alien seeking to enter the United States until such alien has been registered in accordance with section 221(b) [8 USCS § 1201(b)].

(June 27, 1952, ch 477, Title II, Ch 7, § 261, 66 Stat. 223; Nov. 14, 1986, P. L. 99-653, § 8, 100 Stat. 3657; Oct. 24, 1988, P. L. 100-525, § 8(g), 102 Stat. 2617).)

§ 1302. Registration of aliens

(a) It shall be the duty of every alien now [June 27, 1952] or hereafter in the United States, who (1) is fourteen years of age or older, (2) has not been registered and fingerprinted under section 221(b) of this Act [8 USCS § 1201(b)] or section 30 or 31 of the Alien Registration Act, 1940, and (3) remains in the United States for thirty days or longer, to apply for registration and to be fingerprinted before the expiration of such thirty days.

(b) It shall be the duty of every parent or legal guardian of any alien now or hereafter in the United States, who (1) is less than fourteen years of age, (2) has not been registered under section 221(b) of this Act [8 USCS § 1201(b)] or section 30 or 31 of the Alien Registration Act, 1940, and (3) remains in the United States for thirty days or longer, to apply for the registration of such alien before the expiration of such thirty days. Whenever any alien attains his fourteenth birthday in the United States he shall, within thirty days thereafter, apply in person for registration and to be fingerprinted.

(c) The Attorney General may, in his discretion and on the basis of reciprocity pursuant to such regulations as he may prescribe, waive the requirement of fingerprinting specified in subsections (a) and (b) in the case of any nonimmigrant.

(June 27, 1952, ch 477, Title II, Ch 7, § 262, 66 Stat. 224; Nov. 14, 1986, P. L. 99-653, § 9, 100 Stat. 3657; Oct. 24, 1988, P. L. 100-525, § 8(h), 102 Stat. 261; Oct. 25, 1994, P. L. 103-416, Title II, § 219(n), 108 Stat. 4317.)

§ 1303. Registration of special groups

(a) Notwithstanding the provisions of sections 261 and 262 [8 USCS §§ 1301, 1302], the Attorney General is authorized to prescribe special regulations and forms for the registration and fingerprinting of (1) alien crewman, (2) holders of border-crossing identification cards, (3) aliens confined in institutions within the United States, (4) aliens under order of removal, (5) aliens who are or have been on criminal probation or criminal parole within the United States, and (6) aliens of any other class not lawfully admitted to the United States for permanent residence.

(b) The provisions of section 262 [8 USCS § 1302] and of this section shall not be applicable to any alien who is in the United States as a nonimmigrant under section 101(a)(15)(A) or 101(a)(15)(G) [8 USCS § 1101(a)(15)(A) or (G)] until the alien ceases to be entitled to such a nonimmigrant status.

(June 27, 1952, ch 477, Title II, Ch 7, § 263, 66 Stat. 224; Sept. 30, 1996, P. L. 104-208, Div C, Title III, Subtitle A, § 308(e)(1)(J), Subtitle B, § 323, 110 Stat. 3009-619, 3009-629.)

§ 1304. Forms for registration and fingerprinting

(a) Preparation; contents. The Attorney General and the Secretary of State jointly are authorized and directed to prepare forms for the registration of aliens under section 261 of this title [8 USCS § 1301], and the Attorney General is authorized and directed to prepare forms for the registration and fingerprinting of aliens under section 262 of this title [8 USCS § 1302]. Such forms shall contain inquiries with respect to (1) the date and place of entry of the alien into the United States; (2) activities in which he has been and intends to be engaged; (3) the length of time he expects to remain in the United States; (4) the police and criminal record, if any, of such alien; and (5) such additional matters as may be prescribed.

(b) Confidential nature. All registration and fingerprint records made under the provisions of this title shall be confidential, and shall be made available only (1) pursuant to section 287(f)(2) [8 USCS § 1357(f)(2)], and (2) to such persons or agencies as may be designated by the Attorney General.

(c) Information under oath. Every person required to apply for the registration of himself or another under this title shall submit under oath the information required for such registration. Any person authorized under regulations issued by the Attorney General to register aliens under this title shall be authorized to administer oaths for such purpose.

(d) Certificate of alien registration or alien receipt card. Every alien in the United States who has been registered and fingerprinted under the provisions of the Alien Registration Act, 1940, or under the provisions of this Act shall be issued a certificate of alien registration or an alien registration receipt card in such form and manner and at such time as shall be prescribed under regulations issued by the Attorney General.

(e) Personal possession of registration or receipt card; penalties. Every alien, eighteen years of age and over, shall at all times carry with him and have in his personal possession any certificate of alien registration or alien registration receipt card issued to him pursuant to subsection (d). Any alien who fails to comply with the provisions of this subsection shall be guilty of a misdemeanor and shall upon conviction for each offense be fined not to exceed $100 or be imprisoned not more than thirty days, or both.

(f) Inclusion of alien's social security account number. Notwithstanding any other provision of law, the Attorney General is authorized to require any alien to provide the alien's social security account number for purposes of inclusion in any record of the alien maintained by the Attorney General or the Service.

(June 27, 1952, ch 477, Title II, Ch 7, § 264, 66 Stat. 224; Nov. 14, 1986, P. L. 99-653, § 10, 100 Stat. 3657; Nov. 14, 1986, P. L. 99-653, § 10, 100 Stat. 3657; Oct. 24, 1988, P. L. 100-525, § 8(i), 102 Stat. 2517; Nov. 29, 1990, P. L. 101-649, Title V, Subtitle A, § 503(b)(2), 104 Stat. 5049; Sept. 30, 1996, P. L. 104-208, Div C, Title IV, Subtitle B, § 415, 110 Stat. 3009-669.)

§ 1305. Notices of change of address

(a) Notification of change. Each alien required to be registered under this title who is within the United States shall notify the Attorney General in writing of each change of address and new address within ten days from the date of such change and furnish with such notice such additional information as the Attorney General may require by regulation.

(b) Current address of natives of any one or more foreign states. The Attorney General may in his discretion, upon ten days notice, require the natives of any one or more foreign states, or any class or group thereof, who are within the United States and who are required to be registered under this title, to notify the Attorney General of their current addresses and furnish such additional information as the Attorney General may require.

(c) Notice to parent or legal guardian. In the case of an alien for whom a parent or legal guardian is required to apply for registration, the notice required by this section shall be given to such parent or legal guardian.

(June 27, 1952, ch 477, Title II, Ch 7, § 265, 66 Stat. 225; Dec. 29, 1981, P. L. 97-116, § 11, 95 Stat. 1617; Oct. 24, 1988, P. L. 100-525, § 9(o), 102 Stat. 2620.)

§ 1306. Penalties

(a) Willful failure to register. Any alien required to apply for registration and to be fingerprinted in the United States who willfully fails or refuses to make such application or to be fingerprinted, and any parent or legal guardian required to apply for the registration of any alien who willfully fails or refuses to file application for the registration of such alien shall be guilty of a misdemeanor and shall, upon conviction thereof, be fined not to exceed $1,000 or be imprisoned not more than six months, or both.

(b) Failure to notify change of address. Any alien or any parent or legal guardian in the United States of any alien who fails to give written notice to the Attorney General, as required by section 265 of this title [8 USCS § 1305], shall be guilty of a misdemeanor and shall, upon conviction thereof, be fined not to exceed $200 or be imprisoned not more than thirty days, or both. Irrespective of whether an alien is convicted and punished as herein provided, any alien who fails to give written notice to the Attorney General, as required by section 265 [8 USCS § 1305], shall be taken into custody and removed in the manner provided by chapter 4 of this title [8 USCS §§ 1221 et seq.], unless such alien establishes to the satisfaction of the Attorney General that such failure was reasonably excusable or was not willful.

(c) Fraudulent statements. Any alien or any parent or legal guardian of any alien, who files an application for registration containing statements known by him to be false, or who procures or attempts to procure registration of himself or another person through fraud, shall be guilty of a misdemeanor and shall, upon conviction thereof, be fined not to exceed $1,000, or be imprisoned not more than six months, or both; and any alien so convicted shall, upon the warrant of the Attorney General, be taken into custody and be removed in the manner provided in chapter 4 of this title [8 USCS §§ 1221 et seq.].

(d) Counterfeiting. Any person who with unlawful intent photographs, prints, or in any other manner makes, or executes, any engraving, photograph, print, or impression in the likeness of any certificate of alien registration or an alien registration receipt card or any colorable imitation thereof, except when and as authorized under such rules and regulations as may be prescribed by the Attorney General, shall upon conviction be fined not to exceed $5,000 or be imprisoned not more than five years, or both.

(June 27, 1952, ch 477, Title II, Ch 7, § 266, 66 Stat. 225; Sept. 30, 1996, P. L. 104-208, Div C, Title III, Subtitle A, § 308(e)(2)(G), (g)(9)(A), 110 Stat. 3009-620, 3009-624.)

GENERAL PENALTY PROVISIONS

§ 1321. Prevention of unauthorized landing of aliens

(a) Failure to report; penalties [Caution: For inflation-adjusted civil monetary penalties, see 8 CFR 280.53(c).]. It shall be the duty of every person, including the owners, masters, officers, and agents of vessels, aircraft, transportation lines, or international bridges or toll roads, other than transportation lines which may enter into a contract as provided in section 238 [233] [8 USCS § 1223], bringing an alien to, or providing a means for an alien to come to, the United States (including an alien crewman whose case is not covered by section 254(a) [8 USCS § 1284(a)]) to prevent the landing of such alien in the United States at a port of entry other than as designated by the Attorney General or at any time or place other than as designated by the immigration officers. Any such person, owner, master, officer, or agent who fails to comply with the foregoing requirements shall be liable to a penalty to be imposed by the Attorney General of $3,000 for each such violation, which may, in the discretion of the Attorney General, be remitted or mitigated by him in accordance with such proceedings as he shall by regulation prescribe. Such penalty shall be a lien upon the vessel or aircraft whose owner, master, officer, or agent violates the provisions of this section, and such vessel or aircraft may be libeled therefor in the appropriate United States court.

(b) Prima facie evidence. Proof that the alien failed to present himself at the time and place designated by the immigration officers shall be prima facie evidence that such alien has landed in the United States at a time or place other than as designated by the immigration officers.

(c) Liability of owners and operators of international bridges and toll roads.

(1) Any owner or operator of a railroad line, international Any owner or operator of a railroad line, international bridge, or toll road who establishes to the satisfaction of the Attorney General that the person has acted diligently and reasonably to fulfill the duty imposed by subsection (a) shall not be liable for the penalty described in such subsection, notwithstanding the failure of the person to prevent the unauthorized landing of any alien.

(2)(A) At the request of any person described in paragraph (1), At the request of any person described in paragraph (1), the Attorney General shall inspect any facility established, or any method utilized, at a point of entry into the United States by such person for the purpose of complying with subsection (a). The Attorney General shall approve any such facility or method (for such period of time as the Attorney General may prescribe) which the Attorney General determines is satisfactory for such purpose.

(B) Proof that any person described in paragraph (1) has diligently maintained any facility, or utilized any method, which has been approved by the Attorney General under subparagraph (A) (within the period for which the approval is effective) shall be prima facie evidence that such person acted diligently and reasonably to fulfill the duty imposed by subsection (a) (within the meaning of paragraph (1) of this subsection).

(June 27, 1952, ch 477, Title II, subch 8, § 271, 66 Stat. 226; Nov. 6, 1986, P. L. 99-603, Title I, Part B, § 114, 100 Stat. 3383; Nov. 29, 1990, P. L. 101-649, Title V, Subtitle D, § 543(a)(8), 104 Stat. 5058.)

§ 1322. Bringing in aliens subject to denial of admission on a health-related ground; persons liable; clearance papers; exceptions; "person" defined

(a) **[Caution: For inflation-adjusted civil monetary penalties, see 8 CFR 280.53(c).]** Any person who shall bring to the United States an alien (other than an alien crewman) who is inadmissible under section 212(a)(1) [8 USCS § 1182(a)(1)] shall pay Commissioner for each and every alien so afflicted the sum of $3,000 unless (1) the alien was in possession of a valid, unexpired immigrant visa, or (2) the alien was allowed to land in the United States, or (3) the alien was in possession of a valid unexpired nonimmigrant visa or other document authorizing such alien to apply for temporary admission to the United States or an unexpired reentry permit issued to him, and (A) such application was made within one hundred and twenty days of the date of issuance of the visa or other document, or in the case of an alien in possession of a reentry permit, within one hundred and twenty days of the date on which the alien was last examined and admitted by the Service, or (B) in the event the application was made later than one hundred and twenty days of the date of issuance of the visa or other document or such examination and admission, if such person establishes to the satisfaction of the Attorney General that the existence of the condition causing inadmissibility could not have been detected by the exercise of due diligence prior to the alien's embarkation.

(b) No vessel or aircraft shall be granted clearance papers pending determination of the question of liability to the payment of any fine under this section, or while the fines remain unpaid, nor shall such fines be remitted or refunded; but clearance may be granted prior to the determination of such question upon the deposit of a sum sufficient to cover such fines or of a bond with sufficient surety to secure the payment thereof, approved by the Commissioner.

(c) Nothing contained in this section shall be construed to subject transportation companies to a fine for bringing to ports of entry in the United States aliens who are entitled by law to exemption from the provisions of section 212(a) [8 USCS § 1182(a)].

(d) As used in this section, the term "person" means the owner, master, agent, commanding officer, charterer, or consignee of any vessel or aircraft.

(June 27, 1952, ch 477, Title 11, Ch 8, § 272, 66 Stat. 226; Oct. 3, 1965, P. L. 89-236, § 18, 79 Stat. 920; Nov. 29, 1990, P. L. 101-649, Title V, Subtitle D, § 543(a)(9), Title VI, § 603(a)(15), 104 Stat. 5058, 5083; Dec. 12, 1991, P. L. 102-232, Title III, § 307(l)(7), 105 Stat. 1757; Oct. 25, 1994, P. L. 103-416, Title II, § 219(o), 108 Stat. 4317; Sept. 30, 1996, P. L. 104-208, Div C, Title III, Subtitle A, § 308(d)(3)(A), (4)(I)(i), 110 Stat. 3009-617, 3009-618.)

§ 1323. Unlawful bringing of aliens into United States

(a) Persons liable.

(1) It shall be unlawful for any person, including any transportation company, or the owner, master, commanding officer, agent, charterer, or consignee of any vessel or aircraft, to bring to the United States from any place outside thereof (other than from foreign contiguous territory) any alien who does not have a

valid passport and an unexpired visa, if a visa was required under this Act or regulations issued thereunder.

(2) It is unlawful for an owner, agent, master, commanding officer, person in charge, purser, or consignee of a vessel or aircraft who is bringing an alien (except an alien crewmember) to the United States to take any consideration to be kept or returned contingent on whether an alien is admitted to, or ordered removed from, the United States.

(b) Evidence [Caution: For inflation-adjusted civil monetary penalties, see 8 CFR 280.53(c).]. If it appears to the satisfaction of the Attorney General that any alien has been so brought, such person, or transportation company, or the master, commanding officer, agent, owner, charterer, or consignee of any such vessel or aircraft, shall pay to the Commissioner a fine of $3,000 for each alien so brought and, except in the case of any such alien who is admitted, or permitted to land temporarily, in addition, an amount equal to that paid by such alien for his transportation from the initial point of departure, indicated in his ticket, to the port of arrival, such latter fine to be delivered by the Commissioner to the alien on whose account the assessment is made. No vessel or aircraft shall be granted clearance pending the determination of the liability to the payment of such fine or while such fine remains unpaid, except that clearance may be granted prior to the determination of such question upon the deposit of an amount sufficient to cover such fine, or of a bond with sufficient surety to secure the payment thereof approved by the Commissioner.

(c) Remission or refund. Except as provided in subsection (e), such fine shall not be remitted or refunded, unless it appears to the satisfaction of the Attorney General that such person, and the owner, master, commanding officer, agent, charterer, and consignee of the vessel or aircraft, prior to the departure of the vessel or aircraft from the last port outside the United States, did not know, and could not have ascertained, by the exercise of reasonable diligence, that the individual transported was an alien and that a valid passport or visa was required.

(d) [Repealed]

(e) Reduction, refund, or waiver. A fine under this section may be reduced, refunded, or waived under such regulations as the Attorney General shall prescribe in cases in which—

(1) the carrier demonstrates that it had screened all passengers on the vessel or aircraft in accordance with procedures prescribed by the Attorney General, or

(2) circumstances exist that the Attorney General determines would justify such reduction, refund, or waiver.

(June 27, 1952, ch 477, Title II, Ch 8, § 273, 66 Stat. 227; Nov. 29, 1990, P. L. 101-649, Title II, Subtitle A, § 201(b), Title V, Subtitle D, § 543(a)(10), 104 Stat. 5014, 5058; Dec. 12, 1991, P. L. 102-232, Title III, § 306(c)(4)(B), 105 Stat. 1752; Oct. 25, 1994, P. L. 103-416, Title II, §§ 209(a), 216, 219(p), 108 Stat. 4312, 4315, 4317; Sept. 30, 1996, P. L. 104-208, Div C, Title III, Subtitle A, § 308(c)(3), (e)(13), Subtitle F, § 371(b)(8), Title VI, Subtitle E, § 671(b)(6), (7), 110 Stat. 3009-616, 3009-620, 3009-645, 3009-722.)

§ 1324. Bringing in and harboring certain aliens

(a) Criminal penalties.

(1)(A) Any person who—

(i) knowing that a person is an alien, brings to or attempts to bring to the United States in any manner whatsoever such person at a place other than a designated port of entry or place other than as designated by the Commissioner, regardless of whether such alien has received prior official authorization to come to, enter, or reside in the United States and regardless of any future official action which may be taken with respect to such alien;

(ii) knowing or in reckless disregard of the fact that an alien has come to, entered, or remains in the United States in violation of law, transports, or moves or attempts to transport or move such alien within the United States by means of transportation or otherwise, in furtherance of such violation of law;

(iii) knowing or in reckless disregard of the fact that an alien has come to, entered, or remains in the United States in violation of law, conceals, harbors, or shields from detection, or attempts to conceal, harbor, or shield from detection, such alien in any place, including any building or any means of transportation;

(iv) encourages or induces an alien to come to, enter, or reside in the United States, knowing or in reckless disregard of the fact that such coming to, entry, or residence is or will be in violation of law; or

(v)(I) engages in any conspiracy to commit any of the preceding acts, or

(II) aids or abets the commission of any of the preceding acts,

shall be punished as provided in subparagraph (B).

(B) A person who violates subparagraph (A) shall, for each alien in respect to whom such a violation occurs—

(i) in the case of a violation of subparagraph (A)(i) or (v)(I) or in the case of a violation of subparagraph (A)(ii), (iii), or (iv) in which the offense was done for the purpose of commercial advantage or private financial gain, be fined under title 18, United States Code, imprisoned not more than 10 years, or both;

(ii) in the case of a violation of subparagraph (A) (ii), (iii), (iv), or (v)(II), be fined under title 18, United States Code, imprisoned not more than 5 years, or both;

(iii) in the case of a violation of subparagraph (A) (i), (ii), (iii), (iv), or (v) during and in relation to which the person causes serious bodily injury (as defined in section 1365 of title 18, United States Code) to, or places in jeopardy the life of, any person, be fined under title 18, United States Code, imprisoned not more than 20 years, or both; and

(iv) in the case of a violation of subparagraph (A) (i), (ii), (iii), (iv), or (v) resulting in the death of any person, be punished by death or imprisoned for any term of years or for life, fined under title 18, United States Code, or both.

(C) It is not a violation of clauses [clause] (ii) or (iii) of subparagraph (A), or of clause (iv) of subparagraph (A) except where a person encourages or induces an alien to come to or enter the United States, for a religious denomination having a bona fide nonprofit, religious organization in the United States, or the agents or officers of such denomination or organization, to encourage, invite, call, allow, or enable an alien who is present in the United States to perform the vocation of a minister or missionary for the denomination or organization in the United States as a volunteer who is not compensated as an employee, notwithstanding the provision of room, board, travel, medical assistance, and other basic living expenses, provided the minister or missionary has been a member of the denomination for at least one year.

(2) Any person who, knowing or in reckless disregard of the fact that an alien has not received prior official authorization to come to, enter, or reside in the United States, brings to or attempts to bring to the United States in any manner whatsoever, such alien, regardless of any official action which may later be taken with respect to such alien shall, for each alien in respect to whom a violation of this paragraph occurs—

(A) be fined in accordance with title 18, United States Code, or imprisoned not more than 1 year, or both; or

(B) in the case of—

(i) an offense committed with the intent or with reason to believe that the alien unlawfully brought into the United States will commit an offense against the United States or any State punishable by imprisonment for more than 1 year,

(ii) an offense done for the purpose of commercial advantage or private financial gain, or

(iii) an offense in which the alien is not upon arrival immediately brought and presented to an appropriate immigration officer at a designated port of entry,

be fined under title 18, United States Code, and shall be imprisoned, in the case of a first or second violation of subparagraph (B)(iii), not more than 10 years, in the case of a first or second violation of subparagraph (B)(i) or (B)(ii), not less than 3 nor more than 10 years, and for any other violation, not less than 5 nor more than 15 years.

(3)(A) Any person who, during any 12-month period, knowingly hires for employment at least 10 individuals with actual knowledge that the individuals are aliens described in subparagraph (B) shall be fined under title 18, United States Code, or imprisoned for not more than 5 years, or both.

(B) An alien described in this subparagraph is an alien who—

(i) is an unauthorized alien (as defined in section 274A(h)(3) [8 USCS § 1324a(h)(3)]), and

(ii) has been brought into the United States in violation of this subsection.

(4) In the case of a person who has brought aliens into the United States in violation of this subsection, the sentence otherwise provided for may be increased by up to 10 years if—

(A) the offense was part of an ongoing commercial organization or enterprise;

(B) aliens were transported in groups of 10 or more; and

(C)(i) aliens were transported in a manner that endangered their lives; or

(ii) the aliens presented a life-threatening health risk to people in the United States.

(b) Seizure and forfeiture.

(1) In general. Any conveyance, including any vessel, vehicle, or aircraft, that has been or is being used in the commission of a violation of subsection (a), the gross proceeds of such violation, and any property traceable to such conveyance or proceeds, shall be seized and subject to forfeiture.

(2) Applicable procedures. Seizures and forfeitures under this subsection shall be governed by the provisions of chapter 46 of title 18, United States Code [18 USCS §§ 981 et seq.], relating to civil forfeitures, including section 981(d) of such title, except that such duties as are imposed upon the Secretary of the Treasury under the customs laws described in that section shall be performed by such officers, agents, and other persons as may be designated for that purpose by the Attorney General.

(3) Prima facie evidence in determinations of violations. In determining whether a violation of subsection (a) has occurred, any of the following shall be prima facie evidence that an alien involved in the alleged violation had not received prior official authorization to come to, enter, or reside in the United States or that such alien had come to, entered, or remained in the United States in violation of law:

(A) Records of any judicial or administrative proceeding in which that alien's status was an issue and in which it was determined that the alien had not received prior official authorization to come to, enter, or reside in the United States or that such alien had come to, entered, or remained in the United States in violation of law.

(B) Official records of the Service or of the Department of State showing that the alien had not received prior official authorization to come to, enter, or reside in the United States or that such alien had come to, entered, or remained in the United States in violation of law.

(C) Testimony, by an immigration officer having personal knowledge of the facts concerning that alien's status, that the alien had not received prior official authorization to come to, enter, or reside in the United States or that such alien had come to, entered, or remained in the United States in violation of law.

(c) Authority to arrest. No officer or person shall have authority to make any arrest for a violation of any provision of this section except officers and employees of the Service designated by the Attorney General, either individually or as a member of a class, and all other officers whose duty it is to enforce criminal laws.

(d) Admissibility of videotaped witness testimony. Notwithstanding any provision of the Federal Rules of Evidence, the videotaped (or otherwise audiovisually preserved) deposition of a witness to a violation of subsection (a) who has been deported or otherwise expelled from the United States, or is otherwise unable to testify, may be admitted into evidence in an action brought for that violation if the witness was available for cross examination and the deposition otherwise complies with the Federal Rules of Evidence.

(e) Outreach program. The Secretary of Homeland Security, in consultation with the Attorney General and the Secretary of State, as appropriate, shall develop and implement an outreach program to educate the public in the United States and abroad about the penalties for bringing in and harboring aliens in violation of this section.

(June 27, 1952, ch 477, Title II, Ch 8, § 274, 66 Stat. 228; Nov. 2, 1978, P. L. 95-582, § 2, 92 Stat. 2479; Dec. 29, 1981, P. L. 97-116, § 12, 985 Stat. 1617; Nov. 6, 1986, P. L. 99-603, Title I, Part B, § 112, 100 Stat. 3381; Oct. 24, 1988, P. L. 100-525, § 2(d)(1), 102 Stat. 2610; Sept. 13, 1994, P. L. 103-322, Title VI, § 60024, 108 Stat. 1981; Sept. 30, 1996, P. L. 104-208, Div C, Title II, Subtitle A, § 203(a)–(d), Subtitle B, § 219, Title VI, Subtitle E, § 671(a)(1), 110 Stat. 3009-565, 3009-574, 3009-721; April 25, 2000, P. L. 106-185, § 18(a), 114 Stat. 222; Dec. 17, 2004, P. L. 108-458, Title V, Subtitle D, § 5401, 118 Stat. 3737; Nov. 10, 2005, P. L. 109-97, Title VII, § 796, 119 Stat. 2165.)

§ 1324a. Unlawful employment of aliens

(a) Making employment of unauthorized aliens unlawful.

(1) In general. It is unlawful for a person or other entity—

(A) to hire, or to recruit or refer for a fee, for employment in the United States an alien knowing the alien is an unauthorized alien (as defined in subsection (h)(3)) with respect to such employment, or

(B) (i) to hire for employment in the United States an individual without complying with the requirements of subsection (b) or (ii) if the person or entity is an agricultural association, agricultural employer, or farm labor contractor (as defined in section 3 of the Migrant and Seasonal Agricultural Worker Protection Act [29 USCS § 1802], to hire, or to recruit or refer for a fee, for employment in the United States an individual without complying with the requirements of subsection (b).

(2) Continuing employment. It is unlawful for a person or other entity, after hiring an alien for employment in accordance with paragraph (1), to continue to employ the alien in the United States knowing the alien is (or has become) an unauthorized alien with respect to such employment.

(3) Defense. A person or entity that establishes that it has complied in good faith with the requirements of subsection (b) with respect to the hiring, recruiting, or referral for employment of an alien in the United States has established an affirmative defense that the person or entity has not violated paragraph (1)(A) with respect to such hiring, recruiting, or referral.

(4) Use of labor through contract. For purposes of this section, a person or other entity who uses a contract, subcontract, or exchange, entered into, renegotiated, or extended after the date of the enactment of this section, to obtain the labor of an alien in the United States knowing that the alien is an unauthorized alien (as defined in subsection (h)(3)) with respect to performing such labor, shall be considered to have hired the alien for employment in the United States in violation of paragraph (1)(A).

(5) Use of State employment agency documentation. For purposes of paragraphs (1)(B) and (3), a person or entity shall be deemed to have complied with the requirements of subsection (b) with respect to the hiring of an individual who was referred for such employment by a State employment agency (as defined by the Attorney General), if the person or entity has and retains (for the period and in the manner described in subsection (b)(3)) appropriate documentation of such referral by that agency, which documentation certifies that the agency has complied with the procedures specified in subsection (b) with respect to the individual's referral.

(6) Treatment of documentation for certain employees.

(A) In general. For purposes of this section, if—

(i) an individual is a member of a collective-bargaining unit and is employed, under a collective bargaining agreement entered into between one or more employee organizations and an association of two or more employers, by an employer that is a member of such association, and

(ii) within the period specified in subparagraph (B), another employer that is a member of the association (or an agent of such association on behalf of the employer) has complied with the requirements of subsection (b) with respect to the employment of the individual,

the subsequent employer shall be deemed to have complied with the requirements of subsection (b) with respect to the hiring of the employee and shall not be liable for civil penalties described in subsection (e)(5).

(B) Period. The period described in this subparagraph is 3 years, or, if less, the period of time that the individual is authorized to be employed in the United States.

(C) Liability.

(i) In general. If any employer that is a member of an association hires for employment in the United States an individual and relies upon the provisions of subparagraph (A) to comply with the requirements of subsection (b) and the individual is an alien not authorized to work in the United States, then for the purposes of paragraph (1)(A), subject to clause (ii), the employer shall be presumed to have known at the time of hiring or afterward that the individual was an alien not authorized to work in the United States.

(ii) Rebuttal of presumption. The presumption established by clause (i) may be rebutted by the employer only through the presentation of clear and convincing evidence that the employer did not know (and could not reasonably have known) that the individual at the time of hiring or afterward was an alien not authorized to work in the United States.

(iii) Exception. Clause (i) shall not apply in any prosecution under subsection (f)(1).

(7) Application to Federal Government. For purposes of this section, the term "entity" includes an entity in any branch of the Federal Government.

(b) Employment verification system. The requirements referred to in paragraphs (1)(B) and (3) of subsection (a) are, in the case of a person or other entity hiring, recruiting, or referring an individual for employment in the United States, the requirements specified in the following three paragraphs:

(1) Attestation after examination of documentation.

(A) In general. The person or entity must attest, under penalty of perjury and on a form designated or established by the Attorney General by regulation, that it has verified that the individual is not an unauthorized alien by examining—

(i) a document described in subparagraph (B), or

(ii) a document described in subparagraph (C) and a document described in subparagraph (D).

Such attestation may be manifested by either a hand-written or an electronic signature. A person or entity has complied with the requirement of this paragraph with respect to examination of a document if the document reasonably appears on its face to be genuine. If an individual provides a document or combination of documents that reasonably appears on its face to be genuine and that is sufficient to meet the requirements of the first sentence of this paragraph, nothing in this paragraph shall be construed as requiring the person or entity to solicit the production of any other document or as requiring the individual to produce such another document.

(B) Documents establishing both employment authorization and identity. A document described in this subparagraph is an individual's—

(i) United States passport; [or]

(ii) resident alien card, alien registration card, or other document designated by the Attorney General, if the document—

(I) contains a photograph of the individual and such other personal identifying information relating to the individual as the Attorney General finds, by regulation, sufficient for purposes of this subsection,

(II) is evidence of authorization of employment in the United States, and

(III) contains security features to make it resistant to tampering, counterfeiting, and fraudulent use.

(C) Documents evidencing employment authorization. A document described in this subparagraph is an individual's—

(i) social security account number card (other than such a card which specifies on the face that the issuance of the card does not authorize employment in the United States); or

(ii) other documentation evidencing authorization of employment in the United States which the Attorney General finds, by regulation, to be acceptable for purposes of this section.

(D) Documents establishing identity of individual. A document described in this subparagraph is an individual's—

(i) driver's license or similar document issued for the purpose of identification by a State, if it contains a photograph of the individual or such other personal identifying information relating to the individual as the Attorney General finds, by regulation, sufficient for purposes of this section; or

(ii) in the case of individuals under 16 years of age or in a State which does not provide for issuance of an identification document (other than a driver's license) referred to in clause (i), documentation of personal identity of such other type as the Attorney General finds, by regulation, provides a reliable means of identification.

(E) Authority to prohibit use of certain documents. If the Attorney General finds, by regulation, that any document described in subparagraph (B), (C), or (D) as establishing employment authorization or identity does not reliably establish such authorization or identity or is being used fraudulently to an unacceptable degree, the Attorney General may prohibit or place conditions on its use for purposes of this subsection.

(2) Individual attestation of employment authorization. The individual must attest, under penalty of perjury on the form designated or established for purposes of paragraph (1), that the individual is a citizen or national of the United States, an alien lawfully admitted for permanent residence, or an alien who is authorized under this Act or by the Attorney General to be hired, recruited, or referred for such employment. Such attestation may be manifested by either a hand-written or an electronic signature.

(3) Retention of verification form. After completion of such form in accordance with paragraphs (1) and (2), the person or entity must retain a paper, microfiche, microfilm, or electronic version of the form and make it available for inspection by officers of the Service, the Special Counsel for Immigration-Related Unfair Employment Practices or the Department of Labor during a period beginning on the date of the hiring, recruiting, or referral of the individual and ending—

(A) in the case of the recruiting or referral for a fee (without hiring) of an individual, three years after the date of the recruiting or referral, and

(B) in the case of the hiring of an individual—

(i) three years after the date of such hiring, or

(ii) one year after the date the individual's employment is terminated,

whichever is later.

(4) Copying of documentation permitted. Notwithstanding any other provision of law, the person or entity may copy a document presented by an individual pursuant to this subsection and may retain the copy, but only (except as otherwise permitted under law) for the purpose of complying with the requirements of this subsection.

(5) Limitation on use of attestation form. A form designated or established by the Attorney General under this subsection and any information contained in or appended to such form, may not be used for purposes other than for enforcement of this Act and sections 1001, 1028, 1546, and 1621 of title 18, United States Code.

(6) Good faith compliance.

(A) In general. Except as provided in subparagraphs (B) and (C), a person or entity is considered to have complied with a requirement of this subsection notwithstanding a technical or procedural failure to meet such requirement if there was a good faith attempt to comply with the requirement.

(B) Exception if failure to correct after notice. Subparagraph (A) shall not apply if—

(i) the Service (or another enforcement agency) has explained to the person or entity the basis for the failure,

(ii) the person or entity has been provided a period of not less than 10 business days (beginning after the date of the explanation) within which to correct the failure, and

(iii) the person or entity has not corrected the failure voluntarily within such period.

(C) Exception for pattern or practice violators. Subparagraph (A) shall not apply to a person or entity that has or is engaging in a pattern or practice of violations of subsection (a)(1)(A) or (a)(2).

(c) No authorization of national identification cards. Nothing in this section shall be construed to authorize, directly or indirectly, the issuance or use of national identification cards or the establishment of a national identification card.

(d) Evaluation and changes in employment verification system.

(1) Presidential monitoring and improvements in system.

(A) Monitoring. The President shall provide for the monitoring and evaluation of the degree to which the employment verification system established under subsection (b) provides a secure system to determine employment eligibility in the United States and shall examine the suitability of existing Federal and State identification systems for use for this purpose.

(B) Improvements to establish secure system. To the extent that the system established under subsection (b) is found not to be a secure system to determine employment eligibility in the United States, the President shall, subject to paragraph (3) and taking into account the results of any demonstration projects conducted under paragraph (4), implement such changes in (including additions to) the requirements of subsection (b) as may be necessary to establish a secure system to determine employment eligibility in the United States. Such changes in the system may be implemented only if the changes conform to the requirements of paragraph (2).

(2) Restrictions on changes in system. Any change the President proposes to implement under paragraph (1) in the verification system must be designed in a manner so the verification system, as so changed, meets the following requirements:

(A) Reliable determination of identity. The system must be capable of reliably determining whether—

(i) a person with the identity claimed by an employee or prospective employee is eligible to work, and

(ii) the employee or prospective employee is claiming the identity of another individual.

(B) using of counterfeit-resistant documents. If the system requires that a document be presented to or examined by an employer, the document must be in a form which is resistant to counterfeiting and tampering.

(C) Limited use of system. Any personal information utilized by the system may not be made available to Government agencies, employers, and other persons except to the extent necessary to verify that an individual is not an unauthorized alien.

(D) Privacy of information. The system must protect the privacy and security of personal information and identifiers utilized in the system.

(E) Limited denial of verification. A verification that an employee or prospective employee is eligible to be employed in the United States may not be withheld or revoked under the system for any reason other than that the employee or prospective employee is an unauthorized alien.

(F) Limited use for law enforcement purposes. The system may not be used for law enforcement purposes, other than for enforcement of this Act or sections 1001, 1028, 1546, and 1621 of title 18, United States Code.

(G) Restriction on use of new documents. If the system requires individuals to present a new card or other document (designed specifically for use for this purpose) at the time of hiring, recruitment, or referral, then such document may not be required to be presented for any purpose other than under this Act (or enforcement of sections 1001, 1028, 1546, and 1621 of title 18, United States Code) nor to be carried on one's person.

(3) Notice to Congress before implementing changes.

(A) In general. The President may not implement any change under paragraph (1) unless at least—

(i) 60 days,

(ii) one year, in the case of a major change described in subparagraph (D)(iii), or

(iii) two years, in the case of a major change described in clause (i) or (ii) of subparagraph (D),

before the date of implementation of the change, the President has prepared and transmitted to the Committee on the Judiciary of the House of Representatives and to the Committee on the Judiciary of the Senate a written report setting forth the proposed change. If the President proposes to make any change regarding social security account number cards, the President shall transmit to the Committee on Ways and Means of the House of Representatives and to the Committee on Finance of the Senate a written report setting forth the proposed change. The President promptly shall cause to have printed in the Federal Register the substance of any major change (described in subparagraph (D)) proposed and reported to Congress.

(B) Contents of report. In any report under subparagraph (A) the President shall include recommendations for the establishment of civil and criminal sanctions for unauthorized use or disclosure of the information or identifiers contained in such system.

(C) Congressional review of major changes.

(i) Hearings and review. The Committees on the Judiciary of the House of Representatives and of the Senate shall cause to have printed in the Congressional Record the substance of any major change described in subparagraph (D), shall hold hearings respecting the feasibility and desirability of implementing such a change, and, within the two year period before implementation, shall report to their respective Houses findings on whether or not such a change should be implemented.

(ii) Congressional action. No major change may be implemented unless the Congress specifically provides, in an appropriations or other Act, for funds for implementation of the change.

(D) Major changes requiring two years notice and Congressional review. As used in this paragraph, the term "major change" means a change which would—

(i) require an individual to present a new card or other document (designed specifically for use for this purpose) at the time of hiring, recruitment, or referral,

(ii) provide for a telephone verification system under which an employer, recruiter, or referrer must transmit to a Federal official information concerning the immigration status of prospective employees and the official transmits to the person, and the person must record, a verification code, or

(iii) require any change in any card used for accounting purposes under the Social Security Act [42 USCS §§ 301 et seq.], including any change requiring that the only social security account number cards which may be presented in order to comply with subsection (b)(1)(C)(i) are such cards as are in a counterfeit-resistant form consistent with the second sentence of section 205(c)(2)(D) of the Social Security Act [42 USCS § 405(c)(2)(D)].

(E) General revenue funding of Social Security card changes. Any costs incurred in developing and implementing any change described in subparagraph (D)(iii) for purposes of this subsection shall not be paid for out of any trust fund established under the Social Security Act [42 USCS §§ 301 et seq.].

(4) Demonstration projects.

(A) Authority. The President may undertake demonstration projects (consistent with paragraph (2)) of different changes in the requirements of subsection (b). No such project may extend over a period of longer than five years.

(B) Reports on projects. The President shall report to the Congress on the results of demonstration projects conducted under this paragraph.

(e) Compliance [Caution: For inflation-adjusted civil monetary penalties, see 8 CFR 274a.10.].

(1) Complaints and investigations. The Attorney General shall establish procedures—

(A) for individuals and entities to file written, signed complaints respecting potential violations of subsection (a) or (g)(1),

(B) for the investigation of those complaints which, on their face, have a substantial probability of validity,

(C) for the investigation of such other violations of subsection (a) or (g)(1) as the Attorney General determines to be appropriate, and

(D) for the designation in the Service of a unit which has, as its primary duty, the prosecution of cases of violations of subsection (a) or (g)(1) under this subsection.

(2) Authority in investigations. In conducting investigations and hearings under this subsection—

(A) immigration officers and administrative law judges shall have reasonable access to examine evidence of any person or entity being investigated,

(B) administrative law judges may, if necessary, compel by subpoena the attendance of witnesses and the production of evidence at any designated place or hearing, and

(C) immigration officers designated by the Commissioner may compel by subpoena the attendance of witnesses and the production of evidence at any designated place prior to the filing of a complaint in a case under paragraph (2).

In case of contumacy or refusal to obey a subpoena lawfully issued under this paragraph and upon application of the Attorney General, an appropriate district court of the United States may issue an order requiring compliance with such subpoena and any failure to obey such order may be punished by such court as a contempt thereof.

(3) Hearing.

(A) In general. Before imposing an order described in paragraph (4), (5), or (6) against a person or entity under this subsection for a violation of subsection (a) or (g)(1), the Attorney General shall provide the person or entity with notice and, upon request made within a reasonable time (of not less than 30 days, as established by the Attorney General) of the date of the notice, a hearing respecting the violation.

(B) Conduct of hearing. Any hearing so requested shall be conducted before an administrative law judge. The hearing shall be conducted in accordance with the requirements of section 554 of title 5, United States Code. The hearing shall be held at the nearest practicable place to the place where the person or entity resides or of the place where the alleged violation occurred. If no hearing is so requested, the Attorney General's imposition of the order shall constitute a final and unappealable order.

(C) Issuance of orders. If the administrative law judge determines, upon the preponderance of the evidence received, that a person or entity named in the complaint has violated subsection (a) or (g)(1), the administrative law judge shall state his findings of fact and issue and cause to be served on such person or entity an order described in paragraph (4), (5), or (6).

(4) Cease and desist order with civil money penalty for hiring, recruiting, and referral violations. With respect to a violation of subsection (a)(1)(A) or (a)(2), the order under this subsection—

(A) shall require the person or entity to cease and desist from such violations and to pay a civil penalty in an amount of—

(i) not less than $250 and not more than $2,000 for each unauthorized alien with respect to whom a violation of either such subsection occurred,

(ii) not less than $2,000 and not more than $5,000 for each such alien in the case of a person or entity previously subject to one order under this paragraph, or

(iii) not less than $3,000 and not more than $10,000 for each such alien in the case of a person or entity previously subject to more than one order under this paragraph; and

(B) may require the person or entity—

(i) to comply with the requirements of subsection (b) (or subsection (d) if applicable) with respect to individuals hired (or recruited or referred for employment for a fee) during a period of up to three years, and

(ii) to take such other remedial action as is appropriate.

In applying this subsection in the case of a person or entity composed of distinct, physically separate subdivisions each of which provides separately for the hiring, recruiting, or referring for employment, without reference to the practices of, and not under the control of or common control with, another subdivision, each such subdivision shall be considered a separate person or entity.

(5) Order for civil money penalty for paperwork violations. With respect to a violation of subsection (a)(1)(B), the order under this subsection shall require the person or entity to pay a civil penalty in an amount of not less than $100 and not more than $1,000 for each individual with respect to whom such violation occurred. In determining the amount of the penalty, due consideration shall be given to the size of the business of the employer being charged, the good faith of the employer, the seriousness of the violation, whether or not the individual was an unauthorized alien, and the history of previous violations.

(6) Order for prohibited indemnity bonds. With respect to a violation of subsection (g)(1), the order under this subsection may provide for the remedy described in subsection (g)(2).

(7) Administrative appellate review. The decision and order of an administrative law judge shall become the final agency decision and order of the Attorney General unless either (A) within 30 days, an official delegated by regulation to exercise review authority over the decision and order modifies or vacates the decision and order, or (B) within 30 days of the date of such a modification or vacation (or within 60 days of the date of decision and order of an administrative law judge if not so modified or vacated) the decision and order is referred to the Attorney General pursuant to regulations, in which case the decision and order of the Attorney General shall become the final agency decision and order under this subsection. The Attorney General may not delegate the Attorney General's authority under this paragraph to any entity which has review authority over immigration-related matters.

(8) Judicial review. A person or entity adversely affected by a final order respecting an assessment may, within 45 days after the date the final order is issued, file a petition in the Court of Appeals for the appropriate circuit for review of the order.

(9) Enforcement of orders. If a person or entity fails to comply with a final order issued under this subsection against the person or entity, the Attorney General shall file a suit to seek compliance with the order in any appropriate district court of the United States. In any such suit, the validity and appropriateness of the final order shall not be subject to review.

(f) Criminal penalties and injunctions for pattern or practice violations.

(1) Criminal penalty. Any person or entity which engages in a pattern or practice of violations of subsection (a)(1)(A) or (a)(2) shall be fined not more than $3,000 for each unauthorized alien with respect to whom such a violation occurs, imprisoned for not more than six months for the entire pattern or practice, or both, notwithstanding the provisions of any other Federal law relating to fine levels.

(2) Enjoining of pattern or practice violations. Whenever the Attorney General has reasonable cause to believe that a person or entity is engaged in a pattern or practice of employment, recruitment, or referral in violation of paragraph (1)(A) or (2) of subsection (a), the Attorney General may bring a civil action in the appropriate district court of the United States requesting such relief, including a permanent or temporary injunction, restraining order, or other order against the person or entity, as the Attorney General deems necessary.

(g) Prohibition of indemnity bonds.

(1) Prohibition. It is unlawful for a person or other entity, in the hiring, recruiting, or referring for employment of any individual, to require the individual to post a bond or security, to pay or agree to pay an amount, or otherwise to provide a financial guarantee or indemnity, against any potential liability arising under this section relating to such hiring, recruiting, or referring of the individual.

(2) Civil penalty. Any person or entity which is determined, after notice and opportunity for an administrative hearing under subsection (e), to have violated paragraph (1) shall be subject to a civil penalty of $1,000 for each violation and to an administrative order requiring the return of any amounts received in violation of such paragraph to the employee or, if the employee cannot be located, to the general fund of the Treasury.

(h) Miscellaneous provisions.

(1) Documentation. In providing documentation or endorsement of authorization of aliens (other than aliens lawfully admitted for permanent residence) authorized to be employed in the United States, the Attorney General shall provide that any limitations with respect to the period or type of employment or employer shall be conspicuously stated on the documentation or endorsement.

(2) Preemption. The provisions of this section preempt any State or local law imposing civil or criminal sanctions (other than through licensing and similar laws) upon those who employ, or recruit or refer for a fee for employment, unauthorized aliens.

(3) Definition of unauthorized alien. As used in this section, the term "unauthorized alien" means, with respect to the employment of an alien at a particular time, that the alien is not at that time either (A) an alien lawfully admitted for permanent residence, or (B) authorized to be so employed by this Act or by the Attorney General.

(June 27, 1952, ch 477, Title II, Ch 8, § 274A, as added Nov. 6, 1986, P. L. 99-603, Title I, Part A, § 101(a)(1), 100 Stat. 3360; Oct. 24, 1988, P. L. 100-525, § 2(a)(1), 102 Stat. 2609; Nov. 29, 1990, P. L. 101-649, Title V, Subtitle B, § 521(a), Subtitle C, § 538(a), 104 Stat. 5053, 5056; Dec. 12, 1991, P. L. 102-232, Title III, §§ 306(b)(2), 309(b)(11), 105 Stat. 1752, 1759; Oct. 25, 1994, P. L. 103-416, Title II, §§ 213, 219(z)(4), 108 Stat. 4314, 4318; Sept. 30, 1996, P. L. 104-208, Div C, Title III, Subtitle F, § 379(a), Title IV, Subtitle B, §§ 411(a), 412(a)–(d), 416, 110 Stat. 3009-649, 3009-666, 3009-669; Oct. 30, 2004, P. L. 108-390, § 1(a), 118 Stat. 2242.)

§ 1324b. Unfair immigration-related employment practices

(a) Prohibition of discrimination based on national origin or citizenship status.

(1) General rule. It is an unfair immigration-related employment practice for a person or other entity to discriminate against any individual (other than an unauthorized alien, as defined in section 274A(h)(3) [8 USCS § 1324a(h)(3)]) with respect to the hiring, or recruitment or referral for a fee, of the individual for employment or the discharging of the individual from employment-

(A) because of such individual's national origin, or

(B) in the case of a protected individual (as defined in paragraph (3)), because of such individual's citizenship status.

(2) Exceptions. Paragraph (1) shall not apply to—

(A) a person or other entity that employs three or fewer employees,

(B) a person's or entity's discrimination because of an individual's national origin if the discrimination with respect to that person or entity and that individual is covered under section 703 of the Civil Rights Act of 1964 [42 USCS § 2000e-2], or

(C) discrimination because of citizenship status which is otherwise required in order to comply with law, regulation, or executive order, or required by Federal, State, or local government contract, or which the Attorney General determines to be essential for an employer to do business with an agency or department of the Federal, State, or local government.

(3) Definition of protected individual. As used in paragraph (1), the term "protected individual" means an individual who—

(A) is a citizen or national of the United States, or

(B) is an alien who is lawfully admitted for permanent residence, is granted the status of an alien lawfully admitted for temporary residence under section 210(a) or 245A(a)(1) [8 USCS § 1160(a) or 1255a(a)(1)], is admitted as a refugee under section 207 [8 USCS § 1157], or is granted asylum under section 208 [8 USCS § 1158]; but does not include (i) an alien who fails to apply for naturalization within six months of the date the alien first becomes eligible (by virtue of period of lawful permanent residence) to apply for naturalization or, if later, within six months after the date of the enactment of this section and (ii) an alien who has applied on a timely basis, but has not been naturalized as a citizen within 2 years after the date of the application, unless the alien can establish that the alien is actively pursuing naturalization, except that time consumed in the Service's processing the application shall not be counted toward the 2-year period.

(4) Additional exception providing right to prefer equally qualified citizens. Notwithstanding any other provision of this section, it is not an unfair immigration-related employment practice for a person or other entity to prefer to hire, recruit, or refer an individual who is a citizen or national of the United States over another individual who is an alien if the two individuals are equally qualified.

(5) Prohibition of intimidation or retaliation. It is also an unfair immigration-related employment practice for a person or other entity to intimidate, threaten, coerce, or retaliate against any individual for the purpose of interfering with any right or privilege secured under this section or because the individual intends to file or has filed a charge or a complaint, testified, assisted, or participated in an manner in an investigation, proceeding, or hearing under section. An individual so intimidated, threatened, coerced, or retaliated against shall be considered, for purposes of subsections (d) and (g), to have been discriminated against.

(6) Treatment of certain documentary practices as employment practices. A person's or other entity's request, for purposes of satisfying the requirements of section 274A(b) [8 USCS § 1324a(b)], for more or different documents than are required under such section or refusing to honor documents tendered that on their face reasonably appear to be genuine shall be treated as an unfair immigration-related employment practice if made for the purpose or with the intent of discriminating against an individual in violation of paragraph (1).

(b) Charges of violations.

(1) In general. Except as provided in paragraph (2), any person alleging that the person is adversely affected directly by an unfair immigration-related employment practice (or a person on that person's behalf) or an officer of the Service alleging that an unfair immigration-related employment practice has occurred or is occurring may file a charge respecting such practice or violation with the Special Counsel (appointed under subsection (c)). Charges shall be in writing under oath or affirmation and shall contain such information as the Attorney General requires. The Special Counsel by certified mail shall serve a notice of the charge (including the date, place, and circumstances of the alleged unfair immigration-related employment practice) on the person or entity involved within 10 days.

(2) No overlap with EEOC complaints. No charge may be filed respecting an unfair immigration-related employment practice described in subsection (a)(1)(A) if a charge with respect to that practice based on the same set of facts has been filed with the Equal Employment Opportunity Commission under title VII of the Civil Rights Act of 1964 [42 USCS §§ 2000e et seq.], unless the charge is dismissed as being outside the scope of such title [42 USCS §§ 2000e et seq.]. No charge respecting an employment practice may be filed with the Equal Employment Opportunity Commission under such title [42 USCS §§ 2000e et seq.] if a charge with respect to such practice based on the same set of facts has been filed under this subsection, unless the charge is dismissed under this section as being outside the scope of this section.

(c) Special Counsel.

(1) Appointment. The President shall appoint, by and with the advice and consent of the Senate, a Special Counsel for Immigration-Related Unfair Employment Practices (hereinafter in this section referred to as the "Special Counsel") within the Department of Justice to serve for a term of four years. In the case of a vacancy

in the office of the Special Counsel the President may designate the officer or employee who shall act as Special Counsel during such vacancy.

(2) Duties. The Special Counsel shall be responsible for investigation of charges and issuance of complaints under this section and in respect of the prosecution of all such complaints before administrative law judges and the exercise of certain functions under subsection (j)(1).

(3) Compensation. The Special Counsel is entitled to receive compensation at a rate not to exceed the rate now or hereafter provided for grade GS-17 of the General Schedule, under section 5332 of title 5, United States Code [5 USCS § 5332].

(4) Regional offices. The Special Counsel, in accordance with regulations of the Attorney General, shall establish such regional offices as may be necessary to carry out his duties.

(d) Investigation of charges.

(1) By special counsel. The Special Counsel shall investigate each charge received and, within 120 days of the date of the receipt of the charge, determine whether or not there is reasonable cause to believe that the charge is true and whether or not to bring a complaint with respect to the charge before an administrative law judge. The Special Counsel may, on his own initiative, conduct investigations respecting unfair immigration-related employment practices and, based on such an investigation and subject to paragraph (3), file a complaint before such a judge.

(2) Private actions. If the Special Counsel, after receiving such a charge respecting an unfair immigration-related employment practice which alleges knowing and intentional discriminatory activity or a pattern or practice of discriminatory activity, has not filed a complaint before an administrative law judge with respect to such charge within such 120-day period, the Special Counsel shall notify the person making the charge of the determination not to file such a complaint during such period and the person making the charge may (subject to paragraph (3)) file a complaint directly before such a judge within 90 days after the date of receipt of the notice. The Special Counsel's failure to file such a complaint within such 120-day period shall not affect the right of the Special Counsel to investigate the charge or to bring a complaint before an administrative law judge during such 90-day period.

(3) Time limitations on complaints. No complaint may be filed respecting any unfair immigration-related employment practice occurring more than 180 days prior to the date of the filing of the charge with the Special Counsel. This subparagraph shall not prevent the subsequent amending of a charge or complaint under subsection (e)(1).

(e) Hearings.

(1) Notice. Whenever a complaint is made that a person or entity has engaged in or is engaging in any such unfair immigration-related employment practice, an administrative law judge shall have power to issue and cause to be served upon such person or entity a copy of the complaint and a notice of hearing before the judge at a place therein fixed, not less than five days after the serving of the complaint. Any such complaint may be amended by the judge conducting the hearing, upon the motion of the party filing the complaint,in the judge's discretion at any time prior to the issuance of an order based thereon. The person or entity so complained of shall have the right to file an answer to the original or amended complaint and to appear in person or otherwise and give testimony at the place and time fixed in the complaint.

(2) Judges hearing cases. Hearings on complaints under this subsection shall be considered before administrative law judges who are specially designated by the Attorney General as having special training respecting employment discrimination and, to the extent practicable, before such judges who only consider cases under this section.

(3) Complainant as party. Any person filing a charge with the Special Counsel respecting an unfair immigration-related employment practice shall be considered a party to any complaint before an administrative law judge respecting such practice and any subsequent appeal respecting that complaint. In the discretion of the judge conducting the hearing, any other person may be allowed to intervene in the proceeding and to present testimony.

(f) Testimony and authority of hearing officers.

(1) Testimony. The testimony taken by the administrative law judge shall be reduced to writing. Thereafter, the judge, in his discretion, upon notice may provide for the taking of further testimony or hear argument.

(2) Authority of administrative law judges. In conducting investigations and hearings under this subsection and in accordance with regulations of the Attorney General, the Special Counsel and administrative law judges shall have reasonable access to examine evidence of any person or entity being investigated. The administrative law judges by subpoena may compel the attendance of witnesses and the production of evidence at any designated place or hearing. In case of contumacy or refusal to obey a subpoena lawfully issued under this paragraph and upon application of the administrative law judge, an appropriate district court of the United States may issue an order requiring compliance with such subpoena and any failure to obey such order may be punished by such court as a contempt thereof.

(g) Determinations.

(1) Order. The administrative law judge shall issue and cause to be served on the parties to the proceeding an order, which shall be final unless appealed as provided under subsection (i).

(2) Orders finding violations.

(A) In general. If, upon the preponderance of the evidence, an administrative law judge determines that any person or entity named in the complaint has engaged in or is engaging in any such unfair immigration-related employment practice, then the judge shall state his findings of fact and shall issue and cause to be served on such person or entity an order which requires such person or entity to cease and desist from such unfair immigration-related employment practice.

(B) Contents of order. Such an order also may require the person or entity —

(i) to comply with the requirements of section 274A(b) [8 USCS § 1324a(b)] with respect to individuals hired (or recruited or referred for employment for a fee) during a period of up to three years;

(ii) to retain for the period referred to in clause (i) and only for purposes consistent with section 274A(b)(5) [8 USCS § 1324a(b)(5)], the name and address of each individual who applies, in person or in writing, for hiring for an existing position, or for recruiting or referring for a fee, for employment in the United States;

(iii) to hire individuals directly and adversely affected, with or without back pay;

(iv)(I) except as provided in subclauses (II) through (I) through (IV), to pay a civil penalty of not less than $250 and not more than $2,000 for each individual discriminated against,

(II) except as provided in subclauses (III) and (IV), in the case of a person or entity previously subject to a single order under this paragraph, to pay a civil penalty of not less than $2,000 and not more than $5,000 for each individual discriminated against,

(III) except as provided in subclause (IV), in the case of a person or entity previously subject to more than one order under this paragraph, to pay a civil penalty of not less than $3,000 and not more than $10,000 for each individual discriminated against, and

(IV) in the case of an unfair immigration-related employment practice described in subsection (a)(6), to pay a civil penalty of not less than $100 and not more than $1,000 for each individual discriminated against;

(v) to post notices to employees about their rights under this section and employers' obligations under section 274A [8 USCS § 1324a];

(vi) to educate all personnel involved in hiring and complying with this section or section 274A [8 USCS § 1324a] about the requirements of this section or such section;

(vii) to remove (in an appropriate case) a false performance review or false warning from an employees personnel file; and

(viii) to lift (in an appropriate case) any restrictions on any employee's assignments, work shifts, or movements.

(C) Limitation on back pay remedy. In providing a remedy under subparagraph (B)(iii), back pay liability shall not accrue from a date more than two years prior to the date of the filing of a charge with the Special Counsel. Interim earnings or amounts earnable with reasonable diligence by the individual or individuals discriminated against shall operate to reduce the back pay otherwise allowable under such subparagraph. No order shall require the hiring of an individual as an employee or the payment to an individual of any back pay, if the individual was refused employment for any reason other than discrimination on account of national origin or citizenship status.

(D) Treatment of distinct entities. In applying this subsection in the case of a person or entity composed of distinct, physically separate subdivisions each of which provides separately for the hiring, recruiting, or referring for employment, without reference to the practices of, and not under the control of or common control with, another subdivision, each such subdivision shall be considered a separate person or entity.

(3) Orders not finding violations. If upon the preponderance of the evidence an administrative law judge determines that the person or entity named in the complaint has not engaged and is not engaging in any such unfair immigration-related employment practice, then the judge shall state his findings of fact and shall issue an order dismissing the complaint.

(h) Awarding of attorney's fees. In any complaint respecting an unfair immigration-related employment practice, an administrative law judge, in the judge's discretion, may allow a prevailing party, other than the United States, a reasonable attorney's fee, if the losing party's argument is without reasonable foundation in law and fact.

(i) Review of final orders.

(1) In general. Not later than 60 days after the entry of such final order, any person aggrieved by such final order may seek a review of such order in the United States court of appeals for the circuit in which the violation is alleged to have occurred or in which the employer resides or transacts business.

(2) Further review. Upon the filing of the record with the court, the jurisdiction of the court shall be exclusive and its judgment shall be final, except that the same shall be subject to review by the Supreme Court of the United States upon writ of certiorari or certification as provided in section 1254 of title 28, United States Code [28 USCS § 1254].

(j) Court enforcement of administrative orders.

(1) In general. If an order of the agency is not appealed under subsection (i)(1), the Special Counsel (or, if the Special Counsel fails to act, the person filing the charge) may petition the United States district court for the district in which a violation of the order is alleged to have occurred, or in which the respondent resides or transacts business, for the enforcement of the order of the administrative law judge, by filing in such court a written petition praying that such order be enforced.

(2) Court enforcement order. Upon the filing of such petition, the court shall have jurisdiction to make and enter a decree enforcing the order of the administrative law judge. In such a proceeding, the order of the administrative law judge shall not be subject to review.

(3) Enforcement decree in original review. If, upon appeal of an order under subsection (i)(1), the United States court of appeals does not reverse such order, such court shall have the jurisdiction to make and enter a decree enforcing the order of the administrative law judge.

(4) Awarding of attorney's fees. In any judicial proceeding under subsection (i) or this subsection, the court, in its discretion, may allow a prevailing party, other than the United States, a reasonable attorney's fee a part of costs but only if the losing party's argument is without reasonable foundation in law and fact.

(k) Termination dates.

(1) This section shall not apply to discrimination in hiring, recruiting, referring, or discharging of individuals occurring after the date of any termination of the provisions of section 274A [8 USCS § 1324a], under subsection (l) of that section.

(2) The provisions of this section shall terminate 30 calendar days after receipt of the last report required to be transmitted under section 274A(j) if—

(A) the Comptroller General determines, and so reports in such report that—

(i) no significant discrimination has resulted, against citizens or national of the United States or against any eligible workers seeking employment, from the implementation of section 274A [8 USCS § 1324a], or

(ii) such section has created an unreasonable burden on employers hiring such workers; and

(B) there has been enacted, within such period of 30 calendar days, a joint resolution stating in substance that the Congress approves the findings of the Comptroller General contained in such report.

The provisions of subsections (m) and (n) of section 274A [8 USCS § 1324a] shall apply to any joint resolution under subparagraph (B) in the same manner as they apply to a joint resolution under subsection (l) of such section.

(l) Dissemination of information concerning anti-discrimination provisions.

(1) Not later than 3 months after the date of the enactment of this subsection [enacted Nov. 29, 1990], the Special Counsel, in cooperation with the chairman of the Equal Employment Opportunity Commission, the Secretary of Labor, and the Administrator of the Small Business Administration, shall conduct a campaign to disseminate information respecting the rights and remedies prescribed under this section and under title VII of the Civil Rights Act of 1964 [42 USCS §§ 2000e et seq.] in connection with unfair immigration-related employment practices. Such campaign shall be aimed at increasing the knowledge of employers, employees, and the general public concerning employer and employee rights, responsibilities, and remedies under this section and such title [42 USCS §§ 2000e et seq.].

(2) In order to carry out the campaign under this subsection, the Special Counsel—

(A) may, to the extent deemed appropriate and subject to the availability of appropriations, contract with public and private organizations for outreach activities under the campaign, and

(B) shall consult with the Secretary of Labor, the chairman of the Equal Employment Opportunity Commission, and the heads of such other agencies as may be appropriate.

(3) There are authorized to be appropriated to carry out this subsection $10,000,000 for each fiscal year (beginning with fiscal year 1991).

(June 27, 1952, ch 477, Title II, Ch 8, § 274B, as added Nov. 6, 1986, P. L. 99-603, Title I, Part A, § 102(a), 100 Stat. 3374; Oct. 24, 1988, P. L. 100-525, § 2(b), 102 Stat. 2610; Nov. 29, 1990, P. L. 101-649, Title V, Subtitle C, §§ 531, 532(a), 533(a), 534(a), 535(a), 536(a), 537(a), 539(a), 104 Stat. 5054-5056; Dec. 12, 1991, P. L. 102-232, Title III, § 306(b)(1), (2), (c)(1), 105 Stat. 1752; Oct. 25, 1994, P. L. 103-416, Title II, § 219(q), 108 Stat. 4317; Sept. 30, 1996, P. L. 104-208, Div C, Title IV, Subtitle C, § 421(a), Title VI, Subtitle E, § 671(d)(1)(B), 110 Stat. 3009-670, 3990-723.)

§ 1324c. Penalties for document fraud

(a) Activities prohibited. It is unlawful for any person or entity knowingly—

(1) to forge, counterfeit, alter, or falsely make any document for the purpose of satisfying a requirement of this Act or to obtain a benefit under this Act,

(2) to use, attempt to use, possess, obtain, accept, or receive or to provide any forged, counterfeit, altered, or falsely made document in order to satisfy any requirement of this Act or to obtain a benefit under this Act,

(3) to use or attempt to use or to provide or attempt to provide any document lawfully issued to or with respect to a person other than the possessor (including a deceased individual) for the purpose of satisfying a requirement of this Act or obtaining a benefit under this Act,

(4) to accept or receive or to provide any document lawfully issued to or with respect to a person other than the possessor (including a deceased individual) for the purpose of complying with section 274A(b) [8 USCS § 1324a(b)] or obtaining a benefit under this Act, or

(5) to prepare, file, or assist another in preparing or filing, any application for benefits under this Act, or any document required under this Act, or any document submitted in connection with such application or document, with knowledge or in reckless disregard of the fact that such application or document was falsely made or, in whole or in part, does not relate to the person on whose behalf it was or is being submitted, or

(6) (A) to present before boarding a common carrier for the purpose of coming to the United States a document which relates to the alien's eligibility to enter the United States, and (B) to fail to present such document to an immigration officer upon arrival at a United States port of entry.

(b) Exception. This section does not prohibit any lawfully authorized investigative, protective, or intelligence activity of a law enforcement agency of the United States, a State, or a subdivision of a State, or of an intelligence agency of the United States, or any activity authorized under chapter 224 of title 18, United States Code [18 USCS §§ 3521 et seq.].

(c) Construction. Nothing in this section shall be construed to diminish or qualify any of the penalties available for activities by this section but proscribed as well in title 18, United States Code.

(d) Enforcement.

(1) Authority in investigations. In conducting investigations and hearings under this subsection—

(A) immigration officers and administrative law judges shall have reasonable access to examine evidence of any person or entity being investigated,

(B) administrative law judges, may, if necessary, compel by subpoena the attendance of witnesses and the production of evidence at any designated place or hearing, and

(C) immigration officers designated by the Commissioner may compel by subpoena the attendance of witnesses and the production of evidence at any designated place prior to the filing of a complaint in a case under paragraph (2).

In case of contumacy or refusal to obey a subpoena lawfully issued under this paragraph and upon application of the Attorney General, an appropriate district court of the United States may issue an order requiring compliance with such subpoena and any failure to obey such order may be punished by such court as a contempt thereof.

(2) Hearing.

(A) In general. Before imposing an order described in paragraph (3) against a person or entity under this subsection for a violation of subsection (a), the Attorney General shall provide the person or entity with notice and, upon request made within a reasonable time (of not less than 30 days, as established by the Attorney General) of the date of the notice, a hearing respecting the violation.

(B) Conduct of hearing. Any hearing so requested shall be conducted before an administrative law judge. The hearing shall be conducted in accordance with the requirements of section 554 of title 5, United States Code. The hearing shall be held at the nearest practicable place to the place where the person or entity resides or of the place where the alleged violation occurred. If no hearing is so requested, the Attorney General's imposition of the order shall constitute a final and unappealable order.

(C) Issuance of orders. If the administrative law judge determines, upon the preponderance of the evidence received, that a person or entity has violated subsection (a), the administrative law judge shall state his findings of fact and issue and cause to be served on such person or entity an order described in paragraph (3).

(3) Cease and desist order with civil money penalty **[Caution: For inflation-adjusted civil monetary penalties, see 8 CFR 270.3(b)(1)(ii).]**. With respect to a violation of subsection (a), the order under this subsection shall require the person or entity to cease and desist from such violations and to pay a civil penalty in an amount of—

(A) not less than $250 and not more than $2,000 for each document that is the subject of a violation under subsection (a), or

(B) in the case of a person or entity previously subject to an order under this paragraph, not less than $2,000 and not more than $5,000 for each document that is the subject of a violation under subsection (a).

In applying this subsection in the case of a person or entity composed of distinct, physically separate subdivisions each of which provides separately for the hiring, recruiting, or referring for employment, without reference to the practices of, and not under the control of or common control with, another subdivision, each such subdivision shall be considered a separate person or entity.

(4) Administrative appellate review. The decision and order of an administrative law judge shall become the final agency decision and order of the Attorney General unless either (A) within 30 days, an official delegated by regulation to exercise review authority over the decision and order modifies or vacates the decision and order, or (B) within 30 days of the date of such a modification or vacation (or within 60 days of the date of decision and order of an administrative law judge if not so modified or vacated) the decision and order is referred to the Attorney General pursuant to regulations, in which case the decision and order of the Attorney General shall become the final agency decision and order under this subsection.

(5) Judicial review. A person or entity adversely affected by a final order under this section may, within 45 days after the date the final order is issued, file a petition in the Court of Appeals for the appropriate circuit for review of the order.

(6) Enforcement of orders. If a person or entity fails to comply with a final order issued under this section against the person or entity, the Attorney General shall file a suit to seek compliance with the order in any appropriate district court of the United States. In any such suit, the validity and appropriateness of the final order shall not be subject to review.

(7) Waiver by Attorney General. The Attorney General may waive the penalties imposed by this section with respect to an alien who knowingly violates subsection (a)(6) if the alien is granted asylum under section 208 [8 USCS § 1158] or withholding of removal under section 241(b)(3) [8 USCS § 1251(b)(3)].

(e) Criminal penalties for failure to disclose role as document preparer.

(1) Whoever, in any matter within the jurisdiction of the Service, knowingly and willfully fails to disclose, conceals, or covers up the fact that they have, on behalf of any person and for a fee or other remuneration, prepared or assisted in preparing an application which was falsely made (as defined in subsection (f)) for immigration benefits, shall be fined in accordance with title 18, United States Code, imprisoned for not more than 5 years, or both, and prohibited from preparing or assisting in preparing, whether or not for a fee or other remuneration, any other such application.

(2) Whoever, having been convicted of a violation of paragraph (1), knowingly and willfully prepares or assists in preparing an application for immigration benefits pursuant to this Act, or the regulations promulgated thereunder, whether or not for a fee or other remuneration and regardless of whether in any matter within the jurisdiction of the Service, shall be fined in accordance with title 18, United States Code, imprisoned for not more than 15 years, or both, and prohibited from preparing or assisting in preparing any other such application.

(f) Falsely make. For purposes of this section, the term "falsely make" means to prepare or provide an application or document, with knowledge or in reckless disregard of the fact that the application or document contains a false, fictitious, or fraudulent statement or material representation, or has no basis in law or fact, or otherwise fails to state a fact which is material to the purpose for which it was submitted.

(June 27, 1952, ch 477, Title II, Ch 8, § 274C, as added Nov. 29, 1990, P. L. 101-649, Title V, Subtitle D, § 544(a), 104 Stat. 5059; Dec. 12, 1991, P. L. 102-232, Title III, § 306(c)(5)(A), 105 Stat. 1752; Oct. 25, 1994, P. L. 103-416, Title II, § 219(r), 108 Stat. 4317; Sept. 30, 1996, P. L. 104-208, Div C, Title II, Subtitle B, § 212(a)–(d), 213, 220, Title III, Subtitle A, § 308(g)(10)(D), Subtitle F, § 379(a), 110 Stat. 3009-570, 3009-571, 3009-575, 3009-625, 3009-650.)

§ 1324d. Civil penalties for failure to depart

(a) In general. Any alien subject to a final order of removal who—

(1) willfully fails or refuses to—

(A) depart from the United States pursuant to the order,

(B) make timely application in good faith for travel or other documents necessary for departure, or

(C) present for removal at the time and place required by the Attorney General; or

(2) conspires to or takes any action designed to prevent or hamper the alien's departure pursuant to the order,

shall pay a civil penalty of not more than $500 to the Commissioner for each day the alien is in violation of this section.

(b) Construction. Nothing in this section shall be construed to diminish or qualify any penalties to which an alien may be subject for activities proscribed by section 243(a) [8 USCS § 1253(a)] or any other section of this Act.

(June 27, 1952, ch 477, Title II, Ch 8, § 274D, as added Sept. 30, 1996, P. L. 104-208, Div C, Title III, Subtitle F, § 380(a), 110 Stat. 3009-650.)

§ 1325. Improper entry by alien

(a) Improper time or place; avoidance of examination or inspection; misrepresentation and concealment of facts. Any alien who (1) enters or attempts to enter the United States at any time or place other than as designated by immigration officers, or (2) eludes examination or inspection by immigration officers, or (3) attempts to enter or obtains entry to the United States by a willfully false or misleading representation or the willful concealment of a material fact, shall, for the first commission of any such offense, be fined under title 18, United States Code, or imprisoned not more than 6 months, or both, and, for a subsequent commission of any such offense, be fined under title 18, United States Code, or imprisoned not more than 2 years, or both.

(b) Improper time or place; civil penalties. Any alien who is apprehended while entering (or attempting to enter) the United States at a time or place other than as designated by immigration officers shall be subject to a civil penalty of—

(1) at least $50 and not more than $250 for each such entry (or attempted entry); or

(2) twice the amount specified in paragraph (1) in the case of an alien who has been previously subject to a civil penalty under this subsection.

Civil penalties under this subsection are in addition to, and not in lieu of, any criminal or other civil penalties that may be imposed.

(c) Marriage fraud. Any individual who knowingly enters into a marriage for the purpose of evading any provision of the immigration laws shall be imprisoned for not more than 5 years, or fined not more than $250,000, or both.

(d) Immigration-related entrepreneurship fraud. Any individual who knowingly establishes a commercial enterprise for the purpose of evading any provision of the immigration laws shall be imprisoned for not more than 5 years, fined in accordance with title 18, United States Code, or both.

(June 27, 1952, ch 477, Title II, Ch 8, § 275, 66 Stat. 229; Nov. 10, 1986, P. L. 99-639, § 2(d), 100 Stat. 3542; Nov. 29, 1990, P. L. 101-649, Title I, Subtitle B, Part 2, § 121(b)(3), Title V, Subtitle D, § 543(b)(2), 104 Stat. 4994, 5059; Dec. 12, 1991, P. L. 102-232, Title III, § 306(c)(3), 105 Stat. 1752; Sept. 30, 1996, P. L. 104-208, Div C, Title I, Subtitle A, § 105(a), 110 Stat. 3009-556.)

§ 1326. Reentry of removed aliens

(a) In general. Subject to subsection (b), any alien who—

(1) has been denied admission, excluded, deported, or removed or has departed the United States while an order of exclusion, deportation, or removal is outstanding, and thereafter

(2) enters, attempts to enter, or is at any time found in, the United States, unless (A) prior to his reembarkation at a place outside the United States or his application for admission from foreign contiguous territory, the Attorney General has expressly consented to such alien's reapplying for admission; or (B) with respect to an alien previously denied admission and removed, unless such alien shall establish that he was not required to obtain such advance consent under this or any prior Act,

shall be fined under title 18, United States Code, or imprisoned not more than 2 years or both.

(b) Criminal penalties for reentry of certain removed aliens. Notwithstanding subsection (a), in the case of any alien described in such subsection—

(1) whose removal was subsequent to a conviction for commission of three or more misdemeanors involving drugs, crimes against the person, or both, or a felony (other than an aggravated felony), such alien shall be fined under title 18, United States Code, imprisoned not more than 10 years, or both;

(2) whose removal was subsequent to a conviction for commission of an aggravated felony, such alien shall be fined under such title, imprisoned not more than 20 years, or both;

(3) who has been excluded from the United States pursuant to section 235(c) [8 USCS § 1225(c)] because the alien was excludable under section 212(a)(3)(B) [8 USCS § 1182(a)(3)(B)] or who has been removed from the United States pursuant to the provisions of title V [8 USCS §§ 1531 et seq.], and who thereafter, without the permission of the Attorney General, enters the United States, or attempts to do so, shall be fined under title 18, United States Code, and imprisoned for a period of 10 years, which sentence shall not run concurrently with any other sentence.[;] or

(4) who was removed from the United States pursuant to section 241(a)(4)(B) [8 USCS § 1231(a)(4)(B)] who thereafter, without the permission of the Attorney General, enters, attempts to enter, or is at any time found in, the United States (unless the Attorney General has expressly consented to such alien's reentry) shall be fined under title 18, United States Code, imprisoned for not more than 10 years, or both.

For the purposes of this subsection, the term "removal" includes any agreement in which an alien stipulates to removal during (or not during) a criminal trial under either Federal or State law.

(c) Reentry of alien deported prior to completion of term of imprisonment. Any alien deported pursuant to section 242(h)(2) [8 USCS § 1252(h)(2)] who enters, attempts to enter, or is at any time found in, the United States (unless the Attorney General has expressly consented to such alien's reentry) shall be incarcerated for the remainder of the sentence of imprisonment which was pending at the time of deportation without any reduction for parole or supervised release. Such alien shall be subject to such other penalties relating to the reentry of deported aliens as may be available under this section or any other provision of law.

(d) Limitation on collateral attack on underlying deportation order. In a criminal proceeding under this section, an alien may not challenge the validity of the deportation order described in subsection (a)(1) or subsection (b) unless the alien demonstrates that—

(1) the alien exhausted any administrative remedies that may have been available to seek relief against the order;

(2) the deportation proceedings at which the order was issued improperly deprived the alien of the opportunity for judicial review; and

(3) the entry of the order was fundamentally unfair.

(June 27, 1952, ch 477, Title II, Ch 8, § 276, 66 Stat. 229; Nov. 18, 1988, P. L. 100-690, Title VII, Subtitle J, § 7345(a), 102 Stat. 4471; Nov. 29, 1990, P. L. 101-649, Title V, Subtitle D, § 543(b)(3), 104 Stat. 5059; Sept. 13, 1994, P. L. 103-322, Title XIII, § 130001(b), 108 Stat. 2023; April 24, 1996, P. L. 104-132, Title IV, Subtitle A, § 401(c), Subtitle C, §§ 438(b), 441(a), 110 Stat. 1267, 1276, 1279; Sept. 30, 1996, P. L. 104-208, Div C, Title III, Subtitle A, §§ 305(b), 308(d)(4)(J), (e)(1)(K), (14)(A), Subtitle B, § 324(a), (b), 110 Stat. 3009-606, 3009-618, 3009-619, 3009-620, 3009-629.)

§ 1327. Aiding or assisting certain aliens to enter

Any person who knowingly aids or assists any alien inadmissible under section 212(a)(2) [8 USCS § 1182(a)(2)] (insofar as an alien inadmissible under such section has been convicted of an aggravated felony) or 212(a)(3) [8 USCS § 1182(a)(3)] (other than subparagraph (E) thereof) to enter the United States, or who connives or conspires with any person or persons to allow, procure, or permit any such alien to enter the United States, shall be fined under title 18, United States Code, or imprisoned not more than 10 years, or both.

(June 27, 1952, ch 477, Title II, Ch 8, § 277, 66 Stat. 229; Nov. 18, 1988, P. L. 100-690, Title VII, Subtitle J, § 7346(a), (c)(1), 102 Stat. 4471; Nov. 29, 1990, P. L. 101-649, Title V, Subtitle D, § 543(b)(4), Title VI, § 603(a)(16), 104 Stat. 5059, 5084; Sept. 30, 1996, P. L. 104-208, Div C, Title III, Subtitle A, § 308(d)(3)(A), 110 Stat. 3009-617.)

§ 1328. Importation of alien for immoral purpose

The importation into the United States of any alien for the purpose of prostitution, or for any other immoral purpose, is hereby forbidden. Whoever shall, directly or indirectly, import, or attempt to import into the United States any alien for the purpose of prostitution or for any other immoral purpose, or shall hold or attempt to hold any alien for any such purpose in pursuance of such illegal importation, or shall keep, maintain, control, support, employ, or harbor in any house or other place, for the purpose of prostitution or for any other immoral purpose, any alien, in pursuance of such illegal importation, shall be fined under title 18, United States Code, or imprisoned not more than 10 years, or both. The trial and punishment of offenses under this section may be in any district to or into which such alien is brought in pursuance of importation by the person or persons accused, or in any district in which a violation of any of the provisions of this section occurs. In all prosecutions under this section, the testimony of a husband or wife shall be admissible and competent evidence against each other.

(June 27, 1952, ch 477, Title II, Ch 8, § 278, 66 Stat. 230; Nov. 29, 1990, P. L. 101-649, Title V, Subtitle D, § 543(b)(5), 104 Stat. 5059.)

§ 1329. Jurisdiction of district courts

The district courts of the United States shall have jurisdiction of all causes, civil and criminal, brought by the United States that arise under the provisions of this title. It shall be the duty of the United States attorney of the proper district to prosecute every such suit when brought by the United States. Notwithstanding any other law, such prosecutions or suits may be instituted at any place in the United States at which the violation may occur or at which the person charged with a violation under section 275 or 276 [8 USCS § 1325 or 1326] may be apprehended. No suit or proceeding for a violation of any of the provisions of this title shall be settled, compromised, or discontinued without the consent of the court in which it is pending and any such settlement, compromise, or discontinuance shall be entered of record with the reasons therefor. Nothing in this section shall be construed as providing jurisdiction for suits against the United States or its agencies or officers.

(June 27, 1952, ch 477, Title II, Ch 8, § 279, 66 Stat. 230; Sept. 30, 1996, P. L. 104-208, Div C, Title III, Subtitle F, § 381(a), 110 Stat. 3009-650.)

§ 1330. Collection of penalties and expenses

(a) Notwithstanding any other provisions of this title, the withholding or denial of clearance of or a lien upon any vessel or aircraft provided for in section 231, 234, 243(c)(2), 251, 253, 254, 255, 256, 271, 272, or 273 of this title [8 USCS § 1221, 1224, 1253(c)(2), 1281, 1283, 1284, 1285, 1286, 1321, 1322, or 1323] shall not be regarded as the sole and exclusive means or remedy for the enforcement of payments of any fine, penalty or expenses imposed or incurred under such sections, but, in the discretion of the Attorney General, the amount thereof may be recovered by civil suit, in the name of the United States, from any person made liable under any of such sections.

(b)(1) There is established in the general fund of the Treasury a separate account which shall be known as the "Immigration Enforcement Account". Notwithstanding any other section of this title, there shall be deposited as offsetting receipts into the Immigration Enforcement Account amounts described in paragraph (2) to remain available until expended.

(2) The amounts described in this paragraph are the following:

(A) The increase in penalties collected resulting from the amendments made by sections 203(b) and 543(a) of the Immigration Act of 1990.

(B) Civil penalties collected under sections 240B(d), 274C, 274D, and 275(b) [8 USCS §§ 1229c(d), 1324c, 1324d, and 1325(b)].

(3)(A) The Secretary of the Treasury shall refund out of the Immigration Enforcement Account to any appropriation the amount paid out of such appropriation for expenses incurred by the Attorney General for activities that enhance enforcement of provisions of this title. Such activities include—

(i) the identification, investigation, apprehension, detention, and removal of criminal aliens;

(ii) the maintenance and updating of a system to identify and track criminal aliens, deportable aliens, inadmissible aliens, and aliens illegally entering the United States; and

(iii) for the repair, maintenance, or construction on the United States border, in areas experiencing high levels of apprehensions of illegal aliens, of structures to deter illegal entry into the United States.

(B) The amounts which are required to be refunded under subparagraph (A) shall be refunded at least quarterly on the basis of estimates made by the Attorney General of the expenses referred to in subparagraph (A). Proper adjustments shall be made in the amounts subsequently refunded under subparagraph (A) to the extent prior estimates were in excess of, or less than, the amount required to be refunded under subparagraph (A).

(C) The amounts required to be refunded from the Immigration Enforcement Account for fiscal year 1996 and thereafter shall be refunded in accordance with estimates made in the budget request of the Attorney General for those fiscal years. Any proposed changes in the amounts designated in such budget requests shall only be made after notification to the Committees on Appropriations of the House of Representatives and the Senate in accordance with section 605 of Public Law 104-134 [unclassified].

(D) The Attorney General shall prepare and submit annually to the Congress statements of financial condition of the Immigration Enforcement Account, including beginning account balance, revenues, withdrawals, and ending account balance and projection for the ensuing fiscal year.

(June 27, 1952, ch 477, Title II, Ch 8, § 280, 66 Stat. 230; Nov. 29, 1990, P. L. 101-649, Title V, Subtitle D, § 542(a), 104 Stat. 5057; Oct. 25, 1994, P. L. 103-416, Title II, § 219(s), 108 Stat. 4317; Sept. 30, 1996, P. L. 104-208, Div C, Title III, Subtitle A, § 308(g)(4)(C), Subtitle F, § 382(a), 110 Stat. 3009-623, 3009-651.)

MISCELLANEOUS

§ 1351. Nonimmigrant visa fees

The fees for the furnishing and verification of applications for visas by nonimmigrants of each foreign country and for the issuance of visas to nonimmigrants of each foreign country shall be prescribed by the Secretary of State, if practicable, in amounts corresponding to the total of all visa, entry, residence, or other similar fees, taxes, or charges assessed or levied against nationals of the United States by the foreign countries of which such nonimmigrants are nationals or stateless residents: *Provided,* That nonimmigrant visas issued to aliens coming to the United States in transit to and from the headquarters district of the United Nations in accordance with the provisions of the Headquarters Agreement shall be gratis. Subject to such criteria as the Secretary of State may prescribe, including the duration of stay of the alien and the financial burden upon the charitable organization, the Secretary of State shall waive or reduce the fee for application and issuance of a nonimmigrant visa for any alien coming to the United States primarily for, or in activities related to, a charitable purpose involving health or nursing care, the provision of food or housing, job training, or any other similar direct service or assistance to poor or otherwise needy individuals in the United States.

(June 27, 1952, ch 477, Title II, Ch 9, § 281, 66 Stat. 230; Oct. 3, 1965, P. L. 89-236, § 14, 79 Stat. 919; Oct. 21, 1968, P. L. 90-609, § 1, 82 Stat. 1199; Oct. 6, 1997, P. L. 105-54, § 2(a), 111 Stat. 1175.)

§ 1352. Printing of reentry permits and blank forms of manifests and crew lists; sale to public

(a) Reentry permits issued under section 223 [8 USCS § 1203] shall be printed on distinctive safety paper and shall be prepared and issued under regulations prescribed by the Attorney General.

(b) The Public Printer [Director of the Government Publishing Office] is authorized to print for sale to the public by the Superintendent of Documents, upon prepayment, copies of blank forms of manifests and crew lists and such other forms as may be prescribed and authorized by the Attorney General to be sold pursuant to the provisions of this title.

(June 27, 1952, ch 477, Title II, Ch 9, § 282, 66 Stat. 231.)

§ 1353. Travel expenses and expense of transporting remains of officers and employees dying outside of United States

When officers, inspectors, or other employees of the Service are ordered to perform duties in a foreign country, or are transferred from one station to another, in the United States or in a foreign country, or while performing duties in any foreign country become eligible for voluntary retirement and return to the United States, they shall be allowed their traveling expenses in accordance with such regulations as the Attorney General may deem advisable, and they may also be allowed, within the discretion and under written orders of the Attorney General, the expenses incurred for the transfer of their wives and dependent children, their household effects and other personal property, including the expenses for packing, crating, freight, unpacking, temporary storage, and drayage thereof in accordance with subchapter II of chapter 57 of title 5, United States Code [5 USCS §§ 5721 et seq.]. The expense of transporting the remains of such officers, inspectors, or other employees who die while in, or in transit to, a foreign country in the discharge of their official duties to their former homes in this country for interment, and the ordinary and necessary expenses of such interment and of preparation for shipment, are authorized to be paid on the written order of the Attorney General.

(June 27, 1952, ch 477, Title II, Ch 9, § 283, 66 Stat. 231; Oct. 24, 1988, P. L. 100-525, § 9(p), 102 Stat. 2621.)

§ 1353a. Officers and employees; overtime services; extra compensation; length of working day

The Attorney General shall fix a reasonable rate of extra compensation for overtime services of immigration officers and employees of the Immigration and Naturalization Service who may be required to remain on duty between the hours of five o'clock postmeridian and eight o'clock antemeridian, or on Sundays or holidays, to perform duties in connection with the examination and landing of passengers and crews of steamships, trains, airplanes, or other vehicles, arriving in the United States from a foreign port by water, land, or air, such rates to be fixed on a basis of one-half day's additional pay for each two hours or fraction thereof of at least one hour that the overtime extends beyond five o'clock postmeridian (but not to exceed two and one-half days' pay for the full period from five o'clock postmeridian to eight o'clock antemeridian) and two additional days' pay for Sunday and holiday duty; in those ports where the customary working hours are other than those heretofore mentioned, the Attorney General is vested with authority to regulate the hours of immigration employees so as to agree with the prevailing working hours in said ports, but nothing contained in this section shall be construed in any manner to affect or alter the length of a working day for immigration employees or the overtime pay herein fixed.

(March 2, 1931, ch 368, § 1, 46 Stat. 1467; June 27, 1952, ch 477, Title IV, § 402(i)(1), 66 Stat. 278.)

§ 1353b. Extra compensation; payment

The said extra compensation shall be paid by the master, owner, agent, or consignee of such vessel or other conveyance arriving in the United States from a foreign port to the Attorney General, who shall pay the same to the several immigration officers and employees entitled thereto as provided in this Act [this section and 8 USCS § 1353a]. Such extra compensation shall be paid if such officers or employees have been ordered to report for duty and have so reported, whether the actual inspection or examination of passenger or crew takes place or not: *Provided,* That this section shall not apply to the inspection at designated ports of entry of passengers arriving by international ferries, bridges, or tunnels, or by aircraft, railroad trains, or vessels on the Great Lakes and connecting waterways, when operating on regular schedules.

(March 2, 1931, ch 368, § 2, 46 Stat. 1467.)

§ 1353c. Immigration officials; service in foreign contiguous territory

Nothing in section 1914 of Title 18, United States Code, relative to augmenting salaries of Government officials from outside sources shall prevent receiving reimbursements for services of immigration officials incident to the inspection of aliens in foreign contiguous territory, and such reimbursement shall be credited to the appropriation, "Immigration and Naturalization Service—Salaries and Expenses."

(March 4, 1921, ch 161, § 1, 41 Stat. 1424; Sept. 3, 1954, ch 1263, § 6, 68 Stat. 1227.)

§ 1353d. Disposition of money received as extra compensation

Moneys collected on or after July 1, 1941, as extra compensation for overtime service of immigration officers and employees of the Immigration Service [Immigration and Naturalization Service] pursuant to the Act of March 2, 1931 (46 Stat. 1467) [8 USCS §§ 1353a, 1353b], shall be deposited in the Treasury of the United States to the credit of the appropriation for the payment of salaries, field personnel of the Immigration and Naturalization Service, and the appropriation so credited shall be available for the payment of such compensation.

(Aug. 22, 1940, ch 688, 54 Stat. 858; June 27, 1952, ch 477, Title IV, § 402(i)(2), 66 Stat. 278.)

§ 1354. Applicability to members of the armed forces

(a) Nothing contained in this title shall be construed so as to limit, restrict, deny, or affect the coming into or departure from the United States of an alien member of the Armed Forces of the United States who is in the uniform of, or who bears documents identifying him as a member of, such Armed Forces, and who is coming to or departing from the United States under official orders or permit of such Armed Forces: *Provided,* That nothing contained in this section shall be construed to give to or confer upon any such alien any other privileges, rights, benefits, exemptions, or immunities under this Act, which are not otherwise specifically granted by this Act.

(b) If a person lawfully admitted for permanent residence is the spouse or child of a member of the Armed Forces of the United States, is authorized to accompany the member and reside abroad with the member pursuant to the member's official orders, and is so accompanying and residing with the member (in marital union if a spouse), then the residence and physical presence of the person abroad shall not be treated as—

(1) an abandonment or relinquishment of lawful permanent resident status for purposes of clause (i) of section 101(a)(13)(C) [8 USCS § 1101(a)(13)(C)]; or

(2) an absence from the United States for purposes of clause (ii) of such section.

(June 27, 1952, ch 477, Title II, Ch 9, § 284, 66 Stat. 232; Jan. 28, 2008, P. L. 110-181, Div A, Title VI, Subtitle G, § 673, 122 Stat. 185.)

§ 1355. Disposal of privileges at immigrant stations; rentals; retail sale; disposition of receipts

(a) Subject to such conditions and limitations as the Attorney General shall prescribe, all exclusive privileges of exchanging money, transporting passengers or baggage, keeping eating houses, or other like privileges in connection with any United States immigrant station, shall be disposed of to the lowest responsible and capable bidder (other than an alien) in accordance with the provisions of section 3709 of the Revised Statutes, as amended (41 U. S. C. 5) [41 USCS § 6101], and for the use of Government property in connection with the exercise of such exclusive privileges a reasonable rental may be charged. The feeding of aliens, or the furnishing of any other necessary service in connection with any United States immigrant station, may be performed by the Service without regard to the foregoing provisions of this subsection if the Attorney General shall find that it would be advantageous to the Government in terms of economy and efficiency. No intoxicating liquors shall be sold at any immigrant station.

(b) Such articles determined by the Attorney General to be necessary to the health and welfare of aliens detained at any immigrant station, when not otherwise readily procurable by such aliens, may be sold at reasonable prices to such aliens through Government canteens operated by the Service, under such conditions and limitations as the Attorney General shall prescribe.

(c) All rentals or other receipts accruing from the disposal of privileges, and all moneys arising from the sale of articles through Service-operated canteens, authorized by this section, shall be covered into the Treasury to the credit of the appropriation for the enforcement of this title.

(June 27, 1952, ch 477, Title II, Ch 9, § 285, 66 Stat. 232.)

§ 1356. Disposition of moneys collected under the provisions of this title

(a) Detention, transportation, hospitalization, and all other expenses of detained aliens; expenses of landing stations. All moneys paid into the Treasury to reimburse the Service for detention, transportation, hospitalization, and all other expenses of detained aliens paid from the appropriation for the enforcement of this Act, and all moneys paid into the Treasury to reimburse the Service for expenses of landing stations referred to in section 238(b) [233(b)] [8 USCS § 1223(b)] paid by the Service from the appropriation for the enforcement of this Act, shall be credited to the appropriation for the enforcement of this Act for the fiscal year in which the expenses were incurred.

(b) Purchase of evidence. Moneys expended from appropriations for the Service for the purchase of evidence and subsequently recovered shall be reimbursed to the current appropriation for the Service.

(c) Fees and administrative fines and penalties; exception. Except as otherwise provided in subsection (a) and subsection (b), or in any other provision of this title, all moneys received in payment of fees and administrative fines and penalties under this title shall be covered into the Treasury as miscellaneous receipts: *Provided, however,* That all fees received from applicants residing in the Virgin Islands of the United States, and in Guam, required to be paid under section 281 [8 USCS § 1351], shall be paid over to the Treasury of the Virgin Islands and to the Treasury of Guam, respectively.

(d) Schedule of fees. In addition to any other fee authorized by law, the Attorney General shall charge and collect $7 per individual for the immigration inspection of each passenger arriving at a port of entry in the United States, or for the preinspection of a passenger in a place outside of the United States prior to such arrival, aboard a commercial aircraft or commercial vessel.

(e) Limitations on fees.

(1) Except as provided in paragraph (3), no fee shall be charged under subsection (d) for immigration inspection or preinspection provided in connection with the arrival of any passenger, other than aircraft passengers, whose journey originated in the following:

(A) Canada,

(B) Mexico,

(C) a State, territory or possession of the United States, or

(D) any adjacent island (within the meaning of section 101(b)(5) [8 USCS § 1101(b)(5)]).

(2) No fee may be charged under subsection (d) with respect to the arrival of any passenger—

(A) who is in transit to a destination outside the United States, and

(B) for whom immigration inspection services are not provided.

(3) The Attorney General shall charge and collect $3 per individual for the immigration inspection or preinspection of each commercial vessel passenger whose journey originated in the United States or in any place set forth in paragraph (1): *Provided,* That this requirement shall not apply to immigration inspection at designated ports of entry of passengers arriving by ferry, or by Great Lakes vessels on the Great Lakes and connecting waterways when operating on a regular schedule. For the purposes of this paragraph, the term "ferry" means a vessel, in other than ocean or coastwise service, having provisions only for deck passengers and/or vehicles, operating on a short run on a frequent schedule between two points over the most direct water route, and offering a public service of a type normally attributed to a bridge or tunnel.

(f) Collection.

(1) Each person that issues a document or ticket to an individual for transportation by a commercial vessel or commercial aircraft into the United States shall—

(A) collect from that individual the fee charged under subsection (d) at the time the document or ticket is issued; and

(B) identify on that document or ticket the fee charged under subsection (d) as a Federal inspection fee.

(2) If—

(A) a document or ticket for transportation of a passenger into the United States is issued in a foreign country; and

(B) the fee charged under subsection (d) is not collected at the time such document or ticket is issued; the person providing transportation to such passenger shall collect such fee at the time such passenger departs from the United States and shall provide such passenger a receipt for the payment of such fee.

(3) The person who collects fees under paragraph (1) or (2) shall remit those fees to the Attorney General at any time before the date that is thirty-one days after the close of the calendar quarter in which the fees are collected, except the fourth quarter payment for fees collected from airline passengers shall be made on the date that is ten days before the end of the fiscal year, and the first quarter payment shall include any collections made in the preceding quarter that were not remitted with the previous payment. Regulations issued by the Attorney General under this subsection with respect to the collection of the fees charged under subsection (d) and the remittance of such fees to the Treasury of the United States shall be consistent with the regulations issued by the Secretary of the Treasury for the collection and remittance of the taxes imposed by subchapter C of chapter 33 of the Internal Revenue Code of 1986 [26 USCS §§ 4261 et seq.], but only to the extent the regulations issued with respect to such taxes do not conflict with the provisions of this section.

(g) Provision of immigration inspection and preinspection services. Notwithstanding the Act of March 2, 1931, 46 Stat. 1467 (8 U.S.C. 1353b), or any other provision of law, the immigration services required to be provided to passengers upon arrival in the United States on scheduled airline flights shall be adequately provided when needed and at no cost (other than the fees imposed under subsection (d)) to airlines and airline passengers at:

(1) immigration serviced airports, and

(2) places located outside of the United States at which an immigration officer is stationed for the purpose of providing such immigration services.

(h) Disposition of receipts.

(1)(A) There is established in the general fund of the Treasury a separate account which shall be known as the "Immigration User Fee Account". Notwithstanding any other section of this title, there shall be deposited as offsetting receipts into the Immigration User Fee Account all fees collected under subsection (d) of this section, to remain available until expended. At the end of each 2-year period, beginning with the creation of this account, the Attorney General, following a public rulemaking with opportunity for notice and comment, shall submit a report to the Congress concerning the status of the account, including any balances therein, and recommend any adjustment in the prescribed fee that may be required to ensure that the receipts collected from the fee charged for the succeeding two years equal, as closely as possible, the cost of providing these services.

(B) Notwithstanding any other provisions of law, all civil fines or penalties collected pursuant to sections 243(c), 271, and 273 of this title [8 USCS §§ 1253(c), 1321, 1323] and all liquidated damages and expenses collected pursuant to this Act shall be deposited in the Immigration User Fee Account.

(2)(A) The Secretary of the Treasury shall refund out of the Immigration User Fee Account to any appropriation the amount paid out of such appropriation for expenses incurred by the Attorney General in providing immigration inspection and preinspection services for commercial aircraft or vessels and in—

(i) providing overtime immigration inspection services for commercial aircraft or vessels;

(ii) administration of debt recovery, including the establishment and operation of a national collections office;

(iii) expansion, operation and maintenance of information systems for nonimmigrant control and debt collection;

(iv) detection of fraudulent documents used by passengers traveling to the United States, including training of, and technical assistance to, commercial airline personnel regarding such detection;

(v) providing detention and removal services for inadmissible aliens arriving on commercial aircraft and vessels and for any alien who is inadmissible under section 212(a) [8 USCS § 1182(a)] who has attempted illegal entry into the United States through avoidance of immigration inspection at air or sea ports-of-entry; and

(vi) providing removal and asylum proceedings at air or sea ports-of-entry for inadmissible aliens arriving on commercial aircraft and vessels including immigration removal proceedings resulting from presentation of fraudulent documents and failure to present documentation and for any alien who is inadmissible under section 212(a) [8 USCS § 1182(a)] who has attempted illegal entry into the United States through avoidance of immigration inspection at air or sea ports-of-entry.

The Attorney General shall provide for expenditures for training and assistance described in clause (iv) in an amount, for any fiscal year, not less than 5 percent of the total of the expenses incurred that are described in the previous sentence.

(B) The amounts which are required to be refunded under subparagraph (A) shall be refunded at least quarterly on the basis of estimates made by the Attorney General of the expenses referred to in subparagraph (A). Proper adjustments shall be made in the amounts subsequently refunded under subparagraph (A) to the extent prior estimates were in excess of, or less than, the amount required to be refunded under subparagraph (A).

(i) Reimbursement. Notwithstanding any other provision of law, the Attorney General is authorized to receive reimbursement from the owner, operator, or agent of a private or commercial aircraft, train, or vessel, or from any airport, rail line, or seaport authority for expenses incurred by the Attorney General in providing immigration inspection services which are rendered at the request of such person or authority (including the salary and expenses of individuals employed by the Attorney General to provide such immigration inspection services). Reimbursements under this subsection may be collected in advance of the provision of such immigration inspection services. Notwithstanding subsection (h)(1)(B), and only to the extent provided in appropriations Acts, any amounts collected under this subsection shall be credited as offsetting collections to the currently applicable appropriation, account, or fund of U.S. Customs and Border Protection, remain available until expended, and be available for the purposes for which such appropriation, account, or fund is authorized to be used.

(j) Regulations. The Attorney General may prescribe such rules and regulations as may be necessary to carry out the provisions of this section.

(k) Advisory committee. In accordance with the provisions of chapter 10 of title 5, United States Code [5 USCS §§ 1001 et seq.], the Attorney General shall establish an advisory committee, whose membership shall consist of representatives from the airline and other transportation industries who may be subject to any fee or charge authorized by law or proposed by the Immigration and Naturalization Service for the purpose of covering expenses incurred by the Immigration and Naturalization Service. The advisory committee shall meet on a periodic basis and shall advise the Attorney General on issues related to the performance of the inspectional services of the Immigration and Naturalization Service. This advice shall include, but not be limited to, such issues as the time periods during which such services should be performed, the proper number and deployment of inspection officers, the level of fees, and the appropriateness of any proposed fee. The Attorney General shall give substantial consideration to the views of the advisory committee in the exercise of his duties.

(l) Report to Congress. In addition to the reporting requirements established pursuant to subsection (h), the Attorney General shall prepare and submit annually to the Congress, not later than March 31st of each year, a statement of the financial condition of the "Immigration User Fee Account" including beginning account balance, revenues, withdrawals and their purpose, ending balance, projections for the ensuing fiscal year and a full and complete workload analysis showing on a port by port basis the current and projected need for inspectors. The statement shall indicate the success rate of the Immigration and Naturalization Service in meeting the forty-five minute inspection standard and shall provide detailed statistics regarding the number of passengers inspected within the standard, progress that is being made to expand the utilization of United States citizen by-pass, the number of passengers for whom the standard is not met and the length of their delay, locational breakdown of these statistics and the steps being taken to correct any nonconformity.

(m) Immigration Examinations Fee Account. Notwithstanding any other provisions of law, all adjudication fees as are designated by the Attorney General in regulations shall be deposited as offsetting receipts into a separate account entitled "Immigration Examinations Fee Account" in the Treasury of the United States, whether collected directly by the Attorney General or through clerks of courts: *Provided, however,* That all fees received by the Attorney General from applicants residing in the Virgin Islands of the United States, and in Guam, under this subsection shall be paid over to the treasury of the Virgin Islands and to the treasury of Guam: *Provided further,* That fees for providing adjudication and naturalization services may be set at a level that will ensure recovery of the full costs of providing all such services, including the costs of similar services provided without charge to asylum applicants or other immigrants. Such fees may also be set at a level that will recover any additional costs associated with the administration of the fees collected.

(n) Reimbursement of administrative expenses; transfer of deposits to General Fund of United States Treasury. All deposits into the "Immigration Examinations Fee Account" shall remain available until expended to the Attorney General to reimburse any appropriation the amount paid out of such appropriation for expenses in providing immigration adjudication and naturalization services and the collection, safeguarding and accounting for fees deposited in and funds reimbursed from the "Immigration Examinations Fee Account".

(o) Annual financial reports to Congress. The Attorney General shall prepare and submit annually to Congress statements of financial condition of the "Immigration Examinations Fee Account", including beginning account balance, revenues, withdrawals, and ending account balance and projections for the ensuing fiscal year.

(p) Additional effective dates. The provisions set forth in subsections (m), (n), and (o) of this section apply to adjudication and naturalization services performed and to related fees collected on or after October 1, 1988.

(q) Land Border Inspection Fee Account.

(1)(A)(i) Notwithstanding any other provision of law, the Attorney General is authorized to establish, by regulation, not more than 96 projects under which a fee may be charged and collected for inspection services provided at one or more land border points of entry. Such projects may include the establishment of commuter lanes to be made available to qualified United States citizens and aliens, as determined by the Attorney General.

(ii) This subparagraph shall take effect, with respect to any project described in clause (1) [(i)] that was not authorized to be commenced before the date of the enactment of the Illegal Immigration Reform and Immigrant Responsibility Act of 1996 [enacted Sept. 30, 1996], 30 days after submission of a written plan by the Attorney General detailing the proposed implementation of such project.

(iii) The Attorney General shall prepare and submit on a quarterly basis a status report on each land border inspection project implemented under this subparagraph.

(B) The Attorney General, in consultation with the Secretary of the Treasury, may conduct pilot projects to demonstrate the use of designated ports of entry after working hours through the use of card reading machines or other appropriate technology.

(2) All of the fees collected under this subsection, including receipts for services performed in processing forms I-94, I-94W, and I-68, and other similar applications processed at land border ports of entry, shall be deposited as offsetting receipts in a separate account within the general fund of the Treasury of the United States, to remain available until expended. Such account shall be known as the Land Border Inspection Fee Account.

(3)(A) The Secretary of the Treasury shall refund, at least on a quarterly basis amounts to any appropriations for expenses incurred in providing inspection services at land border points of entry. Such expenses shall include—

(i) the providing of overtime inspection services;

(ii) the expansion, operation and maintenance of information systems for nonimmigrant control;

(iii) the hire of additional permanent and temporary inspectors;

(iv) the minor construction costs associated with the addition of new traffic lanes (with the concurrence of the General Services Administration);

(v) the detection of fraudulent documents used by passengers travelling to the United States;

(vi) providing for the administration of said account.

(B) The amounts required to be refunded from the Land Border Inspection Fee Account for fiscal years 1992 and thereafter shall be refunded in accordance with estimates made in the budget request of the Attorney General for those fiscal years: *Provided,* That any proposed changes in the amounts designated in said budget requests shall only be made after notification to the Committees on Appropriations of the House of Representatives and the Senate in accordance with section 606 of Public Law 101-162 [unclassified].

(4) The Attorney General will prepare and submit annually to the Congress statements of financial condition of the Land Border Immigration Fee Account, including beginning account balance, revenues, withdrawals, and ending account balance and projection for the ensuing fiscal year.

(r) Breached Bond/Detention Fund.

(1) Notwithstanding any other provision of law, there is established in the general fund of the Treasury a separate account which shall be known as the Breached Bond/Detention Fund (in this subsection referred to as the "Fund").

(2) There shall be deposited as offsetting receipts into the Fund all breached cash and surety bonds, in excess of $8,000,000, posted under this Act which are recovered by the Department of Justice, and amount [amounts] described in section 245(i)(3)(b) [245(i)(3)(B)] [8 USCS § 1255(i)(3)(B)].

(3) Such amounts as are deposited into the Fund shall remain available until expended and shall be refunded out of the Fund by the Secretary of the Treasury, at least on a quarterly basis, to the Attorney General for the following purposes—

(i) for expenses incurred in the collection of breached bonds, and

(ii) for expenses associated with the detention of illegal aliens.

(4) The amounts required to be refunded from the Fund for fiscal year 1998 and thereafter shall be refunded in accordance with estimates made in the budget request of the President for those fiscal years. Any proposed changes in the amounts designated in such budget requests shall only be made after Congressional reprogramming notification in accordance with the reprogramming guidelines for the applicable fiscal year.

(5) The Attorney General shall prepare and submit annually to the Congress, statements of financial condition of the Fund, including the beginning balance, receipts, refunds to appropriations, transfers to the general fund, and the ending balance.

(6) For fiscal year 1993 only, the Attorney General may transfer up to $1,000,000 from the Immigration User Fee Account to the Fund for initial expenses necessary to enhance collection efforts: *Provided,* That any such transfers shall be refunded from the Fund back to the Immigration User Fee Account by December 31, 1993.

(s) H-1B Nonimmigrant Petitioner Account.

(1) In general. There is established in the general fund of the Treasury a separate account, which shall be known as the "H-1B Nonimmigrant Petitioner Account". Notwithstanding any other section of this title, there shall be deposited as offsetting receipts into the account all fees collected under paragraphs (9) and (11) of section 214(c) [8 USCS § 1184(c)].

(2) Use of fees for job training. 50 percent of amounts deposited into the H-1B Nonimmigrant Petitioner Account shall remain available to the Secretary of Labor until expended for demonstration programs and projects described in section 414(c) of the American Competitiveness and Workforce Improvement Act of 1998 [29 USCS § 2916a].

(3) Use of fees for low-income scholarship program. 30 percent of the amounts deposited into the H-1B Nonimmigrant Petitioner Account shall remain available to the Director of the National Science Foundation until expended for scholarships described in section 414(d) of the American Competitiveness and Workforce Improvement Act of 1998 [42 USCS § 1869c] for low-income students enrolled in a program of study leading to a degree in mathematics, engineering, or computer science.

(4) National Science Foundation competitive grant program for K-12 math, science and technology education.

(A) In general. 10 percent of the amounts deposited into the H-1B Nonimmigrant Petitioner Account shall remain available to the Director of the National Science Foundation until expended to carry out a direct or matching grant program to support private-public partnerships in K-12 education.

(B) Types of programs covered. The Director shall award grants to such programs, including those which support the development and implementation of standards-based instructional materials models and related student assessments that enable K-12 students to acquire an understanding of science, mathematics, and technology, as well as to develop critical thinking skills; provide systemic improvement in training K-12 teachers and education for students in science, mathematics, and technology; support the professional development of K-12 math and science teachers in the use of technology in the classroom; stimulate system-wide K-12 reform of science, mathematics, and technology in rural, economically disadvantaged regions of the United States; provide externships and other opportunities for students to increase their appreciation and understanding of science, mathematics, engineering, and technology (including summer institutes sponsored by an institution of higher education for students in grades 7-12 that provide instruction in such fields); involve partnerships of industry, educational institutions, and community organizations to address the educational needs of disadvantaged communities; provide college preparatory support to expose and prepare students for careers in science, mathematics, engineering, and technology; and provide for carrying out systemic reform activities under section 3(a)(1) of the National Science Foundation Act of 1950 (42 U.S.C. 1862(a)(1)).

(5) Use of fees for duties relating to petitions. 5 percent of the amounts deposited into the H-1B Nonimmigrant Petitioner Account shall remain available to the Secretary of Homeland Security until expended to carry out duties under paragraphs (1) and (9) of section 214(c) [8 USCS § 1184(c)] related to petitions made for nonimmigrants described in section 101(a)(15)(H)(i)(b) [8 USCS § 1101(a)(15)(H)(i)(b)], under paragraph (1) (C) or (D) of section 204 [204(a)] [8 USCS § 1154(a)] related to petitions for immigrants described in section 203(b) [8 USCS § 1153(b)].

(6) Use of fees for application processing and enforcement. For fiscal year 1999, 5 percent [4 percent] of the amounts deposited into the H-1B Nonimmigrant Petitioner Account shall remain available to the Secretary of Labor until expended for decreasing the processing time for applications under section 212(n)(1) [8 USCS § 1182(n)(1)] and for carrying out section 212(n)(2) [8 USCS § 1182(n)(2)]. Beginning with fiscal year 2000, 5 percent of the amounts deposited into the H-1B Nonimmigrant Petitioner Account shall remain available to the Secretary of Labor until expended for decreasing the processing time for applications under section 212(n)(1) [8 USCS § 1182(n)(1)] and section 212(a)(5)(A) [8 USCS § 1182(a)(5)(A)].

(t) Genealogy Fee.

(1) There is hereby established the Genealogy Fee for providing genealogy research and information services. This fee shall be deposited as offsetting collections into the Examinations Fee Account. Fees for such research and information services may be set at a level that will ensure the recovery of the full costs of providing all such services.

(2) The Attorney General will prepare and submit annually to Congress statements of the financial condition of the Genealogy Fee.

(3) Any officer or employee of the Immigration and Naturalization Service shall collect fees prescribed under regulation before disseminating any requested genealogical information.

(u) Premium fee for certain immigration benefit types.

(1) In general. The Secretary of Homeland Security is authorized to establish and collect a premium fee for the immigration benefit types described in paragraph (2). Such fee shall be paid in addition to any other fees authorized by law, deposited as offsetting receipts in the Immigration Examinations Fee Account established under subsection (m), and used for the purposes described in paragraph (4).

(2) Immigration benefit types. Subject to reasonable conditions or limitations, the Secretary shall establish a premium fee under paragraph (1) in connection with—

(A) employment-based nonimmigrant petitions and associated applications for dependents of the beneficiaries of such petitions;

(B) employment-based immigrant petitions filed by or on behalf of aliens described in paragraph (1), (2), or (3) of section 203(b) [8 USCS § 1153(b)];

(C) applications to change or extend nonimmigrant status;

(D) applications for employment authorization; and

(E) any other immigration benefit type that the Secretary deems appropriate for premium processing.

(3) Amount of fee.

(A) In general. Subject to subparagraph (C), with respect to an immigration benefit type designated for premium processing by the Secretary on or before August 1, 2020, the premium fee shall be $2,500, except that the premium fee for a petition for classification of a nonimmigrant described in subparagraph (H)(ii)(b) or (R) of section 101(a)(15) [8 USCS § 1101(a)(15)] shall be $1,500.

(B) Other immigration benefit types. With respect to an immigration benefit type designated for premium processing but not described in subparagraph (A), the initial premium fee shall be established by regulation, which shall include a detailed methodology supporting the proposed premium fee amount.

(C) Biennial adjustment. The Secretary may adjust a premium fee under subparagraph (A) or (B) on a biennial basis by the percentage (if any) by which the Consumer Price Index for All Urban Consumers for the month of June preceding the date on which such adjustment takes effect exceeds the Consumer Price Index for All Urban Consumers for the same month of the second preceding calendar year. The provisions of section 553 of title 5, United States Code, shall not apply to an adjustment authorized under this subparagraph.

(4) Use of fee. Fees collected under this subsection may only be used by U.S. Citizenship and Immigration Services to—

(A) provide the services described in paragraph (5) to premium processing requestors;

(B) make infrastructure improvements in adjudications processes and the provision of information and services to immigration and naturalization benefit requestors;

(C) respond to adjudication demands, including by reducing the number of pending immigration and naturalization benefit requests; and

(D) otherwise offset the cost of providing adjudication and naturalization services.

(5) Premium processing services. The Secretary—

(A) may suspend the availability of premium processing for designated immigration benefit requests only if circumstances prevent the completion of processing of a significant number of such requests within the required period; and

(B) shall ensure that premium processing requestors have direct and reliable access to current case status information as well as the ability to communicate with the premium processing units at each service center or office that provides premium processing services.

(v) Fraud Prevention and Detection Account.

(1) In general. There is established in the general fund of the Treasury a separate account, which shall be known as the "Fraud Prevention and Detection Account". Notwithstanding any other provision of law, there shall be deposited as offsetting receipts into the account all fees collected under paragraph (12) or (13) of section 214(c) [8 USCS § 1184(c)].

(2) Use of fees to combat fraud.

(A) Secretary of State. One-third of the amounts deposited into the Fraud Prevention and Detection Account shall remain available to the Secretary of State until expended for programs and activities at United States embassies and consulates abroad—

(i) to increase the number [of] diplomatic security personnel assigned exclusively or primarily to the function of preventing and detecting fraud by applicants for visas described in subparagraph (H)(i), (H)(ii), or (L) of section 101(a)(15) [8 USCS § 1101(a)(15)];

(ii) otherwise to prevent and detect visa fraud, including primarily fraud by applicants for visas described in subparagraph (H)(i), (H)(ii), or (L) of section 101(a)(15) [8 USCS § 1101(a)(15)], in cooperation with the Secretary of Homeland Security or pursuant to the terms of a memorandum of understanding or other agreement between the Secretary of State and the Secretary of Homeland Security; and

(iii) upon request by the Secretary of Homeland Security, to assist such Secretary in carrying out the fraud prevention and detection programs and activities described in subparagraph (B).

(B) Secretary of Homeland Security. One-third of the amounts deposited into the Fraud Prevention and Detection Account shall remain available to the Secretary of Homeland Security until expended for programs and activities to prevent and detect immigration benefit fraud, including fraud with respect to petitions filed under paragraph (1) or (2)(A) of section 214(c) [8 USCS § 1184(c)] to grant an alien nonimmigrant status described in subparagraph (H) or (L) of section 101(a)(15) [8 USCS § 1101(a)(15)].

(C) Secretary of Labor. One-third of the amounts deposited into the Fraud Prevention and Detection Account shall remain available to the Secretary of Labor until expended for wage and hour enforcement programs and activities otherwise authorized to be conducted by the Secretary of Labor that focus on industries likely to employ nonimmigrants, including enforcement programs and activities described in section 212(n) [8 USCS § 1182(n)] and enforcement programs and activities related to section 214(c)(14)(A)(i) [8 USCS § 1184(c)(14)(A)(i)].

(D) Consultation. The Secretary of State, the Secretary of Homeland Security, and the Secretary of Labor shall consult one another with respect to the use of the funds in the Fraud Prevention and Detection Account or for programs and activities to prevent and detect fraud with respect to petitions under paragraph (1) or (2)(A) of section 214(c) [8 USCS § 1184(c)] to grant an alien nonimmigrant status described in section 101(a)(15)(H)(ii) [8 USCS § 1101(a)(15)(H)(ii)].

(June 27, 1952, ch 477, Title II, Ch 9, § 286, 66 Stat. 232; Dec. 29, 1981, P. L. 97-116, § 13, 95 Stat. 1618; Oct. 18, 1986, P. L. 99-500; Title I, § 101(b) [Title II, § 205(a)], 100 Stat. 3341-53; Oct. 30, 1986, P. L. 100-591, § 101(b) [Title II, § 205(a), 100 Stat. 3341-53 (as amended Oct. 24, 1988, P. L. 100-525, § 4(a)(2)(A), 102 Stat. 2615); Nov. 14, 1986, P. L. 99-653, § 7(d)(1) (as added Oct. 24, 1988, P. L. 100-525, § 8(f), 102 Stat. 2617); July 11, 1987, P. L. 100-71, Title I, ch I, 101 Stat. 394; Oct. 1, 1988, P. L. 100-459, Title II, § 209(a), 102 Stat. 2203; Oct. 24, 1988, P. L. 100-525, § 4(a)(1), 102 Stat. 2614; Nov. 21, 1989, P. L. 101-162, Title II, 103 Stat. 1000; Nov. 5, 1990, P. L. 101-515, Title II, § 210(a), (d), 104 Stat. 2120, 2121; Dec. 12, 1991, P. L. 102-232, Title III, § 309(a)(1)(A)(i), (B), (2), (b)(12), 105 Stat. 1757, 1758, 1759; Oct. 6, 1992, P. L. 102-395, Title I, § 112, 106 Stat. 1843; Oct. 27, 1993, P. L. 103-121, Title I, 107 Stat. 1161; Oct. 25, 1994, P. L. 103-416, Title II, § 219(t), 108 Stat. 4317; Sept. 30, 1996, P. L. 104-208, Div C, Title I, Subtitle B, § 122(a), 124(a)(1), Title III, Subtitle A, § 308(d)(3)(A), (4)(K), (e)(1)(L), Subtitle F, §§ 376(b), 382(b), Title VI, Subtitle E, § 671(b)(11), (e)(5), (6), 110 Stat. 3009-560, 3009-562, 3009-617, 3009-618, 3009-619, 3009-648, 3009-651, 3009-722, 3009-723; Nov. 26, 1997, P. L. 105-119, Title I, § 110(1), (2), 111 Stat. 2458; Oct. 21, 1998, P. L. 105-277, Div A, § 101(b) [Title I, § 114], Div C, Title IV, § 414(b), 112 Stat. 2681-68, 2681-652; Nov. 29, 1999, P. L. 106-113, Div B, § 1000(a)(1), 113 Stat. 1535; Oct. 17, 2000, P. L. 106-313, Title I, §§ 110(a), 113, 114 Stat. 1255, 1261; Dec. 21, 2000, P. L. 106-553, § 1(a)(2), 114 Stat. 2762; Dec. 21, 2000, P. L. 106-554, § 1(a)(1), 114 Stat. 2763; Nov. 28, 2001, P. L. 107-77, Title I, §§ 109, 110, 115 Stat. 765; May 14, 2002, P. L. 107-173, Title IV, § 403(a), 116 Stat. 559; Aug. 2, 2002, P. L. 107-206, Title I, Ch. 2, § 202, 116 Stat. 832; Nov. 2, 2002, P. L. 107-273, Div C, Title I, Subtitle A, § 11016(2), 116 Stat. 1824; Nov. 25, 2002, P. L. 107-296, Title IV, Subtitle E, § 457, 116 Stat. 2201; Feb. 20, 2003, P. L. 108-7, Div B, Title I, § 108, Div L, § 107, 117 Stat. 67, 532; Sept. 3, 2003, P. L. 108-77, Title IV, § 402(d)(2), 117 Stat. 946; Dec. 8, 2004, P. L. 108-447, Div J, Title IV, Subtitle B, §§ 426(b), 427, 118 Stat. 3357, 3358; May 11, 2005, P. L. 109-13, Div A, Title VI, § 6046, Div B, Title IV, § 403(b), 119 Stat. 295, 319; Jan. 11, 2007, P. L. 109-472, § 2, 120 Stat. 3554; Dec. 16, 2009, P. L. 111-117, Div D, Title V, § 524(a), 123 Stat. 3283; Feb. 24, 2016, P. L. 114-125, Title VIII, Subtitle B, § 818(a), 130 Stat. 222; Oct. 5, 2018, P.L. 115-254, Div B, Title V, § 573, 132 Stat. 3389; Oct. 1, 2020, P.L. 116-159, Div D, Title I, § 4102(a), 134 Stat. 738; Dec. 27, 2022, P.L. 117-286, § 4(a)(44), 136 Stat. 4310.)

§ 1357. Powers of immigration officers and employees

(a) Powers without warrant. Any officer or employee of the Service authorized under regulations prescribed by the Attorney General shall have power without warrant—

(1) to interrogate any alien or person believed to be an alien as to his right to be or to remain in the United States;

(2) to arrest any alien who in his presence or view is entering or attempting to enter the United States in violation of any law or regulation made in pursuance of law regulating the admission, exclusion, expulsion, or removal of aliens, or to arrest any alien in the United States, if he has reason to believe that the alien so arrested is in the United States in violation of any such law or regulation and is likely to escape before a warrant can be obtained for his arrest, but the alien arrested shall be taken without unnecessary delay for examination before an officer of the Service having authority to examine aliens as to their right to enter or remain in the United States;

(3) within a reasonable distance from any external boundary of the United States, to board and search for aliens any vessel within the territorial waters of the United States and any railway car, aircraft, conveyance, or vehicle, and within a distance of twenty-five miles from any such external boundary to have access to private lands, but not dwellings, for the purpose of patrolling the border to prevent the illegal entry of aliens into the United States;

(4) to make arrests for felonies which have been committed and which are cognizable under any law of the United States regulating the admission, exclusion, expulsion, or removal of aliens, if he has reason to believe that the person so arrested is guilty of such felony and if there is likelihood of the person escaping before a warrant can be obtained for his arrest, but the person arrested shall be taken without unnecessary delay before the nearest available officer empowered to commit persons charged with offenses against the laws of the United States; and

(5) to make arrests—

(A) for any offense against the United States, if the offense is committed in the officer's or employee's presence, or

(B) for any felony cognizable under the laws of the United States, if the officer or employee has reasonable grounds to believe that the person to be arrested has committed or is committing such felony,

if the officer or employee is performing duties relating to the enforcement of the immigration laws at the time of the arrest and if there is a likelihood of the person escaping before a warrant can be obtained for his arrest.

Under regulations prescribed by the Attorney General, an officer or employee of the Service may carry a firearm and may execute and serve any order, warrant, subpoena, summons, or other process issued under the authority of the United States. The authority to make arrests under paragraph (5)(B) shall only be effective on and after the date on which the Attorney General publishes final regulations which (i) prescribe the categories of officers and employees of the Service who may use force (including deadly force) and the circumstances under which such force may be used, (ii) establish standards with respect to enforcement activities of the Service, (iii) require that any officer or employee of the Service is not authorized to make arrests under paragraph (5)(B) unless the officer or employee has received certification as having completed a training program which covers such arrests and standards described in clause (ii), and (iv) establish an expedited, internal review process for violations of such standards, which process is consistent with standard agency procedure regarding confidentiality of matters related to internal investigations.

(b) Administration of oath; taking of evidence. Any officer or employee of the Service designated by the Attorney General, whether individually or as one of a class, shall have power and authority to administer oaths and to take and consider evidence concerning the privilege of any person to enter, reenter, pass through, or reside in the United States, or concerning any matter which is material or relevant to the enforcement of this Act and the administration of the Service; and any person to whom such oath has been administered (or who has executed an unsworn declaration, certificate, verification, or statement under penalty of perjury as permitted under section 1746 of title 28, United States Code), under the provisions of this Act, who shall knowingly or willfully give false evidence or swear (or subscribe under penalty of perjury as permitted under section 1746 of title 28, United States Code) to any false statement concerning any matter referred to in this subsection shall be guilty of perjury and shall be punished as provided by section 1621, title 18, United States Code.

(c) Search without warrant. Any officer or employee of the Service authorized and designated under regulations prescribed by the Attorney General, whether individually or as one of a class, shall have power to conduct a search, without warrant, of the person, and of the personal effects in the possession of any person seeking admission to the United States, concerning whom such officer or employee may have reasonable cause to suspect that grounds exist for denial of admission to the United States under this Act which would be disclosed by such search.

(d) Detainer of aliens for violation of controlled substances laws. In the case of an alien who is arrested by a Federal, State, or local law enforcement official for a violation of any law relating to controlled substances, if the official (or another official)—

(1) has reason to believe that the alien may not have been lawfully admitted to the United States or otherwise is not lawfully present in the United States,

(2) expeditiously informs an appropriate officer or employee of the Service authorized and designated by the Attorney General of the arrest and of facts concerning the status of the alien, and

(3) requests the Service to determine promptly whether or not to issue a detainer to detain the alien,

the officer or employee of the Service shall promptly determine whether or not to issue such a detainer. If such a detainer is issued and the alien is not otherwise detained by Federal, State, or local officials, the Attorney General shall effectively and expeditiously take custody of the alien.

(e) Restriction on warrantless entry in case of outdoor agricultural operations. Notwithstanding any other provision of this section other than paragraph (3) of subsection (a), an officer or employee of the Service may not enter without the consent of the owner (or agent thereof) or a properly executed warrant onto the premises of a farm or other outdoor agricultural operation for the purpose of interrogating a person believed to be an alien as to the person's right to be or to remain in the United States.

(f) Fingerprinting and photographing of certain aliens.

(1) Under regulations of the Attorney General, the Commissioner shall provide for the fingerprinting and photographing of each alien 14 years of age or older against whom a proceeding is commenced under section 240 [8 USCS § 1229a].

(2) Such fingerprints and photographs shall be made available to Federal, State, and local law enforcement agencies, upon request.

(g) Performance of immigration officer functions by State officers and employees.

(1) Notwithstanding section 1342 of title 31, United States Code, the Attorney General may enter into a written agreement with a State, or any political subdivision of a State, pursuant to which an officer or employee of the State or subdivision, who is determined by the Attorney General to be qualified to perform a function of an immigration officer in relation to the investigation, apprehension, or detention of aliens in the United States (including the transportation of such aliens across State lines to detention centers), may carry out such function at the expense of the State or political subdivision and to the extent consistent with State and local law.

(2) An agreement under this subsection shall require that an officer or employee of a State or political subdivision of a State performing a function under the agreement shall have knowledge of, and adhere to, Federal law relating to the function, and shall contain a written certification that the officers or employees performing the function under the agreement have received adequate training regarding the enforcement of relevant Federal immigration laws.

(3) In performing a function under this subsection, an officer or employee of a State or political subdivision of a State shall be subject to the direction and supervision of the Attorney General.

(4) In performing a function under this subsection, an officer or employee of a State or political subdivision of a State may use Federal property or facilities, as provided in a written agreement between the Attorney General and the State or subdivision.

(5) With respect to each officer or employee of a State or political subdivision who is authorized to perform a function under this subsection, the specific powers and duties that may be, or are required to be, exercised or performed by the individual, the duration of the authority of the individual, and the position of the agency of the Attorney General who is required to supervise and direct the individual, shall be set forth in a written agreement between the Attorney General and the State or political subdivision.

(6) The Attorney General may not accept a service under this subsection if the service will be used to displace any Federal employee.

(7) Except as provided in paragraph (8), an officer or employee of a State or political subdivision of a State performing functions under this subsection shall not be treated as a Federal employee for any purpose other than for purposes of chapter 81 of title 5, United States Code [5 USCS §§ 8101 et seq.] (relating to compensation for injury), and sections 2671 through 2680 of title 28, United States Code (relating to tort claims).

(8) An officer or employee of a State or political subdivision of a State acting under color of authority under this subsection, or any agreement entered into under this subsection, shall be considered to be acting under color of Federal authority for purposes of determining the liability, and immunity from suit, of the officer or employee in a civil action brought under Federal or State law.

(9) Nothing in this subsection shall be construed to require any State or political subdivision of a State to enter into an agreement with the Attorney General under this subsection.

(10) Nothing in this subsection shall be construed to require an agreement under this subsection in order for any officer or employee of a State or political subdivision of a State—

(A) to communicate with the Attorney General regarding the immigration status of any individual, including reporting knowledge that a particular alien is not lawfully present in the United States; or

(B) otherwise to cooperate with the Attorney General in the identification, apprehension, detention, or removal of aliens not lawfully present in the United States.

(h) Protecting abused juveniles. An alien described in section 101(a)(27)(J) of the Immigration and Nationality Act [8 USCS § 1101(a)(27)(J)] who has been battered, abused, neglected, or abandoned, shall not be compelled to contact the alleged abuser (or family member of the alleged abuser) at any stage of applying for special immigrant juvenile status, including after a request for the consent of the Secretary of Homeland Security under section 101(a)(27)(J)(iii)(I) of such Act [8 USCS § 1101(a)(27)(J)(iii)(I)].

(June 27, 1952, ch 477, Title II, Ch 9, § 287, 66 Stat. 233; Oct. 18, 1976, P. L. 94-550, § 7, 90 Stat. 2535; Oct. 27, 1986, P. L. 99-570, Title I, Subtitle M, § 1751(d), 100 Stat. 3207-47; Nov. 6, 1986, P. L. 99-603, Title I, Part B, § 116, 100 Stat. 3384; Oct. 24, 1988, P. L. 100-525, §§ 2(e), 5, 102 Stat. 2610, 2615; Nov. 29, 1990, P. L. 101-649, Title V, Subtitle A, § 503(a), (b)(1), 104 Stat. 5048, 5049; Dec. 12, 1991, P. L. 102-232, Title III, § 306(a)(3), 105 Stat. 1751; Sept. 30, 1996, P. L. 104-208, Div C, Title I, Subtitle C, § 133, Title III, Subtitle A, § 308(d)(4)(L), (e)(1)(M), (g)(5)(A)(i), 110 Stat. 3009-563, 3009-618, 3009-619, 3009-623; Jan. 5, 2006, P. L. 109-162, Title VIII, Subtitle C, §

826, 119 Stat. 3065; Aug. 12, 2006, P. L. 109-271, § 6(g), 120 Stat. 763.)

§ 1358. Local jurisdiction over immigrant stations

The officers in charge of the various immigrant stations shall admit therein the proper State and local officers charged with the enforcement of the laws of the State or Territory of the United States in which any such immigrant station is located in order that such State and local officers may preserve the peace and make arrests for crimes under the laws of the States and Territories. For the purpose of this section the jurisdiction of such State and local officers and of the State and local courts shall extend over such immigrant stations.

(June 27, 1952, ch 477, Title II, Ch 9, § 288, 66 Stat. 234.)

§ 1359. Application to American Indians born in Canada

Nothing in this title shall be construed to affect the right of American Indians born in Canada to pass the borders of the United States, but such right shall extend only to persons who possess at least 50 per centum of blood of the American Indian race.

(June 27, 1952, ch 477, Title II, Ch 9, § 289, 66 Stat. 234.)

§ 1360. Establishment of central file; information from other departments and agencies

(a) Establishment of central file. There shall be established in the office of the Commissioner, for the use of the security and enforcement agencies of the Government of the United States, a central index, which shall contain the names of all aliens heretofore admitted or denied admission to the United States, insofar as such information is available from the existing records of the Service, and the names of all aliens hereafter admitted or denied admission to the United States, the names of their sponsors of record, if any, and such other relevant information as the Attorney General shall require as an aid to the proper enforcement of this Act.

(b) Information from other departments and agencies. Any information in any records kept by any department or agency of the Government as to the identity and location of aliens in the United States shall be made available to the Service upon request made by the Attorney General to the head of any such department or agency.

(c) Reports on social security account numbers and earnings of aliens not authorized to work.

(1) Not later than 3 months after the end of each fiscal year (beginning with fiscal year 1996), the Commissioner of Social Security shall report to the Committees on the Judiciary of the House of Representatives and the Senate on the aggregate quantity of social security account numbers issued to aliens not authorized to be employed, with respect to which, in such fiscal year, earnings were reported to the Social Security Administration.

(2) If earnings are reported on or after January 1, 1997, to the Social Security Administration on a social security account number issued to an alien not authorized to work in the United States, the Commissioner of Social Security shall provide the Attorney General with information regarding the name and address of the alien, the name and address of the person reporting the earnings, and the amount of the earnings. The information shall be provided in an electronic form agreed upon by the Commissioner and the Attorney General.

(d) Certification of search of Service records. A written certification signed by the Attorney General or by any officer of the Service designated by the Attorney General to make such certification, that after diligent search no record or entry of a specified nature is found to exist in the records of the Service, shall be admissible as evidence in any proceeding as evidence that the records of the Service contain no such record or entry, and shall have the same effect as the testimony of a witness given in open court.

(June 27, 1952, ch 477, Title II, Ch 9, § 290, 66 Stat. 234; Oct. 24, 1988, P. L. 100-525, § 9(q), 102 Stat. 2621; Sept. 30, 1996, P. L. 104-208, Div C, Title III, Subtitle A, § 308(d)(4)(M), Title IV, Subtitle B, § 414(a), 110 Stat. 3009-618, 3009-669.)

§ 1361. Burden of proof upon alien

Whenever any person makes application for a visa or any other document required for entry, or makes application for admission, or otherwise attempts to enter the United States, the burden of proof shall be upon such person to establish that he is eligible to receive such visa or such document, or is not inadmissible under any provision of this Act, and, if an alien, that he is entitled to the nonimmigrant, immigrant, special immigrant, immediate relative, or refugee status claimed, as the case may be. If such person fails to establish to the satisfaction of the consular officer that he is eligible to receive a visa or other document required for entry, no visa or other document required for entry shall be issued to such person, nor shall such person be admitted to the United States unless he establishes to the satisfaction of the Attorney General that he is not inadmissible under any provision of this Act. In any removal proceeding under chapter 4 [8 USCS §§ 1221 et seq.] against any person, the burden of proof shall be upon such person to show the time, place, and manner of his entry into the United States, but in presenting such proof he shall be entitled to the production of his visa or other entry document, if any, and of any other documents and records, not considered by the Attorney General to be confidential, pertaining to such entry in the custody of the Service. If such burden of proof is not sustained, such person shall be presumed to be in the United States in violation of law.

(June 27, 1952, ch 477, Title II, Ch 9, § 291, 66 Stat. 234; Dec. 29, 1981, P. L. 97-116, § 18(k)(1), 95 Stat. 1620; Sept. 30, 1996, P. L. 104-208, Div C, Title III, Subtitle A, § 308(d)(4)(N), (e)(1)(N), (g)(9)(A), 110 Stat. 3009-618, 3009-619, 3009-624.)

§ 1362. Right to counsel

In any removal proceedings before an immigration judge and in any appeal proceedings before the Attorney General from any such removal proceedings, the person concerned shall have the privilege of being represented (at no expense to the Government) by such counsel, authorized to practice in such proceedings, as he shall choose.

(June 27, 1952, ch 477, Title II, Ch 9, § 292, 66 Stat. 235; Sept. 30, 1996, P. L. 104-208, Div C, Title III, Subtitle A, § 308(d)(4)(O), Subtitle F, § 371(b)(9), 110 Stat. 3009-619, 3009-645.)

§ 1363. Deposit of and interest on cash received to secure immigration bonds

(a) Cash received by the Attorney General as security on an immigration bond shall be deposited in the Treasury of the United States in trust for the obligor on the bond, and shall bear interest payable at a rate determined by the Secretary of the Treasury, except that in no case shall the interest rate exceed 3 per centum per annum. Such interest shall accrue from date of deposit occurring after April 27, 1966, to and including date of withdrawal or date of breach of the immigration bond, whichever occurs first: *Provided,* That cash received by the Attorney General as security on an immigration bond, and deposited by him in the postal savings system prior to discontinuance of the system, shall accrue interest as provided in this section from the date such cash ceased to accrue interest under the system. Appropriations to the Treasury Department for interest on uninvested funds shall be available for payment of said interest.

(b) The interest accruing on cash received by the Attorney General as security on an immigration bond shall be subject to the same disposition as prescribed for the principal cash, except that interest accruing to the date of breach of the immigration bond shall be paid to the obligor on the bond.

(June 27, 1952, ch 477, Title II, Ch 9, § 293, as added July 10, 1970, P. L. 91-313, § 2, 84 Stat. 413.)

§ 1363a. Undercover investigation authority

(a) In general. With respect to any undercover investigative operation of the Service which is necessary for the detection and prosecution of crimes against the United States—

(1) sums appropriated for the Service may be used for leasing space within the United States and the territories and possessions of the United States without regard to the following provisions of law:

(A) section 3679(a) of the Revised Statutes (31 U.S.C. 1341),

(B) section 3732(a) of the Revised Statutes (41 U.S.C. 11(a)) [41 USCS § 6301],

(C) section 305 of the Act of June 30, 1949 (63 Stat. 396; 41 U.S.C. 255) [41 USCS §§ 4501 et seq.],

(D) the third undesignated paragraph under the heading "Miscellaneous" of the Act of March 3, 1877 (19 Stat. 370; 40 U.S.C. 34) [40 USCS § 8141],

(E) section 3648 of the Revised Statutes (31 U.S.C. 3324),

(F) section 3741 of the Revised Statutes (41 U.S.C. 22) [41 USCS § 6306], and

(G) subsections (a) and (c) of section 304 of the Federal Property and Administrative Services Act of 1949 (63 Stat. 395; 41 U.S.C. 254 (a) and (c)) [41 USCS § 3901];

(2) sums appropriated for the Service may be used to establish or to acquire proprietary corporations or business entities as part of an undercover operation, and to operate such corporations or business entities on a commercial basis, without regard to the provisions of section 304 of the Government Corporation Control Act (31 U.S.C. 9102);

(3) sums appropriated for the Service, and the proceeds from the undercover operation, may be deposited in banks or other financial institutions without regard to the provisions of section 648 of title 18, United States Code, and of section 3639 of the Revised Statutes (31 U.S.C. 3302); and

(4) the proceeds from the undercover operation may be used to offset necessary and reasonable expenses incurred in such operation without regard to the provisions of section 3617 of the Revised Statutes (31 U.S.C. 3302).

The authority set forth in this subsection may be exercised only upon written certification of the Commissioner, in consultation with the Deputy Attorney General, that any action authorized by paragraph (1), (2), (3), or (4) is necessary for the conduct of the undercover operation.

(b) Disposition of proceeds no longer required. As soon as practicable after the proceeds from an undercover investigative operation, carried out under paragraphs (3) and (4) of subsection (a), are no longer necessary for the conduct of the operation, the proceeds or the balance of the proceeds remaining at the time shall be deposited into the Treasury of the United States as miscellaneous receipts.

(c) Disposition of certain corporations and business entities. If a corporation or business entity established or acquired as part of an undercover operation under paragraph (2) of subsection (a) with a net value of over $50,000 is to be liquidated, sold, or otherwise disposed of, the Service, as much in advance as the Commissioner or Commissioner's designee determines practicable, shall report the circumstances to the Attorney General, the Director of the Office of Management and Budget, and the Comptroller General. The proceeds of the liquidation, sale, or other disposition, after obligations are met, shall be deposited in the Treasury of the United States as miscellaneous receipts.

(d) Financial audits. The Service shall conduct detailed financial audits of closed undercover operations on a quarterly basis and shall report the results of the audits in writing to the Deputy Attorney General.

(June 27, 1952, ch 477, Title II, Ch 9, § 294, as added Sept. 30, 1996, P. L. 104-208, Div C, Title II, Subtitle A, § 205(a), 110 Stat. 3009-567.)

§ 1363b. [Repealed]

§ 1364. Triennial comprehensive report on immigration

(a) Triennial report. The President shall transmit to the Congress, not later than January 1, 1989, and not later than January 1 of every third year thereafter, a comprehensive immigration-impact report.

(b) Details in each report. Each report shall include—

(1) the number and classification of aliens admitted (whether as immediate relatives, special immigrants, refugees, or under the preferences classifications, or as nonimmigrants), paroled, or granted asylum, during the relevant period;

(2) a reasonable estimate of the number of aliens who entered the United States during the period without visas or who became deportable during the period under section 241 [237] of the Immigration and Nationality Act [8 USCS § 1227] and

(3) a description of the impact of admissions and other entries of immigrants, refugees, asylees, and parolees into the United States during the period on the economy, labor and housing markets, the educational system, social services, foreign policy, environmental quality and resources, the rate, size, and distribution of population growth in the United States, and the impact on specific States and local units of government of high rates of immigration resettlement.

(c) History and projections. The information (referred to in subsection (b)) contained in each report shall be—

(1) described for the preceding three-year period, and

(2) projected for the succeeding five-year period, based on reasonable estimates substantiated by the best available evidence.

(d) Recommendations. The President also may include in such report any appropriate recommendations on changes in numerical limitations or other policies under title II of the Immigration and Nationality Act bearing on the admission and entry of such aliens to the United States.

(Nov. 6, 1986, P. L. 99-603, Title IV, § 401, 100 Stat. 3440.)

§ 1365. Reimbursement of States for costs of incarcerating illegal aliens and certain Cuban nationals

(a) Reimbursement of States. Subject to the amounts provided in advance in appropriation Acts, the Attorney General shall reimburse a State for the costs incurred by the State for the imprisonment of any illegal alien or Cuban national who is convicted of a felony by such State.

(b) Illegal aliens convicted of a felony. An illegal alien referred to in subsection (a) is any alien who is any alien convicted of a felony who is in the United States unlawfully and—

(1) whose most recent entry into the United States was without inspection, or

(2) whose most recent admission to the United States was as a nonimmigrant and—

(A) whose period of authorized stay as a nonimmigrant expired, or

(B) whose unlawful status was known to the Government, before the date of the commission of the crime for which the alien is convicted.

(c) Marielito Cubans convicted of a felony. A Marielito Cuban convicted of a felony referred to in subsection (a) is a national of Cuba who—

(1) was allowed by the Attorney General to come to the United States in 1980,

(2) after such arrival committed any violation of State or local law for which a term of imprisonment was imposed, and

(3) at the time of such arrival and at the time of such violation was not an alien lawfully admitted to the United States—

(A) for permanent or temporary residence, or

(B) under the terms of an immigrant visa or a nonimmigrant visa issued,

under the laws of the United States.

(d) Authorization of appropriations. There are authorized to be appropriated such sums as are necessary to carry out the purposes of this section.

(e) "State" defined. The term "State" has the meaning given such term in section 101(a)(36) of the Immigration and Nationality Act (8 U.S.C. 1101(a)(36)) [8 USCS § 1101(a)(36)].

(Nov. 6, 1986, P. L. 99-603, Title V, § 501, 100 Stat. 3443.)

§ 1365a. Integrated entry and exit data system

(a) Requirement. The Attorney General shall implement an integrated entry and exit data system.

(b) Integrated entry and exit data system defined. For purposes of this section, the term "integrated entry and exit data system" means an electronic system that—

(1) provides access to, and integrates, alien arrival and departure data that are—

(A) authorized or required to be created or collected under law;

(B) in an electronic format; and

(C) in a data base of the Department of Justice or the Department of State, including those created or used at ports of entry and at consular offices;

(2) uses available data described in paragraph (1) to produce a report of arriving and departing aliens by country of nationality, classification as an immigrant or nonimmigrant, and date of arrival in, and departure from, the United States;

(3) matches an alien's available arrival data with the alien's available departure data;

(4) assists the Attorney General (and the Secretary of State, to the extent necessary to carry out such Secretary's obligations under immigration law) to identify, through on-line searching procedures, lawfully admitted nonimmigrants who may have remained in the United States beyond the period authorized by the Attorney General; and

(5) otherwise uses available alien arrival and departure data described in paragraph (1) to permit the Attorney General to make the reports required under subsection (e).

(c) Construction.

(1) No additional authority to impose documentary or data collection requirements. Nothing in this section

shall be construed to permit the Attorney General or the Secretary of State to impose any new documentary or data collection requirements on any person in order to satisfy the requirements of this section, including—

(A) requirements on any alien for whom the documentary requirements in section 212(a)(7)(B) of the Immigration and Nationality Act (8 U.S.C. 1182(a)(7)(B)) have been waived by the Attorney General and the Secretary of State under section 212(d)(4)(B) of such Act (8 U.S.C. 1182(d)(4)(B)); or

(B) requirements that are inconsistent with the USMCA (as defined in section 3 of the United States-Mexico-Canada Agreement Implementation Act [19 USCS § 4502]).

(2) No reduction of authority. Nothing in this section shall be construed to reduce or curtail any authority of the Attorney General or the Secretary of State under any other provision of law.

(d) Deadlines.

(1) Airports and seaports. Not later than December 31, 2003, the Attorney General shall implement the integrated entry and exit data system using available alien arrival and departure data described in subsection (b)(1) pertaining to aliens arriving in, or departing from, the United States at an airport or seaport. Such implementation shall include ensuring that such data, when collected or created by an immigration officer at an airport or seaport, are entered into the system and can be accessed by immigration officers at other airports and seaports.

(2) High-traffic land border ports of entry. Not later than December 31, 2004, the Attorney General shall implement the integrated entry and exit data system using the data described in paragraph (1) and available alien arrival and departure data described in subsection (b)(1) pertaining to aliens arriving in, or departing from, the United States at the 50 land border ports of entry determined by the Attorney General to serve the highest numbers of arriving and departing aliens. Such implementation shall include ensuring that such data, when collected or created by an immigration officer at such a port of entry, are entered into the system and can be accessed by immigration officers at airports, seaports, and other such land border ports of entry.

(3) Remaining data. Not later than December 31, 2005, the Attorney General shall fully implement the integrated entry and exit data system using all data described in subsection (b)(1). Such implementation shall include ensuring that all such data are available to immigration officers at all ports of entry into the United States.

(e) Reports.

(1) In general. Not later than December 31 of each year following the commencement of implementation of the integrated entry and exit data system, the Attorney General shall use the system to prepare an annual report to the Committees on the Judiciary of the House of Representatives and of the Senate.

(2) Information. Each report shall include the following information with respect to the preceding fiscal year, and an analysis of that information:

(A) The number of aliens for whom departure data was collected during the reporting period, with an accounting by country of nationality of the departing alien.

(B) The number of departing aliens whose departure data was successfully matched to the alien's arrival data, with an accounting by the alien's country of nationality and by the alien's classification as an immigrant or nonimmigrant.

(C) The number of aliens who arrived pursuant to a nonimmigrant visa, or as a visitor under the visa waiver program under section 217 of the Immigration and Nationality Act (8 U.S.C. 1187), for whom no matching departure data have been obtained through the system or through other means as of the end of the alien's authorized period of stay, with an accounting by the alien's country of nationality and date of arrival in the United States.

(D) The number of lawfully admitted nonimmigrants identified as having remained in the United States beyond the period authorized by the Attorney General, with an accounting by the alien's country of nationality.

(f) Authority to provide access to system.

(1) In general. Subject to subsection (d), the Attorney General, in consultation with the Secretary of State, shall determine which officers and employees of the Departments of Justice and State may enter data into, and have access to the data contained in, the integrated entry and exit data system.

(2) Other law enforcement officials. The Attorney General, in the discretion of the Attorney General, may permit other Federal, State, and local law enforcement officials to have access to the data contained in the integrated entry and exit data system for law enforcement purposes.

(g) Use of task force recommendations. The Attorney General shall continuously update and improve the integrated entry and exit data system as technology improves and using the recommendations of the task force established under section 3 of the Immigration and Naturalization Service Data Management Improvement Act of 2000 [note to this section].

(h) Authorization of appropriations. There are authorized to be appropriated to carry out this section such sums as may be necessary for fiscal years 2001 through 2008.

(Sept. 30, 1996, P. L. 104-208, Div C, Title I, Subtitle A, § 110, 110 Stat. 3009-558; Oct. 15, 1998, P. L. 105-259, § 1, 112 Stat. 1918; Oct. 21, 1998, P. L. 105-277, Div A, § 101(b) [Title I, § 116], 112 Stat. 2681-68; June 15, 2000, P. L. 106-215, § 2(a), 114 Stat. 337; Jan. 29, 2020, P.L. 116-113, Title V, § 503(d)(1), 134 Stat. 72.)

§ 1365b. Biometric entry and exit data system

(a) Finding. Consistent with the report of the National Commission on Terrorist Attacks Upon the United States, Congress finds that completing a biometric entry and exit data system as expeditiously as possible is an essential investment in efforts to protect the United States by preventing the entry of terrorists.

(b) Definition. In this section, the term "entry and exit data system" means the entry and exit system required by applicable sections of—

(1) the Illegal Immigration Reform and Immigrant Responsibility Act of 1996 (Public Law 104-208);

(2) the Immigration and Naturalization Service Data Management Improvement Act of 2000 (Public Law 106-205 [106-215]);

(3) the Visa Waiver Permanent Program Act (Public Law 106-396);

(4) the Enhanced Border Security and Visa Entry Reform Act of 2002 (Public Law 107-173); and

(5) the Uniting and Strengthening America by Providing Appropriate Tools Required to Intercept and Obstruct Terrorism (USA PATRIOT ACT) Act of 2001 (Public Law 107-56).

(c) Plan and report.

(1) Development of plan. The Secretary of Homeland Security shall develop a plan to accelerate the full implementation of an automated biometric entry and exit data system.

(2) Report. Not later than 180 days after the date of enactment of this Act [enacted Dec. 17, 2004], the Secretary shall submit a report to Congress on the plan developed under paragraph (1), which shall contain—

(A) a description of the current functionality of the entry and exit data system, including—

(i) a listing of ports of entry and other Department of Homeland Security and Department of State locations with biometric entry data systems in use and whether such screening systems are located at primary or secondary inspection areas;

(ii) a listing of ports of entry and other Department of Homeland Security and Department of State locations with biometric exit data systems in use;

(iii) a listing of databases and data systems with which the entry and exit data system are interoperable;

(iv) a description of—

(I) identified deficiencies concerning the accuracy or integrity of the information contained in the entry and exit data system;

(II) identified deficiencies concerning technology associated with processing individuals through the system; and

(III) programs or policies planned or implemented to correct problems identified in subclause (I) or (II); and

(v) an assessment of the effectiveness of the entry and exit data system in fulfilling its intended purposes, including preventing terrorists from entering the United States;

(B) a description of factors relevant to the accelerated implementation of the biometric entry and exit data system, including—

(i) the earliest date on which the Secretary estimates that full implementation of the biometric entry and exit data system can be completed;

(ii) the actions the Secretary will take to accelerate the full implementation of the biometric entry and exit data system at all ports of entry through which all aliens must pass that are legally required to do so; and

(iii) the resources and authorities required to enable the Secretary to meet the implementation date described in clause (i);

(C) a description of any improvements needed in the information technology employed for the biometric entry and exit data system;

(D) a description of plans for improved or added interoperability with any other databases or data systems; and

(E) a description of the manner in which the Department of Homeland Security's US-VISIT program—

(i) meets the goals of a comprehensive entry and exit screening system, including both entry and exit biometric; and

(ii) fulfills the statutory obligations under subsection (b).

(d) Collection of biometric exit data. The entry and exit data system shall include a requirement for the collection of biometric exit data for all categories of individuals who are required to provide biometric entry data, regardless of the port of entry where such categories of individuals entered the United States.

(e) Integration and interoperability.

(1) Integration of data system. Not later than 2 years after the date of enactment of this Act [enacted Dec. 17, 2004], the Secretary shall fully integrate all databases and data systems that process or contain information on aliens, which are maintained by—

(A) the Department of Homeland Security, at—

(i) the United States Immigration and Customs Enforcement;

(ii) the United States Customs and Border Protection; and

(iii) the United States Citizenship and Immigration Services;

(B) the Department of Justice, at the Executive Office for Immigration Review; and

(C) the Department of State, at the Bureau of Consular Affairs.

(2) Interoperable component. The fully integrated data system under paragraph (1) shall be an interoperable component of the entry and exit data system.

(3) Interoperable data system. Not later than 2 years after the date of enactment of this Act [enacted Dec. 17, 2004], the Secretary shall fully implement an interoperable electronic data system, as required by section 202 of the Enhanced Border Security and Visa Entry Reform Act [of 2002] (8 U.S.C. 1722) to provide current and immediate access to information in the databases of Federal law enforcement agencies and the intelligence community that is relevant to determine—

(A) whether to issue a visa; or

(B) the admissibility or deportability of an alien.

(f) Maintaining accuracy and integrity of entry and exit data system.

(1) Policies and procedures.

(A) Establishment. The Secretary of Homeland Security shall establish rules, guidelines, policies, and operating and auditing procedures for collecting, removing, and updating data maintained in, and adding information to, the entry and exit data system that ensure the accuracy and integrity of the data.

(B) Training. The Secretary shall develop training on the rules, guidelines, policies, and procedures established under subparagraph (A), and on immigration law and procedure. All personnel authorized to access information maintained in the databases and data system shall receive such training.

(2) Data collected from foreign nationals. The Secretary of Homeland Security, the Secretary of State, and the Attorney General, after consultation with directors of the relevant intelligence agencies, shall standardize the information and data collected from foreign nationals, and the procedures utilized to collect such data, to ensure that the information is consistent and valuable to officials accessing that data across multiple agencies.

(3) Data maintenance procedures. Heads of agencies that have databases or data systems linked to the entry and exit data system shall establish rules, guidelines, policies, and operating and auditing procedures for collecting, removing, and updating data maintained in, and adding information to, such databases or data systems that ensure the accuracy and integrity of the data and for limiting access to the information in the databases or data systems to authorized personnel.

(4) Requirements. The rules, guidelines, policies, and procedures established under this subsection shall—

(A) incorporate a simple and timely method for—

(i) correcting errors in a timely and effective manner;

(ii) determining which government officer provided data so that the accuracy of the data can be ascertained; and

(iii) clarifying information known to cause false hits or misidentification errors;

(B) include procedures for individuals to—

(i) seek corrections of data contained in the databases or data systems; and

(ii) appeal decisions concerning data contained in the databases or data systems;

(C) strictly limit the agency personnel authorized to enter data into the system;

(D) identify classes of information to be designated as temporary or permanent entries, with corresponding expiration dates for temporary entries; and

(E) identify classes of prejudicial information requiring additional authority of supervisory personnel before entry.

(5) Centralizing and streamlining correction process.

(A) In general. The President, or agency director designated by the President, shall establish a clearinghouse bureau in the Department of Homeland Security, to centralize and streamline the process through which members of the public can seek corrections to erroneous or inaccurate information contained in agency databases, which is related to immigration status, or which otherwise impedes lawful admission to the United States.

(B) Time schedules. The process described in subparagraph (A) shall include specific time schedules for reviewing data correction requests, rendering decisions on such requests, and implementing appropriate corrective action in a timely manner.

(g) Integrated biometric entry-exit screening system. The biometric entry and exit data system shall facilitate efficient immigration benefits processing by—

(1) ensuring that the system's tracking capabilities encompass data related to all immigration benefits processing, including—

(A) visa applications with the Department of State;

(B) immigration related filings with the Department of Labor;

(C) cases pending before the Executive Office for Immigration Review; and

(D) matters pending or under investigation before the Department of Homeland Security;

(2) utilizing a biometric based identity number tied to an applicant's biometric algorithm established under the entry and exit data system to track all immigration related matters concerning the applicant;

(3) providing that—

(A) all information about an applicant's immigration related history, including entry and exit history, can be queried through electronic means; and

(B) database access and usage guidelines include stringent safeguards to prevent misuse of data;

(4) providing real-time updates to the information described in paragraph (3)(A), including pertinent data from all agencies referred to in paragraph (1); and

(5) providing continuing education in counterterrorism techniques, tools, and methods for all Federal personnel employed in the evaluation of immigration documents and immigration-related policy.

(h) Entry-exit system goals. The Department of Homeland Security shall operate the biometric entry and exit system so that it—

(1) serves as a vital counterterrorism tool;

(2) screens travelers efficiently and in a welcoming manner;

(3) provides inspectors and related personnel with adequate real-time information;

(4) ensures flexibility of training and security protocols to most effectively comply with security mandates;

(5) integrates relevant databases and plans for database modifications to address volume increase and database usage; and

(6) improves database search capacities by utilizing language algorithms to detect alternate names.

(i) Dedicated specialists and front line personnel training. In implementing the provisions of subsections (g) and (h), the Department of Homeland Security and the Department of State shall—

(1) develop cross-training programs that focus on the scope and procedures of the entry and exit data system;

(2) provide extensive community outreach and education on the entry and exit data system's procedures;

(3) provide clear and consistent eligibility guidelines for applicants in low-risk traveler programs; and

(4) establish ongoing training modules on immigration law to improve adjudications at our ports of entry, consulates, and embassies.

(j) Compliance status reports. Not later than 1 year after the date of enactment of this Act [enacted Dec. 17, 2004], the Secretary of Homeland Security, the Secretary of State, the Attorney General, and the head of any other department or agency subject to the requirements of this section, shall issue individual status reports and a joint status report detailing the compliance of the department or agency with each requirement under this section.

(k) Expediting registered travelers across international borders.

(1) Findings. Consistent with the report of the National Commission on Terrorist Attacks Upon the United States, Congress makes the following findings:

(A) Expediting the travel of previously screened and known travelers across the borders of the United States should be a high priority.

(B) The process of expediting known travelers across the borders of the United States can permit inspectors to better focus on identifying terrorists attempting to enter the United States.

(2) Definition. In this subsection, the term "registered traveler program" means any program designed to expedite the travel of previously screened and known travelers across the borders of the United States.

(3) International registered traveler program.

(A) In general. The Secretary of Homeland Security shall establish an international registered traveler program that incorporates available technologies, such as biometrics and e-passports, and security threat assessments to expedite the screening and processing of international travelers, including United States Citizens and residents, who enter and exit the United States. The program shall be coordinated with the United States Visitor and Immigrant Status Indicator Technology program, other pre-screening initiatives, and the Visa Waiver Program.

(B) Fees. The Secretary may impose a fee for the program established under subparagraph (A) and may modify such fee from time to time. The fee may not exceed the aggregate costs associated with the program and shall be credited to the Department of Homeland Security for purposes of carrying out the program. Amounts so credited shall remain available until expended.

(C) Rulemaking. Within 365 days after the date of enactment of this paragraph [enacted Dec. 26, 2007], the Secretary shall initiate a rulemaking to establish the program, criteria for participation, and the fee for the program.

(D) Implementation. Not later than 2 years after the date of enactment of this paragraph [enacted Dec. 26, 2007], the Secretary shall establish a phased-implementation of a biometric-based international registered traveler program in conjunction with the United States Visitor and Immigrant Status Indicator Technology entry and exit system, other pre-screening initiatives, and the Visa Waiver Program at United States airports with the highest volume of international travelers.

(E) Participation. The Secretary shall ensure that the international registered traveler program includes as many participants as practicable by—

(i) establishing a reasonable cost of enrollment;

(ii) making program enrollment convenient and easily accessible; and

(iii) providing applicants with clear and consistent eligibility guidelines.

(4) Report. Not later than 1 year after the date of enactment of this Act [enacted Dec. 17, 2004], the Secretary shall submit to Congress a report describing the Department's progress on the development and implementation of the registered traveler program.

(l) Authorization of appropriations. There are authorized to be appropriated to the Secretary, for each of the fiscal years 2005 through 2009, such sums as may be necessary to carry out the provisions of this section.

(Dec. 17, 2004, P. L. 108-458, Title VII, Subtitle B, § 7208, 118 Stat. 3817; Dec. 26, 2007, P. L. 110-161, Div E, Title V, § 565, 121 Stat. 2091.)

§ 1366. Annual report on criminal aliens

Not later than 12 months after the date of the enactment of this Act [enacted Sept. 30, 1996], and annually thereafter, the Attorney General shall submit to the Committees on the Judiciary of the House of Representatives and of the Senate a report detailing—

(1) the number of illegal aliens incarcerated in Federal and State prisons for having committed felonies, stating the number incarcerated for each type of offense;

(2) the number of illegal aliens convicted of felonies in any Federal or State court, but not sentenced to incarceration, in the year before the report was submitted, stating the number convicted for each type of offense;

(3) programs and plans underway in the Department of Justice to ensure the prompt removal from the United States of criminal aliens subject to removal; and

(4) methods for identifying and preventing the unlawful reentry of aliens who have been convicted of criminal offenses in the United States and removed from the United States.

(Sept. 30, 1996, P. L. 104-208, Div C, Title III, Subtitle B, § 332, 110 Stat. 3009-634.)

§ 1367. Penalties for disclosure of information

(a) In general. Except as provided in subsection (b), in no case may the Attorney General, or any other official or employee of the Department of Justice, the Secretary of Homeland Security, the Secretary of State, or any other official or employee of the Department of Homeland Security or Department of State (including any bureau or agency of either of such Departments)—

(1) make an adverse determination of admissibility or deportability of an alien under the Immigration and Nationality Act using information furnished solely by—

(A) a spouse or parent who has battered the alien or subjected the alien to extreme cruelty,

(B) a member of the spouse's or parent's family residing in the same household as the alien who has battered the alien or subjected the alien to extreme cruelty when the spouse or parent consented to or acquiesced in such battery or cruelty,

(C) a spouse or parent who has battered the alien's child or subjected the alien's child to extreme cruelty (without the active participation of the alien in the battery or extreme cruelty),

(D) a member of the spouse's or parent's family residing in the same household as the alien who has battered the alien's child or subjected the alien's child to extreme cruelty when the spouse or parent consented to or acquiesced in such battery or cruelty and the alien did not actively participate in such battery or cruelty,

(E) in the case of an alien applying for status under section 101(a)(15)(U) of the Immigration and Nationality Act [8 USCS § 1101(a)(15)(U)], the perpetrator of the substantial physical or mental abuse and the criminal activity, [or]

(F) in the case of an alien applying for status under section 101(a)(15)(T) of the Immigration and Nationality Act (8 U.S.C. 1101(a)(15)(T)), under section 107(b)(1)(E)(i)(II)(bb) of the Trafficking Victims Protection Act of 2000 (22 U.S.C. 7105), under section 244(a)(3) of the Immigration and Nationality Act (8 U.S.C. 1254a(a)(3)), as in effect prior to March 31, 1999, or as a VAWA self-petitioner (as defined in section 101(a)(51) of the Immigration and Nationality Act (8 U.S.C. 1101(a)(51))[)], the trafficker or perpetrator, unless the alien has been convicted of a crime or crimes listed in section 237(a)(2) of the Immigration and Nationality Act [8 USCS § 1227(a)(2)]; or

(2) permit use by or disclosure to anyone (other than a sworn officer or employee of the Department, or bureau or agency thereof, for legitimate Department, bureau, or agency purposes) of any information which relates to an alien who is the beneficiary of an application for relief under paragraph (15)(T), (15)(U), or (51) of section 101(a) of the Immigration and Nationality Act [8 USCS § 1101(a)] or section 240A(b)(2) of such Act [8 USCS § 1229b(b)(2)].

The limitation under paragraph (2) ends when the application for relief is denied and all opportunities for appeal of the denial have been exhausted.

(b) Exceptions.

(1) The Secretary of Homeland Security or the Attorney General may provide, in the Secretary's or the Attorney General's discretion, for the disclosure of information in the same manner and circumstances as census information may be disclosed by the Secretary of Commerce under section 8 of title 13, United States Code.

(2) The Secretary of Homeland Security or the Attorney General may provide in the discretion of the Secretary or the Attorney General for the disclosure of information to law enforcement officials to be used solely for a legitimate law enforcement purpose in a manner that protects the confidentiality of such information.

(3) Subsection (a) shall not be construed as preventing disclosure of information in connection with judicial review of a determination in a manner that protects the confidentiality of such information.

(4) Subsection (a)(2) shall not apply if all the battered individuals in the case are adults and they have all waived the restrictions of such subsection.

(5) The Secretary of Homeland Security and the Attorney General are authorized to disclose information, to Federal, State, and local public and private agencies providing benefits, to be used solely in making determinations of eligibility for benefits pursuant to section 431(c) of the Personal Responsibility and Work Opportunity Reconciliation Act of 1996 [8 USCS § 1641(c)].

(6) Subsection (a) may not be construed to prevent the Attorney General and the Secretary of Homeland Security from disclosing to the chairmen and ranking members of the Committee on the Judiciary of the Senate or the Committee on the Judiciary of the House of Representatives, for the exercise of congressional oversight authority, information on closed cases under this section in a manner that protects the confidentiality of such information and that omits personally identifying information (including locational information about individuals).

(7) Government entities adjudicating applications for relief under subsection (a)(2), and government personnel carrying out mandated duties under section 101(i)(1) of the Immigration and Nationality Act [8 USCS § 1101(i)(1)], may, with the prior written consent of the alien involved, communicate with nonprofit, nongovernmental victims' service providers for the sole purpose of assisting victims in obtaining victim services from programs with expertise working with immigrant victims. Agencies receiving referrals are bound by the provisions of this section. Nothing in this paragraph shall be construed as affecting the ability of an applicant to designate a safe organization through whom governmental agencies may communicate with the applicant.

(8) Notwithstanding subsection (a)(2), the Secretary of Homeland Security, the Secretary of State, or the Attorney General may provide in the discretion of either such Secretary or the Attorney General for the disclosure of information to national security officials to be used solely for a national security purpose in a manner that protects the confidentiality of such information.

(c) Penalties for violations. Anyone who willfully uses, publishes, or permits information to be disclosed in violation of this section or who knowingly makes a false certification under section 239(e) of the Immigration and Nationality Act [8 USCS § 1229(e)] shall be subject to appropriate disciplinary action and subject to a civil money penalty of not more than $5,000 for each such violation.

(d) Guidance. The Attorney General, the Secretary of State, and the Secretary of Homeland Security shall provide guidance to officers and employees of the Department of Justice, Department of State, or the Department of Homeland Security who have access to information covered by this section regarding the provisions of this section, including the provisions to protect victims of domestic violence and severe forms of trafficking in persons or criminal activity listed in section 101(a)(15)(U) of the Immigration and Nationality Act (8 U.S.C. 1101(a)(15)(u)) from harm that could result from the inappropriate disclosure of covered information.

(Sept. 30, 1996, P. L. 104-208, Div C, Title III, Subtitle A, § 308(g)(8)(D), Subtitle F, § 384, 110 Stat. 3009-624, 3009-652; Aug. 5, 1997, P. L. 105-33, Title V, Subtitle F, Ch 4, Subch B, § 5572(b), 111 Stat. 641; Oct. 28, 2000, P. L. 106-386, Div B, Title V, § 1513(d), 114 Stat. 1536; Jan. 5, 2006, P. L. 109-162, Title VIII, Subtitle B, § 817, 119 Stat. 3060; Aug. 12, 2006, P. L. 109-271, § 6(h), 120 Stat. 763; March 7, 2013, P. L. 113-4, Title VIII, § 810(a), (b), (d), 127 Stat. 117, 118.)

§ 1368. Increase in INS detention facilities; report on detention space

(a) Increase in detention facilities. Subject to the availability of appropriations, the Attorney General shall provide for an increase in the detention facilities of the Immigration and Naturalization Service to at least 9,000 beds before the end of fiscal year 1997.

(b) Report on detention space.

(1) In general. Not later than 6 months after the date of the enactment of this Act [enacted Sept. 30, 1996], and every 6 months thereafter, the Attorney General shall submit a report to the Committees on the Judiciary of the House of Representatives and of the Senate estimating the amount of detention space that will be required, during the fiscal year in which the report is submitted and the succeeding fiscal year, to detain—

(A) all aliens subject to detention under section 236(c) of the Immigration and Nationality Act [8 USCS § 1226(c)] (as amended by section 303 of this title) and section 241(a) of the Immigration and Nationality Act [8 USCS § 1231(a)] (as inserted by section 305(a)(3) of this title);

(B) all inadmissible or deportable aliens subject to proceedings under section 238 of the Immigration and Nationality Act [8 USCS § 1228] (as redesignated by section 308(b)(5) of this title) or section 235(b)(2)(A) or 240 of the Immigration and Nationality Act [8 USCS § 1225(b)(2)(A) or 1229a]; and

(C) other inadmissible or deportable aliens in accordance with the priorities established by the Attorney General.

(2) Estimate of number of aliens released into the community.

(A) Criminal aliens.

(i) In general. The first report submitted under paragraph (1) shall include an estimate of the number of criminal aliens who, in each of the 3 fiscal years concluded prior to the date of the report—

(I) were released from detention facilities of the Immigration and Naturalization Service (whether operated directly by the Service or through contract with other persons or agencies); or

(II) were not taken into custody or detention by the Service upon completion of their incarceration.

(ii) Aliens convicted of aggravated felonies. The estimate under clause (i) shall estimate separately, with respect to each year described in such clause, the number of criminal aliens described in such clause who were convicted of an aggravated felony.

(B) All inadmissible or deportable aliens. The first report submitted under paragraph (1) shall also estimate the number of inadmissible or deportable aliens who were released into the community due to a lack of detention facilities in each of the 3 fiscal years concluded prior to the date of the report notwithstanding circumstances that the Attorney General believed justified detention (for example, a significant probability that the released alien would not appear, as agreed, at subsequent exclusion or deportation proceedings).

(C) Subsequent reports. Each report under paragraph (1) following the first such report shall include the estimates under subparagraphs (A) and (B), made with respect to the 6-month period immediately preceding the date of the submission of the report.

(Sept. 30, 1996, P. L. 104-208, Div C, Title III, Subtitle A, § 308(g)(10)(G), Subtitle F, § 386, 110 Stat. 3009-625, 3009-653.)

§ 1369. Treatment of expenses subject to emergency medical services exception

(a) In general. Subject to such amounts as are provided in advance in appropriation Acts, each State or political subdivision of a State that provides medical assistance for care and treatment of an emergency medical condition (as defined in subsection (d)) through a public hospital or other public facility (including a nonprofit hospital that is eligible for an additional payment adjustment under section 1886 of the Social Security Act [42 USCS § 1395ww]) or through contract with another hospital or facility to an individual who is an alien not lawfully present in the United States is eligible for payment from the Federal Government of its costs of providing such services, but only to the extent that such costs are not otherwise reimbursed through any other Federal program and cannot be recovered from the alien or another person.

(b) Confirmation of immigration status required. No payment shall be made under this section with respect to services furnished to an individual unless the immigration status of the individual has been verified through appropriate procedures established by the Secretary of Health and Human Services and the Attorney General.

(c) Administration. This section shall be administered by the Attorney General, in consultation with the Secretary of Health and Human Services.

(d) "Emergency medical condition" defined. For purposes of this section, the term "emergency medical condition" means a medical condition (including emergency labor and delivery) manifesting itself by acute symptoms of sufficient severity (including severe pain) such that the absence of immediate medical attention could reasonably be expected to result in—

(1) placing the patient's health in serious jeopardy,

(2) serious impairment to bodily functions, or

(3) serious dysfunction of any bodily organ or part.

(e) Effective date. Subsection (a) shall apply to medical assistance for care and treatment of an emergency medical condition furnished on or after January 1, 1997.

(Sept. 30, 1996, P. L. 104-208, Div C, Title V, Subtitle D, § 562, 110 Stat. 3009-682.)

§ 1370. Reimbursement of States and localities for emergency ambulance services

Subject to the availability of appropriations, the Attorney General shall fully reimburse States and political subdivisions of States for costs incurred by such a State or subdivision for emergency ambulance services provided to any alien who—

(1) is injured while crossing a land or sea border of the United States without inspection or at any time or place other than as designated by the Attorney General; and

(2) is under the custody of the State or subdivision pursuant to a transfer, request, or other action by a Federal authority.

(Sept. 30, 1996, P. L. 104-208, Div C, Title V, Subtitle D, § 563, 110 Stat. 3009-683.)

§ 1371. Reports

Not later than 180 days after the end of each fiscal year, the Attorney General shall submit a report to the Inspector General of the Department of Justice and the Committees on the Judiciary of the House of Representatives and of the Senate describing the following:

(1) Public charge deportations. The number of aliens deported on public charge grounds under section 241(a)(5) [237(a)(5)] of the Immigration and Nationality Act [8 USCS § 1227(a)(5)] during the previous fiscal year.

(2) Indigent sponsors. The number of determinations made under section 421(e) of the Personal Responsibility and Work Opportunity Reconciliation Act of 1996 [8 USCS § 1631(e)] (as added by section 552 of this division) during the previous fiscal year.

(3) Reimbursement actions. The number of actions brought, and the amount of each action, for reimbursement under section 213A of the Immigration and Nationality Act [8 USCS § 1183a] (including private collections) for the costs of providing public benefits.

(Sept. 30, 1996, P. L. 104-208, Div C, Title V, Subtitle D, § 565, 110 Stat. 3009-684.)

§ 1372. Program to collect information relating to nonimmigrant foreign students and other exchange program participants

(a) In general.

(1) Program. The Attorney General, in consultation with the Secretary of State and the Secretary of Education, shall develop and conduct a program to collect from approved institutions of higher education, other approved educational institutions, and designated exchange visitor programs in the United States the information described in subsection (c) with respect to aliens who—

(A) have the status, or are applying for the status, of nonimmigrants under subparagraph (F), (J), or (M) of section 101(a)(15) of the Immigration and Nationality Act [8 USCS § 1101(a)(15)(F), (J), or (M)]; and

(B) are nationals of the countries designated under subsection (b).

(2) Deadline. The program shall commence not later than January 1, 1998.

(3) Aliens for whom a visa is required. The Attorney General, in consultation with the Secretary of State, shall establish an electronic means to monitor and verify—

(A) the issuance of documentation of acceptance of a foreign student by an approved institution of higher education or other approved educational institution, or of an exchange visitor program participant by a designated exchange visitor program;

(B) the transmittal of the documentation referred to in subparagraph (A) to the Department of State for use by the Bureau of Consular Affairs;

(C) the issuance of a visa to a foreign student or an exchange visitor program participant;

(D) the admission into the United States of the foreign student or exchange visitor program participant;

(E) the notification to an approved institution of higher education, other approved educational institution, or exchange visitor program sponsor that the foreign student or exchange visitor participant has been admitted into the United States;

(F) the registration and enrollment of that foreign student in such approved institution of higher education or other approved educational institution, or the participation of that exchange visitor in such designated exchange visitor program, as the case may be; and

(G) any other relevant act by the foreign student or exchange visitor program participant, including a changing of school or designated exchange visitor program and any termination of studies or participation in a designated exchange visitor program.

(4) Reporting requirements. Not later than 30 days after the deadline for registering for classes for an academic term of an approved institution of higher education or other approved educational institution for which documentation is issued for an alien as described in paragraph (3)(A), or the scheduled commencement of participation by an alien in a designated exchange visitor program, as the case may be, the institution or program, respectively, shall report to the Immigration and Naturalization Service any failure of the alien to enroll or to commence participation.

(b) Covered countries. The Attorney General, in consultation with the Secretary of State, shall designate countries for purposes of subsection (a)(1)(B). The Attorney General shall initially designate not less than 5 countries and may designate additional countries at any time while the program is being conducted.

(c) Information to be collected.

(1) In general. The information for collection under subsection (a) with respect to an alien consists of—

(A) the identity and current address in the United States of the alien;

(B) the nonimmigrant classification of the alien and the date on which a visa under the classification was issued or extended or the date on which a change to such classification was approved by the Attorney General;

(C) in the case of a student at an approved institution of higher education, or other approved educational institution,[,] the current academic status of the alien, including whether the alien is maintaining status as a full-time student or, in the case of a participant in a designated exchange visitor program, whether the alien is satisfying the terms and conditions of such program;

(D) in the case of a student at an approved institution of higher education, or other approved educational institution,[,] any disciplinary action taken by the institution against the alien as a result of the alien's being convicted of a crime or, in the case of a participant in a designated exchange visitor program, any change in the alien's participation as a result of the alien's being convicted of a crime; [and]

(E) the date of entry and port of entry;

(F) the date of the alien's enrollment in an approved institution of higher education, other approved educational institution, or designated exchange visitor program in the United States;

(G) the degree program, if applicable, and field of study; and

(H) the date of the alien's termination of enrollment and the reason for such termination (including graduation, disciplinary action or other dismissal, and failure to re-enroll).

(2) FERPA. The Family Educational Rights and Privacy Act of 1974 [20 USCS § 1232g] shall not apply to aliens described in subsection (a) to the extent that the Attorney General determines necessary to carry out the program under subsection (a).

(3) Electronic collection. The information described in paragraph (1) shall be collected electronically, where practicable.

(4) Computer software.

(A) Collecting institutions. To the extent practicable, the Attorney General shall design the program in a manner that permits approved institutions of higher education, other approved educational institutions, and designated exchange visitor programs to use existing software for the collection, storage, and data processing of information described in paragraph (1).

(B) Attorney general. To the extent practicable, the Attorney General shall use or enhance existing software for the collection, storage, and data processing of information described in paragraph (1).

(5) Reporting requirements. The Attorney General shall prescribe by regulation reporting requirements by taking into account the curriculum calendar of the approved institution of higher education, other approved educational institution, or exchange visitor program.

(d) Participation by institutions of higher education and exchange visitor programs.

(1) Condition. The information described in subsection (c) shall be provided by institutions of higher education, other approved educational institutions, or exchange visitor programs as a condition of—

(A) in the case of an approved institution of higher education, or other approved educational institution,[,] the continued approval of the institution under subparagraph (F) or (M) of section 101(a)(15) of the Immigration and Nationality Act [8 USCS § 1101(a)(15)(F) or (M)]; and

(B) in the case of an approved institution of higher education or a designated exchange visitor program, the granting of authority to issue documents to an alien demonstrating the alien's eligibility for a visa under subparagraph (F), (J), or (M) of section 101(a)(15) of such Act [8 USCS § 1101(a)(15)(F), (J), or (M)].

(2) Effect of failure to provide information. If an approved institution of higher education, other approved educational institution, or a designated exchange visitor program fails to provide the specified information, such approvals and such issuance of visas shall be revoked or denied.

(e) Funding.

(1) In general. Beginning on April 1, 1997, the Attorney General shall impose on, and collect from, each alien described in paragraph (3), with respect to whom the institution or program is required by subsection (a) to collect information, a fee established by the Attorney General under paragraph (4) at a time prior to the alien being classified under subparagraph (F), (J), or (M) of section 101(a)(15) of the Immigration and Nationality Act [8 USCS § 1101(a)(15)].

(2) Remittance. The fees collected under paragraph (1) shall be remitted by the alien pursuant to a schedule established by the Attorney General for immediate deposit and availability as described under section 286(m) of the Immigration and Nationality Act [8 USCS § 1356(m)].

(3) Aliens described. An alien referred to in paragraph (1) is an alien who seeks nonimmigrant status under subparagraph (F), (J), or (M) of section 101(a)(15) of the Immigration and Nationality Act [8 USCS § 1101(a)(15)] (other than a nonimmigrant under section 101(a)(15)(J) [8 USCS § 1101(a)(15)(J)] of such Act who seeks to come to the United States as a participant in a program sponsored by the Federal Government).

(4) Amount and use of fees.

(A) Establishment of amount. The Attorney General shall establish the amount of the fee to be imposed on, and collected from, an alien under paragraph (1). Except as provided in subsection (g)(2), the fee imposed on any individual may not exceed $100, except that, in the case of an alien admitted under section 101(a)(15)(J) of the Immigration and Nationality Act [8 USCS § 1101(a)(15)(J)] as an au pair, camp counselor, or participant in a summer work travel program, the fee shall not exceed $40[, except that, in the case of an alien admitted under section 101(a)(15)(J) of the Immigration and Nationality Act as an au pair, camp counselor, or participant in a summer work travel program, the fee shall not exceed $35]. The amount of the fee shall be based on the Attorney General's estimate of the cost per alien of conducting the information collection program described in this section.

(B) Use. Fees collected under paragraph (1) shall be deposited as offsetting receipts into the Immigration Examinations Fee Account (established under section 286(m) of the Immigration and Nationality Act [8 USCS § 1356(m)]) and shall remain available until expended for the Attorney General to reimburse any appropriation the amount paid out of which is for expenses in carrying out this section. Such expenses include, but are not necessarily limited to, those incurred by the Secretary of State in connection with the program under subsection (a).

(5) Proof of payment. The alien shall present proof of payment of the fee before the granting of—

(A) a visa under section 222 of the Immigration and Nationality Act [8 USCS § 1202] or, in the case of an alien who is exempt from the visa requirement described in section 212(d)(4) of the Immigration and Nationality Act [8 USCS § 1182(d)(4)], admission to the United States; or

(B) change of nonimmigrant classification under section 248 of the Immigration and Nationality Act [8

USCS § 1258] to a classification described in paragraph (3).

(6) Implementation. The provisions of section 553 of title 5, United States Code (relating to rule-making) shall not apply to the extent the Attorney General determines necessary to ensure the expeditious, initial implementation of this section.

(f) Joint report. Not later than 4 years after the commencement of the program established under subsection (a), the Attorney General, the Secretary of State, and the Secretary of Education shall jointly submit to the Committees on the Judiciary of the Senate and the House of Representatives a report on the operations of the program and the feasibility of expanding the program to cover the nationals of all countries.

(g) Worldwide applicability of the program.

(1) Expansion of program. Not later than 12 months after the submission of the report required by subsection (f), the Attorney General, in consultation with the Secretary of State and the Secretary of Education, shall commence expansion of the program to cover the nationals of all countries.

(2) Revision of fee. After the program has been expanded, as provided in paragraph (1), the Attorney General may, on a periodic basis, revise the amount of the fee imposed and collected under subsection (e) in order to take into account changes in the cost of carrying out the program.

(h) Definitions. As used in this section:

(1) Approved institution of higher education. The term "approved institution of higher education" means a college or university approved by the Attorney General, in consultation with the Secretary of Education, under subparagraph (F), (J), or (M) of section 101(a)(15) of the Immigration and Nationality Act [8 USCS § 1101(a)(15)(F), (J), or (M)].

(2) Designated exchange visitor program. The term "designated exchange visitor program" means a program that has been—

(A) designated by the Secretary of State for purposes of section 101(a)(15)(J) of the Immigration and Nationality Act [8 USCS § 1101(a)(15)(J)]; and

(B) selected by the Attorney General for purposes of the program under this section.

(3) Other approved educational institution. The term "other approved educational institution" includes any air flight school, language training school, or vocational school, approved by the Attorney General, in consultation with the Secretary of Education and the Secretary of State, under subparagraph (F), (J), or (M) of section 101(a)(15) of the Immigration and Nationality Act [8 USCS § 1101(a)(15)].

(Sept. 30, 1996, P. L. 104-208, Div C, Title VI, Subtitle D, § 641, 110 Stat. 3009-704; Oct. 30, 2000, P. L. 106-396, Title IV, §§ 404–406, 114 Stat. 1649; Dec. 21, 2000, P. L. 106-553, § 1(a)(2), 114 Stat. 2762; Oct. 26, 2001, P. L. 107-56, Title IV, Subtitle B, § 416(c), 115 Stat. 354; May 14, 2002, P. L. 107-173, Title V, § 501(a), 116 Stat. 560.)

§ 1373. Communication between government agencies and the Immigration and Naturalization Service

(a) In general. Notwithstanding any other provision of Federal, State, or local law, a Federal, State, or local government entity or official may not prohibit, or in any way restrict, any government entity or official from sending to, or receiving from, the Immigration and Naturalization Service information regarding the citizenship or immigration status, lawful or unlawful, of any individual.

(b) Additional authority of government entities. Notwithstanding any other provision of Federal, State, or local law, no person or agency may prohibit, or in any way restrict, a Federal, State, or local government entity from doing any of the following with respect to information regarding the immigration status, lawful or unlawful, of any individual:

(1) Sending such information to, or requesting or receiving such information from, the Immigration and Naturalization Service.

(2) Maintaining such information.

(3) Exchanging such information with any other Federal, State, or local government entity.

(c) Obligation to respond to inquiries. The Immigration and Naturalization Service shall respond to an inquiry by a Federal, State, or local government agency, seeking to verify or ascertain the citizenship or immigration status of any individual within the jurisdiction of the agency for any purpose authorized by law, by providing the requested verification or status information.

(Sept. 30, 1996, P. L. 104-208, Div C, Title VI, Subtitle D, § 642, 110 Stat. 3009-707.)

§ 1374. Information regarding female genital mutilation

(a) Provision of information regarding female genital mutilation. The Immigration and Naturalization Service (in cooperation with the Department of State) shall make available for all aliens who are issued immigrant or nonimmigrant visas, prior to or at the time of entry into the United States, the following information:

(1) Information on the severe harm to physical and psychological health caused by female genital mutilation which is compiled and presented in a manner which is limited to the practice itself and respectful to the cultural values of the societies in which such practice takes place.

(2) Information concerning potential legal consequences in the United States for (A) performing female genital mutilation, or (B) allowing a child under his or her care to be subjected to female genital mutilation, under criminal or child protection statutes or as a form of child abuse.

(b) Limitation. In consultation with the Secretary of State, the Commissioner of Immigration and Naturalization shall identify those countries in which female genital mutilation is commonly practiced and, to the extent practicable, limit the provision of information under subsection (a) to aliens from such countries.

(c) "Female genital mutilation" defined. For purposes of this section, the term "female genital mutilation" means the removal or infibulation (or both) of the whole or part of the clitoris, the labia minora, or labia majora.

(Sept. 30, 1996, P. L. 104-208, Div C, Title VI, Subtitle D, § 644, 110 Stat. 3009-708.)

§ 1375. [Repealed]

§ 1375a. Domestic violence information and resources for immigrants and regulation of international marriage brokers

(a) Information for K nonimmigrants on legal rights and resources for immigrant victims of domestic violence.

(1) In general. The Secretary of Homeland Security, in consultation with the Attorney General and the Secretary of State, shall develop an information pamphlet, as described in paragraph (2), on legal rights and resources for immigrant victims of domestic violence and distribute and make such pamphlet available as described in paragraph (5). In preparing such materials, the Secretary of Homeland Security shall consult with nongovernmental organizations with expertise on the legal rights of immigrant victims of battery, extreme cruelty, sexual assault, and other crimes.

(2) Information pamphlet. The information pamphlet developed under paragraph (1) shall include information on the following:

(A) The K nonimmigrant visa application process and the marriage-based immigration process, including conditional residence and adjustment of status.

(B) The illegality of domestic violence, sexual assault, and child abuse in the United States and the dynamics of domestic violence.

(C) Domestic violence and sexual assault services in the United States, including the National Domestic Violence Hotline and the National Sexual Assault Hotline.

(D) The legal rights of immigrant victims of abuse and other crimes in immigration, criminal justice, family law, and other matters, including access to protection orders.

(E) The obligations of parents to provide child support for children.

(F) Marriage fraud under United States immigration laws and the penalties for committing such fraud.

(G) A warning concerning the potential use of K nonimmigrant visas by United States citizens who have a history of committing domestic violence, sexual assault, child abuse, or other crimes and an explanation that such acts may not have resulted in a criminal record for such a citizen.

(H) Notification of the requirement under subsection (d)(3)(A) that international marriage brokers provide foreign national clients with background information gathered on United States clients from searches of the National Sex Offender Public Website and collected from United States clients regarding their marital history and domestic violence or other violent criminal history, but that such information may not be complete or accurate because the United States client may not have a criminal record or may not have truthfully reported their marital or criminal record.

(3) Summaries. The Secretary of Homeland Security, in consultation with the Attorney General and the Secretary of State, shall develop summaries of the pamphlet developed under paragraph (1) that shall be used by Federal officials when reviewing the pamphlet in interviews under subsection (b).

(4) Translation.

(A) In general. In order to best serve the language groups having the greatest concentration of K nonimmigrant visa applicants, the information pamphlet developed under paragraph (1) shall, subject to subparagraph (B), be translated by the Secretary of State into foreign languages, including Russian, Spanish, Tagalog, Vietnamese, Chinese, Ukrainian, Thai, Korean, Polish, Japanese, French, Arabic, Portuguese, Hindi, and such other languages as the Secretary of State, in the Secretary's discretion, may specify.

(B) Revision. Every 2 years, the Secretary of Homeland Security, in consultation with the Attorney General and the Secretary of State, shall determine at least 14 specific languages into which the information pamphlet is translated based on the languages spoken by the greatest concentrations of K nonimmigrant visa applicants.

(5) Availability and distribution. The information pamphlet developed under paragraph (1) shall be made available and distributed as follows:

(A) Mailings to K nonimmigrant visa applicants.

(i) The pamphlet shall be mailed by the Secretary of State to each applicant for a K nonimmigrant visa at the same time that the instruction packet regarding the visa application process is mailed to such applicant. The pamphlet so mailed shall be in the primary language of the applicant or in English if no translation into the applicant's primary language is available.

(ii) The Secretary of Homeland Security shall provide to the Secretary of State, for inclusion in the mailing under clause (i), a copy of the petition submitted by the petitioner for such applicant under subsection (d) or (r) of section 214 of such Act (8 U.S.C. 1184).

(iii) The Secretary of Homeland Security shall provide to the Secretary of State, for inclusion in the mailing described in clause (i), any criminal background information the Secretary of Homeland Security possesses with respect to a petitioner under subsection (d) or (r) of section 214 of such Act (8 U.S.C. 1184). The Secretary of State, in turn, shall share any such criminal background information that is in government records or databases with the K nonimmigrant visa applicant who is the beneficiary of the petition. The visa applicant shall be informed that such criminal background information is based on available records and may not be complete. The Secretary of State also shall provide for the disclosure of such criminal background information to the visa applicant at the consular interview in the primary language of the visa applicant.

(iv) The Secretary of Homeland Security shall conduct a background check of the National Crime Information Center's Protection Order Database on each petitioner for a visa under subsection (d) or (r) of section 214 of the Immigration and Nationality Act (8 U.S.C. 1184). Any appropriate information obtained from such background check—

(I) shall accompany the criminal background information provided by the Secretary of Homeland Security to the Secretary of State and shared by the Secretary of State with a beneficiary of a petition referred to in clause (iii); and

(II) shall not be used or disclosed for any other purpose unless expressly authorized by law.

(v) The Secretary of Homeland Security shall create a cover sheet or other mechanism to accompany the information required to be provided to an applicant for a visa under subsection (d) or (r) of section 214 of the Immigration and Nationality Act (8 U.S.C. 1184) by clauses (i) through (iv) of this paragraph or by clauses (i) and (ii) of subsection (r)(4)(B) of such section 214, that calls to the applicant's attention—

(I) whether the petitioner disclosed a protection order, a restraining order, or criminal history information on the visa petition;

(II) the criminal background information and information about any protection order obtained by the Secretary of Homeland Security regarding the petitioner in the course of adjudicating the petition; and

(III) whether the information the petitioner disclosed on the visa petition regarding any previous petitions filed under subsection (d) or (r) of such section 214 [8 USCS § 1184] is consistent with the information in the multiple visa tracking database of the Department of Homeland Security, as described in subsection (r)(4)(A) of such section 214 [8 USCS § 1184].

(B) Consular access. The pamphlet developed under paragraph (1) shall be made available to the public at all consular posts. The summaries described in paragraph (3) shall be made available to foreign service officers at all consular posts.

(C) Posting on Federal websites. The pamphlet developed under paragraph (1) shall be posted on the websites of the Department of State and the Department of Homeland Security, as well as on the websites of all consular posts processing applications for K nonimmigrant visas.

(D) International marriage brokers and victim advocacy organizations. The pamphlet developed under paragraph (1) shall be made available to any international marriage broker, government agency, or nongovernmental advocacy organization.

(6) Deadline for pamphlet development and distribution. The pamphlet developed under paragraph (1) shall be distributed and made available (including in the languages specified under paragraph (4)) not later than 120 days after the date of the enactment of this Act [enacted Jan. 5, 2006].

(b) Visa and adjustment interviews.

(1) Fiancé(e)s, spouses and their derivatives. During an interview with an applicant for a K nonimmigrant visa, a consular officers shall—

(A) provide information, in the primary language of the visa applicant, on protection orders and criminal convictions collected under subsection (a)(5)(A)(iii);

(B) provide a copy of the pamphlet developed under subsection (a)(1) in English or another appropriate language and provide an oral summary, in the primary language of the visa applicant, of that pamphlet; and

(C) ask the applicant, in the primary language of the applicant, whether an international marriage broker has facilitated the relationship between the applicant and the United States petitioner, and, if so, obtain the identity of the international marriage broker from the applicant and confirm that the international marriage broker provided to the applicant the information and materials required under subsection (d)(3)(A)(iii).

(2) Family-based applicants. The pamphlet developed under subsection (a)(1) shall be distributed directly to applicants for family-based immigration petitions at all consular and adjustment interviews for such visas. The Department of State or Department of Homeland Security officer conducting the interview shall review the summary of the pamphlet with the applicant orally in the applicant's primary language, in addition to distributing the pamphlet to the applicant in English or another appropriate language.

(c) Confidentiality. In fulfilling the requirements of this section, no official of the Department of State or the Department of Homeland Security shall disclose to a nonimmigrant visa applicant the name or contact information of any person who was granted a protection order or restraining order against the petitioner or who was a victim of a crime of violence perpetrated by the petitioner, but shall disclose the relationship of the person to the petitioner.

(d) Regulation of international marriage brokers.

(1) Prohibition on marketing of or to children.

(A) In general. An international marriage broker shall not provide any individual or entity with the personal contact information, photograph, or general information about the background or interests of any individual under the age of 18.

(B) Compliance. To comply with the requirements of subparagraph (A), an international marriage broker shall—

(i) obtain a valid copy of each foreign national client's birth certificate or other proof of age document issued by an appropriate government entity;

(ii) indicate on such certificate or document the date it was received by the international marriage broker;

(iii) retain the original of such certificate or document for 7 years after such date of receipt; and

(iv) produce such certificate or document upon request to an appropriate authority charged with the enforcement of this paragraph.

(2) Requirements of international marriage brokers with respect to mandatory collection of background information.

(A) In general.

(i) Search of sex offender public website. Each international marriage broker shall search the National Sex Offender Website, as required under paragraph (3)(A)(i).

(ii) Collection of background information. Each international marriage broker shall also collect the background information listed in subparagraph (B) about the United States client to whom the personal contact information of a foreign national client would be provided.

(B) Background information. The international marriage broker shall collect a certification signed (in written, electronic, or other form) by the United States client accompanied by documentation or an attestation of the following background information about the United States client:

(i) Any temporary or permanent civil protection order or restraining order issued against the United States client.

(ii) Any Federal, State, or local arrest or conviction of the United States client for homicide, murder, manslaughter, assault, battery, domestic violence, rape, sexual assault, abusive sexual contact, sexual exploitation, incest, child abuse or neglect, torture, trafficking, peonage, holding hostage, involuntary servitude, slave trade, kidnapping, abduction, unlawful criminal restraint, false imprisonment, stalking, or an attempt to commit any such crime.

(iii) Any Federal, State, or local arrest or conviction of the United States client for—

(I) solely, principally, or incidentally engaging in prostitution;

(II) a direct or indirect attempt to procure prostitutes or persons for the purpose of prostitution; or

(III) receiving, in whole or in part, of the proceeds of prostitution.

(iv) Any Federal, State, or local arrest or conviction of the United States client for offenses related to controlled substances or alcohol.

(v) Marital history of the United States client, including whether the client is currently married, whether the client has previously been married and how many times, how previous marriages of the client were terminated and the date of termination, and whether the client has previously sponsored an alien to whom the client was engaged or married.

(vi) The ages of any of the United States client's children who are under the age of 18.

(vii) All States and countries in which the United States client has resided since the client was 18 years of age.

(3) Obligation of international marriage brokers with respect to informed consent.

(A) Limitation on sharing information about foreign national clients. An international marriage broker shall not provide any United States client or representative with the personal contact information of any foreign national client unless and until the international marriage broker has—

(i) performed a search of the National Sex Offender Public Website for information regarding the United States client;

(ii) collected background information about the United States client required under paragraph (2);

(iii) provided to the foreign national client—

(I) in the foreign national client's primary language, a copy of any records retrieved from the search required under paragraph (2)(A)(i) or documentation confirming that such search retrieved no records;

(II) in the foreign national client's primary language, a copy of the signed certification and accompanying documentation or attestation regarding the background information collected under paragraph (2)(B); and

(III) in the foreign national client's primary language (or in English or other appropriate language if there is no translation available into the client's primary language), the pamphlet developed under subsection (a)(1); and

(iv) received from the foreign national client a signed, written consent, in the foreign national client's primary language, to release the foreign national client's personal contact information to the specific United States client.

(B) Confidentiality. In fulfilling the requirements of this paragraph, an international marriage broker shall disclose the relationship of the United States client to individuals who were issued a protection order or restraining order as described in clause (i) of paragraph (2)(B), or of any other victims of crimes as described in clauses (ii) through (iv) of such paragraph, but shall not disclose the name or location information of such individuals.

(C) [Deleted]

(4) Limitation on disclosure. An international marriage broker shall not provide the personal contact information of any foreign national client to any person or entity other than a United States client. Such information shall not be disclosed to potential United States clients or individuals who are being recruited to be United States clients or representatives.

(5) Penalties.

(A) Federal civil penalty.

(i) Violation. An international marriage broker that violates (or attempts to violate) paragraph (1), (2), (3), or (4) is subject to a civil penalty of not less than $5,000 and not more than $25,000 for each such violation.

(ii) Procedures for imposition of penalty. At the discretion of the Attorney General, a penalty may be imposed under clause (i) either by a Federal judge, or by the Attorney General after notice and an opportunity for an agency hearing on the record in accordance with subchapter II of chapter 5 of title 5, United States Code [5 USCS §§ 551 et seq.] (popularly known as the Administrative Procedure Act).

(B) Federal criminal penalties.

(i) Failure of international marriage brokers to comply with obligations. Except as provided in clause (ii), an international marriage broker that, in circumstances in or affecting interstate or foreign commerce, or within the special maritime and territorial jurisdiction of the United States—

(I) except as provided in subclause (II), violates (or attempts to violate) paragraph (1), (2), (3), or (4) shall be fined in accordance with title 18, United States Code, or imprisoned for not more than 1 year, or both; or

(II) knowingly violates or attempts to violate paragraphs (1), (2), (3), or (4) shall be fined in accordance with title 18, United States Code, or imprisoned for not more than 5 years, or both.

(ii) Misuse of information. A person who knowingly discloses, uses, or causes to be used any information obtained by an international marriage broker as a result of a requirement under paragraph (2) or (3) for any purpose other than the disclosures required under paragraph (3) shall be fined in accordance with title 18, United States Code, or imprisoned for not more than 1 year, or both.

(iii) Fraudulent failures of United States clients to make required self-disclosures. A person who knowingly and with intent to defraud another person outside the United States in order to recruit, solicit, entice, or induce that other person into entering a dating or matrimonial relationship, makes false or fraudulent representations regarding the disclosures described in clause (i), (ii), (iii), or (iv) of subsection (d)(2)(B), including by failing to make any such disclosures, shall be fined in accordance with title 18, United States Code, imprisoned for not more than 1 year, or both.

(iv) Relationship to other penalties. The penalties provided in clauses (i), (ii), and (iii) are in addition to any other civil or criminal liability under Federal or State law to which a person may be subject for the misuse of information, including misuse to threaten, intimidate, or harass any individual.

(v) Construction. Nothing in this paragraph or paragraph (3) or (4) may be construed to prevent the disclosure of information to law enforcement or pursuant to a court order.

(C) Additional remedies. The penalties and remedies under this subsection are in addition to any other penalties or remedies available under law including equitable remedies.

(6) Enforcement.

(A) Authority. The Attorney General shall be responsible for the enforcement of the provisions of this section, including the prosecution of civil and criminal penalties provided for by this section.

(B) Consultation. The Attorney General shall consult with the Director of the Office on Violence Against Women of the Department of Justice to develop policies and public education designed to promote enforcement of this section.

(7) Nonpreemption. Nothing in this subsection shall preempt—

(A) any State law that provides additional protections for aliens who are utilizing the services of an international marriage broker; or

(B) any other or further right or remedy available under law to any party utilizing the services of an international marriage broker.

(8) Effective date.

(A) In general. Except as provided in subparagraph (B), this subsection shall take effect on the date that is 60 days after the date of the enactment of this Act [enacted Jan. 5, 2006].

(B) Additional time allowed for information pamphlet. The requirement for the distribution of the pamphlet developed under subsection (a)(1) shall not apply until 30 days after the date of its development and initial distribution under subsection (a)(6).

(e) Definitions. In this section:

(1) Crime of violence. The term "crime of violence" has the meaning given such term in section 16 of title 18, United States Code [18 USCS § 16].

(2) Domestic violence. The term "domestic violence" has the meaning given such term in section 3 of this Act.

(3) Foreign national client. The term "foreign national client" means a person who is not a United States citizen or national or an alien lawfully admitted to the United States for permanent residence and who utilizes the services of an international marriage broker. Such term includes an alien residing in the United States who is in the United States as a result of utilizing the services of an international marriage broker and any alien recruited by an international marriage broker or representative of such broker.

(4) International marriage broker.

(A) In general. The term "international marriage broker" means a corporation, partnership, business, individual, or other legal entity, whether or not organized under any law of the United States, that charges fees for providing dating, matrimonial, matchmaking services, or social referrals between United States citizens or nationals or aliens lawfully admitted to the United States as permanent residents and foreign national clients by providing personal contact information or otherwise facilitating communication between individuals.

(B) Exceptions. Such term does not include—

(i) a traditional matchmaking organization of a cultural or religious nature that operates on a nonprofit basis and otherwise operates in compliance with the laws of the countries in which it operates, including the laws of the United States; or

(ii) an entity that provides dating services if its principal business is not to provide international dating services between United States citizens or United States residents and foreign nationals and it charges comparable rates and offers comparable services to all individuals it serves regardless of the individual's gender or country of citizenship.

(5) K nonimmigrant visa. The term "K nonimmigrant visa" means a nonimmigrant visa under clause (i) or (ii) of section 101(a)(15)(K) of the Immigration and Nationality Act (8 U.S.C. 1101(a)(15)(K)).

(6) Personal contact information.

(A) In general. The term "personal contact information" means information, or a forum to obtain such information, that would permit individuals to contact each other, including—

(i) the name or residential, postal, electronic mail, or instant message address of an individual;

(ii) the telephone, pager, cellphone, or fax number, or voice message mailbox of an individual; or

(iii) the provision of an opportunity for an in-person meeting.

(B) Exception. Such term does not include a photograph or general information about the background or interests of a person.

(7) Representative. The term "representative" means, with respect to an international marriage broker, the person or entity acting on behalf of such broker. Such a representative may be a recruiter, agent, independent contractor, or other international marriage broker or other person conveying information about or to a United States client or foreign national client, whether or not the person or entity receives remuneration.

(8) State. The term "State" includes the District of Columbia, Puerto Rico, the Virgin Islands, Guam, American Samoa, and the Northern Mariana Islands.

(9) United States. The term "United States", when used in a geographic sense, includes all the States.

(10) United States client. The term "United States client" means a United States citizen or other individual who resides in the United States and who utilizes the services of an international marriage broker, if a payment is made or a debt is incurred to utilize such services.

(f) GAO studies and reports.

(1) Study. The Comptroller General of the United States shall conduct a study—

(A) on the impact of this section and section 832 on the K nonimmigrant visa process, including specifically —

(i) annual numerical changes in petitions for K nonimmigrant visas;

(ii) the annual number (and percentage) of such petitions that are denied under subsection (d)(2) or (r) of section 214 of the Immigration and Nationality Act (8 U.S.C. 1184), as amended by this Act;

(iii) the annual number of waiver applications submitted under such a subsection, the number (and percentage) of such applications granted or denied, and the reasons for such decisions;

(iv) the annual number (and percentage) of cases in which the criminal background information collected and provided to the applicant as required by subsection (a)(5)(A)(iii) contains one or more convictions;

(v) the annual number and percentage of cases described in clause (iv) that were granted or were denied waivers under section 214(d)(2) of the Immigration and Nationality Act [8 USCS § 1184(d)(2)], as amended by this Act;

(vi) the annual number of fiancé(e) and spousal K nonimmigrant visa petitions or family-based immigration petitions filed by petitioners or applicants who have previously filed other fiancé(e) or spousal K nonimmigrant visa petitions or family-based immigration petitions;

(vii) the annual number of fiancé(e) and spousal K nonimmigrant visa petitions or family-based immigration petitions filed by petitioners or applicants who have concurrently filed other fiancé(e) or spousal K nonimmigrant visa petitioners or family-based immigration petitions; and

(viii) the annual and cumulative number of petitioners and applicants tracked in the multiple filings database established under paragraph (4) of section 214(r) of the Immigration and Nationality Act [8 USCS § 1184(r)], as added by this Act;

(B) regarding the number of international marriage brokers doing business in the United States, the number of marriages resulting from the services provided, and the extent of compliance with the applicable requirements of this section;

(C) that assesses the accuracy and completeness of information gathered under section 832 and this section from clients and petitioners by international marriage brokers, the Department of State, or the Department of Homeland Security;

(D) that examines, based on the information gathered, the extent to which persons with a history of violence are using either the K nonimmigrant visa process or the services of international marriage brokers, or both, and the extent to which such persons are providing accurate and complete information to the Department of State or the Department of Homeland Security and to international marriage brokers in accordance with subsections (a) and (d)(2)(B); and

(E) that assesses the accuracy and completeness of the criminal background check performed by the Secretary of Homeland Security at identifying past instances of domestic violence.

(2) Report. Not later than 2 years after the date of enactment of this Act [enacted Jan. 5, 2006], the Comptroller General shall submit to the Committee on the Judiciary of the Senate and the Committee on the Judiciary of the House of Representatives a report setting forth the results of the study conducted under paragraph (1).

(3) Data collection. The Secretary of Homeland Security and the Secretary of State shall collect and maintain the data necessary for the Comptroller General of the United States to conduct the study required by paragraph (1).

(4) Continuing impact study and report.

(A) Study. The Comptroller General shall conduct a study on the continuing impact of the implementation of this section and of section of 214 of the Immigration and Nationality Act (8 U.S.C. 1184) on the process for granting K nonimmigrant visas, including specifically a study of the items described in subparagraphs (A) through (E) of paragraph (1).

(B) Report. Not later than 2 years after the date of the enactment of the Violence Against Women Reauthorization Act of 2013 [enacted March 7, 2013], the Comptroller General shall submit to the Committee on the Judiciary of the Senate and the Committee on the Judiciary of the House of Representatives a report setting forth the results of the study conducted under subparagraph (A).

(C) Data collection. The Attorney General, the Secretary of Homeland Security, and the Secretary of State shall collect and maintain the data necessary for the Comptroller General to conduct the study required by paragraph (1)(A).

(g) [Omitted]

(Jan. 5, 2006, P. L. 109-162, Title VIII, Subtitle D, § 833, 119 Stat. 3068; March 7, 2013, P. L. 113-4, Title VIII, §§ 807(b), 808(b)–(d), 127 Stat. 113, 114.)

§ 1375b. Protections for domestic workers and other nonimmigrants

(a) Information pamphlet and video for consular waiting rooms.

(1) Development and distribution. The Secretary of State, in consultation with the Secretary of Homeland Security, the Attorney General, and the Secretary of Labor, shall develop an information pamphlet and video on legal rights and resources for aliens applying for employment- or education-based nonimmigrant visas. The video shall be distributed and shown in consular waiting rooms in embassies and consulates appropriate to the circumstances that are determined to have the greatest concentration of employment or education-based non-immigrant visa applicants, and where sufficient video facilities exist in waiting or other rooms where applicants wait or convene. The Secretary of State is authorized to augment video facilities in such consulates or embassies in order to fulfill the purposes of this section.

(2) Consultation. In developing the information pamphlet under paragraph (1), the Secretary of State shall consult with nongovernmental organizations with expertise on the legal rights of workers and victims of severe forms of trafficking in persons.

(b) Contents. The information pamphlet and video developed under subsection (a) shall include information concerning items such as—

(1) the nonimmigrant visa application processes, including information about the portability of employment;

(2) the legal rights of employment or education-based nonimmigrant visa holders under Federal immigration, labor, and employment law;

(3) the illegality of slavery, peonage, trafficking in persons, sexual assault, extortion, blackmail, and worker exploitation in the United States;

(4) the legal rights of immigrant victims of trafficking in persons and worker exploitation, including—

(A) the right of access to immigrant and labor rights groups;

(B) the right to seek redress in United States courts;

(C) the right to report abuse without retaliation;

(D) the right of the nonimmigrant to relinquish possession of his or her passport to his or her employer;

(E) the requirement of an employment contract between the employer and the nonimmigrant; and

(F) an explanation of the rights and protections included in the contract described in subparagraph (E); and

(5) information about nongovernmental organizations that provide services for victims of trafficking in persons and worker exploitation, including—

(A) anti-trafficking in persons telephone hotlines operated by the Federal Government;

(B) the Operation Rescue and Restore hotline; and

(C) a general description of the types of victims services available for individuals subject to trafficking in persons or worker exploitation.

(c) Translation.

(1) In general. To best serve the language groups having the greatest concentration of employment-based nonimmigrant visas, the Secretary of State shall translate the information pamphlet and produce or dub the video developed under subsection (a) into all relevant foreign languages, to be determined by the Secretary based on the languages spoken by the greatest concentrations of employment- or education-based nonimmigrant visa applicants.

(2) Revision. Every 2 years, the Secretary of State, in consultation with the Attorney General and the Secretary of Homeland Security, shall determine the specific languages into which the information pamphlet will be translated and the video produced or dubbed based on the languages spoken by the greatest concentrations of employment- or education-based nonimmigrant visa applicants.

(d) Availability and distribution.

(1) Posting on Federal websites. The information pamphlet and video developed under subsection (a) shall be posted on the websites of the Department of State, the Department of Homeland Security, the Department of Justice, the Department of Labor, and all United States consular posts processing applications for employment- or education-based nonimmigrant visas.

(2) Other distribution. The information pamphlet and video developed under subsection (a) shall be made available to any—

(A) government agency;

(B) nongovernmental advocacy organization; or

(C) foreign labor broker doing business in the United States.

(3) Deadline for pamphlet development and distribution. Not later than 180 days after the date of the enactment of this Act [enacted Dec. 23, 2008], the Secretary of State shall distribute and make available the information pamphlet developed under subsection (a) in all the languages referred to in subsection (c).

(4) Deadline for video development and distribution. Not later than 1 year after the date of the enactment of the Violence Against Women Reauthorization Act of 2013 [enacted March 7, 2013], the Secretary of State shall make available the video developed under subsection (a) produced or dubbed in all the languages referred to in subsection (c).

(e) Responsibilities of consular officers of the Department of State.

(1) Interviews. A consular officer conducting an interview of an alien for an employment-based nonimmigrant visa shall—

(A)(i) confirm that the alien has received, read, and understood the contents of the pamphlet described in subsections (a) and (b); and

(ii) if the alien has not received, read, or understood the contents of the pamphlet described in subsections (a) and (b), distribute and orally disclose to the alien the information described in paragraphs (2) and (3) in a language that the alien understands; and

(B) offer to answer any questions the alien may have regarding the contents of the pamphlet described in subsections (a) and (b).

(2) Legal rights. The consular officer shall disclose to the alien—

(A) the legal rights of employment-based nonimmigrants under Federal immigration, labor, and employment laws;

(B) the illegality of slavery, peonage, trafficking in persons, sexual assault, extortion, blackmail, and worker exploitation in the United States; and

(C) the legal rights of immigrant victims of trafficking in persons, worker exploitation, and other related crimes, including—

(i) the right of access to immigrant and labor rights groups;

(ii) the right to seek redress in United States courts; and

(iii) the right to report abuse without retaliation.

(3) Victim services. In carrying out the disclosure requirement under this subsection, the consular officer shall disclose to the alien the availability of services for victims of human trafficking and worker exploitation in the United States, including victim services complaint hotlines.

(f) Definitions. In this section:

(1) Employment- or education-based nonimmigrant visa. The term "employment- or education-based nonimmigrant visa" means—

(A) a nonimmigrant visa issued under subparagraph (A)(iii), (G)(v), (H), or (J) of section 101(a)(15) of the Immigration and Nationality Act (8 U.S.C. 1101(a)(15)); and

(B) any nonimmigrant visa issued to a personal or domestic servant who is accompanying or following to join an employer.

(2) Severe forms of trafficking in persons. The term "severe forms of trafficking in persons" has the meaning given the term in section 103 of the Trafficking Victims Protection Act of 2000 (22 U.S.C. 7102).

(3) Secretary. The term "Secretary" means the Secretary of State.

(4) Abusing and exploiting. The term "abusing and exploiting" means any conduct which would constitute a violation of section 1466A, 1589, 1591, 1592, 2251, or 2251A of title 18, United States Code.

(Dec. 23, 2008, P. L. 110-457, Title II, Subtitle A, § 202, 122 Stat. 5055; March 7, 2013, P. L. 113-4, Title XII, Subtitle A, § 1206, 127 Stat. 140.)

§ 1375c. Protections, remedies, and limitations on issuance for A-3 and G-5 visas

(a) Limitations on issuance of A-3 and G-5 visas.

(1) Contract requirement. Notwithstanding any other provision of law, the Secretary of State may not issue—

(A) an A-3 visa unless the applicant is employed, or has signed a contract to be employed containing the requirements set forth in subsection (d)(2), by an officer of a diplomatic mission or consular post; or

(B) a G-5 visa unless the applicant is employed, or has signed a contract to be employed by an employee in an international organization.

(2) Suspension requirement. Notwithstanding any other provision of law, the Secretary shall suspend, for a period of at least 1 year, except if the Secretary determines and reports to the appropriate congressional committees, in advance, the reasons a shorter period is in the national interest,[,] the issuance of A-3 visas or G-5 visas to applicants seeking to work for officials of a diplomatic mission or an international organization, if there is an unpaid default or final civil judgement directly or indirectly related to human trafficking against the employer or a family member assigned to the embassy, or the diplomatic mission or international organization hosting the employer or family member has not responded affirmatively to a request to waive immunity within 6 weeks of the request in a case brought by the United States Government and the country that accredited the employer or family member or, in the case of international organizations, the country of citizenship, has not initiated prosecution against the employer or family member.

(3) Action by diplomatic missions or international organizations. The Secretary may suspend the application of the limitation under paragraph (2) if the Secretary determines and reports to the appropriate congressional committees that, as applicable, the unpaid default judgment or final civil judgement has been resolved, the diplomatic mission or international organization hosting the employer or family member has waived immunity for the employer or family member or the country that accredited the employer or family member or the country of citizenship of the employer or family member completed the prosecution of the employer or family member, and the diplomatic mission or international organization hosting the employer or family member has a mechanism in place to ensure that such abuse or exploitation does not reoccur with respect to any alien employed by an employee of such mission or institution.

(b) Protections and remedies for A-3 and G-5 nonimmigrants employed by diplomats and staff of international organizations.

(1) In general. The Secretary may not issue or renew an A-3 visa or a G-5 visa unless—

(A) the visa applicant has executed a contract with the employer or prospective employer containing provisions described in paragraph (2); and

(B) a consular officer has conducted a personal interview with the applicant outside the presence of the employer or any recruitment agent in which the officer reviewed the terms of the contract and the provisions of the pamphlet required under section 202 [8 USCS § 1375b].

(2) Mandatory contract. The contract between the employer and domestic worker required under paragraph (1) shall include—

(A) an agreement by the employer to abide by all Federal, State, and local laws in the United States;

(B) information on the frequency and form of payment, work duties, weekly work hours, holidays, sick days, and vacation days; and

(C) an agreement by the employer not to withhold the passport, employment contract, or other personal property of the employee.

(3) Training of consular officers. The Secretary shall provide appropriate training to consular officers on the fair labor standards described in the pamphlet required under section 202 [8 USCS § 1375b], trafficking in persons, and the provisions of this section.

(4) Record keeping.

(A) In general. The Secretary shall maintain records on the presence of nonimmigrants holding an A-3 visa or a G-5 visa in the United States, including—

(i) information about when the nonimmigrant entered and permanently exited the country of residence;

(ii) the official title, contact information, and immunity level of the employer; and

(iii) information regarding any allegations of employer abuse received by the Department of State.

(c) Protection from removal during legal actions against former employers.

(1) Remaining in the United States to seek legal redress.

(A) Effect of complaint filing. Except as provided in subparagraph (B), if a nonimmigrant holding an A-3 visa or a G-5 visa working in the United States files a civil action under section 1595 of title 18, United States Code, or a civil action regarding a violation of any of the terms contained in the contract or violation of any other Federal, State, or local law in the United States governing the terms and conditions of employment of the nonimmigrant that are associated with acts covered by such section, the Attorney General and the Secretary of Homeland Security shall permit the nonimmigrant to remain legally in the United States for time sufficient to fully and effectively participate in all legal proceedings related to such action.

(B) Exception. An alien described in subparagraph (A) may be deported before the conclusion of the legal proceedings related to a civil action described in such subparagraph if such alien is—

(i) inadmissible under paragraph (2)(A)(i)(II), (2)(B), (2)(C), (2)(E), (2)(H), (2)(I), (3)(A)(i), (3)(A)(iii), (3)(B), (3)(C), or (3)(F) of section 212(a) of the Immigration and Nationality Act (8 U.S.C. 1182(a)); or

(ii) deportable under paragraph (2)(A)(ii), (2)(A)(iii), (4)(A)(i), (4)(A)(iii), (4)(B), or (4)(C) of section 237(a) of such Act (8 U.S.C. 1227(a)).

(C) Failure to exercise due diligence. If the Secretary of Homeland Security, after consultation with the Attorney General, determines that the nonimmigrant holding an A-3 visa or a G-5 visa has failed to exercise due diligence in pursuing an action described in subparagraph (A), the Secretary may terminate the status of the A-3 or G-5 nonimmigrant.

(2) Authorization to work. The Attorney General and the Secretary of Homeland Security shall authorize any nonimmigrant described in paragraph (1) to engage in employment in the United States during the period the nonimmigrant is in the United States pursuant to paragraph (1).

(d) Study and report.

(1) Investigation report.

(A) In general. Not later than 180 days after the date of the enactment of this Act [enacted Dec. 23, 2008], and every 2 years thereafter for the following 10 years, the Secretary shall submit a report to the appropriate congressional committees on the implementation of this section.

(B) Contents. The report submitted under subparagraph (A) shall include—

(i) an assessment of the actions taken by the Department of State and the Department of Justice to investigate allegations of trafficking or abuse of nonimmigrants holding an A-3 visa or a G-5 visa; and

(ii) the results of such investigations.

(2) Feasibility of oversight of employees of diplomats and representatives of other institutions report. Not later than 180 days after the date of the enactment of this Act [enacted Dec. 23, 2008], the Secretary shall submit a report to the appropriate congressional committees on the feasibility of—

(A) establishing a system to monitor the treatment of nonimmigrants holding an A-3 visa or a G-5 visa who have been admitted to the United States;

(B) a range of compensation approaches, such as a bond program, compensation fund, or insurance scheme, to ensure that such nonimmigrants receive appropriate compensation if their employers violate the terms of their employment contracts; and

(C) with respect to each proposed compensation approach described in subparagraph (B), an evaluation and proposal describing the proposed processes for—

(i) adjudicating claims of rights violations;

(ii) determining the level of compensation; and

(iii) administering the program, fund, or scheme.

(e) Assistance to law enforcement investigations. The Secretary shall cooperate, to the fullest extent possible consistent with the United States obligations under the Vienna Convention on Diplomatic Relations, done at Vienna, April 18, 1961, (23 U.S.T. 3229), with any investigation by United States law enforcement authorities of crimes related to abuse or exploitation of a nonimmigrant holding an A-3 visa or a G-5 visa.

(f) Definitions. In this section:

(1) A-3 visa. The term "A-3 visa" means a nonimmigrant visa issued pursuant to section 101(a)(15)(A)(iii) of the Immigration and Nationality Act (8 U.S.C. 1101(a)(15)(A)(iii)).

(2) G-5 visa. The term "G-5 visa" means a nonimmigrant visa issued pursuant to section 101(a)(15)(G)(v) of the Immigration and Nationality Act (8 U.S.C. 1101(a)(15)(G)(v)).

(3) Secretary. The term "Secretary" means the Secretary of State.

(4) Appropriate congressional committees. The term "appropriate congressional committees" means—

(A) the Committee on Foreign Affairs and the Committee on the Judiciary of the House of Representatives; and

(B) the Committee on Foreign Relations and the Committee on the Judiciary of the Senate.

(Dec. 23, 2008, P. L. 110-457, Title II, Subtitle A, § 203, 122 Stat. 5057; Jan. 8, 2019, P.L. 115-425, Title I, Subtitle C, § 123, 132 Stat. 5479.)

§ 1376. Data on nonimmigrant overstay rates

(a) Collection of data. Not later than the date that is 180 days after the date of the enactment of this Act [enacted April 27, 1998], the Attorney General shall implement a program to collect data, for each fiscal year, regarding the total number of aliens within each of the classes of nonimmigrant aliens described in section 101(a)(15) of the Immigration and Nationality Act (8 U.S.C. 1101(a)(15)) whose authorized period of stay in the United States terminated during the previous fiscal year, but who remained in the United States notwithstanding such termination.

(b) Annual report. Not later than June 30, 1999, and not later than June 30 of each year thereafter, the Attorney General shall submit an annual report to the Congress providing numerical estimates, for each country for the preceding fiscal year, of the number of aliens from the country who are described in subsection (a).

(April 27, 1998, P. L. 105-173, § 2, 112 Stat. 56.)

§ 1377. Collection of data on detained asylum seekers

(a) In general. The Attorney General shall regularly collect data on a nation-wide [nationwide] basis with respect to asylum seekers in detention in the United States, including the following information:

(1) The number of detainees.

(2) An identification of the countries of origin of the detainees.

(3) The percentage of each gender within the total number of detainees.

(4) The number of detainees listed by each year of age of the detainees.

(5) The location of each detainee by detention facility.

(6) With respect to each facility where detainees are held, whether the facility is also used to detain criminals and whether any of the detainees are held in the same cells as criminals.

(7) The number and frequency of the transfers of detainees between detention facilities.

(8) The average length of detention and the number of detainees by category of the length of detention.

(9) The rate of release from detention of detainees for each district of the Immigration and Naturalization Service.

(10) A description of the disposition of cases.

(b) Annual reports. Beginning October 1, 1999, and not later than October 1 of each year thereafter, the Attorney General shall submit to the Committee on the Judiciary of each House of Congress a report setting forth the data collected under subsection (a) for the fiscal year ending September 30 of that year.

(c) Availability to public. Copies of the data collected under subsection (a) shall be made available to members of the public upon request pursuant to such regulations as the Attorney General shall prescribe.

(Oct. 21, 1998, P. L. 105-277, Div A, § 101(h) [Title IX, § 903], 112 Stat. 2681-541.)

§ 1377a. Report on aliens determined to have credible or reasonable fear of persecution or torture

(a) Semimonthly updates. Not later than 30 days after the date of enactment of this Act [enacted Dec. 20, 2019] and updated semimonthly thereafter, the Director of U.S. Citizenship and Immigration Services shall make available, on a publicly accessible website in a downloadable, searchable, and sortable format, a report containing not less than the previous twelve months of semimonthly data on—

(1) the number of aliens determined to have a credible or reasonable fear of—

(A) persecution, as defined in section 235(b)(1)(B)(v) of the Immigration and Nationality Act [8 USCS § 1225(b)(1)(B)(v)]; or

(B) torture, as defined in section 208.30 of title 8, Code of Federal Regulations (as in effect on January 1, 2018);

(2) the total number of cases received by U.S. Citizenship and Immigration Services to adjudicate credible or reasonable fear claims, as described in paragraph (1), and the total number of cases closed.

(b) Disaggregation of data. Such report shall also disaggregate the data described in subsection (a) with respect to the following subsets—

(1) claims submitted by aliens detained at a U.S. Immigration and Customs Enforcement family residential center;

(2) claims submitted by aliens organized by each subdivision of legal or administrative authority under which claims are reviewed; and

(3) the job series of the personnel reviewing the claims.

(Dec. 20, 2019, Div D, Title IV, § 403, 133 Stat. 2524.)

§ 1378. Collection of data on other detained aliens

(a) In general. The Attorney General shall regularly collect data on a nationwide basis on aliens being detained in the United States by the Immigration and Naturalization Service other than the aliens described in section 903 [8 USCS § 1377], including the following information:

(1) The number of detainees who are criminal aliens and the number of detainees who are noncriminal aliens who are not seeking asylum.

(2) An identification of the ages, gender, and countries of origin of detainees within each category described in paragraph (1).

(3) The types of facilities, whether facilities of the Immigration and Naturalization Service or other Federal, State, or local facilities, in which each of the categories of detainees described in paragraph (1) are held.

(b) Length of detention, transfers, and dispositions. With respect to detainees who are criminal aliens and detainees who are noncriminal aliens who are not seeking asylum, the Attorney General shall also collect data concerning—

(1) the number and frequency of transfers between detention facilities for each category of detainee;

(2) the average length of detention of each category of detainee;

(3) for each category of detainee, the number of detainees who have been detained for the same length of time, in 3-month increments;

(4) for each category of detainee, the rate of release from detention for each district of the Immigration and Naturalization Service; and

(5) for each category of detainee, the disposition of detention, including whether detention ended due to deportation, release on parole, or any other release.

(c) Criminal aliens. With respect to criminal aliens, the Attorney General shall also collect data concerning—

(1) the number of criminal aliens apprehended under the immigration laws and not detained by the Attorney General; and

(2) a list of crimes committed by criminal aliens after the decision was made not to detain them, to the extent this information can be derived by cross-checking the list of criminal aliens not detained with other databases accessible to the Attorney General.

(d) Annual reports. Beginning on October 1, 1999, and not later than October 1 of each year thereafter, the Attorney General shall submit to the Committee on the Judiciary of each House of Congress a report setting forth the data collected under subsections (a), (b), and (c) for the fiscal year ending September 30 of that year.

(e) Availability to public. Copies of the data collected under subsections (a), (b), and (c) shall be made available to members of the public upon request pursuant to such regulations as the Attorney General shall prescribe.

(Oct. 21, 1998, P. L. 105-277, Div A, § 101(h) [Title IX, § 904], 112 Stat. 2681-542.)

§ 1378a. Report on aliens detained

Not later than 7 days after the date of enactment of this Act [enacted Dec. 20, 2019] and updated semimonthly thereafter, the Director of U.S. Immigration and Customs Enforcement shall make available a report, on a publicly accessible website in a downloadable, searchable, and sortable format, with not less than the previous twelve months of semimonthly data as of the last date of each such reporting period; on—

(1) aliens detained by such agency, including data disaggregated by single adults and members of family units on—

(A) the average fiscal year-to-date daily populations of aliens detained;

(B) the daily count of aliens detained;

(C) the fiscal year-to-date total for book-ins;

(D) the average lengths of stay, including average postdetermination length of stay in the case of detainees described in subparagraph (F);

(E) the number transferred to the custody of U.S. Immigration and Customs Enforcement by U.S. Customs and Border Protection after being—

(i) deemed inadmissible at a port of entry or after being apprehended within 14 days of entering the United States; or

(ii) arrested by U.S. Immigration and Customs Enforcement;

(F) the number determined to have a credible or reasonable fear of—

(i) persecution, as defined in section 235(b)(1)(B)(v) of the Immigration and Nationality Act [8 USCS § 1225(b)(1)(B)(v)]; or

(ii) torture, as defined in section 208.30 of title 8, Code of Federal Regulations (as in effect on January 1, 2018); and

(G) the number who have been issued a Notice to Appear pursuant to section 239 of the Immigration and Nationality Act [8 USCS § 1229], disaggregated by single adults and members of family units;

(2) the total number of enrollees in the Alternatives to Detention program and the average length of participation, disaggregated by—

(A) single adults and family heads of household;

(B) participants in the family case management program;

(C) level of supervision; and

(D) location of supervision, by field office;

(3) for each facility where aliens are detained by U.S. Immigration and Customs Enforcement—

(A) the address;

(B) the field offices that assign detainees to the facility;

(C) the detailed facility type, as defined in the integrated decision support system;

(D) the gender of aliens detained;

(E) the average daily population of detainees within each detainee classification level, as defined in the integrated decision support system;

(F) the average daily population of individuals within each threat level, as defined in the integrated decision support system;

(G) the average daily population within each criminality category, as defined in the integrated decision support system, disaggregated by gender;

(H) the average length of stay;

(I) the average daily population of individuals whose detention is classified as mandatory;

(J) the performance standards to which the facility is held;

(K) the date of the two most recent inspections, the entity that performed each inspection, and a detailed summary of the results of such inspections; and

(L) the guaranteed minimum detention capacity, if applicable; and

(4) the total number of releases from custody, by condition of release, and total number of removals, disaggregated by adult facilities and family facilities.

(Dec. 20, 2019, P.L. 116-93, Div D, Title II, § 218, 133 Stat. 2514.)

§ 1379. Technology standard to confirm identity

(1) In general. The Attorney General and the Secretary of State jointly, through the National Institute of Standards and Technology (NIST), and in consultation with the Secretary of the Treasury and other Federal law enforcement and intelligence agencies the Attorney General or Secretary of State deems appropriate and in consultation with Congress, shall within 15 months after the date of the enactment of this section [enacted Oct. 26, 2001], develop and certify a technology standard, including appropriate biometric identifier standards, that can be used to verify the identity of persons applying for a United States visa or such persons seeking to enter the United States pursuant to a visa for the purposes of conducting background checks, confirming identity, and ensuring that a person has not received a visa under a different name or such person seeking to enter the United States pursuant to a visa.

(2) Interoperable. The technology standard developed pursuant to paragraph (1), shall be the technological basis for a cross-agency, cross-platform electronic system that is a cost-effective, efficient, fully interoperable means to share law enforcement and intelligence information necessary to confirm the identity of such persons applying for a United States visa or such person seeking to enter the United States pursuant to a visa.

(3) Accessible. The electronic system described in paragraph (2), once implemented, shall be readily and easily accessible to—

(A) all consular officers responsible for the issuance of visas;

(B) all Federal inspection agents at all United States border inspection points; and

(C) all law enforcement and intelligence officers as determined by regulation to be responsible for investigation or identification of aliens admitted to the United States pursuant to a visa.

(4) Report. Not later than one year after the date of the enactment of this Act [enacted Oct. 26, 2001], and every 2 years thereafter, the Attorney General and the Secretary of State shall jointly, in consultation with the Secretary of Treasury, report to Congress describing the development, implementation, efficacy, and privacy implications of the technology standard and electronic database system described in this subsection.

(5) Funding. There is authorized to be appropriated to the Secretary of State, the Attorney General, and the Director of the National Institute of Standards and Technology such sums as may be necessary to carry out the provisions of this subsection [this section].

(Oct. 26, 2001, P. L. 107-56, Title IV, Subtitle A, § 403(c), 115 Stat. 344; May 14, 2002, P. L. 107-173, Title II, §§ 201(c)(5), 202(a)(4)(B), 115 Stat. 548, 549.)

§ 1380. Maintenance of statistics by the Department of Homeland Security

(a) In general. The Department of Homeland Security shall maintain statistics regarding petitions filed, approved, extended, and amended with respect to nonimmigrants described in section 101(a)(15)(L) of the Immigration and Nationality Act (8 U.S.C. 1101(a)(15)(L)), including the number of such nonimmigrants who are classified on the basis of specialized knowledge and the number of nonimmigrants who are classified on the basis of specialized knowledge in order to work primarily at offsite locations.

(b) Applicability. Subsection (a) shall apply to petitions filed on or after the effective date of this subtitle.

(Dec. 8, 2004, P. L. 108-447, Div J, Title IV, Subtitle A, § 414, 118 Stat. 3352.)

§ 1381. Secretary of Labor report

Not later than January 31 of each year, the Secretary of Labor shall report to the Committees on the Judiciary of the Senate and the House of Representatives on the investigations undertaken based on—

(1) the authorities described in clauses (i) and (ii) of section 212(n)(2)(G) of the Immigration and Nationality Act (8 U.S.C. 1182(n)(2)(G)(i) and (ii)); and

(2) the expenditures by the Secretary of Labor described in section 286(v)(2)(D) of the Immigration and Nationality Act (8 U.S.C. 1356(v)(2)(D)).

(Dec. 8, 2004, P. L. 108-447, Div J, Title IV, Subtitle A, § 424(c), 118 Stat. 3356.)

§ 1382. Citizenship Gift and Bequest Account

The Director of U.S. Citizenship and Immigration Services is authorized in fiscal year 2017, and in each fiscal year thereafter, to solicit, accept, administer, and utilize gifts, including donations of property, for the purpose of providing an immigrant integration grants program and related activities to promote citizenship and immigrant integration: *Provided,* That all sums received under this subsection shall be deposited in a separate account in the general fund of the Treasury to be known as the "Citizenship Gift and Bequest Account": *Provided further,* That all funds deposited into the Citizenship Gift and Bequest Account shall remain available until expended, and shall be available in addition to any funds appropriated or otherwise made available for an immigrant integration grants program or other activities to promote citizenship and immigrant integration.

(May 5, 2017, P. L. 115-31, Div F, Title IV, § 404(c), 131 Stat. 422.)

NATIONALITY AND NATURALIZATION

NATIONALITY AT BIRTH AND COLLECTIVE NATURALIZATION

Section

NATIONALITY THROUGH NATURALIZATION

LOSS OF NATIONALITY

MISCELLANEOUS

NATIONALITY AT BIRTH AND COLLECTIVE NATURALIZATION

§ 1401. Nationals and citizens of the United States at birth

The following shall be nationals and citizens of the United States at birth:

(a) a person born in the United States, and subject to the jurisdiction thereof;

(b) a person born in the United States to a member of an Indian, Eskimo, Aleutian, or other aboriginal tribe: *Provided,* That the granting of citizenship under this subsection shall not in any manner impair or otherwise affect the right of such person to tribal or other property;

(c) a person born outside of the United States and its outlying possessions of parents both of whom are citizens of the United States and one of whom has had a residence in the United States or one of its outlying possessions, prior to the birth of such person;

(d) a person born outside of the United States and its outlying possessions of parents one of whom is a citizen of the United States who has been physically present in the United States or one of its outlying possessions for a continuous period of one year prior to the birth of such person, and the other of whom is a national, but not a citizen of the United States;

(e) a person born in an outlying possession of the United States of parents one of whom is a citizen of the United States who has been physically present in the United States or one of its outlying possessions for a continuous period of one year at any time prior to the birth of such person;

(f) a person of unknown parentage found in the United States while under the age of five years, until shown, prior to his attaining the age of twenty-one years, not to have been born in the United States;

(g) a person born outside the geographical limits of the United States and its outlying possessions of parents one of whom is an alien, and the other a citizen of the United States who, prior to the birth of such person, was physically present in the United States or its outlying possessions for a period or periods totaling not less than five years, at least two of which were after attaining the age of fourteen years: *Provided*, That any periods of honorable service in the Armed Forces of the United States, or periods of employment with the United States Government or with an international organization as that term is defined in section 1 of the International Organizations Immunities Act (59 Stat. 669; 22 U.S.C. 288) [22 USCS § 288] by such citizen parent, or any periods during which such citizen parent is physically present abroad as the dependent unmarried son or daughter and a member of the household of a person (A) honorably serving with the Armed Forces of the United States, or (B) employed by the United States Government or an international organization as defined in section 1 of the International Organizations Immunities Act [22 USCS § 288], may be included in order to satisfy the physical-presence requirement of this paragraph. This proviso shall be applicable to persons born on or after December 24, 1952, to the same extent as if it had become effective in its present form on that date; and

(h) a person born before noon (Eastern Standard Time) May 24, 1934, outside the limits and jurisdiction of the United States of an alien father and a mother who is a citizen of the United States who, prior to the birth of such person, had resided in the United States.

(June 27, 1952, ch 477, Title III, Ch 1, § 301, 66 Stat. 235; Nov. 6, 1966, P. L. 89-770, 80 Stat. 1322; Oct. 27, 1972, P. L. 92-584, §§ 1, 3, 86 Stat. 1289; Oct. 10, 1978, P. L. 95-432, §§ 1, 3, 92 Stat. 1046; Nov. 14, 1986, P. L. 99-653, § 12, 100 Stat. 3657; Oct. 25, 1994, P. L. 103-416, Title I, § 101(a), 108 Stat. 4306.)

§ 1401a. Birth abroad before 1952 to service parent

Section 301(g) of the Immigration and Nationality Act [8 USCS § 1401(g)] shall be considered to have been and to be applicable to a child born outside of the United States and its outlying possessions after January 12, 1941, and before December 24, 1952, of parents one of whom is a citizen of the United States who has served in the Armed Forces of the United States after December 31, 1946, and before December 24, 1952, and whose case does not come within the provisions of section 201(g) or (i) of the Nationality Act of 1940.

(March 16, 1956, ch 85, 70 Stat. 50; Dec. 29, 1981, P. L. 97-116, § 18(u)(2), 95 Stat. 1621.)

§ 1401b. [Repealed]

§ 1402. Persons born in Puerto Rico on or after April 11, 1899

All persons born in Puerto Rico on or after April 11, 1899, and prior to January 13, 1941, subject to the jurisdiction of the United States, residing on January 13, 1941, in Puerto Rico or other territory over which the United States exercises rights of sovereignty and not citizens of the United States under any other Act, are hereby declared to be citizens of the United States as of January 13, 1941. All persons born in Puerto Rico on or after January 13, 1941, and subject to the jurisdiction of the United States, are citizens of the United States at birth.

(June 27, 1952, ch 477, Title III, Ch 1, § 302, 66 Stat. 236.)

§ 1403. Persons born in the Canal Zone or Republic of Panama on or after February 26, 1904

(a) Any person born in the Canal Zone on or after February 26, 1904, and whether before or after the effective date of this Act, whose father or mother or both at the time of the birth of such person was or is a citizen of the United States, is declared to be a citizen of the United States.

(b) Any person born in the Republic of Panama on or after February 26, 1904, and whether before or after the effective date of this Act, whose father or mother or both at the time of the birth of such person was or is a citizen of the United States employed by the Government of the United States or by the Panama Railroad Company, or its successor in title, is declared to be a citizen of the United States.

(June 27, 1952, ch 477, Title III, Ch 1, § 303, 66 Stat. 236.)

§ 1404. Persons born in Alaska on or after March 30, 1867

A person born in Alaska on or after March 30, 1867, except a noncitizen Indian, is a citizen of the United States at birth. A noncitizen Indian born in Alaska on or after March 30, 1867, and prior to June 2, 1924, is declared to be a citizen of the United States as of June 2, 1924. An Indian born in Alaska on or after June 2, 1924, is a citizen of the United States at birth.

(June 27, 1952, ch 477, Title III, Ch 1, § 304, 66 Stat. 237.)

§ 1405. Persons born in Hawaii

A person born in Hawaii on or after August 12, 1898, and before April 30, 1900, is declared to be a citizen of the United States as of April 30, 1900. A person born in Hawaii on or after April 30, 1900, is a citizen of the United States at birth. A person who was a citizen of the Republic of Hawaii on August 12, 1898, is declared to be a citizen of the United States as of April 30, 1900.

(June 27, 1952, ch 477, Title III, Ch 1, § 305, 66 Stat. 237.)

§ 1406. Persons living in and born in the Virgin Islands

(a) The following persons and their children born subsequent to January 17, 1917, and prior to February 25, 1927, are declared to be citizens of the United States as of February 25, 1927:

(1) All former Danish citizens who, on January 17, 1917, resided in the Virgin Islands of the United States, and were residing in those islands or in the United States or Puerto Rico on February 25, 1927, and who did not make the declaration required to preserve their Danish citizenship by article 6 of the treaty entered into on August 4, 1916, between the United States and Denmark, or who, having made such a declaration have heretofore renounced or may hereafter renounce it by a declaration before a court of record;

(2) All natives of the Virgin Islands of the United States who, on January 17, 1917, resided in those islands, and were residing in those islands or in the United States or Puerto Rico on February 25, 1927, and who were not on February 25, 1927, citizens or subjects of any foreign country;

(3) All natives of the Virgin Islands of the United States who, on January 17, 1917, resided in the United States, and were residing in those islands on February 25, 1927, and who were not on February 25, 1927, citizens or subjects of any foreign country; and

(4) All natives of the Virgin Islands of the United States who, on June 28, 1932, were residing is continental United States, the Virgin Islands of the United States, Puerto Rico, the Canal Zone, or any other insular possession or territory of the United States, and who, on June 28, 1932, were not citizens or subjects of any foreign country, regardless of their place of residence on January 17, 1917.

(b) All persons born in the Virgin Islands of the United States on or after January 17, 1917, and prior to February 25, 1927, and subject to the jurisdiction of the United States are declared to be citizens of the United States as of February 25, 1927; and all persons born in those islands on or after February 25, 1927, and subject to the jurisdiction of the United States, are declared to be citizens of the United States at birth.

(June 27, 1952, ch 477, Title III, Ch 1, § 306, 66 Stat. 237.)

§ 1407. Persons living in and born in Guam

(a) The following persons, and their children born after April 11, 1899, are declared to be citizens of the United States as of August 1, 1950, if they were residing on August 1, 1950, on the island of Guam or other territory over which the United States exercises rights of sovereignty:

(1) All inhabitants of the island of Guam on April 11, 1899, including those temporarily absent from the island on that date, who were Spanish subjects, who after that date continued to reside in Guam or other territory over which the United States exercises sovereignty, and who have taken no affirmative steps to preserve or acquire foreign nationality; and

(2) All persons born in the island of Guam who resided in Guam on April 11, 1899, including those temporarily absent from the island on that date, who after that date continued to reside in Guam or other territory over which the United States exercises sovereignty, and who have taken no affirmative steps to preserve or acquire foreign nationality.

(b) All persons born in the island of Guam on or after April 11, 1899 (whether before or after August 1, 1950) subject to the jurisdiction of the United States, are hereby declared to be citizens of the United States: *Provided,* That in the case of any person born before August 1, 1950, he has taken no affirmative steps to preserve or acquire foreign nationality.

(c) Any person hereinbefore described who is a citizen or national of a country other than the United States and desires to retain his present political status shall have made, prior to August 1, 1952, a declaration under oath of such desire, said declaration to be in form and executed in the manner prescribed by regulations. From and after the making of such a declaration any such person shall be held not to be a national of the United States by virtue of this Act.

(June 27, 1952, ch 477, Title III, Ch 1, § 307, 66 Stat. 237.)

§ 1408. Nationals but not citizens of the United States at birth

Unless otherwise provided in section 301 of this title [8 USCS § 1401], the following shall be nationals, but not citizens, of the United States at birth:

(1) A person born in an outlying possession of the United States on or after the date of formal acquisition of such possession;

(2) A person born outside the United States and its outlying possessions of parents both of whom are nationals, but not citizens, of the United States, and have had a residence in the United States, or one of its outlying possessions prior to the birth of such person;

(3) A person of unknown parentage found in an outlying possession of the United States while under the age of five years, until shown, prior to his attaining the age of twenty-one years, not to have been born in such outlying possession; and

(4) A person born outside the United States and its outlying possessions of parents one of whom is an alien, and the other a national, but not a citizen, of the United States who, prior to the birth of such person, was physically present in the United States or its outlying possessions for a period or periods totaling not less than seven years in any continuous period of ten years—

(A) during which the national parent was not outside the United States or its outlying possessions for a continuous period of more than one year, and

(B) at least five years of which were after attaining the age of fourteen years.

The proviso of section 301(g) [8 USCS § 1401(g)] shall apply to the national parent under this paragraph in the same manner as it applies to the citizen parent under that section.

(June 27, 1952, ch 477, Title III, Ch 1, § 308, 66 Stat. 238; Aug. 27, 1986, P. L. 99-396, § 15(a), 100 Stat. 842; Aug. 27, 1986, P. L. 99-396, § 15(a), 100 Stat. 842; Oct. 24, 1988, P. L. 100-525, § 3(2), 102 Stat. 2614.)

§ 1409. Children born out of wedlock

(a) The provisions of paragraphs (c), (d), (e), and (g) of section 301 [8 USCS § 1401(c)–(e), (g)], and of paragraph (2) of section 308 [8 USCS § 1408(2)], shall apply as of the date of birth to a person born out of wedlock if—

(1) a blood relationship between the person and the father is established by clear and convincing evidence,

(2) the father had the nationality of the United States at the time of the person's birth,

(3) the father (unless deceased) has agreed in writing to provide financial support for the person until the person reaches the age of 18 years, and

(4) while the person is under the age of 18 years—

(A) the person is legitimated under the law of the person's residence or domicile,

(B) the father acknowledges paternity of the person in writing under oath, or

(C) the paternity of the person is established by adjudication of a competent court.

(b) Except as otherwise provided in section 405 [8 USCS § 1101 note], the provisions of section 301(g) [8 USCS § 1401(g)] shall apply to a child born out of wedlock on or after January 13, 1941, and before December 24, 1952, as of the date of birth, if the paternity of such child is established at any time while such child is under the age of twenty-one years by legitimation.

(c) Notwithstanding the provision of subsection (a) of this section, a person born, after December 23, 1952, outside the United States and out of wedlock shall be held to have acquired at birth the nationality status of his mother, if the mother had the nationality of the United States at the time of such person's birth, and if the mother had previously been physically present in the United States or one of its outlying possessions for a continuous period of one year.

(June 27, 1952, ch 477, Title III, Ch 1, § 309, 66 Stat. 238; Dec. 29, 1981, P. L. 97-116, § 18 (l), 95 Stat. 1620; Nov. 14, 1986, P. L. 99-653, § 13, 100 Stat. 3657; Nov. 14, 1986, P. L. 99-653, § 13, 100 Stat. 3657 (as amended Oct. 24, 1988, P. L. 100-525, § 8(k), 102 Stat. 2617); Oct. 24, 1988, P. L. 100-525, § 9(r), 102 Stat. 2621.)(Act June 27, 1952, ch 477, Title III, Ch 1, § 309, 66 Stat. 238; Dec. 29, 1981, P. L. 97-116, § 18 (l), 95 Stat. 1620; Nov. 14, 1986, P. L. 99-653, § 13, 100 Stat. 3657; Nov. 14, 1986, P. L. 99-653, § 13, 100 Stat. 3657 (as amended Oct. 24, 1988, P. L. 100-525, § 8(k), 102 Stat. 2617); Oct. 24, 1988, P. L. 100-525, § 9(r), 102 Stat. 2621.)

NATIONALITY THROUGH NATURALIZATION

§ 1421. Naturalization authority

(a) Authority in Attorney General. The sole authority to naturalize persons as citizens of the United States is conferred upon the Attorney General.

(b) Court authority to administer oaths.

(1) Jurisdiction. Subject to section 337(c) [8 USCS § 1448(c)]—

(A) General jurisdiction. Except as provided in subparagraph (B), each applicant for naturalization may choose to have the oath of allegiance under section 337(a) [8 USCS § 1448(a)] administered by the Attorney General or by an eligible court described in paragraph (5). Each such eligible court shall have authority to administer such oath of allegiance to persons residing within the jurisdiction of the court.

(B) Exclusive authority. An eligible court described in paragraph (5) that wishes to have exclusive authority to administer the oath of allegiance under section 337(a) [8 USCS § 1448(a)] to persons residing within the jurisdiction of the court during the period described in paragraph (3)(A)(i) shall notify the Attorney General of such wish and, subject to this subsection, shall have such exclusive authority with respect to such persons during such period.

(2) Information.

(A) General information. In the case of a court exercising authority under paragraph (1), in accordance with procedures established by the Attorney General—

(i) the applicant for naturalization shall notify the Attorney General of the intent to be naturalized before the court, and

(ii) the Attorney General—

(I) shall forward to the court (not later than 10 days after the date of approval of an application for naturalization in the case of a court which has provided notice under paragraph (1)(B)) such information as may be necessary to administer the oath of allegiance under section 337(a) [8 USCS § 1448(a)], and

(II) shall promptly forward to the court a certificate of naturalization (prepared by the Attorney General).

(B) Assignment of individuals in the case of exclusive authority. If an eligible court has provided notice under paragraph (1)(B), the Attorney General shall inform each person (residing within the jurisdiction of the court), at the time of the approval of the person's application for naturalization, of—

(i) the court's exclusive authority to administer the oath of allegiance under section 337(a) [8 USCS § 1448(a)] to such a person during the period specified in paragraph (3)(A)(i), and

(ii) the date or dates (if any) under paragraph (3)(B) on which the court has scheduled oath administration ceremonies.

If more than one eligible court in an area has provided notice under paragraph (1)(B), the Attorney General shall permit the person, at the time of the approval, to choose the court to which the information will be forwarded for administration of the oath of allegiance under this section.

(3) Scope of exclusive authority.

(A) Limited period and advance notice required. The exclusive authority of a court to administer the oath of allegiance under paragraph (1)(B) shall apply with respect to a person—

(i) only during the 45-day period beginning on the date on which the Attorney General certifies to the court that an applicant is eligible for naturalization, and

(ii) only if the court has notified the Attorney General, prior to the date of certification of eligibility, of the day or days (during such 45-day period) on which the court has scheduled oath administration ceremonies.

(B) Authority of Attorney General. Subject to subparagraph (C), the Attorney General shall not administer the oath of allegiance to a person under subsection (a) during the period in which exclusive authority to administer the oath of allegiance may be exercised by an eligible court under this subsection with respect to that person.

(C) Waiver of exclusive authority. Notwithstanding the previous provisions of this paragraph, a court may waive exclusive authority to administer the oath of allegiance under section 337(a) [8 USCS § 1448(a)] to a person under this subsection if the Attorney General has not provided the court with the certification described in subparagraph (A)(i) within a reasonable time before the date scheduled by the court for oath administration ceremonies. Upon notification of a court's waiver of jurisdiction, the Attorney General shall promptly notify the applicant.

(4) Issuance of certificates. The Attorney General shall provide for the issuance of certificates of naturalization at the time of administration of the oath of allegiance.

(5) Eligible courts. For purposes of this section, the term "eligible court" means—

(A) a district court of the United States in any State, or

(B) any court of record in any State having a seal, a clerk, and jurisdiction in actions in law or equity, or law and equity, in which the amount in controversy is unlimited.

(c) Judicial review. A person whose application for naturalization under this title is denied, after a hearing before an immigration officer under section 336(a) [8 USCS § 1447(a)], may seek review of such denial before the United States district court or the district in which such person resides in accordance with chapter 7 of title 5, United States Code [5 USCS §§ 701 et seq.]. Such review shall be de novo, and the court shall make its own findings of fact and conclusions of law and shall, at the request of the petitioner, conduct a hearing de novo on the application.

(d) Sole procedure. A person may only be naturalized as a citizen of the United States in the manner and under the conditions prescribed in this title and not otherwise.

(June 27, 1952, ch 477, Title III, Ch 2, § 310, 66 Stat. 239; July 7, 1958, P. L. 85-508, § 25, 72 Stat. 351; March 18, 1959, P. L. 86-3, § 20(c), 73 Stat. 13; Sept. 26, 1961, P. L. 87-301, § 17, 75 Stat. 656; Oct. 24, 1988, P. L. 100-525, § 9(s), 102 Stat. 2621; Nov. 29, 1990, P. L. 101-649, Title IV, § 401(a), 104 Stat. 5038; Dec. 12, 1991, P. L. 102-232, Title I, § 102(a), Title III, § 305(a), 105 Stat. 1734, 1749; Oct. 25, 1994, P. L. 103-416, Title II, § 219(u), 108 Stat. 4318.)

§ 1422. Eligibility for naturalization

The right of a person to become a naturalized citizen of the United States shall not be denied or abridged because of race or sex or because such person is married.

(June 27, 1952, ch 477, Title III, Ch 2, § 311, 66 Stat. 239; Oct. 24, 1988, P. L. 100-525, § 9(t), 102 Stat. 2621.)

§ 1423. Requirements as to understanding the English language, history, principles and form of government of the United States

(a) No person except as otherwise provided in this title shall hereafter be naturalized as a citizen of the United States upon his own application who cannot demonstrate—

(1) an understanding of the English language, including an ability to read, write, and speak words in ordinary usage in the English language: *Provided,* That the requirements of this paragraph relating to ability to read and write shall be met if the applicant can read or write simple words and phrases to the end that a reasonable test of his literacy shall be made and that no extraordinary or unreasonable condition shall be imposed upon the applicant; and

(2) a knowledge and understanding of the fundamentals of the history, and of the principles and form of government, of the United States.

(b)(1) The requirements of subsection (a) shall not apply to any person who is unable because of physical or developmental disability or mental impairment to comply therewith.

(2) The requirement of subsection (a)(1) shall not apply to any person who, on the date of the filing of the person's application for naturalization as provided in section 334 [8 USCS § 1445], either—

(A) is over fifty years of age and has been living in the United States for periods totaling at least twenty years subsequent to a lawful admission for permanent residence, or

(B) is over fifty-five years of age and has been living in the United States for periods totaling at least fifteen years subsequent to a lawful admission for permanent residence.

(3) The Attorney General, pursuant to regulations, shall provide for special consideration, as determined by the Attorney General, concerning the requirement of subsection (a)(2) with respect to any person who, on the date of the filing of the person's application for naturalization as provided in section 334 [8 USCS § 1445], is over sixty-five years of age and has been living in the United States for periods totaling at least twenty years subsequent to a lawful admission for permanent residence.

(June 27, 1952, ch 477, Title III, Ch 2, § 312, 66 Stat. 239; Nov. 2, 1978, P. L. 95-579, § 3, 92 Stat. 2474; Nov. 29, 1990, P. L. 101-649, Title IV, § 403, 104 Stat. 5039; Dec. 12, 1991, P. L. 102-232, Title, § 305(m)(2), 105 Stat. 1750; Oct. 25, 1994, P. L. 103-416, Title I, § 108(a), 108 Stat. 4309.)

§ 1424. Prohibition upon the naturalization of persons opposed to government or law, or who favor totalitarian forms of government

(a) Notwithstanding the provisions of section 405(b) [8 USCS § 1101 note], no person shall hereafter be naturalized as a citizen of the United States—

(1) who advocates or teaches, or who is a member of or affiliated with any organization that advocates or teaches, opposition to all organized government; or

(2) who is a member of or affiliated with (A) the Communist Party of the United States; (B) any other totalitarian party of the United States; (C) the Communist Political Association; (D) the Communist or other totalitarian party of any state of the United States, of any foreign state, or of any political or geographical subdivision of any foreign state; (E) any section, subsidiary, branch, affiliate, or subdivision of any such association or party; or (F) the direct predecessors or successors of any such association or party, regardless of what name such group or organization may have used, may now bear, or may hereafter adopt, unless such alien establishes that he did not have knowledge or reason to believe at the time he became a member of or affiliated with such an organization (and did not thereafter and prior to the date upon which such

organization was so registered or so required to be registered have such knowledge or reason to believe) that such organization was a Communist-front organization; or

(3) who, although not within any of the other provisions of this section, advocates the economic, international, and governmental doctrines of world communism or the establishment in the United States of a totalitarian dictatorship, or who is a member of or affiliated with any organization that advocates the economic, international, and governmental doctrines of world communism or the establishment in the United States of a totalitarian dictatorship, either through its own utterances or through any written or printed publications issued or published by or with the permission or consent of or under authority of such organization or paid for by the funds of such organization; or

(4) who advocates or teaches or who is a member of or affiliated with any organization that advocates or teaches (A) the overthrow by force or violence or other unconstitutional means of the Government of the United States or of all forms of law; or (B) the duty, necessity, or propriety of the unlawful assaulting or killing of any officer or officers (either of specific individuals or of officers generally) of the Government of the United States or of any other organized government because of his or their official character; or (C) the unlawful damage, injury, or destruction of property; or (D) sabotage; or

(5) who writes or publishes or causes to be written or published, or who knowingly circulates, distributes, prints, or displays, or knowingly causes to be circulated, distributed, printed, published, or displayed, or who knowingly has in his possession for the purpose of circulation, publication, distribution, or display, any written or printed matter, advocating or teaching opposition to all organized government, or advocating (A) the overthrow by force, violence, or other unconstitutional means of the Government of the United States or of all forms of law; or (B) the duty, necessity, or propriety of the unlawful assaulting or killing of any officer or officers (either of specific individuals or of officers generally) of the Government of the United States or of any other organized government, because of his or their official character; or (C) the unlawful damage, injury, or destruction of property; or (D) sabotage; or (E) the economic, international, and governmental doctrines of world communism or the establishment in the United States of a totalitarian dictatorship; or

(6) who is a member of or affiliated with any organization that writes, circulates, distributes, prints, publishes, or displays, or causes to be written, circulated, distributed, printed, published, or displayed, or that has in its possession for the purpose of circulation, distribution, publication, issue, or display, any written or printed matter of the character described in subparagraph (5).

(b) The provisions of this section or of any other section of this Act shall not be construed as declaring that any of the organizations referred to in this section or in any other section of this Act do not advocate the overthrow of the Government of the United States by force, violence, or other unconstitutional means.

(c) The provisions of this section shall be applicable to any applicant for naturalization who at any time within a period of ten years immediately preceding the filing of the application for naturalization or after such filing and before taking the final oath of citizenship is, or has been found to be within any of the classes enumerated within this section, notwithstanding that at the time the application is filed he may not be included within such classes.

(d) Any person who is within any of the classes described in subsection (a) solely because of past membership in, or past affiliation with, a party or organization may be naturalized without regard to the provisions of subsection (c) if such person establishes that such membership or affiliation is or was involuntary, or occurred and terminated prior to the attainment by such alien of the age of sixteen years, or that such membership or affiliation is or was by operation of law, or was for purposes of obtaining employment, food rations, or other essentials of living and where necessary for such purposes.

(e) A person may be naturalized under this title [8 USCS §§ 1401 et seq.] without regard to the prohibitions in subsections (a)(2) and (c) of this section if the person—

(1) is otherwise eligible for naturalization;

(2) is within the class described in subsection (a)(2) solely because of past membership in, or past affiliation with, a party or organization described in that subsection;

(3) does not fall within any other of the classes described in that subsection; and

(4) is determined by the Director of Central Intelligence, in consultation with the Secretary of Defense when Department of Defense activities are relevant to the determination, and with the concurrence of the Attorney General and the Secretary of Homeland Security, to have made a contribution to the national security or to the national intelligence mission of the United States.

(June 27, 1952, ch 477, Title III, Ch 2, § 313, 66 Stat. 240; Oct. 24, 1988, P. L. 100-525, § 9(u), 102 Stat. 2621; Nov. 29, 1990, P. L. 101-649, Title IV, § 407(c)(1), 104 Stat. 5041; Dec. 12, 1991, P. L. 102-232, Title III, § 309(b)(13), 105 Stat. 1759; Oct. 25, 1994, P. L. 103-416, Title II, § 219(v), 108 Stat. 4318; Dec. 3, 1999, P. L. 106-120, Title III, § 306, 113 Stat. 1612; Dec. 13, 2003, P. L. 108-177, Title III, Subtitle E, § 373, 117 Stat. 2628.)

§ 1425. Ineligibility to naturalization of deserters from the armed forces

A person who, at any time during which the United States has been or shall be at war, deserted or shall desert the military, air, or naval forces of the United States, or who, having been duly enrolled, departed, or shall depart from the jurisdiction of the district in which enrolled, or who, whether or not having been duly enrolled, went or shall go beyond the limits of the United States, with intent to avoid any draft into the military, air, or naval service, lawfully ordered, shall, upon conviction thereof by a court martial or a court of competent jurisdiction, be permanently ineligible to become a citizen of the United States; and such deserters and evaders shall be forever incapable of holding any office of trust or of profit under the United States, or of exercising any rights of citizens thereof.

(June 27, 1952, ch 477, Title III, Ch 2, § 314, 66 Stat. 241.)

§ 1426. Citizenship denied alien relieved of service in armed forces because of alienage

(a) Permanent ineligibility. Notwithstanding the provisions of section 405(b) [8 USCS § 1101 note] but subject to subsection (c), any alien who applies or has applied for exemption or discharge from training or service in the Armed Forces or in the National Security Training Corps of the United States on the ground that he is an alien, and is or was relieved or discharged from such training or service on such ground, shall be permanently ineligible to become a citizen of the United States.

(b) Conclusiveness of records. The records of the Selective Service System or of the Department of Defense shall be conclusive as to whether an alien was relieved or discharged from such liability for training or service because he was an alien.

(c) Service in armed forces of foreign country. An alien shall not be ineligible for citizenship under this section or otherwise because of an exemption from training or service in the Armed Forces of the United States pursuant to the exercise of rights under a treaty, if before the time of the exercise of such rights the alien served in the Armed Forces of a foreign country of which the alien was a national.

(June 27, 1952, ch 477, Title III, Ch 2, § 315, 66 Stat. 242; Oct. 24, 1988, P. L. 100-525, § 9(v), 102 Stat. 2621; Nov. 29, 1990, P. L. 101-649, Title IV, § 404, 104 Stat. 5039.)

§ 1427. Requirements of naturalization

(a) Residence. No person, except as otherwise provided in this title, shall be naturalized unless such applicant, (1) immediately preceding the date of filing his application for naturalization has resided continuously, after being lawfully admitted for permanent residence, within the United States for at least five years and during the five years immediately preceding the date of filing his application has been physically present therein for periods totaling at least half of that time[,] and who has resided within the State or within the district of the Service in the United States in which the applicant filed the application for at least three months, (2) has resided continuously within the United States from the date of the application up to the time of admission to citizenship, and (3) during all the periods referred to in this subsection has been and still is a person of good moral character, attached to the principles of the Constitution of the United States, and well disposed to the good order and happiness of the United States.

(b) Absences. Absence from the United States of more than six months but less than one year during the period for which continuous residence is required for admission to citizenship, immediately preceding the date of filing the application for naturalization, or during the period between the date of filing the application and the date of any hearing under section 336(a) [8 USCS § 1447(a)], shall break the continuity of such residence, unless the applicant shall establish to the satisfaction of the Attorney General that he did not in fact abandon his residence in the United States during such period.

Absence from the United States for a continuous period of one year or more during the period for which continuous residence is required for admission to citizenship (whether preceding or subsequent to the filing of the application for naturalization) shall break the continuity of such residence, except that in the case of a person who has been physically present and residing in the United States, after being lawfully admitted for permanent residence, for an uninterrupted period of at least one year, and who thereafter is employed by or under contract with the Government of the United States or an American institution of research recognized as such by the Attorney General, or is employed by an American firm or corporation engaged in whole or in part in the development of foreign trade and commerce of the United States, or a subsidiary thereof more than 50 per centum of whose stock is owned by an American firm or corporation, or is employed by a public international organization of which the United States is a member by treaty or statute and by which the alien was not employed until after being lawfully admitted for permanent residence, no period of absence from the United States shall break the continuity of residence if—

(1) prior to the beginning of such period of employment (whether such period begins before or after his departure from the United States), but prior to the expiration of one year of continuous absence from the United States, the person has established to the satisfaction of the Attorney General that his absence from the United States for such period is to be on behalf of such Government, or for the purpose of carrying on scientific research on behalf of such institution, or to be engaged in the development of such foreign trade and commerce or whose residence abroad is necessary to the protection of the property rights in such countries in such firm or corporation, or to be employed by a public international organization of which the United States is a member by treaty or statute and by which the alien was not employed until after being lawfully admitted for permanent residence; and

(2) such person proves to the satisfaction of the Attorney General that his absence from the United States for such period has been for such purpose.

The spouse and dependent unmarried sons and daughters who are members of the household of a person who qualifies for the benefits of this subsection shall also be entitled to such benefits during the period for which they were residing abroad as dependent members of the household of the person.

(c) Physical presence. The granting of the benefits of subsection (b) of this section shall not relieve the applicant from the requirement of physical presence within the United States for the period specified in subsection (a) of this section, except in the case of those persons who are employed by, or under contract with, the Government of the United States. In the case of a person employed by or under contract with Central Intelligence Agency, the requirement in subsection (b) of an uninterrupted period of at least one year of physical presence in the United States may be complied with by such person at any time prior to filing an application for naturalization.

(d) Moral character. No finding by the Attorney General that the applicant is not deportable shall be accepted as conclusive evidence of good moral character.

(e) Determination. In determining whether the applicant has sustained the burden of establishing good moral character and the other qualifications for citizenship specified in subsection (a) of this section, the Attorney General shall not be limited to the applicant's conduct during the five years preceding the filing of the application, but may take into consideration as a basis for such determination the applicant's conduct and acts at any time prior to that period.

(f) Persons making extraordinary contributions to national security.

(1) Whenever the Director of Central Intelligence, the Attorney General and the Commissioner of Immigration determine that an applicant otherwise eligible for naturalization has made an extraordinary contribution to the national security of the United States or to the conduct of United States intelligence activities, the applicant may be naturalized without regard to the residence and physical presence requirements of this section, or to the prohibitions of section 313 of this Act [8 USCS § 1424], and no residence within a particular State or district of the Service in the United States shall be required: *Provided,* That the applicant has continuously resided in the United States for at least one year prior to naturalization: *Provided further,* That the provisions of this subsection shall not apply to any alien described in clauses (i) through (v) of section 208(b)(2)(A) of this Act [8 USCS § 1158(b)(2)(A)].

(2) An applicant for naturalization under this subsection may be administered the oath of allegiance under section 337(a) [8 USCS § 1448(a)] by any district court of the United States, without regard to the residence of the applicant. Proceedings under this subsection shall be conducted in a manner consistent with the protection of intelligence sources, methods and activities.

(3) The number of aliens naturalized pursuant to this subsection in any fiscal year shall not exceed five. The Director of Central Intelligence shall inform the Select Committee on Intelligence and the Committee on the Judiciary of the Senate and the Permanent Select Committee on Intelligence and the Committee on the Judiciary of the House of Representatives within a reasonable time prior to the filing of each application under the provisions of this subsection.

(June 27, 1952, ch 477, Title III, Ch 2, § 316, 66 Stat. 242; Dec. 29, 1981, P. L. 97-116, § 14, 95 Stat. 1619; Dec. 4, 1985, P. L. 99-169, Title VI, § 601, 99 Stat. 1007; Nov. 29, 1990, P. L. 101-649, Title IV, §§ 402, 407(c)(2), (d)(1), (e)(1), 104 Stat. 5038, 5041, 5046; Sept. 30, 1996, P. L. 104-208, Div C, Title III, Subtitle A, § 308(g)(7)(F), 110 Stat. 3009-624; Dec. 30, 2005, P. L. 109-149, Title V, § 518, 119 Stat. 2882.)

§ 1428. Temporary absence of persons performing religious duties

Any person who is authorized to perform the ministerial or priestly functions of a religious denomination having a bona fide organization within the United States, or any person who is engaged solely by a religious denomination or by an interdenominational mission organization having a bona fide organization within the United States as a missionary, brother, nun, or sister, who (1) has been lawfully admitted to the United States for permanent residence, (2) has at any time thereafter and before filing an application for naturalization been physically present and residing within the United States for an uninterrupted period of at least one year, and (3) has heretofore been or may hereafter be absent temporarily from the United States in connection with or for the purpose of performing the ministerial or priestly functions of such religious denomination, or serving as a missionary, brother, nun, or sister, shall be considered as being physically present and residing in the United States for the purpose of naturalization within the meaning of section 316(a) [8 USCS § 1427(a)], notwithstanding any such absence from the United States, if he shall in all other respects comply with the requirements of the naturalization law. Such person shall prove to the satisfaction of the Attorney General that his absence from the United States has been solely for the purpose of performing the ministerial or priestly functions of such religious denomination, or of serving as a missionary, brother, nun, or sister.

(June 27, 1952, ch 477, Title III, Ch 2, § 317, 66 Stat. 243; Nov. 29, 1990, P. L. 101-649, Title IV, § 407(c)(3), (d)(2), 104 Stat. 5041.)

§ 1429. Prerequisite to naturalization; burden of proof

Except as otherwise provided in this title, no person shall be naturalized unless he has been lawfully admitted to the United States for permanent residence in accordance with all applicable provisions of this Act. The burden of proof shall be upon such person to show that he entered the United States lawfully, and the time, place, and manner of such entry into the United States, but in presenting such proof he shall be entitled to the production of his immigrant visa, if any, or of other entry document, if any, and of any other documents and records, not considered by the Attorney General to be confidential, pertaining to such entry, in the custody of the Service. Notwithstanding the provisions of section 405(b) [8 USCS § 1101 note], and except as provided in sections 328 and 329 [8 USCS §§ 1439 and 1440] no person shall be naturalized against whom there is outstanding a final finding of deportability pursuant to a warrant of arrest issued under the provisions of this or any other Act; and no application for naturalization shall be considered by the Attorney General court if there is pending against the applicant a removal proceeding pursuant to a warrant of arrest issued under the provisions of this or any other Act: *Provided,* That the findings of the Attorney General in terminating removal proceedings or in canceling the removal of an alien pursuant to the provisions of this Act, shall not be deemed binding in any way upon the Attorney General with respect to the question of whether such person has established his eligibility for naturalization as required by this title.

(June 27, 1952, ch 477, Title III, Ch 2, § 318, 66 Stat. 244; Oct. 24, 1968, P. L. 90-633, § 4, 82 Stat. 1344; Nov. 29, 1990, P. L. 101-649, Title IV, § 407(c)(4), (d)(3), 104 Stat. 5041; Sept. 30, 1996, P. L. 104-208, Div C, Title III, Subtitle A, § 308(e)(1)(O), (15), 110 Stat. 3009-619, 3009-620.)

§ 1430. Married persons and employees of certain nonprofit organizations

(a) Any person whose spouse is a citizen of the United States, or any person who obtained status as a lawful permanent resident by reason of his or her status as a spouse or child of a United States citizen who battered him or her or subjected him or her to extreme cruelty, may be naturalized upon compliance with all the requirements of this title except the provisions of paragraph (1) of section 316(a) [8 USCS § 1427(a)(1)] if such person immediately preceding the date of filing his application for naturalization has resided continuously, after being lawfully admitted for permanent residence, within the United States for at least three years, and during the three years immediately preceding the date of filing his application has been living in marital union with the citizen spouse (except in the case of a person who has been battered or subjected to extreme cruelty by a United States citizen spouse or parent), who has been a United States citizen during all of such period, and has been physically present in the United States for periods totaling at least half of that time and has resided within the State or the district of the Service in the United States in which the applicant filed his application for at least three months.

(b) Any person, (1) whose spouse is (A) a citizen of the United States, (B) in the employment of the Government of the United States, or of an American institution of research recognized as such by the Attorney General, or of an American firm or corporation engaged in whole or in part in the development of foreign trade and commerce of the United States, or a subsidiary thereof, or of a public international organization in which the United States participates by treaty or statute, or is authorized to perform the ministerial or priestly functions of a religious denomination having a bona fide organization within the United States, or is engaged solely as a missionary by a religious denomination or by an interdenominational mission organization having a bona fide organization within the United States, and (C) regularly stationed abroad in such employment, and (2) who is in the United States at the time of naturalization, and (3) who declares before the Attorney General in good faith an intention to take up residence within the United States immediately upon the termination of such employment abroad of the citizen spouse, may be naturalized upon compliance with all the requirements of the naturalization laws, except that no prior residence or specified period of physical presence within the United States or within a State or a district of the Service in the United States or proof thereof shall be required.

(c) Any person who (1) is employed by a bona fide United States incorporated nonprofit organization which is principally engaged in conducting abroad through communications media the dissemination of information which significantly promotes United States interests abroad and which is recognized as such by the Attorney General, and (2) has been so employed continuously for a period of not less than five years after a lawful admission for permanent residence, and (3) who files his application for naturalization while so employed or within six months following the termination thereof, and (4) who is in the United States at the time of naturalization, and (5) who declares before the Attorney General in good faith an intention to take up residence within the United States immediately upon termination of such employment, may be naturalized upon compliance with all the requirements of this title except that no prior residence or specified period of physical presence within the United States or any State or district of the Service in the United States, or proof thereof, shall be required.

(d) Any person who is the surviving spouse, child, or parent of a United States citizen, whose citizen spouse, parent, or child dies during a period of honorable service in an active duty status in the Armed Forces of the United States and who, in the case of a surviving spouse, was living in marital union with the citizen spouse at the time of his death, may be naturalized upon compliance with all the requirements of this title except that no prior residence or specified physical presence within the United States, or within a State or a district of the Service in the United States shall be required. For purposes of this subsection, the terms "United States citizen" and "citizen spouse" include a person granted posthumous citizenship under section 329A [8 USCS § 1440-1].

(e)(1) In the case of a person lawfully admitted for permanent residence in the United States who is the spouse of a member of the Armed Forces of the United States, is authorized to accompany such member and reside abroad with the member pursuant to the member's official orders, and is so accompanying and residing with the member in marital union, such residence and physical presence abroad shall be treated, for purposes of subsection (a) and section 316(a) [8 USCS § 1427(a)], as residence and physical presence in—

(A) the United States; and

(B) any State or district of the Department of Homeland Security in the United States.

(2) Notwithstanding any other provision of law, a spouse described in paragraph (1) shall be eligible for naturalization proceedings overseas pursuant to section 1701(d) of the National Defense Authorization Act for Fiscal Year 2004 (Public Law 108-136; 8 U.S.C. 1443a).

(June 27, 1952, ch 477, Title III, Ch 2, § 319, 66 Stat. 244; Aug. 20, 1958, P. L. 85-697, § 2, 72 Stat. 687; Dec. 18, 1967, P. L. 90-215, § 1(a), 81 Stat. 661; June 29, 1968, P. L. 90-369, 82 Stat. 279; Nov. 29, 1990, P. L. 101-649, Title IV, §§ 407(b)(1), (c)(5), (d)(4), 104 Stat. 5040, 5041; Oct. 28, 2000, P. L. 106-386, Div B, Title V, § 1503(e), 114 Stat. 1522; Nov. 24, 2003, P. L. 108-136, Div A, Title XVII, § 1703(f)(1), (h), 117 Stat. 1695, 1696; Jan. 28, 2008, P. L. 110-181, Div A, Title VI, Subtitle G, § 674(a), 122 Stat. 185.)

§ 1431. Children born outside the United States and lawfully admitted for permanent residence; conditions under which citizenship automatically acquired

(a) In general. A child born outside of the United States automatically becomes a citizen of the United States when all of the following conditions have been fulfilled:

(1) At least one parent of the child is a citizen of the United States, whether by birth or naturalization.

(2) The child is under the age of eighteen years.

(3) The child is residing in the United States in the legal and physical custody of the citizen parent pursuant to a lawful admission for permanent residence.

(b) Adoption. Subsection (a) shall apply to a child adopted by a United States citizen parent if the child satisfies the requirements applicable to adopted children under section 101(b)(1) [8 USCS § 1101(b)(1)].

(c) Children of military and Federal Government personnel residing abroad. Subsection (a)(3) is deemed satisfied in the case of a child who is lawfully admitted for permanent residence in the United States if—

(1) the child is residing in the legal and physical custody of a citizen parent who is—

(A) stationed and residing abroad as an employee of the Government of the United States; or

(B) residing abroad in marital union with an employee of the Government of the United States who is stationed abroad; or

(2) the child is—

(A) residing in the legal and physical custody of a citizen parent who is—

(i) stationed and residing abroad as a member of the Armed Forces of the United States; or

(ii) authorized to accompany and reside abroad with a member of the Armed Forces of the United States pursuant to the member's official orders, and is so accompanying and residing abroad with the member in marital union; and

(B) authorized to accompany such member and reside abroad with the member pursuant to the member's official orders, and is so accompanying and residing with the member.

(d) Name and birth date. A Certificate of Citizenship or other Federal document issued or requested to be amended under this section shall reflect the child's name and date of birth as indicated on a State court order, birth certificate, certificate of foreign birth, certificate of birth abroad, or similar State vital records document issued by the child's State of residence in the United States after the child has been adopted or readopted in that State.

(June 27, 1952, ch 477, Title III, Ch 2, § 320, 66 Stat. 245; Oct. 5, 1978, P. L. 95-417, § 4, 92 Stat. 917; Dec. 29, 1981, P. L. 97-116, § 18(m), 95 Stat. 1620; Nov. 14, 1986, P. L. 99-653, § 14, 100 Stat. 3657; Oct. 24, 1988, P. L. 100-525, §§ 8(l), 9(w), 102 Stat. 2618, 2621; Oct. 30, 2000, P. L. 106-395, Title I, § 101(a), 114 Stat. 1631; Jan. 16, 2014, P. L. 113-74, § 2, 127 Stat. 1212; Mar. 26, 2020, P.L. 116-133, § 2(a), 134 Stat. 274.)

§ 1432. [Repealed]

§ 1433. Children born and residing outside the United States; conditions for acquiring certificate of citizenship

(a) Application by citizen parents; requirements. A parent who is a citizen of the United States (or, if the citizen parent has died during the preceding 5 years, a citizen grandparent or citizen legal guardian) may apply for naturalization on behalf of a child born outside of the United States who has not acquired citizenship automatically under section 320 [8 USCS § 1431]. The Attorney General shall issue a certificate of citizenship to such applicant upon proof, to the satisfaction of the Attorney General, that the following conditions have been fulfilled:

(1) At least one parent is (or, at the time of his or her death, was) a citizen of the United States, whether by birth or naturalization.

(2) The United States citizen parent—

(A) has (or, at the time of his or her death, had) been physically present in the United States or its outlying possessions for a period or periods totaling not less than five years, at least two of which were after attaining the age of fourteen years; or

(B) has (or, at the time of his or her death, had) a citizen parent who has been physically present in the United States or its outlying possessions for a period or periods totaling not less than five years, at least two of which were after attaining the age of fourteen years.

(3) The child is under the age of eighteen years.

(4) The child is residing outside of the United States in the legal and physical custody of the applicant (or, if the citizen parent is deceased, an individual who does not object to the application).

(5) The child is temporarily present in the United States pursuant to a lawful admission, and is maintaining such lawful status.

(b) Attainment of citizenship status; receipt of certificate. Upon approval of the application (which may be filed from abroad) and, except as provided in the last sentence of section 337(a) [8 USCS § 1448(a)], upon taking and subscribing before an officer of the Service within the United States to the oath of allegiance required by this Act of an applicant for naturalization, the child shall become a citizen of the United States and shall be furnished by the Attorney General with a certificate of citizenship.

(c) Adopted children. Subsections (a) and (b) shall apply to a child adopted by a United States citizen parent if the child satisfies the requirements applicable to adopted children under section 101(b)(1) [8 USCS § 1101(b)(1)].

(d) Overseas naturalization for military chil-

dren. In the case of a child of a member of the Armed Forces of the United States who is authorized to accompany such member and reside abroad with the member pursuant to the member's official orders, and is so accompanying and residing with the member—

(1) any period of time during which the member of the Armed Forces is residing abroad pursuant to official orders shall be treated, for purposes of subsection (a)(2)(A), as physical presence in the United States;

(2) subsection (a)(5) shall not apply; and

(3) the oath of allegiance described in subsection (b) may be subscribed to abroad pursuant to section 1701(d) of the National Defense Authorization Act for Fiscal Year 2004 (Public Law 108-136; 8 U.S.C. 1443a).

(June 27, 1952, ch 477, Title III, Ch 2, § 322, 66 Stat. 246; Oct. 5, 1978, P. L. 95-417, § 6, 92 Stat. 918; Dec. 29, 1981, P. L. 97-116, § 18(m), (n), 95 Stat. 1620, 1621; Nov. 14, 1986, P. L. 99-653, § 16, 100 Stat. 3658; Oct. 24, 1988, P. L. 100-525, § 8(l), 102 Stat. 2618; Nov. 29, 1990, P. L. 101-649, Title IV, § 407(b)(2), (c)(6), (d)(5), 104 Stat. 5040; Dec. 12, 1991, P. L. 102-232, Title III, § 305(m)(3), 105 Stat. 1750; Oct. 25, 1994, P. L. 103-416, Title I, § 102(a), 108 Stat. 4306; Dec. 7, 1999, P. L. 106-139, § 1(b)(2), 113 Stat. 1697; Oct. 30, 2000, P. L. 106-395, Title I, § 102(a), 114 Stat. 1632; Nov. 2, 2002, P. L. 107-273, Div C, Title I, Subtitle A, § 11030B, 116 Stat. 1837; Jan. 28, 2008, P. L. 110-181, Div A, Title VI, Subtitle G, § 674(b), 122 Stat. 186.)

§ 1434. [Repealed]

§ 1435. Former citizens regaining citizenship

(a) Requirements. Any person formerly a citizen of the United States who (1) prior to September 22, 1922, lost United States citizenship by marriage to an alien, or by the loss of United States citizenship of such person's spouse, or (2) on or after September 22, 1922, lost United States citizenship by marriage to an alien ineligible to citizenship, may if no other nationality was acquired by an affirmative act of such person other than by marriage be naturalized upon compliance with all requirements of this title, except—

(1) no period of residence or specified period of physical presence within the United States or within the State or district of the Service in the United States where the application is filed shall be required; and

(2) the application need not set forth that it is the intention of the applicant to reside permanently within the United States.

Such person, or any person who was naturalized in accordance with the provisions of section 317(a) of the Nationality Act of 1940, shall have, from and after her naturalization, the status of a native-born or naturalized citizen of the United States, whichever status existed in the case of such person prior to the loss of citizenship: *Provided,* That nothing contained herein or in any other provision of law shall be construed as conferring United States citizenship retroactively upon such person, or upon any person who was naturalized in accordance with the provisions of section 317(a) of the Nationality Act of 1940, during any period in which such person was not a citizen.

(b) Additional requirements. No person who is otherwise eligible for naturalization in accordance with the provisions of subsection (a) of this section shall be naturalized unless such person shall establish to the satisfaction of the Attorney General that she has been a person of good moral character, attached to the principles of the Constitution of the United States, and well disposed to the good order and happiness of the United States for a period of not less than five years immediately preceding the date of filing an application for naturalization and up to the time of admission to citizenship, and, unless she has resided continuously in the United States since the date of her marriage, has been lawfully admitted for permanent residence prior to filing her petition for naturalization.

(c) Oath of allegiance.

(1) A woman who was a citizen of the United States at birth and (A) who has or is believed to have lost her United States citizenship solely by reason of her marriage prior to September 22, 1922, to an alien, or by her marriage on or after such date to an alien ineligible to citizenship, (B) whose marriage to such alien shall have terminated subsequent to January 12, 1941, and (C) who has not acquired by an affirmative act other than by marriage any other nationality, shall, from and after taking the oath of allegiance required by section 337 of this title [8 USCS § 1448], be a citizen of the United States and have the status of a citizen of the United States by birth, without filing an application for naturalization, and notwithstanding any of the other provisions of this title except the provisions of section 313 [8 USCS § 1424]: *Provided,* That nothing contained herein or in any other provision of law shall be construed as conferring United States citizenship retroactively upon such person, or upon any person who was naturalized in accordance with the provisions of section 317(b) of the Nationality Act of 1940, during any period in which such person was not a citizen.

(2) Such oath of allegiance may be taken abroad before a diplomatic or consular officer of the United States, or in the United States before the Attorney General or the judge or clerk of a court described in section 310(b) [8 USCS § 1421(b)].

(3) Such oath of allegiance shall be entered in the records of the appropriate embassy, legation, consulate, court, or the Attorney General, and upon demand, a certified copy of the proceedings, including a copy of the oath administered, under the seal of the embassy, legation, consulate, court, or the Attorney General, shall be delivered to such woman at a cost not exceeding $5, which certified copy shall be evidence of the facts stated therein before any court of record or judicial tribunal and in any department or agency of the Government of the United States.

(d) Persons losing citizenship for failure to meet physical presence retention requirement.

(1) A person who was a citizen of the United States at birth and lost such citizenship for failure to meet the physical presence retention requirements under section 301(b) [8 USCS § 1401(b)] (as in effect before October 10, 1978), shall, from and after taking the oath of allegiance required by section 337 [8 USCS § 1448] be a citizen of the United States and have the status of a citizen of the United States by birth, without filing an

application for naturalization, and notwithstanding any of the other provisions of this title except the provisions of section 313 [8 USCS § 1424]. Nothing in this subsection or any other provision of law shall be construed as conferring United States citizenship retroactively upon such person during any period in which such person was not a citizen.

(2) The provisions of paragraphs (2) and (3) of subsection (c) shall apply to a person regaining citizenship under paragraph (1) in the same manner as they apply under subsection (c)(1).

(June 27, 1952, ch 477, Title III, Ch 2, § 324, 66 Stat. 246; Oct. 24, 1988, P. L. 100-525, § 9(x), 102 Stat. 2621; Nov. 29, 1990, P. L. 101-649, Title IV, § 407(b)(3), (c)(7), (d)(6), 104 Stat. 5040; Oct. 25, 1994, P. L. 103-416, Title I, § 103(a), 108 Stat. 4307.)

§ 1436. Nationals but not citizens; residence within outlying possessions

A person not a citizen who owes permanent allegiance to the United States, and who is otherwise qualified, may, if he becomes a resident of any State, be naturalized upon compliance with the applicable requirements of this title, except that in applications for naturalization filed under the provisions of this section residence and physical presence within the United States within the meaning of this title shall include residence and physical presence within any of the outlying possessions of the United States.

(June 27, 1952, ch 477, Title III, Ch 2, § 325, 66 Stat. 248; Nov. 29, 1990, P. L. 101-649, Title IV, § 407(c)(8), 104 Stat. 5041.)

§ 1437. Resident Philippine citizens excepted from certain requirements

Any person who (1) was a citizen of the Commonwealth of the Philippines on July 2, 1946, (2) entered the United States prior to May 1, 1934, and (3) has, since such entry, resided continuously in the United States shall be regarded as having been lawfully admitted to the United States for permanent residence for the purpose of applying for naturalization under this title.

(June 27, 1952, ch 477, Title III, Ch 2, § 326, 66 Stat. 248; Nov. 29, 1990, P. L. 101-649, Title IV, § 407(c)(9), 104 Stat. 5041.)

§ 1438. Former citizens losing citizenship by entering the armed forces of foreign countries during World War II

(a) Requirements; oath; certified copies of oath. Any person who, (1) during World War II and while a citizen of the United States, served in the military, air, or naval forces of any country at war with a country with which the United States was at war after December 7, 1941, and before September 2, 1945, and (2) has lost United States citizenship by reason of entering or serving in such forces, or taking an oath or obligation for the purpose of entering such forces, may, upon compliance with all the provisions of title III of this Act, except section 316(a) [8 USCS § 1427(a)], and except as otherwise provided in subsection (b), be naturalized by taking before the Attorney General or before a court described in section 310(b) [8 USCS § 1421(b)] the oath required by section 337 of this title [8 USCS § 1448]. Certified copies of such oath shall be sent by such court to the Department of State and to the Department of Justice and by the Attorney General to the Secretary of State.

(b) Exceptions. No person shall be naturalized under subsection (a) of this section unless he—

(1) is, and has been for a period of at least five years immediately preceding taking the oath required in subsection (a), a person of good moral character, attached to the principles of the Constitution of the United States and well disposed to the good order and happiness of the United States; and

(2) has been lawfully admitted to the United States for permanent residence and intends to reside permanently in the United States.

(c) Status. Any person naturalized in accordance with the provisions of this section, or any person who was naturalized in accordance with the provisions of section 323 of the Nationality Act of 1940, shall have, from and after such naturalization, the status of a native-born or naturalized, citizen of the United States, whichever status existed in the case of such person prior to the loss of citizenship: *Provided,* That nothing contained herein, or in any other provision of law, shall be construed as conferring United States citizenship retroactively upon any such person during any period in which such person was not a citizen.

(d) Span of World War II. For the purpose of this section, World War II shall be deemed to have begun on September 1, 1939, and to have terminated on September 2, 1945.

(e) Inapplicability to certain persons. This section shall not apply to any person who during World War II served in the armed forces of a country while such country was at war with the United States.

(June 27, 1952, ch 477, Title III, Ch 2, § 327, 66 Stat. 248; Nov. 29, 1990, P. L. 101-649, Title IV, § 407(d)(7), 104 Stat. 5042.)

§ 1439. Naturalization through service in the armed forces

(a) Requirements. A person who has served honorably at any time in the armed forces of the United States for a period or periods aggregating one year, and who, if separated from such service, was never separated except under honorable conditions, may be naturalized without having resided, continuously immediately preceding the date of filing such person's application, in the United States for at least five years, and in the State or district of the Service in the United States in which the application for naturalization is filed for at least three months, and without having been physically present in the United States for any specified period, if such petition is filed while the applicant is still in the service or within six months after the termination of such service.

(b) Exceptions. A person filing an applicant under subsection (a) of this section shall comply in all other respects with the requirements of this title, except that—

(1) no residence within a State or district of the Service in the United States shall be required;

(2) notwithstanding section 318 [8 USCS § 1429] insofar as it relates to deportability, such applicant may be naturalized immediately if the applicant be then actually in the Armed Forces of the United States, and if prior to the filing of the applicant shall have appeared before and been examined by a representative of the Service;

(3) the applicant shall furnish to the Secretary of Homeland Security, prior to any hearing upon his application, a certified statement from the proper executive department for each period of his service upon which he relies for the benefits of this section, clearly showing that such service was honorable and that no discharges from service, including periods of service not relied upon by him for the benefits of this section, were other than honorable (the certificate or certificates herein provided for shall be conclusive evidence of such service and discharge); and

(4) notwithstanding any other provision of law, no fee shall be charged or collected from the applicant for filing the application, or for the issuance of a certificate of naturalization upon being granted citizenship, and no clerk of any State court shall charge or collect any fee for such services unless the laws of the State require such charge to be made, in which case nothing more than the portion of the fee required to be paid to the State shall be charged or collected.

(c) Periods when not in service. In the case such applicant's service was not continuous, the applicant's residence in the United States and State or district of the Service in the United States, good moral character, attachment to the principles of the Constitution of the United States, and favorable disposition toward the good order and happiness of the United States, during any period within five years immediately preceding the date of filing such petition between the periods of applicant's service in the Armed Forces, shall be alleged in the application filed under the provisions of subsection (a) of this section, and proved at any hearing thereon. Such allegation and proof shall also be made as to any period between the termination of petitioner's service and the filing of the application for naturalization.

(d) Residence requirements. The applicant shall comply with the requirements of section 316(a) of this title [8 USCS § 1427(a)], if the termination of such service has been more than six months preceding the date of filing the application for naturalization, except that such service within five years immediately preceding the date of filing such application shall be considered as residence and physical presence within the United States.

(e) Moral character. Any such period or periods of service under honorable conditions, and good moral character, attachment to the principles of the Constitution of the United States, and favorable disposition toward the good order and happiness of the United States, during such service, shall be proved by duly authenticated copies of the records of the executive departments having custody of the records of such service, and such authenticated copies of records shall be accepted in lieu of compliance with the provisions of section 316(a) [8 USCS § 1427(a)].

(f) Revocation. Citizenship granted pursuant to this section may be revoked in accordance with section 340 [8 USCS § 1451] if the person is separated from the Armed Forces under other than honorable conditions before the person has served honorably for a period or periods aggregating five years. Such ground for revocation shall be in addition to any other provided by law, including the grounds described in section 340 [8 USCS § 1451]. The fact that the naturalized person was separated from the service under other than honorable conditions shall be proved by a duly authenticated certification from the executive department under which the person was serving at the time of separation. Any period or periods of service shall be proved by duly authenticated copies of the records of the executive departments having custody of the records of such service.

(g), (h) [Repealed]

(June 27, 1952, ch 477, Title III, Ch 2, § 328, 66 Stat. 249; Oct. 24, 1968, P. L. 90-633, § 5, 82 Stat. 1344; Dec. 29, 1981, P. L. 97-116, § 15(e), 95 Stat. 1619; Nov. 29, 1990, P. L. 101-649, Title IV, § 407(b)(4), (c)(10), (d)(8), 104 Stat. 5040; Dec. 12, 1991, P. L. 102-232, Title III, § 305(c), 105 Stat. 1750; Nov. 24, 2003, P. L. 108-136, Div A, Title XVII, § 1701(a), (b)(1), (c)(1)(A), (f), 117 Stat. 1691, 1692; Oct. 9, 2008, P. L. 110-382, §§ 3(a), 4, 122 Stat. 4088, 4089.)

§ 1440. Naturalization through active-duty service in the Armed Forces during World War I, World War II, Korean hostilities, Vietnam hostilities, or other periods of military hostilities

(a) Requirements. Any person who, while an alien or a noncitizen national of the United States, has served honorably as a member of the Selected Reserve of the Ready Reserve or in an active-duty status in the military, air, or naval forces of the United States during either World War I or during a period beginning September 1, 1939, and ending December 31, 1946, or during a period beginning June 25, 1950, and ending July 1, 1955, or during a period beginning February 28, 1961, and ending on a date designated by the President by Executive order as of the date of termination of the Vietnam hostilities, or thereafter during any other period which the President by Executive order shall designate as a period in which Armed Forces of the United States are or were engaged in military operations involving armed conflict with a hostile foreign force, and who, if separated from such service, was separated under honorable conditions, may be naturalized as provided in this section if (1) at the time of enlistment, reenlistment, extension of enlistment, or induction such person shall have been in the United States, the Canal Zone, American Samoa, or Swains Island, or on board a public vessel owned or operated by the United States for noncommercial service, whether or not he has been lawfully admitted to the United States for permanent residence, or (2) at any time subsequent to enlistment or induction such person shall have been lawfully admitted to the United States for permanent residence. The executive department under which such person served shall determine whether persons have served honorably in an active-duty status, and whether separation from such service was under honorable conditions: *Provided, however,* That no person who is or has been separated from such service on account of alienage, or who was a conscientious objector who performed no military, air, or naval duty whatever or refused to wear the uniform, shall be regarded as having served honorably or having been separated under honorable conditions for the purposes of this section. No period of service in the Armed Forces shall be made the basis of an application for naturalization under this section if the applicant has previously been naturalized on the basis of the same period of service.

(b) Exceptions. A person filing an application under subsection (a) of this section shall comply in all other respects with the requirements of this title, except that—

(1) he may be naturalized regardless of age, and notwithstanding the provisions of section 318 [8 USCS § 1429] as they relate to deportability and the provisions of section 331 [8 USCS § 1442];

(2) no period of residence or specified period of physical presence within the United States or any State or district of the Service in the United States shall be required;

(3) service in the military, air, or naval forces of the United States shall be proved by a duly authenticated certification from the executive department under which the applicant served or is serving, which shall state whether the applicant served honorably in active duty status during either World War I or during a period beginning September 1, 1939, and ending December 31, 1946 or during a period beginning June 25, 1950, and ending July 1, 1955, or during a period beginning February 28, 1961, and ending on a date designated by the President by Executive order as the date of termination of the Vietnam hostilities, or thereafter during any other period which the President by Executive order shall designate as a period in which Armed Forces of the United States are or were engaged in military operations involving armed conflict with a hostile foreign force, and was separated from such service under honorable conditions; and

(4) notwithstanding any other provision of law, no fee shall be charged or collected from the applicant for filing a petition for naturalization or for the issuance of a certificate of naturalization upon citizenship being granted to the applicant, and no clerk of any State court shall charge or collect any fee for such services unless the laws of the State require such charge to be made, in which case nothing more than the portion of the fee required to be paid to the State shall be charged or collected.

(c) Revocation. Citizenship granted pursuant to this section may be revoked in accordance with section 340 [8 USCS § 1451] if the person is separated from the Armed Forces under other than honorable conditions before the person has served honorably for a period or periods aggregating five years. Such ground for revocation shall be in addition to any other provided by law, including the grounds described in section 340 [8 USCS § 1451]. The fact that the naturalized person was separated from the service under other than honorable conditions shall be proved by a duly authenticated certification from the executive department under which the person was serving at the time of separation. Any period or periods of service shall be proved by duly authenticated copies of the records of the executive departments having custody of the records of such service.

(June 27, 1952, ch 477, Title III, Ch 2, § 329, 66 Stat. 250; Sept. 26, 1961, P. L. 87-301, § 8, 75 Stat. 654; Oct. 24, 1968, P. L. 90-633, §§ 1, 2, 6, 82 Stat. 1343, 1344; Dec. 29, 1981, P. L. 97-116, § 15(a), 95 Stat. 1619; Oct. 24, 1988, P. L. 100-525, § 9(y), 102 Stat. 2621; Nov. 29, 1990, P. L. 101-649, Title IV, § 407(b)(5), (c)(11), 104 Stat. 5040, 5041; Dec. 12, 1991, P. L. 102-232, Title III, § 305(b), 105 Stat. 1749; Nov. 18, 1997, P. L. 105-85, Div A, Title X, Subtitle G, § 1080(a), 111 Stat. 1916; Nov. 24, 2003, P. L. 108-136, Div A, Title XVII, §§ 1701(b)(2), (c)(1)(B), 1702, 117 Stat. 1691, 1692, 1693.)

§ 1440-1. Posthumous citizenship through death while on active-duty service in the armed forces during World War I, World War II, the Korean hostilities, the Vietnam hostilities, or in other periods of military hostilities

(a) Permitting granting of posthumous citizenship. Notwithstanding any other provision of this title, the Secretary of Homeland Security shall provide, in accordance with this section, for the granting of posthumous citizenship at the time of death to a person described in subsection (b) if the Secretary of Homeland Security approves an application for that posthumous citizenship under subsection (c).

(b) Noncitizens eligible for posthumous citizenship. A person referred to in subsection (a) is a person who, while an alien or a noncitizen national of the United States—

(1) served honorably in an active-duty status in the military, air, or naval forces of the United States during any period described in the first sentence of section 329(a) [8 USCS § 1440(a)],

(2) died as a result of injury or disease incurred in or aggravated by that service, and

(3) satisfied the requirements of clause (1) or (2) of the first sentence of section 329(a) [8 USCS § 1440(a)].

The executive department under which the person so served shall determine whether the person satisfied the requirements of paragraphs (1) and (2).

(c) Requests for posthumous citizenship.

(1) In general. A request for the granting of posthumous citizenship to a person described in subsection (b) may be filed on behalf of that person—

(A) upon locating the next-of-kin, and if so requested by the next-of-kin, by the Secretary of Defense or the Secretary's designee with the Bureau of Citizenship and Immigration Services in the Department of Homeland Security immediately upon the death of that person; or

(B) by the next-of-kin.

(2) Approval. The Director of the Bureau of Citizenship and Immigration Services shall approve a request for posthumous citizenship filed by the next-of-kin in accordance with paragraph (1)(B) if—

(A) the request is filed not later than 2 years after—

(i) the date of enactment of this section; or

(ii) the date of the person's death;

whichever date is later;

(B) the request is accompanied by a duly authenticated certificate from the executive department under which the person served which states that the person satisfied the requirements of paragraphs (1) and (2) of subsection (b); and

(C) the Director finds that the person satisfied the requirement of subsection (b)(3).

(d) Documentation of posthumous citizenship. If the Director of the Bureau of Citizenship and Immigration Services approves the request referred to in subsection (c), the Director shall send to the next-of-kin of the person who is granted citizenship, a suitable document which states that the United States considers the person to have been a citizen of the United States at the time of the person's death.

(June 27, 1952, ch 477, § 329A, as added March 6, 1990, P. L. 101-249, § 2(a), 104 Stat. 94; Nov. 2, 2002, P. L. 107-273, Div C, Title I, Subtitle A, § 11030(b), 116 Stat. 1836; Nov. 24, 2003, P. L. 108-136, Div A, Title XVII, §§ 17032(g), 1704, 117 Stat. 1695, 1696.)

§§ 1440a–1440d. [Omitted]

§ 1440e. Exemption from naturalization fees for aliens naturalized through service during Vietnam hostilities or other subsequent period of military hostilities; report by clerks of courts to Attorney General

Notwithstanding any other provision of law, no clerk of a United States court shall charge or collect a naturalization fee from an alien who has served in the military, air, or naval forces of the United States during a period beginning February 28, 1961, and ending on the date designated by the President by Executive order as the date of termination of the Vietnam hostilities, or thereafter during any other period which the President by Executive order shall designate as a period in which Armed Forces of the United States are or were engaged in military operations involving armed conflict with a hostile foreign force, and who is applying for naturalization during such periods under section 329 of the Immigration and Nationality Act [8 USCS § 1440], as amended by this Act, for filing a petition for naturalization or issuing a certificate of naturalization upon his admission to citizenship, and no clerk of any State court shall charge or collect any fee for such services unless the laws of the State require such charge to be made, in which case nothing more than the portion of the fee required to be paid to the State shall be charged or collected. A report of all transactions under this section shall be made to the Attorney General as in the case of other reports required of clerks of courts by title III of the Immigration and Nationality Act.

(Oct. 24, 1968, P. L. 90-633, § 3, 82 Stat. 1344.)

§ 1440f. Fingerprints and other biometric information for members of the United States Armed Forces

(a) In general. Notwithstanding any other provision of law, including section 552a of title 5, United States Code (commonly referred to as the "Privacy Act of 1974"), the Secretary of Homeland Security shall use the fingerprints provided by an individual at the time the individual enlisted in the United States Armed Forces, or at the time the individual filed an application for adjustment of status, to satisfy any requirement for background and security checks in connection with an application for naturalization if—

(1) the individual may be naturalized pursuant to section 328 or 329 of the Immigration and Nationality Act (8 U.S.C. 1439, 1440);

(2) the individual was fingerprinted and provided other biometric information in accordance with the requirements of the Department of Defense at the time the individual enlisted in the United States Armed Forces;

(3) the individual—

(A) submitted an application for naturalization not later than 24 months after the date on which the individual enlisted in the United States Armed Forces; or

(B) provided the required biometric information to the Department of Homeland Security through a United States Citizenship and Immigration Services Application Support Center at the time of the individual's application for adjustment of status if filed not later than 24 months after the date on which the individual enlisted in the United States Armed Forces; and

(4) the Secretary of Homeland Security determines that the biometric information provided, including fingerprints, is sufficient to conduct the required background and security checks needed for the applicant's naturalization application.

(b) More timely and effective adjudication. Nothing in this section precludes an individual described in subsection (a) from submitting a new set of biometric information, including fingerprints, to the Secretary of Homeland Security with an application for naturalization. If the Secretary determines that submitting a new set of biometric information, including fingerprints, would result in more timely and effective adjudication of the individual's naturalization application, the Secretary shall—

(1) inform the individual of such determination; and

(2) provide the individual with a description of how to submit such biometric information, including fingerprints.

(c) Cooperation. The Secretary of Homeland Security, in consultation with the Secretary of Defense, shall determine the format of biometric information, including fingerprints, acceptable for usage under subsection (a). The Secretary of Defense, or any other official having custody of the biometric information, including fingerprints, referred to in subsection (a), shall—

(1) make such prints available, without charge, to the Secretary of Homeland Security for the purpose described in subsection (a); and

(2) otherwise cooperate with the Secretary of Homeland Security to facilitate the processing of applications for naturalization under subsection (a).

(d) Electronic transmission. Not later than one year after the date of the enactment of this Act [enacted June 26, 2008], the Secretary of Homeland Security shall, in coordination with the Secretary of Defense and the Director of the Federal Bureau of Investigation, implement procedures that will ensure the rapid electronic transmission of biometric information, including fingerprints, from existing repositories of such information needed for military personnel applying for naturalization as described in subsection (a) and that will safeguard privacy and civil liberties.

(e) Centralization and expedited processing.

(1) Centralization. The Secretary of Homeland Security shall centralize the data processing of all applications for naturalization filed by members of the United States Armed Forces on active duty serving abroad.

(2) Expedited processing. The Secretary of Homeland Security, the Director of the Federal Bureau of Investigation, and the Director of National Intelligence shall take appropriate actions to ensure that applications for naturalization by members of the United States Armed Forces described in paragraph (1), and associated background checks, receive expedited processing and are adjudicated within 180 days of the receipt of responses to all background checks.

(June 26, 2008, P. L. 110-251, § 2, 122 Stat. 2319.)

§ 1440g. Provision of information on military naturalization

(a) In general. Not later than 30 days after the effective date of any modification to a regulation related to naturalization under section 328 or 329 of the Immigration and Nationality Act (8 U.S.C. 1439, 1440), the Secretary of Homeland Security shall make appropriate updates to the Internet sites maintained by the Secretary to reflect such modification.

(b) Sense of Congress. It is the sense of Congress that the Secretary of Homeland Security, not later than 180 days after each effective date described in subsection (a), should make necessary updates to the appropriate application forms of the Department of Homeland Security.

(June 26, 2008, P. L. 110-251, § 3, 122 Stat. 2320.)

§ 1441. Constructive residence through service on certain United States vessels

Any periods of time during all of which a person who was previously lawfully admitted for permanent residence has served honorably or with good conduct, in any capacity other than as a member of the Armed Forces of the United States, (A) on board a vessel operated by the United States, or an agency thereof, the full legal and equitable title to which is in the United States; or (B) on board a vessel whose home port is in the United States, and (i) which is registered under the laws of the United States, or (ii) the full legal and equitable title to which is in a citizen of the United States, or a corporation organized under the laws of any of the several States of the United States, shall be deemed residence and physical presence within the United States within the meaning of section 316(a) of this title [8 USCS § 1427(a)], if such service occurred within five years immediately preceding the date such person shall file an application for naturalization. Service on vessels described in clause (A) of this section shall be proved by duly authenticated copies of the records of the executive departments or agency having custody of the records of such service. Service on vessels described in clause (B) of this subsection may be proved by certificates from the masters of such vessels.

(June 27, 1952, ch 477, Title III, Ch 2, § 330, 66 Stat. 251; Oct. 24, 1988, P. L. 100-525, § 9(z), 102 Stat. 2621; Nov. 29, 1990, P. L. 101-649, Title IV, § 407(c)(12), 104 Stat. 5041; Dec. 12, 1991, P. L. 102-232, Title III, § 305(m)(5), 105 Stat. 1750.)

§ 1442. Alien enemies

(a) Naturalization under specified conditions. An alien who is a native, citizen, subject, or denizen of any country, state, or sovereignty with which the United States is at war may, after his loyalty has been fully established upon investigation by the Attorney General, be naturalized as a citizen of the United States if such alien's application for naturalization shall be pending at the beginning of the state of war and the applicant is otherwise entitled to admission to citizenship.

(b) Procedure. An alien embraced within this section shall not have his application for naturalization considered or heard except after 90 days' notice to the Attorney General to be considered at the examination or hearing, and the Attorney General's objection to such consideration shall cause the application to be continued from time to time for so long as the Attorney General may require.

(c) Exceptions from classification. The Attorney General may, in his discretion, upon investigation fully establishing the loyalty of any alien enemy who did not have an application for naturalization pending at the beginning of the state of war, except such alien enemy from the classification of alien enemy for the purposes of this title, and thereupon such alien shall have the privilege of filing an application for naturalization.

(d) Effect of cessation of hostilities. An alien who is a native, citizen, subject, or denizen of any country, state, or sovereignty with which the United States is at war shall cease to be an alien enemy within the meaning of this section upon the determination by proclamation of the President, or by concurrent resolution of the Congress, that hostilities between the United States and such country, state, or sovereignty have ended.

(e) Apprehension and removal. Nothing contained herein shall be taken or construed to interfere with or prevent the apprehension and removal, consistent with law, of any alien enemy at any time prior to the actual naturalization of such alien.

(June 27, 1952, ch 477, Title III, Ch 2, § 331, 66 Stat. 252; Nov. 29, 1990, P. L. 101-649, Title IV, § 407(c)(13), (d)(9), (e)(2), 104 Stat. 5041, 5042, 5046.)

§ 1443. Administration

(a) Rules and regulations governing examination of applicants. The Attorney General shall make such rules and regulations as may be necessary to carry into effect the provisions of this chapter and is authorized to prescribe the scope and nature of the examination of applicants for naturalization as to their admissibility to citizenship. Such examination shall be limited to inquiry concerning the applicant's residence, physical presence in the United States, good moral character, understanding of and attachment to the fundamental principles of the Constitution of the United States, ability to read, write, and speak English, and other qualifications to become a naturalized citizen as required by law, and shall be uniform throughout the United States.

(b) Instruction in citizenship. The Attorney General is authorized to promote instruction and training in citizenship responsibilities of applicants for naturalization including the sending of names of candidates for naturalization to the public schools, preparing and distributing citizenship textbooks to such candidates as are receiving instruction in preparation for citizenship within or under the supervision of the public schools, preparing and distributing monthly an immigration and naturalization bulletin and securing the aid of and cooperating with official State and national organizations, including those concerned with vocational education.

(c) Prescription of forms. The Attorney General shall prescribe and furnish such forms as may be required to give effect to the provisions of this chapter, and only such forms as may be so provided shall be legal. All certificates of naturalization and of citizenship shall be printed on safety paper and shall be consecutively numbered in separate series.

(d) Administration of oaths and depositions. Employees of the Service may be designated by the Attorney General to administer oaths and to take depositions without charge in matters relating to the administration of the naturalization and citizenship laws. In cases where there is a likelihood of unusual delay or of hardship, the Attorney General may, in his discretion, authorize such depositions to be taken before a postmaster without charge, or before a notary public or other person authorized to administer oaths for general purposes.

(e) Issuance of certificate of naturalization or citizenship. A certificate of naturalization or of citizenship issued by the Attorney General under the authority of this title shall have the same effect in all courts, tribunals, and public offices of the United States, at home and abroad, of the District of Columbia, and of each State, Territory, and outlying possession of the United States, as a certificate of naturalization or of citizenship issued by a court having naturalization jurisdiction.

(f) Copies of records. Certifications and certified copies of all papers, documents, certificates, and records required or authorized to be issued, used, filed, recorded, or kept under any and all provisions of this Act shall be admitted in evidence equally with the originals in any and all cases and proceedings under this Act and in all cases and proceedings in which the originals thereof might be admissible as evidence.

(g) Furnished quarters for photographic studios. The officers in charge of property owned or leased by the Government are authorized, upon the recommendation of the Attorney General, to provide quarters, without payment of rent, in any building occupied by the Service, for a photographic studio, operated by welfare organizations without profit and solely for the benefit of persons seeking to comply with requirements under the immigration and nationality laws. Such studio shall be under the supervision of the Attorney General.

(h) Public education regarding naturalization benefits. In order to promote the opportunities and responsibilities of United States citizenship, the Attorney General shall broadly distribute information concerning the benefits which persons may receive under this title and the requirements to obtain such benefits. In carrying out this subsection, the Attorney General shall seek the assistance of appropriate community groups, private voluntary agencies, and other relevant organizations. There are authorized to be appropriated (for each fiscal year beginning with fiscal year 1991) such sums as may be necessary to carry out this subsection.

(June 27, 1952, ch 477, Title III, Ch 2, § 332, 66 Stat. 252; Nov. 29, 1990, P. L. 101-649, Title IV, §§ 406, 407(d)(10), 104 Stat. 5040, 5042; Dec. 12, 1991, P. L. 102-232, Title III, § 305(m)(6), 105 Stat. 1750.)

§ 1443a. Naturalization proceedings overseas for members of the Armed Forces and their spouses and children

Notwithstanding any other provision of law, the Secretary of Homeland Security, the Secretary of State, and the Secretary of Defense shall ensure that any applications, interviews, filings, oaths, ceremonies, or other proceedings under title III of the Immigration and Nationality Act (8 U.S.C. 1401 et seq.) relating to naturalization of members of the Armed Forces, and persons made eligible for naturalization by section 319(e) or 322(d) of such Act [8 USCS § 1430(e) or 1433(d)], are available through United States embassies, consulates, and as practicable, United States military installations overseas.

(Nov. 24, 2003, P. L. 108-136, Div A, Title XVII, § 1701(d), 117 Stat. 1692; Jan. 28, 2008, P. L. 110-181, Div A, Title VI, Subtitle G, § 674(c), 122 Stat. 186.)

§ 1444. Photographs; number

(a) Three identical photographs of the applicant shall be signed by and furnished by each applicant for naturalization or citizenship. One of such photographs shall be affixed by the Attorney General to the original certificate of naturalization issued to the naturalized citizen and one to the duplicate certificate of naturalization required to be forwarded to the Service.

(b) Three identical photographs of the applicant shall be furnished by each applicant for—

(1) a record of lawful admission for permanent residence to be made under section 249 [8 USCS § 1259];

(2) a certificate of derivative citizenship;

(3) a certificate of naturalization or of citizenship;

(4) a special certificate of naturalization;

(5) a certificate of naturalization or of citizenship, in lieu of one lost, mutilated, or destroyed;

(6) a new certificate of citizenship in the new name of any naturalized citizen who, subsequent to naturalization, has had his name changed by order of a court of competent jurisdiction or by marriage; and

(7) a declaration of intention.

One such photograph shall be affixed to each such certificate issued by the Attorney General and one shall be affixed to the copy of such certificate retained by the Service.

(June 27, 1952, ch 477, Title III, Ch 2, § 333, 66 Stat. 253; Nov. 29, 1990, P. L. 101-649, Title IV, § 407(c)(14), (d)(11), 104 Stat. 5041, 5042; Oct. 25, 1994, P. L. 103-416, Title II, § 219(w), 108 Stat. 4318.)

§ 1445. Application for naturalization; declaration of intention

(a) Evidence and form. An applicant for naturalization shall make and file with the Attorney General a sworn application in writing, signed by the applicant in the applicant's own handwriting if physically able to write, which application shall be on a form prescribed by the Attorney General and shall include averments of all facts which in the opinion of the Attorney General may be material to the applicant's naturalization, and required to be proved under this title. In the case of an applicant subject to a requirement of continuous residence under section 316(a) or 319(a) [8 USCS § 1427(a) or 1430(a)], the application for naturalization may be filed up to 3 months before the date the applicant would first otherwise meet such continuous residence requirement.

(b) Who may file. No person shall file a valid application for naturalization unless he shall have attained the age of eighteen years. An application for naturalization by an alien shall contain an averment of lawful admission for permanent residence.

(c) Holding of hearings. Hearings under section 336(a) [8 USCS § 1447(a)] on applications for naturalization shall be held at regular intervals specified by the Attorney General.

(d) Filing of application. Except as provided in subsection (e), an application for naturalization shall be filed in the office of the Attorney General.

(e) Substitute filing place and administering oath other than before Attorney General. A person may file an application for naturalization other than in the office of the Attorney General, and an oath of allegiance administered other than in a public ceremony before the Attorney General or a court, if the Attorney General determines that the person has an illness or other disability which—

(1) is of a permanent nature and is sufficiently serious to prevent the person's personal appearance, or

(2) is of a nature which so incapacitates the person as to prevent him from personally appearing.

(f) Declaration of intention. An alien over 18 years of age who is residing in the United States pursuant to a lawful admission for permanent residence may file with the Attorney General a declaration of intention to become a citizen of the United States. Such a declaration shall be filed in duplicate and in a form prescribed by the Attorney General and shall be accompanied by an application prescribed and approved by the Attorney General. Nothing in this subsection shall be construed as requiring any such alien to make and file a declaration of intention as a condition precedent to filing a petition for naturalization nor shall any such declaration of intention be regarded as conferring or having conferred upon any such alien United States citizenship or nationality or the right to United States citizenship or nationality, nor shall such declaration be regarded as evidence of such alien's lawful admission for permanent residence in any proceeding, action, or matter arising under this or any other Act.

(June 27, 1952, ch 477, Title III, Ch 2, § 334, 66 Stat. 254; Dec. 29, 1981, P. L. 97-116, § 15(b), 95 Stat. 1619; Nov. 29, 1990, P. L. 101-649, Title IV, §§ 401(b), 407(c)(15), (d)(12), 104 Stat. 5038, 5041, 5042; Dec. 12, 1991, P. L. 102-232, Title III, § 305(d), (e), (m)(7), 105 Stat. 1750.)

§ 1446. Investigation of applicants; examination of applications

(a) Waiver. Before a person may be naturalized, an employee of the Service, or of the United States designated by the Attorney General, shall conduct a personal investigation of the person applying for naturalization in the vicinity or vicinities in which such person has maintained his actual place of abode and in the vicinity or vicinities in which such person has been employed or has engaged in business or work for at least five years immediately preceding the filing of his application for naturalization. The Attorney General may, in his discretion, waive a personal investigation in an individual case or in such case or classes of cases as may be designated by him.

(b) Conduct of examinations; authority of designees; record. The Attorney General shall designate employees of the Service to conduct examinations upon petitions for naturalization. For such purposes any such employee so designated is hereby authorized to take testimony concerning any matter touching or in any way affecting the admissibility of any applicant for naturalization, to administer oaths, including the oath of the applicant for naturalization, and to require by subpena the attendance and testimony of witnesses, including applicant, before such employee so designated and the production of relevant books, papers, and documents, and to that end may invoke the aid of any district court of the United States; and any such court may, in the event of neglect or refusal to respond to a subpena issued by any such employee so designated or refusal to testify before such employee so designated issue an order requiring such person to answer before such employee so designated, produce relevant books, papers, and documents if demanded, and testify; and any failure to obey such order of the court may be punished by the court as a contempt thereof. The record of the examination authorized by this subsection shall be admissible as evidence in any hearing conducted by an immigration officer under section 336(a) [8 USCS § 1447(a)]. Any such employee shall, at the examination, inform the petitioner of the remedies available to the petitioner under section 336 [8 USCS § 1447].

(c) Transmittal of record of examination. The record of the examination upon any application for naturalization may, in the discretion of the Attorney General, be transmitted to the Attorney General and the determination with respect thereto of the employee designated to conduct such examination shall when made also be transmitted to the Attorney General.

(d) Determination to grant or deny application. The employee designated to conduct any such examination shall make a determination as to whether the application should be granted or denied, with reasons therefor.

(e) Withdrawal of application. After an application for naturalization has been filed with the Attorney General, the applicant shall not be permitted to withdraw his application, except with the consent of the Attorney General. In cases where the Attorney General does not consent to the withdrawal of the application, the application shall be determined on its merits and a final order determination made accordingly. In cases where the applicant fails to prosecute his application, the application shall be decided on the merits unless the Attorney General dismisses it for lack of prosecution.

(f) Transfer of application. An applicant for naturalization who moves from the district of the Service in the United States in which the application is pending may, at any time thereafter, request the Service to transfer the application to any district of the Service in the United States which may act on the application. The transfer shall not be made without the consent of the Attorney General. In the case of such a transfer, the proceedings on the application shall continue as though the application had originally been filed in the district of the Service to which the application is transferred.

(June 27, 1952, ch 477, Title III, Ch 2, § 335, 66 Stat. 255; Dec. 29, 1981, P. L. 97-116, § 15(c), 95 Stat. 1619; Oct. 24, 1988, P. L. 100-525, § 9(aa), (bb), 102 Stat. 2621; Nov. 29, 1990, P. L. 101-649, Title IV, §§ 401(c), 407(c)(16), (d)(13), 104 Stat. 5038, 5041, 5043; Dec. 12, 1991, P. L. 102-232, Title III, § 305(f), 105 Stat. 1750.)

§ 1447. Hearings on denials of applications for naturalization

(a) Request for hearing before immigration officer. If, after an examination under section 335 [8 USCS § 1446], an application for naturalization is denied, the applicant may request a hearing before an immigration officer.

(b) Request for hearing before district court. If there is a failure to make a determination under section 335 [8 USCS § 1446] before the end of the 120-day period after the date on which the examination is conducted under such section, the applicant may apply to the United States district court for the district in which the applicant resides for a hearing on the matter. Such court has jurisdiction over the matter and may either determine the matter or remand the matter, with appropriate instructions, to the Service to determine the matter.

(c) Appearance of Attorney General. The Attorney General shall have the right to appear before any immigration officer in any naturalization proceedings for the purpose of cross-examining the applicant and the witnesses produced in support of the petition concerning any matter touching or in any way affecting the applicant's right to admission to citizenship, and shall have the right to call witnesses, including the applicant, produce evidence, and be heard in opposition to, or in favor of, the granting of any application in naturalization proceedings.

(d) Subpena of witnesses. The immigration officer shall, if the applicant requests it at the time of filing the request for hearing, issue a subpena for the witnesses named by such petitioner to appear upon the day set for the hearing, but in case such witnesses cannot be produced upon the hearing other witnesses may be summoned upon notice to the Attorney General, in such manner and at such time as the Attorney General may by regulation prescribe. Such subpenas may be enforced in the same manner as subpenas under section 335(b) [8 USCS § 1446(b)] may be enforced.

(e) Change of name. It shall be lawful at the time and as a part of the administration by a court of the oath of allegiance under section 337(a) [8 USCS § 1448(a)], for the court, in its discretion, upon the bona fide prayer of the applicant included in an appropriate petition to the court, to make a decree changing the name of said person, and the certificate of naturalization shall be issued in accordance therewith.

(June 27, 1952, ch 477, Title III, Ch 2, § 336, 66 Stat. 257; Dec. 5, 1969, P. L. 91-136, 83 Stat. 283; Dec. 29, 1981, P. L. 97-116, § 15(d), 95 Stat. 1619; Oct. 24, 1988, P. L. 100-525, § 9(cc), 102 Stat. 2621; Nov. 29, 1990, P. L. 101-649, Title IV, § 407(c)(17), (d)(14), 104 Stat. 5041, 5044; Dec. 12, 1991, P. L. 102-232, Title III, § 305(g), (h), 105 Stat. 1750.)

§ 1448. Oath of renunciation and allegiance

(a) Public ceremony. A person who has applied for naturalization shall, in order to be and before being admitted to citizenship, take in a public ceremony before the Attorney General or a court with jurisdiction under section 310(b) [8 USCS § 1421(b)] an oath (1) to support the Constitution of the United States; (2) to renounce and abjure absolutely and entirely all allegiance and fidelity to any foreign prince, potentate, state, or sovereignty of whom or which the applicant was before a subject or citizen; (3) to support and defend the Constitution and the laws of the United States against all enemies, foreign and domestic; (4) to bear true faith and allegiance to the same; and (5)(A) to bear arms on behalf of the United States when required by the law, or (B) to perform noncombatant service in the

Armed Forces of the United States when required by the law, or (C) to perform work of national importance under civilian direction when required by the law. Any such person shall be required to take an oath containing the substance of clauses (1) through (5) of the preceding sentence, except that a person who shows by clear and convincing evidence to the satisfaction of the Attorney General that he is opposed to the bearing of arms in the Armed Forces of the United States by reason of religious training and belief shall be required to take an oath containing the substance of clauses (1) through (4) and clauses (5)(B) and (5)(C), and a person who shows by clear and convincing evidence to the satisfaction of the Attorney General that he is opposed to any type of service in the Armed Forces of the United States by reason of religious training and belief shall be required to take an oath containing the substance of clauses (1) through (4) and clause (5)(C). The term "religious training and belief" as used in this section shall mean an individual's belief in a relation to a Supreme Being involving duties superior to those arising from any human relation, but does not include essentially political, sociological, or philosophical views or a merely personal moral code. In the case of the naturalization of a child under the provisions of section 322 of this title [8 USCS § 1433] the Attorney General may waive the taking of the oath if in the opinion of the Attorney General the child is unable to understand its meaning. The Attorney General may waive the taking of the oath by a person if in the opinion of the Attorney General the person is unable to understand, or to communicate an understanding of, its meaning because of a physical or developmental disability or mental impairment. If the Attorney General waives the taking of the oath by a person under the preceding sentence, the person shall be considered to have met the requirements of section 316(a)(3) [8 USCS § 1427(a)(3)] with respect to attachment to the principles of the Constitution and well disposition to the good order and happiness of the United States.

(b) Hereditary titles or orders of nobility. In case the person applying for naturalization has borne any hereditary title, or has been of any of the orders of nobility in any foreign state, the petitioner shall in addition to complying with the requirements of subsection (a) of this section, make under oath in the same public ceremony in which the oath of allegiance is administered, an express renunciation of such title or order of nobility, and such renunciation shall be recorded as a part of such proceedings.

(c) Expedited judicial oath administration ceremony. Notwithstanding section 310(b) [8 USCS § 1421(b)], an individual may be granted an expedited judicial oath administration ceremony or administrative naturalization by the Attorney General upon demonstrating sufficient cause. In determining whether to grant an expedited judicial oath administration ceremony, a court shall consider special circumstances (such as serious illness of the applicant or a member of the applicant's immediate family, permanent disability sufficiently incapacitating as to prevent the applicant's personal appearance at the scheduled ceremony, developmental disability or advanced age, or exigent circumstances relating to travel or employment). If an expedited judicial oath administration ceremony is impracticable, the court shall refer such individual to the Attorney General who may provide for immediate administrative naturalization.

(d) Rules and regulations. The Attorney General shall prescribe rules and procedures to ensure that the ceremonies conducted by the Attorney General for the administration of oaths of allegiance under this section are public, conducted frequently and at regular intervals, and are in keeping with the dignity of the occasion.

(June 27, 1952, ch 477, Title III, Ch 2, § 337, 66 Stat. 258; Dec. 29, 1981, P. L. 97-116, § 18(o), 95 Stat. 1621; Nov. 29, 1990, P. L. 101-649, Title IV, § 407(c)(18), (d)(15), 104 Stat. 5041, 5044; Dec. 12, 1991, P. L. 102-232, Title I, §§ 102(b)(2), 305(i), 105 Stat. 1736, 1750; Nov. 6, 2000, P. L. 106-448, § 1, 114 Stat. 1939.)

§ 1448a. Address to newly naturalized citizens

Either at the time of the rendition of the decree of naturalization or at such other time as the judge may fix, the judge or someone designated by him shall address the newly naturalized citizen upon the form and genius of our Government and the privileges and responsibilities of citizenship; it being the intent and purpose of this section to enlist the aid of the judiciary, in cooperation with civil and educational authorities, and patriotic organizations in a continuous effort to dignify and emphasize the significance of citizenship.

(Feb. 29, 1952, ch 49, § 2, 66 Stat. 10.)

§ 1449. Certificate of naturalization; contents

A person admitted to citizenship in conformity with the provisions of this title shall be entitled upon such admission to receive from the Attorney General a certificate of naturalization, which shall contain substantially the following information: Number of application for naturalization; number of certificate of naturalization; date of naturalization; name, signature, place of residence, autographed photograph, and personal description of the naturalized person, including age, sex, marital status, and country of former nationality; location of the district office of the Service in which the application was filed and the title, authority, and location of the official or court administering the oath of allegiance; statement that the Attorney General having found that the petitioner had complied in all respects with all of the applicable provisions of the naturalization laws of the United States, and was entitled to be admitted a citizen of the United States of America, thereupon ordered that the applicant be admitted as a citizen of the United States of America; attestation of an immigration officer; and the seal of the Department of Justice.

(June 27, 1952, ch 477, Title III, Ch 2, § 338, 66 Stat. 259; Nov. 29, 1990, P. L. 101-649, Title IV, § 407(c)(19), (d)(16), 104 Stat. 5041, 5045; Dec. 12, 1991, P. L. 102-232, Title III, § 305(j), 105 Stat. 1750; Oct. 25, 1994, P. L. 103-416, Title 1, § 104(a), Title II, § 219(z)(3), 108 Stat. 4308, 4318.)

§ 1450. Functions and duties of clerks and records of declarations of intention and applications for naturalization

(a) The clerk of each court that administers oaths of allegiance under section 337 [8 USCS § 1448] shall—

(1) deliver to each person administered the oath of allegiance by the court pursuant to section 337(a) [8 USCS § 1448(a)] the certificate of naturalization prepared by the Attorney General pursuant to section 310(b)(2)(A)(ii) [8 USCS § 1421(b)(2)(A)(ii)] ,

(2) forward to the Attorney General a list of applicants actually taking the oath at each scheduled ceremony and information concerning each person to whom such an oath is administered by the court, within 30 days after the close of the month in which the oath was administered,

(3) forward to the Attorney General certified copies of such other proceedings and orders instituted in or issued out of the court affecting or relating to the naturalization of persons as may be required from time to time by the Attorney General; and

(4) be responsible for all blank certificates of naturalization received by them from time to time from the Attorney General and shall account to the Attorney General for them whenever required to do so.

No certificate of naturalization received by any clerk of court which may be defaced or injured in such manner as to prevent its use as herein provided shall in any case be destroyed, but such certificates shall be returned to the Attorney General.

(b) Each district office of the Service in the United States shall maintain, in chronological order, indexed, and consecutively numbered, as part of its permanent records, all declarations of intention and applications for naturalization filed with the office.

(June 27, 1952, ch 477, Title III, Ch 2, § 339, 66 Stat. 259; Nov. 29, 1990, P. L. 101-649, Title IV, § 407(d)(17), 104 Stat. 5045; Dec. 12, 1991, P. L. 102-232, Title I, § 102(b)(1), 105 Stat. 1735.)

§ 1451. Revocation of naturalization

(a) Concealment of material evidence; refusal to testify. It shall be the duty of the United States attorneys for the respective districts, upon affidavit showing good cause therefor, to institute proceedings in any district court of the United States in the judicial district in which the naturalized citizen may reside at the time of bringing suit, for the purpose of revoking and setting aside the order admitting such person to citizenship and canceling the certificate of naturalization on the ground that such order and certificate of naturalization were illegally procured or were procured by concealment of a material fact or by willful misrepresentation, and such revocation and setting aside of the order admitting such person to citizenship and such canceling of certificate of naturalization shall be effective as of the original date of the order and certificate, respectively: *Provided,* That refusal on the part of a naturalized citizen within a period of ten years following his naturalization to testify as a witness in any proceeding before a congressional committee concerning his subversive activities, in a case where such person has been convicted of contempt for such refusal, shall be held to constitute a ground for revocation of such person's naturalization under this subsection as having been procured by concealment of a material fact or by willful misrepresentation. If the naturalized citizen does not reside in any judicial district in the United States at the time of bringing such suit, the proceedings may be instituted in the United States District Court for the District of Columbia or in the United States district court in the judicial district in which such person last had his residence.

(b) Notice to party. The party to whom was granted the naturalization alleged to have been illegally procured or procured by concealment of a material fact or by willful misrepresentation shall, in any such proceedings under subsection (a) of this section, have sixty days' personal notice, unless waived by such party, in which to make answer to the petition of the United States; and if such naturalized person be absent from the United States or from the judicial district in which such person last had his residence, such notice shall be given either by personal service upon him or by publication in the manner provided for the service of summons by publication or upon absentees by the laws of the State or the place where such suit is brought.

(c) Membership in certain organizations; prima facie evidence. If a person who shall have been naturalized after December 24, 1952 shall within five years next following such naturalization become a member of or affiliated with any organization, membership in or affiliation with which at the time of naturalization would have precluded such person from naturalization under the provisions of section 313 [8 USCS § 1424], it shall be considered prima facie evidence that such person was not attached to the principles of the Constitution of the United States and was not well disposed to the good order and happiness of the United States at the time of naturalization, and, in the absence of countervailing evidence, it shall be sufficient in the proper proceeding to authorize the revocation and setting aside of the order admitting such person to citizenship and the cancellation of the certificate of naturalization as having been obtained by concealment of a material fact or by willful misrepresentation, and such revocation and setting aside of the order admitting such person to citizenship and such canceling of certificate of naturalization shall be effective as of the original date of the order and certificate, respectively.

(d) Applicability to citizenship through naturalization of parent or spouse. Any person who claims United States citizenship through the naturalization of a parent or spouse in whose case there is a revocation and setting aside of the order admitting such parent or spouse to citizenship under the provisions of subsection (a) of this section on the ground that the order and certificate of naturalization were procured by concealment of a material fact or by willful misrepresentation shall be deemed to have lost and to lose his citizenship and any right or privilege of citizenship which he may have, now has, or may hereafter acquire under and by virtue of such naturalization of such parent or spouse, regardless of whether such person is residing within or without the United States at the time of the revocation and setting aside of the order admitting such parent or spouse to citizenship. Any person who claims United States citizenship through the naturalization of a parent or spouse in whose case there is a revocation and setting aside of the order admitting such parent or spouse to citizenship and the cancellation of the certificate of naturalization under the provisions of subsection (c) of this section, or under the provisions of section 329(c) of this title [8 USCS § 1440(c)] on any ground other than that the order and certificate of naturalization were procured by concealment of a material fact or by willful misrepresentation, shall be deemed to have lost and to lose his citizenship and any right or privilege of citizenship which would have been enjoyed by such person had there not been a revocation and setting aside of the order admitting such parent or spouse to citizenship and the cancellation of the certificate of naturalization, unless such person is residing in the United States at the time of the revocation and setting aside of the order admitting such parent or spouse to citizenship and the cancellation of the certificate of naturalization.

(e) Citizenship unlawfully procured. When a person shall be convicted under section 1425 of title 18 of the United States Code of knowingly procuring naturalization in violation of law, the court in which such conviction is had shall thereupon revoke, set aside, and declare void the final order admitting such person to citizenship, and shall declare the certificate of naturalization of such person to be canceled. Jurisdiction is hereby conferred on the courts having jurisdiction of the trial of such offense to make such adjudication.

(f) Cancellation of certificate of naturalization. Whenever an order admitting an alien to citizenship shall be revoked and set aside or a certificate of naturalization shall be canceled, or both, as provided in this section, the court in which such judgment or decree is rendered shall make an order canceling such certificate and shall send a certified copy of such order to the Attorney General. The clerk of court shall transmit a copy of such order and judgment to the Attorney General. A person holding a certificate of naturalization or citizenship which has been canceled as provided by this section shall upon notice by the court by which the decree of cancellation was made, or by the Attorney General, surrender the same to the Attorney General.

(g) Applicability to certificates of naturalization and citizenship. The provisions of this section shall apply not only to any naturalization granted and to certificates of naturalization and citizenship issued under the provisions of this title, but to any naturalization heretofore granted by any court, and to all certificates of naturalization and citizenship which may have been issued heretofore by any court or by the Commissioner based upon naturalization granted by any court, or by a designated representative of the Commissioner under the provisions of section 702 of the Nationality Act of 1940, as amended, or by such designated representative under any other act.

(h) Power to correct, reopen, alter, modify or vacate order. Nothing contained in this section shall be regarded as limiting, denying, or restricting the power of the Attorney General to correct, reopen, alter, modify, or vacate an order naturalizing the person.

(June 27, 1952, ch 477, Title III, Ch 2, § 340, 66 Stat. 260; Sept. 3, 1954, ch 1263, § 18, 68 Stat. 1232; Sept. 26, 1961, P. L. 87-301, § 18, 75 Stat. 656; Nov. 14, 1986, P. L. 99-653, § 17, 100 Stat. 3658; Oct. 24, 1988, P. L. 100-525, § 9(dd), 102 Stat. 2621; Nov. 29, 1990, P. L. 101-649, Title IV, § 407(d)(18), 104 Stat. 5046; Dec. 12, 1991, P. L. 102-232, Title III, § 305(k), 105 Stat. 1750; Oct. 25, 1994, P. L. 103-416, Title I, § 104(b), (c), 108 Stat. 4308.)

§ 1452. Certificates of citizenship or U.S. non-citizen national status; procedure

(a) Application to Attorney General for certificate of citizenship; proof; oath of allegiance. A person who claims to have derived United States citizenship through the naturalization of a parent or through the naturalization or citizenship of a husband, or who is a citizen of the United States by virtue of the provisions of section 1993 of the United States Revised Statutes, or of section 1993 of the United States Revised Statutes, as amended by section 1 of the Act of May 24, 1934 (48 Stat. 797), or who is a citizen of the United States by virtue of the provisions of subsection (c), (d), (e), (g), or (i) of section 201 of the Nationality Act of 1940, as amended (54 Stat. 1138; 8 U.S.C. 601), or of the Act of May 7, 1934 (48 Stat. 667), or of paragraph (c), (d), (e), or (g) of section 301 of this title [8 USCS § 1401(c), (d), (e), or (g)], or under the provisions of the Act of August 4, 1937 (50 Stat. 558), or under the provisions of section 203 or 205 of the Nationality Act of 1940 (54 Stat. 1139; 8 U. S. C. 603, 605), or under the provisions of section 303 of this title [8 USCS § 1403], may apply to the Attorney General for a certificate of citizenship. Upon proof to the satisfaction of the Attorney General that the applicant is a citizen, and that the applicant's alleged citizenship was derived as claimed, or acquired, as the case may be, and upon taking and subscribing before a member of the Service within the United States to the oath of allegiance required by this Act of an applicant for naturalization, such individual shall be furnished by the Attorney General with a certificate of citizenship, but only if such individual is at the time within the United States.

(b) Application to Secretary of State for certificate of non-citizen national status; proof; oath of allegiance. A person who claims to be a national, but not a citizen, of the United States may apply to the Secretary of State for a certificate of non-citizen national status. Upon—

(1) proof to the satisfaction of the Secretary of State that the applicant is a national, but not a citizen, of the United States, and

(2) in the case of such a person born outside of the United States or its outlying possessions, taking and subscribing, before an immigration officer within the United States or its outlying possessions, to the oath of allegiance required by this Act of a petitioner for naturalization,

the individual shall be furnished by the Secretary of State with a certificate of non-citizen national status, but only if the individual is at the time within the United States or its outlying possessions.

(June 27, 1952, ch 477, Title III, Ch 2, § 341, 66 Stat. 263; Dec. 29, 1981, P. L. 97-116, § 18(p), 95 Stat. 1621; Aug. 27, 1986, P. L. 99-396, § 16(a), 100 Stat. 843; Nov. 14, 1986, P. L. 99-653, § 22, 100 Stat. 3658; Oct. 24, 1988, P. L. 100-525, § 8(q), 102 Stat. 2618; Dec. 12, 1991, P. L. 102-232, Title III, § 305(m)(8), 105 Stat. 1750; Oct. 25, 1994, P. L. 103-416, Title I, § 102(b), 108 Stat. 4307.)

§ 1453. Cancellation of certificates issued by the Attorney General, the Commissioner or a Deputy Commissioner; action not to affect citizenship status

The Attorney General is authorized to cancel any certificate of citizenship, certificate of naturalization, copy of a declaration of intention, or other certificate, document or record heretofore issued or made by the Commissioner or a Deputy Commissioner or hereafter made by the Attorney General if it shall appear to the Attorney General's satisfaction that such document or record was illegally or fraudulently obtained from, or was created through illegality or by fraud practiced upon, him or the Commissioner or a Deputy Commissioner; but the person for or to whom such document or record has been issued or made shall be given at such person's last-known place of address written notice of the intention to cancel such document or record with the reasons therefor and shall be given at least sixty days in which to show cause why such document or record should not be canceled. The cancellation under this section of any document purporting to show the citizenship status of the person to whom it was issued shall affect only the document and not the citizenship status of the person in whose name the document was issued.

(June 27, 1952, ch 477, Title III, Ch 2, § 342, 66 Stat. 263.)

§ 1454. Documents and copies issued by Attorney General

(a) If any certificate of naturalization or citizenship issued to any citizen or any declaration of intention furnished to any declarant is lost, mutilated, or destroyed, the citizen or declarant may make application to the Attorney General for a new certificate or declaration. If the Attorney General finds that the certificate or declaration is lost, mutilated, or destroyed, he shall issue to the applicant a new certificate or declaration. If the certificate or declaration has been mutilated, it shall be surrendered to the Attorney General before the applicant may receive such new certificate or declaration. If the certification or declaration has been lost, the applicant or any other person who shall have, or may come into possession of it is hereby required to surrender it to the Attorney General.

(b) The Attorney General shall issue for any naturalized citizen, on such citizen's application therefor, a special certificate of naturalization for use by such citizen only for the purpose of obtaining recognition as a citizen of the United States by a foreign state. Such certificate when issued shall be furnished to the Secretary of State for transmission to the proper authority in such foreign state.

(c) If the name of any naturalized citizen has, subsequent to naturalization, been changed by order of any court of competent jurisdiction, or by marriage, the citizen may make application for a new certificate of naturalization in the new name of such citizen. If the Attorney General finds the name of the applicant to have been changed as claimed, the Attorney General shall issue to the applicant a new certificate and shall notify the naturalization court of such action.

(d) The Attorney General is authorized to make and issue certifications of any part of the naturalization records of any court, or of any certificate of naturalization or citizenship, for use in complying with any statute, State or Federal, or in any judicial proceeding. No such certification shall be made by any clerk of court except upon order of the court.

(June 27, 1952, ch 477, Title III, Ch 2, § 343, 66 Stat. 263; Oct. 24, 1988, P. L. 100-235, § 9(ee), 102 Stat. 2621.)

§ 1455. Fiscal provisions

(a) The Attorney General shall charge, collect, and account for fees prescribed by the Attorney General pursuant to section 9701 of title 31, United States Code for the following:

(1) Making, filing, and docketing an application for naturalization, including the hearing on such application, if such hearing be held, and a certificate of naturalization, if the issuance of such certificate is authorized by the Attorney General.

(2) Receiving and filing a declaration of intention, and issuing a duplicate thereof.

(b) Notwithstanding the provisions of this Act or any other law, no fee shall be charged or collected for an application for declaration of intention or a certificate of naturalization in lieu of a declaration or a certificate alleged to have been lost, mutilated, or destroyed, submitted by a person who was a member of the military or naval forces of the United States at any time after April 20, 1898, and before July 5, 1902; or at any time after April 5, 1917, and before November 12, 1918; or who served on the Mexican border as a member of the Regular Army or National Guard between June 1916 and April 1917; or who has served or hereafter serves in the military, air, or naval forces of the United States after September 16, 1940, and who was not at any time during such period or thereafter separated from such forces under other than honorable conditions, who was not a conscientious objector who performed no military duty whatever or refused to wear the uniform, or who was not at any time during such period or thereafter discharged from such military, air, or naval forces on account of alienage.

(c) Except as provided by section 286(q)(2) [8 USCS § 1356(q)(2)] or any other law, all fees collected by the Attorney General shall be deposited by the Attorney General in the Treasury of the United States except that all fees collected or paid over on or after October 1, 1988, shall be deposited in the Immigration Examinations Fee Account established under section 286(m) [8 USCS § 1356(m)]: *Provided, however,* That all fees received by the Attorney General from applicants residing in the Virgin Islands of the United States, and in Guam, under this title, shall be paid over to the treasury of the Virgin Islands and to the treasury of Guam, respectively.

(d) During the time when the United States is at war the Attorney General may not charge or collect a naturalization fee from an alien in the military, air, or naval service of the United States for filing an application for naturalization or issuing a certificate of naturalization upon admission to citizenship.

(e) In addition to the other fees required by this title, the applicant for naturalization shall, upon the filing of a petition for naturalization, deposit with and pay to the Attorney General a sum of money sufficient to cover the expense of subpenaing and paying the legal fees of any witnesses for whom such applicant may request a subpena, and upon the final discharge of such witnesses, they shall receive, if they demand the same from the Attorney General, the customary and usual witness fees from the moneys which the applicant shall have paid to the Attorney General for such purpose, and the residue, if any, shall be returned by the Attorney General to the applicant.

(f)(1) The Attorney General shall pay over to courts administering oaths of allegiance to persons under this title a specified percentage of all fees described in subsection (a)(1) collected by the Attorney General with respect to persons administered the oath of allegiance by the respective courts. The Attorney General, annually and in consultation with the courts, shall determine the specified percentage based on the proportion, of the total costs incurred by the Service and courts for essential services directly related to the naturalization process, which are incurred by courts.

(2) The Attorney General shall provide on an annual basis to the Committees on the Judiciary of the House of Representatives and of the Senate a detailed report on the use of the fees described in paragraph (1) and shall consult with such Committees before increasing such fees.

(June 27, 1952, ch 477, Title III, Ch 2, § 344, 66 Stat. 264; July 7, 1958, P. L. 85-508, § 26, 72 Stat. 351; Oct. 21, 1968, P. L. 90-609, § 3, 82 Stat. 1200; Dec. 29, 1981, P. L. 97-116, § 16, 95 Stat. 1619; Oct. 1, 1988, P. L. 100-459, Title II, § 209(b), 102 Stat. 2203; Oct. 24, 1988, P. L. 100-525, § 9(ff), 102 Stat. 2621; Nov. 29, 1990, P. L. 101-649, Title IV, § 407(c)(20), (d)(19), 104 Stat. 5041, 5046; Dec. 12, 1991, P. L. 102-232, Title , §§ 102(b)(3), 305(l), 309(a)(1)(A)((ii), (b)(14), 105 Stat. 1736, 1750, 1758, 1759; Nov. 2, 2002, P. L. 107-273, Div C, Title I, Subtitle A, § 11016(1), 116 Stat. 1824.)

§ 1456. [Repealed]

§ 1457. Publication and distribution of citizenship textbooks; use of naturalization fees

Authorization is hereby granted for the publication and distribution of the citizenship textbook described in subsection (b) of section 332 [8 USCS § 1443(b)] and for the reimbursement of the appropriation of the Department of Justice upon the records of the Treasury Department from the naturalization fees deposited in the Treasury through the Service for the cost of such publication and distribution, such reimbursement to be made upon statements by the Attorney General of books so published and distributed.

(June 27, 1952, ch 477, Title III, Ch 2, § 346, 66 Stat. 266.)

§ 1458. Compilation of naturalization statistics and payment for equipment

The Attorney General is authorized and directed to prepare from the records in the custody of the Service a report upon those heretofore seeking citizenship to show by nationalities their relation to the numbers of aliens annually arriving and to the prevailing census populations of the foreign-born, their economic, vocational, and other classification, in statistical form, with analytical comment thereon, and to prepare such report annually hereafter. Payment for the equipment used in preparing such compilation shall be made from the appropriation for the enforcement of this Act by the Service.

(June 27, 1952, ch 477, Title III, Ch 2, § 347, 66 Stat. 266.)

§ 1459. [Repealed]

LOSS OF NATIONALITY

§ 1481. Loss of nationality by native-born or naturalized citizen; voluntary action; burden of proof; presumptions

(a) A person who is a national of the United States whether by birth or naturalization, shall lose his nationality by voluntarily performing any of the following acts with the intention of relinquishing United States nationality—

(1) obtaining naturalization in a foreign state upon his own application or upon an application filed by a duly authorized agent, after having attained the age of eighteen years; or

(2) taking an oath or making an affirmation or other formal declaration of allegiance to a foreign state or a political subdivision thereof, after having attained the age of eighteen years; or

(3) entering, or serving in, the armed forces of a foreign state if (A) such armed forces are engaged in hostilities against the United States, or (B) such persons serve as a commissioned or noncommissioned officer; or

(4) (A) accepting, serving in, or performing the duties of any office, post, or employment under the government of a foreign state or a political subdivision thereof, after attaining the age of eighteen years if he has or acquires the nationality of such foreign state; or (B) accepting, serving in, or performing the duties of any office, post, or employment under the government of a foreign state or a political subdivision thereof, after attaining the age of eighteen years for which office, post, or employment an oath, affirmation, or declaration of allegiance is required; or

(5) making a formal renunciation of nationality before a diplomatic or consular officer of the United States

in a foreign state, in such form as may be prescribed by the Secretary of State; or

(6) making in the United States a formal written renunciation of nationality in such form as may be prescribed by, and before such officer as may be designated by, the Attorney General, whenever the United States shall be in a state of war and the Attorney General shall approve such renunciation as not contrary to the interests of national defense; or

(7) committing any act of treason against, or attempting by force to overthrow, or bearing arms against, the United States, violating or conspiring to violate any of the provisions of section 2383 of title 18, United States Code, or willfully performing any act in violation of section 2385 of title 18, United States Code, or violating section 2384 of said title by engaging in a conspiracy to overthrow, put down, or to destroy by force the Government of the United States, or to levy war against them, if and when he is convicted thereof by a court martial or by a court of competent jurisdiction.

(b) Whenever the loss of United States nationality is put in issue in any action or proceeding commenced on or after the enactment of this subsection [enacted Sept. 26, 1961] under, or by virtue of, the provisions of this or any other Act, the burden shall be upon the person or party claiming that such loss occurred, to establish such claim by a preponderance of the evidence. Any person who commits or performs, or who has committed or performed, any act of expatriation under the provisions of this or any other Act shall be presumed to have done so voluntarily, but such presumption may be rebutted upon a showing, by a preponderance of the evidence, that the act or acts committed or performed were not done voluntarily.

(June 27, 1952, ch 477, Title III, Ch 3, § 349, 66 Stat. 267; Sept. 3, 1954, ch 1256, § 2, 68 Stat. 1146; Sept. 26, 1961, P. L. 87-301, § 19, 75 Stat. 656; Sept. 14, 1976, P. L. 94-412, Title V, § 501(a), 90 Stat. 1258; Oct. 10, 1978, P. L. 95-432, §§ 2 in part, 4, 92 Stat. 1046; Dec. 29, 1981, P. L. 97-116, § 18(k)(2), (g), 95 Stat. 1620, 1621; Nov. 14, 1986, P. L. 99-653, §§ 18, 19, 100 Stat. 3658; Oct. 24, 1988, P. L. 100-525, §§ 8(m), (n), 9(hh), 102 Stat. 2618, 2622.)

§ 1482. [Repealed]

§ 1483. Restrictions on loss of nationality

(a) Except as provided in paragraphs (6) and (7) of section 349(a) of this title [8 USCS § 1481(a)(6) and (7)], no national of the United States can lose United States nationality under this Act while within the United States or any of its outlying possessions, but loss of nationality shall result from the performance within the United States or any of its outlying possessions of any of the acts or the fulfillment of any of the conditions specified in this chapter if and when the national thereafter takes up a residence outside the United States and its outlying possessions.

(b) A national who within six months after attaining the age of eighteen years asserts his claim to United States nationality, in such manner as the Secretary of State shall by regulation prescribe, shall not be deemed to have lost United States nationality by the commission, prior to his eighteenth birthday, of any of the acts specified in paragraphs (3), and (5) of section 349(a) of this title.

(June 27, 1952, ch 477, Title III, Ch 3, § 351, 66 Stat. 269; Dec. 29, 1981, P. L. 97-116, § 18(r), 95 Stat. 1621; Nov. 14, 1986, P. L. 99-653, § 20, 100 Stat. 3658; Oct. 24, 1988, P. L. 100-525, § 8(o), 102 Stat. 2618; Oct. 25, 1994, P. L. 103-416, Title I, § 105(a), 108 Stat. 4308; Sept. 30, 1996, P. L. 104-208, Div C, Title VI, Subtitle E, § 671(b)(3), 110 Stat. 3009-721.)

§§ 1484–1487. [Repealed]

§ 1488. Nationality lost solely from performance of acts or fulfillment of conditions

The loss of nationality, under this chapter shall result solely from the performance by a national of the acts or fulfillment of the conditions specified in this chapter.

(June 27, 1952, ch 477, Title III, Ch 3, § 356, 66 Stat. 272.)

§ 1489. Application of treaties; exceptions

Nothing in this title shall be applied in contravention of the provisions of any treaty or convention to which the United States is a party and which has been ratified by the Senate before December 25, 1952: *Provided, however,* That no woman who was a national of the United States shall be deemed to have lost her nationality solely by reason of her marriage to an alien on or after September 22, 1922, or to an alien racially ineligible to citizenship on or after March 3, 1931, or, in the case of a woman who was a United States citizen at birth, through residence abroad following such marriage, notwithstanding the provisions of any existing treaty or convention.

(June 27, 1952, ch 477, Title III, Ch 3, § 357, 66 Stat. 272; Oct. 24, 1988, P. L. 100-525, § 9(ii), 102 Stat. 2622.)

MISCELLANEOUS

§ 1501. Certificate of diplomatic or consular officer of the United States as to loss of American nationality

Whenever a diplomatic or consular officer of the United States has reason to believe that a person while in a foreign state has lost his United States nationality under any provision of chapter 3 of this title, or under any provision of chapter IV of the Nationality Act of 1940, as amended, he shall certify the facts upon which such belief is based to the Department of State, in writing, under regulations prescribed by the Secretary of State. If the report of the diplomatic or consular officer is approved by the Secretary of State, a copy of the certificate shall be forwarded to the Attorney General, for his information, and the diplomatic or consular office in which the report was made shall be directed to forward a copy of the certificate to the person to whom it relates. Approval by the Secretary of State of a certificate under this section shall constitute a final administrative determination of loss of United States nationality under this Act, subject to such procedures for administrative appeal as the Secretary may prescribe by regulation, and also shall constitute a denial of a right or privilege of United States nationality for purposes of section 360 [8 USCS § 1503].

(June 27, 1952, ch 477, Title III, Ch 4, § 358, 66 Stat. 272; Oct. 25, 1994, P. L. 103-416, Title I, § 106, 108 Stat. 4309.)

§ 1502. Certificate of nationality issued by Secretary of State for person not a naturalized citizen of the United States for use in proceedings of a foreign state

The Secretary of State is hereby authorized to issue, in his discretion and in accordance with rules and regulations prescribed by him, a certificate of nationality for any person not a naturalized citizen of the United States who presents satisfactory evidence that he is an American national and that such certificate is needed for use in judicial or administrative proceedings in a foreign state. Such certificate shall be solely for use in the case for which it was issued and shall be transmitted by the Secretary of State through appropriate official channels to the judicial or administrative officers of the foreign state in which it is to be used.

(June 27, 1952, ch 477, Title III, Ch 4, § 359, 66 Stat. 273.)

§ 1503. Denial of rights and privileges as national

(a) Proceedings for declaration of United States nationality. If any person who is within the United States claims a right or privilege as a national of the United States and is denied such right or privilege by any department or independent agency, or official thereof, upon the ground that he is not a national of the United States, such person may institute an action under the provisions of section 2201 of title 28, United States Code, against the head of such department or independent agency for a judgment declaring him to be a national of the United States, except that no such action may be instituted in any case if the issue of such person's status as a national of the United States (1) arose by reason of, or in connection with any removal proceeding under the provisions of this or any other act, or (2) is in issue in any such removal proceeding. An action under this subsection may be instituted only within five years after the final administrative denial of such right or privilege and shall be filed in the district court of the United States for the district in which such person resides or claims a residence, and jurisdiction over such officials in such cases is hereby conferred upon those courts.

(b) Application for certificate of identity; appeal. If any person who is not within the United States claims a right or privilege as a national of the United States and is denied such right or privilege by any department or independent agency, or official thereof, upon the ground that he is not a national of the United States, such person may make application to a diplomatic or consular officer of the United States in the foreign country in which he is residing for a certificate of identity for the purpose of traveling to a port of entry in the United States and applying for admission. Upon proof to the satisfaction of such diplomatic or consular officer that such application is made in good faith and has a substantial basis, he shall issue to such person a certificate of identity. From any denial of an application for such certificate the applicant shall be entitled to an appeal to the Secretary of State, who, if he approves the denial, shall state in writing his reasons for his decision. The Secretary of State shall prescribe rules and regulations for the issuance of certificates of identity as above provided. The provisions of this subsection shall be applicable only to a person who at some time prior to his application for the certificate of identity has been physically present in the United States, or to a person under sixteen years of age who was born abroad of a United States citizen parent.

(c) Application for admission to United States under certificate of identity; revision of determination. A person who has been issued a certificate of identity under the provisions of subsection (b), and while in possession thereof, may apply for admission to the United States at any port of entry, and shall be subject to all the provisions of this Act relating to the conduct of proceedings involving aliens seeking admission to the United States. A final determination by the Attorney General that any such person is not entitled to admission to the United States shall be subject to review by any court of competent jurisdiction in habeas corpus proceedings and not otherwise. Any person described in this section who is finally denied admission to the United States shall be subject to all the provisions of this Act relating to aliens seeking admission to the United States.

(June 27, 1952, ch 477, Title III, Ch 4, § 360, 66 Stat. 273; Sept. 30, 1996, P. L. 104-208, Div C, Title III, Subtitle A, § 308(d)(4)(P), 110 Stat. 3009-619.)

§ 1504. Cancellation of United States passports and Consular Reports of Birth

(a) The Secretary of State is authorized to cancel any United States passport or Consular Report of Birth, or certified copy thereof, if it appears that such document was illegally, fraudulently, or erroneously obtained from, or was created through illegality or fraud practiced upon, the Secretary. The person for or to whom such document has been issued or made shall be given, at such person's last known address, written notice of the cancellation of such document, together with the procedures for seeking a prompt post-cancellation hearing. The cancellation under this section of any document purporting to show the citizenship status of the person to whom it was issued shall affect only the document and not the citizenship status of the person in whose name the document was issued.

(b) For purposes of this section, the term "Consular Report of Birth" refers to the report, designated as a "Report of Birth Abroad of a Citizen of the United States", issued by a consular officer to document a citizen born abroad.

(June 27, 1952, ch 477, Title III, Ch 4, § 361, as added Oct. 25, 1994, P. L. 103-416, Title I, § 107(a), 108 Stat. 4309.)

REFUGEE ASSISTANCE

Section

§ 1521. Office of Refugee Resettlement; establishment; appointment of Director; functions

(a) There is established, within the Department of Health and Human Services, an office to be known as the Office of Refugee Resettlement (hereinafter in this chapter referred to as the "Office"). The head of the Office shall be a Director (hereinafter in this chapter referred to as the "Director"), to be appointed by the Secretary of Health and Human Services (hereinafter in this chapter referred to as the "Secretary").

(b) The function of the Office and its Director is to fund and administer (directly or through arrangements with other Federal agencies), in consultation with the Secretary of State, programs of the Federal Government under this chapter.

(June 27, 1952, ch 477, Title IV, Ch 2, § 411, as added March 17, 1980, P.L. 96-212, Title III, § 311(a)(2), 94 Stat. 111; April 30, 1994, P. L. 103-236, Title I, Part C, § 162(n)(1), 108 Stat. 409.)

§ 1522. Authorization for programs for domestic resettlement of and assistance to refugees

(a) Conditions and considerations.

(1)(A) In providing assistance under this section, the Director shall, to the extent of available appropriations, (i) make available sufficient resources for employment training and placement in order to achieve economic self-sufficiency among refugees as quickly as possible, (ii) provide refugees with the opportunity to acquire sufficient English language training to enable them to become effectively resettled as quickly as possible, (iii) insure that cash assistance is made available to refugees in such a manner as not to discourage their economic self-sufficiency, in accordance with subsection (e)(2), and (iv) insure that women have the same opportunities as men to participate in training and instruction.

(B) It is the intent of Congress that in providing refugee assistance under this section—

(i) employable refugees should be placed on jobs as soon as possible after their arrival in the United States;

(ii) social service funds should be focused on employment-related services, English-as-a-second-language training (in nonwork hours where possible), and case-management services; and

(iii) local voluntary agency activities should be conducted in close cooperation and advance consultation with State and local governments.

(2)(A) The Director and the Federal agency administering subsection (b)(1) shall consult regularly (not less often than quarterly) with State and local governments and private nonprofit voluntary agencies concerning the sponsorship process and the intended distribution of refugees among the States and localities before their placement in those States and localities.

(B) The Director shall develop and implement, in consultation with representatives of voluntary agencies and State and local governments, policies and strategies for the placement and resettlement of refugees within the United States.

(C) Such policies and strategies, to the extent practicable and except under such unusual circumstances as the Director may recognize, shall—

(i) insure that a refugee is not initially placed or resettled in an area highly impacted (as determined under regulations prescribed by the Director after consultation with such agencies and governments) by the presence of refugees or comparable populations unless the refugee has a spouse, parent, sibling, son, or daughter residing in that area,

(ii) provide for a mechanism whereby representatives of local affiliates of voluntary agencies regularly (not less often than quarterly) meet with representatives of State and local governments to plan and coordinate in advance of their arrival the appropriate placement of refugees among the various States and localities, and

(iii) take into account—

(I) the proportion of refugees and comparable entrants in the population in the area,

(II) the availability of employment opportunities, affordable housing, and public and private resources (including educational, health care, and mental health services) for refugees in the area,

(III) the likelihood of refugees placed in the area becoming self-sufficient and free from long-term dependence on public assistance, and

(IV) the secondary migration of refugees to and from the area that is likely to occur.

(D) With respect to the location of placement of refugees within a State, the Federal agency administering subsection (b)(1) shall, consistent with such policies and strategies and to the maximum extent possible, take into account recommendations of the State.

(3) In the provision of domestic assistance under this section, the Director shall make a periodic assessment, based on refugee population and other relevant factors, of the relative needs of refugees for assistance and services under this chapter and the resources available to meet such needs. The Director shall compile and maintain data on secondary migration of refugees within the United States and, by State of residence and nationality, on the proportion of refugees receiving cash or medical assistance described in subsection (e). In allocating resources, the Director shall avoid duplication of services and provide for maximum coordination between agencies providing related services.

(4)(A) No grant or contract may be awarded under this section unless an appropriate proposal and application (including a description of the agency's ability to perform the services specified in the proposal) are submitted to, and approved by, the appropriate administering official. Grants and contracts under this section shall be made to those agencies which the appropriate administering official determines can best perform the services. Payments may be made for activities authorized under this chapter in advance or by way of reimbursement. In carrying out this section, the Director, the Secretary of State, and any such other appropriate administering official are authorized—

(i) to make loans, and

(ii) to accept and use money, funds, property, and services of any kind made available by gift, devise, bequest, grant, or otherwise for the purpose of carrying out this section.

(B) No funds may be made available under this chapter (other than under subsection (b)(1)) to States or political subdivisions in the form of block grants, per capita grants, or similar consolidated grants or contracts. Such funds shall be made available under separate grants or contracts—

(i) for medical screening and initial medical treatment under subsection (b)(5),

(ii) for services for refugees under subsection (c)(1),

(iii) for targeted assistance project grants under subsection (c)(2), and

(iv) for assistance for refugee children under subsection (d)(2).

(C) The Director may not delegate to a State or political subdivision his authority to review or approve grants or contracts under this chapter or the terms under which such grants or contracts are made.

(5) Assistance and services funded under this section shall be provided to refugees without regard to race, religion, nationality, sex, or political opinion.

(6) As a condition for receiving assistance under this section, a State must—

(A) submit to the Director a plan which provides—

(i) a description of how the State intends to encourage effective refugee resettlement and to promote economic self-sufficiency as quickly as possible,

(ii) a description of how the State will insure that language training and employment services are made available to refugees receiving cash assistance,

(iii) for the designation of an individual, employed by the State, who will be responsible for insuring coordination of public and private resources in refugee resettlement,

(iv) for the care and supervision of and legal responsibility for unaccompanied refugee children in the State, and

(v) for the identification of refugees who at the time of resettlement in the State are determined to have medical conditions requiring, or medical histories indicating a need for, treatment or observation and such monitoring of such treatment or observation as may be necessary;

(B) meet standards, goals, and priorities, developed by the Director, which assure the effective resettlement of refugees and which promote their economic self-sufficiency as quickly as possible and the efficient provision of services; and

(C) submit to the Director, within a reasonable period of time after the end of each fiscal year, a report on the uses of funds provided under this chapter which the State is responsible for administering.

(7) The Secretary, together with the Secretary of State with respect to assistance provided by the Secretary of State under subsection (b), shall develop a system of monitoring the assistance provided under this section. This system shall include—

(A) evaluations of the effectiveness of the programs funded under this section and the performance of States, grantees, and contractors;

(B) financial auditing and other appropriate monitoring to detect any fraud, abuse, or mismanagement in the operation of such programs; and

(C) data collection on the services provided and the results achieved.

(8) The Attorney General shall provide the Director with information supplied by refugees in conjunction with their applications to the Attorney General for adjustment of status, and the Director shall compile, summarize, and evaluate such information.

(9) The Secretary, the Secretary of Education, the Attorney General, and the Secretary of State may issue such regulations as each deems appropriate to carry out this chapter.

(10) For purposes of this chapter, the term "refugee" includes any alien described in section 207(c)(2) [8 USCS § 1157(c)(2)].

(b) Program of initial resettlement.

(1)(A) For—

(i) fiscal years 1980 and 1981, the Secretary of State is authorized, and

(ii) fiscal year 1982 and succeeding fiscal years, the Director (except as provided in subparagraph (B)) is authorized,

to make grants to, and contracts with, public or private nonprofit agencies for initial resettlement (including initial reception and placement with sponsors) of refugees in the United States. Grants to, or contracts with, private nonprofit voluntary agencies under this paragraph shall be made consistent with the objectives of this chapter, taking into account the different resettlement approaches and practices of such agencies. Resettlement assistance under this paragraph shall be provided in coordination with the Director's provision of other assistance under this chapter. Funds provided to agencies under such grants and contracts may only be obligated or expended during the fiscal year in which they are provided (or the subsequent fiscal year or such subsequent fiscal period as the Federal contracting agency may approve) to carry out the purposes of this subsection.

(B) If the President determines that the Director should not administer the program under this paragraph, the authority of the Director under the first sentence of subparagraph (A) shall be exercised by such officer as the President shall from time to time specify.

(2) The Director is authorized to develop programs for such orientation, instruction in English, and job training for refugees, and such other education and training of refugees, as facilitates their resettlement in the United States. The Director is authorized to implement such programs, in accordance with the provisions of this section, with respect to refugees in the United States. The Secretary of State is authorized to implement such programs with respect to refugees awaiting entry into the United States.

(3) The Secretary is authorized to make arrangements (including cooperative arrangements with other Federal agencies) for the temporary care of refugees in the United States in emergency circumstances, including the establishment of processing centers, if necessary, without regard to such provisions of law (other than the Renegotiation Act of 1951 and section 414(b) of this chapter [8 USCS § 1524(b)]) regulating the making, performance, amendment, or modification of contracts and the expenditure of funds of the United States Government as the Secretary may specify.

(4) The Secretary shall—

(A) assure that an adequate number of trained staff are available at the location at which the refugees enter the United States to assure that all necessary medical records are available and in proper order;

(B) provide for the identification of refugees who have been determined to have medical conditions affecting the public health and requiring treatment;

(C) assure that State or local health officials at the resettlement destination within the United States of each refugee are promptly notified of the refugee's arrival and provided with all applicable medical records; and

(D) provide for such monitoring of refugees identified under subparagraph (B) as will insure that they receive appropriate and timely treatment.

The Secretary shall develop and implement methods for monitoring and assessing the quality of medical screening and related health services provided to refugees awaiting resettlement in the United States.

(5) The Director is authorized to make grants to, and enter into contracts with, State and local health agencies for payments to meet their costs of providing medical screening and initial medical treatment to refugees.

(6) The Comptroller General shall directly conduct an annual financial audit of funds expended under each grant or contract made under paragraph (1) for fiscal year 1986 and for fiscal year 1987.

(7) Each grant or contract with an agency under paragraph (1) shall require the agency to do the following:

(A) To provide quarterly performance and financial status reports to the Federal agency administering paragraph (1).

(B)(i) To provide, directly or through its local affiliate, not To provide, directly or through its local affiliate, notice to the appropriate county or other local welfare office at the time that the agency becomes aware that a refugee is offered employment and to provide notice to the refugee that such notice has been provided, and

(ii) upon request of such a welfare office to which a refugee has applied for cash assistance, to furnish that office with documentation respecting any cash or other resources provided directly by the agency to the refugee under this subsection.

(C) To assure that refugees, known to the agency as having been identified pursuant to paragraph (4)(B) as having medical conditions affecting the public health and requiring treatment, report to the appropriate county or other health agency upon their resettlement in an area.

(D) To fulfill its responsibility to provide for the basic needs (including food, clothing, shelter, and transportation for job interviews and training) of each refugee resettled and to develop and implement a resettlement plan including the early employment of each refugee resettled and to monitor the implementation of such plan.

(E) To transmit to the Federal agency administering paragraph (1) an annual report describing the following:

(i) The number of refugees placed (by county of placement) and the expenditures made in the year under the grant or contract, including the proportion of such expenditures used for administrative purposes and for provision of services.

(ii) The proportion of refugees placed by the agency in the previous year who are receiving cash or medical assistance described in subsection (e).

(iii) The efforts made by the agency to monitor placement of the refugees and the activities of local affiliates of the agency.

(iv) The extent to which the agency has coordinated its activities with local social service providers in a manner which avoids duplication of activities and has provided notices to local welfare offices and the reporting of medical conditions of certain aliens to local health departments in accordance with subparagraphs (B)(i) and (C).

(v) Such other information as the agency administering paragraph (1) deems to be appropriate in monitoring the effectiveness of agencies in carrying out their functions under such grants and contracts.

The agency administering paragraph (1) shall promptly forward a copy of each annual report transmitted under subparagraph (E) to the Committees on the Judiciary of the House of Representatives and of the Senate.

(8) The Federal agency administering paragraph (1) shall establish criteria for the performance of agencies under grants and contracts under that paragraph, and shall include criteria relating to an agency's—

(A) efforts to reduce welfare dependency among refugees resettled by that agency,

(B) collection of travel loans made to refugees resettled by that agency for travel to the United States,

(C) arranging for effective local sponsorship and other nonpublic assistance for refugees resettled by that agency,

(D) cooperation with refugee mutual assistance associations, local social service providers, health agencies, and welfare offices,

(E) compliance with the guidelines established by the Director for the placement and resettlement of refugees within the United States, and

(F) compliance with other requirements contained in the grant or contract, including the reporting and other requirements under subsection (b)(7).

The Federal administering agency shall use the criteria in the process of awarding or renewing grants and contracts under paragraph (1).

(c) Project grants and controls for services for refugees.

(1)(A) The Director is authorized to make grants to, and enter into contracts with, public or private nonprofit agencies for projects specifically designated—

(i) to assist refugees in obtaining the skills which are necessary for economic self-sufficiency, including projects for job training, employment services, day care, professional refresher training, and other recertification services;

(ii) to provide training in English where necessary (regardless of whether the refugees are employed or receiving cash or other assistance); and

(iii) to provide where specific needs have been shown and recognized by the Director, health (including mental health) services, social services, educational and other services.

(B) The funds available for a fiscal year for grants and contracts under subparagraph (A) shall be allocated among the States based on the total number of refugees (including children and adults) who arrived in the United States not more than 36 months before the beginning of such fiscal year and who are actually residing in each State (taking into account secondary migration) as of the beginning of the fiscal year.

(C) Any limitation which the Director establishes on the proportion of funds allocated to a State under this paragraph that the State may use for services other than those described in subsection (a)(1)(B)(ii) shall not apply if the Director receives a plan (established by or in consultation with local governments) and determines that the plan provides for the maximum appropriate provision of employment-related services for, and the maximum placement of, employable refugees consistent with performance standards established under section 106 of the Job Training Partnership Act [former 29 USCS § 1516].

(2)(A) The Director is authorized to make grants to States for The Director is authorized to make grants to States for assistance to counties and similar areas in the States where, because of factors such as unusually large refugee populations (including secondary migration), high refugee concentrations, and high use of public assistance by refugees, there exists and can be demonstrated a specific need for supplementation of available resources for services to refugees.

(B) Grants shall be made available under this paragraph—

(i) primarily for the purpose of facilitating refugee employment and achievement of self-sufficiency,

(ii) in a manner that does not supplant other refugee program funds and that assures that not less than 95 percent of the amount of the grant award is made available to the county or other local entity.

(d) Assistance for refugee children.

(1) The Secretary of Education is authorized to make grants, and enter into contracts, for payments for projects to provide special educational services (including English language training) to refugee children in elementary and secondary schools were a demonstrated need has been shown.

(2)(A) The Director is authorized to provide assistance, reimbursement to States, and grants to and contracts with public and private nonprofit agencies, for the provision of child welfare services, including foster care maintenance payments and services and health care, furnished to any refugee child (except as provided in subparagraph (B)) during the thirty-six month period beginning with the first month in which such refugee child is in the United States.

(B)(i) In the case of a refugee child who is unaccompanied by a parent or other close adult relative (as defined by the Director), the services described in subparagraph (A) may be furnished until the month after the child attains eighteen years of age (or such higher age as the State's child welfare services plan under part B of title IV of the Social Security Act [42 USCS §§ 620 et seq.] prescribes for the availability of such services to any other child in that State).

(ii) The Director shall attempt to arrange for the placement under the laws of the States of such unaccompanied refugee children, who have been accepted for admission to the United States, before (or as soon as possible after) their arrival in the United States. During any interim period which such a child is in the United States or in transit to the United States but before the child is so placed, the Director shall assume legal responsibility (including financial responsibility) for the child, if necessary, and is authorized to make necessary decisions to provide for the child's immediate care.

(iii) In carrying out the Director's responsibilities under clause (ii), the Director is authorized to enter into contracts with appropriate public or private nonprofit agencies under such conditions as the Director determines to be appropriate.

(iv) The Director shall prepare and maintain a list of (I) all such unaccompanied children who have entered the United States after April 1, 1975, (II) the names and last known residences of their parents (if living) at the time of arrival, and (III) the children's location, status, and progress.

(e) Cash assistance and medical assistance to refugees.

(1) The Director is authorized to provide assistance, reimbursement to States, and grants to, and contracts with, public or private nonprofit agencies for 100 per centum of the cash assistance and medical assistance provided to any refugee during the thirty-six month period beginning with the first month in which such refugee has entered the United States and for the identifiable and reasonable administrative costs of providing this assistance.

(2)(A) Cash assistance provided under this subsection to an employable refugee is conditioned, except for good cause shown—

(i) on the refugee's registration with an appropriate agency providing employment services described in subsection (c)(1)(A)(i), or, if there is no such agency available, with an appropriate State or local employment service;

(ii) on the refugee's participation in any available and appropriate social service or targeted assistance program (funded under subsection (c)) providing job or language training in the area in which the refugee resides; and

(iii) on the refugee's acceptance of appropriate offers of employment.

(B) Cash assistance shall not be made available to refugees who are full-time students in institutions of higher education (as defined by the Director after consultation with the Secretary of Education).

(C) In the case of a refugee who—

(i) refuses an offer of employment which has been determined to be appropriate either by the agency responsible for the initial resettlement of the refugee under subsection (b) or by the appropriate State or local employment service,

(ii) refuses to go to a job interview which has been arranged through such agency or service, or

(iii) refuses to participate in a social service or targeted assistance program referred to in subparagraph (A)(ii) which such agency or service determines to be available and appropriate,

cash assistance to the refugee shall be terminated (after opportunity for an administrative hearing) for a period of three months (for the first such refusal) or for a period of six months (for any subsequent refusal).

(3) The Director shall develop plans to provide English training and other appropriate services and training to refugees receiving cash assistance.

(4) If a refugee is eligible for aid or assistance under a State program funded under part A of title IV or under title XIX [42 USCS §§ 601 et seq. or 1396 et seq.] of the Social Security Act, or for supplemental security income benefits (including State supplementary payments) under the program established under title XVI of that Act [42 USCS §§ 1381 et seq.], funds authorized under this subsection shall only be used for the non-Federal share of such aid or assistance, or for such supplementary payments, with respect to cash and medical assistance provided with respect to such refugee under this paragraph.

(5) The Director is authorized to allow for the provision of medical assistance under paragraph (1) to any refugee, during the one-year period after entry, who does not qualify for assistance under a State plan approved under title XIX of the Social Security Act [42 USCS §§ 1396 et seq.] on account of any resources or income requirement of such plan, but only if the Director determines that—

(A) this will (i) encourage economic self-sufficiency, or (ii) avoid a significant burden on State and local governments; and

(B) the refugee meets such alternative financial resources and income requirements as the Director shall establish.

(6) As a condition for receiving assistance, reimbursement, or a contract under this subsection and notwithstanding any other provision of law, a State or agency must provide assurances that whenever a refugee applies for cash or medical assistance for which assistance or reimbursement is provided under this subsection, the State or agency must notify promptly the agency (or local affiliate) which provided for the initial resettlement of the refugee under subsection (b) of the fact that the refugee has so applied.

(7)(A) The Secretary shall develop and implement alternative projects for refugees who have been in the United States less than thirty-six months, under which refugees are provided interim support, medical services, support services, and case management, as needed, in a manner that encourages self-sufficiency, reduces welfare dependency, and fosters greater coordination among the resettlement agencies and service providers. The Secretary may permit alternative projects to cover specific groups of refugees who have been in the United States 36 months or longer if the Secretary determines that refugees in the group have been significantly and disproportionately dependent on welfare and need the services provided under the project in order to become self-sufficient and that their coverage under the projects would be cost-effective.

(B) Refugees covered under such alternative projects shall be precluded from receiving cash or medical assistance under any other paragraph of this subsection or under title XIX or part A of title IV of the Social Security Act [42 USCS §§ 1396 et seq. or 601 et seq.]

(C) The Secretary shall report to Congress not later than October 31, 1985, on the results of these projects and on any recommendations respecting changes in the refugee assistance program under this section to take into account such results.

(D) To the extent that the use of such funds is consistent with the purposes of such provisions, funds appropriated under section 414(a) of this Act [8 USCS § 1524(a)], part A of title IV of the Social Security Act, or title XIX of such Act [42 USCS §§ 601 et seq. or 1396 et seq.], may be used for the purpose of implementing and evaluating alternative projects under this paragraph.

(8) In its provision of assistance to refugees, a State or political subdivision shall consider the recommendations of, and assistance provided by, agencies with grants or contracts under subsection (b)(1).

(f) Assistance to States and counties for incarceration of certain Cuban nationals; priority for removal and return to Cuba.

(1) The Attorney General shall pay compensation to States and to counties for costs incurred by the States and counties to confine in prisons, during the fiscal year for which such payment is made, nationals of Cuba who—

(A) were paroled into the United States in 1980 by the Attorney General,

(B) after such parole committed any violation of State or county law for which a term of imprisonment was imposed, and

(C) at the time of such parole and such violation were not aliens lawfully admitted to the United States—

(i) for permanent residence, or

(ii) under the terms of an immigrant or a nonimmigrant visa issued,

under this Act [8 USCS §§ 1521 et seq.].

(2) For a State or county to be eligible to receive compensation under this subsection, the chief executive officer of the State or county shall submit to the

Attorney General, in accordance with rules to be issued by the Attorney General, an application containing—

(A) the number and names of the Cuban nationals with respect to whom the State or county is entitled to such compensation, and

(B) such other information as the Attorney General may require.

(3) For a fiscal year the Attorney General shall pay the costs described in paragraph (1) to each State and county determined by the Attorney General to be eligible under paragraph (2); except that if the amounts appropriated for the fiscal year to carry out this subsection are insufficient to cover all such payments, each of such payments shall be ratably reduced so that the total of such payments equals the amounts so appropriated.

(4) The authority of the Attorney General to pay compensation under this subsection shall be effective for any fiscal year only to the extent and in such amounts as may be provided in advance in appropriation Acts.

(5) It shall be the policy of the United States Government that the President, in consultation with the Attorney General and all other appropriate Federal officials and all appropriate State and county officials referred to in paragraph (2), shall place top priority on seeking the expeditious removal from this country and the return to Cuba of Cuban nationals described in paragraph (1) by any reasonable and responsible means, and to this end the Attorney General may use the funds authorized to carry out this subsection to conduct such policy.

(June 27, 1952, ch 477, Title IV, Ch 2, § 412, as added March 17, 1980, P.L. 96-212, Title III, Part B, § 311(a)(2), 94 Stat. 111; Oct. 25, 1982, P. L. 97-363, §§ 3(a), 4–6, 96 Stat. 1734–1736; Nov. 22, 1983, P. L. 98-164, Title X, § 1011(b), 97 Stat. 1061; Oct. 12, 1984, P. L. 98-473, Title I, § 101(d) in part, 98 Stat. 1877; Nov. 6, 1986, P. L. 99-605, §§ 3-5(c), 6(a), (b), (d), 8, 9(a), (b), 10, 12, 13, 100 Stat. 3449, 3453-3455; Oct. 24, 1988, P. L. 100-525, § 6(b), 102 Stat. 2616; April 30, 1994, P. L. 103-236, Title I, Part C, § 162(n)(2), 108 Stat. 409; Oct. 25, 1994, P. L. 103-416, Title II, § 219(x), 108 Stat. 4318; Aug. 22, 1996, P. L. 104-193, Title I, § 110(s)(3), 110 Stat. 2175; Sept. 30, 1996, P. L. 104-208, Div C, Title VI, Subtitle E, § 671(e)(7), 110 Stat. 3009-723.)

§ 1523. Congressional reports

(a) The Secretary shall submit a report on activities under this chapter to the Committees on the Judiciary of the House of Representatives and of the Senate not later than the January 31 following the end of each fiscal year, beginning with fiscal year 1980.

(b) Each such report shall contain—

(1) an updated profile of the employment and labor force statistics for refugees who have entered the United States within the five-fiscal-year period immediately preceding the fiscal year within which the report is to be made and for refugees who entered earlier and who have shown themselves to be significantly and disproportionately dependent on welfare, as well as a description of the extent to which refugees received the forms of assistance or services under this chapter during that period;

(2) a description of the geographic location of refugees;

(3) a summary of the results of the monitoring and evaluation conducted under section 412(a)(7) [8 USCS § 1522(a)(7)] during the period for which the report is submitted;

(4) a description of (A) the activities, expenditures, and policies of the Office under this chapter and of the activities of States, voluntary agencies, and sponsors, and (B) the Director's plans for improvement of refugee resettlement;

(5) evaluations of the extent to which (A) the services provided under this chapter are assisting refugees in achieving economic self-sufficiency, achieving ability in English, and achieving employment commensurate with their skills and abilities, and (B) any fraud, abuse, or mismanagement has been reported in the provisions of services or assistance;

(6) a description of any assistance provided by the Director pursuant to section 412(e)(5) [8 USCS § 1522(e)(5)];

(7) a summary of the location and status of unaccompanied refugee children admitted to the United States; and

(8) a summary of the information compiled and evaluation made under section 412(a)(8) [8 USCS § 1522(a)(8)].

(June 27, 1952, ch 477, Title IV, Ch 2, § 413, as added March 17, 1980, P. L. 96-212, Title III, Part B, § 311(a)(2), 94 Stat. 115; Oct. 25, 1982, P. L. 97-363, §§ 3(b), 7, 96 Stat. 1734, 1737; Nov. 6, 1986, P. L. 99-605, § 11, 100 Stat. 3455; Oct. 24, 1988, P. L. 100-525, § 9(jj), 102 Stat. 2622; April 30, 1994, P. L. 103-236, Title I, Part C, § 162(n)(3), 108 Stat. 409.)

§ 1524. Authorization of appropriations

(a) There are authorized to be appropriated for each of fiscal years 2000 through 2002 such sums as may be necessary to carry out this chapter.

(b) The authority to enter into contracts under this chapter shall be effective for any fiscal year only to such extent or in such amounts as are provided in advance in appropriation Acts.

(June 27, 1952, ch 477, Title IV, Ch 2, § 414, as added March 17, 1980, P.L. 96-212, Title III, Part B, § 311(a)(2), 94 Stat. 116; Oct. 25, 1982, P. L. 97-363, § 2, 96 Stat. 1734; Nov. 6, 1986, P. L. 99-605, § 2, 100 Stat. 3449; Oct. 24, 1988, P. L. 100-525, § 6(a), 102 Stat. 2616; Oct. 1, 1991, P. L. 102-110, § 5, 105 Stat. 558; June 8, 1993, P. L. 103-37, § 1, 107 Stat. 107; Oct. 25, 1994, P. L. 103-416, Title II, § 208, 108 Stat. 4312; Nov. 13, 1997, P. L. 105-78, Title VI, § 604(a), 111 Stat. 1521.; Dec. 2, 1997, P. L. 105-136, § 1(a), 111 Stat. 2639; Nov. 13, 1999, P. L. 106-104, § 3, 113 Stat. 1483.)

§ 1525. [Repealed]

ALIEN TERRORIST REMOVAL PROCEDURES

§ 1531. Definitions

As used in this title [8 USCS §§ 1531 et seq.]—

(1) the term "alien terrorist" means any alien described in section 241(a)(4)(B) [237(a)(4)(B)] [8 USCS § 1227(a)(4)(B)];

(2) the term "classified information" has the same meaning as in section 1(a) of the Classified Information Procedures Act (18 U.S.C. App.);

(3) the term "national security" has the same meaning as in section 1(b) of the Classified Information Procedures Act (18 U.S.C. App.);

(4) the term "removal court" means the court described in section 502 [8 USCS § 1532];

(5) the term "removal hearing" means the hearing described in section 504 [8 USCS § 1534];

(6) the term "removal proceeding" means a proceeding under this title [8 USCS §§ 1531 et seq.]; and

(7) the term "special attorney" means an attorney who is on the panel established under section 502(e) [8 USCS § 1532(e)].

(June 27, 1952, ch 477, Title V, § 501, as added April 24, 1996, P. L. 104-132, Title IV, Subtitle A, § 401(a), 110 Stat. 1259; Sept. 30, 1996, P. L. 104-208, Div C, Title III, Subtitle D, § 354(a)(5), 110 Stat. 3009-643.)

§ 1532. Establishment of removal court

(a) Designation of judges. The Chief Justice of the United States shall publicly designate 5 district court judges from 5 of the United States judicial circuits who shall constitute a court that shall have jurisdiction to conduct all removal proceedings. The Chief Justice may, in the Chief Justice's discretion, designate the same judges under this section as are designated pursuant to section 103(a) of the Foreign Intelligence Surveillance Act of 1978 (50 U.S.C. 1803(a)).

(b) Terms. Each judge designated under subsection (a) shall serve for a term of 5 years and shall be eligible for redesignation, except that of the members first designated—

(1) 1 member shall serve for a term of 1 year;

(2) 1 member shall serve for a term of 2 years;

(3) 1 member shall serve for a term of 3 years; and

(4) 1 member shall serve for a term of 4 years.

(c) Chief judge.

(1) Designation. The Chief Justice shall publicly designate one of the judges of the removal court to be the chief judge of the removal court.

(2) Responsibilities. The chief judge shall—

(A) promulgate rules to facilitate the functioning of the removal court; and

(B) assign the consideration of cases to the various judges on the removal court.

(d) Expeditious and confidential nature of proceedings. The provisions of section 103(c) of the Foreign Intelligence Surveillance Act of 1978 (50 U.S.C. 1803(c)) shall apply to removal proceedings in the same manner as they apply to proceedings under that Act.

(e) Establishment of panel of special attorneys. The removal court shall provide for the designation of a panel of attorneys each of whom—

(1) has a security clearance which affords the attorney access to classified information, and

(2) has agreed to represent permanent resident aliens with respect to classified information under section 504(e)(3) [8 USCS § 1534(e)(3)] in accordance with (and subject to the penalties under) this title [8 USCS §§ 1531 et seq.].

(June 27, 1952, ch 477, Title V, § 502, as added April 24, 1996, P. L. 104-132, Title IV, Subtitle A, § 401(a), 110 Stat. 1259; Sept. 30, 1996, P. L. 104-208, Div C, Title III, Subtitle D, § 354(a)(4), 110 Stat. 3009-643.)

§ 1533. Removal court procedure

(a) Application.

(1) In general. In any case in which the Attorney General has classified information that an alien is an alien terrorist, the Attorney General may seek removal of the alien under this title [8 USCS §§ 1531 et seq.] by filing an application with the removal court that contains—

(A) the identity of the attorney in the Department of Justice making the application;

(B) a certification by the Attorney General or the Deputy Attorney General that the application satisfies the criteria and requirements of this section;

(C) the identity of the alien for whom authorization for the removal proceeding is sought; and

(D) a statement of the facts and circumstances relied on by the Department of Justice to establish probable cause that—

(i) the alien is an alien terrorist;

(ii) the alien is physically present in the United States; and

(iii) with respect to such alien, removal under title II would pose a risk to the national security of the United States.

(2) Filing. An application under this section shall be submitted ex parte and in camera, and shall be filed under seal with the removal court.

(b) Right to dismiss. The Attorney General may dismiss a removal action under this title [8 USCS §§ 1531 et seq.] at any stage of the proceeding.

(c) Consideration of application.

(1) Basis for decision. In determining whether to grant an application under this section, a single judge of the removal court may consider, ex parte and in camera, in addition to the information contained in the application—

(A) other information, including classified information, presented under oath or affirmation; and

(B) testimony received in any hearing on the application, of which a verbatim record shall be kept.

(2) Approval of order. The judge shall issue an order granting the application, if the judge finds that there is probable cause to believe that—

(A) the alien who is the subject of the application has been correctly identified and is an alien terrorist present in the United States; and

(B) removal under title II [8 USCS §§ 1151 et seq.] would pose a risk to the national security of the United States.

(3) Denial of order. If the judge denies the order requested in the application, the judge shall prepare a written statement of the reasons for the denial, taking all necessary precautions not to disclose any classified information contained in the Government's application.

(d) Exclusive provisions. If an order is issued under this section granting an application, the rights of the alien regarding removal and expulsion shall be governed solely by this title [8 USCS §§ 1531 et seq.], and except as they are specifically referenced in this title [8 USCS §§ 1531 et seq.], no other provisions of this Act shall be applicable.

(June 27, 1952, ch 477, Title V, § 503, as added April 24, 1996, P. L. 104-132, Title IV, Subtitle A, § 401(a), 110 Stat. 1259.)

§ 1534. Removal hearing

(a) In general.

(1) Expeditious hearing. In any case in which an application for an order is approved under section 503(c)(2) [8 USCS § 1533(c)(2)], a removal hearing shall be conducted under this section as expeditiously as practicable for the purpose of determining whether the alien to whom the order pertains should be removed from the United States on the grounds that the alien is an alien terrorist.

(2) Public hearing. The removal hearing shall be open to the public.

(b) Notice. An alien who is the subject of a removal hearing under this title [8 USCS §§ 1531 et seq.] shall be given reasonable notice of—

(1) the nature of the charges against the alien, including a general account of the basis for the charges; and

(2) the time and place at which the hearing will be held.

(c) Rights in hearing.

(1) Right of counsel. The alien shall have a right to be present at such hearing and to be represented by counsel. Any alien financially unable to obtain counsel shall be entitled to have counsel assigned to represent the alien. Such counsel shall be appointed by the judge pursuant to the plan for furnishing representation for any person financially unable to obtain adequate representation for the district in which the hearing is conducted, as provided for in section 3006A of title 18, United States Code. All provisions of that section shall apply and, for purposes of determining the maximum amount of compensation, the matter shall be treated as if a felony was charged.

(2) Introduction of evidence. Subject to the limitations in subsection (e), the alien shall have a reasonable opportunity to introduce evidence on the alien's own behalf.

(3) Examination of witnesses. Subject to the limitations in subsection (e), the alien shall have a reasonable opportunity to examine the evidence against the alien and to cross-examine any witness.

(4) Record. A verbatim record of the proceedings and of all testimony and evidence offered or produced at such a hearing shall be kept.

(5) Removal decision based on evidence at hearing. The decision of the judge regarding removal shall be based only on that evidence introduced at the removal hearing.

(d) Subpoenas.

(1) Request. At any time prior to the conclusion of the removal hearing, either the alien or the Department of Justice may request the judge to issue a subpoena for the presence of a named witness (which subpoena may also command the person to whom it is directed to produce books, papers, documents, or other objects designated therein) upon a satisfactory showing that the presence of the witness is necessary for the determination of any material matter. Such a request may be made ex parte except that the judge shall inform the Department of Justice of any request for a subpoena by the alien for a witness or material if compliance with such a subpoena would reveal classified evidence or the source of that evidence. The Department of Justice shall be given a reasonable opportunity to oppose the issuance of such a subpoena.

(2) Payment for attendance. If an application for a subpoena by the alien also makes a showing that the alien is financially unable to pay for the attendance of a witness so requested, the court may order the costs incurred by the process and the fees of the witness so subpoenaed to be paid from funds appropriated for the enforcement of title II [8 USCS §§ 1151 et seq.].

(3) Nationwide service. A subpoena under this subsection may be served anywhere in the United States.

(4) Witness fees. A witness subpoenaed under this subsection shall receive the same fees and expenses as a witness subpoenaed in connection with a civil proceeding in a court of the United States.

(5) No access to classified information. Nothing in this subsection is intended to allow an alien to have access to classified information.

(e) Discovery.

(1) In general. For purposes of this title [8 USCS §§ 1531 et seq.]—

(A) the Government is authorized to use in a removal proceedings [proceeding] the fruits of electronic surveillance and unconsented physical searches authorized under the Foreign Intelligence Surveillance Act of 1978 (50 U.S.C. 1801 et seq.) without regard to subsections (c), (e), (f), (g), and (h) of section 106 of that Act [50 USCS § 1806(c), (e), (f), (g), and (h)] and discovery of information derived pursuant to such Act, or otherwise collected for national security purposes, shall not be authorized if disclosure would present a risk to the national security of the United States;

(B) an alien subject to removal under this title [8 USCS §§ 1531 et seq.] shall not be entitled to suppress evidence that the alien alleges was unlawfully obtained; and

(C) section 3504 of title 18, United States Code, and section 1806(c) of title 50, United States Code, shall not apply if the Attorney General determines that public disclosure would pose a risk to the national security of the United States because it would disclose classified information or otherwise threaten the integrity of a pending investigation.

(2) Protective orders. Nothing in this title [8 USCS §§ 1531 et seq.] shall prevent the United States from seeking protective orders and from asserting privileges ordinarily available to the United States to protect against the disclosure of classified information, including the invocation of the military and State secrets privileges.

(3) Treatment of classified information.

(A) Use. The judge shall examine, ex parte and in camera, any evidence for which the Attorney General determines that public disclosure would pose a risk to the national security of the United States or to the security of any individual because it would disclose classified information and neither the alien nor the public shall be informed of such evidence or its sources other than through reference to the summary provided pursuant to this paragraph. Notwithstanding the previous sentence, the Department of Justice may, in its discretion and, in the case of classified information, after coordination with the originating agency, elect to introduce such evidence in open session.

(B) Submission. With respect to such information, the Government shall submit to the removal court an unclassified summary of the specific evidence that does not pose that risk.

(C) Approval. Not later than 15 days after submission, the judge shall approve the summary if the judge finds that it is sufficient to enable the alien to prepare a defense. The Government shall deliver to the alien a copy of the unclassified summary approved under this subparagraph.

(D) Disapproval.

(i) In general. If an unclassified summary is not approved by the removal court under subparagraph (C), the Government shall be afforded 15 days to correct the deficiencies identified by the court and submit a revised unclassified summary.

(ii) Revised summary. If the revised unclassified summary is not approved by the court within 15 days of its submission pursuant to subparagraph (C), the removal hearing shall be terminated unless the judge makes the findings under clause (iii).

(iii) Findings. The findings described in this clause are, with respect to an alien, that—

(I) the continued presence of the alien in the United States would likely cause serious and irreparable harm to the national security or death or serious bodily injury to any person, and

(II) the provision of the summary would likely cause serious and irreparable harm to the national security or death or serious bodily injury to any person.

(E) Continuation of hearing without summary. If a judge makes the findings described in subparagraph (D)(iii)—

(i) if the alien involved is an alien lawfully admitted for permanent residence, the procedures described in subparagraph (F) shall apply; and

(ii) in all cases the special removal hearing shall continue, the Department of Justice shall cause to be delivered to the alien a statement that no summary is possible, and the classified information submitted in camera and ex parte may be used pursuant to this paragraph.

(F) Special procedures for access and challenges to classified information by special attorneys in case of lawful permanent aliens.

(i) In general. The procedures described in this subparagraph are that the judge (under rules of the removal court) shall designate a special attorney to assist the alien—

(I) by reviewing in camera the classified information on behalf of the alien, and

(II) by challenging through an in camera proceeding the veracity of the evidence contained in the classified information.

(ii) Restrictions on disclosure. A special attorney receiving classified information under clause (i)—

(I) shall not disclose the information to the alien or to any other attorney representing the alien, and

(II) who discloses such information in violation of subclause (I) shall be subject to a fine under title 18, United States Code, imprisoned for not less than 10 years nor more than 25 years, or both.

(f) Arguments. Following the receipt of evidence, the Government and the alien shall be given fair opportunity to present argument as to whether the evidence is sufficient to justify the removal of the alien. The Government shall open the argument. The alien shall be permitted to reply. The Government shall then be permitted to reply in rebuttal. The judge may allow any part of the argument that refers to evidence received in camera and ex parte to be heard in camera and ex parte.

(g) Burden of proof. In the hearing, it is the Government's burden to prove, by the preponderance of the evidence, that the alien is subject to removal because the alien is an alien terrorist.

(h) Rules of Evidence. The Federal Rules of Evidence shall not apply in a removal hearing.

(i) Determination of deportation. If the judge, after considering the evidence on the record as a whole, finds that the Government has met its burden, the judge shall order the alien removed and detained pending removal from the United States. If the alien was released pending the removal hearing, the judge shall order the Attorney General to take the alien into custody.

(j) Written order. At the time of issuing a decision as to whether the alien shall be removed, the judge shall prepare a written order containing a statement of facts found and conclusions of law. Any portion of the order that would reveal the substance or source of information received in camera and ex parte pursuant to subsection (e) shall not be made available to the alien or the public.

(k) No right to ancillary relief. At no time shall the judge consider or provide for relief from removal based on—

(1) asylum under section 208 [8 USCS § 1158];

(2) [by] withholding of removal under section 241(b)(3) [8 USCS § 1251(b)(3)];

(3) suspension of deportation under cancellation of removal under section 240A [8 USCS § 1229b];

(4) voluntary departure under section 244(e);

(5) adjustment of status under section 245 [8 USCS § 1255]; or

(6) registry under section 249 [8 USCS § 1259].

(l) Report on terrorist removal proceedings. Not later than 3 months from the date of the enactment of this subsection [enacted Dec. 28, 2001], the Attorney General shall submit to Congress a report concerning the effect and efficacy of alien terrorist removal proceedings, including the reasons why proceedings pursuant to this section have not been used by the Attorney General in the past and the effect on the use of these proceedings after the enactment of the USA PATRIOT Act of 2001 (Public Law 107-56).

(June 27, 1952, ch 477, Title V, § 504, as added April 24, 1996, P. L. 104-132, Title IV, Subtitle A, § 401(a), 110 Stat. 1260; Sept. 30, 1996, P. L. 104-208, Div C, Title III, Subtitle A, § 308(g)(7)(B), (8)(B), Subtitle D, §§ 354(a)(1), (2), (b), 357, 110 Stat. 3009-623, 3009-624, 3009-641, 3009-643, 3009-644; Dec. 28, 2001, P. L. 107-108, Title III, § 313, 115 Stat. 1401.)

§ 1535. Appeals

(a) Appeal of denial of application for removal proceedings.

(1) In general. The Attorney General may seek a review of the denial of an order sought in an application filed pursuant to section 503 [8 USCS § 1533]. The appeal shall be filed in the United States Court of Appeals for the District of Columbia Circuit by notice of appeal filed not later than 20 days after the date of such denial.

(2) Record on appeal. The entire record of the proceeding shall be transmitted to the Court of Appeals under seal, and the Court of Appeals shall hear the matter ex parte.

(3) Standard of review. The Court of Appeals shall—

(A) review questions of law de novo; and

(B) set aside a finding of fact only if such finding was clearly erroneous.

(b) Appeal of determination regarding summary of classified information.

(1) In general. The United States may take an interlocutory appeal to the United States Court of Appeals for the District of Columbia Circuit of—

(A) any determination by the judge pursuant to section 504(e)(3) [8 USCS § 1534(e)(3)]; or

(B) the refusal of the court to make the findings permitted by section 504(e)(3) [8 USCS § 1534(e)(3)].

(2) Record. In any interlocutory appeal taken pursuant to this subsection, the entire record, including any proposed order of the judge, any classified information and the summary of evidence, shall be transmitted to the Court of Appeals. The classified information shall be transmitted under seal. A verbatim record of such appeal shall be kept under seal in the event of any other judicial review.

(c) Appeal of decision in hearing.

(1) In general. Subject to paragraph (2), the decision of the judge after a removal hearing may be appealed by either the alien or the Attorney General to the United States Court of Appeals for the District of Columbia Circuit by notice of appeal filed not later than 20 days after the date on which the order is issued. The order shall not be enforced during the pendency of an appeal under this subsection.

(2) Automatic appeals in cases of permanent resident aliens in which no summary provided.

(A) In general. Unless the alien waives the right to a review under this paragraph, in any case involving an alien lawfully admitted for permanent residence who is denied a written summary of classified information under section 504(e)(3) [8 USCS § 1534(e)(3)] and with respect to which the procedures described in section 504(e)(3)(F) [8 USCS § 1534(e)(3)(F)] apply, any order issued by the judge shall be reviewed by the Court of Appeals for the District of Columbia Circuit.

(B) Use of special attorney. With respect to any issue relating to classified information that arises in such review, the alien shall be represented only by the special attorney designated under section 504(e)(3)(F)(i) [8 USCS § 1534(e)(3)(F)(i)] on behalf of the alien.

(3) Transmittal of record. In an appeal or review to the Court of Appeals pursuant to this subsection—

(A) the entire record shall be transmitted to the Court of Appeals; and

(B) information received in camera and ex parte, and any portion of the order that would reveal the substance or source of such information, shall be transmitted under seal.

(4) Expedited appellate proceeding. In an appeal or review to the Court of Appeals under this subsection—

(A) the appeal or review shall be heard as expeditiously as practicable and the court may dispense with full briefing and hear the matter solely on the record of the judge of the removal court and on such briefs or motions as the court may require to be filed by the parties;

(B) the Court of Appeals shall issue an opinion not later than 60 days after the date of the issuance of the final order of the district court;

(C) the court shall review all questions of law de novo; and

(D) a finding of fact shall be accorded deference by the reviewing court and shall not be set aside unless such finding was clearly erroneous, except that in the case of a review under paragraph (2) in which an alien lawfully admitted for permanent residence was denied a written summary of classified information under section 504(c)(3) [section 504(e)(3)] [8 USCS § 1534(e)(3)], the Court of Appeals shall review questions of fact de novo.

(d) Certiorari. Following a decision by the Court of Appeals pursuant to subsection (c), the alien or the Attorney General may petition the Supreme Court for a writ of certiorari. In any such case, any information transmitted to the Court of Appeals under seal shall, if such information is also submitted to the Supreme Court, be transmitted under seal. Any order of removal shall not be stayed pending disposition of a writ of certiorari, except as provided by the Court of Appeals or a Justice of the Supreme Court.

(e) Appeal of detention order.

(1) In general. Sections 3145 through 3148 of title 18, United States Code, pertaining to review and appeal of a release or detention order, penalties for failure to appear, penalties for an offense committed while on release, and sanctions for violation of a release condition shall apply to an alien to whom section 507(b)(1) [8 USCS § 1537(b)(1)] applies. In applying the previous sentence—

(A) for purposes of section 3145 of such title an appeal shall be taken to the United States Court of Appeals for the District of Columbia Circuit; and

(B) for purposes of section 3146 of such title the alien shall be considered released in connection with a charge of an offense punishable by life imprisonment.

(2) No review of continued detention. The determinations and actions of the Attorney General pursuant to section 507(b)(2)(C) [8 USCS § 1537(b)(2)(C)] shall not be subject to judicial review, including application for a writ of habeas corpus, except for a claim by the alien that continued detention violates the alien's rights under the Constitution. Jurisdiction over any such challenge shall lie exclusively in the United States Court of Appeals for the District of Columbia Circuit.

(June 27, 1952, ch 477, Title V, § 505, as added April 24, 1996, P. L. 104-132, Title IV, Subtitle A, § 401(a), 110 Stat. 1263; Sept. 30, 1996, P. L. 104-208, Div C, Title III, Subtitle D, § 354(a)(3), 110 Stat. 3009-642.)

§ 1536. Custody and release pending removal hearing

(a) Upon filing application.

(1) In general. Subject to paragraphs (2) and (3), the Attorney General may—

(A) take into custody any alien with respect to whom an application under section 503 [8 USCS § 1533] has been filed; and

(B) retain such an alien in custody in accordance with the procedures authorized by this title [8 USCS §§ 1531 et seq.].

(2) Special rules for permanent resident aliens.

(A) Release hearing. An alien lawfully admitted for permanent residence shall be entitled to a release hearing before the judge assigned to hear the removal hearing. Such an alien shall be detained pending the removal hearing, unless the alien demonstrates to the court that the alien—

(i) is a person lawfully admitted for permanent residence in the United States;

(ii) if released upon such terms and conditions as the court may prescribe (including the posting of any monetary amount), is not likely to flee; and

(iii) will not endanger national security, or the safety of any person or the community, if released.

(B) Information considered. The judge may consider classified information submitted in camera and ex parte in making a determination whether to release an alien pending the removal hearing.

(3) Release if order denied and no review sought.

(A) In general. Subject to subparagraph (B), if a judge of the removal court denies the order sought in an application filed pursuant to section 503 [8 USCS § 1533], and the Attorney General does not seek review of such denial, the alien shall be released from custody.

(B) Application of regular procedures. Subparagraph (A) shall not prevent the arrest and detention of the alien pursuant to title II.

(b) Conditional release if order denied and review sought.

(1) In general. If a judge of the removal court denies the order sought in an application filed pursuant to section 503 [8 USCS § 1533] and the Attorney General seeks review of such denial, the judge shall release the alien from custody subject to the least restrictive condition, or combination of conditions, of release described in section 3142(b) and clauses (i) through (xiv) of section 3142(c)(1)(B) of title 18, United States Code, that—

(A) will reasonably assure the appearance of the alien at any future proceeding pursuant to this title [8 USCS §§ 1531 et seq.]; and

(B) will not endanger the safety of any other person or the community.

(2) No release for certain aliens. If the judge finds no such condition or combination of conditions, as described in paragraph (1), the alien shall remain in custody until the completion of any appeal authorized by this title [8 USCS §§ 1531 et seq.].

(June 27, 1952, ch 477, Title V, § 506, as added April 24, 1996, P. L. 104-132, Title IV, Subtitle A, § 401(a), 110 Stat. 1265.)

§ 1537. Custody and release after removal hearing

(a) Release.

(1) In general. Subject to paragraph (2), if the judge decides that an alien should not be removed, the alien shall be released from custody.

(2) Custody pending appeal. If the Attorney General takes an appeal from such decision, the alien shall remain in custody, subject to the provisions of section 3142 of title 18, United States Code.

(b) Custody and removal.

(1) Custody. If the judge decides that an alien shall be removed, the alien shall be detained pending the outcome of any appeal. After the conclusion of any judicial review thereof which affirms the removal order, the Attorney General shall retain the alien in custody and remove the alien to a country specified under paragraph (2).

(2) Removal.

(A) In general. The removal of an alien shall be to any country which the alien shall designate if such designation does not, in the judgment of the Attorney General, in consultation with the Secretary of State, impair the obligation of the United States under any treaty (including a treaty pertaining to extradition) or otherwise adversely affect the foreign policy of the United States.

(B) Alternate countries. If the alien refuses to designate a country to which the alien wishes to be removed or if the Attorney General, in consultation with the Secretary of State, determines that removal of the alien to the country so designated would impair a treaty obligation or adversely affect United States foreign policy, the Attorney General shall cause the alien to be removed to any country willing to receive such alien.

(C) Continued detention. If no country is willing to receive such an alien, the Attorney General may, notwithstanding any other provision of law, retain the alien in custody. The Attorney General, in coordination with the Secretary of State, shall make periodic efforts to reach agreement with other countries to accept such an alien and at least every 6 months shall provide to the attorney representing the alien at the removal hearing a written report on the Attorney General's efforts. Any alien in custody pursuant to this subparagraph shall be released from custody solely at the discretion of the Attorney General and subject to such conditions as the Attorney General shall deem appropriate.

(D) Fingerprinting. Before an alien is removed from the United States pursuant to this subsection, or pursuant to an order of removal because such alien is inadmissible under section 212(a)(3)(B) [8 USCS § 1182(a)(3)(B)], the alien shall be photographed and fingerprinted, and shall be advised of the provisions of section 276(b) [8 USCS § 1326(b)].

(c) Continued detention pending trial.

(1) Delay in removal. The Attorney General may hold in abeyance the removal of an alien who has been ordered removed, pursuant to this title [8 USCS §§ 1531 et seq.], to allow the trial of such alien on any Federal or State criminal charge and the service of any sentence of confinement resulting from such a trial.

(2) Maintenance of custody. Pending the commencement of any service of a sentence of confinement by an alien described in paragraph (1), such an alien shall remain in the custody of the Attorney General, unless the Attorney General determines that temporary release of the alien to the custody of State authorities for confinement in a State facility is appropriate and would not endanger national security or public safety.

(3) Subsequent removal. Following the completion of a sentence of confinement by an alien described in paragraph (1), or following the completion of State criminal proceedings which do not result in a sentence of confinement of an alien released to the custody of State authorities pursuant to paragraph (2), such an alien shall be returned to the custody of the Attorney General who shall proceed to the removal of the alien under this title [8 USCS §§ 1531 et seq.].

(d) Application of certain provisions relating to escape of prisoners. For purposes of sections 751 and 752 of title 18, United States Code, an alien in the custody of the Attorney General pursuant to this title [8 USCS §§ 1531 et seq.] shall be subject to the penalties provided by those sections in relation to a person committed to the custody of the Attorney General by virtue of an arrest on a charge of a felony.

(e) Rights of aliens in custody.

(1) Family and attorney visits. An alien in the custody of the Attorney General pursuant to this title [8 USCS §§ 1531 et seq.] shall be given reasonable opportunity, as determined by the Attorney General, to communicate with and receive visits from members of the alien's family, and to contact, retain, and communicate with an attorney.

(2) Diplomatic contact. An alien in the custody of the Attorney General pursuant to this title [8 USCS §§ 1531 et seq.] shall have the right to contact an appropriate diplomatic or consular official of the alien's country of citizenship or nationality or of any country providing representation services therefore. The Attorney General shall notify the appropriate embassy, mission, or consular office of the alien's detention.

(June 27, 1952, ch 477, Title V, § 507, as added April 24, 1996, P. L. 104-132, Title IV, Subtitle A, § 401(a), 110 Stat. 1266; Sept. 30, 1996, P. L. 104-208, Div C, Title III, Subtitle A, § 308(d)(4)(Q), 110 Stat. 3009-619.)

CHAPTER 13. IMMIGRATION AND NATURALIZATION SERVICE

ORGANIZATION

§ 1551. Immigration and Naturalization Service

There is created and established in the Department of Justice an Immigration and Naturalization Service.

(Feb. 14, 1903, ch 552, § 4, 32 Stat. 826; June 29, 1906, ch 3592, § 1, 34 Stat. 596; March 4, 1913, ch 141, § 3, 37 Stat. 737.)

§ 1552. Commissioner of Immigration and Naturalization; office

The office of the Commissioner of Immigration and Naturalization is created and established, and the President, by and with the advice and consent of the Senate, is authorized and directed to appoint such officer. The Attorney General shall provide him with a suitable, furnished office in the city of Washington, and with such books of record and facilities for the discharge of the duties of his office as may be necessary.

(March 3, 1891, ch 551, § 7, 26 Stat. 1085; March 2, 1895, ch 177, § 1, 28 Stat. 780; April 28, 1904, No. 34, 33 Stat. 591; March 4, 1913, ch 141, § 3, 37 Stat. 737; Feb. 5, 1917, ch 29, §

23, 39 Stat. 892; March 3, 1917, ch 163, § 1, 39 Stat. 1118; March 28, 1922, ch 117, Title II, 42 Stat. 486; Jan. 5, 1923, ch 24, Title II, 42 Stat. 1127; June 27, 1952, ch 477, Title IV, § 403(a)(4), 66 Stat. 279.)

§ 1553. Assistant commissioners and district director; compensation and salary grade

The compensation of the five assistant commissioners and one district director shall be at the rate of grade GS-16.

(July 20, 1956, ch 414, Title II, § 201, 70 Stat. 307.)

§ 1554. Special immigrant inspectors at Washington

Special immigrant inspectors, not to exceed three, may be detailed for duty in the Bureau [service] at Washington.

(March 2, 1895, ch 177, § 1, 28 Stat. 780.)

§ 1555. Immigration Service expenses

Appropriations now or hereafter provided for the Immigration and Naturalization Service shall be available for payment of (a) hire of privately owned horses for use on official business, under contract with officers or employees of the Service; (b) pay of interpreters and translators who are not citizens of the United States; (c) distribution of citizenship textbooks to aliens without cost to such aliens; (d) payment of allowances (at such rate as may be specified from time to time in the appropriation Act involved) to aliens, while held in custody under the immigration laws, for work performed; and (e) when so specified in the appropriation concerned, expenses of unforeseen emergencies of a confidential character, to be expended under the direction of the Attorney General, who shall make a certificate of the amount of any such expenditure as he may think it advisable not to specify, and every such certificate shall be deemed a sufficient voucher for the sum therein expressed to have been expended.

(July 28, 1950, ch 503, § 6, 64 Stat. 380.)

§ 1556. [Transferred]

§ 1557. Prevention of transportation in foreign commerce of alien women and girls under international agreement; Commissioner designated as authority to receive and preserve information

For the purpose of regulating and preventing the transportation in foreign commerce of alien women and girls for purposes of prostitution and debauchery, and in pursuance of and for the purpose of carrying out the terms of the agreement or project of arrangement for the suppression of the white-slave traffic, adopted July 25, 1902, for submission to their respective governments by the delegates of various powers represented at the Paris Conference and confirmed by a formal agreement signed at Paris on May 18, 1904, and adhered to by the United States on June 6, 1908, as shown by the proclamation of the President of the United States, dated June 15, 1908, the Commissioner General of Immigration [Commissioner of Immigration and Naturalization] is hereby designated as the authority of the United States to receive and centralize information concerning the procuration of alien women and girls with a view to their debauchery, and to exercise supervision over such alien women and girls, receive their declarations, establish their identity, and ascertain from them who induced them to leave their native countries, respectively; and it shall be the duty of said Commissioner General of Immigration [Commissioner of Immigration and Naturalization] to receive and keep on file in his office the statements and declarations which may be made by such alien women and girls, and those which are hereinafter required pertaining to such alien women and girls engaged in prostitution or debauchery in this country, and to furnish receipts for such statements and declarations provided for in this Act to the persons, respectively, making and filing them.

(June 25, 1910, ch 395, § 6(1), 36 Stat. 826.)

IMMIGRATION SERVICES AND INFRASTRUCTURE IMPROVEMENTS

§ 1571. Purposes

(a) Purposes. The purposes of this title [8 USCS §§ 1571 et seq.] are to—

(1) provide the Immigration and Naturalization Service with the mechanisms it needs to eliminate the current backlog in the processing of immigration benefit applications within 1 year after enactment of this Act [enacted Oct. 17, 2000] and to maintain the elimination of the backlog in future years; and

(2) provide for regular congressional oversight of the performance of the Immigration and Naturalization Service in eliminating the backlog and processing delays in immigration benefits adjudications.

(b) Policy. It is the sense of Congress that the processing of an immigration benefit application should be completed not later than 180 days after the initial filing of the application, except that a petition for a nonimmigrant visa under section 214(c) of the Immigration and Nationality Act [8 USCS § 1184(c)] should be processed not later than 30 days after the filing of the petition.

(Oct. 17, 2000, P. L. 106-313, Title II, § 202, 114 Stat. 1262.)

§ 1572. Definitions

In this title [8 USCS §§ 1571 et seq.]:

(1) Backlog. The term "backlog" means, with respect to an immigration benefit application, the period of time in excess of 180 days that such application has been pending before the Immigration and Naturalization Service.

(2) Immigration benefit application. The term "immigration benefit application" means any application or petition to confer, certify, change, adjust, or extend any status granted under the Immigration and Nationality Act.

(Oct. 17, 2000, P. L. 106-313, Title II, § 203, 114 Stat. 1263.)

§ 1573. Immigration services and infrastructure improvement account

(a) Authority of the Attorney General. The Attorney General shall take such measures as may be necessary to—

(1) reduce the backlog in the processing of immigration benefit applications, with the objective of the total elimination of the backlog 1 year after the date of the enactment of the Homeland Security Act of 2002 [enacted Nov. 25, 2002];

(2) make such other improvements in the processing of immigration benefit applications as may be necessary to ensure that a backlog does not develop after such date; and

(3) make such improvements in infrastructure as may be necessary to effectively provide immigration services.

(b) Authorization of appropriations.

(1) In general. There is authorized to be appropriated to the Department of Justice from time to time such sums as may be necessary for the Attorney General to carry out subsection (a).

(2) Designation of account in treasury. Amounts appropriated pursuant to paragraph (1) may be referred to as the "Immigration Services and Infrastructure Improvements Account".

(3) Availability of funds. Amounts appropriated pursuant to paragraph (1) are authorized to remain available until expended.

(4) Limitation on expenditures. None of the funds appropriated pursuant to paragraph (1) may be expended until the report described in section 205(a) [8 USCS § 1574(a)] has been submitted to Congress.

(Oct. 17, 2000, P. L. 106-313, Title II, § 204, 114 Stat. 1263; Nov. 25, 2002, P. L. 107-296, Title IV, Subtitle E, § 458, 116 Stat. 2201.)

§ 1574. Reports to Congress

(a) Backlog elimination plan.

(1) Report required. Not later than 90 days after the date of enactment of this Act [enacted Oct. 17, 2000], the Attorney General shall submit a report to the Committees on the Judiciary and Appropriations of the Senate and the House of Representatives concerning—

(A) the backlogs in immigration benefit applications in existence as of the date of enactment of this title [enacted Oct. 17, 2000]; and

(B) the Attorney General's plan for eliminating such backlogs.

(2) Report elements. The report shall include—

(A) an assessment of the data systems used in adjudicating and reporting on the status of immigration benefit applications, including—

(i) a description of the adequacy of existing computer hardware, computer software, and other mechanisms to comply with the adjudications and reporting requirements of this title [8 USCS §§ 1571 et seq.]; and

(ii) a plan for implementing improvements to existing data systems to accomplish the purpose of this title [8 USCS §§ 1571 et seq.], as described in section 202(a) [8 USCS § 1571(a)];

(B) a description of the quality controls to be put into force to ensure timely, fair, accurate, and complete processing and adjudication of such applications;

(C) the elements specified in subsection (b)(2);

(D) an estimate of the amount of appropriated funds that would be necessary in order to eliminate the backlogs in each category of immigration benefit applications described in subsection (b)(2); and

(E) a detailed plan on how the Attorney General will use any funds in the Immigration Services and Infrastructure Improvements Account to comply with the purposes of this title [8 USCS §§ 1571 et seq.].

(b) Annual reports.

(1) In general. Beginning 90 days after the end of the first fiscal year for which any appropriation authorized by section 204(b) [8 USCS § 1573(b)] is made, and 90 days after the end of each fiscal year thereafter, the Attorney General shall submit a report to the Committees on the Judiciary and Appropriations of the Senate and the House of Representatives concerning the status of—

(A) the Immigration Services and Infrastructure Improvements Account including any unobligated balances of appropriations in the Account; and

(B) the Attorney General's efforts to eliminate backlogs in any immigration benefit application described in paragraph (2).

(2) Report elements. The report shall include—

(A) State-by-State data on—

(i) the number of naturalization cases adjudicated in each quarter of each fiscal year;

(ii) the average processing time for naturalization applications;

(iii) the number of naturalization applications pending for up to 6 months, 12 months, 18 months, 24 months, 36 months, and 48 months or more;

(iv) estimated processing times adjudicating newly submitted naturalization applications;

(v) an analysis of the appropriate processing times for naturalization applications; and

(vi) the additional resources and process changes needed to eliminate the backlog for naturalization adjudications;

(B) the status of applications or, where applicable, petitions described in subparagraph (C), by Immigration and Naturalization Service district, including—

(i) the number of cases adjudicated in each quarter of each fiscal year;

(ii) the average processing time for such applications or petitions;

(iii) the number of applications or petitions pending for up to 6 months, 12 months, 18 months, 24 months, 36 months, and 48 months or more;

(iv) the estimated processing times adjudicating newly submitted applications or petitions;

(v) an analysis of the appropriate processing times for applications or petitions; and

(vi) a description of the additional resources and process changes needed to eliminate the backlog for such processing and adjudications; and

(C) a status report on—

(i) applications for adjustments of status to that of an alien lawfully admitted for permanent residence;

(ii) petitions for nonimmigrant visas under section 214 of the Immigration and Nationality Act [8 USCS § 1184];

(iii) petitions filed under section 204 of such Act [8 USCS § 1154] to classify aliens as immediate relatives or preference immigrants under section 203 of such Act [8 USCS § 1153];

(iv) applications for asylum under section 208 of such Act [8 USCS § 1158];

(v) registrations for Temporary Protected Status under section 244 of such Act [8 USCS § 1254a]; and

(vi) a description of the additional resources and process changes needed to eliminate the backlog for such processing and adjudications.

(3) Absence of appropriated funds. In the event that no funds are appropriated subject to section 204(b) [8 USCS § 1573(b)] in the fiscal year in which this Act is enacted, the Attorney General shall submit a report to Congress not later than 90 days after the end of such fiscal year, and each fiscal year thereafter, containing the elements described in paragraph (2).

(Oct. 17, 2000, P. L. 106-313, Title II, § 205, 114 Stat. 1263.)

TITLE 18.
CRIMES AND CRIMINAL PROCEDURE

(Selected Part)

PART I.
CRIMES

(Selected Chapter)

CHAPTER 7.
ASSAULT

§ 111. Assaulting, resisting, or impeding certain officers or employees

(a) In general. Whoever—

(1) forcibly assaults, resists, opposes, impedes, intimidates, or interferes with any person designated in section 1114 of this title [18 USCS § 1114] while engaged in or on account of the performance of official duties; or

(2) forcibly assaults or intimidates any person who formerly served as a person designated in section 1114 [18 USCS § 1114] on account of the performance of official duties during such person's term of service,

shall, where the acts in violation of this section constitute only simple assault, be fined under this title or imprisoned not more than one year, or both, and where such acts involve physical contact with the victim of that assault or the intent to commit another felony, be fined under this title or imprisoned not more than 8 years, or both.

(b) Enhanced penalty. Whoever, in the commission of any acts described in subsection (a), uses a deadly or dangerous weapon (including a weapon intended to cause death or danger but that fails to do so by reason of a defective component) or inflicts bodily injury, shall be fined under this title or imprisoned not more than 20 years, or both.

(c) Extraterritorial jurisdiction. There is extraterritorial jurisdiction over the conduct prohibited by this section.

(June 25, 1948, ch 645, § 1, 62 Stat. 688; Nov. 18, 1988, P. L. 100-690, Title VI, Subtitle N, § 6487(a), 102 Stat. 4386; Sept. 13, 1994, P. L. 103-322, Title XXXII, Subtitle A, § 320101(a), 108 Stat. 2108; April 24, 1996, P. L. 104-132, Title VII, Subtitle B, § 727(c), 110 Stat. 1302; Nov. 2, 2002, P. L. 107-273, Div C, Title I, Subtitle A, § 11008(b), 116 Stat. 1818; Jan. 7, 2008, P. L. 110-177, Title II, § 208(b), 121 Stat. 2538; Nov. 18, 2021, P.L. 117-59, § 3(1), 135 Stat. 1469.)

§ 112. Protection of foreign officials, official guests, and internationally protected persons

(a) Whoever assaults, strikes, wounds, imprisons, or offers violence to a foreign official, official guest, or internationally protected person or makes any other violent attack upon the person or liberty of such person, or, if likely to endanger his person or liberty, makes a violent attack upon his official premises, private accommodation, or means of transport or attempts to commit any of the foregoing shall be fined under this title or imprisoned not more than three years, or both. Whoever in the commission of any such act uses a deadly or dangerous weapon, or inflicts bodily injury, shall be fined under this title or imprisoned not more than ten years, or both.

(b) Whoever willfully—

(1) intimidates, coerces, threatens, or harasses a foreign official or an official guest or obstructs a foreign official in the performance of his duties;

(2) attempts to intimidate, coerce, threaten, or harass a foreign official or an official guest or obstruct a foreign official in the performance of his duties; or

(3) within the United States and within one hundred feet of any building or premises in whole or in part owned, used, or occupied for official business or for diplomatic, consular, or residential purposes by—

(A) a foreign government, including such use as a mission to an international organization;

(B) an international organization;

(C) a foreign official; or

(D) an official guest;

congregates with two or more other persons with intent to violate any other provision of this section;

shall be fined under this title or imprisoned not more than six months, or both.

(c) For the purpose of this section "foreign government", "foreign official", "internationally protected person", "international organization", "national of the United States", and "official guest" shall have the same meanings as those provided in section 1116(b) of this title [18 USCS § 1116(b)].

(d) Nothing contained in this section shall be construed or applied so as to abridge the exercise of rights guaranteed under the first amendment to the Constitution of the United States.

(e) If the victim of an offense under subsection (a) is an internationally protected person outside the United

States, the United States may exercise jurisdiction over the offense if (1) the victim is a representative, officer, employee, or agent of the United States, (2) an offender is a national of the United States, or (3) an offender is afterwards found in the United States. As used in this subsection, the United States includes all areas under the jurisdiction of the United States including any of the places within the provisions of sections 5 and 7 of this title [18 USCS §§ 5 and 7] and section 46501(2) of title 49.

(f) In the course of enforcement of subsection (a) and any other sections prohibiting a conspiracy or attempt to violate subsection (a), the Attorney General may request assistance from any Federal, State, or local agency, including the Army, Navy, and Air Force, any statute, rule, or regulation to the contrary, notwithstanding.

(June 25, 1948, ch 645, § 1, 62 Stat. 688; Aug. 27, 1964, P. L. 88-493, § 1, 78 Stat. 610; Oct. 24, 1972, P. L. 92-539, Title III, § 301, 86 Stat. 1072; Oct. 8, 1976, P. L. 94-467, § 5, 90 Stat. 1999; Nov. 9, 1977, P. L. 95-163, § 17(b)(1), 91 Stat. 1286; Oct. 24, 1978, P. L. 95-504, § 2(b), 92 Stat. 1705; Nov. 18, 1988, P. L. 100-690, Title VI, Subtitle N, § 6478, 102 Stat. 4381; July 5, 1994, P. L. 103-272, § 5(e)(2), 108 Stat. 1373; Sept. 13, 1994, P. L. 103-322, Title XXXII, Subtitle A, § 320101(b), Title XXXIII, § 330016(1)(G), (K), 108 Stat. 2108, 2147; April 24, 1996, P. L. 104-132, Title VII, Subtitle B, § 721(d), 110 Stat. 1298; Oct. 11, 1996, P. L. 104-294, Title VI, § 604(b)(12)(A), 110 Stat. 3507.)

§ 115. Influencing, impeding, or retaliating against a Federal official by threatening or injuring a family member

(a)(1) Whoever—

(A) assaults, kidnaps, or murders, or attempts or conspires to kidnap or murder, or threatens to assault, kidnap or murder a member of the immediate family of a United States official, a United States judge, a Federal law enforcement officer, or an official whose killing would be a crime under section 1114 of this title [18 USCS § 1114]; or

(B) threatens to assault, kidnap, or murder, a United States official, a United States judge, a Federal law enforcement officer, or an official whose killing would be a crime under such section,

with intent to impede, intimidate, or interfere with such official, judge, or law enforcement officer while engaged in the performance of official duties, or with intent to retaliate against such official, judge, or law enforcement officer on account of the performance of official duties, shall be punished as provided in subsection (b).

(2) Whoever assaults, kidnaps, or murders, or attempts or conspires to kidnap or murder, or threatens to assault, kidnap, or murder, any person who formerly served as a person designated in paragraph (1), or a member of the immediate family of any person who formerly served as a person designated in paragraph (1), with intent to retaliate against such person on account of the performance of official duties during the term of service of such person, shall be punished as provided in subsection (b).

(b)(1) The punishment for an assault in violation of this section is—

(A) a fine under this title; and

(B)(i) if the assault consists of a simple assault, a term of imprisonment for not more than 1 year;

(ii) if the assault involved physical contact with the victim of that assault or the intent to commit another felony, a term of imprisonment for not more than 10 years;

(iii) if the assault resulted in bodily injury, a term of imprisonment for not more than 20 years; or

(iv) if the assault resulted in serious bodily injury (as that term is defined in section 1365 of this title [18 USCS § 1365], and including any conduct that, if the conduct occurred in the special maritime and territorial jurisdiction of the United States, would violate section 2241 or 2242 of this title [18 USCS § 2241 or 2242]) or a dangerous weapon was used during and in relation to the offense, a term of imprisonment for not more than 30 years.

(2) A kidnapping, attempted kidnapping, or conspiracy to kidnap in violation of this section shall be punished as provided in section 1201 of this title [18 USCS § 1201] for the kidnapping or attempted kidnapping of, or a conspiracy to kidnap, a person described in section 1201(a)(5) of this title [18 USCS § 1201(a)(5)].

(3) A murder, attempted murder, or conspiracy to murder in violation of this section shall be punished as provided in sections 1111, 1113, and 1117 of this title [18 USCS §§ 1111, 1113, and 1117].

(4) A threat made in violation of this section shall be punished by a fine under this title or imprisonment for a term of not more than 10 years, or both, except that imprisonment for a threatened assault shall not exceed 6 years.

(c) As used in this section, the term—

(1) "Federal law enforcement officer" means any officer, agent, or employee of the United States authorized by law or by a Government agency to engage in or supervise the prevention, detection, investigation, or prosecution of any violation of Federal criminal law;

(2) "immediate family member" of an individual means—

(A) his spouse, parent, brother or sister, child or person to whom he stands in loco parentis; or

(B) any other person living in his household and related to him by blood or marriage;

(3) "United States judge" means any judicial officer of the United States, and includes a justice of the Supreme Court and a United States magistrate [United States magistrate judge]; and

(4) "United States official" means the President, President-elect, Vice President, Vice President-elect, a Member of Congress, a member-elect of Congress, a member of the executive branch who is the head of a department listed in 5 U.S.C. 101, or the Director of the Central Intelligence Agency.

(d) This section shall not interfere with the investigative authority of the United States Secret Service, as provided under sections 3056, 871, and 879 of this title [18 USCS §§ 3056, 871, and 879].

(e) There is extraterritorial jurisdiction over the conduct prohibited by this section.

(Added Oct. 12, 1984, P. L. 98-473, Title II, Ch X, Part G, § 1008(a), 98 Stat. 2140; Nov. 10, 1986, P. L. 99-646, §§ 37(a), 60, 100 Stat. 3599, 3613; Nov. 18, 1988, P. L. 100-690, Title VI, Subtitle N, § 6487(f), 102 Stat. 4386; Nov. 29, 1990, P. L. 101-647, Title XXXV, § 3508, 104 Stat. 4922; Sept. 13, 1994, P. L. 103-322, Title XXXIII, §§ 330016(2)(C), 330021(1), 108 Stat. 2148, 2150; April 24, 1996, P. L. 104-132, Title VII, Subtitle B, §§ 723(a), 727(b), 110 Stat. 1300, 1302; Nov. 2, 2002, P. L. 107-273, Div B, Title IV, § 4002(b)(9), Div C, Title I, Subtitle A, § 11008(c), 116 Stat. 1808, 1818; Jan. 7, 2008, P. L. 110-177, Title II, § 208(a), 121 Stat. 2538; Nov. 18, 2021, P.L. 117-59, § 3(2), 135 Stat. 1469.)

§ 119. Protection of individuals performing certain official duties

(a) In general. Whoever knowingly makes restricted personal information about a covered person, or a member of the immediate family of that covered person, publicly available—

(1) with the intent to threaten, intimidate, or incite the commission of a crime of violence against that covered person, or a member of the immediate family of that covered person; or

(2) with the intent and knowledge that the restricted personal information will be used to threaten, intimidate, or facilitate the commission of a crime of violence against that covered person, or a member of the immediate family of that covered person,

shall be fined under this title, imprisoned not more than 5 years, or both.

(b) Definitions. In this section—

(1) the term "restricted personal information" means, with respect to an individual, the Social Security number, the home address, home phone number, mobile phone number, personal email, or home fax number of, and identifiable to, that individual;

(2) the term "covered person" means—

(A) an individual designated in section 1114 [18 USCS § 1114];

(B) a grand or petit juror, witness, or other officer in or of, any court of the United States, or an officer who may be, or was, serving at any examination or other proceeding before any United States magistrate judge or other committing magistrate;

(C) an informant or witness in a Federal criminal investigation or prosecution; or

(D) a State or local officer or employee whose restricted personal information is made publicly available because of the participation in, or assistance provided to, a Federal criminal investigation by that officer or employee;

(3) the term "crime of violence" has the meaning given the term in section 16; and

(4) the term "immediate family" has the meaning given the term in section 115(c)(2) [18 USCS § 115(c)(2)].

(Added Jan. 7, 2008, P. L. 110-177, Title II, § 202(a), 121 Stat. 2536.)

CHAPTER 11. BRIBERY, GRAFT, AND CONFLICTS OF INTEREST

Section

§ 201. Bribery of public officials and witnesses

(a) For the purpose of this section—

(1) the term "public official" means Member of Congress, Delegate, or Resident Commissioner, either before or after such official has qualified, or an officer or employee or person acting for or on behalf of the United States, or any department, agency or branch of Government thereof, including the District of Columbia, in any official function, under or by authority of any such department, agency, or branch of Government, or a juror;

(2) the term "person who has been selected to be a public official" means any person who has been nominated or appointed to be a public official, or has been officially informed that such person will be so nominated or appointed; and

(3) the term "official act" means any decision or action on any question, matter, cause, suit, proceeding or controversy, which may at any time be pending, or which may by law be brought before any public official, in such official's official capacity, or in such official's place of trust or profit.

(b) Whoever—

(1) directly or indirectly, corruptly gives, offers or promises anything of value to any public official or person who has been selected to be a public official, or offers or promises any public official or any person who has been selected to be a public official to give anything of value to any other person or entity, with intent—

(A) to influence any official act; or

(B) to influence such public official or person who has been selected to be a public official to commit or aid in committing, or collude in, or allow, any fraud, or make opportunity for the commission of any fraud, on the United States; or

(C) to induce such public official or such person who has been selected to be a public official to do or omit to do any act in violation of the lawful duty of such official or person;

(2) being a public official or person selected to be a public official, directly or indirectly, corruptly demands, seeks, receives, accepts, or agrees to receive or accept anything of value personally or for any other person or entity, in return for:

(A) being influenced in his the performance of any official act;

(B) being influenced to commit or aid in committing, or to collude in, or allow, any fraud, or make opportunity for the commission of any fraud, on the United States; or

(C) being induced to do or omit to do any act in violation of the official duty of such official or person;

(3) directly or indirectly, corruptly gives, offers, or promises anything of value to any person, or offers or promises such person to give anything of value to any other person or entity, with intent to influence the testimony under oath or affirmation of such first-mentioned person as a witness upon a trial, hearing, or other proceeding, before any court, any committee of

either House or both Houses of Congress, or any agency, commission, or officer authorized by the laws of the United States to hear evidence or take testimony, or with intent to influence such person to absent himself therefrom;

(4) directly or indirectly, corruptly demands, seeks, receives, accepts, or agrees to receive or accept anything of value personally or for any other person or entity in return for being influenced in testimony under oath or affirmation as a witness upon any such trial, hearing, or other proceeding, or in return for absenting himself therefrom;

shall be fined under this title or not more than three times the monetary equivalent of the thing of value, whichever is greater, or imprisoned for not more than fifteen years, or both, and may be disqualified from holding any office of honor, trust, or profit under the United States.

(c) Whoever—

(1) otherwise than as provided by law for the proper discharge of official duty—

(A) directly or indirectly gives, offers, or promises anything of value to any public official, former public official, or person selected to be a public official, for or because of any official act performed or to be performed by such public official, former public official, or person selected to be a public official; or

(B) being a public official, former public official, or person selected to be a public official, otherwise than as provided by law for the proper discharge of official duty, directly or indirectly demands, seeks, receives, accepts, or agrees to receive or accept anything of value personally for or because of any official act performed or to be performed by such official or person;

(2) directly or indirectly, gives, offers, or promises anything of value to any person, for or because of the testimony under oath or affirmation given or to be given by such person as a witness upon a trial, hearing, or other proceeding, before any court, any committee of either House or both Houses of Congress, or any agency, commission, or officer authorized by the laws of the United States to hear evidence or take testimony, or for or because of such person's absence therefrom;

(3) directly or indirectly, demands, seeks, receives, accepts, or agrees to receive or accept anything of value personally for or because of the testimony under oath or affirmation given or to be given by such person as a witness upon any such trial, hearing, or other proceeding, or for or because of such person's absence therefrom;

shall be fined under this title or imprisoned for not more than two years, or both.

(d) Paragraphs (3) and (4) of subsection (b) and paragraphs (2) and (3) of subsection (c) shall not be construed to prohibit the payment or receipt of witness fees provided by law, or the payment, by the party upon whose behalf a witness is called and receipt by a witness, of the reasonable cost of travel and subsistence incurred and the reasonable value of time lost in attendance at any such trial, hearing, or proceeding, or, in the case of expert witnesses, a reasonable fee for time spent in the preparation of such opinion, and in appearing and testifying.

(e) The offenses and penalties prescribed in this section are separate from and in addition to those prescribed in sections 1503, 1504, and 1505 [18 USCS §§ 1503, 1504, and 1505] of this title.

(Added Oct. 23, 1962, P. L. 87-849, § 1(a), 76 Stat. 1119; Sept. 22, 1970, P. L. 91-405, Title II, § 204(d)(1), 84 Stat. 853; Nov. 10, 1986, P. L. 99-646, § 46(a)–(l), 100 Stat. 3601; Sept. 13, 1994, P. L. 103-322, Title XXXIII, §§ 330011(b), 330016(2)(D), 108 Stat. 2144, 2148; Dec. 22, 2023, P.L. 118-31, Div E, Title LI, § 5101, 137 Stat. 931; July 30, 2024, P.L. 118-78, § 2(a), 138 Stat. 1512.)

§ 226. Bribery affecting port security

(a) In general. Whoever knowingly—

(1) directly or indirectly, corruptly gives, offers, or promises anything of value to any public or private person, with intent to commit international terrorism or domestic terrorism (as those terms are defined under section 2331 [18 USCS § 2331]), to—

(A) influence any action or any person to commit or aid in committing, or collude in, or allow, any fraud, or make opportunity for the commission of any fraud affecting any secure or restricted area or seaport; or

(B) induce any official or person to do or omit to do any act in violation of the lawful duty of such official or person that affects any secure or restricted area or seaport; or

(2) directly or indirectly, corruptly demands, seeks, receives, accepts, or agrees to receive or accept anything of value personally or for any other person or entity in return for—

(A) being influenced in the performance of any official act affecting any secure or restricted area or seaport; and

(B) knowing that such influence will be used to commit, or plan to commit, international or domestic terrorism,

shall be fined under this title or imprisoned not more than 15 years, or both.

(b) Definition. In this section, the term "secure or restricted area" means an area of a vessel or facility designated as secure in an approved security plan, as required under section 70103 of title 46, United States Code, and the rules and regulations promulgated under that section.

(Added March 9, 2006, P. L. 109-177, Title III, § 309(a), 120 Stat. 241.)

CHAPTER 27. CUSTOMS

Section

USCS—T.18 § 226

§ 541. Entry of goods falsely classified

Whoever knowingly effects any entry of goods, wares, or merchandise, at less than the true weight or measure thereof, or upon a false classification as to quality or value, or by the payment of less than the amount of duty legally due, shall be fined under this title or imprisoned not more than two years, or both.

(June 25, 1948, ch 545, § 1, 62 Stat. 715; Sept. 13, 1994, P. L. 103-322, Title XXXIII, § 330016(1)(K), 108 Stat. 2147.)

§ 542. Entry of goods by means of false statements

Whoever enters or introduces, or attempts to enter or introduce, into the commerce of the United States any imported merchandise by means of any fraudulent or false invoice, declaration, affidavit, letter, paper, or by means of any false statement, written or verbal, or by means of any false or fraudulent practice or appliance, or makes any false statement in any declaration without reasonable cause to believe the truth of such statement, or procures the making of any such false statement as to any matter material thereto without reasonable cause to believe the truth of such statement, whether or not the United States shall or may be deprived of any lawful duties; or

Whoever is guilty of any willful act or omission whereby the United States shall or may be deprived of any lawful duties accruing upon merchandise embraced or referred to in such invoice, declaration, affidavit, letter, paper, or statement, or affected by such act or omission—

Shall be fined for each offense under this title or imprisoned not more than two years, or both.

Nothing in this section shall be construed to relieve imported merchandise from forfeiture under other provisions of law.

The term "commerce of the United States", as used in this section, shall not include commerce with the Virgin Islands, American Samoa, Wake Island, Midway Islands, Kingman Reef, Johnston Island, or Guam.

(June 25, 1948, ch 645, § 1, 62 Stat. 715; June 30, 1955, ch 258, § 2(c), 69 Stat. 242; Sept. 13, 1994, P. L. 103-322, Title XXXIII, §§ 330004(18), 330016(1)(K), 108 Stat. 2142, 2147; Oct. 11, 1996, P. L. 104-294, Title VI, § 604(b)(23), 110 Stat. 3508.)

§ 543. Entry of goods for less than legal duty

Whoever, being an officer of the revenue, knowingly admits to entry, any goods, wares, or merchandise, upon payment of less than the amount of duty legally due, shall be fined under this title or imprisoned not more than two years, or both; and removed from office.

(June 25, 1948, ch 645, § 1, 62 Stat. 716; Sept. 13, 1994, P. L. 103-322, Title XXXIII, § 330016(1)(K), 108 Stat. 2147.)

§ 544. Relanding of goods

If any merchandise entered or withdrawn for exportation without payment of the duties thereon, or with intent to obtain a drawback of the duties paid, or of any other allowances given by law on the exportation thereof, is relanded at any place in the United States without entry having been made, such merchandise shall be considered as having been imported into the United States contrary to law, and each person concerned shall be fined under this title or imprisoned not more than two years, or both; and such merchandise shall be forfeited.

The term "any place in the United States", as used in this section, shall not include the Virgin Islands, American Samoa, Wake Island, Midway Islands, Kingman Reef, Johnston Island, or Guam.

(June 25, 1948, ch 645, § 1, 62 Stat. 716; June 30, 1955, ch 258, § 2(c), 69 Stat. 242; Sept. 13, 1994, P. L. 103-322, Title XXXIII, §§ 330004(18), 330016(1)(K), 108 Stat. 2142, 2147; Oct. 11, 1996, P. L. 104-294, Title VI, § 604(b)(23), 110 Stat. 3508.)

§ 545. Smuggling goods into the United States

Whoever knowingly and willfully, with intent to defraud the United States, smuggles, or clandestinely introduces or attempts to smuggle or clandestinely introduce into the United States any merchandise which should have been invoiced, or makes out or passes, or attempts to pass, through the customhouse any false, forged, or fraudulent invoice, or other document or paper; or

Whoever fraudulently or knowingly imports or brings into the United States, any merchandise contrary to law, or receives, conceals, buys, sells, or in any manner facilitates the transportation, concealment, or sale of such merchandise after importation, knowing the same to have been imported or brought into the United States contrary to law—

Shall be fined under this title or imprisoned not more than 20 years, or both.

Proof of defendant's possession of such goods, unless explained to the satisfaction of the jury, shall be deemed evidence sufficient to authorize conviction for violation of this section.

Merchandise introduced into the United States in violation of this section, or the value thereof, to be recovered from any person described in the first or second paragraph of this section, shall be forfeited to the United States.

The term "United States", as used in this section, shall not include the Virgin Islands, American Samoa, Wake Island, Midway Islands, Kingman Reef, Johnston Island, or Guam.

(June 25, 1948, ch 645, § 1, 62 Stat. 716; Aug. 24, 1954, ch 890, § 1, 68 Stat. 782; Sept. 1, 1954, ch 1213, Title V, § 507, 68 Stat. 1141; June 30, 1955, ch 258, § 2(c), 69 Stat. 242; Sept. 13, 1994, P. L. 103-322, Title XXII, Subtitle I, § 320903(c), Title XXXIII, §§ 330004(18), 330016(1)(L), 108 Stat. 2125, 2142, 2147; Oct. 11, 1996, P. L. 104-294, Title VI, § 604(b)(23), 110 Stat. 3508; March 9, 2006, P. L. 109-177, Title III, § 310, 120 Stat. 242.)

§ 546. Smuggling goods into foreign countries

Any person owning in whole or in part any vessel of the United States who employs, or participates in, or allows the employment of, such vessel for the purpose of smuggling, or attempting to smuggle, or assisting in smuggling, any merchandise into the territory of any foreign government in violation of the laws there in force, if under the laws of such foreign government any penalty or forfeiture is provided for violation of the laws of the United States respecting the customs revenue, and any citizen of, or person domiciled in, or any corporation incorporated in, the United States, controlling or substantially participating in the control of any such vessel, directly or indirectly, whether through ownership of corporate shares or otherwise, and allowing the employment of said vessel for any such purpose, and any person found, or discovered to have been, on board of any such vessel so employed and participating or assisting in any such purpose, shall be fined under this title or imprisoned not more than two years, or both.

It shall constitute an offense under this section to hire out or charter a vessel if the lessor or charterer has knowledge or reasonable grounds for belief that the lessee or person chartering the vessel intends to employ such vessel for any of the purposes described in this section and if such vessel is, during the time such lease or charter is in effect, employed for any such purpose.

(June 25, 1948, ch 645, § 1, 62 Stat. 717; Sept. 13, 1994, P. L. 103-322, Title XXXIII, § 330016(1)(K), 108 Stat. 2147.)

§ 547. Depositing goods in buildings on boundaries

Whoever receives or deposits any merchandise in any building upon the boundary line between the United States and any foreign country, or carries any merchandise through the same, in violation of law, shall be fined under this title or imprisoned not more than two years, or both.

(June 25, 1948, ch 645, § 1, 62 Stat. 717; Sept. 13, 1994, P. L. 103-322, Title XXXIII, § 330016(1)(K), 108 Stat. 2147.)

§ 548. Removing or repacking goods in warehouses

Whoever fraudulently conceals, removes, or repacks merchandise in any bonded warehouse or fraudulently alters, defaces or obliterates any marks or numbers placed upon packages deposited in such warehouse, shall be fined under this title or imprisoned not more than two years, or both.

Merchandise so concealed, removed, or repacked, or packages upon which any marks or numbers have been so altered, defaced, or obliterated, shall be forfeited to the United States.

(June 25, 1948, ch 645, § 1, 62 Stat. 717; Sept. 13, 1994, P. L. 103-322, Title XXXIII, § 330016(1)(K), 108 Stat. 2147.)

§ 549. Removing goods from customs custody; breaking seals

Whoever, without authority, affixes or attaches a customs seal, fastening, or mark, or any seal, fastening, or mark purporting to be a customs seal, fastening, or mark to any vessel, vehicle, warehouse, or package; or

Whoever, without authority, willfully removes, breaks, injures, or defaces any customs seal or other fastening or mark placed upon any vessel, vehicle, warehouse, or package containing merchandise or baggage in bond or in customs custody; or

Whoever maliciously enters any bonded warehouse or any vessel or vehicle laden with or containing bonded merchandise with intent unlawfully to remove therefrom any merchandise or baggage therein, or unlawfully removes any merchandise or baggage in such vessel, vehicle, or bonded warehouse or otherwise in customs custody or control; or

Whoever receives or transports any merchandise or baggage unlawfully removed from any such vessel, vehicle, or warehouse, knowing the same to have been unlawfully removed—

Shall be fined under this title or imprisoned not more than 10 years, or both.

(June 25, 1948, ch 645, § 1, 62 Stat. 717; Sept. 13, 1994, P. L. 103-322, Title XXXIII, § 330016(1)(K), 108 Stat. 2147; March 9, 2006, P. L. 109-177, Title III, § 311(e), 120 Stat. 242.)

§ 550. False claim for refund of duties

Whoever knowingly and willfully files any false or fraudulent entry or claim for the payment of drawback, allowance, or refund of duties upon the exportation of merchandise, or knowingly or willfully makes or files any false affidavit, abstract, record, certificate, or other document, with a view to securing the payment to himself or others of any drawback, allowance, or refund of duties, on the exportation of merchandise, greater than that legally due thereon, shall be fined under this title or imprisoned not more than two years, or both, and such merchandise or the value thereof shall be forfeited.

(June 25, 1948, ch 645, § 1, 62 Stat. 718; Sept. 13, 1994, P. L. 103-322, Title XXXIII, § 330016(1)(K), 108 Stat. 2147.)

§ 551. Concealing or destroying invoices or other papers

Whoever willfully conceals or destroys any invoice, book, or paper relating to any merchandise imported into the United States, after an inspection thereof has been demanded by the collector of any collection district; or

Whoever conceals or destroys at any time any such invoice, book, or paper for the purpose of suppressing any evidence of fraud therein contained—

Shall be fined under this title or imprisoned not more than two years, or both.

(June 25, 1948, ch 645, § 1, 62 Stat. 718; Sept. 13, 1994, P. L. 103-322, Title XXXIII, § 330016(1)(K), 108 Stat. 2147.)

§ 552. Officers aiding importation of obscene or treasonous books and articles

Whoever, being an officer, agent, or employee of the United States, knowingly aids or abets any person engaged in any violation of any of the provisions of law prohibiting importing, advertising, dealing in, exhibiting, or sending or receiving by mail obscene or indecent publications or representations, or books, pamphlets, papers, writings, advertisements, circulars, prints, pictures, or drawings containing any matter advocating or urging treason or insurrection against the United States or forcible resistance to any law of the United States, or containing any threat to take the life of or inflict bodily harm upon any person in the United States, or means for procuring abortion, or other articles of indecent or immoral use or tendency, shall be fined under this title or imprisoned not more than ten years, or both.

(June 25, 1948, ch 645, § 1, 62 Stat. 718; Jan. 8, 1971, P.L. 91-662, § 2, 84 Stat. 1973; Sept. 13, 1994, P. L. 103-322, Title XXXIII, § 330016(1)(K), 108 Stat. 2147.)

§ 553. Importation or exportation of stolen motor vehicles, off-highway mobile equipment, vessels, or aircraft

(a) Whoever knowingly imports, exports, or attempts to import or export—

(1) any motor vehicle, off-highway mobile equipment, vessel, aircraft, or part of any motor vehicle, off-highway mobile equipment, vessel, or aircraft, knowing the same to have been stolen; or

(2) any motor vehicle or off-highway mobile equipment or part of any motor vehicle or off-highway mobile equipment, knowing that the identification number of such motor vehicle, equipment, or part has been removed, obliterated, tampered with, or altered;

shall be fined under this title or imprisoned not more than 10 years, or both.

(b) Subsection (a)(2) shall not apply if the removal, obliteration, tampering, or alteration—

(1) is caused by collision or fire; or

(2)(A) in the case of a motor vehicle, is not a violation of section 511 of this title [18 USCS § 511] (relating to altering or removing motor vehicle identification numbers); or

(B) in the case of off-highway mobile equipment, would not be a violation of section 511 of this title [18 USCS § 511] if such equipment were a motor vehicle.

(c) As used in this section, the term—

(1) "motor vehicle" has the meaning given that term in section 32101 of title 49;

(2) "off-highway mobile equipment" means any self-propelled agricultural equipment, self-propelled construction equipment, and self-propelled special use equipment, used or designed for running on land but not on rail or highway;

(3) "vessel" has the meaning given that term in section 401 of the Tariff Act of 1930 (19 U.S.C. 1401);

(4) "aircraft" has the meaning given that term in section 40102(a) of title 49; and

(5) "identification number"—

(A) in the case of a motor vehicle, has the meaning given that term in section 511 of this title [18 USCS § 511]; and

(B) in the case of any other vehicle or equipment covered by this section, means a number or symbol assigned to the vehicle or equipment, or part thereof, by the manufacturer primarily for the purpose of identifying such vehicle, equipment, or part.

(Added Oct. 25, 1984, P. L. 98-547, Title III, § 301(a), 98 Stat. 2771; Nov. 18, 1988, P. L. 100-690, Title VII, Subtitle B, § 7021, 102 Stat. 4397; Oct. 25, 1992, P. L. 102-519, Title I, Subtitle A, § 102, 106 Stat. 3385; July 5, 1994, P. L. 103-272, § 5(e)(5), 108 Stat. 1374.)

§ 554. Smuggling goods from the United States

(a) In general. Whoever fraudulently or knowingly exports or sends from the United States, or attempts to export or send from the United States, any merchandise, article, or object contrary to any law or regulation of the United States, or receives, conceals, buys, sells, or in any manner facilitates the transportation, concealment, or sale of such merchandise, article or object, prior to exportation, knowing the same to be intended for exportation contrary to any law or regulation of the United States, shall be fined under this title, imprisoned not more than 10 years, or both.

(b) Definition. In this section, the term "United States" has the meaning given that term in section 545 [18 USCS § 545].

(Added March 9, 2006, P. L. 109-177, Title III, § 311(a), 120 Stat. 242.)

§ 555. Border tunnels and passages

(a) Any person who knowingly constructs or finances the construction of a tunnel or subterranean passage that crosses the international border between the United States and another country, other than a lawfully authorized tunnel or passage known to the Secretary of Homeland Security and subject to inspection by Immigration and Customs Enforcement, shall be fined under this title and imprisoned for not more than 20 years.

(b) Any person who knows or recklessly disregards the construction or use of a tunnel or passage described in subsection (a) on land that the person owns or controls shall be fined under this title and imprisoned for not more than 10 years.

(c) Any person who uses a tunnel or passage described in subsection (a) to unlawfully smuggle an alien, goods (in violation of section 545 [18 USCS § 545]), controlled substances, weapons of mass destruction (including biological weapons), or a member of a terrorist organization (as defined in section 2339B(g)(6) [18 USCS § 2339B(g)(6)]) shall be subject to a maximum term of imprisonment that is twice the maximum term of imprisonment that would have otherwise been applicable had the unlawful activity not made use of such a tunnel or passage.

(d) Any person who attempts or conspires to commit any offense under subsection (a) or subsection (c) of this section shall be subject to the same penalties as those prescribed for the offense, the commission of which was the object of the attempt or conspiracy.

(Added Oct. 4, 2006, P. L. 109-295, Title V, § 551(a), 120 Stat. 1389; Dec. 26, 2007, P. L. 110-161, Div E, Title V, § 553(a)(1), 121 Stat. 2082; June 5, 2012, P. L. 112-127, § 3, 126 Stat. 371.)

CHAPTER 35. ESCAPE AND RESCUE

Section

§ 758. High speed flight from immigration checkpoint

Whoever flees or evades a checkpoint operated by the Immigration and Naturalization Service, or any other Federal law enforcement agency, in a motor vehicle and flees Federal, State, or local law enforcement agents in excess of the legal speed limit shall be fined under this title, imprisoned not more than five years, or both.

(Added Sept. 30, 1996, P. L. 104-208, Div C, Title I, Subtitle A, § 108(b)(1), 110 Stat. 3009-557.)

CHAPTER 41. EXTORTION AND THREATS

§ 872. Extortion by officers or employees of the United States

Whoever, being an officer, or employee of the United States or any department or agency thereof, or representing himself to be or assuming to act as such, under color or pretense of office or employment commits or attempts an act of extortion, shall be fined under this title or imprisoned not more than three years, or both; but if the amount so extorted or demanded does not exceed $1,000, he shall be fined under this title or imprisoned not more than one year, or both.

(June 25, 1948, ch 645, § 1, 62 Stat. 740; Oct. 31, 1951, ch 655, § 24(b), 65 Stat. 720; Sept. 13, 1994, P. L. 103-322, Title XXXIII, § 330016(1)(G), (K), 108 Stat. 2147; Oct. 11, 1996, P. L. 104-294, Title VI, § 606(a), 110 Stat. 3511.)

CHAPTER 43. FALSE PERSONATION

§ 911. Citizen of the United States

Whoever falsely and willfully represents himself to be a citizen of the United States shall be fined under this title or imprisoned not more than three years, or both.

(June 25, 1948, ch 645, § 1, 62 Stat. 742; Sept. 13, 1994, P. L. 103-322, Title XXXIII, § 330016(1)(H), 108 Stat. 2147.)

§ 912. Officer or employee of the United States

Whoever falsely assumes or pretends to be an officer or employee acting under the authority of the United States or any department, agency or officer thereof, and acts as such, or in such pretended character demands or obtains any money, paper, document, or thing of value, shall be fined under this title or imprisoned not more than three years, or both.

(June 25, 1948, ch 645, § 1, 62 Stat. 742; Sept. 13, 1994, P. L. 103-322, Title XXXIII, § 330016(1)(H), 108 Stat. 2147.)

§ 913. Impersonator making arrest or search

Whoever falsely represents himself to be an officer, agent, or employee of the United States, and in such assumed character arrests or detains any person or in any manner searches the person, buildings, or other property of any person, shall be fined under this title or imprisoned not more than three years, or both.

(June 25, 1948, ch 645, § 1, 62 Stat. 742; Sept. 13, 1994, P. L. 103-322, Title XXXIII, § 330016(1)(H), 108 Stat. 2147.)

CHAPTER 44. FIREARMS

§ 930. Possession of firearms and dangerous weapons in Federal facilities

(a) Except as provided in subsection (d), whoever knowingly possesses or causes to be present a firearm or other dangerous weapon in a Federal facility (other than a Federal court facility), or attempts to do so, shall be fined under this title or imprisoned not more than 1 year, or both.

(b) Whoever, with intent that a firearm or other dangerous weapon be used in the commission of a crime, knowingly possesses or causes to be present such firearm or dangerous weapon in a Federal facility, or attempts to do so, shall be fined under this title or imprisoned not more than 5 years, or both.

(c) A person who kills any person in the course of a violation of subsection (a) or (b), or in the course of an attack on a Federal facility involving the use of a firearm or other dangerous weapon, or attempts or conspires to do such an act, shall be punished as provided in sections 1111, 1112, 1113, and 1117 [18 USCS §§ 1111, 1112, 1113, and 1117].

(d) Subsection (a) shall not apply to—

(1) the lawful performance of official duties by an officer, agent, or employee of the United States, a State, or a political subdivision thereof, who is authorized by law to engage in or supervise the prevention, detection, investigation, or prosecution of any violation of law;

(2) the possession of a firearm or other dangerous weapon by a Federal official or a member of the Armed Forces if such possession is authorized by law; or

(3) the lawful carrying of firearms or other dangerous weapons in a Federal facility incident to hunting or other lawful purposes.

(e)(1) Except as provided in paragraph (2), whoever knowingly possesses or causes to be present a firearm or other dangerous weapon in a Federal court facility, or attempts to do so, shall be fined under this title, imprisoned not more than 2 years, or both.

(2) Paragraph (1) shall not apply to conduct which is described in paragraph (1) or (2) of subsection (d).

(f) Nothing in this section limits the power of a court of the United States to punish for contempt or to promulgate rules or orders regulating, restricting, or prohibiting the possession of weapons within any building housing such court or any of its proceedings, or upon any grounds appurtenant to such building.

(g) As used in this section:

(1) The term "Federal facility" means a building or part thereof owned or leased by the Federal Government, where Federal employees are regularly present for the purpose of performing their official duties.

(2) The term "dangerous weapon" means a weapon, device, instrument, material, or substance, animate or inanimate, that is used for, or is readily capable of, causing death or serious bodily injury, except that such term does not include a pocket knife with a blade of less than 2½ inches in length.

(3) The term "Federal court facility" means the courtroom, judges' chambers, witness rooms, jury deliberation rooms, attorney conference rooms, prisoner holding cells, offices of the court clerks, the United States attorney, and the United States marshal, probation and parole offices, and adjoining corridors of any court of the United States.

(h) Notice of the provisions of subsections (a) and (b) shall be posted conspicuously at each public entrance to each Federal facility, and notice of subsection (e) shall be posted conspicuously at each public entrance to each Federal court facility, and no person shall be convicted of an offense under subsection (a) or (e) with respect to a Federal facility if such notice is not so posted at such facility, unless such person had actual notice of subsection (a) or (e), as the case may be.

(Added Nov. 18, 1988, P. L. 100-690, Title VI, Subtitle G, § 6215(a), 102 Stat. 4361; Nov. 29, 1990, P. L. 101-647, Title XXII, § 2205(a), 104 Stat. 4858; Sept. 13, 1994, P. L. 103-322, Title VI, § 60014, 108 Stat. 1973; Oct. 11, 1996, P. L. 104-294, Title VI, § 603(t), (u), 110 Stat. 3506; Oct. 26, 2001, P. L. 107-56, Title VIII, § 811(b), 115 Stat. 381; Jan. 7, 2008, P. L. 110-177, Title II, § 203, 121 Stat. 2537.)

CHAPTER 47. FRAUD AND FALSE STATEMENTS

Section

§ 1015. Naturalization, citizenship or alien registry

(a) Whoever knowingly makes any false statement under oath, in any case, proceeding, or matter relating to, or under, or by virtue of any law of the United States relating to naturalization, citizenship, or registry of aliens; or

(b) Whoever knowingly, with intent to avoid any duty or liability imposed or required by law, denies that he has been naturalized or admitted to be a citizen, after having been so naturalized or admitted; or

(c) Whoever uses or attempts to use any certificate of arrival, declaration of intention, certificate of naturalization, certificate of citizenship or other documentary evidence of naturalization or of citizenship, or any duplicate or copy thereof, knowing the same to have been procured by fraud or false evidence or without required appearance or hearing of the applicant in court or otherwise unlawfully obtained; or

(d) Whoever knowingly makes any false certificate, acknowledgment or statement concerning the appearance before him or the taking of an oath or affirmation or the signature, attestation or execution by any person with respect to any application, declaration, petition, affidavit, deposition, certificate of naturalization, certificate of citizenship or other paper or writing required or authorized by the laws relating to immigration, naturalization, citizenship, or registry of aliens; or

(e) Whoever knowingly makes any false statement or claim that he is, or at any time has been, a citizen or national of the United States, with the intent to obtain on behalf of himself, or any other person, any Federal or State benefit or service, or to engage unlawfully in employment in the United States; or

(f) Whoever knowingly makes any false statement or claim that he is a citizen of the United States in order to register to vote or to vote in any Federal, State, or local election (including an initiative, recall, or referendum)—

Shall be fined under this title or imprisoned not more than five years, or both.

Subsection (f) does not apply to an alien if each natural parent of the alien (or, in the case of an adopted alien, each adoptive parent of the alien) is or was a citizen (whether by birth or naturalization), the alien permanently resided in the United States prior to attaining the age of 16, and the alien reasonably believed at the time of making the false statement or claim that he or she was a citizen of the United States.

(June 25, 1948, ch 645, § 1, 62 Stat. 752; Sept. 13, 1994, P. L. 103-322, Title XXXIII, § 330016(1)(K), 108 Stat. 2147; Sept. 30, 1996, P. L. 104-208, Div C, Title II, Subtitle B, § 215, 110 Stat. 3009-572; Oct. 30, 2000, P. L. 106-395, Title II, § 201(d)(2), 114 Stat. 1635.)

CHAPTER 69. NATIONALITY AND CITIZENSHIP

Section

§ 1421. Accounts of court officers

Whoever, being a clerk or assistant clerk of a court, or other person charged by law with a duty to render true accounts of moneys received in any proceeding relating to citizenship, naturalization, or registration of aliens or to pay over any balance of such moneys due to the United States, willfully neglects to do so within thirty days after said payment shall become due and demand therefor has been made, shall be fined under this title or imprisoned not more than five years, or both.

(June 25, 1948, ch 645, § 1, 62 Stat. 766; Sept. 13, 1994, P. L. 103-322, Title XXXIII, § 330016(1)(K), 108 Stat. 2147.)

§ 1422. Fees in naturalization proceedings

Whoever knowingly demands, charges, solicits, collects, or receives, or agrees to charge, solicit, collect, or receive any other or additional fees or moneys in proceedings relating to naturalization or citizenship or the registry of aliens beyond the fees and moneys authorized by law, shall be fined under this title or imprisoned not more than five years, or both.

(June 25, 1948, ch 645, § 1, 62 Stat. 766; Sept. 13, 1994, P. L. 103-322, Title XXXIII, § 330016(1)(K), 108 Stat. 2147.)

§ 1423. Misuse of evidence of citizenship or naturalization

Whoever knowingly uses for any purpose any order, certificate, certificate of naturalization, certificate of citizenship, judgment, decree, or exemplification, unlawfully issued or made, or copies or duplicates thereof, showing any person to be naturalized or admitted to be a citizen, shall be fined under this title or imprisoned not more than five years, or both.

(June 25, 1948, ch 645, § 1, 62 Stat. 766; Sept. 13, 1994, P. L. 103-322, Title XXXIII, § 330016(1)(K), 108 Stat. 2147.)

§ 1424. Personation or misuse of papers in naturalization proceedings

Whoever, whether as applicant, declarant, petitioner, witness or otherwise, in any naturalization or citizenship proceeding, knowingly personates another or appears falsely in the name of a deceased person or in an assumed or fictitious name; or

Whoever knowingly and unlawfully uses or attempts to use, as showing naturalization or citizenship of any person, any order, certificate, certificate of naturalization, certificate of citizenship, judgment, decree, or exemplification, or copies or duplicates thereof, issued to another person, or in a fictitious name or in the name of a deceased person–

Shall be fined under this title or imprisoned not more than five years, or both.

(June 25, 1948, ch 645, § 1, 62 Stat. 766; Sept. 13, 1994, P. L. 103-322, Title XXXIII, § 330016(1)(K), 108 Stat. 2147.)

§ 1425. Procurement of citizenship or naturalization unlawfully

(a) Whoever knowingly procures or attempts to procure, contrary to law, the naturalization of any person, or documentary or other evidence of naturalization or of citizenship; or

(b) Whoever, whether for himself or another person not entitled thereto, knowingly issues, procures or obtains or applies for or otherwise attempts to procure or obtain naturalization, or citizenship, or a declaration of intention to become a citizen, or a certificate of arrival or any certificate or evidence of nationalization or citizenship, documentary or otherwise, or duplicates or copies of any of the foregoing—

Shall be fined under this title or imprisoned not more than 25 years (if the offense was committed to facilitate an act of international terrorism (as defined in section 2331 of this title [18 USCS § 2331])), 20 years (if the offense was committed to facilitate a drug trafficking crime (as defined in section 929(a) of this title [18 USCS § 929(a)])), 10 years (in the case of the first or second such offense, if the offense was not committed to facilitate such an act of international terrorism or a drug trafficking crime), or 15 years (in the case of any other offense), or both.

(June 25, 1948, ch 645, § 1, 62 Stat. 766; Sept. 13, 1994, P. L. 103-322, Title XXXIII, § 330016(1)(K), 108 Stat. 2147; Sept. 30, 1996, P. L. 104-208, Div C, Title II, Subtitle B, § 211(a)(2), 110 Stat. 3009-569; Nov. 2, 2002, P. L. 107-273, Div B, Title IV, § 4002(a)(3), 116 Stat. 1806.)

§ 1426. Reproduction of naturalization or citizenship papers

(a) Whoever falsely makes, forges, alters or counterfeits any oath, notice, affidavit, certificate of arrival, declaration of intention, certificate or documentary evidence of naturalization or citizenship or any order, record, signature, paper or proceeding or any copy thereof, required or authorized by any law relating to naturalization or citizenship or registry of aliens; or

(b) Whoever utters, sells, disposes of or uses as true or genuine, any false, forged, altered, antedated or counterfeited oath, notice, affidavit, certificate of arrival, declaration of intention to become a citizen, certificate or documentary evidence of naturalization or citizenship, or any order, record, signature or other instrument, paper or proceeding required or authorized by any law relating to naturalization or citizenship or registry of aliens, or any copy thereof, knowing the same to be false, forged, altered, antedated or counterfeited; or

(c) Whoever, with intent unlawfully to use the same, possesses any false, forged, altered, antedated or counterfeited certificate of arrival, declaration of intention to become a citizen, certificate or documentary evidence of naturalization or citizenship purporting to have been issued under any law of the United States, or copy thereof, knowing the same to be false, forged, altered, antedated or counterfeited; or

(d) Whoever, without lawul authority, engraves or possesses, sells or brings into the United States any plate in the likeness or similitude of any plate designed, for the printing of a declaration of intention, or certificate or documentary evidence of naturalization or citizenship; or

(e) Whoever, without lawful authority, brings into the United States any document printed therefrom; or

(f) Whoever, without lawful authority, possesses any blank certificate of arrival, blank declaration of intention or blank certificate of naturalization or citizenship provided by the Immigration and Naturalization Service, with intent unlawfully to use the same; or

(g) Whoever, with intent unlawfully to use the same, possesses a distinctive paper adopted by the proper officer or agency of the United States for the printing or engraving of a declaration of intention to become a citizen, or certificate of naturalization or certificate of citizenship; or

(h) Whoever, without lawful authority, prints, photographs, makes or executes any print or impression in the likeness of a certificate of arrival, declaration of intention to become a citizen, or certificate of naturalization or citizenship, or any part thereof—

Shall be fined under this title or imprisoned not more than 25 years (if the offense was committed to facilitate an act of international terrorism (as defined in section 2331 of this title [18 USCS § 2331])), 20 years (if the offense was committed to facilitate a drug trafficking crime (as defined in section 929(a) of this title [18 USCS § 929(a)])), 10 years (in the case of the first or second such offense, if the offense was not committed to facilitate such an act of international terrorism or a drug trafficking crime), or 15 years (in the case of any other offense), or both.

(June 25, 1948, ch 645, § 1, 62 Stat. 767; Sept. 13, 1994, P. L. 103-322, Title XXXIII, § 330016(1)(K), 108 Stat. 2147; Sept. 30, 1996, P. L. 104-208, Div C, Title II, Subtitle B, § 211(a)(2), 110 Stat. 3009-569; Nov. 2, 2002, P. L. 107-273, Div B, Title IV, § 4002(a)(3), 116 Stat. 1806.)

§ 1427. Sale of naturalization or citizenship papers

Whoever unlawfully sells or disposes of a declaration of intention to become a citizen, certificate of naturalization, certificate of citizenship or copies or duplicates or other documentary evidence of naturalization or citizenship, shall be fined under this title or imprisoned not more than 25 years (if the offense was committed to facilitate an act of international terrorism (as defined in section 2331 of this title [18 USCS § 2331])), 20 years (if the offense was committed to facilitate a drug trafficking crime (as defined in section 929(a) of this title [18 USCS § 929(a)])), 10 years (in the case of the first or second such offense, if the offense was not committed to facilitate such an act of international terrorism or a drug trafficking crime), or 15 years (in the case of any other offense), or both.

(June 25, 1948, ch 645, § 1, 62 Stat. 767; Sept. 13, 1994, P. L. 103-322, Title XXXIII, § 330016(1)(K), 108 Stat. 2147; Sept. 30, 1996, P. L. 104-208, Div C, Title II, Subtitle B, § 211(a)(2), 110 Stat. 3009-569; Nov. 2, 2002, P. L. 107-273, Div B, Title IV, § 4002(a)(3), 116 Stat. 1806.)

§ 1428. Surrender of canceled naturalization certificate

Whoever, having in his possession or control a certificate of naturalization or citizenship or a copy thereof which has been canceled as provided by law, fails to surrender the same after at least sixty days' notice by the appropriate court or the Commissioner or Deputy Commissioner of Immigration, shall be fined under this title or imprisoned not more than five years, or both.

(June 25, 1948, ch 645, § 1, 62 Stat. 767; Sept. 13, 1994, P. L. 103-322, Title XXXIII, § 330016(1)(K), 108 Stat. 2147.)

§ 1429. Penalties for neglect or refusal to answer subpena

Any person who has been subpenaed under the provisions of subsection (d) of section 336 of the Immigration and Nationality Act [8 USCS § 1447(d)] to appear at the final hearing of an application for naturalization, and who shall neglect or refuse to so appear and to testify, if in the power of such person to do so, shall be fined under this title or imprisoned not more than five years, or both.

(Added June 27, 1952, ch 477, Title IV, § 402(b), 66 Stat. 276; Dec. 29, 1981, P. L. 97-116, § 18(u)(1), 95 Stat. 1621; Nov. 29, 1990, P. L. 101-649, Title IV, § 407(c)(21), 104 Stat. 5041; Sept. 13, 1994, P. L. 103-322, Title XXXIII, § 330016(1)(K), 108 Stat. 2147.)

CHAPTER 75. PASSPORTS AND VISAS

Section

§ 1541. Issuance without authority

Whoever, acting or claiming to act in any office or capacity under the United States, or a State, without lawful authority grants, issues, or verifies any passport or other instrument in the nature of a passport to or for any person whomsoever; or

Whoever, being a consular officer authorized to grant, issue, or verify passports, knowingly and willfully grants, issues, or verifies any such passport to or for any person not owing allegiance, to the United States, whether a citizen or not—

Shall be fined under this title, imprisoned not more than 25 years (if the offense was committed to facilitate an act of international terrorism (as defined in section 2331 of this title [18 USCS § 2331])), 20 years (if the offense was committed to facilitate a drug trafficking crime (as defined in section 929(a) of this title [18 USCS § 929(a)])), 10 years (in the case of the first or second such offense, if the offense was not committed to facilitate such an act of international terrorism or a drug trafficking crime), or 15 years (in the case of any other offense), or both.

For purposes of this section, the term "State" means a State of the United States, the District of Columbia, and any commonwealth, territory, or possession of the United States.

(June 25, 1948, ch 645, § 1, 62 Stat. 771; Sept. 13, 1994, P. L. 103-322, Title XIII, § 130009(a)(1), Title XXXIII, § 330016(1)(G), 108 Stat. 2030, 2147; Oct. 11, 1996, P. L. 104-294, Title VI, § 607(n), 110 Stat. 3512; Sept. 30, 1996, P. L. 104-208, Div C, Title II, Subtitle B, § 211(a)(2), 110 Stat. 3009-569; Nov. 2, 2002, P. L. 107-273, Div B, Title IV, § 4002(a)(3), 116 Stat. 1806.)

§ 1542. False statement in application and use of passport

Whoever willfully and knowingly makes any false statement in an application for passport with intent to induce or secure the issuance of a passport under the authority of the United States, either for his own use or the use of another, contrary to the laws regulating the issuance of passports or the rules prescribed pursuant to such laws; or

Whoever willfully and knowingly uses or attempts to use, or furnishes to another for use any passport the issue of which was secured in any way by reason of any false statement—

Shall be fined under this title, imprisoned not more than 25 years (if the offense was committed to facilitate an act of international terrorism (as defined in section 2331 of this title [18 USCS § 2331])), 20 years (if the offense was committed to facilitate a drug trafficking crime (as defined in section 929(a) of this title [18 USCS § 929(a)])), 10 years (in the case of the first or second such offense, if the offense was not committed to facilitate such an act of international terrorism or a drug trafficking crime), or 15 years (in the case of any other offense), or both.

(June 25, 1948, ch 645, § 1, 62 Stat. 771; Sept. 13, 1994, P. L. 103-322, Title XIII, § 130009(a)(2), Title XXXIII, § 330016(1)(I), 108 Stat. 2030, 2147; Sept. 30, 1996, P. L. 104-208, Div C, Title II, Subtitle B, § 211(a)(2), 110 Stat. 3009-569; Nov. 2, 2002, P. L. 107-273, Div B, Title IV, § 4002(a)(3), 116 Stat. 1806.)

§ 1543. Forgery or false use of passport

Whoever falsely makes, forges, counterfeits, mutilates, or alters any passport or instrument purporting to be a passport, with intent that the same may be used; or

Whoever willfully and knowingly uses, or attempts to use, or furnishes to another for use any such false, forged, counterfeited, mutilated, or altered passport or instrument purporting to be a passport, or any passport validly issued which has become void by the occurrence of any condition therein prescribed invalidating the same—

Shall be fined under this title, imprisoned not more than 25 years (if the offense was committed to facilitate an act of international terrorism (as defined in section 2331 of this title [18 USCS § 2331])), 20 years (if the offense was committed to facilitate a drug trafficking crime (as defined in section 929(a) of this title [18 USCS § 929(a)])), 10 years (in the case of the first or second such offense, if the offense was not committed to facilitate such an act of international terrorism or a drug trafficking crime), or 15 years (in the case of any other offense), or both.

(June 25, 1948, ch 645, § 1, 62 Stat. 771; Sept. 13, 1994, P. L. 103-322, Title XIII, § 130009(a)(2), Title XXXIII, § 330016(1)(I), 108 Stat. 2030, 2147; Sept. 30, 1996, P. L. 104-208, Div C, Title II, Subtitle B, § 211(a)(2), 110 Stat. 3009-569; Nov. 2, 2002, P. L. 107-273, Div B, Title IV, § 4002(a)(3), 116 Stat. 1806.)

§ 1544. Misuse of passport

Whoever willfully and knowingly uses, or attempts to use, any passport issued or designed for the use of another; or

Whoever willfully and knowingly uses or attempts to use any passport in violation of the conditions or restrictions therein contained, or of the rules prescribed pursuant to the laws regulating the issuance of passports; or

Whoever willfully and knowingly furnishes, disposes of, or delivers a passport to any person, for use by another than the person for whose use it was originally issued and designed—

Shall be fined under this title, imprisoned not more than 25 years (if the offense was committed to facilitate an act of international terrorism (as defined in section 2331 of this title [18 USCS § 2331])), 20 years (if the offense was committed to facilitate a drug trafficking crime (as defined in section 929(a) of this title [18 USCS § 929(a)])), 10 years (in the case of the first or second such offense, if the offense was not committed to facilitate such an act of international terrorism or a drug trafficking crime), or 15 years (in the case of any other offense), or both.

(June 25, 1948, ch 645, § 1, 62 Stat. 771; Sept. 13, 1994, P. L. 103-322, Title XIII, § 130009(a)(2), Title XXXIII, § 330016(1)(I), 108 Stat. 2030, 2147; Sept. 30, 1996, P. L. 104-208, Div C, Title II, Subtitle B, § 211(a)(2), 110 Stat. 3009-569; Nov. 2, 2002, P. L. 107-273, Div B, Title IV, § 4002(a)(3), 116 Stat. 1806.)

§ 1545. Safe conduct violation

Whoever violates any safe conduct or passport duly obtained and issued under authority of the United States shall be fined under this title, imprisoned not more than 10 years, or both.

(June 25, 1948, ch 645, § 1, 62 Stat. 771; Sept. 13, 1994, P. L. 103-322, Title XIII, § 130009(a)(3), Title XXXIII, § 330016(1)(I), 108 Stat. 2030, 2147.)

§ 1546. Fraud and misuse of visas, permits, and other documents

(a) Whoever[,] knowingly forges, counterfeits, alters, or falsely makes any immigrant or nonimmigrant visa, permit, border crossing card, alien registration receipt card, or other document prescribed by statute or regulation for entry into or as evidence of authorized stay or employment in the United States, or utters, uses, attempts to use, possesses, obtains, accepts, or receives any such visa, permit, border crossing card, alien registration receipt card, or other document prescribed by statute or regulation for entry into or as evidence of authorized stay or employment in the United States, knowing it to be forged, counterfeited, altered, or falsely made, or to have been procured by means of any false claim or statement, or to have been otherwise procured by fraud or unlawfully obtained; or

Whoever, except under direction of the Attorney General or the Commissioner of the Immigration and Naturalization Service, or other proper officer, knowingly possesses any blank permit, or engraves, sells, brings into the United States, or has in his control or possession any plate in the likeness of a plate designed for the printing of permits, or makes any print, photograph, or impression in the likeness of any immigrant or nonimmigrant visa, permit or other document required for entry into the United States, or has in his possession a distinctive paper which has been adopted by the Attorney General or the Commissioner of the Immigration and Naturalization Service for the printing of such visas, permits, or documents; or

Whoever, when applying for an immigrant or nonimmigrant visa, permit, or other document required for entry into the United States, or for admission to the United States personates another, or falsely appears in the name of a deceased individual, or evades or attempts to evade the immigration laws by appearing under an assumed or fictitious name without disclosing his true identity, or sells or otherwise disposes of, or offers to sell or otherwise dispose of, or utters, such visa, permit, or other document, to any person not authorized by law to receive such document; or

Whoever knowingly makes under oath, or as permitted under penalty of perjury under section 1746 of title 28, United States Code, knowingly subscribes as true, any false statement with respect to a material fact in any application, affidavit, or other document required by the immigration laws or regulations prescribed thereunder, or knowingly presents any such application, affidavit, or other document which contains any such false statement or which fails to contain any reasonable basis in law or fact—

Shall be fined under this title or imprisoned not more than 25 years (if the offense was committed to facilitate an act of international terrorism (as defined in section 2331 of this title [18 USCS § 2331])), 20 years (if the offense was committed to facilitate a drug trafficking crime (as defined in section 929(a) of this title [18 USCS § 929(a)])), 10 years (in the case of the first or second such offense, if the offense was not committed to facilitate such an act of international terrorism or a drug trafficking crime), or 15 years (in the case of any other offense), or both.

(b) Whoever uses—

(1) an identification document, knowing (or having reason to know) that the document was not issued lawfully for the use of the possessor,

(2) an identification document knowing (or having reason to know) that the document is false, or

(3) a false attestation,

for the purpose of satisfying a requirement of section 274A(b) of the Immigration and Nationality Act [8 USCS § 1324a(b)], shall be fined under this title, imprisoned not more than 5 years, or both.

(c) This section does not prohibit any lawfully authorized investigative, protective, or intelligence activity of a law enforcement agency of the United States, a State, or a subdivision of a State, or of an intelligence agency of the United States, or any activity authorized under title V of the Organized Crime Control Act of 1970 (18 U.S.C. note prec. 3481). For purposes of this section, the term "State" means a State of the United States, the District of Columbia, and any commonwealth, territory, or possession of the United States.

(June 25, 1948, ch 645, § 1, 62 Stat. 771; June 27, 1952, ch 477, Title IV, § 402(a), 66 Stat. 275; Oct. 18, 1976, P.L. 94-550, § 5, 90 Stat. 2535; Nov. 6, 1986, P. L. 99-603, Title I, § 103(a), 100 Stat. 3380; Oct. 24, 1988, P. L. 100-525, § 2(c), 102 Stat. 2610; Nov. 29, 1990, P. L. 101-647, Title XXXV, § 3550, 104 Stat. 4926; Sept. 13, 1994, P. L. 103-322, Title XIII, § 130009(a)(4), (5), Title XXXIII, § 330011(p), 108 Stat. 2030, 2145; Oct. 11, 1996, P. L. 104-294, Title VI, § 607(m), 110 Stat. 3512; Sept. 30, 1996, P. L. 104-208, Div C, Title II, Subtitle B, §§ 211(a)(2), 214, 110 Stat. 3009-569, 3009-572; Nov. 2, 2002, P. L. 107-273, Div B, Title IV, § 4002(a)(3), 116 Stat. 1806.)

§ 1547. Alternative imprisonment maximum for certain offenses

Notwithstanding any other provision of this title, the maximum term of imprisonment that may be imposed for an offense under this chapter (other than an offense under section 1545 [18 USCS § 1545])—

(1) if committed to facilitate a drug trafficking crime (as defined in 929(a) [18 USCS § 929(a)]) is 15 years; and

(2) if committed to facilitate an act of international terrorism (as defined in section 2331 [18 USCS § 2331]) is 20 years.

(Added Sept. 13, 1994, P. L. 103-322, Title XIII, § 130009(a)(6), 108 Stat. 2030.)

CHAPTER 77. PEONAGE, SLAVERY, AND TRAFFICKING IN PERSONS

Section

§ 1581. Peonage; obstructing enforcement

(a) Whoever holds or returns any person to a condition of peonage, or arrests any person with the intent of placing him in or returning him to a condition of peonage, shall be fined under this title or imprisoned not more than 20 years, or both. If death results from the violation of this section, or if the violation includes kidnapping or an attempt to kidnap, aggravated sexual abuse or the attempt to commit aggravated sexual abuse, or an attempt to kill, the defendant shall be fined under this title or imprisoned for any term of years or life, or both.

(b) Whoever obstructs, or attempts to obstruct, or in any way interferes with or prevents the enforcement of this section, shall be liable to the penalties prescribed in subsection (a).

(June 25, 1948, ch 645, § 1, 62 Stat. 772; Sept. 13, 1994, P. L. 103-322, Title XXXIII, § 330016(1)(K), 108 Stat. 2147; Sept. 30, 1996, P. L. 104-208, Div C, Title II, Subtitle B, § 218(a), 110 Stat. 3009-573; Oct. 28, 2000, P. L. 106-386, Div A, § 112(a)(1), 114 Stat. 1486.)

§ 1582. Vessels for slave trade

Whoever, whether as master, factor, or owner, builds, fits out, equips, loads, or otherwise prepares or sends away any vessel, in any port or place within the United States, or causes such vessel to sail from any such port or place, for the purpose of procuring any person from any foreign kingdom or country to be transported and held, sold, or otherwise disposed of as a slave, or held to service or labor, shall be fined under this title or imprisoned not more than seven years, or both.

(June 25, 1948, ch 645, § 1, 62 Stat. 772; Sept. 13, 1994, P. L. 103-322, Title XXXIII, § 330016(1)(K), 108 Stat. 2147.)

§ 1583. Enticement into slavery

(a) Whoever—

(1) kidnaps or carries away any other person, with the intent that such other person be sold into involuntary servitude, or held as a slave;

(2) entices, persuades, or induces any other person to go on board any vessel or to any other place with the intent that he or she may be made or held as a slave, or sent out of the country to be so made or held; or

(3) obstructs, or attempts to obstruct, or in any way interferes with or prevents the enforcement of this section, shall be fined under this title, imprisoned not more than 30 years, or both.

(b) Whoever violates this section shall be fined under this title, imprisoned for any term of years or for life, or both if—

(1) the violation results in the death of the victim; or

(2) the violation includes kidnaping, an attempt to kidnap, aggravated sexual abuse, an attempt to commit aggravated sexual abuse, or an attempt to kill.

(June 25, 1948, ch 645, § 1, 62 Stat. 772; Sept. 13, 1994, P. L. 103-322, Title XXXIII, § 330016(1)(K), 108 Stat. 2147; Sept. 30, 1996, P. L. 104-208, Div C, Title II, Subtitle B, § 218(a), 110 Stat. 3009-573; Oct. 28, 2000, P. L. 106-386, Div A, § 112(a)(1), 114 Stat. 1486; Dec. 23, 2008, P. L. 110-457, Title II, Subtitle C, § 222(b)(1), 122 Stat. 5067; Dec. 21, 2018, P.L. 115-392, § 11(1)(A), 132 Stat. 5255.)

§ 1584. Sale into involuntary servitude

(a) Whoever knowingly and willfully holds to involuntary servitude or sells into any condition of involuntary servitude, any other person for any term, or brings within the United States any person so held, shall be fined under this title or imprisoned not more than 20 years, or both. If death results from the violation of this section, or if the violation includes kidnapping or an attempt to kidnap, aggravated sexual abuse or the attempt to commit aggravated sexual abuse, or an attempt to kill, the defendant shall be fined under this title or imprisoned for any term of years or life, or both.

(b) Whoever obstructs, attempts to obstruct, or in any way interferes with or prevents the enforcement of this section, shall be subject to the penalties described in subsection (a).

(June 25, 1948, ch 645, § 1, 62 Stat. 773; Sept. 13, 1994, P. L. 103-322, Title XXXIII, § 330016(1)(K), 108 Stat. 2147; Sept. 30, 1996, P. L. 104-208, Div C, Title II, Subtitle B, § 218(a), 110 Stat. 3009-573; Oct. 28, 2000, P. L. 106-386, Div A, § 112(a)(1), 114 Stat. 1486; Dec. 23, 2008, P. L. 110-457, Title II, Subtitle C, § 222(b)(2), 122 Stat. 5068.)

§ 1585. Seizure, detention, transportation or sale of slaves

Whoever, being a citizen or resident of the United States and a member of the crew or ship's company of any foreign vessel engaged in the slave trade, or whoever, being of the crew or ship's company of any vessel owned in whole or in part, or navigated for, or in behalf of, any citizen of the United States, lands from such vessel, and on any foreign shore seizes any person with intent to make that person a slave, or decoys, or forcibly brings, carries, receives, confines, detains or transports any person as a slave on board such vessel, or, on board such vessel, offers or attempts to sell any such person as a slave, or on the high seas or anywhere on tide water, transfers or delivers to any other vessel any such person with intent to make such person a slave, or lands or delivers on shore from such vessel any person with intent to sell, or having previously sold, such person as a slave, shall be fined under this title or imprisoned not more than seven years, or both.

(June 25, 1948, ch 645, § 1, 62 Stat. 773; Sept. 13, 1994, P. L. 103-322, Title XXXIII, § 330016(1)(K), 108 Stat. 2147.)

§ 1586. Service on vessels in slave trade

Whoever, being a citizen or resident of the United States, voluntarily serves on board of any vessel employed or made use of in the transportation of slaves from any foreign country or place to another, shall be fined under this title or imprisoned not more than two years, or both.

(June 25, 1948, ch 645, § 1, 62 Stat. 773; Sept. 13, 1994, P. L. 103-322, Title XXXIII, § 330016(1)(I), 108 Stat. 2147.)

§ 1587. Possession of slaves aboard vessel

Whoever, being the captain, master, or commander of any vessel found in any river, port, bay, harbor, or on the high seas within the jurisdiction of the United States, or hovering off the coast thereof, and having on board any person for the purpose of selling such person as a slave, or with intent to land such person for such purpose, shall be fined under this title or imprisoned not more than 10 years, or both.

(June 25, 1948, ch 645, § 1, 62 Stat. 773; Sept. 13, 1994, P. L. 103-322, Title XXXIII, § 330016(1)(L), 108 Stat. 2147; Dec. 21, 2018, P.L. 115-392, § 11(1)(B), 132 Stat. 5255.)

§ 1588. Transportation of slaves from United States

Whoever, being the master or owner or person having charge of any vessel, receives on board any other person with the knowledge or intent that such person is to be carried from any place within the United States to any other place to be held or sold as a slave, or carries away from any place within the United States any such person with the intent that he may be so held or sold as a slave, shall be fined under this title or imprisoned not more than 10 years, or both.

(June 25, 1948, ch 645, § 1, 62 Stat. 773; Sept. 13, 1994, P. L. 103-322, Title XXXIII, § 330016(1)(K), 108 Stat. 2147; Sept. 30, 1996, P. L. 104-208, Div C, Title II, Subtitle B, § 218(a), 110 Stat. 3009-573.)

§ 1589. Forced labor

(a) Whoever knowingly provides or obtains the labor or services of a person by any one of, or by any combination of, the following means—

(1) by means of force, threats of force, physical restraint, or threats of physical restraint to that person or another person;

(2) by means of serious harm or threats of serious harm to that person or another person;

(3) by means of the abuse or threatened abuse of law or legal process; or

(4) by means of any scheme, plan, or pattern intended to cause the person to believe that, if that person did not perform such labor or services, that person or another person would suffer serious harm or physical restraint, shall be punished as provided under subsection (d).

(b) Whoever knowingly benefits, financially or by receiving anything of value, from participation in a venture which has engaged in the providing or obtaining of labor or services by any of the means described in subsection (a), knowing or in reckless disregard of the fact that the venture has engaged in the providing or obtaining of labor or services by any of such means, shall be punished as provided in subsection (d).

(c) In this section:

(1) The term "abuse or threatened abuse of law or legal process" means the use or threatened use of a law or legal process, whether administrative, civil, or criminal, in any manner or for any purpose for which the law was not designed, in order to exert pressure on another person to cause that person to take some action or refrain from taking some action.

(2) The term "serious harm" means any harm, whether physical or nonphysical, including psychological, financial, or reputational harm, that is sufficiently serious, under all the surrounding circumstances, to compel a reasonable person of the same background and in the same circumstances to perform or to continue performing labor or services in order to avoid incurring that harm.

(d) Whoever violates this section shall be fined under this title, imprisoned not more than 20 years, or both. If death results from a violation of this section, or if the violation includes kidnaping, an attempt to kidnap, aggravated sexual abuse, or an attempt to kill, the defendant shall be fined under this title, imprisoned for any term of years or life, or both.

(Added Oct. 28, 2000, P. L. 106-386, Div A, § 112(a)(2), 114 Stat. 1486; Dec. 23, 2008, P. L. 110-457, Title II, Subtitle C, § 222(b)(3), 122 Stat. 5068.)

§ 1590. Trafficking with respect to peonage, slavery, involuntary servitude, or forced labor

(a) Whoever knowingly recruits, harbors, transports, provides, or obtains by any means, any person for labor or services in violation of this chapter shall be fined under this title or imprisoned not more than 20 years, or both. If death results from the violation of this section, or if the violation includes kidnapping or an attempt to kidnap, aggravated sexual abuse, or the attempt to commit aggravated sexual abuse, or an attempt to kill, the defendant shall be fined under this title or imprisoned for any term of years or life, or both.

(b) Whoever obstructs, attempts to obstruct, or in any way interferes with or prevents the enforcement of this section, shall be subject to the penalties under subsection (a).

(Added Oct. 28, 2000, P. L. 106-386, Div A, § 112(a)(2), 114 Stat. 1487; Dec. 23, 2008, P. L. 110-457, Title II, Subtitle C, § 222(b)(4), 122 Stat. 5069.)

§ 1591. Sex trafficking of children or by force, fraud, or coercion

(a) Whoever knowingly—

(1) in or affecting interstate or foreign commerce, or within the special maritime and territorial jurisdiction of the United States, recruits, entices, harbors, transports, provides, obtains, advertises, maintains, patronizes, or solicits by any means a person; or

(2) benefits, financially or by receiving anything of value, from participation in a venture which has engaged in an act described in violation of paragraph (1), knowing, or, except where the act constituting the violation of paragraph (1) is advertising, in reckless disregard of the fact, that means of force, threats of force, fraud, coercion described in subsection (e)(2), or any combination of such means will be used to cause the person to engage in a commercial sex act, or that the person has not attained the age of 18 years and will be caused to engage in a commercial sex act, shall be punished as provided in subsection (b).

(b) The punishment for an offense under subsection (a) is—

(1) if the offense was effected by means of force, threats of force, fraud, or coercion described in subsection (e)(2), or by any combination of such means, or if the person recruited, enticed, harbored, transported, provided, obtained, advertised, patronized, or solicited had not attained the age of 14 years at the time of such offense, by a fine under this title and imprisonment for any term of years not less than 15 or for life; or

(2) if the offense was not so effected, and the person recruited, enticed, harbored, transported, provided, obtained, advertised, patronized, or solicited had attained the age of 14 years but had not attained the age of 18 years at the time of such offense, by a fine under this title and imprisonment for not less than 10 years or for life.

(c) In a prosecution under subsection (a)(1) in which the defendant had a reasonable opportunity to observe the person so recruited, enticed, harbored, transported, provided, obtained, maintained, patronized, or solicited, the Government need not prove that the defendant knew, or recklessly disregarded the fact, that the person had not attained the age of 18 years.

(d) Whoever obstructs, attempts to obstruct, or in any way interferes with or prevents the enforcement of this section, shall be fined under this title, imprisoned for a term not to exceed 25 years, or both.

(e) In this section:

(1) The term "abuse or threatened abuse of law or legal process" means the use or threatened use of a law or legal process, whether administrative, civil, or criminal, in any manner or for any purpose for which the law was not designed, in order to exert pressure on another person to cause that person to take some action or refrain from taking some action.

(2) The term "coercion" means—

(A) threats of serious harm to or physical restraint against any person;

(B) any scheme, plan, or pattern intended to cause a person to believe that failure to perform an act would result in serious harm to or physical restraint against any person; or

(C) the abuse or threatened abuse of law or the legal process.

(3) The term "commercial sex act" means any sex act, on account of which anything of value is given to or received by any person.

(4) The term "participation in a venture" means knowingly assisting, supporting, or facilitating a violation of subsection (a)(1).

(5) The term "serious harm" means any harm, whether physical or nonphysical, including psychological, financial, or reputational harm, that is sufficiently serious, under all the surrounding circumstances, to compel a reasonable person of the same background and in the same circumstances to perform or to continue performing commercial sexual activity in order to avoid incurring that harm.

(6) The term "venture" means any group of two or more individuals associated in fact, whether or not a legal entity.

(Added Oct. 28, 2000, P. L. 106-386, Div A, § 112(a)(2), 114 Stat. 1487; April 30, 2003, P. L. 108-21, Title I, § 103(a)(3), 117 Stat. 653; Dec. 19, 2003, P. L. 108-193, § 5(a), 117 Stat. 2879; July 27, 2006, P. L. 109-248, Title II, § 208, 120 Stat. 615; Dec. 23, 2008, P. L. 110-457, Title II, Subtitle C, § 222(b)(5), 122 Stat. 5069; May 29, 2015, P. L. 114-22, Title I, § 108(a), 118(b), 129 Stat. 238, 247; April 11, 2018, P. L. 115-164, § 5, 132 Stat. 1255; Dec. 21, 2018, P.L. 115-392, § 11(1)(C), 132 Stat. 5255.)

§ 1592. Unlawful conduct with respect to documents in furtherance of trafficking, peonage, slavery, involuntary servitude, or forced labor

(a) Whoever knowingly destroys, conceals, removes, confiscates, or possesses any actual or purported passport or other immigration document, or any other actual or purported government identification document, of another person—

(1) in the course of a violation of section 1581, 1583, 1584, 1589, 1590, 1591, or 1594(a) [18 USCS § 1581, 1583, 1584, 1589, 1590, 1591, or 1594(a)];

(2) with intent to violate section 1581, 1583, 1584, 1589, 1590, or 1591 [18 USCS § 1581, 1583, 1584, 1589, 1590, or 1591]; or

(3) to prevent or restrict or to attempt to prevent or restrict, without lawful authority, the person's liberty to move or travel, in order to maintain the labor or services of that person, when the person is or has been a victim of a severe form of trafficking in persons, as defined in section 103 of the Trafficking Victims Protection Act of 2000 [22 USCS § 7102],

shall be fined under this title or imprisoned for not more than 5 years, or both.

(b) Subsection (a) does not apply to the conduct of a person who is or has been a victim of a severe form of trafficking in persons, as defined in section 103 of the Trafficking Victims Protection Act of 2000 [22 USCS § 7102], if that conduct is caused by, or incident to, that trafficking.

(c) Whoever obstructs, attempts to obstruct, or in any way interferes with or prevents the enforcement of this section, shall be subject to the penalties described in subsection (a).

(Added Oct. 28, 2000, P. L. 106-386, Div A, § 112(a)(2), 114 Stat. 1488; Dec. 23, 2008, P. L. 110-457, Title II, Subtitle C, § 222(b)(6), 122 Stat. 5070.)

§ 1593. Mandatory restitution

(a) Notwithstanding section 3663 or 3663A [18 USCS §§ 3663 and 3663A], and in addition to any other civil or criminal penalties authorized by law, the court shall order restitution for any offense under this chapter [18 USCS §§ 1581 et seq.].

(b)(1) The order of restitution under this section shall direct the defendant to pay the victim (through the appropriate court mechanism) the full amount of the victim's losses, as determined by the court under paragraph (3) of this subsection.

(2) An order of restitution under this section shall be issued and enforced in accordance with section 3664 [18 USCS § 3664] in the same manner as an order under section 3663A [18 USCS § 3663A].

(3) As used in this subsection, the term "full amount of the victim's losses" has the same meaning as provided in section 2259(c)(2) [18 USCS § 2259(c)(2)] and shall in addition include the greater of the gross income or value to the defendant of the victim's services or labor or the value of the victim's labor as guaranteed under the minimum wage and overtime guarantees of the Fair Labor Standards Act (29 U.S.C. 201 et seq.).

(4) The forfeiture of property under this subsection shall be governed by the provisions of section 413 (other than subsection (d) of such section) of the Controlled Substances Act (21 U.S.C. 853).

(c) As used in this section, the term "victim" means the individual harmed as a result of a crime under this chapter [18 USCS §§ 1581 et seq.], including, in the case of a victim who is under 18 years of age, incompetent, incapacitated, or deceased, the legal guardian of the victim or a representative of the victim's estate, or another family member, or any other person appointed as suitable by the court, but in no event shall the defendant be named such representative or guardian.

(Added Oct. 28, 2000, P. L. 106-386, Div A, § 112(a)(2), 114 Stat. 1488; Dec. 23, 2008, P. L. 110-457, Title II, Subtitle C, § 221(1), 122 Stat. 5067; Dec. 7, 2018, P.L. 115-299, § 3(c), 132 Stat. 4385.)

§ 1593A. Benefitting financially from peonage, slavery, and trafficking in persons

Whoever knowingly benefits, financially or by receiving anything of value, from participation in a venture which has engaged in any act in violation of this chapter [18 USCS §§ 1581 et seq.], knowing or in reckless disregard of the fact that the venture has engaged in such violation, shall be fined under this title or imprisoned in the same manner as a completed violation of such section.

(Added Dec. 23, 2008, P. L. 110-457, Title II, Subtitle C, § 222(d)(1), 122 Stat. 5070; Dec. 21, 2018, P.L. 115-393, Title III, § 303(c), 132 Stat. 5273.)

§ 1594. General provisions

(a) Whoever attempts to violate section 1581, 1583, 1584, 1589, 1590, or 1591 [18 USCS § 1581, 1583, 1584, 1589, 1590, or 1591] shall be punishable in the same manner as a completed violation of that section.

(b) Whoever conspires with another to violate section 1581, 1583, 1589, 1590, or 1592 [18 USCS § 1581, 1583, 1589, 1590, or 1592] shall be punished in the same manner as a completed violation of such section.

(c) Whoever conspires with another to violate section 1591 [18 USCS § 1591] shall be fined under this title, imprisoned for any term of years or for life, or both.

(d) The court, in imposing sentence on any person convicted of a violation of this chapter [18 USCS §§ 1581 et seq.], shall order, in addition to any other sentence imposed and irrespective of any provision of State law, that such person shall forfeit to the United States—

(1) such person's interest in any property, real or personal, that was involved in, used, or intended to be used to commit or to facilitate the commission of such violation, and any property traceable to such property; and

(2) any property, real or personal, constituting or derived from, any proceeds that such person obtained, directly or indirectly, as a result of such violation, or any property traceable to such property.

(e)(1) The following shall be subject to forfeiture to the United States and no property right shall exist in them:

(A) Any property, real or personal, involved in, used, or intended to be used to commit or to facilitate the commission of any violation of this chapter [18 USCS §§ 1581 et seq.], and any property traceable to such property.

(B) Any property, real or personal, which constitutes or is derived from proceeds traceable to any violation of this chapter [18 USCS §§ 1581 et seq.].

(2) The provisions of chapter 46 of this title [18 USCS §§ 981 et seq.] relating to civil forfeitures shall extend to any seizure or civil forfeiture under this subsection.

(f) Transfer of forfeited assets.

(1) In general. Notwithstanding any other provision of law, the Attorney General shall transfer assets forfeited pursuant to this section, or the proceeds derived from the sale thereof, to satisfy victim restitution orders arising from violations of this chapter [18 USCS §§ 1581 et seq.].

(2) Priority. Transfers pursuant to paragraph (1) shall have priority over any other claims to the assets or their proceeds.

(3) Use of nonforfeited assets. Transfers pursuant to paragraph (1) shall not reduce or otherwise mitigate the obligation of a person convicted of a violation of this chapter [18 USCS §§ 1581 et seq.] to satisfy the full amount of a restitution order through the use of nonforfeited assets or to reimburse the Attorney General for the value of assets or proceeds transferred under this subsection through the use of nonforfeited assets.

(g) Witness protection. Any violation of this chapter [18 USCS §§ 1581 et seq.] shall be considered an organized criminal activity or other serious offense for the purposes of application of chapter 224 [18 USCS §§ 3521 et seq.] (relating to witness protection).

(Added Oct. 28, 2000, P. L. 106-386, Div A, § 112(a)(2), 114 Stat. 1489; Dec. 23, 2008, P. L. 110-457, Title II, Subtitle C, § 222(c), 122 Stat. 5070, May 29, 2015, P. L. 114-22, Title I, § 105(a), 129 Stat. 236.)

§ 1595. Civil remedy

(a) An individual who is a victim of a violation of this chapter [18 USCS §§ 1581 et seq.] may bring a civil action against the perpetrator (or whoever knowingly benefits, or attempts or conspires to benefit, financially or by receiving anything of value from participation in a venture which that person knew or should have known has engaged in an act in violation of this chapter [18 USCS §§ 1581 et seq.]) in an appropriate district court of the United States and may recover damages and reasonable attorneys fees.

(b)(1) Any civil action filed under subsection (a) shall be stayed during the pendency of any criminal action arising out of the same occurrence in which the claimant is the victim.

(2) In this subsection, a "criminal action" includes investigation and prosecution and is pending until final adjudication in the trial court.

(c) No action may be maintained under subsection (a) unless it is commenced not later than the later of—

(1) 10 years after the cause of action arose; or

(2) 10 years after the victim reaches 18 years of age, if the victim was a minor at the time of the alleged offense.

(d) In any case in which the attorney general of a State has reason to believe that an interest of the residents of that State has been or is threatened or adversely affected by any person who violates section 1591 [18 USCS § 1591], the attorney general of the State, as parens patriae, may bring a civil action against such person on behalf of the residents of the State in an appropriate district court of the United States to obtain appropriate relief.

(Added Dec. 19, 2003, P. L. 108-193, § 4(a)(4)(A), 117 Stat. 2878; Dec. 23, 2008, P. L. 110-457, Title II, Subtitle C, § 221(2), 122 Stat. 5067; May 29, 2015, P. L. 114-22, Title I, § 120, 129 Stat. 247; April 11, 2018, P. L. 115-164, § 6, 132 Stat. 1255; Jan. 5, 2023, P.L. 117-347, Title I, § 102, 136 Stat. 6200.)

§ 1595A. Civil injunctions

(a) In general. Whenever it shall appear that any person is engaged or is about to engage in any act that constitutes or will constitute a violation of this chapter, chapter 110, or chapter 117 [18 USCS §§ 1581 et seq.,

2251 et seq., or 2421 et seq.], or a conspiracy under section 371 [18 USCS § 371] to commit a violation of this chapter, chapter 110, or chapter 117 [18 USCS §§ 1581 et seq., 2251 et seq., or 2421 et seq.], the Attorney General may bring a civil action in a district court of the United States seeking an order to enjoin such act.

(b) Action by court. The court shall proceed as soon as practicable to the hearing and determination of a civil action brought under subsection (a), and may, at any time before final determination, enter such a restraining order or prohibition, or take such other action, as is warranted to prevent a continuing and substantial injury to the United States or to any person or class of persons for whose protection the civil action is brought.

(c) Procedure.

(1) In general. A proceeding under this section shall be governed by the Federal Rules of Civil Procedure, except that, if an indictment has been returned against the respondent, discovery shall be governed by the Federal Rules of Criminal Procedure.

(2) Sealed proceedings. If a civil action is brought under subsection (a) before an indictment is returned against the respondent or while an indictment against the respondent is under seal—

(A) the court shall place the civil action under seal; and

(B) when the indictment is unsealed, the court shall unseal the civil action unless good cause exists to keep the civil action under seal.

(d) Rule of construction. Nothing in this section shall be construed or applied so as to abridge the exercise of rights guaranteed under the First Amendment to the Constitution of the United States.

(Added Dec. 21, 2018, P. L. 115-393, Title II, § 201(a), 132 Stat. 5266.)

§ 1596. Additional jurisdiction in certain trafficking offenses

(a) In general. In addition to any domestic or extra-territorial jurisdiction otherwise provided by law, the courts of the United States have extra-territorial jurisdiction over any offense (or any attempt or conspiracy to commit an offense) under section 1581, 1583, 1584, 1589, 1590, or 1591 [18 USCS § 1581, 1583, 1584, 1589, 1590, or 1591] if—

(1) an alleged offender is a national of the United States or an alien lawfully admitted for permanent residence (as those terms are defined in section 101 of the Immigration and Nationality Act (8 U.S.C. 1101)); or

(2) an alleged offender is present in the United States, irrespective of the nationality of the alleged offender.

(b) Limitation on prosecutions of offenses prosecuted in other countries. No prosecution may be commenced against a person under this section if a foreign government, in accordance with jurisdiction recognized by the United States, has prosecuted or is prosecuting such person for the conduct constituting such offense, except upon the approval of the Attorney General or the Deputy Attorney General (or a person acting in either such capacity), which function of approval may not be delegated.

(Added Dec. 23, 2008, P. L. 110-457, Title II, Subtitle C, § 223(a), 122 Stat. 5071.)

§ 1597. Unlawful conduct with respect to immigration documents

(a) Destruction, concealment, removal, confiscation, or possession of immigration documents. It shall be unlawful for any person to knowingly destroy, conceal, remove, confiscate, or possess, an actual or purported passport or other immigration document of another individual —

(1) in the course of violating section 1351 of this title [18 USCS § 1351] or section 274 of the Immigration and Nationality Act (8 U.S.C. 1324);

(2) with intent to violate section 1351 of this title [18 USCS § 1351] or section 274 of the Immigration and Nationality Act (8 U.S.C. 1324); or

(3) in order to, without lawful authority, maintain, prevent, or restrict the labor of services of the individual.

(b) Penalty. Any person who violates subsection (a) shall be fined under this title, imprisoned for not more than 1 year, or both.

(c) Obstruction. Any person who knowingly obstructs, attempts to obstruct, or in any way interferes with or prevents the enforcement of this section, shall be subject to the penalties described in subsection (b).

(Added March 7, 2013, P. L. 113-4, Title XII, Subtitle B, Part I, § 1211(c)(1), 127 Stat. 142.)

CHAPTER 117. TRANSPORTATION FOR ILLEGAL SEXUAL ACTIVITY AND RELATED CRIMES

Section

§ 2421. Transportation generally

(a) In general. Whoever knowingly transports any individual in interstate or foreign commerce, or in any Territory or Possession of the United States, with intent that such individual engage in prostitution, or in any sexual activity for which any person can be charged with a criminal offense, or attempts to do so, shall be fined under this title or imprisoned not more than 10 years, or both.

(b) Requests to prosecute violations by State Attorneys General.

(1) In general. The Attorney General shall grant a request by a State attorney general that a State or local attorney be cross designated to prosecute a violation of this section unless the Attorney General determines

that granting the request would undermine the administration of justice.

(2) Reason for denial. If the Attorney General denies a request under paragraph (1), the Attorney General shall submit to the State attorney general a detailed reason for the denial not later than 60 days after the date on which a request is received.

(June 25, 1948, ch 645, § 1, 62 Stat. 812; May 24, 1949, ch 139, § 47, 63 Stat. 96; Nov. 7, 1986, P.L. 99-628, § 5(b)(1), 100 Stat. 3511; Oct 30, 1998, P.L. 105-314, Title I, § 106, 112 Stat. 2977; May 29, 2015, P. L. 114-22, Title III, § 303, 129 Stat. 255.)

§ 2421A. Promotion or facilitation of prostitution and reckless disregard of sex trafficking

(a) In general. Whoever, using a facility or means of interstate or foreign commerce or in or affecting interstate or foreign commerce, owns, manages, or operates an interactive computer service (as such term is defined in [defined in] section 230(f) the Communications Act of 1934 (47 U.S.C. 230(f))), or conspires or attempts to do so, with the intent to promote or facilitate the prostitution of another person shall be fined under this title, imprisoned for not more than 10 years, or both.

(b) Aggravated violation. Whoever, using a facility or means of interstate or foreign commerce or in or affecting interstate or foreign commerce, owns, manages, or operates an interactive computer service (as such term is defined in [defined in] section 230(f) the Communications Act of 1934 (47 U.S.C. 230(f))), or conspires or attempts to do so, with the intent to promote or facilitate the prostitution of another person and—

(1) promotes or facilitates the prostitution of 5 or more persons; or

(2) acts in reckless disregard of the fact that such conduct contributed to sex trafficking, in violation of section 1591(a) [18 USCS § 1591(a)],

shall be fined under this title, imprisoned for not more than 25 years, or both.

(c) Civil recovery. Any person injured by reason of a violation of section 2421A(b) [18 USCS § 2421A(b)] may recover damages and reasonable attorneys' fees in an action before any appropriate United States district court.

(d) Mandatory restitution. Notwithstanding sections [section] 3663 or 3663A [18 USCS § 3663 or 3663A] and in addition to any other civil or criminal penalties authorized by law, the court shall order restitution for any violation of subsection (b)(2). The scope and nature of such restitution shall be consistent with section 2327(b) [18 USCS § 2327(b)].

(e) Affirmative defense. It shall be an affirmative defense to a charge of violating subsection (a), or subsection (b)(1) where the defendant proves, by a preponderance of the evidence, that the promotion or facilitation of prostitution is legal in the jurisdiction where the promotion or facilitation was targeted.

(Added April 11, 2018, P. L. 115-164, § 3(a), 132 Stat. 1253.)

§ 2423. Transportation of minors

(a) Transportation with intent to engage in criminal sexual activity. A person who knowingly transports an individual who has not attained the age of 18 years in interstate or foreign commerce, or in any commonwealth, territory or possession of the United States, with intent that the individual engage in prostitution, or in any sexual activity for which any person can be charged with a criminal offense, shall be fined under this title and imprisoned not less than 10 years or for life.

(b) Travel with intent to engage in illicit sexual conduct. A person who travels in interstate commerce or travels into the United States, or a United States citizen or an alien admitted for permanent residence in the United States who travels in foreign commerce, with intent to engage in any illicit sexual conduct with another person shall be fined under this title or imprisoned not more than 30 years, or both.

(c) Engaging in illicit sexual conduct in foreign places. Any United States citizen or alien admitted for permanent residence who travels in foreign commerce or resides, either temporarily or permanently, in a foreign country, and engages in any illicit sexual conduct with another person shall be fined under this title or imprisoned not more than 30 years, or both.

(d) Illicit sexual conduct in connection with certain organizations. Any citizen of the United States or alien admitted for permanent residence who—

(1) is an officer, director, employee, or agent of an organization that affects interstate or foreign commerce;

(2) makes use of the mails or any means or instrumentality of interstate or foreign commerce through the connection or affiliation of the person with such organization; and

(3) commits an act in furtherance of illicit sexual conduct through the connection or affiliation of the person with such organization,

shall be fined under this title, imprisoned for not more than 30 years, or both.

(e) Ancillary offenses. Whoever, for the purpose of commercial advantage or private financial gain, arranges, induces, procures, or facilitates the travel of a person knowing that such a person is traveling in interstate commerce or foreign commerce with intent to engage in any illicit sexual conduct shall be fined under this title, imprisoned not more than 30 years, or both.

(f) Attempt and conspiracy. Whoever attempts or conspires to violate subsection (a), (b), (c), (d), or (e) shall be punishable in the same manner as a completed violation of that subsection.

(g) Definition. As used in this section, the term "illicit sexual conduct" means—

(1) a sexual act (as defined in section 2246 [18 USCS § 2246]) with a person under 18 years of age that would be in violation of chapter 109A [18 USCS §§ 2241 et seq.] if the sexual act occurred in the special maritime and territorial jurisdiction of the United States;

(2) any commercial sex act (as defined in section 1591 [18 USCS § 1591]) with a person under 18 years of age; or

(3) production of child pornography (as defined in section 2256(8) [18 USCS § 2256(8)]).

(h) Rule of construction. As used in this section, the term "intent" shall be construed as any intention to engage in prostitution, sexual activity for which any person can be charged with a criminal offense, or illicit sexual conduct, as applicable, at the time of the transportation or travel.

(i) Defense. In a prosecution under this section based on illicit sexual conduct as defined in subsection (g)(2), it is a defense, which the defendant must establish by clear and convincing evidence, that the defendant reasonably believed that the person with whom the defendant engaged in the commercial sex act had attained the age of 18 years.

(June 25, 1948, ch 645, § 1, 62 Stat. 812; Feb. 6, 1978, P. L. 95-225, § 3(a), 92 Stat. 8; Nov. 7, 1986, P. L. 99-628, § 5(b)(1), 100 Stat. 3511; Dec. 23, 1995, P. L. 104-71, § 5, 109 Stat. 774; Sept. 13, 1994, P. L. 103-322, Title XVI, § 160001(g), 108 Stat. 2037; Dec. 23, 1995, P. L. 104-71, § 5, 109 Stat. 774; Oct. 11, 1996, P. L. 104-294, Title VI, §§ 601(b)(4), 604(b)(33), 110 Stat. 3499, 3508; Oct 30, 1998, P. L. 105-314, Title I, § 103, 112 Stat. 2976; Nov. 2, 2002, P. L. 107-273, Div B, Title IV, § 4002(c)(1), 116 Stat. 1808; April 30, 2003, P. L. 108-21, Title I, §§ 103(a)(2)(C), (b)(2)(B), 105, 117 Stat. 652, 653; July 27, 2006, P. L. 109-248, Title II, § 204, 120 Stat. 613; March 7, 2013, P. L. 113-4, Title XII, Subtitle B, Part I, § 1211(b), 127 Stat. 142; May 29, 2015, P. L. 114-22, Title I, § 111, 129 Stat. 240; Dec. 21, 2018, P.L. 115-392, § 14, 132 Stat. 5256; Dec. 22, 2023, P.L. 118-31, Div E, Title LI, § 5102(c), (d), 137 Stat. 934.)

NOTES TO DECISIONS

III. PROSECUTION AND PUNISHMENT

A. Evidence

2. Sufficiency of evidence

14. Evidence sufficient

17. —Victim's testimony

Service member's conviction under Unif. Code Mil. Justice art. 134, 10 USCS § 934, for violating Mann Act, 18 USCS § 2423, was sufficiently supported by 17-year-old girl's unrebutted testimony that she and married service member had sexual intercourse and that service member brought girl to another state, where she and service member lived and slept together. United States v. Walker, 2006 CCA LEXIS 148 (N-M.C.C.A. June 21, 2006).

§ 2424. Filing factual statement about alien individual

(a) Whoever keeps, maintains, controls, supports, or harbors in any house or place for the purpose of prostitution, or for any other immoral purpose, any individual, knowing or in reckless disregard of the fact that the individual is an alien, shall file with the Commissioner of Immigration and Naturalization a statement in writing setting forth the name of such individual, the place at which that individual is kept, and all facts as to the date of that individual's entry into the United States, the port through which that individual entered, that individual's age, nationality, and parentage, and concerning that individual's procuration to come to this country within the knowledge of such person; and

Whoever fails within five business days after commencing to keep, maintain, control, support, or harbor in any house or place for the purpose of prostitution, or for any other immoral purpose, any alien individual, to file such statement concerning such alien individual with the Commissioner of Immigration and Naturalization; or

Whoever knowingly and willfully states falsely or fails to disclose in such statement any fact within that person's knowledge or belief with reference to the age, nationality, or parentage of any such alien individual, or concerning that individual's procuration to come to this country—

Shall be fined under this title or imprisoned not more than 10 years, or both.

(b) In any prosecution brought under this section, if it appears that any such statement required is not on file in the office of the Commissioner of Immigration and Naturalization, the person whose duty it is to file such statement shall be presumed to have failed to file said statement, unless such person or persons shall prove otherwise. No person shall be excused from furnishing the statement, as required by this section, on the ground or for the reason that the statement so required by that person, or the information therein contained, might tend to criminate that person or subject that person to a penalty or forfeiture, but no information contained in the statement or any evidence which is directly or indirectly derived from such information may be used against any person making such statement in any criminal case, except a prosecution for perjury, giving a false statement or otherwise failing to comply with this section.

(June 25, 1948, ch 645, § 1, 62 Stat. 813; Oct. 15, 1970, P.L. 91-452, Title II, § 226, 84 Stat. 930; Nov. 7, 1986, P. L. 99-628, § 5(c), 100 Stat. 3511; Sept. 13, 1994, P. L. 103-322, Title XXXIII, § 330016(1)(I), 108 Stat. 2147; Sept. 30, 1996, P. L. 104-208, Div C, Title III, Subtitle B, § 325, 110 Stat. 3009-629.)

PART III. PRISONS AND PRISONERS

(Selected Chapter)

Chapter

CHAPTER 306. TRANSFER TO OR FROM FOREIGN COUNTRIES

Section

§ 4113. Status of alien offender transferred to a foreign country

(a) An alien who is deportable from the United States but who has been granted voluntary departure pursuant to section 240B of the Immigration and Nationality Act [8 USCS § 1229c] and who is transferred to a foreign country pursuant to this chapter [18 USCS §§ 4100 et seq.] shall be deemed for all purposes to have voluntarily departed from this country.

(b) An alien who is the subject of an order of removal from the United States pursuant to section 240 of the Immigration and Nationality Act [8 USCS § 1229a] who is transferred to a foreign country pursuant to this chapter [18 USCS §§ 4100 et seq.] shall be deemed for all purposes to have been removed from this country.

(c) An alien who is the subject of an order of removal from the United States pursuant to 240 of the Immigration and Nationality Act [8 USCS § 1229a], who is transferred to a foreign country pursuant to this chapter [18 USCS §§ 4100 et seq.] shall be deemed for all purposes to have been excluded from admission and removed from the United States.

(Added Oct. 28, 1977, P. L. 95-144, § 1, 91 Stat. 1219; Sept. 30, 1996, P. L. 104-208, Div C, Title III, Subtitle A, § 308(d)(4)(U), (e)(1)(Q), (2)(I), (g)(3)(B), (5)(A)(iv), 110 Stat. 3009-619, 3009-620, 3009-622, 3009-623.)

CHAPTER TWO. OFFENSE CONDUCT

HISTORY:
Effective November 1, 1987.

PART L. OFFENSES INVOLVING IMMIGRATION, NATURALIZATION, AND PASSPORTS

1. IMMIGRATION

§ 2L1.1. Smuggling, Transporting, or Harboring an Unlawful Alien

(a) Base Offense Level:

(1) 25, if the defendant was convicted under 8 U.S.C. § 1327 of a violation involving an alien who was inadmissible under 8 U.S.C. § 1182(a)(3);

(2) 23, if the defendant was convicted under 8 U.S.C. § 1327 of a violation involving an alien who previously was deported after a conviction for an aggravated felony; or

(3) 12, otherwise.

(b) Specific Offense Characteristics

(1) If (A) the offense was committed other than for profit, or the offense involved the smuggling, transporting, or harboring only of the defendant's spouse or child (or both the defendant's spouse and child), and (B) the base offense level is determined under subsection (a)(3), decrease by 3 levels.

(2) If the offense involved the smuggling, transporting, or harboring of six or more unlawful aliens, increase as follows:

Number of Unlawful Aliens
Smuggled, Transported, or Harbored — Increase in Level

(A) 6-24 — add 3

(B) 25-99 — add 6

(C) 100 or more — add 9.

(3) If the defendant committed any part of the instant offense after sustaining (A) a conviction for a felony immigration and naturalization offense, increase by 2 levels; or (B) two (or more) convictions for felony immigration and naturalization offenses, each such conviction arising out of a separate prosecution, increase by 4 levels.

(4) If the offense involved the smuggling, transporting, or harboring of a minor who was unaccompanied by the minor's parent, adult relative, or legal guardian, increase by 4 levels.

(5) (Apply the greatest):

(A) If a firearm was discharged, increase by 6 levels, but if the resulting offense level is less than level 22, increase to level 22.

(B) If a dangerous weapon (including a firearm) was brandished or otherwise used, increase by 4 levels, but if the resulting offense level is less than level 20, increase to level 20.

(C) If a dangerous weapon (including a firearm) was possessed, increase by 2 levels, but if the resulting offense level is less than level 18, increase to level 18.

(6) If the offense involved intentionally or recklessly creating a substantial risk of death or serious bodily injury to another person, increase by 2 levels, but if the resulting offense level is less than level 18, increase to level 18.

(7) If any person died or sustained bodily injury, increase the offense level according to the seriousness of the injury:

Death or degree of injury — Increase in level

(A) Bodily Injury — Add 2 levels.

(B) Serious Bodily Injury — Add 4 levels.

(C) Permanent or Life-Threatening Bodily Injury — Add 6 levels.

(D) Death — Add 10 levels.

(8) (Apply the greater):

(A) If an alien was involuntarily detained through coercion or threat, or in connection with a demand for payment, (i) after the alien was smuggled into the United States; or (ii) while the alien was transported or harbored in the United States, increase by 2 levels. If the resulting offense level is less than level 18, increase to level 18.

(B) If (i) the defendant was convicted of alien harboring, (ii) the alien harboring was for the purpose of prostitution, and (iii) the defendant receives an adjustment under § 3B1.1 (Aggravating Role), increase by 2 levels, but if the alien engaging in the prostitution had not attained the age of 18 years, increase by 6 levels.

(9) If the defendant was convicted under 8 U.S.C. § 1324(a)(4), increase by 2 levels.

(c) Cross Reference

(1) If death resulted, apply the appropriate homicide guideline from Chapter Two, Part A, Subpart 1, if the resulting offense level is greater than that determined under this guideline.

Commentary

Statutory Provisions: 8 U.S.C. §§ 1324(a), 1327. For additional statutory provision(s), see Appendix A (Statutory Index).

Application Notes:

1. Definitions. For purposes of this guideline:

"The offense was committed other than for profit" means that there was no payment or expectation of payment for the smuggling, transporting, or harboring of any of the unlawful aliens.

"Number of unlawful aliens smuggled, transported, or harbored" does not include the defendant.

"Aggravated felony" has the meaning given that term in section 101(a)(43) of the Immigration and Nationality Act (8 U.S.C. § 1101(a)(43)), without regard to the date of conviction for the aggravated felony.

"Child" has the meaning set forth in section 101(b)(1) of the Immigration and Nationality Act (8 U.S.C. § 1101(b)(1)).

"Spouse" has the meaning set forth in 101(a)(35) of the Immigration and Nationality Act (8 U.S.C. § 1101(a)(35)).

"Immigration and naturalization offense" means any offense covered by Chapter Two, Part L.

"Minor" means an individual who had not attained the age of 18 years.

"Parent" means (A) a natural mother or father; (B) a stepmother or stepfather; or (C) an adoptive mother or father.

"Bodily injury," "serious bodily injury," and "permanent or life-threatening bodily injury" have the meaning given those terms in the Commentary to § 1B1.1 (Application Instructions).

2. Prior Convictions Under Subsection (b)(3). Prior felony conviction(s) resulting in an adjustment under subsection (b)(3) are also counted for purposes of determining criminal history points pursuant to Chapter Four, Part A (Criminal History).

3. Application of Subsection (b)(6). Reckless conduct to which the adjustment from subsection (b)(6) applies includes a wide variety of conduct (e.g., transporting persons in the trunk or engine compartment of a motor vehicle; carrying substantially more passengers than the rated capacity of a motor vehicle or vessel; harboring persons in a crowded, dangerous, or inhumane condition; or guiding persons through, or abandoning persons in, a dangerous or remote geographic area without adequate food, water, clothing, or protection from the elements). If subsection (b)(6) applies solely on the basis of conduct related to fleeing from a law enforcement officer, do not apply an adjustment from § 3C1.2 (Reckless Endangerment During Flight). Additionally, do not apply the adjustment in subsection (b)(6) if the only reckless conduct that created a substantial risk of death or serious bodily injury is conduct for which the defendant received an enhancement under subsection (b)(5).

4. Application of Subsection (b)(7) to Conduct Constituting Criminal Sexual Abuse. Consistent with Application Note 1(M) of § 1B1.1 (Application Instructions), "serious bodily injury" is deemed to have occurred if the offense involved conduct constituting criminal sexual abuse under 18 U.S.C. § 2241 or § 2242 or any similar offense under state law.

5. Inapplicability of § 3A1.3. If an enhancement under subsection (b)(8)(A) applies, do not apply § 3A1.3 (Restraint of Victim).

6. Interaction with § 3B1.1. For the purposes of § 3B1.1 (Aggravating Role), the aliens smuggled, transported, or harbored are not considered participants unless they actively assisted in the smuggling, transporting, or harboring of others. In large scale smuggling, transporting, or harboring cases, an additional adjustment from § 3B1.1 typically will apply.

7. Upward Departure Provisions. An upward departure may be warranted in any of the following cases:

(A) The defendant smuggled, transported, or harbored an alien knowing that the alien intended to enter the United States to engage in subversive activity, drug trafficking, or other serious criminal behavior.

(B) The defendant smuggled, transported, or harbored an alien the defendant knew was inadmissible for reasons of security and related grounds, as set forth under 8 U.S.C. § 1182(a)(3).

(C) The offense involved substantially more than 100 aliens.

Background: This section includes the most serious immigration offenses covered under the Immigration Reform and Control Act of 1986.

(Effective November 1, 1987. Amended effective January 15, 1988 (see Appendix C, amendments 35, 36, and 37); November 1, 1989 (see Appendix C, amendment 192); November 1, 1990 (see Appendix C, amendment 335); November 1, 1991 (see Appendix C, amendment 375); November 1, 1992 (see Appendix C, amendment 450); May 1, 1997 (see Appendix C, amendment 543); November 1, 1997 (see Appendix C, amendment 561); November 1, 2006 (see Appendix C, amendments 686 and 692); November 1, 2007 (see Appendix C, amendment 702); November 1, 2009 (see Appendix C, amendment 730); November 1, 2014 (see Appendix C, amendment 785); November 1, 2016 (see Appendix C, amendment 802); November 1, 2018 (see Appendix C, amendment 805).)

§ 2L1.2. Unlawfully Entering or Remaining in the United States

(a) Base Offense Level: 8

(b) Specific Offense Characteristics

(1) (Apply the Greater) If the defendant committed the instant offense after sustaining—

(A) a conviction for a felony that is an illegal reentry offense, increase by 4 levels; or

(B) two or more convictions for misdemeanors under 8 U.S.C. § 1325(a), increase by 2 levels.

(2) (Apply the Greatest) If, before the defendant was ordered deported or ordered removed from the United States for the first time, the defendant engaged in criminal conduct that, at any time, resulted in—

(A) a conviction for a felony offense (other than an illegal reentry offense) for which the sentence imposed was five years or more, increase by 10 levels;

(B) a conviction for a felony offense (other than an illegal reentry offense) for which the sentence imposed was two years or more, increase by 8 levels;

(C) a conviction for a felony offense (other than an illegal reentry offense) for which the sentence imposed exceeded one year and one month, increase by 6 levels;

(D) a conviction for any other felony offense (other than an illegal reentry offense), increase by 4 levels; or

(E) three or more convictions for misdemeanors that are crimes of violence or drug trafficking offenses, increase by 2 levels.

(3) (Apply the Greatest) If, after the defendant was ordered deported or ordered removed from the United States for the first time, the defendant engaged in criminal conduct that, at any time, resulted in—

(A) a conviction for a felony offense (other than an illegal reentry offense) for which the sentence imposed was five years or more, increase by 10 levels;

(B) a conviction for a felony offense (other than an illegal reentry offense) for which the sentence imposed was two years or more, increase by 8 levels;

(C) a conviction for a felony offense (other than an illegal reentry offense) for which the sentence imposed exceeded one year and one month, increase by 6 levels;

(D) a conviction for any other felony offense (other than an illegal reentry offense), increase by 4 levels; or

(E) three or more convictions for misdemeanors that are crimes of violence or drug trafficking offenses, increase by 2 levels.

Commentary

Statutory Provisions: 8 U.S.C. § 1253, § 1325(a) (second or subsequent offense only), § 1326. For additional statutory provision(s), see Appendix A (Statutory Index).

Application Notes:

1. In General.

(A) "Ordered Deported or Ordered Removed from the United States for the First Time". For purposes of this guideline, a defendant shall be considered "ordered deported or ordered removed from the United States" if the defendant was ordered deported or ordered removed from the United States based on a final order of exclusion, deportation, or removal, regardless of whether the order was in response to a conviction. "For the first time" refers to the first time the defendant was ever the subject of such an order.

(B) Offenses Committed Prior to Age Eighteen. Subsections (b)(1), (b)(2), and (b)(3) do not apply to a conviction for an offense committed before the defendant was eighteen years of age unless such conviction is classified as an adult conviction under the laws of the jurisdiction in which the defendant was convicted.

2. Definitions. For purposes of this guideline:

"Crime of violence" means any of the following offenses under federal, state, or local law: murder, voluntary manslaughter, kidnapping, aggravated assault, a forcible sex offense, robbery, arson, extortion, the use or unlawful possession of a firearm described in 26 U.S.C. § 5845(a) or explosive material as defined in 18 U.S.C. § 841(c), or any other offense under federal, state, or local law that has as an element the use, attempted use, or threatened use of physical force against the person of another. "Forcible sex offense" includes where consent to the conduct is not given or is not legally valid, such as where consent to the conduct is involuntary, incompetent, or coerced. The offenses of sexual abuse of a minor and statutory rape are included only if the sexual abuse of a minor or statutory rape was (A) an offense described in 18 U.S.C. § 2241(c) or (B) an offense under state law that would have been an offense under section 2241(c) if the offense had occurred within the special maritime and territorial jurisdiction of the United States. "Robbery" is the unlawful taking or obtaining of personal property from the person or in the presence of another, against his will, by means of actual or threatened force, or violence, or fear of injury, immediate or future, to his person or property, or property in his custody or possession, or the person or property of a relative or member of his family or of anyone in his company at the time of the taking or obtaining. The phrase "actual or threatened force" refers to force that is sufficient to overcome a victim's resistance. "Extortion" is obtaining something of value from another by the wrongful use of (A) force, (B) fear of physical injury, or (C) threat of physical injury.

"Drug trafficking offense" means an offense under federal, state, or local law that prohibits the manufacture, import, export, distribution, or dispensing of, or offer to sell a controlled substance (or a counterfeit substance) or the possession of a controlled substance (or a counterfeit substance) with intent to manufacture, import, export, distribute, or dispense.

"Felony" means any federal, state, or local offense punishable by imprisonment for a term exceeding one year.

"Illegal reentry offense" means (A) an offense under 8 U.S.C. § 1253 or § 1326, or (B) a second or subsequent offense under 8 U.S.C. § 1325(a).

"Misdemeanor" means any federal, state, or local offense punishable by a term of imprisonment of one year or less.

"Sentence imposed" has the meaning given the term "sentence of imprisonment" in Application Note 2 and subsection (b) of § 4A1.2 (Definitions and Instructions for Computing Criminal History). The length of the sentence imposed includes any term of imprisonment given upon revocation of probation, parole, or supervised release, regardless of when the revocation occurred.

3. Criminal History Points. For purposes of applying subsections (b)(1), (b)(2), and (b)(3), use only those convictions that receive criminal history points under § 4A1.1(a), (b), or (c). In addition, for purposes of subsections (b)(1)(B), (b)(2)(E), and (b)(3)(E), use only those convictions that are counted separately under § 4A1.2(a)(2).

A conviction taken into account under subsection (b)(1), (b)(2), or (b)(3) is not excluded from consideration of whether that conviction receives criminal history points pursuant to Chapter Four, Part A (Criminal History).

4. Cases in Which Sentences for An Illegal Reentry Offense and Another Felony Offense were Imposed at the Same Time. There may be cases in which the sentences for an illegal reentry offense and another felony offense were imposed at the same time and

treated as a single sentence for purposes of calculating the criminal history score under § 4A1.1(a), (b), and (c). In such a case, use the illegal reentry offense in determining the appropriate enhancement under subsection (b)(1), if it independently would have received criminal history points. In addition, use the prior sentence for the other felony offense in determining the appropriate enhancement under subsection (b)(2) or (b)(3), as appropriate, if it independently would have received criminal history points.

5. Cases in Which the Criminal Conduct Underlying a Prior Conviction Occurred Both Before and After the Defendant Was First Ordered Deported or Ordered Removed. There may be cases in which the criminal conduct underlying a prior conviction occurred both before and after the defendant was ordered deported or ordered removed from the United States for the first time. For purposes of subsections (b)(2) and (b)(3), count such a conviction only under subsection (b)(2).

6. Departure Based on Seriousness of a Prior Offense. There may be cases in which the offense level provided by an enhancement in subsection (b)(2) or (b)(3) substantially understates or overstates the seriousness of the conduct underlying the prior offense, because (A) the length of the sentence imposed does not reflect the seriousness of the prior offense; (B) the prior conviction is too remote to receive criminal history points (see § 4A1.2(e)); or (C) the time actually served was substantially less than the length of the sentence imposed for the prior offense. In such a case, a departure may be warranted.

7. Departure Based on Time Served in State Custody. In a case in which the defendant is located by immigration authorities while the defendant is serving time in state custody, whether pre- or post-conviction, for a state offense, the time served is not covered by an adjustment under § 5G1.3(b) and, accordingly, is not covered by a departure under § 5K2.23 (Discharged Terms of Imprisonment). See § 5G1.3(a). In such a case, the court may consider whether a departure is appropriate to reflect all or part of the time served in state custody, from the time immigration authorities locate the defendant until the service of the federal sentence commences, that the court determines will not be credited to the federal sentence by the Bureau of Prisons. Any such departure should be fashioned to achieve a reasonable punishment for the instant offense.

Such a departure should be considered only in cases where the departure is not likely to increase the risk to the public from further crimes of the defendant. In determining whether such a departure is appropriate, the court should consider, among other things, (A) whether the defendant engaged in additional criminal activity after illegally reentering the United States; (B) the seriousness of any such additional criminal activity, including (1) whether the defendant used violence or credible threats of violence or possessed a firearm or other dangerous weapon (or induced another person to do so) in connection with the criminal activity, (2) whether the criminal activity resulted in death or serious bodily injury to any person, and (3) whether the defendant was an organizer, leader, manager, or supervisor of others in the criminal activity; and (C) the seriousness of the defendant's other criminal history.

8. Departure Based on Cultural Assimilation. There may be cases in which a downward departure may be appropriate on the basis of cultural assimilation. Such a departure should be considered only in cases where (A) the defendant formed cultural ties primarily with the United States from having resided continuously in the United States from childhood, (B) those cultural ties provided the primary motivation for the defendant's illegal reentry or continued presence in the United States, and (C) such a departure is not likely to increase the risk to the public from further crimes of the defendant.

In determining whether such a departure is appropriate, the court should consider, among other things, (1) the age in childhood at which the defendant began residing continuously in the United States, (2) whether and for how long the defendant attended school in the United States, (3) the duration of the defendant's continued residence in the United States, (4) the duration of the defendant's presence outside the United States, (5) the nature and extent of the defendant's familial and cultural ties inside the United States, and the nature and extent of such ties outside the United States, (6) the seriousness of the defendant's criminal history, and (7) whether the defendant engaged in additional criminal activity after illegally reentering the United States.

(Effective November 1, 1987. Amended effective January 15, 1988 (see Appendix C, amendment 38); November 1, 1989 (see Appendix C, amendment 193); November 1, 1991 (see Appendix C, amendment 375); November 1, 1995 (see Appendix C, amendment 523); November 1, 1997 (see Appendix C, amendment 562); November 1, 2001 (see Appendix C, amendment 632); November 1, 2002 (see Appendix C, amendment 637); November 1, 2003 (see Appendix C, amendment 658); November 1, 2007 (see Appendix C, amendment 709); November 1, 2008 (see Appendix C, amendment 722); November 1, 2010 (see Appendix C, amendment 740); November 1, 2011 (see Appendix C, amendment 754); November 1, 2012 (see Appendix C, amendment 764); November 1, 2014 (see Appendix C, amendment 787); November 1, 2015 (see Appendix C, amendment 795); November 1, 2016 (see Appendix C, amendment 802); November 1, 2018 (see Appendix C, amendment 809); November 1, 2023 (see Appendix C, amendment 822).)

2L1.3. [Deleted]

(Section 2L1.3 (Engaging in a Pattern of Unlawful Employment of Aliens), effective November 1, 1987, was deleted effective November 1, 1989 (see Appendix C, amendment 194).)

2. NATURALIZATION AND PASSPORTS

§ 2L2.1. Trafficking in a Document Relating to Naturalization, Citizenship, or Legal Resident Status, or a United States Passport; False Statement in Respect to the Citizenship or Immigration Status of Another; Fraudulent Marriage to Assist Alien to Evade Immigration Law

(a) Base Offense Level: 11

(b) Specific Offense Characteristics

(1) If the offense was committed other than for profit, or the offense involved the smuggling, transporting, or harboring only of the defendant's spouse or child (or both the defendant's spouse and child), decrease by 3 levels.

(2) If the offense involved six or more documents or passports, increase as follows:

Number of
Documents/Passports — Increase in Level
(A) 6-24 — add 3
(B) 25-99 — add 6
(C) 100 or more — add 9.

(3) If the defendant knew, believed, or had reason to believe that a passport or visa was to be used to facilitate the commission of a felony offense, other than an offense involving violation of the immigration laws, increase by 4 levels.

(4) If the defendant committed any part of the instant offense after sustaining (A) a conviction for a felony immigration and naturalization offense, increase by 2 levels; or (B) two (or more) convictions for felony immigration and naturalization offenses, each such conviction arising out of a separate prosecution, increase by 4 levels.

(5) If the defendant fraudulently obtained or used (A) a United States passport, increase by 4 levels; or (B) a foreign passport, increase by 2 levels.

Commentary

Statutory Provisions: 8 U.S.C. §§ 1160(b)(7)(A), 1185(a)(3), (4), 1325(c), (d); 18 U.S.C. §§ 1015, 1028, 1425–1427, 1542, 1544, 1546. For additional statutory provision(s), see Appendix A (Statutory Index).

Application Notes:

1. For purposes of this guideline—

"The offense was committed other than for profit" means that there was no payment or expectation of payment for the smuggling, transporting, or harboring of any of the unlawful aliens.

"Immigration and naturalization offense" means any offense covered by Chapter Two, Part L.

"Child" has the meaning set forth in section 101(b)(1) of the Immigration and Nationality Act (8 U.S.C. § 1101(b)(1)).

"Spouse" has the meaning set forth in section 101(a)(35) of the Immigration and Nationality Act (8 U.S.C. § 1101(a)(35)).

2. Where it is established that multiple documents are part of a set of documents intended for use by a single person, treat the set as one document.

3. Subsection (b)(3) provides an enhancement if the defendant knew, believed, or had reason to believe that a passport or visa was to be used to facilitate the commission of a felony offense, other than an offense involving violation of the immigration laws. If the defendant knew, believed, or had reason to believe that the felony offense to be committed was of an especially serious type, an upward departure may be warranted.

4. Prior felony conviction(s) resulting in an adjustment under subsection (b)(4) are also counted for purposes of determining criminal history points pursuant to Chapter Four, Part A (Criminal History).

5. If the offense involved substantially more than 100 documents, an upward departure may be warranted.

(Effective November 1, 1987. Amended effective November 1, 1989 (see Appendix C, amendment 195); November 1, 1992 (see Appendix C, amendment 450); November 1, 1993 (see Appendix C, amendment 481); November 1, 1995 (see Appendix C, amendment 524); May 1, 1997 (see Appendix C, amendment 544); November 1, 1997 (see Appendix C, amendment 563); November 1, 2006 (see Appendix C, amendment 692); November 1, 2010 (see Appendix C, amendment 746).)

§ 2L2.2. Fraudulently Acquiring Documents Relating to Naturalization, Citizenship, or Legal Resident Status for Own Use; False Personation or Fraudulent Marriage by Alien to Evade Immigration Law; Fraudulently Acquiring or Improperly Using a United States Passport

(a) Base Offense Level: 8

(b) Specific Offense Characteristics

(1) If the defendant is an unlawful alien who has been deported (voluntarily or involuntarily) on one or more occasions prior to the instant offense, increase by 2 levels.

(2) If the defendant committed any part of the instant offense after sustaining (A) a conviction for a felony immigration and naturalization offense, increase by 2 levels; or (B) two (or more) convictions for felony immigration and naturalization offenses, each such conviction arising out of a separate prosecution, increase by 4 levels.

(3) If the defendant fraudulently obtained or used (A) a United States passport, increase by 4 level; or (B) a foreign passport, increase by 2 levels.

(4) (Apply the Greater):

(A) If the defendant committed any part of the instant offense to conceal the defendant's membership in, or authority over, a military, paramilitary, or police organization that was involved in a serious human rights offense during the period in which the defendant was such a member or had such authority, increase by 2 levels. If the resulting offense level is less than level 13, increase to level 13.

(B) If the defendant committed any part of the instant offense to conceal the defendant's participation in

(i) the offense of incitement to genocide, increase by 6 levels; or (ii) any other serious human rights offense, increase by 10 levels. If clause (ii) applies and the resulting offense level is less than level 25, increase to level 25.

(c) Cross Reference

(1) If the defendant used a passport or visa in the commission or attempted commission of a felony offense, other than an offense involving violation of the immigration laws, apply—

(A) § 2X1.1 (Attempt, Solicitation, or Conspiracy) in respect to that felony offense, if the resulting offense level is greater than that determined above; or

(B) if death resulted, the most analogous offense guideline from Chapter Two, Part A, Subpart 1 (Homicide), if the resulting offense level is greater than that determined above.

Commentary

Statutory Provisions: 8 U.S.C. §§ 1160(b)(7)(A), 1185(a)(3), (5), 1325(c), (d); 18 U.S.C. §§ 911, 1015, 1028, 1423–1426, 1542–1544, 1546.

Application Notes:

1. Definition. For purposes of this guideline, "immigration and naturalization offense" means any offense covered by Chapter Two, Part L.

2. Application of Subsection (b)(2). Prior felony conviction(s) resulting in an adjustment under subsection (b)(2) are also counted for purposes of determining criminal history points pursuant to Chapter Four, Part A (Criminal History).

3. Application of Subsection (b)(3). The term "used" is to be construed broadly and includes the attempted renewal of previously-issued passports.

4. Application of Subsection (b)(4). For purposes of subsection (b)(4):

"Serious human rights offense" means (A) violations of federal criminal laws relating to genocide, torture, war crimes, and the use or recruitment of child soldiers under sections 1091, 2340, 2340A, 2441, and 2442 of title 18, United States Code, see 28 U.S.C. § 509B(e); and (B) conduct that would have been a violation of any such law if the offense had occurred within the jurisdiction of the United States or if the defendant or the victim had been a national of the United States.

"The offense of incitement to genocide" means (A) violations of 18 U.S.C. § 1091(c); and (B) conduct that would have been a violation of such section if the offense had occurred within the jurisdiction of the United States or if the defendant or the victim had been a national of the United States.

5. Multiple Counts. For the purposes of Chapter Three, Part D (Multiple Counts), a count of conviction for unlawfully entering or remaining in the United States covered by § 2L1.2 (Unlawfully Entering or Remaining in the United States) arising from the same course of conduct as the count of conviction covered by this guideline shall be considered a closely related count to the count of conviction covered by this guideline, and therefore is to be grouped with the count of conviction covered by this guideline.

6. Upward Departure Provision. If the defendant fraudulently obtained or used a United States passport for the purpose of entering the United States to engage in terrorist activity, an upward departure may be warranted. See Application Note 4 of the Commentary to § 3A1.4 (Terrorism).

(Effective November 1, 1987. Amended effective January 15, 1988 (see Appendix C, amendment 39); November 1, 1989 (see Appendix C, amendment 196); November 1, 1992 (see Appendix C, amendment 450); November 1, 1993 (see Appendix C, amendment 481); November 1, 1995 (see Appendix C, amendment 524); May 1, 1997 (see Appendix C, amendment 544); November 1, 1997 (see Appendix C, amendment 563); November 1, 2004 (see Appendix C, amendment 671); November 1, 2006 (see Appendix C, amendment 692); November 1, 2010 (see Appendix C, amendment 746); November 1, 2012 (see Appendix C, amendment 765).)

2L2.3. [Deleted]

(Section 2L2.3 (Trafficking in a United States Passport), effective November 1, 1987, amended effective November 1, 1989 (see Appendix C, amendment 197) and November 1, 1992 (see Appendix C, amendment 450), was deleted by consolidation with § 2L2.1 effective November 1, 1993 (see Appendix C, amendment 481).)

2L2.4. [Deleted]

(Section 2L2.4 (Fraudulently Acquiring or Improperly Using a United States Passport), effective November 1, 1987, amended effective January 15, 1988 (see Appendix C, amendment 40) and November 1, 1989 (see Appendix C, amendment 198), was deleted by consolidation with § 2L2.2 effective November 1, 1993 (see Appendix C, amendment 481).)

§ 2L2.5. Failure to Surrender Canceled Naturalization Certificate

(a) Base Offense Level: 6

Commentary

Statutory Provision: 18 U.S.C. § 1428.

TITLE 21.
FOOD AND DRUGS

(Selected Chapter)

CHAPTER 13.
DRUG ABUSE PREVENTION AND CONTROL

(Complete Chapter)

CONTROL AND ENFORCEMENT

INTRODUCTORY PROVISIONS

GENERAL PROVISIONS

INTRODUCTORY PROVISIONS

§ 801. Congressional findings and declarations: controlled substances

The Congress makes the following findings and declarations:

(1) Many of the drugs included within this title have a useful and legitimate medical purpose and are necessary to maintain the health and general welfare of the American people.

(2) The illegal importation, manufacture, distribution, and possession and improper use of controlled substances have a substantial and detrimental effect on the health and general welfare of the American people.

(3) A major portion of the traffic in controlled substances flows through interstate and foreign commerce. Incidents of the traffic which are not an integral part of the interstate or foreign flow, such as manufacture, local distribution, and possession, nonetheless have a substantial and direct effect upon interstate commerce because—

(A) after manufacture, many controlled substances are transported in interstate commerce,

(B) controlled substances distributed locally usually have been transported in interstate commerce immediately before their distribution, and

(C) controlled substances possessed commonly flow through interstate commerce immediately prior to such possession.

(4) Local distribution and possession of controlled substances contribute to swelling the interstate traffic in such substances.

(5) Controlled substances manufactured and distributed intrastate cannot be differentiated from controlled substances manufactured and distributed interstate. Thus, it is not feasible to distinguish, in terms of controls, between controlled substances manufactured and distributed interstate and controlled substances manufactured and distributed intrastate.

(6) Federal control of the intrastate incidents of the traffic in controlled substances is essential to the effective control of the interstate incidents of such traffic.

(7) The United States is a party to the Single Convention on Narcotic Drugs, 1961, and other international conventions designed to establish effective control over international and domestic traffic in controlled substances.

(Oct. 27, 1970, P. L. 91-513, Title II, Part A, § 101, 84 Stat. 1242.)

§ 801a. Congressional findings and declarations: psychotropic substances

The Congress makes the following findings and declarations:

(1) The Congress has long recognized the danger involved in the manufacture, distribution, and use of certain psychotropic substances for nonscientific and nonmedical purposes, and has provided strong and effective legislation to control illicit trafficking and to regulate legitimate uses of psychotropic substances in this country. Abuse of psychotropic substances has become a phenomenon common to many countries, however, and is not confined to national borders. It is, therefore, essential that the United States cooperate with other nations in establishing effective controls over international traffic in such substances.

(2) The United States has joined with other countries in executing an international treaty, entitled the Convention on Psychotropic Substances and signed at Vienna, Austria, on February 21, 1971, which is designed to establish suitable controls over the manufacture, distribution, transfer, and use of certain psychotropic substances. The Convention is not self-executing, and the obligations of the United States thereunder may only be performed pursuant to appropriate legislation. It is the intent of the Congress that the amendments made by this Act, together with the existing law, will enable the United States to meet all of its obligations under the Convention and that no further legislation will be necessary for that purpose.

(3) In implementing the Convention on Psychotropic Substances, the Congress intends that, consistent with the obligations of the United States under the Convention, control of psychotropic substances in the United States should be accomplished within the framework of the procedures and criteria for classification of substances provided in the Comprehensive Drug Abuse Prevention and Control Act of 1970. This will insure that (A) the availability of psychotropic substances to manufacturers, distributors, dispensers, and researchers for useful and legitimate medical and scientific purposes will not be unduly restricted; (B) nothing in the Convention will interfere with bona fide research activities; and (C) nothing in the Convention will interfere with ethical medical practice in this country as determined by the Secretary of Health, Education, and Welfare [Secretary of Health and Human Services] on the basis of a consensus of the views of the American medical and scientific community.

(Nov. 10, 1978, P. L. 95-633, Title I, § 101, 92 Stat. 3768.)

§ 802. Definitions

As used in this title:

(1) The term "addict" means any individual who habitually uses any narcotic drug so as to endanger the public morals, health, safety, or welfare, or who is so far addicted to the use of narcotic drugs as to have lost the power of self-control with reference to his addiction.

(2) The term "administer" refers to the direct application of a controlled substance to the body of a patient or research subject by—

(A) a practitioner (or, in his presence, by his authorized agent), or

(B) the patient or research subject at the direction and in the presence of the practitioner, whether such application be by injection, inhalation, ingestion, or any other means.

(3) The term "agent" means an authorized person who acts on behalf of or at the direction of a manufacturer, distributor, or dispenser; except that such term does not include a common or contract carrier, public warehouseman, or employee of the carrier or warehouseman, when acting in the usual and lawful course of the carrier's or warehouseman's business.

(4) The term "Drug Enforcement Administration" means the Drug Enforcement Administration in the Department of Justice.

(5) The term "control" means to add a drug or other substance, or immediate precursor, to a schedule under part B of this title, whether by transfer from another schedule or otherwise.

(6) The term "controlled substance" means a drug or other substance, or immediate precursor, included in schedule I, II, III, IV, or V of part B of this title [21 USCS § 812]. The term does not include distilled spirits, wine, malt beverages, or tobacco, as those terms are defined or used in subtitle E of the Internal Revenue Code of 1954 [26 USCS §§ 5001 et seq.].

(7) The term "counterfeit substance" means a controlled substance which, or the container or labeling of which, without authorization, bears the trademark, trade name, or other identifying mark, imprint, number, or device, or any likeness thereof, of a manufacturer, distributor, or dispenser other than the person or persons who in fact manufactured, distributed, or dispensed such substance and which thereby falsely purports or is represented to be the product of, or to have been distributed by, such other manufacturer, distributor, or dispenser.

(8) The terms "deliver" or "delivery" mean the actual, constructive, or attempted transfer of a controlled substance or a listed chemical, whether or not there exists an agency relationship.

(9) The term "depressant or stimulant substance" means—

(A) a drug which contains any quantity of barbituric acid or any of the salts of barbituric acid; or

(B) a drug which contains any quantity of (i) amphetamine or any of its optical isomers; (ii) any salt of amphetamine or any salt of an optical isomer of amphetamine; or (iii) any substance which the Attorney General, after investigation, has found to be, and by regulation designated as, habit forming because of its stimulant effect on the central nervous system; or

(C) lysergic acid diethylamide; or

(D) any drug which contains any quantity of a substance which the Attorney General, after investigation, has found to have, and by regulation designated as having, a potential for abuse because of its depressant or stimulant effect on the central nervous system or its hallucinogenic effect.

(10) The term "dispense" means to deliver a controlled substance to an ultimate user or research subject by, or pursuant to the lawful order of, a practitioner, including the prescribing and administering of a controlled substance and the packaging, labeling, or compounding necessary to prepare the substance for such delivery. The term "dispenser" means a practitioner who so delivers a controlled substance to an ultimate user or research subject.

(11) The term "distribute" means to deliver (other than by administering or dispensing) a controlled substance or a listed chemical. The term "distributor" means a person who so delivers a controlled substance or a listed chemical.

(12) The term "drug" has the meaning given that term by section 201(g)(1) of the Federal Food, Drug, and Cosmetic Act [21 USCS § 321(g)(1)].

(13) The term "felony" means any Federal or State offense classified by applicable Federal or State law as a felony.

(14) The term "isomer" means the optical isomer, except as used in schedule I(c) and schedule II(a)(4). As used in schedule I(c), the term "isomer" means any optical, positional, or geometric isomer. As used in schedule II(a)(4), the term "isomer" means any optical or geometric isomer.

(15) The term "manufacture" means the production, preparation, propagation, compounding, or processing of a drug or other substance, either directly or indirectly or by extraction from substances of natural origin, or independently by means of chemical synthesis or by a combination of extraction and chemical synthesis, and includes any packaging or repackaging of such substance or labeling or relabeling of its container; except that such term does not include the preparation, compounding, packaging, or labeling of a drug or other substance in conformity with applicable State or local law by a practitioner as an incident to his administration or dispensing of such drug or substance in the course of his professional practice. The term "manufacturer" means a person who manufactures a drug or other substance.

(16)(A) Subject to subparagraph (B), the terms "marihuana" and "marijuana" mean all parts of the plant Cannabis sativa L., whether growing or not; the seeds thereof; the resin extracted from any part of such plant; and every compound, manufacture, salt, derivative, mixture, or preparation of such plant, its seeds or resin.

(B) The terms "marihuana" and "marijuana" do not include—

(i) hemp, as defined in section 297A of the Agricultural Marketing Act of 1946 [7 USCS § 1639o]; or

(ii) the mature stalks of such plant, fiber produced from such stalks, oil or cake made from the seeds of such plant, any other compound, manufacture, salt, derivative, mixture, or preparation of such mature stalks (except the resin extracted therefrom), fiber, oil, or cake, or the sterilized seed of such plant which is incapable of germination.

(17) The term "narcotic drug" means any of the following whether produced directly or indirectly by extraction from substances of vegetable origin, or independently by means of chemical synthesis, or by a combination of extraction and chemical synthesis:

(A) Opium, opiates, derivatives of opium and opiates, including their isomers, esters, ethers, salts, and salts of isomers, esters, and ethers, whenever the existence of such isomers, esters, ethers, and salts is possible within the specific chemical designation. Such term does not include the isoquinoline alkaloids of opium.

(B) Poppy straw and concentrate of poppy straw.

(C) Coca leaves, except coca leaves and extracts of coca leaves from which cocaine, ecgonine, and derivatives of ecgonine or their salts have been removed.

(D) Cocaine, its salts, optical and geometric isomers, and salts of isomers.

(E) Ecgonine, its derivatives, their salts, isomers, and salts of isomers.

(F) Any compound, mixture, or preparation which contains any quantity of any of the substances referred to in subparagraphs (A) through (E).

(18) The term "opiate" or "opioid" means any drug or other substance having an addiction-forming or addiction-sustaining liability similar to morphine or being capable of conversion into a drug having such addiction-forming or addiction-sustaining liability.

(19) The term "opium poppy" means the plant of the species Papaver somniferum L., except the seed thereof.

(20) The term "poppy straw" means all parts, except the seeds, of the opium poppy, after mowing.

(21) The term "practitioner" means a physician, dentist, veterinarian, scientific investigator, pharmacy, hospital, or other person licensed, registered, or otherwise permitted, by the United States or the jurisdiction in which he practices or does research, to distribute, dispense, conduct research with respect to, administer, or use in teaching or chemical analysis, a controlled substance in the course of professional practice or research.

(22) The term "production" includes the manufacture, planting, cultivation, growing, or harvesting of a controlled substance.

(23) The term "immediate precursor" means a substance—

(A) which the Attorney General has found to be and by regulation designated as being the principal compound used, or produced primarily for use, in the manufacture of a controlled substance;

(B) which is an immediate chemical intermediary used or likely to be used in the manufacture of such controlled substance; and

(C) the control of which is necessary to prevent, curtail, or limit the manufacture of such controlled substance.

(24) The term "Secretary," unless the context otherwise indicates, means the Secretary of Health and Human Services.

(25) The term "serious bodily injury" means bodily injury which involves—

(A) a substantial risk of death;

(B) protracted and obvious disfigurement; or

(C) protracted loss or impairment of the function of a bodily member, organ, or mental faculty.

(26) The term "State" means a State of the United States, the District of Columbia, and any commonwealth, territory, or possession of the United States.

(27) The term "ultimate user" means a person who has lawfully obtained, and who possesses, a controlled substance for his own use or for the use of a member of his household or for an animal owned by him or by a member of his household.

(28) The term "United States", when used in a geographic sense, means all places and waters, continental or insular, subject to the jurisdiction of the United States.

(29) The term "maintenance treatment" means the dispensing, for a period in excess of twenty-one days, of a narcotic drug in the treatment of an individual for dependence upon heroin or other morphine-like drugs.

(30) The term "detoxification treatment" means the dispensing, for a period not in excess of one hundred and eighty days, of a narcotic drug in decreasing doses to an individual in order to alleviate adverse physiological or psychological effects incident to withdrawal from the continuous or sustained use of a narcotic drug and as a method of bringing the individual to a narcotic drug-free state within such period.

(31) The term "Convention on Psychotropic Substances" means the Convention on Psychotropic Substances signed at Vienna, Austria, on February 21, 1971; and the term "Single Convention on Narcotic Drugs" means the Single Convention on Narcotic Drugs signed at New York, New York, on March 30, 1961.

(32)(A) Except as provided in subparagraph (C), the term "controlled substance analogue" means a substance—

(i) the chemical structure of which is substantially similar to the chemical structure of a controlled substance in schedule I or II;

(ii) which has a stimulant, depressant, or hallucinogenic effect on the central nervous system that is substantially similar to or greater than the stimulant, depressant, or hallucinogenic effect on the central nervous system of a controlled substance in schedule I or II; or

(iii) with respect to a particular person, which such person represents or intends to have a stimulant, depressant, or hallucinogenic effect on the central nervous system that is substantially similar to or greater than the stimulant, depressant, or hallucinogenic effect on the central nervous system of a controlled substance in schedule I or II.

(B) The designation of gamma butyrolactone or any other chemical as a listed chemical pursuant to paragraph (34) or (35) does not preclude a finding pursuant to subparagraph (A) of this paragraph that the chemical is a controlled substance analogue.

(C) Such term does not include—

(i) a controlled substance;

(ii) any substance for which there is an approved new drug application;

(iii) with respect to a particular person any substance, if an exemption is in effect for investigational use, for that person, under section 505 of the Federal Food, Drug, and Cosmetic Act (21 U.S.C. 355) to the extent conduct with respect to such substance is pursuant to such exemption; or

(iv) any substance to the extent not intended for human consumption before such an exemption takes effect with respect to that substance.

(33) The term "listed chemical" means any list I chemical or any list II chemical.

(34) The term "list I chemical" means a chemical specified by regulation of the Attorney General as a chemical that is used in manufacturing a controlled substance in violation of this title and is important to the manufacture of the controlled substances, and such term includes (until otherwise specified by regulation of the Attorney General, as considered appropriate by the Attorney General or upon petition to the Attorney General by any person) the following:

(A) Anthranilic acid, its esters, and its salts.

(B) Benzyl cyanide.

(C) Ephedrine, its salts, optical isomers, and salts of optical isomers.

(D) Ergonovine and its salts.

(E) Ergotamine and its salts.

(F) N-Acetylanthranilic acid, its esters, and its salts.

(G) Norpseudoephedrine, its salts, optical isomers, and salts of optical isomers.

(H) Phenylacetic acid, its esters, and its salts.

(I) Phenylpropanolamine, its salts, optical isomers, and salts of optical isomers.

(J) Piperidine and its salts.

(K) Pseudoephedrine, its salts, optical isomers, and salts of optical isomers.

(L) 3,4-Methylenedioxyphenyl-2-propanone.

(M) Methylamine.

(N) Ethylamine.

(O) Propionic anhydride.

(P) Isosafrole.

(Q) Safrole.

(R) Piperonal.

(S) N-Methylephedrine.

(T) N-methylpseudoephedrine.

(U) Hydriodic acid.

(V) Benzaldehyde.

(W) Nitroethane.

(X) Gamma butyrolactone.

(Y) Any salt, optical isomer, or salt of an optical isomer of the chemicals listed in subparagraphs (M) through (U) of this paragraph.

(35) The term "list II chemical" means a chemical (other than a list I chemical) specified by regulation of the Attorney General as a chemical that is used in manufacturing a controlled substance in violation of this title, and such term includes (until otherwise specified by regulation of the Attorney General, as considered appropriate by the Attorney General or upon petition to the Attorney General by any person) the following chemicals:

(A) Acetic anhydride.

(B) Acetone.

(C) Benzyl chloride.

(D) Ethyl ether.

(E) [Repealed]

(F) Potassium permanganate.

(G) 2-Butanone (or Methyl Ethyl Ketone).

(H) Toluene.

(I) Iodine.

(J) Hydrochloric gas.

(36) The term "regular customer" means, with respect to a regulated person, a customer with whom the regulated person has an established business relationship that is reported to the Attorney General.

(37) The term "regular importer" means, with respect to a listed chemical, a person that has an established record as an importer of that listed chemical that is reported to the Attorney General.

(38) The term "regulated person" means a person who manufactures, distributes, imports, or exports a listed chemical, a tableting machine, or an encapsulating machine or who acts as a broker or trader for an international transaction involving a listed chemical, a tableting machine, or an encapsulating machine.

(39) The term "regulated transaction" means—

(A) a distribution, receipt, sale, importation, or exportation of, or an international transaction involving shipment of, a listed chemical, or if the Attorney General establishes a threshold amount for a specific listed chemical, a threshold amount, including a cumulative threshold amount for multiple transactions (as determined by the Attorney General, in consultation with the chemical industry and taking into consideration the quantities normally used for lawful purposes), of a listed chemical, except that such term does not include—

(i) a domestic lawful distribution in the usual course of business between agents or employees of a single regulated person;

(ii) a delivery of a listed chemical to or by a common or contract carrier for carriage in the lawful and usual course of the business of the common or contract carrier, or to or by a warehouseman for storage in the lawful and usual course of the business of the warehouseman, except that if the carriage or storage is in connection with the distribution, importation, or exportation of a listed chemical to a third person, this clause does not relieve a distributor, importer, or exporter from compliance with section 310 [21 USCS § 830];

(iii) any category of transaction or any category of transaction for a specific listed chemical or chemicals specified by regulation of the Attorney General as excluded from this definition as unnecessary for enforcement of this title or title III;

(iv) any transaction in a listed chemical that is contained in a drug that may be marketed or distributed lawfully in the United States under the Federal Food, Drug, and Cosmetic Act, subject to clause (v), unless—

(I) the Attorney General has determined under section 204 [21 USCS § 814] that the drug or group of drugs is being diverted to obtain the listed chemical for use in the illicit production of a controlled substance; and

(II) the quantity of the listed chemical contained in the drug included in the transaction or multiple transactions equals or exceeds the threshold established for that chemical by the Attorney General;

(v) any transaction in a scheduled listed chemical product that is a sale at retail by a regulated seller or a distributor required to submit reports under section 310(b)(3) [21 USCS § 830(b)(3)]; or

(vi) any transaction in a chemical mixture which the Attorney General has by regulation designated as exempt from the application of this title and title III based on a finding that the mixture is formulated in such a way that it cannot be easily used in the illicit production of a controlled substance and that the listed chemical or chemicals contained in the mixture cannot be readily recovered; and

(B) a distribution, importation, or exportation of a tableting machine or encapsulating machine.

(40) The term "chemical mixture" means a combination of two or more chemical substances, at least one of which is not a list I chemical or a list II chemical, except that such term does not include any combination of a list I chemical or a list II chemical with another chemical that is present solely as an impurity.

(41)(A) The term "anabolic steroid" means any drug or hormonal substance, chemically and pharmacologically related to testosterone (other than estrogens, progestins, corticosteroids, and dehydroepiandrosterone), and includes—

(i) androstanediol—

(I) 3β,17β-dihydroxy-5α-androstane; and

(II) 3α,17β-dihydroxy-5α-androstane;

(ii) androstanedione (5α-androstan-3,17-dione);

(iii) androstenediol—

(I) 1-androstenediol (3β,17β-dihydroxy-5α-androst-1-ene);

(II) 1-androstenediol (3α,17β-dihydroxy-5α-androst-1-ene);

(III) 4-androstenediol (3β,17β-dihydroxy-androst-4-ene); and

(IV) 5-androstenediol (3β,17β-dihydroxy-androst-5-ene);

(iv) androstenedione—

(I) 1-androstenedione ([5a]-androst-1-en-3,17-dione);

(II) 4-androstenedione (androst-4-en-3,17-dione); and

(III) 5-androstenedione (androst-5-en-3,17-dione);

(v) bolasterone (7α,17α -dimethyl-17β -hydroxyandrost-4-en-3-one);

(vi) boldenone (17β-hydroxyandrost-1,4,-diene-3-one);

(vii) calusterone (7β,17α-dimethyl-17β -hydroxyandrost-4-en-3-one);

(viii) clostebol (4-chloro-17β-hydroxyandrost-4-en-3-one);

(ix) dehydrochloromethyltestosterone (4-chloro-17β -hydroxy-17α-methyl-androst-1, 4-dien-3-one);

(x) D 1-dihydrotestosterone (a.k.a. "1-testosterone") (17β-hydroxy-5α-androst-1-en-3-one);

(xi) 4-dihydrotestosterone (17β-hydroxy-androstan-3-one);

(xii) drostanolone (17β-hydroxy-2α -methyl-5α-androstan-3-one);

(xiii) ethylestrenol (17α-ethyl-17β-hydroxyestr-4-ene);

(xiv) fluoxymesterone (9-fluoro-17α-methyl-11β, 17β-dihydroxyandrost-4-en-3-one);

(xv) formebolone (2-formyl-17α-methyl-11α, 17β-dihydroxyandrost-1,4-dien-3-one);

(xvi) furazabol (17α-methyl-17β -hydroxyandrostano[2,3-c]-furazan);

(xvii) 13β-ethyl-17β-hydroxygon-4-en-3-one;

(xviii) 4-hydroxytestosterone (4,17β-dihydroxy-androst-4-en-3-one);

(xix) 4-hydroxy-19-nortestosterone (4,17β-dihydroxy-estr-4-en-3-one);

(xx) mestanolone (17α-methyl-17β -hydroxy-5α-androstan-3-one);

(xxi) mesterolone (1α-methyl-17β -hydroxy-[5a]-androstan-3-one);

(xxii) methandienone (17α-methyl-17β -hydroxyandrost-1,4-dien-3-one);

(xxiii) methandriol (17α-methyl-3β,17β -dihydroxy-androst-5-ene);

(xxiv) methenolone (1-methyl-17β-hydroxy-5α -androst-1-en-3-one);

(xxv) 17α-methyl-3β, 17β-dihydroxy-5α-androstane;

(xxvi) 17α-methyl-3α, 17β-dihydroxy-5α-androstane;

(xxvii) 17α-methyl-3β, 17β-dihydroxyandrost-4-ene.

(xxviii) 17α-methyl-4-hydroxynandrolone (17α-methyl-4-hydroxy-17β -hydroxyestr-4-en-3-one);

(xxix) methyldienolone (17α-methyl-17β -hydroxyestra-4,9(10)-dien-3-one);

(xxx) methyltrienolone (17α-methyl-17β -hydroxyestra-4,9-11-trien-3-one);

(xxxi) methyltestosterone (17α-methyl-17β -hydroxyandrost-4-en-3-one);

(xxxii) mibolerone (7α,17α-dimethyl-17β -hydroxyestr-4-en-3-one);

(xxxiii) 17α-methyl-D 1-dihydrotestosterone (17β-hydroxy-17α-methyl-5α -androst-1-en-3-one) (a.k.a. "17-α-methyl-1-testosterone");

(xxxiv) nandrolone (17β-hydroxyestr-4-en-3-one);

(xxxv) norandrostenediol—

(I) 19-nor-4-androstenediol (3β, 17β-dihydroxyestr-4-ene);

(II) 19-nor-4-androstenediol (3α, 17β-dihydroxyestr-4-ene);

(III) 19-nor-5-androstenediol (3β, 17β-dihydroxyestr-5-ene); and

(IV) 19-nor-5-androstenediol (3α, 17β-dihydroxyestr-5-ene);

(xxxvi) norandrostenedione—

(I) 19-nor-4-androstenedione (estr-4-en-3,17-dione); and

(II) 19-nor-5-androstenedione (estr-5-en-3,17-dione;

(xxxvii) norbolethone (13β,17α-diethyl-17β -hydroxygon-4-en-3-one);

(xxxviii) norclostebol (4-chloro-17β-hydroxyestr-4-en-3-one);

(xxxix) norethandrolone (17α-ethyl-17β-hydroxyestr-4-en-3-one);

(xl) normethandrolone (17α-methyl-17β-hydroxyestr-4-en-3-one);

(xli) oxandrolone (17α-methyl-17β -hydroxy-2-oxa-[5α] -androstan-3-one);

(xlii) oxymesterone (17α-methyl-4,17β-dihydroxyandrost-4-en-3-one);

(xliii) oxymetholone (17α-methyl-2-hydroxymethylene-17β -hydroxy-[5α] -androstan-3-one);

(xliv) stanozolol (17α-methyl-17β-hydroxy-[5α]-androst-2-eno[3, 2-c]-pyrazole);

(xlv) stenbolone (17β-hydroxy-2-methyl-[5α]-androst-1-en-3-one);

(xlvi) testolactone (13-hydroxy-3-oxo-13,17-secoandrosta-1,4-dien-17-oic acid lactone);

(xlvii) testosterone (17β-hydroxyandrost-4-en-3-one);

(xlviii) tetrahydrogestrinone (13β,17α -diethyl-17β-hydroxygon-4,9, 11-trien-3-one);

(xlix) trenbolone (17β-hydroxyestr-4,9,11-trien-3-one);

(l) 5α-Androstan-3,6,17-trione;

(li) 6-bromo-androstan-3,17-dione;

(lii) 6-bromo-androsta-1,4-diene-3,17-dione;

(liii) 4-chloro-17α-methyl-androsta-1,4-diene-3,17β-diol;

(liv) 4-chloro-17α-methyl-androst-4-ene-3β,17β-diol;

(lv) 4-chloro-17α-methyl-17β-hydroxy-androst-4-en-3-one;

(lvi) 4-chloro-17α-methyl-17β-hydroxy-androst-4-ene-3, 11-dione;

(lvii) 4-chloro-17α-methyl-androsta-1,4-diene-3,17β-diol;

(lviii) 2α,17α-dimethyl-17β-hydroxy-5α-androstan-3-one;

(lix) 2α,17α-dimethyl-17β-hydroxy-5β-androstan-3-one;

(lx) 2α,3α-epithio-17α-methyl-5α-androstan-17β-ol;

(lxi) [3,2-c]-furazan-5α-androstan-17β-ol;

(lxii) 3β-hydroxy-estra-4,9,11-trien-17-one;

(lxiii) 17α-methyl-androst-2-ene-3,17β-diol;

(lxiv) 17α-methyl-androsta-1,4-diene-3,17β-diol;

(lxv) Estra-4,9,11-triene-3,17-dione;

(lxvi) 18a-Homo-3-hydroxy-estra-2,5(10)-dien-17-one;

(lxvii) 6α-Methyl-androst-4-ene-3,17-dione;

(lxviii) 17α-Methyl-androstan-3-hydroxyimine-17β-ol;

(lxix) 17α-Methyl-5α-androstan-17β-ol;

(lxx) 17β-Hydroxy-androstano[2,3-d]isoxazole;

(lxxi) 17β-Hydroxy-androstano[3,2-c]isoxazole;

(lxxii) 4-Hydroxy-androst-4-ene-3,17-dione[3,2-c]pyrazole-5α-androstan-17β-ol;

(lxxiii) [3,2-c]pyrazole-androst-4-en-17β-ol;

(lxxiv) [3,2-c]pyrazole-5α-androstan-17β-ol; and

(lxxv) any salt, ester, or ether of a drug or substance described in this paragraph.

The substances excluded under this subparagraph may at any time be scheduled by the Attorney General in accordance with the authority and requirements of subsections (a) through (c) of section 201 [21 USCS § 811].

(B)(i) Except as provided in clause (ii), such term does not include an anabolic steroid which is expressly intended for administration through implants to cattle or other nonhuman species and which has been approved by the Secretary of Health and Human Services for such administration.

(ii) If any person prescribes, dispenses, or distributes such steroid for human use, such person shall be considered to have prescribed, dispensed, or distributed an anabolic steroid within the meaning of subparagraph (A).

(C)(i) Subject to clause (ii), a drug or hormonal substance (other than estrogens, progestins, corticosteroids, and dehydroepiandrosterone) that is not listed in subparagraph (A) and is derived from, or has a chemical structure substantially similar to, 1 or more anabolic steroids listed in subparagraph (A) shall be considered to be an anabolic steroid for purposes of this Act if—

(I) the drug or substance has been created or manufactured with the intent of producing a drug or other substance that either—

(aa) promotes muscle growth; or

(bb) otherwise causes a pharmacological effect similar to that of testosterone; or

(II) the drug or substance has been, or is intended to be, marketed or otherwise promoted in any manner suggesting that consuming it will promote muscle growth or any other pharmacological effect similar to that of testosterone.

(ii) A substance shall not be considered to be a drug or hormonal substance for purposes of this subparagraph if it—

(I) is—

(aa) an herb or other botanical;

(bb) a concentrate, metabolite, or extract of, or a constituent isolated directly from, an herb or other botanical; or

(cc) a combination of 2 or more substances described in item (aa) or (bb);

(II) is a dietary ingredient for purposes of the Federal Food, Drug, and Cosmetic Act (21 U.S.C. 301 et seq.); and

(III) is not anabolic or androgenic.

(iii) In accordance with section 515(a) [21 USCS § 515(a)], any person claiming the benefit of an exemption or exception under clause (ii) shall bear the burden of going forward with the evidence with respect to such exemption or exception.

(42) The term "international transaction" means a transaction involving the shipment of a listed chemical across an international border (other than a United States border) in which a broker or trader located in the United States participates.

(43) The terms "broker" and "trader" mean a person that assists in arranging an international transaction in a listed chemical by—

(A) negotiating contracts;

(B) serving as an agent or intermediary; or

(C) bringing together a buyer and seller, a buyer and transporter, or a seller and transporter.

(44) The term "felony drug offense" means an offense that is punishable by imprisonment for more than one year under any law of the United States or of a State or foreign country that prohibits or restricts conduct relating to narcotic drugs, marihuana, anabolic steroids, or depressant or stimulant substances.

(45)(A) The term "scheduled listed chemical product" means, subject to subparagraph (B), a product that—

(i) contains ephedrine, pseudoephedrine, or phenylpropanolamine; and

(ii) may be marketed or distributed lawfully in the United States under the Federal, Food, Drug, and Cosmetic Act as a nonprescription drug.
Each reference in clause (i) to ephedrine, pseudoephedrine, or phenylpropanolamine includes each of the salts, optical isomers, and salts of optical isomers of such chemical.

(B) Such term does not include a product described in subparagraph (A) if the product contains a chemical specified in such subparagraph that the Attorney General has under section 201(a) [21 USCS § 811(a)] added to any of the schedules under section 202(c) [21 USCS § 812(c)]. In the absence of such scheduling by the Attorney General, a chemical specified in such subparagraph may not be considered to be a controlled substance.

(46) The term "regulated seller" means a retail distributor (including a pharmacy or a mobile retail vendor), except that such term does not include an employee or agent of such distributor.

(47) The term "mobile retail vendor" means a person or entity that makes sales at retail from a stand that is intended to be temporary, or is capable of being moved from one location to another, whether the stand is located within or on the premises of a fixed facility (such as a kiosk at a shopping center or an airport) or whether the stand is located on unimproved real estate (such as a lot or field leased for retail purposes).

(48) The term "at retail", with respect to the sale or purchase of a scheduled listed chemical product, means a sale or purchase for personal use, respectively.

(49)(A) The term "retail distributor" means a grocery store, general merchandise store, drug store, or other entity or person whose activities as a distributor relating to ephedrine, pseudoephedrine, or phenylpropanolamine products are limited almost exclusively to sales for personal use, both in number of sales and volume of sales, either directly to walk-in customers or in face-to-face transactions by direct sales.

(B) For purposes of this paragraph, entities are defined by reference to the Standard Industrial Classification (SIC) code, as follows:

(i) A grocery store is an entity within SIC code 5411.

(ii) A general merchandise store is an entity within SIC codes 5300 through 5399 and 5499.

(iii) A drug store is an entity within SIC code 5912.

(50) The term "Internet" means collectively the myriad of computer and telecommunications facilities, including equipment and operating software, which comprise the interconnected worldwide network of networks that employ the Transmission Control Protocol/Internet Protocol, or any predecessor or successor protocol to such protocol, to communicate information of all kinds by wire or radio.

(51) The term "deliver, distribute, or dispense by means of the Internet" refers, respectively, to any delivery, distribution, or dispensing of a controlled substance that is caused or facilitated by means of the Internet.

(52) The term "online pharmacy"—

(A) means a person, entity, or Internet site, whether in the United States or abroad, that knowingly or intentionally delivers, distributes, or dispenses, or offers or attempts to deliver, distribute, or dispense, a controlled substance by means of the Internet; and

(B) does not include—

(i) manufacturers or distributors registered under subsection (a), (b), (e), or (f) of section 303 [21 USCS § 823] who do not dispense controlled substances to an unregistered individual or entity;

(ii) nonpharmacy practitioners who are registered under section 303(g) [21 USCS § 823(g)] and whose activities are authorized by that registration;

(iii) any hospital or other medical facility that is operated by an agency of the United States (including the Armed Forces), provided such hospital or other facility is registered under section 303(g) [21 USCS § 823(g)];

(iv) a health care facility owned or operated by an Indian tribe or tribal organization, only to the extent such facility is carrying out a contract or compact under the Indian Self-Determination and Education Assistance Act [25 USCS §§ 450 et seq.];

(v) any agent or employee of any hospital or facility referred to in clause (iii) or (iv), provided such agent or employee is lawfully acting in the usual course of business or employment, and within the scope of the official duties of such agent or employee, with such hospital or facility, and, with respect to agents or employees of health care facilities specified in clause (iv), only to the extent such individuals are furnishing services pursuant to the contracts or compacts described in such clause;

(vi) mere advertisements that do not attempt to facilitate an actual transaction involving a controlled substance;

(vii) a person, entity, or Internet site that is not in the United States and does not facilitate the delivery, distribution, or dispensing of a controlled substance by means of the Internet to any person in the United States;

(viii) a pharmacy registered under section 303(g) [21 USCS § 823(g)] whose dispensing of controlled substances via the Internet consists solely of—

(I) refilling prescriptions for controlled substances in schedule III, IV, or V, as defined in paragraph (55); or

(II) filling new prescriptions for controlled substances in schedule III, IV, or V, as defined in paragraph (56); or

(ix) any other persons for whom the Attorney General and the Secretary have jointly, by regulation, found it to be consistent with effective controls against diversion and otherwise consistent with the public health and safety to exempt from the definition of an "online pharmacy".

(53) The term "homepage" means the opening or main page or screen of the website of an online pharmacy that is viewable on the Internet.

(54) The term "practice of telemedicine" means, for purposes of this title, the practice of medicine in accordance with applicable Federal and State laws by a practitioner (other than a pharmacist) who is at a location remote from the patient and is communicating with the patient, or health care professional who is treating the patient, using a telecommunications sys-

tem referred to in section 1834(m) of the Social Security Act [42 USCS § 1395m(m)], which practice—

(A) is being conducted—

(i) while the patient is being treated by, and physically located in, a hospital or clinic registered under section 303(g) [21 USCS § 823(g)]; and

(ii) by a practitioner—

(I) acting in the usual course of professional practice;

(II) acting in accordance with applicable State law; and

(III) registered under section 303(g) [21 USCS § 823(g)] in the State in which the patient is located, unless the practitioner—

(aa) is exempted from such registration in all States under section 302(d) [21 USCS § 822(d)]; or

(bb) is—

(AA) an employee or contractor of the Department of Veterans Affairs who is acting in the scope of such employment or contract; and

(BB) registered under section 303(g) [21 USCS § 823(g)] in any State or is utilizing the registration of a hospital or clinic operated by the Department of Veterans Affairs registered under section 303(g) [21 USCS § 823(g)];

(B) is being conducted while the patient is being treated by, and in the physical presence of, a practitioner—

(i) acting in the usual course of professional practice;

(ii) acting in accordance with applicable State law; and

(iii) registered under section 303(g) [21 USCS § 823(g)] in the State in which the patient is located, unless the practitioner—

(I) is exempted from such registration in all States under section 302(d) [21 USCS § 822(d)]; or

(II) is—

(aa) an employee or contractor of the Department of Veterans Affairs who is acting in the scope of such employment or contract; and

(bb) registered under section 303(g) [21 USCS § 823(g)] in any State or is using the registration of a hospital or clinic operated by the Department of Veterans Affairs registered under section 303(g) [21 USCS § 823(g)];

(C) is being conducted by a practitioner—

(i) who is an employee or contractor of the Indian Health Service, or is working for an Indian tribe or tribal organization under its contract or compact with the Indian Health Service under the Indian Self-Determination and Education Assistance Act;

(ii) acting within the scope of the employment, contract, or compact described in clause (i); and

(iii) who is designated as an Internet Eligible Controlled Substances Provider by the Secretary under section 311(g)(2) [21 USCS § 831(g)(2)];

(D)(i) is being conducted during a public health emergency declared by the Secretary under section 319 of the Public Health Service Act [42 USCS § 247d]; and

(ii) involves patients located in such areas, and such controlled substances, as the Secretary, with the concurrence of the Attorney General, designates, provided that such designation shall not be subject to the procedures prescribed by subchapter II of chapter 5 of title 5, United States Code [5 USCS §§ 551 et seq.];

(E) is being conducted by a practitioner who has obtained from the Attorney General a special registration under section 311(h) [21 USCS § 831(h)];

(F) is being conducted—

(i) in a medical emergency situation—

(I) that prevents the patient from being in the physical presence of a practitioner registered under section 303(g) [21 USCS § 823(g)] who is an employee or contractor of the Veterans Health Administration acting in the usual course of business and employment and within the scope of the official duties or contract of that employee or contractor;

(II) that prevents the patient from being physically present at a hospital or clinic operated by the Department of Veterans Affairs registered under section 303(g) [21 USCS § 823(g)];

(III) during which the primary care practitioner of the patient or a practitioner otherwise practicing telemedicine within the meaning of this paragraph is unable to provide care or consultation; and

(IV) that requires immediate intervention by a health care practitioner using controlled substances to prevent what the practitioner reasonably believes in good faith will be imminent and serious clinical consequences, such as further injury or death; and

(ii) by a practitioner that—

(I) is an employee or contractor of the Veterans Health Administration acting within the scope of that employment or contract;

(II) is registered under section 303(g) [21 USCS § 823(g)] in any State or is utilizing the registration of a hospital or clinic operated by the Department of Veterans Affairs registered under section 303(g) [21 USCS § 823(g)]; and

(III) issues a controlled substance prescription in this emergency context that is limited to a maximum of a 5-day supply which may not be extended or refilled; or

(G) is being conducted under any other circumstances that the Attorney General and the Secretary have jointly, by regulation, determined to be consistent with effective controls against diversion and otherwise consistent with the public health and safety.

(55) The term "refilling prescriptions for controlled substances in schedule III, IV, or V"—

(A) means the dispensing of a controlled substance in schedule III, IV, or V in accordance with refill instructions issued by a practitioner as part of a valid prescription that meets the requirements of subsections (b) and (c) of section 309 [21 USCS § 829], as appropriate; and

(B) does not include the issuance of a new prescription to an individual for a controlled substance that individual was previously prescribed.

(56) The term "filling new prescriptions for controlled substances in schedule III, IV, or V" means filling a prescription for an individual for a controlled substance in schedule III, IV, or V, if—

(A) the pharmacy dispensing that prescription has previously dispensed to the patient a controlled substance other than by means of the Internet and pursuant to the valid prescription of a practitioner that meets the applicable requirements of subsections (b) and (c) of section 309 [21 USCS § 829] (in this paragraph referred to as the "original prescription");

(B) the pharmacy contacts the practitioner who issued the original prescription at the request of that individual to determine whether the practitioner will authorize the issuance of a new prescription for that individual for the controlled substance described in subparagraph (A); and

(C) the practitioner, acting in the usual course of professional practice, determines there is a legitimate medical purpose for the issuance of the new prescription.

(57) The term "suspicious order" may include, but is not limited to—

(A) an order of a controlled substance of unusual size;

(B) an order of a controlled substance deviating substantially from a normal pattern; and

(C) orders of controlled substances of unusual frequency.

(58) The term "serious drug felony" means an offense described in section 924(e)(2) of title 18, United States Code, for which—

(A) the offender served a term of imprisonment of more than 12 months; and

(B) the offender's release from any term of imprisonment was within 15 years of the commencement of the instant offense.

(59) The term "serious violent felony" means—

(A) an offense described in section 3559(c)(2) of title 18, United States Code, for which the offender served a term of imprisonment of more than 12 months; and

(B) any offense that would be a felony violation of section 113 of title 18, United States Code, if the offense were committed in the special maritime and territorial jurisdiction of the United States, for which the offender served a term of imprisonment of more than 12 months.

(Oct. 27, 1970, P. L. 91-513, Title II, Part A, § 102, 84 Stat. 1242; May 14, 1974, P. L. 93-281, § 2, 88 Stat. 124; Nov. 10, 1978, P. L. 95-633, Title I, § 102(b), 92 Stat. 3772; Nov. 30, 1979, P. L. 96-132, § 16(a), 93 Stat. 1049; Oct. 12, 1984, P. L. 98-473, Title II, Ch V, Part B, § 507, 98 Stat. 2071; Oct. 19, 1984, P. L. 98-509, Title III, § 301(a), 98 Stat. 2364; Oct. 27, 1986, P. L. 99-570, Title I, Subtitle A, § 1003(b), Subtitle E, § 1203, Subtitle Q, § 1870, 100 Stat. 3207-6, 3207-13, 3207-56; Nov. 10, 1986, P. L. 99-646, § 83, 100 Stat. 3619; Nov. 18, 1988, P. L. 100-690, Title VI, Subtitle A, § 6054, 102 Stat. 4316; Nov. 29, 1990, P. L. 101-647, Title XIX, § 1902(b), Title XXIII, § 2301, Title XXXV, § 3599I, 104 Stat. 4852, 4858, 4932; Dec. 17, 1993, P. L. 103-200, §§ 2(a), 7–9(a), 107 Stat. 2333, 2340; Sept. 13, 1994, P. L. 103-322, Title IX, Subtitle A, § 90105(d), Title XXXIII, § 330024(a), (b), (d)(1), 108 Stat. 1988, 2150; Oct. 3, 1996, P. L. 104-237, Title II, §§ 204(a), 209, Title IV, § 401(a), (b), 110 Stat. 3102, 3104, 3107; Oct. 11, 1996, P. L. 104-294, Title VI, §§ 604(b)(4), 607(j), 110 Stat. 3506, 3512; Nov. 21, 1997, P. L. 105-115, Title I, Subtitle B, § 126(c)(3), 111 Stat. 2328; Feb. 18, 2000, P. L. 106-172, §§ 3(c), 5(a), 114 Stat. 9, 10; Oct. 17, 2000, P. L. 106-310, Div B, Title XXXVI, Subtitle A, Part II, § 3622(a), 114 Stat. 1231; Nov. 2, 2002, P. L. 107-273, Div B, Title IV, § 4002(c)(1), 116 Stat. 1808; Oct. 22, 2004, P. L. 108-358, § 2(a), 118 Stat. 1661; Jan. 5, 2006, P. L. 109-162, Title XI, Subtitle C, § 1180, 119 Stat. 3126; March 9, 2006, P. L. 109-177, Title VII, Subtitle A, §§ 711(a)(1), (2)(A), 712(a)(1), 120 Stat. 256, 263; Oct. 15, 2008, P. L. 110-425, § 3(a), 122 Stat. 4821; Dec. 18, 2014, P. L. 113-260, § 2(a), 128 Stat. 2929; July 22, 2016, P. L. 114-198, Title III, § 303(a)(2), 130 Stat. 722; Oct. 24, 2018, P.L. 115-271, Title III, Subtitle B, Ch. 1, § 3202(c), Ch. 9, § 3292(a), 132 Stat. 3945, 3956; Dec. 20, 2018, P.L. 115-334, Title XII, Subtitle F, § 12619(a), 132 Stat. 5018; Dec. 21, 2018, P.L. 115-391, Title IV, § 401(a)(1), 132 Stat. 5220; Dec. 2, 2022, P.L. 117-215, § 2(b), Title I, § 103(b)(1)(A), 136 Stat. 2258, 2262; Dec. 23, 2024, P.L. 118-189, § 1, 138 Stat. 2652.)

§ 803. [Repealed]

AUTHORITY TO CONTROL; STANDARDS AND SCHEDULES

§ 811. Authority and criteria for classification of substances

(a) Rules and regulations of Attorney General; hearing. The Attorney General shall apply the provisions of this title to the controlled substances listed in the schedules established by section 202 of this title [21 USCS § 812] and to any other drug or other substance added to such schedules under this title. Except as provided in subsections (d) and (e), the Attorney General may by rule—

(1) add to such a schedule or transfer between such schedules any drug or other substance if he—

(A) finds that such drug or other substance has a potential for abuse, and

(B) makes with respect to such drug or other substance the findings prescribed by subsection (b) of section 202 [21 USCS § 812(b)] for the schedule in which such drug is to be placed; or

(2) remove any drug or other substance from the schedules if he finds that the drug or other substance does not meet the requirements for inclusion in any schedule.

Rules of the Attorney General under this subsection shall be made on the record after opportunity for a hearing pursuant to the rulemaking procedures prescribed by subchapter II of chapter 5 of title 5 of the United States Code [5 USCS §§ 551 et seq.]. Proceedings for the issuance, amendment, or repeal of such rules may be initiated by the Attorney General (1) on his own motion, (2) at the request of the Secretary, or (3) on the petition of any interested party.

(b) Evaluation of drugs and other substances. The Attorney General shall, before initiating proceedings under subsection (a) to control a drug or other substance or to remove a drug or other substance entirely from the schedules, and after gathering the necessary data, request from the Secretary a scientific and medical evaluation, and his recommendations, as to whether such drug or other substance should be so controlled or removed as a controlled substance. In making such evaluation and recommendations, the Secretary shall consider the factors listed in paragraphs (2), (3), (6), (7), and (8) of subsection (c) and any scientific or medical considerations involved in paragraphs (1), (4), and (5) of such subsection. The recommendations of the Secretary shall include recommendations with respect to the appropriate schedule, if any, under which such drug or other substance should be listed. The evaluation and the recommendations of the Secretary shall be made in writing and submitted to the Attorney General within a reasonable time. The recommendations of the Secretary to the Attorney General shall be binding on the Attorney General as to such scientific and medical matters, and if the Secretary recommends that a drug or other substance not be controlled, the Attorney General shall not control the drug or other substance. If the Attorney General determines that these facts and all other relevant data constitute substantial evidence of potential for abuse such as to warrant control or substantial evidence that the drug or other substance should be removed entirely from the schedules, he shall initiate proceedings for control or removal, as the case may be, under subsection (a).

(c) Factors determinative of control or removal from schedules. In making any finding under subsection (a) of this section or under subsection (b) of section 202 [21 USCS § 812(b)], the Attorney General shall consider the following factors with respect to each drug or other substance proposed to be controlled or removed from the schedules:

(1) Its actual or relative potential for abuse.

(2) Scientific evidence of its pharmacological effect, if known.

(3) The state of current scientific knowledge regarding the drug or other substance.

(4) Its history and current pattern of abuse.

(5) The scope, duration, and significance of abuse.

(6) What, if any, risk there is to the public health.

(7) Its psychic or physiological dependence liability.

(8) Whether the substance is an immediate precursor of a substance already controlled under this title.

(d) International treaties, conventions, and protocols requiring control; procedures respecting changes in drug schedules of Convention on Psychotropic Substances.

(1) If control is required by United States obligations under international treaties, conventions, or protocols in effect on the effective date of this part, the Attorney General shall issue an order controlling such drug under the schedule he deems most appropriate to carry out such obligations, without regard to the findings required by subsection (a) of this section or section 202(b) [21 USCS § 812(b)] and without regard to the procedures prescribed by subsections (a) and (b) of this section.

(2)(A) Whenever the Secretary of State receives notification from the Secretary-General of the United Nations that information has been transmitted by or to the World Health Organization, pursuant to article 2 of the Convention on Psychotropic Substances, which may justify adding a drug or other substance to one of the schedules of the Convention, transferring a drug or substance from one schedule to another, or deleting it from the schedules, the Secretary of State shall immediately transmit the notice to the Secretary of Health, Education, and Welfare [Secretary of Health and Human Services] who shall publish it in the Federal Register and provide opportunity to interested persons to submit to him comments respecting the scientific and medical evaluations which he is to prepare respecting such drug or substance. The Secretary of Health, Education, and Welfare [Secretary of Health and Human Services] shall prepare for transmission through the Secretary of State to the World Health Organization such medical and scientific evaluations as may be appropriate regarding the possible action that could be proposed by the World Health Organization respecting the drug or substance with respect to which a notice was transmitted under this subparagraph.

(B) Whenever the Secretary of State receives information that the Commission on Narcotic Drugs of the United Nations proposes to decide whether to add a drug or other substance to one of the schedules of the Convention, transfer a drug or substance from one schedule to another, or delete it from the schedules, the Secretary of State shall transmit timely notice to the Secretary of Health, Education, and Welfare [Secretary of Health and Human Services] of such information who shall publish a summary of such information in the Federal Register and provide opportunity to interested persons to submit to him comments respecting the recommendation which he is to furnish, pursuant to this subparagraph, respecting such proposal. The Secretary of Health, Education, and Welfare [Secretary of Health and Human Services] shall evaluate the proposal and furnish a recommendation to the Secretary of State which shall be binding on the representative of the United States in discussions and negotiations relating to the proposal.

(3) When the United States receives notification of a scheduling decision pursuant to article 2 of the Convention of Psychotropic Substances that a drug or other substance has been added or transferred to a schedule specified in the notification or receives notification (referred to in this subsection as a "schedule notice") that existing legal controls applicable under this title to a drug or substance and the controls required by the Federal Food, Drug, and Cosmetic Act [21 USCS §§ 301 et seq.] do not meet the requirements of the schedule of the Convention in which such drug or substance has been placed, the Secretary of Health, Education, and Welfare [Secretary of Health and Human Services], after consultation with the Attorney General, shall first determine whether existing legal controls under this title applicable to the drug or substance and the controls required by the Federal Food, Drug, and Cosmetic Act [21 USCS §§ 301 et seq.], meet the requirements of the schedule specified in the notification or schedule notice and shall take the following action:

(A) If such requirements are met by such existing controls but the Secretary of Health, Education, and Welfare [Secretary of Health and Human Services] nonetheless believes that more stringent controls should be applied to the drug or substance, the Secretary shall recommend to the Attorney General that he initiate proceedings for scheduling the drug or substance, pursuant to subsections (a) and (b) of this section, to apply to such controls.

(B) If such requirements are not met by such existing controls and the Secretary of Health, Education, and

Welfare [Secretary of Health and Human Services] concurs in the scheduling decision or schedule notice transmitted by the notification, the Secretary shall recommend to the Attorney General that he initiate proceedings for scheduling the drug or substance under the appropriate schedule pursuant to subsections (a) and (b) of this section.

(C) If such requirements are not met by such existing controls and the Secretary of Health, Education, and Welfare [Secretary of Health and Human Services] does not concur in the scheduling decision or schedule notice transmitted by the notification, the Secretary shall—

(i) if he deems that additional controls are necessary to protect the public health and safety, recommend to the Attorney General that he initiate proceedings for scheduling the drug or substance pursuant to subsections (a) and (b) of this section, to apply such additional controls;

(ii) request the Secretary of State to transmit a notice of qualified acceptance, within the period specified in the Convention, pursuant to paragraph 7 of article 2 of the Convention, to the Secretary-General of the United Nations;

(iii) request the Secretary of State to transmit a notice of qualified acceptance as prescribed in clause (ii) and request the Secretary of State to ask for a review by the Economic and Social Council of the United Nations, in accordance with paragraph 8 of article 2 of the Convention, of the scheduling decision; or

(iv) in the case of a schedule notice, request the Secretary of State to take appropriate action under the Convention to initiate proceedings to remove the drug or substance from the schedules under the Convention or to transfer the drug or substance to a schedule under the Convention different from the one specified in the schedule notice.

(4)(A) If the Attorney General determines, after consultation with the Secretary of Health, Education, and Welfare [Secretary of Health and Human Services], that proceedings initiated under recommendations made under paragraph [subparagraph] (B) or (C)(i) of paragraph (3) will not be completed within the time period required by paragraph 7 of article 2 of the Convention, the Attorney General, after consultation with the Secretary and after providing interested persons opportunity to submit comments respecting the requirements of the temporary order to be issued under this sentence, shall issue a temporary order controlling the drug or substance under schedule IV or V, whichever is most appropriate to carry out the minimum United States obligations under paragraph 7 of article 2 of the Convention. As a part of such order, the Attorney General shall, after consultation with the Secretary, except such drug or substance from the application of any provision of part C of this title [21 USCS §§ 821 et seq.] which he finds is not required to carry out the United States obligations under paragraph 7 of article 2 of the Convention. In the case of proceedings initiated under subparagraph (B) of paragraph (3), the Attorney General, concurrently with the issuance of such order, shall request the Secretary of State to transmit a notice of qualified acceptance to the Secretary-General of the United Nations pursuant to paragraph 7 of article 2 of the Convention. A temporary order issued under this subparagraph controlling a drug or other substance subject to proceedings initiated under subsections (a) and (b) of this section shall expire upon the effective date of the application to the drug or substance of the controls resulting from such proceedings.

(B) After a notice of qualified acceptance of a scheduling decision with respect to a drug or other substance is transmitted to the Secretary-General of the United Nations in accordance with clause (ii) or (iii) of paragraph (3)(C) or after a request has been made under clause (iv) of such paragraph with respect to a drug or substance described in a schedule notice, the Attorney General, after consultation with the Secretary of Health, Education, and Welfare [Secretary of Health and Human Services] and after providing interested persons opportunity to submit comments respecting the requirements of the order to be issued under this sentence, shall issue an order controlling the drug or substance under schedule IV or V, whichever is most appropriate to carry out the minimum United States obligations under paragraph 7 of article 2 of the Convention in the case of a drug or substance for which a notice of qualified acceptance was transmitted or whichever the Attorney General determines is appropriate in the case of a drug or substance described in a schedule notice. As a part of such order, the Attorney General shall, after consultation with the Secretary, except such drug or substance from the application of any provision of part C of this title [21 USCS §§ 821 et seq.] which he finds is not required to carry out the United States obligations under paragraph 7 of article 2 of the Convention. If, as a result of a review under paragraph 8 of article 2 of the Convention of the scheduling decision with respect to which a notice of qualified acceptance was transmitted in accordance with clause (ii) or (iii) of paragraph (3)(C)—

(i) the decision is reversed, and

(ii) the drug or substance subject to such decision is not required to be controlled under schedule IV or V to carry out the minimum United States obligations under paragraph 7 of article 2 of the Convention,

the order issued under this subparagraph with respect to such drug or substance shall expire upon receipt by the United States of the review decision. If, as a result of action taken pursuant to action initiated under a request transmitted under clause (iv) of paragraph (3)(C), the drug or substance with respect to which such action was taken is not required to be controlled under schedule IV or V, the order issued under this paragraph with respect to such drug or substance shall expire upon receipt by the United States of a notice of the action taken with respect to such drug or substance under the Convention.

(C) An order issued under subparagraph (A) or (B) may be issued without regard to the findings required by subsection (a) of this section or by section 202(b) [21 USCS § 812(b)] and without regard to the procedures prescribed by subsection (a) or (b) of this section.

(5) Nothing in the amendments made by the Psychotropic Substances Act of 1978, or the regulations or orders promulgated thereunder shall be construed to preclude requests by the Secretary of Health, Education, and Welfare [Secretary of Health and Human Services] or the Attorney General through the Secretary of State, pursuant to article 2 or other applicable provisions of the Convention, for review of scheduling decisions under such Convention, based on new or additional information.

(e) Immediate precursors. The Attorney General may, without regard to the findings required by subsection (a) of this section or section 202(b) [21 USCS § 812(b)] and without regard to the procedures prescribed by subsections (a) and (b) of this section, place an immediate precursor in the same schedule in which the controlled substance of which it is an immediate precursor is placed or in any other schedule with a higher numerical designation. If the Attorney General designates a substance as an immediate precursor and places it in a schedule, other substances shall not be placed in a schedule solely because they are its precursors.

(f) Abuse potential. If, at the time a new-drug application is submitted to the Secretary for any drug having a stimulant, depressant, or hallucinogenic effect on the central nervous system, it appears that such drug has an abuse potential, such information shall be forwarded by the Secretary to the Attorney General.

(g) Exclusion of non-narcotic substances sold over the counter without a prescription; dextromethorphan; exemption of substances lacking abuse potential.

(1) The Attorney General shall by regulation exclude any nonnarcotic drug which contains a controlled substance from the application of titles II and III of the Comprehensive Drug Abuse Prevention and Control Act (21 U.S.C. 802 et seq.) [21 USCS §§ 801 et seq. and 951 et seq.] if such drug may, under the Federal Food, Drug, and Cosmetic Act [21 USCS §§ 301 et seq.], be lawfully sold over the counter without a prescription.

(2) Dextromethorphan shall not be deemed to be included in any schedule by reason of enactment of this title unless controlled after the date of such enactment [enacted Oct. 27, 1970] pursuant to the foregoing provisions of this section.

(3) The Attorney General may, by regulation, exempt any compound, mixture, or preparation containing a controlled substance from the application of all or any part of this title if he finds such compound, mixture, or preparation meets the requirements of one of the following categories:

(A) A mixture, or preparation containing a nonnarcotic controlled substance, which mixture or preparation is approved for prescription use, and which contains one or more other active ingredients which are not listed in any schedule and which are included therein in such combinations, quantity, proportion, or concentration as to vitiate the potential for abuse.

(B) A compound, mixture, or preparation which contains any controlled substance, which is not for administration to a human being or animal, and which is packaged in such form or concentration, or with adulterants or denaturants, so that as packaged it does not present any significant potential for abuse.

(C) Upon the recommendation of the Secretary of Health and Human Services, a compound, mixture, or preparation which contains any anabolic steroid, which is intended for administration to a human being or an animal, and which, because of its concentration, preparation, formulation or delivery system, does not present any significant potential for abuse.

(h) Temporary scheduling to avoid imminent hazards to public safety.

(1) If the Attorney General finds that the scheduling of a substance in schedule I on a temporary basis is necessary to avoid an imminent hazard to the public safety, he may, by order and without regard to the requirements of subsection (b) relating to the Secretary of Health and Human Services, schedule such substance in schedule I if the substance is not listed in any other schedule in section 202 [21 USCS § 812] or if no exemption or approval is in effect for the substance under section 505 of the Federal Food, Drug, and Cosmetic Act [21 USCS § 355]. Such an order may not be issued before the expiration of thirty days from—

(A) the date of the publication by the Attorney General of a notice in the Federal Register of the intention to issue such order and the grounds upon which such order is to be issued, and

(B) the date the Attorney General has transmitted the notice required by paragraph (4).

(2) The scheduling of a substance under this subsection shall expire at the end of two years from the date of the issuance of the order scheduling such substance, except that the Attorney General may, during the pendency of proceedings under subsection (a)(1) with respect to the substance, extend the temporary scheduling for up to 1 year.

(3) When issuing an order under paragraph (1), the Attorney General shall be required to consider, with respect to the finding of an imminent hazard to the public safety, only those factors set forth in paragraphs (4), (5), and (6) of subsection (c), including actual abuse, diversion from legitimate channels, and clandestine importation, manufacture, or distribution.

(4) The Attorney General shall transmit notice of an order proposed to be issued under paragraph (1) to the Secretary of Health and Human Services. In issuing an order under paragraph (1), the Attorney General shall take into consideration any comments submitted by the Secretary in response to a notice transmitted pursuant to this paragraph.

(5) An order issued under paragraph (1) with respect to a substance shall be vacated upon the conclusion of a subsequent rulemaking proceeding initiated under subsection (a) with respect to such substance.

(6) An order issued under paragraph (1) is not subject to judicial review.

(i) Temporary and permanent scheduling of recently emerged anabolic steroids.

(1) The Attorney General may issue a temporary order adding a drug or other substance to the definition of anabolic steroids if the Attorney General finds that—

(A) the drug or other substance satisfies the criteria for being considered an anabolic steroid under section 102(41) [21 USCS § 802(41)] but is not listed in that section or by regulation of the Attorney General as being an anabolic steroid; and

(B) adding such drug or other substance to the definition of anabolic steroids will assist in preventing abuse or misuse of the drug or other substance.

(2) An order issued under paragraph (1) shall not take effect until 30 days after the date of the publication by the Attorney General of a notice in the Federal Register of the intention to issue such order and the grounds upon which such order is to be issued. The order shall expire not later than 24 months after the date it becomes effective, except that the Attorney General may, during the pendency of proceedings under paragraph (6), extend the temporary scheduling order for up to 6 months.

(3) The Attorney General shall transmit notice of an order proposed to be issued under paragraph (1) to the Secretary of Health and Human Services. In issuing an order under paragraph (1), the Attorney General shall take into consideration any comments submitted by the Secretary in response to a notice transmitted pursuant to this paragraph.

(4) A temporary scheduling order issued under paragraph (1) shall be vacated upon the issuance of a permanent scheduling order under paragraph (6).

(5) An order issued under paragraph (1) is not subject to judicial review.

(6) The Attorney General may, by rule, issue a permanent order adding a drug or other substance to the definition of anabolic steroids if such drug or other substance satisfies the criteria for being considered an anabolic steroid under section 102(41) [21 USCS § 802(41)]. Such rulemaking may be commenced simultaneously with the issuance of the temporary order issued under paragraph (1).

(j) Scheduling of newly approved drugs.

(1) With respect to a drug referred to in subsection (f), if the Secretary of Health and Human Services recommends that the Attorney General control the drug in schedule II, III, IV, or V pursuant to subsections (a) and (b), the Attorney General shall, not later than 90 days after the date described in paragraph (2), issue an interim final rule controlling the drug in accordance with such subsections and section 202(b) [21 USCS § 812(b)] using the procedures described in paragraph (3).

(2) The date described in this paragraph shall be the later of—

(A) the date on which the Attorney General receives the scientific and medical evaluation and the scheduling recommendation from the Secretary of Health and Human Services in accordance with subsection (b); or

(B) the date on which the Attorney General receives notification from the Secretary of Health and Human Services that the Secretary has approved an application under section 505(c), 512, or 571 of the Federal Food, Drug, and Cosmetic Act [21 USCS § 355(c), 360b, or 360ccc] or section 351(a) of the Public Health Service Act [21 USCS § 262(a)], or indexed a drug under section 572 of the Federal Food, Drug, and Cosmetic Act [21 USCS § 360ccc-1], with respect to the drug described in paragraph (1).

(3) A rule issued by the Attorney General under paragraph (1) shall become immediately effective as an interim final rule without requiring the Attorney General to demonstrate good cause therefor. The interim final rule shall give interested persons the opportunity to comment and to request a hearing. After the conclusion of such proceedings, the Attorney General shall issue a final rule in accordance with the scheduling criteria of subsections (b), (c), and (d) of this section and section 202(b) [21 USCS § 812(b)].

(Oct. 27, 1970, P. L. 91-513, Title II, Part B, § 201, 84 Stat. 1245; Nov. 10, 1978, P. L. 95-633, Title I, § 102(a), 92 Stat. 3769; Oct. 12, 1984, P. L. 98-473, Title II, Ch V, Part B, § 509(a), 98 Stat. 2072; Oct. 22, 2004, P. L. 108-358, § 2(b), 118 Stat. 1663; July 9, 2012, P. L. 112-144, Title XI, Subtitle D, § 1153, 126 Stat. 1132; Dec. 18, 2014, P. L. 113-260, § 2(b), 128 Stat. 2930; Nov. 25, 2015, P. L. 114-89, § 2(b), 129 Stat. 700.)

§ 812. Schedules of controlled substances

(a) Establishment. There are established five schedules of controlled substances, to be known as schedules I, II, III, IV, and V. Such schedules shall initially consist of the substances listed in this section. The schedules established by this section shall be updated and republished on a semiannual basis during the two-year period beginning one year after the date of enactment of this title [enacted Oct. 27, 1970] and shall be updated and republished on an annual basis thereafter.

(b) Placement on schedules; findings required. Except where control is required by United States obligations under an international treaty, convention, or protocol, in effect on the effective date of this part, and except in the case of an immediate precursor, a drug or other substance may not be placed in any schedule unless the findings required for such schedule are made with respect to such drug or other substance. The findings required for each of the schedules are as follows:

(1) SCHEDULE I.

(A) The drug or other substance has a high potential for abuse.

(B) The drug or other substance has no currently accepted medical use in treatment in the United States.

(C) There is a lack of accepted safety for use of the drug or other substance under medical supervision.

(2) SCHEDULE II.

(A) The drug or other substance has a high potential for abuse.

(B) The drug or other substance has a currently accepted medical use in treatment in the United States or a currently accepted medical use with severe restrictions.

(C) Abuse of the drug or other substances may lead to severe psychological or physical dependence.

(3) SCHEDULE III.

(A) The drug or other substance has a potential for abuse less than the drugs or other substances in schedules I and II.

(B) The drug or other substance has a currently accepted medical use in treatment in the United States.

(C) Abuse of the drug or other substance may lead to moderate or low physical dependence or high psychological dependence.

(4) SCHEDULE IV.

(A) The drug or other substance has a low potential for abuse relative to the drugs or other substances in schedule III.

(B) The drug or other substance has a currently accepted medical use in treatment in the United States.

(C) Abuse of the drug or other substance may lead to limited physical dependence or psychological dependence relative to the drugs or other substances in schedule III.

(5) SCHEDULE V.

(A) The drug or other substance has a low potential for abuse relative to the drugs or other substances in schedule IV.

(B) The drug or other substance has a currently accepted medical use in treatment in the United States.

(C) Abuse of the drug or other substance may lead to limited physical dependence or psychological dependence relative to the drugs or other substances in schedule IV.

(c) Initial schedules of controlled substances [Caution: For amended schedules, see 21 CFR Part 1308.]. Schedules I, II, III, IV, and V shall, unless and until amended pursuant to section 201 [21 USCS § 811], consist of the following drugs or other substances, by whatever official name, common or usual name, chemical name, or brand name designated:

SCHEDULE I

(a) Unless specifically excepted or unless listed in another schedule, any of the following opiates, including their isomers, esters, ethers, salts, and salts of isomers, esters, and ethers, whenever the existence of such isomers, esters, ethers, and salts is possible within the specific chemical designation:

(1) Acetylmethadol.
(2) Allylprodine.
(3) Alphacetylmathadol [Alphacetylmethadol].
(4) Alphameprodine.
(5) Alphamethadol.
(6) Benzethidine.
(7) Betacetylmethadol.
(8) Betameprodine.
(9) Betamethadol.
(10) Betaprodine.
(11) Clonitazene.
(12) Dextromoramide.
(13) Dextrorphan.
(14) Diampromide.
(15) Diethylthiambutene.
(16) Dimenoxadol.
(17) Dimepheptanol.
(18) Dimethylthiambutene.
(19) Dioxaphetyl butyrate.
(20) Dipipanone.
(21) Ethylmethylthiambutene.
(22) Etonitazene.
(23) Etoxeridine.
(24) Furethidine.
(25) Hydroxypethidine.
(26) Ketobemidone.
(27) Levomoramide.
(28) Levophenacylmorphan.
(29) Morpheridine.
(30) Noracymethadol.
(31) Norlevorphanol.
(32) Normethadone.
(33) Norpipanone.
(34) Phenadoxone.
(35) Phenampromide.
(36) Phenomorphan.
(37) Phenoperidine.
(38) Piritramide.
(39) Proheptazine.
(40) Properidine.
(41) Racemoramide.
(42) Trimeperidine.

(b) Unless specifically excepted or unless listed in another schedule, any of the following opium derivatives, their salts, isomers, and salts of isomers whenever the existence of such salts, isomers, and salts of isomers is possible within the specific chemical designation:

(1) Acetorphine.
(2) Acetyldihydrocodeine.
(3) Benzylmorphine.
(4) Codeine methylbromide.
(5) Codeine-N-Oxide.
(6) Cyprenorphine.
(7) Desomorphine.
(8) Dihydromorphine.
(9) Etorphine.
(10) Heroin.
(11) Hydromorphinol.
(12) Methyldesorphine.
(13) Methylhydromorphine.
(14) Morphine methylbromide.
(15) Morphine methylsulfonate.
(16) Morphine-N-Oxide.
(17) Myrophine.
(18) Nicocodeine.
(19) Nicomorphine.
(20) Normorphine.
(21) Pholcodine.
(22) Thebacon.

(c) Unless specifically excepted or unless listed in another schedule, any material, compound, mixture, or preparation, which contains any quantity of the following hallucinogenic substances, or which contains any of their salts, isomers, and salts of isomers whenever the existence of such salts, isomers, and salts of isomers is possible within the specific chemical designation:

(1) 3, 4-methylenedioxy amphetamine.
(2) 5-methoxy-3, 4-methylenedioxy amphetamine
(3) 3, 4, 5-trimethoxy amphetamine.
(4) Bufotenine.
(5) Diethyltryptamine.
(6) Dimethyltryptamine.
(7) 4-methyl-2, 5-dimethoxyamphetamine.

(8) Ibogaine.
(9) Lysergic acid diethylamide.
(10) Marihuana.
(11) Mescaline.
(12) Peyote.
(13) N-ethyl-3-piperidyl benzilate.
(14) N-methyl-3-piperidyl benzilate.
(15) Psilocybin.
(16) Psilocyn.
(17) Tetrahydrocannabinols, except for tetrahydrocannabinols in hemp (as defined under section 297A of the Agricultural Marketing Act of 1946 [7 USCS § 1639o]).
(18) 4-methylmethcathinone (Mephedrone).
(19) 3,4-methylenedioxypyrovalerone (MDPV).
(20) 2-(2,5-Dimethoxy-4-ethylphenyl)ethanamine (2C-E).
(21) 2-(2,5-Dimethoxy-4-methylphenyl)ethanamine (2C-D).
(22) 2-(4-Chloro-2,5-dimethoxyphenyl)ethanamine (2C-C).
(23) 2-(4-Iodo-2,5-dimethoxyphenyl)ethanamine (2C-I).
(24) 2-[4-(Ethylthio)-2,5-dimethoxyphenyl]ethanamine (2C-T-2).
(25) 2-[4-(Isopropylthio)-2,5-dimethoxyphenyl]ethanamine (2C-T-4).
(26) 2-(2,5-Dimethoxyphenyl)ethanamine (2C-H).
(27) 2-(2,5-Dimethoxy-4-nitro-phenyl)ethanamine (2C-N).
(28) 2-(2,5-Dimethoxy-4-(n)-propylphenyl)ethanamine (2C-P).

(d) Cannabimimetic agents.

(1) Unless specifically exempted or unless listed in another schedule, any material, compound, mixture, or preparation which contains any quantity of cannabimimetic agents, or which contains their salts, isomers, and salts of isomers whenever the existence of such salts, isomers, and salts of isomers is possible within the specific chemical designation.

(2) In paragraph (1):

(A) The term "cannabimimetic agents" means any substance that is a cannabinoid receptor type 1 (CB1 receptor) agonist as demonstrated by binding studies and functional assays within any of the following structural classes:

(i) 2-(3-hydroxycyclohexyl)phenol with substitution at the 5-position of the phenolic ring by alkyl or alkenyl, whether or not substituted on the cyclohexyl ring to any extent.

(ii) 3-(1-naphthoyl)indole or 3-(1-naphthylmethane)indole by substitution at the nitrogen atom of the indole ring, whether or not further substituted on the indole ring to any extent, whether or not substituted on the naphthoyl or naphthyl ring to any extent.

(iii) 3-(1-naphthoyl)pyrrole by substitution at the nitrogen atom of the pyrrole ring, whether or not further substituted in the pyrrole ring to any extent, whether or not substituted on the naphthoyl ring to any extent.

(iv) 1-(1-naphthylmethylene)indene by substitution of the 3-position of the indene ring, whether or not further substituted in the indene ring to any extent, whether or not substituted on the naphthyl ring to any extent.

(v) 3-phenylacetylindole or 3-benzoylindole by substitution at the nitrogen atom of the indole ring, whether or not further substituted in the indole ring to any extent, whether or not substituted on the phenyl ring to any extent.

(B) Such term includes—

(i) 5-(1,1-dimethylheptyl)-2-[(1R,3S)-3-hydroxycyclohexyl]-phenol (CP-47,497);
(ii) 5-(1,1-dimethyloctyl)-2-[(1R,3S)-3-hydroxycyclohexyl]-phenol (cannabicyclohexanol or CP-47,497 C8-homolog);
(iii) 1-pentyl-3-(1-naphthoyl)indole (JWH-018 and AM678);
(iv) 1-butyl-3-(1-naphthoyl)indole (JWH-073);
(v) 1-hexyl-3-(1-naphthoyl)indole (JWH-019);
(vi) 1-[2-(4-morpholinyl)ethyl]-3-(1-naphthoyl)indole (JWH-200);
(vii) 1-pentyl-3-(2-methoxyphenylacetyl)indole (JWH-250);
(viii) 1-pentyl-3-[1-(4-methoxynaphthoyl)]indole (JWH-081);
(ix) 1-pentyl-3-(4-methyl-1-naphthoyl)indole (JWH-122);
(x) 1-pentyl-3-(4-chloro-1-naphthoyl)indole (JWH-398);
(xi) 1-(5-fluoropentyl)-3-(1-naphthoyl)indole (AM2201);
(xii) 1-(5-fluoropentyl)-3-(2-iodobenzoyl)indole (AM694);
(xiii) 1-pentyl-3-[(4-methoxy)-benzoyl]indole (SR-19 and RCS-4);
(xiv) 1-cyclohexylethyl-3-(2-methoxyphenylacetyl-)indole (SR-18 and RCS-8); and
(xv) 1-pentyl-3-(2-chlorophenylacetyl)indole (JWH-203).

SCHEDULE II

(a) Unless specifically excepted or unless listed in another schedule, any of the following substances whether produced directly or indirectly by extraction from substances of vegetable origin, or independently by means of chemical synthesis, or by a combination of extraction and chemical synthesis:

(1) Opium and opiate, and any salt, compound, derivative, or preparation of opium or opiate.

(2) Any salt, compound, derivative, or preparation thereof which is chemically equivalent or identical with any of the substances referred to in clause (1), except that these substances shall not include the isoquinoline alkaloids of opium.

(3) Opium poppy and poppy straw.

(4) coca [Coca] leaves, except coca leaves and extracts of coca leaves from which cocaine, ecgonine, and derivatives of ecgonine or their salts have been removed; cocaine, its salts, optical and geometric isomers, and salts of isomers; ecgonine, its derivatives, their salts, isomers, and salts of isomers; or any compound, mixture, or preparation which contains any quantity of any of the substances referred to in this paragraph.

(b) Unless specifically excepted or unless listed in another schedule, any of the following opiates, including their isomers, esters, ethers, salts, and salts of isomers, esters and ethers, whenever the existence of such isomers, esters, ethers, and salts is possible within the specific chemical designation:

(1) Alphaprodine.
(2) Anileridine.
(3) Bezitramide.
(4) Dihydrocodeine.
(5) Diphenoxylate.
(6) Fentanyl.
(7) Isomethadone.
(8) Levomethorphan.
(9) Levorphanol.
(10) Metazocine.
(11) Methadone.
(12) Methadone-Intermediate, 4-cyano-2-dimethylamino-4, 4-diphenyl butane.
(13) Moramide-Intermediate, 2-methyl-3-morpholino-1, 1-diphenylpropane-carboxylic acid.
(14) Pethidine.
(15) Pethidine-Intermediate-A, 4-cyano-1-methyl-4-phenylpiperidine.
(16) Pethidine-Intermediate-B, ethyl-4-phenylpiperidine-4-carboxylate.
(17) Pethidine-Intermediate-C, 1-methyl-4-phenylpiperidine-4-carboxylic acid.
(18) Phenazocine.
(19) Piminodine.
(20) Racemethorphan.
(21) Racemorphan.

(c) Unless specifically excepted or unless listed in another schedule, any injectable liquid which contains any quantity of methamphetamine, including its salts, isomers, and salts of isomers.

SCHEDULE III

(a) Unless specifically excepted or unless listed in another schedule, any material, compound, mixture, or preparation which contains any quantity of the following substances having a stimulant effect on the central nervous system:

(1) Amphetamine, its salts, optical isomers, and salts of its optical isomers.
(2) Phenmetrazine and its salts.
(3) Any substance (except an injectable liquid) which contains any quantity of methamphetamine, including its salts, isomers, and salts of isomers.
(4) Methylphenidate.

(b) Unless specifically excepted or unless listed in another schedule, any material, compound, mixture, or preparation which contains any quantity of the following substances having a depressant effect on the central nervous system:

(1) Any substance which contains any quantity of a derivative of barbituric acid, or any salt of a derivative of barbituric acid.
(2) Chorhexadol.
(3) Glutethimide.
(4) Lysergic acid.
(5) Lysergic acid amide.
(6) Methyprylon.
(7) Phencyclidine.
(8) Sulfondiethylmethane.
(9) Sulfonethylmethane.
(10) Sulfonmethane.

(c) Nalorphine.

(d) Unless specifically excepted or unless listed in another schedule, any material, compound, mixture, or preparation containing limited quantities of any of the following narcotic drugs, or any salts thereof:

(1) Not more than 1.8 grams of codeine per 100 milliliters or not more than 90 milligrams per dosage unit, with an equal or greater quantity of an isoquinoline alkaloid of opium.

(2) Not more than 1.8 grams of codeine per 100 milliliters or not more than 90 milligrams per dosage unit, with one or more active, nonnarcotic ingredients in recognized therapeutic amounts.

(3) Not more than 300 milligrams of dihydrocodeinone per 100 milliliters or not more than 15 milligrams per dosage unit, with a fourfold or greater quantity of an isoquinoline alkaloid of opium.

(4) Not more than 300 milligrams of dihydrocodeinone per 100 milliliters or not more than 15 milligrams per dosage unit, with one or more active, nonnarcotic ingredients in recognized therapeutic amounts.

(5) Not more than 1.8 grams of dihydrocodeine per 100 milliliters or not more than 90 milligrams per dosage unit, with one or more active, nonnarcotic ingredients in recognized therapeutic amounts.

(6) Not more than 300 milligrams of ethylmorphine per 100 milliliters or not more than 15 milligrams per dosage unit, with one or more active, nonnarcotic ingredients in recognized therapeutic amounts.

(7) Not more than 500 milligrams of opium per 100 milliliters or per 100 grams, or not more than 25 milligrams per dosage unit, with one or more active, nonnarcotic ingredients in recognized therapeutic amounts.

(8) Not more than 50 milligrams of morphine per 100 milliliters or per 100 grams with one or more active, nonnarcotic ingredients in recognized therapeutic amounts.

(e) Anabolic steroids.

SCHEDULE IV

(1) Barbital.
(2) Chloral betaine.
(3) Chloral hydrate.
(4) Ethchlorvynol.
(5) Ethinamate.
(6) Methohexital.
(7) Meprobamate.
(8) Methylphenobarbital.
(9) Paraldehyde.
(10) Petrichloral.
(11) Phenobarbital.

SCHEDULE V

Any compound, mixture, or preparation containing any of the following limited quantities of narcotic drugs, which shall include one or more nonnarcotic active medicinal ingredients in sufficient proportion to confer upon the compound, mixture, or preparation valuable medicinal qualities other than those possessed by the narcotic drug alone:

(1) Not more than 200 milligrams of codeine per 100 milliliters or per 100 grams.

(2) Not more than 100 milligrams of dihydrocodeine per 100 milliliters or per 100 grams.

(3) Not more than 100 milligrams of ethylmorphine per 100 milliliters or per 100 grams.

(4) Not more than 2.5 milligrams of diphenoxylate and not less than 25 micrograms of atropine sulfate per dosage unit.

(5) Not more than 100 milligrams of opium per 100 milliliters or per 100 grams.

(Oct. 27, 1970, P. L. 91-513, Title II, Part B, § 202, 84 Stat. 1247; Nov. 10, 1978, P. L. 95-633, Title I, § 103, 92 Stat. 3772; Oct. 12, 1984, P. L. 98-473, Title II, Ch V, Part B, §§ 507(c), 509(b), 98 Stat. 2071, 2072; Oct. 27, 1986, P. L. 99-570, Title I, Subtitle Q, § 1867, 100 Stat. 3207-55; Nov. 10, 1986, P. L. 99-646, § 84, 100 Stat. 3619; Nov. 29, 1990, P. L. 101-647, Title XIX, § 1902(a), 104 Stat. 4851; July 9, 2012, P. L. 112-144, Title XI, Subtitle D, § 1152, 126 Stat. 1130; Dec. 20, 2018, P.L. 115-334, Title XII, Subtitle F, § 12619(b), 132 Stat. 5018.)

§ 813. Treatment of controlled substance analogues

(a) In general. A controlled substance analogue shall, to the extent intended for human consumption, be treated, for the purposes of any Federal law as a controlled substance in schedule I.

(b) Determination. In determining whether a controlled substance analogue was intended for human consumption under subsection (a), the following factors may be considered, along with any other relevant factors:

(1) The marketing, advertising, and labeling of the substance.

(2) The known efficacy or usefulness of the substance for the marketed, advertised, or labeled purpose.

(3) The difference between the price at which the substance is sold and the price at which the substance it is purported to be or advertised as is normally sold.

(4) The diversion of the substance from legitimate channels and the clandestine importation, manufacture, or distribution of the substance.

(5) Whether the defendant knew or should have known the substance was intended to be consumed by injection, inhalation, ingestion, or any other immediate means.

(6) Any controlled substance analogue that is manufactured, formulated, sold, distributed, or marketed with the intent to avoid the provisions of existing drug laws.

(c) Limitation. For purposes of this section, evidence that a substance was not marketed, advertised, or labeled for human consumption, by itself, shall not be sufficient to establish that the substance was not intended for human consumption.

(Oct. 27, 1970, P. L. 91-513, Title II, Part B, § 203, as added Oct. 27, 1986, P. L. 99-570, Title I, Subtitle E, § 1202, 100 Stat. 3207-13; Nov. 18, 1988, P. L. 100-690, Title VI, Subtitle N, § 6470(c), 102 Stat. 4378; Oct. 24, 2018, P.L. 115-271, Title III, Subtitle B, Ch 5, § 3241, 132 Stat. 3950.)

§ 814. Removal of exemption of certain drugs

(a) Removal of exemption. The Attorney General shall by regulation remove from exemption under section 102(39)(A)(iv) [21 USCS § 802(39)(A)(iv)] a drug or group of drugs that the Attorney General finds is being diverted to obtain a listed chemical for use in the illicit production of a controlled substance.

(b) Factors to be considered. In removing a drug or group of drugs from exemption under subsection (a), the Attorney General shall consider, with respect to a drug or group of drugs that is proposed to be removed from exemption—

(1) the scope, duration, and significance of the diversion;

(2) whether the drug or group of drugs is formulated in such a way that it cannot be easily used in the illicit production of a controlled substance; and

(3) whether the listed chemical can be readily recovered from the drug or group of drugs.

(c) Specificity of designation. The Attorney General shall limit the designation of a drug or a group of drugs removed from exemption under subsection (a) to the most particularly identifiable type of drug or group of drugs for which evidence of diversion exists unless there is evidence, based on the pattern of diversion and other relevant factors, that the diversion will not be limited to that particular drug or group of drugs.

(d) Reinstatement of exemption with respect to particular drug products.

(1) Reinstatement. On application by a manufacturer of a particular drug product that has been removed from exemption under subsection (a), the Attorney General shall by regulation reinstate the exemption with respect to that particular drug product if the Attorney General determines that the particular drug product is manufactured and distributed in a manner that prevents diversion.

(2) Factors to be considered. In deciding whether to reinstate the exemption with respect to a particular drug product under paragraph (1), the Attorney General shall consider—

(A) the package sizes and manner of packaging of the drug product;

(B) the manner of distribution and advertising of the drug product;

(C) evidence of diversion of the drug product;

(D) any actions taken by the manufacturer to prevent diversion of the drug product; and

(E) such other factors as are relevant to and consistent with the public health and safety, including the factors described in subsection (b) as applied to the drug product.

(3) Status pending application for reinstatement. A transaction involving a particular drug product that is the subject of a bona fide pending application for reinstatement of exemption filed with the Attorney General not later than 60 days after a regulation removing the exemption is issued pursuant to subsection (a) shall not be considered to be a regulated

transaction if the transaction occurs during the pendency of the application and, if the Attorney General denies the application, during the period of 60 days following the date on which the Attorney General denies the application, unless—

(A) the Attorney General has evidence that, applying the factors described in subsection (b) to the drug product, the drug product is being diverted; and

(B) the Attorney General so notifies the applicant.

(4) Amendment and modification. A regulation reinstating an exemption under paragraph (1) may be modified or revoked with respect to a particular drug product upon a finding that—

(A) applying the factors described in subsection (b) to the drug product, the drug product is being diverted; or

(B) there is a significant change in the data that led to the issuance of the regulation.

(Oct. 27, 1970, P. L. 91-513, Title II, Part B, § 204, as added Dec. 17, 1993, P. L. 103-200, § 2(b)(1), 107 Stat. 2334; Oct. 3, 1996, P. L. 104-237, Title IV, § 401(c), 110 Stat. 3108; March 9, 2006, P. L. 109-177, Title VII, Subtitle A, § 712(a)(2), 120 Stat. 263.)

REGISTRATION OF MANUFACTURERS, DISTRIBUTORS, AND DISPENSERS OF CONTROLLED SUBSTANCES

§ 821. Rules and regulations

The Attorney General is authorized to promulgate rules and regulations and to charge reasonable fees relating to the registration and control of the manufacture, distribution, and dispensing of controlled substances and to listed chemicals.

(Oct. 27, 1970, P. L. 91-513, Title II, Part C, § 301, 84 Stat. 1253; Dec. 17, 1993, P. L. 103-200, § 3(a), 107 Stat. 2336; Dec. 8, 2004, P. L. 108-447, Div B, Title VI, § 633(b), 118 Stat. 2922.)

§ 822. Persons required to register

(a) Period of registration.

(1) Every person who manufactures or distributes any controlled substance or list I chemical, or who proposes to engage in the manufacture or distribution of any controlled substance or list I chemical, shall obtain annually a registration issued by the Attorney General in accordance with the rules and regulations promulgated by him.

(2) Every person who dispenses, or who proposes to dispense, any controlled substance, shall obtain from the Attorney General a registration issued in accordance with the rules and regulations promulgated by him. The Attorney General shall, by regulation, determine the period of such registrations. In no event, however, shall such registrations be issued for less than one year nor for more than three years.

(3)(A) Except as provided in subparagraph (C), the registration of any registrant under this title to manufacture, distribute, or dispense controlled substances or list I chemicals terminates if and when such registrant—

(i) dies;

(ii) ceases legal existence;

(iii) discontinues business or professional practice; or

(iv) surrenders such registration.

(B) In the case of such a registrant who ceases legal existence or discontinues business or professional practice, such registrant shall promptly notify the Attorney General in writing of such fact.

(C) No registration under this title to manufacture, distribute, or dispense controlled substances or list I chemicals, and no authority conferred thereby, may be assigned or otherwise transferred except upon such conditions as the Attorney General may specify and then only pursuant to written consent. A registrant to whom a registration is assigned or transferred pursuant to the preceding sentence may not manufacture, distribute, or dispense controlled substances or list I chemicals pursuant to such registration until the Attorney General receives such written consent.

(D) In the case of a registrant under this title to manufacture, distribute, or dispense controlled substances or list I chemicals desiring to discontinue business or professional practice altogether or with respect to controlled substances and list I chemicals (without assigning or transferring such business or professional practice to another entity), such registrant shall return to the Attorney General for cancellation—

(i) the registrant's certificate of registration;

(ii) any unexecuted order forms in the registrant's possession; and

(iii) any other documentation that the Attorney General may require.

(b) Authorized activities. Persons registered by the Attorney General under this title to manufacture, distribute, or dispense controlled substances or list I chemicals are authorized to possess, manufacture, distribute, or dispense such substances or chemicals (including any such activity in the conduct of research) to the extent authorized by their registration and in conformity with the other provisions of this title.

(c) Exceptions. The following persons shall not be required to register and may lawfully possess any controlled substance or list I chemical under this title:

(1) An agent or employee of any registered manufacturer, distributor, or dispenser of any controlled substance or list I chemical if such agent or employee is acting in the usual course of his business or employment.

(2) A common or contract carrier or warehouseman, or an employee thereof, whose possession of the controlled substance or list I chemical is in the usual course of his business or employment.

(3) An ultimate user who possesses such substance for a purpose specified in section 102.

(d) Waiver. The Attorney General may, by regulation, waive the requirement for registration of certain manufacturers, distributors, or dispensers if he finds it consistent with the public health and safety.

(e) Separate registration; transport and dispensing of controlled substances in the usual course of veterinary practice.

(1) A separate registration shall be required at each principal place of business or professional practice

where the applicant manufactures, distributes, or dispenses controlled substances or list I chemicals.

(2) Notwithstanding paragraph (1), a registrant who is a veterinarian shall not be required to have a separate registration in order to transport and dispense controlled substances in the usual course of veterinary practice at a site other than the registrant's registered principal place of business or professional practice, so long as the site of transporting and dispensing is located in a State where the veterinarian is licensed to practice veterinary medicine and is not a principal place of business or professional practice.

(3) Notwithstanding paragraph (1), a registrant that is dispensing pursuant to section 303(g) [21 USCS § 823(g)] narcotic drugs to individuals for maintenance treatment or detoxification treatment shall not be required to have a separate registration to incorporate one or more mobile medication units into the registrant's practice to dispense such narcotics at locations other than the registrant's principal place of business or professional practice described in paragraph (1), so long as the registrant meets such standards for operation of a mobile medication unit as the Attorney General may establish.

(f) Inspection. The Attorney General is authorized to inspect the establishment of a registrant or applicant for registration in accordance with the rules and regulations promulgated by him.

(g) Delivery of controlled substances by ultimate users for disposal.

(1) An ultimate user who has lawfully obtained a controlled substance in accordance with this title may, without being registered, deliver the controlled substance to another person for the purpose of disposal of the controlled substance if—

(A) the person receiving the controlled substance is authorized under this title to engage in such activity; and

(B) the disposal takes place in accordance with regulations issued by the Attorney General to prevent diversion of controlled substances.

(2) In developing regulations under this subsection, the Attorney General shall take into consideration the public health and safety, as well as the ease and cost of program implementation and participation by various communities. Such regulations may not require any entity to establish or operate a delivery or disposal program.

(3) The Attorney General may, by regulation, authorize long-term care facilities, as defined by the Attorney General by regulation, to dispose of controlled substances on behalf of ultimate users who reside, or have resided, at such long-term care facilities in a manner that the Attorney General determines will provide effective controls against diversion and be consistent with the public health and safety.

(4) If a person dies while lawfully in possession of a controlled substance for personal use, any person lawfully entitled to dispose of the decedent's property may deliver the controlled substance to another person for the purpose of disposal under the same conditions as provided in paragraph (1) for an ultimate user.

(5)(A) In the case of a person receiving hospice care, an employee of a qualified hospice program, acting within the scope of employment, may handle, without being registered under this section, any controlled substance that was lawfully dispensed to the person receiving hospice care, for the purpose of disposal of the controlled substance so long as such disposal occurs onsite in accordance with all applicable Federal, State, Tribal, and local law and—

(i) the disposal occurs after the death of a person receiving hospice care;

(ii) the controlled substance is expired; or

(iii)(I) the employee is—

(aa) the physician of the person receiving hospice care; and

(bb) registered under section 303(g) [21 USCS § 823(g)]; and

(II) the hospice patient no longer requires the controlled substance because the plan of care of the hospice patient has been modified.

(B) For the purposes of this paragraph:

(i) The terms "hospice care" and "hospice program" have the meanings given to those terms in section 1861(dd) of the Social Security Act [42 USCS § 1395x(dd)].

(ii) The term "employee of a qualified hospice program" means a physician, physician assistant, nurse, or other person who—

(I) is employed by, or pursuant to arrangements made by, a qualified hospice program;

(II)(aa) is licensed to perform medical or nursing services by the jurisdiction in which the person receiving hospice care was located; and

(bb) is acting within the scope of such employment in accordance with applicable State law; and

(III) has completed training through the qualified hospice program regarding the disposal of controlled substances in a secure and responsible manner so as to discourage abuse, misuse, or diversion.

(iii) The term "qualified hospice program" means a hospice program that—

(I) has written policies and procedures for assisting in the disposal of the controlled substances of a person receiving hospice care after the person's death;

(II) at the time when the controlled substances are first ordered—

(aa) provides a copy of the written policies and procedures to the patient or patient representative and family;

(bb) discusses the policies and procedures with the patient or representative and the family in a language and manner that they understand to ensure that these parties are educated regarding the safe disposal of controlled substances; and

(cc) documents in the patient's clinical record that the written policies and procedures were provided and discussed; and

(III) at the time following the disposal of the controlled substances—

(aa) documents in the patient's clinical record the type of controlled substance, dosage, route of administration, and quantity so disposed; and (bb) the time, date, and manner in which that disposal occurred.

(Oct. 27, 1970, P. L. 91-513, Title II, Part C, § 302, 84 Stat. 1253; Oct. 12, 1984, P. L. 98-473, Title II, Ch V, Part B, § 510, 98 Stat. 2072; Dec. 17, 1993, P. L. 103-200, § 3(b), 107 Stat. 2336; Oct. 12, 2010, P. L. 111-273, § 3(a), 124 Stat. 2859; Aug. 1, 2014, P. L. 113-143, § 2, 128 Stat. 1750; Oct. 24, 2018, P.L. 115-271, Title III, Subtitle B, Ch 3, § 3222(a), 132 Stat. 3948; Nov. 10, 2021, P.L. 117-53, § 2, 135 Stat. 411; Dec. 2, 2022, P.L. 117-215, Title I, § 103(b)(1)(B), 136 Stat. 2263; Dec. 29, 2022, P.L. 117-328, Div FF, Title I, Subtitle B, Ch 5, § 1252(a), 136 Stat. 5681.)

§ 822a. Prescription drug take back expansion

(a) Definition of covered entity. In this section, the term "covered entity" means—

(1) a State, local, or tribal law enforcement agency;

(2) a manufacturer, distributor, or reverse distributor of prescription medications;

(3) a retail pharmacy;

(4) a registered narcotic treatment program;

(5) a hospital or clinic with an onsite pharmacy;

(6) an eligible long-term care facility; or

(7) any other entity authorized by the Drug Enforcement Administration to dispose of prescription medications.

(b) Program authorized. The Attorney General, in coordination with the Administrator of the Drug Enforcement Administration, the Secretary of Health and Human Services, and the Director of the Office of National Drug Control Policy, shall coordinate with covered entities in expanding or making available disposal sites for unwanted prescription medications.

(July 22, 2016, P. L. 114-198, Title II, § 203, 130 Stat. 717.)

§ 823. Registration requirements

(a) Manufacturers of controlled substances in schedule I or II. The Attorney General shall register an applicant to manufacture controlled substances in schedule I or II if he determines that such registration is consistent with the public interest and with United States obligations under international treaties, conventions, or protocols in effect on the effective date of this part. In determining the public interest, the following factors shall be considered:

(1) maintenance of effective controls against diversion of particular controlled substances and any controlled substance in schedule I or II compounded therefrom into other than legitimate medical, scientific, research, or industrial channels, by limiting the importation and bulk manufacture of such controlled substances to a number of establishments which can produce an adequate and uninterrupted supply of these substances under adequately competitive conditions for legitimate medical, scientific, research, and industrial purposes;

(2) compliance with applicable State and local law;

(3) promotion of technical advances in the art of manufacturing these substances and the development of new substances;

(4) prior conviction record of applicant under Federal and State laws relating to the manufacture, distribution, or dispensing of such substances;

(5) past experience in the manufacture of controlled substances, and the existence in the establishment of effective control against diversion; and

(6) such other factors as may be relevant to and consistent with the public health and safety.

(b) Distributors of controlled substances in schedule I or II. The Attorney General shall register an applicant to distribute a controlled substance in schedule I or II unless he determines that the issuance of such registration is inconsistent with the public interest. In determining the public interest, the following factors shall be considered:

(1) maintenance of effective control against diversion of particular controlled substances into other than legitimate medical, scientific, and industrial channels;

(2) compliance with applicable State and local law;

(3) prior conviction record of applicant under Federal or State laws relating to the manufacture, distribution, or dispensing of such substances;

(4) past experience in the distribution of controlled substances; and

(5) such other factors as may be relevant to and consistent with the public health and safety.

(c)(1)(A) As it relates to applications to manufacture marijuana for research purposes, when the Attorney General places a notice in the Federal Register to increase the number of entities registered under this Act to manufacture marijuana to supply appropriately registered researchers in the United States, the Attorney General shall, not later than 60 days after the date on which the Attorney General receives a completed application—

(i) approve the application; or

(ii) request supplemental information.

(B) For purposes of subparagraph (A), an application shall be deemed complete when the applicant has submitted documentation showing each of the following:

(i) The requirements designated in the notice in the Federal Register are satisfied.

(ii) The requirements under this Act are satisfied.

(iii) The applicant will limit the transfer and sale of any marijuana manufactured under this subsection—

(I) to researchers who are registered under this Act to conduct research with controlled substances in schedule I; and

(II) for purposes of use in preclinical research or in a clinical investigation pursuant to an investigational new drug exemption under 505(i) of the Federal Food, Drug, and Cosmetic Act (21 U.S.C. 355(i)).

(iv) The applicant will transfer or sell any marijuana manufactured under this subsection only with prior, written consent for the transfer or sale by the Attorney General.

(v) The applicant has completed the application and review process under subsection (a) for the bulk manufacture of controlled substances in schedule I.

(vi) The applicant has established and begun operation of a process for storage and handling of controlled substances in schedule I, including for inventory control and monitoring security in accordance with section

105 of the Medical Marijuana and Cannabidiol Research Expansion Act [note to this section].

(vii) The applicant is licensed by each State in which the applicant will conduct operations under this subsection, to manufacture marijuana, if that State requires such a license.

(C) Not later than 30 days after the date on which the Attorney General receives supplemental information requested under subparagraph (A)(ii) with respect to an application, the Attorney General shall approve or deny the application.

(2) If an application described in this subsection is denied, the Attorney General shall provide a written explanation of the basis of denial to the applicant.

(d) Limits of authorized activities. Registration granted under subsections (a) and (b) of this section shall not entitle a registrant to (1) manufacture or distribute controlled substances in schedule I or II other than those specified in the registration, or (2) manufacture any quantity of those controlled substances in excess of the quota assigned pursuant to section 306 [21 USCS § 826].

(e) Manufacturers of controlled substances in schedule III, IV, or V. The Attorney General shall register an applicant to manufacture controlled substances in schedule III, IV, or V, unless he determines that the issuance of such registration is inconsistent with the public interest. In determining the public interest, the following factors shall be considered:

(1) maintenance of effective controls against diversion of particular controlled substances and any controlled substance in schedule III, IV, or V compounded therefrom into other than legitimate medical, scientific, or industrial channels;

(2) compliance with applicable State and local law;

(3) promotion of technical advances in the art of manufacturing these substances and the development of new substances;

(4) prior conviction record of applicant under Federal or State laws relating to the manufacture, distribution, or dispensing of such substances;

(5) past experience in the manufacture, distribution, and dispensing of controlled substances, and the existence in the establishment of effective controls against diversion; and

(6) such other factors as may be relevant to and consistent with the public health and safety.

(f) Distributors of controlled substances in schedule III, IV, or V. The Attorney General shall register an applicant to distribute controlled substances in schedule III, IV, or V, unless he determines that the issuance of such registration is inconsistent with the public interest. In determining the public interest, the following factors shall be considered:

(1) maintenance of effective controls against diversion of particular controlled substances into other than legitimate medical, scientific, and industrial channels;

(2) compliance with applicable State and local law;

(3) prior conviction record of applicant under Federal or State laws relating to the manufacture, distribution, or dispensing of such substances;

(4) past experience in the distribution of controlled substances; and

(5) such other factors as may be relevant to and consistent with the public health and safety.

(g) Research by practitioners; pharmacies; research applications; construction of Article 7 of the Convention on Psychotropic Substances.

(1) The Attorney General shall register practitioners (including pharmacies, as distinguished from pharmacists) to dispense, or conduct research with, controlled substances in schedule II, III, IV, or V and shall modify the registrations of pharmacies so registered to authorize them to dispense controlled substances by means of the Internet, if the applicant is authorized to dispense, or conduct research with respect to, controlled substances under the laws of the State in which he practices. The Attorney General may deny an application for such registration or such modification of registration if the Attorney General determines that the issuance of such registration or modification would be inconsistent with the public interest. In determining the public interest, the following factors shall be considered:

(A) The recommendation of the appropriate State licensing board or professional disciplinary authority.

(B) The applicant's experience in dispensing, or conducting research with respect to controlled substances.

(C) The applicant's conviction record under Federal or State laws relating to the manufacture, distribution, or dispensing of controlled substances.

(D) Compliance with applicable State, Federal, or local laws relating to controlled substances.

(E) Such other conduct which may threaten the public health and safety.

Separate registration under this part [21 USCS §§ 821 et seq.] for practitioners engaging in research with controlled substances in schedule II, III, IV, or V, who are already registered under this part [21 USCS §§ 821 et seq.] in another capacity, shall not be required.

(2)(A) Registration applications by practitioners wishing to conduct research with controlled substances in schedule I shall be referred to the Secretary, who shall determine the qualifications and competency of each practitioner requesting registration, as well as the merits of the research protocol. The Secretary, in determining the merits of each research protocol, shall consult with the Attorney General as to effective procedures to adequately safeguard against diversion of such controlled substances from legitimate medical or scientific use. Registration for the purpose of bona fide research with controlled substances in schedule I by a practitioner deemed qualified by the Secretary may be denied by the Attorney General only on a ground specified in section 304(a) [21 USCS § 824(a)].

(B)(i) The Attorney General shall register a practitioner to conduct research with marijuana (including any derivative, extract, preparation, and compound thereof) if—

(I) the applicant's research protocol has been reviewed and allowed—

(aa) by the Secretary of Health and Human Services under section 505(i) of the Federal Food, Drug, and Cosmetic Act (21 U.S.C. 355(i));

(bb) by the National Institutes of Health or another Federal agency that funds scientific research; or

(cc) pursuant to sections 1301.18 and 1301.32 of title 21, Code of Federal Regulations, or any successors thereto; and

(II) the applicant has demonstrated to the Attorney General that there are effective procedures in place to adequately safeguard against diversion of the controlled substance for legitimate medical or scientific use pursuant to section 105 of the Medical Marijuana and Cannabidiol Research Expansion Act [21 USCS § 823 note], including demonstrating that the security measures are adequate for storing the quantity of marijuana the applicant would be authorized to possess.

(ii) The Attorney General may deny an application for registration under this subparagraph only if the Attorney General determines that the issuance of the registration would be inconsistent with the public interest. In determining the public interest, the Attorney General shall consider the factors listed in—

(I) subparagraphs (B) through (E) of paragraph (1); and

(II) subparagraph (A) of paragraph (1), if the applicable State requires practitioners conducting research to register with a board or authority described in such subparagraph (A).

(iii)(I) Not later than 60 days after the date on which the Attorney General receives a complete application for registration under this subparagraph, the Attorney General shall—

(aa) approve the application; or

(bb) request supplemental information.

(II) For purposes of subclause (I), an application shall be deemed complete when the applicant has submitted documentation showing that the requirements under clause (i) are satisfied.

(iv) Not later than 30 days after the date on which the Attorney General receives supplemental information as described in clause (iii)(I)(bb) in connection with an application described in this subparagraph, the Attorney General shall approve or deny the application.

(v) If an application described in this subparagraph is denied, the Attorney General shall provide a written explanation of the basis of denial to the applicant.

(vi)(I) If the Attorney General grants an application for registration under clause (i), the registrant may amend or supplement the research protocol without notification to, or review by, the Drug Enforcement Administration if the registrant does not change—

(aa) the quantity or type of marijuana or cannabidiol (including any derivative, extract, preparation, and compound thereof);

(bb) the source of such marijuana or cannabidiol; or

(cc) the conditions under which such marijuana or cannabidiol is stored, tracked, or administered.

(II)(aa) If a registrant under clause (i) seeks to change the type of marijuana or cannabidiol (including any derivative, extract, preparation, and compound thereof), the source of such marijuana or cannabidiol, or the conditions under which such marijuana or cannabidiol is stored, tracked, or administered, the registrant shall notify the Attorney General via registered mail, or an electronic means permitted by the Attorney General, not later than 30 days before implementing an amended or supplemental research protocol.

(bb) A registrant may proceed with an amended or supplemental research protocol described in item (aa) if the Attorney General does not explicitly object during the 30-day period beginning on the date on which the Attorney General receives the notice under item (aa).

(cc) The Attorney General may only object to an amended or supplemental research protocol under this subclause if additional security measures are needed to safeguard against diversion or abuse.

(dd) If a registrant under clause (i) seeks to address additional security measures identified by the Attorney General under item (cc), the registrant shall notify the Attorney General via registered mail, or an electronic means permitted by the Attorney General, not later than 30 days before implementing an amended or supplemental research protocol.

(ee) A registrant may proceed with an amended or supplemental research protocol described in item (dd) if the Attorney General does not explicitly object during the 30-day period beginning on the date on which the Attorney General receives the notice under item (dd).

(III)(aa) If a registrant under clause (i) seeks to change the quantity of marijuana needed for research and the change in quantity does not impact the factors described in item (bb) or (cc) of subclause (I) of this clause, the registrant shall notify the Attorney General via registered mail or using an electronic means permitted by the Attorney General.

(bb) A notification under item (aa) shall include—

(AA) the Drug Enforcement Administration registration number of the registrant;

(BB) the quantity of marijuana or cannabidiol already obtained;

(CC) the quantity of additional marijuana or cannabidiol needed to complete the research; and

(DD) an attestation that the change in quantity does not impact the source of the marijuana or cannabidiol or the conditions under which the marijuana or cannabidiol is stored, tracked, or administered.

(cc) The Attorney General shall ensure that—

(AA) any registered mail return receipt with respect to a notification under item (aa) is submitted for delivery to the registrant providing the notification not later than 3 days after receipt of the notification by the Attorney General; and

(BB) notice of receipt of a notification using an electronic means permitted under item (aa) is provided to the registrant providing the notification not later than 3 days after receipt of the notification by the Attorney General.

(dd)(AA) On and after the date described in subitem (BB), a registrant that submits a notification in accordance with item (aa) may proceed with the research as if the change in quantity has been approved on such date, unless the Attorney General notifies the registrant of an objection described in item (ee).

(BB) The date described in this subitem is the date on which a registrant submitting a notification under item (aa) receives the registered mail return receipt with respect to the notification or the date on which the registrant receives notice that the notification using an electronic means permitted under item (aa) was received by the Attorney General, as the case may be.

(ee) A notification submitted under item (aa) shall be deemed to be approved unless the Attorney General, not later than 10 days after receiving the notification, explicitly objects based on a finding that the change in quantity—

(AA) does impact the source of the marijuana or cannabidiol or the conditions under which the marijuana or cannabidiol is stored, tracked, or administered; or

(BB) necessitates that the registrant implement additional security measures to safeguard against diversion or abuse.

(IV) Nothing in this clause shall limit the authority of the Secretary of Health and Human Services over requirements related to research protocols, including changes in—

(aa) the method of administration of marijuana or cannabidiol;

(bb) the dosing of marijuana or cannabidiol; and

(cc) the number of individuals or patients involved in research.

(3) Article 7 of the Convention on Psychotropic Substances shall not be construed to prohibit, or impose additional restrictions upon, research involving drugs or other substances scheduled under the convention which is conducted in conformity with this subsection and other applicable provisions of this title.

(h) Practitioners dispensing narcotic drugs for narcotic treatment; annual registration; separate registration; qualifications. Practitioners who dispense narcotic drugs (other than narcotic drugs in schedule III, IV, or V) to individuals for maintenance treatment or detoxification treatment or detoxification treatment shall obtain annually a separate registration for that purpose. The Attorney General shall register an applicant to dispense narcotic drugs to individuals for maintenance treatment or detoxification treatment (or both)—

(1) if the applicant is a practitioner who is determined by the Secretary to be qualified (under standards established by the Secretary) to engage in the treatment with respect to which registration is sought;

(2) if the Attorney General determines that the applicant will comply with standards established by the Attorney General respecting (A) security of stocks of narcotic drugs for such treatment, and (B) the maintenance of records (in accordance with section 307 [21 USCS § 827]) on such drugs; and

(3) if the Secretary determines that the applicant will comply with standards established by the Secretary (after consultation with the Attorney General) respecting the quantities of narcotic drugs which may be provided for unsupervised use by individuals in such treatment.

(i) Applicants for distribution of list I chemicals. The Attorney General shall register an applicant to distribute a list I chemical unless the Attorney General determines that registration of the applicant is inconsistent with the public interest. Registration under this subsection shall not be required for the distribution of a drug product that is exempted under clause (iv) or (v) of section 102(39)(A) [21 USCS § 802(39)(A)]. In determining the public interest for the purposes of this subsection, the Attorney General shall consider—

(1) maintenance by the applicant of effective controls against diversion of listed chemicals into other than legitimate channels;

(2) compliance by the applicant with applicable Federal, State, and local law;

(3) any prior conviction record of the applicant under Federal or State laws relating to controlled substances or to chemicals controlled under Federal or State law;

(4) any past experience of the applicant in the manufacture and distribution of chemicals; and

(5) such other factors as are relevant to and consistent with the public health and safety.

(j) Enhancing new drug development.

(1) For purposes of registration to manufacture a controlled substance under subsection (e) for use only in a clinical trial, the Attorney General shall register the applicant, or serve an order to show cause upon the applicant in accordance with section 304(c) [21 USCS § 824(c)], not later than 180 days after the date on which the application is accepted for filing.

(2) For purposes of registration to manufacture a controlled substance under subsection (a) for use only in a clinical trial, the Attorney General shall, in accordance with the regulations issued by the Attorney General, issue a notice of application not later than 90 days after the application is accepted for filing. Not later than 90 days after the date on which the period for comment pursuant to such notice ends, the Attorney General shall register the applicant, or serve an order to show cause upon the applicant in accordance with section 304(c) [21 USCS § 824(c)], unless the Attorney General has granted a hearing on the application under section 1008(i) of the Controlled Substances Import and Export Act [21 USCS § 958(i)].

(k) Emergency medical services that administer controlled substances.

(1) Registration. For the purpose of enabling emergency medical services professionals to administer controlled substances in schedule II, III, IV, or V to ultimate users receiving emergency medical services in accordance with the requirements of this subsection, the Attorney General—

(A) shall register an emergency medical services agency if the agency submits an application demonstrating it is authorized to conduct such activity under the laws of each State in which the agency practices; and

(B) may deny an application for such registration if the Attorney General determines that the issuance of such registration would be inconsistent with the requirements of this subsection or the public interest based on the factors listed in subsection (g).

(2) Option for single registration. In registering an emergency medical services agency pursuant to paragraph (1), the Attorney General shall allow such agency the option of a single registration in each State where

the agency administers controlled substances in lieu of requiring a separate registration for each location of the emergency medical services agency.

(3) Hospital-based agency. If a hospital-based emergency medical services agency is registered under subsection (g), the agency may use the registration of the hospital to administer controlled substances in accordance with this subsection without being registered under this subsection.

(4) Administration outside physical presence of medical director or authorizing medical professional. Emergency medical services professionals of a registered emergency medical services agency may administer controlled substances in schedule II, III, IV, or V outside the physical presence of a medical director or authorizing medical professional in the course of providing emergency medical services if the administration is—

(A) authorized by the law of the State in which it occurs; and

(B) pursuant to—

(i) a standing order that is issued and adopted by one or more medical directors of the agency, including any such order that may be developed by a specific State authority; or

(ii) a verbal order that is—

(I) issued in accordance with a policy of the agency; and

(II) provided by a medical director or authorizing medical professional in response to a request by the emergency medical services professional with respect to a specific patient—

(aa) in the case of a mass casualty incident; or

(bb) to ensure the proper care and treatment of a specific patient.

(5) Delivery. A registered emergency medical services agency may deliver controlled substances from a registered location of the agency to an unregistered location of the agency only if the agency—

(A) designates the unregistered location for such delivery; and

(B) notifies the Attorney General at least 30 days prior to first delivering controlled substances to the unregistered location.

(6) Storage. A registered emergency medical services agency may store controlled substances—

(A) at a registered location of the agency;

(B) at any designated location of the agency or in an emergency services vehicle situated at a registered or designated location of the agency; or

(C) in an emergency medical services vehicle used by the agency that is—

(i) traveling from, or returning to, a registered or designated location of the agency in the course of responding to an emergency; or

(ii) otherwise actively in use by the agency under circumstances that provide for security of the controlled substances consistent with the requirements established by regulations of the Attorney General.

(7) No treatment as distribution. The delivery of controlled substances by a registered emergency medical services agency pursuant to this subsection shall not be treated as distribution for purposes of section 308 [21 USCS § 828].

(8) Restocking of emergency medical services vehicles at a hospital. Notwithstanding paragraph (13)(J), a registered emergency medical services agency may receive controlled substances from a hospital for purposes of restocking an emergency medical services vehicle following an emergency response, and without being subject to the requirements of section 308 [21 USCS § 828], provided all of the following conditions are satisfied:

(A) The registered or designated location of the agency where the vehicle is primarily situated maintains a record of such receipt in accordance with paragraph (9).

(B) The hospital maintains a record of such delivery to the agency in accordance with section 307 [21 USCS § 827].

(C) If the vehicle is primarily situated at a designated location, such location notifies the registered location of the agency within 72 hours of the vehicle receiving the controlled substances.

(9) Maintenance of records.

(A) In general. A registered emergency medical services agency shall maintain records in accordance with subsections (a) and (b) of section 307 [21 USCS § 827] of all controlled substances that are received, administered, or otherwise disposed of pursuant to the agency's registration, without regard to subsection 307(c)(1)(B) [21 USCS § 827(c)(1)(B)].

(B) Requirements. Such records—

(i) shall include records of deliveries of controlled substances between all locations of the agency; and

(ii) shall be maintained, whether electronically or otherwise, at each registered and designated location of the agency where the controlled substances involved are received, administered, or otherwise disposed of.

(10) Other requirements. A registered emergency medical services agency, under the supervision of a medical director, shall be responsible for ensuring that—

(A) all emergency medical services professionals who administer controlled substances using the agency's registration act in accordance with the requirements of this subsection;

(B) the recordkeeping requirements of paragraph (9) are met with respect to a registered location and each designated location of the agency;

(C) the applicable physical security requirements established by regulation of the Attorney General are complied with wherever controlled substances are stored by the agency in accordance with paragraph (6); and

(D) the agency maintains, at a registered location of the agency, a record of the standing orders issued or adopted in accordance with paragraph (9).

(11) Regulations. The Attorney General may issue regulations—

(A) specifying, with regard to delivery of controlled substances under paragraph (5)—

(i) the types of locations that may be designated under such paragraph; and

(ii) the manner in which a notification under paragraph (5)(B) must be made;

(B) specifying, with regard to the storage of controlled substances under paragraph (6), the manner in which such substances must be stored at registered and designated locations, including in emergency medical service vehicles; and

(C) addressing the ability of hospitals, emergency medical services agencies, registered locations, and designated locations to deliver controlled substances to each other in the event of—

(i) shortages of such substances;

(ii) a public health emergency; or

(iii) a mass casualty event.

(12) Rule of construction. Nothing in this subsection shall be construed—

(A) to limit the authority vested in the Attorney General by other provisions of this title [21 USCS §§ 801 et seq.] to take measures to prevent diversion of controlled substances; or

(B) to override the authority of any State to regulate the provision of emergency medical services consistent with this subsection.

(13) Definitions. In this section:

(A) The term "authorizing medical professional" means an emergency or other physician, or another medical professional (including an advanced practice registered nurse or physician assistant)—

(i) who is registered under this Act [21 USCS §§ 801 et seq.];

(ii) who is acting within the scope of the registration; and

(iii) whose scope of practice under a State license or certification includes the ability to provide verbal orders.

(B) The term "designated location" means a location designated by an emergency medical services agency under paragraph (5).

(C) The term "emergency medical services" means emergency medical response and emergency mobile medical services provided outside of a fixed medical facility.

(D) The term "emergency medical services agency" means an organization providing emergency medical services, including such an organization that—

(i) is governmental (including fire-based and hospital-based agencies), nongovernmental (including hospital-based agencies), private, or volunteer-based;

(ii) provides emergency medical services by ground, air, or otherwise; and

(iii) is authorized by the State in which the organization is providing such services to provide emergency medical care, including the administering of controlled substances, to members of the general public on an emergency basis.

(E) The term "emergency medical services professional" means a health care professional (including a nurse, paramedic, or emergency medical technician) licensed or certified by the State in which the professional practices and credentialed by a medical director of the respective emergency medical services agency to provide emergency medical services within the scope of the professional's State license or certification.

(F) The term "emergency medical services vehicle" means an ambulance, fire apparatus, supervisor truck, or other vehicle used by an emergency medical services agency for the purpose of providing or facilitating emergency medical care and transport or transporting controlled substances to and from the registered and designated locations.

(G) The term "hospital-based" means, with respect to an agency, owned or operated by a hospital.

(H) The term "medical director" means a physician who is registered under subsection (g) and provides medical oversight for an emergency medical services agency.

(I) The term "medical oversight" means supervision of the provision of medical care by an emergency medical services agency.

(J) The term "registered emergency medical services agency" means—

(i) an emergency medical services agency that is registered pursuant to this subsection; or

(ii) a hospital-based emergency medical services agency that is covered by the registration of the hospital under subsection (g).

(K) The term "registered location" means a location that appears on the certificate of registration issued to an emergency medical services agency under this subsection or subsection (g), which shall be where the agency receives controlled substances from distributors.

(L) The term "specific State authority" means a governmental agency or other such authority, including a regional oversight and coordinating body, that, pursuant to State law or regulation, develops clinical protocols regarding the delivery of emergency medical services in the geographic jurisdiction of such agency or authority within the State that may be adopted by medical directors.

(M) The term "standing order" means a written medical protocol in which a medical director determines in advance the medical criteria that must be met before administering controlled substances to individuals in need of emergency medical services.

(N) The term "verbal order" means an oral directive that is given through any method of communication including by radio or telephone, directly to an emergency medical services professional, to contemporaneously administer a controlled substance to individuals in need of emergency medical services outside the physical presence of the medical director or authorizing medical professional.

(l) Definition. In this section, the phrase "factors as may be relevant to and consistent with the public health and safety" means factors that are relevant to and consistent with the findings contained in section 101 [21 USCS § 801].

[(m)](l) Required training for prescribers.

(1) Training required. As a condition on registration under this section to dispense controlled substances in schedule II, III, IV, or V, the Attorney General shall require any qualified practitioner, beginning with the

first applicable registration for the practitioner, to meet the following:

(A) If the practitioner is a physician (as defined under section 1861(r) of the Social Security Act [21 USCS § 1395x(r)]) and the practitioner meets one or more of the following conditions:

(i) The physician holds a board certification in addiction psychiatry or addiction medicine from the American Board of Medical Specialties.

(ii) The physician holds a board certification from the American Board of Addiction Medicine.

(iii) The physician holds a board certification in addiction medicine from the American Osteopathic Association.

(iv) The physician has, with respect to the treatment and management of patients with opioid or other substance use disorders, or the safe pharmacological management of dental pain and screening, brief intervention, and referral for appropriate treatment of patients with or at risk of developing opioid or other substance use disorders, completed not less than 8 hours of training (through classroom situations, seminars at professional society meetings, electronic communications, or otherwise) that is provided by—

(I) the American Society of Addiction Medicine, the American Academy of Addiction Psychiatry, the American Medical Association, the American Osteopathic Association, the American Dental Association, the American Association of Oral and Maxillofacial Surgeons, the American Psychiatric Association, or any other organization accredited by the Accreditation Council for Continuing Medical Education (ACCME) or the Commission for Continuing Education Provider Recognition (CCEPR);

(II) any organization accredited by a State medical society accreditor that is recognized by the ACCME or the CCEPR;

(III) any organization accredited by the American Osteopathic Association to provide continuing medical education; or

(IV) any organization approved by the Assistant Secretary for Mental Health and Substance Use, the ACCME, or the CCEPR.

(v) The physician graduated in good standing from an accredited school of allopathic medicine, osteopathic medicine, dental surgery, or dental medicine in the United States during the 5-year period immediately preceding the date on which the physician first registers or renews under this section and has successfully completed a comprehensive allopathic or osteopathic medicine curriculum or accredited medical residency or dental surgery or dental medicine curriculum that included not less than 8 hours of training on—

(I) treating and managing patients with opioid or other substance use disorders, including the appropriate clinical use of all drugs approved by the Food and Drug Administration for the treatment of a substance use disorder; or

(II) the safe pharmacological management of dental pain and screening, brief intervention, and referral for appropriate treatment of patients with or at risk of developing opioid and other substance use disorders.

(B) If the practitioner is not a physician (as defined under section 1861(r) of the Social Security Act [21 USCS § 1395x(r)]), the practitioner is legally authorized by the State to dispense controlled substances under schedule II, III, IV, or V and is dispensing such substances within such State in accordance with all applicable State laws, and the practitioner meets one or more of the following conditions:

(i) The practitioner has completed not fewer than 8 hours of training with respect to the treatment and management of patients with opioid or other substance use disorders (through classroom situations, seminars at professional society meetings, electronic communications, or otherwise) provided by the American Society of Addiction Medicine, the American Academy of Addiction Psychiatry, the American Medical Association, the American Osteopathic Association, the American Nurses Credentialing Center, the American Psychiatric Association, the American Association of Nurse Practitioners, the American Academy of Physician Associates, or any other organization approved or accredited by the Assistant Secretary for Mental Health and Substance Use or the Accreditation Council for Continuing Medical Education.

(ii) The practitioner has graduated in good standing from an accredited physician assistant school or accredited school of advanced practice nursing in the United States during the 5-year period immediately preceding the date on which the practitioner first registers or renews under this section and has successfully completed a comprehensive physician assistant or advanced practice nursing curriculum that included not fewer than 8 hours of training on treating and managing patients with opioid and other substance use disorders, including the appropriate clinical use of all drugs approved by the Food and Drug Administration for the treatment of a substance use disorder.

(2) One-time training.

(A) In general. The Attorney General shall not require any qualified practitioner to complete the training described in clause (iv) or (v) of paragraph (1)(A) or clause (i) or (ii) of paragraph (1)(B) more than once.

(B) Notification. Not later than 90 days after the date of the enactment of the Restoring Hope for Mental Health and Well-Being Act of 2022 [enacted Dec. 29, 2022], the Attorney General shall provide to qualified practitioners a single written, electronic notification of the training described in clauses (iv) and (v) of paragraph (1)(A) or clauses (i) and (ii) of paragraph (1)(B).

(3) Rule of construction. Nothing in this subsection shall be construed—

(A) to preclude the use, by a qualified practitioner, of training received pursuant to this subsection to satisfy registration requirements of a State or for some other lawful purpose; or

(B) to preempt any additional requirements by a State related to the dispensing of controlled substances under schedule II, III, IV, or V.

(4) Definitions. In this section:

(A) First applicable registration. The term "first applicable registration" means the first registration or renewal of registration by a qualified practitioner under this section that occurs on or after the date that is 180 days after the date of enactment of the Restoring Hope for Mental Health and Well-Being Act of 2022 [enacted Dec. 29, 2022].

(B) Qualified practitioner. In this subsection, the term "qualified practitioner" means a practitioner who—

(i) is licensed under State law to prescribe controlled substances; and

(ii) is not solely a veterinarian.

(Oct. 27, 1970, P. L. 91-513, Title II, Part C, § 303, 84 Stat. 1253; May 14, 1974, P. L. 93-281, § 3, 88 Stat. 124, Nov. 10, 1978, P. L. 95-633, Title I, § 109, 92 Stat. 3773; Oct. 12, 1984, P. L. 98-473, Title II, Ch V, Part B, § 511, 98 Stat. 2073; Dec. 17, 1993, P. L. 103-200, § 3(c), 107 Stat. 2336; Oct. 17, 2000, P. L. 106-310, Div B, Title XXXV, § 3502(a), 114 Stat. 1222; Nov. 2, 2002, P. L. 107-273, Div B, Title II, Subtitle E, § 2501, 116 Stat. 1803; Aug. 2, 2005, P. L. 109-56, § 1(a), (b), 119 Stat. 591; March 9, 2006, P. L. 109-177, Title VII, Subtitle A, § 712(a)(3), 120 Stat. 263; Dec. 29, 2006, P. L. 109-469, Title XI, § 1102, 120 Stat. 3540; Oct. 15, 2008, P. L. 110-425, § 3(b), 122 Stat. 4824; Nov. 21, 2015, P. L. 114-89, § 3, 129 Stat. 701; April 19, 2016, P. L. 114-145, § 2(a)(1), 130 Stat. 354; July 22, 2016, P. L. 114-198, Title III, § 303(a)(1), (b), 130 Stat. 720; Nov. 17, 2017, P. L. 115-83, § 2, 131 Stat. 1267; Oct. 24, 2018, P.L. 115-271, Title III, Subtitle B, Ch. 1, §§ 3201(a)-(d), 3202(a), 132 Stat. 3943, 3944; Dec. 2, 2022, P.L. 117-215, Title I, §§ 101, 102(a), 103(a), 136 Stat. 2258, 2260, 2261; Dec. 29, 2022, P.L. 117-328, Div FF, Title I, Subtitle B, Ch 6, §§ 1262(a), 1263(a), 136 Stat. 5681, 5683.)

§ 824. Denial, revocation, or suspension of registration

(a) Grounds. A registration pursuant to section 303 [21 USCS § 823] to manufacture, distribute, or dispense a controlled substance or a list I chemical may be suspended or revoked by the Attorney General upon a finding that the registrant—

(1) has materially falsified any application filed pursuant to or required by this title or title II;

(2) has been convicted of a felony under this title or title III or any other law of the United States, or of any State, relating to any substance defined in this title as a controlled substance or a list I chemical;

(3) has had his State license or registration suspended, revoked, or denied by competent State authority and is no longer authorized by State law to engage in the manufacturing, distribution, or dispensing of controlled substances or list I chemicals or has had the suspension, revocation, or denial of his registration recommended by competent State authority;

(4) has committed such acts as would render his registration under section 303 [21 USCS § 823] inconsistent with the public interest as determined under such section; or

(5) has been excluded (or directed to be excluded) from participation in a program pursuant to section 1128(a) of the Social Security Act [42 USCS § 1320a-7(a)]

A registration pursuant to section 303(h) [21 USCS § 823(h)] to dispense a narcotic drug for maintenance treatment or detoxification treatment may be suspended or revoked by the Attorney General upon a finding that the registrant has failed to comply with any standard referred to in section 303(h) [21 USCS § 823(h)].

(b) Limits of revocation or suspension. The Attorney General may limit revocation or suspension of a registration to the particular controlled substance or list I chemical with respect to which grounds for revocation or suspension exist.

(c) Service of show cause order; proceedings.

(1) Before taking action pursuant to this section, or pursuant to a denial of registration under section 303 [21 USCS § 823], the Attorney General shall serve upon the applicant or registrant an order to show cause why registration should not be denied, revoked, or suspended.

(2) An order to show cause under paragraph (1) shall—

(A) contain a statement of the basis for the denial, revocation, or suspension, including specific citations to any laws or regulations alleged to be violated by the applicant or registrant;

(B) direct the applicant or registrant to appear before the Attorney General at a time and place stated in the order, but not less than 30 days after the date of receipt of the order; and

(C) notify the applicant or registrant of the opportunity to submit a corrective action plan on or before the date of appearance.

(3) Upon review of any corrective action plan submitted by an applicant or registrant pursuant to paragraph (2), the Attorney General shall determine whether denial, revocation, or suspension proceedings should be discontinued, or deferred for the purposes of modification, amendment, or clarification to such plan.

(4) Proceedings to deny, revoke, or suspend shall be conducted pursuant to this section in accordance with subchapter II of chapter 5 of title 5, United States Code [5 USCS §§ 551 et seq.]. Such proceedings shall be independent of, and not in lieu of, criminal prosecutions or other proceedings under this title or any other law of the United States.

(5) The requirements of this subsection shall not apply to the issuance of an immediate suspension order under subsection (d).

(d) Suspension of registration in cases of imminent danger.

(1) The Attorney General may, in his discretion, suspend any registration simultaneously with the institution of proceedings under this section, in cases where he finds that there is an imminent danger to the public health or safety. A failure to comply with a standard referred to in section 303(h) [21 USCS § 823(h)] may be treated under this subsection as grounds for immediate suspension of a registration granted under such section. A suspension under this subsection shall continue in effect until the conclusion of such proceedings, including judicial review thereof, unless sooner withdrawn by the Attorney General or dissolved by a court of competent jurisdiction.

(2) In this subsection, the phrase "imminent danger to the public health or safety" means that, due to the failure of the registrant to maintain effective controls against diversion or otherwise comply with the obliga-

tions of a registrant under this title or title III, there is a substantial likelihood of an immediate threat that death, serious bodily harm, or abuse of a controlled substance will occur in the absence of an immediate suspension of the registration.

(e) Suspension and revocation of quotas. The suspension or revocation of a registration under this section shall operate to suspend or revoke any quota applicable under section 306 [21 USCS § 826].

(f) Disposition of controlled substances or list I chemicals. In the event the Attorney General suspends or revokes a registration granted under section 303 [21 USCS § 823], all controlled substances or list I chemicals owned or possessed by the registrant pursuant to such registration at the time of suspension or the effective date of the revocation order, as the case may be, may, in the discretion of the Attorney General, be placed under seal. No disposition may be made of any controlled substances or list I chemicals under seal until the time for taking an appeal has elapsed or until all appeals have been concluded except that a court, upon application therefor, may at any time order the sale of perishable controlled substances or list I chemicals. Any such order shall require the deposit of the proceeds of the sale with the court. Upon a revocation order becoming final, all such controlled substances or list I chemicals (or proceeds of sale deposited in court) shall be forfeited to the United States; and the Attorney General shall dispose of such controlled substances or list I chemicals in accordance with section 511(e) [21 USCS § 881(e)]. All right, title, and interest in such controlled substances or list I chemicals shall vest in the United States upon a revocation order becoming final.

(g) Seizure or placing under seal of controlled substances or list I chemicals. The Attorney General may, in his discretion, seize or place under seal any controlled substances or list I chemicals owned or possessed by a registrant whose registration has expired or who has ceased to practice or do business in the manner contemplated by his registration. Such controlled substances or list I chemicals shall be held for the benefit of the registrant, or his successor in interest. The Attorney General shall notify a registrant, or his successor in interest, who has any controlled substance or list I chemical seized or placed under seal of the procedures to be followed to secure the return of the controlled substance or list I chemical and the conditions under which it will be returned. The Attorney General may not dispose of any controlled substance or list I chemical seized or placed under seal under this subsection until the expiration of one hundred and eighty days from the date such substance or chemical was seized or placed under seal.

(h) Order to prohibit registration based on prior history. The Attorney General may issue an order to prohibit, conditionally or unconditionally, and permanently or for such period as the Attorney General may determine, any person from being registered under this title to manufacture, distribute, or dispense a controlled substance or a list I chemical, if the Attorney General finds that—

(1) such person meets or has met any of the conditions for suspension or revocation of registration under subsection (a); and

(2) such person has a history of prior suspensions or revocations of registration.

(Oct. 27, 1970, P. L. 91-513, Title II, Part C, § 304, 84 Stat. 1255; May 14, 1974, P. L. 93-281, § 4(a), (b), 88 Stat. 125; Oct. 12, 1984, P. L. 98-473, Title II, Ch III, Part B, § 304, Ch V, Part B, §§ 512, 513, 98 Stat. 2050, 2073; Aug. 18, 1987, P. L. 100-93, § 8(j), 101 Stat. 695; Dec. 17, 1993, P. L. 103-200, § 3(d), 107 Stat. 2337; Sept. 13, 1994, P. L. 103-322, Title XXXIII, § 330024(e), 108 Stat. 2151; Oct. 17, 2000, P. L. 106-310, Div B, Title XXXV, § 3502(b), 114 Stat. 1227; April 19, 2016, P. L. 114-145, § 2(a)(2), (b), 130 Stat. 354; Aug. 6, 2021, P.L. 117-36, § 2, 135 Stat. 328; Dec. 2, 2022, P.L. 117-215, Title I, § 103(b)(1)(C), 136 Stat. 2263; Dec. 29, 2022, P.L. 117-328, Div FF, Title I, Subtitle B, Ch 6, § 1262(b)(1), 136 Stat. 5682.)

§ 825. Labeling and packaging

(a) Symbol. It shall be unlawful to distribute a controlled substance in a commercial container unless such container, when and as required by regulations of the Attorney General, bears a label (as defined in section 201(k) of the Federal Food, Drug, and Cosmetic Act [21 USCS § 321(k)]) containing an identifying symbol for such substance in accordance with such regulations. A different symbol shall be required for each schedule of controlled substances.

(b) Unlawful distribution without identifying symbol. It shall be unlawful for the manufacturer of any controlled substance to distribute such substance unless the labeling (as defined in section 201(m) of the Federal Food, Drug, and Cosmetic Act [21 USCS § 321(m)]) of such substance contains, when and as required by regulations of the Attorney General, the identifying symbol required under subsection (a).

(c) Warning on label. The Secretary shall prescribe regulations under section 503(b) of the Federal Food, Drug, and Cosmetic Act [21 USCS § 353(b)] which shall provide that the label of a drug listed in schedule II, III, or IV shall, when dispensed to or for a patient, contain a clear, concise warning that it is a crime to transfer the drug to any person other than the patient.

(d) Containers to be securely sealed. It shall be unlawful to distribute controlled substances in schedule I or II, and narcotic drugs in schedule III or IV, unless the bottle or other container, stopper, covering, or wrapper thereof is securely sealed as required by regulations of the Attorney General.

(e) False labeling of anabolic steroids.

(1) It shall be unlawful to import, export, manufacture, distribute, dispense, or possess with intent to manufacture, distribute, or dispense, an anabolic steroid or product containing an anabolic steroid, unless the steroid or product bears a label clearly identifying an anabolic steroid or product containing an anabolic steroid by the nomenclature used by the International Union of Pure and Applied Chemistry (IUPAC).

(2)(A) A product described in subparagraph (B) is exempt from the International Union of Pure and Applied Chemistry nomenclature requirement of this subsection if such product is labeled in the manner required under the Federal Food, Drug, and Cosmetic Act.

(B) A product is described in this subparagraph if the product—

(i) is the subject of an approved application as described in section 505(b) or (j) of the Federal Food, Drug, and Cosmetic Act [21 USCS § 355(b) or (j)]; or

(ii) is exempt from the provisions of section 505 of such Act [21 USCS § 355] relating to new drugs because—

(I) it is intended solely for investigational use as described in section 505(i) of such Act [21 USCS § 355(i)]; and

(II) such product is being used exclusively for purposes of a clinical trial that is the subject of an effective investigational new drug application.

(Oct. 27, 1970, P. L. 91-513, Title II, Part C, § 305, 84 Stat. 1256; Dec. 18, 2014, P. L. 113-260, § 3(a), 128 Stat. 2931.)

§ 826. Production quotas for controlled substances

(a) Establishment of total annual needs.

(1) The Attorney General shall determine the total quantity and establish production quotas for each basic class of controlled substance in schedules I and II and for ephedrine, pseudoephedrine, and phenylpropanolamine to be manufactured each calendar year to provide for the estimated medical, scientific, research, and industrial needs of the United States, for lawful export requirements, and for the establishment and maintenance of reserve stocks. Except as provided in paragraph (2), production quotas shall be established in terms of quantities of each basic class of controlled substance and not in terms of individual pharmaceutical dosage forms prepared from or containing such a controlled substance.

(2) The Attorney General may, if the Attorney General determines it will assist in avoiding the overproduction, shortages, or diversion of a controlled substance, establish an aggregate or individual production quota under this subsection, or a procurement quota established by the Attorney General by regulation, in terms of pharmaceutical dosage forms prepared from or containing the controlled substance.

(b) Individual production quotas; revised quotas. The Attorney General shall limit or reduce individual manufacturing quotas to the extent necessary to prevent the aggregate of individual quotas from exceeding the amount determined necessary each year by the Attorney General under subsection (a). The quota of each registered manufacturer for each basic class of controlled substance in schedule I or II or for ephedrine, pseudoephedrine, or phenylpropanolamine shall be revised in the same proportion as the limitation or reduction of the aggregate of the quotas. However, if any registrant, before the issuance of a limitation or reduction in quota, has manufactured in excess of his revised quota, the amount of the excess shall be subtracted from his quota for the following year.

(c) Manufacturing quotas for registered manufacturers. On or before December 1 of each year, upon application therefor by a registered manufacturer, the Attorney General shall fix a manufacturing quota for the basic classes of controlled substances in schedules I and II and for ephedrine, pseudoephedrine, and phenylpropanolamine that the manufacturer seeks to produce. The quota shall be subject to the provisions of subsections (a) and (b) of this section. In fixing such quotas, the Attorney General shall determine the manufacturer's estimated disposal, inventory, and other requirements for the calendar year; and, in making his determination, the Attorney General shall consider the manufacturer's current rate of disposal, the trend of the national disposal rate during the preceding calendar year, the manufacturer's production cycle and inventory position, the economic availability of raw materials, yield and stability problems, emergencies such as strikes and fires, and other factors.

(d) Quotas for registrants who have not manufactured controlled substance during one or more preceding years. The Attorney General shall, upon application and subject to the provisions of subsections (a) and (b) of this section, fix a quota for a basic class of controlled substance in schedule I or II for any registrant who has not manufactured that basic class of controlled substance or ephedrine, pseudoephedrine, or phenylpropanolamine during one or more preceding calendar years. In fixing such quota, the Attorney General shall take into account the registrant's reasonably anticipated requirements for the current year; and, in making his determination of such requirements, he shall consider such factors specified in subsection (c) of this section as may be relevant.

(e) Quota increases. At any time during the year any registrant who has applied for or received a manufacturing quota for a basic class of controlled substance in schedule I or II or for ephedrine, pseudoephedrine, or phenylpropanolamine may apply for an increase in that quota to meet his estimated disposal, inventory, and other requirements during the remainder of that year. In passing upon the application the Attorney General shall take into consideration any occurrences since the filing of the registrant's initial quota application that may require an increased manufacturing rate by the registrant during the balance of the year. In passing upon the application the Attorney General may also take into account the amount, if any, by which the determination of the Attorney General under subsection (a) of this section exceeds the aggregate of the quotas of all registrants under this section.

(f) Incidental production exception. Notwithstanding any other provisions of this title, no registration or quota may be required for the manufacture of such quantities of controlled substances in schedules I and II or ephedrine, pseudoephedrine, or phenylpropanolamine as incidentally and necessarily result from the manufacturing process used for the manufacture of a controlled substance or of ephedrine, pseudoephedrine, or phenylpropanolamine with respect to which its manufacturer is duly registered under this title. The Attorney General may, by regulation, prescribe restrictions on the retention and disposal of such incidentally produced substances or chemicals.

(g) Reference to ephedrine, pseudoephedrine,

or phenylpropanolamine. Each reference in this section to ephedrine, pseudoephedrine, or phenylpropanolamine includes each of the salts, optical isomers, and salts of optical isomers of such chemical.

(h) Quotas applicable to drugs in shortage.

(1) Not later than 30 days after the receipt of a request described in paragraph (2), the Attorney General shall—

(A) complete review of such request; and

(B)(i) as necessary to address a shortage of a controlled substance, increase the aggregate and individual production quotas under this section applicable to such controlled substance and any ingredient therein to the level requested; or

(ii) if the Attorney General determines that the level requested is not necessary to address a shortage of a controlled substance, the Attorney General shall provide a written response detailing the basis for the Attorney General's determination. The Secretary shall make the written response provided under subparagraph (B)(ii) available to the public on the Internet Web site of the Food and Drug Administration.

(2) A request is described in this paragraph if—

(A) the request pertains to a controlled substance on the list of drugs in shortage maintained under section 506E of the Federal Food, Drug, and Cosmetic Act [21 USCS § 356e];

(B) the request is submitted by the manufacturer of the controlled substance; and

(C) the controlled substance is in schedule II.

(i)(1)(A) In establishing any quota under this section, or any procurement quota established by the Attorney General by regulation, for fentanyl, oxycodone, hydrocodone, oxymorphone, or hydromorphone (in this subsection referred to as a "covered controlled substance"), the Attorney General shall estimate the amount of diversion of the covered controlled substance that occurs in the United States.

(B) In estimating diversion under this paragraph, the Attorney General—

(i) shall consider information the Attorney General, in consultation with the Secretary of Health and Human Services, determines reliable on rates of overdose deaths and abuse and overall public health impact related to the covered controlled substance in the United States; and

(ii) may take into consideration whatever other sources of information the Attorney General determines reliable.

(C) After estimating the amount of diversion of a covered controlled substance, the Attorney General shall make appropriate quota reductions, as determined by the Attorney General, from the quota the Attorney General would have otherwise established had such diversion not been considered.

(2)(A) For any year for which the approved aggregate production quota for a covered controlled substance is higher than the approved aggregate production quota for the covered controlled substance for the previous year, the Attorney General, in consultation with the Secretary of Health and Human Services, shall include in the final order an explanation of why the public health benefits of increasing the quota clearly outweigh the consequences of having an increased volume of the covered controlled substance available for sale, and potential diversion, in the United States.

(B) Not later than 1 year after the date of enactment of this subsection [enacted Oct. 24, 2018], and every year thereafter, the Attorney General shall submit to the Committee on the Judiciary, the Committee on Health, Education, Labor, and Pensions, and the Committee on Appropriations of the Senate and the Committee on the Judiciary, the Committee on Energy and Commerce, and the Committee on Appropriations of the House of Representatives the following information with regard to each covered controlled substance:

(i) An anonymized count of the total number of manufacturers issued individual manufacturing quotas that year for the covered controlled substance.

(ii) An anonymized count of how many such manufacturers were issued an approved manufacturing quota that was higher than the quota issued to that manufacturer for the covered controlled substance in the previous year.

(3) Not later than 1 year after the date of enactment of this subsection [enacted Oct. 24, 2018], the Attorney General shall submit to Congress a report on how the Attorney General, when fixing and adjusting production and manufacturing quotas under this section for covered controlled substances, will—

(A) take into consideration changes in the accepted medical use of the covered controlled substances; and

(B) work with the Secretary of Health and Human Services on methods to appropriately and anonymously estimate the type and amount of covered controlled substances that are submitted for collection from approved drug collection receptacles, mail-back programs, and take-back events.

(Oct. 27, 1970, P. L. 91-513, Title II, Part C, § 306, 84 Stat. 1257; April 21, 1976, P. L. 94-273, § 3(16), 90 Stat. 377; March 9, 2006, P. L. 109-177, Title VII, Subtitle A, § 713, 120 Stat. 264; July 9, 2012, P. L. 112-144, Title X, § 1005, 126 Stat. 1105; Oct. 24, 2018, P.L. 115-271, Title III, Subtitle B, Ch. 8, § 3282(a), 132 Stat. 3954.)

§ 826a. Attorney General report on drug shortages

Not later than 6 months after the date of the enactment of this Act [enacted July 9, 2012], and annually thereafter, the Attorney General shall submit to the Committee on Energy and Commerce of the House of Representatives and the Committee on the Judiciary of the Senate a report on drug shortages that—

(1) identifies the number of requests received under section 306(h) of the Controlled Substances Act [21 USCS § 826(h)] (as added by section 1005 of this Act), the average review time for such requests, the number of requests granted and denied under such section, and, for each of the requests denied under such section, the basis for such denial;

(2) describes the coordination between the Drug Enforcement Administration and Food and Drug Administration on efforts to prevent or alleviate drug shortages; and

(3) identifies drugs containing a controlled substance subject to section 306 of the Controlled Substances Act [21 USCS § 826] when such a drug is determined by the Secretary to be in shortage.

(July 9, 2012, P. L. 112-144, Title X, § 1006, 126 Stat. 1105.)

§ 827. Records and reports of registrants

(a) Inventory. Except as provided in subsection (c)—

(1) every registrant under this title shall, on the effective date of this section, or as soon thereafter as such registrant first engages in the manufacture, distribution, or dispensing of controlled substances, and every second year thereafter, make a complete and accurate record of all stocks thereof on hand, except that the regulations prescribed under this section shall permit each such biennial inventory (following the initial inventory required by this paragraph) to be prepared on such registrant's regular general physical inventory date (if any) which is nearest to and does not vary by more than six months from the biennial date that would otherwise apply;

(2) on the effective date of each regulation of the Attorney General controlling a substance that immediately prior to such date was not a controlled substance, each registrant under this title manufacturing, distributing, or dispensing such substance shall make a complete and accurate record of all stocks thereof on hand; and

(3) on and after the effective date of this section, every registrant under this title manufacturing, distributing, or dispensing a controlled substance or substances shall maintain, on a current basis, a complete and accurate record of each such substance manufactured, received, sold, delivered, or otherwise disposed of by him, except that this paragraph shall not require the maintenance of a perpetual inventory.

(b) Availability of records. Every inventory or other record required under this section (1) shall be in accordance with, and contain such relevant information as may be required by, regulations of the Attorney General, (2) shall (A) be maintained separately from all other records of the registrant, or (B) alternatively, in the case of nonnarcotic controlled substances, be in such form that information required by the Attorney General is readily retrievable from the ordinary business records of the registrant, and (3) shall be kept and be available, for at least two years, for inspection and copying by officers or employees of the United States authorized by the Attorney General.

(c) Nonapplicability. The foregoing provisions of this section shall not apply—

(1)(A) to the prescribing of controlled substances in schedule II, III, IV, or V by practitioners acting in the lawful course of their professional practice unless such substance is prescribed in the course of maintenance or detoxification treatment of an individual; or

(B) to the administering of a controlled substance in schedule II, III, IV, or V unless the practitioner regularly engages in the dispensing or administering of controlled substances and charges his patients, either separately or together with charges for other professional services, for substances so dispensed or administered or unless such substance is administered in the course of maintenance treatment or detoxification treatment of an individual;

(2)(A) to the use of controlled substances, at establishments registered under this title which keep records with respect to such substances, in research conducted in conformity with an exemption granted under section 505(i) or 512(j) of the Federal Food, Drug, and Cosmetic Act [21 USCS § 355(i) or 360b(j)];

(B) to the use of controlled substances, at establishments registered under this title which keep records with respect to such substances, in preclinical research or in teaching; or

(3) to the extent of any exemption granted to any person, with respect to all or part of such provisions, by the Attorney General by or pursuant to regulation on the basis of a finding that the application of such provisions (or part thereof) to such person is not necessary for carrying out the purposes of this title.

Nothing in the Convention on Psychotropic Substances shall be construed as superseding or otherwise affecting the provisions of paragraph (1)(B), (2), or (3) of this subsection.

(d) Periodic reports to Attorney General.

(1) Every manufacturer registered under section 303 [21 USCS § 823] shall, at such time or times and in such form as the Attorney General may require, make periodic reports to the Attorney General of every sale, delivery, or other disposal by him of any controlled substance, and each distributor shall make such reports with respect to narcotic controlled substances, identifying by the registration number assigned under this title the person or establishment (unless exempt from registration under section 302(d) [21 USCS § 822(d)]) to whom such sale, delivery, or other disposal was made.

(2) Each pharmacy with a modified registration under section 303(g) [21 USCS § 823(g)] that authorizes the dispensing of controlled substances by means of the Internet shall report to the Attorney General the controlled substances it dispenses, in the amount specified, and in such time and manner as the Attorney General by regulation shall require, except that the Attorney General, under this paragraph, may not require any pharmacy to report any information other than the total quantity of each controlled substance that the pharmacy has dispensed each month. For purposes of this paragraph, no reporting shall be required unless the pharmacy has met 1 of the following thresholds in the month for which the reporting is required:

(A) 100 or more prescriptions dispensed.

(B) 5,000 or more dosage units of all controlled substances combined.

(e) Reporting and recordkeeping requirements of drug conventions. In addition to the reporting and recordkeeping requirements under any other provision of this title, each manufacturer registered under section 303 [21 USCS § 823] shall, with respect to narcotic and nonnarcotic controlled substances manufactured by it, make such reports to the Attorney General, and maintain such records, as the Attorney General may require to enable the United States to meet its obligations under articles 19 and 20 of the Single Convention on Narcotic Drugs and article 16 of the Convention on Psychotropic Substances. The Attorney General shall administer the requirements of this subsection in such a manner as to avoid the unnecessary imposition of duplicative requirements under this title on manufacturers subject to the requirements of this subsection.

(f)(1) The Attorney General shall, not less frequently than quarterly, make the following information available to manufacturer and distributor registrants through the Automated Reports and Consolidated Orders System, or any subsequent automated system developed by the Drug Enforcement Administration to monitor selected controlled substances:

(A) The total number of distributor registrants that distribute controlled substances to a pharmacy or practitioner registrant, aggregated by the name and address of each pharmacy and practitioner registrant.

(B) The total quantity and type of opioids distributed, listed by Administration Controlled Substances Code Number, to each pharmacy and practitioner registrant described in subparagraph (A).

(2) The information required to be made available under paragraph (1) shall be made available not later than the 30th day of the first month following the quarter to which the information relates.

(3)(A) All registered manufacturers and distributors shall be responsible for reviewing the information made available by the Attorney General under this subsection.

(B) In determining whether to initiate proceedings under this title against a registered manufacturer or distributor based on the failure of the registrant to maintain effective controls against diversion or otherwise comply with the requirements of this title or the regulations issued thereunder, the Attorney General may take into account that the information made available under this subsection was available to the registrant.

(g) Investigational uses of drugs; procedures. Regulations under sections 505(i) and 512(j) of the Federal Food, Drug, and Cosmetic Act [21 USCS §§ 355(i) and 360b(j)], relating to investigational use of drugs, shall include such procedures as the Secretary, after consultation with the Attorney General, determines are necessary to insure the security and accountability of controlled substances used in research to which such regulations apply.

(h) Change of address. Every registrant under this title shall be required to report any change of professional or business address in such manner as the Attorney General shall by regulation require.

(i) Reporting requirements for GHB. Reporting requirements for GHB. In the case of a drug product containing gamma hydroxybutyric acid for which an application has been approved under section 505 of the Federal Food, Drug, and Cosmetic Act [21 USCS § 355], the Attorney General may, in addition to any other requirements that apply under this section with respect to such a drug product, establish any of the following as reporting requirements:

(1) That every person who is registered as a manufacturer of bulk or dosage form, as a packager, repackager, labeler, relabeler, or distributor shall report acquisition and distribution transactions quarterly, not later than the 15th day of the month succeeding the quarter for which the report is submitted, and annually report end-of-year inventories.

(2) That all annual inventory reports shall be filed no later than January 15 of the year following that for which the report is submitted and include data on the stocks of the drug product, drug substance, bulk drug, and dosage forms on hand as of the close of business December 31, indicating whether materials reported are in storage or in process of manufacturing.

(3) That every person who is registered as a manufacturer of bulk or dosage form shall report all manufacturing transactions both inventory increases, including purchases, transfers, and returns, and reductions from inventory, including sales, transfers, theft, destruction, and seizure, and shall provide data on material manufactured, manufactured from other material, use in manufacturing other material, and use in manufacturing dosage forms.

(4) That all reports under this section must include the registered person's registration number as well as the registration numbers, names, and other identifying information of vendors, suppliers, and customers, sufficient to allow the Attorney General to track the receipt and distribution of the drug.

(5) That each dispensing practitioner shall maintain for each prescription the name of the prescribing practitioner, the prescribing practitioner's Federal and State registration numbers, with the expiration dates of these registrations, verification that the prescribing practitioner possesses the appropriate registration to prescribe this controlled substance, the patient's name and address, the name of the patient's insurance provider and documentation by a medical practitioner licensed and registered to prescribe the drug of the patient's medical need for the drug. Such information shall be available for inspection and copying by the Attorney General.

(6) That section 310(b)(3) [21 USCS § 830(b)(3)] (relating to mail order reporting) applies with respect to gamma hydroxybutyric acid to the same extent and in the same manner as such section applies with respect to the chemicals and drug products specified in subparagraph (A)(i) of such section.

(j) All of the reports required under this section shall be provided in an electronic format.

(Oct. 27, 1970, P. L. 91-513, Title II, Part C, § 307, 84 Stat. 1258; May 14, 1974, P. L. 93-281, § 5, 88 Stat. 125; Nov. 10, 1978, P. L. 95-633, Title I, §§ 104, 110, 92 Stat. 3772, 3773; Oct. 12, 1984, P. L. 98-473, Title II, Ch V, Part B, §§ 514, 515, 98 Stat. 2074; Feb. 18, 2000, P. L. 106-172, § 4, 114 Stat. 9; Oct. 15, 2008, P. L. 110-425, § 3(c), 122 Stat. 4824; Oct. 24, 2018, P.L. 115-271, Title III, Subtitle B, Ch 7, § 3273(a), 132 Stat. 3952; Dec. 2, 2022, P.L. 117-215, Title I, § 103(b)(1)(D), 136 Stat. 2263.)

§ 828. Order forms

(a) Unlawful distribution of controlled sub-

stances. It shall be unlawful for any person to distribute a controlled substance in schedule I or II to another except in pursuance of a written order of the person to whom such substance is distributed, made on a form to be issued by the Attorney General in blank in accordance with subsection (d) and regulations prescribed by him pursuant to this section.

(b) Nonapplicability of provisions. Nothing in subsection (a) shall apply to—

(1) the exportation of such substances from the United States in conformity with title III;

(2) the delivery of such a substance to or by a common or contract carrier for carriage in the lawful and usual course of its business, or to or by a warehouseman for storage in the lawful and usual course of its business; but where such carriage or storage is in connection with the distribution by the owner of the substance to a third person, this paragraph shall not relieve the distributor from compliance with subsection (a); or

(3) the delivery of such a substance for the purpose of disposal by an ultimate user, long-term care facility, or other person acting in accordance with section 302(g) [21 USCS § 822(g)].

(c) Preservation and availability.

(1) Every person who in pursuance of an order required under subsection (a) distributes a controlled substance shall preserve such order for a period of two years, and shall make such order available for inspection and copying by officers and employees of the United States duly authorized for that purpose by the Attorney General, and by officers or employees of States or their political subdivisions who are charged with the enforcement of State or local laws regulating the production, or regulating the distribution or dispensing, of controlled substances and who are authorized under such laws to inspect such orders.

(2) Every person who gives an order required under subsection (a) shall, at or before the time of giving such order, make or cause to be made a duplicate thereof on a form to be issued by the Attorney General in blank in accordance with subsection (d) and regulations prescribed by him pursuant to this section, and shall, if such order is accepted, preserve such duplicate for a period of two years and make it available for inspection and copying by the officers and employees mentioned in paragraph (1) of this subsection.

(d) Issuance.

(1) The Attorney General shall issue forms pursuant to subsections (a) and (c)(2) only to persons validly registered under section 303 [21 USCS § 823] (or exempted from registration under section 302(d) [21 USCS § 822(d)]). Whenever any such form is issued to a person, the Attorney General shall, before delivery thereof, insert therein the name of such person, and it shall be unlawful for any other person (A) to use such form for the purpose of obtaining controlled substances or (B) to furnish such form to any person with intent thereby to procure the distribution of such substances.

(2) The Attorney General may charge reasonable fees for the issuance of such forms in such amounts as he may prescribe for the purpose of covering the cost to the United States of issuing such forms, and other necessary activities in connection therewith.

(e) Unlawful acts. It shall be unlawful for any person to obtain by means of order forms issued under this section controlled substances for any purpose other than their use, distribution, dispensing, or administration in the conduct of a lawful business in such substances or in the course of his professional practice or research.

(Oct. 27, 1970, P. L. 91-513, Title II, Part C, § 308, 84 Stat. 1259; Oct. 12, 2010, P. L. 111-273, § 3(b), 124 Stat. 2860.)

§ 829. Prescriptions

(a) Schedule II substances. Except when dispensed directly by a practitioner, other than a pharmacist, to an ultimate user, no controlled substance in schedule II, which is a prescription drug as determined under the Federal Food, Drug, and Cosmetic Act [21 USCS §§ 301 et seq.], may be dispensed without the written prescription of a practitioner, except that in emergency situations, as prescribed by the Secretary by regulation after consultation with the Attorney General, such drug may be dispensed upon oral prescription in accordance with section 503(b) of that Act [21 USCS § 353(b)]. Prescriptions shall be retained in conformity with the requirements of section 307 of this title [21 USCS § 827]. No prescription for a controlled substance in schedule II may be refilled.

(b) Schedule III and IV substances. Except when dispensed directly by a practitioner, other than a pharmacist, to an ultimate user, no controlled substance in schedule III or IV, which is a prescription drug as determined under the Federal Food, Drug, and Cosmetic Act [21 USCS §§ 301 et seq.], may be dispensed without a written or oral prescription in conformity with section 503(b) of that Act [21 USCS § 353(b)]. Such prescriptions may not be filled or refilled more than six months after the date thereof or be refilled more than five times after the date of the prescription unless renewed by the practitioner.

(c) Schedule V substances. No controlled substance in schedule V which is a drug may be distributed or dispensed other than for a medical purpose.

(d) Non-prescription drugs with abuse potential. Whenever it appears to the Attorney General that a drug not considered to be a prescription drug under the Federal Food, Drug, and Cosmetic Act [21 USCS §§ 301 et seq.] should be so considered because of its abuse potential, he shall so advise the Secretary and furnish to him all available data relevant thereto.

(e) Controlled substances dispensed by means of the Internet.

(1) No controlled substance that is a prescription drug as determined under the Federal Food, Drug, and Cosmetic Act [21 USCS §§ 301 et seq.] may be delivered, distributed, or dispensed by means of the Internet without a valid prescription.

(2) As used in this subsection:

(A) The term "valid prescription" means a prescription that is issued for a legitimate medical purpose in the usual course of professional practice by—

(i) a practitioner who has conducted at least 1 in-person medical evaluation of the patient; or

(ii) a covering practitioner.

(B)(i) The term "in-person medical evaluation" means a medical evaluation that is conducted with the patient in the physical presence of the practitioner, without regard to whether portions of the evaluation are conducted by other health professionals.

(ii) Nothing in clause (i) shall be construed to imply that 1 in-person medical evaluation demonstrates that a prescription has been issued for a legitimate medical purpose within the usual course of professional practice.

(C) The term "covering practitioner" means, with respect to a patient, a practitioner who conducts a medical evaluation (other than an in-person medical evaluation) at the request of a practitioner who—

(i) has conducted at least 1 in-person medical evaluation of the patient or an evaluation of the patient through the practice of telemedicine, within the previous 24 months; and

(ii) is temporarily unavailable to conduct the evaluation of the patient.

(3) Nothing in this subsection shall apply to—

(A) the delivery, distribution, or dispensing of a controlled substance by a practitioner engaged in the practice of telemedicine; or

(B) the dispensing or selling of a controlled substance pursuant to practices as determined by the Attorney General by regulation, which shall be consistent with effective controls against diversion.

(f) Partial fills of schedule II controlled substances.

(1) Partial fills. A prescription for a controlled substance in schedule II may be partially filled if—

(A) it is not prohibited by State law;

(B) the prescription is written and filled in accordance with this title, regulations prescribed by the Attorney General, and State law;

(C) the partial fill is requested by the patient or the practitioner that wrote the prescription; and

(D) the total quantity dispensed in all partial fillings does not exceed the total quantity prescribed.

(2) Remaining portions.

(A) In general. Except as provided in subparagraph (B), remaining portions of a partially filled prescription for a controlled substance in schedule II—

(i) may be filled; and

(ii) shall be filled not later than 30 days after the date on which the prescription is written.

(B) Emergency situations. In emergency situations, as described in subsection (a), the remaining portions of a partially filled prescription for a controlled substance in schedule II—

(i) may be filled; and

(ii) shall be filled not later than 72 hours after the prescription is issued.

(3) Currently lawful partial fills. Notwithstanding paragraph (1) or (2), in any circumstance in which, as of the day before the date of enactment of this subsection [enacted July 22, 2016], a prescription for a controlled substance in schedule II may be lawfully partially filled, the Attorney General may allow such a prescription to be partially filled.

(Oct. 27, 1970, P. L. 91-513, Title II, Part C, § 309, 84 Stat. 1260; Oct. 15, 2008, P. L. 110-425, § 2, 122 Stat. 4820; July 22, 2016, P. L. 114-198, Title VII, § 702(a), 130 Stat. 740.)

§ 829a. Delivery of a controlled substance by a pharmacy to an administering practitioner

(a) In general. Notwithstanding section 102(10) [21 USCS § 802(10)], a pharmacy may deliver a controlled substance to a practitioner in accordance with a prescription that meets the requirements of this title [21 USCS §§ 811 et seq.] and the regulations issued by the Attorney General under this title [21 USCS §§ 811 et seq.] for the purpose of administering the controlled substance by the practitioner if—

(1) the controlled substance is delivered by the pharmacy to the prescribing practitioner or the practitioner administering the controlled substance, as applicable, at the location listed on the practitioner's certificate of registration issued under this title [21 USCS §§ 811 et seq.];

(2) the controlled substance is a narcotic drug in schedule III, IV, or V to be administered for the purpose of maintenance or detoxification treatment and is to be administered by injection or implantation;

(3) the pharmacy and the practitioner are authorized to conduct the activities specified in this section under the law of the State in which such activities take place;

(4) the prescription is not issued to supply any practitioner with a stock of controlled substances for the purpose of general dispensing to patients;

(5) except as provided in subsection (b), the controlled substance is to be administered only to the patient named on the prescription not later than 45 days after the date of receipt of the controlled substance by the practitioner; and

(6) notwithstanding any exceptions under section 307 [21 USCS § 827] the prescribing practitioner, and the practitioner administering the controlled substance, as applicable, maintain complete and accurate records of all controlled substances delivered, received, administered, or otherwise disposed of under this section, including the persons to whom controlled substances were delivered and such other information as may be required by regulations of the Attorney General.

(b) Modification of number of days before which controlled substance shall be administered.

(1) Initial 2-year period. During the 2-year period beginning on the date of enactment of this section [enacted Oct. 24, 2018], the Attorney General, in coordination with the Secretary, may reduce the number of days described in subsection (a)(5) if the Attorney General determines that such reduction will—

(A) reduce the risk of diversion; or

(B) protect the public health.

(2) Modifications after submission of report. After the date on which the report described in section 3204(b) of the SUPPORT for Patients and Communities Act is submitted, the Attorney General, in coordination

with the Secretary, may modify the number of days described in subsection (a)(5).

(3) Minimum number of days. Any modification under this subsection shall be for a period of not less than 7 days.

(Oct. 27, 1970, P. L. 91-513, Title II, Part C, § 309A, as added Oct. 24, 2018, P. L. 115-271, Title III, Subtitle B, Ch. 1, § 3204(a), 132 Stat. 3945; Dec. 2, 2022, P.L. 117-215, Title I, § 103(b)(1)(E), 136 Stat. 2263; Dec. 29, 2022, P.L. 117-328, Div FF, Title I, Subtitle B, Ch 6, §§ 1262(b)(2), 1264, 136 Stat. 5682, 5685.)

§ 830. Regulation of listed chemicals and certain machines

(a) Record of regulated transactions.

(1) Each regulated person who engages in a regulated transaction involving a listed chemical, a tableting machine, or an encapsulating machine shall keep a record of the transaction for two years after the date of the transaction.

(2) A record under this subsection shall be retrievable and shall include the date of the regulated transaction, the identity of each party to the regulated transaction, a statement of the quantity and form of the listed chemical, a description of the tableting machine or encapsulating machine, and a description of the method of transfer. Such record shall be available for inspection and copying by the Attorney General.

(3) It is the duty of each regulated person who engages in a regulated transaction to identify each other party to the transaction. It is the duty of such other party to present proof of identity to the regulated person. The Attorney General shall specify by regulation the types of documents and other evidence that constitute proof of identity for purposes of this paragraph.

(b) Reports to Attorney General.

(1) Each regulated person shall report to the Attorney General, in such form and manner as the Attorney General shall prescribe by regulation—

(A) any regulated transaction involving an extraordinary quantity of a listed chemical, an uncommon method of payment or delivery, or any other circumstance that the regulated person believes may indicate that the listed chemical will be used in violation of this title;

(B) any proposed regulated transaction with a person whose description or other identifying characteristic the Attorney General furnishes in advance to the regulated person;

(C) any unusual or excessive loss or disappearance of a listed chemical under the control of the regulated person; and

(D) any regulated transaction in a tableting machine or an encapsulating machine.

Each report under subparagraph (A) shall be made at the earliest practicable opportunity after the regulated person becomes aware of the circumstance involved. A regulated person may not complete a transaction with a person whose description or identifying characteristic is furnished to the regulated person under subparagraph (B) unless the transaction is approved by the Attorney General. The Attorney General shall make available to regulated persons guidance documents describing transactions and circumstances for which reports are required under subparagraph (A) and subparagraph (C).

(2) A regulated person that manufactures a listed chemical shall report annually to the Attorney General, in such form and manner and containing such specific data as the Attorney General shall prescribe by regulation, information concerning listed chemicals manufactured by the person. The requirement of the preceding sentence shall not apply to the manufacture of a drug product that is exempted under section 102(39)(A)(iv) [21 USCS § 802(39)(A)(iv)].

(3) Mail order reporting.

(A) As used in this paragraph:

(i) The term "drug product" means an active ingredient in dosage form that has been approved or otherwise may be lawfully marketed under the Food, Drug, and Cosmetic Act [21 USCS §§ 301 et seq.] for distribution in the United States.

(ii) The term "valid prescription" means a prescription which is issued for a legitimate medical purpose by an individual practitioner licensed by law to administer and prescribe the drugs concerned and acting in the usual course of the practitioner's professional practice.

(B) Each regulated person who engages in a transaction with a nonregulated person or who engages in an export transaction which—

(i) involves ephedrine, pseudoephedrine, or phenylpropanolamine (including drug products containing these chemicals); and

(ii) uses or attempts to use the Postal Service or any private or commercial carrier;

shall, on a monthly basis, submit a report of each such transaction conducted during the previous month to the Attorney General in such form, containing such data, and at such times as the Attorney General shall establish by regulation.

(C) The data required for such reports shall include—

(i) the name of the purchaser;

(ii) the quantity and form of the ephedrine, pseudoephedrine, or phenylpropanolamine purchased; and

(iii) the address to which such ephedrine, pseudoephedrine, or phenylpropanolamine was sent.

(D) Except as provided in subparagraph (E), the following distributions to a nonregulated person, and the following export transactions, shall not be subject to the reporting requirement in subparagraph (B):

(i) Distributions of sample packages of drug products when such packages contain not more than two solid dosage units or the equivalent of two dosage units in liquid form, not to exceed 10 milliliters of liquid per package, and not more than one package is distributed to an individual or residential address in any 30-day period.

(ii) Distributions of drug products by retail distributors that may not include face-to-face transactions to the extent that such distributions are consistent with the activities authorized for a retail distributor as specified in section 102(49) [21 USCS § 802(49)], except that this clause does not apply to sales of scheduled listed chemical products at retail.

(iii) Distributions of drug products to a resident of a long term care facility (as that term is defined in regulations prescribed by the Attorney General) or distributions of drug products to a long term care facility for dispensing to or for use by a resident of that facility.

(iv) Distributions of drug products pursuant to a valid prescription.

(v) Exports which have been reported to the Attorney General pursuant to section 1004 or 1018 [21 USCS § 954 or 971] or which are subject to a waiver granted under section 1018(f)(2) [21 USCS § 971(f)(2)].

(vi) Any quantity, method, or type of distribution or any quantity, method, or type of distribution of a specific listed chemical (including specific formulations or drug products) or of a group of listed chemicals (including specific formulations or drug products) which the Attorney General has excluded by regulation from such reporting requirement on the basis that such reporting is not necessary for the enforcement of this title or title III.

(E) The Attorney General may revoke any or all of the exemptions listed in subparagraph (D) for an individual regulated person if he finds that drug products distributed by the regulated person are being used in violation of this title or title III. The regulated person shall be notified of the revocation, which will be effective upon receipt by the person of such notice, as provided in section 1018(c)(1) [21 USCS § 971(c)(1)], and shall have the right to an expedited hearing as provided in section 1018(c)(2) [21 USCS § 971(c)(2)].

(c) Confidentiality of information obtained by Attorney General; non-disclosure; exceptions.

(1) Except as provided in paragraph (2), any information obtained by the Attorney General under this section which is exempt from disclosure under section 552(a) of title 5, United States Code, by reason of section 552(b)(4) of such title, is confidential and may not be disclosed to any person.

(2) Information referred to in paragraph (1) may be disclosed only—

(A) to an officer or employee of the United States engaged in carrying out this title, title III, or the customs laws;

(B) when relevant in any investigation or proceeding for the enforcement of this title, title III, or the custom laws;

(C) when necessary to comply with an obligation of the United States under a treaty or other international agreement; or

(D) to a State or local official or employee in conjunction with the enforcement of controlled substances laws or chemical control laws.

(3) The Attorney General shall—

(A) take such action as may be necessary to prevent unauthorized disclosure of information by any person to whom such information is disclosed under paragraph (2); and

(B) issue guidelines that limit, to the maximum extent feasible, the disclosure of proprietary business information, including the names or identities of United States exporters of listed chemicals, to any person to whom such information is disclosed under paragraph (2).

(4) Any person who is aggrieved by a disclosure of information in violation of this section may bring a civil action against the violator for appropriate relief.

(5) Notwithstanding paragraph (4), a civil action may not be brought under such paragraph against investigative or law enforcement personnel of the Drug Enforcement Administration.

(d) Scheduled listed chemicals; restrictions on sales quantity; requirements regarding nonliquid forms. With respect to ephedrine base, pseudoephedrine base, or phenylpropanolamine base in a scheduled listed chemical product—

(1) the quantity of such base sold at retail in such a product by a regulated seller, or a distributor required to submit reports by subsection (b)(3) may not, for any purchaser, exceed a daily amount of 3.6 grams, without regard to the number of transactions; and

(2) such a seller or distributor may not sell such a product in nonliquid form (including gel caps) at retail unless the product is packaged in blister packs, each blister containing not more than 2 dosage units, or where the use of blister packs is technically infeasible, the product is packaged in unit dose packets or pouches.

(e) Scheduled listed chemicals; behind-the-counter access; logbook requirement; training of sales personnel; privacy protections.

(1) Requirements regarding retail transactions.

(A) In general. Each regulated seller shall ensure that, subject to subparagraph (F), sales by such seller of a scheduled listed chemical product at retail are made in accordance with the following:

(i) In offering the product for sale, the seller places the product such that customers do not have direct access to the product before the sale is made (in this paragraph referred to as "behind-the-counter" placement). For purposes of this paragraph, a behind-the-counter placement of a product includes circumstances in which the product is stored in a locked cabinet that is located in an area of the facility involved to which customers do have direct access.

(ii) The seller delivers the product directly into the custody of the purchaser.

(iii) The seller maintains, in accordance with criteria issued by the Attorney General, a written or electronic list of such sales that identifies the products by name, the quantity sold, the names and addresses of purchasers, and the dates and times of the sales (which list is referred to in this subsection as the "logbook"), except that such requirement does not apply to any purchase by an individual of a single sales package if that package contains not more than 60 milligrams of pseudoephedrine.

(iv) In the case of a sale to which the requirement of clause (iii) applies, the seller does not sell such a product unless the sale is made in accordance with the following:

(I) The prospective purchaser—

(aa) presents an identification card that provides a photograph and is issued by a State or the Federal Government, or a document that, with respect to identification, is considered acceptable for purposes of sections 274a.2(b)(1)(v)(A) and 274a.2(b)(1)(v)(B) of title 8, Code of Federal Regulations (as in effect on or after March 9, 2006); and

(bb) signs the written logbook and enters in the logbook his or her name, address, and the date and time of the sale, or for transactions involving an electronic logbook, the purchaser provides a signature using one of the following means:

(AA) Signing a device presented by the seller that captures signatures in an electronic format. Such device shall display the notice described in clause (v). Any device used shall preserve each signature in a manner that clearly links that signature to the other electronically-captured logbook information relating to the prospective purchaser providing that signature.

(BB) Signing a bound paper book. Such bound paper book shall include, for such purchaser, either (aaa) a printed sticker affixed to the bound paper book at the time of sale which either displays the name of each product sold, the quantity sold, the name and address of the purchaser, and the date and time of the sale, or a unique identifier which can be linked to that electronic information, or (bbb) a unique identifier which can be linked to that information and which is written into the book by the seller at the time of sale. The purchaser shall sign adjacent to the printed sticker or written unique identifier related to that sale. Such bound paper book shall display the notice described in clause (v).

(CC) Signing a printed document that includes, for such purchaser, the name of each product sold, the quantity sold, the name and address of the purchaser, and the date and time of the sale. Such document shall be printed by the seller at the time of the sale. Such document shall contain a clearly identified signature line for a purchaser to sign. Such printed document shall display the notice described in clause (v). Each signed document shall be inserted into a binder or other secure means of document storage immediately after the purchaser signs the document.

(II) The seller enters in the logbook the name of the product and the quantity sold. Such information may be captured through electronic means, including through electronic data capture through bar code reader or similar technology.

(III) The logbook maintained by the seller includes the prospective purchaser's name, address, and the date and time of the sale, as follows:

(aa) If the purchaser enters the information, the seller must determine that the name entered in the logbook corresponds to the name provided on such identification and that the date and time entered are correct.

(bb) If the seller enters the information, the prospective purchaser must verify that the information is correct.

(cc) Such information may be captured through electronic means, including through electronic data capture through bar code reader or similar technology.

(v) The written or electronic logbook includes, in accordance with criteria of the Attorney General, a notice to purchasers that entering false statements or misrepresentations in the logbook, or supplying false information or identification that results in the entry of false statements or misrepresentations, may subject the purchasers to criminal penalties under section 1001 of title 18, United States Code [18 USCS § 1001], which notice specifies the maximum fine and term of imprisonment under such section.

(vi) Regardless of whether the logbook entry is written or electronic, the seller maintains each entry in the logbook for not fewer than 2 years after the date on which the entry is made.

(vii) In the case of individuals who are responsible for delivering such products into the custody of purchasers or who deal directly with purchasers by obtaining payments for the products, the seller has submitted to the Attorney General a self-certification that all such individuals have, in accordance with criteria under subparagraph (B)(ii), undergone training provided by the seller to ensure that the individuals understand the requirements that apply under this subsection and subsection (d).

(viii) The seller maintains a copy of such certification and records demonstrating that individuals referred to in clause (vii) have undergone the training.

(ix) If the seller is a mobile retail vendor:

(I) The seller complies with clause (i) by placing the product in a locked cabinet.

(II) The seller does not sell more than 7.5 grams of ephedrine base, pseudoephedrine base, or phenylpropanolamine base in such products per customer during a 30-day period.

(B) Additional provisions regarding certifications and training.

(i) In general. A regulated seller may not sell any scheduled listed chemical product at retail unless the seller has submitted to the Attorney General the self-certification referred to in subparagraph (A)(vii). The certification is not effective for purposes of the preceding sentence unless, in addition to provisions regarding the training of individuals referred to in such subparagraph, the certification includes a statement that the seller understands each of the requirements that apply under this paragraph and under subsection (d) and agrees to comply with the requirements.

(ii) Issuance of criteria; self-certification. The Attorney General shall by regulation establish criteria for certifications under this paragraph. The criteria shall—

(I) provide that the certifications are self-certifications provided through the program under clause (iii);

(II) provide that a separate certification is required for each place of business at which a regulated seller sells scheduled listed chemical products at retail; and

(III) include criteria for training under subparagraph (A)(vii).

(iii) Program for regulated sellers. The Attorney General shall establish a program regarding such certifications and training in accordance with the following:

(I) The program shall be carried out through an Internet site of the Department of Justice and such other means as the Attorney General determines to be appropriate.

(II) The program shall inform regulated sellers that section 1001 of title 18, United States Code [18 USCS § 1001], applies to such certifications.

(III) The program shall make available to such sellers an explanation of the criteria under clause (ii).

(IV) The program shall be designed to permit the submission of the certifications through such Internet site.

(V) The program shall be designed to automatically provide the explanation referred to in subclause (III), and an acknowledgement that the Department has received a certification, without requiring direct interactions of regulated sellers with staff of the Department (other than the provision of technical assistance, as appropriate).

(iv) Availability of certification to State and local officials. Promptly after receiving a certification under subparagraph (A)(vii), the Attorney General shall make available a copy of the certification to the appropriate State and local officials.

(v) Publication of list of self-certified persons. The Attorney General shall develop and make available a list of all persons who are currently self-certified in accordance with this section. This list shall be made publicly available on the website of the Drug Enforcement Administration in an electronically downloadable format.

(C) Privacy protections. In order to protect the privacy of individuals who purchase scheduled listed chemical products, the Attorney General shall by regulation establish restrictions on disclosure of information in logbooks under subparagraph (A)(iii). Such regulations shall—

(i) provide for the disclosure of the information as appropriate to the Attorney General and to State and local law enforcement agencies; and

(ii) prohibit accessing, using, or sharing information in the logbooks for any purpose other than to ensure compliance with this title or to facilitate a product recall to protect public health and safety.

(D) False statements or misrepresentations by purchasers. For purposes of section 1001 of title 18, United States Code [18 USCS § 1001], entering information in the logbook under subparagraph (A)(iii) shall be considered a matter within the jurisdiction of the executive, legislative, or judicial branch of the Government of the United States.

(E) Good faith protection. A regulated seller who in good faith releases information in a logbook under subparagraph (A)(iii) to Federal, State, or local law enforcement authorities is immune from civil liability for such release unless the release constitutes gross negligence or intentional, wanton, or willful misconduct.

(F) Inapplicability of requirements to certain sales. Subparagraph (A) does not apply to the sale at retail of a scheduled listed chemical product if a report on the sales transaction is required to be submitted to the Attorney General under subsection (b)(3).

(G) Certain measures regarding theft and diversion. A regulated seller may take reasonable measures to guard against employing individuals who may present a risk with respect to the theft and diversion of scheduled listed chemical products, which may include, notwithstanding State law, asking applicants for employment whether they have been convicted of any crime involving or related to such products or controlled substances.

(2) Mail-order reporting; verification of identity of purchaser; 30-day restriction on quantities for individual purchasers. Each regulated person who makes a sale at retail of a scheduled listed chemical product and is required under subsection (b)(3) to submit a report of the sales transaction to the Attorney General is subject to the following:

(A) The person shall, prior to shipping the product, confirm the identity of the purchaser in accordance with procedures established by the Attorney General. The Attorney General shall by regulation establish such procedures.

(B) The person may not sell more than 7.5 grams of ephedrine base, pseudoephedrine base, or phenylpropanolamine base in such products per customer during a 30-day period.

(C) Each regulated person who makes a sale at retail of a scheduled listed chemical product and is required under subsection (b)(3) to submit a report of the sales transaction to the Attorney General may not sell any scheduled listed chemical product at retail unless such regulated person has submitted to the Attorney General a self-certification including a statement that the seller understands each of the requirements that apply under this paragraph and under subsection (d) and agrees to comply with the requirements. The Attorney General shall by regulation establish criteria for certifications of mail-order distributors that are consistent with the criteria established for the certifications of regulated sellers under paragraph (1)(B).

(3) Exemptions for certain products. Upon the application of a manufacturer of a scheduled listed chemical product, the Attorney General may by regulation provide that the product is exempt from the provisions of subsection (d) and paragraphs (1) and (2) of this subsection if the Attorney General determines that the product cannot be used in the illicit manufacture of methamphetamine.

(Oct. 27, 1970, P. L. 91-513, Title II, Part C, § 310, as added Nov. 10, 1978, P. L. 95-633, Title II, § 202(a), 92 Stat. 3774; Nov. 18, 1988, P. L. 100-690, Title VI, Subtitle A, § 6052(a), 102 Stat. 4312; Dec. 17, 1993, P. L. 103-200, §§ 2(c), 10, 107 Stat. 2336, 2341; Oct. 3, 1996, P. L. 104-237, Title II, § 208, Title IV, § 402, 110 Stat. 3104, 3111; Oct. 17, 2000, P. L. 106-310, Div B, Title XXXVI, Subtitle B, § 3652, 114 Stat. 1239; March 9, 2006, P. L. 109-177, Title VII, Subtitle A, §§ 711(a)(2)(B), (b)(1), (c)(1), (2), (d), 716(b)(2), 120 Stat. 257, 261, 267; Oct. 14, 2008, P. L. 110-415, § 2, 122 Stat. 4349; Oct. 12, 2010, P. L. 111-268, §§ 2, 3, 124 Stat. 2847.)

§ 831. Additional requirements relating to online pharmacies and telemedicine

(a) In general. An online pharmacy shall display in a visible and clear manner on its homepage a statement that it complies with the requirements of this section with respect to the delivery or sale or offer for sale of controlled substances and shall at all times display on the homepage of its Internet site a declaration of compliance in accordance with this section.

(b) Licensure. Each online pharmacy shall comply with the requirements of State law concerning the licensure of pharmacies in each State from which it, and in each State to which it, delivers, distributes, or dispenses or offers to deliver, distribute, or dispense controlled substances by means of the Internet, pursuant to applicable licensure requirements, as determined by each such State.

(c) Internet pharmacy site disclosure information. Each online pharmacy shall post in a visible and clear manner on the homepage of each Internet site it operates, or on a page directly linked thereto in which the hyperlink is also visible and clear on the homepage, the following information for each pharmacy that delivers, distributes, or dispenses controlled substances pursuant to orders made on, through, or on behalf of, that website:

(1) The name and address of the pharmacy as it appears on the pharmacy's Drug Enforcement Administration certificate of registration.

(2) The pharmacy's telephone number and email address.

(3) The name, professional degree, and States of licensure of the pharmacist-in-charge, and a telephone number at which the pharmacist-in-charge can be contacted.

(4) A list of the States in which the pharmacy is licensed to dispense controlled substances.

(5) A certification that the pharmacy is registered under this part to deliver, distribute, or dispense by means of the Internet controlled substances.

(6) The name, address, telephone number, professional degree, and States of licensure of any practitioner who has a contractual relationship to provide medical evaluations or issue prescriptions for controlled substances, through referrals from the website or at the request of the owner or operator of the website, or any employee or agent thereof.

(7) The following statement, unless revised by the Attorney General by regulation: This online pharmacy will only dispense a controlled substance to a person who has a valid prescription issued for a legitimate medical purpose based upon a medical relationship with a prescribing practitioner. This includes at least one prior in-person medical evaluation or medical evaluation via telemedicine in accordance with applicable requirements of section 309 [21 USCS § 829]..

(d) Notification.

(1) In general. Thirty days prior to offering a controlled substance for sale, delivery, distribution, or dispensing, the online pharmacy shall notify the Attorney General, in such form and manner as the Attorney General shall determine, and the State boards of pharmacy in any States in which the online pharmacy offers to sell, deliver, distribute, or dispense controlled substances.

(2) Contents. The notification required under paragraph (1) shall include—

(A) the information required to be posted on the online pharmacy's Internet site under subsection (c) and shall notify the Attorney General and the applicable State boards of pharmacy, under penalty of perjury, that the information disclosed on its Internet site under subsection (c) is true and accurate;

(B) the online pharmacy's Internet site address and a certification that the online pharmacy shall notify the Attorney General of any change in the address at least 30 days in advance; and

(C) the Drug Enforcement Administration registration numbers of any pharmacies and practitioners referred to in subsection (c), as applicable.

(3) Existing online pharmacies. An online pharmacy that is already operational as of the effective date of this section, shall notify the Attorney General and applicable State boards of pharmacy in accordance with this subsection not later than 30 days after such date.

(e) Declaration of compliance. On and after the date on which it makes the notification under subsection (d), each online pharmacy shall display on the homepage of its Internet site, in such form as the Attorney General shall by regulation require, a declaration that it has made such notification to the Attorney General.

(f) Reports. Any statement, declaration, notification, or disclosure required under this section shall be considered a report required to be kept under this part.

(g) Notice and designations concerning Indian tribes.

(1) In general. For purposes of sections 102(52) and 512(c)(6)(B) [21 USCS §§ 802(52) and 882(c)(6)(B)], the Secretary shall notify the Attorney General, at such times and in such manner as the Secretary and the Attorney General determine appropriate, of the Indian tribes or tribal organizations with which the Secretary has contracted or compacted under the Indian Self-Determination and Education Assistance Act [25 USCS §§ 450 et seq.] for the tribes or tribal organizations to provide pharmacy services.

(2) Designations.

(A) In general. The Secretary may designate a practitioner described in subparagraph (B) as an Internet Eligible Controlled Substances Provider. Such designations shall be made only in cases where the Secretary has found that there is a legitimate need for the practitioner to be so designated because the population served by the practitioner is in a sufficiently remote location that access to medical services is limited.

(B) Practitioners. A practitioner described in this subparagraph is a practitioner who is an employee or contractor of the Indian Health Service, or is working for an Indian tribe or tribal organization under its contract or compact under the Indian Self-Determination and Education Assistance Act [25 USCS §§ 450 et seq.] with the Indian Health Service.

(h) Special registration for telemedicine.

(1) In general. The Attorney General may issue to a practitioner a special registration to engage in the practice of telemedicine for purposes of section 102(54)(E) [21 USCS § 802(54)(E)] if the practitioner, upon application for such special registration—

(A) demonstrates a legitimate need for the special registration; and

(B) is registered under section 303(g) [21 USCS § 823(g)] in the State in which the patient will be located when receiving the telemedicine treatment, unless the practitioner—

(i) is exempted from such registration in all States under section 302(d) [21 USCS § 822(d)]; or

(ii) is an employee or contractor of the Department of Veterans Affairs who is acting in the scope of such employment or contract and is registered under section 303(g) [21 USCS § 823(g)] in any State or is utilizing the registration of a hospital or clinic operated by the Department of Veterans Affairs registered under section 303(g) [21 USCS § 823(g)].

(2) Regulations. Not later than 1 year after the date of enactment of the SUPPORT for Patients and Communities Act [enacted Oct. 24, 2018], in consultation with the Secretary, the Attorney General shall promulgate final regulations specifying—

(A) the limited circumstances in which a special registration under this subsection may be issued; and

(B) the procedure for obtaining a special registration under this subsection.

(3) Denials. Proceedings to deny an application for registration under this subsection shall be conducted in accordance with section 304(c) [21 USCS § 824(c)].

(i) Reporting of telemedicine by VHA during medical emergency situations.

(1) In general. Any practitioner issuing a prescription for a controlled substance under the authorization to conduct telemedicine during a medical emergency situation described in section 102(54)(F) [21 USCS § 802(54)(F)] shall report to the Secretary of Veterans Affairs the authorization of that emergency prescription, in accordance with such requirements as the Secretary of Veterans Affairs shall, by regulation, establish.

(2) To Attorney General. Not later than 30 days after the date that a prescription described in subparagraph (A) is issued, the Secretary of Veterans Affairs shall report to the Attorney General the authorization of that emergency prescription.

(j) Clarification concerning prescription transfers. Any transfer between pharmacies of information relating to a prescription for a controlled substance shall meet the applicable requirements under regulations promulgated by the Attorney General under this Act.

(Oct. 27, 1970, P. L. 91-513, Title II, Part C, § 311, as added Oct. 15, 2008, P. L. 110-425, § 3(d)(1), 122 Stat. 4825; Oct. 24, 2018, P.L. 115-271, Title III, Subtitle B, Ch 4, § 3232, 132 Stat. 3950; Dec. 2, 2022, P.L. 117-215, Title I, § 103(b)(1)(F), 136 Stat. 2263.)

§ 832. Suspicious orders

(a) Reporting. Each registrant shall—

(1) design and operate a system to identify suspicious orders for the registrant;

(2) ensure that the system designed and operated under paragraph (1) by the registrant complies with applicable Federal and State privacy laws; and

(3) upon discovering a suspicious order or series of orders, notify the Administrator of the Drug Enforcement Administration and the Special Agent in Charge of the Division Office of the Drug Enforcement Administration for the area in which the registrant is located or conducts business.

(b) Suspicious order database.

(1) In general. Not later than 1 year after the date of enactment of this section [enacted Oct. 24, 2018], the Attorney General shall establish a centralized database for collecting reports of suspicious orders.

(2) Satisfaction of reporting requirements. If a registrant reports a suspicious order to the centralized database established under paragraph (1), the registrant shall be considered to have complied with the requirement under subsection (a)(3) to notify the Administrator of the Drug Enforcement Administration and the Special Agent in Charge of the Division Office of the Drug Enforcement Administration for the area in which the registrant is located or conducts business.

(c) Sharing information with the States.

(1) In general. The Attorney General shall prepare and make available information regarding suspicious orders in a State, including information in the database established under subsection (b)(1), to the point of contact for purposes of administrative, civil, and criminal oversight relating to the diversion of controlled substances for the State, as designated by the Governor or chief executive officer of the State.

(2) Timing. The Attorney General shall provide information in accordance with paragraph (1) within a reasonable period of time after obtaining the information.

(3) Coordination. In establishing the process for the provision of information under this subsection, the Attorney General shall coordinate with States to ensure that the Attorney General has access to information, as permitted under State law, possessed by the States relating to prescriptions for controlled substances that will assist in enforcing Federal law.

(Oct. 27, 1970, P. L. 91-513, Title II, Part C, § 312, as added Oct. 24, 2018, P. L. 115-271, Title III, Subtitle B, Ch. 9, § 3292(b), 132 Stat. 3956.)

OFFENSES AND PENALTIES

§ 841. Prohibited acts A

(a) Unlawful acts. Except as authorized by this title, it shall be unlawful for any person knowingly or intentionally—

(1) to manufacture, distribute, or dispense, or possess with intent to manufacture, distribute, or dispense, a controlled substance; or

(2) to create, distribute, or dispense, or possess with intent to distribute or dispense, a counterfeit substance.

(b) Penalties. Except as otherwise provided in section 409, 418, 419, or 420 [21 USCS § 849, 859, 860, or 861], any person who violates subsection (a) of this section shall be sentenced as follows:

(1)(A) In the case of a violation of subsection (a) of this section involving—

(i) 1 kilogram or more of a mixture or substance containing a detectable amount of heroin;

(ii) 5 kilograms or more of a mixture or substance containing a detectable amount of—

(I) coca leaves, except coca leaves and extracts of coca leaves from which cocaine, ecgonine, and derivatives of ecgonine or their salts have been removed;

(II) cocaine, its salts, optical and geometric isomers, and salts of isomers;

(III) ecgonine, its derivatives, their salts, isomers, and salts of isomers; or

(IV) any compound, mixture, or preparation which contains any quantity of any of the substances referred to in subclauses (I) through (III);

(iii) 280 grams or more of a mixture or substance described in clause (ii) which contains cocaine base;

(iv) 100 grams or more of phencyclidine (PCP) or 1 kilogram or more of a mixture or substance containing a detectable amount of phencyclidine (PCP);

(v) 10 grams or more of a mixture or substance containing a detectable amount of lysergic acid diethylamide (LSD);

(vi) 400 grams or more of a mixture or substance containing a detectable amount of N-phenyl-N- [1-(2-phenylethyl)-4-piperidinyl] propanamide or 100 grams or more of a mixture or substance containing a detectable amount of any analogue of N-phenyl-N- [1-(2-phenylethyl)-4-piperidinyl] propanamide;

(vii) 1000 kilograms or more of a mixture or substance containing a detectable amount of marihuana, or 1,000 or more marihuana plants regardless of weight; or

(viii) 50 grams or more of methamphetamine, its salts, isomers, and salts of its isomers or 500 grams or more of a mixture or substance containing a detectable amount of methamphetamine, its salts, isomers, or salts of its isomers;

such person shall be sentenced to a term of imprisonment which may not be less than 10 years or more than life and if death or serious bodily injury results from the use of such substance shall be not less than 20 years or more than life, a fine not to exceed the greater of that authorized in accordance with the provisions of title 18, United States Code, or $10,000,000 if the defendant is an individual or $50,000,000 if the defendant is other than an individual, or both. If any person commits such a violation after a prior conviction for a serious drug felony or serious violent felony has become final, such person shall be sentenced to a term of imprisonment of not less than 15 years and not more than life imprisonment and if death or serious bodily injury results from the use of such substance shall be sentenced to life imprisonment, a fine not to exceed the greater of twice that authorized in accordance with the provisions of title 18, United States Code, or $20,000,000 if the defendant is an individual or $75,000,000 if the defendant is other than an individual, or both. If any person commits a violation of this subparagraph or of section 409, 418, 419, or 420 [21 USCS § 849, 859, 860, or 861] after 2 or more prior convictions for a serious drug felony or serious violent felony have become final, such person shall be sentenced to a term of imprisonment of not less than 25 years and fined in accordance with the preceding sentence. Notwithstanding section 3583 of title 18, any sentence under this subparagraph shall, in the absence of such a prior conviction, impose a term of supervised release of at least 5 years in addition to such term of imprisonment and shall, if there was such a prior conviction, impose a term of supervised release of at least 10 years in addition to such term of imprisonment. Notwithstanding any other provision of law, the court shall not place on probation or suspend the sentence of any person sentenced under this subparagraph. No person sentenced under this subparagraph shall be eligible for parole during the term of imprisonment imposed therein.

(B) In the case of a violation of subsection (a) of this section involving—

(i) 100 grams or more of a mixture or substance containing a detectable amount of heroin;

(ii) 500 grams or more of a mixture or substance containing a detectable amount of—

(I) coca leaves, except coca leaves and extracts of coca leaves from which cocaine, ecgonine, and derivatives of ecgonine or their salts have been removed;

(II) cocaine, its salts, optical and geometric isomers, and salts of isomers;

(III) ecgonine, its derivatives, their salts, isomers, and salts of isomers; or

(IV) any compound, mixture, or preparation which contains any quantity of any of the substances referred to in subclauses (I) through (III);

(iii) 28 grams or more of a mixture or substance described in clause (ii) which contains cocaine base;

(iv) 10 grams or more of phencyclidine (PCP) or 100 grams or more of a mixture or substance containing a detectable amount of phencyclidine (PCP);

(v) 1 gram or more of a mixture or substance containing a detectable amount of lysergic acid diethylamide (LSD);

(vi) 40 grams or more of a mixture or substance containing a detectable amount of N-phenyl-N- [1-(2-phenylethyl)-4-piperidinyl] propanamide or 10 grams or more of a mixture or substance containing a detectable amount of any analogue of N-phenyl-N- [1-(2-phenylethyl)-4-piperidinyl] propanamide;

(vii) 100 kilograms or more of a mixture or substance containing a detectable amount of marihuana, or 100 or more marihuana plants regardless of weight; or

(viii) 5 grams or more of methamphetamine, its salts, isomers, and salts of its isomers or 50 grams or more of a mixture or substance containing a detectable amount of methamphetamine, its salts, isomers, or salts of its isomers;

such person shall be sentenced to a term of imprisonment which may not be less than 5 years and not more than 40 years and if death or serious bodily injury results from the use of such substance shall be not less than 20 years or more than life, a fine not to exceed the greater of that authorized in accordance with the provisions of title 18, United States Code, or $5,000,000 if the defendant is an individual or $25,000,000 if the defendant is other than an individual, or both. If any person commits such a violation after a prior conviction for a serious drug felony or serious violent felony has become final, such person shall be sentenced to a term of imprisonment which may not be less than 10 years and not more than life imprisonment and if death or serious bodily injury results from the use of such substance shall be sentenced to life imprisonment, a fine not to exceed the greater of twice that authorized in accordance with the provisions of title 18, United States Code, or $8,000,000 if the defendant is an individual or $50,000,000 if the defendant is other than an individual, or both. Notwithstanding section 3583 of title 18, any sentence imposed under this subparagraph shall, in the absence of such a prior conviction, include a term of supervised release of at least 4 years in addition to such term of imprisonment and shall, if there was such a prior conviction, include a term of supervised release of at least 8 years in addition to such term of imprisonment. Notwithstanding any other provision of law, the court shall not place on probation or suspend the sentence of any person sentenced under this subparagraph. No person sentenced under this subparagraph shall be eligible for parole during the term of imprisonment imposed therein.

(C) In the case of a controlled substance in schedule I or II, gamma hydroxybutyric acid (including when scheduled as an approved drug product for purposes of section 3(a)(1)(B) of the Hillory J. Farias and Samantha Reid Date-Rape Drug Prohibition Act of 1999 [21 USCS § 812 note]), or 1 gram of flunitrazepam, except as provided in subparagraphs (A), (B), and (D), such person shall be sentenced to a term of imprisonment of not more than 20 years and if death or serious bodily injury results from the use of such substance shall be sentenced to a term of imprisonment of not less than twenty years or more than life, a fine not to exceed the greater of that authorized in accordance with the provisions of title 18, United States Code, or $1,000,000 if the defendant is an individual or $5,000,000 if the defendant is other than an individual, or both. If any person commits such a violation after a prior conviction for a felony drug offense has become final, such person shall be sentenced to a term of imprisonment of not more than 30 years and if death or serious bodily injury results from the use of such substance shall be sentenced to life imprisonment, a fine not to exceed the greater of twice that authorized in accordance with the provisions of title 18, United States Code, or $2,000,000 if the defendant is an individual or $10,000,000 if the defendant is other than an individual, or both. Notwithstanding section 3583 of title 18, any sentence imposing a term of imprisonment under this paragraph shall, in the absence of such a prior conviction, impose a term of supervised release of at least 3 years in addition to such term of imprisonment and shall, if there was such a prior conviction, impose a term of supervised release of at least 6 years in addition to such term of imprisonment. Notwithstanding any other provision of law, the court shall not place on probation or suspend the sentence of any person sentenced under the provisions of this subparagraph which provide for a mandatory term of imprisonment if death or serious bodily injury results, nor shall a person so sentenced be eligible for parole during the term of such a sentence.

(D) In the case of less than 50 kilograms of marihuana, except in the case of 50 or more marihuana plants regardless of weight, 10 kilograms of hashish, or one kilogram of hashish oil, such person shall, except as provided in paragraphs (4) and (5) of this subsection, be sentenced to a term of imprisonment of not more than 5 years, a fine not to exceed the greater of that authorized in accordance with the provisions of title 18, United States Code, or $250,000 if the defendant is an individual or $1,000,000 if the defendant is other than an individual, or both. If any person commits such a violation after a prior conviction for a felony drug offense has become final, such person shall be sentenced to a term of imprisonment of not more than 10 years, a fine not to exceed the greater of twice that authorized in accordance with the provisions of title 18, United States Code, or $500,000 if the defendant is an individual or $2,000,000 if the defendant is other than an individual, or both. Notwithstanding section 3583 of title 18, any sentence imposing a term of imprisonment under this paragraph shall, in the absence of such a prior conviction, impose a term of supervised release of at least 2 years in addition to such term of imprisonment and shall, if there was such a prior conviction, impose a special parole term of at least 4 years in addition to such term of imprisonment.

(E)(i) Except as provided in subparagraphs (C) and (D), in the case of any controlled substance in schedule III, such person shall be sentenced to a term of imprisonment of not more than 10 years and if death or serious bodily injury results from the use of such substance shall be sentenced to a term of imprisonment of not more than 15 years, a fine not to exceed the greater of that authorized in accordance with the provisions of title 18, United States Code, or $500,000 if the defendant is an individual or $2,500,000 if the defendant is other than an individual, or both.

(ii) If any person commits such a violation after a prior conviction for a felony drug offense has become final, such person shall be sentenced to a term of imprisonment of not more than 20 years and if death or serious bodily injury results from the use of such substance shall be sentenced to a term of imprisonment of not more than 30 years, a fine not to exceed the greater of twice that authorized in accordance with the provisions of title 18, United States Code, or $1,000,000 if the defendant is an individual or $5,000,000 if the defendant is other than an individual, or both.

(iii) Any sentence imposing a term of imprisonment under this subparagraph shall, in the absence of such a prior conviction, impose a term of supervised release of at least 2 years in addition to such term of imprisonment and shall, if there was such a prior conviction, impose a term of supervised release of at least 4 years in addition to such term of imprisonment.

(2) In the case of a controlled substance in schedule IV, such person shall be sentenced to a term of imprisonment of not more than 5 years, a fine not to exceed the greater of that authorized in accordance with the provisions of title 18, United States Code, or $250,000 if the defendant is an individual or $1,000,000 if the defendant is other than an individual, or both. If any person commits such a violation after a prior conviction for a felony drug offense has become final, such person shall be sentenced to a term of imprisonment of not more than 10 years, a fine not to exceed the greater of twice that authorized in accordance with the provisions of title 18, United States Code, or $500,000 if the defendant is an individual or $2,000,000 if the defendant is other than an individual, or both. Any sentence imposing a term of imprisonment under this paragraph shall, in the absence of such a prior conviction, impose a term of supervised release of at least one year in addition to such term of imprisonment and shall, if there was such a prior conviction, impose a special parole term of at least 2 years in addition to such term of imprisonment.

(3) In the case of a controlled substance in schedule V, such person shall be sentenced to a term of imprisonment of not more than one year, a fine not to exceed the greater of that authorized in accordance with the provisions of title 18, United States Code, or $100,000 if the defendant is an individual or $250,000 if the defendant is other than an individual, or both. If any person commits such a violation after a prior conviction for a felony drug offense has become final, such person shall be sentenced to a term of imprisonment of not more than 4 years, a fine not to exceed the greater of twice that authorized in accordance with the provisions of title 18, United States Code, or $200,000 if the defendant is an individual or $500,000 if the defendant is other than an individual, or both. Any sentence imposing a term of imprisonment under this paragraph may, if there was a prior conviction, impose a term of supervised release of not more than 1 year, in addition to such term of imprisonment.

(4) Notwithstanding paragraph (1)(D) of this subsection, any person who violates subsection (a) of this section by distributing a small amount of marihuana for no remuneration shall be treated as provided in section 404 [21 USCS § 844] and section 3607 of title 18, United States Code.

(5) Any person who violates subsection (a) of this section by cultivating or manufacturing a controlled substance on Federal property shall be imprisoned as provided in this subsection and shall be fined any amount not to exceed—

(A) the amount authorized in accordance with this section;

(B) the amount authorized in accordance with the provisions of title 18, United States Code;

(C) $500,000 if the defendant is an individual; or

(D) $1,000,000 if the defendant is other than an individual; or both.

(6) Any person who violates subsection (a), or attempts to do so, and knowingly or intentionally uses a poison, chemical, or other hazardous substance on Federal land, and, by such use—

(A) creates a serious hazard to humans, wildlife, or domestic animals,

(B) degrades or harms the environment or natural resources, or

(C) pollutes an aquifer, spring, stream, river, or body of water,

shall be fined in accordance with title 18, United States Code, or imprisoned not more than five years, or both.

(7) Penalties for distribution.

(A) In general. Whoever, with intent to commit a crime of violence, as defined in section 16 of title 18, United States Code (including rape), against an individual, violates subsection (a) by distributing a controlled substance or controlled substance analogue to that individual without that individual's knowledge, shall be imprisoned not more than 20 years and fined in accordance with title 18, United States Code.

(B) Definition. For purposes of this paragraph, the term "without that individual's knowledge" means that the individual is unaware that a substance with the ability to alter that individual's ability to appraise conduct or to decline participation in or communicate unwillingness to participate in conduct is administered to the individual.

(c) Offenses involving listed chemicals. Any person who knowingly or intentionally—

(1) possesses a listed chemical with intent to manufacture a controlled substance except as authorized by this title;

(2) possesses or distributes a listed chemical knowing, or having reasonable cause to believe, that the listed chemical will be used to manufacture a controlled substance except as authorized by this title; or

(3) with the intent of causing the evasion of the recordkeeping or reporting requirements of section 310 [21 USCS § 830], or the regulations issued under that section, receives or distributes a reportable amount of any listed chemical in units small enough so that the making of records or filing of reports under that section is not required;

shall be fined in accordance with title 18, United States Code, or imprisoned not more than 20 years in the case of a violation of paragraph (1) or (2) involving a list I chemical or not more than 10 years in the case of a violation of this subsection other than a violation of paragraph (1) or (2) involving a list I chemical, or both.

(d) Boobytraps on Federal property; penalties; "boobytrap" defined.

(1) Any person who assembles, maintains, places, or causes to be placed a boobytrap on Federal property where a controlled substance is being manufactured, distributed, or dispensed shall be sentenced to a term of imprisonment for not more than 10 years or fined under title 18, United States Code, or both.

(2) If any person commits such a violation after 1 or more prior convictions for an offense punishable under this subsection, such person shall be sentenced to a term of imprisonment of not more than 20 years or fined under title 18, United States Code, or both.

(3) For the purposes of this subsection, the term "boobytrap" means any concealed or camouflaged device designed to cause bodily injury when triggered by any action of any unsuspecting person making contact with the device. Such term includes guns, ammunition, or explosive devices attached to trip wires or other triggering mechanisms, sharpened stakes, and lines or wires with hooks attached.

(e) Ten-year injunction as additional penalty. In addition to any other applicable penalty, any person convicted of a felony violation of this section relating to the receipt, distribution, manufacture, exportation, or importation of a listed chemical may be enjoined from engaging in any transaction involving a listed chemical for not more than ten years.

(f) Wrongful distribution or possession of listed chemicals.

(1) Whoever knowingly distributes a listed chemical in violation of this title (other than in violation of a recordkeeping or reporting requirement of section 310 [21 USCS § 830]) shall, except to the extent that paragraph (12), (13), or (14) of section 402(a) [21 USCS § 842(a)] applies, be fined under title 18, United States Code, or imprisoned not more than 5 years, or both.

(2) Whoever possesses any listed chemical, with knowledge that the recordkeeping or reporting requirements of section 310 [21 USCS § 830] have not been adhered to, if, after such knowledge is acquired, such person does not take immediate steps to remedy the violation shall be fined under title 18, United States Code, or imprisoned not more than one year, or both.

(g) Internet sales of date rape drugs.

(1) Whoever knowingly uses the Internet to distribute a date rape drug to any person, knowing or with reasonable cause to believe that—

(A) the drug would be used in the commission of criminal sexual conduct; or

(B) the person is not an authorized purchaser;

shall be fined under this title or imprisoned not more than 20 years, or both.

(2) As used in this subsection:

(A) The term "date rape drug" means—

(i) gamma hydroxybutyric acid (GHB) or any controlled substance analogue of GHB, including gamma butyrolactone (GBL) or 1,4-butanediol;

(ii) ketamine;

(iii) flunitrazepam; or

(iv) any substance which the Attorney General designates, pursuant to the rulemaking procedures prescribed by section 553 of title 5, United States Code [5 USCS § 553], to be used in committing rape or sexual assault.

The Attorney General is authorized to remove any substance from the list of date rape drugs pursuant to the same rulemaking authority.

(B) The term "authorized purchaser" means any of the following persons, provided such person has acquired the controlled substance in accordance with this Act:

(i) A person with a valid prescription that is issued for a legitimate medical purpose in the usual course of professional practice that is based upon a qualifying medical relationship by a practitioner registered by the Attorney General. A "qualifying medical relationship" means a medical relationship that exists when the practitioner has conducted at least 1 medical evaluation with the authorized purchaser in the physical presence of the practitioner, without regard to whether portions of the evaluation are conducted by other heath [health] professionals. The preceding sentence shall not be construed to imply that 1 medical evaluation demonstrates that a prescription has been issued for a legitimate medical purpose within the usual course of professional practice.

(ii) Any practitioner or other registrant who is otherwise authorized by their registration to dispense, procure, purchase, manufacture, transfer, distribute, import, or export the substance under this Act.

(iii) A person or entity providing documentation that establishes the name, address, and business of the person or entity and which provides a legitimate purpose for using any "date rape drug" for which a prescription is not required.

(3) The Attorney General is authorized to promulgate regulations for record-keeping and reporting by persons handling 1,4-butanediol in order to implement and enforce the provisions of this section. Any record or report required by such regulations shall be considered a record or report required under this Act.

(h) Offenses involving dispensing of controlled substances by means of the Internet.

(1) In general. It shall be unlawful for any person to knowingly or intentionally—

(A) deliver, distribute, or dispense a controlled substance by means of the Internet, except as authorized by this title; or

(B) aid or abet (as such terms are used in section 2 of title 18, United States Code) any activity described in subparagraph (A) that is not authorized by this title.

(2) Examples. Examples of activities that violate paragraph (1) include, but are not limited to, knowingly or intentionally—

(A) delivering, distributing, or dispensing a controlled substance by means of the Internet by an online pharmacy that is not validly registered with a modification authorizing such activity as required by section 303(g) [21 USCS § 823(g)] (unless exempt from such registration);

(B) writing a prescription for a controlled substance for the purpose of delivery, distribution, or dispensation by means of the Internet in violation of section 309(e) [21 USCS § 829(e)];

(C) serving as an agent, intermediary, or other entity that causes the Internet to be used to bring together a buyer and seller to engage in the dispensing of a controlled substance in a manner not authorized by sections [section] 303(g) or 309(e) [21 USCS § 823(g) or 829(e)];

(D) offering to fill a prescription for a controlled substance based solely on a consumer's completion of an online medical questionnaire; and

(E) making a material false, fictitious, or fraudulent statement or representation in a notification or declaration under subsection (d) or (e), respectively, of section 311 [21 USCS § 831].

(3) Inapplicability.

(A) This subsection does not apply to—

(i) the delivery, distribution, or dispensation of controlled substances by nonpractitioners to the extent authorized by their registration under this title;

(ii) the placement on the Internet of material that merely advocates the use of a controlled substance or includes pricing information without attempting to propose or facilitate an actual transaction involving a controlled substance; or

(iii) except as provided in subparagraph (B), any activity that is limited to—

(I) the provision of a telecommunications service, or of an Internet access service or Internet information location tool (as those terms are defined in section 231 of the Communications Act of 1934 [47 USCS § 231]); or

(II) the transmission, storage, retrieval, hosting, formatting, or translation (or any combination thereof) of a communication, without selection or alteration of the content of the communication, except that deletion of a particular communication or material made by another person in a manner consistent with section 230(c) of the Communications Act of 1934 [47 USCS § 230(c)] shall not constitute such selection or alteration of the content of the communication.

(B) The exceptions under subclauses (I) and (II) of subparagraph (A)(iii) shall not apply to a person acting in concert with a person who violates paragraph (1).

(4) Knowing or intentional violation. Any person who knowingly or intentionally violates this subsection shall be sentenced in accordance with subsection (b).

(Oct. 27, 1970, P. L. 91-513, Title II, Part D, § 401, 84 Stat. 1260; Nov. 10, 1978, P. L. 95-633, Title II, § 201, 92 Stat. 3774; Sept. 26, 1980, P. L. 96-359, § 8(c), 94 Stat. 1194; Oct. 12, 1984, P. L. 98-473, Title II, Ch II, § 224(a)(2), Ch V, Subch, Part A, Subpart, §§ 502, 503(b)(1)(2), 98 Stat. 2030, 2068, 2070; Oct. 27, 1986, P. L. 99-570, Title I, Subtitle A, §§ 1002, 1003(a), 1004(a) Subtitle C, § 1103, Title XV, § 15005, 100 Stat. 3207-2, 3207-5, 3207-6, 3207-11, 3207-192; Nov. 18, 1988, P. L. 100-690, Title VI, Subtitle A, § 6055, Subtitle H, §§ 6254(h), 6265(h), Subtitle N, §§ 6452(a), 6470(g), (h), 6479, 102 Stat. 4318, 4366, 4367, 4371, 4378, 4379, 4381; Nov. 29, 1990, P. L. 101-647, Title X, § 1002(e), Title XII, § 1202, Title XXXV, § 3599K, 104 Stat. 4828, 4830, 4932; Sept. 13, 1994, P. L. 103-322, Title IX, Subtitle A, § 90105(a), (c), Title XVIII, Subtitle B, 180201(b)(2)(A), 108 Stat. 1987, 1988, 2047; Oct. 3, 1996, P. L. 104-237, Title II, § 206(a), Title III, § 302(a), 110 Stat. 3103, 3105; Oct. 13, 1996, P. L. 104-305, § 2(a), (b)(1), 110 Stat. 3807; Oct. 21, 1998, P. L. 105-277, Div E, § 2(a), 112 Stat. 2681-759; Feb. 18, 2000, P. L. 106-172, §§ 3(b)(1), 5(b), 9, 114 Stat. 9, 10, 13; Nov. 2, 2002, P. L. 107-273, Div B, Title III, § 3005(a), Title IV, § 4002(d)(2)(A), 116 Stat. 1805, 1809; March 9, 2006, P. L. 109-177, Title VII, Subtitle A, § 711(f)(1)(B), Subtitle C, § 732, 120 Stat. 262, 270; July 27, 2006, P. L. 109-248, Title II, § 201, 120 Stat. 611; Oct. 15, 2008, P. L. 110-425, § 3(e), (f), 122 Stat. 4828; Aug. 3, 2010, P. L. 111-220, §§ 2(a), 4(a), 124 Stat. 2372; Dec. 21, 2018, P.L. 115-391, Title IV, § 401(a)(2), 132 Stat. 5220; Dec. 2, 2022, P.L. 117-215, Title I, § 103(b)(1)(G), 136 Stat. 2263.)

§ 842. Prohibited acts B

(a) Unlawful acts. It shall be unlawful for any person—

(1) who is subject to the requirements of part C [21 USCS §§ 821 et seq.] to distribute or dispense a controlled substance in violation of section 309 [21 USCS § 829];

(2) who is a registrant to distribute or dispense a controlled substance not authorized by his registration to another registrant or other authorized person or to manufacture a controlled substance not authorized by his registration;

(3) who is a registrant to distribute a controlled substance in violation of section 305 of this title [21 USCS § 825];

(4) to remove, alter, or obliterate a symbol or label required by section 305 of this title [21 USCS § 825];

(5) to refuse or negligently fail to make, keep, or furnish any record, report, notification, declaration, order or order form, statement, invoice, or information required under this title or title III;

(6) to refuse any entry into any premises or inspection authorized by this title or title III;

(7) to remove, break, injure, or deface a seal placed upon controlled substances pursuant to section 304(f) or 511 [21 USCS § 824(f) or 881] or to remove or dispose of substances so placed under seal;

(8) to use, to his own advantage, or to reveal, other than to duly authorized officers or employees of the United States, or to the courts when relevant in any judicial proceeding under this title or title III, any information acquired in the course of an inspection authorized by this title concerning any method or process which as a trade secret is entitled to protection, or to use to his own advantage or reveal (other than as authorized by section 310) any information that is confidential under such section;

(9) who is a regulated person to engage in a regulated transaction without obtaining the identification required by [section] 310(a)(3) [21 USCS § 830(a)(3)];

(10) negligently to fail to keep a record or make a report under section 310 [21 USCS § 830] or negligently to fail to self-certify as required under section 310 [21 USCS § 830];

(11) to distribute a laboratory supply to a person who uses, or attempts to use, that laboratory supply to manufacture a controlled substance or a listed chemical, in violation of this title or title III, with reckless disregard for the illegal uses to which such a laboratory supply will be put;

(12) who is a regulated seller, or a distributor required to submit reports under subsection (b)(3) of section 310 [21 USCS § 830]—

(A) to sell at retail a scheduled listed chemical product in violation of paragraph (1) of subsection (d) of such section, knowing at the time of the transaction involved (independent of consulting the logbook under subsection (e)(1)(A)(iii) of such section) that the transaction is a violation; or

(B) to knowingly or recklessly sell at retail such a product in violation of paragraph (2) of such subsection (d);

(13) who is a regulated seller to knowingly or recklessly sell at retail a scheduled listed chemical product in violation of subsection (e) of such section;

(14) who is a regulated seller or an employee or agent of such seller to disclose, in violation of regulations under subparagraph (C) of section 310(e)(1) [21 USCS § 830(e)(1)], information in logbooks under subparagraph (A)(iii) of such section, or to refuse to provide such a logbook to Federal, State, or local law enforcement authorities;

(15) to distribute a scheduled listed chemical product to a regulated seller, or to a regulated person referred to in section 310(b)(3)(B) [21 USCS § 830(b)(3)(B)], unless such regulated seller or regulated person is, at the time of such distribution, currently registered with the Drug Enforcement Administration, or on the list of persons referred to under section 310(e)(1)(B)(v) [21 USCS § 830(e)(1)(B)(v)];

(16) to violate subsection (e) of section 825 of this title [21 USCS § 825]; or

(17) in the case of a registered manufacturer or distributor of opioids, to fail to review the most recent information, directly related to the customers of the manufacturer or distributor, made available by the Attorney General in accordance with section 307(f) [21 USCS § 827(f)].

As used in paragraph (11), the term "laboratory supply" means a listed chemical or any chemical, substance, or item on a special surveillance list published by the Attorney General, which contains chemicals, products, materials, or equipment used in the manufacture of controlled substances and listed chemicals. For purposes of paragraph (11), there is a rebuttable presumption of reckless disregard at trial if the Attorney General notifies a firm in writing that a laboratory supply sold by the firm, or any other person or firm, has been used by a customer of the notified firm, or distributed further by that customer, for the unlawful production of controlled substances or listed chemicals a firm distributes and 2 weeks or more after the notification the notified firm distributes a laboratory supply to the customer. For purposes of paragraph (15), if the distributor is temporarily unable to access the list of persons referred to under section 310(e)(1)(B)(v) [21 USCS § 830(e)(1)(B)(v)], the distributor may rely on a written, faxed, or electronic copy of a certificate of self-certification submitted by the regulated seller or regulated person, provided the distributor confirms within 7 business days of the distribution that such regulated seller or regulated person is on the list referred to under section 310(e)(1)(B)(v) [21 USCS § 830(e)(1)(B)(v)].

(b) Manufacture. It shall be unlawful for any person who is a registrant to manufacture a controlled substance in schedule I or II, or ephedrine, pseudoephedrine, or phenylpropanolamine or any of the salts, optical isomers, or salts of optical isomers of such chemical, which is—

(1) not expressly authorized by his registration and by a quota assigned to him pursuant to section 306 [21 USCS § 826]; or

(2) in excess of a quota assigned to him pursuant to section 306 [21 USCS § 826].

(c) Penalties.

(1)(A) Except as provided in subparagraph (B), (C), or (D) of this paragraph and paragraph (2), any person who violates this section shall, with respect to any such violation, be subject to a civil penalty of not more than $25,000. The district courts of the United States (or, where there is no such court in the case of any territory or possession of the United States, then the court in such territory or possession having the jurisdiction of a district court of the United States in cases arising under the Constitution and laws of the United States) shall have jurisdiction in accordance with section 1355 of title 28 of the United States Code [28 USCS § 1355] to enforce this paragraph.

(B)(i) Except as provided in clause (ii), in the case of a violation of paragraph (5), (10), or (17) of subsection (a), the civil penalty shall not exceed $10,000.

(ii) In the case of a violation described in clause (i) committed by a registered manufacturer or distributor of opioids and related to the reporting of suspicious orders for opioids, failing to maintain effective controls against diversion of opioids, or failing to review the most recent information made available by the Attorney General in accordance with section 307(f) [21 USCS § 827(f)], the penalty shall not exceed $100,000.

(C) In the case of a violation of paragraph (16) of subsection (a) of this section by an importer, exporter, manufacturer, or distributor (other than as provided in subparagraph (D)), up to $500,000 per violation. For purposes of this subparagraph, a violation is defined as each instance of importation, exportation, manufacturing, distribution, or possession with intent to manufacture or distribute, in violation of paragraph (16) of subsection (a).

(D) In the case of a distribution, dispensing, or possession with intent to distribute or dispense in violation of paragraph (16) of subsection (a) of this section at the retail level, up to $1000 per violation. For purposes of this paragraph, the term "at the retail level" refers to products sold, or held for sale, directly to the consumer for personal use. Each package, container or other separate unit containing an anabolic steroid that is distributed, dispensed, or possessed with intent to distribute or dispense at the retail level in violation of such paragraph (16) of subsection (a) shall be considered a separate violation.

(2)(A) If a violation of this section is prosecuted by an information or indictment which alleges that the violation was committed knowingly and the trier of fact specifically finds that the violation was so committed, such person shall, except as otherwise provided in subparagraph (B) or (D) of this paragraph, be sentenced to imprisonment of not more than one year or a fine under title 18, United States Code, or both.

(B) If a violation referred to in subparagraph (A) was committed after one or more prior convictions of the offender for an offense punishable under this paragraph (2), or for a crime under any other provision of this title or title III or other law of the United States relating to narcotic drugs, marihuana, or depressant or stimulant substances, have become final, such person shall be sentenced to a term of imprisonment of not more than 2 years, a fine under title 18, United States Code, or both.

(C) In addition to the penalties set forth elsewhere in this title or title III, any business that violates paragraph (11) of subsection (a) shall, with respect to the first such violation, be subject to a civil penalty of not more than $250,000, but shall not be subject to criminal penalties under this section, and shall, for any succeeding violation, be subject to a civil fine of not more than $250,000 or double the last previously imposed penalty, whichever is greater.

(D) In the case of a violation described in subparagraph (A) that was a violation of paragraph (5), (10), or (17) of subsection (a) committed by a registered manufacturer or distributor of opioids that relates to the reporting of suspicious orders for opioids, failing to maintain effective controls against diversion of opioids, or failing to review the most recent information made available by the Attorney General in accordance with section 307(f) [21 USCS § 827(f)], the criminal fine under title 18, United States Code, shall not exceed $500,000.

(3) Except under the conditions specified in paragraph (2) of this subsection, a violation of this section does not constitute a crime, and a judgment for the United States and imposition of a civil penalty pursuant to paragraph (1) shall not give rise to any disability or legal disadvantage based on conviction for a criminal offense.

(4)(A) If a regulated seller, or a distributor required to submit reports under section 310(b)(3) [21 USCS § 830(b)(3)], violates paragraph (12) of subsection (a) of this section, or if a regulated seller violates paragraph (13) of such subsection, the Attorney General may by order prohibit such seller or distributor (as the case may be) from selling any scheduled listed chemical product. Any sale of such a product in violation of such an order is subject to the same penalties as apply under paragraph (2).

(B) An order under subparagraph (A) may be imposed only through the same procedures as apply under section 304(c) [21 USCS § 824(c)] for an order to show cause.

(Oct. 27, 1970, P. L. 91-513, Title II, Part D, § 402, 84 Stat. 1262; Nov. 10, 1978, P. L. 95-633, Title II, § 202(b)(1), (2), 92 Stat. 3776; Nov. 18, 1988, P. L. 100-690, Title VI, Subtitle A, § 6056, 102 Stat. 4318; Oct. 3, 1996, P. L. 104-237, Title II, § 205, 110 Stat. 3103; Oct. 21, 1998, P. L. 105-277, Div A, § 101(b) [Title I, § 117], 112 Stat. 2681-68; Nov. 2, 2002, P. L. 107-273, Div B, Title IV, § 4002(b)(16), (d)(2)(B), 116 Stat. 1808, 1809; March 9, 2006, P. L. 109-177, Title VII, Subtitle A, §§ 711(f)(1)(A), (2), 714, 120 Stat. 262, 263, 264; Oct. 12, 2010, P. L. 111-268, §§ 4, 5, 124 Stat. 2847; Dec. 18, 2014, P. L. 113-260, § 3(c), 128 Stat. 2931; Oct. 24, 2018, P.L. 115-271, Title III, Subtitle B, Ch 7, § 3273(c), 132 Stat. 3953.)

§ 843. Prohibited acts C

(a) Unlawful acts. It shall be unlawful for any person knowingly or intentionally—

(1) who is a registrant to distribute a controlled substance classified in schedule I or II, in the course of his legitimate business, except pursuant to an order or an order form as required by section 308 of this title [21 USCS § 828];

(2) to use in the course of the manufacture, distribution, or dispensing of a controlled substance, or to use for the purpose of acquiring or obtaining a controlled substance, a registration number which is fictitious, revoked, suspended, expired, or issued to another person;

(3) to acquire or obtain possession of a controlled substance by misrepresentation, fraud, forgery, deception, or subterfuge;

(4) (A) to furnish false or fraudulent material information in, or omit any material information from, any application, report, record, or other document required to be made, kept, or filed under this title or title III, or (B) to present false or fraudulent identification where the person is receiving or purchasing or a listed chemical and the person is required to present identification under section 310(a) [21 USCS § 830(a)];

(5) to make, distribute, or possess any punch, die, plate, stone, or other thing designed to print, imprint, or reproduce the trademark, trade name, or other identifying mark, imprint, or device of another or any likeness of any of the foregoing upon any drug or container or labeling thereof so as to render such drug a counterfeit substance; or

(6) to possess any three-neck round-bottom flask, tableting machine, encapsulating machine, or gelatin capsule, or any equipment, chemical, product, or material which may be used to manufacture a controlled substance or listed chemical, knowing, intending, or having reasonable cause to believe, that it will be used to manufacture a controlled substance or listed chemical in violation of this title or title II;

(7) to manufacture, distribute, export, or import any three-neck round-bottom flask, tableting machine, encapsulating machine, or gelatin capsule, or any equipment, chemical, product, or material which may be used to manufacture a controlled substance or listed chemical, knowing, intending, or having reasonable cause to believe, that it will be used to manufacture a controlled substance or listed chemical in violation of this title or title III or, in the case of an exportation, in violation of this title or title III or of the laws of the country to which it is exported;

(8) to create a chemical mixture for the purpose of evading a requirement of section 310 [21 USCS § 830] or to receive a chemical mixture created for that purpose; or

(9) to distribute, import, or export a list I chemical without the registration required by this title or title II.

(b) Communication facility. It shall be unlawful for any person knowingly or intentionally to use any communication facility in committing or in causing or facilitating the commission of any act or acts constituting a felony under any provision of this title or title III. Each separate use of a communication facility shall be a separate offense under this subsection. For purposes of this subsection, the term "communication facility" means any and all public and private instrumentalities used or useful in the transmission of writing, signs, signals, pictures, or sounds of all kinds and includes mail, telephone, wire, radio, and all other means of communication.

(c) Advertising.

(1) It shall be unlawful for any person to place in any newspaper, magazine, handbill, or other publications, any written advertisement knowing that it has the purpose of seeking or offering illegally to receive, buy, or distribute a Schedule [schedule] I controlled substance. As used in this section the term "advertisement" includes, in addition to its ordinary meaning, such advertisements as those for a catalog of Schedule [schedule] I controlled substances and any similar written advertisement that has the purpose of seeking or offering illegally to receive, buy, or distribute a Schedule [schedule] I controlled substance. The term "advertisement" does not include material which merely advocates the use of a similar material, which advocates a position or practice, and does not attempt to propose or facilitate an actual transaction in a Schedule [schedule] I controlled substance.

(2)(A) It shall be unlawful for any person to knowingly or intentionally use the Internet, or cause the Internet to be used, to advertise the sale of, or to offer to sell, distribute, or dispense, a controlled substance where such sale, distribution, or dispensing is not authorized by this title or by the Controlled Substances Import and Export Act.

(B) Examples of activities that violate subparagraph (A) include, but are not limited to, knowingly or intentionally causing the placement on the Internet of an advertisement that refers to or directs prospective buyers to Internet sellers of controlled substances who are not registered with a modification under section 303(g) [21 USCS § 823(g)].

(C) Subparagraph (A) does not apply to material that either—

(i) merely advertises the distribution of controlled substances by nonpractitioners to the extent authorized by their registration under this title; or

(ii) merely advocates the use of a controlled substance or includes pricing information without attempting to facilitate an actual transaction involving a controlled substance.

(d) Penalties.

(1) Except as provided in paragraph (2), any person who violates this section shall be sentenced to a term of imprisonment of not more than 4 years, a fine under title 18, United States Code, or both; except that if any person commits such a violation after one or more prior convictions of him for violation of this section, or for a felony under any other provision of this title or title III or other law of the United States relating to narcotic drugs, marihuana, or depressant or stimulant substances, have become final, such person shall be sentenced to a term of imprisonment of not more than 8 years, a fine under title 18, United States Code, or both.

(2) Any person who, with the intent to manufacture or to facilitate the manufacture of methamphetamine, violates paragraph (6) or (7) of subsection (a), shall be sentenced to a term of imprisonment of not more than 10 years, a fine under title 18, United States Code, or both; except that if any person commits such a violation after one or more prior convictions of that person—

(A) for a violation of paragraph (6) or (7) of subsection (a);

(B) for a felony under any other provision of this subchapter or subchapter II of this chapter [this title or title III]; or

(C) under any other law of the United States or any State relating to controlled substances or listed chemicals,

has become final, such person shall be sentenced to a term of imprisonment of not more than 20 years, a fine under title 18, United States Code, or both.

(e) Additional penalties. In addition to any other applicable penalty, any person convicted of a felony violation of this section relating to the receipt, distribution, manufacture, exportation, or importation of a listed chemical may be enjoined from engaging in any transaction involving a listed chemical for not more than ten years.

(f) Injunctions.

(1) In addition to any penalty provided in this section, the Attorney General is authorized to commence a civil action for appropriate declaratory or injunctive relief relating to violations of this section, section 402 [21 USCS § 842], or [section] 416 [21 USCS § 856].

(2) Any action under this subsection may be brought in the district court of the United States for the district in which the defendant is located or resides or is doing business.

(3) Any order or judgment issued by the court pursuant to this subsection shall be tailored to restrain violations of this section or section 402 [21 USCS § 842].

(4) The court shall proceed as soon as practicable to the hearing and determination of such an action. An action under this subsection is governed by the Federal Rules of Civil Procedure except that, if an indictment has been returned against the respondent, discovery is governed by the Federal Rules of Criminal Procedure.

(Oct. 27, 1970, P. L. 91-513, Title II, Part D, § 403, 84 Stat. 1263; Nov. 10, 1978, P. L. 95-633, Title II, § 202(b)(3), 92 Stat. 3776; Oct. 12, 1984, P. L. 98-473, Title II, Ch V, Part B, § 516, 98 Stat. 2074; Oct. 27, 1986, P. L. 99-570, Title I, Subtitle Q, § 1866(a), 100 Stat. 3207-54; Nov. 18, 1988, P. L. 100-690, Title VI, Subtitle A, § 6057, 102 Stat. 4319; Dec. 17, 1993, P. L. 103-200, § 3(g), 107 Stat. 2337; Sept. 13, 1994, P. L. 103-322, Title IX, Subtitle A, § 90106, 108 Stat. 1988; Oct. 3, 1996, P. L. 104-237, Title II, §§ 203(a), 206(b), 110 Stat. 3102, 3103; Nov. 2, 2002, P. L. 107-273, Div B, Title IV, § 4002(d)(2)(C), 116 Stat. 1810; April 30, 2003, P. L. 108-21, Title VI, § 608(d), 117 Stat. 691; Oct. 15, 2008, P. L. 110-425, § 3(g), 122 Stat. 4830; Dec. 2, 2022, P.L. 117-215, Title I, § 103(b)(1)(H), 136 Stat. 2263.)

§ 844. Penalty for simple possession

(a) Unlawful acts; penalties. It shall be unlawful for any person knowingly or intentionally to possess a controlled substance unless such substance was obtained directly, or pursuant to a valid prescription or order, from a practitioner, while acting in the course of his professional practice, or except as otherwise authorized by this title or title III. It shall be unlawful for any person knowingly or intentionally to possess any list I chemical obtained pursuant to or under authority of a registration issued to that person under section 303 of this title [21 USCS § 823] or section 1008 of title III [21 USCS § 958] if that registration has been revoked or suspended, if that registration has expired, or if the registrant has ceased to do business in the manner contemplated by his registration. It shall be unlawful for any person to knowingly or intentionally purchase at retail during a 30 day period more than 9 grams of ephedrine base, pseudoephedrine base, or phenylpropanolamine base in a scheduled listed chemical product, except that, of such 9 grams, not more than 7.5 grams may be imported by means of shipping through any private or commercial carrier or the Postal Service. Any person who violates this subsection may be sentenced to a term of imprisonment of not more than 1 year, and shall be fined a minimum of $1,000, or both, except that if he commits such offense after a prior conviction under this title or title III, or a prior conviction for any drug, narcotic, or chemical offense chargeable under the law of any State, has become final, he shall be sentenced to a term of imprisonment for not less than 15 days but not more than 2 years, and shall be fined a minimum of $2,500, except, further, that if he commits such offense after two or more prior convictions under this title or title III, or two or more prior convictions for any drug, narcotic, or chemical offense chargeable under the law of any State, or a combination of two or more such offenses have become final, he shall be sentenced to a term of imprisonment for not less than 90 days but not more than 3 years, and shall be fined a minimum of $5,000. Notwithstanding any penalty provided in this subsection, any person convicted under this subsection for the possession of flunitrazepam shall be imprisoned for not more than 3 years, shall be fined as otherwise provided in this section, or both. The imposition or execution of a minimum sentence required to be imposed under this subsection shall not be suspended or deferred. Further, upon conviction, a person who violates this subsection shall be fined the reasonable costs of the investigation and prosecution of the offense, including the costs of prosecution of an offense as defined in sections 1918 and 1920 of title 28, United States Code, except that this sentence shall not apply and a fine under this section need not be imposed if the court determines under the provision of title 18 that the defendant lacks the ability to pay.

(b) [Repealed]

(c) "Drug, narcotic, or chemical offense" defined. As used in this section, the term " drug, narcotic, or chemical offense" means any offense which proscribes the possession, distribution, manufacture, cultivation, sale, transfer, or the attempt or conspiracy to possess, distribute, manufacture, cultivate, sell or transfer any substance the possession of which is prohibited under this title.

(Oct. 27, 1970, P. L. 91-513, Title II, Part D, § 404, 84 Stat. 1264; Oct. 12, 1984, P. L. 98-473, Title II, Ch II, § 219, 98 Stat. 2027; Oct. 27, 1986, P. L. 99-570, Title I, Subtitle B, § 1052, 100 Stat. 3207-8; Nov. 18, 1988, P. L. 100-690, Title VI, Subtitle L, § 6371, Subtitle N, § 6480, 102 Stat. 4370, 4382; Nov. 29, 1990, P. L. 101-647, Title XII, § 1201, Title XIX, § 1907, 104 Stat. 4829, 4854; Oct. 3, 1996, P. L. 104-237, Title II, § 201(a), 110 Stat. 3101; Oct. 13, 1996, P. L. 104-305, § 2(c), 110 Stat. 3808; March 9, 2006, P. L. 109-177, Title VII, Subtitle A, § 711(e)(1), 120 Stat. 262; Aug. 3, 2010, P. L. 111-220, § 3, 124 Stat. 2372.)

§ 844a. Civil penalty for possession of small amounts of certain controlled substances

(a) In general. Any individual who knowingly possesses a controlled substance that is listed in section 401(b)(1)(A) [21 USCS § 841(b)(1)(A)] in violation of section 404 [21 USCS § 844(b)(1)(A)] in an amount that, as specified by regulation of the Attorney General, is a personal use amount shall be liable to the United States for a civil penalty in an amount not to exceed $10,000 for each such violation.

(b) Income and net assets. The income and net assets of an individual shall not be relevant to the determination whether to assess a civil penalty under this section or to prosecute the individual criminally. However, in determining the amount of a penalty under this section, the income and net assets of an individual shall be considered.

(c) Prior conviction. A civil penalty may not be assessed under this section if the individual previously was convicted of a Federal or State offense relating to a controlled substance.

(d) Limitation on number of assessments. A civil penalty may not be assessed on an individual under this section on more than two separate occasions.

(e) Assessment. A civil penalty under this section may be assessed by the Attorney General only by an order made on the record after opportunity for a hearing in accordance with section 554 of title 5, United States Code. The Attorney General shall provide written notice to the individual who is the subject of the proposed order informing the individual of the opportunity to receive such a hearing with respect to the proposed order. The hearing may be held only if the individual makes a request for the hearing before the expiration of the 30-day period beginning on the date such notice is issued.

(f) Compromise. The Attorney General may compromise, modify, or remit, with or without conditions, any civil penalty imposed under this section.

(g) Judicial review. If the Attorney General issues an order pursuant to subsection (e) after a hearing described in such subsection, the individual who is the subject of the order may, before the expiration of the 30-day period beginning on the date the order is issued, bring a civil action in the appropriate district court of the United States. In such action, the law and the facts of the violation and the assessment of the civil penalty shall be determined de novo, and shall include the right of a trial by jury, the right to counsel, and the right to confront witnesses. The facts of the violation shall be proved beyond a reasonable doubt.

(h) Civil action. If an individual does not request a hearing pursuant to subsection (e) and the Attorney General issues an order pursuant to such subsection, or if an individual does not under subsection (g) seek judicial review of such an order, the Attorney General may commence a civil action in any appropriate district court of the United States for the purpose of recovering the amount assessed and an amount representing interest at a rate computed in accordance with section 1961 of title 28, United States Code. Such interest shall accrue from the expiration of the 30-day period described in subsection (g). In such an action, the decision of the Attorney General to issue the order, and the amount of the penalty assessed by the Attorney General, shall not be subject to review.

(i) Limitation. The Attorney General may not under this subsection [section] commence proceeding against an individual after the expiration of the 5-year period beginning on the date on which the individual allegedly violated subsection (a).

(j) Expungement procedures. The Attorney General shall dismiss the proceedings under this section against an individual upon application of such individual at any time after the expiration of 3 years if—

(1) the individual has not previously been assessed a civil penalty under this section;

(2) the individual has paid the assessment;

(3) the individual has complied with any conditions imposed by the Attorney General;

(4) the individual has not been convicted of a Federal or State offense relating to a controlled substance; and

(5) the individual agrees to submit to a drug test, and such test shows the individual to be drug free.

A nonpublic record of a disposition under this subsection shall be retained by the Department of Justice solely for the purpose of determining in any subsequent proceeding whether the person qualified for a civil penalty or expungement under this section. If a record is expunged under this subsection, an individual concerning whom such an expungement has been made shall not be held thereafter under any provision of law to be guilty of perjury, false swearing, or making a false statement by reason of his failure to recite or acknowledge a proceeding under this section or the results thereof in response to an inquiry made of him for any purpose.

(Oct. 27, 1970, P. L. 91-513, Title II, Part D, § 405, as redesignated by Act Nov. 29, 1990, P. L. 101-647, Title X, § 1002(g)(1), (2), 104 Stat. 4828.)

§ 845. [Transferred]

§ 845a. [Transferred]

§ 845b. [Transferred]

§ 846. Attempt and conspiracy

Any person who attempts or conspires to commit any offense defined in this title shall be subject to the same penalties as those prescribed for the offense, the commission of which was the object of the attempt or conspiracy.

(Oct. 27, 1970, P. L. 91-513, Title II, Part D, § 406, 84 Stat. 1265; Nov. 18, 1988, P. L. 100-690, Title VI, Subtitle N, § 6470(a), 102 Stat. 4377.)

§ 847. Additional penalties

Any penalty imposed for violation of this title shall be in addition to, and not in lieu of, any civil or administrative penalty or sanction authorized by law.

(Oct. 27, 1970, P. L. 91-513, Title II, Part D, § 407, 84 Stat. 1265.)

§ 848. Continuing criminal enterprise

(a) Penalties; forfeitures. Any person who engages in a continuing criminal enterprise shall be sentenced to a term of imprisonment which may not be less than 20 years and which may be up to life imprisonment, to a fine not to exceed the greater of that authorized in accordance with the provisions of title 18, United States Code, or $2,000,000 if the defendant is an individual or $5,000,000 if the defendant is other than an individual, and to the forfeiture prescribed in section 413 of this title [21 USCS § 853]; except that if any person engages in such activity after one or more prior convictions of him under this section have become final, he shall be sentenced to a term of imprisonment which may not be less than 30 years and which may be up to life imprisonment, to a fine not to exceed the greater of twice the amount authorized in accordance with the provisions of title 18, United States Code, or $4,000,000 if the defendant is an individual or $10,000,000 if the defendant is other than an individual, and to the forfeiture prescribed in section 413 of this title [21 USCS § 853].

(b) Life imprisonment for engaging in continuing criminal enterprise. Any person who engages in a continuing criminal enterprise shall be imprisoned for life and fined in accordance with subsection (a), if—

(1) such person is the principal administrator, organizer, or leader of the enterprise or is one of several such principal administrators, organizers, or leaders; and

(2)(A) the violation referred to in subsection (c)(1) involved at least 300 times the quantity of a substance described in subsection 401(b)(1)(B) of this Act [21 USCS § 841(b)(1)(B)], or

(B) the enterprise, or any other enterprise in which the defendant was the principal or one of several principal administrators, organizers, or leaders, received $10 million dollars in gross receipts during any twelve-month period of its existence for the manufacture, importation, or distribution of a substance described in section 401(b)(1)(B) of this Act [21 USCS § 841(b)(1)(B)].

(c) "Continuing criminal enterprise" defined. For purposes of subsection (a), a person is engaged in a continuing criminal enterprise if—

(1) he violates any provision of this title or title III the punishment for which is a felony, and

(2) such violation is a part of a continuing series of violations of this title or title III—

(A) which are undertaken by such person in concert with five or more other persons with respect to whom such person occupies a position of organizer, a supervisory position, or any other position of management, and

(B) from which such person obtains substantial income or resources.

(d) Suspension of sentence and probation prohibited. In the case of any sentence imposed under this section, imposition or execution of such sentence shall not be suspended, probation shall not be granted, and the Act of July 15, 1932 (D. C. Code, secs. 24-203–24-207), shall not apply.

(e) Death penalty.

(1) In addition to the other penalties set forth in this section—

(A) any person engaging in or working in furtherance of a continuing criminal enterprise, or any person engaging in an offense punishable under section 841(b)(1)(A) or section 960(b)(1) [21 USCS § 841(b)(1)(A) or 960(b)(1)] who intentionally kills or counsels, commands, induces, procures, or causes the intentional killing of an individual and such killing results, shall be sentenced to any term of imprisonment, which shall not be less than 20 years, and which may be up to life imprisonment, or may be sentenced to death; and

(B) any person, during the commission of, in furtherance of, or while attempting to avoid apprehension, prosecution or service of a prison sentence for, a felony violation of this title or title III who intentionally kills or counsels, commands, induces, procures, or causes the intentional killing of any Federal, State, or local law enforcement officer engaged in, or on account of, the performance of such officer's official duties and such killing results, shall be sentenced to any term of imprisonment, which shall not be less than 20 years, and which may be up to life imprisonment, or may be sentenced to death.

(2) As used in paragraph (1)(B), the term "law enforcement officer" means a public servant authorized by law or by a Government agency or Congress to conduct or engage in the prevention, investigation, prosecution or adjudication of an offense, and includes those engaged in corrections, probation, or parole functions.

(f) [Not enacted]

(g)–(r) [Repealed]

(s) Special provision for methamphetamine. For the purposes of subsection (b), in the case of continuing criminal enterprise involving methamphetamine or its salts, isomers, or salts of isomers, paragraph (2)(A) shall be applied by substituting "200" for "300", and paragraph (2)(B) shall be applied by substituting "$5,000,000" for "$10 million dollars".

(Oct. 27, 1970, P. L. 91-513, Title II, Part D, § 408, 84 Stat. 1265; Oct. 12, 1984, P. L. 98-473, Title II, Ch II, § 224(b) [(c)], Ch 111, Part B, § 305, 98 Stat. 2030, 2050; Oct. 27, 1986, P. L. 99-570, Title I, Subtitle A, § 1005(b)(2), Subtitle F, §§ 1252, 1253, 100 Stat. 3207-6, 3207-15; Nov. 1, 1988, P. L. 100-690, Title VI, Subtitle N, § 6481, Title VII, Subtitle A, § 7001, 102 Stat. 4382, 4387; Sept. 13, 1994, P. L. 103-322, Title XXXIII, §§ 330003(e), 330009(d), 330014, 108 Stat. 2141, 2143, 2146; April 24, 1996, P. L. 104-132, Title I, § 108, Title IX, § 903(b), 110 Stat. 1226, 1318; March 9, 2006, P. L. 109-177, Title II, Subtitle B, §§ 221, 222(c), Title VII, Subtitle C, § 733, 120 Stat. 231, 232, 270.)

§ 849. Transportation safety offenses

(a) Definitions. In this section—

"safety rest area" means a roadside facility with parking facilities for the rest or other needs of motorists.

"truck stop" means a facility (including any parking lot appurtenant thereto) that—

(A) has the capacity to provide fuel or service, or both, to any commercial motor vehicle (as defined in section 31301 of title 49, United States Code), operating in commerce (as defined in that section); and

(B) is located within 2,500 feet of the National System of Interstate and Defense Highways or the Federal-Aid Primary System.

(b) First offense. A person who violates section 401(a)(1) or section 416 [21 USCS § 841(a)(1) or 856] by distributing or possessing with intent to distribute a controlled substance in or on, or within 1,000 feet of, a truck stop or safety rest area is (except as provided in subsection (b) [(c)]) subject to—

(1) twice the maximum punishment authorized by section 401(b) [21 USCS § 841(b)]; and

(2) twice any term of supervised release authorized by section 401(b) [21 USCS § 841(b)] for a first offense.

(c) Subsequent offense. A person who violates section 401(a)(1) or section 416 [21 USCS § 841(a)(1) or 856] by distributing or possessing with intent to distribute a controlled substance in or on, or within 1,000 feet of, a truck stop or a safety rest area after a prior conviction or convictions under subsection (a) [(b)] have become final is subject to—

(1) 3 times the maximum punishment authorized by section 401(b) [21 USCS § 841(b)]; and

(2) 3 times any term of supervised release authorized by section 401(b) [21 USCS § 841(b)] for a first offense.

(Oct. 27, 1970, P. L. 91-513, Title II, Part D, § 409, as added Sept. 13, 1994, P. L. 103-322, Title XVIII, Subtitle B, § 180201(b)(1), 108 Stat. 2046.)

§ 850. Information for sentencing

Except as otherwise provided in this title or section 303(a) of the Public Health Service Act, no limitation shall be placed on the information concerning the background, character, and conduct of a person convicted of an offense which a court of the United States may receive and consider for the purpose of imposing an appropriate sentence under this title or title III.

(Oct. 27, 1970, P. L. 91-513, Title II, Part D, § 410, 84 Stat. 1269.)

§ 851. Proceedings to establish previous convictions

(a) Information filed by United States Attorney.

(1) No person who stands convicted of an offense under this part [21 USCS §§ 841 et seq.] shall be sentenced to increased punishment by reason of one or more prior convictions, unless before trial, or before entry of a plea of guilty, the United States attorney files an information with the court (and serves a copy of such information on the person or counsel for the person) stating in writing the previous convictions to be relied upon. Upon a showing by the United States attorney that facts regarding prior convictions could not with due diligence be obtained prior to trial or before entry of a plea of guilty, the court may postpone the trial or the taking of the plea of guilty for a reasonable period for the purpose of obtaining such facts. Clerical mistakes in the information may be amended at any time prior to the pronouncement of sentence.

(2) An information may not be filed under this section if the increased punishment which may be imposed is imprisonment for a term in excess of three years unless the person either waived or was afforded prosecution by indictment for the offense for which such increased punishment may be imposed.

(b) Affirmation or denial of previous conviction. If the United States attorney files an information under this section, the court shall after conviction but before pronouncement of sentence inquire of the person with respect to whom the information was filed whether he affirms or denies that he has been previously convicted as alleged in the information, and shall inform him that any challenge to a prior conviction which is not made before sentence is imposed may not thereafter be raised to attack the sentence.

(c) Denial; written response; hearing.

(1) If the person denies any allegation of the information of prior conviction, or claims that any conviction alleged is invalid, he shall file a written response to the information. A copy of the response shall be served upon the United States attorney. The court shall hold a hearing to determine any issues raised by the response which would except the person from increased punishment. The failure of the United States attorney to include in the information the complete criminal record of the person or any facts in addition to the convictions to be relied upon shall not constitute grounds for invalidating the notice given in the information required by subsection (a)(1). The hearing shall be before the court without a jury and either party may introduce evidence. Except as otherwise provided in paragraph (2) of this subsection, the United States attorney shall have the burden of proof beyond a reasonable doubt on any issue of fact. At the request of either party, the court shall enter findings of fact and conclusions of law.

(2) A person claiming that a conviction alleged in the information was obtained in violation of the Constitution of the United States shall set forth his claim, and the factual basis therefor, with particularity in his response to the information. The person shall have the burden of proof by a preponderance of the evidence on any issue of fact raised by the response. Any challenge to a prior conviction, not raised by response to the information before an increased sentence is imposed in reliance thereon, shall be waived unless good cause be shown for failure to make a timely challenge.

(d) Imposition of sentence.

(1) If the person files no response to the information, or if the court determines, after hearing, that the person is subject to increased punishment by reason of prior convictions, the court shall proceed to impose sentence upon him as provided by this part [21 USCS §§ 841 et seq.].

(2) If the court determines that the person has not been convicted as alleged in the information, that a conviction alleged in the information is invalid, or that the person is otherwise not subject to an increased sentence as a matter of law, the court shall, at the request of the United States attorney, postpone sentence to allow an appeal from that determination. If no such request is made, the court shall impose sentence as provided by this part [21 USCS §§ 841 et seq.]. The person may appeal from an order postponing sentence as if sentence had been pronounced and a final judgment of conviction entered.

(e) Statute of limitations. No person who stands convicted of an offense under this part [21 USCS §§ 841 et seq.] may challenge the validity of any prior conviction alleged under this section which occurred more than five years before the date of the information alleging such prior conviction.

(Oct. 27, 1970, P. L. 91-513, Title II, Part D, § 411, 84 Stat. 1269.)

§ 852. Application of treaties and other international agreements

Nothing in the Single Convention on Narcotic Drugs, the Convention on Psychotropic Substances, or other treaties or international agreements shall be construed to limit the provision of treatment, education, or rehabilitation as alternatives to conviction or criminal penalty for offenses involving any drug or other substance subject to control under any such treaty or agreement.

(Oct. 27, 1970, P. L. 91-513, Title II, Part D, § 412, as added Nov. 10, 1978, P. L. 95-633, Title I, § 107(a), 92 Stat. 3773.)

§ 853. Criminal forfeitures

(a) Property subject to criminal forfeiture. Any person convicted of a violation of this title or title III punishable by imprisonment for more than one year shall forfeit to the United States, irrespective of any provision of State law—

(1) any property constituting, or derived from, any proceeds the person obtained, directly or indirectly, as the result of such violation;

(2) any of the person's property used, or intended to be used, in any manner or part, to commit, or to facilitate the commission of, such violation; and

(3) in the case of a person convicted of engaging in a continuing criminal enterprise in violation of section 408 of this title (21 U.S.C. 848), the person shall forfeit, in addition to any property described in paragraph (1) or (2), any of his interest in, claims against, and property or contractual rights affording a source of control over, the continuing criminal enterprise.

The court, in imposing sentence on such person, shall order, in addition to any other sentence imposed pursuant to this title or title III, that the person forfeit to the United States all property described in this subsection. In lieu of a fine otherwise authorized by this part [21 USCS §§ 841 et seq.], a defendant who derives profits or other proceeds from an offense may be fined not more than twice the gross profits or other proceeds.

(b) Meaning of term "property". Property subject to criminal forfeiture under this section includes—

(1) real property, including things growing on, affixed to, and found in land; and

(2) tangible and intangible personal property, including rights, privileges, interests, claims, and securities.

(c) Third party transfers. All right, title, and interest in property described in subsection (a) vests in the United States upon the commission of the act giving rise to forfeiture under this section. Any such property that is subsequently transferred to a person other than the defendant may be the subject of a special verdict of forfeiture and thereafter shall be ordered forfeited to the United States, unless the transferee establishes in a hearing pursuant to subsection (n) that he is a bona fide purchaser for value of such property who at the time of purchase was reasonably without cause to believe that the property was subject to forfeiture under this section.

(d) Rebuttable presumption. There is a rebuttable presumption at trial that any property of a person convicted of a felony under this title or title III is subject to forfeiture under this section if the United States establishes by a preponderance of the evidence that—

(1) such property was acquired by such person during the period of the violation of this title or title III or within a reasonable time after such period; and

(2) there was no likely source for such property other than the violation of this title or title III.

(e) Protective orders.

(1) Upon application of the United States, the court may enter a restraining order or injunction, require the execution of a satisfactory performance bond, or take any other action to preserve the availability of property described in subsection (a) for forfeiture under this section—

(A) upon the filing of an indictment or information charging a violation of this title or title III for which criminal forfeiture may be ordered under this section and alleging that the property with respect to which the order is sought would, in the event of conviction, be subject to forfeiture under this section; or

(B) prior to the filing of such an indictment or information, if, after notice to persons appearing to have an interest in the property and opportunity for a hearing, the court determines that—

(i) there is a substantial probability that the United States will prevail on the issue of forfeiture and that failure to enter the order will result in the property being destroyed, removed from the jurisdiction of the court, or otherwise made unavailable for forfeiture; and

(ii) the need to preserve the availability of the property through the entry of the requested order outweighs the hardship on any party against whom the order is to be entered:

Provided, however, That an order entered pursuant to subparagraph (B) shall be effective for not more than ninety days, unless extended by the court for good cause shown or unless an indictment or information described in subparagraph (A) has been filed.

(2) A temporary restraining order under this subsection may be entered upon application of the United States without notice or opportunity for a hearing when an information or indictment has not yet been filed with respect to the property, if the United States demonstrates that there is probable cause to believe that the property with respect to which the order is sought would, in the event of conviction, be subject to forfeiture under this section and that provision of notice will jeopardize the availability of the property for forfeiture. Such a temporary order shall expire not more than fourteen days after the date on which it is entered, unless extended for good cause shown or unless the party against whom it is entered consents to an extension for a longer period. A hearing requested concerning an order entered under this paragraph shall be held at the earliest possible time and prior to the expiration of the temporary order.

(3) The court may receive and consider, at a hearing held pursuant to this subsection, evidence and information that would be inadmissible under the Federal Rules of Evidence.

(4) Order to repatriate and deposit.

(A) In general. Pursuant to its authority to enter a pretrial restraining order under this section, the court may order a defendant to repatriate any property that may be seized and forfeited, and to deposit that property pending trial in the registry of the court, or with the United States Marshals Service or the Secretary of the Treasury, in an interest-bearing account, if appropriate.

(B) Failure to comply. Failure to comply with an order under this subsection, or an order to repatriate property under subsection (p), shall be punishable as a civil or criminal contempt of court, and may also result in an enhancement of the sentence of the defendant under the obstruction of justice provision of the Federal Sentencing Guidelines.

(f) Warrant of seizure. The Government may request the issuance of a warrant authorizing the seizure of property subject to forfeiture under this section in the same manner as provided for a search warrant. If the court determines that there is probable cause to believe that the property to be seized would, in the event of conviction, be subject to forfeiture and that an order under subsection (e) may not be sufficient to assure the availability of the property for forfeiture, the court shall issue a warrant authorizing the seizure of such property.

(g) Execution. Upon entry of an order of forfeiture under this section, the court shall authorize the Attorney General to seize all property ordered forfeited upon such terms and conditions as the court shall deem proper. Following entry of an order declaring the property forfeited, the court may, upon application of the United States, enter such appropriate restraining orders or injunctions, require the execution of satisfactory performance bonds, appoint receivers, conservators, appraisers, accountants, or trustees, or take any other action to protect the interest of the United States in the property ordered forfeited. Any income accruing to or derived from property ordered forfeited under this section may be used to offset ordinary and necessary expenses to the property which are required by law, or which are necessary to protect the interests of the United States or third parties.

(h) Disposition of property. Following the seizure of property ordered forfeited under this section, the Attorney General shall direct the disposition of the property by sale or any other commercially feasible means, making due provision for the rights of any innocent persons. Any property right or interest not exercisable by, or transferable for value to, the United

States shall expire and shall not revert to the defendant, nor shall the defendant or any person acting in concert with him or on his behalf be eligible to purchase forfeited property at any sale held by the United States. Upon application of a person, other than the defendant or a person acting in concert with him or on his behalf, the court may restrain or stay the sale or disposition of the property pending the conclusion of any appeal of the criminal case giving rise to the forfeiture, if the applicant demonstrates that proceeding with the sale or disposition of the property will result in irreparable injury, harm, or loss to him.

(i) Authority of the Attorney General. With respect to property ordered forfeited under this section, the Attorney General is authorized to—

(1) grant petitions for mitigation or remission of forfeiture, restore forfeited property to victims of a violation of this title, or take any other action to protect the rights of innocent persons which is in the interest of justice and which is not inconsistent with the provisions of this section;

(2) compromise claims arising under this section;

(3) award compensation to persons providing information resulting in a forfeiture under this section;

(4) direct the disposition by the United States, in accordance with the provisions of section 511(e) of this title (21 U.S.C. 881(e)), of all property ordered forfeited under this section by public sale or any other commercially feasible means, making due provision for the rights of innocent persons; and

(5) take appropriate measures necessary to safeguard and maintain property ordered forfeited under this section pending its disposition.

(j) Applicability of civil forfeiture provisions. Except to the extent that they are inconsistent with the provisions of this section, the provisions of section 511(d) of this title (21 U.S.C. 881(d)) shall apply to a criminal forfeiture under this section.

(k) Bar on intervention. Except as provided in subsection (n), no party claiming an interest in property subject to forfeiture under this section may—

(1) intervene in a trial or appeal of a criminal case involving the forfeiture of such property under this section; or

(2) commence an action at law or equity against the United States concerning the validity of his alleged interest in the property subsequent to the filing of an indictment or information alleging that the property is subject to forfeiture under this section.

(l) Jurisdiction to enter orders. The district courts of the United States shall have jurisdiction to enter orders as provided in this section without regard to the location of any property which may be subject to forfeiture under this section or which has been ordered forfeited under this section.

(m) Depositions. In order to facilitate the identification and location of property declared forfeited and to facilitate the disposition of petitions for remission or mitigation of forfeiture, after the entry of an order declaring property forfeited to the United States, the court may, upon application of the United States, order that the testimony of any witness relating to the property forfeited be taken by deposition and that any designated book, paper, document, record, recording, or other material not privileged be produced at the same time and place, in the same manner as provided for the taking of depositions under Rule 15 of the Federal Rules of Criminal Procedure.

(n) Third party interests.

(1) Following the entry of an order of forfeiture under this section, the United States shall publish notice of the order and of its intent to dispose of the property in such manner as the Attorney General may direct. The Government may also, to the extent practicable, provide direct written notice to any person known to have alleged an interest in the property that is the subject of the order of forfeiture as a substitute for published notice as to those persons so notified.

(2) Any person, other than the defendant, asserting a legal interest in property which has been ordered forfeited to the United States pursuant to this section may, within thirty days of the final publication of notice or his receipt of notice under paragraph (1), whichever is earlier, petition the court for a hearing to adjudicate the validity of his alleged interest in the property. The hearing shall be held before the court alone, without a jury.

(3) The petition shall be signed by the petitioner under penalty of perjury and shall set forth the nature and extent of the petitioner's right, title, or interest in the property, the time and circumstances of the petitioner's acquisition of the right, title, or interest in the property, any additional facts supporting the petitioner's claim, and the relief sought.

(4) The hearing on the petition shall, to the extent practicable and consistent with the interests of justice, be held within thirty days of the filing of the petition. The court may consolidate the hearing on the petition with a hearing on any other petition filed by a person other than the defendant under this subsection.

(5) At the hearing, the petitioner may testify and present evidence and witnesses on his own behalf, and cross-examine witnesses who appear at the hearing. The United States may present evidence and witnesses in rebuttal and in defense of its claim to the property and cross-examine witnesses who appear at the hearing. In addition to testimony and evidence presented at the hearing, the court shall consider the relevant portions of the record of the criminal case which resulted in the order of forfeiture.

(6) If, after the hearing, the court determines that the petitioner has established by a preponderance of the evidence that—

(A) the petitioner has a legal right, title, or interest in the property, and such right, title, or interest renders the order of forfeiture invalid in whole or in part because the right, title, or interest was vested in the petitioner rather than the defendant or was superior to any right, title, or interest of the defendant at the time of the commission of the acts which gave rise to the forfeiture of the property under this section; or

(B) the petitioner is a bona fide purchaser for value of the right, title, or interest in the property and was at the time of purchase reasonably without cause to believe that the property was subject to forfeiture under this section;

the court shall amend the order of forfeiture in accordance with its determination.

(7) Following the court's disposition of all petitions filed under this subsection, or if no such petitions are filed following the expiration of the period provided in paragraph (2) for the filing of such petitions, the United States shall have clear title to property that is the subject of the order of forfeiture and may warrant good title to any subsequent purchaser or transferee.

(o) Construction. The provisions of this section shall be liberally construed to effectuate its remedial purposes.

(p) Forfeiture of substitute property.

(1) In general. Paragraph (2) of this subsection shall apply, if any property described in subsection (a), as a result of any act or omission of the defendant—

(A) cannot be located upon the exercise of due diligence;

(B) has been transferred or sold to, or deposited with, a third party;

(C) has been placed beyond the jurisdiction of the court;

(D) has been substantially diminished in value; or

(E) has been commingled with other property which cannot be divided without difficulty.

(2) Substitute property. In any case described in any of subparagraphs (A) through (E) of paragraph (1), the court shall order the forfeiture of any other property of the defendant, up to the value of any property described in subparagraphs (A) through (E) of paragraph (1), as applicable.

(3) Return of property to jurisdiction. In the case of property described in paragraph (1)(C), the court may, in addition to any other action authorized by this subsection, order the defendant to return the property to the jurisdiction of the court so that the property may be seized and forfeited.

(q) Restitution for cleanup of clandestine laboratory sites. The court, when sentencing a defendant convicted of an offense under this title or title III involving the manufacture, the possession, or the possession with intent to distribute, of amphetamine or methamphetamine, shall—

(1) order restitution as provided in sections 3612 and 3664 of title 18, United States Code [18 USCS §§ 3612 and 3664];

(2) order the defendant to reimburse the United States, the State or local government concerned, or both the United States and the State or local government concerned for the costs incurred by the United States or the State or local government concerned, as the case may be, for the cleanup associated with the manufacture of amphetamine or methamphetamine by the defendant, or on premises or in property that the defendant owns, resides, or does business in; and

(3) order restitution to any person injured as a result of the offense as provided in section 3663A of title 18, United States Code [18 USCS § 3663A].

(Oct. 27, 1970, P. L. 91-513, Title II, Part D, § 413, as added Oct. 12, 1984, P. L. 98-473, Title II, Ch III, Part B, § 303 in part, 98 Stat. 2044; Oct. 12, 1984, P. L. 98-473, Title II, Ch XXIII, § 2301(d)–(f), 98 Stat. 2192; Oct. 27, 1986, P. L. 99-570, Title I, Subtitle D, § 1153(b), Subtitle Q, § 1864, 100 Stat. 3207-13, 3207-54; Oct. 3, 1996, P. L. 104-237, Title II, § 207, 110 Stat. 3104; Oct. 17, 2000, P. L. 106-310, Div B, Title XXXVI, Subtitle A, Part I, § 3613(a), 114 Stat. 1229; Oct. 26, 2001, P. L. 107-56, Title III, Subtitle A, § 319(d), 115 Stat. 314; March 9, 2006, P. L. 109-177, Title VII, Subtitle D, § 743(a), 120 Stat. 272; May 7, 2009, P. L. 111-16, § 5, 123 Stat. 1608.)

§ 853a. [Transferred]

§ 854. Investment of illicit drug profits

(a) Prohibition. It shall be unlawful for any person who has received any income derived, directly or indirectly, from a violation of this title or title III punishable by imprisonment for more than one year in which such person has participated as a principal within the meaning of section 2 of title 18, United States Code, to use or invest, directly or indirectly, any part of such income, or the proceeds of such income, in acquisition of any interest in, or the establishment or operation of, any enterprise which is engaged in, or the activities of which affect interstate or foreign commerce. A purchase of securities on the open market for purposes of investment, and without the intention of controlling or participating in the control of the issuer, or of assisting another to do so, shall not be unlawful under this section if the securities of the issuer held by the purchaser, the members of his immediate family, and his or their accomplices in any violation of this title or title III after such purchase do not amount in the aggregate to 1 per centum of the outstanding securities of any one class, and do not confer, either in law or in fact, the power to elect one or more directors of the issuer.

(b) Penalty. Whoever violates this section shall be fined not more than $50,000 or imprisoned not more than ten years, or both.

(c) "Enterprise" defined. As used in this section, the term "enterprise" includes any individual, partnership, corporation, association, or other legal entity, and any union or group of individuals associated in fact although not a legal entity.

(d) Construction. The provisions of this section shall be liberally construed to effectuate its remedial purposes.

(Oct. 27, 1970, P. L. 91-513, Title II, Part D, § 414, as added Oct. 12, 1984, P. L. 98-473, Title II, Ch III Part B, § 303 in part, 98 Stat. 2049.)

§ 855. Alternative fine

In lieu of a fine otherwise authorized by this part [21 USCS §§ 841 et seq.], a defendant who derives profits or other proceeds from an offense may be fined not more than twice the gross profits or other proceeds.

(Oct. 27, 1970, P. L. 91-513, Title II, Part D, § 415, as added Oct. 12, 1984, P. L. 98-473, Title II, Ch XXIII, § 2302, 98 Stat. 2193.)

§ 856. Maintaining drug-involved premises

(a) Unlawful acts. Except as authorized by this title, it shall be unlawful to—

(1) knowingly open, lease, rent, use, or maintain any place, whether permanently or temporarily, for the purpose of manufacturing, distributing, or using any controlled substance;

(2) manage or control any place, whether permanently or temporarily, either as an owner, lessee, agent, employee, occupant, or mortgagee, and knowingly and intentionally rent, lease, profit from, or make available for use, with or without compensation, the place for the purpose of unlawfully manufacturing, storing, distributing, or using a controlled substance.

(b) Criminal penalties. Any person who violates subsection (a) of this section shall be sentenced to a term of imprisonment of not more than 20 years or a fine of not more than $500,000, or both, or a fine of $2,000,000 for a person other than an individual.

(c) Violation as offense against property. A violation of subsection (a) shall be considered an offense against property for purposes of section 3663A(c)(1)(A)(ii) of title 18, United States Code.

(d) Civil penalties.

(1) Any person who violates subsection (a) shall be subject to a civil penalty of not more than the greater of—

(A) $250,000; or

(B) 2 times the gross receipts, either known or estimated, that were derived from each violation that is attributable to the person.

(2) If a civil penalty is calculated under paragraph (1)(B), and there is more than 1 defendant, the court may apportion the penaty between multiple violators, but each violator shall be jointly and severally liable for the civil penalty under this subsection.

(e) Declaratory and injunctive remedies. Any person who violates subsection (a) shall be subject to declaratory and injunctive remedies as set forth in section 403(f) [21 USCS § 843(f)].

(Oct. 27, 1970, P. L. 91-513, Title II, Part D, § 416, as added Oct. 27, 1986, P. L. 99-570, Title I, Subtitle P, § 1841(a), 100 Stat. 3207-52; Oct. 17, 2000, P. L. 106-310, Div B, Title XXXVI, Subtitle A, Part I, § 3613(e), 114 Stat. 1230; April 30, 2003, P. L. 108-21, Title VI, § 608(b)(1), (2), (c), 117 Stat. 691.)

§ 857. [Repealed and Transferred]

§ 858. Endangering human life while illegally manufacturing a controlled substance

Whoever, while manufacturing a controlled substance in violation of this title, or attempting to do so, or transporting or causing to be transported materials, including chemicals, to do so, creates a substantial risk of harm to human life shall be fined in accordance with title 18, United States Code, or imprisoned not more than 10 years, or both.

(Oct. 27, 1970, P. L. 91-513, Title II, Part D, § 417, as added Nov. 18, 1988, P. L. 100-690, Title VI, Subtitle K, § 6301(a), 102 Stat. 4370.)

§ 859. Distribution to persons under age twenty-one

(a) First offense. Except as provided in section 419 [19 USCS § 860], any person at least eighteen years of age who violates section 401(a)(1) [21 USCS § 841(a)(1)] by distributing a controlled substance to a person under twenty-one years of age is (except as provided in subsection (b)) subject to (1) twice the maximum punishment authorized by section 401(b) [21 USCS § 841(b)], and (2) at least twice any term of supervised release authorized by section 401(b) [21 USCS § 841(b)], for a first offense involving the same controlled substance and schedule. Except to the extent a greater minimum sentence is otherwise provided by section 401(b) [21 USCS § 841(b)], a term of imprisonment under this subsection shall be not less than one year. The mandatory minimum sentencing provisions of this subsection shall not apply to offenses involving 5 grams or less of marihuana.

(b) Second offense. Except as provided in section 419 [18 USCS § 860], any person at least eighteen years of age who violates section 401(a)(1) [21 USCS § 841(a)(1)] by distributing a controlled substance to a person under twenty-one years of age after a prior conviction under subsection (a) of this section (or under section 303(b)(2) of the Federal Food, Drug, and Cosmetic Act as in effect prior to the effective date of section 701(b) of this Act) has become final, is subject to (1) three times the maximum punishment authorized by section 401(b) [21 USCS § 841(b)], and (2) at least three times any special parole term authorized by section 401(b) [21 USCS § 841(b)], for a second or subsequent offense involving the same controlled substance and schedule. Except to the extent a greater minimum sentence is otherwise provided by section 401(b) [21 USCS § 841(b)], a term of imprisonment under this subsection shall be not less than one year. Penalties for third and subsequent convictions shall be governed by section 401(b)(1)(A) [21 USCS § 841(b)(1)(A)].

(Oct. 27, 1970, P. L. 91-513, Title II, Part D, § 418 [405], 84 Stat. 1265; Oct. 12, 1984, P. L. 98-473, Title II, Ch II, § 224(b), Ch V, Part A, § 503(b)(3), 98 Stat. 2030, 2070; Oct. 27, 1986, P. L. 99-570, Title I, Subtitle A, § 1005(b)(1), Subtitle C, § 1105(a), (b), 100 Stat. 3207-6, 3207-11; Oct. 27, 1986, P. L. 99-570, Title I, Subtitle A, § 1004(a), 100 Stat. 3207-6; Nov. 18, 1988, P. L. 100-690, Title VI, Subtitle N, §§ 6452(b), 6455, 6456, 102 Stat. 4371, 4372; Nov. 29, 1990, P. L. 101-647, Title X, §§ 1002(a), 1003(a), Title XXXV, § 3599L, 104 Stat. 4827, 4828, 4932.)

§ 860. Distribution or manufacturing in or near schools and colleges

(a) Penalty. Any person who violates section 401(a)(1) or section 416 [21 USCS § 841(a)(1) or 856] by distributing, possessing with intent to distribute, or manufacturing a controlled substance in or on, or within one thousand feet of, the real property comprising a public or private elementary, vocational, or secondary school or a public or private college, junior college, or university, or a playground, or housing facility owned by a public housing authority, or within 100 feet of a public or private youth center, public swimming pool, or video arcade facility, is (except as provided in subsection (b)) subject to (1) twice the maximum punishment authorized by section 401(b) [21 USCS § 841(b)], and (2) at least twice any term of supervised release authorized by section 401(b) [21 USCS § 841(b)] for a first offense. A fine up to twice that authorized by section 401(b) [21 USCS § 841(b)] may be imposed in addition to any term of imprisonment authorized by this subsection. Except to the extent a greater minimum sentence is otherwise provided by section 401(b) [21 USCS § 841(b)], a person shall be sentenced under this subsection to a term of imprisonment of not less than one year. The mandatory minimum sentencing provisions of this paragraph shall not apply to offenses involving 5 grams or less of marihuana.

(b) Second offenders. Any person who violates section 401(a)(1) or section 416 [21 USCS § 841(a)(1) or 856] by distributing, possessing with intent to distribute, or manufacturing a controlled substance in or on, or within one thousand feet of, the real property comprising a public or private elementary, vocational, or secondary school or a public or private college, junior college, or university, or a playground, or housing facility owned by a public housing authority, or within 100 feet of a public or private youth center, public swimming pool, or video arcade facility, after a prior conviction under subsection (a) has become final is punishable (1) by the greater of (A) a term of imprisonment of not less than three years and not more than life imprisonment or (B) three times the maximum punishment authorized by section 401(b) [21 USCS § 841(b)] for a first offense, and (2) at least three times any term of supervised release authorized by section 401(b) of this title [21 USCS § 841(b)] for a first offense. A fine up to three times that authorized by section 401(b) [21 USCS § 841(b)] may be imposed in addition to any term of imprisonment authorized by this subsection. Except to the extent a greater minimum sentence is otherwise provided by section 401(b) [21 USCS § 841(b)], a person shall be sentenced under this subsection to a term of imprisonment of not less than three years. Penalties for third and subsequent convictions shall be governed by section 401(b)(1)(A) [21 USCS § 841(b)(1)(A)].

(c) Employing children to distribute drugs near schools or playgrounds. Notwithstanding any other law, any person at least 21 years of age who knowingly and intentionally—

(1) employs, hires, uses, persuades, induces, entices, or coerces a person under 18 years of age to violate this section; or

(2) employs, hires, uses, persuades, induces, entices, or coerces a person under 18 years of age to assist in avoiding detection or apprehension for any offense under this section by any Federal, State, or local law enforcement official,

is punishable by a term of imprisonment, a fine, or both, up to triple those authorized by section 401 [21 USCS § 841].

(d) Suspension of sentence; probation; parole. In the case of any mandatory minimum sentence imposed under subsection (b) [this section], imposition or execution of such sentence shall not be suspended and probation shall not be granted. An individual convicted under this section shall not be eligible for parole until the individual has served the mandatory minimum term of imprisonment as provided by this section.

(e) Definitions. For the purposes of this section—

(1) The term "playground" means any outdoor facility (including any parking lot appurtenant thereto) intended for recreation, open to the public, and with any portion thereof containing three or more separate apparatus intended for the recreation of children including, but not limited to, sliding boards, swingsets, and teeterboards.

(2) The term "youth center" means any recreational facility and/or gymnasium (including any parking lot appurtenant thereto), intended primarily for use by persons under 18 years of age, which regularly provides athletic, civic, or cultural activities.

(3) The term "video arcade facility" means any facility, legally accessible to persons under 18 years of age, intended primarily for the use of pinball and video machines for amusement containing a minimum of ten pinball and/or video machines.

(4) The term "swimming pool" includes any parking lot appurtenant thereto.

(Oct. 27, 1970, P. L. 91-513, Title II, Part D, § 419 [405A], as added Oct. 12, 1984, P. L. 98-473, Title II, Ch V, Part A, § 503(a), 98 Stat. 2070; Oct. 27, 1986, P. L. 99-570, Title I, Subtitle A, § 1004(a) Subtitle C, §§ 1104, 1105(c), Subtitle P, § 1841(b), Subtitle Q, § 1866(b), (c), 100 Stat. 3207-6, 3207-11, 3207-52, 3207-55; Nov. 10, 1986, P. L. 99-646, § 28, 100 Stat. 3598; Nov. 18, 1988, P. L. 100-690, Title VI, Subtitle N, §§ 6452(b)(1), 6457, 6458, 102 Stat. 4371, 4373; Nov. 29, 1990, P. L. 101-647, Title X, §§ 1002(b), 1003(b), Title XII, § 1214, Title XV, § 1502, Title XXXV, § 3599L, 104 Stat. 4827, 4829, 4833, 4836, 4932; Sept. 13, 1994, P. L. 103-322, Title XIV, § 140006, Title XXXII, Subtitle A, § 320107, Title XXXIII, § 330009(a), 108 Stat. 2032, 2111, 2143.)

§ 860a. Consecutive sentence for manufacturing or distributing, or possessing with intent to manufacture or distribute, methamphetamine on premises where children are present or reside

Whoever violates section 401(a)(1) [21 USCS § 841(a)(1)] by manufacturing or distributing, or possessing with intent to manufacture or distribute, methamphetamine or its salts, isomers or salts of isomers on premises in which an individual who is under the age of 18 years is present or resides, shall, in addition to any other sentence imposed, be imprisoned for a period of any term of years but not more than 20 years, subject to a fine, or both.

(Oct. 27, 1970, P. L. 91-513, Title II, Part D, § 419a, as added March 9, 2006, P. L. 109-177, Title VII, Subtitle C, § 734(a), 120 Stat. 270.)

§ 861. Employment or use of persons under 18 years of age in drug operations

(a) Unlawful acts. It shall be unlawful for any person at least eighteen years of age to knowingly and intentionally—

(1) employ, hire, use, persuade, induce, entice, or coerce, a person under eighteen years of age to violate any provision of this title or title III;

USCS—T.21 § 860a

(2) employ, hire, use, persuade, induce, entice, or coerce, a person under eighteen years of age to assist in avoiding detection or apprehension for any offense of this title or title III by any Federal, State, or local law enforcement official; or

(3) receive a controlled substance from a person under 18 years of age, other than an immediate family member, in violation of this title or title III.

(b) Penalty for first offense. Any person who violates subsection (a) is subject to twice the maximum punishment otherwise authorized and at least twice any term of supervised release otherwise authorized for a first offense. Except to the extent a greater minimum sentence is otherwise provided, a term of imprisonment under this subsection shall not be less than one year.

(c) Penalty for subsequent offenses. Any person who violates subsection (a) after a prior conviction under subsection (a) of this section has become final, is subject to three times the maximum punishment otherwise authorized and at least three times any term of supervised release otherwise authorized for a first offense. Except to the extent a greater minimum sentence is otherwise provided, a term of imprisonment under this subsection shall not be less than one year. Penalties for third and subsequent convictions shall be governed by section 401(b)(1)(A) [21 USCS § 841(b)(1)(A)].

(d) Penalty for providing or distributing controlled substance to underage person. Any person who violates section 405B(a)(1) or (2) [—]

(1) by knowingly providing or distributing a controlled substance or a controlled substance analogue to any person under eighteen years of age; or

(2) if the person employed, hired, or used is fourteen years of age or younger, shall be subject to a term of imprisonment for not more than five years or a fine of not more than $50,000, or both, in addition to any other punishment authorized by this section.

(e) Suspension of sentence; probation; parole. In any case of any sentence imposed under this section, imposition or execution of such sentence shall not be suspended and probation shall not be granted. An individual convicted under this section of an offense for which a mandatory minimum term of imprisonment is applicable shall not be eligible for parole under section 4202 of title 18, United States Code, until the individual has served the mandatory term of imprisonment as enhanced by this section.

(f) Distribution of controlled substance to pregnant individual. Except as authorized by this title, it shall be unlawful for any person to knowingly or intentionally provide or distribute any controlled substance to a pregnant individual in violation of any provision of this title. Any person who violates this subsection shall be subject to the provisions of subsections (b), (c), and (e).

(Oct. 27, 1970, P. L. 91-513, Title II, Part d, § 420 [405B] as added Oct. 27, 1986, P. L. 99-570, Title I, Subtitle C, § 1102, 100 Stat. 3207-10; Nov. 18, 1988, P. L. 100-690, Title VI, Subtitle N, §§ 6452(b)(1), 6459, 6470(b), 102 Stat. 4371, 4373, 4378; Nov. 29, 1990, P. L. 101-647, Title X, §§ 1002(c), 1003(c), Title XXXV, § 3599L, 104 Stat. 4827, 4829, 4932.)

§ 862. Denial of Federal benefits to drug traffickers and possessors

(a) Drug traffickers.

(1) Any individual who is convicted of any Federal or State offense consisting of the distribution of controlled substances shall—

(A) at the discretion of the court, upon the first conviction for such an offense be ineligible for any or all Federal benefits for up to 5 years after such conviction;

(B) at the discretion of the court, upon a second conviction for such an offense be ineligible for any or all Federal benefits for up to 10 years after such conviction; and

(C) upon a third or subsequent conviction for such an offense be permanently ineligible for all Federal benefits.

(2) The benefits which are denied under this subsection shall not include benefits relating to long-term drug treatment programs for addiction for any person who, if there is a reasonable body of evidence to substantiate such declaration, declares himself to be an addict and submits himself to a long-term treatment program for addiction, or is deemed to be rehabilitated pursuant to rules established by the Secretary of Health and Human Services.

(b) Drug possessors.

(1) Any individual who is convicted of any Federal or State offense involving the possession of a controlled substance (as such term is defined for purposes of the Controlled Substances Act) shall—

(A) upon the first conviction for such an offense and at the discretion of the court—

(i) be ineligible for any or all Federal benefits for up to one year;

(ii) be required to successfully complete an approved drug treatment program which includes periodic testing to insure that the individual remains drug free;

(iii) be required to perform appropriate community service; or

(iv) any combination of clauses (i), (ii), or (iii); and

(B) upon a second or subsequent conviction for such an offense be ineligible for all Federal benefits for up to 5 years after such conviction as determined by the court. The court shall continue to have the discretion in subparagraph (A) above. In imposing penalties and conditions under subparagraph (A), the court may require that the completion of the conditions imposed by clause (ii) or (iii) be a requirement for the reinstatement of benefits under clause (i).

(2) The penalties and conditions which may be imposed under this subsection shall be waived in the case of a person who, if there is a reasonable body of evidence to substantiate such declaration, declares himself to be an addict and submits himself to a long-term treatment program for addiction, or is deemed to be rehabilitated pursuant to rules established by the Secretary of Health and Human Services.

(c) Suspension of period of ineligibility. The period of ineligibility referred to in subsections (a) and (b) shall be suspended if the individual—

(A) completes a supervised drug rehabilitation program after becoming ineligible under this section;

(B) has otherwise been rehabilitated; or

(C) has made a good faith effort to gain admission to a supervised drug rehabilitation program, but is unable to do so because of inaccessibility or unavailability of such a program, or the inability of the individual to pay for such a program.

(d) Definitions. As used in this section—

(1) the term "Federal benefit"—

(A) means the issuance of any grant, contract, loan, professional license, or commercial license provided by an agency of the United States or by appropriated funds of the United States; and

(B) does not include any retirement, welfare, Social Security, health, disability, veterans benefit, public housing, or other similar benefit, or any other benefit for which payments or services are required for eligibility; and

(2) the term "veterans benefit" means all benefits provided to veterans, their families, or survivors by virtue of the service of a veteran in the Armed Forces of the United States.

(e) Inapplicability of this section to government witnesses. The penalties provided by this section shall not apply to any individual who cooperates or testifies with the Government in the prosecution of a Federal or State offense or who is in a Government witness protection program.

(f) Indian provision. Nothing in this section shall be construed to affect the obligation of the United States to any Indian or Indian tribe arising out of any treaty, statute, Executive order, or the trust responsibility of the United States owing to such Indian or Indian tribe. Nothing in this subsection shall exempt any individual Indian from the sanctions provided for in this section, provided that no individual Indian shall be denied any benefit under Federal Indian programs comparable to those described in subsection (d)(1)(B) or (d)(2) above.

(g) Presidential report.

(1) On or before May 1, 1989, the President shall transmit to the Congress a report—

(A) delineating the role of State courts in implementing this section;

(B) describing the manner in which Federal agencies will implement and enforce the requirements of this section;

(C) detailing the means by which Federal and State agencies, courts, and law enforcement agencies will exchange and share the data and information necessary to implement and enforce the withholding of Federal benefits; and

(D) recommending any modifications to improve the administration of this section or otherwise achieve the goal of discouraging the trafficking and possession of controlled substances.

(2) No later than September 1, 1989, the Congress shall consider the report of the President and enact such changes as it deems appropriate to further the goals of this section.

(h) Effective date. The denial of Federal benefits set forth in this section shall take effect for convictions occurring after September 1, 1989.

(Oct. 27, 1970, P. L. 91-513, Title II, Part D, § 421, as redesignated by Act Nov. 29, 1990, P. L. 101-647, Title X, § 1002(d)(1), 104 Stat. 4827; Nov. 29, 1990, P. L. 101-647, Title X, § 1002(d)(2), 104 Stat. 4827.)

§ 862a. Denial of assistance and benefits for certain drug-related convictions

(a) In general. An individual convicted (under Federal or State law) of any offense which is classified as a felony by the law of the jurisdiction involved and which has as an element the possession, use, or distribution of a controlled substance (as defined in section 102(6) of the Controlled Substances Act (21 U.S.C. 802(6))) shall not be eligible for—

(1) assistance under any State program funded under part A of title IV of the Social Security Act [42 USCS §§ 601 et seq.], or

(2) benefits under the supplemental nutrition assistance program (as defined in section 3 of the Food and Nutrition Act of 2008 (7 U.S.C. 2012)) or any State program carried out under that Act [7 USCS §§ 2011 et seq.].

(b) Effects on assistance and benefits for others.

(1) Program of temporary assistance for needy families. The amount of assistance otherwise required to be provided under a State program funded under part A of title IV of the Social Security Act [42 USCS §§ 601 et seq.] to the family members of an individual to whom subsection (a) applies shall be reduced by the amount which would have otherwise been made available to the individual under such part.

(2) Benefits under the Food and Nutrition Act of 2008. The amount of benefits otherwise required to be provided to a household under the supplemental nutrition assistance program (as defined in section 3 of the Food and Nutrition Act of 2008 (7 U.S.C. 2012)), or any State program carried out under that Act [7 USCS §§ 2011 et seq.], shall be determined by considering the individual to whom subsection (a) applies not to be a member of such household, except that the income and resources of the individual shall be considered to be income and resources of the household.

(c) Enforcement. A State that has not exercised its authority under subsection (d)(1)(A) shall require each individual applying for assistance or benefits referred to in subsection (a), during the application process, to state, in writing, whether the individual, or any member of the household of the individual, has been convicted of a crime described in subsection (a).

(d) Limitations.

(1) State elections.

(A) Opt out. A State may, by specific reference in a law enacted after the date of the enactment of this Act [enacted Aug. 22, 1996], exempt any or all individuals domiciled in the State from the application of subsection (a).

(B) Limit period of prohibition. A State may, by law enacted after the date of the enactment of this Act [enacted Aug. 22, 1996], limit the period for which subsection (a) shall apply to any or all individuals domiciled in the State.

(2) Inapplicability to convictions occurring on or before enactment. Subsection (a) shall not apply to a conviction if the conviction is for conduct occurring on or before the date of the enactment of this Act [enacted Aug. 22, 1996].

(e) "State" defined. For purposes of this section, the term "State" has the meaning given it—

(1) in section 419(5) of the Social Security Act [42 USCS § 619(5)], when referring to assistance provided under a State program funded under part A of title IV of the Social Security Act [42 USCS §§ 601 et seq.], and

(2) in section 3 of the Food and Nutrition Act of 2008 (7 U.S.C. 2012), when referring to the supplemental nutrition assistance program (as defined in that section) or any State program carried out under that Act [7 USCS §§ 2011 et seq.].

(f) Rule of interpretation. Nothing in this section shall be construed to deny the following Federal benefits:

(1) Emergency medical services under title XIX of the Social Security Act [42 USCS §§ 1396 et seq.].

(2) Short-term, noncash, in-kind emergency disaster relief.

(3)(A) Public health assistance for immunizations.

(B) Public health assistance for testing and treatment of communicable diseases if the Secretary of Health and Human Services determines that it is necessary to prevent the spread of such disease.

(4) Prenatal care.

(5) Job training programs.

(6) Drug treatment programs.

(Aug. 22, 1996, P. L. 104-193, Title I, § 115, 110 Stat. 2180; Aug. 5, 1997, P. L. 105-33, Title V, Subtitle F, Ch 1, § 5516(a), 111 Stat. 620; May 22, 2008, P. L. 110-234, Title IV, Subtitle A, Part III, § 4115(c)(2)(C), 122 Stat. 1109; June 18, 2008, P. L. 110-246, § 4(a), Title IV, Subtitle A, Part III, § 4115(c)(2)(C), 122 Stat. 1664, 1871; Feb. 7, 2014, P. L. 113-79, Title IV, Subtitle A, § 4030(n), 128 Stat. 814.)

§ 862b. Sanctioning for testing positive for controlled substances

Notwithstanding any other provision of law, States shall not be prohibited by the Federal Government from testing welfare recipients for use of controlled substances nor from sanctioning welfare recipients who test positive for use of controlled substances.

(Aug. 22, 1996, P. L. 104-193, Title IX, § 902, 110 Stat. 2347.)

§ 863. Drug paraphernalia

(a) In general. It is unlawful for any person—

(1) to sell or offer for sale drug paraphernalia;

(2) to use the mails or any other facility of interstate commerce to transport drug paraphernalia; or

(3) to import or export drug paraphernalia.

(b) Penalties. Anyone convicted of an offense under subsection (a) of this section shall be imprisoned for not more than three years and fined under title 18, United States Code.

(c) Seizure and forfeiture. Any drug paraphernalia involved in any violation of subsection (a) of this section shall be subject to seizure and forfeiture upon the conviction of a person for such violation. Any such paraphernalia shall be delivered to the Administrator of General Services, General Services Administration, who may order such paraphernalia destroyed or may authorize its use for law enforcement or educational purposes by Federal, State, or local authorities.

(d) "Drug paraphernalia" defined. The term "drug paraphernalia" means any equipment, product, or material of any kind which is primarily intended or designed for use in manufacturing, compounding, converting, concealing, producing, processing, preparing, injecting, ingesting, inhaling, or otherwise introducing into the human body a controlled substance, possession of which is unlawful under the Controlled Substances Act (title II of Public Law 91-513). It includes items primarily intended or designed for use in ingesting, inhaling, or otherwise introducing marijuana [marihuana], cocaine, hashish, hashish oil, PCP, methamphetamine, or amphetamines into the human body, such as—

(1) metal, wooden, acrylic, glass, stone, plastic, or ceramic pipes with or without screens, permanent screens, hashish heads, or punctured metal bowls;

(2) water pipes;

(3) carburetion tubes and devices;

(4) smoking and carburetion masks;

(5) roach clips: meaning objects used to hold burning material, such as a marihuana cigarette, that has become too small or too short to be held in the hand;

(6) miniature spoons with level capacities of one-tenth cubic centimeter or less;

(7) chamber pipes;

(8) carburetor pipes;

(9) electric pipes;

(10) air-driven pipes;

(11) chillums;

(12) bongs;

(13) ice pipes or chillers;

(14) wired cigarette papers; or

(15) cocaine freebase kits.

(e) Matters considered in determination of what constitutes drug paraphernalia. In determining whether an item constitutes drug paraphernalia, in addition to all other logically relevant factors, the following may be considered:

(1) instructions, oral or written, provided with the item concerning its use;

(2) descriptive materials accompanying the item which explain or depict its use;

(3) national and local advertising concerning its use;

(4) the manner in which the item is displayed for sale;

(5) whether the owner, or anyone in control of the item, is a legitimate supplier of like or related items to the community, such as a licensed distributor or dealer of tobacco products;

(6) direct or circumstantial evidence of the ratio of sales of the item(s) to the total sales of the business enterprise;

(7) the existence and scope of legitimate uses of the item in the community; and

(8) expert testimony concerning its use.

(f) Exemptions. This section shall not apply to—

(1) any person authorized by local, State, or Federal law to manufacture, possess, or distribute such items; or

(2) any item that, in the normal lawful course of business, is imported, exported, transported, or sold through the mail or by any other means, and traditionally intended for use with tobacco products, including any pipe, paper, or accessory.

(Oct. 27, 1970, P. L. 91-513, Title II, Part D, § 422, as added Nov. 29, 1990, P. L. 101-647, Title XXIV, § 2401(a), 104 Stat. 4858; Nov. 18, 1988, P. L. 100-690, Title VI, Subtitle IV, § 6485, 102 Stat. 4384; Nov. 29, 1990, P. L. 101-647, Title XXIV, § 2401(b), (c), 104 Stat. 4859; Oct. 17, 2000, P. L. 106-310, Div B, Title XXXVI, Subtitle A, Part I, § 3614, 114 Stat. 1230.)

§ 864. Anhydrous ammonia

(a) It is unlawful for any person—

(1) to steal anhydrous ammonia, or

(2) to transport stolen anhydrous ammonia across State lines,

knowing, intending, or having reasonable cause to believe that such anhydrous ammonia will be used to manufacture a controlled substance in violation of this part [21 USCS §§ 841 et seq.].

(b) Any person who violates subsection (a) shall be imprisoned or fined, or both, in accordance with section 403(d) [21 USCS § 843(d)] as if such violation were a violation of a provision of section 403 [21 USCS § 843].

(Oct. 27, 1970, P. L. 91-513, Title II, Part D, § 423, as added Oct. 17, 2000, P. L. 106-310, Div B, Title XXXVI, Subtitle B, § 3653(a), 114 Stat. 1240.)

§ 864a. Grants to reduce production of methamphetamines from anhydrous ammonia

(a) Definitions. In this section:

(1) Eligible entity. The term "eligible entity" means—

(A) a producer of agricultural commodities;

(B) a cooperative association, a majority of the members of which produce or process agricultural commodities; or

(C) a person in the trade or business of—

(i) selling an agricultural product (including an agricultural chemical) at retail, predominantly to farmers and ranchers; or

(ii) aerial and ground application of an agricultural chemical.

(2) Nurse tank. The term "nurse tank" shall be considered to be a cargo tank (within the meaning of section 173.315(m) of title 49, Code of Federal Regulations, as in effect as of the date of the enactment of this Act).

(b) Grant authority. The Secretary may make a grant to an eligible entity to enable the eligible entity to obtain and add to an anhydrous ammonia fertilizer nurse tank a physical lock or a substance to reduce the amount of methamphetamine that can be produced from any anhydrous ammonia removed from the nurse tank.

(c) Grant amount. The amount of a grant made under this section to an eligible entity shall be the product obtained by multiplying—

(1) an amount not less than $40 and not more than $60, as determined by the Secretary; and

(2) the number of fertilizer nurse tanks of the eligible entity.

(d) Authorization of appropriations. There is authorized to be appropriated to the Secretary to make grants under this section $15,000,000 for the period of fiscal years 2008 through 2012.

(June 18, 2008, P. L. 110-246, Title XIV, Subtitle C, § 14203, 122 Stat. 2220.)

§ 865. Smuggling methamphetamine or methamphetamine precursor chemicals into the United States while using facilitated entry programs

(a) Enhanced prison sentence. The sentence of imprisonment imposed on a person convicted of an offense under the Controlled Substances Act (21 U.S.C. 801 et seq.) or the Controlled Substances Import and Export Act (21 U.S.C. 951 et seq.), involving methamphetamine or any listed chemical that is defined in section 102(33) of the Controlled Substances Act (21 U.S.C. 802(33)[)], shall, if the offense is committed under the circumstance described in subsection (b), be increased by a consecutive term of imprisonment of not more than 15 years.

(b) Circumstances. For purposes of subsection (a), the circumstance described in this subsection is that the offense described in subsection (a) was committed by a person who—

(1) was enrolled in, or who was acting on behalf of any person or entity enrolled in, any dedicated commuter lane, alternative or accelerated inspection system, or other facilitated entry program administered or approved by the Federal Government for use in entering the United States; and

(2) committed the offense while entering the United States, using such lane, system, or program.

(c) Permanent ineligibility. Any person whose term of imprisonment is increased under subsection (a) shall be permanently and irrevocably barred from being eligible for or using any lane, system, or program described in subsection (b)(1).

(March 9, 2006, P. L. 109-177, Title VII, Subtitle C, § 731, 120 Stat. 270.)

ADMINISTRATIVE AND ENFORCEMENT PROVISIONS

§ 871. Attorney General

(a) Delegation of functions. The Attorney General may delegate any of his functions under this title to any officer or employee of the Department of Justice.

(b) Rules and regulations. The Attorney General may promulgate and enforce any rules, regulations, and procedures which he may deem necessary and appropriate for the efficient execution of his functions under this title.

(c) Acceptance of devises, bequests, gifts, and donations. The Attorney General may accept in the name of the Department of Justice any form of devise, bequest, gift, or donation where the donor intends to donate property for the purpose of preventing or controlling the abuse of controlled substances. He may take all appropriate steps to secure possession of such property and may sell, assign, transfer, or convey any such property other than moneys.

(Oct. 27, 1970, P. L. 91-513, Title II, Part E, § 501, 84 Stat. 1270.)

§ 871a. Semiannual reports to Congress

(a) In general. The Attorney General shall, on a semiannual basis, submit to the congressional committees and organizations specified in subsection (b) reports that—

(1) describe the allocation of the resources of the Drug Enforcement Administration and the Federal Bureau of Investigation for the investigation and prosecution of alleged violations of the Controlled Substances Act involving methamphetamine; and

(2) the measures being taken to give priority in the allocation of such resources to such violations involving—

(A) persons alleged to have imported into the United States substantial quantities of methamphetamine or scheduled listed chemicals (as defined pursuant to the amendment made by section 711(a)(1));

(B) persons alleged to have manufactured methamphetamine; and

(C) circumstances in which the violations have endangered children.

(b) Congressional committees. The congressional committees and organizations referred to in subsection (a) are—

(1) in the House of Representatives, the Committee on the Judiciary, the Committee on Energy and Commerce, and the Committee on Government Reform [Oversight and Government Reform]; and

(2) in the Senate, the Committee on the Judiciary, the Committee on Commerce, Science, and Transportation, and the Caucus on International Narcotics Control.

(March 9, 2006, P. L. 109-177, Title VII, Subtitle C, § 736, 120 Stat. 271.)

§ 872. Education and research programs of Attorney General

(a) Authorization. The Attorney General is authorized to carry out educational and research programs directly related to enforcement of the laws under his jurisdiction concerning drugs or other substances which are or may be subject to control under this title. Such programs may include—

(1) educational and training programs on drug abuse and controlled substances law enforcement for local, State, tribal, and Federal personnel;

(2) studies or special projects designed to compare the deterrent effects of various enforcement strategies on drug use and abuse;

(3) studies or special projects designed to assess and detect accurately the presence in the human body of drugs or other substances which are or may be subject to control under this title, including the development of rapid field identification methods which would enable agents to detect microquantities of such drugs or other substances;

(4) studies or special projects designed to evaluate the nature and sources of the supply of illegal drugs throughout the country;

(5) studies or special projects to develop more effective methods to prevent diversion of controlled substances into illegal channels; and

(6) studies or special projects to develop information necessary to carry out his functions under section 201 of this title [21 USCS § 811].

(b) Contracts. The Attorney General may enter into contracts for such educational and research activities without performance bonds and without regard to section 3709 of the Revised Statutes (41 U.S.C. 5) [41 USCS § 6101].

(c) Identification of research populations; authorization to withhold. The Attorney General may authorize persons engaged in research to withhold the names and other identifying characteristics of persons who are the subjects of such research. Persons who obtain this authorization may not be compelled in any Federal, State, tribal, or local civil, criminal, administrative, legislative, or other proceeding to identify the subjects of research for which such authorization was obtained.

(d) Affect of treaties and other international agreements on confidentiality. Nothing in the Single Convention on Narcotic Drugs, the Convention on Psychotropic Substances, or other treaties or international agreements shall be construed to limit, modify, or prevent the protection of the confidentiality of patient records or of the names and other identifying characteristics of research subjects as provided by any Federal, State, or local law or regulation.

(e) Use of controlled substances in research. The Attorney General, on his own motion or at the request of the Secretary, may authorize the possession, distribution, and dispensing of controlled substances by persons engaged in research. Persons who obtain this authorization shall be exempt from State or Federal prosecution for possession, distribution, and dispensing of controlled substances to the extent authorized by the Attorney General.

(f) Program to curtail diversion of precursor and essential chemicals. The Attorney General shall maintain an active program, both domestic and international, to curtail the diversion of precursor chemicals and essential chemicals used in the illicit manufacture of controlled substances.

(Oct. 27, 1970, P. L. 91-513, Title II, Part E, § 502, 84 Stat. 1271; Nov. 10, 1978, P. L. 95-633, Title I, § 108(a), 92 Stat. 3773; Nov. 18, 1988, P. L. 100-690, Title VI, Subtitle A, § 6060, 102 Stat. 4320; July 29, 2010, P. L. 111-211, Title II, Subtitle C, § 232(a), 124 Stat. 2278.)

§ 872a. Public-private education program

(a) Advisory panel. The Attorney General shall establish an advisory panel consisting of an appropriate number of representatives from Federal, State, tribal, and local law enforcement and regulatory agencies with experience in investigating and prosecuting illegal transactions of precursor chemicals. The Attorney General shall convene the panel as often as necessary to develop and coordinate educational programs for wholesale and retail distributors of precursor chemicals and supplies.

(b) Continuation of current efforts. The Attorney General shall continue to—

(1) maintain an active program of seminars and training to educate wholesale and retail distributors of precursor chemicals and supplies regarding the identification of suspicious transactions and their responsibility to report such transactions; and

(2) provide assistance to State, tribal, and local law enforcement and regulatory agencies to facilitate the establishment and maintenance of educational programs for distributors of precursor chemicals and supplies.

(Oct. 3, 1996, P. L. 104-237, Title V, § 503, 110 Stat. 3112; July 29, 2010, P. L. 111-211, Title II, Subtitle C, § 232(b), 124 Stat. 2278.)

§ 873. Cooperative arrangements

(a) Cooperation of Attorney General with local, State, tribal, and Federal agencies. The Attorney General shall cooperate with local, State, tribal, and Federal agencies concerning traffic in controlled substances and in suppressing the abuse of controlled substances. To this end, he is authorized to—

(1) arrange for the exchange of information between governmental officials concerning the use and abuse of controlled substances;

(2) cooperate in the institution and prosecution of cases in the courts of the United States and before the licensing boards and courts of the several States;

(3) conduct training programs on controlled substance law enforcement for local, State, tribal, and Federal personnel;

(4) maintain in the Department of Justice a unit which will accept, catalog, file, and otherwise utilize all information and statistics, including records of controlled substance abusers and other controlled substance law offenders, which may be received from Federal, State, tribal, and local agencies, and make such information available for Federal, State, tribal, and local law enforcement purposes;

(5) conduct programs of eradication aimed at destroying wild or illicit growth of plant species from which controlled substances may be extracted;

(6) assist State, tribal, and local governments in suppressing the diversion of controlled substances from legitimate medical, scientific, and commercial channels by—

(A) making periodic assessments of the capabilities of State, tribal, and local governments to adequately control the diversion of controlled substances;

(B) providing advice and counsel to State, tribal, and local governments on the methods by which such governments may strengthen their controls against diversion; and

(C) establishing cooperative investigative efforts to control diversion; and

(7) notwithstanding any other provision of law, enter into contractual agreements with State, tribal, and local law enforcement agencies to provide for cooperative enforcement and regulatory activities under this Act.

(b) Requests by Attorney General for assistance from Federal agencies or instrumentalities. When requested by the Attorney General, it shall be the duty of any agency or instrumentality of the Federal Government to furnish assistance, including technical advice, to him for carrying out his functions under this title; except that no such agency or instrumentality shall be required to furnish the name of, or other identifying information about, a patient or research subject whose identity it has undertaken to keep confidential.

(c)(1) The Attorney General shall, once every 6 months, prepare and make available to regulatory, licensing, attorneys general, and law enforcement agencies of States a standardized report containing descriptive and analytic information on the actual distribution patterns, as gathered through the Automated Reports and Consolidated Orders System, or any subsequent automated system, pursuant to section 307 [21 USCS § 827] and which includes detailed amounts, outliers, and trends of distributor and pharmacy registrants, in such States for the controlled substances contained in schedule II, which, in the discretion of the Attorney General, are determined to have the highest abuse.

(2) If the Attorney General publishes the report described in paragraph (1) once every 6 months as required under paragraph (1), nothing in this subsection shall be construed to bring an action in any court to challenge the sufficiency of the information or to compel the Attorney General to produce any documents or reports referred to in this subsection.

(d) Grants by Attorney General.

(1) The Attorney General may make grants, in accordance with paragraph (2), to State, tribal, and local governments to assist in meeting the costs of—

(A) collecting and analyzing data on the diversion of controlled substances,

(B) conducting investigations and prosecutions of such diversions,

(C) improving regulatory controls and other authorities to control such diversions,

(D) programs to prevent such diversions,

(E) preventing and detecting forged prescriptions, and

(F) training law enforcement and regulatory personnel to improve the control of such diversions.

(2) No grant may be made under paragraph (1) unless an application therefor is submitted to the Attorney General in such form and manner as the Attorney General may prescribe. No grant may exceed 80 per centum of the costs for which the grant is made, and no grant may be made unless the recipient of the grant provides assurances satisfactory to the Attorney General that it will obligate funds to meet the remaining 20 per centum of such costs. The Attorney General shall review the activities carried out with grants

under paragraph (1) and shall report annually to Congress on such activities.

(3) To carry out this subsection there is authorized to be appropriated $6,000,000 for fiscal year 1985 and $6,000,000 for fiscal year 1986.

(Oct. 27, 1970, P. L. 91-513, Title II, Part E, § 503, 84 Stat. 1271; Sept. 26, 1980, P. L. 96-359, § 8(a), 94 Stat. 1194; Oct. 12, 1984, P. L. 98-473, Title II, Ch V, Part B, § 517, 98 Stat. 2074; Oct. 27, 1986, P. L. 99-570, Title I, Subtitle Q, § 1868, 100 Stat. 3207-55; Nov. 10, 1986, P. L. 99-646, § 85, 100 Stat. 3620; July 29, 2010, P. L. 111-211, Title II, Subtitle C, § 232(c), 124 Stat. 2278; Oct. 24, 2018, P.L. 115-271, Title III, Subtitle B, Ch 7, § 3273(b), 132 Stat. 3953.)

§ 874. Advisory committees

The Attorney General may from time to time appoint committees to advise him with respect to preventing and controlling the abuse of controlled substances. Members of the committees may be entitled to receive compensation at the rate of $100 for each day (including traveltime) during which they are engaged in the actual performance of duties. While traveling on official business in the performance of duties for the committees, members of the committees shall be allowed expenses of travel, including per diem instead of subsistence, in accordance with subchapter I of chapter 57 of title 5, United States Code [5 USCS §§ 5701 et seq.].

(Oct. 27, 1970, P. L. 91-513, Title II, Part E, § 504, 84 Stat. 1272.)

§ 875. Administrative hearings

(a) Power of Attorney General. In carrying out his functions under this title, the Attorney General may hold hearings, sign and issue subpenas, administer oaths, examine witnesses, and receive evidence at any place in the United States.

(b) Procedures applicable. Except as otherwise provided in this title, notice shall be given and hearings shall be conducted under appropriate procedures of subchapter II of chapter 5, title 5, United States Code [5 USCS §§ 551 et seq.].

(Oct. 27, 1970, P. L. 91-513, Title II, Part E, § 505, 84 Stat. 1272.)

§ 876. Subpoenas

(a) Authorization of use by Attorney General. In any investigation relating to his functions under this title with respect to controlled substances, listed chemicals, tableting machines, or encapsulating machines, the Attorney General may subpoena witnesses, compel the attendance and testimony of witnesses, and require the production of any records (including books, papers, documents, and other tangible things which constitute or contain evidence) which the Attorney General finds relevant or material to the investigation. The attendance of witnesses and the production of records may be required from any place in any State or in any territory or other place subject to the jurisdiction of the United States at any designated place of hearing; except that a witness shall not be required to appear at any hearing more than 500 miles distant from the place where he was served with a subpoena. Witnesses summoned under this section shall be paid the same fees and mileage that are paid witnesses in the courts of the United States.

(b) Service. A subpoena issued under this section may be served by any person designated in the subpoena to serve it. Service upon a natural person may be made by personal delivery of the subpoena to him. Service may be made upon a domestic or foreign corporation or upon a partnership or other unincorporated association which is subject to suit under a common name, by delivering the subpoena to an officer, to a managing or general agent, or to any other agent authorized by appointment or by law to receive service of process. The affidavit of the person serving the subpoena entered on a true copy thereof by the person serving it shall be proof of service.

(c) Enforcement. In the case of contumacy by or refusal to obey a subpoena issued to any person, the Attorney General may invoke the aid of any court of the United States within the jurisdiction of which the investigation is carried on or of which the subpoenaed person is an inhabitant, or in which he carries on business or may be found, to compel compliance with the subpoena. The court may issue an order requiring the subpoenaed person to appear before the Attorney General to produce records, if so ordered, or to give testimony touching the matter under investigation. Any failure to obey the order of the court may be punished by the court as a contempt thereof. All process in any such case may be served in any judicial district in which such person may be found.

(Oct. 27, 1970, P. L. 91-513, Title II, Part E, § 506, 84 Stat. 1272; Nov. 18, 1988, P. L. 100-690, Title VI, Subtitle A, § 6058, 102 Stat. 4319.)

§ 877. Judicial review

All final determinations, findings, and conclusions of the Attorney General under this title shall be final and conclusive decisions of the matters involved, except that any person aggrieved by a final decision of the Attorney General may obtain review of the decision in the United States Court of Appeals for the District of Columbia or for the circuit in which his principal place of business is located upon petition filed with the court and delivered to the Attorney General within thirty days after notice of the decision. Findings of fact by the Attorney General, if supported by substantial evidence, shall be conclusive.

(Oct. 27, 1970, P. L. 91-513, Title II, Part E, § 507, 84 Stat. 1273.)

§ 878. Powers of enforcement personnel

(a) Any officer or employee of the Drug Enforcement Administration or any State, tribal, or local law enforcement officer designated by the Attorney General may—

(1) carry firearms;

(2) execute and serve search warrants, arrest warrants, administrative inspection warrants, subpenas, and summonses issued under the authority of the United States;

(3) make arrests without warrant (A) for any offense against the United States committed in his presence, or (B) for any felony, cognizable under the laws of the United States, if he has probable cause to believe that the person to be arrested has committed or is committing a felony;

(4) make seizures of property pursuant to the provisions of this title; and

(5) perform such other law enforcement duties as the Attorney General may designate.

(b) State and local law enforcement officers performing functions under this section shall not be deemed Federal employees and shall not be subject to provisions of law relating to Federal employees, except that such officers shall be subject to section 3374(c) of title 5, United States Code.

(Oct. 27, 1970, P. L. 91-513, Title II, Part E, § 508, 84 Stat. 1273; Nov. 30, 1979, P. L. 96-132, § 16(b), 93 Stat. 1049; Oct. 27, 1986, P. L. 99-570, Title I, Subtitle Q, § 1869, 100 Stat. 3207-55; Nov. 10, 1986, P. L. 99-646, § 86, 100 Stat. 3620; July 29, 2010, P. L. 111-211, Title II, Subtitle C, § 232(d), 124 Stat. 2278.)

§ 879. Search warrants

A search warrant relating to offenses involving controlled substances may be served at any time of the day or night if the judge or United States magistrate [United States magistrate judge] issuing the warrant is satisfied that there is probable cause to believe that grounds exist for the warrant and for its service at such time.

(Oct. 27, 1970, P. L. 91-513, Title II, Part E, § 509, 84 Stat. 1274; Oct. 26, 1974, P. L. 93-481, § 3, 88 Stat. 1455.)

§ 880. Administrative inspections and warrants

(a) "Controlled premises" defined. As used in this section, the term "controlled premises" means—

(1) places where original or other records or documents required under this title are kept or required to be kept, and

(2) places, including factories, warehouses, and other establishments, and conveyances, where persons registered under section 303 [21 USCS § 823] (or exempt from registration under section 302(d) [21 USCS § 822(d)] or by regulation of the Attorney General) or regulated persons may lawfully hold, manufacture, distribute, dispense, administer, or otherwise dispose of controlled substances or listed chemicals or where records relating to those activities are maintained.

(b) Grant of authority; scope of inspection.

(1) For the purpose of inspecting, copying, and verifying the correctness of records, reports, or other documents required to be kept or made under this title and otherwise facilitating the carrying out of his functions under this title, the Attorney General is authorized, in accordance with this section, to enter controlled premises and to conduct administrative inspections thereof, and of the things specified in this section, relevant to those functions.

(2) Such entries and inspections shall be carried out through officers or employees (hereinafter referred to as "inspectors") designated by the Attorney General. Any such inspector, upon stating his purpose and presenting to the owner, operator, or agent in charge of such premises (A) appropriate credentials and (B) a written notice of his inspection authority (which notice in the case of an inspection requiring, or in fact supported by, an administrative inspection warrant shall consist of such warrant), shall have the right to enter such premises and conduct such inspection at reasonable times.

(3) Except as may otherwise be indicated in an applicable inspection warrant, the inspector shall have the right—

(A) to inspect and copy records, reports, and other documents required to be kept or made under this title;

(B) to inspect, within reasonable limits and in a reasonable manner, controlled premises and all pertinent equipment, finished and unfinished drugs, listed chemicals, and other substances or materials, containers, and labeling found therein, and, except as provided in paragraph (4) of this subsection, all other things therein (including records, files, papers, processes, controls, and facilities) appropriate for verification of the records, reports, and documents referred to in clause (A) or otherwise bearing on the provisions of this title; and

(C) to inventory any stock of any controlled substance or listed chemical therein and obtain samples of any such substance or chemical.

(4) Except when the owner, operator, or agent in charge of the controlled premises so consents in writing, no inspection authorized by this section shall extend to—

(A) financial data;

(B) sales data other than shipment data; or

(C) pricing data.

(c) Situations not requiring warrants. A warrant under this section shall not be required for the inspection of books and records pursuant to an administrative subpena issued in accordance with section 506 [21 USCS § 876], nor for entries and administrative inspections (including seizures of property)—

(1) with the consent of the owner, operator, or agent in charge of the controlled premises;

(2) in situations presenting imminent danger to health or safety;

(3) in situations involving inspection of conveyances where there is reasonable cause to believe that the mobility of the conveyance makes it impracticable to obtain a warrant;

(4) in any other exceptional or emergency circumstance where time or opportunity to apply for a warrant is lacking; or

(5) in any other situations where a warrant is not constitutionally required.

(d) Administrative inspection warrants; issuance; execution; probable cause. Issuance and execution of administrative inspection warrants shall be as follows:

(1) Any judge of the United States or of a State court of record, or any United States magistrate [United States magistrate judge], may, within his territorial jurisdiction, and upon proper oath or affirmation showing probable cause, issue warrants for the purpose of

conducting administrative inspections authorized by this title or regulations thereunder, and seizures of property appropriate to such inspections. For the purposes of this section, the term "probable cause" means a valid public interest in the effective enforcement of this title or regulations thereunder sufficient to justify administrative inspections of the area, premises, building, or conveyance, or contents thereof, in the circumstances specified in the application for the warrant.

(2) A warrant shall issue only upon an affidavit of an officer or employee having knowledge of the facts alleged, sworn to before the judge or magistrate [magistrate judge] and establishing the grounds for issuing the warrant. If the judge or magistrate [magistrate judge] is satisfied that grounds for the application exist or that there is probable cause to believe they exist, he shall issue a warrant identifying the area, premises, building, or conveyance to be inspected, the purpose of such inspection, and, where appropriate, the type of property to be inspected, if any. The warrant shall identify the items or types of property to be seized, if any. The warrant shall be directed to a person authorized under subsection (b)(2) to execute it. The warrant shall state the grounds for its issuance and the name of the person or persons whose affidavit has been taken in support thereof. It shall command the person to whom it is directed to inspect the area, premises, building, or conveyance identified for the purpose specified, and, where appropriate, shall direct the seizure of the property specified. The warrant shall direct that it be served during normal business hours. It shall designate the judge or magistrate [magistrate judge] to whom it shall be returned.

(3) A warrant issued pursuant to this section must be executed and returned within ten days of its date unless, upon a showing by the United States of a need therefor, the judge or magistrate [magistrate judge] allows additional time in the warrant. If property is seized pursuant to a warrant, the person executing the warrant shall give to the person from whom or from whose premises the property was taken a copy of the warrant and a receipt for the property taken or shall leave the copy and receipt at the place from which the property was taken. The return of the warrant shall be made promptly and shall be accompanied by a written inventory of any property taken. The inventory shall be made in the presence of the person executing the warrant and of the person from whose possession or premises the property was taken, if they are present or in the presence of at least one credible person other than the person making such inventory, and shall be verified by the person executing the warrant. The judge or magistrate [magistrate judge], upon request, shall deliver a copy of the inventory to the person from whom or from whose premises the property was taken and to the applicant for the warrant.

(4) The judge or magistrate [magistrate judge] who has issued a warrant under this section shall attach to the warrant a copy of the return and all papers filed in connection therewith and shall file them with the clerk of the district court of the United States for the judicial district in which the inspection was made.

(Oct. 27, 1970, P. L. 91-513, Title II, Part E, § 510, 84 Stat. 1274; Nov. 29, 1990, P. L. 101-647, Title XXXV, § 3599M, 104 Stat. 4932; Dec. 17, 1993, P. L. 103-200, § 6, 107 Stat. 2340.)

§ 881. Forfeitures

(a) Subject property. The following shall be subject to forfeiture to the United States and no property right shall exist in them:

(1) All controlled substances which have been manufactured, distributed, dispensed, or acquired in violation of this title.

(2) All raw materials, products, and equipment of any kind which are used, or intended for use, in manufacturing, compounding, processing, delivering, importing, or exporting any controlled substance or listed chemical in violation of this title.

(3) All property which is used, or intended for use, as a container for property described in paragraph (1), (2), or (9).

(4) All conveyances, including aircraft, vehicles, or vessels, which are used, or are intended for use, to transport, or in any manner to facilitate the transportation, sale, receipt, possession, or concealment of property described in paragraph (1), (2), or (9).

(5) All books, records, and research, including formulas, microfilm, tapes, and data which are used, or intended for use, in violation of this title.

(6) All moneys, negotiable instruments, securities, or other things of value furnished or intended to be furnished by any person in exchange for a controlled substance or listed chemical in violation of this title, all proceeds traceable to such an exchange, and all moneys, negotiable instruments, and securities used or intended to be used to facilitate any violation of this title.

(7) All real property, including any right, title, and interest (including any leasehold interest) in the whole of any lot or tract of land and any appurtenances or improvements, which is used, or intended to be used, in any manner or part, to commit, or to facilitate the commission of, a violation of this title punishable by more than one year's imprisonment.

(8) All controlled substances which have been possessed in violation of this title.

(9) All listed chemicals, all drug manufacturing equipment, all tableting machines, all encapsulating machines, and all gelatin capsules, which have been imported, exported, manufactured, possessed, distributed, dispensed, acquired, or intended to be distributed, dispensed, acquired, imported, or exported, in violation of this title or title III.

(10) Any drug paraphernalia (as defined in section 422 [21 USCS § 863]).

(11) Any firearm (as defined in section 921 of title 18, United States Code) used or intended to be used to facilitate the transportation, sale, receipt, possession, or concealment of property described in paragraph (1) or (2) and any proceeds traceable to such property.

(b) Seizure procedures. Any property subject to forfeiture to the United States under this section may be seized by the Attorney General in the manner set forth in section 981(b) of title 18, United States Code.

(c) Custody of Attorney General. Property taken or detained under this section shall not be repleviable, but shall be deemed to be in the custody of the Attorney General, subject only to the orders and decrees of the court or the official having jurisdiction thereof. Whenever property is seized under any of the provisions of this title, the Attorney General may—

(1) place the property under seal;

(2) remove the property to a place designated by him; or

(3) require that the General Services Administration take custody of the property and remove it, if practicable, to an appropriate location for disposition in accordance with law.

(d) Other laws and proceedings applicable. The provisions of law relating to the seizure, summary and judicial forfeiture, and condemnation of property for violation of the customs laws; the disposition of such property or the proceeds from the sale thereof; the remission or mitigation of such forfeitures; and the compromise of claims shall apply to seizures and forfeitures incurred, or alleged to have been incurred, under any of the provisions of this title, insofar as applicable and not inconsistent with the provisions hereof; except that such duties as are imposed upon the customs officer or any other person with respect to the seizure and forfeiture of property under the customs laws shall be performed with respect to seizures and forfeitures of property under this title by such officers, agents, or other persons as may be authorized or designated for that purpose by the Attorney General, except to the extent that such duties arise from seizures and forfeitures effected by any customs officer.

(e) Disposition of forfeited property.

(1) Whenever property is civilly or criminally forfeited under this title the Attorney General may—

(A) retain the property for official use or, in the manner provided with respect to transfers under section 616 of the Tariff Act of 1930, transfer the property to any Federal agency or to any State or local law enforcement agency which participated directly in the seizure or forfeiture of the property;

(B) except as provided in paragraph (4), sell, by public sale or any other commercially feasible means, any forfeited property which is not required to be destroyed by law and which is not harmful to the public;

(C) require that the General Services Administration take custody of the property and dispose of it in accordance with law;

(D) forward it to the Bureau of Narcotics and Dangerous Drugs for disposition (including delivery for medical or scientific use to any Federal or State agency under regulations of the Attorney General); or

(E) transfer the forfeited personal property or the proceeds of the sale of any forfeited personal or real property to any foreign country which participated directly or indirectly in the seizure or forfeiture of the property, if such a transfer—

(i) has been agreed to by the Secretary of State;

(ii) is authorized in an international agreement between the United States and the foreign country; and

(iii) is made to a country which, if applicable, has been certified under section 490(b) of the Foreign Assistance Act of 1961 [22 USCS § 2291j(b)].

(2)(A) The proceeds from any sale under subparagraph (B) of paragraph (1) and any moneys forfeited under this title shall be used to pay—

(i) all property expenses of the proceedings for forfeiture and sale including expenses of seizure, maintenance of custody, advertising, and court costs; and

(ii) awards of up to $100,000 to any individual who provides original information which leads to the arrest and conviction of a person who kills or kidnaps a Federal drug law enforcement agent. Any award paid for information concerning the killing or kidnapping of a Federal drug law enforcement agent, as provided in clause (ii), shall be paid at the discretion of the Attorney General.

(B) The Attorney General shall forward to the Treasurer of the United States for deposit in accordance with section 524(c) of title 28, United States Code, any amounts of such moneys and proceeds remaining after payment of the expenses provided in subparagraph (A), except that, with respect to forfeitures conducted by the Postal Service, the Postal Service shall deposit in the Postal Service Fund, under section 2003(b)(7) of title 39, United States Code, such moneys and proceeds.

(3) The Attorney General shall assure that any property transferred to a State or local law enforcement agency under paragraph (1)(A)—

(A) has a value that bears a reasonable relationship to the degree of direct participation of the State or local agency in the law enforcement effort resulting in the forfeiture, taking into account the total value of all property forfeited and the total law enforcement effort with respect to the violation of law on which the forfeiture is based; and

(B) will serve to encourage further cooperation between the recipient State or local agency and Federal law enforcement agencies.

(4)(A) With respect to real property described in subparagraph (B), if the chief executive officer of the State involved submits to the Attorney General a request for purposes of such subparagraph, the authority established in such subparagraph is in lieu of the authority established in paragraph (1)(B).

(B) In the case of property described in paragraph (1)(B) that is civilly or criminally forfeited under this title, if the property is real property that is appropriate for use as a public area reserved for recreational or historic purposes or for the preservation of natural conditions, the Attorney General, upon the request of the chief executive officer of the State in which the property is located, may transfer title to the property to the State, either without charge or for a nominal charge, through a legal instrument providing that—

(i) such use will be the principal use of the property; and

(ii) title to the property reverts to the United States in the event that the property is used otherwise.

(f) Forfeiture and destruction of schedule I or II substances.

(1) All controlled substances in schedule I or II that are possessed, transferred, sold, or offered for sale in violation of the provisions of this title; all dangerous, toxic, or hazardous raw materials or products subject to forfeiture under subsection (a)(2) of this section; and any equipment or container subject to forfeiture under subsection (a)(2) or (3) which cannot be separated safely from such raw materials or products shall be deemed contraband and seized and summarily forfeited to the United States. Similarly, all substances in schedule I or II, which are seized or come into the possession of the United States, the owners of which are unknown, shall be deemed contraband and summarily forfeited to the United States.

(2) The Attorney General may direct the destruction of all controlled substances in schedule I or II seized for violation of this title; all dangerous, toxic, or hazardous raw materials or products subject to forfeiture under subsection (a)(2) of this section; and any equipment or container subject to forfeiture under subsection (a)(2) or (3) which cannot be separated safely from such raw materials or products under such circumstances as the Attorney General may deem necessary.

(g) Plants.

(1) All species of plants from which controlled substances in schedules I and II may be derived which have been planted or cultivated in violation of this title, or of which the owners or cultivators are unknown, or which are wild growths, may be seized and summarily forfeited to the United States.

(2) The failure, upon demand by the Attorney General or his duly authorized agent, of the person in occupancy or in control of land or premises upon which such species of plants are growing or being stored, to produce an appropriate registration, or proof that he is the holder thereof, shall constitute authority for the seizure and forfeiture.

(3) The Attorney General, or his duly authorized agent, shall have authority to enter upon any lands, or into any dwelling pursuant to a search warrant, to cut, harvest, carry off, or destroy such plants.

(h) Vesting of title in United States. All right, title, and interest in property described in subsection (a) shall vest in the United States upon commission of the act giving rise to forfeiture under this section.

(i) Stay of civil forfeiture proceedings. The provisions of section 981(g) of title 18, United States Code, regarding the stay of a civil forfeiture proceeding shall apply to forfeitures under this section.

(j) Venue. In addition to the venue provided for in section 1395 of title 28, United States Code, or any other provision of law, in the case of property of a defendant charged with a violation that is the basis for forfeiture of the property under this section, a proceeding for forfeiture under this section may be brought in the judicial district in which the defendant owning such property is found or in the judicial district in which the criminal prosecution is brought.

(k) [Not enacted]

(l) Agreement between Attorney General and Postal Service for performance of functions. The functions of the Attorney General under this section shall be carried out by the Postal Service pursuant to such agreement as may be entered into between the Attorney General and the Postal Service.

(Oct. 27, 1970, P. L. 91-513, Title II, Part E, § 511, 84 Stat. 1276; Nov. 10, 1978, P. L. 95-633, Title III, § 301(a), 92 Stat. 3777; Nov. 30, 1979, P. L. 96-132, § 14, 93 Stat. 1048; Oct. 12, 1984, P. L. 98-473, Title II, Ch III, Part B, § 306 Part C, § 309, Ch V, § 518, 98 Stat. 2050, 2051, 2075; Oct. 27, 1986, P. L. 99-570, Title I, Subtitle A, § 1006(c), Subtitle Q, § 1865, Subtitle U. § 1992, 100 Stat. 3207-7, 3207-54, 3207-59; Nov. 10, 1986, P. L. 99-646, § 74, 100 Stat. 3618; Nov. 18, 1988, P. L. 100-690, Title V, Subtitle C, Ch 1, § 5105, Title VI, Subtitle A, § 6059, Subtitle B, §§ 6074, 6075, 6077(a), (b), Subtitle H, § 6253, 102 Stat. 4301, 4320, 4323, 4324, 4363; Nov. 29, 1989, P. L. 101-189, Div A, Title XII, § 1215(a), 103 Stat. 1569; Nov. 29, 1990, P. L. 101-647, Title XX, §§ 2003, 2004, 2007, 2008, 104 Stat. 4855; Dec. 17, 1991, P. L. 102-239, § 2, 105 Stat. 1912; Nov. 2, 1994, P. L. 103-447, Title I, § 102(d), 108 Stat. 4693; Oct. 3, 1996, P. L. 104-237, Title II, § 201(b), 110 Stat. 3101; April 25, 2000, P. L. 106-185, §§ 2(c)(2), 5(b), 8(b), 114 Stat. 210, 214, 216; Nov. 2, 2002, P. L. 107-273, Div B, Title IV, § 4002(e)(3), 116 Stat. 1810.)

§ 881-1. [Transferred]

§ 881a. [Transferred]

§ 882. Injunctions

(a) Jurisdiction. The district courts of the United States and all courts exercising general jurisdiction in the territories and possessions of the United States shall have jurisdiction in proceedings in accordance with the Federal Rules of Civil Procedure to enjoin violations of this title.

(b) Jury trial. In case of an alleged violation of an injunction or restraining order issued under this section, trial shall, upon demand of the accused, be by a jury in accordance with the Federal Rules of Civil Procedure.

(c) State cause of action pertaining to online pharmacies.

(1) In general. In any case in which the State has reason to believe that an interest of the residents of that State has been or is being threatened or adversely affected by the action of a person, entity, or Internet site that violates the provisions of section 303(g), 309(e), or 311 [21 USCS § 823(g), 829(e), or 831], the State may bring a civil action on behalf of such residents in a district court of the United States with appropriate jurisdiction—

(A) to enjoin the conduct which violates this section;

(B) to enforce compliance with this section;

(C) to obtain damages, restitution, or other compensation, including civil penalties under section 402(b) [21 USCS § 842(b)]; and

(D) to obtain such other legal or equitable relief as the court may find appropriate.

(2) Service; intervention.

(A) Prior to filing a complaint under paragraph (1), the State shall serve a copy of the complaint upon the Attorney General and upon the United States Attorney for the judicial district in which the complaint is to be filed. In any case where such prior service is not feasible, the State shall serve the complaint on the Attorney General and the appropriate United States Attorney on the same day that the State's complaint is filed in Federal district court of the United States. Such proceedings shall be independent of, and not in lieu of, criminal prosecutions or any other proceedings under this title or any other laws of the United States.

(B) Upon receiving notice respecting a civil action pursuant to this section, the United States shall have the right to intervene in such action and, upon so intervening, to be heard on all matters arising therein, and to file petitions for appeal.

(C) Service of a State's complaint on the United States as required in this paragraph shall be made in accord with the requirements of rule 4(i)(1) of the Federal Rule [Rules] of Civil Procedure.

(3) Powers conferred by State law. For purposes of bringing any civil action under paragraph (1), nothing in this Act shall prevent an attorney general of a State from exercising the powers conferred on the attorney general of a State by the laws of such State to conduct investigations or to administer oaths or affirmations or to compel the attendance of witnesses of or the production of documentary or other evidence.

(4) Venue. Any civil action brought under paragraph (1) in a district court of the United States may be brought in the district in which the defendant is found, is an inhabitant, or transacts business or wherever venue is proper under section 1391 of title 28, United States Code. Process in such action may be served in any district in which the defendant is an inhabitant or in which the defendant may be found.

(5) No private right of action. No private right of action is created under this subsection.

(6) Limitation. No civil action may be brought under paragraph (1) against—

(A) the United States;

(B) an Indian Tribe or tribal organization, to the extent such tribe or tribal organization is lawfully carrying out a contract or compact under the Indian Self-Determination and Education Assistance Act [25 USCS §§ 450 et seq.]; or

(C) any employee of the United States or such Indian tribe or tribal organization, provided such agent or employee is acting in the usual course of business or employment, and within the scope of the official duties of such agent or employee therewith.

(Oct. 27, 1970, P. L. 91-513, Title II, Part E, § 512, 84 Stat. 1278; Oct. 15, 2008, P. L. 110-425, § 3(h), 122 Stat. 4830; Dec. 2, 2022, P.L. 117-215, Title I, § 103(b)(1)(I), 136 Stat. 2263.)

§ 883. Enforcement proceedings

Before any violation of this title is reported by the Administrator of the Drug Enforcement Administration to any United States attorney for institution of a criminal proceeding, the Administrator may require that the person against whom such proceeding is contemplated be given appropriate notice and an opportunity to present his views, either orally or in writing, with regard to such contemplated proceeding.

(Oct. 27, 1970, P. L. 91-513, Title II, Part E, § 513, 84 Stat. 1278; Nov. 30, 1979, P. L. 96-132, § 16(c), 93 Stat. 1049.)

§ 884. Immunity and privilege

(a) Refusal to testify. Whenever a witness refuses, on the basis of his privilege against self-incrimination, to testify or provide other information in a proceeding before a court or grand jury of the United States, involving a violation of this title, and the person presiding over the proceeding communicates to the witness an order issued under this section, the witness may not refuse to comply with the order on the basis of his privilege against self-incrimination. But no testimony or other information compelled under the order issued under subsection (b) of this section or any information obtained by the exploitation of such testimony or other information, may be used against the witness in any criminal case, including any criminal case brought in a court of a State, except a prosecution for perjury, giving a false statement, or otherwise failing to comply with the order.

(b) Order of United States district court. In the case of any individual who has been or may be called to testify or provide other information at any proceeding before a court or grand jury of the United States, the United States district court for the judicial district in which the proceeding is or may be held shall issue, upon the request of the United States attorney for such district, an order requiring such individual to give any testimony or provide any other information which he refuses to give or provide on the basis of his privilege against self-incrimination.

(c) Request by United States attorney. A United States attorney may, with the approval of the Attorney General or the Deputy Attorney General, the Associate Attorney General, or any Assistant Attorney General designated by the Attorney General, request an order under subsection (b) when in his judgment—

(1) the testimony or other information from such individual may be necessary to the public interest; and

(2) such individual has refused or is likely to refuse to testify or provide other information on the basis of his privilege against self-incrimination.

(Oct. 27, 1970, P. L. 91-513, Title II, Part E, § 514, 84 Stat. 1278; Nov. 18, 1988, P. L. 100-690, Title VII, Subtitle B, § 7020(f), 102 Stat. 4396.)

§ 885. Burden of proof; liabilities

(a) Exemptions and exceptions; presumption in simple possession offenses.

(1) It shall not be necessary for the United States to negative any exemption or exception set forth in this title in any complaint, information, indictment, or other pleading or in any trial, hearing, or other proceeding under this title, and the burden of going forward with the evidence with respect to any such exemption or exception shall be upon the person claiming its benefit.

(2) In the case of a person charged under section 404(a) [21 USCS § 844(a)] with the possession of a controlled substance, any label identifying such substance for purposes of section 503(b)(2) of the Federal Food, Drug, and Cosmetic Act [21 USCS § 353(b)(2)] shall be admissible in evidence and shall be prima facie evidence that such substance was obtained pursuant to

a valid prescription from a practitioner while acting in the course of his professional practice.

(b) Registration and order forms. In the absence of proof that a person is the duly authorized holder of an appropriate registration or order form issued under this title, he shall be presumed not to be the holder of such registration or form, and the burden of going forward with the evidence with respect to such registration or form shall be upon him.

(c) Use of vehicles, vessels, and aircraft. The burden of going forward with the evidence to establish that a vehicle, vessel, or aircraft used in connection with controlled substances in schedule I was used in accordance with the provisions of this title shall be on the persons engaged in such use.

(d) Immunity of Federal, State, local and other officials. Except as provided in sections 2234 and 2235 of title 18, United States Code, no civil or criminal liability shall be imposed by virtue of this title upon any duly authorized Federal officer lawfully engaged in the enforcement of this title, or upon any duly authorized officer of any State, territory, political subdivision thereof, the District of Columbia, or any possession of the United States, who shall be lawfully engaged in the enforcement of any law or municipal ordinance relating to controlled substances.

(Oct. 27, 1970, P. L. 91-513, Title II, Part E, § 515, 84 Stat. 1279.)

§ 886. Payments and advances

(a) Payment to informers. The Attorney General is authorized to pay any person, from funds appropriated for the Drug Enforcement Administration, for information concerning a violation of this title, such sum or sums of money as he may deem appropriate, without reference to any moieties or rewards to which such person may otherwise be entitled by law.

(b) Reimbursement for purchase of controlled substances. Moneys expended from appropriations of the Drug Enforcement Administration for purchase of controlled substances and subsequently recovered shall be reimbursed to the current appropriation for the Bureau [Administration].

(c) Advance of funds for enforcement purposes. The Attorney General is authorized to direct the advance of funds by the Treasury Department in connection with the enforcement of this title.

(d) Drug Pollution Fund.

(1) There is established in the Treasury a trust fund to be known as the "Drug Pollution Fund" (hereinafter referred to in this subsection as the "Fund"), consisting of amounts appropriated or credited to such Fund under section 401(b)(6) [21 USCS § 841(b)(6)].

(2) There are hereby appropriated to the Fund amounts equivalent to the fines imposed under section 401(b)(6) [21 USCS § 841(b)(6)].

(3) Amounts in the Fund shall be available, as provided in appropriations Acts, for the purpose of making payments in accordance with paragraph (4) for the clean up of certain pollution resulting from the actions referred to in section 401(b)(6) [21 USCS § 841(b)(6)].

(4)(A) The Secretary of the Treasury, after consultation with the Attorney General, shall make payments under paragraph (3), in such amounts as the Secretary determines appropriate, to the heads of executive agencies or departments that meet the requirements of subparagraph (B).

(B) In order to receive a payment under paragraph (3), the head of an executive agency or department shall submit an application in such form and containing such information as the Secretary of the Treasury shall by regulation require. Such application shall contain a description of the fine imposed under section 401(b)(6) [21 USCS § 841(b)(6)], the circumstances surrounding the imposition of such fine, and the type and severity of pollution that resulted from the actions to which such fine applies.

(5) For purposes of subchapter B of chapter 98 of the Internal Revenue Code of 1986 [26 USCS §§ 9601 et seq.], the Fund established under this paragraph shall be treated in the same manner as a trust fund established under subchapter A of such chapter [26 USCS §§ 9501 et seq.].

(Oct. 27, 1970, P. L. 91-513, Title II, Part E, § 516, 84 Stat. 1279; Nov. 30, 1979, P. L. 96-132, § 16(b), 93 Stat. 1049; Nov. 18, 1988, P. L. 100-690, Title VI, Subtitle H, § 6254(i), 102 Stat. 4367.)

§ 886a. Diversion Control Fee Account

(1) In general. There is established in the general fund of the Treasury a separate account which shall be known as the Diversion Control Fee Account. For fiscal year 1993 and thereafter:

(A) There shall be deposited as offsetting receipts into that account all fees collected by the Drug Enforcement Administration, in excess of $15,000,000, for the operation of its diversion control program.

(B) Such amounts as are deposited into the Diversion Control Fee Account shall remain available until expended and shall be refunded out of that account by the Secretary of the Treasury, at least on a quarterly basis, to reimburse the Drug Enforcement Administration for expenses incurred in the operation of the diversion control program. Such reimbursements shall be made without distinguishing between expenses related to controlled substance activities and expenses related to chemical activities.

(C) Fees charged by the Drug Enforcement Administration under its diversion control program shall be set at a level that ensures the recovery of the full costs of operating the various aspects of that program.

(D) The amount required to be refunded from the Diversion Control Fee Account for fiscal year 1994 and thereafter shall be refunded in accordance with estimates made in the budget request of the Attorney General for those fiscal years. Any proposed changes in the amounts designated in said budget requests shall only be made after notification to the Committees on Appropriations of the House of Representatives and the Senate fifteen days in advance.

(2) Definitions. In this section:

(A) Diversion control program. The term "diversion control program" means the controlled substance and chemical diversion control activities of the Drug Enforcement Administration.

(B) Controlled substance and chemical diversion control activities. The term "controlled substance and chemical diversion control activities" means those activities related to the registration and control of the manufacture, distribution, dispensing, importation, and exportation of controlled substances and listed chemicals.

(Oct. 6, 1992, P. L. 102-395, Title I, § 111(b), 106 Stat. 1843; Nov. 10, 1998, P. L. 105-362, Title X, § 1001(b), 112 Stat. 3291; Dec. 8, 2004, P. L. 108-447, Div B, Title VI, § 633(a), 118 Stat. 2921.)

§ 887. Coordination and consolidation of post-seizure administration

The Attorney General and the Secretary of the Treasury shall take such action as may be necessary to develop and maintain a joint plan to coordinate and consolidate post-seizure administration of property seized under this title, title III, or provisions of the customs laws relating to controlled substances.

(Oct. 27, 1970, P. L. 91-513, Title II, Part E, § 517, as added Nov. 18, 1988, P. L. 100-690, Title VI, Subtitle B, § 6078(a), 102 Stat. 4325.)

§ 888. [Repealed]

§ 889. Production control of controlled substances

(a) Definitions. As used in this section:

(1) The term "controlled substance" has the same meaning given such term in section 102(6) of the Controlled Substances Act (21 U.S.C. 801(6) [802(6)]).

(2) The term "Secretary" means the Secretary of Agriculture.

(3) The term "State" means each of the fifty States, the District of Columbia, the Commonwealth of Puerto Rico, Guam, the Virgin Islands of the United States, American Samoa, the Commonwealth of the Northern Mariana Islands, or the Trust Territory of the Pacific Islands.

(b) Persons ineligible for Federal agricultural program benefits. Notwithstanding any other provision of law, following the date of enactment of this Act [enacted Dec. 23, 1985], any person who is convicted under Federal or State law of planting, cultivation, growing, producing, harvesting, or storing a controlled substance in any crop year shall be ineligible for—

(1) as to any commodity produced during that crop year, and the four succeeding crop years, by such person—

(A) any price support or payment made available under the Agricultural Act of 1949 (7 U.S.C. 1421 et seq.), the Commodity Credit Corporation Charter Act (15 U.S.C. 714 et seq.), or any other Act;

(B) a farm storage facility loan made under section 4(h) of the Commodity Credit Corporation Charter Act (15 U.S.C. 714b(h));

(C) crop insurance under the Federal Crop Insurance Act (7 U.S.C. 1501 et seq.);

(D) a disaster payment made under the Agricultural Act of 1949 (7 U.S.C. 1421 et seq.); or

(E) a loan made, insured or guaranteed under the Consolidated Farm and Rural Development Act (7 U.S.C. 1921 et seq.) or any other provision of law administered by the Farmers Home Administration; or

(2) a payment made under section 4 or 5 of the Commodity Credit Corporation Charter Act (15 U.S.C. 714b or 714c) for the storage of an agricultural commodity that is—

(A) produced during that crop year, or any of the four succeeding crop years, by such person; and

(B) acquired by the Commodity Credit Corporation.

(c) Regulations. Not later than 180 days after the date of enactment of this Act [enacted Dec. 23, 1985], the Secretary shall issue such regulations as the Secretary determines are necessary to carry out this section, including regulations that—

(1) define the term "person";

(2) govern the determination of persons who shall be ineligible for program benefits under this section; and

(3) protect the interests of tenants and sharecroppers.

(Oct. 27, 1970, P. L. 91-513, Title II, Part E, § 519, as redesignated by Act Nov. 29, 1990, P. L. 101-647, Title X, § 1002(h)(2), 104 Stat. 4828.)

§ 890. Review of Federal sales of chemicals usable to manufacture controlled substances

A Federal department or agency may not sell from the stocks of the department or agency any chemical which, as determined by the Administrator of the Drug Enforcement Administration, could be used in the manufacture of a controlled substance unless the Administrator certifies in writing to the head of the department or agency that there is no reasonable cause to believe that the sale of the chemical would result in the illegal manufacture of a controlled substance.

(Oct. 27, 1970, P. L. 91-513, Title II, Part E, § 520, as added Sept. 23, 1996, P. L. 104-201, Div A, Title X, Subtitle C, § 1034(a), 110 Stat. 2640.)

GENERAL PROVISIONS

§ 901. Severability

If a provision of this Act is held invalid, all valid provisions that are severable shall remain in effect. If a provision of this Act is held invalid in one or more of its applications, the provision shall remain in effect in all its valid applications that are severable.

(Oct. 27, 1970, P. L. 91-513, Title II, Part G, § 706, 84 Stat. 1284.)

§ 902. Saving provisions

Nothing in this Act, except this part and, to the extent of any inconsistency, sections 307(e) and 309 of this title [21 USCS §§ 827(e), 829], shall be construed as in any way affecting, modifying, repealing, or superseding the provisions of the Federal Food, Drug, and Cosmetic Act [21 USCS §§ 301 et seq.].

(Oct. 27, 1970, P. L. 91-513, Title II, Part G, § 707, 84 Stat. 1284.)

§ 903. Application of State law

No provision of this title shall be construed as indicating an intent on the part of the Congress to occupy the field in which that provision operates, including criminal penalties, to the exclusion of any State law on the same subject matter which would otherwise be within the authority of the State, unless there is a positive conflict between that provision of this title and that State law so that the two cannot consistently stand together.

(Oct. 27, 1970, P. L. 91-513, Title II, Part G, § 708, 84 Stat. 1284.)

§ 904. Payment of tort claims

Notwithstanding section 2680(k) of title 28, United States Code, the Attorney General, in carrying out the functions of the Department of Justice under this title, is authorized to pay tort claims in the manner authorized by section 2672 of title 28, United States Code, when such claims arise in a foreign country in connection with the operations of the Drug Enforcement Administration abroad.

(Oct. 27, 1970, P. L. 91-513, Title II, Part G, § 709, 84 Stat. 1284; Oct. 26, 1974, P. L. 93-481, § 1, 88 Stat. 1455; Oct. 18, 1977, P. L. 95-137, § 1(a), 91 Stat. 1169; Nov. 30, 1979, P. L. 96-132, §§ 13, 15, 93 Stat. 1048; Jan. 4, 1983, P. L. 97-414, § 9(g)(1) in part, 96 Stat. 2064.)

IMPORT AND EXPORT

Section

§ 951. Definitions

(a) For purposes of this part [21 USCS §§ 951 et seq.]—

(1) The term "import" means, with respect to any article, any bringing in or introduction of such article into any area (whether or not such bringing in or introduction constitutes an importation within the meaning of the tariff laws of the United States).

(2) The term "customs territory of the United States" has the meaning assigned to such term by general note 2 of the Harmonized Tariff Schedule of the United States (19 U.S.C. 1202).

(b) Each term defined in section 102 of title II [21 USCS § 802] shall have the same meaning for purposes of this title as such term has for purposes of title II.

(Oct. 27, 1970, P. L. 91-513, Title III, Part A, § 1001, 84 Stat. 1285; Aug. 23, 1988, P. L. 100-418, Title I, Subtitle B, § 1214(m), 102 Stat. 1158.)

§ 952. Importation of controlled substances

(a) Controlled substances in schedule I or II and narcotic drugs in schedule III, IV, or V; exceptions. It shall be unlawful to import into the customs territory of the United States from any place outside thereof (but within the United States), or to import into the United States from any place outside thereof, any controlled substance in schedule I or II of title II, or any narcotic drug in schedule III, IV, or V of title II, or ephedrine, pseudoephedrine, or phenylpropanolamine, except that—

(1) such amounts of crude opium, poppy straw, concentrate of poppy straw, and coca leaves, and of ephedrine, pseudoephedrine, and phenylpropanolamine, as the Attorney General finds to be necessary to provide for medical, scientific, or other legitimate purposes, and

(2) such amounts of any controlled substance in schedule I or II or any narcotic drug in schedule III, IV, or V that the Attorney General finds to be necessary to provide for the medical, scientific, or other legitimate needs of the United States—

(A) during an emergency in which domestic supplies of such substance or drug are found by the Attorney General to be inadequate,

(B) in any case in which the Attorney General finds that competition among domestic manufacturers of the controlled substance is inadequate and will not be rendered adequate by the registration of additional manufacturers under section 303 [21 USCS § 823], or

(C) in any case in which the Attorney General finds that such controlled substance is in limited quantities exclusively for scientific, analytical, or research uses,

may be so imported under such regulations as the Attorney General shall prescribe. No crude opium may be so imported for the purpose of manufacturing heroin or smoking opium.

(b) Nonnarcotic controlled substances in schedule III, IV, or V. It shall be unlawful to import into the customs territory of the United States from any place outside thereof (but within the United States), or to import into the United States from any place outside thereof, any nonnarcotic controlled substance in schedule III, IV, or V, unless such nonnarcotic controlled substance—

(1) is imported for medical, scientific, or other legitimate uses, and

(2) is imported pursuant to such notification, or declaration, or in the case of any nonnarcotic controlled substance in schedule III, such import permit, notification, or declaration, as the Attorney General may by regulation prescribe, except that if a nonnarcotic controlled substance in schedule IV or V is also listed in schedule I or II of the Convention on Psychotropic Substances it shall be imported pursuant to such import permit requirements, prescribed by regulation of the Attorney General, as are required by the Convention.

(c) Coca leaves. In addition to the amount of coca leaves authorized to be imported into the United States under subsection (a), the Attorney General may permit the importation of additional amounts of coca leaves. All cocaine and ecgonine (and all salts, derivatives, and preparations from which cocaine or ecgonine may be synthesized or made) contained in such additional amounts of coca leaves imported under this subsection shall be destroyed under the supervision of an authorized representative of the Attorney General.

(d) Application for increased importation of ephedrine, pseudoephedrine, or phenylpropanolamine.

(1) With respect to a registrant under section 1008 [21 USCS § 958] who is authorized under subsection (a)(1) to import ephedrine, pseudoephedrine, or phenylpropanolamine, at any time during the year the registrant may apply for an increase in the amount of such chemical that the registrant is authorized to import, and the Attorney General may approve the application if the Attorney General determines that the approval is necessary to provide for medical, scientific, or other legitimate purposes regarding the chemical.

(2) With respect to the application under paragraph (1):

(A) Not later than 60 days after receiving the application, the Attorney General shall approve or deny the application.

(B) In approving the application, the Attorney General shall specify the period of time for which the approval is in effect, or shall provide that the approval is effective until the registrant involved is notified in writing by the Attorney General that the approval is terminated.

(C) If the Attorney General does not approve or deny the application before the expiration of the 60-day period under subparagraph (A), the application is deemed to be approved, and such approval remains in effect until the Attorney General notifies the registrant in writing that the approval is terminated.

(e) Reference to ephedrine, pseudoephedrine, or phenylpropanolamine. Each reference in this section to ephedrine, pseudoephedrine, or phenylpropanolamine includes each of the salts, optical isomers, and salts of optical isomers of such chemical.

(Oct. 27, 1970, P. L. 91-513, Title III, Part A, § 1002, 84 Stat. 1285; Nov. 10, 1978, P. L. 95-633, Title I, § 105, 92 Stat. 3772; Oct. 12, 1984, P. L. 98-473, Title II, Ch V, Part B, §§ 519-521, 98 Stat. 2075; March 9, 2006, P. L. 109-177, Title VII, Subtitle A, § 715, 120 Stat. 264.)

§ 953. Exportation of controlled substances

(a) Narcotic drugs in schedule I, II, III, or IV. It shall be unlawful to export from the United States any narcotic drug in schedule I, II, III, or IV unless—

(1) it is exported to a country which is a party to—

(A) the International Opium Convention of 1912 for the Suppression of the Abuses of Opium, Morphine, Cocaine, and Derivative Drugs, or to the International Opium Convention signed at Geneva on February 19, 1925; or

(B) the Convention for Limiting the Manufacture and Regulating the Distribution of Narcotic Drugs concluded at Geneva, July 13, 1931, as amended by the protocol signed at Lake Success on December 11, 1946, and the protocol bringing under international control drugs outside the scope of the convention of July 13, 1931, for limiting the manufacture and regulating the distribution of narcotic drugs (as amended by the protocol signed at Lake Success on December 11, 1946), signed at Paris, November 19, 1948; or

(C) the Single Convention on Narcotic Drugs, 1961, signed at New York, March 30, 1961;

(2) such country has instituted and maintains, in conformity with the conventions to which it is a party, a system for the control of imports of narcotic drugs which the Attorney General deems adequate;

(3) the narcotic drug is consigned to a holder of such permits or licenses as may be required under the laws of the country of import, and a permit or license to import such drug has been issued by the country of import;

(4) substantial evidence is furnished to the Attorney General by the exporter that (A) the narcotic drug is to be applied exclusively to medical or scientific uses within the country of import, and (B) there is an actual need for the narcotic drug for medical or scientific uses within such country; and

(5) a permit to export the narcotic drug in each instance has been issued by the Attorney General.

(b) Exception for exportation for special scientific purposes. Notwithstanding subsection (a), the Attorney General may authorize any narcotic drug (including crude opium and coca leaves) in schedule I, II, III, or IV to be exported from the United States to a country which is a party to any of the international instruments mentioned in subsection (a) if the particular drug is to be applied to a special scientific purpose in the country of destination and the authorities of such country will permit the importation of the particular drug for such purpose.

(c) Nonnarcotic controlled substances in schedule I or II. It shall be unlawful to export from the United States any nonnarcotic controlled substance in schedule I or II unless—

(1) it is exported to a country which has instituted and maintains a system which the Attorney General deems adequate for the control of imports of such substances;

(2) the controlled substance is consigned to a holder of such permits or licenses as may be required under the laws of the country of import;

(3) substantial evidence is furnished to the Attorney General that (A) the controlled substance is to be applied exclusively to medical, scientific, or other legitimate uses within the country to which exported, (B) it will not be exported from such country, and (C) there is an actual need for the controlled substance for medical, scientific, or other legitimate uses within the country; and

(4) a permit to export the controlled substance in each instance has been issued by the Attorney General.

(d) Exception for exportation for special scientific purposes. Notwithstanding subsection (c), the Attorney General may authorize any nonnarcotic controlled substance in schedule I or II to be exported from the United States if the particular substance is to be applied to a special scientific purpose in the country of destination and the authorities of such country will permit the importation of the particular drug for such purpose.

(e) Nonnarcotic controlled substances in schedule III or IV; controlled substances in schedule V. It shall be unlawful to export from the United States to any other country any nonnarcotic controlled substance in schedule III or IV or any controlled substances in schedule V unless—

(1) there is furnished (before export) to the Attorney General documentary proof that importation is not contrary to the laws or regulations of the country of destination for consumption for medical, scientific, or other legitimate purposes;

(2) it is exported pursuant to such notification or declaration, or in the case of any nonnarcotic controlled substance in schedule III, such export permit, notification, or declaration as the Attorney General may by regulation prescribe; and

(3) in the case of a nonnarcotic controlled substance in schedule IV or V which is also listed in schedule I or II of the Convention on Psychotropic Substances, it is exported pursuant to such export permit requirements, prescribed by regulation of the Attorney General, as are required by the Convention.

(f) Exception to exportation for subsequent export. Notwithstanding subsections (a)(4) and (c)(3), the Attorney General may authorize any controlled substance that is in schedule I or II, or is a narcotic drug in schedule III or IV, to be exported from the United States to a country for subsequent export from that country to another country, if each of the following conditions is met:

(1) Both the country to which the controlled substance is exported from the United States (referred to in this subsection as the "first country") and the country to which the controlled substance is exported from the first country (referred to in this subsection as the "second country") are parties to the Single Convention on Narcotic Drugs, 1961, and the Convention on Psychotropic Substances, 1971.

(2) The first country and the second country have each instituted and maintain, in conformity with such Conventions, a system of controls of imports of controlled substances which the Attorney General deems adequate.

(3) With respect to the first country, the controlled substance is consigned to a holder of such permits or licenses as may be required under the laws of such country, and a permit or license to import the controlled substance has been issued by the country.

(4) With respect to the second country, substantial evidence is furnished to the Attorney General by the person who will export the controlled substance from the United States that—

(A) the controlled substance is to be consigned to a holder of such permits or licenses as may be required under the laws of such country, and a permit or license to import the controlled substance is to be issued by the country; and

(B) the controlled substance is to be applied exclusively to medical, scientific, or other legitimate uses within the country.

(5)(A) The controlled substance will not be exported from the second country, except that the controlled substance may be exported from a second country that is a member of the European Economic Area to another country that is a member of the European Economic Area, provided that the first country is also a member of the European Economic Area.

(B) Subsequent to any re-exportation described in subparagraph (A), a controlled substance may continue to be exported from any country that is a member of the European Economic Area to any other such country, if—

(i) the conditions applicable with respect to the first country under paragraphs (1), (2), (3), (4), (6), and (7) are met by each subsequent country from which the controlled substance is exported pursuant to this paragraph; and

(ii) the conditions applicable with respect to the second country under paragraphs (1), (2), (3), (4), (6), and (7) are met by each subsequent country to which the controlled substance is exported pursuant to this paragraph.

(6)(A) Within 30 days after the controlled substance is exported from the first country to the second country, the person who exported the controlled substance from the United States delivers to the Attorney General documentation certifying that such export from the first country has occurred.

(B) In the case of re-exportation among members of the European Economic Area, within 30 days after each re-exportation, the person who exported the controlled substance from the United States delivers to the Attorney General—

(i) documentation certifying that such re-exportation has occurred; and

(ii) information concerning the consignee, country, and product.

(7) A permit to export the controlled substance from the United States has been issued by the Attorney General.

(g) Limitation. Subject to paragraphs (5) and (6) of subsection (f) in the case of any controlled substance in schedule I or II or any narcotic drug in schedule III or

IV, the Attorney General shall not promulgate nor enforce any regulation, subregulatory guidance, or enforcement policy which impedes re-exportation of any controlled substance among European Economic Area countries, including by promulgating or enforcing any requirement that—

(1) re-exportation from the first country to the second country or re-exportation from the second country to another country occur within a specified period of time; or

(2) information concerning the consignee, country, and product be provided prior to exportation of the controlled substance from the United States or prior to each re-exportation among members of the European Economic Area.

(Oct. 27, 1970, P. L. 91-513, Title III, Part A, § 1003, 84 Stat. 1286; Nov. 10, 1978, P. L. 95-633, Title I, § 106, 92 Stat. 3772; Oct. 12, 1984, P. L. 98-473, Title II, Ch V, Part B, § 522, 98 Stat. 2076; Aug. 2, 2005, P. L. 109-57, § 1(b), 119 Stat. 592; Nov. 25, 2015, P. L. 114-89, § 4, 129 Stat. 701.)

§ 954. Transshipment and in-transit shipment of controlled substances

Notwithstanding sections 1002, 1003, and 1007 [21 USCS §§ 952, 953, and 957]—

(1) A controlled substance in schedule I may—

(A) be imported into the United States for transshipment to another country, or

(B) be transferred or transshipped from one vessel, vehicle, or aircraft to another vessel, vehicle, or aircraft within the United States for immediate exportation,

if and only if it is so imported, transferred, or transshipped (i) for scientific, medical, or other legitimate purposes in the country of destination, and (ii) with the prior written approval of the Attorney General (which shall be granted or denied within 21 days of the request).

(2) A controlled substance in schedule II, III, or IV may be so imported, transferred, or transshipped if and only if advance notice is given to the Attorney General in accordance with regulations of the Attorney General.

(Oct. 27, 1970, P. L. 91-513, Title III, Part A, § 1004, 84 Stat. 1287.)

§ 955. Possession on board vessels, etc., arriving in or departing from United States

It shall be unlawful for any person to bring or possess on board any vessel or aircraft, or on board any vehicle of a carrier, arriving in or departing from the United States or the customs territory of the United States, a controlled substance in schedule I or II or a narcotic drug in schedule III or IV, unless such substance or drug is a part of the cargo entered in the manifest or part of the official supplies of the vessel, aircraft, or vehicle.

(Oct. 27, 1970, P. L. 91-513, Title III, Part A, § 1005, 84 Stat. 1287.)

§§ 955a–955d. [Transferred]

§ 956. Exemption authority

(a) Individual possessing controlled substance.

(1) Subject to paragraph (2), the Attorney General may by regulation exempt from sections 1002(a) and (b), 1003, 1004, and 1005 [21 USCS §§ 952(a), (b), 953–955] any individual who has a controlled substance (except a substance in schedule I) in his possession for his personal medical use, or for administration to any animal accompanying him, if he lawfully obtained such substance and he makes such declaration (or gives such other notification) as the Attorney General may by regulation require.

(2) Notwithstanding any exemption under paragraph (1), a United States resident who enters the United States through an international land border with a controlled substance (except a substance in schedule I) for which the individual does not possess a valid prescription issued by a practitioner (as defined in section 102 of the Controlled Substances Act (21 U.S.C. 802)) in accordance with applicable Federal and State law (or documentation that verifies the issuance of such a prescription to that individual) may not import the controlled substance into the United States in an amount that exceeds 50 dosage units of the controlled substance.

(b) Compound, mixture, or preparation. The Attorney General may by regulation except any compound, mixture, or preparation containing any depressant or stimulant substance listed in paragraph (a) or (b) of schedule III or in schedule IV or V from the application of all or any part of this title if (1) the compound, mixture, or preparation contains one or more active medicinal ingredients not having a depressant or stimulant effect on the central nervous system, and (2) such ingredients are included therein in such combinations, quantity, proportion, or concentration as to vitiate the potential for abuse of the substances which do have a depressant or stimulant effect on the central nervous system.

(Oct. 27, 1970, P. L. 91-513, Title III, Part A, § 1006, 84 Stat. 1288; Oct. 21, 1998, P. L. 105-277, Div C, Title VIII, Subtitle G, § 872(a), 112 Stat. 2681-707; Nov. 10, 1998, P. L. 105-357, § 2(a), 112 Stat. 3271.)

§ 957. Persons required to register

(a) Coverage. No person may—

(1) import into the customs territory of the United States from any place outside thereof (but within the United States), or import into the United States from any place outside thereof, any controlled substance or list I chemical, or

(2) export from the United States any controlled substance or list I chemical,

unless there is in effect with respect to such person a registration issued by the Attorney General under section 1008 [21 USCS § 958], or unless such person is exempt from registration under subsection (b).

(b) Exemptions.

(1) The following persons shall not be required to register under the provisions of this section and may lawfully possess a controlled substance or list I chemical:

(A) An agent or an employee of any importer or exporter registered under section 1008 [21 USCS § 958] if such agent or employee is acting in the usual course of his business or employment.

(B) A common or contract carrier or warehouseman, or an employee thereof, whose possession of any controlled substance or list I chemical is in the usual course of his business or employment.

(C) An ultimate user who possesses such substance for a purpose specified in section 102(25) and in conformity with an exemption granted under section 1006(a) [21 USCS § 956(a)].

(2) The Attorney General may, by regulation, waive the requirement for registration of certain importers and exporters if he finds it consistent with the public health and safety; and may authorize any such importer or exporter to possess controlled substances or list I chemicals for purposes of importation and exportation.

(Oct. 27, 1970, P. L. 91-513, Title III, Part A, § 1007, 84 Stat. 1288; Oct. 12, 1984, P. L. 98-473, Title II, Ch V, Part B, § 523, 98 Stat. 2076; Dec. 17, 1993, P. L. 103-200, § 3(e), 107 Stat. 2337.)

§ 958. Registration requirements

(a) Applicants to import or export controlled substances in schedule I or II. The Attorney General shall register an applicant to import or export a controlled substance in schedule I or II if he determines that such registration is consistent with the public interest and with United States obligations under international treaties, conventions, or protocols in effect on the effective date of this section [effective May 1, 1971]. In determining the public interest, the factors enumerated in paragraphs (1) through (6) of section 303(a) [21 USCS § 823(a)(1)–(6)] shall be considered.

(b) Activity limited to specified substances. Registration granted under this section shall not entitle a registrant to import or export controlled substances other than specified in the registration.

(c) Applicants to import controlled substances in schedule III, IV, or V or to export controlled substances in schedule III or IV; applicants to import or export list I chemicals.

(1) The Attorney General shall register an applicant to import a controlled substance in schedule III, IV, or V or to export a controlled substance in schedule III or IV, unless he determines that the issuance of such registration is inconsistent with the public interest. In determining the public interest, the factors enumerated in paragraphs (1) through (6) of section 303(e) [21 USCS § 823(e)(1)–(6)] shall be considered.

(2)(A) The Attorney General shall register an applicant to import or export a list I chemical unless the Attorney General determines that registration of the applicant is inconsistent with the public interest. Registration under this subsection shall not be required for the import or export of a drug product that is exempted under section 102(39)(A)(iv) [21 USCS § 802(39)(A)(iv)].

(B) In determining the public interest for the purposes of subparagraph (A), the Attorney General shall consider the factors specified in section 303(i) [21 USCS § 823(i)].

(d) Denial of application.

(1) The Attorney General may deny an application for registration under subsection (a) if he is unable to determine that such registration is consistent with the public interest (as defined in subsection (a)) and with the United States obligations under international treaties, conventions, or protocols in effect on the effective date of this part [effective May 1, 1971].

(2) The Attorney General may deny an application for registration under subsection (c), or revoke or suspend a registration under subsection (a) or (c), if he determines that such registration is inconsistent with the public interest (as defined in subsection (a) or (c)) or with the United States obligations under international treaties, conventions, or protocols in effect on the effective date of this part [effective May 1, 1971].

(3) The Attorney General may limit the revocation or suspension of a registration to the particular controlled substance, or substances, or list I chemical or chemicals, with respect to which grounds for revocation or suspension exist.

(4) Before taking action pursuant to this subsection, the Attorney General shall serve upon the applicant or registrant an order to show cause as to why the registration should not be denied, revoked, or suspended. The order to show cause shall contain a statement of the basis thereof and shall call upon the applicant or registrant to appear before the Attorney General, or his designee, at a time and place stated in the order, but in no event less than thirty days after the date of receipt of the order. Proceedings to deny, revoke, or suspend shall be conducted pursuant to this subsection in accordance with subchapter II of chapter 5 of title 5 of the United States Code [5 USCS §§ 551 et seq.]. Such proceedings shall be independent of, and not in lieu of, criminal prosecutions or other proceedings under this title or any other law of the United States.

(5) The Attorney General may, in his discretion, suspend any registration simultaneously with the institution of proceedings under this subsection, in cases where he finds that there is an imminent danger to the public health and safety. Such suspension shall continue in effect until the conclusion of such proceedings, including judicial review thereof, unless sooner withdrawn by the Attorney General or dissolved by a court of competent jurisdiction.

(6) In the event that the Attorney General suspends or revokes a registration granted under this section, all controlled substances or list I chemicals owned or possessed by the registrant pursuant to such registration at the time of suspension or the effective date of the revocation order, as the case may be, may, in the discretion of the Attorney General, be seized or placed under seal. No disposition may be made of any controlled substances or list I chemicals under seal until the time for taking an appeal has elapsed or until all appeals have been concluded, except that a court, upon application therefor, may at any time order the sale of perishable controlled substances or list I chemicals. Any such order shall require the deposit of the proceeds of the sale with the court. Upon a revocation order becoming final, all such controlled substances or list I chemicals (or proceeds of the sale thereof which have

been deposited with the court) shall be forfeited to the United States; and the Attorney General shall dispose of such controlled substances or list I chemicals in accordance with section 511(e) of the Controlled Substances Act [21 USCS § 881(e)].

(e) Registration period. No registration shall be issued under this part [21 USCS §§ 951 et seq.] for a period in excess of one year. Unless the regulations of the Attorney General otherwise provide, sections 302(f), 305, 307, and 310 [21 USCS §§ 822(f), 825, 827, and 830] shall apply to persons registered under this section to the same extent such sections apply to persons registered under section 303 [21 USCS § 823].

(f) Rules and regulations. The Attorney General is authorized to promulgate rules and regulations and to charge reasonable fees relating to the registration and control of importers and exporters of controlled substances or listed chemicals.

(g) Scope of authorized activity. Persons registered by the Attorney General under this section to import or export controlled substances or list I chemicals may import or export (and, for the purpose of so importing or exporting, may possess) such substances to the extent authorized by their registration and in conformity with the other provisions of this title and title II.

(h) Separate registrations for each principal place of business. A separate registration shall be required at each principal place of business where the applicant imports or exports controlled substances or list I chemicals.

(i) Emergency situations. Except in emergency situations as described in section 1002(a)(2)(A) [21 USCS § 952(a)(2)(A)], prior to issuing a registration under this section to a bulk manufacturer of a controlled substance in schedule I or II, and prior to issuing a regulation under section 1002(a) [21 USCS § 952(a)] authorizing the importation of such a substance, the Attorney General shall give manufacturers holding registrations for the bulk manufacture of the substance an opportunity for a hearing.

(Oct. 27, 1970, P. L. 91-513, Title III, Part A, § 1008, 84 Stat. 1289; Oct. 12, 1984, P. L. 98-473, Title II, Ch V, Part B, § 524, 98 Stat. 2076; Oct. 27, 1986, P. L. 99-570, Title I, Subtitle Q, § 1866(d), 100 Stat. 3207-55; Dec. 17, 1993, P. L. 103-200, § 3(f), 107 Stat. 2337; Dec. 8, 2004, P. L. 108-447, Div B, Title VI, § 633(c), 118 Stat. 2922; Dec. 2, 2022, P.L. 117-215, Title I, § 103(b)(2), 136 Stat. 2263.)

§ 959. Possession, manufacture, or distribution of controlled substance

(a) Manufacture or distribution for purpose of unlawful importation. It shall be unlawful for any person to manufacture or distribute a controlled substance in schedule I or II or flunitrazepam or a listed chemical intending, knowing, or having reasonable cause to believe that such substance or chemical will be unlawfully imported into the United States or into waters within a distance of 12 miles of the coast of the United States.

(b) Manufacture or distribution of listed chemicals for purpose of manufacture or unlawful importation of controlled substance. It shall be unlawful for any person to manufacture or distribute a listed chemical—

(1) intending or knowing that the listed chemical will be used to manufacture a controlled substance; and

(2) intending, knowing, or having reasonable cause to believe that the controlled substance will be unlawfully imported into the United States.

(c) Possession, manufacture, or distribution by person on board aircraft. It shall be unlawful for any United States citizen on board any aircraft, or any person on board an aircraft owned by a United States citizen or registered in the United States, to—

(1) manufacture or distribute a controlled substance or listed chemical; or

(2) possess a controlled substance or listed chemical with intent to distribute.

(d) Acts committed outside territorial jurisdiction of United States. This section is intended to reach acts of manufacture or distribution committed outside the territorial jurisdiction of the United States.

(Oct. 27, 1970, P. L. 91-513, Title III, Part A, § 1009, 84 Stat. 1289; Oct. 27, 1986, P. L. 99-570, Title III, Subtitle B, Part 5, § 3161(a), 100 Stat. 3207-94; Oct. 3, 1996, P. L. 104-237, Title I, § 102(a), (b), 110 Stat. 3100; Oct. 13, 1996, P. L. 104-305, § 2(b)(2)(A), 110 Stat. 3807; May 16, 2016, P. L. 114-154, § 2, 130 Stat. 387; Dec. 12, 2017, P. L. 115-91, Div A, Title X, Subtitle B, § 1012(b), 131 Stat. 1546.)

§ 960. Prohibited acts A

(a) Unlawful acts. Any person who—

(1) contrary to section 305, 1002, 1003, or 1007 [21 USCS § 825, 952, 953 or 957], knowingly or intentionally imports or exports a controlled substance,

(2) contrary to section 1005 [21 USCS § 955], knowingly or intentionally brings or possesses on board a vessel, aircraft, or vehicle a controlled substance, or

(3) contrary to section 1009 [21 USCS § 959], manufactures, possesses with intent to distribute, or distributes a controlled substance,

shall be punished as provided in subsection (b).

(b) Penalties.

(1) In the case of a violation of subsection (a) of this section involving—

(A) 1 kilogram or more of a mixture or substance containing a detectable amount of heroin;

(B) 5 kilograms or more of a mixture or substance containing a detectable amount of—

(i) coca leaves, except coca leaves and extracts of coca leaves from which cocaine, ecgonine, and derivatives of ecgonine or their salts have been removed;

(ii) cocaine, its salts, optical and geometric isomers, and salts or isomers;

(iii) ecgonine, its derivatives, their salts, isomers, and salts of isomers; or

(iv) any compound, mixture, or preparation which contains any quantity of any of the substances referred to in clauses (i) through (iii);

(C) 280 grams or more of a mixture or substance described in subparagraph (B) which contains cocaine base;

(D) 100 grams or more of phencyclidine (PCP) or 1 kilogram or more of a mixture or substance containing a detectable amount of phencyclidine (PCP);

(E) 10 grams or more of a mixture or substance containing a detectable amount of lysergic acid diethylamide (LSD);

(F) 400 grams or more of a mixture or substance containing a detectable amount of N-phenyl-N- [1-(2-phenylethyl)-4-piperidinyl] propanamide or 100 grams or more of a mixture or substance containing a detectable amount of any analogue of N-phenyl-N [1-(2-phenylethyl)-4-piperidinyl] propanamide;

(G) 1000 kilograms or more of a mixture or substance containing a detectable amount of marihuana; or

(H) 50 grams or more of methamphetamine, its salts, isomers, and salts of its isomers or 500 grams or more of a mixture or substance containing a detectable amount of methamphetamine, its salts, isomers, or salts of its isomers.[;]

the person committing such violation shall be sentenced to a term of imprisonment of not less than 10 years and not more than life and if death or serious bodily injury results from the use of such substance shall be sentenced to a term of imprisonment of not less than 20 years and not more than life, a fine not to exceed the greater of that authorized in accordance with the provisions of title 18, United States Code, or $10,000,000 if the defendant is an individual or $50,000,000 if the defendant is other than an individual, or both. If any person commits such a violation after a prior conviction for a serious drug felony or serious violent felony has become final, such person shall be sentenced to a term of imprisonment of not less than 15 years and not more than life imprisonment and if death or serious bodily injury results from the use of such substance shall be sentenced to life imprisonment, a fine not to exceed the greater of twice that authorized in accordance with the provisions of title 18, United States Code, or $20,000,000 if the defendant is an individual or $75,000,000 if the defendant is other than an individual, or both. Notwithstanding section 3583 of title 18, any sentence under this paragraph shall, in the absence of such a prior conviction, impose a term of supervised release of at least 5 years in addition to such term of imprisonment and shall, if there was such a prior conviction, impose a term of supervised release of at least 10 years in addition to such term of imprisonment. Notwithstanding any other provision of law, the court shall not place on probation or suspend the sentence of any person sentenced under this paragraph. No person sentenced under this paragraph shall be eligible for parole during the term of imprisonment imposed therein.

(2) In the case of a violation of subsection (a) of this section involving—

(A) 100 grams or more of a mixture or substance containing a detectable amount of heroin;

(B) 500 grams or more of a mixture or substance containing a detectable amount of—

(i) coca leaves, except coca leaves and extracts of coca leaves from which cocaine, ecgonine, and derivatives of ecgonine or their salts have been removed;

(ii) cocaine, its salts, optical and geometric isomers, and salts or isomers;

(iii) ecgonine, its derivatives, their salts, isomers, and salts of isomers; or

(iv) any compound, mixture, or preparation which contains any quantity of any of the substances referred to in clauses (i) through (iii);

(C) 28 grams or more of a mixture or substance described in subparagraph (B) which contains cocaine base;

(D) 10 grams or more of phencyclidine (PCP) or 100 grams or more of a mixture or substance containing a detectable amount of phencyclidine (PCP);

(E) 1 gram or more of a mixture or substance containing a detectable amount of lysergic acid diethylamide (LSD);

(F) 40 grams or more of a mixture or substance containing a detectable amount of N-phenyl-N- [1-(2-phenylethyl)-4-piperidinyl] propanamide or 10 grams or more of a mixture or substance containing a detectable amount of any analogue of N-phenyl-N- [1-(2-phenylethyl)-4-piperidinyl] propanamide;

(G) 100 kilograms or more of a mixture or substance containing a detectable amount of marihuana; or

(H) 5 grams or more of methamphetamine, its salts, isomers, and salts of its isomers or 50 grams or more of a mixture or substance containing a detectable amount of methamphetamine, its salts, isomers, or salts of its isomers.[;]

the person committing such violation shall be sentenced to a term of imprisonment of not less than 5 years and not more than 40 years and if death or serious bodily injury results from the use of such substance shall be sentenced to a term of imprisonment of not less than twenty years and not more than life, a fine not to exceed the greater of that authorized in accordance with the provisions of title 18, United States Code, or $5,000,000 if the defendant is an individual or $25,000,000 if the defendant is other than an individual, or both. If any person commits such a violation after a prior conviction for a serious drug felony or serious violent felony has become final, such person shall be sentenced to a term of imprisonment of not less than 10 years and not more than life imprisonment and if death or serious bodily injury results from the use of such substance shall be sentenced to life imprisonment, a fine not to exceed the greater of twice that authorized in accordance with the provisions of title 18, United States Code, or $8,000,000 if the defendant is an individual or $50,000,000 if the defendant is other than an individual, or both. Notwithstanding section 3583 of title 18, any sentence imposed under this paragraph shall, in the absence of such a prior conviction, include a term of supervised release of at least 4 years in addition to such term of imprisonment and shall, if there was such a prior conviction, include a term of supervised release of at least 8 years in addition to such term of imprisonment. Notwithstanding any other provision of law, the court shall not place on probation or suspend the sentence of any person sentenced under this paragraph. No person sentenced under this paragraph shall be eligible for parole during the term of imprisonment imposed therein.

(3) In the case of a violation under subsection (a) of this section involving a controlled substance in schedule I or II, gamma hydroxybutyric acid (including when scheduled as an approved drug product for purposes of section 3(a)(1)(B) of the Hillory J. Farias and Samantha Reid Date-Rape Drug Prohibition Act of 1999 [21 USCS § 812 note]), or flunitrazepam, the person committing such violation shall, except as provided in paragraphs (1), (2), and (4), be sentenced to a term of imprisonment of not more than 20 years and if death or serious bodily injury results from the use of such substance shall be sentenced to a term of imprisonment of not less than twenty years and not more than life, a fine not to exceed the greater of that authorized in accordance with the provisions of title 18, United States Code, or $1,000,000 if the defendant is an individual or $5,000,000 if the defendant is other than an individual, or both. If any person commits such a violation after a prior conviction for a felony drug offense has become final, such person shall be sentenced to a term of imprisonment of not more than 30 years and if death or serious bodily injury results from the use of such substance shall be sentenced to life imprisonment, a fine not to exceed the greater of twice that authorized in accordance with the provisions of title 18, United States Code, or $2,000,000 if the defendant is an individual or $10,000,000 if the defendant is other than an individual, or both. Notwithstanding section 3583 of title 18, any sentence imposing a term of imprisonment under this paragraph shall, in the absence of such a prior conviction, impose a term of supervised release of at least 3 years in addition to such term of imprisonment and shall, if there was such a prior conviction, impose a term of supervised release of at least 6 years in addition to such term of imprisonment. Notwithstanding the prior sentence, and notwithstanding any other provision of law, the court shall not place on probation or suspend the sentence of any person sentenced under the provisions of this paragraph which provide for a mandatory term of imprisonment if death or serious bodily injury results.

(4) In the case of a violation under subsection (a) with respect to less than 50 kilograms of marihuana, except in the case of 10 or more marihuana plants regardless of weight, less than 10 kilograms of hashish, or less than one kilogram of hashish oil, the person committing such violation shall be sentenced in accordance with section 401(b)(1)(D) [21 USCS § 841(b)(1)(D)].

(5) In the case of a violation of subsection (a) involving a controlled substance in schedule III, such person shall be sentenced in accordance with section 401(b)(1) [21 USCS § 841(b)(1)].

(6) In the case of a violation of subsection (a) involving a controlled substance in schedule IV, such person shall be sentenced in accordance with section 401(b)(2) [21 USCS § 841(b)(2)].

(7) In the case of a violation of subsection (a) involving a controlled substance in schedule V, such person shall be sentenced in accordance with section 401(b)(3) [21 USCS § 841(b)(3)].

(c) [Repealed]

(d) Penalty for importation or exportation. A person who knowingly or intentionally—

(1) imports or exports a listed chemical with intent to manufacture a controlled substance in violation of this title or title II;

(2) exports a listed chemical in violation of the laws of the country to which the chemical is exported or serves as a broker or trader for an international transaction involving a listed chemical, if the transaction is in violation of the laws of the country to which the chemical is exported;

(3) imports or exports a listed chemical knowing, or having reasonable cause to believe, that the chemical will be used to manufacture a controlled substance in violation of this title or title II;

(4) exports a listed chemical, or serves as a broker or trader for an international transaction involving a listed chemical, knowing, or having reasonable cause to believe, that the chemical will be used to manufacture a controlled substance in violation of the laws of the country to which the chemical is exported;

(5) imports or exports a listed chemical, with the intent to evade the reporting or recordkeeping requirements of section 1018 [21 USCS § 971] applicable to such importation or exportation by falsely representing to the Attorney General that the importation or exportation qualifies for a waiver of the 15-day notification requirement granted pursuant to paragraph (2) or (3) of section 1018(f) [21 USCS § 971(f)] by misrepresenting the actual country of final destination of the listed chemical or the actual listed chemical being imported or exported;

(6) imports a listed chemical in violation of section 1002 [21 USCS § 952], imports or exports such a chemical in violation of section 1007 or 1018 [21 USCS § 957 or 971], or transfers such a chemical in violation of section 1018(d) [21 USCS § 971(d)]; or

(7) manufactures, possesses with intent to distribute, or distributes a listed chemical in violation of section 959 of this title.[,]

shall be fined in accordance with title 18, imprisoned not more than 20 years in the case of a violation of paragraph (1) or (3) involving a list I chemical or not more than 10 years in the case of a violation of this subsection other than a violation of paragraph (1) or (3) involving a list I chemical, or both.

(Oct. 27, 1970, P. L. 91-513, Title III, Part A, § 1010, 84 Stat. 1290; Oct. 12, 1984, P. L. 98-473, Title II, Ch II, § 225 [(a)], Ch V, Part A, § 504, 98 Stat. 2030, 2070; Oct. 27, 1986, P. L. 99-570, Title I, Subtitle A, §§ 1004(a), 1005(c) Subtitle G, § 1302, Subtitle Q, § 1866(e), 100 Stat. 3207-6, 3207-15, 3207-55; Nov. 18, 1988, P. L. 100-690, Title VI, Subtitle A, § 6053(c), Subtitle N, § 6475, 102 Stat. 4315, 4380; Nov. 29, 1990, P. L. 101-647, Title XII, § 1204, Title XXXV, § 3599J, 104 Stat. 4830, 4932; Dec. 17, 1993, P. L. 103-200, §§ 4(b), 5(b), 107 Stat. 2338, 2339; Sept. 13, 1994, P. L. 103-322, Title IX, Subtitle A, § 90105(a), Title XXXIII, § 330024(d)(2), 108 Stat. 1987, 2151; Oct. 3, 1996, P. L. 104-237, Title I, § 102(c), 110 Stat. 3100; Oct. 13, 1996, P. L. 104-305, § 2(b)(1)(B), (C), 110 Stat. 3807; Oct. 21, 1998, P. L. 105-277, Div E, § 2(b), 112 Stat. 2681-759; Feb. 18, 2000, P. L. 106-172, § 3(b)(2), 114 Stat. 9; Nov. 2, 2002, P. L. 107-273, Div B, Title III, § 3005(b), 116 Stat. 1806; March 9, 2006, P. L. 109-177, Title VII, Subtitle A, §§ 716(b)(1)(A), 717, 120 Stat.

267; Oct. 15, 2008, P. L. 110-425, § 3(i), 122 Stat. 4832; Aug. 3, 2010, P. L. 111-220, §§ 2(b), 4(b), 124 Stat. 2372; Dec. 18, 2014, P. L. 113-260, § 3(b), 128 Stat. 2931; Dec. 21, 2018, P.L. 115-391, Title IV, § 401(b)(1), 132 Stat. 5221.)

§ 960a. Foreign terrorist organizations, terrorist persons and groups

(a) Prohibited acts. Whoever engages in conduct that would be punishable under section 841(a) of this title if committed within the jurisdiction of the United States, or attempts or conspires to do so, knowing or intending to provide, directly or indirectly, anything of pecuniary value to any person or organization that has engaged or engages in terrorist activity (as defined in section 212(a)(3)(B) of the Immigration and Nationality Act [8 USCS § 1182(a)(3)(B)]) or terrorism (as defined in section 140(d)(2) of the Foreign Relations Authorization Act, Fiscal Years 1988 and 1989 [22 USCS § 2656f(d)(2)]), shall be sentenced to a term of imprisonment of not less than twice the minimum punishment under section 841(b)(1), and not more than life, a fine in accordance with the provisions of title 18, United States Code, or both. Notwithstanding section 3583 of title 18, United States Code, any sentence imposed under this subsection shall include a term of supervised release of at least 5 years in addition to such term of imprisonment.

(b) Jurisdiction. There is jurisdiction over an offense under this section if—

(1) the prohibited drug activity or the terrorist offense is in violation of the criminal laws of the United States;

(2) the offense, the prohibited drug activity, or the terrorist offense occurs in or affects interstate or foreign commerce;

(3) an offender provides anything of pecuniary value for a terrorist offense that causes or is designed to cause death or serious bodily injury to a national of the United States while that national is outside the United States, or substantial damage to the property of a legal entity organized under the laws of the United States (including any of its States, districts, commonwealths, territories, or possessions) while that property is outside of the United States;

(4) the offense or the prohibited drug activity occurs in whole or in part outside of the United States (including on the high seas), and a perpetrator of the offense or the prohibited drug activity is a national of the United States or a legal entity organized under the laws of the United States (including any of its States, districts, commonwealths, territories, or possessions); or

(5) after the conduct required for the offense occurs an offender is brought into or found in the United States, even if the conduct required for the offense occurs outside the United States.

(c) Proof requirements. To violate subsection (a), a person must have knowledge that the person or organization has engaged or engages in terrorist activity (as defined in section 212(a)(3)(B) of the Immigration and Nationality Act [8 USCS § 1182(a)(3)(B)]) or terrorism (as defined in section 140(d)(2) of the Foreign Relations Authorization Act, Fiscal Years 1988 and 1989 [22 USCS § 2656f(d)(2)]).

(d) Definition. As used in this section, the term "anything of pecuniary value" has the meaning given the term in section 1958(b)(1) of title 18, United States Code.

(Oct. 27, 1970, P. L. 91-513, Title III, Part A, § 1010A, as added March 9, 2006, P. L. 109-177, Title I, § 122, 120 Stat. 225.)

§ 961. Prohibited acts B

Any person who violated section 1004 [21 USCS § 954] or fails to notify the Attorney General of an importation or exportation under section 1018 [21 USCS § 971] shall be subject to the following penalties:

(1) **[Caution: For inflation-adjusted civil monetary penalties, see 28 CFR 85.3.]** Except as provided in paragraph (2), any such person shall, with respect to any such violation, be subject to a civil penalty of not more than $25,000. Sections 402(c)(1) and (c)(3) [21 USCS § 842(c)(1), (3)] shall apply to any civil penalty assessed under this paragraph.

(2) If such a violation is prosecuted by an information or indictment which alleges that the violation was committed knowingly or intentionally and the trier of fact specifically finds that the violation was so committed, such person shall be sentenced to imprisonment for not more than one year or a fine of not more than $25,000 or both.

(Oct. 27, 1970, P. L. 91-513, Title III, Part A, § 1011, 84 Stat. 1290; Nov. 18, 1988, P. L. 100-690, Title VI, Subtitle A, § 6053(d), 102 Stat. 4315.)

§ 962. Second or subsequent offenses

(a) Term of imprisonment and fine. Any person convicted of any offense under this part [21 USCS §§ 951 et seq.] is, if the offense is a second or subsequent offense, punishable by a term of imprisonment twice that otherwise authorized, by twice the fine otherwise authorized, or by both. If the conviction is for an offense punishable under section 1010(b) [21 USCS § 960(b)], and if it is the offender's second or subsequent offense, the court shall impose, in addition to any term of imprisonment and fine, twice the term of supervised release otherwise authorized.

(b) Determination of status. For purposes of this section, a person shall be considered convicted of a second or subsequent offense if, prior to the commission of such offense, one or more prior convictions of such person for a felony drug offense have become final.

(c) Procedures applicable. Section 411 [21 USCS § 851] shall apply with respect to any proceeding to sentence a person under this section.

(Oct. 27, 1970, P. L. 91-513, Title III, Part A, § 1012, 84 Stat. 1290; Oct. 12, 1984, P. L. 98-473, Title II, Ch II, § 225(b), Ch V, Part A, § 505, 98 Stat. 2030, 2070; Oct. 27, 1986, P. L. 99-570, Title I, Subtitle A, §§ 1004(a), 1005(c), 100 Stat. 3207-6; Sept. 13, 1994, P. L. 103-322, Title IX, Subtitle A, § 90105(b), 108 Stat. 1988.)

§ 963. Attempt and conspiracy

Any person who attempts or conspires to commit any offense defined in this title shall be subject to the same penalties as those prescribed for the offense, the commission of which was the object of the attempt or conspiracy.

(Oct. 27, 1970, P. L. 91-513, Title III, Part A, § 1013, 84 Stat. 1291; Nov. 18, 1988, P. L. 100-690, Title VI, Subtitle N, § 6470(a), 102 Stat. 4377.)

§ 964. Additional penalties

Any penalty imposed for violation of this title shall be in addition to, and not in lieu of, any civil or administrative penalty or sanction authorized by law.

(Oct. 27, 1970, P. L. 91-513, Title III, Part A, § 1014, 84 Stat. 1291.)

§ 965. Applicability of 21 USCS §§ 871 et seq.

Part E of title II [21 USCS §§ 871 et seq.] shall apply with respect to functions of the Attorney General (and of officers and employees of the Bureau of Narcotics and Dangerous Drugs) under this title, to administrative and judicial proceedings under this title, and to violations of this title, to the same extent that such part [21 USCS §§ 871 et seq.] applies to functions of the Attorney General (and such officers and employees) under title II, to such proceedings under title II, and to violations of title II. For purposes of the application of this section to section 510 or 511 [21 USCS § 880 or 881], any reference in such section 510 or 511 [21 USCS § 880 or 881] to "this title" shall be deemed to be a reference to title III, any reference to section 303 [21 USCS § 823] shall be deemed to be a reference to section 1008 [21 USCS § 958], and any reference to section 302(d) [21 USCS § 822(d)] shall be deemed to be a reference to section 1007(b)(2) [21 USCS § 957(b)(2)].

(Oct. 27, 1970, P. L. 91-513, Title III, Part A, § 1015, 84 Stat. 1291; Nov. 10, 1978, P. L. 95-633, Title III, § 301(b), 92 Stat. 3778.)

§ 966. Authority of Secretary of Treasury

Nothing in this Act shall derogate from the authority of the Secretary of the Treasury under the customs and related laws.

(Oct. 27, 1970, P. L. 91-513, Title III, Part A, § 1016, 84 Stat. 1291.)

§ 967. Smuggling of controlled substances; investigations; oaths; subpenas; witnesses; evidence; production of records; territorial limits; fees and mileage of witnesses

For the purpose of any investigation which, in the opinion of the Secretary of the Treasury, is necessary and proper to the enforcement of section 545 of title 18 of the United States Code (relating to smuggling goods into the United States) with respect to any controlled substance (as defined in section 102 of the Controlled Substances Act [21 USCS § 802]), the Secretary of the Treasury may administer oaths and affirmations, subpena witnesses, compel their attendance, take evidence, and require the production of records (including books, papers, documents, and tangible things which constitute or contain evidence) relevant or material to the investigation. The attendance of witnesses and the production of records may be required from any place within the customs territory of the United States, except that a witness shall not be required to appear at any hearing distant more then 100 miles from the place where he was served with subpena. Witnesses summoned by the Secretary shall be paid the same fees and mileage that are paid witnesses in the courts of the United States. Oaths and affirmations may be made at any place subject to the jurisdiction of the United States.

(Aug. 11, 1955, ch 800, § 1, 69 Stat. 684; Oct. 27, 1970, P. L. 91-513, Title III, Part B, § 1102(t), 84 Stat. 1294.)

§ 968. Service of subpena; proof of service

A subpena of the Secretary of the Treasury may be served by any person designated in the subpena to serve it. Service upon a natural person may be made by personal delivery of the subpena to him. Service may be made upon a domestic or foreign corporation or upon a partnership or other unincorporated association which is subject to suit under a common name, by delivering the subpena to an officer, a managing or general agent, or to any other agent authorized by appointment or by law to receive service of process. The affidavit of the person serving the subpena entered on a true copy thereof by the person serving it shall be proof of service.

(Aug. 11, 1955, ch 800, § 2, 69 Stat. 685.)

§ 969. Contempt proceedings

In case of contumacy by, or refusal to obey a subpena issued to, any person, the Secretary of the Treasury may invoke the aid of any court of the United States within the jurisdiction of which the investigation is carried on or of which the subpenaed person is an inhabitant, carries on business or may be found, to compel compliance with the subpena of the Secretary of the Treasury. The court may issue an order requiring the subpenaed person to appear before the Secretary of the Treasury there to produce records, if so ordered, or to give testimony touching the matter under investigation. Any failure to obey the order of the court may be punished by the court as a contempt thereof. All process in any such case may be served in the judicial district whereof the subpenaed person is an inhabitant or wherever he may be found.

(Aug. 11, 1955, ch 800, § 3, 69 Stat. 685.)

§ 970. Criminal forfeitures

Section 413 of title II [18 USCS § 853], relating to criminal forfeitures, shall apply in every respect to a violation of this title punishable by imprisonment for more than one year.

(Oct. 27, 1970, P. L. 91-513, Title III, Part A, § 1017, as added Oct. 12, 1984, P. L. 98-473, Title II, Ch III, Part B, § 307, 98 Stat. 2051.)

§ 971. Notification, suspension of shipment, and penalties with respect to importation and exportation of listed chemicals

(a) Notification prior to transaction. Each regulated person who imports or exports a listed chemical shall notify the Attorney General of the importation or exportation not later than 15 days before the transaction is to take place.

(b) Regular customers or importers.

(1) The Attorney General shall provide by regulation for circumstances in which the requirement of subsection (a) does not apply to a transaction between a regulated person and a regular customer or to a transaction that is an importation by a regular importer. At the time of any importation or exportation constituting a transaction referred to in the preceding sentence, the regulated person shall notify the Attorney General of the transaction.

(2) The regulations under this subsection shall provide that the initial notification under subsection (a) with respect to a customer of a regulated person or to an importer shall, upon the expiration of the 15-day period, qualify the customer as a regular customer or the importer as a regular importer, unless the Attorney General otherwise notifies the regulated person in writing.

(c) Suspension of importation or exportation; disqualification of regular customers or importers; hearing.

(1) The Attorney General may order the suspension of any importation or exportation of a listed chemical (other than a regulated transaction to which the requirement of subsection (a) does not apply by reason of subsection (b)) or may disqualify any regular customer or regular importer on the ground that the chemical may be diverted to the clandestine manufacture of a controlled substance (without regard to the form of the chemical that may be diverted, including the diversion of a finished drug product to be manufactured from bulk chemicals to be transferred). From and after the time when the Attorney General provides written notice of the order (including a statement of the legal and factual basis for the order) to the regulated person, the regulated person may not carry out the transaction.

(2) Upon written request to the Attorney General, a regulated person to whom an order applies under paragraph (1) is entitled to an agency hearing on the record in accordance with subchapter II of chapter 5 of title 5, United States Code [5 USCS §§ 551 et seq.]. The hearing shall be held on an expedited basis and not later than 45 days after the request is made, except that the hearing may be held at a later time, if so requested by the regulated person.

(d) Information required in notice; updated notice for change in circumstances.

(1)(A) Information provided in a notice under subsection (a) or (b) shall include the name of the person to whom the importer or exporter involved intends to transfer the listed chemical involved, and the quantity of such chemical to be transferred.

(B) In the case of a notice under subsection (b) submitted by a regular importer, if the transferee identified in the notice is not a regular customer, such importer may not transfer the listed chemical until after the expiration of the 15-day period beginning on the date on which the notice is submitted to the Attorney General.

(C) After a notice under subsection (a) or (b) is submitted to the Attorney General, if circumstances change and the importer or exporter will not be transferring the listed chemical to the transferee identified in the notice, or will be transferring a greater quantity of the chemical than specified in the notice, the importer or exporter shall update the notice to identify the most recent prospective transferee or the most recent quantity or both (as the case may be) and may not transfer the listed chemical until after the expiration of the 15-day period beginning on the date on which the update is submitted to the Attorney General, except that such 15-day restriction does not apply if the prospective transferee identified in the update is a regular customer. The preceding sentence applies with respect to changing circumstances regarding a transferee or quantity identified in an update to the same extent and in the same manner as such sentence applies with respect to changing circumstances regarding a transferee or quantity identified in the original notice under subsection (a) or (b).

(D) In the case of a transfer of a listed chemical that is subject to a 15-day restriction under subparagraph (B) or (C), the transferee involved shall, upon the expiration of the 15-day period, be considered to qualify as a regular customer, unless the Attorney General otherwise notifies the importer or exporter involved in writing.

(2) With respect to a transfer of a listed chemical with which a notice or update referred to in paragraph (1) is concerned:

(A) The Attorney General, in accordance with the same procedures as apply under subsection (c)(2)—

(i) may order the suspension of the transfer of the listed chemical by the importer or exporter involved, except for a transfer to a regular customer, on the ground that the chemical may be diverted to the clandestine manufacture of a controlled substance (without regard to the form of the chemical that may be diverted, including the diversion of a finished drug product to be manufactured from bulk chemicals to be transferred), subject to the Attorney General ordering such suspension before the expiration of the 15-day period referred to in paragraph (1) with respect to the importation or exportation (in any case in which such a period applies); and

(ii) may, for purposes of clause (i) and paragraph (1), disqualify a regular customer on such ground.

(B) From and after the time when the Attorney General provides written notice of the order under subparagraph (A) (including a statement of the legal and factual basis for the order) to the importer or exporter, the importer or exporter may not carry out the transfer.

(3) For purposes of this subsection:

(A) The terms "importer" and "exporter" mean a regulated person who imports or exports a listed chemical, respectively.

(B) The term "transfer", with respect to a listed chemical, includes the sale of the chemical.

(C) The term "transferee" means a person to whom an importer or exporter transfers a listed chemical.

(e) Broker or trader for international transaction in listed chemical. A person located in the United States who is a broker or trader for an international transaction in a listed chemical that is a regulated transaction solely because of that person's involvement as a broker or trader shall, with respect to that transaction, be subject to all of the notification, reporting, recordkeeping, and other requirements placed upon exporters of listed chemicals by this title and title II.

(f) Application of notification requirement to exports of listed chemical; waiver.

(1) The Attorney General may by regulation require that the 15-day notification requirement of subsection (a) apply to all exports of a listed chemical to a specified country, regardless of the status of certain customers in such country as regular customers, if the Attorney General finds that such notification is necessary to support effective chemical diversion control programs or is required by treaty or other international agreement to which the United States is a party.

(2) The Attorney General may by regulation waive the 15-day notification requirement for exports of a listed chemical to a specified country if the Attorney General determines that such notification is not required for effective chemical diversion control. If the notification requirement is waived, exporters of the listed chemical shall be required to submit to the Attorney General reports of individual exportations or periodic reports of such exportation of the listed chemical, at such time or times and containing such information as the Attorney General shall establish by regulation.

(3) The Attorney General may by regulation waive the 15-day notification requirement for the importation of a listed chemical if the Attorney General determines that such notification is not necessary for effective chemical diversion control. If the notification requirement is waived, importers of the listed chemical shall be required to submit to the Attorney General reports of individual importations or periodic reports of the importation of the listed chemical, at such time or times and containing such information as the Attorney General shall establish by regulation.

(g) Return declaration. Within 30 days after a transaction covered by this section is completed, the importer or exporter shall send the Attorney General a return declaration containing particulars of the transaction, including the date, quantity, chemical, container, name of transferees, and such other information as the Attorney General may specify in regulations. For importers, a single return declaration may include the particulars of both the importation and distribution. If the importer has not distributed all chemicals imported by the end of the initial 30-day period, the importer shall file supplemental return declarations no later than 30 days from the date of any further distribution, until the distribution or other disposition of all chemicals imported pursuant to the import notification or any update are accounted for.

(h) Importation and distribution of ephedrine, pseudoephedrine, or phenylpropanolamine.

(1) With respect to a regulated person importing ephedrine, pseudoephedrine, or phenylpropanolamine (referred to in this section as an "importer"), a notice of importation under subsection (a) or (b) shall include all information known to the importer on the chain of distribution of such chemical from the manufacturer to the importer.

(2) For the purpose of preventing or responding to the diversion of ephedrine, pseudoephedrine, or phenylpropanolamine for use in the illicit production of methamphetamine, the Attorney General may, in the case of any person who is a manufacturer or distributor of such chemical in the chain of distribution referred to in paragraph (1) (which person is referred to in this subsection as a "foreign-chain distributor"), request that such distributor provide to the Attorney General information known to the distributor on the distribution of the chemical, including sales.

(3) If the Attorney General determines that a foreign-chain distributor is refusing to cooperate with the Attorney General in obtaining the information referred to in paragraph (2), the Attorney General may, in accordance with procedures that apply under subsection (c), issue an order prohibiting the importation of ephedrine, pseudoephedrine, or phenylpropanolamine in any case in which such distributor is part of the chain of distribution for such chemical. Not later than 60 days prior to issuing the order, the Attorney General shall publish in the Federal Register a notice of intent to issue the order. During such 60-day period, imports of the chemical with respect to such distributor may not be restricted under this paragraph.

(Oct. 27, 1970, P. L. 91-513, Title III, Part A, § 1018, as added Nov. 18, 1988, P. L. 100-690, Title VI, Subtitle A, § 6053(a), 102 Stat. 4314; Dec. 17, 1993, P. L. 103-200, §§ 4(a), 5(a), 9(b), 107 Stat. 2338, 2339, 2340; Sept. 13, 1994, P. L. 103-322, Title XXXIII, § 330024(c), 108 Stat. 2150; March 9, 2006, P. L. 109-177, Title VII, Subtitle A, § 716(a), (b)(1)(B), Subtitle B, § 721, 120 Stat. 265, 267.)

CODE OF FEDERAL REGULATIONS

TITLE 8

ALIENS AND NATIONALITY

(Complete Titles)

CHAPTER I

DEPARTMENT OF HOMELAND SECURITY (IMMIGRATION AND NATURALIZATION)

SUBCHAPTER A

GENERAL PROVISIONS

PART 1

DEFINITIONS

AUTHORITY NOTE APPLICABLE TO ENTIRE PART:

AUTHORITY:

8 U.S.C. 1101; 8 U.S.C. 1103; 5 U.S.C. 301; Pub. L. 107-296, 116 Stat. 2135; 6 U.S.C. 1 et seq.

§ 1.1 Applicability.

This part further defines some of the terms already described in section 101 and other sections of the Immigration and Nationality Act (66 Stat. 163), as amended, and such other enactments as pertain to immigration and nationality. These terms are used consistently by components within the Department of Homeland Security including U.S. Customs and Border Protection, U.S. Immigration and Customs Enforcement, and U.S. Citizenship and Immigration Services.

HISTORY:

[23 FR 9115, Nov. 26, 1958, as amended at 30 FR 14772, Nov. 30, 1965; 34 FR 12213, July 24, 1969; 38 FR 8590, Apr. 4, 1973; 40 FR 23271, May 29, 1975; 48 FR 8039, Feb. 25, 1983, 52 FR 2936, Jan. 29, 1987; 53 FR 30016, Aug. 10, 1988; 61 FR 18900, 18904, Apr. 29, 1996; 62 FR 10312, 10330, Mar. 6, 1997; 63 FR 19382, 19383, Apr. 20, 1998; 68 FR 10922, 10923, Mar. 6, 2003; 68 FR 35273, 35275, June 13, 2003; 71 FR 27585, 27591, May 12, 2006; 74 FR 26933, 26935, June 5, 2009; 74 FR 55726, 55736, Oct. 28, 2009; 75 FR 5225, 5227, Feb. 2, 2010; 76 FR 53764, 53778, Aug. 29, 2011]

§ 1.2 Definitions.

As used in this chapter I, the term:

Act or INA means the Immigration and Nationality Act, as amended.

Aggravated felony means a crime (or a conspiracy or attempt to commit a crime) described in section 101(a)(43) of the Act. This definition applies to any proceeding, application, custody determination, or adjudication pending on or after September 30, 1996, but shall apply under section 276(b) of the Act only to violations of section 276(a) of the Act occurring on or after that date.

Application means benefit request.

Arriving alien means an applicant for admission coming or attempting to come into the United States at a port-of-entry, or an alien seeking transit through the United States at a port-of-entry, or an alien interdicted in international or United States waters and brought into the United States by any means, whether or not to a designated port-of-entry, and regardless of the means of transport. An arriving alien remains an arriving alien even if paroled pursuant to section 212(d)(5) of the Act, and even after any such parole is terminated or revoked. However, an arriving alien who was paroled into the United States before April 1, 1997, or who was paroled into the United States on or after April 1, 1997, pursuant to a grant of advance parole which the alien applied for and obtained in the United States prior to the alien's departure from and return to the United States, will not be treated, solely by reason of that grant of parole, as an arriving alien under section 235(b)(1)(A)(i) of the Act.

Attorney means any person who is eligible to practice law in, and is a member in good standing of the bar of, the highest court of any State, possession, territory, or Commonwealth of the United States, or of the District of Columbia, and is not under any order suspending, enjoining, restraining, disbarring, or otherwise restricting him or her in the practice of law.

Benefit request means any application, petition, motion, appeal, or other request relating to an immigration or naturalization benefit, whether such request is filed on a paper form or submitted in an electronic format, provided such request is submitted in a manner prescribed by DHS for such purpose.

Board means the Board of Immigration Appeals within the Executive Office for Immigration Review, Department of Justice, as defined in 8 CFR 1001.1(e).

Case, unless the context otherwise requires, means any proceeding arising under any immigration or naturalization law, Executive Order, or Presidential proclamation, or preparation for or incident to such proceeding, including preliminary steps by any private person or corporation preliminary to the filing of the application or petition by which any proceeding under the jurisdiction of the Service or the Board is initiated.

CBP means U.S. Customs and Border Protection.

Commissioner means the Commissioner of the Immigration and Naturalization Service prior to March 1, 2003. Unless otherwise specified, references after that date mean the Director of U.S. Citizenship and Immigration Services, the Commissioner of U.S. Customs and Border Protection, and the Director of U.S. Immigration and Customs Enforcement, as appropriate in the context in which the term appears.

Day, when computing the period of time for taking any action provided in this chapter I including the taking of an appeal, shall include Saturdays, Sundays, and legal holidays, except that when the last day of the period computed falls on a Saturday, Sunday, or a legal holiday, the period shall run until the end of the next day which is not a Saturday, Sunday, or a legal holiday.

Department or DHS, unless otherwise noted, means the Department of Homeland Security.

Director or district director prior to March 1, 2003, means the district director or regional service center director, unless otherwise specified. On or after March 1, 2003, pursuant to delegation from the Secretary of Homeland Security or any successive re-delegation, the terms mean, to the extent that authority has been delegated to such official: asylum office director; director, field operations; district director for interior enforcement; district director for services; field office director; service center director; or special agent in charge. The terms also mean such other official, including an official in an acting capacity, within U.S. Citizenship and Immigration Services, U.S. Customs and Border Protection, U.S. Immigration and Customs Enforcement, or other component of the Department of Homeland Security who is delegated the function or authority above for a particular geographic district, region, or area.

EOIR means the Executive Office for Immigration Review within the Department of Justice.

Executed or execute means fully completed.

Form when used in connection with a benefit or other request to be filed with DHS to request an immigration benefit, means a device for the collection of information in a standard format that may be submitted in paper format or in an electronic format as prescribed by USCIS on its official Internet Web site. The term Form followed by an immigration form number includes an approved electronic equivalent of such form as may be prescribed by the appropriate component on its official Internet Web site.

Form instructions means instructions on how to complete and where to file a benefit request, supporting evidence or fees, or any other required or preferred document or instrument with a DHS immigration component. Form instructions prescribed by USCIS or other DHS immigration components on their official Internet Web sites will be considered the currently applicable version, notwithstanding paper or other versions that may be in circulation, and may be issued through non-form guidance such as appendices, exhibits, guidebooks, or manuals.

ICE means U.S. Immigration and Customs Enforcement.

Immigration judge means an immigration judge as defined in 8 CFR 1001.1(l).

Immigration officer means the following employees of the Department of Homeland Security, including senior or supervisory officers of such employees, designated as immigration officers authorized to exercise the powers and duties of such officer as specified by the Act and this chapter I: aircraft pilot, airplane pilot, asylum officer, refugee corps officer, Border Patrol agent, contact representative, deportation officer, detention enforcement officer, detention officer, fingerprint specialist, forensic document analyst, general attorney (except with respect to CBP, only to the extent that the attorney is performing any immigration function), helicopter pilot, immigration agent (investigations), immigration enforcement agent, immigration information officer, immigration inspector, immigration officer, immigration services officer, investigator, intelligence agent, intelligence officer, investigative assistant, special agent, other officer or employee of the Department of Homeland Security or of the United States as designated by the Secretary of Homeland Security as provided in 8 CFR 2.1.

Lawfully admitted for permanent residence means the status of having been lawfully accorded the privilege of residing permanently in the United States as an immigrant in accordance with the immigration laws, such status not having changed. Such status terminates upon entry of a final administrative order of exclusion, deportation, or removal.

Petition. See Benefit request.

Practice means the act or acts of any person appearing in any case, either in person or through the preparation or filing of any brief or other document, paper, application, or petition on behalf of another person or client before or with DHS.

Preparation, constituting practice, means the study of the facts of a case and the applicable laws, coupled with the giving of advice and auxiliary activities, including the incidental preparation of papers, but does not include the lawful functions of a notary public or service consisting solely of assistance in the completion of blank spaces on printed DHS forms, by one whose remuneration, if any, is nominal and who does not hold himself or herself out as qualified in legal matters or in immigration and naturalization procedure.

Representation before DHS includes practice and preparation as defined in this section.

Representative refers to a person who is entitled to represent others as provided in 8 CFR 292.1(a)(2) through (6) and 8 CFR 292.1(b).

Respondent means an alien named in a Notice to Appear issued in accordance with section 239(a) of the Act, or in an Order to Show Cause issued in accordance with 8 CFR 242.1 (1997) as it existed prior to April 1, 1997.

Secretary, unless otherwise noted, means the Secretary of Homeland Security.

Service means U.S. Citizenship and Immigration Services, U.S. Customs and Border Protection, and/or U.S. Immigration and Customs Enforcement, as appropriate in the context in which the term appears.

Service counsel means any immigration officer assigned to represent the Service in any proceeding before an immigration judge or the Board of Immigration Appeals.

Transition program effective date as used with respect to extending the immigration laws to the Commonwealth of the Northern Mariana Islands means November 28, 2009.

USCIS means U.S. Citizenship and Immigration Services.

HISTORY:

[76 FR 53764, 53778, Aug. 29, 2011]

§ 1.3 Lawfully present aliens for purposes of applying for Social Security benefits.

(a) Definition of the term an "alien who is lawfully present in the United States." For the purposes of 8 U.S.C. 1611(b)(2) only, an "alien who is lawfully present in the United States" means:

(1) A qualified alien as defined in 8 U.S.C. 1641(b);

(2) An alien who has been inspected and admitted to the United States and who has not violated the terms of the status under which he or she was admitted or to which he or she has changed after admission;

(3) An alien who has been paroled into the United States pursuant to section 212(d)(5) of the Act for less than 1 year, except:

(i) Aliens paroled for deferred inspection or pending removal proceedings under section 240 of the Act; and

(ii) Aliens paroled into the United States for prosecution pursuant to 8 CFR 212.5(b)(3);

(4) An alien who belongs to one of the following classes of aliens permitted to remain in the United States because DHS has decided for humanitarian or other public policy reasons not to initiate removal proceedings or enforce departure:

(i) Aliens currently in temporary resident status pursuant to section 210 or 245A of the Act;

(ii) Aliens currently under Temporary Protected Status (TPS) pursuant to section 244 of the Act;

(iii) Cuban-Haitian entrants, as defined in section 202(b) of Pub. L. 99-603, as amended;

(iv) Family Unity beneficiaries pursuant to section 301 of Pub. L. 101-649, as amended;

(v) Aliens currently under Deferred Enforced Departure (DED) pursuant to a decision made by the President;

(vi) Aliens currently in deferred action status;

(vii) Aliens who are the spouse or child of a United States citizen whose visa petition has been approved and who have a pending application for adjustment of status;

(5) Applicants for asylum under section 208(a) of the Act and applicants for withholding of removal under section 241(b)(3) of the Act or under the Convention Against Torture who have been granted employment authorization, and such applicants under the age of 14 who have had an application pending for at least 180 days.

(b) Non-issuance of a Notice to Appear and non-enforcement of deportation, exclusion, or removal orders. An alien may not be deemed to be lawfully present solely on the basis of DHS's decision not to, or failure to:

(1) Issue a Notice to Appear; or

(2) Enforce an outstanding order of deportation, exclusion or removal.

HISTORY:

[76 FR 53764, 53778, Aug. 29, 2011]

§ 1.4 Definition of Form I-94

The term Form I-94, as used in this chapter I, includes the collection of arrival/departure and admission or parole information by DHS, whether in paper or electronic format, which is made available to the person about whom the information has been collected, as may be prescribed by DHS. The following terms, when used in the context of the Form I-94, are clarified as to their meaning to accommodate the collection of such information in an electronic format.

(a) The terms "annotate," "note," "indicate on," "stamp," and "endorse," unless used in part 231 of this chapter, include, but are not limited, to DHS amending, including or completing information in its electronic record of admission, or arrival/departure. For purposes of part 231, the term "endorse" includes but is not limited to the submission of electronic departure data to CBP.

(b) The terms "completed," "completely executed" and "completed and signed" include, but are not limited to, DHS completing its collection of information into its electronic record of admission, or arrival/departure.

(c) The terms "issuance" and "given" include, but are not limited to, the creation of an electronic record of admission, or arrival/departure by DHS following an inspection performed by an immigration officer.

(d) The term "original I-94" includes, but is not limited to, any printout or electronic transmission of information from DHS systems containing the electronic record of admission or arrival/departure.

(e) The terms "present," "presentation," or "submission" of a Form I-94, unless they are used in § 231.1 or § 231.2 of this chapter, include, but are not limited to, providing a printout of information from DHS systems containing an electronic record of admission or arrival/departure. For purposes of § 231.1 of this chapter, the terms "present" or "submission" of the Form I-94 includes ensuring that each passenger presents him/herself to a CBP Officer for inspection at a U.S. port-of-entry. For the purposes of § 231.2 of this chapter, the terms "present," "submit," or "submission" of the Form I-94 includes ensuring that each passenger is available for inspection by a CBP Officer upon request.

(f) The term "possession" with respect to a Form I-94 includes, but is not limited to, obtaining a copy or printout of the record of an electronic evidence of admission or arrival/departure from the appropriate CBP systems.

(g) The terms "surrendering," "turning in a Form I-94," and "departure I-94" includes, but is not limited to, complying with any departure controls under 8 CFR part 215 that may be prescribed by CBP in addition to the submission of electronic departure data to CBP by a carrier.

HISTORY:

[78 FR 18457, 18472, Mar. 27, 2013, as confirmed at 81 FR 91646, 91670, Dec. 19, 2016]

PART 2

AUTHORITY OF THE SECRETARY OF HOMELAND SECURITY

AUTHORITY NOTE APPLICABLE TO ENTIRE PART:

AUTHORITY:

8 U.S.C. 1103; 5 U.S.C. 301; Public Law 107-296, 116 Stat. 2135 (6 U.S.C. 1 et seq.).

§ 2.1 Authority of the Secretary of Homeland Security.

All authorities and functions of the Department of Homeland Security to administer and enforce the immigration laws are vested in the Secretary of Homeland Security. The Secretary of Homeland Security may, in the Secretary's discretion, delegate any such authority or function to any official, officer, or employee of the Department of Homeland Security, including delegation through successive redelegation, or to any employee of the United States to the extent authorized by law. Such delegation may be made by regulation, directive, memorandum, or other means as deemed appropriate by the Secretary in the exercise of the Secretary's discretion. A delegation of authority or function may in the Secretary's discretion be published in the Federal Register, but such publication is not required.

HISTORY:

[48 FR 8039, Feb. 25, 1983; 67 FR 48354, 48359, July 24, 2002; 68 FR 10922, 10923, Mar. 6, 2003]

PART 3

EXECUTIVE OFFICE FOR IMMIGRATION REVIEW

AUTHORITY NOTE APPLICABLE TO ENTIRE PART:

AUTHORITY:

5 U.S.C. 301; 8 U.S.C. 1101 note, 1103, 1252 note, 1252b, 1324b, 1362; 28 U.S.C. 509, 510, 1746; sec. 2, Reorg. Plan No. 2 of 1950, 3 CFR, 1949-1953 Comp., p. 1002; section 203 of Pub. L. 105-100, 111 Stat. 2196-200; sections 1506 and 1510 of Pub. L. 106-386; 114 Stat. 1527-29, 1531-32; section 1505 of Pub. L. 106-554, 114 Stat. 2763A-326 to-328.

§ 3.0 Executive Office for Immigration Review

Regulations of the Executive Office for Immigration Review relating to the adjudication of immigration matters before immigration judges (referred to in some regulations as special inquiry officers) and the Board of Immigration Appeals are located in 8 CFR chapter V, part 1003.

HISTORY:

[68 FR 9824, 9831, Feb. 28, 2003]

SUBCHAPTER B

IMMIGRATION REGULATIONS

Part

PART 100

STATEMENT OF ORGANIZATION

AUTHORITY NOTE APPLICABLE TO ENTIRE PART:

AUTHORITY:

8 U.S.C. 1103; 8 U.S.C. 1185 note (section 7209 of Pub. L. 108-458); 8 CFR part 2.

§ 100.1 Introduction.

The following components have been delegated authority under the Immigration and Nationality Act to administer and enforce certain provisions of the Immigration and Nationality Act and all other laws relating to immigration: U.S. Customs and Border Protection (CBP), U.S. Immigration and Customs Enforcement (ICE), and U.S. Citizenship and Immigration Services (USCIS).

HISTORY:

[48 FR 37201, Aug. 17, 1983; 74 FR 26933, 26936, June 5, 2009]

§ 100.2 [This section was removed and reserved. See 74 FR 26933, 26936, June 5, 2009.]

[NO TEXT IN ORIGINAL]

HISTORY:

[48 FR 13147, Mar. 30, 1983; 48 FR 17060, Apr. 21, 1983, as amended at 49 FR 12189, Mar. 29, 1984; 49 FR 13135, Apr. 3, 1984; 49 FR 22768, June 1, 1984; 49 FR 37371, Sept. 24, 1984; 51 FR 19824, June 3, 1986; 52 FR 16191, May 1, 1987; 54 FR 18649, May 2, 1989; 59 FR 60068, Nov. 22, 1994]

AUTHORITY:

(8 U.S.C. 1103; 8 CFR part 2.)

§ 100.3 Places where, and methods whereby, information may be secured or submittals or requests made.

Any person desiring information relative to a matter handled by CBP, ICE or USCIS or any person desiring to make a submittal or request in connection with such a matter, should communicate either orally or in writing, with either CBP, ICE or USCIS as appropriate. When the submittal or request consists of a formal application for one of the documents, privileges, or other benefits provided for in the laws administered by CBP, ICE or USCIS or the regulations implementing those laws, follow the instructions on the form as to preparation and place of submission. Individuals can seek service or assistance from CBP, ICE or USCIS by visiting the CBP, ICE or USCIS Web site or calling CBP, ICE or USCIS.

HISTORY:

[32 FR 9616, July 4, 1967; 74 FR 26933, 26936, June 5, 2009]

§ 100.4 Field Offices.

(a) Ports-of-Entry for aliens arriving by vessel or by land transportation. Subject to the limitations prescribed in this paragraph, the following places are hereby designated as Ports-of-Entry for aliens arriving by any means of travel other than aircraft. The designation of such a Port-of-Entry may be withdrawn whenever, in the judgment of the Commissioner, such action is warranted. The ports are listed according to location by districts and are designated either Class A, B, or C. Class A means that the port is a designated Port-of-Entry for all aliens. Class B means that the port is a designated Port-of-Entry for aliens who at the time of applying for admission are exempt from document requirements by § 212.1(c)(5) of this chapter or who are lawfully in possession of valid Permanent Resident Cards, and nonimmigrant aliens who are citizens of Canada or Bermuda or nationals of Mexico and who at the time of applying for admission are lawfully in possession of all valid documents required for admission as set forth in §§ 212.1(a) and (c) and 235.1(d) and (e) of this chapter and are admissible without further arrival documentation or immigration processing. Class C means that the port is a designated Port-of-Entry only for aliens who are arriving in the United

States as crewmen as that term is defined in section 101(a)(10) of the Act with respect to vessels.

DISTRICT NO. 1 — [RESERVED]

DISTRICT NO. 2 — BOSTON, MASSACHUSETTS

Class A

Boston, MA (the port of Boston includes, among others, the port facilities at Beverly, Braintree, Chelsea, Everett, Hingham, Lynn, Manchester, Marblehead, Milton, Quincy, Revere, Salem, Saugus, and Weymouth, MA)

Gloucester, MA

Hartford, CT (the port at Hartford includes, among others, the port facilities at Bridgeport, Groton, New Haven, and New London, CT)

Providence, RI (the port of Providence includes, among others, the port facilities at Davisville, Melville, Newport, Portsmouth, Quonset Point, Saunderstown, Tiverton, and Warwick, RI; and at Fall River, New Bedford, and Somerset, MA)

Class C

Newburyport, MA

Plymouth, MA

Portsmouth, NH

Provincetown, MA

Sandwich, MA

Woods Hole, MA

DISTRICT NO. 3 — NEW YORK, NEW YORK

Class A

New York, NY (the port of New York includes, among others, the port facilities at Bronx, Brooklyn, Buchanan, Manhattan, Montauk, Northport, Port Jefferson, Queens, Riverhead, Poughkeepsie, the Stapleton Anchorage-Staten Island, Staten Island, Stoney Point, and Yonkers, NY, as well as the East Side Passenger Terminal in Manhattan)

DISTRICT NO. 4 — PHILADELPHIA, PENNSYLVANIA

Class A

Erie Seaport, PA

Philadelphia, PA (the port of Philadelphia includes, among others, the port facilities at Delaware City, Lewes, New Castle, and Wilmington, DE; and at Chester, Essington, Fort Mifflin, Marcus Hook, and Morrisville, PA)

Pittsburgh, PA

DISTRICT NO. 5 — BALTIMORE, MARYLAND

Class A

Baltimore, MD

Patuxent River, MD

Class C

Piney Point, MD

Salisbury, MD

DISTRICT NO. 6 — MIAMI, FLORIDA

Class A

Boca Grande, FL

Fernandina, FL

Fort Lauderdale/Port Everglades, FL, Seaport

Fort Pierce, FL

*Jacksonville, FL

Key West, FL

Miami Marine Unit, FL

Panama City, FL

Pensacola, FL

Port Canaveral, FL

St. Augustine, FL

St. Petersburg, FL

*Tampa, FL (includes Fort Myers)

West Palm Beach, FL

Class C

Manatee, FL

Port Dania, FL

Port St. Joe, FL

DISTRICT NO. 7 — BUFFALO, NEW YORK

Class A

Albany, NY

Alexandria Bay, NY

Buffalo, NY

Cape Vincent, NY

Champlain, NY

Chateaugay, NY

Ft. Covington, NY

Massena, NY

Mooers, NY

Niagara Falls, NY (the port of Niagara Falls includes, among others, the port facilities at Lewiston Bridge, Rainbow Bridge, and Whirlpool Bridge, NY)

Ogdensburg, NY

Peace Bridge, NY

Rochester, NY

Rouses Point, NY

Thousand Islands Bridge, NY

Trout River, NY

Class B

Cannons Corner, NY

Churubusco, NY

Class C

Oswego, NY

DISTRICT NO. 8 — DETROIT, MICHIGAN

Class A

Algonac, MI

Detroit, MI, Detroit and Canada Tunnel

Detroit, MI, Detroit International Bridge (Ambassador Bridge)

Grosse Isle, MI

Isle Royale, MI

Marine City, MI

Port Huron, MI

Sault Ste. Marie, MI

Class B

Alpena, MI

Detour, MI

Grand Rapids, MI

Mackinac Island, MI

Rogers City, MI

Class C

Alpena, MI

Baraga, MI

Bay City, MI

Cheboygan, MI

Detour, MI

Escanaba, MI

Grand Haven, MI

Holland, MI

Houghton, MI

Ludington, MI
Mackinac Island, MI
Manistee, MI
Marquette, MI
Menominee, MI
Monroe, MI
Munising, MI
Muskegon, MI
Pontiac, MI
Port Dolomite, MI
Port Inland, MI
Rogers City (Calcite), MI
Saginaw, MI
South Haven, MI
DISTRICT NO. 9 — CHICAGO, ILLINOIS
Class A
Algoma, WI
Bayfield, WI
Chicago, IL
Green Bay, WI
*Milwaukee, WI
Class C
Ashland, WI
East Chicago, IL
Gary, IN
Kenosha, WI
Manitowoc, WI
Marinette, WI
Michigan City, IN
Racine, WI
Sheboygan, WI
Sturgeon Bay, WI
DISTRICT NO. 10 — ST. PAUL, MINNESOTA
Class A
Ambrose, ND
Antler, ND
Baudette, MN
Carbury, ND
Duluth, MN (the port of Duluth includes, among others, the port facilities at Superior, WI)
Dunseith, ND
Ely, MN
Fortuna, ND
Grand Portage, MN
Hannah, ND
Hansboro, ND
International Falls, MN
Lancaster, MN
Maida, ND
Neche, ND
Noonan, ND
Northgate, ND
Noyes, MN
Pembina, ND
Pine Creek, MN
Portal, ND
Ranier, MN
Roseau, MN
Sarles, ND
Sherwood, ND
St. John, ND
Walhalla, ND
Warroad, MN
Westhope, ND
Class B
Crane Lake, MN
Oak Island, MN
Class C
Grand Marais, MN
Silver Bay, MN
Taconite Harbor, MN
Two Harbors, MN
DISTRICT NO. 11 — KANSAS CITY, MISSOURI
Class A
Kansas City, MO
Class B
Wichita, KS
DISTRICT NO. 12 — SEATTLE, WASHINGTON
Class A
Aberdeen, WA (the port of Aberdeen includes, among others, the port facilities at Raymond and South Bend, WA)
Anacortes, WA
Bellingham, WA
Blaine-Pacific Highway, WA
Blaine-Peach Arch, WA
Boundary, WA
Colville, WA
Danville, WA
Eastport, ID
Ferry, WA
Friday Harbor, WA (the port of Friday Harbor includes, among others, the port facilities at Roche Harbor, WA)
Frontier, WA
Kalama, WA
Laurier, WA
Longview, WA
Lynden, WA
Metaline Falls, WA
Neah Bay, WA
Olympia, WA
Oroville, WA
Point Roberts, WA
Port Angeles, WA
Port Townsend, WA
Porthill, WA
Seattle, WA (the port of Seattle includes, among others, the port facilities at Bangor, Blake Island, Bremerton, Eagle Harbor, Edmonds, Everett, Holmes Harbor, Houghton, Kennydale, Keyport, Kingston, Manchester, Mukilteo, Orchard Point, Point Wells, Port Gamble, Port Ludlow, Port Orchard, Poulsbo, Shuffleton, and Winslow, WA)
Sumas, WA
Tacoma, WA (the port of Tacoma includes, among others, the port facilities at Dupont, WA)
Vancouver, WA
Yakima, WA
Class B
Nighthawk, WA
DISTRICT NO. 13 — SAN FRANCISCO, CALIFORNIA
Class A

San Francisco, CA (the port of San Francisco includes, among others, the port facilities at Antioch, Benicia, Martinez, Oakland, Pittsburgh, Port Chicago Concord Naval Weapon Station, Redwood City, Richmond, Sacramento, San Pablo Bay, and Stockton, CA)

Class C

Eureka, CA

DISTRICT NO. 14 — SAN ANTONIO, TEXAS

Class A

Amistad Dam, TX

Corpus Christi, TX (the port of Corpus Christi includes, among others, the port facilities at Harbor Island, Ingeleside, and Port Lavaca-Point Comfort, TX)

Del Rio, TX

Laredo, TX (the port of Laredo includes, among others, the port facilities at Colombia Bridge, Convent Bridge, and Lincoln-Juarez Bridge, TX)

Maverick, TX

DISTRICT NO. 15 — EL PASO, TEXAS

Class A

Columbus, NM

El Paso, TX (the port of El Paso includes, among others, the port facilities at Bridge of the Americas, Paso Del Norte Bridge, and Ysleta Bridge, TX)

Fabens, TX

Fort Hancock, TX

Presidio, TX

Santa Teresa, NM

Class B

Boquillas, TX

DISTRICT NO. 16 — LOS ANGELES, CALIFORNIA

Class A

Los Angeles, CA (the port of Los Angeles includes, among others, the port facilities at Long Beach, Ontario, Port Hueneme, San Pedro, and Ventura, CA)

San Luis Obispo, CA (the port of San Luis Obispo includes, among others, the port facilities at Avila, Estero Bay, El Capitan, Elwood, Gaviota, Morro Bay, and Santa Barbara, CA)

DISTRICT NO. 17 — HONOLULU, HAWAII

Class A

Agana, Guam, M.I (including the port facilities of Apra Harbor, Guam).

Honolulu, HI, Seaport (including all port facilities on the island of Oahu).

Rota, the Commonwealth of the Northern Mariana Islands.

Saipan, the Commonwealth of the Northern Mariana Islands.

Tinian, the Commonwealth of the Northern Mariana Islands.

Class C

Hilo, HI

Kahului, HI, Kahului Harbor

Nawiliwilli, HI, Nawiliwilli Harbor

Port Allen, HI, Port Allen Harbor

DISTRICT NO. 18 — PHOENIX, ARIZONA

Class A

Douglas, AZ

Lukeville, AZ

Mariposa, AZ

Morley Gate, AZ

Naco, AZ

Nogales, AZ

Sasabe, AZ

San Luis, AZ

DISTRICT NO. 19 — DENVER, COLORADO

Class A

Denver, CO

Grand Junction, CO

Pueblo, CO

Salt Lake City, UT

DISTRICT NO. 20 — [RESERVED]

DISTRICT NO. 21 — NEWARK, NEW JERSEY

Class A

Camden, NJ (the port of Camden includes, among others, the port facilities at Artificial Island, Billingsport, Burlington, Cape May, Deepwater Point, Fisher's Point, Gibbstown, Gloucester City, Paulsboro, Salem, and Trenton, NJ)

Newark, NJ (the port of Newark includes, among others, the port facilities at Bayonne, Carteret, Edgewater, Elizabeth, Jersey City, Leonardo, Linden, Perth Amboy, Port Newark, and Sewaren, NJ)

DISTRICT NO. 22 — PORTLAND, MAINE

Class A

Alburg, VT

Alburg Springs, VT

Bangor, ME (the port of Bangor includes, among others, the port facilities at Bar Harbor, Belfast, Brewer, Bucksport Harbor, Prospect Harbor, Sandypoint, Seal Harbor, Searsport, and South West Harbor, ME)

Beebe Plain, VT

Beecher Falls, VT

Bridgewater, ME

Calais, ME (includes Ferry Point and Milltown Bridges)

Canaan, VT

Coburn Gore, ME

Derby Line, VT

Eastport, ME

East Richford, VT

Fort Fairfield, ME

Fort Kent, ME

Hamlin, ME

Highgate Springs, VT

Houlton, ME

Jackman, ME

Limestone, ME

Lubec, ME

Madawaska, ME

Morses Line, VT

North Troy, VT

Norton, VT

Pittsburgh, NH

Portland, ME

Richford, VT (includes the Pinnacle Port-of-Entry)

*St. Albans, VT

Van Buren, ME

Vanceboro, ME

West Berkshire, VT

Class B

Daaquam, ME

Easton, ME
Eastcourt, ME
Forest City, ME
Monticello, ME
Orient, ME
Robinston, ME
St. Aurelie, ME
St. Pamphile, ME
Class C
Bath, ME
Boothbay Harbor, ME
Kittery, ME
Rockland, ME
Wiscasset, ME
DISTRICT NO. 23 — [RESERVED]
DISTRICT NO. 24 — CLEVELAND, OHIO
Class A
Cincinnati, OH
Cleveland, OH
Columbus, OH
Put-In-Bay, OH
Sandusky, OH
Toledo, OH
Class C
Ashtabula, OH
Conneaut, OH
Fairport, OH
Huron, OH
Lorain, OH
Marblehead, OH
DISTRICT NO. 25 — WASHINGTON, DC
Class A
Hopewell, VA
*Norfolk, VA — (the port of Norfolk includes, among others, the port facilities at Fort Monroe and Newport News, VA)
Richmond, VA
Washington, DC (includes the port facilities at Alexandria, VA)
Yorktown, VA
DISTRICT NO. 26 — ATLANTA, GEORGIA
Class A
Charleston, SC (the port of Charleston includes, among others, the port facilities at Georgetown and Port Royal, SC)
Mobile, AL
Savannah, GA (the port of Savannah includes, among others, the port facilities at Brunswick and St. Mary's Seaport, GA)
Wilmington, NC (the port of Wilmington includes the port facilities at Morehead City, NC)
DISTRICT NO. 27 — SAN JUAN, PUERTO RICO
Class A
Aguadilla, PR
*Charlotte Amalie, St. Thomas, VI
Christiansted, St. Croix, VI
Cruz Bay, St. John, VI
Ensenada, PR
Federiksted, St. Croix, VI
Fajardo, PR
Humacao, PR
Jobos, PR
Mayaguez, PR
Ponce, PR
Red Hook, St. Thomas, VI
Class B
Coral Bay, St. John, VI
DISTRICT NO. 28 — NEW ORLEANS, LOUISIANA
Class A
Baton Rouge, LA
Gulfport, MS
Lake Charles, LA
Memphis, TN
Nashville, TN
New Orleans, LA (the port of New Orleans includes, among others, the port facilities at Avondale, Bell Chasse, Braithwaite, Burnside, Chalmette, Destrahan, Geismar, Gramercy, Gretna, Harvey, Marrero, Norco, Port Sulphur, St. Rose, and Westwego, LA)
Class C
Morgan City, LA
Pascagoula, MS
DISTRICT NO. 29 — OMAHA, NEBRASKA
Class A
Omaha, NE
Des Moines, IA
DISTRICT NO. 30 — HELENA, MONTANA
Class A
Chief Mountain, MT (May-October)
Del Bonita, MT
Morgan, MT
Opheim, MT
Peigan, MT
Raymond, MT
Roosville, MT
Scobey, MT
Sweetgrass, MT
Turner, MT
Wildhorse, MT
Willow Creek, MT
Class B
Goat Haunt, MT
Trail Creek, MT
Whitlash, MT
DISTRICT NO. 31 — PORTLAND, OREGON
Class A
Astoria, OR (the port of Astoria includes, among others, the port facilities at Bradwood, Pacific City, Taft, Tilliamook, (including Bay City and Garibaldi), Warrenton, Wauna, and Westport, OR)
Coos Bay, OR (the port of Coos Bay includes, among others, the port facilities at Bandon, Brookings, Depoe Bay, Florence, Frankfort, Gold Beach, Newport (including Toledo), Port Orford, Reedsport, Waldport, and Yachats, OR)
Portland, OR (the port of Portland includes, among others, the port facilities at Beaver, Columbia City, Prescott, Rainier, and St. Helens, OR)
DISTRICT NO. 32 — ANCHORAGE, ALASKA
Class A
Alcan, AK
Anchorage, AK (the port of Anchorage includes, among others (for out of port inspections only),

Afognak, Barrow, Cold Bay, Cordova, Homer, Kodiak, Kotzebue, Nikiski, Seward, Valdez, and Yakutat, AK)

Dalton's Cache, AK

Dutch Harbor, AK

Fairbanks, AK

Gambell, AK

Juneau, AK

Ketchikan, AK

Nome, AK

Poker Creek, AK

Skagway, AK

Class B

Eagle, AK

Hyder, AK

Class C

Valdez, AK

DISTRICT NO. 38 — HOUSTON, TEXAS

Class A

Galveston, TX (the port of Galveston includes, among others, the port facilities at Freeport, Port Bolivar, and Texas City, TX)

Houston, TX (the port of Houston includes, among others, the port facilities at Baytown, TX)

Port Arthur, TX (the port of Port Arthur includes, among others, the port facilities at Beaumont, Orange, and Sabine, TX)

DISTRICT NO. 39 — SAN DIEGO, CALIFORNIA

Class A

Andrade, CA

Calexico, CA

Otay Mesa, CA

San Ysidro, CA (including the Cross Border Xpress (CBX) facility)

Tecate, CA

DISTRICT NO. 40 — HARLINGEN, TEXAS

Class A

Brownsville, TX (the port of Brownsville includes, among others, the port facilities at Brownsville Seaport, Port Isabel, Padre Island and Harlingen, TX, Ship Channel)

Brownsville, TX, Gateway Bridge and Brownsville/Matamoros Bridge

Falcon Heights, TX

Hidalgo, TX

Los Ebanos, TX

Los Indios, TX

Pharr, TX

Progreso, TX

Rio Grande City, TX

Roma, TX

(b) Ports-of-Entry for aliens arriving by aircraft. In addition to the following international airports which are hereby designated as Ports-of-Entry for aliens arriving by aircraft, other places where permission for certain aircraft to land officially has been given and places where emergency or forced landings are made under part 239 of this chapter shall be regarded as designated for the entry of aliens arriving by such aircraft:

DISTRICT NO. 1 — [RESERVED]

DISTRICT NO. 2 — BOSTON, MASSACHUSETTS

Boston, MA, Logan International Airport

Manchester, NH, Grenier Airport

Portsmouth, NH, Pease Air Force Base

Warwick, RI, T. F. Greene Airport

Windsor Locks, CT, Bradley International Airport

DISTRICT NO. 3 — NEW YORK CITY, NEW YORK

Newburgh, NY, Stewart International Airport

Queens, NY, LaGuardia Airport

Westchester, NY, Westchester County Airport

DISTRICT NO. 4 — PHILADELPHIA, PENNSYLVANIA

Charlestown, WV, Kanahwa Airport

Dover, DE, Dover Air Force Base

Erie, PA, Erie International Airport (USCS)

Harrisburg, PA, Harrisburg International Airport

Philadelphia, PA, Philadelphia International Airport

Pittsburgh, PA, Pittsburgh International Airport

DISTRICT NO. 5 — BALTIMORE, MARYLAND

Baltimore, MD, Baltimore-Washington International Airport

DISTRICT NO. 6 — MIAMI, FLORIDA

Daytona, FL, Daytona International Airport, FL

Fort Lauderdale, FL, Executive Airport

Fort Lauderdale, FL, Fort Lauderdale-Hollywood Airport

Fort Myers, FL, Southwest Regional International Airport

Freeport, Bahamas, Freeport International Airport

Jacksonville, FL, Jacksonville International Airport

Key West, FL, Key West International Airport

Melbourne, FL, Melbourne International Airport

Miami, FL, Chalks Flying Service Seaplane Base

Miami, FL, Miami International Airport

Nassau, Bahamas, Nassau International Airport

Orlando, FL, Orlando International Airport

Palm Beach, FL, Palm Beach International Airport

Paradise Island, Bahamas, Paradise Island Airport

Sanford, FL, Sanford International Airport

Sarasota, FL, Sarasota Airport

St. Petersburg, FL, St. Petersburg/Clearwater International Airport

Tampa, FL, Tampa International Airport

DISTRICT NO. 7 — BUFFALO, NEW YORK

Albany, NY, Albany County Airport

Buffalo, NY, Buffalo Airport

Massena, NY, Massena Airport

Niagara Falls, NY, Niagara Falls International Airport

Ogdensburg, NY, Ogdensburg Municipal Airport

Rochester, NY, Rochester Airport

Syracuse, NY, Hancock International Airport

Watertown, NY, Watertown Municipal Airport

DISTRICT NO. 8 — DETROIT, MICHIGAN

Battle Creek, MI, Battle Creek Airport

Chippewa, MI, Chippewa County International Airport

Detroit, MI, Detroit City Airport

Detroit, MI, Detroit Metropolitan Wayne County Airport

Port Huron, MI, St. Clair County International Airport

Sault Ste. Marie, MI, Sault Ste. Marie Airport

DISTRICT NO. 9 — CHICAGO, ILLINOIS

Chicago, IL, Chicago Midway Airport
Chicago, IL, Chicago O'Hare International Airport
Indianapolis, IN, Indianapolis International Airport
Mitchell, WI, Mitchell International Airport
DISTRICT NO. 10 — ST. PAUL, MINNESOTA
Baudette, MN, Baudette International Airport
Duluth, MN, Duluth International Airport
Duluth, MN, Sky Harbor Airport
Grand Forks, ND, Grand Forks International Airport
International Falls, MN, Falls International Airport
Minneapolis/St. Paul, MN, Minneapolis/St. Paul International Airport
Minot, ND, Minot International Airport
Pembina, ND, Port Pembina Airport
Portal, ND, Portal Airport
Ranier, MN, International Seaplane Base
Warroad, MN, Warroad International Airport
Williston, ND, Sioulin Field (Municipal)
DISTRICT NO. 11 — KANSAS CITY, MISSOURI
Kansas City, MO, Kansas City International Airport
Springfield, MO, Springfield Regional Airport
St. Louis, MO, St. Louis Lambert International Airport
St. Louis, MO, Spirit of St. Louis Airport
DISTRICT NO. 12 — SEATTLE, WASHINGTON
Bellingham, WA, Bellingham Airport
Friday Harbor, WA, Friday Harbor
McChord, WA, McChord Air Force Base
Oroville, WA, Dorothy Scott Municipal Airport
Oroville, WA, Dorothy Scott Seaplane Base
Point Roberts, WA, Point Roberts Airport
Port Townsend, WA, Jefferson County International Airport
SEA-TAC, WA, SEA-TAC International Airport
Seattle, WA, Boeing Municipal Air Field
Seattle, WA, Lake Union
Spokane, WA, Felts Field
Spokane, WA, Spokane International Airport
DISTRICT NO. 13 — SAN FRANCISCO, CALIFORNIA
Alameda, CA, Alemeda Naval Air Station
Oakland, CA, Oakland International Airport
Sacramento, CA, Beale Air Force Base
San Francisco, CA, San Francisco International Airport
San Jose, CA, San Jose International Airport
Travis, CA, Travis Air Force Base
DISTRICT NO. 14 — SAN ANTONIO, TEXAS
Austin, TX, Austin International Airport
Corpus Christi, TX, Corpus Christi Airport
Del Rio, TX, Del Rio International Airport
Laredo, TX, Laredo International Airport
Maverick, TX, Maverick County Airport
San Antonio, TX, San Antonio International Airport
DISTRICT NO. 15 — EL PASO, TEXAS
Albuquerque, NM, Albuquerque International Airport
El Paso, TX, International Airport
Presidio, TX, Presidio Airport
Santa Teresa, NM, Santa Teresa Airport
DISTRICT NO. 16 — LOS ANGELES, CALIFORNIA
Los Angeles, CA, Los Angeles International Airport
Ontario, CA, Ontario International Airport
DISTRICT NO. 17 — HONOLULU, HAWAII
Agana, Guam, Guam International Airport Terminal.
Honolulu, HI, Honolulu International Airport.
Honolulu, HI, Hickam Air Force Base.
Rota, the Commonwealth of the Northern Mariana Islands.
Saipan, the Commonwealth of the Northern Mariana Islands.
Tinian, the Commonwealth of the Northern Mariana Islands.
DISTRICT NO. 18 — PHOENIX, ARIZONA
Douglas, AZ, Bisbee-Douglas Airport
Las Vegas, NV, McCarren International Airport
Nogales, AZ, Nogales International Airport
Phoenix, AZ, Phoenix Sky Harbor International Airport
Reno, NV, Reno Carron International Airport
Tucson, AZ, Tucson International Airport
Yuma, AZ, Yuma International Airport
DISTRICT NO. 19 — DENVER, COLORADO
Colorado Springs, CO, Colorado Springs Airport
Denver, CO, Denver International Airport
Salt Lake City, UT, Salt Lake City Airport
DISTRICT NO. 20 — DALLAS, TEXAS
Dallas, TX, Dallas-Fort Worth International Airport
Oklahoma City, OK, Oklahoma City Airport (includes Altus and Tinker AFBs)
DISTRICT NO. 21 — NEWARK, NEW JERSEY
Atlantic City, NJ, Atlantic City International Airport
Lakehurst, NJ, Lakehurst Naval Air Station
Morristown, NJ, Morristown Airport
Newark, NJ, Newark International Airport
Newark, NJ, Signature Airport
Teterboro, NJ, Teterboro Airport
Wrightstown, NJ, McGuire Air Force Base
DISTRICT NO. 22 — PORTLAND, MAINE
Bangor, ME, Bangor International Airport
Burlington, VT, Burlington International Airport
Caribou, ME, Caribou Municipal Airport
Highgate Springs, VT, Franklin County Regional Airport
Newport, VT, Newport State Airport
DISTRICT NO. 23 — [RESERVED]
DISTRICT NO. 24 — CLEVELAND, OHIO
Akron, OH, Municipal Airport
Cincinnati, OH, Cincinnati International Airport
Cleveland, OH, Cleveland Hopkins Airport
Columbus, OH, Port Columbus International Airport
Sandusky, OH, Griffing/Sandusky Airport
DISTRICT NO. 25 — WASHINGTON, D.C.
Camp Springs, MD, Andrews Air Force Base
Chantilly, VA, Washington Dulles International Airport
Winchester, VA, Winchester Airport
DISTRICT NO. 26 — ATLANTA, GEORGIA
Atlanta, GA, Atlanta Hartsfield International Airport
Charleston, SC, Charleston International Airport
Charleston, SC, Charleston Air Force Base
Charlotte, NC, Charlotte International Airport
Raleigh, NC, Raleigh-Durham International Airport
Savannah, GA, Savannah International Airport

DISTRICT NO. 27 — SAN JUAN, PUERTO RICO
San Juan, PR, San Juan International Airport
DISTRICT NO. 28 — NEW ORLEANS, LOUISIANA
Louisville, KY, Louisville International Airport
New Orleans, LA, New Orleans International Airport
Memphis, TN, Memphis International Airport
Nashville, TN, Nashville International Airport
DISTRICT NO. 29 — OMAHA, NEBRASKA
Des Moines, IA, Des Moines International Airport
Omaha, NE, Eppley International Airport
Omaha, NE, Offutt Air Force Base
DISTRICT NO. 30 — HELENA, MONTANA
Billings, MT, Billings Airport
Boise, ID, Boise Airport
Cut Bank, MT, Cut Bank Airport
Glasgow, MT, Glasgow International Airport
Great Falls, MT, Great Falls International Airport
Havre, MT, Havre-Hill County Airport
Helena, MT, Helena Airport
Kalispel, MT, Kalispel Airport
Missoula, MT, Missoula Airport
DISTRICT NO. 31 — PORTLAND, OREGON
Medford, OR, Jackson County Airport
Portland, OR, Portland International Airport
DISTRICT NO. 32 — ANCHORAGE, ALASKA
Anchorage, AK, Anchorage International Airport
Juneau, AK, Juneau Airport (Seaplane Base Only)
Juneau, AK, Juneau Municipal Airport
Ketchikan, AK, Ketchikan Airport
Wrangell, AK, Wrangell Seaplane Base
DISTRICT NO. 38 — HOUSTON, TEXAS
Galveston, TX, Galveston Airport
Houston, TX, Ellington Field
Houston, TX, Hobby Airport
Houston, TX, Houston Intercontinental Airport
DISTRICT NO. 39 — SAN DIEGO, CALIFORNIA
Calexico, CA, Calexico International Airport
San Diego, CA, San Diego International Airport
San Diego, CA, San Diego Municipal Airport (Lindbergh Field)
DISTRICT NO. 40 — HARLINGEN, TEXAS
Brownsville, TX, Brownsville/South Padre Island International Airport
Harlingen, TX, Valley International Airport
McAllen, TX, McAllen Miller International Airport

(c) Border patrol sectors. Border Patrol Sector Headquarters and Stations are situated at the following locations:

SECTOR NO. 1 — HOULTON, MAINE
Calais, ME
Fort Fairfield, ME
Houlton, ME
Jackman, ME
Rangeley, ME
Van Buren, ME
SECTOR NO. 2 — SWANTON, VERMONT
Beecher Falls, VT
Burke, NY
Champlain, NY
Massena, NY
Newport, VT
Ogdensburg, NY
Richford, VT
Swanton, VT
SECTOR NO. 3 — RAMEY, PUERTO RICO
Ramey, Puerto Rico
SECTOR NO. 4 — BUFFALO, NEW YORK
Buffalo, NY
Fulton, NY
Niagara Falls, NY
Watertown, NY
SECTOR NO. 5 — DETROIT, MICHIGAN
Detroit, MI
Grand Rapids, MI
Port Huron, MI
Sault Ste. Marie, MI
Trenton, MI
SECTOR NO. 6 — GRAND FORKS, NORTH DAKOTA
Bottineau, ND
Duluth, MN
Grand Forks, ND
Grand Marais, MN
International Falls, MN
Pembina, ND
Portal, ND
Warroad, MN
SECTOR NO. 7 — HAVRE, MONTANA
Billings, MT
Havre, MT
Malta, MT
Plentywood, MT
Scobey, MT
Shelby, MT
St. Mary, MT
Sweetgrass, MT
Twin Falls, ID
SECTOR NO. 8 — SPOKANE, WASHINGTON
Bonners Ferry, ID
Colville, WA
Eureka, MT
Oroville, WA
Pasco, WA
Spokane, WA
Wenatchee, WA
Whitefish, MT
SECTOR NO. 9 — BLAINE, WASHINGTON
Bellingham, WA
Blaine, WA
Lynden, WA
Port Angeles, WA
Roseburg, OR
SECTOR NO. 10 — LIVERMORE, CALIFORNIA
Bakersfield, CA
Fresno, CA
Livermore, CA
Oxnard, CA
Sacramento, CA
Salinas, CA
San Luis Obispo, CA
Stockton, CA
SECTOR NO. 11 — SAN DIEGO, CALIFORNIA
Brown Field, CA
Campo, CA (Boulevard, CA)

Chula Vista, CA
El Cajon, CA (San Marcos and Julian, CA)
Imperial Beach, CA
San Clemente, CA
Temecula, CA
SECTOR NO. 12 — EL CENTRO, CALIFORNIA
Calexico, CA
El Centro, CA
Indio, CA
Riverside, CA
SECTOR NO. 13 — YUMA, ARIZONA
Blythe, CA
Boulder City, NV
Wellton, AZ
Yuma, AZ
SECTOR NO. 14 — TUCSON, ARIZONA
Ajo, AZ
Casa Grande, AZ
Douglas, AZ
Naco, AZ
Nogales, AZ
Phoenix, AZ
Sonita, AZ
Tucson, AZ
Willcox, AZ
SECTOR NO. 15 — EL PASO, TEXAS
Alamogordo, NM
Albuquerque, NM
Carlsbad, NM
Deming, NM
El Paso, TX
Fabens, TX
Fort Hancock, TX
Las Cruces, NM,
Lordsburg, NM
Truth or Consequences, NM
Ysleta, TX
SECTOR NO. 16 — MARFA, TEXAS
Alpine, TX
Amarillo, TX
Fort Stockton, TX
Lubbock, TX
Marfa, TX
Midland, TX
Pecos, TX
Presidio, TX
Sanderson, TX
Sierra Blanca, TX
Van Horn, TX
SECTOR NO. 17 — DEL RIO, TEXAS
Abilene, TX
Brackettville, TX
Carrizo Springs, TX
Comstock, TX
Del Rio, TX
Eagle Pass, TX
Llano, TX
Rocksprings, TX
San Angelo, TX
Uvalde, TX
SECTOR NO. 18 — LAREDO, TEXAS
Cotulla, TX
Dallas, TX
Freer, TX
Hebbronville, TX
Laredo North, TX
Laredo South, TX
San Antonio, TX
Zapata, TX
SECTOR NO. 19 — MCALLEN, TEXAS
Brownsville, TX
Corpus Christi, TX
Falfurrias, TX
Harlingen, TX
Kingsville, TX
McAllen, TX
Mercedes, TX
Port Isabel, TX
Rio Grande City, TX
SECTOR NO. 20 — NEW ORLEANS, LOUISIANA
Baton Rouge, LA
Gulfport, MS
Lake Charles, LA
Little Rock, AR
Miami, OK
Mobile, AL
New Orleans, LA
SECTOR NO. 21 — MIAMI, FLORIDA
Jacksonville, FL
Orlando, FL
Pembroke Pines, FL
Tampa, FL
West Palm Beach, FL

HISTORY:

[38 FR 34183, Dec. 12, 1973; 51 FR 34439, 42080, 1986; 52 FR 16191, 22629, 1987; 53 FR 15194, 23603, 43985, 1988; 54 FR 2994, 39336, 29439, 47674, 1989; 56 FR 50811, 1991; 58 FR 471, Jan. 6, 1993.; 58 FR 3487, Jan. 11, 1993; 58 FR 38045, July 15, 1993; 60 FR 57165, 57166, Nov. 14, 1995; 61 FR 25777, 25778, May 23, 1996; 63 FR 70313, 70315, Dec. 21, 1998; 65 FR 39071, 39072, June 23, 2000; 66 FR 29661, 29672, June 1, 2001, as confirmed at 67 FR 38341, 38350, June 4, 2002; 74 FR 2824, 2833, Jan. 16, 2009; 74 FR 26933, 26936, June 5, 2009; 77 FR 75823, 75824, Dec. 26, 2012; 77 FR 76346, 76352, Dec. 28, 2012; 79 FR 42449, 42451, July 22, 2014; 80 FR 75631, 75632, Dec. 3, 2015]

§ 100.5 Regulations.

The regulations of the Department of Homeland Security, published as chapter I of title 8 of the Code of Federal Regulations, contain information which under the provisions of section 552 of title 5 of the United States Code, is required to be published and is subdivided into Subchapter A (General Provisions, parts 1 through 3, inclusive), Subchapter B (Immigration Regulations, parts 100 through 299, inclusive), and Subchapter C (Nationality Regulations, parts 306 through 499, inclusive). Any person desiring information with respect to a particular procedure (other than rule making) under the Immigration and Nationality Act should examine the part or section in chapter I of title 8 of the Code of Federal Regulations dealing with such procedures as well as the section of the Act implemented by such part or section.

HISTORY:

[32 FR 9616, July 4, 1967; 74 FR 26933, 26936, June 5, 2009]

§ 100.6 [This section was removed and reserved. See 74 FR 26933, 26936, June 5, 2009.]

[NO TEXT IN ORIGINAL]

HISTORY:

[32 FR 9616, July 4, 1967]

AUTHORITY:

(8 U.S.C. 1103; 8 CFR part 2.)

§ 100.7 [This section was removed. See 76 FR 53764, 53780, Aug. 29, 2011.]

[NO TEXT IN ORIGINAL]

HISTORY:

[48 FR 37201, Aug. 17, 1983; 73 FR 58023, 58030, Oct. 6, 2008; 74 FR 26933, 26936, June 5, 2009; 76 FR 53764, 53780, Aug. 29, 2011]

PART 101

PRESUMPTION OF LAWFUL ADMISSION

Rule

§ 101.1 Presumption of lawful admission.

A member of the following classes shall be presumed to have been lawfully admitted for permanent residence even though a record of his admission cannot be found, except as otherwise provided in this section, unless he abandoned his lawful permanent resident status or subsequently lost that status by operation of law:

(a) Prior to June 30, 1906. An alien who establishes that he entered the United States prior to June 30, 1906.

(b) United States land borders. An alien who establishes that, while a citizen of Canada or Newfoundland, he entered the United States across the Canadian border prior to October 1, 1906; an alien who establishes that while a citizen of Mexico he entered the United States across the Mexican border prior to July 1, 1908; an alien who establishes that, while a citizen of Mexico, he entered the United States at the port of Presidio, Texas, prior to October 21, 1918, and an alien for whom a record of his actual admission to the United States does not exist but who establishes that he gained admission to the United States prior to July 1, 1924, pursuant to preexamination at a United States immigration station in Canada and that a record of such preexamination exists.

(c) Virgin Islands. An alien who establishes that he entered the Virgin Islands of the United States prior to July 1, 1938, even though a record of his admission prior to that date exists as a non-immigrant under the Immigration Act of 1924.

(d) Asiatic barred zone. An alien who establishes that he is of a race indigenous to, and a native of a country within, the Asiatic zone defined in section 3 of the Act of February 5, 1917, as amended, that he was a member of a class of aliens exempted from exclusion by the provisions of that section, and that he entered the United States prior to July 1, 1924, provided that a record of his admission exists.

(e) Chinese and Japanese aliens—

(1) Prior to July 1, 1924. A Chinese alien for whom there exists a record of his admission to the United States prior to July 1, 1924, under the laws and regulations formerly applicable to Chinese and who establishes that at the time of his admission he was a merchant, teacher, or student, and his son or daughter under 21 or wife accompanying or following to join him; a traveler for curiosity or pleasure and his accompanying son or daughter under 21 or accompanying wife; a wife of a United States citizen; a returning laborer; and a person erroneously admitted as a United States citizen under section 1993 of the Revised Statutes of the United States, as amended, his father not having resided in the United States prior to his birth.

(2) On or after July 1, 1924. A Chinese alien for whom there exists a record of his admission to the United States as a member of one of the following classes; an alien who establishes that he was readmitted between July 1, 1924, and December 16, 1943, inclusive, as a returning Chinese laborer who acquired lawful permanent residence prior to July 1, 1924; a person erroneously admitted between July 1, 1924, and June 6, 1927, inclusive, as a United States citizen under section 1993 of the Revised Statutes of the United States, as amended, his father not having resided in the United States prior to his birth; an alien admitted at any time after June 30, 1924, under section 4 (b) or (d) of the Immigration Act of 1924; an alien wife of a United States citizen admitted between June 13, 1930, and December 16, 1943, inclusive, under section 4(a) of the Immigration Act of 1924; an alien admitted on or after December 17, 1943, under section 4(f) of the Immigration Act of 1924; an alien admitted on or after December 17, 1943, under section 317(c) of the Nationality Act of 1940, as amended; an alien admitted on or after December 17, 1943, as a preference or nonpreference quota immigrant pursuant to section 2 of that act; and a Chinese or Japanese alien admitted to the United States between July 1, 1924, and December 23, 1952, both dates inclusive, as the wife or minor son or daughter of a treaty merchant admitted before July 1, 1924, if the husband-father was lawfully admitted to the United States as a treaty merchant before July 1, 1924, or, while maintaining another status under which he was admitted before that date, and his status changed to that of a treaty merchant or treaty trader

after that date, and was maintaining the changed status at the time his wife or minor son or daughter entered the United States.

(f) Citizens of the Philippine Islands—

(1) Entry prior to May 1, 1934. An alien who establishes that he entered the United States prior to May 1, 1934, and that he was on the date of his entry a citizen of the Philippine Islands, provided that for the purpose of petitioning for naturalization he shall not be regarded as having been lawfully admitted for permanent residence unless he was a citizen of the Commonwealth of the Philippines on July 2, 1946.

(2) Entry between May 1, 1934, and July 3, 1946. An alien who establishes that he entered Hawaii between May 1, 1934, and July 3, 1946, inclusive, under the provisions of the last sentence of section 8(a)(1) of the Act of March 24, 1934, as amended, that he was a citizen of the Philippine Islands when he entered, and that a record of such entry exists.

(g) Temporarily admitted aliens. The following aliens who when admitted expressed an intention to remain in the United States temporarily or to pass in transit through the United States, for whom records of admission exist, but who remained in the United States: An alien admitted prior to June 3, 1921, except if admitted temporarily under the 9th proviso to section 3 of the Immigration Act of 1917, or as an accredited official of a foreign government, his suite, family, or guest, or as a seaman in pursuit of his calling; an alien admitted under the Act of May 19, 1921, as amended, who was admissible for permanent residence under that Act notwithstanding the quota limitation's thereof and his accompanying wife or unmarried son or daughter under 21 who was admissible for permanent residence under that Act notwithstanding the quota limitations thereof; and an alien admitted under the Act of May 19, 1921, as amended, who was charged under that Act to the proper quota at the time of his admission or subsequently and who remained so charged.

(h) Citizens of the Trust Territory of the Pacific Islands who entered Guam prior to December 24, 1952. An alien who establishes that while a citizen of the Trust Territory of the Pacific Islands he entered Guam prior to December 24, 1952, by records, such as Service records subsequent to June 15, 1952, records of the Guamanian Immigration Service, records of the Navy or Air Force, or records of contractors of those agencies, and was residing in Guam on December 24, 1952.

(i) Aliens admitted to Guam. An alien who establishes that he was admitted to Guam prior to December 24, 1952, by records such as Service records subsequent to June 15, 1952, records of the Guamanian Immigration Service, records of the Navy or Air Force, or records of contractors of those agencies; that he was not excludable under the Act of February 5, 1917, as amended; and that he continued to reside in Guam until December 24, 1952, and thereafter was not admitted or readmitted into Guam as a nonimmigrant, provided that the provisions of this paragraph shall not apply to an alien who was exempted from the contract laborer provisions of section 3 of the Immigration Act of February 5, 1917, as amended, through the exercise, expressly or impliedly, of the 4th or 9th provisos to section 3 of that act.

(j) Erroneous admission as United States citizens or as children of citizens.

(1)(i) An alien for whom there exists a record of admission prior to September 11, 1957, as a United States citizen who establishes that at the time of such admission he was the child of a United States citizen parent; he was erroneously issued a United States passport or included in the United States passport of his citizen parent accompanying him or to whom he was destined; no fraud or misrepresentation was practiced by him in the issuance of the passport or in gaining admission; he was otherwise admissible at the time of entry except for failure to meet visa or passport requirements; and he has maintained a residence in the United States since the date of admission, or (ii) an alien who meets all of the foregoing requirements except that if he were, in fact, a citizen of the United States a passport would not have been required, or it had been individually waived, and was erroneously admitted as a United States citizen by a Service officer. For the purposes of all of the foregoing, the terms child and parent shall be defined as in section 101(b) of the Immigration and Nationality Act, as amended.

(ii) an alien who meets all of the foregoing requirements except that if he were, in fact, a citizen of the United States a passport would not have been required, or it had been individually waived, and was erroneously admitted as a United States citizen by a Service officer. For the purposes of all of the foregoing, the terms child and parent shall be defined as in section 101(b) of the Immigration and Nationality Act, as amended.

(2) An alien admitted to the United States before July 1, 1948, in possession of a section 4(a) 1924 Act nonquota immigration visa issued in accordance with State Department regulations, including a child of a United States citizen after he reached the age of 21, in the absence of fraud or misrepresentation; a member of a naturalized person's family who was admitted to the United States as a United States citizen or as a section 4(a) 1924 Act nonquota immigrant on the basis of that naturalization, unless he knowingly participated in the unlawful naturalization of the parent or spouse rendered void by cancellation, or knew at any time prior to his admission to the United States of the cancellation; and a member of a naturalized person's family who knew at any time prior to his admission to the United States of the cancellation of the naturalization of his parent or spouse but was admitted to the United States as a United States citizen pursuant to a State Department or Service determination based upon a then prevailing administrative view, provided the State Department or Service knew of the cancellation.

HISTORY:

[23 FR 9119, Nov. 26, 1958, as amended at 24 FR 2583, Apr. 3, 1959; 24 FR 6476, Aug. 12, 1959; 25 FR 581, Jan. 23, 1960.; 31 FR 535, Jan. 15, 1966]

AUTHORITY:

8 U.S.C. 1103, 8 CFR part 2.

§ 101.2 Presumption of lawful admission; entry under erroneous name or other errors.

An alien who entered the United States as either an immigrant or nonimmigrant under any of the following circumstances shall be regarded as having been lawfully admitted in such status, except as otherwise provided in this part: An alien otherwise admissible whose entry was made and recorded under other than his full true and correct name or whose entry record contains errors in recording sex, names of relatives, or names of foreign places of birth or residence, provided that he establishes by clear, unequivocal, and convincing evidence that the record of the claimed admission relates to him, and, if entry occurred on or after May 22, 1918, if under other than his full, true and correct name that he also establishes that the name was not adopted for the purpose of concealing his identity when obtaining a passport or visa, or for the purpose of using the passport or visa of another person or otherwise evading any provision of the immigration laws, and that the name used at the time of entry was one by which he had been known for a sufficient length of time prior to making application for a passport or visa to have permitted the issuing authority or authorities to have made any necessary investigation concerning him or that his true identity was known to such officials.

HISTORY:

[32 FR 9622, July 4, 1967]

AUTHORITY:

8 U.S.C. 1103, 8 CFR part 2.

§ 101.3 Creation of record of lawful permanent resident status for person born under diplomatic status in the United States.

(a) **Person born to foreign diplomat.**

(1) Status of person. A person born in the United States to a foreign diplomatic officer accredited to the United States, as a matter of international law, is not subject to the jurisdiction of the United States. That person is not a United States citizen under the Fourteenth Amendment to the Constitution. Such a person may be considered a lawful permanent resident at birth.

(2) Definition of foreign diplomatic officer. Foreign diplomatic officer means a person listed in the State Department Diplomatic List, also known as the Blue List. It includes ambassadors, ministers, chargeİs d'affaires, counselors, secretaries and attacheİs of embassies and legations as well as members of the Delegation of the Commission of the European Communities. The term also includes individuals with comparable diplomatic status and immunities who are accredited to the United Nations or to the Organization of American States, and other individuals who are also accorded comparable diplomatic status.

(b) Child born subject to the jurisdiction of the United States. A child born in the United States is born subject to the jurisdiction of the United States and is a United States citizen if the parent is not a "foreign diplomatic officer" as defined in paragraph (a)(2) of this section. This includes, for example, a child born in the United States to one of the following foreign government officials or employees:

(1) Employees of foreign diplomatic missions whose names appear in the State Department list entitled "Employees of Diplomatic Missions Not Printed in the Diplomatic List," also known as the White List; employees of foreign diplomatic missions accredited to the United Nations or the Organization of American States; or foreign diplomats accredited to other foreign states. The majority of these individuals enjoy certain diplomatic immunities, but they are not "foreign diplomatic officers" as defined in paragraph (a)(2) of this section. The immunities, if any, of their family members are derived from the status of the employees or diplomats.

(2) Foreign government employees with limited or no diplomatic immunity such as consular officials named on the State Department list entitled "Foreign Consular Officers in the United States" and their staffs.

(c) Voluntary registration as lawful permanent resident of person born to foreign diplomat. Since a person born in the United States to a foreign diplomatic officer is not subject to the jurisdiction of the United States, his/her registration as a lawful permanent resident of the United States is voluntary. The provisions of section 262 of the Act do not apply to such a person unless and until that person ceases to have the rights, privileges, exemptions, or immunities which may be claimed by a foreign diplomatic officer.

(d) Retention of lawful permanent residence. To be eligible for lawful permanent resident status under paragraph (a) of this section, an alien must establish that he/she has not abandoned his/her residence in the United States. One of the tests for retention of lawful permanent resident status is continuous residence, not continuous physical presence, in the United States. Such a person will not be considered to have abandoned his/her residence in the United States solely by having been admitted to the United States in a nonimmigrant classification under paragraph (15)(A) or (15)(G) of section 101(a) of the Act after a temporary stay in a foreign country or countries on one or several occasions.

HISTORY:

[47 FR 940, Jan. 8, 1982]

AUTHORITY:

(Secs. 101(a)(20), 103, 262, 264 of the Immigration and Nationality Act, as amended; 8 U.S.C. 1101(a)(20), 1103, 1302, 1304)

§ 101.4 Registration procedure.

The procedure for an application for creation of a record of lawful permanent residence and a Permanent Resident Card, Form I-551, for a person eligible for presumption of lawful admission for permanent residence under § 101.1 or § 101.2 or for lawful permanent residence as a person born in the United States to a foreign diplomatic officer under § 101.3 is described in § 264.2 of this chapter.

HISTORY:

[47 FR 941, Jan. 8, 1982.; 63 FR 70313, 70315, Dec. 21, 1998]

AUTHORITY:

(Secs. 101(a)(20), 103, 262, 264 of the Immigration and Nationality Act, as amended; 8 U.S.C. 1101(a)(20), 1103, 1302, 1304)

§ 101.5 Special immigrant status for certain G-4 nonimmigrants.

(a) Application. An application for adjustment to special immigrant status under section 101(a)(27)(I) of the INA shall be made on Form I-485. The application date of the I-485 shall be the date of acceptance by the Service as properly filed. If the application date is other than the fee receipt date it must be noted and initialed by a Service officer. The date of application for adjustment of status is the closing date for computing the residence and physical presence requirement. The applicant must have complied with all requirements as of the date of application.

(b) Documentation. All documents must be submitted in accordance with § 103.2(b) of this chapter. The application shall be accompanied by documentary evidence establishing the aggregate residence and physical presence required. Documentary evidence may include official employment verification, records of official or personnel transactions or recordings of events occurring during the period of claimed residence and physical presence. Affidavits of credible witnesses may also be accepted. Persons unable to furnish evidence in their own names may furnish evidence in the names of parents or other persons with whom they have been living, if affidavits of the parents or other persons are submitted attesting to the claimed residence and physical presence. The claimed family relationship to the principle G-4 international organization officer or employee must be substantiated by the submission of verifiable civil documents.

(c) Residence and physical presence requirements. All applicants applying under sections 101(a)(27)(I) (i), (ii), and (iii) of the INA must have resided and been physically present in the United States for a designated period of time.

For purposes of this section only, an absence from the United States to conduct official business on behalf of the employing organization, or approved customary leave shall not be subtracted from the aggregated period of required residence or physical presence for the current or former G-4 officer or employee or the accompanying spouse and unmarried sons or daughters of such officer or employee, provided residence in the United States is maintained during such absences, and the duty station of the principle G-4 nonimmigrant continues to be in the United States. Absence from the United States by the G-4 spouse or unmarried son or daughter without the principle G-4 shall not be subtracted from the aggregate period of residence and physical presence if on customary leave as recognized by the international organization employer. Absence by the unmarried son or daughter while enrolled in a school outside the United States will not be counted toward the physical presence requirement.

(d) Maintenance of nonimmigrant status. Section 101(a)(27)(I) (i), and (ii) requires the applicant to accrue the required period of residence and physical presence in the United States while maintaining status as a G-4 or N nonimmigrant. Section 101(a)(27)(I)(iii) requires such time accrued only in G-4 nonimmigrant status.

Maintaining G-4 status for this purpose is defined as maintaining qualified employment with a "G" international organization or maintaining the qualifying family relationship with the G-4 international organization officer or employee. Maintaining status as an N nonimmigrant for this purpose requires the qualifying family relationship to remain in effect. Unauthorized employment will not remove an otherwise eligible alien from G-4 status for residence and physical presence requirements, provided the qualifying G-4 status is maintained.

HISTORY:

[54 FR 5927, Feb. 7, 1989]

AUTHORITY:

8 U.S.C. 1103, 8 CFR part 2.

PART 103

IMMIGRATION BENEFIT REQUESTS; USCIS FILING REQUIREMENTS; BIOMETRIC REQUIREMENTS; AVAILABILITY OF RECORDS

Subpart A. Applying for Benefits, Surety Bonds, Fees

Rule

Subpart B. Biometric Requirements

AUTHORITY NOTE APPLICABLE TO ENTIRE PART:

AUTHORITY:

5 U.S.C. 301, 552, 552a; 8 U.S.C. 1101, 1103, 1304, 1356, 1365b, 1372; 31 U.S.C. 9701; 48 U.S.C. 1806; Public Law 107-296, 116 Stat. 2135 (6 U.S.C. 1 et seq.); E.O. 12356, 47 FR 14874, 15557, 3 CFR, 1982 Comp., p. 166; 8 CFR part 2, Pub. L. 112-54, 125 Stat 550; 31 CFR part 223.

Subpart A

Applying for Benefits, Surety Bonds, Fees

§ 103.1 [This section was removed and reserved. See 76 FR 53764, 53780, Aug. 29, 2011.]

[NO TEXT IN ORIGINAL]

HISTORY:

[40 FR 30468, July 21, 1975; 51 FR 19824, 34439, 1986; 52 FR 2985, 16192, 22629, 1987; 53 FR 10064, 35799, 43985, 1988; 54 FR 6876, 18649, 29439, 29441, 29881, 1989; 55 FR 20769, 20774, 12627, 30680, 41988, 43439, 1990; 56 FR 624, 23209, 23496, 60905, 1991.; 57 FR 33861, 1992, as confirmed at 50836, Sept. 29, 1993; 58 FR 42849, Aug. 12, 1993; 58 FR 44608, Aug. 24, 1993, as confirmed at 59 FR 17921, Apr. 15, 1994; 58 FR 69210, Dec. 30, 1993, as confirmed at 63 FR 1331, 1334, Jan. 9, 1998; 59 FR 60070, Nov. 22, 1994; 61 FR 13061, 13072, Mar. 26, 1996; 61 FR 28003, 28010, June 4, 1996; 62 FR 9071, 9074, Feb. 28, 1997; 62 FR 10312, 10336, Mar. 6, 1997; 63 FR 12979, 12984, Mar. 17, 1998; 63 FR 63593, 63595, Nov. 16, 1998; 64 FR 27856, 27875, May 21, 1999; 65 FR 43528, 43531, July 13, 2000, withdrawn at 67 FR 61474, Oct. 1, 2002; 65 FR 67616, 67617, Nov. 13, 2000; 66 FR 32138, 32143, June 13, 2001; 66 FR 49514, Sept. 28, 2001; 67 FR 4784, 4794, Jan. 31, 2002; 67 FR 39255, 39257, June 7, 2002; 67 FR 78667, 78673, Dec. 26, 2002; 68 FR 10922, 10923, Mar. 6, 2003; 68 FR 35273, 35275, June 13, 2003; 69 FR 35229, 35234, June 24, 2004; 76 FR 53764, 53780, Aug. 29, 2011]

AUTHORITY:

(5 U.S.C. 301, 552, 552a; 8 U.S.C. 1101, 1103, 1304, 1356; 31 U.S.C. 9701; 48 U.S.C. 1806; Public Law 107-296, 116 Stat. 2135 (6 U.S.C. 1 et seq.), E.O. 12356, 47 FR 14874, 15557, 3 CFR, 1982 Comp., p. 166; 8 CFR part 2.)

§ 103.2 Submission and adjudication of benefit requests.

(a) **Filing.**

(1) Preparation and submission. Every form, benefit request, or other document must be submitted to DHS and executed in accordance with the form instructions regardless of a provision of 8 CFR chapter I to the contrary. Each form, benefit request, or other document must be filed with the fee(s) required by regulation. Filing fees generally are non-refundable regardless of the outcome of the benefit request, or how much time the adjudication requires, and any decision to refund a fee is at the discretion of USCIS. Except as otherwise provided in this chapter I, fees must be paid when the request is filed or submitted.

(2) Signature. An applicant or petitioner must sign his or her benefit request. However, a parent or legal guardian may sign for a person who is less than 14 years old. A legal guardian may sign for a mentally incompetent person. By signing the benefit request, the applicant or petitioner, or parent or guardian certifies under penalty of perjury that the benefit request, and all evidence submitted with it, either at the time of filing or thereafter, is true and correct. Unless otherwise specified in this chapter, an acceptable signature on a benefit request that is being filed with the USCIS is one that is either handwritten or, for benefit requests filed electronically as permitted by the instructions to the form, in electronic format.

(3) Representation. An applicant or petitioner may be represented by an attorney in the United States, as defined in § 1.2 of this chapter, by an attorney outside the United States as defined in § 292.1(a)(6) of this chapter, or by an accredited representative as defined in § 292.1(a)(4) of this chapter. A beneficiary of a petition is not a recognized party in such a proceeding. A benefit request presented in person by someone who is not the applicant or petitioner, or his or her representative as defined in this paragraph, shall be treated as if received through the mail, and the person advised that the applicant or petitioner, and his or her representative, will be notified of the decision. Where a notice of representation is submitted that is not properly signed, the benefit request will be processed as if the notice had not been submitted.

(4) Oath. Any required oath may be administered by an immigration officer or person generally authorized to administer oaths, including persons so authorized by Article 136 of the Uniform Code of Military Justice.

(5) Translation of name. If a document has been executed in an anglicized version of a name, the native form of the name may also be required.

(6) Where to file. All benefit requests must be filed in accordance with the form instructions.

(7) Benefit requests submitted.

(i) USCIS will consider a benefit request received and will record the receipt date as of the actual date of receipt at the location designated for filing such benefit request whether electronically or in paper format.

(ii) A benefit request which is rejected will not retain a filing date. A benefit request will be rejected if it is not:

(A) Signed with valid signature;

(B) Executed;

(C) Filed in compliance with the regulations governing the filing of the specific application, petition, form, or request; and

(D) Submitted with the correct fee(s). Every form, benefit request, or other document that requires a fee payment must be submitted with the correct fee(s).

(1) If USCIS accepts a benefit request and determines later that the request was not accompanied by the correct fee, USCIS may reject or deny the request. If the benefit request was approved when USCIS determines the correct fee was not paid, the approval may be revoked upon notice.

(2) If a check or other financial instrument used to pay a fee is dishonored, declined, or returned because of insufficient funds, USCIS will resubmit the payment to the remitter institution one time. If the instrument used to pay a fee is dishonored, declined, or returned a second time, the filing may be rejected or denied.

(3) Financial instruments dishonored, declined, or returned for any reason other than insufficient funds, including but not limited to when an applicant, petitioner, or requestor places a stop payment on a financial instrument will not be resubmitted, and any immigration benefit request or request for action filed with USCIS may be rejected or denied regardless of whether USCIS has begun processing the request or already taken action on a case. Credit cards that are declined for any reason will not be resubmitted.

(4) If a check or other financial instrument used to pay a fee is dated more than one year before the request is received, the payment and request may be rejected.

(iii) A rejection of a filing with USCIS may not be appealed.

(iv) Unless otherwise provided in this title, only one of the same benefit request as defined in 8 CFR 1.2 may be submitted at a time or while the same request is pending. If more than one materially identical requests are submitted, USCIS may reject one at its discretion. For purposes of this section, a motion to reopen or reconsider and an appeal that is filed on the same decision will be considered a duplicate request.

(b) Evidence and processing.

(1) Demonstrating eligibility. An applicant or petitioner must establish that he or she is eligible for the requested benefit at the time of filing the benefit request and must continue to be eligible through adjudication. Each benefit request must be properly completed and filed with all initial evidence required by applicable regulations and other USCIS instructions. Any evidence submitted in connection with a benefit request is incorporated into and considered part of the request.

(2) Submitting secondary evidence and affidavits —

(i) General. The non-existence or other unavailability of required evidence creates a presumption of ineligibility. If a required document, such as a birth or marriage certificate, does not exist or cannot be obtained, an applicant or petitioner must demonstrate this and submit secondary evidence, such as church or school records, pertinent to the facts at issue. If secondary evidence also does not exist or cannot be obtained, the applicant or petitioner must demonstrate the unavailability of both the required document and relevant secondary evidence, and submit two or more affidavits, sworn to or affirmed by persons who are not parties to the petition who have direct personal knowledge of the event and circumstances. Secondary evidence must overcome the unavailability of primary evidence, and affidavits must overcome the unavailability of both primary and secondary evidence.

(ii) Demonstrating that a record is not available. Where a record does not exist, the applicant or petitioner must submit an original written statement on government letterhead establishing this from the relevant government or other authority. The statement must indicate the reason the record does not exist, and indicate whether similar records for the time and place are available. However, a certification from an appropriate foreign government that a document does not exist is not required where the Department of State's Foreign Affairs Manual indicates this type of document generally does not exist. An applicant or petitioner who has not been able to acquire the necessary document or statement from the relevant foreign authority may submit evidence that repeated good faith attempts were made to obtain the required document or statement. However, where USCIS finds that such documents or statements are generally available, it may require that the applicant or petitioner submit the required document or statement.

(iii) Evidence provided with a self-petition filed by a spouse or child of abusive citizen or resident. USCIS will consider any credible evidence relevant to a self-petition filed by a qualified spouse or child of an abusive citizen or lawful permanent resident under section 204(a)(1)(A)(iii), 204(a)(1)(A)(iv), 204(a)(1)(B)(ii), or 204(a)(1)(B)(iii) of the Act. The self-petitioner may, but is not required to, demonstrate that preferred primary or secondary evidence is unavailable. The determination of what evidence is credible and the weight to be given that evidence shall be within the sole discretion of USCIS.

(3) Translations. Any document containing foreign language submitted to USCIS shall be accompanied by

a full English language translation which the translator has certified as complete and accurate, and by the translator's certification that he or she is competent to translate from the foreign language into English.

(4) Supporting documents. Original or photocopied documents which are required to support any benefit request must be submitted in accordance with the form instructions.

(5) Request for an original document. USCIS may, at any time, request submission of an original document for review. The request will set a deadline for submission of the original document. Failure to submit the requested original document by the deadline may result in denial or revocation of the underlying benefit request. An original document submitted in response to such a request, when no longer required by USCIS, will be returned to the petitioner or applicant upon completion of the adjudication. If USCIS does not return an original document within a reasonable time after completion of the adjudication, the petitioner or applicant may request return of the original document in accordance with instructions provided by USCIS.

(6) Withdrawal. An applicant or petitioner may withdraw a benefit request at any time until a decision is issued by USCIS or, in the case of an approved petition, until the person is admitted or granted adjustment or change of status, based on the petition. However, a withdrawal may not be retracted.

(7) Testimony. USCIS may require the taking of testimony, and may direct any necessary investigation. When a statement is taken from and signed by a person, he or she shall, upon request, be given a copy without fee. Any allegations made subsequent to filing a benefit request which are in addition to, or in substitution for, those originally made, shall be filed in the same manner as the original benefit request, and acknowledged under oath thereon.

(8) Request for Evidence; Notice of Intent to Deny—

(i) Evidence of eligibility or ineligibility. If the evidence submitted with the benefit request establishes eligibility, USCIS will approve the benefit request, except that in any case in which the applicable statute or regulation makes the approval of a benefit request a matter entrusted to USCIS discretion, USCIS will approve the benefit request only if the evidence of record establishes both eligibility and that the petitioner or applicant warrants a favorable exercise of discretion. If the record evidence establishes ineligibility, the benefit request will be denied on that basis.

(ii) Initial evidence. If all required initial evidence is not submitted with the benefit request or does not demonstrate eligibility, USCIS in its discretion may deny the benefit request for lack of initial evidence or for ineligibility or request that the missing initial evidence be submitted within a specified period of time as determined by USCIS.

(iii) Other evidence. If all required initial evidence has been submitted but the evidence submitted does not establish eligibility, USCIS may: deny the benefit request for ineligibility; request more information or evidence from the applicant or petitioner, to be submitted within a specified period of time as determined by USCIS; or notify the applicant or petitioner of its intent to deny the benefit request and the basis for the proposed denial, and require that the applicant or petitioner submit a response within a specified period of time as determined by USCIS.

(iv) Process. A request for evidence or notice of intent to deny will be communicated by regular or electronic mail and will specify the type of evidence required, and whether initial evidence or additional evidence is required, or the bases for the proposed denial sufficient to give the applicant or petitioner adequate notice and sufficient information to respond. The request for evidence or notice of intent to deny will indicate the deadline for response, but in no case shall the maximum response period provided in a request for evidence exceed twelve weeks, nor shall the maximum response time provided in a notice of intent to deny exceed thirty days. Additional time to respond to a request for evidence or notice of intent to deny may not be granted.

(9) Appearance for interview or biometrics. USCIS may require any applicant, petitioner, sponsor, beneficiary, or individual filing a benefit request, or any group or class of such persons submitting requests, to appear for an interview and/or biometric collection. USCIS may require the payment of the biometric services fee in 8 CFR 106.2 or that the individual obtain a fee waiver. Such appearance and fee may also be required by law, regulation, form instructions, or Federal Register notice applicable to the request type. USCIS will notify the affected person of the date, time and location of any required appearance under this paragraph. Any person required to appear under this paragraph may, before the scheduled date and time of the appearance, either:

(i) Appear before the scheduled date and time;

(ii) For good cause, request that the biometric services appointment be rescheduled; or

(iii) Withdraw the benefit request.

(10) Effect of a request for initial or additional evidence for fingerprinting or interview rescheduling—

(i) Effect on processing. The priority date of a properly filed petition shall not be affected by a request for missing initial evidence or request for other evidence. If a benefit request is missing required initial evidence, or an applicant, petitioner, sponsor, beneficiary, or other individual who requires fingerprinting requests that the fingerprinting appointment or interview be rescheduled, any time period imposed on USCIS processing will start over from the date of receipt of the required initial evidence or request for fingerprint or interview rescheduling. If USCIS requests that the applicant or petitioner submit additional evidence or respond to other than a request for initial evidence, any time limitation imposed on USCIS for processing will be suspended as of the date of request. It will resume at the same point where it stopped when USCIS receives the requested evidence or response, or a request for a decision based on the evidence.

(ii) Effect on interim benefits. Interim benefits will not be granted based on a benefit request held in suspense for the submission of requested initial evidence, except that the applicant or beneficiary will normally be allowed to remain while a benefit request to extend or obtain status while in the United States is pending. USCIS may choose to pursue other actions to seek removal of a person notwithstanding the pending application. Employment authorization previously accorded based on the same status and employment as that requested in the current benefit request may continue uninterrupted as provided in 8 CFR 274a.12(b)(20) during the suspense period.

(11) Responding to a request for evidence or notice of intent to deny. In response to a request for evidence or a notice of intent to deny, and within the period afforded for a response, the applicant or petitioner may: submit a complete response containing all requested information at any time within the period afforded; submit a partial response and ask for a decision based on the record; or withdraw the benefit request. All requested materials must be submitted together at one time, along with the original USCIS request for evidence or notice of intent to deny. Submission of only some of the requested evidence will be considered a request for a decision on the record.

(12) Effect where evidence submitted in response to a request does not establish eligibility at the time of filing. A benefit request shall be denied where evidence submitted in response to a request for evidence does not establish filing eligibility at the time the benefit request was filed. A benefit request shall be denied where any benefit request upon which it was based was filed subsequently.

(13) Effect of failure to respond to a request for evidence or a notice of intent to deny or to appear for interview or biometrics capture—

(i) Failure to submit evidence or respond to a notice of intent to deny. If the petitioner or applicant fails to respond to a request for evidence or to a notice of intent to deny by the required date, the benefit request may be summarily denied as abandoned, denied based on the record, or denied for both reasons. If other requested material necessary to the processing and approval of a case, such as photographs, are not submitted by the required date, the application may be summarily denied as abandoned.

(ii) Failure to appear for biometrics capture, interview or other required in-person process. Except as provided in 8 CFR 335.6, if USCIS requires an individual to appear for biometrics capture, an interview, or other required in-person process but the person does not appear, the benefit request shall be considered abandoned and denied unless by the appointment time USCIS has received a change of address or rescheduling request that the agency concludes warrants excusing the failure to appear.

(14) Effect of request for decision. Where an applicant or petitioner does not submit all requested additional evidence and requests a decision based on the evidence already submitted, a decision shall be issued based on the record. Failure to submit requested evidence which precludes a material line of inquiry shall be grounds for denying the benefit request. Failure to appear for required fingerprinting or for a required interview, or to give required testimony, shall result in the denial of the related benefit request.

(15) Effect of withdrawal or denial due to abandonment. The USCIS acknowledgement of a withdrawal may not be appealed. A denial due to abandonment may not be appealed, but an applicant or petitioner may file a motion to reopen under § 103.5. Withdrawal or denial due to abandonment does not preclude the filing of a new benefit request with a new fee. However, the priority or processing date of a withdrawn or abandoned benefit request may not be applied to a later application petition. Withdrawal or denial due to abandonment shall not itself affect the new proceeding; but the facts and circumstances surrounding the prior benefit request shall otherwise be material to the new benefit request.

(16) Inspection of evidence. An applicant or petitioner shall be permitted to inspect the record of proceeding which constitutes the basis for the decision, except as provided in the following paragraphs.

(i) Derogatory information unknown to petitioner or applicant. If the decision will be adverse to the applicant or petitioner and is based on derogatory information considered by the Service and of which the applicant or petitioner is unaware, he/she shall be advised of this fact and offered an opportunity to rebut the information and present information in his/her own behalf before the decision is rendered, except as provided in paragraphs (b)(16)(ii), (iii), and (iv) of this section. Any explanation, rebuttal, or information presented by or in behalf of the applicant or petitioner shall be included in the record of proceeding.

(ii) Determination of statutory eligibility. A determination of statutory eligibility shall be based only on information contained in the record of proceeding which is disclosed to the applicant or petitioner, except as provided in paragraph (b)(16)(iv) of this section.

(iii) Discretionary determination. Where an application may be granted or denied in the exercise of discretion, the decision to exercise discretion favorably or unfavorably may be based in whole or in part on classified information not contained in the record and not made available to the applicant, provided the USCIS Director or his or her designee has determined that such information is relevant and is classified under Executive Order No. 12356 (47 FR 14874; April 6, 1982) as requiring protection from unauthorized disclosure in the interest of national security.

(iv) Classified information. An applicant or petitioner shall not be provided any information contained in the record or outside the record which is classified under Executive Order No. 12356 (47 FR 14874; April 6, 1982) as requiring protection from unauthorized disclosure in the interest of national security, unless the classifying authority has agreed in writing to such disclosure. Whenever he/she believes he/she can do so consistently with safeguarding both the information and its source, the USCIS Director or his or her designee should direct that the applicant or petitioner be given notice of the general nature of the information and an opportunity to offer opposing evidence. The USCIS Director's or his or her designee's authorization to use such classified information shall be made a part of the record. A decision based in whole or in part on such classified information shall state that the information is material to the decision.

(17) Verifying claimed permanent resident status—

(i) Department records. The status of an applicant or petitioner who claims that he or she is a permanent resident of the United States or was formerly a permanent resident of the United States will be verified from official Department records. These records include alien and other files, arrival manifests, arrival records, Department index cards, Immigrant Identification Cards, Certificates of Registry, Declarations of Intention issued after July 1, 1929, Permanent Resident Cards, or other registration receipt forms (provided that such forms were issued or endorsed to show admission for permanent residence), passports, and reentry permits. An official record of a Department index card must bear a designated immigrant visa symbol and must have been prepared by an authorized official of the Department in the course of processing immigrant admissions or adjustments to permanent resident status. Other cards, certificates, declarations, permits, and passports must have been issued or endorsed to show admission for permanent residence. Except as otherwise provided in 8 CFR part 101, and in the absence of countervailing evidence, such official records will be regarded as establishing lawful admission for permanent residence.

(ii) Assisting self-petitioners who are spousal-abuse victims. If a self-petitioner filing a petition under section 204(a)(1)(A)(iii), 204(a)(1)(A)(iv), 204(a)(1)(B)(ii), or 204(a)(1)(B)(iii) of the Act is unable to present primary or secondary evidence of the abuser's status, USCIS will attempt to electronically verify the abuser's citizenship or immigration status from information contained in the Department's automated or computerized records. Other Department records may also be reviewed at the discretion of the adjudicating officer. If USCIS is unable to identify a record as relating to the abuser, or the record does not establish the abuser's immigration or citizenship status, the self-petition will be adjudicated based on the information submitted by the self-petitioner.

(18) Withholding adjudication. USCIS may authorize withholding adjudication of a visa petition or other application if USCIS determines that an investigation has been undertaken involving a matter relating to eligibility or the exercise of discretion, where applicable, in connection with the benefit request, and that the disclosure of information to the applicant or petitioner in connection with the adjudication of the benefit request would prejudice the ongoing investigation. If an investigation has been undertaken and has not been completed within one year of its inception, USCIS will review the matter and determine whether adjudication of the benefit request should be held in abeyance for six months or until the investigation is completed, whichever comes sooner. If, after six months of USCIS's determination, the investigation has not been completed, the matter will be reviewed again by USCIS and, if it concludes that more time is needed to complete the investigation, adjudication may be held in abeyance for up to another six months. If the investigation is not completed at the end of that time, USCIS may authorize that adjudication be held in abeyance for another six months. Thereafter, if USCIS determines it is necessary to continue to withhold adjudication pending completion of the investigation, it will review that determination every six months.

(19) Notification.

(i) Unrepresented applicants or petitioners. USCIS will only send original notices and documents evidencing lawful status based on the approval of a benefit request directly to the applicant or petitioner if the applicant or petitioner is not represented.

(ii) Represented applicants or petitioners.

(A) Notices. When an applicant or petitioner is represented, USCIS will send original notices both to the applicant or petitioner and his or her authorized attorney or accredited representative. If provided in this title, on the applicable form, or on form instructions, an applicant or petitioner filing a paper application or petition may request that all original notices, such as requests for evidence and notices of decision, only be sent to the official business address of the applicant's or petitioner's authorized attorney or accredited representative, as reflected on a properly executed Notice of Entry of Appearance as Attorney or Accredited Representative. In such instances, a courtesy copy of the original notice will be sent to the applicant or petitioner.

(B) Electronic notices. For applications or petitions filed electronically, USCIS will notify both the applicant or petitioner and the authorized attorney or accredited representative electronically of any notices or decisions. Except as provided in paragraph (b)(19)(ii)(C) of this section, USCIS will not issue paper notices or decisions for electronically-filed applications or petitions, unless:

(1) The option exists for the applicant or petitioner to request to receive paper notices or decisions by mail through the U.S. Postal Service, by indicating this preference in his or her electronic online account profile in USCIS's electronic immigration system; or

(2) USCIS, in its discretion, determines that issuing a paper notice or decision for an electronically-filed application or petition is warranted.

(C) Approval notices with attached Arrival-Departure Records. USCIS will send an original paper approval notice with an attached Arrival-Departure Record, reflecting USCIS's approval of an applicant's request for an extension of stay or change of status, to the official business address of the applicant's or petitioner's attorney or accredited representative, as reflected on a properly executed Notice of Entry of Appearance as Attorney or Accredited Representative or in the address section of the online representative account profile in USCIS's electronic immigration system, unless the applicant specifically requests that the original approval notice with an attached Arrival-Departure Record be sent directly to his or her mailing address.

(iii) Secure identity documents.

(A) USCIS will send secure identification documents, such as a Permanent Resident Card or Employment

Authorization Document, only to the applicant or self-petitioner unless the applicant or self-petitioner specifically consents to having his or her secure identification document sent to a designated agent or their attorney or accredited representative of record, as specified on the form instructions.

(B) The designated agent, or attorney or accredited representative, will be required to provide identification and sign for receipt of the secure document.

(c) — (d) [Reserved]

HISTORY:

[29 FR 11956, Aug. 21, 1964, as amended at 30 FR 14772, Nov. 30, 1965; 32 FR 9622, July 4, 1967; 33 FR 11644, Aug. 16, 1968; 39 FR 43055, Dec. 10, 1974; 44 FR 52169, Sept. 7, 1979; 47 FR 44990, Oct. 13, 1982; 50 FR 11841, Mar. 26, 1985; 52 FR 16192, May 1, 1987; 53 FR 26034, July 11, 1988; 54 FR 29881, July 17, 1989; 56 FR 624, Jan. 7, 1991.; 59 FR 1460, Jan. 11, 1994; 59 FR 33905, July 1, 1994; 61 FR 13061, 13072, Mar. 26, 1996; 61 FR 28803, 28010, June 4, 1996; 61 FR 57583, 57584, Nov. 7, 1996; 63 FR 12979, 12984, Mar. 17, 1998; 63 FR 70313, 70315, Dec. 21, 1998; 66 FR 29661, 29672, 29682, 29685, June 1, 2001, as confirmed at 67 FR 38341, 38350, June 4, 2002; 68 FR 23010, 23012, Apr. 29, 2003, as confirmed and amended at 76 FR 53764, 53778, 53780, Aug. 29, 2011, as corrected at 76 FR 73475, Nov. 29, 2011; 71 FR 29571, 29574, May 23, 2006; 72 FR 19100, 19105, 19106, Apr. 17, 2007; 74 FR 26933, 26936, June 5, 2009; 75 FR 58962, 58986, Sept. 24, 2010; 78 FR 22770, 22771, Apr. 17, 2013; 79 FR 64299, 64305, Oct. 29, 2014; 81 FR 50244, 50275, July 29, 2016; 81 FR 73292, 73328, Oct. 24, 2016; 85 FR 46788, 46914, Aug. 3, 2020; 89 FR 6194, 6384, Jan. 31, 2024]

§ 103.3 Denials, appeals, and precedent decisions.

(a) Denials and appeals —

(1) General —

(i) Denial of application or petition. When a Service officer denies an application or petition filed under § 103.2 of this part, the officer shall explain in writing the specific reasons for denial. If Form I-292 (a denial form including notification of the right of appeal) is used to notify the applicant or petitioner, the duplicate of Form I-292 constitutes the denial order.

(ii) Appealable decisions. Certain unfavorable decisions on applications, petitions, and other types of cases may be appealed. Decisions under the appellate jurisdiction of the Board of Immigration Appeals (Board) are listed in § 3.1(b) of this chapter. Decisions under the appellate jurisdiction of the Associate Commissioner, Examinations, are listed in § 103.1(f)(2) of this part.

(iii) Appeal —

(A) Jurisdiction. When an unfavorable decision may be appealed, the official making the decision shall state the appellate jurisdiction and shall furnish the appropriate appeal form.

(B) Meaning of affected party. For purposes of this section and §§ 103.4 and 103.5 of this part, affected party (in addition to the Service) means the person or entity with legal standing in a proceeding. It does not include the beneficiary of a visa petition. An affected party may be represented by an attorney or representative in accordance with part 292 of this chapter.

(C) Record of proceeding. An appeal and any cross-appeal or briefs become part of the record of proceeding.

(D) Appeal filed by Service officer in case within jurisdiction of Board. If an appeal is filed by a Service officer, a copy must be served on the affected party.

(iv) Function of Administrative Appeals Unit (AAU). The AAU is the appellate body which considers cases under the appellate jurisdiction of the Associate Commissioner, Examinations.

(v) Summary dismissal. An officer to whom an appeal is taken shall summarily dismiss any appeal when the party concerned fails to identify specifically any erroneous conclusion of law or statement of fact for the appeal. The filing by an attorney or representative accredited under 8 CFR 292.2(d) of an appeal which is summarily dismissed under this section may constitute frivolous behavior as defined in 8 CFR 292.3(a)(15). Summary dismissal of an appeal under § 103.3(a)(1)(v) in no way limits the other grounds and procedures for disciplinary action against attorneys or representatives provided in 8 CFR 292.2 or in any other statute or regulation.

(2) AAU appeals in other than special agricultural worker and legalization cases —

(i) Filing appeal. The affected party shall file an appeal on Form I-290B. Except as otherwise provided in this chapter, the affected party must pay the fee required by 8 CFR 106.2. The affected party must submit the complete appeal including any supporting brief as indicated in the applicable form instructions within 30 days after service of the decision.

(ii) Reviewing official. The official who made the unfavorable decision being appealed shall review the appeal unless the affected party moves to a new jurisdiction. In that instance, the official who has jurisdiction over such a proceeding in that geographic location shall review it. In the case of a fee waived or exempt appeal under 8 CFR 106.3, USCIS may forward the appeal for adjudication without requiring a review by the official who made the unfavorable decision.

(iii) Favorable action instead of forwarding appeal to AAU. The reviewing official shall decide whether or not favorable action is warranted. Within 45 days of receipt of the appeal, the reviewing official may treat the appeal as a motion to reopen or reconsider and take favorable action. However, that official is not precluded from reopening a proceeding or reconsidering a decision on his or her own motion under § 103.5(a)(5)(i) of this part in order to make a new decision favorable to the affected party after 45 days of receipt of the appeal.

(iv) Forwarding appeal to AAU. If the reviewing official will not be taking favorable action or decides favorable action is not warranted, that official shall promptly forward the appeal and the related record of proceeding to the AAU in Washington, DC.

(v) Improperly filed appeal —

(A) Appeal filed by person or entity not entitled to file it —

(1) Rejection without refund of filing fee. An appeal filed by a person or entity not entitled to file it must be rejected as improperly filed. In such a case, any filing fee the Service has accepted will not be refunded.

(2) Appeal by attorney or representative without proper Form G-28 —

(i) General. If an appeal is filed by an attorney or representative without a properly executed Notice of Entry of Appearance as Attorney or Representative (Form G-28) entitling that person to file the appeal, the appeal is considered improperly filed. In such a case, any filing fee the Service has accepted will not be refunded regardless of the action taken.

(ii) When favorable action warranted. If the reviewing official decides favorable action is warranted with respect to an otherwise properly filed appeal, that official shall ask the attorney or representative to submit Form G-28 to the official's office within 15 days of the request. If Form G-28 is not submitted within the time allowed, the official may, on his or her own motion, under § 103.5(a)(5)(i) of this part, make a new decision favorable to the affected party without notifying the attorney or representative.

(iii) When favorable action not warranted. If the reviewing official decides favorable action is not warranted with respect to an otherwise properly filed appeal, that official shall ask the attorney or representative to submit Form G-28 directly to the AAU. The official shall also forward the appeal and the relating record of proceeding to the AAU. The appeal may be considered properly filed as of its original filing date if the attorney or representative submits a properly executed Form G-28 entitling that person to file the appeal.

(B) Untimely appeal —

(1) Rejection without refund of filing fee. An appeal which is not filed within the time allowed must be rejected as improperly filed. In such a case, any filing fee the Service has accepted will not be refunded.

(2) Untimely appeal treated as motion. If an untimely appeal meets the requirements of a motion to reopen as described in § 103.5(a)(2) of this part or a motion to reconsider as described in § 103.5(a)(3) of this part, the appeal must be treated as a motion, and a decision must be made on the merits of the case.

(vi) Brief. The affected party may submit a brief with Form I-290B.

(vii) Additional time to submit a brief. The affected party may make a written request to the AAU for additional time to submit a brief. The AAU may, for good cause shown, allow the affected party additional time to submit one.

(viii) Where to submit supporting brief if additional time is granted. If the AAU grants additional time, the affected party shall submit the brief directly to the AAU.

(ix) Withdrawal of appeal. The affected party may withdraw the appeal, in writing, before a decision is made.

(x) Decision on appeal. The decision must be in writing. A copy of the decision must be served on the affected party and the attorney or representative of record, if any.

(3) Denials and appeals of special agricultural worker and legalization applications and termination of lawful temporary resident status under sections 210 and 245A.

(i) Whenever an application for legalization or special agricultural worker status is denied or the status of a lawful temporary resident is terminated, the alien shall be given written notice setting forth the specific reasons for the denial on Form I-692, Notice of Denial. Form I-692 shall also contain advice to the applicant that he or she may appeal the decision and that such appeal must be taken within 30 days after service of the notification of decision accompanied by any additional new evidence, and a supporting brief if desired. The Form I-692 shall additionally provide a notice to the alien that if he or she fails to file an appeal from the decision, the Form I-692 will serve as a final notice of ineligibility.

(ii) Form I-694, Notice of Appeal, in triplicate, shall be used to file the appeal, and must be accompanied by the appropriate fee. Form I-694 shall be furnished with the notice of denial at the time of service on the alien.

(iii) Upon receipt of an appeal, the administrative record will be forwarded to the Administrative Appeals Unit as provided by § 103.1(f)(2) of this part for review and decision. The decision on the appeal shall be in writing, and if the appeal is dismissed, shall include a final notice of ineligibility. A copy of the decision shall be served upon the applicant and his or her attorney or representative of record. No further administrative appeal shall lie from this decision, nor may the application be filed or reopened before an immigration judge or the Board of Immigration Appeals during exclusion or deportation proceedings.

(iv) Any appeal which is filed that:

(A) Fails to state the reason for appeal;

(B) Is filed solely on the basis of a denial for failure to file the application for adjustment of status under section 210 or 245A in a timely manner; or

(C) Is patently frivolous; will be summarily dismissed. An appeal received after the thirty (30) day period has tolled will not be accepted for processing.

(4) Denials and appeal of Replenishment Agricultural Worker petitions and waivers and termination of lawful temporary resident status under section 210A.

(i) Whenever a petition for Replenishment Agricultural Worker status, or a request for a waiver incident to such filing, is denied in accordance with the provisions of part 210a of this title, the alien shall be given written notice setting forth the specific reasons for the denial on Form I-692, Notice of Denial. Form I-692 shall also contain advice to the alien that he or she may appeal the decision and that such appeal must be taken within thirty (30) days after service of the notification of decision accompanied by any additional new evidence, and a supporting brief if desired. The Form I-692 shall additionally provide a notice to the alien that if he or she fails to file an appeal from the decision, the Form I-692 shall serve as a final notice of ineligibility.

(ii) Form I-694, Notice of Appeal, in triplicate, shall be used to file the appeal, and must be accompanied by the appropriate fee. Form I-694 shall be furnished with the notice of denial at the time of service on the alien.

(iii) Upon receipt of an appeal, the administrative record will be forwarded to the Administrative Appeals Unit as provided by § 103.1(f)(2) of this part for review and decision. The decision on the appeal shall be in writing, and if the appeal is dismissed, shall include a final notice of ineligibility. A copy of the decision shall be served upon the petitioner and his or her attorney or representative of record. No further administrative appeal shall lie from this decision, nor may the petition be filed or reopened before an immigration judge or the Board of Immigration Appeals during exclusion or deportation proceedings.

(iv) Any appeal which is filed that: Fails to state the reason for the appeal; is filed solely on the basis of a denial for failure to file the petition for adjustment of status under part 210a of this title in a timely manner; or is patently frivolous, will be summarily dismissed. An appeal received after the thirty (30) day period has tolled will not be accepted for processing.

(b) Oral argument regarding appeal before AAU. —

(1) Request. If the affected party desires oral argument, the affected party must explain in writing specifically why oral argument is necessary. For such a request to be considered, it must be submitted within the time allowed for meeting other requirements.

(2) Decision about oral argument. The Service has sole authority to grant or deny a request for oral argument. Upon approval of a request for oral argument, the AAU shall set the time, date, place, and conditions of oral argument.

(c) Service precedent decisions. The Secretary of Homeland Security, or specific officials of the Department of Homeland Security designated by the Secretary with the concurrence of the Attorney General, may file with the Attorney General decisions relating to the administration of the immigration laws of the United States for publication as precedent in future proceedings, and upon approval of the Attorney General as to the lawfulness of such decision, the Director of the Executive Office for Immigration Review shall cause such decisions to be published in the same manner as decisions of the Board and the Attorney General. In addition to Attorney General and Board decisions referred to in § 1003.1(g) of chapter V, designated Service decisions are to serve as precedents in all proceedings involving the same issue(s). Except as these decisions may be modified or overruled by later precedent decisions, they are binding on all Service employees in the administration of the Act. Precedent decisions must be published and made available to the public as described in 8 CFR 103.10(e).

HISTORY:

[31 FR 3062, Feb. 24, 1966, as amended at 37 FR 927, Jan. 21, 1972.; 48 FR 36441, Aug. 11, 1983; 49 FR 7355, Feb. 29, 1984; 52 FR 16192, May 1, 1987; 54 FR 29881, July 17, 1989; 55 FR 20769, 20775, May 21, 1990; 55 FR 23345, June 7, 1990; 57 FR 11573, Apr. 6, 1992, as confirmed at 1899, Jan. 13, 1994; 68 FR 9824, 9832, Feb. 28, 2003; 76 FR 53764, 53781, Aug. 29, 2011; 5 FR 46788, 46914, Aug. 3, 2020; 89 FR 6194, 6384, Jan. 31, 2024]

§ 103.4 Certifications.

(a) Certification of other than special agricultural worker and legalization cases—

(1) General. The Commissioner or the Commissioner's delegate may direct that any case or class of cases be certified to another Service official for decision. In addition, regional commissioners, regional service center directors, district directors, officers in charge in districts 33 (Bangkok, Thailand), 35 (Mexico City, Mexico), and 37 (Rome, Italy), and the Director, National Fines Office, may certify their decisions to the appropriate appellate authority (as designated in this chapter) when the case involves an unusually complex or novel issue of law or fact.

(2) Notice to affected party. When a case is certified to a Service officer, the official certifying the case shall notify the affected party using a Notice of Certification (Form I-290C). The affected party may submit a brief to the officer to whom the case is certified within 30 days after service of the notice. If the affected party does not wish to submit a brief, the affected party may waive the 30-day period.

(3) Favorable action. The Service officer to whom a case is certified may suspend the 30-day period for submission of a brief if that officer takes action favorable to the affected party.

(4) Initial decision. A case within the appellate jurisdiction of the Associate Commissioner, Examinations, or for which there is no appeal procedure may be certified only after an initial decision is made.

(5) Certification to AAU. A case described in paragraph (a)(4) of this section may be certified to the AAU.

(6) Appeal to Board. In a case within the Board's appellate jurisdiction, an unfavorable decision of the Service official to whom the case is certified (whether made initially or upon review) is the decision which may be appealed to the Board under § 3.1(b) of this chapter.

(7) Other applicable provisions. The provisions of § 103.3(a)(2)(x) of this part also apply to decisions on certified cases. The provisions of § 103.3(b) of this part also apply to requests for oral argument regarding certified cases considered by the AAU.

(b) Certification of denials of special agricultural worker and legalization applications. The Regional Processing Facility director or the district director may, in accordance with paragraph (a) of this section, certify a decision to the Associate Commissioner, Examinations (Administrative Appeals Unit) (the appellate authority designated in § 103.1(f)(2)) of this part, when the case involves an unusually complex or novel question of law or fact.

HISTORY:

[52 FR 661, Jan. 8, 1987, as amended at 53 FR 43985, Oct. 31, 1988; 55 FR 20770, May 21, 1990]

§ 103.5 Reopening or reconsideration.

(a) Motions to reopen or reconsider in other than special agricultural worker and legalization cases —

(1) When filed by affected party —

(i) General. Except where the Board has jurisdiction and as otherwise provided in 8 CFR parts 3, 210, 242 and 245a, when the affected party files a motion, the official having jurisdiction may, for proper cause shown, reopen the proceeding or reconsider the prior decision. Motions to reopen or reconsider are not applicable to proceedings described in § 274a.9 of this chapter. Any motion to reconsider an action by the Service filed by an applicant or petitioner must be filed within 30 days of the decision that the motion seeks to reconsider. Any motion to reopen a proceeding before the Service filed by an applicant or petitioner, must be filed within 30 days of the decision that the motion seeks to reopen, except that failure to file before this period expires, may be excused in the discretion of the Service where it is demonstrated that the delay was reasonable and was beyond the control of the applicant or petitioner.

(ii) Jurisdiction. The official having jurisdiction is the official who made the latest decision in the proceeding unless the affected party moves to a new jurisdiction. In that instance, the new official having jurisdiction is the official over such a proceeding in the new geographical locations.

(iii) Filing Requirements — A motion shall be submitted on Form I-290B and may be accompanied by a brief. It must be:

(A) In writing and signed by the affected party or the attorney or representative of record, if any;

(B) Accompanied by a nonrefundable fee as set forth in 8 CFR 106.2;

(C) Accompanied by a statement about whether or not the validity of the unfavorable decision has been or is the subject of any judicial proceeding and, if so, the court, nature, date, and status or result of the proceeding;

(D) Addressed to the official having jurisdiction; and

(E) Submitted to the office maintaining the record upon which the unfavorable decision was made for forwarding to the official having jurisdiction.

(iv) Effect of motion or subsequent application or petition. Unless the Service directs otherwise, the filing of a motion to reopen or reconsider or of a subsequent application or petition does not stay the execution of any decision in a case or extend a previously set departure date.

(2) Requirements for motion to reopen. A motion to reopen must state the new facts to be provided in the reopened proceeding and be supported by affidavits or other documentary evidence. A motion to reopen an application or petition denied due to abandonment must be filed with evidence that the decision was in error because:

(i) The requested evidence was not material to the issue of eligibility;

(ii) The required initial evidence was submitted with the application or petition, or the request for initial evidence or additional information or appearance was complied with during the allotted period; or

(iii) The request for additional information or appearance was sent to an address other than that on the application, petition, or notice of representation, or that the applicant or petitioner advised the Service, in writing, of a change of address or change of representation subsequent to filing and before the Service's request was sent, and the request did not go to the new address.

(3) Requirements for motion to reconsider. A motion to reconsider must state the reasons for reconsideration and be supported by any pertinent precedent decisions to establish that the decision was based on an incorrect application of law or Service policy. A motion to reconsider a decision on an application or petition must, when filed, also establish that the decision was incorrect based on the evidence of record at the time of the initial decision.

(4) Processing motions in proceedings before the Service. A motion that does not meet applicable requirements shall be dismissed. Where a motion to reopen is granted, the proceeding shall be reopened. The notice and any favorable decision may be combined.

(5) Motion by Service officer —

(i) Service motion with decision favorable to affected party. When a Service officer, on his or her own motion, reopens a Service proceeding or reconsiders a Service decision in order to make a new decision favorable to the affected party, the Service officer shall combine the motion and the favorable decision in one action.

(ii) Service motion with decision that may be unfavorable to affected party. When a Service officer, on his or her own motion, reopens a Service proceeding or reconsiders a Service decision, and the new decision may be unfavorable to the affected party, the officer shall give the affected party 30 days after service of the motion to submit a brief. The officer may extend the time period for good cause shown. If the affected party does not wish to submit a brief, the affected party may waive the 30-day period.

(6) Appeal to AAU from Service decision made as a result of a motion. A field office decision made as a result of a motion may be applied to the AAU only if the original decision was appealable to the AAU.

(7) Other applicable provisions. The provisions of § 103.3(a)(2)(x) of this part also apply to decisions on motions. The provisions of § 103.3(b) of this part also apply to requests for oral argument regarding motions considered by the AAU.

(8) Treating an appeal as a motion. The official who denied an application or petition may treat the appeal from that decision as a motion for the purpose of granting the motion.

(b) Motions to reopen or reconsider denials of special agricultural worker and legalization applications. Upon the filing of an appeal to the Associate Commissioner, Examinations (Administrative Appeals Unit), the Director of a Regional Processing Facility or the consular officer at an Overseas Processing Office may sua sponte reopen any proceeding under his or her jurisdiction opened under part 210 or 245a of this chapter and may reconsider any decision rendered in such proceeding. The new decision must be served on the appellant within 45 days of receipt of any brief and/or new evidence, or upon expiration of the time allowed for the submission of a brief. The Associate Commissioner, Examinations, or the Chief of the Administrative Appeals Unit may sua sponte reopen any proceeding conducted by that Unit under part 210 or 245a of this chapter and reconsider any decision rendered in such proceeding. Motions to reopen a proceeding or reconsider a decision under part 210 or 245a of this chapter shall not be considered.

(c) Motions to reopen or reconsider decisions on replenishment agricultural worker petitions.

(1) The director of a regional processing facility may sua sponte reopen any proceeding under part 210a of this title which is within his or her jurisdiction and may render a new decision. This decision may reverse a prior favorable decision when it is determined that there was fraud during the registration or petition processes and the petitioner was not entitled to the status granted. The petitioner must be given an opportunity to offer evidence in support of the petition and in opposition to the grounds for reopening the petition before a new decision is rendered.

(2) The Associate Commissioner, Examinations or the Chief of the Administrative Appeals Unit may sua sponte reopen any proceeding conducted by that unit under part 210a of this title and reconsider any decision rendered in such proceeding.

(3) Motions to reopen a proceeding or reconsider a decision under part 210a of this title shall not be considered.

HISTORY:

[27 FR 7562, Aug. 1, 1962, as amended at 30 FR 12772, Oct. 7, 1965; 32 FR 271, Jan. 11, 1967.; 52 FR 16193, May 1, 1987; 54 FR 29881, July 17, 1989; 55 FR 20770, 20775, May 21, 1990; 55 FR 25931, June 25, 1990; 56 FR 41782, Aug. 23, 1991; 59 FR 1463, Jan. 11, 1994; 61 FR 18900, 18909, Apr. 29, 1996; 62 FR 10312, 10336, Mar. 6, 1997; 70 FR 50954, 50957, Aug. 29, 2005; 85 FR 46788, 46914, Aug. 3, 2020]

§ 103.5a [This section was redesignated as § 103.8. See 76 FR 53764, 53781, Aug. 29, 2011.]

[NO TEXT IN ORIGINAL]

HISTORY:

[37 FR 11470, June 8, 1972, as amended at 39 FR 23247, June 27, 1974; 62 FR 10312, 10336, Mar. 6, 1997; 64 FR 17943, 17944, Apr. 13, 1999; redesignated at 76 FR 53764, 53781, Aug. 29, 2011]

AUTHORITY:

(5 U.S.C. 301, 552, 552a; 8 U.S.C. 1101, 1103, 1304, 1356; 31 U.S.C. 9701; 48 U.S.C. 1806; Public Law 107-296, 116 Stat. 2135 (6 U.S.C. 1 et seq.), E.O. 12356, 47 FR 14874, 15557, 3 CFR, 1982 Comp., p. 166; 8 CFR part 2.)

§ 103.5b [This section was redesignated as § 103.9. See 76 FR 53764, 53781, Aug. 29, 2011.]

[NO TEXT IN ORIGINAL]

HISTORY:

[59 FR 1463, Jan. 11, 1994; redesignated at 76 FR 53764, 53781, Aug. 29, 2011]

AUTHORITY:

(5 U.S.C. 301, 552, 552a; 8 U.S.C. 1101, 1103, 1304, 1356; 31 U.S.C. 9701; 48 U.S.C. 1806; Public Law 107-296, 116 Stat. 2135 (6 U.S.C. 1 et seq.), E.O. 12356, 47 FR 14874, 15557, 3 CFR, 1982 Comp., p. 166; 8 CFR part 2.)

§ 103.6 Immigration Bonds

(a) Posting of surety bonds. —

(1) Extension agreements; consent of surety; collateral security. All surety bonds posted in immigration cases shall be executed on Form I–352, Immigration Bond, a copy of which, and any rider attached thereto, shall be furnished the obligor. A district director is authorized to approve a bond, a formal agreement to extension of liability of surety, a request for delivery of collateral security to a duly appointed and undischarged administrator or executor of the estate of a deceased depositor, and a power of attorney executed on Form I–312, Designation of Attorney in Fact. All other matters relating to bonds, including a power of attorney not executed on Form I–312 and a request for delivery of collateral security to other than the depositor or his or her approved attorney in fact, shall be forwarded to the regional director for approval.

(2) Bond riders—

(i) General. Bond riders shall be prepared on Form I–351, Bond Riders, and attached to Form I–352. If a condition to be included in a bond is not on Form I–351, a rider containing the condition shall be executed.

(ii) [Reserved]

(b) Acceptable sureties—

(1) Acceptable sureties generally. Immigration bonds may be posted by a company holding a certificate from the Secretary of the Treasury under 31 U.S.C. 9304–9308 as an acceptable surety on Federal bonds (a Treasurycertified surety). They may also be posted by an entity or individual who deposits cash or cash equivalents, such as postal money orders, certified checks, or cashier's checks, in the face amount of the bond.

(2) Authority to decline bonds underwritten by Treasury-certified surety. In its discretion, ICE may decline to accept an immigration bond underwritten by a Treasury-certified surety when—

(i) Ten or more invoices issued to the surety on administratively final breach determinations are past due at the same time;

(ii) The surety owes a cumulative total of $50,000 or more on past-due invoices issued to the surety on administratively final breach determinations, including interest and other fees assessed by law on delinquent debt; or

(iii) The surety has a breach rate of 35 percent or greater in any Federal fiscal year after August 31, 2020.The surety's breach rate will be calculated in the month of January following each Federal fiscal year after the effective date of this rule by dividing the sum of administratively final breach determinations for that surety during the fiscal year by the total of such sum and bond cancellations for that surety during that same year. For example, if 50 bonds posted by a surety company were declared breached from October 1 to September 30, and 50 bonds posted by that same surety were cancelled during the same fiscal year (for a total of 100 bond dispositions), that surety would have a breach rate of 50 percent for that fiscal year.

(iv) Consistent with 31 CFR 223.17(b)(5)(i), ICE may not decline a future bond from a Treasury-certified surety when a court of competent jurisdiction has stayed or enjoined enforcement of a breach determination that would support ICE's decision to decline future bonds. For example, if collection of a past-due invoice has been stayed by a court, it cannot be counted as one of the ten or more invoices under paragraph (b)(1)(i) of this section.

(3) Definitions. For purposes of paragraphs (b)(2)(i) and (ii) of this section—

(i) A breach determination is administratively final when the time to file an appeal with the Administrative Appeals Office (AAO) has expired or when the appeal is dismissed or rejected.

(ii) An invoice is past due if it is delinquent, meaning either that it has not been paid or disputed in writing within 30 days of issuance of the invoice; or, if it is a debt upon which the surety has submitted a written dispute within 30 days of issuance of the invoice, ICE has issued a written explanation to the surety of the agency's determination that the debt is valid, and the debt has not been paid within 30 days of issuance of such written explanation that the debt is valid.

(4) Notice of intention to decline future bonds. When one or more of the for cause standards provided in paragraph (b)(2) of this section applies to a Treasury-certified surety, ICE may, in its discretion, initiate the process to notify the surety that it will decline future bonds. To initiate this process, ICE will issue written notice to the surety stating ICE's intention to decline bonds underwritten by the surety and the reasons for the proposed nonacceptance of the bonds. This notification will inform the surety of its opportunity to rebut the stated reasons set forth in the notice, and its opportunity to cure the stated reasons, i.e., deficient performance.

(5) Surety's response. The Treasurycertified surety must send any response to ICE's notice in writing to the office that sent the notice. The surety's response must be received by the designated office on or before the 30th calendar day following the date the notice was issued. If the surety or agent fails to submit a timely response, the surety will have waived the right to respond, and ICE will decline any future bonds submitted for approval that are underwritten by the surety.

(6) Written determination. After considering any timely response submitted by the Treasury-certified surety to the written notice issued by ICE, ICE will issue a written determination stating whether future bonds issued by the surety will be accepted or declined. This written determination constitutes final agency action. If the written determination concludes that future bonds will be declined from the surety, ICE will decline any future bonds submitted for approval that are underwritten by the surety.

(7) Effect of decision to decline future bonds. Consistent with 31 CFR 223.17(b)(4), ICE will use best efforts to ensure persons conducting business with the agency are aware that future bonds underwritten by the surety will be declined by ICE. For example, ICE will notify any bonding agents who have served as co-obligors with the surety that ICE will decline future bonds underwritten by the surety.

(c) Cancellation and breach—

(1) Public charge bonds. A public charge bond posted for an alien will be cancelled when the alien dies, departs permanently from the United States, or is naturalized, provided the alien did not breach such bond by receiving either public cash assistance for income maintenance or long-term institutionalization at government expense prior to death, permanent departure, or naturalization. USCIS may cancel a public charge bond at any time after determining that the alien is not likely at any time to become a public charge. A bond may also be cancelled in order to allow substitution of another bond. A public charge bond will be cancelled by USCIS upon review following the fifth anniversary of the admission or adjustment of status of the alien, provided that the alien has filed Form I-356, Request for Cancellation of Public Charge Bond, and USCIS finds that the alien did not receive either public cash assistance for income maintenance or long-term institutionalization at government expense prior to the fifth anniversary. If Form I-356 is not filed, the public charge bond will remain in effect until the form is filed and USCIS reviews the evidence supporting the form, and renders a decision regarding the breach of the bond, or a decision to cancel the bond.

(2) Maintenance of status and departure bonds. When the status of a nonimmigrant who has violated the conditions of his admission has been adjusted as a result of administrative or legislative action to that of a permanent resident retroactively to a date prior to the violation, any outstanding maintenance of status and departure bond shall be canceled. If an application for adjustment of status is made by a nonimmigrant while he is in lawful temporary status, the bond shall be canceled if his status is adjusted to that of a lawful permanent resident or if he voluntarily departs within any period granted to him. As used in this paragraph, the term lawful temporary status means that there must not have been a violation of any of the conditions of the alien's nonimmigrant classification by acceptance of unauthorized employment or otherwise during the time he has been accorded such classification, and that from the date of admission to the date of departure or adjustment of status he must have had uninterrupted Service approval of his presence in the United States in the form of regular extensions of stay or dates set by which departure is to occur, or a combination of both. An alien admitted as a nonimmigrant shall not be regarded as having violated his nonimmigrant status by engaging in employment subsequent to his proper filing of an application for adjustment of status under section 245 of the Act and part 245 of this chapter. A maintenance of status and departure bond posted at the request of an American consular officer abroad in behalf of an alien who did not travel to the United States shall be canceled upon receipt of notice from an American consular officer that the alien is outside the United States and the nonimmigrant visa issued pursuant to the posting of the bond has been canceled or has expired.

(3) Substantial performance. Substantial performance of all conditions imposed by the terms of a bond shall release the obligor from liability.

(d) Bond schedules —

(1) Blanketbonds for departure of visitors and transits. The amount of bond required for various numbers of nonimmigrant visitors or transits admitted under bond on Forms I-352 shall be in accordance with the following schedule:

Aliens

1 to 4—$500 each.

5 to 9—$2,500 total bond.

10 to 24—$3,500 total bond.

25 to 49—$5,000 total bond.

50 to 74—$6,000 total bond.

75 to 99—$7,000 total bond.

100 to 124—$8,000 total bond.

125 to 149—$9,000 total bond.

150 to 199—$10,000 total bond.

200 or more—$10,000 plus $50 for each alien over 200.

(2) Blanket bonds for importation of workers classified as nonimmigrants under section 101(a)(15)(H). The following schedule shall be employed by district directors when requiring employers or their agents or representatives to post bond as a condition to importing alien laborers into the United States from the West Indies, the British Virgin Islands, or from Canada:

Less than 500 workers — $ 15 each

500 to 1,000 workers — $ 10 each

1,000 or more workers — $ 5 each

A bond shall not be posted for less than $ 1,000 or for more than $ 12,000 irrespective of the number of workers involved. Failure to comply with conditions of the bond will result in the employer's liability in the amount of $ 200 as liquidated damages for each alien involved.

(3) [Removed]

(e) Breach of bond. A bond is breached when there has been a substantial violation of the stipulated conditions. A final determination that a bond has been breached creates a claim in favor of the United States which may not be released or discharged by a Service officer. The district director having custody of the file containing the immigration bond executed on Form I–352 shall determine whether the bond shall be declared breached or cancelled, and shall notify the obligor on Form I– 323 or Form I–391 of the decision, and, if declared breached, of the reasons therefor, and of the right to appeal in accordance with the provisions of this part.

(f) Appeals of Breached Bonds Issued by Treasury-Certified Sureties.

(1) Final agency action. Consistent with section 10(c) of the Administrative Procedure Act, 5 U.S.C. 704, the AAO's decision on appeal of a breach determination constitutes final agency action. The initial breach determination remains inoperative during the administrative appeal period and while a timely administrative appeal is pending. Dismissal of an appeal is effective upon the date of the AAO decision. Only the granting of a motion to reopen or reconsider by the AAO makes the dismissal decision no longer final.

(2) Exhaustion of administrative remedies. The failure by a Treasury certified surety or its bonding agent to exhaust administrative appellate review before the AAO, or the lapse of time to file an appeal to the AAO without filing an appeal to the AAO, constitutes waiver and forfeiture of all claims, defenses, and arguments involving the bond breach determination. A Treasury certified surety's or its agent's failure to move to reconsider or to reopen a breach decision does not constitute failure to exhaust administrative remedies.

(3) Requirement to raise all issues. A Treasury-certified surety or its bonding agent must raise all issues and present all facts relied upon in the appeal to the AAO. A Treasury-certified surety's or its agent's failure to timely raise any claim, defense, or argument before the AAO in support of reversal or remand of a breach decision waives and forfeits that claim, defense, or argument.

(4) Failure to file a timely administrative appeal. If a Treasury certified surety or its bonding agent does not timely file an appeal with the AAO upon receipt of a breach notice, a claim in favor of ICE is created on the bond breach determination, and ICE may seek to collect the amount due on the breached bond.

(g) Delivery bond notices to surrender aliens. Notwithstanding the requirements of § 103.8 for the service of other notices, ICE may serve demand notices electronically to bond obligors who consent to electronic delivery of service, or by any mail service that allows delivery confirmation to cause an alien who has been released from DHS custody on an immigration bond to appear at an ICE office or an immigration court. An electronic record from the ICE bonds system showing that the bond obligor opened the demand notice will constitute valid proof of service of the notice. If ICE cannot confirm proof of service of the electronic notice, ICE will issue a new demand notice to the bond obligor's last known address using any mail service that allows delivery confirmation.

(h) Bond breach, bond cancellation, and other bond notices. Notwithstanding the service requirements for demand notices in paragraph (g) of this section, ICE may serve any other bond-related notices that pertain to delivery, order of supervision, or voluntary departure immigration bonds, such as bond breach or cancellation notices, electronically to obligors who consent to electronic delivery of service, or by ordinary mail. An electronic record from the ICE bonds system showing that the bond obligor opened the bond-related notice will constitute valid proof of service of the notice. If ICE cannot confirm proof of service of the electronic notice, ICE will reissue another notice to the bond obligor's last known address using ordinary mail.

HISTORY:

[31 FR 11713, Sept. 7, 1966, as amended at 32 FR 9622, July 4, 1967; 33 FR 5255, Apr. 2, 1968; 33 FR 10504, July 24, 1968; 34 FR 1008, Jan. 23, 1969; 34 FR 14760, Sept. 25, 1969; 39 FR 12334, Apr. 5, 1974; 40 FR 42852, Sept. 17, 1975; 48 FR 51144, Nov. 7, 1983; 49 FR 24011, June 11, 1984; 60 FR 21974, May 4, 1995; 62 FR 10312, 10336, March 6, 1997; 84 FR 41292, 41500, Aug. 14, 2019; 85 FR 45968, 45989, July 31, 2020; 86 FR 14221, 14227, Mar. 15, 2021; 87 FR 55472, 55636, Sept. 9, 2022; 88 FR 53358, 53371 Aug. 8, 2023; 90 FR 535, 556, Jan. 6, 2025]

§ 103.7 Fees.

(a) Department of Justice (DOJ) fees. Fees for proceedings before immigration judges and the Board of Immigration Appeals are described in 8 CFR 1003.8, 1003.24, and 1103.7.

(1) USCIS may accept DOJ fees. Except as provided in 8 CFR 1003.8, or as the Attorney General otherwise may provide by regulation, any fee relating to any EOIR proceeding may be paid to USCIS. Payment of a fee under this section does not constitute filing of the document with the Board or with the immigration court. DHS will provide the payer with a receipt for a fee and return any documents submitted with the fee relating to any immigration court proceeding.

(2) DHS–EOIR biometric services fee. Fees paid to and accepted by DHS relating to any immigration proceeding as provided in 8 CFR 1103.7(a) must include an additional $30 for DHS to collect, store, and use biometric information.

(3) Waiver of immigration court fees. An immigration judge may waive any fees prescribed under this chapter for cases under their jurisdiction to the extent provided in 8 CFR 1003.8, 1003.24, and 1103.7.

(b) USCIS fees. USCIS fees will be required as provided in 8 CFR part 106.

(c) Remittances. Remittances to the Board of Immigration Appeals must be made payable to the "United States Department of Justice," in accordance with 8 CFR 1003.8.

(d) Non-USCIS DHS immigration fees. The following fees are applicable to one or more of the immigration components of DHS:

(1) [Removed and reserved.]

(2) Petition for Approval of School for Attendance by Nonimmigrant Student (Form I–17).

(i) For filing a petition for school certification: $3,000 plus, a site visit fee of $655 for each location required to be listed on the form.

(ii) For filing a petition for school recertification: $1,250, plus a site visit fee of $655 for each new location required to be listed on the form.

(3) Form I–68. For application for issuance of the Canadian Border Boat Landing Permit under section 235 of the Act:

(i) $16.00; or

(ii) $32 for a family (applicant, spouse, and unmarried children under 21 years of age, and parents of either spouse).

(4) Form I–94. For issuance of Arrival/Departure Record at a land border port-of-entry: $6.00.

(5) Form I–94W. For issuance of Nonimmigrant Visa Waiver Arrival/Departure Form at a land border port-of-entry under section 217 of the Act: $6.00.

(6) Form I–246. For filing application for stay of deportation under 8 CFR part 243: $155.00. The application fee may be waived by DHS.

(7) Form I–823. For application to a PORTPASS program under section 286 of the Act:

(i) $25.00; or

(ii) $50.00 for a family (applicant, spouse, and minor children).

(iii) The application fee may be waived by DHS.

(iv) If fingerprints are required, the inspector will inform the applicant of the current Federal Bureau of Investigation fee for conducting fingerprint checks before accepting the application fee.

(v) The application fee (if not waived) and fingerprint fee must be paid to CBP before the application will be processed. The fingerprint fee may not be waived.

(vi) For replacement of PORTPASS documentation during the participation period: $25.00.

(vii) For the SENTRI program, see paragraph (d)(16) of this section.

(8) Fee Remittance for F, J, and M Nonimmigrants (Form I–901). The fee for Form I–901 is:

(i) For F and M students: $350.

(ii) For J–1 au pairs, camp counselors, and participants in a summer work or travel program: $35.

(iii) For all other J exchange visitors (except those participating in a program sponsored by the Federal Government): $220.

(iv) There is no Form I–901 fee for J exchange visitors in federally funded programs with a program identifier designation prefix that begins with G–1, G–2, G–3, or G–7.

(9) Special statistical tabulations. The DHS cost of the work involved.

(10) Monthly, semiannual, or annual "Passenger Travel Reports via Sea and Air" tables.

(i) For the years 1975 and before: $7.00.

(ii) For after 1975: Contact: U.S. Department of Transportation, Transportation Systems Center, Kendall Square, Cambridge, MA 02142.

(11) Request for Classification of a citizen of Canada to engage in professional business activities under section 214(e) of the Act (Chapter 16 of the North American Free Trade Agreement). $50.00.

(12) Request for authorization for parole of an alien into the United States. $65.00.

(13) Global Entry. For filing an application for Global Entry—$120. Minors under the age of 18 who apply to the Global Entry program concurrently with a parent or legal guardian, or whose parent or legal guardian is already a participant of Global Entry, are exempt from payment of the application fee.

(14) U.S. Asia-Pacific Economic Cooperation (APEC) Business Travel Card. Application fee: $70.

(15) Notice of Appeal or Motion (Form I–290B) filed with ICE SEVP. For a Form I–290B filed with the Student and Exchange Visitor Program (SEVP): $675.

(16) SENTRI program. For filing an application for the SENTRI program—$120. Minors under the age of 18 who apply to the SENTRI program concurrently with a parent or legal guardian, or whose parent or legal guardian is already a participant of SENTRI, are exempt from payment of the application fee. Registration of one vehicle for use in the SENTRI lanes is included in the $120 application fee and may be done during the initial application or renewal process If an applicant or participant wishes to register more than one vehicle for use in the SENTRI lanes, or the participant registers any vehicle after the initial application

or renewal process, that applicant or participant will be assessed an additional fee of $42 for each vehicle.

HISTORY:

[38 FR 35296, Dec. 27, 1973; 51 FR 8183, 39994, 1986; 52 FR 3, 2939, 16193, 19719, 1987.; 53 FR 43985, 1988; 54 FR 13, 29882, 48231, 13515, 47348, 48577, 51870, 1989.; 55 FR 12629, 20775, 29342, 1990; 56 FR 624, 21919, 22822, 31060, 12649, 23496, 23498, 32501, 49672, 50480, 1991.; 57 FR 39626, 5227, 6182, 34507, 1992; 57 FR 6460, as confirmed at 60 FR 66062, 66067, Dec. 21, 1995; 57 FR 11573, Apr. 16, 1992, as confirmed at 59 FR 1899, Jan. 13, 1994; 58 FR 30699, May 27, 1993, as confirmed at 60 FR 9774, Feb. 22, 1995; 58 FR 31148, June 1, 1993; 58 FR 58937, Nov. 5, 1993; 58 FR 69210, Dec. 30, 1993, as confirmed at 63 FR 1331, 1334, Jan. 9, 1998; 59 FR 26590, May 23, 1994; 59 FR 30518, June 14, 1994; 59 FR 51095, Oct. 7, 1994; 60 FR 21974, May 4, 1995; 60 FR 34090, June 30, 1995; 60 FR 37328, July 20, 1995; 60 FR 40068, Aug. 7, 1995; 60 FR 50386, 50388, Sept. 29, 1995, as confirmed at 61 FR 53830, 53831, Oct. 16, 1996; 61 FR 18900, 18909, Apr. 29, 1996; 61 FR 28003, 28013, June 4, 1996; 61 FR 35597, 35598, July 8, 1996; 61 FR 46373, 46374, Sept. 3, 1996, as corrected at 61 FR 47550, Sept. 9, 1996; 61 FR 53303, 53304, Oct. 11, 1996; 62 FR 10312, 10336, Mar. 6, 1997; 62 FR 39417, 39423, July 23, 1997; 62 FR 45148, 45149, Aug. 26, 1997; 63 FR 12979, 12985, 12986, Mar. 17, 1998; 63 FR 30105, 30108, June 3, 1998; 63 FR 43604, 43609, 43610, Aug. 14, 1998; 63 FR 63593, 63595, Nov. 16, 1998; 63 FR 65657, 65659, Nov. 30, 1998; 64 FR 27856, 27875, May 21, 1999; 64 FR 69883, 69888, Dec. 15, 1999; 65 FR 10678, 10684, Feb. 29, 2000; 65 FR 43528, 43531, July 13, 2000, withdrawn at 67 FR 61474, Oct. 1, 2002; 65 FR 67616, 67617, Nov. 13, 2000; 66 FR 29661, 29672, 29682, 29685, June 1, 2001, as confirmed at 67 FR 38341, 38350, June 4, 2002; 66 FR 49514, Sept. 28, 2001; 66 FR 65811, 65816, Dec. 21, 2001, 67 FR 4784, 4794, Jan. 31, 2002; 67 FR 60107, 60111, Sept. 25, 2002; 67 FR 71443, 71447, Dec. 2, 2002; 67 FR 76256, 76270, Dec. 11, 2002; 68 FR 3798, 3800, Jan. 24, 2003, as confirmed at 69 FR 20528, 20534, Apr. 15, 2004; 68 FR 8989, 8992, Feb. 27, 2003, as confirmed at 69 FR 20528, 20534, Apr. 15, 2004; 68 FR 43901, 43915, July 25, 2003; 69 FR 20528, 20534, Apr. 15, 2004; 69 FR 39814, 39824, July 1, 2004; 70 FR 50954, 50957, Aug. 29, 2005; 72 FR 29851, 29873, May 30, 2007; 72 FR 41888, 41890, Aug. 1, 2007; 72 FR 46142, 46143, Aug. 17, 2007; 72 FR 53014, 53035, Sept. 17, 2007, as corrected at 72 FR 54813, Sept. 27, 2007; 72 FR 56832, 56853, Oct. 4, 2007; 73 FR 28026, 28030, May 15, 2008; 73 FR 55683, 55698, Sept. 26, 2008; 73 FR 75540, 75557, Dec. 12, 2008; 74 FR 2824, Jan. 16, 2009; 74 FR 55094, 55108, Oct. 27, 2009, as confirmed and amended at 76 FR 55502, Sept. 7, 2011; 75 FR 58962, 58986, Sept. 24, 2010, as corrected at 75 FR 69851, Nov. 16, 2010; 75 FR 79264, 79275, Dec. 20, 2010; 76 FR 53764, 53781, Aug. 29, 2011, as corrected at 76 FR 73475, Nov. 29, 2011; 76 FR 69119, Nov. 8, 2011; 77 FR 5681, 5690, Feb. 6, 2012; 78 FR 536, 576, Jan. 3, 2013; 79 FR 27161, 27174, May 13, 2014, as confirmed at 81 FR 84403, 84415, Nov. 23, 2016; 81 FR 73292, 73328, Oct. 24, 2016; 82 FR 5238, 5286, Jan. 17, 2017; 82 FR 31887, July 11, 2017; 83 FR 44449, 44450, Aug. 31, 2018; 84 FR 23930, 23978, May 23, 2019; 84 FR 41292, 41500, Aug. 14, 2019; 84 FR 58303, 58304, Oct. 31, 2019; 84 FR 60307, 60316, Nov. 8, 2019; 85 FR 29264, 29309, May. 14, 2020; 85 FR 46788, 46914, Aug. 3, 2020; 87 FR 18967, 18980, Apr. 1, 2022; 87 FR 41027, 41029, July 11, 2022; 89 FR 6194, 6384, Jan. 31, 2024; 89 FR 22607, 22628, Apr. 2, 2024]

§ 103.8 Service of decisions and other notices.

This section states authorized means of service by the Service on parties and on attorneys and other interested persons of notices, decisions, and other papers (except warrants and subpoenas) in administrative proceedings before Service officers as provided in this chapter.

(a) Types of service—

(1) Routine service.

(i) Routine service consists of mailing the notice by ordinary mail addressed to the affected party and his or her attorney or representative of record at his or her last known address, or

(ii) If so requested by a party, advising the party of such notice by electronic mail and posting the decision to the party's USCIS account.

(2) Personal service. Personal service, which shall be performed by a Government employee, consists of any of the following, without priority or preference:

(i) Delivery of a copy personally;

(ii) Delivery of a copy at a person's dwelling house or usual place of abode by leaving it with some person of suitable age and discretion;

(iii) Delivery of a copy at the office of an attorney or other person, including a corporation, by leaving it with a person in charge;

(iv) Mailing a copy by certified or registered mail, return receipt requested, addressed to a person at his last known address; or

(v) If so requested by a party, advising the party by electronic mail and posting the decision to the party's USCIS account.

(3) Personal service involving notices of intention to fine. In addition to any of the methods of personal service listed in paragraph (a)(2) of this section, personal service of Form I-79, Notice of Intention to Fine, may also consist of delivery of the Form I-79 by a commercial delivery service at the carrier's address on file with the National Fines Office, the address listed on the Form I-849, Record for Notice of Intent to Fine, or to the office of the attorney or agent representing the carrier, provided that such a commercial delivery service requires the addressee or other responsible party accepting the package to sign for the package upon receipt.

(b) Effect of service by mail. Whenever a person has the right or is required to do some act within a prescribed period after the service of a notice upon him and the notice is served by mail, 3 days shall be added to the prescribed period. Service by mail is complete upon mailing.

(c) **When personal service required —**

(1) Generally. In any proceeding which is initiated by the Service, with proposed adverse effect, service of the initiating notice and of notice of any decision by a Service officer shall be accomplished by personal service, except as provided in section 239 of the Act.

(2) Persons confined, minors, and incompetents —

(i) Persons confined. If a person is confined in a penal or mental institution or hospital and is competent to understand the nature of the proceedings initiated against him, service shall be made both upon him and upon the person in charge of the institution or the hospital. If the confined person is not competent to understand, service shall be made only on the person in charge of the institution or hospital in which he is confined, such service being deemed service on the confined person.

(ii) Incompetents and minors. In case of mental incompetency, whether or not confined in an institution, and in the case of a minor under 14 years of age, service shall be made upon the person with whom the incompetent or the minor resides; whenever possible, service shall also be made on the near relative, guardian, committee, or friend.

(d) When personal service not required. Service of other types of papers in proceedings described in paragraph (c) of this section, and service of any type of papers in any other proceedings, may be accomplished either by routine service or by personal service.

HISTORY:

[37 FR 11470, June 8, 1972, as amended at 39 FR 23247, June 27, 1974; 62 FR 10312, 10336, Mar. 6, 1997; 64 FR 17943, 17944, Apr. 13, 1999; redesignated and amended at 76 FR 53764, 53781, Aug. 29, 2011]

§ 103.9 Request for further action on an approved benefit request.

(a) Filing a request. A person may request further action on an approved benefit request as prescribed by the form instructions. Requests for further action may be submitted with the original benefit request or following the approval of such benefit.

(b) Processing. The request will be approved if the requester has demonstrated eligibility for the requested action. There is no appeal from the denial of such request.

HISTORY:

[59 FR 1463, Jan. 11, 1994; redesignated and revised at 76 FR 53764, 53781, Aug. 29, 2011]

§ 103.10 Precedent decisions.

(a) Proceedings before the immigration judges, the Board of Immigration Appeals and the Attorney General are governed by part 1003 of 8 CFR chapter V.

(b) Decisions as precedents. Except as Board decisions may be modified or overruled by the Board or the Attorney General, decisions of the Board, and decisions of the Attorney General, shall be binding on all officers and employees of the Department of Homeland Security or immigration judges in the administration of the immigration laws of the United States. By majority vote of the permanent Board members, selected decisions of the Board rendered by a three-member panel or by the Board en banc may be designated to serve as precedents in all proceedings involving the same issue or issues. Selected decisions designated by the Board, decisions of the Attorney General, and decisions of the Secretary of Homeland Security to the extent authorized in paragraph (i) of this section, shall serve as precedents in all proceedings involving the same issue or issues.

(c) Referral of cases to the Attorney General.

(1) The Board shall refer to the Attorney General for review of its decision all cases which:

(i) The Attorney General directs the Board to refer to him.

(ii) The Chairman or a majority of the Board believes should be referred to the Attorney General for review.

(iii) The Secretary of Homeland Security, or specific officials of the Department of Homeland Security designated by the Secretary with the concurrence of the Attorney General, refers to the Attorney General for review.

(2) In any case the Attorney General decides, the Attorney General's decision shall be stated in writing and shall be transmitted to the Board or Secretary, as appropriate, for transmittal and service as provided in paragraph (c) of this section or 8 CFR 1003.1(h)(2).

(d) Publication of Secretary's precedent decisions. The Secretary of Homeland Security, or specific officials of the Department of Homeland Security designated by the Secretary with the concurrence of the Attorney General, may file with the Attorney General Service precedent decisions as set forth in § 103.3(c).

(e) Precedent decisions. Bound volumes of designated precedent decisions, entitled "Administrative Decisions under Immigration and Nationality Laws of the United States," may be purchased from the Superintendent of Documents, U.S. Government Printing Office. Prior to publication in volume form, current precedent decisions are available from the Department of Justice, Executive Office for Immigration Review's Virtual Law Library at: http://www.justice.gov/eoir/vll/libindex-.html.

(f) [Reserved]

HISTORY:

[68 FR 9824, 9832, Feb. 28, 2003; redesignated and amended at 76 FR 53764, 53781, Aug. 29, 2011]

§ 103.11 [This section was removed. See 76 FR 53764, 53781, Aug. 29, 2011.]

[NO TEXT IN ORIGINAL]

HISTORY:

[58 FR 31149, June 1, 1993; 76 FR 53764, 53781, Aug. 29, 2011]

AUTHORITY:

(5 U.S.C. 301, 552, 552a; 8 U.S.C. 1101, 1103, 1304, 1356; 31 U.S.C. 9701; 48 U.S.C. 1806; Public Law 107-296, 116 Stat. 2135 (6 U.S.C. 1 et seq.), E.O. 12356, 47 FR 14874, 15557, 3 CFR, 1982 Comp., p. 166; 8 CFR part 2.)

§ 103.12 [This section was removed. See 76 FR 53764, 53781, Aug. 29, 2011.]

[NO TEXT IN ORIGINAL]

HISTORY:

[61 FR 47039, 47041, Sept. 6, 1996; 63 FR 63593, 63595, Nov. 16, 1998; 64 FR 8478, 8487, Feb. 19, 1999; 65 FR 82254, 82255, Dec. 28, 2000; 66 FR 7863, Jan. 26, 2001; 76 FR 53764, 53781, Aug. 29, 2011]

AUTHORITY:

(5 U.S.C. 301, 552, 552a; 8 U.S.C. 1101, 1103, 1304, 1356; 31 U.S.C. 9701; 48 U.S.C. 1806; Public Law 107-296, 116 Stat. 2135 (6 U.S.C. 1 et seq.), E.O. 12356, 47 FR 14874, 15557, 3 CFR, 1982 Comp., p. 166; 8 CFR part 2.)

Subpart B Biometric Requirements

§ 103.16 Collection, use and storage of biometric information.

(a) Use of biometric information. An individual may be required to submit biometric information by law, regulation, Federal Register notice or the form instructions applicable to the request type or if required in accordance with 8 CFR 103.2(b)(9). DHS may collect and store for present or future use, by electronic or other means, the biometric information submitted by an individual. DHS may use this biometric information to conduct background and security checks, adjudicate immigration and naturalization benefits, and perform other functions related to administering and enforcing the immigration and naturalization laws.

(b) Individuals residing abroad. An individual who is required to provide biometric information and who is residing outside of the United States must report to a DHS-designated location to have his or her biometric information collected, whether by electronic or non-electronic means.

HISTORY:

[76 FR 53764, 53782, Aug. 29, 2011; 81 FR 73292, 73331, Oct. 24, 2016]

§ 103.17 Biometric service fee.

DHS may charge a fee to collect biometric information, to provide biometric collection services, to conduct required national security and criminal history background checks, to verify an individual's identity, and to store and maintain this biometric information for reuse to support other benefit requests. When a biometric services fee is required, USCIS may reject a benefit request submitted without the correct biometric services fee.

HISTORY:

[76 FR 53764, 53782, Aug. 29, 2011; 81 FR 73292, 73332, Oct. 24, 2016; 85 FR 46788, 46915, Aug 3, 2020; 89 FR 6194, 6385, Jan. 31, 2024]

§ 103.20 [This section was removed and reserved. See 76 FR 53764, 53782, Aug. 29, 2011.]

[NO TEXT IN ORIGINAL]

HISTORY:

[40 FR 44481, Sept. 26, 1975, as amended at 48 FR 49652, Oct. 27, 1983; 58 FR 31149, June 1, 1993; 76 FR 53764, 53782, Aug. 29, 2011, as corrected at 76 FR 73475, Nov. 29, 2011]

AUTHORITY:

(5 U.S.C. 301, 552, 552a; 8 U.S.C. 1101, 1103, 1304, 1356; 31 U.S.C. 9701; 48 U.S.C. 1806; Public Law 107-296, 116 Stat. 2135 (6 U.S.C. 1 et seq.), E.O. 12356, 47 FR 14874, 15557, 3 CFR, 1982 Comp., p. 166; 8 CFR part 2.)

§ 103.21 [This section was removed and reserved. See 76 FR 53764, 53782, Aug. 29, 2011.]

[NO TEXT IN ORIGINAL]

HISTORY:

[40 FR 44481, Sept. 26, 1975; 40 FR 46092, Oct. 6, 1975, as amended at 42 FR 33025, June 29, 1977; 48 FR 49653, Oct. 27, 1983; 58 FR 31149, June 1, 1993; 63 FR 70313, 70315, Dec. 21, 1998; 76 FR 53764, 53782, Aug. 29, 2011, as corrected at 76 FR 73475, Nov. 29, 2011]

AUTHORITY:

(5 U.S.C. 301, 552, 552a; 8 U.S.C. 1101, 1103, 1304, 1356; 31 U.S.C. 9701; 48 U.S.C. 1806; Public Law 107-296, 116 Stat. 2135 (6 U.S.C. 1 et seq.), E.O. 12356, 47 FR 14874, 15557, 3 CFR, 1982 Comp., p. 166; 8 CFR part 2.)

§ 103.22 [This section was removed and reserved. See 76 FR 53764, 53782, Aug. 29, 2011.]

[NO TEXT IN ORIGINAL]

HISTORY:

[40 FR 44481, Sept. 26, 1975, as amended at 48 FR 49653, Oct. 27, 1983; 58 FR 31149, June 1, 1993; 76 FR 53764, 53782, Aug. 29, 2011, as corrected at 76 FR 73475, Nov. 29, 2011]

AUTHORITY:

(5 U.S.C. 301, 552, 552a; 8 U.S.C. 1101, 1103, 1304, 1356; 31 U.S.C. 9701; 48 U.S.C. 1806; Public Law 107-296, 116 Stat. 2135 (6 U.S.C. 1 et seq.), E.O. 12356, 47 FR 14874, 15557, 3 CFR, 1982 Comp., p. 166; 8 CFR part 2.)

§ 103.23 [This section was removed and reserved. See 76 FR 53764, 53782, Aug. 29, 2011.]

[NO TEXT IN ORIGINAL]

HISTORY:

[40 FR 44481, Sept. 26, 1975, as amended at 48 FR 49653, Oct. 27, 1983; 58 FR 31149, 31150, June 1, 1993; 76 FR 53764, 53782, Aug. 29, 2011, as corrected at 76 FR 73475, Nov. 29, 2011]

AUTHORITY:

(5 U.S.C. 301, 552, 552a; 8 U.S.C. 1101, 1103, 1304, 1356; 31 U.S.C. 9701; 48 U.S.C. 1806; Public Law 107-296, 116 Stat. 2135 (6 U.S.C. 1 et seq.), E.O. 12356, 47 FR 14874, 15557, 3 CFR, 1982 Comp., p. 166; 8 CFR part 2.)

§ 103.24 [This section was removed and reserved. See 76 FR 53764, 53782, Aug. 29, 2011.]

[NO TEXT IN ORIGINAL]

HISTORY:

[40 FR 44481, Sept. 26, 1975; 58 FR 31150, June 1, 1993; 76 FR 53764, 53782, Aug. 29, 2011, as corrected at 76 FR 73475, Nov. 29, 2011]

AUTHORITY:

(5 U.S.C. 301, 552, 552a; 8 U.S.C. 1101, 1103, 1304, 1356; 31 U.S.C. 9701; 48 U.S.C. 1806; Public Law 107-296, 116 Stat. 2135 (6 U.S.C. 1 et seq.), E.O. 12356, 47 FR 14874, 15557, 3 CFR, 1982 Comp., p. 166; 8 CFR part 2.)

§ 103.25 [This section was removed and reserved. See 76 FR 53764, 53782, Aug. 29, 2011.]

[NO TEXT IN ORIGINAL.]

HISTORY:

[40 FR 44481, Sept. 26, 1975; 58 FR 31150, June 1, 1993; 76 FR 53764, 53782, Aug. 29, 2011, as corrected at 76 FR 73475, Nov. 29, 2011]

AUTHORITY:

(5 U.S.C. 301, 552, 552a; 8 U.S.C. 1101, 1103, 1304, 1356; 31 U.S.C. 9701; 48 U.S.C. 1806; Public Law 107-296, 116 Stat. 2135 (6 U.S.C. 1 et seq.), E.O. 12356, 47 FR 14874, 15557, 3 CFR, 1982 Comp., p. 166; 8 CFR part 2.)

§ 103.26 [This section was removed and reserved. See 76 FR 53764, 53782, Aug. 29, 2011.]

[NO TEXT IN ORIGINAL.]

HISTORY:

[40 FR 44481, Sept. 26, 1975; 58 FR 31150, June 1, 1993; 76 FR 53764, 53782, Aug. 29, 2011, as corrected at 76 FR 73475, Nov. 29, 2011]

AUTHORITY:

(5 U.S.C. 301, 552, 552a; 8 U.S.C. 1101, 1103, 1304, 1356; 31 U.S.C. 9701; 48 U.S.C. 1806; Public Law 107-296, 116 Stat. 2135 (6 U.S.C. 1 et seq.), E.O. 12356, 47 FR 14874, 15557, 3 CFR, 1982 Comp., p. 166; 8 CFR part 2.)

§ 103.27 [This section was removed and reserved. See 76 FR 53764, 53782, Aug. 29, 2011.]

[NO TEXT IN ORIGINAL]

HISTORY:

[40 FR 44481, Sept. 26, 1975; 58 FR 31150, June 1, 1993; 76 FR 53764, 53782, Aug. 29, 2011, as corrected at 76 FR 73475, Nov. 29, 2011]

AUTHORITY:

(5 U.S.C. 301, 552, 552a; 8 U.S.C. 1101, 1103, 1304, 1356; 31 U.S.C. 9701; 48 U.S.C. 1806; Public Law 107-296, 116 Stat. 2135 (6 U.S.C. 1 et seq.), E.O. 12356, 47 FR 14874, 15557, 3 CFR, 1982 Comp., p. 166; 8 CFR part 2.)

§ 103.28 [This section was removed and reserved. See 76 FR 53764, 53782, Aug. 29, 2011.]

[NO TEXT IN ORIGINAL]

HISTORY:

[40 FR 44481, Sept. 26, 1975, as amended at 48 FR 49653, Oct. 27, 1983; 48 FR 51431, Nov. 9, 1983; 58 FR 31150, June 1, 1993; 76 FR 53764, 53782, Aug. 29, 2011, as corrected at 76 FR 73475, Nov. 29, 2011]

AUTHORITY:

(5 U.S.C. 301, 552, 552a; 8 U.S.C. 1101, 1103, 1304, 1356; 31 U.S.C. 9701; 48 U.S.C. 1806; Public Law 107-296, 116 Stat. 2135 (6 U.S.C. 1 et seq.), E.O. 12356, 47 FR 14874, 15557, 3 CFR, 1982 Comp., p. 166; 8 CFR part 2.)

§ 103.29 [This section was removed and reserved. See 76 FR 53764, 53782, Aug. 29, 2011.]

[NO TEXT IN ORIGINAL]

HISTORY:

[40 FR 44481, Sept. 26, 1975; 76 FR 53764, 53782, Aug. 29, 2011, as corrected at 76 FR 73475, Nov. 29, 2011]

AUTHORITY:

(5 U.S.C. 301, 552, 552a; 8 U.S.C. 1101, 1103, 1304, 1356; 31 U.S.C. 9701; 48 U.S.C. 1806; Public Law 107-296, 116 Stat. 2135 (6 U.S.C. 1 et seq.), E.O. 12356, 47 FR 14874, 15557, 3 CFR, 1982 Comp., p. 166; 8 CFR part 2.)

§ 103.30 [This section was removed and reserved. See 76 FR 53764, 53782, Aug. 29, 2011.]

[NO TEXT IN ORIGINAL]

HISTORY:

[40 FR 44481, Sept. 26, 1975, as amended at 48 FR 49653, Oct. 27, 1983, 58 FR 31150, June 1, 1993; 76 FR 53764, 53782, Aug. 29, 2011, as corrected at 76 FR 73475, Nov. 29, 2011]

AUTHORITY:

(5 U.S.C. 301, 552, 552a; 8 U.S.C. 1101, 1103, 1304, 1356; 31 U.S.C. 9701; 48 U.S.C. 1806; Public Law 107-296, 116 Stat. 2135 (6 U.S.C. 1 et seq.), E.O. 12356, 47 FR 14874, 15557, 3 CFR, 1982 Comp., p. 166; 8 CFR part 2.)

§ 103.31 [This section was removed and reserved. See 76 FR 53764, 53782, Aug. 29, 2011.]

[NO TEXT IN ORIGINAL]

HISTORY:

[40 FR 44481, Sept. 26, 1975; 76 FR 53764, 53782, Aug. 29, 2011, as corrected at 76 FR 73475, Nov. 29, 2011]

AUTHORITY:

(5 U.S.C. 301, 552, 552a; 8 U.S.C. 1101, 1103, 1304, 1356; 31 U.S.C. 9701; 48 U.S.C. 1806; Public Law 107-296, 116 Stat. 2135 (6 U.S.C. 1 et seq.), E.O. 12356, 47 FR 14874, 15557, 3 CFR, 1982 Comp., p. 166; 8 CFR part 2.)

§ 103.32 [This section was removed and reserved. See 76 FR 53764, 53782, Aug. 29, 2011.]

[NO TEXT IN ORIGINAL]

HISTORY:

[40 FR 44481, Sept. 26, 1975; 76 FR 53764, 53782, Aug. 29, 2011, as corrected at 76 FR 73475, Nov. 29, 2011]

AUTHORITY:

(5 U.S.C. 301, 552, 552a; 8 U.S.C. 1101, 1103, 1304, 1356; 31 U.S.C. 9701; 48 U.S.C. 1806; Public Law 107-296, 116 Stat. 2135 (6 U.S.C. 1 et seq.), E.O. 12356, 47 FR 14874, 15557, 3 CFR, 1982 Comp., p. 166; 8 CFR part 2.)

§ 103.33 [This section was removed and reserved. See 76 FR 53764, 53782, Aug. 29, 2011.]

[NO TEXT IN ORIGINAL]

HISTORY:

[40 FR 44481, Sept. 26, 1975; 58 FR 31150, June 1, 1993; 76 FR 53764, 53782, Aug. 29, 2011, as corrected at 76 FR 73475, Nov. 29, 2011]

AUTHORITY:

(5 U.S.C. 301, 552, 552a; 8 U.S.C. 1101, 1103, 1304, 1356; 31 U.S.C. 9701; 48 U.S.C. 1806; Public Law 107-296, 116 Stat. 2135 (6 U.S.C. 1 et seq.), E.O. 12356, 47 FR 14874, 15557, 3 CFR, 1982 Comp., p. 166; 8 CFR part 2.)

§ 103.34 [This section was removed and reserved. See 76 FR 53764, 53782, Aug. 29, 2011.]

[NO TEXT IN ORIGINAL]

HISTORY:

[40 FR 44481, Sept. 26, 1975; 76 FR 53764, 53782, Aug. 29, 2011, as corrected at 76 FR 73475, Nov. 29, 2011]

AUTHORITY:

(5 U.S.C. 301, 552, 552a; 8 U.S.C. 1101, 1103, 1304, 1356; 31 U.S.C. 9701; 48 U.S.C. 1806; Public Law 107-296, 116 Stat. 2135 (6 U.S.C. 1 et seq.), E.O. 12356, 47 FR 14874, 15557, 3 CFR, 1982 Comp., p. 166; 8 CFR part 2.)

§ 103.35 [This section was removed and reserved. See 76 FR 53764, 53782, Aug. 29, 2011.]

[NO TEXT IN ORIGINAL]

HISTORY:

[40 FR 44481, Sept. 26, 1975; 58 FR 31150, June 1, 1993; 76 FR 53764, 53782, Aug. 29, 2011, as corrected at 76 FR 73475, Nov. 29, 2011]

AUTHORITY:

(5 U.S.C. 301, 552, 552a; 8 U.S.C. 1101, 1103, 1304, 1356; 31 U.S.C. 9701; 48 U.S.C. 1806; Public Law 107-296, 116 Stat. 2135 (6 U.S.C. 1 et seq.), E.O. 12356, 47 FR 14874, 15557, 3 CFR, 1982 Comp., p. 166; 8 CFR part 2.)

§ 103.36 [This section was removed and reserved. See 76 FR 53764, 53782, Aug. 29, 2011.]

[NO TEXT IN ORIGINAL]

HISTORY:

[40 FR 44481, Sept. 26, 1975; 58 FR 31150, June 1, 1993; 76 FR 53764, 53782, Aug. 29, 2011, as corrected at 76 FR 73475, Nov. 29, 2011]

AUTHORITY:

(5 U.S.C. 301, 552, 552a; 8 U.S.C. 1101, 1103, 1304, 1356; 31 U.S.C. 9701; 48 U.S.C. 1806; Public Law 107-296, 116 Stat. 2135 (6 U.S.C. 1 et seq.), E.O. 12356, 47 FR 14874, 15557, 3 CFR, 1982 Comp., p. 166; 8 CFR part 2.)

§ 103.37 [This section was redesignated as § 103.10. See 76 FR 53764, 53781, Aug. 29, 2011.]

[NO TEXT IN ORIGINAL]

HISTORY:

[68 FR 9824, 9832, Feb. 28, 2003; redesignated at 76 FR 53764, 53781, Aug. 29, 2011.

AUTHORITY:

(5 U.S.C. 301, 552, 552a; 8 U.S.C. 1101, 1103, 1304, 1356; 31 U.S.C. 9701; 48 U.S.C. 1806; Public Law 107-296, 116 Stat. 2135 (6 U.S.C. 1 et seq.), E.O. 12356, 47 FR 14874, 15557, 3 CFR, 1982 Comp., p. 166; 8 CFR part 2.)

Subpart D

Availability of Records

§ 103.38 Genealogy Program.

(a) Purpose. The Department of Homeland Security, U.S. Citizenship and Immigration Services Genealogy Program is a fee-for-service program designed to provide genealogical and historical records and reference services to genealogists, historians, and others seeking documents maintained within the historical record systems.

(b) Scope and limitations. Sections 103.38 through 103.41 comprise the regulations of the Genealogy Program. These regulations apply only to searches for and retrieval of records from the file series described as historical records in 8 CFR 103.39. These regulations set forth the procedures by which individuals may request searches for historical records and, if responsive records are located, obtain copies of those records.

HISTORY:

[73 FR 28026, 28030, May 15, 2008]

§ 103.39 Historical Records.

Historical Records are files, forms, and documents now located within the following records series:

(a) Naturalization Certificate Files (C-Files), from September 27, 1906 to April 1, 1956. Copies of records relating to all U.S. naturalizations in Federal, State, county, or municipal courts, overseas military naturalizations, replacement of old law naturalization certificates, and the issuance of Certificates of Citizenship in derivative, repatriation, and resumption cases. The majority of C-Files exist only on microfilm. Standard C-Files generally contain at least one application form (Declaration of Intention and/or Petition for Naturalization, or other application) and a duplicate certificate of naturalization or certificate of citizenship. Many files contain additional documents, including correspondence, affidavits, or other records. Only C-Files dating from 1929 onward include photographs.

(b) Microfilmed Alien Registration Forms, from August 1, 1940 to March 31, 1944. Microfilmed copies of 5.5 million Alien Registration Forms (Form AR-2) completed by all aliens age 14 and older, residing in or entering the United States between August 1, 1940 and March 31, 1944. The two-page form called for the following information: Name; name at arrival; other names used; street address; post-office address; date of birth; place of birth; citizenship; sex; marital status; race; height; weight; hair and eye color; date, place, vessel, and class of admission of last arrival in United States; date of first arrival in United States; number of years in United States; usual occupation; present occupation; name, address, and business of present employer; membership in clubs, organizations, or societies; dates and nature of military or naval service; whether citizenship papers filed, and if so date, place, and court for declaration or petition; number of relatives living in the United States; arrest record, including date, place, and disposition of each arrest; whether or not affiliated with a foreign government; signature; and fingerprint.

(c) Visa Files, from July 1, 1924 to March 31, 1944. Original arrival records of immigrants admitted for permanent residence under provisions of the Immigration Act of 1924. Visa forms contain all information normally found on a ship passenger list of the period, as well as the immigrant's places of residence for 5 years prior to emigration, names of both the immigrant's parents, and other data. In most cases, birth records or affidavits are attached to the visa, and in some cases, marriage, military, or police records may also be attached to the visa.

(d) Registry Files, from March 2, 1929 to March 31, 1944. Original records documenting the creation of immigrant arrival records for persons who entered the United States prior to July 1, 1924, and for whom no arrival record could later be found. Most files also include documents supporting the immigrant's claims regarding arrival and residence (e.g., proofs of residence, receipts, and employment records).

(e) Alien-Files numbered below 8 million (A8000000), and documents therein dated prior to May 1, 1951. Individual alien case files (A-files) became the official file for all immigration records created or consolidated after April 1, 1944. The United States issued A-numbers ranging up to approximately 6 million to aliens and immigrants who were within or entered the United States between 1940 and 1945. The United States entered the 6 million and 7 million series of A-numbers between circa 1944 and May 1, 1951. Any documents dated after May 1, 1951, though found in an A-File numbered below 8 million, will remain subject to FOIA/PA restrictions.

HISTORY:

[73 FR 28026, 28030, May 15, 2008]

§ 103.40 Genealogical Research Requests.

(a) Nature of requests. Genealogy requests are requests for searches and/or copies of historical records relating to a deceased person, usually for genealogy and family history research purposes.

(b) Forms. USCIS provides on its website at https://www.uscis.gov/records/genealogy the required forms in electronic versions: Genealogy Index Search Request or Genealogy Records Request.

(c) Required information. Genealogical research requests may be submitted to request one or more separate records relating to an individual. A separate request must be submitted for everyone searched. All requests for records or index searches must include the individual's:

(1) Full name (including variant spellings of the name and/or aliases, if any).

(2) Date of birth, at least as specific as a year.

(3) Place of birth, at least as specific as a country and the country name at the time of the individual's immigration or naturalization if known.

(d) Optional information. To better ensure a successful search, a genealogical research request may include everyone's:

(1) Date of arrival in the United States.

(2) Residence address at time of naturalization.

(3) Names of parents, spouse, and children if applicable and available.

(e) Additional information required to retrieve records. For a Genealogy Records Request, requests for copies of historical records or files must identify the record by number or other specific data used by the Genealogy Program Office to retrieve the record as follows:

(1) C-Files must be identified by a naturalization certificate number.

(2) Forms AR–2 and A-Files numbered below 8 million must be identified by Alien Registration Number.

(3) Visa Files must be identified by the Visa File Number. Registry Files must be identified by the Registry File Number (for example, R–12345).

(f) Information required for release of records.

(1) Documentary evidence must be attached to a Genealogy Records Request or submitted in accordance with the instructions on the Genealogy Records Request form.

(2) Search subjects will be presumed deceased if their birth dates are more than 100 years before the date of the request. In other cases, the subject is presumed to be living until the requestor establishes to the satisfaction of USCIS that the subject is deceased.

(3) Documentary evidence of the subject's death is required (including but not limited to death records, published obituaries or eulogies, published death notices, church or bible records, photographs of gravestones, and/or copies of official documents relating to payment of death benefits).

(g) Index search. Requestors who are unsure whether USCIS has any record of their ancestor, or who suspect a record exists but cannot identify that record by number, may submit a request for index search. An index search will determine the existence of responsive historical records. If no record is found, USCIS will notify the requestor accordingly. If records are found, USCIS will give the requestor electronic copies of records stored in digital format for no additional fee. For records found that are stored in paper format, USCIS will give the requestor the search results, including the type of record found and the file number or other information identifying the record. The requestor can use index search results to submit a Genealogy Records Request.

(h) Processing of paper record copy requests. This service is designed for requestors who can identify a specific record or file to be retrieved, copied, reviewed, and released. Requestors may identify one or more files in a single request.

HISTORY:

[73 FR 28026, 28031, May 15, 2008; 85 FR 46788, 46915, Aug. 3, 2020; 89 FR 6194, 6385, Jan. 31, 2024]

§ 103.41 Genealogy request fees. [This section was removed and reserved, effective October 2, 2020. See 85 FR 46788, 46915, Aug. 3, 2020.]

§ 103.42 Rules relating to the Freedom of Information Act (FOIA) and the Privacy Act.

Immigration-related regulations relating to FOIA and the Privacy Act are located in 6 CFR part 5.

HISTORY:

[76 FR 53764, 53782, Aug. 29, 2011]

PART 106

USCIS FEE SCHEDULE

AUTHORITY:
AUTHORITY NOTE APPLICABLE TO ENTIRE PART:

8 U.S.C. 1101, 1103, 1254a, 1254b, 1304, 1356; Pub. L. 107–609; 48 U.S.C. 1806; Pub. L. 107–296, 116 Stat. 2135 (6 U.S.C. 101 note); Pub. L. 115–218, 132 Stat. 1547; Pub. L. 116–159, 134 Stat. 709.

§ 106.1 Fee requirements.

(a) General. Fees must be submitted with any USCIS request in the amount and subject to the conditions provided in this part and remitted in the manner prescribed in the relevant form instructions, on the USCIS website, or in a Federal Register document. The fees established in this part are associated with the benefit, the adjudication, or the type of request and not solely determined by the form number listed in § 106.2.

(b) Remittance source and method. Fees must be remitted from a bank or other institution located in the United States and payable in U.S. currency. The fee must be paid using the method that USCIS prescribes for the request, office, filing method, or filing location. USCIS will provide at least a 30-day public notice before amending the payment method required for a fee.

(c) Dishonored payments. If a remittance in payment of a fee or any other matter is not honored by the bank or financial institution on which it is drawn:

(1) The provisions of 8 CFR 103.2(a)(7)(ii) apply, no receipt will be issued, and if a receipt was issued, it is void and the benefit request loses its receipt date; and

(2) If the benefit request was approved, the approval may be revoked upon notice, rescinded, or canceled subject to statutory and regulatory requirements applicable to the immigration benefit request. If the approved benefit request requires multiple fees, this paragraph (c) would apply if any fee submitted is not honored, including a fee to request premium processing under § 106.4. Other fees that were paid for a benefit request that is revoked upon notice under this paragraph (c) will be retained and not refunded. A revocation of an approval because the fee submitted is not honored may be appealed in accordance with 8 CFR 103.3, the applicable form instructions, and other statutes or regulations that may apply.

(d) Expired payments. DHS is not responsible for financial instruments that expire before they are deposited. USCIS may reject any filing for which required payment cannot be processed due to expiration of the financial instrument.

(e) Credit and debit card disputes. Fees paid to USCIS using a credit or debit card are not subject to dispute, chargeback, forced refund, or return to the cardholder for any reason except at the discretion of USCIS.

(f) Definitions. For the purposes of this part, the term:

(1) Small employer means a firm or individual that has 25 or fewer full-time equivalent employees in the United States, including any affiliates and subsidiaries.

(2) Nonprofit means not-for-profit primary or secondary educational institutions, or institutions of higher education, as defined in section 101(a) of the Higher Education Act of 1965, 20 U.S.C. 1001(a); organizations organized as tax exempt under the Internal Revenue Code of 1986, section 501(c)(3), 26 U.S.C. 501(c)(3); or governmental research organizations as defined under 8 CFR 214.2(h)(19)(iii)(C).

(3) Means tested benefit means, as determined by USCIS, a public benefit where the agency granting the benefit considers income and resources. Means-tested benefits may be federally, state, or locally funded. In general, for a benefit that was granted based on income, USCIS considers it a means-tested benefit.

(4) Federal Poverty Guidelines means the poverty guidelines updated periodically in the Federal Register by the U.S. Department of Health and Human Services under the authority of 42 U.S.C. 9902(2).

(g) Online filing discount. Unless otherwise provided in this part, the fee for forms filed online with USCIS, using the electronic system prescribed by USCIS, will be an amount that is $50 lower than the fee prescribed in § 106.2.

HISTORY:

[85 FR 46788, 46916, Aug. 3, 2020; 89 FR 6194, 6386, Jan. 31, 2024, as corrected at 89 FR 20101, Mar. 21, 2024]

§ 106.2 Fees

(a) I Forms—

(1) Application to Replace Permanent Resident Card, Form I–90. For filing an application for a Permanent Resident Card, Form I–551, to replace an obsolete card or to replace one lost, mutilated, or destroyed, or for a change in name $465.

(i) If the applicant was issued a card but never received it: No fee.

(ii) If the applicant's card was issued with incorrect information because of DHS error and the applicant is filing for a replacement: No fee.

(iii) If the applicant has reached their 14th birthday and their existing card will expire after their 16th birthday: No fee.

(2) Application for Replacement/Initial Nonimmigrant Arrival-Departure Document, Form I–102. For filing an application for Arrival/Departure Record Form I–94, or Crewman's Landing Permit Form I–95, to replace one lost, mutilated, or destroyed: $560.

(i) For nonimmigrant member of the U.S. armed forces: No fee for initial filing;

(ii) For a nonimmigrant member of the North Atlantic Treaty Organization (NATO) armed forces or civil component: No fee for initial filing;

(iii) For nonimmigrant member of the Partnership for Peace military program under the Status of Forces Agreement (SOFA): No fee for initial filing; and

(iv) For replacement for DHS error: No fee.

(3) Petition or Application for a Nonimmigrant Worker, Form I–129. For filing a petition or application for a nonimmigrant worker:

(i) Petition for H–1B Nonimmigrant Worker or H–1B1 Free Trade Nonimmigrant Worker: $780. For small employers and nonprofits: $460.

(ii) Petition for H–2A Nonimmigrant Worker with 1 to 25 named beneficiaries: $1,090.

(iii) Petition for H–2A Nonimmigrant Worker with only unnamed beneficiaries: $530. For small employers and nonprofits: $460.

(iv) Petition for H–2B Nonimmigrant Worker with 1 to 25 named beneficiaries: $1,080.

(v) Petition for H–2B Nonimmigrant Worker with only unnamed beneficiaries: $580. For small employers and nonprofits: $460.

(vi) Petition for L Nonimmigrant Worker: $1,385.

(vii) Petition for O Nonimmigrant Worker with 1 to 25 named beneficiaries: $1,055.

(viii) Petition or Application for E, H–3, P, Q, R, or TN Nonimmigrant Worker with 1 to 25 named beneficiaries: $1,015.

(ix) For small employers and nonprofits as defined in § 106.1(f), the fees in paragraphs (a)(3)(ii), (a)(3)(iv), (a)(3)(vi), (a)(3)(vii), and (a)(3)(viii) of this section will be one-half the amount in those paragraphs rounded to the nearest $5 increment.

(x) Additional fees in paragraph (c) of this section may apply.

(xi) The online filing discount in § 106.1(g) does not apply to the fee for small employers and nonprofits in paragraphs (a)(3)(i), (a)(3)(iii), (a)(3)(v), and (a)(3)(ix) of this section."

(4) Petition for a CNMI-Only Nonimmigrant Transitional Worker, Form I–129CW.

(i) For an employer to petition on behalf of CW–1 nonimmigrant beneficiaries in the Commonwealth of the Northern Mariana Islands (CNMI): $1,015.

(ii) For small employers and nonprofits: $510. For the Semiannual Report for CW-1 Employers (Form I-129CWR): No fee. The online filing discount in § 106.1(g) does not apply.

(iii) Additional fees in paragraph (c) of this section may apply.

(5) Petition for Alien Fiancé(e), Form I–129F.

(i) For filing a petition to classify a nonimmigrant as a fiancée or fiancé under section 214(d) of the Act: $675.

(ii) For a K–3 spouse as designated in 8 CFR 214.1(a)(2) who is the beneficiary of an immigrant petition filed by a U.S. citizen on a Petition for Alien Relative, Form I–130: No fee.

(6) Petition for Alien Relative, Form I–130. For filing a petition to classify status of a foreign national relative for issuance of an immigrant visa under section 204(a) of the Act. $675.

(7) Application for Travel Document, Form I–131.

(i) Refugee Travel Document for asylee and lawful permanent resident who obtained such status as an asylee 16 years or older: $165.

(ii) Refugee Travel Document for asylee or lawful permanent resident who obtained such status as an asylee under the age of 16: $135.

(iii) Advance Parole, Reentry Permit, and other travel documents: $630.

(iv) There is no fee for a travel document for applicants who filed USCIS Form I–485 on or after July 30, 2007, and before April 1, 2024, and paid the Form I–485 fee, while the I–485 remains pending.

(v) There is no fee for parole requests from current or former U.S. armed forces service members.

(vi) The discount in section 106.1(g) does not apply to paragraphs (a)(7)(i) and (ii) of this section.

(8) Application for Carrier Documentation, Form I–131A. For filing an application to allow an individual who loses their approved travel document to apply for a travel document (carrier documentation) to board an airline or other transportation carrier to return to the United States: $575.

(9) Declaration of Financial Support, Form I–134. To provide financial support to a beneficiary of certain immigration benefits for the duration of their temporary stay in the United States. No fee.

(10) Online Request to be a Supporter and Declaration of Financial Support, Form I–134A. To request to be a supporter and agree to provide financial support to a beneficiary and undergo background checks as part of certain special parole processes. No fee.

(11) Immigrant Petition for Alien Worker, Form I–140. For filing a petition to classify preference status of an alien based on profession or occupation under section 204(a) of the Act: $715.

(12) Application for Relief Under Former Section 212(c) of the Immigration and Nationality Act (INA), Form I–191. For filing an application for discretionary relief under section 212(c) of the Act: $930.

(13) Application for Advance Permission to Enter as a Nonimmigrant, Form I–192. For filing an application for discretionary relief under section 212(d)(3), (13), or (14) of the Act, except in an emergency case or where the approval of the application is in the interest of the U.S. Government: $1,100. The online filing discount in § 106.1(g) applies when this form is submitted to USCIS but does not apply to this paragraph when the form is submitted to CBP.

(14) Application for Waiver of Passport and/or Visa, Form I–193. For filing an application for waiver of passport and/or visa: $695. The discount in § 106.1(g) does not apply to this section when the form is submitted to CBP.

(15) Application for Permission to Reapply for Admission into the United States After Deportation or Removal, Form I–212. For filing an application for permission to reapply for admission by an excluded, deported, or removed alien; an alien who has fallen into distress; an alien who has been removed as an alien enemy; or an alien who has been removed at Government expense: $1,175. The online filing discount in § 106.1(g) does not apply to this section when the form is submitted to CBP.

(16) Notice of Appeal or Motion, Form I–290B. For appealing a decision under the immigration laws in any type of proceeding over which the Board of Immigration Appeals does not have appellate jurisdiction, and for filing a motion to reopen or reconsider a USCIS decision: $800.

(i) The fee will be the same for appeal of or motion on a denial of a benefit request with one or multiple beneficiaries.

(ii) There is no fee for conditional permanent residents who filed a waiver of the joint filing requirement based on battery or extreme cruelty and filed a Notice of Appeal or Motion (Form I–290B) when their Petition to Remove the Conditions on Residence (Form I–751) was denied.

(17) Petition for Amerasian, Widow(er), or Special Immigrant, Form I–360: $515. There is no fee for the following:

(i) A petition seeking classification as an Amerasian;

(ii) A petition seeking immigrant classification as a Violence Against Women Act (VAWA) self-petitioner;

(iii) A petition for Special Immigrant Juvenile classification;

(iv) A petition seeking special immigrant classification as Afghan or Iraqi translator or interpreter, Iraqi national employed by or on behalf of the U.S. Government, or Afghan national employed by or on behalf of the U.S. Government or employed by the International Security Assistance Force (ISAF); or a surviving spouse or child of such a person; or

(v) A petition for a person who served honorably on active duty in the U.S. armed forces filing under section 101(a)(27)(K) of the Act.

(18) Affidavit of Financial Support and Intent to Petition for Legal Custody for Public Law 97–359 Amerasian, Form I–361. Filed in support of Form I–360, Petition to Classify Public Law 97–359 Amerasian as the Child, Son, or Daughter of a United States Citizen. No fee.

(19) Request to Enforce Affidavit of Financial Support and Intent to Petition for Legal Custody for Public Law 97–359 Amerasian, Form I–363. For a beneficiary of a petition for a Public Law 97–359 Amerasian to request enforcement of the guarantee of financial support and legal custody executed by the beneficiary's sponsor. No fee.

(20) Record of Abandonment of Lawful Permanent Resident Status, Form I–407. To voluntarily abandon status as a lawful permanent resident. No fee.

(21) Application to Register Permanent Residence or Adjust Status, Form I–485. For filing an application for permanent resident status or creation of a record of lawful permanent residence:

(i) $1,440 for an applicant 14 years of age or older; or

(ii) $950 for an applicant under the age of 14 years who submits the application concurrently with the Form I–485 of a parent.

(iii) There is no fee for the following:

(A) An applicant who is in deportation, exclusion, or removal proceedings before an immigration judge, and the court waives the application fee.

(B) An applicant who served honorably on active duty in the U.S. armed forces who is filing under section 101(a)(27)(K) of the Act.

(22) Application to Adjust Status under Section 245(i) of the Act, Form I- 485 Supplement A. Supplement A to Form I–485 for persons seeking to adjust status under the provisions of section 245(i) of the Act a sum of $1,000 be paid while the applicant's, "Application to Register Permanent Residence or Adjust Status," is pending, unless payment of the additional sum is not required under section 245(i) of the Act, including:

(i) If applicant is unmarried and under 17 years of age: No fee.

(ii) If the applicant is the spouse or unmarried child under 21 years of age of a legalized alien and attaches a copy of a USCIS receipt or approval notice for a properly filed Form I–817, Application for Family Unity Benefits: No fee.

(23) Confirmation of Bona Fide Job Offer or Request for Job Portability Under INA Section 204(j), Form I–485J. To confirm that the job offered in Form I–140, Immigrant Petition for Alien Workers, remains a bona fide job offer that the beneficiary intends to accept once we approve the Form I–485, Application to Register Permanent Residence or Adjust Status, or request job portability under INA section 204(j) to a new, full-time, permanent job offer that the beneficiary intends to accept once we approve the Form I–485. No fee.

(24) Request for Waiver of Certain Rights, Privileges, Exemptions, and Immunities, Form I–508. To waive certain diplomatic rights privileges, exemptions, and immunities associated with your occupational status. No fee.

(25) Immigrant Petition by Standalone or Regional Center Investor, Forms I–526 and I–526E. To petition USCIS for status as an immigrant to the United States under section 203(b)(5) of the Act.

(i) Immigrant Petition by Standalone Investor, Form I–526: $11,160.

(ii) Immigrant Petition by Regional Center Investor, Form I–526E: $11,160.

(26) Application To Extend/Change Nonimmigrant Status, Form I–539. For certain nonimmigrants to extend their stay or change to another nonimmigrant status, CNMI residents applying for an initial grant of status, F and M nonimmigrants applying for reinstatement, and persons seeking V nonimmigrant status or an extension of stay as a V nonimmigrant. $470. There is no fee for Nonimmigrant A, G, and NATO.

(27) Interagency Record of Request—A, G, or NATO Dependent Employment Authorization or Change/Adjustment To/From A, G, or NATO Status, Form I–566. For dependent employment authorization as an eligible A–1, A–2, G–1, G–3, G–4, or NATO 1–6 dependent; or change or adjustment of status to, or from, A, G or NATO status. No fee.

(28) Application for Asylum and Withholding of Removal, Form I–589. To apply for asylum and withholding of removal. No fee.

(29) Registration for Classification as a Refugee, Form I–590. To determine eligibility for refugee classification and resettlement in the United States. No fee.

(30) Petition to Classify Orphan as an Immediate Relative, Form I–600. For filing a petition to classify an orphan as an immediate relative: $920.

(i) There is no fee for the first Form I–600 filed for a child based on an approved Application for Advance

Processing of an Orphan Petition, Form I–600A, during the Form I–600A approval period.

(ii) If more than one Form I–600 is filed during the Form I–600A approval period on behalf of beneficiaries who are birth siblings, no additional fee is required.

(iii) If more than one Form I–600 is filed during the Form I–600A approval period on behalf of beneficiaries who are not birth siblings, the fee is $920 for the second and each subsequent Form I–600 petition submitted.

(iv) This filing fee is not charged if a new Form I–600 combination filing is filed due to a change in marital status while the prior Form I–600A or Form I–600 combination filing is pending.

(v) This filing fee is charged if a new Form I–600 combination filing is filed due to a change in marital status after the Form I–600A or Form I–600 combination filing suitability determined is approved.

(31) Application for Advance Processing of an Orphan Petition, Form I–600A. For filing an application for determination of suitability and eligibility to adopt an orphan: $920.

(i) This filing fee is not charged if a new Form I–600A is filed due to a change in marital status while the prior Form I–600A is pending.

(ii) This filing fee is charged if a new Form I–600A is filed due to a change in marital status after the Form I–600A is approved.

(32) Request for Action on Approved Form I–600A/I–600, Form I–600A/I–600 Supplement 3. To request an extension of a suitability determination; updated suitability determination; change of non-Convention country; or a duplicate approval notice. $455. This filing fee:

(i) Is not charged to obtain a first or second extension of the approval of Form I–600A, or to obtain a first or second change of non-Hague Adoption Convention country during the Form I–600A approval period.

(ii) Is not charged for a request for a duplicate approval notice.

(iii) Is charged to request a new approval notice based on a significant change and updated home study unless there is also a request for a first or second extension of the Form I–600A approval, or a first or second change of non-Hague Adoption Convention country on the same Supplement 3.

(iv) Is charged for third or subsequent extensions of the approval of the Form I–600A and third or subsequent changes of non-Hague Adoption Convention country.

(33) Application for Waiver of Ground of Inadmissibility, Form I–601. To seek a waiver of grounds of inadmissibility if you are inadmissible to the United States and are seeking an immigrant visa, adjustment of status, certain nonimmigrant statuses, or certain other immigration benefits. $1,050. For applicants for adjustment of status of Indochina refugees under Public Law 95–145. No fee.

(34) Application for Provisional Unlawful Presence Waiver, Form I–601A. To request a provisional waiver of the unlawful presence grounds of inadmissibility under section 212(a)(9)(B) of the Act. $795.

(35) Application by Refugee for Waiver of Grounds of Inadmissibility, Form I–602. For a refugee who has been found inadmissible to the United States to apply for a waiver of inadmissibility for humanitarian reasons, family unity, or national interest. No fee.

(36) Application for Waiver of the Foreign Residence Requirement (under Section 212(e) of the Immigration and Nationality Act, as Amended), Form I–612. For J–1 and J–2 visas holders and their families to apply for a waiver of the two-year foreign residence requirement. $1,100.

(37) Application for Status as a Temporary Resident under Section 245A of the Immigration and Nationality Act, Form I–687. To apply for a waiver of inadmissibility for an applicant for adjustment of status under section 245A or 210 of the Act. $1,240.

(38) Application for Waiver of Grounds of Inadmissibility, Form I–690. For filing an application for waiver of a ground of inadmissibility under section 212(a) of the Act as amended, in conjunction with the application under section 210 or 245A of the Act: $905.

(39) Report of Immigration Medical Examination and Vaccination Record (Form I–693). For adjustment of status applicants to establish they are not inadmissible to the United States on health-related grounds. No fee.

(40) Notice of Appeal of Decision under Sections 245A or 210 of the Immigration and Nationality Act, Form I–694. For appealing the denial of an application under section 210 or 245A of the Act, or a petition under section 210A of the Act: $1,125.

(41) Application to Adjust Status from Temporary to Permanent Resident (Under Section 245A of the INA), Form I–698. For filing an application to adjust status from temporary to permanent resident (under section 245A of Pub. L. 99–603): $1,670.

(42) Refugee/Asylee Relative Petition, Form I–730. For a refugee to request a spouse and unmarried child be approved to join them in the United States. No fee.

(43) Petition to Remove Conditions on Residence, Form I–751. For filing a petition to remove the conditions on residence based on marriage: $750. There is no fee for a conditional permanent resident spouse or child who files a waiver of the joint filing requirement based on battery or extreme cruelty.

(44) Application for Employment Authorization, Form I–765. To request employment authorization and/or an Employment Authorization Document (EAD). $520.

(i) For an applicant who filed USCIS Form I–485 with a fee after April 1, 2024, and their Form I–485 is still pending: $260. The online filing discount in § 106.1(g) does not apply to this paragraph.

(ii) There is no fee for an initial Employment Authorization Document for the following:

(A) An applicant who filed USCIS Form I–485 on or after July 30, 2007, and before April 1, 2024, and paid the Form I–485 fee;

(B) Dependents of certain government and international organizations or NATO personnel;

(C) N–8 (Parent of alien classed as SK3) and N–9 (Child of N–8) nonimmigrants;

(D) Persons granted asylee status (AS1, AS6);

(E) Citizen of Micronesia, Marshall Islands, or Palau;

(F) Persons granted Withholding of Deportation or Removal;

(G) Applicant for Asylum and Withholding of Deportation or Removal including derivatives;

(H) Taiwanese dependents of Taipei Economic and Cultural Representative Office (TECRO) E–1 employees; and

(I) Current or former U.S. armed forces service members.

(iii) Request for replacement Employment Authorization Document based on USCIS error: No fee.

(iv) There is no fee for a renewal or replacement Employment Authorization Document for the following:

(A) Any current Adjustment of Status or Registry applicant who filed for adjustment of status on or after July 30, 2007, and before April 1, 2024, and paid the appropriate Form I–485 filing fee;

(B) Dependent of certain foreign government, international organization, or NATO personnel;

(C) Citizen of Micronesia, Marshall Islands, or Palau; and

(D) Persons granted withholding of deportation or removal.

(E) Current or former U.S. armed forces service members.

(45) Application for Employment Authorization for Abused Nonimmigrant Spouse, Form I–765V. Used for certain abused nonimmigrant spouses to request an employment authorization document (EAD). No fee.

(46) Petition to Classify Convention Adoptee as an Immediate Relative, Form I-800. For filing a petition to classify a Convention adoptee as an immediate relative: $920.

(i) There is no fee for the first Form I–800 filed for a child based on an approved Application for Determination of Suitability to Adopt a Child from a Convention Country, Form I–800A, during the Form I–800A approval period.

(ii) If more than one Form I–800 is filed during the Form I–800A approval period on behalf of beneficiaries who are birth siblings, no additional fee is required.

(iii) If more than one Form I–800 is filed during the Form I–800A approval period on behalf of beneficiaries who are not birth siblings, the fee is $920 for the second and each subsequent Form I–800 petition submitted.

(47) Application for Determination of Suitability to Adopt a Child from a Convention Country, Form I–800A. For filing an application for determination of suitability and eligibility to adopt a child from a Hague Adoption Convention country: $920.

(i) This filing fee is not charged if a new Form I–800A is filed due to a change in marital status while the prior Form I–800A is pending.

(ii) This filing fee is charged if a new Form I–800A is filed due to a change in marital status after the Form I–800A is approved.

(48) Request for Action on Approved Form I–800A, Form I–800A Supplement 3. To request an extension of a suitability determination; updated suitability determination; change in Convention country; or a request for a duplicate approval notice. $455. This filing fee:

(i) Is not charged to obtain a first or second extension of the approval of Form I–800A, or to obtain a first or second change of Hague Adoption Convention country during the Form I–800A approval period.

(ii) Is not charged for a request for a duplicate approval notice.

(iii) Is charged to request a new approval notice based on a significant change and updated home study unless there is a request for a first or second extension of the Form I–800A approval, or a first or second change of Hague Adoption Convention country on the same Supplement 3.

(iv) Is charged for third or subsequent extensions of the Form I–800A approval and third or subsequent changes of Hague Adoption Convention country.

(49) Application for Family Unity Benefits, Form I–817. For filing an application for voluntary departure under the Family Unity Program: $760.

(50) Application for Temporary Protected Status, Form I–821. For an eligible national of a designated country or a person without nationality who last habitually resided in the designated country to apply for Temporary Protected Status (TPS).

(i) For first time applicants: $50 or the maximum permitted by section 244(c)(1)(B) of the Act.

(ii) There is no fee for re-registration.

(iii) A Temporary Protected Status (TPS) applicant or re-registrant must pay $30 for biometric services.

(iv) The online filing discount in § 106.1(g) does not apply to paragraphs (a)(50)(i) and (a)(50)(ii) of this section.

(51) Consideration of Deferred Action for Childhood Arrivals, Form I–821D. To request that USCIS consider granting or renewing deferred action under 8 CFR 236.21–236.25. $85. The online filing discount in § 106.1(g) does not apply to this section.

(52) Application for Action on an Approved Application or Petition, Form I–824. To request additional action on a previously approved benefit request. $590.

(53) Petition by Investor to Remove Conditions on Permanent Resident Status, Form I–829. For a conditional permanent resident who obtained status through qualified investment to remove the conditions on their residence. $9,525.

(54) Inter-Agency Alien Witness and Informant Record, Form I–854. To request an alien witness and/or informant receive classification as an S nonimmigrant. No fee.

(55) Affidavit of Support Under Section 213A of the INA, Form I–864. For immigrants to show they have adequate means of financial support and are not likely to rely on the U.S. government for financial support. No fee.

(i) Contract Between Sponsor and Household Member, Form I–864A. For a household member to promise to support sponsored immigrants. No fee.

(ii) Affidavit of Support Under Section 213A of the INA, Form I–864EZ. To show that the applying immigrant has adequate means of financial support and is not likely to rely on the U.S. government for financial support. No fee.

(iii) Request for Exemption for Intending Immigrant's Affidavit of Support, Form I–864W. To establish that an applicant is exempt from the Form I–864 requirements. No fee.

(iv) Sponsor's Notice of Change of Address, Form I–865. To report a sponsor's new address and/or residence. No fee.

(56) Application for Suspension of Deportation or Special Rule Cancellation of Removal (Pursuant to Section 203 of Pub. L. 105–100), Form I–881. To apply for suspension of deportation or special rule cancellation of removal under the Nicaraguan Adjustment and Central American Relief Act.

(i) $340 for adjudication by DHS.

(ii) $165 for adjudication by EOIR. If the Form I–881 is referred to the immigration court by DHS: No fee.

(iii) If filing Form I–881 as a VAWA self-petitioner, including derivatives, as defined under section 101(a)(51)(F) of the Act: No fee.

(57) Application for Authorization to Issue Certification for Health Care Workers, Form I–905. For an organization to apply for authorization to issue certificates to health care workers. $230.

(58) Request for Premium Processing Service, Form I–907. The Request for Premium Processing Service fee will be as provided in § 106.4. The online filing discount in § 106.1(g) does not apply to a request for premium processing.

(59) Request for Civil Surgeon Designation, Form I–910. To apply for civil surgeon designation. $990.

(60) Request for Fee Waiver, Form I–912. To request a fee waiver. No fee.

(61) Application for T Nonimmigrant Status, Form I–914. To request temporary immigration benefits for a victim of a severe form of trafficking in persons, also known as human trafficking. No fee.

(i) Supplement A to Form I–914, Application for Immigrant Family Member of a T–1 Recipient. To request temporary immigration benefits for eligible family members of a victim of a severe form of trafficking in persons. No fee.

(ii) Supplement B to Form I–914, Declaration of Law Enforcement Officer for Victim of Trafficking in Persons. For a law enforcement agency to certify that a trafficking victim is being helpful to law enforcement during the detection, investigation, or prosecution of the trafficking. No fee.

(62) Petition for U Nonimmigrant Status, Form I–918. For a victim of qualifying criminal activity to petition for temporary immigration benefits. No fee.

(i) Supplement A to Form I–918, Petition for Qualifying Family Member of U–1 Recipient. To request temporary immigration benefits for qualifying family members of a victim of qualifying criminal activity. No fee.

(ii) Supplement B to Form I–918, U Nonimmigrant Status Certification. For a law enforcement agency to certify that an individual is a victim of qualifying criminal activity and has been, is being, or is likely to be helpful to law enforcement in the detection, investigation, or prosecution of the qualifying criminal activity. No fee.

(63) Petition for Qualifying Family Member of a U–1 Nonimmigrant, Form I–929. For a principal U–1 nonimmigrant to request immigration benefits on behalf of a qualifying family member who has never held U nonimmigrant status. No fee.

(64) Application for Entrepreneur Parole, Form I–941. For filing an application for parole for an entrepreneur. $1,200.

(65) Application for Regional Center Designation, Form I–956. To request designation as a regional center or to request an amendment to an approved regional center. $47,695.

(66) Application for Approval of Investment in a Commercial Enterprise, Form I–956F. To request approval of each particular investment offering through an associated new commercial enterprise. $47,695.

(67) Regional Center Annual Statement, Form I–956G. To provide updated information and certify that a Regional Center under the Immigrant Investor Program has maintained its eligibility. $4,470.

(68) Bona Fides of Persons Involved with Regional Center Program, Form I–956H. For each person involved with a regional center to attest to their compliance with section 203(b)(5)(H) of the Act. No fee.

(69) Registration for Direct and Third-Party Promoters, Form I–956K. For each person acting as a direct or third-party promoter (including migration agents) of a regional center, any new commercial enterprises, an affiliated job-creating entity, or an issuer of securities intended to be offered to immigrant investors in connection with a particular capital investment project. No fee.

(b) N Forms.

(1) Application to File Declaration of Intention, Form N–300. For a permanent resident to declare their intent to become a U.S. citizen. $320.

(2) Request for a Hearing on a Decision in Naturalization Proceedings Under Section 336, Form N–336. To request a hearing before an immigration officer on the denial of Form N–400, Application for Naturalization. $830. There is no fee for an applicant who has filed an Application for Naturalization under section 328 or 329 of the Act with respect to military service and whose application has been denied.

(3) Application for Naturalization, Form N–400. To apply for U.S. citizenship. $760. The following exceptions apply:

(i) No fee is charged an applicant who meets the requirements of section 328 or 329 of the Act with respect to military service.

(ii) The fee for an applicant whose documented household income is less than or equal to 400 percent of the Federal Poverty Guidelines: $380. The discount in section 106.1(g) does not apply to this section.

(4) Request for Certification of Military or Naval Service, Form N–426. To request that the Department of Defense verify military or naval service. No fee.

(5) Application to Preserve Residence for Naturalization Purposes, Form N–470. Application for a lawful permanent resident who must leave the United States

to preserve their residence to pursue naturalization. $420.

(6) Application for Replacement Naturalization/Citizenship Document, Form N–565. To apply for a replacement Declaration of Intention; Naturalization Certificate; Certificate of Citizenship; or Repatriation Certificate; or to apply for a special certificate of naturalization as a U.S. citizen to be recognized by a foreign country. $555. There is no fee when this application is submitted under 8 CFR 338.5(a) to request correction of a certificate that contains an error.

(7) Application for Certificate of Citizenship, Form N–600. To apply for a Certificate of Citizenship. $1,385.

(i) There is no fee for any application filed by a current or former member of any branch of the U.S. armed forces on their own behalf.

(ii) There is no fee for an application filed on behalf of an individual who is the subject of a final adoption for immigration purposes and meets (or met before age 18) the definition of child under section 101(b)(1)(E), (F), or (G) of the Act.

(8) Application for Citizenship and Issuance of Certificate Under Section 322, Form N–600K. Application for children who regularly reside outside the United States to apply for citizenship based on a U.S. citizen parent. $1,385. There is no fee for an application filed on behalf of a child who is the subject of a final adoption for immigration purposes and meets the definition of child under section 101(b)(1)(E), (F), or (G) of the Act.

(9) Application for Posthumous Citizenship, Form N–644. To request citizenship for someone who died because of injury or disease incurred in or aggravated by service in an active-duty status with the U.S. armed forces during a specified period of military hostilities. No fee.

(10) Medical Certification for Disability Exceptions, Form N–648. For a naturalization applicant to request an exception to the English and civics testing requirements for naturalization because of physical or developmental disability or mental impairment. No fee.

(c) G Forms, statutory fees, and non-form fees —

(1) Genealogy Index Search Request, Form G–1041. The fee is due regardless of the search results. $80.

(2) Genealogy Records Request, Form G–1041A. USCIS will refund the records request fee when it cannot find any file previously identified in response to the index search request. $80.

(3) USCIS immigrant fee. For DHS domestic processing and issuance of required documents after an immigrant visa is issued by the U.S. Department of State: $235.

(4) American Competitiveness and Workforce Improvement Act (ACWIA) fee. For filing certain H–1B petitions as described in 8 CFR 214.2(h)(19): $1,500 or $750.

(5) Fraud detection and prevention fee.

(i) For filing certain H–1B and L petitions as described in 8 U.S.C. 1184(c): $500.

(ii) For filing H–2B petitions as described in 8 U.S.C. 1184(c): $150.

(6) Fraud detection and prevention fee for Form I–129CW. For filing certain CW–1 petitions as described in Public Law 115–218s: $50.

(7) CNMI education funding fee. For filing certain CW–1 petitions as described in Public Law 115–218 and USCIS form instructions. The fee amount will be as prescribed in the form instructions and:

(i) The employer must pay the fee for each beneficiary and for each year or partial year of requested validity; and

(ii) Beginning in FY 2020, the $200 fee may be adjusted once per year by notice in the Federal Register based on the amount of inflation according to the Consumer Price Index for All Urban Consumers (CPI–U).

(8) 9–11 response and biometric entry-exit fee for H–1B Visa. For certain petitioners who employ 50 or more employees in the United States if more than 50 percent of the petitioner's employees are in H–1B, L–1A, or L–1B nonimmigrant status: $4,000. Collection of this fee is scheduled to end on September 30, 2027.

(9) 9–11 response and biometric entry-exit fee for L–1 Visa. For certain petitioners who employ 50 or more employees in the United States, if more than 50 percent of the petitioner's employees are in H–1B, L–1A, or L–1B nonimmigrant status: $4,500. Collection of this fee is scheduled to end on September 30, 2027.

(10) Claimant under section 289 of the Act. For American Indians who are born in Canada and possess at least 50 percent American Indian blood to request lawful permanent resident status. No fee.

(11) Registration requirement for petitioners seeking to file H-1B petitions on behalf of cap-subject aliens. For each registration submitted to register for the H-1B cap or advanced degree exemption selection process: $215. This fee is not subject to the online discount provided in § 106.1(g).

(12) Request for Certificate of Non-Existence, G–1566. For a certification of non-existence of a naturalization record. $330.

(13) Asylum Program Fee. In addition to the fees required by § 106.2(a)(3), (a)(4) and (a)(11), to fund the asylum program, the Asylum Program Fee must be paid by any petitioner filing a Petition for a Nonimmigrant Worker, Form I–129 under 8 CFR 214.2, Petition for a CNMI-Only Nonimmigrant Transitional Worker, Form I–129CW under 8 CFR 214.2(w), or an Immigrant Petition for Alien Worker, Form I–140 under 8 CFR 204.1(a). $600. For petitions:

(i) Filed by a nonprofit as defined in § 106.1(f): No fee.

(ii) Filed by a small employer as defined in § 106.1(f): $300.

(iii) The online filing discount provided in § 106.1(g) does not apply to this fee.

(d) Inflationary adjustment. The fees prescribed in this section that are not set or limited by statute may be adjusted, but not more often than once per year, by publication of a rule in the Federal Register that:

(1) Is based on the amount of inflation as measured by the difference in the CPI–U as published by the U.S. Department of Labor, U.S. Bureau of Labor Statistics in April of the year of the last fee rule and the year of the adjustment under this section.

(2) Adjusts all fees that are not set by statute based on the amount of inflation.

(3) Rounds the fees calculated by the amount of inflation to the nearest $5 increment.

HISTORY:

[85 FR 46788, 46916, Aug. 3, 2020; 86 FR 14221, 14227, Mar. 15, 2021; 87 FR 53152, 53297, Aug. 30, 2022; 89 FR 6194, 6386, Jan. 31, 2024, as corrected at 89 FR 20101, Mar. 21, 2024]

§ 106.3 Fee waivers and exemptions.

(a) Waiver of fees.

(1) Eligibility. The party requesting the benefit must be unable to pay the prescribed fee. A person demonstrates an inability to pay the fee by establishing at least one of the following criteria:

(i) Receipt of a means-tested benefit as defined in § 106.1(f)(3) at the time of filing;

(ii) Household income at or below 150 percent of the Federal Poverty Guidelines at the time of filing; or

(iii) Extreme financial hardship due to extraordinary expenses or other circumstances that render the individual unable to pay the fee.

(2) Requesting a fee waiver. To request a fee waiver, a person requesting an immigration benefit must submit a written request for permission to have their request processed without payment of a fee with their benefit request. The request must state the person's belief that he or she is entitled to or deserving of the benefit requested, the reasons for his or her inability to pay, and evidence to support the reasons indicated. There is no appeal of the denial of a fee waiver request.

(3) USCIS fees that may be waived. Only the following fees may be waived:

(i) The following fees for the following forms may be waived without condition:

(A) Application to Replace Permanent Resident Card (Form I–90);

(B) Application for Relief Under Former Section 212(c) of the Immigration and Nationality Act (Form I–191);

(C) Petition to Remove the Conditions of Residence (Form I–751);

(D) Application for Family Unity Benefits (Form I–817);

(E) Application for Temporary Protected Status (Form I–821);

(F) Application for Suspension of Deportation or Special Rule Cancellation of Removal (Form I–881) (under section 203 of Pub. L. 105–110);

(G) Application to File Declaration of Intention (Form N–300);

(H) Request for a Hearing on a Decision in Naturalization Proceedings Under Section 336 (Form N–336);

(I) Application for Naturalization (Form N–400);

(J) Application to Preserve Residence for Naturalization Purposes (N–470);

(K) Application for Replacement Naturalization/Citizenship Document (N–565);

(L) Application for Certificate of Citizenship (N–600); and

(M) Application for Citizenship and Issuance of Certificate under section 322 of the Act (N–600K).

(ii) The following form fees may be waived based on the conditions described in paragraphs (a)(3)(ii)(A) through (F) of this section:

(A) Petition for a CNMI-Only Nonimmigrant Transitional Worker (Form I-129CW) for a CW-1, CNMI-only transitional worker. Waiver of the fee for Form I-129CW does not waive the requirement for an employer petitioning for a CW-1, CNMI-only transitional worker to pay any fees in § 106.2(c) that may apply.

(B) An Application to Extend/Change Nonimmigrant Status (Form I–539), only in the case of a noncitizen applying for CW–2 nonimmigrant status;

(C) Application for Travel Document (Form I–131), when filed to request humanitarian parole;

(D) Notice of Appeal or Motion (Form I–290B), when there is no fee for the underlying application or petition or that fee may be waived;

(E) Notice of Appeal of Decision Under Sections 245A or 210 of the Immigration and Nationality Act (Form I–694), if the underlying application or petition was fee exempt, the filing fee was waived, or was eligible for a fee waiver;

(F) Application for Employment Authorization (Form I–765), except persons filing under category (c)(33), Deferred Action for Childhood Arrivals; and

(G) Petition for Nonimmigrant Worker (Form I–129) or Application to Extend/Change Nonimmigrant Status (Form I–539), only in the case of a noncitizen applying for E–2 CNMI Investor for an extension of stay.

(iii) Any fees associated with the filing of any benefit request under 8 U.S.C. 1101(a)(51) and those otherwise self-petitioning under 8 U.S.C. 1154(a)(1) (VAWA self-petitioners), 8 U.S.C. 1101(a)(15)(T) (T nonimmigrant status), 8 U.S.C. 1101(a)(15)(U) (U nonimmigrant status), 8 U.S.C. 1105a (battered spouses of A, G, E–3, or H nonimmigrants), 8 U.S.C. 1229b(b)(2) (special rule cancellation for battered spouse or child), and 8 U.S.C. 1254a(a) (Temporary Protected Status).

(iv) The following fees may be waived only if the person is exempt from the public charge grounds of inadmissibility under section 212(a)(4) of the Act, 8 U.S.C. 1182(a)(4):

(A) Application for Advance Permission to Enter as Nonimmigrant (Form I–192);

(B) Application for Waiver for Passport and/or Visa (Form I–193);

(C) Application to Register Permanent Residence or Adjust Status (Form I–485); and

(D) Application for Waiver of Grounds of Inadmissibility (Form I–601).

(4) Immigration Court fees. The provisions relating to the authority of the immigration judges or the Board to waive fees prescribed in paragraph (b) of this section in cases under their jurisdiction can be found at 8 CFR 1003.8 and 1003.24.

(b) Humanitarian fee exemptions. Persons in the following categories are exempt from paying certain fees as follows:

(1) Persons seeking or granted Special Immigrant Juvenile classification who file the following forms

related to the Special Immigrant Juvenile classification or adjustment of status under section 245(h) of the Act, 8 U.S.C. 1255(h):

(i) Application for Travel Document (Form I–131).

(ii) Notice of Appeal or Motion (Form I–290B), if filed for any benefit request filed before adjustment of status or a motion filed for an Application to Register Permanent Residence or Adjust Status (Form I–485) or an associated ancillary form.

(iii) Application to Register Permanent Residence or Adjust Status (Form I–485).

(iv) Application for Waiver of Ground of Inadmissibility (Form I–601).

(v) Application for Employment Authorization (Form I–765).

(vi) Application for Action on an Approved Application or Petition (Form I–824).

(vii) Application for Provisional Unlawful Presence Waiver (Form I-601A).

(2) Persons seeking or granted T nonimmigrant status who file the following forms related to T nonimmigrant status or adjustment of status under INA section 245(l), 8 U.S.C. 1255(l):

(i) Application for Travel Document (Form I–131).

(ii) Application for Advance Permission to Enter as a Nonimmigrant (Form I–192).

(iii) Application for Waiver of Passport and/or Visa (Form I–193).

(iv) Notice of Appeal or Motion (Form I–290B), if filed for any benefit request filed before adjustment of status or a motion or appeal filed for an Application to Register Permanent Residence or Adjust Status (Form I–485) or an associated ancillary form.

(v) Application to Register Permanent Residence or Adjust Status (Form I–485).

(vi) Application to Extend/Change Nonimmigrant Status (Form I–539).

(vii) Application for Waiver of Ground of Inadmissibility (Form I–601).

(viii) Application for Employment Authorization (Form I–765).

(ix) Application for Action on an Approved Application or Petition (Form I–824).

(3) Persons seeking or granted special immigrant visa or status as Afghan or Iraqi translators or interpreters, Iraqi nationals employed by or on behalf of the U.S. Government, or Afghan nationals employed by or on behalf of the U.S. Government or employed by the ISAF and their derivative beneficiaries, who file the following forms related to the Special Immigrant classification or adjustment of status under such classification:

(i) Application for Travel Document (Form I–131).

(ii) Application for Permission to Reapply for Admission into the U.S. After Deportation or Removal (Form I–212).

(iii) Notice of Appeal or Motion (Form I–290B), if filed for any benefit request filed before adjustment of status or a motion filed for an Application to Register Permanent Residence or Adjust Status (Form I–485) or an associated ancillary form.

(iv) Application to Register Permanent Residence or Adjust Status (Form I–485).

(v) Application for Waiver of Ground of Inadmissibility (Form I–601).

(vi) Application for Employment Authorization (Form I–765).

(vii) Application for Action on an Approved Application or Petition (Form I–824).

(4) Persons seeking or granted adjustment of status as abused spouses and children under the Cuban Adjustment Act (CAA) and the Haitian Refugee Immigration Fairness Act (HRIFA) are exempt from paying the following fees for forms related to those benefits:

(i) Application for Travel Document (Form I–131).

(ii) Application for Permission to Reapply for Admission into the U.S. After Deportation or Removal (Form I–212).

(iii) Notice of Appeal or Motion (Form I–290B), if filed for any benefit request filed before adjustment of status or a motion filed for an Application to Register Permanent Residence or Adjust Status (Form I–485) or an associated ancillary form.

(iv) Application to Register Permanent Residence or Adjust Status (Form I–485).

(v) Application for Waiver of Ground of Inadmissibility (Form I–601).

(vi) Application for Employment Authorization (Form I–765).

(vii) Application for Action on an Approved Application or Petition (Form I–824).

(5) Persons seeking or granted U nonimmigrant status who file the following forms related to U nonimmigrant status or adjustment of status under INA section 245(m), 8 U.S.C. 1255(m):

(i) Application for Travel Document (Form I–131).

(ii) Application for Advance Permission to Enter as a Nonimmigrant (Form I–192).

(iii) Application for Waiver of Passport and/or Visa (Form I–193).

(iv) Notice of Appeal or Motion (Form I–290B), if filed for any benefit request filed before adjustment of status or a motion or appeal filed for an Application to Register Permanent Residence or Adjust Status (Form I–485) or an associated ancillary form.

(v) Application to Register Permanent Residence or Adjust Status (Form I–485).

(vi) Application to Extend/Change Nonimmigrant Status (Form I–539).

(vii) Application for Waiver of Ground of Inadmissibility (Form I–601).

(viii) Application for Employment Authorization (Form I–765).

(ix) Application for Action on an Approved Application or Petition (Form I–824).

(x) Petition for Qualifying Family Member of a U–1 Nonimmigrant (Form I–929).

(6) Persons seeking or granted immigrant classification as VAWA self-petitioners and derivatives as defined in section 101(a)(51)(A) and (B) of the Act or those otherwise self-petitioning for immigrant classification under section 204(a)(1) of the Act, 8 U.S.C. 1154(a)(1),

are exempt from paying the following fees for forms related to the benefit:

(i) Application for Travel Document (Form I–131).

(ii) Application for Permission to Reapply for Admission into the U.S. After Deportation or Removal (Form I–212).

(iii) Notice of Appeal or Motion (Form I–290B) if filed for any benefit request filed before adjustment of status or a motion filed for an Application to Register Permanent Residence or Adjust Status (Form I–485) or an associated ancillary form.

(iv) Application to Register Permanent Residence or Adjust Status (Form I–485).

(v) Application for Waiver of Grounds of Inadmissibility (Form I–601).

(vi) Application for Provisional Unlawful Presence Waiver (Form I–601A).

(vii) Application for Employment Authorization (Form I–765) for initial, renewal, and replacement requests submitted under 8 CFR 274a.12(c)(9) and (14) and section 204(a)(1)(K) of the Act.

(viii) Application for Action on an Approved Application or Petition (Form I–824).

(7) Abused spouses and children applying for benefits under the Nicaraguan Adjustment and Central American Relief Act (NACARA) are exempt from paying the following fees for forms related to the benefit:

(i) Application for Suspension of Deportation or Special Rule Cancellation of Removal (Pursuant to Section 203 of Public Law 105–100 (NACARA)) (Form I–881).

(ii) Application for Waiver of Grounds of Inadmissibility (Form I–601).

(iii) Application for Employment Authorization (Form I–765) submitted under 8 CFR 274a.12(c)(10).

(iv) Application for Action on an Approved Application or Petition (Form I–824).

(8) Battered spouses and children of a lawful permanent resident or U.S. citizen applying for cancellation of removal and adjustment of status under section 240A(b)(2) of the Act are exempt from paying the following fees for forms related to the benefit:

(i) Application for Employment Authorization (Form I–765) under 8 CFR 274a.12(c)(10).

(ii) Application for Action on an Approved Application or Petition (Form I–824).

(9) Refugees, persons paroled as refugees, or lawful permanent residents who obtained such status as refugees in the United States are exempt from paying the following fees:

(i) Application for Travel Document (Form I–131).

(ii) Application for Carrier Documentation (Form I–131A).

(iii) Application for Employment Authorization (Form I–765).

(iv) Application to Register Permanent Residence or Adjust Status (Form I–485).

(c) Director's waiver or exemption exception. The Director of USCIS may authorize the waiver of or exemption from, in whole or in part, a form fee required by § 106.2 that is not otherwise waivable or exempt under this section, if the Director determines that such action is in the public interest and consistent with the applicable law. This discretionary authority may be delegated only to the USCIS Deputy Director.

HISTORY:

[85 FR 46788, 46916, Aug. 3, 2020; 89 FR 6194, 6386, Jan. 31, 2024, as corrected at 89 FR 20101, Mar. 21, 2024; 90 FR 5519, 5519, Jan. 17, 2025]

§ 106.4 Premium processing service.

(a) General. A person may submit a request to USCIS for premium processing of certain immigration benefit requests, subject to processing timeframes and fees, as described in this section.

(b) Submitting a request. A request must be submitted on the form and in the manner prescribed by USCIS in the form instructions. If the request for premium processing is submitted together with the underlying immigration benefit request, all required fees in the correct amount must be paid. The fee to request premium processing service may not be waived and must be paid in addition to other filing fees. USCIS may require the premium processing service fee be paid in a separate remittance from other filing fees and preclude combined payments in the applicable form instructions.

(c) Designated benefit requests and fee amounts. Benefit requests designated for premium processing and the corresponding fees to request premium processing service are as follows:

(1) Application for classification of a nonimmigrant described in section 101(a)(15)(E)(i), (ii), or (iii) of the Act: $2,805.

(2) Petition for classification of a nonimmigrant described in section 101(a)(15)(H)(i)(b) of the Act or section 222(a) of the Immigration Act of 1990, Public Law 101–649: $2,805.

(3) Petition for classification of a nonimmigrant described in section 101(a)(15)(H)(ii)(b) of the Act: $1,685.

(4) Petition for classification of a nonimmigrant described in section 101(a)(15)(H)(iii) of the Act: $2,805.

(5) Petition for classification of a nonimmigrant described in section 101(a)(15)(L) of the Act: $2,805.

(6) Petition for classification of a nonimmigrant described in section 101(a)(15)(O)(i) or (ii) of the Act: $2,805.

(7) Petition for classification of a nonimmigrant described in section 101(a)(15)(P)(i), (ii), or (iii) of the Act: $2,805.

(8) Petition for classification of a nonimmigrant described in section 101(a)(15)(Q) of the Act: $2,805.

(9) Petition for classification of a nonimmigrant described in section 101(a)(15)(R) of the Act: $1,685.

(10) Application for classification of a nonimmigrant described in section 214(e) of the Act: $2,805.

(11) Petition for classification under section 203(b)(1)(A) of the Act: $2,805.

(12) Petition for classification under section 203(b)(1)(B) of the Act: $2,805.

(13) Petition for classification under section 203(b)(2)(A) of the Act not involving a waiver under section 203(b)(2)(B) of the Act: $2,805.

(14) Petition for classification under section 203(b)(3)(A)(i) of the Act: $2,805.

(15) Petition for classification under section 203(b)(3)(A)(ii) of the Act: $2,805.

(16) Petition for classification under section 203(b)(3)(A)(iii) of the Act: $2,805.

(17) Petition for classification under section 203(b)(1)(C) of the Act: $2,805.

(18) Petition for classification under section 203(b)(2) of the Act, involving a waiver under section 203(b)(2)(B) of the Act: $2,805.

(19) Application under section 248 of the Act to change status to a classification described in section 101(a)(15)(F), (J), or (M) of the Act: $1,965.

(20) Application under section 248 of the Act to change status to be classified as a dependent of a nonimmigrant described in section 101(a)(15)(E), (H), (L), (O), (P), or (R) of the Act, or to extend stay in such classification: $1,965.

(21) Application for employment authorization: $1,685.

(d) Fee adjustments. The fee to request premium processing service may be adjusted by notification in the Federal Register on a biennial basis based on the percentage by which the Consumer Price Index for All Urban Consumers for the month of June preceding the date on which such adjustment takes effect exceeds the Consumer Price Index for All Urban Consumers for the same month of the second preceding calendar year.

(e) Processing timeframes. The processing timeframes for a request for premium processing are as follows:

(1) Application for classification of a nonimmigrant described in section 101(a)(15)(E)(i), (ii), or (iii) of the Act: 15 business days.

(2) Petition for classification of a nonimmigrant described in section 101(a)(15)(H)(i)(b) of the Act or section 222(a) of the Immigration Act of 1990, Public Law 101–649: 15 business days.

(3) Petition for classification of a nonimmigrant described in section 101(a)(15)(H)(ii)(b) of the Act: 15 business days.

(4) Petition for classification of a nonimmigrant described in section 101(a)(15)(H)(iii) of the Act: 15 business days.

(5) Petition for classification of a nonimmigrant described in section 101(a)(15)(L) of the Act: 15 business days.

(6) Petition for classification of a nonimmigrant described in section 101(a)(15)(O)(i) or (ii) of the Act: 15 business days.

(7) Petition for classification of a nonimmigrant described in section 101(a)(15)(P)(i), (ii), or (iii) of the Act: 15 business days.

(8) Petition for classification of a nonimmigrant described in section 101(a)(15)(Q) of the Act: 15 business days.

(9) Petition for classification of a nonimmigrant described in section 101(a)(15)(R) of the Act: 15 business days.

(10) Application for classification of a nonimmigrant described in section 214(e) of the Act: 15 business days.

(11) Petition for classification under section 203(b)(1)(A) of the Act: 15 business days.

(12) Petition for classification under section 203(b)(1)(B) of the Act: 15 business days.

(13) Petition for classification under section 203(b)(2)(A) of the Act not involving a waiver under section 203(b)(2)(B) of the Act: 15 business days.

(14) Petition for classification under section 203(b)(3)(A)(i) of the Act: 15 business days.

(15) Petition for classification under section 203(b)(3)(A)(ii) of the Act: 15 business days.

(16) Petition for classification under section 203(b)(3)(A)(iii) of the Act: 15 business days.

(17) Petition for classification under section 203(b)(1)(C) of the Act: 45 business days.

(18) Petition for classification under section 203(b)(2) of the Act involving a waiver under section 203(b)(2)(B) of the Act: 45 business days.

(19) Application under section 248 of the Act to change status to a classification described in section 101(a)(15)(F), (J), or (M) of the Act: 30 business days.

(20) Application under section 248 of the Act I to change status to be classified as a dependent of a nonimmigrant described in section 101(a)(15)(E), (H), (L), (O), (P), or (R) of the Act, or to extend stay in such classification: 30 business days.

(21) Application for employment authorization: 30 business days.

(22) For the purpose of this section a business day is a day that the Federal Government is open for business, and does not include weekends, federally observed holidays, or days on which Federal Government offices are closed, such as for weather-related or other reasons. The closure may be nationwide or in the region where the adjudication of the benefit for which premium processing is sought will take place.

(f) Processing requirements and refunds.

(1) USCIS will issue an approval notice, denial notice, a notice of intent to deny, or a request for evidence within the premium processing timeframe.

(2) Premium processing timeframes will commence:

(i) For those benefits described in paragraphs (e)(1) through (16) of this section, on the date the form prescribed by USCIS, together with the required fee(s), are received by USCIS.

(ii) For those benefits described in paragraphs (e)(17) through (21) of this section, on the date that all prerequisites for adjudication, the form prescribed by USCIS, and fee(s) are received by USCIS.

(3) In the event USCIS issues a notice of intent to deny or a request for evidence of the premium processing timeframe will stop and will recommence with a new timeframe as specified in paragraphs (e)(1) through (21) of this section on the date that USCIS receives a response to the notice of intent to deny or the request for evidence.

(4) Except as provided in paragraph (f)(5) of this section, USCIS will refund the premium processing service fee but continue to process the case if USCIS does not take adjudicative action described in paragraph (f)(1) of this section within the applicable processing timeframe as required in paragraph (e) of this section.

(5) USCIS may retain the premium processing fee and not take an adjudicative action described in paragraph (f)(1) of this section on the request within the applicable processing timeframe, and not notify the person who filed the request, if USCIS opens an investigation for fraud or misrepresentation relating to the immigration benefit request.

(g) Availability.

(1) USCIS will announce by its official internet website, currently https://www.uscis.gov, the benefit requests described in paragraph (c) of this section for which premium processing may be requested, the dates upon which such availability commences or ends, or any conditions that may apply.

(2) USCIS may suspend the availability of premium processing for immigration benefit requests designated for premium processing if circumstances prevent the completion of processing of a significant number of such requests within the applicable processing timeframe.

HISTORY:

[85 FR 46788, 46916, Aug. 3, 2020; 87 FR 18227, 18260, Mar. 30, 2022; 88 FR 89539, 89550, Dec. 28, 2023; 89 FR 6194, 6386, Jan. 31, 2024]

§ 106.5 Authority to certify records.

The Director of USCIS, or such officials as he or she may designate, may certify records when authorized under 5 U.S.C. 552 or any other law to provide such records.

HISTORY:

[85 FR 46788, 46916, Aug. 3, 2020; 89 FR 6194, 6386, Jan. 31, 2024]

§ 106.6 DHS severability.

The provisions of this part are separate and severable from one another. If any provision is stayed or determined to be invalid, or held unenforceable as to any person or circumstance, the remaining provisions and applications will continue in effect.

HISTORY:

[85 FR 46788, 46916, Aug. 3, 2020; 89 FR 6194, 6386, Jan. 31, 2024]

PART 204

IMMIGRANT PETITIONS

Subpart A. Immigrant Visa Petitions

Subpart C. Intercountry Adoption of a Convention Adoptee

AUTHORITY NOTE APPLICABLE TO ENTIRE PART:

AUTHORITY:

8 U.S.C. 1101, 1103, 1151, 1153, 1154, 1182, 1184, 1186a, 1255, 1324a, 1641; 8 CFR part 2.

Subpart A

Immigrant Visa Petitions

§ 204.1 General information about immediate relative and family-sponsored petitions.

(a) Types of petitions. Petitions may be filed for an alien's classification as an immediate relative under section 201(b) of the Act or as a preference immigrant under section 203(a) of the Act based on a qualifying relationship to a citizen or lawful permanent resident of the United States, as follows:

(1) A citizen or lawful permanent resident of the United States petitioning under section 204(a)(1)(A)(i) or 204(a)(1)(B)(i) of the Act for a qualifying relative's classification as an immediate relative under section

201(b) of the Act or as a preference immigrant under section 203(a) of the Act must file a Form I-130, Petition for Alien Relative. These petitions are described in § 204.2;

(2) A widow or widower of a United States citizen self-petitioning under section 204(a)(1)(A)(ii) of the Act as an immediate relative under section 201(b) of the Act must file a Form I-360, Petition for Amerasian, Widow, or Special Immigrant. These petitions are described in § 204.2;

(3) A spouse or child of an abusive citizen or lawful permanent resident of the United States self-petitioning under section 204(a)(1)(A)(iii), 204(a)(1)(A)(iv), 204(a)(1)(B)(ii), or 204(a)(1)(B)(iii) of the Act for classification as an immediate relative under section 201(b) of the Act or as a preference immigrant under section 203(a) of the Act must file a Form I-360, Petition for Amerasian, Widow, or Special Immigrant. These petitions are described in § 204.2;

(4) A U.S. citizen seeking to have USCIS accord immediate relative status to a child based on the citizen's adoption of the child as an orphan, as defined in section 101(b)(1)(F) of the Act, must follow the procedures in § 204.3.

(5) A U.S. citizen seeking to have USCIS accord immediate relative status to a child under section 101(b)(1)(G) of the Act on the basis of a Convention adoption must:

(i) File a Form I-800A, Application to Determine Suitability as Adoptive Parents for a Convention adoptee; and

(ii) After USCIS approves the Form I-800A, file a Form I-800, Petition to Classify Convention adoptee as Immediate Relative, as provided in 8 CFR part 204, subpart C.

(6) Any person filing a petition under section 204(f) of the Act as, or on behalf of, an Amerasian for classification as an immediate relative under section 201(b) of the Act or as a preference immigrant under section 203(a)(1) or 203(a)(3) of the Act must file a Form I-360, Petition for Amerasian, Widow, or Special Immigrant. These petitions are described in § 204.4.

(b) Proper filing. A petition for alien relative and a petition for Amerasian, widow(er), or special immigrant must be filed on the form prescribed by USCIS in accordance with the form instructions, and will be considered properly filed when the petition is filed in accordance with 8 CFR 103.2. The filing date of a petition is the date it is properly filed and received by USCIS. That date will constitute the priority date.

(c) [Reserved]

(d) [Reserved]

(e) [Reserved]

(f) **Supporting documentation.**

(1) Documentary evidence consists of those documents which establish the United States citizenship or lawful permanent resident status of the petitioner and the claimed relationship of the petitioner to the beneficiary. They must be in the form of primary evidence, if available. When it is established that primary evidence is not available, secondary evidence may be accepted. To determine the availability of primary documents, the Service will refer to the Department of State's Foreign Affairs Manual (FAM). When the FAM shows that primary documents are generally available in the country of issue but the petitioner claims that his or her document is unavailable, a letter from the appropriate registrar stating that the document is not available will not be required before the Service will accept secondary evidence. The Service will consider any credible evidence relevant to a self-petition filed by a qualified spouse or child of an abusive citizen or lawful permanent resident under section 204(a)(1)(A)(iii), 204(a)(1)(A)(iv), 204(a)(1)(B)(ii), or 204(a)(1)(B)(iii) of the Act. The self-petitioner may, but is not required to, demonstrate that preferred primary or secondary evidence is unavailable. The determination of what evidence is credible and the weight to be given that evidence shall be within the sole discretion of the Service.

(2) Original documents or legible, true copies of original documents are acceptable. The Service reserves the right to require submission of original documents when deemed necessary. Documents submitted with the petition will not be returned to the petitioner, except when originals are requested by the Service. If original documents are requested by the Service, they will be returned to the petitioner after a decision on the petition has been rendered, unless their validity or authenticity is in question. When an interview is required, all original documents must be presented for examination at the interview.

(3) Foreign language documents must be accompanied by an English translation which has been certified by a competent translator.

(g) Evidence of petitioner's United States citizenship or lawful permanent residence —

(1) Primary evidence. A petition must be accompanied by one of the following:

(i) A birth certificate that was issued by a civil authority and that establishes the petitioner's birth in the United States;

(ii) An unexpired United States passport issued initially for a full ten-year period to a petitioner over the age of eighteen years as a citizen of the United States (and not merely as a noncitizen national);

(iii) An unexpired United States passport issued initially for a full five-year period to the petitioner under the age of eighteen years as a citizen of the United States (and not merely as a noncitizen national);

(iv) A statement executed by a United States consular officer certifying the petitioner to be a United States citizen and the bearer of a currently valid United States passport;

(v) The petitioner's Certificate of Naturalization or Certificate of Citizenship;

(vi) Department of State Form FS-240, Report of Birth Abroad of a Citizen of the United States, relating to the petitioner;

(vii) The petitioner's Form I-551, Permanent Resident Card, or other proof given by the Service as evidence of lawful permanent residence. Photocopies of Form I-551 or of a Certificate of Naturalization or

Certificate of Citizenship may be submitted as evidence of status as a lawfully permanent resident or United States citizen, respectively.

(2) Secondary evidence. If primary evidence is unavailable, the petitioner must present secondary evidence. Any evidence submitted as secondary evidence will be evaluated for authenticity and credibility. Secondary evidence may include, but is not limited to, one or more of the following documents:

(i) A baptismal certificate with the seal of the church, showing the date and place of birth in the United States and the date of baptism;

(ii) Affidavits sworn to by persons who were living at the time and who have personal knowledge of the event to which they attest. The affidavits must contain the affiant's full name and address, date and place of birth, relationship to the parties, if any, and complete details concerning how the affiant acquired knowledge of the event;

(iii) Early school records (preferably from the first school) showing the date of admission to the school, the child's date and place of birth, and the name(s) and place(s) of birth of the parent(s);

(iv) Census records showing the name, place of birth, and date of birth or age of the petitioner; or

(v) If it is determined that it would cause unusual delay or hardship to obtain documentary proof of birth in the United States, a United States citizen petitioner who is a member of the Armed Forces of the United States and who is serving outside the United States may submit a statement from the appropriate authority of the Armed Forces. The statement should attest to the fact that the personnel records of the Armed Forces show that the petitioner was born in the United States on a certain date.

(3) Evidence submitted with a self-petition. If a self-petitioner filing under section 204(a)(1)(A)(iii), 204(a)(1)(A)(iv), 204(a)(1)(B)(ii), or 204(a)(1)(B)(iii) of the Act is unable to present primary or secondary evidence of the abuser's status, the Service will attempt to electronically verify the abuser's citizenship or immigration status from information contained in Service computerized records. Other Service records may also be reviewed at the discretion of the adjudicating officer. If the Service is unable to identify a record as relating to the abuser or the record does not establish the abuser's immigration or citizenship status, the self-petition will be adjudicated based on the information submitted by the self-petitioner.

HISTORY:

[57 FR 41056, Sept. 9, 1992; 58 FR 48778, Sept. 20, 1993; 59 FR 47063, Sept. 14, 1994; 60 FR 14353, Mar. 17, 1995; 61 FR 13061, 13072, 13073, Mar. 26, 1996; 63 FR 70313, 70315, Dec. 21, 1998; 72 FR 19100, 19106, Apr. 17, 2007; 72 FR 56832, 56853, Oct. 4, 2007; 74 FR 26933, 26936, June 5, 2009; 76 FR 28303, 28305, May 17, 2011]

§ 204.2 Petitions for relatives, widows and widowers, and abused spouses and children.

(a) Petition for a spouse —

(1) Eligibility. A United States citizen or alien admitted for lawful permanent residence may file a petition on behalf of a spouse.

(i) Marriage within five years of petitioner's obtaining lawful permanent resident status.

(A) A visa petition filed on behalf of an alien by a lawful permanent resident spouse may not be approved if the marriage occurred within five years of the petitioner being accorded the status of lawful permanent resident based upon a prior marriage to a United States citizen or alien lawfully admitted for permanent residence, unless:

(1) The petitioner establishes by clear and convincing evidence that the marriage through which the petitioner gained permanent residence was not entered into for the purposes of evading the immigration laws; or

(2) The marriage through which the petitioner obtained permanent residence was terminated through death.

(B) Documentation. The petitioner should submit documents which cover the period of the prior marriage. The types of documents which may establish that the prior marriage was not entered into for the purpose of evading the immigration laws include, but are not limited to:

(1) Documentation showing joint ownership of property;

(2) A lease showing joint tenancy of a common residence;

(3) Documentation showing commingling of financial resources;

(4) Birth certificate(s) of child(ren) born to the petitioner and prior spouse;

(5) Affidavits sworn to or affirmed by third parties having personal knowledge of the bona fides of the prior marital relationship. (Each affidavit must contain the full name and address, date and place of birth of the person making the affidavit; his or her relationship, if any, to the petitioner, beneficiary or prior spouse; and complete information and details explaining how the person acquired his or her knowledge of the prior marriage. The affiant may be required to testify before an immigration officer about the information contained in the affidavit. Affidavits should be supported, if possible, by one or more types of documentary evidence listed in this paragraph.); or

(6) Any other documentation which is relevant to establish that the prior marriage was not entered into in order to evade the immigration laws of the United States.

(C) The petitioner must establish by clear and convincing evidence that the prior marriage was not entered into for the purpose of evading the immigration laws. Failure to meet the "clear and convincing evidence" standard will result in the denial of the petition. Such a denial shall be without prejudice to the filing of a new petition once the petitioner has acquired five years of lawful permanent residence. The director may choose to initiate deportation proceedings based upon information gained through the adjudication of the petition; however, failure to initiate such proceedings shall not establish that the petitioner's prior marriage was not entered into for the purpose of evading the immigration laws. Unless the petition is approved, the beneficiary shall not be accorded a filing date within the meaning of section 203(c) of the Act based upon any spousal second preference petition.

(ii) Fraudulent marriage prohibition. Section 204(c) of the Act prohibits the approval of a visa petition filed on behalf of an alien who has attempted or conspired to enter into a marriage for the purpose of evading the immigration laws. The director will deny a petition for immigrant visa classification filed on behalf of any alien for whom there is substantial and probative evidence of such an attempt or conspiracy, regardless of whether that alien received a benefit through the attempt or conspiracy. Although it is not necessary that the alien have been convicted of, or even prosecuted for, the attempt or conspiracy, the evidence of the attempt or conspiracy must be contained in the alien's file.

(iii) Marriage during proceedings — general prohibition against approval of visa petition. A visa petition filed on behalf of an alien by a United States citizen or a lawful permanent resident spouse shall not be approved if the marriage creating the relationship occurred on or after November 10, 1986, and while the alien was in exclusion, deportation, or removal proceedings, or judicial proceedings relating thereto. Determination of commencement and termination of proceedings and exemptions shall be in accordance with § 245.1(c)(8) of this chapter, except that the burden in visa petition proceedings to establish eligibility for the exemption in § 245.1(c)(8)(iii)(F) of this chapter shall rest with the petitioner.

(A) Request for exemption. No application or fee is required to request an exemption. The request must be made in writing and submitted with the Form I-130. The request must state the reason for seeking the exemption and must be supported by documentary evidence establishing eligibility for the exemption.

(B) Evidence to establish eligibility for the bona fide marriage exemption. The petitioner should submit documents which establish that the marriage was entered into in good faith and not entered into for the purpose of procuring the alien's entry as an immigrant. The types of documents the petitioner may submit include, but are not limited to:

(1) Documentation showing joint ownership of property;

(2) Lease showing joint tenancy of a common residence;

(3) Documentation showing commingling of financial resources;

(4) Birth certificate(s) of child(ren) born to the petitioner and beneficiary;

(5) Affidavits of third parties having knowledge of the bona fides of the marital relationship (Such persons may be required to testify before an immigration officer as to the information contained in the affidavit. Affidavits must be sworn to or affirmed by people who have personal knowledge of the marital relationship. Each affidavit must contain the full name and address, date and place of birth of the person making the affidavit and his or her relationship to the spouses, if any. The affidavit must contain complete information and details explaining how the person acquired his or her knowledge of the marriage. Affidavits should be supported, if possible, by one or more types of documentary evidence listed in this paragraph); or

(6) Any other documentation which is relevant to establish that the marriage was not entered into in order to evade the immigration laws of the United States.

(C) Decision. Any petition filed during the prohibited period shall be denied, unless the petitioner establishes eligibility for an exemption from the general prohibition. The petitioner shall be notified in writing of the decision of the director.

(D) Denials. The denial of a petition because the marriage took place during the prohibited period shall be without prejudice to the filing of a new petition after the beneficiary has resided outside the United States for the required period of two years following the marriage. The denial shall also be without prejudice to the consideration of a new petition or a motion to reopen the visa petition proceedings if deportation or exclusion proceedings are terminated after the denial other than by the beneficiary's departure from the United States. Furthermore, the denial shall be without prejudice to the consideration of a new petition or motion to reopen the visa petition proceedings, if the petitioner establishes eligibility for the bona fide marriage exemption contained in this part: Provided, That no motion to reopen visa petition proceedings may be accepted if the approval of the motion would result in the beneficiary being accorded a priority date within the meaning of section 203(c) of the Act earlier than November 29, 1990.

(E) Appeals. The decision of the Board of Immigration Appeals concerning the denial of a relative visa petition because the petitioner failed to establish eligibility for the bona fide marriage exemption contained in this part will constitute the single level of appellate review established by statute.

(F) Priority date. A preference beneficiary shall not be accorded a priority date within the meaning of section 203(c) of the Act based upon any relative petition filed during the prohibited period, unless an exemption contained in this part has been granted. Furthermore, a preference beneficiary shall not be accorded a priority date prior to November 29, 1990, based upon the approval of a request for consideration for the bona fide marriage exemption contained in this part.

(2) Evidence for petition for a spouse. In addition to evidence of United States citizenship or lawful permanent residence, the petitioner must also provide evidence of the claimed relationship. A petition submitted on behalf of a spouse must be accompanied by a recent ADIT-style photograph of the petitioner, a recent ADIT-style photograph of the beneficiary, a certificate of marriage issued by civil authorities, and proof of the legal termination of all previous marriages of both the petitioner and the beneficiary. However, non-ADIT-style photographs may be accepted by the district

director when the petitioner or beneficiary reside(s) in a country where such photographs are unavailable or cost prohibitive.

(3) Decision on and disposition of petition. The approved petition will be forwarded to the Department of State's Processing Center. If the beneficiary is in the United States and is eligible for adjustment of status under section 245 of the Act, the approved petition will be retained by the Service. If the petition is denied, the petitioner will be notified of the reasons for the denial and of the right to appeal in accordance with the provisions of 8 CFR 3.3.

(4) Derivative beneficiaries. No alien may be classified as an immediate relative as defined in section 201(b) of the Act unless he or she is the direct beneficiary of an approved petition for that classification. Therefore, a child of an alien approved for classification as an immediate relative spouse is not eligible for derivative classification and must have a separate petition filed on his or her behalf. A child accompanying or following to join a principal alien under section 203(a)(2) of the Act may be included in the principal alien's second preference visa petition. The child will be accorded second preference classification and the same priority date as the principal alien. However, if the child reaches the age of twenty-one prior to the issuance of a visa to the principal alien parent, a separate petition will be required. In such a case, the original priority date will be retained if the subsequent petition is filed by the same petitioner. Such retention of priority date will be accorded only to a son or daughter previously eligible as a derivative beneficiary under a second preference spousal petition.

(b) Petition by widow or widower of a United States citizen —

(1) Eligibility. A widow or widower of a United States citizen may file a petition and be classified as an immediate relative under section 201(b) of the Act if:

(i) He or she had been married for at least two years to a United States citizen.

(NOTE: The United States citizen is not required to have had the status of United States citizen for the entire two year period, but must have been a United States citizen at the time of death.)

(ii) The petition is filed within two years of the death of the citizen spouse or before November 29, 1992, if the citizen spouse died before November 29, 1990;

(iii) The alien petitioner and the citizen spouse were not legally separated at the time of the citizen's death; and

(iv) The alien spouse has not remarried.

(2) Evidence for petition of widow or widower. If a petition is submitted by the widow or widower of a deceased United States citizen, it must be accompanied by evidence of citizenship of the United States citizen and primary evidence, if available, of the relationship in the form of a marriage certificate issued by civil authorities, proof of the termination of all prior marriages of both husband and wife, and the United States citizen's death certificate issued by civil authorities. To determine the availability of primary documents, the Service will refer to the Department of State's Foreign Affairs Manual (FAM). When the FAM shows that primary documents are generally available in the country at issue but the petitioner claims that his or her document is unavailable, a letter from the appropriate registrar stating that the document is not available will be required before the Service will accept secondary evidence. Secondary evidence will be evaluated for its authenticity and credibility. Secondary evidence may include:

(i) Such evidence of the marriage and termination of prior marriages as religious documents, tribal records, census records, or affidavits; and

(ii) Such evidence of the United States citizen's death as religious documents, funeral service records, obituaries, or affidavits. Affidavits submitted as secondary evidence pursuant to paragraphs (b)(2)(i) and (b)(2)(ii) of this section must be sworn to or affirmed by people who have personal knowledge of the event to which they attest. Each affidavit should contain the full name and address, date and place of birth of the person making the affidavit and his or her relationship, if any, to the widow or widower. Any such affidavit must contain complete information and details explaining how knowledge of the event was acquired.

(3) Decision on and disposition of petition. The approved petition will be forwarded to the Department of State's Processing Center. If the widow or widower is in the United States and is eligible for adjustment of status under section 245 of the Act, the approved petition will be retained by the Service. If the petition is denied, the widow or widower will be notified of the reasons for the denial and of the right to appeal in accordance with the provisions of 8 CFR 3.3.

(4) Derivative beneficiaries. A child of an alien widow or widower classified as an immediate relative is eligible for derivative classification as an immediate relative. Such a child may be included in the principal alien's immediate relative visa petition, and may accompany or follow to join the principal alien to the United States. Derivative benefits do not extend to an unmarried or married son or daughter of an alien widow or widower.

(c) Self-petition by spouse of abusive citizen or lawful permanent resident —

(1) Eligibility —

(i) Basic eligibility requirements. A spouse may file a self-petition under section 204(a)(1)(A)(iii) or 204(a)(1)(B)(ii) of the Act for his or her classification as an immediate relative or as a preference immigrant if he or she:

(A) Is the spouse of a citizen or lawful permanent resident of the United States;

(B) Is eligible for immigrant classification under section 201(b)(2)(A)(i) or 203(a)(2)(A) of the Act based on that relationship;

(C) Is residing in the United States;

(D) Has resided in the United States with the citizen or lawful permanent resident spouse;

(E) Has been battered by, or has been the subject of extreme cruelty perpetrated by, the citizen or lawful permanent resident during the marriage; or is that parent of a child who has been battered by, or has been the subject of extreme cruelty perpetrated by, the citizen or lawful permanent resident during the marriage;

(F) Is a person of good moral character;

(G) Is a person whose deportation would result in extreme hardship to himself, herself, or his or her child; and

(H) Entered into the marriage to the citizen or lawful permanent resident in good faith.

(ii) Legal status of the marriage. The self-petitioning spouse must be legally married to the abuser when the petition is properly filed with the Service. A spousal self-petition must be denied if the marriage to the abuser legally ended through annulment, death, or divorce before that time. After the self-petition has been properly filed, the legal termination of the marriage will have no effect on the decision made on the self-petition. The self-petitioner's remarriage, however, will be a basis for the denial of a pending self-petition.

(iii) Citizenship or immigration status of the abuser. The abusive spouse must be a citizen of the United States or a lawful permanent resident of the United States when the petition is filed and when it is approved. Changes in the abuser's citizenship or lawful permanent resident status after the approval will have no effect on the self-petition. A self-petition approved on the basis of a relationship to an abusive lawful permanent resident spouse will not be automatically upgraded to immediate relative status. The self-petitioner would not be precluded, however, from filing a new self-petition for immediate relative classification after the abuser's naturalization, provided the self-petitioner continues to meet the self-petitioning requirements.

(iv) Eligibility for immigrant classification. A self-petitioner is required to comply with the provisions of section 204(c) of the Act, section 204(g) of the Act, and section 204(a)(2) of the Act.

(v) Residence. A self-petition will not be approved if the self-petitioner is not residing in the United States when the self-petition is filed. The self-petitioner is not required to be living with the abuser when the petition is filed, but he or she must have resided with the abuser in the United States in the past.

(vi) Battery or extreme cruelty. For the purpose of this chapter, the phrase "was battered by or was the subject of extreme cruelty" includes, but is not limited to, being the victim of any act or threatened act of violence, including any forceful detention, which results or threatens to result in physical or mental injury. Psychological or sexual abuse or exploitation, including rape, molestation, incest (if the victim is a minor), or forced prostitution shall be considered acts of violence. Other abusive actions may also be acts of violence under certain circumstances, including acts that, in and of themselves, may not initially appear violent but that are a part of an overall pattern of violence. The qualifying abuse must have been committed by the citizen or lawful permanent resident spouse, must have been perpetrated against the self-petitioner or the self-petitioner's child, and must have taken place during the self-petitioner's marriage to the abuser.

(vii) Good moral character. A self-petitioner will be found to lack good moral character if he or she is a person described in section 101(f) of the Act. Extenuating circumstances may be taken into account if the person has not been convicted of an offense or offenses but admits to the commission of an act or acts that could show a lack of good moral character under section 101(f) of the Act. A person who was subjected to abuse in the form of forced prostitution or who can establish that he or she was forced to engage in other behavior that could render the person excludable under section 212(a) of the Act would not be precluded from being found to be a person of good moral character, provided the person has not been convicted for the commission of the offense or offenses in a court of law. A self-petitioner will also be found to lack good moral character, unless he or she establishes extenuating circumstances, if he or she willfully failed or refused to support dependents; or committed unlawful acts that adversely reflect upon his or her moral character, or was convicted or imprisoned for such acts, although the acts do not require an automatic finding of lack of good moral character. A self-petitioner's claim of good moral character will be evaluated on a case-by-case basis, taking into account the provisions of section 101(f) of the Act and the standards of the average citizen in the community. If the results of record checks conducted prior to the issuance of an immigrant visa or approval of an application for adjustment of status disclose that the self-petitioner is no longer a person of good moral character or that he or she has not been a person of good moral character in the past, a pending self-petition will be denied or the approval of a self-petition will be revoked.

(viii) Extreme hardship. The Service will consider all credible evidence of extreme hardship submitted with a self-petition, including evidence of hardship arising from circumstances surrounding the abuse. The extreme hardship claim will be evaluated on a case-by-case basis after a review of the evidence in the case. Self-petitioners are encouraged to cite and document all applicable factors, since there is no guarantee that a particular reason or reasons will result in a finding that deportation would cause extreme hardship. Hardship to persons other than the self-petitioner or the self-petitioner's child cannot be considered in determining whether a self-petitioning spouse's deportation would cause extreme hardship.

(ix) Good faith marriage. A spousal self-petition cannot be approved if the self-petitioner entered into the marriage to the abuser for the primary purpose of circumventing the immigration laws. A self-petition will not be denied, however, solely because the spouses are not living together and the marriage is no longer viable.

(2) Evidence for a spousal self-petition —

(i) General. Self-petitioners are encouraged to submit primary evidence whenever possible. The Service will consider, however, any credible evidence relevant to the petition. The determination of what evidence is credible and the weight to be given that evidence shall be within the sole discretion of the Service.

(ii) Relationship. A self-petition filed by a spouse must be accompanied by evidence of citizenship of the United States citizen or proof of the immigration status of the lawful permanent resident abuser. It must also be accompanied by evidence of the relationship. Primary evidence of a marital relationship is a marriage certificate issued by civil authorities, and proof of the termination of all prior marriages, if any, of both the self-petitioner and the abuser. If the self-petition is based on a claim that the self-petitioner's child was battered or subjected to extreme cruelty committed by the citizen or lawful permanent resident spouse, the self-petition should also be accompanied by the child's birth certificate or other evidence showing the relationship between the self-petitioner and the abused child.

(iii) Residence. One or more documents may be submitted showing that the self-petitioner and the abuser have resided together in the United States. One or more documents may also be submitted showing that the self-petitioner is residing in the United States when the self-petition is filed. Employment records, utility receipts, school records, hospital or medical records, birth certificates of children born in the United States, deeds, mortgages, rental records, insurance policies, affidavits or any other type of relevant credible evidence of residency may be submitted.

(iv) Abuse. Evidence of abuse may include, but is not limited to, reports and affidavits from police, judges and other court officials, medical personnel, school officials, clergy, social workers, and other social service agency personnel. Persons who have obtained an order of protection against the abuser or have taken other legal steps to end the abuse are strongly encouraged to submit copies of the relating legal documents. Evidence that the abuse victim sought safe-haven in a battered women's shelter or similar refuge may be relevant, as may a combination of documents such as a photograph of the visibly injured self-petitioner supported by affidavits. Other forms of credible relevant evidence will also be considered. Documentary proof of non-qualifying abuses may only be used to establish a pattern of abuse and violence and to support a claim that qualifying abuse also occurred.

(v) Good moral character. Primary evidence of the self-petitioner's good moral character is the self-petitioner's affidavit. The affidavit should be accompanied by a local police clearance or a state-issued criminal background check from each locality or state in the United States in which the self-petitioner has resided for six or more months during the 3-year period immediately preceding the filing of the self-petition. Self-petitioners who lived outside the United States during this time should submit a police clearance, criminal background check, or similar report issued by the appropriate authority in each foreign country in which he or she resided for six or more months during the 3-year period immediately preceding the filing of the self-petition. If police clearances, criminal background checks, or similar reports are not available for some or all locations, the self-petitioner may include an explanation and submit other evidence with his or her affidavit. The Service will consider other credible evidence of good moral character, such as affidavits from responsible persons who can knowledgeably attest to the self-petitioner's good moral character.

(vi) Extreme hardship. Evidence of extreme hardship may include affidavits, birth certificates of children, medical reports, protection orders and other court documents, police reports, and other relevant credible evidence.

(vii) Good faith marriage. Evidence of good faith at the time of marriage may include, but is not limited to, proof that one spouse has been listed as the other's spouse on insurance policies, property leases, income tax forms, or bank accounts; and testimony or other evidence regarding courtship, wedding ceremony, shared residence and experiences. Other types of readily available evidence might include the birth certificates of children born to the abuser and the spouse; police, medical, or court documents providing information about the relationship; and affidavits of persons with personal knowledge of the relationship. All credible relevant evidence will be considered.

(3) Decision on and disposition of the petition —

(i) Petition approved. If the self-petitioning spouse will apply for adjustment of status under section 245 of the Act, the approved petition will be retained by the Service. If the self-petitioner will apply for an immigrant visa abroad, the approved self-petition will be forwarded to the Department of State's National Visa Center.

(ii) Petition denied. If the self-petition is denied, the self-petitioner will be notified in writing of the reasons for the denial and of the right to appeal the decision.

(4) Derivative beneficiaries. A child accompanying or following-to-join the self-petitioning spouse may be accorded the same preference and priority date as the self-petitioner without the necessity of a separate petition, if the child has not been classified as an immigrant based on his or her own self-petition. A derivative child who had been included in a parent's self-petition may later file a self-petition, provided the child meets the self-petitioning requirements. A child who has been classified as an immigrant based on a petition filed by the abuser or another relative may also be derivatively included in a parent's self-petition. The derivative child must be unmarried, less than 21 years old, and otherwise qualify as the self-petitioner's child under section 101(b)(1)(F) of the Act until he or she becomes a lawful permanent resident based on the derivative classification.

(5) Name change. If the self-petitioner's current name is different than the name shown on the documents, evidence of the name change (such as the petitioner's marriage certificate, legal document showing name change, or other similar evidence) must accompany the self-petition.

(6) Prima facie determination —

(i) Upon receipt of a self-petition under paragraph (c)(1) of this section, the Service shall make a determination as to whether the petition and the supporting documentation establish a "prima facie case" for purposes of 8 U.S.C. 1641, as amended by section 501 of Public Law 104-208.

(ii) For purposes of paragraph (c)(6)(i) of this section, a prima facie case is established only if the petitioner submits a completed Form I-360 and other evidence supporting all of the elements required of a self-petitioner in paragraph (c)(1) of this section. A finding of prima facie eligibility does not relieve the petitioner of the burden of providing additional evidence in support of the petition and does not establish eligibility for the underlying petition.

(iii) If the Service determines that a petitioner has made a "prima facie case," the Service shall issue a Notice of Prima Facie Case to the petitioner. Such Notice shall be valid until the Service either grants or denies the petition.

(iv) For purposes of adjudicating the petition submitted under paragraph (c)(1) of this section, a prima facie determination —

(A) Shall not be considered evidence in support of the petition;

(B) Shall not be construed to make a determination of the credibility or probative value of any evidence submitted along with that petition; and,

(C) Shall not relieve the self-petitioner of his or her burden of complying with all of the evidentiary requirements of paragraph (c)(2) of this section.

(d) **Petition for a child or son or daughter —**

(1) Eligibility. A United States citizen may file a petition on behalf of an unmarried child under twenty-one years of age for immediate relative classification under section 201(b) of the Act. A United States citizen may file a petition on behalf of an unmarried son or daughter over twenty-one years of age under section 203(a)(1) or for a married son or daughter for preference classification under section 203(a)(3) of the Act. An alien lawfully admitted for permanent residence may file a petition on behalf of a child or an unmarried son or daughter for preference classification under section 203(a)(2) of the Act.

(2) Evidence to support petition for child or son or daughter. In addition to evidence of United States citizenship or lawful permanent resident, the petitioner must also provide evidence of the claimed relationship.

(i) Primary evidence for a legitimate child or son or daughter. If a petition is submitted by the mother, the birth certificate of the child showing the mother's name must accompany the petition. If the mother's name on the birth certificate is different from her name on the petition, evidence of the name change must also be submitted. If a petition is submitted by the father, the birth certificate of the child, a marriage certificate of the parents, and proof of legal termination of the parents' prior marriages, if any, issued by civil authorities must accompany the petition. If the father's name has been legally changed, evidence of the name change must also accompany the petition.

(ii) Primary evidence for a legitimated child or son or daughter. A child can be legitimated through the marriage of his or her natural parents, by the laws of the country or state of the child's residence or domicile, or by the laws of the country or state of the father's residence or domicile. If the legitimation is based on the natural parents' marriage, such marriage must have taken place while the child was under the age of eighteen. If the legitimation is based on the laws of the country or state of the child's residence or domicile, the law must have taken effect before the child's eighteenth birthday. If the legitimation is based on the laws of the country or state of the father's residence or domicile, the father must have resided — while the child was under eighteen years of age — in the country or state under whose laws the child has been legitimated. Primary evidence of the relationship should consist of the beneficiary's birth certificate and the parents' marriage certificate or other evidence of legitimation issued by civil authorities.

(iii) Primary evidence for an illegitimate child or son or daughter. If a petition is submitted by the mother, the child's birth certificate, issued by civil authorities and showing the mother's name, must accompany the petition. If the mother's name on the birth certificate is different from her name as reflected in the petition, evidence of the name change must also be submitted. If the petition is submitted by the purported father of a child or son or daughter born out of wedlock, the father must show that he is the natural father and that a bona fide parent-child relationship was established when the child or son or daughter was unmarried and under twenty-one years of age. Such a relationship will be deemed to exist or to have existed where the father demonstrates or has demonstrated an active concern for the child's support, instruction, and general welfare. Primary evidence to establish that the petitioner is the child's natural father is the beneficiary's birth certificate, issued by civil authorities and showing the father's name. If the father's name has been legally changed, evidence of the name change must accompany the petition. Evidence of a parent/child relationship should establish more than merely a biological relationship. Emotional and/or financial ties or a genuine concern and interest by the father for the child's support, instruction, and general welfare must be shown. There should be evidence that the father and child actually lived together or that the father held the child out as being his own, that he provided for some or all of the child's needs, or that in general the father's behavior evidenced a genuine concern for the child. The most persuasive evidence for establishing a bona fide parent/child relationship and financial responsibility by the father is documentary evidence which was contemporaneous with the events in question. Such evidence may include, but is not limited to: money order receipts or cancelled checks showing the father's financial support of the beneficiary; the father's income tax returns; the father's medical or insurance records which include the beneficiary as a dependent; school records for the beneficiary; correspondence between the parties; or notarized affidavits of friends, neighbors, school officials, or other associates knowledgeable about the relationship.

(iv) Primary evidence for a stepchild. If a petition is submitted by a stepparent on behalf of a stepchild or stepson or stepdaughter, the petition must be supported by the stepchild's or stepson's or stepdaughter's birth certificate, issued by civil authorities and showing the name of the beneficiary's parent to whom the petitioner is married, a marriage certificate issued by civil authorities which shows that the petitioner and the child's natural parent were married before the stepchild or stepson or stepdaughter reached the age of eighteen; and evidence of the termination of any prior marriages of the petitioner and the natural parent of the stepchild or stepson or stepdaughter.

(v) Secondary evidence. When it is established that primary evidence is not available, secondary evidence may be accepted. To determine the availability of primary documents, the Service will refer to the Department of State's Foreign Affairs Manual (FAM). When the FAM shows that primary documents are generally available in the country at issue but the petitioner claims that his or her document is unavailable, a letter from the appropriate registrar stating that the document is not available will be required before the Service will accept secondary evidence. Secondary evidence will be evaluated for its authenticity and credibility. Secondary evidence may take the form of historical evidence; such evidence must have been issued contemporaneously with the event which it documents any may include, but is not limited to, medical records, school records, and religious documents. Affidavits may also by accepted. When affidavits are submitted, they must be sworn to by persons who were born at the time of and who have personal knowledge of the event to which they attest. Any affidavit must contain the affiant's full name and address, date and place of birth, relationship to the party, if any, and complete details concerning how the affiant acquired knowledge of the event.

(vi) Blood tests. The director may require that a specific Blood Group Antigen Test be conducted of the beneficiary and the beneficiary's father and mother. In general, blood tests will be required only after other forms of evidence have proven inconclusive. If the specific Blood Group Antigen Test is also found not to be conclusive and the director determines that additional evidence is needed, a Human Leucocyte Antigen (HLA) test may be requested. Tests will be conducted, at the expense of the petitioner or beneficiary, by the United States Public Health Service physician who is authorized overseas or by a qualified medical specialist designated by the district director. The results of the test should be reported on Form G-620. Refusal to submit to a Specific Blood Group Antigen or HLA test when requested may constitute a basis for denial of the petition, unless a legitimate religious objection has been established. When a legitimate religious objection is established, alternate forms of evidence may be considered based upon documentation already submitted.

(vii) Primary evidence for an adopted child or son or daughter. A petition may be submitted on behalf of an adopted child or son or daughter by a United States citizen or lawful permanent resident if the adoption took place before the beneficiary's sixteenth birthday, and if the child has been in the legal custody of the adopting parent or parents and has resided with the adopting parent or parents for at least two years. A copy of the adoption decree, issued by the civil authorities, must accompany the petition.

(A) Legal custody means the assumption of responsibility for a minor by an adult under the laws of the state and under the order or approval of a court of law or other appropriate government entity. This provision requires that a legal process involving the courts or other recognized government entity take place. If the adopting parent was granted legal custody by the court or recognized governmental entity prior to the adoption, that period may be counted toward fulfillment of the two-year legal custody requirement. However, if custody was not granted prior to the adoption, the adoption decree shall be deemed to mark the commencement of legal custody. An informal custodial or guardianship document, such as a sworn affidavit signed before a notary public, is insufficient for this purpose.

(B) Evidence must also be submitted to show that the beneficiary resided with the petitioner for at least two years. Generally, such documentation must establish that the petitioner and the beneficiary resided together in a familial relationship. Evidence of parental control may include, but is not limited to, evidence that the adoptive parent owns or maintains the property where the child resides and provides financial support and day-to-day supervision. The evidence must clearly indicate the physical living arrangements of the adopted child, the adoptive parent(s), and the natural parent(s) for the period of time during which the adoptive parent claims to have met the residence requirement. When the adopted child continued to reside in the same household as a natural parent(s) during the period in which the adoptive parent petitioner seeks to establish his or her compliance with this requirement, the petitioner has the burden of establishing that he or she exercised primary parental control during that period of residence.

(C) Legal custody and residence occurring prior to or after the adoption will satisfy both requirements. Legal custody, like residence, is accounted for in the aggregate. Therefore, a break in legal custody or residence will not affect the time already fulfilled. To meet the definition of child contained in sections 101(b)(1)(E) and 101(b)(2) of the Act, the child must have been under 16 years of age when the adoption is finalized.

(D) On or after the Convention effective date, as defined in 8 CFR part 204.301, a United States citizen who is habitually resident in the United States, as determined under 8 CFR 204.303, may not file a Form I-130 under this section on behalf of child who was habitually resident in a Convention country, as determined under 8 CFR 204.303, unless the adoption was completed before the Convention effective date. In the case of any adoption occurring on or after the Convention effective date, a Form I-130 may be filed and approved only if the United States citizen petitioner was not habitually resident in the United States at the time of the adoption.

(E) For purposes of paragraph (d)(2)(vii)(D) of this section, USCIS will deem a United States citizen, 8 CFR 204.303 notwithstanding, to have been habitually resident outside the United States, if the citizen satisfies the 2-year joint residence and custody requirements by residing with the child outside the United States.

(F) For purposes of paragraph (d)(2)(vii)(D) of this section, USCIS will not approve a Form I-130 under section 101(b)(1)(E) of the Act on behalf of an alien child who is present in the United States based on an adoption that is entered on or after the Convention effective date, but whose habitual residence immediately before the child's arrival in the United States was in a Convention country. However, the U.S. citizen seeking the child's adoption may file a Form I-800A and Form I-800 under 8 CFR part 204, subpart C.

(3) Decision on and disposition of petition. The approved petition will be forwarded to the Department of State's Processing Center. If the beneficiary is in the United States and is eligible for adjustment of status under section 245 of the Act, the approved petition will be retained by the Service. If the petition is denied, the petitioner will be notified of the reasons for the denial and of the right to appeal in accordance with the provisions of 8 CFR 3.3.

(4) Derivative beneficiaries. A spouse or child accompanying or following to join a principal alien as used in this section may be accorded the same preference and priority date as the principal alien without the necessity of a separate petition. However, a child of an alien who is approved for classification as an immediate relative is not eligible for derivative classification and must have a separate petition approved on his or her behalf.

(5) Name change. When the petitioner's name does not appear on the child's birth certificate, evidence of the name change (such as the petitioner's marriage certificate, legal document showing name change, or other similar evidence) must accompany the petition. If the beneficiary's name has been legally changed, evidence of the name change must also accompany the petition.

(e) Self-petition by child of abusive citizen or lawful permanent resident —

(1) Eligibility

(i) A child may file a self-petition under section 204(a)(1)(A)(iv) or 204(a)(1)(B)(iii) of the Act if he or she:

(A) Is the child of a citizen or lawful permanent resident of the United States;

(B) Is eligible for immigrant classification under section 201(b)(2)(A)(i) or 203(a)(2)(A) of the Act based on that relationship;

(C) Is residing in the United States;

(D) Has resided in the United States with the citizen or lawful permanent resident parent;

(E) Has been battered by, or has been the subject of extreme cruelty perpetrated by, the citizen or lawful permanent resident parent while residing with that parent;

(F) Is a person of good moral character; and

(G) Is a person whose deportation would result in extreme hardship to himself or herself.

(ii) Parent-child relationship to the abuser. The self-petitioning child must be unmarried, less than 21 years of age, and otherwise qualify as the abuser's child under the definition of child contained in section 101(b)(1) of the Act when the petition is filed and when it is approved. Termination of the abuser's parental rights or a change in legal custody does not alter the self-petitioning relationship provided the child meets the requirements of section 101(b)(1) of the Act.

(iii) Citizenship or immigration status of the abuser. The abusive parent must be a citizen of the United States or a lawful permanent resident of the United States when the petition is filed and when it is approved. Changes in the abuser's citizenship or lawful permanent resident status after the approval will have no effect on the self-petition. A self-petition approved on the basis of a relationship to an abusive lawful permanent resident will not be automatically upgraded to immediate relative status. The self-petitioning child would not be precluded, however, from filing a new self-petition for immediate relative classification after the abuser's naturalization, provided the self-petitioning child continues to meet the self-petitioning requirements.

(iv) Eligibility for immigrant classification. A self-petitioner is required to comply with the provisions of section 204(c) of the Act, section 204(g) of the Act, and section 204(a)(2) of the Act.

(v) Residence. A self-petition will not be approved if the self-petitioner is not residing in the United States when the self-petition is filed. The self-petitioner is not required to be living with the abuser when the petition is filed, but he or she must have resided with the abuser in the United States in the past.

(vi) Battery or extreme cruelty. For the purpose of this chapter, the phrase "was battered by or was the subject of extreme cruelty" includes, but is not limited to, being the victim of any act or threatened act of violence, including any forceful detention, which results or threatens to result in physical or mental injury. Psychological or sexual abuse or exploitation, including rape, molestation, incest (if the victim is a minor), or forced prostitution shall be considered acts of violence. Other abusive actions may also be acts of violence under certain circumstances, including acts that, in and of themselves, may not initially appear violent but are a part of an overall pattern of violence. The qualifying abuse must have been committed by the citizen or lawful permanent resident parent, must have been perpetrated against the self-petitioner, and must have taken place while the self-petitioner was residing with the abuser.

(vii) Good moral character. A self-petitioner will be found to lack good moral character if he or she is a person described in section 101(f) of the Act. Extenuating circumstances may be taken into account if the person has not been convicted of an offense or offenses but admits to the commission of an act or acts that could show a lack of good moral character under section 101(f) of the Act. A person who was subjected to abuse in the form of forced prostitution or who can establish that he or she was forced to engage in other behavior that could render the person excludable under section 212(a) of the Act would not be precluded from being found to be a person of good moral character, provided the person has not been convicted for the commission of the offense or offenses in a court of law. A self-petitioner will also be found to lack good moral character, unless he or she establishes extenuating circumstances, if he or she willfully failed or refused to support dependents; or committed unlawful acts that adversely reflect upon his or her moral character, or was convicted or imprisoned for such acts, although the acts do not require an automatic finding of lack of good moral character. A self-petitioner's claim of good moral character will be evaluated on a case-by-case basis, taking into account the provisions of section 101(f) of the Act and the standards of the average citizen in the community. If the results of record checks conducted prior to the issuance of an immigrant visa or approval of an application for adjustment of status disclose that the self-petitioner is no longer a person of good moral character or that he or she has not been a person of good moral character in the past, a pending self-petition will be denied or the approval of a self-petition will be revoked.

(viii) Extreme hardship. The Service will consider all credible evidence of extreme hardship submitted with a self-petition, including evidence of hardship arising from circumstances surrounding the abuse. The extreme hardship claim will be evaluated on a case-by-case basis after a review of the evidence in the case. Self-petitioners are encouraged to cite and document all applicable factors, since there is no guarantee that a particular reason or reasons will result in a finding that deportation would cause extreme hardship. Hardship to persons other than the self-petitioner cannot be considered in determining whether a self-petitioning child's deportation would cause extreme hardship.

(2) Evidence for a child's self-petition.

(i) General. Self-petitioners are encouraged to submit primary evidence whenever possible. The Service will consider, however, any credible evidence relevant to the petition. The determination of what evidence is credible and the weight to be given that evidence shall be within the sole discretion of the Service.

(ii) Relationship. A self-petition filed by a child must be accompanied by evidence of citizenship of the United States citizen or proof of the immigration status of the lawful permanent resident abuser. It must also be accompanied by evidence of the relationship. Primary evidence of the relationship between:

(A) The self-petitioning child and an abusive biological mother is the self-petitioner's birth certificate issued by civil authorities;

(B) A self-petitioning child who was born in wedlock and an abusive biological father is the child's birth certificate issued by civil authorities, the marriage certificate of the child's parents, and evidence of legal termination of all prior marriages, if any;

(C) A legitimated self-petitioning child and an abusive biological father is the child's birth certificate issued by civil authorities, and evidence of the child's legitimation;

(D) A self-petitioning child who was born out of wedlock and an abusive biological father is the child's birth certificate issued by civil authorities showing the father's name, and evidence that a bona fide parent-child relationship has been established between the child and the parent;

(E) A self-petitioning stepchild and an abusive stepparent is the child's birth certificate issued by civil authorities, the marriage certificate of the child's parent and the stepparent showing marriage before the stepchild reached 18 years of age, and evidence of legal termination of all prior marriages of either parent, if any; and

(F) An adopted self-petitioning child and an abusive adoptive parent is an adoption decree showing that the adoption took place before the child reached 16 years of age, and evidence that the child has been residing with and in the legal custody of the abusive adoptive parent for at least 2 years.

(iii) Residence. One or more documents may be submitted showing that the self-petitioner and the abuser have resided together in the United States. One or more documents may also be submitted showing that the self-petitioner is residing in the United States when the self-petition is filed. Employment records, school records, hospital or medical records, rental records, insurance policies, affidavits or any other type of relevant credible evidence of residency may be submitted.

(iv) Abuse. Evidence of abuse may include, but is not limited to, reports and affidavits from police, judges and other court officials, medical personnel, school officials, clergy, social workers, and other social service agency personnel. Persons who have obtained an order of protection against the abuser or taken other legal steps to end the abuse are strongly encouraged to submit copies of the relating legal documents. Evidence that the abuse victim sought safe-haven in a battered women's shelter or similar refuge may be relevant, as may a combination of documents such as a photograph of the visibly injured self-petitioner supported by affidavits. Other types of credible relevant evidence will also be considered. Documentary proof of non-qualifying abuse may only be used to establish a pattern of abuse and violence and to support a claim that qualifying abuse also occurred.

(v) Good moral character. Primary evidence of the self-petitioner's good moral character is the self-petitioner's affidavit. The affidavit should be accompanied by a local police clearance or a state-issued criminal background check from each locality or state in the United States in which the self-petitioner has resided for six or more months during the 3-year period immediately preceding the filing of the self-petition. Self-petitioners who lived outside the United States during this time should submit a police clearance, criminal background check, or similar report issued by the appropriate authority in the foreign country in which he or she resided for six or more months during the 3-year period immediately preceding the filing of the self-petition. If police clearances, criminal background checks, or similar reports are not available for some or all locations, the self-petitioner may include an explanation and submit other evidence with his or her affidavit. The Service will consider other credible evidence of good moral character, such as affidavits from responsible persons who can knowledgeably attest to the self-petitioner's good moral character. A child who is less than 14 years of age is presumed to be a person of good moral character and is not required to submit affidavits of good moral character, police clearances, criminal background checks, or other evidence of good moral character.

(vi) Extreme hardship. Evidence of extreme hardship may include affidavits, medical reports, protection orders and other court documents, police reports, and other relevant credible evidence.

(3) Decision on and disposition of the petition —

(i) Petition approved. If the self-petitioning child will apply for adjustment of status under section 245 of the Act, the approved petition will be retained by the Service. If the self-petitioner will apply for an immigrant visa abroad, the approved self-petition will be forwarded to the Department of State's National Visa Center.

(ii) Petition denied. If the self-petition is denied, the self-petitioner will be notified in writing of the reasons for the denial and of the right to appeal the decision.

(4) Derivative beneficiaries. A child of a self-petitioning child is not eligible for derivative classification and must have a petition filed on his or her behalf if seeking immigrant classification.

(5) Name change. If the self-petitioner's current name is different than the name shown on the documents, evidence of the name change (such as the petitioner's marriage certificate, legal document showing the name change, or other similar evidence) must accompany the self-petition.

(6) prima facie determination —

(i) Upon receipt of a self-petition under paragraph (e)(1) of this section, the Service shall make a determination as to whether the petition and the supporting documentation establish a "prima facie case" for purposes of 8 U.S.C. 1641, as amended by section 501 of Public Law 104-208.

(ii) For purposes of paragraph (e)(6)(i) of this section, a prima facie case is established only if the petitioner submits a completed Form I-360 and other evidence supporting all of the elements required of a self-petitioner in paragraph (e)(1) of this section. A finding of prima facie eligibility does not relieve the petitioner of the burden of providing additional evidence in support of the petition and does not establish eligibility for the underlying petition.

(iii) If the Service determines that a petitioner has made a "prima facie case" the Service shall issue a Notice of Prima Facie Case to the petitioner. Such Notice shall be valid until the Service either grants or denies the petition.

(iv) For purposes of adjudicating the petition submitted under paragraph (e)(1) of this section, a prima facie determination:

(A) Shall not be considered evidence in support of the petition;

(B) Shall not be construed to make a determination of the credibility or probative value of any evidence submitted along with that petition; and,

(C) Shall not relieve the self-petitioner of his or her burden of complying with all of the evidentiary requirements of paragraph (e)(2) of this section.

(f) **Petition for a parent —**

(1) Eligibility. Only a United States citizen who is twenty-one years of age or older may file a petition on behalf of a parent for classification under section 201(b) of the Act.

(2) Evidence to support a petition for a parent. In addition to evidence of United States citizenship as listed in § 204.1(g) of this part, the petitioner must also provide evidence of the claimed relationship.

(i) Primary evidence if petitioner is a legitimate son or daughter. If a petition is submitted on behalf of the mother, the birth certificate of the petitioner showing the mother's name must accompany the petition. If the mother's name on the birth certificate is different from her name as reflected in the petition, evidence of the name change must also be submitted. If a petition is submitted on behalf of the father, the birth certificate of the petitioner, a marriage certificate of the parents, and proof of legal termination of the parents' prior marriages, if any, issued by civil authorities must accompany the petition. If the father's name on the birth certificate has been legally changed, evidence of the name change must also accompany the petition.

(ii) Primary evidence if petitioner is a legitimated son or daughter. A child can be legitimated through the marriage of his or her natural parents, by the laws of the country or state of the child's residence or domicile, or by the laws of the country or state of the father's residence or domicile. If the legitimation is based on the natural parent's marriage, such marriage must have taken place while the child was under the age of eighteen. If the legitimation is based on the laws of the country or state of the child's residence or domicile, the law must have taken effect before the child's eighteenth birthday. If the legitimation is based on the laws of the country or state of the father's residence or domicile, the father must have resided — while the child was under eighteen years of age — in the country or state under whose laws the child has been legitimated. Primary evidence of the relationship should consist of petitioner's birth certificate and the parents' marriage certificate or other evidence of legitimation issued by civil authorities.

(iii) Primary evidence if the petitioner is an illegitimate son or daughter. If a petition is submitted on behalf of the mother, the petitioner's birth certificate, issued by civil authorities and showing the mother's name, must accompany the petition. If the mother's name on the birth certificate is different from her name as reflected in the petition, evidence of the name change must also be submitted. If the petition is submitted on behalf of the purported father of the petitioner, the petitioner must show that the beneficiary is his or her natural father and that a bona fide parent-child relationship was established when the petitioner was unmarried and under twenty-one years of age. Such a relationship will be deemed to exist or to have existed where the father demonstrates or has demonstrated an active concern for the child's support, instruction, and general welfare. Primary evidence to establish that the beneficiary is the petitioner's natural father is the petitioner's birth certificate, issued by civil authorities and showing the father's name. If the father's name has been legally changed, evidence of the name change must accompany the petition. Evidence of a parent/child relationship should establish more than merely a biological relationship. Emotional and/or financial ties or a genuine concern and interest by the father for the child's support, instruction, and general welfare must be shown. There should be evidence that the father and child actually lived together or that the father held the child out as being his own, that he provided for some or all of the child's needs, or that in general the father's behavior evidenced a genuine concern for the child. The most persuasive evidence for establishing a bona fide parent/child relationship is documentary evidence which was contemporaneous with the events in question. Such evidence may include, but is not limited to: money order receipts or cancelled checks showing the father's financial support of the beneficiary; the father's income tax returns; the father's medical or insurance records which include the petitioner as a dependent; school records for the petitioner; correspondence between the parties; or notarized affidavits of friends, neighbors, school officials, or other associates knowledgeable as to the relationship.

(iv) Primary evidence if petitioner is an adopted son or daughter. A petition may be submitted for an adoptive parent by a United States citizen who is twenty-one years of age or older if the adoption took place before the petitioner's sixteenth birthday and if the two year legal custody and residence requirements have been met. A copy of the adoption decree, issued by the civil authorities, must accompany the petition.

(A) Legal custody means the assumption of responsibility for a minor by an adult under the laws of the state and under the order or approval of a court of law or other appropriate government entity. This provision requires that a legal process involving the courts or other recognized government entity take place. If the adopting parent was granted legal custody by the court or recognized governmental entity prior to the adoption, that period may be counted toward fulfillment of the two-year legal custody requirement. However, if custody was not granted prior to the adoption, the adoption decree shall be deemed to mark the commencement of legal custody. An informal custodial or guardianship document, such as a sworn affidavit signed before a notary public, is insufficient for this purpose.

(B) Evidence must also be submitted to show that the beneficiary resided with the petitioner for at least two years. Generally, such documentation must establish that the petitioner and the beneficiary resided together in a parental relationship. The evidence must clearly indicate the physical living arrangements of the adopted child, the adoptive parent(s), and the natural parent(s) for the period of time during which the adoptive parent claims to have met the residence requirement.

(C) Legal custody and residence occurring prior to or after the adoption will satisfy both requirements. Legal custody, like residence, is accounted for in the aggregate. Therefore, a break in legal custody or residence will not affect the time already fulfilled. To meet the definition of child contained in sections 101(b)(1)(E) and 101(b)(2) of the Act, the child must have been under 16 years of age when the adoption is finalized.

(v) Name change. When the petition is filed by a child for the child's parent, and the parent's name is not on the child's birth certificate, evidence of the name change (such as the parent's marriage certificate, a legal document showing the parent's name change, or other similar evidence) must accompany the petition. If the petitioner's name has been legally changed, evidence of the name change must also accompany the petition.

(3) Decision on and disposition of petition. The approved petition will be forwarded to the Department of State's Processing Center. If the beneficiary is in the United States and is eligible for adjustment of status under section 245 of the Act, the approved petition will be retained by the Service. If the petition is denied, the petitioner will be notified of the reasons for the denial and of the right to appeal in accordance with the provisions of 8 CFR 3.3.

(4) Derivative beneficiaries. A child or a spouse of a principal alien who is approved for classification as an immediate relative is not eligible for derivative classification and must have a separate petition approved on his or her behalf.

(g) **Petition for a brother or sister —**

(1) Eligibility. Only a United States citizen who is twenty-one years of age or older may file a petition of a brother or sister for classification under section 203(a)(4) of the Act.

(2) Evidence to support a petition for brother or sister. In addition to evidence of United States citizenship, the petitioner must also provide evidence of the claimed relationship.

(i) Primary evidence if the siblings share a common mother or are both legitimate children of a common father. If a sibling relationship is claimed through a common mother, the petition must be supported by a birth certificate of the petitioner and a birth certificate of the beneficiary showing a common mother. If the mother's name on one birth certificate is different from her name as reflected on the other birth certificate or in the petition, evidence of the name change must also be submitted. If a sibling relationship is claimed through a common father, the birth certificates of the beneficiary and petitioner, a marriage certificate of the parents' and proof of legal termination of the parents, prior marriage(s), if any, issued by civil authorities must accompany the petition. If the father's name has been legally changed, evidence of the name change must also accompany the petition.

(ii) Primary evidence if either or both siblings are legitimated. A child can be legitimated through the marriage of his or her natural parents, by the laws of the country or state of the child's residence or domicile, or by the laws of the country or state of the father's residence or domicile. If the legitimation is based on the natural parents' marriage, such marriage must have taken place while the child was under the age of eighteen. If the legitimation is based on the laws of the country or state of the child's residence or domicile, the law must have taken effect before the child's eighteenth birthday. If based on the laws of the country or state of the father's residence or domicile, the father must have resided — while the child was under eighteen years of age — in the country or state under whose laws the child has been legitimated. Primary evidence of the relationship should consist of the petitioner's birth certificate, the beneficiary's birth certificate, and the parents' marriage certificate or other evidence of legitimation issued by civil authorities.

(iii) Primary evidence if either sibling is illegitimate. If one or both of the siblings is (are) the illegitimate child(ren) of a common father, the petitioner must show that they are the natural children of the father and that a bona fide parent-child relationship was established when the illegitimate child(ren) was (were) unmarried and under twenty-one years of age. Such a relationship will be deemed to exist or to have existed where the father demonstrates or has demonstrated an active concern for the child's support, instruction, and general welfare. Primary evidence is the petitioner's and beneficiary's birth certificates, issued by civil authorities and showing the father's name, and evidence that the siblings have or had a bona fide parent/child relationship with the natural father. If the father's name has been legally changed, evidence of the name change must accompany the petition. Evidence of a parent/child relationship should establish more than merely a biological relationship. Emotional and/or financial ties or a genuine concern and interest by the father for the child's support, instruction, and general welfare must be shown. There should be evidence that the father and child actually lived together or that the father held the child out as being his own, that he provided for some or all of the child's needs, or that in general the father's behavior evidenced a genuine concern for the child. The most persuasive evidence for establishing a bona fide parent/child relationship is documentary evidence which was contemporaneous with the events in question. Such evidence may include, but is not limited to: money order receipts or canceled checks showing the father's financial support of the beneficiary; the father's income tax returns; the father's medical or insurance records which include the beneficiary as a dependent; school records for the beneficiary; correspondence between the parties; or notarized affidavits of friends, neighbors, school officials, or other associates knowledgeable about the relationship.

(iv) Primary evidence for stepsiblings. If the petition is submitted on behalf of a brother or sister having a common father, the relationship of both the petitioner and the beneficiary to the father must be established as required in paragraphs (g)(2)(ii) and (g)(2)(iii) of this section. If the petitioner and beneficiary are stepsiblings through the marriages of their common father to different mothers, the marriage certificates of the parents and evidence of the termination of any prior marriages of the parents must be submitted.

(3) Decision on and disposition of petition. The approved petition will be forwarded to the Department of State's Processing Center. If the beneficiary is in the United States and is eligible for adjustment of status under section 245 of the Act, the approved petition will be retained by the Service. If the petition is denied, the petitioner will be notified of the reasons for the denial and of the right to appeal in accordance with the provisions of 8 CFR 3.3.

(4) Derivative beneficiaries. A spouse or a child accompanying or following to join a principal alien beneficiary under this section may be accorded the same preference and priority date as the principal alien without the necessity of a separate petition.

(5) Name change. If the name of the petitioner, the beneficiary, or both has been legally changed, evidence showing the name change (such as a marriage certificate, a legal document showing the name change, or other similar evidence) must accompany the petition.

(h) **Validity of approved petitions —**

(1) General. Unless terminated pursuant to section 203(g) of the Act or revoked pursuant to part 205 of this chapter, the approval of a petition to classify an alien as a preference immigrant under paragraphs (a)(1), (a)(2), (a)(3), or (a)(4) of section 203 of the Act, or as an immediate relative under section 201(b) of the Act, shall remain valid for the duration of the relationship to the petitioner and of the petitioner's status as established in the petition.

(2) Subsequent petition by same petitioner for same beneficiary. When a visa petition has been approved, and subsequently a new petition by the same petitioner is approved for the same preference classification on behalf of the same beneficiary, the latter approval shall be regarded as a reaffirmation or reinstatement of the validity of the original petition, except when the original petition has been terminated pursuant to section 203(g) of the Act or revoked pursuant to part 205 of this chapter, or when an immigrant visa has been issued to the beneficiary as a result of the petition approval. A self-petition filed under section 204(a)(1)(A)(iii), 204(a)(1)(A)(iv), 204(a)(1)(B)(ii), 204(a)(1)(B)(iii) of the Act based on the relationship to an abusive citizen or lawful permanent resident of the United States will not be regarded as a reaffirmation or reinstatement of a petition previously filed by the abuser. A self-petitioner who has been the beneficiary of a visa petition filed by the abuser to accord the self-petitioner immigrant classification as his or her spouse or child, however, will be allowed to transfer the visa petition's priority date to the self-petition. The visa petition's priority date may be assigned to the self-petition without regard to the current validity of the visa petition. The burden of proof to establish the existence of and the filing date of the visa petition lies with the self-petitioner, although the Service will attempt to verify a claimed filing through a search of the Service's computerized records or other records deemed appropriate by the adjudicating officer. A new self-petition filed under section 204(a)(1)(A)(iii),

204(a)(1)(A)(iv), 204(a)(1)(B)(ii), or 204(a)(1)(B)(iii) of the Act will not be regarded as a reaffirmation or reinstatement of the original self-petition unless the prior and the subsequent self-petitions are based on the relationship to the same abusive citizen or lawful permanent resident of the United States.

(i) Automatic conversion of preference classification —

(1) By change in beneficiary's marital status

(i) A currently valid petition previously approved to classify the beneficiary as the unmarried son or daughter of a United States citizen under section 203(a)(1) of the Act shall be regarded as having been approved for preference status under section 203(a)(3) of the Act as of the date the beneficiary marries. The beneficiary's priority date is the same as the date the petition for classification under section 203(a)(1) of the Act was properly filed.

(ii) A currently valid petition previously approved to classify a child of a United States citizen as an immediate relative under section 201(b) of the Act shall be regarded as having been approved for preference status under section 203(a)(3) of the Act as of the date the beneficiary marries. The beneficiary's priority date is the same as the date the petition for 201(b) classification was properly filed.

(iii) A currently valid petition classifying the married son or married daughter of a United States citizen for preference status under section 203(a)(3) of the Act shall, upon legal termination of the beneficiary's marriage, be regarded as having been approved under section 203(a)(1) of the Act if the beneficiary is over twenty-one years of age. The beneficiary's priority date is the same as the date the petition for classification under section 203(a)(3) of the Act was properly filed. If the beneficiary is under twenty-one years of age, the petition shall be regarded as having been approved for classification as an immediate relative under section 201(b) of the Act as of the date the petition for classification under section 203(a)(3) of the Act was properly filed.

(iv) A currently valid visa petition previously approved to classify the beneficiary as an immediate relative as the spouse of a United States citizen must be regarded, upon the death of the petitioner, as having been approved as a Form I-360, Petition for Amerasian, Widow(er) or Special Immigrant for classification under paragraph (b) of this section, if, on the date of the petitioner's death, the beneficiary satisfies the requirements of paragraph (b)(1) of this section. If the petitioner dies before the petition is approved, but, on the date of the petitioner's death, the beneficiary satisfies the requirements of paragraph (b)(1) of this section, then the petition shall be adjudicated as if it had been filed as a Form I-360, Petition for Amerasian, Widow(er) or Special Immigrant under paragraph (b) of this section.

(2) By the beneficiary's attainment of the age of twenty-one years. A currently valid petition classifying the child of a United States citizen as an immediate relative under section 201(b) of the Act shall be regarded as having been approved for preference status under section 203(a)(1) of the Act as of the beneficiary's twenty-first birthday. The beneficiary's priority date is the same as the date the petition for section 201(b) classification was filed.

(3) By the petitioner's naturalization. Effective upon the date of naturalization of a petitioner who had been lawfully admitted for permanent residence, a currently valid petition according preference status under section 203(a)(2) of the Act to the petitioner's spouse and unmarried children under twenty-one years of age shall be regarded as having been approved for immediate relative status under section 201(b) of the Act. Similarly, a currently valid petition according preference status under section 203(a)(2) of the Act for the unmarried son or daughter over twenty-one years of age shall be regarded as having been approved under section 203(a)(1) of the Act. In any case of conversion to classification under section 203(a)(1) of the Act, the beneficiary's priority date is the same as the date the petition for classification under section 203(a)(2) of the Act was properly filed. A self-petition filed under section 204(a)(1)(B)(ii) or 204(a)(1)(B)(iii) of the Act based on the relationship to an abusive lawful permanent resident of the United States for classification under section 203(a)(2) of the Act will not be affected by the abuser's naturalization and will not be automatically converted to a petition for immediate relative classification.

HISTORY:

[57 FR 41057, Sept. 9, 1992; 60 FR 34090, June 30, 1995; 60 FR 38948, July 31, 1995, as confirmed at 61 FR 7206, 7207, Feb. 27, 1996; 61 FR 13061, 13073, 13074, 13077, Mar. 26, 1996; 62 FR 10312, 10336, Mar. 6, 1997; 62 FR 60769, 60771, Nov. 13, 1997; 71 FR 35732, 35749, June 21, 2006; 72 FR 19100, 19107, Apr. 17, 2007; 72 FR 56832, 56853, Oct. 4, 2007; 90 FR 4587, 4588, Jan. 15, 2025]

§ 204.3 Orphan cases under section 101(b)(1)(F) of the Act (non-Hague Adoption Convention cases).

(a) This section addresses the immigration classification of alien orphans as provided for in section 101(b)(1)(F) of the Act.

(1) Except as provided in paragraph (a)(2) of this section, a child who meets the definition of orphan contained in section 101(b)(1)(F) of the Act is eligible for classification as the immediate relative of a U.S. citizen if:

(i) The U.S. citizen seeking the child's immigration can document that the citizen (and his or her spouse, if any) are capable of providing, and will provide, proper care for an alien orphan; and

(ii) The child is an orphan under section 101(b)(1)(F) of the Act.

A U.S. citizen may submit the documentation necessary for each of these determinations separately or at one time, depending on when the orphan is identified.

(2) Form I-600A or Form I-600 may not be filed under this section on or after the Convention effective date, as defined in 8 CFR 204.301, on behalf of a child who is habitually resident in a Convention country, as defined in 8 CFR 204.301. On or after the Convention effective

date, USCIS may approve a Form I-600 on behalf of a child who is habitually resident in a Convention country only if the Form I-600A or Form I-600 was filed before the Convention effective date.

(b) Definitions. As used in this section, the term:

Abandonment by both parents means that the parents have willfully forsaken all parental rights, obligations, and claims to the child, as well as all control over and possession of the child, without intending to transfer, or without transferring, these rights to any specific person(s). Abandonment must include not only the intention to surrender all parental rights, obligations, and claims to the child, and control over and possession of the child, but also the actual act of surrendering such rights, obligations, claims, control, and possession. A relinquishment or release by the parents to the prospective adoptive parents or for a specific adoption does not constitute abandonment. Similarly, the relinquishment or release of the child by the parents to a third party for custodial care in anticipation of, or preparation for, adoption does not constitute abandonment unless the third party (such as a governmental agency, a court of competent jurisdiction, an adoption agency, or an orphanage) is authorized under the child welfare laws of the foreign-sending country to act in such a capacity. A child who is placed temporarily in an orphanage shall not be considered to be abandoned if the parents express an intention to retrieve the child, are contributing or attempting to contribute to the support of the child, or otherwise exhibit ongoing parental interest in the child. A child who has been given unconditionally to an orphanage shall be considered to be abandoned.

Adult member of the prospective adoptive parents' household means an individual, other than a prospective adoptive parent, over the age of 18 whose principal or only residence is the home of the prospective adoptive parents. This definition excludes any child of the prospective adoptive parents, whose principal or only residence is the home of the prospective adoptive parents, who reaches his or her eighteenth birthday after the prospective adoptive parents have filed the advanced processing application (or the advanced processing application concurrently with the orphan petition) unless the director has an articulable and substantive reason for requiring an evaluation by a home study preparer and/or fingerprint check.

Advanced processing application means Form I-600A (Application for Advance Processing of an Orphan Petition) completed in accordance with the form's instructions and submitted with the required supporting documentation and the fee as required in 8 CFR 106.2. The application must be signed in accordance with the form's instructions by the married petitioner and spouse, or by the unmarried petitioner.

Application is synonymous with advanced processing application.

Competent authority means a court or governmental agency of a foreign-sending country having jurisdiction and authority to make decisions in matters of child welfare, including adoption.

Desertion by both parents means that the parents have willfully forsaken their child and have refused to carry out their parental rights and obligations and that, as a result, the child has become a ward of a competent authority in accordance with the laws of the foreign-sending country.

Disappearance of both parents means that both parents have unaccountably or inexplicably passed out of the child's life, their whereabouts are unknown, there is no reasonable hope of their reappearance, and there has been a reasonable effort to locate them as determined by a competent authority in accordance with the laws of the foreign-sending country.

Foreign-sending country means the country of the orphan's citizenship, or if he or she is not permanently residing in the country of citizenship, the country of the orphan's habitual residence. This excludes a country to which the orphan travels temporarily, or to which he or she travels either as a prelude to, or in conjunction with, his or her adoption and/or immigration to the United States.

Home study preparer means any party licensed or otherwise authorized under the law of the State of the orphan's proposed residence to conduct the research and preparation for a home study, including the required personal interview(s). This term includes a public agency with authority under that State's law in adoption matters, public or private adoption agencies licensed or otherwise authorized by the laws of that State to place children for adoption, and organizations or individuals licensed or otherwise authorized to conduct the research and preparation for a home study, including the required personal interview(s), under the laws of the State of the orphan's proposed residence. In the case of an orphan whose adoption has been finalized abroad and whose adoptive parents reside abroad, the home study preparer includes any party licensed or otherwise authorized to conduct home studies under the law of any State of the United States, or any party licensed or otherwise authorized by the foreign country's adoption authorities to conduct home studies under the laws of the foreign country.

Incapable of providing proper care means that a sole or surviving parent is unable to provide for the child's basic needs, consistent with the local standards of the foreign sending country.

Loss from both parents means the involuntary severance or detachment of the child from the parents in a permanent manner such as that caused by a natural disaster, civil unrest, or other calamitous event beyond the control of the parents, as verified by a competent authority in accordance with the laws of the foreign sending country.

Orphan petition means Form I-600 (Petition to Classify Orphan as an Immediate Relative). The petition must be completed in accordance with the form's instructions and submitted with the required supporting documentation and, if there is not a pending, or currently valid and approved advanced processing application, the fee as required in 8 CFR 106.2. The petition must be signed in accordance with the form's instructions by the married petitioner and spouse, or the unmarried petitioner.

Overseas site means the Department of State immigrant visa-issuing post having jurisdiction over the orphan's residence, or in foreign countries in which the Services has an office or offices, the Service office having jurisdiction over the orphan's residence.

Petition is synonymous with orphan petition.

Petitioner means a married United States citizen of any age, or an unmarried United States citizen who is at least 24 years old at the time he or she files the advanced processing application and at least 25 years old at the time he or she files the orphan petition. In the case of a married couple, both of whom are United States citizens, either party may be the petitioner.

Prospective adoptive parents means a married United States citizen of any age and his or her spouse of any age, or an unmarried United States citizen who is at least 24 years old at the time he or she files the advanced processing application and at least 25 years old at the time he or she files the orphan petition. The spouse of the United States citizen may be a citizen or an alien. An alien spouse must be in lawful immigration status if residing in the United States.

Separation from both parents means the involuntary severance of the child from his or her parents by action of a competent authority for good cause and in accordance with the laws of the foreign-sending country. The parents must have been properly notified and granted the opportunity to contest such action. The termination of all parental rights and obligations must be permanent and unconditional.

Sole parent means the mother when it is established that the child is illegitimate and has not acquired a parent within the meaning of section 101(b)(2) of the Act. An illegitimate child shall be considered to have a sole parent if his or her father has severed all parental ties, rights, duties, and obligations to the child, or if his or her father has, in writing, irrevocably released the child for emigration and adoption. This definition is not applicable to children born in countries which make no distinction between a child born in or out of wedlock, since all such children are considered to be legitimate. In all cases, a sole parent must be incapable of providing proper care as that term is defined in this section.

Surviving parent means the child's living parent when the child's other parent is dead, and the child has not acquired another parent within the meaning of section 101(b)(2) of the Act. In all cases, a surviving parent must be incapable of providing proper care as that term is defined in this section.

(c) Supporting documentation for an advanced processing application. The prospective adoptive parents may file an advanced processing application before an orphan is identified in order to secure the necessary clearance to file the orphan petition. Any document not in the English language must be accompanied by a certified English translation.

(1) Required supporting documentation that must accompany the advanced processing application. The following supporting documentation must accompany an advanced processing application at the time of filing:

(i) Evidence of the petitioner's United States citizenship as set forth in § 204.1(g) and, if the petitioner is married and the married couple is residing in the United States, evidence of the spouse's United States citizenship or lawful immigration status;

(ii) A copy of the petitioner's marriage certificate to his or her spouse, if the petitioner is currently married;

(iii) Evidence of legal termination of all previous marriages for the petitioner and/or spouse, if previously married; and

(iv) Evidence of compliance with preadoption requirements, if any, of the State of the orphan's proposed residence in cases where it is known that there will be no adoption abroad, or that both members of the married prospective adoptive couple or the unmarried prospective adoptive parent will not personally see the child prior to, or during, the adoption abroad, and/or that the adoption abroad will not be full and final. Any preadoption requirements which cannot be met at the time the advanced processing application is filed because of operation of State law must be noted and explained when the application is filed. Preadoption requirements must be met at the time the petition is filed, except for those which cannot be met until the orphan arrives in the United States.

(2) Home study. The home study must comply with the requirements contained in paragraph (e) of this section. If the home study is not submitted when the advanced processing application is filed, it must be submitted within one year of the filing date of the advanced processing application, or the application will be denied pursuant to paragraph (h)(5) of this section.

(3) After receipt of a properly filed advanced processing application, USCIS will fingerprint each member of the married prospective adoptive couple or the unmarried prospective adoptive parent, as prescribed in 8 CFR 103.16. USCIS will also fingerprint each additional adult member of the prospective adoptive parents' household, as prescribed in 8 CFR 103.16. USCIS may waive the requirement that each additional adult member of the prospective adoptive parents' household be fingerprinted when it determines that such adult is physically unable to be fingerprinted because of age or medical condition.

(d) Supporting documentation for a petition for an identified orphan. Any document not in the English language must be accompanied by a certified English translation. If an orphan has been identified for adoption and the advanced processing application is pending, the prospective adoptive parents may file the orphan petition at the USCIS office where the application is pending. The prospective adoptive parents who have an approved advanced processing application must file an orphan petition and all supporting documents within 15 months of the date of the approval of the advanced processing application. If the prospective adoptive parents fail to file the orphan petition within the approval validity period of the advanced processing application, the advanced processing application will be deemed abandoned under paragraph (h)(7) of this section. If the prospective adoptive parents file the orphan petition after the approval period of the advanced processing application has expired, the petition will be denied under paragraph (h)(13) of this section. Prospective adoptive parents who do not have an advanced processing application approved or pending may file the application and petition concurrently on one Form I-600 if they have identified an orphan for adoption. An orphan petition must be accompanied by full documentation as follows:

(1) Filing an orphan petition after the advanced processing application has been approved. The following supporting documentation must accompany an orphan petition filed after approval of the advanced processing application:

(i) Evidence of approval of the advanced processing application;

(ii) The orphan's birth certificate, or if such a certificate is not available, an explanation together with other proof of identity and age;

(iii) Evidence that the child is an orphan as appropriate to the case:

(A) Evidence that the orphan has been abandoned or deserted by, separated or lost from both parents, or that both parents have disappeared as those terms are defined in paragraph (b) of this section; or

(B) The death certificate(s) of the orphan's parent(s), if applicable;

(C) If the orphan has only a sole or surviving parent, as defined in paragraph (b) of this section, evidence of this fact and evidence that the sole or surviving parent is incapable of providing for the orphan's care and has irrevocably released the orphan for emigration and adoption; and

(iv) Evidence of adoption abroad or that the prospective adoptive parents have, or a person or entity working on their behalf has, custody of the orphan for emigration and adoption in accordance with the laws of the foreign-sending country:

(A) A legible, certified copy of the adoption decree, if the orphan has been the subject of a full and final adoption abroad, and evidence that the unmarried petitioner, or married petitioner and spouse, saw the orphan prior to or during the adoption proceeding abroad; or

(B) If the orphan is to be adopted in the United States because there was no adoption abroad, or the unmarried petitioner, or married petitioner and spouse, did not personally see the orphan prior to or during the adoption proceeding abroad, and/or the adoption abroad was not full and final:

(1) Evidence that the prospective adoptive parents have, or a person or entity working on their behalf has, secured custody of the orphan in accordance with the laws of the foreign-sending country;

(2) An irrevocable release of the orphan for emigration and adoption from the person, organization, or competent authority which had the immediately previous legal custody or control over the orphan if the adoption was not full and final under the laws of the foreign-sending country;

(3) Evidence of compliance with all preadoption requirements, if any, of the State of the orphan's proposed residence. (Any such requirements that cannot be complied with prior to the orphan's arrival in the United States because of State law must be noted and explained); and

(4) Evidence that the State of the orphan's proposed residence allows readoption or provides for judicial recognition of the adoption abroad if there was an adoption abroad which does not meet statutory requirements pursuant to section 101(b)(1)(F) of the Act, because the unmarried petitioner, or married petitioner and spouse, did not personally see the orphan prior to or during the adoption proceeding abroad, and/or the adoption abroad was not full and final.

(2) Filing an orphan petition while the advanced processing application is pending. An orphan petition filed while an advanced processing application is pending must be filed at the Service office where the application is pending. The following supporting documentation must accompany an orphan petition filed while the advanced processing application is pending:

(i) A photocopy of the fee receipt relating to the advanced processing application, or if not available, other evidence that the advanced processing application has been filed, such as a statement including the date when the application was filed;

(ii) The home study, if not already submitted; and

(iii) The supporting documentation for an orphan petition required in paragraph (d)(1) of this section, except for paragraph (d)(1)(i) of this section.

(3) Filing an orphan petition concurrently with the advanced processing application. A petition filed concurrently with the advanced processing application must be submitted on Form I-600, completed and signed in accordance with the form's instructions. (Under this concurrent procedure, Form I-600 serves as both the Forms I-600A and I-600, and the prospective adoptive parents should not file a separate Form I-600A). The following supporting documentation must accompany a petition filed concurrently with the application under this provision:

(i) The supporting documentation for an advanced processing application required in paragraph (c) of this section; and

(ii) The supporting documentation for an orphan petition required in paragraph (d)(1) of this section, except for paragraph (d)(1)(i) of this section.

(e) Home study requirements. For immigration purposes, a home study is a process for screening and preparing prospective adoptive parents who are interested in adopting an orphan from another country. The home study should be tailored to the particular situation of the prospective adoptive parents: for example, a family which previously has adopted children will require different preparation than a family that has no adopted children. If there are any additional adult members of the prospective adoptive parents' household, the home study must address this fact. The home study preparer must interview any additional adult member of the prospective adoptive parents' household and assess him or her in light of the requirements of paragraphs (e)(1), (e)(2)(i), (iii), (iv), and (v) of this section. A home study must be conducted by a home study preparer, as defined in paragraph (b) of this section. The home study, or the most recent update to the home study, must not be more than six months old at the time the home study is submitted to the Service. Only one copy of the home study must be submitted to the Service. Ordinarily, a home study (or a home study and update as discussed above) will not have to be updated after it has been submitted to the Service unless there is a significant change in the household of the prospective adoptive parents such as a change in residence, marital status, criminal history, financial resources, and/or the addition of one or more children or other dependents to the family prior to the orphan's immigration into the United States. In addition to meeting any State, professional, or agency requirements, a home study must include the following:

(1) Personal interview(s) and home visit(s). The home study preparer must conduct at least one interview in person, and at least one home visit, with the prospective adoptive couple or the unmarried prospective adoptive parent. Each additional adult member of the prospective adoptive parents' household must also be interviewed in person at least once. The home study report must state the number of such interviews and visits, and must specify any other contacts with the prospective adoptive parents and any adult member of the prospective adoptive parents' household.

(2) Assessment of the capabilities of the prospective adoptive parents to properly parent the orphan. The home study must include a discussion of the following areas:

(i) Assessment of the physical, mental, and emotional capabilities of the prospective adoptive parents to properly parent the orphan. The home study preparer must make an initial assessment of how the physical, mental, and emotional health of the prospective adoptive parents would affect their ability to properly care for the prospective orphan. If the home study preparer determines that there are areas beyond his or her expertise which need to be addressed, he or she shall refer the prospective adoptive parents to an appropriate licensed professional, such as a physician, psychiatrist, clinical psychologist, or clinical social worker for an evaluation. Some problems may not necessarily disqualify applicants. For example, certain physical limitations may indicate which categories of children may be most appropriately placed with certain prospective adoptive parents. Certain mental and emotional health problems may be successfully treated. The home study must include the home study preparer's assessment of any such potential problem areas, a copy of any outside evaluation(s), and the home study preparer's recommended restrictions, if any, on the characteristics of the child to be placed in the home. Additionally, the home study preparer must apply the requirements of this paragraph to each adult member of the prospective adoptive parents' household.

(ii) Assessment of the finances of the prospective adoptive parents. The financial assessment must include a description of the income, financial resources, debts, and expenses of the prospective adoptive parents. A statement concerning the evidence that was considered to verify the source and amount of income and financial resources must be included. Any income designated for the support of one or more children in the care and custody of the prospective adoptive parents, such as funds for foster care, or any income designated for the support of another member of the household must not be counted towards the financial resources available for the support of a prospective orphan. The Service will not routinely require a detailed financial statement or supporting financial documents. However, should the need arise, the Service reserves the right to ask for such detailed documentation.

(iii) History of abuse and/or violence.

(A) Screening for abuse and violence.

(1) Checking available child abuse registries. The home study preparer must ensure that a check of each prospective adoptive parent and each adult member of the prospective adoptive parents' household has been made with available child abuse registries and must include in the home study the results of the checks including, if applicable, a report that no record was found to exist. Depending on the access allowed by the state of proposed residence of the orphan, the home study preparer must take one of the following courses of action:

(i) If the home study preparer is allowed access to information from the child abuse registries, he or she shall make the appropriate checks for each of the prospective adoptive parents and for each adult member of the prospective adoptive parents' household;

(ii) If the State requires the home study preparer to secure permission from each of the prospective adoptive parents and for each adult member of the prospective adoptive parents' household before gaining access to information in such registries, the home study preparer must secure such permission from those individuals, and make the appropriate checks;

(iii) If the State will only release information directly to each of the prospective adoptive parents and directly to the adult member of the prospective adoptive parents' household, those individuals must secure such information and provide it to the home study preparer. The home study preparer must include the results of these checks in the home study;

(iv) If the State will not release information to either the home study preparer or the prospective adoptive parents and the adult members of the prospective adoptive parents' household, this must be noted in the home study; or

(v) If the State does not have a child abuse registry, this must be noted in the home study.

(2) Inquiring about abuse and violence. The home study preparer must ask each prospective adoptive parent whether he or she has a history of substance abuse, sexual or child abuse, or domestic violence, even if it did not result in an arrest or conviction. The home study preparer must include each prospective adoptive parent's response to the questions regarding abuse and violence. Additionally, the home study preparer must apply the requirements of this paragraph to each adult member of the prospective adoptive parents' household.

(B) Information concerning history of abuse and/or violence. If the petitioner and/or spouse, if married, disclose(s) any history of abuse and/or violence as set forth in paragraph (e)(2)(iii)(A) of this section, or if, in the absence of such disclosure, the home study preparer becomes aware of any of the foregoing, the home study report must contain an evaluation of the suitability of the home for adoptive placement of an orphan in light of this history. This evaluation must include information concerning all arrests or convictions or history of substance abuse, sexual or child abuse, and/or domestic violence and the date of each occurrence. A certified copy of the documentation showing the final disposition of each incident, which resulted in arrest, indictment, conviction, and/or any other judicial or administrative action, must accompany the home study. Additionally, the prospective adoptive parent must submit a signed statement giving details including mitigating circumstances, if any, about each incident. The home study preparer must apply the requirements of this paragraph to each adult member of the prospective adoptive parents' household.

(C) Evidence of rehabilitation. If a prospective adoptive parent has a history of substance abuse, sexual or child abuse, and/or domestic violence, the home study preparer may, nevertheless, make a favorable finding if the prospective adoptive parent has demonstrated appropriate rehabilitation. In such a case, a discussion of such rehabilitation which demonstrates that the prospective adoptive parent is and will be able to provide proper care for the orphan must be included in the home study. Evidence of rehabilitation may include an evaluation of the seriousness of the arrest(s), conviction(s), or history of abuse, the number of such incidents, the length of time since the last incident, and any type of counseling or rehabilitation programs which have been successfully completed. Evidence of rehabilitation may also be provided by an appropriate licensed professional, such as a psychiatrist, clinical psychologist, or clinical social worker. The home study report must include all facts and circumstances which the home study preparer has considered, as well as the preparer's reasons for a favorable decision regarding the prospective adoptive parent. Additionally, if any adult member of the prospective adoptive parents' household has a history of substance abuse, sexual or child abuse, and/or domestic violence, the home study preparer must apply the requirements of this paragraph to that adult member of the prospective adoptive parents' household.

(D) Failure to disclose or cooperate. Failure to disclose an arrest, conviction, or history of substance abuse, sexual or child abuse, and/or domestic violence by the prospective adoptive parents or an adult member of the prospective adoptive parents' household to the home study preparer and to the Service, may result in the denial of the advanced processing application or, if applicable, the application and orphan petition, pursuant to paragraph (h)(4) of this section. Failure by the prospective adoptive parents or an adult member of the prospective adoptive parents' household to cooperate in having available child abuse registries in accordance with paragraphs (e)(2)(iii)(A)(1) and (e)(2)(iii)(A)(1)(i) through (e)(2)(iii)(A)(1)(iii) of this section will result in the denial of the advanced processing application or, if applicable, the application and orphan petition, pursuant to paragraph (h)(4) of this section.

(iv) Previous rejection for adoption or prior unfavorable home study. The home study preparer must ask each prospective adoptive parent whether he or she previously has been rejected as a prospective adoptive parent or has been the subject of an unfavorable home study, and must include each prospective adoptive parent's response to this question in the home study report. If a prospective adoptive parent previously has been rejected or found to be unsuitable, the reasons for such a finding must be set forth as well as the reason(s) why he or she is not being favorably considered as a prospective adoptive parent. A copy of each previous rejection and/or unfavorable home study must be attached to the favorable home study. Additionally, the home study preparer must apply the requirements of this paragraph to each adult member of the prospective adoptive parents' household.

(v) Criminal history. The prospective adoptive parents and the adult members of the prospective adoptive parents' household are expected to disclose to the home study preparer and the Service any history of arrest and/or conviction early in the advanced processing procedure. Failure to do so may result in denial pursuant to paragraph (h)(4) of this section or in delays. Early disclosure provides the prospective adoptive parents with the best opportunity to gather and present evidence, and it gives the home study preparer and the Service the opportunity to properly evaluate the criminal record in light of such evidence. When such information is not presented early in the process, it comes to light when the fingerprint checks are received by the Service. By that time, the prospective adoptive parents are usually well into preadoption proceedings of identifying a child and may even have firm travel plans. At times, the travel plans have to be rescheduled while the issues raised by the criminal record are addressed. It is in the best interests of all parties to have any criminal records disclosed and resolved early in the process.

(3) Living accommodations. The home study must include a detailed description of the living accommodations where the prospective adoptive parents currently reside. If the prospective adoptive parents are planning to move, the home study must include a description of the living accommodations where the child will reside with the prospective adoptive parents, if known. If the prospective adoptive parents are residing abroad at the time of the home study, the home study must include a description of the living accommodations where the child will reside in the United States with the prospective adoptive parents, if known. Each description must include an assessment of the suitability of accommodations for a child and a determination whether such space meets applicable State requirements, if any.

(4) Handicapped or special needs orphan. A home study conducted in conjunction with the proposed adoption of a special needs or handicapped orphan must contain a discussion of the prospective adoptive par-

ents' preparation, willingness, and ability to provide proper care for such an orphan.

(5) Summary of the counseling given and plans for post-placement counseling. The home study must include a summary of the counseling given to prepare the prospective adoptive parents for an international adoption and any plans for post-placement counseling. Such preadoption counseling must include a discussion of the processing, expenses, difficulties, and delays associated with international adoptions.

(6) Specific approval of the prospective adoptive parents for adoption. If the home study preparer's findings are favorable, the home study must contain his or her specific approval of the prospective adoptive parents for adoption and a discussion of the reasons for such approval. The home study must include the number of orphans which the prospective adoptive parents may adopt. The home study must state whether there are any specific restrictions to the adoption such as nationality, age, or gender of the orphan. If the home study preparer has approved the prospective parents for a handicapped or special needs adoption, this fact must be clearly stated.

(7) Home study preparer's certification and statement of authority to conduct home studies. The home study must include a statement in which the home study preparer certifies that he or she is licensed or otherwise authorized by the State of the orphan's proposed residence to research and prepare home studies. In the case of an orphan whose adoption was finalized abroad and whose adoptive parents reside abroad, the home study preparer must certify that he or she is licensed or otherwise authorized to conduct home studies under the law of any State of the United States, or authorized by the adoption authorities of the foreign country to conduct home studies under the laws of the foreign country. In every case, this statement must cite the State or country under whose authority the home study preparer is licensed or authorized, the specific law or regulation authorizing the preparer to conduct home studies, the license number, if any, and the expiration date, if any, of this authorization or license.

(8) Review of home study. If the prospective adoptive parents reside in a State which requires the State to review the home study, such a review must occur and be documented before the home study is submitted to the Service. If the prospective adoptive parents reside abroad, an appropriate public or private adoption agency licensed, or otherwise authorized, by any State of the United States to place children for adoption, must review and favorably recommend the home study before it is submitted to the Service.

(9) Home study updates and amendments —

(i) Updates. If the home study is more than six months old at the time it would be submitted to the Service, the prospective adoptive parents must ensure that it is updated by a home study preparer before it is submitted to the Service. Each update must include screening in accordance with paragraphs (e)(2)(iii) (A) and (B) of this section.

(ii) Amendments. If there have been any significant changes, such as a change in the residence of the prospective adoptive parents, marital status, criminal history, financial resources, and/or the addition of one or more children or other dependents to the family, the prospective adoptive parents must ensure that the home study is amended by a home study preparer to reflect any such changes. If the orphan's proposed State of residence has changed, the home study amendment must contain a recommendation in accordance with paragraph (e)(8) of this section, if required by State law. Any preadoption requirements of the new State must be complied with in the case of an orphan coming to the United States to be adopted.

(10) "Grandfather" provision for home study. A home study properly completed in conformance with the regulations in force prior to September 30, 1994, shall be considered acceptable if submitted to the Service within 90 days of September 30, 1994. Any such home study accepted under this "grandfather" provision must include screening in accordance with paragraphs (e)(2)(iii) (A) and (B) of this section. Additionally, any such home study submitted under this "grandfather" provision which is more than six months old at the time of its submission must be amended or updated pursuant to the requirements of paragraph (e)(9) of this section.

(f) State preadoption requirements —

(1) General. Many States have preadoption requirements which, under the Act, must be complied with in every case in which a child is coming to such a State as an orphan to be adopted in the United States.

(2) Child coming to be adopted in the United States. An orphan is coming to be adopted in the United States if he or she will not be or has not been adopted abroad, or if the unmarried petitioner or both the married petitioner and spouse did not or will not personally see the orphan prior to or during the adoption proceeding abroad, and/or if the adoption abroad will not be, or was not, full and final. If the prospective adoptive parents reside in a State with preadoption requirements and they plan to have the child come to the United States for adoption, they must submit evidence of compliance with the State's preadoption requirements to the Service. Any preadoption requirements which by operation of State law cannot be met before filing the advanced processing application must be noted. Such requirements must be met prior to filing the petition, except for those which cannot be met by operation of State law until the orphan is physically in the United States. Those requirements which cannot be met until the orphan is physically present in the United States must be noted.

(3) Special circumstances. If both members of the prospective adoptive couple or the unmarried prospective adoptive parent intend to travel abroad to see the child prior to or during the adoption, the Act permits the application and/or petition, if otherwise approvable, to be approved without preadoption requirements having been met. However, if plans change and both members of the prospective adoptive couple or the unmarried prospective adoptive parent fail to see the child prior to or during the adoption, then preadoption requirements must be met before the immigrant visa

can be issued, except for those preadoption requirements that cannot be met until the child is physically in the United States because of operation of State law.

(4) Evidence of compliance. In every case where compliance with preadoption requirements is required, the evidence of compliance must be in accordance with applicable State law, regulation, and procedure.

(g) Where to file. Form I-600, Petition to Classify Orphan as an Immediate Relative, and Form I-600A, Application for Advanced Processing of Orphan Petition, must be filed in accordance with the instructions on the form.

(h) Adjudication and decision —

(1) "Grandfather" provision for advanced processing application and/or orphan petition. All applications and petitions filed under prior regulations which are filed before and are still pending on September 30, 1994, shall be processed and adjudicated under the prior regulations.

(2) Director's responsibility to make an independent decision in an advanced processing application. No advanced processing application shall be approved unless the director is satisfied that proper care will be provided for the orphan. If the director has reason to believe that a favorable home study, or update, or both are based on an inadequate or erroneous evaluation of all the facts, he or she shall attempt to resolve the issue with the home study preparer, the agency making the recommendation pursuant to paragraph (e)(8) of this section, if any, and the prospective adoptive parents. If such consultations are unsatisfactory, the director may request a review and opinion from the appropriate State Government authorities.

(3) Advanced processing application approved. If the advanced processing application is approved:

(i) The prospective adoptive parents will be advised in writing. A notice of approval expires 15 months after the approval date.

(ii) USCIS may extend the validity period for the approval of a Form I-600A if requested in accordance with 8 CFR 106.2(a)(32). Form I-600A/I-600 Supplement 3 cannot be used to:

(A) Seek extension of an approval notice more than 90 days before the expiration of the validity period for the Form I-600A approval but must be filed on or before the date on which the validity period expires if the applicant seeks an extension.

(B) Extend eligibility to proceed as a Hague Adoption Convention transition case beyond the first extension once the Convention enters into force for the new Convention country.

(C) Request a change of country to a Hague Adoption Convention transition country for purposes of becoming a transition case if another country was already designated on the Form I-600A or the applicant previously changed countries.

(iii) Form I-600A/I-600 Supplement 3 may only be used to request an increase in the number of children the applicant/petitioner is approved to adopt from a transition country if: the additional child is a birth sibling of a child whom the applicant/petitioner has adopted or is in the process of adopting, as a transition case, and is identified and petitioned for while the Form I-600A approval is valid, unless the new Convention country prohibits such birth sibling cases from proceeding as transition cases.

(iv) If the Form I-600A approval is for more than one orphan, the prospective adoptive parents may file a petition for each of the additional children, to the maximum number approved.

(v) It does not guarantee that the orphan petition will be approved.

(4) Advanced processing application denied for failure to disclose history of abuse and/or violence, or for failure to disclose a criminal history, or for failure to cooperate in checking child abuse registries. Failure to disclose an arrest, conviction, or history of substance abuse, sexual or child abuse, and/or domestic violence, or a criminal history to the home study preparer and to the Service in accordance with paragraphs (e)(2)(iii) (A) and (B) and (e)(2)(v) of this section may result in the denial of the advanced processing application, or if applicable, the application and orphan petition filed concurrently. Failure by the prospective adoptive parents or an adult member of the prospective adoptive parents' household to cooperate in having available child abuse registries checked in accordance with paragraphs (e)(2)(iii)(A)(1) and (e)(2)(iii)(A)(1)(i) through (e)(2)(iii)(A)(1)(iii) of this section will result in the denial of the advanced processing application or, if applicable, the application and orphan petition filed concurrently. Any new application and/or petition filed within a year of such denial will also be denied.

(5) Advanced processing denied for failure to submit home study. If the home study is not submitted within one year of the filing date of the advanced processing application, the application shall be denied. This action shall be without prejudice to a new filing at any time with fee.

(6) Advanced processing application otherwise denied. If the director finds that the prospective adoptive parents have otherwise failed to establish eligibility, the applicable provisions of 8 CFR part 103 regarding a letter of intent to deny, if appropriate, and denial and notification of appeal rights shall govern.

(7) Advanced processing application deemed abandoned for failure to file orphan petition within the approval validity period of the advanced processing application. If an orphan petition is not properly filed within the validity period of the advanced processing application:

(i) The application will be deemed abandoned;

(ii) Supporting documentation will be returned to the prospective adoptive parents, except for documentation submitted by a third party which will be returned to the third party, and documentation relating to the biometric checks;

(iii) The director will dispose of documentation relating to biometrics checks in accordance with current policy; and

(iv) Such abandonment will be without prejudice to a new filing at any time with fee.

(8) Orphan petition approved by a stateside Service office. If the orphan petition is approved by a stateside

Service office, the prospective adoptive parents shall be advised in writing, telegraphic notification shall be sent to the immigrant visa-issuing post pursuant to paragraph (j)(3) of this section, and the petition and supporting documents shall be forwarded to the Department of State.

(9) Orphan petition approved by an overseas Service office. If the orphan petition is approved by an overseas Service office located in the country of the orphan's residence, the prospective adoptive parents shall be advised in writing, and the petition and supporting documents shall be forwarded to the immigrant visa-issuing post having jurisdiction for immigrant visa processing.

(10) Orphan petition approved at an immigrant visa-issuing post. If the orphan petition is approved at an immigrant visa-issuing post, the post shall initiate immigrant visa processing.

(11) Orphan petition found to be "not readily approvable" by a consular officer. If the consular officer adjudicating the orphan petition finds that it is "not readily approvable," he or she shall notify the prospective adoptive parents in his or her consular district and forward the petition, the supporting documents, the findings of the I-604 investigation conducted pursuant to paragraph (k)(1) of this section, and any other relating documentation to the overseas Service office having jurisdiction pursuant to § 100.4(b) of this chapter.

(12) Orphan petition denied: petitioner fails to establish that the child is an orphan. If the director finds that the petitioner has failed to establish that the child is an orphan who is eligible for the benefits sought, the applicable provisions of 8 CFR part 103 regarding a letter of intent to deny and notification of appeal rights shall govern.

(13) Orphan petition denied: petitioner files orphan petition after the approval of the advanced processing application has expired. If the petitioner files the orphan petition after the advanced processing application has expired, the petition will be denied unless it is filed concurrently with a new advanced processing application under 8 CFR 204.3(d)(3). This action will be without prejudice to a new filing at any time with fee.

(14) Revocation.

(i) The approval of an advanced processing application or an orphan petition shall be automatically revoked in accordance with 8 CFR 205.1 if an applicable reason exists. The approval of an advanced processing application or an orphan petition shall be revoked if the director becomes aware of information that would have resulted in denial had it been known at the time of adjudication. Such a revocation or any other revocation on notice shall be made in accordance with 8 CFR 205.2.

(ii) The approval of a Form I-600A or Form I-600 combination filing is automatically revoked if before the final decision on a beneficiary's application for admission with an immigrant visa or for adjustment of status:

(A) The marriage of the applicant terminates; or

(B) An unmarried applicant marries.

(iii) Revocation is without prejudice to the filing of a new Form I-600A or Form I-600 combination filing, with fee, accompanied by a new or updated home study, reflecting the change in marital status. If a Form I-600 had already been filed based on the approval of the prior Form I-600A and a new Form I-600A is filed under this paragraph (h)(14) rather than a Form I-600 combination filing, then a new Form I-600 must also be filed. The new Form I-600 will be adjudicated only if the new Form I-600A is approved.

(i) Child-buying as a ground for denial. An orphan petition must be denied under this section if the prospective adoptive parents or adoptive parent(s), or a person or entity working on their behalf, have given or will given money or other consideration either directly or indirectly to the child's parent(s), agent(s), other individual(s), or entity as payment for the child or as an inducement to release the child. Nothing in this paragraph shall be regarded as precluding reasonable payment for necessary activities such as administrative, court, legal, translation, and/or medical services related to the adoption proceedings.

(j) Telegraphic notifications —

(1) Telegraphic notification of approval of advanced processing application. Unless conditions preclude normal telegraphic transmissions, whenever an advanced processing application is approved in the United States, the director shall send telegraphic notification of the approval to the overseas site if a prospective adoptive parent advises the director that the petitioner intends to travel abroad and file the orphan petition abroad.

(2) Requesting a change in visa-issuing posts. If a prospective adoptive parent is in the United States, he or she may request the director to transfer notification of the approved advanced processing application to another visa-issuing post. Such a request shall be made on Form I-824 (Application for Action on an Approved Application or Petition) with the appropriate fee. The director shall send a Visas 37 telegram to both the previously and the newly designated posts. The following shall be inserted after the last numbered standard entry. "To: [insert name of previously designated visa-issuing post or overseas Service office]. Pursuant to the petitioner's request, the Visas 37 cable previously sent to your post/office in this matter is hereby invalidated. The approval is being transferred to the other post/office addressed in this telegram. Please forward the approved advanced processing application to that destination." Prior to sending such a telegram, the director must ensure that the change in posts does not alter any conditions of the approval.

(3) Telegraphic notification of approval of an orphan petition. Unless conditions preclude normal telegraphic transmissions, whenever a petition is approved by a stateside Service office, the director shall send telegraphic notification of the approval to the immigrant visa-issuing post.

(k) Other considerations —

(1) I-604 investigations. An I-604 investigation must be completed in every orphan case. The investigation must be completed by a consular officer except when the petition is properly filed at a Service office overseas, in

which case it must be completed by a Service officer. An I-604 investigation shall be completed before a petition is adjudicated abroad. When a petition is adjudicated by a stateside Service office, the I-604 investigation is normally completed after the case has been forwarded to visa-issuing post abroad. However, in a case where the director of a stateside Service office adjudicating the petition has articulable concerns that can only be resolved through the I-604 investigation, he or she shall request the investigation prior to adjudication. In any case in which there are significant differences between the facts presented in the approved advanced processing application and/or orphan petition and the facts uncovered by the I-604 investigation, the overseas site may consult directly with the appropriate Service office. In any instance where an I-604 investigation reveals negative information sufficient to sustain a denial or revocation, the investigation report, supporting documentation, and petition shall be forwarded to the appropriate Service office for action. Depending on the circumstances surrounding the case, the I-604 investigation shall include, but shall not necessarily be limited to, document checks, telephonic checks, interview(s) with the natural parent(s), and/or a field investigation.

(2) Authority of consular officers. An American consular officer is authorized to approve an orphan petition if the Service has made a favorable determination on the related advanced processing application, and the petitioner, who has traveled abroad to a country with no Service office in order to locate or adopt an orphan, has properly filed the petition, and the petition is approvable. A consular officer, however, shall refer any petition which is "not clearly approvable" for a decision by the Service office having jurisdiction pursuant to § 100.4(b) of this chapter. The consular officer's adjudication includes all aspects of eligibility for classification as an orphan under section 101(b)(1)(F) of the Act other than the issue of the ability of the prospective adoptive parents to furnish proper care to the orphan. However, if the consular officer has a well-founded and substantive reason to believe that the advanced processing approval was obtained on the basis of fraud or misrepresentation, or has knowledge of a change in material fact subsequent to the approval of the advanced processing application, he or she shall consult with the Service office having jurisdiction pursuant to § 100.4(b) of this chapter.

(3) Child in the United States. A child who is in parole status and who has not been adopted in the United States is eligible for the benefits of an orphan petition when all the requirements of sections 101(b)(1)(F) and 204 (d) and (e) of the Act have been met. A child in the United States either illegally or as a nonimmigrant, however, is ineligible for the benefits of an orphan petition.

(4) Liaison. Each director shall develop and maintain liaison with State Government adoption authorities having jurisdiction within his or her jurisdiction, including the administrator(s) of the Interstate Compact on the Placement of Children, and with other parties with interest in international adoptions. Such parties include, but are not necessarily limited to, adoption agencies, organizations representing adoption agencies, organizations representing adoptive parents, and adoption attorneys.

HISTORY:

[57 FR 41063, Sept. 9, 1992; 59 FR 38881, Aug. 1, 1994, as corrected at 59 FR 42878, Aug. 19, 1994; 63 FR 12979, 12986, Mar. 17, 1998; 68 FR 46925, 46926, Aug. 7, 2003; 72 FR 56832, 56853, Oct. 4, 2007; 74 FR 26933, 26936, June 5, 2009; 76 FR 53764, 53782, Aug. 29, 2011; 85 FR 46788, 46921, Aug. 3, 2020; 89 FR 6194, 6395, Jan. 31, 2024]

§ 204.4 Amerasian child of a United States citizen.

(a) Eligibility. An alien is eligible for benefits under Public Law 97-359 as the Amerasian child or son or daughter of a United States citizen if there is reason to believe that the alien was born in Korea, Vietnam, Laos, Kampuchea, or Thailand after December 31, 1950, and before October 22, 1982, and was fathered by a United States citizen. Such an alien is eligible for classification under sections 201(b), 203(a)(1), or 203(a)(3) of the Act as the Amerasian child or son or daughter of a United States citizen, pursuant to section 204(f) of the Act.

(b) Filing petition. Any alien claiming to be eligible for benefits as an Amerasian under Public Law 97-359, or any person on the alien's behalf, may file a petition, Form I-360, Petition for Amerasian, Widow, or Special Immigrant. Any person filing the petition must either be eighteen years of age or older or be an emancipated minor. In addition, a corporation incorporated in the United States may file the petition on the alien's behalf.

(c) Jurisdiction. The petition must be filed in accordance with the instructions on the form.

(d) **Two-stage processing —**

(1) Preliminary processing. Upon initial submission of a petition with the documentary evidence required in paragraph (f)(1) of this section, the director shall adjudicate the petition to determine whether there is reason to believe the beneficiary was fathered by a United States citizen. If the preliminary processing is completed in a satisfactory manner, the director shall advise the petitioner to submit the documentary evidence required in paragraph (f)(1) of this section and shall fingerprint the sponsor in accordance with 8 CFR 103.16. The petitioner must submit all required documents within one year of the date of the request or the petition will be considered to have been abandoned. To reactivate an abandoned petition, the petitioner must submit a new petition without the previously submitted documentation, to the Service office having jurisdiction over the prior petition.

(2) Final processing. Upon submission of the documentary evidence required in paragraph (f)(1) of this section, the director shall complete the adjudication of the petition.

(e) One-stage processing. If all documentary evidence required in paragraph (f)(1) of this section is available when the petition is initially filed, the petitioner may submit it at that time. In that case, the director shall consider all evidence without using the two-stage processing procedure set out in paragraph (d) of this section.

(f) Evidence to support a petition for an Amerasian child of a United States citizen —

(1) Two-stage processing of petition —

(i) Preliminary processing.

(A) A petition filed by or on behalf of an Amerasian under this section must be accompanied by evidence that the beneficiary was born in Korea, Vietnam, Laos, Kampuchea, or Thailand after December 31, 1950, and before October 22, 1982. If the beneficiary was born in Vietnam, the beneficiary's ID card must be submitted, if available. If it is not available, the petitioner must submit an affidavit explaining why the beneficiary's ID card is not available. Evidence that the beneficiary was fathered by a United States citizen must also be presented. The putative father must have been a United States citizen at the time of the beneficiary's birth or at the time of the father's death, if his death occurred prior to the beneficiary's birth. It is not required that the name of the father be given. Such evidence may include, but need not be limited to:

(1) The beneficiary's birth and baptismal certificates or other religious documents;

(2) Local civil records;

(3) Affidavits from knowledgeable witnesses;

(4) Letters or evidence of financial support from the beneficiary's putative father;

(5) Photographs of the beneficiary's putative father, especially with the beneficiary; and

(6) Evidence of the putative father's United States citizenship.

(B) The beneficiary's photograph must be submitted.

(C) The beneficiary's marriage certificate, if married, and evidence of the termination of any previous marriages, if applicable, is required.

(D) If the beneficiary is under eighteen years of age, a written irrevocable release for emigration must be received from the beneficiary's mother or legal guardian. The mother or legal guardian must authorize the placing agency or agencies to make decisions necessary for the child's immediate care until the sponsor receives custody. Interim costs are the responsibility of the sponsor. The mother or legal guardian must show an understanding of the effects of the release and state before signing the release whether any money was paid or any coercion was used. The signature of the mother or legal guardian must be authenticated by the local registrar, the court of minors, or a United States immigration or consular officer. The release must include the mother's or legal guardian's full name, date and place of birth, and current or permanent address.

(ii) Final processing.

(A) If the director notifies the petitioner that all preliminary processing has been completed in a satisfactory manner, the petitioner must then submit Form I-361, Affidavit of Financial Support and Intent to Petition for Legal Custody for Public Law 97-359 Amerasian, executed by the beneficiary's sponsor, along with the documentary evidence of the sponsor's financial ability required by that form. If the beneficiary is under eighteen years of age, the sponsor must agree to petition the court having jurisdiction, within thirty days of the beneficiary's arrival in the United States, for legal custody under the laws of the state where the beneficiary will reside until the beneficiary is eighteen years of age. The term "legal custody" as used in this section means the assumption of responsibility for a minor by an adult under the laws of the state in a court of law. The sponsor must be a United States citizen or lawful permanent resident who is twenty-one years of age or older and who is of good moral character.

(B) Other documents necessary to support the petition are:

(1) Evidence of the age of the beneficiary's sponsor;

(2) Evidence of United States citizenship or lawful permanent residence of the sponsor as provided in § 204.1(f); and

(C) If the beneficiary is under eighteen years of age, evidence that a public, private, or state agency licensed in the United States to place children and actively involved, with recent experience, in the intercountry placement of children has arranged the beneficiary's placement in the United States. Evidence must also be provided that the sponsor with whom the beneficiary is being placed is able to accept the beneficiary for care in the sponsor's home under the laws of the state of the beneficiary's intended residence. The evidence must demonstrate the agency's capability, including financial capability, to arrange the placement as described in paragraph (f)(1) of this section, either directly or through cooperative agreement with other suitable provider(s) of service.

(iii) Arrangements for placement of beneficiary under eighteen years of age.

(A) If the beneficiary is under eighteen years of age, the petitioner must submit evidence of the placement arrangement required under paragraph (f)(1) of this section. A favorable home study of the sponsor is necessary and must be conducted by an agency in the United States legally authorized to conduct that study. If the sponsor resides outside the United States, a home study of the sponsor must be conducted by an agency legally authorized to conduct home studies in the state of the sponsor's and beneficiary's intended residence in the United States and must be submitted with a favorable recommendation by the agency.

(B) A plan from the agency to provide follow-up services, including mediation and counselling, is required to ensure that the sponsor and the beneficiary have satisfactorily adjusted to the placement and to determine whether the terms of the sponsorship are being observed. A report from the agency concerning the placement, including information regarding any family separation or dislocation abroad that results from the placement, must also be submitted. In addition, the agency must submit to the Director, Outreach Program, Immigration and Naturalization Service, Washington, DC, within 90 days of each occurrence, reports of any breakdowns in sponsorship that occur, and reports of the steps taken to remedy these breakdowns. The petitioner must also submit a statement from the agency:

(1) Indicating that, before signing the sponsorship agreement, the sponsor has been provided a report covering pre-placement screening and evaluation, including a health evaluation, of the beneficiary;

(2) Describing the agency's orientation of both the sponsor and the beneficiary on the legal and cultural aspects of the placement;

(3) Describing the initial facilitation of the placement through introduction, translation, and similar services; and

(4) Describing the contingency plans to place the beneficiary in another suitable home if the initial placement fails. The new sponsor must execute and submit a Form I-361 to the Service office having jurisdiction over the beneficiary's residence in the United States. The original sponsor nonetheless retains financial responsibility for the beneficiary under the terms of the guarantee of financial support and intent to petition for legal custody which that sponsor executed, unless that responsibility is assumed by a new sponsor. In the event that the new sponsor does not comply with the terms of the new guarantee of financial support and intent to petition for legal custody and if, for any reason, that guarantee is not enforced, the original sponsor again becomes financially responsible for the beneficiary.

(2) One-stage processing of petition. If the petitioner chooses to have the petition processed under the one-stage processing procedure described in paragraph (e) of this section, the petitioner must submit all evidence required by paragraph (f)(1) of this section.

(g) **Decision —**

(1) General. The director shall notify the petitioner of the decision and, if the petition is denied, of the reasons for the denial. If the petition is denied, the petitioner may appeal the decision under part 103 of this chapter.

(2) Denial upon completion of preliminary processing. The director may deny the petition upon completion of the preliminary processing under paragraph (d) of this section for:

(i) Failure to establish that there is reason to believe the alien was fathered by a United States citizen; or

(ii) Failure to meet the sponsorship requirements if the fingerprints of the sponsor, required in paragraph (f)(1) of this section, were submitted during the preliminary processing and the completed background check of the sponsor discloses adverse information resulting in a finding that the sponsor is not of good moral character.

(3) Denial upon completion of final processing. The director may deny the petition upon completion of final processing if it is determined that the sponsorship requirements, or one or more of the other applicable requirements, have not been met.

(4) Denial upon completion of one-stage processing. The director may deny the petition upon completion of all processing if any of the applicable requirements in a case being processed under the one-stage processing described in paragraph (e) of this section are not met.

(h) Classification of Public Law 97-359 Amerasian. If the petition is approved the beneficiary is classified as follows:

(1) An unmarried beneficiary under the age of twenty-one is classified as the child of a United States citizen under section 201(b) of the Act;

(2) An unmarried beneficiary twenty-one years of age or older is classified as the unmarried son or daughter of a United States citizen under section 203(a)(1) of the Act; and

(3) A married beneficiary is classified as the married son or daughter of a United States citizen under section 203(a)(3) of the Act.

(i) Enforcement of affidavit of financial support and intent to petition for legal custody. A guarantee of financial support and intent to petition for legal custody on Form I-361 may be enforced against the alien's sponsor in a civil suit brought by the Attorney General in the United States District Court for the district in which the sponsor resides, except that the sponsor's estate is not liable under the guarantee if the sponsor dies or is adjudicated as bankrupt under title 11, United States Code. After admission to the United States, if the beneficiary of a petition requires enforcement of the guarantee of financial support and intent to petition for legal custody executed by the beneficiary's sponsor, the beneficiary may file Form I-363 with USCIS. If the beneficiary is under eighteen years of age, any agency or individual (other than the sponsor) having legal custody of the beneficiary, or a legal guardian acting on the alien's behalf, may file Form I-363.

HISTORY:

[57 FR 41066, Sept. 9, 1992; 63 FR 12979, 12986, Mar. 17, 1998; 74 FR 26933, 26936, June 5, 2009; 76 FR 53764, 53782, Aug. 29, 2011]

§ 204.5 Petitions for employment-based immigrants.

(a) General. A petition to classify an alien under section 203(b)(1), 203(b)(2), or 203(b)(3) of the Act must be filed on Form I-140, Petition for Immigrant Worker. A petition to classify an alien under section 203(b)(4) (as it relates to special immigrants under section 101(a)(27)(C)) must be filed on kForm I-360, Petition for Amerasian, Widow, or Special Immigrant. A separate Form I-140 or I-360 must be filed for each beneficiary, accompanied by the applicable fee. A petition is considered properly filed if it is:

(1) Accepted for processing under the provisions of part 103;

(2) Accompanied by any required individual labor certification, application for Schedule A designation, or evidence that the alien's occupation qualifies as a shortage occupation within the Department of Labor's Labor Market Information Pilot Program; and

(3) Accompanied by any other required supporting documentation.

(b) Jurisdiction. Form I-140 or I-360 must be filed in accordance with the instructions on the form.

(c) Filing petition. Any United States employer desiring and intending to employ an alien may file a petition for classification of the alien under section 203(b)(1)(B), 203(b)(1)(C), 203(b)(2), or 203(b)(3) of the

Act. An alien, or any person in the alien's behalf, may file a petition for classification under section 203(b)(1)(A) or 203(b)(4) of the Act (as it relates to special immigrants under section 101(a)(27)(C) of the Act).

(d) Priority date. The priority date of any petition filed for classification under section 203(b) of the Act which is accompanied by an individual labor certification from the Department of Labor shall be the date the labor certification application was accepted for processing by any office of the Department of Labor. The priority date of any petition filed for a classification under section 203(b) of the Act which does not require a labor certification from the Department of Labor shall be the date the completed, signed petition (including all initial evidence and the correct fee) is properly filed with USCIS. The priority date of any petition filed for classification under section 203(b) of the Act which is accompanied by an application for Schedule A designation shall be the date the completed, signed petition (including all initial evidence and the correct fee) is properly filed with USCIS. The priority date of an alien who filed for classification as a special immigrant under section 203(b)(4) of the Act prior to October 1, 1991, and who is the beneficiary of an approved petition for special immigrant status after October 1, 1991, shall be the date the alien applied for an immigrant visa or adjustment of status.

(e) Retention of section 203(b)(1), (2), or (3) priority date.

(1) A petition approved on behalf of an alien under sections 203(b)(1), (2), or (3) of the Act accords the alien the priority date of the approved petition for any subsequently filed petition for any classification under section 203(b)(1), (2), or (3) of the Act for which the alien may qualify. In the event that the alien is the beneficiary of multiple approved petitions under section 203(b)(1), (2), or (3) of the Act, the alien shall be entitled to the earliest priority date.

(2) The priority date of a petition may not be retained under paragraph (e)(1) of this section if at any time USCIS revokes the approval of the petition because of:

(i) Fraud, or a willful misrepresentation of a material fact;

(ii) Revocation by the Department of Labor of the approved permanent labor certification that accompanied the petition;

(iii) Invalidation by USCIS or the Department of State of the permanent labor certification that accompanied the petition; or

(iv) A determination by USCIS that petition approval was based on a material error.

(3) A denied petition will not establish a priority date.

(4) A priority date is not transferable to another alien.

(5) A petition filed under section 204(a)(1)(F) of the Act for an alien shall remain valid with respect to a new employment offer as determined by USCIS under section 204(j) of the Act and 8 CFR 245.25. An alien will continue to be afforded the priority date of such petition, if the requirements of paragraph (e) of this section are met.

(f) Maintaining the priority date of a third or sixth preference petition filed prior to October 1, 1991—Any petition filed before October 1, 1991, and approved on any date, to accord status under section 203(a)(3) or 203(a)(6) of the Act, as in effect before October 1, 1991, shall be deemed a petition approved to accord status under section 203(b)(2) or within the appropriate classification under section 203(b)(3), respectively, of the Act as in effect on or after October 1, 1991, provided that the alien applies for an immigrant visa or adjustment of status within the two years following notification that an immigrant visa is immediately available for his or her use.

(g) Initial evidence—

(1) General. Specific requirements for initial supporting documents for the various employment-based immigrant classifications are set forth in this section. In general, ordinary legible photocopies of such documents (except for labor certifications from the Department of Labor) will be acceptable for initial filing and approval. However, at the discretion of the director, original documents may be required in individual cases. Evidence relating to qualifying experience or training shall be in the form of letter(s) from current or former employer(s) or trainer(s) and shall include the name, address, and title of the writer, and a specific description of the duties performed by the alien or of the training received. If such evidence is unavailable, other documentation relating to the alien's experience or training will be considered.

(2) Ability of prospective employer to pay wage. Any petition filed by or for an employment-based immigrant which requires an offer of employment must be accompanied by evidence that the prospective United States employer has the ability to pay the proffered wage. The petitioner must demonstrate this ability at the time the priority date is established and continuing until the beneficiary obtains lawful permanent residence. Evidence of this ability shall be either in the form of copies of annual reports, federal tax returns, or audited financial statements. In a case where the prospective United States employer employs 100 or more workers, the director may accept a statement from a financial officer of the organization which establishes the prospective employer's ability to pay the proffered wage. In appropriate cases, additional evidence, such as profit/loss statements, bank account records, or personnel records, may be submitted by the petitioner or requested by the Service.

(h) Aliens with extraordinary ability.

(1) An alien, or any person on behalf of the alien, may file an I-140 visa petition for classification under section 203(b)(1)(A) of the Act as an alien of extraordinary ability in the sciences, arts, education, business, or athletics.

(2) Definition. As used in this section:

Extraordinary ability means a level of expertise indicating that the individual is one of that small percentage who have risen to the very top of the field of endeavor.

(3) Initial evidence. A petition for an alien of extraordinary ability must be accompanied by evidence that the alien has sustained national or international acclaim and that his or her achievements have been recognized in the field of expertise. Such evidence shall include evidence of a one-time achievement (that is, a major, international recognized award), or at least three of the following:

(i) Documentation of the alien's receipt of lesser nationally or internationally recognized prizes or awards for excellence in the field of endeavor;

(ii) Documentation of the alien's membership in associations in the field for which classification is sought, which require outstanding achievements of their members, as judged by recognized national or international experts in their disciplines or fields;

(iii) Published material about the alien in professional or major trade publications or other major media, relating to the alien's work in the field for which classification is sought. Such evidence shall include the title, date, and author of the material, and any necessary translation;

(iv) Evidence of the alien's participation, either individually or on a panel, as a judge of the work of others in the same or an allied field of specification for which classification is sought;

(v) Evidence of the alien's original scientific, scholarly, artistic, athletic, or business-related contributions of major significance in the field;

(vi) Evidence of the alien's authorship of scholarly articles in the field, in professional or major trade publications or other major media;

(vii) Evidence of the display of the alien's work in the field at artistic exhibitions or showcases;

(viii) Evidence that the alien has performed in a leading or critical role for organizations or establishments that have a distinguished reputation;

(ix) Evidence that the alien has commanded a high salary or other significantly high remuneration for services, in relation to others in the field; or

(x) Evidence of commercial successes in the performing arts, as shown by box office receipts or record, cassette, compact disk, or video sales.

(4) If the above standards do not readily apply to the beneficiary's occupation, the petitioner may submit comparable evidence to establish the beneficiary's eligibility.

(5) No offer of employment required. Neither an offer for employment in the United States nor a labor certification is required for this classification; however, the petition must be accompanied by clear evidence that the alien is coming to the United States to continue work in the area of expertise. Such evidence may include letter(s) from prospective employer(s), evidence of prearranged commitments such as contracts, or a statement from the beneficiary detailing plans on how he or she intends to continue his or her work in the United States.

(i) Outstanding professors and researchers.

(1) Any United States employer desiring and intending to employ a professor or researcher who is outstanding in an academic field under section 203(b)(1)(B) of the Act may file an I-140 visa petition for such classification.

(2) Definitions. As used in this section:

Academic field means a body of specialized knowledge offered for study at an accredited United States university or institution of higher education.

Permanent, in reference to a research position, means either tenured, tenure-track, or for a term of indefinite or unlimited duration, and in which the employee will ordinarily have an expectation of continued employment unless there is good cause for termination.

(3) Initial evidence. A petition for an outstanding professor or researcher must be accompanied by:

(i) Evidence that the professor or researcher is recognized internationally as outstanding in the academic field specified in the petition. Such evidence shall consist of at least two of the following:

(A) Documentation of the alien's receipt of major prizes or awards for outstanding achievement in the academic field;

(B) Documentation of the alien's membership in associations in the academic field which require outstanding achievements of their members;

(C) Published material in professional publications written by others about the alien's work in the academic field. Such material shall include the title, date, and author of the material, and any necessary translation;

(D) Evidence of the alien's participation, either individually or on a panel, as the judge of the work of others in the same or an allied academic field;

(E) Evidence of the alien's original scientific or scholarly research contributions to the academic field; or

(F) Evidence of the alien's authorship of scholarly books or articles (in scholarly journals with international circulation) in the academic field;

(ii) If the standards in paragraph (i)(3)(i) of this section do not readily apply, the petitioner may submit comparable evidence to establish the beneficiary's eligibility.

(iii) Evidence that the alien has at least three years of experience in teaching and/or research in the academic field. Experience in teaching or research while working on an advanced degree will only be acceptable if the alien has acquired the degree, and if the teaching duties were such that he or she had full responsibility for the class taught or if the research conducted toward the degree has been recognized within the academic field as outstanding. Evidence of teaching and/or research experience shall be in the form of letter(s) from current or former employer(s) and shall include the name, address, and title of the writer, and a specific description of the duties performed by the alien; and

(iv) An offer of employment from a prospective United States employer. A labor certification is not required for this classification. The offer of employment shall be in the form of a letter from:

(A) A United States university or institution of higher learning offering the alien a tenured or tenure-track teaching position in the alien's academic field;

(B) A United States university or institution of higher learning offering the alien a permanent research position in the alien's academic field; or

(C) A department, division, or institute of a private employer offering the alien a permanent research position in the alien's academic field. The department, division, or institute must demonstrate that it employs at least three persons full-time in research positions, and that it has achieved documented accomplishments in an academic field.

(j) Certain multinational executives and managers.

(1) A United States employer may file a petition on Form I-140 for classification of an alien under section 203(b)(1)(C) of the Act as a multinational executive or manager.

(2) Definitions. As used in this section;

Affiliate means:

(A) One of two subsidiaries both of which are owned and controlled by the same parent or individual;

(B) One of two legal entities owned and controlled by the same group of individuals, each individual owning and controlling approximately the same share or proportion of each entity; or

(C) In the case of a partnership that is organized in the United States to provide accounting services, along with managerial and/or consulting services, and markets its accounting services under an internationally recognized name under an agreement with a worldwide coordinating organization that is owned and controlled by the member accounting firms, a partnership (or similar organization) that is organized outside the United States to provide accounting' services shall be considered to be an affiliate of the United States partnership if it markets its accounting services under the same internationally recognized name under the agreement with the worldwide coordinating organization of which the United States partnership is also a member.

Doing business means the regular, systematic, and continuous provision of goods and/or services by a firm, corporation, or other entity and does not include the mere presence of an agent or office.

Executive capacity means an assignment within an organization in which the employee primarily:

(A) Directs the management of the organization or a major component or function of the organization;

(B) Establishes the goals and policies of the organization, component, or function;

(C) Exercises wide latitude in discretionary decision-making; and

(D) Receives only general supervision or direction from higher level executives, the board of directors, or stockholders of the organization.

Managerial capacity means an assignment within an organization in which the employee primarily:

(A) Manages the organization, or a department, subdivision, function, or component of the organization;

(B) Supervises and controls the work of other supervisory, professional, or managerial employees, or manages an essential function within the organization, or a department or subdivision of the organization;

(C) If another employee or other employees are directly supervised, has the authority to hire and fire or recommend those as well as other personnel actions (such as promotion and leave authorization), or, if no other employee is directly supervised, functions at a senior level within the organizational hierarchy or with respect to the function managed; and

(D) Exercises direction over the day-to-day operations of the activity or function for which the employee has authority.

Multinational means that the qualifying entity, or its affiliate, or subsidiary, conducts business in two or more countries, one of which is the United States.

Subsidiary means a firm, corporation, or other legal entity of which a parent owns, directly or indirectly, more than half of the entity and controls the entity; or owns, directly or indirectly, half of the entity and controls the entity; or owns, directly or indirectly, 50 percent of a 50-50 joint venture and has equal control and veto power over the entity; or owns, directly or indirectly, less than half of the entity, but in fact controls the entity.

(3) Initial evidence –

(i) Required evidence. A petition for a multinational executive or manager must be accompanied by a statement from an authorized official of the petitioning United States employer which demonstrates that:

(A) If the alien is outside the United States, in the three years immediately preceding the filing of the petition the alien has been employed outside the United States for at least one year in a managerial or executive capacity by a firm or corporation, or other legal entity, or by an affiliate or subsidiary of such a firm or corporation or other legal entity; or

(B) If the alien is already in the United States working for the same employer or a subsidiary or affiliate of the firm or corporation, or other legal entity by which the alien was employed overseas, in the three years preceding entry as a nonimmigrant, the alien was employed by the entity abroad for at least one year in a managerial or executive capacity;

(C) The prospective employer in the United States is the same employer or a subsidiary or affiliate of the firm or corporation or other legal entity by which the alien was employed overseas; and

(D) The prospective United States employer has been doing business for at least one year.

(ii) Appropriate additional evidence. In appropriate cases, the director may request additional evidence.

(4) Determining managerial or exectuve capacities --

(i) Supervisors as managers. A first-line supervisor is not considered to be acting in a managerial capacity merely by virtue of his or her supervisory duties unless the employees supervised are professional.

(ii) Staffing levels. If staffing levels are used as a factor in determining whether an individual is acting in a managerial or executive capacity, the reasonable needs of the organization, component, or function, in light of the overall purpose and stage of development of the organization, component, or function, shall be taken into account. An individual shall not be considered to be acting in a managerial or executive capacity merely on the basis of the number of employees that the individual supervises or has supervised or directs or has directed.

(5) Offer of employment. No labor certification is required for this classification; however, the prospective employer in the United States must furnish a job offer in the form of a statement which indicates that the alien is to be employed in the United States in a managerial or executive capacity. Such letter must clearly describe the duties to be performed by the alien.

(k) Aliens who are members of the professions holding advanced degrees or aliens of exceptional ability.

(1) Any United States employer may file a petition on Form I-140 for classification of an alien under section 203(b)(2) of the Act as an alien who is a member of the professions holding an advanced degree or an alien of exceptional ability in the sciences, arts, or business. If an alien is claiming exceptional ability in the sciences, arts, or business and is seeking an exemption from the requirement of a job offer in the United States pursuant to section 203(b)(2)(B) of the Act, then the alien, or anyone in the alien's behalf, may be the petitioner.

(2) Definitions. As used in this section: Advanced degree means any United States academic or professional degree or a foreign equivalent degree above that of baccalaureate. A United States baccalaureate degree or a foreign equivalent degree followed by at least five years of progressive experience in the specialty shall be considered the equivalent of a master's degree. If a doctoral degree is customarily required by the specialty, the alien must have a United States doctorate or a foreign equivalent degree.

Exceptional ability in the sciences, arts, or business means a degree of expertise significantly above that ordinarily encountered in the sciences, arts, or business.

Profession means one of the occupations listed in section 101(a)(32) of the Act, as well as any occupation for which a United States baccalaureate degree or its foreign equivalent is the minimum requirement for entry into the occupation.

(3) Initial evidence. The petition must be accompanied by documentation showing that the alien is a professional holding an advanced degree or an alien of exceptional ability in the sciences, the arts, or business.

(i) To show that the alien is a professional holding an advanced degree, the petition must be accompanied by:

(A) An official academic record showing that the alien has a United States advanced degree or a foreign equivalent degree; or

(B) An official academic record showing that the alien has a United States baccalaureate degree or a foreign equivalent degree, and evidence in the form of letters from current or former employer(s) showing that the alien has at least five years of progressive post-baccalaureate experience in the specialty.

(ii) To show that the alien is an alien of exceptional ability in the sciences, arts, or business, the petition must be accompanied by at least three of the following:

(A) An official academic record showing that the alien has a degree, diploma, certificate, or similar award from a college, university, school, or other institution of learning relating to the area of exceptional ability;

(B) Evidence in the form of letter(s) from current or former employer(s) showing that the alien has at least ten years of full-time experience in the occupation for which he or she is being sought;

(C) A license to practice the profession or certification for a particular profession or occupation;

(D) Evidence that the alien has commanded a salary, or other renumeration for services, which demonstrates exceptional ability;

(E) Evidence of membership in professional associations; or

(F) Evidence of recognition for achievements and significant contributions to the industry or field by peers, governmental entities, or professional or business organizations.

(iii) If the above standards do not readily apply to the beneficiary's occupation, the petitioner may submit comparable evidence to establish the beneficiary's eligibility.

(4) Labor certification or evidence that alien qualifies for Labor Market Information Pilot Program —

(i) General. Every petition under this classification must be accompanied by an individual labor certification from the Department of Labor, by an application for Schedule A designation (if applicable), or by documentation to establish that the alien qualifies for one of the shortage occupations in the Department of Labor's Labor Market Information Pilot Program. To apply for Schedule A designation or to establish that the alien's occupation is within the Labor Market Information Program, a fully executed uncertified Form ETA-750 in duplicate must accompany the petition. The job offer portion of the individual labor certification, Schedule A application, or Pilot Program application must demonstrate that the job requires a professional holding an advanced degree or the equivalent or an alien of exceptional ability.

(ii) Exemption from job offer. The director may exempt the requirement of a job offer, and thus of a labor certification, for aliens of exceptional ability in the sciences, arts, or business if exemption would be in the national interest. To apply for the exemption, the petitioner must submit Form ETA-750B, Statement of Qualifications of Alien, in duplicate, as well as evidence to support the claim that such exemption would be in the national interest.

(*l*) Skilled workers, professionals, and other workers.

(1) Any United States employer may file a petition on Form I-140 for classification of an alien under section 203(b)(3) as a skilled worker, professional, or other (unskilled) worker.

(2) Definitions. As used in this part:

Other worker means a qualified alien who is capable, at the time of petitioning for this classification, of performing unskilled labor (requiring less than two years training or experience), not of a temporary or seasonal nature, for which qualified workers are not available in the United States.

Professional means a qualified alien who holds at least a United States baccalaureate degree or a foreign equivalent degree and who is a member of the professions.

Skilled worker means an alien who is capable, at the time of petitioning for this classification, of performing skilled labor (requiring at least two years training or experience), not of a temporary or seasonal nature, for which qualified workers are not available in the United States. Relevant post-secondary education may be considered as training for the purposes of this provision.

(3) Initial evidence —

(i) Labor certification or evidence that alien qualifies for Labor Market Information Pilot Program. Every petition under this classification must be accompanied by an individual labor certification from the Department of Labor, by an application for Schedule A designation, or by documentation to establish that the alien qualifies for one of the shortage occupations in the Department of Labor's Labor Market Information Pilot Program. To apply for Schedule A designation or to establish that the alien's occupation is a shortage occupation with the Labor Market Pilot Program, a fully executed uncertified Form ETA-750 in duplicate must accompany the petition. The job offer portion of an individual labor certification, Schedule A application, or Pilot Program application for a professional must demonstrate that the job requires the minimum of a baccalaureate degree.

(ii) Other documentation —

(A) General. Any requirements of training or experience for skilled workers, professionals, or other workers must be supported by letters from trainers or employers giving the name, address, and title of the trainer or employer, and a description of the training received or the experience of the alien.

(B) Skilled workers. If the petition is for a skilled worker, the petition must be accompanied by evidence that the alien meets the educational, training or experience, and any other requirements of the individual labor certification, meets the requirements for Schedule A designation, or meets the requirements for the Labor Market Information Pilot Program occupation designation. The minimum requirements for this classification are at least two years of training or experience.

(C) Professionals. If the petition is for a professional, the petition must be accompanied by evidence that the alien holds a United States baccalaureate degree or a foreign equivalent degree and by evidence that the alien is a member of the professions. Evidence of a baccalaureate degree shall be in the form of an official college or university record showing the date the baccalaureate degree was awarded and the area of concentration of study. To show that the alien is a member of the professions, the petitioner must submit evidence showing that the minimum of a baccalaureate degree is required for entry into the occupation.

(D) Other workers. If the petition is for an unskilled (other) worker, it must be accompanied by evidence that the alien meets any educational, training and experience, and other requirements of the labor certification.

(4) Differentiating between skilled and other workers. The determination of whether a worker is a skilled or other worker will be based on the requirements of training and/or experience placed on the job by the prospective employer, as certified by the Department of Labor. In the case of a Schedule A occupation or a shortage occupation within the Labor Market Pilot Program, the petitioner will be required to establish to the director that the job is a skilled job, i.e., one which requires at least two years of training and/or experience.

(m) Religious workers. This paragraph governs classification of an alien as a special immigrant religious worker as defined in section 101(a)(27)(C) of the Act and under section 203(b)(4) of the Act. To be eligible for classification as a special immigrant religious worker, the alien (either abroad or in the United States) must:

(1) For at least the two years immediately preceding the filing of the petition have been a member of a religious denomination that has a bona fide non-profit religious organization in the United States.

(2) Be coming to the United States to work in a full time (average of at least 35 hours per week) compensated position in one of the following occupations as they are defined in paragraph (m)(5) of this section:

(i) Solely in the vocation of a minister of that religious denomination;

(ii) A religious vocation either in a professional or nonprofessional capacity; or

(iii) A religious occupation either in a professional or nonprofessional capacity.

(3) Be coming to work for a bona fide non-profit religious organization in the United States, or a bona fide organization which is affiliated with the religious denomination in the United States.

(4) Have been working in one of the positions described in paragraph (m)(2) of this section, either abroad or in lawful immigration status in the United States, and after the age of 14 years continuously for at least the two-year period immediately preceding the filing of the petition. The prior religious work need not correspond precisely to the type of work to be performed. A break in the continuity of the work during the preceding two years will not affect eligibility so long as:

(i) The alien was still employed as a religious worker;

(ii) The break did not exceed two years; and

(iii) The nature of the break was for further religious training or for sabbatical that did not involve unauthorized work in the United States. However, the alien must have been a member of the petitioner's denomination throughout the two years of qualifying employment.

(5) Definitions. As used in paragraph (m) of this section, the term:

Bona fide non-profit religious organization in the United States means a religious organization exempt from taxation as described in section 501(c)(3) of the Internal Revenue Code of 1986, subsequent amendment or equivalent sections of prior enactments of the Internal Revenue Code, and possessing a currently valid determination letter from the IRS confirming such exemption.

Bona fide organization which is affiliated with the religious denomination means an organization which is closely associated with the religious denomination and which is exempt from taxation as described in section 501(c)(3) of the Internal Revenue Code of 1986, subsequent amendment or equivalent sections of prior enactments of the Internal Revenue Code and possessing a currently valid determination letter from the IRS confirming such exemption.

Denominational membership means membership during at least the two-year period immediately preceding the filing date of the petition, in the same type of religious denomination as the United States religious organization where the alien will work.

Minister means an individual who:

(A) Is fully authorized by a religious denomination, and fully trained according to the denomination's standards, to conduct such religious worship and perform other duties usually performed by authorized members of the clergy of that denomination;

(B) Is not a lay preacher or a person not authorized to perform duties usually performed by clergy;

(C) Performs activities with a rational relationship to the religious calling of the minister; and

(D) Works solely as a minister in the United States, which may include administrative duties incidental to the duties of a minister.

Petition means USCIS Form I-360, Petition for Amerasian, Widow(er), or Special Immigrant, a successor form, or other form as may be prescribed by USCIS, along with a supplement containing attestations required by this section, the fee specified in 8 CFR 106.2, and supporting evidence filed as provided by this part.

Religious denomination means a religious group or community of believers that is governed or administered under a common type of ecclesiastical government and includes one or more of the following:

(A) A recognized common creed or statement of faith shared among the denomination's members;

(B) A common form of worship;

(C) A common formal code of doctrine and discipline;

(D) Common religious services and ceremonies;

(E) Common established places of religious worship or religious congregations; or

(F) Comparable indicia of a bona fide religious denomination.

Religious occupation means an occupation that meets all of the following requirements:

(A) The duties must primarily relate to a traditional religious function and be recognized as a religious occupation within the denomination.

(B) The duties must be primarily related to, and must clearly involve, inculcating or carrying out the religious creed and beliefs of the denomination.

(C) The duties do not include positions that are primarily administrative or support such as janitors, maintenance workers, clerical employees, fund raisers, persons solely involved in the solicitation of donations, or similar positions, although limited administrative duties that are only incidental to religious functions are permissible.

(D) Religious study or training for religious work does not constitute a religious occupation, but a religious worker may pursue study or training incident to status.

Religious vocation means a formal lifetime commitment, through vows, investitures, ceremonies, or similar indicia, to a religious way of life. The religious denomination must have a class of individuals whose lives are dedicated to religious practices and functions, as distinguished from the secular members of the religion. Examples of individuals practicing religious vocations include nuns, monks, and religious brothers and sisters.

Religious worker means an individual engaged in and, according to the denomination's standards, qualified for a religious occupation or vocation, whether or not in a professional capacity, or as a minister.

Tax-exempt organization means an organization that has received a determination letter from the IRS establishing that it, or a group that it belongs to, is exempt from taxation in accordance with sections 501(c)(3) of the Internal Revenue Code of 1986 or subsequent amendments or equivalent sections of prior enactments of the Internal Revenue Code.

(6) Filing requirements. A petition must be filed as provided in the petition form instructions either by the alien or by his or her prospective United States employer. After the date stated in section 101(a)(27)(C) of the Act, immigration or adjustment of status on the basis of this section is limited solely to ministers.

(7) Attestation. An authorized official of the prospective employer of an alien seeking religious worker status must complete, sign and date an attestation prescribed by USCIS and submit it along with the petition. If the alien is a self-petitioner and is also an authorized official of the prospective employer, the self-petitioner may sign the attestation. The prospective employer must specifically attest to all of the following:

(i) That the prospective employer is a bona fide non-profit religious organization or a bona fide organization which is affiliated with the religious denomination and is exempt from taxation;

(ii) The number of members of the prospective employer's organization;

(iii) The number of employees who work at the same location where the beneficiary will be employed and a summary of the type of responsibilities of those employees. USCIS may request a list of all employees, their titles, and a brief description of their duties at its discretion;

(iv) The number of aliens holding special immigrant or nonimmigrant religious worker status currently employed or employed within the past five years by the prospective employer's organization;

(v) The number of special immigrant religious worker and nonimmigrant religious worker petitions and applications filed by or on behalf of any aliens for employment by the prospective employer in the past five years;

(vi) The title of the position offered to the alien, the complete package of salaried or non-salaried compensation being offered, and a detailed description of the alien's proposed daily duties;

(vii) That the alien will be employed at least 35 hours per week;

(viii) The specific location(s) of the proposed employment;

(ix) That the alien has worked as a religious worker for the two years immediately preceding the filing of the application and is otherwise qualified for the position offered;

(x) That the alien has been a member of the denomination for at least two years immediately preceding the filing of the application;

(xi) That the alien will not be engaged in secular employment, and any salaried or non-salaried compensation for the work will be paid to the alien by the attesting employer; and

(xii) That the prospective employer has the ability and intention to compensate the alien at a level at which the alien and accompanying family members will not become public charges, and that funds to pay the alien's compensation do not include any monies obtained from the alien, excluding reasonable donations or tithing to the religious organization.

(8) Evidence relating to the petitioning organization. A petition shall include the following initial evidence relating to the petitioning organization:

(i) A currently valid determination letter from the Internal Revenue Service (IRS) establishing that the organization is a tax-exempt organization; or

(ii) For a religious organization that is recognized as tax-exempt under a group tax-exemption, a currently valid determination letter from the IRS establishing that the group is tax-exempt; or

(iii) For a bona fide organization that is affiliated with the religious denomination, if the organization was granted tax-exempt status under section 501(c)(3) of the Internal Revenue Code of 1986, or subsequent amendment or equivalent sections of prior enactments of the Internal Revenue Code, as something other than a religious organization:

(A) A currently valid determination letter from the IRS establishing that the organization is a tax-exempt organization;

(B) Documentation that establishes the religious nature and purpose of the organization, such as a copy of the organizing instrument of the organization that specifies the purposes of the organization;

(C) Organizational literature, such as books, articles, brochures, calendars, flyers and other literature describing the religious purpose and nature of the activities of the organization; and

(D) A religious denomination certification. The religious organization must complete, sign and date a religious denomination certification certifying that the petitioning organization is affiliated with the religious denomination. The certification is to be submitted by the petitioner along with the petition.

(9) Evidence relating to the qualifications of a minister. If the alien is a minister, the petitioner must submit the following:

(i) A copy of the alien's certificate of ordination or similar documents reflecting acceptance of the alien's qualifications as a minister in the religious denomination; and

(ii) Documents reflecting acceptance of the alien's qualifications as a minister in the religious denomination, as well as evidence that the alien has completed any course of prescribed theological education at an accredited theological institution normally required or recognized by that religious denomination, including transcripts, curriculum, and documentation that establishes that the theological institution is accredited by the denomination, or

(iii) For denominations that do not require a prescribed theological education, evidence of:

(A) The denomination's requirements for ordination to minister;

(B) The duties allowed to be performed by virtue of ordination;

(C) The denomination's levels of ordination, if any; and

(D) The alien's completion of the denomination's requirements for ordination.

(10) Evidence relating to compensation. Initial evidence must include verifiable evidence of how the petitioner intends to compensate the alien. Such compensation may include salaried or non-salaried compensation. This evidence may include past evidence of compensation for similar positions; budgets showing monies set aside for salaries, leases, etc.; verifiable documentation that room and board will be provided; or other evidence acceptable to USCIS. If IRS documentation, such as IRS Form W-2 or certified tax returns, is available, it must be provided. If IRS documentation is not available, an explanation for its absence must be provided, along with comparable, verifiable documentation.

(11) Evidence relating to the alien's prior employment. Qualifying prior experience during the two years immediately preceding the petition or preceding any acceptable break in the continuity of the religious work, must have occurred after the age of 14, and if acquired in the United States, must have been authorized under United States immigration law. If the alien was employed in the United States during the two years immediately preceding the filing of the application and:

(i) Received salaried compensation, the petitioner must submit IRS documentation that the alien received a salary, such as an IRS Form W-2 or certified copies of income tax returns.

(ii) Received non-salaried compensation, the petitioner must submit IRS documentation of the non-salaried compensation if available.

(iii) Received no salary but provided for his or her own support, and provided support for any dependents, the petitioner must show how support was maintained by submitting with the petition additional documents such as audited financial statements, financial institution records, brokerage account statements, trust documents signed by an attorney, or other verifiable evidence acceptable to USCIS.

If the alien was employed outside the United States during such two years, the petitioner must submit comparable evidence of the religious work.

(12) Inspections, evaluations, verifications, and compliance reviews. The supporting evidence submitted may be verified by USCIS through any means determined appropriate by USCIS, up to and including an on-site inspection of the petitioning organization. The inspection may include a tour of the organization's facilities, an interview with the organization's officials, a review of selected organization records relating to compliance with immigration laws and regulations, and an interview with any other individuals or review of any other records that the USCIS considers pertinent to the integrity of the organization. An inspection may include the organization headquarters, satellite locations, or the work locations planned for the applicable employee. If USCIS decides to conduct a pre-approval inspection, satisfactory completion of such inspection will be a condition for approval of any petition.

(n) Closing action —

(1) Approval. An approved employment-based petition will be forwarded to the National Visa Center of the Department of State if the beneficiary resides outside of the United States. If the Form I-140 petition indicates that the alien has filed or will file an application for adjustment to permanent residence in the United States (Form I-485) the approved visa petition (Form I-140), will be retained by the Service for consideration with the application for permanent residence (Form I-485). If a visa is available, and Form I-485 has not been filed, the alien will be instructed on the Form I-797, Notice of Action, (mailed out upon approval of the Form I-140 petition) to file the Form I-485.

(2) Denial. The denial of a petition for classification under section 203(b)(1), 203(b)(2), 203(b)(3), or 203(b)(4) of the Act (as it relates to special immigrants under section 101(a)(27)(C) of the Act) shall be appealable to the Associate Commissioner for Examinations. The petitioner shall be informed in plain language of the reasons for denial and of his or her right to appeal.

(3) Validity of approved petitions. Unless approval is revoked under section 203(g) or 205 of the Act, an employment-based petition is valid indefinitely.

(o) Denial of petitions under section 204 of the Act based on a finding by the Department of Labor. Upon debarment by the Department of Labor pursuant to 20 CFR 655.31, USCIS may deny any employment-based immigrant petition filed by that petitioner for a period of at least 1 year but not more than 5 years. The time period of such bar to petition approval shall be based on the severity of the violation or violations. The decision to deny petitions, the time period for the bar to petitions, and the reasons for the time period will be explained in a written notice to the petitioner.

(p) Eligibility for employment authorization in compelling circumstances —

(1) Eligibility of principal alien. An individual who is the principal beneficiary of an approved immigrant petition for classification under sections 203(b)(1), 203(b)(2) or 203(b)(3) of the Act may be eligible to receive employment authorization, upon application, if:

(i) In the case of an initial request for employment authorization, the individual is in E-3, H-1B, H-1B1, O-1, or L-1 nonimmigrant status, including the periods authorized by § 214.1(l)(l) and (2), as well as any other periods of admission authorized by this chapter before a validity period begins or after the expiration of a validity period, on the date the application for employment authorization (Form I-765) is filed;

(ii) An immigrant visa is not authorized for issuance to the principal beneficiary based on his or her priority date on the date the application for employment authorization is filed; and

(iii) USCIS determines, as a matter of discretion, that the principal beneficiary demonstrates compelling circumstances that justify the issuance of employment authorization.

(2) Eligibility of spouses and children. The family members, as described in section 203(d) of the Act, of a principal beneficiary, who are in nonimmigrant status at the time the principal beneficiary applies for employment authorization under paragraph (p)(1) of this section, are eligible to apply for employment authorization provided that the principal beneficiary has been granted employment authorization under paragraph (p) of this section and such employment authorization has not been terminated or revoked. Such family members may apply for employment authorization concurrently with the principal beneficiary, but cannot be granted employment authorization until the principal beneficiary is so authorized. The validity period of employment authorization granted to family members may not extend beyond the validity period of employment authorization granted to the principal beneficiary.

(3) Eligibility for renewal of employment authorization. An alien may be eligible to renew employment authorization granted under paragraph (p) of this section, upon submission of a new application before the expiration of such employment authorization, if:

(i) He or she is the principal beneficiary of an approved immigrant petition for classification under section 203(b)(1), 203(b)(2) or 203(b)(3) of the Act and either:

(A) An immigrant visa is not authorized for issuance to the principal beneficiary based on his or her priority date on the date the application for employment authorization, (Form I-765) is filed; and USCIS determines, as a matter of discretion that the principal beneficiary demonstrates compelling circumstances that justify the issuance of employment authorization; or

(B) The difference between the principal beneficiary's priority date and the date upon which immigrant visas are authorized for issuance for the principal beneficiary's preference category and country of chargeability is 1 year or less according to the Department of State Visa Bulletin in effect on the date the application for employment authorization (Form I-765), is filed. For example, if the Department of State Visa Bulletin in effect on the date the renewal application is filed indicates immigrant visas are authorized for issuance for the applicable preference category and country of chargeability to individuals with priority dates earlier than November 1, 2000, USCIS may grant a renewal to a principal beneficiary whose priority date is on or between October 31, 1999 and October 31, 2001; or

(ii) He or she is a family member, as described under paragraph (p)(2) of this section, of a principal beneficiary granted a renewal of employment authorization under paragraph (p)(3)(i) that remains valid, except that the family member need not be maintaining nonimmigrant status at the time the principal beneficiary applies for renewal of employment authorization under paragraph (p) of this section. A family member may file an application to renew employment authorization concurrently with an application to renew employment authorization filed by the principal beneficiary or while such application by the principal beneficiary is pending, but the family member's renewal application cannot be approved unless the principal beneficiary's application is granted. The validity period of a renewal of employment authorization granted to family members may not extend beyond the validity period of the renewal of employment authorization granted to the principal beneficiary.

(4) Application for employment authorization.

(i) To request employment authorization, an eligible applicant described in paragraph (p)(1), (2), or (3) of this section must:

(A) File an application for employment authorization with USCIS, in accordance with 8 CFR 274a.13(a) and the form instructions.

(B) Submit biometric information in accordance with the applicable form instructions.

(ii) Employment authorization under this paragraph may be granted solely in 1-year increments.

(5) Ineligibility for employment authorization. An alien is not eligible for employment authorization, including renewal of employment authorization, under this paragraph if the alien has been convicted of any felony or two or more misdemeanors.

HISTORY:

[56 FR 60905, Nov. 29, 1991; 59 FR 502, Jan. 5, 1994, as confirmed at 59 FR 51360, Oct. 11, 1994; 59 FR 27229, May 26, 1994; 60 FR 29753, June 6, 1995; 61 FR 33304, 33305, June 27, 1996, as confirmed at 62 FR 4631, Jan. 31, 1997; 67 FR 49561, 49563, July 31, 2002; 73 FR 72276, 72291, Nov. 26, 2008; 73 FR 78104, 78127, Dec. 19, 2008; 74 FR 26933, 26936, June 5, 2009; 81 FR 2068, 2083, Jan. 15, 2016; 81 FR 82398, 82484, Nov. 18, 2016; 85 FR 46788, 46922, Aug. 3, 2020; 89 FR 6194, 6396, Jan. 31, 2024]

§ 204.6 Petitions for employment creation aliens. [Contingent]

(a) General. A petition to classify an alien under section 203(b)(5) of the Act must be filed on Form I–526, Immigrant Petition by Alien Entrepreneur. The petition must be accompanied by the appropriate fee. Before a petition is considered properly filed, the petition must be signed by the petitioner, and the initial supporting documentation required by this section must be attached. Legible photocopies of supporting documents will ordinarily be acceptable for initial filing and approval. However, at the discretion of the director, original documents may be required.

(b) [Reserved]

(c) Eligibility to file. A petition for classification as an alien entrepreneur may only be filed by any alien on his or her own behalf.

(d) Priority date. The priority date of a petition for classification as an alien entrepreneur is the date the petition is properly filed with the Service or, if filed prior to the effective date of these regulations, the date the Form I–526 was received at the appropriate Service Center.

(e) Definitions. As used in this section:

Capital means cash, equipment, inventory, other tangible property, cash equivalents, and indebtedness secured by assets owned by the alien entrepreneur, provided that the alien entrepreneur is personally and primarily liable and that the assets of the new commercial enterprise upon which the petition is based are not used to secure any of the indebtedness. All capital shall be valued at fair market value in United States dollars. Assets acquired, directly or indirectly, by unlawful means (such as criminal activities) shall not be considered capital for the purposes of section 203(b)(5) of the Act.

Commercial enterprise means any forprofit activity formed for the ongoing conduct of lawful business including, but not limited to, a sole proprietorship, partnership (whether limited or general), holding company, joint venture, corporation, business trust, or other entity which may be publicly or privately owned. This definition includes a commercial enterprise consisting of a holding company and its wholly-owned subsidiaries, provided that each such subsidiary is engaged in a for-profit activity formed for the ongoing conduct of a lawful business. This definition shall not include a noncommercial activity such as owning and operating a personal residence.

Employee means an individual who provides services or labor for the new commercial enterprise and who receives wages or other remuneration directly from the new commercial enterprise. In the case of the Immigrant Investor Pilot Program, "employee" also means an individual who provides services or labor in a job which has been created indirectly through investment in the new commercial enterprise. This definition shall not include independent contractors.

Full-time employment means employment of a qualifying employee by the new commercial enterprise in a position that requires a minimum of 35 working hours per week. In the case of the Immigrant Investor Pilot Program, "full-time employment" also means employment of a qualifying employee in a position that has been created indirectly through revenues generated from increased exports resulting from the Pilot Program that requires a minimum of 35 working hours per week. A job-sharing arrangement whereby two or more qualifying employees share a full-time position shall count as full-time employment provided the hourly requirement per week is met. This definition shall not include combinations of part-time positions even if, when combined, such positions meet the hourly requirement per week.

High employment area means a part of a metropolitan statistical area that at the time of investment:

(i) Is not a targeted employment area; and

(ii) Is an area with an unemployment rate significantly below the national average unemployment rates.

Invest means to contribute capital. A contribution of capital in exchange for a note, bond, convertible debt, obligation, or any other debt arrangement between the alien entrepreneur and the new commercial enterprise does not constitute a contribution of capital for the purposes of this part.

New means established after November 29, 1990.

Qualifying employee means a United States citizen, a lawfully admitted permanent resident, or other immigrant lawfully authorized to be employed in the United States including, but not limited to, a conditional resident, a temporary resident, an asylee, a refugee, or an alien remaining in the United States under suspension of deportation. This definition does not include the alien entrepreneur, the alien entrepreneur's spouse, sons, or daughters, or any nonimmigrant alien.

Regional center means any economic unit, public or private, which is involved with the promotion of economic growth, including increased export sales, improved regional productivity, job creation, and increased domestic capital investment.

Rural area means any area not within either a metropolitan statistical area (as designated by the Office of Management and Budget) or the outer boundary of any city or town having a population of 20,000 or more.

Targeted employment area means an area which, at the time of investment, is a rural area or an area which has experienced unemployment of at least 150 percent of the national average rate.

Troubled business means a business that has been in existence for at least two years, has incurred a net loss for accounting purposes (determined on the basis of generally accepted accounting principles) during the twelveor twenty-four month period prior to the priority date on the alien entrepreneur's Form I–526, and the loss for such period is at least equal to twenty percent of the troubled business's net worth prior to such loss. For purposes of determining whether or not the troubled business has been in existence for two years, successors in interest to the troubled business will be deemed to have been in existence for the same period of time as the business they succeeded.

(f) **Required amounts of capital—**

(1) General. Unless otherwise specified, the amount of capital necessary to make a qualifying investment in the United States is one million United States dollars ($1,000,000).

(2) Targeted employment area. The amount of capital necessary to make a qualifying investment in a targeted employment area within the United States is five hundred thousand United States dollars ($500,000).

(3) High employment area. The amount of capital necessary to make a qualifying investment in a high employment area within the United States, as defined in section 203(b)(5)(C)(iii) of the Act, is one million United States dollars ($1,000,000).

(g) **Multiple investors —**

(1) General. The establishment of a new commercial enterprise may be used as the basis of a petition for classification as an alien entrepreneur by more than one investor, provided each petitioning investor has invested or is actively in the process of investing the required amount for the area in which the new commercial enterprise is principally doing business, and provided each individual investment results in the creation of at least ten full-time positions for qualifying employees. The establishment of a new commercial enterprise may be used as the basis of a petition for classification as an alien entrepreneur even though there are several owners of the enterprise, including persons who are not seeking classification under section 203(b)(5) of the Act and non-natural persons, both foreign and domestic, provided that the source(s) of all capital invested is identified and all invested capital has been derived by lawful means.

(2) Employment creation allocation. The total number of full-time positions created for qualifying employees shall be allocated solely to those alien entrepreneurs who have used the establishment of the new commercial enterprise as the basis of a petition on Form I–526. No allocation need be made among persons not seeking classification under section 203(b)(5) of the Act or among non-natural persons, either foreign or domestic. The Service shall recognize any reasonable agreement made among the alien entrepreneurs in regard to the identification and allocation of such qualifying positions.

(h) Establishment of a new commercial enterprise. The establishment of a new commercial enterprise may consist of:

(1) The creation of an original business;

(2) The purchase of an existing business and simultaneous or subsequent restructuring or reorganization such that a new commercial enterprise results; or

(3) The expansion of an existing business through the investment of the required amount, so that a substantial change in the net worth or number of employees results from the investment of capital. Substantial change means a 40 percent increase either in the net worth, or in the number of employees, so that the new net worth, or number of employees amounts to at least 140 percent of the pre-expansion net worth or number of employees. Establishment of a new commercial enterprise in this manner does not exempt the petitioner from the requirements of 8 CFR 204.6(j) (2) and (3) relating to the required amount of capital investment and the creation of full-time employment for ten qualifying employees. In the case of a capital investment in a troubled business, employment creation may meet the criteria set forth in 8 CFR 204.6(j)(4)(ii).

(i) State designation of a high unemployment area. The state government of any state of the United States may designate a particular geographic or political subdivision located within a metropolitan statistical area or within a city or town having a population of 20,000 or more within such state as an area of high unemployment (at least 150 percent of the national average rate). Evidence of such designation, including a description of the boundaries of the geographic or political subdivision and the method or methods by which the unemployment statistics were obtained, may be provided to a prospective alien entrepreneur for submission with Form I–526. Before any such designation is made, an official of the state must notify the Associate Commissioner for Examinations of the agency, board, or other appropriate governmental body of the state which shall be delegated the authority to certify that the geographic or political subdivision is a high unemployment area.

(j) Initial evidence to accompany petition. A petition submitted for classification as an alien entrepreneur must be accompanied by evidence that the alien has invested or is actively in the process of investing lawfully obtained capital in a new commercial enterprise in the United States which will create full-time positions for not fewer than 10 qualifying employees. In the case of petitions submitted under the Immigrant Investor Pilot Program, a petition must be accompanied by evidence that the alien has invested, or is actively in the process of investing, capital obtained through lawful means within a regional center designated by the Service in accordance with paragraph (m)(4) of this section. The petitioner may be required to submit information or documentation that the Service deems appropriate in addition to that listed below.

(1) To show that a new commercial enterprise has been established by the petitioner in the United States, the petition must be accompanied by:

(i) As applicable, articles of incorporation, certificate of merger or consolidation, partnership agreement, certificate of limited partnership, joint venture agreement, business trust agreement, or other similar organizational document for the new commercial enterprise;

(ii) A certificate evidencing authority to do business in a state or municipality or, if the form of the business does not require any such certificate or the State or municipality does not issue such a certificate, a statement to that effect; or

(iii) Evidence that, as of a date certain after November 29, 1990, the required amount of capital for the area in which an enterprise is located has been transferred to an existing business, and that the investment has resulted in a substantial increase in the net worth or number of employees of the business to which the capital was transferred. This evidence must be in the form of stock purchase agreements, investment agreements, certified financial reports, payroll records, or any similar instruments, agreements, or documents evidencing the investment in the commercial enterprise and the resulting substantial change in the net worth, number of employees.

(2) To show that the petitioner has invested or is actively in the process of investing the required amount of capital, the petition must be accompanied by evidence that the petitioner has placed the required amount of capital at risk for the purpose of generating a return on the capital placed at risk. Evidence of mere intent to invest, or of prospective investment arrangements entailing no present commitment, will not suffice to show that the petitioner is actively in the process of investing. The alien must show actual commitment of the required amount of capital. Such evidence may include, but need not be limited to:

(i) Bank statement(s) showing amount(s) deposited in United States business account(s) for the enterprise;

(ii) Evidence of assets which have been purchased for use in the United States enterprise, including invoices, sales receipts, and purchase contracts containing sufficient information to identify such assets, their purchase costs, date of purchase, and purchasing entity;

(iii) Evidence of property transferred from abroad for use in the United States enterprise, including United States Customs Service commercial entry documents, bills of lading, and transit insurance policies containing ownership information and sufficient information to identify the property and to indicate the fair market value of such property;

(iv) Evidence of monies transferred or committed to be transferred to the new commercial enterprise in exchange for shares of stock (voting or nonvoting, common or preferred). Such stock may not include terms requiring the new commercial enterprise to redeem it at the holder's request; or

(v) Evidence of any loan or mortgage agreement, promissory note, security agreement, or other evidence of borrowing which is secured by assets of the petitioner, other than those of the new commercial enterprise, and for which the petitioner is personally and primarily liable.

(3) To show that the petitioner has invested, or is actively in the process of investing, capital obtained through lawful means, the petition must be accompanied, as applicable, by:

(i) Foreign business registration records;

(ii) Corporate, partnership (or any other entity in any form which has filed in any country or subdivision thereof any return described in this subpart), and personal tax returns including income, franchise, property (whether real, personal, or intangible), or any other tax returns of any kind filed within five years, with any taxing jurisdiction in or outside the United States by or on behalf of the petitioner;

(iii) Evidence identifying any other source(s) of capital; or

(iv) Certified copies of any judgments or evidence of all pending governmental civil or criminal actions, governmental administrative proceedings, and any private civil actions (pending or otherwise) involving monetary judgments against the petitioner from any court in or outside the United States within the past fifteen years.

(4) Job creation —

(i) General. To show that a new commercial enterprise will create not fewer than ten (10) full-time positions for qualifying employees, the petition must be accompanied by:

(A) Documentation consisting of photocopies of relevant tax records, Form I-9, or other similar documents for ten (10) qualifying employees, if such employees have already been hired following the establishment of the new commercial enterprise; or

(B) A copy of a comprehensive business plan showing that, due to the nature and projected size of the new commercial enterprise, the need for not fewer than ten (10) qualifying employees will result, including approximate dates, within the next two years, and when such employees will be hired.

(ii) Troubled business. To show that a new commercial enterprise which has been established through a capital investment in a troubled business meets the statutory employment creation requirement, the petition must be accompanied by evidence that the number of existing employees is being or will be maintained at no less than the pre-investment level for a period of at least two years. Photocopies of tax records, Forms I-9, or other relevant documents for the qualifying employees and a comprehensive business plan shall be submitted in support of the petition.

(iii) Immigrant Investor Pilot Program. To show that the new commercial enterprise located within a regional center approved for participation in the Immigrant Investor Pilot Program meets the statutory employment creation requirement, the petition must be accompanied by evidence that the investment will create full-time positions for not fewer than 10 persons either directly or indirectly through revenues generated from increased exports resulting from the Pilot Program. Such evidence may be demonstrated by reasonable methodologies including those set forth in paragraph (m)(3) of this section.

(5) To show that the petitioner is or will be engaged in the management of the new commercial enterprise, either through the exercise of day-to-day managerial control or through policy formulation, as opposed to maintaining a purely passive role in regard to the investment, the petition must be accompanied by:

(i) A statement of the position title that the petitioner has or will have in the new enterprise and a complete description of the position's duties;

(ii) Evidence that the petitioner is a corporate officer or a member of the corporate board of directors; or

(iii) If the new enterprise is a partnership, either limited or general, evidence that the petitioner is engaged in either direct management or policy making activities. For purposes of this section, if the petitioner is a limited partner and the limited partnership agreement provides the petitioner with certain rights, powers, and duties normally granted to limited partners under the Uniform Limited Partnership Act, the petitioner will be considered sufficiently engaged in the management of the new commercial enterprise.

(6) If applicable, to show that the new commercial enterprise has created or will create employment in a targeted employment area, the petition must be accompanied by:

(i) In the case of a rural area, evidence that the new commercial enterprise is principally doing business within a civil jurisdiction not located within any standard metropolitan statistical area as designated by the Office of Management and Budget, or within any city or town having a population of 20,000 or more as based on the most recent decennial census of the United States; or

(ii) In the case of a high unemployment area:

(A) Evidence that the metropolitan statistical area, the specific county within a metropolitan statistical area, or the county in which a city or town with a population of 20,000 or more is located, in which the new commercial enterprise is principally doing business has experienced an average unemployment rate of 150 percent of the national average rate; or

(B) A letter from an authorized body of the government of the state in which the new commercial enterprise is located which certifies that the geographic or political subdivision of the metropolitan statistical area or of the city or town with a population of 20,000 or more in which the enterprise is principally doing business has been designated a high unemployment area. The letter must meet the requirements of 8 CFR 204.6(i).

(k) Decision. The petitioner will be notified of the decision, and, if the petition is denied, of the reasons for the denial and of the petitioner's right of appeal to the Associate Commissioner for Examinations in accordance with the provisions of part 103 of this chapter. The decision must specify whether or not the new commercial enterprise is principally doing business within a targeted employment area.

(l) [Reserved]

(m) Immigrant Investor Pilot Program.

(1) Scope. The Immigrant Investor Pilot Program is established solely pursuant to the provisions of section 610 of the Departments of Commerce, Justice, and State, the Judiciary, and Related Agencies Appropriation Act, and subject to all conditions and restrictions stipulated in that section. Except as provided herein, aliens seeking to obtain immigration benefits under this paragraph continue to be subject to all conditions and restrictions set forth in section 203(b)(5) of the Act and this section.

(2) Number of immigrant visas allocated. The annual allocation of the visas available under the Immigrant Investor Pilot Program is set at 300 for each of the five fiscal years commencing on October 1, 1993.

(3) Requirements for regional centers. Each regional center wishing to participate in the Immigrant Investor Pilot Program shall submit a proposal to the Assistant Commissioner for Adjudications, which:

(i) Clearly describes how the regional center focuses on a geographical region of the United States, and how it will promote economic growth through increased export sales, improved regional productivity, job creation, and increased domestic capital investment;

(ii) Provides in verifiable detail how jobs will be created indirectly through increased exports;

(iii) Provides a detailed statement regarding the amount and source of capital which has been committed to the regional center, as well as a description of the promotional efforts taken and planned by the sponsors of the regional center;

(iv) Contains a detailed prediction regarding the manner in which the regional center will have a positive impact on the regional or national economy in general as reflected by such factors as increased household earnings, greater demand for business services, utilities, maintenance and repair, and construction both within and without the regional center; and

(v) Is supported by economically or statistically valid forecasting tools, including, but not limited to, feasibility studies, analyses of foreign and domestic markets for the goods or services to be exported, and/or multiplier tables.

(4) Submission of proposals to participate in the Immigrant Investor Pilot Program. On August 24, 1993, the Service will accept proposals from regional centers seeking approval to participate in the Immigrant Investor Pilot Program. Regional centers that have been approved by the Assistant Commissioner for Adjudications will be eligible to participate in the Immigrant Investor Pilot Program.

(5) Decision to participate in the Immigrant Investor Pilot Program. The Assistant Commissioner for Adjudications shall notify the regional center of his or her decision on the request for approval to participate in the Immigrant Investor Pilot Program, and, if the petition is denied, of the reasons for the denial and of the regional center's right of appeal to the Associate Commissioner for Examinations. Notification of denial and appeal rights, and the procedure for appeal shall be the same as those contained in 8 CFR 103.3.

(6) Continued participation requirements for regional centers

(i) Regional centers approved for participation in the program must:

(A) Continue to meet the requirements of section 610(a) of the Appropriations Act.

(B) Provide USCIS with updated information annually, and/or as otherwise requested by USCIS, to demonstrate that the regional center is continuing to promote economic growth, including increased export sales, improved regional productivity, job creation, and increased domestic capital investment in the approved geographic area, using a form designated for this purpose; and

(C) Pay the fee provided by 8 CFR 106.2.

(ii) USCIS will issue a notice of intent to terminate the designation of a regional center in the program if:

(A) A regional center fails to submit the information required in paragraph (m)(6)(i)(B) of this section, or pay the associated fee; or

(B) USCIS determines that the regional center no longer serves the purpose of promoting economic growth, including increased export sales, improved regional productivity, job creation, and increased domestic capital investment.

(iii) A notice of intent to terminate the designation of a regional center will be sent to the regional center and set forth the reasons for termination.

(iv) The regional center will be provided 30 days from receipt of the notice of intent to terminate to rebut the ground or grounds stated in the notice of intent to terminate.

(v) USCIS will notify the regional center of the final decision. If USCIS determines that the regional center's participation in the program should be terminated, USCIS will state the reasons for termination. The regional center may appeal the final termination decision in accordance with 8 CFR 103.3.

(vi) A regional center may elect to withdraw from the program and request a termination of the regional center designation. The regional center must notify USCIS of such election in the form of a letter or as otherwise requested by USCIS. USCIS will notify the regional center of its decision regarding the withdrawal request in writing.

(7) Requirements for alien entrepreneurs. An alien seeking an immigrant visa as an alien entrepreneur under the Immigrant Investor Pilot Program must demonstrate that his or her qualifying investment is within a regional center approved pursuant to paragraph (m)(4) of this section and that such investment will create jobs indirectly through revenues generated from increased exports resulting from the new commercial enterprise.

(i) Exports. For purposes of paragraph (m) of this section, the term "exports" means services or goods which are produced directly or indirectly through revenues generated from a new commercial enterprise and which are transported out of the United States;

(ii) Indirect job creation. To show that 10 or more jobs are actually created indirectly by the business, reasonable methodologies may be used. Such methodologies may include multiplier tables, feasibility studies, analyses of foreign and domestic markets for the goods or services to be exported, and other economically or statistically valid forecasting devices which indicate the likelihood that the business will result in increased employment.

(8) Time for submission of petitions for classification as an alien entrepreneur under the Immigrant Investor Pilot Program. Commencing on October 1, 1993, petitions will be accepted for filing and adjudicated in accordance with the provisions of this section if the alien entrepreneur has invested or is actively in the process of investing within a regional center which has been approved by the Service for participation in the Pilot Program.

(9) Effect of termination of approval of regional center to participate in the Immigrant Investor Pilot Program.

Upon termination of approval of a regional center to participate in the Immigrant Investor Pilot Program, the director shall send a formal written notice to any alien within the regional center who has been granted lawful permanent residence on a conditional basis under the Pilot Program, and who has not yet removed the conditional basis of such lawful permanent residence, of the termination of the alien's permanent resident status, unless the alien can establish continued eligibility for alien entrepreneur classification under section 203(b)(5) of the Act.

HISTORY:

[56 FR 60910, Nov. 29, 1991, as amended at 57 FR 1860, Jan. 16, 1992; 58 FR 44609, Aug. 24, 1993, as confirmed at 59 FR 17921, Apr. 15, 1994; 74 FR 26933, 26937, June 5, 2009; 75 FR 58962, 58990, Sept. 24, 2010; 76 FR 53764, 53782, Aug. 29, 2011; 81 FR 73292, 73332, Oct. 24, 2016; 84 FR 35750, 35808, July 24, 2019; 85 FR 46788, 46922, Aug. 3, 2020]

§ 204.6 Petitions for employment creation aliens. [Effective until contingency met]

(a) General. An EB-5 immigrant petition to classify an alien under section 203(b)(5) of the Act must be properly filed in accordance with the form instructions, with the appropriate fee(s), initial evidence, and any other supporting documentation.

(b) [Reserved]

(c) Eligibility to file and continued eligibility. An alien may file a petition for classification as an investor on his or her own behalf.

(d) Priority date. The priority date of a petition for classification as an investor is the date the completed, signed petition (including all initial evidence and the correct fee) is properly filed. The priority date of an immigrant petition approved for classification as an investor, including immigrant petitions whose approval was revoked on grounds other than those set forth below, will apply to any subsequently filed petition for classification under section 203(b)(5) of the Act for which the alien qualifies. A denied petition will not establish a priority date. A priority date is not transferable to another alien. In the event that the alien is the petitioner of multiple immigrant petitions approved for classification as an investor, the alien shall be entitled to the earliest qualifying priority date. The priority date of an immigrant petition approved for classification as an investor shall not be conferred to a subsequently filed petition if the alien was lawfully admitted to the United States for permanent residence under section 203(b)(5) of the Act using the priority date of the earlier-approved petition or if at any time USCIS revokes the approval of the petition based on:

(1) Fraud or a willful misrepresentation of a material fact by the petitioner; or

(2) A determination by USCIS that the petition approval was based on a material error.

(e) Definitions. As used in this section:

Capital means cash, equipment, inventory, other tangible property, cash equivalents, and indebtedness secured by assets owned by the alien entrepreneur, provided that the alien investor is personally and primarily liable and that the assets of the new commercial enterprise upon which the petition is based are not used to secure any of the indebtedness. All capital shall be valued at fair market value in United States dollars. Assets acquired, directly or indirectly, by unlawful means (such as criminal activities) shall not be considered capital for the purposes of section 203(b)(5) of the Act.

Commercial enterprise means any for-profit activity formed for the ongoing conduct of lawful business including, but not limited to, a sole proprietorship, partnership (whether limited or general), holding company, joint venture, corporation, business trust, or other entity which may be publicly or privately owned. This definition includes a commercial enterprise consisting of a holding company and its wholly-owned subsidiaries, provided that each such subsidiary is engaged in a for-profit activity formed for the ongoing conduct of a lawful business. This definition shall not include a noncommercial activity such as owning and operating a personal residence.

Employee means an individual who provides services or labor for the new commercial enterprise and who receives wages or other remuneration directly from the new commercial enterprise. In the case of the Immigrant Regional Center Program, "employee" also means an individual who provides services or labor in a job which has been created indirectly through investment in the new commercial enterprise. This definition shall not include independent contractors.

Full-time employment means employment of a qualifying employee by the new commercial enterprise in a position that requires a minimum of 35 working hours per week. In the case of the Immigrant Regional Center Program, "full-time employment" also means employment of a qualifying employee in a position that has been created indirectly through revenues generated from increased exports resulting from the Regional Center Program that requires a minimum of 35 working hours per week. A job-sharing arrangement whereby two or more qualifying employees share a full-time position shall count as full-time employment provided the hourly requirement per week is met. This definition shall not include combinations of part-time positions even if, when combined, such positions meet the hourly requirement per week.

High employment area means a part of a metropolitan statistical area that at the time of investment:

(i) Is not a targeted employment area; and

(ii) Is an area with an unemployment rate significantly below the national average unemployment rates.

Invest means to contribute capital. A contribution of capital in exchange for a note, bond, convertible debt, obligation, or any other debt arrangement between the alien investor and the new commercial enterprise does not constitute a contribution of capital for the purposes of this part.

New means established after November 29, 1990.

Qualifying employee means a United States citizen, a lawfully admitted permanent resident, or other immigrant lawfully authorized to be employed in the United States including, but not limited to, a conditional resident, a temporary resident, an asylee, a refugee, or an alien remaining in the United States under suspension of deportation. This definition does not include the alien investor, the alien entrepreneur's spouse, sons, or daughters, or any nonimmigrant alien.

Regional center means any economic unit, public or private, which is involved with the promotion of economic growth, including increased export sales, improved regional productivity, job creation, and increased domestic capital investment.

Regional Center Program means the program established by Public Law 102-395, Section 610, as amended.

Rural area means any area other than an area within a standard metropolitan statistical area (as designated by the Office of Management and Budget) or within the outer boundary of any city or town having a population of 20,000 or more based on the most recent decennial census of the United States.

Targeted employment area means an area that, at the time of investment, is a rural area or is designated as an area that has experienced unemployment of at least 150 percent of the national average rate.

Troubled business means a business that has been in existence for at least two years, has incurred a net loss for accounting purposes (determined on the basis of generally accepted accounting principles) during the twelve- or twenty-four month period prior to the priority date on the alien investor's EB-5 immigrant petition, and the loss for such period is at least equal to twenty percent of the troubled business's net worth prior to such loss. For purposes of determining whether or not the troubled business has been in existence for two years, successors in interest to the troubled business will be deemed to have been in existence for the same period of time as the business they succeeded.

(f) Required amounts of capital.

(1) General. Unless otherwise specified, for EB-5 immigrant petitions filed on or after November 21, 2019, the amount of capital necessary to make a qualifying investment in the United States is one million eight hundred thousand United States dollars ($1,800,000). Beginning on October 1, 2024, and every five years thereafter, this amount will automatically adjust for petitions filed on or after each adjustment's effective date, based on the cumulative annual percentage change in the unadjusted All Items Consumer Price Index for All Urban Consumers (CPI-U) for the U.S. City Average reported by the Bureau of Labor Statistics, as compared to $1,000,000 in 1990. The qualifying investment amount will be rounded down to the nearest hundred thousand. DHS may update this figure by publication of a technical amendment in the Federal Register.

(2) Targeted employment area. Unless otherwise specified, for EB-5 immigrant petitions filed on or after November 21, 2019, the amount of capital necessary to make a qualifying investment in a targeted employment area in the United States is nine hundred thousand United States dollars ($900,000). Beginning on October 1, 2024, and every five years thereafter, this amount will automatically adjust for petitions filed on or after each adjustment's effective date, to be equal to 50 percent of the standard minimum investment amount described in paragraph (f)(1) of this section. DHS may update this figure by publication of a technical amendment in the Federal Register.

(3) High employment area. Unless otherwise specified, for EB-5 immigrant petitions filed on or after November 21, 2019, the amount of capital necessary to make a qualifying investment in a high employment area in the United States is one million eight hundred thousand United States dollars ($1,800,000). Beginning on October 1, 2024, and every five years thereafter, this amount will automatically adjust for petitions filed on or after each adjustment's effective date, based on the cumulative annual percentage change in the unadjusted All Items Consumer Price Index for All Urban Consumers (CPI-U) for the U.S. City Average reported by the Bureau of Labor Statistics as compared to $1,000,000 in 1990. The qualifying investment amount will be rounded down to the nearest hundred thousand. DHS may update this figure by publication of a technical amendment in the Federal Register.

(g) Multiple investors —

(1) General. The establishment of a new commercial enterprise may be used as the basis of a petition for classification as an alien investor by more than one investor, provided each petitioning investor has invested or is actively in the process of investing the required amount for the area in which the new commercial enterprise is principally doing business, and provided each individual investment results in the creation of at least ten full-time positions for qualifying employees. The establishment of a new commercial enterprise may be used as the basis of a petition for classification as an alien investor even though there are several owners of the enterprise, including persons who are not seeking classification under section 203(b)(5) of the Act and non-natural persons, both foreign and domestic, provided that the source(s) of all capital invested is identified and all invested capital has been derived by lawful means.

(2) Employment creation allocation. The total number of full-time positions created for qualifying employees shall be allocated solely to those alien investors who have used the establishment of the new commercial enterprise as the basis for a petition. No allocation must be made among persons not seeking classification under section 203(b)(5) of the Act or among non-natural persons, either foreign or domestic. USCIS will recognize any reasonable agreement made among the alien investors in regard to the identification and allocation of such qualifying positions.

(h) Establishment of a new commercial enterprise. The establishment of a new commercial enterprise may consist of:

(1) The creation of an original business;

(2) The purchase of an existing business and simultaneous or subsequent restructuring or reorganization such that a new commercial enterprise results; or

(3) The expansion of an existing business through the investment of the required amount, so that a substantial change in the net worth or number of employees results from the investment of capital. Substantial change means a 40 percent increase either in the net worth, or in the number of employees, so that the new net worth, or number of employees amounts to at least 140 percent of the pre-expansion net worth or number of employees. Establishment of a new commercial enterprise in this manner does not exempt the petitioner from the requirements of 8 CFR 204.6(j) (2) and (3) relating to the required amount of capital investment and the creation of full-time employment for ten qualifying employees. In the case of a capital investment in a troubled business, employment creation may meet the criteria set forth in 8 CFR 204.6(j)(4)(ii).

(i) Special designation of a high unemployment area. USCIS may designate as an area of high unemployment (at least 150 percent of the national average rate) a census tract or contiguous census tracts in which the new commercial enterprise is principally doing business, and may also include any or all census tracts directly adjacent to such census tract(s). The weighted average of the unemployment rate for the subdivision, based on the labor force employment measure for each census tract, must be at least 150 percent of the national average unemployment rate.

(j) Initial evidence to accompany petition. A petition submitted for classification as an alien entrepreneur must be accompanied by evidence that the alien has invested or is actively in the process of investing lawfully obtained capital in a new commercial enterprise in the United States which will create full-time positions for not fewer than 10 qualifying employees. In the case of petitions submitted under the Immigrant Investor Pilot Program, a petition must be accompanied by evidence that the alien has invested, or is actively in the process of investing, capital obtained through lawful means within a regional center designated by the Service in accordance with paragraph (m)(4) of this section. The petitioner may be required to submit information or documentation that the Service deems appropriate in addition to that listed below.

(1) To show that a new commercial enterprise has been established by the petitioner in the United States, the petition must be accompanied by:

(i) As applicable, articles of incorporation, certificate of merger or consolidation, partnership agreement, certificate of limited partnership, joint venture agreement, business trust agreement, or other similar organizational document for the new commercial enterprise;

(ii) A certificate evidencing authority to do business in a state or municipality or, if the form of the business does not require any such certificate or the State or municipality does not issue such a certificate, a statement to that effect; or

(iii) Evidence that, as of a date certain after November 29, 1990, the required amount of capital for the area in which an enterprise is located has been transferred to an existing business, and that the investment has resulted in a substantial increase in the net worth or number of employees of the business to which the capital was transferred. This evidence must be in the form of stock purchase agreements, investment agreements, certified financial reports, payroll records, or any similar instruments, agreements, or documents evidencing the investment in the commercial enterprise and the resulting substantial change in the net worth, number of employees.

(2) To show that the petitioner has invested or is actively in the process of investing the required amount of capital, the petition must be accompanied by evidence that the petitioner has placed the required amount of capital at risk for the purpose of generating a return on the capital placed at risk. Evidence of mere intent to invest, or of prospective investment arrangements entailing no present commitment, will not suffice to show that the petitioner is actively in the process of investing. The alien must show actual commitment of the required amount of capital. Such evidence may include, but need not be limited to:

(i) Bank statement(s) showing amount(s) deposited in United States business account(s) for the enterprise;

(ii) Evidence of assets which have been purchased for use in the United States enterprise, including invoices, sales receipts, and purchase contracts containing sufficient information to identify such assets, their purchase costs, date of purchase, and purchasing entity;

(iii) Evidence of property transferred from abroad for use in the United States enterprise, including U.S. Customs and Border Protection commercial entry documents, bills of lading, and transit insurance policies containing ownership information and sufficient information to identify the property and to indicate the fair market value of such property;

(iv) Evidence of monies transferred or committed to be transferred to the new commercial enterprise in exchange for shares of stock (voting or nonvoting, common or preferred). Such stock may not include terms requiring the new commercial enterprise to redeem it at the holder's request; or

(v) Evidence of any loan or mortgage agreement, promissory note, security agreement, or other evidence of borrowing which is secured by assets of the petitioner, other than those of the new commercial enterprise, and for which the petitioner is personally and primarily liable.

(3) To show that the petitioner has invested, or is actively in the process of investing, capital obtained through lawful means, the petition must be accompanied, as applicable, by:

(i) Foreign business registration records;

(ii) Corporate, partnership (or any other entity in any form which has filed in any country or subdivision thereof any return described in this subpart), and personal tax returns including income, franchise, property (whether real, personal, or intangible), or any other tax returns of any kind filed within five years, with any taxing jurisdiction in or outside the United States by or on behalf of the petitioner;

(iii) Evidence identifying any other source(s) of capital; or

(iv) Certified copies of any judgments or evidence of all pending governmental civil or criminal actions, governmental administrative proceedings, and any private civil actions (pending or otherwise) involving monetary judgments against the petitioner from any court in or outside the United States within the past fifteen years.

(4) Job creation —

(i) General. To show that a new commercial enterprise will create not fewer than ten (10) full-time positions for qualifying employees, the petition must be accompanied by:

(A) Documentation consisting of photocopies of relevant tax records, Form I-9, or other similar documents for ten (10) qualifying employees, if such employees have already been hired following the establishment of the new commercial enterprise; or

(B) A copy of a comprehensive business plan showing that, due to the nature and projected size of the new commercial enterprise, the need for not fewer than ten (10) qualifying employees will result, including approximate dates, within the next two years, and when such employees will be hired.

(ii) Troubled business. To show that a new commercial enterprise which has been established through a capital investment in a troubled business meets the statutory employment creation requirement, the petition must be accompanied by evidence that the number of existing employees is being or will be maintained at no less than the pre-investment level for a period of at least two years. Photocopies of tax records, Forms I-9, or other relevant documents for the qualifying employees and a comprehensive business plan shall be submitted in support of the petition.

(iii) Immigrant Investor Pilot Program. To show that the new commercial enterprise located within a regional center approved for participation in the Immigrant Investor Pilot Program meets the statutory employment creation requirement, the petition must be accompanied by evidence that the investment will create full-time positions for not fewer than 10 persons either directly or indirectly through revenues generated from increased exports resulting from the Pilot Program. Such evidence may be demonstrated by reasonable methodologies including those set forth in paragraph (m)(3) of this section.

(5) Petitioner engagement. To show that the petitioner is or will be engaged in the new commercial enterprise, either through the exercise of day-to-day managerial control or through policy formulation, the petition must be accompanied by:

(i) A statement of the position title that the petitioner has or will have in the new enterprise and a complete description of the position's duties;

(ii) Evidence that the petitioner is a corporate officer or a member of the corporate board of directors; or

(iii) Evidence that the petitioner is engaged in policy making activities. For purposes of this section, a petitioner will be considered sufficiently engaged in policy making activities if the petitioner is an equity holder in the new commercial enterprise and the organizational documents of the new commercial enterprise provide the petitioner with certain rights, powers, and duties normally granted to equity holders of the new commercial enterprise's type of entity in the jurisdiction in which the new commercial enterprise is organized.

(6) If applicable, to show that the new commercial enterprise has created or will create employment in a targeted employment area, the petition must be accompanied by:

(i) In the case of a rural area, evidence that the new commercial enterprise is principally doing business within an area not located within any standard metropolitan statistical area as designated by the Office of Management and Budget, nor within any city or town having a population of 20,000 or more as based on the most recent decennial census of the United States; or

(ii) In the case of a high unemployment area:

(A) Evidence that the metropolitan statistical area, the specific county within a metropolitan statistical area, the county in which a city or town with a population of 20,000 or more is located, or the city or town with a population of 20,000 or more outside of a metropolitan statistical area, in which the new commercial enterprise is principally doing business has experienced an average unemployment rate of at least 150 percent of the national average rate; or

(B) A description of the boundaries and the unemployment statistics for the area for which designation is sought as set forth in paragraph (i) of this section, and the reliable method or methods by which the unemployment statistics were obtained.

(k) Decision. The petitioner will be notified of the decision, and, if the petition is denied, of the reasons for the denial. The petitioner has the right to appeal the denial to the Administrative Appeals Office in accordance with the provisions of part 103 of this chapter.

(*l*) [Reserved]

(m) Immigrant Investor Pilot Program.

(1) Scope. The Immigrant Investor Pilot Program is established solely pursuant to the provisions of section 610 of the Departments of Commerce, Justice, and State, the Judiciary, and Related Agencies Appropriation Act, and subject to all conditions and restrictions stipulated in that section. Except as provided herein, aliens seeking to obtain immigration benefits under this paragraph continue to be subject to all conditions and restrictions set forth in section 203(b)(5) of the Act and this section.

(2) Number of immigrant visas allocated. The annual allocation of the visas available under the Immigrant Investor Pilot Program is set at 300 for each of the five fiscal years commencing on October 1, 1993.

(3) Requirements for regional centers. Each regional center wishing to participate in the Immigrant Investor Pilot Program shall submit a proposal to the Assistant Commissioner for Adjudications, which:

(i) Clearly describes how the regional center focuses on a geographical region of the United States, and how it will promote economic growth through increased export sales, improved regional productivity, job creation, and increased domestic capital investment;

(ii) Provides in verifiable detail how jobs will be created indirectly through increased exports;

(iii) Provides a detailed statement regarding the amount and source of capital which has been committed to the regional center, as well as a description of the promotional efforts taken and planned by the sponsors of the regional center;

(iv) Contains a detailed prediction regarding the manner in which the regional center will have a positive impact on the regional or national economy in general as reflected by such factors as increased household earnings, greater demand for business services, utilities, maintenance and repair, and construction both within and without the regional center; and

(v) Is supported by economically or statistically valid forecasting tools, including, but not limited to, feasibility studies, analyses of foreign and domestic markets for the goods or services to be exported, and/or multiplier tables.

(4) Submission of proposals to participate in the Immigrant Investor Pilot Program. On August 24, 1993, the Service will accept proposals from regional centers seeking approval to participate in the Immi-

grant Investor Pilot Program. Regional centers that have been approved by the Assistant Commissioner for Adjudications will be eligible to participate in the Immigrant Investor Pilot Program.

(5) Decision to participate in the Immigrant Investor Pilot Program. The Assistant Commissioner for Adjudications shall notify the regional center of his or her decision on the request for approval to participate in the Immigrant Investor Pilot Program, and, if the petition is denied, of the reasons for the denial and of the regional center's right of appeal to the Associate Commissioner for Examinations. Notification of denial and appeal rights, and the procedure for appeal shall be the same as those contained in 8 CFR 103.3.

(6) Continued participation requirements for regional centers

(i) Regional centers approved for participation in the program must:

(A) Continue to meet the requirements of section 610(a) of the Appropriations Act.

(B) Provide USCIS with updated information annually, and/or as otherwise requested by USCIS, to demonstrate that the regional center is continuing to promote economic growth, including increased export sales, improved regional productivity, job creation, and increased domestic capital investment in the approved geographic area, using a form designated for this purpose; and

(C) Pay the fee provided by 8 CFR 106.2.

(ii) USCIS will issue a notice of intent to terminate the designation of a regional center in the program if:

(A) A regional center fails to submit the information required in paragraph (m)(6)(i)(B) of this section, or pay the associated fee; or

(B) USCIS determines that the regional center no longer serves the purpose of promoting economic growth, including increased export sales, improved regional productivity, job creation, and increased domestic capital investment.

(iii) A notice of intent to terminate the designation of a regional center will be sent to the regional center and set forth the reasons for termination.

(iv) The regional center will be provided 30 days from receipt of the notice of intent to terminate to rebut the ground or grounds stated in the notice of intent to terminate.

(v) USCIS will notify the regional center of the final decision. If USCIS determines that the regional center's participation in the program should be terminated, USCIS will state the reasons for termination. The regional center may appeal the final termination decision in accordance with 8 CFR 103.3.

(vi) A regional center may elect to withdraw from the program and request a termination of the regional center designation. The regional center must notify USCIS of such election in the form of a letter or as otherwise requested by USCIS. USCIS will notify the regional center of its decision regarding the withdrawal request in writing.

(7) Requirements for alien entrepreneurs. An alien seeking an immigrant visa as an alien entrepreneur under the Immigrant Investor Pilot Program must demonstrate that his or her qualifying investment is within a regional center approved pursuant to paragraph (m)(4) of this section and that such investment will create jobs indirectly through revenues generated from increased exports resulting from the new commercial enterprise.

(i) Exports. For purposes of paragraph (m) of this section, the term "exports" means services or goods which are produced directly or indirectly through revenues generated from a new commercial enterprise and which are transported out of the United States;

(ii) Indirect job creation. To show that 10 or more jobs are actually created indirectly by the business, reasonable methodologies may be used. Such methodologies may include multiplier tables, feasibility studies, analyses of foreign and domestic markets for the goods or services to be exported, and other economically or statistically valid forecasting devices which indicate the likelihood that the business will result in increased employment.

(8) Time for submission of petitions for classification as an alien entrepreneur under the Immigrant Investor Pilot Program. Commencing on October 1, 1993, petitions will be accepted for filing and adjudicated in accordance with the provisions of this section if the alien entrepreneur has invested or is actively in the process of investing within a regional center which has been approved by the Service for participation in the Pilot Program.

(9) Effect of termination of approval of regional center to participate in the Immigrant Investor Pilot Program. Upon termination of approval of a regional center to participate in the Immigrant Investor Pilot Program, the director shall send a formal written notice to any alien within the regional center who has been granted lawful permanent residence on a conditional basis under the Pilot Program, and who has not yet removed the conditional basis of such lawful permanent residence, of the termination of the alien's permanent resident status, unless the alien can establish continued eligibility for alien entrepreneur classification under section 203(b)(5) of the Act.

(n) Offering amendments or supplements. Amendments or supplements to any offering necessary to maintain compliance with applicable securities laws based upon changes to this section effective on November 21, 2019 shall not independently result in denial or revocation of a petition for classification under section 203(b)(5) of the Act, provided that the petitioner:

(1) Filed the petition for classification under section 203(b)(5) of the Act prior to November 21, 2019;

(2) Was eligible for classification under 203(b)(5) of the Act at the time the petition was filed; and

(3) Is eligible for classification under 203(b)(5) of the Act, including having no right to withdraw or rescind the investment or commitment to invest into such offering, at the time of adjudication of the petition.

HISTORY:

[56 FR 60910, Nov. 29, 1991, as amended at 57 FR 1860, Jan. 16, 1992; 58 FR 44609, Aug. 24, 1993, as confirmed at 59 FR 17921, Apr. 15, 1994; 74 FR 26933, 26937, June 5, 2009; 75 FR 58962, 58990, Sept. 24, 2010; 76 FR 53764, 53782, Aug. 29, 2011; 81 FR

73292, 73332, Oct. 24, 2016; 84 FR 35750, 35808, July 24, 2019; 85 FR 46788, 46922, Aug. 3, 2020]

§ 204.7 Preservation of benefits contained in savings clause of Immigration and Nationality Act Amendments of 1976.

In order to be considered eligible for the benefits of the savings clause contained in section 9 of the Immigration and Nationality Act Amendments of 1976, an alien must show that the facts established prior to January 1, 1977 upon which the entitlement to such benefits was based continue to exist.

HISTORY:
[41 FR 55849, Dec. 23, 1976]

§ 204.8 [This section was removed and reserved. See 74 FR 26933, 26937, June 5, 2009.]

[NO TEXT IN ORIGINAL]

HISTORY:
[56 FR 23210, May 21, 1991, as amended at 57 FR 14792, 14793, Apr. 23, 1992]

AUTHORITY:
(8 U.S.C. 1101, 1103, 1151, 1153, 1154, 1182, 1184, 1186a, 1255, 1641; 8 CFR part 2.)

§ 204.9 Special immigrant status for certain aliens who have served honorably (or are enlisted to serve) in the Armed Forces of the United States for at least 12 years.

(a) Petition for Armed Forces special immigrant. An alien may not be classified as an Armed Forces special immigrant unless the alien is the beneficiary of an approved petition to classify such an alien as a special immigrant under section 101(a)(27)(K) of the Act. The petition must be filed on Form I-360, Petition for Amerasian, Widow or Special Immigrant.

(1) Who may file. An alien Armed Forces enlistee or veteran may file the petition for Armed Forces special immigrant status in his or her own behalf. The person filing the petition is not required to be a citizen or lawful permanent resident of the United States.

(2) Where to file. The petition must be filed in accordance with the instructions on the form.

(b) Eligibility. An alien is eligible for classification as a special immigrant under section 101(a)(27)(K) of the Act if:

(1) The alien has served honorably on active duty in the Armed Forces of the United States after October 15, 1978;

(2) The alien's original lawful enlistment was outside the United States (under a treaty or agreement in effect October 1, 1991) for a period or periods aggregating—

(i) Twelve years, and who, if separated from such service, was never separated except under honorable conditions; or

(ii) Six years, in the case of an immigrant who is on active duty at the time of seeking special immigrant status under this rule and who has reenlisted to incur a total active duty service obligation of at least 12 years;

(3) The alien is a national of an independent state which maintains a treaty or agreement allowing nationals of that state to enlist in the United States Armed Forces each year; and

(4) The executive department under which the alien has served or is serving has recommended the granting of special immigrant status to the immigrant.

(c) Derivative beneficiaries. A spouse or child accompanying or following to join a principal immigrant who has requested benefits under this section may be accorded the same special immigrant classification as the principal alien. This may occur whether or not the spouse or child is named in the petition and without the approval of a separate petition, but only if the executive department under which the immigrant serves or served recommends the granting of special immigrant status to the principal immigrant.

(1) The relationship of spouse and child as defined in section 101(b)(1) of the Act must have existed at the time the principal alien's special immigrant application under section 101(a)(27)(K) of the Act was approved. The spouse or child of an immigrant classified as a section 103(a)(27)(K) special immigrant is entitled to a derivative status corresponding to the classification and priority date of the beneficiary of the petition.

(2) When a spouse or child of an alien granted special immigrant status under section 101(a)(27)(K) of the Act is in the United States but was not included in the principal alien's application, the spouse or child shall file Form I-485, Application to Register Permanent Residence or Adjust Status, in accordance with the instructions on the form, regardless of the status of that spouse or child in the United States. The application must be supported by evidence that the principal alien has been granted special immigrant status under section 101(a)(27)(K) of the Act.

(3) Revocation of derivative status. The termination of special immigrant status for a person who was the principal applicant shall result in termination of the special immigrant status of a spouse or child whose status was based on the special immigrant application of the principal.

(4) [Redesignated as (c)(3). 58 FR 50835, Sept. 29, 1993.]

(d) Documents which must be submitted in support of the petition.

(1) A petition to classify an immigrant as a special immigrant under section 101(a)(27)(K) of the Act must be accompanied by the following:

(i) Certified proof of reenlistment (after 6 years of active duty service), or certification of past active duty status of 12 years, issued by the authorizing official of the executive department in which the applicant serves or has served, which certifies that the applicant has the required honorable active duty service and commitment. The authorizing official need not be at a level above the "local command". The certification must be submitted with Form I-360, Petition for Amerasian, Widow(er), or Special Immigrant; and

(ii) Birth certificate of the applicant establishing that the applicant is a national of an independent state which maintains a treaty or agreement allowing nationals of that state to enlist in the United States Armed Forces each year.

(2) Any documents submitted in support of the petition must meet the evidentiary requirements as set forth in 8 CFR part 103.

(3) Submission of an original Form DD-214, Certificate of Release or Discharge from Active Duty; Form G-325b, Biographic Information; and Form N-426, Request for Certification of Military or Naval Service, is not required for approval of a petition for special immigrant status.

(e) Decision. The petitioner will be notified of the director's decision and, if the petition is denied, of the reasons for the denial. If the petition is denied, the petitioner will also be notified of the petitioner's right to appeal the decision to the Associate Commissioner for Examinations in accordance with 8 CFR part 103.

(f) Revocation under section 205 of the Act. An alien who has been granted special immigrant classification under section 101(a)(27)(K) of the Act must meet the qualifications set forth in the Act at the time he or she is admitted to the United States for lawful permanent residence. If an Armed Forces special immigrant ceases to be a qualified enlistee by failing to complete the required active duty service obligation for reasons other than an honorable discharge prior to entering the United States with an immigrant visa or approval of an application for adjustment of status to that of an alien lawfully admitted for permanent residence, the petition designating his or her classification as a special immigrant is revoked automatically under the general provisions of section 205 of the Act. The Service shall obtain a current Form DD-214, Certificate of Release or Discharge from Active Duty, from the appropriate executive department for verification of the alien's failure to maintain eligibility for the classification under section 101(a)(27)(K) of the Act.

HISTORY:

[57 FR 33861, July 31, 1992, as confirmed and revised at 58 FR 50836, Sept. 29, 1993; 74 FR 26933, 26937, June 5, 2009]

§ 204.10 [This section was removed and reserved. See 76 FR 53764, 53782, Aug. 29, 2011.]

[NO TEXT IN ORIGINAL]

HISTORY:

[58 FR 30701, May 27, 1993; 60 FR 54027, 54030, Oct. 19, 1995, as confirmed at 62 FR 6707, 6708, Feb. 13, 1997; 70 FR 21129, 21131, Apr. 25, 2005, as confirmed and removed at 76 FR 53764, 53778, 53782, Aug. 29, 2011; 74 FR 26933, 26937, June 5, 2009]

AUTHORITY:

(8 U.S.C. 1101, 1103, 1151, 1153, 1154, 1182, 1184, 1186a, 1255, 1641; 8 CFR part 2.)

§ 204.11 Special immigrant juvenile classification.

(a) Definitions. As used in this section, the following definitions apply to a request for classification as a special immigrant juvenile.

Judicial determination means a conclusion of law made by a juvenile court.

Juvenile court means a court located in the United States that has jurisdiction under State law to make judicial determinations about the dependency and/or custody and care of juveniles.

Petition means the form designated by USCIS to request classification as a special immigrant juvenile and the act of filing the request.

Petitioner means the alien seeking special immigrant juvenile classification.

State means the definition set out in section 101(a)(36) of the Act, including an Indian tribe, tribal organization, or tribal consortium, operating a program under a plan approved under 42 U.S.C. 671.

United States means the definition set out in section 101(a)(38) of the Act.

(b) Eligibility. A petitioner is eligible for classification as a special immigrant juvenile under section 203(b)(4) of the Act as described at section 101(a)(27)(J) of the Act, if they meet all of the following requirements:

(1) Is under 21 years of age at the time of filing the petition;

(2) Is unmarried at the time of filing and adjudication;

(3) Is physically present in the United States;

(4) Is the subject of a juvenile court order(s) that meets the requirements under paragraph (c) of this section; and

(5) Obtains consent from the Secretary of Homeland Security to classification as a special immigrant juvenile. For USCIS to consent, the request for SIJ classification must be bona fide, which requires the petitioner to establish that a primary reason the required juvenile court determinations were sought was to obtain relief from parental abuse, neglect, abandonment, or a similar basis under State law. USCIS may withhold consent if evidence materially conflicts with the eligibility requirements in paragraph (b) of this section such that the record reflects that the request for SIJ classification was not bona fide. USCIS approval of the petition constitutes the granting of consent.

(c) Juvenile court order(s).

(1) Court-ordered dependency or custody and parental reunification determination. The juvenile court must have made certain judicial determinations related to the petitioner's custody or dependency and determined that the petitioner cannot reunify with their parent(s) due to abuse, neglect, abandonment, or a similar basis under State law.

(i) The juvenile court must have made at least one of the following judicial determinations related to the petitioner's custodial placement or dependency in accordance with State law governing such determinations:

(A) Declared the petitioner dependent upon the juvenile court; or

(B) Legally committed to or placed the petitioner under the custody of an agency or department of a State, or an individual or entity appointed by a State or juvenile court.

(ii) The juvenile court must have made a judicial determination that parental reunification with one or both parents is not viable due to abuse, abandonment, neglect, or a similar basis under State law. The court is not required to terminate parental rights to determine that parental reunification is not viable.

(2) Best interest determination.

(i) A determination must be made in judicial or administrative proceedings by a court or agency recognized by the juvenile court and authorized by law to make such decisions that it would not be in the petitioner's best interest to be returned to the petitioner's or their parent's country of nationality or last habitual residence.

(ii) Nothing in this part should be construed as altering the standards for best interest determinations that juvenile court judges routinely apply under relevant State law.

(3) Qualifying juvenile court order(s).

(i) The juvenile court must have exercised its authority over the petitioner as a juvenile and made the requisite judicial determinations in this paragraph under applicable State law to establish eligibility.

(ii) The juvenile court order(s) must be in effect on the date the petitioner files the petition and continue through the time of adjudication of the petition, except when the juvenile court's jurisdiction over the petitioner terminated solely because:

(A) The petitioner was adopted, placed in a permanent guardianship, or another child welfare permanency goal was reached, other than reunification with a parent or parents with whom the court previously found that reunification was not viable; or

(B) The petitioner was the subject of a qualifying juvenile court order that was terminated based on age, provided the petitioner was under 21 years of age at the time of filing the petition.

(d) Petition requirements. A petitioner must submit all of the following evidence, as applicable to their petition:

(1) Petition. A petition by or on behalf of a juvenile, filed on the form prescribed by USCIS in accordance with the form instructions.

(2) Evidence of age. Documentary evidence of the petitioner's age, in the form of a valid birth certificate, official government-issued identification, or other document that in USCIS' discretion establishes the petitioner's age. Under no circumstances is the petitioner compelled to submit evidence that would conflict with paragraph (e) of this section.

(3) Juvenile court order(s). Juvenile court order(s) with the judicial determinations required by paragraph (c) of this section. Where the best interest determination was made in administrative proceedings, the determination may be provided in a separate document issued in those proceedings.

(4) Evidence of a similar basis. When the juvenile court determined parental reunification was not viable due to a basis similar to abuse, neglect, or abandonment, the petitioner must provide evidence of how the basis is legally similar to abuse, neglect, or abandonment under State law. Such evidence must include:

(i) The juvenile court's determination as to how the basis is legally similar to abuse, neglect, or abandonment under State law; or

(ii) Other evidence that establishes the juvenile court made a judicial determination that the legal basis is similar to abuse, neglect, or abandonment under State law.

(5) Evidentiary requirements for DHS consent. For USCIS to consent, the juvenile court order(s) and any supplemental evidence submitted by the petitioner must include the following:

(i) The factual basis for the requisite determinations in paragraph (c) of this section; and

(ii) The relief from parental abuse, neglect, abandonment, or a similar basis under State law granted or recognized by the juvenile court. Such relief may include:

(A) The court-ordered custodial placement; or

(B) The court-ordered dependency on the court for the provision of child welfare services and/or other court-ordered or court-recognized protective or remedial relief, including recognition of the petitioner's placement in the custody of the Department of Health and Human Services, Office of Refugee Resettlement.

(6) U.S. Department of Health and Human Services (HHS) consent. The petitioner must provide documentation of specific consent from HHS with the petition when:

(i) The petitioner is, or was previously, in the custody of HHS; and

(ii) While in the custody of HHS, the petitioner obtained a juvenile court order that altered the petitioner's HHS custody or placement status.

(e) No contact. During the petition or interview process, USCIS will take no action that requires a petitioner to contact the person(s) who allegedly battered, abused, neglected, or abandoned the petitioner (or the family member of such person(s)).

(f) Interview. USCIS may interview a petitioner for special immigrant juvenile classification in accordance with 8 CFR 103.2(b). If an interview is conducted, the petitioner may be accompanied by a trusted adult at the interview. USCIS may limit the number of persons present at the interview, except that the petitioner's attorney or accredited representative of record may be present.

(g) Time for adjudication.

(1) In general, USCIS will make a decision on a petition for classification as a special immigrant juvenile within 180 days of receipt of a properly filed petition. The 180 days does not begin until USCIS has received all of the required evidence in paragraph (d), and the time period will be reset or suspended as described in 8 CFR 103.2(b)(10)(i).

(2) When a petition for special immigrant juvenile classification and an application for adjustment of status to lawful permanent resident are pending at the same time, a request for evidence relating to the separate application for adjustment of status will not stop or suspend the 180-day period for USCIS to decide on the petition for SIJ classification.

(h) Decision. USCIS will notify the petitioner of the decision made on the petition, and, if the petition is denied, of the reasons for the denial, pursuant to 8 CFR 103.2(b) and 103.3. If the petition is denied, USCIS will provide notice of the petitioner's right to appeal the decision, pursuant to 8 CFR 103.3.

(i) No parental immigration rights based on special immigrant juvenile classification. The natural or prior adoptive parent(s) of a petitioner granted special immigrant juvenile classification will not be accorded any right, privilege, or status under the Act by virtue of their parentage. This prohibition applies to all of the petitioner's natural and prior adoptive parent(s).

(j) Revocation.

(1) Automatic revocation. USCIS will issue a notice to the beneficiary of an approved petition for special immigrant juvenile classification of an automatic revocation under this paragraph as provided in 8 CFR 205.1. The approval of a petition for classification as a special immigrant juvenile made under this section is revoked as of the date of approval if any one of the following circumstances occurs before the decision on the beneficiary's application for adjustment of status to lawful permanent resident becomes final:

(i) Reunification of the beneficiary with one or both parents by virtue of a juvenile court order, where a juvenile court previously deemed reunification with that parent, or both parents, not viable due to abuse, neglect, abandonment, or a similar basis under State law; or

(ii) Administrative or judicial proceedings determine that it is in the beneficiary's best interest to be returned to the country of nationality or last habitual residence of the beneficiary or of their parent(s).

(2) Revocation on notice. USCIS may revoke an approved petition for classification as a special immigrant juvenile for good and sufficient cause as provided in 8 CFR 205.2.

HISTORY:

[56 FR 23208, May 21, 1991; redesignated at 58 FR 42849, Aug. 12, 1993; 58 FR 42850, Aug. 12, 1993; 74 FR 26933, 26937, June 5, 2009; 87 FR 13066, 13111, Mar. 8, 2022]

§ 204.12 How can second-preference immigrant physicians be granted a national interest waiver based on service in a medically underserved area or VA facility?

(a) Which physicians qualify? Any alien physician (namely doctors of medicine and doctors of osteopathy) for whom an immigrant visa petition has been filed pursuant to section 203(b)(2) of the Act shall be granted a national interest waiver under section 203(b)(2)(B)(ii) of the Act if the physician requests the waiver in accordance with this section and establishes that:

(1) The physician agrees to work full-time (40 hours per week) in a clinical practice for an aggregate of 5 years (not including time served in J-1 nonimmigrant status); and

(2) The service is;

(i) In a geographical area or areas designated by the Secretary of Health and Human Services (HHS) as a Medically Underserved Area, a Primary Medical Health Professional Shortage Area, or a Mental Health Professional Shortage Area, and in a medical speciality that is within the scope of the Secretary's designation for the geographical area or areas; or

(ii) At a health care facility under the jurisdiction of the Secretary of Veterans Affairs (VA); and

(3) A Federal agency or the department of public health of a State, territory of the United States, or the District of Columbia, has previously determined that the physician's work in that area or facility is in the public interest.

(b) Is there a time limit on how long the physician has to complete the required medical service?

(1) If the physician already has authorization to accept employment (other than as a J-1 exchange alien), the beneficiary physician must complete the aggregate 5 years of qualifying full-time clinical practice during the 6-year period beginning on the date of approval of the Form I-140.

(2) If the physician must obtain authorization to accept employment before the physician may lawfully begin working, the physician must complete the aggregate 5 years of qualifying full-time clinical practice during the 6-year period beginning on the date of the Service issues the necessary employment authorization document.

(c) Are there special requirements for these physicians? Petitioners requesting the national interest waiver as described in this section on behalf of a qualified alien physician, or alien physicians self- petitioning for second preference classification, must meet all eligibility requirements found in paragraphs (k)(1) through (k)(3) of § 204.5. In addition, the petitioner or self-petitioner must submit the following evidence with Form I-140 to support the request for a national interest waiver. Physicians planning to divide the practice of full-time clinical medicine between more than one underserved area must submit the following evidence for each area of intended practice.

(1)(i) If the physician will be an employee, a full-time employment contract for the required period of clinical medical practice, or an employment commitment letter from a VA facility. The contract or letter must have been issued and dated within 6 months prior to the date the petition is filed.

(ii) If the physician will establish his or her own practice, the physician's sworn statement committing to the full-time practice of clinical medicine for the required period, and describing the steps the physician has taken or intends to actually take to establish the practice.

(2) Evidence that the physician will provide full-time clinical medical service:

(i) In a geographical area or areas designated by the Secretary of HHS as having a shortage of health care professionals and in a medical speciality that is within the scope of the Secretary's designation for the geographical area or areas; or

(ii) In a facility under the jurisdiction of the Secretary of VA.

(3) A letter (issued and dated within 6 months prior to the date on which the petition is filed) from a Federal agency or from the department of public health (or equivalent) of a State or territory of the United States or the District of Columbia, attesting that the alien physician's work is or will be in the public interest.

(i) An attestation from a Federal agency must reflect the agency's knowledge of the alien's qualifications and the agency's background in making determinations on matters involving medical affairs so as to substantiate the finding that the alien's work is or will be in the public interest.

(ii) An attestation from the public health department of a State, territory, or the District of Columbia must reflect that the agency has jurisdiction over the place where the alien physician intends to practice clinical medicine. If the alien physician intends to practice clinical medicine in more than one underserved area, attestations from each intended area of practice must be included.

(4) Evidence that the alien physician meets the admissibility requirements established by section 212(a)(5)(B) of the Act.

(5) Evidence of the Service-issued waivers, if applicable, of the requirements of sections 212(e) of the Act, if the alien physician has been a J-1 nonimmigrant receiving medical training within the United States.

(d) How will the Service process petitions filed on different dates?

(1) Petitions filed on or after November 12, 1999. For petitions filed on or after November 12, 1999, the Service will approve a national interest waiver provided the petitioner or beneficiary (if self-petitioning) submits the necessary documentation to satisfy the requirements of section 203(b)(2)(B)(ii) of the Act and this section, and the physician is otherwise eligible for classification as a second preference employment-based immigrant. Nothing in this section relieves the alien physician from any other requirement other than that of fulfilling the labor certification process as provided in § 204.5(k)(4).

(2) Petitions pending on November 12, 1999. Section 203(b)(2)(B)(ii) of the Act applies to all petitions that were pending adjudication as of November 12, 1999 before a Service Center, before the associate Commissioner for Examinations, or before a Federal court. Petitioners whose petitions were pending on November 12, 1999, will not be required to submit a new petition, but may be required to submit supplemental evidence noted in paragraph (c) of this section. The requirement that supplemental evidence be issued and dated within 6 months prior to the date on which the petition is filed is not applicable to petitions that were pending as of November 12, 1999. If the case was pending before the Associate Commissioner for Examinations or a Federal court on November 12, 1999, the petitioner should ask for a remand to the proper Service Center for consideration of this new evidence.

(3) Petitions denied on or after November 12, 1999. The Service Center or the Associate Commissioner for Examinations shall reopen any petition affected by the provision of section 203(b)(2)(B)(ii) of the Act that the Service denied on or after November 12, 1999, but prior to the effective date of this rule.

(4) Petitions filed prior to November 1, 1998. For petitions filed prior to November 1, 1998, and still pending as of November 12, 1999, the Service will approve a national interest waiver provided the beneficiary fulfills the evidence requirements of paragraph (c) of this section. Alien physicians that are beneficiaries of pre-November 1, 1998, petitions are only required to work full-time as a physician practicing clinical medicine for an aggregate of 3 years, rather than 5 years, not including time served in J-1 nonimmigrant status, prior to the physician either adjusting status under section 245 of the Act or receiving a visa issued under section 204(b) of the Act. The physician must complete the aggregate of 3 years of medical service within the 4-year period beginning on the date of the approval of the petition, if the physician already has authorization to accept employment (other than as a J-1 exchange alien). If the physician does not already have authorization to accept employment, the physician must perform the service within the 4-year period beginning the date the Service issues the necessary employment authorization document.

(5) Petitions filed and approved before November 12, 1999. An alien physician who obtained approval of a second preference employment-based visa petition and a national interest waiver before November 12, 1999, is not subject to the service requirements imposed in section 203(b)(2)(B)(ii) of the Act. If the physician obtained under section 214(1) of the Act a waiver of the foreign residence requirement imposed under section 212(e) of the Act, he or she must comply with the requirements of section 214(1) of the Act in order to continue to have the benefit of that waiver.

(6) Petitions denied prior to November 12, 1999. If a prior Service decision denying a national interest waiver under section 203(b)(2)(B) of the Act became administratively final before November 12, 1999, an alien physician who believes that he or she is eligible for the waiver under the provisions of section 203(b)(2)(B)(ii) of the Act may file a new Form I-140 petition accompanied by the evidence required in paragraph (c) of this section. The Service must deny any motion to reopen or reconsider a decision denying an immigrant visa petition if the decision became final before November 12, 1999, without prejudice to the filing of a new visa petition with a national interest waiver request that comports with section 203(b)(2)(B)(ii) of the Act.

(e) May physicians file adjustment of status applications? Upon approval of a second preference employment-based immigrant petition, Form I-140, and national interest waiver based on a full-time clinical practice in a shortage area or areas of the United States, an alien physician may submit Form I-485, Application to Register Permanent Residence or Adjust Status, to the appropriate Service Center. The Service will not approve the alien physician's application for adjustment of status until the alien physician submits evidence documenting that the alien physician has completed the period of required service. Specific instructions for alien physicians filing adjustment applications are found in § 245.18 of this chapter.

(f) May a physician practice clinical medicine in a different underserved area? Physicians in receipt of an approved Form I-140 with a national interest waiver based on full-time clinical practice in a designated shortage area and a pending adjustment of status application may apply to the Service if the physician is offered new employment to practice full-time in another underserved area of the United States.

(1) If the physician beneficiary has found a new employer desiring to petition the Service on the physician's behalf, the new petitioner must submit a new Form I-140 (with fee) with all the evidence required in paragraph (c) of this section, including a copy of the approval notice from the initial Form I-140. If approved, the new petition will be matched with the pending adjustment of status application. The beneficiary will retain the priority date from the initial Form I-140. The Service will calculate the amount of time the physician was between employers so as to adjust the count of the aggregate time served in an underserved area. This calculation will be based on the evidence the physician submits pursuant to the requirements of § 245.18(d) of this chapter. An approved change of practice to another underserved area does not constitute a new 6-year period in which the physician must complete the aggregate 5 years of service.

(2) If the physician intends to establish his or her own practice, the physician must submit a new Form I-140 (with fee) will all the evidence required in paragraph (c) of this section, including the special requirement of paragraph (c)(1)(ii) of this section and a copy of the approval notice from the initial Form I-140. If approved, the new petition will be matched with the pending adjustment of status application. The beneficiary will retain the priority date from the initial Form I-140. The Service will calculate the amount of time the physician was between practices so as to adjust the count of the aggregate time served in an underserved area. This calculation will be based on the evidence the physician submits pursuant to the requirements of § 245.18(d) of this chapter. An approved change of practice to another underserved area does not constitute a new 6-year period in which the physician must complete the aggregate 5 years of service.

(g) Do these provisions have any effect on physicians with foreign residence requirements? Because the requirements of section 203(b)(2)(B)(ii) of the Act are not exactly the same as the requirements of section 212(e) or 214(l) of the Act, approval of a national interest waiver under section 203(b)(2)(B)(ii) of the Act and this paragraph does not relieve the alien physician of any foreign residence requirement that the alien physician may have under section 212(e) of the Act.

HISTORY:

[65 FR 53889, 53893, Sept. 6, 2000, as corrected at 65 FR 57861, Sept. 26, 2000]

§ 204.13 How can the International Broadcasting Bureau of the United States Broadcasting Board of Governors petition for a fourth preference special immigrant broadcaster?

(a) Which broadcasters qualify? Under section 203(b)(4) of the Act, the International Broadcasting Bureau of the United States Broadcasting Board of Governors (BBG), or a grantee of the BBG, may petition for an alien (and the alien's accompanying spouse and children) to work as a broadcaster for the BBG or a grantee of the BBG in the United States. For the purposes of this section, the terms:

BBG grantee means Radio Free Asia, Inc (RFA) or Radio Free Europe/Radio Liberty, Inc. (RFE/RL); and

Broadcaster means a reporter, writer, translator, editor, producer or announcer for news broadcasts; hosts for news broadcasts, news analysis, editorial and other broadcast features; or a news analysis specialist. The term broadcaster does not include individuals performing purely technical or support services for the BBG or a BBG grantee.

(b) Is there a yearly limit on the number of visas available for alien broadcasters petitioned by the BBG or a BBG grantee?

(1) Under the provisions of section 203(b)(4) of the Act, a yearly limit of 100 fourth preference special immigrant visas are available to aliens intending to work as broadcasters in the United States for the BBG or a BBG grantee. These 100 visas are available in any fiscal year beginning on or after October 1, 2000.

(2) The alien broadcaster's accompanying spouse and children are not counted towards the 100 special broadcaster visa limit.

(c) What form should the BBG use to petition for these special alien broadcasters? The BBG or a BBG grantee shall use Form I-360, Petition for Amerasian, Widow(er), or Special Immigrant, to petition for an alien broadcaster. The petition must be submitted with the correct fee noted on the form.

(d) Will the BBG need to submit supplemental evidence with Form I-360 for alien broadcasters?

(1) All Form I-360 petitions submitted by the BBG or a BBG grantee on behalf of an alien for a broadcaster position with the BBG or BBG grantee must be accompanied by a signed and dated supplemental attestation that contains the following information about the prospective alien broadcaster:

(i) The job title and a full description of the job to be performed; and

(ii) The broadcasting expertise held by the alien, including how long the alien has been performing duties that relate to the prospective position or a statement as to how the alien possesses the necessary skills that make him or her qualified for the broadcasting-related position within the BBG or BBG grantee.

(2) [Reserved]

HISTORY:

[66 FR 51819, 51821, Oct. 11, 2001, as confirmed at 71 FR 19805, 19806, Apr. 18, 2006; 74 FR 26933, 26937, June 5, 2009]

Subpart C

Intercountry Adoption of a Convention Adoptee

§ 204.300 Scope of this subpart.

(a) Convention adoptees. This subpart governs the adjudication of a Form I-800A or Form I-800 for a Convention adoptee under section 101(b)(1)(G) of the Act. The provisions of this subpart enter into force on the Convention effective date, as defined in 8 CFR 204.301.

(b) Orphan cases. On or after the Convention effective date, no Form I-600A or I-600 may be filed under section 101(b)(1)(F) of the Act and 8 CFR 204.3 in relation to the adoption of a child who is habitually resident in a Convention country. If a Form I-600A or Form I-600 was filed before the Convention effective date, the case will continue to be governed by 8 CFR 204.3, as in effect before the Convention effective date.

(c) Adopted children. This subpart does not apply to the immigrant visa classification of adopted children, as defined in section 101(b)(1)(E) of the Act. For the procedures that govern classification of adopted children as defined in section 101(b)(1)(E) of the Act, see 8 CFR 204.2.

HISTORY:

[72 FR 56832, 56854, Oct. 4, 2007]

§ 204.301 Definitions.

The definitions in 22 CFR 96.2 apply to this subpart C. In addition, as used in this subpart C, the term:

Abandonment means:

(1) That a child's parent has willfully forsaken all parental rights, obligations, and claims to the child, as well as all custody of the child without intending to transfer, or without transferring, these rights to any specific individual(s) or entity.

(2) The child's parent must have actually surrendered such rights, obligations, claims, control, and possession.

(3) That a parent's knowledge that a specific person or persons may adopt a child does not void an abandonment; however, a purported act of abandonment cannot be conditioned on the child's adoption by that specific person or persons.

(4) That if the parent(s) entrusted the child to a third party for custodial care in anticipation of, or preparation for, adoption, the third party (such as a governmental agency, a court of competent jurisdiction, an adoption agency, or an orphanage) must have been authorized under the Convention country's child welfare laws to act in such a capacity.

(5) That, if the parent(s) entrusted the child to an orphanage, the parent(s) did not intend the placement to be merely temporary, with the intention of retaining the parent-child relationship, but that the child is abandoned if the parent(s) entrusted the child permanently and unconditionally to an orphanage.

(6) That, although a written document from the parent(s) is not necessary to prove abandonment, if any written document signed by the parent(s) is presented to prove abandonment, the document must specify whether the parent(s) who signed the document was (were) able to read and understand the language in which the document is written. If the parent is not able to read or understand the language in which the document is written, then the document is not valid unless the document is accompanied by a declaration, signed by an identified individual, establishing that that identified individual is competent to translate the language in the document into a language that the parent understands and that the individual, on the date and at the place specified in the declaration, did in fact read and explain the document to the parent in a language that the parent understands. The declaration must also indicate the language used to provide this explanation. If the person who signed the declaration is an officer or employee of the Central Authority (but not of an agency or entity authorized to perform a Central Authority function by delegation) or any other governmental agency, the person must certify the truth of the facts stated in the declaration. Any other individual who signs a declaration must sign the declaration under penalty of perjury under United States law.

Adoption means the judicial or administrative act that establishes a permanent legal parent-child relationship between a minor and an adult who is not already the minor's legal parent and terminates the legal parent-child relationship between the adoptive child and any former parent(s).

Adult member of the household means:

(1) Any individual other than the applicant, who has the same principal residence as the applicant and who had reached his or her 18th birthday on or before the date a Form I-800A is filed; or

(2) Any person who has not yet reached his or her 18th birthday before the date a Form I-800A is filed, or who does not actually live at the same residence, but whose presence in the residence is relevant to the issue of suitability to adopt, if the officer adjudicating the Form I-800A concludes, based on the facts of the case, that it is necessary to obtain an evaluation of how that person's presence in the home affects the determination whether the applicant is suitable as the adoptive parent(s) of a Convention adoptee.

Applicant means the U.S. citizen (and his or her spouse, if any) who has filed a Form I-800A under this subpart C. The applicant may be an unmarried U.S. citizen who is at least 24 years old when the Form I-800A is filed, or a married U.S. citizen of any age and his or her spouse of any age. Although the singular term "applicant" is used in this subpart, the term includes both a married U.S. citizen and his or her spouse.

Birth parent means a "natural parent" as used in section 101(b)(1)(G) of the Act.

Central Authority means the entity designated as such under Article 6(1) of the Convention by any Convention country or, in the case of the United States, the United States Department of State. Except as specified in this Part, "Central Authority" also means, solely for purposes of this Part, an individual who or entity that is performing a Central Authority function, having been authorized to do so by the designated Central Authority, in accordance with the Convention and the law of the Central Authority's country.

Competent authority means a court or governmental agency of a foreign country that has jurisdiction and authority to make decisions in matters of child welfare, including adoption.

Convention means the Convention on Protection of Children and Co-operation in Respect of Intercountry Adoption, opened for signature at The Hague on May 29, 1993.

Convention adoptee means a child habitually resident in a Convention country who is eligible to immigrate to the United States on the basis of a Convention adoption.

Convention adoption, except as specified in 8 CFR 204.300(b), means the adoption, on or after the Convention effective date, of an alien child habitually resident in a Convention country by a U.S. citizen habitually resident in the United States, when in connection with the adoption the child has moved, or will move, from the Convention country to the United States.

Convention country means a country that is a party to the Convention and with which the Convention is in force for the United States.

Convention effective date means the date on which the Convention enters into force for the United States as announced by the Secretary of State under 22 CFR 96.17.

Custody for purposes of emigration and adoption exists when:

(1) The competent authority of the country of a child's habitual residence has, by a judicial or administrative act (which may be either the act granting custody of the child or a separate judicial or administrative act), expressly authorized the petitioner, or an individual or entity acting on the petitioner's behalf, to take the child out of the country of the child's habitual residence and to bring the child to the United States for adoption in the United States.

(2) If the custody order shows that custody was given to an individual or entity acting on the petitioner's behalf, the custody order must indicate that the child is to be adopted in the United States by the petitioner.

(3) A foreign judicial or administrative act that is called an adoption but that does not terminate the legal parent-child relationship between the former parent(s) and the adopted child and does not create the permanent legal parent-child relationship between the petitioner and the adopted child will be deemed a grant of custody of the child for purposes of this part, but only if the judicial or administrative act expressly authorizes the custodian to take the child out of the country of the child's habitual residence and to bring the child to the United States for adoption in the United States by the petitioner.

Deserted or desertion means that a child's parent has willfully forsaken the child and has refused to carry out parental rights and obligations and that, as a result, the child has become a ward of a competent authority in accordance with the laws of the Convention country.

Disappeared or Disappearance means that a child's parent has unaccountably or inexplicably passed out of the child's life so that the parent's whereabouts are unknown, there is no reasonable expectation of the parent's reappearance, and there has been a reasonable effort to locate the parent as determined by a competent authority in accordance with the laws of the Convention country. A stepparent who under the definition of "Parent" in this section is deemed to be a child's legal parent, may be found to have disappeared if it is established that the stepparent either never knew of the child's existence, or never knew of their legal relationship to the child.

Home study preparer means a person (whether an individual or an agency) authorized under 22 CFR part 96 to conduct home studies for Convention adoption cases, either as a public domestic authority, an accredited agency, a temporarily accredited agency, approved person, supervised provider, or exempted provider and who (if not a public domestic authority) holds any license or other authorization that may be required to conduct adoption home studies under the law of the jurisdiction in which the home study is conducted.

Incapable of providing proper care means that, in light of all the relevant circumstances including but not limited to economic or financial concerns, extreme poverty, medical, mental, or emotional difficulties, or long term-incarceration, the child's two living birth parents are not able to provide for the child's basic needs, consistent with the local standards of the Convention country.

Irrevocable consent means a document which indicates the place and date the document was signed by a child's legal custodian, and which meets the other requirements specified in this definition, in which the legal custodian freely consents to the termination of the legal custodian's legal relationship with the child. If the irrevocable consent is signed by the child's birth mother or any legal custodian other than the birth father, the irrevocable consent must have been signed after the child's birth; the birth father may sign an irrevocable consent before the child's birth if permitted by the law of the child's habitual residence. This provision does not preclude a birth father from giving consent to the termination of his legal relationship to the child before the child's birth, if the birth father is permitted to do so under the law of the country of the child's habitual residence.

(1) To qualify as an irrevocable consent under this definition, the document must specify whether the legal custodian is able to read and understand the language in which the consent is written. If the legal custodian is not able to read or understand the language in which the document is written, then the document does not qualify as an irrevocable consent unless the document is accompanied by a declaration, signed, by an identified individual, establishing that that identified individual is competent to translate the language in the irrevocable consent into a language that the parent understands, and that the individual, on the date and

at the place specified in the declaration, did in fact read and explain the consent to the legal custodian in a language that the legal custodian understands. The declaration must also indicate the language used to provide this explanation. If the person who signed the declaration is an officer or employee of the Central Authority (but not of an agency or entity authorized to perform a Central Authority function by delegation) or any other governmental agency, the person must certify the truth of the facts stated in the declaration. Any other individual who signs a declaration must sign the declaration under penalty of perjury under United States law.

(2) If more than one individual or entity is the child's legal custodian, the consent of each legal custodian may be recorded in one document, or in an additional document, but all documents, taken together, must show that each legal custodian has given the necessary irrevocable consent.

Legal custodian means the individual who, or entity that, has legal custody of a child, as defined in 22 CFR 96.2.

Officer means a USCIS officer with jurisdiction to adjudicate Form I-800A or Form I-800 or a Department of State officer with jurisdiction, by delegation from USCIS, to grant either provisional or final approval of a Form I-800.

Parent means any person who is related to a child as described in section 101(b)(1)(A), (B), (C), (D), (E), (F), or (G) and section 101(b)(2) of the Act, except that a stepparent described in section 101(b)(1)(B) of the Act is not considered a child's parent, solely for purposes of classification of the child as a Convention adoptee, if the petitioner establishes that, under the law of the Convention country, there is no legal parent-child relationship between a stepparent and stepchild. This definition includes a stepparent if the stepparent adopted the child, or if the stepparent, under the law of the Convention country, became the child's legal parent by marrying the other legal parent. A stepparent who is a legal parent may consent to the child's adoption, or may be found to have abandoned or deserted the child, or to have disappeared from the child's life, in the same manner as would apply to any other legal parent.

Petitioner means the U.S. citizen (and his or her spouse, if any) who has filed a Form I-800 under this subpart C. The petitioner may be an unmarried U.S. citizen who is at least 25 years old when the Form I-800 is filed, or a married U.S. citizen of any age and his or her spouse of any age. Although the singular term "petitioner" is used in this subpart, the term includes both a married U.S. citizen and his or her spouse.

Sole parent means:

(1) The child's mother, when the competent authority has determined that the child's father has abandoned or deserted the child, or has disappeared from the child's life; or

(2) The child's father, when the competent authority has determined that the child's mother has abandoned or deserted the child, or has disappeared from the child's life; except that

(3) A child's parent is not a sole parent if the child has acquired another parent within the meaning of section 101(b)(2) of the Act and this section.

Suitability as adoptive parent(s) means that USCIS is satisfied, based on the evidence of record, that it is reasonable to conclude that the applicant is capable of providing, and will provide, proper parental care to an adopted child.

Suitability as adoptive parent(s) means that USCIS is satisfied, based on the evidence of record, that it is to conclude that the applicant is capable of providing, and will provide, proper parental care to an adopted child.

Surviving parent means the child's living parent when the child's other parent is dead, and the child has not acquired another parent within the meaning of section 101(b)(2) of the Act and this section.

HISTORY:

[72 FR 56832, 56854, Oct. 4, 2007]

§ 204.302 Role of service providers.

(a) Who may provide services in Convention adoption cases. Subject to the limitations in paragraph (b) or (c) of this section, a U.S. citizen seeking to file a Form I-800A or I-800 may use the services of any individual or entity authorized to provide services in connection with adoption, except that the U.S. citizen must use the services of an accredited agency, temporarily accredited agency, approved person, supervised provider public domestic authority or exempted provider when required to do so under 22 CFR part 96.

(b) Unauthorized practice of law prohibited. An adoption agency or facilitator, including an individual or entity authorized under 22 CFR part 96 to provide the six specific adoption services identified in 22 CFR 96.2, may not engage in any act that constitutes the legal representation, as defined in 8 CFR 1.2 of the applicant (for a Form I-800A case) or petitioner (for a Form I-800 case) unless authorized to do so as provided in 8 CFR part 292. An individual authorized under 8 CFR part 292 to practice before USCIS may provide legal services in connection with a Form I-800A or I-800 case, but may not provide any of the six specific adoption services identified in 22 CFR 96.2, unless the individual is authorized to do so under 22 CFR part 96 (for services provided in the United States) or under the laws of the country of the child's habitual residence (for services performed outside the United States). The provisions of 8 CFR 292.5 concerning sending notices about a case do not apply to an adoption agency or facilitator that is not authorized under 8 CFR part 292 to engage in representation before USCIS.

(c) Application of the Privacy Act. Except as permitted by the Privacy Act, 5 U.S.C. 552a and the relevant Privacy Act notice concerning the routine use of information, USCIS may not disclose or give access to any information or record relating to any applicant or petitioner who has filed a Form I-800A or Form I-800 to any individual or entity other than that person, including but not limited to an accredited agency, temporarily accredited agency, approved person, public domestic authority, exempted provider, or supervised provider, unless the applicant who filed the Form I-800A or the petitioner who filed Form I-800 has filed a written consent to disclosure, as provided by the Privacy Act, 5 U.S.C. 552a.

HISTORY:

[72 FR 56832, 56854, Oct. 4, 2007; 76 FR 53764, 53782, Aug. 29, 2011]

§ 204.303 Determination of habitual residence.

(a) U.S. Citizens. For purposes of this subpart, a U.S. citizen who is seeking to have an alien classified as the U.S. citizen's child under section 101(b)(1)(G) of the Act is deemed to be habitually resident in the United States if the individual:

(1) Has his or her domicile in the United States, even if he or she is living temporarily abroad; or

(2) Is not domiciled in the United States but establishes by a preponderance of the evidence that:

(i) The citizen will have established a domicile in the United States on or before the date of the child's admission to the United States for permanent residence as a Convention adoptee; or

(ii) The citizen indicates on the Form I-800 that the citizen intends to bring the child to the United States after adopting the child abroad, and before the child's 18th birthday, at which time the child will be eligible for, and will apply for, naturalization under section 322 of the Act and 8 CFR part 322. This option is not available if the child will be adopted in the United States.

(b) Convention adoptees. A child whose classification is sought as a Convention adoptee is, generally, deemed for purposes of this subpart C to be habitually resident in the country of the child's citizenship. If the child's actual residence is outside the country of the child's citizenship, the child will be deemed habitually resident in that other country, rather than in the country of citizenship, if the Central Authority (or another competent authority of the country in which the child has his or her actual residence) has determined that the child's status in that country is sufficiently stable for that country properly to exercise jurisdiction over the child's adoption or custody. This determination must be made by the Central Authority itself, or by another competent authority of the country of the child's habitual residence, but may not be made by a nongovernmental individual or entity authorized by delegation to perform Central Authority functions. The child will not be considered to be habitually resident in any country to which the child travels temporarily, or to which he or she travels either as a prelude to, or in conjunction with, his or her adoption and/or immigration to the United States.

HISTORY:

[72 FR 56832, 56854, Oct. 4, 2007]

§ 204.304 Improper inducement prohibited.

(a) Prohibited payments. Neither the applicant/petitioner, nor any individual or entity acting on behalf of the applicant/petitioner may, directly or indirectly, pay, give, offer to pay, or offer to give to any individual or entity or request, receive, or accept from any individual or entity, any money (in any amount) or anything of value (whether the value is great or small), directly or indirectly, to induce or influence any decision concerning:

(1) The placement of a child for adoption;

(2) The consent of a parent, a legal custodian, individual, or agency to the adoption of a child;

(3) The relinquishment of a child to a competent authority, or to an agency or person as defined in 22 CFR 96.2, for the purpose of adoption; or

(4) The performance by the child's parent or parents of any act that makes the child a Convention adoptee.

(b) Permissible payments. Paragraph (a) of this section does not prohibit an applicant/petitioner, or an individual or entity acting on behalf of an applicant/petitioner, from paying the reasonable costs incurred for the services designated in this paragraph. A payment is not reasonable if it is prohibited under the law of the country in which the payment is made or if the amount of the payment is not commensurate with the costs for professional and other services in the country in which any particular service is provided. The permissible services are:

(1) The services of an adoption service provider in connection with an adoption;

(2) Expenses incurred in locating a child for adoption;

(3) Medical, hospital, nursing, pharmaceutical, travel, or other similar expenses incurred by a mother or her child in connection with the birth or any illness of the child;

(4) Counseling services for a parent or a child for a reasonable time before and after the child's placement for adoption;

(5) Expenses, in an amount commensurate with the living standards in the country of the child's habitual residence, for the care of the birth mother while pregnant and immediately following the birth of the child;

(6) Expenses incurred in obtaining the home study;

(7) Expenses incurred in obtaining the reports on the child as described in 8 CFR 204.313(d)(3) and (4);

(8) Legal services, court costs, and travel or other administrative expenses connected with an adoption, including any legal services performed for a parent who consents to the adoption of a child or relinquishes the child to an agency; and

(9) Any other service the payment for which the officer finds, on the basis of the facts of the case, was reasonably necessary.

(c) Department of State requirements. See 22 CFR 96.34, 96.36 and 96.40 for additional regulatory information concerning fees in relation to Convention adoptions.

HISTORY:

[72 FR 56832, 56854, Oct. 4, 2007]

§ 204.305 State preadoption requirements.

State preadoption requirements must be complied with when a child is coming into the State as a

Convention adoptee to be adopted in the United States. A qualified Convention adoptee is deemed to be coming to be adopted in the United States if either of the following factors exists:

(a) The applicant/petitioner will not complete the child's adoption abroad; or

(b) In the case of a married applicant/petitioner, the child was adopted abroad only by one of the spouses, rather than by the spouses jointly, so that it will be necessary for the other spouse to adopt the child after the child's admission.

HISTORY:

[72 FR 56832, 56854, Oct. 4, 2007]

§ 204.306 Classification as an immediate relative based on a Convention adoption.

(a) Unless 8 CFR 204.309 requires the denial of a Form I-800A or Form I-800, a child is eligible for classification as an immediate relative, as defined in section 201(b)(2)(A)(i) of the Act, on the basis of a Convention adoption, if the U.S. citizen who seeks to adopt the child establishes that:

(1) The United States citizen is (or, if married, the United States citizen and the United States citizen's spouse are) eligible and suitable to adopt; and

(2) The child is a Convention adoptee.

(b) A U.S. citizen seeking to have USCIS classify an alien child as the U.S. citizen's child under section 101(b)(1)(G) of the Act must complete a two-step process:

(1) First, the U.S. citizen must file a Form I-800A under 8 CFR 204.310;

(2) Then, once USCIS has approved the Form I-800A and a child has been identified as an alien who may qualify as a Convention adoptee, the U.S. citizen must file a Form I-800 under 8 CFR 204.313.

HISTORY:

[72 FR 56832, 56854, Oct. 4, 2007]

§ 204.307 Who may file a Form I-800A or Form I-800.

(a) Eligibility to file Form I-800A. Except as provided in paragraph (c) of this section, the following persons may file a Form I-800A:

(1) An unmarried United States citizen who is at least 24 years old and who is habitually resident in the United States, as determined under 8 CFR 204.303(a); or

(2) A married United States citizen, who is habitually resident in the United States, as determined under 8 CFR 204.303(a), and whose spouse will also adopt any child adopted by the citizen based on the approval of a Form I-800A; and

(3) The citizen's spouse must also be either a U.S. citizen, a non-citizen U.S. national, or an alien who, if living in the United States, holds a lawful status under U.S. immigration law. If an alien spouse is present in a lawful status other than the status of an alien lawfully admitted for permanent residence, such status will be a factor evaluated in determining whether the family's situation is sufficiently stable to support a finding that the applicant is suitable as the adoptive parents of a Convention adoptee.

(b) Eligibility to file a Form I-800. Except as provided in paragraph (c) of this section, the following persons may file a Form I-800:

(1) An unmarried United States citizen who is at least 25 years old and who is habitually resident in the United States, as determined under 8 CFR 204.303(a); or

(2) A married United States citizen, who is habitually resident in the United States as determined under 8 CFR 204.303(a), and whose spouse will also adopt the child the citizen seeks to adopt. The spouse must be either a United States citizen or a non-citizen U.S. national or an alien who, if living in the United States, holds a lawful status under U.S. immigration law; and

(3) The person has an approved and unexpired Form I-800A.

(c) Exceptions.

(1) No applicant may file a Form I-800A, and no petitioner may file a Form I-800, if:

(i) The applicant filed a prior Form I-800A that USCIS denied under 8 CFR 204.309(a); or

(ii) The applicant filed a prior Form I-600A under 8 CFR 204.3 that USCIS denied under 8 CFR 204.3(h)(4); or

(iii) The petitioner filed a prior Form I-800 that USCIS denied under 8 CFR 204.309(b)(3); or

(iv) The petitioner filed a prior Form I-600 under 8 CFR 204.3 that USCIS denied under 8 CFR 204.3(i).

(2) This bar against filing a subsequent Form I-800A or Form I-800 expires one year after the date on which the decision denying the prior Form I-800A, I-600A, I-800 or I-600 became administratively final. If the applicant (for a Form I-800A or I-600A case) or the petitioner (for a Form I-800 or I-600 case) does not appeal the prior decision, the one-year period ends one year after the date of the original decision denying the prior Form I-800A, I-600A, I-800 or I-600. Any Form I-800A, or Form I-800 filed during this one-year period will be denied. If the applicant (for a Form I-800A or Form I-600A case) or petitioner (for a Form I-800 or I-600 case) appeals the prior decision, the bar to filing a new Form I-800A or I-800 applies while the appeal is pending and ends one year after the date of an Administrative Appeals Office decision affirming the denial.

(3) Any facts underlying a prior denial of a Form I-800A, I-800, I-600A, or I-600 are relevant to the adjudication of any subsequently filed Form I-800A or Form I-800 that is filed after the expiration of this one year bar.

HISTORY:

[72 FR 56832, 56854, Oct. 4, 2007]

§ 204.308 Where to file Form I-800A or Form I-800.

(a) Form I-800A. An applicant must file a Form I-800A with the USCIS office identified in the instructions that accompany Form I-800A.

(b) Form I-800. After a Form I-800A has been approved, a petitioner may file a Form I-800 on behalf of a Convention adoptee with the stateside or overseas USCIS office identified in the instructions that accompany Form I-800. The petitioner may also file the Form I-800 with a visa-issuing post that would have jurisdiction to adjudicate a visa application filed by or on behalf of the Convention adoptee, when filing with the visa-issuing post is permitted by the instructions that accompany Form I-800.

(c) Final approval of Form I-800. Once a Form I-800 has been provisionally approved under 8 CFR 204.313(g) and the petitioner has either adopted or obtained custody of the child for purposes of emigration and adoption, the Department of State officer with jurisdiction to adjudicate the child's application for an immigrant or nonimmigrant visa has jurisdiction to grant final approval of the Form I-800. The Department of State officer may approve the Form I-800, but may not deny it; the Department of State officer must refer any Form I-800 that is "not clearly approvable" for a decision by a USCIS office having jurisdiction over Form I-800 cases. If the Department of State officer refers the Form I-800 to USCIS because it is "not clearly approvable," then USCIS has jurisdiction to approve or deny the Form I-800. In the case of an alien child who is in the United States and who is eligible both under 8 CFR 204.309(b)(4) for approval of a Form I-800 and under 8 CFR part 245 for adjustment of status, the USCIS office with jurisdiction to adjudicate the child's adjustment of status application also has jurisdiction to grant final approval of the Form I-800.

(d) Use of electronic filing. When, and if, USCIS adopts electronic, internet-based or other digital means for filing Convention cases, the terms "filing a Form I-800A" and "filing a Form I-800" will include an additional option. Rather than filing the Form I-800A or Form I-800 and accompanying evidence in a paper format, the submission of the same required information and accompanying evidence may be filed according to the digital filing protocol that USCIS adopts.

HISTORY:

[72 FR 56832, 56854, Oct. 4, 2007]

§ 204.309 Factors requiring denial of a Form I-800A or Form I-800.

(a) Form I-800A. A USCIS officer must deny a Form I-800A if:

(1) The applicant or any additional adult member of the household failed to disclose to the home study preparer or to USCIS, or concealed or misrepresented, any fact(s) about the applicant or any additional member of the household concerning the arrest, conviction, or history of substance abuse, sexual abuse, child abuse, and/or family violence, or any other criminal history as an offender; the fact that an arrest or conviction or other criminal history has been expunged, sealed, pardoned, or the subject of any other amelioration does not relieve the applicant or additional adult member of the household of the obligation to disclose the arrest, conviction or other criminal history;

(2) The applicant, or any additional adult member of the household, failed to cooperate in having available child abuse registries checked in accordance with 8 CFR 204.311;

(3) The applicant, or any additional adult member of the household, failed to disclose, as required by 8 CFR 204.311, each and every prior adoption home study, whether completed or not, including those that did not favorably recommend for adoption or custodial care, the person(s) to whom the prior home study related; or

(4) The applicant is barred by 8 CFR 204.307(c) from filing the Form I-800A.

(b) Form I-800. A USCIS officer must deny a Form I-800 if:

(1) Except as specified in 8 CFR 204.312(e)(2)(ii) with respect to a new Form I-800 filed with a new Form I-800A to reflect a change in marital status, the petitioner completed the adoption of the child, or acquired legal custody of the child for purposes of emigration and adoption, before the provisional approval of the Form I-800 under 8 CFR 204.313(g). This restriction will not apply if a competent authority in the country of the child's habitual residence voids, vacates, annuls, or terminates the adoption or grant of custody and then, after the provisional approval of the Form I-800, and after receipt of notice under article 5(c) of the Convention that the child is, or will be, authorized to enter and reside permanently in the United States, permits a new grant of adoption or custody. The prior adoption must be voided, vacated, annulled or otherwise terminated before the petitioner files a Form I-800.

(2) Except as specified in 8 CFR 204.312(e)(2)(ii) with respect to a new Form I-800 filed with a new Form I-800A to reflect a change in marital status, the petitioner, or any additional adult member of the household had met with, or had any other form of contact with, the child's parents, legal custodian, or other individual or entity who was responsible for the child's care when the contact occurred, unless the contact was permitted under this paragraph. An authorized adoption service provider's sharing of general information about a possible adoption placement is not "contact" for purposes of this section. Contact is permitted under this paragraph if:

(i) The first such contact occurred only after USCIS had approved the Form I-800A filed by the petitioner, and after the competent authority of the Convention country had determined that the child is eligible for intercountry adoption and that the required consents to the adoption have been given; or

(ii) The competent authority of the Convention country had permitted earlier contact, either in the particular instance or through laws or rules of general application, and the contact occurred only in compliance with the particular authorization or generally applicable laws or rules. If the petitioner first adopted the child without complying with the Convention, the competent authority's decision to permit the adoption to be vacated, and to allow the petitioner to adopt the child again after complying with the Convention, will also constitute approval of any prior contact; or

(iii) The petitioner was already, before the adoption, the father, mother, son, daughter, brother, sister, uncle, aunt, first cousin (that is, the petitioner, or either spouse, in the case of a married petitioner had at least one grandparent in common with the child's parent), second cousin (that is, the petitioner, or either spouse, in the case of a married petitioner, had at least one great-grandparent in common with the child's parent) nephew, niece, husband, former husband, wife, former wife, father-in-law, mother-in-law, son-in-law, daughter-in-law, brother-in-law, sister-in-law, stepfather, stepmother, stepson, stepdaughter, stepbrother, stepsister, half brother, or half sister of the child's parent(s).

(3) The USCIS officer finds that the petitioner, or any individual or entity acting on behalf of the petitioner has engaged in any conduct related to the adoption or immigration of the child that is prohibited by 8 CFR 204.304, or that the petitioner has concealed or misrepresented any material facts concerning payments made in relation to the adoption;

(4) The child is present in the United States, unless the petitioner, after compliance with the requirements of this subpart, either adopt(s) the child in the Convention country, or else, after having obtained custody of the child under the law of the Convention country for purposes of emigration and adoption, adopt(s) the child in the United States. This subpart does not require the child's actual return to the Convention country; whether to permit the child's adoption without the child's return is a matter to be determined by the Central Authority of the country of the child's habitual residence, but approval of a Form I-800 does not relieve an alien child of his or her ineligibility for adjustment of status under section 245 of the Act, if the child is present in the United States without inspection or is otherwise ineligible for adjustment of status. If the child is in the United States but is not eligible for adjustment of status, the Form I-800 may be provisionally approved only if the child will leave the United States after the provisional approval and apply for a visa abroad before the final approval of the Form I-800.

(5) Except as specified in 8 CFR 204.312(e)(2)(ii) with respect to a new Form I-800 filed with a new Form I-800A to reflect a change in marital status, the petitioner files the Form I-800:

(i) Before the approval of a Form I-800A, or

(ii) After the denial of a Form I-800A; or

(iii) After the expiration of the approval of a Form I-800A;

(6) The petitioner is barred by 8 CFR 204.307(c) from filing the Form I-800.

(c) Notice of intent to deny. Before denying a Form I-800A under paragraph (a) or a Form I-800 under paragraph (b) of this section, the USCIS officer will notify the applicant (for a Form I-800A case) or petitioner (for a Form I-800 case) in writing of the intent to deny the Form I-800A or Form I-800 and provide 30 days in which to submit evidence and argument to rebut the claim that this section requires denial of the Form I-800A or Form I-800.

(d) Rebuttal of intent to deny. If USCIS notifies the applicant that USCIS intends to deny a Form I-800A under paragraph (a) of this section, because the applicant or any additional adult member(s) of the household failed to disclose to the home study preparer or to USCIS, or concealed or misrepresented, any fact(s) concerning the arrest, conviction, or history of substance abuse, sexual abuse or child abuse, and/or family violence, or other criminal history, or failed to cooperate in search of child abuse registries, or failed to disclose a prior home study, the applicant may rebut the intent to deny only by establishing, by clear and convincing evidence that:

(1) The applicant or additional adult member of the household did, in fact, disclose the information; or

(2) If it was an additional adult member of the household who failed to cooperate in the search of child abuse registries, or who failed to disclose to the home study preparer or to USCIS, or concealed or misrepresented, any fact(s) concerning the arrest, conviction, or history of substance abuse, sexual abuse or child abuse, and/or family violence, or other criminal history, or failed to disclose a prior home study, that that person is no longer a member of the household and that that person's conduct is no longer relevant to the suitability of the applicant as the adoptive parent of a Convention adoptee.

HISTORY:

[72 FR 56832, 56854, Oct. 4, 2007]

§ 204.310 Filing requirements for Form I-800A.

(a) Completing and filing the Form. A United States citizen seeking to be determined eligible and suitable as the adoptive parent of a Convention adoptee must:

(1) Complete Form I-800A, including a Form I-800A Supplement 1 for each additional adult member of the household, in accordance with the instructions that accompany the Form I-800A.

(2) Sign the Form I-800A personally. One spouse cannot sign for the other, even under a power of attorney or similar agency arrangement.

(3) File the Form I-800A with the USCIS office that has jurisdiction under 8 CFR 204.308(a) to adjudicate the Form I-800A, together with:

(i) The fee specified in 8 CFR 106.2 for the filing of Form I-800A;

(ii) [Removed and Reserved]

(iii) Evidence that the applicant is a United States citizen, as set forth in 8 CFR 204.1(g), or, in the case of a married applicant, evidence either that both spouses are citizens or, if only one spouse is a United States citizen, evidence of that person's citizenship and evidence that the other spouse, if he or she lives in the United States, is either a non-citizen United States national or an alien who holds a lawful status under U.S. immigration law.

(iv) A copy of the current marriage certificate, unless the applicant is not married;

(v) If the applicant has been married previously, a death certificate or divorce or dissolution decree to establish the legal termination of all previous marriages, regardless of current marital status;

(vi) If the applicant is not married, his or her birth certificate, U.S. passport biographical information page, naturalization or citizenship certificate, or other evidence, to establish that he or she is at least 24 years old;

(vii) A written description of the preadoption requirements, if any, of the State of the child's proposed residence in cases where it is known that any child the applicant may adopt will be adopted in the United States, and of the steps that have already been taken or that are planned to comply with these requirements. The written description must include a citation to the State statutes and regulations establishing the requirements. Any preadoption requirements which cannot be met at the time the Form I-800A is filed because of the operation of State law must be noted and explained when the Form I-800A is filed.

(viii) A home study that meets the requirements of 8 CFR 204.311 and that bears the home study preparer's original signature. If the home study is not included with the Form I-800A, the director of the office that has jurisdiction to adjudicate the Form I-800A will make a written request for evidence, directing the applicant to submit the home study. If the applicant fails to submit the home study within the period specified in the request for evidence, the director of the office that has jurisdiction to adjudicate the Form I-800A will deny the Form I-800A. Denial of a Form I-800A under this paragraph for failure to submit a home study is not subject to appeal, but the applicant may file a new Form I-800A, accompanied by a new filing fee.

(b) Biometrics. Upon the proper filing of a Form I-800A, USCIS will arrange for the collection of biometrics from the applicant and each additional adult member of the household, as prescribed in 8 CFR 103.16, but with no upper age limit. It will be necessary to collect the biometrics of each of these persons again, if the initial collection expires before approval of the Form I-800A. USCIS may waive this requirement for any particular individual if USCIS determines that that person is physically unable to comply. However, USCIS will require the submission of affidavits, police clearances, or other evidence relating to whether that person has a criminal history in lieu of collecting the person's biometrics.

(c) Change in marital status. If, while a Form I-800A is pending, an unmarried applicant marries, or the marriage of a married applicant ends, an amended Form I-800A and amended home study must be filed to reflect the change in marital status. No additional filing fee is required to file an amended Form I-800A while the original Form I-800A is still pending. See 8 CFR 204.312(e)(2) concerning the need to file a new Form I-800A if the marital status changes after approval of a Form I-800A.

HISTORY:

[72 FR 56832, 56854, Oct. 4, 2007; 76 FR 53764, 53782, Aug. 29, 2011; 85 FR 46788, 46922, Aug. 3, 2020]

§ 204.311 Convention adoption home study requirements.

(a) Purpose. For immigration purposes, a home study is a process for screening and preparing an applicant who is interested in adopting a child from a Convention country.

(b) Preparer. Only an individual or entity defined under 8 CFR 204.301 as a home study preparer for Convention cases may complete a home study for a Convention adoption. In addition, the individual or entity must be authorized to complete adoption home studies under the law of the jurisdiction in which the home study is conducted.

(c) Study requirements. The home study must:

(1) Be tailored to the particular situation of the applicant and to the specific Convention country in which the applicant intends to seek a child for adoption. For example, an applicant who has previously adopted children will require different preparation than an applicant who has no adopted children. A home study may address the applicant's suitability to adopt in more than one Convention country, but if the home study does so, the home study must separately assess the applicant's suitability as to each specific Convention country.

(2) If there are any additional adult members of the household, identify each of them by name, alien registration number (if the individual has one), and date of birth.

(3) Include an interview by the preparer of any additional adult member of the household and an assessment of him or her in light of the requirements of this section.

(4) Be no more than 6 months old at the time the home study is submitted to USCIS.

(5) Include the home study preparer's assessment of any potential problem areas, a copy of any outside evaluation(s), and the home study preparer's recommended restrictions, if any, on the characteristics of the child to be placed in the home. See 8 CFR 204.309(a) for the consequences of failure to disclose information or cooperate in completion of a home study.

(6) Include the home study preparer's signature, in accordance with paragraph (f) of this section.

(7) State the number of interviews and visits, the participants, date and location of each interview and visit, and the date and location of any other contacts with the applicant and any additional adult member of the household.

(8) Summarize the pre-placement preparation and training already provided to the applicant concerning the issues specified in 22 CFR 96.48(a) and (b), the plans for future preparation and training with respect to those issues, or with respect to a particular child, as specified in 22 CFR 96.48(c), and the plans for post-placement monitoring specified in 22 CFR 96.50, in the event that the child will be adopted in the United States rather than abroad.

(9) Specify whether the home study preparer made any referrals as described in paragraph (g)(4) of this section, and include a copy of the report resulting from

each referral, the home study preparer's assessment of the impact of the report on the suitability of the applicant to adopt, and the home study preparer's recommended restrictions, if any, on the characteristics of the child to be placed in the home.

(10) Include results of the checks conducted in accordance with paragraph (i) of this section including that no record was found to exist, that the State or foreign country will not release information to the home study preparer or anyone in the household, or that the State or foreign country does not have a child abuse registry.

(11) Include each person's response to the questions regarding abuse and violence in accordance with paragraph (j) of this section.

(12) Include a certified copy of the documentation showing the final disposition of each incident which resulted in arrest, indictment, conviction, and/or any other judicial or administrative action for anyone subject to the home study and a written statement submitted with the home study giving details, including any mitigating circumstances about each arrest, signed, under penalty of perjury, by the person to whom the arrest relates.

(13) Contain an evaluation of the suitability of the home for adoptive placement of a child in light of any applicant's or additional adult member of the household's history of abuse and/or violence as an offender, whether this history is disclosed by an applicant or any additional adult member of the household or is discovered by home study preparer, regardless of the source of the home study preparer's discovery. A single incident of sexual abuse, child abuse, or family violence is sufficient to constitute a "history" of abuse and/or violence.

(14) Contain an evaluation of the suitability of the home for adoptive placement of a child in light of disclosure by an applicant, or any additional adult member of the household, of a history of substance abuse. A person has a history of substance abuse if his or her current or past use of alcohol, controlled substances, or other substances impaired or impairs his or her ability to fulfill obligations at work, school, or home, or creates other social or interpersonal problems that may adversely affect the applicant's suitability as an adoptive parent.

(15) Include a general description of the information disclosed in accordance with paragraph (m) of this section concerning the physical, mental, and emotional health of the applicant and of any additional adult member of the household.

(16) Identify the agency involved in each prior or terminated home study in accordance with paragraph (o) of this section, when the prior home study process began, the date the prior home study was completed, and whether the prior home study recommended for or against finding the applicant or additional adult member of the household suitable for adoption, foster care, or other custodial care of a child. If a prior home study was terminated without completion, the current home study must indicate when the prior home study began, the date of termination, and the reason for the termination.

(d) Duty to disclose.

(1) The applicant, and any additional adult members of the household, each has a duty of candor and must:

(i) Give true and complete information to the home study preparer.

(ii) Disclose any arrest, conviction, or other adverse criminal history, whether in the United States or abroad, even if the record of the arrest, conviction or other adverse criminal history has been expunged, sealed, pardoned, or the subject of any other amelioration. A person with a criminal history may be able to establish sufficient rehabilitation.

(iii) Disclose other relevant information, such as physical, mental or emotional health issues, or behavioral issues, as specified in paragraph (m) of this section. Such problems may not necessarily preclude approval of a Form I-800A, if, for example, they have been or are being successfully treated.

(2) This duty of candor is an ongoing duty, and continues while the Form I-800A is pending, after the Form I-800A is approved, and while any subsequent Form I-800 is pending, and until there is a final decision admitting the Convention adoptee to the United States with a visa. The applicant and any additional adult member of the household must notify the home study preparer and USCIS of any new event or information that might warrant submission of an amended or updated home study.

(e) State standards. In addition to the requirements of this section, the home study preparer must prepare the home study according to the requirements that apply to a domestic adoption in the State of the applicant's actual or proposed residence in the United States.

(f) Home study preparer's signature. The home study preparer (or, if the home study is prepared by an entity, the officer or employee who has authority to sign the home study for the entity) must personally sign the home study, and any updated or amended home study. The home study preparer's signature must include a declaration, under penalty of perjury under United States law, that:

(1) The signer personally, and with the professional diligence reasonably necessary to protect the best interests of any child whom the applicant might adopt, either actually conducted or supervised the home study, including personal interview(s), the home visits, and all other aspects of the investigation needed to prepare the home study; if the signer did not personally conduct the home study, the person who actually did so must be identified;

(2) The factual statements in the home study are true and correct, to the best of the signer's knowledge, information and belief; and

(3) The home study preparer has advised the applicant of the duty of candor under paragraph (d) of this section, specifically including the on-going duty under paragraph (d)(2) of this section concerning disclosure of new events or information warranting submission of an updated or amended home study.

(g) Personal interview(s) and home visit(s). The home study preparer must:

(1) Conduct at least one interview in person, and at least one home visit, with the applicant.

(2) Interview, at least once, each additional adult member of the household, as defined in 8 CFR 204.301. The interview with an additional adult mber of the household should also be in person, unless the home study preparer determines that interviewing that individual in person is not reasonably feasible and explains in the home study the reason for this conclusion.

(3) Provide information on and assess the suitability of the applicant as the adoptive parent of a Convention adoptee based on the applicant's background, family and medical history (including physical, mental and emotional health), social environment, reasons for adoption, ability to undertake an intercountry adoption, and the characteristics of the child(ren) for whom they would be qualified to care.

(4) Refer the applicant to an appropriate licensed professional, such as a physician, psychiatrist, clinical psychologist, clinical social worker, or professional substance abuse counselor, for an evaluation and written report, if the home study preparer determines that there are areas beyond his or her expertise that need to be addressed. The home study preparer must also make such a referral if such a referral would be required for a domestic adoption under the law of the State of the applicant's actual or proposed place of residence in the United States.

(5) Apply the requirements of this paragraph to each additional adult member of the household.

(h) Financial considerations.

(1) Assessment of the finances of the applicant must include:

(i) A description of the applicant's income, financial resources, debts, and expenses.

(ii) A statement concerning the evidence that was considered to verify the source and amount of income and financial resources.

(2) Any income designated for the support of one or more children in the applicant's care and custody, such as funds for foster care, or any income designated for the support of another member of the household, must not be counted towards the financial resources available for the support of a prospective adoptive child.

(3) USCIS will not routinely require a detailed financial statement or supporting financial documents. However, should the need arise, USCIS reserves the right to ask for such detailed documentation.

(i) Checking available child abuse registries. The home study preparer must ensure that a check of the applicant, and of each additional adult member of the household, has been made with available child abuse registries in any State or foreign country that the applicant, or any additional adult member of the household, has resided in since that person's 18th birthday. USCIS may also conduct its own check of any child abuse registries to which USCIS has access. Depending on the extent of access to a relevant registry allowed by the State or foreign law, the home study preparer must take one of the following courses of action:

(1) If the home study preparer is allowed access to information from the child abuse registries, he or she must make the appropriate checks for the applicant and each additional adult member of the household;

(2) If the State or foreign country requires the home study preparer to secure permission from the applicant and each additional adult member of the household before gaining access to information in such registries, the home study preparer must secure such permission from those individuals and make the appropriate checks;

(3) If the State or foreign country will only release information directly to an individual to whom the information relates, then the applicant and the additional adult member of the household must secure such information and provide it to the home study preparer.

(4) If the State or foreign country will release information neither to the home study preparer nor to the person to whom the information relates, or has not done so within 6 months of a written request for the information, this unavailability of information must be noted in the home study.

(j) Inquiring about history of abuse or violence as an offender. The home study preparer must ask each applicant and each additional adult member of the household whether he or she has a history as an offender, whether in the United States or abroad, of substance abuse, sexual abuse, or child abuse, or family violence, even if such history did not result in an arrest or conviction. This evaluation must include:

(1) The dates of each arrest or conviction or history of substance abuse, sexual abuse or child abuse, and/or family violence; or,

(2) If not resulting in an arrest, the date or time period (if occurring over an extended period of time) of each occurrence and

(3) Details including any mitigating circumstances about each incident.

Each statement must be signed, under penalty of perjury, by the person to whom the incident relates.

(k) Criminal history. The applicant, and any additional adult members of the household, must also disclose to the home study preparer and USCIS any history, whether in the United States or abroad, of any arrest and/or conviction (other than for minor traffic offenses) in addition to the information that the person must disclose under paragraph (j) of this section. If an applicant or an additional adult member of the household has a criminal record, the officer may still find that the applicant will be suitable as the adoptive parent of a Convention adoptee, if there is sufficient evidence of rehabilitation as described in paragraph (l) of this section.

(*l*) Evidence of rehabilitation. If an applicant, or any additional adult member of the household, has a history of substance abuse, sexual abuse or child abuse, and/or family violence as an offender, or any other criminal history, the home study preparer may, nevertheless, make a favorable finding if the applicant has demonstrated that the person with this adverse history has achieved appropriate rehabilitation. A favorable recommendation cannot be made based on a claim of rehabilitation while an applicant or any additional adult member of the household is on probation, parole, supervised release, or other similar arrangement for any conviction. The home study must include a discussion of the claimed rehabilitation, which demonstrates that the applicant is suitable as the adoptive parent(s) of a Convention adoptee. Evidence of rehabilitation may include:

(1) An evaluation of the seriousness of the arrest(s), conviction(s), or history of abuse, the number of such incidents, the length of time since the last incident, the offender's acceptance of responsibility for his or her conduct, and any type of counseling or rehabilitation programs which have been successfully completed, or

(2) A written opinion from an appropriate licensed professional, such as a psychiatrist, clinical psychologist, or clinical social worker.

(m) Assessment with respect to physical, mental and emotional health or behavioral issues. The home study must address the current physical, mental and emotional health of the applicant, or any additional adult member of the household, as well as any history of illness or of any mental, emotional, psychological, or behavioral instability if the home study preparer determines, in the exercise of reasonable professional judgment, that the suitability of the applicant as an adoptive parent may be affected adversely by such history. Paragraph (g)(4) of this section, regarding referral to professionals, applies to any home study involving prior psychiatric care, or issues arising from sexual abuse, child abuse, or family violence issues if, in the home study preparer's reasonable professional judgment, such referral(s) may be necessary or helpful to the proper completion of the home study.

(n) Prior home study. The home study preparer must ask each applicant, and any additional adult member of the household, whether he or she previously has had a prior home study completed, or began a home study process in relation to an adoption or to any form of foster or other custodial care of a child that was not completed, whether or not the prior home study related to an intercountry adoption, and must include each individual's response to this question in the home study report. A copy of any previous home study that did not favorably recommend the applicant or additional adult member of the household must be attached to any home study submitted with a Form I-800A. If a copy of any prior home study that did not favorably recommend the applicant or additional adult member of the household is no longer available, the current home study must explain why the prior home study is no longer available. The home study preparer must evaluate the relevance of any prior unfavorable or uncompleted home study to the suitability of the applicant as the adoptive parent of a Convention adoptee.

(o) Living accommodations. The home study must include a detailed description of the living accommodations where the applicant currently resides. If the applicant is planning to move, the home study must include a description of the living accommodations where the child will reside with the applicant, if known. If the applicant is residing abroad at the time of the home study, the home study must include a description of the living accommodations where the child will reside in the United States with the applicant, if known. Each description must include an assessment of the suitability of accommodations for a child and a determination whether such space meets applicable State requirements, if any.

(p) Handicapped or special needs child. A home study conducted in conjunction with the proposed adoption of a special needs or handicapped child must contain a discussion of the preparation, willingness, and ability of the applicant to provide proper care for a child with the handicap or special needs. This information will be used to evaluate the suitability of the applicant as the adoptive parent of a special needs or handicapped child. If this information is not included in the home study, an updated or amended home study will be necessary if the applicant seeks to adopt a handicapped or special needs child.

(q) Addressing a Convention country's specific requirements. If the Central Authority of the Convention country has notified the Secretary of State of any specific requirements that must be met in order to adopt in the Convention country, the home study must include a full and complete statement of all facts relevant to the applicant's eligibility for adoption in the Convention country, in light of those specific requirements.

(r) Specific approval for adoption. If the home study preparer's findings are favorable, the home study must contain his or her specific approval of the applicant for adoption of a child from the specific Convention country or countries, and a discussion of the reasons for such approval. The home study must include the number of children the applicant may adopt at the same time. The home study must state whether there are any specific restrictions to the adoption based on the age or gender, or other characteristics of the child. If the home study preparer has approved the applicant for a handicapped or special needs adoption, this fact must be clearly stated.

(s) Home study preparer's authority to conduct home studies. The home study must include a statement in which the home study preparer certifies that he or she is authorized under 22 CFR part 96 to complete home studies for Convention adoption cases. The certification must specify the State or country under whose authority the home study preparer is licensed or authorized, cite the specific law or regulation authorizing the preparer to conduct home studies, and indicate the license number, if any, and the expiration date, if any, of this authorization or license. The certification must also specify the basis under 22 CFR part 96 (public domestic authority, accredited agency, temporarily accredited agency, approved person, exempted provider, or supervised provider) for his or her authorization to conduct Convention adoption home studies.

(t) Review of home study.

(1) If the law of the State in which the applicant resides requires the competent authority in the State to review the home study, such a review must occur and be documented before the home study is submitted to USCIS.

(2) When the home study is not performed in the first instance by an accredited agency or temporarily accredited agency, as defined in 22 CFR part 96, then an accredited agency or temporarily accredited agency, as defined in 22 CFR part 96, must review and approve the home study as specified in 22 CFR 96.47(c) before the home study is submitted to USCIS. This requirement for review and approval by an accredited agency or temporarily accredited agency does not apply to a home study that was actually prepared by a public domestic authority, as defined in 22 CFR 96.2.

(u) Home study updates and amendments.

(1) A new home study amendment or update will be required if there is:

(i) A significant change in the applicant's household, such as a change in residence, marital status, criminal history, financial resources; or

(ii) The addition of one or more children in the applicant's home, whether through adoption or foster care, birth, or any other means. Even if the original home study provided for the adoption of more than one adopted child, the applicant must submit an amended home study recommending adoption of an additional child, because the addition of the already adopted child(ren) to the applicant's household is a significant change in the household that should be assessed before the adoption of any additional child(ren);

(iii) The addition of other dependents or additional adult member(s) of the household to the family prior to the prospective child's immigration into the United States;

(iv) A change resulting because the applicant is seeking to adopt a handicapped or special needs child, if the home study did not already address the applicant's suitability as the adoptive parent of a child with the particular handicap or special need;

(v) A change to a different Convention country. This change requires the updated home study to address suitability under the requirements of the new Convention country;

(vi) A lapse of more than 6 months between the date the home study is completed and the date it is submitted to USCIS; or

(vii) A change to the child's proposed State of residence. The preadoption requirements of the new State must be complied with in the case of a child coming to the United States to be adopted.

(2) Any updated or amended home study must:

(i) Meet the requirements of this section;

(ii) Be accompanied by a copy of the home study that is being updated or amended, including all prior updates and amendments;

(iii) Include a statement from the preparer that he or she has reviewed the home study that is being updated or amended and is personally and fully aware of its contents; and

(iv) Address whether the home study preparer recommends approval of the proposed adoption and the reasons for the recommendation.

(3) If submission of an updated or amended home study becomes necessary before USCIS adjudicates the Form I-800A, the applicant may simply submit the updated or amended home study to the office that has jurisdiction over the Form I-800A.

(4) If it becomes necessary to file an updated or amended home study after USCIS has approved the Form I-800A, the applicant must file a Form I-800A Supplement 3 with the filing fee specified in 8 CFR 103.7(b)(1) and the amended or updated home study. If USCIS determines that the amended or updated home study shows that the applicant remains suitable as the adoptive parent(s) of a Convention adoptee, USCIS will issue a new approval notice that will expire on the same date as the original approval. If the applicant also wants to have USCIS extend the approval period for the Form I-800A, the applicant must submit the updated or amended home study with an extension request under 8 CFR 204.312(e)(3), rather than under this paragraph (u) of this section.

(5) Each update must indicate that the home study preparer has updated the screening of the applicant and any additional adult member of the household under paragraphs (i) through (l) of this section, and must indicate the results of this updated screening.

HISTORY:

[72 FR 56832, 56854, Oct. 4, 2007; 85 FR 46788, 46922, Aug. 3, 2020]

§ 204.312 Adjudication of the Form I-800A.

(a) USCIS action. The USCIS officer must approve a Form I-800A if the officer finds, based on the evidence of record, that the applicant is eligible under 8 CFR 204.307(a) to file a Form I-800A and the USCIS officer is satisfied that the applicant is suitable as the adoptive parent of a child from the specified Convention country. If the applicant sought approval for more than one Convention country, the decision will specify each country for which the Form I-800A is approved, and will also specify whether the Form I-800A is denied with respect to any particular Convention country.

(b) Evaluation of the home study. In determining suitability to adopt, the USCIS officer will give considerable weight to the home study, but is not bound by it. Even if the home study is favorable, the USCIS officer must deny the Form I-800A if, on the basis of the evidence of record, the officer finds, for a specific and articulable reason, that the applicant has failed to establish that he or she is suitable as the adoptive parent of a child from the Convention country. The USCIS officer may consult the accredited agency or temporarily accredited agency that approved the home study, the home study preparer, the applicant, the relevant State or local child welfare agency, or any appropriate licensed professional, as needed to clarify issues concerning whether the applicant is suitable as the adoptive parent of a Convention adoptee. If this consultation yields evidence that is adverse to the applicant, the USCIS officer may rely on the evidence only after complying with the provisions of 8 CFR 103.2(b)(16) relating to the applicant's right to review and rebut adverse information.

(c) Denial of application.

(1) The USCIS officer will deny the Form I-800A if the officer finds that the applicant has failed to establish that the applicant is:

(i) Eligible under 8 CFR 204.307(a) to file Form I-800A; or

(ii) Suitable as the adoptive parent of a child from the Convention country.

(2) Before denying a Form I-800A, the USCIS officer will comply with 8 CFR 103.2(b)(16), if required to do so under that provision, and may issue a request for evidence or a notice of intent to deny under 8 CFR 103.2(b)(8).

(3) A denial will be in writing, giving the reason for the denial and notifying the applicant of the right to appeal, if any, as provided in 8 CFR 204.314.

(4) It is for the Central Authority of the other Convention country to determine how its own adoption requirements, as disclosed in the home study under 8 CFR 204.311(q), should be applied in a given case. For this reason, the fact that the applicant may be ineligible to adopt in the other Convention country under those requirements, will not warrant the denial of a Form I-800A, if USCIS finds that the applicant has otherwise established eligibility and suitability as the adoptive parent of a Convention adoptee.

(d) Approval notice.

(1) If USCIS approves the Form I-800A, USCIS will notify the applicant in writing as well as the Department of State. The notice of approval will specify:

(i) The expiration date for the notice of approval, as determined under paragraph (e) of this section, and

(ii) The name(s) and marital status of the applicant; and

(iii) If the applicant is not married and not yet 25 years old, the applicant's date of birth.

(2) Once USCIS approves the Form I-800A, or extends the validity period for a prior approval under paragraph (e) of this section, any submission of the home study to the Central Authority of the country of the child's habitual residence must consist of the entire and complete text of the same home study and of any updates or amendments submitted to USCIS.

(e) Duration or revocation of approval.

(1) A notice of approval expires 15 months after the date of the approval, unless approval is revoked. USCIS may extend the validity period for the approval of a Form I-800A only as provided in paragraph (e)(3) of this section.

(2)(i) The approval of a Form I-800A is automatically revoked if before the final decision on a Convention adoptee's application for admission with an immigrant visa or for adjustment of status:

(A) The marriage of the applicant terminates; or

(B) An unmarried applicant marries; or

(C) In the case of a married applicant, either spouse files with a USCIS or Department of State officer a written document withdrawing his or her signature on the Form I-800A.

(ii) This revocation is without prejudice to the filing of a new Form I-800A, with fee, accompanied by a new or amended home study, reflecting the change in marital status. If a Form I-800 had already been filed based on the approval of the prior Form I-800A, a new Form I-800 must also be filed with the new Form I-800A under this paragraph. The new Form I-800 will be adjudicated only if the new Form I-800A is approved. The new Form I-800 will not be subject to denial under 8 CFR 204.309(b)(1) or (2), unless the original Form I-800 would have been subject to denial under either of those provisions.

(3)(i) If the validity period for a Form I-800A approval is about to expire, the applicant:

(A) May file Form I-800A Supplement 3 as described in 8 CFR 106.2(a)(48) to request an extension.

(B) May not file a Form I-800A Supplement 3 seeking extension of an approval notice more than 90 days before the expiration of the validity period for the Form I-800A approval but must do so on or before the date on which the validity period expires if the applicant seeks an extension.

(ii) Any Form I-800A Supplement 3 that is filed to obtain an extension or update of the approval of a Form I-800A or to request a change of Hague Convention countries must be accompanied by:

(A) A statement, signed by the applicant under penalty of perjury, detailing any changes to the answers given to the questions on the original Form I-800A;

(B) An updated or amended home study as required under 8 CFR 204.311(u); and

(C) A photocopy of the Form I-800A approval notice.

(iii) If USCIS continues to be satisfied that the applicant remains suitable as the adoptive parent of a Convention adoptee, USCIS will extend the approval of the Form I-800A for the same period of validity as the initial filing.

(iv) There is no limit to the number of extensions that may be requested and granted under this section, so long as each request is supported by an updated or amended home study that continues to recommend approval of the applicant for intercountry adoption and USCIS continues to find that the applicant remain suitable as the adoptive parent(s) of a Convention adoptee.

(4) In addition to the automatic revocation provided for in paragraph (e)(2) of this section, the approval of a Form I-800A may be revoked pursuant to 8 CFR 205.1 or 205.2.

HISTORY:

[72 FR 56832, 56854, Oct. 4, 2007; 85 FR 46788, 46922, Aug. 3, 2020; 89 FR 6194, 6396, Jan. 31, 2024]

§ 204.313 Filing and adjudication of a Form I-800.

(a) When to file. Once a Form I-800A has been approved and the Central Authority has proposed placing a child for adoption by the petitioner, the petitioner may file the Form I-800. The petitioner must complete the Form I-800 in accordance with the instructions that accompany the Form I-800 and sign the Form I-800 personally. In the case of a married petitioner, one spouse cannot sign for the other, even under a power of attorney or similar agency arrangement. The petitioner may then file the Form I-800 with the stateside or overseas USCIS office or the visa issuing post that has jurisdiction under § 204.308(b) to adjudicate the Form I-800, together with the evidence specified in this section and the filing fee specified in 8 CFR 106.2, if more than one Form I-800 is filed for children who are not birth siblings.

(b) What to include on the Form.

(1) The petitioner must specify on the Form I-800 either that:

(i) The child will seek an immigrant visa, if the Form I-800 is approved, because the child will reside in the United States with the petitioner (in the case of a married petitioner, if only one spouse is a United States citizen, with that spouse) after the child's admission to the United States on the basis of the proposed adoption; or

(ii) The child will seek a nonimmigrant visa, in order to travel to the United States to obtain naturalization under section 322 of the Act, because the petitioner intends to complete the adoption abroad and the petitioner and the child will continue to reside abroad immediately following the adoption, rather than residing in the United States with the petitioner. This option is not available if the child will be adopted in the United States.

(2) In applying this paragraph (b), if a petitioner is a United States citizen who is domiciled in the United States, but who is posted abroad temporarily under official orders as a member of the Uniformed Services as defined in 5 U.S.C. 2101, or as a civilian officer or employee of the United States Government, the child will be deemed to be coming to the United States to reside in the United States with that petitioner.

(c) Filing deadline.

(1) The petitioner must file the Form I-800 before the expiration of the notice of the approval of the Form I-800A and before the child's 16th birthday. Paragraphs (c)(2) and (3) of this section provide special rules for determining that this requirement has been met.

(2) If the appropriate Central Authority places the child with the petitioner for intercountry adoption more than 6 months after the child's 15th birthday but before the child's 16th birthday, the petitioner must still file the Form I-800 before the child's 16th birthday. If the evidence required by paragraph (d)(3) or (4) of this section is not yet available, instead of that evidence, the petitioner may submit a statement from the primary provider, signed under penalty of perjury under United States law, confirming that the Central Authority has, in fact, made the adoption placement on the date specified in the statement. Submission of a Form I-800 with this statement will satisfy the statutory requirement that the petition must be submitted before the child's 16th birthday, but no provisional or final approval of the Form I-800 will be granted until the evidence required by paragraph (d)(3) or (4) of this section has been submitted. When submitted, the evidence required by paragraph (d)(3) and (4) must affirmatively show that the Central Authority did, in fact, make the adoption placement decision before the child's 16th birthday.

(3) If the Form I-800A was filed after the child's 15th birthday but before the child's 16th birthday, the filing date of the Form I-800A will be deemed to be the filing date of the Form I-800, provided the Form I-800 is filed not more than 180 days after the initial approval of the Form I-800A.

(d) Required evidence. Except as specified in paragraph (c)(2) of this section, the petitioner must submit the following evidence with the properly completed Form I-800:

(1) The Form I-800A approval notice and, if applicable, proof that the approval period has been extended under 8 CFR 204.312(e);

(2) A statement from the primary provider, as defined in 22 CFR 96.2, signed under penalty of perjury under United States law, indicating that all of the pre-placement preparation and training provided for in 22 CFR 96.48 has been completed;

(3) The report required under article 16 of the Convention, specifying the child's name and date of birth, the reasons for making the adoption placement, and establishing that the competent authority has, as required under article 4 of the Convention:

(i) Established that the child is eligible for adoption;

(ii) Determined, after having given due consideration to the possibility of placing the child for adoption within the Convention country, that intercountry adoption is in the child's best interests;

(iii) Ensured that the legal custodian, after having been counseled as required, concerning the effect of the child's adoption on the legal custodian's relationship to the child and on the child's legal relationship to his or her family of origin, has freely consented in writing to the child's adoption, in the required legal form;

(iv) Ensured that if any individual or entity other than the legal custodian must consent to the child's adoption, this individual or entity, after having been counseled as required concerning the effect of the child's adoption, has freely consented in writing, in the required legal form, to the child's adoption;

(v) Ensured that the child, after having been counseled as appropriate concerning the effects of the adoption; has freely consented in writing, in the required legal form, to the adoption, if the child is of an age that, under the law of the country of the child's habitual residence, makes the child's consent necessary, and that consideration was given to the child's wishes and opinions; and

(vi) Ensured that no payment or inducement of any kind has been given to obtain the consents necessary for the adoption to be completed.

(4) The report under paragraph (d)(3) of this section must be accompanied by:

(i) A copy of the child's birth certificate, or secondary evidence of the child's age; and

(ii) A copy of the irrevocable consent(s) signed by the legal custodian(s) and any other individual or entity who must consent to the child's adoption unless, as permitted under article 16 of the Convention, the law of the country of the child's habitual residence provides that their identities may not be disclosed, so long as the Central Authority of the country of the child's habitual residence certifies in its report that the required documents exist and that they establish the child's age and availability for adoption;

(iii) A statement, signed under penalty of perjury by the primary provider (or an authorized representative if the primary provider is an agency or other juridical person), certifying that the report is a true, correct, and complete copy of the report obtained from the Central Authority of the Convention country;

(iv) A summary of the information provided to the petitioner under 22 CFR 96.49(d) and (f) concerning the child's medical and social history. This summary, or a separate document, must include:

(A) A statement concerning whether, from any examination as described in 22 CFR 96.49(e) or for any other reason, there is reason to believe that the child has any medical condition that makes the child inadmissible under section 212(a)(1) of the Act; if the medical information that is available at the provisional approval stage is not sufficient to assess whether the child may be inadmissible under section 212(a)(1), the submission of this information may be deferred until the petitioner seeks final approval of the Form I-800;

(B) If both of the child's birth parents were the child's legal custodians and signed the irrevocable consent, the factual basis for determining that they are incapable of providing proper care for the child, as defined in 8 CFR 204.301;

(C) Information about the circumstances of the other birth parent's death, if applicable, supported by a copy of the death certificate, unless paragraph (d)(4)(ii) of this section makes it unnecessary to provide a copy of the death certificate;

(D) If a sole birth parent was the legal custodian, the circumstances leading to the determination that the other parent abandoned or deserted the child, or disappeared from the child's life; and

(E) If the legal custodian was the child's prior adoptive parent(s) or any individual or entity other than the child's birth parent(s), the circumstances leading to the custodian's acquisition of custody of the child and the legal basis of that custody.

(v) If the child will be adopted in the United States, the primary provider's written report, signed under penalty of perjury by the primary provider (or an authorized representative if the primary provider is an agency or other juridical person) detailing the primary adoption service provider's plan for post-placement duties, as specified in 22 CFR 96.50; and

(5) If the child may be inadmissible under any provision of section 212(a) for which a waiver is available, a properly completed waiver application for each such ground; and

(6) Either a Form I-864W, Intending Immigrant's I-864 Exemption, or a Form I-864, Affidavit of Support, as specified in 8 CFR 213a.2.

(e) Obtaining the home study and supporting evidence. The materials from the Form I-800A proceeding will be included in the record of the Form I-800 proceeding.

(f) Investigation. An investigation concerning the alien child's status as a Convention adoptee will be completed before the Form I-800 is adjudicated in any case in which the officer with jurisdiction to grant provisional or final approval of the Form I-800 determines, on the basis of specific facts, that completing the investigation will aid in the provisional or final adjudication of the Form I-800. Depending on the circumstances surrounding the case, the investigation may include, but is not limited to, document checks, telephone checks, interview(s) with the birth or prior adoptive parent(s), a field investigation, and any other appropriate investigatory actions. In any case in which there are significant differences between the facts presented in the approved Form I-800A or Form I-800 and the facts uncovered by the investigation, the office conducting the investigation may consult directly with the appropriate USCIS office. In any instance where the investigation reveals negative information sufficient to sustain a denial of the Form I-800 (including a denial of a Form I-800 that had been provisionally approved) or the revocation of the final approval of the Form I-800, the results of the investigation, including any supporting documentation, and the Form I-800 and its supporting documentation will be forwarded to the appropriate USCIS office for action. Although USCIS is not precluded from denying final approval of a Form I-800 based on the results of an investigation under this paragraph, the grant of provisional approval under paragraph (g), and the fact that the Department of State has given the notice contemplated by article 5(c) of the Convention, shall constitute prima facie evidence that the grant of adoption or custody for purposes of adoption will, ordinarily, warrant final approval of the Form I-800. The Form I-800 may still be denied, however, if the Secretary of State declines to issue the certificate provided for under section 204(d)(2) of the Act or if the investigation under this paragraph establishes the existence of facts that clearly warrant denial of the petition.

(g) Provisional approval.

(1) The officer will consider the evidence described in paragraph (d) of this section and any additional evidence acquired as a result of any investigation completed under paragraph (f) of this section, to determine whether the preponderance of the evidence shows that the child qualifies as a Convention adoptee. Unless 8 CFR 204.309(b) prohibits approval of the Form I-800, the officer will serve the petitioner with a written order provisionally approving the Form I-800 if the officer determines that the child does qualify for classification as a "child" under section 101(b)(1)(G), and that the proposed adoption or grant of custody will meet the Convention requirements.

(i) The provisional approval will expressly state that the child will, upon adoption or acquisition of custody, be eligible for classification as a Convention adoptee, adjudicate any waiver application and (if any necessary waiver of inadmissibility is granted) direct the petitioner to obtain and present the evidence required under paragraph (h) of this section in order to obtain final approval of the Form I-800.

(ii) The grant of a waiver of inadmissibility in conjunction with the provisional approval of a Form I-800 is conditioned upon the issuance of an immigrant or nonimmigrant visa for the child's admission to the United States based on the final approval of the same Form I-800. If the Form I-800 is finally denied or the immigrant or nonimmigrant visa application is denied, the waiver is void.

(2) If the petitioner filed the Form I-800 with USCIS and the child will apply for an immigrant or nonimmigrant visa, then, upon provisional approval of the Form I-800, the officer will forward the notice of provisional approval, Form I-800, and all supporting evidence to the Department of State. If the child will apply for adjustment of status, USCIS will retain the record of proceeding.

(h) Final approval.

(1) To obtain final approval of a provisionally approved Form I-800, the petitioner must submit to the Department of State officer who has jurisdiction of the child's application for an immigrant or nonimmigrant visa, or to the USCIS officer who has jurisdiction of the child's adjustment of status application, a copy of the following document(s):

(i) If the child is adopted in the Convention country, the adoption decree or administrative order from the competent authority in the Convention country showing that the petitioner has adopted the child; in the case of a married petitioner, the decree or order must show that both spouses adopted the child; or

(ii) If the child will be adopted in the United States:

(A) The decree or administrative order from the competent authority in the Convention country giving custody of the child for purposes of emigration and adoption to the petitioner or to an individual or entity acting on behalf of the petitioner. In the case of a married petitioner, an adoption decree that shows that the child was adopted only by one spouse, but not by both, will be deemed to show that the petitioner has acquired sufficient custody to bring the child to the United States for adoption by the other spouse;

(B) If not already provided before the provisional approval (because, for example, the petitioner thought the child would be adopted abroad, but that plan has changed so that the child will now be adopted in the United States), a statement from the primary provider, signed under penalty of perjury under United States law, summarizing the plan under 22 CFR 96.50 for monitoring of the placement until the adoption is finalized in the United States;

(C) If not already provided before the provisional approval (because, for example, the petitioner thought the child would be adopted abroad, but that plan has changed so that the child will now be adopted in the United States), a written description of the preadoption requirements that apply to adoptions in the State of the child's proposed residence and a description of when and how, after the child's immigration, the petitioner intends to complete the child's adoption. The written description must include a citation to the relevant State statutes or regulations and specify how the petitioner intends to comply with any requirements that can be satisfied only after the child arrives in the United States.

(2) If the Secretary of State, after reviewing the evidence that the petitioner provides under paragraph (h)(1)(i) or (ii) of this section, issues the certificate required under section 204(d)(2) of the Act, the Department of State officer who has jurisdiction over the child's visa application has authority, on behalf of USCIS, to grant final approval of a Form I-800. In the case of an alien who will apply for adjustment of status, the USCIS officer with jurisdiction of the adjustment application has authority to grant this final approval upon receiving the Secretary of State's certificate under section 204(d)(2) of the Act.

(i) Denial of Form I-800.

(1) A USCIS officer with authority to grant provisional or final approval will deny the Form I-800 if the officer finds that the child does not qualify as a Convention adoptee, or that 8 CFR 204.309(b) of this section requires denial of the Form I-800. Before denying a Form I-800, the officer will comply with the requirements of 8 CFR 103.2(b)(16)), if required to do so under that provision, and may issue a request for evidence or a notice of intent to deny under 8 CFR 103.2(b)(8).

(2) The decision will be in writing, specifying the reason(s) for the denial and notifying the petitioner of the right to appeal, if any, as specified in 8 CFR 204.314.

(3) If a Department of State officer finds, either at the provisional approval stage or the final approval stage, that the Form I-800 is "not clearly approvable," or that 8 CFR 204.309(b) warrants denial of the Form I-800, the Department of State officer will forward the Form I-800 and accompanying evidence to the USCIS office with jurisdiction over the place of the child's habitual residence for review and decision.

HISTORY:

[72 FR 56832, 56854, Oct. 4, 2007; 85 FR 46788, 46922, Aug. 3, 2020; 89 FR 6194, 6396, Jan. 31, 2024]

§ 204.314 Appeal.

(a) Decisions that may be appealed.

(1) Except as provided in paragraph (b) of this section:

(i) An applicant may appeal the denial of a Form I-800A (including the denial of a request to extend the prior approval of a Form I-800A) and

(ii) A petitioner may appeal the denial of a Form I-800.

(2) The provisions of 8 CFR 103.3, concerning how to file an appeal, and how USCIS adjudicates an appeal, apply to the appeal of a decision under this subpart C.

(b) Decisions that may not be appealed. There is no appeal from the denial of:

(1) Form I-800A because the Form I-800A was filed during any period during which 8 CFR 204.307(c) bars the filing of a Form I-800A; or

(2) Form I-800A for failure to timely file a home study as required by 8 CFR 204.310(a)(3)(viii); or

(3) Form I-800 that is denied because the Form I-800 was filed during any period during which 8 CFR 204.307(c) bars the filing of a Form I-800;

(4) Form I-800 filed either before USCIS approved a Form I-800A or after the expiration of the approval of a Form I-800A.

HISTORY:
[72 FR 56832, 56854, Oct. 4, 2007]

PART 205

REVOCATION OF APPROVAL OF PETITIONS

AUTHORITY NOTE APPLICABLE TO ENTIRE PART:

AUTHORITY:
8 U.S.C. 1101, 1103, 1151, 1153, 1154, 1155, 1182, 1186a, and 1324a.

§ 205.1 Automatic revocation.

(a) Reasons for automatic revocation. The approval of a petition or self-petition made under section 204 of the Act and in accordance with part 204 of this chapter is revoked as of the date of approval:

(1) If the Secretary of State shall terminate the registration of the beneficiary pursuant to the provisions of section 203(e) of the Act before October 1, 1991, or section 203(g) of the Act on or after October 1, 1994;

(2) [Reserved.]

(3) If any of the following circumstances occur before the beneficiary's or self-petitioner's journey to the United States commences or, if the beneficiary or self-petitioner is an applicant for adjustment of status to that of a permanent resident, before the decision on his or her adjustment application becomes final:

(i) Immediate relative and family-sponsored petitions, other than Amerasian petitions.

(A) Upon written notice of withdrawal filed by the petitioner or self-petitioner with any officer of the Service who is authorized to grant or deny petitions.

(B) Upon the death of the beneficiary or the self-petitioner.

(C) Upon the death of the petitioner, unless:

(1) The petition is deemed under 8 CFR 204.2(i)(1)(iv) to have been approved as a Form I-360, Petition for Amerasian, Widow(er) or Special Immigrant under 8 CFR 204.2(b); or

(2) U.S. Citizenship and Immigration Services (USCIS) determines, as a matter of discretion exercised for humanitarian reasons in light of the facts of a particular case, that it is inappropriate to revoke the approval of the petition. USCIS may make this determination only if the principal beneficiary of the visa petition asks for reinstatement of the approval of the petition and establishes that a person related to the principal beneficiary in one of the ways described in section 213A(f)(5)(B) of the Act is willing and able to file an affidavit of support under 8 CFR part 213a as a substitute sponsor.

(D) Upon the legal termination of the marriage when a citizen or lawful permanent resident of the United States has petitioned to accord his or her spouse immediate relative or family-sponsored preference immigrant classification under section 201(b) or section 203(a)(2) of the Act. The approval of a spousal self-petition based on the relationship to an abusive citizen or lawful permanent resident of the United States filed under section 204(a)(1)(A)(iii) or 204(a)(1)(B)(ii) of the Act, however, will not be revoked solely because of the termination of the marriage to the abuser.

(E) Upon the remarriage of the spouse of an abusive citizen or lawful permanent resident of the United States when the spouse has self-petitioned under section 204(a)(1)(A)(iii) or 204(a)(1)(B)(ii) of the Act for immediate relative classification under section 201(b) of the Act or for preference classification under section 203(a)(2) of the Act.

(F) Upon a child reaching the age of 21, when he or she has been accorded immediate relative status under section 201(b) of the Act. A petition filed on behalf of a child under section 204(a)(1)(A)(i) of the Act or a self-petition filed by a child of an abusive United States citizen under section 204(a)(1)(A)(iv) of the Act, however, will remain valid for the duration of the relationship to accord preference status under section 203(a)(1) of the Act if the beneficiary remains unmarried, or to accord preference status under section 203(a)(3) of the Act if he or she marries.

(G) Upon the marriage of a child, when he or she has been accorded immediate relative status under section 201(b) of the Act. A petition filed on behalf of the child under section 204(a)(1)(A)(i) of the Act or a self-petition filed by a child of an abusive United States citizen under section 204(a)(1)(A)(iv) of the Act, however, will remain valid for the duration of the relationship to accord preference status under section 203(a)(3) of the Act if he or she marries.

(H) Upon the marriage of a person accorded preference status as a son or daughter of a United States citizen under section 203(a)(1) of the Act. A petition filed on behalf of the son or daughter, however, will remain valid for the duration of the relationship to accord preference status under section 203(a)(3) of the Act.

(I) Upon the marriage of a person accorded status as a son or daughter of a lawful permanent resident alien under section 203(a)(2) of the Act.

(J) Upon legal termination of the petitioner's status as an alien admitted for lawful permanent residence in the United States unless the petitioner became a United States citizen. The provisions of 8 CFR 204.2(i)(3) shall apply if the petitioner became a United States citizen.

(ii) Petition for Pub. L. 97-359 Amerasian.

(A) Upon formal notice of withdrawal filed by the petitioner with the officer who approved the petition.

(B) Upon the death of the beneficiary.

(C) Upon the death or bankruptcy of the sponsor who executed Form I-361, Affidavit of Financial Support and Intent to Petition for Legal Custody for Pub. L. 97-359 Amerasian. In that event, a new petition may be filed in the beneficiary's behalf with the documentary evidence relating to sponsorship and, in the case of a beneficiary under 18 years of age, placement. If the new petition is approved, it will be given the priority date of the previously approved petition.

(D) Upon the death or substitution of the petitioner if other than the beneficiary or sponsor. However, if the petitioner dies or no longer desires or is able to proceed with the petition, and another person 18 years of age or older, an emancipated minor, or a corporation incorporated in the United States desires to be substituted for the deceased or original petitioner, a written request may be submitted to the Service or American consular office where the petition is located to reinstate the petition and restore the original priority date.

(E) Upon the beneficiary's reaching the age of 21 when the beneficiary has been accorded classification under section 201(b) of the Act. Provided that all requirements of section 204(f) of the Act continue to be met, however, the petition is to be considered valid for purposes of according the beneficiary preference classification under section 203(a)(1) of the Act if the beneficiary remains unmarried or under section 203(a)(3) if the beneficiary marries.

(F) Upon the beneficiary's marriage when the beneficiary has been accorded classification under section 201(b) or section 203(a)(1) of the Act. Provided that all requirements of section 204(f) of the Act continue to be met, however, the petition is to be considered valid for purposes of according the beneficiary preference classification under section 203(a)(3) of the Act.

(iii) Petitions under section 203(b), other than special immigrant juvenile petitions.

(A) Upon invalidation pursuant to 20 CFR Part 656 of the labor certification in support of the petition.

(B) Upon the death of the petitioner or beneficiary.

(C) In employment-based preference cases, upon written notice of withdrawal filed by the petitioner to any officer of USCIS who is authorized to grant or deny petitions, where the withdrawal is filed less than 180 days after approval of the employment-based preference petition, unless an associated adjustment of status application has been pending for 180 days or more. A petition that is withdrawn 180 days or more after its approval, or 180 days or more after the associated adjustment of status application has been filed, remains approved unless its approval is revoked on other grounds. If an employment-based petition on behalf of an alien is withdrawn, the job offer of the petitioning employer is rescinded and the alien must obtain a new employment-based preference petition in order to seek adjustment of status or issuance of an immigrant visa as an employment-based immigrant, unless eligible for adjustment of status under section 204(j) of the Act and in accordance with 8 CFR 245.25.

(D) Upon termination of the petitioning employer's business less than 180 days after petition approval under section 203(b)(1)(B), 203(b)(1)(C), 203(b)(2), or 203(b)(3) of the Act, unless an associated adjustment of status application has been pending for 180 days or more. If a petitioning employer's business terminates 180 days or more after petition approval, or 180 days or more after an associated adjustment of status application has been filed, the petition remains approved unless its approval is revoked on other grounds. If a petitioning employer's business terminates the job offer of the petitioning employer is rescinded and the beneficiary must obtain a new employment-based preference petition on his or her behalf in order to seek adjustment of status or issuance of an immigrant visa as an employment-based immigrant, unless eligible for adjustment of status under section 204(j) of the Act and in accordance with 8 CFR 245.25.

(iv) Special immigrant juvenile petitions. An approved petition for classification as a special immigrant juvenile will be revoked as provided in 8 CFR 204.11(j)(1).

(b) Notice. When it shall appear to the director that the approval of a petition has been automatically revoked, he or she shall cause a notice of such revocation to be sent promptly to the consular office having jurisdiction over the visa application and a copy of such notice to be mailed to the petitioner's last known address.

HISTORY:

[41 FR 55849, Dec. 23, 1976, as amended at 48 FR 19156, Apr. 28, 1983; 49 FR 29567, July 23, 1984; 49 FR 30679, Aug. 1, 1984; 53 FR 30017, Aug. 10, 1988; 58 FR 42850, Aug. 12, 1993; 61 FR 13061, 13077, Mar. 26, 1996; 71 FR 35732, 35749, June 21, 2006; 81 FR 73292, 73332, Oct. 24, 2016; 81 FR 82398, 82486, Nov. 18, 2016; 87 FR 13066, 13112, Mar. 8, 2022]

§ 205.2 Revocation on notice.

(a) General. Any Service officer authorized to approve a petition under section 204 of the Act may revoke the approval of that petition upon notice to the petitioner on any ground other than those specified in § 205.1 when the necessity for the revocation comes to the attention of this Service.

(b) Notice of intent. Revocation of the approval of a petition of self-petition under paragraph (a) of this section will be made only on notice to the petitioner or self-petitioner. The petitioner or self-petitioner must be given the opportunity to offer evidence in support of the petition or self-petition and in opposition to the grounds alleged for revocation of the approval.

(c) Notification of revocation. If, upon reconsideration, the approval previously granted is revoked, the director shall provide the petitioner or the self-petitioner with a written notification of the decision that explains the specific reasons for the revocation. The director shall notify the consular officer having jurisdiction over the visa application, if applicable, of the revocation of an approval.

(d) Appeals. The petitioner or self-petitioner may appeal the decision to revoke the approval within 15 days after the service of notice of the revocation. The appeal must be filed as provided in part 3 of this chapter, unless the Associate Commissioner for Examinations exercises appellate jurisdiction over the revocation under part 103 of this chapter. Appeals filed with the Associate Commissioner for Examinations must meet the requirements of part 103 of this chapter.

HISTORY:

[48 FR 19156, Apr. 28, 1983; 58 FR 42851, Aug. 12, 1993; 61 FR 13061, 13078, Mar. 26, 1996]

PART 207
ADMISSION OF REFUGEES

AUTHORITY NOTE APPLICABLE TO ENTIRE PART:

AUTHORITY:

8 U.S.C. 1101, 1103, 1151, 1157, 1159, 1182; 8 CFR part 2.

§ 207.1 Eligibility.

(a) Filing. Any alien who believes he or she is a refugee as defined in section 101(a)(42) of the Act, and is included in a refugee group identified in section 207(a) of the Act, may apply for admission to the United States by submitting an application, including biometric information, in accordance with the form instructions, as defined in 8 CFR 1.2.

(b) Firmly resettled. Any applicant (other than an applicant for derivative refugee status under 8 CFR 207.7) who has become firmly resettled in a foreign country is not eligible for refugee status under this chapter I. A refugee is considered to be "firmly resettled" if he or she has been offered resident status, citizenship, or some other type of permanent resettlement by a country other than the United States and has traveled to and entered that country as a consequence of his or her flight from persecution. Any applicant who claims not to be firmly resettled in a foreign country must establish that the conditions of his or her residence in that country are so restrictive as to deny resettlement. In determining whether or not an applicant is firmly resettled in a foreign country, the officer reviewing the matter shall consider the conditions under which other residents of the country live:

(1) Whether permanent or temporary housing is available to the refugee in the foreign country;

(2) Nature of employment available to the refugee in the foreign country; and

(3) Other benefits offered or denied to the refugee by the foreign country which are available to other residents, such as right to property ownership, travel documentation, education, public welfare, and citizenship.

(c) Immediate relatives and special immigrants. Any applicant for refugee status who qualifies as an immediate relative or as a special immigrant shall not be processed as a refugee unless it is in the public interest. The alien shall be advised to obtain an immediate relative or special immigrant visa and shall be provided with the proper petition forms to send to any prospective petitioners. An applicant who may be eligible for classification under sections 203(a) or 203(b) of the Act, and for whom a visa number is now available, shall be advised of such eligibility but is not required to apply.

HISTORY:

[46 FR 45118, Sept. 10, 1981; 62 FR 10312, 10336, Mar. 6, 1997; 74 FR 26933, 26937, June 5, 2009; 76 FR 53764, 53782, Aug. 29, 2011]

§ 207.2 Applicant processing.

(a) Interview. Each applicant 14 years old or older shall appear in person before an immigration officer for inquiry under oath to determine his or her eligibility for admission as a refugee.

(b) Medical examination. Each applicant shall submit to a medical examination as required by sections 221(d) and 232(b) of the Act.

(c) Sponsorship. Each applicant must be sponsored by a responsible person or organization. Transportation for the applicant from his or her present abode to the place of resettlement in the United States must be guaranteed by the sponsor.

HISTORY:

[46 FR 45118, Sept. 10, 1981; 64 FR 27660, 27661, May 21, 1999, as confirmed and amended 76 FR 53764, 53778, 53783, Aug. 29, 2011]

§ 207.3 Waivers of inadmissibility.

(a) Authority. Section 207(c)(3) of the Act sets forth grounds of inadmissibility under section 212(a) of the Act which are not applicable and those which may be waived in the case of an otherwise qualified refugee and the conditions under which such waivers may be approved.

(b) Filing requirements. An applicant may request a waiver by submitting an application for a waiver in accordance with the form instructions. The burden is on the applicant to show that the waiver should be granted based upon humanitarian grounds, family unity, or the public interest. The applicant shall be notified in writing of the decision, including the reasons for denial if the application is denied. There is no appeal from such decision.

HISTORY:

[46 FR 45118, Sept. 10, 1981; 62 FR 10312, 10336, Mar. 6, 1997; 76 FR 53764, 53783, Aug. 29, 2011]

§ 207.4 Approved application.

Approval of a refugee application by USCIS outside the United States authorizes CBP to admit the applicant conditionally as a refugee upon arrival at the port within four months of the date the refugee application was approved. There is no appeal from a denial of refugee status under this chapter.

HISTORY:

[46 FR 45118, Sept. 10, 1981; 76 FR 53764, 53783, Aug. 29, 2011]

§ 207.5 Waiting lists and priority handling.

Waiting lists are maintained for each designated refugee group of special humanitarian concern. Each applicant whose application is accepted for filing by USCIS shall be registered as of the date of filing. The date of filing is the priority date for purposes of case control. Refugees or groups of refugees may be selected from these lists in a manner that will best support the policies and interests of the United States. The Secretary may adopt appropriate criteria for selecting the refugees and assignment of processing priorities for each designated group based upon such considerations as reuniting families, close association with the United States, compelling humanitarian concerns, and public interest factors.

HISTORY:

[46 FR 45118, Sept. 10, 1981; 76 FR 53764, 53783, Aug. 29, 2011]

§ 207.6 Control over approved refugee numbers.

Current numerical accounting of approved refugees is maintained for each special group designated by the President. As refugee status is authorized for each applicant, the total count is reduced correspondingly from the appropriate group so that information is readily available to indicate how many refugee numbers remain available for issuance.

HISTORY:

46 FR 45118, Sept. 10, 1981.

§ 207.7 Derivatives of refugees.

(a) Eligibility. A spouse, as defined in section 101(a)(35) of the Act, and/or child(ren), as defined in section 101(b)(1)(A), (B), (C), (D), or (E) of the Act, shall be granted refugee status if accompanying or following-to-join the principal alien. An accompanying derivative is a spouse or child of a refugee who is in the physical company of the principal refugee when he or she is admitted to the United States, or a spouse or child of a refugee who is admitted within 4 months following the principal refugee's admission. A following-to-join derivative, on the other hand, is a spouse or child of a refugee who seeks admission more than 4 months after the principal refugee's admission to the United States.

(b) Ineligibility. The following relatives of refugees are ineligible for accompanying or following-to-join benefits:

(1) A spouse or child who has previously been granted asylee or refugee status;

(2) An adopted child, if the adoption took place after the child became 16 years old, or if the child has not been in the legal custody and living with the parent(s) for at least 2 years;

(3) A stepchild, if the marriage that created this relationship took place after the child became 18 years old;

(4) A husband or wife if each/both were not physically present at the marriage ceremony, and the marriage was not consummated (section 101(a)(35) of the Act);

(5) A husband or wife if the Secretary has determined that such alien has attempted or conspired to enter into a marriage for the purpose of evading immigration laws; and

(6) A parent, sister, brother, grandparent, grandchild, nephew, niece, uncle, aunt, cousin or in-law.

(c) Relationship. The relationship of a spouse and child as defined in sections 101(a)(35) and 101(b) (1)(A), (B), (C), (D), or (E), respectively, of the Act, must have existed prior to the refugee's admission to the United States and must continue to exist at the time of filing for accompanying or following-to-join benefits and at the time of the spouse or child's subsequent admission to the United States. If the refugee proves that the refugee is the parent of a child who was born after the refugee's admission as a refugee, but who was in utero on the date of the refugee's admission as a refugee, the child shall be eligible to accompany or follow-to-join the refugee. The child's mother, if not the principal refugee, shall not be eligible to accompany or follow-to-join the principal refugee unless the child's mother was the principal refugee's spouse on the date of the principal refugee's admission as a refugee.

(d) Filing. A refugee may request accompanying or following-to-join benefits for his or her spouse and unmarried, minor child(ren) (whether the spouse and children are inside or outside the United States) by filing a separate Request for Refugee/Asylee Relative in accordance with the form instructions for each qualifying family member. The request may only be filed by the principal refugee. Family members who derived their refugee status are not eligible to request derivative benefits on behalf of their spouse and child(ren). A separate Request for Refugee/Asylee Relative must be filed for each qualifying family member within two years of the refugee's admission to the United States unless USCIS determines that the filing period should be extended for humanitarian reasons. There is no time limit imposed on a family member's travel to the United States once the Request for Refugee/Asylee Relative has been approved, provided that the relationship of spouse or child continues to exist and approval of the Request for Refugee/Asylee Relative has not been subsequently revoked. There is no fee for this benefit request.

(e) Evidence. Documentary evidence consists of those documents which establish that the petitioner is a refugee, and evidence of the claimed relationship of the petitioner to the beneficiary. The burden of proof is on the petitioner to establish by a preponderance of the evidence that any person on whose behalf he/she is making a request under this section is an eligible spouse or unmarried, minor child. Evidence to establish the claimed relationship for a spouse or unmarried, minor child as set forth in 8 CFR part 204 must be submitted with the request for accompanying or following-to-join benefits. Where possible this will consist of the documents specified in § 204.2(a(1)(i)(B), (a)(1)(iii)(B), (a)(2), (d)(2), and (d)(5) of this chapter.

(f) **Approvals.**

(1) Spouse or child in the United States. When a spouse or child of a refugee is in the United States and the Request for Refugee/Asylee Relative is approved, USCIS will notify the refugee of such approval. Employment will be authorized incident to status.

(2) Spouse or child outside the United States. When a spouse or child of a refugee is outside the United States and the Request for Refugee/Asylee Relative is approved, USCIS will notify the refugee of such approval. USCIS will send the approved request to the Department of State for transmission to the U.S. Embassy or Consulate having jurisdiction over the area in which the refugee's spouse or child is located.

(3) Benefits. The approval of the Request for Refugee/Asylee Relative will remain valid for the duration of the relationship to the refugee and, in the case of a child, while the child is under 21 years of age and unmarried, provided also that the principal's status has not been revoked. However, the approved Request for Refugee/Asylee Relative will cease to confer immigration benefits after it has been used by the beneficiary for admission to the United States as a derivative of a refugee. For a derivative inside or arriving in the United States, USCIS will issue a document reflecting the derivative's current status as a refugee to demonstrate employment authorization, or the derivative may apply, under 8 CFR 274a.12(a), for evidence of employment authorization.

(g) Denials. If the spouse or child of a refugee is found to be ineligible for derivative status, a written notice explaining the basis for denial shall be forwarded to the principal refugee. There shall be no appeal from this decision. However, the denial shall be without prejudice to the consideration of a new petition or motion to reopen the refugee or asylee relative petition proceeding, if the refugee establishes eligibility for the accompanying or following-to-join benefits contained in this part.

HISTORY:

[63 FR 3792, 3795, Jan. 27, 1998; 76 FR 53764, 53783, Aug. 29, 2011, as corrected at 76 FR 73475, Nov. 29, 2011]

§ 207.8 Physical presence in the United States.

For the purpose of adjustment of status under section 209(a)(1) of the Act, the required one year physical presence of the applicant in the United States is computed from the date the applicant entered the United States as a refugee.

HISTORY:

[46 FR 45118, Sept. 10, 1981; redesignated at 63 FR 3792, 3795, Jan. 27, 1998]

§ 207.9 Termination of refugee status.

The refugee status of any alien (and of the spouse or child of the alien) admitted to the United States under section 207 of the Act will be terminated by USCIS if the alien was not a refugee within the meaning of section 101(a)(42) of the Act at the time of admission. USCIS will notify the alien in writing of its intent to terminate the alien's refugee status. The alien will have 30 days from the date notice is served upon him or her in accordance with 8 CFR 103.8, to present written or oral evidence to show why the alien's refugee status should not be terminated. There is no appeal under this chapter I from the termination of refugee status by USCIS. Upon termination of refugee status, USCIS will process the alien under sections 235, 240, and 241 of the Act.

HISTORY:

[46 FR 45118, Sept. 10, 1981; 62 FR 10312, 10337, Mar. 6, 1997; redesignated at 63 FR 3792, 3795, Jan. 27, 1998; 76 FR 53764, 53784, Aug. 29, 2011]

PART 208

PROCEDURES FOR ASYLUM AND WITHHOLDING OF REMOVAL

Subpart A. Asylum and Withholding of Removal

Rule

Subpart B. Credible Fear of Persecution

AUTHORITY NOTE APPLICABLE TO ENTIRE PART:

AUTHORITY:

8 U.S.C. 1101, 1103, 1158, 1226, 1252, 1282; Title VII of Pub. L. 110– 229; 8 CFR part 2; Pub. L. 115–218.

Subpart A
Asylum and Withholding of Removal

§ 208.1 General.

(a) **Applicability.**

(1) *General.* Unless otherwise provided in this chapter I, this subpart A shall apply to all applications for asylum under section 208 of the Act or for withholding of deportation or withholding of removal under section 241(b)(3) of the Act, or under the Convention Against Torture, whether before an asylum officer or an immigration judge, regardless of the date of filing. For purposes of this chapter I, withholding of removal shall also mean withholding of deportation under section 243(h) of the Act, as it appeared prior to April 1, 1997, except as provided in § 208.16(d). Such applications are referred to as "asylum applications." The provisions of this part 208 shall not affect the finality or validity of any decision made by a district director, an immigration judge, or the Board of Immigration Appeals in any such case prior to April 1, 1997. No asylum application that was filed with a district director, asylum officer, or immigration judge prior to April 1, 1997, may be reopened or otherwise reconsidered under the provisions of this part 208 except by motion granted in the exercise of discretion by the Board of Immigration Appeals, an immigration judge, or an asylum officer for proper cause shown. Motions to reopen or reconsider must meet the requirements of sections 240(c)(6) and (c)(7) of the Act, and 8 CFR parts 103 and 1003, as applicable.

(2) *Commonwealth of the Northern Mariana Islands.* The provisions of this subpart A shall not apply prior to January 1, 2030, to an alien physically present in or arriving in the Commonwealth of the Northern Mariana Islands seeking to apply for asylum. No application for asylum may be filed prior to January 1, 2030, pursuant to section 208 of the Act by an alien physically present in or arriving in the Commonwealth of the Northern Mariana Islands.

(b) *Training of asylum officers.* The Associate Director of USCIS Refugee, Asylum, and International Operations (RAIO) shall ensure that asylum officers receive special training in international human rights law, nonadversarial interview techniques, and other relevant national and international refugee laws and principles. The Director of International Affairs shall also, in cooperation with the Department of State and other appropriate sources, compile and disseminate to asylum officers information concerning the persecution of persons in other countries on account of race, religion, nationality, membership in a particular social group, or political opinion, torture of persons in other countries, and other information relevant to asylum determinations, and shall maintain a documentation center with information on human rights conditions.

(c) *Particular social group.* For purposes of adjudicating an application for asylum under section 208 of the Act or an application for withholding of removal under section 241(b)(3) of the Act, a particular social group is one that is based on an immutable or fundamental characteristic, is defined with particularity, and is recognized as socially distinct in the society at question. Such a particular social group cannot be defined exclusively by the alleged persecutory acts or harms and must also have existed independently of the alleged persecutory acts or harms that form the basis of the claim. The Secretary, in general, will not favorably adjudicate claims of aliens who claim a fear of persecution on account of membership in a particular social group consisting of or defined by the following circumstances: Past or present criminal activity or association (including gang membership); presence in a country with generalized violence or a high crime rate; being the subject of a recruitment effort by criminal, terrorist, or persecutory groups; the targeting of the applicant for criminal activity for financial gain based on perceptions of wealth or affluence; interpersonal disputes of which governmental authorities were unaware or uninvolved; private criminal acts of which governmental authorities were unaware or uninvolved; past or present terrorist activity or association; past or present persecutory activity or association; or status as an alien returning from the United States. This list is nonexhaustive, and the substance of the alleged particular social group, rather than the precise form of its delineation, shall be considered in determining whether the group falls within one of the categories on the list. No alien shall be found to be a refugee or have it decided that the alien's life or freedom would be threatened based on membership in a particular social group in any case unless that person articulates on the record, or provides a basis on the record for determining, the definition and boundaries of the alleged particular social group. A failure to define, or provide a basis for defining, a formulation of a particular social group before an immigration judge shall waive any such claim for all purposes under the Act, including on appeal. Any waived claim on this basis shall not serve as the basis for any motion to reopen or reconsider for any reason, including a claim of ineffective assistance of counsel unless the alien complies with the procedural requirements for such a motion and demonstrates that counsel's failure to define, or provide a basis for defining, a formulation of a particular social group constituted egregious conduct.

(d) *Political opinion.* For purposes of adjudicating an application for asylum under section 208 of the Act or an application for withholding of removal under section 241(b)(3) of the Act, a political opinion is one expressed by or imputed to an applicant in which the applicant possesses an ideal or conviction in support of the furtherance of a discrete cause related to political control of a State or a unit thereof. The Secretary, in general, will not favorably adjudicate claims of aliens who claim a fear of persecution on account of a political opinion defined solely by generalized disapproval of, disagreement with, or opposition to criminal, terrorist, gang, guerilla, or other non-state organizations absent expressive behavior in furtherance of a cause against such organizations related to efforts by the State to control such organizations or behavior that is antithetical to or otherwise opposes the ruling legal entity of the State or a legal sub-unit of the State. A person who has been forced to abort a pregnancy or to undergo involuntary sterilization, or who has been persecuted for failure or refusal to undergo such a procedure or for other resistance to a coercive population control program, shall be deemed to have been persecuted on account of political opinion, and a person who has a well-founded fear that he or she will be forced to undergo such a procedure or subject to persecution for such failure, refusal, or resistance shall be deemed to have a well-founded fear of persecution on account of political opinion.

(e) *Persecution.* For purposes of screening or adjudicating an application for asylum under section 208 of the Act or an application for withholding of removal under section 241(b)(3) of the Act, persecution requires an intent to target a belief or characteristic, a severe level of harm, and the infliction of a severe level of harm by the government of a country or by persons or an organization that the government was unable or unwilling to control. For purposes of evaluating the severity of the level of harm, persecution is an extreme concept involving a severe level of harm that includes actions so severe that they constitute an exigent threat. Persecution does not encompass the generalized harm that arises out of civil, criminal, or military strife in a country, nor does it encompass all treatment that the United States regards as unfair, offensive, unjust, or even unlawful or unconstitutional. It does not include intermittent harassment, including brief detentions; threats with no actual effort to carry out the threats, except that particularized threats of severe harm of an immediate and menacing nature made by an identified entity may constitute persecution; or, non-severe economic harm or property damage, though this list is nonexhaustive. The existence of laws or government policies that are unenforced or infrequently enforced do not, by themselves, constitute persecution, unless there is credible evidence that those laws or policies have been or would be applied to an applicant personally.

(f) *Nexus.* For purposes of adjudicating an application for asylum under section 208 of the Act or an application or withholding of removal under section 241(b)(3) of the Act, the Secretary, in general, will not favorably adjudicate the claims of aliens who claim persecution based on the following list of nonexhaustive circumstances:

(1) Interpersonal animus or retribution;

(2) Interpersonal animus in which the alleged persecutor has not targeted, or manifested an animus against, other members of an alleged particular social group in addition to the member who has raised the claim at issue;

(3) Generalized disapproval of, disagreement with, or opposition to criminal, terrorist, gang, guerilla, or other non-state organizations absent expressive behavior in furtherance of a discrete cause against such organizations related to control of a State or expressive behavior that is antithetical to the State or a legal unit of the State;

(4) Resistance to recruitment or coercion by guerilla, criminal, gang, terrorist or other non-state organizations;

(5) The targeting of the applicant for criminal activity for financial gain based on wealth or affluence or perceptions of wealth or affluence;

(6) Criminal activity;

(7) Perceived, past or present, gang affiliation; or,

(8) Gender.

(g) *Evidence based on stereotypes.* For purposes of adjudicating an application for asylum under section 208 of the Act or an application for withholding of removal under section 241(b)(3) of the Act, evidence offered in support of such an application which promotes cultural stereotypes about a country, its inhabitants, or an alleged persecutor, including stereotypes based on race, religion, nationality, or gender, shall not be admissible in adjudicating that application, provided that nothing in this paragraph shall be construed as prohibiting the submission of evidence that an alleged persecutor holds stereotypical views of the applicant.

HISTORY:

[55 FR 30680, July 27, 1990; 59 FR 62297, Dec. 5, 1994; 62 FR 10312, 10337, Mar. 6, 1997; 64 FR 8478, 8487, Feb. 19, 1999; 74 FR 55726, 55736, Oct. 28, 2009; 76 FR 53764, 53784, Aug. 29, 2011; 85 FR 29264, 29310, May. 14, 2020; 85 FR 80274, 80385, December 11, 2020]

§ 208.2 Jurisdiction.

(a) Jurisdiction of U.S. Citizenship and Immigration Services (USCIS).

(1) Except as provided in paragraph (b) or (c) of this section, USCIS shall have initial jurisdiction over:

(i) An asylum application filed by an alien physically present in the United States or seeking admission at a port-of-entry; and

(ii) Interviews provided in accordance with section 235(b)(1)(B)(ii) of the Act to further consider the application for asylum of an alien, other than a stowaway or alien physically present in or arriving in the Commonwealth of the Northern Mariana Islands, found to have a credible fear of persecution or torture in accordance with § 208.30(f) and retained by USCIS, or referred to USCIS by an immigration judge pursuant to 8 CFR 1003.42 and 1208.30 after the immigration judge has vacated a negative credible fear determination. Interviews to further consider applications for asylum under this paragraph (a)(1)(ii) are governed by the procedures provided for under § 208.9. Further consideration of an asylum application filed by a stowaway who has received a positive credible fear determination will be under the jurisdiction of an immigration judge pursuant to paragraph (c) of this section.

(2) USCIS shall also have initial jurisdiction over credible fear determinations under § 208.30 and reasonable fear determinations under § 208.31.

(b) Jurisdiction of Immigration Court in general. Immigration judges shall have exclusive jurisdiction over asylum applications filed by an alien who has been served a Form I-221, Order to Show Cause; Form I-122, Notice to Applicant for Admission Detained for a Hearing before an Immigration Judge; or Form I-862, Notice to Appear, after the charging document has been filed with the Immigration Court. Immigration judges shall also have jurisdiction over any asylum applications filed prior to April 1, 1997, by alien crewmembers who have remained in the United States longer than authorized, by applicants for admission under the Visa Waiver Pilot Program, and by aliens who have been admitted to the United States under the Visa Waiver Pilot Program. Immigration judges shall also have the authority to review reasonable fear determinations referred to the Immigration Court under § 208.31, and credible fear determinations referred to the Immigration Court under § 208.30.

(c) Certain aliens not entitled to proceedings under section 240 of the Act.

(1) Asylum applications and withholding of removal applications only. After Form I-863, Notice of Referral to Immigration Judge, has been filed with the Immigration Court, an immigration judge shall have exclusive jurisdiction over any asylum application filed on or after April 1, 1997, by:

(i) An alien crewmember who:

(A) Is an applicant for a landing permit;

(B) Has been refused permission to land under section 252 of the Act; or

(C) On or after April 1, 1997, was granted permission to land under section 252 of the Act, regardless of whether the alien has remained in the United States longer than authorized;

(ii) An alien stowaway who has been found to have a credible fear of persecution or torture pursuant to the procedures set forth in subpart B of this part;

(iii) An alien who is an applicant for admission pursuant to the Visa Waiver Program under section 217 of the Act, except that if such an alien is an applicant for admission to the Commonwealth of the Northern Mariana Islands, then he or she shall not be eligible for asylum prior to January 1, 2030;

(iv) An alien who was admitted to the United States pursuant to the Visa Waiver Program under section 217 of the Act and has remained longer than authorized or has otherwise violated his or her immigration status, except that if such an alien was admitted to the Commonwealth of the Northern Mariana Islands, then he or she shall not be eligible for asylum in the Commonwealth of the Northern Mariana Islands prior to January 1, 2030;

(v) An alien who has been ordered removed under § 235(c) of the Act, as described in § 235.8(a) of this chapter (applicable only in the event that the alien is referred for proceedings under this paragraph by the Regional Director pursuant to section 235.8(b)(2)(ii) of this chapter);

(vi) An alien who is an applicant for admission, or has been admitted, as an alien classified under section 101(a)(15)(S) of the Act (applicable only in the event that the alien is referred for proceedings under this paragraph by the district director);

(vii) An alien who is an applicant for admission to Guam or the Commonwealth of the Northern Mariana Islands pursuant to the Guam-CNMI Visa Waiver Program under section 212(l) of the Act, except that if such an alien is an applicant for admission to the Commonwealth of the Northern Mariana Islands, then he or she shall not be eligible for asylum prior to January 1, 2030;

(viii) An alien who was admitted to Guam or the Commonwealth of the Northern Mariana Islands pursuant to the Guam-CNMI Visa Waiver Program under section 212(l) of the Act and has remained longer than authorized or has otherwise violated his or her immigration status, except that if such an alien was admitted to the Commonwealth of the Northern Mariana Islands, then he or she shall not be eligible for asylum in the Commonwealth of the Northern Mariana Islands prior to January 1, 2030; or

(ix) [Removed and reserved.]

(2) Withholding of removal applications only. After Form I-863, Notice of Referral to Immigration Judge, has been filed with the Immigration Court, an immigration judge shall have exclusive jurisdiction over any application for withholding of removal filed by:

(i) An alien who is the subject of a reinstated removal order pursuant to section 241(a)(5) of the Act; or

(ii) An alien who has been issued an administrative removal order pursuant to section 238 of the Act as an alien convicted of committing an aggravated felony.

(3) Rules of procedure.

(i) General. Except as provided in this section, proceedings falling under the jurisdiction of the immigration judge pursuant to paragraph (c)(1) or (c)(2) of this section shall be conducted in accordance with the same rules of procedure as proceedings conducted under 8 CFR part 240, subpart A. The scope of review in proceedings conducted pursuant to paragraph (c)(1) of this section shall be limited to a determination of whether the alien is eligible for asylum or withholding or deferral of removal, and whether asylum shall be granted in the exercise of discretion. The scope of review in proceedings conducted pursuant to paragraph (c)(2) of this section shall be limited to a determination of whether the alien is eligible for withholding or deferral of removal. During such proceedings, all parties are prohibited from raising or considering any other issues, including but not limited to issues of admissibility, deportability, eligibility for waivers, and eligibility for any other form of relief.

(ii) Notice of hearing procedures and in-absentia decisions. The alien will be provided with notice of the time and place of the proceeding. The request for asylum and withholding of removal submitted by an alien who fails to appear for the hearing shall be denied. The denial of asylum and withholding of removal for failure to appear may be reopened only upon a motion filed with the immigration judge with jurisdiction over the case. Only one motion to reopen may be filed, and it must be filed within 90 days, unless the alien establishes that he or she did not receive notice of the hearing date or was in Federal or State custody on the date directed to appear. The motion must include documentary evidence, which demonstrates that:

(A) The alien did not receive the notice;

(B) The alien was in Federal or State custody and the failure to appear was through no fault of the alien; or

(C) "Exceptional circumstances," as defined in section 240(e)(1) of the Act, caused the failure to appear.

(iii) Relief. The filing of a motion to reopen shall not stay removal of the alien unless the immigration judge issues an order granting a stay pending disposition of the motion. An alien who fails to appear for a proceeding under this section shall not be eligible for relief under section 240A, 240B, 245, 248, or 249 of the Act for a period of 10 years after the date of the denial, unless the applicant can show exceptional circumstances resulted in his or her failure to appear.

HISTORY:

[55 FR 30680, July 27, 1990; 59 FR 62298, Dec. 5, 1994; 60 FR 34090, June 30, 1995; 60 FR 44260, 44264, Aug. 25, 1995; 62 FR 10312, 10337, Mar. 6, 1997, as corrected at 62 FR 15362, Apr. 1, 1997; 64 FR 8478, 8487, Feb. 19, 1999; 65 FR 76121, 76130, Dec. 6, 2000; 74 FR 55726, 55736, Oct. 28, 2009; 76 FR 53764, 53784, Aug. 29, 2011; 85 FR 29264, 29310, May. 14, 2020; 85 FR 80274, 80386, Dec. 11, 2020; 87 FR 18078, 18215, Mar. 29, 2022]

§ 208.3 Form of application.

(a)(1) Except for applicants described in paragraph (a)(2) of this section, an asylum applicant must file Form I-589, Application for Asylum and for Withholding of Removal, together with any additional supporting evidence in accordance with the instructions on the form. The applicant's spouse and children shall be listed on the application and may be included in the request for asylum if they are in the United States. One additional copy of the principal applicant's Form I-589 must be submitted for each dependent included in the principal's application.

(2) For asylum applicants, other than stowaways, who are awaiting further consideration of an asylum application pursuant to section 235(b)(1)(B)(ii) of the Act following a positive credible fear determination, the written record of a positive credible fear finding issued in accordance with § 208.30(f) or 8 CFR 1003.42 or 1208.30 satisfies the application filing requirements in paragraph (a)(1) of this section for purposes of consideration by USCIS pursuant to the jurisdiction provided at § 208.2(a)(1)(ii). The written record of the positive credible fear determination shall be considered a complete asylum application for purposes of §§ 208.4(a), 208.7, and 208.9(a); shall not be subject to the requirements of 8 CFR 103.2; and shall be subject to the conditions and consequences in paragraph (c) of this section upon signature at the asylum interview. The date that the positive credible fear determination is served on the alien shall be considered the date of filing and receipt. Application information collected electronically will be preserved in its native format. The applicant's spouse and children may be included in the request for asylum only if they were included in the credible fear determination pursuant to § 208.30(c), or also presently have an application for asylum pending adjudication with USCIS pursuant to § 208.2(a)(1)(ii). If USCIS does not grant the applicant's asylum application after an interview conducted in accordance with § 208.9 and if a spouse or child who was included in the request for asylum does not separately file an asylum application that is adjudicated by USCIS, the application will also be deemed to satisfy the application filing requirements of 8 CFR 1208.4(b) for a spouse or child who was included in the request for asylum. The biometrics captured during expedited removal for the principal applicant and any dependents may be used to verify identity and for criminal and other background checks for purposes of an asylum application under the jurisdiction of USCIS pursuant to § 208.2(a)(1) and any subsequent immigration benefit.

(b) An asylum application shall be deemed to constitute at the same time an application for withholding of removal, unless adjudicated in deportation or exclusion proceedings commenced prior to April 1, 1997. In such instances, the asylum application shall be deemed to constitute an application for withholding of deportation under section 243(h) of the Act, as that section existed prior to April 1, 1997. Where a determination is made that an applicant is ineligible to apply for asylum under section 208(a)(2) of the Act, an asylum application shall be construed as an application for withholding of removal.

(c) Form I-589 shall be filed under the following conditions and shall have the following consequences:

(1) If the application was filed on or after January 4, 1995, information provided in the application may be used as a basis for the initiation of removal proceedings, or to satisfy any burden of proof in exclusion, deportation, or removal proceedings;

(2) The applicant and anyone other than a spouse, parent, son, or daughter of the applicant who assists the applicant in preparing the application must sign the application under penalty of perjury. The applicant's signature establishes a presumption that the applicant is aware of the contents of the application. A person other than a relative specified in this paragraph

who assists the applicant in preparing the application also must provide his or her full mailing address;

(3) An asylum application that does not include a response to each of the questions contained in the Form I-589, is unsigned, or is unaccompanied by the required materials specified in paragraph (a)(1) of this section is incomplete. The filing of an incomplete application shall not commence the 150-day period after which the applicant may file an application for employment authorization in accordance with § 208.7. An application that is incomplete shall be returned by mail to the applicant within 30 days of the receipt of the application by the Service. If the Service has not mailed the incomplete application back to the applicant within 30 days, it shall be deemed complete. An application returned to the applicant as incomplete shall be resubmitted by the applicant with the additional information if he or she wishes to have the application considered;

(4) Knowing placement of false information on the application may subject the person placing that information on the application to criminal penalties under title 18 of the United States Code and to civil or criminal penalties under section 274C of the Act; and

(5) Knowingly filing a frivolous application on or after April 1, 1997, so long as the applicant has received the notice required by section 208(d)(4) of the Act, shall render the applicant permanently ineligible for any benefits under the Act pursuant to § 208.20.

HISTORY:

[55 FR 30680, July 27, 1990, as amended at 56 FR 50812, Oct. 9, 1991; 59 FR 62298, Dec. 5, 1994; 60 FR 34090, June 30, 1995; 62 FR 10312, 10338, Mar. 6, 1997; 65 FR 76121, 76131, Dec. 6, 2000; 85 FR 38532, 38626, June 26, 2020; 87 FR 18078, 18216, Mar. 29, 2022; 87 FR 57795, 57797, Sept. 22, 2022]

§ 208.4 Filing the application.

Except as prohibited in paragraph (a) of this section, asylum applications shall be filed in accordance with paragraph (b) of this section.

(a) Prohibitions on filing. Section 208(a)(2) of the Act prohibits certain aliens from filing for asylum on or after April 1, 1997, unless the alien can demonstrate to the satisfaction of the Attorney General that one of the exceptions in section 208(a)(2)(D) of the Act applies. Such prohibition applies only to asylum applications under section 208 of the Act and not to applications for withholding of removal under § 208.16. If an applicant files an asylum application and it appears that one or more of the prohibitions contained in section 208(a)(2) of the Act apply, an asylum officer, in an interview, or an immigration judge, in a hearing, shall review the application and give the applicant the opportunity to present any relevant and useful information bearing on any prohibitions on filing to determine if the application should be rejected. For the purpose of making determinations under section 208(a)(2) of the Act, the following rules shall apply:

(1) Authority. Only an asylum officer, an immigration judge, or the Board of Immigration Appeals is authorized to make determinations regarding the prohibitions contained in section 208(a)(2)(B) or (C) of the Act.

(2) One-year filing deadline.

(i) For purposes of section 208(a)(2)(B) of the Act, an applicant has the burden of proving:

(A) By clear and convincing evidence that the application has been filed within 1 year of the date of the alien's arrival in the United States, or

(B) To the satisfaction of the asylum officer, the immigration judge, or the Board that he or she qualifies for an exception to the 1-year deadline.

(ii) The 1-year period shall be calculated from the date of the alien's last arrival in the United States or April 1, 1997, whichever is later. When the last day of the period so computed falls on a Saturday, Sunday, or legal holiday, the period shall run until the end of the next day that is not a Saturday, Sunday, or legal holiday. For the purpose of making determinations under section 208(a)(2)(B) of the Act only, an application is considered to have been filed on the date it is received by the Service, pursuant to § 103.2(a)(7) of this chapter. In a case in which the application has not been received by the Service within 1 year from the applicant's date of entry into the United States, but the applicant provides clear and convincing documentary evidence of mailing the application within the 1-year period, the mailing date shall be considered the filing date. For cases before the Immigration Court in accordance with § 3.13 of this chapter, the application is considered to have been filed on the date it is received by the Immigration Court. For cases before the Board of Immigration Appeals, the application is considered to have been filed on the date it is received by the Board. In the case of an application that appears to have been filed more than a year after the applicant arrived in the United States, the asylum officer, the immigration judge, or the Board will determine whether the applicant qualifies for an exception to the deadline. For aliens present in or arriving in the Commonwealth of the Northern Mariana Islands, the 1-year period shall be calculated from either January 1, 2030 or the date of the alien's last arrival in the United States (including the Commonwealth of the Northern Mariana Islands), whichever is later. No period of physical presence in the Commonwealth of the Northern Mariana Islands prior to January 1, 2030, shall count toward the 1-year period. After November 28, 2009, any travel to the Commonwealth of the Northern Mariana Islands from any other State shall not re-start the calculation of the 1-year period.

(3) Prior denial of application. For purposes of section 208(a)(2)(C) of the Act, an asylum application has not been denied unless denied by an immigration judge or the Board of Immigration Appeals.

(4) Changed circumstances.

(i) The term "changed circumstances" in section 208(a)(2)(D) of the Act shall refer to circumstances materially affecting the applicant's eligibility for asylum. They may include, but are not limited to:

(A) Changes in conditions in the applicant's country of nationality or, if the applicant is stateless, country of last habitual residence;

(B) Changes in the applicant's circumstances that materially affect the applicant's eligibility for asylum, including changes in applicable U.S. law and activities the applicant becomes involved in outside the country of feared persecution that place the applicant at risk; or

(C) In the case of an alien who had previously been included as a dependent in another alien's pending asylum application, the loss of the spousal or parent-child relationship to the principal applicant through marriage, divorce, death, or attainment of age 21.

(ii) The applicant shall file an asylum application within a reasonable period given those "changed circumstances." If the applicant can establish that he or she did not become aware of the changed circumstances until after they occurred, such delayed awareness shall be taken into account in determining what constitutes a "reasonable period."

(5) The term "extraordinary circumstances" in section 208(a)(2)(D) of the Act shall refer to events or factors directly related to the failure to meet the 1-year deadline. Such circumstances may excuse the failure to file within the 1-year period as long as the alien filed the application within a reasonable period given those circumstances. The burden of proof is on the applicant to establish to the satisfaction of the asylum officer, the immigration judge, or the Board of Immigration Appeals that the circumstances were not intentionally created by the alien through his or her own action or inaction, that those circumstances were directly related to the alien's failure to file the application within the 1-year period, and that the delay was reasonable under the circumstances. Those circumstances may include but are not limited to:

(i) Serious illness or mental or physical disability, including any effects of persecution or violent harm suffered in the past, during the 1-year period after arrival;

(ii) Legal disability (e.g., the applicant was an unaccompanied minor or suffered from a mental impairment) during the 1-year period after arrival;

(iii) Ineffective assistance of counsel, provided that:

(A) The alien files an affidavit setting forth in detail the agreement that was entered into with counsel with respect to the actions to be taken and what representations counsel did or did not make to the respondent in this regard;

(B) The counsel whose integrity or competence is being impugned has been informed of the allegations leveled against him or her and given an opportunity to respond; and

(C) The alien indicates whether a complaint has been filed with appropriate disciplinary authorities with respect to any violation of counsel's ethical or legal responsibilities, and if not, why not;

(iv) The applicant maintained Temporary Protected Status, lawful immigrant or nonimmigrant status, or was given parole, until a reasonable period before the filing of the asylum application;

(v) The applicant filed an asylum application prior to the expiration of the 1-year deadline, but that application was rejected by the Service as not properly filed, was returned to the applicant for corrections, and was refiled within a reasonable period thereafter; and

(vi) The death or serious illness or incapacity of the applicant's legal representative or a member of the applicant's immediate family.

(6) Asylum Cooperative Agreements. Immigration officers have authority to apply section 208(a)(2)(A) of the Act, relating to the determination that the alien may be removed to a third country pursuant to a bilateral or multilateral agreement, as provided in § 208.30(e). For provisions relating to the authority of immigration judges with respect to section 208(a)(2)(A), see 8 CFR 1240.11(g) and (h).

(b) Amending an application after filing.

(1) For applications being considered by USCIS pursuant to § 208.2(a)(1)(i), upon the request of the alien, and as a matter of discretion, the asylum officer or immigration judge with jurisdiction may permit an asylum applicant to amend or supplement the application. Any delay in adjudication or in proceedings caused by a request to amend or supplement the application will be treated as a delay caused by the applicant for purposes of § 208.7 and 8 CFR 274a.12(c)(8).

(2) For applications being considered by USCIS pursuant to § 208.2(a)(1)(ii), the asylum applicant may subsequently amend or correct the biographic or credible fear information in the Form I-870, Record of Determination/Credible Fear Worksheet, or supplement the information collected during the process that concluded with a positive credible fear determination, provided the information is submitted directly to the asylum office no later than 7 calendar days prior to the scheduled asylum interview, or for documents submitted by mail, postmarked no later than 10 calendar days prior to the scheduled asylum interview. The asylum officer, finding good cause in an exercise of USCIS's discretion, may consider amendments or supplements submitted after the 7- or 10-day (depending on the method of submission) deadline or may grant the applicant an extension of time during which the applicant may submit additional evidence, subject to the limitation on extensions described at § 208.9(e)(2). Any amendment, correction, or supplement shall be included in the record.

HISTORY:

[55 FR 30680, July 27, 1990, as amended at 56 FR 50812, Oct. 9, 1991; 59 FR 62298, Dec. 5, 1994; 60 FR 34090, June 30, 1995; 62 FR 10312, 10338, Mar. 6, 1997; 64 FR 8478, 8488, Feb. 19, 1999, as corrected at 64 FR 13881, Mar. 23, 1999; 65 FR 76121, 76131, Dec. 6, 2000; 69 FR 69480, 69488, Nov. 29, 2004; 74 FR 26933, 26937, June 5, 2009; 74 FR 55726, 55737, Oct. 28, 2009; 84 FR 63994, 64008, Nov. 19, 2019; 85 FR 29264, 29310, May. 14, 2020; 85 FR 38532, 38626, June 26, 2020; 87 FR 18078, 18216, Mar. 29, 2022]

§ 208.5 Special duties toward aliens in custody of DHS.

(a) General. When an alien in the custody of DHS requests asylum or withholding of removal, or expresses a fear of persecution or harm upon return to his or her country of origin or to agents thereof, DHS shall make available the appropriate application forms and shall provide the applicant with the information required by section 208(d)(4) of the Act, including in the case of an alien who is in custody with a positive credible fear or reasonable fear determination under 8 CFR 208.30 or 208.31, and except in the case of an alien who is in custody pending a credible fear determination under 8 CFR 208.30 or a reasonable fear determination pursuant to 8 CFR 208.31. Although DHS does not have a duty in the case of an alien who is in custody pending a credible fear or reasonable fear determination under either 8 CFR 208.30 or 8 CFR 208.31, DHS may provide the appropriate forms, upon request. Where possible, expedited consideration shall be given to applications of detained aliens. Except as provided in paragraph (c) of this section, such alien shall not be excluded, deported, or removed before a decision is rendered on his or her asylum application. Furthermore, except as provided in paragraph (c) of this section, an alien physically present in or arriving in the Commonwealth of the Northern Mariana Islands shall not be excluded, deported, or removed before a decision is rendered on his or her application for withholding of removal pursuant to section 241(b)(3) of the Act and withholding of removal under the Convention Against Torture. No application for asylum may be filed prior to January 1, 2030, under section 208 of the Act by an alien physically present in or arriving in the Commonwealth of the Northern Mariana Islands.

(b) Certain aliens aboard vessels.

(1) If an alien crewmember or alien stowaway on board a vessel or other conveyance alleges, claims, or otherwise makes known to an immigration inspector or other official making an examination on the conveyance that he or she is unable or unwilling to return to his or her country of nationality or last habitual residence (if not a national of any country) because of persecution or a fear of persecution in that country on account of race, religion, nationality, membership in a particular social group, or political opinion, or if the alien expresses a fear of torture upon return to that country, the alien shall be promptly removed from the conveyance. If the alien makes such fear known to an official while off such conveyance, the alien shall not be returned to the conveyance but shall be retained in or transferred to the custody of the Service.

(i) An alien stowaway will be referred to an asylum officer for a credible fear determination under § 208.30.

(ii) An alien crewmember shall be provided the appropriate application forms and information required by section 208(d)(4) of the Act and may then have 10 days within which to submit an asylum application in accordance with the instructions on the form. DHS may extend the 10-day filing period for good cause. Once the application has been filed, DHS shall serve Form I-863 on the alien and immediately forward any such application to the appropriate Immigration Court with a copy of the Form I-863 being filed with that court.

(iii) An alien crewmember physically present in or arriving in the Commonwealth of the Northern Mariana Islands can request withholding of removal pursuant to section 241(b)(3) of the Act and withholding of removal under the Convention Against Torture. However, such an alien crewmember is not eligible to request asylum pursuant to section 208 of the Act prior to January 1, 2030.

(2) Pending adjudication of the application, and, in the case of a stowaway the credible fear determination and any review thereof, the alien may be detained by the Service or otherwise paroled in accordance with § 212.5 of this chapter. However, pending the credible fear determination, parole of an alien stowaway may be permitted only when the Secretary determines, in the exercise of discretion, that parole is required to meet a medical emergency or is necessary for a legitimate law enforcement objective.

(c) Exception to prohibition on removal. A motion to reopen or an order to remand accompanied by an asylum application pursuant to § 208.4(b)(3)(iii) shall not stay execution of a final exclusion, deportation, or removal order unless such stay is specifically granted by the Board of Immigration Appeals or the immigration judge having jurisdiction over the motion.

HISTORY:

[55 FR 30680, July 27, 1990; 62 FR 10312, 10339, Mar. 6, 1997; 64 FR 8478, 8488, Feb. 19, 1999; 65 FR 76121, 76132, Dec. 6, 2000; 74 FR 26933, 26937, June 5, 2009; 74 FR 55726, 55737, Oct. 28, 2009; 76 FR 53764, 53784, Aug. 29, 2011; 85 FR 29264, 29310, May. 14, 2020; 85 FR 80274, 80386, Dec. 11, 2020]

§ 208.6 Disclosure to third parties.

(a) Information contained in or pertaining to any application for refugee admission, asylum, withholding of removal under section 241(b)(3) of the Act, or protection under regulations issued pursuant to the Convention Against Torture's implementing legislation, records pertaining to any credible fear determination conducted pursuant to § 208.30, and records pertaining to any reasonable fear determination conducted pursuant to § 208.31, shall not be disclosed without the written consent of the applicant, except as permitted by this section or at the discretion of the Secretary.

(b) The confidentiality of other records kept by DHS and the Executive Office for Immigration Review that indicate that a specific alien has applied for refugee admission, asylum, withholding of removal under section 241(b)(3) of the Act, or protection under regulations issued pursuant to the Convention Against Torture's implementing legislation, or has received a credible fear or reasonable fear interview, or received a credible fear or reasonable fear review shall also be protected from disclosure, except as permitted in this section. DHS will coordinate with the Department of State to ensure that the confidentiality of those records is maintained if they are transmitted to Department of State offices in other countries.

(c) This section shall not apply to any disclosure to:

(1) Any United States Government official or contractor having a need to examine information in connection with:

(i) The adjudication of asylum applications;

(ii) The consideration of a request for a credible fear or reasonable fear interview, or a credible fear or reasonable fear review;

(iii) The defense of any legal action arising from the adjudication of, or failure to adjudicate, the asylum application, or from a credible fear determination or reasonable fear determination under § 208.30 or § 208.31;

(iv) The defense of any legal action of which the asylum application, credible fear determination, or reasonable fear determination is a part; or

(v) Any United States Government investigation concerning any criminal or civil matter; or

(2) Any Federal, State, or local court in the United States considering any legal action:

(i) Arising from the adjudication of, or failure to adjudicate, the asylum application, or from a credible fear or reasonable fear determination under § 208.30 or § 208.31; or

(ii) Arising from the proceedings of which the asylum application, credible fear determination, or reasonable fear determination is a part.

(d)(1) Any information contained in an application for refugee admission, asylum, withholding of removal under section 241(b)(3) of the Act, or protection under regulations issued pursuant to the Convention Against Torture's implementing legislation, any relevant and applicable information supporting that application, any information regarding an alien who has filed such an application, and any relevant and applicable information regarding an alien who has been the subject of a reasonable fear or credible fear determination may be disclosed:

(i) As part of an investigation or adjudication of the merits of that application or of any other application under the immigration laws,

(ii) As part of any State or Federal criminal investigation, proceeding, or prosecution;

(iii) Pursuant to any State or Federal mandatory reporting requirement;

(iv) To deter, prevent, or ameliorate the effects of child abuse;

(v) As part of any proceeding arising under the immigration laws, including proceedings arising under the Act; and

(vi) As part of the Government's defense of any legal action relating to the alien's immigration or custody status including petitions for review filed in accordance with 8 U.S.C. 1252.

(2) If information may be disclosed under paragraph (d)(1) of this section, the disclosure provisions in paragraphs (a), (b), and (c) of this section shall not apply.

(e) Nothing in this section shall be construed as prohibiting the disclosure of information contained in an application for refugee admission, asylum, withholding of removal under section 241(b)(3)(B) of the Act, or protection under regulations issued pursuant to the Convention Against Torture's implementing legislation, information supporting that application, information regarding an alien who has filed such an application, or information regarding an alien who has been the subject of a reasonable fear or credible fear determination:

(1) Among employees and officers of the Department of Justice, the Department of Homeland Security, the Department of State, the Department of Health and Human Services, the Department of Labor, or a U.S. national security agency having a need to examine the information for an official purpose; or

(2) Where a United States Government employee or contractor has a good faith and reasonable belief that disclosure is necessary to prevent the commission of a crime, the furtherance of an ongoing crime, or to ameliorate the effects of a crime.

HISTORY:

[55 FR 30680, July 27, 1990; 62 FR 10312, 10340, Mar. 6, 1997; 65 FR 76121, 76133, Dec. 6, 2000; 85 FR 80274, 80386, Dec. 11, 2020]

§ 208.7 Employment authorization.

(a) Application and approval.

(1) Subject to the restrictions contained in sections 208(d) and 236(a) of the Act, an applicant for asylum who is not an aggravated felon shall be eligible pursuant to §§ 274a.12(c)(8) and 274a.13(a) of this chapter to request employment authorization. Except in the case of an alien whose asylum application has been recommended for approval, or in the case of an alien who filed an asylum application prior to January 4, 1995, the application shall be submitted no earlier than 150 days after the date on which a complete asylum application submitted in accordance with §§ 208.3 and 208.4 has been received. In the case of an applicant whose asylum application has been recommended for approval, the applicant may apply for employment authorization when he or she receives notice of the recommended approval. If an asylum application has been returned as incomplete in accordance with § 208.3(c)(3), the 150-day period will commence upon receipt by the Service of a complete asylum application. An applicant whose asylum application has been denied by an asylum officer or by an immigration judge within the 150-day period shall not be eligible to apply for employment authorization. If an asylum application is denied prior to a decision on the application for employment authorization, the application for employment authorization shall be denied. If the asylum application is not so denied, the Service shall have 30 days from the date of filing of the request employment authorization to grant or deny that application, except that no employment authorization shall be issued to an asylum applicant prior to the expiration of the 180-day period following the filing of the asylum application filed on or after April 1, 1997.

(2) The time periods within which the alien may not apply for employment authorization and within which USCIS must respond to any such application and within which the asylum application must be adjudicated pursuant to section 208(d)(5)(A)(iii) of the Act shall begin when the alien has filed a complete asylum application in accordance with §§ 208.3 and 208.4. Any delay requested or caused by the applicant shall not be counted as part of these time periods, including delays caused by failure without good cause to follow the requirements for fingerprint processing. Such time periods shall also be extended by the equivalent of the time between issuance of a request for evidence pursu-

ant to § 103.2(b)(8) of this chapter and the receipt of the applicant's response to such request.

(3) The provisions of paragraphs (a)(1) and (a)(2) of this section apply to applications for asylum filed on or after January 4, 1995.

(4) Employment authorization pursuant to § 274a.12(c)(8) of this chapter may not be granted to an alien who fails to appear for a scheduled interview before an asylum officer or a hearing before an immigration judge, unless the applicant demonstrates that the failure to appear was the result of exceptional circumstances.

(b) Renewal and termination. Employment authorization shall be renewable, in increments to be determined by USCIS, for the continuous period of time necessary for the asylum officer or immigration judge to decide the asylum application and, if necessary, for completion of any administrative or judicial review.

(1) If the asylum application is denied by the asylum officer, the employment authorization shall terminate at the expiration of the employment authorization document or 60 days after the denial of asylum, whichever is longer.

(2) If the application is denied by the immigration judge, the Board of Immigration Appeals, or a Federal court, the employment authorization terminates upon the expiration of the employment authorization document, unless the applicant has filed an appropriate request for administrative or judicial review.

(c) Supporting evidence for renewal of employment authorization. In order for employment authorization to be renewed under this section, the alien must request employment authorization in accordance with the form instructions. USCIS may require that an alien establish that he or she has continued to pursue an asylum application before an immigration judge or sought administrative or judicial review. For purposes of employment authorization, pursuit of an asylum application is established by presenting one of the following, depending on the stage of the alien's immigration proceedings:

(1) If the alien's case is pending in proceedings before the immigration judge, and the alien wishes to continue to pursue his or her asylum application, a copy of any asylum denial, referral notice, or charging document placing the alien in such proceedings;

(2) If the immigration judge has denied asylum, a copy of the document issued by the Board of Immigration Appeals to show that a timely appeal has been filed from a denial of the asylum application by the immigration judge; or

(3) If the Board of Immigration Appeals has dismissed the alien's appeal of a denial of asylum, or sustained an appeal by the Service of a grant of asylum, a copy of the petition for judicial review or for habeas corpus pursuant to section 242 of the Act, date stamped by the appropriate court.

(d) In order for employment authorization to be renewed before its expiration, the application for renewal must be received by the Service 90 days prior to expiration of the employment authorization.

HISTORY:

[55 FR 30680, July 27, 1990; 58 FR 12148, Mar. 3, 1993, as corrected at 58 FR 14145, Mar. 16, 1993; 59 FR 62298, Dec. 5, 1994; 60 FR 21974, May 4, 1995; 60 FR 34090, June 30, 1995; 62 FR 10312, 10340, Mar. 6, 1997; 63 FR 12979, 12986, Mar. 17, 1998; 76 FR 53764, 53784, Aug. 29, 2011; 85 FR 37502, 37545, June 22, 2020; 85 FR 38532, 38626, June 26, 2020; 87 FR 57795, 57797, Sept. 22, 2022]

§ 208.8 Limitations on travel outside the United States.

(a) An applicant who leaves the United States without first obtaining advance parole under § 212.5(f) of this chapter shall be presumed to have abandoned his or her application under this section.

(b) An applicant who leaves the United States pursuant to advance parole under § 212.5(f) of this chapter and returns to the country of claimed persecution shall be presumed to have abandoned his or her application, unless the applicant is able to establish compelling reasons for such return.

HISTORY:

[55 FR 30680, July 27, 1990; 59 FR 62299, Dec. 5, 1994; 62 FR 10312, 10341, Mar. 6, 1997; 65 FR 82254, 82255, Dec. 28, 2000; 66 FR 7863, Jan. 26, 2001]

§ 208.9 Procedure for interview before an asylum officer.

(a) Claims adjudicated. USCIS shall adjudicate the claim of each asylum applicant whose application is complete within the meaning of § 208.3(a)(2) or (c)(3), when applicable, and is within the jurisdiction of USCIS pursuant to § 208.2(a). In all cases, such proceedings shall be conducted in accordance with section 208 of the Act.

(1) Timing of interview. For interviews on asylum applications within the jurisdiction of USCIS pursuant to § 208.2(a)(1)(ii), USCIS shall not schedule the interview to take place fewer than 21 days after the applicant has been served with a record of the positive credible fear determination pursuant to § 208.30(f), unless the applicant requests in writing that an interview be scheduled sooner. The asylum officer shall conduct the interview within 45 days of the applicant being served with a positive credible fear determination made by an asylum officer pursuant to § 208.30(f) or made by an immigration judge pursuant to 8 CFR 1208.30, subject to the need to reschedule an interview due to exigent circumstances, such as the unavailability of an asylum officer to conduct the interview, the inability of the applicant to attend the interview due to illness, the inability to timely secure an appropriate interpreter pursuant to paragraph (g)(2) of this section, or the closure of the asylum office.

(2) [Reserved]

(b) Conduct and purpose of interview. The asylum officer shall conduct the interview in a nonadversarial manner and, except at the request of the applicant, separate and apart from the general public. The purpose of the interview shall be to elicit all relevant and useful information bearing on the applicant's eligibility for asylum. For interviews on applications within the jurisdiction of USCIS pursuant to § 208.2(a)(1)(ii), the asylum officer shall also elicit all relevant and useful information bearing on the applicant's eligibility for withholding of removal under the Act and protection under the Convention Against Torture, and, as appropriate, elicit sufficient information to make a determination whether there is a significant possibility that the applicant's spouse or child, if included in the request for asylum, has experienced or fears harm that would be an independent basis for asylum, withholding of removal under the Act, or protection under the Convention Against Torture in the event that the principal applicant is not granted asylum. If the asylum officer determines that there is a significant possibility that the applicant's spouse or child has experienced or fears harm that would be an independent basis for asylum, withholding of removal under the Act, or protection under the Convention Against Torture, the asylum officer shall inform the spouse or child of that determination. At the time of the interview, the applicant must provide complete information regarding the applicant's identity, including name, date and place of birth, and nationality, and may be required to register this identity. The applicant may have counsel or a representative present, may present witnesses, and may submit affidavits of witnesses and other evidence.

(c) Authority of asylum officer. The asylum officer shall have authority to administer oaths, verify the identity of the applicant (including through the use of electronic means), verify the identity of any interpreter, present evidence, receive evidence, and question the applicant and any witnesses.

(d) Completion of the interview. Upon completion of the interview before an asylum officer:

(1) The applicant or the applicant's representative will have an opportunity to make a statement or comment on the evidence presented. The representative will also have the opportunity to ask follow-up questions of the applicant and any witness. The asylum officer may, in the asylum officer's discretion, limit the length of any statement or comment and may require its submission in writing.

(2) USCIS shall inform the applicant that the applicant must appear in person to receive and to acknowledge receipt of the decision of the asylum officer and any other accompanying material at a time and place designated by the asylum officer, except as otherwise provided by the asylum officer. An applicant's failure to appear to receive and acknowledge receipt of the decision will be treated as delay caused by the applicant for purposes of § 208.7.

(e) Extensions. The asylum officer will consider evidence submitted by the applicant together with the applicant's asylum application.

(1) For applications being considered under § 208.2(a)(1)(i), the applicant must submit any documentary evidence at least 14 calendar days in advance of the interview date. As a matter of discretion, the asylum officer may consider evidence submitted within the 14-day period prior to the interview date or may grant the applicant a brief extension of time during which the applicant may submit additional evidence. Any such extension will be treated as a delay caused by the applicant for purposes of § 208.7.

(2) For applications being considered under § 208.2(a)(1)(ii), the asylum officer may grant the applicant a brief extension of time during which the applicant may submit additional evidence, but the asylum officer shall not grant any extension to submit additional evidence that would prevent a decision from being issued on the application within 60 days of service of the positive credible fear determination made by an asylum officer pursuant to § 208.30(f) or made by an immigration judge pursuant to 8 CFR 1208.30 except when the interview has been rescheduled due to exigent circumstances pursuant to paragraph (a)(1) of this section.

(f) Record.

(1) The asylum application, as defined in § 208.3(a), all supporting information provided by the applicant, any comments submitted by the Department of State or by DHS, and any other unclassified information considered by the asylum officer in the written decision shall comprise the record.

(2) For interviews on asylum applications within the jurisdiction of USCIS pursuant to § 208.2(a)(1)(ii), except for statements made off the record with the permission of the asylum officer, the interview shall be recorded. A verbatim transcript of the interview shall be prepared and included in the referral package to the immigration judge as described in § 208.14(c)(1), with a copy also provided to the applicant.

(g) Interpreters.

(1) Except as provided in paragraph (g)(2) of this section, an applicant unable to proceed with the interview in English must provide, at no expense to USCIS, a competent interpreter fluent in both English and the applicant's native language or any other language in which the applicant is fluent. The interpreter must be at least 18 years of age. Neither the applicant's attorney or representative of record, a witness testifying on the applicant's behalf, nor a representative or employee of the applicant's country of nationality, or if stateless, country of last habitual residence, may serve as the applicant's interpreter. Failure without good cause to comply with this paragraph (g)(1) may be considered a failure to appear for the interview for purposes of § 208.10.

(2) Notwithstanding paragraph (h) of this section, for interviews on asylum applications within the jurisdiction of USCIS pursuant to § 208.2(a)(1)(ii), if the applicant is unable to proceed effectively in English, the asylum officer shall arrange for the assistance of an interpreter in conducting the interview. The interpreter must be at least 18 years of age. Neither the applicant's attorney or representative of record, a witness testifying on the applicant's behalf, nor a representative or employee of the applicant's country of nationality, or if stateless, country of last habitual residence, may serve as the applicant's interpreter. If a USCIS interpreter is unavailable, USCIS will attribute any resulting delay to USCIS for the purposes of employment authorization pursuant to § 208.7.

(h) [Reserved]

(i) Dependents of applicants being considered under § 208.2(a)(1)(ii). This paragraph (i) governs when an applicant whose application for asylum is being considered under § 208.2(a)(1)(ii) is not granted asylum pursuant to § 208.14(c) and has included a spouse or children within their request for asylum. The asylum officer will make a determination whether there is a significant possibility that the spouse or child has experienced or fears harm that would be an independent basis for asylum, withholding of removal under the Act, or protection under the Convention Against Torture, based on the information elicited pursuant to paragraph (b) of this section. This determination will be included in the record, as otherwise described in paragraph (f) of this section. Referral of the principal applicant's application to an immigration judge, along with the appropriate charging documents, will not be made until any pending application by the spouse or child as a principal applicant is adjudicated.

HISTORY:

[55 FR 30680, July 27, 1990; 59 FR 62299, Dec. 5, 1994; 62 FR 10312, 10341, Mar. 6, 1997; 65 FR 76121, 76133, Dec. 6, 2000; 76 FR 53764, 53784, Aug. 29, 2011; 85 FR 38532, 38627, June 26, 2020; 85 FR 59655, 59660, Sept. 23, 2020; 86 FR 15072, 15076, Mar. 22, 2021; 86 FR 51781, 51788, Sept. 17, 2021; 87 FR 14757, Mar. 16, 2022; 87 FR 14757, 14763, Mar. 16, 2022; 87 FR 18078, 18216, Mar. 29, 2022; 88 FR 16372, Mar. 17, 2023; 88 FR 16372, 16378, Mar. 17, 2023]

§ 208.10 Failure to appear at an interview before an asylum officer or failure to follow requirements for fingerprint processing.

Failure to appear for a scheduled interview without prior authorization may result in dismissal of the application or waiver of the right to an interview. Failure to comply with fingerprint processing requirements without good cause may result in dismissal of the application or waiver of the right to an adjudication by an asylum officer. Failure to appear shall be excused if the notice of the interview or fingerprint appointment was not mailed to the applicant's current address and such address had been provided to the USCIS by the applicant prior to the date of mailing in accordance with section 265 of the Act and regulations promulgated thereunder, unless the asylum officer determines that the applicant received reasonable notice of the interview or fingerprinting appointment. Failure to appear at the interview or fingerprint appointment will be excused if the applicant demonstrates that such failure was the result of exceptional circumstances.

HISTORY:

[55 FR 30680, July 27, 1990; 59 FR 62300, Dec. 5, 1994; 62 FR 10312, 10341, Mar. 6, 1997; 63 FR 12979, 12986, Mar. 17, 1998; 76 FR 53764, 53784, Aug. 29, 2011; 85 FR 38532, 38627, June 26, 2020; 87 FR 57795, 57798, Sept. 22, 2022]

§ 208.11 Comments from the Department of State.

(a) U.S. Citizenship and Immigration Services (USCIS) may request, at its discretion, specific comments from the Department of State regarding individual cases or types of claims under consideration, or such other information as USCIS deems appropriate.

(b) With respect to any asylum application, the Department of State may provide, at its discretion, to USCIS:

(1) Detailed country conditions information relevant to eligibility for asylum or withholding of removal;

(2) An assessment of the accuracy of the applicant's assertions about conditions in his or her country of nationality or habitual residence and his or her particular situation;

(3) Information about whether persons who are similarly situated to the applicant are persecuted or tortured in the applicant's country of nationality or habitual residence and the frequency of such persecution or torture; or

(4) Such other information as it deems relevant.

(c) Any comments received pursuant to paragraph (b) of this section shall be made part of the record. Unless the comments are classified under the applicable Executive Order, the applicant shall be provided an opportunity to review and respond to such comments prior to the issuance of any decision to deny the application.

HISTORY:

[55 FR 30680, July 27, 1990; 59 FR 62300, Dec. 5, 1994; 62 FR 10312, 10341, Mar. 6, 1997; 64 FR 8478, 8488, Feb. 19, 1999; 74 FR 15367, 15369, Apr. 6, 2009]

§ 208.12 Reliance on information compiled by other sources.

(a) In deciding an asylum application, or in deciding whether the alien has a credible fear of persecution or torture pursuant to § 208.30 of this part, or a reasonable fear of persecution or torture pursuant to § 208.31, the asylum officer may rely on material provided by the Department of State, other USCIS offices or other credible sources, such as international organizations, private voluntary agencies, news organizations, or academic institutions.

(b) Nothing in this part shall be construed to entitle the applicant to conduct discovery directed toward the records, officers, agents, or employees of the Service, the Department of Justice, or the Department of State. Persons may continue to seek documents available through a Freedom of Information Act (FOIA) request pursuant to 8 CFR part 103.

HISTORY:

[55 FR 30680, July 27, 1990; 59 FR 62300, Dec. 4, 1995; 62 FR 10312, 10342, Mar. 6, 1997; 64 FR 8478, 8488, Feb. 19, 1999; 65 FR 76121, 76133, Dec. 6, 2000; 76 FR 53764, 53784, Aug. 29, 2011]

§ 208.13 Establishing asylum eligibility. [Effective until December 31, 2025]

(a) Burden of proof. The burden of proof is on the applicant for asylum to establish that he or she is a refugee as defined in section 101(a)(42) of the Act. The testimony of the applicant, if credible, may be sufficient to sustain the burden of proof without corroboration. The fact that the applicant previously established a credible fear of persecution for purposes of section 235(b)(1)(B) of the Act does not relieve the alien of the additional burden of establishing eligibility for asylum.

(b) Eligibility. The applicant may qualify as a refugee either because he or she has suffered past persecution or because he or she has a well-founded fear of future persecution.

(1) Past persecution. An applicant shall be found to be a refugee on the basis of past persecution if the applicant can establish that he or she has suffered persecution in the past in the applicant's country of nationality or, if stateless, in his or her country of last habitual residence, on account of race, religion, nationality, membership in a particular social group, or political opinion, and is unable or unwilling to return to, or avail himself or herself of the protection of, that country owing to such persecution. An applicant who has been found to have established such past persecution shall also be presumed to have a well-founded fear of persecution on the basis of the original claim. That presumption may be rebutted if an asylum officer or immigration judge makes one of the findings described in paragraph (b)(1)(i) of this section. If the applicant's fear of future persecution is unrelated to the past persecution, the applicant bears the burden of establishing that the fear is well-founded.

(i) Discretionary referral or denial. Except as provided in paragraph (b)(1)(iii) of this section, an asylum officer shall, in the exercise of his or her discretion, refer or deny, or an immigration judge, in the exercise of his or her discretion, shall deny the asylum application of an alien found to be a refugee on the basis of past persecution if any of the following is found by a preponderance of the evidence:

(A) There has been a fundamental change in circumstances such that the applicant no longer has a well-founded fear of persecution in the applicant's country of nationality or, if stateless, in the applicant's country of last habitual residence, on account of race, religion, nationality, membership in a particular social group, or political opinion; or

(B) The applicant could avoid future persecution by relocating to another part of the applicant's country of nationality or, if stateless, another part of the applicant's country of last habitual residence, and under all the circumstances, it would be reasonable to expect the applicant to do so.

(ii) Burden of proof. In cases in which an applicant has demonstrated past persecution under paragraph (b)(1) of this section, the Service shall bear the burden of establishing by a preponderance of the evidence the requirements of paragraphs (b)(1)(i)(A) or (B) of this section.

(iii) Grant in the absence of well-founded fear of persecution. An applicant described in paragraph (b)(1)(i) of this section who is not barred from a grant of asylum under paragraph (c) of this section, may be granted asylum, in the exercise of the decision-maker's discretion, if:

(A) The applicant has demonstrated compelling reasons for being unwilling or unable to return to the country arising out of the severity of the past persecution; or

(B) The applicant has established that there is a reasonable possibility that he or she may suffer other serious harm upon removal to that country.

(2) Well-founded fear of persecution

(i) An applicant has a well-founded fear of persecution if:

(A) The applicant has a fear of persecution in his or her country of nationality or, if stateless, in his or her country of last habitual residence, on account of race, religion, nationality, membership in a particular social group, or political opinion;

(B) There is a reasonable possibility of suffering such persecution if he or she were to return to that country; and

(C) He or she is unable or unwilling to return to, or avail himself or herself of the protection of, that country because of such fear.

(ii) An applicant does not have a well-founded fear of persecution if the applicant could avoid persecution by relocating to another part of the applicant's country of nationality or, if stateless, another part of the applicant's country of last habitual residence, if under all the circumstances it would be reasonable to expect the applicant to do so.

(iii) In evaluating whether the applicant has sustained the burden of proving that he or she has a well-founded fear of persecution, the asylum officer or immigration judge shall not require the applicant to provide evidence that there is a reasonable possibility he or she would be singled out individually for persecution if:

(A) The applicant establishes that there is a pattern or practice in his or her country of nationality or, if stateless, in his or her country of last habitual residence, of persecution of a group of persons similarly situated to the applicant on account of race, religion, nationality, membership in a particular social group, or political opinion; and

(B) The applicant establishes his or her own inclusion in, and identification with, such group of persons such that his or her fear of persecution upon return is reasonable.

(3) Reasonableness of internal relocation. For purposes of determinations under paragraphs (b)(1)(i) and (ii) and (b)(2) of this section, adjudicators should consider the totality of the relevant circumstances regarding an applicant's prospects for relocation, including the size of the country of nationality or last habitual residence, the geographic locus of the alleged persecution, the size, reach, or numerosity of the alleged persecutor, and the applicant's demonstrated ability to relocate to the United States in order to apply for asylum.

(i) In cases in which the applicant has not established past persecution, the applicant shall bear the burden of establishing that it would not be reasonable for him or her to relocate, unless the persecution is by a government or is government-sponsored.

(ii) In cases in which the persecutor is a government or is governmentsponsored, it shall be presumed that internal relocation would not be reasonable, unless DHS establishes by a preponderance of the evidence that, under all the circumstances, it would be reasonable for the applicant to relocate.

(iii) Regardless of whether an applicant has established persecution in the past, in cases in which the persecutor is not the government or a government-sponsored actor, or otherwise is a private actor, there shall be a presumption that internal relocation would be reasonable unless the applicant establishes, by a preponderance of the evidence, that it would be unreasonable to relocate.

(iv) For purposes of determinations under paragraphs (b)(3)(ii) and (iii) of this section, persecutors who are private actors-including persecutors who are gang members, officials acting outside their official capacity, family members who are not themselves government officials, or neighbors who are not themselves government officials-shall not be considered to be persecutors who are the government or government-sponsored absent evidence that the government sponsored the persecution.

(c) Mandatory denials —

(1) Applications filed on or after April 1, 1997. For applications filed on or after April 1, 1997, an applicant shall not qualify for asylum if section 208(a)(2) or 208(b)(2) of the Act applies to the applicant. If the applicant is found to be ineligible for asylum under either section 208(a)(2) or 208(b)(2) of the Act, the applicant shall be considered for eligibility for withholding of removal under section 241(b)(3) of the Act. The applicant shall also be considered for eligibility for withholding of removal under the Convention Against Torture if the applicant requests such consideration or if the evidence presented by the alien indicates that the alien may be tortured in the country of removal.

(2) Applications filed before April 1, 1997

(i) An immigration judge or asylum officer shall not grant asylum to any applicant who filed his or her application before April 1, 1997, if the alien:

(A) Having been convicted by a final judgment of a particularly serious crime in the United States, constitutes a danger to the community;

(B) Has been firmly resettled within the meaning of § 208.15;

(C) Can reasonably be regarded as a danger to the security of the United States;

(D) Has been convicted of an aggravated felony, as defined in section 101(a)(43) of the Act; or

(E) Ordered, incited, assisted, or otherwise participated in the persecution of any person on account of race, religion, nationality, membership in a particular social group, or political opinion.

(F) Is described within section 212(a)(3)(B)(i)(I),(II), and (III) of the Act as it existed prior to April 1, 1997, and as amended by the Anti-terrorist and Effective Death Penalty Act of 1996 (AEDPA), unless it is determined that there are no reasonable grounds to believe that the individual is a danger to the security of the United States.

(ii) If the evidence indicates that one of the above grounds apply to the applicant, he or she shall have the burden of proving by a preponderance of the evidence that he or she did not so act.

(3) [Removed and reserved.]

(4) [Removed and reserved.]

(5) [Removed and reserved.]

(6) Additional limitations on eligibility for asylum. For applications filed on or after November 20, 2020, an alien shall be found ineligible for asylum if:

(i) The alien has been convicted on or after such date of an offense arising under sections 274(a)(1)(A), 274(a)(2), or 276 of the Act;

(ii) The alien has been convicted on or after such date of a Federal, State, tribal, or local crime that the asylum officer knows or has reason to believe was committed in support, promotion, or furtherance of the activity of a criminal street gang as that term is defined either under the jurisdiction where the conviction occurred or in section 521(a) of title 18;

(iii) The alien has been convicted on or after such date of an offense for driving while intoxicated or impaired as those terms are defined under the jurisdiction where the conviction occurred (including a conviction for driving while under the influence of or impaired by alcohol or drugs) without regard to whether the conviction is classified as a misdemeanor or felony under Federal, State, tribal, or local law, in which such impaired driving was a cause of serious bodily injury or death of another person;

(iv)(A) The alien has been convicted on or after such date of a second or subsequent offense for driving while intoxicated or impaired as those terms are defined under the jurisdiction where the conviction occurred (including a conviction for driving while under the influence of or impaired by alcohol or drugs) without regard to whether the conviction is classified as a misdemeanor or felony under Federal, State, tribal, or local law;

(B) A finding under paragraph (c)(6)(iv)(A) of this section does not require the asylum officer to find the first conviction for driving while intoxicated or impaired (including a conviction for driving while under the influence of or impaired by alcohol or drugs) as a predicate offense. The asylum officer need only make a factual determination that the alien was previously convicted for driving while intoxicated or impaired as those terms are defined under the jurisdiction where the convictions occurred (including a conviction for driving while under the influence of or impaired by alcohol or drugs).

(v)(A) The alien has been convicted on or after such date of a crime that involves conduct amounting to a crime of stalking; or a crime of child abuse, child neglect, or child abandonment; or that involves conduct amounting to a domestic assault or battery offense, including a misdemeanor crime of domestic violence, as described in section 922(g)(9) of title 18, a misdemeanor crime of domestic violence as described in section 921(a)(33) of title 18, a crime of domestic violence as described in section 12291(a)(8) of title 34, or any crime based on conduct in which the alien harassed, coerced, intimidated, voluntarily or recklessly used (or threatened to use) force or violence against, or inflicted physical injury or physical pain, however slight, upon a person, and committed by:

(1) An alien who is a current or former spouse of the person;

(2) An alien with whom the person shares a child in common;

(3) An alien who is cohabiting with or has cohabited with the person as a spouse;

(4) An alien similarly situated to a spouse of the person under the domestic or family violence laws of the jurisdiction where the offense occurs; or

(5) Any other alien against a person who is protected from that alien's acts under the domestic or family violence laws of the United States or any State, tribal government, or unit of local government.

(B) In making a determination under paragraph (c)(6)(v)(A) of this section, including in determining the existence of a domestic relationship between the alien and the victim, the underlying conduct of the crime may be considered and the asylum officer is not limited to facts found by the criminal court or provided in the underlying record of conviction.

(C) An alien who was convicted of offenses described in paragraph (c)(6)(v)(A) of this section is not subject to ineligibility for asylum on that basis if the alien would be described in section 237(a)(7)(A) of the Act were the crimes or conduct considered grounds for deportability under section 237(a)(2)(E)(i) through (ii) of the Act.

(vi) The alien has been convicted on or after such date of—

(A) Any felony under Federal, State, tribal, or local law;

(B) Any misdemeanor offense under Federal, State, tribal, or local law involving:

(1) The possession or use of an identification document, authentication feature, or false identification document without lawful authority, unless the alien can establish that the conviction resulted from circumstances showing that the document was presented before boarding a common carrier, that the document related to the alien's eligibility to enter the United States, that the alien used the document to depart a country in which the alien has claimed a fear of persecution, and that the alien claimed a fear of persecution without delay upon presenting himself or herself to an immigration officer upon arrival at a United States port of entry;

(2) The receipt of Federal public benefits, as defined in 8 U.S.C. 1611(c), from a Federal entity, or the receipt of similar public benefits from a State, tribal, or local entity, without lawful authority; or

(3) Possession or trafficking of a controlled substance or controlledsubstance paraphernalia, other than a single offense involving possession for one's own use of 30 grams or less of marijuana.

(vii) The asylum officer knows or has reason to believe that the alien has engaged on or after such date in acts of battery or extreme cruelty as defined in 8 CFR 204.2(c)(1)(vi), upon a person, and committed by:

(A) An alien who is a current or former spouse of the person;

(B) An alien with whom the person shares a child in common;

(C) An alien who is cohabiting with or has cohabited with the person as a spouse;

(D) An alien similarly situated to a spouse of the person under the domestic or family violence laws of the jurisdiction where the offense occurs; or

(E) Any other alien against a person who is protected from that alien's acts under the domestic or family violence laws of the United States or any State, tribal government, or unit of local government, even if the acts did not result in a criminal conviction;

(F) Except that an alien who was convicted of offenses or engaged in conduct described in paragraph (c)(6)(vii) of this section is not subject to ineligibility for asylum on that basis if the alien would be described in section 237(a)(7)(A) of the Act were the crimes or conduct considered grounds for deportability under section 237(a)(2)(E)(i)–(ii) of the Act.

(7) For purposes of paragraph (c)(6) of this section:

(i) The term "felony" means any crime defined as a felony by the relevant jurisdiction (Federal, State, tribal, or local) of conviction, or any crime punishable by more than one year of imprisonment.

(ii) The term "misdemeanor" means any crime defined as a misdemeanor by the relevant jurisdiction (Federal, State, tribal, or local) of conviction, or any crime not punishable by more than one year of imprisonment.

(iii) Whether any activity or conviction also may constitute a basis for removability under the Act is immaterial to a determination of asylum eligibility.

(iv) All references to a criminal offense or criminal conviction shall be deemed to include any attempt, conspiracy, or solicitation to commit the offense or any other inchoate form of the offense.

(v) No order vacating a conviction, modifying a sentence, clarifying a sentence, or otherwise altering a conviction or sentence, shall have any effect unless the asylum officer determines that—

(A) The court issuing the order had jurisdiction and authority to do so; and

(B) The order was not entered for rehabilitative purposes or for purposes of ameliorating the immigration consequences of the conviction or sentence.

(8) For purposes of paragraph (c)(7)(v)(B) of this section, the order shall be presumed to be for the purpose of ameliorating immigration consequences if:

(i) The order was entered after the initiation of any proceeding to remove the alien from the United States; or

(ii) The alien moved for the order more than one year after the date of the original order of conviction or sentencing.

(9) An asylum officer is authorized to look beyond the face of any order purporting to vacate a conviction, modify a sentence, or clarify a sentence to determine whether the requirements of paragraph (c)(7)(v) of this section have been met in order to determine whether such order should be given any effect under this section.

(d) Discretion. Factors that fall short of grounds of mandatory denial of an asylum application may constitute discretionary considerations.

(1) The following are significant adverse discretionary factors that a decision-maker shall consider, if applicable, in determining whether an alien merits a grant of asylum in the exercise of discretion:

(i) An alien's unlawful entry or unlawful attempted entry into the United States unless such entry or attempted entry was made in immediate flight from persecution in a contiguous country or unless such entry or attempted entry was made by an alien under the age of 18 at the time the entry or attempted entry was made;

(ii) The failure of an alien to apply for protection from persecution or torture in at least one country outside the alien's country of citizenship, nationality, or last lawful habitual residence through which the alien transited before entering the United States unless:

(A) The alien received a final judgment denying the alien protection in such country;

(B) The alien demonstrates that he or she satisfies the definition of "victim of a severe form of trafficking in persons" provided in 8 CFR 214.11; or

(C) Such country or all such countries were, at the time of the transit, not parties to the 1951 Convention relating to the Status of Refugees, the 1967 Protocol relating to the Status of Refugees, or the Convention Against Torture and Other Cruel, Inhuman or Degrading Treatment or Punishment; and

(iii) An alien's use of fraudulent documents to enter the United States, unless the alien arrived in the United States by air, sea, or land directly from the applicant's home country without transiting through any other country.

(2)(i) The Secretary, except as provided in paragraph (d)(2)(ii) of this section, will not favorably exercise discretion under section 208 of the Act for an alien who:

(A) Immediately prior to his arrival in the United States or en route to the United States from the alien's country of citizenship, nationality, or last lawful habitual residence, spent more than 14 days in any one country unless:

(1) The alien demonstrates that he or she applied for protection from persecution or torture in such country and the alien received a final judgment denying the alien protection in such country;

(2) The alien demonstrates that he or she satisfies the definition of "victim of a severe form of trafficking in persons" provided in 8 CFR 214.11; or

(3) Such country was, at the time of the transit, not a party to the 1951 Convention relating to the Status of Refugees, the 1967 Protocol relating to the Status of Refugees, or the Convention against Torture and Other Cruel, Inhuman or Degrading Treatment or Punishment;

(B) Transits through more than one country between his country of citizenship, nationality, or last habitual residence and the United States unless:

(1) The alien demonstrates that he or she applied for protection from persecution or torture in at least one such country and received a final judgment denying the alien protection in that country;

(2) The alien demonstrates that he or she satisfies the definition of "victim of a severe form of trafficking in persons" provided in 8 CFR 214.11; or

(3) All such countries were, at the time of the transit, not parties to the 1951 Convention relating to the Status of Refugees, the 1967 Protocol relating to the Status of Refugees, or the Convention against Torture and Other Cruel, Inhuman or Degrading Treatment or Punishment;

(C) Would otherwise be subject to § 208.13(c) but for the reversal, vacatur, expungement, or modification of a conviction or sentence, unless the alien was found not guilty;

(D) Accrued more than one year of unlawful presence in the United States, as defined in sections 212(a)(9)(B)(ii) and (iii) of the Act, prior to filing an application for asylum;

(E) At the time the asylum application is filed with DHS has:

(1) Failed to timely file (or timely file a request for an extension of time to file) any required Federal, State, or local income tax returns;

(2) Failed to satisfy any outstanding Federal, State, or local tax obligations; or

(3) Has income that would result in tax liability under section 1 of the Internal Revenue Code of 1986 and that was not reported to the Internal Revenue Service;

(F) Has had two or more prior asylum applications denied for any reason;

(G) Has withdrawn a prior asylum application with prejudice or been found to have abandoned a prior asylum application;

(H) Failed to attend an interview regarding his asylum application with DHS, unless the alien shows by a preponderance of the evidence that:

(1) Exceptional circumstances prevented the alien from attending the interview; or

(2) The interview notice was not mailed to the last address provided by the alien or his or her representative and neither the alien nor the alien's representative received notice of the interview; or

(I) Was subject to a final order of removal, deportation, or exclusion and did not file a motion to reopen to seek asylum based on changed country conditions within one year of those changes in country conditions.

(ii) Where one or more of the adverse discretionary factors set forth in paragraph (d)(2)(i) of this section are present, the Secretary, in extraordinary circumstances, such as those involving national security or foreign policy considerations, or cases in which an alien, by clear and convincing evidence, demonstrates that the denial or referral (which may result in the denial by an immigration judge) of the application for asylum would result in exceptional and extremely unusual hardship to the alien, may favorably exercise discretion under section 208 of the Act, notwithstanding the applicability of paragraph (d)(2)(i). Depending on the gravity of the circumstances underlying the application of paragraph (d)(2)(i), a showing of extraordinary circumstances might still be insufficient to warrant a favorable exercise of discretion under section 208 of the Act.

(e) [Reserved]

(f) Lawful pathways condition. For applications filed by aliens who entered the United States between May 11, 2023, and May 11, 2025, also refer to the provisions on asylum eligibility described in § 208.33.

(g) Entry during emergency border circumstances. For an alien who entered the United States across the southern border (as that term is described in section 4(d) of the Presidential Proclamation of June 3, 2024, as defined in paragraph (h) of this section) between the dates described in section 1 and section 2(a) of such Proclamation (or the revocation of such Proclamation, whichever is earlier), or between the dates described in section 2(b) and section 2(a) of such Proclamation (or the revocation of such Proclamation, whichever is earlier), refer to the provisions on asylum eligibility described in § 208.35.

(h) References to the Presidential Proclamation of June 3, 2024. For purposes of paragraph (g) of this section and this chapter, the Presidential Proclamation of June 3, 2024, refers to Proclamation 10773 of June 3, 2024, as amended by the Presidential Proclamation of September 27, 2024. The Department intends that in the event the Presidential Proclamation of September 27, 2024, or the portions of this chapter referring to it are rendered inoperative by court order, this chapter shall continue to operate as if the references to that Proclamation have been stricken.

HISTORY:

[55 FR 30680, July 27, 1990; 59 FR 62300, Dec. 5, 1994; 62 FR 10312, 10342, Mar. 6, 1997; 64 FR 8478, 8488, Feb. 19, 1999; 65 FR 76121, 76133, Dec. 6, 2000; 83 FR 55934, 55952, Nov. 9, 2018; 84 FR 33829, 33843, July 16, 2019; 85 FR 67202, 67259, Oct. 21, 2020; 85 FR 80274, 80387, Dec. 11, 2020; 85 FR 82260, 82289, Dec. 17, 2020; 85 FR 84160, 84193, Dec. 23, 2020; 86 FR 6847, Jan. 25, 2021; 86 FR 15069, Mar. 22, 2021; 86 FR 73615, Dec. 28, 2021; 87 FR 79789, Dec. 28, 2022; 88 FR 31314, 31449, May 16, 2023; 89 FR 48710, 48769, June 7, 2024, as confirmed at 89 FR 81156, Oct. 7, 2024; 89 FR 81156, 81284, Oct. 7, 2024; 89 FR 105386, Dec. 27, 2024]

§ 208.13 Establishing asylum eligibility. [Effective December 31, 2025]

(a) Burden of proof. The burden of proof is on the applicant for asylum to establish that he or she is a refugee as defined in section 101(a)(42) of the Act. The testimony of the applicant, if credible, may be sufficient to sustain the burden of proof without corroboration. The fact that the applicant previously established a credible fear of persecution for purposes of section 235(b)(1)(B) of the Act does not relieve the alien of the additional burden of establishing eligibility for asylum.

(b) Eligibility. The applicant may qualify as a refugee either because he or she has suffered past persecution or because he or she has a well-founded fear of future persecution.

(1) Past persecution. An applicant shall be found to be a refugee on the basis of past persecution if the applicant can establish that he or she has suffered persecution in the past in the applicant's country of nationality or, if stateless, in his or her country of last habitual residence, on account of race, religion, nationality, membership in a particular social group, or political opinion, and is unable or unwilling to return to, or avail himself or herself of the protection of, that country owing to such persecution. An applicant who has been found to have established such past persecution shall also be presumed to have a well-founded fear of persecution on the basis of the original claim. That presumption may be rebutted if an asylum officer or immigration judge makes one of the findings described in paragraph (b)(1)(i) of this section. If the applicant's fear of future persecution is unrelated to the past persecution, the applicant bears the burden of establishing that the fear is well-founded.

(i) Discretionary referral or denial. Except as provided in paragraph (b)(1)(iii) of this section, an asylum officer shall, in the exercise of his or her discretion, refer or deny, or an immigration judge, in the exercise of his or her discretion, shall deny the asylum application of an alien found to be a refugee on the basis of past persecution if any of the following is found by a preponderance of the evidence:

(A) There has been a fundamental change in circumstances such that the applicant no longer has a well-founded fear of persecution in the applicant's country of nationality or, if stateless, in the applicant's country of last habitual residence, on account of race, religion, nationality, membership in a particular social group, or political opinion; or

(B) The applicant could avoid future persecution by relocating to another part of the applicant's country of nationality or, if stateless, another part of the applicant's country of last habitual residence, and under all the circumstances, it would be reasonable to expect the applicant to do so.

(ii) Burden of proof. In cases in which an applicant has demonstrated past persecution under paragraph (b)(1) of this section, the Service shall bear the burden of establishing by a preponderance of the evidence the requirements of paragraphs (b)(1)(i)(A) or (B) of this section.

(iii) Grant in the absence of well-founded fear of persecution. An applicant described in paragraph (b)(1)(i) of this section who is not barred from a grant of asylum under paragraph (c) of this section, may be granted asylum, in the exercise of the decision-maker's discretion, if:

(A) The applicant has demonstrated compelling reasons for being unwilling or unable to return to the country arising out of the severity of the past persecution; or

(B) The applicant has established that there is a reasonable possibility that he or she may suffer other serious harm upon removal to that country.

(2) Well-founded fear of persecution

(i) An applicant has a well-founded fear of persecution if:

(A) The applicant has a fear of persecution in his or her country of nationality or, if stateless, in his or her country of last habitual residence, on account of race, religion, nationality, membership in a particular social group, or political opinion;

(B) There is a reasonable possibility of suffering such persecution if he or she were to return to that country; and

(C) He or she is unable or unwilling to return to, or avail himself or herself of the protection of, that country because of such fear.

(ii) An applicant does not have a well-founded fear of persecution if the applicant could avoid persecution by relocating to another part of the applicant's country of nationality or, if stateless, another part of the applicant's country of last habitual residence, if under all the circumstances it would be reasonable to expect the applicant to do so.

(iii) In evaluating whether the applicant has sustained the burden of proving that he or she has a well-founded fear of persecution, the asylum officer or immigration judge shall not require the applicant to provide evidence that there is a reasonable possibility he or she would be singled out individually for persecution if:

(A) The applicant establishes that there is a pattern or practice in his or her country of nationality or, if stateless, in his or her country of last habitual residence, of persecution of a group of persons similarly situated to the applicant on account of race, religion, nationality, membership in a particular social group, or political opinion; and

(B) The applicant establishes his or her own inclusion in, and identification with, such group of persons such that his or her fear of persecution upon return is reasonable.

(3) Reasonableness of internal relocation. For purposes of determinations under paragraphs (b)(1)(i) and (ii) and (b)(2) of this section, adjudicators should consider the totality of the relevant circumstances regarding an applicant's prospects for relocation, including the size of the country of nationality or last habitual residence, the geographic locus of the alleged persecution, the size, reach, or numerosity of the alleged persecutor, and the applicant's demonstrated ability to relocate to the United States in order to apply for asylum.

(i) In cases in which the applicant has not established past persecution, the applicant shall bear the burden of establishing that it would not be reasonable for him or her to relocate, unless the persecution is by a government or is government-sponsored.

(ii) In cases in which the persecutor is a government or is governmentsponsored, it shall be presumed that internal relocation would not be reasonable, unless DHS establishes by a preponderance of the evidence that, under all the circumstances, it would be reasonable for the applicant to relocate.

(iii) Regardless of whether an applicant has established persecution in the past, in cases in which the persecutor is not the government or a government-sponsored actor, or otherwise is a private actor, there shall be a presumption that internal relocation would be reasonable unless the applicant establishes, by a preponderance of the evidence, that it would be unreasonable to relocate.

(iv) For purposes of determinations under paragraphs (b)(3)(ii) and (iii) of this section, persecutors who are private actors-including persecutors who are gang members, officials acting outside their official capacity, family members who are not themselves government officials, or neighbors who are not themselves government officials-shall not be considered to be persecutors who are the government or government-sponsored absent evidence that the government sponsored the persecution.

(c) Mandatory denials —

(1) Applications filed on or after April 1, 1997. For applications filed on or after April 1, 1997, an applicant shall not qualify for asylum if section 208(a)(2) or 208(b)(2) of the Act applies to the applicant. If the applicant is found to be ineligible for asylum under either section 208(a)(2) or 208(b)(2) of the Act, the applicant shall be considered for eligibility for withholding of removal under section 241(b)(3) of the Act. The applicant shall also be considered for eligibility for withholding of removal under the Convention Against Torture if the applicant requests such consideration or if the evidence presented by the alien indicates that the alien may be tortured in the country of removal.

(2) Applications filed before April 1, 1997

(i) An immigration judge or asylum officer shall not grant asylum to any applicant who filed his or her application before April 1, 1997, if the alien:

(A) Having been convicted by a final judgment of a particularly serious crime in the United States, constitutes a danger to the community;

(B) Has been firmly resettled within the meaning of § 208.15;

(C) Can reasonably be regarded as a danger to the security of the United States;

(D) Has been convicted of an aggravated felony, as defined in section 101(a)(43) of the Act; or

(E) Ordered, incited, assisted, or otherwise participated in the persecution of any person on account of race, religion, nationality, membership in a particular social group, or political opinion.

(F) Is described within section 212(a)(3)(B)(i)(I),(II), and (III) of the Act as it existed prior to April 1, 1997, and as amended by the Anti-terrorist and Effective Death Penalty Act of 1996 (AEDPA), unless it is determined that there are no reasonable grounds to believe that the individual is a danger to the security of the United States.

(ii) If the evidence indicates that one of the above grounds apply to the applicant, he or she shall have the burden of proving by a preponderance of the evidence that he or she did not so act.

(3) [Removed and reserved.]

(4) [Removed and reserved.]

(5) [Removed and reserved.]

(6) Additional limitations on eligibility for asylum. For applications filed on or after November 20, 2020, an alien shall be found ineligible for asylum if:

(i) The alien has been convicted on or after such date of an offense arising under sections 274(a)(1)(A), 274(a)(2), or 276 of the Act;

(ii) The alien has been convicted on or after such date of a Federal, State, tribal, or local crime that the asylum officer knows or has reason to believe was committed in support, promotion, or furtherance of the activity of a criminal street gang as that term is defined either under the jurisdiction where the conviction occurred or in section 521(a) of title 18;

(iii) The alien has been convicted on or after such date of an offense for driving while intoxicated or impaired as those terms are defined under the jurisdiction where the conviction occurred (including a conviction for driving while under the influence of or impaired by alcohol or drugs) without regard to whether the conviction is classified as a misdemeanor or felony under Federal, State, tribal, or local law, in which such impaired driving was a cause of serious bodily injury or death of another person;

(iv)(A) The alien has been convicted on or after such date of a second or subsequent offense for driving while intoxicated or impaired as those terms are defined under the jurisdiction where the conviction occurred (including a conviction for driving while under the influence of or impaired by alcohol or drugs) without regard to whether the conviction is classified as a misdemeanor or felony under Federal, State, tribal, or local law;

(B) A finding under paragraph (c)(6)(iv)(A) of this section does not require the asylum officer to find the first conviction for driving while intoxicated or impaired (including a conviction for driving while under the influence of or impaired by alcohol or drugs) as a predicate offense. The asylum officer need only make a factual determination that the alien was previously convicted for driving while intoxicated or impaired as those terms are defined under the jurisdiction where the convictions occurred (including a conviction for driving while under the influence of or impaired by alcohol or drugs).

(v)(A) The alien has been convicted on or after such date of a crime that involves conduct amounting to a crime of stalking; or a crime of child abuse, child neglect, or child abandonment; or that involves conduct amounting to a domestic assault or battery offense, including a misdemeanor crime of domestic violence, as described in section 922(g)(9) of title 18, a misdemeanor crime of domestic violence as described in section 921(a)(33) of title 18, a crime of domestic violence as described in section 12291(a)(8) of title 34, or any crime based on conduct in which the alien harassed, coerced, intimidated, voluntarily or recklessly used (or threatened to use) force or violence against, or inflicted physical injury or physical pain, however slight, upon a person, and committed by:

(1) An alien who is a current or former spouse of the person;

(2) An alien with whom the person shares a child in common;

(3) An alien who is cohabiting with or has cohabited with the person as a spouse;

(4) An alien similarly situated to a spouse of the person under the domestic or family violence laws of the jurisdiction where the offense occurs; or

(5) Any other alien against a person who is protected from that alien's acts under the domestic or family violence laws of the United States or any State, tribal government, or unit of local government.

(B) In making a determination under paragraph (c)(6)(v)(A) of this section, including in determining the existence of a domestic relationship between the alien and the victim, the underlying conduct of the crime may be considered and the asylum officer is not limited to facts found by the criminal court or provided in the underlying record of conviction.

(C) An alien who was convicted of offenses described in paragraph (c)(6)(v)(A) of this section is not subject to ineligibility for asylum on that basis if the alien would be described in section 237(a)(7)(A) of the Act were the crimes or conduct considered grounds for deportability under section 237(a)(2)(E)(i) through (ii) of the Act.

(vi) The alien has been convicted on or after such date of—

(A) Any felony under Federal, State, tribal, or local law;

(B) Any misdemeanor offense under Federal, State, tribal, or local law involving:

(1) The possession or use of an identification document, authentication feature, or false identification document without lawful authority, unless the alien can establish that the conviction resulted from circumstances showing that the document was presented before boarding a common carrier, that the document related to the alien's eligibility to enter the United States, that the alien used the document to depart a country in which the alien has claimed a fear of persecution, and that the alien claimed a fear of persecution without delay upon presenting himself or herself to an immigration officer upon arrival at a United States port of entry;

(2) The receipt of Federal public benefits, as defined in 8 U.S.C. 1611(c), from a Federal entity, or the receipt of similar public benefits from a State, tribal, or local entity, without lawful authority; or

(3) Possession or trafficking of a controlled substance or controlledsubstance paraphernalia, other than a single offense involving possession for one's own use of 30 grams or less of marijuana.

(vii) The asylum officer knows or has reason to believe that the alien has engaged on or after such date in acts of battery or extreme cruelty as defined in 8 CFR 204.2(c)(1)(vi), upon a person, and committed by:

(A) An alien who is a current or former spouse of the person;

(B) An alien with whom the person shares a child in common;

(C) An alien who is cohabiting with or has cohabited with the person as a spouse;

(D) An alien similarly situated to a spouse of the person under the domestic or family violence laws of the jurisdiction where the offense occurs; or

(E) Any other alien against a person who is protected from that alien's acts under the domestic or family violence laws of the United States or any State, tribal government, or unit of local government, even if the acts did not result in a criminal conviction;

(F) Except that an alien who was convicted of offenses or engaged in conduct described in paragraph (c)(6)(vii) of this section is not subject to ineligibility for asylum on that basis if the alien would be described in section 237(a)(7)(A) of the Act were the crimes or conduct considered grounds for deportability under section 237(a)(2)(E)(i)–(ii) of the Act.

(7) For purposes of paragraph (c)(6) of this section:

(i) The term "felony" means any crime defined as a felony by the relevant jurisdiction (Federal, State, tribal, or local) of conviction, or any crime punishable by more than one year of imprisonment.

(ii) The term "misdemeanor" means any crime defined as a misdemeanor by the relevant jurisdiction (Federal, State, tribal, or local) of conviction, or any crime not punishable by more than one year of imprisonment.

(iii) Whether any activity or conviction also may constitute a basis for removability under the Act is immaterial to a determination of asylum eligibility.

(iv) All references to a criminal offense or criminal conviction shall be deemed to include any attempt, conspiracy, or solicitation to commit the offense or any other inchoate form of the offense.

(v) No order vacating a conviction, modifying a sentence, clarifying a sentence, or otherwise altering a conviction or sentence, shall have any effect unless the asylum officer determines that—

(A) The court issuing the order had jurisdiction and authority to do so; and

(B) The order was not entered for rehabilitative purposes or for purposes of ameliorating the immigration consequences of the conviction or sentence.

(8) For purposes of paragraph (c)(7)(v)(B) of this section, the order shall be presumed to be for the purpose of ameliorating immigration consequences if:

(i) The order was entered after the initiation of any proceeding to remove the alien from the United States; or

(ii) The alien moved for the order more than one year after the date of the original order of conviction or sentencing.

(9) An asylum officer is authorized to look beyond the face of any order purporting to vacate a conviction, modify a sentence, or clarify a sentence to determine whether the requirements of paragraph (c)(7)(v) of this section have been met in order to determine whether such order should be given any effect under this section.

(10) Aliens who pose a danger to the security of the United States—

(i) Public health emergencies. If a communicable disease has triggered an ongoing declaration of a public health emergency under Federal law, such as under section 319 of the Public Health Service Act, 42 U.S.C. 247d, or section 564 of the Food, Drug, and Cosmetic Act, 21 U.S.C. 360bbb–3, then an alien is ineligible for asylum under section 208 of the Act on the basis of there being reasonable grounds for regarding the alien as a danger to the security of the United States under section 208(b)(2)(A)(iv) of the Act if the alien:

(A) Exhibits symptoms indicating that he or she is afflicted with the disease, per guidance issued by the Secretary or the Attorney General, as appropriate, or

(B) Has come into contact with the disease within the number of days equivalent to the longest known incubation and contagion period for the disease, per guidance issued by the Secretary or the Attorney General, as appropriate.

(ii) Danger to the public health caused by an epidemic outside of the United States. If, regarding a communicable disease of public health significance as defined at 42 CFR 34.2(b), the Secretary and the Attorney General, in consultation with the Secretary of Health and Human Services, have jointly—

(A) Determined that the physical presence in the United States of aliens who are coming from a country or countries (or one or more subdivisions or regions thereof), or have embarked at a place or places, where such disease is prevalent or epidemic (or had come from that country or countries (or one or more subdivisions or regions thereof), or had embarked at that place or places, during a period in which the disease was prevalent or epidemic there) would cause a danger to the public health in the United States; and

(B) Designated the foreign country or countries (or one or more subdivisions or regions thereof), or place or places, and the period of time or circumstances under which they jointly deem it necessary for the public health that aliens or classes of aliens described in paragraph (c)(10)(ii)(A) of this section who are still within the number of days equivalent to the longest known incubation and contagion period for the disease be regarded as a danger to the security of the United States under section 208(b)(2)(A)(iv) of the Act, including any relevant exceptions as appropriate, then—

(C) An alien or class of aliens are ineligible for asylum under section 208 of the Act on the basis of there being reasonable grounds for regarding the alien or class of aliens as a danger to the security of the United States under section 208(b)(2)(A)(iv) of the Act if the alien or class of aliens are described in (c)(10)(ii)(A) of this section and are regarded as a danger to the security of the United States as provided for in paragraph (c)(10)(ii)(B) of this section.

(iii) The grounds for mandatory denial described in paragraphs (c)(10)(i) and (ii) of this section shall not apply to an alien who is applying for asylum or withholding of removal in the United States upon return from Canada to the United States and pursuant to the Agreement Between the Government of the United States and the Government of Canada for Cooperation in the Examination of Refugee Status Claims from Nationals of Third Countries.

(d) Discretion. Factors that fall short of grounds of mandatory denial of an asylum application may constitute discretionary considerations.

(1) The following are significant adverse discretionary factors that a decision-maker shall consider, if applicable, in determining whether an alien merits a grant of asylum in the exercise of discretion:

(i) An alien's unlawful entry or unlawful attempted entry into the United States unless such entry or attempted entry was made in immediate flight from persecution in a contiguous country or unless such entry or attempted entry was made by an alien under the age of 18 at the time the entry or attempted entry was made;

(ii) The failure of an alien to apply for protection from persecution or torture in at least one country outside the alien's country of citizenship, nationality, or last lawful habitual residence through which the alien transited before entering the United States unless:

(A) The alien received a final judgment denying the alien protection in such country;

(B) The alien demonstrates that he or she satisfies the definition of "victim of a severe form of trafficking in persons" provided in 8 CFR 214.11; or

(C) Such country or all such countries were, at the time of the transit, not parties to the 1951 Convention relating to the Status of Refugees, the 1967 Protocol relating to the Status of Refugees, or the Convention Against Torture and Other Cruel, Inhuman or Degrading Treatment or Punishment; and

(iii) An alien's use of fraudulent documents to enter the United States, unless the alien arrived in the United States by air, sea, or land directly from the applicant's home country without transiting through any other country.

(2)(i) The Secretary, except as provided in paragraph (d)(2)(ii) of this section, will not favorably exercise discretion under section 208 of the Act for an alien who:

(A) Immediately prior to his arrival in the United States or en route to the United States from the alien's country of citizenship, nationality, or last lawful habitual residence, spent more than 14 days in any one country unless:

(1) The alien demonstrates that he or she applied for protection from persecution or torture in such country and the alien received a final judgment denying the alien protection in such country;

(2) The alien demonstrates that he or she satisfies the definition of "victim of a severe form of trafficking in persons" provided in 8 CFR 214.11; or

(3) Such country was, at the time of the transit, not a party to the 1951 Convention relating to the Status of Refugees, the 1967 Protocol relating to the Status of Refugees, or the Convention against Torture and Other Cruel, Inhuman or Degrading Treatment or Punishment;

(B) Transits through more than one country between his country of citizenship, nationality, or last habitual residence and the United States unless:

(1) The alien demonstrates that he or she applied for protection from persecution or torture in at least one such country and received a final judgment denying the alien protection in that country;

(2) The alien demonstrates that he or she satisfies the definition of "victim of a severe form of trafficking in persons" provided in 8 CFR 214.11; or

(3) All such countries were, at the time of the transit, not parties to the 1951 Convention relating to the Status of Refugees, the 1967 Protocol relating to the Status of Refugees, or the Convention against Torture and Other Cruel, Inhuman or Degrading Treatment or Punishment;

(C) Would otherwise be subject to § 208.13(c) but for the reversal, vacatur, expungement, or modification of a conviction or sentence, unless the alien was found not guilty;

(D) Accrued more than one year of unlawful presence in the United States, as defined in sections 212(a)(9)(B)(ii) and (iii) of the Act, prior to filing an application for asylum;

(E) At the time the asylum application is filed with DHS has:

(1) Failed to timely file (or timely file a request for an extension of time to file) any required Federal, State, or local income tax returns;

(2) Failed to satisfy any outstanding Federal, State, or local tax obligations; or

(3) Has income that would result in tax liability under section 1 of the Internal Revenue Code of 1986 and that was not reported to the Internal Revenue Service;

(F) Has had two or more prior asylum applications denied for any reason;

(G) Has withdrawn a prior asylum application with prejudice or been found to have abandoned a prior asylum application;

(H) Failed to attend an interview regarding his asylum application with DHS, unless the alien shows by a preponderance of the evidence that:

(1) Exceptional circumstances prevented the alien from attending the interview; or

(2) The interview notice was not mailed to the last address provided by the alien or his or her representative and neither the alien nor the alien's representative received notice of the interview; or

(I) Was subject to a final order of removal, deportation, or exclusion and did not file a motion to reopen to seek asylum based on changed country conditions within one year of those changes in country conditions.

(ii) Where one or more of the adverse discretionary factors set forth in paragraph (d)(2)(i) of this section are present, the Secretary, in extraordinary circumstances, such as those involving national security or foreign policy considerations, or cases in which an alien, by clear and convincing evidence, demonstrates that the denial or referral (which may result in the denial by an immigration judge) of the application for asylum would result in exceptional and extremely unusual hardship to the alien, may favorably exercise discretion under section 208 of the Act, notwithstanding the applicability of paragraph (d)(2)(i). Depending on the gravity of the circumstances underlying the application of paragraph (d)(2)(i), a showing of extraordinary circumstances might still be insufficient to warrant a favorable exercise of discretion under section 208 of the Act.

(e) [Reserved]

(f) Lawful pathways condition. For applications filed by aliens who entered the United States between May 11, 2023, and May 11, 2025, also refer to the provisions on asylum eligibility described in § 208.33.

(g) Entry during emergency border circumstances. For an alien who entered the United States across the southern border (as that term is described in section 4(d) of the Presidential Proclamation of June 3, 2024, as defined in paragraph (h) of this section) between the dates described in section 1 and section 2(a) of such

Proclamation (or the revocation of such Proclamation, whichever is earlier), or between the dates described in section 2(b) and section 2(a) of such Proclamation (or the revocation of such Proclamation, whichever is earlier), refer to the provisions on asylum eligibility described in § 208.35.

(h) References to the Presidential Proclamation of June 3, 2024. For purposes of paragraph (g) of this section and this chapter, the Presidential Proclamation of June 3, 2024, refers to Proclamation 10773 of June 3, 2024, as amended by the Presidential Proclamation of September 27, 2024. The Department intends that in the event the Presidential Proclamation of September 27, 2024, or the portions of this chapter referring to it are rendered inoperative by court order, this chapter shall continue to operate as if the references to that Proclamation have been stricken.

HISTORY:

[55 FR 30680, July 27, 1990; 59 FR 62300, Dec. 5, 1994; 62 FR 10312, 10342, Mar. 6, 1997; 64 FR 8478, 8488, Feb. 19, 1999; 65 FR 76121, 76133, Dec. 6, 2000; 83 FR 55934, 55952, Nov. 9, 2018; 84 FR 33829, 33843, July 16, 2019; 85 FR 67202, 67259, Oct. 21, 2020; 85 FR 80274, 80387, Dec. 11, 2020; 85 FR 82260, 82289, Dec. 17, 2020; 85 FR 84160, 84193, Dec. 23, 2020; 86 FR 6847, Jan. 25, 2021; 86 FR 15069, Mar. 22, 2021; 86 FR 73615, Dec. 28, 2021; 87 FR 79789, Dec. 28, 2022; 88 FR 31314, 31449, May 16, 2023; 89 FR 48710, 48769, June 7, 2024, as confirmed at 89 FR 81156, Oct. 7, 2024; 89 FR 81156, 81284, Oct. 7, 2024; 89 FR 105386, Dec. 27, 2024]

§ 208.14 Approval, denial, referral, or dismissal of application.

(a) By an immigration judge. Unless otherwise prohibited in § 208.13(c), an immigration judge may grant or deny asylum in the exercise of discretion to an applicant who qualifies as a refugee under section 101(a)(42) of the Act.

(b) Approval by an asylum officer. In any case within the jurisdiction of USCIS, unless otherwise prohibited in § 208.13(c), an asylum officer, subject to review within USCIS, may grant, in the exercise of his or her discretion, asylum to an applicant who qualifies as a refugee under section 101(a)(42) of the Act, and whose identity has been checked pursuant to section 208(d)(5)(A)(i) of the Act.

(c) Denial, referral, or dismissal by an asylum officer. If the asylum officer, subject to review within USCIS, does not grant asylum to an applicant after an interview conducted in accordance with § 208.9, or if, as provided in § 208.10, the applicant is deemed to have waived the applicant's right to an interview or an adjudication by an asylum officer, the asylum officer shall deny, refer, or dismiss the application as follows:

(1) Inadmissible or deportable aliens. Except for applicants described in paragraph (c)(4)(ii) of this section who have not already been subject to proceedings in accordance with § 235.3(b) of this chapter, in the case of an applicant who appears to be inadmissible or deportable under section 212(a) or 237(a) of the Act, the asylum officer shall refer the application to an immigration judge, together with the appropriate charging document, for adjudication in removal proceedings (or, where charging documents may not be issued, shall dismiss the application).

(2) Alien in valid status. In the case of an applicant who is maintaining valid immigrant, nonimmigrant, or Temporary Protected Status at the time the application is decided, the asylum officer shall deny the application for asylum.

(3) Alien with valid parole. If an applicant has been paroled into the United States and the parole has not expired or been terminated by the Service, the asylum officer shall deny the application for asylum.

(4) Alien paroled into the United States whose parole has expired or is terminated.

(i) Alien paroled prior to April 1, 1997, or with advance authorization for parole. In the case of an applicant who was paroled into the United States prior to April 1, 1997, or who, prior to departure from the United States, had received an advance authorization for parole, the asylum officer shall refer the application, together with the appropriate charging documents, to an immigration judge for adjudication in removal proceedings if the parole has expired, the Service has terminated parole, or the Service is terminating parole through issuance of the charging documents, pursuant to § 212.5(d)(2)(i) of this chapter.

(ii) Alien paroled on or after April 1, 1997, without advance authorization for parole. In the case of an applicant who is an arriving alien or is otherwise subject to removal under § 235.3(b) of this chapter, and was paroled into the United States on or after April 1, 1997, without advance authorization for parole prior to departure from the United States, the asylum officer will take the following actions, if the parole has expired or been terminated:

(A) Inadmissible under section 212(a)(6)(C) or 212(a)(7) of the Act. If the applicant appears inadmissible to the United States under section 212(a)(6)(C) or 212(a)(7) of the Act and the asylum officer does not intend to lodge any additional charges of inadmissibility, the asylum officer shall proceed in accordance with § 235.3(b) of this chapter. If such applicant is found to have a credible fear of persecution or torture based on information elicited from the asylum interview, an asylum officer may refer the applicant directly to an immigration judge in removal proceedings under section 240 of the Act, without conducting a separate credible fear interview pursuant to § 208.30. If such applicant is not found to have a credible fear based on information elicited at the asylum interview, an asylum officer will conduct a credible fear interview and the applicant will be subject to the credible fear process specified at § 208.30(b).

(B) Inadmissible on other grounds. In the case of an applicant who was paroled into the United States on or after April 1, 1997, and will be charged as inadmissible to the United States under provisions of the Act other than, or in addition to, sections 212(a)(6)(C) or 212(a)(7), the asylum officer shall refer the application to an immigration judge for adjudication in removal proceedings.

(d) Applicability of § 103.2(b) of this chapter. No application for asylum or withholding of deportation shall be subject to denial pursuant to § 103.2(b) of this chapter.

(e) Duration. If the applicant is granted asylum, the grant will be effective for an indefinite period, subject to termination as provided in § 208.24.

(f) Effect of denial of principal's application on separate applications by dependents. The denial of an asylum application filed by a principal applicant for asylum shall also result in the denial of asylum status to any dependents of that principal applicant who are included in that same application. Such denial shall not preclude a grant of asylum for an otherwise eligible dependent who has filed a separate asylum application, nor shall such denial result in an otherwise eligible dependent becoming ineligible to apply for asylum due to the provisions of section 208(a)(2)(C) of the Act.

(g) Applicants granted lawful permanent residence status. If an asylum applicant is granted adjustment of status to lawful permanent resident, the Service may provide written notice to the applicant that his or her asylum application will be presumed abandoned and dismissed without prejudice, unless the applicant submits a written request within 30 days of the notice, that the asylum application be adjudicated. If an applicant does not respond within 30 days of the date the written notice was sent or served, the Service may presume the asylum application abandoned and dismiss it without prejudice.

HISTORY:

[55 FR 30680, July 27, 1990; 59 FR 62300, Dec. 5, 1994; 62 FR 10312, 10342, Mar. 6, 1997; 63 FR 12979, 12986, Mar. 17, 1998; 64 FR 27856, 27875, May 21, 1999; 65 FR 76121, 76134, Dec. 6, 2000; 76 FR 53764, 53784, Aug. 29, 2011; 87 FR 18078, 18217, Mar. 29, 2022]

§ 208.15 Definition of "firm resettlement."

(a) An alien is considered to be firmly resettled if, after the events giving rise to the alien's asylum claim:

(1) The alien resided in a country through which the alien transited prior to arriving in or entering the United States and —

(i) Received or was eligible for any permanent legal immigration status in that country;

(ii) Resided in such a country with any non-permanent but indefinitely renewable legal immigration status (including asylee, refugee, or similar status but excluding status such as of a tourist); or

(iii) Resided in such a country and could have applied for and obtained any non-permanent but indefinitely renewable legal immigration status in that country;

(2) The alien physically resided voluntarily, and without continuing to suffer persecution or torture, in any one country for one year or more after departing his country of nationality or last habitual residence and prior to arrival in or entry into the United States, provided that time spent in Mexico by an alien who is not a native or citizen of Mexico solely as a direct result of being returned to Mexico pursuant to section 235(b)(2)(C) of the Act or of being subject to metering would not be counted for purposes of this paragraph; or

(3)(i) The alien is a citizen of a country other than the one where the alien alleges a fear of persecution and the alien was present in that country after departing his country of nationality or last habitual residence and prior to arrival in or entry into the United States; or

(ii) The alien was a citizen of a country other than the one where the alien alleges a fear of persecution, the alien was present in that country after departing his country of nationality or last habitual residence and prior to arrival in or entry into the United States, and the alien renounced that citizenship after arriving in the United States.

(b) The provisions of 8 CFR 1240.8(d) shall apply when the evidence of record indicates that the firm resettlement bar may apply. In such cases, the alien shall bear the burden of proving the bar does not apply. Either DHS or the immigration judge may raise the issue of the application of the firm resettlement bar based on the evidence of record. The firm resettlement of an alien's parent(s) shall be imputed to the alien if the resettlement occurred before the alien turned 18 and the alien resided with the alien's parents at the time of the firm resettlement unless the alien establishes that he or she could not have derived any permanent legal immigration status or any non-permanent but indefinitely renewable legal immigration status (including asylee, refugee, or similar status but excluding status such as of a tourist) from the alien's parent.

HISTORY:

[55 FR 30680, July 27, 1990; 62 FR 10312, 10343, Mar. 6, 1997; 65 FR 76121, 76135, Dec. 6, 2000; 85 FR 80274, 80388, Dec. 11, 2020]

§ 208.16 Withholding of removal under section 241(b)(3)(B) of the Act and withholding of removal under the Convention Against Torture. [Effective until December 31, 2025]

(a) Consideration of application for withholding of removal. An asylum officer shall not determine whether an alien is eligible for withholding of the exclusion, deportation, or removal of the alien to a country where the alien's life or freedom would be threatened, except in the case of an alien who is determined to be an applicant for admission under section 235(b)(1) of the Act, who is found to have a credible fear of persecution or torture, whose case is subsequently retained by or referred to USCIS pursuant to the jurisdiction provided at § 208.2(a)(1)(ii) to consider the application for asylum, and whose application for asylum is not granted; or in the case of the spouse or child of such an alien who is included in the alien's asylum application and who files a separate application for asylum with USCIS that is not granted. In such cases, the asylum officer will determine, based on the record before USCIS, whether the applicant is eligible for statutory withholding of removal under paragraph (b) of this section or withholding or deferral of removal pursuant to the Convention Against Torture under paragraph (c) of this section. Even if the asylum officer determines that the applicant has established eligibility for withholding of removal under paragraph (b) or (c) of this section, the asylum officer shall proceed with referring the application to the immigration judge for a hearing pursuant to § 208.14(c)(1). In exclusion, deportation, or removal proceedings, an immigration judge may adjudicate both an asylum claim and a request for withholding of removal whether or not asylum is granted.

(b) Eligibility for withholding of removal under section 241(b)(3) of the Act; burden of proof. The burden of proof is on the applicant for withholding of removal under section 241(b)(3) of the Act to establish that his or her life or freedom would be threatened in the proposed country of removal on account of race, religion, nationality, membership in a particular social group, or political opinion. The testimony of the applicant, if credible, may be sufficient to sustain the burden of proof without corroboration. The evidence shall be evaluated as follows:

(1) Past threat to life or freedom

(i) If the applicant is determined to have suffered past persecution in the proposed country of removal on account of race, religion, nationality, membership in a particular social group, or political opinion, it shall be presumed that the applicant's life or freedom would be threatened in the future in the country of removal on the basis of the original claim. This presumption may be rebutted if an asylum officer or immigration judge finds by a preponderance of the evidence.

(A) There has been a fundamental change in circumstances such that the applicant's life or freedom would not be threatened on account of any of the five grounds mentioned in this paragraph upon the applicant's removal to that country; or

(B) The applicant could avoid a future threat to his or her life or freedom by relocating to another part of the proposed country of removal and, under all the circumstances, it would be reasonable to expect the applicant to do so.

(ii) In cases in which the applicant has established past persecution, the Service shall bear the burden of establishing by a preponderance of the evidence the requirements of paragraphs (b)(1)(i)(A) or (b)(1)(i)(B) of this section.

(iii) If the applicant's fear of future threat to life or freedom is unrelated to the past persecution, the applicant bears the burden of establishing that it is more likely than not that he or she would suffer such harm.

(2) Future threat to life or freedom. An applicant who has not suffered past persecution may demonstrate that his or her life or freedom would be threatened in the future in a country if he or she can establish that it is more likely than not that he or she would be persecuted on account of race, religion, nationality, membership in a particular social group, or political opinion upon removal to that country. Such an applicant cannot demonstrate that his or her life or freedom would be threatened if the asylum officer or immigration judge finds that the applicant could avoid a future threat to his or her life or freedom by relocating to another part of the proposed country of removal and, under all the circumstances, it would be reasonable to expect the applicant to do so. In evaluating whether it is more likely than not that the applicant's life or freedom would be threatened in a particular country on account of race, religion, nationality, membership in a particular social group, or political opinion, the asylum officer or immigration judge shall not require the applicant to provide evidence that he or she would be singled out individually for such persecution if:

(i) The applicant establishes that in that country there is a pattern or practice of persecution of a group of persons similarly situated to the applicant on account of race, religion, nationality, membership in a particular social group, or political opinion; and

(ii) The applicant establishes his or her own inclusion in and identification with such group of persons such that it is more likely than not that his or her life or freedom would be threatened upon return to that country.

(3) Reasonableness of internal relocation. For purposes of determinations under paragraphs (b)(1) and (2) of this section, adjudicators should consider the totality of the relevant circumstances regarding an applicant's prospects for relocation, including the size of the country of nationality or last habitual residence, the geographic locus of the alleged persecution, the size, reach, or numerosity of the alleged persecutor, and the applicant's demonstrated ability to relocate to the United States in order to apply for withholding of removal.

(i) In cases in which the applicant has not established past persecution, the applicant shall bear the burden of establishing that it would not be reasonable for him or her to relocate, unless the persecutor is a government or is government-sponsored.

(ii) In cases in which the persecutor is a government or is government-sponsored, it shall be presumed that internal relocation would not be reasonable, unless DHS establishes by a preponderance of the evidence that, under the totality of the circumstances, it would be reasonable for the applicant to relocate.

(iii) Regardless of whether an applicant has established persecution in the past, in cases in which the persecutor is not the government or a government-sponsored actor, or otherwise is a private actor, there shall be a presumption that internal relocation would be reasonable unless the applicant establishes, by a preponderance of the evidence, that it would be unreasonable to relocate.

(iv) For purposes of determinations under paragraphs (b)(3)(ii) and (iii) of this section, persecutors who are private actors, including but not limited to persecutors who are gang members, public officials who are not acting under color of law, or family members who are not themselves government officials or neighbors who are not themselves government officials, shall not be considered to be persecutors who are the government or government-sponsored absent evidence that the government sponsored the persecution.

(c) Eligibility for withholding of removal under the Convention Against Torture.

(1) For purposes of regulations under Title II of the Act, "Convention Against Torture" shall refer to the United Nations Convention Against Torture and Other Cruel, Inhuman or Degrading Treatment or Punish-

ment, subject to any reservations, understandings, declarations, and provisos contained in the United States Senate resolution of ratification of the Convention, as implemented by section 2242 of the Foreign Affairs Reform and Restructuring Act of 1998 (Pub. L. 105-277, 112 Stat. 2681, 2681-821). The definition of torture contained in § 208.18(a) of this part shall govern all decisions made under regulations under Title II of the Act about the applicability of Article 3 of the Convention Against Torture.

(2) The burden of proof is on the applicant for withholding of removal under this paragraph to establish that it is more likely than not that he or she would be tortured if removed to the proposed country of removal. The testimony of the applicant, if credible, may be sufficient to sustain the burden of proof without corroboration.

(3) In assessing whether it is more likely than not that an applicant would be tortured in the proposed country of removal, all evidence relevant to the possibility of future torture shall be considered, including, but not limited to:

(i) Evidence of past torture inflicted upon the applicant;

(ii) Evidence that the applicant could relocate to a part of the country of removal where he or she is not likely to be tortured;

(iii) Evidence of gross, flagrant or mass violations of human rights within the country of removal, where applicable; and

(iv) Other relevant information regarding conditions in the country of removal.

(4) In considering an application for withholding of removal under the Convention Against Torture, the adjudicator shall first determine whether the alien is more likely than not to be tortured in the country of removal. If the adjudicator determines that the alien is more likely than not to be tortured in the country of removal, the alien is eligible for protection under the Convention Against Torture, and the adjudicator shall determine whether protection under the Convention Against Torture should be granted either in the form of withholding of removal or in the form of deferral of removal. The adjudicator shall state that an alien eligible for such protection is eligible for withholding of removal unless the alien is subject to mandatory denial of withholding of removal under paragraph (d)(2) or (3) of this section. If an alien eligible for such protection is subject to mandatory denial of withholding of removal under paragraph (d)(2) or (3) of this section, the adjudicator shall state that the alien is eligible for deferral of removal under § 208.17(a). For cases under the jurisdiction of USCIS pursuant to § 208.2(a)(1)(ii), the asylum officer may make such a determination based on the application and the record before USCIS; however, the asylum officer shall not issue an order granting either withholding of removal or deferral of removal because that is referred to the immigration judge pursuant to § 208.14(c)(1) and 8 CFR 1240.17.

(d) Approval or denial of application.

(1) General. Subject to paragraphs (d)(2) and (d)(3) of this section, an application for withholding of deportation or removal to a country of proposed removal shall be granted if the applicant's eligibility for withholding is established pursuant to paragraphs (b) or (c) of this section.

(2) Mandatory denials. Except as provided in paragraph (d)(3) of this section, an application for withholding of removal under section 241(b)(3) of the Act or under the Convention Against Torture shall be denied if the applicant falls within section 241(b)(3)(B) of the Act or, for applications for withholding of deportation adjudicated in proceedings commenced prior to April 1, 1997, within section 243(h)(2) of the Act as it appeared prior to that date. For purposes of section 241(b)(3)(B)(ii) of the Act, or section 243(h)(2)(B) of the Act as it appeared prior to April 1, 1997, an alien who has been convicted of a particularly serious crime shall be considered to constitute a danger to the community. If the evidence indicates the applicability of one or more of the grounds for denial of withholding enumerated in the Act, the applicant shall have the burden of proving by a preponderance of the evidence that such grounds do not apply.

(3) Exception to the prohibition on withholding of deportation in certain cases. Section 243(h)(3) of the Act, as added by section 413 of Pub. L. 104-132 (110 Stat. 1214), shall apply only to applications adjudicated in proceedings commenced before April 1, 1997, and in which final action had not been taken before April 24, 1996. The discretion permitted by that section to override section 243(h)(2) of the Act shall be exercised only in the case of an applicant convicted of an aggravated felony (or felonies) where he or she was sentenced to an aggregate term of imprisonment of less than 5 years and the immigration judge determines on an individual basis that the crime (or crimes) of which the applicant was convicted does not constitute a particularly serious crime. Nevertheless, it shall be presumed that an alien convicted of an aggravated felony has been convicted of a particularly serious crime. Except in the cases specified in this paragraph, the grounds for denial of withholding of deportation in section 243(h)(2) of the Act as it appeared prior to April 1, 1997, shall be deemed to comply with the Protocol Relating to the Status of Refugees, Jan. 31, 1967, T.I.A.S. No. 6577.

(e) [Removed and reserved].

(f) Removal to third country. Nothing in this section or §208.17 shall prevent the Service from removing an alien to a third country other than the country to which removal has been withheld or deferred.

HISTORY:

[55 FR 30680, July 27, 1990; 59 FR 62301, Dec. 5, 1994; 60 FR 44260, 44264, Aug. 25, 1995; 62 FR 10312, 10343, Mar. 6, 1997; 64 FR 8478, 8488, Feb. 19, 1999; 65 FR 76121, 76135, Dec. 6, 2000; 85 FR 67202, 67259, Oct. 21, 2020; 85 FR 80274, 80388, Dec. 11, 2020; 85 FR 84160, 84193, Dec. 23, 2020; 86 FR 6847, Jan. 25, 2021; 86 FR 15069, Mar. 22, 2021; 86 FR 73615, Dec. 28, 2021; 87 FR 18078, 18218, Mar. 29, 2022; 87 FR 79789, Dec. 28, 2022; 89 FR 105386, Dec. 27, 2024]

§ 208.16 Withholding of removal under section 241(b)(3)(B) of the Act and withholding of removal under the Convention Against Torture. [Effective December 31, 2025]

(a) Consideration of application for withholding of

removal. An asylum officer shall not determine whether an alien is eligible for withholding of the exclusion, deportation, or removal of the alien to a country where the alien's life or freedom would be threatened, except in the case of an alien who is determined to be an applicant for admission under section 235(b)(1) of the Act, who is found to have a credible fear of persecution or torture, whose case is subsequently retained by or referred to USCIS pursuant to the jurisdiction provided at § 208.2(a)(1)(ii) to consider the application for asylum, and whose application for asylum is not granted; or in the case of the spouse or child of such an alien who is included in the alien's asylum application and who files a separate application for asylum with USCIS that is not granted. In such cases, the asylum officer will determine, based on the record before USCIS, whether the applicant is eligible for statutory withholding of removal under paragraph (b) of this section or withholding or deferral of removal pursuant to the Convention Against Torture under paragraph (c) of this section. Even if the asylum officer determines that the applicant has established eligibility for withholding of removal under paragraph (b) or (c) of this section, the asylum officer shall proceed with referring the application to the immigration judge for a hearing pursuant to § 208.14(c)(1). In exclusion, deportation, or removal proceedings, an immigration judge may adjudicate both an asylum claim and a request for withholding of removal whether or not asylum is granted.

(b) Eligibility for withholding of removal under section 241(b)(3) of the Act; burden of proof. The burden of proof is on the applicant for withholding of removal under section 241(b)(3) of the Act to establish that his or her life or freedom would be threatened in the proposed country of removal on account of race, religion, nationality, membership in a particular social group, or political opinion. The testimony of the applicant, if credible, may be sufficient to sustain the burden of proof without corroboration. The evidence shall be evaluated as follows:

(1) Past threat to life or freedom

(i) If the applicant is determined to have suffered past persecution in the proposed country of removal on account of race, religion, nationality, membership in a particular social group, or political opinion, it shall be presumed that the applicant's life or freedom would be threatened in the future in the country of removal on the basis of the original claim. This presumption may be rebutted if an asylum officer or immigration judge finds by a preponderance of the evidence:

(A) There has been a fundamental change in circumstances such that the applicant's life or freedom would not be threatened on account of any of the five grounds mentioned in this paragraph upon the applicant's removal to that country; or

(B) The applicant could avoid a future threat to his or her life or freedom by relocating to another part of the proposed country of removal and, under all the circumstances, it would be reasonable to expect the applicant to do so.

(ii) In cases in which the applicant has established past persecution, the Service shall bear the burden of establishing by a preponderance of the evidence the requirements of paragraphs (b)(1)(i)(A) or (b)(1)(i)(B) of this section.

(iii) If the applicant's fear of future threat to life or freedom is unrelated to the past persecution, the applicant bears the burden of establishing that it is more likely than not that he or she would suffer such harm.

(2) Future threat to life or freedom. An applicant who has not suffered past persecution may demonstrate that his or her life or freedom would be threatened in the future in a country if he or she can establish that it is more likely than not that he or she would be persecuted on account of race, religion, nationality, membership in a particular social group, or political opinion upon removal to that country. Such an applicant cannot demonstrate that his or her life or freedom would be threatened if the asylum officer or immigration judge finds that the applicant could avoid a future threat to his or her life or freedom by relocating to another part of the proposed country of removal and, under all the circumstances, it would be reasonable to expect the applicant to do so. In evaluating whether it is more likely than not that the applicant's life or freedom would be threatened in a particular country on account of race, religion, nationality, membership in a particular social group, or political opinion, the asylum officer or immigration judge shall not require the applicant to provide evidence that he or she would be singled out individually for such persecution if:

(i) The applicant establishes that in that country there is a pattern or practice of persecution of a group of persons similarly situated to the applicant on account of race, religion, nationality, membership in a particular social group, or political opinion; and

(ii) The applicant establishes his or her own inclusion in and identification with such group of persons such that it is more likely than not that his or her life or freedom would be threatened upon return to that country.

(3) Reasonableness of internal relocation. For purposes of determinations under paragraphs (b)(1) and (2) of this section, adjudicators should consider the totality of the relevant circumstances regarding an applicant's prospects for relocation, including the size of the country of nationality or last habitual residence, the geographic locus of the alleged persecution, the size, reach, or numerosity of the alleged persecutor, and the applicant's demonstrated ability to relocate to the United States in order to apply for withholding of removal.

(i) In cases in which the applicant has not established past persecution, the applicant shall bear the burden of establishing that it would not be reasonable for him or her to relocate, unless the persecutor is a government or is government-sponsored.

(ii) In cases in which the persecutor is a government or is government-sponsored, it shall be presumed that internal relocation would not be reasonable, unless DHS establishes by a preponderance of the evidence that, under the totality of the circumstances, it would be reasonable for the applicant to relocate.

(iii) Regardless of whether an applicant has established persecution in the past, in cases in which the persecutor is not the government or a government-sponsored actor, or otherwise is a private actor, there shall be a presumption that internal relocation would be reasonable unless the applicant establishes, by a preponderance of the evidence, that it would be unreasonable to relocate.

(iv) For purposes of determinations under paragraphs (b)(3)(ii) and (iii) of this section, persecutors who are private actors, including but not limited to persecutors who are gang members, public officials who are not acting under color of law, or family members who are not themselves government officials or neighbors who are not themselves government officials, shall not be considered to be persecutors who are the government or government-sponsored absent evidence that the government sponsored the persecution.

(c) Eligibility for withholding of removal under the Convention Against Torture.

(1) For purposes of regulations under Title II of the Act, "Convention Against Torture" shall refer to the United Nations Convention Against Torture and Other Cruel, Inhuman or Degrading Treatment or Punishment, subject to any reservations, understandings, declarations, and provisos contained in the United States Senate resolution of ratification of the Convention, as implemented by section 2242 of the Foreign Affairs Reform and Restructuring Act of 1998 (Pub. L. 105-277, 112 Stat. 2681, 2681-821). The definition of torture contained in § 208.18(a) of this part shall govern all decisions made under regulations under Title II of the Act about the applicability of Article 3 of the Convention Against Torture.

(2) The burden of proof is on the applicant for withholding of removal under this paragraph to establish that it is more likely than not that he or she would be tortured if removed to the proposed country of removal. The testimony of the applicant, if credible, may be sufficient to sustain the burden of proof without corroboration.

(3) In assessing whether it is more likely than not that an applicant would be tortured in the proposed country of removal, all evidence relevant to the possibility of future torture shall be considered, including, but not limited to:

(i) Evidence of past torture inflicted upon the applicant;

(ii) Evidence that the applicant could relocate to a part of the country of removal where he or she is not likely to be tortured;

(iii) Evidence of gross, flagrant or mass violations of human rights within the country of removal, where applicable; and

(iv) Other relevant information regarding conditions in the country of removal.

(4) In considering an application for withholding of removal under the Convention Against Torture, the adjudicator shall first determine whether the alien is more likely than not to be tortured in the country of removal. If the adjudicator determines that the alien is more likely than not to be tortured in the country of removal, the alien is eligible for protection under the Convention Against Torture, and the adjudicator shall determine whether protection under the Convention Against Torture should be granted either in the form of withholding of removal or in the form of deferral of removal. The adjudicator shall state that an alien eligible for such protection is eligible for withholding of removal unless the alien is subject to mandatory denial of withholding of removal under paragraph (d)(2) or (3) of this section. If an alien eligible for such protection is subject to mandatory denial of withholding of removal under paragraph (d)(2) or (3) of this section, the adjudicator shall state that the alien is eligible for deferral of removal under § 208.17(a). For cases under the jurisdiction of USCIS pursuant to § 208.2(a)(1)(ii), the asylum officer may make such a determination based on the application and the record before USCIS; however, the asylum officer shall not issue an order granting either withholding of removal or deferral of removal because that is referred to the immigration judge pursuant to § 208.14(c)(1) and 8 CFR 1240.17.

(d) Approval or denial of application.

(1) General. Subject to paragraphs (d)(2) and (d)(3) of this section, an application for withholding of deportation or removal to a country of proposed removal shall be granted if the applicant's eligibility for withholding is established pursuant to paragraphs (b) or (c) of this section.

(2) Mandatory denials—

(i) In general. Except as provided in paragraph (d)(3) of this section, an application for withholding of removal under section 241(b)(3) of the Act or under the regulations issued pursuant to the legislation implementing the Convention Against Torture shall be denied if the applicant falls within section 241(b)(3)(B) of the Act or, for applications for withholding of deportation adjudicated in proceedings commenced prior to April 1, 1997, within section 243(h)(2) of the Act as it appeared prior to that date. For purposes of section 241(b)(3)(B)(ii) of the Act, or section 243(h)(2)(B) of the Act as it appeared prior to April 1, 1997, an alien who has been convicted of a particularly serious crime shall be considered to constitute a danger to the community. If the evidence indicates the applicability of one or more of the grounds for denial of withholding enumerated in the Act, the applicant shall have the burden of proving by a preponderance of the evidence that such grounds do not apply.

(ii) Public health emergencies. If a communicable disease has triggered an ongoing declaration of a public health emergency under Federal law, such as under section 319 of the Public Health Service Act, 42 U.S.C. 247d, or section 564 of the Food, Drug, and Cosmetic Act, 21 U.S.C. 360bbb–3, then an alien is ineligible for withholding of removal under section 241(b)(3) of the Act and under the regulations issued pursuant to the legislation implementing the Convention Against Torture on the basis of there being reasonable grounds for regarding the alien as a danger to the security of the United States under section 241(b)(3)(B)(iv) of the Act if the alien

(A) Exhibits symptoms indicating that he or she is afflicted with the disease, per guidance issued by the Secretary or the Attorney General, as appropriate, or

(B) Has come into contact with the disease within the number of days equivalent to the longest known incubation and contagion period for the disease, per guidance issued by the Secretary or the Attorney General, as appropriate.

(iii) Danger to the Public Health Caused by an Epidemic Outside of the United States. If, regarding a communicable disease of public health significance as defined at 42 CFR 34.2(b), the Secretary and the Attorney General, in consultation with the Secretary of Health and Human Services, have jointly

(A) Determined that the physical presence in the United States of aliens who are coming from a country or countries (or one or more subdivisions or regions thereof), or have embarked at a place or places, where such disease is prevalent or epidemic (or had come from that country or countries (or one or more subdivisions or regions thereof), or had embarked at that place or places, during a period in which the disease was prevalent or epidemic there) would cause a danger to the public health in the United States, and

(B) Designated the foreign country or countries (or one or more subdivisions or regions thereof), or place or places, and the period of time or circumstances under which they jointly deem it necessary for the public health that aliens or classes of aliens described in paragraph (d)(2)(ii)(A) of this section who are still within the number of days equivalent to the longest known incubation and contagion period for the disease be regarded as a danger to the security of the United States under section 241(b)(3)(B)(iv) of the Act, including any relevant exceptions as appropriate, then—

(C) An alien or class of aliens are ineligible for withholding of removal under section 241(b)(3) of the Act and under the regulations issued pursuant to the legislation implementing the Convention Against Torture on the basis of there being reasonable grounds for regarding the alien or class of aliens as a danger to the security of the United States under section 241(b)(3)(B)(iv) of the Act if the alien or class of aliens are described in paragraph (d)(2)(ii)(A) of this section and are regarded as a danger to the security of the United States as provided for in paragraph (d)(2)(ii)(B) of this section.

(iv) The grounds for mandatory denial described in paragraphs (d)(2)(ii) and (iii) of this section shall not apply to an alien who is applying for asylum or withholding of removal in the United States upon return from Canada to the United States and pursuant to the Agreement Between the Government of the United States and the Government of Canada for Cooperation in the Examination of Refugee Status Claims from Nationals of Third Countries.

(3) Exception to the prohibition on withholding of deportation in certain cases. Section 243(h)(3) of the Act, as added by section 413 of Pub. L. 104-132 (110 Stat. 1214), shall apply only to applications adjudicated in proceedings commenced before April 1, 1997, and in which final action had not been taken before April 24, 1996. The discretion permitted by that section to override section 243(h)(2) of the Act shall be exercised only in the case of an applicant convicted of an aggravated felony (or felonies) where he or she was sentenced to an aggregate term of imprisonment of less than 5 years and the immigration judge determines on an individual basis that the crime (or crimes) of which the applicant was convicted does not constitute a particularly serious crime. Nevertheless, it shall be presumed that an alien convicted of an aggravated felony has been convicted of a particularly serious crime. Except in the cases specified in this paragraph, the grounds for denial of withholding of deportation in section 243(h)(2) of the Act as it appeared prior to April 1, 1997, shall be deemed to comply with the Protocol Relating to the Status of Refugees, Jan. 31, 1967, T.I.A.S. No. 6577.

(e) [Removed and reserved.]

(f) Removal to third country.

(1) Nothing in this section or § 208.17 shall prevent the Department from removing an alien requesting protection to a third country other than a country to which removal is currently withheld or deferred.

(2) If an alien requests withholding or deferral of removal to his or her home country or another specific country, nothing in this section or § 208.17 precludes the Department from removing the alien to a third country prior to a determination or adjudication of the alien's initial request for withholding or deferral of removal if, after being notified of the identity of the prospective third country of removal and provided an opportunity to demonstrate that he or she is more likely than not to be tortured in that third country, the alien fails to establish that they are more likely than not to be tortured there. However, such a removal shall be executed only if the alien was:

(i) Advised at the time of requesting withholding or deferral of removal of the possibility of being removed to a third country prior to a determination or adjudication of the same under the conditions set forth in this paragraph; and

(ii) Provided, but did not accept, an opportunity to withdraw the request for withholding or deferral of removal in order to prevent such removal and, instead, proceed to removal pursuant to section 241(b) of the Act, as appropriate.

HISTORY:

[55 FR 30680, July 27, 1990; 59 FR 62301, Dec. 5, 1994; 60 FR 44260, 44264, Aug. 25, 1995; 62 FR 10312, 10343, Mar. 6, 1997; 64 FR 8478, 8488, Feb. 19, 1999; 65 FR 76121, 76135, Dec. 6, 2000; 85 FR 67202, 67259, Oct. 21, 2020; 85 FR 80274, 80388, Dec. 11, 2020; 85 FR 84160, 84193, Dec. 23, 2020; 86 FR 6847, Jan. 25, 2021; 86 FR 15069, Mar. 22, 2021; 86 FR 73615, Dec. 28, 2021; 87 FR 18078, 18218, Mar. 29, 2022; 87 FR 79789, Dec. 28, 2022; 89 FR 105386, Dec. 27, 2024]

§ 208.17 Deferral of removal under the Convention Against Torture.

(a) Grant of deferral of removal. An alien who: has been ordered removed; has been found under § 208.16(c)(3) to be entitled to protection under the Convention Against Torture; and is subject to the provisions for mandatory denial of withholding of removal under § 208.16(d)(2) or (d)(3), shall be granted deferral of removal to the country where he or she is more likely than not to be tortured.

(b) Notice to Alien.

(1) After an immigration judge orders an alien described in paragraph (a) of this section removed, the immigration judge shall inform the alien that his or her removal to the country where he or she is more likely than not to be tortured shall be deferred until such time as the deferral is terminated under this section. The immigration judge shall inform the alien that deferral of removal:

(i) Does not confer upon the alien any lawful or permanent immigration status in the United States;

(ii) Will not necessarily result in the alien being released from the custody of the Service if the alien is subject to such custody;

(iii) Is effective only until terminated; and

(iv) Is subject to review and termination if the immigration judge determines that it is not likely that the alien would be tortured in the country to which removal has been deferred, or if the alien requests that deferral be terminated.

(2) The immigration judge shall also inform the alien that removal has been deferred only to the country in which it has been determined that the alien is likely to be tortured, and that the alien may be removed at any time to another country where he or she is not likely to be tortured.

(c) Detention of an alien granted deferral of removal under this section. Nothing in this section shall alter the authority of the Service to detain an alien whose removal has been deferred under this section and who is otherwise subject to detention. In the case of such an alien, decisions about the alien's release shall be made according to part 241 of this chapter.

(d) Termination of deferral of removal.

(1) At any time while deferral of removal is in effect, the INS District Counsel for the District with jurisdiction over an alien whose removal has been deferred under paragraph (a) of this section may file a motion with the Immigration Court having administrative control pursuant to § 3.11 of this chapter to schedule a hearing to consider whether deferral of removal should be terminated. The Service motion shall be granted if it is accompanied by evidence that is relevant to the possibility that the alien would be tortured in the country to which removal has been deferred and that was not presented at the previous hearing. The Service motion shall not be subject to the requirements for reopening in §§ 3.2 and 3.23 of this chapter.

(2) The Immigration Court shall provide notice to the alien and the Service of the time, place, and date of the termination hearing. Such notice shall inform the alien that the alien may supplement the information in his or her initial application for withholding of removal under the Convention Against Torture and shall provide that the alien must submit any such supplemental information within 10 calendar days of service of such notice (or 13 calendar days if service of such notice was by mail). At the expiration of this 10 or 13 day period, the Immigration Court shall forward a copy of the original application, and any supplemental information the alien or the Service has submitted, to the Department of State, together with notice to the Department of State of the time, place and date of the termination hearing. At its option, the Department of State may provide comments on the case, according to the provisions of § 208.11 of this part.

(3) The immigration judge shall conduct a hearing and make a de novo determination, based on the record of proceeding and initial application in addition to any new evidence submitted by the Service or the alien, as to whether the alien is more likely than not to be tortured in the country to which removal has been deferred. This determination shall be made under the standards for eligibility set out in § 208.16(c). The burden is on the alien to establish that it is more likely than not that he or she would be tortured in the country to which removal has been deferred.

(4) If the immigration judge determines that the alien is more likely than not to be tortured in the country to which removal has been deferred, the order of deferral shall remain in place. If the immigration judge determines that the alien has not established that he or she is more likely than not to be tortured in the country to which removal has been deferred, the deferral of removal shall be terminated and the alien may be removed to that country. Appeal of the immigration judge's decision shall lie to the Board.

(e) Termination at the request of the alien.

(1) At any time while deferral of removal is in effect, the alien may make a written request to the Immigration Court having administrative control pursuant to § 3.11 of this chapter to terminate the deferral order. If satisfied on the basis of the written submission that the alien's request is knowing and voluntary, the immigration judge shall terminate the order of deferral and the alien may be removed.

(2) If necessary the immigration judge may calendar a hearing for the sole purpose of determining whether the alien's request is knowing and voluntary. If the immigration judge determines that the alien's request is knowing and voluntary, the order of deferral shall be terminated. If the immigration judge determines that the alien's request is not knowing and voluntary, the alien's request shall not serve as the basis for terminating the order of deferral.

(f) Termination pursuant to § 208.18(c). At any time while deferral of removal is in effect, the Attorney General may determine whether deferral should be terminated based on diplomatic assurances forwarded by the Secretary of State pursuant to the procedures in § 208.18(c).

HISTORY:

[55 FR 30680, July 27, 1990; 59 FR 62301, Dec. 5, 1994; 62 FR 10312, 10344, Mar. 6, 1997; 64 FR 8478, 8489, Feb. 19, 1999]

§ 208.18 Implementation of the Convention Against Torture.

(a) Definitions. The definitions in this subsection incorporate the definition of torture contained in Article 1 of the Convention Against Torture, subject to the reservations, understandings, declarations, and provisos contained in the United States Senate resolution of ratification of the Convention.

(1) Torture is defined as any act by which severe pain or suffering, whether physical or mental, is intentionally inflicted on a person for such purposes as obtaining from him or her or a third person information or a confession, punishing him or her for an act he or she or a third person has committed or is suspected of having committed, or intimidating or coercing him or her or a third person, or for any reason based on discrimination of any kind, when such pain or suffering is inflicted by or at the instigation of or with the consent or acquiescence of a public official acting in an official capacity or other person acting in an official capacity. Pain or suffering inflicted by a public official who is not acting under color of law shall not constitute pain or suffering inflicted by or at the instigation of or with the consent or acquiescence of a public official acting in an official capacity or other person acting in an official capacity, although a different public official acting in an official capacity or other person acting in an official capacity could instigate, consent to, or acquiesce in the pain or suffering inflicted by the public official who is not acting under color of law.

(2) Torture is an extreme form of cruel and inhuman treatment and does not include lesser forms of cruel, inhuman or degrading treatment or punishment that do not amount to torture.

(3) Torture does not include pain or suffering arising only from, inherent in or incidental to lawful sanctions. Lawful sanctions include judicially imposed sanctions and other enforcement actions authorized by law, including the death penalty, but do not include sanctions that defeat the object and purpose of the Convention Against Torture to prohibit torture.

(4) In order to constitute torture, mental pain or suffering must be prolonged mental harm caused by or resulting from:

(i) The intentional infliction or threatened infliction of severe physical pain or suffering;

(ii) The administration or application, or threatened administration or application, of mind altering substances or other procedures calculated to disrupt profoundly the senses or the personality;

(iii) The threat of imminent death; or

(iv) The threat that another person will imminently be subjected to death, severe physical pain or suffering, or the administration or application of mind altering substances or other procedures calculated to disrupt profoundly the sense or personality.

(5) In order to constitute torture, an act must be specifically intended to inflict severe physical or mental pain or suffering. An act that results in unanticipated or unintended severity of pain and suffering is not torture.

(6) In order to constitute torture an act must be directed against a person in the offender's custody or physical control.

(7) Acquiescence of a public official requires that the public official, prior to the activity constituting torture, have awareness of such activity and thereafter breach his or her legal responsibility to intervene to prevent such activity. Such awareness requires a finding of either actual knowledge or willful blindness. Willful blindness means that the public official acting in an official capacity or other person acting in an official capacity was aware of a high probability of activity constituting torture and deliberately avoided learning the truth; it is not enough that such public official acting in an official capacity or other person acting in an official capacity was mistaken, recklessly disregarded the truth, or negligently failed to inquire. In order for a public official to breach his or her legal responsibility to intervene to prevent activity constituting torture, the official must have been charged with preventing the activity as part of his or her duties and have failed to intervene. No person will be deemed to have breached a legal responsibility to intervene if such person is unable to intervene, or if the person intervenes but is unable to prevent the activity that constitutes torture.

(8) Noncompliance with applicable legal procedural standards does not per se constitute torture.

(b) Applicability of §§ 208.16(c) and 208.17(a).

(1) Aliens in proceedings on or after March 22, 1999. An alien who is in exclusion, deportation, or removal proceedings on or after March 22, 1999 may apply for withholding of removal under § 208.16(c), and, if applicable, may be considered for deferral of removal under § 208.17(a).

(2) Aliens who were ordered removed, or whose removal orders became final, before March 22, 1999. An alien under a final order of deportation, exclusion, or removal that became final prior to March 22, 1999 may move to reopen proceedings for the sole purpose of seeking protection under § 208.16(c). Such motions shall be governed by §§ 3.23 and 3.2 of this chapter, except that the time and numerical limitations on motions to reopen shall not apply and the alien shall not be required to demonstrate that the evidence sought to be offered was unavailable and could not have been discovered or presented at the former hearing. The motion to reopen shall not be granted unless:

(i) The motion is filed within June 21, 1999; and

(ii) The evidence sought to be offered establishes a prima facie case that the applicant's removal must be withheld or deferred under §§ 208.16(c) or 208.17(a).

(3) Aliens who, on March 22, 1999, have requests pending with the Service for protection under Article 3 of the Convention Against Torture.

(i) Except as otherwise provided, after March 22, 1999, the Service will not:

(A) Consider, under its pre-regulatory administrative policy to ensure compliance with the Convention Against Torture, whether Article 3 of that Convention prohibits the removal of an alien to a particular country, or

(B) Stay the removal of an alien based on a request filed with the Service for protection under Article 3 of that Convention.

(ii) For each alien who, on or before March 22, 1999, filed a request with the Service for protection under Article 3 of the Convention Against Torture, and whose request has not been finally decided by the Service, the Service shall provide written notice that, after March 22, 1999, consideration for protection under Article 3 can be obtained only through the provisions of this rule.

(A) The notice shall inform an alien who is under an order of removal issued by EOIR that, in order to seek consideration of a claim under §§ 208.16(c) or 208.17(a), such an alien must file a motion to reopen with the immigration court or the Board of Immigration Appeals. This notice shall be accompanied by a stay of removal, effective until 30 days after service of the notice on the alien. A motion to reopen filed under this paragraph for the limited purpose of asserting a claim under §§ 208.16(c) or 208.17(a) shall not be subject to the requirements for reopening in §§ 3.2 and 3.23 of this chapter. Such a motion shall be granted if it is accompanied by a copy of the notice described in paragraph (b)(3)(ii) or by other convincing evidence that the alien had a request pending with the Service for protection under Article 3 of the Convention Against Torture on March 22, 1999. The filing of such a motion shall extend the stay of removal during the pendency of the adjudication of this motion.

(B) The notice shall inform an alien who is under an administrative order of removal issued by the Service under section 238(b) of the Act or an exclusion, deportation, or removal order reinstated by the Service under section 241(a)(5) of the Act that the alien's claim to withholding of removal under § 208.16(c) or deferral of removal under § 208.17(a) will be considered under § 208.31.

(C) The notice shall inform an alien who is under an administrative order of removal issued by the Service under section 235(c) of the Act that the alien's claim to protection under the Convention Against Torture will be decided by the Service as provided in § 208.18(d) and 235.8(b)(4) and will not be considered under the provisions of this part relating to consideration or review by an immigration judge, the Board of Immigration Appeals, or an asylum officer.

(4) Aliens whose claims to protection under the Convention Against Torture were finally decided by the Service prior to March 22, 1999. Sections 208.16(c) and 208.17 (a) and paragraphs (b)(1) through (b)(3) of this section do not apply to cases in which, prior to March 22, 1999, the Service has made a final administrative determination about the applicability of Article 3 of the Convention Against Torture to the case of an alien who filed a request with the Service for protection under Article 3. If, prior to March 22, 1999, the Service determined that an applicant cannot be removed consistent with the Convention Against Torture, the alien shall be considered to have been granted withholding of removal under § 208.16(c), unless the alien is subject to mandatory denial of withholding of removal under § 208.16(d)(2) or (d)(3), in which case the alien will be considered to have been granted deferral of removal under 208.17(a). If, prior to March 22, 1999, the Service determined that an alien can be removed consistent with the Convention Against Torture, the alien will be considered to have been finally denied withholding of removal under § 208.16(c) and deferral of removal under § 208.17(a).

(c) Diplomatic assurances against torture obtained by the Secretary of State.

(1) The Secretary of State may forward to the Attorney General assurances that the Secretary has obtained from the government of a specific country that an alien would not be tortured there if the alien were removed to that country.

(2) If the Secretary of State forwards assurances described in paragraph (c)(1) of this section to the Attorney General for consideration by the Attorney General or her delegates under this paragraph, the Attorney General shall determine, in consultation with the Secretary of State, whether the assurances are sufficiently reliable to allow the alien's removal to that country consistent with Article 3 of the Convention Against Torture. The Attorney General's authority under this paragraph may be exercised by the Deputy Attorney General or by the Commissioner, Immigration and Naturalization Service, but may not be further delegated.

(3) Once assurances are provided under paragraph (c)(2) of this section, the alien's claim for protection under the Convention Against Torture shall not be considered further by an immigration judge, the Board of Immigration Appeals, or an asylum officer.

(d) Cases involving aliens ordered removed under section 235(c) of the Act. With respect to an alien terrorist or other alien subject to administrative removal under section 235(c) of the Act who requests protection under Article 3 of the Convention Against Torture, the Service will assess the applicability of Article 3 through the removal process to ensure that a removal order will not be executed under circumstances that would violate the obligations of the United States under Article 3. In such cases, the provisions of Part 208 relating to consideration or review by an immigration judge, the Board of Immigration Appeals, or an asylum officer shall not apply.

(e) Judicial review of claims for protection from removal under Article 3 of the Convention Against Torture.

(1) Pursuant to the provisions of section 2242(d) of the Foreign Affairs Reform and Restructuring Act of 1998, there shall be no judicial appeal or review of any action, decision, or claim raised under the Convention or that section, except as part of the review of a final order of removal pursuant to section 242 of the Act; provided however, that any appeal or petition regarding an action, decision, or claim under the Convention or under section 2242 of the Foreign Affairs Reform and Restructuring Act of 1998 shall not be deemed to include or authorize the consideration of any administrative order or decision, or portion thereof, the appeal or review of which is restricted or prohibited by the Act.

(2) Except as otherwise expressly provided, nothing in this paragraph shall be construed to create a private right of action or to authorize the consideration or issuance of administrative or judicial relief.

HISTORY:

[64 FR 8478, 8490, Feb. 19, 1999, as corrected at 64 FR 13881, Mar. 23, 1999; 85 FR 80274, 80389, Dec. 11, 2020]

§ 208.19 Decisions.

The decision of an asylum officer to grant or to deny asylum or to refer an asylum application, in accordance with § 208.14(b) or (c), shall be communicated in writing to the applicant. Pursuant to § 208.9(d), an applicant must appear in person to receive and to acknowledge receipt of the decision to grant or deny asylum, or to refer an asylum application unless, in the discretion of the asylum office director, service by mail is appropriate. A letter communicating denial of asylum or referral of the application shall state the basis for denial or referral and include an assessment of the applicant's credibility.

HISTORY:

[65 FR 76121, 76136, Dec. 6, 2000]

§ 208.20 Determining if an asylum application is frivolous.

(a) For applications filed on or after April 1, 1997, and before January 11, 2021, an applicant is subject to the provisions of section 208(d)(6) of the Act only if the alien received the notice required by section 208(d)(4)(A) of the Act and a final order by an immigration judge or the Board of Immigration Appeals specifically finds that the alien knowingly filed a frivolous asylum application. An application is frivolous if:

(1) Any of the material elements in the asylum application is deliberately fabricated, and the immigration judge or the Board is satisfied that the applicant, during the course of the proceedings, has had sufficient opportunity to account for any discrepancies or implausible aspects of the claim.

(2) Paragraphs (b) through (f) of this section shall only apply to applications filed on or after January 11, 2021.

(b) For applications filed on or after January 11, 2021, an asylum officer may determine that the applicant knowingly filed a frivolous asylum application and may refer the applicant to an immigration judge on that basis, so long as the applicant has received the notice required by section 208(d)(4)(A) of the Act. For any application referred to an immigration judge, an asylum officer's determination that an application is frivolous will not render an applicant permanently ineligible for immigration benefits unless an immigration judge or the Board makes a finding of frivolousness as described in paragraph 1208.20(c).

(c) For applications filed on or after January 11, 2021, an asylum application is frivolous if it:

(1) Contains a fabricated material element;

(2) Is premised upon false or fabricated evidence unless the application would have been granted without the false or fabricated evidence;

(3) Is filed without regard to the merits of the claim; or

(4) Is clearly foreclosed by applicable law.

(d) If the alien has been provided the warning required by section 208(d)(4)(A) of the Act, he or she need not be given any additional or further opportunity to account for any issues with his or her claim prior to the entry of a frivolousness finding.

(e) An asylum application may be found frivolous even if it was untimely filed.

(f) A withdrawn asylum application may also be found frivolous unless:

(1) The alien wholly disclaims the application and withdraws it with prejudice;

(2) The alien is eligible for and agrees to accept voluntary departure for a period of no more than 30 days pursuant to section 240B(a) of the Act;

(3) The alien withdraws any and all other applications for relief or protection with prejudice; and

(4) The alien waives his right to appeal and any rights to file, for any reason, a motion to reopen or reconsider.

(g) For purposes of this section, a finding that an alien knowingly filed a frivolous asylum application shall not preclude the alien from seeking withholding of removal under section 241(b)(3) of the Act or protection under the regulations issued pursuant to the Convention Against Torture's implementing legislation.

HISTORY:

[55 FR 30680, July 27, 1990; 60 FR 34090, June 30, 1995; 61 FR 18900, 18909, Apr. 29, 1996; 62 FR 10312, 10344, Mar. 6, 1997; 63 FR 3792, 3796, Jan. 27, 1998; redesignated and revised at 64 FR 8478, 8490, 8492, Feb. 19, 1999; redesignated at 65 FR 76121, 76136, Dec. 6, 2000; 85 FR 80274, 80389, Dec. 11, 2020]

§ 208.21 Admission of the asylee's spouse and children.

(a) Eligibility. In accordance with section 208(b)(3) of the Act, a spouse, as defined in section 101(a)(35) of the Act, 8 U.S.C. 1101(a)(35), or child, as defined in section 101(b)(1) of the Act, also may be granted asylum if accompanying, or following to join, the principal alien who was granted asylum, unless it is determined that the spouse or child is ineligible for asylum under section 208(b)(2)(A)(i), (ii), (iii), (iv) or (v) of the Act for applications filed on or after April 1, 1997, or under § 208.13(c)(2)(i)(A), (C), (D), (E), or (F) for applications filed before April 1, 1997.

(1) The spouse or child ordered, incited, assisted, or otherwise participated in the persecution of any persons on account of race, religion, nationality, membership in a particular social group, or political opinion;

(2) The spouse or child, having been convicted by a final judgment of a particularly serious crime in the United States, constitutes a danger to the community of the United States;

(3) The spouse or child has been convicted of an aggravated felony, as defined in section 101(a)(43) of the Act; or

(4) There are reasonable grounds for regarding the spouse or child a danger to the security of the United States.

(b) Relationship. The relationship of spouse and child as defined in sections 101(a)(35) and 101(b)(1) of the Act must have existed at the time the principal alien's asylum application was approved and must continue to exist at the time of filing for accompanying or following-to-join benefits and at the time of the spouse or child's subsequent admission to the United States. If the asylee proves that the asylee is the parent of a child who was born after asylum was granted, but who was in utero on the date of the asylum grant, the child shall be eligible to accompany or follow-to-join the asylee. The child's mother, if not the principal asylee, shall not be eligible to accompany or follow-to-join the principal asylee unless the child's mother was the principal asylee's spouse on the date the principal asylee was granted asylum.

(c) Spouse or child in the United States. When a spouse or child of an alien granted asylum is in the United States, but was not included in the asylee's benefit request, the asylee may request accompanying or following-to-join benefits for his or her spouse or child, by filing for each qualifying family member a Request for Refugee/Asylee Relative, with supporting evidence, and in accordance with the form instructions, regardless of the status of that spouse or child in the United States. A separate Request for Refugee/Asylee Relative must be filed by the asylee for each qualifying family member within two years of the date in which he or she was granted asylum status, unless it is determined by USCIS that this period should be extended for humanitarian reasons. Upon approval of the Request for Refugee/Asylee Relative, USCIS will notify the asylee of such approval. Employment will be authorized incident to status. To demonstrate employment authorization, USCIS will issue a document reflecting the derivative's current status as an asylee, or the derivative may apply, under 8 CFR 274a.12(a), for employment authorization. The approval of the Request for Refugee/Asylee Relative will remain valid for the duration of the relationship to the asylee and, in the case of a child, while the child is under 21 years of age and unmarried, provided also that the principal's status has not been revoked. However, the approved Request for Refugee/Asylee Relative will cease to confer immigration benefits after it has been used by the beneficiary for admission to the United States as a derivative of an asylee.

(d) Spouse or child outside the United States. When a spouse or child of an alien granted asylum is outside the United States, the asylee may request accompanying or following-to-join benefits for his or her spouse or child(ren) by filing a separate Request for Refugee/Asylee Relative for each qualifying family member in accordance with the form instructions. A separate Request for Refugee/Asylee Relative for each qualifying family member must be filed within two years of the date in which the asylee was granted asylum, unless USCIS determines that the filing period should be extended for humanitarian reasons. When the Request for Refugee/Asylee Relative is approved, USCIS will notify the asylee of such approval. USCIS also will send the approved request to the Department of State for transmission to the U.S. Embassy or Consulate having jurisdiction over the area in which the asylee's spouse or child is located. The approval of the Request for Refugee/Asylee Relative will remain valid for the duration of the relationship to the asylee and, in the case of a child, while the child is under 21 years of age and unmarried, provided also that the principal's status has not been revoked. However, the approved Request for Refugee/Asylee Relative will cease to confer immigration benefits after it has been used by the beneficiary for admission to the United States as a derivative of an asylee.

(e) Denial. If the spouse or child is found to be ineligible for the status accorded under section 208(c) of the Act, a written notice stating the basis for denial shall be forwarded to the principal alien. No appeal shall lie from this decision.

(f) Burden of proof. To establish the claimed relationship of spouse or child as defined in sections 101(a)(35) and 101(b)(1) of the Act, evidence must be submitted with the request as set forth in part 204 of this chapter. Where possible this will consist of the documents specified in § 204.2 (a)(1)(i)(B), (a)(1)(iii)(B), (a)(2), (d)(2), and (d)(5) of this chapter. The burden of proof is on the principal alien to establish by a preponderance of the evidence that any person on whose behalf he or she is making a request under this section is an eligible spouse or child.

(g) Duration. The spouse or child qualifying under section 208(c) of the Act shall be granted asylum for an indefinite period unless the principal's status is revoked.

HISTORY:

[55 FR 30680, July 27, 1990; 60 FR 34090, June 30, 1995; 61 FR 18900, 18909, Apr. 29, 1996; 62 FR 10312, 10344, Mar. 6, 1997; 63 FR 3792, 3796, Jan. 27, 1998; redesignated at 64 FR 8478, 8490, Feb. 19, 1999; redesignated and amended at 65 FR 76121, 76136, Dec. 6, 2000; 76 FR 53764, 53784, Aug. 29, 2011, as corrected at 76 FR 73475, Nov. 29, 2011]

§ 208.22 Effect on exclusion, deportation, and removal proceedings.

An alien who has been granted asylum may not be deported or removed unless his or her asylum status is terminated pursuant to § 208.24. An alien in exclusion, deportation, or removal proceedings who is granted withholding of removal or deportation, or deferral of removal, may not be deported or removed to the country to which his or her deportation or removal is ordered withheld or deferred unless the withholding order is terminated pursuant to § 208.24 or deferral is terminated pursuant to § 208.17(d) or (e).

HISTORY:

[55 FR 30680, July 27, 1990; 59 FR 62301, Dec. 5, 1994; 62 FR 10312, 10344, Mar. 6, 1997; redesignated and revised at 64 FR 8478, 8490, 8492, Feb. 19, 1999; redesignated and revised at 65 FR 76121, 76136, Dec. 6, 2000]

§ 208.23 Restoration of status.

An alien who was maintaining his or her nonimmigrant status at the time of filing an asylum application and has such application denied may continue in or be restored to that status, if it has not expired.

HISTORY:

[55 FR 30680, July 27, 1990; 59 FR 62301, Dec. 5, 1994; 62 FR

10312, 10344, Mar. 6, 1997; redesignated at 64 FR 8478, 8490, Feb. 19, 1999; redesignated at 65 FR 76121, 76136, Dec. 6, 2000]

§ 208.24 Termination of asylum or withholding of removal or deportation.

(a) Termination of asylum by USCIS. Except as provided in paragraph (e) of this section, an asylum officer may terminate a grant of asylum made under the jurisdiction of USCIS if, following an interview, the asylum officer determines that:

(1) There is a showing of fraud in the alien's application such that he or she was not eligible for asylum at the time it was granted;

(2) As to applications filed on or after April 1, 1997, one or more of the conditions described in section 208(c)(2) of the Act exist; or

(3) As to applications filed before April 1, 1997, the alien no longer has a well-founded fear of persecution upon return due to a change of country conditions in the alien's country of nationality or habitual residence or the alien has committed any act that would have been grounds for denial of asylum under § 208.13(c)(2).

(b) Termination of withholding of deportation or removal by USCIS. Except as provided in paragraph (e) of this section, an asylum officer may terminate a grant of withholding of deportation or removal made under the jurisdiction of USCIS if the asylum officer determines, following an interview, that:

(1) The alien is no longer entitled to withholding of deportation or removal because, owing to a fundamental change in circumstances relating to the original claim, the alien's life or freedom no longer would be threatened on account of race, religion, nationality, membership in a particular social group, or political opinion in the country from which deportation or removal was withheld.

(2) There is a showing of fraud in the alien's application such that the alien was not eligible for withholding of removal at the time it was granted;

(3) The alien has committed any other act that would have been grounds for denial of withholding of removal under section 241(b)(3)(B) of the Act had it occurred prior to the grant of withholding of removal; or

(4) For applications filed in proceedings commenced before April 1, 1997, the alien has committed any act that would have been grounds for denial of withholding of deportation under section 243(h)(2) of the Act.

(c) Procedure. Prior to the termination of a grant of asylum or withholding of deportation or removal, the alien shall be given notice of intent to terminate, with the reasons therefor, at least 30 days prior to the interview specified in paragraph (a) of this section before an asylum officer. The alien shall be provided the opportunity to present evidence showing that he or she is still eligible for asylum or withholding of deportation or removal. If the asylum officer determines that the alien is no longer eligible for asylum or withholding of deportation or removal, the alien shall be given written notice that asylum status or withholding of deportation or removal and any employment authorization issued pursuant thereto, are terminated.

(d) Termination of derivative status. The termination of asylum status for a person who was the principal applicant shall result in termination of the asylum status of a spouse or child whose status was based on the asylum application of the principal. Such termination shall not preclude the spouse or child of such alien from separately asserting an asylum or withholding of deportation or removal claim.

(e) Removal proceedings. When an alien's asylum status or withholding of removal or deportation is terminated under this section, the Service shall initiate removal proceedings, as appropriate, if the alien is not already in exclusion, deportation, or removal proceedings. Removal proceedings may take place in conjunction with a termination hearing scheduled under § 208.24(f).

(f) Termination of asylum, or withholding of deportation or removal, by an immigration judge or the Board of Immigration Appeals. An immigration judge or the Board of Immigration Appeals may reopen a case pursuant to 8 CFR 1003.2 and 8 CFR 1003.23 for the purpose of terminating a grant of asylum, or a withholding of deportation or removal. In such a reopened proceeding, the Service must establish, by a preponderance of evidence, one or more of the grounds set forth in paragraphs (a) or (b) of this section. In addition, an immigration judge may terminate a grant of asylum, or a withholding of deportation or removal, made under the jurisdiction of USCIS at any time after the alien has been provided a notice of intent to terminate by USCIS. Any termination under this paragraph may occur in conjunction with an exclusion, deportation, or removal proceeding.

(g) Termination of asylum for arriving aliens. If the Service determines that an applicant for admission who had previously been granted asylum in the United States falls within conditions set forth in § 208.24 and is inadmissible, the Service shall issue a notice of intent to terminate asylum and initiate removal proceedings under section 240 of the Act. The alien shall present his or her response to the intent to terminate during proceedings before the immigration judge.

HISTORY:

[55 FR 30680, July 27, 1990; 62 FR 10312, 10344, Mar. 6, 1997; redesignated at 64 FR 8478, 8490, Feb. 19, 1999; redesignated and amended at 65 FR 76121, 76136, Dec. 6, 2000; 76 FR 53764, 53785, Aug. 29, 2011; 78 FR 22770, 22771, Apr. 17, 2013]

§ 208.25 Severability.

The provisions of part 208 are separate and severable from one another. In the event that any provision in part 208 is stayed, enjoined, not implemented, or otherwise held invalid, the remaining provisions shall nevertheless be implemented as an independent rule and continue in effect.

HISTORY:

85 FR 80274, 80389, Dec. 11, 2020]

§§ 208.26 — 208.29 [Reserved]

[NO TEXT IN ORIGINAL]

Subpart B

Credible Fear of Persecution

§ 208.30 Credible fear determinations involving stowaways and applicants for admission found inadmissible pursuant to section 212(a)(6)(C) or 212(a)(7) of the Act. [Effective until December 31, 2025]

(a) *Jurisdiction*. The provisions of this subpart B apply to aliens subject to sections 235(a)(2) and 235(b)(1) of the Act. Pursuant to section 235(b)(1)(B) of the Act, DHS has exclusive jurisdiction to make the determinations described in this subpart B. Except as otherwise provided in this subpart B, paragraphs (b) through (g) of this section are the exclusive procedures applicable to stowaways and applicants for admission who are found inadmissible pursuant to section 212(a)(6)(C) or 212(a)(7) of the Act and who receive fear interviews, determinations, and reviews under section 235(b)(1)(B) of the Act. Prior to January 1, 2030, an alien physically present in or arriving in the Commonwealth of the Northern Mariana Islands is ineligible to apply for asylum and may only establish eligibility for withholding of removal pursuant to section 241(b)(3) of the Act or withholding or deferral of removal under the regulations issued pursuant to the Convention Against Torture's implementing legislation.

(b) Process and authority. If an alien subject to section 235(a)(2) or 235(b)(1) of the Act indicates an intention to apply for asylum, or expresses a fear of persecution or torture, or a fear of return to his or her country, the inspecting officer shall not proceed further with removal of the alien until the alien has been referred for an interview by a USCIS asylum officer in accordance with this section. A USCIS asylum officer shall then screen the alien for a credible fear of persecution or torture. An asylum officer, as defined in section 235(b)(1)(E) of the Act, has the authorities described in § 208.9(c). If in exercising USCIS's discretion, it is determined that circumstances so warrant, the asylum officer, after supervisory concurrence, may refer the alien for proceedings under section 240 of the Act without making a credible fear determination.

(c) Treatment of family units.

(1) A spouse or child of a principal alien who arrived in the United States concurrently with the principal alien shall be included in that alien's positive credible fear evaluation and determination, unless the principal alien or the spouse or child declines such inclusion. Any alien may have his or her evaluation and determination made separately, if that alien expresses such a desire. The option for members of a family unit to have their evaluations and determinations made separately shall be communicated to all family members at the beginning of the interview process.

(2) The asylum officer in the officer's discretion may also include other accompanying family members who arrived in the United States concurrently with a principal alien in that alien's positive fear evaluation and determination for purposes of family unity.

(d) Interview. A USCIS asylum officer will conduct the credible fear interview in a nonadversarial manner, separate and apart from the general public. The purpose of the interview shall be to elicit all relevant and useful information bearing on whether the alien can establish a credible fear of persecution or torture. The information provided during the interview may form the basis of an asylum application pursuant to paragraph (f) of this section and § 208.3(a)(2). The asylum officer shall conduct the interview as follows:

(1) If the officer conducting the interview determines that the alien is unable to participate effectively in the interview because of illness, fatigue, or other impediments, the officer may reschedule the interview.

(2) At the time of the interview, the asylum officer shall verify that the alien has received in writing the relevant information regarding the fear determination process. The officer shall also determine that the alien has an understanding of the fear determination process.

(3) The alien may be required to register his or her identity.

(4) The alien may consult with a person or persons of the alien's choosing prior to the interview or any review thereof, and may present other evidence, if available. Such consultation shall be at no expense to the Government and shall not unreasonably delay the process. Any person or persons with whom the alien chooses to consult may be present at the interview and may be permitted, in the discretion of the asylum officer, to present a statement at the end of the interview. The asylum officer, in his or her discretion, may place reasonable limits on the number of persons who may be present at the interview and on the length of the statement.

(5) If the alien is unable to proceed effectively in English, and if the asylum officer is unable to proceed competently in a language the alien speaks and understands, the asylum officer shall arrange for the assistance of an interpreter in conducting the interview. The interpreter must be at least 18 years of age and may not be the alien's attorney or representative of record, a witness testifying on the alien's behalf, a representative or employee of the alien's country of nationality, or, if the alien is stateless, the alien's country of last habitual residence.

(6) The asylum officer shall create a summary of the material facts as stated by the alien. At the conclusion of the interview, the officer shall review the summary with the alien and provide the alien with an opportunity to correct any errors therein.

(e) Determination.

(1) The asylum officer shall create a written record of the officer's determination, including a summary of the material facts as stated by the applicant, any additional facts relied on by the officer, and the officer's determination of whether, in light of such facts, the alien has established a credible fear of persecution or torture.

(2) An alien will be found to have a credible fear of persecution if there is a significant possibility, taking into account the credibility of the statements made by the alien in support of the alien's claim and such other facts as are known to the officer, that the alien can establish eligibility for asylum under section 208 of the Act or for withholding of removal under section 241(b)(3) of the Act, including that the alien is not subject to a mandatory bar, if considered under paragraph (e)(5)(ii) of this section. However, prior to January 1, 2030, in the case of an alien physically present in or arriving in the Commonwealth of the Northern Mariana Islands, the officer may only find a credible fear of persecution if there is a significant possibility that the alien can establish eligibility for withholding of removal pursuant to section 241(b)(3) of the Act.

(3) An alien will be found to have a credible fear of torture if the alien shows that there is a significant possibility that the alien is eligible for withholding of removal or deferral of removal under the Convention Against Torture, pursuant to § 208.16 or § 208.17.

(4) In all cases, the asylum officer will create a written record of his or her determination, including a summary of the material facts as stated by the alien, any additional facts relied on by the officer, and the officer's determination of whether, in light of such facts, the alien has established a credible fear of persecution, reasonable possibility of persecution, reasonable possibility of torture or that it is more likely than not that he or she would be tortured in the prospective country of removal. In determining whether the alien has a credible fear of persecution, as defined in section 235(b)(1)(B)(v) of the Act, a reasonable possibility of persecution or torture, or that it is more likely than not that he or she would be tortured in the prospective country of removal, the asylum officer shall consider whether the alien's case presents novel or unique issues that merit consideration in a full hearing before an immigration judge.

(5) Except as provided in paragraph (e)(6) or (7) of this section:

(i) If an alien is able to establish a credible fear of persecution or torture but appears to be subject to one or more of the mandatory bars to applying for, or being granted, asylum contained in section 208(a)(2) and (b)(2)(A)(vi) of the Act, the Department of Homeland Security shall nonetheless issue a Notice to Appear or retain jurisdiction over the alien's case for further consideration of the alien's claim pursuant to paragraph (f) of this section, if the alien is not a stowaway.

(ii) If an alien, who is unable to establish a credible fear of torture, is able to establish a credible fear of persecution but appears to be subject to one or more of the mandatory bars to being granted either asylum or withholding of removal, as set forth in section 208(b)(2)(A)(i) through (v) of the Act or section 241(b)(3)(B) of the Act, respectively, the asylum officer may consider the applicability of such bar(s) as part of the asylum officer's credible fear determination.

(A) The asylum officer shall issue a negative credible fear finding with regard to the alien's eligibility for asylum or withholding of removal under the Act if the asylum officer determines there is not a significant possibility that, in a proceeding on the merits, the alien would be able to establish by a preponderance of the evidence that such bar(s) do not apply.

(B) The asylum officer shall issue a Notice to Appear or retain jurisdiction over the alien's case for further consideration of the alien's claim pursuant to paragraph (f) of this section, if the asylum officer finds that there is a significant possibility that, in a proceeding on the merits, the alien would be able to establish by a preponderance of the evidence that such bar(s) do not apply.

(iii) In all cases, if the alien is a stowaway and the Department would otherwise initiate proceedings under paragraphs (e)(5)(i) and (ii) of this section, the Department shall place the alien in proceedings for consideration of the alien's claim pursuant to § 208.2(c)(3) and shall not retain jurisdiction over the case for further consideration nor issue a Notice to Appear.

(6) Prior to any determination concerning whether an alien arriving in the United States at a U.S.-Canada land border port-of-entry or in transit through the United States during removal by Canada or an alien who, on or after 12:01 a.m. on Saturday, March 25, 2023, entered the United States by crossing the U.S.-Canada land border between the ports-of-entry, including a crossing of the border in those waters as mutually designated by the United States and Canada, and who made an asylum or other protection claim relating to fear of persecution or torture within 14 days after such crossing, has a credible fear of persecution or torture, the asylum officer shall conduct a threshold screening interview to determine whether such an alien is ineligible to apply for asylum pursuant to section 208(a)(2)(A) of the Act and subject to removal to Canada by operation of the Agreement Between the Government of the United States and the Government of Canada for Cooperation in the Examination of Refugee Status Claims from Nationals of Third Countries ("Agreement"), which includes the Additional Protocol of 2022 to the Agreement Between the Government of the United States of America and the Government of Canada For Cooperation in the Examination of Refugee Status Claims from Nationals of Third Countries ("Additional Protocol of 2022"). In conducting this threshold screening interview, the asylum officer shall apply all relevant interview procedures outlined in paragraph (d) of this section, provided however, that paragraph (d)(2) of this section shall not apply to aliens described in this paragraph (e)(6). The asylum officer shall advise the alien of the exceptions contained in the Agreement, which includes the Additional Protocol of 2022, and question the alien as to applicability of any of these exceptions to the alien's case.

(i) If the asylum officer, with concurrence from a supervisory asylum officer, determines that an alien is subject to the Agreement, which includes the Additional Protocol of 2022, and that an alien does not qualify for an exception under the Agreement, which includes the Additional Protocol of 2022, during this threshold screening interview, the alien is ineligible to apply for asylum in the United States. After the asylum officer's documented finding is reviewed by a supervisory asylum officer, the alien shall be advised that the alien will be removed to Canada in order to pursue the alien's claims relating to a fear of persecution or torture under Canadian law. Aliens found ineligible to apply for asylum under this paragraph shall be removed to Canada.

(ii) If the alien establishes by a preponderance of the evidence that the alien qualifies for an exception under the terms of the Agreement, which includes the Additional Protocol of 2022, the asylum officer shall make a written notation of the basis of the exception, and then proceed immediately to a determination concerning whether the alien has a credible fear of persecution or torture under paragraph (d) of this section.

(iii) An alien qualifies for an exception to the Agreement, which includes the Additional Protocol of 2022, if the alien is not being removed from Canada in transit through the United States and:

(A) Is a citizen of Canada or, not having a country of nationality, is a habitual resident of Canada;

(B) Has in the United States a spouse, son, daughter, parent, legal guardian, sibling, grandparent, grandchild, aunt, uncle, niece, or nephew who has been granted asylum, refugee, or other lawful status in the United States, provided, however, that this exception shall not apply to an alien whose relative maintains only nonimmigrant visitor status, as defined in section 101(a)(15)(B) of the Act, or whose relative maintains only visitor status based on admission to the United States pursuant to the Visa Waiver Program;

(C) Has in the United States a spouse, son, daughter, parent, legal guardian, sibling, grandparent, grandchild, aunt, uncle, niece, or nephew who is at least 18 years of age and has an asylum application pending before U.S. Citizenship and Immigration Services, the Executive Office for Immigration Review, or on appeal in federal court in the United States;

(D) Is unmarried, under 18 years of age, and does not have a parent or legal guardian in either Canada or the United States;

(E) Arrived in the United States with a validly issued visa or other valid admission document, other than for transit, issued by the United States to the alien, or, being required to hold a visa to enter Canada, was not required to obtain a visa to enter the United States; or

(F) The Director of USCIS, or the Director's designee, determines, in the exercise of unreviewable discretion, that it is in the public interest to allow the alien to pursue a claim for asylum, withholding of removal, or protection under the Convention Against Torture, in the United States.

(iv) As used in paragraphs (e)(6)(iii)(B), (C), and (D) of this section only, "legal guardian" means a person currently vested with legal custody of such an alien or vested with legal authority to act on the alien's behalf, provided that such an alien is both unmarried and less than 18 years of age, and provided further that any dispute with respect to whether an individual is a legal guardian will be resolved on the basis of U.S. law.

(7) When an immigration officer has made an initial determination that an alien, other than an alien described in paragraph (e)(6) of this section and regardless of whether the alien is arriving at a port of entry, appears to be subject to the terms of an agreement authorized by section 208(a)(2)(A) of the Act, and seeks the alien's removal consistent with that provision, prior to any determination concerning whether the alien has a credible fear of persecution, reasonable possibility of persecution, or a reasonable possibility of torture, the asylum officer shall conduct a threshold screening interview to determine whether the alien is ineligible to apply for asylum in the United States and is subject to removal to a country ("receiving country") that is a signatory to the applicable agreement authorized by section 208(a)(2)(A) of the Act, other than the U.S.-Canada Agreement, which includes the Additional Protocol of 2022. In conducting this threshold screening interview, the asylum officer shall apply all relevant interview procedures outlined in paragraph (d) of this section, except that paragraphs (d)(2) and (4) of this section shall not apply to aliens described in this paragraph (e)(7). The asylum officer shall advise the alien of the applicable agreement's exceptions and question the alien as to applicability of any of these exceptions to the alien's case. The alien shall be provided written notice that if the alien fears removal to the prospective receiving country because of the likelihood of persecution on account of a protected ground or torture in that country and wants the officer to determine whether it is more likely than not that the alien would be persecuted on account of a protected ground or tortured in that country, the alien should affirmatively state to the officer such a fear of removal. If the alien affirmatively states such a fear, the asylum officer will determine whether the individual has demonstrated that it is more likely than not that the alien would be persecuted on account of a protected ground or tortured in that country.

(i)(A) If the asylum officer, with concurrence from a supervisory asylum officer, determines during the threshold screening interview that an alien does not qualify for an exception under the applicable agreement, and, if applicable, that the alien has not demonstrated that it is more likely than not that he or she would be persecuted on account of a protected ground or tortured in the receiving country, the alien is ineligible to apply for asylum in the United States. Subject to paragraph (e)(7)(i)(B) of this section, after the asylum officer's documented finding is reviewed by a supervisory asylum officer, the alien shall be advised that he or she will be removed to the receiving country, as appropriate under the applicable agreement, in order to pursue his or her claims relating to a fear of persecution or torture under the law of the receiving country. Prior to removal to a receiving country under an agreement authorized by section 208(a)(2)(A), the alien shall be informed that, in the receiving country, the alien will have an opportunity to pursue the alien's claim for asylum or equivalent temporary protection.

(B) Aliens found ineligible to apply for asylum under this paragraph (e)(7) shall be removed to the receiving country, depending on the applicable agreement, unless the alien voluntarily withdraws his or her request for asylum.

(ii) If the alien establishes by a preponderance of the evidence that he or she qualifies for an exception under the terms of the applicable agreement, or would more likely than not be persecuted on account of his or her race, religion, nationality, membership in a particular social group, or tortured, in the receiving country, the asylum officer shall make a written notation to that effect, and may then proceed to determine whether any other agreement is applicable to the alien under the procedures set forth in this paragraph (e)(7). If the alien establishes by a preponderance of the evidence that he or she qualifies for an exception under the terms of each of the applicable agreements, or would more likely than not be persecuted on account of his or her race, religion, nationality, membership in a particular social group, or tortured, in each of the prospective receiving countries, the asylum officer shall make a written notation to that effect, and then proceed immediately to a determination concerning whether the alien has a credible fear of persecution, reasonable possibility of persecution, or a reasonable possibility of torture, under paragraph (d) of this section.

(iii) An exception to an applicable agreement is defined under the terms of the agreement itself. Each agreement, including any exceptions, will be announced in a Federal Register document. If the asylum officer determines that an alien is within one of the classes covered by a section 208(a)(2)(A) agreement, the officer shall next determine whether the alien meets any of the applicable agreement's exceptions. Regardless of whether the text of the applicable agreement provides for the following exceptions, all such agreements, by operation of section 208(a)(2)(A) of the Act, and as applicable to the United States, are deemed to contain the following provisions:

(A) No alien may be removed, pursuant to an agreement authorized by section 208(a)(2)(A), to the alien's country of nationality, or, if the alien has no nationality, to the alien's country of last habitual residence; and

(B) No alien may be removed, pursuant to an agreement authorized by section 208(a)(2)(A), where the Director of USCIS, or the Director's designee, determines, in the exercise of unreviewable discretion, that it is in the public interest for the alien to receive asylum in the United States, and that the alien therefore may apply for asylum, withholding of removal, or protection under the Convention Against Torture, in the United States.

(iv) If the asylum officer determines the alien meets an exception under the applicable agreement, or would more likely than not be persecuted on account of a protected ground or tortured in the prospective receiving country, the officer may consider whether the alien is subject to another agreement and its exceptions or would more likely than not be persecuted on account of a protected ground or tortured in another receiving country. If another section 208(a)(2)(A) agreement may not be applied to the alien, the officer should immediately proceed to a credible fear interview.

(8) An asylum officer's determination shall not become final until reviewed by a supervisory asylum officer.

(f) Procedures for a positive fear determination. If, pursuant to paragraph (e) of this section, an alien stowaway or an alien subject to expedited removal establishes either a credible fear of persecution, reasonable possibility of persecution, a reasonable possibility of torture, or that it is more likely than not that they would be tortured in the prospective country of removal:

(1) Except as provided in paragraphs (e)(5)(iii) through (iv) of this section, DHS shall issue a Notice of Referral to Immigration Judge for asylum-and-withholding-only proceedings under 8 CFR 208.2(c)(1).

(2) Parole of the alien may be considered only in accordance with section 212(d)(5) of the Act and 8 CFR 212.5 of this chapter.

(g) *Procedures for a negative fear determination.*

(1) If, pursuant to paragraphs (e) and (f) of this section, an alien does not establish a credible fear of persecution, reasonable possibility of persecution, reasonable possibility of torture, or that he or she is more likely than not to be tortured in the prospective country of removal, DHS shall provide the alien with a written notice of decision and inquire whether the alien wishes to have an immigration judge review the negative determination, in accordance with section 235(b)(1)(B)(iii)(III) of the Act and this § 208.30. The alien must indicate whether he or she desires such review on a Record of Negative Fear Finding and Request for Review by Immigration Judge. If the alien refuses to make an indication, DHS shall consider such a response as a decision to decline review.

(i) If the alien requests such review, DHS shall arrange for detention of the alien and serve him or her with a Notice of Referral to Immigration Judge, for review of the negative fear determination in accordance with paragraph (g)(2) of this section.

(ii) If the alien is not a stowaway and does not request a review by an immigration judge, DHS shall order the alien removed with a Notice and Order of Expedited Removal, after review by a supervisory officer.

(iii) If the alien is a stowaway and the alien does not request a review by an immigration judge, DHS shall complete removal proceedings in accordance with section 235(a)(2) of the Act. (2) Review by immigration judge of a negative fear determination.

(2) Review by immigration judge of a negative fear determination.

(i) Immigration judges shall review negative fear determinations as provided in 8 CFR 1208.30(g). DHS, however, may reconsider a negative credible fear finding that has been concurred upon by an immigration judge after providing notice of its reconsideration to the immigration judge.

(ii) DHS shall provide the record of any negative fear determinations being reviewed, including copies of the Notice of Referral to Immigration Judge, the asylum officer's notes, the summary of the material facts, and other materials upon which the determination was based, to the immigration judge with the negative fear determination.

HISTORY:

[62 FR 10312, 10345, Mar. 6, 1997; 64 FR 8478, 8492, Feb. 19, 1999; 65 FR 76121, 76136, Dec. 6, 2000; 69 FR 69480, 69488, Nov. 29, 2004; 74 FR 55726, 55737, Oct. 28, 2009; 76 FR 53764, 53785, Aug. 29, 2011; 83 FR 55934, 55952, Nov. 9, 2018; 84 FR 33829, 33843, July 16, 2019; 84 FR 63994, 64008, Nov. 19, 2019; 85 FR 29264, 29310, May. 14, 2020; 85 FR 80274, 80389, Dec. 11, 2020; 85 FR 84160, 84194, Dec. 23, 2020; 86 FR 6847, Jan. 25, 2021; 86 FR 15069, Mar. 22, 2021; 86 FR 73615, Dec. 28, 2021; 87 FR 18078, 18218, Mar. 29, 2022; 87 FR 79789, Dec. 28, 2022; 88 FR 18227, 18239, Mar. 28, 2023; 88 FR 23329, 23330, Apr. 17, 2023; 88 FR 31314, 31449, May 16, 2023; 89 FR 103370, 103413, Dec. 18, 2024; 89 FR 105386, Dec. 27, 2024]

§ 208.30 Credible fear determinations involving stowaways and applicants for admission found inadmissible pursuant to section 212(a)(6)(C) or 212(a)(7) of the Act. [Effective December 31, 2025]

(a) *Jurisdiction*. The provisions of this subpart B apply to aliens subject to sections 235(a)(2) and 235(b)(1) of the Act. Pursuant to section 235(b)(1)(B) of the Act, DHS has exclusive jurisdiction to make the determinations described in this subpart B. Except as otherwise provided in this subpart B, paragraphs (b) through (g) of this section are the exclusive procedures applicable to stowaways and applicants for admission who are found inadmissible pursuant to section 212(a)(6)(C) or 212(a)(7) of the Act and who receive fear interviews, determinations, and reviews under section 235(b)(1)(B) of the Act. Prior to January 1, 2030, an alien physically present in or arriving in the Commonwealth of the Northern Mariana Islands is ineligible to apply for asylum and may only establish eligibility for withholding of removal pursuant to section 241(b)(3) of the Act or withholding or deferral of removal under the regulations issued pursuant to the Convention Against Torture's implementing legislation.

(b) Process and authority. If an alien subject to section 235(a)(2) or 235(b)(1) of the Act indicates an intention to apply for asylum, or expresses a fear of persecution or torture, or a fear of return to his or her country, the inspecting officer shall not proceed further with removal of the alien until the alien has been referred for an interview by a USCIS asylum officer in accordance with this section. A USCIS asylum officer shall then screen the alien for a credible fear of persecution or torture. An asylum officer, as defined in section 235(b)(1)(E) of the Act, has the authorities described in § 208.9(c). If in exercising USCIS's discretion, it is determined that circumstances so warrant, the asylum officer, after supervisory concurrence, may refer the alien for proceedings under section 240 of the Act without making a credible fear determination.

(c) Treatment of family units.

(1) A spouse or child of a principal alien who arrived in the United States concurrently with the principal alien shall be included in that alien's positive credible fear evaluation and determination, unless the principal alien or the spouse or child declines such inclusion. Any alien may have his or her evaluation and determination made separately, if that alien expresses such a desire. The option for members of a family unit to have their evaluations and determinations made separately shall be communicated to all family members at the beginning of the interview process.

(2) The asylum officer in the officer's discretion may also include other accompanying family members who arrived in the United States concurrently with a principal alien in that alien's positive fear evaluation and determination for purposes of family unity.

(d) Interview. A USCIS asylum officer will conduct the credible fear interview in a nonadversarial manner, separate and apart from the general public. The purpose of the interview shall be to elicit all relevant and useful information bearing on whether the alien can establish a credible fear of persecution or torture. The information provided during the interview may form the basis of an asylum application pursuant to paragraph (f) of this section and § 208.3(a)(2). The asylum officer shall conduct the interview as follows:

(1) If the officer conducting the interview determines that the alien is unable to participate effectively in the interview because of illness, fatigue, or other impediments, the officer may reschedule the interview.

(2) At the time of the interview, the asylum officer shall verify that the alien has received in writing the relevant information regarding the fear determination process. The officer shall also determine that the alien has an understanding of the fear determination process.

(3) The alien may be required to register his or her identity.

(4) The alien may consult with a person or persons of the alien's choosing prior to the interview or any review thereof, and may present other evidence, if available. Such consultation shall be at no expense to the Government and shall not unreasonably delay the process. Any person or persons with whom the alien chooses to consult may be present at the interview and may be permitted, in the discretion of the asylum officer, to present a statement at the end of the interview. The asylum officer, in his or her discretion, may place reasonable limits on the number of persons who may be present at the interview and on the length of the statement.

(5) If the alien is unable to proceed effectively in English, and if the asylum officer is unable to proceed competently in a language the alien speaks and understands, the asylum officer shall arrange for the assistance of an interpreter in conducting the interview. The interpreter must be at least 18 years of age and may not be the alien's attorney or representative of record, a witness testifying on the alien's behalf, a representative or employee of the alien's country of nationality, or, if the alien is stateless, the alien's country of last habitual residence.

(6) The asylum officer shall create a summary of the material facts as stated by the alien. At the conclusion of the interview, the officer shall review the summary with the alien and provide the alien with an opportunity to correct any errors therein.

(e) Determination.

(1) The asylum officer shall create a written record of the officer's determination, including a summary of the material facts as stated by the applicant, any additional facts relied on by the officer, and the officer's determination of whether, in light of such facts, the alien has established a credible fear of persecution or torture.

(2) An alien will be found to have a credible fear of persecution if there is a significant possibility, taking into account the credibility of the statements made by the alien in support of the alien's claim and such other facts as are known to the officer, that the alien can establish eligibility for asylum under section 208 of the Act or for withholding of removal under section 241(b)(3) of the Act. However, prior to January 1, 2030, in the case of an alien physically present in or arriving in the Commonwealth of the Northern Mariana Islands, the officer may only find a credible fear of persecution if there is a significant possibility that the alien can establish eligibility for withholding of removal pursuant to section 241(b)(3) of the Act.

(3) An alien will be found to have a credible fear of torture if the alien shows that there is a significant possibility that the alien is eligible for withholding of removal or deferral of removal under the Convention Against Torture, pursuant to § 208.16 or § 208.17.

(4) In all cases, the asylum officer will create a written record of his or her determination, including a summary of the material facts as stated by the alien, any additional facts relied on by the officer, and the officer's determination of whether, in light of such facts, the alien has established a credible fear of persecution, reasonable possibility of persecution, reasonable possibility of torture or that it is more likely than not that he or she would be tortured in the prospective country of removal. In determining whether the alien has a credible fear of persecution, as defined in section 235(b)(1)(B)(v) of the Act, a reasonable possibility of persecution or torture, or that it is more likely than not that he or she would be tortured in the prospective country of removal, the asylum officer shall consider whether the alien's case presents novel or unique issues that merit consideration in a full hearing before an immigration judge.

(5) Except as provided in paragraph (e)(6) or (7) of this section, if an alien is able to establish a credible fear of persecution or torture but appears to be subject to one or more of the mandatory bars to applying for, or being granted, asylum contained in section 208(a)(2) and (b)(2) of the Act, or to withholding of removal contained in section 241(b)(3)(B) of the Act, the Department of Homeland Security shall nonetheless issue a Notice to Appear or retain the alien for further consideration of the alien's claim pursuant to paragraph (f) of this section, if the alien is not a stowaway. If the alien is a stowaway, the Department shall place the alien in proceedings for consideration of the alien's claim pursuant to § 208.2(c)(3).

(6) Prior to any determination concerning whether an alien arriving in the United States at a U.S.-Canada land border port-of-entry or in transit through the United States during removal by Canada or an alien who, on or after 12:01 a.m. on Saturday, March 25, 2023, entered the United States by crossing the U.S.-Canada land border between the ports-of-entry, including a crossing of the border in those waters as mutually designated by the United States and Canada, and who made an asylum or other protection claim relating to fear of persecution or torture within 14 days after such crossing, has a credible fear of persecution or torture, the asylum officer shall conduct a threshold screening interview to determine whether such an alien is ineligible to apply for asylum pursuant to section 208(a)(2)(A) of the Act and subject to removal to Canada by operation of the Agreement Between the Government of the United States and the Government of Canada for Cooperation in the Examination of Refugee Status Claims from Nationals of Third Countries ("Agreement"), which includes the Additional Protocol of 2022 to the Agreement Between the Government of the United States of America and the Government of Canada For Cooperation in the Examination of Refugee Status Claims from Nationals of Third Countries ("Additional Protocol of 2022"). In conducting this threshold screening interview, the asylum officer shall apply all relevant interview procedures outlined in paragraph (d) of this section, provided however, that paragraph (d)(2) of this section shall not apply to aliens described in this paragraph (e)(6). The asylum officer shall advise the alien of the exceptions contained in the Agreement, which includes the Additional Protocol of 2022, and question the alien as to applicability of any of these exceptions to the alien's case.

(i) If the asylum officer, with concurrence from a supervisory asylum officer, determines that an alien is subject to the Agreement, which includes the Additional Protocol of 2022, and that an alien does not qualify for an exception under the Agreement, which includes the Additional Protocol of 2022, during this threshold screening interview, the alien is ineligible to apply for asylum in the United States. After the asylum officer's documented finding is reviewed by a supervisory asylum officer, the alien shall be advised that the alien will be removed to Canada in order to pursue the alien's claims relating to a fear of persecution or torture under Canadian law. Aliens found ineligible to apply for asylum under this paragraph shall be removed to Canada.

(ii) If the alien establishes by a preponderance of the evidence that the alien qualifies for an exception under the terms of the Agreement, which includes the Additional Protocol of 2022, the asylum officer shall make a written notation of the basis of the exception, and then proceed immediately to a determination concerning whether the alien has a credible fear of persecution or torture under paragraph (d) of this section.

(iii) An alien qualifies for an exception to the Agreement, which includes the Additional Protocol of 2022, if the alien is not being removed from Canada in transit through the United States and:

(A) Is a citizen of Canada or, not having a country of nationality, is a habitual resident of Canada;

(B) Has in the United States a spouse, son, daughter, parent, legal guardian, sibling, grandparent, grandchild, aunt, uncle, niece, or nephew who has been granted asylum, refugee, or other lawful status in the United States, provided, however, that this exception shall not apply to an alien whose relative maintains only nonimmigrant visitor status, as defined in section 101(a)(15)(B) of the Act, or whose relative maintains only visitor status based on admission to the United States pursuant to the Visa Waiver Program;

(C) Has in the United States a spouse, son, daughter, parent, legal guardian, sibling, grandparent, grandchild, aunt, uncle, niece, or nephew who is at least 18 years of age and has an asylum application pending before U.S. Citizenship and Immigration Services, the Executive Office for Immigration Review, or on appeal in federal court in the United States;

(D) Is unmarried, under 18 years of age, and does not have a parent or legal guardian in either Canada or the United States;

(E) Arrived in the United States with a validly issued visa or other valid admission document, other than for transit, issued by the United States to the alien, or, being required to hold a visa to enter Canada, was not required to obtain a visa to enter the United States; or

(F) The Director of USCIS, or the Director's designee, determines, in the exercise of unreviewable discretion, that it is in the public interest to allow the alien to pursue a claim for asylum, withholding of removal, or protection under the Convention Against Torture, in the United States.

(iv) As used in paragraphs (e)(6)(iii)(B), (C), and (D) of this section only, "legal guardian" means a person currently vested with legal custody of such an alien or vested with legal authority to act on the alien's behalf, provided that such an alien is both unmarried and less than 18 years of age, and provided further that any dispute with respect to whether an individual is a legal guardian will be resolved on the basis of U.S. law.

(7) When an immigration officer has made an initial determination that an alien, other than an alien described in paragraph (e)(6) of this section and regardless of whether the alien is arriving at a port of entry, appears to be subject to the terms of an agreement authorized by section 208(a)(2)(A) of the Act, and seeks the alien's removal consistent with that provision, prior to any determination concerning whether the alien has a credible fear of persecution, reasonable possibility of persecution, or a reasonable possibility of torture, the asylum officer shall conduct a threshold screening interview to determine whether the alien is ineligible to apply for asylum in the United States and is subject to removal to a country ("receiving country") that is a signatory to the applicable agreement authorized by section 208(a)(2)(A) of the Act, other than the U.S.-Canada Agreement, which includes the Additional Protocol of 2022. In conducting this threshold screening interview, the asylum officer shall apply all relevant interview procedures outlined in paragraph (d) of this section, except that paragraphs (d)(2) and (4) of this section shall not apply to aliens described in this paragraph (e)(7). The asylum officer shall advise the alien of the applicable agreement's exceptions and question the alien as to applicability of any of these exceptions to the alien's case. The alien shall be provided written notice that if the alien fears removal to the prospective receiving country because of the likelihood of persecution on account of a protected ground or torture in that country and wants the officer to determine whether it is more likely than not that the alien would be persecuted on account of a protected ground or tortured in that country, the alien should affirmatively state to the officer such a fear of removal. If the alien affirmatively states such a fear, the asylum officer will determine whether the individual has demonstrated that it is more likely than not that the alien would be persecuted on account of a protected ground or tortured in that country.

(i)(A) If the asylum officer, with concurrence from a supervisory asylum officer, determines during the threshold screening interview that an alien does not qualify for an exception under the applicable agreement, and, if applicable, that the alien has not demonstrated that it is more likely than not that he or she would be persecuted on account of a protected ground or tortured in the receiving country, the alien is ineligible to apply for asylum in the United States. Subject to paragraph (e)(7)(i)(B) of this section, after the asylum officer's documented finding is reviewed by a supervisory asylum officer, the alien shall be advised that he or she will be removed to the receiving country, as appropriate under the applicable agreement, in order to pursue his or her claims relating to a fear of persecution or torture under the law of the receiving country. Prior to removal to a receiving country under an agreement authorized by section 208(a)(2)(A), the alien shall be informed that, in the receiving country, the alien will have an opportunity to pursue the alien's claim for asylum or equivalent temporary protection.

(B) Aliens found ineligible to apply for asylum under this paragraph (e)(7) shall be removed to the receiving country, depending on the applicable agreement, unless the alien voluntarily withdraws his or her request for asylum.

(ii) If the alien establishes by a preponderance of the evidence that he or she qualifies for an exception under the terms of the applicable agreement, or would more likely than not be persecuted on account of his or her race, religion, nationality, membership in a particular social group, or tortured, in the receiving country, the asylum officer shall make a written notation to that effect, and may then proceed to determine whether any other agreement is applicable to the alien under the procedures set forth in this paragraph (e)(7). If the alien establishes by a preponderance of the evidence that he or she qualifies for an exception under the terms of each of the applicable agreements, or would more likely than not be persecuted on account of his or her race, religion, nationality, membership in a particular social group, or tortured, in each of the prospective receiving countries, the asylum officer shall make a written notation to that effect, and then proceed immediately to a determination concerning whether the alien has a credible fear of persecution, reasonable possibility of persecution, or a reasonable possibility of torture, under paragraph (d) of this section.

(iii) An exception to an applicable agreement is defined under the terms of the agreement itself. Each agreement, including any exceptions, will be announced in a Federal Register document. If the asylum officer determines that an alien is within one of the classes covered by a section 208(a)(2)(A) agreement, the officer shall next determine whether the alien meets any of the applicable agreement's exceptions. Regardless of whether the text of the applicable agreement provides for the following exceptions, all such agreements, by operation of section 208(a)(2)(A) of the Act, and as applicable to the United States, are deemed to contain the following provisions:

(A) No alien may be removed, pursuant to an agreement authorized by section 208(a)(2)(A), to the alien's country of nationality, or, if the alien has no nationality, to the alien's country of last habitual residence; and

(B) No alien may be removed, pursuant to an agreement authorized by section 208(a)(2)(A), where the Director of USCIS, or the Director's designee, determines, in the exercise of unreviewable discretion, that it is in the public interest for the alien to receive asylum in the United States, and that the alien therefore may apply for asylum, withholding of removal, or protection under the Convention Against Torture, in the United States.

(iv) If the asylum officer determines the alien meets an exception under the applicable agreement, or would more likely than not be persecuted on account of a protected ground or tortured in the prospective receiving country, the officer may consider whether the alien is subject to another agreement and its exceptions or would more likely than not be persecuted on account of a protected ground or tortured in another receiving country. If another section 208(a)(2)(A) agreement may not be applied to the alien, the officer should immediately proceed to a credible fear interview.

(8) An asylum officer's determination shall not become final until reviewed by a supervisory asylum officer.

(f) Procedures for a positive fear determination. If, pursuant to paragraph (e) of this section, an alien stowaway or an alien subject to expedited removal establishes either a credible fear of persecution, reasonable possibility of persecution, a reasonable possibility of torture, or that it is more likely than not that they would be tortured in the prospective country of removal:

(1) Except as provided in paragraphs (e)(5)(iii) through (iv) of this section, DHS shall issue a Notice of Referral to Immigration Judge for asylum-and-withholding-only proceedings under 8 CFR 208.2(c)(1).

(2) Parole of the alien may be considered only in accordance with section 212(d)(5) of the Act and 8 CFR 212.5 of this chapter.

(g) *Procedures for a negative fear determination.*

(1) If, pursuant to paragraphs (e) and (f) of this section, an alien does not establish a credible fear of persecution, reasonable possibility of persecution, reasonable possibility of torture, or that he or she is more likely than not to be tortured in the prospective country of removal, DHS shall provide the alien with a written notice of decision and inquire whether the alien wishes to have an immigration judge review the negative determination, in accordance with section 235(b)(1)(B)(iii)(III) of the Act and this § 208.30. The alien must indicate whether he or she desires such review on a Record of Negative Fear Finding and Request for Review by Immigration Judge. If the alien refuses to make an indication, DHS shall consider such a response as a decision to decline review.

(i) If the alien requests such review, DHS shall arrange for detention of the alien and serve him or her with a Notice of Referral to Immigration Judge, for review of the negative fear determination in accordance with paragraph (g)(2) of this section.

(ii) If the alien is not a stowaway and does not request a review by an immigration judge, DHS shall order the alien removed with a Notice and Order of Expedited Removal, after review by a supervisory officer.

(iii) If the alien is a stowaway and the alien does not request a review by an immigration judge, DHS shall complete removal proceedings in accordance with section 235(a)(2) of the Act. (2) Review by immigration judge of a negative fear determination.

(2) Review by immigration judge of a negative fear determination.

(i) Immigration judges shall review negative fear determinations as provided in 8 CFR 1208.30(g). DHS, however, may reconsider a negative credible fear finding that has been concurred upon by an immigration judge after providing notice of its reconsideration to the immigration judge.

(ii) DHS shall provide the record of any negative fear determinations being reviewed, including copies of the Notice of Referral to Immigration Judge, the asylum officer's notes, the summary of the material facts, and other materials upon which the determination was based, to the immigration judge with the negative fear determination.

HISTORY:

[62 FR 10312, 10345, Mar. 6, 1997; 64 FR 8478, 8492, Feb. 19, 1999; 65 FR 76121, 76136, Dec. 6, 2000; 69 FR 69480, 69488, Nov. 29, 2004; 74 FR 55726, 55737, Oct. 28, 2009; 76 FR 53764, 53785, Aug. 29, 2011; 83 FR 55934, 55952, Nov. 9, 2018; 84 FR 33829, 33843, July 16, 2019; 84 FR 63994, 64008, Nov. 19, 2019; 85 FR 29264, 29310, May. 14, 2020; 85 FR 80274, 80389, Dec. 11, 2020; 85 FR 84160, 84194, Dec. 23, 2020; 86 FR 6847, Jan. 25, 2021; 86 FR 15069, Mar. 22, 2021; 86 FR 73615, Dec. 28, 2021; 87 FR 18078, 18218, Mar. 29, 2022; 87 FR 79789, Dec. 28, 2022; 88 FR 18227, 18239, Mar. 28, 2023; 88 FR 23329, 23330, Apr. 17, 2023; 88 FR 31314, 31449, May 16, 2023; 89 FR 103370, 103413, Dec. 18, 2024; 89 FR 105386, Dec. 27, 2024]

§ 208.31 Reasonable fear of persecution or torture determinations involving aliens ordered removed under section 238(b) of the Act and aliens whose removal is reinstated under section 241(a)(5) of the Act.

(a) Jurisdiction. This section shall apply to any alien ordered removed under section 238(b) of the Act or whose deportation, exclusion, or removal order is reinstated under section 241(a)(5) of the Act who, in the course of the administrative removal or reinstatement process, expresses a fear of returning to the country of removal. USCIS has exclusive jurisdiction to make reasonable fear determinations, and EOIR has exclusive jurisdiction to review such determinations.

(b) Initiation of reasonable fear determination process. Upon issuance of a Final Administrative Removal Order under § 238.1 of this chapter, or notice under § 241.8(b) of this chapter that an alien is subject to removal, an alien described in paragraph (a) of this section shall be referred to an asylum officer for a reasonable fear determination. In the absence of exceptional circumstances, this determination will be conducted within 10 days of the referral.

(c) Interview and procedure. The asylum officer shall conduct the interview in a non-adversarial manner, separate and apart from the general public. At the time of the interview, the asylum officer shall determine that the alien has an understanding of the reasonable fear determination process. The alien may be represented by counsel or an accredited representative at the interview, at no expense to the Government, and may present evidence, if available, relevant to the possibility of persecution or torture. The alien's representative may present a statement at the end of the interview. The asylum officer, in his or her discretion, may place reasonable limits on the number of persons who may be present at the interview and the length of the statement. If the alien is unable to proceed effectively in English, and if the asylum officer is unable to proceed competently in a language chosen by the alien, the asylum officer shall arrange for the assistance of an interpreter in conducting the interview. The interpreter may not be a representative or employee of the applicant's country or nationality, or if the applicant is stateless, the applicant's country of last habitual residence. The asylum officer shall create a summary of the material facts as stated by the applicant. At the conclusion of the interview, the officer shall review the summary with the alien and provide the alien with an opportunity to correct errors therein. The asylum officer shall create a written record of his or her determination, including a summary of the material facts as stated by the applicant, any additional facts relied on by the officers, and the officer's determination of whether, in light of such facts, the alien has established a reasonable fear of persecution or torture. The alien shall be determined to have a reasonable fear of persecution if the alien establishes a reasonable possibility that he or she would be persecuted on account of his or her race, religion, nationality, membership in a particular social group or political opinion, unless the alien appears to be subject to one or more of the mandatory bars to being granted withholding of removal under the Act contained in section 241(b)(3)(B) of the Act and the alien fails to show that there is a reasonable possibility that no mandatory bar applies, if the asylum officer considers such bars. The alien shall be determined to have a reasonable fear of torture if the alien establishes a reasonable possibility that he or she would be tortured in the country of removal.

(d) Authority. Asylum officers conducting screening determinations under this section shall have the authority described in § 208.9(c).

(e) Referral to Immigration Judge. If an asylum officer determines that an alien described in this section has a reasonable fear of persecution or torture, the officer shall so inform the alien and issue a Form I-863, Notice of Referral to the Immigration Judge, for full consideration of the request for withholding of removal only. Such cases shall be adjudicated by the immigration judge in accordance with the provisions of § 208.16. Appeal of the immigration judge's decision shall lie to the Board of Immigration Appeals.

(f) Removal of aliens with no reasonable fear of persecution or torture. If the asylum officer determines that the alien has not established a reasonable fear of persecution or torture, the asylum officer shall inform the alien in writing of the decision and shall inquire whether the alien wishes to have an immigration judge review the negative decision, using the Record of Negative Reasonable Fear Finding and Request for Review by Immigration Judge, on which the alien must indicate whether he or she desires such review. If the alien refuses to make an indication, DHS shall consider such a response as a decision to decline review.

(g) Review by immigration judge. The asylum officer's negative decision regarding reasonable fear shall be subject to review by an immigration judge upon the alien's request. If the alien requests such review, the asylum officer shall serve him or her with a Notice of Referral to Immigration Judge. The record of determination, including copies of the Notice of Referral to Immigration Judge, the asylum officer's notes, the summary of the material facts, and other materials upon which the determination was based shall be provided to the immigration judge with the negative determination. The immigration judge's review shall proceed under the procedures set forth in 8 CFR 1208.31(g).

HISTORY:

[64 FR 8478, 8493, Feb. 19, 1999, as corrected at 64 FR 13881, Mar. 23, 1999; 76 FR 53764, 53785, Aug. 29, 2011; 85 FR 80274, 80392, Dec. 11, 2020; 89 FR 103370, 103413, Dec. 18, 2024]

Subpart C

Lawful Pathways and Asylum Eligibility for Certain Aliens Who Entered Between May 11, 2023, and May 11, 2025

§ 208.33 Lawful pathways condition on asylum eligibility.

Notwithstanding any contrary section of this part, including §§ 208.2, 208.13, and 208.30—

(a) Condition on eligibility.

(1) Applicability. A rebuttable presumption of ineligibility for asylum applies to an alien who enters the United States from Mexico at the southwest land border or adjacent coastal borders without documents sufficient for lawful admission as described in section 212(a)(7) of the Act and whose entry was:

(i) Between May 11, 2023, and May 11, 2025,

(ii) Subsequent to the end of implementation of the Title 42 public health Order issued on August 2, 2021, and related prior orders issued pursuant to the authorities in sections 362 and 365 of the Public Health Service Act (42 U.S.C. 265, 268) and the implementing regulation at 42 CFR 71.40, and

(iii) After the alien traveled through a country other than the alien's country of citizenship, nationality, or, if stateless, last habitual residence, that is a party to the 1951 United Nations Convention relating to the Status of Refugees or the 1967 Protocol relating to the Status of Refugees.

(2) Exceptions to applicability of the rebuttable presumption. The rebuttable presumption described in paragraph (a)(1) of this section does not apply if:

(i) The alien was, at the time of entry, an unaccompanied alien child as defined in 6 U.S.C. 279(g)(2); or

(ii) The alien, or a member of the alien's family as described in § 208.30(c) with whom the alien is traveling:

(A) Was provided appropriate authorization to travel to the United States to seek parole, pursuant to a DHS-approved parole process;

(B) Presented at a port of entry, pursuant to a pre-scheduled time and place, or presented at a port of entry without a pre-scheduled time and place, if the alien demonstrates by a preponderance of the evidence that it was not possible to access or use the DHS scheduling system due to language barrier, illiteracy, significant technical failure, or other ongoing and serious obstacle; or

(C) Sought asylum or other protection in a country through which the alien traveled and received a final decision denying that application. A final decision includes any denial by a foreign government of the applicant's claim for asylum or other protection through one or more of that government's pathways for that claim. A final decision does not include a determination by a foreign government that the alien abandoned the claim.

(3) Rebuttal of the presumption.

(i) An alien subject to the presumption described in paragraph (a)(1) of this section can rebut the presumption by demonstrating by a preponderance of the evidence that exceptionally compelling circumstances exist, including if the alien demonstrates that, at the time of entry, the alien or a member of the alien's family as described in § 208.30(c) with whom the alien is traveling:

(A) Faced an acute medical emergency;

(B) Faced an imminent and extreme threat to life or safety, such as an imminent threat of rape, kidnapping, torture, or murder; or

(C) Satisfied the definition of "victim of a severe form of trafficking in persons" provided in § 214.201 of this chapter.

(ii) An alien who demonstrates by a preponderance of the evidence any of the circumstances in paragraph (a)(3)(i) of this section shall necessarily rebut the presumption in paragraph (a)(1) of this section.

(b) Application in credible fear determinations —

(1) Initial determination. The asylum officer shall first determine whether the alien is covered by the presumption in paragraph (a)(1) of this section and, if so, whether the alien has rebutted the presumption in accordance with paragraph (a)(3) of this section.

(i) If the alien is covered by the presumption in paragraph (a)(1) of this section and fails to rebut the presumption in accordance with paragraph (a)(3) of this section, then the asylum officer shall enter a negative credible fear determination with respect to the alien's asylum claim and continue to consider the alien's claim under paragraph (b)(2) of this section.

(ii) If the alien is not covered by the presumption in paragraph (a)(1) of this section or has rebutted the presumption in accordance with paragraph (a)(3) of this section, the asylum officer shall follow the procedures in § 208.30.

(2) Additional procedures.

(i) In cases in which the asylum officer enters a negative credible fear determination under paragraph (b)(1)(i) of this section, the asylum officer will assess whether the alien has established a reasonable possibility of persecution (meaning a reasonable possibility of being persecuted because of their race, religion, nationality, membership in a particular social group, or political opinion) or torture, with respect to the identified country or countries of removal identified pursuant to section 241(b) of the Act. As part of this reasonable possibility determination, if there is evidence that the alien is subject to one or more of the mandatory bars to being granted withholding of removal under the Act contained in section 241(b)(3)(B) of the Act, the asylum officer may consider the applicability of such bar(s).

(ii) In cases described in paragraph (b)(2)(i) of this section, if the alien establishes a reasonable possibility of persecution with respect to the identified country or countries of removal and, to the extent bars are considered, that there is a reasonable possibility that no mandatory bar applies, the Department will issue a Form I-862, Notice to Appear. If the alien establishes a reasonable possibility of torture with respect to the identified country or countries of removal, the Department will issue a Form I-862, Notice to Appear.

(iii) In cases described in paragraph (b)(2)(i) of this section, if an alien fails to establish a reasonable possibility of persecution with respect to the identified country or countries of removal or, to the extent bars are considered, fails to establish that there is a reasonable possibility that no mandatory bar applies, and fails to establish a reasonable possibility of torture with respect to the identified country or countries of removal, the asylum officer will provide the alien with a written notice of decision and inquire whether the alien wishes to have an immigration judge review the negative credible fear determination.

(iv) The alien must indicate whether he or she desires such review on a Record of Negative Fear Finding and Request for Review by Immigration Judge.

(v) Only if the alien requests such review by so indicating on the Record of Negative Fear shall the asylum officer serve the alien with a Notice of Referral to Immigration Judge. The record of determination, including copies of the Notice of Referral to Immigration Judge, the asylum officer's notes, the summary of the material facts, and other materials upon which the determination was based shall be provided to the immigration judge with the negative determination. Immigration judges will evaluate the case as provided in 8 CFR 1208.33(b). The case shall then proceed as set forth in paragraphs (b)(2)(v)(A) through (C) of this section.

(A) Where the immigration judge issues a positive credible fear determination under 8 CFR 1208.33(b)(2)(i), the case shall proceed under 8 CFR 1208.30(g)(2)(iv)(B).

(B) Where the immigration judge issues a positive credible fear determination under 8 CFR 1208.33(b)(2)(ii), DHS shall issue a Form I-862, Notice to Appear, to commence removal proceedings under section 240 of the Act.

(C) Where the immigration judge issues a negative credible fear determination, the case shall be returned to DHS for removal of the alien. No appeal shall lie from the immigration judge's decision and no request for reconsideration may be submitted to USCIS. Nevertheless, USCIS may, in its sole discretion, reconsider a negative determination.

(c) Continuing applicability of condition on eligibility.

(1) Subject to paragraph (c)(2) of this section, the condition on asylum eligibility in paragraph (a)(1) of this section shall apply to any asylum application filed by an alien who entered the United States during the time and in the manner specified in paragraph (a)(1) of this section and who is not covered by an exception in paragraph (a)(2) of this section, regardless of when the application is filed and adjudicated.

(2) The conditions on asylum eligibility in paragraph (a)(1) of this section shall not apply to an asylum application filed by an alien described in paragraph (c)(1) of this section if the asylum application is filed after May 11, 2025, the alien was under the age of 18 at the time of the entry referenced in paragraph (c)(1) of this section, and the alien is applying for asylum as a principal applicant.

(d) Severability. The Department intends that any provision of this section held to be invalid or unenforceable by its terms, or as applied to any person or circumstance, should be construed so as to continue to give the maximum effect to the provision permitted by law, unless such holding is that the provision is wholly invalid and unenforceable, in which event the provision should be severed from the remainder of this section and the holding should not affect the remainder of this section or the application of the provision to persons not similarly situated or to dissimilar circumstances.

HISTORY:

[88 FR 31314, 31449, May 16, 2023; 89 FR 81156, 81284, Oct. 7, 2024; 89 FR 103370, 103414, Dec. 18, 2024]

Subpart D

Eligibility for Aliens Who Enter the United States During Emergency Border Circumstances

208.35 Limitation on asylum eligibility and credible fear procedures for those who enter the United States during emergency border circumstances.

Notwithstanding any contrary section of this part, including §§ 208.2, 208.13, 208.30, and 208.33—

(a) Limitation on eligibility.

(1) Applicability. An alien who is described in § 208.13(g) and who is not described in section 3(b) of the Presidential Proclamation of June 3, 2024, as defined in 8 CFR 208.13(h), is ineligible for asylum.

(2) Exceptions.

(i) This limitation on eligibility does not apply if the alien demonstrates by a preponderance of the evidence that exceptionally compelling circumstances exist, including if the alien, or the alien's family member as described in § 208.30(c) with whom the alien is traveling, demonstrates by a preponderance of the evidence that, at the time of entry, the alien or a member of the alien's family as described in § 208.30(c) with whom the alien is traveling:

(A) Faced an acute medical emergency;

(B) Faced an imminent and extreme threat to life or safety, such as an imminent threat of rape, kidnapping, torture, or murder; or

(C) Satisfied the definition of "victim of a severe form of trafficking in persons" provided in § 214.201 of this chapter.

(ii) An alien who demonstrates by a preponderance of the evidence any of the circumstances in paragraph (a)(2)(i) of this section shall necessarily establish exceptionally compelling circumstances.

(iii) An alien described in section 3(b) of the Presidential Proclamation of June 3, 2024, as defined in 8 CFR 208.13(h), or who establishes exceptionally compelling circumstances under paragraph (a)(2)(i) of this section has established exceptionally compelling circumstances under § 208.33(a)(3).

(b) Application in credible fear determinations.

(1) Initial determination. The asylum officer shall first determine whether the alien is subject to the limitation on asylum eligibility under paragraph (a) of this section.

(i) Where the asylum officer determines that the alien is subject to the limitation on asylum eligibility under paragraph (a) of this section, then the asylum officer shall enter a negative credible fear determination with respect to the alien's asylum claim and continue to consider the alien's claim under paragraph (b)(2) of this section.

(ii) Where the asylum officer determines that the alien is not subject to the limitation on asylum eligibility under paragraph (a) of this section because the alien is not described in § 208.13(g), the asylum officer shall follow the procedures in § 208.33(b).

(iii) Where the asylum officer determines that the alien is not subject to the limitation on asylum eligibility under paragraph (a) of this section because the alien is described in section 3(b) of the Presidential Proclamation of June 3, 2024, as defined in 8 CFR 208.13(h), or is excepted from the limitation on asylum eligibility under paragraph (a)(2) of this section, the asylum officer shall follow the procedures in § 208.30.

(2) Protection eligibility screening.

(i) In cases in which the asylum officer enters a negative credible fear determination under paragraph (b)(1)(i) or (b)(3) of this section, the asylum officer will assess the alien under the procedures set forth in § 208.33(b)(2)(i) except that the asylum officer will apply a reasonable probability standard. For purposes of this section, reasonable probability means substantially more than a reasonable possibility, but somewhat less than more likely than not.

(ii) In cases described in paragraph (b)(2)(i) or (b)(3) of this section, if the alien establishes a reasonable probability of persecution or torture with respect to the designated country or countries of removal, the Department will issue a positive credible fear determination and follow the procedures in § 208.30(f). For any case in which USCIS retains jurisdiction over the application for asylum pursuant to § 208.2(a)(1)(ii) for further consideration in an interview pursuant to § 208.9, USCIS may require aliens who received a negative credible fear determination with respect to their asylum claim under paragraph (b)(1)(i) of this section to submit a Form I-589, Application for Asylum and for Withholding of Removal, together with any additional supporting evidence in accordance with the instructions on the form, to USCIS within 30 days from the date of service of the positive credible fear determination. The date of service of the positive credible fear determination remains the date of filing and receipt of the asylum application under § 208.3(a)(2); however, for any case in which USCIS requires the alien to submit a Form I-589, it may extend the timelines in § 208.9(a)(1) and (e)(2) by up to 15 days. If USCIS requires the alien to submit a Form I-589 and the alien fails to do so within the applicable timeline, USCIS shall issue a Form I-862, Notice to Appear.

(iii) In cases described in paragraph (b)(2)(i) or (b)(3) of this section, if the alien fails to establish a reasonable probability of persecution or torture with respect to all designated countries of removal, the asylum officer will provide the alien with a written notice of decision and inquire whether the alien wishes to have an immigration judge review the negative credible fear determinations.

(iv) The alien must indicate whether he or she desires such review on a Record of Negative Fear Finding and Request for Review by Immigration Judge.

(v) Only if the alien requests such review by so indicating on the Record of Negative Fear shall the asylum officer serve the alien with a Notice of Referral to Immigration Judge. The record of determination, including copies of the Notice of Referral to Immigration Judge, the asylum officer's notes, the summary of the material facts, and other materials upon which the determination was based shall be provided to the immigration judge with the negative determination. Immigration judges will evaluate the case as provided in 8 CFR 1208.35(b). The case shall then proceed as set forth in paragraphs (b)(2)(v)(A) and (B) of this section.

(A) Where the immigration judge issues a positive credible fear determination under 8 CFR 1208.35(b)(2)(iii) or (b)(4), the case shall proceed under 8 CFR 1208.30(g)(2)(iv)(B).

(B) Where the immigration judge issues a negative credible fear determination, the case shall be returned to the Department for removal of the alien. No appeal shall lie from the immigration judge's decision and no request for reconsideration may be submitted to USCIS. Nevertheless, USCIS may, in its sole discretion, reconsider a negative determination.

(3) Procedures in the absence of the limitation on asylum eligibility. If the limitation on asylum eligibility in paragraph (a) of this section is held to be invalid or unenforceable by its terms, or as applied to any person or circumstance, then during the period(s) described in § 208.13(g), the asylum officer shall, as applicable, apply a reasonable probability screening standard for any protection screening under § 208.33(b)(2).

(c) Family unity in the asylum merits process. In cases where the Department retains jurisdiction over the application for asylum pursuant to § 208.2(a)(1)(ii), where a principal asylum applicant is found eligible for withholding of removal under section 241(b)(3) of the Act or withholding of removal under § 208.16(c)(2) and would be granted asylum but for the limitation on asylum in paragraph (a)(1) of this section or § 208.33(a), or both, and where an accompanying spouse or child as defined in section 208(b)(3)(A) of the Act does not independently qualify for asylum or other protection from removal or the principal asylum applicant has a spouse or child who would be eligible to follow to join that applicant as described in section 208(b)(3)(A) of the Act, the asylum officer may deem the principal applicant to have established exceptionally compelling circumstances under paragraph (a)(2)(i) of this section and § 208.33(a)(3)(i).

(d) Continuing applicability of limitation on eligibility.

(1) Subject to paragraph (d)(2) of this section, the limitation on asylum eligibility in paragraph (a) of this section shall apply to any asylum application filed by an alien who entered the United States during the time and in the manner described in § 208.13(g) and who is not covered by an exception in paragraph (d)(2) of this section, regardless of when the application is filed and adjudicated.

(2) The limitation on asylum eligibility in paragraph (a) of this section shall not apply to an alien who was under the age of 18 at the time of the alien's entry, if—

(i) The alien is applying for asylum as a principal applicant; and

(ii) The asylum application is filed after the period of time in 208.13(g) during which the alien entered.

(e) Severability. The Department intends that in the event that any provision of this section, § 235.15, or the Presidential Proclamation of June 3, 2024, as defined in 8 CFR 208.13(h), is held to be invalid or unenforceable by its terms, or as applied to any person or circumstance, the provisions of this section and § 235.15 should be construed so as to continue to give the maximum effect to those provisions permitted by law, unless such holding is that a provision is wholly invalid and unenforceable, in which event the provision should be severed from the remainder of this section and the holding should not affect the remainder of this section or the application of the provision to persons not similarly situated or to dissimilar circumstances.

HISTORY:

[89 FR 48710, 48769, June 7, 2024, as confirmed at 89 FR 81156, Oct. 7, 2024; 89 FR 81156, 81284, Oct. 7, 2024]

PART 209

ADJUSTMENT OF STATUS OF REFUGEES AND ALIENS GRANTED ASYLUM

Rule

AUTHORITY NOTE APPLICABLE TO ENTIRE PART:

AUTHORITY:

8 U.S.C. 1101, 1103, 1157, 1158, 1159, 1228, 1252, 1282; Title VII of Pub. L. 110–229; 8 CFR part 2; Pub. L. 115– 218.

§ 209.1 Adjustment of status of refugees.

The provisions of this section shall provide the sole and exclusive procedure for adjustment of status by a refugee admitted under section 207 of the Act whose application is based on his or her refugee status.

(a) Eligibility.

(1) Every alien in the United States who is classified as a refugee under 8 CFR part 207, whose status has not been terminated, is required to apply to USCIS one year after entry in order for USCIS to determine his or her admissibility under section 212 of the Act, without regard to paragraphs (4), (5), and (7)(A) of section 212(a) of the Act.

(2) Every alien processed by the Immigration and Naturalization Service abroad and paroled into the United States as a refugee after April 1, 1980, and before May 18, 1980, shall be considered as having entered the United States as a refugee under section 207(a) of the Act.

(b) Application. Upon admission to the United States, every refugee entrant will be notified of the requirement to submit an application for permanent residence one year after entry. An application for the benefits of section 209(a) of the Act must be submitted along with the biometrics required by 8 CFR 103.16 and in accordance with the applicable form instructions.

(c) Medical examination. A refugee seeking adjustment of status under section 209(a) of the Act is not required to repeat the medical examination performed under § 207.2(c), unless there were medical grounds of inadmissibility applicable at the time of admission. The refugee is, however, required to establish compliance with the vaccination requirements described under section 212(a)(1)(A)(ii) of the Act.

(d) Interview. USCIS will determine, on a case-by-case basis, whether an interview by an immigration officer is necessary to determine the applicant's admissibility for permanent resident status under this part.

(e) Decision. USCIS will notify the applicant in writing of the decision on his or her application. There is no appeal of a denial, but USCIS will notify an applicant of the right to renew the request for permanent residence in removal proceedings under section 240 of the Act. If the applicant is found to be admissible for permanent residence under section 209(a) of the Act, USCIS will approve the application, admit the applicant for lawful permanent residence as of the date of the alien's arrival in the United States, and issue proof of such status.

(f) Inadmissible Alien. An applicant who is inadmissible to the United States as described in 8 CFR 209.1(a)(1), may, under section 209(c) of the Act, have the grounds of inadmissibility waived by USCIS except for those grounds under sections 212(a)(2)(C) and 212(a)(3)(A), (B), (C), or (E) of the Act for humanitarian purposes, to ensure family unity, or when it is otherwise in the public interest. An application for the waiver may be requested with the application for adjustment, in accordance with the form instructions.

HISTORY:

[46 FR 45119, Sept. 10, 1981; 62 FR 10312, 10346, March 6, 1997; 63 FR 12979, 12986, Mar. 17, 1998; 63 FR 30105, 30109, June 3, 1998; 76 FR 53764, 53785, Aug. 29, 2011]

§ 209.2 Adjustment of status of alien granted asylum.

The provisions of this section shall be the sole and exclusive procedure for adjustment of status by an asylee admitted under section 208 of the Act whose application is based on his or her asylee status.

(a) Eligibility.

(1) Except as provided in paragraph (a)(2) or (a)(3) of this section, the status of any alien who has been granted asylum in the United States may be adjusted by USCIS to that of an alien lawfully admitted for permanent residence, provided the alien:

(i) Applies for such adjustment;

(ii) Has been physically present in the United States for at least one year after having been granted asylum;

(iii) Continues to be a refugee within the meaning of section 101(a)(42) of the Act, or is the spouse or child of a refugee;

(iv) Has not been firmly resettled in any foreign country; and

(v) Is admissible to the United States as an immigrant under the Act at the time of examination for adjustment without regard to paragraphs (4), (5)(A), (5)(B), and (7)(A)(i) of section 212(a) of the Act, and (vi) has a refugee number available under section 207(a) of the Act.

(2) An alien, who was granted asylum in the United States prior to November 29, 1990 (regardless of whether or not such asylum has been terminated under section 208(b) of the Act), and is no longer a refugee due to a change in circumstances in the foreign state where he or she feared persecution, may also have his or her status adjusted by USCIS to that of an alien lawfully admitted for permanent residence even if he or she is no longer able to demonstrate that he or she continues to be a refugee within the meaning of section 10l(a)(42) of the Act, or to be a spouse or child of such a refugee or to have been physically present in the United States for at least one year after being granted asylum, so long as he or she is able to meet the requirements noted in paragraphs (a)(1)(i), (iv), and (v) of this section.

(3) No alien arriving in or physically present in the Commonwealth of the Northern Mariana Islands may apply to adjust status under section 209(b) of the Act in the Commonwealth of the Northern Mariana Islands prior to January 1, 2030.

(b) Inadmissible alien. An applicant who is not admissible to the United States as described in 8 CFR 209.2(a)(1)(v), may, under section 209(c) of the Act, have the grounds of inadmissibility waived by USCIS except for those grounds under sections 212(a)(2)(C) and 212(a)(3)(A), (B), (C), or (E) of the Act for humanitarian purposes, to ensure family unity, or when it is otherwise in the public interest. An application for the waiver may be requested with the application for adjustment, in accordance with the form instructions. An applicant for adjustment under this part who has had the status of an exchange alien nonimmigrant under section 101(a)(15)(J) of the Act, and who is subject to the foreign resident requirement of section 212(e) of the Act, shall be eligible for adjustment without regard to the foreign residence requirement if otherwise eligible for adjustment.

(c) Application. An application for the benefits of section 209(b) of the Act may be filed in accordance with the form instructions. If an alien has been placed in removal, deportation, or exclusion proceedings, the application can be filed and considered only in proceedings under section 240 of the Act.

(d) Medical examination. For an alien seeking adjustment of status under section 209(b) of the Act, the alien shall submit a medical examination to determine whether any grounds of inadmissibility described under section 212(a)(1)(A) of the Act apply. The asylee is also required to establish compliance with the vaccination requirements described under section 212(a)(1)(A)(ii) of the Act.

(e) Interview. USCIS will determine, on a case-by-case basis, whether an interview by an immigration officer is necessary to determine the applicant's admissibility for permanent resident status under this part.

(f) Decision. USCIS will notify the applicant in writing of the decision on his or her application. There is no appeal of a denial, but USCIS will notify an applicant of the right to renew the request in removal proceedings under section 240 of the Act. If the application is approved, USCIS will record the alien's admission for lawful permanent residence as of the date one year before the date of the approval of the application, but not earlier than the date of the approval for asylum in the case of an applicant approved under paragraph (a)(2) of this section.

HISTORY:

[46 FR 45119, Sept. 10, 1981, as amended at 56 FR 26898, June 12, 1991; 57 FR 42883, 42884, Sept. 17, 1992; 58 FR 12149, Mar. 3, 1993, as corrected at 58 FR 14145, Mar. 16, 1993; 62 FR 10312, 10346, Mar. 6, 1997; 63 FR 12979, 12986, Mar. 17, 1998; 63 FR 30105, 30109, June 3, 1998; 74 FR 55726, 55737, Oct. 28, 2009; 76 FR 53764, 53785, Aug. 29, 2011; 77 FR 76352, Dec. 28, 2012; 85 FR 29264, 29310, May 14, 2020]

PART 210

SPECIAL AGRICULTURAL WORKERS

Rule

§ 210.1 Definition of terms used in this part.

(a) Act. The Immigration and Nationality Act, as amended by the Immigration Reform and Control Act of 1986.

(b) ADIT. Alien Documentation, Identification and Telecommunications card, Form I-89. Used to collect key data concerning an alien. When processed together with an alien's photographs, fingerprints and signature, this form becomes the source document for generation of Form I-551, Permanent Resident Card.

(c) Application period. The 18-month period during which an application for adjustment of status to that of a temporary resident may be accepted, begins on June 1, 1987, and ends on November 30, 1988.

(d) Complete application. A complete application consists of an executed Form I-700, Application for Temporary Resident Status as a Special Agricultural Worker, evidence of qualifying agricultural employment and residence, a report of medical examination, and the prescribed number of photographs. An application is not complete until the required fee has been paid and recorded.

(e) Determination process. Determination process as used in this part means reviewing and evaluating all information provided pursuant to an application for the benefit sought and making a determination thereon. If fraud, willful misrepresentation of a material fact, a false writing or document, or any other activity prohibited by section 210(b)(7) of the Act is discovered during the determination process the Service shall refer the case to a U.S. Attorney for possible prosecution.

(f) Family unity. The term "family unity" as used in section 210(c)(2)(B)(i) of the Act means maintaining the family group without deviation or change. The family group shall include the spouse, unmarried minor children who are not members of some other household, and parents who reside regularly in the household of the family group.

(g) Group 1. Special agricultural workers who have performed qualifying agricultural employment in the United States for at least 90 man-days in the aggregate in each of the twelve-month periods ending on May 1, 1984, 1985, and 1986, and who have resided in the United States for six months in the aggregate in each of those twelve-month periods.

(h) Group 2. Special agricultural workers who during the twelve-month period ending on May 1, 1986 have performed at least 90 man-days in the aggregate of qualifying agricultural employment in the United States.

(i) Legalization Office. Legalization offices are local offices of the Immigration and Naturalization Service which accept and process applications for legalization or special agricultural worker status, under the authority of the district directors in whose districts such offices are located.

(j) Man-day. The term "man-day" means the performance during any day of not less than one hour of qualifying agricultural employment for wages paid. If employment records relating to an alien applicant show only piece rate units completed, then any day in which piece rate work was performed shall be counted as a man-day. Work for more than one employer in a single day shall be counted as no more than one man-day for the purposes of this part.

(k) Nonfrivolous application. A complete application will be determined to be nonfrivolous at the time the applicant appears for an interview at a legalization or overseas processing office if it contains:

(1) Evidence or information which shows on its face that the applicant is admissible to the United States or, if inadmissible, that the applicable grounds of excludability may be waived under the provisions of section 210(c)(2)(i) of the Act,

(2) Evidence or information which shows on its face that the applicant performed at least 90 man-days of qualifying employment in seasonal agricultural services during the twelve-month period from May 1, 1985 through May 1, 1986, and

(3) Documentation which establishes a reasonable inference of the performance of the seasonal agricultural services claimed by the applicant.

(l) Overseas processing office. Overseas processing offices are offices outside the United States at which applications for adjustment to temporary resident status as a special agricultural worker are received, processed, referred to the Service for adjudication or denied. The Secretary of State has designated for this purpose the United States Embassy at Mexico City, and in all other countries the immigrant visa issuing of office at which the alien, if an applicant for an immigrant visa, would make such application. Consular officers assigned to such offices are authorized to recommend approval of an application for special agricultural worker status to the Service if the alien establishes eligibility for approval and to deny such an application if the alien fails to establish eligibility for approval or is found to have committed fraud or misrepresented facts in the application process.

(m) Preliminary application. A preliminary application is defined as a fully completed and signed application with fee and photographs which contains specific information concerning the performance of qualifying employment in the United States, and identifies documentary evidence which the applicant intends to submit as proof of such employment. The applicant must be otherwise admissible to the United States and must establish to the satisfaction of the examining officer during an interview that his or her claim to eligibility for special agriculture worker status is credible.

(n) Public cash assistance. Public cash assistance means income or needs-based monetary assistance. This includes but is not limited to supplemental security income received by the alien or his immediate family members through federal, state, or local programs designed to meet subsistence levels. It does not include assistance in kind, such as food stamps, public housing, or other non-cash benefits, nor does it include work-related compensation or certain types of medical assistance (Medicare, Medicaid, emergency treatment, services to pregnant women or children under 18 years of age, or treatment in the interest of public health).

(o) Qualified designated entity. A qualified designated entity is any state, local, church, community, or voluntary agency, farm labor organization, association of agricultural employers or individual designated by the Service to assist aliens in the preparation of applications for Legalization and/or Special Agricultural Worker status.

(p) Qualifying agricultural employment. Qualifying agricultural employment means the performance of "seasonal agricultural services" described at section 210(h) of the Act as that term is defined in regulations by the Secretary of Agriculture at 7 CFR part 1d.

(q) Regional processing facility. Regional Processing Facilities are Service offices established in each of the four Service regions to adjudicate, under the authority of the Directors of the Regional Processing Facilities, applications for adjustment of status under sections 210 and 245a of the Act.

(r) Service. The Immigration and Naturalization Service (INS).

(s) Special agricultural worker. Any individual granted temporary resident status in the Group 1 or Group 2 classification or permanent resident status under section 210(a) of the Act.

HISTORY:

[53 FR 10064, Mar. 29, 1988, as amended at 54 FR 50339, Dec. 6, 1989; 63 FR 70313, 70315, Dec. 21, 1998]

AUTHORITY:

8 U.S.C. 1103, 1160, 8 CFR part 2.

§ 210.2 Application for temporary resident status.

(a)(1) Application for temporary resident status. An alien agricultural worker who believes that he or she is eligible for adjustment of status under the provisions of

§ 210.3 of this part may file an application for such adjustment at a qualified designated entity, at a legalization office, or at an overseas processing office outside the United States. Such application must be filed within the application period.

(2) Application for Group 1 status. An alien who believes that he or she qualifies for Group 1 status as defined in § 210.1(f) of this part and who desires to apply for that classification must so endorse his or her application at the time of filing. Applications not so endorsed will be regarded as applications for Group 2 status as defined in § 210.1(g) of this part.

(3) Numerical limitations. The numerical limitations of sections 201 and 202 of the Act do not apply to the adjustment of aliens to lawful temporary or permanent resident status under section 210 of the Act. No more than 350,000 aliens may be granted temporary resident status in the Group 1 classification. If more than 350,000 aliens are determined to be eligible for Group 1 classification, the first 350,000 applicants (in chronological order by date the application is filed at a legalization or overseas processing office) whose applications are approved for Group 1 status shall be accorded that classification. Aliens admitted to the United States under the transitional admission standard placed in effect between July 1, 1987, and November 1, 1987, and under the preliminary application standard at § 210.2(c)(4) who claim eligibility for Group 1 classification shall be registered as applicants for that classification on the date of submission to a legalization office of a complete application as defined in § 210.1(c) of this part. Other applicants who may be eligible for Group 1 classification shall be classified as Group 2 aliens. There is no limitation on the number of aliens whose resident status may be adjusted from temporary to permanent in Group 2 classification.

(b) Filing date of application —

(1) General. The date the alien submits an application to a qualified designated entity, legalization office or overseas processing office shall be considered the filing date of the application, provided that in the case of an application filed at a qualified designated entity the alien has consented to have the entity forward the application to a legalization office. Qualified designated entities are required to forward completed applications to the appropriate legalization office within 60 days after the applicant gives consent for such forwarding.

(2) [Reserved]

(c) **Filing of application —**

(1) General. The application must be filed on Form I-700 at a qualified designated entity, at a legalization office, at a designated port of entry, or at an overseas processing office within the eighteen-month period beginning on June 1, 1987 and ending on November 30, 1988.

(2) Applications in the United States.

(i) The application must be filed on Form I-700 with the required fee and, if the applicant is 14 years or older, the application must be accompanied by a completed Form FD-258 (Fingerprint Card).

(ii) All fees for applications filed in the United States, other than those within the provisions of § 210.2(c)(4), must be submitted in the exact amount in the form of a money order, cashier's check, or bank check made payable to the Immigration and Naturalization Service. No personal checks or currency will be accepted. Fees will not be waived or refunded under any circumstances.

(iii) In the case of an application filed at a legalization office, including an application received from a qualified designated entity, the district director may, at his or her discretion, require filing either by mail or in person, or may permit filing in either manner.

(iv) Each applicant, regardless of age, must appear at the appropriate Service legalization office and must be fingerprinted for the purpose of issuance of Form I-688A. Each applicant shall be interviewed by an immigration officer, except that the interview may be waived when it is impractical because of the health of the applicant.

(3) Filing at overseas processing offices.

(i) The application must be filed on Form I-700 and must include a completed State Department Form OF-179 (Biographic Data for Visa Purposes).

(ii) Every applicant must appear at the appropriate overseas processing office to be interviewed by a consular officer. The overseas processing office will inform each applicant of the date and time of the interview. At the time of the interview every applicant shall submit the required fee.

(iii) All fees for applications submitted to an overseas processing office shall be submitted in United States currency, or in the currency of the country in which the overseas processing office is located. Fees will not be waived or refunded under any circumstances.

(iv) An applicant at an overseas processing office whose application is recommended for approval shall be provided with an entry document attached to the applicant's file. Upon admission to the United States, the applicant shall proceed to a legalization office for presentation or completion of Form FD-258 (Fingerprint Card), presentation of the applicant's file and issuance of the employment authorization Form I-688A.

(4) Border processing. The Commissioner will designate specific ports of entry located on the southern land border to accept and process applications under this part. Ports of entry so designated will process preliminary applications as defined at § 210.1(l) under the authority of the district directors in whose districts they are located. The ports of entry at Calexico, California, Otay Mesa, California, and Laredo, Texas have been designated to conduct preliminary application processing. Designated ports of entry may be closed or added at the discretion of the Commissioner.

(i) Admission standard. The applicant must present a fully completed and signed Form I-700, Application for Temporary Resident Status with the required fee and photographs at a designated port of entry. The application must contain specific information concerning the performance of qualifying employment in the United States and identify documentary evidence which the applicant intends to submit as proof of such employment. The applicant must establish to the satisfaction of the examining officer during an interview that his or her claim to eligibility for special agricultural worker classification is credible, and that he or she is otherwise admissible to the United States under the provisions of § 210.3(e) of this part including, if required, approval of an application for waiver of grounds of excludability.

(ii) Procedures. The fee for any application under this paragraph including applications for waivers of grounds of excludability, must be submitted in United States currency. Application fees shall not be collected until the examining immigration officer has determined that the applicant has presented a preliminary application and is admissible to the United States including, if required, approval of an application for waiver of grounds of excludability as provided in this paragraph. Applicants at designated ports of entry must present proof of identity in the form of a valid passport, a "cartilla" (Mexican military service registration booklet), a Form 13 ("Forma trece" — Mexican lieu passport identity document), or a certified copy of a birth certificate accompanied by additional evidence of identity bearing a photograph and/or fingerprint of the applicant. Upon a determination by an immigration officer at a designated port of entry that an applicant has presented a preliminary application, the applicant shall be admitted to the United States as an applicant for special agricultural worker status. All preliminary applicants shall be considered as prospective applicants for the Group 2 classification. However, such applicants may later submit a complete application for either the Group 1 or Group 2 classification to a legalization office. Preliminary applicants are not required to pay the application fee a second time when submitting the complete application to a legalization office.

(iii) Conditions of admission. Aliens who present a preliminary application shall be admitted to the United States for a period of ninety (90) days with authorization to accept employment, if they are determined by an immigration officer to be admissible to the United States. Such aliens are required, within that ninety-day period, to submit evidence of eligibility which meets the provisions of § 210.3 of this part; to complete Form FD-258 (Fingerprint Card); to obtain a report of medical examination in accordance with § 210.2(d) of this part; and to submit to a legalization office a complete application as defined at § 210.1(c) of this part. The INS may, for good cause, extend the ninety-day period and grant further authorization to accept employment in the United States if an alien demonstrates he or she was unable to perfect an application within the initial period. If an alien described in this paragraph fails to submit a complete application to a legalization office within ninety days or within such additional period as may have been authorized, his or her application may be denied for lack of prosecution, without prejudice.

(iv) Deportation is not stayed for an alien subject to deportation and removal under the INA, notwithstanding a claim to eligibility for SAW status, unless that alien has filed a nonfrivolous application.

(d) Medical examination. An applicant under this part must be examined at no expense to the government by a designated civil surgeon or, in the case of an applicant abroad, by a physician or clinic designated to perform medical examinations of immigrant visa applicants. The medical report setting forth the findings concerning the mental and physical condition of the applicant shall be incorporated into the record. Any applicant certified under paragraph (1), (2), (3), (4), or (5) of section 212(a) of the Act may appeal to a Board of Medical Officers of the U.S. Public Health Service as provided in section 234 of the Act and part 235 of this chapter.

(e) **Limitation on access to information and confidentiality.**

(1) Except for consular officials engaged in the processing of applications overseas and employees of a qualified designated entity where an application is filed with that entity, no person other than a sworn officer or employee of the Department of Justice or bureau or agency thereof, or contract personnel employed by the Service to work in connection with the legalization program, will be permitted to examine individual applications.

(2) Files and records prepared by qualified designated entities under this section are confidential. The Attorney General and the Service shall not have access to these files and records without the consent of the alien.

(3) All information furnished pursuant to an application for temporary resident status under this part including documentary evidence filed with the application shall be used only in the determination process, including a determination under § 210.4(d) of this part, or to enforce the provisions of section 210(b)(7) of the Act, relating to prosecutions for fraud and false statements made in connection with applications, as provided in paragraph (e)(4) of this section.

(4) If a determination is made by the Service that the alien has, in connection with his or her application, engaged in fraud or willful misrepresentation or concealment of a material fact, knowingly provided a false writing or document in making his or her application, knowingly made a false statement or representation, or engaged in any other activity prohibited by section 210(b)(7) of the Act, the Service shall refer the matter to the U.S. Attorney for prosecution of the alien or any person who created or supplied a false writing or document for use in an application for adjustment of status under this part.

(f) Decision. The applicant shall be notified in writing of the decision and, if the application is denied, of the reason(s) therefor. An adverse decision under this part including an overseas application may be appealed to the Associate Commissioner, Examinations (Administrative Appeals Unit) on Form I-694. The appeal with the required fee shall be filed with the Regional Processing Facility in accordance with the provisions of § 103.3(a)(2) of this chapter. An applicant for Group 1 status as defined in § 210.1(f) of this part who is determined to be ineligible for that status may be classified as a temporary resident under Group 2 as defined in § 210.1(g) of this part if otherwise eligible for Group 2 status. In such a case the applicant shall be notified of the decision to accord him or her Group 2 status and to deny Group 1 status. He or she is entitled to file an appeal in accordance with the provisions of § 103.3(a)(2) of this chapter from that portion of the decision denying Group 1 status. In the case of an applicant who is represented in the application process in accordance with 8 CFR part 292, the applicant's representative shall also receive notification of decision specified in this section.

(g) Motions. In accordance with the provisions of § 103.5(b) of this chapter, the director of a regional processing facility or a consular officer at an overseas processing office may sua sponte reopen any proceeding under this part under his or her jurisdiction and reverse any adverse decision in such proceeding when appeal is taken under § 103.3(a)(2) of this part from such adverse decision; the Associate Commissioner, Examinations, and the Chief of the Administrative Appeals Unit may sua sponte reopen any proceeding conducted by that unit under this part and reconsider any decision rendered in such proceeding. The decision must be served on the appealing party within forty-five (45) days of receipt of any briefs and/or new evidence, or upon expiration of the time allowed for the submission of any briefs. Motions to reopen a proceeding or reconsider a decision shall not be considered under this part.

(h) Certifications. The regional processing facility director may, in accordance with § 103.4 of this chapter, certify a decision to the Associate Commissioner, Examinations when the case involves an unusually complex or novel question of law or fact. A consular officer assigned to an overseas processing office is authorized to certify a decision in the same manner and upon the same basis.

HISTORY:

[53 FR 10064, Mar. 29, 1988, as amended at 55 FR 12629, Apr. 5, 1990; 60 FR 21975, May 4, 1995]

AUTHORITY:

8 U.S.C. 1103, 1160, 8 CFR part 2.

§ 210.3 Eligibility.

(a) General. An alien who, during the twelve-month period ending on May 1, 1986, has engaged in qualifying agricultural employment in the United States for at least 90 man-days is eligible for status as an alien lawfully admitted for temporary residence if otherwise admissible under the provisions of section 210(c) of the Act and if he or she is not ineligible under the provisions of paragraph (d) of this section.

(b) Proof of eligibility—

(1) Burden of proof. An alien applying for adjustment of status under this part has the burden of proving by a preponderance of the evidence that he or she has worked the requisite number of man-days, is admissible to the United States under the provisions of section 210(c) of the Act, is otherwise eligible for adjustment of status under this section and in the case of a Group 1 applicant, has resided in the United States for the requisite periods. If the applicant cannot provide documentation which shows qualifying employment for each of the requisite man-days, or in the case of a Group 1 applicant, which meets the residence requirement, the applicant may meet his or her burden of proof by providing documentation sufficient to establish the requisite employment or residence as a matter of just and reasonable inference. The inference to be drawn from the documentation provided shall depend on the extent of the documentation, its credibility and amenability to verification as set forth in paragraphs (b)(2) and (3) of this section. If an applicant establishes that he or she has in fact performed the requisite qualifying agricultural employment by producing sufficient evidence to show the extent of that employment as a matter of just and reasonable inference, the burden then shifts to the Service to disprove the applicant's evidence by showing that the inference drawn from the evidence is not reasonable.

(2) Evidence. The sufficiency of all evidence produced by the applicant will be judged according to its probative value and credibility. Original documents will be given greater weight than copies. To meet his or her burden of proof, an applicant must provide evidence of eligibility apart from his or her own testimony. Analysis of evidence submitted will include consideration of the fact that work performed by minors and spouses is sometimes credited to a principal member of a family.

(3) Verification. Personal testimony by an applicant which is not corroborated, in whole or in part, by other credible evidence (including testimony of persons other than the applicant) will not serve to meet an applicant's burden of proof. All evidence of identity, qualifying employment, admissibility, and eligibility submitted by an applicant for adjustment of status under this part will be subject to verification by the Service. Failure by an applicant to release information protected by the Privacy Act or related laws when such information is essential to the proper adjudication of an application may result in denial of the benefit sought. The Service may solicit from agricultural producers, farm labor contractors, collective bargaining organizations and other groups or organizations which maintain records of employment, lists of workers against which evidence of qualifying employment can be checked. If such corroborating evidence is not available and the evidence provided is deemed insufficient, the application may be denied.

(4) Securing SAW employment records. When a SAW applicant alleges that an employer or farm labor contractor refuses to provide him or her with records relating to his or her employment and the applicant has reason to believe such records exist, the Service shall attempt to secure such records. However, prior to any attempt by the Service to secure the employment records, the following conditions must be met: a SAW application (Form I-700) must have been filed; an interview must have been conducted; the applicant's testimony must support credibly his or her claim; and, the Service must determine that the application cannot be approved in the absence of the employer or farm labor contractor records. Provided each of these conditions has been met, and after unsuccessful attempts by the Service for voluntary compliance, the District Di-

rectors shall utilize section 235 of the Immigration and Nationality Act and issue a subpoena in accordance with 8 CFR 287.4, in such cases where the employer or farm labor contractor refuses to release the needed employment records.

(c) Documents. A complete application for adjustment of status must be accompanied by proof of identity, evidence of qualifying employment, evidence of residence and such evidence of admissibility or eligibility as may be requested by the examining immigration officer in accordance with requirements specified in this part. At the time of filing, certified copies of documents may be submitted in lieu of originals. However, at the time of the interview, wherever possible, the original documents must be presented except for the following: Official government records; employment or employment related records maintained by employers, unions, or collective bargaining organizations; medical records; school records maintained by a school or school board; or other records maintained by a party other than the applicant. Copies of records maintained by parties other than the applicant which are submitted in evidence must be certified as true and correct by such parties and must bear their seal or signature or the signature and title of persons authorized to act in their behalf. If at the time of the interview the return of original documents is desired by the applicant, they must be accompanied by notarized copies or copies certified true and correct by a qualified designated entity or by the alien's representative in the format prescribed in § 204.2(j)(1) or (2) of this chapter. At the discretion of the district director or consular officer, original documents, even if accompanied by certified copies, may be temporarily retained for further examination.

(1) Proof of identity. Evidence to establish identity is listed below in descending order of preference:

(i) Passport;

(ii) Birth certificate;

(iii) Any national identity document from a foreign country bearing a photo and/or fingerprint (e.g., "cedula", "cartilla", "carte d'identite," etc.);

(iv) Driver's license or similar document issued by a state if it contains a photo;

(v) Baptismal record or marriage certificate;

(vi) Affidavits, or

(vii) Such other documentation which may establish the identity of the applicant.

(2) Assumed names—

(i) General. In cases where an applicant claims to have met any of the eligibility criteria under an assumed name, the applicant has the burden of proving that the applicant was in fact the person who used that name.

(ii) Proof of common identity. The most persuasive evidence is a document issued in the assumed name which identifies the applicant by photograph, fingerprint or detailed physical description. Other evidence which will be considered are affidavit(s) by a person or persons other than the applicant, made under oath, which identify the affiant by name and address and state the affiant's relationship to the applicant and the basis of the affiant's knowledge of the applicant's use of the assumed name. Affidavits accompanied by a photograph which has been identified by the affiant as the individual known to the affiant under the assumed name in question will carry greater weight. Other documents showing the assumed name may serve to establish the common identity when substantiated by corroborating detail.

(3) Proof of employment. The applicant may establish qualifying employment through government employment records, or records maintained by agricultural producers, farm labor contractors, collective bargaining organizations and other groups or organizations which maintain records of employment, or such other evidence as worker identification issued by employers or collective bargaining organizations, union membership cards or other union records such as dues receipts or records of the applicant's involvement or that of his or her immediate family with organizations providing services to farmworkers, or work records such as pay stubs, piece work receipts, W-2 Forms or certification of the filing of Federal income tax returns on IRS Form 6166, or state verification of the filing of state income tax returns. Affidavits may be submitted under oath, by agricultural producers, foremen, farm labor contractors, union officials, fellow employees, or other persons with specific knowledge of the applicant's employment. The affiant must be identified by name and address; the name of the applicant and the relationship of the affiant to the applicant must be stated; and the source of the information in the affidavit (e.g. personal knowledge, reliance on information provided by others, etc.) must be indicated. The affidavit must also provide information regarding the crop and the type of work performed by the applicant and the period during which such work was performed. The affiant must provide a certified copy of corroborating records or state the affiant's willingness to personally verify the information provided. The weight and probative value of any affidavit accepted will be determined on the basis of the substance of the affidavit and any documents which may be affixed thereto which may corroborate the information provided.

(4) Proof of residence. Evidence to establish residence in the United States during the requisite period(s) includes: Employment records as described in paragraph (c)(3) of this section; utility bills (gas, electric, phone, etc.), receipts, or letters from companies showing the dates during which the applicant received service; school records (letters, report cards, etc.) from the schools that the applicant or his or her children have attended in the United States showing the name of school, name and, if available, address of student, and periods of attendance, and hospital or medical records showing similar information; attestations by churches, unions, or other organizations to the applicant's residence by letter which: Identify applicant by name, are signed by an official (whose title is shown), show inclusive dates of membership, state the address where applicant resided during the membership period, include the seal of the organization impressed on the letter, establish how the author knows the applicant,

and the origin of the information; and additional documents that could show that the applicant was in the United States at a specific time, such as: Money order receipts for money sent out of the country; passport entries; birth certificates of children born in the United States; bank books with dated transactions; letters of correspondence between the applicant and another person or organization; Social Security card; Selective Service card; automobile license receipts, title, vehicle registration, etc.; deeds, mortgages, contracts to which applicant has been a party; tax receipts; insurance policies, receipts, or letters; and any other document that will show that applicant was in the United States at a specific time. For Group 2 eligibility, evidence of performance of the required 90 man-days of seasonal agricultural services shall constitute evidence of qualifying residence.

(5) Proof of financial responsibility. Generally, the evidence of employment submitted under paragraph (c)(3) of this section will serve to demonstrate the alien's financial responsibility. If it appears that the applicant may be inadmissible under section 212(a)(15) of the Act, he or she may be required to submit documentation showing a history of employment without reliance on public cash assistance for all periods of residence in the United States.

(d) Ineligible classes. The following classes of aliens are ineligible for temporary residence under this part:

(1) An alien who at any time was a nonimmigrant exchange visitor under section 101(a)(15)(J) of the Act who is subject to the two-year foreign residence requirement unless the alien has complied with that requirement or the requirement has been waived pursuant to the provisions of section 212(e) of the Act;

(2) An alien excludable under the provisions of section 212(a) of the Act whose grounds of excludability may not be waived, pursuant to section 210(c)(2)(B)(ii) of the Act;

(3) An alien who has been convicted of a felony, or three or more misdemeanors.

(e) Exclusion grounds—

(1) Grounds of exclusion not to be applied. Sections (14), (20), (21), (25), and (32) of section 212(a) of the Act shall not apply to applicants applying for temporary resident status.

(2) Waiver of grounds for exclusion. Except as provided in paragraph (e)(3) of this section, the Service may waive any other provision of section 212(a) of the Act only in the case of individual aliens for humanitarian purposes, to assure family unity, or when the granting of such a waiver is in the public interest. If an alien is excludable on grounds which may be waived as set forth in this paragraph, he or she shall be advised of the procedures for applying for a waiver of grounds of excludability on Form I-690. When an application for waiver of grounds of excludability is submitted in conjunction with an application for temporary residence under this section, it shall be accepted for processing at the legalization office, overseas processing office, or designated port of entry. If an application for waiver of grounds of excludability is submitted after the alien's preliminary interview at the legalization office it shall be forwarded to the appropriate regional processing facility. All applications for waivers of grounds of excludability must be accompanied by the correct fee in the exact amount. All fees for applications filed in the United States other than those within the provisions of § 210.2(c)(4) must be in the form of a money order, cashier's check, or bank check. No personal checks or currency will be accepted. Fees for waiver applications filed at the designated port of entry under the preliminary application standard must be submitted in United States currency. Fees will not be waived or refunded under any circumstances. Generally, an application for waiver of grounds of excludability under this part submitted at a legalization office or overseas processing office will be approved or denied by the director of the regional processing facility in whose jurisdiction the applicant's application for adjustment of status was filed. However, in cases involving clear statutory ineligibility or admitted fraud, such application for a waiver may be denied by the district director in whose jurisdiction the application is filed; in cases filed at overseas processing offices, such application for a waiver may be denied by a consular officer; or, in cases returned to a legalization office for reinterview, such application may be approved at the discretion of the district director. Waiver applications filed at the port of entry under the preliminary application standard will be approved or denied by the district director having jurisdiction over the port of entry. The applicant shall be notified of the decision and, if the application is denied, of the reason(s) therefor. The applicant may appeal the decision within 30 days after the service of the notice pursuant to the provisions of § 103.3(a)(2) of this chapter.

(3) Grounds of exclusion that may not be waived. The following provisions of section 212(a) of the Act may not be waived:

(i) Paragraphs (9) and (10) (criminals);

(ii) Paragraph (15) (public charge) except as provided in paragraph (c)(4) of this section.

(iii) Paragraph (23) (narcotics) except for a single offense of simple possession of thirty grams or less of marijuana.

(iv) Paragraphs (27), (prejudicial to the public interest), (28), (communists), and (29) (subversive);

(v) Paragraph (33) (Nazi persecution).

(4) Special Rule for determination of public charge. An applicant who has a consistent employment history which shows the ability to support himself and his or her family, even though his income may be below the poverty level, is not excludable under paragraph (e)(3)(ii) of this section. The applicant's employment history need not be continuous in that it is uninterrupted. It should be continuous in the sense that the applicant shall be regularly attached to the workforce, has an income over a substantial period of the applicable time, and has demonstrated the capacity to exist on his or her income and maintain his or her family without reliance on public cash assistance. This regulation is prospective in that the Service shall determine, based on the applicant's history, whether he or she is likely to become a public charge. Past acceptance

of public cash assistance within a history of consistent employment will enter into this decision. The weight given in considering applicability of the public charge provisions will depend on many factors, but the length of time an applicant has received public cash assistance will constitute a significant factor.

HISTORY:

[53 FR 10064, Mar. 29, 1988, as amended at 53 FR 27335, July 20, 1988; 54 FR 4757, Jan. 31, 1989; 55 FR 12629, Apr. 5, 1990]

AUTHORITY:

8 U.S.C. 1103, 1160, 8 CFR part 2.

§ 210.4 Status and benefits.

(a) Date of adjustment. The status of an alien whose application for temporary resident status is approved shall be adjusted to that of a lawful temporary resident as of the date on which the fee was paid at a legalization office, except that the status of an alien who applied for such status at an overseas processing office whose application has been recommended for approval by that office shall be adjusted as of the date of his or her admission into the United States.

(b) **Employment and travel authorization —**

(1) General. Authorization for employment and travel abroad for temporary resident status applicants under section 210 of the Act be granted by the INS. In the case of an application which has been filed with a qualified designated entity, employment authorization may only be granted after a nonfrivolous application has been received at a legalization office, and receipt of the fee has been recorded.

(2) Employment and travel authorization prior to the granting of temporary resident status. Permission to travel abroad and to accept employment will be granted to the applicant after an interview has been conducted in connection with a nonfrivolous application at a Service office. If an interview appointment cannot be scheduled within 30 days from the date an application is filed at a Service office, authorization to accept employment will be granted, valid until the scheduled appointment date. Employment authorization, both prior and subsequent to an interview, will be restricted to increments not exceeding 1 year, pending final determination on the application for temporary resident status. If a final determination has not been made prior to the expiration date on the Employment Authorization Document (Form I-766, Form I-688A or Form I-688B) that date may be extended upon return of the employment authorization document by the applicant to the appropriate Service office. Persons submitting applications who currently have work authorization incident to status as defined in § 274a.12(b) of this chapter shall be granted work authorization by the Service effective on the date the alien's prior work authorization expires. Permission to travel abroad shall be granted in accordance with the Service's advance parole provisions contained in § 212.5(f) of this chapter.

(3) Employment and travel authorization upon grant of temporary resident status. Upon the granting of an application for adjustment to temporary resident status, the service center will forward a notice of approval to the applicant at his or her last known address and to his or her qualified designated entity or representative. The applicant may appear at any Service office, and upon surrender of the previously issued Employment Authorization Document, will be issued Form I-688, Temporary Resident Card. An alien whose status is adjusted to that of a lawful temporary resident under section 210 of the Act has the right to reside in the United States, to travel abroad (including commuting from a residence abroad), and to accept employment in the United States in the same manner as aliens lawfully admitted to permanent residence.

(c) Ineligibility for immigration benefits. An alien whose status is adjusted to that of a lawful temporary resident under section 210 of the Act is not entitled to submit a petition pursuant to section 203(a)(2) of the Act or to any other benefit or consideration accorded under the Act to aliens lawfully admitted for permanent residence, except as provided in paragraph (b)(3) of this section.

(d) **Termination of temporary resident status —**

(1) General. The temporary resident status of a special agricultural worker is terminated automatically and without notice under section 210(a)(3) of the Act upon entry of a final order of deportation by an immigration judge based on a determination that the alien is deportable under section 241 of the Act.

(2) The status of an alien lawfully admitted for temporary residence under section 210(a)(2) of the Act, may be terminated before the alien becomes eligible for adjustment of status under § 210.5 of this part, upon the occurrence of any of the following:

(i) It is determined by a preponderance of the evidence that the adjustment to temporary resident status was the result of fraud or willful misrepresentation as provided in section 212(a)(19) of the Act;

(ii) The alien commits an act which renders him or her inadmissible as an immigrant, unless a waiver is secured pursuant to § 210.3(e)(2) of this part;

(iii) The alien is convicted of any felony, or three or more misdemeanors in the United States.

(3) Procedure.

(i) Termination of an alien's status under paragraph (d)(2) of this section will be made only on notice to the alien sent by certified mail directed to his or her last known address, and to his or her representative. The alien must be given an opportunity to offer evidence in opposition to the grounds alleged for termination of his or her status. Evidence in opposition must be submitted within thirty (30) days after the service of the Notice of Intent to Terminate. If the alien's status is terminated, the director of the regional processing facility shall notify the alien of the decision and the reasons for the termination, and further notify the alien that any Service Form I-94 (see § 1.4), Arrival-Departure Record or other official Service document issued to the alien authorizing employment and/or travel abroad, or any Form I-688, Temporary Resident Card previously issued to the alien will be declared void by the director of the regional processing facility within thirty (30) days if no appeal of the termination decision is filed within that period. The alien may appeal the decision to the Associate Commissioner, Examinations (Administrative Appeals Unit) using Form I-694. Any appeal with the required fee shall be filed with the regional processing facility within thirty (30) days after the service of the notice of termination. If no appeal is filed within that period, the Forms I-94, I-688 or other official Service document shall be deemed void, and must be surrendered without delay to an immigration officer or to the issuing office of the Service.

(ii) Termination proceedings must be commenced before the alien becomes eligible for adjustment of status under § 210.5 of this part. The timely commencement of termination proceedings will preclude the alien from becoming a lawful permanent resident until a final determination is made in the proceedings, including any appeal.

HISTORY:

[53 FR 10064, Mar. 29, 1988, as amended at 55 FR 12629, Apr. 5, 1990; 60 FR 21975, May 4, 1995; 61 FR 46534, 46536, Sept. 4, 1996; 65 FR 82254, 82255, Dec. 28, 2000; 66 FR 7863, Jan. 26, 2001; 78 FR 18457, 18472, Mar. 27, 2013, as confirmed at 81 FR 91646, 91670, Dec. 19, 2016]

AUTHORITY:

8 U.S.C. 1103, 1160, 8 CFR part 2.

§ 210.5 Adjustment to permanent resident status.

(a) Eligibility and date of adjustment to permanent resident status. The status of an alien lawfully admitted to the United States for temporary residence under section 210(a)(1) of the Act, if the alien has otherwise maintained such status as required by the Act, shall be adjusted to that of an alien lawfully admitted to the United States for permanent residence as of the following dates:

(1) Group 1. Aliens determined to be eligible for Group 1 classification, whose adjustment to temporary residence occurred prior to November 30, 1988, shall be adjusted to lawful permanent residence as of December 1, 1989. Those aliens whose adjustment to temporary residence occurred after November 30, 1988 shall be adjusted to lawful permanent residence one year from the date of the adjustment to temporary residence.

(2) Group 2. Aliens determined to be eligible for Group 2 classification whose adjustment to temporary residence occurred prior to November 30, 1988, shall be adjusted to lawful permanent residence as of December 1, 1990. Those aliens whose adjustment to temporary residence occurred after November 30, 1988 shall be adjusted to lawful permanent residence two years from the date of the adjustment to temporary residence.

(b) **ADIT processing —**

(1) General. To obtain proof of permanent resident status an alien described in paragraph (a) of this section must appear at a legalization or Service office designated for this purpose for preparation of Form I-551, Permanent Resident Card. Such appearance may be prior to the date of adjustment, but only upon invitation by the Service. Form I-551 shall be issued subsequent to the date of adjustment.

(2) Upon appearance at a Service office for preparation of Form I-551, an alien must present proof of identity, suitable ADIT photographs, and a fingerprint and signature must be obtained from the alien on Form I-89.

HISTORY:

[53 FR 10064, Mar. 29, 1988, as amended at 54 FR 50339, Dec. 6, 1989; 63 FR 70313, 70315, Dec. 21, 1998]

AUTHORITY:

8 U.S.C. 1103, 1160, 8 CFR part 2.

PART 211

DOCUMENTARY REQUIREMENTS: IMMIGRANTS; WAIVERS

Rule

AUTHORITY NOTE APPLICABLE TO ENTIRE PART:

AUTHORITY:

8 U.S.C. 1101, 1103, 1181, 1182, 1203, 1225, 1257; 8 CFR part 2.

§ 211.1 Visas.

(a) General. Except as provided in paragraph (b)(1) of this section, each arriving alien applying for admission (or boarding the vessel or aircraft on which he or she arrives) into the United States for lawful permanent residence, or as a lawful permanent resident returning to an unrelinquished lawful permanent residence in the United States, shall present one of the following:

(1) A valid, unexpired immigrant visa;

(2) A valid, unexpired Form I-551, Permanent Resident Card, if seeking readmission after a temporary absence of less than 1 year, or in the case of a crewmember regularly serving on board a vessel or aircraft of United States registry seeking readmission after any temporary absence connected with his or her duties as a crewman;

(3) A valid, unexpired Form I-327, Permit to Reenter the United States;

(4) A valid, unexpired Form I-571, Refugee Travel Document, properly endorsed to reflect admission as a lawful permanent resident;

(5) An expired Form I-551, Permanent Resident Card, accompanied by a filing receipt issued within the previous 6 months for either a Form I-751, Petition to Remove the Conditions on Residence, or Form I-829, Petition by Entrepreneur to Remove Conditions, if seeking admission or readmission after a temporary absence of less than 1 year;

(6) A Form I-551, whether or not expired, presented by a civilian or military employee of the United States

Government who was outside the United States pursuant to official orders, or by the spouse or child of such employee who resided abroad while the employee or serviceperson was on overseas duty and who is preceding, accompanying or following to join within 4 months the employee, returning to the United States; or

(7) Form I-551, whether or not expired, or a transportation letter issued by an American consular officer, presented by an employee of the American University of Beirut, who was so employed immediately preceding travel to the United States, returning temporarily to the United States before resuming employment with the American University of Beirut, or resuming permanent residence in the United States.

(b) Waivers.

(1) A waiver of the visa required in paragraph (a) of this section shall be granted without fee or application by the district director, upon presentation of the child's birth certificate, to a child born subsequent to the issuance of an immigrant visa to his or her accompanying parent who applies for admission during the validity of such a visa; or a child born during the temporary visit abroad of a mother who is a lawful permanent resident alien, or a national, of the United States, provided that the child's application for admission to the United States is made within 2 years of birth, the child is accompanied by the parent who is applying for readmission as a permanent resident upon the first return of the parent to the United States after the birth of the child, and the accompanying parent is found to be admissible to the United States.

(2) For an alien described in paragraph (b)(1) of this section, recordation of the child's entry shall be on Form I-181, Memorandum of Creation of Record of Admission for Lawful Permanent Residence. The carrier of such alien shall not be liable for a fine pursuant to section 273 of the Act.

(3) If an immigrant alien returning to an unrelinquished lawful permanent residence in the United States after a temporary absence abroad believes that good cause exists for his or her failure to present an unexpired immigrant visa, permanent resident card, or reentry permit, the alien may file an application for a waiver of this requirement with the DHS officer with jurisdiction over the port of entry where the alien arrives. To apply for this waiver, the alien must file the designated form with the fee prescribed in 8 CFR 106.2. If the alien's permanent resident card was lost or stolen and the alien has been absent for less than one year, rather than the waiver application the alien must apply for a replacement card as described in 8 CFR 264.5. In the exercise of discretion, the DHS officer who has jurisdiction over the port of entry where the alien arrives may waive the alien's lack of an immigrant visa, permanent resident card, or reentry permit and admit the alien as a returning resident if DHS is satisfied that the alien has established good cause for the alien's failure to present an immigrant visa, permanent resident card, or reentry permit. Filing a request to replace a lost or stolen card will serve as both application for replacement and as application for waiver of passport and visa, without the obligation to file a separate waiver application.

(c) Immigrants having occupational status defined in section 101(a)(15) (A), (E), or (G) of the Act. An immigrant visa, reentry permit, or Form I-551 shall be invalid when presented by an alien who has an occupational status under section 101(a)(15) (A), (E), or (G) of the Act, unless he or she has previously submitted, or submits at the time he or she applies for admission to the United States, the written waiver required by section 247(b) of the Act and 8 CFR part 247.

HISTORY:

[31 FR 13387, Oct. 15, 1966, as amended at 42 FR 19478, Apr. 14, 1977; 45 FR 30062, 30063, May 7, 1980; 45 FR 32657, May 19, 1980; 46 FR 25597, May 8, 1981; 46 FR 37240, July 20, 1981; 50 FR 49921, Dec. 6, 1985; 52 FR 16193, May 1, 1987; 53 FR 30017, Aug. 10, 1988; 54 FR 30369, July 20, 1989; 58 FR 48778, Sept. 20, 1993; 59 FR 26590, May 23, 1994; 59 FR 47063, Sept. 14, 1994; 60 FR 14353, Mar. 17, 1995; 62 FR 10312, 10346, March 6, 1997; 63 FR 39217, 39218, July 22, 1998; 63 FR 70313, 70315, Dec. 21, 1998; 74 FR 26933, 26937, June 5, 2009; 76 FR 53764, 53786, Aug. 29, 2011; 85 FR 46788, 46922, Aug 3, 2020]

§ 211.2 Passports.

(a) A passport valid for the bearer's entry into a foreign country at least 60 days beyond the expiration date of his or her immigrant visa shall be presented by each immigrant except an immigrant who:

(1) Is the parent, spouse, or unmarried son or daughter of a United States citizen or of an alien lawful permanent resident of the United States;

(2) Is entering under the provisions of § 211.1(a)(2) through (a)(7);

(3) Is a child born during the temporary visit abroad of a mother who is a lawful permanent resident alien, or a national, of the United States, provided that the child's application for admission to the United States is made within 2 years of birth, the child is accompanied by the parent who is applying for readmission as a permanent resident upon the first return of the parent to the United States after the birth of the child, and the accompanying parent is found to be admissible to the United States;

(4) Is a stateless person or a person who because of his or her opposition to Communism is unwilling or unable to obtain a passport from the country of his or her nationality, or is the accompanying spouse or unmarried son or daughter of such immigrant; or

(5) Is a member of the Armed Forces of the United States.

(b) Except as provided in paragraph (a) of this section, if an alien seeking admission as an immigrant with an immigrant visa believes that good cause exists for his or her failure to present a passport, the alien may file an application for a waiver of this requirement with the DHS officer who has jurisdiction over the port of entry where the alien arrives. To apply for this waiver, the alien must apply on the form specified by USCIS, with the fee prescribed in 8 CFR 106.2. In the exercise of discretion, the DHS officer with jurisdiction over the port of entry, may waive the alien's lack of passport and admit the alien as an immigrant, if DHS is satisfied that the alien has established good cause for his or her failure to present a passport.

HISTORY:

[29 FR 10578, July 30, 1964, as amended at 30 FR 14776, Nov. 30, 1965; 62 FR 10312, 10347, Mar. 6, 1997; 74 FR 26933, 26937, June 5, 2009; 76 FR 53764, 53786, Aug. 29, 2011; 85 FR 46788, 46922, Aug. 3, 2020]

§ 211.3 Expiration of immigrant visa or other travel document.

An immigrant visa, reentry permit, refugee travel document, or a permanent resident card shall be regarded as unexpired if the rightful holder embarked or enplaned before the expiration of his or her immigrant visa, reentry permit, or refugee travel document, or with respect to a permanent resident card, before the first anniversary of the date on which he or she departed from the United States, provided that the vessel or aircraft on which he or she so embarked or enplaned arrives in the United States or foreign contiguous territory on a continuous voyage. The continuity of the voyage shall not be deemed to have been interrupted by scheduled or emergency stops of the vessel or aircraft en route to the United States or foreign contiguous territory, or by a layover in foreign contiguous territory necessitated solely for the purpose of effecting a transportation connection to the United States.

HISTORY:

[29 FR 10578, July 30, 1964, as amended at 38 FR 8238, Mar. 30, 1973; 45 FR 32657, May 19, 1980; 58 FR 48778, Sept. 20, 1993; 59 FR 47063, Sept. 14, 1994; 60 FR 14353, Mar. 17, 1995; 62 FR 10312, 10347, Mar. 6, 1997; 76 FR 53764, 53786, Aug. 29, 2011]

§ 211.4 Waiver of documents for returning residents.

(a) Pursuant to the authority contained in section 211(b) of the Act, an alien previously lawfully admitted to the United States for permanent residence who, upon return from a temporary absence was inadmissible because of failure to have or to present a valid passport, immigrant visa, reentry permit, border crossing card, or other document required at the time of entry, may be granted a waiver of such requirement in the discretion of the district director if the district director determines that such alien:

(1) Was not otherwise inadmissible at the time of entry, or having been otherwise inadmissible at the time of entry is with respect thereto qualified for an exemption from deportability under section 237(a)(1)(H) of the Act; and

(2) Is not otherwise subject to removal.

(b) Denial of a waiver by the district director is not appealable but shall be without prejudice to renewal of an application and reconsideration in proceedings before the immigration judge.

HISTORY:

[32 FR 9625, July 4, 1967. Redesignated at 41 FR 55849, Dec. 23, 1976; 62 FR 10312, 10347, Mar. 6, 1997]

§ 211.5 Alien commuters.

(a) General. An alien lawfully admitted for permanent residence or a special agricultural worker lawfully admitted for temporary residence under section 210 of the Act may commence or continue to reside in foreign contiguous territory and commute as a special immigrant defined in section 101(a)(27)(A) of the Act to his or her place of employment in the United States. An alien commuter engaged in seasonal work will be presumed to have taken up residence in the United States if he or she is present in this country for more than 6 months, in the aggregate, during any continuous 12-month period. An alien commuter's address report under section 265 of the Act must show his or her actual residence address even though it is not in the United States.

(b) Loss of residence status. An alien commuter who has been out of regular employment in the United States for a continuous period of 6 months shall be deemed to have lost residence status, notwithstanding temporary entries in the interim for other than employment purposes. An exception applies when employment in the United States was interrupted for reasons beyond the individual's control other than lack of a job opportunity or the commuter can demonstrate that he or she has worked 90 days in the United States in the aggregate during the 12-month period preceding the application for admission into the United States. Upon loss of status, the alien's permanent resident card becomes invalid and must be surrendered to an immigration officer.

(c) Eligibility for benefits under the immigration and nationality laws. Until he or she has taken up residence in the United States, an alien commuter cannot satisfy the residence requirements of the naturalization laws and cannot qualify for any benefits under the immigration laws on his or her own behalf or on behalf of his or her relatives other than as specified in paragraph (a) of this section. When an alien commuter takes up residence in the United States, he or she shall no longer be regarded as a commuter. He or she may facilitate proof of having taken up such residence by notifying the Service as soon as possible, preferably at the time of his or her first reentry for that purpose. Application for issuance of a new Permanent Resident Card to show that he or she has taken up residence in the United States shall be made in accordance with 8 CFR 264.5.

HISTORY:

[40 FR 34106, Aug. 14, 1975. Redesignated and amended at 41 FR 55849, Dec. 23, 1976; 45 FR 32657, May 19, 1980; 46 FR 4858, Jan. 19, 1981; 52 FR 16193, May 1, 1987; 53 FR 18260, May 23, 1988; 54 FR 8184, Feb. 27, 1989; 58 FR 48778, Sept. 20, 1993; 59 FR 47063, Sept. 14, 1994; 60 FR 14353, Mar. 17, 1995; 62 FR 10312,

10348, Mar. 6, 1997; 63 FR 70313, 70315, Dec. 21, 1998; 76 FR 53764, 53786, Aug. 29, 2011]

PART 212

DOCUMENTARY REQUIREMENTS: NONIMMIGRANTS; WAIVERS; ADMISSION OF CERTAIN INADMISSIBLE ALIENS; PAROLE

Rule

AUTHORITY NOTE APPLICABLE TO ENTIRE PART:

AUTHORITY:

6 U.S.C. 111, 202(4) and 271; 8 U.S.C. 1101 and note, 1102, 1103, 1182 and note, 1184, 1187, 1223, 1225, 1226, 1227, 1255, 1359; section 7209 of Pub. L. 108-458 (8 U.S.C. 1185 note); Title VII of Pub. L. 110-229 (8 U.S.C. 1185 note); Pub. L. 115-218; 8 CFR part 2.

§ 212.0 Definitions.

For purposes of § 212.1 and § 235.1 of this chapter:

Adjacent islands means Bermuda and the islands located in the Caribbean Sea, except Cuba.

Cruise ship means a passenger vessel over 100 gross tons, carrying more than 12 passengers for hire, making a voyage lasting more than 24 hours any part of which is on the high seas, and for which passengers are embarked or disembarked in the United States or its territories.

Ferry means any vessel operating on a pre-determined fixed schedule and route, which is being used solely to provide transportation between places that are no more than 300 miles apart and which is being used to transport passengers, vehicles, and/or railroad cars.

Pleasure vessel means a vessel that is used exclusively for recreational or personal purposes and not to transport passengers or property for hire.

United States means "United States" as defined in section 215(c) of the Immigration and Nationality Act of 1952, as amended (8 U.S.C. 1185(c)).

U.S. citizen means a United States citizen or a U.S. non-citizen national.

United States qualifying tribal entity means a tribe, band, or other group of Native Americans formally recognized by the United States Government which agrees to meet WHTI document standards.

HISTORY:

[73 FR 18384, 18415, Apr. 3, 2008]

§ 212.1 Documentary requirements for nonimmigrants.

A valid unexpired visa that meets the requirements of part 215, subpart B, of this chapter, if applicable, and an unexpired passport, shall be presented by each arriving nonimmigrant alien except that the passport validity period for an applicant for admission who is a member of a class described in section 102 of the Act is not required to extend beyond the date of his application for admission if so admitted, and except as otherwise provided in the Act, this chapter, and for the following classes:

(a) Citizens of Canada or Bermuda, Bahamian nationals or British subjects resident in certain islands.

(1) Canadian citizens. A visa is generally not required for Canadian citizens, except those Canadians that fall under nonimmigrant visa categories E, K, S, or V as provided in paragraphs (h), (l), and (m) of this section and 22 CFR 41.2. A valid unexpired passport is required for Canadian citizens arriving in the United States, except when meeting one of the following requirements:

(i) NEXUS Program. A Canadian citizen who is traveling as a participant in the NEXUS program, and who is not otherwise required to present a passport and visa as provided in paragraphs (h), (l), and (m) of this section and 22 CFR 41.2, may present a valid unexpired NEXUS program card when using a NEXUS Air kiosk or when entering the United States from contiguous territory or adjacent islands at a land or sea port-of-entry. A Canadian citizen who enters the United States by pleasure vessel from Canada under the remote inspection system may present a valid unexpired NEXUS program card.

(ii) FAST Program. A Canadian citizen who is traveling as a participant in the FAST program, and who is not otherwise required to present a passport and visa as provided in paragraphs (h), (l), and (m) of this section and 22 CFR 41.2, may present a valid unexpired FAST card at a land or sea port-of-entry prior to entering the United States from contiguous territory or adjacent islands.

(iii) SENTRI Program. A Canadian citizen who is traveling as a participant in the SENTRI program, and who is not otherwise required to present a passport and visa as provided in paragraphs (h), (l), and (m) of this section and 22 CFR 41.2, may present a valid unexpired SENTRI card at a land or sea port-of-entry prior to entering the United States from contiguous territory or adjacent islands.

(iv) Canadian Indians. If designated by the Secretary of Homeland Security, a Canadian citizen holder of a Indian and Northern Affairs Canada ("INAC") card issued by the Canadian Department of Indian Affairs and North Development, Director of Land and Trust Services ("LTS") in conformance with security standards agreed upon by the Governments of Canada and the United States, and containing a machine readable zone and who is arriving from Canada may present the card prior to entering the United States at a land port-of-entry.

(v) Children. A child who is a Canadian citizen arriving from contiguous territory may present for admission to the United States at sea or land ports-of-entry certain other documents if the arrival meets the requirements described below.

(A) Children Under Age 16. A Canadian citizen who is under the age of 16 is permitted to present an original or a copy of his or her birth certificate, a Canadian Citizenship Card, or a Canadian Naturalization Certificate when arriving in the United States from contiguous territory at land or sea ports-of-entry.

(B) Groups of Children Under Age 19. A Canadian citizen, under age 19 who is traveling with a public or private school group, religious group, social or cultural organization, or team associated with a youth sport organization is permitted to present an original or a copy of his or her birth certificate, a Canadian Citizenship Card, or a Canadian Naturalization Certificate when arriving in the United States from contiguous territory at land or sea ports-of-entry, when the group, organization or team is under the supervision of an adult affiliated with the organization and when the child has parental or legal guardian consent to travel. For purposes of this paragraph, an adult is considered to be a person who is age 19 or older.

The following requirements will apply:

(1) The group, organization, or team must provide to CBP upon crossing the border, on organizational letterhead:

(i) The name of the group, organization or team, and the name of the supervising adult;

(ii) A trip itinerary, including the stated purpose of the trip, the location of the destination, and the length of stay;

(iii) A list of the children on the trip;

(iv) For each child, the primary address, primary phone number, date of birth, place of birth, and name of a parent or legal guardian.

(2) The adult leading the group, organization, or team must demonstrate parental or legal guardian consent by certifying in the writing submitted in paragraph (a)(1)(v)(B)(1) of this section that he or she has obtained for each child the consent of at least one parent or legal guardian.

(3) The inspection procedure described in this paragraph is limited to members of the group, organization, or team who are under age 19. Other members of the group, organization, or team must comply with other applicable document and/or inspection requirements found in this part or parts 211 or 235 of this subchapter.

(2) Citizens of the British Overseas Territory of Bermuda. A visa is generally not required for Citizens of the British Overseas Territory of Bermuda, except those Bermudians that fall under nonimmigrant visa categories E, K, S, or V as provided in paragraphs (h), (l), and (m) of this section and 22 CFR 41.2. A passport is required for Citizens of the British Overseas Territory of Bermuda arriving in the United States.

(3) Bahamian nationals or British subjects resident in the Bahamas. A passport is required. A visa required of such an alien unless, prior to or at the time of embarkation for the United States on a vessel or aircraft, the alien satisfied the examining U.S. immigration officer at the Bahamas, that he or she is clearly and beyond a doubt entitled to admission, under section 212(a) of the Immigration and Nationality Act, in all other respects.

(4) British subjects resident in the Cayman Islands or in the Turks and Caicos Islands. A passport is required. A visa is required of such an alien unless he or she arrives directly from the Cayman Islands or the Turks and Caicos Islands and presents a current certificate from the Clerk of Court of the Cayman Islands or the Turks and Caicos Islands indicating no criminal record.

(b) Nationals of the British Virgin Islands. A visa is not required of a national of the British Virgin Islands who has his or her residence in the British Virgin Islands, if:

(1) The alien is seeking admission solely to visit the Virgin Islands of the United States; or

(2) At the time of embarking on an aircraft at St. Thomas, U.S. Virgin Islands, the alien meets each of the following requirements:

(i) The alien is traveling to any other part of the United States by aircraft as a nonimmigrant visitor for business or pleasure (as described in section 101(a)(15)(B) of the Act);

(ii) The alien satisfies the examining U.S. immigration officer at the port-of-entry that he or she is clearly and beyond doubt entitled to admission in all other respects; and

(iii) The alien presents a current certificate issued by the Royal Virgin Islands Police Force indicating that he or she has no criminal record.

(c) Mexican nationals.

(1) A visa and a passport are not required of a Mexican national who:

(i) Is applying for admission as a temporary visitor for business or pleasure from Mexico at a land port-of-entry, or arriving by pleasure vessel or ferry, if the national is in possession of a Form DSP-150, B-1/B-2 Visa and Border Crossing Card issued by the Department of State, containing a machine-readable biometric identifier; or.

(ii) Is applying for admission from contiguous territory or adjacent islands at a land or sea port-of-entry, if the national is a member of the Texas Band of Kickapoo Indians or Kickapoo Tribe of Oklahoma who is in possession of a Form I-872 American Indian Card.

(2) A visa shall not be required of a Mexican national who:

(i) Is in possession of a Form DSP-150, with a biometric identifier, issued by the DOS, and a passport, and is applying for admission as a temporary visitor for business or pleasure from other than contiguous territory;

(ii) Is a crew member employed on an aircraft belonging to a Mexican company owned carrier authorized to engage in commercial transportation into the United States; or

(iii) Bears a Mexican diplomatic or official passport and who is a military or civilian official of the Federal Government of Mexico entering the United States for 6 months or less for a purpose other than on assignment as a permanent employee to an office of the Mexican Federal Government in the United States, and the official's spouse or any of the official's dependent family members under 19 years of age, bearing diplomatic or official passports, who are in the actual company of such official at the time of admission into the United States. This provision does not apply to the spouse or any of the official's family members classifiable under section 101(a)(15)(F) or (M) of the Act.

(3) A Mexican national who presents a BCC at a POE must present the DOS-issued DSP-150 containing a machine-readable biometric identifier. The alien will not be permitted to cross the border into the United States unless the biometric identifier contained on the card matches the appropriate biometric characteristic of the alien.

(4) Mexican nationals presenting a combination B-1/B-2 nonimmigrant visa and border crossing card (or similar stamp in a passport), issued by DOS prior to April 1, 1998, that does not contain a machine-readable biometric identifier, may be admitted on the basis of the nonimmigrant visa only, provided it has not expired and the alien remains admissible. A passport is also required.

(5) Aliens entering pursuant to International Boundary and Water Commission Treaty. A visa and a passport are not required of an alien employed either directly or indirectly on the construction, operation, or maintenance of works in the United States undertaken in accordance with the treaty concluded on February 3, 1944, between the United States and Mexico regarding the functions of the International Boundary and Water Commission, and entering the United States temporarily in connection with such employment.

(d) Citizens of the Freely Associated States, formerly Trust Territory of the Pacific Islands. Citizens of the Republic of the Marshall Islands and the Federated States of Micronesia may enter into, lawfully engage in employment, and establish residence in the United States and its territories and possessions without regard to paragraphs (14), (20) and (26) of section 212(a) of the Act pursuant to the terms of Pub. L. 99-239. Pending issuance by the aforementioned governments of travel documents to eligible citizens, travel documents previously issued by the Trust Territory of the Pacific Islands will continue to be accepted for purposes of identification and to establish eligibility for admission into the United States, its territories and possessions.

(e) Aliens entering Guam pursuant to section 14 of Pub. L. 99-396, "Omnibus Territories Act."

(1) Until November 28, 2009, a visa is not required of an alien who is a citizen of a country enumerated in paragraph (e)(3) of this section who:

(i) Is classifiable as a vistor for business or pleasure;

(ii) Is solely entering and staying on Guam for a period not to exceed fifteen days;

(iii) Is in possession of a round-trip nonrefundable and nontransferable transportation ticket bearing a confirmed departure date not exceeding fifteen days from the date of admission to Guam;

(iv) Is in possession of a completed and signed Visa Waiver Information Form (Form I-736);

(v) Waives any right to review or appeal the immigration officer's determination of admissibility at the port of entry at Guam; and

(vi) Waives any right to contest any action for deportation, other than on the basis of a request for asylum.

(2) An alien is eligible for the waiver provision if all of the eligibility criteria in paragraph (e)(1) of this section have been met prior to embarkation and the alien is a citizen of a country that:

(i) Has a visa refusal rate of 16.9% or less, or a country whose visa refusal rate exceeds 16.9% and has an established preinspection or preclearance program, pursuant to a bilateral agreement with the United States under which its citizens traveling to Guam without a valid United States visa are inspected by the Immigration and Naturalization Service prior to departure from that country;

(ii) Is within geographical proximity to Guam, unless the country has a substantial volume of nonimmigrant admissions to Guam as determined by the Commissioner and extends reciprocal privileges to citizens of the United States;

(iii) Is not designated by the Department of State as being of special humanitarian concern; and

(iv) Poses no threat to the welfare, safety or security of the United States, its territories, or commonwealths.

Any potential threats to the welfare, safety, or security of the United States, its territories, or commonwealths will be dealt with on a country by country basis, and a determination by the Commissioner of the Immigration and Naturalization Service that a threat exists will result in the immediate deletion of that country from the listing in paragraph (e)(3) of this section.

(3)(i) The following geographic areas meet the eligibility criteria as stated in paragraph (e)(2) of this section: Australia, Brunei, Indonesia, Japan, Malaysia, Nauru, New Zealand, Papua New Guinea, Republic of Korea, Singapore, Solomon Islands, Taiwan (residents thereof who begin their travel in Taiwan and who travel on direct flights from Taiwan to Guam without an intermediate layover or stop except that the flights may stop in a territory of the United States enroute), the United Kingdom (including the citizens of the colony of Hong Kong), Vanuatu, and Western Samoa. The provision that flights transporting residents of Taiwan to Guam may stop at a territory of the United States enroute may be rescinded whenever the number of inadmissible passengers arriving in Guam who have transited a territory of the United States enroute to Guam exceeds 20 percent of all the inadmissible passengers arriving in Guam within any consecutive two-month period. Such rescission will be published in the FEDERAL REGISTER.

(ii) For the purposes of this section, the term citizen of a country as used in 8 CFR 212.1(e)(1) when applied to Taiwan refers only to residents of Taiwan who are in possession of Taiwan National Identity Cards and a valid Taiwan passport with a valid re-entry permit issued by the Taiwan Ministry of Foreign Affairs. It does not refer to any other holder of a Taiwan passport or a passport issued by the People's Republic of China.

(4) Admission under this section renders an alien ineligible for:

(i) Adjustment of status to that of a temporary resident or, except as provided by section 245(i) of the Act or as an immediate relative as defined in section 201(b) of the Act, to that of a lawful permanent resident.

(ii) Change of nonimmigrant status; or

(iii) Extension of stay.

(5) A transportation line bringing any alien to Guam pursuant to this section shall:

(i) Enter into a contract on Form I-760, made by the Commissioner of the Immigration and Naturalization Service in behalf of the government;

(ii) Transport only an alien who is a citizen and in possession of a valid passport of a country enumerated in paragraph (e)(3) of this section;

(iii) Transport only an alien in possession of a round-trip, nontransferable transportation ticket:

(A) Bearing a confirmed departure date not exceeding fifteen days from the date of admission to Guam,

(B) Valid for a period of not less than one year,

(C) Nonrefundable except in the country in which issued or in the country of the alien's nationality or residence,

(D) Issued by a carrier which has entered into an agreement described in part (5)(i) of this section, and

(E) Which the carrier will unconditionally honor when presented for return passage; and

(iv) Transport only an alien in possession of a completed and signed Visa Waiver Information Form I-736.

(f) Direct transits

(1) — (2) [Reserved]

(3) Foreign government officials in transit. If an alien is of the class described in section 212(d)(8) of the Act, only a valid unexpired visa and a travel document valid for entry into a foreign country for at least 30 days from the date of admission to the United States are required.

(g) Unforeseen emergency. A nonimmigrant seeking admission to the United States must present an unexpired visa and passport valid for the amount of time set forth in section 212(a)(7)(B)(i) of the Act, 8 U.S.C. 1182(a)(7)(B)(i), or a valid biometric border crossing card issued by the DOS on Form DSP-150, at the time of application for admission, unless the nonimmigrant satisfies the requirements described in one or more of paragraphs (a) through (f) or (i), (o), or (p) of this section. Upon a nonimmigrant's application on Form I-193, or successor form, "Application for Waiver of Passport and/or Visa," a district director may, in the exercise of its discretion, on a case-by-case basis, waive either or both of the documentary requirements of section 212(a)(7)(B)(i) if satisfied that the nonimmigrant cannot present the required documents because of an unforeseen emergency. The district director may at any time revoke a waiver previously authorized pursuant to this paragraph and notify the nonimmigrant in writing to that effect.

(h) Nonimmigrant spouses, fiancees, fiances, and children of U.S. citizens. Notwithstanding any of the provisions of this part, an alien seeking admission as a spouse, fiancee, fiance, or child of a U.S. citizen, or as a child of the spouse, fiane, or finacee of a U.S. citizen, pursuant to section 101(a)(15)(K) of the Act shall be in possession of an unexpired nonimmigrant visa issued by an American consular officer classifying the alien under that section, or be inadmissible under section 212(a)(7)(B) of the Act.

(i) Visa Waiver Program. A visa is not required of any alien who is eligible to apply for admission to the United States as a Visa Waiver Program applicant pursuant to the provisions of section 217 of the Act and part 217 of this chapter if such alien is a national of a country designated under the Visa Waiver Program, who seeks admission to the United States for a period of 90 days or less as a visitor for business or pleasure.

(j) Officers authorized to act upon recommendations of United States consular officers for waiver of visa and passport requirements. All district directors, the officers in charge are authorized to act upon recommendations made by United States consular officers or by officers of the Visa Office, Department of State, pursuant to the provisions of 22 CFR 41.7 for waiver of visa and passport requirements under the provisions of section 212(d)(4)(A) of the Act. The District Director at Washington, DC, has jurisdiction in such cases recommended to the Service at the seat of Government level by the Department of State. Neither an application nor fee are required if the concurrence in a passport or visa waiver is requested by a U.S. consular officer or by an officer of the Visa Office. The district director or the Deputy Commissioner, may at any time revoke a waiver previously authorized pursuant to this paragraph and notify the nonimmigrant alien in writing to that effect.

(k) Cancellation of nonimmigrant visas by immigration officers. Upon receipt of advice from the Department of State that a nonimmigrant visa has been revoked or invalidated, and request by that Department for such action, immigration officers shall place an appropriate endorsement thereon.

(*l*) Treaty traders and investors. Notwithstanding any of the provisions of this part, an alien seeking admission as a treaty trader or investor under the provisions of Chapter 16 of the Agreement Between the United States of America, the United Mexican States, and Canada (USMCA) pursuant to section 101(a)(15)(E) of the Act, shall be in possession of a nonimmigrant visa issued by an American consular officer classifying the alien under that section.

(m) Aliens in S classification. Notwithstanding any of the provisions of this part, an alien seeking admission pursuant to section 101(a)(15)(S) of the Act must be in possession of appropriate documents issued by a United States consular officer classifying the alien under that section.

(n) [Reserved]

(o) Alien in T-2 through T-6 classification. USCIS may apply paragraph (g) of this section to individuals seeking T-2, T-3, T-4, T-5, or T-6 nonimmigrant status upon request by the applicant.

(p) Alien in U-1 through U-5 classification. Individuals seeking U-1 through U-5 nonimmigrant status may avail themselves of the provisions of paragraph (g) of this section, except that the authority to waive documentary requirements resides with the director of the USCIS office having jurisdiction over the adjudication of Form I-918, "Petition for U Nonimmigrant Status."

(q) Aliens admissible under the Guam-CNMI Visa Waiver Program.

(1) Eligibility for Program. In accordance with Public Law 110-229, beginning November 28, 2009, the Secretary, in consultation with the Secretaries of the Departments of Interior and State, may waive the visa requirement in the case of a nonimmigrant alien who seeks admission to Guam or to the Commonwealth of the Northern Mariana Islands (CNMI) under the Guam-CNMI Visa Waiver Program. To be admissible under the Guam-CNMI Visa Waiver Program, prior to embarking on a carrier for travel to Guam or the CNMI, each nonimmigrant alien must:

(i) Be a national of a country or geographic area listed in paragraph (q)(2) of this section;

(ii) Be classifiable as a visitor for business or pleasure;

(iii) Be solely entering and staying on Guam or the CNMI for a period not to exceed forty-five days;

(iv) On or after November 29, 2024, receive electronic travel authorization pursuant to paragraph (q)(9) of this section; prior to this date, receive electronic travel authorization pursuant to paragraph (q)(9) of this section or be in possession of a completed and signed Guam-CNMI Visa Waiver Information Form (CBP Form I-736);

(v) Be in possession of a completed and signed Guam-CNMI Visa Waiver Information Form (CBP Form I-736);

(vi) Be in possession of a completed and signed I-94 (see § 1.4), Arrival-Departure Record (CBP Form I-94);

(vii) Be in possession of a valid unexpired ICAO compliant, machine readable passport issued by a country that meets the eligibility requirements of paragraph (q)(2) of this section;

(viii) Have not previously violated the terms of any prior admissions. Prior admissions include those under the Guam-CNMI Visa Waiver Program, the prior Guam Visa Waiver Program, the Visa Waiver Program as described in section 217(a) of the Act and admissions pursuant to any immigrant or nonimmigrant visa;

(ix) Waive any right to review or appeal an immigration officer's determination of admissibility at the port of entry into Guam or the CNMI;

(x) Waive any right to contest any action for deportation or removal, other than on the basis of: An application for withholding of removal under section 241(b)(3) of the INA; withholding or deferral of removal under the regulations implementing Article 3 of the United Nations Convention Against Torture and Other Cruel, Inhuman or Degrading Treatment or Punishment; or, an application for asylum if permitted under section 208 of the Act.

(2) Program Countries and Geographic Areas

(i) General Eligibility Criteria.

(A) A country or geographic area may not participate in the Guam-CNMI Visa Waiver Program if the country or geographic area poses a threat to the welfare, safety or security of the United States, its territories, or commonwealths;

(B) A country or geographic area may not participate in the Guam-CNMI Visa Waiver Program if it has been designated a Country of Particular Concern under the International Religious Freedom Act of 1998 by the Department of State, or identified by the Department of State as a source country of refugees designated of special humanitarian concern to the United States;

(C) A country or geographic area may not participate in the Guam-CNMI Visa Waiver Program if that country, not later than three weeks after the issuance of a final order of removal, does not accept for repatriation any citizen, former citizen, or national of the country against whom a final executable order of removal is issued. Nothing in this subparagraph creates any duty for the United States or any right for any alien with respect to removal or release. Nothing in this subparagraph gives rise to any cause of action or claim under this paragraph or any other law against any official of the United States or of any State to compel the release, removal or reconsideration for release or removal of any alien.

(D) DHS may make a determination regarding a country's eligibility based on other factors including, but not limited to, rate of refusal for nonimmigrant visas, rate of overstays, cooperation in information exchange with the United States, electronic travel authorizations, and any other factors deemed relevant by DHS.

(ii) Eligible Countries and Geographic Areas. Nationals of the following countries are eligible to participate in the Guam-CNMI Visa Waiver Program for purposes of admission to both Guam and the CNMI: Australia, Brunei, Japan, Malaysia, Nauru, New Zealand, Papua New Guinea, Republic of Korea, Singapore, and the United Kingdom. Travelers with a connection to one of the following geographic areas — the Hong Kong Special Administrative Region (Hong Kong) or Taiwan — may also be eligible to participate in the Guam-CNMI Visa Waiver Program for purposes of admission to both Guam and the CNMI, see paragraphs (q)(2)(ii)(A) and (q)(2)(ii)(B) respectively.

(A) Hong Kong Special Administrative Region (Hong Kong). To be eligible to participate in the program as a result of a connection to Hong Kong, the following documentation is required: A Hong Kong Special Administrative Region (SAR) passport with a Hong Kong identification card; or a British National (Overseas) (BN(O)) passport with a Hong Kong identification card.

(B) Taiwan. To be eligible to participate in the program as a result of a connection to Taiwan, one must be a resident of Taiwan who begins his or her travel in Taiwan and who travels on direct flights from Taiwan to Guam or the CNMI without an intermediate layover or stop, except that the flights may stop in a territory of the United States en route, and must be in possession of a Taiwan National Identity Card and a valid Taiwan passport with a valid re-entry permit issued by the Taiwan Ministry of Foreign Affairs.

(iii) Significant Economic Benefit Criteria. If, in addition to the considerations enumerated under paragraph (q)(2)(i) of this section, DHS determines that the CNMI has received a significant economic benefit from the number of visitors for pleasure from particular countries during the period of May 8, 2007 through May 8, 2008, those countries are eligible to participate in the Guam-CNMI Visa Waiver Program unless the Secretary of Homeland Security determines that such country's inclusion in the Guam-CNMI Visa Waiver Program would represent a threat to the welfare, safety, or security of the United States and its territories.

(iv) Additional Eligible Countries or Geographic Areas Based on Significant Economic Benefit. [Reserved.]

(3) Suspension of Program Countries or Geographic Areas.

(i) Suspension of a country or geographic area from the Guam-CNMI Visa Waiver Program may be made on a country-by-country basis for good cause including, but not limited to if: The admissions of visitors from a country have resulted in an unacceptable number of visitors from a country remaining unlawfully in Guam or the CNMI, unlawfully obtaining entry to other parts of the United States, or seeking withholding of removal or seeking asylum; or that visitors from a country pose a risk to law enforcement or security interests, including the enforcement of immigration laws of Guam, the CNMI, or the United States.

(ii) A country or geographic area may be suspended from the Guam-CNMI Visa Waiver Program if that country or geographic area is designated as a Country of Particular Concern under the International Religious Freedom Act of 1998 by the Department of State, or identified by the Department of State as a source country of refugees designated of special humanitarian concern to the United States, pending an evaluation and determination by the Secretary.

(iii) A country or geographic area may be suspended from the Guam-CNMI Visa Waiver Program by the Secretary of Homeland Security, in consultation with the Secretary of the Interior and the Secretary of State, based on the evaluation of all factors the Secretary deems relevant including, but not limited to, electronic travel authorization, procedures for reporting lost and stolen passports, repatriation of aliens, rates of refusal for nonimmigrant visitor visas, overstays, exit systems and information exchange.

(4) Ineligibility due to admission under the Guam-CNMI Visa Waiver Program. Admission under this section renders an alien ineligible for:

(i) Adjustment of status to that of a temporary resident or, except as provided by section 245(i) of the Act or as an immediate relative as defined in section 201(b) of the Act, to that of a lawful permanent resident.

(ii) Change of nonimmigrant status; or

(iii) Extension of stay.

(5) Requirements for transportation lines. A transportation line bringing any alien to Guam or the CNMI pursuant to this section must:

(i) Enter into a contract on CBP Form I-760, made by the Commissioner of Customs and Border Protection on behalf of the government;

(ii) Transport an alien who is a citizen or national and in possession of a valid unexpired ICAO compliant, machine readable passport of a country enumerated in paragraph (q)(2) of this section;

(iii) Transport an alien only if the alien is in possession of a round trip ticket as defined in paragraph (q)(1)(iv) of this section bearing a confirmed departure date not exceeding forty-five days from the date of admission to Guam or the CNMI which the carrier will unconditionally honor when presented for return passage. This ticket must be:

(A) Valid for a period of not less than one year,

(B) Nonrefundable except in the country in which issued or in the country of the alien's nationality or residence, and

(C) Issued by a carrier which has entered into an agreement described in paragraph (q)(5) of this section.

(iv) On or after November 29, 2024, transport an alien who has received electronic travel authorization pursuant to paragraph (q)(9) of this section; prior to this date, transport an alien who has received electronic travel authorization pursuant to paragraph (q)(9) of this section or an alien in possession of a completed and signed Guam-CNMI Visa Waiver Information Form (CBP Form I-736), and

(v) Transport an alien in possession of completed I-94, Arrival-Departure Record (CBP Form I-94) (see § 1.4).

(6) [Removed and reserved.]

(7) Maintenance of status—satisfactory departure.

If an emergency prevents an alien admitted under the Guam-CNMI Visa Waiver Program, as set forth in this paragraph (q), from departing from Guam or the CNMI within the alien's period of authorized stay, an immigration officer having jurisdiction over the place of the alien's temporary stay may, in the officer's discretion, grant a period of satisfactory departure not to exceed 15 days. If departure is accomplished during that period, the alien is to be regarded as having satisfactorily accomplished the visit without overstaying the allotted time.

(8) Inadmissibility and Deportability

(i) Determinations of inadmissibility.

(A) An alien who applies for admission under the provisions of the Guam-CNMI Visa Waiver Program, who is determined by an immigration officer to be inadmissible to Guam or the CNMI under one or more of the grounds of inadmissibility listed in section 212 of the Act (other than for lack of a visa), or who is in possession of and presents fraudulent or counterfeit travel documents, will be refused admission into Guam or the CNMI and removed. Such refusal and removal shall be effected without referral of the alien to an immigration judge for further inquiry, examination, or hearing, except that an alien who presents himself or herself as an applicant for admission to Guam under the Guam-CNMI Visa Waiver Program, who applies for asylum, withholding of removal under section 241(b)(3) of the INA or withholding or deferral of removal under the regulations implementing Article 3 of the United Nations Convention Against Torture and Other Cruel, Inhuman or Degrading Treatment or Punishment must be issued a Form I-863, Notice of Referral to Immigration Judge, for a proceeding in accordance with 8 CFR 208.2(c)(1) and (2). The provisions of 8 CFR subpart 208 subpart A shall not apply to an alien present or arriving in the CNMI seeking to apply for asylum prior to January 1, 2030. No application for asylum may be filed pursuant to section 208 of the Act by an alien present or arriving in the CNMI prior to January 1, 2030; however, aliens physically present in the CNMI during the transition period who express a fear of persecution or torture only may establish eligibility for withholding of removal pursuant to INA 241(b)(3) or pursuant to the regulations implementing Article 3 of the United Nations Convention Against Torture and Other Cruel, Inhuman or Degrading Treatment or Punishment.

(B) The removal of an alien under this section may be deferred if the alien is paroled into the custody of a Federal, State, or local law enforcement agency for criminal prosecution or punishment. This section in no way diminishes the discretionary authority of the Secretary enumerated in section 212(d) of the Act.

(C) Refusal of admission under this paragraph shall not constitute removal for purposes of the Act.

(ii) Determination of deportability.

(A) An alien who has been admitted to either Guam or the CNMI under the provisions of this section who is determined by an immigration officer to be deportable from either Guam or the CNMI under one or more of the grounds of deportability listed in section 237 of the Act, shall be removed from either Guam or the CNMI to the alien's country of nationality or last residence. Such removal will be determined by DHS authority that has jurisdiction over the place where the alien is found, and will be effected without referral of the alien to an immigration judge for a determination of deportability, except that an alien admitted to Guam under the Guam-CNMI Visa Waiver Program who applies for asylum or other form of protection from persecution or torture must be issued a Form I-863 for a proceeding in accordance with 8 CFR 208.2(c)(1) and (2). The provisions of 8 CFR part 208 subpart A shall not apply to an alien present or arriving in the CNMI seeking to apply for asylum prior to January 1, 2030. No application for asylum may be filed pursuant to section 208 of the INA by an alien present or arriving in the CNMI prior to January 1, 2030; however, aliens physically present or arriving in the CNMI prior to January 1, 2030, may apply for withholding of removal under section 241(b)(3) of the Act and withholding and deferral of removal under the regulations implementing Article 3 of the United Nations Convention Against Torture, Inhuman or Degrading Treatment or Punishment.

(B) Removal by DHS under paragraph (q)(8)(ii)(A) of this section is equivalent in all respects and has the same consequences as removal after proceedings conducted under section 240 of the Act.

(iii) Removal of inadmissible aliens who arrived by air or sea. Removal of an alien from Guam or the CNMI under this section may be effected using the return portion of the round trip passage presented by the alien at the time of entry to Guam and the CNMI. Such removal shall be on the first available means of transportation to the alien's point of embarkation to Guam or the CNMI. Nothing in this part absolves the carrier of the responsibility to remove any inadmissible or deportable alien at carrier expense, as provided in the carrier agreement.

(9) Electronic Travel Authorization —

(i) Travel authorization required. Each nonimmigrant alien intending to travel to Guam or the CNMI under the Guam-CNMI Visa Waiver Program on or after November 29, 2024, must, within the time specified in paragraph (q)(9)(ii) of this section, receive a travel authorization, which is a positive determination of eligibility to travel to the United States under the Guam-CNMI Visa Waiver Program, from CBP. In order to receive a travel authorization, each nonimmigrant alien intending to travel to Guam or the CNMI under the Guam-CNMI Visa Waiver Program must provide the data elements set forth in paragraph (q)(9)(iii) of this section to CBP, in English, in the manner specified herein. Prior to this date, travelers must either receive an electronic travel authorization pursuant to this subparagraph or provide the required information via a completed and signed paper Guam-CNMI Visa Waiver Information Form (CBP Form I-736) upon arrival.

(ii) Time. Each alien falling within the provisions of paragraph (q)(9)(i) of this section must receive a travel authorization prior to embarking on a carrier for travel to Guam or the CNMI.

(iii) Required elements. CBP will collect such information as the Secretary deems necessary to issue a travel authorization, as reflected by the electronic Guam-CNMI Visa Waiver Information Form (Form I-736).

(iv) Duration —

(A) General rule. A travel authorization issued under the Guam-CNMI Visa Waiver Program will be valid for a period of two years from the date of issuance, unless the passport of the authorized alien will expire in less than two years, in which case the authorization will be valid until the date of expiration of the passport.

(B) Exception. For travelers from countries or geographic areas which have not entered into agreements with the United States whereby their passports are recognized as valid for the return of the bearer to the country or geographic area of the foreign-issuing authority for a period of six months beyond the expiration date specified in the passport, a travel authorization issued under the Guam-CNMI Visa Waiver Program is not valid beyond the six months prior to the expiration date of the passport. Travelers from these countries or geographic areas whose passports will expire in six months or less will not receive a travel authorization.

(C) Changes to the validity period. The Secretary, in consultation with the Secretary of State, may increase or decrease the Guam-CNMI Visa Waiver Program travel authorization validity period otherwise authorized by subparagraph (A) for a designated Guam-CNMI Visa Waiver Program country or geographic area. Notice of any change to the Guam-CNMI Visa Waiver Program travel authorization validity periods will be published in the Federal Register. The Guam-CNMI Visa Waiver Program website will be updated to reflect the specific Guam-CNMI Visa Waiver Program travel authorization validity period for each Guam-CNMI Visa Waiver Program country or geographic area.

(v) New travel authorization required. A new travel authorization is required if any of the following occurs:

(A) The alien is issued a new passport;

(B) The alien's name changes;

(C) The alien's gender changes;

(D) The alien's country of citizenship changes; or

(E) The circumstances underlying the alien's previous responses to any of the Guam-CNMI Visa Waiver Information Form (Form I-736) questions requiring a "yes" or "no" response (eligibility questions) have changed.

(vi) Limitations —

(A) Current authorization period. A travel authorization under the Guam-CNMI Visa Waiver Program is a positive determination that an alien is eligible, and grants the alien permission, to travel to Guam or the CNMI under the Guam-CNMI Visa Waiver Program and to apply for admission under the Guam-CNMI Visa Waiver Program during the period of time the travel authorization is valid. A travel authorization under the Guam-CNMI Visa Waiver Program is not a determination that the alien is admissible to Guam, the CNMI, or the United States. A determination of admissibility is made only after an applicant for admission is inspected by a CBP officer at a U.S. port of entry in Guam or the CNMI.

(B) Not a determination of visa eligibility. A determination under the Guam-CNMI Visa Waiver Program that an alien is not eligible to travel to Guam or the CNMI under the Guam-CNMI Visa Waiver Program is not a determination that the alien is ineligible for a visa to travel to Guam, the CNMI, or the United States and does not preclude the alien from applying for a visa before a United States consular officer.

(C) Revocation. A determination under the Guam-CNMI Visa Waiver Program that an alien is eligible to travel to Guam or the CNMI to apply for admission under the Guam-CNMI Visa Waiver Program may be revoked at the discretion of the Secretary.

(10) Severability. The provisions of paragraphs (q) and (r) of this section are separate and severable from one another. If any provision is stayed or determined to be invalid, the remaining provisions shall continue in effect.

(r) Aliens admissible under the Commonwealth of the Northern Mariana Islands (CNMI) Economic Vitality & Security Travel Authorization Program (EVS-TAP)—

(1) Description. In accordance with Public Law 110-229, the Secretary, in consultation with the Secretaries of the Departments of the Interior and State, may waive the visa requirement in the case of a nonimmigrant alien who seeks admission to Guam or the Commonwealth of the Northern Mariana Islands (CNMI). The requirements for the Guam-CNMI Visa Waiver program are set forth in paragraph (q) of this section. Also in accordance with Public Law 110-229 and the process provided therein, the Secretary may add countries to the list of those whose nationals may obtain a visa waiver, with any special requirements the Secretary may impose. The CNMI Economic Vitality & Security Travel Authorization Program (EVS-TAP) is a restricted travel authorization sub-program of the Guam-CNMI Visa Waiver Program that allows a nonimmigrant alien who is a national of the People's Republic of China (PRC) to be admitted to the CNMI only without a visa in specified circumstances. A visa is still required for a nonimmigrant alien who is a national of the PRC seeking to be admitted to Guam.

(2) Eligibility. To be admissible under the CNMI EVS-TAP, prior to embarking on a carrier for travel to the CNMI, the nonimmigrant alien must:

(i) Be a national of the PRC;

(ii) Be classifiable as a visitor for business or pleasure;

(iii) Be solely entering and staying on the CNMI for a period not to exceed 14 days;

(iv) Be in possession of a round trip ticket that is nonrefundable and nontransferable and bears a confirmed departure date not exceeding 14 days from the date of admission to the CNMI. "Round trip ticket" includes any return trip transportation ticket issued by a participating carrier, electronic ticket record, airline employee passes indicating return passage, individual vouchers for return passage, group vouchers for return passage for charter flights, or military travel orders which include military dependents for return to duty stations outside the United States on U.S. military flights;

(v) Receive an electronic travel authorization from CBP pursuant to paragraph (r)(9) of this section;

(vi) Be in possession of a completed and signed I-94 (see § 1.4), Arrival-Departure Record (CBP Form I-94);

(vii) Be in possession of a valid unexpired ICAO compliant, machine readable passport issued by the PRC;

(viii) Have not previously violated the terms of any prior admissions or parole;

(ix) Waive any right to review or appeal an immigration officer's determination of admissibility at the port of entry into the CNMI; and

(x) Waive any right to contest any action for deportation or removal, other than on the basis of: an application for withholding of removal under section 241(b)(3) of the INA; withholding or deferral of removal under the regulations implementing Article 3 of the United Nations Convention Against Torture and Other Cruel, Inhuman or Degrading Treatment or Punishment; or, after December 31, 2029, an application for asylum if permitted under section 208 of the Act.

(3) Suspension or Discontinuation of Program.

(i) The Secretary may suspend the CNMI EVS-TAP for good cause including, but not limited to the following circumstances:

(A) The admissions of visitors from the PRC have resulted in an unacceptable number of visitors from the PRC remaining unlawfully in the CNMI, unlawfully obtaining entry to other parts of the United States, or seeking withholding of removal or asylum; or

(B) Visitors from the PRC pose a risk to law enforcement or security interests, including the enforcement of immigration laws of the CNMI or the United States.

(ii) The Secretary, in consultation with the Secretary of the Interior and the Secretary of State, may also discontinue the CNMI EVS-TAP based on the evaluation of all factors the Secretary deems relevant including, but not limited to, electronic travel authorization, procedures for reporting lost and stolen passports, repatriation of aliens, rates of refusal for nonimmigrant visitor visas, overstays, exit systems, and information exchange.

(4) Ineligibility due to admission under the CNMI EVS-TAP. Admission under this section renders an alien ineligible for:

(i) Adjustment of status to that of a temporary resident or, except as provided by section 245(i) of the Act or as an immediate relative as defined in section 201(b) of the Act, to that of a lawful permanent resident.

(ii) Change of nonimmigrant status; or

(iii) Extension of stay.

(5) Requirements for transportation lines. A transportation line bringing any alien to the CNMI pursuant to this section must:

(i) Enter into a contract on CBP Form I-760, made by the Commissioner of U.S. Customs and Border Protection on behalf of the government;

(ii) Transport an alien only if the alien is a national of the PRC and is in possession of a valid unexpired ICAO compliant, machine readable passport issued by the PRC;

(iii) Transport an alien only if the alien is in possession of a round trip ticket as defined in paragraph (r)(2)(iv) of this section bearing a confirmed departure date not exceeding 14 days from the date of admission to the CNMI which the carrier will unconditionally honor when presented for return passage. This ticket must be:

(A) Valid for a period of not less than one year,

(B) Nonrefundable except in the country in which issued or in the country of the alien's nationality or residence, and

(C) Issued by a carrier which has entered into an agreement described in paragraph (r)(5) of this section.

(iv) Transport an alien only if the alien has received electronic travel authorization from CBP pursuant to paragraph (r)(9) of this section.

(6) [Reserved.]

(7) Maintenance of status — satisfactory departure. If an emergency prevents an alien admitted under the CNMI EVS-TAP, as set forth in this paragraph (r), from departing from the CNMI within the alien's period of authorized stay, an immigration officer having jurisdiction over the place of the alien's temporary stay may, in the officer's discretion, grant a period of satisfactory departure not to exceed 15 days. If departure is accomplished during that period, the alien is to be regarded as having satisfactorily accomplished the visit without overstaying the allotted time.

(8) Inadmissibility and Deportability —

(i) Determinations of inadmissibility.

(A) An alien who applies for admission under the provisions of the CNMI EVS-TAP, who is determined by an immigration officer to be inadmissible to the CNMI under one or more of the grounds of inadmissibility listed in section 212 of the Act (other than for lack of a visa), or who is in possession of and presents fraudulent or counterfeit travel documents, will be refused admission into the CNMI and removed. Such refusal and removal shall be effected without referral of the alien to an immigration judge for further inquiry, examination, or hearing. The provisions of 8 CFR subpart 208 subpart A shall not apply to an alien present or arriving in the CNMI seeking to apply for asylum prior to January 1, 2030. No application for asylum may be filed pursuant to section 208 of the Act by an alien present or arriving in the CNMI prior to January 1, 2030; however, aliens physically present in the CNMI during the transition period who express a fear of persecution or torture only may establish eligibility for withholding of removal pursuant to INA 241(b)(3) or pursuant to the regulations implementing Article 3 of the United Nations Convention Against Torture and Other Cruel, Inhuman or Degrading Treatment or Punishment.

(B) The removal of an alien under this section may be deferred if the alien is paroled into the custody of a Federal, State, or local law enforcement agency for criminal prosecution or punishment. This section in no way diminishes the discretionary authority of the Secretary enumerated in section 212(d) of the Act.

(C) Refusal of admission under this paragraph shall not constitute removal for purposes of the Act.

(ii) Determination of deportability.

(A) An alien who has been admitted to the CNMI under the provisions of this section who is determined by an immigration officer to be deportable from the

CNMI under one or more of the grounds of deportability listed in section 237 of the Act, shall be removed from the CNMI to the alien's country of nationality or last residence. Such removal will be determined by DHS authority that has jurisdiction over the place where the alien is found, and will be effected without referral of the alien to an immigration judge for a determination of deportability. The provisions of 8 CFR part 208 subpart A shall not apply to an alien present or arriving in the CNMI seeking to apply for asylum prior to January 1, 2030. No application for asylum may be filed pursuant to section 208 of the INA by an alien present or arriving in the CNMI prior to January 1, 2030; however, aliens physically present or arriving in the CNMI prior to January 1, 2030, may apply for withholding of removal under section 241(b)(3) of the Act and withholding and deferral of removal under the regulations implementing Article 3 of the United Nations Convention Against Torture, Inhuman or Degrading Treatment or Punishment.

(B) Removal by DHS under paragraph (r)(8)(ii)(A) of this section is equivalent in all respects and has the same consequences as removal after proceedings conducted under section 240 of the Act.

(iii) Removal of inadmissible aliens who arrived by air or sea. Removal of an alien from the CNMI under this section may be effected using the return portion of the round trip passage presented by the alien at the time of entry to the CNMI. Such removal shall be on the first available means of transportation to the alien's point of embarkation to the CNMI. Nothing in this part absolves the carrier of the responsibility to remove any inadmissible or deportable alien at carrier expense, as provided in the carrier agreement.

(9) Electronic Travel Authorization —

(i) Travel authorization required. Each nonimmigrant alien intending to travel to the CNMI under the CNMI EVS-TAP as described in paragraph (r)(1) of this section must, within the time specified in paragraph (r)(9)(ii) of this section, receive a travel authorization from CBP, which is a positive determination of eligibility to travel to the United States under the CNMI EVS-TAP. In order to receive a travel authorization, each nonimmigrant alien intending to travel to the CNMI under the CNMI EVS-TAP must provide the information set forth in paragraph (r)(9)(iii) of this section electronically to CBP, in English, in the manner specified herein.

(ii) Time. Each alien falling within the provisions of paragraph (r)(9)(i) of this section must receive a travel authorization prior to embarking on a carrier for travel to the CNMI.

(iii) Required elements. CBP will collect such information as the Secretary deems necessary to issue a travel authorization, as reflected by the electronic CNMI EVS-TAP application questions.

(iv) Duration —

(A) General rule. A travel authorization issued under the CNMI EVS-TAP will be valid for a period of one year from the date of issuance.

(B) Exceptions. If the passport of the authorized alien will expire in less than one year but greater than six months, the authorization will be valid until six months prior to the expiration date of the passport. Travelers whose passports will expire in six months or less will not receive a travel authorization.

(C) Changes to the validity period. The Secretary, in consultation with the Secretary of State, may increase or decrease the CNMI EVS-TAP travel authorization validity period otherwise authorized by paragraph (r)(9)(iv)(A) of this section. Notice of any change to the CNMI EVS-TAP travel authorization validity period will be published in the Federal Register. The CNMI EVS-TAP website will be updated to reflect the travel authorization validity period.

(v) New travel authorization required. A new travel authorization is required if any of the following occurs:

(A) The alien is issued a new passport;

(B) The alien's name changes;

(C) The alien's gender changes;

(D) The alien's country of citizenship changes; or

(E) The circumstances underlying the alien's previous responses to any of the CNMI EVS-TAP questions requiring a "yes" or "no" response (eligibility questions) have changed.

(vi) Limitations —

(A) Current authorization period. A travel authorization under the CNMI EVS-TAP is a positive determination that an alien is eligible, and grants the alien permission, to travel to the CNMI under the CNMI EVS-TAP and to apply for admission under the CNMI EVS-TAP during the period of time the travel authorization is valid. A travel authorization under the CNMI EVS-TAP is not a determination that the alien is admissible to the CNMI. A determination of admissibility is made only after an applicant for admission is inspected by a CBP officer at a U.S. port of entry in the CNMI.

(B) Not a determination of visa eligibility. A determination under the CNMI EVS-TAP that an alien is not eligible to travel to the CNMI under the CNMI EVS-TAP is not a determination that the alien is ineligible for a visa to travel to the CNMI and does not preclude the alien from applying for a visa before a United States consular officer.

(C) Revocation. A determination under the CNMI EVS-TAP that an alien is eligible to travel to the CNMI to apply for admission under the CNMI EVS-TAP may be revoked at the discretion of the Secretary.

(10) Severability. The provisions of paragraphs (q) and (r) of this section are separate and severable from one another. If any provision is stayed or determined to be invalid, the remaining provisions shall continue in effect.

(11) Implementation date. The requirements of this paragraph will take effect 45 days after the publication by the Secretary of notification in the Federal Register announcing the implementation of CNMI EVS-TAP.

HISTORY:

[26 FR 12066, Dec. 16, 1961; 51 FR 18769, 44783; 52 FR 48083, 1987; 53 FR 24900, 1988; 54 FR 13, 48577, 1989.; 55 FR 36259, 1990; 58 FR 4891, Jan. 19, 1993; 58 FR 38046, July 15, 1993, as confirmed at 59 FR 35615, July 13, 1994; 58 FR 43438, Aug. 16, 1993; 58 FR 69210, Dec. 30, 1993, as corrected at 59 FR 1992, Jan.

13, 1994, and confirmed at 63 FR 1331, 1334, Jan. 9, 1998; 59 FR 1467, Jan. 11, 1994; 59 FR 35615, July 13, 1994; 59 FR 51095, Oct. 7, 1994; 60 FR 44260, 44264, Aug. 25, 1995; 61 FR 11717, 11720, Mar. 22, 1996; 64 FR 7989, 7990, Feb. 18, 1999; 65 FR 14774, 14777, Mar. 17, 2000; 66 FR 235, 236, Jan. 3, 2001, as confirmed at 66 FR 51821, 51822, Oct. 11, 2001; 66 FR 1017, 1018, Jan. 5, 2001; 66 FR 8743, Feb. 2, 2001; 66 FR 17321, 17322, Mar. 30, 2001; 66 FR 32529, 32530, June 15, 2001; 66 FR 42587, 42593, Aug. 14, 2001; 67 FR 4784, 4795, Jan. 31, 2002; 67 FR 71443, 71447, Dec. 2, 2002; 68 FR 5190, 5193, Jan. 31, 2003; 68 FR 46926, 46928, Aug. 7, 2003; 71 FR 68412, 68429, Nov. 24, 2006; 72 FR 53014, 53035, Sept. 17, 2007; 73 FR 18384, 18416, Apr. 3, 2008; 74 FR 2824, 2833, Jan. 16, 2009; 74 FR 25387, 25388, May 28, 2009; 74 FR 55726, 55738, Oct. 28, 2009; 76 FR 16231, 16232, Mar. 23, 2011; 76 FR 53764, 53786, Aug. 29, 2011; 78 FR 18457, 18472, Mar. 27, 2013, as confirmed at 81 FR 91646, 91670, Dec. 19, 2016; 81 FR 6430, 6433, Feb. 8, 2016, as confirmed at 83 FR 31447, 31450, July 6, 2018; 81 FR 72481, 72491, Oct. 20, 2016; 81 FR 92266, 92304, Dec. 19, 2016; 82 FR 41867, 41873, Sept. 5, 2017; 85 FR 29264, 29311, May 14, 2020; 87 FR 18967, 18980, Apr. 1, 2022; 87 FR 41027, 41029, July 11, 2022; 89 FR 3299, 3327, Jan. 18, 2024]

AUTHORITY:

Section 212.1(q) and (r) also issued under section 702, Pub. L. 110-229, 122 Stat. 754, 854.

§ 212.2 Consent to reapply for admission after deportation, removal or departure at Government expense.

(a) Evidence. Any alien who has been deported or removed from the United States is inadmissible to the United States unless the alien has remained outside of the United States for five consecutive years since the date of deportation or removal. If the alien has been convicted of an aggravated felony, he or she must remain outside of the United States for twenty consecutive years from the deportation date before he or she is eligible to re-enter the United States. Any alien who has been deported or removed from the United States and is applying for a visa, admission to the United States, or adjustment of status, must present proof that he or she has remained outside of the United States for the time period required for re-entry after deportation or removal. The examining consular or immigration officer must be satisfied that since the alien's deportation or removal, the alien has remained outside the United States for more than five consecutive years, or twenty consecutive years in the case of an alien convicted of an aggravated felony as defined in section 101(a)(43) of the Act. Any alien who does not satisfactorily present proof of absence from the United States for more than five consecutive years, or twenty consecutive years in the case of an alien convicted of an aggravated felony, to the consular or immigration officer, and any alien who is seeking to enter the United States prior to the completion of the requisite five- or twenty-year absence, must apply for permission to reapply for admission to the United States as provided under this part. A temporary stay in the United States under section 212(d)(3) of the Act does not interrupt the five or twenty consecutive year absence requirement.

(b) Alien applying to consular officer for nonimmigrant visa or nonresident alien border crossing card.

(1) An alien who is applying to a consular officer for a nonimmigrant visa or a nonresident alien border crossing card, must request permission to reapply for admission to the United States if five years, or twenty years if the alien's deportation was based upon a conviction for an aggravated felony, have not elapsed since the date of deportation or removal. This permission shall be requested in the manner prescribed through the consular officer, and may be granted only in accordance with sections 212(a)(9)(A) and 212(d)(3)(A) of the Act and 8 CFR 212.4. However, the alien may apply for such permission by submitting an application on the form designated by USCIS with the fee prescribed in 8 CFR 106.2, in accordance with the form instructions, to the consular officer if that officer is willing to accept the application, and recommends to the district director that the alien be permitted to apply.

(2) The consular officer shall forward the application to the district director with jurisdiction over the place where the deportation or removal proceedings were held.

(c) Special provisions for an applicant for nonimmigrant visa under section 101(a)(15)(K) of the Act.

(1) An applicant for a nonimmigrant visa under section 101(a)(15)(K) must:

(i) Be the beneficiary of a valid visa petition approved by the Service; and

(ii) File the application on the form designated by USCIS with the fee prescribed in 8 CFR 106.2, in accordance with the form instructions with the consular officer for permission to reapply for admission to the United States after deportation or removal.

(2) The consular officer must forward the application to the designated USCIS office. If the alien is ineligible on grounds which, upon the applicant's marriage to the United States citizen petitioner, may be waived under section 212 (g), (h), or (i) of the Act, the consular officer must also forward a recommendation as to whether the waiver should be granted.

(d) Applicant for immigrant visa. Except as provided in paragraph (g)(2) of this section, an applicant for an immigrant visa who is not physically present in the United States and who requires permission to reapply must file the waiver request on the form designated by USCIS. Except as provided in paragraph (g)(2) of this section, if the applicant also requires a waiver under section 212(g), (h), or (i) of the Act, he or she must file both waiver requests simultaneously on the forms designated by USCIS with the fees prescribed in 8 CFR 106.2 and in accordance with the form instructions.

(e) Applicant for adjustment of status. An applicant for adjustment of status under section 245 of the Act and part 245 of this chapter must request permission to reapply for entry in conjunction with his or her application for adjustment of status. This request is made by filing the application on the form designated by USCIS. If the application under section 245 of the Act has been initiated, renewed, or is pending in a proceeding before an immigration judge, the district director must refer the application to the immigration judge for adjudication.

(f) Applicant for admission at port of entry. An alien may request permission at a port of entry to reapply for admission to the United States within 5 years of the deportation or removal, or 20 years in the case of an alien deported, or removed 2 or more times, or at any time after deportation or removal in the case of an alien convicted of an aggravated felony. The alien must file the application, where required, with the DHS officer having jurisdiction over the port of entry.

(g) Other applicants.

(1) Any applicant for permission to reapply for admission under circumstances other than those described in paragraphs (b) through (f) of this section must apply on the form designated by USCIS with the fee prescribed in 8 CFR 106.2 and in accordance with the form instructions.

(2) An alien who is an applicant for parole authorization under 8 CFR 245.15(t)(2) or 8 CFR 245.13(k)(2) and requires consent to reapply for admission after deportation, removal, or departure at Government expense, or a waiver under section 212(g), 212(h), or 212(i) of the Act, must file the requisite waiver form concurrently with the parole request.

(h) Decision. An applicant who has submitted a request for consent to reapply for admission after deportation or removal must be notified of the decision. If the application is denied, the applicant must be notified of the reasons for the denial and of his or her right to appeal as provided in part 103 of this chapter. Except in the case of an applicant seeking to be granted advance permission to reapply for admission prior to his or her departure from the United States, the denial of the application shall be without prejudice to the renewal of the application in the course of proceedings before an immigration judge under section 242 of the Act and this chapter.

(i) Retroactive approval.

(1) If the alien filed the application when seeking admission at a port of entry, the approval of the application shall be retroactive to either:

(i) The date on which the alien embarked or reembarked at a place outside the United States; or

(ii) The date on which the alien attempted to be admitted from foreign contiguous territory.

(2) If the alien filed the application in conjunction with an application for adjustment of status under section 245 of the Act, the approval of the application shall be retroactive to the date on which the alien embarked or reembarked at a place outside the United States.

(j) Advance approval. An alien whose departure will execute an order of deportation shall receive a conditional approval depending upon his or her satisfactory departure. However, the grant of permission to reapply does not waive inadmissibility under section 212(a)(9)(A) of the Act resulting from exclusion, deportation, or removal proceedings which are instituted subsequent to the date permission to reapply is granted.

HISTORY:

[56 FR 23212, May 21, 1991; 64 FR 25756, 25766, May 12, 1999, as confirmed and amended at 65 FR 15846, 15854, Mar. 24, 2000; 74 FR 26933, 26937, June 5, 2009; 76 FR 53764, 53786, Aug. 29, 2011, as corrected at 76 FR 73475, Nov. 29, 2011; 85 FR 46788, 46922, Aug. 3, 2020; 89 FR 65165, 65165, Aug. 9, 2024]

§ 212.3 Application for the exercise of discretion under section 212(c).

(a) Jurisdiction. An application for the exercise of discretion under section 212(c) of the Act must be submitted on the form designated by USCIS with the fee prescribed in 8 CFR 106.2 and in accordance with the form instructions. If the application is made in the course of proceedings under sections 235, 236, or 242 of the Act, the application shall be made to the Immigration Court.

(b) Filing of application. The application may be filed prior to, at the time of, or at any time after the applicant's departure from or arrival into the United States. All material facts and/or circumstances which the applicant knows or believes apply to the grounds of excludability or deportability must be described. The applicant must also submit all available documentation relating to such grounds.

(c) Decision of the District Director. A district director may grant or deny an application for advance permission to return to an unrelinquished domicile under section 212(c) of the Act, in the exercise of discretion, unless otherwise prohibited by paragraph (f) of this section. The applicant shall be notified of the decision and, if the application is denied, of the reason(s) for denial. No appeal shall lie from denial of the application, but the application may be renewed before an Immigration Judge as provided in paragraph (e) of this section.

(d) Validity. Once an application is approved, that approval is valid indefinitely. However, the approval covers only those specific grounds of excludability or deportability that were described in the application. An application who failed to describe any other grounds of excludability or deportability, or failed to disclose material facts existing at the time of the approval of the application, remains excludable or deportable under the previously unidentified grounds. If at a later date, the applicant becomes subject to exclusion or deportation based upon these previously unidentified grounds or upon new ground(s), a new application must be filed.

(e) Filing or renewal of applications before an Immigration Judge.

(1) An application for the exercise of discretion under section 212(c) of the Act may be renewed or submitted in proceedings before an Immigration Judge under sections 235, 236, or 242 of the Act, and under this chapter. Such application shall be adjudicated by the Immigration Judge, without regard to whether the applicant previously has made application to the district director.

(2) The Immigration Judge may grant or deny an application for advance permission to return to an unrelinquished domicile under section 212(c) of the Act, in the exercise of discretion, unless otherwise prohibited by paragraph (f) of this section.

(3) An alien otherwise entitled to appeal to the Board of Immigration Appeals may appeal the denial by the Immigration Judge of this application in accordance with the provisions of § 3.36 of this chapter.

(f) Limitations on discretion to grant an application under section 212(c) of the Act. An application for advance permission to enter under section 212 of the Act shall be denied if:

(1) The alien has not been lawfully admitted for permanent residence;

(2) The alien has not maintained lawful domicile in the United States, as either a lawful permanent resident or a lawful temporary resident pursuant to section 245A or section 210 of the Act, for at least seven consecutive years immediately preceding the filing of the application;

(3) The alien is subject to exclusion from the United States under paragraphs (3)(A), (3)(B), (3)(C), or (3)(E) of section 212(a) of the Act;

(4) The alien has been convicted of an aggravated felony, as defined by section 101(a)(43) of the Act, and has served a term of imprisonment of at least five years for such conviction; or

(5) The alien applies for relief under section 212(c) within five years of the barring act as enumerated in one or more sections of section 242B(e) (1) through (4) of the Act.

(g) Relief for certain aliens who were in deportation proceedings before April 24, 1996. Section 440(d) of Antiterrorism and Effective Death Penalty Act of 1996 (AEDPA) shall not apply to any applicant for relief under this section whose deportation proceedings were commenced before the Immigration Court before April 24, 1996.

HISTORY:

[56 FR 50034, Oct. 3, 1991; 60 FR 34090, June 30, 1995; 61 FR 59824, 59825, Nov. 25, 1996, as confirmed at 62 FR 43466, 43467, Aug. 14, 1997; 66 FR 6436, 6446, Jan. 22, 2001; 74 FR 26933, 26938, June 5, 2009; 76 FR 53764, 53787, Aug. 29, 2011; 85 FR 46788, 46922, Aug. 3, 2020]

§ 212.4 Applications for the exercise of discretion under section 212(d)(1) and 212(d)(3).

(a) Applications under section 212(d)(3)(A) —

(1) General. District directors and officers in charge outside the United States in the districts of Bangkok, Thailand; Mexico City, Mexico; and Rome, Italy are authorized to act upon recommendations made by consular officers for the exercise of discretion under section 212(d)(3)(A) of the Act. The District Director, Washington, DC, has jurisdiction in such cases recommended to the Service at the seat-of-government level by the Department of State. When a consular officer or other State Department official recommends that the benefits of section 212(d)(3)(A) of the Act be accorded an alien, neither an application nor fee shall be required. The recommendation shall specify:

(i) The reasons for inadmissibility and each section of law under which the alien is inadmissible;

(ii) Each intended date of arrival;

(iii) The length of each proposed stay in the United States;

(iv) The purpose of each stay;

(v) The number of entries which the alien intends to make; and

(vi) The justification for exercising the authority contained in section 212(d)(3) of the Act.

If the alien desires to make multiple entries and the consular officer or other State Department official believes that the circumstances justify the issuance of a visa valid for multiple entries rather than for a specified number of entries, and recommends that the alien be accorded an authorization valid for multiple entries, the information required by items (ii) and (iii) shall be furnished only with respect to the initial entry. Item (ii) does not apply to a bona fide crewman. The consular officer or other State Department official shall be notified of the decision on his recommendation. No appeal by the alien shall lie from an adverse decision made by a Service officer on the recommendation of a consular officer or other State Department official.

(2) Authority of consular officers to approve section 212(d)(3)(A) recommendations pertaining to aliens inadmissible under section 212(a)(28)(C). In certain categories of visa cases defined by the Secretary of State, United States consular officers assigned to visa-issuing posts abroad may, on behalf of the Attorney General pursuant to section 212(d)(3)(A) of the Act, approve a recommendation by another consular officer that an alien be admitted temporarily despite visa ineligibility solely because the alien is of the class of aliens defined at section 212(a)(28)(C) of the Act, as a result of presumed or actual membership in, or affiliation with, an organization described in that section. Authorizations for temporary admission granted by consular officers shall be subject to the terms specified in § 212.4(c) of this chapter. Any recommendation which is not clearly approvable shall, and any recommendation may, be presented to the appropriate official of the Immigration and Naturalization Service for a determination.

(b) Applications under section 212(d)(3)(B). An application for the exercise of discretion under section 212(d)(3)(B) of the Act shall be submitted on the form designated by USCIS with the fee prescribed in 8 CFR 106.2, and in accordance with the form instructions. (For Department of State procedure when a visa is required, see 22 CFR 41.95 and paragraph (a) of this section.) If the application is made because the applicant may be inadmissible due to present or past membership in or affiliation with any Communist or other totalitarian party or organization, there shall be attached to the application a written statement of the history of the applicant's membership or affiliation, including the period of such membership or affiliation, whether the applicant held any office in the organization, and whether his membership or affiliation was voluntary or involuntary. If the applicant alleges that his membership or affiliation was involuntary, the statement shall include the basis for that allegation. When the application is made because the applicant may be inadmissible due to disease, mental or physical defect, or disability of any kind, the application shall describe the disease, defect, or disability. If the purpose of seeking admission to the United States is for treatment, there shall be attached to the application statements in writing to establish that satisfactory treatment cannot be obtained outside the United States; that arrangements have been completed for treatment, and where and from whom treatment will be received; what financial arrangements for payment of expenses incurred in connection with the treatment have been made, and that a bond will be available if required. When the application is made because the applicant may be inadmissible due to the conviction of one or more crimes, the designation of each crime, the date and place of its commission and of the conviction thereof, and the sentence or other judgment of the court shall be stated in the application; in such a case the application shall be supplemented by the official record of each conviction, and any other documents relating to commutation of sentence, parole, probation, or pardon. If the application is made at the time of the applicant's arrival to the district director at a port of entry, the applicant shall establish that he was not aware of the ground of inadmissibility and that it could not have been ascertained by the exercise of reasonable diligence, and he shall be in possession of a passport and visa, if required, or have been granted a waiver thereof. The applicant shall be notified of the decision and if the application is denied of the reasons therefor and of his right to appeal to the Board within 15 days after the mailing of the notification of decision in accordance with the Provisions of part 3 of this chapter. If denied, the denial shall be without prejudice to renewal of the application in the course of proceedings before a special inquiry officer under sections 235 and 236 of the Act and this chapter. When an appeal may not be taken from a decision of a special inquiry officer excluding an alien but the alien has applied for the exercise of discretion under section 212(d)(3)(B) of the Act, the alien may appeal to the Board from a denial of such application in accordance with the provisions of § 236.5(b) of this chapter.

(c) Terms of authorization.

(1) General. Except as provided in paragraph (c)(2) of this section, each authorization under section 212(d)(3)(A) or (B) of the Act shall specify:

(i) Each section of law under which the alien is inadmissible;

(ii) The intended date of each arrival, unless the applicant is a bona fide crewman. However, if the authorization is valid for multiple entries rather than for a specified number of entries, this information shall be specified only with respect to the initial entry;

(iii) The length of each stay authorized in the United States, which shall not exceed the period justified and shall be subject to limitations specified in 8 CFR part 214. However, if the authorization is valid for multiple entries rather than for a specified number of entries, this information shall be specified only with respect to the initial entry;

(iv) The purpose of each stay;

(v) The number of entries for which the authorization is valid;

(vi) Subject to the conditions set forth in paragraph (c)(2) of this section, the dates on or between which each application for admission at POEs in the United States is valid;

(vii) The justification for exercising the authority contained in section 212(d)(3) of the Act; and

(viii) That the authorization is subject to revocation at any time.

(2) Conditions of admission.

(i) For aliens issued an authorization for temporary admission in accordance with this section, admissions pursuant to section 212(d)(3) of the Act shall be subject to the terms and conditions set forth in the authorization.

(ii) The period for which the alien's admission is authorized pursuant to this section shall not exceed the period justified, or the limitations specified, in 8 CFR part 214 for each class of nonimmigrant, whichever is less.

(3) Validity.

(i) Authorizations granted to crew members may be valid for a maximum period of 2 years for application for admission at U.S. POEs and may be valid for multiple entries.

(ii) An authorization issued in conjunction with an application for a Form DSP-150, B-1/B-2 Visa and Border Crossing Card, issued by the DOS shall be valid for a period not to exceed the validity of the biometric BCC for applications for admission at U.S. POEs and shall be valid for multiple entries.

(iii) A multiple entry authorization for a person other than a crew member or applicant for a Form DSP-150 may be made valid for a maximum period of 5 years for applications for admission at U.S. POEs.

(iv) An authorization that was previously issued in conjunction with Form I-185, Nonresident Alien Canadian Border Crossing Card, and that is noted on the card may remain valid. Although the waiver may remain valid, the non-biometric border crossing card portion of this document is not valid after that date. This waiver authorization shall cease if otherwise revoked or voided.

(v) A single-entry authorization to apply for admission at a U.S. POE shall not be valid for more than 6 months from the date the authorization is issued.

(vi) An authorization may not be revalidated. Upon expiration of the authorization, a new application and authorization are required.

(d) Admission of groups inadmissible under section 212(a)(28) for attendance at international conferences. When the Secretary of State recommends that a group of nonimmigrant aliens and their accompanying family members be admitted to attend international conferences notwithstanding their inadmissibility under section 212(a)(28) of the Act, the Deputy Commissioner, may enter an order pursuant to the authority contained in section 212(d)(3)(A) of the Act specifying the terms and conditions of their admission and stay.

(e) Inadmissibility under section 212(a)(1)(A)(iii). Pursuant to the authority contained in section 212(d)(3) of the Act, the temporary admission of a nonimmigrant visitor is authorized notwithstanding inadmissibility under section 212(a)(1)(A)(iii)(I) or (II) of the Act due to a mental disorder and associated threatening or harmful behavior, if such alien is accompanied by a member of his/her family, or a guardian who will be responsible for him/her during the period of admission authorized.

(f) Inadmissibility under section 212(a)(1) for aliens inadmissible due to HIV.

(1) General. Pursuant to the authority in section 212(d)(3)(A)(i) of the Act, any alien who is inadmissible under section 212(a)(1)(A)(i) of the Act due to infection with the etiologic agent for acquired immune deficiency syndrome (HIV infection) may be issued a B-1 (business visitor) or B-2 (visitor for pleasure) nonimmigrant visa by a consular officer or the Secretary of State, and be authorized for temporary admission into the United States for a period not to exceed 30 days, subject to authorization of an additional period or periods under paragraph (f)(5) of this section, provided that the authorization is granted in accordance with paragraphs (f)(2) through (f)(7) of this section. Application under this paragraph (f) may not be combined with any other waiver of inadmissibility.

(2) Conditions. An alien who is HIV-positive who applies for a nonimmigrant visa before a consular officer may be issued a B-1 (business visitor) or B-2 (visitor for pleasure) nonimmigrant visa and admitted to the United States for a period not to exceed 30 days, provided that the applicant establishes that:

(i) The applicant has tested positive for HIV;

(ii) The applicant is not currently exhibiting symptoms indicative of an active, contagious infection associated with acquired immune deficiency syndrome;

(iii) The applicant is aware of, has been counseled on, and understands the nature, severity, and the communicability of his or her medical condition;

(iv) The applicant's admission poses a minimal risk of danger to the public health in the United States and poses a minimal risk of danger of transmission of the infection to any other person in the United States;

(v) The applicant will have in his or her possession, or will have access to, as medically appropriate, an adequate supply of antiretroviral drugs for the anticipated stay in the United States and possesses sufficient assets, such as insurance that is accepted in the United States, to cover any medical care that the applicant may require in the event of illness at any time while in the United States;

(vi) The applicant's admission will not create any cost to the United States, or a state or local government, or any agency thereof, without the prior written consent of the agency;

(vii) The applicant is seeking admission solely for activities that are consistent with the B-1 (business visitor) or B-2 (visitor for pleasure) nonimmigrant classification;

(viii) The applicant is aware that no single admission to the United States will be for a period that exceeds 30 days (subject to paragraph (f)(5) of this section);

(ix) The applicant is otherwise admissible to the United States and no other ground of inadmissibility applies;

(x) The applicant is aware that he or she cannot be admitted under section 217 of the Act (Visa Waiver Program);

(xi) The applicant is aware that any failure to comply with any condition of admission set forth under this paragraph (f) will thereafter make him or her ineligible for authorization under this paragraph; and

(xii) The applicant, for the purpose of admission pursuant to authorization under this paragraph (f), waives any opportunity to apply for an extension of nonimmigrant stay (except as provided in paragraph (f)(5) of this section), a change of nonimmigrant status, or adjustment of status to that of permanent resident.

(A) Nothing in this paragraph (f) precludes an alien admitted under this paragraph (f) from applying for asylum pursuant to section 208 of the Act.

(B) Any alien admitted under this paragraph (f) who applies for adjustment of status under section 209 of the Act after being granted asylum must establish his or her eligibility to adjust status under all applicable provisions of the Act and 8 CFR part 209. Any applicable ground of inadmissibility must be waived by approval of an appropriate waiver(s) under section 209(c) of the Act and 8 CFR 209.2(b).

(C) Nothing within this paragraph (f) constitutes a waiver of inadmissibility under section 209 of the Act or 8 CFR part 209.

(3) Nonimmigrant visa. A nonimmigrant visa issued to the applicant for purposes of temporary admission under section 212(d)(3)(A)(i) of the Act and this paragraph (f) may not be valid for more than 12 months or for more than two applications for admission during the 12-month period. The authorized period of stay will be for 30 calendar days calculated from the initial admission under this visa.

(4) Application at U.S. port. If otherwise admissible, a holder of the nonimmigrant visa issued under section 212(d)(3)(A)(i) of the Act and this paragraph (f) is authorized to apply for admission at a United States port of entry at any time during the period of validity of the visa in only the B-1 (business visitor) or B-2 (visitor for pleasure) nonimmigrant categories.

(5) Admission limited; satisfactory departure. Notwithstanding any other provision of this chapter, no single period of admission under section 212(d)(3)(A)(i) of the Act and this paragraph (f) may be authorized for more than 30 days; if an emergency prevents a nonimmigrant alien admitted under this paragraph (f) from departing from the United States within his or her period of authorized stay, the director (or other appropriate official) having jurisdiction over the place of the alien's temporary stay may, in his or her discretion, grant an additional period (or periods) of satisfactory departure, each such period not to exceed 30 days. If departure is accomplished during that period, the alien is to be regarded as having satisfactorily accomplished the visit without overstaying the allotted time.

(6) Failure to comply. No authorization under section 212(d)(3)(A)(i) of the Act and this paragraph (f) may be provided to any alien who has previously failed to comply with any condition of an admission authorized under this paragraph.

(7) Additional limitations. The Secretary of Homeland Security or the Secretary of State may require additional evidence or impose additional conditions on granting authorization for temporary admissions under

this paragraph (f) as international (or other relevant) conditions may indicate.

(8) Option for case-by-case determination. If the applicant does not meet the criteria under this paragraph (f), or does not wish to agree to the conditions for the streamlined 30-day visa under this paragraph (f), the applicant may elect to utilize the process described in either paragraph (a) or (b) of this section, as applicable.

(g) Action upon alien's arrival. Upon admitting an alien who has been granted the benefits of section 212(d)(3)(A) of the Act, the immigration officer shall be guided by the conditions and limitations imposed in the authorization and noted by the consular officer in the alien's passport. When admitting any alien who has been granted the benefits of section 212(d)(3)(B) of the Act, the Immigration officer shall note on the arrival-departure record, Form I-94 (see § 1.4), or crewman's landing permit, Form I-95, issued to the alien, the conditions and limitations imposed in the authorization.

(h) Authorizations issued to crewmen without limitation as to period of validity. When a crewman who has a valid section 212(d)(3) authorization without any time limitation comes to the attention of the Service, his travel document shall be endorsed to show that the validity of his section 212(d)(3) authorization expires as of a date six months thereafter, and any previously-issued Form I 184 shall be lifted and Form I-95 shall be issued in its place and similarly endorsed.

(i) Revocation. The Deputy Commissioner or the district director may at any time revoke a waiver previously authorized under section 212(d)(3) of the Act and shall notify the nonimmigrant in writing to that effect.

(j) Alien witnesses and informants. —

(1) Waivers under section 212(d)(1) of the Act. Upon the application of a federal or state law enforcement authority ("LEA"), which shall include a state or federal court or United States Attorney's Office, pursuant to the filing, for nonimmigrant classification described in section 101(a)(15)(S) of the Act, USCIS will determine whether a ground of exclusion exists with respect to the alien for whom classification is sought and, if so, whether it is in the national interest to exercise the discretion to waive the ground of excludability, other than section 212(a)(3)(E) of the Act. USCIS may at any time revoke a waiver previously authorized under section 212(d)(1) of the Act. In the event USCIS decides to revoke a previously authorized waiver for an S nonimmigrant, the Assistant Attorney General, Criminal Division, and the relevant LEA shall be notified in writing to that effect. The Assistant Attorney General, Criminal Division, shall concur in or object to the decision. Unless the Assistant Attorney General, Criminal Division, objects within 7 days, he or she shall be deemed to have concurred in the decision. In the event of an objection by the Assistant Attorney General, Criminal Division, the matter will be expeditiously referred to the Deputy Attorney General for a final resolution. In no circumstances shall the alien or the relevant LEA have a right of appeal from any decision to revoke.

(2) Grounds of removal. Nothing shall prohibit the Service from removing from the United States an alien classified pursuant to section 101(a)(15)(S) of the Act for conduct committed after the alien has been admitted to the United States as an S nonimmigrant, or after the alien's change to S classification, or for conduct or a condition undisclosed to the Attorney General prior to the alien's admission in, or change to, S classification, unless such conduct or condition is waived prior to admission and classification. In the event USCIS decides to remove an S nonimmigrant from the United States, the Assistant Attorney General, Criminal Division, and the relevant LEA shall be notified in writing to that effect. The Assistant Attorney General, Criminal Division, shall concur in or object to that decision. Unless the Assistant Attorney General, Criminal Division, objects within 7 days, he or she shall be deemed to have concurred in the decision. In the event of an objection by the Assistant Attorney General, Criminal Division, the matter will be expeditiously referred to the Deputy Attorney General for a final resolution. In no circumstances shall the alien or the relevant LEA have a right of appeal from any decision to remove.

HISTORY:

[29 FR 15252, Nov. 13, 1964, as amended at 30 FR 12330, Sept. 28, 1965; 31 FR 10413, Aug. 3, 1966; 32 FR 15469, Nov. 7, 1967; 35 FR 3065, Feb. 17, 1970; 35 FR 7637, May 16, 1970; 40 FR 30470, July 21, 1975; 51 FR 32295, Sept. 10, 1986; 53 FR 40867, Oct. 19, 1988; 60 FR 44260, 44264, Aug. 25, 1995, as corrected at 60 FR 52248, Oct. 5, 1995; 67 FR 71443, 71448, Dec. 2, 2002; 73 FR 58023, 58030, Oct. 6, 2008; 76 FR 53764, 53787, Aug. 29, 2011; 78 FR 18457, 18472, Mar. 27, 2013, as confirmed at 81 FR 91646, 91670, Dec. 19, 2016; 85 FR 46788, 46923, Aug. 3, 2020]

§ 212.5 Parole of aliens into the United States.

(a) The authority of the Secretary to continue an alien in custody or grant parole under section 212(d)(5)(A) of the Act shall be exercised by the Assistant Commissioner, Office of Field Operations; Director, Detention and Removal; directors of field operations; port directors; special agents in charge; deputy special agents in charge; associate special agents in charge; assistant special agents in charge; resident agents in charge; field office directors; deputy field office directors; chief patrol agents; district directors for services; and those other officials as may be designated in writing, subject to the parole and detention authority of the Secretary or his designees. The Secretary or his designees may invoke, in the exercise of discretion, the authority under section 212(d)(5)(A) of the Act.

(b) Parole from custody. The parole of aliens within the following groups who have been or are detained in accordance with § 235.3(b) or (c) of this chapter would generally be justified only on a case-by-case basis for "urgent humanitarian reasons" or "significant public benefit," provided the aliens present neither a security risk nor a risk of absconding:

(c) In the case of all other arriving aliens, except those detained under § 235.3(b) or (c) of this chapter and paragraph (b) of this section, those officials listed in paragraph (a) of this section may, after review of the individual case, parole into the United States temporarily in accordance with section 212(d)(5)(A) of the Act, any alien applicant for admission, under such terms and conditions, including those set forth in paragraph (d) of this section, as he or she may deem appropriate. An alien who arrives at a port-of-entry and applies for parole into the United States for the sole purpose of seeking adjustment of status under section 245A of the Act, without benefit of advance authorization as described in paragraph (f) of this section shall be denied parole and detained for removal in accordance with the provisions of § 235.3(b) or (c) of this chapter. An alien seeking to enter the United States for the sole purpose of applying for adjustment of status under section 210 of the Act shall be denied parole and detained for removal under § 235.3(b) or (c) of this chapter, unless the alien has been recommended for approval of such application for adjustment by a consular officer at an Overseas Processing Office.

(d) Conditions. In any case where an alien is paroled under paragraph (b) or (c) of this section, those officials listed in paragraph (a) of this section may require reasonable assurances that the alien will appear at all hearings and/or depart the United States when required to do so. Not all factors listed need be present for parole to be exercised. Those officials should apply reasonable discretion. The consideration of all relevant factors includes:

(1) The giving of an undertaking by the applicant, counsel, or a sponsor to ensure appearances or departure, and a bond may be required on Form I-352 in such amount as may be deemed appropriate;

(2) Community ties such as close relatives with known addresses; and

(3) Agreement to reasonable conditions (such as periodic reporting of whereabouts).

(e) Termination of parole —

(1) Automatic. Parole shall be automatically terminated without written notice (i) upon the departure from the United States of the alien, or, (ii) if not departed, at the expiration of the time for which parole was authorized, and in the latter case the alien shall be processed in accordance with paragraph (e)(2) of this section except that no written notice shall be required.

(2)(i) On notice. In cases not covered by paragraph (e)(1) of this section, upon accomplishment of the purpose for which parole was authorized or when in the opinion of one of the officials listed in paragraph (a) of this section, neither humanitarian reasons nor public benefit warrants the continued presence of the alien in the United States, parole shall be terminated upon written notice to the alien and he or she shall be restored to the status that he or she had at the time of parole. When a charging document is served on the alien, the charging document will constitute written notice of termination of parole, unless otherwise specified. Any further inspection or hearing shall be conducted under section 235 or 240 of the Act and this chapter, or any order of exclusion, deportation, or removal previously entered shall be executed. If the exclusion, deportation, or removal order cannot be executed within a reasonable time, the alien shall again be released on parole unless in the opinion of the official listed in paragraph (a) of this section the public interest requires that the alien be continued in custody.

(ii) An alien who is granted parole into the United States after enactment of the Immigration Reform and Control Act of 1986 for other than the specific purpose of applying for adjustment of status under section 245A of the Act shall not be permitted to avail him or herself of the privilege of adjustment thereunder. Failure to abide by this provision through making such an application will subject the alien to termination of parole status and institution of proceedings under sections 235 and 236 of the Act without the written notice of termination required by § 212.5(e)(2)(i) of this chapter.

(iii) Any alien granted parole into the United States so that he or she may transit through the United States in the course of removal from Canada shall have his or her parole status terminated upon notice, as specified in 8 CFR 212.5(e)(2)(i), if he or she makes known to an immigration officer of the United States a fear of persecution or an intention to apply for asylum. Upon termination of parole, any such alien shall be regarded as an arriving alien, and processed accordingly by the Department of Homeland Security.

(f) Advance authorization. When parole is authorized for an alien who will travel to the United States without a visa, the alien shall be issued an appropriate document authorizing travel.

(g) Parole for certain Cuban nationals. Notwithstanding any other provision respecting parole, the determination whether to release on parole, or to revoke the parole of, a native of Cuba who last came to the United States between April 15, 1980, and October 20, 1980, shall be governed by the terms of § 212.12.

(h) Effect of parole of Cuban and Haitian nationals.

(1) Except as provided in paragraph (h)(2) of this section, any national of Cuba or Haiti who was paroled into the United States on or after October 10, 1980, shall be considered to have been paroled in the special status for nationals of Cuba or Haiti, referred to in section 501(e)(1) of the Refugee Education Assistance Act of 1980, Public Law 96-422, as amended (8 U.S.C. 1522 note).

(2) A national of Cuba or Haiti shall not be considered to have been paroled in the special status for nationals of Cuba or Haiti, referred to in section 501(e)(1) of the Refugee Education Assistance Act of 1980, Public Law 96-422, as amended, if the individual was paroled into the United States:

(i) In the custody of a Federal, State or local law enforcement or prosecutorial authority, for purposes of criminal prosecution in the United States; or

(ii) Solely to testify as a witness in proceedings before a judicial, administrative, or legislative body in the United States.

HISTORY:

[47 FR 30045, July 9, 1982, as amended at 47 FR 46494, Oct. 19, 1982; 52 FR 16194, May 1, 1987; 52 FR 48802, Dec. 28, 1987; 53 FR 17450, May 17, 1988; 61 FR 36610, 36611, July 12, 1996, as confirmed at 63 FR 31895, 31896, June 11, 1998; 62 FR 10312, 10348, Mar. 6, 1997; 65 FR 80281, 80294, Dec. 21, 2000; 65 FR 82254, 82255, Dec. 28, 2000; 66 FR 7863, Jan. 26, 2001; 67 FR 39255, 39257, June 7, 2002; 68 FR 35151, 35152, June 12, 2003; 69 FR 69480, 69489, Nov. 29, 2004; 76 FR 53764, 53787, Aug. 29, 2011; 84 FR 44392, 44525, Aug. 23, 2019; 87 FR 18078, 18220, Mar. 29, 2022]

§ 212.6 Border crossing identification cards.

(a) Application for Form DSP-150, B-1/B-2 Visa and Border Crossing Card, issued by the Department of State. A citizen of Mexico, who seeks to travel temporarily to the United States for business or pleasure without a visa and passport, must apply to the DOS on Form DS-156, Visitor Visa Application, to obtain a Form DSP-150 in accordance with the applicable DOS regulations at 22 CFR 41.32 and/or instructions.

(b) Use.

(1) Application for admission with Non-resident Canadian Border Crossing Card, Form I-185, containing separate waiver authorization; Canadian residents bearing DOS-issued combination B-1/B-2 visa and border crossing card (or similar stamp in a passport).

(i) A Canadian citizen or other person sharing common nationality with Canada and residing in Canada who presents a Form I-185 that contains a separate notation of a waiver authorization issued pursuant to § 212.4 may be admitted on the basis of the waiver, provided the waiver has not expired or otherwise been revoked or voided. Although the waiver may remain valid on or after October 1, 2002, the non-biometric border crossing card portion of the document is not valid after that date.

(ii) A Canadian resident who presents a combination B-1/B-2 visa and border crossing card (or similar stamp in a passport) issued by the DOS prior to April 1, 1998, that does not contain a machine-readable biometric identifier, may be admitted on the basis of the nonimmigrant visa only, provided it has not expired and the alien remains otherwise admissible.

(2) Application for admission by a national of Mexico-Form DSP-150 issued by the DOS; DOS-issued combination B-1/B-2 visa and border crossing card (or similar stamp in a passport).

(i) The rightful holder of a Form DSP-150 issued by the DOS may be admitted under § 235.1(f) of this chapter if found otherwise admissible and if the biometric identifier contained on the card matches the appropriate biometric characteristic of the alien.

(ii) The bearer of a combination B-1/B-2 nonimmigrant visa and border crossing card (or similar stamp in a passport) issued by DOS prior to April 1, 1998, that does not contain a machine-readable biometric identifier, may be admitted on the basis of the nonimmigrant visa only, provided it has not expired and the alien remains otherwise admissible. A passport is also required.

(iii) Any alien seeking admission as a visitor for business or pleasure, must also present a valid passport with his or her border crossing card, and shall be issued a Form I-94 (see § 1.4) if the alien is applying for admission from:

(A) A country other than Mexico or Canada, or

(B) Canada if the alien has been in a country other than the United States or Canada since leaving Mexico.

(c) Validity. Forms I-185, I-186, and I-586 are invalid on or after October 1, 2002. If presented on or after that date, these documents will be voided at the POE.

(d) Voidance for reasons other than expiration of the validity of the form.

(1) At a POE.

(i) In accordance with 22 CFR 41.122, a Form DSP-150 or combined B-1/B-2 visitor visa and non-biometric border crossing identification card or (a similar stamp in a passport), issued by the DOS, may be physically cancelled and voided by a supervisory immigration officer at a POE if it is considered void pursuant to section 222(g) of the Act when presented at the time of application for admission, or as the alien departs the United States. If the card is considered void and if the applicant for admission is not otherwise subject to expedited removal in accordance with 8 CFR part 235, the applicant shall be advised in writing that he or she may request a hearing before an immigration judge. The purpose of the hearing shall be to determine his/her admissibility in accordance with § 235.6 of this chapter. The applicant may be represented at this hearing by an attorney of his/her own choice at no expense to the Government. He or she shall also be advised of the availability of free legal services provided by organizations and attorneys qualified under 8 CFR part 3, and organizations recognized under § 292.2 of this chapter located in the district where the removal hearing is to be held. If the applicant requests a hearing, the Form DSP-150 or combined B-1/B-2 visitor visa and non-biometric border crossing identification card (or similar stamp in a passport), issued by the DOS, shall be held by the Service for presentation to the immigration judge.

(ii) If the applicant chooses not to have a hearing, the Form DSP-150 or combined B-1/B-2 visitor visa and non-biometric BCC (or similar stamp in a passport) issued by the DOS, shall be voided and physically cancelled. The alien to whom the card or stamp was issued by the DOS shall be notified of the action taken and the reasons for such action by means of Form I-275, Withdrawal of Application for Admission/Consular Notification, delivered in person or by mailing the Form I-275 to the last known address. The DOS shall be notified of the cancellation of the biometric Form DSP-150 or combined B-1/B-2 visitor visa and non-biometric BCC (or similar stamp in a passport) issued by DOS, by means of a copy of the original Form I-275. Nothing in this paragraph limits the Service's ability to remove an alien pursuant to 8 CFR part 235 where applicable.

(2) Within the United States. In accordance with former section 242 of the Act (before amended by section 306 of the IIRIRA of 1996, Div. C, Public Law 104-208, 110 Stat. 3009 (Sept. 30, 1996,) or current sections 235(b), 238, and 240 of the Act, if the holder of a Form DSP-150, or other combined B-1/B-2 visa and BCC, or (similar stamp in a passport) issued by the DOS, is placed under removal proceedings, no action to cancel the card or stamp shall be taken pending the outcome of the hearing. If the alien is ordered removed or granted voluntary departure, the card or stamp shall be physically cancelled and voided by an immigration officer. In the case of an alien holder of a BCC who is granted voluntary departure without a hearing, the card shall be declared void and physically cancelled by an immigration officer who is authorized to issue a Notice to Appear or to grant voluntary departure.

(3) In Mexico or Canada. Forms I-185, I-186 or I-586 issued by the Service and which are now invalid, or a Form DSP-150 or combined B-1/B-2 visitor visa and non-biometric BCC, or (similar stamp in a passport) issued by the DOS may be declared void by United States consular officers or United States immigration officers in Mexico or Canada.

(4) Grounds. Grounds for voidance of a Form I-185, I-186, I-586, a DOS-issued non-biometric BCC, or the biometric Form DSP-150 shall be that the holder has violated the immigration laws; that he/she is inadmissible to the United States; that he/she has abandoned his/her residence in the country upon which the card was granted; or if the BCC is presented for admission on or after October 1, 2002, it does not contain a machine-readable biometric identifier corresponding to the bearer and is invalid on or after October 1, 2002.

(e) Replacement. If a valid Border Crossing Card (Forms I-185, I-186, or I-586) previously issued by the Service, a non-biometric border crossing card issued by the DOS before April 1998, or a Form DSP-150 issued by the DOS has been lost, stolen, mutilated, or destroyed, the person to whom the card was issued may apply for a new card as provided for in the DOS regulations found at 22 CFR 41.32 and 22 CFR 41.103.

HISTORY:

[30 FR 10184, Aug. 17, 1965, as amended at 34 FR 129, Jan. 4, 1969.; 35 FR 3065, Feb. 17, 1970; 37 FR 7584, Apr. 18, 1972; 37 FR 8061, Apr. 25, 1972; 45 FR 11114, Feb. 20, 1980; 46 FR 25082, May 5, 1981; 48 FR 35349, Aug. 4, 1983; 60 FR 40068, Aug. 7, 1995; 62 FR 9071, 9074, Feb. 28, 1997; 62 FR 10312, 10349, Mar. 6, 1997; 67 FR 71443, 71448, Dec. 2, 2002; 78 FR 18457, 18472, Mar. 27, 2013, as confirmed at 81 FR 91646, 91670, Dec. 19, 2016]

§ 212.7 Waiver of certain grounds of inadmissibility.

(a)(1) Application. Except as provided by 8 CFR 212.7(e), an applicant for an immigrant visa, adjustment of status, or a K or V nonimmigrant visa who is inadmissible under any provision of section 212(a) of the Act for which a waiver is available under section 212 of the Act may apply for the related waiver by filing the form designated by USCIS, with the fee prescribed in 8 CFR 106.2, and in accordance with the form instructions. Certain immigrants may apply for a provisional unlawful presence waiver of inadmissibility as specified in 8 CFR 212.7(e).

(2) Termination of application for lack of prosecution. An applicant may withdraw the application at any time prior to the final decision, whereupon the case will be closed and the consulate notified. If the applicant fails to prosecute the application within a reasonable time either before or after interview the applicant shall be notified that if he or she fails to prosecute the application within 30 days the case will be closed subject to being reopened at the applicant's request. If no action has been taken within the 30-day period immediately thereafter, the case will be closed and the appropriate consul notified.

(3) Decision. If the waiver application is denied, USCIS will provide a written decision and notify the applicant and his or her attorney or accredited representative and will advise the applicant of appeal procedures, if any, in accordance with 8 CFR 103.3. The denial of a provisional unlawful presence waiver is governed by 8 CFR 212.7(e).

(4) Validity.

(i) A provisional unlawful presence waiver granted according to paragraph (e) of this section is valid subject to the terms and conditions as specified in paragraph (e) of this section. In any other case, approval of an immigrant waiver of inadmissibility under this section applies only to the grounds of inadmissibility, and the related crimes, events, or incidents that are specified in the application for waiver.

(ii) Except for K-1 and K-2 nonimmigrants and aliens lawfully admitted for permanent residence on a conditional basis, an immigrant waiver of inadmissibility is valid indefinitely, even if the applicant later abandons or otherwise loses lawful permanent resident status.

(iii) For a K-1 or K-2 nonimmigrant, approval of the waiver is conditioned on the K-1 nonimmigrant marrying the petitioner; if the K-1 nonimmigrant marries the K nonimmigrant petitioner, the waiver becomes valid indefinitely, subject to paragraph (a)(4)(iv) of this section, even if the applicant later abandons or otherwise loses lawful permanent resident status. If the K-1 does not marry the K nonimmigrant petitioner, the K-1 and K-2 nonimmigrants remain inadmissible for purposes of any application for a benefit on any basis other than the proposed marriage between the K-1 and the K nonimmigrant petitioner.

(iv) For an alien lawfully admitted for permanent residence on a conditional basis under section 216 of the Act, removal of the conditions on the alien's status renders the waiver valid indefinitely, even if the applicant later abandons or otherwise loses lawful permanent resident status. Termination of the alien's status as an alien lawfully admitted for permanent residence on a conditional basis also terminates the validity of a waiver of inadmissibility based on sections 212(h) or 212(i) of the Act that was granted to the alien. Separate notification of the termination of the waiver is not required when an alien is notified of the termination of residence under section 216 of the Act, and no appeal will lie from the decision to terminate the waiver on this basis. If the alien challenges the termination in removal proceedings, and the removal proceedings end in the restoration of the alien's status, the waiver will become effective again.

(v) Nothing in this subsection precludes USCIS from reopening and reconsidering a decision if the decision is determined to have been made in error.

(b) Section 212(g) waivers for certain medical conditions.

(1) Application. Any alien who is inadmissible under section 212(a)(1)(A)(i), (ii), or (iii) of the Act and who is eligible for a waiver under section 212(g) of the Act may file an application as described in paragraph (a)(1) of this section. The family member specified in section 212(g) of the Act may file the waiver application for the

applicant if the applicant is incompetent to file the waiver personally.

(2) Section 212(a) (1) or (3) (certain mental conditions) —

(i) Arrangements for submission of medical report. If the alien is excludable under section 212(a)(1)(A)(iii) of the Act he or his sponsoring family member shall submit a waiver request with a statement that arrangements have been made for the submission to that office of a medical report. The medical report shall contain a complete medical history of the alien, including details of any hospitalization or institutional care or treatment for any physical or mental condition; findings as to the current physical condition of the alien, including reports of chest X-ray examination and of serologic test for syphilis if the alien is 15 years of age or over, and other pertinent diagnostic tests; and findings as to the current mental condition of the alien, with information as to prognosis and life expectancy and with a report of a psychiatric examination conducted by a psychiatrist who shall, in case of mental retardation, also provide an evaluation of the alien's intelligence. For an alien with a past history of mental illness, the medical report shall also contain available information on which the U.S. Public Health Service can base a finding as to whether the alien has been free of such mental illness for a period of time sufficient in the light of such history to demonstrate recovery.

(ii) Submission of statement. Upon being notified that the medical report has been reviewed by the U.S. Public Health Service and determined to be acceptable, the alien or the alien's sponsoring family member shall submit a statement to the consular or Service office. The statement must be from a clinic, hospital, institution, specialized facility, or specialist in the United States approved by the U.S. Public Health Service. The alien or alien's sponsor may be referred to the mental retardation or mental health agency of the state of proposed residence for guidance in selecting a post-arrival medical examining authority who will complete the evaluation and provide an evaluation report to the Centers for Disease Control. The statement must specify the name and address of the specialized facility, or specialist, and must affirm that:

(A) The specified facility or specialist agrees to evaluate the alien's mental status and prepare a complete report of the findings of such evaluation.

(B) The alien, the alien's sponsoring family member, or another responsible person has made complete financial arrangements for payment of any charges that may be incurred after arrival for studies, care, training and service;

(C) The Director, Division of Quarantine, Center for Prevention Services, Centers for Disease Control, Atlanta, GA. 30333 shall be furnished:

(1) The report evaluating the alien's mental status within 30 days after the alien's arrival; and

(2) Prompt notification of the alien's failure to report to the facility or specialist within 30 days after being notified by the U.S. Public Health Service that the alien has arrived in the United States.

(D) The alien shall be in an outpatient, inpatient, study, or other specified status as determined by the responsible local physcian or specialist during the initial evaluation.

(3) Assurances: Bonds. In all cases under paragraph (b) of this section the alien or his or her sponsoring family member shall also submit an assurance that the alien will comply with any special travel requirements as may be specified by the U.S. Public Health Service and that, upon the admission of the alien into the United States, he or she will proceed directly to the facility or specialist specified for the initial evaluation, and will submit to such further examinations or treatment as may be required, whether in an outpatient, inpatient, or other status. The alien, his or her sponsoring family member, or other responsible person shall provide such assurances or bond as may be required to assure that the necessary expenses of the alien will be met and that he or she will not become a public charge. For procedures relating to cancellation or breaching of bonds, see part 103 of this chapter.

(c) Section 212(e).

(1) An alien who was admitted to the United States as an exchange visitor, or who acquired that status after admission, is subject to the foreign residence requirement of section 212(e) of the Act if his or her participation in an exchange program was financed in whole or in part, directly or indirectly, by a United States government agency or by the government of the country of his or her nationality or last foreign residence.

(2) An alien is also subject to the foreign residence requirement of section 212(e) of the Act if at the time of admission to the United States as an exchange visitor or at the time of acquisition of exchange visitor status after admission to the United States, the alien was a national or lawful permanent resident of a country which the Director of the United States Information Agency had designated, through public notice in the Federal Register, as clearly requiring the services of persons engaged in the field of specialized knowledge or skill in which the alien was to engage in his or her exchange visitor program.

(3) An alien is also subject to the foreign residence requirement of section 212(e) of the Act if he or she was admitted to the United States as an exchange visitor on or after January 10, 1977 to receive graduate medical education or training, or following admission, acquired such status on or after that date for that purpose. However, an exchange visitor already participating in an exchange program of graduate medical education or training as of January 9, 1977 who was not then subject to the foreign residence requirement of section 212(e) and who proceeds or has proceeded abroad temporarily and is returning to the United States to participate in the same program, continues to be exempt from the foreign residence requirement.

(4) A spouse or child admitted to the United States or accorded status under section 101(a)(15)(J) of the Act to accompany or follow to join an exchange visitor who is subject to the foreign residence requirement of section 212(e) of the Act is also subject to that requirement.

(5) An alien who is subject to the foreign residence requirement and who believes that compliance therewith would impose exceptional hardship upon his/her spouse or child who is a citizen of the United States or a lawful permanent resident alien, or that he or she cannot return to the country of his or her nationality or last residence because he or she will be subject to persecution on account of race, religion, or political opinion, may apply for a waiver on the form designated by USCIS. The alien's spouse and minor children, if also subject to the foreign residence requirement, may be included in the application, provided the spouse has not been a participant in an exchange program.

(6) Each application based upon a claim to exceptional hardship must be accompanied by the certificate of marriage between the applicant and his or her spouse and proof of legal termination of all previous marriages of the applicant and spouse; the birth certificate of any child who is a United States citizen or lawful permanent resident alien, if the application is based upon a claim of exceptional hardship to a child, and evidence of the United States citizenship of the applicant's spouse or child, when the application is based upon a claim of exceptional hardship to a spouse or child who is a citizen of the United States.

(7) Evidence of United States citizenship and of status as a lawful permanent resident shall be in the form provided in part 204 of this chapter. An application based upon exceptional hardship shall be supported by a statement, dated and signed by the applicant, giving a detailed explanation of the basis for his or her belief that his or her compliance with the foreign residence requirement of section 212(e) of the Act, as amended, would impose exceptional hardship upon his or her spouse or child who is a citizen of the United States or a lawful permanent resident thereof. The statement shall include all pertinent information concerning the incomes and savings of the applicant and spouse. If exceptional hardship is claimed upon medical grounds, the applicant shall submit a medical certificate from a qualified physician setting forth in terms understandable to a layman the nature and effect of the illness and prognosis as to the period of time the spouse or child will require care or treatment.

(8) An application based upon the applicant's belief that he or she cannot return to the country of his or her nationality or last residence because the applicant would be subject to persecution on account of race, religion, or political opinion, must be supported by a statement, dated and signed by the applicant, setting forth in detail why the applicant believes he or she would be subject to persecution.

(9) Waivers under Pub. L. 103-416 based on a request by a State Department of Public Health (or equivalent). In accordance with section 220 of Pub. L. 103-416, an alien admitted to the United States as a nonimmigrant under section 101(a)(15)(J) of the Act, or who acquired status under section 101(a)(15)(J) of the Act after admission to the United States, to participate in an exchange program of graduate medical education or training (as of January 9, 1977), may apply for a waiver of the 2-year home country residence and physical presence requirement (the "2-year requirement") under section 212(e)(iii) of the Act based on a request by a State Department of Pubic Health, or its equivalent. To initiate the application for a waiver under Pub. L. 103-416, the Department of Public Health, or its equivalent, or the State in which the foreign medical graduate seeks to practice medicine, must request the Director of USIA to recommend a waiver to the Service. The waiver may be granted only if the Director of USIA provides the Service with a favorable waiver recommendation. Only the Service, however, may grant or deny the waiver application. If granted, such a waiver shall be subject to the terms and conditions imposed under section 214(l) of the Act (as redesignated by section 671(a)(3)(A) of Pub. L. 104-208). Although the alien is not required to submit a separate waiver application to the Service, the burden rests on the alien to establish eligibility for the waiver. If the Service approves a waiver request made under Pub. L. 103-416, the foreign medical graduate (and accompanying dependents) may apply for change of nonimmigrant status, from J-1 to H-1B and, in the case of dependents of such a foreign medical graduate, from J-2 to H-4. Aliens receiving waivers under section 220 of Pub. L. 103-416 are subject, in all cases, to the provisions of section 214(g)(1)(A) of the Act.

(i) Eligiblity criteria. J-1 foreign medical graduates (with accompanying J-2 dependents) are eligible to apply for a waiver of the 2-year requirement under Pub. L. 103-416 based on a request by a State Department of Public Health (or its equivalent) if:

(A) They were admitted to the United States under section 101(a)(15)(J) of the Act, or acquired J nonimmigrant status before June 1, 2002, to pursue graduate medical education or training in the United States.

(B) They have entered into a bona fide, full-time employment contract for 3 years to practice medicine at a health care facility located in an area or areas designated by the Secretary of Health and Human Services as having a shortage of health care professionals ("HHS-designated shortage area");

(C) They agree to commence employment within 90 days of receipt of the waiver under this section and agree to practice medicine for 3 years at the facility named in the waiver application and only in HHS-designated shortage areas. The health care facility named in the waiver application may be operated by:

(1) An agency of the Government of the United States or of the State in which it is located; or

(2) A charitable, educational, or other not-for-profit organization; or

(3) Private medical practitioners.

(D) The Department of Public Health, or its equivalent, in the State where the health care facility is located has requested the Director, USIA, to recommend the waiver, and the Director, USIA, submits a favorable waiver recommendation to the Service; and

(E) Approval of the waiver will not cause the number of waivers granted pursuant to Pub. L. 103-416 and this section to foreign medical graduates who will practice medicine in the same state to exceed 20 during the current fiscal year.

(ii) Decision on waivers under Pub. L. 103-416 and notification to the alien —

(A) Approval. If the Director of USIA submits a favorable waiver recommendation on behalf of a foreign medical graduate pursuant to Pub. L. 103-416, and the Service grants the waiver, the alien shall be notified of the approval on Form I-797 (or I-797A or I-797B, as appropriate). The approval notice shall clearly state the terms and conditions imposed on the waiver, and the Service's records shall be noted accordingly.

(B) Denial. If the Director of USIA issues a favorable waiver recommendation under Pub. L. 103-416 and the Service denies the waiver, the alien shall be notified of the decision and of the right to appeal under 8 CFR part 103. However, no appeal shall lie where the basis for denial is that the number of waivers granted to the State in which the foreign medical graduate will be employed would exceed 20 for that fiscal year.

(iii) Conditions. The foreign medical graduate must agree to commence employment for the health care facility specified in the waiver application within 90 days of receipt of the waiver under Pub. L. 103-416. The foreign medical graduate may only fulfill the requisite 3-year employment contract as an H-1B nonimmigrant. A foreign medical graduate who receives a waiver under Pub. L. 103-416 based on a request by a State Department of Public Health (or equivalent), and changes his or her nonimmigrant classification from J-1 to H-1B, may not apply for permanent residence or for any other change of nonimmigrant classification unless he or she has fulfilled the 3-year employment contract with the health care facility and in the specified HHS-designated shortage area named in the waiver application.

(iv) Failure to fulfill the three-year employment contract due to extenuating circumstances. A foreign medical graduate who fails to meet the terms and conditions imposed on the waiver under section 214(l) of the Act and this paragraph will once again become subject to the 2-year requirement under section 212(e) of the Act.

Under section 214(l)(1)(B) of the Act, however, the Service, in the exercise of discretion, may excuse early termination of the foreign medical graduate's 3-year period of employment with the health care facility named in the waiver application due to extenuating circumstances. Extenuating circumstances may include, but are not limited to, closure of the health care facility or hardship to the alien. In determining whether to excuse such early termination of employment, the Service shall base its decision on the specific facts of each case. In all cases, the burden of establishing eligibility for a favorable exercise of discretion rests with the foreign medical graduate. Depending on the circumstances, closure of the health care facility named in the waiver application may, but need not, be considered an extenuating circumstance excusing early termination of employment. Under no circumstances will a foreign medical graduate be eligible to apply for change of status to another nonimmigrant category, for an immigrant visa or for status as a lawful permanent resident prior to completing the requisite 3-year period of employment for a health care facility located in an HHS-designated shortage area.

(v) Required evidence. A foreign medical graduate who seeks to have early termination of employment excused due to extenuating circumstances shall submit documentary evidence establishing such a claim. In all cases, the foreign medical graduate shall submit an employment contract with another health care facility located in an HHS-designated shortage area for the balance of the required 3-year period of employment. A foreign medical graduate claiming extenuating circumstances based on hardship shall also submit evidence establishing that such hardship was caused by unforeseen circumstances beyond his or her control. A foreign medical graduate claiming extenuating circumstances based on closure of the health care facility named in the waiver application shall also submit evidence that the facility has closed or is about to be closed.

(vi) Notification requirements. A J-1 foreign medical graduate who has been granted a waiver of the 2-year requirement pursuant to Pub. L. 103-416, is required to comply with the terms and conditions specified in section 214(l) of the Act and the implementing regulations in this section. If the foreign medical graduate subsequently applies for and receives H-1B status, he or she must also comply with the terms and conditions of that nonimmigrant status. Such compliance shall also include notifying USCIS of any material change in the terms and conditions of the H-1B employment, by filing either an amended or a new H-1B petition, as required, under §§ 214.2(h)(2)(i)(D), 214.2(h)(2)(i)(E), and 214.2(h)(11) of this chapter.

(A) Amended H-1B petitions. The health care facility named in the waiver application and H-1B petition shall file an amended H-1B petition, as required under § 214.2(h)(2)(i)(E) of this chapter, if there are any material changes in the terms and conditions of the beneficiary's employment or eligibility as specified in the waiver application filed under Pub. L. 103-416 and in the subsequent H-1B petition. In such a case, an amended H-1B petition shall be accompanied by evidence that the alien will continue practicing medicine with the original employer in an HHS-designated shortage area.

(B) New H-1B petitions. A health care facility seeking to employ a foreign medical graduate who has been granted a waiver under Pub. L. 103-416 (prior to the time the alien has completed his or her 3-year contract with the facility named in the waiver application and original H-1B petition), shall file a new H-1B petition, as required under §§ 214.2(h)(2)(i) (D) and (E) of this chapter. Although a new waiver application need not be filed, the new H-1B petition shall be accompanied by the documentary evidence generally required under § 214.2(h) of this chapter, and the following additional documents:

(1) A copy of the USCIS approval notice relating to the waiver and nonimmigrant H status granted under Pub. L. 103-416;

(2) An explanation from the foreign medical graduate, with supporting evidence, establishing that ex-

tenuating circumstances necessitate a change in employment;

(3) An employment contract establishing that the foreign medical graduate will practice medicine at the health care facility named in the new H-1B petition for the balance of the required 3-year period; and

(4) Evidence that the geographic area or areas of intended employment indicated in the new H-1B petition are in HHS-designated shortage areas.

(C) Review of amended and new H-1B petitions for foreign medical graduates granted waivers under Pub. L. 103-416 and who seek to have early termination of employment excused due to extenuating circumstances —

(1) Amended H-1B petitions. The waiver granted under Pub. L. 103-416 may be affirmed, and the amended H-1B petition may be approved, if the petitioning health care facility establishes that the foreign medical graduate otherwise remains eligible for H-1B classification and that he or she will continue practicing medicine in an HHS-designated shortage area.

(2) New H-1B petitions. The Service shall review a new H-1B petition filed on behalf of a foreign medical graduate who has not yet fulfilled the required 3-year period of employment with the health care facility named in the waiver application and in the original H-1B petition to determine whether extenuating circumstances exist which warrant a change in employment, and whether the waiver granted under Pub. L. 103-416 should be affirmed. In conducting such a review, the Service shall determine whether the foreign medical graduate will continue practicing medicine in an HHS-designated shortage area, and whether the new H-1B petitioner and the foreign medical graduate have satisfied the remaining H-1B eligibility criteria described under section 101(a)(15)(H) of the Act and § 214.2(h) of this chapter. If these criteria have been satisfied, the waiver granted to the foreign medical graduate under Pub. L. 103-416 may be affirmed, and the new H1-B petition may be approved in the exercise of discretion, thereby permitting the foreign medical graduate to serve the balance of the requisite 3-year employment period at the health care facility named in the new H-1B petition.

(D) Failure to notify the Service of any material changes in employment. Foreign medical graduates who have been granted a waiver of the 2-year requirement and who have obtained H-1B status under Pub. L. 103-416 but fail tonotify the Service of any material change in the terms and conditions of their H-1B employment, by having their employer file an amended or a new H-1B petition in accordance with this section and § 214.2(h) of this chapter; or establish continued eligibility for the waiver and H-1B status, shall (together with their dependents) again become subject to the 2-year requirement. Such foreign medical graduates and their accompanying H-4 dependents also become subject to deportation under section 241(a)(1)(C)(i) of the Act.

(10) The applicant and his or her spouse may be interviewed by an immigration officer in connection with the application and consultation may be had with the Director, United States Information Agency and the sponsor of any exchange program in which the applicant has been a participant.

(11) The applicant shall be notified of the decision, and if the application is denied, of the reasons therefor and of the right of appeal in accordance with the provisions of part 103 of this chapter. However, no appeal shall lie from the denial of an application for lack of a favorable recommendation from the Secretary of State. When an interested United States Government agency requests a waiver of the two-year foreign-residence requirement and the Director, United States Information Agency had made a favorable recommendation, the interested agency shall be notified of the decision on its request and, if the request is denied, of the reasons thereof, and of the right of appeal. If the foreign country of the alien's nationality or last residence has furnished statement in writing that it has no objection to his/her being granted a waiver of the foreign residence requirement and the Director, United States Information Agency has made a favorable recommendation, the Director shall be notified of the decision and, if the foreign residence requirement is not waived, of the reasons therefor and of the foregoing right of appeal. However, this "no objection" provision is not applicable to the exchange visitor admitted to the United States on or after January 10, 1977 to receive graduate medical education or training, or who acquired such status on or after that date for such purpose; except that the alien who commenced a program before January 10, 1977 and who was readmitted to the United States on or after that date to continue participation in the same program, is eligible for the "no objection" waiver.

(d) Criminal grounds of inadmissibility involving violent or dangerous crimes. The Attorney General, in general, will not favorably exercise discretion under section 212(h)(2) of the Act (8 U.S.C. 1182(h)(2)) to consent to an application or reapplication for a visa, or admission to the United States, or adjustment of status, with respect to immigrant aliens who are inadmissible under section 212(a)(2) of the Act in cases involving violent or dangerous crimes, except in extraordinary circumstances, such as those involving national security or foreign policy considerations, or cases in which an alien clearly demonstrates that the denial of the application for adjustment of status or an immigrant visa or admission as an immigrant would result in exceptional and extremely unusual hardship. Moreover, depending on the gravity of the alien's underlying criminal offense, a showing of extraordinary circumstances might still be insufficient to warrant a favorable exercise of discretion under section 212(h)(2) of the Act.

(e) Provisional unlawful presence waivers of inadmissibility. The provisions of this paragraph (e) apply to certain aliens who are pursuing consular immigrant visa processing.

(1) Jurisdiction. USCIS has exclusive jurisdiction to grant a provisional unlawful presence waiver under this paragraph (e). An alien applying for a provisional unlawful presence waiver must file with USCIS the

form designated by USCIS, with the fees prescribed in 8 CFR 106.2, and in accordance with the form instructions.

(2) Provisional unlawful presence waiver; in general.

(i) USCIS may adjudicate applications for a provisional unlawful presence waiver of inadmissibility based on section 212(a)(9)(B)(v) of the Act filed by eligible aliens described in paragraph (e)(3) of this section. USCIS will only approve such provisional unlawful presence waiver applications in accordance with the conditions outlined in paragraph (e) of this section. Consistent with section 212(a)(9)(B)(v) of the Act, the decision whether to approve a provisional unlawful presence waiver application is discretionary. A pending or approved provisional unlawful presence waiver does not constitute a grant of a lawful immigration status or a period of stay authorized by the Secretary.

(ii) A pending or an approved provisional unlawful presence waiver does not support the filing of any application for interim immigration benefits, such as employment authorization or an advance parole document. Any application for an advance parole document or employment authorization that is submitted in connection with a provisional unlawful presence waiver application will be rejected.

(3) Eligible aliens. Except as provided in paragraph (e)(4) of this section, an alien may be eligible to apply for and receive a provisional unlawful presence waiver for the grounds of inadmissibility under section 212(a)(9)(B)(i)(I) or (II) of the Act if he or she meets the requirements in this paragraph. An alien may be eligible to apply for and receive a waiver if he or she:

(i) Is present in the United States at the time of filing the application for a provisional unlawful presence waiver;

(ii) Provides biometrics to USCIS at a location in the United States designated by USCIS;

(iii) Upon departure, would be inadmissible only under section 212(a)(9)(B)(i) of the Act at the time of the immigrant visa interview;

(iv) Has a case pending with the Department of State, based on:

(A) An approved immigrant visa petition, for which the Department of State immigrant visa processing fee has been paid; or

(B) Selection by the Department of State to participate in the Diversity Visa Program under section 203(c) of the Act for the fiscal year for which the alien registered;

(v) Will depart from the United States to obtain the immigrant visa; and

(vi) Meets the requirements for a waiver provided in section 212(a)(9)(B)(v) of the Act.

(4) Ineligible aliens. Notwithstanding paragraph (e)(3) of this section, an alien is ineligible for a provisional unlawful presence waiver under paragraph (e) of this section if:

(i) The alien is under the age of 17;

(ii) The alien does not have a case pending with the Department of State, based on:

(A) An approved immigrant visa petition, for which the Department of State immigrant visa processing fee has been paid; or

(B) Selection by the Department of State to participate in the Diversity Visa program under section 203(c) of the Act for the fiscal year for which the alien registered;

(iii) The alien is in removal proceedings, in which no final order has been entered, unless the removal proceedings are administratively closed and have not been recalendared at the time of filing the application for a provisional unlawful presence waiver;

(iv) The alien is subject to an administratively final order of removal, deportation, or exclusion under any provision of law (including an in absentia order under section 240(b)(5) of the Act), unless the alien has already filed and USCIS has already granted, before the alien applies for a provisional unlawful presence waiver under 8 CFR 212.7(e), an application for consent to reapply for admission under section 212(a)(9)(A)(iii) of the Act and 8 CFR 212.2(j);

(v) CBP or ICE, after service of notice under 8 CFR 241.8, has reinstated a prior order of removal under section 241(a)(5) of the Act, either before the filing of the provisional unlawful presence waiver application or while the provisional unlawful presence waiver application is pending; or

(vi) The alien has a pending application with USCIS for lawful permanent resident status.

(5) Filing.

(i) An alien must file an application for a provisional unlawful presence waiver of the unlawful presence inadmissibility bars under section 212(a)(9)(B)(i)(I) or (II) of the Act on the form designated by USCIS, in accordance with the form instructions, with the fee prescribed in 8 CFR 106.2, and with the evidence required by the form instructions.

(ii) An application for a provisional unlawful presence waiver will be rejected and the fee and package returned to the alien if the alien:

(A) Fails to pay the required filing fee or correct filing fee for the provisional unlawful presence waiver application;

(B) Fails to sign the provisional unlawful presence waiver application;

(C) Fails to provide his or her family name, domestic home address, and date of birth;

(D) Is under the age of 17;

(E) Does not include evidence of:

(1) An approved immigrant visa petition;

(2) Selection by the Department of State to participate in the Diversity Visa Program under section 203(c) of the Act for the fiscal year for which the alien registered; or

(3) Eligibility as a derivative beneficiary of an approved immigrant visa petition or of an alien selected for participation in the Diversity Visa Program as provided in this section and outlined in section 203(d) of the Act.

(F) Fails to include documentation evidencing:

(1) That the alien has paid the immigrant visa processing fee to the Department of State for the immigrant visa application upon which the alien's approved immigrant visa petition is based; or

(2) In the case of a diversity immigrant, that the Department of State selected the alien to participate in the Diversity Visa Program for the fiscal year for which the alien registered.

(6) Biometrics.

(i) All aliens who apply for a provisional unlawful presence waiver under this section will be required to provide biometrics in accordance with 8 CFR 103.16 and 103.17, as specified on the form instructions.

(ii) Failure to appear for biometric services. If an alien fails to appear for a biometric services appointment or fails to provide biometrics in the United States as directed by USCIS, a provisional unlawful presence waiver application will be considered abandoned and denied under 8 CFR 103.2(b)(13). The alien may not appeal or file a motion to reopen or reconsider an abandonment denial under 8 CFR 103.5.

(7) Burden and standard of proof. The alien has the burden to establish, by a preponderance of the evidence, eligibility for a provisional unlawful presence waiver as described in this paragraph, and under section 212(a)(9)(B)(v) of the Act, including that the alien merits a favorable exercise of discretion.

(8) Adjudication. USCIS will adjudicate a provisional unlawful presence waiver application in accordance with this paragraph and section 212(a)(9)(B)(v) of the Act. If USCIS finds that the alien is not eligible for a provisional unlawful presence waiver, or if USCIS determines in its discretion that a waiver is not warranted, USCIS will deny the waiver application. Notwithstanding 8 CFR 103.2(b)(16), USCIS may deny an application for a provisional unlawful presence waiver without prior issuance of a request for evidence or notice of intent to deny.

(9) Notice of decision.

(i) USCIS will notify the alien and the alien's attorney of record or accredited representative of the decision in accordance with 8 CFR 103.2(b)(19). USCIS may notify the Department of State of the denial of an application for a provisional unlawful presence waiver. A denial is without prejudice to the alien's filing another provisional unlawful presence waiver application under this paragraph (e), provided the alien meets all of the requirements in this part, including that the alien's case must be pending with the Department of State. An alien also may elect to file a waiver application under paragraph (a)(1) of this section after departing the United States, appearing for his or her immigrant visa interview at the U.S. Embassy or consulate abroad, and after the Department of State determines the alien's admissibility and eligibility for an immigrant visa.

(ii) Denial of an application for a provisional unlawful presence waiver is not a final agency action for purposes of section 10(c) of the Administrative Procedure Act, 5 U.S.C. 704.

(10) Withdrawal of waiver applications. An alien may withdraw his or her application for a provisional unlawful presence waiver at any time before USCIS makes a final decision. Once the case is withdrawn, USCIS will close the case and notify the alien and his or her attorney or accredited representative. The alien may file a new application for a provisional unlawful presence waiver, in accordance with the form instructions and required fees, provided that the alien meets all of the requirements included in this paragraph (e).

(11) Appeals and motions to reopen. There is no administrative appeal from a denial of a request for a provisional unlawful presence waiver under this section. The alien may not file, pursuant to 8 CFR 103.5, a motion to reopen or reconsider a denial of a provisional unlawful presence waiver application under this section.

(12) Approval and conditions. A provisional unlawful presence waiver granted under this section:

(i) Does not take effect unless, and until, the alien who applied for and obtained the provisional unlawful presence waiver:

(A) Departs from the United States;

(B) Appears for an immigrant visa interview at a U.S. Embassy or consulate; and

(C) Is determined to be otherwise eligible for an immigrant visa by the Department of State in light of the approved provisional unlawful presence waiver.

(ii) Waives, upon satisfaction of the conditions described in paragraph (e)(12)(i), the alien's inadmissibility under section 212(a)(9)(B) of the Act only for purposes of the application for an immigrant visa and admission to the United States as an immigrant based on the approved immigrant visa petition upon which a provisional unlawful presence waiver application is based or selection by the Department of State to participate in the Diversity Visa Program under section 203(c) of the Act for the fiscal year for which the alien registered, with such selection being the basis for the alien's provisional unlawful presence waiver application;

(iii) Does not waive any ground of inadmissibility other than, upon satisfaction of the conditions described in paragraph (e)(12)(i), the grounds of inadmissibility under section 212(a)(9)(B)(i)(I) or (II) of the Act.

(13) Validity. Until the provisional unlawful presence waiver takes full effect as provided in paragraph (e)(12) of this section, USCIS may reopen and reconsider its decision at any time. Once a provisional unlawful presence waiver takes full effect as defined in paragraph (e)(12) of this section, the period of unlawful presence for which the provisional unlawful presence waiver is granted is waived indefinitely, in accordance with and subject to paragraph (a)(4) of this section.

(14) Automatic revocation. The approval of a provisional unlawful presence waiver is revoked automatically if:

(i) The Department of State denies the immigrant visa application after completion of the immigrant visa interview based on a finding that the alien is ineligible to receive an immigrant visa for any reason other than inadmissibility under section 212(a)(9)(B)(i)(I) or (II) of the Act. This automatic revocation does not prevent the alien from applying for a waiver of inadmissibility for unlawful presence under section 212(a)(9)(B)(v) of the Act and 8 CFR 212.7(a) or for any other relief from inadmissibility on any other ground for which a waiver is available and for which the alien may be eligible;

(ii) The immigrant visa petition approval associated with the provisional unlawful presence waiver is at any time revoked, withdrawn, or rendered invalid but not otherwise reinstated for humanitarian reasons or converted to a widow or widower petition;

(iii) The immigrant visa registration is terminated in accordance with section 203(g) of the Act, and has not been reinstated in accordance with section 203(g) of the Act; or

(iv) The alien enters or attempts to reenter the United States without inspection and admission or parole at any time after the alien files the provisional unlawful presence waiver application and before the approval of the provisional unlawful presence waiver takes effect in accordance with paragraph (e)(12) of this section.

HISTORY:

[29 FR 12584, Sept. 4, 1964, and 29 FR 13242; Sept. 24, 1964, as amended at 30 FR 14776, Nov. 30, 1965; 32 FR 2500, Feb. 7, 1967; 37 FR 22725, Oct. 31, 1972; 46 FR 45327, Sept. 11, 1981; 47 FR 44235, Oct. 7, 1982; 48 FR 20684, May 9, 1983; 48 FR 23159, May 24, 1983; 48 FR 30610, July 5, 1983; 49 FR 48530, Dec. 13, 1984; 53 FR 30017, Aug. 10, 1988; 60 FR 26681, May 18, 1995, as confirmed and amended at 62 FR 18506, 18508, Apr. 16, 1997; 64 FR 25756, 25766, May 12, 1999, as confirmed and amended at 65 FR 15835, 15844, 15846, 15854, Mar. 24, 2000; 66 FR 42587, 42593, Aug. 14, 2001; 67 FR 78675, 78678, Dec. 26, 2002; 74 FR 26933, 26938, June 5, 2009; 76 FR 53764, 53787, Aug. 29, 2011, as corrected at 76 FR 73475, Nov. 29, 2011; 78 FR 536, 376, Jan. 3, 2013; 81 FR 50244, 50275, July 29, 2016]; 85 FR 46788, 46923, Aug. 3, 2020]

AUTHORITY:

(Secs. 103, 203, 212 of the Immigration and Nationality Act, as amended by secs. 4, 5, 18 of Pub. L. 97-116, 95 Stat. 1611, 1620, (8 U.S.C. 1103, 1153, 1182)

§ 212.8 [This section was removed and reserved. See 76 FR 53764, 53787, Aug. 29, 2011.]

[NO TEXT IN ORIGINAL]

HISTORY:

[31 FR 10021, July 23, 1966; 31 FR 10355, Aug. 22, 1966, as amended at 34 FR 5326, Mar. 18, 1969; 38 FR 31166, Nov. 12, 1973; 41 FR 37566, Sept. 7, 1976; 41 FR 55850, Dec. 23, 1976; 47 FR 44990, Oct. 13, 1982; 48 FR 19157, Apr. 28, 1983; 76 FR 53764, 53787, Aug. 29, 2011]

AUTHORITY:

(8 U.S.C. 1101 and note, 1102, 1103, 1182 and note, 1184, 1187, 1223, 1225, 1226, 1227, 1255, 1359; 8 U.S.C. 1185 note (section 7209 of Pub. L. 108-458); 8 CFR part 2.)

§ 212.9 [This section was removed and reserved. See 76 FR 53764, 53787, Aug. 29, 2011.]

[NO TEXT IN ORIGINAL]

HISTORY:

[45 FR 63836, Sept. 26, 1980; 76 FR 53764, 53787, Aug. 29, 2011]

AUTHORITY:

(Secs. 103, 203(a)(8), and 212(a)(32), 8 U.S.C 1103, 1153(a)(8), and 1182(a)(32))

§ 212.10 Section 212(k) waiver.

Any applicant for admission who is in possession of an immigrant visa, and who is inadmissible under section 212(a)(5)(A) or 212(a)(7)(A)(i) of the Act, may apply at the port of entry for a waiver under section 212(k) of the Act. If the application for waiver is denied, the application may be renewed in removal proceedings before an immigration judge as provided in 8 CFR part 1240.

HISTORY:

[47 FR 44236, Oct. 7, 1982; 76 FR 53764, 53787, Aug. 29, 2011]

§ 212.11 [This section was removed and reserved. See 76 FR 53764, 53787, Aug. 29, 2011.]

[NO TEXT IN ORIGINAL]

HISTORY:

[53 FR 9282, Mar. 22, 1988; 76 FR 53764, 53787, Aug. 29, 2011]

AUTHORITY:

(8 U.S.C. 1101 and note, 1102, 1103, 1182 and note, 1184, 1187, 1223, 1225, 1226, 1227, 1255, 1359; 8 U.S.C. 1185 note (section 7209 of Pub. L. 108-458); 8 CFR part 2.)

§ 212.12 Parole determinations and revocations respecting Mariel Cubans.

(a) Scope. This section applies to any native of Cuba who last came to the United States between April 15, 1980, and October 20, 1980 (hereinafter referred to as Mariel Cuban) and who is being detained by the Immigration and Naturalization Service (hereinafter referred to as the Service) pending his or her exclusion hearing, or pending his or her return to Cuba or to another country. It covers Mariel Cubans who have never been paroled as well as those Mariel Cubans whose previous parole has been revoked by the Service. It also applies to any Mariel Cuban, detained under the authority of the Immigration and Nationality Act in any facility, who has not been approved for release or who is currently awaiting movement to a Service or Bureau Of Prisons (BOP) facility. In addition, it covers the revocation of parole for those Mariel Cubans who have been released on parole at any time.

(b) Parole authority and decision. The authority to grant parole under section 212(d)(5) of the Act to a detained Mariel Cuban shall be exercised by the Commissioner, acting through the Associate Commissioner for Enforcement, as follows:

(1) Parole decisions. The Associate Commissioner for Enforcement may, in the exercise of discretion, grant parole to a detained Mariel Cuban for emergent reasons or for reasons deemed strictly in the public interest. A decision to retain in custody shall briefly set forth the reasons for the continued detention. A decision to release on parole may contain such special conditions as are considered appropriate. A copy of any decision to parole or to detain, with an attached copy translated into Spanish, shall be provided to the detainee. Parole documentation for Mariel Cubans shall be issued by the district director having jurisdiction over the alien, in accordance with the parole determination made by the Associate Commissioner for Enforcement.

(2) Additional delegation of authority. All references to the Commissioner and Associate Commissioner for

Enforcement in this section shall be deemed to include any person or persons (including a committee) designated in writing by the Commissioner or Associate Commissioner for Enforcement to exercise powers under this section.

(c) Review Plan Director. The Associate Commissioner for Enforcement shall appoint a Director of the Cuban Review Plan. The Director shall have authority to establish and maintain appropriate files respecting each Mariel Cuban to be reviewed for possible parole, to determine the order in which the cases shall be reviewed, and to coordinate activities associated with these reviews.

(d) Recommendations to the Associate Commissioner for Enforcement. Parole recommendations for detained Mariel Cubans shall be developed in accordance with the following procedures.

(1) Review Panels. The Director shall designate a panel or panels to make parole recommendations to the Associate Commissioner for Enforcement. A Cuban Review Panel shall, except as otherwise provided, consist of two persons. Members of a Review Panel shall be selected from the professional staff of the Service. All recommendations by a two-member Panel shall be unanimous. If the vote of a two-member Panel is split, it shall adjourn its deliberations concerning that particular detainee until a third Panel member is added. A recommendation by a three-member Panel shall be by majority vote. The third member of any Panel shall be the Director of the Cuban Review Plan or his designee.

(2) Criteria for Review. Before making any recommendation that a detainee be granted parole, a majority of the Cuban Review Panel members, or the Director in case of a record review, must conclude that:

(i) The detainee is presently a nonviolent person;

(ii) The detainee is likely to remain nonviolent;

(iii) The detainee is not likely to pose a threat to the community following his release; and

(iv) The detainee is not likely to violate the conditions of his parole.

(3) Factors for consideration. The following factors should be weighed in considering whether to recommend further detention or release on parole of a detainee:

(i) The nature and number of disciplinary infractions or incident reports received while in custody;

(ii) The detainee's past history of criminal behavior;

(iii) Any psychiatric and psychological reports pertaining to the detainee's mental health;

(iv) Institutional progress relating to participation in work, educational and vocational programs;

(v) His ties to the United States, such as the number of close relatives residing lawfully here;

(vi) The likelihood that he may abscond, such as from any sponsorship program; and

(vii) Any other information which is probative of whether the detainee is likely to adjust to life in a community, is likely to engage in future acts of violence, is likely to engage in future criminal activity, or is likely to violate the conditions of his parole.

(4) Procedure for review. The following procedures will govern the review process:

(i) Record review. Initially, the Director or a Panel shall review the detainee's file. Upon completion of this record review, the Director or the Panel shall issue a written recommendation that the detainee be released on parole or scheduled for a personal interview.

(ii) Personal interview. If a recommendation to grant parole after only a record review is not accepted or if the detainee is not recommended for release, a Panel shall personally interview the detainee. The scheduling of such interviews shall be at the discretion of the Director. The detainee may be accompanied during the interview by a person of his choice, who is able to attend at the time of the scheduled interview, to assist in answering any questions. The detainee may submit to the Panel any information, either orally or in writing, which he believes presents a basis for release on parole.

(iii) Panel recommendation. Following completion of the interview and its deliberations, the Panel shall issue a written recommendation that the detainee be released on parole or remain in custody pending deportation or pending further observation and subsequent review. This written recommendation shall include a brief statement of the factors which the Panel deems material to its recommendation. The recommendation and appropriate file material shall be forwarded to the Associate Commissioner for Enforcement, to be considered in the exercise of discretion pursuant to § 212.12(b).

(e) Withdrawal of parole approval. The Associate Commissioner for Enforcement may, in his or her discretion, withdraw approval for parole of any detainee prior to release when, in his or her opinion, the conduct of the detainee, or any other circumstance, indicates that parole would no longer be appropriate.

(f) Sponsorship. No detainee may be released on parole until suitable sponsorship or placement has been found for the detainee. The paroled detainee must abide by the parole conditions specified by the Service in relation to his sponsorship or placement. The following sponsorships and placements are suitable:

(1) Placement by the Public Health Service in an approved halfway house or mental health project;

(2) Placement by the Community Relations Service in an approved halfway house or community project; and

(3) Placement with a close relative such as a parent, spouse, child, or sibling who is a lawful permanent resident or a citizen of the United States.

(g) Timing of reviews. The timing of review shall be in accordance with the following guidelines.

(1) Parole revocation cases. The Director shall schedule the review process in the case of a new or returning detainee whose previous immigration parole has been revoked. The review process will commence with a scheduling of a file review, which will ordinarily be expected to occur within approximately three months after parole is revoked. In the case of a Mariel Cuban who is in the custody of the Service, the Cuban Review Plan Director may, in his or her discretion, suspend or postpone the parole review process if such detainee's prompt deportation is practicable and proper.

(2) Continued detention cases. A subsequent review shall be commenced for any detainee within one year of a refusal to grant parole under § 212.12(b), unless a shorter interval is specified by the Director.

(3) Discretionary reviews. The Cuban Review Plan Director, in his discretion, may schedule a review of a detainee at any time when the Director deems such a review to be warranted.

(h) Revocation of parole. The Associate Commissioner for Enforcement shall have authority, in the exercise of discretion, to revoke parole in respect to Mariel Cubans. A district director may also revoke parole when, in the district director's opinion, revocation is in the public interest and circumstances do not reasonably permit referral of the case to the Associate Commissioner. Parole may be revoked in the exercise of discretion when, in the opinion of the revoking official:

(1) The purposes of parole have been served;

(2) The Mariel Cuban violates any condition of parole;

(3) It is appropriate to enforce an order of exclusion or to commence proceedings against a Mariel Cuban; or

(4) The period of parole has expired without being renewed.

HISTORY:

[52 FR 48802, Dec. 28, 1987; 59 FR 13870, March 24, 1994; 65 FR 80281, 80294, Dec. 21, 2000]

§ 212.13 [Reserved]

[NO TEXT IN ORIGINAL]

§ 212.14 Parole determinations for alien witnesses and informants for whom a law enforcement authority ("LEA") will request S classification.

(a) Parole authority. Parole authorization under section 212(d)(5) of the Act for aliens whom LEAs seek to bring to the United States as witnesses or informants in criminal/counter terrorism matters and to apply for S classification shall be exercised as follows:

(1) Grounds of eligibility. The Commissioner may, in the exercise of discretion, grant parole to an alien (and the alien's family members) needed for law enforcement purposes provided that a state or federal LEA:

(i) Establishes its intention to file, within 30 days after the alien's arrival in the United States, an application for S nonimmigrant status on the form designated for such purposes, with the Assistant Attorney General, Criminal Division, Department of Justice, in accordance with the instructions on or attached to the form, which will include the names of qualified family members for whom parole is sought;

(ii) Specifies the particular operational reasons and basis for the request, and agrees to assume responsibility for the alien during the period of the alien's temporary stay in the United States, including maintaining control and supervision of the alien and the alien's whereabouts and activities, and further specifies any other terms and conditions specified by the Service during the period for which the parole is authorized;

(iii) Agrees to advise the Service of the alien's failure to report quarterly any criminal conduct by the alien, or any other activity or behavior on the alien's part that may constitute a ground of excludability or deportability;

(iv) Assumes responsibility for ensuring the alien's departure on the date of termination of the authorized parole (unless the alien has been admitted in S nonimmigrant classification pursuant to the terms of paragraph (a)(2) of this section), provides any and all assistance needed by the Service, if necessary, to ensure departure, and verifies departure in a manner acceptable to the Service;

(v) Provide LEA seat-of-government certification that parole of the alien is essential to an investigation or prosecution, is in the national interest, and is requested pursuant to the terms and authority of section 212(d)(5) of the Act;

(vi) Agrees that no promises may be, have been, or will be made by the LEA to the alien that the alien will or may:

(A) Remain in the United States in parole status or any other nonimmigrant classification;

(B) Adjust status to that of lawful permanent resident; or

(C) Otherwise attempt to remain beyond the authorized parole. The alien (and any family member of the alien who is 18 years of age or older) shall sign a statement acknowledging an awareness that parole only authorizes a temporary stay in the United States and does not convey the benefits of S nonimmigrant classification, any other nonimmigrant classification, or any entitlement to further benefits under the Act; and

(vii) Provides, in the case of a request for the release of an alien from Service custody, certification that the alien is eligible for parole pursuant to § 235.3 of this chapter.

(2) Authorization.

(i) Upon approval of the request for parole, the Commissioner shall notify the Assistant Attorney General, Criminal Division, of the approval.

(ii) Upon notification of approval of a request for parole, the LEA will advise the Commissioner of the date, time, and place of the arrival of the alien. The Commissioner will coordinate the arrival of the alien in parole status with the port director prior to the time of arrival.

(iii) Parole will be authorized for a period of thirty (30) days to commence upon the alien's arrival in the United States in order for the LEA to submit the completed application to the Assistant Attorney General, Criminal Division. Upon the submission to the Assistant Attorney General of the completed application for S classification, the period of parole will be automatically extended while the request is being reviewed. The Assistant Attorney General, Criminal Division, will notify the Commissioner of the submission of the application.

(b) **Termination of parole —**

(1) General. The Commissioner may terminate parole for any alien (including a member of the alien's family) in parole status under this section where ter-

mination is in the public interest. A district director may also terminate parole when, in the district director's opinion, termination is in the public interest and circumstances do not reasonably permit referral of the case to the Commissioner. In such a case, the Commissioner shall be notified immediately. In the event the Commissioner, or in the appropriate case, a district director, decides to terminate the parole of a alien witness or informant authorized under the terms of this paragraph, the Assistant Attorney General, Criminal Division, and the relevant LEA shall be notified in writing to that effect. The Assistant Attorney General, Criminal Division, shall concur in or object to that decision. Unless the Assistant Attorney General, Criminal Division, objects within 7 days, he or she shall be deemed to have concurred in the decision. In the event of an objection by the Assistant Attorney General, Criminal Division, the matter will be expeditiously referred to the Deputy Attorney General for a final resolution. In no circumstances shall the alien or the relevant LEA have a right of appeal from any decision to terminate parole.

(2) Termination of parole and admission in S classification. When an LEA has filed a request for an alien in authorized parole status to be admitted in S nonimmigrant classification and that request has been approved by the Commissioner pursuant to the procedures outlines in 8 CFR 214.2(t), the Commissioner may, in the exercise of discretion:

(i) Terminate the alien's parole status;

(ii) Determine eligibility for waivers; and

(iii) Admit the alien in S nonimmigrant classification pursuant to the terms and conditions of section 101(a)(15(S) of the Act and 8 CFR 214.2(t).

(c) Departure. If the alien's parole has been terminated and the alien has been ordered excluded from the United States, the LEA shall ensure departure from the United States and so inform the district director in whose jurisdiction the alien has last resided. The district director, if necessary, shall oversee the alien's departure from the United States and, in any event, shall notify the Commissioner of the alien's departure. The Commissioner shall be notified in writing of the failure of any alien authorized parole under this paragraph to depart in accordance with an order of exclusion and deportation entered after parole authorized under this paragraph has been terminated.

(d) Failure to comply with procedures. Any failure to adhere to the parole procedures contained in this section shall immediately be brought to the attention of the Commissioner, who will notify the Attorney General.

HISTORY:

[60 FR 44260, 44265, Aug. 25, 1995; 76 FR 53764, 53787, Aug. 29, 2011]

§ 212.15 Certificates for foreign health care workers.

(a) General certification requirements.

(1) Except as provided in paragraph (b) or paragraph (d)(1) of this section, any alien who seeks admission to the United States as an immigrant or as a nonimmigrant for the primary purpose of performing labor in a health care occupation listed in paragraph (c) of this section is inadmissible unless the alien presents a certificate from a credentialing organization, listed in paragraph (e) of this section.

(2) In the alternative, an eligible alien who seeks to enter the United States for the primary purpose of performing labor as a nurse may present a certified statement as provided in paragraph (h) of this section.

(3) A certificate or certified statement described in this section does not constitute professional authorization to practice in that health care occupation.

(b) Inapplicability of the ground of inadmissibility. This section does not apply to:

(1) Physicians;

(2) Aliens seeking admission to the United States to perform services in a non-clinical health care occupation. A non-clinical care occupation is one in which the alien is not required to perform direct or indirect patient care. Occupations which are considered to be non-clinical include, but are not limited to, medical teachers, medical researchers, and managers of health care facilities;

(3) Aliens coming to the United States to receive training as an H-3 nonimmigrant, or receiving training as part of an F or J nonimmigrant program.

(4) The spouse and dependent children of any immigrant or nonimmigrant alien;

(5) Any alien applying for adjustment of status to that of a permanent resident under any provision of law other than under section 245 of the Act, or any alien who is seeking adjustment of status under section 245 of the Act on the basis of a relative visa petition approved under section 203(a) of the Act, or any alien seeking adjustment of status under section 245 of the Act on the basis of an employment-based petition approved pursuant to section 203(b) of the Act for employment that does not fall under one of the covered health care occupations listed in paragraph (c) of this section.

(c) Covered health care occupations. With the exception of the aliens described in paragraph (b) of this section, this paragraph (c) applies to any alien seeking admission to the United States to perform labor in one of the following health care occupations, regardless of where he or she received his or her education or training:

(1) Licensed Practical Nurses, Licensed Vocational Nurses, and Registered Nurses.

(2) Occupational Therapists.

(3) Physical Therapists.

(4) Speech Language Pathologists and Audiologists.

(5) Medical Technologists (Clinical Laboratory Scientists).

(6) Physician Assistants.

(7) Medical Technicians (Clinical Laboratory Technicians)

(d) Presentation of certificate or certified statements.

(1) Aliens required to obtain visas. Except as provided in paragraph (n) of this section, if 8 CFR 212.1 requires an alien who is described in paragraph (a) of

this section and who is applying for admission as a nonimmigrant seeking to perform labor in a health care occupation as described in this section to obtain a nonimmigrant visa, the alien must present a certificate or certified statement to a consular officer at the time of visa issuance and to the Department of Homeland Security (DHS) at the time of admission. The certificate or certified statement must be valid at the time of visa issuance and admission at a port-of-entry. An alien who has previously presented a foreign health care worker certification or certified statement for a particular health care occupation will be required to present it again at the time of visa issuance or each admission to the United States.

(2) Aliens not requiring a nonimmigrant visa. Except as provided in paragraph (n) of this section, an alien described in paragraph (a) of this section who, pursuant to 8 CFR 212.1, is not required to obtain a nonimmigrant visa to apply for admission to the United States must present a certificate or certified statement as provided in this section to an immigration officer at the time of initial application for admission to the United States to perform labor in a particular health care occupation. An alien who has previously presented a foreign health care worker certification or certified statement for a particular health care occupation will be required to present it again at the time of each application for admission.

(e) Approved credentialing organizations for health care workers. An alien may present a certificate from any credentialing organization listed in this paragraph (e) with respect to a particular health care field. In addition to paragraphs (e)(1) through (e)(3) of this section, the DHS will notify the public of additional credentialing organizations through the publication of notices in the FEDERAL REGISTER.

(1) The Commission on Graduates of Foreign Nursing Schools (CGFNS) is authorized to issue certificates under section 212(a)(5)(C) of the Act for nurses, physical therapists, occupational therapists, speech-language pathologists and audiologists, medical technologists (also known as clinical laboratory scientists), medical technicians (also known as clinical laboratory technicians), and physician assistants.

(2) The National Board for Certification in Occupational Therapy (NBCOT) is authorized to issue certificates in the field of occupational therapy pending final adjudication of its credentialing status under this part.

(3) The Foreign Credentialing Commission on Physical Therapy (FCCPT) is authorized to issue certificates in the field of physical therapy pending final adjudication of its credentialing status under this part.

(f) Requirements for issuance of health care certification.

(1) Prior to issuing a certification to an alien, the organization must verify the following:

(i) That the alien's education, training, license, and experience are comparable with that required for an American health care worker of the same type;

(ii) That the alien's education, training, license, and experience are authentic and, in the case of a license, unencumbered;

(iii) That the alien's education, training, license, and experience meet all applicable statutory and regulatory requirements for admission into the United States. This verification is not binding on the DHS; and

(iv) Either that the alien has passed a test predicting success on the occupation's licensing or certification examination, provided such a test is recognized by a majority of states licensing the occupation for which the certification is issued, or that the alien has passed the occupation's licensing or certification examination.

(2) A certificate issued under section 212(a)(5)(C) of the Act must contain the following:

(i) The name, address, and telephone number of the credentialing organization, and a point of contact to verify the validity of the certificate;

(ii) The date the certificate was issued;

(iii) The health care occupation for which the certificate was issued; and

(iv) The alien's name, and date and place of birth.

(g) English language requirements.

(1) With the exception of those aliens described in paragraph (g)(2) of this section, every alien must meet certain English language requirements in order to obtain a certificate. The Secretary of HHS has sole authority to set standards for these English language requirements, and has determined that an alien must have a passing score on one of the three tests listed in paragraph (g)(3) of this section before he or she can be granted a certificate. HHS will notify The Department of Homeland Security of additions or deletions to this list, and The Department of Homeland Security will publish such changes in the FEDERAL REGISTER.

(2) The following aliens are exempt from the English language requirements:

(i) Alien nurses who are presenting a certified statement under section 212(r) of the Act; and

(ii) Aliens who have graduated from a college, university, or professional training school located in Australia, Canada (except Quebec), Ireland, New Zealand, the United Kingdom, or the United States.

(3) The following English testing services have been approved by the Secretary of HHS:

(i) Educational Testing Service (ETS).

(ii) Test of English in International Communication (TOEIC) Service International.

(iii) International English Language Testing System (IELTS).

(4) Passing English test scores for various occupations.

(i) Occupational and physical therapists. An alien seeking to perform labor in the United States as an occupational or physical therapist must obtain the following scores on the English tests administered by ETS: Test Of English as a Foreign Language (TOEFL): Paper-Based 560, Computer-Based 220; Test of Written English (TWE): 4.5; Test of Spoken English (TSE): 50. The certifying organizations shall not accept the results of the TOEIC, or the IELTS for the occupation of occupational therapy or physical therapy.

(ii) Registered nurses and other health care workers requiring the attainment of a baccalaureate degree. An alien coming to the United States to perform labor as a registered nurse (other than a nurse presenting a certified statement under section 212(r) of the Act) or to perform labor in another health care occupation requiring a baccalaureate degree (other than occupational or physical therapy) must obtain one of the following combinations of scores to obtain a certificate:

(A) ETS: TOEFL: Paper-Based 540, Computer-Based 207; TWE: 4.0; TSE: 50;

(B) TOEIC Service International: TOEIC: 725; plus TWE: 4.0 and TSE: 50; or

(C) IELTS: 6.5 overall with a spoken band score of 7.0. This would require the Academic module.

(iii) Occupations requiring less than a baccalaureate degree. An alien coming to the United States to perform labor in a health care occupation that does not require a baccalaureate degree must obtain one of the following combinations of scores to obtain a certificate:

(A) ETS: TOEFL: Paper-Based 530, Computer-Based 197; TWE: 4.0; TSE: 50;

(B) TOEIC Service International: TOEIC: 700; plus TWE 4.0 and TSE: 50; or

(C) IELTS: 6.0 overall with a spoken band score of 7.0. This would allow either the Academic or the General module.

(h) Alternative certified statement for certain nurses.

(1) CGFNS is authorized to issue certified statements under section 212(r) of the Act for aliens seeking to enter the United States to perform labor as nurses. The DHS will notify the public of new organizations that are approved to issue certified statements through notices published in the FEDERAL REGISTER.

(2) An approved credentialing organization may issue a certified statement to an alien if each of the following requirements is satisfied:

(i) The alien has a valid and unrestricted license as a nurse in a state where the alien intends to be employed and such state verifies that the foreign licenses of alien nurses are authentic and unencumbered;

(ii) The alien has passed the National Council Licensure Examination for registered nurses (NCLEX-RN);

(iii) The alien is a graduate of a nursing program in which the language of instruction was English;

(iv) The nursing program was located in Australia, Canada (except Quebec), Ireland, New Zealand, South Africa, the United Kingdom, or the United States; or in any other country designated by unanimous agreement of CGFNS and any equivalent credentialing organizations which have been approved for the certification of nurses and which are listed at paragraph (e) of this section; and

(v) The nursing program was in operation on or before November 12, 1999, or has been approved by unanimous agreement of CGFNS and any equivalent credentialing organizations that have been approved for the certification of nurses.

(3) An individual who obtains a certified statement need not comply with the certificate requirements of paragraph (f) or the English language requirements of paragraph (g) of this section.

(4) A certified statement issued to a nurse under section 212(r) of the Act must contain the following information:

(i) The name, address, and telephone number of the credentialing organization, and a point of contact to verify the validity of the certified statement;

(ii) The date the certified statement was issued; and

(iii) The alien's name, and date and place of birth.

(i) Streamlined certification process.

(1) Nurses. An alien nurse who has graduated from an entry level program accredited by the National League for Nursing Accreditation Commission (NLNAC) or the Commission on Collegiate Nursing Education (CCNE) is exempt from the educational comparability review and English language proficiency testing.

(2) Occupational Therapists. An alien occupational therapist who has graduated from a program accredited by the Accreditation Council for Occupational Therapy Education (ACOTE) of the American Occupational Therapy Association (AOTA) is exempt from the educational comparability review and English language proficiency testing.

(3) Physical therapists. An alien physical therapist who has graduated from a program accredited by the Commission on Accreditation in Physical Therapy Education (CAPTE) of the American Physical Therapy Association (APTA) is exempt from the educational comparability review and English language proficiency testing.

(4) Speech language pathologists and audiologists. An alien speech language pathologists and/or audiologist who has graduated from a program accredited by the Council on Academic Accreditation in Audiology and Speech Language Pathology (CAA) of the American Speech-Language-Hearing Association (ASHA) is exempt from the educational comparability review and English language proficiency testing.

(j) Application process for credentialing organizations.

(1) Organizations other than CGFNS. An organization, other than CGFNS, seeking to obtain approval to issue certificates to health care workers, or certified statements to nurses must apply on the form designated by USCIS in accordance with the form instructions. An organization seeking authorization to issue certificates or certified statements must agree to submit all evidence required by the DHS and, upon request, allow the DHS to review the organization's records related to the certification process. The application must:

(i) Clearly describe and identify the organization seeking authorization to issue certificates;

(ii) List the occupations for which the organization desires to provide certificates;

(iii) Describe how the organization substantially meets the standards described at paragraph (k) of this section;

(iv) Describe the organization's expertise, knowledge, and experience in the health care occupation(s) for which it desires to issue certificates;

(v) Provide a point of contact;

(vi) Describe the verification procedure the organization has designed in order for the DHS to verify the validity of a certificate; and

(vii) Describe how the organization will process and issue in a timely manner the certificates.

(2) Applications filed by CGFNS.

(i) CGFNS must apply to ensure that it will be in compliance with the regulations governing the issuance and content of certificates to nurses, physical therapists, occupational therapists, speech-language pathologists and audiologists, medical technologists (also known as clinical laboratory scientists), medical technicians (also known as clinical laboratory technicians), and physician assistants under section 212(a)(5)(C) of the Act, or issuing certified statements to nurses under section 212(r) of the Act.

(ii) Prior to issuing certificates for any other health care occupations, CGFNS must apply on the form designated by USCIS with the fee prescribed in 8 CFR 106.2 and in accordance with the form instructions for authorization to issue such certificates. The DHS will evaluate CGFNS' expertise with respect to the particular health care occupation for which authorization to issue certificates is sought, in light of CGFNS' statutory designation as a credentialing organization.

(3) Procedure for review of applications by credentialing organizations.

(i) USCIS will forward a copy of the application and supporting documents to the Secretary of HHS in order to obtain an opinion on the merits of the application. The DHS will not render a decision on the request until the Secretary of HHS provides an opinion. The DHS shall accord the Secretary of HHS' opinion great weight in reaching its decision. The DHS may deny the organization's request notwithstanding the favorable recommendation from the Secretary of HHS, on grounds unrelated to the credentialing of health care occupations or health care services.

(ii) The DHS will notify the organization of the decision on its application in writing and, if the request is denied, of the reasons for the denial. Approval of authorization to issue certificates to foreign health care workers or certified statements to nurses will be made in 5-year increments, subject to the review process described at paragraph (l) of this section.

(iii) If the application is denied, the decision may be appealed pursuant to 8 CFR 103.3.

(k) Standards for credentialing organizations. The DHS will evaluate organizations, including CGFNS, seeking to obtain approval from the DHS to issue certificates for health care workers, or certified statements for nurses. Any organization meeting the standards set forth in paragraph (k)(1) of this section can be eligible for authorization to issue certificates. While CGFNS has been specifically listed in the statute as an entity authorized to issue certificates, it is not exempt from governmental oversight. All organizations will be reviewed, including CGFNS, to guarantee that they continue to meet the standards required of all certifying organizations, under the following:

(1) Structure of the organization.

(i) The organization shall be incorporated as a legal entity.

(ii)(A) The organization shall be independent of any organization that functions as a representative of the occupation or profession in question or serves as or is related to a recruitment/placement organization.

(B) The DHS shall not approve an organization that is unable to render impartial advice regarding an individual's qualifications regarding training, experience, and licensure.

(C) The organization must also be independent in all decision making matters pertaining to evaluations and/or examinations that it develops including, but not limited to: policies and procedures; eligibility requirements and application processing; standards for granting certificates and their renewal; examination content, development, and administration; examination cut-off scores, excluding those pertaining to English language requirements; grievance and disciplinary processes; governing body and committee meeting rules; publications about qualifying for a certificate and its renewal; setting fees for application and all other services provided as part of the screening process; funding, spending, and budget authority related to the operation of the certification organization; ability to enter into contracts and grant arrangements; ability to demonstrate adequate staffing and management resources to conduct the program(s) including the authority to approve selection of, evaluate, and initiate dismissal of the chief staff member.

(D) An organization whose fees are based on whether an applicant receives a visa may not be approved.

(iii) The organization shall include the following representation in the portion of its organization responsible for overseeing certification and, where applicable, examinations:

(A) Individuals from the same health care discipline as the alien health care worker being evaluated who are eligible to practice in the United States; and

(B) At least one voting public member to represent the interests of consumers and protect the interests of the public at large. The public member shall not be a member of the discipline or derive significant income from the discipline, its related organizations, or the organization issuing the certificate.

(iv) The organization must have a balanced representation such that the individuals from the same health care discipline, the voting public members, and any other appointed individuals have an equal say in matters relating to credentialing and/or examinations.

(v) The organization must select representatives of the discipline using one of the following recommended methods, or demonstrate that it has a selection process that meets the intent of these methods:

(A) Be selected directly by members of the discipline eligible to practice in the United States;

(B) Be selected by members of a membership organization representing the discipline or by duly elected representatives of a membership organization; or

(C) Be selected by a membership organization representing the discipline from a list of acceptable candidates supplied by the credentialing body.

(vi) The organization shall use formal procedures for the selection of members of the governing body that prohibit the governing body from selecting a majority of its successors. Not-for-profit corporations which have difficulty meeting this requirement may provide in their applications evidence that the organization is independent, and free of material conflicts of interest regarding whether an alien receives a visa.

(vii) The organization shall be separate from the accreditation and educational functions of the discipline, except for those entities recognized by the Department of Education as having satisfied the requirement of independence.

(viii) The organization shall publish and make available a document which clearly defines the responsibilities of the organization and outlines any other activities, arrangements, or agreements of the organization that are not directly related to the certification of health care workers.

(2) Resources of the organization.

(i) The organization shall demonstrate that its staff possess the knowledge and skills necessary to accurately assess the education, work experience, licensure of health care workers, and the equivalence of foreign educational institutions, comparable to those of United States-trained health care workers and institutions.

(ii) The organization shall demonstrate the availability of financial and material resources to effectively and thoroughly conduct regular and ongoing evaluations on an international basis.

(iii) If the health care field is one for which a majority of the states require a predictor test, the organization shall demonstrate the ability to conduct examinations in those countries with educational and evaluation systems comparable to the majority of states.

(iv) The organization shall have the resources to publish and make available general descriptive materials on the procedures used to evaluate and validate credentials, including eligibility requirements, determination procedures, examination schedules, locations, fees, reporting of results, and disciplinary and grievance procedures.

(3) Candidate evaluation and testing mechanisms.

(i) The organization shall publish and make available a comprehensive outline of the information, knowledge, or functions covered by the evaluation/examination process, including information regarding testing for English language competency.

(ii) The organization shall use reliable evaluation/examination mechanisms to evaluate individual credentials and competence that is objective, fair to all candidates, job related, and based on knowledge and skills needed in the discipline.

(iii) The organization shall conduct ongoing studies to substantiate the reliability and validity of the evaluation/examination mechanisms.

(iv) The organization shall implement a formal policy of periodic review of the evaluation/examination mechanism to ensure ongoing relevance of the mechanism with respect to knowledge and skills needed in the discipline.

(v) The organization shall use policies and procedures to ensure that all aspects of the evaluation/examination procedures, as well as the development and administration of any tests, are secure.

(vi) The organization shall institute procedures to protect against falsification of documents and misrepresentation, including a policy to request each applicant's transcript(s) and degree(s) directly from the educational licensing authorities.

(vii) The organization shall establish policies and procedures that govern the length of time the applicant's records must be kept in their original format.

(viii) The organization shall publish and make available, at least annually, a summary of all screening activities for each discipline including, at least, the number of applications received, the number of applicants evaluated, the number receiving certificates, the number who failed, and the number receiving renewals.

(4) Responsibilities to applicants applying for an initial certificate or renewal.

(i) The organization shall not discriminate among applicants as to age, sex, race, religion, national origin, disability, or marital status and shall include a statement of nondiscrimination in announcements of the evaluation/examination procedures and renewal certification process.

(ii) The organization shall provide all applicants with copies of formalized application procedures for evaluation/examination and shall uniformly follow and enforce such procedures for all applicants. Instructions shall include standards regarding English language requirements.

(iii) The organization shall implement a formal policy for the periodic review of eligibility criteria and application procedures to ensure that they are fair and equitable.

(iv) Where examinations are used, the organization shall provide competently proctored examination sites at least once annually.

(v) The organization shall report examination results to applicants in a uniform and timely fashion.

(vi) The organization shall provide applicants who failed either the evaluation or examination with information on general areas of deficiency.

(vii) The organization shall implement policies and procedures to ensure that each applicant's examination results are held confidential and delineate the circumstances under which the applicant's certification status may be made public.

(viii) The organization shall have a formal policy for renewing the certification if an individual's original certification has expired before the individual first seeks admission to the United States or applies for adjustment of status. Such procedures shall be restricted to updating information on licensure to determine the existence of any adverse actions and the need to re-establish English competency.

(ix) The organization shall publish due process policies and procedures for applicants to question eligibility determinations, examination or evaluation results, and eligibility status.

(x) The organization shall provide all qualified applicants with a certificate in a timely manner.

(5) Maintenance of comprehensive and current information.

(i) The organization shall maintain comprehensive and current information of the type necessary to evaluate foreign educational institutions and accrediting bodies for purposes of ensuring that the quality of foreign educational programs is equivalent to those training the same occupation in the United States. The organization shall examine, evaluate, and validate the academic and clinical requirements applied to each country's accrediting body or bodies, or in countries not having such bodies, of the educational institution itself.

(ii) The organization shall also evaluate the licensing and credentialing system(s) of each country or licensing jurisdiction to determine which systems are equivalent to that of the majority of the licensing jurisdictions in the United States.

(6) Ability to conduct examinations fairly and impartially. An organization undertaking the administration of a predictor examination, or a licensing or certification examination shall demonstrate the ability to conduct such examination fairly and impartially.

(7) Criteria for awarding and governing certificate holders.

(i) The organization shall issue a certificate after the education, experience, license, and English language competency have been evaluated and determined to be equivalent to their United States counterparts. In situations where a United States nationally recognized licensure or certification examination, or a test predicting the success on the licensure or certification examination, is offered overseas, the applicant must pass the examination or the predictor test prior to receiving certification. Passage of a test predicting the success on the licensure or certification examination may be accepted only if a majority of states (and Washington, DC) licensing the profession in which the alien intends to work recognize such a test.

(ii) The organization shall have policies and procedures for the revocation of certificates at any time if it is determined that the certificate holder was not eligible to receive the certificate at the time that it was issued. If the organization revokes an individual's certificate, it must notify the DHS, via the Nebraska Service Center, and the appropriate state regulatory authority with jurisdiction over the individual's health care profession. The organization may not reissue a certificate to an individual whose certificate has been revoked.

(8) Criteria for maintaining accreditation.

(i) The organization shall advise the DHS of any changes in purpose, structure, or activities of the organization or its program(s).

(ii) The organization shall advise the DHS of any major changes in the evaluation of credentials and examination techniques, if any, or in the scope or objectives of such examinations.

(iii) The organization shall, upon the request of the DHS, submit to the DHS, or any organization designated by the DHS, information requested of the organization and its programs for use in investigating allegations of non-compliance with standards and for general purposes of determining continued approval as an independent credentialing organization.

(iv) The organization shall establish performance outcome measures that track the ability of the certificate holders to pass United States licensure or certification examinations. The purpose of the process is to ensure that certificate holders pass United States licensure or certification examinations at the same pass rate as graduates of United States programs. Failure to establish such measures, or having a record showing an inability of persons granted certificates to pass United States licensure examinations at the same rate as graduates of United States programs, may result in a ground for termination of approval. Information regarding the passage rates of certificate holders shall be maintained by the organization and provided to HHS on an annual basis, to the DHS as part of the 5-year reauthorization application, and at any other time upon request by HHS or the DHS.

(v) The organization shall be in ongoing compliance with other policies specified by the DHS.

(*l*) DHS review of the performance of certifying organizations. The DHS will review credentialing organizations every 5 years to ensure continued compliance with the standards described in this section. Such review will occur concurrent with the adjudication of a request for reauthorization to issue health care worker certificates. The DHS will notify the credentialing organization in writing of the results of the review and request for reauthorization. The DHS may conduct a review of the approval of any request for authorization to issue certificates at any time within the 5-year period of authorization for any reason. If at any time the DHS determines that an organization is not complying with the terms of its authorization or if other adverse information relating to eligibility to issue certificates is developed, the DHS may initiate termination proceedings.

(m) Termination of certifying organizations.

(1) If the DHS determines that an organization has been convicted, or the directors or officers of an authorized credentialing organization have individually been convicted of the violation of state or federal laws, or other information is developed such that the fitness of the organization to continue to issue certificates or certified statements is called into question, the DHS shall automatically terminate authorization for that organization to issue certificates or certified statements by issuing to the organization a notice of termination of authorization to issue certificates to foreign health care workers. The notice shall reference the specific conviction that is the basis of the automatic termination.

(2) If the DHS determines that an organization is not complying with the terms of its authorization or other adverse information relating to eligibility to issue certificates is uncovered during the course of a review or otherwise brought to the DHS' attention, or if the DHS determines that an organization currently authorized to issue certificates or certified statements has not submitted an application or provided all information required on the request within 6 months of July 25, 2003, the DHS will issue a Notice of Intent to Terminate authorization to issue certificates to the creden-

tialing organization. The Notice shall set forth reasons for the proposed termination.

(i) The credentialing organization shall have 30 days from the date of the Notice of Intent to Terminate authorization to rebut the allegations, or to cure the noncompliance identified in the DHS's notice of intent to terminate.

(ii) DHS will forward to HHS upon receipt any information received in response to a Notice of Intent to Terminate an entity's authorization to issue certificates. Thirty days after the date of the Notice of Intent to Terminate, the DHS shall forward any additional evidence and shall request an opinion from HHS regarding whether the organization's authorization should be terminated. The DHS shall accord HHS' opinion great weight in determining whether the authorization should be terminated. After consideration of the rebuttal evidence, if any, and consideration of HHS' opinion, the DHS will promptly provide the organization with a written decision. If termination of credentialing status is made, the written decision shall set forth the reasons for the termination.

(3) An adverse decision may be appealed pursuant to 8 CFR 103.3 to the Associate Commissioner for Examinations. Termination of credentialing status shall remain in effect until and unless the terminated organization reapplies for credentialing status and is approved, or its appeal of the termination decision is sustained by the Administrative Appeals Office. There is no waiting period for an organization to re-apply for credentialing status.

(n) Transition.

(1) One year waiver

(i) Pursuant to section 212(d)(3) of the Act (and, for cases described in paragraph (d)(1) of this section, upon the recommendation of the Secretary of State), the Secretary has determined that until July 26, 2004 (or until July 26, 2005, in the case of a citizen of Canada or Mexico who, before September 23, 2003, was employed as a TN or TC nonimmigrant health care worker and held a valid license from a U.S. jurisdiction), DHS, subject to the conditions in paragraph (n)(2) of this section, may in its discretion admit, extend the period of authorized stay, or change the nonimmigrant status of an alien described in paragraph (d)(1) or paragraph (d)(2) of this section, despite the alien's inadmissibility under section 212(a)(5)(C) of the Act, provided the alien is not otherwise inadmissible.

(ii) After July 26, 2004 (or, after July 26, 2005, in the case of a citizen of Canada or Mexico, who, before September 23, 2003, was employed as a TN or TC nonimmigrant health care worker and held a valid license from a U.S. jurisdiction), such discretion shall be applied on a case-by-case basis.

(2) Conditions. Until July 26, 2004 (or until July 26, 2005, in the case of a citizen of Canada or Mexico, who, before September 23, 2003, was employed as a TN or TC nonimmigrant health care worker and held a valid license from a U.S. jurisdiction), the temporary admission, extension of stay, or change of status of an alien described in 8 CFR part 212(d)(1) or (d)(2) of this section that is provided for under this paragraph (n) is subject to the following conditions:

(i) The admission, extension of stay, or change of status may not be for a period longer than 1 year from the date of the decision, even if the relevant provision of 8 CFR 214.2 would ordinarily permit the alien's admission for a longer period;

(ii) The alien must obtain the certification required by paragraph (a) of this section within 1 year of the date of decision to admit the alien or to extend the alien's stay or change the alien's status; and,

(iii) Any subsequent petition or application to extend the period of the alien's authorized stay or change the alien's nonimmigrant status must include proof that the alien has obtained the certification required by paragraph (a) of this section, if the extension or stay or change of status is sought for the primary purpose of the alien's performing labor in a health care occupation listed in paragraph (c) of this section.

(3) Immigrant aliens. An alien described in paragraph (a) of this section, who is coming to the United States as an immigrant or is applying for adjustment of status pursuant to section 245 of the Act (8 U.S.C. 1255), to perform labor in a health care occupation described in paragraph (c) of this section, must submit the certificate or certified statement as provided in this section at the time of visa issuance or adjustment of status.

(4) Expiration of certificate or certified statement. The individual's certification or certified statement must be used for any admission into the United States, change of status within the United States, or adjustment of status within 5 years of the date that it is issued.

(5) Revocation of certificate or certified statement. When a credentialing organization notifies the DHS, via the Nebraska Service Center, that an individual's certification or certified statement has been revoked, the DHS will take appropriate action, including, but not limited to, revocation of approval of any related petitions, consistent with the Act and DHS regulations at 8 CFR 205.2, 8 CFR 214.2(h)(11)(iii), and 8 CFR 214.6(d)(5)(iii).

HISTORY:

[63 FR 55007, 55011, Oct. 14, 1998; 64 FR 23174, 23177, Apr. 30, 1999; 66 FR 3440, 3444, Jan. 16, 2001; 68 FR 43901, 43915, July 25, 2003; 69 FR 43729, 43731, July 22, 2004; 74 FR 26933, 26938, June 5, 2009; 76 FR 53764, 53788, Aug. 29, 2011, as corrected at 76 FR 73475, Nov. 29, 2011]; 85 FR 46788, 46923, Aug. 3, 2020]

§ 212.16 Applications for exercise of discretion relating to T nonimmigrant status.

(a) Requesting the waiver. An applicant requesting a waiver of inadmissibility under section 212(d)(3)(A)(ii) or (d)(13) of the Act must submit an Application for Advance Permission to Enter as a Nonimmigrant, or successor form as designated by USCIS in accordance with 8 CFR 103.2.

(b) Treatment of waiver request. USCIS, in its discretion, may grant a waiver request based on section 212(d)(13) of the Act of the applicable ground(s) of inadmissibility, except USCIS may not waive a ground of inadmissibility based on section 212(a)(3), (a)(10)(C), or (a)(10)(E) of the Act. An applicant for T nonimmigrant status is not subject to the ground of inadmissibility based on section 212(a)(4) of the Act (public charge) and is not required to file a waiver form for the public charge ground. Waiver requests are subject to a determination of national interest and connection to victimization as follows.

(1) National interest. USCIS, in its discretion, may grant a waiver of inadmissibility request if it determines that it is in the national interest to exercise discretion to waive the applicable ground(s) of inadmissibility.

(2) Connection to victimization. An applicant requesting a waiver under section 212(d)(13) of the Act on grounds other than the health-related grounds described in section 212(a)(1) of the Act must establish that the activities rendering them inadmissible were caused by, or were incident to, the victimization described in section 101(a)(15)(T)(i)(I) of the Act.

(3) Criminal grounds. In exercising its discretion, USCIS will consider the number and seriousness of the criminal offenses and convictions that render an applicant inadmissible under the criminal and related grounds in section 212(a)(2) of the Act. In cases involving violent or dangerous crimes, USCIS will only exercise favorable discretion in extraordinary circumstances, unless the criminal activities were caused by, or were incident to, the victimization described under section 101(a)(15)(T)(i)(I) of the Act.

(c) No appeal. There is no appeal of a decision to deny a waiver request. Nothing in this section is intended to prevent an applicant from re-filing a request for a waiver of a ground of inadmissibility in appropriate cases.

(d) Revocation. USCIS, at any time, may revoke a waiver previously authorized under section 212(d) of the Act. There is no appeal of a decision to revoke a waiver.

HISTORY:

[67 FR 4784, 4795, Jan. 31, 2002; 76 FR 53764, 53788, Aug. 29, 2011; 81 FR 92266, 92304, Dec. 19, 2016; 89 FR 34864, 34930, Apr. 30, 2024]

§ 212.17 Applications for the exercise of discretion relating to U nonimmigrant status.

(a) Filing the waiver application. An alien applying for a waiver of inadmissibility under section 212(d)(3)(B) or (d)(14) of the Act (waivers of inadmissibility), 8 U.S.C. 1182(d)(3)(B) or (d)(14), in connection with a petition for U nonimmigrant status being filed pursuant to 8 CFR 214.14, must submit the waiver request and the petition for U nonimmigrant status on the forms designated by USCIS in accordance with the form instructions. An alien in U nonimmigrant status who is seeking a waiver of section 212(a)(9)(B) of the Act, 8 U.S.C. 1182(a)(9)(B) (unlawful presence ground of inadmissibility triggered by departure from the United States), must file the waiver request prior to his or her application for reentry to the United States in accordance with the form instructions.

(b) **Treatment of waiver application.**

(1) USCIS, in its discretion, may grant the waiver based on section 212(d)(14) of the Act, 8 U.S.C. 1182(d)(14), if it determines that it is in the public or national interest to exercise discretion to waive the applicable ground(s) of inadmissibility. USCIS may not waive a ground of inadmissibility based upon section 212(a)(3)(E) of the Act, 8 U.S.C. 1182(a)(3)(E). USCIS, in its discretion, may grant the waiver based on section 212(d)(3) of the Act, 8 U.S.C. 1182(d)(3), except where the ground of inadmissibility arises under sections 212(a)(3)(A)(i)(I), (3)(A)(ii), (3)(A)(iii), (3)(C), or (3)(E) of the Act, 8 U.S.C. 1182(a)(3)(A)(i)(I), (3)(A)(ii), (3)(A)(iii), (3)(C), or (3)(E).

(2) In the case of applicants inadmissible on criminal or related grounds, in exercising its discretion USCIS will consider the number and severity of the offenses of which the applicant has been convicted. In cases involving violent or dangerous crimes or inadmissibility based on the security and related grounds in section 212(a)(3) of the Act, USCIS will only exercise favorable discretion in extraordinary circumstances.

(3) There is no appeal of a decision to deny a waiver. However, nothing in this paragraph is intended to prevent an applicant from re-filing a request for a waiver of ground of inadmissibility in appropriate cases.

(c) Revocation. The Secretary of Homeland Security, at any time, may revoke a waiver previously authorized under section 212(d) of the Act, 8 U.S.C. 118(d). Under no circumstances will the alien or any party acting on his or her behalf have a right to appeal from a decision to revoke a waiver.

HISTORY:

[72 FR 53014, 53035, Sept. 17, 2007; 76 FR 53764, 53788, Aug. 29, 2011]

§ 212.18 Application for Waivers of inadmissibility in connection with an application for adjustment of status by T nonimmigrant status holders

(a) Filing the waiver application. An alien applying for a waiver of inadmissibility under section 245(l)(2) of the Act in connection with an application for adjustment of status under 8 CFR 245.23(a) or (b) must submit:

(1) A completed Form I-485 application package;

(2) The appropriate fee in accordance with 8 CFR 106.2 or an application for a fee waiver; and, as applicable,

(3) Form I-601, Application for Waiver of Grounds of Excludability.

(b) Treatment of waiver application.

(1) USCIS may not waive an applicant's inadmissibility under sections 212(a)(3), 212(a)(10)(C), or 212(a)(10)(E) of the Act.

(2) If an applicant is inadmissible under section 212(a)(1) of the Act, USCIS may waive such inadmissi-

bility if it determines that granting a waiver is in the national interest.

(3) If any other applicable provision of section 212(a) renders the applicant inadmissible, USCIS may grant a waiver of inadmissibility if the activities rendering the applicant inadmissible were caused by or were incident to the victimization and USCIS determines that it is in the national interest to waive the applicable ground or grounds of inadmissibility.

(c) Other waivers. Nothing in this section shall be construed as limiting an alien's ability to apply for any other waivers of inadmissibility for which he or she may be eligible.

(d) Revocation. The Secretary of Homeland Security may, at any time, revoke a waiver previously granted through the procedures described in 8 CFR 103.5.

HISTORY:

[73 FR 75540, 75557, Dec. 12, 2008; 84 FR 41292, 41501, Aug. 14, 2019; 85 FR 46788, 46923, Aug. 3, 2020; 86 FR 14221, 14227, Mar. 15, 2021; 87 FR 55472, 55636, Sept. 9, 2022]

§ 212.19 Parole for entrepreneurs.

(a) Definitions. For purposes of this section, the following definitions apply:

(1) Entrepreneur means an alien who possesses a substantial ownership interest in a start-up entity and has a central and active role in the operations of that entity, such that the alien is well-positioned, due to his or her knowledge, skills, or experience, to substantially assist the entity with the growth and success of its business. For purposes of this section, an alien may be considered to possess a substantial ownership interest if he or she possesses at least a 10 percent ownership interest in the start-up entity at the time of adjudication of the initial grant of parole and possesses at least a 5 percent ownership interest in the start-up entity at the time of adjudication of a subsequent period of re-parole. During the period of initial parole, the entrepreneur may continue to reduce his or her ownership interest in the start-up entity, but must, at all times during the period of initial parole, maintain at least a 5 percent ownership interest in the entity. During the period of re-parole, the entrepreneur may continue to reduce his or her ownership interest in the start-up entity, but must, at all times during the period of parole, maintain an ownership interest in the entity.

(2) Start-up entity means a U.S. business entity that was recently formed, has lawfully done business during any period of operation since its date of formation, and has substantial potential for rapid growth and job creation. An entity that is the basis for a request for parole under this section may be considered recently formed if it was created within the 5 years immediately preceding the filing date of the alien's initial parole request. For purposes of paragraphs (a)(3) and (5) of this section, an entity may be considered recently formed if it was created within the 5 years immediately preceding the receipt of the relevant grant(s), award(s), or investment(s).

(3) Qualified government award or grant means an award or grant for economic development, research and development, or job creation (or other similar monetary award typically given to start-up entities) made by a federal, state, or local government entity (not including foreign government entities) that regularly provides such awards or grants to start-up entities. This definition excludes any contractual commitment for goods or services.

(4) Qualified investment means an investment made in good faith, and that is not an attempt to circumvent any limitations imposed on investments under this section, of lawfully derived capital in a start-up entity that is a purchase from such entity of its equity, convertible debt, or other security convertible into its equity commonly used in financing transactions within such entity's industry. Such an investment shall not include an investment, directly or indirectly, from the entrepreneur; the parents, spouse, brother, sister, son, or daughter of such entrepreneur; or any corporation, limited liability company, partnership, or other entity in which such entrepreneur or the parents, spouse, brother, sister, son, or daughter of such entrepreneur directly or indirectly has any ownership interest.

(5) Qualified investor means an individual who is a U.S. citizen or lawful permanent resident of the United States, or an organization that is located in the United States and operates through a legal entity organized under the laws of the United States or any state, that is majority owned and controlled, directly and indirectly, by U.S. citizens or lawful permanent residents of the United States, provided such individual or organization regularly makes substantial investments in start-up entities that subsequently exhibit substantial growth in terms of revenue generation or job creation. The term "qualified investor" shall not include an individual or organization that has been permanently or temporarily enjoined from participating in the offer or sale of a security or in the provision of services as an investment adviser, broker, dealer, municipal securities dealer, government securities broker, government securities dealer, bank, transfer agent or credit rating agency, barred from association with any entity involved in the offer or sale of securities or provision of such services, or otherwise found to have participated in the offer or sale of securities or provision of such services in violation of law. For purposes of this section, such an individual or organization may be considered a qualified investor if, during the preceding 5 years:

(i) The individual or organization made investments in start-up entities in exchange for equity, convertible debt, or other security convertible into equity commonly used in financing transactions within their respective industries comprising a total in such 5-year period of no less than $746,571; and

(ii) Subsequent to such investment by such individual or organization, at least 2 such entities each created at least 5 qualified jobs or generated at least $622,142 in revenue with average annualized revenue growth of at least 20 percent.

(6) Qualified job means full-time employment located in the United States that has been filled for at least 1 year by one or more qualifying employees.

(7) Qualifying employee means a U.S. citizen, a lawful permanent resident, or other immigrant lawfully authorized to be employed in the United States, who is not an entrepreneur of the relevant start-up entity or the parent, spouse, brother, sister, son, or daughter of such an entrepreneur. This definition shall not include independent contractors.

(8) Full-time employment means paid employment in a position that requires a minimum of 35 working hours per week. This definition does not include combinations of part-time positions even if, when combined, such positions meet the hourly requirement per week.

(9) U.S. business entity means any corporation, limited liability company, partnership, or other entity that is organized under federal law or the laws of any state, and that conducts business in the United States, that is not an investment vehicle primarily engaged in the offer, purchase, sale or trading of securities, futures contracts, derivatives or similar instruments.

(10) Material change means any change in facts that could reasonably affect the outcome of the determination whether the entrepreneur provides, or continues to provide, a significant public benefit to the United States. Such changes include, but are not limited to, the following: Any criminal charge, conviction, plea of no contest, or other judicial determination in a criminal case concerning the entrepreneur or start-up entity; any complaint, settlement, judgment, or other judicial or administrative determination concerning the entrepreneur or start-up entity in a legal or administrative proceeding brought by a government entity; any settlement, judgment, or other legal determination concerning the entrepreneur or start-up entity in a legal proceeding brought by a private individual or organization other than proceedings primarily involving claims for damages not exceeding 10 percent of the current assets of the entrepreneur or start-up entity; a sale or other disposition of all or substantially all of the start-up entity's assets; the liquidation, dissolution or cessation of operations of the start-up entity; the voluntary or involuntary filing of a bankruptcy petition by or against the start-up entity; a significant change with respect to ownership and control of the start-up entity; and a cessation of the entrepreneur's qualifying ownership interest in the start-up entity or the entrepreneur's central and active role in the operations of that entity.

(b) Initial parole —

(1) Filing of initial parole request form. An alien seeking an initial grant of parole as an entrepreneur of a start-up entity must file Form I-941, Application for Entrepreneur Parole, with USCIS, with the required fee, and supporting documentary evidence in accordance with this section and the form instructions, demonstrating eligibility as provided in paragraph (b)(2) of this section.

(2) Criteria for consideration —

(i) In general. An alien may be considered for parole under this section if the alien demonstrates that a grant of parole will provide a significant public benefit to the United States based on his or her role as an entrepreneur of a start-up entity.

(ii) General criteria. An alien may meet the standard described in paragraph (b)(2)(i) of this section by providing a detailed description, along with supporting evidence:

(A) Demonstrating that the alien is an entrepreneur as defined in paragraph (a)(1) of this section and that his or her entity is a start-up entity as defined in paragraph (a)(2) of this section; and

(B) Establishing that the alien's entity has:

(1) Received, within 18 months immediately preceding the filing of an application for initial parole, a qualified investment amount of at least $311,071 from one or more qualified investors; or

(2) Received, within 18 months immediately preceding the filing of an application for initial parole, an amount of at least $124,429 through one or more qualified government awards or grants.

(iii) Alternative criteria. An alien who satisfies the criteria in paragraph (b)(2)(ii)(A) of this section and partially meets one or both of the criteria in paragraph (b)(2)(ii)(B) of this section may alternatively meet the standard described in paragraph (b)(2)(i) of this section by providing other reliable and compelling evidence of the start-up entity's substantial potential for rapid growth and job creation.

(c) Additional periods of parole

(1) Filing of re-parole request form. Before expiration of the initial period of parole, an entrepreneur parolee may request an additional period of parole based on the same start-up entity that formed the basis for his or her initial period of parole granted under this section. To request such parole, an entrepreneur parolee must timely file an application for entrepreneur parole with USCIS on the form prescribed by USCIS with the required fee and supporting documentation in accordance with the form instructions, demonstrating eligibility as provided in paragraph (c)(2) of this section.

(2) Criteria for consideration —

(i) In general. An alien may be considered for re-parole under this section if the alien demonstrates that a grant of parole will continue to provide a significant public benefit to the United States based on his or her role as an entrepreneur of a start-up entity.

(ii) General criteria. An alien may meet the standard described in paragraph (c)(2)(i) of this section by providing a detailed description, along with supporting evidence:

(A) Demonstrating that the alien continues to be an entrepreneur as defined in paragraph (a)(1) of this section and that his or her entity continues to be a start-up entity as defined in paragraph (a)(2) of this section; and

(B) Establishing that the alien's entity has:

(1) Received at least $622,142 in qualifying investments, qualified government grants or awards, or a combination of such funding, during the initial parole period;

(2) Created at least 5 qualified jobs with the start-up entity during the initial parole period; or

(3) Reached at least $622,142 in annual revenue in the United States and averaged 20 percent in annual revenue growth during the initial parole period.

(iii) Alternative criteria. An alien who satisfies the criteria in paragraph (c)(2)(ii)(A) of this section and partially meets one or more of the criteria in paragraph (c)(2)(ii)(B) of this section may alternatively meet the standard described in paragraph (c)(2)(i) of this section by providing other reliable and compelling evidence of the start-up entity's substantial potential for rapid growth and job creation.

(d) Discretionary authority; decision; appeals and motions to reopen —

(1) Discretionary authority. DHS may grant parole under this section in its sole discretion on a case-by-case basis if the Department determines, based on the totality of the evidence, that an applicant's presence in the United States will provide a significant public benefit and that he or she otherwise merits a favorable exercise of discretion. In determining whether an alien's presence in the United States will provide a significant public benefit and whether the alien warrants a favorable exercise of discretion, USCIS will consider and weigh all evidence, including any derogatory evidence or information, such as but not limited to, evidence of criminal activity or national security concerns.

(2) Initial parole. DHS may grant an initial period of parole based on the start-up entity listed in the request for parole for a period of up to 30 months from the date the individual is initially paroled into the United States. Approval by USCIS of such a request must be obtained before the alien may appear at a port of entry to be granted parole, in lieu of admission.

(3) Re-parole. DHS may re-parole an entrepreneur for one additional period of up to 30 months from the date of the expiration of the initial parole period. If the entrepreneur is in the United States at the time that USCIS approves the request for re-parole, such approval shall be considered a grant of re-parole. If the alien is outside the United States at the time that USCIS approves the request for re-parole, the alien must appear at a port of entry to be granted parole, in lieu of admission.

(4) Appeals and motions to reopen. There is no appeal from a denial of parole under this section. USCIS will not consider a motion to reopen or reconsider a denial of parole under this section. On its own motion, USCIS may reopen or reconsider a decision to deny the Application for Entrepreneur Parole (Form I-941), in accordance with 8 CFR 103.5(a)(5).

(e) Collection of biometric information. An alien seeking an initial grant of parole or re-parole will be required to submit biometric information.

(f) Limitations. No more than three entrepreneurs may be granted parole under this section based on the same start-up entity. An alien shall not receive more than one initial grant of entrepreneur parole or more than one additional grant of entrepreneur re-parole based on the same start-up entity, for a maximum period of parole of five years.

(g) Employment authorization. An entrepreneur who is paroled into the United States pursuant to this section is authorized for employment with the start-up entity incident to the conditions of his or her parole.

(h) Spouse and children.

(1) The entrepreneur's spouse and children who are seeking parole as derivatives of such entrepreneur must individually file Form I-131, Application for Travel Document. Such application must also include evidence that the derivative has a qualifying relationship to the entrepreneur and otherwise merits a grant of parole in the exercise of discretion. Such spouse or child will be required to appear for collection of biometrics in accordance with the form instructions or upon request.

(2) The spouse and children of an entrepreneur granted parole under this section may be granted parole under this section for no longer than the period of parole granted to such entrepreneur.

(3) The spouse of the entrepreneur parolee, after being paroled into the United States, may be eligible for employment authorization on the basis of parole under this section. To request employment authorization, an eligible spouse paroled into the United States must file an Application for Employment Authorization (Form I-765), in accordance with 8 CFR 274a.13 and form instructions. An Application for Employment Authorization must be accompanied by documentary evidence establishing eligibility, including evidence of the spousal relationship.

(4) Notwithstanding 8 CFR 274a.12(c)(11), a child of the entrepreneur parolee may not be authorized for and may not accept employment on the basis of parole under this section.

(i) Conditions on parole. As a condition of parole under this section, a parolee must maintain household income that is greater than 400 percent of the federal poverty line for his or her household size as defined by the Department of Health and Human Services. USCIS may impose other such reasonable conditions in its sole discretion with respect to any alien approved for parole under this section, and it may request verification of the parolee's compliance with any such condition at any time. Violation of any condition of parole may lead to termination of the parole in accordance with paragraph (k) of this section or denial of re-parole.

(j) Reporting of material changes. An alien granted parole under this section must immediately report any material change(s) to USCIS. If the entrepreneur will continue to be employed by the start-up entity and maintain a qualifying ownership interest in the start-up entity, the entrepreneur must submit a form prescribed by USCIS, with any applicable fee in accordance with the form instructions to notify USCIS of the material change(s). The entrepreneur parolee must immediately notify USCIS in writing if they will no longer be employed by the start-up entity or ceases to possess a qualifying ownership stake in the start-up entity.

(k) Termination of parole —

(1) In general. DHS, in its discretion, may terminate parole granted under this section at any time and

without prior notice or opportunity to respond if it determines that the alien's continued parole in the United States no longer provides a significant public benefit. Alternatively, DHS, in its discretion, may provide the alien notice and an opportunity to respond prior to terminating the alien's parole under this section.

(2) Automatic termination. Parole granted under this section will be automatically terminated without notice upon the expiration of the time for which parole was authorized, unless the alien timely files a non-frivolous application for re-parole. Parole granted under this section may be automatically terminated when USCIS receives written notice from the entrepreneur parolee that he or she will no longer be employed by the start-up entity or ceases to possess a qualifying ownership stake in the start-up entity in accordance with paragraph (j) of this section. Additionally, parole of the spouse or child of the entrepreneur will be automatically terminated without notice if the parole of the entrepreneur has been terminated. If parole is terminated, any employment authorization based on that parole is automatically revoked.

(3) Termination on notice. USCIS may terminate on notice or provide the entrepreneur or his or her spouse or children, as applicable, written notice of its intent to terminate parole if USCIS believes that:

(i) The facts or information contained in the request for parole were not true and accurate;

(ii) The alien failed to timely file or otherwise comply with the material change reporting requirements in this section;

(iii) The entrepreneur parolee is no longer employed in a central and active role by the start-up entity or ceases to possess a qualifying ownership stake in the start-up entity;

(iv) The alien otherwise violated the terms and conditions of parole; or

(v) Parole was erroneously granted.

(4) Notice and decision. A notice of intent to terminate issued under this paragraph should generally identify the grounds for termination of the parole and provide a period of up to 30 days for the alien's written rebuttal. The alien may submit additional evidence in support of his or her rebuttal, when applicable, and USCIS will consider all relevant evidence presented in deciding whether to terminate the alien's parole. Failure to timely respond to a notice of intent to terminate will result in termination of the parole. When a charging document is served on the alien, the charging document will constitute written notice of termination of parole (if parole has not already been terminated), unless otherwise specified. Any further immigration and removal actions will be conducted in accordance with the Act and this chapter. The decision to terminate parole may not be appealed. USCIS will not consider a motion to reopen or reconsider a decision to terminate parole under this section. On its own motion, USCIS may reopen or reconsider a decision to terminate.

(*l*) Increase of investment and revenue amount requirements. The investment and revenue amounts in this section will be automatically adjusted every 3 years by the Consumer Price Index and posted on the USCIS Web site at https://www.uscis.gov/. Investment and revenue amounts adjusted under this paragraph will apply to all applications filed on or after the beginning of the fiscal year for which the adjustment is made.

HISTORY:

[82 FR 5238, 5286, Jan. 17, 2017; 82 FR 31887, July 11, 2017]; 85 FR 46788, 46923, Aug. 3, 2020; 86 FR 50839, 50841, Sept. 13, 2021; 89 FR 6194, 6396, Jan. 31, 2024; 89 FR 60298, 60301, July 25, 2024]

§ 212.20 Applicability of public charge inadmissibility.

8 CFR 212.20 through 212.23 address the public charge ground of inadmissibility under section 212(a)(4) of the Act. Unless the alien requesting the immigration benefit or classification has been exempted from section 212(a)(4) of the Act as listed in § 212.23(a), the provisions of §§ 212.20 through 212.23 of this part apply to an applicant for admission or adjustment of status to that of a lawful permanent resident.

HISTORY:

[84 FR 41292, 41501, Aug. 14, 2019; 86 FR 14221, 14227, Mar. 15, 2021; 87 FR 55472, 55636, Sept. 9, 2022]

§ 212.21 Definitions.

For the purposes of §§ 212.20 through 212.23, the following definitions apply:

(a) Likely at any time to become a public charge means likely at any time to become primarily dependent on the government for subsistence, as demonstrated by either the receipt of public cash assistance for income maintenance or long-term institutionalization at government expense.

(b) Public cash assistance for income maintenance means:

(1) Supplemental Security Income (SSI), 42 U.S.C. 1381 et seq.;

(2) Cash assistance for income maintenance under the Temporary Assistance for Needy Families (TANF) program, 42 U.S.C. 601 et seq.; or

(3) State, Tribal, territorial, or local cash benefit programs for income maintenance (often called "General Assistance" in the State context, but which also exist under other names).

(c) Long-term institutionalization at government expense means government assistance for long-term institutionalization (in the case of Medicaid, limited to institutional services under section 1905(a) of the Social Security Act) received by a beneficiary, including in a nursing facility or mental health institution. Long-term institutionalization does not include imprisonment for conviction of a crime or institutionalization for short periods for rehabilitation purposes.

(d) Receipt (of public benefits). An individual's receipt of public benefits occurs when a public benefit-granting agency provides either public cash assistance for income maintenance or long-term institutionalization at government expense to the individual, where the individual is listed as a beneficiary of such benefits. An individual's application for a public benefit on their own behalf or on behalf of another does not constitute receipt of public benefits by such individual. Approval for future receipt of a public benefit that an individual applied for on their own behalf or on behalf of another does not constitute receipt of public benefits by such an individual. An individual's receipt of public benefits solely on behalf of a third party (including a member of the alien's household as defined in paragraph (f) of this section) does not constitute receipt of public benefits by such individual. The receipt of public benefits solely by a third party (including a member of the alien's household as defined in paragraph (f) of this section), even if an individual assists with the application process, does not constitute receipt for such individual.

(e) Government means any Federal, State, Tribal, territorial, or local government entity or entities of the United States.

(f) Household: The alien's household includes:

(1) The alien;

(2) The alien's spouse, if physically residing with the alien;

(3) If physically residing with the alien, the alien's parents, the alien's unmarried siblings under 21 years of age, and the alien's children as defined in section 101(b)(1) of the Act;

(4) Any other individuals (including a spouse or child as defined in section 101(b)(1) of the Act not physically residing with the alien) who are listed as dependents on the alien's federal income tax return; and

(5) Any other individual(s) who lists the alien as a dependent on their federal income tax return.

HISTORY:

[84 FR 41292, 41501, Aug. 14, 2019, as corrected at 84 FR 52357, 52362, Oct. 2, 2019; 86 FR 14221, 14227, Mar. 15, 2021; 87 FR 55472, 55636, Sept. 9, 2022]

§ 212.22 Public charge inadmissibility determination.

(a) Factors to consider—

(1) Consideration of minimum factors: For purposes of a public charge inadmissibility determination, DHS will consider the alien's:

(i) Age;

(ii) Health, as evidenced by a report of an immigration medical examination performed by a civil surgeon or panel physician where such examination is required (to which DHS will generally defer absent evidence that such report is incomplete);

(iii) Family status, as evidenced by the alien's household size, based on the definition of household in § 212.21(f);

(iv) Assets, resources, and financial status, as evidenced by the alien's household's income, assets, and liabilities (excluding any income from public benefits listed in § 212.21(b) and income or assets from illegal activities or sources such as proceeds from illegal gambling or drug sales); and

(v) Education and skills, as evidenced by the alien's degrees, certifications, licenses, skills obtained through work experience or educational programs, and educational certificates.

(2) Consideration of affidavit of support. DHS will favorably consider an Affidavit of Support Under Section 213A of the INA, when required under section 212(a)(4)(C) or (D) of the Act, that meets the requirements of section 213A of the Act and 8 CFR part 213a, in making a public charge inadmissibility determination.

(3) Consideration of current and/or past receipt of public benefits: DHS will consider the alien's current and/or past receipt of public cash assistance for income maintenance or long-term institutionalization at government expense (consistent with § 212.21(c)). DHS will consider such receipt in the totality of the circumstances, along with the other factors. DHS will consider the amount and duration of receipt, as well as how recently the alien received the benefits, and for long-term institutionalization at government expense, evidence submitted by the alien that the alien's institutionalization violates federal law, including the Americans with Disabilities Act or the Rehabilitation Act. However, current and/or past receipt of these benefits will not alone be a sufficient basis to determine whether the alien is likely at any time to become a public charge. DHS will not consider receipt of, or certification or approval for future receipt of, public benefits not referenced in § 212.21(b) and (c)), such as Supplemental Nutrition Assistance Program (SNAP) or other nutrition programs, Children's Health Insurance Program (CHIP), Medicaid (other than for long-term use of institutional services under section 1905(a) of the Social Security Act), housing benefits, any benefits related to immunizations or testing for communicable diseases, or other supplemental or special-purpose benefits.

(4) Disability alone not sufficient. A finding that an alien has a disability, as defined by Section 504 of the Rehabilitation Act, will not alone be a sufficient basis to determine whether the alien is likely at any time to become a public charge.

(b) Totality of the circumstances. The determination of an alien's likelihood of becoming a public charge at any time in the future must be based on the totality of the alien's circumstances. No one factor outlined in paragraph (a) of this section, other than the lack of a sufficient Affidavit of Support Under Section 213A of the INA, if required, should be the sole criterion for determining if an alien is likely to become a public charge. DHS may periodically issue guidance to adjudicators to inform the totality of the circumstances assessment. Such guidance will consider how these factors affect the likelihood that the alien will become a public charge at any time based on an empirical analysis of the best-available data as appropriate.

(c) Denial Decision. Every written denial decision issued by USCIS based on the totality of the circumstances set forth in paragraph (b) of this section will reflect consideration of each of the factors outlined in paragraph (a) of this section and specifically articulate the reasons for the officer's determination.

(d) Receipt of public benefits while an alien is in an immigration category exempt from public charge inadmissibility. In an adjudication for an immigration benefit for which the public charge ground of inadmissibility applies, DHS will not consider any public benefits received by an alien during periods in which the alien was present in the United States in an immigration category that is exempt from the public charge ground of inadmissibility, as set forth in § 212.23(a), or for which the alien received a waiver of public charge inadmissibility, as set forth in § 212.23(c).

(e) Receipt of benefits available to refugees. DHS will not consider any public benefits that were received by an alien who, while not a refugee admitted under section 207 of the Act, is eligible for resettlement assistance, entitlement programs, and other benefits available to refugees admitted under section 207 of the Act, including services described under section 412(d)(2) of the Act provided to an unaccompanied alien child as defined under 6 U.S.C. 279(g)(2).

HISTORY:

[84 FR 41292, 41501, Aug. 14, 2019, as corrected at 84 FR 52357, 52363, Oct. 2, 2019; 86 FR 14221, 14227, Mar. 15, 2021; 87 FR 55472, 55636, Sept. 9, 2022]

§ 212.23 Exemptions and waivers for public charge ground of inadmissibility.

(a) Exemptions. The public charge ground of inadmissibility under section 212(a)(4) of the Act does not apply, based on statutory or regulatory authority, to the following categories of aliens:

(1) Refugees at the time of admission under section 207 of the Act and at the time of adjustment of status to lawful permanent resident under section 209 of the Act;

(2) Asylees at the time of grant under section 208 of the Act and at the time of adjustment of status to lawful permanent resident under section 209 of the Act;

(3) Amerasian immigrants at the time of application for admission as described in sections 584 of the Foreign Operations, Export Financing, and Related Programs Appropriations Act of 1988, Public Law 100-202, 101 Stat. 1329-183, section 101(e) (Dec. 22, 1987), as amended, 8 U.S.C. 1101 note;

(4) Afghan and Iraqi Interpreters, or Afghan or Iraqi nationals employed by or on behalf of the U.S. Government as described in section 1059(a)(2) of the National Defense Authorization Act for Fiscal Year 2006 Public Law 109-163 (Jan. 6, 2006), as amended, and section 602(b) of the Afghan Allies Protection Act of 2009, Public Law 111-8, title VI (Mar. 11, 2009), as amended, 8 U.S.C. 1101 note, and section 1244(g) of the National Defense Authorization Act for Fiscal Year 2008, as amended, Public Law 110-181 (Jan. 28, 2008);

(5) Cuban and Haitian entrants applying for adjustment of status under section 202 of the Immigration Reform and Control Act of 1986 (IRCA), Public Law 99-603, 100 Stat. 3359 (Nov. 6, 1986), as amended, 8 U.S.C. 1255a note;

(6) Aliens applying for adjustment of status under the Cuban Adjustment Act, Public Law 89-732 (Nov. 2, 1966), as amended, 8 U.S.C. 1255 note;

(7) Nicaraguans and other Central Americans applying for adjustment of status under section 202(a) and section 203 of the Nicaraguan Adjustment and Central American Relief Act (NACARA), Public Law 105-100, 111 Stat. 2193 (Nov. 19, 1997), as amended, 8 U.S.C. 1255 note;

(8) Haitians applying for adjustment of status under section 902 of the Haitian Refugee Immigration Fairness Act of 1998, Public Law 105-277, 112 Stat. 2681 (Oct. 21, 1998), as amended, 8 U.S.C. 1255 note;

(9) Lautenberg parolees as described in section 599E of the Foreign Operations, Export Financing, and Related Programs Appropriations Act of 1990, Public Law 101-167, 103 Stat. 1195, title V (Nov. 21, 1989), as amended, 8 U.S.C. 1255 note;

(10) Special immigrant juveniles as described in section 245(h) of the Act;

(11) Aliens who entered the United States prior to January 1, 1972, and who meet the other conditions for being granted lawful permanent residence under section 249 of the Act and 8 CFR part 249 (Registry);

(12) Aliens applying for or reregistering for Temporary Protected Status as described in section 244 of the Act in accordance with section 244(c)(2)(A)(ii) of the Act and 8 CFR 244.3(a);

(13) Nonimmigrants described in section 101(a)(15)(A)(i) and (ii) of the Act (Ambassador, Public Minister, Career Diplomat or Consular Officer, or Immediate Family or Other Foreign Government Official or Employee, or Immediate Family), in accordance with section 102 of the Act and 22 CFR 41.21(d);

(14) Nonimmigrants classifiable as C-2 (alien in transit to U.N. Headquarters) or C-3 (foreign government official), 22 CFR 41.21(d);

(15) Nonimmigrants described in section 101(a)(15)(G)(i), (ii), (iii), and (iv), of the Act (Principal Resident Representative of Recognized Foreign Government to International Organization, and related categories), in accordance with section 102 of the Act and 22 CFR 41.21(d);

(16) Nonimmigrants classifiable as NATO-1, NATO-2, NATO-3, NATO-4 (NATO representatives), and NATO-6 in accordance with 22 CFR 41.21(d);

(17) Applicants for nonimmigrant status under section 101(a)(15)(T) of the Act, in accordance with § 212.16(b);

(18) Except as provided in paragraph (b) of this section, individuals who are seeking an immigration benefit for which admissibility is required, including but not limited to adjustment of status under section 245(a) of the Act and section 245(l) of the Act and who:

(i) Have a pending application that sets forth a prima facie case for eligibility for nonimmigrant status under section 101(a)(15)(T) of the Act, or

(ii) Have been granted nonimmigrant status under section 101(a)(15)(T) of the Act, provided that the individual is in valid T nonimmigrant status at the time the benefit request is properly filed with USCIS and at the time the benefit request is adjudicated;

(19) Except as provided in paragraph (b) of this section:

(i) Petitioners for nonimmigrant status under section 101(a)(15)(U) of the Act, in accordance with section 212(a)(4)(E)(ii) of the Act; or

(ii) Individuals who are granted nonimmigrant status under section 101(a)(15)(U) of the Act in accordance with section 212(a)(4)(E)(ii) of the Act, who are seeking an immigration benefit for which admissibility is required, including, but not limited to, adjustment of status under section 245(a) of the Act, provided that the individuals are in valid U nonimmigrant status at the time the benefit request is properly filed with USCIS and at the time the benefit request is adjudicated;

(20) Except as provided in paragraph (b) of this section, any aliens who are VAWA self-petitioners under section 212(a)(4)(E)(i) of the Act;

(21) Except as provided in paragraph (b) of this section, qualified aliens described in section 431(c) of the Personal Responsibility and Work Opportunity Reconciliation Act of 1996, 8 U.S.C. 1641(c), under section 212(a)(4)(E)(iii) of the Act;

(22) Applicants adjusting status who qualify for a benefit under section 1703 of the National Defense Authorization Act, Public Law 108-136, 117 Stat. 1392 (Nov. 24, 2003), 8 U.S.C. 1151 note (posthumous benefits to surviving spouses, children, and parents);

(23) American Indians born in Canada determined to fall under section 289 of the Act;

(24) Texas Band of Kickapoo Indians of the Kickapoo Tribe of Oklahoma, Public Law 97-429 (Jan. 8, 1983);

(25) Nationals of Vietnam, Cambodia, and Laos applying for adjustment of status under section 586 of Public Law 106-429 under 8 CFR 245.21;

(26) Polish and Hungarian Parolees who were paroled into the United States from November 1, 1989 to December 31, 1991, under section 646(b) of the IIRIRA, Public Law 104-208, Div. C, Title VI, Subtitle D (Sept. 30, 1996), 8 U.S.C. 1255 note;

(27) Applicants adjusting status who qualify for a benefit under Section 7611 of the National Defense Authorization Act for Fiscal Year 2020, Public Law 116-92, 113 Stat. 1198, 2309 (December 20, 2019) (Liberian Refugee Immigration Fairness), later extended by Section 901 of Division O, Title IX of the Consolidated Appropriations Act, 2021, Public Law 116-260 (December 27, 2020) (Adjustment of Status for Liberian Nationals Extension);

(28) Certain Syrian nationals adjusting status under Public Law 106-378; and

(29) Any other categories of aliens exempt under any other law from the public charge ground of inadmissibility provisions under section 212(a)(4) of the Act.

(b) Limited Exemption. Aliens described in paragraphs (a)(18) through (21) of this section must submit an Affidavit of Support Under Section 213A of the INA if they are applying for adjustment of status based on an employment-based petition that requires such an affidavit of support as described in section 212(a)(4)(D) of the Act.

(c) Waivers. A waiver for the public charge ground of inadmissibility may be authorized based on statutory or regulatory authority, for the following categories of aliens:

(1) Applicants for admission as nonimmigrants under 101(a)(15)(S) of the Act;

(2) Nonimmigrants admitted under section 101(a)(15)(S) of the Act applying for adjustment of status under section 245(j) of the Act (witnesses or informants); and

(3) Any other category of aliens who are eligible to receive a waiver of the public charge ground of inadmissibility.

HISTORY:

[84 FR 41292, 41501, Aug. 14, 2019, as corrected at 84 FR 52357, 52363, Oct. 2, 2019; 86 FR 14221, 14227, Mar. 15, 2021; 87 FR 55472, 55636, Sept. 9, 2022]

PART 213

PUBLIC CHARGE BONDS

AUTHORITY NOTE APPLICABLE TO ENTIRE PART:

AUTHORITY:

8 U.S.C. 1103; 1183; 8 CFR part 2.

PART 213A

AFFIDAVITS OF SUPPORT ON BEHALF OF IMMIGRANTS

Rule

AUTHORITY NOTE APPLICABLE TO ENTIRE PART:

AUTHORITY:

8 U.S.C. 1183a; 8 CFR part 2.

§ 213a.1 Definitions.

As used in this part, the term:

Domicile means the place where a sponsor has his or her principal residence, as defined in section 101(a)(33) of the Act, with the intention to maintain that residence for the foreseeable future.

Federal poverty line means the level of income equal to the poverty guidelines as issued by the Secretary of Health and Human Services in accordance with 42 U.S.C. 9902 that is applicable to a household of the size involved. For purposes of considering the Form I-864, Affidavit of Support Under Section 213A of the Act, the Service and Consular Posts will use the most recent income-poverty guidelines published in the Federal Register by the Department of Health and Human Services. These guidelines are updated annually, and the Service and Consular Posts will begin to use updated guidelines on the first day of the second month after the date the guidelines are published in the Federal Register.

Household income means the income used to determine whether the sponsor meets the minimum income requirements under sections 213A(f)(1)(E), 213A(f)(3), or 213A(f)(5) of the Act. It includes the income of the sponsor, and of the sponsor's spouse and any other person included in determining the sponsor's household size, if the spouse or other person is at least 18 years old and has signed the form designated by USCIS for this purpose, on behalf of the sponsor and intending immigrants. The "household income" may not, however, include the income of an intending immigrant, unless the intending immigrant is either the sponsor's spouse or has the same principal residence as the sponsor and the preponderance of the evidence shows that the intending immigrant's income results from the intending immigrant's lawful employment in the United States or from some other lawful source that will continue to be available to the intending immigrant after he or she acquires permanent resident status. The prospect of employment in the United States that has not yet actually begun will not be sufficient to meet this requirement.

Household size means the number obtained by adding the number of persons specified in this definition. In calculating household size, no individual shall be counted more than once. If the intending immigrant's spouse or child is a citizen or already holds the status of an alien lawfully admitted for permanent residence, then the sponsor should not include that spouse or child in determining the total household size, unless the intending immigrant's spouse or child is a dependent of the sponsor.

(1) In all cases, the household size includes the sponsor, the sponsor's spouse and all of the sponsor's children, as defined in section 101(b)(1) of the Act (other than a stepchild who meets the requirements of section 101(b)(1)(B) of the Act, if the stepchild does not reside with the sponsor, is not claimed by the sponsor as a dependent for tax purposes, and is not seeking to immigrate based on the stepparent/stepchild relationship), unless these children have reached the age of majority under the law of the place of domicile and the sponsor did not claim them as dependents on the sponsor's Federal income tax return for the most recent tax year. The following persons must also be included in calculating the sponsor's household size: Any other persons (whether related to the sponsor or not) whom the sponsor has claimed as dependents on the sponsor's Federal income tax return for the most recent tax year, even if such persons do not have the same principal residence as the sponsor, plus the number of aliens the sponsor has sponsored under any other affidavit of support for whom the sponsor's support obligation has not terminated, plus the number of aliens to be sponsored under the current affidavit of support, even if such aliens do not or will not have the same principal residence as the sponsor. If a child, as defined in section 101(b)(1) of the Act, or spouse of the principal intending immigrant is an alien who does not currently reside in the United States and who either is not seeking to immigrate at the same time as, or will not seek to immigrate within six months of the principal intending immigrant's immigration, the sponsor may exclude that child or spouse in calculating the sponsor's household size.

(2) If the sponsor chooses to do so, the sponsor may add to the number of persons specified in the first part of this definition the number of relatives (as defined in this section) of the sponsor who have the same principal residence as the sponsor and whose income will be relied on to meet the requirements of section 213A of the Act and this part.

Immigration Officer, solely for purposes of this part, includes a Consular Officer, as defined by section 101(a)(9) of the Act, as well as an Immigration Officer, as defined by § 103.1(j) of this chapter.

Income means an individual's total income (adjusted gross income for those who file IRS Form 1040EZ) for purposes of the individual's U.S. Federal income tax liability, including a joint income tax return (e.g., line 22 on the 2004 IRS Form 1040, line 15 on the 2004 IRS Form 1040A, or line 4 on the 2004 IRS Form 1040EZ or the corresponding line on any future revision of these IRS Forms). Only an individual's Federal income tax return — that is, neither a state or territorial income tax return nor an income tax return filed with a foreign government — shall be filed with an affidavit of support, unless the individual had no duty to file a Federal income tax return, and claims that his or her state, territorial or foreign taxable income is sufficient to establish the sufficiency of the affidavit of support.

Intending immigrant means any beneficiary of an immigrant visa petition filed under section 204 of the Act, including any alien who will accompany or follow-to-join the principal beneficiary.

Joint sponsor means any individual who meets the requirements of section 213A(f)(1)(A), (B), (C), and (E) of the Act and 8 CFR 213a.2(c)(1)(i), and who, as permitted by section 213A(f)(5)(A) of the Act, is willing to submit an affidavit of support and accept joint and several liability with the sponsor or substitute sponsor, in any case in which the sponsor's or substitute sponsor's household income is not sufficient to satisfy the requirements of section 213A of the Act.

Means-tested public benefit means either a Federal means-tested public benefit, which is any public benefit funded in whole or in part by funds provided by the Federal Government that the Federal agency administering the Federal funds has determined to be a Federal means-tested public benefit under the Personal Responsibility and Work Opportunity Reconciliation Act of 1996, Public Law 104-193, or a State means-tested public benefit, which is any public benefit for which no Federal funds are provided that a State, State agency, or political subdivision of a State has determined to be a means-tested public benefit. No benefit shall be considered to be a means-tested public benefit if it is a benefit described in sections 401(b), 411(b), 422(b) or 423(d) of Public Law 104-193.

Program official means the officer or employee of any Federal, State, or local government agency or of any private agency that administers any means-tested public benefit program who has authority to act on the agency's behalf in seeking reimbursement of means-tested public benefits.

Relative means a husband, wife, father, mother, child, adult son, adult daughter, brother, or sister.

Significant ownership interest means an ownership interest of 5 percent or more in a for-profit entity that filed an immigrant visa petition to accord a prospective employee an immigrant status under section 203(b) of the Act.

Sponsor means an individual who is either required to execute or has executed an affidavit of support under this part.

Sponsored immigrant means any alien who was an intending immigrant, once that person has been lawfully admitted for permanent residence, so that the affidavit of support filed for that person under this part has entered into force.

Substitute sponsor means an individual who meets the requirements of section 213A(f)(1)(A), (B), (C), and (E) of the Act and 8 CFR 213a.2(c)(1)(i), who is related to the principal intending immigrant in one of the ways described in section 213A(f)(5)(B) of the Act, and who is willing to sign the affidavit of support in place of the now-deceased person who filed a relative or fiance(e) petition that provides the basis for the intending immigrant's ability to seek permanent residence.

HISTORY:

[62 FR 54346, 54352, Oct. 20, 1997, as confirmed and amended at 71 FR 35732, 35749, June 21, 2006; 76 FR 53764, 53788, Aug. 29, 2011]

§ 213a.2 Use of affidavit of support.

(a) Applicability of section 213a affidavit of support.

(1)(i)(A) In any case specified in paragraph (a)(2) of this section, an intending immigrant is inadmissible as an alien likely to become a public charge, unless the qualified sponsor specified in paragraph (b) of this section or a substitute sponsor and, if necessary, a joint sponsor, has executed on behalf of the intending immigrant an affidavit of support on the applicable form designated by USCIS in accordance with the requirements of section 213A of the Act and the form instructions. Each reference in this section to the affidavit of support or the form is deemed to be a reference to all such forms designated by USCIS for use by a sponsor for compliance with section 213A of the Act.

(B) If the intending immigrant claims that, under paragraph (a)(2)(ii)(A), (C), or (E) of this section, the intending immigrant is exempt from the requirement to file an affidavit of support, the intending immigrant must include with his or her application for an immigrant visa or adjustment of status an exemption request on the form designated by USCIS for this purpose.

(ii) An affidavit of support is executed when a sponsor signs and submits the appropriate forms in accordance with the form instructions to USCIS or the Department of State, as appropriate.

(iii) A separate affidavit of support is required for each principal beneficiary.

(iv) Each immigrant who will accompany the principal intending immigrant must be included on the affidavit. See paragraph (f) of this section for further information concerning immigrants who intend to accompany or follow the principal intending immigrant to the United States.

(v)(A) Except as provided for under paragraph (a)(1)(v)(B) of this section, the Department of State consular officer, immigration officer, or immigration judge will determine the sufficiency of the affidavit of support based on the sponsor's, substitute sponsor's, or joint sponsor's reasonably expected household income in the year in which the intending immigrant filed the application for an immigrant visa or for adjustment of status, and based on the evidence submitted with the affidavit of support and the Poverty Guidelines in effect when the intending immigrant filed the application for an immigrant visa or adjustment of status.

(B) If more than one year passes between the filing of the affidavit of support or required affidavit of support attachment form and the hearing, interview, or examination of the intending immigrant concerning the intending immigrant's application for an immigrant visa or adjustment of status, and the Department of State officer, immigration officer or immigration judge determines, in the exercise of discretion, that the particular facts of the case make the submission of additional evidence necessary to the proper adjudication of the case, then the Department of State officer, immigration officer or immigration judge may direct the intending immigrant to submit additional evidence. A Department of State officer or immigration officer shall make the request in writing, and provide the intending immigrant not less than 30 days to submit the additional evidence. An immigration judge may direct the intending immigrant to submit additional evidence and also set the deadline for submission of the initial evidence in any manner permitted under subpart C of 8 CFR part 1003 and any local rules of the Immigration Court. If additional evidence is required under this paragraph, an intending immigrant must submit additional evidence (including copies or transcripts of any income tax returns for the most recent tax year) concerning the income or employment of the sponsor, substitute sponsor, joint sponsor, or household member in the year in which the Department of State officer, immigration officer, or immigration judge makes the request for additional evidence. In this case, the sufficiency of the affidavit of support and any required affidavit of support attachment will be determined based on the sponsor's, substitute sponsor's, or joint sponsor's reasonably expected household income in the year the Department of State officer, immigration officer or immigration judge makes the request for additional evidence, and based on the evidence submitted in response to the request for additional evidence and on the Poverty Guidelines in effect when the request for evidence was issued.

(2)(i) Except for cases specified in paragraph (a)(2)(ii) of this section, paragraph (a)(1) of this section applies to any application for an immigrant visa or for adjustment of status filed on or after December 19, 1997, in which an intending immigrant seeks an immigrant visa, admission as an immigrant, or adjustment of status as:

(A) An immediate relative under section 201(b)(2)(A)(i) of the Act, including orphans and any alien admitted as a K nonimmigrant when the alien seeks adjustment of status;

(B) A family-based immigrant under section 203(a) of the Act; or

(C) An employment-based immigrant under section 203(b) of the Act, if a relative (as defined in 8 CFR 213a.1) of the intending immigrant is a citizen or an alien lawfully admitted for permanent residence who either filed the employment-based immigrant petition or has a significant ownership interest in the entity that filed the immigrant visa petition on behalf of the intending immigrant. An affidavit of support under this section is not required, however, if the relative is a brother or sister of the intending immigrant, unless the brother or sister is a citizen.

(ii) Paragraph (a)(1) of this section shall not apply if the intending immigrant:

(A) Filed a visa petition on his or her own behalf pursuant to section 204(a)(1)(A)(ii), (iii), or (iv) or section 204(a)(1)(B)(ii) or (iii) of the Act, or who seeks to accompany or follow-to-join an immigrant who filed a visa petition on his or his own behalf pursuant to section 204(a)(1)(A)(ii), (iii), or (iv) or section 204(a)(1)(B)(ii) or (iii) of the Act;

(B) Seeks admission as an immigrant on or after December 19, 1997, in a category specified in paragraph (a)(2)(i) of this section with an immigrant visa issued on the basis of an immigrant visa application filed with the Department of State officer before December 19, 1997;

(C) Establishes, on the basis of the alien's own Social Security Administration record or those of his or her spouse or parent(s), that he or she has already worked, or under section 213A(a)(3)(B) of the Act, can already be credited with, 40 qualifying quarters of coverage as defined under title II of the Social Security Act, 42 U.S.C. 401, et seq;

(D) Is a child admitted under section 211(a) of the Act and 8 CFR 211.1(b)(1); or

(E) Is the child of a citizen, if the child is not likely to become a public charge (other than because of the provision of section 212(a)(4)(C) of the Act), and the child's lawful admission for permanent residence will result automatically in the child's acquisition of citizenship under section 320 of the Act, as amended. This exception applies to an alien orphan if the citizen parent(s) has (or have) legally adopted the alien orphan before the alien orphan's acquisition of permanent residence, and if both adoptive parents personally saw and observed the alien orphan before or during the foreign adoption proceeding. An affidavit of support under this part is still required if the citizen parent(s) will adopt the alien orphan in the United States only after the alien orphan's acquisition of permanent residence. If the citizen parent(s) adopted the alien orphan abroad, but at least one of the adoptive parents did not see and observe the alien orphan before or during the foreign adoption proceeding, then an affidavit of support under this part is still required, unless the citizen parent establishes that, under the law of the State of the alien orphan's intended residence in the United States, the foreign adoption decree is entitled to recognition without the need for a formal administrative or judicial proceeding in the State of proposed residence. In the case of a child who immigrates as a Convention adoptee, as defined in 8 CFR 204.301, this exception applies if the child was adopted by the petitioner in the Convention country. An affidavit of support under this part is still required in the case of a child who immigrates as a Convention adoptee if the petitioner will adopt the child in the United States only after the child's acquisition of permanent residence.

(b) Affidavit of support sponsors. The following individuals must execute an affidavit of support on behalf of the intending immigrant in order for the intending immigrant to be found admissible on public charge grounds:

(1) For immediate relatives and family-based immigrants. The person who filed a relative, orphan or fiance(e) petition, the approval of which forms the basis of the intending immigrant's eligibility to apply for an immigrant visa or adjustment of status as an immediate relative or a family-based immigrant, must execute an affidavit of support on behalf of the intending immigrant. If the intending immigrant is the beneficiary of more than one approved immigrant visa petition, it is the person who filed the petition that is actually the basis for the intending immigrant's eligibility to apply for an immigrant visa or adjustment of status who must file an affidavit of support.

(2) For employment-based immigrants. A relative of an intending immigrant seeking an immigrant visa under section 203(b) of the Act must file an affidavit of support if the relative either filed the immigrant visa petition on behalf of the intending immigrant or owns a significant ownership interest in an entity that filed an immigrant visa petition on behalf of the intending immigrant, but only if the relative is a citizen or an alien lawfully admitted for permanent residence. If the intending immigrant is the beneficiary of more than one relative's employment-based immigrant visa petition, it is the relative who filed the petition that is actually the basis for the intending immigrant's eligibility to apply for an immigrant visa or adjustment of status who must file an affidavit of support.

(c) Sponsorship requirements.

(1)(i) General. A sponsor must be:

(A) At least 18 years of age;

(B) Domiciled in the United States or any territory or possession of the United States; and

(C)(1) A citizen or an alien lawfully admitted for permanent residence in the case described in paragraph (a)(2)(i) of this section; or

(2) A citizen or national or an alien lawfully admitted for permanent residence if the individual is a substitute sponsor or joint sponsor.

(ii) Determination of domicile.

(A) If the sponsor is residing abroad, but only temporarily, the sponsor bears the burden of proving, by a preponderance of the evidence, that the sponsor's domicile (as that term is defined in 8 CFR 213a.1) remains in the United States, provided, that a permanent resident who is living abroad temporarily is considered to be domiciled in the United States if the permanent resident has applied for and obtained the preservation of residence benefit under section 316(b) or section 317 of the Act, and provided further, that a citizen who is living abroad temporarily is considered to be domiciled in the United States if the citizen's employment abroad meets the requirements of section 319(b)(1) of the Act.

(B) If the sponsor is not domiciled in the United States, the sponsor can still sign and submit an affidavit of support so long as the sponsor satisfies the Department of State officer, immigration officer, or immigration judge, by a preponderance of the evidence, that the sponsor will establish a domicile in the United States on or before the date of the principal intending immigrant's admission or adjustment of status. The intending immigrant will be inadmissible under section 212(a)(4) of the Act, and the immigration officer or immigration judge must deny the intending immigrant's application for admission or adjustment of status, if the sponsor has not, in fact, established a domicile in the United States on or before the date of the decision on the principal intending immigrant's application for admission or adjustment of status. In the case of a sponsor who comes to the United States intending to establish his or her principal residence in the United States at the same time as the principal intending immigrant's arrival and application for admission at a port-of-entry, the sponsor shall be deemed to have established a domicile in the United States for purposes of this paragraph, unless the sponsor is also a permanent resident alien and the sponsor's own application for admission is denied and the sponsor leaves the United States under a removal order or as a result of the sponsor's withdrawal of the application for admission.

(2) Demonstration of ability to support intending immigrants. In order for the intending immigrant to overcome the public charge ground of inadmissibility, the sponsor must demonstrate the means to maintain the intending immigrant at an annual income of at least 125 percent of the Federal poverty line. If the sponsor is on active duty in the Armed Forces of the United States (other than active duty for training) and the intending immigrant is the sponsor's spouse or child, the sponsor's ability to maintain income must equal at least 100 percent of the Federal poverty line.

(i) Proof of income.

(A) The sponsor must include with an affidavit of support either a photocopy or an Internal Revenue Service-issued transcript of his or her complete Federal income tax return for the most recent taxable year (counting from the date of the signing, rather than the filing, of an affidavit of support). However, the sponsor may, at his or her option, submit tax returns for the three most recent years if the sponsor believes that these additional tax returns may help in establishing the sponsor's ability to maintain his or her income at the applicable threshold set forth in the Poverty Guidelines. Along with each transcript or photocopy, the sponsor must also submit as initial evidence copies of all schedules filed with each return and (if the sponsor submits a photocopy, rather than an IRS transcript of the tax return(s)) all Forms W-2 (if the sponsor relies on income from employment) and Forms 1099 (if the sponsor relies on income from sources documented on Forms 1099) in meeting the income threshold. The sponsor may also include as initial evidence: Letter(s) evidencing his or her current employment and income, paycheck stub(s) (showing earnings for the most recent six months, financial statements, or other evidence of the sponsor's anticipated household income for the year in which the intending immigrant files the application for an immigrant visa or adjustment of status. By executing an affidavit of support, the sponsor certifies under penalty of perjury under United States law that the evidence of his or her current household income is true and correct and that each transcript or photocopy of each income tax return is a true and correct transcript or photocopy of the return that the sponsor filed with the Internal Revenue Service for that taxable year.

(B) If the sponsor had no legal duty to file a Federal income tax return for the most recent tax year, the sponsor must explain why he or she had no legal duty to a file a Federal income tax return for that year. If the sponsor claims he or she had no legal duty to file for any reason other than the level of the sponsor's income for that year, the initial evidence submitted with an affidavit of support must also include any evidence of the amount and source of the income that the sponsor claims was exempt from taxation and a copy of the provisions of any statute, treaty, or regulation that supports the claim that he or she had no duty to file an income tax return with respect to that income. If the sponsor had no legal obligation to file a Federal income tax return, he or she may submit other evidence of annual income. The fact that a sponsor had no duty to file a Federal income tax return does not relieve the sponsor of the duty to file an affidavit of support.

(C)(1) The sponsor's ability to meet the income requirement will be determined based on the sponsor's household income. In establishing the household income, the sponsor may rely entirely on his or her personal income, if it is sufficient to meet the income requirement. The sponsor may also rely on the income of the sponsor's spouse and of any other person included in determining the sponsor's household size, if the spouse or other person is at least 18 years old and has completed and signed an affidavit of support attachment. A person does not need to be a U.S. citizen, national, or alien lawfully admitted for permanent residence in order to sign an affidavit of support attachment.

(2) Each individual who signs an affidavit of support attachment agrees, in consideration of the sponsor's signing of an affidavit of support, to provide to the sponsor as much financial assistance as may be necessary to enable the sponsor to maintain the intending immigrants at the annual income level required by section 213A(a)(1)(A) of the Act, to be jointly and severally liable for any reimbursement obligation that the sponsor may incur, and to submit to the personal jurisdiction of any court that has subject matter juris-

diction over a civil suit to enforce the contract or the affidavit of support. The sponsor, as a party to the contract, may bring suit to enforce the contract. The intending immigrants and any Federal, state, or local agency or private entity that provides a means-tested public benefit to an intending immigrant are third party beneficiaries of the contract between the sponsor and the other individual or individuals on whose income the sponsor relies and may bring an action to enforce the contract in the same manner as third party beneficiaries of other contracts.

(3) If there is no spouse or child immigrating with the intending immigrant, then there will be no need for the intending immigrant to sign an affidavit of support attachment, even if the sponsor will rely on the continuing income of the intending immigrant to meet the income requirement. If, however, the sponsor seeks to rely on an intending immigrant's continuing income to establish the sponsor's ability to support the intending immigrant's spouse or children, then the intending immigrant whose income is to be relied on must sign an affidavit of support attachment.

(4) If the sponsor relies on the income of any individual who has signed an affidavit of support attachment, the sponsor must also include with an affidavit of support and an affidavit of support attachment, with respect to the person who signed an affidavit of support attachment, the initial evidence required under paragraph (c)(2)(i)(A) of this section. The household member's tax return(s) must be for the same tax year as the sponsor's tax return(s). An individual who signs an affidavit of support attachment certifies, under penalty of perjury, that the submitted transcript or photocopy of the tax return is a true and correct transcript or photocopy of the Federal income tax return filed with the Internal Revenue Service, and that the information concerning that person's employment and income is true and correct.

(5) If the person who signs an affidavit of support attachment is not an intending immigrant, and is any person other than the sponsor's spouse or a claimed dependent of the sponsor, the sponsor must also attach proof that the person is a relative (as defined in 8 CFR 213a.1) of the sponsor and that an affidavit of support attachment signer has the same principal residence as the sponsor. If an intending immigrant signs an affidavit of support attachment, the sponsor must also provide proof that the sponsored immigrant has the same principal residence as the sponsor, unless the sponsored immigrant is the sponsor's spouse.

(D) Effect of failure to file income tax returns. If a sponsor, substitute sponsor, joint sponsor, or household member did not file a Federal income tax return for the year for which a transcript or photocopy must be provided, an affidavit of support or an affidavit of support attachment will not be considered sufficient to satisfy the requirements of section 213A of the Act, even if the household income meets the requirements of section 213A of the Act, unless the sponsor, substitute sponsor, joint sponsor, or household member proves, by a preponderance of the evidence, that he or she had no duty to file. If the sponsor, substitute sponsor, joint sponsor or household member cannot prove that he or she had no duty to file, then an affidavit of support or an affidavit of support attachment will not be considered sufficient to satisfy the requirements of section 213A of the Act until the sponsor, substitute sponsor, joint sponsor, or household member proves that he or she has satisfied the obligation to file the tax return and provides a transcript or copy of the return.

(ii) Determining the sufficiency of an affidavit of support. The sufficiency of an affidavit of support shall be determined in accordance with this paragraph.

(A) Income. The sponsor must first calculate the total income attributable to the sponsor under paragraph (c)(2)(i)(C) of this section for the year in which the intending immigrant filed the application for an immigrant visa or adjustment of status.

(B) Number of persons to be supported. The sponsor must then determine his or her household size as defined in 8 CFR 213a.1.

(C) Sufficiency of income. Except as provided in this paragraph, or in paragraph (a)(1)(v)(B) of this section, the sponsor's affidavit of support shall be considered sufficient to satisfy the requirements of section 213A of the Act and this section if the reasonably expected household income for the year in which the intending immigrant filed the application for an immigrant visa or adjustment of status, calculated under paragraph (c)(2)(iii)(A) of this section, would equal at least 125 percent of the Federal poverty line for the sponsor's household size as defined in 8 CFR 213a.1, under the Poverty Guidelines in effect when the intending immigrant filed the application for an immigrant visa or for adjustment of status, except that the sponsor's income need only equal at least 100 percent of the Federal poverty line for the sponsor's household size, if the sponsor is on active duty (other than for training) in the Armed Forces of the United States and the intending immigrant is the sponsor's spouse or child. The sponsor's household income for the year in which the intending immigrant filed the application for an immigrant visa or adjustment of status shall be given the greatest evidentiary weight; any tax return and other information relating to the sponsor's financial history will serve as evidence tending to show whether the sponsor is likely to be able to maintain his or her income in the future. If the projected household income for the year in which the intending immigrant filed the application for an immigrant visa or adjustment of status meets the applicable income threshold, the affidavit of support may be held to be insufficient on the basis of the household income but only if, on the basis of specific facts, including a material change in employment or income history of the sponsor, substitute sponsor, joint sponsor or household member, the number of aliens included in an affidavit of support that the sponsor has signed but that have not yet entered into force in accordance with paragraph (e) of this section, or other relevant facts, it is reasonable to infer that the sponsor will not be able to maintain his or her household income at a level sufficient to meet his or her support obligations.

(iii) Inability to meet income requirement.

(A) If the sponsor is unable to meet the minimum income requirement in paragraph (c)(2)(iii) of this section, the intending immigrant is inadmissible under section 212(a)(4) of the Act unless:

(1) The sponsor, the intending immigrant or both, can meet the significant assets provision of paragraph (c)(2)(iv)(B) of this section; or

(2) A joint sponsor executes a separate affidavit of support.

(B) Significant assets. The sponsor may submit evidence of the sponsor's ownership of significant assets, such as savings accounts, stocks, bonds, certificates of deposit, real estate, or other assets. An intending immigrant may submit evidence of the intending immigrant's assets as a part of the affidavit of support, even if the intending immigrant is not required to sign an affidavit of support attachment. The assets of any person who has signed an affidavit of support attachment may also be considered in determining whether the assets are sufficient to meet this requirement. To qualify as "significant assets" the combined cash value of all the assets (the total value of the assets less any offsetting liabilities) must exceed:

(1) If the intending immigrant is the spouse or child of a United States citizen (and the child has reached his or her 18th birthday), three times the difference between the sponsor's household income and the Federal poverty line for the sponsor's household size (including all immigrants sponsored in any affidavit of support in force or submitted under this section);

(2) If the intending immigrant is an alien orphan who will be adopted in the United States after the alien orphan acquires permanent residence (or in whose case the parents will need to seek a formal recognition of a foreign adoption under the law of the State of the intending immigrant's proposed residence because at least one of the parents did not see the child before or during the adoption), and who will, as a result of the adoption or formal recognition of the foreign adoption, acquire citizenship under section 320 of the Act, the difference between the sponsor's household income and the Federal poverty line for the sponsor's household size (including all immigrants sponsored in any affidavit of support in force or submitted under this section);

(3) In all other cases, five times the difference between the sponsor's household income and the Federal poverty line for the sponsor's household size (including all immigrants sponsored in any affidavit of support in force or submitted under this section).

(C) Joint sponsor. A joint sponsor must execute a separate affidavit of support on behalf of the intending immigrant(s) and be willing to accept joint and several liabilities with the sponsor or substitute sponsor. A joint sponsor must meet all the eligibility requirements under paragraph (c)(1) of this section, except that the joint sponsor is not required to file a visa petition on behalf of the intending immigrant. The joint sponsor must demonstrate his or her ability to support the intending immigrant in the manner specified in paragraph (c)(2) of this section. A joint sponsor's household income must meet or exceed the income requirement in paragraph (c)(2)(iii) of this section unless the joint sponsor can demonstrate significant assets as provided in paragraph (c)(2)(iv)(A) of this section. The joint sponsor's household income must equal at least 125 percent of the Poverty Guidelines for the joint sponsor's household size, unless the joint sponsor is on active duty in the Armed Forces and the intending immigrant is the joint sponsor's spouse or child, in which case the joint sponsor's household income is sufficient if it equals at least 100 percent of the Poverty Guidelines for the joint sponsor's household size. An intending immigrant may not have more than one joint sponsor, but, if the joint sponsor's household income is not sufficient to meet the income requirement with respect to the principal intending immigrant, any spouse and all the children who, under section 203(d) of the Act, seek to accompany the principal intending immigrant, then the joint sponsor may specify on the affidavit that it is submitted only on behalf of the principal intending immigrant and those accompanying family members specifically listed on the affidavit. The remaining accompanying family members will then be inadmissible under section 212(a)(4) of the Act unless a second joint sponsor submits an affidavit(s) on behalf of all the remaining family members who seek to accompany the principal intending immigrant and who are not included in the first joint sponsor's affidavit. There may not be more than two joint sponsors for the family group consisting of the principal intending immigrant and the accompanying spouse and children.

(D) Substitute sponsor. In a family-sponsored case, if the visa petitioner dies after approval of the visa petition, but the U.S. Citizenship and Immigration Services determines, under 8 CFR 205.1(a)(3)(i)(C), that for humanitarian reasons it would not be appropriate to revoke approval of the visa petition, then a substitute sponsor, as defined in 8 CFR 213a.1, may sign an affidavit of support. The substitute sponsor must meet all the requirements of this section that would have applied to the visa petitioner, had the visa petitioner survived and been the sponsor. The substitute sponsor's household income must equal at least 125% of the Poverty Guidelines for the substitute sponsor's household size, unless the intending immigrant is the substitute sponsor's spouse or child and the substitute sponsor is on active duty in the Armed Forces (other than active duty for training), in which case the substitute sponsor's household income is sufficient if it equals at least 100% of the Poverty Guidelines for the substitute sponsor's household size. If the substitute sponsor's household income is not sufficient to meet the requirements of section 213A(a)(f)(1)(E) of the Act and paragraph (c)(2) of this section, the alien will be inadmissible unless a joint sponsor signs an affidavit of support.

(iv) Remaining inadmissibility on public charge grounds. Notwithstanding the filing of a sufficient affidavit of support under section 213A of the Act and this section, an alien may be found to be inadmissible under section 212(a)(4) of the Act if the alien's case includes evidence of specific facts that, when considered in light of section 212(a)(4)(B) of the Act, support a reasonable inference that the alien is likely at any time to become a public charge.

(v) Verification of employment, income, and assets. The Federal Government may pursue verification of any information provided on or with an affidavit of support, including information on employment, income, or assets, with the employer, financial or other institutions, the Internal Revenue Service, or the Social Security Administration. To facilitate this verification process, the sponsor, joint sponsor, substitute sponsor, or household member must sign and submit any necessary waiver form when directed to do so by the immigration officer, immigration judge, or Department of State officer who has jurisdiction to adjudicate the case to which an affidavit of support or an affidavit of support attachment relates. A sponsor's, substitute sponsor's, joint sponsor's, or household member's failure or refusal to sign any waiver needed to verify the information when directed to do so constitutes a withdrawal of an affidavit of support or an affidavit of support attachment, so that, in adjudicating the intending immigrant's application for an immigrant visa or adjustment of status, an affidavit of support or an affidavit of support attachment will be deemed not to have been filed.

(vi) Effect of fraud or material concealment or misrepresentation. An affidavit of support or an affidavit of support attachment is insufficient to satisfy the requirements of section 213A of the Act and this part, and the affidavit of support shall be found insufficient to establish that the intending immigrant is not likely to become a public charge, if the Department of State officer, immigration officer or immigration judge finds that an affidavit of support or an affidavit of support attachment is forged, counterfeited, or otherwise falsely executed, or if an affidavit of support or an affidavit of support attachment conceals or misrepresents facts concerning household size, household income, employment history, or any other material fact. Any person who knowingly participated in the forgery, counterfeiting, or false production of an affidavit of support or an affidavit of support attachment, or in any concealment or misrepresentation of any material fact, may be subject to a civil penalty under section 274C of the Act, to criminal prosecution, or to both, to the extent permitted by law. If the person is an alien, the person may also be subject to removal from the United States.

(d) Legal effect of affidavit of support. Execution of an affidavit of support under this section creates a contract between the sponsor and the U.S. Government for the benefit of the sponsored immigrant, and of any Federal, State, or local governmental agency or private entity that administers any means-tested public benefits program. The sponsored immigrant, or any Federal, State, or local governmental agency or private entity that provides any means-tested public benefit to the sponsored immigrant after the sponsored immigrant acquires permanent resident status, may seek enforcement of the sponsor's obligations through an appropriate civil action.

(e) **Commencement and termination of support obligation.**

(1) With respect to any intending immigrant, the support obligation and change of address obligation imposed on a sponsor, substitute sponsor, or joint sponsor under an affidavit of support, and any household member's support obligation under an affidavit of support attachment, all begin when the immigration officer or the immigration judge grants the intending immigrant's application for admission as an immigrant or for adjustment of status on the basis of an application for admission or adjustment that included an affidavit of support or an affidavit of support attachment. Any person completing and submitting an affidavit of support as a joint sponsor or an affidavit of support attachment as a household member is not bound to any obligations under section 213A of the Act if, notwithstanding his or her signing of an affidavit of support or an affidavit of support attachment, the Department of State officer (in deciding an application for an immigrant visa) or the immigration officer or immigration judge (in deciding an application for admission or adjustment of status) includes in the decision a specific finding that the sponsor or substitute sponsor's own household income is sufficient to meet the income requirements under section 213A of the Act.

(2)(i) The support obligation and the change of address reporting requirement imposed on a sponsor, substitute sponsor and joint sponsor under an affidavit of support, and any household member's support obligation under an affidavit of support attachment, all terminate by operation of law when the sponsored immigrant:

(A) Becomes a citizen of the United States;

(B) Has worked, or can be credited with, 40 qualifying quarters of coverage under title II of the Social Security Act, 42 U.S.C. 401, et seq., provided that the sponsored immigrant is not credited with any quarter beginning after December 31, 1996, during which the sponsored immigrant receives or received any Federal means-tested public benefit;

(C) Ceases to hold the status of an alien lawfully admitted for permanent residence and departs the United States (if the sponsored immigrant has not abandoned permanent resident status, executing the form designated by USCIS for recording such action, this provision will apply only if the sponsored immigrant is found in a removal proceeding to have abandoned that status while abroad);

(D) Obtains in a removal proceeding a new grant of adjustment of status as relief from removal (in this case, if the sponsored immigrant is still subject to the affidavit of support requirement under this part, then any individual(s) who signed an affidavit of support or an affidavit of support attachment in relation to the new adjustment application will be subject to the obligations of this part, rather than those who signed an affidavit of support or an affidavit of support attachment in relation to an earlier grant of admission as an immigrant or of adjustment of status); or

(E) Dies.

(ii) The support obligation under an affidavit of support also terminates if the sponsor, substitute sponsor or joint sponsor dies. A household member's obligation under an affidavit of support attachment terminates when the household member dies. The death of one person who had a support obligation under an affidavit of support or an affidavit of support attachment does not terminate the support obligation of any other sponsor, substitute sponsor, joint sponsor, or household member with respect to the same sponsored immigrant.

(3) The termination of the sponsor's, substitute sponsor's, or joint sponsor's obligations under an affidavt of support or of a household member's obligations under an affidavit of support attachment does not relieve the sponsor, substitute sponsor, joint sponsor, or household member (or their respective estates) of any reimbursement obligation under section 213A(b) of the Act and this section that accrued before the support obligation terminated.

(f) **Withdrawal of affidavit of support and any required attachments.**

(1) In an immigrant visa case, once the sponsor, substitute sponsor, joint sponsor, household member, or intending immigrant has presented a signed affidavit of support and any required attachments to a Department of State officer, the sponsor, substitute sponsor, joint sponsor, or household member may disavow his or her agreement to act as sponsor, substitute sponsor, joint sponsor, or household member if he or she does so in writing and submits the document to the Department of State officer before the actual issuance of an immigrant visa to the intending immigrant. Once the intending immigrant has obtained an immigrant visa, a sponsor, substitute sponsor, joint sponsor, or household member cannot disavow his or her agreement to act as a sponsor, joint sponsor, or household member unless the person or entity who filed the visa petition withdraws the visa petition in writing, as specified in 8 CFR 205.1(a)(3)(i)(A) or 8 CFR 205.1(a)(3)(iii)(C), and also notifies the Department of State officer who issued the visa of the withdrawal of the petition.

(2) In an adjustment of status case, once the sponsor, substitute sponsor, joint sponsor, household member, or intending immigrant has presented a signed affidavit of support and any required attachments to an immigration officer or immigration judge, the sponsor, substitute sponsor, joint sponsor, or household member may disavow his or her agreement to act as sponsor, substitute sponsor, joint sponsor, or household member only if he or she does so in writing and submits the document to the immigration officer or immigration judge before the decision on the adjustment application.

(g) **Aliens who accompany or follow-to-join a principal intending immigrant.**

(1) To avoid inadmissibility under section 212(a)(4) of the Act, an alien who applies for an immigrant visa, admission, or adjustment of status as an alien who is accompanying, as defined in 22 CFR 40.1, a principal intending immigrant must submit clear and true photocopies of any relevant affidavit(s) and attachments filed on behalf of the principal intending immigrant.

(2)(i) To avoid inadmissibility under section 212(a)(4) of the Act, an alien who applies for an immigrant visa, admission, or adjustment of status as an alien who is following-to-join a principal intending immigrant must submit a new affidavit(s) of support, together with all documents or other evidence necessary to prove that the new affidavits comply with the requirements of section 213A of the Act and 8 CFR part 213a.

(ii) When paragraph (g)(2)(i) of this section requires the filing of a new affidavit for an alien who seeks to follow-to-join a principal sponsored immigrant, the same sponsor who filed the visa petition and affidavit of support for the principal sponsored immigrant must file the new affidavit on behalf of the alien seeking to follow-to-join. If that person has died, then the alien seeking to follow-to-join is inadmissible unless a substitute sponsor, as defined by 8 CFR 213a.1, signs a new affidavit that meets the requirements of this section. Persons other than the person or persons who signed the original joint affidavits on behalf of the principal sponsored immigrant may sign a new joint affidavit on behalf of an alien who seeks to follow-to-join a principal sponsored immigrant.

(iii) If a joint sponsor is needed in the case of an alien who seeks to follow-to-join a principal sponsored immigrant, and the principal sponsored immigrant also required a joint sponsor when the principal sponsored immigrant immigrated, that same person may, but is not required to be, the joint sponsor for the alien who seeks to follow-to-join the principal sponsored immigrant.

HISTORY:

[62 FR 54346, 54353, Oct. 20, 1997, as corrected at 62 FR 60122, Nov. 6, 1997 and 62 FR 64048, Dec. 3, 1997, and as confirmed and amended at 71 FR 35732, 35749, 35750, June 21, 2006; 72 FR 56832, 56867, Oct. 4, 2007; 76 FR 53764, 53788, Aug. 29, 2011, as corrected at 76 FR 73475, Nov. 29, 2011]

§ 213a.3 Change of address.

(a) **Submission of address change.**

(1) Filing requirements. If the address of a sponsor (including a substitute sponsor or joint sponsor) changes while the sponsor's support obligation is in effect, the sponsor shall file a change of address notice within 30 days, in a manner as prescribed by USCIS on its address change form instructions.

(2) Proof of mailing. USCIS will accept a photocopy of the change of address form together with proof of the form's delivery to USCIS as evidence that the sponsor has complied with this requirement.

(3) Electronic notices. USCIS will provide the sponsor with a receipt notice for an address change.

(4) Alien sponsors. If the sponsor is an alien, the sponsor must still comply with the requirements of 8 CFR 265.1 to notify USCIS of his or her change of address.

(b) Civil penalty. If the sponsor fails to give notice in accordance with paragraph (a) of this section, DHS may impose on the sponsor a civil penalty in an amount within the penalty range established in section 213A(d)(2)(A) of the Act. Except, if the sponsor, knowing that the sponsored immigrant has received any means-tested public benefit, fails to give notice in accordance with paragraph (a) of this section, DHS may impose on the sponsor a civil penalty in an amount within the penalty range established in section 213A(d)(2)(B) of the Act. The procedure for imposing a civil penalty is established at 8 CFR part 280.

HISTORY:

[62 FR 54346, 54355, Oct. 20, 1997, as confirmed and amended at 71 FR 35732, 35749, 35755, June 21, 2006; 76 FR 53764, 53789, Aug. 29, 2011]

§ 213a.4 Actions for reimbursement, public notice, and congressional reports.

(a) Requests for reimbursement; commencement of civil action.

(1) By agencies.

(i) If an agency that provides a means-tested public benefit to a sponsored immigrant wants to seek reimbursement from a sponsor, household member, or joint sponsor, the program official must arrange for service of a written request for reimbursement upon the sponsor, household member, or joint sponsor, by personal service, as defined by 8 CFR 103.8(a)(2), except that the person making personal service need not be a Federal Government officer or employee.

(ii) The request for reimbursement must specify the date the sponsor, household member, or joint sponsor's support obligation commenced (this is the date the sponsored immigrant became a permanent resident), the sponsored immigrant's name, alien registration number, address, and date of birth, as well as the types of means-tested public benefit(s) that the sponsored immigrant received, the dates the sponsored immigrant received the means-tested public benefit(s), and the total amount of the means-tested public benefit(s) received.

(iii) It is not necessary to make a separate request for each type of means-tested public benefit, nor for each separate payment. The agency may instead aggregate in a single request all benefit payments the agency has made as of the date of the request. A state or local government may make a single reimbursement request on behalf of all of the state or local government agencies that have provided means-tested public benefits.

(iv) So that the sponsor, household member, or joint sponsor may verify the accuracy of the request, the request for reimbursement must include an itemized statement supporting the claim for reimbursement. The request for reimbursement must also include a notification to the sponsor, household member, or joint sponsor that the sponsor, household member, or joint sponsor must, within 45 days of the date of service, respond to the request for reimbursement either by paying the reimbursement or by arranging to commence payments pursuant to a payment schedule that is agreeable to the program official.

(v) Prior to filing a lawsuit against a sponsor, household member, or joint sponsor to enforce the sponsor, household member, or joint sponsor's support obligation under section 213A(b)(2) of the Act, a Federal, state, or local governmental agency or a private entity must wait 45 days from the date it serves a written request for reimbursement in accordance with this section.

(2) By the sponsored immigrant. Section 213A(b) of the Act does not require a sponsored immigrant to request the sponsor or joint sponsor to comply with the support obligation, before bringing an action to compel compliance.

(3) Role of USCIS and DHS. Upon the receipt of a duly issued subpoena, USCIS may provide a certified copy of an affidavit of support that has been filed on behalf of a specific alien for use as evidence in a civil action to enforce the affidavit of support, and may also disclose the last known address and social security number of the sponsor, substitute sponsor, or joint sponsor. Requesting information through the Systematic Alien Verification for Entitlement (SAVE) Program is sufficient, and a subpoena is not required, to obtain the sponsored immigrant's current immigration or citizenship status or the name, social security number and last known address of a sponsor, substitute sponsor, or joint sponsor.

(b) Designation of means-tested public benefits. Federal, State, and local government agencies should issue public notice of determinations regarding which benefits are considered "means-tested public benefits" prior to December 19, 1997, the date the new affidavit of support goes into effect, or as soon as possible thereafter. Additional notices should be issued whenever an agency revises its determination of which benefits are considered "means-tested public benefits." A sponsor, joint sponsor, or household member is not liable to reimburse any agency for any benefit with respect to which a public notice of the determination that the benefit is a means-tested public benefit was not published until after the date the benefit was first provided to the immigrant.

(c) **Congressional reports.**

(1) For purposes of section 213A(i)(3) of the Act, USCIS will consider a sponsor or joint sponsor to be in compliance with the financial obligations of section 213A of the Act unless a party that has obtained a final judgment enforcing the sponsor or joint sponsor's obligations under section 213A(a)(1)(A) or 213A(b) of the Act has provided a copy of the final judgment to the USCIS by mailing a certified copy to the address listed in paragraph (c)(3) of this section. The copy should be accompanied by a cover letter that includes the reference "Civil Judgments for Congressional Reports under section 213A(i)(3) of the Act." Failure to file a certified copy of the final civil judgment in accordance with this section has no effect on the plaintiff's ability to collect on the judgment pursuant to law.

(2) If a Federal, state, or local agency or private entity that administers any means-tested public benefit makes a determination under section 421(e) of the Personal Responsibility and Work Opportunity Reconciliation Act of 1996 in the case of any sponsored immigrant, the program official shall send written notice of the determination, including the name of the sponsored immigrant and of the sponsor, to the address listed in paragraph (c)(3) of this section. The written notice should include the reference "Determinations under 421(e) of the Personal Responsibility and Work Opportunity Reconciliation Act of 1996."

(3) The address referred to in paragraphs (c)(1) and (c)(2) of this section is: Office of Program and Regulation Development, U.S. Citizenship and Immigration Services, 20 Massachusetts Avenue, NW., Washington, DC, 20529.

HISTORY:

[62 FR 54346, 54355, Oct. 20, 1997, as confirmed and amended at 71 FR 35732, 35749, 35755, June 21, 2006; 76 FR 53764, 53790, Aug. 29, 2011]

§ 213a.5 Relationship of this part to other affidavits of support.

Nothing in this part precludes the continued use of other affidavits of support provided by USCIS in a case other than a case described in § 213a.2(a)(2). The obligations of section 213A of the Act do not bind a person who executes such other USCIS affidavits of support. Persons sponsoring an Amerasian alien described in section 204(f)(2) of the Act remain subject to the provisions of section 204(f)(4)(B) of the Act and 8 CFR 204.4(i), as appropriate.

HISTORY:

[62 FR 54346, 54355, Oct. 20, 1997, as confirmed at 71 FR 35732, 35749, June 21, 2006; 76 FR 53764, 53790, Aug. 29, 2011]

PART 214
NONIMMIGRANT CLASSES

Subpart A. Classes A through S

Rule

Rule

Subpart C. Noncitizen Victims of Severe Forms of Trafficking in Persons

AUTHORITY NOTE APPLICABLE TO ENTIRE PART:

AUTHORITY:

6 U.S.C. 202, 236; 8 U.S.C. 1101, 1102, 1103, 1182, 1184, 1186a, 1187, 1221, 1281, 1282, 1301-1305, 1357, and 1372; sec. 643, Pub. L. 104-208, 110 Stat. 3009-708; Pub. L. 106-386, 114 Stat. 1477-1480; section 141 of the Compacts of Free Association with the Federated States of Micronesia and the Republic of the Marshall Islands, and with the Government of Palau, 48 U.S.C. 1901 note and 1931 note, respectively; 48 U.S.C. 1806; 8 CFR part 2; Pub. L. 115-218, 132 Stat. 1547 (48 U.S.C. 1806).

Subpart A
Classes A through S

§ 214.1 Requirements for admission, extension, and maintenance of status.

(a) General.

(1) Nonimmigrant classes. For the purpose of administering the nonimmigrant provisions of the Act, the following administrative subclassifications of nonimmigrant classifications as defined in section 101(a)(15) of the Act are established:

(i) Section 101(a)(15)(B) is divided into (B)(i) for visitors for business and (B)(ii) for visitors for pleasure;

(ii) Section 101(a)(15)(C) is divided into (C)(i) for aliens who are not diplomats and are in transit through the United States; (C)(ii) for aliens in transit to and from the United Nations Headquarters District; and (C)(iii) for alien diplomats in transit through the United States;

(iii) Section 101(a)(15)(H) is divided to create an (H)(iv) subclassification for the spouse and children of a nonimmigrant classified under section 101(a)(15) (H) (i), (ii), or (iii);

(iv) Section 101(a)(15)(J) is divided into (J)(i) for principal aliens and (J)(ii) for such alien's spouse and children;

(v) Section 101(a)(15)(K) is divided into (K)(i) for the fiance(e), (K)(ii) for the spouse, and (K)(iii) for the children of either;

(vi) Section 101(a)(15)(L) is divided into (L)(i) for principal aliens and (L)(ii) for such alien's spouse and children;

(vii) Section 101(a)(15)(Q)(ii) is divided to create a (Q)(iii) for subclassification for the spouse and children of a nonimmigrant classified under section 101(a)(15)(Q)(ii) of the Act;

(viii) Section 101(a)(15)(T)(ii) is divided into (T)(ii), (T)(iii), (T)(iv), and (T)(v) for the spouse, child, parent, and unmarried sibling under 18 years of age, respectively, of a principal nonimmigrant classified under section 101(a)(15)(T)(i); and T(vi) for the adult or minor child of a derivative nonimmigrant classified under section 101(a)(15)(T)(ii); and

(ix) Section 101(a)(15)(U)(ii) is divided into (U)(ii), (U)(iii), (U)(iv), and (U)(v) for the spouse, child, parent, and siblings, respectively, of a nonimmigrant classified under section 101(a)(15)(U)(i); and

(2) Classification designations. For the purpose of this chapter the following nonimmigrant designations are established. The designation in the second column may be used to refer to the appropriate nonimmigrant classification.

Section	Designation
101(a)(15)(A)(i)	A-1.
101(a)(15)(A)(ii)	A-2.
101(a)(15)(A)(iii)	A-3.
101(a)(15)(B)(i)	B-1.
101(a)(15)(B)(ii)	B-2.
101(a)(15)(C)(i)	C-1.
101(a)(15)(C)(ii)	C-2.
101(a)(15)(C)(iii)	C-3.
101(a)(15)(D)(i)	D-1.
101(a)(15)(D)(ii)	D-2.
101(a)(15)(E)(i)	E-1.
101(a)(15)(E)(ii)	E-2.
101(a)(15)(F)(i)	F-1.
101(a)(15)(F)(ii)	F-2.
101(a)(15)(G)(i)	G-1.
101(a)(15)(G)(ii)	G-2.
101(a)(15)(G)(iii)	G-3.
101(a)(15)(G)(iv)	G-4.
101(a)(15)(g)(v)	G-5.
101(a)(15)(H)(i)(B)	H-1B.
101(a)(15)(H)(i)(C)	H-1C.
101(a)(15)(H)(ii)(A)	H-2A.
101(a)(15)(H)(ii)(B)	H-2B.
101(a)(15)(H)(iii)	H-3.
101(a)(15)(H)(iv)	H-4.
101(a)(15)(I)	I.
101(a)(15)(J)(i)	J-1.
101(a)(15)(J)(ii)	J-2.
101(a)(15)(K)(i)	K-1.
101(a)(15)(K)(ii)	K-3.
101(a)(15)(K)(iii)	K-2; K-4.
101(a)(15)(L)(i)	L-1.
101(a)(15)(L)(ii)	L-2.
101(a)(15)(M)(i)	M-1.
101(a)(15)(M)(ii)	M-2.
101(a)(15)(N)(i)	N-8.
101(a)(15)(N)(ii)	N-9.
101(a)(15)(O)(i)	O-1.
101(a)(15)(O)(ii)	O-2.
101(a)(15)(O)(iii)	O-3.
101(a)(15)(P)(i)	P-1.
101(a)(15)(P)(ii)	P-2.
101(a)(15)(P)(iii)	P-3.
101(a)(15)(P)(iv)	P-4.
101(a)(15)(Q)(i)	Q-1.
101(a)(15)(Q)(ii)	Q-2.
101(a)(15)(Q)(iii)	Q-3.
101(a)(15)(R)(i)	R-1.
101(a)(15)(R)(ii)	R-2.
101(a)(15)(S)(i)	S-5.
101(a)(15)(S)(ii)	S-6.
101(a)(15)(S) qualified family members	S-7.
101(a)(15)(T)(i)	T-1
101(a)(15)(T)(ii)	T-2
101(a)(15)(T)(iii)	T-3
101(a)(15)(T)(iv)	T-4
101(a)(15)(T)(v)	T-5
101(a)(15)(T)(vi)	T-6
101(a)(15)(U)(i)	U-1
101(a)(15)(U)(ii)	U-2, U-3, U-4, U-5
101(a)(15)(V)	V-1, V-2, or V-3
USMCA, Principal	TN.
USMCA, Dependent	TD.
Visa Waiver, Business	WB.
Visa Waiver, Tourist	WT.

Note 1: The classification designation K-2 is for the child of a K-1. The classification designation K-4 is for the child of a K-3.

Note 2: The classification designation V-1 is for the spouse of a lawful permanent resident; the classification designation V-2 is for the principal beneficiary of an I-130 who is the child of an LPR; the classification V-3 is for the derivative child of a V-1 or V-2 alien.

(3) General requirements.

(i) Every nonimmigrant alien who applies for admission to, or an extension of stay in, the United States, must establish that he or she is admissible to the United States, or that any ground of inadmissibility has been waived under section 212(d)(3) of the Act. Upon application for admission, the alien must present a valid passport and valid visa unless either or both documents have been waived. A nonimmigrant alien's admission to the United States is conditioned on compliance with any inspection requirement in § 235.1(d) or of this chapter, as well as compliance with part 215, subpart B, of this chapter, if applicable. The passport of an alien applying for admission must be valid for a minimum of six months from the expiration date of the contemplated period of stay, unless otherwise provided in this chapter, and the alien must agree to abide by the terms and conditions of his or her admission. An alien applying for extension of stay must present a passport only if requested to do so by the Department of Homeland Security. The passport of an alien applying for extension of stay must be valid at the time of application for extension, unless otherwise provided in this chapter, and the alien must agree to maintain the validity of his or her passport and to abide by all the terms and conditions of his extension.

(ii) At the time of admission or extension of stay, every nonimmigrant alien must also agree to depart the United States at the expiration of his or her authorized period of admission or extension of stay, or upon abandonment of his or her authorized nonimmigrant status, and to comply with the departure procedures at section 215.8 of this chapter if such procedures apply to the particular alien. The nonimmigrant alien's failure to comply with those departure requirements, including any requirement that the alien provide biometric identifiers, may constitute a failure of the alien to maintain the terms of his or her nonimmigrant status.

(iii) At the time a nonimmigrant alien applies for admission or extension of stay, he or she must post a bond on Form I-352 in the sum of not less than $ 500, to ensure the maintenance of his or her nonimmigrant status and departure from the United States, if required to do so by the Commissioner of CBP, the Director of U.S. Citizenship and Immigration Services, an immigration judge, or the Board of Immigration Appeals.

(b) Readmission of nonimmigrants under section 101(a)(15) (F), (J), (M), or (Q)(ii) to complete unexpired periods of previous admission or extension of stay —

(1) Section 101(a)(15)(F). The inspecting immigration officer shall readmit for duration of status as defined in § 214.2(f)(5)(i), any nonimmigrant alien whose nonimmigrant visa is considered automatically revalidated pursuant to 22 CFR 41.112(d) and who is applying for readmission under section 101(a)(15)(F) of the Act, if the alien:

(i) Is admissible;

(ii) Is applying for readmission after an absence from the United States not exceeding thirty days solely in contiguous territory or adjacent islands;

(iii) Is in possession of a valid passport unless exempt from the requirement for presentation of a passport; and

(iv) Presents, or is the accompanying spouse or child of an alien who presents, an Arrival-Departure Record, Form I-94 (see § 1.4 of this chapter), issued to the alien in connection with the previous admission or stay and either:

(A) A properly endorsed Form I-20 or successor form if there has been no substantive change in the information on the student's most recent Form I-20 or successor form since the form was initially issued; or

(B) A new Form I-20 or successor form if there has been any substantive change in the information on the student's most recent Form I-20 or successor form since the form was initially issued.

(2) Section 101(a)(15)(J). The inspecting immigration officer shall readmit for the unexpired period of stay authorized prior to the alien's departure, any nonimmigrant alien whose nonimmigrant visa is considered automatically revalidated pursuant to 22 CFR 41.112(d) and who is applying for readmission under section 101(a)(15)(J) of the Act, if the alien:

(i) Is admissible;

(ii) Is applying for readmission after an absence from the United States not exceeding thirty days solely in contiguous territory or adjacent islands;

(iii) Is in possession of a valid passport unless exempt from the requirement for the presentation of a passport; and

(iv) Presents, or is the accompanying spouse or child of an alien who presents, Form I-94 issued to the alien in connection with the previous admission or stay or the last Form IAP-66 issued to the alien. Form I-94 or Form DS-2019 must show the unexpired period of the alien's stay properly endorsed.

(3) Section 101(a)(15)(M). The inspecting immigration officer shall readmit for the unexpired period of stay authorized prior to the alien's departure, any nonimmigrant alien whose nonimmigrant visa is considered automatically revalidated pursuant to 22 CFR 41.112(d) and who is applying for readmission under section 101(a)(15)(M) of the Act, if the alien:

(i) Is admissible;

(ii) Is applying for readmission after an absence not exceeding thirty days solely in contiguous territory;

(iii) Is in possession of a valid passport unless exempt from the requirement for presentation of a passport; and

(iv) Presents, or is the accompanying spouse or child of an alien who presents, Form I–94 issued to the alien in connection with the previous admission or stay, and the alien's properly endorsed Form I-20 or successor form.

(4) Section 101(a)(15)(Q)(ii). The inspecting immigration officer shall readmit for the unexpired period of stay authorized prior to the alien's departure, if the alien:

(i) Is admissible;

(ii) Is applying for readmission after an absence from the United States not exceeding 30 days solely in contiguous territory or adjacent islands;

(iii) Is in possession of a valid passport;

(iv) Presents, or is the accompanying spouse or child of an alien who presents, an Arrival-Departure Record, Form I-94, issued to the alien in connection with the previous admission or stay. The principal alien must also present a Certification Letter issued by the Department of State's Program Administrator.

(c) Extensions of stay.

(1) Extension or amendment of stay for certain employment-based nonimmigrant workers. An applicant or petitioner seeking the services of an E– 1, E–2, E–3, H–1B, H–1B1, H–2A, H–2B, H–3, L–1, O–1, O–2, P–1, P–2, P–3, P– 1S, P–2S, P–3S, Q–1, R–1, or TN nonimmigrant beyond the period previously granted, or seek-

ing to amend the terms and conditions of the nonimmigrant's stay without a request for additional time, must file for an extension of stay or amendment of stay, on Form I–129, with the fee prescribed in 8 CFR 106.2, with the initial evidence specified in § 214.2, and in accordance with the form instructions. Dependents holding derivative status may be included in the petition if it is for only one worker and the form version specifically provides for their inclusion. In all other cases, dependents of the worker should file extensions of stay using Form I–539.

(2) Filing on Form I-539. Any other nonimmigrant alien, except an alien in F or J status who has been granted duration of status, who seeks to extend his or her stay beyond the currently authorized period of admission, must apply for an extension of stay on Form I-539 with the fee required in 8 CFR 106.2 together with any initial evidence specified in the applicable provisions of § 214.2, and on the application form. More than one person may be included in an application where the co-applicants are all members of a single family group and either all hold the same nonimmigrant status or one holds a nonimmigrant status and the other co-applicants are his or her spouse and/or children who hold derivative nonimmigrant status based on his or her status. Extensions granted to members of a family group must be for the same period of time. The shortest period granted to any member of the family shall be granted to all members of the family. In order to be eligible for an extension of stay, nonimmigrant aliens in K-3/K-4 status must do so in accordance with § 214.2(k)(10).

(3) Ineligible for extension of stay. A nonimmigrant in any of the following classes is ineligible for an extension of stay:

(i) B-1 or B-2 where admission was pursuant to the Visa Waiver Pilot Program;

(ii) C-1, C-2, C-3;

(iii) D-1, D-2;

(iv) K-1, K-2;

(v) Any nonimmigrant admitted for duration of status, other than as provided in § 214.2(f)(7);

(vi) Any nonimmigrant who is classified pursuant to section 101(a)(15)(S) of the Act beyond a total of 3 years; or

(vii) Any nonimmigrant who is classified according to section 101(a)(15)(Q)(ii) of the Act beyond a total of 3 years.

(viii) Any nonimmigrant admitted pursuant to the Guam-CNMI Visa Waiver Program, or its sub-program, the CNMI Economic Vitality & Security Travel Authorization Program (EVS-TAP), as provided in section 212(*l*) of the Act.

(4) Timely filing and maintenance of status.

(i) An extension or amendment of stay may not be approved for an applicant or beneficiary who failed to maintain the previously accorded status or where such status expired before the application or petition was filed, except that USCIS may excuse the late filing in its discretion where it is demonstrated at the time of filing that:

(A) The delay was due to extraordinary circumstances beyond the control of the applicant or petitioner, and USCIS finds the delay commensurate with the circumstances;

(B) The applicant or beneficiary has not otherwise violated their nonimmigrant status;

(C) The applicant or beneficiary remains a bona fide nonimmigrant; and

(D) The applicant or beneficiary is not the subject of deportation proceedings under section 242 of the Act (prior to April 1, 1997) or removal proceedings under section 240 of the Act.

(ii) If USCIS excuses the late filing of an extension of stay or amendment of stay request, it will do so without requiring the filing of a separate application or petition and will grant the extension of stay from the date the previously authorized stay expired, or the amendment of stay from the date the petition was filed.

(5) Deference to prior USCIS determinations of eligibility. When adjudicating a request filed on Form I–129 involving the same parties and the same underlying facts, USCIS gives deference to its prior determination of the petitioner's, applicant's, or beneficiary's eligibility. However, USCIS need not give deference to a prior approval if: there was a material error involved with a prior approval; there has been a material change in circumstances or eligibility requirements; or there is new, material information that adversely impacts the petitioner's, applicant's, or beneficiary's eligibility.

(6) Evidence of maintenance of status. When requesting an extension or amendment of stay on Form I–129, an applicant or petitioner must submit supporting evidence to establish that the applicant or beneficiary maintained the previously accorded nonimmigrant status before the extension or amendment request was filed. Evidence of such maintenance of status may include, but is not limited to: copies of paystubs, W–2 forms, quarterly wage reports, tax returns, contracts, and work orders.

(7) Decision on extension or amendment of stay request. Where an applicant or petitioner demonstrates eligibility for a requested extension or amendment of stay, USCIS may grant the extension or amendment in its discretion. The denial of an extension or amendment of stay request may not be appealed.

(d) Termination of status. Within the period of initial admission or extension of stay, the nonimmigrant status of an alien shall be terminated by the revocation of a waiver authorized on his or her behalf under section 212(d) (3) or (4) of the Act; by the introduction of a private bill to confer permanent resident status on such alien; or, pursuant to notification in the FEDERAL REGISTER, on the basis of national security, diplomatic, or public safety reasons.

(e) Employment. A nonimmigrant in the United States in a class defined in section 101(a)(15)(B) of the Act as a temporary visitor for pleasure, or section 101(a)(15)(C) of the Act as an alien in transit through this country, may not engage in any employment. Any other nonimmigrant in the United States may not engage in any employment unless he has been accorded a nonimmigrant classification which authorizes employment or he has been granted permission to engage in employment in accordance with the provisions of this chapter. A nonimmigrant who is permitted to engage in employment may engage only in such employment as has been authorized. Any unauthorized employment by a nonimmigrant constitutes a failure to maintain status within the meaning of section 241(a)(1)(C)(i) of the Act.

(f) False information. A condition of a nonimmigrant's admission and continued stay in the United States is the full and truthful disclosure of all information requested by DHS. A nonimmigrant's willful failure to provide full and truthful information requested by DHS (regardless of whether or not the information requested was material) constitutes a failure to maintain nonimmigrant status under section 237(a)(1)(C)(i) of the Act.

(g) Criminal activity. A condition of a nonimmigrant's admission and continued stay in the United States is obedience to all laws of United States jurisdictions which prohibit the commission of crimes of violence and for which a sentence of more than one year imprisonment may be imposed. A nonimmigrant's conviction in a jurisdiction in the United States for a crime of violence for which a sentence of more than one year imprisonment may be imposed (regardless of whether such sentence is in fact imposed) constitutes a failure to maintain status under section 241(a)(1)(C)(i) of the Act.

(h) Education privacy and F, J, and M nonimmigrants. As authorized by section 641(c)(2) of Division C of Pub. L. 104-208, 8 U.S.C. 1372, and § 2.1 of this chapter, DHS has determined that, with respect to F and M nonimmigrant students and J nonimmigrant exchange visitors, waiving the provisions of the Family Educational Rights and Privacy Act (FERPA), 20 U.S.C. 1232g, is necessary for the proper implementation of 8 U.S.C. 1372. An educational agency or institution may not refuse to report information concerning an F or M nonimmigrant student or a J nonimmigrant exchange visitor that the educational agency or institution is required to report under 8 U.S.C. 1372 and § 214.3(g) (or any corresponding Department of State regulation concerning J nonimmigrants) on the basis of FERPA and any regulation implementing FERPA. The waiver of FERPA under this paragraph authorizes and requires an educational agency or institution to report information concerning an F, J or M nonimmigrant that would ordinarily be protected by FERPA, but only to the extent that 8 U.S.C. 1372 and § 214.3(g) (or any corresponding Department of State regulation concerning J nonimmigrants) requires the educational agency or institution to report information.

(i) Employment in a health care occupation.

(1) Except as provided in 8 CFR 212.15(n), any alien described in 8 CFR 212.15(a) who is coming to the United States to perform labor in a health care occupation described in 8 CFR 212.15(c) must obtain a certificate from a credentialing organization described in 8 CFR 212.15(e). The certificate or certified statement must be presented to the Department of Homeland Security in accordance with 8 CFR 212.15(d). In the alternative, an eligible alien seeking admission as a nurse may obtain a certified statement as provided in 8 CFR 212.15(h).

(2) A TN nonimmigrant may establish that he or she is eligible for a waiver described at 8 CFR 212.15(n) by providing evidence that his or her initial admission as a TN (or TC) nonimmigrant health care worker occurred before September 23, 2003, and he or she was licensed and employed in the United States as a health care worker before September 23, 2003. Evidence may include, but is not limited to, copies of TN or TC approval notices, copies of Form I-94 Arrival/Departure Records, employment verification letters and/or pay-stubs or other employment records, and state health care worker licenses.

(j) Extension of stay or change of status for health care worker. In the case of any alien admitted temporarily as a nonimmigrant under section 212(d)(3) of the Act and 8 CFR 212.15(n) for the primary purpose of the providing labor in a health care occupation described in 8 CFR 212.15(c), the petitioning employer may file an application or petition to extend the approval period for the alien's classification for the nonimmigrant status. If the alien is in the United States and is eligible for an extension of stay or change of status, the application or petition also serves as an application to extend the period of the alien's authorized stay or to change the alien's status. Although the application or petition may be approved, as it relates to the employer's request to classify the alien, the application for an extension of stay or change of status shall be denied if:

(1) The petitioner or applicant fails to submit the certification required by 8 CFR 212.15(a) with the petition or application to extend the alien's stay or change the alien's status; or

(2) The petition or application to extend the alien's stay or change the alien's status does include the certification required by 8 CFR 212.15(a), but the alien obtained the certification more than 1 year after the date of the alien's admission under section 212(d)(3) of the Act and 8 CFR 212.15(n). While DHS may admit, extend the period of authorized stay, or change the status of a nonimmigrant health care worker for a period of 1 year if the alien does not have certification on or before July 26, 2004 (or on or before July 26, 2005, in the case of a citizen of Canada or Mexico, who, before September 23, 2003, was employed as a TN or TC nonimmigrant health care worker and held a valid license from a U.S. jurisdiction), the alien will not be eligible for a subsequent admission, change of status, or extension of stay as a health care worker if the alien has not obtained the requisite certification 1 year after the initial date of admission, change of status, or extension of stay as a health care worker.

(k) Denial of petitions under section 214(c) of the Act based on a finding by the Department of Labor. Upon debarment by the Department of Labor pursuant to 20 CFR part 655, USCIS may deny any petition filed by that petitioner for nonimmigrant status under section 101(a)(15)(H) (except for status under sections 101(a)(15)(H)(i)(b1)), (L), (O), and (P)(i) of the Act) for a period of at least 1 year but not more than 5 years. The length of the period shall be based on the severity of the violation or violations. The decision to deny petitions, the time period for the bar to petitions, and the reasons for the time period will be explained in a written notice to the petitioner.

(*l*) Period of stay.

(1) An alien admissible in E-1, E-2, E-3, H-1B, L-1, or TN classification and his or her dependents may be admitted to the United States or otherwise provided such status for the validity period of the petition, or for a validity period otherwise authorized for the E-1, E-2, E-3, and TN classifications, plus an additional period of up to 10 days before the validity period begins and 10 days after the validity period ends. Unless authorized under 8 CFR 274a.12, the alien may not work except during the validity period.

(2) An alien admitted or otherwise provided status in E-1, E-2, E-3, H-1B, H-1B1, L-1, O-1 or TN classification and his or her dependents shall not be considered to have failed to maintain nonimmigrant status solely on the basis of a cessation of the employment on which the alien's classification was based, for up to 60 consecutive days or until the end of the authorized validity period, whichever is shorter, once during each authorized validity period. DHS may eliminate or shorten this 60-day period as a matter of discretion. Unless otherwise authorized under 8 CFR 274a.12, the alien may not work during such a period.

(3) An alien in any authorized period described in paragraph (l) of this section may apply for and be granted an extension of stay under paragraph (c)(4) of this section or change of status under 8 CFR 248.1, if otherwise eligible.

HISTORY:

[26 FR 12067, Dec. 16, 1961, as amended at 36 FR 8048, Apr. 29, 1971; 37 FR 14288, June 19, 1972; 43 FR 12674, Mar. 27, 1978; 44 FR 65727, Nov. 14, 1979; 48 FR 14582, Apr. 5, 1983; 48 FR 20685, May 9, 1983; 48 FR 30350, July 1, 1983; 52 FR 45446, Nov. 30, 1987; 56 FR 38333, Aug. 13, 1991, as confirmed at 59 FR 26594, May 23, 1994; 59 FR 1463, Jan. 11, 1994; 60 FR 44260, 44266, Aug. 25, 1995, as corrected at 60 FR 52248, Oct. 5, 1995; 62 FR 10312, 10349, Mar. 6, 1997; 65 FR 14774, 14777, Mar. 17, 2000; 65 FR 43528, 43531, July 13, 2000, withdrawn at 67 FR 61474, Oct. 1, 2002; 65 FR 67616, 67617, Nov. 13, 2000; 66 FR 31107, 31112, June 11, 2001; 66 FR 42587, 42593, Aug. 14, 2001; 66 FR 46697, 46702, Sept. 7, 2001; 66 FR 49514, Sept. 28, 2001; 67 FR 4784, 4795, Jan. 31, 2002; 67 FR 52584, 52591, Aug. 12, 2002; 67 FR 76256, 76270, Dec. 11, 2002; 68 FR 43901, 43920, July 25, 2003; 69 FR 468, 480, Jan. 5, 2004; 69 FR 43729, 43732, July 22, 2004; 72 FR 53014, 53036, Sept. 17, 2007; 73 FR 61332, 61334, Oct. 16, 2008; 73 FR 78104, 78127, Dec. 19, 2008; 74 FR 2824, 2835, Jan. 16, 2009; 78 FR 18457, 18472, Mar. 27, 2013, as confirmed at 81 FR 91646, 91670, Dec. 19, 2016; 80 FR 24042, 24108, Apr. 29, 2015; 81 FR 2068, 2083, Jan. 15, 2016; 81 FR 72481, 72491, Oct. 20, 2016; 81 FR 82398, 82486, Nov. 18, 2016; 81 FR 92266, 92304, Dec. 19, 2016; 81 FR 94231, 94234, Dec. 23, 2016; 84 FR 41292, 41507, Aug. 14, 2019; 85 FR 46788, 46923, Aug. 3, 2020, as corrected at 53645, August 31, 2020; 86 FR 14221, 14228, Mar. 15, 2021; 87 FR 41027, 41029, July 11, 2022; 87 FR 75891, 75902, Dec. 12, 2022; 88 FR 53761, Aug. 9, 2023; 89 FR 3299, 3330, Jan. 18, 2024; 89 FR 6194, 6397, Jan. 31, 2024; redesignated at 89 FR 34864, 34931, Apr. 30, 2024; 89 FR 103054, 103195, Dec. 18, 2024]

§ 214.2 Special requirements for admission, extension, and maintenance of status. [Effective until November 27, 2026]

Table 1 to § 214.2—Section Contents

The general requirements in § 214.1 are modified for the following nonimmigrant classes:

(a) Foreign government officials —

(1) General. The determination by a consular officer prior to admission and the recognition by the Secretary of State subsequent to admission is evidence of the proper classification of a nonimmigrant under section 101(a)(15)(A) of the Act. An alien who has a nonimmigrant status under section 101(a)(15)(A)(i) or (ii) of the Act is to be admitted for the duration of the period for which the alien continues to be recognized by the Secretary of State as being entitled to that status. An alien defined in section (101)(a)(15)(A)(iii) of the Act is to be admitted for an initial period of not more than three years, and may be granted extensions of temporary stay in increments of not more than two years. In addition, the application for extension of temporary stay must be accompanied by a statement signed by the employing official stating that he/she intends to continue to employ the applicant and describing the type of work the applicant will perform.

(2) Definition of A-1 or A-2 dependent. For purposes of employment in the United States, the term dependent of an A-1 or A-2 principal alien, as used in § 214.2(a), means any of the following immediate members of the family habitually residing in the same

household as the principal alien who is an officer or employee assigned to a diplomatic or consular office in the United States:

(i) Spouse;

(ii) Unmarried children under the age of 21;

(iii) Unmarried sons or daughters under the age of 23 who are in full-time attendance as students at post-secondary educational institutions;

(iv) Unmarried sons or daughters under the age of 25 who are in full-time attendance as students at post-secondary educational institutions if a formal bilateral employment agreement permitting their employment in the United States was signed prior to November 21, 1988, and such bilateral employment agreement does not specify 23 as the maximum age for employment of such sons and daughters. The Office of Protocol of the Department of State shall maintain a listing of foreign states with which the United States has such bilateral employment agreements;

(v) Unmarried sons or daughters who are physically or mentally disabled to the extent that they cannot adequately care for themselves or cannot establish, maintain or re-establish their own households. The Department of State or the Service may require certification(s) as it deems sufficient to document such mental or physical disability; or

(vi) An immediate family member of an A-1 or A-2 principal alien described in 22 CFR 41.21(a)(3)(i) to (iv) with A-1 or A-2 nonimmigrant status, who falls within a category of aliens recognized by the Department of State as qualifying dependents.

(3) Applicability of a formal bilateral agreement or an informal de facto arrangement for A-1 or A-2 dependents. The applicability of a formal bilateral agreement shall be based on the foreign state which employs the principal alien and not on the nationality of the principal alien or dependent. The applicability of an informal de facto arrangement shall be based on the foreign state which employs the principal alien, but under a de facto arrangement the principal alien also must be a national of the foreign state which employs him/her in the United States.

(4) Income tax, Social Security liability; non-applicability of certain immunities. Dependents who are granted employment authorization under this section are responsible for payment of all federal, state and local income, employment and related taxes and Social Security contributions on any remuneration received. In addition, immunity from civil or administrative jurisdiction in accordance with Article 37 of the Vienna Convention on Diplomatic Relations or other international agreements does not apply to these dependents with respect to matters arising out of their employment.

(5) Dependent employment pursuant to formal bilateral employment agreements and informal de facto reciprocal arrangements.

(i) The Office of Protocol shall maintain a listing of foreign states which have entered into formal bilateral employment agreements. Dependents of an A-1 or A-2 principal alien assigned to official duty in the United States may accept or continue in unrestricted employment based on such formal bilateral agreements upon favorable recommendation by the Department of State and issuance of employment authorization documentation by the Service in accordance with 8 CFR part 274a. The application procedures are set forth in paragraph (a)(6) of this section.

(ii) For purposes of this section, an informal de facto reciprocal arrangement exists when the Department of State determines that a foreign state allows appropriate employment on the local economy for dependents of certain United States officials assigned to duty in that foreign state. The Office of Protocol shall maintain a listing of countries with which such reciprocity exists. Dependents of an A-1 or A-2 principal alien assigned to official duty in the United States may be authorized to accept or continue in employment based upon informal de facto arrangements upon favorable recommendation by the Department of State and issuance of employment authorization by the Service in accordance with 8 CFR part 274a. Additionally, the procedures set forth in paragraph (a)(6) of this section must be complied with, and the following conditions must be met:

(A) Both the principal alien and the dependent desiring employment are maintaining A-1 or A-2 status as appropriate;

(B) The principal's assignment in the United States is expected to last more than six months;

(C) Employment of a similar nature for dependents of United States Government officials assigned to official duty in the foreign state employing the principal alien is not prohibited by that foreign state's government;

(D) The proposed employment is not in an occupation listed in the Department of Labor Schedule B (20 CFR part 656), or otherwise determined by the Department of Labor to be one for which there is an oversupply of qualified U.S. workers in the area of proposed employment. This Schedule B restriction does not apply to a dependent son or daughter who is a full-time student if the employment is part-time, consisting of not more than 20 hours per week, and/or if it is temporary employment of not more than 12 weeks during school holiday periods; and

(E) The proposed employment is not contrary to the interest of the United States. Employment contrary to the interest of the United States includes, but is not limited to, the employment of A-1 or A-2 dependents: who have criminal records; who have violated United States immigration laws or regulations, or visa laws or regulations; who have worked illegally in the United States; and/or who cannot establish that they have paid taxes and social security on income from current or previous United States employment.

(6) Application procedures. The following procedures are applicable to dependent employment applications under bilateral agreements and de facto arrangements:

(i) The dependent must submit a completed Form I-566 to the Department of State through the office, mission, or organization which employs his/her principal alien. A dependent applying under paragraph (a)(2)(iii) or (iv) of this section must submit a certified statement from the post-secondary educational institution confirming that he/she is pursuing studies on a full-time basis. A dependent applying under paragraph (a)(2)(v) of this section must submit medical certification regarding his/her condition. The certification should identify the dependent and the certifying physician and give the physician's phone number; identify the condition, describe the symptoms and provide a prognosis; and certify that the dependent is unable to maintain a home of his or her own. Additionally, a dependent applying under the terms of a de facto arrangement must attach a statement from the prospective employer which includes the dependent's name; a description of the position offered and the duties to be performed; the salary offered; and verification that the dependent possesses the qualifications for the position.

(ii) The Department of State reviews and verifies the information provided, makes its determination, and endorses the Form I-566.

(iii) If the Department of State's endorsement is favorable, the dependent may apply to USCIS for employment authorization. When applying to USCIS for employment authorization, the dependent must present his or her Form I-566 with a favorable endorsement from the Department of State and any additional documentation as may be required by the Secretary.

(7) Period of time for which employment may be authorized. If approved, an application to accept or continue employment under this section shall be granted in increments of not more than three years each.

(8) No appeal. There shall be no appeal from a denial of permission to accept or continue employment under this section.

(9) Dependents or family members of principal aliens classified A-3. A dependent or family member of a principal alien classified A-3 may not be employed in the United States under this section.

(10) Unauthorized employment. An alien classified under section 101(a)(15)(A) of the Act who is not a principal alien and who engages in employment outside the scope of, or in a manner contrary to this section, may be considered in violation of section 241(a)(1)(C)(i) of the Act. An alien who is classified under section 101(a)(15)(A) of the Act who is a principal alien and who engages in employment outside the scope of his/her official position may be considered in violation of section 241(a)(1)(C)(i) of the Act.

(b) Visitors —

(1) General. any B-1 visitor for business or B-2 visitor for pleasure may be admitted for not more than one year and may be granted extensions of temporary stay in increments of not more than six months each, except that alien members of a religious denomination coming temporarily and solely to do missionary work in behalf of a religious denomination may be granted extensions of not more than one year each, provided that such work does not involve the selling of articles or the solicitation or acceptance of donations. Those B-1 and B-2 visitors admitted pursuant to the waiver provided at § 212.1(e) of this chapter may be admitted to and stay on Guam for period not to exceed fifteen days and are not eligible for extensions of stay.

(2) Minimum six month admissions. Any B-2 visitor who is found otherwise admissible and is issued a Form I-94 (see § 1.4), will be admitted for a minimum period of six months, regardless of whether less time is requested, provided, that any required passport is valid as specified in section 212(a)(26) of the Act. Exceptions to the minimum six month admission may be made only in individual cases upon the specific approval of the district director for good cause.

(3) Visa Waiver Pilot Program. Special requirements for admission and maintenance of status for visitors admitted to the United States under the Visa Waiver Pilot Program are set forth in section 217 of the Act and part 217 of this chapter.

(4) Admission of aliens pursuant to the Agreement Between the United States of America, the United Mexican States, and Canada (USMCA). A citizen of Canada or Mexico seeking temporary entry for purposes set forth in paragraph (b)(4)(i) of this section, who otherwise meets the requirements under section 101(a)(15)(B) of the Act, including but not limited to requirements regarding the source of remuneration, shall be admitted upon presentation of proof of such citizenship in the case of Canadian applicants, and valid, unexpired entry documents such as a passport and visa, or a passport and BCC in the case of Mexican applicants, a description of the purpose for which the alien is seeking admission, and evidence demonstrating that he or she is engaged in one of the occupations or professions set forth in paragraph (b)(4)(i) of this section.

(i) Occupations and professions set forth in Section B of Appendix 1 of Chapter 16 of the USMCA —

(A) Research and design. Technical, scientific and statistical researchers conducting independent research or research for an enterprise located in the territory of another Party.

(B) Growth, manufacture, and production.

(1) Harvester owner supervising a harvesting crew admitted under applicable law. (Applies only to harvesting of agricultural crops: Grain, fiber, fruit and vegetables.)

(2) Purchasing and production management personnel conducting commercial transactions for an enterprise located in the territory of another Party.

(C) Marketing.

(1) Market researchers and analysts conducting independent research or analysis, or research or analysis for an enterprise located in the territory of another Party.

(2) Trade fair and promotional personnel attending a trade convention.

(D) Sales.

(1) Sales representatives and agents taking orders or negotiating contracts for goods or services for an enterprise located in the territory of another Party but not delivering goods or supplying services.

(2) Buyers purchasing for an enterprise located in the territory of another Party.

(E) Distribution.

(1) Transportation operators transporting goods or passengers to the United States from the territory of another Party or loading and transporting goods or passengers from the United States, with no unloading in the United States, to the territory of another Party. (These operators may make deliveries in the United States if all goods or passengers to be delivered were loaded in the territory of another Party. Furthermore, they may load from locations in the United States if all goods or passengers to be loaded will be delivered in the territory of another Party. Purely domestic service or solicitation, in competition with the United States operators, is not permitted.)

(2) Customs brokers performing brokerage duties associated with the export of goods from the United States to or through Canada.

(F) After-sales services. Installers, repair and maintenance personnel, and supervisors, possessing specialized knowledge essential to the seller's contractual obligation, performing services or training workers to perform services, pursuant to a warranty or other service contract incidental to the sale of commercial or industrial equipment or machinery, including computer software, purchased from an enterprise located outside the United States, during the life of the warranty or service agreement. (For the purposes of this provision, the commercial or industrial equipment or machinery, including computer software, must have been manufactured outside the United States.)

(G) General service. Professionals engaging in a business activity at a professional level in a profession set out in Appendix 2 to Annex 16-A of Chapter 16 of the USMCA, but receiving no salary or other remuneration from a United States source (other than an expense allowance or other reimbursement for expenses incidental to the temporary stay) and otherwise satisfying the requirements of Section A to Annex 16-A of the USMCA.

(H) Commercial transactions.

(1) Management and supervisory personnel engaging in commercial transactions for an enterprise located in the territory of another Party.

(2) Financial services personnel (insurers, bankers or investment brokers) engaging in commercial transactions for an enterprise located in the territory of another Party.

(I) Public relations and advertising. Public relations and advertising personnel consulting with business associates, or attending or participating in conventions.

(J) Tourism. Tourism personnel (tour and travel agents, tour guides or tour operators) attending or participating in conventions or conducting a tour that has begun in the territory of another Party. (The tour may begin in the United States; but must terminate in foreign territory, and a significant portion of the tour must be conducted in foreign territory. In such a case, an operator may enter the United States with an empty conveyance and a tour guide may enter on his or her own and join the conveyance.)

(K) Tour bus operation. Tour bus operators entering the United States:

(1) With a group of passengers on a bus tour that has begun in, and will return to, the territory of another Party.

(2) To meet a group of passengers on a bus tour that will end, and the predominant portion of which will take place, in the territory of another Party.

(3) With a group of passengers on a bus tour to be unloaded in the United States and returning with no passengers or reloading with the group for transportation to the territory of another Party.

(L) Translation. Translators or interpreters performing services as employees of an enterprise located in the territory of another Party.

(ii) Occupations and professions not listed in Section B of Appendix 1 of Chapter 16 of the USMCA. Nothing in paragraph (b)(4) of this section shall preclude a business person engaged in an occupation or profession other than those listed in Section B of Appendix 1 of Chapter 16 of the USMCA from temporary entry under section 101(a)(15)(B) of the Act, if such person otherwise meets the requirements for admission as prescribed by the Attorney General.

(5) Construction workers not admissible. Aliens seeking to enter the country to perform building or construction work, whether on-site or in-plant, are not eligible for classification or admission as B-1 nonimmigrants under section 101(a)(15)(B) of the Act. However, alien nonimmigrants otherwise qualified as B-1 nonimmigrants may be issued visas and may enter for the purpose of supervision or training of others engaged in building or construction work, but not for the purpose of actually performing any such building or construction work themselves.

(6) [Reserved]

(7) Enrollment in a course of study prohibited. An alien who is admitted as, or changes status to, a B-1 or B-2 nonimmigrant on or after April 12, 2002, or who files a request to extend the period of authorized stay in B-1 or B-2 nonimmigrant status on or after such date, violates the conditions of his or her B-1 or B-2 status if the alien enrolls in a course of study. Such an alien who desires to enroll in a course of study must either obtain an F-1 or M-1 nonimmigrant visa from a consular officer abroad and seek readmission to the United States, or apply for and obtain a change of status under section 248 of the Act and 8 CFR part 248. The alien may not enroll in the course of study until the Service has admitted the alien as an F-1 or M-1 nonimmigrant or has approved the alien's application under part 248 of this chapter and changed the alien's status to that of an F-1 or M-1 nonimmigrant.

(c) Transits.

(1) [Reserved]

(2) United Nations Headquarters District. An alien of the class defined in section 101(a)(15)(C) of the Act, whose visa is limited to transit to and from the United Nations Headquarters District, if otherwise admissible, shall be admitted on the additional conditions that he proceed directly to the immediate vicinity of the United Nations Headquarters District, and remain there continuously, departing therefrom only if required in connection with his departure from the United States, and

that he have a document establishing his ability to enter some country other than the United States following his sojourn in the United Nations Headquarters District. The immediate vicinity of the United Nations Headquarters District is that area lying within a twenty-five mile radius of Columbus Circle, New York, NY.

(3) Others. The period of admission of an alien admitted under section 101(a)(15)(C) of the Act shall not exceed 29 days.

(d) Crewmen.

(1) The provisions of parts 251, 252, 253, and 258 of this chapter shall govern the landing of crewmen as nonimmigrants of the class defined in section 101(a)(15)(D) of the Act. An alien in this status may be employed only in a crewman capacity on the vessel or aircraft of arrival, or on a vessel or aircraft of the same transportation company, and may not be employed in connection with domestic flights or movements of a vessel or aircraft. However, nonimmigrant crewmen may perform crewmember duties through stopovers on an international flight for any United States carrier where such flight uses a single aircraft and has an origination or destination point outside the United States.

(2) Denial of crewman status in the case of certain labor disputes (D nonimmigrants)

(i) An alien shall be denied D crewman status as described in section 101(a)(15)(D) of the Act if:

(A) The alien intends to land for the purpose of performing service on a vessel of the United States (as defined in 46 U.S.C. 2101(46)) or an aircraft of an air carrier (as defined in section 101(3) of the Federal Aviation Act of 1958); and

(B) A labor dispute consisting of a strike or lockout exists in the bargaining unit of the employer in which the alien intends to perform such service; and

(C) The alien is not already an employee of the company (as described in paragraph (d)(2)(iv) of this section).

(ii) Refusal to land. Any alien (except a qualified current employee as described in paragraph (d)(2)(iv) of this section) who the examining immigration officer determines has arrived in the United States for the purpose of performing service on board a vessel or an aircraft of the United States when a strike or lockout is under way in the bargaining unit of the employer, shall be refused a conditional landing permit under section 252 of the Act.

(iii) Ineligibility for parole. An alien described in paragraph (d)(2)(i) of this section may not be paroled into the United States under section 212(d)(5) of the Act for the purpose of performing crewmember duties unless the Attorney General determines that the parole of such alien is necessary to protect the national security of the United States. This paragraph does not prohibit the granting of parole for other purposes, such as medical emergencies.

(iv) Qualified current employees.

(A) Paragraphs (d)(2)(i), (d)(2)(ii), and (d)(2)(iii) of this section do not apply to an alien who is already an employee of the owner or operator of the vessel or air carrier and who at the time of inspection presents true copies of employer work records which satisfy the examining immigration officer that the alien:

(1) Has been an employee of such employer for a period of not less than one year preceding the date that a strike or lawful lockout commenced;

(2) Has served as a qualified crewman for such employer at least once in three different months during the 12-month period preceding the date that the strike or lockout commenced; and

(3) Shall continue to provide the same crewman services that he or she previously provided to the employer.

(B) An alien crewman who qualifies as a current employee under this paragraph remains subject to the restrictions on his or her employment in the United States contained in paragraph (d)(1) of this section.

(v) Strike or lockout determination. These provisions will take effect if the Attorney General, through the Commissioner of the Immigration and Naturalization Service or his or her designee, after consultation with the National Mediation Board, determines that a strike, lockout, or labor dispute involving a work stoppage is in progress in the bargaining unit of the employer for whom the alien intends to perform such service.

(e) Treaty traders and investors —

(1) Treaty trader. An alien, if otherwise admissible, may be classified as a nonimmigrant treaty trader (E-1) under the provisions of section 101(a)(15)(E)(i) of the Act if the alien:

(i) Will be in the United States solely to carry on trade of a substantial nature, which is international in scope, either on the alien's behalf or as an employee of a foreign person or organization engaged in trade principally between the United States and the treaty country of which the alien is a national, taking into consideration any conditions in the country of which the alien is a national which may affect the alien's ability to carry on such substantial trade; and

(ii) Intends to depart the United States upon the expiration or termination of treaty trader (E-1) status.

(2) Treaty investor. An alien, if otherwise admissible, may be classified as a nonimmigrant treaty investor (E-2) under the provision of section 101(a)(15)(E)(ii) of the Act if the alien:

(i) Has invested or is actively in the process of investing a substantial amount of capital in a bona fide enterprise in the United States, as distinct from a relatively small amount of capital in a marginal enterprise solely for the purpose of earning a living;

(ii) Is seeking entry solely to develop and direct the enterprise; and

(iii) Intends to depart the United States upon the expiration or termination of treaty investor (E-2) status.

(3) Employee of treaty trader or treaty investor. An alien employee of a treaty trader, if otherwise admissible, may be classified as E-1, and an alien employee of a treaty investor, if otherwise admissible, may be classified as E-2 if the employee is in or is coming to the United States to engage in duties of an executive or

supervisory character, or, if employed in a lesser capacity, the employee has special qualifications that make the alien's services essential to the efficient operation of the enterprise. The employee must have the same nationality as the principal alien employer. In addition, the employee must intend to depart the United States upon the expiration or termination of E-1 or E-2 status. The principal alien employer must be:

(i) A person in the United States having the nationality of the treaty country and maintaining nonimmigrant treaty trader or treaty investor status or, if not in the United States, would be classifiable as a treaty trader or treaty investor; or

(ii) An enterprise or organization at least 50 percent owned by persons in the United States having the nationality of the treaty country and maintaining nonimmigrant treaty trader or treaty investor status or who, if not in the United States, would be classifiable as treaty traders or treaty investors.

(4) Spouse and children of treaty trader or treaty investor. The spouse and child of a treaty trader or treaty investor accompanying or following to join the principal alien, if otherwise admissible, may receive the same classification as the principal alien. The nationality of a spouse or child of a treaty trader or treaty investor is not material to the classification of the spouse or child under the provisions of section 101(a)(15)(E) of the Act.

(5) Nonimmigrant intent. An alien classified under section 101(a)(15)(E) of the Act shall maintain an intention to depart the United States upon the expiration or termination of E-1 or E-2 status. However, an application for initial admission, change of status, or extension of stay in E classification may not be denied solely on the basis of an approved request for permanent labor certification or a filed or approved immigrant visa preference petition.

(6) Treaty country. A treaty country is, for purposes of this section, a foreign state with which a qualifying Treaty of Friendship, Commerce, or Navigation or its equivalent exists with the United States. A treaty country includes a foreign state that is accorded treaty visa privileges under section 101(a)(15)(E) of the Act by specific legislation.

(7) Treaty country nationality. The nationality of an individual treaty trader or treaty investor is determined by the authorities of the foreign state of which the alien is a national. In the case of an enterprise or organization, ownership must be traced as best as is practicable to the individuals who are ultimately its owners.

(8) Terms and conditions of E treaty status —

(i) Limitations on employment. The Service determines the terms and conditions of E treaty status at the time of admission or approval of a request to change nonimmigrant status to E classification. A treaty trader, treaty investor, or treaty employee may engage only in employment which is consistent with the terms and conditions of his or her status and the activity forming the basis for the E treaty status.

(ii) Subsidiary employment. Treaty employees may perform work for the parent treaty organization or enterprise, or any subsidiary of the parent organization or enterprise. Performing work for subsidiaries of a common parent enterprise or organization will not be deemed to constitute a substantive change in the terms and conditions of the underlying E treaty employment if, at the time the E treaty status was determined, the applicant presented evidence establishing:

(A) The enterprise or organization, and any subsidiaries thereof, where the work will be performed; the requisite parent-subsidiary relationship; and that the subsidiary independently qualifies as a treaty organization or enterprise under this paragraph;

(B) In the case of an employee of a treaty trader or treaty investor, the work to be performed requires executive, supervisory, or essential skills; and

(C) The work is consistent with the terms and conditions of the activity forming the basis of the classification.

(iii) Substantive changes. Approval of USCIS must be obtained where there will be a substantive change in the terms or conditions of E status. The treaty alien must file a new application in accordance with the instructions on the form prescribed by USCIS requesting extension of stay in the United States, plus evidence of continued eligibility for E classification in the new capacity. Or the alien may obtain a visa reflecting the new terms and conditions and subsequently apply for admission at a port-of-entry. USCIS will deem there to have been a substantive change necessitating the filing of a new application where there has been a fundamental change in the employing entity's basic characteristics, such as a merger, acquisition, or sale of the division where the alien is employed.

(iv) Non-substantive changes. Neither prior approval nor a new application is required if there is no substantive, or fundamental, change in the terms or conditions of the alien's employment that would affect the alien's eligibility for E classification. Further, prior approval is not required if corporate changes occur which do not affect the previously approved employment relationship or are otherwise non-substantive. To facilitate admission, the alien may:

(A) Present a letter from the treaty-qualifying company through which the alien attained E classification explaining the nature of the change;

(B) Request a new approval notice reflecting the non-substantive change by filing an application with a description of the change; or

(C) Apply directly to Department of State for a new E visa reflecting the change. An alien who does not elect one of the three options contained in paragraphs (e)(8)(iv)(A) through (C) of this section, is not precluded from demonstrating to the satisfaction of the immigration officer at the port-of-entry in some other manner, his or her admissibility under section 101(a)(15)(E) of the Act.

(v) Advice. To request advice from USCIS as to whether a change is substantive, an alien may file an application with a complete description of the change. In cases involving multiple employees, an alien may request that USCIS determine if a merger or other corporate restructuring requires the filing of separate applications by filing a single application and attaching a list of the related receipt numbers for the employees involved and an explanation of the change or changes.

(vi) Advice. To request advice from USCIS as to whether a change is substantive, an alien may file an application with a complete description of the change. In cases involving multiple employees, an alien may request that USCIS determine if a merger or other corporate restructuring requires the filing of separate applications by filing a single application and attaching a list of the related receipt numbers for the employees involved and an explanation of the change or changes.

(vii) An unauthorized change of employment to a new employer will constitute a failure to maintain status within the meaning of section 237(a)(1)(C)(i) of the Act. In all cases where the treaty employee will be providing services to a subsidiary under this paragraph, the subsidiary is required to comply with the terms of 8 CFR part 274a.

(9) Trade — definitions. For purposes of this paragraph: Items of trade include but are not limited to goods, services, international banking, insurance, monies, transportation, communications, data processing, advertising, accounting, design and engineering, management consulting, tourism, technology and its transfer, and some news-gathering activities. For purposes of this paragraph, goods are tangible commodities or merchandise having extrinsic value. Further, as used in this paragraph, services are legitimate economic activities which provide other than tangible goods.

Trade is the existing international exchange of items of trade for consideration between the United States and the treaty country. Existing trade includes successfully negotiated contracts binding upon the parties which call for the immediate exchange of items of trade. Domestic trade or the development of domestic markets without international exchange does not constitute trade for purposes of section 101(a)(15)(E) of the Act. This exchange must be traceable and identifiable. Title to the trade item must pass from one treaty party to the other.

(10) Substantial trade. Substantial trade is an amount of trade sufficient to ensure a continuous flow of international trade items between the United States and the treaty country. This continuous flow contemplates numerous transactions over time. Treaty trader status may not be established or maintained on the basis of a single transaction, regardless of how protracted or monetarily valuable the transaction. Although the monetary value of the trade item being exchanged is a relevant consideration, greater weight will be given to more numerous exchanges of larger value. There is no minimum requirement with respect to the monetary value or volume of each individual transaction. In the case of smaller businesses, an income derived from the value of numerous transactions which is sufficient to support the treaty trader and his or her family constitutes a favorable factor in assessing the existence of substantial trade.

(11) Principal trade. Principal trade between the United States and the treaty country exists when over 50 percent of the volume of international trade of the treaty trader is conducted between the United States and the treaty country of the treaty trader's nationality.

(12) Investment. An investment is the treaty investor's placing of capital, including funds and other assets (which have not been obtained, directly or indirectly, through criminal activity), at risk in the commercial sense with the objective of generating a profit. The treaty investor must be in possession of and have control over the capital invested or being invested. The capital must be subject to partial or total loss if investment fortunes reverse. Such investment capital must be the investor's unsecured personal business capital or capital secured by personal assets. Capital in the process of being invested or that has been invested must be irrevocably committed to the enterprise. The alien has the burden of establishing such irrevocable commitment. The alien may use any legal mechanism available, such as the placement of invested funds in escrow pending admission in, or approval of, E classification, that would not only irrevocably commit funds to the enterprise, but might also extend personal liability protection to the treaty investor in the event the application for E classification is denied.

(13) Bona fide enterprise. The enterprise must be a real, active, and operating commercial or entrepreneurial undertaking which produces services or goods for profit. The enterprise must meet applicable legal requirements for doing business in the particular jurisdiction in the United States.

(14) Substantial amount of capital. A substantial amount of capital constitutes an amount which is:

(i) Substantial in relationship to the total cost of either purchasing an established enterprise or creating the type of enterprise under consideration;

(ii) Sufficient to ensure the treaty investor's financial commitment to the successful operation of the enterprise; and

(iii) Of a magnitude to support the likelihood that the treaty investor will successfully develop and direct the enterprise. Generally, the lower the cost of the enterprise, the higher, proportionately, the investment must be to be considered a substantial amount of capital.

(15) Marginal enterprise. For purposes of this section, an enterprise may not be marginal. A marginal enterprise is an enterprise that does not have the present or future capacity to generate more than enough income to provide a minimal living for the treaty investor and his or her family. An enterprise that does not have the capacity to generate such income, but that has a present or future capacity to make a significant economic contribution is not a marginal enterprise. The projected future income-generating capacity should generally be realizable within 5 years from the date the alien commences the normal business activity of the enterprise.

(16) Solely to develop and direct. An alien seeking classification as a treaty investor (or, in the case of an employee of a treaty investor, the owner of the treaty enterprise) must demonstrate that he or she does or will develop and direct the investment enterprise. Such an applicant must establish that he or she controls the

enterprise by demonstrating ownership of at least 50 percent of the enterprise, by possessing operational control through a managerial position or other corporate device, or by other means.

(17) Executive and supervisory character. The applicant's position must be principally and primarily, as opposed to incidentally or collaterally, executive or supervisory in nature. Executive and supervisory duties are those which provide the employee ultimate control and responsibility for the enterprise's overall operation or a major component thereof. In determining whether the applicant has established possession of the requisite control and responsibility, a Service officer shall consider, where applicable:

(i) That an executive position is one which provides the employee with great authority to determine the policy of, and the direction for, the enterprise;

(ii) That a position primarily of supervisory character provides the employee supervisory responsibility for a significant proportion of an enterprise's operations and does not generally involve the direct supervision of low-level employees, and;

(iii) Whether the applicant possesses executive and supervisory skills and experience; a salary and position title commensurate with executive or supervisory employment; recognition or indicia of the position as one of authority and responsibility in the overall organizational structure; responsibility for making discretionary decisions, setting policies, directing and managing business operations, supervising other professional and supervisory personnel; and that, if the position requires some routine work usually performed by a staff employee, such functions may only be of an incidental nature.

(18) Special qualifications. Special qualifications are those skills and/or aptitudes that an employee in a lesser capacity brings to a position or role that are essential to the successful or efficient operation of the treaty enterprise. In determining whether the skills possessed by the alien are essential to the operation of the employing treaty enterprise, a Service officer must consider, where applicable:

(i) The degree of proven expertise of the alien in the area of operations involved; whether others possess the applicant's specific skill or aptitude; the length of the applicant's experience and/or training with the treaty enterprise; the period of training or other experience necessary to perform effectively the projected duties; the relationship of the skill or knowledge to the enterprise's specific processes or applications, and the salary the special qualifications can command; that knowledge of a foreign language and culture does not, by itself, meet the special qualifications requirement, and;

(ii) Whether the skills and qualifications are readily available in the United States. In all cases, in determining whether the applicant possesses special qualifications which are essential to the treaty enterprise, a Service officer must take into account all the particular facts presented. A skill that is essential at one point in time may become commonplace at a later date. Skills that are needed to start up an enterprise may no longer be essential after initial operations are complete and running smoothly. Some skills are essential only in the short-term for the training of locally hired employees. Under certain circumstances, an applicant may be able to establish his or her essentiality to the treaty enterprise for a longer period of time, such as, in connection with activities in the areas of product improvement, quality control, or the provision of a service not yet generally available in the United States. Where the treaty enterprise's need for the applicant's special qualifications, and therefore, the applicant's essentiality, is time-limited, Service officers may request that the applicant provide evidence of the period for which skills will be needed and a reasonable projected date for completion of start-up or replacement of the essential skilled workers.

(19) Period of admission. Periods of admission are as follows:

(i) A treaty trader or treaty investor may be admitted for an initial period of not more than 2 years.

(ii) The spouse and minor children accompanying or following to join a treaty trader or treaty investor shall be admitted for the period during which the principal alien is in valid treaty trader or investor status. The temporary departure from the United States of the principal trader or investor shall not affect the derivative status of the dependent spouse and minor unmarried children, provided the familial relationship continues to exist and the principal remains eligible for admission as an E nonimmigrant to perform the activity.

(iii) Unless otherwise provided for in this chapter, an alien shall not be admitted in E classification for a period of time extending more than 6 months beyond the expiration date of the alien's passport.

(20) Extensions of stay. Requests for extensions of stay may be granted in increments of not more than 2 years. A treaty trader or treaty investor in valid E status may apply for an extension of stay by filing an application for extension of stay on the form prescribed by USCIS, with required accompanying documents, in accordance with § 214.1 and the instructions on that form.

(i) For purposes of eligibility for an extension of stay, the alien must prove that he or she:

(A) Has at all times maintained the terms and conditions of his or her E nonimmigrant classification;

(B) Was physically present in the United States at the time of filing the application for extension of stay; and

(C) Has not abandoned his or her extension request.

(ii) With limited exceptions, it is presumed that employees of treaty enterprises with special qualifications who are responsible for start-up operations should be able to complete their objectives within 2 years. Absent special circumstances, therefore, such employees will not be eligible to obtain an extension of stay.

(iii) Subject to paragraph (e)(5) of this section and the presumption noted in paragraph (e)(22)(ii) of this section, there is no specified number of extensions of stay that a treaty trader or treaty investor may be granted.

(21) Change of nonimigrant status.

(i) An alien in another valid nonimmigrant status may apply for change of status to E classification by filing an application for change of status on the form prescribed by USCIS, with required accompanying documents establishing eligibility for a change of status and E classification, in accordance with 8 CFR part 248 and the instructions on the form prescribed by USCIS.

(ii) The spouse or minor children of an applicant seeking a change of status to that of treaty trader or treaty investor alien shall file concurrent applications for change of status to derivative treaty classification on the appropriate Service form. Applications for derivative treaty status shall:

(A) Be approved only if the principal treaty alien is granted treaty alien status and continues to maintain that status;

(B) Be approved for the period of admission authorized in paragraph (e)(20) of this section.

(22) Denial of treaty trader or treaty investor status to citizens of Canada or Mexico in the case of certain labor disputes.

(i) A citizen of Canada or Mexico may be denied E treaty trader or treaty investor status as described in section 101(a)(15)(E) of the Act and Section B of Annex 16-A of Chapter 16 of the USMCA if:

(A) The Secretary of Labor certifies to or otherwise informs the Commissioner that a strike or other labor dispute involving a work stoppage of workers in the alien's occupational classification is in progress at the place where the alien is or intends to be employed; and

(B) Temporary entry of that alien may affect adversely either:

(1) The settlement of any labor dispute that is in progress at the place or intended place of employment, or

(2) The employment of any person who is involved in such dispute.

(ii) If the alien has already commenced employment in the United States and is participating in a strike or other labor dispute involving a work stoppage of workers, whether or not such strike or other labor dispute has been certified by the Secretary of Labor, or whether the Service has been otherwise informed that such a strike or labor dispute is in progress, the alien shall not be deemed to be failing to maintain his or her status solely on account of past, present, or future participation in a strike or other labor dispute involving a work stoppage of workers, but is subject to the following terms and conditions:

(A) The alien shall remain subject to all applicable provisions of the Immigration and Nationality Act, and regulations promulgated in the same manner as all other E nonimmigrants; and

(B) The status and authorized period of stay of such an alien is not modified or extended in any way by virtue of his or her participation in a strike or other labor dispute involving a work stoppage of workers.

(iii) Although participation by an E nonimmigrant alien in a strike or other labor dispute involving a work stoppage of workers will not constitute a ground for deportation, any alien who violates his or her status or who remains in the United States after his or her authorized period of stay has expired will be subject to deportation.

(iv) If there is a strike or other labor dispute involving a work stoppage of workers in progress, but such strike or other labor dispute is not certified under paragraph (e)(22)(i) of this section, or the Service has not otherwise been informed by the Secretary that such a strike or labor dispute is in progress, the Commissioner shall not deny entry to an applicant for E status.

(23) Special procedures for classifying foreign investors in the Commonwealth of the Northern Mariana Islands (CNMI) as E-2 nonimmigrant treaty investors under title VII of the Consolidated Natural Resources Act of 2008 (Pub. L. 110-229), 48 U.S.C. 1806.

(i) E-2 CNMI Investor eligibility. During the period ending on January 18, 2013, an alien may, upon application to the Secretary of Homeland Security, be classified as a CNMI-only nonimmigrant treaty investor (E-2 CNMI Investor) under section 101(a)(15)(E)(ii) of the Act if the alien:

(A) Was lawfully admitted to the CNMI in long-term investor status under the immigration laws of the CNMI before the transition program effective date and had that status on the transition program effective date;

(B) Has continuously maintained residence in the CNMI;

(C) Is otherwise admissible to the United States; and

(D) Maintains the investment or investments that formed the basis for such long-term investment status.

(ii) Definitions. For purposes of paragraph (e)(23) of this section, the following definitions apply:

(A) Approved investment or residence means an investment or residence approved by the CNMI government.

(B) Approval letter means a letter issued by the CNMI government certifying the acceptance of an approved investment subject to the minimum investment criteria and standards provided in 4 N. Mar. I. Code section 5941 et seq. (long-term business certificate), 4 N. Mar. I. Code section 5951 et seq. (foreign investor certificate), and 4 N. Mar. I. Code section 50101 et seq. (foreign retiree investment certificate).

(C) Certificate means a certificate or certification issued by the CNMI government to an applicant whose application has been approved by the CNMI government.

(D) Continuously maintained residence in the CNMI means that the alien has maintained his or her residence within the CNMI since being lawfully admitted as a long-term investor and has been physically present therein for periods totaling at least half of that time. Absence from the CNMI for any continuous period of more than six months but less than one year after such lawful admission shall break the continuity of such residence, unless the subject alien establishes to the satisfaction of DHS that he or she did not in fact abandon residence in the CNMI during such period. Absence from the CNMI for any period of one year or more during the period for which continuous residence is required shall break the continuity of such residence.

(E) Public organization means a CNMI public corporation or an agency of the CNMI government.

(F) Transition period means the period beginning on the transition program effective date and ending on December 31, 2029.

(iii) Long-term investor status. Long-term investor status under the immigration laws of the CNMI includes only the following investor classifications under CNMI immigration laws as in effect on or before November 27, 2009:

(A) Long-term business investor. An alien who has an approved investment of at least $ 50,000 in the CNMI, as evidenced by a Long-Term Business Certificate.

(B) Foreign investor. An alien in the CNMI who has invested either a minimum of $ 100,000 in an aggregate approved investment in excess of $ 2,000,000, or a minimum of $ 250,000 in a single approved investment, as evidenced by a Foreign Investment Certificate.

(C) Retiree investor. An alien in the CNMI who:

(1) Is over the age of 55 years and has invested a minimum of $ 100,000 in an approved residence on Saipan or $ 75,000 in an approved residence on Tinian or Rota, as evidenced by a Foreign Retiree Investment Certification; or

(2) Is over the age of 55 years and has invested a minimum of $ 150,000 in an approved residence to live in the CNMI, as evidenced by a Foreign Retiree Investment Certificate.

(iv) Maintaining investments. An alien in long-term investor status under the immigration laws of the CNMI is maintaining his or her investments if that alien investor is in compliance with the terms upon which the investor certificate was issued.

(v) Filing procedures. An alien seeking classification under E-2 CNMI Investor nonimmigrant status must file an application for E-2 CNMI investor nonimmigrant status, along with accompanying evidence, with USCIS in accordance with the form instructions before January 18, 2013. An application filed after the filing date deadline will be rejected.

(vi) Appropriate documents. Documentary evidence establishing eligibility for E-2 CNMI nonimmigrant investor status is required.

(A) Required evidence of admission includes a valid unexpired foreign passport and a properly endorsed CNMI admission document (e.g., entry permit or certificate) reflecting lawful admission to the CNMI in long-term business investor, foreign investor, or retiree foreign investor status.

(B) Required evidence of long-term investor status includes:

(1) An unexpired Long-Term Business Certificate, in the case of an alien in long-term business investor status.

(2) An unexpired Foreign Investment Certificate, in the case of an alien in foreign investor status.

(3) A Foreign Retiree Investment Certification or a Foreign Retiree Investment Certificate, in the case of an alien in retiree investor status.

(C) Required evidence that the long-term investor is maintaining his or her investment includes all of the following, as applicable:

(1) An approval letter issued by the CNMI government.

(2) Evidence that capital has been invested, including bank statements showing amounts deposited in CNMI business accounts, invoices, receipts or contracts for assets purchased, stock purchase transaction records, loan or other borrowing agreements, land leases, financial statements, business gross tax receipts, or any other agreements supporting the application.

(3) Evidence that the applicant has invested at least the minimum amount required, including evidence of assets which have been purchased for use in the enterprise, evidence of property transferred from abroad for use in the enterprise, evidence of monies transferred or committed to be transferred to the new or existing enterprise in exchange for shares of stock, any loan or mortgage, promissory note, security agreement, or other evidence of borrowing which is secured by assets of the applicant.

(4) A comprehensive business plan for new enterprises.

(5) Articles of incorporation, by-laws, partnership agreements, joint venture agreements, corporate minutes and annual reports, affidavits, declarations, or certifications of paid-in capital.

(6) Current business licenses.

(7) Foreign business registration records, recent tax returns of any kind, evidence of other sources of capital.

(8) A listing of all resident and nonresident employees.

(9) A listing of all holders of business certificates for the business establishment.

(10) A listing of all corporations in which the applicant has a controlling interest.

(11) In the case of a holder of a certificate of foreign investment, copies of annual reports of investment activities in the CNMI containing sufficient information to determine whether the certificate holder is under continuing compliance with the standards of issuance, accompanied by annual financial audit reports performed by an independent certified public accountant.

(12) In the case of an applicant who is a retiree investor, evidence that he or she has an interest in property in the CNMI (e.g., lease agreement), evidence of the value of the property interest (e.g., an appraisal regarding the value of the property), and, as applicable, evidence of the value of the improvements on the property (e.g., receipts or invoices of the costs of construction, the amount paid for a preexisting structure, or an appraisal of improvements).

(vii) Physical presence in the CNMI. Physical presence in the CNMI at the time of filing or during the pendency of the application is not required, but an application may not be filed by, or E-2 CNMI Investor status granted to, any alien present in U.S. territory other than in the CNMI. If an alien with CNMI long-term investor status departs the CNMI on or after the transition program effective date but before being granted E-2 CNMI Investor status, he or she may not be re-admitted to the CNMI without a visa or appropriate inadmissibility waiver under the U.S. immigration laws. If USCIS grants E-2 CNMI Investor nonimmigrant classification to an alien who is not physically present in the CNMI at the time of the grant, such alien must obtain an E-2 CNMI Investor nonimmigrant visa at a consular office abroad in order to seek admission to the CNMI in E-2 CNMI Investor status.

(viii) Information for background checks. USCIS may require an applicant for E-2 CNMI Investor status, including but not limited to any applicant for derivative status as a spouse or child, to submit biometrics as required under 8 CFR 103.16.

(ix) Denial. A grant of E-2 CNMI Investor status is a discretionary determination, and the application may be denied for failure of the applicant to demonstrate eligibility or for other good cause. Denial of the application may be appealed to the USCIS Administrative Appeals Office or any successor body.

(x) Spouse and children of an E-2 CNMI Investor.

(A) Classification. The spouse and children of an E-2 CNMI Investor accompanying or following-to-join the principal alien, if otherwise admissible, may receive the same classification as the principal alien. The nationality of a spouse or child of an E-2 CNMI investor is not material to the classification of the spouse or child.

(B) Employment authorization. The spouse of an E-2 CNMI Investor lawfully admitted in the CNMI in E-2 CNMI Investor nonimmigrant status, other than the spouse of an E-2 CNMI investor who obtained such status based upon a Foreign Retiree Investment Certificate, is eligible to apply for employment authorization under 8 CFR 274a.12(c)(12) while in E-2 CNMI Investor nonimmigrant status. Employment authorization acquired under this paragraph is limited to employment in the CNMI only.

(xi) Terms and conditions of E-2 CNMI Investor nonimmigrant status.

(A) Nonimmigrant status. E-2 CNMI Investor nonimmigrant status and any derivative status are only applicable in the CNMI. Entry, employment, and residence in the rest of the United States (including Guam) require the appropriate visa or visa waiver eligibility. An E-2 CNMI Investor who enters, attempts to enter or attempts to travel to any other part of the United States without the appropriate visa or visa waiver eligibility, or who violates conditions of nonimmigrant stay applicable to any such authorized status in any other part of the United States, will be deemed to have violated the terms and conditions of his or her E-2 CNMI Investor status. An E-2 CNMI Investor who departs the CNMI will require an E-2 CNMI investor visa for readmission to the CNMI as an E-2 CNMI Investor.

(B) Employment authorization. An alien with E-2 CNMI Investor nonimmigrant status is only employment authorized in the CNMI for the enterprise that is the basis for his or her CNMI Foreign Investment Certificate or Long-Term Business Certificate, to the extent that such Certificate authorized such activity. An alien with E-2 CNMI Investor nonimmigrant status based upon a Foreign Retiree Investor Certificate is not employment authorized.

(C) Changes in E-2 CNMI investor nonimmigrant status. If there are any substantive changes to an alien's compliance with the terms and conditions of qualification for E-2 CNMI Investor nonimmigrant status, the alien must file a new application for E-2 CNMI Investor nonimmigrant status, in accordance with the appropriate form instructions to request an extension of stay in the United States. Prior approval is not required if corporate changes occur that do not affect a previously approved employment relationship, or are otherwise non-substantive.

(D) Unauthorized change of employment. An unauthorized change of employment to a new employer will constitute a failure to maintain status within the meaning of section 237(a)(1)(C)(i) of the Act.

(E) Periods of admission.

(1) An E-2 CNMI Investor may be admitted for an initial period of not more than two years.

(2) The spouse and children accompanying or following-to-join an E-2 CNMI Investor may be admitted for the period during which the principal alien is in valid E-2 CNMI Investor nonimmigrant status. The temporary departure from the United States of the principal E-2 CNMI Investor shall not affect the derivative status of the dependent spouse and children, provided the familial relationship continues to exist and the principal alien remains eligible for admission as an E-2 CNMI Investor.

(xii) Extensions of stay. Requests for extensions of E-2 CNMI Investor nonimmigrant status may be granted in increments of not more than two years, until the end of the transition period. To request an extension of stay, an E-2 CNMI Investor must file with USCIS an application for extension of stay, with required accompanying documents, in accordance with the appropriate form instructions. To qualify for an extension of E-2 CNMI Investor nonimmigrant status, each alien must demonstrate:

(A) Continuous maintenance of the terms and conditions of E-2 CNMI Investor nonimmigrant status;

(B) Physical presence in the CNMI at the time of filing the application for extension of stay; and

(C) That he or she did not leave during the pendency of the application.

(xiii) Change of status. An alien lawfully admitted to the United States in another valid nonimmigrant status who is continuing to maintain that status may apply to change nonimmigrant status to E-2 CNMI Investor in accordance with paragraph (e)(21) of this section, if otherwise eligible, including but not limited to having been in CNMI long-term investor status on the transition date and within the period provided by paragraph (e)(23)(v) of this section.

(xiv) Expiration of the transition period. Upon expiration of the transition period, the E–2 CNMI Investor nonimmigrant status will automatically terminate.

(xv) [Removed and Reserved]

(xvi) Waiver of inadmissibility for applicants present in the CNMI. An applicant for E-2 CNMI Investor nonimmigrant status, who is otherwise eligible for such status and otherwise admissible to the United States, and who has provided all appropriate documents as described in paragraph (e)(23)(vi) of this section, may be granted a waiver of inadmissibility under section 212(d)(3)(A)(ii) of the Act, including the grounds of inadmissibility described in sections 212(a)(6)(A)(i) (to the extent such grounds arise solely because of the alien's presence in the CNMI on November 28, 2009) and 212(a)(7)(B)(i)(II) of the Act, for the purpose of granting the E-2 CNMI Investor nonimmigrant status. Such waiver may be granted without additional form or fee required. In the case of an application by a spouse or child as described in paragraph (e)(23)(x) of this section who is present in the CNMI, the appropriate documents required for such waiver are a valid unexpired passport and evidence that the spouse or child is lawfully present in the CNMI under section 1806(e) of title 48, U.S. Code (which may include evidence of a grant of parole by USCIS or by the Department of Homeland Security pursuant to a grant of advance parole by USCIS in furtherance of section 1806(e) of title 48, U.S. Code).

(f) Students in colleges, universities, seminaries, conservatories, academic high schools, elementary schools, other academic institutions, and in language training programs.

Table 2 to Paragraph (f)—Paragraph Contents

(1) Admission of student.
(2) Form I-20 or successor form.
(3) Admission of the spouse and minor children of an F-1 student.
(4) Temporary absence.
(5) Duration of status.
(6) Full course of study.
(7) Extension of stay.
(8) School transfer.
(9) Employment.
(10) Practical training.
(11) OPT application and approval process.
(12) Reporting while on optional practical training.
(13) Temporary absence from the United States of F-1 student granted employment authorization.
(14) Effect of strike or other labor dispute.
(15) Spouse and children of F-1 student.
(16) Reinstatement to student status.
(17) Current name and address.
(18) Special rules for certain border commuter students.
(19) Remittance of the fee.

(1) Admission of student —

(i) Eligibility for admission. A nonimmigrant student may be admitted into the United States in nonimmigrant status under section 101(a)(15)(F) of the Act, if:

(A) The student presents a Form I-20 or successor form issued in the student's name by a school certified by the Student and Exchange Visitor Program (SEVP) for attendance by F-1 foreign students;

(B) The student has documentary evidence of financial support in the amount indicated on the Form I-20 or successor form;

(C) For students seeking initial admission only, the student intends to attend the school specified in the student's visa (or, where the student is exempt from the requirement for a visa, the school indicated on the Form I-20 or successor form); and

(D) In the case of a student who intends to study at a public secondary school, the student has demonstrated that he or she has reimbursed the local educational agency that administers the school for the full, unsubsidized per capita cost of providing education at the school for the period of the student's attendance.

(ii) Form I-20 or successor form requirements at the port-of-entry. When an F-1 student applies for admission with a complete Form I-20 or successor form, the inspecting officer will:

(A) Transcribe the student's admission number from Form I-94 onto the student's Form I-20 or successor form (for students seeking initial admission only);

(B) Endorse the Form I-20 or successor form; and

(C) Return the Form I-20 or successor form to the student.

(iii) Use of the Student and Exchange Visitor Information System (SEVIS). Schools must issue a Form I-20 or successor form in SEVIS to any current student requiring a reportable action (e.g., extension of stay, practical training, and requests for employment authorization), or to any alien who must obtain a new nonimmigrant student visa.

(2) Student maintenance of Form I-20 or successor form. An F-1 student is expected to retain for safekeeping the initial Form I-20 or successor form bearing the admission number and any subsequent Form I-20 issued to them. Should the student lose their current Form I-20 or successor form, a replacement copy bearing the same information as the lost copy, including any endorsement for employment and notations, should be issued by the designated school official (DSO) as defined in § 214.3(l)(1).

(3) Admission of the spouse and minor children of an F-1 student. The spouse and minor children accompanying an F-1 student are eligible for admission in F-2 status if the student is admitted in F-1 status. The spouse and minor children following-to-join an F-1 student are eligible for admission to the United States in F-2 status if they are able to demonstrate that the F-1 student has been admitted and is, or will be within 30 days, enrolled in a full course of study, or engaged in approved practical training following completion of studies. In either case, at the time they seek admission, the eligible spouse and minor children of an F-1 student must individually present a Form I-20 or successor form in the name of each F-2 dependent issued by a school certified by SEVP for attendance by F-1 students. A new Form I-20 or successor form is required for a dependent where there has been any substantive change in the F-1 student's current information.

(4) Temporary absence. An F-1 student returning to the United States from a temporary absence of five months or less may be readmitted for attendance at an SEVP-certified educational institution, if the student presents:

(i) A current Form I-20 or successor form properly endorsed by the DSO for reentry if there has been no substantive change to the most recent Form I-20 or successor form information; or

(ii) An updated Form I-20 or successor form if there has been a substantive change in the information on the student's most recent Form I-20 or successor form, such as in the case of a student who has changed the major area of study, who intends to transfer to another SEVP-certified institution, or who has advanced to a higher level of study.

(5) Duration of status —

(i) General. Duration of status is defined as the time during which an F-1 student is pursuing a full course of study at an educational institution certified by SEVP for attendance by foreign students, or engaging in authorized practical training following completion of studies, except that an F-1 student who is admitted to attend a public high school is restricted to an aggregate of 12 months of study at any public high school(s). An F-1 student may be admitted for a period up to 30 days before the indicated report date or program start date listed on the Form I-20 or successor form. The student is considered to be maintaining status if the student is making normal progress toward completing a course of study.

(ii) Change in educational levels. An F-1 student who continues from one educational level to another is considered to be maintaining status, provided that the transition to the new educational level is accomplished according to transfer procedures outlined in paragraph (f)(8) of this section.

(iii) Annual vacation. An F-1 student at an academic institution is considered to be in status during the annual (or summer) vacation if the student is eligible and intends to register for the next term. A student attending a school on a quarter or trimester calendar who takes only one vacation a year during any one of the quarters or trimesters instead of during the summer is considered to be in status during that vacation, if the student has completed the equivalent of an academic year prior to taking the vacation.

(iv) Preparation for departure. An F-1 student who has completed a course of study and any authorized practical training following completion of studies will be allowed an additional 60-day period to prepare for departure from the United States or to transfer in accordance with paragraph (f)(8) of this section. An F-1 student authorized by the DSO to withdraw from classes will be allowed a 15-day period for departure from the United States. However, an F-1 student who fails to maintain a full course of study without the approval of the DSO or otherwise fails to maintain status is not eligible for an additional period for departure.

(v) Emergent circumstances as determined by the Secretary. Where the Secretary has suspended the applicability of any or all of the requirements for on-campus or off-campus employment authorization for specified students pursuant to paragraphs (f)(9)(i) or (ii) of this section by notice in the Federal Register , an affected student who needs to reduce their full course of study as a result of accepting employment authorized by such notice in the Federal Register will be considered to be in status during the authorized employment, subject to any other conditions specified in the notice, provided that, for the duration of the authorized employment, the student is registered for the number of semester or quarter hours of instruction per academic term specified in the notice, which in no event shall be less than six semester or quarter hours of instruction per academic term if the student is at the undergraduate level or less than three semester or quarter hours of instruction per academic term if the student is at the graduate level, and is continuing to make progress toward completing the course of study.

(vi) Extension of duration of status and grant of employment authorization.

(A) The duration of status, and any employment authorization granted under 8 CFR 274a.12(c)(3)(i)(B) or (C), of an F–1 student who is the beneficiary of an H–1B petition subject to section 214(g)(1)(A) of the Act (8 U.S.C. 1184(g)(1)(A)) requesting a change of status will be automatically extended until April 1 of the fiscal year for which such H–1B status is being requested or until the validity start date of the approved petition, whichever is earlier, where such petition:

(1) Has been timely filed;

(2) Requests an H–1B employment start date in the fiscal year for which such H–1B status is being requested consistent with paragraph (h)(2)(i)(I) of this section; and

(3) Is nonfrivolous.

(B) The automatic extension of an F-1 student's duration of status and employment authorization under paragraph (f)(5)(vi)(A) of this section shall automatically terminate upon the rejection, denial, revocation, or withdrawal of the H-1B petition filed on such F-1 student's behalf or upon the denial or withdrawal of the request for change of nonimmigrant status, even if the H-1B petition filed on the F-1 student's behalf is approved for consular processing.

(C) In order to obtain the automatic extension of stay and employment authorization under paragraph (f)(5)(vi)(A) of this section, the F-1 student, consistent with 8 CFR part 248, must not have violated the terms or conditions of his or her nonimmigrant status.

(D) An automatic extension of an F-1 student's duration of status under paragraph (f)(5)(vi)(A) of this section also applies to the duration of status of any F-2 dependent aliens.

(6) Full course of study —

(i) General. Successful completion of the full course of study must lead to the attainment of a specific educational or professional objective. A course of study at an institution not certified for attendance by foreign students as provided in § 214.3(a)(3) does not satisfy the requirement of this paragraph (f)(6)(i). A "full course of study" as required by section 101(a)(15)(F)(i) of the Act means:

(A) Postgraduate study or postdoctoral study at a college or university, or undergraduate or postgraduate study at a conservatory or religious seminary, certified by a DSO as a full course of study;

(B) Undergraduate study at a college or university, certified by a school official to consist of at least 12 semester or quarter hours of instruction per academic term in those institutions using standard semester, trimester, or quarter hour systems, where all undergraduate students who are enrolled for a minimum of 12 semester or quarter hours are charged full-time tuition or are considered full-time for other administrative purposes, or its equivalent (as determined by SEVP in the school certification process), except when the student needs a lesser course load to complete the course of study during the current term;

(C) Study in a postsecondary language, liberal arts, fine arts, or other non-vocational program at a school which confers upon its graduates recognized associate or other degrees or has established that its credits have been and are accepted unconditionally by at least three other institutions of higher learning which are either:

(1) A school (or school system) owned and operated as a public educational institution by the United States or a State or political subdivision thereof; or

(2) a school accredited by a nationally recognized accrediting body; and which has been certified by a designated school official to consist of at least 12 clock hours of instruction a week, or its equivalent as determined by SEVP in the school certification process;

(D) Study in any other language, liberal arts, fine arts, or other nonvocational training program, certified by a designated school official to consist of at least eighteen clock hours of attendance a week if the dominant part of the course of study consists of classroom instruction, or to consist of at least twenty-two clock hours a week if the dominant part of the course of study consists of laboratory work; or

(E) Study in a curriculum at a certified private elementary or middle school or public or private academic high school which is certified by a designated school official to consist of class attendance for not less than the minimum number of hours a week prescribed by the school for normal progress toward graduation.

(F) Notwithstanding paragraphs (f)(6)(i)(A) and (B) of this section, an alien who has been granted employment authorization pursuant to the terms of a document issued by the Secretary under paragraphs (f)(9)(i) or (ii) of this section and published in the Federal Register shall be deemed to be engaged in a "full course of study" if he or she remains registered for no less than the number of semester or quarter hours of instruction per academic term specified by the Secretary in the notice for the validity period of such employment authorization.

(G) For F-1 students enrolled in classes for credit or classroom hours, no more than the equivalent of one class or three credits per session, term, semester, trimester, or quarter may be counted toward the full course of study requirement if the class is taken on-line or through distance education and does not require the student's physical attendance for classes, examination or other purposes integral to completion of the class. An on-line or distance education course is a course that is offered principally through the use of television, audio, or computer transmission including open broadcast, closed circuit, cable, microwave, or satellite, audio conferencing, or computer conferencing. If the F-1 student's course of study is in a language study program, no on-line or distance education classes may be considered to count toward a student's full course of "study requirement.

(H) On-campus employment pursuant to the terms of a scholarship, fellowship, or assistantship is deemed to be part of the academic program of a student otherwise taking a full course of study.

(ii) Institution of higher learning. For purposes of this paragraph, a college or university is an institution of higher learning which awards recognized associate, bachelor's, master's, doctorate, or professional degrees. Schools which devote themselves exclusively or primarily to vocational, business, or language instruction are not included in the category of colleges or universities. Vocational or business schools which are classifiable as M-1 schools are provided for by regulations under 8 CFR 214.2(m).

(iii) Reduced course load. The designated school official may allow an F-1 student to engage in less than a full course of study as provided in this paragraph (f)(6)(iii). Except as otherwise noted, a reduced course load must consist of at least six semester or quarter hours, or half the clock hours required for a full course of study. A student who drops below a full course of study without the prior approval of the DSO will be considered out of status. On-campus employment pursuant to the terms of a scholarship, fellowship, or assistantship is deemed to be part of the academic program of a student otherwise taking a full course of study.

(A) Academic difficulties. The DSO may authorize a reduced course load on account of a student's initial difficulty with the English language or reading requirements, unfamiliarity with U.S. teaching methods, or improper course level placement. The student must resume a full course of study at the next available term, session, or semester, excluding a summer session, in order to maintain student status. A student previously authorized to drop below a full course of study due to academic difficulties is not eligible for a second authorization by the DSO due to academic difficulties while pursuing a course of study at that program level. A student authorized to drop below a full course of study for academic difficulties while pursuing a course of study at a particular program level may still be authorized for a reduced course load due to an illness medical condition as provided for in paragraph (B) of this section.

(B) Medical conditions. The DSO may authorize a reduced course load (or, if necessary, no course load) due to a student's temporary illness or medical condition for a period of time not to exceed an aggregate of 12 months while the student is pursuing a course of study at a particular program level. In order to authorize a reduced course load based upon a medical condition, the student must provide medical documentation from a licensed medical doctor, a licensed doctor of osteopathy, a licensed psychologist, or a licensed clinical psychologist to the DSO to substantiate the illness or medical condition. The student must provide current medical documentation and the DSO must reauthorize the drop below full course of study each new term, session, or semester. A student previously authorized to drop below a full course of study due to illness or medical condition for an aggregate of 12 months may not be authorized by a DSO to reduce their course load on subsequent occasions while pursuing a course of study at the same program level. A student may be authorized to reduce course load for a reason of illness or medical condition on more than one occasion while pursuing a course of study, so long as the aggregate period of that authorization does not exceed 12 months.

(C) Completion of course of study. The DSO may authorize a reduced course load in the student's final term, semester, or session if fewer courses are needed to complete the course of study. If the student is not required to take any additional courses to satisfy the requirements for completion, but continues to be enrolled for administrative purposes, the student is considered to have completed the course of study and must take action to maintain status. Such action may include application for change of status or departure from the U.S.

(D) [Removed and reserved.]

(E) Reporting requirements. In order for a student to be authorized to drop below a full course of study, the DSO must update SEVIS prior to the student reducing their course load. The DSO must update SEVIS with the date, reason for authorization, and the start date of the next term or session. The DSO must also notify SEVIS within 21 days of the student's commencement of a full course of study. If an extension of the program end date is required due to the student dropping below a full course of study, the DSO must update SEVIS by completing a new Form I-20 or successor form with the new program end date in accordance with paragraph (f)(7) of this section.

(iv) Concurrent enrollment. An F-1 student may be enrolled in two different SEVP-certified schools at one time as long as the combined enrollment amounts to a full course of study. In cases where a student is concurrently enrolled, the school from which the student will earn their degree or certification should issue the Form I-20 or successor form, and conduct subsequent certifications and updates to the Form I-20 or successor form. The DSO from this school is also responsible for all of the reporting requirements to SEVP. In instances where a student is enrolled in programs with different full course of study requirements (e.g., clock hours vs. credit hours), the DSO is permitted to determine what constitutes a full course of study.

(7) Extension of stay—

(i) General. An F-1 student who is admitted for duration of status is not required to apply for extension of stay as long as the student is maintaining status and making normal progress toward completion of their educational objective. An F-1 student who is currently maintaining status and making normal progress toward completing their educational objective, but who is unable to complete their course of study by the program end date on the Form I-20 or successor form, must apply prior to the program end date for a program extension pursuant to paragraph (f)(7)(iii) of this section.

(ii) Report date and program completion date on Form I-20 or successor form. When determining the report date on the Form I-20 or successor form, the DSO may choose a reasonable date to accommodate a student's need to be in attendance for required activities at the school prior to the actual start of classes. Such required activities may include, but are not limited to, research projects and orientation sessions. However, for purposes of employment, the DSO may not indicate a report date more than 30 days prior to the start of classes. When determining the program completion date on Form I-20 or successor form, the DSO should make a reasonable estimate based upon the time an average student would need to complete a similar program in the same discipline.

(iii) Program extension for students in lawful status. An F-1 student who is unable to meet the program completion date on the Form I-20 or successor form may be granted an extension by the DSO if the DSO certifies that the student has continually maintained status and that the delays are caused by compelling academic or medical reasons, such as changes of major or research topics, unexpected research problems, or documented illnesses. Delays caused by academic probation or suspension are not acceptable reasons for program extensions. A DSO may not grant an extension if the student did not apply for an extension until after the program end date noted on the Form I-20 or successor form. An F-1 student who is unable to complete the educational program within the time listed on Form I-20 or successor form and who is ineligible for program extension pursuant to this paragraph (f)(7) is considered out of status. If eligible, the student may apply for reinstatement under the provisions of paragraph (f)(16) of this section.

(iv) SEVIS update. A DSO may grant a program extension only by updating SEVIS and issuing a new Form I-20 or successor form reflecting the current program end date. A DSO may grant an extension any time prior to the program end date listed on the student's Form I-20 or successor form.

(8) School transfer —

(i) General. A student who is maintaining status may transfer to another SEVP-certified school by following the notification procedure prescribed in paragraph (f)(8)(ii) of this section. However, an F-1 student is not permitted to remain in the United States when transferring between schools or programs unless the student will begin classes at the transfer school or program within five months of transferring out of the current school or within 5 months of the program completion date on their current Form I-20 or successor form, whichever is earlier. In the case of an F-1 student authorized to engage in post-completion optional practical training (OPT), the student must be able resume classes within 5 months of transferring out of the school that recommended OPT or the date the OPT authorization ends, whichever is earlier. An F-1 student who was not pursuing a full course of study at the school he or she was last authorized to attend is ineligible for school transfer and must apply for reinstatement under the provisions of paragraph (f)(16) of this section, or, in the alternative, may depart the country and return as an initial entry in a new F-1 nonimmigrant status.

(ii) Transfer procedure. To transfer schools, the student must first notify their current school (the "transfer-out" school) of the intent to transfer and indicate the school to which the student intends to transfer (the "transfer-in" school). Upon notification by the student, the transfer-out school must update SEVIS to show the student is transferring out, indicate the transfer-in school, and input the transfer release date. The release date will be the current semester or session completion date, or the date of expected transfer if earlier than the established academic cycle. The transfer-out school will retain control over the student's record in SEVIS until the student completes the current term or reaches the release date. At the request of the student, the DSO of the transfer-out school may cancel the transfer request at any time prior to the release date. As of the release date specified by the transfer-out DSO, the transfer-in school will be granted full access to the student's SEVIS record and then becomes responsible for that student. The transfer-out school conveys authority and responsibility over that student to the transfer-in school and relinquishes its SEVIS access to that student's record. As such, a transfer request may not be cancelled by the transfer-out DSO after the release date has been reached. After the release date, the transfer-in DSO must complete the transfer of the student's record in SEVIS and may issue a Form I-20 or successor form. The student is then required to contact the DSO at the transfer-in school within 15 days of the program start date listed on the Form I-20 or successor form. Upon notification that the student is enrolled in classes, the transfer-in DSO must update SEVIS to reflect the student's registration and current address, thereby acknowledging that the student has completed the transfer process. The transfer is completed when the transfer-in school notifies SEVIS that the student has enrolled in classes in accordance with the 30 days required by § 214.3(g)(2)(iii).

(iii) [Removed and reserved.]

(9) Employment —

(i) On-campus employment. On-campus employment must either be performed on the school's premises, (including on-location commercial firms which provide services for students on campus, such as the school bookstore or cafeteria), or at an off-campus location that is educationally affiliated with the school. Employment with on-site commercial firms, such as a construction company building a school building, which do not provide direct student services is not deemed on-campus employment for the purposes of this paragraph (f)(9)(i). In the case of off-campus locations, the educational affiliation must be associated with the school's established curriculum or related to contractually funded research projects at the post-graduate level. In any event, the employment must be an integral part of the student's educational program. Employment authorized under this paragraph (f)(9)(i) must not exceed 20 hours a week while school is in session, unless the Secretary suspends the applicability of this limitation due to emergent circumstances, as determined by the Secretary, by means of notice in the Federal Register , the student demonstrates to the DSO that the employment is necessary to avoid severe economic hardship resulting from the emergent circumstances, and the DSO notates the Form I-20 or successor form in accordance with the Federal Register document. An F-1 student may, however, work on campus full-time when school is not in session or during the annual vacation. A student who has been issued a Form I-20 or successor form to begin a new program in accordance with the provision of § 214.3(k) and who intends to enroll for the next regular academic year, term, or session at the institution that issued the Form I-20 or successor form may continue on-campus employment incident to status. Otherwise, an F-1 student may not engage in on-campus employment after completing a course of study, except employment for practical training as authorized under paragraph (f)(10) of this section. An F-1 student may engage in any on-campus employment authorized under this paragraph (f)(9)(i) which will not displace United States residents. In the case of a transfer in SEVIS, the student may only engage in on-campus employment at the school having jurisdiction over the student's SEVIS record. Upon initial entry to begin a new course of study, an F-1 student may not begin on-campus employment more than 30 days prior to the actual start of classes.

(ii) Off-campus work authorization —

(A) General. An F-1 student may be authorized to work off-campus on a part-time basis in accordance with paragraph (f)(9)(ii)(C) of this section after having been in F-1 status for one full academic year provided that the student is in good academic standing as determined by the DSO. Part-time off-campus employment authorized under this section is limited to no more than 20 hours a week when school is in session. A student who is granted off-campus employment authorization may work full-time during holidays or school vacation. The employment authorization is automatically terminated whenever the student fails to maintain status. In emergent circumstances as determined by the Secretary, the Secretary may suspend the applicability of any or all of the requirements of paragraph (f)(9)(ii) of this section by notice in the Federal Register .

(B) [Reserved]

(C) Severe economic hardship. If other employment opportunities are not available or are otherwise insufficient, an eligible F-1 student may request off-campus employment work authorization based upon severe economic hardship caused by unforeseen circumstances beyond the student's control. These circumstances may include loss of financial aid or on-campus employment without fault on the part of the student, substantial fluctuations in the value of currency or exchange rate, inordinate increases in tuition and/or living costs, unexpected changes in the financial condition of the student's source of support, medical bills, or other substantial and unexpected expenses.

(D) Procedure for off-campus employment authorization due to severe economic hardship. The student must request a recommendation from the DSO for off-campus employment. The DSO must complete such certification in SEVIS. The DSO may recommend the student for work off-campus for one-year intervals by certifying that:

(1) The student has been in F-1 status for one full academic year;

(2) The student is in good standing as a student and is carrying a full course of study as defined in paragraph (f)(6) of this section;

(3) The student has demonstrated that acceptance of employment will not interfere with the student's carrying a full course of study; and

(4) The student has demonstrated that the employment is necessary to avoid severe economic hardship due to unforeseen circumstances beyond the student's control pursuant to paragraph (f)(9)(ii)(C) of this section and has demonstrated that employment under paragraph (f)(9)(i) of this section is unavailable or otherwise insufficient to meet the needs that have arisen as a result of the unforeseen circumstances.

(E) [Reserved]

(F) Severe economic hardship application.

(1) The applicant should submit the economic hardship application for employment authorization on Form I-765 or successor form, with the fee required by 8 CFR 106.2, and any other supporting materials such as affidavits which further detail the unforeseen circumstances that require the student to seek employment authorization and the unavailability or insufficiency of employment under paragraph (f)(9)(i) of this section to USCIS. Students should submit the Form I-20 or successor form with the employment page demonstrating the DSO's comments and certification. USCIS will adjudicate the application for work authorization based upon severe economic hardship on the basis of Form I-20 and Form I-765 or successor forms, and any additional supporting materials. If employment is authorized, the adjudicating officer will issue an employment authorization document (EAD). USCIS will notify the student of the decision, and, if the application is denied, of the reason or reasons for the denial. No appeal will lie from a decision to deny a request for employment authorization under this section. The employment authorization may be granted in one-year intervals up to the expected date of completion of the student's current course of study. A student has permission to engage in off-campus employment only if the student receives the EAD endorsed to that effect. Off-campus employment authorization may be renewed by USCIS only if the student is maintaining status and good academic standing. The employment authorization is automatically terminated whenever the student fails to maintain status.

(2) [Removed and reserved.]

(iii) Internship with an international organization. A bona fide F-1 student who has been offered employment by a recognized international organization within the meaning of the International Organization Immunities Act (59 Stat. 669) must apply for employment authorization with USCIS. A student seeking employment authorization under this provision is required to present a written certification from the international organization that the proposed employment is within the scope of the organization's sponsorship, Form I-20 or successor form with employment page completed by DSO certifying eligibility for employment, and a completed Form I-765 or successor form, with the fee required by 8 CFR 106.2(a)(32).

(10) Practical training. Practical training may be authorized to an F-1 student who has been lawfully enrolled on a full-time basis, in an approved SEVP-certified college, university, conservatory, or seminary for one full academic year. This paragraph (f)(10) also includes students who, during their course of study, were enrolled in a study abroad program, if the student had spent at least one full academic term enrolled in a full course of study in the United States prior to studying abroad. A student may be authorized 12 months of practical training, and becomes eligible for another 12 months of practical training when they change to a higher educational level. Students in English language training programs are ineligible for practical training. An eligible student may request employment authorization for practical training in a position that is directly related to their major area of study. There are two types of practical training available:

(i) Curricular practical training. An F-1 student may be authorized by the DSO to participate in a curricular practical training program that is an integral part of an established curriculum. Curricular practical training is defined to be alternative work/study, internship, cooperative education or any other type of required internship or practicum that is offered by sponsoring employers through cooperative agreements with the school. Students who have received one year or more of full time curricular practical training are ineligible for post-completion academic training. Exceptions to the one academic year requirement are provided for students enrolled in graduate studies that require immediate participation in curricular practical training. A request for authorization for curricular practical training must be made to the DSO. A student may begin curricular practical training only after receiving their Form I-20 or successor form with the DSO endorsement. To grant authorization for a student to engage in curricular practical training, a DSO will update the student's record in SEVIS as being authorized for curricular practical training that is directly related to the student's major area of study. The DSO will indicate whether the training is full-time or part-time, the employer and location, and the employment start and end date. The DSO must sign, date, and return the Form I-20 or successor form to the student prior to the student's commencement of employment indicating that curricular practical training has been approved.

(ii) Optional practical training —

(A) General. Consistent with the application and approval process in paragraph (f)(11) of this section, a student may apply to USCIS for authorization for temporary employment for optional practical training directly related to the student's major area of study. The student may not begin optional practical training until the date indicated on his or her employment authorization document, Form I-766. A student may be granted authorization to engage in temporary employment for optional practical training:

(1) During the student's annual vacation and at other times when school is not in session, if the student

is currently enrolled, and is eligible for registration and intends to register for the next term or session;

(2) While school is in session, provided that practical training does not exceed 20 hours a week while school is in session; or

(3) After completion of the course of study, or, for a student in a bachelor's, master's, or doctoral degree program, after completion of all course requirements for the degree (excluding thesis or equivalent). Continued enrollment, for the school's administrative purposes, after all requirements for the degree have been met does not preclude eligibility for optional practical training. A student must complete all practical training within a 14-month period following the completion of study, except that a 24-month extension pursuant to paragraph (f)(10)(ii)(C) of this section does not need to be completed within such 14-month period.

(B) Termination of practical training. Authorization to engage in optional practical training employment is automatically terminated when the student transfers to another school or begins study at another educational level.

(C) 24-month extension of post-completion OPT for a science, technology, engineering, or mathematics (STEM) degree. Consistent with paragraph (f)(11)(i)(C) of this section, a qualified student may apply for an extension of OPT while in a valid period of post-completion OPT authorized under 8 CFR 274a.12(c)(3)(i)(B). An extension will be for 24 months for the first qualifying degree for which the student has completed all course requirements (excluding thesis or equivalent), including any qualifying degree as part of a dual degree program, subject to the requirement in paragraph (f)(10)(ii)(C)(3) of this section that previously obtained degrees must have been conferred. If a student completes all such course requirements for another qualifying degree at a higher degree level than the first, the student may apply for a second -month extension of OPT while in a valid period of post-completion OPT authorized under 8 CFR 274a.12(c)(3)(i)(B). In no event may a student be authorized for more than two lifetime STEM OPT extensions. A student who was granted a 17-month OPT extension under the rule issued at 73 FR 18944, whether or not such student requests an additional 7-month period of STEM OPT under 8 CFR 214.16, is considered to have been authorized for one STEM OPT extension, and may be eligible for only one more STEM OPT extension. Any subsequent application for an additional 24-month OPT extension under this paragraph (f)(10)(ii)(C) must be based on a degree at a higher degree level than the degree that was the basis for the student's first OPT extension. In order to qualify for an extension of post-completion OPT based upon a STEM degree, all of the following requirements must be met.

(1) Accreditation. The degree that is the basis for the 24-month OPT extension is from a U.S. educational institution accredited by an accrediting agency recognized by the Department of Education at the time of application.

(2) DHS-approved degree. The degree that is the basis for the 24-month OPT extension is a bachelor's, master's, or doctoral degree in a field determined by the Secretary, or his or her designee, to qualify within a science, technology, engineering, or mathematics field.

(i) The term "science, technology, engineering or mathematics field" means a field included in the Department of Education's Classification of Instructional Programs taxonomy within the two-digit series or successor series containing engineering, biological sciences, mathematics, and physical sciences, or a related field. In general, related fields will include fields involving research, innovation, or development of new technologies using engineering, mathematics, computer science, or natural sciences (including physical, biological, and agricultural sciences).

(ii) The Secretary, or his or her designee, will maintain the STEM Designated Degree Program List, which will be a complete list of qualifying degree program categories, published on the Student and Exchange Visitor Program Web site at http://www.ice.gov/sevis. Changes that are made to the Designated Degree Program List may also be published in a notice in the Federal Register . All program categories included on the list must be consistent with the definition set forth in paragraph (f)(10)(ii)(C)(2)(i) of this section.

(iii) At the time the DSO recommends a 24-month OPT extension under this paragraph (f)(10)(ii)(C) in SEVIS, the degree that is the basis for the application for the OPT extension must be contained within a category on the STEM Designated Degree Program List.

(3) Previously obtained STEM degree(s). The degree that is the basis for the 24-month OPT extension under this paragraph (f)(10)(ii)(C) may be, but is not required to be, the degree that is the basis for the post-completion OPT period authorized under 8 CFR 274a.12(c)(3)(i)(B). If an application for a 24-month OPT extension under this paragraph (f)(10)(ii)(C) is based upon a degree obtained previous to the degree that provided the basis for the period of post-completion OPT authorized under 8 CFR 274a.12(c)(3)(i)(B), that previously obtained degree must have been conferred from a U.S. educational institution that is accredited and SEVP-certified at the time the student's DSO recommends the student for the 24-month OPT extension and must be in a degree program category included on the current STEM Designated Degree Program List at the time of the DSO recommendation. That previously obtained degree must have been conferred within the 10 years preceding the date the DSO recommends the student for the 24-month OPT extension.

(4) Eligible practical training opportunity. The STEM practical training opportunity that is the basis for the 24-month OPT extension under this paragraph (f)(10)(ii)(C) must be directly related to the degree that qualifies the student for such extension, which may be the previously obtained degree described in paragraph (f)(10)(ii)(C)(3) of this section.

(5) Employer qualification. The student's employer is enrolled in E-Verify, as evidenced by either a valid E-Verify Company Identification number or, if the employer is using an employer agent to create its E-Verify cases, a valid E-Verify Client Company Identification

number, and the employer remains a participant in good standing with E-Verify, as determined by USCIS. An employer must also have an employer identification number (EIN) used for tax purposes.

(6) Employer reporting. A student may not be authorized for employment with an employer pursuant to paragraph (f)(10)(ii)(C)(2) of this section unless the employer agrees, by signing the Training Plan for STEM OPT Students, Form I-983 or successor form, to report the termination or departure of an OPT student to the DSO at the student's school, if the termination or departure is prior to the end of the authorized period of OPT. Such reporting must be made within five business days of the termination or departure. An employer shall consider a student to have departed when the employer knows the student has left the practical training opportunity, or if the student has not reported for his or her practical training for a period of five consecutive business days without the consent of the employer, whichever occurs earlier.

(7) Training Plan for STEM OPT Students, Form I-983 or successor form.

(i) A student must fully complete an individualized Form I-983 or successor form and obtain requisite signatures from an appropriate individual in the employer's organization on the form, consistent with form instructions, before the DSO may recommend a 24-month OPT extension under paragraph (f)(10)(ii)(C)(2) of this section in SEVIS. A student must submit the Form I-983 or successor form, which includes a certification of adherence to the training plan completed by an appropriate individual in the employer's organization who has signatory authority for the employer, to the student's DSO, prior to the new DSO recommendation. A student must present his or her signed and completed Form I-983 or successor form to a DSO at the educational institution of his or her most recent enrollment. A student, while in F-1 student status, may also be required to submit the Form I-983 or successor form to ICE and/or USCIS upon request or in accordance with form instructions.

(ii) The training plan described in the Form I-983 or successor form must identify goals for the STEM practical training opportunity, including specific knowledge, skills, or techniques that will be imparted to the student, and explain how those goals will be achieved through the work-based learning opportunity with the employer; describe a performance evaluation process; and describe methods of oversight and supervision. Employers may rely on their otherwise existing training programs or policies to satisfy the requirements relating to performance evaluation and oversight and supervision, as applicable.

(iii) The training plan described in the Form I-983 or successor form must explain how the training is directly related to the student's qualifying STEM degree.

(iv) If a student initiates a new practical training opportunity with a new employer during his or her 24-month OPT extension, the student must submit, within 10 days of beginning the new practical training opportunity, a new Form I-983 or successor form to the student's DSO, and subsequently obtain a new DSO recommendation.

(8) Duties, hours, and compensation for training. The terms and conditions of a STEM practical training opportunity during the period of the 24-month OPT extension, including duties, hours, and compensation, must be commensurate with terms and conditions applicable to the employer's similarly situated U.S. workers in the area of employment. A student may not engage in practical training for less than 20 hours per week, excluding time off taken consistent with leave-related policies applicable to the employer's similarly situated U.S. workers in the area of employment. If the employer does not employ and has not recently employed more than two similarly situated U.S. workers in the area of employment, the employer nevertheless remains obligated to attest that the terms and conditions of a STEM practical training opportunity are commensurate with the terms and conditions of employment for other similarly situated U.S. workers in the area of employment. "Similarly situated U.S. workers" includes U.S. workers performing similar duties subject to similar supervision and with similar educational backgrounds, industry expertise, employment experience, levels of responsibility, and skill sets as the student. The duties, hours, and compensation of such students are "commensurate" with those offered to U.S. workers employed by the employer in the same area of employment when the employer can show that the duties, hours, and compensation are consistent with the range of such terms and conditions the employer has offered or would offer to similarly situated U.S. employees. The student must disclose his or her compensation, including any adjustments, as agreed to with the employer, on the Form I-983 or successor form.

(9) Evaluation requirements and Training Plan modifications.

(i) A student may not be authorized for employment with an employer pursuant to paragraph (f)(10)(ii)(C)(2) of this section unless the student submits a self-evaluation of the student's progress toward the training goals described in the Form I-983 or successor form. All required evaluations must be completed prior to the conclusion of a STEM practical training opportunity, and the student and an appropriate individual in the employer's organization must sign each evaluation to attest to its accuracy. All STEM practical training opportunities require an initial evaluation within 12 months of the approved starting date on the employment authorization document granted pursuant to the student's 24-month OPT extension application, and a concluding evaluation. The student is responsible for ensuring the DSO receives his or her 12-month evaluation and final evaluation no later than 10 days following the conclusion of the reporting period or conclusion of his or her practical training opportunity, respectively.

(ii) If any material change to or deviation from the training plan described in the Form I-983 or successor form occurs, the student and employer must sign a modified Form I-983 or successor form reflecting the material change(s) or deviation(s). Material changes and deviations relating to training may include, but are not limited to, any change of Employer Identification Number resulting from a corporate restructuring, any reduction in compensation from the amount previously submitted on the Form I-983 or successor form that is not tied to a reduction in hours worked, any significant decrease in hours per week that a student engages in a STEM training opportunity, and any decrease in hours worked below the minimum hours for the 24-month extension as described in paragraph (f)(10)(ii)(C)(8) of this section. Material changes and deviations also include any change or deviation that renders an employer attestation inaccurate, or renders inaccurate the information in the Form I-983 or successor form on the nature, purpose, oversight, or assessment of the student's practical training opportunity. The student and employer must ensure that the modified Form I-983 or successor form is submitted to the student's DSO at the earliest available opportunity.

(iii) The educational institution whose DSO is responsible for duties associated with the student's latest OPT extension under paragraph (f)(10)(ii)(C)(2) of this section is responsible for ensuring the Student and Exchange Visitor Program has access to each individualized Form I-983 or successor form and associated student evaluations (electronic or hard copy), including through SEVIS if technologically available, beginning within 30 days after the document is submitted to the DSO and continuing for a period of three years following the completion of each STEM practical training opportunity.

(10) Additional STEM opportunity obligations. A student may only participate in a STEM practical training opportunity in which the employer attests, including by signing the Form I-983 or successor form, that:

(i) The employer has sufficient resources and personnel available and is prepared to provide appropriate training in connection with the specified opportunity at the location(s) specified in the Form I-983 or successor form;

(ii) The student on a STEM OPT extension will not replace a full- or part-time, temporary or permanent U.S. worker; and

(iii) The student's opportunity assists the student in reaching his or her training goals.

(11) Site visits. DHS, at its discretion, may conduct a site visit of any employer. The purpose of the site visit is for DHS to ensure that each employer possesses and maintains the ability and resources to provide structured and guided work-based learning experiences consistent with any Form I-983 or successor form completed and signed by the employer. DHS will provide notice to the employer 48 hours in advance of any site visit, except notice may not be provided if the visit is triggered by a complaint or other evidence of noncompliance with the regulations in this paragraph (f)(10)(ii)(C).

(D) Duration of status while on post-completion OPT. For a student with approved post-completion OPT, the duration of status is defined as the period beginning on the date that the student's application for OPT was properly filed and pending approval, including the authorized period of post-completion OPT, and ending 60 days after the OPT employment authorization expires.

(E) Periods of unemployment during post-completion OPT. During post-completion OPT, F-1 status is dependent upon employment. Students may not accrue an aggregate of more than 90 days of unemployment during any post-completion OPT period described in 8 CFR 274a.12(c)(3)(i)(B). Students granted a 24-month OPT extension under paragraph (f)(10)(ii)(C)(2) of this section may not accrue an aggregate of more than 150 days of unemployment during a total OPT period, including any post-completion OPT period described in 8 CFR 274a.12(c)(3)(i)(B) and any subsequent 24-month extension period.

(11) OPT application and approval process —

(i) Student responsibilities. A student must initiate the OPT application process by requesting a recommendation for OPT from his or her DSO. Upon making the recommendation, the DSO will provide the student a signed Form I-20 indicating that recommendation.

(A) Applications for employment authorization. The student must properly file an Application for Employment Authorization, Form I-765 or successor form, with USCIS, accompanied by the required fee, and the supporting documents, as described in the form's instructions.

(B) Applications and filing deadlines for pre-completion OPT and post-completion OPT—

(1) Pre-completion OPT. For pre-completion OPT, the student may properly file his or her Form I-765 or successor form up to 90 days before being enrolled for one full academic year, provided that the period of employment will not start prior to the completion of the full academic year.

(2) Post-completion OPT. For post-completion OPT, not including a 24-month OPT extension under paragraph (f)(10)(ii)(C)(2) of this section, the student may properly file his or her Form I-765 or successor form up to 90 days prior to his or her program end date and no later than 60 days after his or her program end date. The student must also file his or her Form I-765 or successor form with USCIS within 30 days of the date the DSO enters the recommendation for OPT into his or her SEVIS record.

(C) Applications and filing deadlines for 24-month OPT extension. A student meeting the eligibility requirements for a 24-month OPT extension under paragraph (f)(10)(ii)(C) of this section may request an extension of employment authorization by filing Form I-765 or successor form, with the required fee and supporting documents, up to 90 days prior to the expiration date of the student's current OPT employment authorization. The student seeking such 24-month OPT extension must properly file his or her Form I-765 or successor form with USCIS within 60 days of the date the DSO enters the recommendation for the OPT extension into his or her SEVIS record. If a student timely and properly files an application for such 24-month OPT extension and timely and properly requests a DSO recommendation, including by submitting the fully executed Form I-983 or successor form to his or her DSO, but the Employment Authorization Document, Form I-766 or successor form, currently in the student's possession expires prior to the decision on the student's application for the OPT extension, the student's Form I-766 or successor form is extended automatically pursuant to the terms and conditions specified in 8 CFR 274a.12(b)(6)(iv).

(D) Start of OPT employment. A student may not begin OPT employment prior to the approved start date on his or her Employment Authorization Document, Form I-766 or successor form, except as described in paragraph (f)(11)(i)(C) of this section. A student may not request a start date that is more than 60 days after the student's program end date. Employment authorization will begin on the date requested or the date the employment authorization is adjudicated, whichever is later.

(ii) Additional DSO responsibilities. A student must have a recommendation from his or her DSO in order to apply for OPT. When a DSO recommends a student for OPT, the school assumes the added responsibility for maintaining the SEVIS record of that student for the entire period of authorized OPT, consistent with paragraph (f)(12) of this section.

(A) Prior to making a recommendation, the DSO at the educational institution of the student's most recent enrollment must ensure that the student is eligible for the given type and period of OPT and that the student is aware of the student's responsibilities for maintaining status while on OPT. Prior to recommending a 24-month OPT extension under paragraph (f)(10)(ii)(C) of this section, the DSO at the educational institution of the student's most recent enrollment must certify that the student's degree being used to qualify that student for the 24-month OPT extension, as shown in SEVIS or official transcripts, is a bachelor's, master's, or doctorate degree with a degree code that is contained within a category on the current STEM Designated Degree Program List at the time the recommendation is made. A DSO may recommend a student for a 24-month OPT extension under paragraph (f)(10)(ii)(C) of this section only if the Form I-983 or successor form described in paragraph (f)(10)(ii)(C)(7) of this section has been properly completed and executed by the student and prospective employer. A DSO may not recommend a student for an OPT extension under paragraph (f)(10)(ii)(C) of this section if the practical training would be conducted by an employer who has failed to meet the requirements under paragraphs (f)(10)(ii)(C)(5) through (9) of this section or has failed to provide the required assurances of paragraph (f)(10)(ii)(C)(10) of this section.

(B) The DSO must update the student's SEVIS record with the DSO's recommendation for OPT before the student can apply to USCIS for employment authorization. The DSO will indicate in SEVIS whether the OPT employment is to be full-time or part-time, or for a student seeking a recommendation for a 24-month OPT extension under paragraph (f)(10)(ii)(C) of this section whether the OPT employment meets the minimum hours requirements described in paragraph (f)(10)(ii)(C)(8) of this section, and note in SEVIS the OPT start and end dates.

(C) The DSO must provide the student with a signed, dated Form I-20 or successor form indicating that OPT has been recommended.

(iii) Decision on application for OPT employment authorization. USCIS will adjudicate a student's Form I-765 or successor form on the basis of the DSO's recommendation and other eligibility considerations.

(A) If granted, the employment authorization period for post-completion OPT begins on the requested date of commencement or the date the Form I-765 or successor form is approved, whichever is later, and ends at the conclusion of the remaining time period of post-completion OPT eligibility. The employment authorization period for a 24-month OPT extension under paragraph (f)(10)(ii)(C) of this section begins on the day after the expiration of the initial post-completion OPT employment authorization and ends 24 months thereafter, regardless of the date the actual extension is approved.

(B) USCIS will notify the applicant of the decision on the Form I-765 or successor form in writing, and, if the application is denied, of the reason or reasons for the denial.

(C) The applicant may not appeal the decision.

(12) Reporting while on optional practical training—

(i) General. An F-1 student who is granted employment authorization by USCIS to engage in optional practical training is required to report any change of name or address, or interruption of such employment to the DSO for the duration of the optional practical training. A DSO who recommends a student for OPT is responsible for updating the student's record to reflect these reported changes for the duration of the time that training is authorized.

(ii) Additional reporting obligations for students with an approved 24-month OPT extension. Students with an approved 24-month OPT extension under paragraph (f)(10)(ii)(C) of this section have additional reporting obligations. Compliance with these reporting requirements is required to maintain F-1 status. The reporting obligations are:

(A) Within 10 days of the change, the student must report to the student's DSO a change of legal name, residential or mailing address, employer name, employer address, and/or loss of employment.

(B) The student must complete a validation report, confirming that the information required by paragraph (f)(12)(ii)(A) of this section has not changed, every six months. The requirement for validation reporting starts on the date the 24-month OPT extension begins and ends when the student's F-1 status expires or the 24-month OPT extension concludes, whichever is first. The validation report is due to the student's DSO within 10 business days of each reporting date.

(13) Temporary absence from the United States of F-1 student granted employment authorization.

(i) A student returning from a temporary trip abroad with an unexpired off-campus employment authorization on their Form I-20 or successor form may resume employment only if the student is readmitted to attend the same school that granted the employment authorization.

(ii) An F-1 student who has an unexpired EAD issued for post-completion practical training and who is otherwise admissible may return to the United States to resume employment after a period of temporary absence. The EAD must be used in combination with a Form I-20 or successor form endorsed for reentry by the DSO within the last six months.

(14) Effect of strike or other labor dispute. Any employment authorization, whether or not part of an academic program, is automatically suspended upon certification by the Secretary of Labor or the Secretary's designee to the Secretary of Homeland Security or the Secretary's designee, that a strike or other labor dispute involving a work stoppage of workers is in progress in the occupation at the place of employment. As used in this paragraph, "place of employment" means the facility or facilities where a labor dispute exists. The employer is prohibited from transferring F-1 students working at other facilities to the facility where the work stoppage is occurring.

(15) Spouse and children of F-1 student. The F-2 spouse and minor children of an F-1 student will each be issued an individual Form I-20 or successor form in accordance with the provisions of § 214.3(k).

(i) Employment. The F-2 spouse and children of an F-1 student may not accept employment.

(ii) Study—

(A) F-2 post-secondary/vocational study —

(1) Authorized study at SEVP-certified schools. An F-2 spouse or F-2 child may enroll in less than a full course of study, as defined in paragraphs (f)(6)(i)(A) through (D) and (m)(9)(i) through (iv), in any course of study described in paragraphs (f)(6)(i)(A) through (D) or (m)(9)(i) through (iv) of this section at an SEVP-certified school. Notwithstanding paragraphs (f)(6)(i)(B) and (m)(9)(i) of this section, study at an undergraduate college or university or at a community college or junior college is not a full course of study solely because the F-2 nonimmigrant is engaging in a lesser course load to complete a course of study during the current term. An F-2 spouse or F-2 child enrolled in less than a full course of study is not eligible to engage in employment pursuant to paragraphs (f)(9) and (10) of this section or pursuant to paragraph (m)(14) of this section.

(2) Full course of study. Subject to paragraphs (f)(15)(ii)(B) and (f)(18) of this section, an F-2 spouse and child may engage in a full course of study only by applying for and obtaining a change of status to F-1, M-1 or J-1 nonimmigrant status, as appropriate, before beginning a full course of study. An F-2 spouse and child may engage in study that is avocational or recreational in nature, up to and including on a full-time basis.

(B) F-2 elementary or secondary study. An F-2 child may engage in full-time study, including any full course of study, in any elementary or secondary school (kindergarten through twelfth grade).

(C) An F-2 spouse and child violates his or her nonimmigrant status by enrolling in any study except as provided in paragraph (f)(15)(ii)(A) or (B) of this section.

(16) Reinstatement to student status. —

(i) General. USCIS may consider reinstating a student who makes a request for reinstatement on Form I-539, Application to Extend/Change Nonimmigrant Status, accompanied by a properly completed Form I-20 or successor form indicating the DSO's recommendation for reinstatement. USCIS may consider granting the request if the student:

(A) Has not been out of status for more than 5 months at the time of filing the request for reinstatement (or demonstrates that the failure to file within the 5 month period was the result of exceptional circumstances and that the student filed the request for reinstatement as promptly as possible under these exceptional circumstances);

(B) Does not have a record of repeated or willful violations of DHS regulations;

(C) Is currently pursuing, or intending to pursue, a full course of study in the immediate future at the school which issued the Form I-20 or successor form;

(D) Has not engaged in unauthorized employment;

(E) Is not deportable on any ground other than section 237(a)(1)(B) or (C)(i) of the Act; and

(F) Establishes to the satisfaction of USCIS, by a detailed showing, either that:

(1) The violation of status resulted from circumstances beyond the student's control. Such circumstances might include serious injury or illness, closure of the institution, a natural disaster, or inadvertence, oversight, or neglect on the part of the DSO, but do not include instances where a pattern of repeated violations or where a willful failure on the part of the student resulted in the need for reinstatement; or

(2) The violation relates to a reduction in the student's course load that would have been within a DSO's power to authorize, and that failure to approve reinstatement would result in extreme hardship to the student.

(ii) Decision. The adjudicating officer will update SEVIS to reflect USCIS' decision. If USCIS does not reinstate the student, the student may not appeal the decision.

(17) Current name and address. A student must inform DHS and the DSO of any legal changes to the student's name or of any change of address, within 10 days of the change, in a manner prescribed by the school. A student can satisfy the requirement in 8 CFR 265.1 of notifying DHS by providing a notice of a change of address within 10 days to the DSO, and the DSO in turn must enter the information in SEVIS within 21 days of notification by the student. Except in the case of a student who cannot receive mail where the student resides, the address provided by the student must be the actual physical location where the student resides rather than a mailing address. In cases where a student provides a mailing address, the school must maintain a record of, and must provide upon request from DHS, the actual physical location where the student resides.

(18) Special rules for certain border commuter students —

(i) Applicability. For purposes of the special rules in this paragraph (f)(18), the term "border commuter student" means a national of Canada or Mexico who is admitted to the United States as an F-1 nonimmigrant student to enroll in a full course of study, albeit on a part-time basis, in an approved school located within 75 miles of a United States land border. A border commuter student must maintain actual residence and place of abode in the student's country of nationality, and seek admission to the United States at a land border port-of-entry. These special rules do not apply to a national of Canada or Mexico who is:

(A) Residing in the United States while attending a certified school as an F-1 student, or

(B) Enrolled in a full course of study as defined in paragraph (f)(6) of this section.

(ii) Full course of study. The border commuter student must be enrolled in a full course of study at the school that leads to the attainment of a specific educational or professional objective, albeit on a part-time basis. A designated school official at the school may authorize an eligible border commuter student to enroll in a course load below that otherwise required for a full course of study under paragraph (f)(6) of this section, provided that the reduced course load is consistent with the border commuter student's certified course of study.

(iii) Period of admission. An F-1 nonimmigrant student who is admitted as a border commuter student under this paragraph (f)(18) will be admitted until a date certain. The DSO is required to specify a completion date on the Form I-20 that reflects the actual semester or term dates for the commuter student's current term of study. A new Form I-20 will be required for each new semester or term that the border commuter student attends at the school. The provisions of paragraphs (f)(5) and (f)(7) of this section, relating to duration of status and extension of stay, are not applicable to a border commuter student.

(iv) Employment. A border commuter student may not be authorized to accept any employment in connection with his or her F-1 student status, except for curricular practical training as provided in paragraph (f)(10)(i) of this section or post-completion optional practical training as provided in paragraph (f)(10)(ii)(A)(3) of this section.

(19) Remittance of the fee. An alien who applies for F-1 or F-3 nonimmigrant status in order to enroll in a program of study at an SEVP-certified educational institution is required to pay the Student and Exchange Visitor Information System (SEVIS) fee to DHS, pursuant to 8 CFR 214.13, except as otherwise provided in that section.

(g) Representatives to international organizations —

(1) General. The determination by a consular officer prior to admission and the recognition by the Secretary of State subsequent to admission is evidence of the proper classification of a nonimmigrant under section 101(a)(15)(G) of the Act. An alien who has a nonimmigrant status under section 101(a)(15)(G) (i), (ii), (iii) or (iv) of the Act is to be admitted for the duration of the period for which the alien continues to be recognized by the Secretary of State as being entitled to that status. An alien defined in section (101)(a)(15)(G)(v) of the Act is to be admitted for an initial period of not more than three years, and may be granted extensions of temporary stay in increments of not more than two years. In addition, the application for extension of temporary stay must be accompanied by a statement signed by the employing official stating that he or she intends to continue to employ the applicant and describing the type of work the applicant will perform.

(2) Definition of G-1, G-3, or G-4 dependent. For purposes of employment in the United States, the term dependent of a G-1, G-3, or G-4 principal alien, as used in § 214.2(g), means any of the following immediate members of the family habitually residing in the same household as the principal alien who is an officer or employee assigned to a mission, to an international organization, or is employed by an international organization in the United States:

(i) Spouse;

(ii) Unmarried children under the age of 21;

(iii) Unmarried sons or daughters under the age of 23 who are in full-time attendance as students at post-secondary educational institutions;

(iv) Unmarried sons or daughters under the age of 25 who are in full-time attendance as students at post-secondary educational institutions if a formal bilateral employment agreement permitting their employment in the United States was signed prior to November 21, 1988, and such bilateral employment agreement does not specify 23 as the maximum age for employment of such sons and daughters. The Office of Protocol of the Department of State shall maintain a listing of foreign states which the United States has such bilateral employment agreements. The provisions of this paragraph apply only to G-1 and G-3 dependents under certain bilateral agreements and are not applicable to G-4 dependents;

(v) Unmarried sons or daughters who are physically or mentally disabled to the extent that they cannot adequately care for themselves or cannot establish, maintain, or re-establish their own households. The Department of State or the Service may require certification(s) as it deems sufficient to document such mental or physical disability; or

(vi) An immediate family member of a G-1, G-3, or G-4 principal alien described in 22 CFR 41.21(a)(3)(i) to (iv) with G-1, G-3, or G-4 nonimmigrant status who falls within a category of aliens designated by the Department of State as qualifying dependents.

(3) Applicability of a formal bilateral agreement or an informal de facto arrangement for G-1 and G-3 dependents. The applicability of a formal bilateral agreement shall be based on the foreign state which employs the principal alien and not on the nationality of the principal alien or dependent. The applicability of an informal de facto arrangement shall be based on the foreign state which employs the principal alien, but under a de facto arrangement the principal alien also must be a national of the foreign state which employs him or her in the United States.

(4) Income tax, Social Security liability; non-applicability of certain immunities. Dependents who are granted employment authorization under this section are responsible for payment of all federal, state and

local income, employment and related taxes and Social Security contributions on any remuneration received. In addition, immunity from civil or administrative jurisdiction in accordance with Article 37 of the Vienna Convention on Diplomatic Relations or other international agreements does not apply to these dependents with respect to matters arising out of their employment.

(5) G-1 and G-3 dependent employment pursuant to formal bilateral employment agreements and informal de facto reciprocal arrangements, and G-4 dependent employment.

(i) The Office of Protocol shall maintain a listing of foreign states which have entered into formal bilateral employment agreements. Dependents of a G-1 or G-3 principal alien assigned to official duty in the United States may accept or continue in unrestricted employment based on such formal bilateral agreements, if the applicable agreement includes persons in G-1 or G-3 visa status, upon favorable recommendation by the Department of State and issuance of employment authorization documentation by the Service in accordance with 8 CFR part 274a. The application procedures are set forth in paragraph (g)(6) of this section.

(ii) For purposes of this section, an informal de facto reciprocal arrangement exists when the Department of State determines that a foreign state allows appropriate employment on the local economy for dependents of certain United States officials assigned to duty in that foreign state. The Office of Protocol shall maintain a listing of countries with which such reciprocity exists. Dependents of a G-1 or G-3 principal alien assigned to official duty in the United States may be authorized to accept or continue in employment based upon informal de facto arrangements, and dependents of a G-4 principal alien assigned to official duty in the United States may be authorized to accept or continue in employment upon favorable recommendation by the Department of State and issuance of employment authorization by the Service in accordance with 8 CFR part 274a. Additionally, the procedures set forth in paragraph (g)(6) of this section must be complied with, and the following conditions must be met:

(A) Both the principal alien and the dependent desiring employment are maintaining G-1, G-3, or G-4 status as appropriate;

(B) The principal's assignment in the United States is expected to last more than six months;

(C) Employment of a similar nature for dependents of United States Government officials assigned to official duty in the foreign state employing the principal alien is not prohibited by that foreign government. The provisions of this paragraph apply only to G-1 and G-3 dependents;

(D) The proposed employment is not in an occupation listed in the Department of Labor Schedule B (20 CFR part 656), or otherwise determined by the Department of Labor to be one for which there is an oversupply of qualified U.S. workers in the area of proposed employment. This Schedule B restriction does not apply to a dependent son or daughter who is a full-time student if the employment is part-time, consisting of not more than 20 hours per week, and/or if it is temporary employment of not more than 12 weeks during school holiday periods; and

(E) The proposed employment is not contrary to the interest of the United States. Employment contrary to the interest of the United States includes, but is not limited to, the employment of G-1, G-3, or G-4 dependents: who have criminal records; who have violated United States immigration laws or regulations, or visa laws or regulations; who have worked illegally in the United States; and/or who cannot establish that they have paid taxes and social security on income from current or previous United States employment. Additionally, the Department of State may determine a G-4 dependent's employment is contrary to the interest of the United States when the principal alien's country of nationality has one or more components of an international organization or international organizations within its borders and does not allow the employment of dependents of United States citizens employed by such component(s) or organization(s).

(6) Application procedures. The following procedures are applicable to G-1 and G-3 dependent employment applications under bilateral agreements and de facto arrangements, as well as to G-4 dependent employment applications:

(i) The dependent must submit a completed Form I-566 to the Department of State through the office, mission, or organization which employs his or her principal alien. If the principal is assigned to or employed by the United Nations, the Form I-566 must be submitted to the U.S. Mission to the United Nations. All other applications must be submitted to the Office of Protocol of the Department of State. A dependent applying under paragraph (g)(2) (iii) or (iv) of this section must submit a certified statement from the post-secondary educational institution confirming that he or she is pursuing studies on a full-time basis. A dependent applying under paragraph (g)(2)(v) of this section must submit medical certification regarding his or her condition. The certification should identify the dependent and the certifying physician and give the physician's phone number; identify the condition, describe the symptoms and provide a prognosis; certify that the dependent is unable to establish, re-establish, and maintain a home or his or her own. Additionally, a G-1 or G-3 dependent applying under the terms of a de facto arrangement or a G-4 dependent must attach a statement from the prospective employer which includes the dependent's name; a description of the position offered and the duties to be performed; the salary offered; and verification that the dependent possesses the qualifications for the position.

(ii) The Department of State reviews and verifies the information provided, makes its determination, and endorses the Form I-566.

(iii) If the Department of State's endorsement is favorable, the dependent may apply to USCIS for employment authorization. When applying to USCIS for employment authorization, the dependent must present his or her Form I-566 with a favorable endorsement from the Department of State and any additional documentation as may be required by the Secretary.

(7) Period of time for which employment may be authorized. If approved, an application to accept or continue employment under this section shall be granted in increments of not more than three years each.

(8) No appeal. There shall be no appeal from a denial of permission to accept or continue employment under this section.

(9) Dependents or family members of principal aliens classified G-2 or G-5. A dependent or family member of a principal alien classified G-2 or G-5 may not be employed in the United States under this section.

(10) Unauthorized employment. An alien classified under section 101(a)(15)(G) of the Act who is not a principal alien and who engages in employment outside the scope of, or in a manner contrary to this section, may be considered in violation of section 241(a)(1)(C)(i) of the Act. An alien who is classified under section 101(a)(15)(G) of the Act who is a principal alien and who engages in employment outside the scope of his/her official position may be considered in violation of section 241(a)(1)(C)(i) of the Act.

(11) Special provision. As of February 16, 1990 no new employment authorization will be granted and no pre-existing employment authorization will be extended for a G 1 dependent absent an appropriate bilateral agreement or de facto arrangement. However, a G-1 dependent who has been granted employment authorization by the Department of State prior to the effective date of this section and who meets the definition of dependent under § 214.2(g)(2) (i), (ii), (iii) or (v) of this part but is not covered by the terms of a bilateral agreement or de facto arrangement may be allowed to continue in employment until whichever of the following occurs first:

(i) The employment authorization by the Department of State expires; or

(ii) He or she no longer qualifies as a dependent as that term is defined in this section; or

(iii) March 19, 1990.

(h) Temporary employees.

Table 3 to Paragraph (h)—Paragraph Contents

(1) Admission of temporary employees.
(2) Petitions.
(3) Petition for registered nurse (H-1C).
(4) Petition for alien to perform services in a specialty occupation, services relating to a DOD cooperative research and development project or coproduction project, or services of distinguished merit and ability in the field of fashion modeling (H-1B).
(5) Petition for alien to perform agricultural labor or services of a temporary or seasonal nature (H-2A).
(6) Petition for alien to perform temporary nonagricultural services or labor (H-2B).
(7) Petition for alien trainee or participant in a special education exchange visitor program (H-3).
(8) Numerical limits.
(9) Approval and validity of petition.
(10) Denial of petition.
(11) Revocation of approval of petition.
(12) Appeal of a denial or a revocation of a petition.
(13) Admission.
(14) Extension of visa petition validity.
(15) Extension of stay.
(16) Effect of approval of a permanent labor certification or filing of a preference petition on H classification.
(17) Effect of a strike.
(18) Use of approval notice, Form I-797.
(19) Additional fee for filing certain H-1B petitions.
(20) Retaliatory action claims.
(21) Change of employers during COVID-19 National Emergency (August 19, 2020 through December 17, 2020).
(22) Change of employers during COVID-19 National Emergency (December 18, 2020 through June 16, 2021).
(23) Change of employers and extensions beyond 3 years during COVID-19 National Emergency for H-2B aliens essential to the U.S. food supply chain.
(24) Severability.
(25) [Reserved].
(26) Change of employers and portability for H-2B workers (May 25, 2021 through November 22, 2021).
(27) Change of employers and portability for H-2B workers (January 28, 2022 through July 27, 2022).
(28) Change of employers and portability for H-2B workers (July 28, 2022 through January 24, 2023).
(29) [Effective Dec. 15, 2022 through Dec. 15, 2025] Change of employers and portability for H-2B workers (January 25, 2023 through January 24, 2024).
(30) [Effective Nov. 17, 2023 through Nov. 17, 2026] [Reserved]
(31) [Effective Nov. 17, 2023 through Nov. 17, 2026] Change of employers and portability for H-2B workers (January 25, 2024 through January 24, 2025).
(32) [Effective Dec. 2, 2024 through Dec. 2, 2027] Change of employers and portability for H-2B workers (January 25, 2025 through January 24, 2026).

(1) Admission of temporary employees —

(i) General. Under section 101(a)(15)(H) of the Act, an alien may be authorized to come to the United States temporarily to perform services or labor for, or to receive training from, an employer, if petitioned for by that employer. Under this nonimmigrant category, the alien may be classified as follows: under section 101(a)(15)(H)(i)(c) of the Act as a registered nurse; under section 101(a)(15)(H)(i)(b) of the Act as an alien who is coming to perform services in a specialty occupation, services relating to a Department of Defense (DOD) cooperative research and development project or coproduction project, or services as a fashion model who is of distinguished merit and ability; under section 101(a)(15)(H)(ii)(a) of the Act as an alien who is coming to perform agricultural labor or services of a temporary or seasonal nature; under section 101(a)(15)(H)(ii)(b) of the Act as an alien coming to perform other temporary services or labor; or under section 101(a)(15)(H)(iii) of the Act as an alien who is coming as a trainee or as a participant in a special education exchange visitor program. These classifications are called H-1C, H-1B, H-2A, H-2B, and H-3, respectively. The employer must file a petition with the Service for review of the services or training and for determination of the alien's eligibility for classification as a temporary employee or trainee, before the alien may apply for a visa or seek admission to the United States. This paragraph sets forth the standards and procedures applicable to these classifications.

(ii) Description of classification.

(A) An H-1C classification applies to an alien who is coming temporarily to the United States to perform services as a registered nurse, meets the requirements of section 212(m)(1) of the Act, and will perform services at a facility (as defined at section 212(m)(6) of the Act) for which the Secretary of Labor has determined and certified to the Attorney General that an unexpired attestation is on file and in effect under section 212(m)(2) of the Act. This classification will expire 4 years from June 11, 2001.

(B) An H-1B classification applies to an alien who is coming temporarily to the United States:

(1) To perform services in a specialty occupation (except agricultural workers, and aliens described in section 101(a)(15) (O) and (P) of the Act) described in section 214(i)(1) of the Act, that meets the requirements of section 214(i)(2) of the Act, and for whom the Secretary of Labor has determined and certified to the Attorney General that the prospective employer has filed a labor condition application under section 212(n)(1) of the Act;

(2) To perform services of an exceptional nature requiring exceptional merit and ability relating to a cooperative research and development project or a coproduction project provided for under a Government-to-Government agreement administered by the Secretary of Defense;

(3) To perform services as a fashion model of distinguished merit and ability and for whom the Secretary of Labor has determined and certified to the Attorney General that the prospective employer has filed a labor condition application under section 212(n)(1) of the Act.

(C) An H-2A classification applies to an alien who is coming temporarily to the United States to perform agricultural work of a temporary or seasonal nature.

(D) An H-2B classification applies to an alien who is coming temporarily to the United States to perform nonagricultural work of a temporary or seasonal nature, if there are not sufficient workers who are able, willing, qualified, and available at the time of application for a visa and admission to the United States and at the place where the alien is to perform such services or labor. This classification does not apply to graduates of medical schools coming to the United States to perform services as members of the medical profession. The temporary or permanent nature of the services or labor described on the approved temporary labor certification are subject to review by USCIS. This classification requires a temporary labor certification issued by the Secretary of Labor or the Governor of Guam prior to the filing of a petition with USCIS.

(E) An H-3 classification applies to an alien who is coming temporarily to the United States:

(1) As a trainee, other than to receive graduate medical education or training, or training provided primarily at or by an academic or vocational institution, or

(2) As a participant in a special education exchange visitor program which provides for practical training and experience in the education of children with physical, mental, or emotional disabilities.

(2) Petitions —

(i) Filing of petitions —

(A) General. A United States employer seeking to classify an alien as an H-1B, H-2A, H-2B, or H-3 temporary employee must file a petition on the form prescribed by USCIS in accordance with the form instructions.

(B) [Removed and reserved.]

(C) Services or training for more than one employer. If the beneficiary will perform nonagricultural services for, or receive training from, more than one employer, each employer must file a separate petition with USCIS as provided in the form instructions.

(D) Change of employers. If the alien is in the United States and seeks to change employers, the prospective new employer must file a petition for a nonimmigrant worker requesting classification and an extension of the alien's stay in the United States. If the new petition is approved, the extension of stay may be granted for the validity of the approved petition. The validity of the petition and the alien's extension of stay must conform to the limits on the alien's temporary stay that are prescribed in paragraph (h)(13) of this section. Except as provided in paragraph (h)(2)(i)(I) of this section, 8 CFR 274a.12(b)(21), or section 214(n) of the Act, 8 U.S.C. 1184(n), the alien is not authorized to begin the employment with the new petitioner until the petition is approved. An H–1C nonimmigrant alien may not change employers.

(E) Amended or new petition—

(1) General provisions. The petitioner must file an amended or new petition, with the appropriate fee and in accordance with the form instructions, to reflect any material changes in the terms and conditions of employment or training or the beneficiary's eligibility as specified in the original approved petition. An amended or new H–1B, H–2A, or H–2B petition must be accompanied by a current or new Department of Labor determination. In the case of an H–1B petition, this requirement includes a current or new certified labor condition application.

(2) Additional H–1B provisions. The amended or new petition must be properly filed before the material change(s) takes place. The beneficiary is not authorized to work under the materially changed terms and conditions of employment until the new or amended H–1B petition is approved and takes effect, unless the beneficiary is eligible for H–1B portability pursuant to paragraph (h)(2)(i)(H) of this section. Any change in the place of employment to a geographical area that requires a corresponding labor condition application to be certified to USCIS is considered a material change and requires an amended or new petition to be filed with USCIS before the H–1B worker may begin work at the new place of employment. Provided there are no material changes in the terms and conditions of the H–1B worker's employment, a petitioner does not need to file an amended or new petition when:

(i) Moving a beneficiary to a new job location within the same area of intended employment as listed on the labor condition application certified to USCIS in support of the current H–1B petition approval authorizing the H–1B nonimmigrant's employment.

(ii) Placing a beneficiary at a shortterm placements(s) or assignment(s) at any worksite(s) outside of the area of intended employment for a total of 30 days or less in a 1-year period, or for a total of 60 days or less in a 1-year period where the H–1B beneficiary continues to maintain an office or work station at their permanent worksite, the beneficiary spends a substantial amount of time at the permanent worksite in a 1-year period, and the beneficiary's residence is located in the area of the permanent worksite and not in the area of the short-term worksite(s); or

(iii) An H–1B beneficiary is going to a non-worksite location to participate in employee development, will be spending little time at any one location, or when the job is peripatetic in nature, in that the normal duties of the beneficiary's occupation (rather than the nature of the employer's business) requires frequent travel (local or nonlocal) from location to location. Peripatetic jobs include situations where the job is primarily at one location, but the beneficiary occasionally travels for short periods to other locations on a casual, short-term basis, which can be recurring but not excessive (i.e., not exceeding 5 consecutive workdays for any one visit by a peripatetic worker, or 10 consecutive workdays for any one visit by a worker who spends most work time at one location and travels occasionally to other locations). (F) Agents as petitioners. A United States agent may file a petition in cases involving workers who are traditionally self-employed or workers who use agents to arrange short-term employment on their behalf with numerous employers, and in cases where a foreign employer authorizes the agent to act on its behalf. A United States agent may be: the actual employer of the beneficiary; the representative of both the employer and the beneficiary; or a person or entity authorized by the employer to act for, or in place of, the employer as its agent. The burden is on the agent to explain the terms and conditions of the employment and to provide any required documentation. In questionable cases, a contract between the employers and the beneficiary or beneficiaries may be required.

(1) An agent performing the function of an employer must guarantee the wages and other terms and conditions of employment by contractual agreement with the beneficiary or beneficiaries of the petition.

(2) A foreign employer who, through a United States agent, files a petition for an H nonimmigrant alien is responsible for complying with all of the employer sanctions provisions of section 274A of the Act and 8 CFR part 274a.

(F) Agents as petitioners. A United States agent may file a petition in cases involving workers who are traditionally self-employed or workers who use agents to arrange short-term employment on their behalf with numerous employers, and in cases where a foreign employer authorizes the agent to act on its behalf. A United States agent may be: the actual employer of the beneficiary, the representative of both the employer and the beneficiary, or, a person or entity authorized by the employer to act for, or in place of, the employer as it agent. A petition filed by a United States agent is subject to the following conditions;

(1) An agent performing the function of an employer must guarantee the wages and other terms and conditions of employment by contractual agreement with the beneficiary or beneficiaries of the petition. The agent/employer must also provide an itinerary of definite employment and information on any other services planned for the period of time requested.

(2) A person or company in business as an agent may file the H petition involving multiple employers as the representative of both the employers and the beneficiary or beneficiaries if the supporting documentation includes a complete itinerary of services or engagements. The itinerary shall specify the dates of each service or engagement, the names and addresses of the actual employers, and the names and addresses of the establishment, venues, or locations where the services will be performed. In questionable cases, a contract between the employers and the beneficiary or beneficiaries may be required. The burden is on the agent to explain the terms and conditions of the employment and to provide any required documentation.

(3) A foreign employer who, through a United States agent, files a petition for an H nonimmigrant alien is responsible for complying with all of the employer sanctions provisions of section 274A of the Act and 8 CFR part 274a.

(G) Multiple H-1B petitions. An employer may not file, in the same fiscal year, more than one H-1B petition on behalf of the same alien if the alien is subject to the numerical limitations of section 214(g)(1)(A) of the Act or is exempt from those limitations under section 214(g)(5)(C) of the Act. If an H-1B petition is denied, on a basis other than fraud or misrepresentation, the employer may file a subsequent H-1B petition on behalf of the same alien in the same fiscal year, provided that the numerical limitation has not been reached or if the filing qualifies as exempt from the numerical limitation. Otherwise, filing more than one H-1B petition by an employer on behalf of the same alien in the same fiscal year will result in the denial or revocation of all such petitions. If USCIS believes that related entities (such as a parent company, subsidiary, or affiliate) may not have a legitimate business need to file more than one H-1B petition on behalf of the same alien subject to the numerical limitations of section 214(g)(1)(A) of the Act or otherwise eligible for an exemption under section 214(g)(5)(C) of the Act, USCIS may issue a request for additional evidence or notice of intent to deny, or notice of intent to revoke each petition. If any of the related entities fail to demonstrate a legitimate business need to file an H-1B petition on behalf of the same alien, all petitions filed on that alien's behalf by the related entities will be denied or revoked.

(H) H-1B portability. An eligible H-1B nonimmigrant is authorized to start concurrent or new employment under section 214(n) of the Act upon the filing, in accordance with 8 CFR 103.2(a), of a nonfrivolous H-1B petition on behalf of such alien, or as of the requested start date, whichever is later.

(1) Eligible H-1B nonimmigrant. For H-1B portability purposes, an eligible H-1B nonimmigrant is defined as an alien:

(i) Who has been lawfully admitted into the United States in, or otherwise provided, H-1B nonimmigrant status;

(ii) On whose behalf a nonfrivolous H-1B petition for new employment has been filed, including a petition for new employment with the same employer, with a request to amend or extend the H-1B nonimmigrant's stay, before the H-1B nonimmigrant's period of stay authorized by the Secretary of Homeland Security expires; and

(iii) Who has not been employed without authorization in the United States from the time of last admission through the filing of the petition for new employment.

(2) Length of employment. Employment authorized under paragraph (h)(2)(i)(H) of this section automatically ceases upon the adjudication of the H-1B petition described in paragraph (h)(2)(i)(H)(1)(ii) of this section.

(3) Successive H-1B portability petitions.

(i) An alien maintaining authorization for employment under paragraph (h)(2)(i)(H) of this section, whose status, as indicated on the Arrival-Departure Record (Form I-94), has expired, shall be considered to be in a period of stay authorized by the Secretary of Homeland Security for purposes of paragraph (h)(2)(i)(H)(1)(ii) of this section. If otherwise eligible under paragraph (h)(2)(i)(H) of this section, such alien may begin working in a subsequent position upon the filing of another H-1B petition or from the requested start date, whichever is later, notwithstanding that the previous H-1B petition upon which employment is authorized under paragraph (h)(2)(i)(H) of this section remains pending and regardless of whether the validity period of an approved H-1B petition filed on the alien's behalf expired during such pendency.

(ii) A request to amend the petition or for an extension of stay in any successive H-1B portability petition cannot be approved if a request to amend the petition or for an extension of stay in any preceding H-1B portability petition in the succession is denied, unless the beneficiary's previously approved period of H-1B status remains valid.

(iii) Denial of a successive portability petition does not affect the ability of the H-1B beneficiary to continue or resume working in accordance with the terms of an H-1B petition previously approved on behalf of the beneficiary if that petition approval remains valid and the beneficiary has maintained H-1B status or been in a period of authorized stay and has not been employed in the United States without authorization.

(I) H–2A and H–2B portability. An eligible H–2A or H–2B nonimmigrant is authorized to start new employment upon the proper filing, in accordance with 8 CFR 103.2(a), of a nonfrivolous H–2A or H–2B petition on behalf of such alien requesting the same classification that the nonimmigrant alien currently holds, or as of the requested start date, whichever is later.

(1) Eligible H–2A or H–2B nonimmigrant. For H–2A and H–2B portability purposes, an eligible H–2A or H–2B nonimmigrant is defined as an alien:

(i) Who has been lawfully admitted into the United States in, or otherwise provided, H–2A or H–2B nonimmigrant status;

(ii) On whose behalf a nonfrivolous H–2A or H–2B petition for new employment has been properly filed, including a petition for new employment with the same employer, with a request to amend or extend the H–2A or H–2B nonimmigrant's stay in the same classification that the nonimmigrant currently holds, before the H–2A or H–2B nonimmigrant's period of stay authorized by the Secretary of Homeland Security expires; and

(iii) Who has not been employed without authorization in the United States from the time of last admission through the filing of the petition for new employment.

(2) Length of employment. Employment authorized under this paragraph (h)(2)(i)(I) automatically ceases upon the adjudication or withdrawal of the H–2A or H–2B petition described in paragraph (h)(2)(i)(I)(1)(ii) of this section.

(3) Application of H–2A or H–2B program requirements during the pendency of the petition. The petitioner and any employer is required to comply with all H–2A or H–2B program requirements, as applicable under the relevant program, with respect to an alien who has commenced new employment with that petitioner or employer based on a properly filed nonfrivolous petition and while that petition is pending, even if the petition is subsequently denied or withdrawn. During the pendency of the petition, the alien will not be considered to have been in a period of unauthorized stay or employed in the United States without authorization solely on the basis of employment pursuant to the new petition, even if the petition is subsequently denied or withdrawn.

(4) Successive H–2A or H–2B portability petitions.

(i) An alien maintaining authorization for employment under this paragraph (h)(2)(i)(I), whose status, as indicated on the Arrival–Departure Record (Form I–94), has expired, will be considered to be in a period of stay authorized by the Secretary of Homeland Security for purposes of paragraph (h)(2)(i)(I)(1)(ii) of this section. If otherwise eligible under this paragraph (h)(2)(i)(I), such alien may begin working in a subsequent position upon the filing of another H– 2A or H–2B petition in the same classification that the nonimmigrant alien currently holds or from the requested start date, whichever is later, notwithstanding that the previous H–2A or H–2B petition upon which employment is authorized under this paragraph (h)(2)(i)(I) remains pending and regardless of whether the validity period of an approved H–2A or H–2B petition filed on the alien's behalf expired during such pendency.

(ii) A request to amend the petition or for an extension of stay in any successive H–2A or H–2B portability petition requesting the same classification that the nonimmigrant alien currently holds cannot be approved if a request to amend the petition or for an extension of stay in any preceding H–2A or H–2B portability petition in the succession is denied, unless the beneficiary's previously approved period of H–2A or H–2B status remains valid.

(iii) Denial of a successive portability petition does not affect the ability of the H–2A or H–2B beneficiary to continue or resume working in accordance with the terms of an H–2A or H–2B petition previously approved on behalf of the beneficiary if that petition approval remains valid, and the beneficiary has either maintained H–2A or H–2B status, as appropriate, or been in a period of authorized stay and has not been employed in the United States without authorization.

(J) Time of filing. A petition filed under section 101(a)(15)(H) of the Act may not be filed earlier than 6 months before the date of actual need for the beneficiary's services or training.

(ii) Multiple beneficiaries. Up to 25 named beneficiaries may be included in an H-1C, H-2A, H-2B, or H-3 petition if the beneficiaries will be performing the same service, or receiving the same training, for the same period, and in the same location. If more than 25 named beneficiaries are being petitioned for, an additional petition is required. Petitions for H-2A and H-2B workers from countries not designated in accordance with paragraph (h)(6)(i)(E) of this section must be filed separately. Multiple beneficiaries. Up to 25 named beneficiaries may be included in an H–1C, H–2A, H–2B, or H–3 petition if the beneficiaries will be performing the same service, or receiving the same training, for the same period, and in the same location. If more than 25 named beneficiaries are being petitioned for, an additional petition is required.

(iii) Naming beneficiaries. H–1B, H– 1C, and H–3 petitions must include the name of each beneficiary. Except as provided in this paragraph (h), all H–2A and H–2B petitions must include the name of each beneficiary who is currently in the United States, but need not name any beneficiary who is not currently in the United States. Unnamed beneficiaries must be shown on the petition by total number. USCIS may require the petitioner to name H–2B beneficiaries where the name is needed to establish eligibility for H–2B nonimmigrant status. If all of the beneficiaries covered by an H–2A or H– 2B temporary labor certification have not been identified at the time a petition is filed, multiple petitions for subsequent beneficiaries may be filed at different times but must include a copy of the same temporary labor certification. Each petition must reference all previously filed petitions associated with that temporary labor certification.

(iv) [Reserved]

(v) H-2A Petitions. Special criteria for admission, extension, and maintenance of status apply to H-2A petitions and are specified in paragraph (h)(5) of this section. The other provisions of § 214.2(h) apply to H-2A only to the extent that they do not conflict with the special agricultural provisions in paragraph (h)(5) of this section.

(3) Petition for registered nurse (H-1C) —

(i) General.

(A) For purposes of H-1C classification, the term "registered nurse" means a person who is or will be authorized by a State Board of Nursing to engage in registered nurse practice in a state or U.S. territory or possession, and who is or will be practicing at a facility which provides health care services.

(B) A United States employer which provides health care services is referred to as a facility. A facility may file an H-1C petition for an alien nurse to perform the services of a registered nurse, if the facility meets the eligibility standards of 20 CFR 655.1111 and the other requirements of the Department of Labor's regulations in 20 CFR part 655, subpart L.

(C) The position must involve nursing practice and require licensure or other authorization to practice as a registered nurse from the State Board of Nursing in the state of intended employment.

(ii) [Reserved]

(iii) Beneficiary requirements. An H-1C petition for a nurse shall be accompanied by evidence that the nurse:

(A) Has obtained a full and unrestricted license to practice nursing in the country where the alien obtained nursing education, or has received nursing education in the United States;

(B) Has passed the examination given by the Commission on Graduates of Foreign Nursing Schools (CGFNS), or has obtained a full and unrestricted (permanent) license to practice as a registered nurse in the state of intended employment, or has obtained a full and unrestricted (permanent) license in any state or territory of the United States and received temporary authorization to practice as a registered nurse in the state of intended employment; and

(C) Is fully qualified and eligible under the laws (including such temporary or interim licensing requirements which authorize the nurse to be employed) governing the place of intended employment to practice as a registered nurse immediately upon admission to the United States, and is authorized under such laws to be employed by the employer. For purposes of this paragraph, the temporary or interim licensing may be obtained immediately after the alien enters the United States.

(iv) Petitioner requirements. The petitioning facility shall submit the following with an H-1C petition:

(A) A current copy of the DOL's notice of acceptance of the filing of its attestation on Form ETA 9081;

(B) A statement describing any limitations which the laws of the state or jurisdiction of intended employment place on the alien's services; and

(C) Evidence that the alien(s) named on the petition meets the definition of a registered nurse as defined at 8 CFR 214.2(h)(3)(i)(A), and satisfies the requirements contained in section 212(m)(1) of the Act.

(v) Licensure requirements.

(A) A nurse who is granted H-1C classification based on passage of the CGFNS examination must, upon admission to the United States, be able to obtain temporary licensure or other temporary authorization to practice as a registered nurse from the State Board of Nursing in the state of intended employment.

(B) An alien who was admitted as an H-1C nonimmigrant on the basis of a temporary license or authorization to practice as a registered nurse must comply with the licensing requirements for registered nurses in the state of intended employment. An alien admitted as an H-1C nonimmigrant is required to obtain a full and unrestricted license if required by the state of intended employment. The Service must be notified pursuant to § 214.2(h)(11) when an H-1C nurse is no longer licensed as a registered nurse in the state of intended employment.

(C) A nurse shall automatically lose his or her eligibility for H-1C classification if he or she is no longer performing the duties of a registered professional nurse. Such a nurse is not authorized to remain in employment unless he or she otherwise receives authorization from the Service.

(vi) Other requirements.

(A) If the Secretary of Labor notifies the Service that a facility which employs H-1C nonimmigrant nurses has failed to meet a condition in its attestation, or that there was a misrepresentation of a material fact in the attestation, the Service shall not approve petitions for H-1C nonimmigrant nurses to be employed by the facility for a period of at least 1 year from the date of receipt of such notice. The Secretary of Labor shall make a recommendation with respect to the length of debarment. If the Secretary of Labor recommends a longer period of debarment, the Service will give considerable weight to that recommendation.

(B) If the facility's attestation expires, or is suspended or invalidated by DOL, the Service will not suspend or revoke the facility's approved petitions for nurses, if the facility has agreed to comply with the terms of the attestation under which the nurses were admitted or subsequent attestations accepted by DOL for the duration of the nurses' authorized stay.

(4) Petition for alien to perform services in a specialty occupation, services relating to a DOD cooperative research and development project or coproduction project, or services of distinguished merit and ability in the ield of fashion modeling (H-1B) —

(i)(A) Types of H-1B classification. An H-1B classification may be granted to an alien who:

(1) Will perform services in a specialty occupation which requires theoretical and practical application of a body of highly specialized knowledge and attainment of a baccalaureate or higher degree or its equivalent as a minimum requirement for entry into the occupation in the United States, and who is qualified to perform services in the specialty occupation because he or she has attained a baccalaureate or higher degree or its equivalent in the specialty occupation;

(2) Based on reciprocity, will perform services of an exceptional nature requiring exceptional merit and ability relating to a DOD cooperative research and development project or a coproduction project provided for under a Government-to-Government agreement administered by the Secretary of Defense;

(3) Will perform services in the field of fashion modeling and who is of distinguished merit and ability.

(B) General requirements for petitions involving a specialty occupation—

(1) Labor condition application requirements.

(i) Before filing a petition for H–1B classification in a specialty occupation, the petitioner must obtain a certified labor condition application from the Department of Labor in the occupational specialty in which the alien(s) will be employed.

(ii) Certification by the Department of Labor of a labor condition application in an occupational classification does not constitute a determination by the agency that the occupation in question is a specialty occupation. USCIS will determine whether the labor condition application involves a specialty occupation as defined in section 214(i)(1) of the Act and properly corresponds with the petition. USCIS will also determine whether all other eligibility requirements have been met, such as whether the alien for whom H– 1B classification is sought qualifies to perform services in the specialty occupation as prescribed in section 214(i)(2) of the Act.

(iii) If all of the beneficiaries covered by an H–1B labor condition application have not been identified at the time a petition is filed, petitions for newly identified beneficiaries may be filed at any time during the validity of the labor condition application using copies of the same certified labor condition application. Each petition must refer by file number to all previously approved petitions for that labor condition application.

(iv) When petitions have been approved for the total number of workers specified in the labor condition application, substitution of aliens against previously approved openings cannot be made. A new labor condition application will be required.

(v) If the Secretary of Labor notifies USCIS that the petitioning employer has failed to meet a condition of paragraph (B) of section 212(n)(1) of the Act, has substantially failed to meet a condition of paragraphs (C) or (D) of section 212(n)(1) of the Act, has willfully failed to meet a condition of paragraph (A) of section 212(n)(1) of the Act, or has misrepresented any material fact in the application, USCIS will not approve petitions filed with respect to that employer under section 204 or 214(c) of the Act for a period of at least 1 year from the date of receipt of such notice. (vi) If the employer's labor condition application is suspended or invalidated by the Department of Labor, USCIS will not suspend or revoke the employer's approved petitions for aliens already employed in specialty occupations if the employer has certified to the Department of Labor that it will comply with the terms of the labor condition application for the duration of the authorized stay of aliens it employs.

(2) Inspections, evaluations, verifications, and compliance reviews.

(i) The information provided on an H– 1B petition and the evidence submitted in support of such petition may be verified by USCIS through lawful means as determined by USCIS, including telephonic and electronic verifications and on-site inspections. Such verifications and inspections may include, but are not limited to: electronic validation of a petitioner's or third party's basic business information; visits to the petitioner's or third party's facilities; interviews with the petitioner's or third party's officials; reviews of the petitioner's or third party's records related to compliance with immigration laws and regulations; and interviews with any other individuals possessing pertinent information, as determined by USCIS, which may be conducted in the absence of the employer or the employer's representatives; and reviews of any other records that USCIS may lawfully obtain and that it considers pertinent to verify facts related to the adjudication of the H–1B petition, such as facts relating to the petitioner's and beneficiary's H– 1B eligibility and compliance. The interviews may be conducted on the employer's property, or as feasible, at a neutral location agreed to by the interviewee and USCIS away from the employer's property. An inspection may be conducted at locations including the petitioner's headquarters, satellite locations, or the location where the beneficiary works, has worked, or will work, including third party worksites, as applicable. USCIS may commence verification or inspection under this paragraph (h)(4)(i)(B)(2) for any petition and at any time after an H–1B petition is filed, including any time before or after the final adjudication of the petition. The commencement of such verification and inspection before the final adjudication of the petition does not preclude the ability of USCIS to complete final adjudication of the petition before the verification and inspection are completed.

(ii) USCIS conducts on-site inspections or other compliance reviews to verify facts related to the adjudication of the petition and compliance with H– 1B petition requirements. If USCIS is unable to verify facts, including due to the failure or refusal of the petitioner or a third party to cooperate in an inspection or other compliance review, then such inability to verify facts, including due to failure or refusal to cooperate, may result in denial or revocation of any H–1B petition for H–1B workers performing services at the location or locations that are a subject of inspection or compliance review, including any third party worksites.

(3) Third party requirements. If the beneficiary will be staffed to a third party, meaning they will be contracted to fill a position in a third party's organization and becomes part of that third party's organizational hierarchy by filling a position in that hierarchy (and not merely providing services to the third party), the actual work to be performed by the beneficiary must be in a specialty occupation. When staffed to a third party, it is the requirements of that third party, and not the petitioner, that are most relevant when determining whether the position is a specialty occupation.

(C) General requirements for petitions involving an alien of distinguished merit and ability in the field of fashion modeling — H-1B classification may be granted to an alien who is of distinguished merit and ability in the field of fashion modeling. An alien of distinguished merit and ability in the field of fashion modeling is one who is prominent in the field of fashion modeling. The alien must also be coming to the United States to perform services which require a fashion model of prominence.

(ii) Definitions.

Employer-employee relationship means the conventional master-servant relationship consistent with the common law. The petitioner must establish that its offer of employment as stated in the petition is based on a valid employer-employee relationship that exists or will exist. In considering whether the petitioner has established that a valid "employer-employee relationship" exists or will exist, USCIS will assess and weigh all relevant aspects of the relationship with no one factor being determinative.

(1) In cases where the H–1B beneficiary does not possess an ownership interest in the petitioning organization or entity, the factors that USCIS may consider to determine if a valid employment relationship will exist or continue to exist include, but are not limited to:

(i) Whether the petitioner supervises the beneficiary and, if so, where such supervision takes place;

(ii) Where the supervision is not at the petitioner's worksite, how the petitioner maintains such supervision;

(iii) Whether the petitioner has the right to control the work of the beneficiary on a day-to-day basis and to assign projects;

(iv) Whether the petitioner provides the tools or instrumentalities needed for the beneficiary to perform the duties of employment;

(v) Whether the petitioner hires, pays, and has the ability to fire the beneficiary;

(vi) Whether the petitioner evaluates the work-product of the beneficiary;

(vii) Whether the petitioner claims the beneficiary as an employee for tax purposes;

(viii) Whether the petitioner provides the beneficiary any type of employee benefits;

(ix) Whether the beneficiary uses proprietary information of the petitioner in order to perform the duties of employment;

(x) Whether the beneficiary produces an end-product that is directly linked to the petitioner's line of business; and

(xi) Whether the petitioner has the ability to control the manner and means in which the work product of the beneficiary is accomplished.

(2) In cases where the H–1B beneficiary possesses an ownership interest in the petitioning organization or entity, additional factors that USCIS may consider to determine if a valid employment relationship will exist or continue to exist include, but are not limited to:

(i) Whether the petitioning entity can hire or fire the beneficiary or set the rules and parameters of the beneficiary's work;

(ii) Whether and, if so, to what extent the petitioner supervises the beneficiary's work;

(iii) Whether the beneficiary reports to someone higher in the petitioning entity;

(iv) Whether and, if so, to what extent the beneficiary is able to influence the petitioning entity;

(v) Whether the parties intended that the beneficiary be an employee, as expressed in written agreements or contracts; and

(vi) Whether the beneficiary shares in the profits, losses, and liabilities of the organization or entity.

Prominence means a high level of achievement in the field of fashion modeling evidenced by a degree of skill and recognition substantially above that ordinarily encountered to the extent that a person described as prominent is renowned, leading, or well-known in the field of fashion modeling.

Recognized authority means a person or an organization with expertise in a particular field, special skills or knowledge in that field, and the expertise to render the type of opinion requested. Such an opinion must state:

(1) The writer's qualifications as an expert;

(2) The writer's experience giving such opinions, citing specific instances where past opinions have been accepted as authoritative and by whom;

(3) How the conclusions were reached; and

(4) The basis for the conclusions supported by copies or citations of any research material used.

Specialty occupation means an occupation which requires theoretical and practical application of a body of highly specialized knowledge in fields of human endeavor including, but not limited to, architecture, engineering, mathematics, physical sciences, social sciences, medicine and health, education, business specialties, accounting, law, theology, and the arts, and which requires the attainment of a bachelor's degree or higher in a directly related specific specialty, or its equivalent, as a minimum for entry into the occupation in the United States. A position is not a specialty occupation if attainment of a general degree, without further specialization, is sufficient to qualify for the position. A position may allow for a range of qualifying degree fields, provided that each of those fields is directly related to the duties of the position. Directly related means there is a logical connection between the required degree, or its equivalent, and the duties of the position.

Third-party worksite means a worksite, other than the beneficiary's residence in the United States, that is not owned or leased, and not operated, by the petitioner.

United States employer means a person, firm, corporation, contractor, or other association, or organization in the United States that:

(1) Has a bona fide job offer for the beneficiary to work within the United States, which may include telework, remote work, or other off-site work within the United States;

(2) Has a legal presence in the United States and is amenable to service of process in the United States; and

(3) Has an Internal Revenue Service Tax identification number.

(4) If the H–1B beneficiary possesses a controlling interest in the petitioner, meaning the beneficiary owns more than 50 percent of the petitioner or has majority voting rights in the petitioner, such a beneficiary may perform duties that are directly related to owning and directing the petitioner's business as long as the beneficiary will perform specialty occupation duties a majority of the time, consistent with the terms of the H–1B petition.

Worksite means the physical location where the work actually is performed by the H–1B nonimmigrant. A "worksite" will not include any location that would not be considered a "worksite" for Labor Condition Application (LCA) purposes.

(iii) General H–1B requirements—

(A) Criteria for specialty occupation position. A position does not meet the definition of specialty occupation in paragraph (h)(4)(ii) of this section unless it also satisfies at least one of the following criteria at paragraphs (h)(4)(iii)(A)(1) through (4) of this section:

(1) A U.S. baccalaureate or higher degree in a directly related specific specialty, or its equivalent, is normally the minimum requirement for entry into the particular occupation;

(2) A U.S. baccalaureate or higher degree in a directly related specific specialty, or its equivalent, is normally required to perform job duties in parallel positions among similar organizations in the employer's industry in the United States;

(3) The employer, or third party if the beneficiary will be staffed to that third party, normally requires a U.S. baccalaureate or higher degree in a directly related specific specialty, or its equivalent, to perform the job duties of the position; or

(4) The specific duties of the proffered position are so specialized, complex, or unique that the knowledge required to perform them is normally associated with the attainment of a U.S. baccalaureate or higher degree in a directly related specific specialty, or its equivalent.

(5) For purposes of the criteria at paragraphs (h)(4)(iii)(A)(1) through (4) of this section, normally means conforming to a type, standard, or regular pattern, and is characterized by that which is considered usual, typical, common, or routine. Normally does not mean always.

(B) Petitioner requirements. The petitioner shall submit the following with an H-1B petition involving a specialty occupation:

(1) A certification from the Secretary of Labor that the petitioner has filed a labor condition application with the Secretary,

(2) A statement that it will comply with the terms of the labor condition application for the duration of the alien's authorized period of stay,

(3) Evidence that the alien qualifies to perform services in the specialty occupation as described in paragraph (h)(4)(iii)(A) of this section, and

(C) Beneficiary qualifications. To qualify to perform services in a specialty occupation, the alien must meet one of the following criteria:

(1) Hold a United States baccalaureate or higher degree required by the specialty occupation from an accredited college or university;

(2) Hold a foreign degree determined to be equivalent to a United States baccalaureate or higher degree required by the specialty occupation from an accredited college or university;

(3) Hold an unrestricted State license, registration or certification which authorizes him or her to fully prac-

tice the specialty occupation and be immediately engaged in that specialty in the state of intended employment; or

(4) Have education, specialized training, and/or progressively responsible experience that is equivalent to completion of a United States baccalaureate or higher degree in the specialty occupation, and have recognition of expertise in the specialty through progressively responsible positions directly related to the specialty.

(D) Equivalence to completion of a college degree. For purposes of paragraph (h)(4)(iii)(C)(4) of this section, equivalence to completion of a United States baccalaureate or higher degree shall mean achievement of a level of knowledge, competence, and practice in the specialty occupation that has been determined to be equal to that of an individual who has a baccalaureate or higher degree in the specialty and shall be determined by one or more of the following:

(1) An evaluation from an official who has authority to grant college-level credit for training and/or experience in the specialty at an accredited college or university which has a program for granting such credit based on an individual's training and/or work experience;

(2) The results of recognized college-level equivalency examinations or special credit programs, such as the College Level Examination Program (CLEP), or Program on Noncollegiate Sponsored Instruction (PONSI);

(3) An evaluation of education by a reliable credentials evaluation service which specializes in evaluating foreign educational credentials;

(4) Evidence of certification or registration from a nationally-recognized professional association or society for the specialty that is known to grant certification or registration to persons in the occupational specialty who have achieved a certain level of competence in the specialty;

(5) A determination by the Service that the equivalent of the degree required by the specialty occupation has been acquired through a combination of education, specialized training, and/or work experience in areas related to the specialty and that the alien has achieved recognition of expertise in the specialty occupation as a result of such training and experience. For purposes of determining equivalency to a baccalaureate degree in the specialty, three years of specialized training and/or work experience must be demonstrated for each year of college-level training the alien lacks. For equivalence to an advanced (or Masters) degree, the alien must have a baccalaureate degree followed by at least five years of experience in the specialty. If required by a specialty, the alien must hold a Doctorate degree or its foreign equivalent. It must be clearly demonstrated that the alien's training and/or work experience included the theoretical and practical application of specialized knowledge required by the specialty occupation; that the alien's experience was gained while working with peers, supervisors, or subordinates who have a degree or its equivalent in the specialty occupation; and that the alien has recognition of expertise in the specialty evidenced by at least one type of documentation such as:

(i) Recognition of expertise in the specialty occupation by at least two recognized authorities in the same specialty occupation;

(ii) Membership in a recognized foreign or United States association or society in the specialty occupation;

(iii) Published material by or about the alien in professional publications, trade journals, books, or major newspapers;

(iv) Licensure or registration to practice the specialty occupation in a foreign country; or

(v) Achievements which a recognized authority has determined to be significant contributions to the field of the specialty occupation.

(E) Liability for transportation costs. The employer will be liable for the reasonable costs of return transportation of the alien abroad if the alien is dismissed from employment by the employer before the end of the period of authorized admission pursuant to section 214(c)(5) of the Act. If the beneficiary voluntarily terminates his or her employment prior to the expiration of the validity of the petition, the alien has not been dismissed. If the beneficiary believes that the employer has not complied with this provision, the beneficiary shall advise the Service Center which adjudicated the petition in writing. The complaint will be retained in the file relating to the petition. Within the context of this paragraph, the term "abroad" refers to the alien's last place of foreign residence. This provision applies to any employer whose offer of employment became the basis for an alien obtaining or continuing H-1B status.

(F) Bona fide position in a specialty occupation. At the time of filing, the petitioner must establish that it has a bona fide position in a specialty occupation available for the beneficiary as of the start date of the validity period as requested on the petition. A petitioner is not required to establish specific day-to-day assignments for the entire time requested in the petition.

(iv) General documentary requirements for H–1B classification in a specialty occupation. Except as specified in paragraph (h)(4)(iv)(C) of this section, an H–1B petition involving a specialty occupation must be accompanied by:

(A) Documentation, certifications, affidavits, declarations, degrees, diplomas, writings, reviews, or any other required evidence sufficient to establish that the beneficiary is qualified to perform services in a specialty occupation as described in paragraph (h)(4)(i) of this section and that the services the beneficiary is to perform are in a specialty occupation. The evidence shall conform to the following:

(1) School records, diplomas, degrees, affidavits, declarations, contracts, and similar documentation submitted must reflect periods of attendance, courses of study, and similar pertinent data, be executed by the person in charge of the records of the educational or other institution, firm, or establishment where education or training was acquired.

(2) Affidavits or declarations made under penalty of perjury submitted by present or former employers or recognized authorities certifying as to the recognition and expertise of the beneficiary shall specifically describe the beneficiary's recognition and ability in fac-

tual terms and must set forth the expertise of the affiant and the manner in which the affiant acquired such information.

(B) Copies of any written contracts between the petitioner and beneficiary, or a summary of the terms of the oral agreement under which the beneficiary will be employed, if there is no written contract.

(C) In accordance with 8 CFR 103.2(b) and paragraph (h)(9) of this section, USCIS may request evidence such as contracts, work orders, or other similar evidence between all parties in a contractual relationship showing the bona fide nature of the beneficiary's position and the minimum educational requirements to perform the duties.

(v) Licensure for H classification —

(A) General. If an occupation requires a state or local license for an individual to fully perform the duties of the occupation, an alien (except an H-1C nurse) seeking H classification in that occupation must have that license prior to approval of the petition to be found qualified to enter the United States and immediately engage in employment in the occupation.

(B) Temporary licensure. If a temporary license is available and the alien is allowed to perform the duties of the occupation without a permanent license, the director shall examine the nature of the duties, the level at which the duties are performed, the degree of supervision received, and any limitations placed on the alien. If an analysis of the facts demonstrates that the alien under supervision is authorized to fully perform the duties of the occupation, H classification may be granted.

(C) Duties without licensure.

(1) In certain occupations which generally require licensure, a state may allow an individual without licensure to fully practice the occupation under the supervision of licensed senior or supervisory personnel in that occupation. In such cases, USCIS shall examine the nature of the duties and the level at which they are performed, as well as evidence provided by the petitioner as to the identity, physical location, and credentials of the individual(s) who will supervise the alien, and evidence that the petitioner is complying with state requirements. If the facts demonstrate that the alien under supervision will fully perform the duties of the occupation, H classification may be granted.

(2) An H-1B petition filed on behalf of an alien who does not have a valid state or local license, where a license is otherwise required to fully perform the duties in that occupation, may be approved for a period of up to 1 year if:

(i) The license would otherwise be issued provided the alien was in possession of a valid Social Security number, was authorized for employment in the United States, or met a similar technical requirement; and

(ii) The petitioner demonstrates, through evidence from the state or local licensing authority, that the only obstacle to the issuance of a license to the beneficiary is the lack of a Social Security number, a lack of employment authorization in the United States, or a failure to meet a similar technical requirement that precludes the issuance of the license to an individual who is not yet in H-1B status. The petitioner must demonstrate that the alien is fully qualified to receive the state or local license in all other respects, meaning that all educational, training, experience, and other substantive requirements have been met. The alien must have filed an application for the license in accordance with applicable state and local rules and procedures, provided that state or local rules or procedures do not prohibit the alien from filing the license application without provision of a Social Security number or proof of employment authorization or without meeting a similar technical requirement.

(3) An H-1B petition filed on behalf of an alien who has been previously accorded H-1B classification under paragraph (h)(4)(v)(C)(2) of this section may not be approved unless the petitioner demonstrates that the alien has obtained the required license, is seeking to employ the alien in a position requiring a different license, or the alien will be employed in that occupation in a different location which does not require a state or local license to fully perform the duties of the occupation.

(D) H-1C nurses. For purposes of licensure, H-1C nurses must provide the evidence required in paragraph (h)(3)(iii) of this section.

(E) Limitation on approval of petition. Where licensure is required in any occupation, including registered nursing, the H petition may only be approved for a period of one year or for the period that the temporary license is valid, whichever is longer, unless the alien already has a permanent license to practice the occupation. An alien who is accorded H classification in an occupation which requires licensure may not be granted an extension of stay or accorded a new H classification after the one year unless he or she has obtained a permanent license in the state of intended employment or continues to hold a temporary license valid in the same state for the period of the requested extension.

(vi) Criteria and documentary requirements for H-1B petitions involving DOD cooperative research and development projects or coproduction projects —

(A) General.

(1) For purposes of H-1B classification, services of an exceptional nature relating to DOD cooperative research and development projects or coproduction projects shall be those services which require a baccalaureate or higher degree, or its equivalent, to perform the duties. The existence of this special program does not preclude the DOD from utilizing the regular H-1B provisions provided the required guidelines are met.

(2) The requirements relating to a labor condition application from the Department of Labor shall not apply to petitions involving DOD cooperative research and development projects or coproduction projects.

(B) Petitioner requirements.

(1) The petition must be accompanied by a verification letter from the DOD project manager for the particular project stating that the alien will be working on a cooperative research and development project or a coproduction project under a reciprocal Government-to-

Government agreement administered by DOD. Details about the specific project are not required.

(2) The petitioner shall provide a general description of the alien's duties on the particular project and indicate the actual dates of the alien's employment on the project.

(3) The petitioner shall submit a statement indicating the names of aliens currently employed on the project in the United States and their dates of employment. The petitioner shall also indicate the names of aliens whose employment on the project ended within the past year.

(C) Beneficiary requirement. The petition shall be accompanied by evidence that the beneficiary has a baccalaureate or higher degree or its equivalent in the occupational field in which he or she will be performing services in accordance with paragraph (h)(4)(iii)(C) and/or (h)(4)(iii)(D) of this section.

(vii) Criteria and documentary requirements for H-1B petitions for aliens of distinguished merit and ability in the field of fashion modeling —

(A) General. Prominence in the field of fashion modeling may be established in the case of an individual fashion model. The work which a prominent alien is coming to perform in the United States must require the services of a prominent alien. A petition for an H-1B alien of distinguished merit and ability in the field of fashion modeling shall be accompanied by:

(1) Documentation, certifications, affidavits, writings, reviews, or any other required evidence sufficient to establish that the beneficiary is a fashion model of distinguished merit and ability. Affidavits submitted by present or former employers or recognized experts certifying to the recognition and distinguished ability of the beneficiary shall specifically describe the beneficiary's recognition and ability in factual terms and must set forth the expertise of the affiant and the manner in which the affiant acquired such information.

(2) Copies of any written contracts between the petitioner and beneficiary, or a summary of the terms of the oral agreement under which the beneficiary will be employed, if there is no written contract.

(B) Petitioner's requirements. To establish that a position requires prominence, the petitioner must establish that the position meets one of the following criteria:

(1) The services to be performed involve events or productions which have a distinguished reputation;

(2) The services are to be performed for an organization or establishment that has a distinguished reputation for, or record of, employing prominent persons.

(C) Beneficiary's requirements. A petitioner may establish that a beneficiary is a fashion model of distinguished merit and ability by the submission of two of the following forms of documentation showing that the alien:

(1) Has achieved national or international recognition and acclaim for outstanding achievement in his or her field as evidenced by reviews in major newspapers, trade journals, magazines, or other published material;

(2) Has performed and will perform services as a fashion model for employers with a distinguished reputation;

(3) Has received recognition for significant achievements from organizations, critics, fashion houses, modeling agencies, or other recognized experts in the field; or

(4) Commands a high salary or other substantial remuneration for services evidenced by contracts or other reliable evidence.

(viii) Criteria and documentary requirements for H-1B petitions for physicians —

(A) Beneficiary's requirements. An H-1B petition for a physician shall be accompanied by evidence that the physician:

(1) Has a license or other authorization required by the state of intended employment to practice medicine, or is exempt by law therefrom, if the physician will perform direct patient care and the state requires the license or authorization, and

(2) Has a full and unrestricted license to practice medicine in a foreign state or has graduated from a medical school in the United States or in a foreign state.

(B) Petitioner's requirements. The petitioner must establish that the alien physician:

(1) Is coming to the United States primarily to teach or conduct research, or both, at or for a public or nonprofit private educational or research institution or agency, and that no patient care will be performed, except that which is incidental to the physician's teaching or research; or

(2) The alien has passed the Federation Licensing Examination (or an equivalent examination as determined by the Secretary of Health and Human Services) or is a graduate of a United States medical school; and

(i) Has competency in oral and written English which shall be demonstrated by the passage of the English language proficiency test given by the Educational Commission for Foreign Medical Graduates; or

(ii) Is a graduate of a school of medicine accredited by a body or bodies approved for that purpose by the Secretary of Education.

(C) Exception for physicians of national or international renown. A physician who is a graduate of a medical school in a foreign state and who is of national or international renown in the field of medicine is exempt from the requirements of paragraph (h)(4)(viii)(B) of this section.

(5) Petition for alien to perform agricultural labor or services of a temporary or seasonal nature (H-2A) —

(i) Filing a petition --

(A) General. An H-2A petition must be filed on the form prescribed by USCIS with a single valid temporary agricultural labor certification. The petition may be filed by either the employer listed on the temporary labor certification, the employer's agent, or the association of United States agricultural producers named as a joint employer on the temporary labor certification.

(B) Multiple beneficiaries. The total number of beneficiaries of a petition or series of petitions based on the same temporary labor certification may not exceed the number of workers indicated on that document. A single petition can include more than one named beneficiary if the total number is 25 or fewer and does not exceed the number of positions indicated on the relating temporary labor certification.

(C) [Reserved]

(D) Evidence. An H-2A petitioner must show that the proposed employment qualifies as a basis for H-2A status, and that any named beneficiary qualifies for that employment. A petition will be automatically denied if filed without the certification evidence required in paragraph (h)(5)(i)(A) of this section and, for each named beneficiary, the initial evidence required in paragraph (h)(5)(v) of this section.

(E) Special filing requirements. Where a certification shows joint employers, a petition must be filed with an attachment showing that each employer has agreed to the conditions of H-2A eligibility. A petition filed by an agent must be filed with an attachment in which the employer has authorized the agent to act on its behalf, has assumed full responsibility for all representations made by the agent on its behalf, and has agreed to the conditions of H-2A eligibility.

(ii) Effect of the labor certification process. The temporary agricultural labor certification process determines whether employment is as an agricultural worker, whether it is open to U.S. workers, if qualified U.S. workers are available, the adverse impact of employment of a qualified alien, and whether employment conditions, including housing, meet applicable requirements. In petition proceedings a petitioner must establish that the employment and beneficiary meet the requirements of paragraph (h)(5) of this section.

(iii) Ability and intent to meet a job offer --

(A) Eligibility requirements. An H-2A petitioner must establish that each beneficiary will be employed in accordance with the terms and conditions of the certification, which includes that the principal duties to be performed are those on the certification, with other duties minor and incidental.

(B) [Removed and reserved.]

(C) Initial evidence. Representations required for the purpose of labor certification are initial evidence of intent.

(iv) Temporary and seasonal employment --

(A) Eligibility requirements. An H-2A petitioner must establish that the employment proposed in the certification is of a temporary or seasonal nature. Employment is of a seasonal nature where it is tied to a certain time of year by an event or pattern, such as a short annual growing cycle or a specific aspect of a longer cycle, and requires labor levels far above those necessary for ongoing operations. Employment is of a temporary nature where the employer's need to fill the position with a temporary worker will, except in extraordinary circumstances, last no longer than one year.

(B) Effect of Department of Labor findings. In temporary agricultural labor certification proceedings the Department of Labor separately tests whether employment qualifies as temporary or seasonal. Its finding that employment qualifies is normally sufficient for the purpose of an H-2A petition, However, notwithstanding that finding, employment will be found not to be temporary or seasonal where an application for permanent labor certification has been filed for the same alien, or for another alien to be employed in the same position, by the same employer or by its parent, subsidiary or affiliate. This can only be overcome by the petitioner's demonstration that there will be at least a six month interruption of employment in the United States after H-2A status ends. Also, eligibility will not be found, notwithstanding the issuance of a temporary agricultural labor certification, where there is substantial evidence that the employment is not temporary or seasonal.

(v) The beneficiary's qualifications --

(A) Eligibility requirements. An H-2A petitioner must establish that any named beneficiary met the stated minimum requirements and was fully able to perform the stated duties when the application for certification was filed. It must be established at time of application for an H-2A visa, or for admission if a visa is not required, that any unnamed beneficiary either met these requirements when the certification was applied for or passed any certified aptitude test at any time prior to visa issuance, or prior to admission if a visa is not required.

(B) Evidence of employment/job training. For petitions with named beneficiaries, a petition must be filed with evidence that the beneficiary met the certification's minimum employment and job training requirements, if any are prescribed, as of the date of the filing of the labor certification application. For petitions with unnamed beneficiaries, such evidence must be submitted at the time of a visa application or, if a visa is not required, at the time the applicant seeks admission to the United States. Evidence must be in the form of the past employer or employers' detailed statement(s) or actual employment documents, such as company payroll or tax records. Alternately, a petitioner must show that such evidence cannot be obtained, and submit affidavits from persons who worked with the beneficiary that demonstrate the claimed employment or job training.

(C) Evidence of education and other training. For petitions with named beneficiaries, a petition must be filed with evidence that the beneficiary met all of the certification's post-secondary education and other formal training requirements, if any are prescribed in the labor certification application as of date of the filing of the labor certification application. For petitions with unnamed beneficiaries, such evidence must be submitted at the time of a visa application or, if a visa is not required, at the time the applicant seeks admission to the United States. Evidence must be in the form of documents, issued by the relevant institution(s) or organization(s), that show periods of attendance, majors and degrees or certificates accorded.

(vi) Petitioner consent and notification requirements—

(A) Consent. In filing an H–2A petition, a petitioner and each employer consents to allow Government access to all sites where the labor is being or will be performed and where workers are or will be housed and agrees to fully cooperate with any compliance review, evaluation, verification, or inspection conducted by US-

CIS, including an on-site inspection of the employer's facilities, review of the employer's records related to the compliance with immigration laws and regulations, and interview of the employer's employees and any other individuals possessing pertinent information, which may be conducted in the absence of the employer or the employer's representatives, as a condition for the approval of the petition. The interviews may be conducted on the employer's property, or as feasible, at a neutral location agreed to by the employee and USCIS away from the employer's property. If USCIS is unable to verify facts, including due to the failure or refusal of the petitioner or employer to cooperate in an inspection or other compliance review, then such inability to verify facts, including due to failure or refusal to cooperate, may result in denial or revocation of any H–2A petition for H– 2A workers performing services at the location or locations that are a subject of inspection or compliance review.

(B) Agreements. The petitioner agrees to the following requirements:

(1) To notify DHS, within 2 workdays, and beginning on a date and in a manner specified in a notice published in the Federal Register if:

(i) An H–2A worker does not report for work within 5 workdays of the employment start date on the H–2A petition or within 5 workdays of the start date established by their employer, whichever is later;

(ii) The agricultural labor or services for which H–2A workers were hired is completed more than 30 days earlier than the employment end date stated on the H–2A petition; or

(iii) The H–2A worker does not report for work for a period of 5 consecutive workdays without the consent of the employer or is terminated prior to the completion of agricultural labor or services for which they were hired.

(2) To retain evidence of such notification and make it available for inspection by DHS officers for a 1-year period beginning on the date of the notification. To retain evidence of a different employment start date if it is changed from that on the petition by the employer and make it available for inspection by DHS officers for the 1-year period beginning on the newlyestablished employment start date.

(3) To pay $10 in liquidated damages for each instance where the employer cannot demonstrate that it has complied with the notification requirements, unless, in the case of an untimely notification, the employer demonstrates with such notification that good cause existed for the untimely notification, and DHS, in its discretion, waives the liquidated damages amount.

(C) Process. If DHS has determined that the petitioner has violated the notification requirements in paragraph (h)(5)(vi)(B)(1) of this section and has not received the required notification, the petitioner will be given written notice and 30 days to reply before being given written notice of the assessment of liquidated damages. (D) Failure to pay liquidated damages. If liquidated damages are not paid within 10 days of assessment, an H–2A petition may not be processed for that petitioner or any joint employer shown on the petition until such damages are paid.

(vii) Validity. An approved H–2A petition is valid through the expiration of the relating certification for the purpose of allowing a beneficiary to seek issuance of an H–2A nonimmigrant visa, admission or an extension of stay for the purpose of engaging in the specific certified employment.

(viii) Admission --

(A) Effect of violations of status. An alien may not be accorded H-2A status who, at any time during the past 5 years, USCIS finds to have violated, other than through no fault of his or her own (e.g., due to an employer's illegal or inappropriate conduct), any of the terms or conditions of admission into the United States as an H-2A nonimmigrant, including remaining beyond the specific period of authorized stay or engaging in unauthorized employment.

(B) Period of admission. An alien admissible as an H–2A nonimmigrant will be admitted for the period of the approved petition. Such alien will be admitted for an additional period of up to 10 days before the beginning of the approved period for the purpose of travel to the worksite, and up to 30 days subject to the 3-year limitation in paragraph (h)(5)(viii)(C) of this section following the expiration of the H–2A petition for the purpose of departure or to seek an extension based on a subsequent offer of employment. Unless authorized under 8 CFR 274a.12, the alien may not work except during the validity period of the petition.

(C) Limits on an individual's stay. Except as provided in paragraph (h)(5)(viii)(B) of this section, an alien's stay as an H–2A nonimmigrant is limited by the period of time stated in an approved petition. An alien may remain longer to engage in other qualifying temporary agricultural employment by obtaining an extension of stay. However, an individual who has held H–2A or H–2B status for a total of 3 years may not again be granted H–2A status until such time as they remain outside the United States for an uninterrupted period of at least 60 days. Eligibility under this paragraph (h)(5)(viii)(C) will be determined during adjudication of a request for admission, change of status or extension. An alien found eligible for a shorter period of H– 2A status than that indicated by the petition due to the application of this paragraph (h)(5)(viii)(C) will only be admitted for that shorter period.

(D) Period of absence. An absence from the United States for an uninterrupted period of at least 60 days at any time will result in the alien becoming eligible for a new 3-year maximum period of H–2 stay. To qualify, the petitioner must provide evidence documenting the alien's relevant absence(s) from the United States, such as, but not limited to, arrival and departure records, copies of tax returns, and records of employment abroad.

(ix) Substitution of beneficiaries after admission. An H–2A petition may be filed to replace H–2A workers whose employment was terminated earlier than the end date stated on the H–2A petition and before the completion of work; who do not report for work within 5 workdays of the employment start date on the H–2A petition or within 5 workdays of the start date established by their employer, whichever is later; or who do not report for work for a period of 5 consecutive workdays without the consent of the employer. The petition must be filed with a copy of the temporary labor certification, a copy of the approval notice covering the workers for which replacements are sought, and other evidence required by paragraph (h)(5)(i)(D) of this section. It must also be filed with a statement giving the name, date and country of birth, termination date, and the reason for termination, if applicable, for such worker and the date that USCIS was notified that the worker was terminated or did not report for work for a period of 5 consecutive workdays without the consent of the employer. A petition for a replacement will not be approved where the requirements of paragraph (h)(5)(vi) of this section have not been met. A petition for replacements does not constitute the notification required by paragraph (h)(5)(vi)(B)(1) of this section.

(x) Extensions in emergent circumstances. In emergent circumstances, as determined by USCIS, a single H-2A petition may be extended for a period not to exceed 2 weeks without an additional approved labor certification if filed on behalf of one or more beneficiaries who will continue to be employed by the same employer that previously obtained an approved petition on the beneficiary's behalf, so long as the employee continues to perform the same duties and will be employed for no longer than 2 weeks after the expiration of previously-approved H-2A petition. The previously approved H-2A petition must have been based on an approved temporary labor certification, which shall be considered to be extended upon the approval of the extension of H-2A status.

(xi) Treatment of petitions and alien beneficiaries upon a determination that fees were collected from alien beneficiaries—

(A) Denial or revocation of petition for prohibited fees. As a condition of approval of an H–2A petition, no job placement fee, fee or penalty for breach of contract, or other fee, penalty, or compensation (either direct or indirect), related to the H–2A employment (collectively, "prohibited fees") may be collected at any time from a beneficiary of an H–2A petition or any person acting on the beneficiary's behalf by a petitioner, a petitioner's employee, agent, attorney, facilitator, recruiter, or similar employment service, or by any employer (if different from the petitioner) or any joint employer, including a member employer if the petitioner is an association of U.S. agricultural producers. The term "similar employment service" refers to any person or entity that recruits or solicits prospective beneficiaries of the H–2A petition. The passing of a cost to the beneficiary that, by statute or applicable regulations, is the responsibility of the petitioner, constitutes the collection of a prohibited fee. This provision does not prohibit petitioners (including their employees), employers or any joint employers, agents, attorneys, facilitators, recruiters, or similar employment services from receiving reimbursement from the beneficiary for costs that are the responsibility and primarily for the benefit of the worker, such as government-required passport fees. This provision does not prohibit employers from allowing workers to initially incur fees or expenses that the employers are required to subsequently reimburse, where such arrangement is specifically permitted by, and performed in compliance with statute or regulations governing the H–2A program.

(1) If USCIS determines that the petitioner or any of its employees, whether before or after the filing of the H–2A petition, has collected, or entered into an agreement to collect, a prohibited fee related to the H–2A employment, USCIS will deny or revoke the H–2A petition filed on or after January 17, 2025 on notice unless the petitioner demonstrates through clear and convincing evidence that: the petitioner made ongoing, good faith, reasonable efforts to prevent and learn of the prohibited fee collection or agreement by its employees throughout the recruitment, hiring, and employment process; extraordinary circumstances beyond the petitioner's control resulted in its failure to prevent collection or entry into agreement for collection of prohibited fees; the petitioner took immediate remedial action as soon as it became aware of the payment of or agreement to pay the prohibited fee; and the petitioner fully reimbursed all affected beneficiaries or, only if such beneficiaries cannot be located or are deceased, it fully reimbursed the beneficiaries' designees.

(2) If USCIS determines that the beneficiary has paid or agreed to pay a prohibited fee related to the H–2A employment, whether before or after the filing of the H–2A petition, to any agent, attorney, employer, facilitator, recruiter, or similar employment service, or any joint employer, including a member employer if the petitioner is an association of U.S. agricultural producers, USCIS will deny or revoke the H–2A petition filed on or after January 17, 2025 on notice unless the petitioner demonstrates to USCIS through clear and convincing evidence that: the petitioner made ongoing, good faith, reasonable efforts to prevent and learn of the prohibited fee collection or agreement by such parties throughout the recruitment, hiring, and employment process; the petitioner took immediate remedial action as soon as it became aware of the payment of or agreement to pay the prohibited fee; and that all affected beneficiaries, or their designees only if such beneficiaries cannot be located or are deceased, have been fully reimbursed. A written contract between the petitioner and the agent, attorney, facilitator, recruiter, similar employment service, or member employer stating that such fees were prohibited will not, by itself, be sufficient to meet this standard of proof.

(3) For purposes of paragraph (h)(5)(xi) of this section, a designee must be an individual or entity for whom the beneficiary has provided the petitioner or its successor in interest prior written authorization to receive such reimbursement, as long as the petitioner or its successor in interest, or its agent, employer, or any joint employer, attorney, facilitator, recruiter, or similar employment service would not act as such designee or derive any financial benefit, either directly or indirectly, from the reimbursement.

(B) One-year denial period of subsequent H–2A petitions. USCIS will deny any H–2A petition filed by the same petitioner or a successor in interest within 1 year after the decision denying or revoking on notice an

H–2B or H–2A petition on the basis of paragraph (h)(6)(i)(B) or (h)(5)(xi)(A), respectively, of this section, provided that the denied or revoked petition was filed on or after January 17, 2025. In addition, USCIS will deny any H–2A petition filed by the same petitioner or successor in interest within 1 year after withdrawal of an H–2A or H–2B petition filed on or after January 17, 2025, that was withdrawn following USCIS issuance of a request for evidence or notice of intent to deny or revoke the petition on the basis of paragraph (h)(5)(xi)(A) or (h)(6)(i)(B), respectively, of this section.

(C) Reimbursement as condition of approval of future H–2A petitions—

(1) Additional 3-year denial period of subsequent H–2A petitions. For an additional 3 years after the 1-year period described in paragraph (h)(5)(xi)(B) of this section, USCIS will deny any H–2A petition filed by the same petitioner or successor in interest, unless the petitioner or successor in interest demonstrates to USCIS that the petitioner, successor in interest, or the petitioner's or successor in interest's agent, facilitator, recruiter, or similar employment service, or any joint employer, including a member employer if the petitioner is an association of U.S. agricultural producers, reimbursed in full each beneficiary, or the beneficiary's designee only if such beneficiary cannot be located or is deceased, of the denied or revoked petition from whom a prohibited fee was collected. USCIS will deny H–2A petitions under this provision based on the denial or revocation decision(s) issued pursuant to paragraph (h)(5)(xi)(A) or (h)(6)(i)(B) of this section on a prior petition filed on or after January 17, 2025.

(2) Successor in interest. For the purposes of paragraphs (h)(5)(xi)(B) and (C) of this section, successor in interest means an employer that is controlling and carrying on the business of a previous employer regardless of whether such successor in interest has succeeded to all of the rights and liabilities of the predecessor entity. The following factors may be considered by USCIS in determining whether an employer is a successor in interest; no one factor is dispositive, but all of the circumstances will be considered as a whole:

(i) Substantial continuity of the same business operations;

(ii) Use of the same facilities;

(iii) Substantial continuity of the work force;

(iv) Similarity of jobs and working conditions;

(v) Similarity of supervisory personnel;

(vi) Whether the former management or owner retains a direct or indirect interest in the new enterprise;

(vii) Similarity in machinery, equipment, production methods, or assets required to conduct business;

(viii) Similarity of products and services;

(ix) Familial or close personal relationships between predecessor and successor owners of the entity; and

(x) Use of the same or related remittance sources for business payments.

(6) Petition for alien to perform temporary nonagricultural services or labor (H-2B) --

(i) Petition.

(A) H–2B nonagricultural temporary worker. An H–2B nonagricultural temporary worker is an alien who is coming temporarily to the United States to perform temporary services or labor without displacing qualified United States workers available to perform such services or labor and whose employment is not adversely affecting the wages and working conditions of United States workers.

(B) Denial or revocation of petition for prohibited fees. As a condition of approval of an H–2B petition, no job placement fee, fee or penalty for breach of contract, or other fee, penalty, or compensation (either direct or indirect), related to the H–2B employment (collectively, "prohibited fees") may be collected at any time from a beneficiary of an H–2B petition or any person acting on the beneficiary's behalf by a petitioner, a petitioner's employee, agent, attorney, facilitator, recruiter, or similar employment service, or any employer (if different from the petitioner). The term "similar employment service" refers to any person or entity that recruits or solicits prospective beneficiaries of the H–2B petition. The passing of a cost to the beneficiary that, by statute or applicable regulations is the responsibility of the petitioner, constitutes the collection of a prohibited fee. This provision does not prohibit petitioners (including their employees), employers, agents, attorneys, facilitators, recruiters, or similar employment services from receiving reimbursement from the beneficiary for costs that are the responsibility and primarily for the benefit of the worker, such as government-required passport fees. This provision does not prohibit employers from allowing workers to initially incur fees or expenses that the employers are required to subsequently reimburse, where such arrangement is specifically permitted by, and performed in compliance with, statute or regulations governing the H–2B program.

(1) If USCIS determines that the petitioner or any of its employees, whether before or after the filing of the H–2B petition, has collected or entered into an agreement to collect a prohibited fee related to the H–2B employment, USCIS will deny or revoke the H–2B petition filed on or after January 17, 2025 on notice unless the petitioner demonstrates through clear and convincing evidence that: the petitioner made ongoing, good faith, reasonable efforts to prevent and learn of the prohibited fee collection or agreement throughout the recruitment, hiring, and employment process; extraordinary circumstances beyond the petitioner's control resulted in its failure to prevent collection or entry into agreement for collection of prohibited fees; the petitioner took immediate remedial action as soon as it became aware of the payment of or agreement to pay the prohibited fee; and the petitioner fully reimbursed all affected beneficiaries or, only if such beneficiaries cannot be located or are deceased, it fully reimbursed their designees.

(2) If USCIS determines that the beneficiary has paid or agreed to pay any employer, agent, attorney, facilitator, recruiter, or similar employment service a prohibited fee related to the H–2B employment, whether before or after the filing of the H–2B petition, USCIS will deny or revoke the H–2B petition filed on or after January 17, 2025 on notice unless the petitioner demonstrates to USCIS through clear and convincing

evidence that: the petitioner made ongoing, good faith, reasonable efforts to prevent and learn of the prohibited fee(s) collection or agreement by such parties throughout the recruitment, hiring, and employment process; the petitioner took immediate remedial action as soon as it became aware of the payment of the prohibited fee or agreement; and all affected beneficiaries, or their designees only if such beneficiaries cannot be located or are deceased, have been fully reimbursed. A written contract between the petitioner and the facilitator, recruiter, or similar employment service stating that such fees were prohibited will not, by itself, be sufficient to meet this standard of proof.

(3) For purposes of paragraph (h)(6)(i) of this section, a designee must be an individual or entity for whom the beneficiary has provided the petitioner or its successor in interest prior written authorization to receive such reimbursement, as long as the petitioner or its successor in interest, or its agent, employer, attorney, facilitator, recruiter, or similar employment service would not act as such designee or derive any financial benefit, either directly or indirectly, from the reimbursement.

(C) One-year denial period of subsequent H–2B petitions. USCIS will deny any H–2B petition filed by the same petitioner or a successor in interest within 1 year after the decision denying or revoking on notice an H–2B or H–2A petition on the basis of paragraph (h)(6)(i)(B) or (h)(5)(xi)(A), respectively, of this section, provided that the denied or revoked petition was filed on or after January 17, 2025. In addition, USCIS will deny any H–2B petition filed by the same petitioner or successor in interest within 1 year after withdrawal of an H–2B or H–2A petition filed on or after January 17, 2025, that was withdrawn following USCIS issuance of a request for evidence or notice of intent to deny or revoke the petition on the basis of paragraph (h)(6)(i)(B) or (h)(5)(xi)(A), respectively, of this section.

(D) Reimbursement as condition of approval of future H–2B petitions—

(1) Additional 3-year denial period of subsequent H–2B petitions. For an additional 3 years after the 1-year period described in paragraph (h)(6)(i)(C) of this section, USCIS will deny any H–2B petition filed by the same petitioner or successor in interest, unless the petitioner or successor in interest demonstrates to USCIS that the petitioner or successor in interest, or the petitioner's or successor in interest's agent, facilitator, recruiter, or similar employment service, reimbursed in full each beneficiary, or the beneficiary's designee only if such beneficiary cannot be located or is deceased, of the denied or revoked petition from whom a prohibited fee was collected. USCIS will deny H–2B petitions under this provision based on the denial or revocation decision(s) issued pursuant to paragraph (h)(6)(i)(B) or (h)(5)(xi)(A) of this section on a prior petition filed on or after January 17, 2025.

(2) Successor in interest. For the purposes of paragraphs (h)(6)(i)(C) and (D) of this section, successor in interest means an employer that is controlling and carrying on the business of a previous employer regardless of whether such successor in interest has succeeded to all of the rights and liabilities of the predecessor entity. The following factors may be considered by USCIS in determining whether an employer is a successor in interest; no one factor is dispositive, but all of the circumstances will be considered as a whole:

(i) Substantial continuity of the same business operations;

(ii) Use of the same facilities;

(iii) Substantial continuity of the work force;

(iv) Similarity of jobs and working conditions;

(v) Similarity of supervisory personnel;

(vi) Whether the former management or owner retains a direct or indirect interest in the new enterprise;

(vii) Similarity in machinery, equipment, production methods, or assets required to conduct business;

(viii) Similarity of products and services;

(ix) Familial or close personal relationships between predecessor and successor owners of the entity; and

(x) Use of the same or related remittance sources for business payments.

(E) [Reserved]

(1) H-2B petitions may be approved for nationals of countries that the Secretary of Homeland Security has designated as participating countries, with the concurrence of the Secretary of State, in a notice published in the Federal Register, taking into account factors, including but not limited to:

(i) The country's cooperation with respect to issuance of travel documents for citizens, subjects, nationals and residents of that country who are subject to a final order of removal;

(ii) The number of final and unexecuted orders of removal against citizens, subjects, nationals, and residents of that country;

(iii) The number of orders of removal executed against citizens, subjects, nationals and residents of that country; and

(iv) Such other factors as may serve the U.S. interest.

(2) A national from a country not on the list described in paragraph (h)(6)(i)(E)(1) of this section may be a beneficiary of an approved H-2B petition upon the request of a petitioner or potential H-2B petitioner, if the Secretary of Homeland Security, in his sole and unreviewable discretion, determines that it is in the U.S. interest for that alien to be a beneficiary of such petition. Determination of such a U.S. interest will take into account factors, including but not limited to:

(i) Evidence from the petitioner demonstrating that a worker with the required skills is not available from among foreign workers from a country currently on the list described in paragraph (h)(6)(i)(E)(1) of this section;

(ii) Evidence that the beneficiary has been admitted to the United States previously in H-2B status;

(iii) The potential for abuse, fraud, or other harm to the integrity of the H-2B visa program through the potential admission of a beneficiary from a country not currently on the list; and

(iv) Such other factors as may serve the U.S. interest.

(3) Once published, any designation of participating countries pursuant to paragraph (h)(6)(i)(E)(1) of this section shall be effective for one year after the date of

publication in the Federal Register and shall be without effect at the end of that one-year period.

(F) Petitioner agreements and notification requirements—

(1) Agreements. The petitioner must notify DHS, within 2 workdays, and beginning on a date and in a manner specified in a notice published in the Federal Register if: An H–2B worker does not report for work within 5 workdays after the employment start date stated on the petition; the nonagricultural labor or services for which H–2B workers were hired were completed more than 30 days early; or an H–2B worker does not report for work for a period of 5 consecutive workdays without the consent of the employer or is terminated prior to the completion of the nonagricultural labor or services for which they were hired. The petitioner must also retain evidence of such notification and make it available for inspection by DHS officers for a 1-year period beginning on the date of the notification.

(2) Consent. In filing an H–2B petition, the petitioner and each employer (if different from the petitioner) consent to allow Government access to all sites where the labor is being or will be performed and agrees to fully cooperate with any compliance review, evaluation, verification, or inspection conducted by USCIS, including an on-site inspection of the employer's facilities, review of the employer's records related to the compliance with immigration laws and regulations, and interview of the employer's employees and any other individuals possessing pertinent information, which may be conducted in the absence of the employer or the employer's representatives, as a condition for the approval of the petition. The interviews may be conducted on the employer's property, or as feasible, at a neutral location agreed to by the employee and USCIS away from the employer's property. If USCIS is unable to verify facts, including due to the failure or refusal of the petitioner or employer to cooperate in an inspection or other compliance review, then such inability to verify facts, including due to failure or refusal to cooperate, may result in denial or revocation of any H–2B petition for H– 2B workers performing services at the location or locations that are a subject of inspection or compliance review.

(ii) Temporary services or labor --

(A) Definition. Temporary services or labor under the H-2B classification refers to any job in which the petitioner's need for the duties to be performed by the employee(s) is temporary, whether or not the underlying job can be described as permanent or temporary.

(B) Nature of petitioner's need. Employment is of a temporary nature when the employer needs a worker for a limited period of time. The employer must establish that the need for the employee will end in the near, definable future. Generally, that period of time will be limited to one year or less, but in the case of a one-time event could last up to 3 years. The petitioner's need for the services or labor shall be a one-time occurrence, a seasonal need, a peak load need, or an intermittent need.

(1) One-time occurence. The petitioner must establish that it has not employed workers to perform the services or labor in the past and that it will not need workers to perform the services or labor in the future, or that it has an employment situation that is otherwise permanent, but a temporary event of short duration has created the need for a temporary worker.

(2) Seasonal need. The petitioner must establish that the services or labor is traditionally tied to a season of the year by an event or pattern and is of a recurring nature. The petitioner shall specify the period(s) of time during each year in which it does not need the services or labor. The employment is not seasonal if the period during which the services or labor is not needed is unpredictable or subject to change or is considered a vacation period for the petitioner's permanent employees.

(3) Peakload need. The petitoner must establish that it regularly employs permanent workers to perform the services or labor at the place of employment and that it needs to supplement its permanent staff at the place of employment on a temporary basis due to a seasonal or short-term demand and that the temporary additions to staff will not become a part of the petitioner's regular operation.

(4) Intermittent need. The petitioner must establish that it has not employed permanent or full-time workers to perform the services or labor, but occasionally or intermittently needs temporary workers to perform services or labor for short periods.

(iii) Procedures.

(A) Prior to filing a petition with the director to classify an alien as an H-2B worker, the petitioner shall apply for a temporary labor certification with the Secretary of Labor for all areas of the United States, except the Territory of Guam. In the Territory of Guam, the petitioning employer shall apply for a temporary labor certification with the Governor of Guam. The labor certification shall be advice to the director on whether or not United States workers capable of performing the temporary services or labor are available and whether or not the alien's employment will adversely affect the wages and working conditions of similarly employed United States workers.

(B) An H-2B petitioner shall be a United States employer, a United States agent, or a foreign employer filing through a United States agent. For purposes of paragraph (h) of this section, a foreign employer is any employer who is not amenable to service of process in the United States. A foreign employer may not directly petition for an H-2B nonimmigrant but must use the services of a United States agent to file a petition for an H-2B nonimmigrant. A United States agent petitioning on behalf of a foreign employer must be authorized to file the petition, and to accept service of process in the United States in proceedings under section 274A of the Act, on behalf of the employer. The petitioning employer shall consider available United States workers for the temporary services or labor, and shall offer terms and conditions of employment which are consistent with the nature of the occupation, activity, and industry in the United States.

(C) The petitioner may not file an H-2B petition unless the United States petitioner has applied for a labor certification with the Secretary of Labor or the Governor of Guam within the time limits prescribed or accepted by each, and has obtained a favorable labor certification determination as required by paragraph (h)(6)(iv) or (h)(6)(v) of this section.

(D) The Governor of Guam shall separately establish procedures for administering the temporary labor program under his or her jurisdiction. The Secretary of Labor shall separately establish for the temporary labor program under his or her jurisdiction, by regulation at 20 CFR 655, procedures for administering that temporary labor program under his or her jurisdiction, and shall determine the prevailing wage applicable to an application for temporary labor certification for that temporary labor program in accordance with the Secretary of Labor's regulation at 20 CFR 655.10.

(E) After obtaining a favorable determination from the Secretary of Labor or the Governor of Guam, as appropriate, the petitioner shall file a petition on the form prescribed by USCIS, accompanied by the labor certification determination and supporting documents, with the director having jurisdiction in the area of intended employment.

(iv) Labor certifications, except Guam --

(A) Secretary of Labor's determination. An H-2B petition for temporary employment in the United States, except for temporary employment on Guam, shall be accompanied by an approved temporary labor certification from the Secretary of Labor stating that qualified workers in the United States are not available and that the alien's employment will not adversely affect wages and working conditions of similarly employed United States workers.

(B) Validity of the labor certification. The Secretary of Labor may issue a temporary labor certification for a period of up to one year.

(C) U.S. Virgin Islands. Temporary labor certifications filed under section 101(a)(15)(H)(ii)(b) of the Act for employment in the United States Virgin Islands may be approved only for entertainers and athletes and only for periods not to exceed 45 days.

(D) Employment start date. Beginning with petitions filed for workers for fiscal year 2010, an H-2B petition must state an employment start date that is the same as the date of need stated on the approved temporary labor certification. A petitioner filing an amended H-2B petition due to the unavailability of originally requested workers may state an employment start date later than the date of need stated on the previously approved temporary labor certification accompanying the amended H-2B petition.

(v) Labor certification for Guam --

(A) Governor of Guam's determination. An H-2B petition for temporary employment on Guam shall be accompanied by an approved temporary labor certification issued by the Governor of Guam stating that qualified workers in the United States are not available to perform the required services, and that the alien's employment will not adversely affect the wages and working conditions of United States resident workers who are similarly employed on Guam.

(B) Validity of labor certification. The Governor of Guam may issue a temporary labor certification for a period up to one year.

(C) [Reserved]

(D) [Reserved]

(E) Criteria for Guam labor certifications. The Governor of Guam shall, in consultation with the Service, establish systematic methods for determining the prevailing wage rates and working conditions for individual occupations on Guam and for making determinations as to availability of qualified United States residents.

(1) Prevailing wage and working conditions. The system to determine wages and working conditions must provide for consideration of wage rates and employment conditions for occupations in both the private and public sectors, in Guam and/or in the United States (as defined in section 101(a)(38) of the Act), and may not consider wages and working conditions outside of the United States. If the system includes utilitzation of advisory opinions and consultations, the opinions must be provided by officially sanctioned groups which reflect a balance of the interests of the private and public sectors, government, unions and management.

(2) Availability of United States workers. The system for determining availability of qualified United States workers must require the prospective employer to:

(i) Advertise the availability of the position for a minimum of three consecutive days in the newspaper with the largest daily circulation on Guam;

(ii) Place a job offer with an appropriate agency of the Territorial Government which operates as a job referral service at least 30 days in advance of the need for the services to commence, except that for applications from the armed forces of the United States and those in the entertainment industry, the 30-day period may be reduced by the Governor to 10 days;

(iii) Conduct appropriate recruitment in other areas of the United States and its territories if sufficient qualified United States construction workers are not available on Guam to fill a job. The Governor of Guam may require a job order to be placed more than 30 days in advance of need to accommodate such recruitment;

(iv) Report to the appropriate agency the names of all United States resident workers who applied for the position, indicating those hired and the job-related reasons for not hiring;

(v) Offer all special considerations, such as housing and transportation expenses, to all United States resident workers who applied for the position, indicating those hired and the job-related reasons for not hiring;

(vi) Meet the prevailing wage rates and working conditions determined under the wages and working conditions system by the Governor; and

(vii) Agree to meet all Federal and Territorial requirements relating to employment, such as nondiscrimination, occupational safety, and minimum wage requirements.

(F) Approval and publication of employment systems on Guam --

(1) Systems. The Commissioner of Immigration and Naturalization must approve the system to determine prevailing wages and working conditions and the system to determine availability of United States resident workers and any future modifications of the systems prior to implementation. If the Commissioner, in consultation with the Secretary of Labor, finds that the systems or modified systems meet the requirements of this section, the Commissioner shall publish them as a notice in the FEDERAL REGISTER and the Governor shall publish them as a public record in Guam.

(2) Approval of construction wage rates. The Commissioner must approve specific wage data and rates used for construction occupations on Guam prior to implementation of new rates. The Governor shall submit new wage survey data and proposed rates to the Commissioner for approval at least eight weeks before authority to use existing rates expires. Surveys shall be conducted at least every two years, unless the Commissioner prescribes a lesser period.

(G) Reporting. The Governor shall provide the Commissioner statistical data on temporary labor certification workload and determinations. This information shall be submitted quarterly no later than 30 days after the quarter ends.

(H) Invalidation of temporary labor certification issued by the Governor of Guam --

(1) General. A temporary labor certification issued by the Governor of Guam may be invalidated by a director if it is determined by the director or a court of law that the certification request involved fraud or willful misrepresentation. A temporary labor certification may also be invalidated if the director determines that the certification involved gross error.

(2) Notice of intent to invalidate. If the director intends to invalidate a temporary labor certification, a notice of intent shall be served upon the employer, detailing the reasons for the intended invalidation. The employer shall have 30 days in which to file a written response in rebuttal to the notice of intent. The director shall consider all evidence submitted upon rebuttal in reaching a decision.

(3) Appeal of invalidation. An employer may appeal the invalidation of a temporary labor certification in accordance with part 103 of this chapter.

(vi) Evidence for H-2B petitions. An H-2B petition shall be accompanied by:

(A) Labor certification. An approved temporary labor certification issued by the Secretary of Labor or the Governor of Guam, as appropriate;

(B) [Reserved]

(C) Alien's qualifications. In petitions where the temporary labor certification application requires certain education, training, experience, or special requirements of the beneficiary who is present in the United States, documentation that the alien qualifies for the job offer as specified in the application for such temporary labor certification. This requirement also applies to the named beneficiary who is abroad on the basis of special provisions stated in paragraph (h)(2)(iii) of this section;

(D) Statement of need. A statement describing in detail the temporary situation or conditions which make it necessary to bring the alien to the United States and whether the need is a one-time occurrence, seasonal, peakload, or intermittent. If the need is seasonal, peakload, or intermittent, the statement shall indicate whether the situation or conditions are expected to be recurrent; or

(E) Liability for transportation costs. The employer will be liable for the reasonable costs of return transportation of the alien abroad, if the alien is dismissed from employment for any reason by the employer before the end of the period of authorized admission pursuant to section 214(c)(5) of the Act. If the beneficiary voluntarily terminates his or her employment prior to the expiration of the validity of the petition, the alien has not been dismissed. If the beneficiary believes that the employer has not complied with this provision, the beneficiary shall advise the Service Center which adjudicated the petition in writing. The complaint will be retained in the file relating to the petition. Within the context of this paragraph, the term "abroad" means the alien's last place of foreign residence. This provision applies to any employer whose offer of employment became the basis for the alien obtaining or continuing H-2B status.

(vii) Admission—

(A) Period of admission. An alien admissible as an H– 2B nonimmigrant will be admitted for the period of the approved petition. Such alien will be admitted for an additional period of up to 10 days before the beginning of the approved period for the purpose of travel to the worksite, and up to 30 days subject to the 3-year limitation in paragraph (h)(6)(vii)(B) of this section following the expiration of the H–2B petition for the purpose of departure or to seek an extension based on a subsequent offer of employment. Unless authorized under 8 CFR 274a.12, the alien may not work except during the validity period of the petition.

(B) Limits on an individual's stay. Except as provided in paragraph (h)(6)(vii)(A) of this section, an alien's stay as an H–2B nonimmigrant is limited by the period of time stated in an approved petition. An alien may remain longer to engage in other qualifying temporary nonagricultural employment by obtaining an extension of stay. However, an individual who has held H–2A or H–2B status for a total of 3 years may not again be granted H–2B status until such time as they remain outside the United States for an uninterrupted period of at least 60 days. Eligibility under this paragraph (h)(6)(vii)(B) will be determined during adjudication of a request for admission, change of status or extension of stay. An alien found eligible for a shorter period of H–2B status than that indicated by the petition due to the application of this paragraph (h)(6)(vii)(B) will only be admitted for that shorter period.

(C) Period of absence. An absence from the United States for an uninterrupted period of at least 60 days at any time will result in the alien becoming eligible for a new 3-year maximum period of H–2 stay. The limitation in paragraph (h)(6)(vii)(B) of this section will not apply to H–2B aliens who did not reside continually in the United States and whose employment in the United States was seasonal or intermittent or was for an aggregate of 6 months or less per year. In addition, the limitation in paragraph (h)(6)(vii)(B) of this section will not apply to aliens who reside abroad and regularly commute to the United States to engage in part-time employment. To qualify, the petitioner must provide evidence documenting the alien's relevant absence(s) from the United States, such as, but not limited to, arrival and departure records, copies of tax returns, and records of employment abroad.

(D) Traded professional H–2B athletes. In the case of a professional H– 2B athlete who is traded from one organization to another organization, employment authorization for the player will automatically continue for a period of 30 days after the player's acquisition by the new organization, within which time the new organization is expected to file a new application or petition for H– 2B nonimmigrant classification. If a new application or petition is not filed within 30 days, employment authorization will cease. If a new application or petition is filed within 30 days, the professional athlete will be deemed to be in valid H–2B status, and employment will continue to be authorized, until the petition is adjudicated. If the new petition is denied, employment authorization will cease.

(viii) Substitution of beneficiaries. Beneficiaries of H-2B petitions that are approved for named or unnamed beneficiaries who have not been admitted may be substituted only if the employer can demonstrate that the total number of beneficiaries will not exceed the number of beneficiaries certified in the original temporary labor certification. Beneficiaries who were admitted to the United States may not be substituted without a new petition accompanied by a newly approved temporary labor certification.

(A) To substitute beneficiaries who were previously approved for consular processing but have not been admitted with aliens who are outside of the United States, the petitioner shall, by letter and a copy of the petition approval notice, notify the consular office at which the alien will apply for a visa or the port of entry where the alien will apply for admission. The petitioner shall also submit evidence of the qualifications of beneficiaries to the consular office or port of entry prior to issuance of a visa or admission, if applicable.

(B) To substitute beneficiaries who were previously approved for consular processing but have not been admitted with aliens who are currently in the United States, the petitioner shall file an amended petition with fees at the USCIS Service Center where the original petition was filed, with a copy of the original petition approval notice, a statement explaining why the substitution is necessary, evidence of the qualifications of beneficiaries, if applicable, evidence of the beneficiaries' current status in the United States, and evidence that the number of beneficiaries will not exceed the number allocated on the approved temporary labor certification, such as employment records or other documentary evidence to establish that the number of visas sought in the amended petition were not already issued. The amended petition must retain a period of employment within the same half of the same fiscal year as the original petition. Otherwise, a new temporary labor certification issued by DOL or the Governor of Guam and subsequent H-2B petition are required.

(ix) Enforcement. The Secretary of Labor may investigate employers to enforce compliance with the conditions of a petition and Department of Labor-approved temporary labor certification to admit or otherwise provide status to an H-2B worker.

(x) [Effective May 25, 2021 through May 28, 2024.] Special requirements for additional cap allocations under the Consolidated Appropriations Act, 2021, Public Law 116-260—

(A) Public Law 116-260—

(1) Supplemental allocation for returning workers. Notwithstanding the numerical limitations set forth in paragraph (h)(8)(i)(C) of this section, for fiscal year 2021 only, the Secretary has authorized up to an additional 16,000 visas for aliens who may receive H-2B nonimmigrant visas pursuant to section 105 of Division O of the Consolidated Appropriations Act, 2021, Public Law 116-260. An alien may be eligible to receive an H-2B nonimmigrant visa under this paragraph (h)(6)(x)(A)(1) if she or he is a returning worker. The term "returning worker" under this paragraph (h)(6)(x)(A)(1) means a person who was issued an H-2B visa or was otherwise granted H-2B status in fiscal year 2018, 2019, or 2020. Notwithstanding § 248.2 of this chapter, an alien may not change status to H-2B nonimmigrant under this paragraph (h)(6)(x)(A)(1).

(2) Supplemental allocation for nationals of Guatemala, El Salvador, and Honduras (Northern Triangle countries). Notwithstanding the numerical limitations set forth in paragraph (h)(8)(i)(C) of this section, for fiscal year 2021 only, and in addition to the allocation described in paragraph (h)(6)(x)(A)(1) of this section, the Secretary has authorized up to an additional 6,000 aliens who are nationals of Guatemala, El Salvador, or Honduras (Northern Triangle countries) who may receive H-2B nonimmigrant visas pursuant to section 105 of Division O of the Consolidated Appropriations Act, 2021, Public Law 116-260. Such workers are not subject to the returning worker requirement in paragraph (h)(6)(x)(A)(1). Petitioners must request such workers in an H-2B petition that is separate from H-2B petitions that request returning workers under paragraph (h)(6)(x)(A)(1) and must declare that they are requesting these workers in the attestation required under 20 CFR 655.68(a)(1). Notwithstanding § 248.2 of this chapter, an alien may not change status to H-2B nonimmigrant under this paragraph (h)(6)(x)(A)(2).

(i) Petitions submitted under this paragraph (h)(6)(x)(A)(2) must be received by July 8, 2021. H-2B petitions under the supplemental allocation for nationals of Northern Triangle countries received after that date will be rejected.

(ii) If USCIS determines that it has received fewer petitions by July 8, 2021 than needed to reach the USCIS projections for the Northern Triangle countries supplemental allocation in this paragraph (h)(6)(x)(A)(2), it will make the remainder of the allocation available as a separate allocation described in paragraph (h)(6)(x)(A)(3) of this section.

(3) Availability of remainder of supplemental allocation. If USCIS determines that fewer petitions have been received by July 8, 2021 than needed to meet the additional allocation described in paragraph (h)(6)(x)(A)(2) of this section, USCIS will make the remainder of the allocation available as a separate allocation to returning workers as described in paragraph (h)(6)(x)(A)(1) of this section and will announce the availability of the remainder of the allocation on the USCIS website at uscis.gov no later than July 23, 2021. Such announcement, if made, will specify the date on which petitioners may begin to file H-2B petitions under this paragraph (h)(6)(x)(A)(3).

(B) Eligibility. In order to file a petition with USCIS under this paragraph (h)(6)(x), the petitioner must:

(1) Comply with all other statutory and regulatory requirements for H-2B classification, including, but not limited to, requirements in this section, under part 103 of this chapter, and under 20 CFR part 655 and 29 CFR part 503; and

(2) Submit to USCIS, at the time the employer files its petition, a U.S. Department of Labor attestation, in compliance with this section and 20 CFR 655.64, evidencing that:

(i) Without the ability to employ all of the H-2B workers requested on the petition filed pursuant to this paragraph (h)(6)(x), its business is likely to suffer irreparable harm (that is, permanent and severe financial loss);

(ii) All workers requested and/or instructed to apply for a visa have been issued an H-2B visa or otherwise granted H-2B status in fiscal year 2018, 2019, or 2020, unless the H-2B worker is a national of Guatemala, El Salvador, or Honduras and is counted towards the 6,000 cap described in paragraph (h)(6)(x)(A)(2) of this section;

(iii) The employer will comply with all Federal, State, and local employment-related laws and regulations, including health and safety laws and laws related to COVID-19 worker protections, any right to time off or paid time off for COVID-19 vaccination, and that the employer will notify any H-2B workers approved under the supplemental cap in paragraph (h)(6)(x)(A)(2) of this section, in a language understood by the worker, as necessary or reasonable, that all persons in the United States, including nonimmigrants, have equal access to COVID-19 vaccines and vaccine distribution sites;

(iv) The employer will comply with obligations and additional recruitment requirements outlined in 20 CFR 655.64(a)(3) through (5);

(v) The employer will provide documentary evidence of the facts in paragraphs (h)(6)(x)(B)(2)(i) through (iv) of this section to DHS or DOL upon request; and

(vi) The employer will agree to fully cooperate with any compliance review, evaluation, verification, or inspection conducted by DHS, including an on-site inspection of the employer's facilities, interview of the employer's employees and any other individuals possessing pertinent information, and review of the employer's records related to the compliance with immigration laws and regulations, including but not limited to evidence pertaining to or supporting the eligibility criteria for the FY 2021 supplemental allocations outlined in paragraph (h)(6)(x)(B) of this section, as a condition for the approval of the petition.

(vii) The employer must attest on Form ETA-9142-B-CAA-4 that it will fully cooperate with any audit, investigation, compliance review, evaluation, verification or inspection conducted by DOL, including an on-site inspection of the employer's facilities, interview of the employer's employees and any other individuals possessing pertinent information, and review of the employer's records related to the compliance with applicable laws and regulations, including but not limited to evidence pertaining to or supporting the eligibility criteria for the FY 2021 supplemental allocations outlined in 20 CFR 655.64(a) and 655.68(a), as a condition for the approval of the H-2B petition. The employer must further attest on Form ETA-9142-B-CAA-4 that it will not impede, interfere, or refuse to cooperate with an employee of the Secretary of the U.S. Department of Labor who is exercising or attempting to exercise DOL's audit or investigative authority pursuant to 20 CFR part 655, subpart A, and 29 CFR 503.25.

(C) Processing. USCIS will reject petitions filed pursuant to paragraph (h)(6)(x)(A)(1) or (3) of this section that are received after the applicable numerical limitation has been reached or after September 15, 2021, whichever is sooner. USCIS will reject petitions filed pursuant to paragraph (h)(6)(x)(A)(2) of this section that are received after the applicable numerical limitation has been reached or after July 8, 2021, whichever is sooner. USCIS will not approve a petition filed pursuant to this paragraph (h)(6)(x) on or after October 1, 2021.

(D) Numerical limitations under paragraphs (h)(6)(x)(A)(1), (2), and (3) of this section. When calculating the numerical limitations under paragraphs (h)(6)(x)(A)(1), (2), and (3) of this section as authorized under Public Law 116-260, USCIS will make numbers for each allocation available to petitions in the order in which the petitions subject to the respective limitation are received. USCIS will make projections of the number of petitions necessary to achieve the numerical limit of approvals, taking into account historical data related to approvals, denials, revocations, and other relevant factors. USCIS will monitor the number of petitions (including the number of workers requested when necessary) received and will notify the public of the dates that USCIS has received the necessary number of petitions (the "final receipt dates") under paragraph (h)(6)(x)(A)(1) or paragraphs (h)(6)(x)(A)(2) and (3). The day the public is notified will not control the final receipt dates. When necessary to ensure the fair and orderly allocation of numbers subject to the numerical limitations in paragraphs (h)(6)(x)(A)(1), (2), and (3), USCIS may randomly select from among the petitions received on the final receipt dates the remaining number of petitions deemed necessary to generate the numerical limit of approvals. This random selection will be made via computer-generated selection. Petitions subject to a numerical limitation not randomly selected or that were received after the final receipt dates that may be applicable under paragraph (h)(6)(x)(A)(1), (2), or (3) will be rejected. If the final receipt date is any of the first 5 business days on which petitions subject to the applicable numerical limits described in paragraph (h)(6)(x)(A)(1), (2), or (3) may be received (in other words, if any of the numerical limits described in paragraph (h)(6)(x)(A)(1), (2), or (3) is reached on any one of the first 5 business days that filings can be made), USCIS will randomly apply all of the numbers among the petitions received on any of those 5 business days.

(E) Sunset. This paragraph (h)(6)(x) expires on October 1, 2021.

(F) Non-severability. The requirement to file an attestation under paragraph (h)(6)(x)(B)(2) of this section is intended to be non-severable from the remainder of this paragraph (h)(6)(x), including, but not limited to, the numerical allocation provisions at paragraphs (h)(6)(x)(A)(1), (2), and (3) of this section in their entirety. In the event that any part of this paragraph (h)(6)(x) is enjoined or held to be invalid by any court of competent jurisdiction, the remainder of this paragraph (h)(6)(x) is also intended to be enjoined or held to be invalid in such jurisdiction, without prejudice to workers already present in the United States under this paragraph (h)(6)(x), as consistent with law.

(xi) [Effective Jan. 28, 2022 through Jan. 28, 2025.] Special requirements for additional cap allocations under Public Laws 116-260, 117-43 and 117-70 —

(A) Public Law 116-260, and sections 101 and 106(3) of Division A of Public Law 117-43, Continuing Appropriations Act, 2022, and section 101 of Division A of Public Law 117-70, Further Continuing Appropriations Act, 2022 through February 18, 2022 —

(1) Supplemental allocation for returning workers. Notwithstanding the numerical limitations set forth in paragraph (h)(8)(i)(C) of this section, for fiscal year 2022 only, the Secretary has authorized up to an additional 13,500 visas for aliens who may receive H-2B nonimmigrant visas pursuant to section 105 of Division O of the Consolidated Appropriations Act, 2021, Public Law 116-260, sections 101 and 106(3) of Division A of Public Law 117-43, Continuing Appropriations Act, 2022, and section 101 of Division A of Public Law 117-70, Further Continuing Appropriations Act, 2022 through February 18, 2022 based on petitions requesting FY 2022 employment start dates on or before March 31, 2022. An alien may be eligible to receive an H-2B nonimmigrant visa under this paragraph (h)(6)(xi)(A)(1) if she or he is a returning worker. The term "returning worker" under this paragraph (h)(6)(xi)(A)(1) means a person who was issued an H-2B visa or was otherwise granted H-2B status in fiscal year 2019, 2020, or 2021. Notwithstanding § 248.2 of this chapter, an alien may not change status to H-2B nonimmigrant under this paragraph (h)(6)(xi)(A)(1).

(2) Supplemental allocation for nationals of Guatemala, El Salvador, Honduras (Northern Triangle countries), or Haiti. Notwithstanding the numerical limitations set forth in paragraph (h)(8)(i)(C) of this section, for fiscal year 2022 only, and in addition to the allocation described in paragraph (h)(6)(xi)(A)(1) of this section, the Secretary has authorized up to an additional 6,500 aliens who are nationals of Guatemala, El Salvador, Honduras (Northern Triangle countries), or of Haiti who may receive H-2B nonimmigrant visas pursuant to section 105 of Division O of the Consolidated Appropriations Act, 2021, Public Law 116-260, and Public Laws 117-43 and 117-70, based on petitions with FY 2022 employment start dates on or before March 31, 2022. Such workers are not subject to the returning worker requirement in paragraph (h)(6)(xi)(A)(1). Petitioners must request such workers in an H-2B petition that is separate from H-2B petitions that request returning workers under paragraph (h)(6)(xi)(A)(1) and must declare that they are requesting these workers in the attestation required under 20 CFR 655.69(a)(1). A petition requesting returning workers under paragraph (h)(6)(xi)(A)(1), which is accompanied by an attestation indicating that the petitioner is requesting nationals of Northern Triangle countries or Haiti, will be rejected, denied or, in the case of a non-frivolous petition, will be approved solely for the number of beneficiaries that are from the Northern Triangle or Haiti. Notwithstanding § 248.2 of this chapter, an alien may not change status to H-2B nonimmigrant under this paragraph (h)(6)(xi)(A)(2).

(B) Eligibility. In order to file a petition with USCIS under this paragraph (h)(6)(xi), the petitioner must:

(1) Comply with all other statutory and regulatory requirements for H-2B classification, including, but not limited to, requirements in this section, under part 103 of this chapter, and under 20 CFR part 655 and 29 CFR part 503; and

(2) Submit to USCIS, at the time the employer files its petition, a U.S. Department of Labor attestation, in compliance with this section and 20 CFR 655.64, evidencing that:

(i) Its business is suffering irreparable harm or will suffer impending irreparable harm (that is, permanent and severe financial loss) without the ability to employ all of the H-2B workers requested on the petition filed pursuant to this paragraph (h)(6)(xi);

(ii) All workers requested and/or instructed to apply for a visa have been issued an H-2B visa or otherwise granted H-2B status in fiscal year 2019, 2020, or 2021, unless the H-2B worker is a national of Guatemala, El Salvador, Honduras, or Haiti who is counted towards the 6,500 cap described in paragraph (h)(6)(xi)(A)(2) of this section;

(iii) The employer will comply with all Federal, State, and local employment-related laws and regulations, including, where applicable, health and safety laws and laws related to COVID-19 worker protections; any right to time off or paid time off for COVID-19 vaccination, or to reimbursement for travel to and from the nearest available vaccination site; and that the employer will notify any H-2B workers approved under the supplemental cap in paragraph (h)(6)(xi)(A)(2) of this section, in a language understood by the worker as necessary or reasonable, that all persons in the United States, including nonimmigrants, have equal access to COVID-19 vaccines and vaccine distribution sites;

(iv) The employer will comply with obligations and additional recruitment requirements outlined in 20 CFR 655.64(a)(3) through (5);

(v) The employer will provide documentary evidence of the facts in paragraphs (h)(6)(xi)(B)(2)(i) through (iv) of this section to DHS or DOL upon request; and

(vi) The employer will agree to fully cooperate with any compliance review, evaluation, verification, or inspection conducted by DHS, including an on-site inspection of the employer's facilities, interview of the employer's employees and any other individuals possessing pertinent information, and review of the employer's records related to the compliance with immigration laws and regulations, including but not limited to evidence pertaining to or supporting the eligibility criteria for the FY 2022 supplemental allocations outlined in paragraph (h)(6)(xi)(B) of this section, as a condition for the approval of the petition.

(vii) The employer must attest on Form ETA-9142-B-CAA-5 that it will fully cooperate with any audit, investigation, compliance review, evaluation, verification or inspection conducted by DOL, including an on-site inspection of the employer's facilities, interview of the employer's employees and any other individuals possessing pertinent information, and review of the employer's records related to the compliance with applicable laws and regulations, including but not limited to evidence pertaining to or supporting the eligibility criteria for the FY 2022 supplemental allocations outlined in 20 CFR 655.64(a) and 655.69(a), as a condition for the approval of the H-2B petition. The employer must further attest on Form ETA-9142-B-CAA-5 that it will not impede, interfere, or refuse to cooperate with an employee of the Secretary of the U.S. Department of Labor who is exercising or attempting to exercise DOL's audit or investigative authority pursuant to 20 CFR part 655, subpart A, and 29 CFR 503.25.

(C) Processing. USCIS will reject petitions filed pursuant to paragraph (h)(6)(xi)(A)(1) or (2) of this section that are received after the applicable numerical limitation has been reached or after March 31, 2022, whichever is sooner. USCIS will not approve a petition filed pursuant to this paragraph (h)(6)(xi) on or after October 1, 2022.

(D) Numerical limitations under paragraphs (h)(6)(xi)(A)(1) and (2) of this section. When calculating the numerical limitations under paragraphs (h)(6)(xi)(A)(1) and (2) of this section as authorized under Public Law 116-260, as extended by Public Law 117-43, and Public Law 117-70, USCIS will make numbers for each allocation available to petitions in the order in which the petitions subject to the respective limitation are received. USCIS will make projections of the number of petitions necessary to achieve the numerical limit of approvals, taking into account historical data related to approvals, denials, revocations, and other relevant factors. USCIS will monitor the number of petitions received (including the number of workers requested when necessary) and will notify the public of the dates that USCIS has received the necessary number of petitions (the "final receipt dates") under paragraph (h)(6)(xi)(A)(1) or (2). The day the public is notified will not control the final receipt dates. When necessary to ensure the fair and orderly allocation of numbers subject to the numerical limitations in paragraphs (h)(6)(xi)(A)(1) and (2), USCIS may randomly select from among the petitions received on the final receipt dates the remaining number of petitions deemed necessary to generate the numerical limit of approvals. This random selection will be made via computer-generated selection. Petitions subject to a numerical limitation not randomly selected or that were received after the final receipt dates that may be applicable under paragraph (h)(6)(xi)(A)(1) or (2) will be rejected. If the final receipt date is any of the first 5 business days on which petitions subject to the applicable numerical limits described in paragraph (h)(6)(xi)(A)(1) or (2) may be received (in other words, if either of the numerical limits described in paragraph (h)(6)(xi)(A)(1) or (2) is reached on any one of the first 5 business days that filings can be made), USCIS will randomly apply all of the numbers among the petitions received on any of those 5 business days.

(E) Sunset. This paragraph (h)(6)(xi) expires on October 1, 2022.

(F) Non-severability. The requirement to file an attestation under paragraph (h)(6)(xi)(B)(2) of this section is intended to be non-severable from the remainder of this paragraph (h)(6)(xi), including, but not limited to, the numerical allocation provisions at paragraphs (h)(6)(xi)(A)(1) and (2) of this section in their entirety. In the event that any part of this paragraph (h)(6)(xi) is enjoined or held to be invalid by any court of competent jurisdiction, the remainder of this paragraph (h)(6)(xi) is also intended to be enjoined or held to be invalid in such jurisdiction, without prejudice to workers already present in the United States under this paragraph (h)(6)(xi), as consistent with law.

(xii) [Effective May 18, 2022 through May 18, 2025] Special requirements for additional cap allocations under the Consolidated Appropriations Act, 2022, Public Law 117-103—

(A) Public Law 117-103 —

(1) Supplemental allocation for returning workers. Notwithstanding the numerical limitations set forth in paragraph (h)(8)(i)(C) of this section, for fiscal year 2022 only, the Secretary has authorized up to an additional 23,500 visas for aliens who may receive H-2B nonimmigrant visas pursuant to section 204 of Division O of the Consolidated Appropriations Act, 2022, Public Law 117-103, based on petitions requesting FY 2022 employment start dates on or after April 1, 2022 through September 30, 2022. An alien may be eligible to receive an H-2B nonimmigrant visa under this paragraph (h)(6)(xii)(A)(1) if she or he is a returning worker. The term "returning worker" under this paragraph (h)(6)(xii)(A)(1) means a person who was issued an H-2B visa or was otherwise granted H-2B status in fiscal year 2019, 2020, or 2021. Notwithstanding § 248.2 of this chapter, an alien may not change status to H-2B nonimmigrant under this paragraph (h)(6)(xii)(A)(1).

(2) Supplemental allocation for nationals of Guatemala, El Salvador, Honduras (Northern Central Ameri-

can countries), or Haiti. Notwithstanding the numerical limitations set forth in paragraph (h)(8)(i)(C) of this section, for fiscal year 2022 only, and in addition to the allocation described in paragraph (h)(6)(xii)(A)(1) of this section, the Secretary has authorized up to an additional 11,500 aliens who are nationals of Guatemala, El Salvador, Honduras (Northern Central American countries), or of Haiti who may receive H-2B nonimmigrant visas pursuant to section 204 of Division O of the Consolidated Appropriations Act, 2022, Public Law 117-103, based on petitions with FY 2022 employment start dates on or after April 1, 2022 through September 30, 2022. Such workers are not subject to the returning worker requirement in paragraph (h)(6)(xii)(A)(1). Petitioners must request such workers in an H-2B petition that is separate from H-2B petitions that request returning workers under paragraph (h)(6)(xii)(A)(1) and must declare that they are requesting these workers in the attestation required under 20 CFR 655.66(a)(1). A petition requesting returning workers under paragraph (h)(6)(xii)(A)(1), which is accompanied by an attestation indicating that the petitioner is requesting nationals of Northern Central American countries or Haiti, will be rejected, denied or, in the case of a non-frivolous petition, will be approved solely for the number of beneficiaries that are from the Northern Central American countries or Haiti. Notwithstanding § 248.2 of this chapter, an alien may not change status to H-2B nonimmigrant under this paragraph (h)(6)(xii)(A)(2).

(B) Eligibility. In order to file a petition with USCIS under this paragraph (h)(6)(xii), the petitioner must:

(1) Comply with all other statutory and regulatory requirements for H-2B classification, including, but not limited to, requirements in this section, under part 103 of this chapter, and under 20 CFR part 655 and 29 CFR part 503; and

(2) Submit to USCIS, at the time the employer files its petition, a U.S. Department of Labor attestation, in compliance with this section and 20 CFR 655.65, evidencing that:

(i) Its business is suffering irreparable harm or will suffer impending irreparable harm (that is, permanent and severe financial loss) without the ability to employ all of the H-2B workers requested on the petition filed pursuant to this paragraph (h)(6)(xii);

(ii) All workers requested and/or instructed to apply for a visa have been issued an H-2B visa or otherwise granted H-2B status in fiscal year 2019, 2020, or 2021, unless the H-2B worker is a national of Guatemala, El Salvador, Honduras, or Haiti who is counted towards the 11,500 cap described in paragraph (h)(6)(xii)(A)(2) of this section;

(iii) The employer will comply with all Federal, State, and local employment-related laws and regulations, including, where applicable, health and safety laws and laws related to COVID-19 worker protections; any right to time off or paid time off for COVID-19 vaccination, or to reimbursement for travel to and from the nearest available vaccination site; and that the employer will notify any H-2B workers approved under the supplemental cap in paragraph (h)(6)(xii)(A)(2) of this section, in a language understood by the worker as necessary or reasonable, that all persons in the United States, including nonimmigrants, have equal access to COVID-19 vaccines and vaccine distribution sites;

(iv) The employer will comply with obligations and additional recruitment requirements outlined in 20 CFR 655.65(a)(3) through (5);

(v) The employer will provide documentary evidence of the facts in paragraphs (h)(6)(xii)(B)(2)(i) through (iv) of this section to DHS or DOL upon request; and

(vi) The employer will agree to fully cooperate with any compliance review, evaluation, verification, or inspection conducted by DHS, including an on-site inspection of the employer's facilities, interview of the employer's employees and any other individuals possessing pertinent information, and review of the employer's records related to the compliance with immigration laws and regulations, including but not limited to evidence pertaining to or supporting the eligibility criteria for the FY 2022 supplemental allocations outlined in paragraph (h)(6)(xii)(B) of this section, as a condition for the approval of the petition.

(vii) The employer must attest on Form ETA-9142-B-CAA-6 that it will fully cooperate with any audit, investigation, compliance review, evaluation, verification or inspection conducted by DOL, including an on-site inspection of the employer's facilities, interview of the employer's employees and any other individuals possessing pertinent information, and review of the employer's records related to the compliance with applicable laws and regulations, including but not limited to evidence pertaining to or supporting the eligibility criteria for the FY 2022 supplemental allocations outlined in 20 CFR 655.65(a) and 655.66(a), as a condition for the approval of the H-2B petition. The employer must further attest on Form ETA-9142-B-CAA-6 that it will not impede, interfere, or refuse to cooperate with an employee of the Secretary of the U.S. Department of Labor who is exercising or attempting to exercise DOL's audit or investigative authority pursuant to 20 CFR part 655, subpart A, and 29 CFR 503.25.

(C) Processing. USCIS will reject petitions filed pursuant to paragraph (h)(6)(xii)(A)(1) or (2) of this section that are received after the applicable numerical limitation has been reached or after September 15, 2022, whichever is sooner. USCIS will not approve a petition filed pursuant to this paragraph (h)(6)(xii) on or after October 1, 2022.

(D) Numerical limitations under paragraphs (h)(6)(xii)(A)(1) and (2) of this section. When calculating the numerical limitations under paragraphs (h)(6)(xii)(A)(1) and (2) of this section as authorized under Public Law 117-103, USCIS will make numbers for each allocation available to petitions in the order in which the petitions subject to the respective limitation are received. USCIS will make projections of the number of petitions necessary to achieve the numerical limit of approvals, taking into account historical data related to approvals, denials, revocations, and other relevant factors. USCIS will monitor the number of petitions received (including the number of workers requested when necessary) and will notify the public of the dates that USCIS has received the necessary number of petitions (the "final receipt dates") under paragraph (h)(6)(xii)(A)(1) or (2). The day the public is notified will not control the final receipt dates. When necessary to ensure the fair and orderly allocation of numbers subject to the numerical limitations in paragraphs (h)(6)(xii)(A)(1) and (2), USCIS may randomly select from among the petitions received on the final receipt dates the remaining number of petitions deemed necessary to generate the numerical limit of approvals. This random selection will be made via computer-generated selection. Petitions subject to a numerical limitation not randomly selected or that were received after the final receipt dates that may be applicable under paragraph (h)(6)(xii)(A)(1) or (2) will be rejected. If the final receipt date is any of the first 5 business days on which petitions subject to the applicable numerical limits described in paragraph (h)(6)(xii)(A)(1) or (2) may be received (in other words, if either of the numerical limits described in paragraph (h)(6)(xii)(A)(1) or (2) is reached on any one of the first 5 business days that filings can be made), USCIS will randomly apply all of the numbers among the petitions received on any of those 5 business days.

(E) Sunset. This paragraph (h)(6)(xii) expires on October 1, 2022.

(F) Non-severability. The requirement to file an attestation under paragraph (h)(6)(xii)(B)(2) of this section is intended to be non-severable from the remainder of this paragraph (h)(6)(xii), including, but not limited to, the numerical allocation provisions at paragraphs (h)(6)(xii)(A)(1) and (2) of this section in their entirety. In the event that any part of this paragraph (h)(6)(xii) is enjoined or held to be invalid by any court of competent jurisdiction, the remainder of this paragraph (h)(6)(xii) is also intended to be enjoined or held to be invalid in such jurisdiction, without prejudice to workers already present in the United States under this paragraph (h)(6)(xii), as consistent with law.

(xiii) [Effective Dec. 15, 2022 through Dec. 15, 2025] Special requirements for additional cap allocations under Public Laws 117-103 and 117-180—

(A) Public Law 117-103 and section 101(6) of Division A of Public Law 117-180, Continuing Appropriations and Ukraine Supplemental Appropriations Act, 2023 —

(1) Supplemental allocation for returning workers. Notwithstanding the numerical limitations set forth in paragraph (h)(8)(i)(C) of this section, for fiscal year 2023 only, the Secretary has authorized up to an additional 64,716 visas for aliens who may receive H-2B nonimmigrant visas pursuant to section 204 of Division O of Public Law 117-103, the Consolidated Appropriations Act, 2022, and section 101(6) of Division A of Public Law 117-180, Continuing Appropriations and Ukraine Supplemental Appropriations Act, 2023. An alien may be eligible to receive an H-2B nonimmigrant visa under this paragraph (h)(6)(xiii)(A)(1) if she or he is a returning worker. The term "returning worker" under this paragraph (h)(6)(xiii)(A)(1) means a person who was issued an H-2B visa or was otherwise granted H-2B status in fiscal year 2020, 2021, or 2022. Notwithstanding § 248.2 of this chapter, an alien may not change status to H-2B nonimmigrant under this paragraph (h)(6)(xiii)(A)(1). The additional H-2B visas authorized under this paragraph will be made available to returning workers as follows:

(i) Up to an additional 18,216 visas for aliens who may receive H-2B nonimmigrant visas based on petitions requesting FY 2023 employment start dates on or before March 31, 2023.

(ii) Up to an additional 16,500 visas for aliens who may receive H-2B nonimmigrant visas based on petitions requesting FY 2023 employment start dates from April 1, 2023 to May 14, 2023.

(iii) Up to an additional 10,000 visas available for aliens with employment start dates from May 15, 2023 to September 30, 2023.

(2) Supplemental allocation for nationals of Guatemala, El Salvador, Honduras (Northern Central American countries), or Haiti. Notwithstanding the numerical limitations set forth in paragraph (h)(8)(i)(C) of this section, for fiscal year 2023 only, and in addition to the allocation described in paragraph (h)(6)(xiii)(A)(1) of this section, the Secretary has authorized up to an additional 20,000 visas for aliens who are nationals of Guatemala, El Salvador, Honduras (Northern Central American countries), or Haiti, who may receive H-2B nonimmigrant visas pursuant section 204 of Division O of the Consolidated Appropriations Act, 2022, Public Law 117-103, and section 101(6) of Division A of Public Law 117-180 Continuing Appropriations and Ukraine Supplemental Appropriations Act, 2023, based on petitions with FY 2023 employment start dates. Such workers are not subject to the returning worker requirement in paragraph (h)(6)(xiii)(A)(1). Petitioners must request such workers in an H-2B petition that is separate from H-2B petitions that request returning workers under paragraph (h)(6)(xiii)(A)(1) and must declare that they are requesting these workers in the attestation required under 20 CFR 655.67(a)(1). A petition requesting returning workers under paragraph (h)(6)(xiii)(A)(1), which is accompanied by an attestation indicating that the petitioner is requesting nationals of Northern Central American countries or Haiti, will be rejected, denied or, in the case of a non-frivolous petition, will be approved solely for the number of beneficiaries that are from the Northern Central American countries or Haiti. Notwithstanding § 248.2 of this chapter, an alien may not change status to H-2B nonimmigrant under this paragraph (h)(6)(xiii)(A)(2).

(B) Eligibility. In order to file a petition with USCIS under this paragraph (h)(6)(xiii), the petitioner must:

(1) Comply with all other statutory and regulatory requirements for H-2B classification, including, but not limited to, requirements in this section, under part 103 of this chapter, and under 20 CFR part 655 and 29 CFR part 503; and

(2) Submit to USCIS, at the time the employer files its petition, a U.S. Department of Labor attestation, in compliance with this section and 20 CFR 655.65, evidencing that:

(i) Its business is suffering irreparable harm or will suffer impending irreparable harm (that is, permanent and severe financial loss) without the ability to employ all of the H-2B workers requested on the petition filed pursuant to this paragraph (h)(6)(xiii);

(ii) All workers requested and/or instructed to apply for a visa have been issued an H-2B visa or otherwise granted H-2B status in fiscal year 2020, 2021, or 2022, unless the H-2B worker is a national of Guatemala, El Salvador, Honduras, or Haiti who is counted towards the 20,000 cap described in paragraph (h)(6)(xiii)(A)(2) of this section;

(iii) The employer will comply with all Federal, State, and local employment-related laws and regulations, including, where applicable, health and safety laws and laws related to COVID-19 worker protections and any right to time off or paid time off for COVID-19 vaccination, or to reimbursement for travel to and from the nearest available vaccination site; and that the employer will notify any H-2B workers approved under the supplemental cap in paragraph (h)(6)(xiii)(A)(2) of this section, in a language understood by the worker as necessary or reasonable, that all persons in the United States, including nonimmigrants, have equal access to COVID-19 vaccines and vaccine distribution sites;

(iv) The employer will comply with obligations and additional recruitment requirements outlined in 20 CFR 655.65(a)(3) through (5);

(v) The employer will provide documentary evidence of the facts in paragraphs (h)(6)(xiii)(B)(2)(i) through (iv) of this section to DHS or DOL upon request; and

(vi) The employer will agree to fully cooperate with any compliance review, evaluation, verification, or inspection conducted by DHS, including an on-site inspection of the employer's facilities, interview of the employer's employees and any other individuals possessing pertinent information, and review of the employer's records related to the compliance with immigration laws and regulations, including but not limited to evidence pertaining to or supporting the eligibility criteria for the FY 2023 supplemental allocations outlined in paragraph (h)(6)(xiii)(B) of this section, as a condition for the approval of the petition.

(vii) The employer will fully cooperate with any audit, investigation, compliance review, evaluation, verification or inspection conducted by DOL, including an on-site inspection of the employer's facilities, interview of the employer's employees and any other individuals possessing pertinent information, and review of the employer's records related to the compliance with applicable laws and regulations, including but not limited to evidence pertaining to or supporting the eligibility criteria for the FY 2023 supplemental allocations outlined in 20 CFR 655.65(a) and 655.67(a), as a condition for the approval of the H-2B petition. The employer must attest to this on Form ETA-9142-B-CAA-7 and must further attest on Form ETA-9142-B-CAA-7 that it will not impede, interfere, or refuse to cooperate with an employee of the Secretary of the U.S. Department of Labor who is exercising or attempting to exercise DOL's audit or investigative authority pursuant to 20 CFR part 655, subpart A, and 29 CFR 503.25.

(C) Processing—

(1) Petitions filed pursuant to paragraph (h)(6)(xiii)(A)(1)(i) requesting FY 2023 employment start dates on or before March 31, 2023. USCIS will reject petitions filed pursuant to paragraph (h)(6)(xiii)(A)(1)(i) of this section requesting employment start dates on or before March 31, 2023 that are received after the applicable numerical limitation has been reached or after September 15, 2023.

(2) Petitions filed pursuant to paragraph (h)(6)(xiii)(A)(1)(ii) requesting FY 2023 employment start dates from April 1, 2023 to May 14, 2023. USCIS will reject petitions filed pursuant to paragraph (h)(6)(xiii)(A)(1)(ii) of this section requesting employment start dates from April 1, 2023 to May 14, 2023 that are received earlier than 15 days after the INA section 214(g) cap for the second half FY 2023 has been met or after the applicable numerical limitation has been reached or after September 15, 2023.

(3) Petitions filed pursuant to paragraph (h)(6)(xiii)(A)(1)(iii) of this section requesting FY 2023 employment start dates from May 15, 2023 and September 30, 2023. USCIS will reject petitions filed pursuant to paragraph (h)(6)(xiii)(A)(1)(iii) of this section requesting employment start dates from May 15, 2023 to September 30, 2023, that are received earlier than 45 days after the INA section 214(g) cap for the second half FY 2023 has been met, or after the applicable numerical limitation has been reached or after September 15, 2023.

(4) Petitions filed pursuant to paragraph (h)(6)(xiii)(A)(2) of this section requesting nationals of Guatemala, El Salvador, Honduras (Northern Central American countries), or Haiti with FY 2023 employment start dates. USCIS will reject petitions filed pursuant to paragraph (h)(6)(xiii)(A)(2) of this section that have a date of need on or after April 1, 2023 and are received earlier than 15 days after the INA section 214(g) cap for the second half of FY 2023 is met, or after the applicable numerical limitation has been reached or after September 15, 2023.

(5) USCIS will not approve a petition filed pursuant to paragraph (h)(6)(xiii) of this section on or after October 1, 2023.

(D) Numerical limitations under paragraphs (h)(6)(xiii)(A)(1) and (2) of this section. When calculating the numerical limitations under paragraphs (h)(6)(xiii)(A)(1) and (2) of this section as authorized under Public Law 117-103, as extended by Public Law 117-180, USCIS will make numbers for each allocation available to petitions in the order in which the petitions subject to the respective limitation are received. USCIS will make projections of the number of petitions necessary to achieve the numerical limit of approvals, taking into account historical data related to approvals, denials, revocations, and other relevant factors. USCIS will monitor the number of petitions received (including the number of workers requested when necessary) and will notify the public of the dates that USCIS has received the necessary number of petitions (the "final receipt dates") under paragraph (h)(6)(xiii)(A)(1) or (2) of this section. The day the public is notified will not control the final receipt dates. When necessary to ensure the fair and orderly allocation of numbers subject to the numerical limitations in paragraphs (h)(6)(xiii)(A)(1) and (2) of this section, USCIS may randomly select from among the petitions received on the final receipt dates the remaining number of petitions deemed necessary to generate the numerical limit of approvals. This random selection will be made via computer-generated selection. Petitions subject to a numerical limitation not randomly selected or that were received after the final receipt dates that may be applicable under paragraph (h)(6)(xiii)(A)(1) or (2) of this section will be rejected. If the final receipt date is any of the first 5 business days on which petitions subject to the applicable numerical limits described in paragraph (h)(6)(xiii)(A)(1) or (2) of this section may be received (in other words, if either of the numerical limits described in paragraph (h)(6)(xiii)(A)(1) or (2) of this section is reached on any one of the first 5 business days that filings can be made), USCIS will randomly apply all of the numbers among the petitions received on any of those 5 business days.

(E) Sunset. This paragraph (h)(6)(xiii) expires on October 1, 2023.

(F) Non-severability. The requirement to file an attestation under paragraph (h)(6)(xiii)(B)(2) of this section is intended to be non-severable from the remainder of paragraph (h)(6)(xiii), including, but not limited to, the numerical allocation provisions at paragraphs (h)(6)(xiii)(A)(1) and (2) of this section in their entirety. In the event that any part of this paragraph (h)(6)(xiii) is enjoined or held to be invalid by any court of competent jurisdiction, the remainder of this paragraph (h)(6)(xiii) is also intended to be enjoined or held to be invalid in such jurisdiction, without prejudice to workers already present in the United States under this paragraph (h)(6)(xiii), as consistent with law.

(xiv) Special requirements for additional cap allocations under Public Laws 117-328 and 118-15—

(A) Public Law 117-328 and section 101(6) of Division A of Public Law 118-15, Continuing Appropriations Act, 2024 and Other Extensions Act —

(1) Supplemental allocation for returning workers. Notwithstanding the numerical limitations set forth in paragraph (h)(8)(i)(C) of this section, for fiscal year 2024 only, the Secretary has authorized up to an additional 64,716 visas for aliens who may receive H-2B nonimmigrant visas pursuant to section 303 of Division O of Public Law 117-328, the Consolidated Appropriations Act, 2023, and section 101(6) of Division A of Public Law 118-15, Continuing Appropriations Act, 2024 and Other Extensions Act. An alien may be eligible to receive an H-2B nonimmigrant visa under this paragraph (h)(6)(xiv)(A)(1) if she or he is a returning worker. The term "returning worker" under this paragraph (h)(6)(xiv)(A)(1) means a person who was issued an H-2B visa or was otherwise granted H-2B status in fiscal year 2021, 2022, or 2023. Notwithstanding § 248.2 of this chapter, an alien may not change status to H-2B nonimmigrant under this paragraph (h)(6)(xiv)(A)(1). The additional H-2B visas authorized under this paragraph will be made available to returning workers as follows:

(i) Up to an additional 20,716 visas for aliens who may receive H-2B nonimmigrant visas based on petitions requesting FY 2024 employment start dates on or before March 31, 2024.

(ii) Up to an additional 19,000 visas for aliens who may receive H-2B nonimmigrant visas based on petitions requesting FY 2024 employment start dates from April 1, 2024 to May 14, 2024.

(iii) Up to an additional 5,000 visas available for aliens with employment start dates from May 15, 2024 to September 30, 2024.

(2) Supplemental allocation for nationals of Guatemala, El Salvador, Honduras, Haiti, Colombia, Ecuador, or Costa Rica. Notwithstanding the numerical limitations set forth in paragraph (h)(8)(i)(C) of this section, for fiscal year 2024 only, and in addition to the allocation described in paragraph (h)(6)(xiv)(A)(1) of this section, the Secretary has authorized up to an additional 20,000 visas for aliens who are nationals of Guatemala, El Salvador, Honduras, Haiti, Colombia, Ecuador, or Costa Rica, who may receive H-2B nonimmigrant visas pursuant section 303 of Division O of the Consolidated Appropriations Act, 2023, Public Law 117-328, and section 101(6) of Division A of Public Law 118-15 Continuing Appropriations Act, 2024 and Other Extensions Act, based on petitions with FY 2024 employment start dates. Such workers are not subject to the returning worker requirement in paragraph (h)(6)(xiv)(A)(1). Petitioners must request such workers in an H-2B petition that is separate from H-2B petitions that request returning workers under paragraph (h)(6)(xiv)(A)(1) and must declare that they are requesting these workers in the attestation Form ETA-9142-B-CAA-8 required under 20 CFR 655.65(a)(1). A petition requesting returning workers under paragraph (h)(6)(xiv)(A)(1), which is accompanied by an attestation indicating that the petitioner is requesting nationals of Guatemala, El Salvador, Honduras, Haiti, Colombia, Ecuador, or Costa Rica, will be rejected, denied or, in the case of a non-frivolous petition, approved solely for the number of beneficiaries that are from the Guatemala, El Salvador, Honduras, Haiti, Colombia, Ecuador, or Costa Rica. Notwithstanding § 248.2 of this chapter, an alien may not change status to H-2B nonimmigrant under this paragraph (h)(6)(xiv)(A)(2).

(B) Eligibility. In order to file a petition with USCIS under this paragraph (h)(6)(xiv), the petitioner must:

(1) Comply with all other statutory and regulatory requirements for H-2B classification, including, but not limited to, requirements in this section, under part 103 of this chapter, and under 20 CFR part 655 and 29 CFR part 503; and

(2) Submit to USCIS, at the time the employer files its petition, a U.S. Department of Labor attestation, in compliance with this section and 20 CFR 655.64, evidencing that:

(i) Its business is suffering irreparable harm or will suffer impending irreparable harm (that is, permanent and severe financial loss) without the ability to employ all of the H-2B workers requested on the petition filed pursuant to this paragraph (h)(6)(xiv);

(ii) All workers requested and/or instructed to apply for a visa have been issued an H-2B visa or otherwise granted H-2B status in fiscal year 2021, 2022, or 2023, unless the H-2B worker is a national of Guatemala, El Salvador, Honduras, Haiti, Colombia, Ecuador, or Costa Rica who is counted towards the 20,000 cap described in paragraph (h)(6)(xiv)(A)(2) of this section;

(iii) The employer will comply with obligations and additional recruitment requirements outlined in 20 CFR 655.64(a)(3) through (5);

(iv) The employer will provide documentary evidence of the facts in paragraphs (h)(6)(xiv)(B)(2)(i) through (iii) of this section to DHS and/or DOL upon request; and

(v) The employer will agree to fully cooperate with any compliance review, evaluation, verification, or inspection conducted by DHS, including an on-site inspection of the employer's facilities, interview of the employer's employees and any other individuals possessing pertinent information, and review of the employer's records related to the compliance with immigration laws and regulations, including but not limited to evidence pertaining to or supporting the eligibility criteria for the FY 2024 supplemental allocations outlined in paragraph (h)(6)(xiv)(B) of this section, as a condition for the approval of the petition.

(vi) The employer will fully cooperate with any audit, investigation, compliance review, evaluation, verification or inspection conducted by DOL, including an on-site inspection of the employer's facilities, interview of the employer's employees and any other individuals possessing pertinent information, and review of the employer's records related to the compliance with applicable laws and regulations, including but not limited to evidence pertaining to or supporting the eligibility criteria for the FY 2024 supplemental allocations outlined in 20 CFR 655.64(a) and 655.65(a), as a condition for the approval of the H-2B petition. The employer must attest to this on Form ETA-9142-B-CAA-8 and must further attest on Form ETA-9142-B-CAA-8 that it will not impede, interfere, or refuse to cooperate with an employee of the Secretary of the U.S. Department of Labor who is exercising or attempting to exercise DOL's audit or investigative authority pursuant to 20 CFR part 655, subpart A, and 29 CFR 503.25.

(C) Processing—

(1) Petitions filed pursuant to paragraph (h)(6)(xiv)(A)(1)(a) requesting FY 2024 employment start dates on or before March 31, 2024. USCIS will reject petitions filed pursuant to paragraph (h)(6)(xiv)(A)(1)(a) of this section requesting employment start dates on or before March 31, 2024 that are received after the applicable numerical limitation has been reached or after September 16, 2024.

(2) Petitions filed pursuant to paragraph (h)(6)(xiv)(A)(1)(ii) of this section requesting FY 2024 employment start dates from April 1, 2024 to May 14, 2024. USCIS will reject petitions filed pursuant to paragraph (h)(6)(xiv)(A)(1)(ii) of this section requesting employment start dates from April 1, 2024 to May 14, 2024 that are received earlier than 15 days after the INA section 214(g) cap for the second half FY 2024 has been met, or after the applicable numerical limitation has been reached or after September 16, 2024.

(3) Petitions filed pursuant to paragraph (h)(6)(xiv)(A)(1)(iii) of this section requesting FY 2024 employment start dates from May 15, 2024 and September 30, 2024. USCIS will reject petitions filed pursuant to paragraph (h)(6)(xiv)(A)(1)(iii) of this section requesting employment start dates from May 15, 2024 to September 30, 2024 that are received earlier than 45 days after the INA section 214(g) cap for the second half FY 2024 has been met, or after the applicable numerical limitation has been reached or after September 16, 2024.

(4) Petitions filed pursuant to paragraph (h)(6)(xiv)(A)(2) requesting nationals of Guatemala, El Salvador, Honduras, Haiti, Colombia, Ecuador, or Costa Rica with FY 2024 employment start dates. USCIS will reject petitions filed pursuant to paragraph (h)(6)(xiv)(A)(2) of this section that have a date of need on or after April 1, 2024 and are received earlier than 15 days after the INA section 214(g) cap for the second half of FY 2024 is met, or after the applicable numerical limitation has been reached or after September 16, 2024.

(5) USCIS will not approve a petition filed pursuant to this paragraph (h)(6)(xiv) on or after October 1, 2024.

(D) Numerical limitations under paragraphs (h)(6)(xiv)(A)(1) and (2) of this section. When calculating the numerical limitations under paragraphs (h)(6)(xiv)(A)(1) and (2) of this section as authorized under Public Law 117-328, as extended by Public Law 118-15, USCIS will make numbers for each allocation available to petitions in the order in which the petitions subject to the respective limitation are received. USCIS will make projections of the number of petitions necessary to achieve the numerical limit of approvals, taking into account historical data related to approvals, denials, revocations, and other relevant factors. USCIS will monitor the number of petitions received (including the number of workers requested when necessary) and will notify the public of the dates that USCIS has received the necessary number of petitions (the "final receipt dates") under paragraph (h)(6)(xiv)(A)(1) or (2). The day the public is notified will not control the final receipt dates. When necessary to ensure the fair and orderly allocation of numbers subject to the numerical limitations in paragraphs (h)(6)(xiv)(A)(1) and (2), USCIS may randomly select from among the petitions received on the final receipt dates the remaining number of petitions deemed necessary to generate the numerical limit of approvals. This random selection will be made via computer-generated selection. Petitions subject to a numerical limitation not randomly selected or that were received after the final receipt dates that may be applicable under paragraph (h)(6)(xiv)(A)(1) or (2) will be rejected. If the final receipt date is any of the first 5 business days on which petitions subject to the applicable numerical limits described in paragraph (h)(6)(xiv)(A)(1) or (2) may be received (in other words, if either of the numerical limits described in paragraph (h)(6)(xiv)(A)(1) or (2) is reached on any one of the first 5 business days that filings can be made), USCIS will randomly apply all of the numbers among the petitions received on any of those 5 business days.

(E) Sunset. This paragraph (h)(6)(xiv) expires on October 1, 2024.

(F) Non-severability. The requirement to file an attestation under paragraph (h)(6)(xiv)(B)(2) of this section is intended to be non-severable from the remainder of this paragraph (h)(6)(xiv), including, but not limited to, the numerical allocation provisions at paragraphs (h)(6)(xiv)(A)(1) and (2) of this section in their entirety. In the event that any part of this paragraph (h)(6)(xiv) is enjoined or held to be invalid by any court of competent jurisdiction, the remainder of this paragraph (h)(6)(xiv) is also intended to be enjoined or held to be invalid in such jurisdiction, without prejudice to workers already present in the United States under this paragraph (h)(6)(xiv), as consistent with law.

(xv) Special requirements for additional cap allocations under Public Laws 118-47 and 118-83—

(A) Public Law 118-47 and sections 101(6) and 106, Division A, Title I of Public Law 118-83 —

(1) Supplemental allocation for returning workers. Notwithstanding the numerical limitations set forth in paragraph (h)(8)(i)(C) of this section, for fiscal year 2025 only, the Secretary has authorized up to an additional 64,716 visas for aliens who may receive H-2B nonimmigrant visas pursuant to section 105 of Division G, Title I of Public Law 118-47, the Further Consolidated Appropriations Act, 2024, and sections 101(6) and 106, Division A, Title I of the Continuing Appropriations and Extensions Act, 2025, Public Law 118-83. An alien may be eligible to receive an H-2B nonimmigrant visa under this paragraph (h)(6)(xv)(A)(1) if she or he is a returning worker. The term "returning worker" under this paragraph (h)(6)(xv)(A)(1) means a person who was issued an H-2B visa or was otherwise granted H-2B status in fiscal year 2022, 2023, or 2024. Notwithstanding § 248.2 of this chapter, an alien may not change status to H-2B nonimmigrant under this paragraph (h)(6)(xv)(A)(1). The additional H-2B visas authorized under this paragraph will be made available to returning workers as follows:

(i) Up to an additional 20,716 visas for aliens who may receive H-2B nonimmigrant visas based on petitions requesting FY 2025 employment start dates on or before March 31, 2025.

(ii) Up to an additional 19,000 visas for aliens who may receive H-2B nonimmigrant visas based on petitions requesting FY 2025 employment start dates from April 1, 2025 to May 14, 2025.

(iii) Up to an additional 5,000 visas available for aliens with employment start dates from May 15, 2025 to September 30, 2025.

(2) Supplemental allocation for nationals of Guatemala, El Salvador, Honduras, Haiti, Colombia, Ecuador, or Costa Rica. Notwithstanding the numerical limitations set forth in paragraph (h)(8)(i)(C) of this section, for fiscal year 2025 only, and in addition to the allocation described in paragraph (h)(6)(xv)(A)(1) of this section, the Secretary has authorized up to an additional 20,000 visas for aliens who are nationals of Guatemala, El Salvador, Honduras, Haiti, Colombia, Ecuador, or Costa Rica, who may receive H-2B nonimmigrant visas pursuant to section 105 of Division G, Title I of Public Law 118-47, the Further Consolidated Appropriations Act, 2024, and sections 101(6) and 106 of Division A, Title I of the Continuing Appropriations and Extensions Act, 2025, Public Law 118-83, based on petitions with FY 2025 employment start dates. Such workers are not subject to the returning worker requirement in paragraph (h)(6)(xv)(A)(1). Petitioners must request such workers in an H-2B petition that is separate from H-2B petitions that request returning workers under paragraph (h)(6)(xv)(A)(1) and must declare that they are requesting these workers in the attestation Form ETA-9142-B-CAA-9 required under 20 CFR 655.68(a)(1). A petition requesting returning workers under paragraph (h)(6)(xv)(A)(1), which is accompanied by an attestation indicating that the petitioner is requesting nationals of Guatemala, El Salvador, Honduras, Haiti, Colombia, Ecuador, or Costa Rica, will be rejected, denied or, in the case of a non-frivolous petition, approved solely for the number of beneficiaries that are from Guatemala, El Salvador, Honduras, Haiti, Colombia, Ecuador, or Costa Rica. Notwithstanding § 248.2 of this chapter, an alien may not change status to H-2B nonimmigrant under this paragraph (h)(6)(xv)(A)(2).

(B) Eligibility. In order to file a petition with USCIS under this paragraph (h)(6)(xv), the petitioner must:

(1) Comply with all other statutory and regulatory requirements for H-2B classification, including, but not limited to, requirements in this section, under part 103 of this chapter, and under 20 CFR part 655 and 29 CFR part 503; and (2) Submit to USCIS, at the time the employer files its petition, a U.S. Department of Labor attestation, in compliance with this section and 20 CFR 655.64, evidencing that:

(i) Its business is suffering irreparable harm or will suffer impending irreparable harm (that is, permanent and severe financial loss) without the ability to employ all of the H-2B workers requested on the petition filed pursuant to this paragraph (h)(6)(xv);

(ii) All workers requested and/or instructed to apply for a visa have been issued an H-2B visa or otherwise granted H-2B status in fiscal year 2022, 2023, or 2024, unless the H-2B worker is a national of Guatemala, El Salvador, Honduras, Haiti, Colombia, Ecuador, or Costa Rica who is counted towards the 20,000 cap described in paragraph (h)(6)(xv)(A)(2) of this section;

(iii) The employer will comply with obligations and additional recruitment requirements outlined in 20 CFR 655.64(a)(3) through (5);

(iv) The employer will provide documentary evidence of the facts in paragraphs (h)(6)(xv)(B)(2)(i) through (iii) of this section to DHS and/or DOL upon request; and

(v) The employer will agree to fully cooperate with any compliance review, evaluation, verification, or inspection conducted by DHS, including an on-site inspection of the employer's facilities, interview of the employer's employees and any other individuals possessing pertinent information, and review of the employer's records related to the compliance with immigration laws and regulations, including but not limited to evidence pertaining to or supporting the eligibility criteria for the FY 2025 supplemental allocations outlined in paragraph (h)(6)(xv)(B) of this section, as a condition for the approval of the petition.

(vi) The employer will fully cooperate with any audit, investigation, compliance review, evaluation, verification or inspection conducted by DOL, including an on-site inspection of the employer's facilities, interview of the employer's employees and any other individuals possessing pertinent information, and review of the employer's records related to the compliance with applicable laws and regulations, including but not limited to evidence pertaining to or supporting the eligibility criteria for the FY 2025 supplemental allocations outlined in 20 CFR 655.64(a) and 655.68(a), as a condition for the approval of the H-2B petition. The employer must attest to this on Form ETA-9142-B-CAA-9 and must further attest on Form ETA-9142-B-CAA-9 that it will not impede, interfere, or refuse to cooperate with an employee of the Secretary of the U.S. Department of Labor who is exercising or attempting to exercise DOL's audit or investigative authority pursuant to 20 CFR part 655, subpart A, and 29 CFR 503.25.

(C) Processing—

(1) Petitions filed pursuant to paragraph (h)(6)(xv)(A)(1)(i) of this section requesting FY 2025 employment start dates on or before March 31, 2025. USCIS will reject petitions filed pursuant to paragraph (h)(6)(xv)(A)(1)(i) of this section requesting employment start dates on or before March 31, 2025 that are received after the applicable numerical limitation has been reached or after September 15, 2025.

(2) Petitions filed pursuant to paragraph (h)(6)(xv)(A)(1)(ii) of this section requesting FY 2025 employment start dates from April 1, 2025 to May 14, 2025. USCIS will reject petitions filed pursuant to paragraph (h)(6)(xv)(A)(1)(ii) of this section requesting employment start dates from April 1, 2025 to May 14, 2025 that are received earlier than 15 days after the INA section 214(g) cap for the second half FY 2024 has been met, or after the applicable numerical limitation has been reached or after September 15, 2025.

(3) Petitions filed pursuant to paragraph (h)(6)(xv)(A)(1)(iii) of this section requesting FY 2025 employment start dates from May 15, 2025 and September 30, 2025. USCIS will reject petitions filed pursuant to paragraph (h)(6)(xv)(A)(1)(iii) of this section requesting employment start dates from May 15, 2025 to September 30, 2025 that are received earlier than 45 days after the INA section 214(g) cap for the second half FY 2025 has been met, or after the applicable numerical limitation has been reached or after September 15, 2025.

(4) Petitions filed pursuant to paragraph (h)(6)(xv)(A)(2) requesting nationals of Guatemala, El Salvador, Honduras, Haiti, Colombia, Ecuador, or Costa Rica with FY 2025 employment start dates. USCIS will reject petitions filed pursuant to paragraph (h)(6)(xv)(A)(2) of this section that have a date of need on or after April 1, 2025, and are received earlier than 15 days after the INA section 214(g) cap for the second half of FY 2025 is met, or after the applicable numerical limitation has been reached or after September 15, 2025.

(5) USCIS will not approve a petition filed pursuant to this paragraph (h)(6)(xv) on or after October 1, 2025.

(D) Numerical limitations under paragraphs (h)(6)(xv)(A)(1) and (2) of this section. When calculating the numerical limitations under paragraphs (h)(6)(xv)(A)(1) and (2) of this section as authorized under section 105 of Division G, Title I of Public Law 118-47, the Further Consolidated Appropriations Act, 2024, and sections 101(6) and 106 of Division A, Title I of the Continuing Appropriations and Extensions Act, 2025, Public Law 118-83, USCIS will make numbers for each allocation available to petitions in the order in which the petitions subject to the respective limitation are received. USCIS will make projections of the number of petitions necessary to achieve the numerical limit of approvals, taking into account historical data related to approvals, denials, revocations, and other relevant factors. USCIS will monitor the number of petitions received (including the number of workers requested when necessary) and will notify the public of the dates that USCIS has received the necessary number of petitions (the "final receipt dates") under paragraph (h)(6)(xv)(A)(1) or (2). The day the public is notified will not control the final receipt dates. When necessary to ensure the fair and orderly allocation of numbers subject to the numerical limitations in paragraphs (h)(6)(xv)(A)(1) and (2), USCIS may randomly select from among the petitions received on the final receipt dates the remaining number of petitions deemed necessary to generate the numerical limit of approvals. This random selection will be made via computer-generated selection. Petitions subject to a numerical limitation not randomly selected or that were received after the final receipt dates that may be applicable under paragraph (h)(6)(xv)(A)(1) or (2) will be rejected. If the final receipt date is any of the first 5 business days on which petitions subject to the applicable numerical limits described in paragraph (h)(6)(xv)(A)(1) or (2) may be received (in other words, if either of the numerical limits described in paragraph (h)(6)(xv)(A)(1) or (2) is reached on any one of the first 5 business days that filings can be made), USCIS will randomly apply all of the numbers among the petitions received on any of those 5 business days.

(E) Sunset. This paragraph (h)(6)(xv) expires on October 1, 2025.

(F) Non-severability. The requirement to file an attestation under paragraph (h)(6)(xv)(B)(2) of this section is intended to be non-severable from the remainder of this paragraph (h)(6)(xv), including, but not limited to, the entirety of the numerical allocation provisions at paragraphs (h)(6)(xv)(A)(1) and (2) of this section. In the event that any part of this paragraph (h)(6)(xv) is enjoined or held to be invalid by any court of competent jurisdiction, the remainder of this paragraph (h)(6)(xv) is also intended to be enjoined or held to be invalid in such jurisdiction, without prejudice to workers already present in the United States under this paragraph (h)(6)(xv), as consistent with law.

(7) Petition for alien trainee or participant in a special education exchange visitor program (H-3) --

(i) Alien trainee. The H-3 trainee is a nonimmigrant who seeks to enter the United States at the invitation of an organization or individual for the purpose of receiving training in any field of endeavor, such as agriculture, commerce, communications, finance, government, transportation, or the professions, as well as training in a purely industrial establishment. This category shall not apply to physicians, who are statutorily ineligible to use H-3 classification in order to receive any type of graduate medical education or training.

(A) Externs. A hospital approved by the American Medical Association or the American Osteopathic Association for either an internship or residency program may petition to classify as an H-3 trainee a medical student attending a medical school abroad, if the alien will engage in employment as an extern during his/her medical school vacation.

(B) Nurses. A petitioner may seek H-3 classification for a nurse who is not H-1 if it can be established that there is a genuine need for the nurse to receive a brief period of training that is unavailable in the alien's native country and such training is designed to benefit the nurse and the overseas employer upon the nurse's return to the country of origin, if:

(1) The beneficiary has obtained a full and unrestricted license to practice professional nursing in the country where the beneficiary obtained a nursing education, or such education was obtained in the United States or Canada; and

(2) The petitioner provides a statement certifying that the beneficiary is fully qualified under the laws governing the place where the training will be received to engage in such training, and that under those laws the petitioner is authorized to give the beneficiary the desired training.

(ii) Evidence required for petition involving alien trainee --

(A) Conditions. The petitioner is required to demonstrate that:

(1) The proposed training is not available in the alien's own country;

(2) The beneficiary will not be placed in a position which is in the normal operation of the business and in which citizens and resident workers are regularly employed;

(3) The beneficiary will not engage in productive employment unless such employment is incidental and necessary to the training; and

(4) The training will benefit the beneficiary in pursuing a career outside the United States.

(B) Description of training program. Each petition for a trainee must include a statement which:

(1) Describes the type of training and supervision to be given, and the structure of the training program;

(2) Sets forth the proportion of time that will be devoted to productive employment;

(3) Shows the number of hours that will be spent, respectively, in classroom instruction and in on-the-job training;

(4) Describes the career abroad for which the training will prepare the alien;

(5) Indicates the reasons why such training cannot be obtained in the alien's country and why it is necessary for the alien to be trained in the United States; and

(6) Indicates the source of any remuneration received by the trainee and any benefit which will accrue to the petitioner for providing the training.

(iii) Restrictions on training program for alien trainee. A training program may not be approved which:

(A) Deals in generalities with no fixed schedule, objectives, or means of evaluation;

(B) Is incompatible with the nature of the petitioner's business or enterprise;

(C) Is on behalf of a beneficiary who already possesses substantial training and expertise in the proposed field of training;

(D) Is in a field in which it is unlikely that the knowledge or skill will be used outside the United States;

(E) Will result in productive employment beyond that which is incidental and necessary to the training;

(F) Is designed to recruit and train aliens for the ultimate staffing of domestic operations in the United States;

(G) Does not establish that the petitioner has the physical plant and sufficiently trained manpower to provide the training specified; or

(H) Is designed to extend the total allowable period of practical training previously authorized a nonimmigrant student.

(iv) Petition for participant in a special education exchange visitor program --

(A) General Requirements.

(1) The H-3 participant in a special education training program must be coming to the United States to participate in a structured program which provides for practical training and experience in the education of children with physical, mental, or emotional disabilities.

(2) The petition must be filed by a facility which has professionally trained staff and a structured program for providing education to children with disabilities, and for providing training and hands-on experience to participants in the special education exchange visitor program.

(3) The requirements in this section for alien trainees shall not apply to petitions for participants in a special education exchange visitor program.

(B) Evidence. An H-3 petition for a participant in a special education exchange visitor program shall be accompanied by:

(1) A description of the training program and the facility's professional staff and details of the alien's participation in the training program (any custodial care of children must be incidental to the training), and

(2) Evidence that the alien participant is nearing completion of a baccalaureate or higher degree in special education, or already holds such a degree, or has extensive prior training and experience in teaching

children with physical, mental, or emotional disabilities.

(8) Numerical limits --

(i) Limits on affected categories. During each fiscal year, the total number of aliens who can be provided nonimmigrant classification is limited as follows:

(A) Aliens classified as H-1B nonimmigrants, excluding those involved in Department of Defense research and development projects or coproduction projects, may not exceed the limits identified in section 214(g)(1)(A) of the Act.

(B) Aliens classified as H-1B nonimmigrants to work for DOD research and development projects or coproduction projects may not exceed 100 at any time.

(C) Aliens classified as H-2B nonimmigrants may not exceed 66,000.

(D) Aliens classified as H-3 nonimmigrant participants in a special education exchange visitor program may not exceed 50.

(E) Aliens classified as H-1C nonimmigrants may not exceed 500 in a fiscal year.

(ii) Procedures.

(A) Each alien issued a visa or otherwise provided nonimmigrant status under sections 101(a)(15)(H)(i)(b), 101(a)(15)(H)(i)(c), or 101(a)(15)(H)(ii) of the Act shall be counted for purposes of any applicable numerical limit, unless otherwise exempt from such numerical limit. Requests for petition extension or extension of an alien's stay shall not be counted for the purpose of the numerical limit. The spouse and children of principal H aliens are classified as H-4 nonimmigrants and shall not be counted against numerical limits applicable to principals.

(B) When an approved petition is not used because the beneficiary(ies) does not apply for admission to the United States, the petitioner shall notify the Service Center Director who approved the petition that the number(s) has not been used. The petition shall be revoked pursuant to paragraph (h)(11)(ii) of this section and USCIS will take into account the unused number during the appropriate fiscal year.

(C) If the total numbers available in a fiscal year are used, new petitions and the accompanying fee shall be rejected and returned with a notice that numbers are unavailable for the particular nonimmigrant classification until the beginning of the next fiscal year. Petitions received after the total numbers available in a fiscal year are used stating that the alien beneficiaries are exempt from the numerical limitation will be denied and filing fees will not be returned or refunded if USCIS later determines that such beneficiaries are subject to the numerical limitation.

(iii) H-1B numerical limitations--

(A) Registration —

(1) Registration requirement. Except as provided in paragraph (h)(8)(iv) of this section, before a petitioner can file an H-1B cap-subject petition for a beneficiary who may be counted under section 214(g)(1)(A) of the Act ("H-1B regular cap") or eligible for exemption under section 214(g)(5)(C) of the Act ("H-1B advanced degree exemption"), the petitioner must register to file a petition on behalf of a beneficiary electronically through the USCIS website (www.uscis.gov). To be eligible to file a petition for a beneficiary who may be counted against the H-1B regular cap or the H-1B advanced degree exemption for a particular fiscal year, a registration must be properly submitted in accordance with 8 CFR 103.2(a)(1), paragraph (h)(8)(iii) of this section, and the form instructions, for the same fiscal year.

(2) Limitation on beneficiaries. A prospective petitioner must electronically submit a separate registration for each beneficiary it seeks to register, and each beneficiary must be named. A petitioner may only submit one registration per beneficiary in any fiscal year. If a petitioner submits more than one registration per beneficiary in the same fiscal year, all registrations filed by that petitioner relating to that beneficiary for that fiscal year may be considered invalid, and USCIS may deny or revoke the approval of any H-1B petition filed for the beneficiary based on those registrations. If USCIS determines that registrations were submitted for the same beneficiary by the same or different registrants, but using different identifying information, USCIS may find those registrations invalid and deny or revoke the approval of any H-1B petition filed based on those registrations. Petitioners will be given notice and the opportunity to respond before USCIS denies or revokes the approval of a petition.

(3) Initial registration period. The annual initial registration period will last a minimum of 14 calendar days and will start at least 14 calendar days before the earliest date on which H-1B cap-subject petitions may be filed for a particular fiscal year, consistent with paragraph (h)(2)(i)(I) of this section. USCIS will announce the start and end dates of the initial registration period on the USCIS website at www.uscis.gov for each fiscal year. USCIS will announce the start of the initial registration period at least 30 calendar days in advance of such date.

(4) Selecting registrations based on unique beneficiaries. Registrations will be counted based on the number of unique beneficiaries who are registered. USCIS will separately notify each registrant that their registration on behalf of a beneficiary has been selected, and that the petitioner(s) may file a petition(s) for that beneficiary. A petitioner may file an H-1B cap-subject petition on behalf of a registered beneficiary only after their properly submitted registration for that beneficiary has been selected for that fiscal year.

(i) Should a random selection be necessary, as provided in paragraphs (h)(8)(iii)(A)(5)(ii), (h)(8)(iii)(A)(6)(ii), and (h)(8)(iii)(A)(7) of this section, each unique beneficiary will only be counted once towards the random selection of registrations, regardless of how many registrations were submitted for that beneficiary.

(ii) Registrations must include the beneficiary's valid passport information or valid travel document information, as specified in the form instructions. Each beneficiary must only be registered under one passport or travel document, and if or when the beneficiary is abroad, the passport information or travel document information must correspond to the passport or travel document the beneficiary intends to use to enter the United States.

(5) Regular cap selection. In determining whether there are enough registrations for unique beneficiaries to meet the H-1B regular cap, USCIS will consider all properly submitted registrations relating to beneficiaries that may be counted under section 214(g)(1)(A) of the Act, including those that may also be eligible for exemption under section 214(g)(5)(C) of the Act. Registrations will be counted based on the number of unique beneficiaries that are registered.

(i) Fewer registrations than needed to meet the H-1B regular cap. At the end of the annual initial registration period, if USCIS determines that it has received fewer registrations for unique beneficiaries than needed to meet the H-1B regular cap, USCIS will notify all petitioners that have properly registered that their registrations have been selected. USCIS will keep the registration period open beyond the initial registration period, until it determines that it has received a sufficient number of registrations for unique beneficiaries to meet the H-1B regular cap. Once USCIS has received a sufficient number of registrations for unique beneficiaries to meet the H-1B regular cap, USCIS will no longer accept registrations for petitions subject to the H-1B regular cap under section 214(g)(1)(A) of the Act. USCIS will monitor the number of registrations received and will notify the public of the date that USCIS has received the necessary number of registrations for unique beneficiaries (the "final registration date"). The day the public is notified will not control the applicable final registration date. When necessary to ensure the fair and orderly allocation of numbers under section 214(g)(1)(A) of the Act, USCIS may randomly select the remaining number of registrations for unique beneficiaries deemed necessary to meet the H-1B regular cap from among the registrations received on the final registration date. This random selection will be made via computer-generated selection, based on the unique beneficiary.

(ii) Sufficient registrations to meet the H-1B regular cap during initial registration period. At the end of the initial registration period, if USCIS determines that it has received more than sufficient registrations for unique beneficiaries to meet the H-1B regular cap, USCIS will no longer accept registrations under section 214(g)(1)(A) of the Act and will notify the public of the final registration date. USCIS will randomly select from among the registrations properly submitted during the initial registration period the number of registrations for unique beneficiaries deemed necessary to meet the H-1B regular cap. This random selection will be made via computer-generated selection, based on the unique beneficiary.

(6) Advanced degree exemption selection. After USCIS has determined it will no longer accept registrations under section 214(g)(1)(A) of the Act, USCIS will determine whether there is a sufficient number of remaining registrations to meet the H-1B advanced degree exemption.

(i) Fewer registrations than needed to meet the H-1B advanced degree exemption numerical limitation. If USCIS determines that it has received fewer registrations for unique beneficiaries than needed to meet the H-1B advanced degree exemption numerical limitation, USCIS will notify all petitioners that have properly registered that their registrations have been selected. USCIS will continue to accept registrations to file petitions for beneficiaries that may be eligible for the H-1B advanced degree exemption under section 214(g)(5)(C) of the Act until USCIS determines that it has received enough registrations for unique beneficiaries to meet the H-1B advanced degree exemption numerical limitation. USCIS will monitor the number of registrations received and will notify the public of the date that USCIS has received the necessary number of registrations for unique beneficiaries (the "final registration date"). The day the public is notified will not control the applicable final registration date. When necessary to ensure the fair and orderly allocation of numbers under sections 214(g)(1)(A) and 214(g)(5)(C) of the Act, USCIS may randomly select the remaining number of registrations for unique beneficiaries deemed necessary to meet the H-1B advanced degree exemption numerical limitation from among the registrations properly submitted on the final registration date. This random selection will be made via computer-generated selection, based on the unique beneficiary.

(ii) Sufficient registrations to meet the H-1B advanced degree exemption numerical limitation. If USCIS determines that it has received more than enough registrations for unique beneficiaries to meet the H-1B advanced degree exemption numerical limitation, USCIS will no longer accept registrations that may be eligible for exemption under section 214(g)(5)(C) of the Act and will notify the public of the final registration date. USCIS will randomly select the number of registrations for unique beneficiaries needed to meet the H-1B advanced degree exemption numerical limitation from among the remaining registrations for unique beneficiaries who may be counted against the advanced degree exemption numerical limitation. This random selection will be made via computer-generated selection, based on the unique beneficiary.

(7) Increase to the number of beneficiaries projected to meet the H-1B regular cap or advanced degree exemption allocations in a fiscal year. Unselected registrations will remain on reserve for the applicable fiscal year. If USCIS determines that it needs to increase the number of registrations for unique beneficiaries projected to meet the H-1B regular cap or advanced degree exemption allocation, and select additional registrations for unique beneficiaries, USCIS will select from among the registrations that are on reserve a sufficient number to meet the H-1B regular cap or advanced degree exemption numerical limitation, as applicable. If all of the registrations on reserve are selected and there are still fewer registrations than needed to meet the H-1B regular cap or advanced degree exemption numerical limitation, as applicable, USCIS may reopen the applicable registration period until USCIS determines that it has received a sufficient number of registrations for unique beneficiaries projected as needed to meet the H-1B regular cap or

advanced degree exemption numerical limitation. USCIS will monitor the number of registrations received and will notify the public of the date that USCIS has received the necessary number of registrations (the new "final registration date"). The day the public is notified will not control the applicable final registration date. When necessary to ensure the fair and orderly allocation of numbers, USCIS may randomly select the remaining number of registrations for unique beneficiaries deemed necessary to meet the H-1B regular cap or advanced degree exemption numerical limitation from among the registrations properly submitted on the final registration date. If the registration period will be reopened, USCIS will announce the start of the reopened registration period on the USCIS website at https://www.uscis.gov/.

(B) Confirmation. Petitioners will receive electronic notification that USCIS has accepted a registration for processing.

(C) Notification to file H-1B cap-subject petitions. USCIS will notify all petitioners with selected registrations that the petitioner is eligible to file an H-1B cap-subject petition on behalf of the beneficiary named in the notice within the filing period indicated on the notice.

(D) H-1B cap-subject petition filing following registration —

(1) Filing procedures. In addition to any other applicable requirements, a petitioner may file an H-1B petition for a beneficiary who may be counted under section 214(g)(1)(A) of the Act or eligible for exemption under section 214(g)(5)(C) of the Act only if the petition is based on a valid registration, which means that the registration was properly submitted in accordance with 8 CFR 103.2(a)(1), paragraph (h)(8)(iii) of this section, and the registration tool instructions; and was submitted by the petitioner, or its designated representative, on behalf of the beneficiary who was selected for that cap season by USCIS. A petitioner may not substitute the beneficiary named in the original registration or transfer the registration to another petitioner. Any H-1B petition filed on behalf of a beneficiary must contain and be supported by the same identifying information provided in the selected registration. Petitioners must submit evidence of the passport or travel document used at the time of registration to identify the beneficiary. In its discretion, USCIS may find that a change in identifying information in some circumstances would be permissible. Such circumstances could include, but are not limited to, a legal name change due to marriage, change in gender identity, or a change in passport number or expiration date due to renewal or replacement of a stolen passport, in between the time of registration and filing the petition. USCIS may deny or revoke the approval of an H-1B petition that does not meet these requirements.

(2) Registration fee. USCIS may deny or revoke the approval of an H-1B petition if it determines that the fee associated with the registration is declined, not reconciled, disputed, or otherwise invalid after submission. The registration fee is non-refundable and due at the time the registration is submitted.

(3) Filing period. An H-1B cap-subject petition must be properly filed within the filing period indicated on the relevant selection notice. The filing period for filing the H-1B cap-subject petition will be at least 90 days. If petitioners do not meet the requirements of this paragraph (h)(8)(iii)(D), USCIS may deny or reject the H-1B cap-subject petition.

(E) Calculating the number of registrations needed to meet the H-1B regular cap and H-1B advanced degree exemption allocation. When calculating the number of registrations for unique beneficiaries needed to meet the H-1B regular cap and the H-1B advanced degree exemption numerical limitation for a given fiscal year, USCIS will take into account historical data related to approvals, denials, revocations, and other relevant factors. If necessary, USCIS may increase those numbers throughout the fiscal year.

(F) Cap exemptions under sections 214(g)(5)(A) and (B) of the Act. An alien is not subject to the numerical limitations identified in section 214(g)(1)(A) of the Act if the alien qualifies for an exemption under section 214(g)(5) of the Act. For purposes of section 214(g)(5)(A) and (B) of the Act:

(1) "Institution of higher education" has the same definition as described at section 101(a) of the Higher Education Act of 1965 (20 U.S.C. 1001(a)).

(2) A nonprofit entity shall be considered to be related to or affiliated with an institution of higher education if it satisfies any one of the following conditions:

(i) The nonprofit entity is connected to or associated with an institution of higher education through shared ownership or control by the same board or federation;

(ii) The nonprofit entity is operated by an institution of higher education;

(iii) The nonprofit entity is attached to an institution of higher education as a member, branch, cooperative, or subsidiary; or

(iv) The nonprofit entity has entered into a formal written affiliation agreement with an institution of higher education that establishes an active working relationship between the nonprofit entity and the institution of higher education for the purposes of research or education, and a fundamental activity of the nonprofit entity is to directly contribute to the research or education mission of the institution of higher education. A nonprofit entity may engage in more than one fundamental activity.

(3) An entity is considered a "nonprofit entity" if it meets the definition described at paragraph (h)(19)(iv) of this section. "Nonprofit research organization" and "governmental research organization" have the same definitions as described at paragraph (h)(19)(iii)(C) of this section.

(4) An H–1B beneficiary who is not directly employed by a qualifying institution, organization, or entity identified in section 214(g)(5)(A) or (B) of the Act will qualify for an exemption under such section if the H–1B beneficiary will spend at least half of their work time performing job duties at a qualifying institution, organization, or entity and those job duties directly further an activity that supports or advances one of the funda-

mental purposes, missions, objectives, or functions of the qualifying institution, organization, or entity, namely, either higher education, nonprofit research, or government research. Work performed "at" the qualifying institution may include work performed in the United States through telework, remote work, or other off-site work. When considering whether a position is cap-exempt, USCIS will focus on the job duties to be performed, rather than where the duties are physically performed.

(5) If cap-exempt employment ceases, and if the alien is not the beneficiary of a new cap-exempt petition, then the alien will be subject to the cap if not previously counted within the 6-year period of authorized admission to which the cap-exempt employment applied. If cap-exempt employment converts to cap-subject employment subject to the numerical limitations in section 214(g)(1)(A) of the Act, USCIS may revoke the petition authorizing such employment consistent with paragraph (h)(11)(iii) of this section.

(6) Concurrent H-1B employment in a cap-subject position of an alien that qualifies for an exemption under section 214(g)(5)(A) or (B) of the Act shall not subject the alien to the numerical limitations in section 214(g)(1)(A) of the Act. When petitioning for concurrent cap-subject H-1B employment, the petitioner must demonstrate that the H- B beneficiary is employed in valid H-1B status under a cap exemption under section 214(g)(5)(A) or (B) of the Act, the beneficiary's employment with the cap-exempt employer is expected to continue after the new cap-subject petition is approved, and the beneficiary can reasonably and concurrently perform the work described in each employer's respective positions.

(i) Validity of a petition for concurrent cap-subject H-1B employment approved under paragraph (h)(8)(iii)(F)(6) of this section cannot extend beyond the period of validity specified for the cap-exempt H-1B employment.

(ii) If H-1B employment subject to a cap exemption under section 214(g)(5)(A) or (B) of the Act is terminated by a petitioner, or otherwise ends before the end of the validity period listed on the approved petition filed on the alien's behalf, the alien who is concurrently employed in a cap-subject position becomes subject to the numerical limitations in section 214(g)(1)(A) of the Act, unless the alien was previously counted with respect to the 6-year period of authorized H-1B admission to which the petition applies or another exemption applies. If such an alien becomes subject to the numerical limitations in section 214(g)(1)(A) of the Act, USCIS may revoke the cap-subject petition described in paragraph (h)(8)(iii)(F)(6) of this section consistent with paragraph (h)(11)(iii) of this section.

(iv) Suspension of registration requirement--

(A) Determination to suspend registration requirement. USCIS may suspend the H-1B registration requirement, in its discretion, if it determines that the registration process is inoperable for any reason. If USCIS suspends the registration requirement, USCIS will make an announcement of the suspension on its website (http://www.uscis.gov) along with the opening date of the applicable H-1B cap-subject petition-filing period.

(B) Petition-based cap-subject selections in event of suspended registration process. In any year in which USCIS suspends the H-1B registration process for cap-subject petitions, USCIS will allow for the submission of H-1B petitions notwithstanding paragraph (h)(8)(iii) of this section and conduct a cap-subject selection process based on the petitions that are received. USCIS will deny petitions indicating that they are exempt from the H-1B regular cap and the H-1B advanced degree exemption if USCIS determines, after the final receipt date, that they are not eligible for the exemption sought. If USCIS determines, on or before the final receipt date, that the petition is not eligible for the exemption sought, USCIS may consider the petition under the applicable numerical allocation and proceed with processing of the petition. If a petition is denied under this paragraph (h)(8)(iv)(B), USCIS will not return or refund filing fees.

(1) H-1B regular cap selection in event of suspended registration process. In determining whether there are enough H-1B cap-subject petitions to meet the H-1B regular cap, USCIS will consider all petitions properly submitted in accordance with 8 CFR 103.2 relating to beneficiaries that may be counted under section 214(g)(1)(A) of the Act, including those that may be eligible for exemption under section 214(g)(5)(C) of the Act. When calculating the number of petitions needed to meet the H-1B regular cap USCIS will take into account historical data related to approvals, denials, revocations, and other relevant factors. USCIS will monitor the number of petitions received and will announce on its website the date that it receives the number of petitions projected as needed to meet the H-1B regular cap (the "final receipt date"). The date the announcement is posted will not control the final receipt date. If the final receipt date is any of the first five business days on which petitions subject to the H–1B regular cap may be received, USCIS will select from among all the petitions properly submitted during the first five business days the number of petitions deemed necessary to meet the H–1B regular cap. If USCIS has received more petitions than necessary to meet the numerical limitation for the H–1B regular cap, USCIS will rank and select the petitions received on the basis of the highest Occupational Employment Statistics (OES) wage level that the proffered wage equals or exceeds for the relevant Standard Occupational Classification (SOC) code in the area of intended employment, beginning with OES wage level IV and proceeding in descending order with OES wage levels III, II, and I. Where there is no current OES prevailing wage information for the proffered position, USCIS will rank and select petitions based on the appropriate wage level that corresponds to the requirements of the proffered position. If the final receipt date is any of the first five business days on which petitions subject to the H–1B regular cap may be received, USCIS will select from among all the petitions properly submitted during the first five business days the number of petitions deemed necessary to meet the H–1B regular cap. If USCIS has

received more petitions than necessary to meet the numerical limitation for the H–1B regular cap, USCIS will rank and select the petitions received on the basis of the highest Occupational Employment Statistics (OES) wage level that the proffered wage equals or exceeds for the relevant Standard Occupational Classification (SOC) code in the area of intended employment, beginning with OES wage level IV and proceeding in descending order with OES wage levels III, II, and I. Where there is no current OES prevailing wage information for the proffered position, USCIS will rank and select petitions based on the appropriate wage level that corresponds to the requirements of the proffered position. If the wage falls below an OES wage level I, USCIS will rank the petition in the same category as OES wage level I. USCIS will rank the petition in the same manner even if, instead of obtaining an OES prevailing wage, a petitioner elects to obtain a prevailing wage using another legitimate source (other than OES) or an independent authoritative source. If USCIS receives and ranks more petitions at a particular wage level than the projected number needed to meet the numerical limitation, USCIS will randomly select from among all eligible petitions within that particular wage level a sufficient number of petitions needed to reach the numerical limitation.

(2) Advanced degree exemption selection in event of suspended registration process. After USCIS has received a sufficient number of petitions to meet the H–1B regular cap and, as applicable, completed the selection process of petitions for the H–1B regular cap, USCIS will determine whether there is a sufficient number of remaining petitions to meet the H–1B advanced degree exemption numerical limitation. When calculating the number of petitions needed to meet the H–1B advanced degree exemption numerical limitation USCIS will take into account historical data related to approvals, denials, revocations, and other relevant factors. USCIS will monitor the number of petitions received and will announce on its website the date that it receives the number of petitions projected as needed to meet the H–1B advanced degree exemption numerical limitation (the "final receipt date"). The date the announcement is posted will not control the final receipt date. If the final receipt date is any of the first five business days on which petitions subject to the H–1B advanced degree exemption may be received (in other words, if the numerical limitation is reached on any one of the first five business days that filings can be made), USCIS will select from among all the petitions properly submitted during the first five business days the number of petitions deemed necessary to meet the H–1B advanced degree exemption numerical limitation. If USCIS has received more petitions than necessary to meet the numerical limitation for the H–1B advanced degree exemption, USCIS will rank and select the petitions received on the basis of the highest Occupational Employment Statistics (OES) wage level that the proffered wage equals or exceeds for the relevant Standard Occupational Classification (SOC) code in the area of intended employment, beginning with OES wage level IV and proceeding with OES wage levels III, II, and I. Where there is no current OES prevailing wage information for the proffered position, USCIS will rank and select petitions based on the appropriate wage level that corresponds to the requirements of the proffered position. If the proffered wage is below an OES wage level I, USCIS will rank the petition in the same category as OES wage level I. USCIS will rank the petition in the same manner even if, instead of obtaining an OES prevailing wage, a petitioner elects to obtain a prevailing wage using another legitimate source (other than OES) or an independent authoritative source. If USCIS receives and ranks more petitions at a particular wage level than necessary to meet the numerical limitation for the H–1B advanced degree exemption, USCIS will randomly select from among all eligible petitions within that particular wage level a sufficient number of petitions needed to reach the numerical limitation.

(v) Severability.

(A) The requirement to submit a registration for an H-1B cap-subject petition and the selection process based on properly submitted registrations under paragraph (h)(8)(iii) of this section are intended to be severable from paragraph (h)(8)(iv) of this section. In the event paragraph (h)(8)(iii) of this section is not implemented, or in the event that paragraph (h)(8)(iv) of this section is not implemented, DHS intends that either of those provisions be implemented as an independent rule, without prejudice to petitioners in the United States under this regulation, as consistent with law.

(B) DHS intends that the provisions governing the beneficiary centric selection process in paragraph (h)(8)(iii) of this section, the elimination of the requirement that the requested start date for the beneficiary be the first day for the applicable fiscal year in (h)(8)(iii)(A)(4), and the provisions governing the denial or revocation of H-1B petitions based on inaccurate, fraudulent, or misrepresented material facts in the H-1B petition, H-1B registration, temporary labor certification, or labor condition application in paragraphs (h)(10)(ii) and (iii) and (h)(11)(iii) of this section, respectively, published on February 2, 2024 be severable from one another. In the event that any of these provision(s) is held to be invalid or unenforceable by its terms, or as applied to any person or circumstance, it should be construed so as to continue to give the maximum effect to the provision(s) permitted by law, unless any such provision is held to be wholly invalid and unenforceable, in which event the provision(s) should be severed from the remainder of this section and the holding should not affect the remainder of this section or the application of the other provisions to persons not similarly situated or to dissimilar circumstances.

(vi) H-1C numerical limitations. The 500 H-1C nonimmigrant visas issued each fiscal year shall be allocated in the following manner:

(A) For each fiscal year, the number of visas issued to the states of California, Florida, Illinois, Michigan, New York, Ohio, Pennsylvania, and Texas shall not exceed 50 each (except as provided for in paragraph (h)(8)(vi)(C) of this section).

(B) For each fiscal year, the number of visas issued to the states not listed in paragraph "(h)(8)(vi)(A) of this section shall not exceed 25 each (except as provided for in paragraph (h)(8)(vi)(C) of this section).

(C) If the total number of visas available during the first three quarters of a fiscal year exceeds the number of approvable H-1C petitions during those quarters, visas may be issued during the last quarter of the fiscal year to nurses who will be working in a state whose cap has already been reached for that fiscal year.

(D) When an approved H-1C petition is not used because the alien(s) does not obtain H-1C classification, e.g., the alien is never admitted to the United States, or the alien never worked for the facility, the facility must notify the Service according to the instructions contained in paragraph (h)(11)(ii) of this section. The Service will subtract H-1C petitions approved in the current fiscal year that are later revoked from the total count of approved H-1C petitions, provided that the alien never commenced employment with the facility.

(E) If the number of alien nurses included in an H-1C petition exceeds the number available for the remainder of a fiscal year, the Service shall approve the petition for the beneficiaries to the allowable amount in the order that they are listed on the petition. The remaining beneficiaries will be considered for approval in the subsequent fiscal year.

(F) Once the 500 cap has been reached, the Service will reject any new petitions subsequently filed requesting a work start date prior to the first day of the next fiscal year.

(vii) H-2B numerical limitations. When calculating the numerical limitations under section 214(g)(1)(B) and 214(g)(10) of the Act for a given fiscal year, USCIS will make numbers available to petitions in the order in which the petitions are filed. USCIS will make projections of the number of petitions necessary to achieve the numerical limit of approvals, taking into account historical data related to approvals, denials, revocations, and other relevant factors. USCIS will monitor the number of petitions (including the number of beneficiaries requested when necessary) received and will notify the public of the date that USCIS has received the necessary number of petitions (the "final receipt date"). The day the public is notified will not control the final receipt date. When necessary to ensure the fair and orderly allocation of numbers subject to the numerical limitations in 214(g)(1)(B) and 214(g)(10) of the Act, USCIS may randomly select from among the petitions received on the final receipt date the remaining number of petitions deemed necessary to generate the numerical limit of approvals. This random selection will be made via computer-generated selection. Petitions subject to a numerical limitation not randomly selected or that were received after the final receipt date will be rejected. Petitions indicating that they are exempt from the numerical limitation but that are determined by USCIS after the final receipt date to be subject to the numerical limit will be denied and filing fees will not be returned or refunded. If the final receipt date is any of the first five business days on which petitions subject to the applicable numerical limit may be received (i.e., if the numerical limit is reached on any one of the first five business days that filings can be made), USCIS will randomly apply all of the numbers among the petitions received on any of those five business days.

(9) Approval and validity of petition --

(i) Approval.

(A) USCIS will consider all the evidence submitted and any other evidence independently required to assist in adjudication. USCIS will notify the petitioner of the approval of the petition on a Notice of Action. The approval notice will include the beneficiary's (or beneficiaries') name(s) and classification and the petition's period of validity. A petition for more than one beneficiary and/or multiple services may be approved in whole or in part. The approval notice will cover only those beneficiaries approved for classification under section 101(a)(15)(H) of the Act.

(B) Where an H–1B petition is approved for less time than requested on the petition, the approval notice will provide or be accompanied by a brief explanation for the validity period granted.

(ii) Recording the validity of petitions. Procedures for recording the validity period of petitions are:

(A) If a new H petition is approved before the date the petitioner indicates that the services or training will begin, the approved petition and approval notice shall show the actual dates requested by the petitoner as the validity period, not to exceed the limits specified by paragraph (h)(9)(iii) of this section or other Service policy.

(B) If a new H petition is approved after the date the petitioner indicates that the services or training will begin, the aproved petition and approval notice shall show a validity period commencing with the date of approval and ending with the date requested by the petitioner, as long as that date does not exceed either the limits specified by paragraph (h)(9)(iii) of this section or other Service policy.

(C) If the period of services or training requested by the petitioner exceeds the limit specified in paragraph (h)(9)(iii) of this section, the petition shall be approved only up to the limit specified in that paragraph.

(D)(1) If an H–1B petition is adjudicated and deemed approvable after the initially requested validity period end-date or end-date for which eligibility is established, the officer may issue a request for evidence (RFE) asking the petitioner whether they want to update the requested dates of employment. Factors that inform whether USCIS issues an RFE could include, but would not be limited to: additional petitions filed or approved on the beneficiary's behalf, or the beneficiary's eligibility for additional time in H–1B status. If the new requested period exceeds the validity period of the labor condition application already submitted with the H–1B petition, the petitioner must submit a certified labor condition application with a new validity period that properly corresponds to the new requested validity period on the petition and an updated prevailing or proffered wage, if applicable, except that the petitioner may not reduce the proffered wage from that originally indicated in their petition. This labor condition application may be certified after the date the H–1B petition was filed with USCIS. The request for new dates of employment and submission of a labor condition application corresponding with the new dates of employment, absent other changes, will not be considered a material change. An increase to the proffered wage will not be considered a material change, as long as there are no other material changes to the position.

(2) If USCIS does not issue an RFE concerning the requested dates of employment, if the petitioner does not respond, or the RFE response does not support new dates of employment, the petition will be approved, if otherwise approvable, for the originally requested period or until the end-date eligibility has been established, as appropriate. However, the petition will not be forwarded to the Department of State nor will any accompanying request for a change of status, an extension of stay, or amendment of stay, be granted.

(iii) Validity. The initial approval period of an H petition shall conform to the limits prescribed as follows:

(A)(1) H–1B petition in a specialty occupation. The maximum validity period for an approved petition classified under section 101(a)(15)(H)(i)(b) of the Act for an alien in a specialty occupation is 3 years. However, where the beneficiary will be working at a third-party worksite, the maximum validity period for an approved petition is 1 year. In all instances, the approved petition may not exceed the validity period of the labor condition application.

(2) H-1B petition involving a DOD research and development or coproduction project. An approved petition classified under section 101(a)(15)(H)(i)(b) of the Act for an alien involved in a DOD research and development project or a coproduction project shall be valid for a period of up to five years.

(3) H-1B petition involving an alien of distinguished merit and ability in the field of fashion modeling. An approved petition classified under section 101(a)(15)(H)(i)(b) of the Act for an alien of distinguished merit and ability in the field of fashion modeling shall be valid for a period of up to three years.

(B) H-2B petition. The approval of the petition to accord an alien a classification under section 101(a)(15)(H)(ii)(b) of the Act shall be valid for the period of the approved temporary labor certification.

(C)(1) H-3 petition for alien trainee. An approved petition for an alien trainee classified under section 101(a)(15)(H)(iii) of the Act shall be valid for a period of up to two years.

(2) H-3 petition for alien participant in a special education training program. An approved petition for an alien classified under section 101(a)(15)(H)(iii) of the Act as a participant in a special education exchange visitor program shall be valid for a period of up to 18 months.

(D) H-1C petition for a registered nurse. An approved petition for an alien classified under section 101(a)(15)(H)(i)(c) of the Act shall be valid for a period of 3 years.

(E) H–1B petition for certain beneficiary-owned entities. The initial approval of a petition filed by a United States employer in which the H–1B beneficiary possesses a controlling interest in the petitioning organization or entity, meaning the beneficiary owns more than 50 percent of the petitioner or has majority voting rights in the petitioner, will be limited to a validity period of up to 18 months. The first extension (including an amended petition with a request for an extension of stay) of such a petition will also be limited to a validity period of up to 18 months.

(iv) H-4 dependents. The spouse and children of an H nonimmigrant, if they are accompanying or following to join such H nonimmigrant in the United States, may be admitted, if otherwise admissible, as H-4 nonimmigrants for the same period of admission or extension as the principal spouse or parent. H-4 nonimmigrant status does not confer eligibility for employment authorization incident to status. An H-4 nonimmigrant spouse of an H-1B nonimmigrant may be eligible for employment authorization only if the H-1B nonimmigrant is the beneficiary of an approved Immigrant Petition for Alien Worker, or successor form, or the H-1B nonimmigrant's period of stay in H-1B status is authorized in the United States under sections 106(a) and (b) of the American Competitiveness in the Twenty-first Century Act of 2000 (AC21), Public Law 106-313, as amended by the 21st Century Department of Justice Appropriations Authorization Act, Public Law 107-273 (2002). To request employment authorization, an eligible H-4 nonimmigrant spouse must file an Application for Employment Authorization, or a successor form, in accordance with 8 CFR 274a.13 and the form instructions. An Application for Employment Authorization must be accompanied by documentary evidence establishing eligibility, including evidence of the spousal relationship and that the principal H-1B is the beneficiary of an approved Immigrant Petition for Alien Worker or has been provided H-1B status under sections 106(a) and (b) of AC21, as amended by the 21st Century Department of Justice Appropriations Authorization Act, the H-1B beneficiary is currently in H-1B status, and the H-4 nonimmigrant spouse is currently in H-4 status.

(10) Denial of petition --

(i) Multiple beneficiaries. A petition for multiple beneficiaries may be denied in whole or in part.

(ii) Denial for statement of facts on the petition, H-1B registration, temporary labor certification, labor condition application, or invalid H-1B registration. The petition will be denied if it is determined that the statements on the petition, H-1B registration (if applicable), the application for a temporary labor certification, or the labor condition application, were inaccurate, fraudulent, or misrepresented a material fact, including if the attestations on the registration are determined to be false. An H-1B cap-subject petition also will be denied if it is not based on a valid registration submitted by the petitioner (or its designated representative), or a successor in interest, for the beneficiary named or identified in the petition.

(iii) Notice of denial. The petitioner will be notified of the reasons for the denial and of the right to appeal the denial of the petition under 8 CFR part 103. There is no appeal from a decision to deny an extension of stay to the alien.

(iv) H–2A and H–2B violators.

(A) USCIS will deny any H–2A or H–2B petition filed by a petitioner, or the successor in interest of a petitioner as defined in paragraphs (h)(5)(xi)(C)(2) and (h)(6)(i)(D)(2) of this section, that has been the subject of one or more of the following actions:

(1) A final administrative determination by the Secretary of Labor under 20 CFR part 655, subpart A or B, or 29 CFR part 501 or 503 debarring the petitioner from filing or receiving a future labor certification, or a final administrative determination by the Governor of Guam debarring the petitioner from issuance of future labor certifications under applicable Guam regulations and rules, if the petition is filed on or after January 17, 2025 and during the debarment period, or if the debarment occurs during the pendency of the petition filed on or after January 17, 2025, and the final administrative determination debarring the petitioner is made on or after January 17, 2025; or

(2) A final USCIS denial or revocation decision issued during the pendency of the petition or within 3 years prior to filing the petition that includes a finding of fraud or willful misrepresentation of a material fact with respect to a previously filed H–2A or H– 2B petition. This provision will only apply if the final denial or revocation decision was issued on a petition filed on or after January 17, 2025; or

(3) A final determination of violation(s) under section 274(a) of the Act during the pendency of the petition or within 3 years prior to filing the petition if the final determination of violation(s) under section 274(a) of the Act is made on or after January 17, 2025 and the petition is filed on or after January 17, 2025.

(B) Except as provided in paragraph (h)(10)(iv)(A) of this section, USCIS may deny any H–2A or H–2B petition filed by a petitioner, or the successor in interest of a petitioner as defined in paragraphs (h)(5)(xi)(C)(2) and (h)(6)(i)(D)(2) of this section on or after January 17, 2025, that has been the subject of one or more of the following actions during the pendency of the petition or within 3 years prior to filing the petition, regardless of whether the action(s) or underlying violation(s) occurred before, on, or after January 17, 2025. USCIS may deny such a petition if it determines that the petitioner or successor has not established its intention and/or ability to comply with H–2A or H–2B program requirements. The violation(s) underlying the following actions that may call into question a petitioner's or successor's intention and/or ability to comply include:

(1) A final administrative determination by the Secretary of Labor or the Governor of Guam with respect to a prior H–2A or H–2B temporary labor certification that includes:

(i) Revocation of an approved temporary labor certification under 20 CFR part 655, subpart A or B, or applicable Guam regulations and rules;

(ii) Debarment under 20 CFR part 655, subpart A or B, or 29 CFR part 501 or 503, or applicable Guam regulations and rules, if the debarment period has concluded prior to filing the petition; or (iii) Any other administrative sanction or remedy under 29 CFR part 501 or 503, or applicable Guam regulations and rules, including assessment of civil money penalties as described in those parts. (2) A final USCIS decision revoking the approval of a prior petition that includes one or more of the following findings: the beneficiary was not employed by the petitioner in the capacity specified in the petition; the statement of facts contained in the petition or on the application for a temporary labor certification was not true and correct, or was inaccurate; the petitioner violated terms and conditions of the approved petition; or the petitioner violated requirements of section 101(a)(15)(H) of the Act or this paragraph (h); or (3) Any final administrative or judicial determination (other than one described in paragraph (h)(10)(iv)(A) of this section) that the petitioner violated any applicable employment-related laws or regulations, including health and safety laws or regulations.

(C) In determining whether the underlying violation(s) in paragraph (h)(10)(iv)(B) of this section calls into question the intention and/or ability of the petitioner or its successor in interest to comply with H–2A or H–2B program requirements, USCIS will consider all relevant factors, including, but not limited to:

(1) The recency and number of violations;

(2) The egregiousness of the violation(s), including how many workers were affected, and whether it involved a risk to the health or safety of workers;

(3) Overall history or pattern of prior violations;

(4) The severity or monetary amount of any penalties imposed;

(5) Whether the final determination, decision, or conviction included a finding of willfulness;

(6) The extent to which the violator achieved a financial gain due to the violation(s), or the potential financial loss or potential financial injury to the workers;

(7) Timely compliance with all penalties and remedies ordered under the final determination(s), decision(s), or conviction(s); and

(8) Other corrective actions taken by the petitioner or its successor in interest to cure its violation(s) or prevent future violations.

(D) For purposes of paragraph (h)(10)(iv) of this section, a criminal conviction or final administrative or judicial determination against any one of the following individuals will be treated as a conviction or final administrative or judicial determination against the petitioner or successor in interest:

(1) An individual acting on behalf of the petitioning entity, which could include, among others, the petitioner's owner, employee, or contractor; or

(2) With respect to paragraph (h)(10)(iv)(B) of this section, an employee of the petitioning entity who a reasonable person in the H–2A or H– 2B worker's position would believe is acting on behalf of the petitioning entity.

(E)(1) With respect to denials under paragraph (h)(10)(iv)(A) of this section, USCIS will inform the petitioner of the right to appeal the denial under 8 CFR 103.3, and indicate in the denial notice that the mandatory ground of denial will also apply in the adjudication of any other pending or future H–2 petition filed by the petitioner or a successor in interest during the applicable time period.

(2) With respect to denials under paragraph (h)(10)(iv)(B) of this section, USCIS will inform the petitioner of the right to appeal the denial under 8 CFR 103.3, and indicate in the denial notice that the discretionary ground of denial may also apply in the adjudication of any other pending or future H–2 petition filed by the petitioner or a successor in interest during the applicable time period.

(F) If USCIS has determined in the course of a prior adjudication that a petitioner (or the preceding entity, if the petitioner is a successor in interest) has established its intention and ability to comply with H–2A or H–2B program requirements notwithstanding relevant violation determination(s) under paragraph (h)(10)(iv)(B) of this section, USCIS will not seek to deny a subsequent petition under paragraph (h)(10)(iv)(B) based on the same previous violation determination(s) unless USCIS becomes aware of a new material fact or finds that its previous determination was based on a material error of law

(11) Revocation of approval of petition --

(i) General.

(A) The petitioner shall immediately notify the Service of any changes in the terms and conditions of employment of a beneficiary which may affect eligibility under section 101(a)(15)(H) of the Act and paragraph (h) of this section. An amended petition on the form prescribed by USCIS should be filed when the petitioner continues to employ the beneficiary. If the petitioner no longer employs the beneficiary, the petitioner shall send a letter explaining the change(s) to the director who approved the petition. However, H-2A and H-2B petitioners must send notification to DHS pursuant to paragraphs (h)(5)(vi) and (h)(6)(i)(F) of this section respectively.

(B) The director may revoke a petition at any time, even after the expiration of the petition.

(ii) Immediate and automatic revocation. The approval of any petition is immediately and automatically revoked if the petitioner goes out of business, files a written withdrawal of the petition, or the Department of Labor revokes the labor certification upon which the petition is based. The approval of an H–1B petition is also immediately and automatically revoked upon notification from the H–1B petitioner that the beneficiary is no longer employed.

(iii) Revocation on notice --

(A) Grounds for revocation. The director shall send to the petitioner a notice of intent to revoke the petition in relevant part if he or she finds that:

(1) The beneficiary is no longer employed by the petitioner in the capacity specified in the petition, or if the beneficiary is no longer receiving training as specified in the petition; or

(2) The statement of facts contained in the petition, H-1B registration (if applicable), the application for a temporary labor certification, or the labor condition application, was not true and correct, inaccurate, fraudulent, or misrepresented a material fact, including if the attestations on the registration are determined to be false; or

(3) The petitioner, or a related entity, filed a new or amended petition on behalf of the same beneficiary, if USCIS determines that the filing of the new or amended petition is part of the petitioner's attempt to unfairly increase the odds of selection during the registration or petition selection process, as applicable, such as by reducing the proffered wage to an amount that would be equivalent to a lower wage level than that indicated on the registration, or the original petition if the registration process was suspended. USCIS will not revoke approval of such an amended or new petition solely on the basis of a different proffered wage if that wage does not correspond to a lower OES wage level than the wage level on which the registration or petition selection, as applicable, was based; or

(4) The petitioner violated terms and conditions of the approved petition; or

(5) The approval of the petition violated paragraph (h) of this section or involved gross error; or

(6) The H-1B cap-subject petition was not based on a valid registration submitted by the petitioner (or its designated representative), or a successor in interest, for the beneficiary named or identified in the petition; or

(7) The petitioner failed to timely file an amended petition notifying USCIS of a material change or otherwise failed to comply with the material change reporting requirements in paragraph (h)(2)(i)(E) of this section.

(B) Notice and decision. The notice of intent to revoke shall contain a detailed statement of the grounds for the revocation and the time period allowed for the petitioner's rebuttal. The petitioner may submit evidence in rebuttal within 30 days of receipt of the notice. The director shall consider all relevant evidence presented in deciding whether to revoke the petition in whole or in part. If the petition is revoked in part, the remainder of the petition shall remain approved and a revised approval notice shall be sent to the petitioner with the revocation notice.

(iv) Effect of H–2A or H–2B petition revocation. Upon revocation of the approval of an employer's H–2A or H– 2B petition, the beneficiary and their dependents will not be considered to have failed to maintain nonimmigrant status, and will not accrue any period of unlawful presence under section 212(a)(9) of the Act (8 U.S.C. 1182(a)(9)), solely on the basis of the petition revocation for a 60-day period following the date of the revocation, or until the end of the authorized period of admission, whichever is shorter. During such a period, the alien may only work as otherwise authorized under 8 CFR 274a.12. The employer will be liable for the alien beneficiary's reasonable costs of return transportation to their last place of foreign residence abroad, unless such alien obtains an extension of stay based on an approved petition in the same classification filed by a different employer.

(12) Appeal of a denial or a revocation of a petition --

(i) Denial. A petition denied in whole or in part may be appealed under part 103 of this chapter.

(ii) Revocation. A petition that has been revoked on notice in whole or in part may be appealed under part 103 of this chapter. Automatic revocations may not be appealed.

(13) Admission --

(i) General.

(A) An H–3 beneficiary will be admitted to the United States for the validity period of the petition, plus a period of up to 10 days before the validity period begins and 10 days after the validity period ends. The beneficiary may not work except during the validity period of the petition.

(B) When an alien in an H classification has spent the maximum allowable period of stay in the United States, a new petition under section 101(a)(15)(H) or (L) of the Act may not be approved unless that alien has resided and been physically present outside the United States, except for brief trips for business or pleasure, for the time limit imposed on the particular H classification. Brief trips to the United States for business or pleasure during the required time abroad are not interruptive, but do not count toward fulfillment of the required time abroad. A certain period of absence from the United States of H–2A and H–2B aliens, as set forth in 8 CFR 214.2(h)(5)(viii)(D) and 8 CFR 214.2(h)(6)(vii)(C), respectively, will provide a new total of 3 years that H–2A or H–2B status may be granted. The petitioner must provide information about the alien's employment, place of residence, and the dates and purposes of any trips to the United States during the period that the alien was required to reside abroad.

(C) An alien admitted or otherwise provided status in H–2A or H–2B classification and their dependents will not be considered to have failed to maintain nonimmigrant status, and will not accrue any period of unlawful presence under section 212(a)(9) of the Act (8 U.S.C. 1182(a)(9)), solely on the basis of a cessation of the employment on which the alien's classification was based, for 60 consecutive days or until the end of the authorized period of admission, whichever is shorter, once during each authorized period of admission. During such a period, the alien may only work as otherwise authorized under 8 CFR 274a.12.

(D) An alien in any authorized period described in paragraph (C) of this section may apply for and be granted an extension of stay under 8 CFR 214.1(c)(4) or change of status under 8 CFR 248.1, if otherwise eligible.

(ii) H-1C limitation on admission. The maximum period of admission for an H-1C nonimmigrant alien is 3 years. The maximum period of admission for an H-1C alien begins on the date the H-1C alien is admitted to the United and ends on the third anniversary of the alien's admission date. Periods of time spent out of the United States for business or personal reasons during the validity period of the H-1C petition count towards the alien's maximum period of admission. When an H-1C alien has reached the 3-year maximum period of admission, the H-1C alien is no longer eligible for admission to the United States as an H-1C nonimmigrant alien.

(iii) H-1B limitation on admission.

(A) Alien in a specialty occupation or an alien of distinguished merit and ability in the field of fashion modeling. An H-1B alien in a specialty occupation or an alien of distinguished merit and ability who has spent six years in the United States under section 101(a)(15)(H) and/or (L) of the Act may not seek extension, change status, or be readmitted to the United States under section 101(a)(15) (H) or (L) of the Act unless the alien has resided and been physically present outside the United States, except for brief trips for business or pleasure, for the immediate prior year.

(B) Alien involved in a DOD research and development or coproduction project. An H-1B alien involved in a DOD research and development or coproduction project who has spent 10 years in the United States under section 101(a)(15) (H) and/or (L) of the Act may not seek extension, change status, or be readmitted to the United States under section 101(a)(15) (H) or (L) of the Act to perform services involving a DOD research and development project or coproduction project. A new petition or change of status under section 101(a)(15) (H) or (L) of the Act may not be approved for such an alien unless the alien has resided and been physically present outside the United States, except for brief trips for business or pleasure, for the immediate prior year.

(C) Calculating the maximum H-1B admission period. Time spent physically outside the United States exceeding 24 hours by an alien during the validity of an H-1B petition that was approved on the alien's behalf shall not be considered for purposes of calculating the alien's total period of authorized admission under section 214(g)(4) of the Act, regardless of whether such time meaningfully interrupts the alien's stay in H-1B status and the reason for the alien's absence. Accordingly, such remaining time may be recaptured in a subsequent H-1B petition on behalf of the alien, at any time before the alien uses the full period of H-1B admission described in section 214(g)(4) of the Act.

(1) It is the H-1B petitioner's burden to request and demonstrate the specific amount of time for recapture on behalf of the beneficiary. The beneficiary may provide appropriate evidence, such as copies of passport stamps, Arrival-Departure Records (Form I-94), or airline tickets, together with a chart, indicating the dates spent outside of the United States, and referencing the relevant independent documentary evidence, when seeking to recapture the alien's time spent outside the United States. Based on the evidence provided, USCIS may grant all, part, or none of the recapture period requested.

(2) If the beneficiary was previously counted toward the H-1B numerical cap under section 214(g)(1) of the Act with respect to the 6-year maximum period of H-1B admission from which recapture is sought, the H-1B petition seeking to recapture a period of stay as an H-1B nonimmigrant will not subject the beneficiary to the H-1B numerical cap, whether or not the alien has been physically outside the United States for 1 year or more and would be otherwise eligible for a new period of admission under such section of the Act. An H-1B petitioner may either seek such recapture on behalf of the alien or, consistent with paragraph (h)(13)(iii) of

this section, seek a new period of admission on behalf of the alien under section 214(g)(1) of the Act.

(D) Lengthy adjudication delay exemption from 214(g)(4) of the Act.

(1) An alien who is in H-1B status or has previously held H-1B status is eligible for H-1B status beyond the 6-year limitation under section 214(g)(4) of the Act, if at least 365 days have elapsed since:

(i) The filing of a labor certification with the Department of Labor on the alien's behalf, if such certification is required for the alien to obtain status under section 203(b) of the Act; or

(ii) The filing of an immigrant visa petition with USCIS on the alien's behalf to accord classification under section 203(b) of the Act.

(2) H-1B approvals under paragraph (h)(13)(iii)(D) of this section may be granted in up to 1-year increments until either the approved permanent labor certification expires or a final decision has been made to:

(i) Deny the application for permanent labor certification, or, if approved, to revoke or invalidate such approval;

(ii) Deny the immigrant visa petition, or, if approved, revoke such approval;

(iii) Deny or approve the alien's application for an immigrant visa or application to adjust status to lawful permanent residence; or

(iv) Administratively or otherwise close the application for permanent labor certification, immigrant visa petition, or application to adjust status.

(3) No final decision while appeal available or pending. A decision to deny or revoke an application for labor certification, or to deny or revoke the approval of an immigrant visa petition, will not be considered final under paragraph (h)(13)(iii)(D)(2)(i) or (ii) of this section during the period authorized for filing an appeal of the decision, or while an appeal is pending.

(4) Substitution of beneficiaries. An alien who has been replaced by another alien, on or before July 16, 2007, as the beneficiary of an approved permanent labor certification may not rely on that permanent labor certification to establish eligibility for H-1B status based on this lengthy adjudication delay exemption. Except for a substitution of a beneficiary that occurred on or before July 16, 2007, an alien establishing eligibility for this lengthy adjudication delay exemption based on a pending or approved labor certification must be the named beneficiary listed on the permanent labor certification.

(5) Advance filing. A petitioner may file an H-1B petition seeking a lengthy adjudication delay exemption under paragraph (h)(13)(iii)(D) of this section within 6 months of the requested H-1B start date. The petition may be filed before 365 days have elapsed since the labor certification application or immigrant visa petition was filed with the Department of Labor or USCIS, respectively, provided that the application for labor certification or immigrant visa petition must have been filed at least 365 days prior to the date the period of admission authorized under this exemption will take effect. The petitioner may request any time remaining to the beneficiary under the maximum period of admission described at section 214(g)(4) of the Act along with the exemption request, but in no case may the approved H-1B period of validity exceed the limits specified by paragraph (h)(9)(iii) of this section. Time remaining to the beneficiary under the maximum period of admission described at section 214(g)(4) of the Act may include any request to recapture unused H-1B, L-1A, or L-1B time spent outside of the United States.

(6) Petitioners seeking exemption. The H-1B petitioner need not be the employer that filed the application for labor certification or immigrant visa petition that is used to qualify for this exemption.

(7) Subsequent exemption approvals after the 7th year. The qualifying labor certification or immigrant visa petition need not be the same as that used to qualify for the initial exemption under paragraph (h)(13)(iii)(D) of this section.

(8) Aggregation of time not permitted. A petitioner may not aggregate the number of days that have elapsed since the filing of one labor certification or immigrant visa petition with the number of days that have elapsed since the filing of another such application or petition to meet the 365-day requirement.

(9) Exemption eligibility. Only a principal beneficiary of a nonfrivolous labor certification application or immigrant visa petition filed on his or her behalf may be eligible under paragraph (h)(13)(iii)(D) of this section for an exemption to the maximum period of admission under section 214(g)(4) of the Act.

(10) Limits on future exemptions from the lengthy adjudication delay. An alien is ineligible for the lengthy adjudication delay exemption under paragraph (h)(13)(iii)(D) of this section if the alien is the beneficiary of an approved petition under section 203(b) of the Act and fails to file an adjustment of status application or apply for an immigrant visa within 1 year of an immigrant visa being authorized for issuance based on his or her preference category and country of chargeability. If the accrual of such 1-year period is interrupted by the unavailability of an immigrant visa, a new 1-year period shall be afforded when an immigrant visa again becomes immediately available. USCIS may excuse a failure to file in its discretion if the alien establishes that the failure to apply was due to circumstances beyond his or her control. The limitations described in this paragraph apply to any approved immigrant visa petition under section 203(b) of the Act, including petitions withdrawn by the petitioner or those filed by a petitioner whose business terminates 180 days or more after approval.

(E) Per-country limitation exemption from section 214(g)(4) of the Act. An alien who currently maintains or previously held H-1B status, who is the beneficiary of an approved immigrant visa petition for classification under section 203(b)(1), (2), or (3) of the Act, and who is eligible to be granted that immigrant status but for application of the per country limitation, is eligible for H-1B status beyond the 6-year limitation under section 214(g)(4) of the Act. The petitioner must demonstrate such visa unavailability as of the date the H-1B petition is filed with USCIS.

(1) Validity periods. USCIS may grant validity periods for petitions approved under this paragraph in increments of up to 3 years for as long as the alien remains eligible for this exemption.

(2) H-1B approvals under paragraph (h)(13)(iii)(E) of this section may be granted until a final decision has been made to:

(i) Revoke the approval of the immigrant visa petition; or

(ii) Approve or deny the alien's application for an immigrant visa or application to adjust status to lawful permanent residence.

(3) Current H-1B status not required. An alien who is not in H-1B status at the time the H-1B petition on his or her behalf is filed, including an alien who is not in the United States, may seek an exemption of the 6-year limitation under 214(g)(4) of the Act under this clause, if otherwise eligible.

(4) Subsequent petitioners may seek exemptions. The H-1B petitioner need not be the employer that filed the immigrant visa petition that is used to qualify for this exemption. An H-1B petition may be approved under paragraph (h)(13)(iii)(E) of this section with respect to any approved immigrant visa petition, and a subsequent H-1B petition may be approved with respect to a different approved immigrant visa petition on behalf of the same alien.

(5) Advance filing. A petitioner may file an H-1B petition seeking a per-country limitation exemption under paragraph (h)(13)(iii)(E) of this section within 6 months of the requested H-1B start date. The petitioner may request any time remaining to the beneficiary under the maximum period of admission described in section 214(g)(4) of the Act along with the exemption request, but in no case may the H-1B approval period exceed the limits specified by paragraph (h)(9)(iii) of this section.

(6) Exemption eligibility. Only the principal beneficiary of an approved immigrant visa petition for classification under section 203(b)(1), (2), or (3) of the Act may be eligible under paragraph (h)(13)(iii)(E) of this section for an exemption to the maximum period of admission under section 214(g)(4) of the Act.

(iv) H–3 limitation on admission. An H–3 alien participant in a special education program who has spent 18 months in the United States under sections 101(a)(15)(H) and/or (L) of the Act; and an H–3 alien trainee who has spent 24 months in the United States under sections 101(a)(15)(H) and/or (L) of the Act may not seek extension, change status, or be readmitted to the United States under sections 101(a)(15)(H) and/or (L) of the Act unless the alien has resided and been physically present outside the United States for the immediate prior 6 months.

(v) Exceptions. The limitations in paragraphs (h)(13)(iii) and (iv) of this section will not apply to H–1B and H– 3 aliens who did not reside continually in the United States and whose employment in the United States was seasonal or intermittent or was for an aggregate of 6 months or less per year. In addition, the limitations will not apply to aliens who reside abroad and regularly commute to the United States to engage in part-time employment. To qualify for this exception, the petitioner and the alien must provide clear and convincing proof that the alien qualifies for such an exception. Such proof shall consist of evidence such as arrival and departure records, copies of tax returns, and records of employment abroad.

(14) Extension of visa petition validity. The petitioner must file a request for a petition extension on the Form I–129 to extend the validity of the original petition under section 101(a)(15)(H) of the Act. A request for a petition extension generally may be filed only if the validity of the original petition has not expired.

(15) Extension of stay --

(i) General. The petitioner shall apply for extension of an alien's stay in the United States by filing a petition extension on the form prescribed by USCIS accompanied by the documents described for the particular classification in paragraph (h)(15)(ii) of this section. The petitioner must also request a petition extension. The dates of extension shall be the same for the petition and the beneficiary's extension of stay. The beneficiary must be physically present in the United States at the time of the filing of the extension of stay. Even though the requests to extend the petition and the alien's stay are combined on the petition, the director shall make a separate determination on each. If the alien is required to leave the United States for business or personal reasons while the extension requests are pending, the petitioner may request the director to cable notification of approval of the petition extension to the consular office abroad where the alien will apply for a visa. When the total period of stay in an H classification has been reached, no further extensions may be granted.

(ii) Extension periods --

(A) H-1C extension of stay. The maximum period of admission for an H-1C alien is 3 years. An H-1C alien who was initially admitted to the United States for less than 3 years may receive an extension of stay up to the third anniversary date of his or her initial admission. An H-1C nonimmigrant may not receive an extension of stay beyond the third anniversary date of his or her initial admission to the United States.

(B) H-1B extension of stay --

(1) Alien in a specialty occupation or an alien of distinguished merit and ability in the field of fashion modeling. An extension of stay may be authorized for a period of up to three years for a beneficiary of an H-1B petition in a specialty occupation or an alien of distinguished merit and ability. The alien's total period of stay may not exceed six years. The request for extension must be accompanied by either a new or a photocopy of the prior certification from the Department of Labor that the petitioner continues to have on file a labor condition application valid for the period of time requested for the occupation.

(2) Alien in a DOD research and development or coproduction project. An extension of stay may be authorized for a period up to five years for the beneficiary of an H-1B petition involving a DOD research and

development project or coproduction project. The total period of stay may not exceed 10 years.

(C) H-2A or H-2B extension of stay. An extension of stay for the beneficiary of an H-2A or H-2B petition may be authorized for the validity of the labor certification or for a period of up to one year, except as provided for in paragraph (h)(5)(x) of this section. The alien's total period of stay as an H-2A or H-2B worker may not exceed three years, except that in the Virgin Islands, the alien's total period of stay may not exceed 45 days.

(D) H-3 extension of stay. An extension of stay may be authorized for the length of the training program for a total period of stay as an H-3 trainee not to exceed two years, or for a total period of stay as a participant in a special education training program not to exceed 18 months.

(16) Effect of approval of a permanent labor certification or filing of a preference petition on H classification --

(i) H-1B or H-1C classification. The approval of a permanent labor certification or the filing of a preference petition for an alien shall not be a basis for denying an H-1C or H-1B petition or a request to extend such a petition, or the alien's admission, change of status, or extension of stay. The alien may legitimately come to the United States for a temporary period as an H-1C or H-1B nonimmigrant and depart voluntarily at the end of his or her authorized stay and, at the same time, lawfully seek to become a permanent resident of the United States.

(ii) H–2A or H–2B classification. The approval of a permanent labor certification, the filing of an immediate relative or preference petition for or by an alien or a diversity visa petition with the Department of State, or an application by an alien to seek lawful permanent residence or an immigrant visa, will not, standing alone, be the basis for denying an H–2 petition, a request to extend such a petition, or an application for admission in, change of status to, or extension of stay in H–2 status. The approval of a permanent labor certification, filing of an immediate relative petition, preference petition, or diversity visa petition, or filing of an application for adjustment of status or an immigrant visa will be considered, together with all other facts presented, in determining whether the H–2 nonimmigrant is maintaining his or her H–2 status and whether the alien has a residence in a foreign country which he or she has no intention of abandoning.

(iii) H–3 classification. The approval of a permanent labor certification, or the filing of a preference petition for an alien currently employed by or in a training position with the same petitioner, will be a reason, by itself, to deny the alien's extension of stay.

(17) Effect of a strike --

(i) If the Secretary of Labor certifies to the Commissioner that a strike or other labor dispute involving a work stoppage of workers is in progress in the occupation and at the place where the beneficiary is to be employed or trained, and that the employment of training of the beneficiary would adversely affect the wages and working conditions of U.S. citizens and lawful resident workers:

(A) A petition to classify an alien as a nonimmigrant as defined in section 101(a)(15)(H) of the Act shall be denied.

(B) If a petition has already been approved, but the alien has not yet entered the United States, or has entered the United States but has not commenced the employment, the approval of the petition is automatically suspended, and the application for admission on the basis of the petition shall be denied.

(ii) If there is a strike or other labor dispute involving a work stoppage of workers in progress, but such strike or other labor dispute is not certified under paragraph (h)(17)(i), the Commissioner shall not deny a petition or suspend an approved petition.

(iii) If the alien has already commenced employment in the United States under an approved petition and is participating in a strike or other labor dispute involving a work stoppage of workers, whether or not such strike or other labor dispute has been certified by the Department of Labor, the alien shall not be deemed to be failing to maintain his or her status solely on account of past, present, or future participation in a strike or other labor dispute involving a work stoppage of workers, but is subject to the following terms and conditions:

(A) The alien shall remain subject to all applicable provisions of the Immigration and Nationality Act, and regulations promulgated in the same manner as all other H nonimmigrants;

(B) The status and authorized period of stay of such an alien is not modified or extended in any way by virtue of his or her participation in a strike or other labor dispute involving a work stoppage of workers; and

(C) Although participation by an H nonimmigrant alien in a strike or other labor dispute involving a work stoppage of workers will not constitute a ground for deportation, any alien who violates his or her status or who remains in the United States after his or her authorized period of stay has expired will be subject to deportation.

(18) Use of approval notice, Form I-797. The Service shall notify the petitioner on Form I-797 whenever a visa petition, an extension of a visa petition, or an alien's extension of stay is approved under the H classification. The beneficiary of an H petition who does not require a nonimmigrant visa may present a copy of the approval notice at a port of entry to facilitate entry into the United States. A beneficiary who is required to present a visa for admission and whose visa will have expired before the date of his or her intended return may use a copy of Form I-797 to apply for a new or revalidated visa during the validity period of the petition. The copy of Form I-797 shall be retained by the beneficiary and presented during the validity of the petition when reentering the United States to resume the same employment with the same petitioner.

(19) Additional fee for filing certain H-1B petitions --

(i) A United States employer (other than an exempt employer defined in paragraph (h)(19)(iii) of this section, or an employer filing a petition described in paragraph (h)(19)(v) of this section) who files a petition or application must include the additional American

Competitiveness and Workforce Improvement Act (ACWIA) fee referenced in 8 CFR 106.2, if the petition is filed for any of the following purposes:

(A) An initial grant of H-1B status under section 101(a)(15)(H)(i)(b) of the Act;

(B) An initial extension of stay, as provided in paragraph (h)(15)(i) of this section; or

(C) Authorization for a change in employers, as provided in paragraph (h)(2)(i)(D) of this section.

(ii) A petitioner must submit with the petition the ACWIA fee, and any other applicable fees, in accordance with § 103.7 of this chapter, and form instructions. Payment of all applicable fees must be made at the same time, but the petitioner may submit separate checks. USCIS will accept payment of the ACWIA fee only from the United States employer or its representative of record, as defined in 8 CFR 103.2(a) and 8 CFR part 292.

(iii) The following exempt organizations are not required to pay the additional fee:

(A) An institution of higher education, as defined in section 101(a) of the Higher Education Act of 1965;

(B) An affiliated or related nonprofit entity. A nonprofit entity shall be considered to be related to or affiliated with an institution of higher education if it satisfies any one of the following conditions:

(1) The nonprofit entity is connected to or associated with an institution of higher education through shared ownership or control by the same board or federation;

(2) The nonprofit entity is operated by an institution of higher education;

(3) The nonprofit entity is attached to an institution of higher education as a member, branch, cooperative, or subsidiary; or

(4) The nonprofit entity has entered into a formal written affiliation agreement with an institution of higher education that establishes an active working relationship between the nonprofit entity and the institution of higher education for the purposes of research or education, and a fundamental activity of the nonprofit entity is to directly contribute to the research or education mission of the institution of higher education. A nonprofit entity may engage in more than one fundamental activity;

(C) A nonprofit research organization or government research organization. When a fundamental activity of a nonprofit organization is engaging in basic research and/or applied research, that organization is a nonprofit research organization. When a fundamental activity of a governmental organization is the performance or promotion of basic research and/or applied research, that organization is a government research organization. A governmental research organization may be a Federal, State, or local entity. A nonprofit research organization or governmental research organization may perform or promote more than one fundamental activity. Basic research is general research to gain more comprehensive knowledge or understanding of the subject under study, without specific applications in mind. Basic research is also research that advances scientific knowledge but does not have specific immediate commercial objectives although it may be in fields of present or potential commercial interest. Applied research is research to gain knowledge or understanding to determine the means by which a specific, recognized need may be met. Applied research includes investigations oriented to discovering new scientific knowledge that has specific commercial objectives with respect to products, processes, or services. Both basic research and applied research may include research and investigation in the sciences, social sciences, or humanities and may include designing, analyzing, and directing the research of others if on an ongoing basis and throughout the research cycle;

(D) A primary or secondary education institution; or

(E) A nonprofit entity which engages in an established curriculum-related clinical training of students registered at an institution of higher education.

(iv) Nonprofit or tax exempt organizations. For purposes of paragraphs (h)(19)(iii)(B) and (C) of this section, a nonprofit organization or entity must be determined by the Internal Revenue Service to be a tax exempt organization under the Internal Revenue Code of 1986, section 501(c)(3), (c)(4), or (c)(6), 26 U.S.C. 501(c)(3), (c)(4), or (c)(6).

(v) Filing situations where the American Competitiveness and Workforce Improvement Act of 1998 (ACWIA) fee is not required. The ACWIA fee is not required if:

(A) The petition is an amended H-1B petition that does not contain any requests for an extension of stay;

(B) The petition is an H-1B petition filed for the sole purpose of correcting a Service error; or

(C) The petition is the second or subsequent request for an extension of stay filed by the employer regardless of when the first extension of stay was filed or whether the ACWIA fee was paid on the initial petition or the first extension of stay.

(vi) ACWIA fee exemption evidence.

(A) Employer claiming to be exempt. An employer claiming to be exempt from the ACWIA fee must file the form prescribed by USCIS, in accordance with the form instructions, including supporting evidence establishing that it meets one of the exemptions described at paragraph (h)(19)(iii) of this section. A United States employer claiming an exemption from the ACWIA fee on the basis that it is a non-profit research organization must submit evidence that it has tax exempt status under the Internal Revenue Code of 1986, section 501(c)(3), (c)(4) or (c)(6), 26 U.S.C. 501(c)(3), (c)(4) or (c)(6). All other employers claiming an exemption must submit a statement describing why the organization or entity is exempt.

(B) Exempt filing situations. Any non-exempt employer who claims that the ACWIA fee does not apply with respect to a particular filing for one of the reasons described in paragraph (h)(19)(v) of this section must indicate why the ACWIA fee is not required.

(20) Retaliatory action claims.

(i) If credible documentary evidence is provided in support of a petition seeking an extension of H–1B stay in or change of status to another classification indicating that the beneficiary faced retaliatory action from their employer based on a report regarding a violation of that employer's labor condition application obligations under section 212(n)(2)(C)(iv) of the Act, USCIS may consider a loss or failure to maintain H- 1B status by the beneficiary related to such violation as due to, and commensurate with, "extraordinary circumstances" as defined by 8 CFR 214.1(c)(4) and 8 CFR 248.1(b).

(ii) If credible documentary evidence is provided in support of a petition seeking an extension of H–2A or H–2B stay in or change of status to another classification indicating that the beneficiary faced retaliatory action from their employer based on a reasonable claim of a violation or potential violation of any applicable program requirements or based on engagement in another protected activity, USCIS may consider a loss or failure to maintain H- 2A or H–2B status by the beneficiary related to such violation as due to, and commensurate with, "extraordinary circumstances" as defined by 8 CFR 214.1(c)(4) and 8 CFR 248.1(b). USCIS will determine the reasonableness of any claim from the perspective of a reasonable person in the H–2A or H–2B worker's position.

(21) [Effective Aug. 19, 2020 through Aug. 19, 2023.] Change of employers during COVID-19 National Emergency (August 19, 2020 through December 17, 2020).

(i) If an H–2A nonimmigrant who is physically present in the United States seeks to change employers during the COVID–19 National Emergency, the prospective new H–2A employer may file an H–2A petition on Form I–129 or Form I– 129H2A, accompanied by a valid temporary agricultural labor certification, requesting an extension of the alien's stay in the United States. To be approved under this paragraph (h)(21), an H–2A petition must be received on or after August 19, 2020 but no later than December 17, 2020. If the new petition is approved, the extension of stay may be granted for the validity of the approved petition for a period not to exceed the validity period of the temporary agricultural labor certification. Notwithstanding paragraph (h)(2)(i)(D) of this section and 8 CFR 274a.12(b)(21), an alien in valid H–2A nonimmigrant status on August 19, 2020, or lawfully obtaining such status thereafter pursuant to this paragraph (h)(21), is authorized to begin employment with the new petitioner after the petition described in this paragraph (h)(21) is received by USCIS, but no earlier than the start date of employment, indicated in the H–2A petition. The H–2A worker is authorized to commence employment with the petitioner before the petition is approved and subject to the requirements of 8 CFR 274a.12(b)(26) for a period of up to 45 days beginning on the Received Date on Form I–797 (Notice of Action) or, if the start date of employment occurs after the I–797 Received Date, 45 days beginning on the start date of employment indicated in the H–2A petition. If USCIS adjudicates the petition prior to the expiration of this 45-day period and denies the petition for extension of stay, or if the petition is withdrawn by the petitioner before the expiration of the 45-day period, the employment authorization associated with the filing of that petition under 8 CFR 274a.12(b)(26) will automatically terminate 15 days after the date of the denial decision or the date on which the petition is withdrawn.

(ii) Authorization to initiate employment changes pursuant to this paragraph (h)(21) begins at 12 a.m. on August 19, 2020, and ends at the end of December 17, 2020.

(22) [Effective Dec. 18, 2020 through Dec. 18, 2023.] Change of employers during COVID-19 National Emergency (December 18, 2020 through June 16, 2021).

(i) If an H–2A nonimmigrant who is physically present in the United States seeks to change employers during the COVID–19 National Emergency, the prospective new H–2A employer may file an H–2A petition on Form I–129, accompanied by a valid temporary agricultural labor certification, requesting an extension of the alien's stay in the United States. To be approved under this paragraph (h)(22), an H–2A petition must be received on or after December 18, 2020 but no later than June 16, 2021. If the new petition is approved, the extension of stay may be granted for the validity of the approved petition for a period not to exceed the validity period of the temporary agricultural labor certification. Notwithstanding paragraph (h)(2)(i)(D) of this section and 8 CFR 274a.12(b)(21), an alien in valid H–2A nonimmigrant status on December 18, 2020, or lawfully obtaining such status thereafter pursuant to this paragraph (h)(22), is authorized to begin employment with the new petitioner after the petition described in this paragraph (h)(22) is received by USCIS, but no earlier than the start date of employment, indicated in the H–2A petition. The H–2A worker is authorized to commence employment with the petitioner before the petition is approved and subject to the requirements of 8 CFR 274a.12(b)(28) for a period of up to 45 days beginning on the Received Date on Form I–797 (Notice of Action) or, if the start date of employment occurs after the I–797 Received Date, 45 days beginning on the start date of employment indicated in the H–2A petition. If USCIS adjudicates the petition prior to the expiration of this 45-day period and denies the petition for extension of stay, or if the petition is withdrawn by the petitioner before the expiration of the 45-day period, the employment authorization associated with the filing of that petition under 8 CFR 274a.12(b)(28) will automatically terminate 15 days after the date of the denial decision or the date on which the petition is withdrawn.

(ii) Authorization to initiate employment changes pursuant to this paragraph (h)(22) begins at 12 a.m. on December 18, 2020, and ends at the end of June 16, 2021.

(23) [Effective May 14, 2020 through May 15, 2023.] Change of employers and extensions beyond 3 years during COVID-19 National Emergency for H-2B aliens essential to the U.S. food supply chain.

(i) This paragraph (h)(23) relates to certain H-2B workers providing temporary nonagricultural services or labor essential to the U.S. food supply chain.

(ii) A prospective new H-2B employer or U.S. agent who is seeking to employ an H-2B alien to provide temporary nonagricultural services or labor essential to the U.S. food supply chain under this paragraph (h)(23) may file an H-2B petition on Form I-129, accompanied by an approved temporary labor certification and attestation described in paragraph (h)(23)(v)(A) of this section, requesting an extension of the alien's stay in the United States. If the new petition is approved, the extension of stay may be granted for the validity of the approved petition for a period not to exceed the validity period of the temporary labor certification. Notwithstanding paragraph (h)(2)(i)(D) of this section, an alien in valid H-2B nonimmigrant status on or after March 1, 2020:

(A) Whose new petitioner files an H-2B petition on or after May 14, 2020, is authorized to begin employment with the new petitioner to perform work that is essential to the U.S. food supply chain after the petition described in this paragraph (h)(23), including the attestation described in paragraph (h)(23)(v)(A) of this section, is received by USCIS and before the H-2B petition is approved, but no earlier than the start date of employment indicated in the H-2B petition; or

(B) Whose new petitioner filed an H-2B petition on or after March 1, 2020 and the petition was pending on or after May 14, 2020, is authorized to begin employment with the new petitioner to perform work that is essential to the U.S. food supply chain after the attestation described in paragraph (h)(23)(v)(A) is received by USCIS and before the H-2B petition is approved.

(iii)(A) With respect to a petition described in paragraph (h)(23)(ii)(A) of this section, and subject to the requirements of 8 CFR 274a.12(b)(27), the new period of employment described in paragraph (h)(23)(ii) may last for up to 60 days beginning on the Received Date on Form I-797 (Notice of Action) or, if the start date of employment occurs after the I-797 Received Date, for a period of up to 60 days beginning on the start date of employment indicated in the H-2B petition. Employment is not authorized under this paragraph (h)(23) if USCIS does not receive the attestation described in paragraph (h)(23)(v)(A) of this section.

(B) With respect to a petition described in paragraph (h)(23)(ii)(B) of this section, the new period of employment described in paragraph (h)(23)(ii) may last for up to 60 days beginning on the date that USCIS acknowledges in writing the receipt of a properly filed attestation described paragraph (h)(23)(v). Employment under this paragraph (h)(23) is not authorized if USCIS does not receive the attestation described in paragraph (h)(23)(v)(A) of this section.

(C) With respect to either type of petition, if USCIS adjudicates the petition prior to the expiration of this 60-day period and denies the petition for extension of stay, or if the petition is withdrawn by the petitioner before the expiration of the 60-day period, the employment authorization associated with the filing of that petition under 8 CFR 274a.12(b)(27) will automatically terminate 15 days after the date of the denial decision or 15 days after the date on which the petition is withdrawn. Nothing in this paragraph (h)(23) is intended to alter the availability of employment authorization related to professional H-2B athletes who are traded between organizations pursuant to paragraph (h)(6)(vii) of this section and 8 CFR 274a.12(b)(9).

(iv) Notwithstanding paragraphs (h)(13)(i)(B), (h)(13)(iv) and (v), and (h)(15)(ii)(C) of this section, an H-2B petition seeking an extension of stay for H-2B aliens who are essential to the U.S. food supply chain to work, and submitted with an approved temporary labor certification, may be approved on the basis of this paragraph (h)(23), even if any of the aliens requested in the H-2B petition have otherwise exhausted the applicable 3-year maximum period of stay in the United States and have not thereafter been absent from the United States for an uninterrupted period of 3 months, or if any such aliens would exceed the 3-year limit as a consequence of the approval of the extension.

(v) In addition to meeting all other requirements for the H-2B classification, to commence employment and be approved under this paragraph (h)(23):

(A) The H-2B petitioner must submit an attestation indicating that the H-2B alien will be performing work that is essential to the U.S. food supply chain;

(B) The alien must have been in valid H-2B nonimmigrant status on or after March 1, 2020; and

(C) The H-2B petition must have been—

(1) Received on or after March 1, 2020, and pending as of May 14, 2020, so long as the H-2B worker did not begin work with the new employer before May 14, 2020, or

(2) Received on or after May 14, 2020, but no later than September 11, 2020.

(vi) Authorization to initiate employment changes pursuant to paragraphs (h)(23)(ii) and (iii) of this section, or be approved for employment exceeding 3 years in duration pursuant to paragraph (h)(23)(iv) of this section, begins on May 14, 2020, and ends at the end of September 11, 2020.

(24) Severability.

(i) The requirement to submit a registration for an H–1B capsubject petition and the selection process based on properly submitted registrations under paragraph (h)(8)(iii) of this section are intended to be severable from paragraph (h)(8)(iv) of this section. In the event paragraph (h)(8)(iii) is not implemented, or in the event that paragraph (h)(8)(iv) is not implemented, DHS intends that either of those provisions be implemented as an independent rule, without prejudice to petitioners in the United States under this section, as consistent with law.

(ii) The following provisions added or revised by the changes made to the H– 1B nonimmigrant visa classification program, as of December 7, 2020, are intended to be implemented as separate and severable from one another: paragraphs (h)(2)(i), (h)(4)(i)(B)(7), (h)(4)(ii) (definitions of employer-employee, specialty occupation, third-party worksite, U.S. employer, and worksite), (h)(4)(iii)(A), (h)(4)(iv)(C), (h)(9)(i)(B), and (h)(9)(iii)(A)(1) of this section. If one or more of the paragraphs in the preceding sentence is not implemented, DHS intends that the remaining paragraphs will remain valid and be implemented to the greatest extent possible.

(25) [Reserved effective May 25, 2021 through May 28, 2024.]

(26) [Effective May 25, 2021 through May 28, 2024.] Change of employers and portability for H-2B workers (May 25, 2021 through November 22, 2021).

(i) This paragraph (h)(26) relates to H-2B workers seeking to change employers during the time period specified in paragraph (h)(26)(iv) of this section. Notwithstanding paragraph (h)(2)(i)(D) of this section, an alien in valid H-2B nonimmigrant status:

(A) Whose new petitioner files a non-frivolous H-2B petition requesting an extension of the alien's stay on or after May 25, 2021, is authorized to begin employment with the new petitioner after the petition described in this paragraph (h)(26) is received by USCIS and before the new H-2B petition is approved, but no earlier than the start date indicated in the new H-2B petition; or

(B) Whose new petitioner filed a non-frivolous H-2B petition requesting an extension of the alien's stay before May 25, 2021 that remains pending on May 25, 2021, is authorized to begin employment with the new petitioner before the new H-2B petition is approved, but no earlier than the start date of employment indicated on the new H-2B petition.

(ii)(A) With respect to a new petition described in paragraph (h)(26)(i)(A) of this section, and subject to the requirements of 8 CFR 274a.12(b)(30), the new period of employment described in paragraph (h)(26)(i) of this section may last for up to 60 days beginning on the Received Date on Form I-797 (Notice of Action) or, if the start date of employment occurs after the I-797 Received Date, for a period of up to 60 days beginning on the start date of employment indicated in the H-2B petition.

(B) With respect to a new petition described in paragraph (h)(26)(i)(B) of this section, the new period of employment described in paragraph (h)(26)(i) of this section may last for up to 60 days beginning on the later of either May 25, 2021 or the start date of employment indicated in the H-2B petition.

(C) With respect to either type of new petition, if USCIS adjudicates the new petition before the expiration of this 60-day period and denies the petition, or if the new petition is withdrawn by the petitioner before the expiration of the 60-day period, the employment authorization associated with the filing of that petition under 8 CFR 274a.12(b)(30) will automatically terminate 15 days after the date of the denial decision or 15 days after the date on which the new petition is withdrawn. Nothing in this paragraph (h)(26) is intended to alter the availability of employment authorization related to professional H-2B athletes who are traded between organizations pursuant to paragraph (h)(6)(vii) of this section and 8 CFR 274a.12(b)(9).

(iii) In addition to meeting all other requirements in paragraph (h)(6) of this section for the H-2B classification, to commence employment and be approved under this paragraph (h)(26):

(A) The alien must have been in valid H-2B nonimmigrant status on or after May 25, 2021;

(B) The new H-2B petition must have been—

(1) Pending as of May 25, 2021; or

(2) Received on or after May 25, 2021, but no later than November 22, 2021;

(C) The petitioner must comply with all Federal, State, and local employment-related laws and regulations, including health and safety laws, laws related to COVID-19 worker protections, and any right to time off or paid time off for COVID-19 vaccination; and

(D) The petitioner may not impede, interfere, or refuse to cooperate with an employee of the Secretary of the U.S. Department of Labor who is exercising or attempting to exercise DOL's audit or investigative authority under 20 CFR part 655, subpart A, and 29 CFR 503.25.

(iv) Authorization to initiate employment changes pursuant to this paragraph (h)(26) begins at 12 a.m. on May 25, 2021, and ends at the end of November 22, 2021.

(27) [Effective Jan. 28, 2022 through Jan. 28, 2025.] Change of employers and portability for H-2B workers (January 28, 2022 through July 27, 2022).

(i) This paragraph (h)(27) relates to H-2B workers seeking to change employers during the time period specified in paragraph (h)(27)(iv) of this section. Notwithstanding paragraph (h)(2)(i)(D) of this section:

(A) An alien in valid H-2B nonimmigrant status whose new petitioner files a non-frivolous H-2B petition requesting an extension of the alien's stay on or after January 28, 2022, is authorized to begin employment with the new petitioner after the petition described in this paragraph (h)(27) is received by USCIS and before the new H-2B petition is approved, but no earlier than the start date indicated in the new H-2B petition; or

(B) An alien whose new petitioner filed a non-frivolous H-2B petition requesting an extension of the alien's stay before January 28, 2022 that remains pending on January 28, 2022, is authorized to begin employment with the new petitioner before the new H-2B petition is approved, but no earlier than the start date of employment indicated on the new H-2B petition.

(ii)(A) With respect to a new petition described in paragraph (h)(27)(i)(A) of this section, and subject to the requirements of 8 CFR 274a.12(b)(30), the new period of employment described in paragraph (h)(27)(i) of this section may last for up to 60 days beginning on the Received Date on Form I-797 (Notice of Action) or, if the start date of employment occurs after the I-797 Received Date, for a period of up to 60 days beginning on the start date of employment indicated in the H-2B petition.

(B) With respect to a new petition described in paragraph (h)(27)(i)(B) of this section, the new period of employment described in paragraph (h)(27)(i) of this section may last for up to 60 days beginning on the later of either January 28, 2022 or the start date of employment indicated in the H-2B petition.

(C) With respect to either type of new petition, if USCIS adjudicates the new petition before the expiration of this 60-day period and denies the petition, or if the new petition is withdrawn by the petitioner before the expiration of the 60-day period, the employment authorization associated with the filing of that petition under 8 CFR 274a.12(b)(30) will automatically terminate 15 days after the date of the denial decision or 15 days after the date on which the new petition is withdrawn. Nothing in this paragraph (h)(27) is intended to alter the availability of employment authorization related to professional H-2B athletes who are traded between organizations pursuant to paragraph (h)(6)(vii) of this section and 8 CFR 274a.12(b)(9).

(iii) In addition to meeting all other requirements in paragraph (h)(6) of this section for the H-2B classification, to commence employment and be approved under this paragraph (h)(27), the alien must either:

(A) Have been in valid H-2B nonimmigrant status on or after January 28, 2022 and be the beneficiary of a non-frivolous H-2B petition requesting an extension of the alien's stay that is received on or after January 28, 2022, but no later than July 27, 2022; or

(B) Be the beneficiary of a non-frivolous H-2B petition requesting an extension of the alien's stay that is pending as of January 28, 2022.

(C) The petitioner must comply with all Federal, State, and local employment-related laws and regulations, including, where applicable, health and safety laws, laws related to COVID-19 worker protections, any right to time off or paid time off for COVID-19 vaccination, or to reimbursement for travel to and from the nearest available vaccination site; and

(D) The petitioner may not impede, interfere, or refuse to cooperate with an employee of the Secretary of the U.S. Department of Labor who is exercising or attempting to exercise DOL's audit or investigative authority under 20 CFR part 655, subpart A, and 29 CFR 503.25.

(iv) Authorization to initiate employment changes pursuant to this paragraph (h)(27) begins at 12 a.m. on January 28, 2022, and ends at the end of July 27, 2022.

(28) [Effective May 18, 2022 through May 18, 2025] Change of employers and portability for H-2B workers (July 28, 2022 through January 24, 2023).

(i) This paragraph (h)(28) relates to H-2B workers seeking to change employers during the time period specified in paragraph (h)(28)(iv) of this section. Notwithstanding paragraph (h)(2)(i)(D) of this section:

(A) An alien in valid H-2B nonimmigrant status whose new petitioner files a non-frivolous H-2B petition requesting an extension of the alien's stay on or after July 28, 2022, is authorized to begin employment with the new petitioner after the petition described in this paragraph (h)(28) is received by USCIS and before the new H-2B petition is approved, but no earlier than the start date indicated in the new H-2B petition; or

(B) An alien whose new petitioner filed a non-frivolous H-2B petition requesting an extension of the alien's stay before July 28, 2022 that remains pending on July 28, 2022, is authorized to begin employment with the new petitioner before the new H-2B petition is approved, but no earlier than the start date of employment indicated on the new H-2B petition.

(ii)(A) With respect to a new petition described in paragraph (h)(28)(i)(A) of this section, and subject to the requirements of 8 CFR 274a.12(b)(30), the new period of employment described in paragraph (h)(28)(i) of this section may last for up to 60 days beginning on the Received Date on Form I-797 (Notice of Action) or, if the start date of employment occurs after the I-797 Received Date, for a period of up to 60 days beginning on the start date of employment indicated in the H-2B petition.

(B) With respect to a new petition described in paragraph (h)(28)(i)(B) of this section, the new period of employment described in paragraph (h)(28)(i) of this section may last for up to 60 days beginning on the later of either July 28, 2022 or the start date of employment indicated in the H-2B petition.

(C) With respect to either type of new petition, if USCIS adjudicates the new petition before the expiration of this 60-day period and denies the petition, or if the new petition is withdrawn by the petitioner before the expiration of the 60-day period, the employment authorization associated with the filing of that petition under 8 CFR 274a.12(b)(30) will automatically terminate 15 days after the date of the denial decision or 15 days after the date on which the new petition is withdrawn. Nothing in this paragraph (h)(28) is intended to alter the availability of employment authorization related to professional H-2B athletes who are traded between organizations pursuant to paragraph (h)(6)(vii) of this section and 8 CFR 274a.12(b)(9).

(iii) In addition to meeting all other requirements in paragraph (h)(6) of this section for the H-2B classification, to commence employment and be approved under this paragraph (h)(28):

(A) The alien must either (1) have been in valid H-2B nonimmigrant status on or after July 28, 2022 and be the beneficiary of a non-frivolous H-2B petition requesting an extension of the alien's stay that is received on or after July 28, 2022, but no later than January 24, 2023; or (2) be the beneficiary of a non-frivolous H-2B petition requesting an extension of the alien's stay that is pending as of July 28, 2022.

(B) The petitioner must comply with all Federal, State, and local employment-related laws and regulations, including, where applicable, health and safety laws, laws related to COVID-19 worker protections, any right to time off or paid time off for COVID-19 vaccination, or to reimbursement for travel to and from the nearest available vaccination site; and

(C) The petitioner may not impede, interfere, or refuse to cooperate with an employee of the Secretary of the U.S. Department of Labor who is exercising or attempting to exercise DOL's audit or investigative authority under 20 CFR part 655, subpart A, and 29 CFR 503.25.

(iv) Authorization to initiate employment changes pursuant to this paragraph (h)(28) begins at 12 a.m. on July 28, 2022, and ends at the end of January 24, 2023.

(29) [Effective Dec. 15, 2022 through Dec. 15, 2025] Change of employers and portability for H-2B workers.

(i) This paragraph (h)(29) relates to H-2B workers seeking to change employers during the time period specified in paragraph (h)(29)(iv) of this section. Notwithstanding paragraph (h)(2)(i)(D) of this section:

(A) An alien in valid H-2B nonimmigrant status whose new petitioner files a non-frivolous H-2B petition requesting an extension of the alien's stay on or after January 25, 2023, is authorized to begin employment with the new petitioner after the petition described in this paragraph (h)(29) is received by USCIS and before the new H-2B petition is approved, but no earlier than the start date indicated in the new H-2B petition; or

(B) An alien whose new petitioner filed a non-frivolous H-2B petition requesting an extension of the alien's stay before January 25, 2023 that remains pending on January 25, 2023, is authorized to begin employment with the new petitioner before the new H-2B petition is approved, but no earlier than the start date of employment indicated on the new H-2B petition.

(ii)(A) With respect to a new petition described in paragraph (h)(29)(i)(A) of this section, and subject to the requirements of 8 CFR 274a.12(b)(33), the new period of employment described in paragraph (h)(29)(i) of this section may last for up to 60 days beginning on the Received Date on Form I-797 (Notice of Action) or, if the start date of employment occurs after the I-797 Received Date, for a period of up to 60 days beginning on the start date of employment indicated in the H-2B petition.

(B) With respect to a new petition described in paragraph (h)(29)(i)(B) of this section, the new period of employment described in paragraph (h)(29)(i) of this section may last for up to 60 days beginning on the later of either January 25, 2023 or the start date of employment indicated in the H-2B petition.

(C) With respect to either type of new petition, if USCIS adjudicates the new petition before the expiration of this 60-day period and denies the petition, or if the new petition is withdrawn by the petitioner before the expiration of the 60-day period, the employment authorization associated with the filing of that petition under 8 CFR 274a.12(b)(33) will automatically terminate 15 days after the date of the denial decision or 15 days after the date on which the new petition is withdrawn. Nothing in this paragraph (h)(29) is intended to alter the availability of employment authorization related to professional H-2B athletes who are traded between organizations pursuant to paragraph (h)(6)(vii) of this section and 8 CFR 274a.12(b)(9).

(iii) In addition to meeting all other requirements in paragraph (h)(6) of this section for the H-2B classification, to commence employment under this paragraph (h)(29):

(A) The alien must either have been in valid H-2B nonimmigrant status on or after January 25, 2023 and be the beneficiary of a non-frivolous H-2B petition requesting an extension of the alien's stay that is received on or after January 25, 2023, but no later than January 24, 2024; or be the beneficiary of a non-frivolous H-2B petition requesting an extension of the alien's stay that is pending as of January 25, 2023.

(B) The petitioner must comply with all Federal, State, and local employment-related laws and regulations, including, where applicable, health and safety laws, laws related to COVID-19 worker protections, any right to time off or paid time off for COVID-19 vaccination, or to reimbursement for travel to and from the nearest available vaccination site; and

(C) The petitioner may not impede, interfere, or refuse to cooperate with an employee of the Secretary of the U.S. Department of Labor who is exercising or attempting to exercise DOL's audit or investigative authority under 20 CFR part 655, subpart A, and 29 CFR 503.25.

(iv) Authorization to initiate employment changes pursuant to this paragraph (h)(29) begins at 12 a.m. on January 25, 2023, and ends at the end of January 24, 2024.

(30) Severability. The Department intends that should any of the revisions effective on January 17, 2025, to provisions in paragraphs (h)(2), (5), (6), (10), (11), (13), (16) and (20) of this section or to the provision in 8 CFR 274a.12(b)(21) be held to be invalid or unenforceable by their terms or as applied to any person or circumstance they should nevertheless be construed so as to continue to give the maximum effect to the provision(s) permitted by law, unless any such provision is held to be wholly invalid and unenforceable, in which event the provision(s) should be severed from the remainder of the provisions and the holding should not affect the other provisions or the application of those other provisions to persons not similarly situated or to dissimilar circumstances.

(31) Change of employers and portability for H-2B workers.

(i) This paragraph (h)(31) relates to H-2B workers seeking to change employers during the time period specified in paragraph (h)(31)(iv) of this section. Notwithstanding paragraph (h)(2)(i)(D) of this section:

(A) An alien in valid H-2B nonimmigrant status whose new petitioner files a non-frivolous H-2B petition requesting an extension of the alien's stay on or after January 25, 2024, is authorized to begin employment with the new petitioner after the petition described in this paragraph (h)(31) is received by USCIS and before the new H-2B petition is approved, but no earlier than the start date indicated in the new H-2B petition; or

(B) An alien whose new petitioner filed a non-frivolous H-2B petition requesting an extension of the alien's stay before January 25, 2024, that remains pending on January 25, 2024, is authorized to begin employment with the new petitioner before the new H-2B petition is approved, but no earlier than the start date of employment indicated on the new H-2B petition.

(ii)(A) With respect to a new petition described in paragraph (h)(31)(i)(A) of this section, and subject to the requirements of 8 CFR 274a.12(b)(34), the new period of employment described in paragraph (h)(31)(i) of this section may last for up to 60 days beginning on the Received Date on Form I-797 (Notice of Action) or, if the start date of employment occurs after the I-797 Received Date, for a period of up to 60 days beginning on the start date of employment indicated in the H-2B petition.

(B) With respect to a new petition described in paragraph (h)(31)(i)(B) of this section, the new period of employment described in paragraph (h)(31)(i) of this section may last for up to 60 days beginning on the later of either January 25, 2024, or the start date of employment indicated in the H-2B petition.

(C) With respect to either type of new petition, if USCIS adjudicates the new petition before the expiration of this 60-day period and denies the petition, or if the new petition is withdrawn by the petitioner before the expiration of the 60-day period, the employment authorization associated with the filing of that petition under 8 CFR 274a.12(b)(34) will automatically terminate 15 days after the date of the denial decision or 15 days after the date on which the new petition is withdrawn. Nothing in this paragraph (h)(31) is intended to alter the availability of employment authorization related to professional H-2B athletes who are traded between organizations pursuant to paragraph (h)(6)(vii) of this section and 8 CFR 274a.12(b)(9).

(iii) In addition to meeting all other requirements in paragraph (h)(6) of this section for the H-2B classification, to commence employment under this paragraph (h)(31):

(A) The alien must either:

(1) Have been in valid H-2B nonimmigrant status on or after January 25, 2024 and be the beneficiary of a non-frivolous H-2B petition requesting an extension of the alien's stay that is received on or after January 25, 2024, but no later than January 24, 2025; or

(2) Be the beneficiary of a non-frivolous H-2B petition requesting an extension of the alien's stay that is pending as of January 25, 2024; and

(B) The petitioner may not impede, interfere, or refuse to cooperate with an employee of the Secretary of the U.S. Department of Labor who is exercising or attempting to exercise DOL's audit or investigative authority under 20 CFR part 655, subpart A, and 29 CFR 503.25.

(iv) Authorization to initiate employment changes pursuant to this paragraph (h)(31) begins at 12 a.m. on January 25, 2024, and ends at the end of January 24, 2025.

(32) Change of employers and portability for H-2B workers.

(i) This paragraph (h)(32) relates to H-2B workers seeking to change employers during the time period specified in paragraph (h)(32)(iv) of this section. Notwithstanding paragraph (h)(2)(i)(D) of this section:

(A) An alien in valid H-2B nonimmigrant status whose new petitioner files a non-frivolous H-2B petition requesting an extension of the alien's stay on or after January 25, 2025, is authorized to begin employment with the new petitioner after the petition described in this paragraph (h)(32) is received by USCIS and before the new H-2B petition is approved, but no earlier than the start date indicated in the new H-2B petition; or

(B) An alien whose new petitioner filed a non-frivolous H-2B petition requesting an extension of the alien's stay before January 25, 2025, that remains pending on January 25, 2025, is authorized to begin employment with the new petitioner before the new H-2B petition is approved, but no earlier than the start date of employment indicated on the new H-2B petition.

(ii)(A) With respect to a new petition described in paragraph (h)(32)(i)(A) of this section, and subject to the requirements of 8 CFR 274a.12(b)(35), the new period of employment described in paragraph (h)(32)(i) of this section may last for up to 60 days beginning on the Received Date on Form I-797 (Notice of Action) or, if the start date of employment occurs after the I-797 Received Date, for a period of up to 60 days beginning on the start date of employment indicated in the H-2B petition.

(B) With respect to a new petition described in paragraph (h)(32)(i)(B) of this section, the new period of employment described in paragraph (h)(32)(i) of this section may last for up to 60 days beginning on the later of either January 25, 2025, or the start date of employment indicated in the H-2B petition.

(C) With respect to either type of new petition, if USCIS adjudicates the new petition before the expiration of this 60-day period and denies the petition, or if the new petition is withdrawn by the petitioner before the expiration of the 60-day period, the employment authorization associated with the filing of that petition under 8 CFR 274a.12(b)(35) will automatically terminate 15 days after the date of the denial decision or 15 days after the date on which the new petition is withdrawn. Nothing in this paragraph (h)(32) is intended to alter the availability of employment authorization related to professional H-2B athletes who are traded between organizations pursuant to paragraph (h)(6)(vii) of this section and 8 CFR 274a.12(b)(9).

(iii) In addition to meeting all other requirements in paragraph (h)(6) of this section for the H-2B classification, to commence employment under this paragraph (h)(32):

(A) The alien must either:

(1) Have been in valid H-2B nonimmigrant status on or after January 25, 2025 and be the beneficiary of a non-frivolous H-2B petition requesting an extension of the alien's stay that is received on or after January 25, 2025, but no later than January 24, 2026; or

(2) Be the beneficiary of a non-frivolous H-2B petition requesting an extension of the alien's stay that is pending as of January 25, 2025; and

(B) The petitioner may not impede, interfere, or refuse to cooperate with an employee of the Secretary of the U.S. Department of Labor who is exercising or attempting to exercise DOL's audit or investigative authority under 20 CFR part 655, subpart A, and 29 CFR 503.25.

(iv) Authorization to initiate employment changes pursuant to this paragraph (h)(32) begins at 12 a.m. on January 25, 2025, and ends at the end of January 24, 2026.

(33) Severability. The Department intends that should any of the revisions effective on January 17, 2025, to provisions in paragraphs (f)(5), (h)(2), (4) through (6), (8), (9), (11), (14), and (19), (l)(14), (o)(11), and (p)(13) of this section or to the provisions in 8 CFR 214.1(c)(1) and (4) through (7) be held to be invalid or unenforceable by their terms or as applied to any person or circumstance they should nevertheless be construed so as to continue to give the maximum effect to the provision(s) permitted by law, unless any such provision is held to be wholly invalid and unenforceable, in which event the provision(s) should be severed from the remainder of the provisions and the holding should not affect the other provisions or the application of those other provisions to persons not similarly situated or to dissimilar circumstances.

(i) Representatives of information media—

(1) In general. The admission of an alien of the class defined in section 101(a)(15)(I) of the Act constitutes an agreement by the alien not to change the information medium or his or her employer until he or she obtains permission to do so from the district director having jurisdiction over his or her residence. An alien classified as an information media nonimmigrant (I) may be admitted in or otherwise granted I nonimmigrant status for:

(i) The duration of employment, except as provided in paragraph (i)(1)(ii) of this section; or

(ii) In the case of an alien who presents a passport issued by the People's Republic of China (PRC) (other than a Hong Kong Special Administrative Region passport or a Macau Special Administrative Region passport), until the activities or assignments consistent with the I classification are completed, not to exceed the maximum period of stay as determined by the Secretary. The Secretary of Homeland Security may determine the maximum period of stay when the Secretary determines an adjustment is needed, with such maximum period to be no longer than one year. In determining the maximum period of stay and whether an adjustment is needed, the Secretary will consider factors including, but not limited to, the average authorized period of stay and press credential validity for U.S. journalists in the PRC, the treatment of U.S. journalists in the PRC, any input from the U.S. Department of State, and such other factors as may affect the U.S. interest. Such determination will be published in the Federal Register as a notice and will remain in effect until the Secretary of Homeland Security publishes a new determination under this paragraph.

(2) Extension of stay. An alien in I status who is described in paragraph (i)(1)(ii) of this section may be eligible for extensions of stay, each of up to the maximum period of stay determined by the Secretary pursuant to paragraph (i)(1)(ii) of this section or until the activities or assignments consistent with the I classification are completed (whichever date is earlier).

(i) Notwithstanding 8 CFR 274a.12(b)(20), an alien in I status who is described in paragraph (i)(1)(ii) of this section whose status has expired, but who timely filed an application for an extension of stay, is authorized to stay in the United States and continue employment with the same employer for a period not to exceed 90 days beginning on the date of the expiration of the authorized period of stay. However, if USCIS adjudicates the application prior to the expiration of the 90-day period, and denies the application for an extension of stay, the alien must immediately depart the United States.

(ii) To request an extension of stay, an alien in I status must file an application to extend his or her stay by submitting the form designated by USCIS, in accordance with that form's instructions, and with the required fee, including any biometrics required by 8 CFR 103.16, as appropriate. Requests for extensions of stay will be adjudicated consistent with international legal obligations, including the United Nations Headquarters Agreement and Organization of American States Headquarters Agreement.

(3) Change of status. An alien seeking to change from a different nonimmigrant status to, if eligible, an I status described in paragraph (i)(1)(ii) of this section, may be granted a period of stay until the activities or assignments consistent with the I classification are completed, not to exceed the maximum period of stay determined by the Secretary pursuant to paragraph (i)(1)(ii) of this section. To request a change from a different nonimmigrant status to an I status described in paragraph (i)(1)(ii), an alien must file an application to change his or her status by submitting the form designated by USCIS, in accordance with that form's instructions, and with the required fee, including any biometrics required by 8 CFR 103.16, as appropriate.

(4) Applicable maximum period of stay. Any change in the maximum period of stay announced by a Federal Register notice pursuant to paragraph (i)(1)(ii) of this section applies to applications for an extension of stay or a change of status, filed under paragraphs (i)(2) and (3) of this section respectively, that are pending with USCIS on the effective date of the Federal Register notice.

(j) Exchange aliens —

(1) General —

(i) Eligibility for admission. A nonimmigrant exchange visitor and his or her accompanying spouse and minor children may be admitted into the United States in J-1 and J-2 classifications under section 101(a)(15)(J) of the Act, if the exchange visitor and his or her accompanying spouse and children each presents a SEVIS Form DS-2019 issued in his or her own name by a program approved by the Department of State for participation by J-1 exchange visitors. Prior to August 1, 2003, if exigent circumstances are demonstrated, the Service will allow the dependent of an exchange visitor possessing a SEVIS Form DS-2019 to enter the United States using a copy of the exchange visitor's SEVIS Form DS-2019. However, where the exchange visitor presents a properly completed Form DS-2019, Certificate of Eligibility for Exchange Visitor (J-1) Status, which was issued to the J-1 exchange visitor by a program approved by the Department of State for participation by exchange visitors and which remains valid for the admission of the exchange visitor, the accompanying spouse and children may be admitted on the basis of the J-1's non-SEVIS Form DS-2019.

(ii) Admission period. An exchange alien, and J-2 spouse and children, may be admitted for a period up to 30 days before the report date or start of the approved program listed on Form DS-2019. The initial admission of an exchange visitor, spouse and children may not exceed the period specified on Form DS-2019, plus a period of 30 days for the purposes of travel or for the period designated by the Commissioner as provided in paragraph (j)(1)(vi) of this section. Regulations of the Department of State published at 22 CFR part 62 give general limitations on the stay of the various classes of exchange visitors. A spouse or child may not be admitted for longer than the principal exchange visitor.

(iii) Readmission. An exchange alien may be readmitted to the United States for the remainder of the time authorized on Form I-94, without presenting Form IAP-66, if the alien is returning from a visit solely to foreign contiguous territory or adjacent islands after an absence of less than 30 days and if the original Form I-94 is presented. All other exchange aliens must present a valid Form IAP-66. An original Form IAP-66 or copy three (the pink copy) of a previously issued form presented by an exchange alien returning from a temporary absence shall be retained by the exchange alien for re-entries during the balance of the alien's stay.

(iv) Extensions of Stay. If an exchange alien requires an extension beyond the initial admission period, the alien shall apply by submitting a new Form DS-2019 which indicates the date to which the alien's program is extended. The extension may not exceed the period specified on Form DS-2019, plus a period of 30 days for the purpose of travel. Extensions of stay for the alien's spouse and children require, as an attachment to Form DS-2019, Form I-94 for each dependent, and a list containing the names of the applicants, dates and places of birth, passport numbers, issuing countries, and expiration dates. An accompanying spouse or child may not be granted an extension of stay for longer than the principal exchange alien.

(v) Employment.

(A) The accompanying spouse and minor children of a J-1 exchange visitor may accept employment only with authorization by the Immigration and Naturalization Service. A request for employment authorization must be made on Form I-765, Application for Employment Authorization, with fee, as required by the Service, to the district director having jurisdiction over the J-1 exchange visitor's temporary residence in the United States. Income from the spouse's or dependent's employment may be used to support the family's customary recreational and cultural activities and related travel, among other things. Employment will not be authorized if this income is needed to support the J-1 principal alien.

(B) J-2 employment may be authorized for the duration of the J-1 principal alien's authorized stay as indicated on Form I-94 or a period of four years, whichever is shorter. The employment authorization is valid only if the J-1 is maintaining status. Where a J-2 spouse or dependent child has filed a timely application for extension of stay, only upon approval of the request for extension of stay may he or she apply for a renewal of the employment authorization on a Form I-765 with the required fee.

(vi) Extension of duration of status. The Commissioner may, by notice in the FEDERAL REGISTER, at any time she determines that the H-1B numerical limitation as described in section 214(g)(1)(A) of the Act will likely be reached prior to the end of a current fiscal year, extend for such a period of time as the Commissioner deems necessary to complete the adjudication of the H-1B application, the duration of status of any J-1 alien on behalf of whom an employer has timely filed an application for change of status to H-1B. The alien, in accordance with 8 CFR part 248, must not have violated the terms of his or her nonimmigrant stay and is not subject to the 2-year foreign residence requirement at 212(e) of the Act. Any J-1 student whose duration of status has been extended shall be considered to be maintaining lawful nonimmigrant status for all purposes under the Act, provided that the alien does not violate the terms and conditions of his or her J nonimmigrant stay. An extension made under this paragraph also applies to the J-2 dependent aliens.

(vii) Use of SEVIS. At a date to be established by the Department of State, the use of the Student and Exchange Visitor Information System (SEVIS) will become mandatory for designated program sponsors. After that date, which will be announced by publication in the FEDERAL REGISSTER all designated program sponsors must begin issuance of the SEVIS Form DS-2019.

(viii) Current name and address. A J-1 exchange visitor must inform the Service and the responsible officer of the exchange visitor program of any legal changes to his or her name or of any change of address, within 10 days of the change, in a manner prescribed by the program sponsor. A J-1 exchange visitor enrolled in a SEVIS program can satisfy the requirement in 8 CFR 265.1 of notifying the Service by providing a notice of a change of address within 10 days to the responsible officer, who in turn shall enter the information in SEVIS within 21 days of notification by the exchange visitor. A J-1 exchange visitor enrolled at a non-SEVIS program must submit a change of address to the Service, as provided in 8 CFR 265.1, within 10 days of the change. Except in the case of an exchange visitor who cannot receive mail where he or she resides, the address provided by the exchange visitor must be the actual physical location where the exchange visitor resides rather than a mailing address. In cases where an exchange visitor provides a mailing address, the exchange visitor program must maintain a record of, and must provide upon request from the Service, the actual physical location where the exchange visitor resides.

(2) Special reporting requirement. Each exchange alien participating in a program of graduate medical education or training shall file Form I-644 (Supplementary Statement for Graduate Medical Trainees) annually with the Service attesting to the conditions as specified on the form. The exchange alien shall also submit Form I-644 as an attachment to a completed Form DS-2019 when applying for an extension of stay.

(3) Alien in cancelled programs. When the approval of an exchange visitor program is withdrawn by the Director of the United States Information Agency, the district director shall send a notice of the withdrawal to each participant in the program and a copy of each such notice shall be sent to the program sponsor. If the exchange visitor is currently engaged in activities authorized by the cancelled program, the participant is authorized to remain in the United States to engage in those activities until expiration of the period of stay previously authorized. The district director shall notify participants in cancelled programs that permission to remain in the United States as an exchange visitor, or

extension of stay may be obtained if the participant is accepted in another approved program and a Form DS-2019, executed by the new program sponsor, is submitted. In this case, a release from the sponsor of the cancelled program will not be required.

(4) Eligibility requirements for section 101(a)(15)(J) classification for aliens desiring to participate in programs under which they will receive graduate medical education or training —

(i) Requirements. Any alien coming to the United States as an exchange visitor to participate in a program under which the alien will receive graduate medical education or training, or any alien seeking to change nonimmigrant status to that of an exchange visitor on Form I-506 for that purpose, must have passed parts of I and II of the National Board of Medical Examiners Examination (or an equivalent examination as determined by the Secretary of Health and Human Services), and must be competent in oral and written English, and shall submit a completely executed and valid Form DS-2019.

(ii) Exemptions. From January 10, 1978 until December 31, 1983, any alien who has come to or seeks to come to the United States as an exchange visitor to participate in an accredited program of graduate medical education or training, or any alien who seeks to change nonimmigrant status for that purpose, may be admitted to participate in such program without regard to the requirements stated in subparagraphs (A) and (B)(ii)(I) of section 212(j)(1) of the Act if a substantial disruption in the health services provided by such program would result from not permitting the alien to participate in the program: Provided that the exemption will not increase the total number of aliens then participating in such programs to a level greater than that participating on January 10, 1978.

(5) Remittance of the fee. An alien who applies for J-1 nonimmigrant status in order to commence participation in a Department of State-designated exchange visitor program is required to pay the SEVIS fee to DHS, pursuant to 8 CFR 214.13, except as otherwise provided in that section.

(k) Spouses, Fiancees, and Fiances of United States Citizens. —

(1) Petition and supporting documents. To be classified as a fiance or fiancee as defined in section 101(a)(15)(K)(i) of the Act, an alien must be the beneficiary of an approved visa petition filed on Form I-129F. A copy of a document submitted in support of a visa petition filed pursuant to section 214(d) of the Act and this paragraph may be accepted, though unaccompanied by the original, if the copy bears a certification by an attorney, typed or rubber-stamped, in the language set forth in § 204.2(j) of this chapter. However, the original document shall be submitted if requested by the Service.

(2) Requirement that petitioner and K-1 beneficiary have met. The petitioner shall establish to the satisfaction of the director that the petitioner and K-1 beneficiary have met in person within the two years immediately preceding the filing of the petition. As a matter of discretion, the director may exempt the petitioner from this requirement only if it is established that compliance would result in extreme hardship to the petitioner or that compliance would violate strict and long-established customs of the K-1 beneficiary's foreign culture or social practice, as where marriages are traditionally arranged by the parents of the contracting parties and the prospective bride and groom are prohibited from meeting subsequent to the arrangement and prior to the wedding day. In addition to establishing that the required meeting would be a violation of custom or practice, the petitioner must also establish that any and all other aspects of the traditional arrangements have been or will be met in accordance with the custom or practice. Failure to establish that the petitioner and K-1 beneficiary have met within the required period or that compliance with the requirement should be waived shall result in the denial of the petition. Such denial shall be without prejudice to the filing of a new petition once the petitioner and K-1 beneficiary have met in person.

(3) Children of beneficiary. Without the approval of a separate petition on his or her behalf, a child of the beneficiary (as defined in section 101(b)(1)(A), (B), (C), (D), or (E) of the Act) may be accorded the same nonimmigrant classification as the beneficiary if accompanying or following to join him or her.

(4) Notification. The petitioner shall be notified of the decision and, if the petition is denied, of the reasons therefor and of the right to appeal in accordance with the provisions of part 103 of this chapter.

(5) Validity. The approval of a petition under this paragraph shall be valid for a period of four months. A petition which has expired due to the passage of time may be revalidated by a director or a consular officer for a period of four months from the date of revalidation upon a finding that the petitioner and K-1 beneficiary are free to marry and intend to marry each other within 90 days of the beneficiary's entry into the United States. The approval of any petition is automatically terminated when the petitioner dies or files a written withdrawal of the petition before the beneficiary arrives in the United States.

(6) Adjustment of status from nonimmigrant to immigrant —

(i) [Reserved]

(ii) Nonimmigrant visa issued on or after November 10, 1986. Upon contracting a valid marriage to the petitioner within 90 days of his or her admission as a nonimmigrant pursuant to a valid K-1 visa issued on or after November 10, 1986, the K-1 beneficiary and his or her minor children may apply for adjustment of status to lawful permanent resident under section 245 of the Act. Upon approval of the application the director shall record their lawful admission for permanent residence in accordance with that section and subject to the conditions prescribed in section 216 of the Act.

(7) Eligibility, petition and supporting documents for K-3/K-4 classification. To be classified as a K-3 spouse as defined in section 101(a)(15)(k)(ii) of the Act, or the K-4 child of such alien defined in section 101(a)(15)(K)(iii) of the Act, the alien spouse must be the beneficiary of an immigrant visa petition filed by a

U.S. citizen on Form I-130, Petition for Alien Relative, and the beneficiary of an approved petition for a K-3 nonimmigrant visa filed on Form I-129F.

(8) Period of admission for K3/K-4 status. Aliens entering the United States as a K-3 shall be admitted for a period of 2 years. Aliens entering the United States as a K-4 shall be admitted for a period of 2 years or until that alien's 21st birthday, whichever is shorter.

(9) Employment authorization. An alien admitted to the United States as a nonimmigrant under section 101(a)(15)(K) of the Act shall be authorized to work incident to status for the period of authorized stay. K-1/K-2 aliens seeking work authorization must apply, with fee, to the Service for work authorization pursuant to § 274a.12(a)(6) of this chapter. K-3/K-4 aliens must apply to the Service for a document evidencing employment authorization pursuant to § 274a.12(a)(9) of this chapter. Employment authorization documents issued to K-3/K-4 aliens may be renewed only upon a showing that the applicant has an application or petition awaiting approval, equivalent to the showing required for an extension of stay pursuant to § 214.2(k)(10).

(10) Extension of stay for K-3/K-4 status.

(i) General. A K-3/K-4 alien may apply for extension of stay, on Form I-539, Application to Extend/Change Nonimmigrant Status, 120 days prior to the expiration of his or her authorized stay. Extensions for K-4 status must be filed concurrently with the alien's parent's K-3 status extension application. In addition, the citizen parent of a K-4 alien filing for extension of K status should file Form I-130 on their behalf. Extension will be granted in 2-year intervals upon a showing of eligibility pursuant to section 101(a)(15)(K)(ii) or (iii) of the Act. Aliens wishing to extend their period of stay as a K-3 or K-4 alien pursuant to § 214.1(c)(2) must show that one of the following has been filed with the Service or the Department of State, as applicable, and is awaiting approval:

(A) The Form I-130, Petition for Alien Relative, filed by the K-3's U.S. citizen spouse who filed the Form I-129F;

(B) An application for an immigrant visa based on a Form I-130 described in § 214.2(K)(10)(i);

(C) A Form I-485, Application for Adjustment to that of Permanent Residence, based on a Form I-130 described in § 214.2(k)(10)(i);

(ii) "Good Cause" showing. Aliens may file for an extension of stay as a K-3/K-4 nonimmigrant after a Form I-130 filed on their behalf has been approved, without filing either an application for adjustment of status or an immigrant visa upon a showing of "good cause." A showing of "good cause" may include an illness, a job loss, or some other catastrophic event that has prevented the filing of an adjustment of status application by the K-3/K-4 alien. The event or events must have taken place since the alien entered the United States as a K-3/K-4 nonimmigrant. The burden of establishing "good cause" rests solely with the applicant. Whether the applicant has shown "good cause" is a purely discretionary decision by the Service from which there is no appeal.

(11) Termination of K-3/K-4 status. The status of an alien admitted to the United States as a K-3/K-4 under section 101(a)(15)(K)(ii) or (iii) of the Act, shall be automatically terminated 30 days following the occurrence of any of the following:

(i) The denial or revocation of the Form I-130 filed on behalf of that alien;

(ii) The denial or revocation of the immigrant visa application filed by that alien;

(iii) The denial or revocation of the alien's application for adjustment of status to that of lawful permanent residence;

(iv) The K-3 spouse's divorce from the U.S. citizen becomes final;

(v) The marriage of an alien in K-4 status.

(vi) The denial of any of these petitions or applications to a K-3 also results in termination of a dependent K-4's status. For purposes of this section, there is no denial or revocation of a petition or application until the administrative appeal applicable to that application or petition has been exhausted.

(*l*) Intracompany transferees —

(1) Admission of intracompany transferees —

(i) General. Under section 101(a)(15)(L) of the Act, an alien who within the preceding three years has been employed abroad for one continuous year by a qualifying organization may be admitted temporarily to the United States to be employed by a parent, branch, affiliate, or subsidiary of that employer in a managerial or executive capacity, or in a position requiring specialized knowledge. An alien transferred to the United States under this nonimmigrant classification is referred to as an intracompany transferee and the organization which seeks the classification of an alien as an intracompany transferee is referred to as the petitioner. The Service has responsibility for determining whether the alien is eligible for admission and whether the petitioner is a qualifying organization. These regulations set forth the standards applicable to these classifications. They also set forth procedures for admission of intracompany transferees and appeal of adverse decisions. Certain petitioners seeking the classification of aliens as intracompany transferees may file blanket petitions with the Service. Under the blanket petition process, the Service is responsible for determining whether the petitioner and its parent, branches, affiliates, or subsidiaries specified are qualifying organizations. The Department of State or, in certain cases, the Service is responsible for determining the classification of the alien.

(ii) Definitions —

(A) Intracompany transferee means an alien who, within three years preceding the time of his or her application for admission into the United States, has been employed abroad continuously for one year by a firm or corporation or other legal entity or parent, branch, affiliate, or subsidiary thereof, and who seeks to enter the United States temporarily in order to render his or her services to a branch of the same employer or a parent, affiliate, or subsidiary thereof in a capacity that is managerial, executive, or involves specialized knowledge. Periods spent in the United

States in lawful status for a branch of the same employer or a parent, affiliate, or subsidiary thereof and brief trips to the United States for business or pleasure shall not be interruptive of the one year of continuous employment abroad but such periods shall not be counted toward fulfillment of that requirement.

(B) Managerial capacity means an assignment within an organization in which the employee primarily:

(1) Manages the organization, or a department, subdivision, function, or component of the organization;

(2) Supervises and controls the work of other supervisory, professional, or managerial employees, or manages an essential function within the organization, or a department or subdivision of the organization;

(3) Has the authority to hire and fire or recommend those as well as other personnel actions (such as promotion and leave authorization) if another employee or other employees are directly supervised; if no other employee is directly supervised, functions at a senior level within the organizational hierarchy or with respect to the function managed; and

(4) Exercises discretion over the day-to-day operations of the activity or function for which the employee has authority. A first-line supervisor is not considered to be acting in a managerial capacity merely by virtue of the supervisor's supervisory duties unless the employees supervised are professional.

(C) Executive capacity means an assignment within an organization in which the employee primarily:

(1) Directs the management of the organization or a major component or function of the organization;

(2) Establishes the goals and policies of the organization, component, or function;

(3) Exercises wide latitude in discretionary decision-making; and

(4) Receives only general supervision or direction from higher level executives, the board of directors, or stockholders of the organization.

(D) Specialized knowledge means special knowledge possessed by an individual of the petitioning organization's product, service, research, equipment, techniques, management, or other interests and its application in international markets, or an advanced level of knowledge or expertise in the organization's processes and procedures.

(E) Specialized knowledge professional means an individual who has specialized knowledge as defined in paragraph (l)(1)(ii)(D) of this section and is a member of the professions as defined in section 101(a)(32) of the Immigration and Nationality Act.

(F) New office means an organization which has been doing business in the United States through a parent, branch, affiliate, or subsidiary for less than one year.

(G) Qualifying organization means a United States or foreign firm, corporation, or other legal entity which:

(1) Meets exactly one of the qualifying relationships specified in the definitions of a parent, branch, affiliate or subsidiary specified in paragraph (l)(1)(ii) of this section;

(2) Is or will be doing business (engaging in international trade is not required) as an employer in the United States and in at least one other country directly or through a parent, branch, affiliate, or subsidiary for the duration of the alien's stay in the United States as an intracompany transferee; and

(3) Otherwise meets the requirements of section 101(a)(15)(L) of the Act.

(H) Doing business means the regular, systematic, and continuous provision of goods and/or services by a qualifying organization and does not include the mere presence of an agent or office of the qualifying organization in the United States and abroad.

(I) Parent means a firm, corporation, or other legal entity which has subsidiaries.

(J) Branch means an operating division or office of the same organization housed in a different location.

(K) Subsidiary means a firm, corporation, or other legal entity of which a parent owns, directly or indirectly, more than half of the entity and controls the entity; or owns, directly or indirectly, half of the entity and controls the entity; or owns, directly or indirectly, 50 percent of a 50-50 joint venture and has equal control and veto power over the entity; or owns, directly or indirectly, less than half of the entity, but in fact controls the entity.

(L) Affiliate means

(1) One of two subsidiaries both of which are owned and controlled by the same parent or individual, or

(2) One of two legal entities owned and controlled by the same group of individuals, each individual owning and controlling approximately the same share or proportion of each entity, or

(3) In the case of a partnership that is organized in the United States to provide accounting services along with managerial and/or consulting services and that markets its accounting services under an internationally recognized name under an agreement with a worldwide coordinating organization that is owned and controlled by the member accounting firms, a partnership (or similar organization) that is organized outside the United States to provide accounting services shall be considered to be an affiliate of the United States partnership if it markets its accounting services under the same internationally recognized name under the agreement with the worldwide coordinating organization of which the United States partnership is also a member.

(M) Director means a Service Center director with delegated authority at 8 CFR 103.1.

(2) Filing of petitions —

(i) Except as provided in paragraph (l)(2)(ii) and (l)(17) of this section, a petitioner seeking to classify an alien as an intracompany transferee must file a petition on the form prescribed by USCIS. The petitioner shall advise USCIS whether a previous petition for the same beneficiary has been filed, and certify that another petition for the same beneficiary will not be filed unless the circumstances and conditions in the initial petition have changed. Failure to make a full disclosure of previous petitions filed may result in a denial of the petition.

(ii) A United States petitioner which meets the requirements of paragraph (l)(4) of this section and seeks continuing approval of itself and its parent, branches, specified subsidiaries and affiliates as qualifying organizations and, later, classification under section 101(a)(15)(L) of the Act multiple numbers of aliens employed by itself, its parent, or those branches, subsidiaries, or affiliates may file a blanket petition on the form prescribed by USCIS. The blanket petition shall be maintained at the adjudicating office. The petitioner shall be the single representative for the qualifying organizations with which USCIS will deal regarding the blanket petition.

(3) Evidence for individual petitions. An individual petition filed on the form prescribed by USCIS shall be accompanied by:

(i) Evidence that the petitioner and the organization which employed or will employ the alien are qualifying organizations as defined in paragraph (l)(1)(ii)(G) of this section.

(ii) Evidence that the alien will be employed in an executive, managerial, or specialized knowledge capacity, including a detailed description of the services to be performed.

(iii) Evidence that the alien has at least one continuous year of full-time employment abroad with a qualifying organization within the three years preceding the filing of the petition.

(iv) Evidence that the alien's prior year of employment abroad was in a position that was managerial, executive, or involved specialized knowledge and that the alien's prior education, training, and employment qualifies him/her to perform the intended services in the United States; however, the work in the United States need not be the same work which the alien performed abroad.

(v) If the petition indicates that the beneficiary is coming to the United States as a manager or executive to open or to be employed in a new office in the United States, the petitioner shall submit evidence that:

(A) Sufficient physical premises to house the new office have been secured;

(B) The beneficiary has been employed for one continuous year in the three year period preceding the filing of the petition in an executive or managerial capacity and that the proposed employment involved executive or managerial authority over the new operation; and

(C) The intended United States operation, within one year of the approval of the petition, will support an executive or managerial position as defined in paragraphs (l)(1)(ii) (B) or (C) of this section, supported by information regarding:

(1) The proposed nature of the office describing the scope of the entity, its organizational structure, and its financial goals;

(2) The size of the United States investment and the financial ability of the foreign entity to remunerate the beneficiary and to commence doing business in the United States; and

(3) The organizational structure of the foreign entity.

(vi) If the petition indicates that the beneficiary is coming to the United States in a specialized knowledge capacity to open or to be employed in a new office, the petitioner shall submit evidence that:

(A) Sufficient physical premises to house the new office have been secured;

(B) The business entity in the United States is or will be a qualifying organization as defined in paragraph (l)(1)(ii)(G) of this section; and

(C) The petitioner has the financial ability to remunerate the beneficiary and to commence doing business in the United States.

(vii) If the beneficiary is an owner or major stockholder of the company, the petition must be accompanied by evidence that the beneficiary's services are to be used for a temporary period and evidence that the beneficiary will be transferred to an assignment abroad upon the completion of the temporary services in the United States.

(viii) Such other evidence as the director, in his or her discretion, may deem necessary.

(4) Blanket petitions —

(i) A petitioner which meets the following requirements may file a blanket petition seeking continuing approval of itself and some or all of its parent, branches, subsidiaries, and affiliates as qualifying organizations if:

(A) The petitioner and each of those entities are engaged in commercial trade or services;

(B) The petitioner has an office in the United States that has been doing business for one year or more;

(C) The petitioner has three or more domestic and foreign branches, subsidiaries, or affiliates; and

(D) The petitioner and the other qualifying organizations have obtained approval of petitions for at least ten "L" managers, executives, or specialized knowledge professionals during the previous 12 months; or have U.S. subsidiaries or affiliates with combined annual sales of at least $ 25 million; or have a United States work force of at least 1,000 employees.

(ii) Managers, executives, and specialized knowledge professionals employed by firms, corporations, or other entities which have been found to be qualifying organizations pursuant to an approved blanket petition may be classified as intracompany transferees and admitted to the United States as provided in paragraphs (l) (5) and (11) of this section.

(iii) When applying for a blanket petition, the petitioner shall include in the blanket petition all of its branches, subsidiaries, and affiliates which plan to seek to transfer aliens to the United States under the blanket petition. An individual petition may be filed by the petitioner or organizations in lieu of using the blanket petition procedure. However, the petitioner and other qualifying organizations may not seek L classification for the same alien under both procedures, unless a consular officer first denies eligibility. Whenever a petitioner which has blanket L approval files an individual petition to seek L classification for a manager, executive, or specialized knowledge professional, the petitioner shall advise the Service that it has blanket L approval and certify that the beneficiary has not and will not apply to a consular officer for L classification under the approved blanket petition.

(iv) Evidence. A blanket petition filed on the form prescribed by USCIS shall be accompanied by:

(A) Evidence that the petitioner meets the requirements of paragraph (l)(4)(i) of this section.

(B) Evidence that all entities for which approval is sought are qualifying organizations as defined in subparagraph (l)(1)(ii)(G) of this section.

(C) Such other evidence as the director, in his or her discretion, deems necessary in a particular case.

(5) Certification and admission procedures for beneficiaries under blanket petition.

(i) Jurisdiction. United States consular officers shall have authority to determine eligibility of individual beneficiaries outside the United States seeking L classification under blanket petitions, except for visa-exempt nonimmigrants. An application for a visa-exempt nonimmigrant seeking L classification under a blanket petition or by an alien in the United States applying for change of status to L classification under a blanket petition shall be filed with the Service office at which the blanket petition was filed.

(ii) Procedures.

(A) When one qualifying organization listed in an approved blanket petition wishes to transfer an alien outside the United States to a qualifying organization in the United States and the alien requires a visa to enter the United States, that organization shall complete Form I-129S, Certificate of Eligibility for Intracompany Transferee under a Blanket Petition, in an original and three copies. The qualifying organization shall retain one copy for its records and send the original and two copies to the alien. A copy of the approved Form I-797 must be attached to the original and each copy of Form I-129S.

(B) After receipt of Form I-797 and Form I-129S, a qualified employee who is being transferred to the United States may use these documents to apply for visa issuance with the consular officer within six months of the date on Form I-129S.

(C) When the alien is a visa-exempt nonimmigrant seeking L classification under a blanket petition, or when the alien is in the United States and is seeking a change of status from another nonimmigrant classification to L classification under a blanket petition, the petitioner shall submit Form I-129S, Certificate of Eligibility, and a copy of the approval notice, Form I-797, to the USCIS office with which the blanket petition was filed.

(D) The consular or Service officer shall determine whether the position in which the alien will be employed in the United States is with an organization named in the approved petition and whether the specific job is for a manager, executive, or specialized knowledge professional. The consular or Service officer shall determine further whether the alien's immediate prior year of continuous employment abroad was with an organization named in the petition and was in a position as manager, executive, or specialized knowledge professional.

(E) Consular officers may grant "L" classification only in clearly approvable applications. If the consular officer determines that the alien is eligible for L classification, the consular officer may issue a nonimmigrant visa, noting the visa classification "Blanket L-1" for the principal alien and "Blanket L-2" for any accompanying or following to join spouse and children. The consular officer shall also endorse all copies of the alien's Form I-129S with the blanket L-1 visa classification and return the original and one copy to the alien. When the alien is inspected for entry into the United States, both copies of the Form I-129S shall be stamped to show a validity period not to exceed three years and the second copy collected and sent to the appropriate Regional Service Center for control purposes. Service officers who determine eligibility of aliens for L-1 classification under blanket petitions shall endorse both copies of Form I-129S with the blanket L-1 classification and the validity period not to exceed three years and retain the second copy for Service records.

(F) If the consular officer determines that the alien is ineligible for L classification under a blanket petition, the consular officer's decision shall be final. The consular officer shall record the reasons for the denial on Form I-129S, retain one copy, return the original of I-129S to the USCIS office which approved the blanket petition, and provide a copy to the alien. In such a case, an individual petition may be filed for the alien on the form prescribed by USCIS. The petition shall state the reason the alien was denied L classification and specify the consular office which made the determination and the date of the determination.

(G) An alien admitted under an approved blanket petition may be reassigned to any organization listed in the approved petition without referral to the Service during his/her authorized stay if the alien will be performing virtually the same job duties. If the alien will be performing different job duties, the petitioner shall complete a new Certificate of Eligibility and send it for approval to the director who approved the blanket petition.

(6) Copies of supporting documents. The petitioner may submit a legible photocopy of a document in support of the visa petition, in lieu of the original document. However, the original document shall be submitted if requested by the Service.

(7) Approval of petition —

(i) General. The director shall notify the petitioner of the approval of an individual or a blanket petition within 30 days after the date a completed petition has been filed. If additional information is required from the petitioner, the 30 day processing period shall begin again upon receipt of the information. The original Form I-797 received from the USCIS with respect to an approved individual or blanket petition may be duplicated by the petitioner for the beneficiary's use as described in paragraph (l)(13) of this section.

(A) Individual petition —

(1) Form I-797 shall include the beneficiary's name and classification and the petition's period of validity.

(2) An individual petition approved under this paragraph shall be valid for the period of established need for the beneficiary's services, not to exceed three years, except where the beneficiary is coming to the United States to open or to be employed in a new office.

(3) If the beneficiary is coming to the United States to open or be employed in a new office, the petition may

be approved for a period not to exceed one year, after which the petitioner shall demonstrate as required by paragraph (l)(14)(ii) of this section that it is doing business as defined in paragraph (l) (1)(ii)(H) of this section to extend the validity of the petition.

(B) Blanket petition —

(1) Form I-797 shall identify the approved organizations included in the petition and the petition's period of validity.

(2) A blanket petition approved under this paragraph shall be valid initially for a period of three years and may be extended indefinitely thereafter if the qualifying organizations have complied with these regulations.

(3) A blanket petition may be approved in whole or in part and shall cover only qualifying organizations.

(C) Amendments. The petitioner must file an amended petition, with fee, at the USCIS office where the original petition was filed to reflect changes in approved relationships, additional qualifying organizations under a blanket petition, change in capacity of employment (i.e., from a specialized knowledge position to a managerial position), or any information which would affect the beneficiary's eligibility under section 101(a)(15)(L) of the Act.

(ii) Spouse and dependents. The spouse and unmarried minor children of the beneficiary are entitled to L nonimmigrant classification, subject to the same period of admission and limits as the beneficiary, if the spouse and unmarried minor children are accompanying or following to join the beneficiary in the United States. Neither the spouse nor any child may accept employment unless he or she has been granted employment authorization.

(8) Denial of petition —

(i) Individual petition. If an individual is denied, the petitioner shall be notified within 30 days after the date a completed petition has been filed of the denial, the reasons for the denial, and the right to appeal the denial.

(ii) Blanket petition. If a blanket petition is denied in whole or in part, the petitioner shall be notified within 30 days after the date a completed petition has been filed of the denial, the reasons for the denial, and the right to appeal the denial. If the petition is denied in part, the USCIS office issuing the denial shall forward to the petitioner, along with the denial, a Form I-797 listing those organizations which were found to quality. If the decision to deny is reversed on appeal, a new Form I-797 shall be sent to the petitioner to reflect the changes made as a result of the appeal.

(9) Revocation of approval of individual and blanket petitions —

(i) General. The director may revoke a petition at any time, even after the expiration of the petition.

(ii) Automatic revocation. The approval of any individual or blanket petition is automatically revoked if the petitioner withdraws the petition or the petitioner fails to request indefinite validity of a blanket petition.

(iii) Revocation on notice.

(A) The director shall send to the petitioner a notice of intent to revoke the petition in relevant part if he/she finds that:

(1) One or more entities are no longer qualifying organizations;

(2) The alien is no longer eligible under section 101(a)(15)(L) of the Act;

(3) A qualifying organization(s) violated requirements of section 101(a)(15)(L) and these regulations;

(4) The statement of facts contained in the petition was not true and correct; or

(5) Approval of the petition involved gross error; or

(6) None of the qualifying organizations in a blanket petition have used the blanket petition procedure for three consecutive years.

(B) The notice of intent to revoke shall contain a detailed statement of the grounds for the revocation and the time period allowed for the petitioner's rebuttal. Upon receipt of this notice, the petitioner may submit evidence in rebuttal within 30 days of the notice. The director shall consider all relevant evidence presented in deciding whether to revoke the petition in whole or in part. If a blanket petition is revoked in part, the remainder of the petition shall remain approved, and a revised Form I-797 shall be sent to the petitioner with the revocation notice.

(iv) Status of beneficiaries. If an individual petition is revoked, the beneficiary shall be required to leave the United States, unless the beneficiary has obtained other work authorization from the Service. If a blanket petition is revoked and the petitioner and beneficiaries already in the United States are otherwise eligible for L classification, the director shall extend the blanket petition for a period necessary to support the stay of those blanket L beneficiaries. The approval notice, Form I-171C, shall include only the names of qualifying organizations and covered beneficiaries. No new beneficiaries may be classified or admitted under this limited extension.

(10) Appeal of denial or revocation of individual or blanket petition —

(i) A petition denied in whole or in part may be appealed under 8 CFR part 103. Since the determination on the Certificate of Eligibility, Form I-129S, is part of the petition process, a denial or revocation of approval of an I-129S is appealable in the same manner as the petition.

(ii) A petition that has been revoked on notice in whole or in part may be appealed under part 103 of this chapter. Automatic revocations may not be appealed.

(11) Admission. A beneficiary may apply for admission to the United States only while the individual or blanket petition is valid. The beneficiary of an individual petition shall not be admitted for a date past the validity period of the petition. The beneficiary of a blanket petition may be admitted for three years even though the initial validity period of the blanket petition may expire before the end of the three-year period. If the blanket petition will expire while the alien is in the United States, the burden is on the petitioner to file for indefinite validity of the blanket petition or to file an individual petition in the alien's behalf to support the alien's status in the United States. The admission period for any alien under section 101(a)(15)(L) shall

not exceed three years unless an extension of stay is granted pursuant to paragraph (l)(15) of this section.

(12) L-1 limitation on period of stay —

(i) Limits. An alien who has spent five years in the United States in a specialized knowledge capacity or seven years in the United States in a managerial or executive capacity under section 101(a)(15) (L) and/or (H) of the Act may not be readmitted to the United States under section 101(a)(15) (L) or (H) of the Act unless the alien has resided and been physically present outside the United States, except for brief visits for business or pleasure, for the immediate prior year. Such visits do not interrupt the one year abroad, but do not count towards fulfillment of that requirement. In view of this restriction, a new individual petition may not be approved for an alien who has spent the maximum time period in the United States under section 101(a)(15) (L) and/or (H) of the Act, unless the alien has resided and been physically present outside the United States, except for brief visits for business or pleasure, for the immediate prior year. The petitioner shall provide information about the alien's employment, place of residence, and the dates and purpose of any trips to the United States for the previous year. A consular or Service officer may not grant L classification under a blanket petition to an alien who has spent five years in the United States as a professional with specialized knowledge or seven years in the United States as a manager or executive, unless the alien has met the requirements contained in this paragraph.

(ii) Exceptions. The limitations of paragraph (l)(12)(i) of this section shall not apply to aliens who do not reside continually in the United States and whose employment in the United States is seasonal, intermittent, or consists of an aggregate of six months or less per year. In addition, the limitations will not apply to aliens who reside abroad and regularly commute to the United States to engage in part-time employment. The petitioner and the alien must provide clear and convincing proof that the alien qualifies for an exception. Clear and convincing proof shall consist of evidence such as arrival and departure records, copies of tax returns, and records of employment abroad.

(13) Beneficiary's use of Form I-797 and Form I-129S —

(i) Beneficiary of an individual petition. The beneficiary of an individual petition who does not require a nonimmigrant visa may present a copy of Form I-797 at a port of entry to facilitate entry into the United States. The copy of Form I-797 shall be retained by the beneficiary and presented during the validity of the petition (provided that the beneficiary is entering or reentering the United States) for entry and reentry to resume the same employment with the same petitioner (within the validity period of the petition) and to apply for an extension of stay. A beneficiary who is required to present a visa for admission and whose visa will have expired before the date of his or her intended return may use an original Form I-797 to apply for a new or revalidated visa during the validity period of the petition and to apply for an extension of stay.

(ii) Beneficiary of a blanket petition. Each alien seeking L classification and admission under a blanket petition shall present a copy of Form I-797 and a Form I-129S from the petitioner which identifies the position and organization from which the employee is transferring, the new organization and position to which the employee is destined, a description of the employee's actual duties for both the new and former positions, and the positions, dates, and locations of previous L stays in the United States. A current copy of Form I-797 and Form I-129S should be retained by the beneficiary and used for leaving and reentering the United States to resume employment with a qualifying organization during his/her authorized period of stay, for applying for a new or revalidated visa, and for applying for readmission at a port of entry. The alien may be readmitted even though reassigned to a different organization named on the Form I-797 than the one shown on Form I-129S if the job duties are virtually the same.

(14) Extension of visa petition validity —

(i) Individual petition. The petitioner must file a petition extension on Form I–129 to extend an individual petition under section 101(a)(15)(L) of the Act. A petition extension generally may be filed only if the validity of the original petition has not expired.

(ii) New offices. A visa petition under section 101(a)(15)(L) which involved the opening of a new office may be extended by filing a new application or petition, accompanied by the following:

(A) Evidence that the United States and foreign entities are still qualifying organizations as defined in paragraph (l)(1)(ii)(G) of this section;

(B) Evidence that the United States entity has been doing business as defined in paragraph (l)(1)(ii)(H) of this section for the previous year;

(C) A statement of the duties performed by the beneficiary for the previous year and the duties the beneficiary will perform under the extended petition;

(D) A statement describing the staffing of the new operation, including the number of employees and types of positions held accompanied by evidence of wages paid to employees when the beneficiary will be employed in a managerial or executive capacity; and

(E) Evidence of the financial status of the United States operation.

(iii) Blanket petitions —

(A) Extension procedure. A blanket petition may only be extended indefinitely by filing a new Form I-129 with a copy of the previous approval notice and a report of admissions during the preceding three years. The report of admissions shall include a list of the aliens admitted under the blanket petition during the preceding three years, including positions held during that period, the employing entity, and the dates of initial admission and final departure of each alien. The petitioner shall state whether it still meets the criteria for filing a blanket petition and shall document any changes in approved relationships and additional qualifying organizations.

(B) Other conditions. If the petitioner in an approved blanket petition fails to request indefinite validity or if indefinite validity is denied, the petitioner and its other qualifying organizations shall seek L classification by filing individual petitions until another three years have expired; after which the petitioner may seek approval of a new blanket petition.

(15) Extension of stay.

(i) In individual petitions, the petitioner must apply for the petition extension and the alien's extension of stay concurrently on Form I-129. When the alien is a beneficiary under a blanket petition, a new certificate of eligibility, accompanied by a copy of the previous approved certificate of eligibility, shall be filed by the petitioner to request an extension of the alien's stay. The petitioner must also request a petition extension. The dates of extension shall be the same for the petition and the beneficiary's extension of stay. The beneficiary must be physically present in the United States at the time the extension of stay is filed. Even though the requests to extend the visa petition and the alien's stay are combined on the petition, the director shall make a separate determination on each. If the alien is required to leave the United States for business or personal reasons while the extension requests are pending, the petitioner may request the director to cable notification of approval of the petition extension to the consular office abroad where the alien will apply for a visa.

(ii) An extension of stay may be authorized in increments of up to two years for beneficiaries of individual and blanket petitions. The total period of stay may not exceed five years for aliens employed in a specialized knowledge capacity. The total period of stay for an alien employed in a managerial or executive capacity may not exceed seven years. No further extensions may be granted. When an alien was initially admitted to the United States in a specialized knowledge capacity and is later promoted to a managerial or executive position, he or she must have been employed in the managerial or executive position for at least six months to be eligible for the total period of stay of seven years. The change to managerial or executive capacity must have been approved by the Service in an amended, new, or extended petition at the time that the change occurred.

(16) Effect of filing an application for or approval of a permanent labor certification, preference petition, or filing of an application for adjustment of status on L-1 classification. An alien may legitimately come to the United States for a temporary period as an L-1 nonimmigrant and, at the same time, lawfully seek to become a permanent resident of the United States provided he or she intends to depart voluntarily at the end of his or her authorized stay. The filing of an application for or approval of a permanent labor certification, an immigrant visa preference petition, or the filing of an application of readjustment of status for an L-1 nonimmigrant shall not be the basis for denying:

(i) An L-1 petition filed on behalf of the alien,

(ii) A request to extend an L-1 petition which had previously been filed on behalf of the alien;

(iii) An application for admission as an L-1 nonimmigrant by the alien, or as an L-2 nonimmigrant by the spouse or child of such alien;

(iv) An application for change of status to H-1 or L-2 nonimmigrant filed by the alien, or to H-1, H-4, or L-1 status filed by the L-2 spouse or child of such alien;

(v) An application for change of status to H-4 nonimmigrant filed by the L-1 nonimmigrant, if his or her spouse has been approved for classification as an H-1; or

(vi) An application for extension of stay filed by the alien, or by the L-2 spouse or child of such alien.

(17) Filing of individual petitions and certifications under blanket petitions for citizens of Canada under the Agreement Between the United States of America, the United Mexican States, and Canada (USMCA).

(i) Individual petitions. Except as provided in paragraph (1)(2)(ii) of this section (filing of blanket petitions), a United States or foreign employer seeking to classify a citizen of Canada as an intracompany transferee may file an individual petition in duplicate on the form prescribed by USCIS in conjunction with an application for admission of the citizen of Canada. Such filing may be made with an immigration officer at a Class A port of entry located on the United States-Canada land border or at a United States pre-clearance/pre-flight station in Canada. The petitioning employer need not appear, but Form I-129 must bear the authorized signature of the petitioner.

(ii) Certification of eligibility for intracompany transferree under the blanket petition. An immigration officer at a location identified in paragraph (1)(17)(i) of this section may determine eligibility of individual citizens of Canada seeking L classification under approved blanket petitions. At these locations, such citizens of Canada shall present the original and two copies of Form I-129S, Intracompany Transferee Certificate of Eligibility, prepared by the approved organization, as well as three copies of Form I-797, Notice of Approval of Nonimmigrant Visa Petition.

(iii) Nothing in this section shall preclude or discourage the advance filing of petitions and certificates of eligibility in accordance with paragraph (l)(2) of this section.

(iv) Deficient or deniable petitions or certificates of eligibility. If a petition or certificate of eligibility submitted concurrently with an application for admission is lacking necessary supporting documentation or is otherwise deficient, the inspecting immigration officer shall return it to the applicant for admission in order to obtain the necessary documentation from the petitioner or for the deficiency to be overcome. The fee to file the petition will be remitted at such time as the documentary or other deficiency is overcome. If the petition or certificate of eligibility is clearly deniable, the immigration officer will accept the petition (with fee) and the petitioner shall be notified of the denial, the reasons for denial, and the right of appeal. If a formal denial order cannot be issued by the port of entry, the petition with a recommendation for denial shall be forwarded to the appropriate Service Center for final action. For the purposes of this provision, the appropriate Service Center will be the one within the same Service region as the location where the application for admission is made.

(v) Spouse and dependent minor children accompanying or following to join.

(A) The Canadian citizen spouse and Canadian citizen unmarried minor children of a Canadian citizen admitted under this paragraph shall be entitled to the same nonimmigrant classification and same length of stay subject to the same limits as the principal alien. They shall not be required to present visas, and they shall be admitted under the classification symbol L-2.

(B) A non-Canadian citizen spouse or non-Canadian citizen unmarried minor child shall be entitled to the same nonimmigrant classification and the same length of stay subject to the same limits as the principal, but shall be required to present a visa upon application for admission as an L-2 unless otherwise exempt under § 212.1 of this chapter.

(C) The spouse and dependent minor children shall not accept employment in the United States unless otherwise authorized under the Act.

(18) Denial of intracompany transferee status to citizens of Canada or Mexico in the case of certain labor disputes.

(i) If the Secretary of Labor certifies to or otherwise informs the Commissioner that a strike or other labor dispute involving a work stoppage of workers is in progress where the beneficiary is to be employed, and the temporary entry of the beneficiary may affect adversely the settlement of such labor dispute or the employment of any person who is involved in such dispute, a petition to classify a citizen of Mexico or Canada as an L-1 intracompany transferee may be denied. If a petition has already been approved, but the alien has not yet entered the United States, or has entered the United States but not yet commenced employment, the approval of the petition may be suspended, and an application for admission on the basis of the petition may be denied.

(ii) If there is a strike or other labor dispute involving a work stoppage of workers in progress, but such strike or other labor dispute is not certified under paragraph (l)(18)(i) of this section, or the Service has not otherwise been informed by the Secretary that such a strike or labor dispute is in progress, the Commissioner shall not deny a petition or suspend an approved petition.

(iii) If the alien has already commended employment in the United States under an approved petition and is participating in a strike or other labor dispute involving a work stoppage of workers, whether or not such strike or other labor dispute has been certified by the Department of Labor, the alien shall not be deemed to be failing to maintain his or her status solely on account of past, present, or future participation in a strike or other labor dispute involving a work stoppage of workers, but is subject to the following terms and conditions.

(A) The alien shall remain subject to all applicable provisions of the Immigration and Nationality Act, and regulations promulgated in the same manner as all other L nonimmigrants;

(B) The status and authorized period of stay of such an alien is not modified or extended in any way by virtue of his or her participation in a strike or other labor dispute involving work stoppage of workers; and

(C) Although participation by an L nonimmigrant alien in a strike or other labor dispute involving a work stoppage of workers will not constitute a ground for deportation, any alien who violates his or her status or who remains in the United States after his or her authorized period of stay has expired will be subject to deportation.

(m) Students in established vocational or other recognized nonacademic institutions, other than in language training programs.

Table 4 to Paragraph (m)—Paragraph Contents

(1) Admission of student.
(2) Form I-20 ID copy.
(3) Admission of the spouse and minor children of an M-1 student.
(4) Temporary absence.
(5) Period of stay.
(6)-(8) [Reserved].
(9) Full course of study.
(10) Extension of stay.
(11) School transfer.
(12) Change in educational objective.
(13) Employment.
(14) Practical training.
(15) Decision on application for extension, permission to transfer to another school, or permission to accept employment for practical training.
(16) Reinstatement to student status.
(17) Spouse and children of M-1 student.
(18) Current name and address.
(19) Special rules for certain border commuter students.
(20) Remittance of the fee.

(1) Admission of student.

(i) Eligibility for admission. A nonimmigrant student may be admitted into the United States in nonimmigrant status under section 101(a)(15)(M) of the Act, if:

(A) The student presents a Form I-20 or successor form issued in the student's own name by a school certified by SEVP for attendance by M-1 foreign students;

(B) The student has documentary evidence of financial support in the amount indicated on the Form 1-20 or successor form; and

(C) For students seeking initial admission only, the student intends to attend the school specified in the student's visa (or, where the student is exempt from the requirement for a visa, the school indicated on the Form I-20 or successor form.

(ii) [Removed and reserved.]

(iii) Use of SEVIS. Schools must issue a Form I-20 or successor form in SEVIS to any current student requiring a reportable action (e.g., extension of stay, practical training, and requests for employment authorization) or a new Form I-20 or successor form, or for any aliens who must obtain a new nonimmigrant student visa.

(2) Student maintenance of Form I-20 or successor form. An M-1 student is expected to retain for safekeeping the initial Form I-20 or successor form bearing the admission number and any subsequent Form I-20 or successor form issued to the student. Should the student lose their current Form I-20 or successor form, a replacement copy bearing the same information as the

lost copy, including any endorsement for employment and notations, should be issued by the DSO as defined in § 214.3(*l*)(1).

(3) Admission of the spouse and minor children of an M-1 student. The spouse and minor children accompanying an M-1 student are eligible for admission in M-2 status if the student is admitted in M-1 status. The spouse and minor children following-to-join an M-1 student are eligible for admission to the United States in M-2 status if they are able to demonstrate that the M-1 student has been admitted and is, or will be within 30 days, enrolled in a full course of study, or engaged in approved practical training following completion of studies. In either case, at the time they seek admission, the eligible spouse and minor children of an M-1 student must individually present a Form I-20 or successor form issued in the name of each M-2 dependent issued by a school certified by SEVP for attendance by M-1 students. A new Form I-20 or successor form is required for a dependent where there has been any substantive change in the M-1 student's current information.

(i) A properly endorsed page 4 of Form I-20M-N if there has been no substantive change in the information on the student's most recent Form I-20M since the form was initially issued; or

(ii) A new Form I-20M-N if there has been any substantive change in the information on the student's most recent Form I-20M since the form was initially issued.

(4) Temporary absence —

(i) General. An M-1 student returning to the United States from a temporary absence to attend the school which the student was previously authorized to attend must present either —

(A) A properly endorsed Form I-20 or successor form if there has been no substantive change in the information on the student's most recent Form I-20 or successor form since the form was initially issued; or

(B) A new Form I-20 or successor form if there has been any substantive change in the information on the student's most recent Form I-20 or successor form since the form was initially issued.

(ii) Student who transferred between schools. If an M-1 student has been authorized to transfer between schools and is returning to the United States from a temporary absence in order to attend the school to which transfer was authorized as indicated on the student's Form I-20 or successor form, the name of the transfer-in school does not need to be specified in the student's visa.

(5) Period of stay. A student in M nonimmigrant status is admitted for a fixed time period, which is the period necessary to complete the course of study indicated on the Form 1-20 or successor form, plus practical training following completion of the course of study, plus an additional 30 days to depart the United States, but not to exceed a total period of one year. An M-1 student may be admitted for a period up to 30 days before the report date or start date of the course of study listed on the Form 1-20 or successor form. An M-1 student who fails to maintain a full course of study or otherwise fails to maintain status is not eligible for the additional 30-day period of stay.

(6) [Reserved]

(7) [Reserved]

(8) [Reserved]

(9) Full course of study. Successful completion of the course of study must lead to the attainment of a specific educational or vocational objective. A course of study at an institution not certified for attendance by foreign students as provided in § 214.3(a)(3) does not satisfy this requirement. A "full course of study" as required by section 101(a)(15)(M)(i) of the Act means—

(i) Community college or junior college. Study at a community college or junior college, certified by a school official to consist of at least twelve semester or quarter hours of instruction per academic term in those institutions using standard semester, trimester, or quarter-hour systems, where all students enrolled for a minimum of twelve semester or quarter hours are charged full-time tuition or considered full-time for other administrative purposes, or its equivalent (as determined by SEVP in the school certification process) except when the student needs a lesser course load to complete the course of study during the current term;

(ii) Postsecondary vocational or business school. Study at a postsecondary vocational or business school, other than in a language training program except as provided in § 214.3(a)(2)(iv), which confers upon its graduates recognized associate or other degrees or has established that its credits have been and are accepted unconditionally by at least three other institutions of higher learning which are either:

(A) A school (or school system) owned and operated as a public educational institution by the United States or a State or political subdivision thereof; or

(B) A school accredited by a nationally recognized accrediting body; and which has been certified by a designated school official to consist of at least 12 clock hours of instruction a week, or its equivalent as determined by SEVP in the school certification process;

(iii) Study in a vocational or other nonacademic curriculum, other than in a language training program except as provided in § 214.3(a)(2)(iv), certified by a designated school official to consist of at least eighteen clock hours of attendance a week if the dominant part of the course of study consists of classroom instruction, or at least twenty-two clock hours a week if the dominant part of the course of study consists of shop or laboratory work; or

(iv) Study in a vocational or other nonacademic high school curriculum, certified by a designated school official to consist of class attendance for not less than the minimum number of hours a week prescribed by the school for normal progress towards graduation.

(v) On-line courses/distance education programs. No on-line or distance education classes may be considered to count toward an M-1 student's full course of study requirement if such classes do not require the student's physical attendance for classes, examination or other purposes integral to completion of the class. An on-line or distance education course is a course that is offered principally through the use of television, audio, or computer transmission including open broadcast, closed circuit, cable, microwave, or satellite, audio conferencing, or computer conferencing.

(vi) Reduced course load. The designated school official may authorize an M-1 student to engage in less than a full course of study only where the student has been compelled by illness or a medical condition that has been documented by a licensed medical doctor, a licensed doctor of osteopathy, a licensed psychologist, or a licensed clinical psychologist to interrupt or reduce their course of study. A DSO may not authorize a reduced course load for more than an aggregate of 5 months per course of study. An M-1 student previously authorized to drop below a full course of study due to illness or medical condition for an aggregate of 5 months, may not be authorized by the DSO to reduce their course load on subsequent occasions during their particular course of study.

(A) [Reserved]

(B) Reporting requirements. In order for a student to be authorized to drop below a full course of study, the DSO must update SEVIS prior to the student reducing their load.

(10) Extension of stay.

(i) Eligibility. The cumulative time of extensions that can be granted to an M-1 student is limited to a period of 3 years from the M-1 student's original start date, plus 30 days. No extension can be granted to an M-1 student if the M-1 student is unable to complete the course of study within 3 years of the original program start date. This limit includes extensions that have been granted due to a drop below full course of study, a transfer of schools, or reinstatement. An M-1 student may be granted an extension of stay if it is established that:

(A) He or she is a bona fide nonimmigrant currently maintaining student status;

(B) Compelling educational or medical reasons have resulted in a delay to his or her course of study. Delays caused by academic probation or suspension are not acceptable reasons for program extension; and

(C) He or she is able to, and in good faith intends to, continue to maintain that status for the period for which the extension is granted.

(ii) Application. A student must apply to USCIS for an extension on Form I-539, Application to Extend/Change Nonimmigrant Status or successor form. A student's M-2 spouse and children seeking an extension of stay must be included in the application. The student must submit the application at least 15 days but not more than 60 days before the program end date on the student's Form I-20 or successor form. The application must also be accompanied by the student's Form I-20 or successor form and the Form I-94 of the student's spouse and children, if applicable.

(iii) Period of stay. If an application for extension is granted, the student and the student's spouse and children, if applicable, are to be given an extension of stay for the period of time necessary to complete the course of study, plus 30 days within which to depart from the United States, or for a total period of one year, whichever is less. A student's M-2 spouse and children are not eligible for an extension unless the M-1 student is granted an extension of stay, or for a longer period than is granted to the M-1 student.

(iv) SEVIS update. The Form I-20 or successor form must be endorsed with the recommendation and new program end date for submission to USCIS, with Form I-539 or successor form, and Form I-94 if applicable.

(11) School transfer —

(i) Eligibility. An M-1 student may not transfer to another school after six months from the date the student is first admitted as, or changes nonimmigrant classification to that of, an M-1 student unless the student is unable to remain at the school to which the student was initially admitted due to circumstances beyond the student's control. An M-1 student may be otherwise eligible to transfer to another school if the student —

(A) Is a bona fide nonimmigrant;

(B) Has been pursuing a full course of study at the school the student was last authorized to attend;

(C) Intends to pursue a full course of study at the school to which the student intends to transfer; and

(D) Is financially able to attend the school to which the student intends to transfer.

(ii) Transfer procedure. A student must apply to USCIS on Form I-539 or successor form, for permission to transfer between schools. Upon application for school transfer, a student may affect the transfer subject to approval of the application. A student who transfers without complying with this requirement or whose application is denied after transfer (pursuant to this section) is considered to be out of status. If the application is approved, the approval date of the transfer will be determined to be the program start date listed on the Form I-20 or successor form, and the student will be granted an extension of stay for the period of time necessary to complete the new course of study plus 30 days, or for a total period of one year, whichever is less. The student must first notify their current school (the "transfer-out" school) of the intent to transfer and indicate the school to which the student intends to transfer (the "transfer-in" school). Upon notification by the student, the transfer-out school must update SEVIS to show the student is transferring out, indicate the transfer-in school, and input the transfer release date. Once SEVIS is updated, the transfer-in school may generate a Form I-20 or successor form for transfer. However, the transfer-in school will not gain access to the student's SEVIS record until the release date. Upon receipt of the Form I-20 or successor form from the transfer-in school, the student must submit Form I-539 or successor form in accordance with this paragraph (m)(11). The student may enroll in the transfer-in school at the next available term or session and is required to notify the DSO of the transfer-in school immediately upon beginning attendance. The transfer-in school must update the student's registration record in SEVIS in accordance with § 214.3(g)(2)(iii). Upon approval of the transfer application, USCIS will transmit the approval of the transfer to SEVIS. If the application for transfer is denied, the student is out of status, and the student's record must be terminated in SEVIS.

(iii) Student who has not been pursuing a full course of study. If an M-1 student who has not been pursuing a full course of study at the school the student was last authorized to attend desires to attend a different school, the student must apply for reinstatement to student status under paragraph (m)(16) of this section.

(12) Change in educational objective. An M-1 student may not change educational objective.

(13) Employment. Except as provided in paragraph (m)(14) of this section, a student may not accept employment.

(14) Practical training —

(i) When practical training may be authorized. Temporary employment for practical training may be authorized only after completion of the student's course of study.

(A) The proposed employment is recommended for the purpose of practical training;

(B) The proposed employment is related to the student's course of study; and

(C) Upon the designated school official's information and belief, employment comparable to the proposed employment is not available to the student in the country of the student's foreign residence.

(ii) Application. An M-1 student must apply for permission to accept employment for practical training on Form I-765, with fee as contained in 8 CFR part 106, accompanied by a properly endorsed Form I-20 by the designated school official for practical training. The application must be submitted before the program end date listed on the student's Form I-20 but not more than 90 days before the program end date. The designated school official must certify on Form I-538 that:

(A) The proposed employment is recommended for the purpose of practical training;

(B) The proposed employment is related to the student's course of study; and

(C) Upon the designated school official's information and belief, employment comparable to the proposed employment is not available to the student in the country of the student's foreign residence.

(iii) Duration of practical training. When the student is authorized to engage in employment for practical training, they will be issued an EAD. The M-1 student may not begin employment until he or she has been issued an EAD by USCIS. One month of employment authorization will be granted for each four months of full-time study that the M-1 student has completed. However, an M-1 student may not engage in more than six months of practical training in the aggregate. The student will not be granted employment authorization if he or she cannot complete the requested practical training within six months.

(iv) Temporary absence of M-1 student granted practical training. An M-1 student who has been granted permission to accept employment for practical training and who temporarily departs from the United States, may be readmitted for the remainder of the authorized period indicated on the student's Form I-20 or successor form. The student must be returning to the United States to perform the authorized practical training. A student may not be readmitted to begin practical training which was not authorized prior to the student's departure from the United States.

(v) Effect of strike or other labor dispute. Authorization for all employment for practical training is automatically suspended upon certification by the Secretary of Labor or the Secretary's designee to the Secretary of Homeland Security or the Secretary's designee that a strike or other labor dispute involving a work stoppage of workers is in progress in the occupation at the place of employment. As used in this paragraph (m)(14)(v), "place of employment" means wherever the employer or joint employer does business.

(vi) SEVIS process. The DSO must update the student's record in SEVIS to recommend that USCIS approve the student for practical training, and generate a SEVIS Form I-20 with the recommendation, for the student to submit to USCIS with Form I-765 as provided in this paragraph (m)(14).

(15) Decision on application for extension, permission to transfer to another school, or permission to accept employment for practical training. USCIS will notify the applicant of the decision and, if the application is denied, of the reason(s) for the denial. The applicant may not appeal the decision.

(16) Reinstatement to student status.

(i) General. USCIS may consider reinstating a student who makes a request for reinstatement on Form I-539, Application to Extend/Change Nonimmigrant Status or successor form, accompanied by a properly completed Form I-20 or successor form indicating the DSO's recommendation for reinstatement. USCIS may consider granting the request only if the student:

(A) Has not been out of status for more than 5 months at the time of filing the request for reinstatement (or demonstrates that the failure to file within the 5 month period was the result of exceptional circumstances and that the student filed the request for reinstatement as promptly as possible under these exceptional circumstances);

(B) Does not have a record of repeated or willful violations of DHS regulations;

(C) Is currently pursuing, or intends to pursue, a full course of study at the school which issued the Form I-20 or successor form;

(D) Has not engaged in unlawful employment;

(E) Is not deportable on any ground other than section 237(a)(1)(B) or (C)(i) of the Act; and

(F) Establishes to the satisfaction of USCIS, by a detailed showing, either that:

(1) The violation of status resulted from circumstances beyond the student's control. Such circumstances might include serious injury or illness, closure of the institution, a natural disaster, or inadvertence, oversight or neglect on the part of the DSO, but do not include instances where a pattern of repeated violations or where a willful failure on the part of the student resulted in the need for reinstatement; or

(2) The violation relates to a reduction in the student's course load that would have been within a DSO's power to authorize, and that failure to approve rein-

statement would result in extreme hardship to the student.

(ii) Decision. The adjudicating officer will update SEVIS to reflect USCIS's decision. If USCIS does not reinstate the student, the student may not appeal the decision.

(17) Spouse and children of M-1 student. The M-2 spouse and minor children of an M-1 student will each be issued an individual Form I-20 or successor form in accordance with the provisions of § 214.3(k).

(i) Employment. The M-2 spouse and children may not accept employment.

(ii) Study —

(A) M-2 post-secondary/vocational study—

(1) Authorized study at SEVP-certified schools. An M-2 spouse or M-2 child may enroll in less than a full course of study, as defined in paragraphs (f)(6)(i)(A) through (D) or (m)(9)(i) through (v), in any course of study described in paragraphs (f)(6)(i)(A) through (D) or (m)(9)(i) through (v) of this section at an SEVP-certified school. Notwithstanding paragraphs (f)(6)(i)(B) and (m)(9)(i) of this section, study at an undergraduate college or university or at a community college or junior college is not a full course of study solely because the M-2 nonimmigrant is engaging in a lesser course load to complete a course of study during the current term. An M-2 spouse or M-2 child enrolled in less than a full course of study is not eligible to engage in employment pursuant to paragraph (m)(14) of this section or pursuant to paragraphs (f)(9) through (10) of this section.

(2) Full course of study. Subject to paragraph (m)(17)(ii)(B) of this section, an M-2 spouse and child may engage in a full course of study only by applying for and obtaining a change of status to F-1, M-1, or J-1 status, as appropriate, before beginning a full course of study. An M-2 spouse and M-2 child may engage in study that is avocational or recreational in nature, up to and including on a full-time basis.

(B) M-2 elementary or secondary study. An M-2 child may engage in full-time study, including any full course of study, in any elementary or secondary school (kindergarten through twelfth grade).

(C) An M-2 spouse or child violates his or her nonimmigrant status by enrolling in any study except as provided in paragraph (m)(17)(ii)(A) or (B) of this section.

(18) Current name and address. A student must inform DHS and the DSO of any legal changes to the student's name or of any change of address, within 10 days of the change, in a manner prescribed by the school. A student can satisfy the requirement in 8 CFR 265.1 of notifying DHS by providing a notice of a change of address within 10 days to the DSO, and the DSO in turn must enter the information in SEVIS within 21 days of notification by the student. Except in the case of a student who cannot receive mail where the student resides, the address provided by the student must be the actual physical location where the student resides rather than a mailing address. In cases where a student provides a mailing address, the school must maintain a record of, and must provide upon request from DHS, the actual physical location where the student resides.

(19) Special rules for certain border commuter students.

(i) Applicability. For purposes of the special rules in this paragraph (m)(19), the term "border commuter student" means a national of Canada or Mexico who is admitted to the United States as an M-1 student to enroll in a full course of study, albeit on a part-time basis, in a certified school located within 75 miles of a United States land border. The border commuter student must maintain actual residence and place of abode in the student's country of nationality, and seek admission to the United States at a land border port-of-entry. These special rules do not apply to a national of Canada or Mexico who is:

(A) Residing in the United States while attending a certified school as an M-1 student; or

(B) Enrolled in a full course of study as defined in paragraph (m)(9) of this section.

(ii) Full course of study. A designated school official at the school may authorize an eligible border commuter student to enroll in a course load below that otherwise required for a full course of study under paragraph (m)(9) of this section, provided that the reduced course load is consistent with the border commuter student's certified course of study.

(iii) Period of stay. An M-1 border commuter student is not entitled to an additional 30-day period of stay otherwise available under paragraph (m)(5) of this section.

(iv) Employment. A border commuter student may not be authorized to accept any employment in connection with his or her M-1 student status, except for practical training as provided in paragraph (m)(14) of this section.

(20) Remittance of the fee. An alien who applies for M-1 or M-3 nonimmigrant status in order to enroll in a program of study at an SEVP-certified vocational educational institution is required to pay the SEVIS fee to DHS, pursuant to § 214.13, except as otherwise provided in that section.

(n) Certain parents and children of section 101(a)(27)(I) special immigrants —

(1) Parent of special immigrant. Upon application, a parent of a child accorded special immigrant status under section 101(a)(27)(I)(i) of the Act may be granted status under section 101(a)(15)(N)(i) of the Act as long as the permanent resident child through whom eligibility is derived remains a child as defined in section 101(b)(1) of the Act.

(2) Child of section 101(a)(27)(I) special immigrants and section 101(a)(15)(N)(i) nonimmigrants. Children of parents granted nonimmigrant status under section 101(a)(15)(N)(i) of the Act, or of parents who have been granted special immigrant status under section 101(a)(27)(I) (ii), (iii) or (iv) of the Act may be granted status under section 101(a)(15)(N)(ii) of the Act for such time as each remains a child as defined in section 101(b)(1) of the Act.

(3) Admission and extension of stay. A nonimmigrant granted (N) status shall be admitted for not to exceed three years with extensions in increments up to but not to exceed three years. Status as an (N) nonimmigrant

shall terminate on the date the child described in paragraph (n)(1) or (n)(2) of this section no longer qualifies as a child as defined in section 101(b)(1) of the Act.

(4) Employment. A nonimmigrant admitted in or granted (N) status is authorized employment incident to (N) status without restrictions as to location or type of employment.

(o) Aliens of extraordinary ability or achievement —

(1) Classifications —

(i) General. Under section 101(a)(15)(O) of the Act, a qualified alien may be authorized to come to the United States to perform services relating to an event or events if petitioned for by an employer. Under this nonimmigrant category, the alien may be classified under section 101(a)(15)(O)(i) of the Act as an alien who has extraordinary ability in the sciences, arts, education, business, or athletics, or who has a demonstrated record of extraordinary achievement in the motion picture or television industry. Under section 101(a)(15)(O)(ii) of the Act, an alien having a residence in a foreign country which he or she has no intention of abandoning may be classified as an accompanying alien who is coming to assist in the artistic or athletic performance of an alien admitted under section 101(a)(15)(O)(i) of the Act. The spouse or child of an alien described in section 101(a)(15)(O)(i) or (ii) of the Act who is accompanying or following to join the alien is entitled to classification pursuant to section 101(a)(15)(O)(iii) of the Act. These classifications are called the O-1, O-2, and O-3 categories, respectively. The petitioner must file a petition with the Service for a determination of the alien's eligibility for O-1 or O-2 classification before the alien may apply for a visa or seek admission to the United States. This paragraph sets forth the standards and procedures applicable to these classifications.

(ii) Description of classifications —

(A) An O-1 classification applies to:

(1) An individual alien who has extraordinary ability in the sciences, arts, education, business, or athletics which has been demonstrated by sustained national or international acclaim and who is coming temporarily to the United States to continue work in the area of extraordinary ability; or

(2) An alien who has a demonstrated record of extraordinary achievement in motion picture and/or television productions and who is coming temporarily to the United States to continue work in the area of extraordinary achievement.

(B) An O-2 classification applies to an accompanying alien who is coming temporarily to the United States solely to assist in the artistic or athletic performance by an O-1. The O-2 alien must:

(1) Be an integral part of the actual performances or events and posses critical skills and experience with the O-1 alien that are not of a general nature and which are not possessed by others; or

(2) In the case of a motion picture or television production, have skills and experience with the O-1 alien which are not of a general nature and which are critical, either based on a pre-existing and longstanding working relationship or, if in connection with a specific production only, because significant production (including pre- and post-production) will take place both inside and outside the United States and the continuing participation of the alien is essential to the successful completion of the production.

(2) Filing of petitions —

(i) General. Except as provided for in paragraph (o)(2)(iv)(A) of this section, a petitioner seeking to classify an alien as an O-1 or O-2 nonimmigrant shall file a petition on the form prescribed by USCIS. The petition may not be filed more than one year before the actual need for the alien's services. An O-1 or O-2 petition shall be adjudicated at the appropriate Service Center, even in emergency situations. Only one beneficiary may be included on an O-1 petition. O-2 aliens must be filed for on a separate petition from the O-1 alien. An O-1 or O-2 petition may only be filed by a United States employer, a United States agent, or a foreign employer through a United States agent. For purposes of paragraph (o) of this section, a foreign employer is any employer who is not amenable to service of process in the United States. A foreign employer may not directly petition for an O nonimmigrant alien but instead must use the services of a United States agent to file a petition for an O nonimmigrant alien. A United States agent petitioning on behalf of a foreign employer must be authorized to file the petition, and to accept services of process in the United States in proceedings under section 274A of the Act, on behalf of the foreign employer. An O alien may not petition for himself or herself.

(ii) Evidence required to accompany a petition. Petitions for O aliens shall be accompanied by the following:

(A) The evidence specified in the particular section for the classification;

(B) Copies of any written contracts between the petitioner and the alien beneficiary or, if there is no written contract, a summary of the terms of the oral agreement under which the alien will be employed;

(C) An explanation of the nature of the events or activities, the beginning and ending dates for the events or activities, and a copy of any itinerary for the events or activities; and

(D) A written advisory opinion(s) from the appropriate consulting entity or entities.

(iii) Form of documentation. The evidence submitted with an O petition shall conform to the following:

(A) Affidavits, contracts, awards, and similar documentation must reflect the nature of the alien's achievement and be executed by an officer or responsible person employed by the institution, firm, establishment, or organization where the work was performed.

(B) Affidavits written by present or former employers or recognized experts certifying to the recognition and extraordinary ability, or in the case of a motion picture or television production, the extraordinary achievement of the alien, shall specifically describe the alien's recognition and ability or achievement in factual terms and set forth the expertise of the affiant and the manner in which the affiant acquired such information.

(C) A legible photocopy of a document in support of the petition may be submitted in lieu of the original. However, the original document shall be submitted if requested by the Director.

(iv) Other filing situations —

(A) Services in more than one location. A petition which requires the alien to work in more than one location must include an itinerary with the dates and locations of work.

(B) Services for more than one employer. If the beneficiary will work concurrently for more than one employer within the same time period, each employer must file a separate petition, unless an established agent files the petition.

(C) Change of employer. If an O-1 or O-2 alien in the United States seeks to change employers, the new employer must file a petition and a request to extend the alien's stay. An O-2 alien may change employers only in conjunction with a change of employers by the principal O-1 alien. If the O-1 or O-2 petition was filed by an agent, an amended petition must be filed with evidence relating to the new employer and a request for an extension of stay.

(D) Amended petition. The petitioner shall file an amended petition on the form prescribed by USCIS, with fee, to reflect any material changes in the terms and conditions of employment or the beneficiary's eligibility as specified in the original approved petition. In the case of a petition filed for an artist or entertainer, a petitioner may add additional performances or engagements during the validity period of the petition without filing an amended petition, provided the additional performances or engagements require an alien of O-1 caliber.

(E) Agents as petitioners. A United States agent may file a petition in cases involving workers who are traditionally self-employed or workers who use agents to arrange short-term employment on their behalf with numerous employers, and in cases where a foreign employer authorizes the agent to act in its behalf. A United States agent may be: The actual employer of the beneficiary, the representative of both the employer and the beneficiary; or, a person or entity authorized by the employer to act for, or in place of, the employer as its agent. A petition filed by an agent is subject to the following conditions:

(1) An agent performing the function of an employer must provide the contractual agreement between the agent and the beneficiary which specifies the wage offered and the other terms and conditions of employment of the beneficiary.

(2) A person or company in business as an agent may file the petition involving multiple employers as the representative of both the employers and the beneficiary, if the supporting documentation includes a complete itinerary of the event or events. The itinerary must specify the dates of each service or engagement, the names and addresses of the actual employers, and the names and addresses of the establishments, venues, or locations where the services will be performed. A contract between the employers and the beneficiary is required. The burden is on the agent to explain the terms and conditions of the employment and to provide any required documentation.

(3) A foreign employer who, through a United States agent, files a petition for an O nonimmigrant alien is responsible for complying with all of the employer sanctions provisions of section 274A of the Act and 8 CFR part 274a.

(F) Multiple beneficiaries. More than one O-2 accompanying alien may be included on a petition if they are assisting the same O-1 alien for the same events or performances, during the same period, and in the same location. Up to 25 named beneficiaries may be included per petition.

(G) Traded professional O-1 athletes. In the case of a professional O-1 athlete who is traded from one organization to another organization, employment authorization for the player will automatically continue for a period of 30 days after acquisition by the new organization, within which time the new organization is expected to file a new application or petition. If a new application or petition is not filed within 30 days, employment authorization will cease. If a new application or petition is filed within 30 days, the professional athlete shall be deemed to be in valid O-1 status, and employment shall continue to be authorized, until the petition is adjudicated. If the new petition is denied, employment authorization will cease.

(3) Petition for alien of extraordinary ability or achievement (O-1) —

(i) General. Extraordinary ability in the sciences, arts, education, business, or athletics, or extraordinary achievement in the case of an alien in the motion picture or television industry, must be established for an individual alien. An O-1 petition must be accompanied by evidence that the work which the alien is coming to the United States to continue is in the area of extraordinary ability, and that the alien meets the criteria in paragraph (o)(3)(iii) or (iv) of this section.

(ii) Definitions. As used in this paragraph, the term:

Arts includes any field of creative activity or endeavor such as, but not limited to, fine arts, visual arts, culinary arts, and performing arts. Aliens engaged in the field of arts include not only the principal creators and performers but other essential persons such as, but not limited to, directors, set designers, lighting designers, sound designers, choreographers, choreologists, conductors, orchestrators, coaches, arrangers, musical supervisors, costume designers, makeup artists, flight masters, stage technicians, and animal trainers.

Event means an activity such as, but not limited to, a scientific project, conference, convention, lecture series, tour, exhibit, business project, academic year, or engagement. Such activity may include short vacations, promotional appearances, and stopovers which are incidental and/or related to the event. A group of related activities may also be considered to be an event. In the case of an O-1 athlete, the event could be the alien's contract.

Extraordinary ability in the field of arts means distinction. Distinction means a high level of achievement in the field of arts evidenced by a degree of skill and recognition substantially above that ordinarily encountered to the extent that a person described as prominent is renowned, leading, or well-known in the field of arts.

Extraordinary ability in the field of science, education, business, or athletics means a level of expertise indicating that the person is one of the small percentage who have arisen to the very top of the field of endeavor.

Extraordinary achievement with respect to motion picture and television productions, as commonly defined in the industry, means a very high level of accomplishment in the motion picture or television industry evidenced by a degree of skill and recognition significantly above that ordinarily encountered to the extent that the person is recognized as outstanding, notable, or leading in the motion picture or television field.

Peer group means a group or organization which is comprised of practitioners of the alien's occupation. If there is a collective bargaining representative of an employer's employees in the occupational classification for which the alien is being sought, such a representative may be considered the appropriate peer group for purposes of consultation.

(iii) *Evidentiary criteria for an O-1 alien of extraordinary ability in the fields of science, education, business, or athletics.* An alien of extraordinary ability in the fields of science, education, business, or athletics must demonstrate sustained national or international acclaim and recognition for achievements in the field of expertise by providing evidence of:

(A) Receipt of a major, internationally recognized award, such as the Nobel Prize; or

(B) At least three of the following forms of documentation:

(*1*) Documentation of the alien's receipt of nationally or internationally recognized prizes or awards for excellence in the field of endeavor;

(*2*) Documentation of the alien's membership in associations in the field for which classification is sought, which require outstanding achievements of their members, as judged by recognized national or international experts in their disciplines or fields;

(*3*) Published material in professional or major trade publications or major media about the alien, relating to the alien's work in the field for which classification is sought, which shall include the title, date, and author of such published material, and any necessary translation;

(*4*) Evidence of the alien's participation on a panel, or individually, as a judge of the work of others in the same or in an allied field of specialization to that for which classification is sought;

(*5*) Evidence of the alien's original scientific, scholarly, or business-related contributions of major significance in the field;

(*6*) Evidence of the alien's authorship of scholarly articles in the field, in professional journals, or other major media;

(*7*) Evidence that the alien has been employed in a critical or essential capacity for organizations and establishments that have a distinguished reputation;

(*8*) Evidence that the alien has either commanded a high salary or will command a high salary or other remuneration for services, evidenced by contracts or other reliable evidence.

(C) If the criteria in paragraph (o)(3)(iii) of this section do not readily apply to the beneficiary's occupation, the petitioner may submit comparable evidence in order to establish the beneficiary's eligibility.

(iv) *Evidentiary criteria for an O-1 alien of extraordinary ability in the arts.* To qualify as an alien of extraordinary ability in the field of arts, the alien must be recognized as being prominent in his or her field of endeavor as demonstrated by the following:

(A) Evidence that the alien has been nominated for, or has been the recipient of, significant national or international awards or prizes in the particular field such as an Academy Award, an Emmy, a Grammy, or a Director's Guild Award; or

(B) At least three of the following forms of documentation:

(*1*) Evidence that the alien has performed, and will perform, services as a lead or starring participant in productions or events which have a distinguished reputation as evidenced by critical reviews, advertisements, publicity releases, publications contracts, or endorsements;

(*2*) Evidence that the alien has achieved national or international recognition for achievements evidenced by critical reviews or other published materials by or about the individual in major newspapers, trade journals, magazines, or other publications;

(*3*) Evidence that the alien has performed, and will perform, in a lead, starring, or critical role for organizations and establishments that have a distinguished reputation evidenced by articles in newspapers, trade journals, publications, or testimonials;

(*4*) Evidence that the alien has a record of major commercial or critically acclaimed successes as evidenced by such indicators as title, rating, standing in the field, box office receipts, motion pictures or television ratings, and other occupational achievements reported in trade journals, major newspapers, or other publications;

(*5*) Evidence that the alien has received significant recognition for achievements from organizations, critics, government agencies, or other recognized experts in the field in which the alien is engaged. Such testimonials must be in a form which clearly indicates the author's authority, expertise, and knowledge of the alien's achievements; or

(*6*) Evidence that the alien has either commanded a high salary or will command a high salary or other substantial remuneration for services in relation to others in the field, as evidenced by contracts or other reliable evidence; or

(C) If the criteria in paragraph (o)(3)(iv) of this section do not readily apply to the beneficiary's occupation, the petitioner may submit comparable evidence in order to establish the beneficiary's eligibility.

(v) *Evidentiary criteria for an alien of extraordinary achievement in the motion picture or television industry.* To qualify as an alien of extraordinary achievement in the motion picture or television industry, the alien must be recognized as having a demonstrated record of extraordinary achievement as evidenced by the following:

(A) Evidence that the alien has been nominated for, or has been the recipient of, significant national or international awards or prizes in the particular field such as an Academy Award, an Emmy, a Grammy, or a Director's Guild Award; or

(B) At least three of the following forms of documentation:

(1) Evidence that the alien has performed, and will perform, services as a lead or starring participant in productions or events which have a distinguished reputation as evidenced by critical reviews, advertisements, publicity releases, publications contracts, or endorsements;

(2) Evidence that the alien has achieved national or international recognition for achievements evidenced by critical reviews or other published materials by or about the individual in major newspapers, trade journals, magazines, or other publications;

(3) Evidence that the alien has performed, and will perform, in a lead, starring, or critical role for organizations and establishments that have a distinguished reputation evidenced by articles in newspapers, trade journals, publications, or testimonials;

(4) Evidence that the alien has a record of major commercial or critically acclaimed successes as evidenced by such indicators as title, rating, standing in the field, box office receipts, motion picture or television ratings, and other occupational achievements reported in trade journals, major newspapers, or other publications;

(5) Evidence that the alien has received significant recognition for achievements from organizations, critics, government agencies, or other recognized experts in the field in which the alien is engaged. Such testimonials must be in a form which clearly indicates the author's authority, expertise, and knowledge of the alien's achievements; or

(6) Evidence that the alien has either commanded a high salary or will command a high salary or other substantial remuneration for services in relation to other in the field, as evidenced by contracts or other reliable evidence.

(4) Petition for an O-2 accompanying alien —

(i) General. An O-2 accompanying alien provides essential support to an O-1 artist or athlete. Such aliens may not accompany O-1 aliens in the fields of science, business, or education. Although the O-2 alien must obtain his or her own classification, this classification does not entitle him or her to work separate and apart from the O-1 alien to whom he or she provides support. An O-2 alien must be petitioned for in conjunction with the services of the O-1 alien.

(ii) Evidentiary criteria for qualifying as an O-2 accompanying alien —

(A) Alien accompanying an O-1 artist or athlete of extraordinary ability. To qualify as an O-2 accompanying alien, the alien must be coming to the United States to assist in the performance of the O-1 alien, be an integral part of the actual performance, and have critical skills and experience with the O-1 alien which are not of a general nature and which are not possessed by a U.S. worker.

(B) Alien accompanying an O-1 alien of extraordinary achievement. To qualify as an O-2 alien accompanying and O-1 alien involved in a motion picture or television production, the alien must have skills and experience with the O-1 alien which are not of a general nature and which are critical based on a pre-existing longstanding working relationship or, with respect to the specific production, because significant production (including pre- and post-production work) will take place both inside and outside the United States and the continuing participation of the alien is essential to the successful completion of the production.

(C) The evidence shall establish the current essentiality, critical skills, and experience of the O-2 alien with the O-1 alien and that the alien has substantial experience performing the critical skills and essential support services for the O-1 alien. In the case of a specific motion picture or television production, the evidence shall establish that significant production has taken place outside the United States, and will take place inside the United States, and that the continuing participation of the alien is essential to the successful completion of the production.

(5) Consultation —

(i) General.

(A) Consultation with an appropriate U.S. peer group (which could include a person or persons with expertise in the field), labor and/or management organization regarding the nature of the work to be done and the alien's qualifications is mandatory before a petition for an O-1 or O-2 classification can be approved.

(B) Except as provided in paragraph (o)(5)(i)(E) of this section, evidence of consultation shall be in the form of a written advisory opinion from a peer group (which could include a person or persons with expertise in the field), labor and/or management organization with expertise in the specific field involved.

(C) Except as provided in paragraph (o)(5)(i)(E) of this section, the petitioner shall obtain a written advisory opinion from a peer group (which could include a person or persons with expertise in the field), labor, and/or management organization with expertise in the specific field involved. The advisory opinion shall be submitted along with the petition when the petition is filed. If the advisory opinion is not favorable to the petitioner, the advisory opinion must set forth a specific statement of facts which supports the conclusion reached in the opinion. Advisory opinions must be submitted in writing and must be signed by an authorized official of the group or organization.

(D) Except as provided in paragraph (o)(5)(i)(E) and (G) of this section, written evidence of consultation shall be included in the record in every approved O petition. Consultations are advisory and are not binding on the Service.

(E) In a case where the alien will be employed in the field of arts, entertainment, or athletics, and the Service has determined that a petition merits expeditious handling, the Service shall contact the appropriate labor and/or management organization and request an advisory opinion if one is not submitted by the petitioner. The labor and/or management organization shall have 24 hours to respond to the Service's request. The Service shall adjudicate the petition after receipt of the response from the consulting organization. The labor and/or management organization shall then furnish the Service with a written advisory opinion within 5 days of the initiating request. If the labor and/or management organization fails to respond within 24 hours, the Service shall render a decision on the petition without the advisory opinion.

(F) In a routine processing case where the petition is accompanied by a written opinion from a peer group, but the peer group is not a labor organization, the Director will forward a copy of the petition and all supporting documentation to the national office of the appropriate labor organization within 5 days of receipt of the petition. If there is a collective bargaining representative of an employer's employees in the occupational classification for which the alien is being sought, that representative shall be the appropriate labor organization for purposes of this section. The labor organization will then have 15 days from receipt of the petition and supporting documents to submit to the Service a written advisory opinion, comment, or letter of no objection. Once the 15-day period has expired, the Director shall adjudicate the petition in no more than 14 days. The Director may shorten this time in his or her discretion for emergency reasons, if no unreasonable burden would be imposed on any participant in the process. If the labor organization does not respond within 15 days, the Director will render a decision on the record without the advisory opinion.

(G) In those cases where it is established by the petitioner that an appropriate peer group, including a labor organization, does not exist, the Service shall render a decision on the evidence of record.

(ii) Consultation requirements for an O-1 alien for extraordinary ability —

(A) Content. Consultation with a peer group in the area of the alien's ability (which may include a labor organization), or a person or persons with expertise in the area of the alien's ability, is required in an O-1 petition for an alien of extraordinary ability. If the advisory opinion is not favorable to the petitioner, the advisory opinion must set forth a specific statement of facts which supports the conclusion reached in the opinion. If the advisory opinion is favorable to the petitioner, it should describe the alien's ability and achievements in the field of endeavor, describe the nature of the duties to be performed, and state whether the position requires the services of an alien of extraordinary ability. A consulting organization may also submit a letter of no objection in lieu of the above if it has no objection to the approval of the petition.

(B) Waiver of consultation of certain aliens of extraordinary ability in the field of arts. Consultation for an alien of extraordinary ability in the field of arts shall be waived by the Director in those instances where the alien seeks readmission to the United States to perform similar services within 2 years of the date of a previous consultation. The director shall, within 5 days of granting the waiver, forward a copy of the petition and supporting documentation to the national office of an appropriate labor organization. Petitioners desiring to avail themselves of the waiver should submit a copy of the prior consultation with the petition and advise the Director of the waiver request.

(iii) Consultation requirements for an O-1 alien of extraordinary achievement. In the case of an alien of extraordinary achievement who will be working on a motion picture or television production, consultation shall be made with the appropriate union representing the alien's occupational peers and a management organization in the area of the alien's ability. If an advisory opinion is not favorable to the petitioner, the advisory opinion must set forth a specific statement of facts which supports the conclusion reached in the opinion. If the advisory opinion is favorable to the petitioner, the written advisory opinion from the labor and management organizations should describe the alien's achievements in the motion picture or television field and state whether the position requires the services of an alien of extraordinary achievement. If a consulting organization has no objection to the approval of the petition, the organization may submit a letter of no objection in lieu of the above.

(iv) Consultation requirements for an O-2 accompanying alien. Consultation with a labor organization with expertise in the skill area involved is required for an O-2 alien accompanying an O-1 alien of extraordinary ability. In the case of an O-2 alien seeking entry for a motion picture or television production, consultation with a labor organization and a management organization in the area of the alien's ability is required. If an advisory opinion is not favorable to the petitioner, the advisory opinion must set forth a specific statement of facts which supports the conclusion reached in the opinion. If the advisory opinion is favorable to the petitioner, the opinion provided by the labor and/or management organization should describe the alien's essentiality to, and working relationship with, the O-1 artist or athlete and state whether there are available U.S. workers who can perform the support services. If the alien will accompany an O-1 alien involved in a motion picture or television production, the advisory opinion should address the alien's skills and experience wit the O-1 alien and whether the alien has a pre-existing longstanding working relationship with the O-1 alien, or whether significant production will take place in the United States and abroad and if the continuing participation of the alien is essential to the successful completion of the production. A consulting organization may also submit a letter of no objection in lieu of the above if it has no objection to the approval of the petition.

(v) Organizations agreeing to provide advisory opinions. The Service will list in its Operations Instructions for O classification those peer groups, labor organizations, and/or management organizations which have agreed to provide advisory opinions to the Service and/or petitioners. The list will not be an exclusive or exhaustive list. The Service and petitioners may use other sources, such as publications, to identify appropriate peer groups, labor organizations, and management organizations. Additionally, the Service will list in its Operations Instructions those occupations or fields of endeavor where the nonexistence of an appropriate consulting entity has been verified.

(6) Approval and validity of petition —

(1) Approval. The Director shall consider all of the evidence submitted and such other evidence as may be independently required to assist in the adjudication. The Director shall notify the petitioner of the approval of the petition on Form I-797, Notice of Action. The approval notice shall include the alien beneficiary name, the classification, and the petition's period of validity.

(ii) Recording the validity of petitions. Procedures for recording the validity period of petitions are as follows;

(A) If a new O petition is approved before the date the petitioner indicates the services will begin, the approved petition and approval notice shall show the actual dates requested by the petitioner, not to exceed the limit specified by paragraph (o)(6)(iii) of this section or other Service policy.

(B) If a new 0 petition is approved after the date the petitioner indicates the services will begin, the approved petition and approval notice shall generally show a validity period commencing with the date of approval and ending with the date requested by the petitioner, not to exceed the limit specified by paragraph (o)(6)(iii) of this section or other Service policy.

(C) If the period of services requested by the petitioner exceeds the limit specified in paragraph (o)(6)(iii) of this section, the petition shall be approved only up to the limit specified in that paragraph.

(iii) Validity —

(A) O-1 petition. An approved petition for an alien classified under section 101(a)(15)(O)(i) of the Act shall be valid for a period of time determined by the Director to be necessary to accomplish the event or activity, not to exceed 3 years.

(B) O-2 petition. An approved petition for an alien classified under section 101(a)(15)(O)(ii) of the Act shall be valid for a period of time determined to be necessary to assist the O-1 alien to accomplish the event or activity, not to exceed 3 years.

(iv) Spouse and dependents. The spouse and unmarried minor children of the O-1 or O-2 alien beneficiary are entitled to O-3 nonimmigrant classification, subject to the same period of admission and limitations as the alien beneficiary, if they are accompanying or following to join the alien beneficiary in the United States. Neither the spouse nor a child of the alien beneficiary may accept employment unless he or she has been granted employment authorization.

(7) The petitioner shall be notified of the decision, the reasons for the denial, and the right to appeal the denial under 8 CFR part 103.

(8) Revocation of approval of petition —

(i) General.

(A) The petitioner shall immediately notify the Service of any changes in the terms and conditions of employment of a beneficiary which may affect eligibility under section 101(a)(15)(O) of the Act and paragraph (o) of this section. An amended petition should be filed when the petitioner continues to employ the beneficiary. If the petitioner no longer employs the beneficiary, the petitioner shall send a letter explaining the change(s) to the Director who approved the petition.

(B) The Director may revoke a petition at any time, even after the validity of the petition has expired.

(ii) Automatic revocation. The approval of an unexpired petition is automatically revoked if the petitioner, or the named employer in a petition filed by an agent, goes out of business, files a written withdrawal of the petition, or notifies the Service that the beneficiary is no longer employed by the petitioner.

(iii) Revocation on notice —

(A) Grounds for revocation. The Director shall send to the petitioner a notice of intent to revoke the petition in relevant part if is determined that:

(1) The beneficiary is no longer employed by the petitioner in the capacity specified in the petition;

(2) The statement of facts contained in the petition was not true and correct;

(3) The petitioner violated the terms or conditions of the approved petition;

(4) The petitioner violated the requirements of section 101(a)(15)(O) of the Act or paragraph (o) of this section; or

(5) The approval of the petition violated paragraph (o) of this section or involved gross error.

(B) Notice and decision. The notice of intent to revoke shall contain a detailed statement of the grounds for the revocation and the time period allowed for the petitioner's rebuttal. The petitioner may submit evidence in rebuttal within 30 days of the date of the notice. The Director shall consider all relevant evidence presented in deciding whether to revoke the petition.

(9) Appeal of a denial or a revocation of a petition —

(i) Denial. A denied petition may be appealed under 8 CFR part 103.

(ii) Revocation. A petition that has been revoked on notice may be appealed under 8 CFR part 103. Automatic revocations may not be appealed.

(10) Admission. A beneficiary may be admitted to the United States for the validity period of the petition, plus a period of up to 10 days before the validity period begins and 10 days after the validity period ends. The beneficiary may only engage in employment during the validity period of the petition.

(11) Extension of visa petition validity. The petitioner must file a request to extend the validity of the original petition under section 101(a)(15)(O) of the Act on the form prescribed by USCIS, in order to continue or complete the same activities or events specified in the original petition. A petition extension generally may be filed only if the validity of the original petition has not expired.

(12) Extension of stay —

(i) Extension procedure. The petitioner shall request extension of the alien's stay to continue or complete the same event or activity by filing an application or petition, accompanied by a statement explaining the reasons for the extension. The petitioner must also request a petition extension. The dates of extension shall be the same for the petition and the beneficiary's extension of stay. The alien beneficiary must be physically present in the United States at the time of filing of the extension of stay. Even though the request to extend the petition and the alien's stay are combined on the petition, the Director shall make a separate determination on each. If the alien leaves the United States for business or personal reasons while the extension requests are pending, the petitioner may request the Director to cable notification of approval of the petition extension to the consular office abroad where the alien will apply for a visa.

(ii) Extension period. An extension of stay may be authorized in increments of up to 1 year for an O-1 or O-2 beneficiary to continue or complete the same event or activity for which he or she was admitted plus an additional 10 days to allow the beneficiary to get his or her personal affairs in order.

(iii) Denial of an extension of stay. The denial of the request for the alien's extension of temporary stay may not be appealed.

(13) Effect of approval of a permanent labor certification or filing of a preference petition on O classification. The approval of a permanent labor certification or the filing of a preference petition for an alien shall not be a basis for denying an O-1 petition, a request to extend such a petition, or the alien's application for admission, change of status, or extension of stay. The alien may legitimately come to the United States for a temporary period as an O-1 nonimmigrant and depart voluntarily at the end of his or her authorized stay and, at the same time, lawfully seek to become a permanent resident of the United States.

(14) Effect of a strike —

(i) If the Secretary of Labor certifies to the Commissioner that a strike or other labor dispute involving a work stoppage of workers is in progress in the occupation at the place where the beneficiary is to be employed, and that the employment of the beneficiary would adversely affect the wages and working conditions of U.S. citizens and lawful resident workers:

(A) A petition to classify an alien as a nonimmigrant as defined in section 101(a)(15)(O) of the Act shall be denied; or

(B) If a petition has been approved, but the alien has not yet entered the United States, or has entered the United States but has not commenced employment, the approval of the petition is automatically suspended, and the application for admission on the basis of the petition shall be denied.

(ii) If there is a strike or other labor dispute involving a work stoppage of workers in progress, but such strike or other labor dispute is not certified under paragraph (o)(14)(i) of this section, the Commissioner shall not deny a petition or suspend an approved petition.

(iii) If the alien has already commenced employment in the United States under an approved petition and is participating in a strike or labor dispute involving a work stoppage of workers, whether or not such strike or other labor dispute has been certified by the Secretary of Labor, the alien shall not be deemed to be failing to maintain his or her status solely on account of past, present, or future participation in a strike or other labor dispute involving a work stoppage of workers but is subject to the following terms and conditions:

(A) The alien shall remain subject to all applicable provisions of the Immigration and Nationality Act and regulations promulgated thereunder in the same manner as are all other O nonimmigrants;

(B) The status and authorized period of stay of such an alien is not modified or extended in any way by virtue of his or her participation in a strike or other labor dispute involving a work stoppage of workers; and

(C) Although participation by an O nonimmigrant alien in a strike or other labor dispute involving a work stoppage of workers will not constitute a ground for deportation, and alien who violates his or her status or who remains in the United States after his or her authorized period of stay has expired will be subject to deportation.

(15) Use of approval notice, Form I-797. The Service shall notify the petitioner of Form I-797 whenever a visa petition or an extension of a visa petition is approved under the O classification. The beneficiary of an O petition who does not require a nonimmigrant visa may present a copy of the approval notice at a Port-of-Entry to facilitate entry into the United States. A beneficiary who is required to present a visa for admission, and who visa will have expired before the date of his or her intended return, may use Form I-797 to apply for a new or revalidated visa during the validity period of the petition. A copy of Form I-797 shall be retained by the beneficiary and presented during the validity of the petition when reentering the United States to resume the same employment with the same petitioner.

(16) Return transportation requirement. In the case of an alien who enters the United States under section 101(a)(15(O) of the Act and whose employment terminates for reasons other than voluntary resignation, the employer whose offer of employment formed the basis of such nonimmigrant status and the petitioner are jointly and severally liable for the reasonable cost of return transportation of the alien abroad. For the purposes of this paragraph, the term "abroad" means the alien's last place of residence prior to his or her entry into the United States.

(p) Artists, athletes, and entertainers —

(1) Classifications —

(i) General. Under section 101(a)(15)(P) of the Act, an alien having a residence in a foreign country which he or she has not intention or abandoning may be authorized to come to the United States temporarily to perform services for an employer or a sponsor. Under the nonimmigrant category, the alien may be classified under section 101(a)(15)(P)(i) of the Act as an alien who is coming to the United States to perform services as an internationally recognized athlete, individually or as part of a group or team, or member of an internationally recognized entertainment group; under section

101(a)(15)(P)(ii) of the Act, who is coming to perform as an artist or entertainer under a reciprocal exchange program; under section 101(a)(15)(P)(iii) of the Act, as an alien who is coming solely to perform, teach, or coach under a program that is culturally unique; or under section 101(a)(15)(P)(iv) of the Act, as the spouse or child of an alien described in section 101(a)(15)(P) (i), (ii), or (iii) of the Act who is accompanying or following to join the alien. These classifications are called P-1, P-2, P-3, and P-4 respectively. The employer or sponsor must file a petition with the Service for review of the services to be performed and for determination of the alien's eligibility for P-1, P-2, or P-3 classification before the alien may apply for a visa or seek admission to the United States. This paragraph sets forth the standards and procedures applicable to these classifications.

(ii) Description of classification —

(A) A P-1 classification applies to an alien who is coming temporarily to the United States:

(1) To perform at specific athletic competition as an athlete, individually or as part of a group or team, at an internationally recognized level or performance, or

(2) To perform with, or as an integral and essential part of the performance of, and entertainment group that has been recognized internationally as being outstanding in the discipline for a sustained and substantial period of time, and who has had a sustained and substantial relationship with the group (ordinarily for at least 1 year) and provides functions integral to the performance of the group.

(B) A P-2 classification applies to an alien who is coming temporarily to the United States to perform as an artist or entertainer, individually or as part of a group, or to perform as an integral part of the performance of such a group, and who seeks to perform under a reciprocal exchange program which is between an organization or organizations in the United States and an organization or organizations in one or more foreign states, and which provides for the temporary exchange of artists and entertainers, or groups of artists and entertainers.

(C) A P-3 classification applies to an alien artist or entertainer who is coming temporarily to the United States, either individually or as part of a group, or as an integral part of the performance of the group, to perform, teach, or coach under a commercial or noncommercial program that is culturally unique.

(2) Filing of petitions —

(i) General. A P-1 petition for an athlete or entertainment group shall be filed by a United States employer, a United States sponsoring organization, a United States agent, or a foreign employer through a United States agent. For purposes of paragraph (p) of this section, a foreign employer is any employer who is not amenable to service of process in the United States. Foreign employers seeking to employ a P-1 alien may not directly petition for the alien but must use a United States agent. A United States agent petitioning on behalf of a foreign employer must be authorized to file the petition, and to accept service of process in the United States in proceedings under section 274A of the Act, on behalf of the foreign employer. A P-2 petition for an artist or entertainer in a reciprocal exchange program shall be filed by the United States labor organization which negotiated the reciprocal exchange agreement, the sponsoring organization, or a United States employer. A P-3 petition for an artist or entertainer in a culturally unique program shall be filed by the sponsoring organization or a United States employer. Essential support personnel may not be included on the petition filed for the principal alien(s). These aliens require a separate petition. The petitioner must file a P petition on the form prescribed by USCIS. The petition may not be filed more than one year before the actual need for the alien's services. A P-1, P-2, or P-3 petition shall be adjudicated at the appropriate Service Center, even in emergency situations.

(ii) Evidence required to accompany a petition for a P nonimmigrant. Petitions for P nonimmigrant aliens shall be accompanied by the following:

(A) The evidence specified in the specific section of this part for the classification;

(B) Copies of any written contracts between the petitioner and the alien beneficiary or, if there is no written contract, a summary of the terms of the oral agreement under which the alien(s) will be employed;

(C) An explanation of the nature of the events or activities, the beginning and ending dates for the events or activities, and a copy of any itinerary for the events or activities; and

(D) A written consultation from a labor organization.

(iii) Form of documentation. The evidence submitted with an P petition should conform to the following:

(A) Affidavits, contracts, awards, and similar documentation must reflect the nature of the alien's achievement and be executed by an officer or responsible person employed by the institution, establishment, or organization where the work has performed.

(B) Affidavits written by present or former employers or recognized experts certifying to the recognition and extraordinary ability, or, in the case of a motion picture or television production, the extraordinary achievement of the alien, which shall specifically describe the alien's recognition and ability or achievement in factual terms. The affidavit must also set forth the expertise of the affiant and the manner in which the affiant acquired such information.

(C) A legible copy of a document in support of the petition may be submitted in lieu of the original. However, the original document shall be submitted if requested by the Director.

(iv) Other filing situations —

(A) Services in more than one location. A petition which requires the alien to work in more than one location (e.g., a tour) must include an itinerary with the dates and locations of the performances and must be filed with the Service Center which has jurisdiction in the area where the petitioner is located. The address which the petitioner specifies as its location on the petition shall be where the petitioner is located for purposes of this paragraph.

(B) Services for more than one employer. If the beneficiary or beneficiaries will work for more than one employer within the same time period, each employer must file a separate petition unless an agent files the petition pursuant to paragraph (p)(2)(iv)(E) of this section.

(C) Change of employer —

(1) General. If a P-1, P-2, or P-3 alien in the United States seeks to change employers or sponsors, the new employer or sponsor must file both a petition and a request to extend the alien's stay in the United States. The alien may not commence employment with the new employer or sponsor until the petition and request for extension have been approved.

(2) Traded professional P-1 athletes. In the case of a professional P-1 athlete who is traded from one organization to another organization, employment authorization for the player will automatically continue for a period of 30 days after acquisition by the new organization, within which time the new organization is expected to file a new application or petition for P-1 nonimmigrant classification. If a new application or petition is not filed within 30 days, employment authorization will cease. If a new application or petition is filed within 30 days, the professional athlete shall be deemed to be in valid P-1 status, and employment shall continue to be authorized, until the petition is adjudicated. If the new petition is denied, employment authorization will cease.

(D) Amended petition. The petitioner shall file an amended petition, with fee, with the Service Center where the original petition was filed to reflect any material changes in the terms and conditions of employment or the beneficiary's eligibility as specified in the original approved petition. A petitioner may add additional, similar or comparable performance, engagements, or competitions during the validity period of the petition without filing an amended petition.

(E) Agents as petitioners. A United States agent may file a petition in cases involving workers who are traditionally self-employed or workers who use agents to arrange short-term employment on their behalf with numerous employers, and in cases where a foreign employer authorizes the agent to act on its behalf. A United States agent may be: the actual employer of the beneficiary; the representative of both the employer and the beneficiary; or, a person or entity authorized by the employer to act for, or in place of, the employer as its agent. A petition filed by an United States agent is subject to the following conditions:

(1) An agent performing the function of an employer must specify the wage offered and the other terms and conditions of employment by contractual agreement with the beneficiary or beneficiaries. The agent/employer must also provide an itinerary of definite employment and information on any other services planned for the period of time requested.

(2) A person or company in business as an agent may file the P petition involving multiple employers as the representative of both the employers and the beneficiary or beneficiaries if the supporting documentation includes a complete itinerary of services or engagements. The itinerary shall specify the dates of each service or engagement, the names and addresses of the actual employers, the names and addresses of the establishment, venues, or locations where the services will be performed. In questionable cases, a contract between the employer(s) and the beneficiary or beneficiaries may be required. The burden is on the agent to explain the terms and conditions of the employment and to provide any required documentation.

(3) A foreign employer who, through a United States agent, files a petition for a P nonimmigrant alien is responsible for complying with all of the employer sanctions provisions of section 274A of the Act and 8 CFR part 274a.

(F) Multiple beneficiaries. More than one beneficiary may be included in a P petition if they are members of a team or group, or if they will provide essential support to P-1, P-2, or P-3 beneficiaries performing in the same location and in the same occupation. Up to 25 named beneficiaries may be included per petition.

(G) Named beneficiaries. Petitions for P classification must include the names of beneficiaries and other required information at the time of filing.

(H) Substitution of beneficiaries. A petitioner may request substitution of beneficiaries in approved P-1, P-2, and P-3 petitions for groups. To request substitution, the petitioner shall submit a letter requesting such substitution, along with a copy of the petitioner's approval notice, to the consular office at which the alien will apply for a visa or the Port-of-Entry where the alien will apply for admission. Essential support personnel may not be substituted at consular offices or at Ports-of-entry. In order to add additional new essential support personnel, a new Form application or petition must be filed.

(3) Definitions. As used in this paragraph, the term:

Arts includes fields of creative activity or endeavor such as, but not limited to, fine arts, visual arts, and performing arts.

Competition, event, or performance means an activity such as an athletic competition, athletic season, tournament, tour, exhibit, project, entertainment event, or engagement. Such activity could include short vacations, promotional appearances for the petitioning employer relating to the competition, event, or performance, and stopovers which are incidental and/or related to the activity. An athletic competition or entertainment event could include an entire season of performances A group of related activities will also be considered an event. In the case of a P-2 petition, the event may be the duration of the reciprocal exchange agreement. In the case of a P-1 athlete, the event may be the duration of the alien's contract.

Contract means the written agreement between the petitioner and the beneficiary(ies) that explains the terms and conditions of employment. The contract shall describe the services to be performed, and specify the wages, hours of work, working conditions, and any fringe benefits.

Culturally unique means a style of artistic expression, methodology, or medium which is unique to a particular country, nation, society, class, ethnicity, religion, tribe, or other group of persons.

Essential support alien means a highly skilled, essential person determined by the Director to be an integral part of the performance of a P-1, P-2, or P-3 alien because he or she performs support services which cannot be readily performed by a United States worker and which are essential to the successful performance of services by the P-1, P-2, alien. Such alien must have appropriate qualifications to perform the services, critical knowledge of the specific services to be performed, and experience in providing such support to the P-1, P-2, or P-3 alien.

Group means two or more persons established as one entity or unit to perform or to provide a service.

Internationally recognized means having a high level of achievement in a field evidenced by a degree of skill and recognition substantially above that ordinarily encountered, to the extent that such achievement is renowned, leading, or well-known in more than one country.

Member of a group means a person who is actually performing the entertainment services.

Sponsor means an established organization in the United States which will not directly employ a P-1, P-2, or P-3 alien but will assume responsibility for the accuracy of the terms and conditions specified in the petition.

Team means two or more persons organized to perform together as a competitive unit in a competitive event.

(4) Petition for an internationally recognized athlete or member of an internationally recognized entertainment group (P-1) —

(i) Types of classification.

(A) P-1 classification as an athlete in an individual capacity. A P-1 classification may be granted to an alien who is an internationally recognized athlete based on his or her own reputation and achievements as an individual. The alien must be coming to the United States to perform services which require an internationally recognized athlete.

(B) P-1 classification as a member of an entertainment group or an athletic team. An entertainment group or athletic team consists of two or more persons who function as a unit. The entertainment group or athletic team as a unit must be internationally recognized as outstanding in the discipline and must be coming to perform services which require an internationally recognized entertainment group or athletic team. A person who is a member of an internationally recognized entertainment group or athletic team may be granted P-1 classification based on that relationship, but may not perform services separate and apart from the entertainment group or athletic team. An entertainment group must have been established for a minimum of 1 year, and 75 percent of the members of the group must have been performing entertainment services for the group for a minimum of 1 year.

(ii) Criteria and documentary requirements for P-1 athletes —

(A) General. A P-1 athlete must have an internationally recognized reputation as an international athlete or he or she must be a member of a foreign team that is internationally recognized. The athlete or team must be coming to the United States to participate in an athletic competition which has a distinguished reputation and which requires participation of an athlete or athletic team that has an international reputation.

(B) Evidentiary requirements for an internationally recognized athlete or athletic team. A petition for an athletic team must be accompanied by evidence that the team as a unit has achieved international recognition in the sport. Each member of the team is accorded P-1 classification based on the international reputation of the team. A petition for an athlete who will compete individually or as a member of a U.S. team must be accompanied by evidence that the athlete has achieved international recognition in the sport based on his or her reputation. A petition for a P-1 athlete or athletic team shall include:

(1) A tendered contract with a major United States sports league or team, or a tendered contract in an individual sport commensurate with international recognition in that sport, if such contracts are normally executed in the sport, and

(2) Documentation of at least two of the following:

(i) Evidence of having participated to a significant extent in a prior season with a major United States sports league;

(ii) Evidence of having participated in international competition with a national team;

(iii) Evidence of having participated to a significant extent in a prior season for a U.S. college or university in intercollegiate competition;

(iv) A written statement from an official of the governing body of the sport which details how the alien or team is internationally recognized;

(v) A written statement from a member of the sports media or a recognized expert in the sport which details how the alien or team is internationally recognized;

(vi) Evidence that the individual or team is ranked if the sport has international rankings; or

(vii) Evidence that the alien or team has received a significant honor or award in the sport.

(iii) Criteria and documentary requirements for members of an internationally recognized entertainment group —

(A) General. A P-1 classification shall be accorded to an entertainment group to perform as a unit based on the international reputation of the group. Individual entertainers shall not be accorded P-1 classification to perform separate and apart from a group. Except as provided in paragraph (p)(4)(iii)(C)(2) of this section, it must be established that the group has been internationally recognized as outstanding in the discipline for a sustained and substantial period of time. Seventy-five percent of the members of the group must have had a sustained and substantial relationship with the group for at least 1 year and must provide functions integral to the group's performance.

(B) Evidentiary criteria for members of internationally recognized entertainment groups. A petition for P-1 classification for the members of an entertainment group shall be accompanied by:

(1) Evidence that the group has been established and performing regularly for a period of at least 1 year;

(2) A statement from the petitioner listing each member of the group and the exact dates for which each member has been employed on a regular basis by the group; and

(3) Evidence that the group has been internationally recognized in the discipline for a sustained and substantial period of time. This may be demonstrated by the submission of evidence of the group's nomination or receipt of significant international awards or prices for outstanding achievement in its field or by three of the following different types of documentation:

(i) Evidence that the group has performed, and will perform, as a starring or leading entertainment group in productions or events which have a distinguished reputation as evidenced by critical reviews, advertisements, publicity releases, publications, contracts, or endorsements;

(ii) Evidence that the group has achieved international recognition and acclaim for outstanding achievement in its field as evidenced by reviews in major newspapers, trade journals, magazines, or other published material;

(iii) Evidence that the group has performed, and will perform, services as a leading or starring group for organizations and establishments that have a distinguished reputation evidenced by articles in newspapers, trade journals, publications, or testimonials;

(iv) Evidence that the group has a record of major commercial or critically acclaimed successes, as evidenced by such indicators as ratings; standing in the field; box office receipts; record, cassette, or video sales; and other achievements in the field as reported in trade journals, major newspapers, or other publications;

(v) Evidence that the group has achieved significant recognition for achievements from organizations, critics, government agencies, or other recognized experts in the field. Such testimonials must be in a form that clearly indicates the author's authority, expertise, and knowledge of the alien's achievements; or

(vi) Evidence that the group has either commanded a high salary or will command a high salary or other substantial remuneration for services comparable to other similarly situated in the field as evidenced by contracts or other reliable evidence.

(C) Special provisions for certain entertainment groups —

(1) Alien circus personnel. The 1-year group membership requirement and the international recognition requirement are not applicable to alien circus personnel who perform as part of a circus or circus group, or who constitute an integral and essential part of the performance of such circus or circus group, provided that the alien or aliens are coming to join a circus that has been recognized nationally as outstanding for a sustained and substantial period of time or as part of such a circus.

(2) Certain nationally known entertainment groups. The Director may waive the international recognition requirement in the case of an entertainment group which has been recognized nationally as being outstanding in its discipline for a sustained and substantial period of time in consideration of special circumstances. An example of a special circumstances would be when an entertainment group may find it difficult to demonstrate recognition in more than one country due to such factors as limited access to news media or consequences of geography.

(3) Waiver of 1-year relationship in exigent circumstances. The Director may waive the 1-year relationship requirement for an alien who, because of illness or unanticipated and exigent circumstances, replaces an essential member of a P-1 entertainment group or an alien who augments the group by performing a critical role. The Department of State is hereby delegated the authority to waive the 1-year relationship requirement in the case of consular substitutions involving P-1 entertainment groups.

(iv) P-1 classification as an essential support alien —

(A) General. An essential support alien as defined in paragraph (p)(3) of this section may be granted P-1 classification based on a support relationship with an individual P-1 athlete, P-1 athletic team, or a P-1 entertainment group.

(B) Evidentiary criteria for a P-1 essential support petition. A petition for P-1 essential support personnel must be accompanied by:

(1) A consultation from a labor organization with expertise in the area of the alien's skill;

(2) A statement describing the alien(s) prior essentiality, critical skills, and experience with the principal alien(s); and

(3) A copy of the written contract or a summary of the terms of the oral agreement between the alien(s) and the employer.

(5) Petition for an artist or entertainer under a reciprocal exchange program (P-2) —

(i) General.

(A) A P-2 classification shall be accorded to artists or entertainers, individually or as a group, who will be performing under a reciprocal exchange program which is between an organization or organizations in the United States, which may include a management organization, and an organization or organizations in one or more foreign states and which provides for the temporary exchange of artists and entertainers, or groups of artists and entertainers.

(B) The exchange of artists or entertainers shall be similar in terms of caliber of artists or entertainers, terms and conditions of employment, such as length of employment, and numbers of artists or entertainers involved in the exchange. However, this requirement does not preclude an individual for group exchange.

(C) An alien who is an essential support person as defined in paragraph (p)(3) of this section may be accorded P-2 classification based on a support relationship to a P-2 artist or entertainer under a reciprocal exchange program.

(ii) Evidentiary requirements for petition involving a reciprocal exchange program. A petition for P-2 classification shall be accompanied by:

(A) A copy of the formal reciprocal exchange agreement between the U.S. organization or organizations which sponsor the aliens and an organization or organizations in a foreign country which will receive the U.S. artist or entertainers;

(B) A statement from the sponsoring organization describing the reciprocal exchange of U.S. artists or entertainers as it relates to the specific petition for which P-2 classification is being sought;

(C) Evidence that an appropriate labor organization in the United States was involved in negotiating, or has concurred with, the reciprocal exchange of U.S. and foreign artists or entertainers; and

(D) Evidence that the aliens for whom P-2 classification is being sought and the U.S. artists or entertainers subject to the reciprocal exchange agreement are artists or entertainers with comparable skills, and that the terms and conditions of employment are similar.

(iii) P-2 classification as an essential support alien —

(A) General. An essential support alien as defined in paragraph (p)(3) of this section may be granted P-2 classification based on a support relationship with a P-2 entertainer or P-2 entertainment group.

(B) Evidentiary criteria for a P-2 essential support petition. A petition for P-2 essential support personnel must be accompanied by:

(1) A consultation from a labor organization with expertise in the area of the alien's skill;

(2) A statement describing the alien(s) prior essentiality, critical skills, and experience with the principal alien(s); and

(3) A copy of the written contract or a summary of the terms of the oral agreement between the alien(s) and the employer.

(6) Petition for an artist or entertainer under a culturally unique program —

(i) General.

(A) A P-3 classification may be accorded to artists or entertainers, individually or as a group, coming to the United States for the purpose of developing, interpreting, representing, coaching, or teaching a unique or traditional ethnic, folk, cultural, musical, theatrical, or artistic performance or presentation.

(B) The artist or entertainer must be coming to the United States to participate in a cultural event or events which will further the understanding or development of his or her art form. The program may be of a commercial or noncommercial nature.

(ii) Evidentiary criteria for a petition involving a culturally unique program. A petition for P-3 classification shall be accompanied by:

(A) Affidavits, testimonials, or letters from recognized experts attesting to the authenticity of the alien's or the group's skills in performing, presenting, coaching, or teaching the unique or traditional art form and giving the credentials of the expert, including the basis of his or her knowledge of the alien's or group's skill, or

(B) Documentation that the performance of the alien or group is culturally unique, as evidence by reviews in newspapers, journals, or other published materials; and

(C) Evidence that all of the performances or presentations will be culturally unique events.

(iii) P-3 classification as an essential support alien —

(A) General. An essential support alien as defined in paragraph (p)(3) of this section may be granted P-3 classification based on a support relationship with a P-3 entertainer or P-3 entertainment group.

(B) Evidentiary criteria for a P-3 essential support petition. A petition for P-3 essential support personnel must be accompanied by:

(1) A consultation from a labor organization with expertise in the area of the alien's skill;

(2) A statement describing the alien(s) prior essentiality, critical skills and experience with the principal alien(s); and

(3) A copy of the written contract or a summary of the terms of the oral agreement between the alien(s) and the employer.

(7) Consultation —

(i) General.

(A) Consultation with an appropriate labor organization regarding the nature of the work to be done and the alien's qualifications is mandatory before a petition for P-1, P-2, or P-3 classification can be approved.

(B) Except as provided in paragraph (p)(7)(i)(E) of this section, evidence of consultation shall be a written advisory opinion from an appropriate labor organization.

(C) Except as provided in paragraph (p)(7)(i)(E) of this section, the petitioner shall obtain a written advisory opinion from an appropriate labor organization. The advisory opinion shall be submitted along with the petition when the petition is filed. If the advisory opinion is not favorable to the petitioner, the advisory opinion must set forth a specific statement of facts which support the conclusion reached in the opinion. Advisory opinions must be submitted in writing and signed by an authorized official of the organization.

(D) Except as provided in paragraph (p)(7)(i)(E) and (F) of this section, written evidence of consultation shall be included in the record of every approved petition. Consultations are advisory and are not binding on the Service.

(E) In a case where the Service has determined that a petition merits expeditious handling, the Service shall contact the labor organization and request an advisory opinion if one is not submitted by the petitioner. The labor organization shall have 24 hours to respond to the Service's request. The Service shall adjudicate the petition after receipt of the response from the labor organization. The labor organization shall then furnish the Service with a written advisory opinion within 5 working days of the request. If the labor organization fails to respond within 24 hours, the Service shall render a decision on the petition without the advisory opinion.

(F) In those cases where it is established by the petitioner that an appropriate labor organization does not exist, the Service shall render a decision on the evidence of record.

(ii) Consultation requirements for P-1 athletes and entertainment groups. Consultation with a labor organization that has expertise in the area of the alien's sport or entertainment field is required in the case of a P-1 petition. If the advisory opinion is not favorable to the petitioner, the advisory opinion must set forth a specific statement of facts which support the conclusion reached in the opinion. If the advisory opinion provided by the labor organization is favorable to the petitioner it should evaluate and/or describe the alien's or group's ability and achievements in the field of endeavor, comment on whether the alien or group is internationally recognized for achievements, and state whether the services the alien or group is coming to perform are appropriate for an internationally recognized athlete or entertainment group. In lieu of the above, a labor organization may submit a letter of no objection if it has no objection to the approval of the petition.

(iii) Consultation requirements for P-1 circus personnel. The advisory opinion provided by the labor organization should comment on whether the circus which will employ the alien has national recognition as well as any other aspect of the beneficiary's or beneficiaries' qualifications which the labor organization deems appropriate. If the advisory opinion is not favorable to the petitioner, it must set forth a specific statement of facts which support the conclusion reached in the opinion. In lieu of the above, a labor organization may submit a letter of no objection if it has no objection to the approval of the petition.

(iv) Consultation requirements for P-2 alien in a reciprocal exchange program. In P-2 petitions where an artist or entertainer is coming to the United States under a reciprocal exchange program, consultation with the appropriate labor organization is required to verify the existence of a viable exchange program. The advisory opinion from the labor organization shall comment on the bona fides of the reciprocal exchange program and specify whether the exchange meets the requirements of paragraph (p)(5) of this section. If the advisory opinion is not favorable to the petitioner, it must also set forth a specific statement of facts which support the conclusion reached in the opinion.

(v) Consultation requirements for P-3 in a culturally unique program. Consultation with an appropriate labor organization is required for P-3 petitions involving aliens in culturally unique programs. If the advisory opinion is favorable to the petitioner, it should evaluate the cultural uniqueness of the alien's skills, state whether the events are cultural in nature, and state whether the event or activity is appropriate for P-3 classification. If the advisory opinion is not favorable to the petitioner, it must also set forth a specific statement of facts which support the conclusion reached in the opinion. In lieu of the above, a labor organization may submit a letter of no objection if it has no objection to the approval of the petition.

(vi) Consultation requirements for essential support aliens. Written consultation on petitions for P-1, P-2, or P-3 essential support aliens must be made with a labor organization with expertise in the skill area involved. If the advisory opinion provided by the labor organization is favorable to the petitioner, it must evaluate the alien's essentiality to and working relationship with the artist or entertainer, and state whether United States workers are available who can perform the support services. If the advisory opinion is not favorable to the petitioner, it must also set forth a specific statement of facts which support the conclusion reached in the opinion. A labor organization may submit a letter of no objection if it has no objection to the approval of the petition.

(vii) Labor organizations agreeing to provide consultations. The Service shall list in its Operations Instructions for P classification those organizations which have agreed to provide advisory opinions to the Service and/or petitioners. The list will not be an exclusive or exhaustive list. The Service and petitioners may use other sources, such as publications, to identify appropriate labor organizations. The Service will also list in its Operations Instructions those occupations or fields of endeavor where it has been determined by the Service that no appropriate labor organization exists.

(8) Approval and validity of petition —

(i) Approval. The Director shall consider all the evidence submitted and such other evidence as he or she may independently require to assist in his or her adjudication. The Director shall notify the petitioner of the approval of the petition on Form I-797, Notice of Action. The approval notice shall include the alien beneficiary's name and classification and the petition's period of validity.

(ii) Recording the validity of petitions. Procedures for recording the validity period of petitions are:

(A) If a new P petition is approved before the date the petitioner indicates the services will begin, the approved petition and approval notice shall show the actual dates requested by the petitioner as the validity period, not to exceed the limit specified in paragraph (p)(8)(iii) of this section or other Service policy.

(B) If a new P petition is approved after the date the petitioner indicates the services will begin, the approved petition and approval notice shall generally show a validity period commencing with the date of approval and ending with the date requested by the petitioner, not to exceed the limit specified in paragraph (p)(8)(iii) of this section or other Service policy.

(C) If the period of services requested by the petitioner exceeds the limit specified in paragraph (p)(8)(iii) of this section, the petition shall be approved only up to the limit specified in that paragraph.

(iii) Validity. The approval period of a P petition shall conform to the limits prescribed as follows:

(A) P-1 petition for athletes. An approved petition for an individual athlete classified under section 101(a)(15)(P)(i) of the Act shall be valid for a period up to 5 years. An approved petition for an athletic team classified under section 101(a)(15)(P)(i) of the Act shall be valid for a period of time determined by the Director to complete the competition or event for which the alien team is being admitted, not to exceed 1 year.

(B) P-1 petition for an entertainment group. An approved petition for an entertainment group classified under section 101(a)(15)(P)(i) of the Act shall be valid for a period of time determined by the Director to be necessary to complete the performance or event for which the group is being admitted, not to exceed 1 year.

(C) P-2 and P-3 petitions for artists or entertainers. An approved petition for an artist or entertainer under section 101(a)(15)(P)(ii) or (iii) of the Act shall be valid for a period of time determined by the Director to be necessary to complete the event, activity, or performance for which the P-2 or P-3 alien is admitted, not to exceed 1 year.

(D) Spouse and dependents. The spouse and unmarried minor children of a P-1, P-2, or P-3 alien beneficiary are entitled to P-4 nonimmigrant classification, subject to the same period of admission and limitations as the alien beneficiary, if they are accompanying or following to join the alien beneficiary in the United States. Neither the spouse nor a child of the alien beneficiary may accept employment unless he or she has been granted employment authorization.

(E) Essential support aliens. Petitions for essential support personnel to P-1, P-2, and P-3 aliens shall be valid for a period of time determined by the Director to be necessary to complete the event, activity, or performance for which the P-1, P-2, or P-3 alien is admitted, not to exceed 1 year.

(9) The petitioner shall be notified of the decision, the reasons for the denial, and the right to appeal the denial under 8 CFR part 103. There is no appeal from a decision to deny an extension of stay to the alien or a change of nonimmigrant status.

(10) Revocation of approval of petition —

(i) General.

(A) The petitioner shall immediately notify the Service of any changes in the terms and conditions of employment of a beneficiary which may affect eligibility under section 101(a)(15)(P) of the Act and paragraph (p) of this section. An amended petition should be filed when the petitioner continues to employ the beneficiary. If the petitioner no longer employs the beneficiary, the petitioner shall send a letter explaining the change(s) to the Director who approved the petition.

(B) The Director may revoke a petition at any time, even after the validity of the petition has expired.

(ii) Automatic revocation. The approval of an unexpired petition is automatically revoked if the petitioner, or the employer in a petition filed by an agent, goes out of business, files a written withdrawal of the petition, or notifies the Service that the beneficiary is no longer employed by the petitioner.

(iii) Revocation on notice —

(A) Grounds for revocation. The Director shall send to the petitioner a notice of intent to revoke the petition in relevant part if he or she finds that:

(1) The beneficiary is no longer employed by the petitioner in the capacity specified in the petition;

(2) The statement of facts contained in the petition were not true and correct;

(3) The petitioner violated the terms or conditions of the approved petition;

(4) The petitioner violated requirements of section 101(a)(15)(P) of the Act or paragraph (p) of this section; or

(5) The approval of the petition violated paragraph (p) of this section or involved gross error.

(B) Notice and decision. The notice of intent to revoke shall contain a detailed statement of the grounds for the revocation and the time period allowed for the petitioner's rebuttal. The petitioner may submit evidence in rebuttal within 30 days of the date of the notice. The Director shall consider all relevant evidence presented in deciding whether to revoke the petition.

(11) Appeal of a denial or a revocation of a petition —

(i) Denial. A denied petition may be appealed under 8 CFR part 103.

(ii) Revocation. A petition that has been revoked on notice may be appealed under 8 CFR part 103. Automatic revocations may not be appealed.

(12) Admission. A beneficiary may be admitted to the United States for the validity period of the petition, plus a period of up to 10 days before the validity period begins and 10 days after the validity period ends. The beneficiary may not work except during the validity period of the petition.

(13) Extension of visa petition validity. The petitioner must file a request to extend the validity of the original petition under section 101(a)(15)(P) of the Act on the form prescribed by USCIS in order to continue or complete the same activity or event specified in the original petition. A petition extension generally may be filed only if the validity of the original petition has not expired.

(14) Extension of stay —

(i) Extension procedure. The petitioner shall request extension of the alien's stay to continue or complete the same event or activity by filing Form I-129, accompanied by a statement explaining the reasons for the extension. The petitioner must also request a petition extension. The extension dates shall be the same for the petition and the beneficiary's stay. The beneficiary must be physically present in the United States at the time the extension of stay is filed. Even though the requests to extend the petition and the alien's stay are combined on the petition, the Director shall make a separate determination on each. If the alien leaves the United States for business or personal reasons while the extension requests are pending, the petitioner may request the Director to cable notification of approval of the petition extension to the consular office abroad where the alien will apply for a visa.

(ii) Extension periods —

(A) P-1 individual athlete. An extension of stay for a P-1 individual athlete and his or her essential support personnel may be authorized for a period up to 5 years for a total period of stay not to exceed 10 years.

(B) Other P-1, P-2, and P-3 aliens. An extension of stay may be authorized in increments of 1 year for P-1 athletic teams, entertainment groups, aliens in reciprocal exchange programs, aliens in culturally unique programs, and their essential support personnel to continue or complete the same event or activity for which they were admitted.

(15) Effect of approval of a permanent labor certification or filing of a preference petition on P classification. The approval of a permanent labor certification or the filing of a preference petition for an alien shall not be a basis for denying a P petition, a request to extend such a petition, or the alien's admission, change of status, or extension of stay. The alien may legitimately come to the United States for a temporary period as a P

nonimmigrant and depart voluntarily at the end of his or her authorized stay and, at the same time, lawfully seek to become a permanent resident of the United States. This provision does not include essential support personnel.

(16) Effect of a strike —

(i) If the Secretary of Labor certifies to the Commissioner that a strike or other labor dispute involving a work stoppage of workers is in progress in the occupation at the place where the beneficiary is to be employed, and that the employment of the beneficiary would adversely affect the wages and working conditions of U.S. citizens and lawful resident workers:

(A) A petition to classify an alien as a nonimmigrant as defined in section 101(a)(15)(P) of the Act shall be denied; or

(B) If a petition has been approved, but the alien has not yet entered the United States, or has entered the United States but has not commenced employment, the approval of the petition is automatically suspended, and the application for admission of the basis of the petition shall be denied.

(ii) If there is a strike or other labor dispute involving a work stoppage of workers in progress, but such strike or other labor dispute is not certified under paragraph (p)(16)(i) of this section, the Commissioner shall not deny a petition or suspend an approved petition.

(iii) If the alien has already commenced employment in the United States under an approved petition and is participating in a strike or labor dispute involving a work stoppage of workers, whether or not such strike or other labor dispute has been certified by the Secretary of Labor, the alien shall not be deemed to be failing to maintain his or her status solely on account of past, present, or future participation in a strike or other labor dispute involving a work stoppage of workers but is subject to the following terms and conditions:

(A) The alien shall remain subject to all applicable provisions of the Immigration and Nationality Act and regulations promulgated thereunder in the same manner as all other P nonimmigrant aliens;

(B) The status and authorized period of stay of such an alien is not modified or extended in any way by virtue of his or her participation in a strike or other labor dispute involving a work stoppage of workers; and

(C) Although participation by a P nonimmigrant alien in a strike or other labor dispute involving a work stoppages of workers will not constitute a ground for deportation, an alien who violates his or her status or who remains in the United States after his or her authorized period of stay has expired, will be subject to deportation.

(17) Use of approval of notice, Form I-797. The Service has notify the petitioner on Form I-797 whenever a visa petition or an extension of a visa petition is approved under the P classification. The beneficiary of a P petition who does not require a nonimmigrant visa may present a copy of the approved notice at a Port-of-Entry to facilitate entry into the United States. A beneficiary who is required to present a visa for admission, and whose visa expired before the date of his or her intended return, may use Form I-797 to apply for a new or revalidated visa during the validity period of the petition. The copy of Form I-797 shall be retained by the beneficiary and present during the validity of the petition when reentering the United States to resume the same employment with the same petitioner.

(18) Return transportation requirement. In the case of an alien who enters the United States under section 101(a)(15)(P) of the Act and whose employment terminates for reasons other than voluntary resignation, the employer whose offer of employment formed the basis of suh nonimmigrant status and the petitioner are jointly and severally liable for the reasonable cost of return transportation of the alien abroad. For the purposes of this paragraph, the term "abroad" means the alien's last place of residence prior to his or her entry into the United States.

(q) Cultural visitors —

(1)(i) International cultural exchange visitors program. Paragraphs (q)(2) through (q)(11) of this section provide the rules governing nonimmigrant aliens who are visiting the United States temporarily in an international cultural exchange visitors program (Q-1).

(ii) Irish peace process cultural and training program. Paragraph (q)(15) of this section provides the rules governing nonimmigrant aliens who are visiting the United States temporarily under the Irish peace process cultural and training program (Q-2) and their dependents (Q-3).

(iii) Definitions. As used in this section:

Country of nationality means the country of which the participant was a national at the time of the petition seeking international cultural exchange visitor status for him or her.

Doing business means the regular, systematic, and continuous provision of goods and/or services (including lectures, seminars and other types of cultural programs) by a qualified employer which has employees, and does not include the mere presence of an agent or office of the qualifying employer.

Duration of program means the time in which a qualified employer is conducting an approved international cultural exchange program in the manner as established by the employer's petition for program approval, provided that the period of time does not exceed 15 months.

International cultural exchange visitor means an alien who has a residence in a foreign country which he or she has no intention of abandoning, and who is coming temporarily to the United States to take part in an international cultural exchange program approved by the Attorney General.

Petitioner means the employer or its designated agent who has been employed by the qualified employer on a permanent basis in an executive or managerial capacity. The designated agent must be a United States citizen, an alien lawfully admitted for permanent residence, or an alien provided temporary residence status under sections 210 or 245A of the Act.

Qualified employer means a United States or foreign firm, corporation, non-profit organization, or other legal entity (including its U.S. branches, subsidiaries, affiliates, and franchises) which administers an international cultural exchange program designated by the Attorney General in accordance with the provisions of section 101(a)(15)(Q)(i) of the Act.

(2) Admission of international cultural exchange visitor —

(i) General. A nonimmigrant alien may be authorized to enter the United States as a participant in an international cultural exchange program approved by the Attorney General for the purpose of providing practical training, employment, and the sharing of the history, culture, and traditions of the country of the alien's nationality. The period of admission is the duration of the approved international cultural exchange program or fifteen (15) months, whichever is shorter. A nonimmigrant alien admitted under this provision is classifiable as an international cultural exchange visitor in Q-1 status.

(ii) Limitation on admission. Any alien who has been admitted into the United States as an international cultural exchange visitor under section 101(a)(15)(Q)(i) of the Act shall not be readmittted in Q-1 status unless the alien has resided and been physically present outside the United States for the immediate prior year. Brief trips to the United States for pleasure or business during the immediate prior year do not break the continuity of the one-year foreign residency.

(3) International cultural exchange program —

(i) General. A United States employer shall petition the Attorney General on the form prescribed by USCIS, for approval of an international cultural exchange program which is designed to provide an opportunity for the American public to learn about foreign cultures. The United States employer must simultaneously petition on the same application or petition for the authorization for one or more individually identified nonimmigrant aliens to be admitted in Q-1 status. These aliens are to be admitted to engage in employment or training of which the essential element is the sharing with the American public, or a segment of the public sharing a common cultural interest, of the culture of the alien's country of nationality. The international cultural exchange visitor's eligibility for admission will be considered only if the international cultural exchange program is approved.

(ii) Program validity. Each petition for an international cultural exchange program will be approved for the duration of the program, which may not exceed 15 months, plus 30 days to allow time for the participants to make travel arrangements. Subsequent to the approval of the initial petition, a new petition must be filed each time the qualified employer wishes to bring in additional cultural visitors. A qualified employer may replace or substitute a participant named on a previously approved petition for the remainder of the program in accordance with paragraph (q)(6) of this section. The replacement or substituting alien may be admitted in Q-1 status until the expiration date of the approved petition.

(iii) Requirements for program approval. An international cultural exchange program must meet all of the following requirements:

(A) Accessibility to the public. The international cultural exchange program must take place in a school, museum, business or other establishment where the American public, or a segment of the public sharing a common cultural interest, is exposed to aspects of a foreign culture as part of a structured program. Activities that take place in a private home or an isolated business setting to which the American public, or a segment of the public sharing a common cultural interest, does not have direct access do not qualify.

(B) Cultural component. The international cultural exchange program must have a cultural component which is an essential and integral part of the international cultural exchange visitor's employment or training. The cultural component must be designed, on the whole, to exhibit or explain the attitude, customs, history, heritage, philosophy, or traditions of the international cultural exchange visitor's country of nationality. A cultural component may include structured instructional activities such as seminars, courses, lecture series, or language camps.

(C) Work component. The international cultural exchange visitor's employment or training in the United States may not be independent of the cultural component of the international cultural exchange program. The work component must serve as the vehicle to achieve the objectives of the cultural component. The sharing of the culture of the international cultural exchange visitor's country of nationality must result from his or her employment or training with the qualified employer in the United States.

(iv) Requirements for international cultural exchange visitors. To be eligible for international cultural exchange visitor status, an alien must be a bona fide nonimmigrant who:

(A) Is at least 18 years of age at the time the petition is filed;

(B) Is qualified to perform the service or labor or receive the type of training stated in the petition;

(C) Has the ability to communicate effectively about the cultural attributes of his or her country of nationality to the American public; and

(D) Has resided and been physically present outside of the United States for the immediate prior year, if he or she was previously admitted as an international cultural exchange visitor.

(4) Supporting documentation —

(i) Documentation by the employer. To establish eligibility as a qualified employer, the petitioner must submit with the completed application or petition appropriate evidence that the employer:

(A) Maintains an established international cultural exchange program in accordance with the requirements set forth in paragraph (q)(3) of this section;

(B) Has designated a qualified employee as a representative who will be responsible for administering the international cultural exchange program and who will serve as liaison with the Immigration and Naturalization Service;

(C) Is actively doing business in the United States;

(D) Will offer the alien(s) wages and working conditions comparable to those accorded local domestic workers similarly employed; and

(E) Has the financial ability to remunerate the participant(s).

(ii) Certification by petitioner.

(A) The petitioner must give the date of birth, country of nationality, level of education, position title, and a brief job description for each international cultural exchange visitor included in the petition. The petitioner must verify and certify that the prospective participants are qualified to perform the service or labor, or receive the type of training, described in the petition.

(B) The petitioner must report the international cultural exchange visitors' wages and certify that such cultural exchange visitors are offered wages and working conditions comparable to those accorded to local domestic workers similarly employed.

(iii) Supporting documentation as prescribed in paragraphs (q)(4)(i) and (q)(4)(ii) of this section must accompany a petition filed on the form prescribed by USCIS in all cases except where the employer files multiple petitions in the same calendar year. When petitioning to repeat a previously approved international cultural exchange program, a copy of the initial program approval notice may be submitted in lieu of the documentation required under paragraph (q)(4)(i) of this section. The Service will request additional documentation only when clarification is needed.

(5) Filing of petitions for international cultural exchange visitor program —

(i) General. A United States employer seeking to bring in international cultural exchange visitors must file a petition on the form prescribed by USCIS, with the applicable fee, along with appropriate documentation. A new petition on the form prescribed by USCIS, with the applicable fee, must be filed with the appropriate service center each time a qualified employer wants to bring in additional international cultural exchange visitors. Each person named on an approved petition will be admitted only for the duration of the approved program. Replacement or substitution may be made for any person named on an approved petition as provided in paragraph (q)(6) of this section, but only for the remainder of the approved program.

(ii) Petition for multiple participants. The petitioner may include up to 25 named participants on a petition. The petitioner shall include the name, date of birth, nationality, and other identifying information required on the petition for each participant. The petitioner must also indicate the United States consulate at which each participant will apply for a Q-1 visa. For participants who are visa-exempt under 8 CFR 212.1(a), the petitioner must indicate the port of entry at which each participant will apply for admission to the United States.

(iii) Service, labor, or training in more than one location. A petition which requires the international cultural exchange visitor to engage in employment or training (with the same employer) in more than one location must include an itinerary with the dates and locations of the services, labor, or training.

(iv) Services, labor, or training for more than one employer. If the international cultural exchange visitor will perform services or labor for, or receive training from, more than one employer, each employer must file a separate petition. The international cultural exchange visitor may work part-time for multiple employers provided that each employer has an approved petition for the alien.

(v) Change of employers. If an international cultural exchange visitor is in the United States under section 101(a)(15)(Q)(i) of the Act and decides to change employers, the new employer must file a petition. However, the total period of time the international cultural exchange visitor may stay in the United States remains limited to fifteen (15) months.

(6) Substitution or replacements of participants in an international cultural exhange visitor program. The petitioner may substitute for or replace a person named on a previously approved petition for the remainder of the program without filing a new application or petition. The substituting international cultural exchange visitor must meet the qualification requirements prescribed in paragraph (q)(3)(iv) of this section. To request substitution or replacement, the petitioner shall, by letter, notify the consular office at which the alien will apply for a visa or, in the case of visa-exempt aliens, the Service office at the port of entry where the alien will apply for admission. A copy of the petition's approval notice must be included with the letter. The petitioner must state the date of birth, country of nationality, level of education, and position title of each prospective international cultural exchange visitor and must certify that each is qualified to perform the service or labor or receive the type of training described in the approved petition. The petitioner must also indicate each international cultural exchange visitor's wages and certify that the international cultural exchange visitor is offered wages and working conditions comparable to those accorded to local domestic workers in accordance with paragraph (q)(11)(ii) of this section.

(7) Approval of petition for international cultural exchange visitor program —

(i) The director shall consider all the evidence submitted and request other evidence as he or she may deem necessary.

(ii) The director shall notify the petitioner and the appropriate United States consulate(s) of the approval of a petition. For participants who are visa-exempt under 8 CFR 212.1(a), the director shall give notice of the approval to the director of the port of entry at which each such participant will apply for admission to the United States. The notice of approval shall include the name of the international cultural exchange visitors, their classification, and the petition's period of validity.

(iii) An approved petition for an alien classified under section 101(a)(15)(Q)(i) of the Act is valid for the length of the approved program or fifteen (15) months, whichever is shorter.

(iv) A petition shall not be approved for an alien who has an aggregate of fifteen (15) months in the United States under section 101(a)(15)(Q)(i) of the Act, unless the alien has resided and been physically present outside the United States for the immediate prior year.

(8) Denial of the petition —

(i) Notice of denial. The petitioner shall be notified of the denial of a petition, the reasons for the denial, and the right to appeal the denial under part 103 of this chapter.

(ii) Multiple participants. A petition for multiple international cultural exchange visitors may be denied in whole or in part.

(9) Revocation of approval of petition —

(i) General. The petitioner shall immediately notify the appropriate Service center of any changes in the employment of a participant which would affect eligibility under section 101(a)(15)(Q)(i) of the Act.

(ii) Automatic revocation. The approval of any petition is automatically revoked if the qualifying employer goes out of business, files a written withdrawal of the petition, or terminates the approved international cultural exchange program prior to its expiration date. No further action or notice by the Service is necessary in the case of automatic revocation. In any other case, the Service shall follow the revocation procedures in paragraphs (q)(9) (iii) through (v) of this section.

(iii) Revocation on notice. The director shall send the petitioner a notice of intent to revoke the petition in whole or in part if he or she finds that:

(A) The international cultural exchange visitor is no longer employed by the petitioner in the capacity specified in the petition, or if the international cultural exchange visitor is no longer receiving training as specified in the petition;

(B) The statement of facts contained in the petition was not true and correct;

(C) The petitioner violated the terms and conditions of the approved petition; or

(D) The Service approved the petition in error.

(iv) Notice and decision. The notice of intent to revoke shall contain a detailed statement of the grounds for the revocation and the period of time allowed for the petitioner's rebuttal. The petitioner may submit evidence in rebuttal within 30 days of receipt of the notice. The director shall consider all relevant evidence presented in deciding whether to revoke the petition in whole or in part. If the petition is revoked in part, the remainder of the petition shall remain approved and a revised approval notice shall be sent to the petitioner with the revocation notice.

(v) Appeal of a revocation of a petition. Revocation with notice of a petition in whole or in part may be appealed to the Associate Commissioner for Examinations under part 103 of this chapter. Automatic revocation may not be appealed.

(10) Extension of stay. An alien's total period of stay in the United States under section 101(a)(15)(Q)(i) of the Act cannot exceed fifteen (15) months. The authorized stay of an international cultural exchange visitor may be extended within the 15-month limit if he or she is the beneficiary of a new petition filed in accordance with paragraph (q)(3) of this section. The new petition, if filed by the same employer, should include a copy of the previous petition's approval notice and a letter from the petitioner indicating any terms and conditions of the previous petition that have changed.

(11) Employment provisions —

(i) General. An alien classified under section 101(a)(15)(Q)(i) of the Act may be employed only by the qualified employer through which the alien attained Q-1 nonimmigrant status. An alien in this class is not required to apply for an employment authorization document. Employment outside the specific program violates the terms of the alien's Q-1 nonimmigrant status within the meaning of section 237(a)(1)(C)(i) of the Act.

(ii) Wages and working conditions. The wages and working conditions of an international cultural exchange visitor must be comparable to those accorded to domestic workers similarly employed in the geographical area of the alien's employment. The employer must certify on the petition that such conditions are met as in accordance with paragraph (q)(4)(iii)(B) of this section.

(12) (Reserved)

(13) (Reserved)

(14) (Reserved)

(15) Irish peace process cultural and training program visitors (Q-2) and their dependents (Q-3) —

(i) General. An Irish Peace Process Cultural and Training Program (IPPCTP) visitor is a nonimmigrant alien coming to the United States temporarily to gain or upgrade work skills through training and temporary employment and to experience living in a diverse and peaceful environment.

(ii) What are the requirements for participation?

(A) The principal alien must have been physically resident in either Northern Ireland or the counties of Louth, Monaghan, Cavan, Leitrim, Sligo, and Donegal in the Republic of Ireland, for at least 3 months immediately preceding application to the program and must show that he or she has no intention of abandoning this residence.

(B) The principal alien must be between the ages of 18 and 35.

(C) The principal alien must:

(1) Be unemployed for at least 3 months, or have completed or currently be enrolled in a training/employment program sponsored by the Training and Employment Agency of Northern Ireland (T&EA) or by the Training and Employment Authority of Ireland (FAS), or by other such publicly funded programs, or have been made redundant from employment (i.e., lost their job), or have received a notice of redundancy (termination of employment); or

(2) Be a currently employed person whose employer has nominated him/her to participate in this program for additional training or job experience that is to benefit both the participant and his/her employer upon returning home.

(D) The principal alien must intend to come to the United States temporarily, for a period not to exceed 36 months, in order to obtain training, employment, and the experience of coexistence and conflict resolution in a diverse society.

(iii) Are there any limitations on admissions ?

(A) No more than 4,000 participants, including spouses and any minor children of principal aliens, may be admitted annually for 3 consecutive program years, beginning with FY 2000 (October 1, 1999, through September 30, 2000).

(B) For each alien admitted under section 101(a)(15)(Q)(ii) of the Act, the number of aliens admitted under section 101(a)(15)(H)(ii)(b) of the Act is reduced by one for that fiscal year or the subsequent fiscal year.

(C) This program expires on October 1, 2005.

(iv) What are the requirements for initial admission to the United States?

(A) Principal aliens, their spouses, and minor children of principal aliens must present valid passports and either a Q-2 or Q-3 visa at the time of inspection.

(B) Initial admission for those principal and dependent aliens in this program who received their visas at either the U.S. Embassy in Dublin or the U.S. Consulate in Belfast must take place at the Service's Pre-Flight Inspection facilities at either the Shannon or Dublin airports in the Republic of Ireland.

(C) The principal alien will be required to present a Certification Letter issued by the Department of State's (DOS') Program Administrator documenting him or her as an individual selected for participation in the IP-PCTP. Eligible dependents may be requested to present written documentation certifying their relationship to the principal.

(v) May the principal alien and dependents make brief visits outside the United States?

(A) The principal alien, spouse, and any minor children of the principal alien may make brief departures, for periods not to exceed 3 consecutive months, and may be readmitted without having to obtain a new visa. However, such periods of time spent outside the United States will not be added to the end of stay, which is not to exceed a total of 3 years from the initial date of entry of the principal alien.

(B) Those participants or dependents who remain outside the United States in excess of 3 consecutive months will not be readmitted by the Service on their initial Q-2 or Q-3 visa. Instead, any such individual and eligible dependents wishing to rejoin the program will be required to reapply to the program and be in receipt of a new Q-2 or Q-3 visa and a Certification Letter issued by the DOS' Program Administrator, prior to any subsequent admission to the United States.

(vi) How long may a Q-2 or Q-3 visa holder remain in the United States under this program?

(A) The principal alien and any accompanying, or following-to-join, spouse or minor children of the principal alien are admitted for the duration of the principal alien's planned cultural and training program or 36 months, whichever is shorter.

(B) Those participants and eligible dependents admitted for specific periods less than 36 months may extend their period of stay through the Service so that their total period of stay is 36 months, provided the extension of stay is related to employment or training certified by the DOS' Program Administrator.

(vii) How is employment authorized under this program?

(A) Following endorsement of his/her Form I-94, Arrival-Departure Record, by a Service officer, any principal alien admitted under section 101(a)(15)(Q)(ii) of the Act is permitted to work for an employer or employers listed on the Certification Letter issued by the DOS' Program Administrator.

(B) The accompanying spouse and minor children of the principal alien may not accept employment, unless the spouse has also been designated as a principal alien (Q-2) in this program and has been issued a Certification Letter by the DOS' Program Administrator.

(viii) May the principal alien change employers? Principal aliens wishing to change employers must request such a change through the DOS' Program Administrator to the Service. Following review and consideration of the request by the Service, the Service will inform the participant of the decision. The Service will grant such approval of employers only if the new employer has been approved by DOS in accordance with its regulations and such approval is communicated to the Service through the DOS' Program Administrator. If approved, the participant's Form I-94 will be annotated to show the new employer. If denied, there is no appeal under this section.

(ix) May the principal alien hold other jobs during his/her U.S. visit? No; any principal alien classified as an Irish peace process cultural and training program visitor may only engage in employment that has been certified by the DOS' Program Administrator and approved by the DOS or the Service as endorsed on the Form I-94. An alien who engages in unauthorized employment violates the terms of the Q-2 visa and will be considered to have violated section 237(a)(1)(C)(i) of the Act.

(x) What happens if a principal alien loses his/her job? A principal alien, who loses his or her job, will have 30 days from his/her last date of employment to locate appropriate employment or training, to have the job offer certified by the DOS' Program Administrator in accordance with the DOS' regulations and to have it approved by the Service. If appropriate employment or training cannot be found within this 30-day-period, the principal alien and any accompany family members will be required to depart the United States.

(r) Religious workers. This paragraph governs classification of an alien as a nonimmigrant religious worker (R-1).

(1) To be approved for temporary admission to the United States, or extension and maintenance of status, for the purpose of conducting the activities of a religious worker for a period not to exceed five years, an alien must:

(i) Be a member of a religious denomination having a bona fide non-profit religious organization in the United States for at least two years immediately preceding the time of application for admission;

(ii) Be coming to the United States to work at least in a part time position (average of at least 20 hours per week);

(iii) Be coming solely as a minister or to perform a religious vocation or occupation as defined in paragraph (r)(3) of this section (in either a professional or nonprofessional capacity);

(iv) Be coming to or remaining in the United States at the request of the petitioner to work for the petitioner; and

(v) Not work in the United States in any other capacity, except as provided in paragraph (r)(2) of this section.

(2) An alien may work for more than one qualifying employer as long as each qualifying employer submits a petition plus all additional required documentation as prescribed by USCIS regulations.

(3) Definitions. As used in this section, the term:

Bona fide non-profit religious organization in the United States means a religious organization exempt from taxation as described in section 501(c)(3) of the Internal Revenue Code of 1986, subsequent amendment or equivalent sections of prior enactments of the Internal Revenue Code, and possessing a currently valid determination letter from the Internal Revenue Service (IRS) confirming such exemption.

Bona fide organization which is affiliated with the religious denomination means an organization which is closely associated with the religious denomination and which is exempt from taxation as described in section 501(c)(3) of the Internal Revenue Code of 1986, or subsequent amendment or equivalent sections of prior enactments of the Internal Revenue Code, and possessing a currently valid determination letter from the IRS confirming such exemption.

Denominational membership means membership during at least the two-year period immediately preceding the filing date of the petition, in the same type of religious denomination as the United States religious organization where the alien will work.

Minister means an individual who:

(A) Is fully authorized by a religious denomination, and fully trained according to the denomination's standards, to conduct religious worship and perform other duties usually performed by authorized members of the clergy of that denomination;

(B) Is not a lay preacher or a person not authorized to perform duties usually performed by clergy;

(C) Performs activities with a rational relationship to the religious calling of the minister; and

(D) Works solely as a minister in the United States which may include administrative duties incidental to the duties of a minister.

Petition means the form or as may be prescribed by USCIS, a supplement containing attestations required by this section, and the supporting evidence required by this part.

Religious denomination means a religious group or community of believers that is governed or administered under a common type of ecclesiastical government and includes one or more of the following:

(A) A recognized common creed or statement of faith shared among the denomination's members;

(B) A common form of worship;

(C) A common formal code of doctrine and discipline;

(D) Common religious services and ceremonies;

(E) Common established places of religious worship or religious congregations; or

(F) Comparable indicia of a bona fide religious denomination.

Religious occupation means an occupation that meets all of the following requirements:

(A) The duties must primarily relate to a traditional religious function and be recognized as a religious occupation within the denomination;

(B) The duties must be primarily related to, and must clearly involve, inculcating or carrying out the religious creed and beliefs of the denomination;

(C) The duties do not include positions which are primarily administrative or support such as janitors, maintenance workers, clerical employees, fund raisers, persons solely involved in the solicitation of donations, or similar positions, although limited administrative duties that are only incidental to religious functions are permissible; and

(D) Religious study or training for religious work does not constitute a religious occupation, but a religious worker may pursue study or training incident to status.

Religious vocation means a formal lifetime commitment, through vows, investitures, ceremonies, or similar indicia, to a religious way of life. The religious denomination must have a class of individuals whose lives are dedicated to religious practices and functions, as distinguished from the secular members of the religion. Examples of vocations include nuns, monks, and religious brothers and sisters.

Religious worker means an individual engaged in and, according to the denomination's standards, qualified for a religious occupation or vocation, whether or not in a professional capacity, or as a minister.

Tax-exempt organization means an organization that has received a determination letter from the IRS establishing that it, or a group it belongs to, is exempt from taxation in accordance with sections 501(c)(3) of the Internal Revenue Code of 1986, or subsequent amendments or equivalent sections of prior enactments of the Internal Revenue Code.

(4) Requirements for admission/change of status; time limits —

(i) Principal applicant (R-1 nonimmigrant). If otherwise admissible, an alien who meets the requirements of section 101(a)(15)(R) of the Act may be admitted as an R-1 alien or changed to R-1 status for an initial period of up to 30 months from date of initial admission. If visa-exempt, the alien must present original documentation of the petition approval.

(ii) Spouse and children (R-2 status). The spouse and unmarried children under the age of 21 of an R-1 alien may be accompanying or following to join the R-1 alien, subject to the following conditions:

(A) R-2 status is granted for the same period of time and subject to the same limits as the principal, regardless of the time such spouse and children may have spent in the United States in R-2 status;

(B) Neither the spouse nor children may accept employment while in the United States in R-2 status; and

(C) The primary purpose of the spouse or children coming to the United States must be to join or accompany the principal R-1 alien.

(5) Extension of stay or readmission. An R-1 alien who is maintaining status or is seeking readmission and who satisfies the eligibility requirements of this section may be granted an extension of R-1 stay or readmission in R-1 status for the validity period of the petition, up to 30 months, provided the total period spent in R-1 status does not exceed a maximum of 5 years. A Petition for a Nonimmigrant Worker to request an extension of R-1 status must be filed by the employer with a supplement prescribed by USCIS containing attestations required by this section, the fee specified in 8 CFR part 106, and the supporting evidence, in accordance with the applicable form instructions.

(6) Limitation on total stay. An alien who has spent five years in the United States in R-1 status may not be readmitted to or receive an extension of stay in the United States under the R visa classification unless the alien has resided abroad and has been physically present outside the United States for the immediate prior year. The limitations in this paragraph shall not apply to R-1 aliens who did not reside continually in the United States and whose employment in the United States was seasonal or intermittent or was for an aggregate of six months or less per year. In addition, the limitations shall not apply to aliens who reside abroad and regularly commute to the United States to engage in part-time employment. To qualify for this exception, the petitioner and the alien must provide clear and convincing proof that the alien qualifies for such an exception. Such proof shall consist of evidence such as arrival and departure records, transcripts of processed income tax returns, and records of employment abroad.

(7) Jurisdiction and procedures for obtaining R-1 status. An employer in the United States seeking to employ a religious worker, by initial petition or by change of status, shall file a petition in accordance with the applicable form instructions.

(8) Attestation. An authorized official of the prospective employer of an R-1 alien must complete, sign and date an attestation prescribed by USCIS and submit it along with the petition. The prospective employer must specifically attest to all of the following:

(i) That the prospective employer is a bona fide non-profit religious organization or a bona fide organization which is affiliated with the religious denomination and is exempt from taxation;

(ii) That the alien has been a member of the denomination for at least two years and that the alien is otherwise qualified for the position offered;

(iii) The number of members of the prospective employer's organization;

(iv) The number of employees who work at the same location where the beneficiary will be employed and a summary of the type of responsibilities of those employees. USCIS may request a list of all employees, their titles, and a brief description of their duties at its discretion;

(v) The number of aliens holding special immigrant or nonimmigrant religious worker status currently employed or employed within the past five years by the prospective employer's organization;

(vi) The number of special immigrant religious worker and nonimmigrant religious worker petitions and applications filed by or on behalf of any aliens for employment by the prospective employer in the past five years;

(vii) The title of the position offered to the alien and a detailed description of the alien's proposed daily duties;

(viii) Whether the alien will receive salaried or non-salaried compensation and the details of such compensation;

(ix) That the alien will be employed at least 20 hours per week;

(x) The specific location(s) of the proposed employment; and

(xi) That the alien will not be engaged in secular employment.

(9) Evidence relating to the petitioning organization. A petition shall include the following initial evidence relating to the petitioning organization:

(i) A currently valid determination letter from the IRS showing that the organization is a tax-exempt organization; or

(ii) For a religious organization that is recognized as tax-exempt under a group tax-exemption, a currently valid determination letter from the IRS establishing that the group is tax-exempt; or

(iii) For a bona fide organization that is affiliated with the religious denomination, if the organization was granted tax-exempt status under section 501(c)(3), or subsequent amendment or equivalent sections of prior enactments, of the Internal Revenue Code, as something other than a religious organization:

(A) A currently valid determination letter from the IRS establishing that the organization is a tax-exempt organization;

(B) Documentation that establishes the religious nature and purpose of the organization, such as a copy of the organizing instrument of the organization that specifies the purposes of the organization;

(C) Organizational literature, such as books, articles, brochures, calendars, flyers, and other literature describing the religious purpose and nature of the activities of the organization; and

(D) A religious denomination certification. The religious organization must complete, sign and date a statement certifying that the petitioning organization is affiliated with the religious denomination. The statement must be submitted by the petitioner along with the petition.

(10) Evidence relating to the qualifications of a minister. If the alien is a minister, the petitioner must submit the following:

(i) A copy of the alien's certificate of ordination or similar documents reflecting acceptance of the alien's qualifications as a minister in the religious denomination; and

(ii) Documents reflecting acceptance of the alien's qualifications as a minister in the religious denomination, as well as evidence that the alien has completed any course of prescribed theological education at an accredited theological institution normally required or recognized by that religious denomination, including transcripts, curriculum, and documentation that establishes that the theological education is accredited by the denomination, or

(iii) For denominations that do not require a prescribed theological education, evidence of:

(A) The denomination's requirements for ordination to minister;

(B) The duties allowed to be performed by virtue of ordination;

(C) The denomination's levels of ordination, if any; and

(D) The alien's completion of the denomination's requirements for ordination.

(11) Evidence relating to compensation. Initial evidence must state how the petitioner intends to compensate the alien, including specific monetary or in-kind compensation, or whether the alien intends to be self-supporting. In either case, the petitioner must submit verifiable evidence explaining how the petitioner will compensate the alien or how the alien will be self-supporting. Compensation may include:

(i) Salaried or non-salaried compensation. Evidence of compensation may include past evidence of compensation for similar positions; budgets showing monies set aside for salaries, leases, etc.; verifiable documentation that room and board will be provided; or other evidence acceptable to USCIS. IRS documentation, such as IRS Form W-2 or certified tax returns, must be submitted, if available. If IRS documentation is unavailable, the petitioner must submit an explanation for the absence of IRS documentation, along with comparable, verifiable documentation.

(ii) Self support.

(A) If the alien will be self-supporting, the petitioner must submit documentation establishing that the position the alien will hold is part of an established program for temporary, uncompensated missionary work, which is part of a broader international program of missionary work sponsored by the denomination.

(B) An established program for temporary, uncompensated work is defined to be a missionary program in which:

(1) Foreign workers, whether compensated or uncompensated, have previously participated in R-1 status;

(2) Missionary workers are traditionally uncompensated;

(3) The organization provides formal training for missionaries; and

(4) Participation in such missionary work is an established element of religious development in that denomination.

(C) The petitioner must submit evidence demonstrating:

(1) That the organization has an established program for temporary, uncompensated missionary work;

(2) That the denomination maintains missionary programs both in the United states and abroad;

(3) The religious worker's acceptance into the missionary program;

(4) The religious duties and responsibilities associated with the traditionally uncompensated missionary work; and

(5) Copies of the alien's bank records, budgets documenting the sources of self-support (including personal or family savings, room and board with host families in the United States, donations from the denomination's churches), or other verifiable evidence acceptable to USCIS.

(12) Evidence of previous R-1 employment. Any request for an extension of stay as an R-1 must include initial evidence of the previous R-1 employment. If the beneficiary:

(i) Received salaried compensation, the petitioner must submit IRS documentation that the alien received a salary, such as an IRS Form W-2 or certified copies of filed income tax returns, reflecting such work and compensation for the preceding two years.

(ii) Received non-salaried compensation, the petitioner must submit IRS documentation of the non-salaried compensation if available. If IRS documentation is unavailable, an explanation for the absence of IRS documentation must be provided, and the petitioner must provide verifiable evidence of all financial support, including stipends, room and board, or other support for the beneficiary by submitting a description of the location where the beneficiary lived, a lease to establish where the beneficiary lived, or other evidence acceptable to USCIS.

(iii) Received no salary but provided for his or her own support, and that of any dependents, the petitioner must show how support was maintained by submitting with the petition verifiable documents such as audited financial statements, financial institution records, brokerage account statements, trust documents signed by an attorney, or other evidence acceptable to USCIS.

(13) Change or addition of employers. An R-1 alien may not be compensated for work for any religious organization other than the one for which a petition has been approved or the alien will be out of status. A different or additional employer seeking to employ the alien may obtain prior approval of such employment through the filing of a separate petition and appropriate supplement, supporting documents, and fee prescribed in 8 CFR 106.2.

(14) Employer obligations. When an R-1 alien is working less than the required number of hours or has been released from or has otherwise terminated employment before the expiration of a period of authorized R-1 stay, the R-1 alien's approved employer must notify DHS within 14 days using procedures set forth in the instructions to the petition or otherwise prescribed by USCIS on the USCIS Internet Web site at www.uscis.gov.

(15) Nonimmigrant intent. An alien classified under section 101(a)(15)(R) of the Act shall maintain an intention to depart the United States upon the expiration or termination of R-1 or R-2 status. However, a nonimmigrant petition, application for initial admission, change of status, or extension of stay in R classification may not be denied solely on the basis of a filed or an approved request for permanent labor certifica-

tion or a filed or approved immigrant visa preference petition.

(16) Inspections, evaluations, verifications, and compliance reviews. The supporting evidence submitted may be verified by USCIS through any means determined appropriate by USCIS, up to and including an on-site inspection of the petitioning organization. The inspection may include a tour of the organization's facilities, an interview with the organization's officials, a review of selected organization records relating to compliance with immigration laws and regulations, and an interview with any other individuals or review of any other records that the USCIS considers pertinent to the integrity of the organization. An inspection may include the organization headquarters, or satellite locations, or the work locations planned for the applicable employee. If USCIS decides to conduct a pre-approval inspection, satisfactory completion of such inspection will be a condition for approval of any petition.

(17) Denial and appeal of petition. USCIS will provide written notification of the reasons for the denial under 8 CFR 103.3(a)(1). The petitioner may appeal the denial under 8 CFR 103.3.

(18) Revocation of approved petitions —

(i) Director discretion. The director may revoke a petition at any time, even after the expiration of the petition.

(ii) Automatic revocation. The approval of any petition is automatically revoked if the petitioner ceases to exist or files a written withdrawal of the petition.

(iii) Revocation on notice —

(A) Grounds for revocation. The director shall send to the petitioner a notice of intent to revoke the petition in relevant part if he or she finds that:

(1) The beneficiary is no longer employed by the petitioner in the capacity specified in the petition;

(2) The statement of facts contained in the petition was not true and correct;

(3) The petitioner violated terms and conditions of the approved petition;

(4) The petitioner violated requirements of section 101(a)(15)(R) of the Act or paragraph (r) of this section; or

(5) The approval of the petition violated paragraph (r) of this section or involved gross error.

(B) Notice and decision. The notice of intent to revoke shall contain a detailed statement of the grounds for the revocation and the time period allowed for the petitioner's rebuttal. The petitioner may submit evidence in rebuttal within 30 days of receipt of the notice. The director shall consider all relevant evidence presented in deciding whether to revoke the petition.

(19) Appeal of a revocation of a petition. A petition that has been revoked on notice in whole or in part may be appealed under 8 CFR 103.3. Automatic revocations may not be appealed.

(s) NATO nonimmigrant aliens —

(1) General —

(i) Background. The North Atlantic Treaty Organization (NATO) is constituted of nations signatory to the North Atlantic Treaty. The Agreement Between the Parties to the North Atlantic Treaty Regarding the Status of Their Forces, signed in London, June 1951 (NATO Status of Forces Agreement), is the agreement between those nations that defines the terms of the status of their armed forces while serving abroad.

(A) Nonimmigrant aliens classified as NATO-1 through NATO-5 are officials, employees, or persons associated with NATO, and members of their immediate families, who may enter the United States in accordance with the NATO Status of Forces Agreement or the Protocol on the Status of International Military Headquarters set up pursuant to the North Atlantic Treaty (Paris Protocol). The following specific classifications shall be assigned to such NATO nonimmigrants:

(1)NATO-1 — A principal permanent representative of a Member State to NATO (including any of its subsidiary bodies) resident in the United States and resident members of permanent representative's official staff; Secretary General, Deputy Secretary General, Assistant Secretaries General and Executive Secretary of NATO; other permanent NATO officials of similar rank; and the members of the immediate family of such persons.

(2)NATO-2 — Other representatives of Member States to NATO (including any of its subsidiary bodies) including representatives, advisers and technical experts of delegations, and the members of the immediate family of such persons; dependents of members of a force entering in accordance with the provisions of the NATO Status of Forces Agreement or in accordance with the provisions of the Paris Protocol; members of such a force, if issued visas.

(3)NATO-3 — Official clerical staff accompanying a representative of a Member State to NATO (including any of its subsidiary bodies) and the members of the immediate family of such persons.

(4)NATO-4 — Officials of NATO (other than those classifiable under NATO-1) and the members of their immediate family

(5)NATO-5 — Experts, other than NATO officials classifiable under NATO-4, employed on missions on behalf of NATO and their dependents.

(B) Nonimmigrant aliens classified as NATO-6 are civilians, and members of their immediate families, who may enter the United States as employees of a force entering in accordance with the NATO Status of Forces Agreement, or as members of a civilian component attached to or employed by NATO Headquarters, Supreme Allied Commander, Atlantic (SACLANT), set up pursuant to the Paris Protocol.

(C) Nonimmigrant aliens classified as NATO-7 are attendants, servants, or personal employees of nonimmigrant aliens classified as NATO-1, NATO-2, NATO-3, NATO-4, NATO-5, and NATO-6, who are authorized to work only for the NATO-1 through NATO-6 nonimmigrant from whom they derive status, and members of their immediate families.

(ii) Admission and extension of stay. NATO-1, NATO-2, NATO-3, NATO-4, and NATO-5 aliens are normally exempt from inspection under 8 CFR 235.1(c). NATO-6 aliens may be authorized admission for duration of status. NATO-7 aliens may be admitted for not more than 3 years and may be granted extensions of temporary stay in increments of not more than 2 years. In addition, an application for extension of temporary stay for a NATO-7 alien must be accompanied by a statement signed by the employing official stating that he or she intends to continue to employ the NATO-7 applicant, describing the work the applicant will perform, and acknowledging that this is, and will be, the sole employment of the NATO-7 applicant.

(2) Definition of a dependent of a NATO-1, NATO-2, NATO-3, NATO-4, NATO-5, or NATO-6. For purposes of employment in the United States, the term dependent of a NATO-1, NATO-2, NATO-3, NATO-4, NATO-5, or NATO-6 principal alien, as used in this section, means any of the following immediate members of the family habitually residing in the same household as the NATO-1, NATO-2, NATO-3, NATO-4, NATO-5, or NATO-6 principal alien assigned to official duty in the United States:

(i) Spouse;

(ii) Unmarried children under the age of 21;

(iii) Unmarried sons or daughters under the age of 23 who are in full-time attendance as students at post-secondary educational institutions;

(iv) Unmarried sons or daughters under the age of 25 who are in full-time attendance as students at post-secondary educational institutions if a formal bilateral employment agreement permitting their employment in the United States was signed prior to November 21, 1988, and such bilateral employment agreements do not specify under the age of 23 as the maximum age for employment of such sons and daughters;

(v) Unmarried sons or daughters who are physically or mentally disabled to the extent that they cannot adequately care for themselves or cannot establish, maintain, or re-establish their own households. The Service may require medical certification(s) as it deems necessary to document such mental or physical disability.

(3) Dependent employment requirements based on formal bilateral employment agreements and informal de facto reciprocal arrangements —

(i) Formal bilateral employment agreements. The Department of State's Family Liaison office (FLO) shall maintain all listing of NATO Member States which have entered into formal bilateral employment agreements that include NATO personnel. A dependent of a NATO-1, NATO-2, NATO-3, NATO-4, NATO-5, or NATO-6 principal alien assigned to official duty in the United States may accept, or continue in, unrestricted employment based on such formal bilateral agreement upon favorable recommendation by SACLANT, pursuant to paragraph (s)(5) of this section, and issuance of employment authorization documentation by the Service in accordance with 8 CFR part 274a. The application procedures are set forth in paragraph (s)(5) of this section.

(ii) Informal de facto reciprocal arrangements. For purposes of this section, an informal de facto reciprocal arrangement exists when the Office of the Secretary of Defense, Foreign Military Rights Affairs (OSD/FMRA), certifies, with State Department concurrence, that a NATO Member State allows appropriate employment in the local economy for dependents of members of the force and members of the civilian component of the United States assigned to duty in the NATO Member State. OSD/FMRA and State's FLO shall maintain a listing of countries with which such reciprocity exists. Dependents of a NATO-1, NATO-2, NATO-3, NATO-4, NATO-5, or NATO-6 principal alien assigned to official duty in the United States may be authorized to accept, or continue in, employment based upon informal de facto arrangements upon favorable recommendation by SACLANT, pursuant to paragraph (s)(5) of this section, and issuance of employment authorization by the Service in accordance with 8 CFR part 274a. Additionally, the application procedures set forth in paragraph (s)(5) of this section must be complied with, and the following conditions must be met:

(A) Both the principal alien and the dependent requesting employment are maintaining NATO-1, NATO-2, NATO-3, NATO-4, NATO-5, or NATO-6 status, as appropriate;

(B) The principal alien's total length of assignment in the United States is expected to last more than 6 months;

(C) Employment of a similar nature for dependents of members of the force and members of the civilian component of the United States assigned to official duty in the NATO Member State employing the principal alien is not prohibited by the NATO Member State;

(D) The proposed employment is not in an occupation listed in the Department of Labor's Schedule B (20 CFR part 656), or otherwise determined by the Department of Labor to be one for which there is an oversupply of qualified United States workers in the area of proposed employment. This Schedule B restriction does not apply to a dependent son or daughter who is a full-time student if the employment is part-time, consisting of not more than 20 hours per week, of if it is temporary employment of not more than 12 weeks during school holiday periods; and

(E) The proposed employment is not contrary to the interest of the United States. Employment contrary to the interest of the United States includes, but is not limited to, the employment of NATO-1, NATO-2, NATO-3, NATO-4, NATO-5, or NATO-6 dependents who have criminal records; who have violated United States immigration laws or regulations, or visa laws or regulations; who have worked illegally in the United States; or who cannot establish that they have paid taxes and social security on income from current or previous United States employment.

(iii) State's FLO shall inform the Service, by contacting Headquarters, Adjudications, Attention: Chief, Business and Trade Services Branch, 425 I Street, NW., Washington, DC 20536, of any additions or changes to the formal bilateral employment agreements and informal de facto reciprocal arrangements.

(4) Applicability of a formal bilateral agreement or an informal de facto arrangement for NATO-1, NATO-2, NATO-3, NATO-4, NATO-5, or NATO-6 dependents. The applicability of a formal bilateral agreement shall be based on the NATO Member State which

employs the principal alien and not on the nationality of the principal alien or dependent. The applicability of an informal de facto arrangement shall be based on the NATO Member State which employs the principal alien, and the principal alien also must be a national of the NATO Member State which employs him or her in the United States. Dependents of SACLANT employees receive bilateral agreement or de facto arrangement employment privileges as appropriate based upon the nationality of the SACLANT employee (principal alien).

(5) Application procedures. The following procedures are required for dependent employment applications under bilateral agreements and de facto arrangements:

(i) The dependent of a NATO alien shall submit a complete application for employment authorization, including Form I-765 and Form I-566, completed in accordance with the instructions on, or attached to, those forms. The complete application shall be submitted to SACLANT for certification of the Form I-566 and forwarding to the Service.

(ii) In a case where a bilateral dependent employment agreement containing a numerical limitation on the number of dependents authorized to work is applicable, the certifying officer of SACLANT shall not forward the application for employment authorization to the Service unless, following consultation with State's Office of Protocol, the certifying officer has confirmed that this numerical limitation has not been reached. The countries with such limitations are indicated on the bilateral/de facto dependent employment listing issued by State's FLO.

(iii) SACLANT shall keep copies of each application and certified Form I-566 for 3 years from the date of the certification.

(iv) A dependent applying under the terms of a de facto arrangement must also attach a statement from the prospective employer which includes the dependent's name, a description of the position offered, the duties to be performed, the hours to be worked, the salary offered, and verification that the dependent possesses the qualifications for the position.

(v) A dependent applying under paragraph (s)(2) (iii) or (iv) of this section must also submit a certified statement from the post-secondary educational institution confirming that he or she is pursuing studies on a full-time basis.

(vi) A dependent applying under paragraph (s)(2)(v) of this section must also submit medical certification regarding his or her condition. The certification should identify both the dependent and the certifying physician, give the physician's phone number, identify the condition, describe the symptoms, provide a clear prognosis, and certify that the dependent is unable to maintain a home of his or her own.

(vii) The Service may require additional supporting documentation, but only after consultation with SACLANT.

(6) Period of time for which employment may be authorized. If approved, an application to accept or continue employment under this paragraph shall be granted in increments of not more than 3 years.

(7) Income tax and Social Security liability. Dependents who are granted employment authorization under this paragraph are responsible for payment of all Federal, state, and local income taxes, employment and related taxes and Social Security contributions on any remuneration received.

(8) No appeal. There shall be no appeal from a denial of permission to accept or continue employment under this paragraph.

(9) Unauthorized employment. An alien classified as a NATO-1, NATO-2, NATO-3, NATO-4, NATO-5, NATO-6, or NATO-7 who is not a NATO principal alien and who engages in employment outside the scope of, or in a manner contrary to, this paragraph may be considered in violation of status pursuant to section 237(a)(1)(C)(i) of the Act. A NATO principal alien in those classifications who engages in employment outside the scope of his or her official position may be considered in violation of status pursuant to section 237(a)(1)(C)(i) of the Act.

(t) Alien witnesses and informants —

(1) Alien witness or informant in criminal matter. An alien may be classified as an S-5 alien witness or informant under the provisions of section 101(a)(15)(S)(i) of the Act if, in the exercise of discretion pursuant to an application on Form I-854 by an interested federal or state law enforcement authority ("LEA"), it is determined by the Commissioner that the alien:

(i) Possesses critical reliable information concerning a criminal organization or enterprise;

(ii) Is willing to supply, or has supplied, such information to federal or state LEA; and

(iii) Is essential to the success of an authorized criminal investigation or the successful prosecution of an individual involved in the criminal organization or enterprise.

(2) Alien witness or informant in counterterrorism matter. An alien may be classified as an S-6 alien counterterrorism witness or informant under the provisions of section 101(a)(15)(S)(ii) of the Act if it is determined by the Secretary of State and the Commissioner acting jointly, in the exercise of their discretion, pursuant to an application on Form I-854 by an interested federal LEA, that the alien:

(i) Possesses critical reliable information concerning a terrorist organization, enterprise, or operation;

(ii) Is willing to supply or has supplied such information to a federal LEA;

(iii) Is in danger or has been placed in danger as a result of providing such information; and

(iv) Is eligible to receive a reward under section 36(a) of the State Department Basic Authorities Act of 1956, 22 U.S.C. 2708(a).

(3) Spouse, married and unmarried sons and daughters, and parents of alien witness or informant in criminal or counterterrorism matter. An alien spouse, married or unmarried son or daughter, or parent of an alien witness or informant may be granted derivative S classification (S-7) when accompanying, or following to join, the alien witness or informant if, in the exercise of discretion by, with respect to paragraph (t)(1) of this

section, the Commissioner, or, with respect to paragraph (t)(2) of this section, the Secretary of State and the Commissioner acting jointly, consider it to be appropriate. A nonimmigrant in such derivative S-7 classification shall be subject to the same period of admission, limitations, and restrictions as the alien witness or informant and must be identified by the requesting LEA on the application Form I-854 in order to qualify for S nonimmigrant classification. Family members not identified on the Form I-854 application will not be eligible for S nonimmigrant classification.

(4) Request for S nonimmigrant classification. An application on Form I-854, requesting S nonimmigrant classification for a witness or informant, may only be filed by a federal or state LEA (which shall include a federal or state court or a United States Attorney's Office) directly in need of the information to be provided by the alien witness or informant. The completed application is filed with the Assistant Attorney General, Criminal Division, Department of Justice, who will forward only properly certified applications that fall within the numerical limitation to the Commissioner, Immigration and Naturalization Service, for approval, pursuant to the following process.

(i) Filing request. For an alien to qualify for status as an S nonimmigrant, S nonimmigrant classification must be requested by an LEA. The LEA shall recommend an alien for S nonimmigrant classification by: Completing Form I-854, with all necessary endorsements and attachments, in accordance with the instructions on, or attached to, that form, and agreeing, as a condition of status, that no promises may be, have been, or will be made by the LEA that the alien will or may remain in the United States in S or any other nonimmigrant classification or parole, adjust status to that of lawful permanent resident, or otherwise attempt to remain beyond a 3-year period other than by the means authorized by section 101(a)(15)(S) of the Act. The alien, including any derivative beneficiary who is 18 years or older, shall sign a statement, that is part of or affixed to Form I-854, acknowledging awareness that he or she is restricted by the terms of S nonimmigrant classification to the specific terms of section 101(a)(15)(S) of the Act as the exclusive means by which he or she may remain permanently in the United States.

(A) District director referral. Any district director or Service officer who receives a request by an alien, an eligible LEA, or other entity seeking S nonimmigrant classification shall advise the requestor of the process and the requirements for applying for S nonimmigrant classification. Eligible LEAs seeking S nonimmigrant classification shall be referred to the Commissioner.

(B) United States Attorney certification. The United States Attorney with jurisdiction over a prosecution or investigation that forms the basis for a request for S nonimmigrant classification must certify and endorse the application on Form I-854 and agree that no promises may be, have been, or will be made that the alien will or may remain in the United States in S or any other nonimmigrant classification or parole, adjust status to lawful permanent resident, or attempt to remain beyond the authorized period of admission.

(C) LEA certification. LEA certifications on Form I-854 must be made at the seat-of-government level, if federal, or the highest level of the state LEA involved in the matter. With respect to the alien for whom S nonimmigrant classification is sought, the LEA shall provide evidence in the form of attachments establishing the nature of the alien's cooperation with the government, the need for the alien's presence in the United States, all conduct or conditions which may constitute a ground or grounds of excludability, and all factors and considerations warranting a favorable exercise of discretionary waiver authority by the Attorney General on the alien's behalf. The attachments submitted with a request for S nonimmigrant classification may be in the form of affidavits, statements, memoranda, or similar documentation. The LEA shall review Form I-854 for accuracy and ensure the alien understands the certifications made on Form I-854.

(D) Filing procedure. Upon completion of Form I-854, the LEA shall forward the form and all required attachments to the Assistant Attorney General, Criminal Division, United States Department of Justice, at the address listed on the form.

(ii) Assistant Attorney General, Criminal Division review —

(A) Review of information. Upon receipt of a complete application for S nonimmigrant classification on Form I-854, with all required attachments, the Assistant Attorney General, Criminal Division, shall ensure that all information relating to the basis of the application, the need for the witness or informant, and grounds of excludability under section 212 of the Act has been provided to the Service on Form I-854, and shall consider the negative and favorable factors warranting an exercise of discretion on the alien's behalf. No application may be acted on by the Assistant Attorney General unless the eligible LEA making the request has proceeded in accordance with the instructions on, or attached to, Form I-854 and agreed to all provisions therein.

(B) Advisory panel. Where necessary according to procedures established by the Assistant Attorney General, Criminal Division, an advisory panel, composed of representatives of the Service, Marshals Service, Federal Bureau of Investigation, Drug Enforcement Administration, Criminal Division, and the Department of State, and those representatives of other LEAs, including state and federal courts designated by the Attorney General, will review the completed application and submit a recommendation to the Assistant Attorney General, Criminal Division, regarding requests for S nonimmigrant classification. The function of this advisory panel is to prioritize cases in light of the numerical limitation in order to determine which cases will be forwarded to the Commissioner.

(C) Assistant Attorney General certification. The certification of the Assistant Attorney General, Criminal Division, to the Commissioner recommending approval of the application for S nonimmigrant classification shall contain the following:

(1) All information and attachments that may constitute, or relate to, a ground or grounds of excludability under section 212(a) of the Act;

(2) Each section of law under which the alien appears to be inadmissible;

(3) The reasons that waiver(s) of inadmissibility are considered to be justifiable and in the national interest;

(4) A detailed statement that the alien is eligible for S nonimmigrant classification, explaining the nature of the alien's cooperation with the government and the government's need for the alien's presence in the United States;

(5) The intended date of arrival;

(6) The length of the proposed stay in the United States;

(7) The purpose of the proposed stay; and

(8) A statement that the application falls within the statutorily specified numerical limitation.

(D) Submission of certified requests for S nonimmigrant classification to Service.

(1) The Assistant Attorney General, Criminal Division, shall forward to the Commissioner only qualified applications for S-5 nonimmigrant classification that have been certified in accordance with the provisions of this paragraph and that fall within the annual numerical limitation.

(2) The Assistant Attorney General Criminal Division, shall forward to the Commissioner applications for S-6 nonimmigrant classification that have been certified in accordance with the provisions of this paragraph, certified by the Secretary of State or eligibility for S-6 classification, and that fall within the annual numerical limitation.

(5) Decision on application.

(i) The Attorney General's authority to waive grounds of excludability pursuant to section 212 of the Act is delegated to the Commissioner and shall be exercised with regard to S nonimmigrant classification only upon the certification of the Assistant Attorney General, Criminal Division. Such certification is nonreviewable as to the matter's significance, importance, and/or worthwhileness to law enforcement. The Commissioner shall make the final decision to approve or deny a request for S nonimmigrant classification certified by the Assistant Attorney General, Criminal Division.

(ii) Decision to approve application. Upon approval of the application on Form I-854, the Commissioner shall notify the Assistant Attorney General, Criminal Division, the Secretary of State, and Service officers as appropriate. Admission shall be authorized for a period not to exceed 3 years.

(iii) Decision to deny application. In the event the Commissioner decides to deny an application for S nonimmigrant classification on Form I-854, the Assistant Attorney General, Criminal Division, and the relevant LEA shall be notified in writing to that effect. The Assistant Attorney General, Criminal Division, shall concur in or object to that decision. Unless the Assistant Attorney General, Criminal Division, objects within 7 days, he or she shall be deemed to have concurred in the decision. In the event of an objection by the Assistant Attorney General, Criminal Division, the matter will be expeditiously referred to the Deputy Attorney General for a final resolution. In no circumstances shall the alien or the relevant LEA have a right of appeal from any decision to deny.

(6) Submission of requests for S nonimmigrant visa classification to Secretary of State. No request for S nonimmigrant visa classification may be presented to the Secretary of State unless it is approved and forwarded by the Commissioner.

(7) Conditions of status. An alien witness or informant is responsible for certifying and fulfilling the terms and conditions specified on Form I-854 as a condition of status. The LEA that assumes responsibility for the S nonimmigrant must:

(i) Ensure that the alien:

(A) Reports quarterly to the LEA on his or her whereabouts and activities, and as otherwise specified on Form I-854 or pursuant to the terms of his or her S nonimmigrant classification;

(B) Notifies the LEA of any change of home or work address and phone numbers or any travel plans;

(C) Abides by the law and all specified terms, limitations, or restrictions on the visa, Form I-854, or any waivers pursuant to classification; and

(D) Cooperates with the responsible LEA in accordance with the terms of his or her classification and any restrictions on Form I-854;

(ii) Provide the Assistant Attorney General, Criminal Division, with the name of the control agent on an ongoing basis and provide a quarterly report indicating the whereabouts, activities, and any other control information required on Form I-854 or by the Assistant Attorney General;

(iii) Report immediately to the Service any failure on the alien's part to:

(A) Report quarterly;

(B) Cooperate with the LEA;

(C) Comply with the terms and conditions of the specific S nonimmigrant classification; or

(D) Refrain from criminal activity that may render the alien deportable, which information shall also be forwarded to the Assistant Attorney General, Criminal Division; and

(iv) Report annually to the Assistant Attorney General, Criminal Division, on whether the alien's S nonimmigrant classification and cooperation resulted in either:

(A) A successful criminal prosecution or investigation or the failure to produce a successful resolution of the matter; or

(B) The prevention or frustration of terrorist acts or the failure to prevent such acts.

(v) Assist the alien in his or her application to the Service for employment authorization.

(8) Annual report. The Assistant Attorney General, Criminal Division, in consultation with the Commissioner, shall compile the statutorily mandated annual report to the Committee on the Judiciary of the House of Representatives and the Committee on the Judiciary of the Senate.

(9) Admission. The responsible LEA will coordinate the admission of an alien in S nonimmigrant classification with the Commissioner as to the date, time, place, and manner of the alien's arrival.

(10) Employment. An alien classified under section 101(a)(15)(S) of the Act may apply for employment authorization by filing Form I-765, Application for Employment Authorization, with fee, in accordance with the instructions on, or attached to, that form pursuant to § 274a.12(c)(21) of this chapter.

(11) Failure to maintain status. An alien classified under section 101(a)(15)(S) of the Act shall abide by all the terms and conditions of his or her S nonimmigrant classification imposed by the Attorney General. If the terms and conditions of S nonimmigrant classification will not be or have not been met, or have been violated, the alien is convicted of any criminal offense punishable by a term of imprisonment of 1 year or more, is otherwise rendered deportable, or it is otherwise appropriate or in the public interest to do so, the Commissioner shall proceed to deport an alien pursuant to the terms of 8 CFR 242.26. In the event the Commissioner decides to deport an alien witness or informant in S nonimmigrant classification, the Assistant Attorney General, Criminal Division, and the relevant LEA shall be notified in writing to that effect. The Assistant Attorney General, Criminal Division, shall concur in or object to that decision. Unless the Assistant Attorney General, Criminal Division, objects within 7 days, he or she shall be deemed to have concurred in the decision. In the event of an objection by the Assistant Attorney General, Criminal Division, the matter will be expeditiously referred to the Deputy Attorney General for a final resolution. In no circumstances shall the alien or the relevant LEA have a right of appeal from any decision to deport.

(12) Change of classification.

(i) An alien in S nonimmigrant classification is prohibited from changing to any other nonimmigrant classification.

(ii) An LEA may request that any alien lawfully admitted to the United States and maintaining status in accordance with the provisions of § 248.1 of this chapter, except for those aliens enumerated in 8 CFR 248.2, have his or her nonimmigrant classification changed to that of an alien classified pursuant to section 101(a)(15)(S) of the Act as set forth in 8 CFR 248.3(h).

(u) [Reserved]

(v) Certain spouses and children of LPRs. Section 214.15 of this chapter provides the procedures and requirements pertaining to V nonimmigrant status.

(w) CNMI-Only Transitional Worker (CW-1).

Table 5 to Paragraph (w)—Paragraph Contents

(1) Definitions.
(2) Eligible aliens.
(3) Derivative beneficiaries—CW-2 nonimmigrant classification.
(4) Eligible employers.
(5) Petition requirements.
(6) Appropriate documents.
(7) Change of employers.
(8) Amended or new petition.
(9) Multiple beneficiaries.
(10) Named beneficiaries.
(11) Early termination.
(12) Approval.
(13) Petition validity.
(14) Validity of the labor certification.
(15) How to apply for CW-1 or CW-2 status.
(16) Biometrics and other information.
(17) Period of admission.
(18) Extension of petition validity and extension of stay.
(19) Change or adjustment of status.
(20) Effect of filing an application for or approval of a permanent labor certification, preference petition, or filing of an application for adjustment of status on CW-1 or CW-2 classification.
(21) Rejection.
(22) Denial.
(23) Terms and conditions of CW Nonimmigrant status.
(24) Expiration of status.
(25) Waivers of inadmissibility for applicants lawfully present in the CNMI.
(26) Semiannual report.
(27) Revocation of approval of petition.
(28) Appeal of a revocation of a petition.
(29) Notice to DOL.

(1) Definitions. The following definitions apply to petitions for and maintenance of CW status in the Commonwealth of the Northern Mariana Islands (the CNMI or the Commonwealth):

(i) CW–1 Application for Temporary Employment Certification means the Office of Management and Budget (OMB)-approved Form ETA–9142C (or successor form) and the appropriate appendices, a valid prevailing wage determination (Form ETA–9141C, or successor form), and all supporting documentation submitted by an employer, as set forth in the U.S. Department of Labor's (DOL) regulations at 20 CFR 655.420 through 655.422, to secure a temporary labor certification determination from DOL's Office of Foreign Labor Certification (OFLC) Administrator.

(ii) Direct Guam transit means travel from the CNMI to a foreign place by an alien in CW status, or from a foreign place to the CNMI by an alien with a valid CW visa, on a direct itinerary involving a flight stopover or connection in Guam (and no other place).

(iii) Doing business means the regular, systematic, and continuous provision of goods or services by an employer as defined in this paragraph and does not include the mere presence of an agent or office of the employer in the CNMI.

(iv) Employer means a person, firm, corporation, contractor, or other association, or organization which:

(A) Engages a person to work within the CNMI; and

(B) Has or will have an employer-employee relationship with the CW–1 nonimmigrant being petitioned for.

(v) Employer-employee relationship means that the employer will hire, pay, fire, supervise, and control the work of the employee.

(vi) Lawfully present in the CNMI means that the alien was lawfully admitted or paroled into the CNMI under the immigration laws on or after the transition program effective date, other than an alien admitted or paroled as a visitor for business or pleasure (B– 1 or B–2, under any visa-free travel provision or parole of certain visitors from Russia and the People's Republic of China), and remains in a lawful immigration status or if paroled into the CNMI, the authorized parole period has not expired.

(vii) Legitimate business, as determined by DHS, means a real, active, and operating commercial or entrepreneurial undertaking that:

(A) Produces services or goods for profit, or is a governmental, charitable or other validly recognized nonprofit entity;

(B) Meets applicable legal requirements for doing business in the CNMI;

(C) Has substantially complied with wage and hour laws, occupational safety and health requirements, nondiscrimination, and all other Federal, CNMI, and local requirements relating to employment during the fiveyear period immediately preceding the date of filing the petition, and continues to be in substantial compliance with such requirements;

(D) Does not directly or indirectly engage in, or knowingly benefit from, prostitution, human trafficking, or any other activity that is illegal under Federal, CNMI, or local law;

(E) Is a participant in good standing in the E-Verify program;

(F) Does not have, as an owner, investor, manager, operator, or person meaningfully involved with the undertaking, any individual who has been an owner, investor, manager, operator, or person otherwise meaningfully involved with an undertaking that was not in compliance with paragraph (w)(1)(vii)(C) of this section at the time of the individual's involvement and within the five years immediately preceding the date of filing the petition; or that was not in compliance with clause paragraph (w)(1)(vii)(D) of this section at any time during which the individual was involved with the undertaking, or is an agent of such individual; and

(G) Is not a successor in interest to an undertaking that has not complied with paragraphs (C) or (D).

(viii) Long-term worker means an alien who was admitted to the CNMI, or otherwise granted status, as a CW–1 nonimmigrant during fiscal year 2015, and during each of fiscal years 2016 through 2018.

(ix) Minor child means a child as defined in section 101(b)(1) of the Act who is under 18 years of age.

(x) Numerical limitation means the maximum number of persons who may be granted CW–1 status in a given fiscal year, as follows:

(A) For fiscal years 2018 through the first quarter of fiscal year 2030, the numerical limitations are:

(1) 9,998 for fiscal year 2018;

(2) 13,000 for fiscal year 2019;

(3) 12,500 for fiscal year 2020;

(4) 12,000 for fiscal year 2021;

(5) 11,500 for fiscal year 2022;

(6) 11,000 for fiscal year 2023;

(7) 10,000 for fiscal year 2024;

(8) 9,000 for fiscal year 2025;

(9) 8,000 for fiscal year 2026;

(10) 7,000 for fiscal year 2027;

(11) 6,000 for fiscal year 2028;

(12) 5,000 for fiscal year 2029; and

(13) 1,000 for the first quarter of fiscal year 2030.

(B) A long-term worker granted CW– 1 nonimmigrant status for a period exceeding one year shall be counted toward the numerical limitation, and toward any reservation of CW–1 numbers, as described in paragraph (w)(1)(x)(D)(1) of this section, if applicable, for each fiscal year within the period of petition validity.

(C) For each petition revoked entirely or in part in a fiscal year, the numerical limitation for the next fiscal year shall be increased by the number of beneficiaries of such petitions subject to such revocation before the end of the validity period of the petition.

(D)(1) Within the numerical limitations described in paragraph (w)(1)(x)(A) of this section, the following reservations of CW–1 numbers for specified occupational categories shall apply:

(i) 200 for occupational categories 29– 0000 (Healthcare Practitioners and Technical Occupations) and 31–0000 (Healthcare Support Occupations); and

(ii) 60 for occupational categories related to the operations of the CNMI public utilities services, including, but not limited to, 17–2081 (Water/Waste Water Engineers), 17–2071 (Electrical Engineers), 17–2141 (Mechanical Engineers), and Trades Technicians.

(2) Reserved CW–1 numbers described in paragraph (w)(1)(x)(D)(1) of this section will be made available to eligible petitioners requesting such numbers for a fiscal year in order of filing, separately under either paragraph (w)(1)(x)(D)(1)(i) or (ii) of this section, until exhausted. Unused reserved numbers under either paragraph (w)(1)(x)(D)(1)(i) or (ii) of this section will not be available to other petitioners.

(3) DHS may adjust the reservation of numbers for specified occupational categories for a fiscal year or other period via publication of a notice in the Federal Register, as long as such adjustment is consistent with paragraph (w)(1)(x)(A) of this section. DHS will base any such adjustment on factors including: The level of past demand for reserved numbers compared to supply; whether a reservation of numbers has resulted in unused numbers; reservation of numbers compared to overall numerical limitation in a fiscal year; and any recommendation received from the Governor of the CNMI regarding the adjustment of the reservation of numbers.

(E) If the numerical limitation is not reached for a specified fiscal year, unused numbers do not carry over to the next fiscal year.

(F) If USCIS receives a sufficient number of petitions to meet the numerical limitation in paragraph (w)(1)(x)(A) of this section in a fiscal year, USCIS will cease processing further cap-subject petitions in that fiscal year, and DOL may cease processing cap-subject applications for temporary labor certification for that fiscal year.

(xi) Occupational category means those employment activities that DHS has determined require alien workers to supplement the resident workforce and includes:

(A) Professional, technical, or management occupations;

(B) Clerical and sales occupations;

(C) Service occupations;

(D) Agricultural, fisheries, forestry, and related occupations;

(E) Processing occupations;

(F) Machine trade occupations;

(G) Benchwork occupations;

(H) Structural work occupations; and

(I) Miscellaneous occupations.

(xii) Participant in good standing in the E-Verify program means an employer, as defined in paragraph (w)(1)(iv) of this section, that has enrolled in E-Verify with respect to all hiring sites in the United States as of the time of filing a petition; is in compliance with all requirements of the E-Verify program, including but not limited to verifying the employment eligibility of newly hired employees in the United States; and continues to be a participant in good standing in EVerify at any time during which the employer employs any CW–1 nonimmigrant.

(xiii) Petition means USCIS Form I– 129CW, Petition for a CNMI–Only Nonimmigrant Transitional Worker, a successor form, other form, or electronic equivalent, any supplemental information requested by USCIS, and additional evidence as may be prescribed or requested by USCIS.

(xiv) Successor in interest means an employer that is controlling and carrying on the business of a previous employer. The following factors may be considered in determining whether an employer is a successor in interest; no one factor is dispositive, but all of the circumstances will be considered as a whole:

(A) Substantial continuity of the same business operations;

(B) Use of the same facilities;

(C) Continuity of the work force;

(D) Similarity of jobs and working conditions;

(E) Similarity of supervisory personnel;

(F) Whether the former management or owner retains a direct or indirect interest in the new enterprise;

(G) Similarity in machinery, equipment, and production methods;

(H) Similarity of products and services; and

(I) The ability of the predecessor to provide relief.

(xv) Temporary Labor Certification or TLC means the certification made by the DOL OFLC Administrator, based on the CW–1 Application for Temporary Employment Certification, and all supporting documentation, with respect to an employer seeking to file with a CW–1 petition.

(xvi) Transition period means the period beginning on the transition program effective date and ending on December 31, 2029.

(xvii) United States worker means a citizen or national of the United States, an alien lawfully admitted for permanent residence, or a citizen of the Federated States of Micronesia, the Republic of the Marshall Islands, or the Republic of Palau who is eligible for nonimmigrant admission and is employment-authorized under the Compacts of Free Association between the United States and those nations.

(2) Eligible aliens. Subject to the numerical limitation, an alien may be classified as a CW–1 nonimmigrant if, during the transition period, the alien:

(i) Will enter or remain in the CNMI for the purpose of employment within the transition period in an occupational category that DHS has designated as requiring alien workers to supplement the resident workforce;

(ii) Is petitioned for by an employer;

(iii) Is not present in the United States, other than the CNMI;

(iv) If present in the CNMI, is lawfully present in the CNMI;

(v) Is not inadmissible to the United States as a nonimmigrant or has been granted a waiver of each applicable ground of inadmissibility;

(vi) Is ineligible for status in a nonimmigrant worker classification under section 101(a)(15) of the Act; and

(vii) Will not be employed in a Construction and Extraction Occupation (as defined by the U.S. Department of Labor as Standard Occupational Classification Group 47–0000 or successor provision) unless the alien is a long-term worker.

(3) Derivative beneficiaries—CW–2 nonimmigrant classification. The spouse or minor child of a CW–1 nonimmigrant may accompany or follow the alien as a CW–2 nonimmigrant if the alien:

(i) Is not present in the United States, other than the CNMI;

(ii) If present in the CNMI, is lawfully present in the CNMI; and

(iii) Is not inadmissible to the United States as a nonimmigrant or has been granted a waiver of each applicable ground of inadmissibility.

(4) Eligible employers. To be eligible to petition for a CW–1 nonimmigrant worker, an employer must:

(i) Be engaged in legitimate business;

(ii) Obtain a TLC from DOL and consider all available United States workers for the position being filled by the CW–1 worker;

(iii) Offer terms and conditions of employment which are consistent with the nature of the petitioner's business and the nature of the occupation, activity, and industry in the CNMI; and

(iv) Comply with all Federal and Commonwealth requirements relating to employment, including but not limited to nondiscrimination, occupational safety, and minimum wage requirements.

(5) Petition requirements. An employer who seeks to classify an alien as a CW-1 worker must file a petition with USCIS and pay the requisite petition fee plus the CNMI education funding fee and the fraud prevention and detection fee as prescribed in 8 CFR part 106. If the beneficiary will perform services for more than one employer, each employer must file a separate petition with fees with USCIS.

(6) Appropriate documents. Documentary evidence establishing eligibility for CW status is required. A petition must be accompanied by:

(i) Evidence demonstrating the petitioner meets the definition of eligible employer in this section;

(ii) An attestation by the petitioner certified as true and accurate by an appropriate official of the petitioner, of the following:

(A) The employer has not displaced and will not displace a United States worker in order to employ the beneficiary as agreed to in the CW–1 Application for Temporary Employment Certification;

(B) The employer is doing business as defined in paragraph (w)(1)(iii) of this section;

(C) The employer is a legitimate business as defined in paragraph (w)(1)(vii) of this section;

(D) The employer is an eligible employer as described in paragraph (w)(4) of this section and will continue to comply with the requirements for an eligible employer until such time as the employer no longer employs the CW–1 nonimmigrant worker;

(E) The beneficiary meets the qualifications for the position;

(F) The beneficiary, if present in the CNMI, is lawfully present in the CNMI;

(G) The position is not temporary or seasonal employment, and the petitioner does not reasonably believe it to qualify as eligible for any other nonimmigrant worker classification, including H–2A or H–2B;

(H) The position falls within the list of occupational categories designated by DHS;

(I) The petitioner will pay the beneficiary a wage that is not less than the greater of—

(1) The CNMI minimum wage;

(2) The Federal minimum wage; or

(3) The prevailing wage in the CNMI for the occupation in which the beneficiary will be employed as established by the U.S. Department of Labor; and

(J) The petitioner will comply with the reporting and retention requirements in paragraph 26.

(iii) Evidence of licensure if an occupation requires a Commonwealth or local license for an individual to fully perform the duties of the occupation. Categories of valid licensure for CW–1 classification are:

(A) Licensure. An alien seeking CW– 1 classification in that occupation must have that license prior to approval of the petition to be found qualified to enter the CNMI and immediately engage in employment in the occupation.

(B) Temporary licensure. If a temporary license is available and allowed for the occupation with a temporary license, USCIS may grant the petition at its discretion after considering the duties performed, the degree of supervision received, and any limitations placed on the alien by the employer and/or pursuant to the temporary license.

(C) Duties without licensure. If the CNMI allows an individual to fully practice the occupation that usually requires a license without a license under the supervision of licensed senior or supervisory personnel in that occupation, USCIS may grant CW–1 status at its discretion after considering the duties performed, the degree of supervision received, and any limitations placed on the alien if the facts demonstrate that the alien under supervision could fully perform the duties of the occupation.

(iv) For any petition requesting an employment start date on or after October 1, 2019, including both new petitions and petitions for renewal of an existing permit, a TLC approved by DOL, confirming that there are not sufficient United States workers in the CNMI who are able, willing, qualified, and available at the time and place needed to perform the services or labor involved in the petition, and that the employment of the CW–1 nonimmigrant will not adversely affect the wages and working conditions of similarly employed United States workers. If the TLC accepts certain education, training, experience, or special requirements of the beneficiary, the petition must also be accompanied by documentation that the CW–1 nonimmigrant worker qualifies for the job offer as specified in the TLC.

(7) Change of employers. A change of employment to a new employer inconsistent with paragraphs (w)(7)(i) and (ii) of this section will constitute a failure to maintain status within the meaning of section 237(a)(1)(C)(i) of the Act. A CW–1 nonimmigrant may change employers if:

(i) The prospective new employer files a petition to classify the alien as a CW–1 worker in accordance with paragraph (w)(5) of this section, and

(ii) An extension of the alien's stay is requested if necessary for the validity period of the petition.

(iii) A CW–1 worker may work for a prospective new employer after the prospective new employer files a Form I–129CW petition on the employee's behalf if:

(A) The prospective employer has filed a nonfrivolous petition for new employment before the date of expiration of the CW–1 worker's authorized period of stay; and

(B) Subsequent to his or her lawful admission, the CW–1 worker has not been employed without authorization in the United States.

(iv) Employment authorization shall continue for such alien until the new petition is adjudicated. If the new petition is denied, such authorization shall cease.

(v) If a CW–1 worker's employment has been terminated prior to the filing of a petition by a prospective new employer consistent with paragraphs (w)(7)(i) and (ii), or if the CW–1's current petition has been revoked (other than for the reason described in paragraph (w)(27)(iii)(A)(7) of this section) the CW–1 worker will not be considered to be in violation of his or her CW–1 status during the 30-day period immediately following the date on which the CW–1 worker's employment terminated if a nonfrivolous petition for new employment is filed consistent with this paragraph within that 30-day period and the CW–1 worker does not otherwise violate the terms and conditions of his or her status during that 30-day period.

(8) Amended or new petition. If there are any material changes in the terms and conditions of employment, the petitioner must file an amended or new petition to reflect the changes. An amended or new petition must be submitted with a new TLC approved by DOL.

(9) Multiple beneficiaries. A petitioning employer may include more than one beneficiary in a CW–1 petition if the beneficiaries will be working in the same occupational category, under the same terms and conditions, for the same period of time, and in the same location.

(10) Named beneficiaries. The petition must include the name of the beneficiary and other required information, as indicated in the form instructions, at the time of filing. Unnamed beneficiaries are not permitted.

(11) Early termination. The petitioning employer must pay the reasonable cost of return transportation of the alien to the alien's last place of foreign residence if the alien is dismissed from employment for any reason by the employer before the end of the period of authorized admission.

(12) Approval. USCIS will consider all the evidence submitted and such other evidence required in the form instructions to adjudicate the petition. USCIS will notify the petitioner of the approval of the petition on Form I–797, Notice of Action, or in another form as USCIS may prescribe.

(i) The approval notice will include the CW–1 classification and name of the beneficiary or beneficiaries and the petition's period of validity. A petition for more than one beneficiary may be approved in whole or in part.

(ii) The application for a TLC may not be filed with DOL earlier than 120 days before the date of actual need for the beneficiary's services for an initial petition for CW–1 status, or 180 days before the date of expiration of CW–1 status in the case of an extension petition described in paragraph (w)(18) of this section. The petition may then be filed with USCIS after the TLC is approved. If DOL debars an employer from obtaining a CW–1 TLC, USCIS may not approve future petitions during the debarment period.

(13) Petition validity. An approved petition will be valid for a period of up to one year, unless the beneficiary is a long-term worker in which case an approved petition will be valid for a period of up to three years.

(14) Validity of the labor certification. A TLC is valid only for the period of employment as approved on the CW–1 Application for Temporary Employment Certification. The TLC expires on the last day of authorized employment.

(15) How to apply for CW–1 or CW– 2 status.

(i) Upon approval of the petition, a beneficiary, his or her eligible spouse, and his or her minor child(ren) outside the CNMI will be informed in the approval notice of where they may apply for a visa authorizing admission in CW–1 or CW–2 status.

(ii) If the beneficiary is present in the CNMI, the petition also serves as the application for a grant of status as a CW–1.

(iii) If the eligible spouse and/or minor child(ren) are present in the CNMI, the spouse or child(ren) may apply for CW-2 dependent status on Form I-539 (or such alternative form as USCIS may designate) in accordance with the form instructions. The CW-2 status may not be approved until approval of the CW-1 petition.

(16) Biometrics and other information. The beneficiary of a CW-1 petition or the spouse or child applying for a grant or extension of CW-2 status, or a change of status to CW-2 status, must submit biometric information as requested by USCIS.

(17) Period of admission.

(i) A CW–1 nonimmigrant will be admitted for the period of petition validity, plus up to 10 days before the validity period begins and 10 days after the validity period ends. The CW–1 nonimmigrant may not work except during the validity period of the petition. A CW–2 spouse will be admitted for the same period as the principal alien. A CW–2 minor child will be admitted for the same period as the principal alien, but such admission will not extend beyond the child's 18th birthday.

(ii) The temporary departure from the CNMI of the CW–1 nonimmigrant will not affect the derivative status of the CW–2 spouse and minor children, provided the familial relationship continues to exist and the principal remains eligible for admission as a CW– 1 nonimmigrant.

(18) Extension of petition validity and extension of stay.

(i) The petitioner may request an extension of an employee's CW–1 nonimmigrant status by filing a new petition.

(ii) A request for a petition extension may be filed only if the validity of the original petition has not expired.

(iii) Extensions of CW–1 status may be granted for a period of up to 1 year (or a period of up to 3 years if the beneficiary is a long-term worker) until the end of the transition period, subject to any numerical limitation.

(iv) To qualify for an extension of stay, the petitioner must demonstrate that the beneficiary or beneficiaries:

(A) Continuously maintained the terms and conditions of CW–1 status;

(B) Remains admissible to the United States; and

(C) Remains eligible for CW–1 classification.

(v) A beneficiary (other than a longterm worker) may not be granted CW– 1 status beyond three consecutive petition validity periods unless the beneficiary has departed and remained outside of the United States for a continuous period of at least 30 days after the expiration of the third petition validity period and before the filing of any new petition on behalf of the beneficiary.

(vi) The derivative CW–2 nonimmigrant may file an application for extension of nonimmigrant stay on Form I–539 (or such alternative form as USCIS may designate) in accordance with the form instructions. The CW–2 status extension may not be approved until approval of the CW–1 extension petition.

(19) Change or adjustment of status. A CW–1 or CW–2 nonimmigrant can apply to change nonimmigrant status under section 248 of the Act or apply for adjustment of status under section 245 of the Act, if otherwise eligible. During the transition period, CW–1 or CW–2 nonimmigrants may be the beneficiary of a petition for or may apply for any nonimmigrant or

immigrant visa classification for which they may qualify.

(20) Effect of filing an application for or approval of a permanent labor certification, preference petition, or filing of an application for adjustment of status on CW–1 or CW–2 classification. An alien may be granted, be admitted in and maintain lawful CW–1 or CW–2 nonimmigrant status while, at the same time, lawfully seeking to become a lawful permanent resident of the United States, provided he or she intends to depart the CNMI voluntarily at the end of the period of authorized stay. The filing of an application for or approval of a permanent labor certification or an immigrant visa preference petition, the filing of an application for adjustment of status, or the lack of residence abroad will not be the basis for denying:

(i) A CW–1 petition filed on behalf of the alien;

(ii) A request to extend a CW–1 status pursuant to a petition previously filed on behalf of the alien;

(iii) An application for CW–2 classification filed by an alien;

(iv) A request to extend CW–2 status pursuant to the extension of a related CW–1 alien's extension; or

(v) An application for admission as a CW–1 or CW–2 nonimmigrant.

(21) Rejection. USCIS may reject an employer's petition for new or extended CW–1 status if any numerical limitation has been met. In that case, the petition and accompanying fee will be rejected and returned with the notice that numbers are unavailable for the CW nonimmigrant classification. The beneficiary's application for admission based upon an approved petition will not be rejected based upon the numerical limitation.

(22) Denial. The ultimate decision to grant or deny CW–1 or CW–2 classification or status is a discretionary determination, and the petition or the application may be denied for failure of the petitioner or the applicant to demonstrate eligibility or for other good cause. The denial of a petition to classify an alien as a CW–1 may be appealed to the USCIS Administrative Appeals Office or any successor body. The denial of CW–1 or CW–2 status within the CNMI, or of an application for change or extension of status filed under this section, may not be appealed.

(23) Terms and conditions of CW Nonimmigrant status—

(i) Geographical limitations. CW–1 and CW–2 statuses are only applicable in the CNMI. Entry, employment and residence in the rest of the United States (including Guam) require the appropriate visa or visa waiver and nonimmigrant classification. Except as provided in paragraph (w)(23)(iii) of this section, an alien with CW–1 or CW–2 status who enters or attempts to enter, or travels or attempts to travel to any other part of the United States without an appropriate visa or visa waiver, or who violates conditions of nonimmigrant stay applicable to any such authorized status in any other part of the United States, will be deemed to have violated CW–1 or CW–2 status.

(ii) Re-entry. An alien with CW–1 or CW–2 status who travels abroad from the CNMI will require a CW–1 or CW– 2 or other appropriate visa to be readmitted to the CNMI.

(iii) Travel outside the CNMI—

(A) Direct Guam transit from the CNMI. An alien with CW–1 or CW–2 status may travel to a foreign place via a direct Guam transit without being deemed to violate that status.

(B) Travel from a foreign place to the CNMI. An alien with a valid CW–1 or CW–2 visa, who is admissible to the CNMI in such status, may be admitted to the United States in CW–1 or CW–2 status in Guam for the purpose of a direct Guam transit to the CNMI. An alien who violates the terms of direct Guam transit violates his or her CW–1 or CW–2 status.

(iv) Employment authorization. An alien with CW–1 nonimmigrant status is only authorized employment in the CNMI for the petitioning employer. An alien with CW–2 status is not authorized to be employed.

(24) Expiration of status. CW–1 status expires when the alien violates his or her CW–1 status (or in the case of a CW– 1 status violation caused solely by termination of the alien's employment, at the end of the 30 day period described in paragraph (w)(7)(v) of this section), 10 days after the end of the petition's validity period, when the petition is revoked, or at the end of the transitional worker program, whichever is earlier. CW–2 nonimmigrant status expires when the status of the related CW–1 alien expires, on a CW 2 minor child's 18th birthday, when the alien violates his or her status, or at the end of the transitional worker program, whichever is earlier. No alien will be eligible for admission to the CNMI in CW–1 or CW–2 status, and no CW–1 or CW–2 visa will be valid for travel to the CNMI, after the transitional worker program ends.

(25) Waivers of inadmissibility for applicants lawfully present in the CNMI. An applicant for CW–1 or CW–2 nonimmigrant status, who is otherwise eligible for such status and otherwise admissible to the United States, and who possesses appropriate documents demonstrating that the applicant is lawfully present in the CNMI, may be granted a waiver of inadmissibility under section 212(d)(3)(A)(ii) of the Act, including the grounds of inadmissibility described in sections 212(a)(6)(A)(i) and 212(a)(7)(B)(i)(II) of the Act, as a matter of discretion for the purpose of granting the CW–1 or CW–2 nonimmigrant status. Such waiver may be granted without additional form or fee. Appropriate documents required for such a waiver include a valid unexpired passport and other documentary evidence demonstrating that the applicant is lawfully present in the CNMI, such as a DHS-issued Form I–94. Evidence that the applicant possesses appropriate documents may be provided by an employer to accompany a petition, by an eligible spouse or minor child to accompany the Form I–539 (or such alternative form as USCIS may designate), or in such other manner as USCIS may designate.

(26) Semiannual report—

(i) Filing. During the validity period of the petition, an employer whose petition has been approved for an employment start date on or after October 1, 2019 and for a validity period of six months or more, shall file a semiannual report, every six months after the petition validity start date up to and including the sixth month preceding the petition's validity end date. The semiannual report must be filed within a 60 day window surrounding the six month anniversary of the petition validity start date, with the filing window opening 30 days before and closing 30 days after the six month anniversary of the petition validity start date. The semiannual report must be filed with USCIS in the form and containing such evidence as USCIS may direct, to verify the continuing employment and payment of the beneficiary under the terms and conditions of the approved petition.

(ii) Use. DHS may provide such semiannual reports to other federal partners, including DOL for investigative or other use as the DOL may deem appropriate. Failure to comply with the requirements of paragraph (w)(26) of this section may be a basis for revocation of an approved petition as provided in paragraph (w)(27) of this section, or for denial of subsequent petitions filed by the employer.

(iii) Document retention.

(A) An employer must retain all documents and records in support of an approved petition, and any semiannual report. An employer must retain evidence that supports the semiannual report including, but not limited to:

(1) Personnel records for each CW–1 worker including the name, address of current residence in the Commonwealth, age, domicile, citizenship, point of hire, and approved employment contract termination date;

(2) Payroll records for each CW–1 worker including the O*NET job classification; wage rate or salary, number of hours worked each week, gross compensation, itemized deductions, and evidence of net payments made and received biweekly; and

(3) Direct evidence of payment of wages and overtime, such as receipts for cash payments, cancelled checks or deposit records. Petitioners must provide such documents and records to DHS and DOL at any time, during the retention period specified in paragraph (w)(26)(iii)(B) of this section.

(B) An employer must retain documents and records until the date that is three years after the ending date of the petition validity period.

(27) Revocation of approval of petition—

(i) General.

(A) The petitioner shall immediately notify USCIS of any changes in the terms and conditions of employment of a beneficiary which may affect eligibility under this paragraph (w). To notify USCIS of such changes, an amended petition shall be filed when the petitioner continues to employ the beneficiary. If the petitioner no longer employs the beneficiary, the petitioner shall send a letter to the office at which the CW–1 petition was filed explaining the basis on which the specific CW–1 nonimmigrant is no longer employed.

(B) USCIS may revoke a petition at any time, even after the expiration of the petition.

(ii) Immediate and automatic revocation. The approval of any petition is immediately and automatically revoked if the petitioner ceases operations, files a written withdrawal of the petition, or the U.S. Department of Labor revokes the temporary labor certification upon which the petition is based.

(iii) Revocation on notice—

(A) Grounds for revocation. USCIS may in its discretion send to the petitioner a notice of intent to revoke the petition in relevant part, for good cause, including, if it finds that:

(1) The beneficiary is no longer employed by the petitioner in the capacity specified in the petition;

(2) The facts contained in the petition or on the application for a temporary labor certification was not true and correct, inaccurate, fraudulent, or misrepresented a material fact;

(3) The petitioner violated terms and conditions of the approved petition;

(4) The petitioner violated a requirement of paragraph (w) of this section;

(5) The approval of the petition violated paragraph (w) this section or involved gross error;

(6) The petitioner failed to maintain the continuous employment of the CW– 1 nonimmigrant, failed to pay the nonimmigrant, failed to timely file a semiannual report described in paragraph (w)(26) of this section, committed any other violation of the terms and conditions of employment, or otherwise ceased to operate as a legitimate business;

(7) The beneficiary did not apply for admission to the CNMI within 10 days after the beginning of the petition validity period if the petition has been approved for consular processing; or

(8) The employer failed to provide a former, current, or prospective CW–1 nonimmigrant, not later than 21 business days after a written request from such individual, with the original (or a certified copy of the original) of all petitions, notices, and other written communication related to the worker (other than sensitive financial or proprietary information of the employer which may be redacted) that has been exchanged between the employer and the Department of Labor, the Department of Homeland Security, or any other Federal agency or department.

(B) Notice and decision. The notice of intent to revoke shall state the grounds for the revocation. The petitioner may submit evidence in rebuttal within 30 days of receipt of the notice. USCIS shall consider all relevant evidence presented in deciding whether to revoke the petition in whole or in part. If the petition is revoked in part, the remainder of the petition shall remain approved and a revised approval notice shall be sent to the petitioner with the revocation notice.

(28) Appeal of a revocation of a petition. A petition that has been revoked on notice in whole or in part may be appealed under part 103 of this chapter. Automatic revocations may not be appealed.

(29) Notice to DOL. USCIS will provide notice to DOL of CW–1 petition revocations.

HISTORY:

[38 FR 35425, Dec. 28, 1973; 48 FR 14575, Apr. 5, 1983; 51 FR 44267, 1986; 52 FR 5750, 7063, 13226, 20555, 30329, 48084, 1987;

53 FR 3331, 24900, 26231, 30017, 46852, 1988; 54 FR 14, 10979, 48577, 51816, 1989.; 55 FR 2621, 5573, 7881, 7882, 34897, 34900, 34901, 1990; 56 FR 480, 41624, 482, 2841, 11916, 11917, 26017, 31305, 33371, 38333, 55613, 61119, 61127, 61130, 66967, 1991.; 57 FR 749, 6184, 10978, 12178, 12181, 12182, 12186, 12190, 29193, 31955, 31956, 33426, 40832, 42884, 55060, 1992.; 58 FR 49905, Sept. 24, 1993; 58 FR 58097, Oct. 29, 1993; 58 FR 69210, Dec. 30, 1993, as confirmed and amended at 63 FR 1331, 1334, Jan. 9, 1998; 59 FR 1470, Jan. 11, 1994; 59 FR 41830, Aug. 15, 1994; as corrected at 59 FR 42487, Aug. 18, 1994 and as corrected at 59 FR 55910, Nov. 9, 1994; 59 FR 51102, Oct. 7, 1994; 60 FR 21975, May 4, 1995; 60 FR 44260, 44266, Aug. 25, 1995, as corrected at 60 FR 52248, Oct. 5, 1995; 60 FR 49195, Sept. 22, 1995; 60 FR 62021, 62022, Dec. 4, 1995; 61 FR 35934, 35935, July 9, 1996; 62 FR 10422, 10424, Mar. 7, 1997; 62 FR 18508, 18511, 18512, Apr. 16, 1997; 62 FR 48138, 48146, Sept. 12, 1997, as corrected at 62 FR 50435, Sept. 25, 1997, and 62 FR 60122, Nov. 6, 1997; 63 FR 31872, 31873, 31874, June 10, 1998; 63 FR 32113, 32115, June 12, 1998; 63 FR 65657, 65659, Nov. 30, 1998, as corrected at 63 FR 71342, Dec. 24, 1998; 64 FR 29208, 29211, June 1, 1999, as corrected at 64 FR 30103, June 4, 1999; 64 FR 32146, 32147, June 15, 1999, as corrected at 64 FR 33346, June 22, 1999 and as corrected at 64 FR 36423, July 6, 1999; 65 FR 7715, Feb. 16, 2000; 65 FR 10678, 10684, Feb. 29, 2000; 65 FR 14774, 14778, 14779, Mar. 17, 2000, as corrected at 65 FR 18432, Apr. 7, 2000; 65 FR 43528, 43531, July 13, 2000, withdrawn at 67 FR 61474, Oct. 1, 2002; 65 FR 67616, 67617, Nov. 13, 2000; 66 FR 31107, 31112, June 11, 2001; 66 FR 42587, 42593, Aug. 14, 2001; 66 FR 46697, 46702, Sept. 7, 2001; 66 FR 49514, Sept. 28, 2001; 67 FR 18062, 18063, Apr. 12, 2002; 67 FR 54941, 54945, Aug. 27, 2002; 67 FR 71443, 71449, Dec. 2, 2002; 67 FR 76256, 76270, 76276, Dec. 11, 2002; 68 FR 46926, 46929, Aug. 7, 2003; 69 FR 39814, 39825, July 1, 2004; 70 FR 23775, 23783, May 5, 2005, as confirmed at 76 FR 53764, 53778, Aug. 29, 2011; 72 FR 18856, 18860, Apr. 16, 2007; 72 FR 19100, 19107, Apr. 17, 2007; 73 FR 15389, 15394, Mar. 24, 2008; 73 FR 18944, 18954, Apr. 8, 2008; 73 FR 72276, 72293, Nov. 26, 2008; 73 FR 76891, 76911, Dec. 18, 2008; 73 FR 78104, 78127, Dec. 19, 2008, as corrected at 74 FR 2837, Jan. 16, 2009; 74 FR 26514, 26515, June 3, 2009; 74 FR 26933, 26938, June 5, 2009; 74 FR 55094, 55109, Oct. 27, 2009, as confirmed and amended at 76 FR 55502, Sept. 7, 2011; 75 FR 47699, 47701, Aug. 9, 2010; 75 FR 79264, 79275, Dec. 20, 2010; 77 FR 76353, Dec. 28, 2012; 78 FR 18457, 18472, Mar. 27, 2013, as confirmed at 81 FR 91646, 91670, Dec. 19, 2016; 78 FR 24047, 24061, Apr. 24, 2013, as confirmed at 80 FR 24146, 24183, Apr. 29, 2015; 80 FR 10284, 10311, Feb. 25, 2015; 80 FR 23680, 23688, Apr. 29, 2015; 80 FR 24042, 24108, Apr. 29, 2015; 81 FR 13040, 13117, Mar. 11, 2016; 81 FR 82398, 82486, Nov. 18, 2016; 82 FR 32987, 32998, July 19, 2017; 83 FR 24905, 24917, May 31, 2018; 84 FR 888, 954, Jan. 31, 2019; 84 FR 20005, 20020, May 8, 2019; 84 FR 52357, 52363, Oct. 2, 2019; 85 FR 21739, 21744, Apr. 20, 2020; 85 FR 27645, 27649, May 11, 2020; 85 FR 28843, 28850, May 14, 2020; 85 FR 29264, 29311, May 14, 2020; 85 FR 46788, 46923, Aug. 3, 2020, as corrected at 85 FR 53645, Aug. 31, 2020; 85 FR 51304, 51311, Aug. 20, 2020; 85 FR 63918, 63963, Oct. 8, 2020; 85 FR 82291, 82298, Dec. 18, 2020; 86 FR 1676, 1732, Jan. 8, 2021, withdrawn at 86 FR 72516, Dec. 22, 2021; 86 FR 8543, Feb. 8, 2021; 86 FR 14221, 14228, Mar. 15, 2021; 86 FR 27027, May 19, 2021; 86 FR 28198, 28230, May 25, 2021; 87 FR 4722, 4758, Jan. 28, 2022; 87 FR 30334, 30375, May 18, 2022; 87 FR 41027, 41029, July 11, 2022; 87 FR 61959, 61963, Oct. 13, 2022; 87 FR 62721, 62722, Oct. 17, 2022; 87 FR 75891, 75902, Dec. 12, 2022; 87 FR 76816, 76874, Dec. 15, 2022; 87 FR 77979, 77979, Dec. 21 , 2022; 88 FR 53761, Aug. 9, 2023; 88 FR 80394, 80456, Nov. 17, 2023; 89 FR 6194, 6397, Jan. 31, 2024; 89 FR 7456, 7491, Feb. 2, 2024, as corrected at 89 FR 20101, Mar. 21, 2024; 89 FR 22903, 22912, Apr. 3, 2024; redesignated at 89 FR 34864, 34931, Apr. 30, 2024; 89 FR 95626, 95681, Dec. 2, 2024; 89 FR 103054, 103196, Dec. 18, 2024; 89 FR 103202, 103327, Dec. 18, 2024]

§ 214.2 Special requirements for admission, extension, and maintenance of status. [Effective November 17, 2026]

Table 1 to § 214.2—Section Contents

(a) Foreign government officials.
(b) Visitors.
(c) Transits.
(d) Crewmen.
(e) Treaty traders and investors.
(f) Students in colleges, universities, seminaries, conservatories, academic high schools, elementary schools, other academic institutions, and in language training programs.
(g) Representatives to international organizations.
(h) Temporary employees.
(i) Representatives of information media.
(j) Exchange aliens.
(k) Spouses, Fiancées, and Fiancés of United States Citizens.
(l) Intracompany transferees.
(m) Students in established vocational or other recognized nonacademic institutions, other than in language training programs.
(n) Certain parents and children of section 101(a)(27)(I) special immigrants.
(o) Aliens of extraordinary ability or achievement.
(p) Artists, athletes, and entertainers.
(q) Cultural visitors.
(r) Religious workers.
(s) NATO nonimmigrant aliens.
(t) Alien witnesses and informants.
(u) [Reserved].
(v) Certain spouses and children of LPRs.
(w) CNMI-Only Transitional Worker (CW-1).

The general requirements in § 214.1 are modified for the following nonimmigrant classes:

(a) Foreign government officials —

(1) General. The determination by a consular officer prior to admission and the recognition by the Secretary of State subsequent to admission is evidence of the proper classification of a nonimmigrant under section 101(a)(15)(A) of the Act. An alien who has a nonimmigrant status under section 101(a)(15)(A)(i) or (ii) of the Act is to be admitted for the duration of the period for which the alien continues to be recognized by the Secretary of State as being entitled to that status. An alien defined in section (101)(a)(15)(A)(iii) of the Act is to be admitted for an initial period of not more than three years, and may be granted extensions of temporary stay in increments of not more than two years. In addition, the application for extension of temporary stay must be accompanied by a statement signed by the employing official stating that he/she intends to continue to employ the applicant and describing the type of work the applicant will perform.

(2) Definition of A-1 or A-2 dependent. For purposes of employment in the United States, the term dependent of an A-1 or A-2 principal alien, as used in § 214.2(a), means any of the following immediate members of the family habitually residing in the same

household as the principal alien who is an officer or employee assigned to a diplomatic or consular office in the United States:

(i) Spouse;

(ii) Unmarried children under the age of 21;

(iii) Unmarried sons or daughters under the age of 23 who are in full-time attendance as students at post-secondary educational institutions;

(iv) Unmarried sons or daughters under the age of 25 who are in full-time attendance as students at post-secondary educational institutions if a formal bilateral employment agreement permitting their employment in the United States was signed prior to November 21, 1988, and such bilateral employment agreement does not specify 23 as the maximum age for employment of such sons and daughters. The Office of Protocol of the Department of State shall maintain a listing of foreign states with which the United States has such bilateral employment agreements;

(v) Unmarried sons or daughters who are physically or mentally disabled to the extent that they cannot adequately care for themselves or cannot establish, maintain or re-establish their own households. The Department of State or the Service may require certification(s) as it deems sufficient to document such mental or physical disability; or

(vi) An immediate family member of an A-1 or A-2 principal alien described in 22 CFR 41.21(a)(3)(i) to (iv) with A-1 or A-2 nonimmigrant status, who falls within a category of aliens recognized by the Department of State as qualifying dependents.

(3) Applicability of a formal bilateral agreement or an informal de facto arrangement for A-1 or A-2 dependents. The applicability of a formal bilateral agreement shall be based on the foreign state which employs the principal alien and not on the nationality of the principal alien or dependent. The applicability of an informal de facto arrangement shall be based on the foreign state which employs the principal alien, but under a de facto arrangement the principal alien also must be a national of the foreign state which employs him/her in the United States.

(4) Income tax, Social Security liability; non-applicability of certain immunities. Dependents who are granted employment authorization under this section are responsible for payment of all federal, state and local income, employment and related taxes and Social Security contributions on any remuneration received. In addition, immunity from civil or administrative jurisdiction in accordance with Article 37 of the Vienna Convention on Diplomatic Relations or other international agreements does not apply to these dependents with respect to matters arising out of their employment.

(5) Dependent employment pursuant to formal bilateral employment agreements and informal de facto reciprocal arrangements.

(i) The Office of Protocol shall maintain a listing of foreign states which have entered into formal bilateral employment agreements. Dependents of an A-1 or A-2 principal alien assigned to official duty in the United States may accept or continue in unrestricted employment based on such formal bilateral agreements upon favorable recommendation by the Department of State and issuance of employment authorization documentation by the Service in accordance with 8 CFR part 274a. The application procedures are set forth in paragraph (a)(6) of this section.

(ii) For purposes of this section, an informal de facto reciprocal arrangement exists when the Department of State determines that a foreign state allows appropriate employment on the local economy for dependents of certain United States officials assigned to duty in that foreign state. The Office of Protocol shall maintain a listing of countries with which such reciprocity exists. Dependents of an A-1 or A-2 principal alien assigned to official duty in the United States may be authorized to accept or continue in employment based upon informal de facto arrangements upon favorable recommendation by the Department of State and issuance of employment authorization by the Service in accordance with 8 CFR part 274a. Additionally, the procedures set forth in paragraph (a)(6) of this section must be complied with, and the following conditions must be met:

(A) Both the principal alien and the dependent desiring employment are maintaining A-1 or A-2 status as appropriate;

(B) The principal's assignment in the United States is expected to last more than six months;

(C) Employment of a similar nature for dependents of United States Government officials assigned to official duty in the foreign state employing the principal alien is not prohibited by that foreign state's government;

(D) The proposed employment is not in an occupation listed in the Department of Labor Schedule B (20 CFR part 656), or otherwise determined by the Department of Labor to be one for which there is an oversupply of qualified U.S. workers in the area of proposed employment. This Schedule B restriction does not apply to a dependent son or daughter who is a full-time student if the employment is part-time, consisting of not more than 20 hours per week, and/or if it is temporary employment of not more than 12 weeks during school holiday periods; and

(E) The proposed employment is not contrary to the interest of the United States. Employment contrary to the interest of the United States includes, but is not limited to, the employment of A-1 or A-2 dependents: who have criminal records; who have violated United States immigration laws or regulations, or visa laws or regulations; who have worked illegally in the United States; and/or who cannot establish that they have paid taxes and social security on income from current or previous United States employment.

(6) Application procedures. The following procedures are applicable to dependent employment applications under bilateral agreements and de facto arrangements:

(i) The dependent must submit a completed Form I-566 to the Department of State through the office, mission, or organization which employs his/her principal alien. A dependent applying under paragraph (a)(2)(iii) or (iv) of this section must submit a certified statement from the post-secondary educational institution confirming that he/she is pursuing studies on a full-time basis. A dependent applying under paragraph (a)(2)(v) of this section must submit medical certification regarding his/her condition. The certification should identify the dependent and the certifying physician and give the physician's phone number; identify the condition, describe the symptoms and provide a prognosis; and certify that the dependent is unable to maintain a home of his or her own. Additionally, a dependent applying under the terms of a de facto arrangement must attach a statement from the prospective employer which includes the dependent's name; a description of the position offered and the duties to be performed; the salary offered; and verification that the dependent possesses the qualifications for the position.

(ii) The Department of State reviews and verifies the information provided, makes its determination, and endorses the Form I-566.

(iii) If the Department of State's endorsement is favorable, the dependent may apply to USCIS for employment authorization. When applying to USCIS for employment authorization, the dependent must present his or her Form I-566 with a favorable endorsement from the Department of State and any additional documentation as may be required by the Secretary.

(7) Period of time for which employment may be authorized. If approved, an application to accept or continue employment under this section shall be granted in increments of not more than three years each.

(8) No appeal. There shall be no appeal from a denial of permission to accept or continue employment under this section.

(9) Dependents or family members of principal aliens classified A-3. A dependent or family member of a principal alien classified A-3 may not be employed in the United States under this section.

(10) Unauthorized employment. An alien classified under section 101(a)(15)(A) of the Act who is not a principal alien and who engages in employment outside the scope of, or in a manner contrary to this section, may be considered in violation of section 241(a)(1)(C)(i) of the Act. An alien who is classified under section 101(a)(15)(A) of the Act who is a principal alien and who engages in employment outside the scope of his/her official position may be considered in violation of section 241(a)(1)(C)(i) of the Act.

(b) Visitors —

(1) General. any B-1 visitor for business or B-2 visitor for pleasure may be admitted for not more than one year and may be granted extensions of temporary stay in increments of not more than six months each, except that alien members of a religious denomination coming temporarily and solely to do missionary work in behalf of a religious denomination may be granted extensions of not more than one year each, provided that such work does not involve the selling of articles or the solicitation or acceptance of donations. Those B-1 and B-2 visitors admitted pursuant to the waiver provided at § 212.1(e) of this chapter may be admitted to and stay on Guam for period not to exceed fifteen days and are not eligible for extensions of stay.

(2) Minimum six month admissions. Any B-2 visitor who is found otherwise admissible and is issued a Form I-94 (see § 1.4), will be admitted for a minimum period of six months, regardless of whether less time is requested, provided, that any required passport is valid as specified in section 212(a)(26) of the Act. Exceptions to the minimum six month admission may be made only in individual cases upon the specific approval of the district director for good cause.

(3) Visa Waiver Pilot Program. Special requirements for admission and maintenance of status for visitors admitted to the United States under the Visa Waiver Pilot Program are set forth in section 217 of the Act and part 217 of this chapter.

(4) Admission of aliens pursuant to the Agreement Between the United States of America, the United Mexican States, and Canada (USMCA). A citizen of Canada or Mexico seeking temporary entry for purposes set forth in paragraph (b)(4)(i) of this section, who otherwise meets the requirements under section 101(a)(15)(B) of the Act, including but not limited to requirements regarding the source of remuneration, shall be admitted upon presentation of proof of such citizenship in the case of Canadian applicants, and valid, unexpired entry documents such as a passport and visa, or a passport and BCC in the case of Mexican applicants, a description of the purpose for which the alien is seeking admission, and evidence demonstrating that he or she is engaged in one of the occupations or professions set forth in paragraph (b)(4)(i) of this section.

(i) Occupations and professions set forth in Section B of Appendix 1 of Chapter 16 of the USMCA —

(A) Research and design. Technical, scientific and statistical researchers conducting independent research or research for an enterprise located in the territory of another Party.

(B) Growth, manufacture, and production.

(1) Harvester owner supervising a harvesting crew admitted under applicable law. (Applies only to harvesting of agricultural crops: Grain, fiber, fruit and vegetables.)

(2) Purchasing and production management personnel conducting commercial transactions for an enterprise located in the territory of another Party.

(C) Marketing.

(1) Market researchers and analysts conducting independent research or analysis, or research or analysis for an enterprise located in the territory of another Party.

(2) Trade fair and promotional personnel attending a trade convention.

(D) Sales.

(1) Sales representatives and agents taking orders or negotiating contracts for goods or services for an enterprise located in the territory of another Party but not delivering goods or supplying services.

(2) Buyers purchasing for an enterprise located in the territory of another Party.

(E) Distribution.

(1) Transportation operators transporting goods or passengers to the United States from the territory of another Party or loading and transporting goods or passengers from the United States, with no unloading in the United States, to the territory of another Party. (These operators may make deliveries in the United States if all goods or passengers to be delivered were loaded in the territory of another Party. Furthermore, they may load from locations in the United States if all goods or passengers to be loaded will be delivered in the territory of another Party. Purely domestic service or solicitation, in competition with the United States operators, is not permitted.)

(2) Customs brokers performing brokerage duties associated with the export of goods from the United States to or through Canada.

(F) After-sales services. Installers, repair and maintenance personnel, and supervisors, possessing specialized knowledge essential to the seller's contractual obligation, performing services or training workers to perform services, pursuant to a warranty or other service contract incidental to the sale of commercial or industrial equipment or machinery, including computer software, purchased from an enterprise located outside the United States, during the life of the warranty or service agreement. (For the purposes of this provision, the commercial or industrial equipment or machinery, including computer software, must have been manufactured outside the United States.)

(G) General service. Professionals engaging in a business activity at a professional level in a profession set out in Appendix 2 to Annex 16-A of Chapter 16 of the USMCA, but receiving no salary or other remuneration from a United States source (other than an expense allowance or other reimbursement for expenses incidental to the temporary stay) and otherwise satisfying the requirements of Section A to Annex 16-A of the USMCA.

(H) Commercial transactions.

(1) Management and supervisory personnel engaging in commercial transactions for an enterprise located in the territory of another Party.

(2) Financial services personnel (insurers, bankers or investment brokers) engaging in commercial transactions for an enterprise located in the territory of another Party.

(I) Public relations and advertising. Public relations and advertising personnel consulting with business associates, or attending or participating in conventions.

(J) Tourism. Tourism personnel (tour and travel agents, tour guides or tour operators) attending or participating in conventions or conducting a tour that has begun in the territory of another Party. (The tour may begin in the United States; but must terminate in foreign territory, and a significant portion of the tour must be conducted in foreign territory. In such a case, an operator may enter the United States with an empty conveyance and a tour guide may enter on his or her own and join the conveyance.)

(K) Tour bus operation. Tour bus operators entering the United States:

(1) With a group of passengers on a bus tour that has begun in, and will return to, the territory of another Party.

(2) To meet a group of passengers on a bus tour that will end, and the predominant portion of which will take place, in the territory of another Party.

(3) With a group of passengers on a bus tour to be unloaded in the United States and returning with no passengers or reloading with the group for transportation to the territory of another Party.

(L) Translation. Translators or interpreters performing services as employees of an enterprise located in the territory of another Party.

(ii) Occupations and professions not listed in Section B of Appendix 1 of Chapter 16 of the USMCA. Nothing in paragraph (b)(4) of this section shall preclude a business person engaged in an occupation or profession other than those listed in Section B of Appendix 1 of Chapter 16 of the USMCA from temporary entry under section 101(a)(15)(B) of the Act, if such person otherwise meets the requirements for admission as prescribed by the Attorney General.

(5) Construction workers not admissible. Aliens seeking to enter the country to perform building or construction work, whether on-site or in-plant, are not eligible for classification or admission as B-1 nonimmigrants under section 101(a)(15)(B) of the Act. However, alien nonimmigrants otherwise qualified as B-1 nonimmigrants may be issued visas and may enter for the purpose of supervision or training of others engaged in building or construction work, but not for the purpose of actually performing any such building or construction work themselves.

(6) [Reserved]

(7) Enrollment in a course of study prohibited. An alien who is admitted as, or changes status to, a B-1 or B-2 nonimmigrant on or after April 12, 2002, or who files a request to extend the period of authorized stay in B-1 or B-2 nonimmigrant status on or after such date, violates the conditions of his or her B-1 or B-2 status if the alien enrolls in a course of study. Such an alien who desires to enroll in a course of study must either obtain an F-1 or M-1 nonimmigrant visa from a consular officer abroad and seek readmission to the United States, or apply for and obtain a change of status under section 248 of the Act and 8 CFR part 248. The alien may not enroll in the course of study until the Service has admitted the alien as an F-1 or M-1 nonimmigrant or has approved the alien's application under part 248 of this chapter and changed the alien's status to that of an F-1 or M-1 nonimmigrant.

(c) Transits.

(1) [Reserved]

(2) United Nations Headquarters District. An alien of the class defined in section 101(a)(15)(C) of the Act, whose visa is limited to transit to and from the United Nations Headquarters District, if otherwise admissible, shall be admitted on the additional conditions that he proceed directly to the immediate vicinity of the United Nations Headquarters District, and remain there continuously, departing therefrom only if required in connection with his departure from the United States, and

that he have a document establishing his ability to enter some country other than the United States following his sojourn in the United Nations Headquarters District. The immediate vicinity of the United Nations Headquarters District is that area lying within a twenty-five mile radius of Columbus Circle, New York, NY.

(3) Others. The period of admission of an alien admitted under section 101(a)(15)(C) of the Act shall not exceed 29 days.

(d) Crewmen.

(1) The provisions of parts 251, 252, 253, and 258 of this chapter shall govern the landing of crewmen as nonimmigrants of the class defined in section 101(a)(15)(D) of the Act. An alien in this status may be employed only in a crewman capacity on the vessel or aircraft of arrival, or on a vessel or aircraft of the same transportation company, and may not be employed in connection with domestic flights or movements of a vessel or aircraft. However, nonimmigrant crewmen may perform crewmember duties through stopovers on an international flight for any United States carrier where such flight uses a single aircraft and has an origination or destination point outside the United States.

(2) Denial of crewman status in the case of certain labor disputes (D nonimmigrants).

(i) An alien shall be denied D crewman status as described in section 101(a)(15)(D) of the Act if:

(A) The alien intends to land for the purpose of performing service on a vessel of the United States (as defined in 46 U.S.C. 2101(46)) or an aircraft of an air carrier (as defined in section 101(3) of the Federal Aviation Act of 1958); and

(B) A labor dispute consisting of a strike or lockout exists in the bargaining unit of the employer in which the alien intends to perform such service; and

(C) The alien is not already an employee of the company (as described in paragraph (d)(2)(iv) of this section).

(ii) Refusal to land. Any alien (except a qualified current employee as described in paragraph (d)(2)(iv) of this section) who the examining immigration officer determines has arrived in the United States for the purpose of performing service on board a vessel or an aircraft of the United States when a strike or lockout is under way in the bargaining unit of the employer, shall be refused a conditional landing permit under section 252 of the Act.

(iii) Ineligibility for parole. An alien described in paragraph (d)(2)(i) of this section may not be paroled into the United States under section 212(d)(5) of the Act for the purpose of performing crewmember duties unless the Attorney General determines that the parole of such alien is necessary to protect the national security of the United States. This paragraph does not prohibit the granting of parole for other purposes, such as medical emergencies.

(iv) Qualified current employees.

(A) Paragraphs (d)(2)(i), (d)(2)(ii), and (d)(2)(iii) of this section do not apply to an alien who is already an employee of the owner or operator of the vessel or air carrier and who at the time of inspection presents true copies of employer work records which satisfy the examining immigration officer that the alien:

(1) Has been an employee of such employer for a period of not less than one year preceding the date that a strike or lawful lockout commenced;

(2) Has served as a qualified crewman for such employer at least once in three different months during the 12-month period preceding the date that the strike or lockout commenced; and

(3) Shall continue to provide the same crewman services that he or she previously provided to the employer.

(B) An alien crewman who qualifies as a current employee under this paragraph remains subject to the restrictions on his or her employment in the United States contained in paragraph (d)(1) of this section.

(v) Strike or lockout determination. These provisions will take effect if the Attorney General, through the Commissioner of the Immigration and Naturalization Service or his or her designee, after consultation with the National Mediation Board, determines that a strike, lockout, or labor dispute involving a work stoppage is in progress in the bargaining unit of the employer for whom the alien intends to perform such service.

(e) Treaty traders and investors —

(1) Treaty trader. An alien, if otherwise admissible, may be classified as a nonimmigrant treaty trader (E-1) under the provisions of section 101(a)(15)(E)(i) of the Act if the alien:

(i) Will be in the United States solely to carry on trade of a substantial nature, which is international in scope, either on the alien's behalf or as an employee of a foreign person or organization engaged in trade principally between the United States and the treaty country of which the alien is a national, taking into consideration any conditions in the country of which the alien is a national which may affect the alien's ability to carry on such substantial trade; and

(ii) Intends to depart the United States upon the expiration or termination of treaty trader (E-1) status.

(2) Treaty investor. An alien, if otherwise admissible, may be classified as a nonimmigrant treaty investor (E-2) under the provision of section 101(a)(15)(E)(ii) of the Act if the alien:

(i) Has invested or is actively in the process of investing a substantial amount of capital in a bona fide enterprise in the United States, as distinct from a relatively small amount of capital in a marginal enterprise solely for the purpose of earning a living;

(ii) Is seeking entry solely to develop and direct the enterprise; and

(iii) Intends to depart the United States upon the expiration or termination of treaty investor (E-2) status.

(3) Employee of treaty trader or treaty investor. An alien employee of a treaty trader, if otherwise admissible, may be classified as E-1, and an alien employee of a treaty investor, if otherwise admissible, may be classified as E-2 if the employee is in or is coming to the United States to engage in duties of an executive or

supervisory character, or, if employed in a lesser capacity, the employee has special qualifications that make the alien's services essential to the efficient operation of the enterprise. The employee must have the same nationality as the principal alien employer. In addition, the employee must intend to depart the United States upon the expiration or termination of E-1 or E-2 status. The principal alien employer must be:

(i) A person in the United States having the nationality of the treaty country and maintaining nonimmigrant treaty trader or treaty investor status or, if not in the United States, would be classifiable as a treaty trader or treaty investor; or

(ii) An enterprise or organization at least 50 percent owned by persons in the United States having the nationality of the treaty country and maintaining nonimmigrant treaty trader or treaty investor status or who, if not in the United States, would be classifiable as treaty traders or treaty investors.

(4) Spouse and children of treaty trader or treaty investor. The spouse and child of a treaty trader or treaty investor accompanying or following to join the principal alien, if otherwise admissible, may receive the same classification as the principal alien. The nationality of a spouse or child of a treaty trader or treaty investor is not material to the classification of the spouse or child under the provisions of section 101(a)(15)(E) of the Act.

(5) Nonimmigrant intent. An alien classified under section 101(a)(15)(E) of the Act shall maintain an intention to depart the United States upon the expiration or termination of E-1 or E-2 status. However, an application for initial admission, change of status, or extension of stay in E classification may not be denied solely on the basis of an approved request for permanent labor certification or a filed or approved immigrant visa preference petition.

(6) Treaty country. A treaty country is, for purposes of this section, a foreign state with which a qualifying Treaty of Friendship, Commerce, or Navigation or its equivalent exists with the United States. A treaty country includes a foreign state that is accorded treaty visa privileges under section 101(a)(15)(E) of the Act by specific legislation.

(7) Treaty country nationality. The nationality of an individual treaty trader or treaty investor is determined by the authorities of the foreign state of which the alien is a national. In the case of an enterprise or organization, ownership must be traced as best as is practicable to the individuals who are ultimately its owners.

(8) Terms and conditions of E treaty status —

(i) Limitations on employment. The Service determines the terms and conditions of E treaty status at the time of admission or approval of a request to change nonimmigrant status to E classification. A treaty trader, treaty investor, or treaty employee may engage only in employment which is consistent with the terms and conditions of his or her status and the activity forming the basis for the E treaty status.

(ii) Subsidiary employment. Treaty employees may perform work for the parent treaty organization or enterprise, or any subsidiary of the parent organization or enterprise. Performing work for subsidiaries of a common parent enterprise or organization will not be deemed to constitute a substantive change in the terms and conditions of the underlying E treaty employment if, at the time the E treaty status was determined, the applicant presented evidence establishing:

(A) The enterprise or organization, and any subsidiaries thereof, where the work will be performed; the requisite parent-subsidiary relationship; and that the subsidiary independently qualifies as a treaty organization or enterprise under this paragraph;

(B) In the case of an employee of a treaty trader or treaty investor, the work to be performed requires executive, supervisory, or essential skills; and

(C) The work is consistent with the terms and conditions of the activity forming the basis of the classification.

(iii) Substantive changes. Approval of USCIS must be obtained where there will be a substantive change in the terms or conditions of E status. The treaty alien must file a new application in accordance with the instructions on the form prescribed by USCIS requesting extension of stay in the United States, plus evidence of continued eligibility for E classification in the new capacity. Or the alien may obtain a visa reflecting the new terms and conditions and subsequently apply for admission at a port-of-entry. USCIS will deem there to have been a substantive change necessitating the filing of a new application where there has been a fundamental change in the employing entity's basic characteristics, such as a merger, acquisition, or sale of the division where the alien is employed.

(iv) Non-substantive changes. Neither prior approval nor a new application is required if there is no substantive, or fundamental, change in the terms or conditions of the alien's employment that would affect the alien's eligibility for E classification. Further, prior approval is not required if corporate changes occur which do not affect the previously approved employment relationship or are otherwise non-substantive. To facilitate admission, the alien may:

(A) Present a letter from the treaty-qualifying company through which the alien attained E classification explaining the nature of the change;

(B) Request a new approval notice reflecting the non-substantive change by filing an application with a description of the change; or

(C) Apply directly to Department of State for a new E visa reflecting the change. An alien who does not elect one of the three options contained in paragraphs (e)(8)(iv)(A) through (C) of this section, is not precluded from demonstrating to the satisfaction of the immigration officer at the port-of-entry in some other manner, his or her admissibility under section 101(a)(15)(E) of the Act.

(v) Advice. To request advice from USCIS as to whether a change is substantive, an alien may file an application with a complete description of the change. In cases involving multiple employees, an alien may request that USCIS determine if a merger or other corporate restructuring requires the filing of separate applications by filing a single application and attaching a list of the related receipt numbers for the employees involved and an explanation of the change or changes.

(vi) Advice. To request advice from USCIS as to whether a change is substantive, an alien may file an application with a complete description of the change. In cases involving multiple employees, an alien may request that USCIS determine if a merger or other corporate restructuring requires the filing of separate applications by filing a single application and attaching a list of the related receipt numbers for the employees involved and an explanation of the change or changes.

(vii) An unauthorized change of employment to a new employer will constitute a failure to maintain status within the meaning of section 237(a)(1)(C)(i) of the Act. In all cases where the treaty employee will be providing services to a subsidiary under this paragraph, the subsidiary is required to comply with the terms of 8 CFR part 274a.

(9) Trade — definitions. For purposes of this paragraph: Items of trade include but are not limited to goods, services, international banking, insurance, monies, transportation, communications, data processing, advertising, accounting, design and engineering, management consulting, tourism, technology and its transfer, and some news-gathering activities. For purposes of this paragraph, goods are tangible commodities or merchandise having extrinsic value. Further, as used in this paragraph, services are legitimate economic activities which provide other than tangible goods.

Trade is the existing international exchange of items of trade for consideration between the United States and the treaty country. Existing trade includes successfully negotiated contracts binding upon the parties which call for the immediate exchange of items of trade. Domestic trade or the development of domestic markets without international exchange does not constitute trade for purposes of section 101(a)(15)(E) of the Act. This exchange must be traceable and identifiable. Title to the trade item must pass from one treaty party to the other.

(10) Substantial trade. Substantial trade is an amount of trade sufficient to ensure a continuous flow of international trade items between the United States and the treaty country. This continuous flow contemplates numerous transactions over time. Treaty trader status may not be established or maintained on the basis of a single transaction, regardless of how protracted or monetarily valuable the transaction. Although the monetary value of the trade item being exchanged is a relevant consideration, greater weight will be given to more numerous exchanges of larger value. There is no minimum requirement with respect to the monetary value or volume of each individual transaction. In the case of smaller businesses, an income derived from the value of numerous transactions which is sufficient to support the treaty trader and his or her family constitutes a favorable factor in assessing the existence of substantial trade.

(11) Principal trade. Principal trade between the United States and the treaty country exists when over 50 percent of the volume of international trade of the treaty trader is conducted between the United States and the treaty country of the treaty trader's nationality.

(12) Investment. An investment is the treaty investor's placing of capital, including funds and other assets (which have not been obtained, directly or indirectly, through criminal activity), at risk in the commercial sense with the objective of generating a profit. The treaty investor must be in possession of and have control over the capital invested or being invested. The capital must be subject to partial or total loss if investment fortunes reverse. Such investment capital must be the investor's unsecured personal business capital or capital secured by personal assets. Capital in the process of being invested or that has been invested must be irrevocably committed to the enterprise. The alien has the burden of establishing such irrevocable commitment. The alien may use any legal mechanism available, such as the placement of invested funds in escrow pending admission in, or approval of, E classification, that would not only irrevocably commit funds to the enterprise, but might also extend personal liability protection to the treaty investor in the event the application for E classification is denied.

(13) Bona fide enterprise. The enterprise must be a real, active, and operating commercial or entrepreneurial undertaking which produces services or goods for profit. The enterprise must meet applicable legal requirements for doing business in the particular jurisdiction in the United States.

(14) Substantial amount of capital. A substantial amount of capital constitutes an amount which is:

(i) Substantial in relationship to the total cost of either purchasing an established enterprise or creating the type of enterprise under consideration;

(ii) Sufficient to ensure the treaty investor's financial commitment to the successful operation of the enterprise; and

(iii) Of a magnitude to support the likelihood that the treaty investor will successfully develop and direct the enterprise. Generally, the lower the cost of the enterprise, the higher, proportionately, the investment must be to be considered a substantial amount of capital.

(15) Marginal enterprise. For purposes of this section, an enterprise may not be marginal. A marginal enterprise is an enterprise that does not have the present or future capacity to generate more than enough income to provide a minimal living for the treaty investor and his or her family. An enterprise that does not have the capacity to generate such income, but that has a present or future capacity to make a significant economic contribution is not a marginal enterprise. The projected future income-generating capacity should generally be realizable within 5 years from the date the alien commences the normal business activity of the enterprise.

(16) Solely to develop and direct. An alien seeking classification as a treaty investor (or, in the case of an employee of a treaty investor, the owner of the treaty enterprise) must demonstrate that he or she does or will develop and direct the investment enterprise. Such an applicant must establish that he or she controls the

enterprise by demonstrating ownership of at least 50 percent of the enterprise, by possessing operational control through a managerial position or other corporate device, or by other means.

(17) Executive and supervisory character. The applicant's position must be principally and primarily, as opposed to incidentally or collaterally, executive or supervisory in nature. Executive and supervisory duties are those which provide the employee ultimate control and responsibility for the enterprise's overall operation or a major component thereof. In determining whether the applicant has established possession of the requisite control and responsibility, a Service officer shall consider, where applicable:

(i) That an executive position is one which provides the employee with great authority to determine the policy of, and the direction for, the enterprise;

(ii) That a position primarily of supervisory character provides the employee supervisory responsibility for a significant proportion of an enterprise's operations and does not generally involve the direct supervision of low-level employees, and;

(iii) Whether the applicant possesses executive and supervisory skills and experience; a salary and position title commensurate with executive or supervisory employment; recognition or indicia of the position as one of authority and responsibility in the overall organizational structure; responsibility for making discretionary decisions, setting policies, directing and managing business operations, supervising other professional and supervisory personnel; and that, if the position requires some routine work usually performed by a staff employee, such functions may only be of an incidental nature.

(18) Special qualifications. Special qualifications are those skills and/or aptitudes that an employee in a lesser capacity brings to a position or role that are essential to the successful or efficient operation of the treaty enterprise. In determining whether the skills possessed by the alien are essential to the operation of the employing treaty enterprise, a Service officer must consider, where applicable:

(i) The degree of proven expertise of the alien in the area of operations involved; whether others possess the applicant's specific skill or aptitude; the length of the applicant's experience and/or training with the treaty enterprise; the period of training or other experience necessary to perform effectively the projected duties; the relationship of the skill or knowledge to the enterprise's specific processes or applications, and the salary the special qualifications can command; that knowledge of a foreign language and culture does not, by itself, meet the special qualifications requirement, and;

(ii) Whether the skills and qualifications are readily available in the United States. In all cases, in determining whether the applicant possesses special qualifications which are essential to the treaty enterprise, a Service officer must take into account all the particular facts presented. A skill that is essential at one point in time may become commonplace at a later date. Skills that are needed to start up an enterprise may no longer be essential after initial operations are complete and running smoothly. Some skills are essential only in the short-term for the training of locally hired employees. Under certain circumstances, an applicant may be able to establish his or her essentiality to the treaty enterprise for a longer period of time, such as, in connection with activities in the areas of product improvement, quality control, or the provision of a service not yet generally available in the United States. Where the treaty enterprise's need for the applicant's special qualifications, and therefore, the applicant's essentiality, is time-limited, Service officers may request that the applicant provide evidence of the period for which skills will be needed and a reasonable projected date for completion of start-up or replacement of the essential skilled workers.

(19) Period of admission. Periods of admission are as follows:

(i) A treaty trader or treaty investor may be admitted for an initial period of not more than 2 years.

(ii) The spouse and minor children accompanying or following to join a treaty trader or treaty investor shall be admitted for the period during which the principal alien is in valid treaty trader or investor status. The temporary departure from the United States of the principal trader or investor shall not affect the derivative status of the dependent spouse and minor unmarried children, provided the familial relationship continues to exist and the principal remains eligible for admission as an E nonimmigrant to perform the activity.

(iii) Unless otherwise provided for in this chapter, an alien shall not be admitted in E classification for a period of time extending more than 6 months beyond the expiration date of the alien's passport.

(20) Extensions of stay. Requests for extensions of stay may be granted in increments of not more than 2 years. A treaty trader or treaty investor in valid E status may apply for an extension of stay by filing an application for extension of stay on the form prescribed by USCIS, with required accompanying documents, in accordance with § 214.1 and the instructions on that form.

(i) For purposes of eligibility for an extension of stay, the alien must prove that he or she:

(A) Has at all times maintained the terms and conditions of his or her E nonimmigrant classification;

(B) Was physically present in the United States at the time of filing the application for extension of stay; and

(C) Has not abandoned his or her extension request.

(ii) With limited exceptions, it is presumed that employees of treaty enterprises with special qualifications who are responsible for start-up operations should be able to complete their objectives within 2 years. Absent special circumstances, therefore, such employees will not be eligible to obtain an extension of stay.

(iii) Subject to paragraph (e)(5) of this section and the presumption noted in paragraph (e)(22)(ii) of this section, there is no specified number of extensions of stay that a treaty trader or treaty investor may be granted.

(21) Change of nonimigrant status.

(i) An alien in another valid nonimmigrant status may apply for change of status to E classification by filing an application for change of status on the form prescribed by USCIS, with required accompanying documents establishing eligibility for a change of status and E classification, in accordance with 8 CFR part 248 and the instructions on the form prescribed by USCIS.

(ii) The spouse or minor children of an applicant seeking a change of status to that of treaty trader or treaty investor alien shall file concurrent applications for change of status to derivative treaty classification on the appropriate Service form. Applications for derivative treaty status shall:

(A) Be approved only if the principal treaty alien is granted treaty alien status and continues to maintain that status;

(B) Be approved for the period of admission authorized in paragraph (e)(20) of this section.

(22) Denial of treaty trader or treaty investor status to citizens of Canada or Mexico in the case of certain labor disputes.

(i) A citizen of Canada or Mexico may be denied E treaty trader or treaty investor status as described in section 101(a)(15)(E) of the Act and Section B of Annex 16-A of Chapter 16 of the USMCA if:

(A) The Secretary of Labor certifies to or otherwise informs the Commissioner that a strike or other labor dispute involving a work stoppage of workers in the alien's occupational classification is in progress at the place where the alien is or intends to be employed; and

(B) Temporary entry of that alien may affect adversely either:

(1) The settlement of any labor dispute that is in progress at the place or intended place of employment, or

(2) The employment of any person who is involved in such dispute.

(ii) If the alien has already commenced employment in the United States and is participating in a strike or other labor dispute involving a work stoppage of workers, whether or not such strike or other labor dispute has been certified by the Secretary of Labor, or whether the Service has been otherwise informed that such a strike or labor dispute is in progress, the alien shall not be deemed to be failing to maintain his or her status solely on account of past, present, or future participation in a strike or other labor dispute involving a work stoppage of workers, but is subject to the following terms and conditions:

(A) The alien shall remain subject to all applicable provisions of the Immigration and Nationality Act, and regulations promulgated in the same manner as all other E nonimmigrants; and

(B) The status and authorized period of stay of such an alien is not modified or extended in any way by virtue of his or her participation in a strike or other labor dispute involving a work stoppage of workers.

(iii) Although participation by an E nonimmigrant alien in a strike or other labor dispute involving a work stoppage of workers will not constitute a ground for deportation, any alien who violates his or her status or who remains in the United States after his or her authorized period of stay has expired will be subject to deportation.

(iv) If there is a strike or other labor dispute involving a work stoppage of workers in progress, but such strike or other labor dispute is not certified under paragraph (e)(22)(i) of this section, or the Service has not otherwise been informed by the Secretary that such a strike or labor dispute is in progress, the Commissioner shall not deny entry to an applicant for E status.

(23) Special procedures for classifying foreign investors in the Commonwealth of the Northern Mariana Islands (CNMI) as E-2 nonimmigrant treaty investors under title VII of the Consolidated Natural Resources Act of 2008 (Pub. L. 110-229), 48 U.S.C. 1806.

(i) E-2 CNMI Investor eligibility. During the period ending on January 18, 2013, an alien may, upon application to the Secretary of Homeland Security, be classified as a CNMI-only nonimmigrant treaty investor (E-2 CNMI Investor) under section 101(a)(15)(E)(ii) of the Act if the alien:

(A) Was lawfully admitted to the CNMI in long-term investor status under the immigration laws of the CNMI before the transition program effective date and had that status on the transition program effective date;

(B) Has continuously maintained residence in the CNMI;

(C) Is otherwise admissible to the United States; and

(D) Maintains the investment or investments that formed the basis for such long-term investment status.

(ii) Definitions. For purposes of paragraph (e)(23) of this section, the following definitions apply:

(A) Approved investment or residence means an investment or residence approved by the CNMI government.

(B) Approval letter means a letter issued by the CNMI government certifying the acceptance of an approved investment subject to the minimum investment criteria and standards provided in 4 N. Mar. I. Code section 5941 et seq. (long-term business certificate), 4 N. Mar. I. Code section 5951 et seq. (foreign investor certificate), and 4 N. Mar. I. Code section 50101 et seq. (foreign retiree investment certificate).

(C) Certificate means a certificate or certification issued by the CNMI government to an applicant whose application has been approved by the CNMI government.

(D) Continuously maintained residence in the CNMI means that the alien has maintained his or her residence within the CNMI since being lawfully admitted as a long-term investor and has been physically present therein for periods totaling at least half of that time. Absence from the CNMI for any continuous period of more than six months but less than one year after such lawful admission shall break the continuity of such residence, unless the subject alien establishes to the satisfaction of DHS that he or she did not in fact abandon residence in the CNMI during such period. Absence from the CNMI for any period of one year or more during the period for which continuous residence is required shall break the continuity of such residence.

(E) Public organization means a CNMI public corporation or an agency of the CNMI government.

(F) Transition period means the period beginning on the transition program effective date and ending on December 31, 2029.

(iii) Long-term investor status. Long-term investor status under the immigration laws of the CNMI includes only the following investor classifications under CNMI immigration laws as in effect on or before November 27, 2009:

(A) Long-term business investor. An alien who has an approved investment of at least $ 50,000 in the CNMI, as evidenced by a Long-Term Business Certificate.

(B) Foreign investor. An alien in the CNMI who has invested either a minimum of $ 100,000 in an aggregate approved investment in excess of $ 2,000,000, or a minimum of $ 250,000 in a single approved investment, as evidenced by a Foreign Investment Certificate.

(C) Retiree investor. An alien in the CNMI who:

(1) Is over the age of 55 years and has invested a minimum of $ 100,000 in an approved residence on Saipan or $ 75,000 in an approved residence on Tinian or Rota, as evidenced by a Foreign Retiree Investment Certification; or

(2) Is over the age of 55 years and has invested a minimum of $ 150,000 in an approved residence to live in the CNMI, as evidenced by a Foreign Retiree Investment Certificate.

(iv) Maintaining investments. An alien in long-term investor status under the immigration laws of the CNMI is maintaining his or her investments if that alien investor is in compliance with the terms upon which the investor certificate was issued.

(v) Filing procedures. An alien seeking classification under E-2 CNMI Investor nonimmigrant status must file an application for E-2 CNMI investor nonimmigrant status, along with accompanying evidence, with USCIS in accordance with the form instructions before January 18, 2013. An application filed after the filing date deadline will be rejected.

(vi) Appropriate documents. Documentary evidence establishing eligibility for E-2 CNMI nonimmigrant investor status is required.

(A) Required evidence of admission includes a valid unexpired foreign passport and a properly endorsed CNMI admission document (e.g., entry permit or certificate) reflecting lawful admission to the CNMI in long-term business investor, foreign investor, or retiree foreign investor status.

(B) Required evidence of long-term investor status includes:

(1) An unexpired Long-Term Business Certificate, in the case of an alien in long-term business investor status.

(2) An unexpired Foreign Investment Certificate, in the case of an alien in foreign investor status.

(3) A Foreign Retiree Investment Certification or a Foreign Retiree Investment Certificate, in the case of an alien in retiree investor status.

(C) Required evidence that the long-term investor is maintaining his or her investment includes all of the following, as applicable:

(1) An approval letter issued by the CNMI government.

(2) Evidence that capital has been invested, including bank statements showing amounts deposited in CNMI business accounts, invoices, receipts or contracts for assets purchased, stock purchase transaction records, loan or other borrowing agreements, land leases, financial statements, business gross tax receipts, or any other agreements supporting the application.

(3) Evidence that the applicant has invested at least the minimum amount required, including evidence of assets which have been purchased for use in the enterprise, evidence of property transferred from abroad for use in the enterprise, evidence of monies transferred or committed to be transferred to the new or existing enterprise in exchange for shares of stock, any loan or mortgage, promissory note, security agreement, or other evidence of borrowing which is secured by assets of the applicant.

(4) A comprehensive business plan for new enterprises.

(5) Articles of incorporation, by-laws, partnership agreements, joint venture agreements, corporate minutes and annual reports, affidavits, declarations, or certifications of paid-in capital.

(6) Current business licenses.

(7) Foreign business registration records, recent tax returns of any kind, evidence of other sources of capital.

(8) A listing of all resident and nonresident employees.

(9) A listing of all holders of business certificates for the business establishment.

(10) A listing of all corporations in which the applicant has a controlling interest.

(11) In the case of a holder of a certificate of foreign investment, copies of annual reports of investment activities in the CNMI containing sufficient information to determine whether the certificate holder is under continuing compliance with the standards of issuance, accompanied by annual financial audit reports performed by an independent certified public accountant.

(12) In the case of an applicant who is a retiree investor, evidence that he or she has an interest in property in the CNMI (e.g., lease agreement), evidence of the value of the property interest (e.g., an appraisal regarding the value of the property), and, as applicable, evidence of the value of the improvements on the property (e.g., receipts or invoices of the costs of construction, the amount paid for a preexisting structure, or an appraisal of improvements).

(vii) Physical presence in the CNMI. Physical presence in the CNMI at the time of filing or during the pendency of the application is not required, but an application may not be filed by, or E-2 CNMI Investor status granted to, any alien present in U.S. territory other than in the CNMI. If an alien with CNMI long-term investor status departs the CNMI on or after the transition program effective date but before being granted E-2 CNMI Investor status, he or she may not be re-admitted to the CNMI without a visa or appropriate inadmissibility waiver under the U.S. immigration laws. If USCIS grants E-2 CNMI Investor nonimmigrant classification to an alien who is not physically present in the CNMI at the time of the grant, such alien must obtain an E-2 CNMI Investor nonimmigrant visa at a consular office abroad in order to seek admission to the CNMI in E-2 CNMI Investor status.

(viii) Information for background checks. USCIS may require an applicant for E-2 CNMI Investor status, including but not limited to any applicant for derivative status as a spouse or child, to submit biometrics as required under 8 CFR 103.16.

(ix) Denial. A grant of E-2 CNMI Investor status is a discretionary determination, and the application may be denied for failure of the applicant to demonstrate eligibility or for other good cause. Denial of the application may be appealed to the USCIS Administrative Appeals Office or any successor body.

(x) Spouse and children of an E-2 CNMI Investor.

(A) Classification. The spouse and children of an E-2 CNMI Investor accompanying or following-to-join the principal alien, if otherwise admissible, may receive the same classification as the principal alien. The nationality of a spouse or child of an E-2 CNMI investor is not material to the classification of the spouse or child.

(B) Employment authorization. The spouse of an E-2 CNMI Investor lawfully admitted in the CNMI in E-2 CNMI Investor nonimmigrant status, other than the spouse of an E-2 CNMI investor who obtained such status based upon a Foreign Retiree Investment Certificate, is eligible to apply for employment authorization under 8 CFR 274a.12(c)(12) while in E-2 CNMI Investor nonimmigrant status. Employment authorization acquired under this paragraph is limited to employment in the CNMI only.

(xi) Terms and conditions of E-2 CNMI Investor nonimmigrant status.

(A) Nonimmigrant status. E-2 CNMI Investor nonimmigrant status and any derivative status are only applicable in the CNMI. Entry, employment, and residence in the rest of the United States (including Guam) require the appropriate visa or visa waiver eligibility. An E-2 CNMI Investor who enters, attempts to enter or attempts to travel to any other part of the United States without the appropriate visa or visa waiver eligibility, or who violates conditions of nonimmigrant stay applicable to any such authorized status in any other part of the United States, will be deemed to have violated the terms and conditions of his or her E-2 CNMI Investor status. An E-2 CNMI Investor who departs the CNMI will require an E-2 CNMI investor visa for readmission to the CNMI as an E-2 CNMI Investor.

(B) Employment authorization. An alien with E-2 CNMI Investor nonimmigrant status is only employment authorized in the CNMI for the enterprise that is the basis for his or her CNMI Foreign Investment Certificate or Long-Term Business Certificate, to the extent that such Certificate authorized such activity. An alien with E-2 CNMI Investor nonimmigrant status based upon a Foreign Retiree Investor Certificate is not employment authorized.

(C) Changes in E-2 CNMI investor nonimmigrant status. If there are any substantive changes to an alien's compliance with the terms and conditions of qualification for E-2 CNMI Investor nonimmigrant status, the alien must file a new application for E-2 CNMI Investor nonimmigrant status, in accordance with the appropriate form instructions to request an extension of stay in the United States. Prior approval is not required if corporate changes occur that do not affect a previously approved employment relationship, or are otherwise non-substantive.

(D) Unauthorized change of employment. An unauthorized change of employment to a new employer will constitute a failure to maintain status within the meaning of section 237(a)(1)(C)(i) of the Act.

(E) Periods of admission.

(*1*) An E-2 CNMI Investor may be admitted for an initial period of not more than two years.

(*2*) The spouse and children accompanying or following-to-join an E-2 CNMI Investor may be admitted for the period during which the principal alien is in valid E-2 CNMI Investor nonimmigrant status. The temporary departure from the United States of the principal E-2 CNMI Investor shall not affect the derivative status of the dependent spouse and children, provided the familial relationship continues to exist and the principal alien remains eligible for admission as an E-2 CNMI Investor.

(xii) Extensions of stay. Requests for extensions of E-2 CNMI Investor nonimmigrant status may be granted in increments of not more than two years, until the end of the transition period. To request an extension of stay, an E-2 CNMI Investor must file with USCIS an application for extension of stay, with required accompanying documents, in accordance with the appropriate form instructions. To qualify for an extension of E-2 CNMI Investor nonimmigrant status, each alien must demonstrate:

(A) Continuous maintenance of the terms and conditions of E-2 CNMI Investor nonimmigrant status;

(B) Physical presence in the CNMI at the time of filing the application for extension of stay; and

(C) That he or she did not leave during the pendency of the application.

(xiii) Change of status. An alien lawfully admitted to the United States in another valid nonimmigrant status who is continuing to maintain that status may apply to change nonimmigrant status to E-2 CNMI Investor in accordance with paragraph (e)(21) of this section, if otherwise eligible, including but not limited to having been in CNMI long-term investor status on the transition date and within the period provided by paragraph (e)(23)(v) of this section.

(xiv) Expiration of the transition period. Upon expiration of the transition period, the E–2 CNMI Investor nonimmigrant status will automatically terminate.

(xv) [Removed and Reserved]

(xvi) Waiver of inadmissibility for applicants present in the CNMI. An applicant for E-2 CNMI Investor nonimmigrant status, who is otherwise eligible for such status and otherwise admissible to the United States, and who has provided all appropriate documents as described in paragraph (e)(23)(vi) of this section, may be granted a waiver of inadmissibility under section 212(d)(3)(A)(ii) of the Act, including the grounds of inadmissibility described in sections 212(a)(6)(A)(i) (to the extent such grounds arise solely because of the alien's presence in the CNMI on November 28, 2009) and 212(a)(7)(B)(i)(II) of the Act, for the purpose of granting the E-2 CNMI Investor nonimmigrant status. Such waiver may be granted without additional form or fee required. In the case of an application by a spouse or child as described in paragraph (e)(23)(x) of this section who is present in the CNMI, the appropriate documents required for such waiver are a valid unexpired passport and evidence that the spouse or child is lawfully present in the CNMI under section 1806(e) of title 48, U.S. Code (which may include evidence of a grant of parole by USCIS or by the Department of Homeland Security pursuant to a grant of advance parole by USCIS in furtherance of section 1806(e) of title 48, U.S. Code).

(f) Students in colleges, universities, seminaries, conservatories, academic high schools, elementary schools, other academic institutions, and in language training programs.

Table 2 to Paragraph (f)—Paragraph Contents

(1) Admission of student.
(2) Form I-20 or successor form.
(3) Admission of the spouse and minor children of an F-1 student.
(4) Temporary absence.
(5) Duration of status.
(6) Full course of study.
(7) Extension of stay.
(8) School transfer.
(9) Employment.
(10) Practical training.
(11) OPT application and approval process.
(12) Reporting while on optional practical training.
(13) Temporary absence from the United States of F-1 student granted employment authorization.
(14) Effect of strike or other labor dispute.
(15) Spouse and children of F-1 student.
(16) Reinstatement to student status.
(17) Current name and address.
(18) Special rules for certain border commuter students.
(19) Remittance of the fee.

(1) Admission of student —

(i) Eligibility for admission. A nonimmigrant student may be admitted into the United States in nonimmigrant status under section 101(a)(15)(F) of the Act, if:

(A) The student presents a Form I-20 or successor form issued in the student's name by a school certified by the Student and Exchange Visitor Program (SEVP) for attendance by F-1 foreign students;

(B) The student has documentary evidence of financial support in the amount indicated on the Form I-20 or successor form;

(C) For students seeking initial admission only, the student intends to attend the school specified in the student's visa (or, where the student is exempt from the requirement for a visa, the school indicated on the Form I-20 or successor form); and

(D) In the case of a student who intends to study at a public secondary school, the student has demonstrated that he or she has reimbursed the local educational agency that administers the school for the full, unsubsidized per capita cost of providing education at the school for the period of the student's attendance.

(ii) Form I-20 or successor form requirements at the port-of-entry. When an F-1 student applies for admission with a complete Form I-20 or successor form, the inspecting officer will:

(A) Transcribe the student's admission number from Form I-94 onto the student's Form I-20 or successor form (for students seeking initial admission only);

(B) Endorse the Form I-20 or successor form; and

(C) Return the Form I-20 or successor form to the student.

(iii) Use of the Student and Exchange Visitor Information System (SEVIS). Schools must issue a Form I-20 or successor form in SEVIS to any current student requiring a reportable action (e.g., extension of stay, practical training, and requests for employment authorization), or to any alien who must obtain a new nonimmigrant student visa.

(2) Student maintenance of Form I-20 or successor form. An F-1 student is expected to retain for safekeeping the initial Form I-20 or successor form bearing the admission number and any subsequent Form I-20 issued to them. Should the student lose their current Form I-20 or successor form, a replacement copy bearing the same information as the lost copy, including any endorsement for employment and notations, should be issued by the designated school official (DSO) as defined in § 214.3(l)(1).

(3) Admission of the spouse and minor children of an F-1 student. The spouse and minor children accompanying an F-1 student are eligible for admission in F-2 status if the student is admitted in F-1 status. The spouse and minor children following-to-join an F-1 student are eligible for admission to the United States in F-2 status if they are able to demonstrate that the F-1 student has been admitted and is, or will be within 30 days, enrolled in a full course of study, or engaged in approved practical training following completion of studies. In either case, at the time they seek admission, the eligible spouse and minor children of an F-1 student must individually present a Form I-20 or successor form in the name of each F-2 dependent issued by a school certified by SEVP for attendance by F-1 students. A new Form I-20 or successor form is required for a dependent where there has been any substantive change in the F-1 student's current information.

(4) Temporary absence. An F-1 student returning to the United States from a temporary absence of five months or less may be readmitted for attendance at an SEVP-certified educational institution, if the student presents:

(i) A current Form I-20 or successor form properly endorsed by the DSO for reentry if there has been no substantive change to the most recent Form I-20 or successor form information; or

(ii) An updated Form I-20 or successor form if there has been a substantive change in the information on the student's most recent Form I-20 or successor form, such as in the case of a student who has changed the major area of study, who intends to transfer to another SEVP-certified institution, or who has advanced to a higher level of study.

(5) Duration of status —

(i) General. Duration of status is defined as the time during which an F-1 student is pursuing a full course of study at an educational institution certified by SEVP for attendance by foreign students, or engaging in authorized practical training following completion of studies, except that an F-1 student who is admitted to attend a public high school is restricted to an aggregate of 12 months of study at any public high school(s). An F-1 student may be admitted for a period up to 30 days before the indicated report date or program start date listed on the Form I-20 or successor form. The student is considered to be maintaining status if the student is making normal progress toward completing a course of study.

(ii) Change in educational levels. An F-1 student who continues from one educational level to another is considered to be maintaining status, provided that the transition to the new educational level is accomplished according to transfer procedures outlined in paragraph (f)(8) of this section.

(iii) Annual vacation. An F-1 student at an academic institution is considered to be in status during the annual (or summer) vacation if the student is eligible and intends to register for the next term. A student attending a school on a quarter or trimester calendar who takes only one vacation a year during any one of the quarters or trimesters instead of during the summer is considered to be in status during that vacation, if the student has completed the equivalent of an academic year prior to taking the vacation.

(iv) Preparation for departure. An F-1 student who has completed a course of study and any authorized practical training following completion of studies will be allowed an additional 60-day period to prepare for departure from the United States or to transfer in accordance with paragraph (f)(8) of this section. An F-1 student authorized by the DSO to withdraw from classes will be allowed a 15-day period for departure from the United States. However, an F-1 student who fails to maintain a full course of study without the approval of the DSO or otherwise fails to maintain status is not eligible for an additional period for departure.

(v) Emergent circumstances as determined by the Secretary. Where the Secretary has suspended the applicability of any or all of the requirements for on-campus or off-campus employment authorization for specified students pursuant to paragraphs (f)(9)(i) or (ii) of this section by notice in the Federal Register , an affected student who needs to reduce their full course of study as a result of accepting employment authorized by such notice in the Federal Register will be considered to be in status during the authorized employment, subject to any other conditions specified in the notice, provided that, for the duration of the authorized employment, the student is registered for the number of semester or quarter hours of instruction per academic term specified in the notice, which in no event shall be less than six semester or quarter hours of instruction per academic term if the student is at the undergraduate level or less than three semester or quarter hours of instruction per academic term if the student is at the graduate level, and is continuing to make progress toward completing the course of study.

(vi) Extension of duration of status and grant of employment authorization.

(A) The duration of status, and any employment authorization granted under 8 CFR 274a.12(c)(3)(i)(B) or (C), of an F–1 student who is the beneficiary of an H–1B petition subject to section 214(g)(1)(A) of the Act (8 U.S.C. 1184(g)(1)(A)) requesting a change of status will be automatically extended until April 1 of the fiscal year for which such H–1B status is being requested or until the validity start date of the approved petition, whichever is earlier, where such petition:

(1) Has been timely filed;

(2) Requests an H–1B employment start date in the fiscal year for which such H–1B status is being requested consistent with paragraph (h)(2)(i)(I) of this section; and

(3) Is nonfrivolous.

(B) The automatic extension of an F-1 student's duration of status and employment authorization under paragraph (f)(5)(vi)(A) of this section shall automatically terminate upon the rejection, denial, revocation, or withdrawal of the H-1B petition filed on such F-1 student's behalf or upon the denial or withdrawal of the request for change of nonimmigrant status, even if the H-1B petition filed on the F-1 student's behalf is approved for consular processing.

(C) In order to obtain the automatic extension of stay and employment authorization under paragraph (f)(5)(vi)(A) of this section, the F-1 student, consistent with 8 CFR part 248, must not have violated the terms or conditions of his or her nonimmigrant status.

(D) An automatic extension of an F-1 student's duration of status under paragraph (f)(5)(vi)(A) of this section also applies to the duration of status of any F-2 dependent aliens.

(6) Full course of study —

(i) General. Successful completion of the full course of study must lead to the attainment of a specific educational or professional objective. A course of study at an institution not certified for attendance by foreign students as provided in § 214.3(a)(3) does not satisfy the requirement of this paragraph (f)(6)(i). A "full course of study" as required by section 101(a)(15)(F)(i) of the Act means:

(A) Postgraduate study or postdoctoral study at a college or university, or undergraduate or postgraduate study at a conservatory or religious seminary, certified by a DSO as a full course of study;

(B) Undergraduate study at a college or university, certified by a school official to consist of at least 12 semester or quarter hours of instruction per academic term in those institutions using standard semester, trimester, or quarter hour systems, where all undergraduate students who are enrolled for a minimum of 12 semester or quarter hours are charged full-time tuition or are considered full-time for other administrative purposes, or its equivalent (as determined by SEVP in the school certification process), except when the student needs a lesser course load to complete the course of study during the current term;

(C) Study in a postsecondary language, liberal arts, fine arts, or other non-vocational program at a school which confers upon its graduates recognized associate or other degrees or has established that its credits have been and are accepted unconditionally by at least three other institutions of higher learning which are either:

(1) A school (or school system) owned and operated as a public educational institution by the United States or a State or political subdivision thereof; or

(2) a school accredited by a nationally recognized accrediting body; and which has been certified by a designated school official to consist of at least 12 clock hours of instruction a week, or its equivalent as determined by SEVP in the school certification process;

(D) Study in any other language, liberal arts, fine arts, or other nonvocational training program, certified by a designated school official to consist of at least eighteen clock hours of attendance a week if the dominant part of the course of study consists of classroom instruction, or to consist of at least twenty-two clock hours a week if the dominant part of the course of study consists of laboratory work; or

(E) Study in a curriculum at a certified private elementary or middle school or public or private academic high school which is certified by a designated school official to consist of class attendance for not less than the minimum number of hours a week prescribed by the school for normal progress toward graduation.

(F) Notwithstanding paragraphs (f)(6)(i)(A) and (B) of this section, an alien who has been granted employment authorization pursuant to the terms of a document issued by the Secretary under paragraphs (f)(9)(i) or (ii) of this section and published in the Federal Register shall be deemed to be engaged in a "full course of study" if he or she remains registered for no less than the number of semester or quarter hours of instruction per academic term specified by the Secretary in the notice for the validity period of such employment authorization.

(G) For F-1 students enrolled in classes for credit or classroom hours, no more than the equivalent of one class or three credits per session, term, semester, trimester, or quarter may be counted toward the full course of study requirement if the class is taken on-line or through distance education and does not require the student's physical attendance for classes, examination or other purposes integral to completion of the class. An on-line or distance education course is a course that is offered principally through the use of television, audio, or computer transmission including open broadcast, closed circuit, cable, microwave, or satellite, audio conferencing, or computer conferencing. If the F-1 student's course of study is in a language study program, no on-line or distance education classes may be considered to count toward a student's full course of "study requirement.

(H) On-campus employment pursuant to the terms of a scholarship, fellowship, or assistantship is deemed to be part of the academic program of a student otherwise taking a full course of study.

(ii) Institution of higher learning. For purposes of this paragraph, a college or university is an institution of higher learning which awards recognized associate, bachelor's, master's, doctorate, or professional degrees. Schools which devote themselves exclusively or primarily to vocational, business, or language instruction are not included in the category of colleges or universities. Vocational or business schools which are classifiable as M-1 schools are provided for by regulations under 8 CFR 214.2(m).

(iii) Reduced course load. The designated school official may allow an F-1 student to engage in less than a full course of study as provided in this paragraph (f)(6)(iii). Except as otherwise noted, a reduced course load must consist of at least six semester or quarter hours, or half the clock hours required for a full course of study. A student who drops below a full course of study without the prior approval of the DSO will be considered out of status. On-campus employment pursuant to the terms of a scholarship, fellowship, or assistantship is deemed to be part of the academic program of a student otherwise taking a full course of study.

(A) Academic difficulties. The DSO may authorize a reduced course load on account of a student's initial difficulty with the English language or reading requirements, unfamiliarity with U.S. teaching methods, or improper course level placement. The student must resume a full course of study at the next available term, session, or semester, excluding a summer session, in order to maintain student status. A student previously authorized to drop below a full course of study due to academic difficulties is not eligible for a second authorization by the DSO due to academic difficulties while pursuing a course of study at that program level. A student authorized to drop below a full course of study for academic difficulties while pursuing a course of study at a particular program level may still be authorized for a reduced course load due to an illness medical condition as provided for in paragraph (B) of this section.

(B) Medical conditions. The DSO may authorize a reduced course load (or, if necessary, no course load) due to a student's temporary illness or medical condition for a period of time not to exceed an aggregate of 12 months while the student is pursuing a course of study at a particular program level. In order to authorize a reduced course load based upon a medical condition, the student must provide medical documentation from a licensed medical doctor, a licensed doctor of osteopathy, a licensed psychologist, or a licensed clinical psychologist to the DSO to substantiate the illness or medical condition. The student must provide current medical documentation and the DSO must reauthorize the drop below full course of study each new term, session, or semester. A student previously authorized to drop below a full course of study due to illness or medical condition for an aggregate of 12 months may not be authorized by a DSO to reduce their course load on subsequent occasions while pursuing a course of study at the same program level. A student may be authorized to reduce course load for a reason of illness or medical condition on more than one occasion while pursuing a course of study, so long as the aggregate period of that authorization does not exceed 12 months.

(C) Completion of course of study. The DSO may authorize a reduced course load in the student's final term, semester, or session if fewer courses are needed to complete the course of study. If the student is not required to take any additional courses to satisfy the requirements for completion, but continues to be enrolled for administrative purposes, the student is considered to have completed the course of study and must take action to maintain status. Such action may include application for change of status or departure from the U.S.

(D) [Removed and reserved.]

(E) Reporting requirements. In order for a student to be authorized to drop below a full course of study, the DSO must update SEVIS prior to the student reducing their course load. The DSO must update SEVIS with the date, reason for authorization, and the start date of the next term or session. The DSO must also notify SEVIS within 21 days of the student's commencement of a full course of study. If an extension of the program end date is required due to the student dropping below a full course of study, the DSO must update SEVIS by completing a new Form I-20 or successor form with the new program end date in accordance with paragraph (f)(7) of this section.

(iv) Concurrent enrollment. An F-1 student may be enrolled in two different SEVP-certified schools at one time as long as the combined enrollment amounts to a full course of study. In cases where a student is concurrently enrolled, the school from which the student will earn their degree or certification should issue the Form I-20 or successor form, and conduct subsequent certifications and updates to the Form I-20 or successor form. The DSO from this school is also responsible for all of the reporting requirements to SEVP. In instances where a student is enrolled in programs with different full course of study requirements (e.g., clock hours vs. credit hours), the DSO is permitted to determine what constitutes a full course of study.

(7) Extension of stay—

(i) General. An F-1 student who is admitted for duration of status is not required to apply for extension of stay as long as the student is maintaining status and making normal progress toward completion of their educational objective. An F-1 student who is currently maintaining status and making normal progress toward completing their educational objective, but who is unable to complete their course of study by the program end date on the Form I-20 or successor form, must apply prior to the program end date for a program extension pursuant to paragraph (f)(7)(iii) of this section.

(ii) Report date and program completion date on Form I-20 or successor form. When determining the report date on the Form I-20 or successor form, the DSO may choose a reasonable date to accommodate a student's need to be in attendance for required activities at the school prior to the actual start of classes. Such required activities may include, but are not limited to, research projects and orientation sessions. However, for purposes of employment, the DSO may not indicate a report date more than 30 days prior to the start of classes. When determining the program completion date on Form I-20 or successor form, the DSO should make a reasonable estimate based upon the time an average student would need to complete a similar program in the same discipline.

(iii) Program extension for students in lawful status. An F-1 student who is unable to meet the program completion date on the Form I-20 or successor form may be granted an extension by the DSO if the DSO certifies that the student has continually maintained status and that the delays are caused by compelling academic or medical reasons, such as changes of major or research topics, unexpected research problems, or documented illnesses. Delays caused by academic probation or suspension are not acceptable reasons for program extensions. A DSO may not grant an extension if the student did not apply for an extension until after the program end date noted on the Form I-20 or successor form. An F-1 student who is unable to complete the educational program within the time listed on Form I-20 or successor form and who is ineligible for program extension pursuant to this paragraph (f)(7) is considered out of status. If eligible, the student may apply for reinstatement under the provisions of paragraph (f)(16) of this section.

(iv) SEVIS update. A DSO may grant a program extension only by updating SEVIS and issuing a new Form I-20 or successor form reflecting the current program end date. A DSO may grant an extension any time prior to the program end date listed on the student's Form I-20 or successor form.

(8) School transfer —

(i) General. A student who is maintaining status may transfer to another SEVP-certified school by following the notification procedure prescribed in paragraph (f)(8)(ii) of this section. However, an F-1 student is not permitted to remain in the United States when transferring between schools or programs unless the student will begin classes at the transfer school or program within five months of transferring out of the current school or within 5 months of the program completion date on their current Form I-20 or successor form, whichever is earlier. In the case of an F-1 student authorized to engage in post-completion optional practical training (OPT), the student must be able resume classes within 5 months of transferring out of the school that recommended OPT or the date the OPT authorization ends, whichever is earlier. An F-1 student who was not pursuing a full course of study at the school he or she was last authorized to attend is ineligible for school transfer and must apply for reinstatement under the provisions of paragraph (f)(16) of this section, or, in the alternative, may depart the country and return as an initial entry in a new F-1 nonimmigrant status.

(ii) Transfer procedure. To transfer schools, the student must first notify their current school (the "transfer-out" school) of the intent to transfer and indicate the school to which the student intends to transfer (the "transfer-in" school). Upon notification by the student, the transfer-out school must update SEVIS to show the student is transferring out, indicate the transfer-in school, and input the transfer release date. The release date will be the current semester or session completion date, or the date of expected transfer if earlier than the established academic cycle. The transfer-out school will retain control over the student's record in SEVIS until the student completes the current term or reaches the release date. At the request of the student, the DSO of the transfer-out school may cancel the transfer request at any time prior to the release date. As of the release date specified by the transfer-out DSO, the transfer-in school will be granted full access to the student's SEVIS record and then becomes responsible for that student. The transfer-out school conveys authority and responsibility over that student to the transfer-in school and relinquishes its SEVIS access to that student's record. As such, a transfer request may not be cancelled by the transfer-out DSO after the release date has been reached. After the release date, the transfer-in DSO must complete the transfer of the student's record in SEVIS and may issue a Form I-20 or successor form. The student is then required to contact the DSO at the transfer-in school within 15 days of the program start date listed on the Form I-20 or successor form. Upon notification that the student is enrolled in classes, the transfer-in DSO must update SEVIS to reflect the student's registration and current address, thereby acknowledging that the student has completed the transfer process. The transfer is completed when the transfer-in school notifies SEVIS that the student has enrolled in classes in accordance with the 30 days required by § 214.3(g)(2)(iii).

(iii) [Removed and reserved.]

(9) Employment —

(i) On-campus employment. On-campus employment must either be performed on the school's premises, (including on-location commercial firms which provide services for students on campus, such as the school bookstore or cafeteria), or at an off-campus location that is educationally affiliated with the school. Employment with on-site commercial firms, such as a construction company building a school building, which do not provide direct student services is not deemed on-campus employment for the purposes of this paragraph (f)(9)(i). In the case of off-campus locations, the educational affiliation must be associated with the school's established curriculum or related to contractually funded research projects at the post-graduate level. In any event, the employment must be an integral part of the student's educational program. Employment authorized under this paragraph (f)(9)(i) must not exceed 20 hours a week while school is in session, unless the Secretary suspends the applicability of this limitation due to emergent circumstances, as determined by the Secretary, by means of notice in the Federal Register , the student demonstrates to the DSO that the employment is necessary to avoid severe economic hardship resulting from the emergent circumstances, and the DSO notates the Form I-20 or successor form in accordance with the Federal Register document. An F-1 student may, however, work on campus full-time when school is not in session or during the annual vacation. A student who has been issued a Form I-20 or successor form to begin a new program in accordance with the provision of § 214.3(k) and who intends to enroll for the next regular academic year, term, or session at the institution that issued the Form I-20 or successor form may continue on-campus employment incident to status. Otherwise, an F-1 student may not engage in on-campus employment after completing a course of study, except employment for practical training as authorized under paragraph (f)(10) of this section. An F-1 student may engage in any on-campus employment authorized under this paragraph (f)(9)(i) which will not displace United States residents. In the case of a transfer in SEVIS, the student may only engage in on-campus employment at the school having jurisdiction over the student's SEVIS record. Upon initial entry to begin a new course of study, an F-1 student may not begin on-campus employment more than 30 days prior to the actual start of classes.

(ii) Off-campus work authorization —

(A) General. An F-1 student may be authorized to work off-campus on a part-time basis in accordance with paragraph (f)(9)(ii)(C) of this section after having been in F-1 status for one full academic year provided that the student is in good academic standing as determined by the DSO. Part-time off-campus employment authorized under this section is limited to no more than 20 hours a week when school is in session. A student who is granted off-campus employment authorization may work full-time during holidays or school vacation. The employment authorization is automatically terminated whenever the student fails to maintain status. In emergent circumstances as determined by the Secretary, the Secretary may suspend the applicability of any or all of the requirements of paragraph (f)(9)(ii) of this section by notice in the Federal Register .

(B) [Reserved]

(C) Severe economic hardship. If other employment opportunities are not available or are otherwise insufficient, an eligible F-1 student may request off-campus employment work authorization based upon severe economic hardship caused by unforeseen circumstances beyond the student's control. These circumstances may include loss of financial aid or on-campus employment without fault on the part of the student, substantial fluctuations in the value of currency or exchange rate, inordinate increases in tuition and/or living costs, unexpected changes in the financial condition of the student's source of support, medical bills, or other substantial and unexpected expenses.

(D) Procedure for off-campus employment authorization due to severe economic hardship. The student must request a recommendation from the DSO for off-campus employment. The DSO must complete such certification in SEVIS. The DSO may recommend the student for work off-campus for one-year intervals by certifying that:

(1) The student has been in F-1 status for one full academic year;

(2) The student is in good standing as a student and is carrying a full course of study as defined in paragraph (f)(6) of this section;

(3) The student has demonstrated that acceptance of employment will not interfere with the student's carrying a full course of study; and

(4) The student has demonstrated that the employment is necessary to avoid severe economic hardship due to unforeseen circumstances beyond the student's control pursuant to paragraph (f)(9)(ii)(C) of this section and has demonstrated that employment under paragraph (f)(9)(i) of this section is unavailable or otherwise insufficient to meet the needs that have arisen as a result of the unforeseen circumstances.

(E) [Reserved]

(F) Severe economic hardship application.

(1) The applicant should submit the economic hardship application for employment authorization on Form I-765 or successor form, with the fee required by 8 CFR 106.2, and any other supporting materials such as affidavits which further detail the unforeseen circumstances that require the student to seek employment authorization and the unavailability or insufficiency of employment under paragraph (f)(9)(i) of this section to USCIS. Students should submit the Form I-20 or successor form with the employment page demonstrating the DSO's comments and certification. USCIS will adjudicate the application for work authorization based upon severe economic hardship on the basis of Form I-20 and Form I-765 or successor forms, and any additional supporting materials. If employment is authorized, the adjudicating officer will issue an employment authorization document (EAD). USCIS will notify the student of the decision, and, if the application is denied, of the reason or reasons for the denial. No appeal will lie from a decision to deny a request for employment authorization under this section. The employment authorization may be granted in one-year intervals up to the expected date of completion of the student's current course of study. A student has permission to engage in off-campus employment only if the student receives the EAD endorsed to that effect. Off-campus employment authorization may be renewed by USCIS only if the student is maintaining status and good academic standing. The employment authorization is automatically terminated whenever the student fails to maintain status.

(2) [Removed and reserved.]

(iii) Internship with an international organization. A bona fide F-1 student who has been offered employment by a recognized international organization within the meaning of the International Organization Immunities Act (59 Stat. 669) must apply for employment authorization with USCIS. A student seeking employment authorization under this provision is required to present a written certification from the international organization that the proposed employment is within the scope of the organization's sponsorship, Form I-20 or successor form with employment page completed by DSO certifying eligibility for employment, and a completed Form I-765 or successor form, with the fee required by 8 CFR 106.2(a)(32).

(10) Practical training. Practical training may be authorized to an F-1 student who has been lawfully enrolled on a full-time basis, in an approved SEVP-certified college, university, conservatory, or seminary for one full academic year. This paragraph (f)(10) also includes students who, during their course of study, were enrolled in a study abroad program, if the student had spent at least one full academic term enrolled in a full course of study in the United States prior to studying abroad. A student may be authorized 12 months of practical training, and becomes eligible for another 12 months of practical training when they change to a higher educational level. Students in English language training programs are ineligible for practical training. An eligible student may request employment authorization for practical training in a position that is directly related to their major area of study. There are two types of practical training available:

(i) Curricular practical training. An F-1 student may be authorized by the DSO to participate in a curricular practical training program that is an integral part of an established curriculum. Curricular practical training is defined to be alternative work/study, internship, cooperative education or any other type of required internship or practicum that is offered by sponsoring employers through cooperative agreements with the school. Students who have received one year or more of full time curricular practical training are ineligible for post-completion academic training. Exceptions to the one academic year requirement are provided for students enrolled in graduate studies that require immediate participation in curricular practical training. A request for authorization for curricular practical training must be made to the DSO. A student may begin curricular practical training only after receiving their Form I-20 or successor form with the DSO endorsement. To grant authorization for a student to engage in curricular practical training, a DSO will update the student's record in SEVIS as being authorized for curricular practical training that is directly related to the student's major area of study. The DSO will indicate whether the training is full-time or part-time, the employer and location, and the employment start and end date. The DSO must sign, date, and return the Form I-20 or successor form to the student prior to the student's commencement of employment indicating that curricular practical training has been approved.

(ii) Optional practical training —

(A) General. Consistent with the application and approval process in paragraph (f)(11) of this section, a student may apply to USCIS for authorization for temporary employment for optional practical training directly related to the student's major area of study. The student may not begin optional practical training until the date indicated on his or her employment authorization document, Form I-766. A student may be granted authorization to engage in temporary employment for optional practical training:

(1) During the student's annual vacation and at other times when school is not in session, if the student

is currently enrolled, and is eligible for registration and intends to register for the next term or session;

(2) While school is in session, provided that practical training does not exceed 20 hours a week while school is in session; or

(3) After completion of the course of study, or, for a student in a bachelor's, master's, or doctoral degree program, after completion of all course requirements for the degree (excluding thesis or equivalent). Continued enrollment, for the school's administrative purposes, after all requirements for the degree have been met does not preclude eligibility for optional practical training. A student must complete all practical training within a 14-month period following the completion of study, except that a 24-month extension pursuant to paragraph (f)(10)(ii)(C) of this section does not need to be completed within such 14-month period.

(B) Termination of practical training. Authorization to engage in optional practical training employment is automatically terminated when the student transfers to another school or begins study at another educational level.

(C) 24-month extension of post-completion OPT for a science, technology, engineering, or mathematics (STEM) degree. Consistent with paragraph (f)(11)(i)(C) of this section, a qualified student may apply for an extension of OPT while in a valid period of post-completion OPT authorized under 8 CFR 274a.12(c)(3)(i)(B). An extension will be for 24 months for the first qualifying degree for which the student has completed all course requirements (excluding thesis or equivalent), including any qualifying degree as part of a dual degree program, subject to the requirement in paragraph (f)(10)(ii)(C)(3) of this section that previously obtained degrees must have been conferred. If a student completes all such course requirements for another qualifying degree at a higher degree level than the first, the student may apply for a second -month extension of OPT while in a valid period of post-completion OPT authorized under 8 CFR 274a.12(c)(3)(i)(B). In no event may a student be authorized for more than two lifetime STEM OPT extensions. A student who was granted a 17-month OPT extension under the rule issued at 73 FR 18944, whether or not such student requests an additional 7-month period of STEM OPT under 8 CFR 214.16, is considered to have been authorized for one STEM OPT extension, and may be eligible for only one more STEM OPT extension. Any subsequent application for an additional 24-month OPT extension under this paragraph (f)(10)(ii)(C) must be based on a degree at a higher degree level than the degree that was the basis for the student's first OPT extension. In order to qualify for an extension of post-completion OPT based upon a STEM degree, all of the following requirements must be met.

(1) Accreditation. The degree that is the basis for the 24-month OPT extension is from a U.S. educational institution accredited by an accrediting agency recognized by the Department of Education at the time of application.

(2) DHS-approved degree. The degree that is the basis for the 24-month OPT extension is a bachelor's, master's, or doctoral degree in a field determined by the Secretary, or his or her designee, to qualify within a science, technology, engineering, or mathematics field.

(i) The term "science, technology, engineering or mathematics field" means a field included in the Department of Education's Classification of Instructional Programs taxonomy within the two-digit series or successor series containing engineering, biological sciences, mathematics, and physical sciences, or a related field. In general, related fields will include fields involving research, innovation, or development of new technologies using engineering, mathematics, computer science, or natural sciences (including physical, biological, and agricultural sciences).

(ii) The Secretary, or his or her designee, will maintain the STEM Designated Degree Program List, which will be a complete list of qualifying degree program categories, published on the Student and Exchange Visitor Program Web site at http://www.ice.gov/sevis. Changes that are made to the Designated Degree Program List may also be published in a notice in the Federal Register . All program categories included on the list must be consistent with the definition set forth in paragraph (f)(10)(ii)(C)(2)(i) of this section.

(iii) At the time the DSO recommends a 24-month OPT extension under this paragraph (f)(10)(ii)(C) in SEVIS, the degree that is the basis for the application for the OPT extension must be contained within a category on the STEM Designated Degree Program List.

(3) Previously obtained STEM degree(s). The degree that is the basis for the 24-month OPT extension under this paragraph (f)(10)(ii)(C) may be, but is not required to be, the degree that is the basis for the post-completion OPT period authorized under 8 CFR 274a.12(c)(3)(i)(B). If an application for a 24-month OPT extension under this paragraph (f)(10)(ii)(C) is based upon a degree obtained previous to the degree that provided the basis for the period of post-completion OPT authorized under 8 CFR 274a.12(c)(3)(i)(B), that previously obtained degree must have been conferred from a U.S. educational institution that is accredited and SEVP-certified at the time the student's DSO recommends the student for the 24-month OPT extension and must be in a degree program category included on the current STEM Designated Degree Program List at the time of the DSO recommendation. That previously obtained degree must have been conferred within the 10 years preceding the date the DSO recommends the student for the 24-month OPT extension.

(4) Eligible practical training opportunity. The STEM practical training opportunity that is the basis for the 24-month OPT extension under this paragraph (f)(10)(ii)(C) must be directly related to the degree that qualifies the student for such extension, which may be the previously obtained degree described in paragraph (f)(10)(ii)(C)(3) of this section.

(5) Employer qualification. The student's employer is enrolled in E-Verify, as evidenced by either a valid E-Verify Company Identification number or, if the employer is using an employer agent to create its E-Verify cases, a valid E-Verify Client Company Identification

number, and the employer remains a participant in good standing with E-Verify, as determined by USCIS. An employer must also have an employer identification number (EIN) used for tax purposes.

(6) Employer reporting. A student may not be authorized for employment with an employer pursuant to paragraph (f)(10)(ii)(C)(2) of this section unless the employer agrees, by signing the Training Plan for STEM OPT Students, Form I-983 or successor form, to report the termination or departure of an OPT student to the DSO at the student's school, if the termination or departure is prior to the end of the authorized period of OPT. Such reporting must be made within five business days of the termination or departure. An employer shall consider a student to have departed when the employer knows the student has left the practical training opportunity, or if the student has not reported for his or her practical training for a period of five consecutive business days without the consent of the employer, whichever occurs earlier.

(7) Training Plan for STEM OPT Students, Form I-983 or successor form.

(i) A student must fully complete an individualized Form I-983 or successor form and obtain requisite signatures from an appropriate individual in the employer's organization on the form, consistent with form instructions, before the DSO may recommend a 24-month OPT extension under paragraph (f)(10)(ii)(C)(2) of this section in SEVIS. A student must submit the Form I-983 or successor form, which includes a certification of adherence to the training plan completed by an appropriate individual in the employer's organization who has signatory authority for the employer, to the student's DSO, prior to the new DSO recommendation. A student must present his or her signed and completed Form I-983 or successor form to a DSO at the educational institution of his or her most recent enrollment. A student, while in F-1 student status, may also be required to submit the Form I-983 or successor form to ICE and/or USCIS upon request or in accordance with form instructions.

(ii) The training plan described in the Form I-983 or successor form must identify goals for the STEM practical training opportunity, including specific knowledge, skills, or techniques that will be imparted to the student, and explain how those goals will be achieved through the work-based learning opportunity with the employer; describe a performance evaluation process; and describe methods of oversight and supervision. Employers may rely on their otherwise existing training programs or policies to satisfy the requirements relating to performance evaluation and oversight and supervision, as applicable.

(iii) The training plan described in the Form I-983 or successor form must explain how the training is directly related to the student's qualifying STEM degree.

(iv) If a student initiates a new practical training opportunity with a new employer during his or her 24-month OPT extension, the student must submit, within 10 days of beginning the new practical training opportunity, a new Form I-983 or successor form to the student's DSO, and subsequently obtain a new DSO recommendation.

(8) Duties, hours, and compensation for training. The terms and conditions of a STEM practical training opportunity during the period of the 24-month OPT extension, including duties, hours, and compensation, must be commensurate with terms and conditions applicable to the employer's similarly situated U.S. workers in the area of employment. A student may not engage in practical training for less than 20 hours per week, excluding time off taken consistent with leave-related policies applicable to the employer's similarly situated U.S. workers in the area of employment. If the employer does not employ and has not recently employed more than two similarly situated U.S. workers in the area of employment, the employer nevertheless remains obligated to attest that the terms and conditions of a STEM practical training opportunity are commensurate with the terms and conditions of employment for other similarly situated U.S. workers in the area of employment. "Similarly situated U.S. workers" includes U.S. workers performing similar duties subject to similar supervision and with similar educational backgrounds, industry expertise, employment experience, levels of responsibility, and skill sets as the student. The duties, hours, and compensation of such students are "commensurate" with those offered to U.S. workers employed by the employer in the same area of employment when the employer can show that the duties, hours, and compensation are consistent with the range of such terms and conditions the employer has offered or would offer to similarly situated U.S. employees. The student must disclose his or her compensation, including any adjustments, as agreed to with the employer, on the Form I-983 or successor form.

(9) Evaluation requirements and Training Plan modifications.

(i) A student may not be authorized for employment with an employer pursuant to paragraph (f)(10)(ii)(C)(2) of this section unless the student submits a self-evaluation of the student's progress toward the training goals described in the Form I-983 or successor form. All required evaluations must be completed prior to the conclusion of a STEM practical training opportunity, and the student and an appropriate individual in the employer's organization must sign each evaluation to attest to its accuracy. All STEM practical training opportunities require an initial evaluation within 12 months of the approved starting date on the employment authorization document granted pursuant to the student's 24-month OPT extension application, and a concluding evaluation. The student is responsible for ensuring the DSO receives his or her 12-month evaluation and final evaluation no later than 10 days following the conclusion of the reporting period or conclusion of his or her practical training opportunity, respectively.

(ii) If any material change to or deviation from the training plan described in the Form I-983 or successor form occurs, the student and employer must sign a modified Form I-983 or successor form reflecting the material change(s) or deviation(s). Material changes and deviations relating to training may include, but are not limited to, any change of Employer Identification Number resulting from a corporate restructuring, any reduction in compensation from the amount previously submitted on the Form I-983 or successor form that is not tied to a reduction in hours worked, any significant decrease in hours per week that a student engages in a STEM training opportunity, and any decrease in hours worked below the minimum hours for the 24-month extension as described in paragraph (f)(10)(ii)(C)(8) of this section. Material changes and deviations also include any change or deviation that renders an employer attestation inaccurate, or renders inaccurate the information in the Form I-983 or successor form on the nature, purpose, oversight, or assessment of the student's practical training opportunity. The student and employer must ensure that the modified Form I-983 or successor form is submitted to the student's DSO at the earliest available opportunity.

(iii) The educational institution whose DSO is responsible for duties associated with the student's latest OPT extension under paragraph (f)(10)(ii)(C)(2) of this section is responsible for ensuring the Student and Exchange Visitor Program has access to each individualized Form I-983 or successor form and associated student evaluations (electronic or hard copy), including through SEVIS if technologically available, beginning within 30 days after the document is submitted to the DSO and continuing for a period of three years following the completion of each STEM practical training opportunity.

(10) Additional STEM opportunity obligations. A student may only participate in a STEM practical training opportunity in which the employer attests, including by signing the Form I-983 or successor form, that:

(i) The employer has sufficient resources and personnel available and is prepared to provide appropriate training in connection with the specified opportunity at the location(s) specified in the Form I-983 or successor form;

(ii) The student on a STEM OPT extension will not replace a full- or part-time, temporary or permanent U.S. worker; and

(iii) The student's opportunity assists the student in reaching his or her training goals.

(11) Site visits. DHS, at its discretion, may conduct a site visit of any employer. The purpose of the site visit is for DHS to ensure that each employer possesses and maintains the ability and resources to provide structured and guided work-based learning experiences consistent with any Form I-983 or successor form completed and signed by the employer. DHS will provide notice to the employer 48 hours in advance of any site visit, except notice may not be provided if the visit is triggered by a complaint or other evidence of noncompliance with the regulations in this paragraph (f)(10)(ii)(C).

(D) Duration of status while on post-completion OPT. For a student with approved post-completion OPT, the duration of status is defined as the period beginning on the date that the student's application for OPT was properly filed and pending approval, including the authorized period of post-completion OPT, and ending 60 days after the OPT employment authorization expires.

(E) Periods of unemployment during post-completion OPT. During post-completion OPT, F-1 status is dependent upon employment. Students may not accrue an aggregate of more than 90 days of unemployment during any post-completion OPT period described in 8 CFR 274a.12(c)(3)(i)(B). Students granted a 24-month OPT extension under paragraph (f)(10)(ii)(C)(2) of this section may not accrue an aggregate of more than 150 days of unemployment during a total OPT period, including any post-completion OPT period described in 8 CFR 274a.12(c)(3)(i)(B) and any subsequent 24-month extension period.

(11) OPT application and approval process —

(i) Student responsibilities. A student must initiate the OPT application process by requesting a recommendation for OPT from his or her DSO. Upon making the recommendation, the DSO will provide the student a signed Form I-20 indicating that recommendation.

(A) Applications for employment authorization. The student must properly file an Application for Employment Authorization, Form I-765 or successor form, with USCIS, accompanied by the required fee, and the supporting documents, as described in the form's instructions.

(B) Applications and filing deadlines for pre-completion OPT and post-completion OPT—

(1) Pre-completion OPT. For pre-completion OPT, the student may properly file his or her Form I-765 or successor form up to 90 days before being enrolled for one full academic year, provided that the period of employment will not start prior to the completion of the full academic year.

(2) Post-completion OPT. For post-completion OPT, not including a 24-month OPT extension under paragraph (f)(10)(ii)(C)(2) of this section, the student may properly file his or her Form I-765 or successor form up to 90 days prior to his or her program end date and no later than 60 days after his or her program end date. The student must also file his or her Form I-765 or successor form with USCIS within 30 days of the date the DSO enters the recommendation for OPT into his or her SEVIS record.

(C) Applications and filing deadlines for 24-month OPT extension. A student meeting the eligibility requirements for a 24-month OPT extension under paragraph (f)(10)(ii)(C) of this section may request an extension of employment authorization by filing Form I-765 or successor form, with the required fee and supporting documents, up to 90 days prior to the expiration date of the student's current OPT employment authorization. The student seeking such 24-month OPT extension must properly file his or her Form I-765 or successor form with USCIS within 60 days of the date the DSO enters the recommendation for the OPT extension into his or her SEVIS record. If a student timely and properly files an application for such 24-month OPT extension and timely and properly requests a DSO recommendation, including by submitting the fully executed Form I-983 or successor form to his or her DSO, but the Employment Authorization Document, Form I-766 or successor form, currently in the student's possession expires prior to the decision on the student's application for the OPT extension, the student's Form I-766 or successor form is extended automatically pursuant to the terms and conditions specified in 8 CFR 274a.12(b)(6)(iv).

(D) Start of OPT employment. A student may not begin OPT employment prior to the approved start date on his or her Employment Authorization Document, Form I-766 or successor form, except as described in paragraph (f)(11)(i)(C) of this section. A student may not request a start date that is more than 60 days after the student's program end date. Employment authorization will begin on the date requested or the date the employment authorization is adjudicated, whichever is later.

(ii) Additional DSO responsibilities. A student must have a recommendation from his or her DSO in order to apply for OPT. When a DSO recommends a student for OPT, the school assumes the added responsibility for maintaining the SEVIS record of that student for the entire period of authorized OPT, consistent with paragraph (f)(12) of this section.

(A) Prior to making a recommendation, the DSO at the educational institution of the student's most recent enrollment must ensure that the student is eligible for the given type and period of OPT and that the student is aware of the student's responsibilities for maintaining status while on OPT. Prior to recommending a 24-month OPT extension under paragraph (f)(10)(ii)(C) of this section, the DSO at the educational institution of the student's most recent enrollment must certify that the student's degree being used to qualify that student for the 24-month OPT extension, as shown in SEVIS or official transcripts, is a bachelor's, master's, or doctorate degree with a degree code that is contained within a category on the current STEM Designated Degree Program List at the time the recommendation is made. A DSO may recommend a student for a 24-month OPT extension under paragraph (f)(10)(ii)(C) of this section only if the Form I-983 or successor form described in paragraph (f)(10)(ii)(C)(7) of this section has been properly completed and executed by the student and prospective employer. A DSO may not recommend a student for an OPT extension under paragraph (f)(10)(ii)(C) of this section if the practical training would be conducted by an employer who has failed to meet the requirements under paragraphs (f)(10)(ii)(C)(5) through (9) of this section or has failed to provide the required assurances of paragraph (f)(10)(ii)(C)(10) of this section.

(B) The DSO must update the student's SEVIS record with the DSO's recommendation for OPT before the student can apply to USCIS for employment authorization. The DSO will indicate in SEVIS whether the OPT employment is to be full-time or part-time, or for a student seeking a recommendation for a 24-month OPT extension under paragraph (f)(10)(ii)(C) of this section whether the OPT employment meets the minimum hours requirements described in paragraph (f)(10)(ii)(C)(8) of this section, and note in SEVIS the OPT start and end dates.

(C) The DSO must provide the student with a signed, dated Form I-20 or successor form indicating that OPT has been recommended.

(iii) Decision on application for OPT employment authorization. USCIS will adjudicate a student's Form I-765 or successor form on the basis of the DSO's recommendation and other eligibility considerations.

(A) If granted, the employment authorization period for post-completion OPT begins on the requested date of commencement or the date the Form I-765 or successor form is approved, whichever is later, and ends at the conclusion of the remaining time period of post-completion OPT eligibility. The employment authorization period for a 24-month OPT extension under paragraph (f)(10)(ii)(C) of this section begins on the day after the expiration of the initial post-completion OPT employment authorization and ends 24 months thereafter, regardless of the date the actual extension is approved.

(B) USCIS will notify the applicant of the decision on the Form I-765 or successor form in writing, and, if the application is denied, of the reason or reasons for the denial.

(C) The applicant may not appeal the decision.

(12) Reporting while on optional practical training—

(i) General. An F-1 student who is granted employment authorization by USCIS to engage in optional practical training is required to report any change of name or address, or interruption of such employment to the DSO for the duration of the optional practical training. A DSO who recommends a student for OPT is responsible for updating the student's record to reflect these reported changes for the duration of the time that training is authorized.

(ii) Additional reporting obligations for students with an approved 24-month OPT extension. Students with an approved 24-month OPT extension under paragraph (f)(10)(ii)(C) of this section have additional reporting obligations. Compliance with these reporting requirements is required to maintain F-1 status. The reporting obligations are:

(A) Within 10 days of the change, the student must report to the student's DSO a change of legal name, residential or mailing address, employer name, employer address, and/or loss of employment.

(B) The student must complete a validation report, confirming that the information required by paragraph (f)(12)(ii)(A) of this section has not changed, every six months. The requirement for validation reporting starts on the date the 24-month OPT extension begins and ends when the student's F-1 status expires or the 24-month OPT extension concludes, whichever is first. The validation report is due to the student's DSO within 10 business days of each reporting date.

(13) Temporary absence from the United States of F-1 student granted employment authorization.

(i) A student returning from a temporary trip abroad with an unexpired off-campus employment authorization on their Form I-20 or successor form may resume employment only if the student is readmitted to attend the same school that granted the employment authorization.

(ii) An F-1 student who has an unexpired EAD issued for post-completion practical training and who is otherwise admissible may return to the United States to resume employment after a period of temporary absence. The EAD must be used in combination with a Form I-20 or successor form endorsed for reentry by the DSO within the last six months.

(14) Effect of strike or other labor dispute. Any employment authorization, whether or not part of an academic program, is automatically suspended upon certification by the Secretary of Labor or the Secretary's designee to the Secretary of Homeland Security or the Secretary's designee, that a strike or other labor dispute involving a work stoppage of workers is in progress in the occupation at the place of employment. As used in this paragraph, "place of employment" means the facility or facilities where a labor dispute exists. The employer is prohibited from transferring F-1 students working at other facilities to the facility where the work stoppage is occurring.

(15) Spouse and children of F-1 student. The F-2 spouse and minor children of an F-1 student will each be issued an individual Form I-20 or successor form in accordance with the provisions of § 214.3(k).

(i) Employment. The F-2 spouse and children of an F-1 student may not accept employment.

(ii) Study—

(A) F-2 post-secondary/vocational study —

(1) Authorized study at SEVP-certified schools. An F-2 spouse or F-2 child may enroll in less than a full course of study, as defined in paragraphs (f)(6)(i)(A) through (D) and (m)(9)(i) through (iv), in any course of study described in paragraphs (f)(6)(i)(A) through (D) or (m)(9)(i) through (iv) of this section at an SEVP-certified school. Notwithstanding paragraphs (f)(6)(i)(B) and (m)(9)(i) of this section, study at an undergraduate college or university or at a community college or junior college is not a full course of study solely because the F-2 nonimmigrant is engaging in a lesser course load to complete a course of study during the current term. An F-2 spouse or F-2 child enrolled in less than a full course of study is not eligible to engage in employment pursuant to paragraphs (f)(9) and (10) of this section or pursuant to paragraph (m)(14) of this section.

(2) Full course of study. Subject to paragraphs (f)(15)(ii)(B) and (f)(18) of this section, an F-2 spouse and child may engage in a full course of study only by applying for and obtaining a change of status to F-1, M-1 or J-1 nonimmigrant status, as appropriate, before beginning a full course of study. An F-2 spouse and child may engage in study that is avocational or recreational in nature, up to and including on a full-time basis.

(B) F-2 elementary or secondary study. An F-2 child may engage in full-time study, including any full course of study, in any elementary or secondary school (kindergarten through twelfth grade).

(C) An F-2 spouse and child violates his or her nonimmigrant status by enrolling in any study except as provided in paragraph (f)(15)(ii)(A) or (B) of this section.

(16) Reinstatement to student status. —

(i) General. USCIS may consider reinstating a student who makes a request for reinstatement on Form I-539, Application to Extend/Change Nonimmigrant Status, accompanied by a properly completed Form I-20 or successor form indicating the DSO's recommendation for reinstatement. USCIS may consider granting the request if the student:

(A) Has not been out of status for more than 5 months at the time of filing the request for reinstatement (or demonstrates that the failure to file within the 5 month period was the result of exceptional circumstances and that the student filed the request for reinstatement as promptly as possible under these exceptional circumstances);

(B) Does not have a record of repeated or willful violations of DHS regulations;

(C) Is currently pursuing, or intending to pursue, a full course of study in the immediate future at the school which issued the Form I-20 or successor form;

(D) Has not engaged in unauthorized employment;

(E) Is not deportable on any ground other than section 237(a)(1)(B) or (C)(i) of the Act; and

(F) Establishes to the satisfaction of USCIS, by a detailed showing, either that:

(1) The violation of status resulted from circumstances beyond the student's control. Such circumstances might include serious injury or illness, closure of the institution, a natural disaster, or inadvertence, oversight, or neglect on the part of the DSO, but do not include instances where a pattern of repeated violations or where a willful failure on the part of the student resulted in the need for reinstatement; or

(2) The violation relates to a reduction in the student's course load that would have been within a DSO's power to authorize, and that failure to approve reinstatement would result in extreme hardship to the student.

(ii) Decision. The adjudicating officer will update SEVIS to reflect USCIS' decision. If USCIS does not reinstate the student, the student may not appeal the decision.

(17) Current name and address. A student must inform DHS and the DSO of any legal changes to the student's name or of any change of address, within 10 days of the change, in a manner prescribed by the school. A student can satisfy the requirement in 8 CFR 265.1 of notifying DHS by providing a notice of a change of address within 10 days to the DSO, and the DSO in turn must enter the information in SEVIS within 21 days of notification by the student. Except in the case of a student who cannot receive mail where the student resides, the address provided by the student must be the actual physical location where the student resides rather than a mailing address. In cases where a student provides a mailing address, the school must maintain a record of, and must provide upon request from DHS, the actual physical location where the student resides.

(18) Special rules for certain border commuter students —

(i) Applicability. For purposes of the special rules in this paragraph (f)(18), the term "border commuter student" means a national of Canada or Mexico who is admitted to the United States as an F-1 nonimmigrant student to enroll in a full course of study, albeit on a part-time basis, in an approved school located within 75 miles of a United States land border. A border commuter student must maintain actual residence and place of abode in the student's country of nationality, and seek admission to the United States at a land border port-of-entry. These special rules do not apply to a national of Canada or Mexico who is:

(A) Residing in the United States while attending a certified school as an F-1 student, or

(B) Enrolled in a full course of study as defined in paragraph (f)(6) of this section.

(ii) Full course of study. The border commuter student must be enrolled in a full course of study at the school that leads to the attainment of a specific educational or professional objective, albeit on a part-time basis. A designated school official at the school may authorize an eligible border commuter student to enroll in a course load below that otherwise required for a full course of study under paragraph (f)(6) of this section, provided that the reduced course load is consistent with the border commuter student's certified course of study.

(iii) Period of admission. An F-1 nonimmigrant student who is admitted as a border commuter student under this paragraph (f)(18) will be admitted until a date certain. The DSO is required to specify a completion date on the Form I-20 that reflects the actual semester or term dates for the commuter student's current term of study. A new Form I-20 will be required for each new semester or term that the border commuter student attends at the school. The provisions of paragraphs (f)(5) and (f)(7) of this section, relating to duration of status and extension of stay, are not applicable to a border commuter student.

(iv) Employment. A border commuter student may not be authorized to accept any employment in connection with his or her F-1 student status, except for curricular practical training as provided in paragraph (f)(10)(i) of this section or post-completion optional practical training as provided in paragraph (f)(10)(ii)(A)(3) of this section.

(19) Remittance of the fee. An alien who applies for F-1 or F-3 nonimmigrant status in order to enroll in a program of study at an SEVP-certified educational institution is required to pay the Student and Exchange Visitor Information System (SEVIS) fee to DHS, pursuant to 8 CFR 214.13, except as otherwise provided in that section.

(g) Representatives to international organizations —

(1) General. The determination by a consular officer prior to admission and the recognition by the Secretary of State subsequent to admission is evidence of the proper classification of a nonimmigrant under section 101(a)(15)(G) of the Act. An alien who has a nonimmigrant status under section 101(a)(15)(G) (i), (ii), (iii) or (iv) of the Act is to be admitted for the duration of the period for which the alien continues to be recognized by the Secretary of State as being entitled to that status. An alien defined in section (101)(a)(15)(G)(v) of the Act is to be admitted for an initial period of not more than three years, and may be granted extensions of temporary stay in increments of not more than two years. In addition, the application for extension of temporary stay must be accompanied by a statement signed by the employing official stating that he or she intends to continue to employ the applicant and describing the type of work the applicant will perform.

(2) Definition of G-1, G-3, or G-4 dependent. For purposes of employment in the United States, the term dependent of a G-1, G-3, or G-4 principal alien, as used in § 214.2(g), means any of the following immediate members of the family habitually residing in the same household as the principal alien who is an officer or employee assigned to a mission, to an international organization, or is employed by an international organization in the United States:

(i) Spouse;

(ii) Unmarried children under the age of 21;

(iii) Unmarried sons or daughters under the age of 23 who are in full-time attendance as students at post-secondary educational institutions;

(iv) Unmarried sons or daughters under the age of 25 who are in full-time attendance as students at post-secondary educational institutions if a formal bilateral employment agreement permitting their employment in the United States was signed prior to November 21, 1988, and such bilateral employment agreement does not specify 23 as the maximum age for employment of such sons and daughters. The Office of Protocol of the Department of State shall maintain a listing of foreign states which the United States has such bilateral employment agreements. The provisions of this paragraph apply only to G-1 and G-3 dependents under certain bilateral agreements and are not applicable to G-4 dependents;

(v) Unmarried sons or daughters who are physically or mentally disabled to the extent that they cannot adequately care for themselves or cannot establish, maintain, or re-establish their own households. The Department of State or the Service may require certification(s) as it deems sufficient to document such mental or physical disability; or

(vi) An immediate family member of a G-1, G-3, or G-4 principal alien described in 22 CFR 41.21(a)(3)(i) to (iv) with G-1, G-3, or G-4 nonimmigrant status who falls within a category of aliens designated by the Department of State as qualifying dependents.

(3) Applicability of a formal bilateral agreement or an informal de facto arrangement for G-1 and G-3 dependents. The applicability of a formal bilateral agreement shall be based on the foreign state which employs the principal alien and not on the nationality of the principal alien or dependent. The applicability of an informal de facto arrangement shall be based on the foreign state which employs the principal alien, but under a de facto arrangement the principal alien also must be a national of the foreign state which employs him or her in the United States.

(4) Income tax, Social Security liability; non-applicability of certain immunities. Dependents who are granted employment authorization under this section are responsible for payment of all federal, state and

local income, employment and related taxes and Social Security contributions on any remuneration received. In addition, immunity from civil or administrative jurisdiction in accordance with Article 37 of the Vienna Convention on Diplomatic Relations or other international agreements does not apply to these dependents with respect to matters arising out of their employment.

(5) G-1 and G-3 dependent employment pursuant to formal bilateral employment agreements and informal de facto reciprocal arrangements, and G-4 dependent employment.

(i) The Office of Protocol shall maintain a listing of foreign states which have entered into formal bilateral employment agreements. Dependents of a G-1 or G-3 principal alien assigned to official duty in the United States may accept or continue in unrestricted employment based on such formal bilateral agreements, if the applicable agreement includes persons in G-1 or G-3 visa status, upon favorable recommendation by the Department of State and issuance of employment authorization documentation by the Service in accordance with 8 CFR part 274a. The application procedures are set forth in paragraph (g)(6) of this section.

(ii) For purposes of this section, an informal de facto reciprocal arrangement exists when the Department of State determines that a foreign state allows appropriate employment on the local economy for dependents of certain United States officials assigned to duty in that foreign state. The Office of Protocol shall maintain a listing of countries with which such reciprocity exists. Dependents of a G-1 or G-3 principal alien assigned to official duty in the United States may be authorized to accept or continue in employment based upon informal de facto arrangements, and dependents of a G-4 principal alien assigned to official duty in the United States may be authorized to accept or continue in employment upon favorable recommendation by the Department of State and issuance of employment authorization by the Service in accordance with 8 CFR part 274a. Additionally, the procedures set forth in paragraph (g)(6) of this section must be complied with, and the following conditions must be met:

(A) Both the principal alien and the dependent desiring employment are maintaining G-1, G-3, or G-4 status as appropriate;

(B) The principal's assignment in the United States is expected to last more than six months;

(C) Employment of a similar nature for dependents of United States Government officials assigned to official duty in the foreign state employing the principal alien is not prohibited by that foreign government. The provisions of this paragraph apply only to G-1 and G-3 dependents;

(D) The proposed employment is not in an occupation listed in the Department of Labor Schedule B (20 CFR part 656), or otherwise determined by the Department of Labor to be one for which there is an oversupply of qualified U.S. workers in the area of proposed employment. This Schedule B restriction does not apply to a dependent son or daughter who is a full-time student if the employment is part-time, consisting of not more than 20 hours per week, and/or if it is temporary employment of not more than 12 weeks during school holiday periods; and

(E) The proposed employment is not contrary to the interest of the United States. Employment contrary to the interest of the United States includes, but is not limited to, the employment of G-1, G-3, or G-4 dependents: who have criminal records; who have violated United States immigration laws or regulations, or visa laws or regulations; who have worked illegally in the United States; and/or who cannot establish that they have paid taxes and social security on income from current or previous United States employment. Additionally, the Department of State may determine a G-4 dependent's employment is contrary to the interest of the United States when the principal alien's country of nationality has one or more components of an international organization or international organizations within its borders and does not allow the employment of dependents of United States citizens employed by such component(s) or organization(s).

(6) Application procedures. The following procedures are applicable to G-1 and G-3 dependent employment applications under bilateral agreements and de facto arrangements, as well as to G-4 dependent employment applications:

(i) The dependent must submit a completed Form I-566 to the Department of State through the office, mission, or organization which employs his or her principal alien. If the principal is assigned to or employed by the United Nations, the Form I-566 must be submitted to the U.S. Mission to the United Nations. All other applications must be submitted to the Office of Protocol of the Department of State. A dependent applying under paragraph (g)(2) (iii) or (iv) of this section must submit a certified statement from the post-secondary educational institution confirming that he or she is pursuing studies on a full-time basis. A dependent applying under paragraph (g)(2)(v) of this section must submit medical certification regarding his or her condition. The certification should identify the dependent and the certifying physician and give the physician's phone number; identify the condition, describe the symptoms and provide a prognosis; certify that the dependent is unable to establish, re-establish, and maintain a home or his or her own. Additionally, a G-1 or G-3 dependent applying under the terms of a de facto arrangement or a G-4 dependent must attach a statement from the prospective employer which includes the dependent's name; a description of the position offered and the duties to be performed; the salary offered; and verification that the dependent possesses the qualifications for the position.

(ii) The Department of State reviews and verifies the information provided, makes its determination, and endorses the Form I-566.

(iii) If the Department of State's endorsement is favorable, the dependent may apply to USCIS for employment authorization. When applying to USCIS for employment authorization, the dependent must present his or her Form I-566 with a favorable endorsement from the Department of State and any additional documentation as may be required by the Secretary.

(7) Period of time for which employment may be authorized. If approved, an application to accept or continue employment under this section shall be granted in increments of not more than three years each.

(8) No appeal. There shall be no appeal from a denial of permission to accept or continue employment under this section.

(9) Dependents or family members of principal aliens classified G-2 or G-5. A dependent or family member of a principal alien classified G-2 or G-5 may not be employed in the United States under this section.

(10) Unauthorized employment. An alien classified under section 101(a)(15)(G) of the Act who is not a principal alien and who engages in employment outside the scope of, or in a manner contrary to this section, may be considered in violation of section 241(a)(1)(C)(i) of the Act. An alien who is classified under section 101(a)(15)(G) of the Act who is a principal alien and who engages in employment outside the scope of his/her official position may be considered in violation of section 241(a)(1)(C)(i) of the Act.

(11) Special provision. As of February 16, 1990 no new employment authorization will be granted and no pre-existing employment authorization will be extended for a G-1 dependent absent an appropriate bilateral agreement or de facto arrangement. However, a G-1 dependent who has been granted employment authorization by the Department of State prior to the effective date of this section and who meets the definition of dependent under § 214.2(g)(2) (i), (ii), (iii) or (v) of this part but is not covered by the terms of a bilateral agreement or de facto arrangement may be allowed to continue in employment until whichever of the following occurs first:

(i) The employment authorization by the Department of State expires; or

(ii) He or she no longer qualifies as a dependent as that term is defined in this section; or

(iii) March 19, 1990.

(h) Temporary employees.

Table 3 to Paragraph (h)—Paragraph Contents

(1) Admission of temporary employees.
(2) Petitions.
(3) Petition for registered nurse (H-1C).
(4) Petition for alien to perform services in a specialty occupation, services relating to a DOD cooperative research and development project or coproduction project, or services of distinguished merit and ability in the field of fashion modeling (H-1B).
(5) Petition for alien to perform agricultural labor or services of a temporary or seasonal nature (H-2A).
(6) Petition for alien to perform temporary nonagricultural services or labor (H-2B).
(7) Petition for alien trainee or participant in a special education exchange visitor program (H-3).
(8) Numerical limits.
(9) Approval and validity of petition.
(10) Denial of petition.
(11) Revocation of approval of petition.
(12) Appeal of a denial or a revocation of a petition.
(13) Admission.
(14) Extension of visa petition validity.
(15) Extension of stay.
(16) Effect of approval of a permanent labor certification or filing of a preference petition on H classification.
(17) Effect of a strike.
(18) Use of approval notice, Form I-797.
(19) Additional fee for filing certain H-1B petitions.
(20) Retaliatory action claims.
(21) Change of employers during COVID-19 National Emergency (August 19, 2020 through December 17, 2020).
(22) Change of employers during COVID-19 National Emergency (December 18, 2020 through June 16, 2021).
(23) Change of employers and extensions beyond 3 years during COVID-19 National Emergency for H-2B aliens essential to the U.S. food supply chain.
(24) Severability.
(25) [Reserved].
(26) Change of employers and portability for H-2B workers (May 25, 2021 through November 22, 2021).
(27) Change of employers and portability for H-2B workers (January 28, 2022 through July 27, 2022).
(28) Change of employers and portability for H-2B workers (July 28, 2022 through January 24, 2023).
(29) [Effective Dec. 15, 2022 through Dec. 15, 2025] Change of employers and portability for H-2B workers (January 25, 2023 through January 24, 2024).
(30) [Effective Nov. 17, 2023 through Nov. 17, 2026] [Reserved]
(31) [Effective Nov. 17, 2023 through Nov. 17, 2026] Change of employers and portability for H-2B workers (January 25, 2024 through January 24, 2025).
(32) [Effective Dec. 2, 2024 through Dec. 2, 2027] Change of employers and portability for H-2B workers (January 25, 2025 through January 24, 2026).

(1) Admission of temporary employees —

(i) General. Under section 101(a)(15)(H) of the Act, an alien may be authorized to come to the United States temporarily to perform services or labor for, or to receive training from, an employer, if petitioned for by that employer. Under this nonimmigrant category, the alien may be classified as follows: under section 101(a)(15)(H)(i)(c) of the Act as a registered nurse; under section 101(a)(15)(H)(i)(b) of the Act as an alien who is coming to perform services in a specialty occupation, services relating to a Department of Defense (DOD) cooperative research and development project or coproduction project, or services as a fashion model who is of distinguished merit and ability; under section 101(a)(15)(H)(ii)(a) of the Act as an alien who is coming to perform agricultural labor or services of a temporary or seasonal nature; under section 101(a)(15)(H)(ii)(b) of the Act as an alien coming to perform other temporary services or labor; or under section 101(a)(15)(H)(iii) of the Act as an alien who is coming as a trainee or as a participant in a special education exchange visitor program. These classifications are called H-1C, H-1B, H-2A, H-2B, and H-3, respectively. The employer must file a petition with the Service for review of the services or training and for determination of the alien's eligibility for classification as a temporary employee or trainee, before the alien may apply for a visa or seek admission to the United States. This paragraph sets forth the standards and procedures applicable to these classifications.

(ii) Description of classification.

(A) An H-1C classification applies to an alien who is coming temporarily to the United States to perform services as a registered nurse, meets the requirements of section 212(m)(1) of the Act, and will perform services at a facility (as defined at section 212(m)(6) of the Act) for which the Secretary of Labor has determined and certified to the Attorney General that an unexpired attestation is on file and in effect under section 212(m)(2) of the Act. This classification will expire 4 years from June 11, 2001.

(B) An H-1B classification applies to an alien who is coming temporarily to the United States:

(1) To perform services in a specialty occupation (except agricultural workers, and aliens described in section 101(a)(15) (O) and (P) of the Act) described in section 214(i)(1) of the Act, that meets the requirements of section 214(i)(2) of the Act, and for whom the Secretary of Labor has determined and certified to the Attorney General that the prospective employer has filed a labor condition application under section 212(n)(1) of the Act;

(2) To perform services of an exceptional nature requiring exceptional merit and ability relating to a cooperative research and development project or a coproduction project provided for under a Government-to-Government agreement administered by the Secretary of Defense;

(3) To perform services as a fashion model of distinguished merit and ability and for whom the Secretary of Labor has determined and certified to the Attorney General that the prospective employer has filed a labor condition application under section 212(n)(1) of the Act.

(C) An H-2A classification applies to an alien who is coming temporarily to the United States to perform agricultural work of a temporary or seasonal nature.

(D) An H-2B classification applies to an alien who is coming temporarily to the United States to perform nonagricultural work of a temporary or seasonal nature, if there are not sufficient workers who are able, willing, qualified, and available at the time of application for a visa and admission to the United States and at the place where the alien is to perform such services or labor. This classification does not apply to graduates of medical schools coming to the United States to perform services as members of the medical profession. The temporary or permanent nature of the services or labor described on the approved temporary labor certification are subject to review by USCIS. This classification requires a temporary labor certification issued by the Secretary of Labor or the Governor of Guam prior to the filing of a petition with USCIS.

(E) An H-3 classification applies to an alien who is coming temporarily to the United States:

(1) As a trainee, other than to receive graduate medical education or training, or training provided primarily at or by an academic or vocational institution, or

(2) As a participant in a special education exchange visitor program which provides for practical training and experience in the education of children with physical, mental, or emotional disabilities.

(2) Petitions —

(i) Filing of petitions —

(A) General. A United States employer seeking to classify an alien as an H-1B, H-2A, H-2B, or H-3 temporary employee must file a petition on the form prescribed by USCIS in accordance with the form instructions.

(B) [Removed and reserved.]

(C) Services or training for more than one employer. If the beneficiary will perform nonagricultural services for, or receive training from, more than one employer, each employer must file a separate petition with USCIS as provided in the form instructions.

(D) Change of employers. If the alien is in the United States and seeks to change employers, the prospective new employer must file a petition for a nonimmigrant worker requesting classification and an extension of the alien's stay in the United States. If the new petition is approved, the extension of stay may be granted for the validity of the approved petition. The validity of the petition and the alien's extension of stay must conform to the limits on the alien's temporary stay that are prescribed in paragraph (h)(13) of this section. Except as provided in paragraph (h)(2)(i)(I) of this section, 8 CFR 274a.12(b)(21), or section 214(n) of the Act, 8 U.S.C. 1184(n), the alien is not authorized to begin the employment with the new petitioner until the petition is approved. An H–1C nonimmigrant alien may not change employers.

(E) Amended or new petition—

(1) General provisions. The petitioner must file an amended or new petition, with the appropriate fee and in accordance with the form instructions, to reflect any material changes in the terms and conditions of employment or training or the beneficiary's eligibility as specified in the original approved petition. An amended or new H–1B, H–2A, or H–2B petition must be accompanied by a current or new Department of Labor determination. In the case of an H–1B petition, this requirement includes a current or new certified labor condition application.

(2) Additional H–1B provisions. The amended or new petition must be properly filed before the material change(s) takes place. The beneficiary is not authorized to work under the materially changed terms and conditions of employment until the new or amended H–1B petition is approved and takes effect, unless the beneficiary is eligible for H–1B portability pursuant to paragraph (h)(2)(i)(H) of this section. Any change in the place of employment to a geographical area that requires a corresponding labor condition application to be certified to USCIS is considered a material change and requires an amended or new petition to be filed with USCIS before the H–1B worker may begin work at the new place of employment. Provided there are no material changes in the terms and conditions of the H–1B worker's employment, a petitioner does not need to file an amended or new petition when:

(i) Moving a beneficiary to a new job location within the same area of intended employment as listed on the labor condition application certified to USCIS in support of the current H–1B petition approval authorizing the H–1B nonimmigrant's employment.

(ii) Placing a beneficiary at a shortterm placements(s) or assignment(s) at any worksite(s) outside of the area of intended employment for a total of 30 days or less in a 1-year period, or for a total of 60 days or less in a 1-year period where the H–1B beneficiary continues to maintain an office or work station at their permanent worksite, the beneficiary spends a substantial amount of time at the permanent worksite in a 1-year period, and the beneficiary's residence is located in the area of the permanent worksite and not in the area of the short-term worksite(s); or

(iii) An H–1B beneficiary is going to a non-worksite location to participate in employee development, will be spending little time at any one location, or when the job is peripatetic in nature, in that the normal duties of the beneficiary's occupation (rather than the nature of the employer's business) requires frequent travel (local or nonlocal) from location to location. Peripatetic jobs include situations where the job is primarily at one location, but the beneficiary occasionally travels for short periods to other locations on a casual, short-term basis, which can be recurring but not excessive (i.e., not exceeding 5 consecutive workdays for any one visit by a peripatetic worker, or 10 consecutive workdays for any one visit by a worker who spends most work time at one location and travels occasionally to other locations). (F) Agents as petitioners. A United States agent may file a petition in cases involving workers who are traditionally self-employed or workers who use agents to arrange short-term employment on their behalf with numerous employers, and in cases where a foreign employer authorizes the agent to act on its behalf. A United States agent may be: the actual employer of the beneficiary; the representative of both the employer and the beneficiary; or a person or entity authorized by the employer to act for, or in place of, the employer as its agent. The burden is on the agent to explain the terms and conditions of the employment and to provide any required documentation. In questionable cases, a contract between the employers and the beneficiary or beneficiaries may be required.

(1) An agent performing the function of an employer must guarantee the wages and other terms and conditions of employment by contractual agreement with the beneficiary or beneficiaries of the petition.

(2) A foreign employer who, through a United States agent, files a petition for an H nonimmigrant alien is responsible for complying with all of the employer sanctions provisions of section 274A of the Act and 8 CFR part 274a.

(F) Agents as petitioners. A United States agent may file a petition in cases involving workers who are traditionally self-employed or workers who use agents to arrange short-term employment on their behalf with numerous employers, and in cases where a foreign employer authorizes the agent to act on its behalf. A United States agent may be: the actual employer of the beneficiary, the representative of both the employer and the beneficiary, or, a person or entity authorized by the employer to act for, or in place of, the employer as it agent. A petition filed by a United States agent is subject to the following conditions;

(1) An agent performing the function of an employer must guarantee the wages and other terms and conditions of employment by contractual agreement with the beneficiary or beneficiaries of the petition. The agent/employer must also provide an itinerary of definite employment and information on any other services planned for the period of time requested.

(2) A person or company in business as an agent may file the H petition involving multiple employers as the representative of both the employers and the beneficiary or beneficiaries if the supporting documentation includes a complete itinerary of services or engagements. The itinerary shall specify the dates of each service or engagement, the names and addresses of the actual employers, and the names and addresses of the establishment, venues, or locations where the services will be performed. In questionable cases, a contract between the employers and the beneficiary or beneficiaries may be required. The burden is on the agent to explain the terms and conditions of the employment and to provide any required documentation.

(3) A foreign employer who, through a United States agent, files a petition for an H nonimmigrant alien is responsible for complying with all of the employer sanctions provisions of section 274A of the Act and 8 CFR part 274a.

(G) Multiple H-1B petitions. An employer may not file, in the same fiscal year, more than one H-1B petition on behalf of the same alien if the alien is subject to the numerical limitations of section 214(g)(1)(A) of the Act or is exempt from those limitations under section 214(g)(5)(C) of the Act. If an H-1B petition is denied, on a basis other than fraud or misrepresentation, the employer may file a subsequent H-1B petition on behalf of the same alien in the same fiscal year, provided that the numerical limitation has not been reached or if the filing qualifies as exempt from the numerical limitation. Otherwise, filing more than one H-1B petition by an employer on behalf of the same alien in the same fiscal year will result in the denial or revocation of all such petitions. If USCIS believes that related entities (such as a parent company, subsidiary, or affiliate) may not have a legitimate business need to file more than one H-1B petition on behalf of the same alien subject to the numerical limitations of section 214(g)(1)(A) of the Act or otherwise eligible for an exemption under section 214(g)(5)(C) of the Act, USCIS may issue a request for additional evidence or notice of intent to deny, or notice of intent to revoke each petition. If any of the related entities fail to demonstrate a legitimate business need to file an H-1B petition on behalf of the same alien, all petitions filed on that alien's behalf by the related entities will be denied or revoked.

(H) H-1B portability. An eligible H-1B nonimmigrant is authorized to start concurrent or new employment under section 214(n) of the Act upon the filing, in accordance with 8 CFR 103.2(a), of a nonfrivolous H-1B petition on behalf of such alien, or as of the requested start date, whichever is later.

(1) Eligible H-1B nonimmigrant. For H-1B portability purposes, an eligible H-1B nonimmigrant is defined as an alien:

(i) Who has been lawfully admitted into the United States in, or otherwise provided, H-1B nonimmigrant status;

(ii) On whose behalf a nonfrivolous H-1B petition for new employment has been filed, including a petition for new employment with the same employer, with a request to amend or extend the H-1B nonimmigrant's stay, before the H-1B nonimmigrant's period of stay authorized by the Secretary of Homeland Security expires; and

(iii) Who has not been employed without authorization in the United States from the time of last admission through the filing of the petition for new employment.

(2) Length of employment. Employment authorized under paragraph (h)(2)(i)(H) of this section automatically ceases upon the adjudication of the H-1B petition described in paragraph (h)(2)(i)(H)(1)(ii) of this section.

(3) Successive H-1B portability petitions.

(i) An alien maintaining authorization for employment under paragraph (h)(2)(i)(H) of this section, whose status, as indicated on the Arrival-Departure Record (Form I-94), has expired, shall be considered to be in a period of stay authorized by the Secretary of Homeland Security for purposes of paragraph (h)(2)(i)(H)(1)(ii) of this section. If otherwise eligible under paragraph (h)(2)(i)(H) of this section, such alien may begin working in a subsequent position upon the filing of another H-1B petition or from the requested start date, whichever is later, notwithstanding that the previous H-1B petition upon which employment is authorized under paragraph (h)(2)(i)(H) of this section remains pending and regardless of whether the validity period of an approved H-1B petition filed on the alien's behalf expired during such pendency.

(ii) A request to amend the petition or for an extension of stay in any successive H-1B portability petition cannot be approved if a request to amend the petition or for an extension of stay in any preceding H-1B portability petition in the succession is denied, unless the beneficiary's previously approved period of H-1B status remains valid.

(iii) Denial of a successive portability petition does not affect the ability of the H-1B beneficiary to continue or resume working in accordance with the terms of an H-1B petition previously approved on behalf of the beneficiary if that petition approval remains valid and the beneficiary has maintained H-1B status or been in a period of authorized stay and has not been employed in the United States without authorization.

(I) H–2A and H–2B portability. An eligible H–2A or H–2B nonimmigrant is authorized to start new employment upon the proper filing, in accordance with 8 CFR 103.2(a), of a nonfrivolous H–2A or H–2B petition on behalf of such alien requesting the same classification that the nonimmigrant alien currently holds, or as of the requested start date, whichever is later.

(1) Eligible H–2A or H–2B nonimmigrant. For H–2A and H–2B portability purposes, an eligible H–2A or H–2B nonimmigrant is defined as an alien:

(i) Who has been lawfully admitted into the United States in, or otherwise provided, H–2A or H–2B nonimmigrant status;

(ii) On whose behalf a nonfrivolous H–2A or H–2B petition for new employment has been properly filed, including a petition for new employment with the same employer, with a request to amend or extend the H–2A or H–2B nonimmigrant's stay in the same classification that the nonimmigrant currently holds, before the H–2A or H–2B nonimmigrant's period of stay authorized by the Secretary of Homeland Security expires; and

(iii) Who has not been employed without authorization in the United States from the time of last admission through the filing of the petition for new employment.

(2) Length of employment. Employment authorized under this paragraph (h)(2)(i)(I) automatically ceases upon the adjudication or withdrawal of the H–2A or H–2B petition described in paragraph (h)(2)(i)(I)(1)(ii) of this section.

(3) Application of H–2A or H–2B program requirements during the pendency of the petition. The petitioner and any employer is required to comply with all H–2A or H–2B program requirements, as applicable under the relevant program, with respect to an alien who has commenced new employment with that petitioner or employer based on a properly filed nonfrivolous petition and while that petition is pending, even if the petition is subsequently denied or withdrawn. During the pendency of the petition, the alien will not be considered to have been in a period of unauthorized stay or employed in the United States without authorization solely on the basis of employment pursuant to the new petition, even if the petition is subsequently denied or withdrawn.

(4) Successive H–2A or H–2B portability petitions.

(i) An alien maintaining authorization for employment under this paragraph (h)(2)(i)(I), whose status, as indicated on the Arrival–Departure Record (Form I–94), has expired, will be considered to be in a period of stay authorized by the Secretary of Homeland Security for purposes of paragraph (h)(2)(i)(I)(1)(ii) of this section. If otherwise eligible under this paragraph (h)(2)(i)(I), such alien may begin working in a subsequent position upon the filing of another H– 2A or H–2B petition in the same classification that the nonimmigrant alien currently holds or from the requested start date, whichever is later, notwithstanding that the previous H–2A or H–2B petition upon which employment is authorized under this paragraph (h)(2)(i)(I) remains pending and regardless of whether the validity period of an approved H–2A or H–2B petition filed on the alien's behalf expired during such pendency.

(ii) A request to amend the petition or for an extension of stay in any successive H–2A or H–2B portability petition requesting the same classification that the nonimmigrant alien currently holds cannot be approved if a request to amend the petition or for an extension of stay in any preceding H–2A or H–2B portability petition in the succession is denied, unless the beneficiary's previously approved period of H–2A or H–2B status remains valid.

(iii) Denial of a successive portability petition does not affect the ability of the H–2A or H–2B beneficiary to continue or resume working in accordance with the terms of an H–2A or H–2B petition previously approved on behalf of the beneficiary if that petition approval remains valid, and the beneficiary has either maintained H–2A or H–2B status, as appropriate, or been in a period of authorized stay and has not been employed in the United States without authorization.

(J) Time of filing. A petition filed under section 101(a)(15)(H) of the Act may not be filed earlier than 6 months before the date of actual need for the beneficiary's services or training.

(ii) Multiple beneficiaries. Up to 25 named beneficiaries may be included in an H-1C, H-2A, H-2B, or H-3 petition if the beneficiaries will be performing the same service, or receiving the same training, for the same period, and in the same location. If more than 25 named beneficiaries are being petitioned for, an additional petition is required. Petitions for H-2A and H-2B workers from countries not designated in accordance with paragraph (h)(6)(i)(E) of this section must be filed separately. Multiple beneficiaries. Up to 25 named beneficiaries may be included in an H–1C, H–2A, H–2B, or H–3 petition if the beneficiaries will be performing the same service, or receiving the same training, for the same period, and in the same location. If more than 25 named beneficiaries are being petitioned for, an additional petition is required.

(iii) Naming beneficiaries. H–1B, H– 1C, and H–3 petitions must include the name of each beneficiary. Except as provided in this paragraph (h), all H–2A and H–2B petitions must include the name of each beneficiary who is currently in the United States, but need not name any beneficiary who is not currently in the United States. Unnamed beneficiaries must be shown on the petition by total number. USCIS may require the petitioner to name H–2B beneficiaries where the name is needed to establish eligibility for H–2B nonimmigrant status. If all of the beneficiaries covered by an H–2A or H– 2B temporary labor certification have not been identified at the time a petition is filed, multiple petitions for subsequent beneficiaries may be filed at different times but must include a copy of the same temporary labor certification. Each petition must reference all previously filed petitions associated with that temporary labor certification.

(iv) [Reserved]

(v) H-2A Petitions. Special criteria for admission, extension, and maintenance of status apply to H-2A petitions and are specified in paragraph (h)(5) of this section. The other provisions of § 214.2(h) apply to H-2A only to the extent that they do not conflict with the special agricultural provisions in paragraph (h)(5) of this section.

(3) Petition for registered nurse (H-1C) —

(i) General.

(A) For purposes of H-1C classification, the term "registered nurse" means a person who is or will be authorized by a State Board of Nursing to engage in registered nurse practice in a state or U.S. territory or possession, and who is or will be practicing at a facility which provides health care services.

(B) A United States employer which provides health care services is referred to as a facility. A facility may file an H-1C petition for an alien nurse to perform the services of a registered nurse, if the facility meets the eligibility standards of 20 CFR 655.1111 and the other requirements of the Department of Labor's regulations in 20 CFR part 655, subpart L.

(C) The position must involve nursing practice and require licensure or other authorization to practice as a registered nurse from the State Board of Nursing in the state of intended employment.

(ii) [Reserved]

(iii) Beneficiary requirements. An H-1C petition for a nurse shall be accompanied by evidence that the nurse:

(A) Has obtained a full and unrestricted license to practice nursing in the country where the alien obtained nursing education, or has received nursing education in the United States;

(B) Has passed the examination given by the Commission on Graduates of Foreign Nursing Schools (CGFNS), or has obtained a full and unrestricted (permanent) license to practice as a registered nurse in the state of intended employment, or has obtained a full and unrestricted (permanent) license in any state or territory of the United States and received temporary authorization to practice as a registered nurse in the state of intended employment; and

(C) Is fully qualified and eligible under the laws (including such temporary or interim licensing requirements which authorize the nurse to be employed) governing the place of intended employment to practice as a registered nurse immediately upon admission to the United States, and is authorized under such laws to be employed by the employer. For purposes of this paragraph, the temporary or interim licensing may be obtained immediately after the alien enters the United States.

(iv) Petitioner requirements. The petitioning facility shall submit the following with an H-1C petition:

(A) A current copy of the DOL's notice of acceptance of the filing of its attestation on Form ETA 9081;

(B) A statement describing any limitations which the laws of the state or jurisdiction of intended employment place on the alien's services; and

(C) Evidence that the alien(s) named on the petition meets the definition of a registered nurse as defined at 8 CFR 214.2(h)(3)(i)(A), and satisfies the requirements contained in section 212(m)(1) of the Act.

(v) Licensure requirements.

(A) A nurse who is granted H-1C classification based on passage of the CGFNS examination must, upon admission to the United States, be able to obtain temporary licensure or other temporary authorization to practice as a registered nurse from the State Board of Nursing in the state of intended employment.

(B) An alien who was admitted as an H-1C nonimmigrant on the basis of a temporary license or authorization to practice as a registered nurse must comply with the licensing requirements for registered nurses in the state of intended employment. An alien admitted as an H-1C nonimmigrant is required to obtain a full and unrestricted license if required by the state of intended employment. The Service must be notified pursuant to § 214.2(h)(11) when an H-1C nurse is no longer licensed as a registered nurse in the state of intended employment.

(C) A nurse shall automatically lose his or her eligibility for H-1C classification if he or she is no longer performing the duties of a registered professional nurse. Such a nurse is not authorized to remain in employment unless he or she otherwise receives authorization from the Service.

(vi) Other requirements.

(A) If the Secretary of Labor notifies the Service that a facility which employs H-1C nonimmigrant nurses has failed to meet a condition in its attestation, or that there was a misrepresentation of a material fact in the attestation, the Service shall not approve petitions for H-1C nonimmigrant nurses to be employed by the facility for a period of at least 1 year from the date of receipt of such notice. The Secretary of Labor shall make a recommendation with respect to the length of debarment. If the Secretary of Labor recommends a longer period of debarment, the Service will give considerable weight to that recommendation.

(B) If the facility's attestation expires, or is suspended or invalidated by DOL, the Service will not suspend or revoke the facility's approved petitions for nurses, if the facility has agreed to comply with the terms of the attestation under which the nurses were admitted or subsequent attestations accepted by DOL for the duration of the nurses' authorized stay.

(4) Petition for alien to perform services in a specialty occupation, services relating to a DOD cooperative research and development project or coproduction project, or services of distinguished merit and ability in the ield of fashion modeling (H-1B) —

(i)(A) Types of H-1B classification. An H-1B classification may be granted to an alien who:

(1) Will perform services in a specialty occupation which requires theoretical and practical application of a body of highly specialized knowledge and attainment of a baccalaureate or higher degree or its equivalent as a minimum requirement for entry into the occupation in the United States, and who is qualified to perform services in the specialty occupation because he or she has attained a baccalaureate or higher degree or its equivalent in the specialty occupation;

(2) Based on reciprocity, will perform services of an exceptional nature requiring exceptional merit and ability relating to a DOD cooperative research and development project or a coproduction project provided for under a Government-to-Government agreement administered by the Secretary of Defense;

(3) Will perform services in the field of fashion modeling and who is of distinguished merit and ability.

(B) General requirements for petitions involving a specialty occupation—

(1) Labor condition application requirements.

(i) Before filing a petition for H–1B classification in a specialty occupation, the petitioner must obtain a certified labor condition application from the Department of Labor in the occupational specialty in which the alien(s) will be employed.

(ii) Certification by the Department of Labor of a labor condition application in an occupational classification does not constitute a determination by the agency that the occupation in question is a specialty occupation. USCIS will determine whether the labor condition application involves a specialty occupation as defined in section 214(i)(1) of the Act and properly corresponds with the petition. USCIS will also determine whether all other eligibility requirements have been met, such as whether the alien for whom H– 1B classification is sought qualifies to perform services in the specialty occupation as prescribed in section 214(i)(2) of the Act.

(iii) If all of the beneficiaries covered by an H–1B labor condition application have not been identified at the time a petition is filed, petitions for newly identified beneficiaries may be filed at any time during the validity of the labor condition application using copies of the same certified labor condition application. Each petition must refer by file number to all previously approved petitions for that labor condition application.

(iv) When petitions have been approved for the total number of workers specified in the labor condition application, substitution of aliens against previously approved openings cannot be made. A new labor condition application will be required.

(v) If the Secretary of Labor notifies USCIS that the petitioning employer has failed to meet a condition of paragraph (B) of section 212(n)(1) of the Act, has substantially failed to meet a condition of paragraphs (C) or (D) of section 212(n)(1) of the Act, has willfully failed to meet a condition of paragraph (A) of section 212(n)(1) of the Act, or has misrepresented any material fact in the application, USCIS will not approve petitions filed with respect to that employer under section 204 or 214(c) of the Act for a period of at least 1 year from the date of receipt of such notice. (vi) If the employer's labor condition application is suspended or invalidated by the Department of Labor, USCIS will not suspend or revoke the employer's approved petitions for aliens already employed in specialty occupations if the employer has certified to the Department of Labor that it will comply with the terms of the labor condition application for the duration of the authorized stay of aliens it employs.

(2) Inspections, evaluations, verifications, and compliance reviews.

(i) The information provided on an H– 1B petition and the evidence submitted in support of such petition may be verified by USCIS through lawful means as determined by USCIS, including telephonic and electronic verifications and on-site inspections. Such verifications and inspections may include, but are not limited to: electronic validation of a petitioner's or third party's basic business information; visits to the petitioner's or third party's facilities; interviews with the petitioner's or third party's officials; reviews of the petitioner's or third party's records related to compliance with immigration laws and regulations; and interviews with any other individuals possessing pertinent information, as determined by USCIS, which may be conducted in the absence of the employer or the employer's representatives; and reviews of any other records that USCIS may lawfully obtain and that it considers pertinent to verify facts related to the adjudication of the H–1B petition, such as facts relating to the petitioner's and beneficiary's H– 1B eligibility and compliance. The interviews may be conducted on the employer's property, or as feasible, at a neutral location agreed to by the interviewee and USCIS away from the employer's property. An inspection may be conducted at locations including the petitioner's headquarters, satellite locations, or the location where the beneficiary works, has worked, or will work, including third party worksites, as applicable. USCIS may commence verification or inspection under this paragraph (h)(4)(i)(B)(2) for any petition and at any time after an H–1B petition is filed, including any time before or after the final adjudication of the petition. The commencement of such verification and inspection before the final adjudication of the petition does not preclude the ability of USCIS to complete final adjudication of the petition before the verification and inspection are completed.

(ii) USCIS conducts on-site inspections or other compliance reviews to verify facts related to the adjudication of the petition and compliance with H– 1B petition requirements. If USCIS is unable to verify facts, including due to the failure or refusal of the petitioner or a third party to cooperate in an inspection or other compliance review, then such inability to verify facts, including due to failure or refusal to cooperate, may result in denial or revocation of any H–1B petition for H–1B workers performing services at the location or locations that are a subject of inspection or compliance review, including any third party worksites.

(3) Third party requirements. If the beneficiary will be staffed to a third party, meaning they will be contracted to fill a position in a third party's organization and becomes part of that third party's organizational hierarchy by filling a position in that hierarchy (and not merely providing services to the third party), the actual work to be performed by the beneficiary must be in a specialty occupation. When staffed to a third party, it is the requirements of that third party, and not the petitioner, that are most relevant when determining whether the position is a specialty occupation.

(C) General requirements for petitions involving an alien of distinguished merit and ability in the field of fashion modeling — H-1B classification may be granted to an alien who is of distinguished merit and ability in the field of fashion modeling. An alien of distinguished merit and ability in the field of fashion modeling is one who is prominent in the field of fashion modeling. The alien must also be coming to the United States to perform services which require a fashion model of prominence.

(ii) Definitions.

Employer-employee relationship means the conventional master-servant relationship consistent with the common law. The petitioner must establish that its offer of employment as stated in the petition is based on a valid employer-employee relationship that exists or will exist. In considering whether the petitioner has established that a valid "employer-employee relationship" exists or will exist, USCIS will assess and weigh all relevant aspects of the relationship with no one factor being determinative.

(1) In cases where the H–1B beneficiary does not possess an ownership interest in the petitioning organization or entity, the factors that USCIS may consider to determine if a valid employment relationship will exist or continue to exist include, but are not limited to:

(i) Whether the petitioner supervises the beneficiary and, if so, where such supervision takes place;

(ii) Where the supervision is not at the petitioner's worksite, how the petitioner maintains such supervision;

(iii) Whether the petitioner has the right to control the work of the beneficiary on a day-to-day basis and to assign projects;

(iv) Whether the petitioner provides the tools or instrumentalities needed for the beneficiary to perform the duties of employment;

(v) Whether the petitioner hires, pays, and has the ability to fire the beneficiary;

(vi) Whether the petitioner evaluates the work-product of the beneficiary;

(vii) Whether the petitioner claims the beneficiary as an employee for tax purposes;

(viii) Whether the petitioner provides the beneficiary any type of employee benefits;

(ix) Whether the beneficiary uses proprietary information of the petitioner in order to perform the duties of employment;

(x) Whether the beneficiary produces an end-product that is directly linked to the petitioner's line of business; and

(xi) Whether the petitioner has the ability to control the manner and means in which the work product of the beneficiary is accomplished.

(2) In cases where the H–1B beneficiary possesses an ownership interest in the petitioning organization or entity, additional factors that USCIS may consider to determine if a valid employment relationship will exist or continue to exist include, but are not limited to:

(i) Whether the petitioning entity can hire or fire the beneficiary or set the rules and parameters of the beneficiary's work;

(ii) Whether and, if so, to what extent the petitioner supervises the beneficiary's work;

(iii) Whether the beneficiary reports to someone higher in the petitioning entity;

(iv) Whether and, if so, to what extent the beneficiary is able to influence the petitioning entity;

(v) Whether the parties intended that the beneficiary be an employee, as expressed in written agreements or contracts; and

(vi) Whether the beneficiary shares in the profits, losses, and liabilities of the organization or entity.

Prominence means a high level of achievement in the field of fashion modeling evidenced by a degree of skill and recognition substantially above that ordinarily encountered to the extent that a person described as prominent is renowned, leading, or well-known in the field of fashion modeling.

Recognized authority means a person or an organization with expertise in a particular field, special skills or knowledge in that field, and the expertise to render the type of opinion requested. Such an opinion must state:

(1) The writer's qualifications as an expert;

(2) The writer's experience giving such opinions, citing specific instances where past opinions have been accepted as authoritative and by whom;

(3) How the conclusions were reached; and

(4) The basis for the conclusions supported by copies or citations of any research material used.

Specialty occupation means an occupation which requires theoretical and practical application of a body of highly specialized knowledge in fields of human endeavor including, but not limited to, architecture, engineering, mathematics, physical sciences, social sciences, medicine and health, education, business specialties, accounting, law, theology, and the arts, and which requires the attainment of a bachelor's degree or higher in a directly related specific specialty, or its equivalent, as a minimum for entry into the occupation in the United States. A position is not a specialty occupation if attainment of a general degree, without further specialization, is sufficient to qualify for the position. A position may allow for a range of qualifying degree fields, provided that each of those fields is directly related to the duties of the position. Directly related means there is a logical connection between the required degree, or its equivalent, and the duties of the position.

Third-party worksite means a worksite, other than the beneficiary's residence in the United States, that is not owned or leased, and not operated, by the petitioner.

United States employer means a person, firm, corporation, contractor, or other association, or organization in the United States that:

(1) Has a bona fide job offer for the beneficiary to work within the United States, which may include telework, remote work, or other off-site work within the United States;

(2) Has a legal presence in the United States and is amenable to service of process in the United States; and

(3) Has an Internal Revenue Service Tax identification number.

(4) If the H–1B beneficiary possesses a controlling interest in the petitioner, meaning the beneficiary owns more than 50 percent of the petitioner or has majority voting rights in the petitioner, such a beneficiary may perform duties that are directly related to owning and directing the petitioner's business as long as the beneficiary will perform specialty occupation duties a majority of the time, consistent with the terms of the H–1B petition.

Worksite means the physical location where the work actually is performed by the H–1B nonimmigrant. A "worksite" will not include any location that would not be considered a "worksite" for Labor Condition Application (LCA) purposes.

(iii) General H–1B requirements—

(A) Criteria for specialty occupation position. A position does not meet the definition of specialty occupation in paragraph (h)(4)(ii) of this section unless it also satisfies at least one of the following criteria at paragraphs (h)(4)(iii)(A)(1) through (4) of this section:

(1) A U.S. baccalaureate or higher degree in a directly related specific specialty, or its equivalent, is normally the minimum requirement for entry into the particular occupation;

(2) A U.S. baccalaureate or higher degree in a directly related specific specialty, or its equivalent, is normally required to perform job duties in parallel positions among similar organizations in the employer's industry in the United States;

(3) The employer, or third party if the beneficiary will be staffed to that third party, normally requires a U.S. baccalaureate or higher degree in a directly related specific specialty, or its equivalent, to perform the job duties of the position; or

(4) The specific duties of the proffered position are so specialized, complex, or unique that the knowledge required to perform them is normally associated with the attainment of a U.S. baccalaureate or higher degree in a directly related specific specialty, or its equivalent.

(5) For purposes of the criteria at paragraphs (h)(4)(iii)(A)(1) through (4) of this section, normally means conforming to a type, standard, or regular pattern, and is characterized by that which is considered usual, typical, common, or routine. Normally does not mean always.

(B) Petitioner requirements. The petitioner shall submit the following with an H-1B petition involving a specialty occupation:

(1) A certification from the Secretary of Labor that the petitioner has filed a labor condition application with the Secretary,

(2) A statement that it will comply with the terms of the labor condition application for the duration of the alien's authorized period of stay,

(3) Evidence that the alien qualifies to perform services in the specialty occupation as described in paragraph (h)(4)(iii)(A) of this section, and

(C) Beneficiary qualifications. To qualify to perform services in a specialty occupation, the alien must meet one of the following criteria:

(1) Hold a United States baccalaureate or higher degree required by the specialty occupation from an accredited college or university;

(2) Hold a foreign degree determined to be equivalent to a United States baccalaureate or higher degree required by the specialty occupation from an accredited college or university;

(3) Hold an unrestricted State license, registration or certification which authorizes him or her to fully prac-

tice the specialty occupation and be immediately engaged in that specialty in the state of intended employment; or

(4) Have education, specialized training, and/or progressively responsible experience that is equivalent to completion of a United States baccalaureate or higher degree in the specialty occupation, and have recognition of expertise in the specialty through progressively responsible positions directly related to the specialty.

(D) Equivalence to completion of a college degree. For purposes of paragraph (h)(4)(iii)(C)(4) of this section, equivalence to completion of a United States baccalaureate or higher degree shall mean achievement of a level of knowledge, competence, and practice in the specialty occupation that has been determined to be equal to that of an individual who has a baccalaureate or higher degree in the specialty and shall be determined by one or more of the following:

(1) An evaluation from an official who has authority to grant college-level credit for training and/or experience in the specialty at an accredited college or university which has a program for granting such credit based on an individual's training and/or work experience;

(2) The results of recognized college-level equivalency examinations or special credit programs, such as the College Level Examination Program (CLEP), or Program on Noncollegiate Sponsored Instruction (PONSI);

(3) An evaluation of education by a reliable credentials evaluation service which specializes in evaluating foreign educational credentials;

(4) Evidence of certification or registration from a nationally-recognized professional association or society for the specialty that is known to grant certification or registration to persons in the occupational specialty who have achieved a certain level of competence in the specialty;

(5) A determination by the Service that the equivalent of the degree required by the specialty occupation has been acquired through a combination of education, specialized training, and/or work experience in areas related to the specialty and that the alien has achieved recognition of expertise in the specialty occupation as a result of such training and experience. For purposes of determining equivalency to a baccalaureate degree in the specialty, three years of specialized training and/or work experience must be demonstrated for each year of college-level training the alien lacks. For equivalence to an advanced (or Masters) degree, the alien must have a baccalaureate degree followed by at least five years of experience in the specialty. If required by a specialty, the alien must hold a Doctorate degree or its foreign equivalent. It must be clearly demonstrated that the alien's training and/or work experience included the theoretical and practical application of specialized knowledge required by the specialty occupation; that the alien's experience was gained while working with peers, supervisors, or subordinates who have a degree or its equivalent in the specialty occupation; and that the alien has recognition of expertise in the specialty evidenced by at least one type of documentation such as:

(i) Recognition of expertise in the specialty occupation by at least two recognized authorities in the same specialty occupation;

(ii) Membership in a recognized foreign or United States association or society in the specialty occupation;

(iii) Published material by or about the alien in professional publications, trade journals, books, or major newspapers;

(iv) Licensure or registration to practice the specialty occupation in a foreign country; or

(v) Achievements which a recognized authority has determined to be significant contributions to the field of the specialty occupation.

(E) Liability for transportation costs. The employer will be liable for the reasonable costs of return transportation of the alien abroad if the alien is dismissed from employment by the employer before the end of the period of authorized admission pursuant to section 214(c)(5) of the Act. If the beneficiary voluntarily terminates his or her employment prior to the expiration of the validity of the petition, the alien has not been dismissed. If the beneficiary believes that the employer has not complied with this provision, the beneficiary shall advise the Service Center which adjudicated the petition in writing. The complaint will be retained in the file relating to the petition. Within the context of this paragraph, the term "abroad" refers to the alien's last place of foreign residence. This provision applies to any employer whose offer of employment became the basis for an alien obtaining or continuing H-1B status.

(F) Bona fide position in a specialty occupation. At the time of filing, the petitioner must establish that it has a bona fide position in a specialty occupation available for the beneficiary as of the start date of the validity period as requested on the petition. A petitioner is not required to establish specific day-to-day assignments for the entire time requested in the petition.

(iv) General documentary requirements for H–1B classification in a specialty occupation. Except as specified in paragraph (h)(4)(iv)(C) of this section, an H–1B petition involving a specialty occupation must be accompanied by:

(A) Documentation, certifications, affidavits, declarations, degrees, diplomas, writings, reviews, or any other required evidence sufficient to establish that the beneficiary is qualified to perform services in a specialty occupation as described in paragraph (h)(4)(i) of this section and that the services the beneficiary is to perform are in a specialty occupation. The evidence shall conform to the following:

(1) School records, diplomas, degrees, affidavits, declarations, contracts, and similar documentation submitted must reflect periods of attendance, courses of study, and similar pertinent data, be executed by the person in charge of the records of the educational or other institution, firm, or establishment where education or training was acquired.

(2) Affidavits or declarations made under penalty of perjury submitted by present or former employers or recognized authorities certifying as to the recognition and expertise of the beneficiary shall specifically describe the beneficiary's recognition and ability in fac-

tual terms and must set forth the expertise of the affiant and the manner in which the affiant acquired such information.

(B) Copies of any written contracts between the petitioner and beneficiary, or a summary of the terms of the oral agreement under which the beneficiary will be employed, if there is no written contract.

(C) In accordance with 8 CFR 103.2(b) and paragraph (h)(9) of this section, USCIS may request evidence such as contracts, work orders, or other similar evidence between all parties in a contractual relationship showing the bona fide nature of the beneficiary's position and the minimum educational requirements to perform the duties.

(v) Licensure for H classification —

(A) General. If an occupation requires a state or local license for an individual to fully perform the duties of the occupation, an alien (except an H-1C nurse) seeking H classification in that occupation must have that license prior to approval of the petition to be found qualified to enter the United States and immediately engage in employment in the occupation.

(B) Temporary licensure. If a temporary license is available and the alien is allowed to perform the duties of the occupation without a permanent license, the director shall examine the nature of the duties, the level at which the duties are performed, the degree of supervision received, and any limitations placed on the alien. If an analysis of the facts demonstrates that the alien under supervision is authorized to fully perform the duties of the occupation, H classification may be granted.

(C) Duties without licensure.

(1) In certain occupations which generally require licensure, a state may allow an individual without licensure to fully practice the occupation under the supervision of licensed senior or supervisory personnel in that occupation. In such cases, USCIS shall examine the nature of the duties and the level at which they are performed, as well as evidence provided by the petitioner as to the identity, physical location, and credentials of the individual(s) who will supervise the alien, and evidence that the petitioner is complying with state requirements. If the facts demonstrate that the alien under supervision will fully perform the duties of the occupation, H classification may be granted.

(2) An H-1B petition filed on behalf of an alien who does not have a valid state or local license, where a license is otherwise required to fully perform the duties in that occupation, may be approved for a period of up to 1 year if:

(i) The license would otherwise be issued provided the alien was in possession of a valid Social Security number, was authorized for employment in the United States, or met a similar technical requirement; and

(ii) The petitioner demonstrates, through evidence from the state or local licensing authority, that the only obstacle to the issuance of a license to the beneficiary is the lack of a Social Security number, a lack of employment authorization in the United States, or a failure to meet a similar technical requirement that precludes the issuance of the license to an individual who is not yet in H-1B status. The petitioner must demonstrate that the alien is fully qualified to receive the state or local license in all other respects, meaning that all educational, training, experience, and other substantive requirements have been met. The alien must have filed an application for the license in accordance with applicable state and local rules and procedures, provided that state or local rules or procedures do not prohibit the alien from filing the license application without provision of a Social Security number or proof of employment authorization or without meeting a similar technical requirement.

(3) An H-1B petition filed on behalf of an alien who has been previously accorded H-1B classification under paragraph (h)(4)(v)(C)(2) of this section may not be approved unless the petitioner demonstrates that the alien has obtained the required license, is seeking to employ the alien in a position requiring a different license, or the alien will be employed in that occupation in a different location which does not require a state or local license to fully perform the duties of the occupation.

(D) H-1C nurses. For purposes of licensure, H-1C nurses must provide the evidence required in paragraph (h)(3)(iii) of this section.

(E) Limitation on approval of petition. Where licensure is required in any occupation, including registered nursing, the H petition may only be approved for a period of one year or for the period that the temporary license is valid, whichever is longer, unless the alien already has a permanent license to practice the occupation. An alien who is accorded H classification in an occupation which requires licensure may not be granted an extension of stay or accorded a new H classification after the one year unless he or she has obtained a permanent license in the state of intended employment or continues to hold a temporary license valid in the same state for the period of the requested extension.

(vi) Criteria and documentary requirements for H-1B petitions involving DOD cooperative research and development projects or coproduction projects —

(A) General.

(1) For purposes of H-1B classification, services of an exceptional nature relating to DOD cooperative research and development projects or coproduction projects shall be those services which require a baccalaureate or higher degree, or its equivalent, to perform the duties. The existence of this special program does not preclude the DOD from utilizing the regular H-1B provisions provided the required guidelines are met.

(2) The requirements relating to a labor condition application from the Department of Labor shall not apply to petitions involving DOD cooperative research and development projects or coproduction projects.

(B) Petitioner requirements.

(1) The petition must be accompanied by a verification letter from the DOD project manager for the particular project stating that the alien will be working on a cooperative research and development project or a coproduction project under a reciprocal Government-to-

Government agreement administered by DOD. Details about the specific project are not required.

(2) The petitioner shall provide a general description of the alien's duties on the particular project and indicate the actual dates of the alien's employment on the project.

(3) The petitioner shall submit a statement indicating the names of aliens currently employed on the project in the United States and their dates of employment. The petitioner shall also indicate the names of aliens whose employment on the project ended within the past year.

(C) Beneficiary requirement. The petition shall be accompanied by evidence that the beneficiary has a baccalaureate or higher degree or its equivalent in the occupational field in which he or she will be performing services in accordance with paragraph (h)(4)(iii)(C) and/or (h)(4)(iii)(D) of this section.

(vii) Criteria and documentary requirements for H-1B petitions for aliens of distinguished merit and ability in the field of fashion modeling —

(A) General. Prominence in the field of fashion modeling may be established in the case of an individual fashion model. The work which a prominent alien is coming to perform in the United States must require the services of a prominent alien. A petition for an H-1B alien of distinguished merit and ability in the field of fashion modeling shall be accompanied by:

(1) Documentation, certifications, affidavits, writings, reviews, or any other required evidence sufficient to establish that the beneficiary is a fashion model of distinguished merit and ability. Affidavits submitted by present or former employers or recognized experts certifying to the recognition and distinguished ability of the beneficiary shall specifically describe the beneficiary's recognition and ability in factual terms and must set forth the expertise of the affiant and the manner in which the affiant acquired such information.

(2) Copies of any written contracts between the petitioner and beneficiary, or a summary of the terms of the oral agreement under which the beneficiary will be employed, if there is no written contract.

(B) Petitioner's requirements. To establish that a position requires prominence, the petitioner must establish that the position meets one of the following criteria:

(1) The services to be performed involve events or productions which have a distinguished reputation;

(2) The services are to be performed for an organization or establishment that has a distinguished reputation for, or record of, employing prominent persons.

(C) Beneficiary's requirements. A petitioner may establish that a beneficiary is a fashion model of distinguished merit and ability by the submission of two of the following forms of documentation showing that the alien:

(1) Has achieved national or international recognition and acclaim for outstanding achievement in his or her field as evidenced by reviews in major newspapers, trade journals, magazines, or other published material;

(2) Has performed and will perform services as a fashion model for employers with a distinguished reputation;

(3) Has received recognition for significant achievements from organizations, critics, fashion houses, modeling agencies, or other recognized experts in the field; or

(4) Commands a high salary or other substantial remuneration for services evidenced by contracts or other reliable evidence.

(viii) Criteria and documentary requirements for H-1B petitions for physicians —

(A) Beneficiary's requirements. An H-1B petition for a physician shall be accompanied by evidence that the physician:

(1) Has a license or other authorization required by the state of intended employment to practice medicine, or is exempt by law therefrom, if the physician will perform direct patient care and the state requires the license or authorization, and

(2) Has a full and unrestricted license to practice medicine in a foreign state or has graduated from a medical school in the United States or in a foreign state.

(B) Petitioner's requirements. The petitioner must establish that the alien physician:

(1) Is coming to the United States primarily to teach or conduct research, or both, at or for a public or nonprofit private educational or research institution or agency, and that no patient care will be performed, except that which is incidental to the physician's teaching or research; or

(2) The alien has passed the Federation Licensing Examination (or an equivalent examination as determined by the Secretary of Health and Human Services) or is a graduate of a United States medical school; and

(i) Has competency in oral and written English which shall be demonstrated by the passage of the English language proficiency test given by the Educational Commission for Foreign Medical Graduates; or

(ii) Is a graduate of a school of medicine accredited by a body or bodies approved for that purpose by the Secretary of Education.

(C) Exception for physicians of national or international renown. A physician who is a graduate of a medical school in a foreign state and who is of national or international renown in the field of medicine is exempt from the requirements of paragraph (h)(4)(viii)(B) of this section.

(5) Petition for alien to perform agricultural labor or services of a temporary or seasonal nature (H-2A) —

(i) Filing a petition --

(A) General. An H-2A petition must be filed on the form prescribed by USCIS with a single valid temporary agricultural labor certification. The petition may be filed by either the employer listed on the temporary labor certification, the employer's agent, or the association of United States agricultural producers named as a joint employer on the temporary labor certification.

(B) Multiple beneficiaries. The total number of beneficiaries of a petition or series of petitions based on the same temporary labor certification may not exceed the number of workers indicated on that document. A single petition can include more than one named beneficiary if the total number is 25 or fewer and does not exceed the number of positions indicated on the relating temporary labor certification.

(C) [Reserved]

(D) Evidence. An H-2A petitioner must show that the proposed employment qualifies as a basis for H-2A status, and that any named beneficiary qualifies for that employment. A petition will be automatically denied if filed without the certification evidence required in paragraph (h)(5)(i)(A) of this section and, for each named beneficiary, the initial evidence required in paragraph (h)(5)(v) of this section.

(E) Special filing requirements. Where a certification shows joint employers, a petition must be filed with an attachment showing that each employer has agreed to the conditions of H-2A eligibility. A petition filed by an agent must be filed with an attachment in which the employer has authorized the agent to act on its behalf, has assumed full responsibility for all representations made by the agent on its behalf, and has agreed to the conditions of H-2A eligibility.

(ii) Effect of the labor certification process. The temporary agricultural labor certification process determines whether employment is as an agricultural worker, whether it is open to U.S. workers, if qualified U.S. workers are available, the adverse impact of employment of a qualified alien, and whether employment conditions, including housing, meet applicable requirements. In petition proceedings a petitioner must establish that the employment and beneficiary meet the requirements of paragraph (h)(5) of this section.

(iii) Ability and intent to meet a job offer --

(A) Eligibility requirements. An H-2A petitioner must establish that each beneficiary will be employed in accordance with the terms and conditions of the certification, which includes that the principal duties to be performed are those on the certification, with other duties minor and incidental.

(B) [Removed and reserved.]

(C) Initial evidence. Representations required for the purpose of labor certification are initial evidence of intent.

(iv) Temporary and seasonal employment --

(A) Eligibility requirements. An H-2A petitioner must establish that the employment proposed in the certification is of a temporary or seasonal nature. Employment is of a seasonal nature where it is tied to a certain time of year by an event or pattern, such as a short annual growing cycle or a specific aspect of a longer cycle, and requires labor levels far above those necessary for ongoing operations. Employment is of a temporary nature where the employer's need to fill the position with a temporary worker will, except in extraordinary circumstances, last no longer than one year.

(B) Effect of Department of Labor findings. In temporary agricultural labor certification proceedings the Department of Labor separately tests whether employment qualifies as temporary or seasonal. Its finding that employment qualifies is normally sufficient for the purpose of an H-2A petition, However, notwithstanding that finding, employment will be found not to be temporary or seasonal where an application for permanent labor certification has been filed for the same alien, or for another alien to be employed in the same position, by the same employer or by its parent, subsidiary or affiliate. This can only be overcome by the petitioner's demonstration that there will be at least a six month interruption of employment in the United States after H-2A status ends. Also, eligibility will not be found, notwithstanding the issuance of a temporary agricultural labor certification, where there is substantial evidence that the employment is not temporary or seasonal.

(v) The beneficiary's qualifications --

(A) Eligibility requirements. An H-2A petitioner must establish that any named beneficiary met the stated minimum requirements and was fully able to perform the stated duties when the application for certification was filed. It must be established at time of application for an H-2A visa, or for admission if a visa is not required, that any unnamed beneficiary either met these requirements when the certification was applied for or passed any certified aptitude test at any time prior to visa issuance, or prior to admission if a visa is not required.

(B) Evidence of employment/job training. For petitions with named beneficiaries, a petition must be filed with evidence that the beneficiary met the certification's minimum employment and job training requirements, if any are prescribed, as of the date of the filing of the labor certification application. For petitions with unnamed beneficiaries, such evidence must be submitted at the time of a visa application or, if a visa is not required, at the time the applicant seeks admission to the United States. Evidence must be in the form of the past employer or employers' detailed statement(s) or actual employment documents, such as company payroll or tax records. Alternately, a petitioner must show that such evidence cannot be obtained, and submit affidavits from persons who worked with the beneficiary that demonstrate the claimed employment or job training.

(C) Evidence of education and other training. For petitions with named beneficiaries, a petition must be filed with evidence that the beneficiary met all of the certification's post-secondary education and other formal training requirements, if any are prescribed in the labor certification application as of date of the filing of the labor certification application. For petitions with unnamed beneficiaries, such evidence must be submitted at the time of a visa application or, if a visa is not required, at the time the applicant seeks admission to the United States. Evidence must be in the form of documents, issued by the relevant institution(s) or organization(s), that show periods of attendance, majors and degrees or certificates accorded.

(vi) Petitioner consent and notification requirements—

(A) Consent. In filing an H–2A petition, a petitioner and each employer consents to allow Government access to all sites where the labor is being or will be performed and where workers are or will be housed and agrees to fully cooperate with any compliance review, evaluation, verification, or inspection conducted by US-

CIS, including an on-site inspection of the employer's facilities, review of the employer's records related to the compliance with immigration laws and regulations, and interview of the employer's employees and any other individuals possessing pertinent information, which may be conducted in the absence of the employer or the employer's representatives, as a condition for the approval of the petition. The interviews may be conducted on the employer's property, or as feasible, at a neutral location agreed to by the employee and USCIS away from the employer's property. If USCIS is unable to verify facts, including due to the failure or refusal of the petitioner or employer to cooperate in an inspection or other compliance review, then such inability to verify facts, including due to failure or refusal to cooperate, may result in denial or revocation of any H–2A petition for H– 2A workers performing services at the location or locations that are a subject of inspection or compliance review.

(B) Agreements. The petitioner agrees to the following requirements:

(1) To notify DHS, within 2 workdays, and beginning on a date and in a manner specified in a notice published in the Federal Register if:

(i) An H–2A worker does not report for work within 5 workdays of the employment start date on the H–2A petition or within 5 workdays of the start date established by their employer, whichever is later;

(ii) The agricultural labor or services for which H–2A workers were hired is completed more than 30 days earlier than the employment end date stated on the H–2A petition; or

(iii) The H–2A worker does not report for work for a period of 5 consecutive workdays without the consent of the employer or is terminated prior to the completion of agricultural labor or services for which they were hired.

(2) To retain evidence of such notification and make it available for inspection by DHS officers for a 1-year period beginning on the date of the notification. To retain evidence of a different employment start date if it is changed from that on the petition by the employer and make it available for inspection by DHS officers for the 1-year period beginning on the newlyestablished employment start date.

(3) To pay $10 in liquidated damages for each instance where the employer cannot demonstrate that it has complied with the notification requirements, unless, in the case of an untimely notification, the employer demonstrates with such notification that good cause existed for the untimely notification, and DHS, in its discretion, waives the liquidated damages amount.

(C) Process. If DHS has determined that the petitioner has violated the notification requirements in paragraph (h)(5)(vi)(B)(1) of this section and has not received the required notification, the petitioner will be given written notice and 30 days to reply before being given written notice of the assessment of liquidated damages. (D) Failure to pay liquidated damages. If liquidated damages are not paid within 10 days of assessment, an H–2A petition may not be processed for that petitioner or any joint employer shown on the petition until such damages are paid.

(vii) Validity. An approved H–2A petition is valid through the expiration of the relating certification for the purpose of allowing a beneficiary to seek issuance of an H–2A nonimmigrant visa, admission or an extension of stay for the purpose of engaging in the specific certified employment.

(viii) Admission --

(A) Effect of violations of status. An alien may not be accorded H-2A status who, at any time during the past 5 years, USCIS finds to have violated, other than through no fault of his or her own (e.g., due to an employer's illegal or inappropriate conduct), any of the terms or conditions of admission into the United States as an H-2A nonimmigrant, including remaining beyond the specific period of authorized stay or engaging in unauthorized employment.

(B) Period of admission. An alien admissible as an H–2A nonimmigrant will be admitted for the period of the approved petition. Such alien will be admitted for an additional period of up to 10 days before the beginning of the approved period for the purpose of travel to the worksite, and up to 30 days subject to the 3-year limitation in paragraph (h)(5)(viii)(C) of this section following the expiration of the H–2A petition for the purpose of departure or to seek an extension based on a subsequent offer of employment. Unless authorized under 8 CFR 274a.12, the alien may not work except during the validity period of the petition.

(C) Limits on an individual's stay. Except as provided in paragraph (h)(5)(viii)(B) of this section, an alien's stay as an H–2A nonimmigrant is limited by the period of time stated in an approved petition. An alien may remain longer to engage in other qualifying temporary agricultural employment by obtaining an extension of stay. However, an individual who has held H–2A or H–2B status for a total of 3 years may not again be granted H–2A status until such time as they remain outside the United States for an uninterrupted period of at least 60 days. Eligibility under this paragraph (h)(5)(viii)(C) will be determined during adjudication of a request for admission, change of status or extension. An alien found eligible for a shorter period of H– 2A status than that indicated by the petition due to the application of this paragraph (h)(5)(viii)(C) will only be admitted for that shorter period.

(D) Period of absence. An absence from the United States for an uninterrupted period of at least 60 days at any time will result in the alien becoming eligible for a new 3-year maximum period of H–2 stay. To qualify, the petitioner must provide evidence documenting the alien's relevant absence(s) from the United States, such as, but not limited to, arrival and departure records, copies of tax returns, and records of employment abroad.

(ix) Substitution of beneficiaries after admission. An H–2A petition may be filed to replace H–2A workers whose employment was terminated earlier than the end date stated on the H–2A petition and before the completion of work; who do not report for work within 5 workdays of the employment start date on the H–2A petition or within 5 workdays of the start date established by their employer, whichever is later; or who do not report for work for a period of 5 consecutive workdays without the consent of the employer. The petition must be filed with a copy of the temporary labor certification, a copy of the approval notice covering the workers for which replacements are sought, and other evidence required by paragraph (h)(5)(i)(D) of this section. It must also be filed with a statement giving the name, date and country of birth, termination date, and the reason for termination, if applicable, for such worker and the date that USCIS was notified that the worker was terminated or did not report for work for a period of 5 consecutive workdays without the consent of the employer. A petition for a replacement will not be approved where the requirements of paragraph (h)(5)(vi) of this section have not been met. A petition for replacements does not constitute the notification required by paragraph (h)(5)(vi)(B)(1) of this section.

(x) Extensions in emergent circumstances. In emergent circumstances, as determined by USCIS, a single H-2A petition may be extended for a period not to exceed 2 weeks without an additional approved labor certification if filed on behalf of one or more beneficiaries who will continue to be employed by the same employer that previously obtained an approved petition on the beneficiary's behalf, so long as the employee continues to perform the same duties and will be employed for no longer than 2 weeks after the expiration of previously-approved H-2A petition. The previously approved H-2A petition must have been based on an approved temporary labor certification, which shall be considered to be extended upon the approval of the extension of H-2A status.

(xi) Treatment of petitions and alien beneficiaries upon a determination that fees were collected from alien beneficiaries—

(A) Denial or revocation of petition for prohibited fees. As a condition of approval of an H–2A petition, no job placement fee, fee or penalty for breach of contract, or other fee, penalty, or compensation (either direct or indirect), related to the H–2A employment (collectively, "prohibited fees") may be collected at any time from a beneficiary of an H–2A petition or any person acting on the beneficiary's behalf by a petitioner, a petitioner's employee, agent, attorney, facilitator, recruiter, or similar employment service, or by any employer (if different from the petitioner) or any joint employer, including a member employer if the petitioner is an association of U.S. agricultural producers. The term "similar employment service" refers to any person or entity that recruits or solicits prospective beneficiaries of the H–2A petition. The passing of a cost to the beneficiary that, by statute or applicable regulations, is the responsibility of the petitioner, constitutes the collection of a prohibited fee. This provision does not prohibit petitioners (including their employees), employers or any joint employers, agents, attorneys, facilitators, recruiters, or similar employment services from receiving reimbursement from the beneficiary for costs that are the responsibility and primarily for the benefit of the worker, such as government-required passport fees. This provision does not prohibit employers from allowing workers to initially incur fees or expenses that the employers are required to subsequently reimburse, where such arrangement is specifically permitted by, and performed in compliance with statute or regulations governing the H–2A program.

(1) If USCIS determines that the petitioner or any of its employees, whether before or after the filing of the H–2A petition, has collected, or entered into an agreement to collect, a prohibited fee related to the H–2A employment, USCIS will deny or revoke the H–2A petition filed on or after January 17, 2025 on notice unless the petitioner demonstrates through clear and convincing evidence that: the petitioner made ongoing, good faith, reasonable efforts to prevent and learn of the prohibited fee collection or agreement by its employees throughout the recruitment, hiring, and employment process; extraordinary circumstances beyond the petitioner's control resulted in its failure to prevent collection or entry into agreement for collection of prohibited fees; the petitioner took immediate remedial action as soon as it became aware of the payment of or agreement to pay the prohibited fee; and the petitioner fully reimbursed all affected beneficiaries or, only if such beneficiaries cannot be located or are deceased, it fully reimbursed the beneficiaries' designees.

(2) If USCIS determines that the beneficiary has paid or agreed to pay a prohibited fee related to the H–2A employment, whether before or after the filing of the H–2A petition, to any agent, attorney, employer, facilitator, recruiter, or similar employment service, or any joint employer, including a member employer if the petitioner is an association of U.S. agricultural producers, USCIS will deny or revoke the H–2A petition filed on or after January 17, 2025 on notice unless the petitioner demonstrates to USCIS through clear and convincing evidence that: the petitioner made ongoing, good faith, reasonable efforts to prevent and learn of the prohibited fee collection or agreement by such parties throughout the recruitment, hiring, and employment process; the petitioner took immediate remedial action as soon as it became aware of the payment of or agreement to pay the prohibited fee; and that all affected beneficiaries, or their designees only if such beneficiaries cannot be located or are deceased, have been fully reimbursed. A written contract between the petitioner and the agent, attorney, facilitator, recruiter, similar employment service, or member employer stating that such fees were prohibited will not, by itself, be sufficient to meet this standard of proof.

(3) For purposes of paragraph (h)(5)(xi) of this section, a designee must be an individual or entity for whom the beneficiary has provided the petitioner or its successor in interest prior written authorization to receive such reimbursement, as long as the petitioner or its successor in interest, or its agent, employer, or any joint employer, attorney, facilitator, recruiter, or similar employment service would not act as such designee or derive any financial benefit, either directly or indirectly, from the reimbursement.

(B) One-year denial period of subsequent H–2A petitions. USCIS will deny any H–2A petition filed by the same petitioner or a successor in interest within 1 year after the decision denying or revoking on notice an

H–2B or H–2A petition on the basis of paragraph (h)(6)(i)(B) or (h)(5)(xi)(A), respectively, of this section, provided that the denied or revoked petition was filed on or after January 17, 2025. In addition, USCIS will deny any H–2A petition filed by the same petitioner or successor in interest within 1 year after withdrawal of an H–2A or H–2B petition filed on or after January 17, 2025, that was withdrawn following USCIS issuance of a request for evidence or notice of intent to deny or revoke the petition on the basis of paragraph (h)(5)(xi)(A) or (h)(6)(i)(B), respectively, of this section.

(C) Reimbursement as condition of approval of future H–2A petitions—

(1) Additional 3-year denial period of subsequent H–2A petitions. For an additional 3 years after the 1-year period described in paragraph (h)(5)(xi)(B) of this section, USCIS will deny any H–2A petition filed by the same petitioner or successor in interest, unless the petitioner or successor in interest demonstrates to USCIS that the petitioner, successor in interest, or the petitioner's or successor in interest's agent, facilitator, recruiter, or similar employment service, or any joint employer, including a member employer if the petitioner is an association of U.S. agricultural producers, reimbursed in full each beneficiary, or the beneficiary's designee only if such beneficiary cannot be located or is deceased, of the denied or revoked petition from whom a prohibited fee was collected. USCIS will deny II–2A petitions under this provision based on the denial or revocation decision(s) issued pursuant to paragraph (h)(5)(xi)(A) or (h)(6)(i)(B) of this section on a prior petition filed on or after January 17, 2025.

(2) Successor in interest. For the purposes of paragraphs (h)(5)(xi)(B) and (C) of this section, successor in interest means an employer that is controlling and carrying on the business of a previous employer regardless of whether such successor in interest has succeeded to all of the rights and liabilities of the predecessor entity. The following factors may be considered by USCIS in determining whether an employer is a successor in interest; no one factor is dispositive, but all of the circumstances will be considered as a whole:

(i) Substantial continuity of the same business operations;

(ii) Use of the same facilities;

(iii) Substantial continuity of the work force;

(iv) Similarity of jobs and working conditions;

(v) Similarity of supervisory personnel;

(vi) Whether the former management or owner retains a direct or indirect interest in the new enterprise;

(vii) Similarity in machinery, equipment, production methods, or assets required to conduct business;

(viii) Similarity of products and services;

(ix) Familial or close personal relationships between predecessor and successor owners of the entity; and

(x) Use of the same or related remittance sources for business payments.

(6) Petition for alien to perform temporary nonagricultural services or labor (H-2B) --

(i) Petition.

(A) H–2B nonagricultural temporary worker. An H–2B nonagricultural temporary worker is an alien who is coming temporarily to the United States to perform temporary services or labor without displacing qualified United States workers available to perform such services or labor and whose employment is not adversely affecting the wages and working conditions of United States workers.

(B) Denial or revocation of petition for prohibited fees. As a condition of approval of an H–2B petition, no job placement fee, fee or penalty for breach of contract, or other fee, penalty, or compensation (either direct or indirect), related to the H–2B employment (collectively, "prohibited fees") may be collected at any time from a beneficiary of an H–2B petition or any person acting on the beneficiary's behalf by a petitioner, a petitioner's employee, agent, attorney, facilitator, recruiter, or similar employment service, or any employer (if different from the petitioner). The term "similar employment service" refers to any person or entity that recruits or solicits prospective beneficiaries of the H–2B petition. The passing of a cost to the beneficiary that, by statute or applicable regulations is the responsibility of the petitioner, constitutes the collection of a prohibited fee. This provision does not prohibit petitioners (including their employees), employers, agents, attorneys, facilitators, recruiters, or similar employment services from receiving reimbursement from the beneficiary for costs that are the responsibility and primarily for the benefit of the worker, such as government-required passport fees. This provision does not prohibit employers from allowing workers to initially incur fees or expenses that the employers are required to subsequently reimburse, where such arrangement is specifically permitted by, and performed in compliance with, statute or regulations governing the H–2B program.

(1) If USCIS determines that the petitioner or any of its employees, whether before or after the filing of the H–2B petition, has collected or entered into an agreement to collect a prohibited fee related to the H–2B employment, USCIS will deny or revoke the H–2B petition filed on or after January 17, 2025 on notice unless the petitioner demonstrates through clear and convincing evidence that: the petitioner made ongoing, good faith, reasonable efforts to prevent and learn of the prohibited fee collection or agreement throughout the recruitment, hiring, and employment process; extraordinary circumstances beyond the petitioner's control resulted in its failure to prevent collection or entry into agreement for collection of prohibited fees; the petitioner took immediate remedial action as soon as it became aware of the payment of or agreement to pay the prohibited fee; and the petitioner fully reimbursed all affected beneficiaries or, only if such beneficiaries cannot be located or are deceased, it fully reimbursed their designees.

(2) If USCIS determines that the beneficiary has paid or agreed to pay any employer, agent, attorney, facilitator, recruiter, or similar employment service a prohibited fee related to the H–2B employment, whether before or after the filing of the H–2B petition, USCIS will deny or revoke the H–2B petition filed on or after January 17, 2025 on notice unless the petitioner demonstrates to USCIS through clear and convincing

evidence that: the petitioner made ongoing, good faith, reasonable efforts to prevent and learn of the prohibited fee(s) collection or agreement by such parties throughout the recruitment, hiring, and employment process; the petitioner took immediate remedial action as soon as it became aware of the payment of the prohibited fee or agreement; and all affected beneficiaries, or their designees only if such beneficiaries cannot be located or are deceased, have been fully reimbursed. A written contract between the petitioner and the facilitator, recruiter, or similar employment service stating that such fees were prohibited will not, by itself, be sufficient to meet this standard of proof.

(3) For purposes of paragraph (h)(6)(i) of this section, a designee must be an individual or entity for whom the beneficiary has provided the petitioner or its successor in interest prior written authorization to receive such reimbursement, as long as the petitioner or its successor in interest, or its agent, employer, attorney, facilitator, recruiter, or similar employment service would not act as such designee or derive any financial benefit, either directly or indirectly, from the reimbursement.

(C) One-year denial period of subsequent H–2B petitions. USCIS will deny any H–2B petition filed by the same petitioner or a successor in interest within 1 year after the decision denying or revoking on notice an H–2B or H–2A petition on the basis of paragraph (h)(6)(i)(B) or (h)(5)(xi)(A), respectively, of this section, provided that the denied or revoked petition was filed on or after January 17, 2025. In addition, USCIS will deny any H–2B petition filed by the same petitioner or successor in interest within 1 year after withdrawal of an H–2B or H–2A petition filed on or after January 17, 2025, that was withdrawn following USCIS issuance of a request for evidence or notice of intent to deny or revoke the petition on the basis of paragraph (h)(6)(i)(B) or (h)(5)(xi)(A), respectively, of this section.

(D) Reimbursement as condition of approval of future H–2B petitions—

(1) Additional 3-year denial period of subsequent H–2B petitions. For an additional 3 years after the 1-year period described in paragraph (h)(6)(i)(C) of this section, USCIS will deny any H–2B petition filed by the same petitioner or successor in interest, unless the petitioner or successor in interest demonstrates to USCIS that the petitioner or successor in interest, or the petitioner's or successor in interest's agent, facilitator, recruiter, or similar employment service, reimbursed in full each beneficiary, or the beneficiary's designee only if such beneficiary cannot be located or is deceased, of the denied or revoked petition from whom a prohibited fee was collected. USCIS will deny H–2B petitions under this provision based on the denial or revocation decision(s) issued pursuant to paragraph (h)(6)(i)(B) or (h)(5)(xi)(A) of this section on a prior petition filed on or after January 17, 2025.

(2) Successor in interest. For the purposes of paragraphs (h)(6)(i)(C) and (D) of this section, successor in interest means an employer that is controlling and carrying on the business of a previous employer regardless of whether such successor in interest has succeeded to all of the rights and liabilities of the predecessor entity. The following factors may be considered by USCIS in determining whether an employer is a successor in interest; no one factor is dispositive, but all of the circumstances will be considered as a whole:

(i) Substantial continuity of the same business operations;

(ii) Use of the same facilities;

(iii) Substantial continuity of the work force;

(iv) Similarity of jobs and working conditions;

(v) Similarity of supervisory personnel;

(vi) Whether the former management or owner retains a direct or indirect interest in the new enterprise;

(vii) Similarity in machinery, equipment, production methods, or assets required to conduct business;

(viii) Similarity of products and services;

(ix) Familial or close personal relationships between predecessor and successor owners of the entity; and

(x) Use of the same or related remittance sources for business payments.

(E) [Reserved]

(1) H-2B petitions may be approved for nationals of countries that the Secretary of Homeland Security has designated as participating countries, with the concurrence of the Secretary of State, in a notice published in the Federal Register, taking into account factors, including but not limited to:

(i) The country's cooperation with respect to issuance of travel documents for citizens, subjects, nationals and residents of that country who are subject to a final order of removal;

(ii) The number of final and unexecuted orders of removal against citizens, subjects, nationals, and residents of that country;

(iii) The number of orders of removal executed against citizens, subjects, nationals and residents of that country; and

(iv) Such other factors as may serve the U.S. interest.

(2) A national from a country not on the list described in paragraph (h)(6)(i)(E)(1) of this section may be a beneficiary of an approved H-2B petition upon the request of a petitioner or potential H-2B petitioner, if the Secretary of Homeland Security, in his sole and unreviewable discretion, determines that it is in the U.S. interest for that alien to be a beneficiary of such petition. Determination of such a U.S. interest will take into account factors, including but not limited to:

(i) Evidence from the petitioner demonstrating that a worker with the required skills is not available from among foreign workers from a country currently on the list described in paragraph (h)(6)(i)(E)(1) of this section;

(ii) Evidence that the beneficiary has been admitted to the United States previously in H-2B status;

(iii) The potential for abuse, fraud, or other harm to the integrity of the H-2B visa program through the potential admission of a beneficiary from a country not currently on the list; and

(iv) Such other factors as may serve the U.S. interest.

(3) Once published, any designation of participating countries pursuant to paragraph (h)(6)(i)(E)(1) of this section shall be effective for one year after the date of

publication in the Federal Register and shall be without effect at the end of that one-year period.

(F) Petitioner agreements and notification requirements—

(1) Agreements. The petitioner must notify DHS, within 2 workdays, and beginning on a date and in a manner specified in a notice published in the Federal Register if: An H–2B worker does not report for work within 5 workdays after the employment start date stated on the petition; the nonagricultural labor or services for which H–2B workers were hired were completed more than 30 days early; or an H–2B worker does not report for work for a period of 5 consecutive workdays without the consent of the employer or is terminated prior to the completion of the nonagricultural labor or services for which they were hired. The petitioner must also retain evidence of such notification and make it available for inspection by DHS officers for a 1-year period beginning on the date of the notification.

(2) Consent. In filing an H–2B petition, the petitioner and each employer (if different from the petitioner) consent to allow Government access to all sites where the labor is being or will be performed and agrees to fully cooperate with any compliance review, evaluation, verification, or inspection conducted by USCIS, including an on-site inspection of the employer's facilities, review of the employer's records related to the compliance with immigration laws and regulations, and interview of the employer's employees and any other individuals possessing pertinent information, which may be conducted in the absence of the employer or the employer's representatives, as a condition for the approval of the petition. The interviews may be conducted on the employer's property, or as feasible, at a neutral location agreed to by the employee and USCIS away from the employer's property. If USCIS is unable to verify facts, including due to the failure or refusal of the petitioner or employer to cooperate in an inspection or other compliance review, then such inability to verify facts, including due to failure or refusal to cooperate, may result in denial or revocation of any H–2B petition for H– 2B workers performing services at the location or locations that are a subject of inspection or compliance review.

(ii) Temporary services or labor --

(A) Definition. Temporary services or labor under the H-2B classification refers to any job in which the petitioner's need for the duties to be performed by the employee(s) is temporary, whether or not the underlying job can be described as permanent or temporary.

(B) Nature of petitioner's need. Employment is of a temporary nature when the employer needs a worker for a limited period of time. The employer must establish that the need for the employee will end in the near, definable future. Generally, that period of time will be limited to one year or less, but in the case of a one-time event could last up to 3 years. The petitioner's need for the services or labor shall be a one-time occurrence, a seasonal need, a peak load need, or an intermittent need.

(1) One-time occurence. The petitioner must establish that it has not employed workers to perform the services or labor in the past and that it will not need workers to perform the services or labor in the future, or that it has an employment situation that is otherwise permanent, but a temporary event of short duration has created the need for a temporary worker.

(2) Seasonal need. The petitioner must establish that the services or labor is traditionally tied to a season of the year by an event or pattern and is of a recurring nature. The petitioner shall specify the period(s) of time during each year in which it does not need the services or labor. The employment is not seasonal if the period during which the services or labor is not needed is unpredictable or subject to change or is considered a vacation period for the petitioner's permanent employees.

(3) Peakload need. The petitoner must establish that it regularly employs permanent workers to perform the services or labor at the place of employment and that it needs to supplement its permanent staff at the place of employment on a temporary basis due to a seasonal or short-term demand and that the temporary additions to staff will not become a part of the petitioner's regular operation.

(4) Intermittent need. The petitioner must establish that it has not employed permanent or full-time workers to perform the services or labor, but occasionally or intermittently needs temporary workers to perform services or labor for short periods.

(iii) Procedures.

(A) Prior to filing a petition with the director to classify an alien as an H-2B worker, the petitioner shall apply for a temporary labor certification with the Secretary of Labor for all areas of the United States, except the Territory of Guam. In the Territory of Guam, the petitioning employer shall apply for a temporary labor certification with the Governor of Guam. The labor certification shall be advice to the director on whether or not United States workers capable of performing the temporary services or labor are available and whether or not the alien's employment will adversely affect the wages and working conditions of similarly employed United States workers.

(B) An H-2B petitioner shall be a United States employer, a United States agent, or a foreign employer filing through a United States agent. For purposes of paragraph (h) of this section, a foreign employer is any employer who is not amenable to service of process in the United States. A foreign employer may not directly petition for an H-2B nonimmigrant but must use the services of a United States agent to file a petition for an H-2B nonimmigrant. A United States agent petitioning on behalf of a foreign employer must be authorized to file the petition, and to accept service of process in the United States in proceedings under section 274A of the Act, on behalf of the employer. The petitioning employer shall consider available United States workers for the temporary services or labor, and shall offer terms and conditions of employment which are consistent with the nature of the occupation, activity, and industry in the United States.

(C) The petitioner may not file an H-2B petition unless the United States petitioner has applied for a labor certification with the Secretary of Labor or the Governor of Guam within the time limits prescribed or accepted by each, and has obtained a favorable labor certification determination as required by paragraph (h)(6)(iv) or (h)(6)(v) of this section.

(D) The Governor of Guam shall separately establish procedures for administering the temporary labor program under his or her jurisdiction. The Secretary of Labor shall separately establish for the temporary labor program under his or her jurisdiction, by regulation at 20 CFR 655, procedures for administering that temporary labor program under his or her jurisdiction, and shall determine the prevailing wage applicable to an application for temporary labor certification for that temporary labor program in accordance with the Secretary of Labor's regulation at 20 CFR 655.10.

(E) After obtaining a favorable determination from the Secretary of Labor or the Governor of Guam, as appropriate, the petitioner shall file a petition on the form prescribed by USCIS, accompanied by the labor certification determination and supporting documents, with the director having jurisdiction in the area of intended employment.

(iv) Labor certifications, except Guam --

(A) Secretary of Labor's determination. An H-2B petition for temporary employment in the United States, except for temporary employment on Guam, shall be accompanied by an approved temporary labor certification from the Secretary of Labor stating that qualified workers in the United States are not available and that the alien's employment will not adversely affect wages and working conditions of similarly employed United States workers.

(B) Validity of the labor certification. The Secretary of Labor may issue a temporary labor certification for a period of up to one year.

(C) U.S. Virgin Islands. Temporary labor certifications filed under section 101(a)(15)(H)(ii)(b) of the Act for employment in the United States Virgin Islands may be approved only for entertainers and athletes and only for periods not to exceed 45 days.

(D) Employment start date. Beginning with petitions filed for workers for fiscal year 2010, an H-2B petition must state an employment start date that is the same as the date of need stated on the approved temporary labor certification. A petitioner filing an amended H-2B petition due to the unavailability of originally requested workers may state an employment start date later than the date of need stated on the previously approved temporary labor certification accompanying the amended H-2B petition.

(v) Labor certification for Guam --

(A) Governor of Guam's determination. An H-2B petition for temporary employment on Guam shall be accompanied by an approved temporary labor certification issued by the Governor of Guam stating that qualified workers in the United States are not available to perform the required services, and that the alien's employment will not adversely affect the wages and working conditions of United States resident workers who are similarly employed on Guam.

(B) Validity of labor certification. The Governor of Guam may issue a temporary labor certification for a period up to one year.

(C) [Reserved]

(D) [Reserved]

(E) Criteria for Guam labor certifications. The Governor of Guam shall, in consultation with the Service, establish systematic methods for determining the prevailing wage rates and working conditions for individual occupations on Guam and for making determinations as to availability of qualified United States residents.

(1) Prevailing wage and working conditions. The system to determine wages and working conditions must provide for consideration of wage rates and employment conditions for occupations in both the private and public sectors, in Guam and/or in the United States (as defined in section 101(a)(38) of the Act), and may not consider wages and working conditions outside of the United States. If the system includes utilitzation of advisory opinions and consultations, the opinions must be provided by officially sanctioned groups which reflect a balance of the interests of the private and public sectors, government, unions and management.

(2) Availability of United States workers. The system for determining availability of qualified United States workers must require the prospective employer to:

(i) Advertise the availability of the position for a minimum of three consecutive days in the newspaper with the largest daily circulation on Guam;

(ii) Place a job offer with an appropriate agency of the Territorial Government which operates as a job referral service at least 30 days in advance of the need for the services to commence, except that for applications from the armed forces of the United States and those in the entertainment industry, the 30-day period may be reduced by the Governor to 10 days;

(iii) Conduct appropriate recruitment in other areas of the United States and its territories if sufficient qualified United States construction workers are not available on Guam to fill a job. The Governor of Guam may require a job order to be placed more than 30 days in advance of need to accommodate such recruitment;

(iv) Report to the appropriate agency the names of all United States resident workers who applied for the position, indicating those hired and the job-related reasons for not hiring;

(v) Offer all special considerations, such as housing and transportation expenses, to all United States resident workers who applied for the position, indicating those hired and the job-related reasons for not hiring;

(vi) Meet the prevailing wage rates and working conditions determined under the wages and working conditions system by the Governor; and

(vii) Agree to meet all Federal and Territorial requirements relating to employment, such as nondiscrimination, occupational safety, and minimum wage requirements.

(F) Approval and publication of employment systems on Guam --

(1) Systems. The Commissioner of Immigration and Naturalization must approve the system to determine prevailing wages and working conditions and the system to determine availability of United States resident workers and any future modifications of the systems prior to implementation. If the Commissioner, in consultation with the Secretary of Labor, finds that the systems or modified systems meet the requirements of this section, the Commissioner shall publish them as a notice in the FEDERAL REGISTER and the Governor shall publish them as a public record in Guam.

(2) Approval of construction wage rates. The Commissioner must approve specific wage data and rates used for construction occupations on Guam prior to implementation of new rates. The Governor shall submit new wage survey data and proposed rates to the Commissioner for approval at least eight weeks before authority to use existing rates expires. Surveys shall be conducted at least every two years, unless the Commissioner prescribes a lesser period.

(G) Reporting. The Governor shall provide the Commissioner statistical data on temporary labor certification workload and determinations. This information shall be submitted quarterly no later than 30 days after the quarter ends.

(H) Invalidation of temporary labor certification issued by the Governor of Guam --

(1) General. A temporary labor certification issued by the Governor of Guam may be invalidated by a director if it is determined by the director or a court of law that the certification request involved fraud or willful misrepresentation. A temporary labor certification may also be invalidated if the director determines that the certification involved gross error.

(2) Notice of intent to invalidate. If the director intends to invalidate a temporary labor certification, a notice of intent shall be served upon the employer, detailing the reasons for the intended invalidation. The employer shall have 30 days in which to file a written response in rebuttal to the notice of intent. The director shall consider all evidence submitted upon rebuttal in reaching a decision.

(3) Appeal of invalidation. An employer may appeal the invalidation of a temporary labor certification in accordance with part 103 of this chapter.

(vi) Evidence for H-2B petitions. An H-2B petition shall be accompanied by:

(A) Labor certification. An approved temporary labor certification issued by the Secretary of Labor or the Governor of Guam, as appropriate;

(B) [Reserved]

(C) Alien's qualifications. In petitions where the temporary labor certification application requires certain education, training, experience, or special requirements of the beneficiary who is present in the United States, documentation that the alien qualifies for the job offer as specified in the application for such temporary labor certification. This requirement also applies to the named beneficiary who is abroad on the basis of special provisions stated in paragraph (h)(2)(iii) of this section;

(D) Statement of need. A statement describing in detail the temporary situation or conditions which make it necessary to bring the alien to the United States and whether the need is a one-time occurrence, seasonal, peakload, or intermittent. If the need is seasonal, peakload, or intermittent, the statement shall indicate whether the situation or conditions are expected to be recurrent; or

(E) Liability for transportation costs. The employer will be liable for the reasonable costs of return transportation of the alien abroad, if the alien is dismissed from employment for any reason by the employer before the end of the period of authorized admission pursuant to section 214(c)(5) of the Act. If the beneficiary voluntarily terminates his or her employment prior to the expiration of the validity of the petition, the alien has not been dismissed. If the beneficiary believes that the employer has not complied with this provision, the beneficiary shall advise the Service Center which adjudicated the petition in writing. The complaint will be retained in the file relating to the petition. Within the context of this paragraph, the term "abroad" means the alien's last place of foreign residence. This provision applies to any employer whose offer of employment became the basis for the alien obtaining or continuing H-2B status.

(vii) Admission—

(A) Period of admission. An alien admissible as an H– 2B nonimmigrant will be admitted for the period of the approved petition. Such alien will be admitted for an additional period of up to 10 days before the beginning of the approved period for the purpose of travel to the worksite, and up to 30 days subject to the 3-year limitation in paragraph (h)(6)(vii)(B) of this section following the expiration of the H–2B petition for the purpose of departure or to seek an extension based on a subsequent offer of employment. Unless authorized under 8 CFR 274a.12, the alien may not work except during the validity period of the petition.

(B) Limits on an individual's stay. Except as provided in paragraph (h)(6)(vii)(A) of this section, an alien's stay as an H–2B nonimmigrant is limited by the period of time stated in an approved petition. An alien may remain longer to engage in other qualifying temporary nonagricultural employment by obtaining an extension of stay. However, an individual who has held H–2A or H–2B status for a total of 3 years may not again be granted H–2B status until such time as they remain outside the United States for an uninterrupted period of at least 60 days. Eligibility under this paragraph (h)(6)(vii)(B) will be determined during adjudication of a request for admission, change of status or extension of stay. An alien found eligible for a shorter period of H–2B status than that indicated by the petition due to the application of this paragraph (h)(6)(vii)(B) will only be admitted for that shorter period.

(C) Period of absence. An absence from the United States for an uninterrupted period of at least 60 days at any time will result in the alien becoming eligible for a new 3-year maximum period of H–2 stay. The limitation in paragraph (h)(6)(vii)(B) of this section will not apply to H–2B aliens who did not reside continually in the United States and whose employment in the United States was seasonal or intermittent or was for an aggregate of 6 months or less per year. In addition, the limitation in paragraph (h)(6)(vii)(B) of this section will not apply to aliens who reside abroad and regularly commute to the United States to engage in part-time employment. To qualify, the petitioner must provide evidence documenting the alien's relevant absence(s) from the United States, such as, but not limited to, arrival and departure records, copies of tax returns, and records of employment abroad.

(D) Traded professional H–2B athletes. In the case of a professional H– 2B athlete who is traded from one organization to another organization, employment authorization for the player will automatically continue for a period of 30 days after the player's acquisition by the new organization, within which time the new organization is expected to file a new application or petition for H– 2B nonimmigrant classification. If a new application or petition is not filed within 30 days, employment authorization will cease. If a new application or petition is filed within 30 days, the professional athlete will be deemed to be in valid H–2B status, and employment will continue to be authorized, until the petition is adjudicated. If the new petition is denied, employment authorization will cease.

(viii) Substitution of beneficiaries. Beneficiaries of H-2B petitions that are approved for named or unnamed beneficiaries who have not been admitted may be substituted only if the employer can demonstrate that the total number of beneficiaries will not exceed the number of beneficiaries certified in the original temporary labor certification. Beneficiaries who were admitted to the United States may not be substituted without a new petition accompanied by a newly approved temporary labor certification.

(A) To substitute beneficiaries who were previously approved for consular processing but have not been admitted with aliens who are outside of the United States, the petitioner shall, by letter and a copy of the petition approval notice, notify the consular office at which the alien will apply for a visa or the port of entry where the alien will apply for admission. The petitioner shall also submit evidence of the qualifications of beneficiaries to the consular office or port of entry prior to issuance of a visa or admission, if applicable.

(B) To substitute beneficiaries who were previously approved for consular processing but have not been admitted with aliens who are currently in the United States, the petitioner shall file an amended petition with fees at the USCIS Service Center where the original petition was filed, with a copy of the original petition approval notice, a statement explaining why the substitution is necessary, evidence of the qualifications of beneficiaries, if applicable, evidence of the beneficiaries' current status in the United States, and evidence that the number of beneficiaries will not exceed the number allocated on the approved temporary labor certification, such as employment records or other documentary evidence to establish that the number of visas sought in the amended petition were not already issued. The amended petition must retain a period of employment within the same half of the same fiscal year as the original petition. Otherwise, a new temporary labor certification issued by DOL or the Governor of Guam and subsequent H-2B petition are required.

(ix) Enforcement. The Secretary of Labor may investigate employers to enforce compliance with the conditions of a petition and Department of Labor-approved temporary labor certification to admit or otherwise provide status to an H-2B worker.

(x) [Effective May 25, 2021 through May 28, 2024.] Special requirements for additional cap allocations under the Consolidated Appropriations Act, 2021, Public Law 116-260—

(A) Public Law 116-260—

(1) Supplemental allocation for returning workers. Notwithstanding the numerical limitations set forth in paragraph (h)(8)(i)(C) of this section, for fiscal year 2021 only, the Secretary has authorized up to an additional 16,000 visas for aliens who may receive H-2B nonimmigrant visas pursuant to section 105 of Division O of the Consolidated Appropriations Act, 2021, Public Law 116-260. An alien may be eligible to receive an H-2B nonimmigrant visa under this paragraph (h)(6)(x)(A)(1) if she or he is a returning worker. The term "returning worker" under this paragraph (h)(6)(x)(A)(1) means a person who was issued an H-2B visa or was otherwise granted H-2B status in fiscal year 2018, 2019, or 2020. Notwithstanding § 248.2 of this chapter, an alien may not change status to H-2B nonimmigrant under this paragraph (h)(6)(x)(A)(1).

(2) Supplemental allocation for nationals of Guatemala, El Salvador, and Honduras (Northern Triangle countries). Notwithstanding the numerical limitations set forth in paragraph (h)(8)(i)(C) of this section, for fiscal year 2021 only, and in addition to the allocation described in paragraph (h)(6)(x)(A)(1) of this section, the Secretary has authorized up to an additional 6,000 aliens who are nationals of Guatemala, El Salvador, or Honduras (Northern Triangle countries) who may receive H-2B nonimmigrant visas pursuant to section 105 of Division O of the Consolidated Appropriations Act, 2021, Public Law 116-260. Such workers are not subject to the returning worker requirement in paragraph (h)(6)(x)(A)(1). Petitioners must request such workers in an H-2B petition that is separate from H-2B petitions that request returning workers under paragraph (h)(6)(x)(A)(1) and must declare that they are requesting these workers in the attestation required under 20 CFR 655.68(a)(1). Notwithstanding § 248.2 of this chapter, an alien may not change status to H-2B nonimmigrant under this paragraph (h)(6)(x)(A)(2).

(i) Petitions submitted under this paragraph (h)(6)(x)(A)(2) must be received by July 8, 2021. H-2B petitions under the supplemental allocation for nationals of Northern Triangle countries received after that date will be rejected.

(ii) If USCIS determines that it has received fewer petitions by July 8, 2021 than needed to reach the USCIS projections for the Northern Triangle countries supplemental allocation in this paragraph (h)(6)(x)(A)(2), it will make the remainder of the allocation available as a separate allocation described in paragraph (h)(6)(x)(A)(3) of this section.

(3) Availability of remainder of supplemental allocation. If USCIS determines that fewer petitions have been received by July 8, 2021 than needed to meet the additional allocation described in paragraph (h)(6)(x)(A)(2) of this section, USCIS will make the remainder of the allocation available as a separate allocation to returning workers as described in paragraph (h)(6)(x)(A)(1) of this section and will announce the availability of the remainder of the allocation on the USCIS website at uscis.gov no later than July 23, 2021. Such announcement, if made, will specify the date on which petitioners may begin to file H-2B petitions under this paragraph (h)(6)(x)(A)(3).

(B) Eligibility. In order to file a petition with USCIS under this paragraph (h)(6)(x), the petitioner must:

(1) Comply with all other statutory and regulatory requirements for H-2B classification, including, but not limited to, requirements in this section, under part 103 of this chapter, and under 20 CFR part 655 and 29 CFR part 503; and

(2) Submit to USCIS, at the time the employer files its petition, a U.S. Department of Labor attestation, in compliance with this section and 20 CFR 655.64, evidencing that:

(i) Without the ability to employ all of the H-2B workers requested on the petition filed pursuant to this paragraph (h)(6)(x), its business is likely to suffer irreparable harm (that is, permanent and severe financial loss);

(ii) All workers requested and/or instructed to apply for a visa have been issued an H-2B visa or otherwise granted H-2B status in fiscal year 2018, 2019, or 2020, unless the H-2B worker is a national of Guatemala, El Salvador, or Honduras and is counted towards the 6,000 cap described in paragraph (h)(6)(x)(A)(2) of this section;

(iii) The employer will comply with all Federal, State, and local employment-related laws and regulations, including health and safety laws and laws related to COVID-19 worker protections, any right to time off or paid time off for COVID-19 vaccination, and that the employer will notify any H-2B workers approved under the supplemental cap in paragraph (h)(6)(x)(A)(2) of this section, in a language understood by the worker, as necessary or reasonable, that all persons in the United States, including nonimmigrants, have equal access to COVID-19 vaccines and vaccine distribution sites;

(iv) The employer will comply with obligations and additional recruitment requirements outlined in 20 CFR 655.64(a)(3) through (5);

(v) The employer will provide documentary evidence of the facts in paragraphs (h)(6)(x)(B)(2)(i) through (iv) of this section to DHS or DOL upon request; and

(vi) The employer will agree to fully cooperate with any compliance review, evaluation, verification, or inspection conducted by DHS, including an on-site inspection of the employer's facilities, interview of the employer's employees and any other individuals possessing pertinent information, and review of the employer's records related to the compliance with immigration laws and regulations, including but not limited to evidence pertaining to or supporting the eligibility criteria for the FY 2021 supplemental allocations outlined in paragraph (h)(6)(x)(B) of this section, as a condition for the approval of the petition.

(vii) The employer must attest on Form ETA-9142-B-CAA-4 that it will fully cooperate with any audit, investigation, compliance review, evaluation, verification or inspection conducted by DOL, including an on-site inspection of the employer's facilities, interview of the employer's employees and any other individuals possessing pertinent information, and review of the employer's records related to the compliance with applicable laws and regulations, including but not limited to evidence pertaining to or supporting the eligibility criteria for the FY 2021 supplemental allocations outlined in 20 CFR 655.64(a) and 655.68(a), as a condition for the approval of the H-2B petition. The employer must further attest on Form ETA-9142-B-CAA-4 that it will not impede, interfere, or refuse to cooperate with an employee of the Secretary of the U.S. Department of Labor who is exercising or attempting to exercise DOL's audit or investigative authority pursuant to 20 CFR part 655, subpart A, and 29 CFR 503.25.

(C) Processing. USCIS will reject petitions filed pursuant to paragraph (h)(6)(x)(A)(1) or (3) of this section that are received after the applicable numerical limitation has been reached or after September 15, 2021, whichever is sooner. USCIS will reject petitions filed pursuant to paragraph (h)(6)(x)(A)(2) of this section that are received after the applicable numerical limitation has been reached or after July 8, 2021, whichever is sooner. USCIS will not approve a petition filed pursuant to this paragraph (h)(6)(x) on or after October 1, 2021.

(D) Numerical limitations under paragraphs (h)(6)(x)(A)(1), (2), and (3) of this section. When calculating the numerical limitations under paragraphs (h)(6)(x)(A)(1), (2), and (3) of this section as authorized under Public Law 116-260, USCIS will make numbers for each allocation available to petitions in the order in which the petitions subject to the respective limitation are received. USCIS will make projections of the number of petitions necessary to achieve the numerical limit of approvals, taking into account historical data related to approvals, denials, revocations, and other relevant factors. USCIS will monitor the number of petitions (including the number of workers requested when necessary) received and will notify the public of the dates that USCIS has received the necessary number of petitions (the "final receipt dates") under paragraph (h)(6)(x)(A)(1) or paragraphs (h)(6)(x)(A)(2) and (3). The day the public is notified will not control the final receipt dates. When necessary to ensure the fair and orderly allocation of numbers subject to the numerical limitations in paragraphs (h)(6)(x)(A)(1), (2), and (3), USCIS may randomly select from among the petitions received on the final receipt dates the remaining number of petitions deemed necessary to generate the numerical limit of approvals. This random selection will be made via computer-generated selection. Petitions subject to a numerical limitation not randomly selected or that were received after the final receipt dates that may be applicable under paragraph (h)(6)(x)(A)(1), (2), or (3) will be rejected. If the final receipt date is any of the first 5 business days on which petitions subject to the applicable numerical limits described in paragraph (h)(6)(x)(A)(1), (2), or (3) may be received (in other words, if any of the numerical limits described in paragraph (h)(6)(x)(A)(1), (2), or (3) is reached on any one of the first 5 business days that filings can be made), USCIS will randomly apply all of the numbers among the petitions received on any of those 5 business days.

(E) Sunset. This paragraph (h)(6)(x) expires on October 1, 2021.

(F) Non-severability. The requirement to file an attestation under paragraph (h)(6)(x)(B)(2) of this section is intended to be non-severable from the remainder of this paragraph (h)(6)(x), including, but not limited to, the numerical allocation provisions at paragraphs (h)(6)(x)(A)(1), (2), and (3) of this section in their entirety. In the event that any part of this paragraph (h)(6)(x) is enjoined or held to be invalid by any court of competent jurisdiction, the remainder of this paragraph (h)(6)(x) is also intended to be enjoined or held to be invalid in such jurisdiction, without prejudice to workers already present in the United States under this paragraph (h)(6)(x), as consistent with law.

(xi) [Effective Jan. 28, 2022 through Jan. 28, 2025.] Special requirements for additional cap allocations under Public Laws 116-260, 117-43 and 117-70 —

(A) Public Law 116-260, and sections 101 and 106(3) of Division A of Public Law 117-43, Continuing Appropriations Act, 2022, and section 101 of Division A of Public Law 117-70, Further Continuing Appropriations Act, 2022 through February 18, 2022 —

(1) Supplemental allocation for returning workers. Notwithstanding the numerical limitations set forth in paragraph (h)(8)(i)(C) of this section, for fiscal year 2022 only, the Secretary has authorized up to an additional 13,500 visas for aliens who may receive H-2B nonimmigrant visas pursuant to section 105 of Division O of the Consolidated Appropriations Act, 2021, Public Law 116-260, sections 101 and 106(3) of Division A of Public Law 117-43, Continuing Appropriations Act, 2022, and section 101 of Division A of Public Law 117-70, Further Continuing Appropriations Act, 2022 through February 18, 2022 based on petitions requesting FY 2022 employment start dates on or before March 31, 2022. An alien may be eligible to receive an H-2B nonimmigrant visa under this paragraph (h)(6)(xi)(A)(1) if she or he is a returning worker. The term "returning worker" under this paragraph (h)(6)(xi)(A)(1) means a person who was issued an H-2B visa or was otherwise granted H-2B status in fiscal year 2019, 2020, or 2021. Notwithstanding § 248.2 of this chapter, an alien may not change status to H-2B nonimmigrant under this paragraph (h)(6)(xi)(A)(1).

(2) Supplemental allocation for nationals of Guatemala, El Salvador, Honduras (Northern Triangle countries), or Haiti. Notwithstanding the numerical limitations set forth in paragraph (h)(8)(i)(C) of this section, for fiscal year 2022 only, and in addition to the allocation described in paragraph (h)(6)(xi)(A)(1) of this section, the Secretary has authorized up to an additional 6,500 aliens who are nationals of Guatemala, El Salvador, Honduras (Northern Triangle countries), or of Haiti who may receive H-2B nonimmigrant visas pursuant to section 105 of Division O of the Consolidated Appropriations Act, 2021, Public Law 116-260, and Public Laws 117-43 and 117-70, based on petitions with FY 2022 employment start dates on or before March 31, 2022. Such workers are not subject to the returning worker requirement in paragraph (h)(6)(xi)(A)(1). Petitioners must request such workers in an H-2B petition that is separate from H-2B petitions that request returning workers under paragraph (h)(6)(xi)(A)(1) and must declare that they are requesting these workers in the attestation required under 20 CFR 655.69(a)(1). A petition requesting returning workers under paragraph (h)(6)(xi)(A)(1), which is accompanied by an attestation indicating that the petitioner is requesting nationals of Northern Triangle countries or Haiti, will be rejected, denied or, in the case of a non-frivolous petition, will be approved solely for the number of beneficiaries that are from the Northern Triangle or Haiti. Notwithstanding § 248.2 of this chapter, an alien may not change status to H-2B nonimmigrant under this paragraph (h)(6)(xi)(A)(2).

(B) Eligibility. In order to file a petition with USCIS under this paragraph (h)(6)(xi), the petitioner must:

(1) Comply with all other statutory and regulatory requirements for H-2B classification, including, but not limited to, requirements in this section, under part 103 of this chapter, and under 20 CFR part 655 and 29 CFR part 503; and

(2) Submit to USCIS, at the time the employer files its petition, a U.S. Department of Labor attestation, in compliance with this section and 20 CFR 655.64, evidencing that:

(i) Its business is suffering irreparable harm or will suffer impending irreparable harm (that is, permanent and severe financial loss) without the ability to employ all of the H-2B workers requested on the petition filed pursuant to this paragraph (h)(6)(xi);

(ii) All workers requested and/or instructed to apply for a visa have been issued an H-2B visa or otherwise granted H-2B status in fiscal year 2019, 2020, or 2021, unless the H-2B worker is a national of Guatemala, El Salvador, Honduras, or Haiti who is counted towards the 6,500 cap described in paragraph (h)(6)(xi)(A)(2) of this section;

(iii) The employer will comply with all Federal, State, and local employment-related laws and regulations, including, where applicable, health and safety laws and laws related to COVID-19 worker protections; any right to time off or paid time off for COVID-19 vaccination, or to reimbursement for travel to and from the nearest available vaccination site; and that the employer will notify any H-2B workers approved under the supplemental cap in paragraph (h)(6)(xi)(A)(2) of this section, in a language understood by the worker as necessary or reasonable, that all persons in the United States, including nonimmigrants, have equal access to COVID-19 vaccines and vaccine distribution sites;

(iv) The employer will comply with obligations and additional recruitment requirements outlined in 20 CFR 655.64(a)(3) through (5);

(v) The employer will provide documentary evidence of the facts in paragraphs (h)(6)(xi)(B)(2)(i) through (iv) of this section to DHS or DOL upon request; and

(vi) The employer will agree to fully cooperate with any compliance review, evaluation, verification, or inspection conducted by DHS, including an on-site inspection of the employer's facilities, interview of the employer's employees and any other individuals possessing pertinent information, and review of the employer's records related to the compliance with immigration laws and regulations, including but not limited to evidence pertaining to or supporting the eligibility criteria for the FY 2022 supplemental allocations outlined in paragraph (h)(6)(xi)(B) of this section, as a condition for the approval of the petition.

(vii) The employer must attest on Form ETA-9142-B-CAA-5 that it will fully cooperate with any audit, investigation, compliance review, evaluation, verification or inspection conducted by DOL, including an on-site inspection of the employer's facilities, interview of the employer's employees and any other individuals possessing pertinent information, and review of the employer's records related to the compliance with applicable laws and regulations, including but not limited to evidence pertaining to or supporting the eligibility criteria for the FY 2022 supplemental allocations outlined in 20 CFR 655.64(a) and 655.69(a), as a condition for the approval of the H-2B petition. The employer must further attest on Form ETA-9142-B-CAA-5 that it will not impede, interfere, or refuse to cooperate with an employee of the Secretary of the U.S. Department of Labor who is exercising or attempting to exercise DOL's audit or investigative authority pursuant to 20 CFR part 655, subpart A, and 29 CFR 503.25.

(C) Processing. USCIS will reject petitions filed pursuant to paragraph (h)(6)(xi)(A)(1) or (2) of this section that are received after the applicable numerical limitation has been reached or after March 31, 2022, whichever is sooner. USCIS will not approve a petition filed pursuant to this paragraph (h)(6)(xi) on or after October 1, 2022.

(D) Numerical limitations under paragraphs (h)(6)(xi)(A)(1) and (2) of this section. When calculating the numerical limitations under paragraphs (h)(6)(xi)(A)(1) and (2) of this section as authorized under Public Law 116-260, as extended by Public Law 117-43, and Public Law 117-70, USCIS will make numbers for each allocation available to petitions in the order in which the petitions subject to the respective limitation are received. USCIS will make projections of the number of petitions necessary to achieve the numerical limit of approvals, taking into account historical data related to approvals, denials, revocations, and other relevant factors. USCIS will monitor the number of petitions received (including the number of workers requested when necessary) and will notify the public of the dates that USCIS has received the necessary number of petitions (the "final receipt dates") under paragraph (h)(6)(xi)(A)(1) or (2). The day the public is notified will not control the final receipt dates. When necessary to ensure the fair and orderly allocation of numbers subject to the numerical limitations in paragraphs (h)(6)(xi)(A)(1) and (2), USCIS may randomly select from among the petitions received on the final receipt dates the remaining number of petitions deemed necessary to generate the numerical limit of approvals. This random selection will be made via computer-generated selection. Petitions subject to a numerical limitation not randomly selected or that were received after the final receipt dates that may be applicable under paragraph (h)(6)(xi)(A)(1) or (2) will be rejected. If the final receipt date is any of the first 5 business days on which petitions subject to the applicable numerical limits described in paragraph (h)(6)(xi)(A)(1) or (2) may be received (in other words, if either of the numerical limits described in paragraph (h)(6)(xi)(A)(1) or (2) is reached on any one of the first 5 business days that filings can be made), USCIS will randomly apply all of the numbers among the petitions received on any of those 5 business days.

(E) Sunset. This paragraph (h)(6)(xi) expires on October 1, 2022.

(F) Non-severability. The requirement to file an attestation under paragraph (h)(6)(xi)(B)(2) of this section is intended to be non-severable from the remainder of this paragraph (h)(6)(xi), including, but not limited to, the numerical allocation provisions at paragraphs (h)(6)(xi)(A)(1) and (2) of this section in their entirety. In the event that any part of this paragraph (h)(6)(xi) is enjoined or held to be invalid by any court of competent jurisdiction, the remainder of this paragraph (h)(6)(xi) is also intended to be enjoined or held to be invalid in such jurisdiction, without prejudice to workers already present in the United States under this paragraph (h)(6)(xi), as consistent with law.

(xii) [Effective May 18, 2022 through May 18, 2025] Special requirements for additional cap allocations under the Consolidated Appropriations Act, 2022, Public Law 117-103—

(A) Public Law 117-103 —

(1) Supplemental allocation for returning workers. Notwithstanding the numerical limitations set forth in paragraph (h)(8)(i)(C) of this section, for fiscal year 2022 only, the Secretary has authorized up to an additional 23,500 visas for aliens who may receive H-2B nonimmigrant visas pursuant to section 204 of Division O of the Consolidated Appropriations Act, 2022, Public Law 117-103, based on petitions requesting FY 2022 employment start dates on or after April 1, 2022 through September 30, 2022. An alien may be eligible to receive an H-2B nonimmigrant visa under this paragraph (h)(6)(xii)(A)(1) if she or he is a returning worker. The term "returning worker" under this paragraph (h)(6)(xii)(A)(1) means a person who was issued an H-2B visa or was otherwise granted H-2B status in fiscal year 2019, 2020, or 2021. Notwithstanding § 248.2 of this chapter, an alien may not change status to H-2B nonimmigrant under this paragraph (h)(6)(xii)(A)(1).

(2) Supplemental allocation for nationals of Guatemala, El Salvador, Honduras (Northern Central Ameri-

can countries), or Haiti. Notwithstanding the numerical limitations set forth in paragraph (h)(8)(i)(C) of this section, for fiscal year 2022 only, and in addition to the allocation described in paragraph (h)(6)(xii)(A)(1) of this section, the Secretary has authorized up to an additional 11,500 aliens who are nationals of Guatemala, El Salvador, Honduras (Northern Central American countries), or of Haiti who may receive H-2B nonimmigrant visas pursuant to section 204 of Division O of the Consolidated Appropriations Act, 2022, Public Law 117-103, based on petitions with FY 2022 employment start dates on or after April 1, 2022 through September 30, 2022. Such workers are not subject to the returning worker requirement in paragraph (h)(6)(xii)(A)(1). Petitioners must request such workers in an H-2B petition that is separate from H-2B petitions that request returning workers under paragraph (h)(6)(xii)(A)(1) and must declare that they are requesting these workers in the attestation required under 20 CFR 655.66(a)(1). A petition requesting returning workers under paragraph (h)(6)(xii)(A)(1), which is accompanied by an attestation indicating that the petitioner is requesting nationals of Northern Central American countries or Haiti, will be rejected, denied or, in the case of a non-frivolous petition, will be approved solely for the number of beneficiaries that are from the Northern Central American countries or Haiti. Notwithstanding § 248.2 of this chapter, an alien may not change status to H-2B nonimmigrant under this paragraph (h)(6)(xii)(A)(2).

(B) Eligibility. In order to file a petition with USCIS under this paragraph (h)(6)(xii), the petitioner must:

(1) Comply with all other statutory and regulatory requirements for H-2B classification, including, but not limited to, requirements in this section, under part 103 of this chapter, and under 20 CFR part 655 and 29 CFR part 503; and

(2) Submit to USCIS, at the time the employer files its petition, a U.S. Department of Labor attestation, in compliance with this section and 20 CFR 655.65, evidencing that:

(i) Its business is suffering irreparable harm or will suffer impending irreparable harm (that is, permanent and severe financial loss) without the ability to employ all of the H-2B workers requested on the petition filed pursuant to this paragraph (h)(6)(xii);

(ii) All workers requested and/or instructed to apply for a visa have been issued an H-2B visa or otherwise granted H-2B status in fiscal year 2019, 2020, or 2021, unless the H-2B worker is a national of Guatemala, El Salvador, Honduras, or Haiti who is counted towards the 11,500 cap described in paragraph (h)(6)(xii)(A)(2) of this section;

(iii) The employer will comply with all Federal, State, and local employment-related laws and regulations, including, where applicable, health and safety laws and laws related to COVID-19 worker protections; any right to time off or paid time off for COVID-19 vaccination, or to reimbursement for travel to and from the nearest available vaccination site; and that the employer will notify any H-2B workers approved under the supplemental cap in paragraph (h)(6)(xii)(A)(2) of this section, in a language understood by the worker as necessary or reasonable, that all persons in the United States, including nonimmigrants, have equal access to COVID-19 vaccines and vaccine distribution sites;

(iv) The employer will comply with obligations and additional recruitment requirements outlined in 20 CFR 655.65(a)(3) through (5);

(v) The employer will provide documentary evidence of the facts in paragraphs (h)(6)(xii)(B)(2)(i) through (iv) of this section to DHS or DOL upon request; and

(vi) The employer will agree to fully cooperate with any compliance review, evaluation, verification, or inspection conducted by DHS, including an on-site inspection of the employer's facilities, interview of the employer's employees and any other individuals possessing pertinent information, and review of the employer's records related to the compliance with immigration laws and regulations, including but not limited to evidence pertaining to or supporting the eligibility criteria for the FY 2022 supplemental allocations outlined in paragraph (h)(6)(xii)(B) of this section, as a condition for the approval of the petition.

(vii) The employer must attest on Form ETA-9142-B-CAA-6 that it will fully cooperate with any audit, investigation, compliance review, evaluation, verification or inspection conducted by DOL, including an on-site inspection of the employer's facilities, interview of the employer's employees and any other individuals possessing pertinent information, and review of the employer's records related to the compliance with applicable laws and regulations, including but not limited to evidence pertaining to or supporting the eligibility criteria for the FY 2022 supplemental allocations outlined in 20 CFR 655.65(a) and 655.66(a), as a condition for the approval of the H-2B petition. The employer must further attest on Form ETA-9142-B-CAA-6 that it will not impede, interfere, or refuse to cooperate with an employee of the Secretary of the U.S. Department of Labor who is exercising or attempting to exercise DOL's audit or investigative authority pursuant to 20 CFR part 655, subpart A, and 29 CFR 503.25.

(C) Processing. USCIS will reject petitions filed pursuant to paragraph (h)(6)(xii)(A)(1) or (2) of this section that are received after the applicable numerical limitation has been reached or after September 15, 2022, whichever is sooner. USCIS will not approve a petition filed pursuant to this paragraph (h)(6)(xii) on or after October 1, 2022.

(D) Numerical limitations under paragraphs (h)(6)(xii)(A)(1) and (2) of this section. When calculating the numerical limitations under paragraphs (h)(6)(xii)(A)(1) and (2) of this section as authorized under Public Law 117-103, USCIS will make numbers for each allocation available to petitions in the order in which the petitions subject to the respective limitation are received. USCIS will make projections of the number of petitions necessary to achieve the numerical limit of approvals, taking into account historical data related to approvals, denials, revocations, and other relevant factors. USCIS will monitor the number of petitions received (including the number of workers requested when necessary) and will notify the public of the dates that USCIS has received the necessary number of petitions (the "final receipt dates") under paragraph (h)(6)(xii)(A)(1) or (2). The day the public is notified will not control the final receipt dates. When necessary to ensure the fair and orderly allocation of numbers subject to the numerical limitations in paragraphs (h)(6)(xii)(A)(1) and (2), USCIS may randomly select from among the petitions received on the final receipt dates the remaining number of petitions deemed necessary to generate the numerical limit of approvals. This random selection will be made via computer-generated selection. Petitions subject to a numerical limitation not randomly selected or that were received after the final receipt dates that may be applicable under paragraph (h)(6)(xii)(A)(1) or (2) will be rejected. If the final receipt date is any of the first 5 business days on which petitions subject to the applicable numerical limits described in paragraph (h)(6)(xii)(A)(1) or (2) may be received (in other words, if either of the numerical limits described in paragraph (h)(6)(xii)(A)(1) or (2) is reached on any one of the first 5 business days that filings can be made), USCIS will randomly apply all of the numbers among the petitions received on any of those 5 business days.

(E) Sunset. This paragraph (h)(6)(xii) expires on October 1, 2022.

(F) Non-severability. The requirement to file an attestation under paragraph (h)(6)(xii)(B)(2) of this section is intended to be non-severable from the remainder of this paragraph (h)(6)(xii), including, but not limited to, the numerical allocation provisions at paragraphs (h)(6)(xii)(A)(1) and (2) of this section in their entirety. In the event that any part of this paragraph (h)(6)(xii) is enjoined or held to be invalid by any court of competent jurisdiction, the remainder of this paragraph (h)(6)(xii) is also intended to be enjoined or held to be invalid in such jurisdiction, without prejudice to workers already present in the United States under this paragraph (h)(6)(xii), as consistent with law.

(xiii) [Effective Dec. 15, 2022 through Dec. 15, 2025] Special requirements for additional cap allocations under Public Laws 117-103 and 117-180—

(A) Public Law 117-103 and section 101(6) of Division A of Public Law 117-180, Continuing Appropriations and Ukraine Supplemental Appropriations Act, 2023 —

(1) Supplemental allocation for returning workers. Notwithstanding the numerical limitations set forth in paragraph (h)(8)(i)(C) of this section, for fiscal year 2023 only, the Secretary has authorized up to an additional 64,716 visas for aliens who may receive H-2B nonimmigrant visas pursuant to section 204 of Division O of Public Law 117-103, the Consolidated Appropriations Act, 2022, and section 101(6) of Division A of Public Law 117-180, Continuing Appropriations and Ukraine Supplemental Appropriations Act, 2023. An alien may be eligible to receive an H-2B nonimmigrant visa under this paragraph (h)(6)(xiii)(A)(1) if she or he is a returning worker. The term "returning worker" under this paragraph (h)(6)(xiii)(A)(1) means a person who was issued an H-2B visa or was otherwise granted H-2B status in fiscal year 2020, 2021, or 2022. Notwithstanding § 248.2 of this chapter, an alien may not change status to H-2B nonimmigrant under this paragraph (h)(6)(xiii)(A)(1). The additional H-2B visas authorized under this paragraph will be made available to returning workers as follows:

(i) Up to an additional 18,216 visas for aliens who may receive H-2B nonimmigrant visas based on petitions requesting FY 2023 employment start dates on or before March 31, 2023.

(ii) Up to an additional 16,500 visas for aliens who may receive H-2B nonimmigrant visas based on petitions requesting FY 2023 employment start dates from April 1, 2023 to May 14, 2023.

(iii) Up to an additional 10,000 visas available for aliens with employment start dates from May 15, 2023 to September 30, 2023.

(2) Supplemental allocation for nationals of Guatemala, El Salvador, Honduras (Northern Central American countries), or Haiti. Notwithstanding the numerical limitations set forth in paragraph (h)(8)(i)(C) of this section, for fiscal year 2023 only, and in addition to the allocation described in paragraph (h)(6)(xiii)(A)(1) of this section, the Secretary has authorized up to an additional 20,000 visas for aliens who are nationals of Guatemala, El Salvador, Honduras (Northern Central American countries), or Haiti, who may receive H-2B nonimmigrant visas pursuant section 204 of Division O of the Consolidated Appropriations Act, 2022, Public Law 117-103, and section 101(6) of Division A of Public Law 117-180 Continuing Appropriations and Ukraine Supplemental Appropriations Act, 2023, based on petitions with FY 2023 employment start dates. Such workers are not subject to the returning worker requirement in paragraph (h)(6)(xiii)(A)(1). Petitioners must request such workers in an H-2B petition that is separate from H-2B petitions that request returning workers under paragraph (h)(6)(xiii)(A)(1) and must declare that they are requesting these workers in the attestation required under 20 CFR 655.67(a)(1). A petition requesting returning workers under paragraph (h)(6)(xiii)(A)(1), which is accompanied by an attestation indicating that the petitioner is requesting nationals of Northern Central American countries or Haiti, will be rejected, denied or, in the case of a non-frivolous petition, will be approved solely for the number of beneficiaries that are from the Northern Central American countries or Haiti. Notwithstanding § 248.2 of this chapter, an alien may not change status to H-2B nonimmigrant under this paragraph (h)(6)(xiii)(A)(2).

(B) Eligibility. In order to file a petition with USCIS under this paragraph (h)(6)(xiii), the petitioner must:

(1) Comply with all other statutory and regulatory requirements for H-2B classification, including, but not limited to, requirements in this section, under part 103 of this chapter, and under 20 CFR part 655 and 29 CFR part 503; and

(2) Submit to USCIS, at the time the employer files its petition, a U.S. Department of Labor attestation, in compliance with this section and 20 CFR 655.65, evidencing that:

(i) Its business is suffering irreparable harm or will suffer impending irreparable harm (that is, permanent and severe financial loss) without the ability to employ all of the H-2B workers requested on the petition filed pursuant to this paragraph (h)(6)(xiii);

(ii) All workers requested and/or instructed to apply for a visa have been issued an H-2B visa or otherwise granted H-2B status in fiscal year 2020, 2021, or 2022, unless the H-2B worker is a national of Guatemala, El Salvador, Honduras, or Haiti who is counted towards the 20,000 cap described in paragraph (h)(6)(xiii)(A)(2) of this section;

(iii) The employer will comply with all Federal, State, and local employment-related laws and regulations, including, where applicable, health and safety laws and laws related to COVID-19 worker protections and any right to time off or paid time off for COVID-19 vaccination, or to reimbursement for travel to and from the nearest available vaccination site; and that the employer will notify any H-2B workers approved under the supplemental cap in paragraph (h)(6)(xiii)(A)(2) of this section, in a language understood by the worker as necessary or reasonable, that all persons in the United States, including nonimmigrants, have equal access to COVID-19 vaccines and vaccine distribution sites;

(iv) The employer will comply with obligations and additional recruitment requirements outlined in 20 CFR 655.65(a)(3) through (5);

(v) The employer will provide documentary evidence of the facts in paragraphs (h)(6)(xiii)(B)(2)(i) through (iv) of this section to DHS or DOL upon request; and

(vi) The employer will agree to fully cooperate with any compliance review, evaluation, verification, or inspection conducted by DHS, including an on-site inspection of the employer's facilities, interview of the employer's employees and any other individuals possessing pertinent information, and review of the employer's records related to the compliance with immigration laws and regulations, including but not limited to evidence pertaining to or supporting the eligibility criteria for the FY 2023 supplemental allocations outlined in paragraph (h)(6)(xiii)(B) of this section, as a condition for the approval of the petition.

(vii) The employer will fully cooperate with any audit, investigation, compliance review, evaluation, verification or inspection conducted by DOL, including an on-site inspection of the employer's facilities, interview of the employer's employees and any other individuals possessing pertinent information, and review of the employer's records related to the compliance with applicable laws and regulations, including but not limited to evidence pertaining to or supporting the eligibility criteria for the FY 2023 supplemental allocations outlined in 20 CFR 655.65(a) and 655.67(a), as a condition for the approval of the H-2B petition. The employer must attest to this on Form ETA-9142-B-CAA-7 and must further attest on Form ETA-9142-B-CAA-7 that it will not impede, interfere, or refuse to cooperate with an employee of the Secretary of the U.S. Department of Labor who is exercising or attempting to exercise DOL's audit or investigative authority pursuant to 20 CFR part 655, subpart A, and 29 CFR 503.25.

(C) Processing—

(1) Petitions filed pursuant to paragraph (h)(6)(xiii)(A)(1)(i) requesting FY 2023 employment start dates on or before March 31, 2023. USCIS will reject petitions filed pursuant to paragraph (h)(6)(xiii)(A)(1)(i) of this section requesting employment start dates on or before March 31, 2023 that are received after the applicable numerical limitation has been reached or after September 15, 2023.

(2) Petitions filed pursuant to paragraph (h)(6)(xiii)(A)(1)(ii) requesting FY 2023 employment start dates from April 1, 2023 to May 14, 2023. USCIS will reject petitions filed pursuant to paragraph (h)(6)(xiii)(A)(1)(ii) of this section requesting employment start dates from April 1, 2023 to May 14, 2023 that are received earlier than 15 days after the INA section 214(g) cap for the second half FY 2023 has been met or after the applicable numerical limitation has been reached or after September 15, 2023.

(3) Petitions filed pursuant to paragraph (h)(6)(xiii)(A)(1)(iii) of this section requesting FY 2023 employment start dates from May 15, 2023 and September 30, 2023. USCIS will reject petitions filed pursuant to paragraph (h)(6)(xiii)(A)(1)(iii) of this section requesting employment start dates from May 15, 2023 to September 30, 2023, that are received earlier than 45 days after the INA section 214(g) cap for the second half FY 2023 has been met, or after the applicable numerical limitation has been reached or after September 15, 2023.

(4) Petitions filed pursuant to paragraph (h)(6)(xiii)(A)(2) of this section requesting nationals of Guatemala, El Salvador, Honduras (Northern Central American countries), or Haiti with FY 2023 employment start dates. USCIS will reject petitions filed pursuant to paragraph (h)(6)(xiii)(A)(2) of this section that have a date of need on or after April 1, 2023 and are received earlier than 15 days after the INA section 214(g) cap for the second half of FY 2023 is met, or after the applicable numerical limitation has been reached or after September 15, 2023.

(5) USCIS will not approve a petition filed pursuant to paragraph (h)(6)(xiii) of this section on or after October 1, 2023.

(D) Numerical limitations under paragraphs (h)(6)(xiii)(A)(1) and (2) of this section. When calculating the numerical limitations under paragraphs (h)(6)(xiii)(A)(1) and (2) of this section as authorized under Public Law 117-103, as extended by Public Law 117-180, USCIS will make numbers for each allocation available to petitions in the order in which the petitions subject to the respective limitation are received. USCIS will make projections of the number of petitions necessary to achieve the numerical limit of approvals, taking into account historical data related to approvals, denials, revocations, and other relevant factors. USCIS will monitor the number of petitions received (including the number of workers requested when necessary) and will notify the public of the dates that USCIS has received the necessary number of petitions (the "final receipt dates") under paragraph (h)(6)(xiii)(A)(1) or (2) of this section. The day the public is notified will not control the final receipt dates. When necessary to ensure the fair and orderly allocation of numbers subject to the numerical limitations in paragraphs (h)(6)(xiii)(A)(1) and (2) of this section, USCIS may randomly select from among the petitions received on the final receipt dates the remaining number of petitions deemed necessary to generate the numerical limit of approvals. This random selection will be made via computer-generated selection. Petitions subject to a numerical limitation not randomly selected or that were received after the final receipt dates that may be applicable under paragraph (h)(6)(xiii)(A)(1) or (2) of this section will be rejected. If the final receipt date is any of the first 5 business days on which petitions subject to the applicable numerical limits described in paragraph (h)(6)(xiii)(A)(1) or (2) of this section may be received (in other words, if either of the numerical limits described in paragraph (h)(6)(xiii)(A)(1) or (2) of this section is reached on any one of the first 5 business days that filings can be made), USCIS will randomly apply all of the numbers among the petitions received on any of those 5 business days.

(E) Sunset. This paragraph (h)(6)(xiii) expires on October 1, 2023.

(F) Non-severability. The requirement to file an attestation under paragraph (h)(6)(xiii)(B)(2) of this section is intended to be non-severable from the remainder of paragraph (h)(6)(xiii), including, but not limited to, the numerical allocation provisions at paragraphs (h)(6)(xiii)(A)(1) and (2) of this section in their entirety. In the event that any part of this paragraph (h)(6)(xiii) is enjoined or held to be invalid by any court of competent jurisdiction, the remainder of this paragraph (h)(6)(xiii) is also intended to be enjoined or held to be invalid in such jurisdiction, without prejudice to workers already present in the United States under this paragraph (h)(6)(xiii), as consistent with law.

(xiv) Special requirements for additional cap allocations under Public Laws 117-328 and 118-15—

(A) Public Law 117-328 and section 101(6) of Division A of Public Law 118-15, Continuing Appropriations Act, 2024 and Other Extensions Act —

(1) Supplemental allocation for returning workers. Notwithstanding the numerical limitations set forth in paragraph (h)(8)(i)(C) of this section, for fiscal year 2024 only, the Secretary has authorized up to an additional 64,716 visas for aliens who may receive H-2B nonimmigrant visas pursuant to section 303 of Division O of Public Law 117-328, the Consolidated Appropriations Act, 2023, and section 101(6) of Division A of Public Law 118-15, Continuing Appropriations Act, 2024 and Other Extensions Act. An alien may be eligible to receive an H-2B nonimmigrant visa under this paragraph (h)(6)(xiv)(A)(1) if she or he is a returning worker. The term "returning worker" under this paragraph (h)(6)(xiv)(A)(1) means a person who was issued an H-2B visa or was otherwise granted H-2B status in fiscal year 2021, 2022, or 2023. Notwithstanding § 248.2 of this chapter, an alien may not change status to H-2B nonimmigrant under this paragraph (h)(6)(xiv)(A)(1). The additional H-2B visas authorized under this paragraph will be made available to returning workers as follows:

(i) Up to an additional 20,716 visas for aliens who may receive H-2B nonimmigrant visas based on petitions requesting FY 2024 employment start dates on or before March 31, 2024.

(ii) Up to an additional 19,000 visas for aliens who may receive H-2B nonimmigrant visas based on petitions requesting FY 2024 employment start dates from April 1, 2024 to May 14, 2024.

(iii) Up to an additional 5,000 visas available for aliens with employment start dates from May 15, 2024 to September 30, 2024.

(2) Supplemental allocation for nationals of Guatemala, El Salvador, Honduras, Haiti, Colombia, Ecuador, or Costa Rica. Notwithstanding the numerical limitations set forth in paragraph (h)(8)(i)(C) of this section, for fiscal year 2024 only, and in addition to the allocation described in paragraph (h)(6)(xiv)(A)(1) of this section, the Secretary has authorized up to an additional 20,000 visas for aliens who are nationals of Guatemala, El Salvador, Honduras, Haiti, Colombia, Ecuador, or Costa Rica, who may receive H-2B nonimmigrant visas pursuant section 303 of Division O of the Consolidated Appropriations Act, 2023, Public Law 117-328, and section 101(6) of Division A of Public Law 118-15 Continuing Appropriations Act, 2024 and Other Extensions Act, based on petitions with FY 2024 employment start dates. Such workers are not subject to the returning worker requirement in paragraph (h)(6)(xiv)(A)(1). Petitioners must request such workers in an H-2B petition that is separate from H-2B petitions that request returning workers under paragraph (h)(6)(xiv)(A)(1) and must declare that they are requesting these workers in the attestation Form ETA-9142-B-CAA-8 required under 20 CFR 655.65(a)(1). A petition requesting returning workers under paragraph (h)(6)(xiv)(A)(1), which is accompanied by an attestation indicating that the petitioner is requesting nationals of Guatemala, El Salvador, Honduras, Haiti, Colombia, Ecuador, or Costa Rica, will be rejected, denied or, in the case of a non-frivolous petition, approved solely for the number of beneficiaries that are from the Guatemala, El Salvador, Honduras, Haiti, Colombia, Ecuador, or Costa Rica. Notwithstanding § 248.2 of this chapter, an alien may not change status to H-2B nonimmigrant under this paragraph (h)(6)(xiv)(A)(2).

(B) Eligibility. In order to file a petition with USCIS under this paragraph (h)(6)(xiv), the petitioner must:

(1) Comply with all other statutory and regulatory requirements for H-2B classification, including, but not limited to, requirements in this section, under part 103 of this chapter, and under 20 CFR part 655 and 29 CFR part 503; and

(2) Submit to USCIS, at the time the employer files its petition, a U.S. Department of Labor attestation, in compliance with this section and 20 CFR 655.64, evidencing that:

(i) Its business is suffering irreparable harm or will suffer impending irreparable harm (that is, permanent and severe financial loss) without the ability to employ all of the H-2B workers requested on the petition filed pursuant to this paragraph (h)(6)(xiv);

(ii) All workers requested and/or instructed to apply for a visa have been issued an H-2B visa or otherwise granted H-2B status in fiscal year 2021, 2022, or 2023, unless the H-2B worker is a national of Guatemala, El Salvador, Honduras, Haiti, Colombia, Ecuador, or Costa Rica who is counted towards the 20,000 cap described in paragraph (h)(6)(xiv)(A)(2) of this section;

(iii) The employer will comply with obligations and additional recruitment requirements outlined in 20 CFR 655.64(a)(3) through (5);

(iv) The employer will provide documentary evidence of the facts in paragraphs (h)(6)(xiv)(B)(2)(i) through (iii) of this section to DHS and/or DOL upon request; and

(v) The employer will agree to fully cooperate with any compliance review, evaluation, verification, or inspection conducted by DHS, including an on-site inspection of the employer's facilities, interview of the employer's employees and any other individuals possessing pertinent information, and review of the employer's records related to the compliance with immigration laws and regulations, including but not limited to evidence pertaining to or supporting the eligibility criteria for the FY 2024 supplemental allocations outlined in paragraph (h)(6)(xiv)(B) of this section, as a condition for the approval of the petition.

(vi) The employer will fully cooperate with any audit, investigation, compliance review, evaluation, verification or inspection conducted by DOL, including an on-site inspection of the employer's facilities, interview of the employer's employees and any other individuals possessing pertinent information, and review of the employer's records related to the compliance with applicable laws and regulations, including but not limited to evidence pertaining to or supporting the eligibility criteria for the FY 2024 supplemental allocations outlined in 20 CFR 655.64(a) and 655.65(a), as a condition for the approval of the H-2B petition. The employer must attest to this on Form ETA-9142-B-CAA-8 and must further attest on Form ETA-9142-B-CAA-8 that it will not impede, interfere, or refuse to cooperate with an employee of the Secretary of the U.S. Department of Labor who is exercising or attempting to exercise DOL's audit or investigative authority pursuant to 20 CFR part 655, subpart A, and 29 CFR 503.25.

(C) Processing—

(1) Petitions filed pursuant to paragraph (h)(6)(xiv)(A)(1)(a) requesting FY 2024 employment start dates on or before March 31, 2024. USCIS will reject petitions filed pursuant to paragraph (h)(6)(xiv)(A)(1)(a) of this section requesting employment start dates on or before March 31, 2024 that are received after the applicable numerical limitation has been reached or after September 16, 2024.

(2) Petitions filed pursuant to paragraph (h)(6)(xiv)(A)(1)(ii) of this section requesting FY 2024 employment start dates from April 1, 2024 to May 14, 2024. USCIS will reject petitions filed pursuant to paragraph (h)(6)(xiv)(A)(1)(ii) of this section requesting employment start dates from April 1, 2024 to May 14, 2024 that are received earlier than 15 days after the INA section 214(g) cap for the second half FY 2024 has been met, or after the applicable numerical limitation has been reached or after September 16, 2024.

(3) Petitions filed pursuant to paragraph (h)(6)(xiv)(A)(1)(iii) of this section requesting FY 2024 employment start dates from May 15, 2024 and September 30, 2024. USCIS will reject petitions filed pursuant to paragraph (h)(6)(xiv)(A)(1)(iii) of this section requesting employment start dates from May 15, 2024 to September 30, 2024 that are received earlier than 45 days after the INA section 214(g) cap for the second half FY 2024 has been met, or after the applicable numerical limitation has been reached or after September 16, 2024.

(4) Petitions filed pursuant to paragraph (h)(6)(xiv)(A)(2) requesting nationals of Guatemala, El Salvador, Honduras, Haiti, Colombia, Ecuador, or Costa Rica with FY 2024 employment start dates. USCIS will reject petitions filed pursuant to paragraph (h)(6)(xiv)(A)(2) of this section that have a date of need on or after April 1, 2024 and are received earlier than 15 days after the INA section 214(g) cap for the second half of FY 2024 is met, or after the applicable numerical limitation has been reached or after September 16, 2024.

(5) USCIS will not approve a petition filed pursuant to this paragraph (h)(6)(xiv) on or after October 1, 2024.

(D) Numerical limitations under paragraphs (h)(6)(xiv)(A)(1) and (2) of this section. When calculating the numerical limitations under paragraphs (h)(6)(xiv)(A)(1) and (2) of this section as authorized under Public Law 117-328, as extended by Public Law 118-15, USCIS will make numbers for each allocation available to petitions in the order in which the petitions subject to the respective limitation are received. USCIS will make projections of the number of petitions necessary to achieve the numerical limit of approvals, taking into account historical data related to approvals, denials, revocations, and other relevant factors. USCIS will monitor the number of petitions received (including the number of workers requested when necessary) and will notify the public of the dates that USCIS has received the necessary number of petitions (the "final receipt dates") under paragraph (h)(6)(xiv)(A)(1) or (2). The day the public is notified will not control the final receipt dates. When necessary to ensure the fair and orderly allocation of numbers subject to the numerical limitations in paragraphs (h)(6)(xiv)(A)(1) and (2), USCIS may randomly select from among the petitions received on the final receipt dates the remaining number of petitions deemed necessary to generate the numerical limit of approvals. This random selection will be made via computer-generated selection. Petitions subject to a numerical limitation not randomly selected or that were received after the final receipt dates that may be applicable under paragraph (h)(6)(xiv)(A)(1) or (2) will be rejected. If the final receipt date is any of the first 5 business days on which petitions subject to the applicable numerical limits described in paragraph (h)(6)(xiv)(A)(1) or (2) may be received (in other words, if either of the numerical limits described in paragraph (h)(6)(xiv)(A)(1) or (2) is reached on any one of the first 5 business days that filings can be made), USCIS will randomly apply all of the numbers among the petitions received on any of those 5 business days.

(E) Sunset. This paragraph (h)(6)(xiv) expires on October 1, 2024.

(F) Non-severability. The requirement to file an attestation under paragraph (h)(6)(xiv)(B)(2) of this section is intended to be non-severable from the remainder of this paragraph (h)(6)(xiv), including, but not limited to, the numerical allocation provisions at paragraphs (h)(6)(xiv)(A)(1) and (2) of this section in their entirety. In the event that any part of this paragraph (h)(6)(xiv) is enjoined or held to be invalid by any court of competent jurisdiction, the remainder of this paragraph (h)(6)(xiv) is also intended to be enjoined or held to be invalid in such jurisdiction, without prejudice to workers already present in the United States under this paragraph (h)(6)(xiv), as consistent with law.

(xv) Special requirements for additional cap allocations under Public Laws 118-47 and 118-83—

(A) Public Law 118-47 and sections 101(6) and 106, Division A, Title I of Public Law 118-83 —

(1) Supplemental allocation for returning workers. Notwithstanding the numerical limitations set forth in paragraph (h)(8)(i)(C) of this section, for fiscal year 2025 only, the Secretary has authorized up to an additional 64,716 visas for aliens who may receive H-2B nonimmigrant visas pursuant to section 105 of Division G, Title I of Public Law 118-47, the Further Consolidated Appropriations Act, 2024, and sections 101(6) and 106, Division A, Title I of the Continuing Appropriations and Extensions Act, 2025, Public Law 118-83. An alien may be eligible to receive an H-2B nonimmigrant visa under this paragraph (h)(6)(xv)(A)(1) if she or he is a returning worker. The term "returning worker" under this paragraph (h)(6)(xv)(A)(1) means a person who was issued an H-2B visa or was otherwise granted H-2B status in fiscal year 2022, 2023, or 2024. Notwithstanding § 248.2 of this chapter, an alien may not change status to H-2B nonimmigrant under this paragraph (h)(6)(xv)(A)(1). The additional H-2B visas authorized under this paragraph will be made available to returning workers as follows:

(i) Up to an additional 20,716 visas for aliens who may receive H-2B nonimmigrant visas based on petitions requesting FY 2025 employment start dates on or before March 31, 2025.

(ii) Up to an additional 19,000 visas for aliens who may receive H-2B nonimmigrant visas based on petitions requesting FY 2025 employment start dates from April 1, 2025 to May 14, 2025.

(iii) Up to an additional 5,000 visas available for aliens with employment start dates from May 15, 2025 to September 30, 2025.

(2) Supplemental allocation for nationals of Guatemala, El Salvador, Honduras, Haiti, Colombia, Ecuador, or Costa Rica. Notwithstanding the numerical limitations set forth in paragraph (h)(8)(i)(C) of this section, for fiscal year 2025 only, and in addition to the allocation described in paragraph (h)(6)(xv)(A)(1) of this section, the Secretary has authorized up to an additional 20,000 visas for aliens who are nationals of Guatemala, El Salvador, Honduras, Haiti, Colombia, Ecuador, or Costa Rica, who may receive H-2B nonimmigrant visas pursuant to section 105 of Division G, Title I of Public Law 118-47, the Further Consolidated Appropriations Act, 2024, and sections 101(6) and 106 of Division A, Title I of the Continuing Appropriations and Extensions Act, 2025, Public Law 118-83, based on petitions with FY 2025 employment start dates. Such workers are not subject to the returning worker requirement in paragraph (h)(6)(xv)(A)(1). Petitioners must request such workers in an H-2B petition that is separate from H-2B petitions that request returning workers under paragraph (h)(6)(xv)(A)(1) and must declare that they are requesting these workers in the attestation Form ETA-9142-B-CAA-9 required under 20 CFR 655.68(a)(1). A petition requesting returning workers under paragraph (h)(6)(xv)(A)(1), which is accompanied by an attestation indicating that the petitioner is requesting nationals of Guatemala, El Salvador, Honduras, Haiti, Colombia, Ecuador, or Costa Rica, will be rejected, denied or, in the case of a non-frivolous petition, approved solely for the number of beneficiaries that are from Guatemala, El Salvador, Honduras, Haiti, Colombia, Ecuador, or Costa Rica. Notwithstanding § 248.2 of this chapter, an alien may not change status to H-2B nonimmigrant under this paragraph (h)(6)(xv)(A)(2).

(B) Eligibility. In order to file a petition with USCIS under this paragraph (h)(6)(xv), the petitioner must:

(1) Comply with all other statutory and regulatory requirements for H-2B classification, including, but not limited to, requirements in this section, under part 103 of this chapter, and under 20 CFR part 655 and 29 CFR part 503; and (2) Submit to USCIS, at the time the employer files its petition, a U.S. Department of Labor attestation, in compliance with this section and 20 CFR 655.64, evidencing that:

(i) Its business is suffering irreparable harm or will suffer impending irreparable harm (that is, permanent and severe financial loss) without the ability to employ all of the H-2B workers requested on the petition filed pursuant to this paragraph (h)(6)(xv);

(ii) All workers requested and/or instructed to apply for a visa have been issued an H-2B visa or otherwise granted H-2B status in fiscal year 2022, 2023, or 2024, unless the H-2B worker is a national of Guatemala, El Salvador, Honduras, Haiti, Colombia, Ecuador, or Costa Rica who is counted towards the 20,000 cap described in paragraph (h)(6)(xv)(A)(2) of this section;

(iii) The employer will comply with obligations and additional recruitment requirements outlined in 20 CFR 655.64(a)(3) through (5);

(iv) The employer will provide documentary evidence of the facts in paragraphs (h)(6)(xv)(B)(2)(i) through (iii) of this section to DHS and/or DOL upon request; and

(v) The employer will agree to fully cooperate with any compliance review, evaluation, verification, or inspection conducted by DHS, including an on-site inspection of the employer's facilities, interview of the employer's employees and any other individuals possessing pertinent information, and review of the employer's records related to the compliance with immigration laws and regulations, including but not limited to evidence pertaining to or supporting the eligibility criteria for the FY 2025 supplemental allocations outlined in paragraph (h)(6)(xv)(B) of this section, as a condition for the approval of the petition.

(vi) The employer will fully cooperate with any audit, investigation, compliance review, evaluation, verification or inspection conducted by DOL, including an on-site inspection of the employer's facilities, interview of the employer's employees and any other individuals possessing pertinent information, and review of the employer's records related to the compliance with applicable laws and regulations, including but not limited to evidence pertaining to or supporting the eligibility criteria for the FY 2025 supplemental allocations outlined in 20 CFR 655.64(a) and 655.68(a), as a condition for the approval of the H-2B petition. The employer must attest to this on Form ETA-9142-B-CAA-9 and must further attest on Form ETA-9142-B-CAA-9 that it will not impede, interfere, or refuse to cooperate with an employee of the Secretary of the U.S. Department of Labor who is exercising or attempting to exercise DOL's audit or investigative authority pursuant to 20 CFR part 655, subpart A, and 29 CFR 503.25.

(C) Processing—

(1) Petitions filed pursuant to paragraph (h)(6)(xv)(A)(1)(i) of this section requesting FY 2025 employment start dates on or before March 31, 2025. USCIS will reject petitions filed pursuant to paragraph (h)(6)(xv)(A)(1)(i) of this section requesting employment start dates on or before March 31, 2025 that are received after the applicable numerical limitation has been reached or after September 15, 2025.

(2) Petitions filed pursuant to paragraph (h)(6)(xv)(A)(1)(ii) of this section requesting FY 2025 employment start dates from April 1, 2025 to May 14, 2025. USCIS will reject petitions filed pursuant to paragraph (h)(6)(xv)(A)(1)(ii) of this section requesting employment start dates from April 1, 2025 to May 14, 2025 that are received earlier than 15 days after the INA section 214(g) cap for the second half FY 2024 has been met, or after the applicable numerical limitation has been reached or after September 15, 2025.

(3) Petitions filed pursuant to paragraph (h)(6)(xv)(A)(1)(iii) of this section requesting FY 2025 employment start dates from May 15, 2025 and September 30, 2025. USCIS will reject petitions filed pursuant to paragraph (h)(6)(xv)(A)(1)(iii) of this section requesting employment start dates from May 15, 2025 to September 30, 2025 that are received earlier than 45 days after the INA section 214(g) cap for the second half FY 2025 has been met, or after the applicable numerical limitation has been reached or after September 15, 2025.

(4) Petitions filed pursuant to paragraph (h)(6)(xv)(A)(2) requesting nationals of Guatemala, El Salvador, Honduras, Haiti, Colombia, Ecuador, or Costa Rica with FY 2025 employment start dates. USCIS will reject petitions filed pursuant to paragraph (h)(6)(xv)(A)(2) of this section that have a date of need on or after April 1, 2025, and are received earlier than 15 days after the INA section 214(g) cap for the second half of FY 2025 is met, or after the applicable numerical limitation has been reached or after September 15, 2025.

(5) USCIS will not approve a petition filed pursuant to this paragraph (h)(6)(xv) on or after October 1, 2025.

(D) Numerical limitations under paragraphs (h)(6)(xv)(A)(1) and (2) of this section. When calculating the numerical limitations under paragraphs (h)(6)(xv)(A)(1) and (2) of this section as authorized under section 105 of Division G, Title I of Public Law 118-47, the Further Consolidated Appropriations Act, 2024, and sections 101(6) and 106 of Division A, Title I of the Continuing Appropriations and Extensions Act, 2025, Public Law 118-83, USCIS will make numbers for each allocation available to petitions in the order in which the petitions subject to the respective limitation are received. USCIS will make projections of the number of petitions necessary to achieve the numerical limit of approvals, taking into account historical data related to approvals, denials, revocations, and other relevant factors. USCIS will monitor the number of petitions received (including the number of workers requested when necessary) and will notify the public of the dates that USCIS has received the necessary number of petitions (the "final receipt dates") under paragraph (h)(6)(xv)(A)(1) or (2). The day the public is notified will not control the final receipt dates. When necessary to ensure the fair and orderly allocation of numbers subject to the numerical limitations in paragraphs (h)(6)(xv)(A)(1) and (2), USCIS may randomly select from among the petitions received on the final receipt dates the remaining number of petitions deemed necessary to generate the numerical limit of approvals. This random selection will be made via computer-generated selection. Petitions subject to a numerical limitation not randomly selected or that were received after the final receipt dates that may be applicable under paragraph (h)(6)(xv)(A)(1) or (2) will be rejected. If the final receipt date is any of the first 5 business days on which petitions subject to the applicable numerical limits described in paragraph (h)(6)(xv)(A)(1) or (2) may be received (in other words, if either of the numerical limits described in paragraph (h)(6)(xv)(A)(1) or (2) is reached on any one of the first 5 business days that filings can be made), USCIS will randomly apply all of the numbers among the petitions received on any of those 5 business days.

(E) Sunset. This paragraph (h)(6)(xv) expires on October 1, 2025.

(F) Non-severability. The requirement to file an attestation under paragraph (h)(6)(xv)(B)(2) of this section is intended to be non-severable from the remainder of this paragraph (h)(6)(xv), including, but not limited to, the entirety of the numerical allocation provisions at paragraphs (h)(6)(xv)(A)(1) and (2) of this section. In the event that any part of this paragraph (h)(6)(xv) is enjoined or held to be invalid by any court of competent jurisdiction, the remainder of this paragraph (h)(6)(xv) is also intended to be enjoined or held to be invalid in such jurisdiction, without prejudice to workers already present in the United States under this paragraph (h)(6)(xv), as consistent with law.

(7) Petition for alien trainee or participant in a special education exchange visitor program (H-3) --

(i) Alien trainee. The H-3 trainee is a nonimmigrant who seeks to enter the United States at the invitation of an organization or individual for the purpose of receiving training in any field of endeavor, such as agriculture, commerce, communications, finance, government, transportation, or the professions, as well as training in a purely industrial establishment. This category shall not apply to physicians, who are statutorily ineligible to use H-3 classification in order to receive any type of graduate medical education or training.

(A) Externs. A hospital approved by the American Medical Association or the American Osteopathic Association for either an internship or residency program may petition to classify as an H-3 trainee a medical student attending a medical school abroad, if the alien will engage in employment as an extern during his/her medical school vacation.

(B) Nurses. A petitioner may seek H-3 classification for a nurse who is not H-1 if it can be established that there is a genuine need for the nurse to receive a brief period of training that is unavailable in the alien's native country and such training is designed to benefit the nurse and the overseas employer upon the nurse's return to the country of origin, if:

(1) The beneficiary has obtained a full and unrestricted license to practice professional nursing in the country where the beneficiary obtained a nursing education, or such education was obtained in the United States or Canada; and

(2) The petitioner provides a statement certifying that the beneficiary is fully qualified under the laws governing the place where the training will be received to engage in such training, and that under those laws the petitioner is authorized to give the beneficiary the desired training.

(ii) Evidence required for petition involving alien trainee --

(A) Conditions. The petitioner is required to demonstrate that:

(1) The proposed training is not available in the alien's own country;

(2) The beneficiary will not be placed in a position which is in the normal operation of the business and in which citizens and resident workers are regularly employed;

(3) The beneficiary will not engage in productive employment unless such employment is incidental and necessary to the training; and

(4) The training will benefit the beneficiary in pursuing a career outside the United States.

(B) Description of training program. Each petition for a trainee must include a statement which:

(1) Describes the type of training and supervision to be given, and the structure of the training program;

(2) Sets forth the proportion of time that will be devoted to productive employment;

(3) Shows the number of hours that will be spent, respectively, in classroom instruction and in on-the-job training;

(4) Describes the career abroad for which the training will prepare the alien;

(5) Indicates the reasons why such training cannot be obtained in the alien's country and why it is necessary for the alien to be trained in the United States; and

(6) Indicates the source of any remuneration received by the trainee and any benefit which will accrue to the petitioner for providing the training.

(iii) Restrictions on training program for alien trainee. A training program may not be approved which:

(A) Deals in generalities with no fixed schedule, objectives, or means of evaluation;

(B) Is incompatible with the nature of the petitioner's business or enterprise;

(C) Is on behalf of a beneficiary who already possesses substantial training and expertise in the proposed field of training;

(D) Is in a field in which it is unlikely that the knowledge or skill will be used outside the United States;

(E) Will result in productive employment beyond that which is incidental and necessary to the training;

(F) Is designed to recruit and train aliens for the ultimate staffing of domestic operations in the United States;

(G) Does not establish that the petitioner has the physical plant and sufficiently trained manpower to provide the training specified; or

(H) Is designed to extend the total allowable period of practical training previously authorized a nonimmigrant student.

(iv) Petition for participant in a special education exchange visitor program --

(A) General Requirements.

(1) The H-3 participant in a special education training program must be coming to the United States to participate in a structured program which provides for practical training and experience in the education of children with physical, mental, or emotional disabilities.

(2) The petition must be filed by a facility which has professionally trained staff and a structured program for providing education to children with disabilities, and for providing training and hands-on experience to participants in the special education exchange visitor program.

(3) The requirements in this section for alien trainees shall not apply to petitions for participants in a special education exchange visitor program.

(B) Evidence. An H-3 petition for a participant in a special education exchange visitor program shall be accompanied by:

(1) A description of the training program and the facility's professional staff and details of the alien's participation in the training program (any custodial care of children must be incidental to the training), and

(2) Evidence that the alien participant is nearing completion of a baccalaureate or higher degree in special education, or already holds such a degree, or has extensive prior training and experience in teaching

children with physical, mental, or emotional disabilities.

(8) Numerical limits --

(i) Limits on affected categories. During each fiscal year, the total number of aliens who can be provided nonimmigrant classification is limited as follows:

(A) Aliens classified as H-1B nonimmigrants, excluding those involved in Department of Defense research and development projects or coproduction projects, may not exceed the limits identified in section 214(g)(1)(A) of the Act.

(B) Aliens classified as H-1B nonimmigrants to work for DOD research and development projects or coproduction projects may not exceed 100 at any time.

(C) Aliens classified as H-2B nonimmigrants may not exceed 66,000.

(D) Aliens classified as H-3 nonimmigrant participants in a special education exchange visitor program may not exceed 50.

(E) Aliens classified as H-1C nonimmigrants may not exceed 500 in a fiscal year.

(ii) Procedures.

(A) Each alien issued a visa or otherwise provided nonimmigrant status under sections 101(a)(15)(H)(i)(b), 101(a)(15)(H)(i)(c), or 101(a)(15)(H)(ii) of the Act shall be counted for purposes of any applicable numerical limit, unless otherwise exempt from such numerical limit. Requests for petition extension or extension of an alien's stay shall not be counted for the purpose of the numerical limit. The spouse and children of principal H aliens are classified as H-4 nonimmigrants and shall not be counted against numerical limits applicable to principals.

(B) When an approved petition is not used because the beneficiary(ies) does not apply for admission to the United States, the petitioner shall notify the Service Center Director who approved the petition that the number(s) has not been used. The petition shall be revoked pursuant to paragraph (h)(11)(ii) of this section and USCIS will take into account the unused number during the appropriate fiscal year.

(C) If the total numbers available in a fiscal year are used, new petitions and the accompanying fee shall be rejected and returned with a notice that numbers are unavailable for the particular nonimmigrant classification until the beginning of the next fiscal year. Petitions received after the total numbers available in a fiscal year are used stating that the alien beneficiaries are exempt from the numerical limitation will be denied and filing fees will not be returned or refunded if USCIS later determines that such beneficiaries are subject to the numerical limitation.

(iii) H-1B numerical limitations--

(A) Registration —

(1) Registration requirement. Except as provided in paragraph (h)(8)(iv) of this section, before a petitioner can file an H-1B cap-subject petition for a beneficiary who may be counted under section 214(g)(1)(A) of the Act ("H-1B regular cap") or eligible for exemption under section 214(g)(5)(C) of the Act ("H-1B advanced degree exemption"), the petitioner must register to file a petition on behalf of a beneficiary electronically through the USCIS website (www.uscis.gov). To be eligible to file a petition for a beneficiary who may be counted against the H-1B regular cap or the H-1B advanced degree exemption for a particular fiscal year, a registration must be properly submitted in accordance with 8 CFR 103.2(a)(1), paragraph (h)(8)(iii) of this section, and the form instructions, for the same fiscal year.

(2) Limitation on beneficiaries. A prospective petitioner must electronically submit a separate registration for each beneficiary it seeks to register, and each beneficiary must be named. A petitioner may only submit one registration per beneficiary in any fiscal year. If a petitioner submits more than one registration per beneficiary in the same fiscal year, all registrations filed by that petitioner relating to that beneficiary for that fiscal year may be considered invalid, and USCIS may deny or revoke the approval of any H-1B petition filed for the beneficiary based on those registrations. If USCIS determines that registrations were submitted for the same beneficiary by the same or different registrants, but using different identifying information, USCIS may find those registrations invalid and deny or revoke the approval of any H-1B petition filed based on those registrations. Petitioners will be given notice and the opportunity to respond before USCIS denies or revokes the approval of a petition.

(3) Initial registration period. The annual initial registration period will last a minimum of 14 calendar days and will start at least 14 calendar days before the earliest date on which H-1B cap-subject petitions may be filed for a particular fiscal year, consistent with paragraph (h)(2)(i)(I) of this section. USCIS will announce the start and end dates of the initial registration period on the USCIS website at www.uscis.gov for each fiscal year. USCIS will announce the start of the initial registration period at least 30 calendar days in advance of such date.

(4) Selecting registrations based on unique beneficiaries. Registrations will be counted based on the number of unique beneficiaries who are registered. USCIS will separately notify each registrant that their registration on behalf of a beneficiary has been selected, and that the petitioner(s) may file a petition(s) for that beneficiary. A petitioner may file an H-1B cap-subject petition on behalf of a registered beneficiary only after their properly submitted registration for that beneficiary has been selected for that fiscal year.

(i) Should a random selection be necessary, as provided in paragraphs (h)(8)(iii)(A)(5)(ii), (h)(8)(iii)(A)(6)(ii), and (h)(8)(iii)(A)(7) of this section, each unique beneficiary will only be counted once towards the random selection of registrations, regardless of how many registrations were submitted for that beneficiary.

(ii) Registrations must include the beneficiary's valid passport information or valid travel document information, as specified in the form instructions. Each beneficiary must only be registered under one passport or travel document, and if or when the beneficiary is abroad, the passport information or travel document information must correspond to the passport or travel document the beneficiary intends to use to enter the United States.

(5) Regular cap selection. In determining whether there are enough registrations for unique beneficiaries to meet the H-1B regular cap, USCIS will consider all properly submitted registrations relating to beneficiaries that may be counted under section 214(g)(1)(A) of the Act, including those that may also be eligible for exemption under section 214(g)(5)(C) of the Act. Registrations will be counted based on the number of unique beneficiaries that are registered.

(i) Fewer registrations than needed to meet the H-1B regular cap. At the end of the annual initial registration period, if USCIS determines that it has received fewer registrations for unique beneficiaries than needed to meet the H-1B regular cap, USCIS will notify all petitioners that have properly registered that their registrations have been selected. USCIS will keep the registration period open beyond the initial registration period, until it determines that it has received a sufficient number of registrations for unique beneficiaries to meet the H-1B regular cap. Once USCIS has received a sufficient number of registrations for unique beneficiaries to meet the H-1B regular cap, USCIS will no longer accept registrations for petitions subject to the H-1B regular cap under section 214(g)(1)(A) of the Act. USCIS will monitor the number of registrations received and will notify the public of the date that USCIS has received the necessary number of registrations for unique beneficiaries (the "final registration date"). The day the public is notified will not control the applicable final registration date. When necessary to ensure the fair and orderly allocation of numbers under section 214(g)(1)(A) of the Act, USCIS may randomly select the remaining number of registrations for unique beneficiaries deemed necessary to meet the H-1B regular cap from among the registrations received on the final registration date. This random selection will be made via computer-generated selection, based on the unique beneficiary.

(ii) Sufficient registrations to meet the H-1B regular cap during initial registration period. At the end of the initial registration period, if USCIS determines that it has received more than sufficient registrations for unique beneficiaries to meet the H-1B regular cap, USCIS will no longer accept registrations under section 214(g)(1)(A) of the Act and will notify the public of the final registration date. USCIS will randomly select from among the registrations properly submitted during the initial registration period the number of registrations for unique beneficiaries deemed necessary to meet the H-1B regular cap. This random selection will be made via computer-generated selection, based on the unique beneficiary.

(6) Advanced degree exemption selection. After USCIS has determined it will no longer accept registrations under section 214(g)(1)(A) of the Act, USCIS will determine whether there is a sufficient number of remaining registrations to meet the H-1B advanced degree exemption.

(i) Fewer registrations than needed to meet the H-1B advanced degree exemption numerical limitation. If USCIS determines that it has received fewer registrations for unique beneficiaries than needed to meet the H-1B advanced degree exemption numerical limitation, USCIS will notify all petitioners that have properly registered that their registrations have been selected. USCIS will continue to accept registrations to file petitions for beneficiaries that may be eligible for the H-1B advanced degree exemption under section 214(g)(5)(C) of the Act until USCIS determines that it has received enough registrations for unique beneficiaries to meet the H-1B advanced degree exemption numerical limitation. USCIS will monitor the number of registrations received and will notify the public of the date that USCIS has received the necessary number of registrations for unique beneficiaries (the "final registration date"). The day the public is notified will not control the applicable final registration date. When necessary to ensure the fair and orderly allocation of numbers under sections 214(g)(1)(A) and 214(g)(5)(C) of the Act, USCIS may randomly select the remaining number of registrations for unique beneficiaries deemed necessary to meet the H-1B advanced degree exemption numerical limitation from among the registrations properly submitted on the final registration date. This random selection will be made via computer-generated selection, based on the unique beneficiary.

(ii) Sufficient registrations to meet the H-1B advanced degree exemption numerical limitation. If USCIS determines that it has received more than enough registrations for unique beneficiaries to meet the H-1B advanced degree exemption numerical limitation, USCIS will no longer accept registrations that may be eligible for exemption under section 214(g)(5)(C) of the Act and will notify the public of the final registration date. USCIS will randomly select the number of registrations for unique beneficiaries needed to meet the H-1B advanced degree exemption numerical limitation from among the remaining registrations for unique beneficiaries who may be counted against the advanced degree exemption numerical limitation. This random selection will be made via computer-generated selection, based on the unique beneficiary.

(7) Increase to the number of beneficiaries projected to meet the H-1B regular cap or advanced degree exemption allocations in a fiscal year. Unselected registrations will remain on reserve for the applicable fiscal year. If USCIS determines that it needs to increase the number of registrations for unique beneficiaries projected to meet the H-1B regular cap or advanced degree exemption allocation, and select additional registrations for unique beneficiaries, USCIS will select from among the registrations that are on reserve a sufficient number to meet the H-1B regular cap or advanced degree exemption numerical limitation, as applicable. If all of the registrations on reserve are selected and there are still fewer registrations than needed to meet the H-1B regular cap or advanced degree exemption numerical limitation, as applicable, USCIS may reopen the applicable registration period until USCIS determines that it has received a sufficient number of registrations for unique beneficiaries projected as needed to meet the H-1B regular cap or

advanced degree exemption numerical limitation. USCIS will monitor the number of registrations received and will notify the public of the date that USCIS has received the necessary number of registrations (the new "final registration date"). The day the public is notified will not control the applicable final registration date. When necessary to ensure the fair and orderly allocation of numbers, USCIS may randomly select the remaining number of registrations for unique beneficiaries deemed necessary to meet the H-1B regular cap or advanced degree exemption numerical limitation from among the registrations properly submitted on the final registration date. If the registration period will be reopened, USCIS will announce the start of the reopened registration period on the USCIS website at https://www.uscis.gov/.

(B) Confirmation. Petitioners will receive electronic notification that USCIS has accepted a registration for processing.

(C) Notification to file H-1B cap-subject petitions. USCIS will notify all petitioners with selected registrations that the petitioner is eligible to file an H-1B cap-subject petition on behalf of the beneficiary named in the notice within the filing period indicated on the notice.

(D) H-1B cap-subject petition filing following registration —

(1) Filing procedures. In addition to any other applicable requirements, a petitioner may file an H-1B petition for a beneficiary who may be counted under section 214(g)(1)(A) of the Act or eligible for exemption under section 214(g)(5)(C) of the Act only if the petition is based on a valid registration, which means that the registration was properly submitted in accordance with 8 CFR 103.2(a)(1), paragraph (h)(8)(iii) of this section, and the registration tool instructions; and was submitted by the petitioner, or its designated representative, on behalf of the beneficiary who was selected for that cap season by USCIS. A petitioner may not substitute the beneficiary named in the original registration or transfer the registration to another petitioner. Any H-1B petition filed on behalf of a beneficiary must contain and be supported by the same identifying information provided in the selected registration. Petitioners must submit evidence of the passport or travel document used at the time of registration to identify the beneficiary. In its discretion, USCIS may find that a change in identifying information in some circumstances would be permissible. Such circumstances could include, but are not limited to, a legal name change due to marriage, change in gender identity, or a change in passport number or expiration date due to renewal or replacement of a stolen passport, in between the time of registration and filing the petition. USCIS may deny or revoke the approval of an H-1B petition that does not meet these requirements.

(2) Registration fee. USCIS may deny or revoke the approval of an H-1B petition if it determines that the fee associated with the registration is declined, not reconciled, disputed, or otherwise invalid after submission. The registration fee is non-refundable and due at the time the registration is submitted.

(3) Filing period. An H-1B cap-subject petition must be properly filed within the filing period indicated on the relevant selection notice. The filing period for filing the H-1B cap-subject petition will be at least 90 days. If petitioners do not meet the requirements of this paragraph (h)(8)(iii)(D), USCIS may deny or reject the H-1B cap-subject petition.

(E) Calculating the number of registrations needed to meet the H-1B regular cap and H-1B advanced degree exemption allocation. When calculating the number of registrations for unique beneficiaries needed to meet the H-1B regular cap and the H-1B advanced degree exemption numerical limitation for a given fiscal year, USCIS will take into account historical data related to approvals, denials, revocations, and other relevant factors. If necessary, USCIS may increase those numbers throughout the fiscal year.

(F) Cap exemptions under sections 214(g)(5)(A) and (B) of the Act. An alien is not subject to the numerical limitations identified in section 214(g)(1)(A) of the Act if the alien qualifies for an exemption under section 214(g)(5) of the Act. For purposes of section 214(g)(5)(A) and (B) of the Act:

(1) "Institution of higher education" has the same definition as described at section 101(a) of the Higher Education Act of 1965 (20 U.S.C. 1001(a)).

(2) A nonprofit entity shall be considered to be related to or affiliated with an institution of higher education if it satisfies any one of the following conditions:

(i) The nonprofit entity is connected to or associated with an institution of higher education through shared ownership or control by the same board or federation;

(ii) The nonprofit entity is operated by an institution of higher education;

(iii) The nonprofit entity is attached to an institution of higher education as a member, branch, cooperative, or subsidiary; or

(iv) The nonprofit entity has entered into a formal written affiliation agreement with an institution of higher education that establishes an active working relationship between the nonprofit entity and the institution of higher education for the purposes of research or education, and a fundamental activity of the nonprofit entity is to directly contribute to the research or education mission of the institution of higher education. A nonprofit entity may engage in more than one fundamental activity.

(3) An entity is considered a "nonprofit entity" if it meets the definition described at paragraph (h)(19)(iv) of this section. "Nonprofit research organization" and "governmental research organization" have the same definitions as described at paragraph (h)(19)(iii)(C) of this section.

(4) An H–1B beneficiary who is not directly employed by a qualifying institution, organization, or entity identified in section 214(g)(5)(A) or (B) of the Act will qualify for an exemption under such section if the H–1B beneficiary will spend at least half of their work time performing job duties at a qualifying institution, organization, or entity and those job duties directly further an activity that supports or advances one of the funda-

mental purposes, missions, objectives, or functions of the qualifying institution, organization, or entity, namely, either higher education, nonprofit research, or government research. Work performed "at" the qualifying institution may include work performed in the United States through telework, remote work, or other off-site work. When considering whether a position is cap-exempt, USCIS will focus on the job duties to be performed, rather than where the duties are physically performed.

(5) If cap-exempt employment ceases, and if the alien is not the beneficiary of a new cap-exempt petition, then the alien will be subject to the cap if not previously counted within the 6-year period of authorized admission to which the cap-exempt employment applied. If cap-exempt employment converts to cap-subject employment subject to the numerical limitations in section 214(g)(1)(A) of the Act, USCIS may revoke the petition authorizing such employment consistent with paragraph (h)(11)(iii) of this section.

(6) Concurrent H-1B employment in a cap-subject position of an alien that qualifies for an exemption under section 214(g)(5)(A) or (B) of the Act shall not subject the alien to the numerical limitations in section 214(g)(1)(A) of the Act. When petitioning for concurrent cap-subject H-1B employment, the petitioner must demonstrate that the H- B beneficiary is employed in valid H-1B status under a cap exemption under section 214(g)(5)(A) or (B) of the Act, the beneficiary's employment with the cap-exempt employer is expected to continue after the new cap-subject petition is approved, and the beneficiary can reasonably and concurrently perform the work described in each employer's respective positions.

(i) Validity of a petition for concurrent cap-subject H-1B employment approved under paragraph (h)(8)(iii)(F)(6) of this section cannot extend beyond the period of validity specified for the cap-exempt H-1B employment.

(ii) If H-1B employment subject to a cap exemption under section 214(g)(5)(A) or (B) of the Act is terminated by a petitioner, or otherwise ends before the end of the validity period listed on the approved petition filed on the alien's behalf, the alien who is concurrently employed in a cap-subject position becomes subject to the numerical limitations in section 214(g)(1)(A) of the Act, unless the alien was previously counted with respect to the 6-year period of authorized H-1B admission to which the petition applies or another exemption applies. If such an alien becomes subject to the numerical limitations in section 214(g)(1)(A) of the Act, USCIS may revoke the cap-subject petition described in paragraph (h)(8)(iii)(F)(6) of this section consistent with paragraph (h)(11)(iii) of this section.

(iv) Suspension of registration requirement--

(A) Determination to suspend registration requirement. USCIS may suspend the H-1B registration requirement, in its discretion, if it determines that the registration process is inoperable for any reason. If USCIS suspends the registration requirement, USCIS will make an announcement of the suspension on its website (http://www.uscis.gov) along with the opening date of the applicable H-1B cap-subject petition-filing period.

(B) Petition-based cap-subject selections in event of suspended registration process. In any year in which USCIS suspends the H-1B registration process for cap-subject petitions, USCIS will allow for the submission of H-1B petitions notwithstanding paragraph (h)(8)(iii) of this section and conduct a cap-subject selection process based on the petitions that are received. USCIS will deny petitions indicating that they are exempt from the H-1B regular cap and the H-1B advanced degree exemption if USCIS determines, after the final receipt date, that they are not eligible for the exemption sought. If USCIS determines, on or before the final receipt date, that the petition is not eligible for the exemption sought, USCIS may consider the petition under the applicable numerical allocation and proceed with processing of the petition. If a petition is denied under this paragraph (h)(8)(iv)(B), USCIS will not return or refund filing fees.

(1) H-1B regular cap selection in event of suspended registration process. In determining whether there are enough H-1B cap-subject petitions to meet the H-1B regular cap, USCIS will consider all petitions properly submitted in accordance with 8 CFR 103.2 relating to beneficiaries that may be counted under section 214(g)(1)(A) of the Act, including those that may be eligible for exemption under section 214(g)(5)(C) of the Act. When calculating the number of petitions needed to meet the H-1B regular cap USCIS will take into account historical data related to approvals, denials, revocations, and other relevant factors. USCIS will monitor the number of petitions received and will announce on its website the date that it receives the number of petitions projected as needed to meet the H-1B regular cap (the "final receipt date"). The date the announcement is posted will not control the final receipt date. If the final receipt date is any of the first five business days on which petitions subject to the H–1B regular cap may be received, USCIS will select from among all the petitions properly submitted during the first five business days the number of petitions deemed necessary to meet the H–1B regular cap. If USCIS has received more petitions than necessary to meet the numerical limitation for the H–1B regular cap, USCIS will rank and select the petitions received on the basis of the highest Occupational Employment Statistics (OES) wage level that the proffered wage equals or exceeds for the relevant Standard Occupational Classification (SOC) code in the area of intended employment, beginning with OES wage level IV and proceeding in descending order with OES wage levels III, II, and I. Where there is no current OES prevailing wage information for the proffered position, USCIS will rank and select petitions based on the appropriate wage level that corresponds to the requirements of the proffered position. If the final receipt date is any of the first five business days on which petitions subject to the H–1B regular cap may be received, USCIS will select from among all the petitions properly submitted during the first five business days the number of petitions deemed necessary to meet the H–1B regular cap. If USCIS has

received more petitions than necessary to meet the numerical limitation for the H–1B regular cap, USCIS will rank and select the petitions received on the basis of the highest Occupational Employment Statistics (OES) wage level that the proffered wage equals or exceeds for the relevant Standard Occupational Classification (SOC) code in the area of intended employment, beginning with OES wage level IV and proceeding in descending order with OES wage levels III, II, and I. Where there is no current OES prevailing wage information for the proffered position, USCIS will rank and select petitions based on the appropriate wage level that corresponds to the requirements of the proffered position. If the wage falls below an OES wage level I, USCIS will rank the petition in the same category as OES wage level I. USCIS will rank the petition in the same manner even if, instead of obtaining an OES prevailing wage, a petitioner elects to obtain a prevailing wage using another legitimate source (other than OES) or an independent authoritative source. If USCIS receives and ranks more petitions at a particular wage level than the projected number needed to meet the numerical limitation, USCIS will randomly select from among all eligible petitions within that particular wage level a sufficient number of petitions needed to reach the numerical limitation.

(2) Advanced degree exemption selection in event of suspended registration process. After USCIS has received a sufficient number of petitions to meet the H–1B regular cap and, as applicable, completed the selection process of petitions for the H–1B regular cap, USCIS will determine whether there is a sufficient number of remaining petitions to meet the H–1B advanced degree exemption numerical limitation. When calculating the number of petitions needed to meet the H–1B advanced degree exemption numerical limitation USCIS will take into account historical data related to approvals, denials, revocations, and other relevant factors. USCIS will monitor the number of petitions received and will announce on its website the date that it receives the number of petitions projected as needed to meet the H–1B advanced degree exemption numerical limitation (the "final receipt date"). The date the announcement is posted will not control the final receipt date. If the final receipt date is any of the first five business days on which petitions subject to the H–1B advanced degree exemption may be received (in other words, if the numerical limitation is reached on any one of the first five business days that filings can be made), USCIS will select from among all the petitions properly submitted during the first five business days the number of petitions deemed necessary to meet the H–1B advanced degree exemption numerical limitation. If USCIS has received more petitions than necessary to meet the numerical limitation for the H–1B advanced degree exemption, USCIS will rank and select the petitions received on the basis of the highest Occupational Employment Statistics (OES) wage level that the proffered wage equals or exceeds for the relevant Standard Occupational Classification (SOC) code in the area of intended employment, beginning with OES wage level IV and proceeding with OES wage levels III, II, and I. Where there is no current OES prevailing wage information for the proffered position, USCIS will rank and select petitions based on the appropriate wage level that corresponds to the requirements of the proffered position. If the proffered wage is below an OES wage level I, USCIS will rank the petition in the same category as OES wage level I. USCIS will rank the petition in the same manner even if, instead of obtaining an OES prevailing wage, a petitioner elects to obtain a prevailing wage using another legitimate source (other than OES) or an independent authoritative source. If USCIS receives and ranks more petitions at a particular wage level than necessary to meet the numerical limitation for the H–1B advanced degree exemption, USCIS will randomly select from among all eligible petitions within that particular wage level a sufficient number of petitions needed to reach the numerical limitation.

(v) Severability.

(A) The requirement to submit a registration for an H-1B cap-subject petition and the selection process based on properly submitted registrations under paragraph (h)(8)(iii) of this section are intended to be severable from paragraph (h)(8)(iv) of this section. In the event paragraph (h)(8)(iii) of this section is not implemented, or in the event that paragraph (h)(8)(iv) of this section is not implemented, DHS intends that either of those provisions be implemented as an independent rule, without prejudice to petitioners in the United States under this regulation, as consistent with law.

(B) DHS intends that the provisions governing the beneficiary centric selection process in paragraph (h)(8)(iii) of this section, the elimination of the requirement that the requested start date for the beneficiary be the first day for the applicable fiscal year in (h)(8)(iii)(A)(4), and the provisions governing the denial or revocation of H-1B petitions based on inaccurate, fraudulent, or misrepresented material facts in the H-1B petition, H-1B registration, temporary labor certification, or labor condition application in paragraphs (h)(10)(ii) and (iii) and (h)(11)(iii) of this section, respectively, published on February 2, 2024 be severable from one another. In the event that any of these provision(s) is held to be invalid or unenforceable by its terms, or as applied to any person or circumstance, it should be construed so as to continue to give the maximum effect to the provision(s) permitted by law, unless any such provision is held to be wholly invalid and unenforceable, in which event the provision(s) should be severed from the remainder of this section and the holding should not affect the remainder of this section or the application of the other provisions to persons not similarly situated or to dissimilar circumstances.

(vi) H-1C numerical limitations. The 500 H-1C nonimmigrant visas issued each fiscal year shall be allocated in the following manner:

(A) For each fiscal year, the number of visas issued to the states of California, Florida, Illinois, Michigan, New York, Ohio, Pennsylvania, and Texas shall not exceed 50 each (except as provided for in paragraph (h)(8)(vi)(C) of this section).

(B) For each fiscal year, the number of visas issued to the states not listed in paragraph "(h)(8)(vi)(A) of this section shall not exceed 25 each (except as provided for in paragraph (h)(8)(vi)(C) of this section).

(C) If the total number of visas available during the first three quarters of a fiscal year exceeds the number of approvable H-1C petitions during those quarters, visas may be issued during the last quarter of the fiscal year to nurses who will be working in a state whose cap has already been reached for that fiscal year.

(D) When an approved H-1C petition is not used because the alien(s) does not obtain H-1C classification, e.g., the alien is never admitted to the United States, or the alien never worked for the facility, the facility must notify the Service according to the instructions contained in paragraph (h)(11)(ii) of this section. The Service will subtract H-1C petitions approved in the current fiscal year that are later revoked from the total count of approved H-1C petitions, provided that the alien never commenced employment with the facility.

(E) If the number of alien nurses included in an H-1C petition exceeds the number available for the remainder of a fiscal year, the Service shall approve the petition for the beneficiaries to the allowable amount in the order that they are listed on the petition. The remaining beneficiaries will be considered for approval in the subsequent fiscal year.

(F) Once the 500 cap has been reached, the Service will reject any new petitions subsequently filed requesting a work start date prior to the first day of the next fiscal year.

(vii) H-2B numerical limitations. When calculating the numerical limitations under section 214(g)(1)(B) and 214(g)(10) of the Act for a given fiscal year, USCIS will make numbers available to petitions in the order in which the petitions are filed. USCIS will make projections of the number of petitions necessary to achieve the numerical limit of approvals, taking into account historical data related to approvals, denials, revocations, and other relevant factors. USCIS will monitor the number of petitions (including the number of beneficiaries requested when necessary) received and will notify the public of the date that USCIS has received the necessary number of petitions (the "final receipt date"). The day the public is notified will not control the final receipt date. When necessary to ensure the fair and orderly allocation of numbers subject to the numerical limitations in 214(g)(1)(B) and 214(g)(10) of the Act, USCIS may randomly select from among the petitions received on the final receipt date the remaining number of petitions deemed necessary to generate the numerical limit of approvals. This random selection will be made via computer-generated selection. Petitions subject to a numerical limitation not randomly selected or that were received after the final receipt date will be rejected. Petitions indicating that they are exempt from the numerical limitation but that are determined by USCIS after the final receipt date to be subject to the numerical limit will be denied and filing fees will not be returned or refunded. If the final receipt date is any of the first five business days on which petitions subject to the applicable numerical limit may be received (i.e., if the numerical limit is reached on any one of the first five business days that filings can be made), USCIS will randomly apply all of the numbers among the petitions received on any of those five business days.

(9) Approval and validity of petition --

(i) Approval.

(A) USCIS will consider all the evidence submitted and any other evidence independently required to assist in adjudication. USCIS will notify the petitioner of the approval of the petition on a Notice of Action. The approval notice will include the beneficiary's (or beneficiaries') name(s) and classification and the petition's period of validity. A petition for more than one beneficiary and/or multiple services may be approved in whole or in part. The approval notice will cover only those beneficiaries approved for classification under section 101(a)(15)(H) of the Act.

(B) Where an H–1B petition is approved for less time than requested on the petition, the approval notice will provide or be accompanied by a brief explanation for the validity period granted.

(ii) Recording the validity of petitions. Procedures for recording the validity period of petitions are:

(A) If a new H petition is approved before the date the petitioner indicates that the services or training will begin, the approved petition and approval notice shall show the actual dates requested by the petitoner as the validity period, not to exceed the limits specified by paragraph (h)(9)(iii) of this section or other Service policy.

(B) If a new H petition is approved after the date the petitioner indicates that the services or training will begin, the aproved petition and approval notice shall show a validity period commencing with the date of approval and ending with the date requested by the petitioner, as long as that date does not exceed either the limits specified by paragraph (h)(9)(iii) of this section or other Service policy.

(C) If the period of services or training requested by the petitioner exceeds the limit specified in paragraph (h)(9)(iii) of this section, the petition shall be approved only up to the limit specified in that paragraph.

(D)(1) If an H–1B petition is adjudicated and deemed approvable after the initially requested validity period end-date or end-date for which eligibility is established, the officer may issue a request for evidence (RFE) asking the petitioner whether they want to update the requested dates of employment. Factors that inform whether USCIS issues an RFE could include, but would not be limited to: additional petitions filed or approved on the beneficiary's behalf, or the beneficiary's eligibility for additional time in H–1B status. If the new requested period exceeds the validity period of the labor condition application already submitted with the H–1B petition, the petitioner must submit a certified labor condition application with a new validity period that properly corresponds to the new requested validity period on the petition and an updated prevailing or proffered wage, if applicable, except that the petitioner may not reduce the proffered wage from that originally indicated in their petition. This labor condition application may be certified after the date the H–1B petition was filed with USCIS. The request for new dates of employment and submission of a labor condition application corresponding with the new dates of employment, absent other changes, will not be considered a material change. An increase to the proffered wage will not be considered a material change, as long as there are no other material changes to the position.

(2) If USCIS does not issue an RFE concerning the requested dates of employment, if the petitioner does not respond, or the RFE response does not support new dates of employment, the petition will be approved, if otherwise approvable, for the originally requested period or until the end-date eligibility has been established, as appropriate. However, the petition will not be forwarded to the Department of State nor will any accompanying request for a change of status, an extension of stay, or amendment of stay, be granted.

(iii) Validity. The initial approval period of an H petition shall conform to the limits prescribed as follows:

(A)(1) H–1B petition in a specialty occupation. The maximum validity period for an approved petition classified under section 101(a)(15)(H)(i)(b) of the Act for an alien in a specialty occupation is 3 years. However, where the beneficiary will be working at a third-party worksite, the maximum validity period for an approved petition is 1 year. In all instances, the approved petition may not exceed the validity period of the labor condition application.

(2) H-1B petition involving a DOD research and development or coproduction project. An approved petition classified under section 101(a)(15)(H)(i)(b) of the Act for an alien involved in a DOD research and development project or a coproduction project shall be valid for a period of up to five years.

(3) H-1B petition involving an alien of distinguished merit and ability in the field of fashion modeling. An approved petition classified under section 101(a)(15)(H)(i)(b) of the Act for an alien of distinguished merit and ability in the field of fashion modeling shall be valid for a period of up to three years.

(B) H-2B petition. The approval of the petition to accord an alien a classification under section 101(a)(15)(H)(ii)(b) of the Act shall be valid for the period of the approved temporary labor certification.

(C)(1) H-3 petition for alien trainee. An approved petition for an alien trainee classified under section 101(a)(15)(H)(iii) of the Act shall be valid for a period of up to two years.

(2) H-3 petition for alien participant in a special education training program. An approved petition for an alien classified under section 101(a)(15)(H)(iii) of the Act as a participant in a special education exchange visitor program shall be valid for a period of up to 18 months.

(D) H-1C petition for a registered nurse. An approved petition for an alien classified under section 101(a)(15)(H)(i)(c) of the Act shall be valid for a period of 3 years.

(E) H–1B petition for certain beneficiary-owned entities. The initial approval of a petition filed by a United States employer in which the H–1B beneficiary possesses a controlling interest in the petitioning organization or entity, meaning the beneficiary owns more than 50 percent of the petitioner or has majority voting rights in the petitioner, will be limited to a validity period of up to 18 months. The first extension (including an amended petition with a request for an extension of stay) of such a petition will also be limited to a validity period of up to 18 months.

(iv) H-4 dependents. The spouse and children of an H nonimmigrant, if they are accompanying or following to join such H nonimmigrant in the United States, may be admitted, if otherwise admissible, as H-4 nonimmigrants for the same period of admission or extension as the principal spouse or parent. H-4 nonimmigrant status does not confer eligibility for employment authorization incident to status. An H-4 nonimmigrant spouse of an H-1B nonimmigrant may be eligible for employment authorization only if the H-1B nonimmigrant is the beneficiary of an approved Immigrant Petition for Alien Worker, or successor form, or the H-1B nonimmigrant's period of stay in H-1B status is authorized in the United States under sections 106(a) and (b) of the American Competitiveness in the Twenty-first Century Act of 2000 (AC21), Public Law 106-313, as amended by the 21st Century Department of Justice Appropriations Authorization Act, Public Law 107-273 (2002). To request employment authorization, an eligible H-4 nonimmigrant spouse must file an Application for Employment Authorization, or a successor form, in accordance with 8 CFR 274a.13 and the form instructions. An Application for Employment Authorization must be accompanied by documentary evidence establishing eligibility, including evidence of the spousal relationship and that the principal H-1B is the beneficiary of an approved Immigrant Petition for Alien Worker or has been provided H-1B status under sections 106(a) and (b) of AC21, as amended by the 21st Century Department of Justice Appropriations Authorization Act, the H-1B beneficiary is currently in H-1B status, and the H-4 nonimmigrant spouse is currently in H-4 status.

(10) Denial of petition --

(i) Multiple beneficiaries. A petition for multiple beneficiaries may be denied in whole or in part.

(ii) Denial for statement of facts on the petition, H-1B registration, temporary labor certification, labor condition application, or invalid H-1B registration. The petition will be denied if it is determined that the statements on the petition, H-1B registration (if applicable), the application for a temporary labor certification, or the labor condition application, were inaccurate, fraudulent, or misrepresented a material fact, including if the attestations on the registration are determined to be false. An H-1B cap-subject petition also will be denied if it is not based on a valid registration submitted by the petitioner (or its designated representative), or a successor in interest, for the beneficiary named or identified in the petition.

(iii) Notice of denial. The petitioner will be notified of the reasons for the denial and of the right to appeal the denial of the petition under 8 CFR part 103. There is no appeal from a decision to deny an extension of stay to the alien.

(iv) H–2A and H–2B violators.

(A) USCIS will deny any H–2A or H–2B petition filed by a petitioner, or the successor in interest of a petitioner as defined in paragraphs (h)(5)(xi)(C)(2) and (h)(6)(i)(D)(2) of this section, that has been the subject of one or more of the following actions:

(1) A final administrative determination by the Secretary of Labor under 20 CFR part 655, subpart A or B, or 29 CFR part 501 or 503 debarring the petitioner from filing or receiving a future labor certification, or a final administrative determination by the Governor of Guam debarring the petitioner from issuance of future labor certifications under applicable Guam regulations and rules, if the petition is filed on or after January 17, 2025 and during the debarment period, or if the debarment occurs during the pendency of the petition filed on or after January 17, 2025, and the final administrative determination debarring the petitioner is made on or after January 17, 2025; or

(2) A final USCIS denial or revocation decision issued during the pendency of the petition or within 3 years prior to filing the petition that includes a finding of fraud or willful misrepresentation of a material fact with respect to a previously filed H–2A or H– 2B petition. This provision will only apply if the final denial or revocation decision was issued on a petition filed on or after January 17, 2025; or

(3) A final determination of violation(s) under section 274(a) of the Act during the pendency of the petition or within 3 years prior to filing the petition if the final determination of violation(s) under section 274(a) of the Act is made on or after January 17, 2025 and the petition is filed on or after January 17, 2025.

(B) Except as provided in paragraph (h)(10)(iv)(A) of this section, USCIS may deny any H–2A or H–2B petition filed by a petitioner, or the successor in interest of a petitioner as defined in paragraphs (h)(5)(xi)(C)(2) and (h)(6)(i)(D)(2) of this section on or after January 17, 2025, that has been the subject of one or more of the following actions during the pendency of the petition or within 3 years prior to filing the petition, regardless of whether the action(s) or underlying violation(s) occurred before, on, or after January 17, 2025. USCIS may deny such a petition if it determines that the petitioner or successor has not established its intention and/or ability to comply with H–2A or H–2B program requirements. The violation(s) underlying the following actions that may call into question a petitioner's or successor's intention and/or ability to comply include:

(1) A final administrative determination by the Secretary of Labor or the Governor of Guam with respect to a prior H–2A or H–2B temporary labor certification that includes:

(i) Revocation of an approved temporary labor certification under 20 CFR part 655, subpart A or B, or applicable Guam regulations and rules;

(ii) Debarment under 20 CFR part 655, subpart A or B, or 29 CFR part 501 or 503, or applicable Guam regulations and rules, if the debarment period has concluded prior to filing the petition; or (iii) Any other administrative sanction or remedy under 29 CFR part 501 or 503, or applicable Guam regulations and rules, including assessment of civil money penalties as described in those parts. (2) A final USCIS decision revoking the approval of a prior petition that includes one or more of the following findings: the beneficiary was not employed by the petitioner in the capacity specified in the petition; the statement of facts contained in the petition or on the application for a temporary labor certification was not true and correct, or was inaccurate; the petitioner violated terms and conditions of the approved petition; or the petitioner violated requirements of section 101(a)(15)(H) of the Act or this paragraph (h); or (3) Any final administrative or judicial determination (other than one described in paragraph (h)(10)(iv)(A) of this section) that the petitioner violated any applicable employment-related laws or regulations, including health and safety laws or regulations.

(C) In determining whether the underlying violation(s) in paragraph (h)(10)(iv)(B) of this section calls into question the intention and/or ability of the petitioner or its successor in interest to comply with H–2A or H–2B program requirements, USCIS will consider all relevant factors, including, but not limited to:

(1) The recency and number of violations;

(2) The egregiousness of the violation(s), including how many workers were affected, and whether it involved a risk to the health or safety of workers;

(3) Overall history or pattern of prior violations;

(4) The severity or monetary amount of any penalties imposed;

(5) Whether the final determination, decision, or conviction included a finding of willfulness;

(6) The extent to which the violator achieved a financial gain due to the violation(s), or the potential financial loss or potential financial injury to the workers;

(7) Timely compliance with all penalties and remedies ordered under the final determination(s), decision(s), or conviction(s); and

(8) Other corrective actions taken by the petitioner or its successor in interest to cure its violation(s) or prevent future violations.

(D) For purposes of paragraph (h)(10)(iv) of this section, a criminal conviction or final administrative or judicial determination against any one of the following individuals will be treated as a conviction or final administrative or judicial determination against the petitioner or successor in interest:

(1) An individual acting on behalf of the petitioning entity, which could include, among others, the petitioner's owner, employee, or contractor; or

(2) With respect to paragraph (h)(10)(iv)(B) of this section, an employee of the petitioning entity who a reasonable person in the H–2A or H– 2B worker's position would believe is acting on behalf of the petitioning entity.

(E)(1) With respect to denials under paragraph (h)(10)(iv)(A) of this section, USCIS will inform the petitioner of the right to appeal the denial under 8 CFR 103.3, and indicate in the denial notice that the mandatory ground of denial will also apply in the adjudication of any other pending or future H–2 petition filed by the petitioner or a successor in interest during the applicable time period.

(2) With respect to denials under paragraph (h)(10)(iv)(B) of this section, USCIS will inform the petitioner of the right to appeal the denial under 8 CFR 103.3, and indicate in the denial notice that the discretionary ground of denial may also apply in the adjudication of any other pending or future H–2 petition filed by the petitioner or a successor in interest during the applicable time period.

(F) If USCIS has determined in the course of a prior adjudication that a petitioner (or the preceding entity, if the petitioner is a successor in interest) has established its intention and ability to comply with H–2A or H–2B program requirements notwithstanding relevant violation determination(s) under paragraph (h)(10)(iv)(B) of this section, USCIS will not seek to deny a subsequent petition under paragraph (h)(10)(iv)(B) based on the same previous violation determination(s) unless USCIS becomes aware of a new material fact or finds that its previous determination was based on a material error of law

(11) Revocation of approval of petition --

(i) General.

(A) The petitioner shall immediately notify the Service of any changes in the terms and conditions of employment of a beneficiary which may affect eligibility under section 101(a)(15)(H) of the Act and paragraph (h) of this section. An amended petition on the form prescribed by USCIS should be filed when the petitioner continues to employ the beneficiary. If the petitioner no longer employs the beneficiary, the petitioner shall send a letter explaining the change(s) to the director who approved the petition. However, H-2A and H-2B petitioners must send notification to DHS pursuant to paragraphs (h)(5)(vi) and (h)(6)(i)(F) of this section respectively.

(B) The director may revoke a petition at any time, even after the expiration of the petition.

(ii) Immediate and automatic revocation. The approval of any petition is immediately and automatically revoked if the petitioner goes out of business, files a written withdrawal of the petition, or the Department of Labor revokes the labor certification upon which the petition is based. The approval of an H–1B petition is also immediately and automatically revoked upon notification from the H–1B petitioner that the beneficiary is no longer employed.

(iii) Revocation on notice --

(A) Grounds for revocation. The director shall send to the petitioner a notice of intent to revoke the petition in relevant part if he or she finds that:

(1) The beneficiary is no longer employed by the petitioner in the capacity specified in the petition, or if the beneficiary is no longer receiving training as specified in the petition; or

(2) The statement of facts contained in the petition, H-1B registration (if applicable), the application for a temporary labor certification, or the labor condition application, was not true and correct, inaccurate, fraudulent, or misrepresented a material fact, including if the attestations on the registration are determined to be false; or

(3) The petitioner, or a related entity, filed a new or amended petition on behalf of the same beneficiary, if USCIS determines that the filing of the new or amended petition is part of the petitioner's attempt to unfairly increase the odds of selection during the registration or petition selection process, as applicable, such as by reducing the proffered wage to an amount that would be equivalent to a lower wage level than that indicated on the registration, or the original petition if the registration process was suspended. USCIS will not revoke approval of such an amended or new petition solely on the basis of a different proffered wage if that wage does not correspond to a lower OES wage level than the wage level on which the registration or petition selection, as applicable, was based; or

(4) The petitioner violated terms and conditions of the approved petition; or

(5) The approval of the petition violated paragraph (h) of this section or involved gross error; or

(6) The H-1B cap-subject petition was not based on a valid registration submitted by the petitioner (or its designated representative), or a successor in interest, for the beneficiary named or identified in the petition; or

(7) The petitioner failed to timely file an amended petition notifying USCIS of a material change or otherwise failed to comply with the material change reporting requirements in paragraph (h)(2)(i)(E) of this section.

(B) Notice and decision. The notice of intent to revoke shall contain a detailed statement of the grounds for the revocation and the time period allowed for the petitioner's rebuttal. The petitioner may submit evidence in rebuttal within 30 days of receipt of the notice. The director shall consider all relevant evidence presented in deciding whether to revoke the petition in whole or in part. If the petition is revoked in part, the remainder of the petition shall remain approved and a revised approval notice shall be sent to the petitioner with the revocation notice.

(iv) Effect of H–2A or H–2B petition revocation. Upon revocation of the approval of an employer's H–2A or H– 2B petition, the beneficiary and their dependents will not be considered to have failed to maintain nonimmigrant status, and will not accrue any period of unlawful presence under section 212(a)(9) of the Act (8 U.S.C. 1182(a)(9)), solely on the basis of the petition revocation for a 60-day period following the date of the revocation, or until the end of the authorized period of admission, whichever is shorter. During such a period, the alien may only work as otherwise authorized under 8 CFR 274a.12. The employer will be liable for the alien beneficiary's reasonable costs of return transportation to their last place of foreign residence abroad, unless such alien obtains an extension of stay based on an approved petition in the same classification filed by a different employer.

(12) Appeal of a denial or a revocation of a petition --

(i) Denial. A petition denied in whole or in part may be appealed under part 103 of this chapter.

(ii) Revocation. A petition that has been revoked on notice in whole or in part may be appealed under part 103 of this chapter. Automatic revocations may not be appealed.

(13) Admission --

(i) General.

(A) An H–3 beneficiary will be admitted to the United States for the validity period of the petition, plus a period of up to 10 days before the validity period begins and 10 days after the validity period ends. The beneficiary may not work except during the validity period of the petition.

(B) When an alien in an H classification has spent the maximum allowable period of stay in the United States, a new petition under section 101(a)(15)(H) or (L) of the Act may not be approved unless that alien has resided and been physically present outside the United States, except for brief trips for business or pleasure, for the time limit imposed on the particular H classification. Brief trips to the United States for business or pleasure during the required time abroad are not interruptive, but do not count toward fulfillment of the required time abroad. A certain period of absence from the United States of H–2A and H–2B aliens, as set forth in 8 CFR 214.2(h)(5)(viii)(D) and 8 CFR 214.2(h)(6)(vii)(C), respectively, will provide a new total of 3 years that H–2A or H–2B status may be granted. The petitioner must provide information about the alien's employment, place of residence, and the dates and purposes of any trips to the United States during the period that the alien was required to reside abroad.

(C) An alien admitted or otherwise provided status in H–2A or H–2B classification and their dependents will not be considered to have failed to maintain nonimmigrant status, and will not accrue any period of unlawful presence under section 212(a)(9) of the Act (8 U.S.C. 1182(a)(9)), solely on the basis of a cessation of the employment on which the alien's classification was based, for 60 consecutive days or until the end of the authorized period of admission, whichever is shorter, once during each authorized period of admission. During such a period, the alien may only work as otherwise authorized under 8 CFR 274a.12.

(D) An alien in any authorized period described in paragraph (C) of this section may apply for and be granted an extension of stay under 8 CFR 214.1(c)(4) or change of status under 8 CFR 248.1, if otherwise eligible.

(ii) H-1C limitation on admission. The maximum period of admission for an H-1C nonimmigrant alien is 3 years. The maximum period of admission for an H-1C alien begins on the date the H-1C alien is admitted to the United and ends on the third anniversary of the alien's admission date. Periods of time spent out of the United States for business or personal reasons during the validity period of the H-1C petition count towards the alien's maximum period of admission. When an H-1C alien has reached the 3-year maximum period of admission, the H-1C alien is no longer eligible for admission to the United States as an H-1C nonimmigrant alien.

(iii) H-1B limitation on admission.

(A) Alien in a specialty occupation or an alien of distinguished merit and ability in the field of fashion modeling. An H-1B alien in a specialty occupation or an alien of distinguished merit and ability who has spent six years in the United States under section 101(a)(15)(H) and/or (L) of the Act may not seek extension, change status, or be readmitted to the United States under section 101(a)(15) (H) or (L) of the Act unless the alien has resided and been physically present outside the United States, except for brief trips for business or pleasure, for the immediate prior year.

(B) Alien involved in a DOD research and development or coproduction project. An H-1B alien involved in a DOD research and development or coproduction project who has spent 10 years in the United States under section 101(a)(15) (H) and/or (L) of the Act may not seek extension, change status, or be readmitted to the United States under section 101(a)(15) (H) or (L) of the Act to perform services involving a DOD research and development project or coproduction project. A new petition or change of status under section 101(a)(15) (H) or (L) of the Act may not be approved for such an alien unless the alien has resided and been physically present outside the United States, except for brief trips for business or pleasure, for the immediate prior year.

(C) Calculating the maximum H-1B admission period. Time spent physically outside the United States exceeding 24 hours by an alien during the validity of an H-1B petition that was approved on the alien's behalf shall not be considered for purposes of calculating the alien's total period of authorized admission under section 214(g)(4) of the Act, regardless of whether such time meaningfully interrupts the alien's stay in H-1B status and the reason for the alien's absence. Accordingly, such remaining time may be recaptured in a subsequent H-1B petition on behalf of the alien, at any time before the alien uses the full period of H-1B admission described in section 214(g)(4) of the Act.

(1) It is the H-1B petitioner's burden to request and demonstrate the specific amount of time for recapture on behalf of the beneficiary. The beneficiary may provide appropriate evidence, such as copies of passport stamps, Arrival-Departure Records (Form I-94), or airline tickets, together with a chart, indicating the dates spent outside of the United States, and referencing the relevant independent documentary evidence, when seeking to recapture the alien's time spent outside the United States. Based on the evidence provided, USCIS may grant all, part, or none of the recapture period requested.

(2) If the beneficiary was previously counted toward the H-1B numerical cap under section 214(g)(1) of the Act with respect to the 6-year maximum period of H-1B admission from which recapture is sought, the H-1B petition seeking to recapture a period of stay as an H-1B nonimmigrant will not subject the beneficiary to the H-1B numerical cap, whether or not the alien has been physically outside the United States for 1 year or more and would be otherwise eligible for a new period of admission under such section of the Act. An H-1B petitioner may either seek such recapture on behalf of the alien or, consistent with paragraph (h)(13)(iii) of

this section, seek a new period of admission on behalf of the alien under section 214(g)(1) of the Act.

(D) Lengthy adjudication delay exemption from 214(g)(4) of the Act.

(1) An alien who is in H-1B status or has previously held H-1B status is eligible for H-1B status beyond the 6-year limitation under section 214(g)(4) of the Act, if at least 365 days have elapsed since:

(i) The filing of a labor certification with the Department of Labor on the alien's behalf, if such certification is required for the alien to obtain status under section 203(b) of the Act; or

(ii) The filing of an immigrant visa petition with USCIS on the alien's behalf to accord classification under section 203(b) of the Act.

(2) H-1B approvals under paragraph (h)(13)(iii)(D) of this section may be granted in up to 1-year increments until either the approved permanent labor certification expires or a final decision has been made to:

(i) Deny the application for permanent labor certification, or, if approved, to revoke or invalidate such approval;

(ii) Deny the immigrant visa petition, or, if approved, revoke such approval;

(iii) Deny or approve the alien's application for an immigrant visa or application to adjust status to lawful permanent residence; or

(iv) Administratively or otherwise close the application for permanent labor certification, immigrant visa petition, or application to adjust status.

(3) No final decision while appeal available or pending. A decision to deny or revoke an application for labor certification, or to deny or revoke the approval of an immigrant visa petition, will not be considered final under paragraph (h)(13)(iii)(D)(2)(i) or (ii) of this section during the period authorized for filing an appeal of the decision, or while an appeal is pending.

(4) Substitution of beneficiaries. An alien who has been replaced by another alien, on or before July 16, 2007, as the beneficiary of an approved permanent labor certification may not rely on that permanent labor certification to establish eligibility for H-1B status based on this lengthy adjudication delay exemption. Except for a substitution of a beneficiary that occurred on or before July 16, 2007, an alien establishing eligibility for this lengthy adjudication delay exemption based on a pending or approved labor certification must be the named beneficiary listed on the permanent labor certification.

(5) Advance filing. A petitioner may file an H-1B petition seeking a lengthy adjudication delay exemption under paragraph (h)(13)(iii)(D) of this section within 6 months of the requested H-1B start date. The petition may be filed before 365 days have elapsed since the labor certification application or immigrant visa petition was filed with the Department of Labor or USCIS, respectively, provided that the application for labor certification or immigrant visa petition must have been filed at least 365 days prior to the date the period of admission authorized under this exemption will take effect. The petitioner may request any time remaining to the beneficiary under the maximum period of admission described at section 214(g)(4) of the Act along with the exemption request, but in no case may the approved H-1B period of validity exceed the limits specified by paragraph (h)(9)(iii) of this section. Time remaining to the beneficiary under the maximum period of admission described at section 214(g)(4) of the Act may include any request to recapture unused H-1B, L-1A, or L-1B time spent outside of the United States.

(6) Petitioners seeking exemption. The H-1B petitioner need not be the employer that filed the application for labor certification or immigrant visa petition that is used to qualify for this exemption.

(7) Subsequent exemption approvals after the 7th year. The qualifying labor certification or immigrant visa petition need not be the same as that used to qualify for the initial exemption under paragraph (h)(13)(iii)(D) of this section.

(8) Aggregation of time not permitted. A petitioner may not aggregate the number of days that have elapsed since the filing of one labor certification or immigrant visa petition with the number of days that have elapsed since the filing of another such application or petition to meet the 365-day requirement.

(9) Exemption eligibility. Only a principal beneficiary of a nonfrivolous labor certification application or immigrant visa petition filed on his or her behalf may be eligible under paragraph (h)(13)(iii)(D) of this section for an exemption to the maximum period of admission under section 214(g)(4) of the Act.

(10) Limits on future exemptions from the lengthy adjudication delay. An alien is ineligible for the lengthy adjudication delay exemption under paragraph (h)(13)(iii)(D) of this section if the alien is the beneficiary of an approved petition under section 203(b) of the Act and fails to file an adjustment of status application or apply for an immigrant visa within 1 year of an immigrant visa being authorized for issuance based on his or her preference category and country of chargeability. If the accrual of such 1-year period is interrupted by the unavailability of an immigrant visa, a new 1-year period shall be afforded when an immigrant visa again becomes immediately available. USCIS may excuse a failure to file in its discretion if the alien establishes that the failure to apply was due to circumstances beyond his or her control. The limitations described in this paragraph apply to any approved immigrant visa petition under section 203(b) of the Act, including petitions withdrawn by the petitioner or those filed by a petitioner whose business terminates 180 days or more after approval.

(E) Per-country limitation exemption from section 214(g)(4) of the Act. An alien who currently maintains or previously held H-1B status, who is the beneficiary of an approved immigrant visa petition for classification under section 203(b)(1), (2), or (3) of the Act, and who is eligible to be granted that immigrant status but for application of the per country limitation, is eligible for H-1B status beyond the 6-year limitation under section 214(g)(4) of the Act. The petitioner must demonstrate such visa unavailability as of the date the H-1B petition is filed with USCIS.

(1) Validity periods. USCIS may grant validity periods for petitions approved under this paragraph in increments of up to 3 years for as long as the alien remains eligible for this exemption.

(2) H-1B approvals under paragraph (h)(13)(iii)(E) of this section may be granted until a final decision has been made to:

(i) Revoke the approval of the immigrant visa petition; or

(ii) Approve or deny the alien's application for an immigrant visa or application to adjust status to lawful permanent residence.

(3) Current H-1B status not required. An alien who is not in H-1B status at the time the H-1B petition on his or her behalf is filed, including an alien who is not in the United States, may seek an exemption of the 6-year limitation under 214(g)(4) of the Act under this clause, if otherwise eligible.

(4) Subsequent petitioners may seek exemptions. The H-1B petitioner need not be the employer that filed the immigrant visa petition that is used to qualify for this exemption. An H-1B petition may be approved under paragraph (h)(13)(iii)(E) of this section with respect to any approved immigrant visa petition, and a subsequent H-1B petition may be approved with respect to a different approved immigrant visa petition on behalf of the same alien.

(5) Advance filing. A petitioner may file an H-1B petition seeking a per-country limitation exemption under paragraph (h)(13)(iii)(E) of this section within 6 months of the requested H-1B start date. The petitioner may request any time remaining to the beneficiary under the maximum period of admission described in section 214(g)(4) of the Act along with the exemption request, but in no case may the H-1B approval period exceed the limits specified by paragraph (h)(9)(iii) of this section.

(6) Exemption eligibility. Only the principal beneficiary of an approved immigrant visa petition for classification under section 203(b)(1), (2), or (3) of the Act may be eligible under paragraph (h)(13)(iii)(E) of this section for an exemption to the maximum period of admission under section 214(g)(4) of the Act.

(iv) H–3 limitation on admission. An H–3 alien participant in a special education program who has spent 18 months in the United States under sections 101(a)(15)(H) and/or (L) of the Act; and an H–3 alien trainee who has spent 24 months in the United States under sections 101(a)(15)(H) and/or (L) of the Act may not seek extension, change status, or be readmitted to the United States under sections 101(a)(15)(H) and/or (L) of the Act unless the alien has resided and been physically present outside the United States for the immediate prior 6 months.

(v) Exceptions. The limitations in paragraphs (h)(13)(iii) and (iv) of this section will not apply to H–1B and H– 3 aliens who did not reside continually in the United States and whose employment in the United States was seasonal or intermittent or was for an aggregate of 6 months or less per year. In addition, the limitations will not apply to aliens who reside abroad and regularly commute to the United States to engage in part-time employment. To qualify for this exception, the petitioner and the alien must provide clear and convincing proof that the alien qualifies for such an exception. Such proof shall consist of evidence such as arrival and departure records, copies of tax returns, and records of employment abroad.

(14) Extension of visa petition validity. The petitioner must file a request for a petition extension on the Form I–129 to extend the validity of the original petition under section 101(a)(15)(H) of the Act. A request for a petition extension generally may be filed only if the validity of the original petition has not expired.

(15) Extension of stay --

(i) General. The petitioner shall apply for extension of an alien's stay in the United States by filing a petition extension on the form prescribed by USCIS accompanied by the documents described for the particular classification in paragraph (h)(15)(ii) of this section. The petitioner must also request a petition extension. The dates of extension shall be the same for the petition and the beneficiary's extension of stay. The beneficiary must be physically present in the United States at the time of the filing of the extension of stay. Even though the requests to extend the petition and the alien's stay are combined on the petition, the director shall make a separate determination on each. If the alien is required to leave the United States for business or personal reasons while the extension requests are pending, the petitioner may request the director to cable notification of approval of the petition extension to the consular office abroad where the alien will apply for a visa. When the total period of stay in an H classification has been reached, no further extensions may be granted.

(ii) Extension periods --

(A) H-1C extension of stay. The maximum period of admission for an H-1C alien is 3 years. An H-1C alien who was initially admitted to the United States for less than 3 years may receive an extension of stay up to the third anniversary date of his or her initial admission. An H-1C nonimmigrant may not receive an extension of stay beyond the third anniversary date of his or her initial admission to the United States.

(B) H-1B extension of stay --

(1) Alien in a specialty occupation or an alien of distinguished merit and ability in the field of fashion modeling. An extension of stay may be authorized for a period of up to three years for a beneficiary of an H-1B petition in a specialty occupation or an alien of distinguished merit and ability. The alien's total period of stay may not exceed six years. The request for extension must be accompanied by either a new or a photocopy of the prior certification from the Department of Labor that the petitioner continues to have on file a labor condition application valid for the period of time requested for the occupation.

(2) Alien in a DOD research and development or coproduction project. An extension of stay may be authorized for a period up to five years for the beneficiary of an H-1B petition involving a DOD research and

development project or coproduction project. The total period of stay may not exceed 10 years.

(C) H-2A or H-2B extension of stay. An extension of stay for the beneficiary of an H-2A or H-2B petition may be authorized for the validity of the labor certification or for a period of up to one year, except as provided for in paragraph (h)(5)(x) of this section. The alien's total period of stay as an H-2A or H-2B worker may not exceed three years, except that in the Virgin Islands, the alien's total period of stay may not exceed 45 days.

(D) H-3 extension of stay. An extension of stay may be authorized for the length of the training program for a total period of stay as an H-3 trainee not to exceed two years, or for a total period of stay as a participant in a special education training program not to exceed 18 months.

(16) Effect of approval of a permanent labor certification or filing of a preference petition on H classification --

(i) H-1B or H-1C classification. The approval of a permanent labor certification or the filing of a preference petition for an alien shall not be a basis for denying an H-1C or H-1B petition or a request to extend such a petition, or the alien's admission, change of status, or extension of stay. The alien may legitimately come to the United States for a temporary period as an H-1C or H-1B nonimmigrant and depart voluntarily at the end of his or her authorized stay and, at the same time, lawfully seek to become a permanent resident of the United States.

(ii) H–2A or H–2B classification. The approval of a permanent labor certification, the filing of an immediate relative or preference petition for or by an alien or a diversity visa petition with the Department of State, or an application by an alien to seek lawful permanent residence or an immigrant visa, will not, standing alone, be the basis for denying an H–2 petition, a request to extend such a petition, or an application for admission in, change of status to, or extension of stay in H–2 status. The approval of a permanent labor certification, filing of an immediate relative petition, preference petition, or diversity visa petition, or filing of an application for adjustment of status or an immigrant visa will be considered, together with all other facts presented, in determining whether the H–2 nonimmigrant is maintaining his or her H–2 status and whether the alien has a residence in a foreign country which he or she has no intention of abandoning.

(iii) H–3 classification. The approval of a permanent labor certification, or the filing of a preference petition for an alien currently employed by or in a training position with the same petitioner, will be a reason, by itself, to deny the alien's extension of stay.

(17) Effect of a strike --

(i) If the Secretary of Labor certifies to the Commissioner that a strike or other labor dispute involving a work stoppage of workers is in progress in the occupation and at the place where the beneficiary is to be employed or trained, and that the employment of training of the beneficiary would adversely affect the wages and working conditions of U.S. citizens and lawful resident workers:

(A) A petition to classify an alien as a nonimmigrant as defined in section 101(a)(15)(H) of the Act shall be denied.

(B) If a petition has already been approved, but the alien has not yet entered the United States, or has entered the United States but has not commenced the employment, the approval of the petition is automatically suspended, and the application for admission on the basis of the petition shall be denied.

(ii) If there is a strike or other labor dispute involving a work stoppage of workers in progress, but such strike or other labor dispute is not certified under paragraph (h)(17)(i), the Commissioner shall not deny a petition or suspend an approved petition.

(iii) If the alien has already commenced employment in the United States under an approved petition and is participating in a strike or other labor dispute involving a work stoppage of workers, whether or not such strike or other labor dispute has been certified by the Department of Labor, the alien shall not be deemed to be failing to maintain his or her status solely on account of past, present, or future participation in a strike or other labor dispute involving a work stoppage of workers, but is subject to the following terms and conditions:

(A) The alien shall remain subject to all applicable provisions of the Immigration and Nationality Act, and regulations promulgated in the same manner as all other H nonimmigrants;

(B) The status and authorized period of stay of such an alien is not modified or extended in any way by virtue of his or her participation in a strike or other labor dispute involving a work stoppage of workers; and

(C) Although participation by an H nonimmigrant alien in a strike or other labor dispute involving a work stoppage of workers will not constitute a ground for deportation, any alien who violates his or her status or who remains in the United States after his or her authorized period of stay has expired will be subject to deportation.

(18) Use of approval notice, Form I-797. The Service shall notify the petitioner on Form I-797 whenever a visa petition, an extension of a visa petition, or an alien's extension of stay is approved under the H classification. The beneficiary of an H petition who does not require a nonimmigrant visa may present a copy of the approval notice at a port of entry to facilitate entry into the United States. A beneficiary who is required to present a visa for admission and whose visa will have expired before the date of his or her intended return may use a copy of Form I-797 to apply for a new or revalidated visa during the validity period of the petition. The copy of Form I-797 shall be retained by the beneficiary and presented during the validity of the petition when reentering the United States to resume the same employment with the same petitioner.

(19) Additional fee for filing certain H-1B petitions --

(i) A United States employer (other than an exempt employer defined in paragraph (h)(19)(iii) of this section, or an employer filing a petition described in paragraph (h)(19)(v) of this section) who files a petition or application must include the additional American

Competitiveness and Workforce Improvement Act (ACWIA) fee referenced in 8 CFR 106.2, if the petition is filed for any of the following purposes:

(A) An initial grant of H-1B status under section 101(a)(15)(H)(i)(b) of the Act;

(B) An initial extension of stay, as provided in paragraph (h)(15)(i) of this section; or

(C) Authorization for a change in employers, as provided in paragraph (h)(2)(i)(D) of this section.

(ii) A petitioner must submit with the petition the ACWIA fee, and any other applicable fees, in accordance with § 103.7 of this chapter, and form instructions. Payment of all applicable fees must be made at the same time, but the petitioner may submit separate checks. USCIS will accept payment of the ACWIA fee only from the United States employer or its representative of record, as defined in 8 CFR 103.2(a) and 8 CFR part 292.

(iii) The following exempt organizations are not required to pay the additional fee:

(A) An institution of higher education, as defined in section 101(a) of the Higher Education Act of 1965;

(B) An affiliated or related nonprofit entity. A nonprofit entity shall be considered to be related to or affiliated with an institution of higher education if it satisfies any one of the following conditions:

(1) The nonprofit entity is connected to or associated with an institution of higher education through shared ownership or control by the same board or federation;

(2) The nonprofit entity is operated by an institution of higher education;

(3) The nonprofit entity is attached to an institution of higher education as a member, branch, cooperative, or subsidiary; or

(4) The nonprofit entity has entered into a formal written affiliation agreement with an institution of higher education that establishes an active working relationship between the nonprofit entity and the institution of higher education for the purposes of research or education, and a fundamental activity of the nonprofit entity is to directly contribute to the research or education mission of the institution of higher education. A nonprofit entity may engage in more than one fundamental activity;

(C) A nonprofit research organization or government research organization. When a fundamental activity of a nonprofit organization is engaging in basic research and/or applied research, that organization is a nonprofit research organization. When a fundamental activity of a governmental organization is the performance or promotion of basic research and/or applied research, that organization is a government research organization. A governmental research organization may be a Federal, State, or local entity. A nonprofit research organization or governmental research organization may perform or promote more than one fundamental activity. Basic research is general research to gain more comprehensive knowledge or understanding of the subject under study, without specific applications in mind. Basic research is also research that advances scientific knowledge but does not have specific immediate commercial objectives although it may be in fields of present or potential commercial interest. Applied research is research to gain knowledge or understanding to determine the means by which a specific, recognized need may be met. Applied research includes investigations oriented to discovering new scientific knowledge that has specific commercial objectives with respect to products, processes, or services. Both basic research and applied research may include research and investigation in the sciences, social sciences, or humanities and may include designing, analyzing, and directing the research of others if on an ongoing basis and throughout the research cycle;

(D) A primary or secondary education institution; or

(E) A nonprofit entity which engages in an established curriculum-related clinical training of students registered at an institution of higher education.

(iv) Nonprofit or tax exempt organizations. For purposes of paragraphs (h)(19)(iii)(B) and (C) of this section, a nonprofit organization or entity must be determined by the Internal Revenue Service to be a tax exempt organization under the Internal Revenue Code of 1986, section 501(c)(3), (c)(4), or (c)(6), 26 U.S.C. 501(c)(3), (c)(4), or (c)(6).

(v) Filing situations where the American Competitiveness and Workforce Improvement Act of 1998 (ACWIA) fee is not required. The ACWIA fee is not required if:

(A) The petition is an amended H-1B petition that does not contain any requests for an extension of stay;

(B) The petition is an H-1B petition filed for the sole purpose of correcting a Service error; or

(C) The petition is the second or subsequent request for an extension of stay filed by the employer regardless of when the first extension of stay was filed or whether the ACWIA fee was paid on the initial petition or the first extension of stay.

(vi) ACWIA fee exemption evidence.

(A) Employer claiming to be exempt. An employer claiming to be exempt from the ACWIA fee must file the form prescribed by USCIS, in accordance with the form instructions, including supporting evidence establishing that it meets one of the exemptions described at paragraph (h)(19)(iii) of this section. A United States employer claiming an exemption from the ACWIA fee on the basis that it is a non-profit research organization must submit evidence that it has tax exempt status under the Internal Revenue Code of 1986, section 501(c)(3), (c)(4) or (c)(6), 26 U.S.C. 501(c)(3), (c)(4) or (c)(6). All other employers claiming an exemption must submit a statement describing why the organization or entity is exempt.

(B) Exempt filing situations. Any non-exempt employer who claims that the ACWIA fee does not apply with respect to a particular filing for one of the reasons described in paragraph (h)(19)(v) of this section must indicate why the ACWIA fee is not required.

(20) Retaliatory action claims.

(i) If credible documentary evidence is provided in support of a petition seeking an extension of H–1B stay in or change of status to another classification indicating that the beneficiary faced retaliatory action from their employer based on a report regarding a violation of that employer's labor condition application obligations under section 212(n)(2)(C)(iv) of the Act, USCIS may consider a loss or failure to maintain H– 1B status by the beneficiary related to such violation as due to, and commensurate with, "extraordinary circumstances" as defined by 8 CFR 214.1(c)(4) and 8 CFR 248.1(b).

(ii) If credible documentary evidence is provided in support of a petition seeking an extension of H–2A or H–2B stay in or change of status to another classification indicating that the beneficiary faced retaliatory action from their employer based on a reasonable claim of a violation or potential violation of any applicable program requirements or based on engagement in another protected activity, USCIS may consider a loss or failure to maintain H– 2A or H–2B status by the beneficiary related to such violation as due to, and commensurate with, "extraordinary circumstances" as defined by 8 CFR 214.1(c)(4) and 8 CFR 248.1(b). USCIS will determine the reasonableness of any claim from the perspective of a reasonable person in the H–2A or H–2B worker's position.

(21) [Effective Aug. 19, 2020 through Aug. 19, 2023.] Change of employers during COVID-19 National Emergency (August 19, 2020 through December 17, 2020).

(i) If an H–2A nonimmigrant who is physically present in the United States seeks to change employers during the COVID–19 National Emergency, the prospective new H–2A employer may file an H–2A petition on Form I–129 or Form I– 129H2A, accompanied by a valid temporary agricultural labor certification, requesting an extension of the alien's stay in the United States. To be approved under this paragraph (h)(21), an H–2A petition must be received on or after August 19, 2020 but no later than December 17, 2020. If the new petition is approved, the extension of stay may be granted for the validity of the approved petition for a period not to exceed the validity period of the temporary agricultural labor certification. Notwithstanding paragraph (h)(2)(i)(D) of this section and 8 CFR 274a.12(b)(21), an alien in valid H–2A nonimmigrant status on August 19, 2020, or lawfully obtaining such status thereafter pursuant to this paragraph (h)(21), is authorized to begin employment with the new petitioner after the petition described in this paragraph (h)(21) is received by USCIS, but no earlier than the start date of employment, indicated in the H–2A petition. The H–2A worker is authorized to commence employment with the petitioner before the petition is approved and subject to the requirements of 8 CFR 274a.12(b)(26) for a period of up to 45 days beginning on the Received Date on Form I–797 (Notice of Action) or, if the start date of employment occurs after the I–797 Received Date, 45 days beginning on the start date of employment indicated in the H–2A petition. If USCIS adjudicates the petition prior to the expiration of this 45-day period and denies the petition for extension of stay, or if the petition is withdrawn by the petitioner before the expiration of the 45-day period, the employment authorization associated with the filing of that petition under 8 CFR 274a.12(b)(26) will automatically terminate 15 days after the date of the denial decision or the date on which the petition is withdrawn.

(ii) Authorization to initiate employment changes pursuant to this paragraph (h)(21) begins at 12 a.m. on August 19, 2020, and ends at the end of December 17, 2020.

(22) [Effective Dec. 18, 2020 through Dec. 18, 2023.] Change of employers during COVID-19 National Emergency (December 18, 2020 through June 16, 2021).

(i) If an H–2A nonimmigrant who is physically present in the United States seeks to change employers during the COVID–19 National Emergency, the prospective new H–2A employer may file an H–2A petition on Form I–129, accompanied by a valid temporary agricultural labor certification, requesting an extension of the alien's stay in the United States. To be approved under this paragraph (h)(22), an H–2A petition must be received on or after December 18, 2020 but no later than June 16, 2021. If the new petition is approved, the extension of stay may be granted for the validity of the approved petition for a period not to exceed the validity period of the temporary agricultural labor certification. Notwithstanding paragraph (h)(2)(i)(D) of this section and 8 CFR 274a.12(b)(21), an alien in valid H–2A nonimmigrant status on December 18, 2020, or lawfully obtaining such status thereafter pursuant to this paragraph (h)(22), is authorized to begin employment with the new petitioner after the petition described in this paragraph (h)(22) is received by USCIS, but no earlier than the start date of employment, indicated in the H–2A petition. The H–2A worker is authorized to commence employment with the petitioner before the petition is approved and subject to the requirements of 8 CFR 274a.12(b)(28) for a period of up to 45 days beginning on the Received Date on Form I–797 (Notice of Action) or, if the start date of employment occurs after the I–797 Received Date, 45 days beginning on the start date of employment indicated in the H–2A petition. If USCIS adjudicates the petition prior to the expiration of this 45-day period and denies the petition for extension of stay, or if the petition is withdrawn by the petitioner before the expiration of the 45-day period, the employment authorization associated with the filing of that petition under 8 CFR 274a.12(b)(28) will automatically terminate 15 days after the date of the denial decision or the date on which the petition is withdrawn.

(ii) Authorization to initiate employment changes pursuant to this paragraph (h)(22) begins at 12 a.m. on December 18, 2020, and ends at the end of June 16, 2021.

(23) [Effective May 14, 2020 through May 15, 2023.] Change of employers and extensions beyond 3 years during COVID-19 National Emergency for H-2B aliens essential to the U.S. food supply chain.

(i) This paragraph (h)(23) relates to certain H-2B workers providing temporary nonagricultural services or labor essential to the U.S. food supply chain.

(ii) A prospective new H-2B employer or U.S. agent who is seeking to employ an H-2B alien to provide temporary nonagricultural services or labor essential to the U.S. food supply chain under this paragraph (h)(23) may file an H-2B petition on Form I-129, accompanied by an approved temporary labor certification and attestation described in paragraph (h)(23)(v)(A) of this section, requesting an extension of the alien's stay in the United States. If the new petition is approved, the extension of stay may be granted for the validity of the approved petition for a period not to exceed the validity period of the temporary labor certification. Notwithstanding paragraph (h)(2)(i)(D) of this section, an alien in valid H-2B nonimmigrant status on or after March 1, 2020:

(A) Whose new petitioner files an H-2B petition on or after May 14, 2020, is authorized to begin employment with the new petitioner to perform work that is essential to the U.S. food supply chain after the petition described in this paragraph (h)(23), including the attestation described in paragraph (h)(23)(v)(A) of this section, is received by USCIS and before the H-2B petition is approved, but no earlier than the start date of employment indicated in the H-2B petition; or

(B) Whose new petitioner filed an H-2B petition on or after March 1, 2020 and the petition was pending on or after May 14, 2020, is authorized to begin employment with the new petitioner to perform work that is essential to the U.S. food supply chain after the attestation described in paragraph (h)(23)(v)(A) is received by USCIS and before the H-2B petition is approved.

(iii)(A) With respect to a petition described in paragraph (h)(23)(ii)(A) of this section, and subject to the requirements of 8 CFR 274a.12(b)(27), the new period of employment described in paragraph (h)(23)(ii) may last for up to 60 days beginning on the Received Date on Form I-797 (Notice of Action) or, if the start date of employment occurs after the I-797 Received Date, for a period of up to 60 days beginning on the start date of employment indicated in the H-2B petition. Employment is not authorized under this paragraph (h)(23) if USCIS does not receive the attestation described in paragraph (h)(23)(v)(A) of this section.

(B) With respect to a petition described in paragraph (h)(23)(ii)(B) of this section, the new period of employment described in paragraph (h)(23)(ii) may last for up to 60 days beginning on the date that USCIS acknowledges in writing the receipt of a properly filed attestation described paragraph (h)(23)(v). Employment under this paragraph (h)(23) is not authorized if USCIS does not receive the attestation described in paragraph (h)(23)(v)(A) of this section.

(C) With respect to either type of petition, if USCIS adjudicates the petition prior to the expiration of this 60-day period and denies the petition for extension of stay, or if the petition is withdrawn by the petitioner before the expiration of the 60-day period, the employment authorization associated with the filing of that petition under 8 CFR 274a.12(b)(27) will automatically terminate 15 days after the date of the denial decision or 15 days after the date on which the petition is withdrawn. Nothing in this paragraph (h)(23) is intended to alter the availability of employment authorization related to professional H-2B athletes who are traded between organizations pursuant to paragraph (h)(6)(vii) of this section and 8 CFR 274a.12(b)(9).

(iv) Notwithstanding paragraphs (h)(13)(i)(B), (h)(13)(iv) and (v), and (h)(15)(ii)(C) of this section, an H-2B petition seeking an extension of stay for H-2B aliens who are essential to the U.S. food supply chain to work, and submitted with an approved temporary labor certification, may be approved on the basis of this paragraph (h)(23), even if any of the aliens requested in the H-2B petition have otherwise exhausted the applicable 3-year maximum period of stay in the United States and have not thereafter been absent from the United States for an uninterrupted period of 3 months, or if any such aliens would exceed the 3-year limit as a consequence of the approval of the extension.

(v) In addition to meeting all other requirements for the H-2B classification, to commence employment and be approved under this paragraph (h)(23):

(A) The H-2B petitioner must submit an attestation indicating that the H-2B alien will be performing work that is essential to the U.S. food supply chain;

(B) The alien must have been in valid H-2B nonimmigrant status on or after March 1, 2020; and

(C) The H-2B petition must have been—

(1) Received on or after March 1, 2020, and pending as of May 14, 2020, so long as the H-2B worker did not begin work with the new employer before May 14, 2020, or

(2) Received on or after May 14, 2020, but no later than September 11, 2020.

(vi) Authorization to initiate employment changes pursuant to paragraphs (h)(23)(ii) and (iii) of this section, or be approved for employment exceeding 3 years in duration pursuant to paragraph (h)(23)(iv) of this section, begins on May 14, 2020, and ends at the end of September 11, 2020.

(24) Severability.

(i) The requirement to submit a registration for an H–1B capsubject petition and the selection process based on properly submitted registrations under paragraph (h)(8)(iii) of this section are intended to be severable from paragraph (h)(8)(iv) of this section. In the event paragraph (h)(8)(iii) is not implemented, or in the event that paragraph (h)(8)(iv) is not implemented, DHS intends that either of those provisions be implemented as an independent rule, without prejudice to petitioners in the United States under this section, as consistent with law.

(ii) The following provisions added or revised by the changes made to the H– 1B nonimmigrant visa classification program, as of December 7, 2020, are intended to be implemented as separate and severable from one another: paragraphs (h)(2)(i), (h)(4)(i)(B)(7), (h)(4)(ii) (definitions of employer-employee, specialty occupation, third-party worksite, U.S. employer, and worksite), (h)(4)(iii)(A), (h)(4)(iv)(C), (h)(9)(i)(B), and (h)(9)(iii)(A)(1) of this section. If one or more of the paragraphs in the preceding sentence is not implemented, DHS intends that the remaining paragraphs will remain valid and be implemented to the greatest extent possible.

(25) [Reserved effective May 25, 2021 through May 28, 2024.]

(26) [Effective May 25, 2021 through May 28, 2024.] Change of employers and portability for H-2B workers (May 25, 2021 through November 22, 2021).

(i) This paragraph (h)(26) relates to H-2B workers seeking to change employers during the time period specified in paragraph (h)(26)(iv) of this section. Notwithstanding paragraph (h)(2)(i)(D) of this section, an alien in valid H-2B nonimmigrant status:

(A) Whose new petitioner files a non-frivolous H-2B petition requesting an extension of the alien's stay on or after May 25, 2021, is authorized to begin employment with the new petitioner after the petition described in this paragraph (h)(26) is received by USCIS and before the new H-2B petition is approved, but no earlier than the start date indicated in the new H-2B petition; or

(B) Whose new petitioner filed a non-frivolous H-2B petition requesting an extension of the alien's stay before May 25, 2021 that remains pending on May 25, 2021, is authorized to begin employment with the new petitioner before the new H-2B petition is approved, but no earlier than the start date of employment indicated on the new H-2B petition.

(ii)(A) With respect to a new petition described in paragraph (h)(26)(i)(A) of this section, and subject to the requirements of 8 CFR 274a.12(b)(30), the new period of employment described in paragraph (h)(26)(i) of this section may last for up to 60 days beginning on the Received Date on Form I-797 (Notice of Action) or, if the start date of employment occurs after the I-797 Received Date, for a period of up to 60 days beginning on the start date of employment indicated in the H-2B petition.

(B) With respect to a new petition described in paragraph (h)(26)(i)(B) of this section, the new period of employment described in paragraph (h)(26)(i) of this section may last for up to 60 days beginning on the later of either May 25, 2021 or the start date of employment indicated in the H-2B petition.

(C) With respect to either type of new petition, if USCIS adjudicates the new petition before the expiration of this 60-day period and denies the petition, or if the new petition is withdrawn by the petitioner before the expiration of the 60-day period, the employment authorization associated with the filing of that petition under 8 CFR 274a.12(b)(30) will automatically terminate 15 days after the date of the denial decision or 15 days after the date on which the new petition is withdrawn. Nothing in this paragraph (h)(26) is intended to alter the availability of employment authorization related to professional H-2B athletes who are traded between organizations pursuant to paragraph (h)(6)(vii) of this section and 8 CFR 274a.12(b)(9).

(iii) In addition to meeting all other requirements in paragraph (h)(6) of this section for the H-2B classification, to commence employment and be approved under this paragraph (h)(26):

(A) The alien must have been in valid H-2B nonimmigrant status on or after May 25, 2021;

(B) The new H-2B petition must have been—

(1) Pending as of May 25, 2021; or

(2) Received on or after May 25, 2021, but no later than November 22, 2021;

(C) The petitioner must comply with all Federal, State, and local employment-related laws and regulations, including health and safety laws, laws related to COVID-19 worker protections, and any right to time off or paid time off for COVID-19 vaccination; and

(D) The petitioner may not impede, interfere, or refuse to cooperate with an employee of the Secretary of the U.S. Department of Labor who is exercising or attempting to exercise DOL's audit or investigative authority under 20 CFR part 655, subpart A, and 29 CFR 503.25.

(iv) Authorization to initiate employment changes pursuant to this paragraph (h)(26) begins at 12 a.m. on May 25, 2021, and ends at the end of November 22, 2021.

(27) [Effective Jan. 28, 2022 through Jan. 28, 2025.] Change of employers and portability for H-2B workers (January 28, 2022 through July 27, 2022).

(i) This paragraph (h)(27) relates to H-2B workers seeking to change employers during the time period specified in paragraph (h)(27)(iv) of this section. Notwithstanding paragraph (h)(2)(i)(D) of this section:

(A) An alien in valid H-2B nonimmigrant status whose new petitioner files a non-frivolous H-2B petition requesting an extension of the alien's stay on or after January 28, 2022, is authorized to begin employment with the new petitioner after the petition described in this paragraph (h)(27) is received by USCIS and before the new H-2B petition is approved, but no earlier than the start date indicated in the new H-2B petition; or

(B) An alien whose new petitioner filed a non-frivolous H-2B petition requesting an extension of the alien's stay before January 28, 2022 that remains pending on January 28, 2022, is authorized to begin employment with the new petitioner before the new H-2B petition is approved, but no earlier than the start date of employment indicated on the new H-2B petition.

(ii)(A) With respect to a new petition described in paragraph (h)(27)(i)(A) of this section, and subject to the requirements of 8 CFR 274a.12(b)(30), the new period of employment described in paragraph (h)(27)(i) of this section may last for up to 60 days beginning on the Received Date on Form I-797 (Notice of Action) or, if the start date of employment occurs after the I-797 Received Date, for a period of up to 60 days beginning on the start date of employment indicated in the H-2B petition.

(B) With respect to a new petition described in paragraph (h)(27)(i)(B) of this section, the new period of employment described in paragraph (h)(27)(i) of this section may last for up to 60 days beginning on the later of either January 28, 2022 or the start date of employment indicated in the H-2B petition.

(C) With respect to either type of new petition, if USCIS adjudicates the new petition before the expiration of this 60-day period and denies the petition, or if the new petition is withdrawn by the petitioner before the expiration of the 60-day period, the employment authorization associated with the filing of that petition under 8 CFR 274a.12(b)(30) will automatically terminate 15 days after the date of the denial decision or 15 days after the date on which the new petition is withdrawn. Nothing in this paragraph (h)(27) is intended to alter the availability of employment authorization related to professional H-2B athletes who are traded between organizations pursuant to paragraph (h)(6)(vii) of this section and 8 CFR 274a.12(b)(9).

(iii) In addition to meeting all other requirements in paragraph (h)(6) of this section for the H-2B classification, to commence employment and be approved under this paragraph (h)(27), the alien must either:

(A) Have been in valid H-2B nonimmigrant status on or after January 28, 2022 and be the beneficiary of a non-frivolous H-2B petition requesting an extension of the alien's stay that is received on or after January 28, 2022, but no later than July 27, 2022; or

(B) Be the beneficiary of a non-frivolous H-2B petition requesting an extension of the alien's stay that is pending as of January 28, 2022.

(C) The petitioner must comply with all Federal, State, and local employment-related laws and regulations, including, where applicable, health and safety laws, laws related to COVID-19 worker protections, any right to time off or paid time off for COVID-19 vaccination, or to reimbursement for travel to and from the nearest available vaccination site; and

(D) The petitioner may not impede, interfere, or refuse to cooperate with an employee of the Secretary of the U.S. Department of Labor who is exercising or attempting to exercise DOL's audit or investigative authority under 20 CFR part 655, subpart A, and 29 CFR 503.25.

(iv) Authorization to initiate employment changes pursuant to this paragraph (h)(27) begins at 12 a.m. on January 28, 2022, and ends at the end of July 27, 2022.

(28) [Effective May 18, 2022 through May 18, 2025] Change of employers and portability for H-2B workers (July 28, 2022 through January 24, 2023).

(i) This paragraph (h)(28) relates to H-2B workers seeking to change employers during the time period specified in paragraph (h)(28)(iv) of this section. Notwithstanding paragraph (h)(2)(i)(D) of this section:

(A) An alien in valid H-2B nonimmigrant status whose new petitioner files a non-frivolous H-2B petition requesting an extension of the alien's stay on or after July 28, 2022, is authorized to begin employment with the new petitioner after the petition described in this paragraph (h)(28) is received by USCIS and before the new H-2B petition is approved, but no earlier than the start date indicated in the new H-2B petition; or

(B) An alien whose new petitioner filed a non-frivolous H-2B petition requesting an extension of the alien's stay before July 28, 2022 that remains pending on July 28, 2022, is authorized to begin employment with the new petitioner before the new H-2B petition is approved, but no earlier than the start date of employment indicated on the new H-2B petition.

(ii)(A) With respect to a new petition described in paragraph (h)(28)(i)(A) of this section, and subject to the requirements of 8 CFR 274a.12(b)(30), the new period of employment described in paragraph (h)(28)(i) of this section may last for up to 60 days beginning on the Received Date on Form I-797 (Notice of Action) or, if the start date of employment occurs after the I-797 Received Date, for a period of up to 60 days beginning on the start date of employment indicated in the H-2B petition.

(B) With respect to a new petition described in paragraph (h)(28)(i)(B) of this section, the new period of employment described in paragraph (h)(28)(i) of this section may last for up to 60 days beginning on the later of either July 28, 2022 or the start date of employment indicated in the H-2B petition.

(C) With respect to either type of new petition, if USCIS adjudicates the new petition before the expiration of this 60-day period and denies the petition, or if the new petition is withdrawn by the petitioner before the expiration of the 60-day period, the employment authorization associated with the filing of that petition under 8 CFR 274a.12(b)(30) will automatically terminate 15 days after the date of the denial decision or 15 days after the date on which the new petition is withdrawn. Nothing in this paragraph (h)(28) is intended to alter the availability of employment authorization related to professional H-2B athletes who are traded between organizations pursuant to paragraph (h)(6)(vii) of this section and 8 CFR 274a.12(b)(9).

(iii) In addition to meeting all other requirements in paragraph (h)(6) of this section for the H-2B classification, to commence employment and be approved under this paragraph (h)(28):

(A) The alien must either (1) have been in valid H-2B nonimmigrant status on or after July 28, 2022 and be the beneficiary of a non-frivolous H-2B petition requesting an extension of the alien's stay that is received on or after July 28, 2022, but no later than January 24, 2023; or (2) be the beneficiary of a non-frivolous H-2B petition requesting an extension of the alien's stay that is pending as of July 28, 2022.

(B) The petitioner must comply with all Federal, State, and local employment-related laws and regulations, including, where applicable, health and safety laws, laws related to COVID-19 worker protections, any right to time off or paid time off for COVID-19 vaccination, or to reimbursement for travel to and from the nearest available vaccination site; and

(C) The petitioner may not impede, interfere, or refuse to cooperate with an employee of the Secretary of the U.S. Department of Labor who is exercising or attempting to exercise DOL's audit or investigative authority under 20 CFR part 655, subpart A, and 29 CFR 503.25.

(iv) Authorization to initiate employment changes pursuant to this paragraph (h)(28) begins at 12 a.m. on July 28, 2022, and ends at the end of January 24, 2023.

(29) [Effective Dec. 15, 2022 through Dec. 15, 2025] Change of employers and portability for H-2B workers.

(i) This paragraph (h)(29) relates to H-2B workers seeking to change employers during the time period specified in paragraph (h)(29)(iv) of this section. Notwithstanding paragraph (h)(2)(i)(D) of this section:

(A) An alien in valid H-2B nonimmigrant status whose new petitioner files a non-frivolous H-2B petition requesting an extension of the alien's stay on or after January 25, 2023, is authorized to begin employment with the new petitioner after the petition described in this paragraph (h)(29) is received by USCIS and before the new H-2B petition is approved, but no earlier than the start date indicated in the new H-2B petition; or

(B) An alien whose new petitioner filed a non-frivolous H-2B petition requesting an extension of the alien's stay before January 25, 2023 that remains pending on January 25, 2023, is authorized to begin employment with the new petitioner before the new H-2B petition is approved, but no earlier than the start date of employment indicated on the new H-2B petition.

(ii)(A) With respect to a new petition described in paragraph (h)(29)(i)(A) of this section, and subject to the requirements of 8 CFR 274a.12(b)(33), the new period of employment described in paragraph (h)(29)(i) of this section may last for up to 60 days beginning on the Received Date on Form I-797 (Notice of Action) or, if the start date of employment occurs after the I-797 Received Date, for a period of up to 60 days beginning on the start date of employment indicated in the H-2B petition.

(B) With respect to a new petition described in paragraph (h)(29)(i)(B) of this section, the new period of employment described in paragraph (h)(29)(i) of this section may last for up to 60 days beginning on the later of either January 25, 2023 or the start date of employment indicated in the H-2B petition.

(C) With respect to either type of new petition, if USCIS adjudicates the new petition before the expiration of this 60-day period and denies the petition, or if the new petition is withdrawn by the petitioner before the expiration of the 60-day period, the employment authorization associated with the filing of that petition under 8 CFR 274a.12(b)(33) will automatically terminate 15 days after the date of the denial decision or 15 days after the date on which the new petition is withdrawn. Nothing in this paragraph (h)(29) is intended to alter the availability of employment authorization related to professional H-2B athletes who are traded between organizations pursuant to paragraph (h)(6)(vii) of this section and 8 CFR 274a.12(b)(9).

(iii) In addition to meeting all other requirements in paragraph (h)(6) of this section for the H-2B classification, to commence employment under this paragraph (h)(29):

(A) The alien must either have been in valid H-2B nonimmigrant status on or after January 25, 2023 and be the beneficiary of a non-frivolous H-2B petition requesting an extension of the alien's stay that is received on or after January 25, 2023, but no later than January 24, 2024; or be the beneficiary of a non-frivolous H-2B petition requesting an extension of the alien's stay that is pending as of January 25, 2023.

(B) The petitioner must comply with all Federal, State, and local employment-related laws and regulations, including, where applicable, health and safety laws, laws related to COVID-19 worker protections, any right to time off or paid time off for COVID-19 vaccination, or to reimbursement for travel to and from the nearest available vaccination site; and

(C) The petitioner may not impede, interfere, or refuse to cooperate with an employee of the Secretary of the U.S. Department of Labor who is exercising or attempting to exercise DOL's audit or investigative authority under 20 CFR part 655, subpart A, and 29 CFR 503.25.

(iv) Authorization to initiate employment changes pursuant to this paragraph (h)(29) begins at 12 a.m. on January 25, 2023, and ends at the end of January 24, 2024.

(30) Severability. The Department intends that should any of the revisions effective on January 17, 2025, to provisions in paragraphs (h)(2), (5), (6), (10), (11), (13), (16) and (20) of this section or to the provision in 8 CFR 274a.12(b)(21) be held to be invalid or unenforceable by their terms or as applied to any person or circumstance they should nevertheless be construed so as to continue to give the maximum effect to the provision(s) permitted by law, unless any such provision is held to be wholly invalid and unenforceable, in which event the provision(s) should be severed from the remainder of the provisions and the holding should not affect the other provisions or the application of those other provisions to persons not similarly situated or to dissimilar circumstances.

(31) Change of employers and portability for H-2B workers.

(i) This paragraph (h)(31) relates to H-2B workers seeking to change employers during the time period specified in paragraph (h)(31)(iv) of this section. Notwithstanding paragraph (h)(2)(i)(D) of this section:

(A) An alien in valid H-2B nonimmigrant status whose new petitioner files a non-frivolous H-2B petition requesting an extension of the alien's stay on or after January 25, 2024, is authorized to begin employment with the new petitioner after the petition described in this paragraph (h)(31) is received by USCIS and before the new H-2B petition is approved, but no earlier than the start date indicated in the new H-2B petition; or

(B) An alien whose new petitioner filed a non-frivolous H-2B petition requesting an extension of the alien's stay before January 25, 2024, that remains pending on January 25, 2024, is authorized to begin employment with the new petitioner before the new H-2B petition is approved, but no earlier than the start date of employment indicated on the new H-2B petition.

(ii)(A) With respect to a new petition described in paragraph (h)(31)(i)(A) of this section, and subject to the requirements of 8 CFR 274a.12(b)(34), the new period of employment described in paragraph (h)(31)(i) of this section may last for up to 60 days beginning on the Received Date on Form I-797 (Notice of Action) or, if the start date of employment occurs after the I-797 Received Date, for a period of up to 60 days beginning on the start date of employment indicated in the H-2B petition.

(B) With respect to a new petition described in paragraph (h)(31)(i)(B) of this section, the new period of employment described in paragraph (h)(31)(i) of this section may last for up to 60 days beginning on the later of either January 25, 2024, or the start date of employment indicated in the H-2B petition.

(C) With respect to either type of new petition, if USCIS adjudicates the new petition before the expiration of this 60-day period and denies the petition, or if the new petition is withdrawn by the petitioner before the expiration of the 60-day period, the employment authorization associated with the filing of that petition under 8 CFR 274a.12(b)(34) will automatically terminate 15 days after the date of the denial decision or 15 days after the date on which the new petition is withdrawn. Nothing in this paragraph (h)(31) is intended to alter the availability of employment authorization related to professional H-2B athletes who are traded between organizations pursuant to paragraph (h)(6)(vii) of this section and 8 CFR 274a.12(b)(9).

(iii) In addition to meeting all other requirements in paragraph (h)(6) of this section for the H-2B classification, to commence employment under this paragraph (h)(31):

(A) The alien must either:

(1) Have been in valid H-2B nonimmigrant status on or after January 25, 2024 and be the beneficiary of a non-frivolous H-2B petition requesting an extension of the alien's stay that is received on or after January 25, 2024, but no later than January 24, 2025; or

(2) Be the beneficiary of a non-frivolous H-2B petition requesting an extension of the alien's stay that is pending as of January 25, 2024; and

(B) The petitioner may not impede, interfere, or refuse to cooperate with an employee of the Secretary of the U.S. Department of Labor who is exercising or attempting to exercise DOL's audit or investigative authority under 20 CFR part 655, subpart A, and 29 CFR 503.25.

(iv) Authorization to initiate employment changes pursuant to this paragraph (h)(31) begins at 12 a.m. on January 25, 2024, and ends at the end of January 24, 2025.

(32) Change of employers and portability for H-2B workers.

(i) This paragraph (h)(32) relates to H-2B workers seeking to change employers during the time period specified in paragraph (h)(32)(iv) of this section. Notwithstanding paragraph (h)(2)(i)(D) of this section:

(A) An alien in valid H-2B nonimmigrant status whose new petitioner files a non-frivolous H-2B petition requesting an extension of the alien's stay on or after January 25, 2025, is authorized to begin employment with the new petitioner after the petition described in this paragraph (h)(32) is received by USCIS and before the new H-2B petition is approved, but no earlier than the start date indicated in the new H-2B petition; or

(B) An alien whose new petitioner filed a non-frivolous H-2B petition requesting an extension of the alien's stay before January 25, 2025, that remains pending on January 25, 2025, is authorized to begin employment with the new petitioner before the new H-2B petition is approved, but no earlier than the start date of employment indicated on the new H-2B petition.

(ii)(A) With respect to a new petition described in paragraph (h)(32)(i)(A) of this section, and subject to the requirements of 8 CFR 274a.12(b)(35), the new period of employment described in paragraph (h)(32)(i) of this section may last for up to 60 days beginning on the Received Date on Form I-797 (Notice of Action) or, if the start date of employment occurs after the I-797 Received Date, for a period of up to 60 days beginning on the start date of employment indicated in the H-2B petition.

(B) With respect to a new petition described in paragraph (h)(32)(i)(B) of this section, the new period of employment described in paragraph (h)(32)(i) of this section may last for up to 60 days beginning on the later of either January 25, 2025, or the start date of employment indicated in the H-2B petition.

(C) With respect to either type of new petition, if USCIS adjudicates the new petition before the expiration of this 60-day period and denies the petition, or if the new petition is withdrawn by the petitioner before the expiration of the 60-day period, the employment authorization associated with the filing of that petition under 8 CFR 274a.12(b)(35) will automatically terminate 15 days after the date of the denial decision or 15 days after the date on which the new petition is withdrawn. Nothing in this paragraph (h)(32) is intended to alter the availability of employment authorization related to professional H-2B athletes who are traded between organizations pursuant to paragraph (h)(6)(vii) of this section and 8 CFR 274a.12(b)(9).

(iii) In addition to meeting all other requirements in paragraph (h)(6) of this section for the H-2B classification, to commence employment under this paragraph (h)(32):

(A) The alien must either:

(1) Have been in valid H-2B nonimmigrant status on or after January 25, 2025 and be the beneficiary of a non-frivolous H-2B petition requesting an extension of the alien's stay that is received on or after January 25, 2025, but no later than January 24, 2026; or

(2) Be the beneficiary of a non-frivolous H-2B petition requesting an extension of the alien's stay that is pending as of January 25, 2025; and

(B) The petitioner may not impede, interfere, or refuse to cooperate with an employee of the Secretary of the U.S. Department of Labor who is exercising or attempting to exercise DOL's audit or investigative authority under 20 CFR part 655, subpart A, and 29 CFR 503.25.

(iv) Authorization to initiate employment changes pursuant to this paragraph (h)(32) begins at 12 a.m. on January 25, 2025, and ends at the end of January 24, 2026.

(33) Severability. The Department intends that should any of the revisions effective on January 17, 2025, to provisions in paragraphs (f)(5), (h)(2), (4) through (6), (8), (9), (11), (14), and (19), (l)(14), (o)(11), and (p)(13) of this section or to the provisions in 8 CFR 214.1(c)(1) and (4) through (7) be held to be invalid or unenforceable by their terms or as applied to any person or circumstance they should nevertheless be construed so as to continue to give the maximum effect to the provision(s) permitted by law, unless any such provision is held to be wholly invalid and unenforceable, in which event the provision(s) should be severed from the remainder of the provisions and the holding should not affect the other provisions or the application of those other provisions to persons not similarly situated or to dissimilar circumstances.

(i) Representatives of information media—

(1) In general. The admission of an alien of the class defined in section 101(a)(15)(I) of the Act constitutes an agreement by the alien not to change the information medium or his or her employer until he or she obtains permission to do so from the district director having jurisdiction over his or her residence. An alien classified as an information media nonimmigrant (I) may be admitted in or otherwise granted I nonimmigrant status for:

(i) The duration of employment, except as provided in paragraph (i)(1)(ii) of this section; or

(ii) In the case of an alien who presents a passport issued by the People's Republic of China (PRC) (other than a Hong Kong Special Administrative Region passport or a Macau Special Administrative Region passport), until the activities or assignments consistent with the I classification are completed, not to exceed the maximum period of stay as determined by the Secretary. The Secretary of Homeland Security may determine the maximum period of stay when the Secretary determines an adjustment is needed, with such maximum period to be no longer than one year. In determining the maximum period of stay and whether an adjustment is needed, the Secretary will consider factors including, but not limited to, the average authorized period of stay and press credential validity for U.S. journalists in the PRC, the treatment of U.S. journalists in the PRC, any input from the U.S. Department of State, and such other factors as may affect the U.S. interest. Such determination will be published in the Federal Register as a notice and will remain in effect until the Secretary of Homeland Security publishes a new determination under this paragraph.

(2) Extension of stay. An alien in I status who is described in paragraph (i)(1)(ii) of this section may be eligible for extensions of stay, each of up to the maximum period of stay determined by the Secretary pursuant to paragraph (i)(1)(ii) of this section or until the activities or assignments consistent with the I classification are completed (whichever date is earlier).

(i) Notwithstanding 8 CFR 274a.12(b)(20), an alien in I status who is described in paragraph (i)(1)(ii) of this section whose status has expired, but who timely filed an application for an extension of stay, is authorized to stay in the United States and continue employment with the same employer for a period not to exceed 90 days beginning on the date of the expiration of the authorized period of stay. However, if USCIS adjudicates the application prior to the expiration of the 90-day period, and denies the application for an extension of stay, the alien must immediately depart the United States.

(ii) To request an extension of stay, an alien in I status must file an application to extend his or her stay by submitting the form designated by USCIS, in accordance with that form's instructions, and with the required fee, including any biometrics required by 8 CFR 103.16, as appropriate. Requests for extensions of stay will be adjudicated consistent with international legal obligations, including the United Nations Headquarters Agreement and Organization of American States Headquarters Agreement.

(3) Change of status. An alien seeking to change from a different nonimmigrant status to, if eligible, an I status described in paragraph (i)(1)(ii) of this section, may be granted a period of stay until the activities or assignments consistent with the I classification are completed, not to exceed the maximum period of stay determined by the Secretary pursuant to paragraph (i)(1)(ii) of this section. To request a change from a different nonimmigrant status to an I status described in paragraph (i)(1)(ii), an alien must file an application to change his or her status by submitting the form designated by USCIS, in accordance with that form's instructions, and with the required fee, including any biometrics required by 8 CFR 103.16, as appropriate.

(4) Applicable maximum period of stay. Any change in the maximum period of stay announced by a Federal Register notice pursuant to paragraph (i)(1)(ii) of this section applies to applications for an extension of stay or a change of status, filed under paragraphs (i)(2) and (3) of this section respectively, that are pending with USCIS on the effective date of the Federal Register notice.

(j) Exchange aliens —

(1) General —

(i) Eligibility for admission. A nonimmigrant exchange visitor and his or her accompanying spouse and minor children may be admitted into the United States in J-1 and J-2 classifications under section 101(a)(15)(J) of the Act, if the exchange visitor and his or her accompanying spouse and children each presents a SEVIS Form DS-2019 issued in his or her own name by a program approved by the Department of State for participation by J-1 exchange visitors. Prior to August 1, 2003, if exigent circumstances are demonstrated, the Service will allow the dependent of an exchange visitor possessing a SEVIS Form DS-2019 to enter the United States using a copy of the exchange visitor's SEVIS Form DS-2019. However, where the exchange visitor presents a properly completed Form DS-2019, Certificate of Eligibility for Exchange Visitor (J-1) Status, which was issued to the J-1 exchange visitor by a program approved by the Department of State for participation by exchange visitors and which remains valid for the admission of the exchange visitor, the accompanying spouse and children may be admitted on the basis of the J-1's non-SEVIS Form DS-2019.

(ii) Admission period. An exchange alien, and J-2 spouse and children, may be admitted for a period up to 30 days before the report date or start of the approved program listed on Form DS-2019. The initial admission of an exchange visitor, spouse and children may not exceed the period specified on Form DS-2019, plus a period of 30 days for the purposes of travel or for the period designated by the Commissioner as provided in paragraph (j)(1)(vi) of this section. Regulations of the Department of State published at 22 CFR part 62 give general limitations on the stay of the various classes of exchange visitors. A spouse or child may not be admitted for longer than the principal exchange visitor.

(iii) Readmission. An exchange alien may be readmitted to the United States for the remainder of the time authorized on Form I-94, without presenting Form IAP-66, if the alien is returning from a visit solely to foreign contiguous territory or adjacent islands after an absence of less than 30 days and if the original Form I-94 is presented. All other exchange aliens must present a valid Form IAP-66. An original Form IAP-66 or copy three (the pink copy) of a previously issued form presented by an exchange alien returning from a temporary absence shall be retained by the exchange alien for re-entries during the balance of the alien's stay.

(iv) Extensions of Stay. If an exchange alien requires an extension beyond the initial admission period, the alien shall apply by submitting a new Form DS-2019 which indicates the date to which the alien's program is extended. The extension may not exceed the period specified on Form DS-2019, plus a period of 30 days for the purpose of travel. Extensions of stay for the alien's spouse and children require, as an attachment to Form DS-2019, Form I-94 for each dependent, and a list containing the names of the applicants, dates and places of birth, passport numbers, issuing countries, and expiration dates. An accompanying spouse or child may not be granted an extension of stay for longer than the principal exchange alien.

(v) Employment.

(A) The accompanying spouse and minor children of a J-1 exchange visitor may accept employment only with authorization by the Immigration and Naturalization Service. A request for employment authorization must be made on Form I-765, Application for Employment Authorization, with fee, as required by the Service, to the district director having jurisdiction over the J-1 exchange visitor's temporary residence in the United States. Income from the spouse's or dependent's employment may be used to support the family's customary recreational and cultural activities and related travel, among other things. Employment will not be authorized if this income is needed to support the J-1 principal alien.

(B) J-2 employment may be authorized for the duration of the J-1 principal alien's authorized stay as indicated on Form I-94 or a period of four years, whichever is shorter. The employment authorization is valid only if the J-1 is maintaining status. Where a J-2 spouse or dependent child has filed a timely application for extension of stay, only upon approval of the request for extension of stay may he or she apply for a renewal of the employment authorization on a Form I-765 with the required fee.

(vi) Extension of duration of status. The Commissioner may, by notice in the FEDERAL REGISTER, at any time she determines that the H-1B numerical limitation as described in section 214(g)(1)(A) of the Act will likely be reached prior to the end of a current fiscal year, extend for such a period of time as the Commissioner deems necessary to complete the adjudication of the H-1B application, the duration of status of any J-1 alien on behalf of whom an employer has timely filed an application for change of status to H-1B. The alien, in accordance with 8 CFR part 248, must not have violated the terms of his or her nonimmigrant stay and is not subject to the 2-year foreign residence requirement at 212(e) of the Act. Any J-1 student whose duration of status has been extended shall be considered to be maintaining lawful nonimmigrant status for all purposes under the Act, provided that the alien does not violate the terms and conditions of his or her J nonimmigrant stay. An extension made under this paragraph also applies to the J-2 dependent aliens.

(vii) Use of SEVIS. At a date to be established by the Department of State, the use of the Student and Exchange Visitor Information System (SEVIS) will become mandatory for designated program sponsors. After that date, which will be announced by publication in the FEDERAL REGISSTER all designated program sponsors must begin issuance of the SEVIS Form DS-2019.

(viii) Current name and address. A J-1 exchange visitor must inform the Service and the responsible officer of the exchange visitor program of any legal changes to his or her name or of any change of address, within 10 days of the change, in a manner prescribed by the program sponsor. A J-1 exchange visitor enrolled in a SEVIS program can satisfy the requirement in 8 CFR 265.1 of notifying the Service by providing a notice of a change of address within 10 days to the responsible officer, who in turn shall enter the information in SEVIS within 21 days of notification by the exchange visitor. A J-1 exchange visitor enrolled at a non-SEVIS program must submit a change of address to the Service, as provided in 8 CFR 265.1, within 10 days of the change. Except in the case of an exchange visitor who cannot receive mail where he or she resides, the address provided by the exchange visitor must be the actual physical location where the exchange visitor resides rather than a mailing address. In cases where an exchange visitor provides a mailing address, the exchange visitor program must maintain a record of, and must provide upon request from the Service, the actual physical location where the exchange visitor resides.

(2) Special reporting requirement. Each exchange alien participating in a program of graduate medical education or training shall file Form I-644 (Supplementary Statement for Graduate Medical Trainees) annually with the Service attesting to the conditions as specified on the form. The exchange alien shall also submit Form I-644 as an attachment to a completed Form DS-2019 when applying for an extension of stay.

(3) Alien in cancelled programs. When the approval of an exchange visitor program is withdrawn by the Director of the United States Information Agency, the district director shall send a notice of the withdrawal to each participant in the program and a copy of each such notice shall be sent to the program sponsor. If the exchange visitor is currently engaged in activities authorized by the cancelled program, the participant is authorized to remain in the United States to engage in those activities until expiration of the period of stay previously authorized. The district director shall notify participants in cancelled programs that permission to remain in the United States as an exchange visitor, or

extension of stay may be obtained if the participant is accepted in another approved program and a Form DS-2019, executed by the new program sponsor, is submitted. In this case, a release from the sponsor of the cancelled program will not be required.

(4) Eligibility requirements for section 101(a)(15)(J) classification for aliens desiring to participate in programs under which they will receive graduate medical education or training —

(i) Requirements. Any alien coming to the United States as an exchange visitor to participate in a program under which the alien will receive graduate medical education or training, or any alien seeking to change nonimmigrant status to that of an exchange visitor on Form I-506 for that purpose, must have passed parts of I and II of the National Board of Medical Examiners Examination (or an equivalent examination as determined by the Secretary of Health and Human Services), and must be competent in oral and written English, and shall submit a completely executed and valid Form DS-2019.

(ii) Exemptions. From January 10, 1978 until December 31, 1983, any alien who has come to or seeks to come to the United States as an exchange visitor to participate in an accredited program of graduate medical education or training, or any alien who seeks to change nonimmigrant status for that purpose, may be admitted to participate in such program without regard to the requirements stated in subparagraphs (A) and (B)(ii)(I) of section 212(j)(1) of the Act if a substantial disruption in the health services provided by such program would result from not permitting the alien to participate in the program: Provided that the exemption will not increase the total number of aliens then participating in such programs to a level greater than that participating on January 10, 1978.

(5) Remittance of the fee. An alien who applies for J-1 nonimmigrant status in order to commence participation in a Department of State-designated exchange visitor program is required to pay the SEVIS fee to DHS, pursuant to 8 CFR 214.13, except as otherwise provided in that section.

(k) Spouses, Fiancees, and Fiances of United States Citizens. —

(1) Petition and supporting documents. To be classified as a fiance or fiancee as defined in section 101(a)(15)(K)(i) of the Act, an alien must be the beneficiary of an approved visa petition filed on Form I-129F. A copy of a document submitted in support of a visa petition filed pursuant to section 214(d) of the Act and this paragraph may be accepted, though unaccompanied by the original, if the copy bears a certification by an attorney, typed or rubber-stamped, in the language set forth in § 204.2(j) of this chapter. However, the original document shall be submitted if requested by the Service.

(2) Requirement that petitioner and K-1 beneficiary have met. The petitioner shall establish to the satisfaction of the director that the petitioner and K-1 beneficiary have met in person within the two years immediately preceding the filing of the petition. As a matter of discretion, the director may exempt the petitioner from this requirement only if it is established that compliance would result in extreme hardship to the petitioner or that compliance would violate strict and long-established customs of the K-1 beneficiary's foreign culture or social practice, as where marriages are traditionally arranged by the parents of the contracting parties and the prospective bride and groom are prohibited from meeting subsequent to the arrangement and prior to the wedding day. In addition to establishing that the required meeting would be a violation of custom or practice, the petitioner must also establish that any and all other aspects of the traditional arrangements have been or will be met in accordance with the custom or practice. Failure to establish that the petitioner and K-1 beneficiary have met within the required period or that compliance with the requirement should be waived shall result in the denial of the petition. Such denial shall be without prejudice to the filing of a new petition once the petitioner and K-1 beneficiary have met in person.

(3) Children of beneficiary. Without the approval of a separate petition on his or her behalf, a child of the beneficiary (as defined in section 101(b)(1)(A), (B), (C), (D), or (E) of the Act) may be accorded the same nonimmigrant classification as the beneficiary if accompanying or following to join him or her.

(4) Notification. The petitioner shall be notified of the decision and, if the petition is denied, of the reasons therefor and of the right to appeal in accordance with the provisions of part 103 of this chapter.

(5) Validity. The approval of a petition under this paragraph shall be valid for a period of four months. A petition which has expired due to the passage of time may be revalidated by a director or a consular officer for a period of four months from the date of revalidation upon a finding that the petitioner and K-1 beneficiary are free to marry and intend to marry each other within 90 days of the beneficiary's entry into the United States. The approval of any petition is automatically terminated when the petitioner dies or files a written withdrawal of the petition before the beneficiary arrives in the United States.

(6) Adjustment of status from nonimmigrant to immigrant —

(i) [Reserved]

(ii) Nonimmigrant visa issued on or after November 10, 1986. Upon contracting a valid marriage to the petitioner within 90 days of his or her admission as a nonimmigrant pursuant to a valid K-1 visa issued on or after November 10, 1986, the K-1 beneficiary and his or her minor children may apply for adjustment of status to lawful permanent resident under section 245 of the Act. Upon approval of the application the director shall record their lawful admission for permanent residence in accordance with that section and subject to the conditions prescribed in section 216 of the Act.

(7) Eligibility, petition and supporting documents for K-3/K-4 classification. To be classified as a K-3 spouse as defined in section 101(a)(15)(k)(ii) of the Act, or the K-4 child of such alien defined in section 101(a)(15)(K)(iii) of the Act, the alien spouse must be the beneficiary of an immigrant visa petition filed by a

U.S. citizen on Form I-130, Petition for Alien Relative, and the beneficiary of an approved petition for a K-3 nonimmigrant visa filed on Form I-129F.

(8) Period of admission for K3/K-4 status. Aliens entering the United States as a K-3 shall be admitted for a period of 2 years. Aliens entering the United States as a K-4 shall be admitted for a period of 2 years or until that alien's 21st birthday, whichever is shorter.

(9) Employment authorization. An alien admitted to the United States as a nonimmigrant under section 101(a)(15)(K) of the Act shall be authorized to work incident to status for the period of authorized stay. K-1/K-2 aliens seeking work authorization must apply, with fee, to the Service for work authorization pursuant to § 274a.12(a)(6) of this chapter. K-3/K-4 aliens must apply to the Service for a document evidencing employment authorization pursuant to § 274a.12(a)(9) of this chapter. Employment authorization documents issued to K-3/K-4 aliens may be renewed only upon a showing that the applicant has an application or petition awaiting approval, equivalent to the showing required for an extension of stay pursuant to § 214.2(k)(10).

(10) Extension of stay for K-3/K-4 status.

(i) General. A K-3/K-4 alien may apply for extension of stay, on Form I-539, Application to Extend/Change Nonimmigrant Status, 120 days prior to the expiration of his or her authorized stay. Extensions for K-4 status must be filed concurrently with the alien's parent's K-3 status extension application. In addition, the citizen parent of a K-4 alien filing for extension of K status should file Form I-130 on their behalf. Extension will be granted in 2-year intervals upon a showing of eligibility pursuant to section 101(a)(15)(K)(ii) or (iii) of the Act. Aliens wishing to extend their period of stay as a K-3 or K-4 alien pursuant to § 214.1(c)(2) must show that one of the following has been filed with the Service or the Department of State, as applicable, and is awaiting approval:

(A) The Form I-130, Petition for Alien Relative, filed by the K-3's U.S. citizen spouse who filed the Form I-129F;

(B) An application for an immigrant visa based on a Form I-130 described in § 214.2(K)(10)(i);

(C) A Form I-485, Application for Adjustment to that of Permanent Residence, based on a Form I-130 described in § 214.2(k)(10)(i);

(ii) "Good Cause" showing. Aliens may file for an extension of stay as a K-3/K-4 nonimmigrant after a Form I-130 filed on their behalf has been approved, without filing either an application for adjustment of status or an immigrant visa upon a showing of "good cause." A showing of "good cause" may include an illness, a job loss, or some other catastrophic event that has prevented the filing of an adjustment of status application by the K-3/K-4 alien. The event or events must have taken place since the alien entered the United States as a K-3/K-4 nonimmigrant. The burden of establishing "good cause" rests solely with the applicant. Whether the applicant has shown "good cause" is a purely discretionary decision by the Service from which there is no appeal.

(11) Termination of K-3/K-4 status. The status of an alien admitted to the United States as a K-3/K-4 under section 101(a)(15)(K)(ii) or (iii) of the Act, shall be automatically terminated 30 days following the occurrence of any of the following:

(i) The denial or revocation of the Form I-130 filed on behalf of that alien;

(ii) The denial or revocation of the immigrant visa application filed by that alien;

(iii) The denial or revocation of the alien's application for adjustment of status to that of lawful permanent residence;

(iv) The K-3 spouse's divorce from the U.S. citizen becomes final;

(v) The marriage of an alien in K-4 status.

(vi) The denial of any of these petitions or applications to a K-3 also results in termination of a dependent K-4's status. For purposes of this section, there is no denial or revocation of a petition or application until the administrative appeal applicable to that application or petition has been exhausted.

(*l*) Intracompany transferees —

(1) Admission of intracompany transferees —

(i) General. Under section 101(a)(15)(L) of the Act, an alien who within the preceding three years has been employed abroad for one continuous year by a qualifying organization may be admitted temporarily to the United States to be employed by a parent, branch, affiliate, or subsidiary of that employer in a managerial or executive capacity, or in a position requiring specialized knowledge. An alien transferred to the United States under this nonimmigrant classification is referred to as an intracompany transferee and the organization which seeks the classification of an alien as an intracompany transferee is referred to as the petitioner. The Service has responsibility for determining whether the alien is eligible for admission and whether the petitioner is a qualifying organization. These regulations set forth the standards applicable to these classifications. They also set forth procedures for admission of intracompany transferees and appeal of adverse decisions. Certain petitioners seeking the classification of aliens as intracompany transferees may file blanket petitions with the Service. Under the blanket petition process, the Service is responsible for determining whether the petitioner and its parent, branches, affiliates, or subsidiaries specified are qualifying organizations. The Department of State or, in certain cases, the Service is responsible for determining the classification of the alien.

(ii) Definitions —

(A) Intracompany transferee means an alien who, within three years preceding the time of his or her application for admission into the United States, has been employed abroad continuously for one year by a firm or corporation or other legal entity or parent, branch, affiliate, or subsidiary thereof, and who seeks to enter the United States temporarily in order to render his or her services to a branch of the same employer or a parent, affiliate, or subsidiary thereof in a capacity that is managerial, executive, or involves specialized knowledge. Periods spent in the United

States in lawful status for a branch of the same employer or a parent, affiliate, or subsidiary thereof and brief trips to the United States for business or pleasure shall not be interruptive of the one year of continuous employment abroad but such periods shall not be counted toward fulfillment of that requirement.

(B) Managerial capacity means an assignment within an organization in which the employee primarily:

(1) Manages the organization, or a department, subdivision, function, or component of the organization;

(2) Supervises and controls the work of other supervisory, professional, or managerial employees, or manages an essential function within the organization, or a department or subdivision of the organization;

(3) Has the authority to hire and fire or recommend those as well as other personnel actions (such as promotion and leave authorization) if another employee or other employees are directly supervised; if no other employee is directly supervised, functions at a senior level within the organizational hierarchy or with respect to the function managed; and

(4) Exercises discretion over the day-to-day operations of the activity or function for which the employee has authority. A first-line supervisor is not considered to be acting in a managerial capacity merely by virtue of the supervisor's supervisory duties unless the employees supervised are professional.

(C) Executive capacity means an assignment within an organization in which the employee primarily:

(1) Directs the management of the organization or a major component or function of the organization;

(2) Establishes the goals and policies of the organization, component, or function;

(3) Exercises wide latitude in discretionary decision-making; and

(4) Receives only general supervision or direction from higher level executives, the board of directors, or stockholders of the organization.

(D) Specialized knowledge means special knowledge possessed by an individual of the petitioning organization's product, service, research, equipment, techniques, management, or other interests and its application in international markets, or an advanced level of knowledge or expertise in the organization's processes and procedures.

(E) Specialized knowledge professional means an individual who has specialized knowledge as defined in paragraph (l)(1)(ii)(D) of this section and is a member of the professions as defined in section 101(a)(32) of the Immigration and Nationality Act.

(F) New office means an organization which has been doing business in the United States through a parent, branch, affiliate, or subsidiary for less than one year.

(G) Qualifying organization means a United States or foreign firm, corporation, or other legal entity which:

(1) Meets exactly one of the qualifying relationships specified in the definitions of a parent, branch, affiliate or subsidiary specified in paragraph (l)(1)(ii) of this section;

(2) Is or will be doing business (engaging in international trade is not required) as an employer in the United States and in at least one other country directly or through a parent, branch, affiliate, or subsidiary for the duration of the alien's stay in the United States as an intracompany transferee; and

(3) Otherwise meets the requirements of section 101(a)(15)(L) of the Act.

(H) Doing business means the regular, systematic, and continuous provision of goods and/or services by a qualifying organization and does not include the mere presence of an agent or office of the qualifying organization in the United States and abroad.

(I) Parent means a firm, corporation, or other legal entity which has subsidiaries.

(J) Branch means an operating division or office of the same organization housed in a different location.

(K) Subsidiary means a firm, corporation, or other legal entity of which a parent owns, directly or indirectly, more than half of the entity and controls the entity; or owns, directly or indirectly, half of the entity and controls the entity; or owns, directly or indirectly, 50 percent of a 50-50 joint venture and has equal control and veto power over the entity; or owns, directly or indirectly, less than half of the entity, but in fact controls the entity.

(L) Affiliate means

(1) One of two subsidiaries both of which are owned and controlled by the same parent or individual, or

(2) One of two legal entities owned and controlled by the same group of individuals, each individual owning and controlling approximately the same share or proportion of each entity, or

(3) In the case of a partnership that is organized in the United States to provide accounting services along with managerial and/or consulting services and that markets its accounting services under an internationally recognized name under an agreement with a worldwide coordinating organization that is owned and controlled by the member accounting firms, a partnership (or similar organization) that is organized outside the United States to provide accounting services shall be considered to be an affiliate of the United States partnership if it markets its accounting services under the same internationally recognized name under the agreement with the worldwide coordinating organization of which the United States partnership is also a member.

(M) Director means a Service Center director with delegated authority at 8 CFR 103.1.

(2) Filing of petitions —

(i) Except as provided in paragraph (l)(2)(ii) and (l)(17) of this section, a petitioner seeking to classify an alien as an intracompany transferee must file a petition on the form prescribed by USCIS. The petitioner shall advise USCIS whether a previous petition for the same beneficiary has been filed, and certify that another petition for the same beneficiary will not be filed unless the circumstances and conditions in the initial petition have changed. Failure to make a full disclosure of previous petitions filed may result in a denial of the petition.

(ii) A United States petitioner which meets the requirements of paragraph (l)(4) of this section and seeks continuing approval of itself and its parent, branches, specified subsidiaries and affiliates as qualifying organizations and, later, classification under section 101(a)(15)(L) of the Act multiple numbers of aliens employed by itself, its parent, or those branches, subsidiaries, or affiliates may file a blanket petition on the form prescribed by USCIS. The blanket petition shall be maintained at the adjudicating office. The petitioner shall be the single representative for the qualifying organizations with which USCIS will deal regarding the blanket petition.

(3) Evidence for individual petitions. An individual petition filed on the form prescribed by USCIS shall be accompanied by:

(i) Evidence that the petitioner and the organization which employed or will employ the alien are qualifying organizations as defined in paragraph (l)(1)(ii)(G) of this section.

(ii) Evidence that the alien will be employed in an executive, managerial, or specialized knowledge capacity, including a detailed description of the services to be performed.

(iii) Evidence that the alien has at least one continuous year of full-time employment abroad with a qualifying organization within the three years preceding the filing of the petition.

(iv) Evidence that the alien's prior year of employment abroad was in a position that was managerial, executive, or involved specialized knowledge and that the alien's prior education, training, and employment qualifies him/her to perform the intended services in the United States; however, the work in the United States need not be the same work which the alien performed abroad.

(v) If the petition indicates that the beneficiary is coming to the United States as a manager or executive to open or to be employed in a new office in the United States, the petitioner shall submit evidence that:

(A) Sufficient physical premises to house the new office have been secured;

(B) The beneficiary has been employed for one continuous year in the three year period preceding the filing of the petition in an executive or managerial capacity and that the proposed employment involved executive or managerial authority over the new operation; and

(C) The intended United States operation, within one year of the approval of the petition, will support an executive or managerial position as defined in paragraphs (l)(1)(ii) (B) or (C) of this section, supported by information regarding:

(1) The proposed nature of the office describing the scope of the entity, its organizational structure, and its financial goals;

(2) The size of the United States investment and the financial ability of the foreign entity to remunerate the beneficiary and to commence doing business in the United States; and

(3) The organizational structure of the foreign entity.

(vi) If the petition indicates that the beneficiary is coming to the United States in a specialized knowledge capacity to open or to be employed in a new office, the petitioner shall submit evidence that:

(A) Sufficient physical premises to house the new office have been secured;

(B) The business entity in the United States is or will be a qualifying organization as defined in paragraph (l)(1)(ii)(G) of this section; and

(C) The petitioner has the financial ability to remunerate the beneficiary and to commence doing business in the United States.

(vii) If the beneficiary is an owner or major stockholder of the company, the petition must be accompanied by evidence that the beneficiary's services are to be used for a temporary period and evidence that the beneficiary will be transferred to an assignment abroad upon the completion of the temporary services in the United States.

(viii) Such other evidence as the director, in his or her discretion, may deem necessary.

(4) Blanket petitions —

(i) A petitioner which meets the following requirements may file a blanket petition seeking continuing approval of itself and some or all of its parent, branches, subsidiaries, and affiliates as qualifying organizations if:

(A) The petitioner and each of those entities are engaged in commercial trade or services;

(B) The petitioner has an office in the United States that has been doing business for one year or more;

(C) The petitioner has three or more domestic and foreign branches, subsidiaries, or affiliates; and

(D) The petitioner and the other qualifying organizations have obtained approval of petitions for at least ten "L" managers, executives, or specialized knowledge professionals during the previous 12 months; or have U.S. subsidiaries or affiliates with combined annual sales of at least $ 25 million; or have a United States work force of at least 1,000 employees.

(ii) Managers, executives, and specialized knowledge professionals employed by firms, corporations, or other entities which have been found to be qualifying organizations pursuant to an approved blanket petition may be classified as intracompany transferees and admitted to the United States as provided in paragraphs (l) (5) and (11) of this section.

(iii) When applying for a blanket petition, the petitioner shall include in the blanket petition all of its branches, subsidiaries, and affiliates which plan to seek to transfer aliens to the United States under the blanket petition. An individual petition may be filed by the petitioner or organizations in lieu of using the blanket petition procedure. However, the petitioner and other qualifying organizations may not seek L classification for the same alien under both procedures, unless a consular officer first denies eligibility. Whenever a petitioner which has blanket L approval files an individual petition to seek L classification for a manager, executive, or specialized knowledge professional, the petitioner shall advise the Service that it has blanket L approval and certify that the beneficiary has not and will not apply to a consular officer for L classification under the approved blanket petition.

(iv) Evidence. A blanket petition filed on the form prescribed by USCIS shall be accompanied by:

(A) Evidence that the petitioner meets the requirements of paragraph (l)(4)(i) of this section.

(B) Evidence that all entities for which approval is sought are qualifying organizations as defined in subparagraph (l)(1)(ii)(G) of this section.

(C) Such other evidence as the director, in his or her discretion, deems necessary in a particular case.

(5) Certification and admission procedures for beneficiaries under blanket petition.

(i) Jurisdiction. United States consular officers shall have authority to determine eligibility of individual beneficiaries outside the United States seeking L classification under blanket petitions, except for visa-exempt nonimmigrants. An application for a visa-exempt nonimmigrant seeking L classification under a blanket petition or by an alien in the United States applying for change of status to L classification under a blanket petition shall be filed with the Service office at which the blanket petition was filed.

(ii) Procedures.

(A) When one qualifying organization listed in an approved blanket petition wishes to transfer an alien outside the United States to a qualifying organization in the United States and the alien requires a visa to enter the United States, that organization shall complete Form I-129S, Certificate of Eligibility for Intracompany Transferee under a Blanket Petition, in an original and three copies. The qualifying organization shall retain one copy for its records and send the original and two copies to the alien. A copy of the approved Form I-797 must be attached to the original and each copy of Form I-129S.

(B) After receipt of Form I-797 and Form I-129S, a qualified employee who is being transferred to the United States may use these documents to apply for visa issuance with the consular officer within six months of the date on Form I-129S.

(C) When the alien is a visa-exempt nonimmigrant seeking L classification under a blanket petition, or when the alien is in the United States and is seeking a change of status from another nonimmigrant classification to L classification under a blanket petition, the petitioner shall submit Form I-129S, Certificate of Eligibility, and a copy of the approval notice, Form I-797, to the USCIS office with which the blanket petition was filed.

(D) The consular or Service officer shall determine whether the position in which the alien will be employed in the United States is with an organization named in the approved petition and whether the specific job is for a manager, executive, or specialized knowledge professional. The consular or Service officer shall determine further whether the alien's immediate prior year of continuous employment abroad was with an organization named in the petition and was in a position as manager, executive, or specialized knowledge professional.

(E) Consular officers may grant "L" classification only in clearly approvable applications. If the consular officer determines that the alien is eligible for L classification, the consular officer may issue a nonimmigrant visa, noting the visa classification "Blanket L-1" for the principal alien and "Blanket L-2" for any accompanying or following to join spouse and children. The consular officer shall also endorse all copies of the alien's Form I-129S with the blanket L-1 visa classification and return the original and one copy to the alien. When the alien is inspected for entry into the United States, both copies of the Form I-129S shall be stamped to show a validity period not to exceed three years and the second copy collected and sent to the appropriate Regional Service Center for control purposes. Service officers who determine eligibility of aliens for L-1 classification under blanket petitions shall endorse both copies of Form I-129S with the blanket L-1 classification and the validity period not to exceed three years and retain the second copy for Service records.

(F) If the consular officer determines that the alien is ineligible for L classification under a blanket petition, the consular officer's decision shall be final. The consular officer shall record the reasons for the denial on Form I-129S, retain one copy, return the original of I-129S to the USCIS office which approved the blanket petition, and provide a copy to the alien. In such a case, an individual petition may be filed for the alien on the form prescribed by USCIS. The petition shall state the reason the alien was denied L classification and specify the consular office which made the determination and the date of the determination.

(G) An alien admitted under an approved blanket petition may be reassigned to any organization listed in the approved petition without referral to the Service during his/her authorized stay if the alien will be performing virtually the same job duties. If the alien will be performing different job duties, the petitioner shall complete a new Certificate of Eligibility and send it for approval to the director who approved the blanket petition.

(6) Copies of supporting documents. The petitioner may submit a legible photocopy of a document in support of the visa petition, in lieu of the original document. However, the original document shall be submitted if requested by the Service.

(7) Approval of petition —

(i) General. The director shall notify the petitioner of the approval of an individual or a blanket petition within 30 days after the date a completed petition has been filed. If additional information is required from the petitioner, the 30 day processing period shall begin again upon receipt of the information. The original Form I-797 received from the USCIS with respect to an approved individual or blanket petition may be duplicated by the petitioner for the beneficiary's use as described in paragraph (l)(13) of this section.

(A) Individual petition —

(1) Form I-797 shall include the beneficiary's name and classification and the petition's period of validity.

(2) An individual petition approved under this paragraph shall be valid for the period of established need for the beneficiary's services, not to exceed three years, except where the beneficiary is coming to the United States to open or to be employed in a new office.

(3) If the beneficiary is coming to the United States to open or be employed in a new office, the petition may

be approved for a period not to exceed one year, after which the petitioner shall demonstrate as required by paragraph (l)(14)(ii) of this section that it is doing business as defined in paragraph (l) (1)(ii)(H) of this section to extend the validity of the petition.

(B) Blanket petition —

(1) Form I-797 shall identify the approved organizations included in the petition and the petition's period of validity.

(2) A blanket petition approved under this paragraph shall be valid initially for a period of three years and may be extended indefinitely thereafter if the qualifying organizations have complied with these regulations.

(3) A blanket petition may be approved in whole or in part and shall cover only qualifying organizations.

(C) Amendments. The petitioner must file an amended petition, with fee, at the USCIS office where the original petition was filed to reflect changes in approved relationships, additional qualifying organizations under a blanket petition, change in capacity of employment (i.e., from a specialized knowledge position to a managerial position), or any information which would affect the beneficiary's eligibility under section 101(a)(15)(L) of the Act.

(ii) Spouse and dependents. The spouse and unmarried minor children of the beneficiary are entitled to L nonimmigrant classification, subject to the same period of admission and limits as the beneficiary, if the spouse and unmarried minor children are accompanying or following to join the beneficiary in the United States. Neither the spouse nor any child may accept employment unless he or she has been granted employment authorization.

(8) Denial of petition —

(i) Individual petition. If an individual is denied, the petitioner shall be notified within 30 days after the date a completed petition has been filed of the denial, the reasons for the denial, and the right to appeal the denial.

(ii) Blanket petition. If a blanket petition is denied in whole or in part, the petitioner shall be notified within 30 days after the date a completed petition has been filed of the denial, the reasons for the denial, and the right to appeal the denial. If the petition is denied in part, the USCIS office issuing the denial shall forward to the petitioner, along with the denial, a Form I-797 listing those organizations which were found to quality. If the decision to deny is reversed on appeal, a new Form I-797 shall be sent to the petitioner to reflect the changes made as a result of the appeal.

(9) Revocation of approval of individual and blanket petitions —

(i) General. The director may revoke a petition at any time, even after the expiration of the petition.

(ii) Automatic revocation. The approval of any individual or blanket petition is automatically revoked if the petitioner withdraws the petition or the petitioner fails to request indefinite validity of a blanket petition.

(iii) Revocation on notice.

(A) The director shall send to the petitioner a notice of intent to revoke the petition in relevant part if he/she finds that:

(1) One or more entities are no longer qualifying organizations;

(2) The alien is no longer eligible under section 101(a)(15)(L) of the Act;

(3) A qualifying organization(s) violated requirements of section 101(a)(15)(L) and these regulations;

(4) The statement of facts contained in the petition was not true and correct; or

(5) Approval of the petition involved gross error; or

(6) None of the qualifying organizations in a blanket petition have used the blanket petition procedure for three consecutive years.

(B) The notice of intent to revoke shall contain a detailed statement of the grounds for the revocation and the time period allowed for the petitioner's rebuttal. Upon receipt of this notice, the petitioner may submit evidence in rebuttal within 30 days of the notice. The director shall consider all relevant evidence presented in deciding whether to revoke the petition in whole or in part. If a blanket petition is revoked in part, the remainder of the petition shall remain approved, and a revised Form I-797 shall be sent to the petitioner with the revocation notice.

(iv) Status of beneficiaries. If an individual petition is revoked, the beneficiary shall be required to leave the United States, unless the beneficiary has obtained other work authorization from the Service. If a blanket petition is revoked and the petitioner and beneficiaries already in the United States are otherwise eligible for L classification, the director shall extend the blanket petition for a period necessary to support the stay of those blanket L beneficiaries. The approval notice, Form I-171C, shall include only the names of qualifying organizations and covered beneficiaries. No new beneficiaries may be classified or admitted under this limited extension.

(10) Appeal of denial or revocation of individual or blanket petition —

(i) A petition denied in whole or in part may be appealed under 8 CFR part 103. Since the determination on the Certificate of Eligibility, Form I-129S, is part of the petition process, a denial or revocation of approval of an I-129S is appealable in the same manner as the petition.

(ii) A petition that has been revoked on notice in whole or in part may be appealed under part 103 of this chapter. Automatic revocations may not be appealed.

(11) Admission. A beneficiary may apply for admission to the United States only while the individual or blanket petition is valid. The beneficiary of an individual petition shall not be admitted for a date past the validity period of the petition. The beneficiary of a blanket petition may be admitted for three years even though the initial validity period of the blanket petition may expire before the end of the three-year period. If the blanket petition will expire while the alien is in the United States, the burden is on the petitioner to file for indefinite validity of the blanket petition or to file an individual petition in the alien's behalf to support the alien's status in the United States. The admission period for any alien under section 101(a)(15)(L) shall

not exceed three years unless an extension of stay is granted pursuant to paragraph (l)(15) of this section.

(12) L-1 limitation on period of stay —

(i) Limits. An alien who has spent five years in the United States in a specialized knowledge capacity or seven years in the United States in a managerial or executive capacity under section 101(a)(15) (L) and/or (H) of the Act may not be readmitted to the United States under section 101(a)(15) (L) or (H) of the Act unless the alien has resided and been physically present outside the United States, except for brief visits for business or pleasure, for the immediate prior year. Such visits do not interrupt the one year abroad, but do not count towards fulfillment of that requirement. In view of this restriction, a new individual petition may not be approved for an alien who has spent the maximum time period in the United States under section 101(a)(15) (L) and/or (H) of the Act, unless the alien has resided and been physically present outside the United States, except for brief visits for business or pleasure, for the immediate prior year. The petitioner shall provide information about the alien's employment, place of residence, and the dates and purpose of any trips to the United States for the previous year. A consular or Service officer may not grant L classification under a blanket petition to an alien who has spent five years in the United States as a professional with specialized knowledge or seven years in the United States as a manager or executive, unless the alien has met the requirements contained in this paragraph.

(ii) Exceptions. The limitations of paragraph (l)(12)(i) of this section shall not apply to aliens who do not reside continually in the United States and whose employment in the United States is seasonal, intermittent, or consists of an aggregate of six months or less per year. In addition, the limitations will not apply to aliens who reside abroad and regularly commute to the United States to engage in part-time employment. The petitioner and the alien must provide clear and convincing proof that the alien qualifies for an exception. Clear and convincing proof shall consist of evidence such as arrival and departure records, copies of tax returns, and records of employment abroad.

(13) Beneficiary's use of Form I-797 and Form I-129S —

(i) Beneficiary of an individual petition. The beneficiary of an individual petition who does not require a nonimmigrant visa may present a copy of Form I-797 at a port of entry to facilitate entry into the United States. The copy of Form I-797 shall be retained by the beneficiary and presented during the validity of the petition (provided that the beneficiary is entering or reentering the United States) for entry and reentry to resume the same employment with the same petitioner (within the validity period of the petition) and to apply for an extension of stay. A beneficiary who is required to present a visa for admission and whose visa will have expired before the date of his or her intended return may use an original Form I-797 to apply for a new or revalidated visa during the validity period of the petition and to apply for an extension of stay.

(ii) Beneficiary of a blanket petition. Each alien seeking L classification and admission under a blanket petition shall present a copy of Form I-797 and a Form I-129S from the petitioner which identifies the position and organization from which the employee is transferring, the new organization and position to which the employee is destined, a description of the employee's actual duties for both the new and former positions, and the positions, dates, and locations of previous L stays in the United States. A current copy of Form I-797 and Form I-129S should be retained by the beneficiary and used for leaving and reentering the United States to resume employment with a qualifying organization during his/her authorized period of stay, for applying for a new or revalidated visa, and for applying for readmission at a port of entry. The alien may be readmitted even though reassigned to a different organization named on the Form I-797 than the one shown on Form I-129S if the job duties are virtually the same.

(14) Extension of visa petition validity —

(i) Individual petition. The petitioner must file a petition extension on Form I–129 to extend an individual petition under section 101(a)(15)(L) of the Act. A petition extension generally may be filed only if the validity of the original petition has not expired.

(ii) New offices. A visa petition under section 101(a)(15)(L) which involved the opening of a new office may be extended by filing a new application or petition, accompanied by the following:

(A) Evidence that the United States and foreign entities are still qualifying organizations as defined in paragraph (l)(1)(ii)(G) of this section;

(B) Evidence that the United States entity has been doing business as defined in paragraph (l)(1)(ii)(H) of this section for the previous year;

(C) A statement of the duties performed by the beneficiary for the previous year and the duties the beneficiary will perform under the extended petition;

(D) A statement describing the staffing of the new operation, including the number of employees and types of positions held accompanied by evidence of wages paid to employees when the beneficiary will be employed in a managerial or executive capacity; and

(E) Evidence of the financial status of the United States operation.

(iii) Blanket petitions —

(A) Extension procedure. A blanket petition may only be extended indefinitely by filing a new Form I-129 with a copy of the previous approval notice and a report of admissions during the preceding three years. The report of admissions shall include a list of the aliens admitted under the blanket petition during the preceding three years, including positions held during that period, the employing entity, and the dates of initial admission and final departure of each alien. The petitioner shall state whether it still meets the criteria for filing a blanket petition and shall document any changes in approved relationships and additional qualifying organizations.

(B) Other conditions. If the petitioner in an approved blanket petition fails to request indefinite validity or if indefinite validity is denied, the petitioner and its other qualifying organizations shall seek L classification by filing individual petitions until another three years have expired; after which the petitioner may seek approval of a new blanket petition.

(15) Extension of stay.

(i) In individual petitions, the petitioner must apply for the petition extension and the alien's extension of stay concurrently on Form I-129. When the alien is a beneficiary under a blanket petition, a new certificate of eligibility, accompanied by a copy of the previous approved certificate of eligibility, shall be filed by the petitioner to request an extension of the alien's stay. The petitioner must also request a petition extension. The dates of extension shall be the same for the petition and the beneficiary's extension of stay. The beneficiary must be physically present in the United States at the time the extension of stay is filed. Even though the requests to extend the visa petition and the alien's stay are combined on the petition, the director shall make a separate determination on each. If the alien is required to leave the United States for business or personal reasons while the extension requests are pending, the petitioner may request the director to cable notification of approval of the petition extension to the consular office abroad where the alien will apply for a visa.

(ii) An extension of stay may be authorized in increments of up to two years for beneficiaries of individual and blanket petitions. The total period of stay may not exceed five years for aliens employed in a specialized knowledge capacity. The total period of stay for an alien employed in a managerial or executive capacity may not exceed seven years. No further extensions may be granted. When an alien was initially admitted to the United States in a specialized knowledge capacity and is later promoted to a managerial or executive position, he or she must have been employed in the managerial or executive position for at least six months to be eligible for the total period of stay of seven years. The change to managerial or executive capacity must have been approved by the Service in an amended, new, or extended petition at the time that the change occurred.

(16) Effect of filing an application for or approval of a permanent labor certification, preference petition, or filing of an application for adjustment of status on L-1 classification. An alien may legitimately come to the United States for a temporary period as an L-1 nonimmigrant and, at the same time, lawfully seek to become a permanent resident of the United States provided he or she intends to depart voluntarily at the end of his or her authorized stay. The filing of an application for or approval of a permanent labor certification, an immigrant visa preference petition, or the filing of an application of readjustment of status for an L-1 nonimmigrant shall not be the basis for denying:

(i) An L-1 petition filed on behalf of the alien,

(ii) A request to extend an L-1 petition which had previously been filed on behalf of the alien;

(iii) An application for admission as an L-1 nonimmigrant by the alien, or as an L-2 nonimmigrant by the spouse or child of such alien;

(iv) An application for change of status to H-1 or L-2 nonimmigrant filed by the alien, or to H-1, H-4, or L-1 status filed by the L-2 spouse or child of such alien;

(v) An application for change of status to H-4 nonimmigrant filed by the L-1 nonimmigrant, if his or her spouse has been approved for classification as an H-1; or

(vi) An application for extension of stay filed by the alien, or by the L-2 spouse or child of such alien.

(17) Filing of individual petitions and certifications under blanket petitions for citizens of Canada under the Agreement Between the United States of America, the United Mexican States, and Canada (USMCA).

(i) Individual petitions. Except as provided in paragraph (l)(2)(ii) of this section (filing of blanket petitions), a United States or foreign employer seeking to classify a citizen of Canada as an intracompany transferee may file an individual petition in duplicate on the form prescribed by USCIS in conjunction with an application for admission of the citizen of Canada. Such filing may be made with an immigration officer at a Class A port of entry located on the United States-Canada land border or at a United States pre-clearance/pre-flight station in Canada. The petitioning employer need not appear, but Form I-129 must bear the authorized signature of the petitioner.

(ii) Certification of eligibility for intracompany transferree under the blanket petition. An immigration officer at a location identified in paragraph (l)(17)(i) of this section may determine eligibility of individual citizens of Canada seeking L classification under approved blanket petitions. At these locations, such citizens of Canada shall present the original and two copies of Form I-129S, Intracompany Transferee Certificate of Eligibility, prepared by the approved organization, as well as three copies of Form I-797, Notice of Approval of Nonimmigrant Visa Petition.

(iii) Nothing in this section shall preclude or discourage the advance filing of petitions and certificates of eligibility in accordance with paragraph (l)(2) of this section.

(iv) Deficient or deniable petitions or certificates of eligibility. If a petition or certificate of eligibility submitted concurrently with an application for admission is lacking necessary supporting documentation or is otherwise deficient, the inspecting immigration officer shall return it to the applicant for admission in order to obtain the necessary documentation from the petitioner or for the deficiency to be overcome. The fee to file the petition will be remitted at such time as the documentary or other deficiency is overcome. If the petition or certificate of eligibility is clearly deniable, the immigration officer will accept the petition (with fee) and the petitioner shall be notified of the denial, the reasons for denial, and the right of appeal. If a formal denial order cannot be issued by the port of entry, the petition with a recommendation for denial shall be forwarded to the appropriate Service Center for final action. For the purposes of this provision, the appropriate Service Center will be the one within the same Service region as the location where the application for admission is made.

(v) Spouse and dependent minor children accompanying or following to join.

(A) The Canadian citizen spouse and Canadian citizen unmarried minor children of a Canadian citizen admitted under this paragraph shall be entitled to the same nonimmigrant classification and same length of stay subject to the same limits as the principal alien. They shall not be required to present visas, and they shall be admitted under the classification symbol L-2.

(B) A non-Canadian citizen spouse or non-Canadian citizen unmarried minor child shall be entitled to the same nonimmigrant classification and the same length of stay subject to the same limits as the principal, but shall be required to present a visa upon application for admission as an L-2 unless otherwise exempt under § 212.1 of this chapter.

(C) The spouse and dependent minor children shall not accept employment in the United States unless otherwise authorized under the Act.

(18) Denial of intracompany transferee status to citizens of Canada or Mexico in the case of certain labor disputes.

(i) If the Secretary of Labor certifies to or otherwise informs the Commissioner that a strike or other labor dispute involving a work stoppage of workers is in progress where the beneficiary is to be employed, and the temporary entry of the beneficiary may affect adversely the settlement of such labor dispute or the employment of any person who is involved in such dispute, a petition to classify a citizen of Mexico or Canada as an L-1 intracompany transferee may be denied. If a petition has already been approved, but the alien has not yet entered the United States, or has entered the United States but not yet commenced employment, the approval of the petition may be suspended, and an application for admission on the basis of the petition may be denied.

(ii) If there is a strike or other labor dispute involving a work stoppage of workers in progress, but such strike or other labor dispute is not certified under paragraph (l)(18)(i) of this section, or the Service has not otherwise been informed by the Secretary that such a strike or labor dispute is in progress, the Commissioner shall not deny a petition or suspend an approved petition.

(iii) If the alien has already commended employment in the United States under an approved petition and is participating in a strike or other labor dispute involving a work stoppage of workers, whether or not such strike or other labor dispute has been certified by the Department of Labor, the alien shall not be deemed to be failing to maintain his or her status solely on account of past, present, or future participation in a strike or other labor dispute involving a work stoppage of workers, but is subject to the following terms and conditions.

(A) The alien shall remain subject to all applicable provisions of the Immigration and Nationality Act, and regulations promulgated in the same manner as all other L nonimmigrants;

(B) The status and authorized period of stay of such an alien is not modified or extended in any way by virtue of his or her participation in a strike or other labor dispute involving work stoppage of workers; and

(C) Although participation by an L nonimmigrant alien in a strike or other labor dispute involving a work stoppage of workers will not constitute a ground for deportation, any alien who violates his or her status or who remains in the United States after his or her authorized period of stay has expired will be subject to deportation.

(m) Students in established vocational or other recognized nonacademic institutions, other than in language training programs.

Table 4 to Paragraph (m)—Paragraph Contents

(1) Admission of student.
(2) Form I-20 ID copy.
(3) Admission of the spouse and minor children of an M-1 student.
(4) Temporary absence.
(5) Period of stay.
(6)-(8) [Reserved].
(9) Full course of study.
(10) Extension of stay.
(11) School transfer.
(12) Change in educational objective.
(13) Employment.
(14) Practical training.
(15) Decision on application for extension, permission to transfer to another school, or permission to accept employment for practical training.
(16) Reinstatement to student status.
(17) Spouse and children of M-1 student.
(18) Current name and address.
(19) Special rules for certain border commuter students.
(20) Remittance of the fee.

(1) Admission of student.

(i) Eligibility for admission. A nonimmigrant student may be admitted into the United States in nonimmigrant status under section 101(a)(15)(M) of the Act, if:

(A) The student presents a Form I-20 or successor form issued in the student's own name by a school certified by SEVP for attendance by M-1 foreign students;

(B) The student has documentary evidence of financial support in the amount indicated on the Form 1-20 or successor form; and

(C) For students seeking initial admission only, the student intends to attend the school specified in the student's visa (or, where the student is exempt from the requirement for a visa, the school indicated on the Form I-20 or successor form.

(ii) [Removed and reserved.]

(iii) Use of SEVIS. Schools must issue a Form I-20 or successor form in SEVIS to any current student requiring a reportable action (e.g., extension of stay, practical training, and requests for employment authorization) or a new Form I-20 or successor form, or for any aliens who must obtain a new nonimmigrant student visa.

(2) Student maintenance of Form I-20 or successor form. An M-1 student is expected to retain for safekeeping the initial Form I-20 or successor form bearing the admission number and any subsequent Form I-20 or successor form issued to the student. Should the student lose their current Form I-20 or successor form, a replacement copy bearing the same information as the

lost copy, including any endorsement for employment and notations, should be issued by the DSO as defined in § 214.3(*l*)(1).

(3) Admission of the spouse and minor children of an M-1 student. The spouse and minor children accompanying an M-1 student are eligible for admission in M-2 status if the student is admitted in M-1 status. The spouse and minor children following-to-join an M-1 student are eligible for admission to the United States in M-2 status if they are able to demonstrate that the M-1 student has been admitted and is, or will be within 30 days, enrolled in a full course of study, or engaged in approved practical training following completion of studies. In either case, at the time they seek admission, the eligible spouse and minor children of an M-1 student must individually present a Form I-20 or successor form issued in the name of each M-2 dependent issued by a school certified by SEVP for attendance by M-1 students. A new Form I-20 or successor form is required for a dependent where there has been any substantive change in the M-1 student's current information.

(i) A properly endorsed page 4 of Form I-20M-N if there has been no substantive change in the information on the student's most recent Form I-20M since the form was initially issued; or

(ii) A new Form I-20M-N if there has been any substantive change in the information on the student's most recent Form I-20M since the form was initially issued.

(4) Temporary absence —

(i) General. An M-1 student returning to the United States from a temporary absence to attend the school which the student was previously authorized to attend must present either —

(A) A properly endorsed Form I-20 or successor form if there has been no substantive change in the information on the student's most recent Form I-20 or successor form since the form was initially issued; or

(B) A new Form I-20 or successor form if there has been any substantive change in the information on the student's most recent Form I-20 or successor form since the form was initially issued.

(ii) Student who transferred between schools. If an M-1 student has been authorized to transfer between schools and is returning to the United States from a temporary absence in order to attend the school to which transfer was authorized as indicated on the student's Form I-20 or successor form, the name of the transfer-in school does not need to be specified in the student's visa.

(5) Period of stay. A student in M nonimmigrant status is admitted for a fixed time period, which is the period necessary to complete the course of study indicated on the Form 1-20 or successor form, plus practical training following completion of the course of study, plus an additional 30 days to depart the United States, but not to exceed a total period of one year. An M-1 student may be admitted for a period up to 30 days before the report date or start date of the course of study listed on the Form 1-20 or successor form. An M-1 student who fails to maintain a full course of study or otherwise fails to maintain status is not eligible for the additional 30-day period of stay.

(6) [Reserved]

(7) [Reserved]

(8) [Reserved]

(9) Full course of study. Successful completion of the course of study must lead to the attainment of a specific educational or vocational objective. A course of study at an institution not certified for attendance by foreign students as provided in § 214.3(a)(3) does not satisfy this requirement. A "full course of study" as required by section 101(a)(15)(M)(i) of the Act means—

(i) Community college or junior college. Study at a community college or junior college, certified by a school official to consist of at least twelve semester or quarter hours of instruction per academic term in those institutions using standard semester, trimester, or quarter-hour systems, where all students enrolled for a minimum of twelve semester or quarter hours are charged full-time tuition or considered full-time for other administrative purposes, or its equivalent (as determined by SEVP in the school certification process) except when the student needs a lesser course load to complete the course of study during the current term;

(ii) Postsecondary vocational or business school. Study at a postsecondary vocational or business school, other than in a language training program except as provided in § 214.3(a)(2)(iv), which confers upon its graduates recognized associate or other degrees or has established that its credits have been and are accepted unconditionally by at least three other institutions of higher learning which are either:

(A) A school (or school system) owned and operated as a public educational institution by the United States or a State or political subdivision thereof; or

(B) A school accredited by a nationally recognized accrediting body; and which has been certified by a designated school official to consist of at least 12 clock hours of instruction a week, or its equivalent as determined by SEVP in the school certification process;

(iii) Study in a vocational or other nonacademic curriculum, other than in a language training program except as provided in § 214.3(a)(2)(iv), certified by a designated school official to consist of at least eighteen clock hours of attendance a week if the dominant part of the course of study consists of classroom instruction, or at least twenty-two clock hours a week if the dominant part of the course of study consists of shop or laboratory work; or

(iv) Study in a vocational or other nonacademic high school curriculum, certified by a designated school official to consist of class attendance for not less than the minimum number of hours a week prescribed by the school for normal progress towards graduation.

(v) On-line courses/distance education programs. No on-line or distance education classes may be considered to count toward an M-1 student's full course of study requirement if such classes do not require the student's physical attendance for classes, examination or other purposes integral to completion of the class. An on-line or distance education course is a course that is offered principally through the use of television, audio, or computer transmission including open broadcast, closed circuit, cable, microwave, or satellite, audio conferencing, or computer conferencing.

(vi) Reduced course load. The designated school official may authorize an M-1 student to engage in less than a full course of study only where the student has been compelled by illness or a medical condition that has been documented by a licensed medical doctor, a licensed doctor of osteopathy, a licensed psychologist, or a licensed clinical psychologist to interrupt or reduce their course of study. A DSO may not authorize a reduced course load for more than an aggregate of 5 months per course of study. An M-1 student previously authorized to drop below a full course of study due to illness or medical condition for an aggregate of 5 months, may not be authorized by the DSO to reduce their course load on subsequent occasions during their particular course of study.

(A) [Reserved]

(B) Reporting requirements. In order for a student to be authorized to drop below a full course of study, the DSO must update SEVIS prior to the student reducing their load.

(10) Extension of stay.

(i) Eligibility. The cumulative time of extensions that can be granted to an M-1 student is limited to a period of 3 years from the M-1 student's original start date, plus 30 days. No extension can be granted to an M-1 student if the M-1 student is unable to complete the course of study within 3 years of the original program start date. This limit includes extensions that have been granted due to a drop below full course of study, a transfer of schools, or reinstatement. An M-1 student may be granted an extension of stay if it is established that:

(A) He or she is a bona fide nonimmigrant currently maintaining student status;

(B) Compelling educational or medical reasons have resulted in a delay to his or her course of study. Delays caused by academic probation or suspension are not acceptable reasons for program extension; and

(C) He or she is able to, and in good faith intends to, continue to maintain that status for the period for which the extension is granted.

(ii) Application. A student must apply to USCIS for an extension on Form I-539, Application to Extend/Change Nonimmigrant Status or successor form. A student's M-2 spouse and children seeking an extension of stay must be included in the application. The student must submit the application at least 15 days but not more than 60 days before the program end date on the student's Form I-20 or successor form. The application must also be accompanied by the student's Form I-20 or successor form and the Form I-94 of the student's spouse and children, if applicable.

(iii) Period of stay. If an application for extension is granted, the student and the student's spouse and children, if applicable, are to be given an extension of stay for the period of time necessary to complete the course of study, plus 30 days within which to depart from the United States, or for a total period of one year, whichever is less. A student's M-2 spouse and children are not eligible for an extension unless the M-1 student is granted an extension of stay, or for a longer period than is granted to the M-1 student.

(iv) SEVIS update. The Form I-20 or successor form must be endorsed with the recommendation and new program end date for submission to USCIS, with Form I-539 or successor form, and Form I-94 if applicable.

(11) School transfer —

(i) Eligibility. An M-1 student may not transfer to another school after six months from the date the student is first admitted as, or changes nonimmigrant classification to that of, an M-1 student unless the student is unable to remain at the school to which the student was initially admitted due to circumstances beyond the student's control. An M-1 student may be otherwise eligible to transfer to another school if the student —

(A) Is a bona fide nonimmigrant;

(B) Has been pursuing a full course of study at the school the student was last authorized to attend;

(C) Intends to pursue a full course of study at the school to which the student intends to transfer; and

(D) Is financially able to attend the school to which the student intends to transfer.

(ii) Transfer procedure. A student must apply to USCIS on Form I-539 or successor form, for permission to transfer between schools. Upon application for school transfer, a student may affect the transfer subject to approval of the application. A student who transfers without complying with this requirement or whose application is denied after transfer (pursuant to this section) is considered to be out of status. If the application is approved, the approval date of the transfer will be determined to be the program start date listed on the Form I-20 or successor form, and the student will be granted an extension of stay for the period of time necessary to complete the new course of study plus 30 days, or for a total period of one year, whichever is less. The student must first notify their current school (the "transfer-out" school) of the intent to transfer and indicate the school to which the student intends to transfer (the "transfer-in" school). Upon notification by the student, the transfer-out school must update SEVIS to show the student is transferring out, indicate the transfer-in school, and input the transfer release date. Once SEVIS is updated, the transfer-in school may generate a Form I-20 or successor form for transfer. However, the transfer-in school will not gain access to the student's SEVIS record until the release date. Upon receipt of the Form I-20 or successor form from the transfer-in school, the student must submit Form I-539 or successor form in accordance with this paragraph (m)(11). The student may enroll in the transfer-in school at the next available term or session and is required to notify the DSO of the transfer-in school immediately upon beginning attendance. The transfer-in school must update the student's registration record in SEVIS in accordance with § 214.3(g)(2)(iii). Upon approval of the transfer application, USCIS will transmit the approval of the transfer to SEVIS. If the application for transfer is denied, the student is out of status, and the student's record must be terminated in SEVIS.

(iii) Student who has not been pursuing a full course of study. If an M-1 student who has not been pursuing a full course of study at the school the student was last authorized to attend desires to attend a different school, the student must apply for reinstatement to student status under paragraph (m)(16) of this section.

(12) Change in educational objective. An M-1 student may not change educational objective.

(13) Employment. Except as provided in paragraph (m)(14) of this section, a student may not accept employment.

(14) Practical training —

(i) When practical training may be authorized. Temporary employment for practical training may be authorized only after completion of the student's course of study.

(A) The proposed employment is recommended for the purpose of practical training;

(B) The proposed employment is related to the student's course of study; and

(C) Upon the designated school official's information and belief, employment comparable to the proposed employment is not available to the student in the country of the student's foreign residence.

(ii) Application. An M-1 student must apply for permission to accept employment for practical training on Form I-765, with fee as contained in 8 CFR part 106, accompanied by a properly endorsed Form I-20 by the designated school official for practical training. The application must be submitted before the program end date listed on the student's Form I-20 but not more than 90 days before the program end date. The designated school official must certify on Form I-538 that:

(A) The proposed employment is recommended for the purpose of practical training;

(B) The proposed employment is related to the student's course of study; and

(C) Upon the designated school official's information and belief, employment comparable to the proposed employment is not available to the student in the country of the student's foreign residence.

(iii) Duration of practical training. When the student is authorized to engage in employment for practical training, they will be issued an EAD. The M-1 student may not begin employment until he or she has been issued an EAD by USCIS. One month of employment authorization will be granted for each four months of full-time study that the M-1 student has completed. However, an M-1 student may not engage in more than six months of practical training in the aggregate. The student will not be granted employment authorization if he or she cannot complete the requested practical training within six months.

(iv) Temporary absence of M-1 student granted practical training. An M-1 student who has been granted permission to accept employment for practical training and who temporarily departs from the United States, may be readmitted for the remainder of the authorized period indicated on the student's Form I-20 or successor form. The student must be returning to the United States to perform the authorized practical training. A student may not be readmitted to begin practical training which was not authorized prior to the student's departure from the United States.

(v) Effect of strike or other labor dispute. Authorization for all employment for practical training is automatically suspended upon certification by the Secretary of Labor or the Secretary's designee to the Secretary of Homeland Security or the Secretary's designee that a strike or other labor dispute involving a work stoppage of workers is in progress in the occupation at the place of employment. As used in this paragraph (m)(14)(v), "place of employment" means wherever the employer or joint employer does business.

(vi) SEVIS process. The DSO must update the student's record in SEVIS to recommend that USCIS approve the student for practical training, and generate a SEVIS Form I-20 with the recommendation, for the student to submit to USCIS with Form I-765 as provided in this paragraph (m)(14).

(15) Decision on application for extension, permission to transfer to another school, or permission to accept employment for practical training. USCIS will notify the applicant of the decision and, if the application is denied, of the reason(s) for the denial. The applicant may not appeal the decision.

(16) Reinstatement to student status.

(i) General. USCIS may consider reinstating a student who makes a request for reinstatement on Form I-539, Application to Extend/Change Nonimmigrant Status or successor form, accompanied by a properly completed Form I-20 or successor form indicating the DSO's recommendation for reinstatement. USCIS may consider granting the request only if the student:

(A) Has not been out of status for more than 5 months at the time of filing the request for reinstatement (or demonstrates that the failure to file within the 5 month period was the result of exceptional circumstances and that the student filed the request for reinstatement as promptly as possible under these exceptional circumstances);

(B) Does not have a record of repeated or willful violations of DHS regulations;

(C) Is currently pursuing, or intends to pursue, a full course of study at the school which issued the Form I-20 or successor form;

(D) Has not engaged in unlawful employment;

(E) Is not deportable on any ground other than section 237(a)(1)(B) or (C)(i) of the Act; and

(F) Establishes to the satisfaction of USCIS, by a detailed showing, either that:

(1) The violation of status resulted from circumstances beyond the student's control. Such circumstances might include serious injury or illness, closure of the institution, a natural disaster, or inadvertence, oversight or neglect on the part of the DSO, but do not include instances where a pattern of repeated violations or where a willful failure on the part of the student resulted in the need for reinstatement; or

(2) The violation relates to a reduction in the student's course load that would have been within a DSO's power to authorize, and that failure to approve rein-

statement would result in extreme hardship to the student.

(ii) Decision. The adjudicating officer will update SEVIS to reflect USCIS's decision. If USCIS does not reinstate the student, the student may not appeal the decision.

(17) Spouse and children of M-1 student. The M-2 spouse and minor children of an M-1 student will each be issued an individual Form I-20 or successor form in accordance with the provisions of § 214.3(k).

(i) Employment. The M-2 spouse and children may not accept employment.

(ii) Study —

(A) M-2 post-secondary/vocational study—

(1) Authorized study at SEVP-certified schools. An M-2 spouse or M-2 child may enroll in less than a full course of study, as defined in paragraphs (f)(6)(i)(A) through (D) or (m)(9)(i) through (v), in any course of study described in paragraphs (f)(6)(i)(A) through (D) or (m)(9)(i) through (v) of this section at an SEVP-certified school. Notwithstanding paragraphs (f)(6)(i)(B) and (m)(9)(i) of this section, study at an undergraduate college or university or at a community college or junior college is not a full course of study solely because the M-2 nonimmigrant is engaging in a lesser course load to complete a course of study during the current term. An M-2 spouse or M-2 child enrolled in less than a full course of study is not eligible to engage in employment pursuant to paragraph (m)(14) of this section or pursuant to paragraphs (f)(9) through (10) of this section.

(2) Full course of study. Subject to paragraph (m)(17)(ii)(B) of this section, an M-2 spouse and child may engage in a full course of study only by applying for and obtaining a change of status to F-1, M-1, or J-1 status, as appropriate, before beginning a full course of study. An M-2 spouse and M-2 child may engage in study that is avocational or recreational in nature, up to and including on a full-time basis.

(B) M-2 elementary or secondary study. An M-2 child may engage in full-time study, including any full course of study, in any elementary or secondary school (kindergarten through twelfth grade).

(C) An M-2 spouse or child violates his or her nonimmigrant status by enrolling in any study except as provided in paragraph (m)(17)(ii)(A) or (B) of this section.

(18) Current name and address. A student must inform DHS and the DSO of any legal changes to the student's name or of any change of address, within 10 days of the change, in a manner prescribed by the school. A student can satisfy the requirement in 8 CFR 265.1 of notifying DHS by providing a notice of a change of address within 10 days to the DSO, and the DSO in turn must enter the information in SEVIS within 21 days of notification by the student. Except in the case of a student who cannot receive mail where the student resides, the address provided by the student must be the actual physical location where the student resides rather than a mailing address. In cases where a student provides a mailing address, the school must maintain a record of, and must provide upon request from DHS, the actual physical location where the student resides.

(19) Special rules for certain border commuter students.

(i) Applicability. For purposes of the special rules in this paragraph (m)(19), the term "border commuter student" means a national of Canada or Mexico who is admitted to the United States as an M-1 student to enroll in a full course of study, albeit on a part-time basis, in a certified school located within 75 miles of a United States land border. The border commuter student must maintain actual residence and place of abode in the student's country of nationality, and seek admission to the United States at a land border port-of-entry. These special rules do not apply to a national of Canada or Mexico who is:

(A) Residing in the United States while attending a certified school as an M-1 student; or

(B) Enrolled in a full course of study as defined in paragraph (m)(9) of this section.

(ii) Full course of study. A designated school official at the school may authorize an eligible border commuter student to enroll in a course load below that otherwise required for a full course of study under paragraph (m)(9) of this section, provided that the reduced course load is consistent with the border commuter student's certified course of study.

(iii) Period of stay. An M-1 border commuter student is not entitled to an additional 30-day period of stay otherwise available under paragraph (m)(5) of this section.

(iv) Employment. A border commuter student may not be authorized to accept any employment in connection with his or her M-1 student status, except for practical training as provided in paragraph (m)(14) of this section.

(20) Remittance of the fee. An alien who applies for M-1 or M-3 nonimmigrant status in order to enroll in a program of study at an SEVP-certified vocational educational institution is required to pay the SEVIS fee to DHS, pursuant to § 214.13, except as otherwise provided in that section.

(n) Certain parents and children of section 101(a)(27)(I) special immigrants —

(1) Parent of special immigrant. Upon application, a parent of a child accorded special immigrant status under section 101(a)(27)(I)(i) of the Act may be granted status under section 101(a)(15)(N)(i) of the Act as long as the permanent resident child through whom eligibility is derived remains a child as defined in section 101(b)(1) of the Act.

(2) Child of section 101(a)(27)(I) special immigrants and section 101(a)(15)(N)(i) nonimmigrants. Children of parents granted nonimmigrant status under section 101(a)(15)(N)(i) of the Act, or of parents who have been granted special immigrant status under section 101(a)(27)(I) (ii), (iii) or (iv) of the Act may be granted status under section 101(a)(15)(N)(ii) of the Act for such time as each remains a child as defined in section 101(b)(1) of the Act.

(3) Admission and extension of stay. A nonimmigrant granted (N) status shall be admitted for not to exceed three years with extensions in increments up to but not to exceed three years. Status as an (N) nonimmigrant

shall terminate on the date the child described in paragraph (n)(1) or (n)(2) of this section no longer qualifies as a child as defined in section 101(b)(1) of the Act.

(4) Employment. A nonimmigrant admitted in or granted (N) status is authorized employment incident to (N) status without restrictions as to location or type of employment.

(o) Aliens of extraordinary ability or achievement —

(1) Classifications —

(i) General. Under section 101(a)(15)(O) of the Act, a qualified alien may be authorized to come to the United States to perform services relating to an event or events if petitioned for by an employer. Under this nonimmigrant category, the alien may be classified under section 101(a)(15)(O)(i) of the Act as an alien who has extraordinary ability in the sciences, arts, education, business, or athletics, or who has a demonstrated record of extraordinary achievement in the motion picture or television industry. Under section 101(a)(15)(O)(ii) of the Act, an alien having a residence in a foreign country which he or she has no intention of abandoning may be classified as an accompanying alien who is coming to assist in the artistic or athletic performance of an alien admitted under section 101(a)(15)(O)(i) of the Act. The spouse or child of an alien described in section 101(a)(15)(O)(i) or (ii) of the Act who is accompanying or following to join the alien is entitled to classification pursuant to section 101(a)(15)(O)(iii) of the Act. These classifications are called the O-1, O-2, and O-3 categories, respectively. The petitioner must file a petition with the Service for a determination of the alien's eligibility for O-1 or O-2 classification before the alien may apply for a visa or seek admission to the United States. This paragraph sets forth the standards and procedures applicable to these classifications.

(ii) Description of classifications —

(A) An O-1 classification applies to:

(1) An individual alien who has extraordinary ability in the sciences, arts, education, business, or athletics which has been demonstrated by sustained national or international acclaim and who is coming temporarily to the United States to continue work in the area of extraordinary ability; or

(2) An alien who has a demonstrated record of extraordinary achievement in motion picture and/or television productions and who is coming temporarily to the United States to continue work in the area of extraordinary achievement.

(B) An O-2 classification applies to an accompanying alien who is coming temporarily to the United States solely to assist in the artistic or athletic performance by an O-1. The O-2 alien must:

(1) Be an integral part of the actual performances or events and posses critical skills and experience with the O-1 alien that are not of a general nature and which are not possessed by others; or

(2) In the case of a motion picture or television production, have skills and experience with the O-1 alien which are not of a general nature and which are critical, either based on a pre-existing and longstanding working relationship or, if in connection with a specific production only, because significant production (including pre- and post-production) will take place both inside and outside the United States and the continuing participation of the alien is essential to the successful completion of the production.

(2) Filing of petitions —

(i) General. Except as provided for in paragraph (o)(2)(iv)(A) of this section, a petitioner seeking to classify an alien as an O-1 or O-2 nonimmigrant shall file a petition on the form prescribed by USCIS. The petition may not be filed more than one year before the actual need for the alien's services. An O-1 or O-2 petition shall be adjudicated at the appropriate Service Center, even in emergency situations. Only one beneficiary may be included on an O-1 petition. O-2 aliens must be filed for on a separate petition from the O-1 alien. An O-1 or O-2 petition may only be filed by a United States employer, a United States agent, or a foreign employer through a United States agent. For purposes of paragraph (o) of this section, a foreign employer is any employer who is not amenable to service of process in the United States. A foreign employer may not directly petition for an O nonimmigrant alien but instead must use the services of a United States agent to file a petition for an O nonimmigrant alien. A United States agent petitioning on behalf of a foreign employer must be authorized to file the petition, and to accept services of process in the United States in proceedings under section 274A of the Act, on behalf of the foreign employer. An O alien may not petition for himself or herself.

(ii) Evidence required to accompany a petition. Petitions for O aliens shall be accompanied by the following:

(A) The evidence specified in the particular section for the classification;

(B) Copies of any written contracts between the petitioner and the alien beneficiary or, if there is no written contract, a summary of the terms of the oral agreement under which the alien will be employed;

(C) An explanation of the nature of the events or activities, the beginning and ending dates for the events or activities, and a copy of any itinerary for the events or activities; and

(D) A written advisory opinion(s) from the appropriate consulting entity or entities.

(iii) Form of documentation. The evidence submitted with an O petition shall conform to the following:

(A) Affidavits, contracts, awards, and similar documentation must reflect the nature of the alien's achievement and be executed by an officer or responsible person employed by the institution, firm, establishment, or organization where the work was performed.

(B) Affidavits written by present or former employers or recognized experts certifying to the recognition and extraordinary ability, or in the case of a motion picture or television production, the extraordinary achievement of the alien, shall specifically describe the alien's recognition and ability or achievement in factual terms and set forth the expertise of the affiant and the manner in which the affiant acquired such information.

(C) A legible photocopy of a document in support of the petition may be submitted in lieu of the original. However, the original document shall be submitted if requested by the Director.

(iv) Other filing situations —

(A) Services in more than one location. A petition which requires the alien to work in more than one location must include an itinerary with the dates and locations of work.

(B) Services for more than one employer. If the beneficiary will work concurrently for more than one employer within the same time period, each employer must file a separate petition, unless an established agent files the petition.

(C) Change of employer. If an O-1 or O-2 alien in the United States seeks to change employers, the new employer must file a petition and a request to extend the alien's stay. An O-2 alien may change employers only in conjunction with a change of employers by the principal O-1 alien. If the O-1 or O-2 petition was filed by an agent, an amended petition must be filed with evidence relating to the new employer and a request for an extension of stay.

(D) Amended petition. The petitioner shall file an amended petition on the form prescribed by USCIS, with fee, to reflect any material changes in the terms and conditions of employment or the beneficiary's eligibility as specified in the original approved petition. In the case of a petition filed for an artist or entertainer, a petitioner may add additional performances or engagements during the validity period of the petition without filing an amended petition, provided the additional performances or engagements require an alien of O-1 caliber.

(E) Agents as petitioners. A United States agent may file a petition in cases involving workers who are traditionally self-employed or workers who use agents to arrange short-term employment on their behalf with numerous employers, and in cases where a foreign employer authorizes the agent to act in its behalf. A United States agent may be: The actual employer of the beneficiary, the representative of both the employer and the beneficiary; or, a person or entity authorized by the employer to act for, or in place of, the employer as its agent. A petition filed by an agent is subject to the following conditions:

(1) An agent performing the function of an employer must provide the contractual agreement between the agent and the beneficiary which specifies the wage offered and the other terms and conditions of employment of the beneficiary.

(2) A person or company in business as an agent may file the petition involving multiple employers as the representative of both the employers and the beneficiary, if the supporting documentation includes a complete itinerary of the event or events. The itinerary must specify the dates of each service or engagement, the names and addresses of the actual employers, and the names and addresses of the establishments, venues, or locations where the services will be performed. A contract between the employers and the beneficiary is required. The burden is on the agent to explain the terms and conditions of the employment and to provide any required documentation.

(3) A foreign employer who, through a United States agent, files a petition for an O nonimmigrant alien is responsible for complying with all of the employer sanctions provisions of section 274A of the Act and 8 CFR part 274a.

(F) Multiple beneficiaries. More than one O-2 accompanying alien may be included on a petition if they are assisting the same O-1 alien for the same events or performances, during the same period, and in the same location. Up to 25 named beneficiaries may be included per petition.

(G) Traded professional O-1 athletes. In the case of a professional O-1 athlete who is traded from one organization to another organization, employment authorization for the player will automatically continue for a period of 30 days after acquisition by the new organization, within which time the new organization is expected to file a new application or petition. If a new application or petition is not filed within 30 days, employment authorization will cease. If a new application or petition is filed within 30 days, the professional athlete shall be deemed to be in valid O-1 status, and employment shall continue to be authorized, until the petition is adjudicated. If the new petition is denied, employment authorization will cease.

(3) Petition for alien of extraordinary ability or achievement (O-1) —

(i) General. Extraordinary ability in the sciences, arts, education, business, or athletics, or extraordinary achievement in the case of an alien in the motion picture or television industry, must be established for an individual alien. An O-1 petition must be accompanied by evidence that the work which the alien is coming to the United States to continue is in the area of extraordinary ability, and that the alien meets the criteria in paragraph (o)(3)(iii) or (iv) of this section.

(ii) Definitions. As used in this paragraph, the term:

Arts includes any field of creative activity or endeavor such as, but not limited to, fine arts, visual arts, culinary arts, and performing arts. Aliens engaged in the field of arts include not only the principal creators and performers but other essential persons such as, but not limited to, directors, set designers, lighting designers, sound designers, choreographers, choreologists, conductors, orchestrators, coaches, arrangers, musical supervisors, costume designers, makeup artists, flight masters, stage technicians, and animal trainers.

Event means an activity such as, but not limited to, a scientific project, conference, convention, lecture series, tour, exhibit, business project, academic year, or engagement. Such activity may include short vacations, promotional appearances, and stopovers which are incidental and/or related to the event. A group of related activities may also be considered to be an event. In the case of an O-1 athlete, the event could be the alien's contract.

Extraordinary ability in the field of arts means distinction. Distinction means a high level of achievement in the field of arts evidenced by a degree of skill and recognition substantially above that ordinarily encountered to the extent that a person described as prominent is renowned, leading, or well-known in the field of arts.

Extraordinary ability in the field of science, education, business, or athletics means a level of expertise indicating that the person is one of the small percentage who have arisen to the very top of the field of endeavor.

Extraordinary achievement with respect to motion picture and television productions, as commonly defined in the industry, means a very high level of accomplishment in the motion picture or television industry evidenced by a degree of skill and recognition significantly above that ordinarily encountered to the extent that the person is recognized as outstanding, notable, or leading in the motion picture or television field.

Peer group means a group or organization which is comprised of practitioners of the alien's occupation. If there is a collective bargaining representative of an employer's employees in the occupational classification for which the alien is being sought, such a representative may be considered the appropriate peer group for purposes of consultation.

(iii) *Evidentiary criteria for an O-1 alien of extraordinary ability in the fields of science, education, business, or athletics.* An alien of extraordinary ability in the fields of science, education, business, or athletics must demonstrate sustained national or international acclaim and recognition for achievements in the field of expertise by providing evidence of:

(A) Receipt of a major, internationally recognized award, such as the Nobel Prize; or

(B) At least three of the following forms of documentation:

(*1*) Documentation of the alien's receipt of nationally or internationally recognized prizes or awards for excellence in the field of endeavor;

(*2*) Documentation of the alien's membership in associations in the field for which classification is sought, which require outstanding achievements of their members, as judged by recognized national or international experts in their disciplines or fields;

(*3*) Published material in professional or major trade publications or major media about the alien, relating to the alien's work in the field for which classification is sought, which shall include the title, date, and author of such published material, and any necessary translation;

(*4*) Evidence of the alien's participation on a panel, or individually, as a judge of the work of others in the same or in an allied field of specialization to that for which classification is sought;

(*5*) Evidence of the alien's original scientific, scholarly, or business-related contributions of major significance in the field;

(*6*) Evidence of the alien's authorship of scholarly articles in the field, in professional journals, or other major media;

(*7*) Evidence that the alien has been employed in a critical or essential capacity for organizations and establishments that have a distinguished reputation;

(*8*) Evidence that the alien has either commanded a high salary or will command a high salary or other remuneration for services, evidenced by contracts or other reliable evidence.

(C) If the criteria in paragraph (o)(3)(iii) of this section do not readily apply to the beneficiary's occupation, the petitioner may submit comparable evidence in order to establish the beneficiary's eligibility.

(iv) *Evidentiary criteria for an O-1 alien of extraordinary ability in the arts.* To qualify as an alien of extraordinary ability in the field of arts, the alien must be recognized as being prominent in his or her field of endeavor as demonstrated by the following:

(A) Evidence that the alien has been nominated for, or has been the recipient of, significant national or international awards or prizes in the particular field such as an Academy Award, an Emmy, a Grammy, or a Director's Guild Award; or

(B) At least three of the following forms of documentation:

(*1*) Evidence that the alien has performed, and will perform, services as a lead or starring participant in productions or events which have a distinguished reputation as evidenced by critical reviews, advertisements, publicity releases, publications contracts, or endorsements;

(*2*) Evidence that the alien has achieved national or international recognition for achievements evidenced by critical reviews or other published materials by or about the individual in major newspapers, trade journals, magazines, or other publications;

(*3*) Evidence that the alien has performed, and will perform, in a lead, starring, or critical role for organizations and establishments that have a distinguished reputation evidenced by articles in newspapers, trade journals, publications, or testimonials;

(*4*) Evidence that the alien has a record of major commercial or critically acclaimed successes as evidenced by such indicators as title, rating, standing in the field, box office receipts, motion pictures or television ratings, and other occupational achievements reported in trade journals, major newspapers, or other publications;

(*5*) Evidence that the alien has received significant recognition for achievements from organizations, critics, government agencies, or other recognized experts in the field in which the alien is engaged. Such testimonials must be in a form which clearly indicates the author's authority, expertise, and knowledge of the alien's achievements; or

(*6*) Evidence that the alien has either commanded a high salary or will command a high salary or other substantial remuneration for services in relation to others in the field, as evidenced by contracts or other reliable evidence; or

(C) If the criteria in paragraph (o)(3)(iv) of this section do not readily apply to the beneficiary's occupation, the petitioner may submit comparable evidence in order to establish the beneficiary's eligibility.

(v) *Evidentiary criteria for an alien of extraordinary achievement in the motion picture or television industry.* To qualify as an alien of extraordinary achievement in the motion picture or television industry, the alien must be recognized as having a demonstrated record of extraordinary achievement as evidenced by the following:

(A) Evidence that the alien has been nominated for, or has been the recipient of, significant national or international awards or prizes in the particular field such as an Academy Award, an Emmy, a Grammy, or a Director's Guild Award; or

(B) At least three of the following forms of documentation:

(1) Evidence that the alien has performed, and will perform, services as a lead or starring participant in productions or events which have a distinguished reputation as evidenced by critical reviews, advertisements, publicity releases, publications contracts, or endorsements;

(2) Evidence that the alien has achieved national or international recognition for achievements evidenced by critical reviews or other published materials by or about the individual in major newspapers, trade journals, magazines, or other publications;

(3) Evidence that the alien has performed, and will perform, in a lead, starring, or critical role for organizations and establishments that have a distinguished reputation evidenced by articles in newspapers, trade journals, publications, or testimonials;

(4) Evidence that the alien has a record of major commercial or critically acclaimed successes as evidenced by such indicators as title, rating, standing in the field, box office receipts, motion picture or television ratings, and other occupational achievements reported in trade journals, major newspapers, or other publications;

(5) Evidence that the alien has received significant recognition for achievements from organizations, critics, government agencies, or other recognized experts in the field in which the alien is engaged. Such testimonials must be in a form which clearly indicates the author's authority, expertise, and knowledge of the alien's achievements; or

(6) Evidence that the alien has either commanded a high salary or will command a high salary or other substantial remuneration for services in relation to other in the field, as evidenced by contracts or other reliable evidence.

(4) Petition for an O-2 accompanying alien —

(i) General. An O-2 accompanying alien provides essential support to an O-1 artist or athlete. Such aliens may not accompany O-1 aliens in the fields of science, business, or education. Although the O-2 alien must obtain his or her own classification, this classification does not entitle him or her to work separate and apart from the O-1 alien to whom he or she provides support. An O-2 alien must be petitioned for in conjunction with the services of the O-1 alien.

(ii) Evidentiary criteria for qualifying as an O-2 accompanying alien —

(A) Alien accompanying an O-1 artist or athlete of extraordinary ability. To qualify as an O-2 accompanying alien, the alien must be coming to the United States to assist in the performance of the O-1 alien, be an integral part of the actual performance, and have critical skills and experience with the O-1 alien which are not of a general nature and which are not possessed by a U.S. worker.

(B) Alien accompanying an O-1 alien of extraordinary achievement. To qualify as an O-2 alien accompanying and O-1 alien involved in a motion picture or television production, the alien must have skills and experience with the O-1 alien which are not of a general nature and which are critical based on a pre-existing longstanding working relationship or, with respect to the specific production, because significant production (including pre- and post-production work) will take place both inside and outside the United States and the continuing participation of the alien is essential to the successful completion of the production.

(C) The evidence shall establish the current essentiality, critical skills, and experience of the O-2 alien with the O-1 alien and that the alien has substantial experience performing the critical skills and essential support services for the O-1 alien. In the case of a specific motion picture or television production, the evidence shall establish that significant production has taken place outside the United States, and will take place inside the United States, and that the continuing participation of the alien is essential to the successful completion of the production.

(5) Consultation —

(i) General.

(A) Consultation with an appropriate U.S. peer group (which could include a person or persons with expertise in the field), labor and/or management organization regarding the nature of the work to be done and the alien's qualifications is mandatory before a petition for an O-1 or O-2 classification can be approved.

(B) Except as provided in paragraph (o)(5)(i)(E) of this section, evidence of consultation shall be in the form of a written advisory opinion from a peer group (which could include a person or persons with expertise in the field), labor and/or management organization with expertise in the specific field involved.

(C) Except as provided in paragraph (o)(5)(i)(E) of this section, the petitioner shall obtain a written advisory opinion from a peer group (which could include a person or persons with expertise in the field), labor, and/or management organization with expertise in the specific field involved. The advisory opinion shall be submitted along with the petition when the petition is filed. If the advisory opinion is not favorable to the petitioner, the advisory opinion must set forth a specific statement of facts which supports the conclusion reached in the opinion. Advisory opinions must be submitted in writing and must be signed by an authorized official of the group or organization.

(D) Except as provided in paragraph (o)(5)(i)(E) and (G) of this section, written evidence of consultation shall be included in the record in every approved O petition. Consultations are advisory and are not binding on the Service.

(E) In a case where the alien will be employed in the field of arts, entertainment, or athletics, and the Service has determined that a petition merits expeditious handling, the Service shall contact the appropriate labor and/or management organization and request an advisory opinion if one is not submitted by the petitioner. The labor and/or management organization shall have 24 hours to respond to the Service's request. The Service shall adjudicate the petition after receipt of the response from the consulting organization. The labor and/or management organization shall then furnish the Service with a written advisory opinion within 5 days of the initiating request. If the labor and/or management organization fails to respond within 24 hours, the Service shall render a decision on the petition without the advisory opinion.

(F) In a routine processing case where the petition is accompanied by a written opinion from a peer group, but the peer group is not a labor organization, the Director will forward a copy of the petition and all supporting documentation to the national office of the appropriate labor organization within 5 days of receipt of the petition. If there is a collective bargaining representative of an employer's employees in the occupational classification for which the alien is being sought, that representative shall be the appropriate labor organization for purposes of this section. The labor organization will then have 15 days from receipt of the petition and supporting documents to submit to the Service a written advisory opinion, comment, or letter of no objection. Once the 15-day period has expired, the Director shall adjudicate the petition in no more than 14 days. The Director may shorten this time in his or her discretion for emergency reasons, if no unreasonable burden would be imposed on any participant in the process. If the labor organization does not respond within 15 days, the Director will render a decision on the record without the advisory opinion.

(G) In those cases where it is established by the petitioner that an appropriate peer group, including a labor organization, does not exist, the Service shall render a decision on the evidence of record.

(ii) Consultation requirements for an O-1 alien for extraordinary ability —

(A) Content. Consultation with a peer group in the area of the alien's ability (which may include a labor organization), or a person or persons with expertise in the area of the alien's ability, is required in an O-1 petition for an alien of extraordinary ability. If the advisory opinion is not favorable to the petitioner, the advisory opinion must set forth a specific statement of facts which supports the conclusion reached in the opinion. If the advisory opinion is favorable to the petitioner, it should describe the alien's ability and achievements in the field of endeavor, describe the nature of the duties to be performed, and state whether the position requires the services of an alien of extraordinary ability. A consulting organization may also submit a letter of no objection in lieu of the above if it has no objection to the approval of the petition.

(B) Waiver of consultation of certain aliens of extraordinary ability in the field of arts. Consultation for an alien of extraordinary ability in the field of arts shall be waived by the Director in those instances where the alien seeks readmission to the United States to perform similar services within 2 years of the date of a previous consultation. The director shall, within 5 days of granting the waiver, forward a copy of the petition and supporting documentation to the national office of an appropriate labor organization. Petitioners desiring to avail themselves of the waiver should submit a copy of the prior consultation with the petition and advise the Director of the waiver request.

(iii) Consultation requirements for an O-1 alien of extraordinary achievement. In the case of an alien of extraordinary achievement who will be working on a motion picture or television production, consultation shall be made with the appropriate union representing the alien's occupational peers and a management organization in the area of the alien's ability. If an advisory opinion is not favorable to the petitioner, the advisory opinion must set forth a specific statement of facts which supports the conclusion reached in the opinion. If the advisory opinion is favorable to the petitioner, the written advisory opinion from the labor and management organizations should describe the alien's achievements in the motion picture or television field and state whether the position requires the services of an alien of extraordinary achievement. If a consulting organization has no objection to the approval of the petition, the organization may submit a letter of no objection in lieu of the above.

(iv) Consultation requirements for an O-2 accompanying alien. Consultation with a labor organization with expertise in the skill area involved is required for an O-2 alien accompanying an O-1 alien of extraordinary ability. In the case of an O-2 alien seeking entry for a motion picture or television production, consultation with a labor organization and a management organization in the area of the alien's ability is required. If an advisory opinion is not favorable to the petitioner, the advisory opinion must set forth a specific statement of facts which supports the conclusion reached in the opinion. If the advisory opinion is favorable to the petitioner, the opinion provided by the labor and/or management organization should describe the alien's essentiality to, and working relationship with, the O-1 artist or athlete and state whether there are available U.S. workers who can perform the support services. If the alien will accompany an O-1 alien involved in a motion picture or television production, the advisory opinion should address the alien's skills and experience wit the O-1 alien and whether the alien has a pre-existing longstanding working relationship with the O-1 alien, or whether significant production will take place in the United States and abroad and if the continuing participation of the alien is essential to the successful completion of the production. A consulting organization may also submit a letter of no objection in lieu of the above if it has no objection to the approval of the petition.

(v) Organizations agreeing to provide advisory opinions. The Service will list in its Operations Instructions for O classification those peer groups, labor organizations, and/or management organizations which have agreed to provide advisory opinions to the Service and/or petitioners. The list will not be an exclusive or exhaustive list. The Service and petitioners may use other sources, such as publications, to identify appropriate peer groups, labor organizations, and management organizations. Additionally, the Service will list in its Operations Instructions those occupations or fields of endeavor where the nonexistence of an appropriate consulting entity has been verified.

(6) Approval and validity of petition —

(1) Approval. The Director shall consider all of the evidence submitted and such other evidence as may be independently required to assist in the adjudication. The Director shall notify the petitioner of the approval of the petition on Form I-797, Notice of Action. The approval notice shall include the alien beneficiary name, the classification, and the petition's period of validity.

(ii) Recording the validity of petitions. Procedures for recording the validity period of petitions are as follows;

(A) If a new O petition is approved before the date the petitioner indicates the services will begin, the approved petition and approval notice shall show the actual dates requested by the petitioner, not to exceed the limit specified by paragraph (o)(6)(iii) of this section or other Service policy.

(B) If a new 0 petition is approved after the date the petitioner indicates the services will begin, the approved petition and approval notice shall generally show a validity period commencing with the date of approval and ending with the date requested by the petitioner, not to exceed the limit specified by paragraph (o)(6)(iii) of this section or other Service policy.

(C) If the period of services requested by the petitioner exceeds the limit specified in paragraph (o)(6)(iii) of this section, the petition shall be approved only up to the limit specified in that paragraph.

(iii) Validity —

(A) O-1 petition. An approved petition for an alien classified under section 101(a)(15)(O)(i) of the Act shall be valid for a period of time determined by the Director to be necessary to accomplish the event or activity, not to exceed 3 years.

(B) O-2 petition. An approved petition for an alien classified under section 101(a)(15)(O)(ii) of the Act shall be valid for a period of time determined to be necessary to assist the O-1 alien to accomplish the event or activity, not to exceed 3 years.

(iv) Spouse and dependents. The spouse and unmarried minor children of the O-1 or O-2 alien beneficiary are entitled to O-3 nonimmigrant classification, subject to the same period of admission and limitations as the alien beneficiary, if they are accompanying or following to join the alien beneficiary in the United States. Neither the spouse nor a child of the alien beneficiary may accept employment unless he or she has been granted employment authorization.

(7) The petitioner shall be notified of the decision, the reasons for the denial, and the right to appeal the denial under 8 CFR part 103.

(8) Revocation of approval of petition —

(i) General.

(A) The petitioner shall immediately notify the Service of any changes in the terms and conditions of employment of a beneficiary which may affect eligibility under section 101(a)(15)(O) of the Act and paragraph (o) of this section. An amended petition should be filed when the petitioner continues to employ the beneficiary. If the petitioner no longer employs the beneficiary, the petitioner shall send a letter explaining the change(s) to the Director who approved the petition.

(B) The Director may revoke a petition at any time, even after the validity of the petition has expired.

(ii) Automatic revocation. The approval of an unexpired petition is automatically revoked if the petitioner, or the named employer in a petition filed by an agent, goes out of business, files a written withdrawal of the petition, or notifies the Service that the beneficiary is no longer employed by the petitioner.

(iii) Revocation on notice —

(A) Grounds for revocation. The Director shall send to the petitioner a notice of intent to revoke the petition in relevant part if is determined that:

(1) The beneficiary is no longer employed by the petitioner in the capacity specified in the petition;

(2) The statement of facts contained in the petition was not true and correct;

(3) The petitioner violated the terms or conditions of the approved petition;

(4) The petitioner violated the requirements of section 101(a)(15)(O) of the Act or paragraph (o) of this section; or

(5) The approval of the petition violated paragraph (o) of this section or involved gross error.

(B) Notice and decision. The notice of intent to revoke shall contain a detailed statement of the grounds for the revocation and the time period allowed for the petitioner's rebuttal. The petitioner may submit evidence in rebuttal within 30 days of the date of the notice. The Director shall consider all relevant evidence presented in deciding whether to revoke the petition.

(9) Appeal of a denial or a revocation of a petition —

(i) Denial. A denied petition may be appealed under 8 CFR part 103.

(ii) Revocation. A petition that has been revoked on notice may be appealed under 8 CFR part 103. Automatic revocations may not be appealed.

(10) Admission. A beneficiary may be admitted to the United States for the validity period of the petition, plus a period of up to 10 days before the validity period begins and 10 days after the validity period ends. The beneficiary may only engage in employment during the validity period of the petition.

(11) Extension of visa petition validity. The petitioner must file a request to extend the validity of the original petition under section 101(a)(15)(O) of the Act on the form prescribed by USCIS, in order to continue or complete the same activities or events specified in the original petition. A petition extension generally may be filed only if the validity of the original petition has not expired.

(12) Extension of stay —

(i) Extension procedure. The petitioner shall request extension of the alien's stay to continue or complete the same event or activity by filing an application or petition, accompanied by a statement explaining the reasons for the extension. The petitioner must also request a petition extension. The dates of extension shall be the same for the petition and the beneficiary's extension of stay. The alien beneficiary must be physically present in the United States at the time of filing of the extension of stay. Even though the request to extend the petition and the alien's stay are combined on the petition, the Director shall make a separate determination on each. If the alien leaves the United States for business or personal reasons while the extension requests are pending, the petitioner may request the Director to cable notification of approval of the petition extension to the consular office abroad where the alien will apply for a visa.

(ii) Extension period. An extension of stay may be authorized in increments of up to 1 year for an O-1 or O-2 beneficiary to continue or complete the same event or activity for which he or she was admitted plus an additional 10 days to allow the beneficiary to get his or her personal affairs in order.

(iii) Denial of an extension of stay. The denial of the request for the alien's extension of temporary stay may not be appealed.

(13) Effect of approval of a permanent labor certification or filing of a preference petition on O classification. The approval of a permanent labor certification or the filing of a preference petition for an alien shall not be a basis for denying an O-1 petition, a request to extend such a petition, or the alien's application for admission, change of status, or extension of stay. The alien may legitimately come to the United States for a temporary period as an O-1 nonimmigrant and depart voluntarily at the end of his or her authorized stay and, at the same time, lawfully seek to become a permanent resident of the United States.

(14) Effect of a strike —

(i) If the Secretary of Labor certifies to the Commissioner that a strike or other labor dispute involving a work stoppage of workers is in progress in the occupation at the place where the beneficiary is to be employed, and that the employment of the beneficiary would adversely affect the wages and working conditions of U.S. citizens and lawful resident workers:

(A) A petition to classify an alien as a nonimmigrant as defined in section 101(a)(15)(O) of the Act shall be denied; or

(B) If a petition has been approved, but the alien has not yet entered the United States, or has entered the United States but has not commenced employment, the approval of the petition is automatically suspended, and the application for admission on the basis of the petition shall be denied.

(ii) If there is a strike or other labor dispute involving a work stoppage of workers in progress, but such strike or other labor dispute is not certified under paragraph (o)(14)(i) of this section, the Commissioner shall not deny a petition or suspend an approved petition.

(iii) If the alien has already commenced employment in the United States under an approved petition and is participating in a strike or labor dispute involving a work stoppage of workers, whether or not such strike or other labor dispute has been certified by the Secretary of Labor, the alien shall not be deemed to be failing to maintain his or her status solely on account of past, present, or future participation in a strike or other labor dispute involving a work stoppage of workers but is subject to the following terms and conditions:

(A) The alien shall remain subject to all applicable provisions of the Immigration and Nationality Act and regulations promulgated thereunder in the same manner as are all other O nonimmigrants;

(B) The status and authorized period of stay of such an alien is not modified or extended in any way by virtue of his or her participation in a strike or other labor dispute involving a work stoppage of workers; and

(C) Although participation by an O nonimmigrant alien in a strike or other labor dispute involving a work stoppage of workers will not constitute a ground for deportation, and alien who violates his or her status or who remains in the United States after his or her authorized period of stay has expired will be subject to deportation.

(15) Use of approval notice, Form I-797. The Service shall notify the petitioner of Form I-797 whenever a visa petition or an extension of a visa petition is approved under the O classification. The beneficiary of an O petition who does not require a nonimmigrant visa may present a copy of the approval notice at a Port-of-Entry to facilitate entry into the United States. A beneficiary who is required to present a visa for admission, and who visa will have expired before the date of his or her intended return, may use Form I-797 to apply for a new or revalidated visa during the validity period of the petition. A copy of Form I-797 shall be retained by the beneficiary and presented during the validity of the petition when reentering the United States to resume the same employment with the same petitioner.

(16) Return transportation requirement. In the case of an alien who enters the United States under section 101(a)(15(O) of the Act and whose employment terminates for reasons other than voluntary resignation, the employer whose offer of employment formed the basis of such nonimmigrant status and the petitioner are jointly and severally liable for the reasonable cost of return transportation of the alien abroad. For the purposes of this paragraph, the term "abroad" means the alien's last place of residence prior to his or her entry into the United States.

(p) Artists, athletes, and entertainers —

(1) Classifications —

(i) General. Under section 101(a)(15)(P) of the Act, an alien having a residence in a foreign country which he or she has not intention or abandoning may be authorized to come to the United States temporarily to perform services for an employer or a sponsor. Under the nonimmigrant category, the alien may be classified under section 101(a)(15)(P)(i) of the Act as an alien who is coming to the United States to perform services as an internationally recognized athlete, individually or as part of a group or team, or member of an internationally recognized entertainment group; under section

101(a)(15)(P)(ii) of the Act, who is coming to perform as an artist or entertainer under a reciprocal exchange program; under section 101(a)(15)(P)(iii) of the Act, as an alien who is coming solely to perform, teach, or coach under a program that is culturally unique; or under section 101(a)(15)(P)(iv) of the Act, as the spouse or child of an alien described in section 101(a)(15)(P) (i), (ii), or (iii) of the Act who is accompanying or following to join the alien. These classifications are called P-1, P-2, P-3, and P-4 respectively. The employer or sponsor must file a petition with the Service for review of the services to be performed and for determination of the alien's eligibility for P-1, P-2, or P-3 classification before the alien may apply for a visa or seek admission to the United States. This paragraph sets forth the standards and procedures applicable to these classifications.

(ii) Description of classification —

(A) A P-1 classification applies to an alien who is coming temporarily to the United States:

(1) To perform at specific athletic competition as an athlete, individually or as part of a group or team, at an internationally recognized level or performance, or

(2) To perform with, or as an integral and essential part of the performance of, and entertainment group that has been recognized internationally as being outstanding in the discipline for a sustained and substantial period of time, and who has had a sustained and substantial relationship with the group (ordinarily for at least 1 year) and provides functions integral to the performance of the group.

(B) A P-2 classification applies to an alien who is coming temporarily to the United States to perform as an artist or entertainer, individually or as part of a group, or to perform as an integral part of the performance of such a group, and who seeks to perform under a reciprocal exchange program which is between an organization or organizations in the United States and an organization or organizations in one or more foreign states, and which provides for the temporary exchange of artists and entertainers, or groups of artists and entertainers.

(C) A P-3 classification applies to an alien artist or entertainer who is coming temporarily to the United States, either individually or as part of a group, or as an integral part of the performance of the group, to perform, teach, or coach under a commercial or noncommercial program that is culturally unique.

(2) Filing of petitions —

(i) General. A P-1 petition for an athlete or entertainment group shall be filed by a United States employer, a United States sponsoring organization, a United States agent, or a foreign employer through a United States agent. For purposes of paragraph (p) of this section, a foreign employer is any employer who is not amenable to service of process in the United States. Foreign employers seeking to employ a P-1 alien may not directly petition for the alien but must use a United States agent. A United States agent petitioning on behalf of a foreign employer must be authorized to file the petition, and to accept service of process in the United States in proceedings under section 274A of the Act, on behalf of the foreign employer. A P-2 petition for an artist or entertainer in a reciprocal exchange program shall be filed by the United States labor organization which negotiated the reciprocal exchange agreement, the sponsoring organization, or a United States employer. A P-3 petition for an artist or entertainer in a culturally unique program shall be filed by the sponsoring organization or a United States employer. Essential support personnel may not be included on the petition filed for the principal alien(s). These aliens require a separate petition. The petitioner must file a P petition on the form prescribed by USCIS. The petition may not be filed more than one year before the actual need for the alien's services. A P-1, P-2, or P-3 petition shall be adjudicated at the appropriate Service Center, even in emergency situations.

(ii) Evidence required to accompany a petition for a P nonimmigrant. Petitions for P nonimmigrant aliens shall be accompanied by the following:

(A) The evidence specified in the specific section of this part for the classification;

(B) Copies of any written contracts between the petitioner and the alien beneficiary or, if there is no written contract, a summary of the terms of the oral agreement under which the alien(s) will be employed;

(C) An explanation of the nature of the events or activities, the beginning and ending dates for the events or activities, and a copy of any itinerary for the events or activities; and

(D) A written consultation from a labor organization.

(iii) Form of documentation. The evidence submitted with an P petition should conform to the following:

(A) Affidavits, contracts, awards, and similar documentation must reflect the nature of the alien's achievement and be executed by an officer or responsible person employed by the institution, establishment, or organization where the work has performed.

(B) Affidavits written by present or former employers or recognized experts certifying to the recognition and extraordinary ability, or, in the case of a motion picture or television production, the extraordinary achievement of the alien, which shall specifically describe the alien's recognition and ability or achievement in factual terms. The affidavit must also set forth the expertise of the affiant and the manner in which the affiant acquired such information.

(C) A legible copy of a document in support of the petition may be submitted in lieu of the original. However, the original document shall be submitted if requested by the Director.

(iv) Other filing situations —

(A) Services in more than one location. A petition which requires the alien to work in more than one location (e.g., a tour) must include an itinerary with the dates and locations of the performances and must be filed with the Service Center which has jurisdiction in the area where the petitioner is located. The address which the petitioner specifies as its location on the petition shall be where the petitioner is located for purposes of this paragraph.

(B) Services for more than one employer. If the beneficiary or beneficiaries will work for more than one employer within the same time period, each employer must file a separate petition unless an agent files the petition pursuant to paragraph (p)(2)(iv)(E) of this section.

(C) Change of employer —

(1) General. If a P-1, P-2, or P-3 alien in the United States seeks to change employers or sponsors, the new employer or sponsor must file both a petition and a request to extend the alien's stay in the United States. The alien may not commence employment with the new employer or sponsor until the petition and request for extension have been approved.

(2) Traded professional P-1 athletes. In the case of a professional P-1 athlete who is traded from one organization to another organization, employment authorization for the player will automatically continue for a period of 30 days after acquisition by the new organization, within which time the new organization is expected to file a new application or petition for P-1 nonimmigrant classification. If a new application or petition is not filed within 30 days, employment authorization will cease. If a new application or petition is filed within 30 days, the professional athlete shall be deemed to be in valid P-1 status, and employment shall continue to be authorized, until the petition is adjudicated. If the new petition is denied, employment authorization will cease.

(D) Amended petition. The petitioner shall file an amended petition, with fee, with the Service Center where the original petition was filed to reflect any material changes in the terms and conditions of employment or the beneficiary's eligibility as specified in the original approved petition. A petitioner may add additional, similar or comparable performance, engagements, or competitions during the validity period of the petition without filing an amended petition.

(E) Agents as petitioners. A United States agent may file a petition in cases involving workers who are traditionally self-employed or workers who use agents to arrange short-term employment on their behalf with numerous employers, and in cases where a foreign employer authorizes the agent to act on its behalf. A United States agent may be: the actual employer of the beneficiary; the representative of both the employer and the beneficiary; or, a person or entity authorized by the employer to act for, or in place of, the employer as its agent. A petition filed by an United States agent is subject to the following conditions:

(1) An agent performing the function of an employer must specify the wage offered and the other terms and conditions of employment by contractual agreement with the beneficiary or beneficiaries. The agent/employer must also provide an itinerary of definite employment and information on any other services planned for the period of time requested.

(2) A person or company in business as an agent may file the P petition involving multiple employers as the representative of both the employers and the beneficiary or beneficiaries if the supporting documentation includes a complete itinerary of services or engagements. The itinerary shall specify the dates of each service or engagement, the names and addresses of the actual employers, the names and addresses of the establishment, venues, or locations where the services will be performed. In questionable cases, a contract between the employer(s) and the beneficiary or beneficiaries may be required. The burden is on the agent to explain the terms and conditions of the employment and to provide any required documentation.

(3) A foreign employer who, through a United States agent, files a petition for a P nonimmigrant alien is responsible for complying with all of the employer sanctions provisions of section 274A of the Act and 8 CFR part 274a.

(F) Multiple beneficiaries. More than one beneficiary may be included in a P petition if they are members of a team or group, or if they will provide essential support to P-1, P-2, or P-3 beneficiaries performing in the same location and in the same occupation. Up to 25 named beneficiaries may be included per petition.

(G) Named beneficiaries. Petitions for P classification must include the names of beneficiaries and other required information at the time of filing.

(H) Substitution of beneficiaries. A petitioner may request substitution of beneficiaries in approved P-1, P-2, and P-3 petitions for groups. To request substitution, the petitioner shall submit a letter requesting such substitution, along with a copy of the petitioner's approval notice, to the consular office at which the alien will apply for a visa or the Port-of-Entry where the alien will apply for admission. Essential support personnel may not be substituted at consular offices or at Ports-of-entry. In order to add additional new essential support personnel, a new Form application or petition must be filed.

(3) Definitions. As used in this paragraph, the term:

Arts includes fields of creative activity or endeavor such as, but not limited to, fine arts, visual arts, and performing arts.

Competition, event, or performance means an activity such as an athletic competition, athletic season, tournament, tour, exhibit, project, entertainment event, or engagement. Such activity could include short vacations, promotional appearances for the petitioning employer relating to the competition, event, or performance, and stopovers which are incidental and/or related to the activity. An athletic competition or entertainment event could include an entire season of performances A group of related activities will also be considered an event. In the case of a P-2 petition, the event may be the duration of the reciprocal exchange agreement. In the case of a P-1 athlete, the event may be the duration of the alien's contract.

Contract means the written agreement between the petitioner and the beneficiary(ies) that explains the terms and conditions of employment. The contract shall describe the services to be performed, and specify the wages, hours of work, working conditions, and any fringe benefits.

Culturally unique means a style of artistic expression, methodology, or medium which is unique to a particular country, nation, society, class, ethnicity, religion, tribe, or other group of persons.

Essential support alien means a highly skilled, essential person determined by the Director to be an integral part of the performance of a P-1, P-2, or P-3 alien because he or she performs support services which cannot be readily performed by a United States worker and which are essential to the successful performance of services by the P-1, P-2, alien. Such alien must have appropriate qualifications to perform the services, critical knowledge of the specific services to be performed, and experience in providing such support to the P-1, P-2, or P-3 alien.

Group means two or more persons established as one entity or unit to perform or to provide a service.

Internationally recognized means having a high level of achievement in a field evidenced by a degree of skill and recognition substantially above that ordinarily encountered, to the extent that such achievement is renowned, leading, or well-known in more than one country.

Member of a group means a person who is actually performing the entertainment services.

Sponsor means an established organization in the United States which will not directly employ a P-1, P-2, or P-3 alien but will assume responsibility for the accuracy of the terms and conditions specified in the petition.

Team means two or more persons organized to perform together as a competitive unit in a competitive event.

(4) Petition for an internationally recognized athlete or member of an internationally recognized entertainment group (P-1) —

(i) Types of classification.

(A) P-1 classification as an athlete in an individual capacity. A P-1 classification may be granted to an alien who is an internationally recognized athlete based on his or her own reputation and achievements as an individual. The alien must be coming to the United States to perform services which require an internationally recognized athlete.

(B) P-1 classification as a member of an entertainment group or an athletic team. An entertainment group or athletic team consists of two or more persons who function as a unit. The entertainment group or athletic team as a unit must be internationally recognized as outstanding in the discipline and must be coming to perform services which require an internationally recognized entertainment group or athletic team. A person who is a member of an internationally recognized entertainment group or athletic team may be granted P-1 classification based on that relationship, but may not perform services separate and apart from the entertainment group or athletic team. An entertainment group must have been established for a minimum of 1 year, and 75 percent of the members of the group must have been performing entertainment services for the group for a minimum of 1 year.

(ii) Criteria and documentary requirements for P-1 athletes —

(A) General. A P-1 athlete must have an internationally recognized reputation as an international athlete or he or she must be a member of a foreign team that is internationally recognized. The athlete or team must be coming to the United States to participate in an athletic competition which has a distinguished reputation and which requires participation of an athlete or athletic team that has an international reputation.

(B) Evidentiary requirements for an internationally recognized athlete or athletic team. A petition for an athletic team must be accompanied by evidence that the team as a unit has achieved international recognition in the sport. Each member of the team is accorded P-1 classification based on the international reputation of the team. A petition for an athlete who will compete individually or as a member of a U.S. team must be accompanied by evidence that the athlete has achieved international recognition in the sport based on his or her reputation. A petition for a P-1 athlete or athletic team shall include:

(1) A tendered contract with a major United States sports league or team, or a tendered contract in an individual sport commensurate with international recognition in that sport, if such contracts are normally executed in the sport, and

(2) Documentation of at least two of the following:

(i) Evidence of having participated to a significant extent in a prior season with a major United States sports league;

(ii) Evidence of having participated in international competition with a national team;

(iii) Evidence of having participated to a significant extent in a prior season for a U.S. college or university in intercollegiate competition;

(iv) A written statement from an official of the governing body of the sport which details how the alien or team is internationally recognized;

(v) A written statement from a member of the sports media or a recognized expert in the sport which details how the alien or team is internationally recognized;

(vi) Evidence that the individual or team is ranked if the sport has international rankings; or

(vii) Evidence that the alien or team has received a significant honor or award in the sport.

(iii) Criteria and documentary requirements for members of an internationally recognized entertainment group —

(A) General. A P-1 classification shall be accorded to an entertainment group to perform as a unit based on the international reputation of the group. Individual entertainers shall not be accorded P-1 classification to perform separate and apart from a group. Except as provided in paragraph (p)(4)(iii)(C)(2) of this section, it must be established that the group has been internationally recognized as outstanding in the discipline for a sustained and substantial period of time. Seventy-five percent of the members of the group must have had a sustained and substantial relationship with the group for at least 1 year and must provide functions integral to the group's performance.

(B) Evidentiary criteria for members of internationally recognized entertainment groups. A petition for P-1 classification for the members of an entertainment group shall be accompanied by:

(1) Evidence that the group has been established and performing regularly for a period of at least 1 year;

(2) A statement from the petitioner listing each member of the group and the exact dates for which each member has been employed on a regular basis by the group; and

(3) Evidence that the group has been internationally recognized in the discipline for a sustained and substantial period of time. This may be demonstrated by the submission of evidence of the group's nomination or receipt of significant international awards or prices for outstanding achievement in its field or by three of the following different types of documentation:

(i) Evidence that the group has performed, and will perform, as a starring or leading entertainment group in productions or events which have a distinguished reputation as evidenced by critical reviews, advertisements, publicity releases, publications, contracts, or endorsements;

(ii) Evidence that the group has achieved international recognition and acclaim for outstanding achievement in its field as evidenced by reviews in major newspapers, trade journals, magazines, or other published material;

(iii) Evidence that the group has performed, and will perform, services as a leading or starring group for organizations and establishments that have a distinguished reputation evidenced by articles in newspapers, trade journals, publications, or testimonials;

(iv) Evidence that the group has a record of major commercial or critically acclaimed successes, as evidenced by such indicators as ratings; standing in the field; box office receipts; record, cassette, or video sales; and other achievements in the field as reported in trade journals, major newspapers, or other publications;

(v) Evidence that the group has achieved significant recognition for achievements from organizations, critics, government agencies, or other recognized experts in the field. Such testimonials must be in a form that clearly indicates the author's authority, expertise, and knowledge of the alien's achievements; or

(vi) Evidence that the group has either commanded a high salary or will command a high salary or other substantial remuneration for services comparable to other similarly situated in the field as evidenced by contracts or other reliable evidence.

(C) Special provisions for certain entertainment groups —

(1) Alien circus personnel. The 1-year group membership requirement and the international recognition requirement are not applicable to alien circus personnel who perform as part of a circus or circus group, or who constitute an integral and essential part of the performance of such circus or circus group, provided that the alien or aliens are coming to join a circus that has been recognized nationally as outstanding for a sustained and substantial period of time or as part of such a circus.

(2) Certain nationally known entertainment groups. The Director may waive the international recognition requirement in the case of an entertainment group which has been recognized nationally as being outstanding in its discipline for a sustained and substantial period of time in consideration of special circumstances. An example of a special circumstances would be when an entertainment group may find it difficult to demonstrate recognition in more than one country due to such factors as limited access to news media or consequences of geography.

(3) Waiver of 1-year relationship in exigent circumstances. The Director may waive the 1-year relationship requirement for an alien who, because of illness or unanticipated and exigent circumstances, replaces an essential member of a P-1 entertainment group or an alien who augments the group by performing a critical role. The Department of State is hereby delegated the authority to waive the 1-year relationship requirement in the case of consular substitutions involving P-1 entertainment groups.

(iv) P-1 classification as an essential support alien —

(A) General. An essential support alien as defined in paragraph (p)(3) of this section may be granted P-1 classification based on a support relationship with an individual P-1 athlete, P-1 athletic team, or a P-1 entertainment group.

(B) Evidentiary criteria for a P-1 essential support petition. A petition for P-1 essential support personnel must be accompanied by:

(1) A consultation from a labor organization with expertise in the area of the alien's skill;

(2) A statement describing the alien(s) prior essentiality, critical skills, and experience with the principal alien(s); and

(3) A copy of the written contract or a summary of the terms of the oral agreement between the alien(s) and the employer.

(5) Petition for an artist or entertainer under a reciprocal exchange program (P-2) —

(i) General.

(A) A P-2 classification shall be accorded to artists or entertainers, individually or as a group, who will be performing under a reciprocal exchange program which is between an organization or organizations in the United States, which may include a management organization, and an organization or organizations in one or more foreign states and which provides for the temporary exchange of artists and entertainers, or groups of artists and entertainers.

(B) The exchange of artists or entertainers shall be similar in terms of caliber of artists or entertainers, terms and conditions of employment, such as length of employment, and numbers of artists or entertainers involved in the exchange. However, this requirement does not preclude an individual for group exchange.

(C) An alien who is an essential support person as defined in paragraph (p)(3) of this section may be accorded P-2 classification based on a support relationship to a P-2 artist or entertainer under a reciprocal exchange program.

(ii) Evidentiary requirements for petition involving a reciprocal exchange program. A petition for P-2 classification shall be accompanied by:

(A) A copy of the formal reciprocal exchange agreement between the U.S. organization or organizations which sponsor the aliens and an organization or organizations in a foreign country which will receive the U.S. artist or entertainers;

(B) A statement from the sponsoring organization describing the reciprocal exchange of U.S. artists or entertainers as it relates to the specific petition for which P-2 classification is being sought;

(C) Evidence that an appropriate labor organization in the United States was involved in negotiating, or has concurred with, the reciprocal exchange of U.S. and foreign artists or entertainers; and

(D) Evidence that the aliens for whom P-2 classification is being sought and the U.S. artists or entertainers subject to the reciprocal exchange agreement are artists or entertainers with comparable skills, and that the terms and conditions of employment are similar.

(iii) P-2 classification as an essential support alien —

(A) General. An essential support alien as defined in paragraph (p)(3) of this section may be granted P-2 classification based on a support relationship with a P-2 entertainer or P-2 entertainment group.

(B) Evidentiary criteria for a P-2 essential support petition. A petition for P-2 essential support personnel must be accompanied by:

(1) A consultation from a labor organization with expertise in the area of the alien's skill;

(2) A statement describing the alien(s) prior essentiality, critical skills, and experience with the principal alien(s); and

(3) A copy of the written contract or a summary of the terms of the oral agreement between the alien(s) and the employer.

(6) Petition for an artist or entertainer under a culturally unique program —

(i) General.

(A) A P-3 classification may be accorded to artists or entertainers, individually or as a group, coming to the United States for the purpose of developing, interpreting, representing, coaching, or teaching a unique or traditional ethnic, folk, cultural, musical, theatrical, or artistic performance or presentation.

(B) The artist or entertainer must be coming to the United States to participate in a cultural event or events which will further the understanding or development of his or her art form. The program may be of a commercial or noncommercial nature.

(ii) Evidentiary criteria for a petition involving a culturally unique program. A petition for P-3 classification shall be accompanied by:

(A) Affidavits, testimonials, or letters from recognized experts attesting to the authenticity of the alien's or the group's skills in performing, presenting, coaching, or teaching the unique or traditional art form and giving the credentials of the expert, including the basis of his or her knowledge of the alien's or group's skill, or

(B) Documentation that the performance of the alien or group is culturally unique, as evidence by reviews in newspapers, journals, or other published materials; and

(C) Evidence that all of the performances or presentations will be culturally unique events.

(iii) P-3 classification as an essential support alien —

(A) General. An essential support alien as defined in paragraph (p)(3) of this section may be granted P-3 classification based on a support relationship with a P-3 entertainer or P-3 entertainment group.

(B) Evidentiary criteria for a P-3 essential support petition. A petition for P-3 essential support personnel must be accompanied by:

(1) A consultation from a labor organization with expertise in the area of the alien's skill;

(2) A statement describing the alien(s) prior essentiality, critical skills and experience with the principal alien(s); and

(3) A copy of the written contract or a summary of the terms of the oral agreement between the alien(s) and the employer.

(7) Consultation —

(i) General.

(A) Consultation with an appropriate labor organization regarding the nature of the work to be done and the alien's qualifications is mandatory before a petition for P-1, P-2, or P-3 classification can be approved.

(B) Except as provided in paragraph (p)(7)(i)(E) of this section, evidence of consultation shall be a written advisory opinion from an appropriate labor organization.

(C) Except as provided in paragraph (p)(7)(i)(E) of this section, the petitioner shall obtain a written advisory opinion from an appropriate labor organization. The advisory opinion shall be submitted along with the petition when the petition is filed. If the advisory opinion is not favorable to the petitioner, the advisory opinion must set forth a specific statement of facts which support the conclusion reached in the opinion. Advisory opinions must be submitted in writing and signed by an authorized official of the organization.

(D) Except as provided in paragraph (p)(7)(i)(E) and (F) of this section, written evidence of consultation shall be included in the record of every approved petition. Consultations are advisory and are not binding on the Service.

(E) In a case where the Service has determined that a petition merits expeditious handling, the Service shall contact the labor organization and request an advisory opinion if one is not submitted by the petitioner. The labor organization shall have 24 hours to respond to the Service's request. The Service shall adjudicate the petition after receipt of the response from the labor organization. The labor organization shall then furnish the Service with a written advisory opinion within 5 working days of the request. If the labor organization fails to respond within 24 hours, the Service shall render a decision on the petition without the advisory opinion.

(F) In those cases where it is established by the petitioner that an appropriate labor organization does not exist, the Service shall render a decision on the evidence of record.

(ii) Consultation requirements for P-1 athletes and entertainment groups. Consultation with a labor organization that has expertise in the area of the alien's sport or entertainment field is required in the case of a P-1 petition. If the advisory opinion is not favorable to the petitioner, the advisory opinion must set forth a specific statement of facts which support the conclusion reached in the opinion. If the advisory opinion provided by the labor organization is favorable to the petitioner it should evaluate and/or describe the alien's or group's ability and achievements in the field of endeavor, comment on whether the alien or group is internationally recognized for achievements, and state whether the services the alien or group is coming to perform are appropriate for an internationally recognized athlete or entertainment group. In lieu of the above, a labor organization may submit a letter of no objection if it has no objection to the approval of the petition.

(iii) Consultation requirements for P-1 circus personnel. The advisory opinion provided by the labor organization should comment on whether the circus which will employ the alien has national recognition as well as any other aspect of the beneficiary's or beneficiaries' qualifications which the labor organization deems appropriate. If the advisory opinion is not favorable to the petitioner, it must set forth a specific statement of facts which support the conclusion reached in the opinion. In lieu of the above, a labor organization may submit a letter of no objection if it has no objection to the approval of the petition.

(iv) Consultation requirements for P-2 alien in a reciprocal exchange program. In P-2 petitions where an artist or entertainer is coming to the United States under a reciprocal exchange program, consultation with the appropriate labor organization is required to verify the existence of a viable exchange program. The advisory opinion from the labor organization shall comment on the bona fides of the reciprocal exchange program and specify whether the exchange meets the requirements of paragraph (p)(5) of this section. If the advisory opinion is not favorable to the petitioner, it must also set forth a specific statement of facts which support the conclusion reached in the opinion.

(v) Consultation requirements for P-3 in a culturally unique program. Consultation with an appropriate labor organization is required for P-3 petitions involving aliens in culturally unique programs. If the advisory opinion is favorable to the petitioner, it should evaluate the cultural uniqueness of the alien's skills, state whether the events are cultural in nature, and state whether the event or activity is appropriate for P-3 classification. If the advisory opinion is not favorable to the petitioner, it must also set forth a specific statement of facts which support the conclusion reached in the opinion. In lieu of the above, a labor organization may submit a letter of no objection if it has no objection to the approval of the petition.

(vi) Consultation requirements for essential support aliens. Written consultation on petitions for P-1, P-2, or P-3 essential support aliens must be made with a labor organization with expertise in the skill area involved. If the advisory opinion provided by the labor organization is favorable to the petitioner, it must evaluate the alien's essentiality to and working relationship with the artist or entertainer, and state whether United States workers are available who can perform the support services. If the advisory opinion is not favorable to the petitioner, it must also set forth a specific statement of facts which support the conclusion reached in the opinion. A labor organization may submit a letter of no objection if it has no objection to the approval of the petition.

(vii) Labor organizations agreeing to provide consultations. The Service shall list in its Operations Instructions for P classification those organizations which have agreed to provide advisory opinions to the Service and/or petitioners. The list will not be an exclusive or exhaustive list. The Service and petitioners may use other sources, such as publications, to identify appropriate labor organizations. The Service will also list in its Operations Instructions those occupations or fields of endeavor where it has been determined by the Service that no appropriate labor organization exists.

(8) Approval and validity of petition —

(i) Approval. The Director shall consider all the evidence submitted and such other evidence as he or she may independently require to assist in his or her adjudication. The Director shall notify the petitioner of the approval of the petition on Form I-797, Notice of Action. The approval notice shall include the alien beneficiary's name and classification and the petition's period of validity.

(ii) Recording the validity of petitions. Procedures for recording the validity period of petitions are:

(A) If a new P petition is approved before the date the petitioner indicates the services will begin, the approved petition and approval notice shall show the actual dates requested by the petitioner as the validity period, not to exceed the limit specified in paragraph (p)(8)(iii) of this section or other Service policy.

(B) If a new P petition is approved after the date the petitioner indicates the services will begin, the approved petition and approval notice shall generally show a validity period commencing with the date of approval and ending with the date requested by the petitioner, not to exceed the limit specified in paragraph (p)(8)(iii) of this section or other Service policy.

(C) If the period of services requested by the petitioner exceeds the limit specified in paragraph (p)(8)(iii) of this section, the petition shall be approved only up to the limit specified in that paragraph.

(iii) Validity. The approval period of a P petition shall conform to the limits prescribed as follows:

(A) P-1 petition for athletes. An approved petition for an individual athlete classified under section 101(a)(15)(P)(i) of the Act shall be valid for a period up to 5 years. An approved petition for an athletic team classified under section 101(a)(15)(P)(i) of the Act shall be valid for a period of time determined by the Director to complete the competition or event for which the alien team is being admitted, not to exceed 1 year.

(B) P-1 petition for an entertainment group. An approved petition for an entertainment group classified under section 101(a)(15)(P)(i) of the Act shall be valid for a period of time determined by the Director to be necessary to complete the performance or event for which the group is being admitted, not to exceed 1 year.

(C) P-2 and P-3 petitions for artists or entertainers. An approved petition for an artist or entertainer under section 101(a)(15)(P)(ii) or (iii) of the Act shall be valid for a period of time determined by the Director to be necessary to complete the event, activity, or performance for which the P-2 or P-3 alien is admitted, not to exceed 1 year.

(D) Spouse and dependents. The spouse and unmarried minor children of a P-1, P-2, or P-3 alien beneficiary are entitled to P-4 nonimmigrant classification, subject to the same period of admission and limitations as the alien beneficiary, if they are accompanying or following to join the alien beneficiary in the United States. Neither the spouse nor a child of the alien beneficiary may accept employment unless he or she has been granted employment authorization.

(E) Essential support aliens. Petitions for essential support personnel to P-1, P-2, and P-3 aliens shall be valid for a period of time determined by the Director to be necessary to complete the event, activity, or performance for which the P-1, P-2, or P-3 alien is admitted, not to exceed 1 year.

(9) The petitioner shall be notified of the decision, the reasons for the denial, and the right to appeal the denial under 8 CFR part 103. There is no appeal from a decision to deny an extension of stay to the alien or a change of nonimmigrant status.

(10) Revocation of approval of petition —

(i) General.

(A) The petitioner shall immediately notify the Service of any changes in the terms and conditions of employment of a beneficiary which may affect eligibility under section 101(a)(15)(P) of the Act and paragraph (p) of this section. An amended petition should be filed when the petitioner continues to employ the beneficiary. If the petitioner no longer employs the beneficiary, the petitioner shall send a letter explaining the change(s) to the Director who approved the petition.

(B) The Director may revoke a petition at any time, even after the validity of the petition has expired.

(ii) Automatic revocation. The approval of an unexpired petition is automatically revoked if the petitioner, or the employer in a petition filed by an agent, goes out of business, files a written withdrawal of the petition, or notifies the Service that the beneficiary is no longer employed by the petitioner.

(iii) Revocation on notice —

(A) Grounds for revocation. The Director shall send to the petitioner a notice of intent to revoke the petition in relevant part if he or she finds that:

(1) The beneficiary is no longer employed by the petitioner in the capacity specified in the petition;

(2) The statement of facts contained in the petition were not true and correct;

(3) The petitioner violated the terms or conditions of the approved petition;

(4) The petitioner violated requirements of section 101(a)(15)(P) of the Act or paragraph (p) of this section; or

(5) The approval of the petition violated paragraph (p) of this section or involved gross error.

(B) Notice and decision. The notice of intent to revoke shall contain a detailed statement of the grounds for the revocation and the time period allowed for the petitioner's rebuttal. The petitioner may submit evidence in rebuttal within 30 days of the date of the notice. The Director shall consider all relevant evidence presented in deciding whether to revoke the petition.

(11) Appeal of a denial or a revocation of a petition —

(i) Denial. A denied petition may be appealed under 8 CFR part 103.

(ii) Revocation. A petition that has been revoked on notice may be appealed under 8 CFR part 103. Automatic revocations may not be appealed.

(12) Admission. A beneficiary may be admitted to the United States for the validity period of the petition, plus a period of up to 10 days before the validity period begins and 10 days after the validity period ends. The beneficiary may not work except during the validity period of the petition.

(13) Extension of visa petition validity. The petitioner must file a request to extend the validity of the original petition under section 101(a)(15)(P) of the Act on the form prescribed by USCIS in order to continue or complete the same activity or event specified in the original petition. A petition extension generally may be filed only if the validity of the original petition has not expired.

(14) Extension of stay —

(i) Extension procedure. The petitioner shall request extension of the alien's stay to continue or complete the same event or activity by filing Form I-129, accompanied by a statement explaining the reasons for the extension. The petitioner must also request a petition extension. The extension dates shall be the same for the petition and the beneficiary's stay. The beneficiary must be physically present in the United States at the time the extension of stay is filed. Even though the requests to extend the petition and the alien's stay are combined on the petition, the Director shall make a separate determination on each. If the alien leaves the United States for business or personal reasons while the extension requests are pending, the petitioner may request the Director to cable notification of approval of the petition extension to the consular office abroad where the alien will apply for a visa.

(ii) Extension periods —

(A) P-1 individual athlete. An extension of stay for a P-1 individual athlete and his or her essential support personnel may be authorized for a period up to 5 years for a total period of stay not to exceed 10 years.

(B) Other P-1, P-2, and P-3 aliens. An extension of stay may be authorized in increments of 1 year for P-1 athletic teams, entertainment groups, aliens in reciprocal exchange programs, aliens in culturally unique programs, and their essential support personnel to continue or complete the same event or activity for which they were admitted.

(15) Effect of approval of a permanent labor certification or filing of a preference petition on P classification. The approval of a permanent labor certification or the filing of a preference petition for an alien shall not be a basis for denying a P petition, a request to extend such a petition, or the alien's admission, change of status, or extension of stay. The alien may legitimately come to the United States for a temporary period as a P

nonimmigrant and depart voluntarily at the end of his or her authorized stay and, at the same time, lawfully seek to become a permanent resident of the United States. This provision does not include essential support personnel.

(16) Effect of a strike —

(i) If the Secretary of Labor certifies to the Commissioner that a strike or other labor dispute involving a work stoppage of workers is in progress in the occupation at the place where the beneficiary is to be employed, and that the employment of the beneficiary would adversely affect the wages and working conditions of U.S. citizens and lawful resident workers:

(A) A petition to classify an alien as a nonimmigrant as defined in section 101(a)(15)(P) of the Act shall be denied; or

(B) If a petition has been approved, but the alien has not yet entered the United States, or has entered the United States but has not commenced employment, the approval of the petition is automatically suspended, and the application for admission of the basis of the petition shall be denied.

(ii) If there is a strike or other labor dispute involving a work stoppage of workers in progress, but such strike or other labor dispute is not certified under paragraph (p)(16)(i) of this section, the Commissioner shall not deny a petition or suspend an approved petition.

(iii) If the alien has already commenced employment in the United States under an approved petition and is participating in a strike or labor dispute involving a work stoppage of workers, whether or not such strike or other labor dispute has been certified by the Secretary of Labor, the alien shall not be deemed to be failing to maintain his or her status solely on account of past, present, or future participation in a strike or other labor dispute involving a work stoppage of workers but is subject to the following terms and conditions:

(A) The alien shall remain subject to all applicable provisions of the Immigration and Nationality Act and regulations promulgated thereunder in the same manner as all other P nonimmigrant aliens;

(B) The status and authorized period of stay of such an alien is not modified or extended in any way by virtue of his or her participation in a strike or other labor dispute involving a work stoppage of workers; and

(C) Although participation by a P nonimmigrant alien in a strike or other labor dispute involving a work stoppages of workers will not constitute a ground for deportation, an alien who violates his or her status or who remains in the United States after his or her authorized period of stay has expired, will be subject to deportation.

(17) Use of approval of notice, Form I-797. The Service has notify the petitioner on Form I-797 whenever a visa petition or an extension of a visa petition is approved under the P classification. The beneficiary of a P petition who does not require a nonimmigrant visa may present a copy of the approved notice at a Port-of-Entry to facilitate entry into the United States. A beneficiary who is required to present a visa for admission, and whose visa expired before the date of his or her intended return, may use Form I-797 to apply for a new or revalidated visa during the validity period of the petition. The copy of Form I-797 shall be retained by the beneficiary and present during the validity of the petition when reentering the United States to resume the same employment with the same petitioner.

(18) Return transportation requirement. In the case of an alien who enters the United States under section 101(a)(15)(P) of the Act and whose employment terminates for reasons other than voluntary resignation, the employer whose offer of employment formed the basis of suh nonimmigrant status and the petitioner are jointly and severally liable for the reasonable cost of return transportation of the alien abroad. For the purposes of this paragraph, the term "abroad" means the alien's last place of residence prior to his or her entry into the United States.

(q) Cultural visitors —

(1)(i) International cultural exchange visitors program. Paragraphs (q)(2) through (q)(11) of this section provide the rules governing nonimmigrant aliens who are visiting the United States temporarily in an international cultural exchange visitors program (Q-1).

(ii) Irish peace process cultural and training program. Paragraph (q)(15) of this section provides the rules governing nonimmigrant aliens who are visiting the United States temporarily under the Irish peace process cultural and training program (Q-2) and their dependents (Q-3).

(iii) Definitions. As used in this section:

Country of nationality means the country of which the participant was a national at the time of the petition seeking international cultural exchange visitor status for him or her.

Doing business means the regular, systematic, and continuous provision of goods and/or services (including lectures, seminars and other types of cultural programs) by a qualified employer which has employees, and does not include the mere presence of an agent or office of the qualifying employer.

Duration of program means the time in which a qualified employer is conducting an approved international cultural exchange program in the manner as established by the employer's petition for program approval, provided that the period of time does not exceed 15 months.

International cultural exchange visitor means an alien who has a residence in a foreign country which he or she has no intention of abandoning, and who is coming temporarily to the United States to take part in an international cultural exchange program approved by the Attorney General.

Petitioner means the employer or its designated agent who has been employed by the qualified employer on a permanent basis in an executive or managerial capacity. The designated agent must be a United States citizen, an alien lawfully admitted for permanent residence, or an alien provided temporary residence status under sections 210 or 245A of the Act.

Qualified employer means a United States or foreign firm, corporation, non-profit organization, or other legal entity (including its U.S. branches, subsidiaries, affiliates, and franchises) which administers an international cultural exchange program designated by the Attorney General in accordance with the provisions of section 101(a)(15)(Q)(i) of the Act.

(2) Admission of international cultural exchange visitor —

(i) General. A nonimmigrant alien may be authorized to enter the United States as a participant in an international cultural exchange program approved by the Attorney General for the purpose of providing practical training, employment, and the sharing of the history, culture, and traditions of the country of the alien's nationality. The period of admission is the duration of the approved international cultural exchange program or fifteen (15) months, whichever is shorter. A nonimmigrant alien admitted under this provision is classifiable as an international cultural exchange visitor in Q-1 status.

(ii) Limitation on admission. Any alien who has been admitted into the United States as an international cultural exchange visitor under section 101(a)(15)(Q)(i) of the Act shall not be readmittted in Q-1 status unless the alien has resided and been physically present outside the United States for the immediate prior year. Brief trips to the United States for pleasure or business during the immediate prior year do not break the continuity of the one-year foreign residency.

(3) International cultural exchange program —

(i) General. A United States employer shall petition the Attorney General on the form prescribed by USCIS, for approval of an international cultural exchange program which is designed to provide an opportunity for the American public to learn about foreign cultures. The United States employer must simultaneously petition on the same application or petition for the authorization for one or more individually identified nonimmigrant aliens to be admitted in Q-1 status. These aliens are to be admitted to engage in employment or training of which the essential element is the sharing with the American public, or a segment of the public sharing a common cultural interest, of the culture of the alien's country of nationality. The international cultural exchange visitor's eligibility for admission will be considered only if the international cultural exchange program is approved.

(ii) Program validity. Each petition for an international cultural exchange program will be approved for the duration of the program, which may not exceed 15 months, plus 30 days to allow time for the participants to make travel arrangements. Subsequent to the approval of the initial petition, a new petition must be filed each time the qualified employer wishes to bring in additional cultural visitors. A qualified employer may replace or substitute a participant named on a previously approved petition for the remainder of the program in accordance with paragraph (q)(6) of this section. The replacement or substituting alien may be admitted in Q-1 status until the expiration date of the approved petition.

(iii) Requirements for program approval. An international cultural exchange program must meet all of the following requirements:

(A) Accessibility to the public. The international cultural exchange program must take place in a school, museum, business or other establishment where the American public, or a segment of the public sharing a common cultural interest, is exposed to aspects of a foreign culture as part of a structured program. Activities that take place in a private home or an isolated business setting to which the American public, or a segment of the public sharing a common cultural interest, does not have direct access do not qualify.

(B) Cultural component. The international cultural exchange program must have a cultural component which is an essential and integral part of the international cultural exchange visitor's employment or training. The cultural component must be designed, on the whole, to exhibit or explain the attitude, customs, history, heritage, philosophy, or traditions of the international cultural exchange visitor's country of nationality. A cultural component may include structured instructional activities such as seminars, courses, lecture series, or language camps.

(C) Work component. The international cultural exchange visitor's employment or training in the United States may not be independent of the cultural component of the international cultural exchange program. The work component must serve as the vehicle to achieve the objectives of the cultural component. The sharing of the culture of the international cultural exchange visitor's country of nationality must result from his or her employment or training with the qualified employer in the United States.

(iv) Requirements for international cultural exchange visitors. To be eligible for international cultural exchange visitor status, an alien must be a bona fide nonimmigrant who:

(A) Is at least 18 years of age at the time the petition is filed;

(B) Is qualified to perform the service or labor or receive the type of training stated in the petition;

(C) Has the ability to communicate effectively about the cultural attributes of his or her country of nationality to the American public; and

(D) Has resided and been physically present outside of the United States for the immediate prior year, if he or she was previously admitted as an international cultural exchange visitor.

(4) Supporting documentation —

(i) Documentation by the employer. To establish eligibility as a qualified employer, the petitioner must submit with the completed application or petition appropriate evidence that the employer:

(A) Maintains an established international cultural exchange program in accordance with the requirements set forth in paragraph (q)(3) of this section;

(B) Has designated a qualified employee as a representative who will be responsible for administering the international cultural exchange program and who will serve as liaison with the Immigration and Naturalization Service;

(C) Is actively doing business in the United States;

(D) Will offer the alien(s) wages and working conditions comparable to those accorded local domestic workers similarly employed; and

(E) Has the financial ability to remunerate the participant(s).

(ii) Certification by petitioner.

(A) The petitioner must give the date of birth, country of nationality, level of education, position title, and a brief job description for each international cultural exchange visitor included in the petition. The petitioner must verify and certify that the prospective participants are qualified to perform the service or labor, or receive the type of training, described in the petition.

(B) The petitioner must report the international cultural exchange visitors' wages and certify that such cultural exchange visitors are offered wages and working conditions comparable to those accorded to local domestic workers similarly employed.

(iii) Supporting documentation as prescribed in paragraphs (q)(4)(i) and (q)(4)(ii) of this section must accompany a petition filed on the form prescribed by USCIS in all cases except where the employer files multiple petitions in the same calendar year. When petitioning to repeat a previously approved international cultural exchange program, a copy of the initial program approval notice may be submitted in lieu of the documentation required under paragraph (q)(4)(i) of this section. The Service will request additional documentation only when clarification is needed.

(5) Filing of petitions for international cultural exchange visitor program —

(i) General. A United States employer seeking to bring in international cultural exchange visitors must file a petition on the form prescribed by USCIS, with the applicable fee, along with appropriate documentation. A new petition on the form prescribed by USCIS, with the applicable fee, must be filed with the appropriate service center each time a qualified employer wants to bring in additional international cultural exchange visitors. Each person named on an approved petition will be admitted only for the duration of the approved program. Replacement or substitution may be made for any person named on an approved petition as provided in paragraph (q)(6) of this section, but only for the remainder of the approved program.

(ii) Petition for multiple participants. The petitioner may include up to 25 named participants on a petition. The petitioner shall include the name, date of birth, nationality, and other identifying information required on the petition for each participant. The petitioner must also indicate the United States consulate at which each participant will apply for a Q-1 visa. For participants who are visa-exempt under 8 CFR 212.1(a), the petitioner must indicate the port of entry at which each participant will apply for admission to the United States.

(iii) Service, labor, or training in more than one location. A petition which requires the international cultural exchange visitor to engage in employment or training (with the same employer) in more than one location must include an itinerary with the dates and locations of the services, labor, or training.

(iv) Services, labor, or training for more than one employer. If the international cultural exchange visitor will perform services or labor for, or receive training from, more than one employer, each employer must file a separate petition. The international cultural exchange visitor may work part-time for multiple employers provided that each employer has an approved petition for the alien.

(v) Change of employers. If an international cultural exchange visitor is in the United States under section 101(a)(15)(Q)(i) of the Act and decides to change employers, the new employer must file a petition. However, the total period of time the international cultural exchange visitor may stay in the United States remains limited to fifteen (15) months.

(6) Substitution or replacements of participants in an international cultural exhange visitor program. The petitioner may substitute for or replace a person named on a previously approved petition for the remainder of the program without filing a new application or petition. The substituting international cultural exchange visitor must meet the qualification requirements prescribed in paragraph (q)(3)(iv) of this section. To request substitution or replacement, the petitioner shall, by letter, notify the consular office at which the alien will apply for a visa or, in the case of visa-exempt aliens, the Service office at the port of entry where the alien will apply for admission. A copy of the petition's approval notice must be included with the letter. The petitioner must state the date of birth, country of nationality, level of education, and position title of each prospective international cultural exchange visitor and must certify that each is qualified to perform the service or labor or receive the type of training described in the approved petition. The petitioner must also indicate each international cultural exchange visitor's wages and certify that the international cultural exchange visitor is offered wages and working conditions comparable to those accorded to local domestic workers in accordance with paragraph (q)(11)(ii) of this section.

(7) Approval of petition for international cultural exchange visitor program —

(i) The director shall consider all the evidence submitted and request other evidence as he or she may deem necessary.

(ii) The director shall notify the petitioner and the appropriate United States consulate(s) of the approval of a petition. For participants who are visa-exempt under 8 CFR 212.1(a), the director shall give notice of the approval to the director of the port of entry at which each such participant will apply for admission to the United States. The notice of approval shall include the name of the international cultural exchange visitors, their classification, and the petition's period of validity.

(iii) An approved petition for an alien classified under section 101(a)(15)(Q)(i) of the Act is valid for the length of the approved program or fifteen (15) months, whichever is shorter.

(iv) A petition shall not be approved for an alien who has an aggregate of fifteen (15) months in the United States under section 101(a)(15)(Q)(i) of the Act, unless the alien has resided and been physically present outside the United States for the immediate prior year.

(8) Denial of the petition —

(i) Notice of denial. The petitioner shall be notified of the denial of a petition, the reasons for the denial, and the right to appeal the denial under part 103 of this chapter.

(ii) Multiple participants. A petition for multiple international cultural exchange visitors may be denied in whole or in part.

(9) Revocation of approval of petition —

(i) General. The petitioner shall immediately notify the appropriate Service center of any changes in the employment of a participant which would affect eligibility under section 101(a)(15)(Q)(i) of the Act.

(ii) Automatic revocation. The approval of any petition is automatically revoked if the qualifying employer goes out of business, files a written withdrawal of the petition, or terminates the approved international cultural exchange program prior to its expiration date. No further action or notice by the Service is necessary in the case of automatic revocation. In any other case, the Service shall follow the revocation procedures in paragraphs (q)(9) (iii) through (v) of this section.

(iii) Revocation on notice. The director shall send the petitioner a notice of intent to revoke the petition in whole or in part if he or she finds that:

(A) The international cultural exchange visitor is no longer employed by the petitioner in the capacity specified in the petition, or if the international cultural exchange visitor is no longer receiving training as specified in the petition;

(B) The statement of facts contained in the petition was not true and correct;

(C) The petitioner violated the terms and conditions of the approved petition; or

(D) The Service approved the petition in error.

(iv) Notice and decision. The notice of intent to revoke shall contain a detailed statement of the grounds for the revocation and the period of time allowed for the petitioner's rebuttal. The petitioner may submit evidence in rebuttal within 30 days of receipt of the notice. The director shall consider all relevant evidence presented in deciding whether to revoke the petition in whole or in part. If the petition is revoked in part, the remainder of the petition shall remain approved and a revised approval notice shall be sent to the petitioner with the revocation notice.

(v) Appeal of a revocation of a petition. Revocation with notice of a petition in whole or in part may be appealed to the Associate Commissioner for Examinations under part 103 of this chapter. Automatic revocation may not be appealed.

(10) Extension of stay. An alien's total period of stay in the United States under section 101(a)(15)(Q)(i) of the Act cannot exceed fifteen (15) months. The authorized stay of an international cultural exchange visitor may be extended within the 15-month limit if he or she is the beneficiary of a new petition filed in accordance with paragraph (q)(3) of this section. The new petition, if filed by the same employer, should include a copy of the previous petition's approval notice and a letter from the petitioner indicating any terms and conditions of the previous petition that have changed.

(11) Employment provisions —

(i) General. An alien classified under section 101(a)(15)(Q)(i) of the Act may be employed only by the qualified employer through which the alien attained Q-1 nonimmigrant status. An alien in this class is not required to apply for an employment authorization document. Employment outside the specific program violates the terms of the alien's Q-1 nonimmigrant status within the meaning of section 237(a)(1)(C)(i) of the Act.

(ii) Wages and working conditions. The wages and working conditions of an international cultural exchange visitor must be comparable to those accorded to domestic workers similarly employed in the geographical area of the alien's employment. The employer must certify on the petition that such conditions are met as in accordance with paragraph (q)(4)(iii)(B) of this section.

(12) (Reserved)

(13) (Reserved)

(14) (Reserved)

(15) Irish peace process cultural and training program visitors (Q-2) and their dependents (Q-3) —

(i) General. An Irish Peace Process Cultural and Training Program (IPPCTP) visitor is a nonimmigrant alien coming to the United States temporarily to gain or upgrade work skills through training and temporary employment and to experience living in a diverse and peaceful environment.

(ii) What are the requirements for participation?

(A) The principal alien must have been physically resident in either Northern Ireland or the counties of Louth, Monaghan, Cavan, Leitrim, Sligo, and Donegal in the Republic of Ireland, for at least 3 months immediately preceding application to the program and must show that he or she has no intention of abandoning this residence.

(B) The principal alien must be between the ages of 18 and 35.

(C) The principal alien must:

(1) Be unemployed for at least 3 months, or have completed or currently be enrolled in a training/employment program sponsored by the Training and Employment Agency of Northern Ireland (T&EA) or by the Training and Employment Authority of Ireland (FAS), or by other such publicly funded programs, or have been made redundant from employment (i.e., lost their job), or have received a notice of redundancy (termination of employment); or

(2) Be a currently employed person whose employer has nominated him/her to participate in this program for additional training or job experience that is to benefit both the participant and his/her employer upon returning home.

(D) The principal alien must intend to come to the United States temporarily, for a period not to exceed 36 months, in order to obtain training, employment, and the experience of coexistence and conflict resolution in a diverse society.

(iii) Are there any limitations on admissions ?

(A) No more than 4,000 participants, including spouses and any minor children of principal aliens, may be admitted annually for 3 consecutive program years, beginning with FY 2000 (October 1, 1999, through September 30, 2000).

(B) For each alien admitted under section 101(a)(15)(Q)(ii) of the Act, the number of aliens admitted under section 101(a)(15)(H)(ii)(b) of the Act is reduced by one for that fiscal year or the subsequent fiscal year.

(C) This program expires on October 1, 2005.

(iv) What are the requirements for initial admission to the United States?

(A) Principal aliens, their spouses, and minor children of principal aliens must present valid passports and either a Q-2 or Q-3 visa at the time of inspection.

(B) Initial admission for those principal and dependent aliens in this program who received their visas at either the U.S. Embassy in Dublin or the U.S. Consulate in Belfast must take place at the Service's Pre-Flight Inspection facilities at either the Shannon or Dublin airports in the Republic of Ireland.

(C) The principal alien will be required to present a Certification Letter issued by the Department of State's (DOS') Program Administrator documenting him or her as an individual selected for participation in the IP-PCTP. Eligible dependents may be requested to present written documentation certifying their relationship to the principal.

(v) May the principal alien and dependents make brief visits outside the United States?

(A) The principal alien, spouse, and any minor children of the principal alien may make brief departures, for periods not to exceed 3 consecutive months, and may be readmitted without having to obtain a new visa. However, such periods of time spent outside the United States will not be added to the end of stay, which is not to exceed a total of 3 years from the initial date of entry of the principal alien.

(B) Those participants or dependents who remain outside the United States in excess of 3 consecutive months will not be readmitted by the Service on their initial Q-2 or Q-3 visa. Instead, any such individual and eligible dependents wishing to rejoin the program will be required to reapply to the program and be in receipt of a new Q-2 or Q-3 visa and a Certification Letter issued by the DOS' Program Administrator, prior to any subsequent admission to the United States.

(vi) How long may a Q-2 or Q-3 visa holder remain in the United States under this program?

(A) The principal alien and any accompanying, or following-to-join, spouse or minor children of the principal alien are admitted for the duration of the principal alien's planned cultural and training program or 36 months, whichever is shorter.

(B) Those participants and eligible dependents admitted for specific periods less than 36 months may extend their period of stay through the Service so that their total period of stay is 36 months, provided the extension of stay is related to employment or training certified by the DOS' Program Administrator.

(vii) How is employment authorized under this program?

(A) Following endorsement of his/her Form I-94, Arrival-Departure Record, by a Service officer, any principal alien admitted under section 101(a)(15)(Q)(ii) of the Act is permitted to work for an employer or employers listed on the Certification Letter issued by the DOS' Program Administrator.

(B) The accompanying spouse and minor children of the principal alien may not accept employment, unless the spouse has also been designated as a principal alien (Q-2) in this program and has been issued a Certification Letter by the DOS' Program Administrator.

(viii) May the principal alien change employers? Principal aliens wishing to change employers must request such a change through the DOS' Program Administrator to the Service. Following review and consideration of the request by the Service, the Service will inform the participant of the decision. The Service will grant such approval of employers only if the new employer has been approved by DOS in accordance with its regulations and such approval is communicated to the Service through the DOS' Program Administrator. If approved, the participant's Form I-94 will be annotated to show the new employer. If denied, there is no appeal under this section.

(ix) May the principal alien hold other jobs during his/her U.S. visit? No; any principal alien classified as an Irish peace process cultural and training program visitor may only engage in employment that has been certified by the DOS' Program Administrator and approved by the DOS or the Service as endorsed on the Form I-94. An alien who engages in unauthorized employment violates the terms of the Q-2 visa and will be considered to have violated section 237(a)(1)(C)(i) of the Act.

(x) What happens if a principal alien loses his/her job? A principal alien, who loses his or her job, will have 30 days from his/her last date of employment to locate appropriate employment or training, to have the job offer certified by the DOS' Program Administrator in accordance with the DOS' regulations and to have it approved by the Service. If appropriate employment or training cannot be found within this 30-day-period, the principal alien and any accompany family members will be required to depart the United States.

(r) Religious workers. This paragraph governs classification of an alien as a nonimmigrant religious worker (R-1).

(1) To be approved for temporary admission to the United States, or extension and maintenance of status, for the purpose of conducting the activities of a religious worker for a period not to exceed five years, an alien must:

(i) Be a member of a religious denomination having a bona fide non-profit religious organization in the United States for at least two years immediately preceding the time of application for admission;

(ii) Be coming to the United States to work at least in a part time position (average of at least 20 hours per week);

(iii) Be coming solely as a minister or to perform a religious vocation or occupation as defined in paragraph (r)(3) of this section (in either a professional or nonprofessional capacity);

(iv) Be coming to or remaining in the United States at the request of the petitioner to work for the petitioner; and

(v) Not work in the United States in any other capacity, except as provided in paragraph (r)(2) of this section.

(2) An alien may work for more than one qualifying employer as long as each qualifying employer submits a petition plus all additional required documentation as prescribed by USCIS regulations.

(3) Definitions. As used in this section, the term:

Bona fide non-profit religious organization in the United States means a religious organization exempt from taxation as described in section 501(c)(3) of the Internal Revenue Code of 1986, subsequent amendment or equivalent sections of prior enactments of the Internal Revenue Code, and possessing a currently valid determination letter from the Internal Revenue Service (IRS) confirming such exemption.

Bona fide organization which is affiliated with the religious denomination means an organization which is closely associated with the religious denomination and which is exempt from taxation as described in section 501(c)(3) of the Internal Revenue Code of 1986, or subsequent amendment or equivalent sections of prior enactments of the Internal Revenue Code, and possessing a currently valid determination letter from the IRS confirming such exemption.

Denominational membership means membership during at least the two-year period immediately preceding the filing date of the petition, in the same type of religious denomination as the United States religious organization where the alien will work.

Minister means an individual who:

(A) Is fully authorized by a religious denomination, and fully trained according to the denomination's standards, to conduct religious worship and perform other duties usually performed by authorized members of the clergy of that denomination;

(B) Is not a lay preacher or a person not authorized to perform duties usually performed by clergy;

(C) Performs activities with a rational relationship to the religious calling of the minister; and

(D) Works solely as a minister in the United States which may include administrative duties incidental to the duties of a minister.

Petition means the form or as may be prescribed by USCIS, a supplement containing attestations required by this section, and the supporting evidence required by this part.

Religious denomination means a religious group or community of believers that is governed or administered under a common type of ecclesiastical government and includes one or more of the following:

(A) A recognized common creed or statement of faith shared among the denomination's members;

(B) A common form of worship;

(C) A common formal code of doctrine and discipline;

(D) Common religious services and ceremonies;

(E) Common established places of religious worship or religious congregations; or

(F) Comparable indicia of a bona fide religious denomination.

Religious occupation means an occupation that meets all of the following requirements:

(A) The duties must primarily relate to a traditional religious function and be recognized as a religious occupation within the denomination;

(B) The duties must be primarily related to, and must clearly involve, inculcating or carrying out the religious creed and beliefs of the denomination;

(C) The duties do not include positions which are primarily administrative or support such as janitors, maintenance workers, clerical employees, fund raisers, persons solely involved in the solicitation of donations, or similar positions, although limited administrative duties that are only incidental to religious functions are permissible; and

(D) Religious study or training for religious work does not constitute a religious occupation, but a religious worker may pursue study or training incident to status.

Religious vocation means a formal lifetime commitment, through vows, investitures, ceremonies, or similar indicia, to a religious way of life. The religious denomination must have a class of individuals whose lives are dedicated to religious practices and functions, as distinguished from the secular members of the religion. Examples of vocations include nuns, monks, and religious brothers and sisters.

Religious worker means an individual engaged in and, according to the denomination's standards, qualified for a religious occupation or vocation, whether or not in a professional capacity, or as a minister.

Tax-exempt organization means an organization that has received a determination letter from the IRS establishing that it, or a group it belongs to, is exempt from taxation in accordance with sections 501(c)(3) of the Internal Revenue Code of 1986, or subsequent amendments or equivalent sections of prior enactments of the Internal Revenue Code.

(4) Requirements for admission/change of status; time limits —

(i) Principal applicant (R-1 nonimmigrant). If otherwise admissible, an alien who meets the requirements of section 101(a)(15)(R) of the Act may be admitted as an R-1 alien or changed to R-1 status for an initial period of up to 30 months from date of initial admission. If visa-exempt, the alien must present original documentation of the petition approval.

(ii) Spouse and children (R-2 status). The spouse and unmarried children under the age of 21 of an R-1 alien may be accompanying or following to join the R-1 alien, subject to the following conditions:

(A) R-2 status is granted for the same period of time and subject to the same limits as the principal, regardless of the time such spouse and children may have spent in the United States in R-2 status;

(B) Neither the spouse nor children may accept employment while in the United States in R-2 status; and

(C) The primary purpose of the spouse or children coming to the United States must be to join or accompany the principal R-1 alien.

(5) Extension of stay or readmission. An R-1 alien who is maintaining status or is seeking readmission and who satisfies the eligibility requirements of this section may be granted an extension of R-1 stay or readmission in R-1 status for the validity period of the petition, up to 30 months, provided the total period spent in R-1 status does not exceed a maximum of 5 years. A Petition for a Nonimmigrant Worker to request an extension of R-1 status must be filed by the employer with a supplement prescribed by USCIS containing attestations required by this section, the fee specified in 8 CFR part 106, and the supporting evidence, in accordance with the applicable form instructions.

(6) Limitation on total stay. An alien who has spent five years in the United States in R-1 status may not be readmitted to or receive an extension of stay in the United States under the R visa classification unless the alien has resided abroad and has been physically present outside the United States for the immediate prior year. The limitations in this paragraph shall not apply to R-1 aliens who did not reside continually in the United States and whose employment in the United States was seasonal or intermittent or was for an aggregate of six months or less per year. In addition, the limitations shall not apply to aliens who reside abroad and regularly commute to the United States to engage in part-time employment. To qualify for this exception, the petitioner and the alien must provide clear and convincing proof that the alien qualifies for such an exception. Such proof shall consist of evidence such as arrival and departure records, transcripts of processed income tax returns, and records of employment abroad.

(7) Jurisdiction and procedures for obtaining R-1 status. An employer in the United States seeking to employ a religious worker, by initial petition or by change of status, shall file a petition in accordance with the applicable form instructions.

(8) Attestation. An authorized official of the prospective employer of an R-1 alien must complete, sign and date an attestation prescribed by USCIS and submit it along with the petition. The prospective employer must specifically attest to all of the following:

(i) That the prospective employer is a bona fide non-profit religious organization or a bona fide organization which is affiliated with the religious denomination and is exempt from taxation;

(ii) That the alien has been a member of the denomination for at least two years and that the alien is otherwise qualified for the position offered;

(iii) The number of members of the prospective employer's organization;

(iv) The number of employees who work at the same location where the beneficiary will be employed and a summary of the type of responsibilities of those employees. USCIS may request a list of all employees, their titles, and a brief description of their duties at its discretion;

(v) The number of aliens holding special immigrant or nonimmigrant religious worker status currently employed or employed within the past five years by the prospective employer's organization;

(vi) The number of special immigrant religious worker and nonimmigrant religious worker petitions and applications filed by or on behalf of any aliens for employment by the prospective employer in the past five years;

(vii) The title of the position offered to the alien and a detailed description of the alien's proposed daily duties;

(viii) Whether the alien will receive salaried or non-salaried compensation and the details of such compensation;

(ix) That the alien will be employed at least 20 hours per week;

(x) The specific location(s) of the proposed employment; and

(xi) That the alien will not be engaged in secular employment.

(9) Evidence relating to the petitioning organization. A petition shall include the following initial evidence relating to the petitioning organization:

(i) A currently valid determination letter from the IRS showing that the organization is a tax-exempt organization; or

(ii) For a religious organization that is recognized as tax-exempt under a group tax-exemption, a currently valid determination letter from the IRS establishing that the group is tax-exempt; or

(iii) For a bona fide organization that is affiliated with the religious denomination, if the organization was granted tax-exempt status under section 501(c)(3), or subsequent amendment or equivalent sections of prior enactments, of the Internal Revenue Code, as something other than a religious organization:

(A) A currently valid determination letter from the IRS establishing that the organization is a tax-exempt organization;

(B) Documentation that establishes the religious nature and purpose of the organization, such as a copy of the organizing instrument of the organization that specifies the purposes of the organization;

(C) Organizational literature, such as books, articles, brochures, calendars, flyers, and other literature describing the religious purpose and nature of the activities of the organization; and

(D) A religious denomination certification. The religious organization must complete, sign and date a statement certifying that the petitioning organization is affiliated with the religious denomination. The statement must be submitted by the petitioner along with the petition.

(10) Evidence relating to the qualifications of a minister. If the alien is a minister, the petitioner must submit the following:

(i) A copy of the alien's certificate of ordination or similar documents reflecting acceptance of the alien's qualifications as a minister in the religious denomination; and

(ii) Documents reflecting acceptance of the alien's qualifications as a minister in the religious denomination, as well as evidence that the alien has completed any course of prescribed theological education at an accredited theological institution normally required or recognized by that religious denomination, including transcripts, curriculum, and documentation that establishes that the theological education is accredited by the denomination, or

(iii) For denominations that do not require a prescribed theological education, evidence of:

(A) The denomination's requirements for ordination to minister;

(B) The duties allowed to be performed by virtue of ordination;

(C) The denomination's levels of ordination, if any; and

(D) The alien's completion of the denomination's requirements for ordination.

(11) Evidence relating to compensation. Initial evidence must state how the petitioner intends to compensate the alien, including specific monetary or in-kind compensation, or whether the alien intends to be self-supporting. In either case, the petitioner must submit verifiable evidence explaining how the petitioner will compensate the alien or how the alien will be self-supporting. Compensation may include:

(i) Salaried or non-salaried compensation. Evidence of compensation may include past evidence of compensation for similar positions; budgets showing monies set aside for salaries, leases, etc.; verifiable documentation that room and board will be provided; or other evidence acceptable to USCIS. IRS documentation, such as IRS Form W-2 or certified tax returns, must be submitted, if available. If IRS documentation is unavailable, the petitioner must submit an explanation for the absence of IRS documentation, along with comparable, verifiable documentation.

(ii) Self support.

(A) If the alien will be self-supporting, the petitioner must submit documentation establishing that the position the alien will hold is part of an established program for temporary, uncompensated missionary work, which is part of a broader international program of missionary work sponsored by the denomination.

(B) An established program for temporary, uncompensated work is defined to be a missionary program in which:

(1) Foreign workers, whether compensated or uncompensated, have previously participated in R-1 status;

(2) Missionary workers are traditionally uncompensated;

(3) The organization provides formal training for missionaries; and

(4) Participation in such missionary work is an established element of religious development in that denomination.

(C) The petitioner must submit evidence demonstrating:

(1) That the organization has an established program for temporary, uncompensated missionary work;

(2) That the denomination maintains missionary programs both in the United states and abroad;

(3) The religious worker's acceptance into the missionary program;

(4) The religious duties and responsibilities associated with the traditionally uncompensated missionary work; and

(5) Copies of the alien's bank records, budgets documenting the sources of self-support (including personal or family savings, room and board with host families in the United States, donations from the denomination's churches), or other verifiable evidence acceptable to USCIS.

(12) Evidence of previous R-1 employment. Any request for an extension of stay as an R-1 must include initial evidence of the previous R-1 employment. If the beneficiary:

(i) Received salaried compensation, the petitioner must submit IRS documentation that the alien received a salary, such as an IRS Form W-2 or certified copies of filed income tax returns, reflecting such work and compensation for the preceding two years.

(ii) Received non-salaried compensation, the petitioner must submit IRS documentation of the non-salaried compensation if available. If IRS documentation is unavailable, an explanation for the absence of IRS documentation must be provided, and the petitioner must provide verifiable evidence of all financial support, including stipends, room and board, or other support for the beneficiary by submitting a description of the location where the beneficiary lived, a lease to establish where the beneficiary lived, or other evidence acceptable to USCIS.

(iii) Received no salary but provided for his or her own support, and that of any dependents, the petitioner must show how support was maintained by submitting with the petition verifiable documents such as audited financial statements, financial institution records, brokerage account statements, trust documents signed by an attorney, or other evidence acceptable to USCIS.

(13) Change or addition of employers. An R-1 alien may not be compensated for work for any religious organization other than the one for which a petition has been approved or the alien will be out of status. A different or additional employer seeking to employ the alien may obtain prior approval of such employment through the filing of a separate petition and appropriate supplement, supporting documents, and fee prescribed in 8 CFR 106.2.

(14) Employer obligations. When an R-1 alien is working less than the required number of hours or has been released from or has otherwise terminated employment before the expiration of a period of authorized R-1 stay, the R-1 alien's approved employer must notify DHS within 14 days using procedures set forth in the instructions to the petition or otherwise prescribed by USCIS on the USCIS Internet Web site at www.uscis.gov.

(15) Nonimmigrant intent. An alien classified under section 101(a)(15)(R) of the Act shall maintain an intention to depart the United States upon the expiration or termination of R-1 or R-2 status. However, a nonimmigrant petition, application for initial admission, change of status, or extension of stay in R classification may not be denied solely on the basis of a filed or an approved request for permanent labor certifica-

tion or a filed or approved immigrant visa preference petition.

(16) Inspections, evaluations, verifications, and compliance reviews. The supporting evidence submitted may be verified by USCIS through any means determined appropriate by USCIS, up to and including an on-site inspection of the petitioning organization. The inspection may include a tour of the organization's facilities, an interview with the organization's officials, a review of selected organization records relating to compliance with immigration laws and regulations, and an interview with any other individuals or review of any other records that the USCIS considers pertinent to the integrity of the organization. An inspection may include the organization headquarters, or satellite locations, or the work locations planned for the applicable employee. If USCIS decides to conduct a pre-approval inspection, satisfactory completion of such inspection will be a condition for approval of any petition.

(17) Denial and appeal of petition. USCIS will provide written notification of the reasons for the denial under 8 CFR 103.3(a)(1). The petitioner may appeal the denial under 8 CFR 103.3.

(18) Revocation of approved petitions —

(i) Director discretion. The director may revoke a petition at any time, even after the expiration of the petition.

(ii) Automatic revocation. The approval of any petition is automatically revoked if the petitioner ceases to exist or files a written withdrawal of the petition.

(iii) Revocation on notice —

(A) Grounds for revocation. The director shall send to the petitioner a notice of intent to revoke the petition in relevant part if he or she finds that:

(1) The beneficiary is no longer employed by the petitioner in the capacity specified in the petition;

(2) The statement of facts contained in the petition was not true and correct;

(3) The petitioner violated terms and conditions of the approved petition;

(4) The petitioner violated requirements of section 101(a)(15)(R) of the Act or paragraph (r) of this section; or

(5) The approval of the petition violated paragraph (r) of this section or involved gross error.

(B) Notice and decision. The notice of intent to revoke shall contain a detailed statement of the grounds for the revocation and the time period allowed for the petitioner's rebuttal. The petitioner may submit evidence in rebuttal within 30 days of receipt of the notice. The director shall consider all relevant evidence presented in deciding whether to revoke the petition.

(19) Appeal of a revocation of a petition. A petition that has been revoked on notice in whole or in part may be appealed under 8 CFR 103.3. Automatic revocations may not be appealed.

(s) NATO nonimmigrant aliens —

(1) General —

(i) Background. The North Atlantic Treaty Organization (NATO) is constituted of nations signatory to the North Atlantic Treaty. The Agreement Between the Parties to the North Atlantic Treaty Regarding the Status of Their Forces, signed in London, June 1951 (NATO Status of Forces Agreement), is the agreement between those nations that defines the terms of the status of their armed forces while serving abroad.

(A) Nonimmigrant aliens classified as NATO-1 through NATO-5 are officials, employees, or persons associated with NATO, and members of their immediate families, who may enter the United States in accordance with the NATO Status of Forces Agreement or the Protocol on the Status of International Military Headquarters set up pursuant to the North Atlantic Treaty (Paris Protocol). The following specific classifications shall be assigned to such NATO nonimmigrants:

(1)NATO-1 — A principal permanent representative of a Member State to NATO (including any of its subsidiary bodies) resident in the United States and resident members of permanent representative's official staff; Secretary General, Deputy Secretary General, Assistant Secretaries General and Executive Secretary of NATO; other permanent NATO officials of similar rank; and the members of the immediate family of such persons.

(2)NATO-2 — Other representatives of Member States to NATO (including any of its subsidiary bodies) including representatives, advisers and technical experts of delegations, and the members of the immediate family of such persons; dependents of members of a force entering in accordance with the provisions of the NATO Status of Forces Agreement or in accordance with the provisions of the Paris Protocol; members of such a force, if issued visas.

(3)NATO-3 — Official clerical staff accompanying a representative of a Member State to NATO (including any of its subsidiary bodies) and the members of the immediate family of such persons.

(4)NATO-4 — Officials of NATO (other than those classifiable under NATO-1) and the members of their immediate family

(5)NATO-5 — Experts, other than NATO officials classifiable under NATO-4, employed on missions on behalf of NATO and their dependents.

(B) Nonimmigrant aliens classified as NATO-6 are civilians, and members of their immediate families, who may enter the United States as employees of a force entering in accordance with the NATO Status of Forces Agreement, or as members of a civilian component attached to or employed by NATO Headquarters, Supreme Allied Commander, Atlantic (SACLANT), set up pursuant to the Paris Protocol.

(C) Nonimmigrant aliens classified as NATO-7 are attendants, servants, or personal employees of nonimmigrant aliens classified as NATO-1, NATO-2, NATO-3, NATO-4, NATO-5, and NATO-6, who are authorized to work only for the NATO-1 through NATO-6 nonimmigrant from whom they derive status, and members of their immediate families.

(ii) Admission and extension of stay. NATO-1, NATO-2, NATO-3, NATO-4, and NATO-5 aliens are normally exempt from inspection under 8 CFR 235.1(c). NATO-6 aliens may be authorized admission for duration of status. NATO-7 aliens may be admitted for not more than 3 years and may be granted extensions of temporary stay in increments of not more than 2 years. In addition, an application for extension of temporary stay for a NATO-7 alien must be accompanied by a statement signed by the employing official stating that he or she intends to continue to employ the NATO-7 applicant, describing the work the applicant will perform, and acknowledging that this is, and will be, the sole employment of the NATO-7 applicant.

(2) Definition of a dependent of a NATO-1, NATO-2, NATO-3, NATO-4, NATO-5, or NATO-6. For purposes of employment in the United States, the term dependent of a NATO-1, NATO-2, NATO-3, NATO-4, NATO-5, or NATO-6 principal alien, as used in this section, means any of the following immediate members of the family habitually residing in the same household as the NATO-1, NATO-2, NATO-3, NATO-4, NATO-5, or NATO-6 principal alien assigned to official duty in the United States:

(i) Spouse;

(ii) Unmarried children under the age of 21;

(iii) Unmarried sons or daughters under the age of 23 who are in full-time attendance as students at post-secondary educational institutions;

(iv) Unmarried sons or daughters under the age of 25 who are in full-time attendance as students at post-secondary educational institutions if a formal bilateral employment agreement permitting their employment in the United States was signed prior to November 21, 1988, and such bilateral employment agreements do not specify under the age of 23 as the maximum age for employment of such sons and daughters;

(v) Unmarried sons or daughters who are physically or mentally disabled to the extent that they cannot adequately care for themselves or cannot establish, maintain, or re-establish their own households. The Service may require medical certification(s) as it deems necessary to document such mental or physical disability.

(3) Dependent employment requirements based on formal bilateral employment agreements and informal de facto reciprocal arrangements —

(i) Formal bilateral employment agreements. The Department of State's Family Liaison office (FLO) shall maintain all listing of NATO Member States which have entered into formal bilateral employment agreements that include NATO personnel. A dependent of a NATO-1, NATO-2, NATO-3, NATO-4, NATO-5, or NATO-6 principal alien assigned to official duty in the United States may accept, or continue in, unrestricted employment based on such formal bilateral agreement upon favorable recommendation by SACLANT, pursuant to paragraph (s)(5) of this section, and issuance of employment authorization documentation by the Service in accordance with 8 CFR part 274a. The application procedures are set forth in paragraph (s)(5) of this section.

(ii) Informal de facto reciprocal arrangements. For purposes of this section, an informal de facto reciprocal arrangement exists when the Office of the Secretary of Defense, Foreign Military Rights Affairs (OSD/FMRA), certifies, with State Department concurrence, that a NATO Member State allows appropriate employment in the local economy for dependents of members of the force and members of the civilian component of the United States assigned to duty in the NATO Member State. OSD/FMRA and State's FLO shall maintain a listing of countries with which such reciprocity exists. Dependents of a NATO-1, NATO-2, NATO-3, NATO-4, NATO-5, or NATO-6 principal alien assigned to official duty in the United States may be authorized to accept, or continue in, employment based upon informal de facto arrangements upon favorable recommendation by SACLANT, pursuant to paragraph (s)(5) of this section, and issuance of employment authorization by the Service in accordance with 8 CFR part 274a. Additionally, the application procedures set forth in paragraph (s)(5) of this section must be complied with, and the following conditions must be met:

(A) Both the principal alien and the dependent requesting employment are maintaining NATO-1, NATO-2, NATO-3, NATO-4, NATO-5, or NATO-6 status, as appropriate;

(B) The principal alien's total length of assignment in the United States is expected to last more than 6 months;

(C) Employment of a similar nature for dependents of members of the force and members of the civilian component of the United States assigned to official duty in the NATO Member State employing the principal alien is not prohibited by the NATO Member State;

(D) The proposed employment is not in an occupation listed in the Department of Labor's Schedule B (20 CFR part 656), or otherwise determined by the Department of Labor to be one for which there is an oversupply of qualified United States workers in the area of proposed employment. This Schedule B restriction does not apply to a dependent son or daughter who is a full-time student if the employment is part-time, consisting of not more than 20 hours per week, of if it is temporary employment of not more than 12 weeks during school holiday periods; and

(E) The proposed employment is not contrary to the interest of the United States. Employment contrary to the interest of the United States includes, but is not limited to, the employment of NATO-1, NATO-2, NATO-3, NATO-4, NATO-5, or NATO-6 dependents who have criminal records; who have violated United States immigration laws or regulations, or visa laws or regulations; who have worked illegally in the United States; or who cannot establish that they have paid taxes and social security on income from current or previous United States employment.

(iii) State's FLO shall inform the Service, by contacting Headquarters, Adjudications, Attention: Chief, Business and Trade Services Branch, 425 I Street, NW., Washington, DC 20536, of any additions or changes to the formal bilateral employment agreements and informal de facto reciprocal arrangements.

(4) Applicability of a formal bilateral agreement or an informal de facto arrangement for NATO-1, NATO-2, NATO-3, NATO-4, NATO-5, or NATO-6 dependents. The applicability of a formal bilateral agreement shall be based on the NATO Member State which

employs the principal alien and not on the nationality of the principal alien or dependent. The applicability of an informal de facto arrangement shall be based on the NATO Member State which employs the principal alien, and the principal alien also must be a national of the NATO Member State which employs him or her in the United States. Dependents of SACLANT employees receive bilateral agreement or de facto arrangement employment privileges as appropriate based upon the nationality of the SACLANT employee (principal alien).

(5) Application procedures. The following procedures are required for dependent employment applications under bilateral agreements and de facto arrangements:

(i) The dependent of a NATO alien shall submit a complete application for employment authorization, including Form I-765 and Form I-566, completed in accordance with the instructions on, or attached to, those forms. The complete application shall be submitted to SACLANT for certification of the Form I-566 and forwarding to the Service.

(ii) In a case where a bilateral dependent employment agreement containing a numerical limitation on the number of dependents authorized to work is applicable, the certifying officer of SACLANT shall not forward the application for employment authorization to the Service unless, following consultation with State's Office of Protocol, the certifying officer has confirmed that this numerical limitation has not been reached. The countries with such limitations are indicated on the bilateral/de facto dependent employment listing issued by State's FLO.

(iii) SACLANT shall keep copies of each application and certified Form I-566 for 3 years from the date of the certification.

(iv) A dependent applying under the terms of a de facto arrangement must also attach a statement from the prospective employer which includes the dependent's name, a description of the position offered, the duties to be performed, the hours to be worked, the salary offered, and verification that the dependent possesses the qualifications for the position.

(v) A dependent applying under paragraph (s)(2) (iii) or (iv) of this section must also submit a certified statement from the post-secondary educational institution confirming that he or she is pursuing studies on a full-time basis.

(vi) A dependent applying under paragraph (s)(2)(v) of this section must also submit medical certification regarding his or her condition. The certification should identify both the dependent and the certifying physician, give the physician's phone number, identify the condition, describe the symptoms, provide a clear prognosis, and certify that the dependent is unable to maintain a home of his or her own.

(vii) The Service may require additional supporting documentation, but only after consultation with SACLANT.

(6) Period of time for which employment may be authorized. If approved, an application to accept or continue employment under this paragraph shall be granted in increments of not more than 3 years.

(7) Income tax and Social Security liability. Dependents who are granted employment authorization under this paragraph are responsible for payment of all Federal, state, and local income taxes, employment and related taxes and Social Security contributions on any remuneration received.

(8) No appeal. There shall be no appeal from a denial of permission to accept or continue employment under this paragraph.

(9) Unauthorized employment. An alien classified as a NATO-1, NATO-2, NATO-3, NATO-4, NATO-5, NATO-6, or NATO-7 who is not a NATO principal alien and who engages in employment outside the scope of, or in a manner contrary to, this paragraph may be considered in violation of status pursuant to section 237(a)(1)(C)(i) of the Act. A NATO principal alien in those classifications who engages in employment outside the scope of his or her official position may be considered in violation of status pursuant to section 237(a)(1)(C)(i) of the Act.

(t) Alien witnesses and informants —

(1) Alien witness or informant in criminal matter. An alien may be classified as an S-5 alien witness or informant under the provisions of section 101(a)(15)(S)(i) of the Act if, in the exercise of discretion pursuant to an application on Form I-854 by an interested federal or state law enforcement authority ("LEA"), it is determined by the Commissioner that the alien:

(i) Possesses critical reliable information concerning a criminal organization or enterprise;

(ii) Is willing to supply, or has supplied, such information to federal or state LEA; and

(iii) Is essential to the success of an authorized criminal investigation or the successful prosecution of an individual involved in the criminal organization or enterprise.

(2) Alien witness or informant in counterterrorism matter. An alien may be classified as an S-6 alien counterterrorism witness or informant under the provisions of section 101(a)(15)(S)(ii) of the Act if it is determined by the Secretary of State and the Commissioner acting jointly, in the exercise of their discretion, pursuant to an application on Form I-854 by an interested federal LEA, that the alien:

(i) Possesses critical reliable information concerning a terrorist organization, enterprise, or operation;

(ii) Is willing to supply or has supplied such information to a federal LEA;

(iii) Is in danger or has been placed in danger as a result of providing such information; and

(iv) Is eligible to receive a reward under section 36(a) of the State Department Basic Authorities Act of 1956, 22 U.S.C. 2708(a).

(3) Spouse, married and unmarried sons and daughters, and parents of alien witness or informant in criminal or counterterrorism matter. An alien spouse, married or unmarried son or daughter, or parent of an alien witness or informant may be granted derivative S classification (S-7) when accompanying, or following to join, the alien witness or informant if, in the exercise of discretion by, with respect to paragraph (t)(1) of this

section, the Commissioner, or, with respect to paragraph (t)(2) of this section, the Secretary of State and the Commissioner acting jointly, consider it to be appropriate. A nonimmigrant in such derivative S-7 classification shall be subject to the same period of admission, limitations, and restrictions as the alien witness or informant and must be identified by the requesting LEA on the application Form I-854 in order to qualify for S nonimmigrant classification. Family members not identified on the Form I-854 application will not be eligible for S nonimmigrant classification.

(4) Request for S nonimmigrant classification. An application on Form I-854, requesting S nonimmigrant classification for a witness or informant, may only be filed by a federal or state LEA (which shall include a federal or state court or a United States Attorney's Office) directly in need of the information to be provided by the alien witness or informant. The completed application is filed with the Assistant Attorney General, Criminal Division, Department of Justice, who will forward only properly certified applications that fall within the numerical limitation to the Commissioner, Immigration and Naturalization Service, for approval, pursuant to the following process.

(i) Filing request. For an alien to qualify for status as an S nonimmigrant, S nonimmigrant classification must be requested by an LEA. The LEA shall recommend an alien for S nonimmigrant classification by: Completing Form I-854, with all necessary endorsements and attachments, in accordance with the instructions on, or attached to, that form, and agreeing, as a condition of status, that no promises may be, have been, or will be made by the LEA that the alien will or may remain in the United States in S or any other nonimmigrant classification or parole, adjust status to that of lawful permanent resident, or otherwise attempt to remain beyond a 3-year period other than by the means authorized by section 101(a)(15)(S) of the Act. The alien, including any derivative beneficiary who is 18 years or older, shall sign a statement, that is part of or affixed to Form I-854, acknowledging awareness that he or she is restricted by the terms of S nonimmigrant classification to the specific terms of section 101(a)(15)(S) of the Act as the exclusive means by which he or she may remain permanently in the United States.

(A) District director referral. Any district director or Service officer who receives a request by an alien, an eligible LEA, or other entity seeking S nonimmigrant classification shall advise the requestor of the process and the requirements for applying for S nonimmigrant classification. Eligible LEAs seeking S nonimmigrant classification shall be referred to the Commissioner.

(B) United States Attorney certification. The United States Attorney with jurisdiction over a prosecution or investigation that forms the basis for a request for S nonimmigrant classification must certify and endorse the application on Form I-854 and agree that no promises may be, have been, or will be made that the alien will or may remain in the United States in S or any other nonimmigrant classification or parole, adjust status to lawful permanent resident, or attempt to remain beyond the authorized period of admission.

(C) LEA certification. LEA certifications on Form I-854 must be made at the seat-of-government level, if federal, or the highest level of the state LEA involved in the matter. With respect to the alien for whom S nonimmigrant classification is sought, the LEA shall provide evidence in the form of attachments establishing the nature of the alien's cooperation with the government, the need for the alien's presence in the United States, all conduct or conditions which may constitute a ground or grounds of excludability, and all factors and considerations warranting a favorable exercise of discretionary waiver authority by the Attorney General on the alien's behalf. The attachments submitted with a request for S nonimmigrant classification may be in the form of affidavits, statements, memoranda, or similar documentation. The LEA shall review Form I-854 for accuracy and ensure the alien understands the certifications made on Form I-854.

(D) Filing procedure. Upon completion of Form I-854, the LEA shall forward the form and all required attachments to the Assistant Attorney General, Criminal Division, United States Department of Justice, at the address listed on the form.

(ii) Assistant Attorney General, Criminal Division review —

(A) Review of information. Upon receipt of a complete application for S nonimmigrant classification on Form I-854, with all required attachments, the Assistant Attorney General, Criminal Division, shall ensure that all information relating to the basis of the application, the need for the witness or informant, and grounds of excludability under section 212 of the Act has been provided to the Service on Form I-854, and shall consider the negative and favorable factors warranting an exercise of discretion on the alien's behalf. No application may be acted on by the Assistant Attorney General unless the eligible LEA making the request has proceeded in accordance with the instructions on, or attached to, Form I-854 and agreed to all provisions therein.

(B) Advisory panel. Where necessary according to procedures established by the Assistant Attorney General, Criminal Division, an advisory panel, composed of representatives of the Service, Marshals Service, Federal Bureau of Investigation, Drug Enforcement Administration, Criminal Division, and the Department of State, and those representatives of other LEAs, including state and federal courts designated by the Attorney General, will review the completed application and submit a recommendation to the Assistant Attorney General, Criminal Division, regarding requests for S nonimmigrant classification. The function of this advisory panel is to prioritize cases in light of the numerical limitation in order to determine which cases will be forwarded to the Commissioner.

(C) Assistant Attorney General certification. The certification of the Assistant Attorney General, Criminal Division, to the Commissioner recommending approval of the application for S nonimmigrant classification shall contain the following:

(1) All information and attachments that may constitute, or relate to, a ground or grounds of excludability under section 212(a) of the Act;

(2) Each section of law under which the alien appears to be inadmissible;

(3) The reasons that waiver(s) of inadmissibility are considered to be justifiable and in the national interest;

(4) A detailed statement that the alien is eligible for S nonimmigrant classification, explaining the nature of the alien's cooperation with the government and the government's need for the alien's presence in the United States;

(5) The intended date of arrival;

(6) The length of the proposed stay in the United States;

(7) The purpose of the proposed stay; and

(8) A statement that the application falls within the statutorily specified numerical limitation.

(D) Submission of certified requests for S nonimmigrant classification to Service.

(1) The Assistant Attorney General, Criminal Division, shall forward to the Commissioner only qualified applications for S-5 nonimmigrant classification that have been certified in accordance with the provisions of this paragraph and that fall within the annual numerical limitation.

(2) The Assistant Attorney General Criminal Division, shall forward to the Commissioner applications for S-6 nonimmigrant classification that have been certified in accordance with the provisions of this paragraph, certified by the Secretary of State or eligibility for S-6 classification, and that fall within the annual numerical limitation.

(5) Decision on application.

(i) The Attorney General's authority to waive grounds of excludability pursuant to section 212 of the Act is delegated to the Commissioner and shall be exercised with regard to S nonimmigrant classification only upon the certification of the Assistant Attorney General, Criminal Division. Such certification is nonreviewable as to the matter's significance, importance, and/or worthwhileness to law enforcement. The Commissioner shall make the final decision to approve or deny a request for S nonimmigrant classification certified by the Assistant Attorney General, Criminal Division.

(ii) Decision to approve application. Upon approval of the application on Form I-854, the Commissioner shall notify the Assistant Attorney General, Criminal Division, the Secretary of State, and Service officers as appropriate. Admission shall be authorized for a period not to exceed 3 years.

(iii) Decision to deny application. In the event the Commissioner decides to deny an application for S nonimmigrant classification on Form I-854, the Assistant Attorney General, Criminal Division, and the relevant LEA shall be notified in writing to that effect. The Assistant Attorney General, Criminal Division, shall concur in or object to that decision. Unless the Assistant Attorney General, Criminal Division, objects within 7 days, he or she shall be deemed to have concurred in the decision. In the event of an objection by the Assistant Attorney General, Criminal Division, the matter will be expeditiously referred to the Deputy Attorney General for a final resolution. In no circumstances shall the alien or the relevant LEA have a right of appeal from any decision to deny.

(6) Submission of requests for S nonimmigrant visa classification to Secretary of State. No request for S nonimmigrant visa classification may be presented to the Secretary of State unless it is approved and forwarded by the Commissioner.

(7) Conditions of status. An alien witness or informant is responsible for certifying and fulfilling the terms and conditions specified on Form I-854 as a condition of status. The LEA that assumes responsibility for the S nonimmigrant must:

(i) Ensure that the alien:

(A) Reports quarterly to the LEA on his or her whereabouts and activities, and as otherwise specified on Form I-854 or pursuant to the terms of his or her S nonimmigrant classification;

(B) Notifies the LEA of any change of home or work address and phone numbers or any travel plans;

(C) Abides by the law and all specified terms, limitations, or restrictions on the visa, Form I-854, or any waivers pursuant to classification; and

(D) Cooperates with the responsible LEA in accordance with the terms of his or her classification and any restrictions on Form I-854;

(ii) Provide the Assistant Attorney General, Criminal Division, with the name of the control agent on an ongoing basis and provide a quarterly report indicating the whereabouts, activities, and any other control information required on Form I-854 or by the Assistant Attorney General;

(iii) Report immediately to the Service any failure on the alien's part to:

(A) Report quarterly;

(B) Cooperate with the LEA;

(C) Comply with the terms and conditions of the specific S nonimmigrant classification; or

(D) Refrain from criminal activity that may render the alien deportable, which information shall also be forwarded to the Assistant Attorney General, Criminal Division; and

(iv) Report annually to the Assistant Attorney General, Criminal Division, on whether the alien's S nonimmigrant classification and cooperation resulted in either:

(A) A successful criminal prosecution or investigation or the failure to produce a successful resolution of the matter; or

(B) The prevention or frustration of terrorist acts or the failure to prevent such acts.

(v) Assist the alien in his or her application to the Service for employment authorization.

(8) Annual report. The Assistant Attorney General, Criminal Division, in consultation with the Commissioner, shall compile the statutorily mandated annual report to the Committee on the Judiciary of the House of Representatives and the Committee on the Judiciary of the Senate.

(9) Admission. The responsible LEA will coordinate the admission of an alien in S nonimmigrant classification with the Commissioner as to the date, time, place, and manner of the alien's arrival.

(10) Employment. An alien classified under section 101(a)(15)(S) of the Act may apply for employment authorization by filing Form I-765, Application for Employment Authorization, with fee, in accordance with the instructions on, or attached to, that form pursuant to § 274a.12(c)(21) of this chapter.

(11) Failure to maintain status. An alien classified under section 101(a)(15)(S) of the Act shall abide by all the terms and conditions of his or her S nonimmigrant classification imposed by the Attorney General. If the terms and conditions of S nonimmigrant classification will not be or have not been met, or have been violated, the alien is convicted of any criminal offense punishable by a term of imprisonment of 1 year or more, is otherwise rendered deportable, or it is otherwise appropriate or in the public interest to do so, the Commissioner shall proceed to deport an alien pursuant to the terms of 8 CFR 242.26. In the event the Commissioner decides to deport an alien witness or informant in S nonimmigrant classification, the Assistant Attorney General, Criminal Division, and the relevant LEA shall be notified in writing to that effect. The Assistant Attorney General, Criminal Division, shall concur in or object to that decision. Unless the Assistant Attorney General, Criminal Division, objects within 7 days, he or she shall be deemed to have concurred in the decision. In the event of an objection by the Assistant Attorney General, Criminal Division, the matter will be expeditiously referred to the Deputy Attorney General for a final resolution. In no circumstances shall the alien or the relevant LEA have a right of appeal from any decision to deport.

(12) Change of classification.

(i) An alien in S nonimmigrant classification is prohibited from changing to any other nonimmigrant classification.

(ii) An LEA may request that any alien lawfully admitted to the United States and maintaining status in accordance with the provisions of § 248.1 of this chapter, except for those aliens enumerated in 8 CFR 248.2, have his or her nonimmigrant classification changed to that of an alien classified pursuant to section 101(a)(15)(S) of the Act as set forth in 8 CFR 248.3(h).

(u) [Reserved]

(v) Certain spouses and children of LPRs. Section 214.15 of this chapter provides the procedures and requirements pertaining to V nonimmigrant status.

(w) CNMI-Only Transitional Worker (CW-1).

Table 5 to Paragraph (w)—Paragraph Contents

(1) Definitions.
(2) Eligible aliens.
(3) Derivative beneficiaries—CW-2 nonimmigrant classification.
(4) Eligible employers.
(5) Petition requirements.
(6) Appropriate documents.
(7) Change of employers.
(8) Amended or new petition.
(9) Multiple beneficiaries.
(10) Named beneficiaries.
(11) Early termination.
(12) Approval.
(13) Petition validity.
(14) Validity of the labor certification.
(15) How to apply for CW-1 or CW-2 status.
(16) Biometrics and other information.
(17) Period of admission.
(18) Extension of petition validity and extension of stay.
(19) Change or adjustment of status.
(20) Effect of filing an application for or approval of a permanent labor certification, preference petition, or filing of an application for adjustment of status on CW-1 or CW-2 classification.
(21) Rejection.
(22) Denial.
(23) Terms and conditions of CW Nonimmigrant status.
(24) Expiration of status.
(25) Waivers of inadmissibility for applicants lawfully present in the CNMI.
(26) Semiannual report.
(27) Revocation of approval of petition.
(28) Appeal of a revocation of a petition.
(29) Notice to DOL.

(1) Definitions. The following definitions apply to petitions for and maintenance of CW status in the Commonwealth of the Northern Mariana Islands (the CNMI or the Commonwealth):

(i) CW–1 Application for Temporary Employment Certification means the Office of Management and Budget (OMB)-approved Form ETA–9142C (or successor form) and the appropriate appendices, a valid prevailing wage determination (Form ETA–9141C, or successor form), and all supporting documentation submitted by an employer, as set forth in the U.S. Department of Labor's (DOL) regulations at 20 CFR 655.420 through 655.422, to secure a temporary labor certification determination from DOL's Office of Foreign Labor Certification (OFLC) Administrator.

(ii) Direct Guam transit means travel from the CNMI to a foreign place by an alien in CW status, or from a foreign place to the CNMI by an alien with a valid CW visa, on a direct itinerary involving a flight stopover or connection in Guam (and no other place).

(iii) Doing business means the regular, systematic, and continuous provision of goods or services by an employer as defined in this paragraph and does not include the mere presence of an agent or office of the employer in the CNMI.

(iv) Employer means a person, firm, corporation, contractor, or other association, or organization which:

(A) Engages a person to work within the CNMI; and

(B) Has or will have an employer-employee relationship with the CW–1 nonimmigrant being petitioned for.

(v) Employer-employee relationship means that the employer will hire, pay, fire, supervise, and control the work of the employee.

(vi) Lawfully present in the CNMI means that the alien was lawfully admitted or paroled into the CNMI under the immigration laws on or after the transition program effective date, other than an alien admitted or paroled as a visitor for business or pleasure (B– 1 or B–2, under any visa-free travel provision or parole of certain visitors from Russia and the People's Republic of China), and remains in a lawful immigration status or if paroled into the CNMI, the authorized parole period has not expired.

(vii) Legitimate business, as determined by DHS, means a real, active, and operating commercial or entrepreneurial undertaking that:

(A) Produces services or goods for profit, or is a governmental, charitable or other validly recognized nonprofit entity;

(B) Meets applicable legal requirements for doing business in the CNMI;

(C) Has substantially complied with wage and hour laws, occupational safety and health requirements, nondiscrimination, and all other Federal, CNMI, and local requirements relating to employment during the fiveyear period immediately preceding the date of filing the petition, and continues to be in substantial compliance with such requirements;

(D) Does not directly or indirectly engage in, or knowingly benefit from, prostitution, human trafficking, or any other activity that is illegal under Federal, CNMI, or local law;

(E) Is a participant in good standing in the E-Verify program;

(F) Does not have, as an owner, investor, manager, operator, or person meaningfully involved with the undertaking, any individual who has been an owner, investor, manager, operator, or person otherwise meaningfully involved with an undertaking that was not in compliance with paragraph (w)(1)(vii)(C) of this section at the time of the individual's involvement and within the five years immediately preceding the date of filing the petition; or that was not in compliance with clause paragraph (w)(1)(vii)(D) of this section at any time during which the individual was involved with the undertaking, or is an agent of such individual; and

(G) Is not a successor in interest to an undertaking that has not complied with paragraphs (C) or (D).

(viii) Long-term worker means an alien who was admitted to the CNMI, or otherwise granted status, as a CW–1 nonimmigrant during fiscal year 2015, and during each of fiscal years 2016 through 2018.

(ix) Minor child means a child as defined in section 101(b)(1) of the Act who is under 18 years of age.

(x) Numerical limitation means the maximum number of persons who may be granted CW–1 status in a given fiscal year, as follows:

(A) For fiscal years 2018 through the first quarter of fiscal year 2030, the numerical limitations are:

(1) 9,998 for fiscal year 2018;

(2) 13,000 for fiscal year 2019;

(3) 12,500 for fiscal year 2020;

(4) 12,000 for fiscal year 2021;

(5) 11,500 for fiscal year 2022;

(6) 11,000 for fiscal year 2023;

(7) 10,000 for fiscal year 2024;

(8) 9,000 for fiscal year 2025;

(9) 8,000 for fiscal year 2026;

(10) 7,000 for fiscal year 2027;

(11) 6,000 for fiscal year 2028;

(12) 5,000 for fiscal year 2029; and

(13) 1,000 for the first quarter of fiscal year 2030.

(B) A long-term worker granted CW– 1 nonimmigrant status for a period exceeding one year shall be counted toward the numerical limitation, and toward any reservation of CW–1 numbers, as described in paragraph (w)(1)(x)(D)(1) of this section, if applicable, for each fiscal year within the period of petition validity.

(C) For each petition revoked entirely or in part in a fiscal year, the numerical limitation for the next fiscal year shall be increased by the number of beneficiaries of such petitions subject to such revocation before the end of the validity period of the petition.

(D)(1) Within the numerical limitations described in paragraph (w)(1)(x)(A) of this section, the following reservations of CW–1 numbers for specified occupational categories shall apply:

(i) 200 for occupational categories 29– 0000 (Healthcare Practitioners and Technical Occupations) and 31–0000 (Healthcare Support Occupations); and

(ii) 60 for occupational categories related to the operations of the CNMI public utilities services, including, but not limited to, 17–2081 (Water/Waste Water Engineers), 17–2071 (Electrical Engineers), 17–2141 (Mechanical Engineers), and Trades Technicians.

(2) Reserved CW–1 numbers described in paragraph (w)(1)(x)(D)(1) of this section will be made available to eligible petitioners requesting such numbers for a fiscal year in order of filing, separately under either paragraph (w)(1)(x)(D)(1)(i) or (ii) of this section, until exhausted. Unused reserved numbers under either paragraph (w)(1)(x)(D)(1)(i) or (ii) of this section will not be available to other petitioners.

(3) DHS may adjust the reservation of numbers for specified occupational categories for a fiscal year or other period via publication of a notice in the Federal Register, as long as such adjustment is consistent with paragraph (w)(1)(x)(A) of this section. DHS will base any such adjustment on factors including: The level of past demand for reserved numbers compared to supply; whether a reservation of numbers has resulted in unused numbers; reservation of numbers compared to overall numerical limitation in a fiscal year; and any recommendation received from the Governor of the CNMI regarding the adjustment of the reservation of numbers.

(E) If the numerical limitation is not reached for a specified fiscal year, unused numbers do not carry over to the next fiscal year.

(F) If USCIS receives a sufficient number of petitions to meet the numerical limitation in paragraph (w)(1)(x)(A) of this section in a fiscal year, USCIS will cease processing further cap-subject petitions in that fiscal year, and DOL may cease processing cap-subject applications for temporary labor certification for that fiscal year.

(xi) Occupational category means those employment activities that DHS has determined require alien workers to supplement the resident workforce and includes:

(A) Professional, technical, or management occupations;

(B) Clerical and sales occupations;

(C) Service occupations;

(D) Agricultural, fisheries, forestry, and related occupations;

(E) Processing occupations;

(F) Machine trade occupations;

(G) Benchwork occupations;

(H) Structural work occupations; and

(I) Miscellaneous occupations.

(xii) Participant in good standing in the E-Verify program means an employer, as defined in paragraph (w)(1)(iv) of this section, that has enrolled in E-Verify with respect to all hiring sites in the United States as of the time of filing a petition; is in compliance with all requirements of the E-Verify program, including but not limited to verifying the employment eligibility of newly hired employees in the United States; and continues to be a participant in good standing in EVerify at any time during which the employer employs any CW–1 nonimmigrant.

(xiii) Petition means USCIS Form I– 129CW, Petition for a CNMI–Only Nonimmigrant Transitional Worker, a successor form, other form, or electronic equivalent, any supplemental information requested by USCIS, and additional evidence as may be prescribed or requested by USCIS.

(xiv) Successor in interest means an employer that is controlling and carrying on the business of a previous employer. The following factors may be considered in determining whether an employer is a successor in interest; no one factor is dispositive, but all of the circumstances will be considered as a whole:

(A) Substantial continuity of the same business operations;

(B) Use of the same facilities;

(C) Continuity of the work force;

(D) Similarity of jobs and working conditions;

(E) Similarity of supervisory personnel;

(F) Whether the former management or owner retains a direct or indirect interest in the new enterprise;

(G) Similarity in machinery, equipment, and production methods;

(H) Similarity of products and services; and

(I) The ability of the predecessor to provide relief.

(xv) Temporary Labor Certification or TLC means the certification made by the DOL OFLC Administrator, based on the CW–1 Application for Temporary Employment Certification, and all supporting documentation, with respect to an employer seeking to file with a CW–1 petition.

(xvi) Transition period means the period beginning on the transition program effective date and ending on December 31, 2029.

(xvii) United States worker means a citizen or national of the United States, an alien lawfully admitted for permanent residence, or a citizen of the Federated States of Micronesia, the Republic of the Marshall Islands, or the Republic of Palau who is eligible for nonimmigrant admission and is employment-authorized under the Compacts of Free Association between the United States and those nations.

(2) Eligible aliens. Subject to the numerical limitation, an alien may be classified as a CW–1 nonimmigrant if, during the transition period, the alien:

(i) Will enter or remain in the CNMI for the purpose of employment within the transition period in an occupational category that DHS has designated as requiring alien workers to supplement the resident workforce;

(ii) Is petitioned for by an employer;

(iii) Is not present in the United States, other than the CNMI;

(iv) If present in the CNMI, is lawfully present in the CNMI;

(v) Is not inadmissible to the United States as a nonimmigrant or has been granted a waiver of each applicable ground of inadmissibility;

(vi) Is ineligible for status in a nonimmigrant worker classification under section 101(a)(15) of the Act; and

(vii) Will not be employed in a Construction and Extraction Occupation (as defined by the U.S. Department of Labor as Standard Occupational Classification Group 47–0000 or successor provision) unless the alien is a long-term worker.

(3) Derivative beneficiaries—CW–2 nonimmigrant classification. The spouse or minor child of a CW–1 nonimmigrant may accompany or follow the alien as a CW–2 nonimmigrant if the alien:

(i) Is not present in the United States, other than the CNMI;

(ii) If present in the CNMI, is lawfully present in the CNMI; and

(iii) Is not inadmissible to the United States as a nonimmigrant or has been granted a waiver of each applicable ground of inadmissibility.

(4) Eligible employers. To be eligible to petition for a CW–1 nonimmigrant worker, an employer must:

(i) Be engaged in legitimate business;

(ii) Obtain a TLC from DOL and consider all available United States workers for the position being filled by the CW–1 worker;

(iii) Offer terms and conditions of employment which are consistent with the nature of the petitioner's business and the nature of the occupation, activity, and industry in the CNMI; and

(iv) Comply with all Federal and Commonwealth requirements relating to employment, including but not limited to nondiscrimination, occupational safety, and minimum wage requirements.

(5) Petition requirements. An employer who seeks to classify an alien as a CW-1 worker must file a petition with USCIS and pay the requisite petition fee plus the CNMI education funding fee and the fraud prevention and detection fee as prescribed in 8 CFR part 106. If the beneficiary will perform services for more than one employer, each employer must file a separate petition with fees with USCIS.

(6) Appropriate documents. Documentary evidence establishing eligibility for CW status is required. A petition must be accompanied by:

(i) Evidence demonstrating the petitioner meets the definition of eligible employer in this section;

(ii) An attestation by the petitioner certified as true and accurate by an appropriate official of the petitioner, of the following:

(A) The employer has not displaced and will not displace a United States worker in order to employ the beneficiary as agreed to in the CW–1 Application for Temporary Employment Certification;

(B) The employer is doing business as defined in paragraph (w)(1)(iii) of this section;

(C) The employer is a legitimate business as defined in paragraph (w)(1)(vii) of this section;

(D) The employer is an eligible employer as described in paragraph (w)(4) of this section and will continue to comply with the requirements for an eligible employer until such time as the employer no longer employs the CW–1 nonimmigrant worker;

(E) The beneficiary meets the qualifications for the position;

(F) The beneficiary, if present in the CNMI, is lawfully present in the CNMI;

(G) The position is not temporary or seasonal employment, and the petitioner does not reasonably believe it to qualify as eligible for any other nonimmigrant worker classification, including H–2A or H–2B;

(H) The position falls within the list of occupational categories designated by DHS;

(I) The petitioner will pay the beneficiary a wage that is not less than the greater of—

(1) The CNMI minimum wage;

(2) The Federal minimum wage; or

(3) The prevailing wage in the CNMI for the occupation in which the beneficiary will be employed as established by the U.S. Department of Labor; and

(J) The petitioner will comply with the reporting and retention requirements in paragraph 26.

(iii) Evidence of licensure if an occupation requires a Commonwealth or local license for an individual to fully perform the duties of the occupation. Categories of valid licensure for CW–1 classification are:

(A) Licensure. An alien seeking CW– 1 classification in that occupation must have that license prior to approval of the petition to be found qualified to enter the CNMI and immediately engage in employment in the occupation.

(B) Temporary licensure. If a temporary license is available and allowed for the occupation with a temporary license, USCIS may grant the petition at its discretion after considering the duties performed, the degree of supervision received, and any limitations placed on the alien by the employer and/or pursuant to the temporary license.

(C) Duties without licensure. If the CNMI allows an individual to fully practice the occupation that usually requires a license without a license under the supervision of licensed senior or supervisory personnel in that occupation, USCIS may grant CW–1 status at its discretion after considering the duties performed, the degree of supervision received, and any limitations placed on the alien if the facts demonstrate that the alien under supervision could fully perform the duties of the occupation.

(iv) For any petition requesting an employment start date on or after October 1, 2019, including both new petitions and petitions for renewal of an existing permit, a TLC approved by DOL, confirming that there are not sufficient United States workers in the CNMI who are able, willing, qualified, and available at the time and place needed to perform the services or labor involved in the petition, and that the employment of the CW–1 nonimmigrant will not adversely affect the wages and working conditions of similarly employed United States workers. If the TLC accepts certain education, training, experience, or special requirements of the beneficiary, the petition must also be accompanied by documentation that the CW–1 nonimmigrant worker qualifies for the job offer as specified in the TLC.

(7) Change of employers. A change of employment to a new employer inconsistent with paragraphs (w)(7)(i) and (ii) of this section will constitute a failure to maintain status within the meaning of section 237(a)(1)(C)(i) of the Act. A CW–1 nonimmigrant may change employers if:

(i) The prospective new employer files a petition to classify the alien as a CW–1 worker in accordance with paragraph (w)(5) of this section, and

(ii) An extension of the alien's stay is requested if necessary for the validity period of the petition.

(iii) A CW–1 worker may work for a prospective new employer after the prospective new employer files a Form I–129CW petition on the employee's behalf if:

(A) The prospective employer has filed a nonfrivolous petition for new employment before the date of expiration of the CW–1 worker's authorized period of stay; and

(B) Subsequent to his or her lawful admission, the CW–1 worker has not been employed without authorization in the United States.

(iv) Employment authorization shall continue for such alien until the new petition is adjudicated. If the new petition is denied, such authorization shall cease.

(v) If a CW–1 worker's employment has been terminated prior to the filing of a petition by a prospective new employer consistent with paragraphs (w)(7)(i) and (ii), or if the CW–1's current petition has been revoked (other than for the reason described in paragraph (w)(27)(iii)(A)(7) of this section) the CW–1 worker will not be considered to be in violation of his or her CW–1 status during the 30-day period immediately following the date on which the CW–1 worker's employment terminated if a nonfrivolous petition for new employment is filed consistent with this paragraph within that 30-day period and the CW–1 worker does not otherwise violate the terms and conditions of his or her status during that 30-day period.

(8) Amended or new petition. If there are any material changes in the terms and conditions of employment, the petitioner must file an amended or new petition to reflect the changes. An amended or new petition must be submitted with a new TLC approved by DOL.

(9) Multiple beneficiaries. A petitioning employer may include more than one beneficiary in a CW–1 petition if the beneficiaries will be working in the same occupational category, under the same terms and conditions, for the same period of time, and in the same location.

(10) Named beneficiaries. The petition must include the name of the beneficiary and other required information, as indicated in the form instructions, at the time of filing. Unnamed beneficiaries are not permitted.

(11) Early termination. The petitioning employer must pay the reasonable cost of return transportation of the alien to the alien's last place of foreign residence if the alien is dismissed from employment for any reason by the employer before the end of the period of authorized admission.

(12) Approval. USCIS will consider all the evidence submitted and such other evidence required in the form instructions to adjudicate the petition. USCIS will notify the petitioner of the approval of the petition on Form I–797, Notice of Action, or in another form as USCIS may prescribe.

(i) The approval notice will include the CW–1 classification and name of the beneficiary or beneficiaries and the petition's period of validity. A petition for more than one beneficiary may be approved in whole or in part.

(ii) The application for a TLC may not be filed with DOL earlier than 120 days before the date of actual need for the beneficiary's services for an initial petition for CW–1 status, or 180 days before the date of expiration of CW–1 status in the case of an extension petition described in paragraph (w)(18) of this section. The petition may then be filed with USCIS after the TLC is approved. If DOL debars an employer from obtaining a CW–1 TLC, USCIS may not approve future petitions during the debarment period.

(13) Petition validity. An approved petition will be valid for a period of up to one year, unless the beneficiary is a long-term worker in which case an approved petition will be valid for a period of up to three years.

(14) Validity of the labor certification. A TLC is valid only for the period of employment as approved on the CW–1 Application for Temporary Employment Certification. The TLC expires on the last day of authorized employment.

(15) How to apply for CW–1 or CW– 2 status.

(i) Upon approval of the petition, a beneficiary, his or her eligible spouse, and his or her minor child(ren) outside the CNMI will be informed in the approval notice of where they may apply for a visa authorizing admission in CW–1 or CW–2 status.

(ii) If the beneficiary is present in the CNMI, the petition also serves as the application for a grant of status as a CW–1.

(iii) If the eligible spouse and/or minor child(ren) are present in the CNMI, the spouse or child(ren) may apply for CW-2 dependent status on Form I-539 (or such alternative form as USCIS may designate) in accordance with the form instructions. The CW-2 status may not be approved until approval of the CW-1 petition.

(16) Biometrics and other information. The beneficiary of a CW-1 petition or the spouse or child applying for a grant or extension of CW-2 status, or a change of status to CW-2 status, must submit biometric information as requested by USCIS.

(17) Period of admission.

(i) A CW–1 nonimmigrant will be admitted for the period of petition validity, plus up to 10 days before the validity period begins and 10 days after the validity period ends. The CW–1 nonimmigrant may not work except during the validity period of the petition. A CW–2 spouse will be admitted for the same period as the principal alien. A CW–2 minor child will be admitted for the same period as the principal alien, but such admission will not extend beyond the child's 18th birthday.

(ii) The temporary departure from the CNMI of the CW–1 nonimmigrant will not affect the derivative status of the CW–2 spouse and minor children, provided the familial relationship continues to exist and the principal remains eligible for admission as a CW– 1 nonimmigrant.

(18) Extension of petition validity and extension of stay.

(i) The petitioner may request an extension of an employee's CW–1 nonimmigrant status by filing a new petition.

(ii) A request for a petition extension may be filed only if the validity of the original petition has not expired.

(iii) Extensions of CW–1 status may be granted for a period of up to 1 year (or a period of up to 3 years if the beneficiary is a long-term worker) until the end of the transition period, subject to any numerical limitation.

(iv) To qualify for an extension of stay, the petitioner must demonstrate that the beneficiary or beneficiaries:

(A) Continuously maintained the terms and conditions of CW–1 status;

(B) Remains admissible to the United States; and

(C) Remains eligible for CW–1 classification.

(v) A beneficiary (other than a longterm worker) may not be granted CW– 1 status beyond three consecutive petition validity periods unless the beneficiary has departed and remained outside of the United States for a continuous period of at least 30 days after the expiration of the third petition validity period and before the filing of any new petition on behalf of the beneficiary.

(vi) The derivative CW–2 nonimmigrant may file an application for extension of nonimmigrant stay on Form I–539 (or such alternative form as USCIS may designate) in accordance with the form instructions. The CW–2 status extension may not be approved until approval of the CW–1 extension petition.

(19) Change or adjustment of status. A CW–1 or CW–2 nonimmigrant can apply to change nonimmigrant status under section 248 of the Act or apply for adjustment of status under section 245 of the Act, if otherwise eligible. During the transition period, CW–1 or CW–2 nonimmigrants may be the beneficiary of a petition for or may apply for any nonimmigrant or

immigrant visa classification for which they may qualify.

(20) Effect of filing an application for or approval of a permanent labor certification, preference petition, or filing of an application for adjustment of status on CW–1 or CW–2 classification. An alien may be granted, be admitted in and maintain lawful CW–1 or CW–2 nonimmigrant status while, at the same time, lawfully seeking to become a lawful permanent resident of the United States, provided he or she intends to depart the CNMI voluntarily at the end of the period of authorized stay. The filing of an application for or approval of a permanent labor certification or an immigrant visa preference petition, the filing of an application for adjustment of status, or the lack of residence abroad will not be the basis for denying:

(i) A CW–1 petition filed on behalf of the alien;

(ii) A request to extend a CW–1 status pursuant to a petition previously filed on behalf of the alien;

(iii) An application for CW–2 classification filed by an alien;

(iv) A request to extend CW–2 status pursuant to the extension of a related CW–1 alien's extension; or

(v) An application for admission as a CW–1 or CW–2 nonimmigrant.

(21) Rejection. USCIS may reject an employer's petition for new or extended CW–1 status if any numerical limitation has been met. In that case, the petition and accompanying fee will be rejected and returned with the notice that numbers are unavailable for the CW nonimmigrant classification. The beneficiary's application for admission based upon an approved petition will not be rejected based upon the numerical limitation.

(22) Denial. The ultimate decision to grant or deny CW–1 or CW–2 classification or status is a discretionary determination, and the petition or the application may be denied for failure of the petitioner or the applicant to demonstrate eligibility or for other good cause. The denial of a petition to classify an alien as a CW–1 may be appealed to the USCIS Administrative Appeals Office or any successor body. The denial of CW–1 or CW–2 status within the CNMI, or of an application for change or extension of status filed under this section, may not be appealed.

(23) Terms and conditions of CW Nonimmigrant status—

(i) Geographical limitations. CW–1 and CW–2 statuses are only applicable in the CNMI. Entry, employment and residence in the rest of the United States (including Guam) require the appropriate visa or visa waiver and nonimmigrant classification. Except as provided in paragraph (w)(23)(iii) of this section, an alien with CW–1 or CW–2 status who enters or attempts to enter, or travels or attempts to travel to any other part of the United States without an appropriate visa or visa waiver, or who violates conditions of nonimmigrant stay applicable to any such authorized status in any other part of the United States, will be deemed to have violated CW–1 or CW–2 status.

(ii) Re-entry. An alien with CW–1 or CW–2 status who travels abroad from the CNMI will require a CW–1 or CW– 2 or other appropriate visa to be readmitted to the CNMI.

(iii) Travel outside the CNMI—

(A) Direct Guam transit from the CNMI. An alien with CW–1 or CW–2 status may travel to a foreign place via a direct Guam transit without being deemed to violate that status.

(B) Travel from a foreign place to the CNMI. An alien with a valid CW–1 or CW–2 visa, who is admissible to the CNMI in such status, may be admitted to the United States in CW–1 or CW–2 status in Guam for the purpose of a direct Guam transit to the CNMI. An alien who violates the terms of direct Guam transit violates his or her CW–1 or CW–2 status.

(iv) Employment authorization. An alien with CW–1 nonimmigrant status is only authorized employment in the CNMI for the petitioning employer. An alien with CW–2 status is not authorized to be employed.

(24) Expiration of status. CW–1 status expires when the alien violates his or her CW–1 status (or in the case of a CW– 1 status violation caused solely by termination of the alien's employment, at the end of the 30 day period described in paragraph (w)(7)(v) of this section), 10 days after the end of the petition's validity period, when the petition is revoked, or at the end of the transitional worker program, whichever is earlier. CW–2 nonimmigrant status expires when the status of the related CW–1 alien expires, on a CW–2 minor child's 18th birthday, when the alien violates his or her status, or at the end of the transitional worker program, whichever is earlier. No alien will be eligible for admission to the CNMI in CW–1 or CW–2 status, and no CW–1 or CW–2 visa will be valid for travel to the CNMI, after the transitional worker program ends.

(25) Waivers of inadmissibility for applicants lawfully present in the CNMI. An applicant for CW–1 or CW–2 nonimmigrant status, who is otherwise eligible for such status and otherwise admissible to the United States, and who possesses appropriate documents demonstrating that the applicant is lawfully present in the CNMI, may be granted a waiver of inadmissibility under section 212(d)(3)(A)(ii) of the Act, including the grounds of inadmissibility described in sections 212(a)(6)(A)(i) and 212(a)(7)(B)(i)(II) of the Act, as a matter of discretion for the purpose of granting the CW–1 or CW–2 nonimmigrant status. Such waiver may be granted without additional form or fee. Appropriate documents required for such a waiver include a valid unexpired passport and other documentary evidence demonstrating that the applicant is lawfully present in the CNMI, such as a DHS-issued Form I–94. Evidence that the applicant possesses appropriate documents may be provided by an employer to accompany a petition, by an eligible spouse or minor child to accompany the Form I–539 (or such alternative form as USCIS may designate), or in such other manner as USCIS may designate.

(26) Semiannual report—

(i) Filing. During the validity period of the petition, an employer whose petition has been approved for an employment start date on or after October 1, 2019 and for a validity period of six months or more, shall file a semiannual report, every six months after the petition validity start date up to and including the sixth month preceding the petition's validity end date. The semiannual report must be filed within a 60 day window surrounding the six month anniversary of the petition validity start date, with the filing window opening 30 days before and closing 30 days after the six month anniversary of the petition validity start date. The semiannual report must be filed with USCIS in the form and containing such evidence as USCIS may direct, to verify the continuing employment and payment of the beneficiary under the terms and conditions of the approved petition.

(ii) Use. DHS may provide such semiannual reports to other federal partners, including DOL for investigative or other use as the DOL may deem appropriate. Failure to comply with the requirements of paragraph (w)(26) of this section may be a basis for revocation of an approved petition as provided in paragraph (w)(27) of this section, or for denial of subsequent petitions filed by the employer.

(iii) Document retention.

(A) An employer must retain all documents and records in support of an approved petition, and any semiannual report. An employer must retain evidence that supports the semiannual report including, but not limited to:

(1) Personnel records for each CW–1 worker including the name, address of current residence in the Commonwealth, age, domicile, citizenship, point of hire, and approved employment contract termination date;

(2) Payroll records for each CW–1 worker including the O*NET job classification; wage rate or salary, number of hours worked each week, gross compensation, itemized deductions, and evidence of net payments made and received biweekly; and

(3) Direct evidence of payment of wages and overtime, such as receipts for cash payments, cancelled checks or deposit records. Petitioners must provide such documents and records to DHS and DOL at any time, during the retention period specified in paragraph (w)(26)(iii)(B) of this section.

(B) An employer must retain documents and records until the date that is three years after the ending date of the petition validity period.

(27) Revocation of approval of petition—

(i) General.

(A) The petitioner shall immediately notify USCIS of any changes in the terms and conditions of employment of a beneficiary which may affect eligibility under this paragraph (w). To notify USCIS of such changes, an amended petition shall be filed when the petitioner continues to employ the beneficiary. If the petitioner no longer employs the beneficiary, the petitioner shall send a letter to the office at which the CW–1 petition was filed explaining the basis on which the specific CW–1 nonimmigrant is no longer employed.

(B) USCIS may revoke a petition at any time, even after the expiration of the petition.

(ii) Immediate and automatic revocation. The approval of any petition is immediately and automatically revoked if the petitioner ceases operations, files a written withdrawal of the petition, or the U.S. Department of Labor revokes the temporary labor certification upon which the petition is based.

(iii) Revocation on notice—

(A) Grounds for revocation. USCIS may in its discretion send to the petitioner a notice of intent to revoke the petition in relevant part, for good cause, including, if it finds that:

(1) The beneficiary is no longer employed by the petitioner in the capacity specified in the petition;

(2) The facts contained in the petition or on the application for a temporary labor certification was not true and correct, inaccurate, fraudulent, or misrepresented a material fact;

(3) The petitioner violated terms and conditions of the approved petition;

(4) The petitioner violated a requirement of paragraph (w) of this section;

(5) The approval of the petition violated paragraph (w) this section or involved gross error;

(6) The petitioner failed to maintain the continuous employment of the CW– 1 nonimmigrant, failed to pay the nonimmigrant, failed to timely file a semiannual report described in paragraph (w)(26) of this section, committed any other violation of the terms and conditions of employment, or otherwise ceased to operate as a legitimate business;

(7) The beneficiary did not apply for admission to the CNMI within 10 days after the beginning of the petition validity period if the petition has been approved for consular processing; or

(8) The employer failed to provide a former, current, or prospective CW–1 nonimmigrant, not later than 21 business days after a written request from such individual, with the original (or a certified copy of the original) of all petitions, notices, and other written communication related to the worker (other than sensitive financial or proprietary information of the employer which may be redacted) that has been exchanged between the employer and the Department of Labor, the Department of Homeland Security, or any other Federal agency or department.

(B) Notice and decision. The notice of intent to revoke shall state the grounds for the revocation. The petitioner may submit evidence in rebuttal within 30 days of receipt of the notice. USCIS shall consider all relevant evidence presented in deciding whether to revoke the petition in whole or in part. If the petition is revoked in part, the remainder of the petition shall remain approved and a revised approval notice shall be sent to the petitioner with the revocation notice.

(28) Appeal of a revocation of a petition. A petition that has been revoked on notice in whole or in part may be appealed under part 103 of this chapter. Automatic revocations may not be appealed.

(29) Notice to DOL. USCIS will provide notice to DOL of CW–1 petition revocations.

HISTORY:

[38 FR 35425, Dec. 28, 1973; 48 FR 14575, Apr. 5, 1983; 51 FR 44267, 1986; 52 FR 5750, 7063, 13226, 20555, 30329, 48084, 1987;

53 FR 3331, 24900, 26231, 30017, 46852, 1988; 54 FR 14, 10979, 48577, 51816, 1989.; 55 FR 2621, 5573, 7881, 7882, 34897, 34900, 34901, 1990; 56 FR 480, 41624, 482, 2841, 11916, 11917, 26017, 31305, 33371, 38333, 55613, 61119, 61127, 61130, 66967, 1991.; 57 FR 749, 6184, 10978, 12178, 12181, 12182, 12186, 12190, 29193, 31955, 31956, 33426, 40832, 42884, 55060, 1992.; 58 FR 49905, Sept. 24, 1993; 58 FR 58097, Oct. 29, 1993; 58 FR 69210, Dec. 30, 1993, as confirmed and amended at 63 FR 1331, 1334, Jan. 9, 1998; 59 FR 1470, Jan. 11, 1994; 59 FR 41830, Aug. 15, 1994; as corrected at 59 FR 42487, Aug. 18, 1994 and as corrected at 59 FR 55910, Nov. 9, 1994; 59 FR 51102, Oct. 7, 1994; 60 FR 21975, May 4, 1995; 60 FR 44260, 44266, Aug. 25, 1995, as corrected at 60 FR 52248, Oct. 5, 1995; 60 FR 49195, Sept. 22, 1995; 60 FR 62021, 62022, Dec. 4, 1995; 61 FR 35934, 35935, July 9, 1996; 62 FR 10422, 10424, Mar. 7, 1997; 62 FR 18508, 18511, 18512, Apr. 16, 1997; 62 FR 48138, 48146, Sept. 12, 1997, as corrected at 62 FR 50435, Sept. 25, 1997, and 62 FR 60122, Nov. 6, 1997; 63 FR 31872, 31873, 31874, June 10, 1998; 63 FR 32113, 32115, June 12, 1998; 63 FR 65657, 65659, Nov. 30, 1998, as corrected at 63 FR 71342, Dec. 24, 1998; 64 FR 29208, 29211, June 1, 1999, as corrected at 64 FR 30103, June 4, 1999; 64 FR 32146, 32147, June 15, 1999, as corrected at 64 FR 33346, June 22, 1999 and as corrected at 64 FR 36423, July 6, 1999; 65 FR 7715, Feb. 16, 2000; 65 FR 10678, 10684, Feb. 29, 2000; 65 FR 14774, 14778, 14779, Mar. 17, 2000, as corrected at 65 FR 18432, Apr. 7, 2000; 65 FR 43528, 43531, July 13, 2000, withdrawn at 67 FR 61474, Oct. 1, 2002; 65 FR 67616, 67617, Nov. 13, 2000; 66 FR 31107, 31112, June 11, 2001; 66 FR 42587, 42593, Aug. 14, 2001; 66 FR 46697, 46702, Sept. 7, 2001; 66 FR 49514, Sept. 28, 2001; 67 FR 18062, 18063, Apr. 12, 2002; 67 FR 54941, 54945, Aug. 27, 2002; 67 FR 71443, 71449, Dec. 2, 2002; 67 FR 76256, 76270, 76276, Dec. 11, 2002; 68 FR 46926, 46929, Aug. 7, 2003; 69 FR 39814, 39825, July 1, 2004; 70 FR 23775, 23783, May 5, 2005, as confirmed at 76 FR 53764, 53778, Aug. 29, 2011; 72 FR 18856, 18860, Apr. 16, 2007; 72 FR 19100, 19107, Apr. 17, 2007; 73 FR 15389, 15394, Mar. 24, 2008; 73 FR 18944, 18954, Apr. 8, 2008; 73 FR 72276, 72293, Nov. 26, 2008; 73 FR 76891, 76911, Dec. 18, 2008; 73 FR 78104, 78127, Dec. 19, 2008, as corrected at 74 FR 2837, Jan. 16, 2009; 74 FR 26514, 26515, June 3, 2009; 74 FR 26933, 26938, June 5, 2009; 74 FR 55094, 55109, Oct. 27, 2009, as confirmed and amended at 76 FR 55502, Sept. 7, 2011; 75 FR 47699, 47701, Aug. 9, 2010; 75 FR 79264, 79275, Dec. 20, 2010; 77 FR 76353, Dec. 28, 2012; 78 FR 18457, 18472, Mar. 27, 2013, as confirmed at 81 FR 91646, 91670, Dec. 19, 2016; 78 FR 24047, 24061, Apr. 24, 2013, as confirmed at 80 FR 24146, 24183, Apr. 29, 2015; 80 FR 10284, 10311, Feb. 25, 2015; 80 FR 23680, 23688, Apr. 29, 2015; 80 FR 24042, 24108, Apr. 29, 2015; 81 FR 13040, 13117, Mar. 11, 2016; 81 FR 82398, 82486, Nov. 18, 2016; 82 FR 32987, 32998, July 19, 2017; 83 FR 24905, 24917, May 31, 2018; 84 FR 888, 954, Jan. 31, 2019; 84 FR 20005, 20020, May 8, 2019; 84 FR 52357, 52363, Oct. 2, 2019; 85 FR 21739, 21744, Apr. 20, 2020; 85 FR 27645, 27649, May 11, 2020; 85 FR 28843, 28850, May 14, 2020; 85 FR 29264, 29311, May 14, 2020; 85 FR 46788, 46923, Aug. 3, 2020, as corrected at 85 FR 53645, Aug. 31, 2020; 85 FR 51304, 51311, Aug. 20, 2020; 85 FR 63918, 63963, Oct. 8, 2020; 85 FR 82291, 82298, Dec. 18, 2020; 86 FR 1676, 1732, Jan. 8, 2021, withdrawn at 86 FR 72516, Dec. 22, 2021; 86 FR 8543, Feb. 8, 2021; 86 FR 14221, 14228, Mar. 15, 2021; 86 FR 27027, May 19, 2021; 86 FR 28198, 28230, May 25, 2021; 87 FR 4722, 4758, Jan. 28, 2022; 87 FR 30334, 30375, May 18, 2022; 87 FR 41027, 41029, July 11, 2022; 87 FR 61959, 61963, Oct. 13, 2022; 87 FR 62721, 62722, Oct. 17, 2022; 87 FR 75891, 75902, Dec. 12, 2022; 87 FR 76816, 76874, Dec. 15, 2022; 87 FR 77979, 77979, Dec. 21 , 2022; 88 FR 53761, Aug. 9, 2023; 88 FR 80394, 80456, Nov. 17, 2023; 89 FR 6194, 6397, Jan. 31, 2024; 89 FR 7456, 7491, Feb. 2, 2024, as corrected at 89 FR 20101, Mar. 21, 2024; 89 FR 22903, 22912, Apr. 3, 2024; redesignated at 89 FR 34864, 34931, Apr. 30, 2024; 89 FR 95626, 95681, Dec. 2, 2024; 89 FR 103054, 103196, Dec. 18, 2024; 89 FR 103202, 103327, Dec. 18, 2024]

§ 214.3 Certification and recertification of schools for enrollment of F and M nonimmigrants.

(a) Filing petition —

(1) General. A school or school system seeking certification or recertification for attendance by nonimmigrant students under sections 101(a)(15)(F) or 101(a)(15)(M) of the Act, or both, must file a petition for certification or recertification with SEVP, using the Student and Exchange Visitor Information System (SEVIS), in accordance with the procedures at paragraph (h) of this section. The petition must state whether the school or school system is seeking certification or recertification for attendance of nonimmigrant students under section 101(a)(15)(F) or 101(a)(15)(M) of the Act or both. The petition must identify by name and address each location of the school that is included in the petition for certification or recertification, specifically including any physical location in which a nonimmigrant can attend classes through the school (i.e., campus, extension campuses, satellite campuses, etc.).

(i) School systems. A school system, as used in this section, means public school (grades 9-12) or private school (grades kindergarten-12). A petition by a school system must include a list of the names and addresses of those schools included in the petition with the supporting documents.

(ii) Submission requirements. Certification and recertification petitions require that a complete Form I-17, Petition for Approval of School for Attendance by Nonimmigrant Student, bearing signatures, be included with the school's submission of supporting documentation. In submitting the Form I-17, a school certifies that the designated school officials (DSOs) signing the form have read and understand DHS regulations relating to: nonimmigrant students at § 214.1, 214.2(f), and/or 214.2(m); change of nonimmigrant classification for students at 8 CFR part 248; school certification and recertification under this section; withdrawal of school certification under this section and §§ 214.4; that both the school and its DSOs intend to comply with these regulations at all times; and that, to the best of its knowledge, the school is eligible for SEVP certification. Willful misstatements may constitute perjury (18 U.S.C. 1621).

(2) Certification for F-1 or M-1 classification, or both—

(i) F-1 classification. The following schools may be certified for attendance by nonimmigrant students under section 101(a)(15)(F) of the Act:

(A) A college or university, i.e., an institution of higher learning which awards recognized bachelor's, master's, doctor's or professional degrees.

(B) A community college or junior college which provides instruction in the liberal arts or in the professions and which awards recognized associate degrees.

(C) A seminary.

(D) A conservatory.

(E) An academic high school.

(F) A private elementary or middle school.

(G) An institution which provides language training, instruction in the liberal arts or fine arts, instruction in the professions, or instruction or training in more than one of these disciplines.

(ii) M-1 classification. The following schools are considered to be vocational or nonacademic institutions and may be certified for attendance by nonimmigrant students under section 101(a)(15)(M) of the Act:

(A) A community college or junior college which provides vocational or technical training and which awards recognized associate degrees.

(B) A vocational high school.

(C) A school which provides vocational or nonacademic training other than language training.

(iii) Both F-1 and M-1 classification. A school may be certified for attendance by nonimmigrant students under both sections 101(a)(15)(F) and 101(a)(15)(M) of the Act if it has both instruction in the liberal arts, fine arts, language, religion, or the professions and vocational or technical training. In that case, a student whose primary intent is to pursue studies in liberal arts, fine arts, language, religion, or the professions at the school is classified as a nonimmigrant under section 101(a)(15)(F) of the Act. A student whose primary intent is to pursue vocational or technical training at the school is classified as a nonimmigrant under section 101(a)(15)(M) of the Act.

(iv) English language training for a vocational student. A student whose primary intent is to pursue vocational or technical training who takes English language training at the same school solely for the purpose of being able to understand the vocational or technical course of study is classified as a nonimmigrant under section 101(a)(15)(M) of the Act.

(v) Schools not qualified for attendance. The following may not be certified for attendance by foreign students:

(A) A home school,

(B) A public elementary or middle school; or

(C) An adult education program, as defined by section 203(1) of the Adult Education and Family Literacy Act, Public Law 113-128, as amended, U.S.C. 3272(1), if the adult education program is funded in whole or in part by a grant under the Adult Education and Family Literacy Act, or by any other Federal, State, county, or municipal funding.

(3) Eligibility

(i) The petitioner, to be eligible for certification, must establish at the time of filing that it:

(A) Is a bona fide school;

(B) Is an established institution of learning or other recognized place of study;

(C) Possesses the necessary facilities, personnel, and finances to conduct instruction in recognized courses; and

(D) Is, in fact, engaged in instruction in those courses.

(ii) The petitioner, to be eligible for recertification, must establish at the time of filing that it:

(A) Remains eligible for certification in accordance with paragraph (a)(3)(i) of this section; and

(B) Has complied during its previous period of certification or recertification with recordkeeping, retention, and reporting requirements and all other requirements of paragraphs (g), (j), (k), and (l) of this section.

(b) Supporting documents. Schools petitioning for certification or recertification must submit the following supporting documents:

(1) Licensure, approval, and accreditation documents. A charter will not be considered a license, approval, or accreditation.

(i) Public Schools. A petitioning school or school system owned and operated as a public educational institution or system by the United States or a State or a political subdivision thereof must submit a certification to that effect signed by the authorized public official. The official must certify that they are authorized to do so.

(ii) Private elementary, middle, or secondary schools. A petitioning private elementary, middle, or secondary school or school system must submit a certification signed by the authorized public official that it meets the requirements of the State or local public educational system. The official must certify that they are authorized to do so.

(iii) Any other school. Any other petitioning school not included under paragraph (b)(1)(i) or (ii) of this section must submit a certification that—

(A) The school is licensed, approved, or accredited by the authorized official, who must certify that they are authorized to do so; or

(B) If the school offers courses recognized by a State-approving agency as appropriate for study for veterans under the provisions of 38 U.S.C. 3675 and 3676, in lieu of such certification provided in paragraph (b)(1)(i)(A) of this section, the school may submit a statement of recognition signed by the authorized official of the State approving agency, who must certify that they are authorized to do so.

(2) School operations information. Private schools that are not accredited by a nationally recognized accrediting body or operated as part of a school that is accredited by a nationally recognized accrediting body must submit a school catalog, if one is issued. If not included in the catalog, or if a catalog is not issued, the school must furnish a written statement containing the following information listed in paragraphs (b)(2)(i) through (vii) of this section:

(i) Size of its physical facilities;

(ii) Nature of its facilities for study and training;

(iii) Educational, vocational, or professional qualifications of the teaching staff;

(iv) Salaries of the teachers;

(v) Attendance and scholastic grading policy;

(vi) Amount and character of supervisory and consultative services available to students and trainees; and

(vii) Finances, including a certified copy of the accountant's last statement of school's net worth, income, and expenses.

(c) Additional evidence—

(1) Vocational, business, and language schools, and American institutions of research. A petitioning vocational, business, or language school, or an American institution of research recognized as such by the Secretary of Homeland Security, must submit evidence that its courses of study are accepted as fulfilling the requirements for the attainment of an educational, professional, or vocational objective, and have not been

designated avocational or recreational through the appropriate licensing or approval officials.

(2) Unaccredited private elementary, middle, and secondary schools. A petitioning private elementary, middle, or secondary school that is not accredited by a nationally recognized accrediting body or operated by a school that is accredited by a nationally recognized accrediting body must submit evidence that attendance at the petitioning school—

(i) Satisfies the compulsory attendance requirements of the State in which it is located; and

(ii) Qualifies graduates for acceptance by schools of a higher educational level by a public school, a school accredited by a nationally recognized accrediting body, or a secondary school operated by a school that is accredited by a nationally recognized accrediting agency.

(3) Unaccredited private institutions of higher learning. A private institution of higher learning that is not accredited by a nationally recognized accrediting body must submit evidence that—

(i) It confers upon its graduates recognized bachelor, master, doctor, professional or divinity degrees; or

(ii) If it does not confer such degrees, its credits have been and are accepted unconditionally by at least three other institutions of higher learning that are public or accredited by a nationally recognized accredited body.

(d) Interview of petitioner. The petitioner or an authorized representative of the petitioner may be required to appear in person before or be interviewed by telephone by a DHS representative prior to the adjudication of a petition for certification or recertification. The interview will be conducted under oath.

(e) Notices to schools related to certification or recertification petitions or to out-of-cycle review—

(1) General. All notices from SEVP to schools or school systems related to school certification, recertification, or out-of-cycle review (including, but not limited to, notices related to the collection of evidence, testimony, and appearance pertaining to petitions for recertification encompassing compliance with the recordkeeping, retention and reporting, and other requirements of paragraphs (f), (g), (j), (k), and (l) of this section, as well as to eligibility) will be served in accordance with the procedures at 8 CFR 103.2(b)(1), (4)-(16), (18) and (19), with the exception that all procedures will be conducted by SEVP, the SEVP Director, and the Assistant Secretary, ICE, as appropriate, and except as provided in this section. All such notices will be served (i.e., generated and transmitted) through SEVIS and/or by e-mail. The date of service is the date of transmission of the e-mail notice. DSOs must maintain current contact information, including current e-mail addresses, at all times. Failure of a school to receive SEVP notices due to inaccurate DSO e-mail addresses in SEVIS or blockages of the school's e-mail system caused by spam filters is not grounds for appeal of a denial or withdrawal. The term "in writing" means either a paper copy bearing original signatures or an electronic copy bearing electronic signatures.

(2) SEVP approval notification and SEVIS updating by certified schools. SEVP will notify the petitioner by updating SEVIS to reflect approval of the petition and by e-mail upon approval of a certification or recertification petition. The certification or recertification is valid only for the type of program and nonimmigrant classification specified in the certification or recertification approval notice. The certification must be recertified every two years and may be subject to out-of-cycle review at any time. Approval may be withdrawn in accordance with 8 CFR 214.4.

(3) Modifications to Form I-17 while a school is SEVP-certified. Any modification made by an SEVP-certified school on the Form I-17 at any time after certification and for the duration of a school's authorization to enroll F and/or M students must be reported to SEVP and will be processed by SEVP in accordance with the provisions of paragraphs (f)(1), (g)(2) and (h)(3)(i) of this section.

(4) Notice of Intent to Withdraw (NOIW) SEVP certification—

(i) Automatic withdrawal. SEVP will serve the school with an NOIW 30 days prior to a school's SEVP certification expiration date if the school has not submitted to SEVP a completed recertification petition, in accordance with paragraph (h)(2) of this section. The school will be automatically withdrawn immediately, in accordance with 8 CFR 214.4(a)(3), if it has not submitted a completed recertification petition by the school's certification expiration date.

(ii) Withdrawal on notice. SEVP will serve a Withdrawal on Notice, in accordance with 8 CFR 214.4(b), if SEVP determines that a school reviewed out-of-cycle has failed to sustain eligibility or has failed to comply with the recordkeeping, retention, reporting and other requirements of paragraphs (f), (g), (j), (k), and (l) of this section. When a school fails to file an answer to an NOIW within the 30-day period, SEVP will withdraw the school's certification and notify the DSOs of the decision, in accordance with 8 CFR 214.4(d). A withdrawal for failure to respond to a notice of intent may not be appealed.

(5) Notice of Denial. A Notice of Denial will be served to a school when SEVP denies a petition for certification or recertification. The notice will address appeals options. Schools denied recertification must comply with 8 CFR 214.4(i).

(6) Notice of Automatic Withdrawal. Schools that relinquish SEVP certification for any of the reasons cited in 8 CFR 214.4(a)(3) will be served a Notice of Automatic Withdrawal.

(7) Notice of Withdrawal. A school found to be ineligible for continued SEVP certification as a result of an out-of-cycle review will receive a Notice of Withdrawal. Schools withdrawn must comply with 8 CFR 214.4(i).

(8) Notice of SEVIS Access Termination Date. The Notice of SEVIS Access Termination Date gives the official date for the school's denial or withdrawal to be final and SEVIS access to be terminated. In most situations, SEVP will not adjust a SEVIS access termination date for that school when the appeals process has concluded and the denial or withdrawal has been upheld, in accordance with § 214.4(i)(2). The school will no longer be able to access SEVIS and SEVP will

automatically terminate any remaining Active SEVIS records for that school on that date.

(f) Adjudication of a petition for SEVP certification or recertification—

(1) Approval. The school is required to immediately report through SEVIS any change to its school information upon approval of a petition for SEVP certification or recertification. Modification to school information listed in paragraph (h)(3) of this section will require a determination of continued eligibility for certification. The certification or recertification is valid only for the type of program and student specified in the approval notice. The certification may be withdrawn in accordance with the provisions of 8 CFR 214.4, is subject to review at any time, and will be reviewed every two years.

(2) Denial. The petitioner will be notified of the reasons for the denial and appeal rights, in accordance with the provisions of 8 CFR part 103 and 8 CFR 214.4, if SEVP denies a petition for certification or recertification.

(g) Recordkeeping and reporting requirements —

(1) Student records. An SEVP-certified school must keep records containing certain specific information and documents relating to each F-1 or M-1 student to whom it has issued a Form I-20 or successor form, while the student is attending the school and until the school notifies SEVP, in accordance with the requirements of paragraphs (g)(1) and (2) of this section, that the student is no longer pursuing a full course of study at that school. Student information not required for entry in SEVIS may be kept in the school's student system of records, but must be accessible to DSOs. The school must keep a record of having complied with the reporting requirements for at least three years after the student is no longer pursuing a full course of study at that school. The school must maintain records on the student in accordance with paragraphs (g)(1) and (2) of this section if a school recommends reinstatement for a student who is out of status. The school must maintain records on the student for three years from the date of the denial if the reinstatement is denied. The DSO must make the information and documents required by this paragraph (g)(1) available, including academic transcripts, and must furnish them to DHS representatives upon request. Schools must maintain and be able to provide an academic transcript or other routinely maintained student records that reflect the total, unabridged academic history of the student at the institution, in accordance with paragraph (g)(1)(iv) of this section. All courses must be recorded in the academic period in which the course was taken and graded. The information and documents that the school must keep on each student are as follows:

(i) Identification of the school, to include name and full address.

(ii) Identification of the student, to include name while in attendance (record any legal name change), date and place of birth, country of citizenship, and school's student identification number.

(iii) Current address where the student and his or her dependents physically reside. In the event the student or his or her dependents cannot receive mail at such physical residence, the school must provide a mailing address in SEVIS. If the mailing address and the physical address are not the same, the school must maintain a record of both mailing and physical addresses and provide the physical location of residence of the student and his or her dependents to DHS upon request.

(iv) Record of coursework. Identify the student's degree program and field of study. For each course, give the periods of enrollment, course identification code and course title; the number of credits or contact hours, and the grade; the number of credits or clock hours, and for credit hour courses the credit unit; the term unit (semester hour, quarter hour, etc.). Include the date of withdrawal if the student withdrew from a course. Show the grade point average for each session or term. Show the cumulative credits or clock hours and cumulative grade point average. Narrative evaluation will be accepted in lieu of grades when the school uses no other type of grading.

(v) Record of transfer credit or clock hours accepted. Type of hours, course identification, grades.

(vi) Academic status. Include the effective date or period if suspended, dismissed, placed on probation, or withdrawn.

(vii) Whether the student has been certified for practical training, and the beginning and end dates of certification.

(viii) Statement of graduation (if applicable). Title of degree or credential received, date conferred, program of study or major.

(ix) Termination date and reason.

(x) The documents referred to in paragraph (k) of this section.

Note to paragraph (g)(1): A DHS officer may request any or all of the data in paragraphs (g)(1)(i) through (x) of this section on any individual student or class of students upon notice. This notice will be in writing if requested by the school. The school will have three work days to respond to any request for information concerning an individual student, and ten work days to respond to any request for information concerning a class of students. The school will respond orally on the same day the request for information is made if DHS requests information on a student who is being held in custody, and DHS will provide a written notification that the request was made after the fact, if the school so desires. DHS will first attempt to gain information concerning a class of students from DHS record systems.

(2) Reporting changes in student and school information.

(i) Schools must update SEVIS with the current information within 21 days of a change in any of the information contained in paragraphs (f)(1) and (h)(3) of this section.

(ii) Schools are also required to report within 21 days any change of the information contained in paragraph (g)(1) or the occurrence of the following events:

(A) Any student who has failed to maintain status or complete his or her program;

(B) A change of the student's or dependent's legal name or U.S. address;

(C) Any student who has graduated early or prior to the program end date listed on SEVIS Form I-20;

(D) Any disciplinary action taken by the school against the student as a result of the student being convicted of a crime; and

(E) Any other notification request not covered by paragraph (g)(1) of this section made by DHS with respect to the current status of the student.

(F) For F-1 students authorized by USCIS to engage in a 24-month extension of OPT under 8 CFR 214.2(f)(10)(ii)(C):

(1) Any change that the student reports to the school concerning legal name, residential or mailing address, employer name, or employer address; and

(2) The end date of the student's employment reported by a former employer in accordance with 8 CFR 214.2(f)(10)(ii)(C)(6).

(iii) Each term or session and no later than 30 days after the deadline for registering for classes, schools are required to report the following registration information:

(A) Whether the student has enrolled at the school, dropped below a full course of study without prior authorization by the DSO, or failed to enroll;

(B) The current address of each enrolled student; and

(C) The start date of the student's next session, term, semester, trimester, or quarter. For initial students, the start date is the "program start date" or "report date." (These terms are used interchangeably.) The DSO may choose a reasonable date to accommodate a student's need to be in attendance for required activities at the school prior to the actual start of classes when determining the report date on the Form I-20. Such required activities may include, but are not limited to, research projects and orientation sessions. The DSO may not, however, indicate a report date more than 30 days prior to the start of classes. The next session start date is the start of classes for continuing students.

(D) Adjustment to the program completion date. Any factors that influence the student's progress toward program completion (e.g., deferred attendance, authorized drop below, program extension) must be reflected by making an adjustment updating the program completion date.

(3) Administrative correction of a student's record. In instances where technological or computer problems on the part of SEVIS cause an error in the student's record, the DSO may request the SEVIS system administrator, without fee, to administratively correct the student's record.

(h) SEVP certification, recertification, out-of-cycle review, and oversight of schools.

(1) Certification. A school seeking SEVP certification for attendance by nonimmigrants under section 101(a)(15)(F) or 101(a)(15)(M) of the Act must use SEVIS to file an electronic petition (which compiles the data for the Form I-17) and must submit the nonrefundable certification petition fee on-line.

(i) Filing a petition. The school must access the SEVP website at https://www.ice.gov/sevis to file a certification petition in SEVIS. The school will be issued a temporary SEVIS user ID and password in order to access SEVIS to complete and submit an electronic Form I-17. The school must submit the proper nonrefundable certification petition fee as provided in 8 CFR 103.7(d)(2).

(ii) Site visit, petition adjudication and school notification. SEVP will conduct a site visit for each petitioning school and its additional schools or campuses. SEVP will contact the school to arrange the site visit. The school must comply with and complete the visit within 30 days after the date SEVP contacts the school to arrange the visit, or the petition for certification will be denied as abandoned. DSOs and school officials that have signed the school's Form I-17 petition must be able to demonstrate to DHS representatives how they obtain access to the regulations cited in the certification petition as part of the site visit. Paper or electronic access is acceptable. DSOs must be able to extract pertinent citations within the regulations related to their requirements and responsibilities. SEVP will serve a notice of approval and SEVIS will be updated to reflect the school's certification if SEVP authorizes the school's certification petition.

(iii) Certification denial. SEVP will serve a notice of denial in accordance with paragraph (f)(2) of this section if a school's petition for certification is denied.

(2) Recertification. Schools are required to file a completed petition for SEVP recertification before the school's certification expiration date, which is 2 years from the date of their previous SEVP certification or recertification expiration date. The school must submit the proper nonrefundable recertification petition fee as provided in 8 CFR 103.7(d)(2). SEVP will review a petitioning school's compliance with the recordkeeping, retention, and reporting, and other requirements of paragraphs (f), (g), (j), (k), and (l) of this section, as well as continued eligibility for certification, pursuant to paragraph (a)(3) of this section.

(i) Filing of petition for recertification. Schools must submit a completed Form I-17 (including any supplements and bearing signatures of all officials) using SEVIS. SEVP will notify all DSOs of a previously certified school 180 days prior to the school's certification expiration date that the school may submit a petition for recertification. A school may file its recertification petition at any time after receipt of this notification. A school must submit a complete recertification petition package, as outlined in the submission guidelines, by its certification expiration date. SEVP will send a notice of confirmation of complete filing or rejection to the school upon receipt of any filing of a petition for recertification.

(A) Notice of confirmation assures a school of uninterrupted access to SEVIS while SEVP adjudicates the school's petition for recertification. A school that has complied with the petition submission requirements will continue to have SEVIS access after its certification expiration date while the adjudication for recertification is pending. The school is required to comply with all regulatory recordkeeping, retention and reporting, and other requirements of paragraphs (f), (g), (j), (k), and (l) of this section during the period the petition is pending.

(B) Notice of rejection informs a school that it must take prompt corrective action in regard to its recertification petition prior to its certification expiration date to ensure that its SEVIS access will not be terminated and its petition for recertification will be accepted for adjudication.

(ii) Consequence of failure to petition. SEVP will serve an NOIW to the school 30 days prior to a school's certification expiration date. SEVP will no longer accept a petition for recertification from the school and will immediately withdraw the school's certification if the school does not petition for recertification, abandons its petition, or does not submit a complete recertification petition package by the certification expiration date, in accordance with the automatic withdrawal criteria in 8 CFR 214.4(a)(3). The school must comply with 8 CFR 214.4(i) upon withdrawal.

(iii) School recertification process —

(A) General. School recertification reaffirms the petitioning school's eligibility for SEVP certification and the school's compliance with recordkeeping, retention, reporting and other requirements of paragraphs (f), (g), (j), (k), and (l) of this section since its previous certification.

(B) Compliance. Assessment by SEVP of a school petitioning for recertification will focus primarily on overall school compliance, but may also include examination of individual DSO compliance as data and circumstances warrant. Past performance of these individuals, whether or not they continue to serve as principal designated school officials (PDSOs) or DSOs, will be considered in any petition for recertification of the school.

(C) On-site review for recertification. All schools are subject to on-site review, at the discretion of SEVP, in conjunction with recertification. The school must comply with and complete an on-site review within 30 days of the notification by a DHS representative of a school that it has been selected for an on-site review for recertification, or the petition for recertification will be denied as abandoned, resulting in the school's withdrawal from SEVIS.

(iv) Recertification approval. SEVP will serve a notice of approval if a school's petition for recertification is approved. The date of the subsequent recertification review will be two years after the school's certification expiration date from this petition cycle.

(v) Recertification denial. SEVP will serve a notice of denial if a school's petition for recertification is denied, in accordance with 8 CFR 103.3(a)(1)(i).

(vi) Adjustment of certification expiration date. Schools eligible for recertification before March 25, 2009 will, at a minimum, have their certification expiration date extended to March 25, 2009. SEVP may extend the certification expiration date beyond this date during the first cycle of recertification.

(3) Out-of-cycle review and oversight of SEVP-certified schools

(i) SEVP will determine if out-of-cycle review is required upon receipt in SEVIS of any changes from an SEVP-certified school to its Form I-17 information. The Form I-17 information that requires out-of-cycle review when changed includes:

(A) Approval for attendance of students (F/M/both);

(B) Name of school system; name of main campus;

(C) Mailing address of the school;

(D) Location of the school;

(E) School type;

(F) Public/private school indicator;

(G) Private school owner name;

(H) The school is engaged in;

(I) The school operates under the following Federal, State, Local or other authorization;

(J) The school has been approved by the following national, regional, or state accrediting association or agency;

(K) Areas of study;

(L) Degrees available from the school;

(M) If the school is engaged in elementary or secondary education;

(N) If the school is engaged in higher education;

(O) If the school is engaged in vocational or technical education;

(P) If the school is engaged in English language training;

(Q) Adding or deleting campuses;

(R) Campus name;

(S) Campus mailing address; and

(T) Campus location address.

(ii) SEVP may request a school to electronically update all Form I-17 fields in SEVIS and provide SEVP with documentation supporting the update. The school must complete such updates in SEVIS and submit the supporting documentation to SEVP within 10 business days of the request from SEVP.

(iii) SEVP may review a school's certification at any time to verify the school's compliance with the recordkeeping, retention, reporting and other requirements of paragraphs (f), (g), (j), (k), and (l) of this section to verify the school's continued eligibility for SEVP certification pursuant to paragraph (a)(3) of this section. SEVP may initiate remedial action with the school, as appropriate, and may initiate withdrawal proceedings against the school pursuant to 8 CFR 214.4(b) if noncompliance or ineligibility of a school is identified.

(iv) On-site review. SEVP-certified schools are subject to on-site review at any time. SEVP will initiate withdrawal proceedings against a certified school, pursuant to 8 CFR 214.4(b), if the certified school selected for on-site review prior to its certification expiration date fails to comply with and complete the review within 30 days of the date SEVP contacted the school to arrange the review.

(v) Notice of Continued Eligibility. SEVP will serve the school a notice of continued eligibility if, upon completion of an out-of-cycle review, SEVP determines that the school remains eligible for certification. Such notice will not change the school's previously-determined certification expiration date unless specifically notified by SEVP.

(vi) Withdrawal of certification. SEVP will institute withdrawal proceedings in accordance with 8 CFR 214.4(b) if, upon completion of an out-of-cycle review, SEVP determines that a school or its programs are no longer eligible for certification.

(vii) Voluntary withdrawal. A school can voluntarily withdraw from SEVP certification at any time or in lieu of complying with an out-of-cycle review or request. Failure of a school to comply with an out-of-cycle review or request by SEVP will be treated as a voluntary withdrawal. A school must initiate voluntary withdrawal by sending a request for withdrawal on official school letterhead to SEVP.

(i) Administration of student regulations. DHS officials may conduct out-of-cycle, on-site reviews on the campuses of SEVP-certified schools to determine whether nonimmigrant students on those campuses are complying with DHS regulations pertaining to them, including the requirement that each maintains a valid passport. DHS officers will take appropriate action regarding violations of the regulations by nonimmigrant students.

(j) Advertising. In any advertisement, catalogue, brochure, pamphlet, literature, or other material hereafter printed or reprinted by or for an SEVP-certified school, any statement which may appear in such material concerning certification for attendance by nonimmigrant students shall be limited solely to the following: This school is authorized under Federal law to enroll nonimmigrant alien students.

(k) Issuance of Certificate of Eligibility. A DSO of an SEVP-certified school must sign any completed Form I-20 issued for either a prospective or continuing student or a dependent. A Form I-20 issued by a certified school system must state which school within the system the student will attend. Only a DSO of an SEVP-certified school may issue a Form I-20 to a prospective student and his or her dependents, and only after the following conditions are met:

(1) The prospective student has made a written application to the school.

(2) The written application, the student's transcripts or other records of courses taken, proof of financial responsibility for the student, and other supporting documents have been received, reviewed, and evaluated at the school's location in the United States.

(3) The appropriate school authority has determined that the prospective student's qualifications meet all standards for admission.

(4) The official responsible for admission at the school has accepted the prospective student for enrollment in a full course of study.

(*l*) Designated official —

(1) Meaning of term Designated Official. As used in §§ 214.2(f) and (m), 214.3 and 214.4, a Designated Official, Designated School Official (DSO), or Principal Designated School Official (PDSO), means a regularly employed member of the school administration whose office is located at the school and whose compensation does not come from commissions for recruitment of foreign students. An individual whose principal obligation to the school is to recruit foreign students for compensation does not qualify as a designated official. The PDSO and any other DSO must be named by the president, owner, or head of a school or school system. The PDSO and DSO may not delegate this designation to any other person.

(i) A PDSO and DSO must be either a citizen or lawful permanent resident of the United States.

(ii) Each campus must have one PDSO. The PDSO is responsible for updating SEVIS to reflect the addition or deletion of any DSO on their associated campus. SEVP will use the PDSO at the main campus at the main campusas the point of contact on any issues that relate to the school's compliance with the regulations, as well as any system alerts generated by SEVIS. SEVP may also designate certain functions in SEVIS for use by the PDSO only. The PDSO of the main campus is the only DSO authorized to submit a Form I-17 for recertification. The PDSO and DSO will share the same responsibilities in all other respects.

(iii) School officials may nominate as many DSOs in addition to PDSOs as they determine necessary to adequately provide recommendations to F and/or M students enrolled at the school regarding maintenance of nonimmigrant status and to support timely and complete recordkeeping and reporting to DHS, as required by this section. School officials must not permit a DSO or PDSO nominee access to SEVIS until DHS approves the nomination.

(2) Name, title, and signature. Petitions for SEVP certification, review and recertification must include the names, titles, and signatures of designated officials. An SEVP-certified school must update SEVIS upon any changes to the persons who are principal or designated officials, and furnish the name, title and e-mail address of any new official within 21 days of the change. Any changes to the PDSO or DSO must be made by the PDSO within 21 days of the change. DHS may, at its discretion, reject the submission of any individual as a DSO or withdraw a previous submission by a school of an individual.

(3) Statement of designated officials. A petition for school certification must include a statement by each designated official certifying that the official is familiar with DHS regulations relating to the requirements for admission and maintenance of status of nonimmigrant students, change of nonimmigrant status under part 248 of this chapter, and school approval under §§ 214.3 and 214.4, and affirming the official's intent to comply with these regulations. At the time a new designated official is added, the designated official must make the same certification.

HISTORY:

[30 FR 919, Jan. 29, 1965.; 52 FR 13229, 1987; 54 FR 19544, 1989; 58 FR 58098, Oct. 29, 1993; 67 FR 60107, 60111, Sept. 25, 2002; 67 FR 76256, 76279, Dec. 11, 2002; 73 FR 18944, 18956, Apr. 8, 2008; 73 FR 55683, 55698, Sept. 26, 2008; 80 FR 23680, 23689, Apr. 29, 2015; 81 FR 13040, 13117, Mar. 11, 2016; 84 FR 23930, 23978, May 23, 2019; 85 FR 46788, 46925, Aug. 3, 2020; 87 FR 75891, 75908, Dec. 12, 2022; 88 FR 53761, Aug. 9, 2023; redesignated at 89 FR 34864, 34931, Apr. 30, 2024.]

§ 214.4 Denial of certification, denial of recertification, or withdrawal of SEVP certification.

(a) General —

(1) Denial of certification. The petitioning school will be notified of the reasons and its appeal rights if a petition for certification is denied, in accordance with the provisions of 8 CFR 103.3(a)(1)(iii). A petitioning school denied certification may file a new petition for certification at any time.

(2) Denial of recertification or withdrawal on notice. The school must wait at least one calendar year from the date of denial of recertification or withdrawal on notice before being eligible to petition again for SEVP certification if a school's petition for recertification is denied by SEVP pursuant to § 214.3(h)(2)(v), or its certification is withdrawn on notice pursuant to paragraph (b) of this section. Eligibility to re-petition will be at the discretion of the Director of SEVP. SEVP certification of a school or school system for the attendance of nonimmigrant students, pursuant to sections 101(a)(15)(F) and/or 101(a)(15)(M) of the Immigration and Nationality Act, will be withdrawn on notice subsequent to out-of-cycle review, or recertification denied, if the school or school system is determined to no longer be entitled to certification for any valid and substantive reason including, but not limited to, the following:

(i) Failure to comply with 8 CFR 214.3(g)(1) without a subpoena.

(ii) Failure to comply with 8 CFR 214.3(g)(2).

(iii) Failure of a DSO to notify SEVP of the attendance of an F-1 transfer student as required by 8 CFR 214.2(f)(8)(ii).

(iv) Failure of a DSO to identify on the Form I-20 or successor form which school within the system the student must attend, in compliance with 8 CFR 214.3(k).

(v) Willful issuance by a DSO of a false statement, including wrongful certification of a statement by signature, in connection with a student's school transfer or application for employment or practical training.

(vi) Conduct on the part of a DSO that does not comply with the regulations.

(vii) The designation as a DSO of an individual who does not meet the requirements of 8 CFR 214.3(l)(1).

(viii) Failure to provide SEVP with the school's Form I-17 bearing the names, titles, and signatures of DSOs as required by 8 CFR 214.3(l)(2).

(ix) Failure to submit statements of DSOs as required by 8 CFR 214.3(l)(3).

(x) Issuance of Form I-20 or successor form or successor form to students without receipt of proof that the students have met scholastic, language, or financial requirements as required by 8 CFR 214.3(k)(2).

(xi) Issuance of Form I-20 or successor form or successor form to aliens who will not be enrolled in or carry full courses of study, as defined in 8 CFR 214.2(f)(6) or 214.2(m)(9).

(xii) Failure to operate as a bona fide institution of learning.

(xiii) Failure to employ adequate qualified professional personnel.

(xiv) Failure to limit advertising in the manner prescribed in 8 CFR 214.3(j).

(xv) Failure to maintain proper facilities for instruction.

(xvi) Failure to maintain accreditation or licensing necessary to qualify graduates as represented in the school's Form I-17.

(xvii) Failure to maintain the physical plant, curriculum, and teaching staff in the manner represented in the Form I-17.

(xviii) Failure to comply with the procedures for issuance of Form I-20 or successor form or successor form as set forth in 8 CFR 214.3(k).

(xix) Failure of a DSO to notify SEVP of material changes, such as changes to the school's name, address, or curricular changes that represent material change to the scope of institution offerings (e.g., addition of a program, class or course for which the school is issuing Form I-20 or successor form or successor form, but which does not have Form I-17 approval), as required by 8 CFR 214.3(f)(1).

(3) Automatic withdrawal. A school that is automatically withdrawn and subsequently wishes to enroll nonimmigrant students in the future may file a new petition for SEVP certification at any time. The school must use the certification petition procedures described in § 214.3(h) to gain access to SEVIS for submitting its petition. Past compliance with the recordkeeping, retention, reporting and other requirements of 8 CFR 214.3(f), (g), (j), (k), and (*l*), and with the requirements for transition of students under paragraph (i) of this section will be considered in the evaluation of a school's subsequent petition for certification. SEVP certification will be automatically withdrawn:

(i) As of the date of termination of operations, if an SEVP-certified school terminates its operations.

(ii) As of a school's certification expiration date, if an SEVP-certified school does not submit a completed recertification petition in the manner required by 8 CFR 214.3(h)(2).

(iii) Sixty days after the occurrence of the change of ownership if the school failed to update its information in accordance with § 214.3(h)(1) or properly file a new petition, SEVP will review the petition if the school properly files such petition to determine whether the school still meets the eligibility requirements of § 214.3(a)(3) and is still in compliance with the recordkeeping, retention, reporting and other requirements of § 214.3(f), (g), (j), (k), and (*l*). SEVP will institute withdrawal proceedings in accordance with paragraph (b) of this section if, upon completion of the review, SEVP finds that the school is no longer eligible for certification, or is not in compliance with the recordkeeping, retention, reporting and other requirements of § 214.3(f), (g), (j), (k), and (*l*), or failed to file a new petition within the allowable 60-day timeframe.

(iv) If an SEVP-certified school voluntarily withdraws from its certification.

(b) Withdrawal on notice. SEVP will initiate an out-of-cycle review and serve the school with an NOIW if SEVP has information that a school or school system may no longer be entitled to SEVP certification prior to the school being due for its two-year recertification. The NOIW will inform the school of:

(1) The grounds for withdrawing SEVP certification.

(2) The 30-day deadline from the date of the service of the NOIW for the school to submit sworn statements, and documentary or other evidence, to rebut the grounds for withdrawal of certification in the NOIW. An NOIW is not a means for the school to submit evidence that it should have previously submitted as a part of its established reporting requirements.

(3) The school's right to submit a written request (including e-mail) within 30 days of the date of service of the NOIW for a telephonic interview in support of its response to the NOIW.

(c) Assistance of counsel. The school or school system shall also be informed in the notice of intent to withdraw certification that it may be assisted or represented by counsel of its choice qualified under part 292 of this chapter, at no expense to the Government, in preparation of its answer or in connection with the interview.

(d) Allegations admitted or no answer filed. If the school or school system admits all of the allegations in the notice of intent to withdraw certification, or if the school or school system fails to file an answer within the 30-day period, SEVP will withdraw the certification previously granted and notify the designated school official of the decision. No appeal of SEVP's decision will be accepted if all allegations are admitted or no answer is filed within the 30-day period.

(e) Allegations denied. If the school or school system denies the allegations in the notice of intent to withdraw certification, then the school or school system shall, in its answer, provide all information or evidence on which the answer is based.

(f) Interview requested.

(1) If in its answer to the notice of intent to withdraw certification the school or school system requests an interview, the school or school system will be given notice of the date set for the interview.

(2) A summary of the information provided by the school or school system at the interview will be prepared and included in the record. At the discretion of SEVP, the interview may be recorded.

(g) Decision. The decision of SEVP will be in accordance with 8 CFR 103.3(a)(1).

(h) Appeals. A school may file an appeal of a denial or withdrawal no later than 15 days after the service of the decision by ICE. The appeal must state the reasons and grounds for contesting the denial or withdrawal. The appeal must be accompanied by the fee as provided in 8 CFR 103.7(d)(15).

(i) Operations at a school when SEVP certification is relinquished or withdrawn, or whose recertification is denied and on the SEVIS access termination date.

(1) General. A school whose certification is relinquished or withdrawn, or whose recertification is denied may, at SEVP discretion, no longer be able to create Initial student records or issue new Form I-20, Certificate of Eligibility for Nonimmigrant Student Status, or successor form, for initial attendance. Schools must comply with the instructions given in the notice of withdrawal or denial with regard to management of status for their Initial and continuing F and/or M students. All other SEVIS functionality, including event reporting for students, will remain unchanged until the school's SEVIS access termination date. The school must continue to comply with the recordkeeping, retention, reporting and other requirements of 8 CFR 214.3(f), (g), (j), (k), and (l) until its SEVIS access termination date.

(2) SEVIS access termination. In determining the SEVIS access termination date, SEVP will consider the impact that such date will have upon SEVP, the school, and the school's nonimmigrant students in determining the SEVIS access termination date. In most situations, SEVP will not determine a SEVIS access termination date for that school until the appeals process has concluded and the denial or withdrawal has been upheld unless a school whose certification is withdrawn or whose recertification is denied is suspected of criminal activity or poses a potential national security threat. The school will no longer be able to access SEVIS, and SEVP will automatically terminate any remaining Active SEVIS records for that school on the SEVIS access termination date.

(3) Legal obligations and ramifications for a school and its DSOs when a school is having SEVP certification denied or withdrawn. Schools are obligated to their students to provide the programs of study to which they have committed themselves in the students' application for enrollment and acceptance process. Schools are obligated to the U.S. government to comply with the recordkeeping, retention, reporting and other requirements contained in 8 CFR 214.3. With any new petition for SEVP certification, SEVP will consider the extent to which a school has fulfilled these obligations to students and the U.S. government during any previous period of SEVP certification.

HISTORY:

[37 FR 17463, Aug. 29, 1972, as amended at 48 FR 14592, Apr. 5, 1983; 48 FR 19867, May 3, 1983; 48 FR 22131, May 17, 1983; 49 FR 41015, Oct. 19, 1984; 50 FR 9991, Mar. 13, 1985; 54 FR 19544, May 8, 1989; 55 FR 41988, Oct. 17, 1990; 67 FR 60107, 60112, Sept. 25, 2002; 73 FR 55683, 55702, Sept. 26, 2008; 84 FR 23930, 23979, May 23, 2019; 87 FR 75891, 75911, Dec. 12, 2022; 88 FR 53761, Aug. 9, 2023; redesignated at 89 FR 34864, 34931, Apr. 30, 2024]

§ 214.5 Libyan and third country nationals acting on behalf of Libyan entities.

(a) Notwithstanding any other provision of this Title, the nonimmigrant status of any Libyan national, or of any other foreign national acting on behalf of a Libyan entity, who is engaging in aviation maintenance, flight operations, or nuclear-related studies or training is terminated.

(b) Notwithstanding any other provision of this chapter, the following benefits will not be available to any Libyan national or any other foreign national acting on behalf of a Libyan entity where the purpose is to engage in, or seek to obtain aviation maintenance, flight operations or nuclear-related studies or training:

(1) Application for school transfer.

(2) Application for extension of stay.

(3) Employment authorization or practical training.

(4) Request for reinstatement of student status.

(5) Application for change of nonimmigrant status.

HISTORY:

[48 FR 10297, Mar. 3, 1983; [redesignated at 89 FR 34864, 34931, Apr. 30, 2024]

AUTHORITY:

(Secs. 103, 212, 214, 248; 8 U.S.C. 1103, 1182, 1184, 1258)

§ 214.6 Citizens of Canada or Mexico seeking temporary entry under USMCA to engage in business activities at a professional level.

(a) General. Under section 214(e) of the Act, a citizen of Canada or Mexico who seeks temporary entry as a business person to engage in business activities at a professional level may be admitted to the United States in accordance with the Agreement Between the United States of America, the United Mexican States, and Canada (USMCA).

(b) Definitions. As used in this section, the terms:

Business activities at a professional level means those undertakings which require that, for successful completion, the individual has a least a baccalaureate degree or appropriate credentials demonstrating status as a professional in a profession set forth in Appendix 2 to Annex 16-A of Chapter 16 of the USMCA.

Business person, as defined in the USMCA, means a citizen of Canada or Mexico who is engaged in the trade of goods, the supply of services, or the conduct of investment activities.

Engage in business activities at a professional level means the performance of prearranged business activities for a United States entity, including an individual. It does not authorize the establishment of a business or practice in the United States in which the professional will be, in substance, self-employed. A professional will be deemed to be self-employed if he or she will be rendering services to a corporation or entity of which the professional is the sole or controlling shareholder or owner.

Temporary entry, as defined in the USMCA, means entry without the intent to establish permanent residence. The alien must satisfy the inspecting immigration officer that the proposed stay is temporary. A temporary period has a reasonable, finite end that does not equate to permanent residence. In order to establish that the alien's entry will be temporary, the alien must demonstrate to the satisfaction of the inspecting immigration officer that his or her work assignment in the United States will end at a predictable time and that he or she will depart upon completion of the assignment.

(c) Appendix 2 to Annex 16-A of Chapter 16 of the USMCA. Pursuant to the USMCA, an applicant seeking admission under this section shall demonstrate business activity at a professional level in one of the professions set forth in Appendix 2 to Annex 16-A of Chapter 16. The professions in Appendix 2 to Annex 16-A and the minimum requirements for qualification for each are as follows:[1]

Appendix 2 to Annex 16-A of Chapter 16 (Annotated)

General

—Accountant—Baccalaureate or Licenciatura Degree; or C.P.A., C.A., C.G.A., or C.M.A.

—Architect—Baccalaureate or Licenciatura Degree; or state/provincial license.[2]

—Computer Systems Analyst—Baccalaureate or Licenciatura Degree; or Post-Secondary Diploma[3] or Post-Secondary Certificate,[4] and three years experience.

—Disaster Relief Insurance Claims Adjuster (claims adjuster employed by an insurance company located in the territory of a Party, or an independent claims adjuster)—Baccalaureate or Licenciatura Degree, and successful completion of training in the appropriate areas of insurance adjustment pertaining to disaster relief claims; or three years experience in claims adjustment and successful completion of training in the appropriate areas of insurance adjustment pertaining to disaster relief claims.

—Economist—Baccalaureate or Licenciatura Degree.

—Engineer—Baccalaureate or Licenciatura Degree; or state/provincial license.

—Forester—Baccalaureate or Licenciatura Degree; or state/provincial license.

—Graphic Designer—Baccalaureate or Licenciatura Degree; or Post-Secondary Diploma or Post-Secondary Certificate, and three years experience.

—Hotel Manager—Baccalaureate or Licenciatura Degree in hotel/restaurant management; or Post-Secondary Diploma or Post-Secondary Certificate in hotel/restaurant management, and three years experience in hotel/restaurant management.

—Industrial Designer—Baccalaureate or Licenciatura Degree; or Post-Secondary Diploma or Post-Secondary Certificate, and three years experience.

—Interior Designer—Baccalaureate or Licenciatura Degree; or Post-Secondary Diploma or Post-Secondary Certificate, and three years experience.

—Land Surveyor—Baccalaureate or Licenciatura Degree; or state/provincial/federal license.

—Landscape Architect—Baccalaureate or Licenciatura Degree.

[1]A business person seeking temporary employment under this Appendix may also perform training functions relating to the profession, including conducting seminars.

[2]The terms "state/provincial license" and "state/provincial/federal license" mean any document issued by a state, provincial, or federal government, as the case may be, or under its authority, but not by a local government, that permits a person to engage in a regulated activity or profession.

[3] "Post-Secondary Diploma" means a credential issued, on completion of two or more years of postsecondary education, by an accredited academic institution in Canada or the United States.

[4]"Post-Secondary Certificate" means a certificate issued, on completion of two or more years of postsecondary education at an academic institution, by the federal government of Mexico or a state government in Mexico, an academic institution recognized by the federal government or a state government, or an academic institution created by federal or state law.

—Lawyer (including Notary in the province of Quebec)—L.L.B., J.D., L.L.L., B.C.L., or Licenciatura Degree (five years); or membership in a state/provincial bar.

—Librarian—M.L.S. or B.L.S. (for which another Baccalaureate or Licenciatura Degree was a prerequisite).

—Management Consultant—Baccalaureate or Licenciatura Degree; or equivalent professional experience as established by statement or professional credential attesting to five years experience as a management consultant, or five years experience in a field of specialty related to the consulting agreement.

—Mathematician (including Statistician)—Baccalaureate or Licenciatura Degree.[5]

—Range Manager/Range Conservationist—Baccalaureate or Licenciatura Degree.

—Research Assistant (working in a post-secondary educational institution)—Baccalaureate or Licenciatura Degree.

—Scientific Technician/Technologist[6]—Possession of (a) theoretical knowledge of any of the following disciplines: agricultural sciences, astronomy, biology, chemistry, engineering, forestry, geology, geophysics, meteorology, or physics; and (b) the ability to solve practical problems in any of those disciplines, or the ability to apply principles of any of those disciplines to basic or applied research.

—Social Worker—Baccalaureate or Licenciatura Degree.

—Sylviculturist (including Forestry Specialist)—Baccalaureate or Licenciatura Degree.

—Technical Publications Writer—Baccalaureate or Licenciatura Degree; or Post-Secondary Diploma or Post-Secondary Certificate, and three years experience.

—Urban Planner (including Geographer)—Baccalaureate or Licenciatura Degree.

—Vocational Counselor—Baccalaureate or Licenciatura Degree.

Medical/Allied Professionals

—Dentist—D.D.S., D.M.D., Doctor en Odontologia or Doctor en Cirugia Dental; or state/provincial license.

—Dietitian—Baccalaureate or Licenciatura Degree; or state/provincial license.

—Medical Laboratory Technologist (Canada)/Medical Technologist (Mexico and the United States)[7]—Baccalaureate or Licenciatura Degree; or Post-Secondary Diploma or Post-Secondary Certificate, and three years experience.

—Nutritionist—Baccalaureate or Licenciatura Degree.

—Occupational Therapist—Baccalaureate or Licenciatura Degree; or state/provincial license.

—Pharmacist—Baccalaureate or Licenciatura Degree; or state/provincial license.

—Physician (teaching or research only)—M.D. or Doctor en Medicina; or state/provincial license.

—Physiotherapist/Physical Therapist—Baccalaureate or Licenciatura Degree; or state/provincial license.

—Psychologist—State/provincial license; or Licenciatura Degree.

—Recreational Therapist—Baccalaureate or Licenciatura Degree.

—Registered Nurse—State/provincial license; or Licenciatura Degree.

—Veterinarian—D.V.M., D.M.V., or Doctor en Veterinaria; or state/provincial license.

Scientist

—Agriculturist (including Agronomist)—Baccalaureate or Licenciatura Degree.

—Animal Breeder—Baccalaureate or Licenciatura Degree.

—Animal Scientist—Baccalaureate or Licenciatura Degree.

—Apiculturist—Baccalaureate or Licenciatura Degree.

—Astronomer—Baccalaureate or Licenciatura Degree.

—Biochemist—Baccalaureate or Licenciatura Degree.

—Biologist—Baccalaureate or Licenciatura Degree.[8]

—Chemist—Baccalaureate or Licenciatura Degree.

—Dairy Scientist—Baccalaureate or Licenciatura Degree.

—Entomologist—Baccalaureate or Licenciatura Degree.

—Epidemiologist—Baccalaureate or Licenciatura Degree.

—Geneticist—Baccalaureate or Licenciatura Degree.

—Geochemist—Baccalaureate or Licenciatura Degree.

—Geologist—Baccalaureate or Licenciatura Degree.

—Geophysicist (including Oceanographer in Mexico and the United States)—Baccalaureate or Licenciatura Degree.

—Horticulturist—Baccalaureate or Licenciatura Degree.

—Meteorologist—Baccalaureate or Licenciatura Degree.

—Pharmacologist—Baccalaureate or Licenciatura Degree.

—Physicist (including Oceanographer in Canada)—Baccalaureate or Licenciatura Degree.

—Plant Breeder—Baccalaureate or Licenciatura Degree.

—Poultry Scientist—Baccalaureate or Licenciatura Degree.

[5]The term "Mathematician" includes the profession of Actuary. An Actuary must satisfy the necessary requirements to be recognized as an actuary by a professional actuarial association or society. A professional actuarial association or society means a professional actuarial association or society operating in the territory of at least one of the Parties.

[6]A business person in this category must be seeking temporary entry for work in direct support of professionals in agricultural sciences, astronomy, biology, chemistry, engineering, forestry, geology, geophysics, meteorology or physics.

[7]A business person in this category must be seeking temporary entry to perform in a laboratory, chemical, biological, hematological, immunologic, microscopic or bacteriological tests and analyses for diagnosis, treatment, or prevention of diseases.

[8]The term "Biologist" includes the profession of Plant Pathologist.

—Soil Scientist—Baccalaureate or Licenciatura Degree.

—Zoologist—Baccalaureate or Licenciatura Degree.

Teacher

—College—Baccalaureate or Licenciatura Degree.

—Seminary—Baccalaureate or Licenciatura Degree.

—University—Baccalaureate or Licenciatura Degree.

(d) Classification of citizens of Canada or Mexico as TN professionals under the USMCA—

(1) Citizens of Mexico. A citizen of Mexico who seeks temporary entry as a business person to engage in business activities at a professional level may be admitted to the United States in accordance with USMCA upon presentation of a valid passport and valid TN nonimmigrant visa at a United States Class A port-of-entry, at a United States airport handling international traffic, or at a United States pre-clearance/pre-flight station.

(2) Citizens of Canada. A citizen of Canada seeking temporary entry as a business person to engage in business activities at a professional level shall make application for admission with a Department officer at the United States Class A port-of-entry, at a United States airport handling international traffic, or at a United States pre-clearance/pre-flight station.

(3) Documentation. Upon application for a visa at a United States consular office, or, in the case of a citizen of Canada making application for admission at a port-of-entry, an applicant under this section shall present the following:

(i) Proof of citizenship. A Mexican citizen applying for admission as a TN nonimmigrant must establish such citizenship by presenting a valid passport. Canadian citizens, while not required to present a valid passport for admission unless traveling from outside the Western hemisphere, must establish Canadian citizenship.

(ii) Documentation demonstrating engagement in business activities at a professional level and demonstrating professional qualifications. The applicant must present documentation sufficient to satisfy the consular officer (in the case of a Mexican citizen) or the Department officer (in the case of a Canadian citizen) that the applicant is seeking entry to the United States to engage in business activities for a United States employer(s) or entity(ies) at a professional level, and that the applicant meets the criteria to perform at such a professional level. This documentation may be in the form of a letter from the prospective employer(s) in the United States or from the foreign employer, and must be supported by diplomas, degrees or membership in a professional organization. Degrees received by the applicant from an educational institution not located within Canada, Mexico, or the United States must be accompanied by an evaluation by a reliable credentials evaluation service which specializes in evaluating foreign educational credentials. The documentation shall fully affirm:

(A) The profession of the applicant under Appendix 2 to Annex 16-A of Chapter 16 of the USMCA;

(B) A description of the professional activities, including a brief summary of daily job duties, if appropriate, in which the applicant will engage in for the United States employer/entity;

(C) The anticipated length of stay;

(D) The educational qualifications or appropriate credentials which demonstrate that the Canadian or Mexican citizen has professional level status; and

(E) The arrangements for remuneration for services to be rendered.

(e) Procedures for admission. A citizen of Canada or Mexico who qualifies for admission under this section shall be provided confirming documentation and shall be admitted under the classification symbol TN for a period not to exceed three years. The conforming document provided shall bear the legend "multiple entry." The fee prescribed under 8 CFR 103.7(b)(1) shall be remitted by Canadian Citizens upon admission to the United States pursuant to the terms and conditions of the USMCA. Upon remittance of the prescribed fee, the TN applicant for admission shall be provided a DHS-issued receipt on the appropriate form.

(f) Reserved.

(g) Readmission.

(1) With a Form I-94. An alien may be readmitted to the United States in TN classification for the remainder of the authorized period of TN admission on Form I-94 (see § 1.4), without presentation of the letter or supporting documentation described in paragraph (d)(3) of this section, and without the prescribed fee set forth in 8 CFR 106.2, provided that the original intended professional activities and employer(s) have not changed, and the Form I-94 has not expired.

(2) Without a valid I-94. If the alien seeking readmission to the United States in TN classification is no longer in possession of a valid, unexpired Form I-94, and the period of initial admission in TN classification has not lapsed, then a new Form I-94 may be issued for the period of validity that remains on the TN nonimmigrant's original Form I-94 with the legend "multiple entry" and the alien can then be readmitted in TN status if the alien presents alternate evidence as follows:

(i) For Canadian citizens, alternate evidence may include, but is not limited to, a fee receipt for admission as a TN or a previously issued admission stamp as TN in a passport, and a confirming letter from the United States employer(s).

(ii) For Mexican citizens seeking readmission as TN nonimmigrants, alternate evidence shall consist of presentation of a valid unexpired TN visa and evidence of a previous admission.

(h) Extension of stay.

(1) Filing. A United States employer of a citizen of Canada or Mexico who is currently maintaining valid TN nonimmigrant status, or a United States entity (in the case of a citizen of Canada or Mexico who is currently maintaining valid TN nonimmigrant status and is employed by a foreign employer), may request an extension of stay, subject to the following conditions:

(i) An extension of stay must be requested by filing the appropriate form with the fee provided at 8 CFR

106.2, in accordance with the form instructions with USCIS.

(ii) The beneficiary must be physically present in the United States at the time of the filing of the appropriate form requesting an extension of stay as a TN nonimmigrant. If the alien is required to leave the United States for any reason while the petition is pending, the petitioner may request that USCIS notify the consular office where the beneficiary is required to apply for a visa or, if visa exempt, a DHS-designated port-of-entry where the beneficiary will apply for admission to the United States, of the approval.

(iii) An extension of stay in TN status may be approved by USCIS for a maximum period of three years.

(iv) There is no specific limit on the total period of time an alien may be in TN status provided the alien continues to be engaged in TN business activities for a U.S. employer or entity at a professional level, and otherwise continues to properly maintain TN nonimmigrant status.

(2) Readmission at the border. Nothing in paragraph (h)(1) of this section shall preclude a citizen of Canada or Mexico who has previously been admitted to the United States in TN status, and who has not violated such status while in the United States, from applying at a DHS-designated port-of-entry, prior to the expiration date of the previous period of admission, for a new three-year period of admission. The application for a new period of admission must be supported by a new letter from the United States employer or the foreign employer, in the case of a citizen of Canada who is providing prearranged services to a United States entity, which meets the requirements of paragraph (d) of this section, together with the appropriate filing fee as noted in 8 CFR 106.2. Citizens of Mexico must present a valid passport and a valid, unexpired TN nonimmigrant visa when applying for readmission, as outlined in paragraph (d)(1) of this section.

(i) Request for change or addition of United States employers —

(1) Filing at the service center. A citizen of Canada or Mexico admitted into the United States as a TN nonimmigrant who seeks to change or add a United States employer during the period of admission must have the new employer file a Form I-129 with appropriate supporting documentation, including a letter from the new employer describing the services to be performed, the time needed to render such services, and the terms of remuneration for services. Employment with a different or with an additional employer is not authorized prior to Department approval of the request.

(2) Readmission at the border. Nothing in paragraph (i)(1) of those section precludes a citizen of Canada or Mexico from applying for readmission to the United States for the purpose of presenting documentation from a different or additional United States or foreign employer. Such documentation shall meet the requirements prescribed in paragraph (d) of this section. The fee prescribed under 8 CFR 106.2 shall be remitted by Canadian citizens upon admission to the United States pursuant to the terms and conditions of the USMCA. Citizens of Mexico may present documentation from a different or additional United States or foreign employer to a consular officer as evidence in support of a new nonimmigrant TN visa application.

(3) No action shall be required on the part of a citizen of Canada or Mexico in TN status who is transferred to another location by the same United States employer to perform the same services. Such an acceptable transfer would be to a branch or office of the employer. In a case of a transfer to a separately incorporated subsidiary or affiliate, the requirements of paragraphs (i)(1) and (i)(2) of this section will apply.

(j) Spouse and unmarried minor children accompanying or following to join.

(1) The spouse or unmarried minor children of a citizen of Canada or Mexico admitted in TN nonimmigrant status, if otherwise admissible, may be admitted initially, readmitted, or granted a change of nonimmigrant status or an extension of his or her period of stay for the same period of time granted to the TN nonimmigrant. Such spouse or unmarried minor children shall, upon approval of an application for admission, readmission, change of status or extension of stay be classified as TD nonimmigrants. A request for a change of status to TD or an extension of stay of a TD nonimmigrant may be made on the appropriate form together with appropriate filing fees and evidence of the principal alien's current TN status.

(2) The spouse or unmarried minor children of a citizen of Canada or Mexico admitted in TN nonimmigrant status shall be required to present a valid, unexpired TD nonimmigrant visa unless otherwise exempt under 8 CFR 212.1.

(3) The spouse and unmarried minor children of a citizen of Canada or Mexico admitted in TN nonimmigrant status shall be issued confirming documentation bearing the legend "multiple entry." There shall be no fee required for admission of the spouse and unmarried minor children.

(4) The spouse and unmarried minor children of a citizen of Canada or Mexico admitted in TN nonimmigrant status shall not accept employment in the United States unless otherwise authorized under the Act.

(k) Effect of a strike.

(1) If the Secretary of Labor certifies or otherwise informs the Director of USCIS that a strike or other labor dispute involving a work stoppage of workers is in progress, and the temporary entry of a citizen of Mexico or Canada in TN nonimmigrant status may adversely affect the settlement of any labor dispute or the employment of any person who is involved in such dispute, the United States may refuse to issue an immigration document authorizing the entry or employment of such an alien.

(2) If the alien has already commenced employment in the United States and is participating in a strike or other labor dispute involving a work stoppage of workers, whether or not such strike or other labor dispute has been certified by the Department of Labor, or whether USCIS has been otherwise informed that such a strike or labor dispute is in progress, the alien shall not be deemed to be failing to maintain his or her status solely on account of past, present, or future participa-

tion in a strike or other labor dispute involving a work stoppage of workers, but is subject to the following terms and conditions:

(i) The alien shall remain subject to all applicable provisions of the Immigration and Nationality Act and regulations promulgated in the same manner as all other TN nonimmigrants;

(ii) The status and authorized period of stay of such an alien is not modified or extended in any way by virtue of his or her participation in a strike or other labor dispute involving a work stoppage of workers; and

(iii) Although participation by a TN nonimmigrant alien in a strike or other labor dispute involving a work stoppage of workers will not constitute a ground for removal, any alien who violates his or her status or who remains in the United States after his or her authorized period of stay has expired will be subject to removal.

(3) If there is a strike or other labor dispute involving a work stoppage of workers in progress but such strike or other labor dispute is not certified under paragraph (k)(1) of this section, or USCIS has not otherwise been informed by the Secretary that such a strike or labor dispute is in progress, Director of USCIS shall not deny a petition or deny entry to an applicant for TN status based upon such strike or other labor dispute.

HISTORY:

[54 FR 48579, Nov. 24, 1989, as amended at 56 FR 482, Jan. 7, 1991.; 57 FR 33273, July 28, 1992; 58 FR 69212, Dec. 30, 1993, as confirmed and amended at 63 FR 1331, 1334, 1335, Jan. 9, 1998; 69 FR 11287, 11289, Mar. 10, 2004, as confirmed at 76 FR 53764, 53778, Aug. 29, 2011; 69 FR 60939, 60941, Oct. 13, 2004; 73 FR 61332, 61334, Oct. 16, 2008; 78 FR 18457, 18472, Mar. 27, 2013, as confirmed at 81 FR 91646, 91670, Dec. 19, 2016; 85 FR 46788, 46925, Aug. 3, 2020; 87 FR 41027, 41030, July 11, 2022; redesignated at 89 FR 34864, 34931, Apr. 30, 2024]

§ 214.7 Habitual residence in the territories and possessions of the United States and consequences thereof.

(a) Definitions. As used in this section, the term:

(1) Compacts means the agreements of free association between the United States and the governments of the Republic of the Marshall Islands, the Federated States of Micronesia, and Palau, approved by Public Law 99-239 with respect to the governments of the Republic of the Marshall Islands and the Federated States of Micronesia, and by Public Law 99-658, with respect to Palau.

(2) Freely associated states (FAS) means the following parts of the former Trust Territories of the Pacific Islands, namely, the Republic of the Marshall Islands, the Federated States of Micronesia, and Palau.

(3) Territories and possessions of the United States means all territories and possessions of the United States to which the Act applies, including those commonwealths of the United States that are not States. It does not include American Samoa, as long as the Act does not apply to it.

(4)(i) Habitual resident means a citizen of the FAS who has been admitted to a territory or possession of the United States (other than American Samoa, as long as the Act is not applicable to it) pursuant to section 141(a) of the Compacts and who occupies in such territory or possession a habitual residence as that term is defined in section 461 of the Compacts, namely a place of general abode or a principal, actual dwelling place of a continuing or lasting nature. The term "habitual resident" does not apply to:

(A) A person who has established a continuing residence in a territory or possession of the United States, but whose cumulative physical presence in the United States amounts to less than 365 days; or

(B) A dependent of a resident representative described in section 152 of the Compacts; or

(C) A person who entered the United States for the purpose of full-time studies as long as such person maintains that status.

(ii) Since the term "habitual" resident requires that the person have entered the United States pursuant to section 141(a) of the Compacts, the term does not apply to FAS citizens whose presence in the territories or possessions is based on an authority other than section 141(a), such as:

(A) Members of the Armed Forces of the United States described in 8 CFR § 235.1(c);

(B) Persons lawfully admitted for permanent residence in the United States; or

(C) Persons having nonimmigrant status whose entry into the United States is based on provisions of the Compacts or the Act other than section 141(a) of the Compacts.

(5) Dependent means a citizen of the FAS, as defined in section 141(a) of the Compacts, who:

(i) Is a habitual resident;

(ii) Resides with a principal habitual resident;

(iii) Relies for financial support on that principal habitual resident; and

(iv) Is either the parent, spouse, or unmarried child under the age of 21 of the principal habitual resident or the parent or child of the spouse of the principal habitual resident.

(6) Principal habitual resident means a habitual resident with whom one or more dependents reside and on whom dependent(s) rely for financial support.

(7) Self-supporting means:

(i) Having a lawful occupation of a current and continuing nature that provides 40 hours of gainful employment each week. A part-time student attending an accredited college or institution of higher learning in a territory or possession of the United States receives for each college or graduate credit-hour of study a three-hour credit toward the 40-hour requirement; or

(ii) If the person cannot meet the 40-hour employment requirement, having lawfully derived funds that meet or exceed 100 percent of the official poverty guidelines for Hawaii for a family unit of the appropriate size as published annually by the Department of Health and Human Services.

(8) Receipt of unauthorized public benefits means the acceptance of public benefits by fraud or willful misrepresentation in violation of section 401 or 411 of the Personal Responsibility and Work Opportunity Reconciliation Act of 1996, Public Law 104-193, 110 Stat. 2261, 2268, as amended by sections 5561 and 5565 of

the Balanced Budget Act of 1997, Public Law 105-33, 111 Stat. 638. 639.

(b) Where do these rules regarding habitual residence apply? The rules in this section apply to habitual residents living in a territory or possession of the United States to which the Act applies. Those territories and possessions are at present Guam, the Commonwealth of Puerto Rico, the American Virgin Islands, and the Commonwealth of the Northern Mariana Islands. These rules do not apply to habitual residents living in American Samoa as long as the Act does not extend to it. These rules are not applicable to habitual residents living in the fifty States or the District of Columbia.

(c) **When is an arriving FAS citizen presumed to be a habitual resident?**

(1) An arriving FAS citizen will be subject to the rebuttable presumption that he or she is a habitual resident if the Service has reason to believe that the arriving FAS citizen was previously admitted to the territory or possession more than one year ago; and

(2) That the arriving FAS citizen either;

(i) Failed to turn in his or her Form I-94 (see § 1.4) when he or she previously departed from the United States; or

(ii) Failed to apply for a replacement Form I-94.

(d) What rights do habitual residents have? Habitual residents have the right to enter, reside, study, and work in the United States, its territories or possessions, in nonimmigrant status without regard to the requirements of sections 212(a)(5)(A) and 212(a)(7)(A) and (B) of the Act.

(e) What are the limitations on the rights of habitual residents? (1) A habitual resident who is not a dependent is subject to removal if he or she:

(1) Is not and has not been self-supporting for a period exceeding 60 consecutive days for reasons other than a lawful strike or other labor dispute involving work stoppage; or

(i) Is not and has not been self-supporting for a period exceeding 60 consecutive days for reasons other than a lawful strike or other labor dispute involving work stoppage; or

(ii) Has received unauthorized public benefits by fraud or willful misrepresentation; or

(iii) Is subject to removal pursuant to section 237 of the Act, or any other provision of the Act.

(2) Any dependent is removable from a territory or possession of the United States if:

(i) The principal habitual resident who financially supports him or her and with whom he or she resides, becomes subject to removal unless the dependent establishes that he or she has become a dependent of another habitual resident or becomes self-supporting; or

(ii) The dependent, as an individual, receives unauthorized public benefits by fraud or willful misrepresentation; or

(iii) The dependent, as an individual, is subject to removal pursuant to section 237 of the Act, or any other provision of the Act.

HISTORY:

[65 FR 56463, 56465, Sept. 19, 2000; 74 FR 55726, 55738, Oct. 28, 2009; 78 FR 18457, 18472, Mar. 27, 2013, as confirmed at 81 FR 91646, 91670, Dec. 19, 2016; redesignated at 89 FR 34864, 34931, Apr. 30, 2024]

§ 214.8 [Reserved]

HISTORY:

[redesignated at 89 FR 34864, 34931, Apr. 30, 2024]

§ 214.9 [Reserved]

HISTORY:

[redesignated at 89 FR 34864, 34931, Apr. 30, 2024]

§ 214.10 [Reserved]

HISTORY:

[redesignated at 89 FR 34864, 34931, Apr. 30, 2024]

§ 214.11 Former regulations for noncitizen victims of severe forms of trafficking in persons.

For DHS and USCIS regulations governing Noncitizen Victims of Severe Forms of Trafficking in Persons, see subpart C of this part.

HISTORY:

[67 FR 4784, 4795, Jan. 31, 2002, 72 FR 19100, 19107, Apr. 17, 2007; 73 FR 75540, 75558, Dec. 12, 2008; 74 FR 55726, 55738, Oct. 28, 2009; 81 FR 92266, 92304, Dec. 19, 2016; 85 FR 46788, 46925, Aug. 3, 2020, as corrected at 85 FR 49941, Aug. 17, 2020, effective Oct. 2, 2020.; 89 FR 34864, 34931, Apr. 30, 2024; redesignated at 89 FR 34864, 34931, Apr. 30, 2024]

§ 214.12 Preliminary enrollment of schools in the Student and Exchange Visitor Information System (SEVIS). [This section was removed and reserved, effective Dec. 12, 2022. See 87 FR 75891, 75911, Dec. 12, 2022.]

§ 214.13 SEVIS fee for certain F, J, and M nonimmigrants.

(a) Applicability. The aliens in paragraphs (a)(1) through (3) of this section are required to submit a payment in the amount indicated for their status to the Student and Exchange Visitor Program (SEVP) in advance of obtaining nonimmigrant status as an F or M student or J exchange visitor, in addition to any other applicable fees, except as otherwise provided for in this section:

(1) An alien who applies for F-1 or F-3 status in order to enroll in a program of study at an SEVP-certified institution of higher education, as defined in section 101(a) of the Higher Education Act of 1965, as amended, or in a program of study at any other SEVP-certified academic or language training institution, including private elementary, middle, and secondary schools and public secondary schools, the amount of $350;

(2) An alien who applies for J-1 status in order to commence participation in an exchange visitor program

designated by the Department of State, the amount of $220, with a reduced fee for certain exchange visitor categories as provided in paragraphs (b)(1) and (c) of this section; and

(3) An alien who applies for M-1 or M-3 status in order to enroll in a program of study at an SEVP-certified vocational educational institution, including a flight school, in the amount of $350.

(b) Aliens not subject to a fee. No SEVIS fee is required with respect to:

(1) A J-1 exchange visitor who is coming to the United States as a participant in an exchange visitor program sponsored by the Federal government, identified by a program identifier designation prefix of G-1, G-2, G-3, or G-7;

(2) Dependents of F, M, or J nonimmigrants. The principal alien must pay the fee, when required under this section, in order for his/her qualifying dependents to obtain F-2, J-2, or M-2 status. However, an F-2, J-2, or M-2 dependent is not required to pay a separate fee under this section in order to obtain that status or during the time he/she remains in that status.

(c) Special Fee for Certain J-1 Nonimmigrants. A J-1 exchange visitor coming to the United States as an au pair, camp counselor, or participant in a summer work/travel program is subject to a fee of $ 35.

(d) Time for payment of SEVIS fee. An alien who is subject to payment of the SEVIS fee must remit the fee directly to DHS as follows:

(1) An alien seeking an F-1, F-3, J-1, M-1, or M-3 visa from a consular officer abroad for initial attendance at an SEVP-certified school or to commence participation in a Department of State-designated exchange visitor program, must pay the fee to DHS before issuance of the visa.

(2) An alien who is exempt from the visa requirement described in section 212(d)(4) of the Act must pay the fee to DHS before the alien applies for admission at a U.S. port-of-entry to begin initial attendance at an SEVP-certified school or initial participation in a Department of State-designated exchange visitor program.

(3) A nonimmigrant alien in the United States seeking a change of status to F-1, F-3, J-1, M-1, or M-3 must pay the fee to DHS before the alien is granted the change of nonimmigrant status, except as provided in paragraph (e)(4) of this section.

(4) A J-1 nonimmigrant who is applying for a change of program category within the United States, in accordance with 22 CFR 62.42, must pay the fee associated with that new category, if any, prior to being granted such a change.

(5) A J-1 nonimmigrant initially granted J-1 status to participate in a program sponsored by the Federal government, as defined in paragraph (b)(1) of this section, and transferring in accordance with 22 CFR 62.42 to a program that is not similarly sponsored, must pay the fee associated with the new program prior to completing the transfer.

(6) A J-1 nonimmigrant who is applying for reinstatement after a substantive violation of status, or who has been out of program status for longer than 120 days but less than 270 days during the course of his/her program must pay a new fee to DHS, if applicable, prior to being granted a reinstatement to valid J-1 status.

(7) An F or M student who is applying for reinstatement of student status because of a violation of status, and who has been out of status for a period of time that exceeds the presumptive ineligibility deadline set forth in 8 CFR 214.2(f)(16)(i)(A) or (m)(16)(i)(A), must pay a new fee to DHS prior to being granted a return to valid status.

(8) An F-1, F-3, M-1, or M-3 nonimmigrant who has been absent from the United States for a period that exceeds 5 months in duration, and wishes to reenter the United States to engage in further study in the same course of study, with the exception of students who have been working toward completion of a U.S. course of study in authorized overseas study, must pay a new fee to DHS prior to being granted student status.

(e) Circumstances where no new fee is required.

(1) Extension of stay, transfer, or optional practical training for students. An F-1, F-3, M-1, or M-3 nonimmigrant is not required to pay a new fee in connection with:

(i) An application for an extension of stay, as provided in 8 CFR 214.2(f)(7) or (m)(10);

(ii) An application for transfer, as provided in 8 CFR 214.2(f)(8) or (m)(11);

(iii) A change in educational level, as provided in 8 CFR 214.2(f)(5)(ii); or

(iv) An application for post-completion practical training, as provided in 8 CFR 214.2(f)(10)(ii) or (m)(14).

(2) Extension of program or transfer for exchange visitors. A J-1 nonimmigrant is not required to pay a new fee in connection with:

(i) An application for an extension of program, as provided in 22 CFR 62.43; or

(ii) An application for transfer of program, as provided in 22 CFR 62.42.

(3) Visa issuance for a continuation of study. An F-1, F-3, J-1, M-1, or M-3 nonimmigrant who has previously paid the fee is not required to pay a new fee in order to be granted a visa to return to the United States as a continuing student or exchange visitor in a single course of study, so long as the nonimmigrant is not otherwise required to pay a new fee in accordance with the other provisions in this section.

(4) Certain changes in student classification.

(i) No fee is required for changes between the F-1 and F-3 classifications, and no fee is required for changes between the M-1 and M-3 classifications.

(ii) Institutional reclassification. DHS retains the discretionary authority to waive the additional fee requirement when a nonimmigrant changes classification between F and M, if the change of status is due solely to institutional reclassification by the Student and Exchange Visitor Program during that nonimmigrant's course of study.

(5) Re-application following denial of application by consular officer. An alien who fully paid a SEVIS fee in connection with an initial application for an F-1, F-3, M-1, or M-3 visa, or a J-1 visa in a particular program

category, whose initial application was denied, and who is reapplying for the same status, or the same J-1 exchange visitor category, within 12 months following the initial notice of denial is not required to repay the SEVIS fee.

(6) Re-application following denial of an application for a change of status. A nonimmigrant who fully paid a SEVIS fee in connection with an initial application for a change of status within in the United States to F-1, F-3, M-1, or M-3 classification, or for a change of status to a particular J-1 exchange visitor category, whose initial application was denied, and who is granted a motion to reopen the denied case is not required to repay the SEVIS fee if the motion to reopen is granted within 12 months of receipt of initial notice of denial.

(f) [Reserved]

(g) Procedures for payment of the SEVIS fee.

(1) Options for payment. An alien subject to payment of a fee under this section may pay the fee by any procedure approved by DHS, including:

(i) Submission of Form I-901, to DHS by mail, along with the proper fee paid by check, money order, or foreign draft drawn on a financial institution in the United States and payable in United States currency, as provided by 8 CFR 103.7(d)(8);

(ii) Electronic submission of Form I-901 to DHS using a credit card or other electronic means of payment accepted by DHS; or,

(iii) A designated payment service and receipt mechanism approved and set forth in future guidance by DHS.

(2) Receipts. DHS will provide a receipt for each fee payment under paragraph (g)(1) of this section until such time as DHS issues a notice in the Federal Register that paper receipts will no longer be necessary. Further receipt provisions include:

(i) DHS will provide for an expedited delivery of the receipt, upon request and receipt of an additional fee;

(ii) If payment was made electronically, both DHS and the Department of State will accept a properly completed receipt that is printed-out electronically, in lieu of the receipt generated by DHS;

(iii) If payment was made through an approved payment service, DHS and the Department of State will accept a properly completed receipt issued by the payment service, in lieu of the receipt generated by DHS.

(3) Electronic record of fee payment. DHS will maintain an electronic record of payment for the alien as verification of receipt of the required fee under this section. If DHS records indicate that the fee has been paid, an alien who has lost or did not receive a receipt for a fee payment under this section will not be denied an immigration benefit, including visa issuance or admission to the United States, solely because of a failure to present a paper receipt of fee payment.

(4) Third-party payments. DHS will accept payment of the required fee for an alien from a certified school or a designated exchange visitor program sponsor, or from another source, in accordance with procedures approved by DHS.

(h) Failure to pay the fee. The failure to pay the required fee is grounds for denial of F, M, or J nonimmigrant status or status-related benefits. Payment of the fee does not preserve the lawful status of any F, J, or M nonimmigrant that has violated his or her status in some other manner.

(1) For purposes of reinstatement to F or M status, failure to pay the required fee will be considered a "willful violation" under 8 CFR 214.2(f)(16) or (m)(16), unless DHS determines that there are sufficient extenuating circumstances (as determined at the discretion of the Student and Exchange Visitor Program).

(2) For purposes of reinstatement to valid J program status, failure to pay the required fee will not be considered a "minor or technical infraction" under 22 CFR 62.45.

HISTORY:

[69 FR 39814, 39825, July 1, 2004, as corrected at 69 FR 41388, July 9, 2004; 73 FR 55683, 55704, Sept. 26, 2008; 84 FR 23930, 23979, May 23, 2019; 87 FR 75891, 75911, Dec. 12, 2022; redesignated at 89 FR 34864, 34931, Apr. 30, 2024]

§ 214.14 Alien victims of certain qualifying criminal activity.

(a) Definitions. As used in this section, the term:

(1) BIWPA means Battered Immigrant Women Protection Act of 2000 of the Victims of Trafficking and Violence Protection Act of 2000, div. B, Violence Against Women Act of 2000, tit. V, Pub. L. 106-386, 114 Stat. 1464, (2000), amended by Violence Against Women and Department of Justice Reauthorization Act of 2005, tit. VIII, Pub. L. 109-162, 119 Stat. 2960 (2006), amended by Violence Against Women and Department of Justice Reauthorization Act — Technical Corrections, Pub. L. 109-271, 120 Stat. 750 (2006).

(2) Certifying agency means a Federal, State, or local law enforcement agency, prosecutor, judge, or other authority, that has responsibility for the investigation or prosecution of a qualifying crime or criminal activity. This definition includes agencies that have criminal investigative jurisdiction in their respective areas of expertise, including, but not limited to, child protective services, the Equal Employment Opportunity Commission, and the Department of Labor.

(3) Certifying official means:

(i) The head of the certifying agency, or any person(s) in a supervisory role who has been specifically designated by the head of the certifying agency to issue U nonimmigrant status certifications on behalf of that agency; or

(ii) A Federal, State, or local judge.

(4) Indian Country is defined as:

(i) All land within the limits of any Indian reservation under the jurisdiction of the United States Government, notwithstanding the issuance of any patent, and including rights-of-way running through the reservation;

(ii) All dependent Indian communities within the borders of the United States whether within the original or subsequently acquired territory thereof, and whether within or without the limits of a state; and

(iii) All Indian allotments, the Indian titles to which have not been extinguished, including rights-of-way running through such allotments.

(5) Investigation or prosecution refers to the detection or investigation of a qualifying crime or criminal activity, as well as to the prosecution, conviction, or sentencing of the perpetrator of the qualifying crime or criminal activity.

(6) Military Installation means any facility, base, camp, post, encampment, station, yard, center, port, aircraft, vehicle, or vessel under the jurisdiction of the Department of Defense, including any leased facility, or any other location under military control.

(7) Next friend means a person who appears in a lawsuit to act for the benefit of an alien under the age of 16 or incapacitated or incompetent, who has suffered substantial physical or mental abuse as a result of being a victim of qualifying criminal activity. The next friend is not a party to the legal proceeding and is not appointed as a guardian.

(8) Physical or mental abuse means injury or harm to the victim's physical person, or harm to or impairment of the emotional or psychological soundness of the victim.

(9) Qualifying crime or qualifying criminal activity includes one or more of the following or any similar activities in violation of Federal, State or local criminal law of the United States: Rape; torture; trafficking; incest; domestic violence; sexual assault; abusive sexual contact; prostitution; sexual exploitation; female genital mutilation; being held hostage; peonage; involuntary servitude; slave trade; kidnapping; abduction; unlawful criminal restraint; false imprisonment; blackmail; extortion; manslaughter; murder; felonious assault; witness tampering; obstruction of justice; perjury; or attempt, conspiracy, or solicitation to commit any of the above mentioned crimes. The term "any similar activity" refers to criminal offenses in which the nature and elements of the offenses are substantially similar to the statutorily enumerated list of criminal activities.

(10) Qualifying family member means, in the case of an alien victim 21 years of age or older who is eligible for U nonimmigrant status as described in section 101(a)(15)(U) of the Act, 8 U.S.C. 1101(a)(15)(U), the spouse or child(ren) of such alien; and, in the case of an alien victim under the age of 21 who is eligible for U nonimmigrant status as described in section 101(a)(15)(U) of the Act, qualifying family member means the spouse, child(ren), parents, or unmarried siblings under the age of 18 of such an alien.

(11) Territories and Possessions of the United States means American Samoa, Swains Island, Bajo Nuevo (the Petrel Islands), Baker Island, Howland Island, Jarvis Island, Johnston Atoll, Kingman Reef, Midway Atoll, Navassa Island, Palmyra Atoll, Serranilla Bank, and Wake Atoll.

(12) U nonimmigrant status certification means Form I-918, Supplement B, "U Nonimmigrant Status Certification," which confirms that the petitioner has been helpful, is being helpful, or is likely to be helpful in the investigation or prosecution of the qualifying criminal activity of which he or she is a victim.

(13) U interim relief refers to the interim benefits that were provided by USCIS to petitioners for U nonimmigrant status, who requested such benefits and who were deemed prima facie eligible for U nonimmigrant status prior to the publication of the implementing regulations.

(14) Victim of qualifying criminal activity generally means an alien who has suffered direct and proximate harm as a result of the commission of qualifying criminal activity.

(i) The alien spouse, children under 21 years of age and, if the direct victim is under 21 years of age, parents and unmarried siblings under 18 years of age, will be considered victims of qualifying criminal activity where the direct victim is deceased due to murder or manslaughter, or is incompetent or incapacitated, and therefore unable to provide information concerning the criminal activity or be helpful in the investigation or prosecution of the criminal activity. For purposes of determining eligibility under this definition, USCIS will consider the age of the victim at the time the qualifying criminal activity occurred.

(ii) A petitioner may be considered a victim of witness tampering, obstruction of justice, or perjury, including any attempt, solicitation, or conspiracy to commit one or more of those offenses, if:

(A) The petitioner has been directly and proximately harmed by the perpetrator of the witness tampering, obstruction of justice, or perjury; and

(B) There are reasonable grounds to conclude that the perpetrator committed the witness tampering, obstruction of justice, or perjury offense, at least in principal part, as a means:

(1) To avoid or frustrate efforts to investigate, arrest, prosecute, or otherwise bring to justice the perpetrator for other criminal activity; or

(2) To further the perpetrator's abuse or exploitation of or undue control over the petitioner through manipulation of the legal system.

(iii) A person who is culpable for the qualifying criminal activity being investigated or prosecuted is excluded from being recognized as a victim of qualifying criminal activity.

(b) Eligibility. An alien is eligible for U-1 nonimmigrant status if he or she demonstrates all of the following in accordance with paragraph (c) of this section:

(1) The alien has suffered substantial physical or mental abuse as a result of having been a victim of qualifying criminal activity. Whether abuse is substantial is based on a number of factors, including but not limited to: The nature of the injury inflicted or suffered; the severity of the perpetrator's conduct; the severity of the harm suffered; the duration of the infliction of the harm; and the extent to which there is permanent or serious harm to the appearance, health, or physical or mental soundness of the victim, including aggravation of pre-existing conditions. No single factor is a prerequisite to establish that the abuse suffered was substantial. Also, the existence of one or more of the factors automatically does not create a presumption that the abuse suffered was substantial. A series of acts taken together may be considered to constitute substantial

physical or mental abuse even where no single act alone rises to that level;

(2) The alien possesses credible and reliable information establishing that he or she has knowledge of the details concerning the qualifying criminal activity upon which his or her petition is based. The alien must possess specific facts regarding the criminal activity leading a certifying official to determine that the petitioner has, is, or is likely to provide assistance to the investigation or prosecution of the qualifying criminal activity. In the event that the alien has not yet reached 16 years of age on the date on which an act constituting an element of the qualifying criminal activity first occurred, a parent, guardian or next friend of the alien may possess the information regarding a qualifying crime. In addition, if the alien is incapacitated or incompetent, a parent, guardian, or next friend may possess the information regarding the qualifying crime;

(3) The alien has been helpful, is being helpful, or is likely to be helpful to a certifying agency in the investigation or prosecution of the qualifying criminal activity upon which his or her petition is based, and since the initiation of cooperation, has not refused or failed to provide information and assistance reasonably requested. In the event that the alien has not yet reached 16 years of age on the date on which an act constituting an element of the qualifying criminal activity first occurred, a parent, guardian or next friend of the alien may provide the required assistance. In addition, if the petitioner is incapacitated or incompetent and, therefore, unable to be helpful in the investigation or prosecution of the qualifying criminal activity, a parent, guardian, or next friend may provide the required assistance; and

(4) The qualifying criminal activity occurred in the United States (including Indian country and U.S. military installations) or in the territories or possessions of the United States, or violated a U.S. federal law that provides for extraterritorial jurisdiction to prosecute the offense in a U.S. federal court.

(c) Application procedures for U nonimmigrant status —

(1) Filing a petition. USCIS has sole jurisdiction over all petitions for U nonimmigrant status. An alien seeking U-1 nonimmigrant status must submit a Petition for U Nonimmigrant Status on the form prescribed by USCIS, and initial evidence to USCIS in accordance with this paragraph (c)(1) and the form instructions. A petitioner who received interim relief is not required to submit initial evidence with a Petition for U Nonimmigrant Status if he or she is relying on the law enforcement certification and other evidence that was submitted with the request for interim relief.

(i) Petitioners in pending immigration proceedings. An alien who is in removal proceedings under section 240 of the Act, 8 U.S.C. 1229a, or in exclusion or deportation proceedings initiated under former sections 236 or 242 of the Act, 8 U.S.C. 1226 and 1252 (as in effect prior to April 1, 1997), and who would like to apply for U nonimmigrant status must file a Form I-918 directly with USCIS. U.S. Immigration and Customs Enforcement (ICE) counsel may agree, as a matter of discretion, to file, at the request of the alien petitioner, a joint motion to terminate proceedings without prejudice with the immigration judge or Board of Immigration Appeals, whichever is appropriate, while a petition for U nonimmigrant status is being adjudicated by USCIS.

(ii) Petitioners with final orders of removal, deportation, or exclusion. An alien who is the subject of a final order of removal, deportation, or exclusion is not precluded from filing a petition for U-1 nonimmigrant status directly with USCIS. The filing of a petition for U-1 nonimmigrant status has no effect on ICE's authority to execute a final order, although the alien may file a request for a stay of removal pursuant to 8 CFR 241.6(a) and 8 CFR 1241.6(a). If the alien is in detention pending execution of the final order, the time during which a stay is in effect will extend the period of detention (under the standards of 8 CFR 241.4) reasonably necessary to bring about the petitioner's removal.

(2) Initial evidence. Form I-918 must include the following initial evidence:

(i) Form I-918, Supplement B, "U Nonimmigrant Status Certification," signed by a certifying official within the six months immediately preceding the filing of Form I-918. The certification must state that: the person signing the certificate is the head of the certifying agency, or any person(s) in a supervisory role who has been specifically designated by the head of the certifying agency to issue U nonimmigrant status certifications on behalf of that agency, or is a Federal, State, or local judge; the agency is a Federal, State, or local law enforcement agency, or prosecutor, judge or other authority, that has responsibility for the detection, investigation, prosecution, conviction, or sentencing of qualifying criminal activity; the applicant has been a victim of qualifying criminal activity that the certifying official's agency is investigating or prosecuting; the petitioner possesses information concerning the qualifying criminal activity of which he or she has been a victim; the petitioner has been, is being, or is likely to be helpful to an investigation or prosecution of that qualifying criminal activity; and the qualifying criminal activity violated U.S. law, or occurred in the United States, its territories, its possessions, Indian country, or at military installations abroad.

(ii) Any additional evidence that the petitioner wants USCIS to consider to establish that: the petitioner is a victim of qualifying criminal activity; the petitioner has suffered substantial physical or mental abuse as a result of being a victim of qualifying criminal activity; the petitioner (or, in the case of a child under the age of 16 or petitioner who is incompetent or incapacitated, a parent, guardian or next friend of the petitioner) possesses information establishing that he or she has knowledge of the details concerning the qualifying criminal activity of which he or she was a victim and upon which his or her application is based; the petitioner (or, in the case of a child under the age of 16 or petitioner who is incompetent or incapacitated, a parent, guardian or next friend of the petitioner) has been helpful, is being helpful, or is likely to be helpful to a Federal, State, or local law enforcement agency, prosecutor, or authority, or Federal or State judge, investigating or prosecuting the criminal activity of which the petitioner is a victim; or the criminal activity is qualifying and occurred in the United States (including Indian country and U.S. military installations) or in the territories or possessions of the United States, or violates a U.S. federal law that provides for extraterritorial jurisdiction to prosecute the offense in a U.S. federal court;

(iii) A signed statement by the petitioner describing the facts of the victimization. The statement also may include information supporting any of the eligibility requirements set out in paragraph (b) of this section. When the petitioner is under the age of 16, incapacitated, or incompetent, a parent, guardian, or next friend may submit a statement on behalf of the petitioner; and

(iv) If the petitioner is inadmissible, Form I-192, "Application for Advance Permission to Enter as Non-Immigrant," in accordance with 8 CFR 212.17.

(3) Biometric capture. All petitioners for U-1 nonimmigrant status must submit to biometric capture and pay a biometric capture fee. USCIS will notify the petitioner of the proper time and location to appear for biometric capture after the petitioner files Form I-918.

(4) Evidentiary standards and burden of proof. The burden shall be on the petitioner to demonstrate eligibility for U-1 nonimmigrant status. The petitioner may submit any credible evidence relating to his or her Form I-918 for consideration by USCIS. USCIS shall conduct a de novo review of all evidence submitted in connection with Form I-918 and may investigate any aspect of the petition. Evidence previously submitted for this or other immigration benefit or relief may be used by USCIS in evaluating the eligibility of a petitioner for U-1 nonimmigrant status. However, USCIS will not be bound by its previous factual determinations. USCIS will determine, in its sole discretion, the evidentiary value of previously or concurrently submitted evidence, including Form I-918, Supplement B, "U Nonimmigrant Status Certification."

(5) Decision. After completing its de novo review of the petition and evidence, USCIS will issue a written decision approving or denying Form I-918 and notify the petitioner of this decision. USCIS will include in a decision approving Form I-918 a list of nongovernmental organizations to which the petitioner can refer regarding his or her options while in the United States and available resources.

(i) Approval of Form I-918, generally. If USCIS determines that the petitioner has met the requirements for U-1 nonimmigrant status, USCIS will approve Form I-918. For a petitioner who is within the United States, USCIS also will concurrently grant U-1 nonimmigrant status, subject to the annual limitation as provided in paragraph (d) of this section. For a petitioner who is subject to an order of exclusion, deportation, or removal issued by the Secretary, the order will be deemed canceled by operation of law as of the date of USCIS' approval of Form I-918. A petitioner who is subject to an order of exclusion, deportation, or removal issued by an immigration judge or the Board may seek cancellation of such order by filing, with the immigration judge or the Board, a motion to reopen and terminate removal proceedings. ICE counsel may agree, as a matter of discretion, to join such a motion to overcome any applicable time and numerical limitations of 8 CFR 1003.2 and 1003.23.

(A) Notice of Approval of Form I-918 for U-1 petitioners within the United States. After USCIS approves Form I-918 for an alien who filed his or her petition from within the United States, USCIS will notify the alien of such approval on Form I-797, "Notice of Action," and include Form I-94 (see § 1.4), "Arrival-Departure Record," indicating U-1 nonimmigrant status.

(B) Notice of Approval of Form I-918 for U-1 petitioners outside the United States. After USCIS approves Form I-918 for an alien who filed his or her petition from outside the United States, USCIS will notify the alien of such approval on Form I-797, "Notice of Action," and will forward notice to the Department of State for delivery to the U.S. Embassy or Consulate having jurisdiction over the area in which the alien is located, or, for a visa exempt alien, to the appropriate port of entry.

(ii) Denial of Form I-918. USCIS will provide written notification to the petitioner of the reasons for the denial. The petitioner may appeal a denial of Form I-918 to the Administrative Appeals Office (AAO) in accordance with the provisions of 8 CFR 103.3. For petitioners who appeal a denial of their Form I-918 to the AAO, the denial will not be deemed administratively final until the AAO issues a decision affirming the denial. Upon USCIS' final denial of a petition for a petitioner who was in removal proceedings that were terminated pursuant to 8 CFR 214.14(c)(1)(i), DHS may file a new Notice to Appear (see section 239 of the Act, 8 U.S.C. 1229) to place the individual in proceedings again. For petitioners who are subject to an order of removal, deportation, or exclusion and whose order has been stayed, USCIS' denial of the petition will result in the stay being lifted automatically as of the date the denial becomes administratively final.

(6) Petitioners granted U interim relief. Petitioners who were granted U interim relief as defined in paragraph (a)(13) of this section and whose Form I-918 is approved will be accorded U-1 nonimmigrant status as of the date that a request for U interim relief was initially approved.

(7) Employment authorization. An alien granted U-1 nonimmigrant status is employment authorized incident to status. USCIS automatically will issue an initial Employment Authorization Document (EAD) to such aliens who are in the United States. For principal aliens who applied from outside the United States, the initial EAD will not be issued until the petitioner has been admitted to the United States in U nonimmigrant status. After admission, the alien may receive an initial EAD, upon request and submission of a copy of his or her Form I-94, "Arrival-Departure Record," to the USCIS office having jurisdiction over the adjudication of petitions for U nonimmigrant status. No additional fee is required. An alien granted U-1 nonimmigrant status seeking to renew his or her expiring EAD or replace an

EAD that was lost, stolen, or destroyed, must file Form I-765 in accordance with the instructions to the form.

(d) Annual cap on U-1 nonimmigrant status —

(1) General. In accordance with section 214(p)(2) of the Act, 8 U.S.C. 1184(p)(2), the total number of aliens who may be issued a U-1 nonimmigrant visa or granted U-1 nonimmigrant status may not exceed 10,000 in any fiscal year.

(2) Waiting list. All eligible petitioners who, due solely to the cap, are not granted U-1 nonimmigrant status must be placed on a waiting list and receive written notice of such placement. Priority on the waiting list will be determined by the date the petition was filed with the oldest petitions receiving the highest priority. In the next fiscal year, USCIS will issue a number to each petition on the waiting list, in the order of highest priority, providing the petitioner remains admissible and eligible for U nonimmigrant status. After U-1 nonimmigrant status has been issued to qualifying petitioners on the waiting list, any remaining U-1 nonimmigrant numbers for that fiscal year will be issued to new qualifying petitioners in the order that the petitions were properly filed. USCIS will grant deferred action or parole to U-1 petitioners and qualifying family members while the U-1 petitioners are on the waiting list. USCIS, in its discretion, may authorize employment for such petitioners and qualifying family members.

(3) Unlawful presence. During the time a petitioner for U nonimmigrant status who was granted deferred action or parole is on the waiting list, no accrual of unlawful presence under section 212(a)(9)(B) of the INA, 8 U.S.C. 1182(a)(9)(B), will result. However, a petitioner may be removed from the waiting list, and the deferred action or parole may be terminated at the discretion of USCIS.

(e) Restrictions on use and disclosure of information relating to petitioners for U nonimmigrant classification —

(1) General. The use or disclosure (other than to a sworn officer or employee of DHS, the Department of Justice, the Department of State, or a bureau or agency of any of those departments, for legitimate department, bureau, or agency purposes) of any information relating to the beneficiary of a pending or approved petition for U nonimmigrant status is prohibited unless the disclosure is made:

(i) By the Secretary of Homeland Security, at his discretion, in the same manner and circumstances as census information may be disclosed by the Secretary of Commerce under 13 U.S.C. 8;

(ii) By the Secretary of Homeland Security, at his discretion, to law enforcement officials to be used solely for a legitimate law enforcement purpose;

(iii) In conjunction with judicial review of a determination in a manner that protects the confidentiality of such information;

(iv) After adult petitioners for U nonimmigrant status or U nonimmigrant status holders have provided written consent to waive the restrictions prohibiting the release of information;

(v) To Federal, State, and local public and private agencies providing benefits, to be used solely in making determinations of eligibility for benefits pursuant to 8 U.S.C. 1641(c);

(vi) After a petition for U nonimmigrant status has been denied in a final decision;

(vii) To the chairmen and ranking members of the Committee on the Judiciary of the Senate or the Committee on the Judiciary of the House of Representatives, for the exercise of congressional oversight authority, provided the disclosure relates to information about a closed case and is made in a manner that protects the confidentiality of the information and omits personally identifying information (including locational information about individuals);

(viii) With prior written consent from the petitioner or derivative family members, to nonprofit, nongovernmental victims' service providers for the sole purpose of assisting the victim in obtaining victim services from programs with expertise working with immigrant victims; or

(ix) To federal prosecutors to comply with constitutional obligations to provide statements by witnesses and certain other documents to defendants in pending federal criminal proceedings.

(2) Agencies receiving information under this section, whether governmental or non-governmental, are bound by the confidentiality provisions and other restrictions set out in 8 U.S.C. 1367.

(3) Officials of the Department of Homeland Security are prohibited from making adverse determinations of admissibility or deportability based on information obtained solely from the perpetrator of substantial physical or mental abuse and the criminal activity.

(f) Admission of qualifying family members —

(1) Eligibility. An alien who has petitioned for or has been granted U-1 nonimmigrant status (i.e., principal alien) may petition for the admission of a qualifying family member in a U-2 (spouse), U-3 (child), U-4 (parent of a U-1 alien who is a child under 21 years of age), or U-5 (unmarried sibling under the age of 18) derivative status, if accompanying or following to join such principal alien. A qualifying family member who committed the qualifying criminal activity in a family violence or trafficking context which established the principal alien's eligibility for U nonimmigrant status shall not be granted U-2, U-3, U-4, or U-5 nonimmigrant status. To be eligible for U-2, U-3, U-4, or U-5 nonimmigrant status, it must be demonstrated that:

(i) The alien for whom U-2, U-3, U-4, or U-5 status is being sought is a qualifying family member, as defined in paragraph (a)(10) of this section; and

(ii) The qualifying family member is admissible to the United States.

(2) Filing procedures. A petitioner for U-1 nonimmigrant status may apply for derivative U nonimmigrant status on behalf of qualifying family members by submitting a Form I-918, Supplement A, "Petition for Qualifying Family Member of U-1 Recipient," for each family member either at the same time the petition for U-1 nonimmigrant status is filed, or at a later date. An alien who has been granted U-1 nonimmigrant status

may apply for derivative U nonimmigrant status on behalf of qualifying family members by submitting Form I-918, Supplement A for each family member. All Forms I-918, Supplement A must be accompanied by initial evidence and the required fees specified in the instructions to the form. Forms I-918, Supplement A that are not filed at the same time as Form I-918 but are filed at a later date must be accompanied by a copy of the Form I-918 that was filed by the principal petitioner or a copy of his or her Form I-94 demonstrating proof of U-1 nonimmigrant status, as applicable.

(i) Qualifying family members in pending immigration proceedings. The principal alien of a qualifying family member who is in removal proceedings under section 240 of the Act, 8 U.S.C. 1229a, or in exclusion or deportation proceedings initiated under former sections 236 or 242 of the Act, 8 U.S.C. 1226 and 1252 (as in effect prior to April 1, 1997), and who is seeking U nonimmigrant status, must file a Form I-918, Supplement A directly with USCIS. ICE counsel may agree to file, at the request of the qualifying family member, a joint motion to terminate proceedings without prejudice with the immigration judge or Board of Immigration Appeals, whichever is appropriate, while the petition for U nonimmigrant status is being adjudicated by USCIS.

(ii) Qualifying family members with final orders of removal, deportation, or exclusion. An alien who is the subject of a final order of removal, deportation, or exclusion is not precluded from filing a petition for U-2, U-3, U-4, or U-5 nonimmigrant status directly with USCIS. The filing of a petition for U-2, U-3, U-4, or U-5 nonimmigrant status has no effect on ICE's authority to execute a final order, although the alien may file a request for a stay of removal pursuant to 8 CFR 241.6(a) and 8 CFR 1241.6(a). If the alien is in detention pending execution of the final order, the time during which a stay is in effect will extend the period of detention (under the standards of 8 CFR 241.4) reasonably necessary to bring about the alien's removal.

(3) Initial evidence. Form I-918, Supplement A, must include the following initial evidence:

(i) Evidence demonstrating the relationship of a qualifying family member, as provided in paragraph (f)(4) of this section;

(ii) If the qualifying family member is inadmissible, Form I-192, "Application for Advance Permission to Enter as a Non-Immigrant," in accordance with 8 CFR 212.17.

(4) Relationship. Except as set forth in paragraphs (f)(4)(i) and (ii) of this section, the relationship between the U-1 principal alien and the qualifying family member must exist at the time Form I-918 was filed, and the relationship must continue to exist at the time Form I-918, Supplement A is adjudicated, and at the time of the qualifying family member's subsequent admission to the United States.

(i) If the U-1 principal alien proves that he or she has become the parent of a child after Form I-918 was filed, the child shall be eligible to accompany or follow to join the U-1 principal alien.

(ii) If the principal alien was under 21 years of age at the time he or she filed Form I-918, and filed Form I-918, Supplement A for an unmarried sibling under the age of 18, USCIS will continue to consider such sibling as a qualifying family member for purposes of U nonimmigrant status even if the principal alien is no longer under 21 years of age at the time of adjudication, and even if the sibling is no longer under 18 years of age at the time of adjudication.

(5) Biometric capture and evidentiary standards. The provisions for biometric capture and evidentiary standards in paragraphs (c)(3) and (c)(4) of this section also are applicable to petitions for qualifying family members.

(6) Decision. USCIS will issue a written decision approving or denying Form I-918, Supplement A and send notice of this decision to the U-1 principal petitioner. USCIS will include in a decision approving Form I-918 a list of nongovernmental organizations to which the qualifying family member can refer regarding his or her options while in the United States and available resources. For a qualifying family member who is subject to an order of exclusion, deportation, or removal issued by the Secretary, the order will be deemed canceled by operation of law as of the date of USCIS' approval of Form I-918, Supplement A. A qualifying family member who is subject to an order of exclusion, deportation, or removal issued by an immigration judge or the Board may seek cancellation of such order by filing, with the immigration judge or the Board, a motion to reopen and terminate removal proceedings. ICE counsel may agree, as a matter of discretion, to join such a motion to overcome any applicable time and numerical limitations of 8 CFR 1003.2 and 1003.23.

(i) Approvals for qualifying family members within the United States. When USCIS approves a Form I-918, Supplement A for a qualifying family member who is within the United States, it will concurrently grant that alien U-2, U-3, U-4, or U-5 nonimmigrant status. USCIS will notify the principal of such approval on Form I-797, "Notice of Action," with Form I-94, "Arrival-Departure Record," indicating U-2, U-3, U-4, or U-5 nonimmigrant status. Aliens who were previously granted U interim relief as defined in paragraph (a)(13) of this section will be accorded U nonimmigrant status as of the date that the request for U interim relief was approved. Aliens who are granted U-2, U-3, U-4, or U-5 nonimmigrant status are not subject to an annual numerical limit. USCIS may not approve Form I-918, Supplement A unless it has approved the principal alien's Form I-918.

(ii) Approvals for qualifying family members outside the United States. When USCIS approves Form I-918, Supplement A for a qualifying family member who is outside the United States, USCIS will notify the principal alien of such approval on Form I-797. USCIS will forward the approved Form I-918, Supplement A to the Department of State for delivery to the U.S. Embassy or Consulate having jurisdiction over the area in which the qualifying family member is located, or, for a visa exempt alien, to the appropriate port of entry.

(iii) Denial of the Form I-918, Supplement A. In accordance with 8 CFR 103.3(a)(1), USCIS will provide written notification of the reasons for the denial. The principal alien may appeal the denial of Form I-918, Supplement A to the Administrative Appeals Office in accordance with the provisions of 8 CFR 103.3. Upon USCIS' final denial of Form I-918, Supplement A for a qualifying family member who was in removal proceedings that were terminated pursuant to 8 CFR 214.14(f)(2)(i), DHS may file a new Notice to Appear (see section 239 of the INA, 8 U.S.C. 1229) to place the individual in proceedings again. For qualifying family members who are subject to an order of removal, deportation, or exclusion and whose order has been stayed, USCIS' denial of the petition will result in the stay being lifted automatically as of the date the denial becomes administratively final.

(7) Employment authorization. An alien granted U-2, U-3, U-4, or U-5 nonimmigrant status is employment authorized incident to status. To obtain an Employment Authorization Document (EAD), such alien must file Form I-765, "Application for Employment Authorization," with the appropriate fee or a request for a fee waiver, in accordance with the instructions to the form. For qualifying family members within the United States, the Form I-765 may be filed concurrently with Form I-918, Supplement A, or at any time thereafter. For qualifying family members who are outside the United States, Form I-765 only may be filed after admission to the United States in U nonimmigrant status.

(g) Duration of U nonimmigrant status —

(1) In general. U nonimmigrant status may be approved for a period not to exceed 4 years in the aggregate. A qualifying family member granted U-2, U-3, U-4, and U-5 nonimmigrant status will be approved for an initial period that does not exceed the expiration date of the initial period approved for the principal alien.

(2) Extension of status.

(i) Where a U nonimmigrant's approved period of stay on Form I-94 is less than 4 years, he or she may file Form I-539, "Application to Extend/Change Nonimmigrant Status," to request an extension of U nonimmigrant status for an aggregate period not to exceed 4 years. USCIS may approve an extension of status for a qualifying family member beyond the date when the U-1 nonimmigrant's status expires when the qualifying family member is unable to enter the United States timely due to delays in consular processing, and an extension of status is necessary to ensure that the qualifying family member is able to attain at least 3 years in nonimmigrant status for purposes of adjusting status under section 245(m) of the Act, 8 U.S.C. 1255.

(ii) Extensions of U nonimmigrant status beyond the 4-year period are available upon attestation by the certifying official that the alien's presence in the United States continues to be necessary to assist in the investigation or prosecution of qualifying criminal activity. In order to obtain an extension of U nonimmigrant status based upon such an attestation, the alien must file Form I-539 and a newly executed Form I-918, Supplement B in accordance with the instructions to Form I-539.

(h) Revocation of approved petitions for U nonimmigrant status —

(1) Automatic revocation. An approved petition for U-1 nonimmigrant status will be revoked automatically if, pursuant to 8 CFR 214.14(d)(1), the beneficiary of the approved petition notifies the USCIS office that approved the petition that he or she will not apply for admission to the United States and, therefore, the petition will not be used.

(2) Revocation on notice

(i) USCIS may revoke an approved petition for U nonimmigrant status following a notice of intent to revoke. USCIS may revoke an approved petition for U nonimmigrant status based on one or more of the following reasons:

(A) The certifying official withdraws the U nonimmigrant status certification referred to in 8 CFR 214.14(c)(2)(i) or disavows the contents in writing;

(B) Approval of the petition was in error;

(C) Where there was fraud in the petition;

(D) In the case of a U-2, U-3, U-4, or U-5 nonimmigrant, the relationship to the principal petitioner has terminated; or

(E) In the case of a U-2, U-3, U-4, or U-5 nonimmigrant, the principal U-1's nonimmigrant status is revoked.

(ii) The notice of intent to revoke must be in writing and contain a statement of the grounds for the revocation and the time period allowed for the U nonimmigrant's rebuttal. The alien may submit evidence in rebuttal within 30 days of the date of the notice. USCIS shall consider all relevant evidence presented in deciding whether to revoke the approved petition for U nonimmigrant status. The determination of what is relevant evidence and the weight to be given to that evidence will be within the sole discretion of USCIS. If USCIS revokes approval of a petition and thereby terminates U nonimmigrant status, USCIS will provide the alien with a written notice of revocation that explains the specific reasons for the revocation.

(3) Appeal of a revocation of approval. A revocation on notice may be appealed to the Administrative Appeals Office in accordance with 8 CFR 103.3 within 30 days after the date of the notice of revocation. Automatic revocations may not be appealed.

(4) Effects of revocation of approval. Revocation of a principal alien's approved Form I-918 will result in termination of status for the principal alien, as well as in the denial of any pending Form I-918, Supplement A filed for qualifying family members seeking U-2, U-3, U-4, or U-5 nonimmigrant status. Revocation of a qualifying family member's approved Form I-918, Supplement A will result in termination of status for the qualifying family member. Revocation of an approved Form I-918 or Form I-918, Supplement A also revokes any waiver of inadmissibility granted in conjunction with such petition.

(i) Removal proceedings. Nothing in this section prohibits USCIS from instituting removal proceedings under section 240 of the Act, 8 U.S.C. 1229(a), for conduct committed after admission, for conduct or a condition that was not disclosed to USCIS prior to the granting of U nonimmigrant status, for misrepresentations of material facts in Form I-918 or Form I-918, Supplement A and supporting documentation, or after revocation of U nonimmigrant status.

HISTORY:

[72 FR 53014, 53036, Sept. 17, 2007, as corrected at 72 FR 54813, Sept. 27, 2007; 74 FR 55726, 55738, Oct. 28, 2009; 78 FR 18457, 18472, Mar. 27, 2013, as confirmed at 81 FR 91646, 91670, Dec. 19, 2016; 85 FR 46788, 46925, Aug. 3, 2020; 89 FR 6194, 6398, Jan. 31, 2024; redesignated at 89 FR 34864, 34931, Apr. 30, 2024]

§ 214.15 Certain spouses and children of lawful permanent residents.

(a) Aliens abroad. Under section 101(a)(15)(v) of the Act, certain eligible spouses and children of lawful permanent residents may apply for a V nonimmigrant visa at a consular office abroad and be admitted to the United States in V-1 (spouse), V-2 (child), or V-3 (dependent child of the spouse or child who is accompanying or following to join the principal beneficiary) nonimmigrant status to await the approval of:

(1) A relative visa petition;

(2) The availability of an immigrant visa number; or

(3) Lawful permanent resident (LPR) status through adjustment of status or an immigrant visa.

(b) Aliens already in the United States. Eligible aliens already in the United States may apply to the Service to obtain V nonimmigrant status for the same purpose. Aliens in the United States in V nonimmigrant status are entitled to reside in the United States as V nonimmigrants and obtain employment authorization.

(c) Eligibility. Subject to section 214(o) of the Act, an alien who is the beneficiary (including a child of the principal alien, if eligible to receive a visa under section 203(d) of the Act) of an immigrant visa petition to accord a status under section 203(a)(2)(A) of the Act that was filed with the Service under section 204 of the Act on or before December 21, 2000, may apply for V nonimmigrant status if:

(1) Such immigrant visa petition has been pending for 3 years or more; or

(2) Such petition has been approved, and 3 or more years have passed since such filing date, in either of the following circumstances:

(i) An immigrant visa is not immediately available to the alien because of a waiting list of applicants for visas under section 203(a)(2)(A) of the Act; or

(ii) The alien's application for an immigrant visa, or the alien's application for adjustment of status under section 245 of the Act, pursuant to the approval of such petition, remains pending.

(d) The definition of "pending petition." For purposes of this section, a pending petition is defined as a petition to accord a status under section 203(a)(2)(A) of the Act that was filed with USCIS under section 204 of the Act on or before December 21, 2000, and has not been adjudicated. In addition, the petition must have been properly filed according to 8 CFR 103.2(a), and if, subsequent to filing, USCIS returns the petition to the applicant for any reason or makes a request for evidence or issues a notice of intent to deny under 8 CFR 103.2(b), the petitioner must comply with the request within the time period set by USCIS. If USCIS denies a petition but the petitioner appeals that decision, the petition will be considered pending until the administrative appeal is decided by USCIS. A petition rejected by USCIS as not properly filed is not considered to be pending.

(e) Classification process for aliens outside the United States.

(1) V nonimmigrant visa. An eligible alien may obtain a V nonimmigrant visa from the Department of State at a consular office abroad pursuant to the procedures set forth in 22 CFR 41.86.

(2) Aliens applying for admission to the United States as a V nonimmigrant at a port-of-entry. Aliens applying under section 235 of the Act for admission to the United States at a port-of-entry as a V nonimmigrant must have a visa in the appropriate category. Such aliens are exempt from the ground of inadmissibility under section 212(a)(9)(B) of the Act.

(f) Application by aliens in the United States. An alien described in paragraph (c) of this section who is in the United States may apply to the Service to obtain V nonimmigrant status pursuant to the procedures set forth in this section and 8 CFR part 248. The alien must be admissible to the United States, except that, in determining the alien's admissibility in V nonimmigrant status, sections 212(a)(6)(A), (a)(7), and (a)(9)(B) of the Act do not apply.

(1) Contents of application. To apply for V nonimmigrant status, an eligible alien must submit:

(i) Form I-539, Application to Extend/Change Nonimmigrant Status, with the fee required by § 103.7(b)(1) of this chapter;

(ii) The fingerprint fee as required by § 103.2(e)(4) of this chapter;

(iii) Form I-693, Medical Examination of Aliens Seeking Adjustment of Status, without the vaccination supplement; and

(iv) Evidence of eligibility as described by Supplement A to Form I-539 and in paragraph (f)(2) of this section.

(2) Evidence. Supplement A to Form I-539 provides instructions regarding the submission of evidence. An alien applying for V nonimmigrant status with the Service should submit proof of filing of the immigrant petition that qualifies the alien for V status. Proof of filing may include Form I-797, Notice of Action, which serves as a receipt of the petition or as a notice of approval, or a receipt for a filed petition or notice of approval issued by a local district office. If the alien does not have such proof, the Service will review other forms of evidence, such as correspondence to or from the Service regarding a pending petition. If the alien does not have any of the items previously mentioned in this paragraph, but believes he or she is eligible for V nonimmigrant status, he or she should state where and when the petition was filed, the name and alien number

of the petitioner, and the names of all beneficiaries (if known).

(g) Period of admission.

(1) Spouse of an LPR. An alien admitted to the United States in V-1 nonimmigrant status (or whose status in the United States is changed to V-1) will be granted a period of admission not to exceed 2 years.

(2) Child of an LPR or derivative child. An alien admitted to the United States in V-2 or V-3 nonimmigrant status (or whose status in the United States is changed to V-2 or V-3) will be granted a period of admission not to exceed 2 years or the day before the alien's 21st birthday, whichever comes first.

(3) Extension of status. An alien may apply to the Service for an extension of V nonimmigrant status pursuant to this part and 8 CFR part 248. Aliens may apply for the extension of V nonimmigrant status, submitting Form I-539, and the associated filing fee, on or before 120 days before the expiration of their status. If approved, the Service will grant an extension of status to aliens in V nonimmigrant status who remain eligible for V nonimmigrant status for a period not to exceed 2 years, or in the case of a child in V-2 or V-3 status, the day before the alien's 21st birthday, whichever comes first.

(4) Special rules. The following special rules apply with respect to aliens who have a current priority date in the United States, but do not have a pending application for an immigrant visa abroad or an application to adjust status.

(i) For an otherwise eligible alien who applies for admission to the United States in a V nonimmigrant category at a designated Port-of-Entry and has a current priority date but does not have a pending immigrant visa abroad or application for adjustment of status in the United States, the Service will admit the alien for a 6-month period (or to the date of the day before the alien's 21st birthday, as appropriate).

(ii) For such an alien in the United States who applies for extension of V nonimmigrant status, the Service will grant a one-time extension not to exceed 6 months.

(iii) If the alien has not filed an application, either for adjustment of status or for an immigrant visa within that 6-month period, the alien cannot extend or be admitted or readmitted to V nonimmigrant status. If the alien does file an application, either for adjustment of status or for an immigrant visa within the time allowed, the alien will continue to be eligible for further extensions of V nonimmigrant status as provided in this section while that application remains pending.

(h) Employment authorization. An alien in V nonimmigrant status may apply to the Service for employment authorization pursuant to this section and § 274a.12(a)(15) of this chapter. An alien must file Form I-765, Application for Employment Authorization, with the fee required by 8 CFR 103.7. The Service will grant employment authorization to aliens in V nonimmigrant status who remain eligible for V nonimmigrant status valid for a period equal to the alien's authorized admission as a V nonimmigrant.

(i) **Travel abroad; unlawful presence. —**

(1) V nonimmigrant status in the United States. An alien who applies for and obtains V nonimmigrant status in the United States will be issued Form I-797, Notice of Action, indicating the alien's V status in the United States. Form I-797 does not serve as a travel document. If such an alien departs the United States, he or she must obtain a V visa from a consular office abroad in order to be readmitted to the United States as a V nonimmigrant. This visa requirement, however, does not apply if the alien traveled to contiguous territory or adjacent islands, possesses another valid visa, and is eligible for automatic revalidation.

(2) V nonimmigrants with a pending Form I-485. An alien in V nonimmigrant status with a pending Form I-485 (Application to Register Permanent Residence or Adjust Status) that was properly filed with the Service does not have to obtain advance parole in order to prevent the abandonment of that application when the alien departs the United States.

(3) Unlawful presence. —

(i) Nonimmigrant admission. An alien otherwise eligible for admission as a V nonimmigrant is not subject to the ground of inadmissibility under section 212(a)(9)(B) of the Act. This is true even if the alien had accrued more than 180 days of unlawful presence in the United States and is applying for admission as a nonimmigrant after travel abroad.

(ii) Permanent resident status. A V nonimmigrant alien is subject to the ground of inadmissibility under section 212(a)(9)(B) of the Act when applying for an immigrant visa or for adjustment of status to that of a lawful permanent resident. Therefore, a departure from the United States at any time after having accrued more than 180 days of unlawful presence will render the alien inadmissible under that section for the purpose of adjustment of status or admission as an immigrant, unless he or she has obtained a waiver under section 212(a)(9)(B)(v) of the Act or falls within one of the exceptions in section 212(a)(9)(B)(iii) of the Act.

(j) **Termination of status. —**

(1) General. The status of an alien admitted to the United States as a V nonimmigrant under section 101(a)(15)(V) of the Act shall be automatically terminated 30 days following the occurrence of any of the following:

(i) The denial, withdrawal, or revocation of the Form I-130, Petition for Immediate Relative, filed on behalf of that alien;

(ii) The denial or withdrawal of the immigrant visa application filed by that alien;

(iii) The denial or withdrawal of the alien's application for adjustment of status to that of lawful permanent residence;

(iv) The V-1 spouse's divorce from the LPR becomes final; or

(v) The marriage of an alien in V-2 or V-3 status.

(2) Dependents. When a principal alien's V nonimmigrant status is terminated, the V nonimmigrant status of any alien listed as a V-3 dependent or who is seeking derivative benefits is also terminated.

(3) Appeals. If the denial of the immigrant visa petition is appealed, the alien's V nonimmigrant status does not terminate until 30 days after the administrative appeal is dismissed.

(4) Violations of status. Nothing in this section precludes the Service from immediately initiating removal proceedings for other violations of an alien's V nonimmigrant status.

(k) Naturalization of the petitioner. If the lawful permanent resident who filed the qualifying Form I-130 immigrant visa petition subsequently naturalizes, the V nonimmigrant status of the spouse and any children will terminate after his or her current period of admission ends. However, in such a case, the alien spouse or child will be considered an immediate relative of a U.S. citizen as defined in section 201(b) of the Act and will immediately be eligible to apply for adjustment of status and related employment authorization. If the V-1 spouse or V-2 child had already filed an application for adjustment of status by the time the LPR naturalized, a new application for adjustment will not be required.

(l) Aliens in proceedings. An alien who is already in immigration proceedings and believes that he or she may have become eligible to apply for V nonimmigrant status should request before the immigration judge or the Board, as appropriate, that the proceedings be administratively closed (or before the Board that a previously-filed motion for reopening or reconsideration be indefinitely continued) in order to allow the alien to pursue an application for V nonimmigrant status with the Service. If the alien appears eligible for V nonimmigrant status, the immigration judge or the Board, whichever has jurisdiction, shall administratively close the proceeding or continue the motion indefinitely. In the event that the Service finds an alien eligible for V nonimmigrant status, the Service can adjudicate the change of status under this section. In the event that the Service finds an alien ineligible for V nonimmigrant status, the Service shall recommence proceedings by filing a motion to re-calendar.

HISTORY:

[66 FR 46697, 46702, Sept. 7, 2001; 72 FR 19100, 19107, Apr. 17, 2007; redesignated at 89 FR 34864, 34931, Apr. 30, 2024]

Subpart B

[Subpart B was added and reserved, effective Aug. 28, 2024. See 89 FR 34864, 34931, Apr. 30, 2024.]

Subpart C

Noncitizen Victims of Severe Forms of Trafficking in Persons

§ 214.200 Scope of this subpart.

This subpart governs the submission and adjudication of an Application for T Nonimmigrant Status, including a request by a principal applicant on behalf of an eligible family member for derivative status.

HISTORY:

[89 FR 34864, 34931, Apr. 30, 2024]

§ 214.201 Definitions.

Where applicable, USCIS will apply the definitions provided in section 103 and 107(e) of the Trafficking Victims Protection Act (TVPA), 22 U.S.C. 7102, and 8 U.S.C. 1101, 1182(d), and 1184, with due regard for the definitions and application of these terms in 28 CFR part 1100 and the provisions of 18 U.S.C. 77. As used in this section the term:

Abuse or threatened abuse of the legal process means the use or threatened use of a law or legal process whether administrative, civil, or criminal, in any manner or for any purpose for which the law was not designed, in order to exert pressure on another person to cause that person to take some action or refrain from taking some action.

Application for Derivative T Nonimmigrant Status means a request by a principal applicant on behalf of an eligible family member for derivative T-2, T-3, T-4, T-5, or T-6 nonimmigrant status on an Application for T Nonimmigrant Status.

Application for T Nonimmigrant Status means a request by a principal applicant for T-1 nonimmigrant status on the form designated by USCIS for that purpose.

Child means a person described in section 101(b)(1) of the Act.

Coercion means threats of serious harm to or physical restraint against any person; any scheme, plan, or pattern intended to cause a person to believe that failure to perform an act would result in serious harm to or physical restraint against any person; or the abuse or threatened abuse of the legal process.

Commercial sex act means any sex act on account of which anything of value is given to or received by any person.

Debt bondage means the status or condition of a debtor arising from a pledge by the debtor of their personal services or those of a person under their control as a security for debt, if the value of those services as reasonably assessed is not applied toward the liquidation of the debt or the length and nature of those services are not respectively limited and defined.

Derivative T nonimmigrant means an eligible family member who has been granted T-2, T-3, T-4, T-5, or T-6 derivative status. A family member outside of the United States is not a derivative T nonimmigrant until they are issued a T-2, T-3, T-4, T-5, or T-6 visa by the Department of State and they are admitted to the United States in derivative T nonimmigrant status.

Eligible family member means:

(1) A family member eligible for derivative T nonimmigrant status based on their relationship to a principal applicant or T-1 nonimmigrant and, if required, upon a showing of a present danger of retaliation;

(2) In the case of a principal applicant or T-1 nonimmigrant who is 21 years of age or older, the spouse and children of such applicant;

(3) In the case of a principal applicant or T-1 nonimmigrant under 21 years of age, the spouse, children, unmarried siblings under 18 years of age, and parents of such applicant; and

(4) Regardless of the age of a principal applicant or T-1 nonimmigrant, any parent or unmarried sibling under 18 years of age, or adult or minor child of a derivative of such principal applicant or T-1 nonimmigrant where the family member faces a present danger of retaliation as a result of the principal applicant or T-1 nonimmigrant's escape from a severe form of trafficking in persons or cooperation with law enforcement.

Involuntary servitude, for the purposes of this part:

(1) Means a condition of servitude induced by means of any scheme, plan, or pattern intended to cause a person to believe that, if the person did not enter into or continue in such condition, that person or another person would suffer serious harm or physical restraint; or a condition of servitude induced by the abuse or threatened abuse of legal process; and

(2) Includes a condition of servitude in which the victim is forced to work for the trafficker by the use or threat of physical restraint or physical injury, or by the use or threat of coercion through the law or the legal process. This definition encompasses those cases in which the trafficker holds the victim in servitude by placing the victim in fear of such physical restraint or injury or legal coercion.

Law Enforcement Agency (LEA) means a Federal, State, Tribal, or local law enforcement agency, prosecutor, judge, labor agency, children's protective services agency, adult protective services agency, or other authority that has the responsibility and authority for the detection, investigation, and/or prosecution of severe forms of trafficking in persons under any administrative, civil, criminal, or Tribal laws. Federal LEAs include but are not limited to the following: Department of Justice (including U.S. Attorneys' Offices, Civil Rights Division, Criminal Division, U.S. Marshals Service, Federal Bureau of Investigation (FBI)); U.S. Immigration and Customs Enforcement (ICE), U.S. Customs and Border Protection (CBP); Department of State (including Diplomatic Security Service); Department of Labor (DOL); Equal Employment Opportunity Commission (EEOC); National Labor Relations Board (NLRB); Offices of Inspectors General (OIG); Bureau of Indian Affairs (BIA) Police, and Offices for Civil Rights and Civil Liberties.

Law Enforcement Agency (LEA) declaration means an official LEA declaration submitted on the Declaration for Trafficking Victim.

Law enforcement involvement, for purposes of establishing physical presence, means law enforcement action beyond receiving the applicant's reporting and may include the LEA interviewing the applicant or otherwise becoming involved in detecting, investigating, or prosecuting the acts of trafficking.

Peonage means a status or condition of involuntary servitude based upon real or alleged indebtedness.

Principal applicant means a noncitizen who has filed an Application for T Nonimmigrant Status.

Request for assistance means a request made by an LEA to a victim to assist in the detection, investigation, or prosecution of the acts of trafficking in persons or the investigation of a crime where acts of trafficking are at least one central reason for the commission of that crime. The reasonableness of the request is assessed using the factors delineated at § 214.208(c).

Serious harm means any harm, whether physical or nonphysical, including psychological, financial, or reputational harm, that is sufficiently serious, under all the surrounding circumstances, to compel a reasonable person of the same background and in the same circumstances to perform or to continue performing labor or services in order to avoid incurring that harm.

Severe form of trafficking in persons means sex trafficking in which a commercial sex act is induced by force, fraud, or coercion, or in which the person induced to perform such act is under the age of 18 years; or the recruitment, harboring, transportation, provision, or obtaining of a person for labor or services through the use of force, fraud, or coercion for the purpose of subjection to involuntary servitude, peonage, debt bondage, or slavery.

Sex trafficking means the recruitment, harboring, transportation, provision, obtaining, patronizing, or soliciting of a person for the purpose of a commercial sex act.

T-1 nonimmigrant means the victim of a severe form of trafficking in persons who has been granted T-1 nonimmigrant status.

United States means the fifty States of the United States, the District of Columbia, the Commonwealth of Puerto Rico, the U.S. Virgin Islands, Guam, and the Commonwealth of the Northern Mariana Islands.

Victim of a severe form of trafficking in persons (victim) means a noncitizen who is or has been subjected to a severe form of trafficking in persons.

HISTORY:

[89 FR 34864, 34931, Apr. 30, 2024]

§ 214.202 Eligibility for T-1 nonimmigrant status.

An applicant is eligible for T-1 nonimmigrant status under section 101(a)(15)(T)(i) of the Act if they demonstrate all of the following, subject to section 214(o) of the Act:

(a) Victim. The applicant is or has been a victim of a severe form of trafficking in persons, according to § 214.206.

(b) Physical presence. The applicant is physically present in the United States, American Samoa, the Commonwealth of the Northern Mariana Islands, or at a port-of-entry thereto, according to § 214.207.

(c) Compliance with any reasonable request for assistance. The applicant has complied with any reasonable request for assistance from law enforcement or meets one of the conditions described below. The reasonableness of the request is assessed using the factors delineated at § 214.208(c).

(1) Exemption for minor victims. An applicant who was under 18 years of age at the time at least one act of trafficking occurred is not required to comply with any reasonable request for assistance.

(2) Exception for trauma. An applicant who, due to physical or psychological trauma, is unable to cooperate with a reasonable request for assistance from law enforcement is not required to comply with such reasonable request.

(d) Hardship. The applicant would suffer extreme hardship involving unusual and severe harm upon removal, according to § 214.209.

(e) Prohibition against traffickers in persons. No applicant will be eligible to receive T nonimmigrant status if there is substantial reason to believe that the applicant has committed an act of a severe form of trafficking in persons.

HISTORY:

[89 FR 34864, 34931, Apr. 30, 2024]

§ 214.203 Period of admission.

(a) T-1 Principal. T-1 nonimmigrant status may be approved for a period not to exceed 4 years, except as provided in section 214(o)(7) of the Act.

(b) Derivative family members. A derivative family member who is otherwise eligible for admission may be granted T-2, T-3, T-4, T-5, or T-6 nonimmigrant status for an initial period that does not exceed the expiration date of the initial period approved for the T-1 principal applicant, except as provided in section 214(o)(7) of the Act.

(c) Notice. At the time an applicant is approved for T nonimmigrant status or receives an extension of T nonimmigrant status, USCIS will notify the applicant when their T nonimmigrant status will expire. USCIS also will notify the applicant that the failure to apply for adjustment of status to lawful permanent resident during the period of T nonimmigrant status, as set forth in 8 CFR 245.23, will result in termination of the applicant's T nonimmigrant status in the United States at the end of the 4-year period or any extension.

HISTORY:

[89 FR 34864, 34931, Apr. 30, 2024]

§ 214.204 Application.

(a) Jurisdiction. USCIS has sole jurisdiction over all applications for T nonimmigrant status.

(b) Filing an application. An applicant seeking T-1 nonimmigrant status must submit an Application for T Nonimmigrant Status on the form designated by USCIS in accordance with 8 CFR 103.2 and with the evidence described in paragraph (c) of this section.

(1) Applicants in pending immigration proceedings.

(i) An applicant in removal proceedings under section 240 of the Act, or in exclusion or deportation proceedings under former sections 236 or 242 of the Act (as in effect prior to April 1, 1997), and who wishes to apply for T-1 nonimmigrant status must file an Application for T Nonimmigrant Status directly with USCIS.

(ii) In its discretion, ICE may exercise prosecutorial discretion, as appropriate, while USCIS adjudicates the Application for T Nonimmigrant Status, including applications for derivatives.

(2) Applicants with final orders of removal, deportation, or exclusion. An applicant subject to a final order of removal, deportation, or exclusion may file an Application for T Nonimmigrant Status directly with USCIS.

(i) The filing of an Application for T Nonimmigrant Status has no effect on DHS authority or discretion to execute a final order of removal, although the applicant may request an administrative stay of removal pursuant to 8 CFR 241.6(a).

(ii) If the applicant is in detention pending execution of the final order, the period of detention (under the standards of 8 CFR 241.4) reasonably necessary to bring about the applicant's removal will be extended during the period the stay is in effect.

(iii) If USCIS subsequently determines under the procedures in § 214.205 that the application is bona fide, the final order of removal, deportation, or exclusion will be automatically stayed, and the stay will remain in effect until a final decision is made on the Application for T Nonimmigrant Status.

(3) Referral of applicants for removal proceedings. USCIS generally will not refer an applicant for T nonimmigrant status for removal proceedings while the application is pending or following denial of the application, absent serious aggravating circumstances, such as the existence of an egregious criminal history, a threat to national security, or where the applicant is complicit in committing an act of trafficking.

(4) Minor applicants. When USCIS receives an application from a principal applicant under the age of 18, USCIS will notify the Department of Health and Human Services to facilitate the provision of interim assistance.

(c) Initial evidence. An Application for T Nonimmigrant Status must include:

(1) A detailed, signed personal statement from the applicant, in their own words, addressing:

(i) The circumstances surrounding the applicant's victimization, including:

(A) The nature of the victimization; and

(B) To the extent possible, the following:

(1) When the victimization occurred;

(2) How long the trafficking lasted;

(3) How and when they escaped, were rescued, or otherwise became separated from the traffickers;

(4) The events surrounding the trafficking;

(5) Who was responsible for the trafficking; and

(6) The circumstances surrounding their entry into the United States, if related to the trafficking;

(ii) How the applicant's physical presence in the United States relates to the trafficking;

(iii) The hardship, including harm or mistreatment the applicant fears if they are removed from the United States; and

(iv) Whether they have complied with any reasonable law enforcement request for assistance and whether any criminal, civil or administrative records relating to the acts of trafficking exist, if known, (or if applicable, why the age exemption or trauma exception applies); and

(2) Any credible evidence that supports any of the eligibility requirements set out in §§ 214.206 through 214.209.

(d) Inadmissible applicants. If an applicant is inadmissible to the United States, they must submit a request for a waiver of inadmissibility on the Application for Advance Permission to Enter as a Nonimmigrant, or successor form as designated by USCIS accordance with 8 CFR 103.2, in accordance with form instructions and 8 CFR 212.16, and accompanied by supporting evidence.

(e) Evidence from law enforcement. An applicant may wish to submit evidence from an LEA to help establish eligibility, including victimization and the compliance with reasonable requests for assistance. An LEA declaration:

(1) Is optional evidence;

(2) Is not given any special evidentiary weight;

(3) Does not grant an immigration benefit and does not lead to automatic approval of the Application for T Nonimmigrant Status;

(4) Must be submitted on the "Declaration for Trafficking Victim," and must be signed by a supervising official responsible for the detection, investigation, or prosecution of severe forms of trafficking in persons;

(5) Is completed at the discretion of the certifying official; and

(6) Does not require that a formal investigation or prosecution be initiated.

(f) Any credible evidence. All evidence demonstrating cooperation with law enforcement will be considered under the any credible evidence standard.

(g) USCIS determination. USCIS, not the LEA, will determine if the applicant was or is a victim of a severe form of trafficking in persons, and otherwise meets the eligibility requirements for T nonimmigrant status.

(h) Disavowed or withdrawn LEA declaration. An LEA may disavow or withdraw the contents of a previously submitted declaration and should provide a detailed explanation of its reasoning in writing. After disavowal or withdrawal, the LEA declaration generally will no longer be considered as evidence of the applicant's compliance with requests for assistance in the LEA's detection, investigation, or prosecution, but may be considered for other purposes.

(i) Continued Presence. An applicant granted Continued Presence under 28 CFR 1100.35 should submit documentation of the grant of Continued Presence. If revoked, the grant of Continued Presence will generally no longer be considered as evidence of the applicant's compliance with requests for assistance in the LEA's investigation or prosecution but may be considered for other purposes.

(j) Other evidence. An applicant may also submit any evidence regarding entry or admission into the United States or permission to remain in the United States. An applicant may also note that such evidence is contained in their immigration file.

(k) Biometric services. All applicants for T-1 nonimmigrant status must submit biometrics in accordance with 8 CFR 103.16.

(l) Evidentiary standards, standard of proof, and burden of proof.

(1) The burden is on the applicant to demonstrate eligibility for T-1 nonimmigrant status by a preponderance of the evidence. The applicant may submit any credible evidence relating to a T nonimmigrant application for consideration by USCIS.

(2) USCIS will conduct a review of all evidence and may investigate any aspect of the application.

(3) Evidence previously submitted by the applicant for any immigration benefit request or relief may be used by USCIS in evaluating the eligibility of an applicant for T-1 nonimmigrant status. USCIS will not be bound by previous factual determinations made in connection with a prior application or petition for any immigration benefit or relief. USCIS will determine, in its sole discretion, the evidentiary value of previously or concurrently submitted evidence.

(4) USCIS will consider the totality of the evidence the applicant submitted and other evidence available to USCIS in evaluating an Application for T Nonimmigrant Status.

(m) Bona fide determination. Once an applicant submits an Application for T Nonimmigrant Status or Application for Derivative T Nonimmigrant Status, USCIS will conduct an initial review to determine if the application is bona fide under the provisions of § 214.205. USCIS will conduct an initial review of an eligible family member's Application for Derivative T Nonimmigrant Status to determine if the application is bona fide if the principal's Application for T Nonimmigrant Status has been deemed bona fide.

(n) Decision. After completing its review of the application and evidence, USCIS will issue a decision approving or denying the application in accordance with 8 CFR 103.3.

(o) Approval. If USCIS determines that the applicant is eligible for T-1 nonimmigrant status, USCIS will approve the application and grant T-1 nonimmigrant status, subject to the annual limitation as provided in § 214.210. USCIS will provide the applicant with evidence of T-1 nonimmigrant status. USCIS may also notify other parties and entities of the approval as it determines appropriate, including any LEA providing an LEA declaration and the Department of Health and Human Service's Office of Refugee Resettlement, consistent with 8 U.S.C. 1367.

(1) Applicants with an outstanding order of removal, deportation, or exclusion issued by DHS. For an applicant who is the subject of an order of removal, deportation, or exclusion issued by DHS, the order will be deemed cancelled by operation of law as of the date of the USCIS approval of the application.

(2) Applicants with an outstanding order of removal, deportation, or exclusion issued by the Department of Justice. An applicant who is the subject of an order of removal, deportation or exclusion issued by an immigration judge or the Board of Immigration Appeals (Board) may seek rescission of such order by filing a

motion to reopen and terminate removal proceedings with the immigration judge or the Board. ICE may agree, as a matter of discretion, to join such motion to overcome any applicable time and numerical limitations of 8 CFR 1003.2 and 1003.23.

(3) Employment authorization. An individual granted T-1 nonimmigrant status is authorized to work incident to status. An applicant does not need to file a separate Application for Employment Authorization to be granted employment authorization. USCIS will issue an initial Employment Authorization Document (EAD) to such T-1 nonimmigrants for the duration of the T-1 nonimmigrant status. An applicant granted T-1 nonimmigrant status seeking to replace an EAD that was lost, stolen, or destroyed must file an Application for Employment Authorization in accordance with form instructions.

(p) Travel abroad. In order to return to the United States after travel abroad and continue to hold T-1 nonimmigrant status, a T-1 nonimmigrant must be granted advance parole pursuant to section 212(d)(5) of the Act prior to departing the United States.

(q) Denial. Upon denial of an application, USCIS will notify the applicant in accordance with 8 CFR 103.3. USCIS may also notify any LEA providing an LEA declaration and the Department of Health and Human Service's Office of Refugee Resettlement. If an applicant appeals a denial in accordance with 8 CFR 103.3, the denial will not become final until the administrative appeal is decided.

(1) Effect on bona fide determination. Upon denial of an application, any benefits derived from a bona fide determination will automatically be revoked when the denial becomes final.

(2) Applicants previously in removal proceedings. In the case of an applicant who was previously in removal proceedings that were terminated on the basis of a pending Application for T Nonimmigrant Status, once a denial becomes final, DHS may file a new Notice to Appear to place the individual in removal proceedings again.

(3) Applicants subject to an order of removal, deportation, or exclusion. In the case of an applicant who is subject to an order of removal, deportation, or exclusion that had been stayed due to the pending Application for T Nonimmigrant Status, the stay will be automatically lifted as of the date the denial becomes final.

HISTORY:

[89 FR 34864, 34931, Apr. 30, 2024, as corrected at 89 FR 68081, Aug. 23, 2024]

§ 214.205 Bona fide determination.

(a) Bona fide determinations for principal applicants for T nonimmigrant status. If an Application for T Nonimmigrant Status is submitted on or after August 28, 2024, USCIS will conduct an initial review to determine if the application is bona fide.

(1) Request for evidence. If an Application for T Nonimmigrant Status was pending as of August 28, 2024, and additional evidence is required to establish eligibility for principal T nonimmigrant status, USCIS will issue a request for evidence, and conduct a bona fide review based on available evidence.

(2) Initial review criteria. After initial review, USCIS will deem an Application for T Nonimmigrant Status bona fide if:

(i) The applicant has submitted a properly filed and complete Application for T Nonimmigrant Status;

(ii) The applicant has submitted a signed personal statement; and

(iii) The results of initial background checks are complete, have been reviewed, and do not present national security concerns.

(3) Secondary review criteria. If initial review does not establish an Application for T Nonimmigrant Status is bona fide, USCIS will conduct a full T nonimmigrant status eligibility review. An Application for T Nonimmigrant Status that meets all eligibility requirements will be approved, or if the statutory cap has been reached, will receive a bona fide determination.

(b) Bona fide determinations for eligible family members in the United States. Once a principal applicant's application has been deemed bona fide, USCIS will conduct an initial review for any eligible family members in the United States who have filed an Application for Derivative T Nonimmigrant Status to determine whether their applications are bona fide.

(1) If an Application for Derivative T Nonimmigrant Status was pending as of August 28, 2024, and additional evidence is required to establish eligibility for derivative T nonimmigrant status, USCIS will issue a request for evidence and conduct a bona fide review based on available evidence.

(2) After initial review, USCIS will determine an Application for Derivative T Nonimmigrant Status is bona fide if:

(i) The eligible family member is in the United States at the time of the bona fide determination;

(ii) The principal applicant or T-1 nonimmigrant has submitted a properly filed and complete Application for Derivative T Nonimmigrant Status;

(iii) The Application for Derivative T Nonimmigrant Status is supported by credible evidence that the derivative applicant qualifies as an eligible family member; and

(iv) Initial background checks are complete, have been reviewed, and do not present national security concerns.

(3) If initial review does not establish an Application for Derivative T Nonimmigrant Status is bona fide, USCIS will conduct a full T nonimmigrant status eligibility review. An Application for Derivative T Nonimmigrant Status that meets all eligibility requirements during this secondary review will be approved, or if the statutory cap has been reached, will receive a bona fide determination.

(c) Notice of USCIS determination. If USCIS determines that the Application for T Nonimmigrant Status or Application for Derivative T Nonimmigrant Status is bona fide under this section, USCIS will issue written notice of that determination, and inform the applicant that they may be considered for deferred action and may file an Application for Employment Authorization if they have not already filed one. The notice will also inform the applicant that any final order of removal, deportation, or exclusion is automatically stayed as set forth in paragraph (g) of this section. An application will be treated as a bona fide application as of the date of the notice.

(d) Not considered bona fide. If an application is incomplete or presents national security concerns, it will not be considered bona fide. There are no motion or appeal rights for a bona fide determination upon initial review under this section.

(1) For applications found not to be bona fide upon initial review, USCIS will proceed to full T nonimmigrant status eligibility review as described in paragraphs (a)(3) and (b)(3) of this section, generally in order of application receipt date.

(2) If an application is found through this review not to establish eligibility for T nonimmigrant status, the application will be denied in accordance with § 214.204(q).

(e) Exercise of discretion.

(1) Once USCIS deems an Application for T Nonimmigrant Status or Application for Derivative T Nonimmigrant Status bona fide, USCIS may consider the applicant for deferred action.

(2) If, after review of the available information including background checks, USCIS determines that deferred action is warranted in a particular case as an exercise of enforcement discretion, USCIS will then proceed to adjudication of the Application for Employment Authorization, if one has been filed.

(3) There are no motion or appeal rights for the exercise of enforcement discretion under this section.

(f) Bona fide determinations for applicants in removal proceedings. This section applies to applicants whose Applications for T Nonimmigrant Status or Applications for Derivative T Nonimmigrant Status have been deemed bona fide and who are in removal proceedings under section 240 of the Act, or in exclusion or deportation proceedings under former sections 236 or 242 of the Act (as in effect prior to April 1, 1997). In such cases, ICE may exercise prosecutorial discretion, as appropriate, while USCIS adjudicates an Application for T Nonimmigrant Status or an Application for Derivative T Nonimmigrant Status.

(g) Stay of final order of removal, deportation, or exclusion.

(1) If USCIS determines that an application is bona fide it automatically stays the execution of any final order of removal, deportation, or exclusion.

(2) This administrative stay will remain in effect until any adverse decision becomes final.

(3) Neither an immigration judge nor the Board has jurisdiction to adjudicate an application for a stay of removal, deportation, or exclusion on the basis of the filing of an Application for T Nonimmigrant Status or Application for Derivative T Nonimmigrant Status.

HISTORY:

[89 FR 34864, 34931, Apr. 30, 2024, as corrected at 89 FR 68081, Aug. 23, 2024; 90 FR 2921, Jan. 14, 2025]

§ 214.206 Victim of a severe form of trafficking in persons.

(a) Evidence. The applicant must submit evidence that demonstrates:

(1) That they are or have been a victim of a severe form of trafficking in persons. Except in instances of sex trafficking involving victims under 18 years of age, severe forms of trafficking in persons must involve both a particular means (force, fraud, or coercion) and a particular end or a particular intended end (sex trafficking, involuntary servitude, peonage, debt bondage, or slavery); or

(2) If an applicant has not performed labor or services, or a commercial sex act, they must establish that they were recruited, transported, harbored, provided, or obtained for the purposes of subjection to sex trafficking, involuntary servitude, peonage, debt bondage, or slavery, or patronized or solicited for the purposes of subjection to sex trafficking.

(3) The applicant may satisfy the requirements under paragraph (a)(1) or (2) of this section by submitting:

(i) The applicant's personal statement, which should describe the circumstances of the victimization suffered. For more information regarding the personal statement, see § 214.204(c).

(ii) Any other credible evidence, including but not limited to:

(A) Trial transcripts;

(B) Court documents;

(C) Police reports or other documentation from an LEA;

(D) News articles;

(E) Copies of reimbursement forms for travel to and from court;

(F) Affidavits from case managers, therapists, medical professionals, witnesses, or other victims in the same trafficking scheme;

(G) Correspondence or other documentation from the trafficker;

(H) Documents used in furtherance of the trafficking scheme such as recruitment materials, advertisements, pay stubs, logbooks, or contracts;

(I) Photographs or images;

(J) An LEA declaration as described in § 214.204(c); or

(K) Documentation of a grant of Continued Presence under 28 CFR 1100.35.

(b) [Reserved]

HISTORY:

[89 FR 34864, 34931, Apr. 30, 2024]

§ 214.207 Physical presence.

(a) Requirement. To be eligible for T-1 nonimmigrant status, an applicant must be physically present in the United States, American Samoa, the Commonwealth of the Northern Mariana Islands, or at a port-of-entry thereto on account of such trafficking. USCIS considers the applicant's presence in the United States at the time of application. An applicant must demonstrate that they are physically present under one of the following grounds:

(1) Are currently being subjected to a severe form of trafficking in persons;

(2) Were liberated from a severe form of trafficking in persons by an LEA, at any time prior to filing the Application for T Nonimmigrant Status;

(3) Escaped a severe form of trafficking in persons before an LEA was involved, at any time prior to filing the Application for T Nonimmigrant Status;

(4) Were subject to a severe form of trafficking in persons at some point in the past and their current presence in the United States is directly related to the original trafficking in persons, regardless of the length of time that has passed between the trafficking and filing of the Application for T Nonimmigrant Status; or

(5) Have been allowed entry into the United States for participation in the detection, investigation, prosecution, or judicial processes associated with an act or perpetrator of trafficking.

(i) An applicant will be deemed physically present under this provision regardless of where such trafficking occurred.

(ii) To demonstrate that the applicant's physical presence is for participation in an investigative or judicial process, the applicant must submit documentation to show valid entry into the United States and evidence that this valid entry is for participation in investigative or judicial processes associated with an act or perpetrator of trafficking.

(b) Departure from the United States. An applicant who has voluntarily departed from or has been removed from the United States at any time after the act of a severe form of trafficking in persons is deemed not to be present in the United States as a result of such trafficking in persons unless:

(1) The applicant's reentry into the United States was the result of the continued victimization of the applicant;

(2) The applicant is a victim of a new incident of a severe form of trafficking in persons;

(3) The applicant has been allowed reentry into the United States for participation in the detection, investigation, prosecution, or judicial process associated with an act or a perpetrator of trafficking. An applicant will be deemed physically present under this provision regardless of where such trafficking occurred. To demonstrate that the applicant's physical presence is for participation in an investigative or judicial process, the applicant must submit documentation to show valid entry into the United States and evidence that this valid entry is for participation in investigative or judicial processes associated with an act or perpetrator of trafficking;

(4) The applicant's presence in the United States is on account of their past or current participation in investigative or judicial processes associated with an act or perpetrator of trafficking, regardless of where such trafficking occurred. The applicant may satisfy physical presence under this provision regardless of the length of time that has passed between their participation in an investigative or judicial process associated with an act or perpetrator of trafficking and the filing of the Application for T Nonimmigrant Status; or

(5) The applicant returned to the United States and received treatment or services related to their victimization that cannot be provided in their home country or last place of residence outside the United States.

(c) Evidence. The applicant must submit evidence that demonstrates that their physical presence in the United States, American Samoa, the Commonwealth of the Northern Mariana Islands, or at a port-of-entry thereto, is on account of trafficking in persons. USCIS will consider any credible evidence presented to determine the physical presence requirement, including but not limited to:

(1) A detailed personal statement describing the applicant's current presence in the United States on account of the trafficking, including:

(i) The circumstances describing the victimization, including when the events took place, the length and severity of the trafficking, how and when the applicant escaped, was rescued, or otherwise became separated from the traffickers, when the trafficking ended, and when and how the applicant learned that they were a victim of human trafficking;

(ii) An explanation of any physical health effects or psychological trauma the applicant has suffered as a result of the trafficking and a description of how this trauma impacts the applicant's life at the time of filing;

(iii) The financial impact of the victimization;

(iv) The applicant's ability to access mental health services, social services, and legal services;

(v) Any relevant description of the applicant's cooperation with law enforcement at the time of filing;

(vi) A description of how the victimization relates to the applicant's current presence in the U.S., if relevant.

(2) Affidavits, evaluations, diagnoses, or other records from the applicant's service providers (including therapists, psychologists, psychiatrists, and social workers) documenting the therapeutic, psychological, or medical services the applicant has sought or is currently accessing as a result of victimization and that describe how the applicant's life is being impacted by the trauma at the time of filing, and describing any mental health conditions resulting from the trafficking;

(3) Documentation of any stabilizing services and benefits, including financial, language, housing, or legal resources, the applicant is accessing or has accessed as a result of being trafficked. For those services and benefits not currently being accessed, the record should demonstrate how those past services and benefits related to trauma the applicant is experiencing at the time of filing;

(4) An LEA declaration as described in § 214.204(c) or other statements from LEAs documenting the cooperation between the applicant and the LEA or law enforcement involvement in liberating the applicant;

(5) Documentation of a grant of Continued Presence under 28 CFR 1100.35;

(6) Any other documentation of entry into the United States or permission to remain in the United States, such as parole under section 212(d)(5) of the Act, or a

notation that such evidence is contained in the applicant's immigration file;

(7) Copies of news reports, law enforcement records, or court records; or

(8) Any other credible evidence to establish the applicant's current presence in the United States is on account of the trafficking victimization.

HISTORY:

[89 FR 34864, 34931, Apr. 30, 2024]

§ 214.208 Compliance with any reasonable request for assistance in the detection, investigation, or prosecution of an act of trafficking.

(a) Requirement. To be eligible for T-1 nonimmigrant status, an applicant must have complied with any reasonable request for assistance from an LEA in the detection, investigation, or prosecution of acts of trafficking or the investigation of a crime where acts of trafficking are at least one central reason for the commission of that crime, unless the applicant meets an exception or exemption described in paragraph (e) of this section.

(b) Applicability. An applicant must, at a minimum, contact an LEA with proper jurisdiction to report the acts of a severe form of trafficking in persons. Credible evidence documenting a single contact with an LEA may suffice. Reporting may be telephonic, electronic, or through other means. An applicant who has never had contact with an LEA regarding the acts of a severe form of trafficking in persons will not be eligible for T-1 nonimmigrant status, unless they meet an exemption or exception as described in paragraph (e) of this section.

(c) Reasonable requests. An applicant need only show compliance with reasonable requests made by an LEA for assistance in the investigation or prosecution of the acts of trafficking in persons. The reasonableness of the request depends on the totality of the circumstances. Factors to consider include, but are not limited to:

(1) General law enforcement and prosecutorial practices;

(2) The nature of the victimization;

(3) The specific circumstances of the victim;

(4) The victim's capacity, competency, or lack thereof;

(5) Trauma suffered (both mental and physical) or whether the request would cause further trauma;

(6) Access to support services;

(7) The safety of the victim or the victim's family;

(8) Compliance with previous requests and the extent of such compliance;

(9) Whether the request would yield essential information;

(10) Whether the information could be obtained without the victim's compliance;

(11) Whether a qualified interpreter or attorney was present to ensure the victim understood the request;

(12) Cultural, religious, or moral objections to the request;

(13) The time the victim had to comply with the request;

(14) The age, health, and maturity of the victim; and

(15) Any other relevant circumstances surrounding the request.

(d) Evidence. An applicant must submit evidence that demonstrates that they have complied with any reasonable request for assistance in a Federal, State, Tribal, or local detection, investigation, or prosecution of trafficking in persons, or a crime where trafficking in persons is at least one central reason for the commission of that crime. In the alternative, an applicant can submit evidence to demonstrate that they should be exempt under paragraph (e) of this section. If USCIS has any question about whether the applicant has complied with a reasonable request for assistance, USCIS may contact the LEA. The applicant may satisfy this requirement by submitting any of the following:

(1) An LEA declaration as described in § 214.204(c);

(2) Documentation of a grant of Continued Presence under 28 CFR 1100.35; or

(3) Any other evidence, including affidavits of witnesses. In the victim's statement prescribed by § 214.204(c), the applicant should show that an LEA that has responsibility and authority for the detection, investigation, or prosecution of severe forms of trafficking in persons has information about such trafficking in persons, that the victim has complied with any reasonable request for assistance in the investigation or prosecution of such acts of trafficking, and, if the victim did not report the crime, why the crime was not previously reported.

(e) Exception or exemption. An applicant who has not had contact with an LEA or who has not complied with any reasonable request may be excepted or exempt from the requirement to comply with any reasonable request for assistance in an investigation or prosecution if either of the following circumstances apply:

(1) Trauma. The applicant is unable to cooperate with a reasonable request for assistance from an LEA in the detection, investigation, or prosecution of acts of trafficking in persons due to physical or psychological trauma. An applicant must submit credible evidence of the trauma experienced. The applicant may satisfy this exception by submitting:

(i) A personal statement describing the trauma and explaining the circumstances surrounding the trauma the applicant experienced, including their age, background, maturity, health, disability, and any history of abuse or exploitation;

(ii) A signed statement from a qualified professional, such as a medical professional, mental health professional, social worker, or victim advocate, who attests to the victim's mental state or medical condition;

(iii) Medical or psychological records documenting the trauma or its impact;

(iv) Witness statements;

(v) Photographs;

(vi) Police reports;

(vii) Court records and court orders;

(viii) Disability determinations;

(ix) Government agency findings; or

(x) Any other credible evidence.

(2) Age. The applicant was under 18 years of age at the time of victimization. An applicant who was under 18 years of age at the time at least one of the acts of trafficking occurred is exempt from the requirement to comply with any reasonable request for assistance in the detection, investigation, or prosecution, but they must submit evidence of their age at the time of the victimization. Where available, an applicant should include an official copy of their birth certificate, a passport, or a certified medical opinion. USCIS will also consider any other credible evidence submitted regarding the age of the applicant.

(f) Exception or exemption established. When an applicant has established that the exception or exemption applies, they are not required to have had any contact with law enforcement or comply with future requests for assistance, including reporting the trafficking. USCIS reserves the authority and discretion to contact the LEA involved in the case, if appropriate.

HISTORY:

[89 FR 34864, 34931, Apr. 30, 2024]

§ 214.209 Extreme hardship involving unusual and severe harm.

To be eligible for T-1 nonimmigrant status, an applicant must demonstrate that removal from the United States would subject the applicant to extreme hardship involving unusual and severe harm.

(a) Standard. A finding of extreme hardship involving unusual and severe harm may be based on the following factors.

(b) Factors. Factors that may be considered in evaluating whether removal would result in extreme hardship involving unusual and severe harm should include both traditional extreme hardship factors and factors associated with having been a victim of a severe form of trafficking in persons. These factors include, but are not limited to:

(1) The age, maturity, and personal circumstances of the applicant;

(2) Any physical or psychological issues the applicant has that necessitate medical or psychological care not reasonably available in the foreign country to which the applicant would be returned;

(3) The nature and extent of the physical and psychological consequences of having been a victim of a severe form of trafficking in persons;

(4) The impact of the loss of access to the United States courts and the criminal justice system for purposes relating to the incident of a severe form of trafficking in persons or other crimes perpetrated against the applicant, including criminal and civil redress for acts of trafficking in persons, criminal prosecution, restitution, and protection;

(5) The reasonable expectation that the existence of laws, social practices, or customs in the foreign country to which the applicant would be returned would penalize the applicant severely for having been the victim of a severe form of trafficking in persons;

(6) The likelihood of re-victimization and the need, ability, and willingness of foreign authorities to protect the applicant;

(7) The likelihood that the trafficker or others acting on behalf of the trafficker in the foreign country would cause the applicant harm;

(8) The likelihood that the applicant's individual safety would be threatened by the existence of civil unrest or armed conflict; or

(9) Current or likelihood of future economic harm.

(c) Evidence.

(1) An applicant is encouraged to describe and document all factors that may be relevant to the case, as there is no guarantee that a particular reason(s) will satisfy the requirement.

(2) Hardship to persons other than the applicant may be considered in determining whether an applicant will suffer the requisite hardship only if the related evidence demonstrates specifically that the applicant will suffer extreme hardship upon removal as a result of hardship to persons other than the applicant.

(3) The applicant may satisfy this requirement by submitting any credible evidence regarding the nature and scope of the hardship if the applicant was removed from the United States, including evidence of hardship arising from circumstances surrounding the victimization and any other circumstances.

(4) An applicant may submit a personal statement or other evidence, including evidence from relevant country condition reports and any other public or private sources of information.

HISTORY:

[89 FR 34864, 34931, Apr. 30, 2024]

§ 214.210 Annual numerical limit.

(a) 5,000 per fiscal year. DHS may not grant T-1 nonimmigrant status to more than 5,000 principal applicants in any fiscal year.

(b) Waiting list. If the numerical limit prevents further grants of T-1 nonimmigrant status, USCIS will place applicants who receive a bona fide determination pursuant to § 214.205 on a waiting list. USCIS:

(1) Will assign priority on the waiting list based on the date the application was properly filed, with the oldest applications receiving the highest priority for processing;

(2) Will in the next fiscal year, issue a number to each application on the waiting list, in the order of the highest priority; and

(3) After T-1 nonimmigrant status has been issued to eligible applicants on the waiting list, USCIS will issue any remaining T-1 nonimmigrant numbers for that fiscal year to new eligible applicants in the order the applications were filed.

(c) Unlawful presence. While an applicant for T nonimmigrant status in the United States is on the waiting list, the applicant will not accrue unlawful presence under section 212(a)(9)(B) of the Act.

(d) Removal from the waiting list. An applicant may be removed from the waiting list consistent with law and policy. Applicants on the waiting list must remain admissible to the United States and otherwise eligible for T nonimmigrant status. If at any time prior to final adjudication USCIS receives information that an applicant is no longer eligible for T nonimmigrant status, the applicant may be removed from the waiting list. USCIS will provide notice to the applicant of that decision.

HISTORY:

[89 FR 34864, 34931, Apr. 30, 2024]

§ 214.211 Application for eligible family members.

(a) Eligibility.Subject to section 214(o) of the Act, an applicant who has applied for or has been granted T-1 nonimmigrant status (principal applicant) may apply for the admission of an eligible family member, who is otherwise admissible to the United States, in derivative T nonimmigrant status if accompanying or following to join the principal applicant.

(1) Principal applicant 21 years of age or older. For a principal applicant who is 21 years of age or over, eligible family member means a T-2 (spouse) or T-3 (child).

(2) Principal applicant under 21 years of age. For a principal applicant who is under 21 years of age, eligible family member means a T-2 (spouse), T-3 (child), T-4 (parent), or T-5 (unmarried sibling under the age of 18).

(3) Family member facing danger of retaliation. Regardless of the age of the principal applicant, if the eligible family member faces a present danger of retaliation as a result of the principal applicant's escape from the severe form of trafficking or cooperation with law enforcement, in consultation with the law enforcement agency investigating a severe form of trafficking, eligible family member means a T-4 (parent), T-5 (unmarried sibling under the age of 18), or T-6 (adult or minor child of a derivative of the principal applicant). In cases where the LEA has not investigated the acts of trafficking after the applicant has reported the crime, USCIS will evaluate any credible evidence demonstrating derivatives' present danger of retaliation.

(4) Admission requirements. The principal applicant must demonstrate that the applicant for whom derivative T nonimmigrant status is being sought is an eligible family member of the T-1 principal applicant, as defined in § 214.201, and is otherwise eligible for that status.

(b) Application.

(1) Application submission. A T-1 principal applicant may submit an Application for Derivative T Nonimmigrant Status in accordance with the form instructions.

(i) The Application for Derivative T Nonimmigrant Status for an eligible family member may be filed with the T-1 application, or separately.

(ii) T nonimmigrant status for eligible family members is dependent on the principal applicant having been granted T-1 nonimmigrant status and the principal applicant maintaining T-1 nonimmigrant status.

(iii) If a T-1 nonimmigrant cannot maintain status due to their death, the provisions of section 204(l) of the Act may apply.

(2) Eligible family members in pending immigration proceedings.

(i) If an eligible family member is in removal proceedings under section 240 of the Act, or in exclusion or deportation proceedings under former sections 236 or 242 of the Act (as in effect prior to April 1, 1997), the principal applicant or T-1 nonimmigrant must file an Application for Derivative T Nonimmigrant Status directly with USCIS.

(ii) At the request of the eligible family member, ICE may exercise prosecutorial discretion, as appropriate, while USCIS adjudicates an Application for Derivative T Nonimmigrant Status.

(3) Eligible family members with final orders of removal, deportation, or exclusion.

(i) If an eligible family member is the subject of a final order of removal, deportation, or exclusion, the principal applicant must file an Application for Derivative T Nonimmigrant Status directly with USCIS.

(ii) The filing of an Application for Derivative T Nonimmigrant Status has no effect on ICE's authority or discretion to execute a final order, although the applicant may file a request for an administrative stay of removal pursuant to 8 CFR 241.6(a).

(iii) If the eligible family member is in detention pending execution of the final order, the period of detention (under the standards of 8 CFR 241.4) will be extended while a stay is in effect for the period reasonably necessary to bring about the applicant's removal.

(c) Required supporting evidence. In addition to the form, an Application for Derivative T Nonimmigrant Status must include the following:

(1) Biometrics.

(2) Evidence demonstrating the relationship of an eligible family member, as provided in § 214.211(d).

(3) In the case of an applicant seeking derivative T nonimmigrant status based on danger of retaliation, evidence demonstrating this danger as provided in § 214.211.

(4) If an eligible family member is inadmissible based on a ground that may be waived, a request for a waiver of inadmissibility under section 212(d)(13) or section 212(d)(3) of the Act must be filed in accordance with § 212.16 of this subchapter and submitted with the completed application package.

(d) Relationship. Except as described in paragraph (e) of this section, the family relationship must exist at the time:

(1) The Application for T Nonimmigrant Status is filed;

(2) The Application for T Nonimmigrant Status is adjudicated;

(3) The Application for Derivative T Nonimmigrant Status is filed;

(4) The Application for Derivative T Nonimmigrant Status is adjudicated; and

(5) The eligible family member is admitted to the United States if residing abroad.

(e) Relationship and age-out protections—

(1) Protection for new child of a principal applicant. If the T-1 principal applicant establishes that they have become a parent of a child after filing the application for T-1 nonimmigrant status, the child will be deemed to be an eligible family member eligible to accompany or follow to join the T-1 principal applicant.

(2) Age-out protection for eligible family members of a principal applicant under 21 years of age.

(i) If the T-1 principal applicant was under 21 years of age when they applied for T-1 nonimmigrant status but reached 21 years of age while the principal application was still pending, USCIS will continue to consider a parent or unmarried sibling as an eligible family member.

(ii) A parent or unmarried sibling will remain eligible even if the principal applicant turns 21 years of age before adjudication of the application for T-1 nonimmigrant status.

(iii) An unmarried sibling will remain eligible even if the unmarried sibling is over 18 years of age at the time of adjudication of the T-1 application, so long as the unmarried sibling was under 18 years of age at the time the T-1 application was filed.

(iv) The age of an unmarried sibling when USCIS adjudicates the T-1 application, when the principal applicant or T-1 nonimmigrant files the Application for Derivative T Nonimmigrant Status, when USCIS adjudicates the derivative application, or when the unmarried sibling is admitted to the United States does not affect eligibility.

(3) Age-out protection for child of a principal applicant.

(i) USCIS will continue to consider a child as an eligible family member if the child was under 21 years of age at the time the principal filed the Application for T Nonimmigrant Status, but reached 21 years of age while the principal's application was still pending.

(ii) The child will remain eligible even if the child is over 21 years of age at the time of adjudication of the T-1 application.

(iii) As long as the child is under age 21 when the Application for T Nonimmigrant Status is filed and reaches age 21 while such application is pending, the age of the child when the principal applicant or T-1 nonimmigrant files the Application for Derivative T Nonimmigrant Status, when USCIS adjudicates the Application for Derivative T Nonimmigrant Status, or when the child is admitted to the United States does not affect eligibility.

(4) Marriage of an eligible family member.

(i) An eligible family member seeking T-3 or T-5 status must be unmarried when the principal applicant files an Application for T Nonimmigrant Status, when USCIS adjudicates the Application for T Nonimmigrant Status, when the principal applicant or T-1 nonimmigrant files the Application for Derivative T Nonimmigrant Status, when USCIS adjudicates the Derivative T Nonimmigrant Status, and if relevant, when the family member is admitted to the United States.

(ii) Principal applicants who marry while their Application for T Nonimmigrant Status is pending may file an Application for Derivative T Nonimmigrant Status on behalf of their spouse, even if the relationship did not exist at the time they filed their Application for T Nonimmigrant Status.

(iii) Similarly, the principal applicant may apply for a stepparent or stepchild if the qualifying relationship was created after they filed their Application for T Nonimmigrant Status but before it was approved.

(iv) USCIS evaluates whether the marriage creating the qualifying spousal relationship or stepchild and stepparent relationship exists at the time of adjudication of the principal's application and through completion of the adjudication of the derivative's application.

(f) Evidence demonstrating a present danger of retaliation. A principal applicant or T-1 nonimmigrant seeking derivative T nonimmigrant status for an eligible family member on the basis of facing a present danger of retaliation as a result of the principal applicant's or T-1 nonimmigrant's escape from a severe form of trafficking or cooperation with law enforcement, must demonstrate the basis of this danger. USCIS may contact the LEA involved, if appropriate. An applicant may satisfy this requirement by submitting:

(1) Documentation of a previous grant of advance parole to an eligible family member;

(2) A signed statement from a law enforcement agency describing the danger of retaliation;

(3) A personal statement from the principal applicant or derivative applicant describing the danger the family member faces and how the danger is linked to the victim's escape or cooperation with law enforcement; and/or

(4) Any other credible evidence, including trial transcripts, court documents, police reports, news articles, copies of reimbursement forms for travel to and from court, and affidavits from other witnesses. This evidence may be from the United States or any country in which the eligible family member is facing danger of retaliation.

(g) Biometric submission; evidentiary standards. The provisions for biometric submission and evidentiary standards described in § 214.204(b) and (d) apply to an eligible family member's Application for Derivative T Nonimmigrant Status.

(h) Review and decision. USCIS will review the application and issue a decision in accordance with paragraph (d) of this section.

(i) Derivative approvals. A noncitizen whose Application for Derivative T Nonimmigrant Status is approved is not subject to the annual limit described in § 214.210. USCIS will not approve an Application for Derivative T Nonimmigrant Status unless and until it has approved T-1 nonimmigrant status for the principal applicant.

(1) Approvals for eligible family members in the United States. When USCIS approves an Application for Derivative T Nonimmigrant Status for an eligible family member in the United States, USCIS will concurrently approve T nonimmigrant status for the eligible family member. USCIS will notify the T-1 nonimmigrant of such approval and provide evidence of T nonimmigrant status to the derivative.

(2) Approvals for eligible family members outside the United States. When USCIS approves an application

for an eligible family member outside the United States, USCIS will notify the T-1 nonimmigrant of such approval and provide the necessary documentation to the Department of State for consideration of visa issuance.

(3) Employment authorization.

(i) A noncitizen granted derivative T nonimmigrant status may apply for employment authorization by filing an Application for Employment Authorization in accordance with form instructions.

(ii) For derivatives in the United States, the Application for Employment Authorization may be filed concurrently with the Application for Derivative T Nonimmigrant Status or at any later time.

(iii) For derivatives outside the United States, an Application for Employment Authorization based on their T nonimmigrant status may only be filed after admission to the United States in T nonimmigrant status.

(iv) If the Application for Employment Authorization is approved, the derivative T nonimmigrant will be granted employment authorization pursuant to 8 CFR 274a.12(c)(25) for the period remaining in derivative T nonimmigrant status.

(4) Travel abroad. In order to return to the United States after travel abroad and continue to hold derivative T nonimmigrant status, a noncitizen granted derivative T nonimmigrant status must either be granted advance parole pursuant to section 212(d)(5) of the Act and 8 CFR 223 or obtain a T nonimmigrant visa (unless visa exempt under 8 CFR 212.1) and be admitted as a T nonimmigrant at a designated port of entry.

HISTORY:

[89 FR 34864, 34931, Apr. 30, 2024, as corrected at 89 FR 68081, Aug. 23, 2024]

§ 214.212 Extension of T nonimmigrant status.

(a) Eligibility. USCIS may grant extensions of T-1 nonimmigrant status beyond 4 years from the date of approval in 1-year periods from the date the T-1 nonimmigrant status ends if:

(1) An LEA detecting, investigating, or prosecuting activity related to acts of trafficking certifies that the presence of the applicant in the United States is necessary to assist in the detection, investigation, or prosecution of such activity; or

(2) USCIS determines that an extension is warranted due to exceptional circumstances.

(b) Application for a discretionary extension of status. Upon application, USCIS may extend T-1 nonimmigrant status based on law enforcement need or exceptional circumstances. A T-1 nonimmigrant may apply for an extension by submitting the form designated by USCIS in accordance with form instructions. A derivative T nonimmigrant may file for an extension of status independently if the T-1 nonimmigrant remains in valid T nonimmigrant status, or the T-1 nonimmigrant may file for an extension of T-1 status and request that this extension be applied to the derivative family members in accordance with the form instructions.

(c) Timely filing. An applicant should file the application to extend nonimmigrant status before the expiration of T nonimmigrant status. If T nonimmigrant status has expired, the applicant must explain in writing the reason for the untimely filing. USCIS may exercise its discretion to approve an untimely filed application for extension of T nonimmigrant status.

(d) Evidence. In addition to the application, a T nonimmigrant must include evidence to support why USCIS should grant an extension of T nonimmigrant status. The nonimmigrant bears the burden of establishing eligibility for an extension of status and that a favorable exercise of discretion is warranted.

(e) Evidence of law enforcement need. An applicant may demonstrate law enforcement need by submitting evidence that comes directly from an LEA, including:

(1) A new LEA declaration;

(2) Evidence from a law enforcement official, prosecutor, judge, or other authority who can detect, investigate, or prosecute acts of trafficking, such as a letter on the agency's letterhead, email, or fax; or

(3) Any other credible evidence.

(f) Exceptional circumstances.

(1) USCIS may, in its discretion, extend status beyond the 4-year period if it determines the extension of the period of such nonimmigrant status is warranted due to exceptional circumstances as described in section 214(o)(7)(iii) of the Act.

(2) USCIS may approve an extension of status for a principal applicant, based on exceptional circumstances, when an approved eligible family member is awaiting initial issuance of a T visa by an embassy or consulate and the principal applicant's T-1 nonimmigrant status is soon to expire.

(g) Evidence of exceptional circumstances.An applicant may demonstrate exceptional circumstances by submitting:

(1) The applicant's affirmative statement; or

(2) Any other credible evidence, including but not limited to:

(i) Medical records;

(ii) Police or court records;

(iii) News articles;

(iv) Correspondence with an embassy or consulate; and

(v) Affidavits from individuals with direct knowledge of or familiarity with the applicant's circumstances.

(h) Mandatory extensions of status for adjustment of status applicants. USCIS will automatically extend T nonimmigrant status when a T nonimmigrant properly files an application for adjustment of status during the period of T nonimmigrant status, in accordance with 8 CFR 245.23. No separate application for extension of T nonimmigrant status, or supporting evidence, is required.

HISTORY:

[89 FR 34864, 34931, Apr. 30, 2024]

§ 214.213 Revocation of approved T nonimmigrant status.

(a) Automatic revocation of derivative status. An approved Application for Derivative T Nonimmigrant

Status will be revoked automatically if the family member with an approved derivative application notifies USCIS that they will not apply for admission to the United States. An automatic revocation cannot be appealed.

(b) Revocation on notice/grounds for revocation. USCIS may revoke an approved Application for T Nonimmigrant Status following issuance of a notice of intent to revoke if:

(1) The approval of the application violated the requirements of section 101(a)(15)(T) of the Act or this subpart or involved error in preparation, procedure, or adjudication that led to the approval;

(2) In the case of a T-2 spouse, the applicant's divorce from the T-1 principal applicant has become final;

(3) In the case of a T-1 principal applicant, an LEA with jurisdiction to detect, investigate, or prosecute the acts of severe forms of trafficking in persons notifies USCIS that the applicant has refused to comply with a reasonable request to assist with the detection, investigation, or prosecution of the trafficking in persons and provides USCIS with a detailed explanation in writing; or

(4) The LEA that signed the LEA declaration withdraws it or disavows its contents and notifies USCIS and provides a detailed explanation of its reasoning in writing.

(c) Procedures.

(1) USCIS may revoke an approved application for T nonimmigrant status following a notice of intent to revoke.

(i) The notice of intent to revoke must be in writing and contain a statement of the grounds for the revocation and the time period allowed for the T nonimmigrant's rebuttal.

(ii) The T nonimmigrant may submit evidence in rebuttal within 30 days of the notice.

(iii) USCIS will consider all relevant evidence in determining whether to revoke the approved application for T nonimmigrant status.

(2) If USCIS revokes approval of the previously granted T nonimmigrant status application, USCIS:

(i) Will provide written notice to the applicant; and

(ii) May notify the LEA who signed the LEA declaration, any consular officer having jurisdiction over the applicant, or the Office of Refugee Resettlement of the Department of Health and Human Services.

(3) If an applicant appeals the revocation, the decision will not become final until the administrative appeal is decided in accordance with 8 CFR 103.3.

(d) Effect of revocation. Revocation of T-1 nonimmigrant status will terminate the principal's status as a T nonimmigrant and result in automatic termination of any derivative T nonimmigrant status. If a derivative application is pending at the time of revocation of T-1 nonimmigrant status, such pending applications will be denied. Revocation of a T-1 nonimmigrant status or derivative T nonimmigrant status also revokes any waiver of inadmissibility granted in conjunction with such application. The revocation of T-1 nonimmigrant status will have no effect on the annual numerical limit described in § 214.210.

HISTORY:
[89 FR 34864, 34931, Apr. 30, 2024]

§ 214.214 Removal proceedings.

(a) Nothing in this section prohibits DHS from instituting removal proceedings for conduct committed after admission, or for conduct or a condition that was not disclosed prior to the granting of T nonimmigrant status, including misrepresentations of material facts in the Application for T-1 Nonimmigrant Status or in an Application for Derivative T Nonimmigrant Status, or after revocation of T nonimmigrant status.

(b) ICE will maintain a policy regarding the exercise of discretion toward all applicants for T nonimmigrant status and T nonimmigrants. This policy will address, but need not be limited to, ICE's discretionary decision-making in proceedings before the Executive Office for Immigration Review and considerations related to ICE's immigration enforcement actions involving T visa applicants and T nonimmigrants.

HISTORY:
[89 FR 34864, 34931, Apr. 30, 2024]

§ 214.215 USCIS employee referral.

(a) Any USCIS employee who, while carrying out their official duties, comes into contact with a noncitizen believed to be a victim of a severe form of trafficking in persons and is not already working with an LEA may consult, as necessary, with the ICE officials responsible for victim protection, trafficking investigations and prevention, and deterrence.

(b) The ICE office may, in turn, refer the victim to another LEA with responsibility for detecting, investigating, or prosecuting acts of trafficking.

(c) If the noncitizen has a credible claim to victimization, USCIS may advise the individual that they can submit an Application for T Nonimmigrant Status and seek any other benefit or protection for which they may be eligible, provided doing so would not compromise the noncitizen's safety.

HISTORY:
[89 FR 34864, 34931, Apr. 30, 2024]

§ 214.216 Restrictions on use and disclosure of information relating to applicants for T nonimmigrant classification.

(a) The use or disclosure (other than to a sworn officer or employee of DHS, the Department of Justice, the Department of State, or a bureau or agency of any of those departments, for legitimate department, bureau, or agency purposes) of any information relating to the beneficiary of a pending or approved Application for T Nonimmigrant Status is prohibited unless the disclosure is made in accordance with an exception described in 8 U.S.C. 1367(b).

(b) Information protected under 8 U.S.C. 1367(a)(2) may be disclosed to Federal prosecutors to comply with constitutional obligations to provide statements by witnesses and certain other documents to defendants in pending Federal criminal proceedings.

(c) Agencies receiving information under this section, whether governmental or non-governmental, are bound by the confidentiality provisions and other restrictions set out in 8 U.S.C. 1367.

(d) DHS officials are prohibited from making adverse determinations of admissibility or deportability based on information obtained solely from the trafficker, unless the applicant has been convicted of a crime or crimes listed in section 237(a)(2) of the Act.

HISTORY:

[89 FR 34864, 34931, Apr. 30, 2024]

PART 215

CONTROLS OF ALIENS DEPARTING FROM THE UNITED STATES; ELECTRONIC VISA UPDATE SYSTEM

AUTHORITY NOTE APPLICABLE TO ENTIRE PART:

AUTHORITY:

6 U.S.C. 202(4), 236; 8 U.S.C. 1101, 1103, 1104, 1184, 1185 (pursuant to Executive Order 13323 (Dec. 30, 2003)), 1365a note, 1379, 1731-32; and 8 CFR part 2.

Subpart A

Controls of Aliens Departing from the United States

§ 215.1 Definitions.

For the purpose of this subpart:

(a) The term alien means any person who is not a citizen or national of the United States.

(b) The term Commissioner means the Commissioner of Immigration and Naturalization.

(c) The term regional commissioner means an officer of the Immigration and Naturalization Service duly appointed or designated as a regional commissioner, or an officer who has been designated to act as a regional commissioner.

(d) The term district director means an officer of the Immigration and Naturalization Service duly appointed or designated as a district director, or an officer who has been designated to act as a district director.

(e) The term United States means the several States, the District of Columbia, Puerto Rico, the Virgin Islands, Guam, American Samoa, Swains Island, the Commonwealth of the Northern Mariana Islands (beginning November 28, 2009), and all other territory and waters, continental and insular, subject to the jurisdiction of the United States.

(f) The term continental United States means the District of Columbia and the several States, except Alaska and Hawaii.

(g) The term geographical part of the United States means:

(1) The continental United States,

(2) Alaska,

(3) Hawaii,

(4) Puerto Rico,

(5) The Virgin Islands,

(6) Guam,

(7) American Samoa,

(8) Swains Island, or

(9) The Commonwealth of the Northern Mariana Islands (beginning November 28, 2009).

(h) The term depart from the United States means depart by land, water, or air: (1) From the United States for any foreign place, or (2) from one geographical part of the United States for a separate geographical part of the United States: Provided, That a trip or journey upon a public ferry, passenger vessel sailing coastwise on a fixed schedule, excursion vessel, or aircraft, having both termini in the continental United States or in any one of the other geographical parts of the United States and not touching any territory or waters under the jurisdiction or control of a foreign power, shall not be deemed a departure from the United States.

(i) The term departure-control officer means any immigration officer as defined in the regulations of the Immigration and Naturalization Service who is designated to supervise the departure of aliens, or any officer or employee of the United States designated by the Governor of the Canal Zone, the High Commissioner of the Trust Territory of the Pacific Islands, or the governor of an outlying possession of the United States, to supervise the departure of aliens.

(j) The term port of departure means a port in the continental United States, Alaska, Guam, Hawaii, Puerto Rico, the Commonwealth of the Northern Mariana Islands (beginning November 28, 2009), or the Virgin Islands, designated as a port of entry by the

Secretary, or in exceptional circumstances such other place as the departure-control officer may, in his discretion, designate in an individual case, or a port in American Samoa, or Swains Island, designated as a port of entry by the chief executive officer thereof.

(k) The term special inquiry officer shall have the meaning ascribed thereto in section 101(b)(4) of the Immigration and Nationality Act.

HISTORY:

[45 FR 65516, Oct. 3, 1980; 74 FR 2824, 2836, Jan. 16, 2009; 74 FR 25387, 25388, May 28, 2009; 81 FR 72481, 72491, Oct. 20, 2016]

§ 215.2 Authority of departure-control officer to prevent alien's departure from the United States.

(a) No alien shall depart, or attempt to depart, from the United States if his departure would be prejudicial to the interests of the United States under the provisions of § 215.3. Any departure-control officer who knows or has reason to believe that the case of an alien in the United States comes within the provisions of § 215.3 shall temporarily prevent the departure of such alien from the United States and shall serve him with a written temporary order directing him not to depart, or attempt to depart, from the United States until notified of the revocation of the order.

(b) The written order temporarily preventing an alien, other than an enemy alien, from departing from the United States shall become final 15 days after the date of service thereof upon the alien, unless prior thereto the alien requests a hearing as hereinafter provided. At such time as the alien is served with an order temporarily preventing his departure from the United States, he shall be notified in writing concerning the provisions of this paragraph, and shall be advised of his right to request a hearing if entitled thereto under § 215.4. In the case of an enemy alien, the written order preventing departure shall become final on the date of its service upon the alien.

(c) Any alien who seeks to depart from the United States may be required, in the discretion of the departure-control officer, to be examined under oath and to submit for official inspection all documents, articles, and other property in his possession which are being removed from the United States upon, or in connection with, the alien's departure. The departure-control officer may permit certain other persons, including officials of the Department of State and interpreters, to participate in such examination or inspection and may exclude from presence at such examination or inspection any person whose presence would not further the objectives of such examination or inspection. The departure-control officer shall temporarily prevent the departure of any alien who refuses to submit to such examination or inspection, and may, if necessary to the enforcement of this requirement, take possession of the alien's passport or other travel document.

HISTORY:

[45 FR 65516, Oct. 3, 1980]

§ 215.3 Aliens whose departure is deemed prejudicial to the interests of the United States.

The departure from the United States of any alien within one or more of the following categories shall be deemed prejudicial to the interests of the United States.

(a) Any alien who is in possession of, and who is believed likely to disclose to unauthorized persons, information concerning the plans, preparation, equipment, or establishments for the national defense and security of the United States.

(b) Any alien who seeks to depart from the United States to engage in, or who is likely to engage in, activities of any kind designed to obstruct, impede, retard, delay or counteract the effectiveness of the national defense of the United States or the measures adopted by the United States or the United Nations for the defense of any other country.

(c) Any alien who seeks to depart from the United States to engage in, or who is likely to engage in, activities which would obstruct, impede, retard, delay, or counteract the effectiveness of any plans made or action taken by any country cooperating with the United States in measures adopted to promote the peace, defense, or safety of the United States or such other country.

(d) Any alien who seeks to depart from the United States for the purpose of organizing, directing, or participating in any rebellion, insurrection, or violent uprising in or against the United States or a country allied with the United States, or of waging war against the United States or its allies, or of destroying, or depriving the United States of sources of supplies or materials vital to the national defense of the United States, or to the effectiveness of the measures adopted by the United States for its defense, or for the defense of any other country allied with the United States.

(e) Any alien who is subject to registration for training and service in the Armed Forces of the United States and who fails to present a Registration Certificate (SSS Form No. 2) showing that he has complied with his obligation to register under the Universal Military Training and Service Act, as amended.

(f) Any alien who is a fugitive from justice on account of an offense punishable in the United States.

(g) Any alien who is needed in the United States as a witness in, or as a party to, any criminal case under investigation or pending in a court in the United States: Provided, That any alien who is a witness in, or a party to, any criminal case pending in any criminal court proceeding may be permitted to depart from the United States with the consent of the appropriate prosecuting authority, unless such alien is otherwise prohibited from departing under the provisions of this part.

(h) Any alien who is needed in the United States in connection with any investigation or proceeding being, or soon to be, conducted by any official executive, legislative, or judicial agency in the United States or by any governmental committee, board, bureau, commission, or body in the United States, whether national, state, or local.

(i) Any alien whose technical or scientific training and knowledge might be utilized by an enemy or a potential enemy of the United States to undermine and defeat the military and defensive operations of the United States or of any nation cooperating with the United States in the interests of collective security.

(j) Any alien, where doubt exists whether such alien is departing or seeking to depart from the United States voluntarily except an alien who is departing or seeking to depart subject to an order issued in extradition, exclusion, or deportation proceedings.

(k) Any alien whose case does not fall within any of the categories described in paragraphs (a) to (j), inclusive, of this section, but which involves circumstances of a similar character rendering the alien's departure prejudicial to the interests of the United States.

HISTORY:
[45 FR 65516, Oct. 3, 1980]

§ 215.4 Procedure in case of alien prevented from departing from the United States.

(a) Any alien, other than an enemy alien, whose departure has been temporarily prevented under the provisions of § 215.2, may, within 15 days of the service upon him of the written order temporarily preventing his departure, request a hearing before a special in quiry officer. The alien's request for a hearing shall be made in writing and shall be addressed to the district director having administrative jurisdiction over the alien's place of residence. If the alien's request for a hearing is timely made, the district director shall schedule a hearing before a special inquiry officer, and notice of such hearing shall be given to the alien. The notice of hearing shall, as specifically as security considerations permit, inform the alien of the nature of the case against him, shall fix the time and place of the hearing, and shall inform the alien of his right to be represented, at no expense to the Government, by counsel of his own choosing.

(b) Every alien for whom a hearing has been scheduled under paragraph (a) of this section shall be entitled: (1) To appear in person before the special inquiry officer, (2) to be represented by counsel of his own choice, (3) to have the opportunity to be heard and to present evidence, (4) to cross-examine the witnesses who appear at the hearing, except that if, in the course of the examination, it appears that further examination may divulge information of a confidential or security nature, the special inquiry officer may, in his discretion, preclude further examination of the witness with respect to such matters, (5) to examine any evidence in possession of the Government which is to be considered in the disposition of the case, provided that such evidence is not of a confidential or security nature the disclosure of which would be prejudicial to the interests of the United States, (6) to have the time and opportunity to produce evidence and witnesses on his own behalf, and (7) to reasonable continuances, upon request, for good cause shown.

(c) Any special inquiry officer who is assigned to conduct the hearing provided for in this section shall have the authority to: (1) Administer oaths and affirmations, (2) present and receive evidence, (3) interrogate, examine, and cross examine under oath or affirmation both the alien and witnesses, (4) rule upon all objections to the introduction of evidence or motions made during the course of the hearing, (5) take or cause depositions to be taken, (6) issue subpoenas, and (7) take any further action consistent with applicable provisions of law, Executive orders, proclamations, and regulations.

HISTORY:
[45 FR 65516, Oct. 3, 1980]

§ 215.5 Hearing procedure before special inquiry officer.

(a) The hearing before the special inquiry officer shall be conducted in accordance with the following procedure:

(1) The special inquiry officer shall advise the alien of the rights and privileges accorded him under the provisions of § 215.4.

(2) The special inquiry officer shall enter of record: (i) A copy of the order served upon the alien temporarily preventing his departure from the United States, and (ii) a copy of the notice of hearing furnished the alien.

(3) The alien shall be interrogated by the special inquiry officer as to the matters considered pertinent to the proceeding, with opportunity reserved to the alien to testify thereafter in his own behalf, if he so chooses.

(4) The special inquiry officer shall present on behalf of the Government such evidence, including the testimony of witnesses and the certificates or written statements of Government officials or other persons, as may be necessary and available. In the event such certificates or statements are received in evidence, the alien may request and, in the discretion of the special inquiry officer, be given an opportunity to interrogate such officials or persons, by deposition or otherwise, at a time and place and in a manner fixed by the special inquiry officer: Provided, That when in the judgment of the special inquiry officer any evidence relative to the disposition of the case is of a confidential or security nature the disclosure of which would be prejudicial to the interests of the United States, such evidence shall not be presented at the hearing but shall be taken into consideration in arriving at a decision in the case.

(5) The alien may present such additional evidence, including the testimony of witnesses, as is pertinent and available.

(b) A complete verbatim transcript of the hearing, except statements made off the record shall be recorded. The alien shall be entitled, upon request, to the loan of a copy of the transcript, without cost, subject to reasonable conditions governing its use.

(c) Following the completion of the hearing, the special inquiry officer shall make and render a recommended decision in the case, which shall be governed by and based upon the evidence presented at the hearing and any evidence of a confidential or security nature which the Government may have in its possession. The decision of the special inquiry officer shall recommend: (1) That the temporary order preventing the departure of the alien from the United States be made final, or (2) that the temporary order preventing the departure of the alien from the United States be revoked. This recommended decision of the special inquiry officer shall be made in writing and shall set forth the officer's reasons for such decision. The alien concerned shall at his request be furnished a copy of the recommended decision of the special inquiry officer, and shall be allowed a reasonable time, not to exceed 10 days, in which to submit representations with respect thereto in writing.

(d) As soon as practicable after the completion of the hearing and the rendering of a decision by the special inquiry officer, the district director shall forward the entire record of the case, including the recommended decision of the special inquiry officer and any written representations submitted by the alien, to the regional commissioner having jurisdiction over his district. After reviewing the record, the regional commissioner shall render a decision in the case, which shall be based upon the evidence in the record and on any evidence or information of a confidential or security nature which he deems pertinent. Whenever any decision is based in whole or in part on confidential or security information not included in the record, the decision shall state that such information was considered. A copy of the regional commissioner's decision shall be furnished the alien, or his attorney or representative. No administrative appeal shall lie from the regional commissioner's decision.

(e) Notwithstanding any other provision of this part, the Administrator of the Bureau of Security and Consular Affairs referred to in section 104(b) of the Immigration and Nationality Act, or such other officers of the Department of State as he may designate, after consultation with the Commissioner, or such other officers of the Immigration and Naturalization Service as he may designate, may at any time permit the departure of an individual alien or of a group of aliens from the United States if he determines that such action would be in the national interest. If the Administrator specifically requests the Commissioner to prevent the departure of a particular alien or of a group of aliens, the Commissioner shall not permit the departure of such alien or aliens until he has consulted with the Administrator.

(f) In any case arising under §§ 215.1 to 215.7, the Administrator shall, at his request, be kept advised, in as much detail as he may indicate is necessary, of the facts and of any action taken or proposed.

HISTORY:

[45 FR 65516, Oct. 3, 1980]

§ 215.6 Departure from the Canal Zone, the Trust Territory of the Pacific Islands, or outlying possessions of the United States.

(a) In addition to the restrictions and prohibitions imposed by the provisions of this part upon the departure of aliens from the United States, any alien who seeks to depart from the Canal Zone, the Trust Territory of the Pacific Islands, or an outlying possession of the United States shall comply with such other restrictions and prohibitions as may be imposed by regulations prescribed, with the concurrence of the Administrator of the Bureau of Security and Consular Affairs and the Commissioner, by the Governor of the Canal Zone, the High Commissioner of the Trust Territory of the Pacific Islands, or by the governor of an outlying possession of the United States, respectively. No alien shall be prevented from departing from such zone, territory, or possession without first being accorded a hearing as provided in §§ 215.4 and 215.5.

(b) The Governor of the Canal Zone, the High Commissioner of the Trust Territory of the Pacific Islands, or the governor of any outlying possession of the United States shall have the authority to designate any employee or class of employees of the United States as hearing officers for the purpose of conducting the hearing referred to in paragraph (a) of this section. The hearing officer so designated shall exercise the same powers, duties, and functions as are conferred upon special inquiry officers under the provisions of this part. The chief executive officer of such zone, territory, or possession shall, in lieu of the regional commissioner, review the recommended decision of the hearing officer, and shall render a decision in any case referred to him, basing it on evidence in the record and on any evidence or information of a confidential or a security nature which he deems pertinent.

HISTORY:

[45 FR 65516, Oct. 3, 1980]

§ 215.7 Instructions from the Administrator required in certain cases.

In the absence of appropriate instructions from the Administrator of the Bureau of Security and Consular Affairs, departure-control officers shall not exercise the authority conferred by § 215.2 in the case of any alien who seeks to depart from the United States in the status of a nonimmigrant under section 101(a)(15) (A) or (G) of the Immigration and Nationality Act, or in the status of a nonimmigrant under section 11(3), 11(4), or 11(5) of the Agreement between the United Nations and the United States of America regarding the Headquarters of the United Nations (61 Stat. 756): Provided, That in cases of extreme urgency, where the national security so requires, a departure-control officer may preliminarily exercise the authority conferred by § 215.2 pending the outcome of consultation with the Administrator, which shall be undertaken immediately. In all cases arising under this section, the decision of the Administrator shall be controlling: Provided, That any decision to prevent the departure of an alien shall be based upon a hearing and record as prescribed in this part.

HISTORY:

[45 FR 65516, Oct. 3, 1980]

§ 215.8 Requirements for biometric identifiers from aliens on departure from the United States.

(a)(1) The Secretary of Homeland Security, or his designee, may establish pilot programs at land border ports of entry, and at up to fifteen air or sea ports of entry, designated through notice in the Federal Register, through which the Secretary or his delegate may require an alien admitted to or paroled into the United States, other than aliens exempted under paragraph (a)(2) of this section or Canadian citizens under section 101(a)(15)(B) of the Act who were not otherwise required to present a visa or have been issued Form I-94 (see § 1.4) or Form I-95 upon arrival at the United States, who departs the United States from a designated port of entry, to provide fingerprints, photograph(s) or other specified biometric identifiers, documentation of his or her immigration status in the United States, and such other evidence as may be requested to determine the alien's identity and whether he or she has properly maintained his or her status while in the United States.

(2) The requirements of paragraph (a)(1) shall not apply to:

(i) Aliens younger than 14 or older than 79 on date of departure;

(ii) Aliens admitted on A-1, A-2, C-3 (except for attendants, servants, or personal employees of accredited officials), G-1, G-2, G-3, G-4, NATO-1, NATO-2, NATO-3, NATO-4, NATO-5, or NATO-6 visas, and certain Taiwan officials who hold E-1 visas and members of their immediate families who hold E-1 visas who are maintaining such status at time of departure, unless the Secretary of State and the Secretary of Homeland Security jointly determine that a class of such aliens should be subject to the requirements of paragraph (a)(1);

(iii) Classes of aliens to whom the Secretary of Homeland Security and the Secretary of State jointly determine it shall not apply; or

(iv) An individual alien to whom the Secretary of Homeland Security, the Secretary of State, or the Director of Central Intelligence determines it shall not apply.

(b) An alien who is required to provide biometric identifiers at departure pursuant to paragraph (a)(1) and who fails to comply with the departure requirements may be found in violation of the terms of his or her admission, parole, or other immigration status. In addition, failure of a covered alien to comply with the departure requirements could be a factor in support of a determination that the alien is ineligible to receive a future visa or other immigration status documentation, or to be admitted to the United States. In making this determination, the officer will consider the totality of the circumstances, including, but not limited to, all positive and negative factors related to the alien's ability to comply with the departure procedures.

(c) A covered alien who leaves the United States without complying with the departure requirements in this section may be found to have overstayed the period of his or her last admission where the available evidence clearly indicates that the alien did not depart the United States within the time period authorized at his or her last admission or extension of stay. A determination that the alien previously overstayed the terms of his admission may result in a finding of inadmissibility for accruing prior unlawful presence in the United States under section 212(a)(9) of the Immigration and Nationality Act or that the alien is otherwise ineligible for a visa or other authorization to reenter the United States, provided that all other requirements of section 212(a)(9) have been met. A determination that an alien who was admitted on the basis of a nonimmigrant visa has remained in the United States beyond his or her authorized period of stay may result in such visa being deemed void pursuant to section 222(g) of the Act (8 U.S.C. 1202(g)) where all other requirements of that section are also met.

HISTORY:

[69 FR 468, 480, Jan. 5, 2004; 69 FR 53318, 53333, Aug. 31, 2004, as corrected at 69 FR 58037, Sept. 29, 2004; 73 FR 77473, 77491, Dec. 19, 2008; 78 FR 18457, 18472, Mar. 27, 2013, as confirmed at 81 FR 91646, 91670, Dec. 19, 2016]

§ 215.9 Temporary Worker Visa Exit Program.

An alien admitted on certain temporary worker visas at a port of entry participating in the Temporary Worker Visa Exit Program must also depart at the end of his or her authorized period of stay through a port of entry participating in the program and must present designated biographic and/or biometric information upon departure. U.S. Customs and Border Protection will publish a Notice in the Federal Register designating which temporary workers must participate in the Temporary Worker Visa Exit Program, which ports of entry are participating in the program, which biographical and/or biometric information would be required, and the format for submission of that information by the departing designated temporary workers.

HISTORY:

[73 FR 76891, 76914, Dec. 18, 2008; 73 FR 78104, 78130, Dec. 19, 2008]

Subpart B

Electronic Visa Update System

§ 215.21 Purpose.

The purpose of this subpart is to establish an electronic visa update system for nonimmigrant aliens who hold a passport issued by an identified country containing a U.S. nonimmigrant visa of a designated category.

HISTORY:

[81 FR 72481, 72491, Oct. 20, 2016]

§ 215.22 Applicability.

This subpart is applicable to nonimmigrant aliens who hold a passport issued by an identified country containing a U.S. nonimmigrant visa of a designated category. The Secretary, in the Secretary's discretion and in consultation with the Secretary of State, may identify countries and designate nonimmigrant visa categories for purposes of this subpart. Notice of the identified countries and designated nonimmigrant visa categories will be published in the Federal Register .

HISTORY:

[81 FR 72481, 72491, Oct. 20, 2016]

§ 215.23 Definitions.

The following definitions apply for purposes of this subpart.

(a) Covered alien. A covered alien is a nonimmigrant alien who holds a passport issued by an EVUS country (as defined in paragraph (c) of this section) containing a U.S. nonimmigrant visa of a designated category.

(b) Electronic Visa Update System (EVUS). The Electronic Visa Update System (EVUS) is the electronic system used by a covered alien to provide required information to DHS after the receipt of his or her visa of a designated category.

(c) EVUS country. An EVUS country is a country that has been identified for inclusion in EVUS, through publication of a notice in the Federal Register, by the Secretary after consultation with the Secretary of State.

(d) Notification of compliance. A notification of compliance is a verification from CBP that a covered alien has successfully enrolled in EVUS. A notification of compliance is a positive determination that an alien's visa is:

(1) Not automatically provisionally revoked pursuant to 22 CFR 41.122(b)(3); and

(2) Is considered valid for travel to the United States as of the time of notification.

HISTORY:

[81 FR 72481, 72491, Oct. 20, 2016]

§ 215.24 Electronic Visa Update System (EVUS) requirements.

(a) Enrollment required. Each covered alien must initially enroll in EVUS, in accordance with paragraph (c)(1) of this section, by providing the information set forth in paragraph (d) of this section electronically through EVUS. Each covered alien who intends to travel to the United States must have a valid notification of compliance as set forth in paragraph (c)(2) of this section. Upon each successful enrollment or re-enrollment, CBP will issue a notification of compliance.

(b) Validity period of notification of compliance —

(1) General validity period. A notification of compliance will generally be valid for a period of two years from the date the notification of compliance is issued, except as provided in paragraph (b)(2) or (3) of this section.

(2) Exception. If the nonimmigrant alien's passport or nonimmigrant visa will expire in less than two years from the date the notification of compliance is issued, the notification will be valid until the date of expiration of the passport or nonimmigrant visa, whichever is sooner.

(3) Change in validity period of notification of compliance. The Secretary, in consultation with the Secretary of State, may increase or decrease the notification of compliance validity period otherwise authorized by paragraph (b)(1) of this section for an EVUS country. Any such increase or decrease would apply to subsequently issued notifications of compliance. Any changes to the validity period will be done through rulemaking. The EVUS Web site will be updated to reflect the specific duration of notification of compliance validity periods for each EVUS country.

(4) Relation to nonimmigrant visa validity. A notification of compliance is not valid unless the alien's nonimmigrant visa also is valid.

(c) Schedule for EVUS enrollment —

(1) Initial EVUS enrollment —

(i) Visas received prior to November 29, 2016. Each covered alien who received his or her nonimmigrant visa of a designated category prior to November 29, 2016 must initially enroll in EVUS by December 14, 2016, unless the covered alien intends to travel to the United States before that date, in which case the requirements for EVUS enrollment outlined in paragraph (c)(2) of this section apply.

(ii) Visas received on or after November 29, 2016. Each covered alien who received his or her nonimmigrant visa of a designated category on or after November 29, 2016 must initially enroll in EVUS upon receipt of such visa.

(2) EVUS re-enrollment requirements prior to travel to the United States—

(i) Individuals arriving at air or sea ports of entry. Each covered alien who intends to travel by air or sea to the United States on a nonimmigrant visa of a designated category must have a notification of compliance that is valid, as described in paragraph (b) of this section, prior to boarding a carrier destined for travel to the United States through the date when the covered alien will arrive at a U.S. port of entry.

(ii) Individuals arriving at land ports of entry. Each covered alien who intends to travel by land to the United States on a nonimmigrant visa of a designated category must have a notification of compliance that is valid, as described in paragraph (b) of this section, through the date of application for admission to the United States.

(d) Required EVUS enrollment elements. DHS will collect such information from covered aliens as DHS deems necessary in its discretion, after consultation with the Department of State. The required information will be reflected in the EVUS enrollment questions.

(e) EVUS re-enrollment required. Each covered alien must re-enroll in EVUS and obtain a new notification of compliance from CBP if any of the following occurs:

(1) The alien is issued a new passport or new nonimmigrant visa of a designated category;

(2) The alien changes his or her name;

(3) The alien changes his or her gender;

(4) There is any change to the alien's country of citizenship or nationality, including becoming a dual national; or

(5) The circumstances underlying the alien's previous responses to any of the EVUS enrollment questions requiring a "yes" or "no" response (eligibility questions) have changed.

(f) Limitation. A notification of compliance is not a determination that the covered alien is admissible to the United States. A determination of admissibility is made after an applicant for admission is inspected by a CBP officer at a U.S. port of entry.

(g) Noncompliance, expiration of notification of compliance, and change in EVUS status resulting in rescission of notification of compliance —

(1) Initial EVUS enrollment. Failure to initially enroll in EVUS in accordance with paragraph (c)(1) of this section will result in the automatic provisional revocation of the covered alien's nonimmigrant visa pursuant to 22 CFR 41.122(b)(3), pending enrollment.

(2) Expiration of notification of compliance. Upon expiration of a notification of compliance, as described in paragraph (b) of this section, the covered alien's nonimmigrant visa will be automatically provisionally revoked pursuant to 22 CFR 41.122(b)(3), pending re-enrollment. To prevent the automatic provisional revocation of his or her nonimmigrant visa due to the expiration of the notification of compliance, each covered alien must re-enroll in EVUS prior to such expiration.

(3) Unsuccessful EVUS enrollment. If a covered alien's EVUS enrollment or re-enrollment is unsuccessful, his or her nonimmigrant visa will be automatically provisionally revoked pursuant to 22 CFR 41.122(b)(3), pending successful enrollment or re-enrollment.

(4) Change in EVUS status after receipt of a notification of compliance. In the event that irreconcilable errors are discovered after the issuance of a notification of compliance, or other circumstances occur including but not limited to a change in the validity period of the notification of compliance as provided in paragraph (b) of this section, CBP may rescind the notification of compliance. If a covered alien's notification of compliance is rescinded, his or her nonimmigrant visa will be automatically provisionally revoked pursuant to 22 CFR 41.122(b)(3), pending successful enrollment. CBP will attempt to provide notification of a change in EVUS status to the covered alien through the provided email address.

(h) Reversal of an automatically provisionally revoked visa and steps to address an unsuccessful EVUS enrollment or rescission of a notification of compliance —

(1) Reversal of an automatically provisionally revoked visa. If a covered alien's nonimmigrant visa has been automatically provisionally revoked as described in paragraph (g)(1) or (2) of this section, the revocation of the alien's visa will be automatically reversed, following compliance with EVUS, if the visa remains valid and was not also revoked on other grounds. After a reversal of the revocation the visa will immediately resume the validity provided for on its face, pursuant to 22 CFR 41.122(b)(3), after the alien enrolls in EVUS and receives a notification of compliance.

(2) Unsuccessful EVUS enrollment. If a covered alien's EVUS enrollment is unsuccessful per paragraph (g)(3) of this section, the covered alien may re-attempt enrollment or contact CBP.

(3) Rescission of notification of compliance. If a covered alien's nonimmigrant visa has been automatically provisionally revoked as described in paragraph (g)(4) of this section, the covered alien may re-attempt enrollment or contact CBP.

HISTORY:

[81 FR 72481, 72491, Oct. 20, 2016]

PART 216

CONDITIONAL BASIS OF LAWFUL PERMANENT RESIDENCE STATUS

Rule

AUTHORITY NOTE APPLICABLE TO ENTIRE PART:

AUTHORITY:

8 U.S.C. 1101, 1103, 1154, 1184, 1186a, 1186b, and 8 CFR part 2.

§ 216.1 Definition of conditional permanent resident.

A conditional permanent resident is an alien who has been lawfully admitted for permanent residence within the meaning of section 101(a)(20) of the Act, except that a conditional permanent resident is also subject to the conditions and responsibilities set forth in section 216 or 216A of the Act, whichever is applicable, and part 216 of this chapter. Unless otherwise specified, the rights, privileges, responsibilities and duties which apply to all other lawful permanent residents apply equally to conditional permanent residents, including but not limited to the right to apply for naturalization (if otherwise eligible), the right to file petitions on behalf of qualifying relatives, the privilege of residing permanently in the United States as an immigrant in accordance with the immigration laws, such status not having changed; the duty to register with the Selective Service System, when required; and the responsibility for complying with all laws and regulations of the United States. All references within this chapter to lawful permanent residents apply equally to conditional permanent residents, unless otherwise specified. The conditions of section 216 of the Act shall not apply to lawful permanent resident status based on a self-petitioning relationship under section 204(a)(1)(A)(iii), 204(a)(1)(A)(iv), 204(a)(1)(b)(ii), or 204(a)(1)(B)(iii) of the Act or based on eligibility as the derivative child of a self-petitioning spouse under section 204(a)(1)(A)(iii) or 204(a)(1)(B)(ii) of the Act, regardless of the date on which the marriage to the abusive citizen or lawful permanent resident occurred.

HISTORY:

[53 FR 30018, Aug. 10, 1988; 59 FR 26590, May 23, 1994; 61 FR 13061, 13079, March 26, 1996]

§ 216.2 Notification requirements.

(a) When alien acquires status of conditional permanent resident. At the time an alien acquires conditional permanent residence through admission to the United States with an immigrant visa or adjustment of status under section 245 of the Act, the Service shall notify the alien of the conditional basis of the alien's status, of the requirement that the alien apply for removal of the conditions within the ninety days immediately preceding the second anniversary of the alien's having been granted such status, and that failure to apply for removal of the conditions will result in automatic termination of the alien's lawful status in the United States.

(b) When alien is required to apply for removal of the conditional basis of lawful permanent resident status. Approximately 90 days before the second anniversary of the date on which the alien obtained conditional permanent residence, the Service should notify the alien a second time of the requirement that the alien and the petitioning spouse or the alien entrepreneur must file a petition to remove the conditional basis of the alien's lawful permanent residence. Such notification shall be mailed to the alien's last known address.

(c) Effect of failure to provide notification. Failure of the Service to provide notification as required by either paragraph (a) or (b) of this section does not relieve the alien and the petitioning spouse, or the alien entrepreneur of the requirement to file a petition to remove conditions within the 90 days immediately preceding the second anniversary of the date on which the alien obtained permanent residence.

HISTORY:

[53 FR 30018, Aug. 10, 1988; 59 FR 26590, May 23, 1994]

§ 216.3 Termination of conditional resident status.

(a) During the two-year conditional period. The director shall send a formal written notice to the conditional permanent resident of the termination of the alien's conditional permanent resident status if the director determines that any of the conditions set forth in section 216(b)(1) or 216A(b)(1) of the Act, whichever is applicable, are true, or it becomes known to the government that an alien entrepreneur who was admitted pursuant to section 203(b)(5) of the Act obtained his or her investment capital through other than legal means (such as through the sale of illegal drugs). If the Service issues a notice of intent to terminate an alien's conditional resident status, the director shall not adjudicate Form I-751 or Form I-829 until it has been determined that the alien's status will not be terminated. During this time, the alien shall continue to be a lawful conditional permanent resident with all the rights, privileges, and responsibilities provided to persons possessing such status. Prior to issuing the notice of termination, the director shall provide the alien with an opportunity to review and rebut the evidence upon which the decision is to be based, in accordance with § 103.2(b)(2) of this chapter. The termination of status, and all of the rights and privileges concomitant thereto (including authorization to accept or continue in employment in this country), shall take effect as of the date of such determination by the director, although the alien may request a review of such determination in removal proceedings. In addition to the notice of termination, the director shall issue a notice to appear in accordance with 8 CFR part 239. During the ensuing removal proceedings, the alien may submit evidence to rebut the determination of the director. The burden of proof shall be on the Service to establish, by a preponderance of the evidence, that one or more of the conditions in section 216(b)(1) or 216A(b)(1) of the Act, whichever is applicable, are true, or that an alien entrepreneur who was admitted pursuant to section 203(b)(5) of the Act obtained his or her investment capital through other than legal means (such as through the sale of illegal drugs).

(b) Determination of fraud after two years. If, subsequent to the removal of the conditional basis of an alien's permanent resident status, the director determines that an alien spouse obtained permanent resident status through a marriage which was entered into for the purpose of evading the immigration laws or an alien entrepreneur obtained permanent resident status through a commercial enterprise which was improper under section 216A(b)(1) of the Act, the director may institute rescission proceedings pursuant to section 246 of the Act (if otherwise appropriate) or removal proceedings under section 240 of the Act.

HISTORY:

[53 FR 30018, Aug. 10, 1988; 59 FR 26590, May 23, 1994; 62 FR 10312, 10349, March 6, 1997]

§ 216.4 Joint petition to remove conditional basis of lawful permanent resident status for alien spouse.

(a) **Filing the petition —**

(1) General procedures. Within the 90-day period immediately preceding the second anniversary of the date on which the alien obtained permanent residence, the alien and the alien's spouse who filed the original immigrant visa petition or fiance/fiancee petition through which the alien obtained permanent residence must file a Petition to Remove the Conditions on Residence (Form I-751) with the Service. The petition shall be filed within this time period regardless of the

amount of physical presence which the alien has accumulated in the United States. Before Form I-751 may be considered as properly filed, it must be accompanied by the fee required under 8 CFR 106.2 and by documentation as described in paragraph (a)(5) of this section, and it must be properly signed by the alien and the alien's spouse. If the joint petition cannot be filed due to the termination of the marriage through annulment, divorce, or the death of the petitioning spouse, or if the petitioning spouse refuses to join in the filing of the petition, the conditional permanent resident may apply for a waiver of the requirement to file the joint petition in accordance with the provisions of § 216.5 of this part. Upon receipt of a properly filed Form I-751, the alien's conditional permanent resident status shall be extended automatically, if necessary, until such time as the director has adjudicated the petition.

(2) Dependent children. Dependent children of a conditional permanent resident who acquired conditional permanent resident status concurrently with the parent may be included in the joint petition filed by the parent and the parent's petitioning spouse. A child shall be deemed to have acquired conditional residence status concurrently with the parent if the child's residence was acquired on the same date or within 90 days thereafter. Children who cannot be included in a joint petition filed by the parent and parent's petitioning spouse due to the child's not having acquired conditional resident status concurrently with the parent, the death of the parent, or other reasons may file a separate Petition to Remove the Conditions on Residence (Form I-751).

(3) [Reserved]

(4) Physical presence at time of filing. A petition may be filed regardless of whether the alien is physically present in the United States. However, if the alien is outside the United States at the time of filing, he or she must return to the United States, with his or her spouse and dependent children, to comply with the interview requirements contained in the Act. Furthermore, if the documentation submitted in support of the petition includes affidavits of third parties having knowledge of the bona fides of the marital relationship, the petitioner must arrange for the affiants to be present at the interview, at no expense to the government. Once the petition has been properly filed, the alien may travel outside the United States and return if in possession of documentation as set forth in § 211.1(b)(1) of this chapter, provided the alien and the petitioning spouse comply with the interview requirements described in § 216.4(b). An alien who is not physically present in the United States during the filing period but subsequently applies for admission to the United States shall be processed in accordance with § 235.11 of this chapter.

(5) Documentation. Form I-751 shall be accompanied by evidence that the marriage was not entered into for the purpose of evading the immigration laws of the United States. Such evidence may include:

(i) Documentation showing joint ownership of property;

(ii) Lease showing joint tenancy of a common residence;

(iii) Documentation showing commingling of financial resources;

(iv) Birth certificates of children born to the marriage;

(v) Affidavits of third parties having knowledge of the bona fides of the marital relationship, or

(vi) Other documentation establishing that the marriage was not entered into in order to evade the immigration laws of the United States.

(6) Termination of status for failure to file petition. Failure to properly file Form I-751 within the 90-day period immediately preceding the second anniversary of the date on which the alien obtained lawful permanent residence on a conditional basis shall result in the automatic termination of the alien's permanent residence status and the initiation of proceedings to remove the alien from the United States. In such proceedings the burden shall be on the alien to establish that he or she complied with the requirement to file the joint petition within the designated period. Form I-751 may be filed after the expiration of the 90-day period only if the alien establishes to the satisfaction of the director, in writing, that there was good cause for the failure to file Form I-751 within the required time period. If the joint petition is filed prior to the jurisdiction vesting with the immigration judge in removal proceedings and the director excuses the late filing and approves the petition, he or she shall restore the alien's permanent residence status, remove the conditional basis of such status and cancel any outstanding notice to appear in accordance with § 239.2 of this chapter. If the joint petition is not filed until after jurisdiction vests with the immigration judge, the immigration judge may terminate the matter upon joint motion by the alien and the Service.

(b) **Interview —**

(1) Authority to waive interview. The director of the regional service center shall review the Form I-751 filed by the alien and the alien's spouse to determine whether to waive the interview required by the Act. If satisfied that the marriage was not for the purpose of evading the immigration laws, the regional service center director may waive the interview and approve the petition. If not so satisfied, then the regional service center director shall forward the petition to the district director having jurisdiction over the place of the alien's residence so that an interview of both the alien and the alien's spouse may be conducted. The director must either waive the requirement for an interview and adjudicate the petition or arrange for an interview within 90 days of the date on which the petition was properly filed.

(2) Location of interview. Unless waived, an interview on the Form I-751 shall be conducted by an immigration examiner or other officer so designated by the district director at the district office, files control office or suboffice having jurisdiction over the residence of the joint petitioners.

(3) Termination of status for failure to appear for interview. If the conditional resident alien and/or the

petitioning spouse fail to appear for an interview in connection with the joint petition required by section 216(c) of the Act, the alien's permanent residence status will be automatically terminated as of the second anniversary of the date on which the alien obtained permanent residence. The alien shall be provided with written notification of the termination and the reasons therefor, and a notice to appear shall be issued placing the alien under removal proceedings. The alien may seek review of the decision to terminate his or her status in such proceedings, but the burden shall be on the alien to establish compliance with the interview requirements. If the alien submits a written request that the interview be rescheduled or that the interview be waived, and the director determines that there is good cause for granting the request, the interview may be rescheduled or waived, as appropriate. If the interview is rescheduled at the request of the petitioners, the Service shall not be required to conduct the interview within the 90-day period following the filing of the petition.

(c) Adjudication of petition. The director shall adjudicate the petition within 90 days of the date of the interview, unless the interview is waived in accordance with paragraph (b)(1) of this section. In adjudicating the petition the director shall determine whether —

(1) The qualifying marriage was entered into in accordance with the laws of the place where the marriage took place;

(2) The qualifying marriage has been judicially annulled or terminated, other than through the death of a spouse;

(3) The qualifying marriage was entered into for the purpose of procuring permanent residence status for the alien; or

(4) A fee or other consideration was given (other than a fee or other consideration to an attorney for assistance in preparation of a lawful petition) in connection with the filing of the petition through which the alien obtained conditional permanent residence. If derogatory information is determined regarding any of these issues, the director shall offer the petitioners the opportunity to rebut such information. If the petitioners fail to overcome such derogatory information the director may deny the joint petition, terminate the alien's permanent residence, and issue a notice to appear to initiate removal proceedings. If derogatory information not relating to any of these issues is determined during the course of the interview, such information shall be forwarded to the investigations unit for appropriate action. If no unresolved derogatory information is determined relating to these issues, the petition shall be approved and the conditional basis of the alien's permanent residence status removed, regardless of any action taken or contemplated regarding other possible grounds for removal.

(d) **Decision —**

(1) Approval. If the director approves the joint petition he or she shall provide written notice of the decision to the alien and shall require the alien to report to the appropriate office of the Service for processing for a new Permanent Resident Card (if necessary), at which time the alien shall surrender any Permanent Resident Card previously issued.

(2) Denial. If the director denies the joint petition, he or she shall provide written notice to the alien of the decision and the reason(s) therefor and shall issue a notice to appear under section 239 of the Act and 8 CFR part 239. The alien's lawful permanent resident status shall be terminated as of the date of the director's written decision. The alien shall also be instructed to surrender any Permanent Resident Card previously issued by the Service. No appeal shall lie from the decision of the director; however, the alien may seek review of the decision in removal proceedings. In such proceedings the burden of proof shall be on the Service to establish, by a preponderance of the evidence, that the facts and information set forth by the petitioners are not true or that the petition was properly denied.

HISTORY:

[53 FR 30018, Aug. 10, 1988, as amended at 54 FR 30369, July 20, 1989; 59 FR 26590, 26591, May 23, 1994; 62 FR 10312, 10349, March 6, 1997; 63 FR 70313, 70315, Dec. 21, 1998; 74 FR 26933, 26939, June 5, 2009; 85 FR 46788, 46925, Aug. 3, 2020]

§ 216.5 Waiver of requirement to file joint petition to remove conditions by alien spouse.

(a) General.

(1) A conditional resident alien who is unable to meet the requirements under section 216 of the Act for a joint petition for removal of the conditional basis of his or her permanent resident status may file Form I-751, Petition to Remove the Conditions on Residence, if the alien requests a waiver, was not at fault in failing to meet the filing requirement, and the conditional resident alien is able to establish that:

(i) Deportation or removal from the United States would result in extreme hardship;

(ii) The marriage upon which his or her status was based was entered into in good faith by the conditional resident alien, but the marriage was terminated other than by death, and the conditional resident was not at fault in failing to file a timely petition; or

(iii) The qualifying marriage was entered into in good faith by the conditional resident but during the marriage the alien spouse or child was battered by or subjected to extreme cruelty committed by the citizen or permanent resident spouse or parent.

(2) A conditional resident who is in exclusion, deportation, or removal proceedings may apply for the waiver only until such time as there is a final order of exclusion, deportation or removal.

(b) Fee. Form I-751 shall be accompanied by the appropriate fee required under 8 CFR 106.2.

(c) [Reserved]

(d) Interview. The service center director may refer the application to the appropriate local office and require that the alien appear for an interview in connection with the application for a waiver. The director shall deny the application and initiate removal proceedings if the alien fails to appear for the interview as required, unless the alien establishes good cause for such failure and the interview is rescheduled.

(e) **Adjudication of waiver application.**

(1) Application based on claim of hardship. In considering an application for a waiver based upon an alien's claim that extreme hardship would result from the alien's removal from the United States, the director shall take into account only those factors that arose subsequent to the alien's entry as a conditional permanent resident. The director shall bear in mind that any removal from the United States is likely to result in a certain degree of hardship, and that only in those cases where the hardship is extreme should the application for a waiver be granted. The burden of establishing that extreme hardship exists rests solely with the applicant.

(2) Application for waiver based upon the alien's claim that the marriage was entered into in good faith. In considering whether an alien entered into a qualifying marriage in good faith, the director shall consider evidence relating to the amount of commitment by both parties to the marital relationship. Such evidence may include —

(i) Documentation relating to the degree to which the financial assets and liabilities of the parties were combined;

(ii) Documentation concerning the length of time during which the parties cohabited after the marriage and after the alien obtained permanent residence;

(iii) Birth certificates of children born to the marriage; and

(iv) Other evidence deemed pertinent by the director.

(3) Application for waiver based on alien's claim of having been battered or subjected to extreme mental cruelty. A conditional resident who entered into the qualifying marriage in good faith, and who was battered or was the subject of extreme cruelty or whose child was battered by or was the subject of extreme cruelty perpetrated by the United States citizen or permanent resident spouse during the marriage, may request a waiver of the joint filing requirement. The conditional resident parent of a battered or abused child may apply for the waiver regardless of the child's citizenship or immigration status.

(i) For the purpose of this chapter the phrase "was battered by or was the subject of extreme cruelty" includes, but is not limited to, being the victim of any act or threatened act of violence, including any forceful detention, which results or threatens to result in physical or mental injury. Psychological or sexual abuse or exploitation, including rape, molestation, incest (if the victim is a minor) or forced prostitution shall be considered acts of violence.

(ii) A conditional resident or former conditional resident who has not departed the United States after termination of resident status may apply for the waiver. The conditional resident may apply for the waiver regardless of his or her present marital status. The conditional resident may still be residing with the citizen or permanent resident spouse, or may be divorced or separated.

(iii) Evidence of physical abuse may include, but is not limited to, expert testimony in the form of reports and affidavits from police, judges, medical personnel, school officials and social service agency personnel. The Service must be satisfied with the credibility of the sources of documentation submitted in support of the application.

(iv) The Service is not in a position to evaluate testimony regarding a claim of extreme mental cruelty provided by unlicensed or untrained individuals. Therefore, all waiver applications based upon claims of extreme mental cruelty must be supported by the evaluation of a professional recognized by the Service as an expert in the field. An evaluation which was obtained in the course of the divorce proceedings may be submitted if it was provided by a professional recognized by the Service as an expert in the field.

(v) The evaluation must contain the professional's full name, professional address and license number. It must also identify the licensing, certifying, or registering authority. The Service retains the right to verify the professional's license.

(vi) The Service's decision on extreme mental cruelty waivers will be based upon the evaluation of the recognized professional. The Service reserves the right to request additional evaluations from expert witnesses chosen by the Service. Requests for additional evaluations must be authorized by the Assistant Regional Commissioner for Adjudications.

(vii) Licensed clinical social workers, psychologists, and psychiatrists are professionals recognized by the Service for the purpose of this section. A clinical social worker who is not licensed only because the state in which he or she practices does not provide for licensing will be considered a licensed professional recognized by the Service if he or she is included in the Register of Clinical Social Workers published by the National Association of Social Workers or is certified by the American Board of Examiners in Clinical Social Work.

(viii) As directed by the statute, the information contained in the application and supporting documents shall not be released without a court order or the written consent of the applicant; or, in the case of a child, the written consent of the parent or legal guardian who filed the waiver application on the child's behalf. Information may be released only to the applicant, his or her authorized representative, an officer of the Department of Justice, or any federal or State law enforcement agency. Any information provided under this part may be used for the purposes of enforcement of the Act or in any criminal proceeding.

(f) Decision. The director shall provide the alien with written notice of the decision on the application for waiver. If the decision is adverse, the director shall advise the alien of the reasons therefor, notify the alien of the termination of his or her permanent residence status, instruct the alien to surrender any Permanent Resident Card issued by the Service and issue a notice to appear placing the alien in removal proceedings. No appeal shall lie from the decision of the director; however, the alien may seek review of such decision in removal proceedings.

HISTORY:

[53 FR 30018, Aug. 10, 1988, as amended at 56 FR 22637, May 16, 1991; 59 FR 26591, May 23, 1994; 62 FR 10312, 10350, March

6, 1997; 63 FR 70313, 70315, Dec. 21, 1998; 74 FR 26933, 26939, June 5, 2009; 85 FR 46788, 46925, Aug. 3, 2020]

§ 216.6 Petition by entrepreneur to remove conditional basis of lawful permanent resident status. [Contingent]

(a) Filing the petition —

(1) General procedures. A petition to remove the conditional basis of the permanent resident status of an alien accorded conditional permanent residence pursuant to section 203(b)(5) of the Act must be filed by the alien entrepreneur on Form I–829, Petition by Entrepreneur to Remove Conditions. The alien entrepreneur must file Form I–829 within the 90-day period preceding the second anniversary of his or her admission to the United States as a conditional permanent resident. Before Form I–829 may be considered as properly filed, it must be accompanied by the fee required under § 103.7(b)(1) of this chapter, and by documentation as described in paragraph (a)(4) of this section, and it must be properly signed by the alien. Upon receipt of a properly filed Form I–829, the alien's conditional permanent resident status shall be extended automatically, if necessary, until such time as the director has adjudicated the petition. The entrepreneur's spouse and children should be included in the petition to remove conditions. Children who have reached the age of twenty-one or who have married during the period of conditional permanent residence and the former spouse of an entrepreneur, who was divorced from the entrepreneur during the period of conditional permanent residence, may be included in the alien entrepreneur's petition or may file a separate petition.

(2) [Reserved]

(3) Physical presence at time of filing. A petition may be filed regardless of whether the alien is physically present in the United States. However, if the alien is outside the United States at the time of filing, he or she must return to the United States, with his or her spouse and children, if necessary, to comply with the interview requirements contained in the Act. Once the petition has been properly filed, the alien may travel outside the United States and return if in possession of documentation as set forth in § 211.1(b)(1) of this chapter, provided the alien complies with the interview requirements described in paragraph (b) of this section. An alien who is not physically present in the United States during the filing period but subsequently applies for admission to the United States shall be processed in accordance with § 235.11 of this chapter.

(4) Documentation. The petition for removal of conditions must be accompanied by the following evidence:

(i) Evidence that a commercial enterprise was established by the alien. Such evidence may include, but is not limited to, Federal income tax returns;

(ii) Evidence that the alien invested or was actively in the process of investing the requisite capital. Such evidence may include, but is not limited to, an audited financial statement or other probative evidence; and

(iii) Evidence that the alien sustained the actions described in paragraph (a)(4)(i) and (a)(4)(ii) of this section throughout the period of the alien's residence in the United States. The alien will be considered to have sustained the actions required for removal of conditions if he or she has, in good faith, substantially met the capital investment requirement of the statute and continuously maintained his or her capital investment over the two years of conditional residence. Such evidence may include, but is not limited to, bank statements, invoices, receipts, contracts, business licenses, Federal or State income tax returns, and Federal or State quarterly tax statements.

(iv) Evidence that the alien created or can be expected to create within a reasonable time ten full-time jobs for qualifying employees. In the case of a "troubled business" as defined in 8 CFR 204.6(j)(4)(ii), the alien entrepreneur must submit evidence that the commercial enterprise maintained the number of existing employees at no less than the pre-investment level for the period following his or her admission as a conditional permanent resident. Such evidence may include payroll records, relevant tax documents, and Forms I–9.

(5) Termination of status for failure to file petition. Failure to properly file Form I–829 within the 90-day period immediately preceding the second anniversary of the date on which the alien obtained lawful permanent residence on a conditional basis shall result in the automatic termination of the alien's permanent resident status and the initiation of deportation proceedings. The director shall send a written notice of termination and an order to show cause to an alien entrepreneur who fails to timely file a petition for removal of conditions. No appeal shall lie from this decision; however, the alien may request a review of the determination during deportation proceedings. In deportation proceedings, the burden of proof shall rest with the alien to show by a preponderance of the evidence that he or she complied with the requirement to file the petition within the designated period. The director may deem the petition to have been filed prior to the second anniversary of the alien's obtaining conditional permanent resident status and accept and consider a late petition if the alien demonstrates to the director's satisfaction that failure to file a timely petition was for good cause and due to extenuating circumstances. If the late petition is filed prior to jurisdiction vesting with the immigration judge in deportation proceedings and the director excuses the late filing and approves the petition, he or she shall restore the alien's permanent resident status, remove the conditional basis of such status, and cancel any outstanding order to show cause in accordance with § 242.7 of this chapter. If the petition is not filed until after jurisdiction vests with the immigration judge, the immigration judge may terminate the matter upon joint motion by the alien and the Service.

(6) Death of entrepreneur and effect on spouse and children. If an entrepreneur dies during the prescribed two-year period of conditional permanent residence, the spouse and children of the entrepreneur will be eligible for removal of conditions if it can be demonstrated that the conditions set forth in paragraph (a)(4) of this section have been met.

(b) Petition review—

(1) Authority to waive interview. USCIS shall review the petition to remove conditions and the supporting documents to determine whether to waive the interview required by the Act. If satisfied that the requirements set forth in paragraph (c)(1) of this section have been met, USCIS may waive the interview and approve the petition. If not so satisfied, then USCIS may require that an interview of the investor be conducted.

(2) Location of interview. Unless waived, an interview relating to the petition to remove conditions for investors shall be conducted by a USCIS immigration officer at the office that has jurisdiction over either the location of the investor's commercial enterprise in the United States, the investor's residence in the United States, or the location of the adjudication of the petition, at the agency's discretion.

(3) Termination of status for failure to appear for interview. If the investor fails to appear for an interview in connection with the petition when requested by USCIS, the investor's permanent resident status will be automatically terminated as of the second anniversary of the date on which the investor obtained permanent residence. The investor will be provided with written notification of the termination and the reasons therefore, and a notice to appear shall be issued placing the investor in removal proceedings. The investor may seek review of the decision to terminate his or her status in such proceedings, but the burden shall be on the investor to establish by a preponderance of the evidence that he or she complied with the interview requirements. If the investor has failed to appear for a scheduled interview, he or she may submit a written request to USCIS asking that the interview be rescheduled or that the interview be waived. That request should explain his or her failure to appear for the scheduled interview, and if a request for waiver of the interview, the reasons such waiver should be granted. If USCIS determines that there is good cause for granting the request, the interview may be rescheduled or waived, as appropriate. If USCIS waives the interview, USCIS shall restore the investor's conditional permanent resident status, cancel any outstanding notice to appear in accordance with 8 CFR 239.2, and proceed to adjudicate the investor's petition. If USCIS reschedules that investor's interview, USCIS shall restore the investor's conditional permanent resident status, and cancel any outstanding notice to appear in accordance with 8 CFR 239.2.

(c) Adjudication of petition.

(1) The decision on the petition shall be made within 90 days of the date of filing or within 90 days of the interview, whichever is later. In adjudicating the petition, the director shall determine whether:

(i) A commercial enterprise was established by the alien;

(ii) The alien invested or was actively in the process of investing the requisite capital; and

(iii) The alien sustained the actions described in paragraphs (c)(1)(i) and (c)(1)(ii) of this section throughout the period of the alien's residence in the United States. The alien will be considered to have sustained the actions required for removal of conditions if he or she has, in good faith, substantially met the capital investment requirement of the statute and continuously maintained his or her capital investment over the two years of conditional residence.

(iv) The alien created or can be expected to create within a reasonable period of time ten full-time jobs to qualifying employees. In the case of a "troubled business" as defined in 8 CFR 204.6(j)(4)(ii), the alien maintained the number of existing employees at no less than the pre-investment level for the previous two years.

(2) If derogatory information is determined regarding any of these issues or it becomes known to the government that the entrepreneur obtained his or her investment funds through other than legal means (such as through the sale of illegal drugs), the director shall offer the alien entrepreneur the opportunity to rebut such information. If the alien entrepreneur fails to overcome such derogatory information or evidence the investment funds were obtained through other than legal means, the director may deny the petition, terminate the alien's permanent resident status, and issue an order to show cause. If derogatory information not relating to any of these issues is determined during the course of the interview, such information shall be forwarded to the investigations unit for appropriate action. If no unresolved derogatory information is determined relating to these issues, the petition shall be approved and the conditional basis of the alien's permanent resident status removed, regardless of any action taken or contemplated regarding other possible grounds for deportation.

(d) Decision—

(1) Approval. If, after initial review or after the interview, the director approves the petition, he or she will remove the conditional basis of the alien's permanent resident status as of the second anniversary of the alien's entry as a conditional permanent resident. He or she shall provide written notice of the decision to the alien and shall require the alien to report to the appropriate district office for processing for a new Permanent Resident Card, Form I–551, at which time the alien shall surrender any Permanent Resident Card previously issued.

(2) Denial. If, after initial review or after the interview, the director denies the petition, he or she shall provide written notice to the alien of the decision and the reason(s) therefor, and shall issue an order to show cause why the alien should not be deported from the United States. The alien's lawful permanent resident status and that of his or her spouse and any children shall be terminated as of the date of the director's written decision. The alien shall also be instructed to surrender any Permanent Resident Card previously issued by the Service. No appeal shall lie from this decision; however, the alien may seek review of the decision in deportation proceedings. In deportation proceedings, the burden shall rest with the Service to establish by a preponderance of the evidence that the facts and information in the alien's petition for removal

of conditions are not true and that the petition was properly denied.

HISTORY:

[59 FR 26591, May 23, 1994; 63 FR 70313, 70315, Dec. 21, 1998; 74 FR 26933, 26939, June 5, 2009; 84 FR 35750, 35809, July 24, 2019; 85 FR 46788, 46925, Aug. 3, 2020]

§ 216.6 Petition by investor to remove conditional basis of lawful permanent resident status. [Effective until contingency met]

(a) Filing the petition —

(1) General procedures

(i) A petition to remove the conditional basis of the permanent resident status of an investor accorded conditional permanent residence pursuant to section 203(b)(5) of the Act must be filed by the investor with the appropriate fee. The investor must file within the 90-day period preceding the second anniversary of the date on which the investor acquired conditional permanent residence. Before the petition may be considered as properly filed, it must be accompanied by the fee required under 8 CFR 106.2, and by documentation as described in paragraph (a)(4) of this section, and it must be properly signed by the investor. Upon receipt of a properly filed petition, the investor's conditional permanent resident status shall be extended automatically, if necessary, until such time as USCIS has adjudicated the petition.

(ii) The investor's spouse and children may be included in the investor's petition to remove conditions. Where the investor's spouse and children are not included in the investor's petition to remove conditions, the spouse and each child must each file his or her own petition to remove the conditions on their permanent resident status, unless the investor is deceased. If the investor is deceased, the spouse and children may file separate petitions or may be included in one petition. A child who reached the age of 21 or who married during the period of conditional permanent residence, or a former spouse who became divorced from the investor during the period of conditional permanent residence, may be included in the investor's petition or must each file a separate petition.

(2) [Reserved]

(3) Physical presence at time of filing. A petition may be filed regardless of whether the alien is physically present in the United States. However, if the alien is outside the United States at the time of filing, he or she must return to the United States, with his or her spouse and children, if necessary, to comply with the interview requirements contained in the Act. Once the petition has been properly filed, the alien may travel outside the United States and return if in possession of documentation as set forth in § 211.1(b)(1) of this chapter, provided the alien complies with the interview requirements described in paragraph (b) of this section. An alien who is not physically present in the United States during the filing period but subsequently applies for admission to the United States shall be processed in accordance with § 235.11 of this chapter.

(4) Documentation. The petition for removal of conditions must be accompanied by the following evidence:

(i) [Reserved]

(ii) Evidence that the alien invested or was actively in the process of investing the requisite capital. Such evidence may include, but is not limited to, an audited financial statement or other probative evidence; and

(iii) Evidence that the alien sustained the actions described in paragraph (a)(4)(i) and (a)(4)(ii) of this section throughout the period of the alien's residence in the United States. The alien will be considered to have sustained the actions required for removal of conditions if he or she has, in good faith, substantially met the capital investment requirement of the statute and continuously maintained his or her capital investment over the two years of conditional residence. Such evidence may include, but is not limited to, bank statements, invoices, receipts, contracts, business licenses, Federal or State income tax returns, and Federal or State quarterly tax statements.

(iv) Evidence that the alien created or can be expected to create within a reasonable time ten full-time jobs for qualifying employees. In the case of a "troubled business" as defined in 8 CFR 204.6(j)(4)(ii), the alien investor must submit evidence that the commercial enterprise maintained the number of existing employees at no less than the pre-investment level for the period following his or her admission as a conditional permanent resident. Such evidence may include payroll records, relevant tax documents, and Forms I-9.

(5) Termination of status for failure to file petition. Failure to properly file the petition to remove conditions within the 90-day period immediately preceding the second anniversary of the date on which the investor obtained lawful permanent residence on a conditional basis shall result in the automatic termination of the investor's permanent resident status and the initiation of removal proceedings. USCIS shall send a written notice of termination and a notice to appear to an investor who fails to timely file a petition for removal of conditions. No appeal shall lie from this decision; however, the investor may request a review of the determination during removal proceedings. In proceedings, the burden of proof shall rest with the investor to show by a preponderance of the evidence that he or she complied with the requirement to file the petition within the designated period. USCIS may deem the petition to have been filed prior to the second anniversary of the investor's obtaining conditional permanent resident status and accept and consider a late petition if the investor demonstrates to USCIS' satisfaction that failure to file a timely petition was for good cause and due to extenuating circumstances. If the late petition is filed prior to jurisdiction vesting with the immigration judge in proceedings and USCIS excuses the late filing and approves the petition, USCIS shall restore the investor's permanent resident status, remove the conditional basis of such status, and cancel any outstanding notice to appear in accordance with 8 CFR 239.2. If the petition is not filed until after jurisdiction vests with the immigration judge, the immigration judge

may terminate the matter upon joint motion by the investor and DHS.

(6) Death of investor and effect on spouse and children. If an investor dies during the prescribed 2-year period of conditional permanent residence, the spouse and children of the investor will be eligible for removal of conditions if it can be demonstrated that the conditions set forth in paragraph (a)(4) of this section have been met.

(b) Petition review—

(1) Authority to waive interview. USCIS shall review the petition to remove conditions and the supporting documents to determine whether to waive the interview required by the Act. If satisfied that the requirements set forth in paragraph (c)(1) of this section have been met, USCIS may waive the interview and approve the petition. If not so satisfied, then USCIS may require that an interview of the investor be conducted.

(2) Location of interview. Unless waived, an interview relating to the petition to remove conditions for investors shall be conducted by a USCIS immigration officer at the office that has jurisdiction over either the location of the investor's commercial enterprise in the United States, the investor's residence in the United States, or the location of the adjudication of the petition, at the agency's discretion.

(3) Termination of status for failure to appear for interview. If the investor fails to appear for an interview in connection with the petition when requested by USCIS, the investor's permanent resident status will be automatically terminated as of the second anniversary of the date on which the investor obtained permanent residence. The investor will be provided with written notification of the termination and the reasons therefore, and a notice to appear shall be issued placing the investor in removal proceedings. The investor may seek review of the decision to terminate his or her status in such proceedings, but the burden shall be on the investor to establish by a preponderance of the evidence that he or she complied with the interview requirements. If the investor has failed to appear for a scheduled interview, he or she may submit a written request to USCIS asking that the interview be rescheduled or that the interview be waived. That request should explain his or her failure to appear for the scheduled interview, and if a request for waiver of the interview, the reasons such waiver should be granted. If USCIS determines that there is good cause for granting the request, the interview may be rescheduled or waived, as appropriate. If USCIS waives the interview, USCIS shall restore the investor's conditional permanent resident status, cancel any outstanding notice to appear in accordance with 8 CFR 239.2, and proceed to adjudicate the investor's petition. If USCIS reschedules that investor's interview, USCIS shall restore the investor's conditional permanent resident status, and cancel any outstanding notice to appear in accordance with 8 CFR 239.2.

(c) Adjudication of petition.

(1) The decision on the petition shall be made within 90 days of the date of filing or within 90 days of the interview, whichever is later. In adjudicating the petition, the director shall determine whether:

(i) [Reserved]

(ii) The alien invested or was actively in the process of investing the requisite capital; and

(iii) The alien sustained the actions described in paragraphs (c)(1)(i) and (c)(1)(ii) of this section throughout the period of the alien's residence in the United States. The alien will be considered to have sustained the actions required for removal of conditions if he or she has, in good faith, substantially met the capital investment requirement of the statute and continuously maintained his or her capital investment over the two years of conditional residence.

(iv) The alien created or can be expected to create within a reasonable period of time ten full-time jobs to qualifying employees. In the case of a "troubled business" as defined in 8 CFR 204.6(j)(4)(ii), the alien maintained the number of existing employees at no less than the pre-investment level for the previous two years.

(2) If derogatory information is determined regarding any of these issues or it becomes known to the government that the investor obtained his or her investment funds through other than legal means, USCIS shall offer the investor the opportunity to rebut such information. If the investor fails to overcome such derogatory information or evidence that the investment funds were obtained through other than legal means, USCIS may deny the petition, terminate the investor's permanent resident status, and issue a notice to appear. If derogatory information not relating to any of these issues is determined during the course of the interview, such information shall be forwarded to the investigations unit for appropriate action. If no unresolved derogatory information is determined relating to these issues, the petition shall be approved and the conditional basis of the investor's permanent resident status removed, regardless of any action taken or contemplated regarding other possible grounds for removal.

(d) Decision—

(1) Approval. If, after initial review or after the interview, USCIS approves the petition, USCIS will remove the conditional basis of the investor's permanent resident status as of the second anniversary of the date on which the investor acquired conditional permanent residence. USCIS shall provide written notice of the decision to the investor. USCIS may request the investor and derivative family members to appear for biometrics at a USCIS facility for processing for a new Permanent Resident Card.

(2) Denial. If, after initial review or after the interview, USCIS denies the petition, USCIS will provide written notice to the investor of the decision and the reason(s) therefore, and shall issue a notice to appear. The investor's lawful permanent resident status and that of his or her spouse and any children shall be terminated as of the date of USCIS' written decision. The investor shall also be instructed to surrender any Permanent Resident Card previously issued by USCIS. No appeal shall lie from this decision; however, the

investor may seek review of the decision in removal proceedings. In proceedings, the burden shall rest with USCIS to establish by a preponderance of the evidence that the facts and information in the investor's petition for removal of conditions are not true and that the petition was properly denied.

HISTORY:

[59 FR 26591, May 23, 1994; 63 FR 70313, 70315, Dec. 21, 1998; 74 FR 26933, 26939, June 5, 2009; 84 FR 35750, 35809, July 24, 2019; 85 FR 46788, 46925, Aug. 3, 2020]

PART 217
VISA WAIVER PROGRAM

Rule

AUTHORITY NOTE APPLICABLE TO ENTIRE PART:

AUTHORITY:

8 U.S.C. 1103, 1187; 8 CFR part 2.

§ 217.1 Scope.

The Visa Waiver Program (VWP) described in this section is established pursuant to the provisions of section 217 of the Act.

HISTORY:

[53 FR 24901, June 30, 1988; 62 FR 10312, 10351, March 6, 1997; 87 FR 18967, 18980, Apr. 1, 2022]

§ 217.2 Eligibility.

(a) Definitions. As used in this part, the term:

Carrier refers to the owner, charterer, lessee, or authorized agent of any commercial vessel or commercial aircraft engaged in transporting passengers to the United States from a foreign place.

Designated country refers to any country currently designated by the Secretary for participation in the Visa Waiver Program. DHS maintains a list of designated countries at https://www.dhs.gov/visa-waiver-program.

Round trip ticket means any return trip transportation ticket in the name of an arriving Visa Waiver Program applicant on a participating carrier valid for at least 1 year, electronic ticket record, airline employee passes indicating return passage, individual vouchers for return passage, group vouchers for return passage for charter flights, and military travel orders which include military dependents for return to duty stations outside the United States on U.S. military flights. A period of validity of 1 year need not be reflected on the ticket itself, provided that the carrier agrees that it will honor the return portion of the ticket at any time, as provided in Form I-775, Visa Waiver Program Agreement.

(b) Special program requirements. —

(1) General. In addition to meeting all of the requirements for the Visa Waiver Program specified in section 217 of the Act, each applicant must possess a valid, unexpired passport issued by a designated country and obtain a travel authorization via the Electronic System for Travel Authorization (ESTA) as provided in § 217.5.

(2) Persons previously removed as deportable aliens. Aliens who have been deported or removed from the United States, after having been determined deportable, require the consent of the Attorney General to apply for admission to the United States pursuant to section 212(a)(9)(A)(iii) of the Act. Such persons may not be admitted to the United States under the provisions of this part notwithstanding the fact that the required consent of the Attorney General may have been secured. Such aliens must secure a visa in order to be admitted to the United States as nonimmigrants, unless otherwise exempt.

(c) Restrictions on manner of arrival. —

(1) Applicants arriving by air and sea. Applicants must arrive on a carrier that is signatory to a Visa Waiver Program Agreement and at the time of arrival must have a round trip ticket that will transport the traveler out of the United States to any other foreign port or place as long as the trip does not terminate in contiguous territory or an adjacent island; except that the round trip ticket may transport the traveler to contiguous territory or an adjacent island, if the traveler is a resident of the country of destination.

(2) Applicants arriving at land border ports of entry. Any Visa Waiver Program applicant arriving at a land border port of entry must provide evidence to the CBP officer of financial solvency and a domicile abroad to which the applicant intends to return. An applicant arriving at a land border port of entry will be charged a fee as prescribed in § 103.7(d)(5) of this chapter for issuance of Form I-94W, Nonimmigrant Visa Waiver Arrival/Departure Form. A round-trip transportation ticket is not required.

(d) Aliens in transit. An alien who is in transit through the United States is eligible to apply for admission under the Visa Waiver Program, provided the applicant meets all other program requirements.

HISTORY:

[53 FR 24901, June 30, 1988, as amended at 53 FR 50160, Dec. 13, 1988; 56 FR 32953, July 18, 1991; 60 FR 40068, Aug. 7, 1995; 62 FR 10312, 10351, March 6, 1997; 62 FR 50998, 50999, Sept. 30, 1997, as confirmed at 63 FR 71726, 71727, Dec. 30, 1998; 64 FR 42006, 42007, Aug. 3, 1999; 67 FR 7943, 7945, Feb. 21, 2002; 68 FR 10954, 10957, Mar. 7, 2003; 73 FR 67711, 67712, Nov. 17, 2008; 73 FR 79595, 79597, Dec. 30, 2008; 75 FR 15991, 15992, Mar. 31, 2010; 77 FR 64409, 64411, Oct. 22, 2012; 79 FR 17852, 17854, Mar. 31, 2014; 84 FR 60316, 60318, Nov. 8, 2019; 85 FR 46788, 46925, Aug. 3, 2020; 86 FR 54029, 54031, Sept. 30, 2021; 87 FR 18967, 18980, Apr. 1, 2022; 88 FR 67063, 67065, Sept. 29, 2023; 89 FR 78783, 78785, Sept. 26, 2024; 89 FR 105391, 105392, Dec. 27, 2024]

§ 217.3 Maintenance of status.

(a) Satisfactory departure. If an emergency prevents an alien admitted under this part from departing from the United States within his or her period of authorized stay, the district director having jurisdiction over the place of the alien's temporary stay may, in his or her discretion, grant a period of satisfactory departure not to exceed 30 days. If departure is accomplished during that period, the alien is to be regarded as having satisfactorily accomplished the visit without overstaying the allotted time.

(b) Readmission after departure to contiguous territory or adjacent island. An alien admitted to the United States under this part may be readmitted to the United States after a departure to foreign contiguous territory or adjacent island for the balance of his or her original Visa Waiver Program admission period if he or she is otherwise admissible and meets all the conditions of this part with the exception of arrival on a signatory carrier.

HISTORY:

[53 FR 24901, June 30, 1988, as amended at 53 FR 50160, Dec. 13, 1988; 59 FR 51095, Oct. 7, 1994; 62 FR 10312, 10351, March 6, 1997; 87 FR 18967, 18980, Apr. 1, 2022]

§ 217.4 Inadmissibility and deportability.

(a) **Determinations of inadmissibility.**

(1) An alien who applies for admission under the provisions of section 217 of the Act, who is determined by an immigration officer not to be eligible for admission under that section or to be inadmissible to the United States under one or more of the grounds of inadmissibility listed in section 212 of the Act (other than for lack of a visa), or who is in possession of and presents fraudulent or counterfeit travel documents, will be refused admission into the United States and removed. Such refusal and removal shall be made at the level of the port director or officer-in-charge, or an officer acting in that capacity, and shall be effected without referral of the alien to an immigration judge for further inquiry, examination, or hearing, except that an alien who presents himself or herself as an applicant for admission under section 217 of the Act and applies for asylum in the United States must be issued a Form I-863, Notice of Referral to Immigration Judge, for a proceeding in accordance with 8 CFR 208.2(c)(1) and (c)(2).

(2) The removal of an alien under this section may be deferred if the alien is paroled into the custody of a Federal, State, or local law enforcement agency for criminal prosecution or punishment. This section in no way diminishes the discretionary authority of the Attorney General enumerated in section 212(d) of the Act.

(3) Refusal of admission under paragraph (a)(1) of this section shall not constitute removal for purposes of the Act.

(b) **Determination of deportability.**

(1) An alien who has been admitted to the United States under the provisions of section 217 of the Act and of this part who is determined by an immigration officer to be deportable from the United States under one or more of the grounds of deportability listed in section 237 of the Act shall be removed from the United States to his or her country of nationality or last residence. Such removal shall be determined by the district director who has jurisdiction over the place where the alien is found, and shall be effected without referral of the alien to an immigration judge for a determination of deportability, except that an alien who was admitted as a Visa Waiver Program visitor who applies for asylum in the United States must be issued a Form I-863 for a proceeding in accordance with 8 CFR 208.2(c)(1) and (c)(2).

(2) Removal by the district director under paragraph (b)(1) of this section is equivalent in all respects and has the same consequences as removal after proceedings conducted under section 240 of the Act.

(c)(1) Removal of inadmissible aliens who arrived by air or sea. Removal of an alien from the United States under this section may be effected using the return portion of the round trip passage presented by the alien at the time of entry to the United States as required by section 217(a)(7) of the Act. Such removal shall be on the first available means of transportation to the alien's point of embarkation to the United States. Nothing in this part absolves the carrier of the responsibility to remove any inadmissible or deportable alien at carrier expense, as provided in the carrier agreement.

(2) Removal of inadmissible and deportable aliens who arrived at land border ports-of-entry. Removal under this section will be by the first available means of transportation deemed appropriate by the district director.

HISTORY:

[53 FR 24901, June 30, 1988, as amended at 56 FR 32953, July 18, 1991; 62 FR 10312, 10351, March 6, 1997; 74 FR 55726, 55738, Oct. 28, 2009]

§ 217.5 Electronic System for Travel Authorization.

(a) Travel authorization required. Each nonimmigrant alien intending to travel by air, sea, or land to the United States under the Visa Waiver Program (VWP) must, within the time specified in paragraph (b) of this section, receive a travel authorization, which is a positive determination of eligibility to travel to the United States under the VWP via the Electronic System for Travel Authorization (ESTA), from CBP. In order to receive a travel authorization, each nonimmigrant alien intending to travel to the United States by air, sea, or land under the VWP must provide the data elements set forth in paragraph (c) of this section to CBP, in English, in the manner specified herein, and must pay a fee as described in paragraph (h) of this section.

(b) Time —

(1) Applicants arriving at air or sea ports of entry. Each alien falling within the provisions of paragraph (a) of this section and intending to travel by air or sea to the United States under the VWP must receive a travel authorization via ESTA prior to boarding a carrier destined for travel to the United States.

(2) Applicants arriving at land ports of entry. Each alien falling within the provisions of paragraph (a) of this section and intending to travel by land to the

United States under the VWP must receive a travel authorization via ESTA prior to application for admission to the United States.

(c) Required elements. CBP will collect such information as the Secretary deems necessary to issue a travel authorization as reflected in the ESTA application.

(d) Duration.

(1) General Rule. A travel authorization issued under ESTA will be valid for a period of two years from the date of issuance, unless the passport of the authorized alien will expire in less than two years, in which case the authorization will be valid until the date of expiration of the passport.

(2) Exception. For travelers from countries which have not entered into agreements with the United States whereby their passports are recognized as valid for the return of the bearer to the country of the foreign-issuing authority for a period of six months beyond the expiration date specified in the passport, a travel authorization issued under ESTA is not valid beyond the six months prior to the expiration date of the passport. Travelers from these countries whose passports will expire in six months or less will not receive a travel authorization.

(3) The Secretary, in consultation with the Secretary of State, may increase or decrease ESTA travel authorization validity period otherwise authorized by subparagraph (1) for a designated VWP country. Notice of any change to ESTA travel authorization validity periods will be published in the Federal Register. The ESTA Web site will be updated to reflect the specific ESTA travel authorization validity period for each VWP country.

(e) New travel authorization required. A new travel authorization is required if any of the following occur:

(1) The alien is issued a new passport;

(2) The alien changes his or her name;

(3) The alien changes his or her gender;

(4) The alien's country of citizenship changes; or

(5) The circumstances underlying the alien's previous responses to any of the ESTA application questions requiring a "yes" or "no" response (eligibility questions) have changed.

(f) Limitations.

(1) Current authorization period. An authorization under ESTA is a positive determination that an alien is eligible, and grants the alien permission, to travel to the United States under the VWP and to apply for admission under the VWP during the period of time the travel authorization is valid. An authorization under ESTA is not a determination that the alien is admissible to the United States. A determination of admissibility is made only after an applicant for admission is inspected by a CBP Officer at a U.S. port of entry.

(2) Not a determination of visa eligibility. A determination under ESTA that an alien is not eligible to travel to the United States under the VWP is not a determination that the alien is ineligible for a visa to travel to the United States and does not preclude the alien from applying for a visa before a United States consular officer.

(3) Judicial review. Notwithstanding any other provision of law, a determination under ESTA is not subject to judicial review pursuant to 8 U.S.C. 217(h)(3)(C)(iv).

(4) Revocation. A determination under ESTA that an alien is eligible to travel to the United States to apply for admission under the VWP may be revoked at the discretion of the Secretary.

(g) [Removed and Reserved]

(h) Fee.

(1) Through September 30, 2027, the fee for an approved ESTA is $21, which is the sum of two amounts: A $17 travel promotion fee to fund the Corporation for Travel Promotion and a $4 operational fee to at least ensure recovery of the full costs of providing and administering the system. In the event the ESTA application is denied, the fee is $4 to cover the operational costs.

(2) Beginning October 1, 2027, the fee for using ESTA is an operational fee of $4 to at least ensure recovery of the full costs of providing and administering the system.

HISTORY:

[73 FR 32440, 32452, June 9, 2008; 75 FR 47701, 47708, Aug. 9, 2010; 80 FR 32267, 32294, June 8, 2015; 87 FR 18967, 18980, Apr. 1, 2022; 87 FR 30769, 30773, May 20, 2022]

§ 217.6 Carrier agreements.

(a) General. The carrier agreements referred to in section 217(e) of the Act shall be made by the Commissioner on behalf of the Attorney General and shall be on Form I-775, Visa Waiver Pilot Program Agreement.

(b) Termination of agreements. The Commissioner, on behalf of the Attorney General, may terminate any carrier agreement under this part, with 5 days notice to a carrier, for the carrier's failure to meet the terms of such agreement. As a matter of discretion, the Commissioner may notify a carrier of the existence of a basis for termination of a carrier agreement under this part and allow the carrier a period not to exceed 15 days within which the carrier may bring itself into compliance with the terms of the carrier agreement. The agreement shall be subject to cancellation by either party for any reason upon 15 days' written notice to the other party.

HISTORY:

[53 FR 24901, June 30, 1988, as amended at 56 FR 32954, July 18, 1991; 62 FR 10312, 10352, March 6, 1997]

§ 217.7 Electronic data transmission requirement.

(a) An alien who applies for admission under the provisions of section 217 of the Act after arriving via sea or air at a port of entry will not be admitted under the Visa Waiver Program unless an appropriate official of the carrier transporting the alien electronically transmitted to Customs and Border Protection (CBP) passenger arrival manifest data relative to that alien passenger in accordance with 19 CFR 4.7b or 19 CFR 122.49a. Upon departure from the United States by sea or air of an alien admitted under the Visa Waiver Program, an appropriate official of the transporting carrier must electronically transmit to CBP departure manifest data relative to that alien passenger in accordance with 19 CFR 4.64 and 19 CFR 122.75a.

(b) If a carrier fails to submit the required electronic arrival or departure manifests specified in paragraph (a) of this section, CBP will evaluate the carrier's compliance with immigration requirements as a whole. CBP will inform the carrier of any noncompliance and then may revoke any contract agreements between CBP and the carrier. The carrier may also be subject to fines for failure to comply with manifest requirements or other statutory provisions. CBP will also review each Visa Waiver Program applicant who applies for admission and, on a case-by-case basis, may authorize a waiver under current CBP policy and guidelines or deny the applicant admission into the United States.

HISTORY:

[67 FR 63246, 63249, Oct. 11, 2002; 70 FR 17820, 17848, Apr. 7, 2005]

PART 221

ADMISSION OF VISITORS OR STUDENTS

Rule

AUTHORITY NOTE APPLICABLE TO ENTIRE PART:

AUTHORITY:

8 U.S.C. 1101, 1103, 1201; 8 CFR part 2.

§ 221.1 Admission under bond.

The district director having jurisdiction over the intended place of residence of an alien may accept a bond on behalf of an alien defined in section 101(a)(15)(B) or (F) of the Act prior to the issuance of a visa to the alien or upon receipt of a request directly from a U.S. consular officer or upon presentation by an interested person of a notification from the consular officer requiring such a bond; such a bond also may be accepted by the district director with jurisdiction over the port of entry or preinspection station where inspection of the alien takes place. Upon acceptance of such a bond, the district director shall notify the United States consular officer who requested the bond, giving the date and place of acceptance and amount of the bond. All bonds given as a condition of admission of an alien under section 221(g) of the Act shall be executed on Form I-352. For procedures relating to bond riders, acceptable sureties, cancellation, or breaching of bonds, see § 103.6 of this chapter.

HISTORY:

[32 FR 9626, July 4, 1967, as amended at 34 FR 1008, Jan. 23, 1969; 62 FR 10312, 10352, March 6, 1997]

PART 223

REENTRY PERMITS, REFUGEE TRAVEL DOCUMENTS, AND ADVANCE PAROLE DOCUMENTS

Rule

AUTHORITY NOTE APPLICABLE TO ENTIRE PART:

AUTHORITY:

8 U.S.C. 1103, 1181, 1182, 1186a, 1203, 1225, 1226, 1227, 1251; Protocol Relating to the Status of Refugees, November 1, 1968, 19 U.S.T. 6223 (TIAS) 6577; 8 CFR part 2.

§ 223.1 Purpose of documents.

(a) Reentry permit. A reentry permit allows a permanent resident to apply for admission to the United States upon return from abroad during the period of the permit's validity without the necessity of obtaining a returning resident visa.

(b) Refugee travel document. A refugee travel document is issued pursuant to this part and article 28 of the United Nations Convention of July 29, 1951, for the purpose of travel. Except as provided in § 223.3(d)(2)(i), a person who holds refugee status pursuant to section 207 of the Act, or asylum status pursuant to section 208 of the Act, must have a refugee travel document to return to the United States after temporary travel abroad unless he or she is in possession of a valid advance parole document.

HISTORY:

[51 FR 12596, Apr. 14, 1986; 58 FR 48778, Sept. 20, 1993; 59 FR 1464, Jan. 11, 1994; 62 FR 10312, 10352, March 6, 1997]

§ 223.2 Processing.

(a) Application. An applicant must submit an application for a reentry permit, refugee travel document, or advance parole on the form designated by USCIS with the fee prescribed in 8 CFR 106.2 and in accordance with the form instructions.

(b) **Filing eligibility.**

(1) Reentry permit. An applicant for a reentry permit must file such application while in the United States and in status as a lawful permanent resident or conditional permanent resident.

(2) Refugee travel document.

(i) Except as provided in paragraph (b)(2)(ii) of this section, an applicant for a refugee travel document must submit the application while in the United States and in valid refugee status under section 207 of the Act, valid asylum status under section 208 of the Act or is a permanent resident who received such status as a direct result of his or her asylum or refugee status.

(ii) Discretionary authority to accept a refugee travel document application from an alien not within the United States. As a matter of discretion, the Service office with jurisdiction over a port-of-entry or pre-flight inspection location where the alien is seeking admission, or the overseas Service office where the alien is physically present, may accept and adjudicate an application for a refugee travel document from an alien who previously had been admitted to the United States as a refugee, or who previously had been granted asylum status in the United States, and who departed from the United States without having applied for such refugee travel document, provided the officer:

(A) Is satisfied that the alien did not intend to abandon his or her refugee or asylum status at the time of departure from the United States;

(B) The alien did not engage in any activities while outside the United States that would be inconsistent with continued refugee or asylum status; and

(C) The alien has been outside the United States for less than 1 year since his or her last departure.

(c) **Ineligibility.**

(1) Prior document still valid. An application for a reentry permit or refugee travel document will be denied if the applicant was previously issued a reentry permit or refugee travel document which is still valid, unless it was returned to USCIS or it is demonstrated that it was lost.

(2) Extended absences. A reentry permit issued to a person who, since becoming a permanent resident or during the last five years, whichever is less, has been outside the United States for more than four years in the aggregate, shall be limited to a validity of one year, except that a permit with a validity of two years may be issued to:

(i) A permanent resident described in 8 CFR 211.1(a)(6) or (a)(7);

(ii) A permanent resident employed by a public international organization of which the United States is a member by treaty or statute, and his or her permanent resident spouse and children; or

(iii) A permanent resident who is a professional athlete who regularly competes in the United States and worldwide.

(3) Permanent resident entitled to nonimmigrant diplomatic or treaty status. A permanent resident entitled to nonimmigrant status under section 101(a)(15)(A), (E), or (G) of the Act because of occupational status may only be issued a reentry permit if the applicant executes and submits with the application, or has previously executed and submitted, a written waiver as required by 8 CFR part 247.

(d) Effect of travel before a decision is made. Departure from the United States before a decision is made on an application for a reentry permit or refugee travel document will not affect the application.

(e) Processing. USCIS may approve or deny a request for a reentry permit or refugee travel document as an exercise of discretion. If it approves the application, USCIS will issue an appropriate document.

(f) Effect on proceedings. Issuance of a reentry permit or refugee travel document to a person in exclusion, deportation, or removal proceedings shall not affect those proceedings.

(g) Appeal. Denial of an application for a reentry permit or refugee travel document may be appealed in accordance with 8 CFR 103.3.

HISTORY:

[53 FR 30021, Aug. 10, 1988; 59 FR 1465, Jan. 11, 1994; 62 FR 10312, 10352, March 6, 1997; 76 FR 53764, 53790, Aug. 29, 2011; 85 FR 46788, 46926, Aug. 3, 2020]

§ 223.3 Validity and effect on admissibility.

(a) **Validity.**

(1) Reentry permit. Except as provided in § 223.2(c)(2), a reentry permit issued to a permanent resident shall be valid for 2 years from the date of issuance. A reentry permit issued to a conditional permanent resident shall be valid for 2 years from the date of issuance, or to the date the conditional permanent resident must apply for removal of the conditions on his or her status, whichever comes first.

(2) Refugee travel document. A refugee travel document shall be valid for 1 year, or to the date the refugee or asylee status expires, whichever comes first.

(b) Invalidation. A document issued under this part is invalid if obtained through material false representation or concealment, or if the person is ordered excluded or deported. A refugee travel document is also invalid if the United Nations Convention of July 28, 1951, ceases to apply or does not apply to the person as provided in Article 1C, D, E, or F of the convention.

(c) Extension. A reentry permit or refugee travel document may not be extended.

(d) **Effect on admissibility.**

(1) Reentry permit. A permanent resident or conditional permanent resident in possession of a valid reentry permit who is otherwise admissible shall not be deemed to have abandoned status based solely on the duration of an absence or absences while the permit is valid.

(2) Refugee travel document.

(i) Inspection and immigration status. Upon arrival in the United States, an alien who presents a valid unexpired refugee travel document, or who has been allowed to file an application for a refugee travel document and this application has been approved under the procedure set forth in § 223.2(b)(2)(ii), shall be examined as to his or her admissibility under the Act. An alien shall be accorded the immigration status endorsed in his or her refugee travel document, or (in the case of an alien discussed in § 223.2(b)(2)(ii)) which will be endorsed in such document, unless he or she is no longer eligible for that status, or he or she applies for and is found eligible for some other immigration status.

(ii) Inadmissibility. If an alien who presents a valid unexpired refugee travel document appears to the examining immigration officer to be inadmissible, he or she shall be referred for proceedings under section 240 of the Act. Section 235(c) of the Act shall not be applicable.

HISTORY:

[47 FR 44239, Oct. 7, 1982; 59 FR 1465, Jan. 11, 1994; 62 FR 10312, 10353, March 6, 1997]

PART 231

ARRIVAL AND DEPARTURE MANIFESTS

AUTHORITY NOTE APPLICABLE TO ENTIRE PART:

AUTHORITY:
8 U.S.C. 1101, 1103, 1182, 1221, 1228, 1229; 8 CFR part 2.

§ 231.1 Electronic manifest and I-94 requirement for passengers and crew onboard arriving vessels and aircraft.

(a) Electronic submission of manifests. Provisions setting forth requirements applicable to commercial carriers regarding the electronic transmission of arrival manifests covering passengers and crew members under section 231 of the Act are set forth in 19 CFR 4.7b (passengers and crew members onboard vessels) and in 19 CFR 122.49a (passengers onboard aircraft) and 122.49b (crew members onboard aircraft).

(b) **Submission of Form I-94.**

(1) General requirement. In addition to the electronic manifest transmission requirement specified in paragraph (a) of this section, and subject to the exception of paragraph (2) of this paragraph (b), the master or commanding officer, or authorized agent, owner or consignee, of each commercial vessel or aircraft arriving in the United States from any place outside the United States must present to a Customs and Border Protection (CBP) officer at the port of entry a properly completed Arrival/Departure Record, Form I-94 (see § 1.4), for each arriving passenger.

(2) Exceptions. The Form I-94 requirement of paragraph (1) of this paragraph (b) does not apply to United States citizens, lawful permanent residents of the United States, immigrants to the United States, or passengers in transit through the United States; nor does it apply to vessels or aircraft arriving directly from Canada on a trip originating in that country or arriving in the Virgin Islands of the United States directly from a trip originating in the British Virgin Islands.

(c) Progressive clearance. Inspection of arriving passengers may be deferred at the request of the carrier to an onward port of debarkation. However, verification of transmission of the electronic manifest referred to in paragraph (a) of this section must occur at the first port of arrival. Authorization for this progressive clearance may be granted by the Director, Field Operations, at the first port of arrival. When progressive clearance is requested, the carrier must present the Form I-92 referred to in paragraph (d) of this section in duplicate at the initial port of entry. The original Form I-92 will be processed at the initial port of entry, and the duplicate will be noted and returned to the carrier for presentation at the onward port of debarkation.

(d) Aircraft/Vessel Report. A properly completed Aircraft/Vessel Report, Form I-92, must be completed for each arriving aircraft and vessel that is transporting passengers. Submission of the Form I-92 to the CBP officer must be accomplished on the day of arrival.

HISTORY:
[48 FR 21548, May 13, 1983, as amended at 48 FR 36093, Aug. 9, 1983; 48 FR 40209, Sept. 6, 1983; 68 FR 5190, 5193, Jan. 31, 2003; 68 FR 46926, 46929, Aug. 7, 2003; 70 FR 17820, 17849, Apr. 7, 2005; 78 FR 18457, 18472, Mar. 27, 2013, as confirmed at 81 FR 91646, 91670, Dec. 19, 2016]

§ 231.2 Electronic manifest and I-94 requirement for passengers and crew onboard departing vessels and aircraft.

(a) Electronic submission of manifests. Provisions setting forth requirements applicable to commercial carriers regarding the electronic transmission of departure manifests covering passengers and crew members under section 231 of the Act are set forth in 19 CFR 4.64 (passengers and crew members onboard vessels) and in 19 CFR 122.75a (passengers onboard aircraft) and 122.75b (crew members onboard aircraft).

(b) **Submission of Form I-94.**

(1) General requirement. In addition to the electronic manifest transmission requirement specified in paragraph (a) of this section, and subject to the exception of paragraph (2) of this paragraph (b), the master or commanding officer, or authorized agent, owner, or consignee, of each commercial vessel or aircraft departing from the United States to any place outside the United States must present a properly completed departure portion of an Arrival/Departure Record, Form I-94 (see § 1.4), to the Customs and Border Protection (CBP) officer at the port of departure for each person on board. Whenever possible, the departure Form I-94 presented must be the same form given to the alien at the time of arrival in the United States. The carrier must endorse the I-94 with the departure information on the reverse of the form. Submission of the I-94 to the CBP officer must be accomplished within 48 hours of the departure, exclusive of Saturdays, Sundays, and legal holidays. Failure to submit the departure I-94 within this period may be regarded as a failure to comply with section 231(g) of the Act, unless prior authorization for delayed delivery is obtained from CBP. A non-immigrant alien departing on an aircraft proceeding directly to Canada on a flight terminating in that country must surrender any Form I-94 in his/her possession to the airline agent at the port of departure.

(2) Exceptions. The form I-94 requirement of paragraph (1) of this paragraph (b) does not apply to United States citizens, lawful permanent residents of the United States, or passengers in transit through the United States; nor does it apply to a vessel or aircraft departing on a trip directly for and terminating in Canada or departing from the United States Virgin

Islands directly to the British Virgin Islands on a trip terminating there.

(c) Aircraft/Vessel Report. A properly completed Aircraft/Vessel Report, Form I-92, must be completed for each departing aircraft and vessel that is transporting passengers. Submission of the Form I-92 to the CBP officer must be accomplished on the day of departure.

HISTORY:

[48 FR 21548, May 13, 1983; 70 FR 17820, 17849, Apr. 7, 2005; 78 FR 18457, 18472, Mar. 27, 2013, as confirmed at 81 FR 91646, 91670, Dec. 19, 2016]

§ 231.3 Exemptions for private vessels and aircraft.

The provision of this part relating to the presentation of arrival and departure manifests shall not apply to a private vessel or private aircraft. Private aircraft as defined in 19 CFR 122.1(h) are subject to the arrival and departure manifest presentation requirements set forth in 19 CFR 122.22.

HISTORY:

[32 FR 9627, July 4, 1967; 73 FR 68295, 68309, Nov. 18, 2008]

PART 232

DETENTION OF ALIENS FOR PHYSICAL AND MENTAL EXAMINATION

AUTHORITY NOTE APPLICABLE TO ENTIRE PART:

AUTHORITY:

8 U.S.C. 1103, 1222, 1224, 1252; 8 CFR part 2.

§ 232.1 General.

The manner in which the physical and mental examination of aliens shall be conducted is set forth in 42 CFR part 34.

HISTORY:

[38 FR 33061, Nov. 30, 1973, as amended at 38 FR 34315, Dec. 13, 1973; redesignated at 62 FR 10312, 10353, March 6, 1997]

§ 232.2 Examination in the United States of alien applicants for benefits under the immigration laws and other aliens.

(a) General. When a medical examination is required of an alien who files an application for status as a permanent resident under section 245 of the Act or part 245 of this chapter, it shall be made by a selected civil surgeon. Such examination shall be performed in accordance with 42 CFR part 34 and any additional instructions and guidelines as may be considered necessary by the U.S. Public Health Service. In any other case in which the Service requests a medical examination of an alien, the examination shall be made by a medical officer of the U.S. Public Health Service, or by a civil surgeon if a medical officer of the U.S. Public Health Service is not located within a reasonable distance or is otherwise not available.

(b) Selection of civil surgeons. When a civil surgeon is to perform the examination, he shall be selected by the district director having jurisdiction over the area of the alien's residence. The district director shall select as many civil surgeons, including clinics and local, county and state health departments employing qualified civil surgeons, as he determines to be necessary to serve the needs of the Service in a locality under his jurisdiction. Each civil surgeon selected shall be a licensed physician with no less than 4 years' professional experience. Under usual circumstances physicians will be required to meet the 4 year professional experience criteria. However, at the district director's discretion other physicians with less experience can be designated to address unusual or unforeseen situations as the need arises. Officers of local health departments and medical societies may be consulted to obtain the names of competent surgeons and clinics willing to make the examinations. An understanding shall be reached with respect to the fee which the surgeon or clinic will charge for the examination. The alien shall pay the fee agreed upon directly to the surgeon making the examination.

(c) Civil surgeon reports —

(1) Applicants for status of permanent resident.

(i) When an applicant for status as a permanent resident is found upon examination to be free of any defect, disease, or disability listed in section 212(a) of the Act, the civil surgeon shall endorse Form I-486A, Medical Examination and Immigration Interview, and forward it with the X-ray and other pertinent laboratory reports to the immigration office from which the alien was referred, The immigration office may return the X-ray and laboratory reports to the alien. If the applicant is found to be afflicted with a defect, disease or disability listed under section 212(a) of the Act, the civil surgeon shall complete Form OF-157 in duplicate, and forward it with Form I-486A, X-ray, and other pertinent laboratory reports to the immigration office from which the alien was referred.

(ii) If the applicant is found to be afflicted with active tuberculosis and a waiver is granted under section 212(g) of the Act, the immigration office will forward a copy of the completed Form I-601 (Application for Waiver of Grounds of Excludability) and a copy of the Form OF-157 to the Director, Division of Quarantine, Center for Prevention Sevices, Centers for Disease Control, Atlanta, GA 30333.

(iii) If an alien who if found to be mentally retarded or to have had one or more previous attacks of insanity, applies for a waiver of excludability under section 212(g) of the Act, the immigration office will submit to the Director, Division of Quarantine, Center for Prevention Services, Centers for Disease Control, Atlanta, GA

30333, the completed Form I-601, including a copy of the medical report specified in the instructions attached to that form, and a copy of Form OF-157. This official shall review the medical report and advise the Service whether it is acceptable, in accordance with § 212.7(b)(4)(ii) of this chapter.

(iv) In any other case where the applicant has been found to be afflicted with active or inactive tuberculosis or an infectious or noninfectious leprosy condition, the immigration office will forward a copy of Form OF-157 with the applicant's address endorsed on the reverse to the Director, Division of Quarantine, Center for Prevention Services, Centers for Disease Control, Atlanta, GA 30333.

(2) Other aliens. The results of the examination of an alien who is not an applicant for status as a permanent resident shall be entered on Form I-141, Medical Certificate, in duplicate. This form shall be returned to the Service office by which the alien was referred.

(d) U.S. Public Health Service hospital and outpatient clinic reports. When an applicant for a benefit under the immigration laws, other than an applicant for status as a permanent resident, is examined by a medical officer of the U.S. Public Health Service, the results of the examination shall be entered on Form I-141, Medical Certificate, in duplicate. The form shall be returned to the Service office by which the alien was referred.

HISTORY:

[38 FR 33061, Nov. 30, 1973, as amended at 48 FR 30610, July 5, 1983; 52 FR 16194, May 1, 1987; redesignated at 62 FR 10312, 10353, March 6, 1997]

§ 232.3 Arriving aliens.

When a district director has reasonable grounds for believing that persons arriving in the United States should be detained for reasons specified in section 232 of the Act, he or she shall, after consultation with the United States Public Health Service at the port-of-entry, notify the master or agent of the arriving vessel or aircraft of his or her intention to effect such detention by serving on the master or agent Form I-259 in accordance with § 235.3(a) of this chapter.

HISTORY:

[54 FR 101, Jan. 4, 1989.; redesignated and revised at 62 FR 10312, 10353, March 6, 1997]

PART 233

CONTRACTS WITH TRANSPORTATION LINES

Rule

Rule

AUTHORITY NOTE APPLICABLE TO ENTIRE PART:

AUTHORITY:

8 U.S.C. 1101, 1103, 1182, 1221, 1228, 1229, 8 CFR part 2.

§ 233.1 Contracts.

The contracts with transportation lines referred to in section 233(c) of the Act may be entered into by the Executive Associate Commissioner for Programs, or by an immigration officer designated by the Executive Associate Commissioner for Programs on behalf of the government and shall be documented on Form I-420. The contracts with transportation lines referred to in section 233(a) of the Act shall be made by the Commissioner on behalf of the government and shall be documented on Form I-426. The contracts with transportation lines desiring their passengers to be preinspected at places outside the United States shall be made by the Commissioner on behalf of the government and shall be documented on Form I-425; except that contracts for irregularly operated charter flights may be entered into by the Associate Commissioner for Examinations or an immigration officer designated by the Executive Associate Commissioner for Programs and having jurisdiction over the location where the inspection will take place.

HISTORY:

[57 FR 59907, Dec. 17, 1992; redesignated and revised at 62 FR 10312, 10353, March 6, 1997]

§ 233.2 Transportation lines bringing aliens to the United States from or through foreign contiguous territory or adjacent islands.

Form I-420 shall be signed in duplicate and forwarded to the Headquarters Office of Inspections. After acceptance, each Regional Office of Inspections, the district office and the carrier will be furnished with one copy of the agreement. The transmittal letter to the Headquarters Office of Inspections shall indicate whether the signatory to the agreement is a subsidiary or affiliate of a line which has already signed a similar agreement. Correspondence regarding ancillary contracts for office space and other facilities to be furnished by transportation lines at Service stations in Canada shall be similarly handled.

HISTORY:

[57 FR 59907, Dec. 17, 1992; redesignated at 62 FR 10312, 10353, March 6, 1997]

§ 233.3 [This section was removed and reserved. See 68 FR 46926, 46929, Aug. 7, 2003.]

[NO TEXT IN ORIGINAL]

HISTORY:

[32 FR 9630, July 4, 1967; 59 FR 1617, Jan. 12, 1994; 60 FR 30457, June 9, 1995; redesignated and amended at 62 FR 10312, 10353, March 6, 1997]

AUTHORITY:

(8 U.S.C. 1103, 1228; 8 CFR part 2.)

§ 233.4 Preinspection outside the United States.

(a) Form I-425 agreements. A transportation line bringing applicants for admission to the United States through preinspection sites outside the United States shall enter into an agreement on Form I-425. Such an agreement shall be negotiated directly by the Service's Headquarters Office of Inspections and the head office of the transportation line.

(b) Signatory lines. A list of transportation lines with currently valid transportation agreements on Form I-425 is maintained by the Service's Headquarters Office of Inspections and is available upon written request.

HISTORY:

[32 FR 9630, July 4, 1967; 59 FR 1618, Jan. 12, 1994; 60 FR 30457, June 9, 1995; redesignated and revised at 62 FR 10312, 10353, March 6, 1997]

§ 233.5 Aliens entering Guam pursuant to section 14 of Public Law 99-396, "Omnibus Territories Act.'

A transportation line bringing aliens to Guam under the visa waiver provisions of § 212.1(e) of this chapter shall enter into an agreement on Form I-760. Such agreements shall be negotiated directly by the Service's Headquarters and head offices of the transportation lines.

HISTORY:

[52 FR 48084, Dec. 18, 1987; redesignated and revised at 62 FR 10312, 10353, March 6, 1997]

§ 233.6 Aliens entering Guam or the Commonwealth of the Northern Mariana Islands pursuant to Title VII of Public Law 110-229, "Consolidated Natural Resources Act of 2008."

A transportation line bringing aliens to Guam or the Commonwealth of the Northern Mariana Islands under the visa waiver provisions of § 212.1(q) of this chapter or to the Commonwealth of the Northern Mariana Islands under the visa waiver provisions of § 212.1(r) of this chapter must enter into an agreement on CBP Form I-760. Such agreements must be negotiated directly by U.S. Customs and Border Protection and head offices of the transportation lines.

HISTORY:

[74 FR 2824, 2836, Jan. 16, 2009; 89 FR 3299, 3331, Jan. 18, 2024]

PART 234

DESIGNATION OF PORTS OF ENTRY FOR ALIENS ARRIVING BY CIVIL AIRCRAFT

Rule

AUTHORITY NOTE APPLICABLE TO ENTIRE PART:

AUTHORITY:

8 U.S.C. 1103, 1221, 1229; 8 CFR part 2.

§ 234.1 Definitions.

(a) Scheduled Airline. This term means any individual, partnership, corporation, or association engaged in air transportation upon regular schedules to, over, or away from the United States, or from one place to another in the United States, and holding a Foreign Air Carrier permit or a Certificate of Public Convenience and Necessity issued pursuant to the Federal Aviation Act of 1958 (72 Stat. 731).

(b) International Airport. An international airport is one designated by the Commissioner for the entry of aliens with the prior approval of the Secretary of Commerce, Secretary of the Treasury and the Secretary of Health and Human Services.

(c) Landing Rights Airport. An airport, although not designated as international, at which permission to land has been granted to aircraft operated by scheduled airlines by the Commissioner of Customs.

HISTORY:

[49 FR 50018, Dec. 26, 1984; redesignated at 62 FR 10312, 10353, March 6, 1997]

§ 234.2 Landing requirements.

(a) Place of landing. Aircraft carrying passengers or crew required to be inspected under the Act must land at the international air ports of entry enumerated in part 100 of this chapter unless permission to land elsewhere is first obtained from the Commissioner of U.S. Customs and Border Protection (CBP) in the case of aircraft operated by scheduled airlines, and in all other cases from the port director of CBP or other CBP officer having jurisdiction over the CBP port of entry nearest the intended place of landing.

(b) Advance notice of arrival. Aircraft carrying passengers or crew required to be inspected under the Immigration and Nationality Act, except aircraft of a scheduled airline arriving in accordance with the regular schedule filed with the Service at the place of landing, shall furnish notice of the intended flight to the immigration officer at or nearest the intended place of landing, or shall furnish similar notice to the district director of Customs or other Customs officer in charge at such place. Such notice shall specify the type of aircraft, the registration marks thereon, the name of the aircraft commander, the place of last departure, the airport of entry, or other place at which landing has been authorized, number of alien passengers, number of citizen passengers, and the estimated time of arrival. The notice shall be sent in sufficient time to enable the officers designated to inspect the aircraft to reach the airport of entry or such other place of landing prior to the arrival of the aircraft.

(c) Permission to discharge or depart. Aircraft carrying passengers or crew required to be inspected under the Immigration and Nationality Act shall not discharge or permit to depart any passenger or crewman without permission from an immigration officer.

(d) Emergency or forced landing. Should any aircraft carrying passengers or crew required to be inspected under the Immigration and Nationality Act make a forced landing in the United States, the commanding officer or person in command shall not allow any passenger or crewman thereon to depart from the landing place without permission of an immigration officer, unless such departure is necessary for purposes of safety or the preservation of life or property. As soon as practicable, the commanding officer or person in command, or the owner of the aircraft, shall communicate with the nearest immigration officer and make a full report of the circumstances of the flight and of the emergency or forced landing.

HISTORY:

[22 FR 9795, Dec. 6, 1957, as amended at 32 FR 9631, July 4, 1967; 45 FR 29243, May 1, 1980; 49 FR 50019, Dec. 26, 1984; 54 FR 102, Jan. 4, 1989.; 54 FR 1050, Jan. 11, 1989; redesignated at 62 FR 10312, 10353, March 6, 1997; 65 FR 58902, 58903, Oct. 3, 2000; 76 FR 5058, 5060, Jan. 28, 2011; 81 FR 14948, 14953, Mar. 21, 2016]

§ 234.3 Aircraft; how considered.

Except as otherwise specifically provided in the Immigration and Nationality Act and this chapter, aircraft arriving in or departing from the continental United States or Alaska directly from or to foreign contiguous territory or the French island of St. Pierre or Miquelon shall be regarded for the purposes of the Immigration and Nationality Act and this chapter as other transportation lines or companies arriving or departing over the land borders of the United States.

HISTORY:

[22 FR 9795, Dec. 6, 1957; redesignated and amended at 62 FR 10312, 10353, March 6, 1997]

§ 234.4 International airports for entry of aliens.

International airports for the entry of aliens shall be those airports designated as such by the Commissioner. An application for designation of an airport as an international airport for the entry of aliens shall be made to the Commissioner and shall state whether the airport: (a) Has been approved by the Secretary of Commerce as a properly equipped airport, (b) has been designated by the Secretary of the Treasury as a port of entry for aircraft arriving in the United States from any place outside thereof and for the merchandise carried thereon, and (c) has been designated by the Secretary of Health, Education, and Welfare as a place for quarantine inspection. An airport shall not be so designated by the Commissioner without such prior approval and designation, and unless it appears to the satisfaction of the Commissioner that conditions render such designation necessary or advisable, and unless adequate facilities have been or will be provided at such airport without cost to the Federal Government for the proper inspection and disposition of aliens, including office space and such temporary detention quarters as may be found necessary. The designation of an airport as an international airport for the entry of aliens may be withdrawn whenever, in the judgment of the Commissioner, there appears just cause for such action.

HISTORY:

[22 FR 9795, Dec. 6, 1957; redesignated at 62 FR 10312, 10353, March 6, 1997]

PART 235

INSPECTION OF PERSONS APPLYING FOR ADMISSION

Rule

AUTHORITY NOTE APPLICABLE TO ENTIRE PART:

AUTHORITY:

6 U.S.C. 218 and note; 8 U.S.C. 1101 and note, 1103, 1158, 1182, 1183, 1185 (pursuant to E.O. 13323, 69 FR 241, 3 CFR, 2004 Comp., p.278), 1185 note, 1201, 1224, 1225, 1226, 1228, 1365a note, 1365b, 1379, 1731-32; 48 U.S.C 1806 and note; Pub. L. 115-218.

§ 235.1 Scope of examination.

(a) General. Application to lawfully enter the United States shall be made in person to an immigration officer at a U.S. port-of-entry when the port is open for inspection, or as otherwise designated in this section.

(b) U.S. Citizens. A person claiming U.S. citizenship must establish that fact to the examining officer's satisfaction and must present a U.S. passport or alternative documentation as required by 22 CFR part 53. If such applicant for admission fails to satisfy the examining immigration officer that he or she is a U.S. citizen, he or she shall thereafter be inspected as an alien. A U.S. citizen must present a valid unexpired U.S. passport book upon entering the United States, unless he or she presents one of the following documents:

(1) Passport Card. A U.S. citizen who possesses a valid unexpired United States passport card, as defined in 22 CFR 53.1, may present the passport card when entering the United States from contiguous territory or adjacent islands at land or sea ports-of-entry.

(2) Merchant Mariner Document. A U.S. citizen who holds a valid Merchant Mariner Document (MMD) issued by the U.S. Coast Guard may present an unexpired MMD used in conjunction with official maritime business when entering the United States.

(3) Military Identification. Any U.S. citizen member of the U.S. Armed Forces who is in the uniform of, or bears documents identifying him or her as a member of, such Armed Forces, and who is coming to or departing from the United States under official orders or permit of such Armed Forces, may present a military identification card and the official orders when entering the United States.

(4) Trusted Traveler Programs. A U.S. citizen who travels as a participant in the NEXUS, FAST, or SENTRI programs may present a valid NEXUS program card when using a NEXUS Air kiosk or a valid NEXUS, FAST, or SENTRI card at a land or sea port-of-entry prior to entering the United States from contiguous territory or adjacent islands. A U.S. citizen who enters the United States by pleasure vessel from Canada using the remote inspection system may present a NEXUS program card.

(5) Certain Cruise Ship Passengers. A U.S. citizen traveling entirely within the Western Hemisphere is permitted to present a government-issued photo identification document in combination with either an original or a copy of his or her birth certificate, a Consular Report of Birth Abroad issued by the Department of State, or a Certificate of Naturalization issued by U.S. Citizenship and Immigration Services for entering the United States when the United States citizen:

(i) Boards a cruise ship at a port or place within the United States; and,

(ii) Returns on the return voyage of the same cruise ship to the same United States port or place from where he or she originally departed.

On such cruises, U.S. Citizens under the age of 16 may present an original or a copy of a birth certificate, a Consular Report of Birth Abroad, or a Certificate of Naturalization issued by U.S. Citizenship and Immigration Services.

(6) Native American Holders of an American Indian Card. A Native American holder of a Form I-872 American Indian Card arriving from contiguous territory or adjacent islands may present the Form I-872 card prior to entering the United States at a land or sea port-of-entry.

(7) Native American Holders of Tribal Documents. A U.S. citizen holder of a tribal document issued by a United States qualifying tribal entity or group of United States qualifying tribal entities, as provided in paragraph (e) of this section, who is arriving from contiguous territory or adjacent islands may present the tribal document prior to entering the United States at a land or sea port-of-entry.

(8) Children. A child who is a United States citizen entering the United States from contiguous territory at a sea or land ports-of-entry may present certain other documents, if the arrival falls under subsection (i) or (ii).

(i) Children Under Age 16. A U.S. citizen who is under the age of 16 is permitted to present either an original or a copy of his or her birth certificate, a Consular Report of Birth Abroad issued by the Department of State, or a Certificate of Naturalization issued by U.S. Citizenship and Immigration Services when entering the United States from contiguous territory at land or sea ports-of-entry.

(ii) Groups of Children Under Age 19. A U.S. citizen, who is under age 19 and is traveling with a public or private school group, religious group, social or cultural organization, or team associated with a youth sport organization is permitted to present either an original or a copy of his or her birth certificate, a Consular Report of Birth Abroad issued by the Department of State, or a Certificate of Naturalization issued by U.S. Citizenship and Immigration Services when arriving from contiguous territory at land or sea ports-of-entry, when the group, organization, or team is under the supervision of an adult affiliated with the group, organization, or team and when the child has parental or legal guardian consent to travel. For purposes of this paragraph, an adult is considered to be a person age 19 or older. The following requirements will apply:

(A) The group or organization must provide to CBP upon crossing the border, on organizational letterhead:

(1) The name of the group, organization or team, and the name of the supervising adult;

(2) A list of the children on the trip;

(3) For each child, the primary address, primary phone number, date of birth, place of birth, and name of a parent or legal guardian.

(B) The adult leading the group, organization, or team must demonstrate parental or legal guardian consent by certifying in the writing submitted in paragraph (b)(8)(ii)(A) of this section that he or she has obtained for each child the consent of at least one parent or legal guardian.

(C) The inspection procedure described in this paragraph is limited to members of the group, organization, or team who are under age 19. Other members of the group, organization, or team must comply with other applicable document and/or inspection requirements found in this part.

(c) Alien members of United States Armed Forces and members of a force of a NATO country. Any alien member of the United States Armed Forces who is in the uniform of, or bears documents identifying him or her as a member of, such Armed Forces, and who is coming to or departing from the United States under official orders or permit of such Armed Forces is not subject to the removal provisions of the Act. A member of the force of a NATO country signatory to Article III of the Status of Forces Agreement seeking to enter the United States under official orders is exempt from the control provision of the Act. Any alien who is a member of either of the foregoing classes may, upon request, be inspected and his or her entry as an alien may be recorded. If the alien does not appear to the examining immigration officer to be clearly and beyond a doubt entitled to enter the United States under the provisions of the Act, the alien shall be so informed and his or her entry shall not be recorded.

(d) Enhanced Driver's License Projects; alternative requirements. Upon the designation by the Secretary of Homeland Security of an enhanced driver's license as an acceptable document to denote identity and citizenship for purposes of entering the United States, U.S. and Canadian citizens may be permitted to present these documents in lieu of a passport upon entering or seeking admission to the United States according to the terms of the agreements entered between the Secretary of Homeland Security and the entity. The Secretary of Homeland Security will announce, by publication of a notice in the Federal Register, documents designated under this paragraph. A list of the documents designated under this paragraph will also be made available to the public.

(e) Native American Tribal Cards; alternative requirements. Upon the designation by the Secretary of Homeland Security of a United States qualifying tribal entity document as an acceptable document to denote identity and citizenship for purposes of entering the United States, Native Americans may be permitted to present tribal cards upon entering or seeking admission to the United States according to the terms of the voluntary agreement entered between the Secretary of Homeland Security and the tribe. The Secretary of Homeland Security will announce, by publication of a notice in the Federal Register, documents designated under this paragraph. A list of the documents designated under this paragraph will also be made available to the public.

(f) Alien applicants for admission.

(1) Each alien seeking admission at a United States port-of-entry must present whatever documents are required and must establish to the satisfaction of the inspecting officer that the alien is not subject to removal under the immigration laws, Executive Orders, or Presidential Proclamations, and is entitled, under all of the applicable provisions of the immigration laws and this chapter, to enter the United States.

(i) A person claiming to have been lawfully admitted for permanent residence must establish that fact to the satisfaction of the inspecting officer and must present proper documents in accordance with § 211.1 of this chapter.

(ii) The Secretary of Homeland Security or his designee may require any alien, other than aliens exempted under paragraph (iv) of this section or Canadian citizens under section 101(a)(15)(B) of the Act who are not otherwise required to present a visa or be issued Form I-94 (see § 1.4) or Form I-95 for admission or parole into the United States, to provide fingerprints, photograph(s) or other specified biometric identifiers, documentation of his or her immigration status in the United States, and such other evidence as may be requested to determine the alien's identity and whether he or she has properly maintained his or her status while in the United States and/or whether he or she is admissible. The failure of an alien at the time of inspection to comply with any requirement to provide biometric identifiers may result in a determination that the alien is inadmissible under section 212(a) of the Immigration and Nationality Act or any other law.

(iii) Aliens who are required under paragraph (d)(1)(ii) to provide biometric identifier(s) at inspection may also be subject to the departure requirements for biometrics contained in § 215.8 of this chapter, unless otherwise exempted.

(iv) The requirements of paragraph (d)(1)(ii) shall not apply to:

(A) Aliens younger than 14 or older than 79 on date of admission;

(B) Aliens admitted on A-1, A-2, C-3 (except for attendants, servants, or personal employees of accredited officials), G-1, G-2, G-3, G-4, NATO-1, NATO-2, NATO-3, NATO-4, NATO-5, or NATO-6 visas, and certain Taiwan officials who hold E-1 visas and members of their immediate families who hold E-1 visas unless the Secretary of State and the Secretary of Homeland Security jointly determine that a class of such aliens should be subject to the requirements of paragraph (d)(1)(ii);

(C) Classes of aliens to whom the Secretary of Homeland Security and the Secretary of State jointly determine it shall not apply; or

(D) An individual alien to whom the Secretary of Homeland Security, the Secretary of State, or the Director of Central Intelligence determines it shall not apply.

(2) An alien present in the United States who has not been admitted or paroled or an alien who seeks entry at other than an open, designated port-of-entry, except as otherwise permitted in this section, is subject to the provisions of section 212(a) of the Act and to removal under section 235(b) or 240 of the Act.

(3) An alien who is brought to the United States, whether or not to a designated port-of-entry and regardless of the means of transportation, after having been interdicted in international or United States waters, is considered an applicant for admission and shall be examined under section 235(b) of the Act.

(4) An alien stowaway is not an applicant for admission and may not be admitted to the United States. A stowaway shall be removed from the United States under section 235(a)(2) of the Act. The provisions of section 240 of the Act are not applicable to stowaways, nor is the stowaway entitled to further hearing or review of the removal, except that an alien stowaway who indicates an intention to apply for asylum, or expresses a fear of persecution, a fear of torture, or a fear of return to the country of proposed removal shall be referred to an asylum officer for a determination of credible fear of persecution or torture in accordance

with section 235(b)(1)(B) of the Act and § 208.30 of this chapter. An alien stowaway who is determined to have a credible fear of persecution or torture shall have his or her asylum application adjudicated in accordance with § 208.2(b)(2) of this chapter.

(g) U.S. citizens, lawful permanent residents of the United States, and other aliens, entering the United States along the northern border, other than at a port-of-entry. A citizen of Canada or a permanent resident of Canada who is a national of a country listed in § 217.2(a) of this chapter may, if in possession of a valid, unexpired, Canadian Border Boat Landing Permit (Form I-68) or evidence of enrollment in any other Service Alternative Inspections program (e.g., the Immigration and Naturalization Service Passenger Accelerated Service System (INSPASS) or the Port Passenger Accelerated Service System (PORTPASS)), enter the United States by means of a pleasure craft along the northern border of the United States from time-to-time without further inspection. No persons other than those described in this paragraph may participate in this program. Permanent residents of Canada who are nationals of a designated Visa Waiver Program country listed in § 217.2(a) of this chapter must be in possession of a valid, unexpired passport issued by his or her country of nationality, and an unexpired multiple entry Form I-94W, Nonimmigrant Visa Waiver Arrival/Departure Form, or an unexpired passport, valid unexpired United States visa and I-94 Arrival/Departure Form. When an entry to the United States is made by a person who is a Canadian citizen or a permanent resident of Canada who is a national of a designated Visa Waiver Program country listed in § 217.2(a) of this chapter, entry may be made under this program only for a purpose as described in section 101(a)(15)(B)(ii) of the Act as a visitor for pleasure. Persons seeking to enter the United States for any other purpose must do so at a port-of-entry staffed by immigration inspectors. Persons aboard a vessel which has crossed the international boundary between the United States and Canada and who do not intend to land in the United States, other than at a staffed port-of-entry, are not required to be in possession of Form I-68, Canadian Border Boat Landing Permit, or evidence of enrollment in an Alternative Inspections program merely because they have crossed the international boundary. However, the Service retains the right to conduct inspections or examinations of all persons applying for admission or readmission to or seeking transit through the United States in accordance with the Act.

(1) Application. An eligible applicant may apply for a Canadian Border Boat Landing Permit by completing the Form I-68 in triplicate. Application forms will be made readily available through the Internet, from a Service office, or by mail. A family may apply on a single application. For the purposes of this paragraph, a family is defined as a husband, wife, unmarried children under the age of 21, and the parents of either husband or wife, who reside at the same address. In order for the I-68 application to be considered complete, it must be accompanied by the following:

(i) For each person included on the application, evidence of citizenship, and, if not a citizen of the Untied States or Canada, evidence of legal permanent resident status in either the United States or Canada. Evidence of residency must be submitted by all applicants. It is not required that all persons on the application be of the same nationality; however, they must all be individually eligible to participate in this program.

(ii) If multiple members of a family, as defined in paragraph (e)(1) of this section, are included on a single application, evidence of the familial relationship.

(iii) A fee as prescribed in 8 CFR 103.7(d)(3).

(iv) A copy of any previously approved Form I-68.

(v) A permanent resident of Canada who is a national of a Visa Waiver Program may apply for admission simultaneously with the Form I-68 application and thereby obtain a Form I-94 or I-94W.

(2) Submission of Form I-68. Except as indicated in this paragraph, Form I-68 shall be properly completed and submitted in person, along with the documentary evidence and the required fee as specified in 8 CFR 103.7(d)(3), to a United States immigration officer at a Canadian border Port-of-Entry located within the district having jurisdiction over the applicant's residence or intended place of landing. Persons previously granted Form I-68 approval may apply by mail to the issuing Service office for renewal if a copy of the previous Form I-68 is included in the application. At the discretion of the district director concerned, any applicant for renewal of Form I-68 may be required to appear for an interview in person if the applicant does not appear to be clearly eligible for renewal.

(3) Denial of Form I-68. If the applicant has committed a violation of any immigration or customs regulation or, in the case of an alien, is inadmissible to the United States, approval of the Form I-68 shall be denied. However, if, in the exercise of discretion, the district director waives under section 212(d)(3) of the Act all applicable grounds of inadmissibility, the I-68 application may be approved for such non-citizens. If the Form I-68 application is denied, the applicant shall be given written notice of and the reasons for the denial by letter from the district director. There is no appeal from the denial of the Form I-68 application, but the denial is without prejudice to a subsequent application for this program or any other Service benefit, except that the applicant may not submit a subsequent Form I-68 application for 90 days after the date of the last denial.

(4) Validity. Form I-68 shall be valid for 1 year from the date of issuance, or until revoked or violated by the Service.

(5) Conditions for participation in the I-68 program. Upon being inspected and positively identified by an immigration officer and found admissible and eligible for participation in the I-68 program, a participant must agree to abide by the following conditions:

(i) Form I-68 may be used only when entering the United States by means of a vessel exclusively used for pleasure, including chartered vessels when such vessel has been chartered by an approved Form I-68 holder. When used by a person who is a not a citizen or a lawful permanent resident of the United States, admission shall be for a period not to exceed 72 hours to visit within 25 miles of the shore line along the northern border of the United States, including the shore line of Lake Michigan and Puget Sound.

(ii) Participants must be in possession of any authorization documents issued for participation in this program or another Service Alternative Inspections program (INSPASS or PORTPASS). Participants over the age of 15 years and who are not in possession of an INSPASS or PORTPASS enrollment card must also be in possession of a photographic identification document issued by a governmental agency. Participants who are permanent residents of Canada who are nationals of a Visa Waiver Program country listed in § 217.2(a) of this chapter must also be in possession of proper documentation as described in paragraph (e) of this section.

(iii) Participants may not import merchandise or transport controlled or restricted items while entering the United States under this program. The entry of any merchandise or goods must be in accordance with the laws and regulations of all Federal Inspection Services.

(iv) Participants must agree to random checks or inspections that may be conducted by the Service, at any time and at any location, to ensure compliance.

(v) Participants must abide by all Federal, state, and local laws regarding the importation of alcohol or agricultural products or the importation or possession of controlled substances as defined in section 101 of the Controlled Substance Act (21 U.S.C. 802).

(vi) Participants acknowledge that all devices, decals, cards, or other Federal Government supplied identification or technology used to identify or inspect persons or vessels seeking entry via this program remain the property of the United States Government at all times, and must be surrendered upon request by a Border Patrol Agent or any other officer of a Federal Inspection Service.

(vii) The captain, charterer, master, or owner (if aboard) of each vessel bringing persons into the United States is responsible for determining that all persons aboard the vessel are in possession of a valid, unexpired Form I-68 or other evidence of participation in a Service Alternative Inspections program (INSPASS or PORTPASS) prior to entry into the territorial waters of the United States. If any person on board is not in possession of such evidence, the captain, charterer, master, or owner must transport such person to a staffed United States Port-of-Entry for an in-person immigration inspection.

(6) Revocation. The district director, the chief patrol agent, or their designated representatives may revoke the designation of any participant who violates any condition of this program, as contained in paragraph (e)(5) of this section, or who has violated any immigration law or regulation, or a law or regulation of the United States Customs Service or other Federal Inspection Service, has abandoned his or her residence in the United States or Canada, is inadmissible to the United States, or who is otherwise determined by an immigration officer to be ineligible for continued participation in this program. Such persons may be subject to other applicable sanctions, such as criminal and/or administrative prosecution or deportation, as well as possible seizure of goods and/or vessels. If permission to participate is revoked, a written request to the district director for restoration of permission to participate may be made. The district director will notify the person of his or her decision and the reasons therefore in writing.

(7) Compliance checking. Participation in this program does not relieve the holder from responsibility to comply with all other aspects of United States Immigration, Customs, or other Federal inspection service laws or regulations. To prevent abuse, the United States Immigration and Naturalization Service retains the right to conduct inspections or examinations of all persons applying for admission or readmission to or seeking transit through the United States in accordance with the Immigration and Nationality Act.

(h) Form I-94, Arrival-Departure Record.

(1) Unless otherwise exempted, each arriving nonimmigrant who is admitted to the United States will be issued a Form I-94 as evidence of the terms of admission. For land border admission, a Form I-94 will be issued only upon payment of a fee, and will be considered issued for multiple entries unless specifically annotated for a limited number of entries. A Form I-94 issued at other than a land border port-of-entry, unless issued for multiple entries, must be surrendered upon departure from the United States in accordance with the instructions on the form. Form I-94 is not required by:

(i) Any nonimmigrant alien described in § 212.1(a) of this chapter and 22 CFR 41.33 who is admitted as a visitor for business or pleasure or admitted to proceed in direct transit through the United States;

(ii) Any nonimmigrant alien residing in the British Virgin Islands who was admitted only to the U.S. Virgin Islands as a visitor for business or pleasure under § 212.1(b) of this chapter;

(iii) Except as provided in paragraph (h)(1)(v) of this section, any Mexican national admitted as a nonimmigrant visitor who is:

(A) Exempt from a visa and passport pursuant to § 212.1(c)(1) of this chapter and is admitted for a period not to exceed 30 days to visit within 25 miles of the border; or

(B) In possession of a valid visa and passport and is admitted for a period not to exceed 72 hours to visit within 25 miles of the border;

(iv) Bearers of Mexican diplomatic or official passports described in § 212.1(c) of this chapter; or

(v) Any Mexican national admitted as a nonimmigrant visitor who is:

(A) Exempt from a visa and passport pursuant to § 212.1(c)(1) of this chapter and is admitted at the Mexican border POEs in the State of Arizona at Sasabe, Nogales, Mariposa, Naco or Douglas to visit within the State of Arizona within 75 miles of the border for a period not to exceed 30 days; or

(B) In possession of a valid visa and passport and is admitted at the Mexican border POEs in the State of Arizona at Sasabe, Nogales, Mariposa, Naco or Douglas to visit within the State of Arizona within 75 miles of the border for a period not to exceed 72 hours; or

(C) Exempt from visa and passport pursuant to § 212.1(c)(1) of this chapter and is admitted for a period not to exceed 30 days to visit within the State of New Mexico within 55 miles of the border or the area south of and including Interstate Highway I-10, whichever is further north; or

(D) In possession of a valid visa and passport and is admitted for a period not to exceed 72 hours to visit within the State of New Mexico within 55 miles of the border or the area south of and including Interstate Highway I-10, whichever is further north.

(2) Paroled aliens. Any alien paroled into the United States under section 212(d)(5) of the Act, including any alien crewmember, shall be issued a completely executed Form I-94, endorsed with the parole stamp.

HISTORY:

[32 FR 9627, July 4, 1967, as amended at 32 FR 11628, Aug. 11, 1967; 45 FR 70428, Oct. 24, 1980; 46 FR 43826, Sept. 1, 1981; 47 FR 49953, Nov. 4, 1982; 49 FR 33434, Aug. 23, 1984; 58 FR 69217, Dec. 30, 1993, as confirmed at 63 FR 1331, 1334, Jan. 9, 1998; 60 FR 40068, Aug. 7, 1995; 60 FR 50386, 50389, Sept. 29, 1995, as confirmed at 61 FR 53830, 53831, Oct. 16, 1996; 62 FR 10312, 10353, Mar. 6, 1997; 62 FR 47449, 47751, Sept. 11, 1997, as confirmed and amended at 64 FR 36559, 36561, July 7, 1999; 64 FR 8478, 8494, Feb. 19, 1999; 64 FR 68616, 68617, Dec. 8, 1999; 67 FR 71443, 71449, Dec. 2, 2002; 68 FR 5190, 5193, Jan. 31, 2003; 69 FR 468, 480, Jan. 5, 2004; 69 FR 50051, 50053, Aug. 13, 2004; 69 FR 53318, 53333, Aug. 31, 2004, as corrected at 69 FR 58037, Sept. 29, 2004; 71 FR 68412, 68429, Nov. 24, 2006; 73 FR 18384, 18416, Apr. 3, 2008; 73 FR 77473, 77491, Dec. 19, 2008, as corrected at 74 FR 2837, Jan. 16, 2009; 78 FR 18457, 18472, Mar. 27, 2013, as confirmed at 81 FR 91646, 91670, Dec. 19, 2016; 78 FR 35103, 35107, June 12, 2013; 85 FR 46788, 46926, Aug. 3, 2020]

§ 235.2 Parole for deferred inspection.

(a) A district director may, in his or her discretion, defer the inspection of any vessel or aircraft, or of any alien, to another Service office or port-of-entry. Any alien coming to a United States port from a foreign port, from an outlying possession of the United States, from Guam, Puerto Rico, or the Virgin Islands of the United States, or from another port of the United States at which examination under this part was deferred, shall be regarded as an applicant for admission at that onward port.

(b) An examining immigration officer may defer further examination and refer the alien's case to the district director having jurisdiction over the place where the alien is seeking admission, or over the place of the alien's residence or destination in the United States, if the examining immigration officer has reason to believe that the alien can overcome a finding of inadmissibility by:

(1) Posting a bond under section 213 of the Act;

(2) Seeking and obtaining a waiver under section 211 or 212(d)(3) or (4) of the Act; or

(3) Presenting additional evidence of admissibility not available at the time and place of the initial examination.

(c) Such deferral shall be accomplished pursuant to the provisions of section 212(d)(5) of the Act for the period of time necessary to complete the deferred inspection.

(d) Refusal of a district director to authorize admission under section 213 of the Act, or to grant an application for the benefits of section 211 or section 212(d) (3) or (4) of the Act, shall be without prejudice to the renewal of such application or the authorizing of such admission by the immigration judge without additional fee.

(e) Whenever an alien on arrival is found or believed to be suffering from a disability that renders it impractical to proceed with the examination under the Act, the examination of such alien, members of his or her family concerning whose admissibility it is necessary to have such alien testify, and any accompanying aliens whose protection or guardianship will be required should such alien be found inadmissible shall be deferred for such time and under such conditions as the district director in whose district the port is located imposes.

HISTORY:

[22 FR 9791, Dec. 6, 1957; 62 FR 10312, 10355, March 6, 1997]

§ 235.3 Inadmissible aliens and expedited removal.

(a) Detention prior to inspection. All persons arriving at a port-of-entry in the United States by vessel or aircraft shall be detained aboard the vessel or at the airport of arrival by the owner, agent, master, commanding officer, person in charge, purser, or consignee of such vessel or aircraft until admitted or otherwise permitted to land by an officer of the Service. Notice or order to detain shall not be required. The owner, agent, master, commanding officer, person in charge, purser, or consignee of such vessel or aircraft shall deliver every alien requiring examination to an immigration officer for inspection or to a medical officer for examination. The Service will not be liable for any expenses related to such detention or presentation or for any expenses of a passenger who has not been presented for inspection and for whom a determination has not been made concerning admissibility by a Service officer.

(b) Expedited removal —

(1) Applicability. The expedited removal provisions shall apply to the following classes of aliens who are determined to be inadmissible under section 212(a)(6)(C) or (7) of the Act:

(i) Arriving aliens, as defined in 8 CFR 1.2;

(ii) As specifically designated by the Commissioner, aliens who arrive in, attempt to enter, or have entered the United States without having been admitted or paroled following inspection by an immigration officer at a designated port-of-entry, and who have not established to the satisfaction of the immigration officer that they have been physically present in the United States continuously for the 2-year period immediately prior to the date of determination of inadmissibility. The Commissioner shall have the sole discretion to apply the provisions of section 235(b)(1) of the Act, at any time, to any class of aliens described in this section. The Commissioner's designation shall become effective upon publication of a notice in the Federal Register. However, if the Commissioner determines, in the exercise of discretion, that the delay caused by publication would adversely affect the interests of the United States or the effective enforcement of the immigration laws, the Commissioner's designation shall become effective immediately upon issuance, and shall be published in the Federal Register as soon as practicable thereafter. When these provisions are in effect for aliens who enter without inspection, the burden of proof rests with the alien to affirmatively show that he or she has the required continuous physical presence in the United States. Any absence from the United States shall serve to break the period of continuous physical presence. An alien who was not inspected and admitted or paroled into the United States but who establishes that he or she has been continuously physically present in the United States for the 2-year period immediately prior to the date of determination of inadmissibility shall be detained in accordance with section 235(b)(2) of the Act for a proceeding under section 240 of the Act.

(2) Determination of inadmissibility —

(i) Record of proceeding. An alien who is arriving in the United States, or other alien as designated pursuant to paragraph (b)(1)(ii) of this section, who is determined to be inadmissible under section 212(a)(6)(C) or 212(a)(7) of the Act (except an alien for whom documentary requirements are waived under § 211.1(b)(3) or § 212.1 of this chapter), shall be ordered removed from the United States in accordance with section 235(b)(1) of the Act. In every case in which the expedited removal provisions will be applied and before removing an alien from the United States pursuant to this section, the examining immigration officer shall create a record of the facts of the case and statements made by the alien. This shall be accomplished by means of a sworn statement using Form I-867AB, Record of Sworn Statement in Proceedings under Section 235(b)(1) of the Act. The examining immigration officer shall read (or have read) to the alien all information contained on Form I-867A. Following questioning and recording of the alien's statement regarding identity, alienage, and inadmissibility, the examining immigration officer shall record the alien's response to the questions contained on Form I-867B, and have the alien read (or have read to him or her) the statement, and the alien shall sign and initial each page of the statement and each correction. The examining immigration officer shall advise the alien of the charges against him or her on Form I-860, Notice and Order of Expedited Removal, and the alien shall be given an opportunity to respond to those charges in the sworn statement. After obtaining supervisory concurrence in accordance with paragraph (b)(7) of this section, the examining immigration official shall serve the alien with Form I-860 and the alien shall sign the reverse of the form acknowledging receipt. Interpretative assistance shall be used if necessary to communicate with the alien.

(ii) No entitlement to hearings and appeals. Except as otherwise provided in this section, such alien is not entitled to a hearing before an immigration judge in proceedings conducted pursuant to section 240 of the Act, or to an appeal of the expedited removal order to the Board of Immigration Appeals.

(iii) Detention and parole of alien in expedited removal. An alien whose inadmissibility is being considered under this section or who has been ordered removed pursuant to this section shall be detained pending determination and removal. Parole of such alien shall only be considered in accordance with section 212(d)(5) of the Act and § 212.5(b) of this chapter. A grant of parole would be for the limited purpose of parole out of custody and cannot serve as an independent basis for employment authorization under § 274a.12(c)(11) of this chapter.

(3) Additional charges of inadmissibility. In the expedited removal process, the Service may not charge an alien with any additional grounds of inadmissibility other than section 212(a)(6)(C) or 212(a)(7) of the Act. If an alien appears to be inadmissible under other grounds contained in section 212(a) of the Act, and if the Service wishes to pursue such additional grounds of inadmissibility, the alien shall be detained and referred for a removal hearing before an immigration judge pursuant to sections 235(b)(2) and 240 of the Act for inquiry into all charges. Once the alien is in removal proceedings under section 240 of the Act, the Service is not precluded from lodging additional charges against the alien. Nothing in this paragraph shall preclude the Service from pursuing such additional grounds of inadmissibility against the alien in any subsequent attempt to reenter the United States, provided the additional grounds of inadmissibility still exist.

(4) Claim of asylum or fear of persecution or torture. If an alien subject to the expedited removal provisions indicates an intention to apply for asylum, or expresses a fear of persecution or torture, or a fear of return to his or her country, the inspecting officer shall not proceed further with removal of the alien until the alien has been referred for an interview by an asylum officer in accordance with 8 CFR 208.30. The examining immigration officer shall record sufficient information in the sworn statement to establish and record that the alien has indicated such intention, fear, or concern, and to establish the alien's inadmissibility.

(i) Referral. The referring officer shall provide the alien with a written disclosure on Form M-444, Information About Credible Fear Interview, describing:

(A) The purpose of the referral and description of the credible fear interview process;

(B) The right to consult with other persons prior to the interview and any review thereof at no expense to the United States Government;

(C) The right to request a review by an immigration judge of the asylum officer's credible fear determination; and

(D) The consequences of failure to establish a credible fear of persecution or torture.

(ii) Detention pending credible fear interview. Pending the credible fear determination by an asylum officer and any review of that determination by an immigration judge, the alien shall be detained. Parole of such alien shall only be considered in accordance with section 212(d)(5) of the Act and § 212.5(b) of this chapter. A grant of parole would be for the limited purpose of parole out of custody and cannot serve as an independent basis for employment authorization under § 274a.12(c)(11) of this chapter. Prior to the interview, the alien shall be given time to contact and consult with any person or persons of the alien's choosing. If the alien is detained, such consultation shall be made available in accordance with the policies and procedures of the detention facility where the alien is detained, shall be at no expense to the Government, and shall not unreasonably delay the process.

(5) Claim to lawful permanent resident, refugee, or asylee status or U.S. citizenship —

(i) Verification of status. If an applicant for admission who is subject to expedited removal pursuant to section 235(b)(1) of the Act claims to have been lawfully admitted for permanent residence, admitted as a refugee under section 207 of the Act, granted asylum under section 208 of the Act, or claims to be a U.S. citizen, the immigration officer shall attempt to verify the alien's claim. Such verification shall include a check of all available Service data systems and any other means available to the officer. An alien whose claim to lawful permanent resident, refugee, asylee status, or U.S. citizen status cannot be verified will be advised of the penalties for perjury, and will be placed under oath or allowed to make a declaration as permitted under 28 U.S.C. 1746, concerning his or her lawful admission for permanent residence, admission as a refugee under section 207 of the Act, grant of asylum status under section 208 of the Act, or claim to U.S. citizenship. A written statement shall be taken from the alien in the alien's own language and handwriting, stating that he or she declares, certifies, verifies, or states that the claim is true and correct. The immigration officer shall issue an expedited order of removal under section 235(b)(1)(A)(i) of the Act and refer the alien to the immigration judge for review of the order in accordance with paragraph (b)(5)(iv) of this section and § 235.6(a)(2)(ii). The person shall be detained pending review of the expedited removal order under this section. Parole of such person, in accordance with section 212(d)(5) of the Act, may be permitted only when the Attorney General determines, in the exercise of discretion, that parole is required to meet a medical emergency or is necessary for a legitimate law enforcement objective.

(ii) Verified lawful permanent residents. If the claim to lawful permanent resident status is verified, and such status has not been terminated in exclusion, deportation, or removal proceedings, the examining immigration officer shall not order the alien removed pursuant to section 235(b)(1) of the Act. The examining immigration officer will determine in accordance with section 101(a)(13)(C) of the Act whether the alien is considered to be making an application for admission. If the alien is determined to be seeking admission and the alien is otherwise admissible, except that he or she is not in possession of the required documentation, a discretionary waiver of documentary requirements may be considered in accordance with section 211(b) of the Act and § 211.1(b)(3) of this chapter or the alien's inspection may be deferred to an onward office for presentation of the required documents. If the alien appears to be inadmissible, the immigration officer may initiate removal proceedings against the alien under section 240 of the Act.

(iii) Verified refugees and asylees. If a check of Service records or other means indicates that the alien has been granted refugee status or asylee status, and such status has not been terminated in deportation, exclusion, or removal proceedings, the immigration officer shall not order the alien removed pursuant to section 235(b)(1) of the Act. If the alien is not in possession of a valid, unexpired refugee travel document, the examining immigration officer may accept an application for a refugee travel document in accordance with § 223.2(b)(2)(ii) of this chapter. If accepted, the immigration officer shall readmit the refugee or asylee in accordance with § 223.3(d)(2)(i) of this chapter. If the alien is determined not to be eligible to file an application for a refugee travel document the immigration officer may initiate removal proceedings against the alien under section 240 of the Act.

(iv) Review of order for claimed lawful permanent residents, refugees, asylees, or U.S. citizens. A person whose claim to U.S. citizenship has been verified may not be ordered removed. When an alien whose status has not been verified but who is claiming under oath or under penalty of perjury to be a lawful permanent resident, refugee, asylee, or U.S. citizen is ordered removed pursuant to section 235(b)(1) of the Act, the case will be referred to an immigration judge for review of the expedited removal order under section 235(b)(1)(C) of the Act and § 235.6(a)(2)(ii). If the immigration judge determines that the alien has never been admitted as a lawful permanent resident or as a refugee, granted asylum status, or is not a U.S. citizen, the order issued by the immigration officer will be affirmed and the Service will remove the alien. There is no appeal from the decision of the immigration judge. If the immigration judge determines that the alien was once so admitted as a lawful permanent resident or as a refugee, or was granted asylum status, or is a U.S. citizen, and such status has not been terminated by final administrative action, the immigration judge will terminate proceedings and vacate the expedited removal order. The Service may initiate removal proceedings against such an alien, but not against a person determined to be a U.S. citizen, in proceedings under section 240 of the Act. During removal proceedings, the immigration judge may consider any waivers, exceptions, or requests for relief for which the alien is eligible.

(6) Opportunity for alien to establish that he or she was admitted or paroled into the United States. If the Commissioner determines that the expedited removal provisions of section 235(b)(1) of the Act shall apply to any or all aliens described in paragraph (b)(2)(ii) of this section, such alien will be given a reasonable opportunity to establish to the satisfaction of the examining immigration officer that he or she was admitted or paroled into the United States following inspection at a port-of-entry. The alien will be allowed to present

evidence or provide sufficient information to support the claim. Such evidence may consist of documentation in the possession of the alien, the Service, or a third party. The examining immigration officer will consider all such evidence and information, make further inquiry if necessary, and will attempt to verify the alien's status through a check of all available Service data systems. The burden rests with the alien to satisfy the examining immigration officer of the claim of lawful admission or parole. If the alien establishes that he or she was lawfully admitted or paroled, the case will be examined to determine if grounds of deportability under section 237(a) of the Act are applicable, or if paroled, whether such parole has been, or should be, terminated, and whether the alien is inadmissible under section 212(a) of the Act. An alien who cannot satisfy the examining officer that he or she was lawfully admitted or paroled will be ordered removed pursuant to section 235(b)(1) of the Act.

(7) Review of expedited removal orders. Any removal order entered by an examining immigration officer pursuant to section 235(b)(1) of the Act must be reviewed and approved by the appropriate supervisor before the order is considered final. Such supervisory review shall not be delegated below the level of the second line supervisor, or a person acting in that capacity. The supervisory review shall include a review of the sworn statement and any answers and statements made by the alien regarding a fear of removal or return. The supervisory review and approval of an expedited removal order for an alien described in section 235(b)(1)(A)(iii) of the Act must include a review of any claim of lawful admission or parole and any evidence or information presented to support such a claim, prior to approval of the order. In such cases, the supervisor may request additional information from any source and may require further interview of the alien.

(8) Removal procedures relating to expedited removal. An alien ordered removed pursuant to section 235(b)(1) of the Act shall be removed from the United States in accordance with section 241(c) of the Act and 8 CFR part 241.

(9) Waivers of documentary requirements. Nothing in this section limits the discretionary authority of the Attorney General, including authority under sections 211(b) or 212(d) of the Act, to waive the documentary requirements for arriving aliens.

(10) Applicant for admission under section 217 of the Act. The provisions of § 235.3(b) do not apply to an applicant for admission under section 217 of the Act.

(c) Arriving aliens placed in proceedings under section 240 of the Act or aliens referred for an asylum merits interview under § 208.2(a)(1)(ii) of this chapter.

(1) Except as otherwise provided in this chapter, any arriving alien who appears to the inspecting officer to be inadmissible, and who is placed in removal proceedings pursuant to section 240 of the Act shall be detained in accordance with section 235(b) of the Act. Parole of such alien shall only be considered in accordance with § 212.5(b) of this chapter. This paragraph (c) shall also apply to any alien who arrived before April 1, 1997, and who was placed in exclusion proceedings.

(2) Except as otherwise provided in this chapter, any alien over whom USCIS exercises jurisdiction pursuant to § 208.2(a)(1)(ii) of this chapter after being found to have a credible fear of persecution or torture shall be detained in accordance with section 235(b) of the Act. Parole of such alien shall only be considered in accordance with § 212.5(b) of this chapter.

(d) Service custody. The Service will assume custody of any alien subject to detention under paragraph (b) or (c) of this section. In its discretion, the Service may require any alien who appears inadmissible and who arrives at a land border port-of-entry from Canada or Mexico, to remain in that country while awaiting a removal hearing. Such alien shall be considered detained for a proceeding within the meaning of section 235(b) of the Act and may be ordered removed in absentia by an immigration judge if the alien fails to appear for the hearing.

(e) Detention in non-Service facility. Whenever an alien is taken into Service custody and detained at a facility other than at a Service Processing Center, the public or private entities contracted to perform such service shall have been approved for such use by the Service's Jail Inspection Program or shall be performing such service under contract in compliance with the Standard Statement of Work for Contract Detention Facilities. Both programs are administered by the Detention and Deportation section having jurisdiction over the alien's place of detention. Under no circumstances shall an alien be detained in facilities not meeting the four mandatory criteria for usage. These are:

(1) 24-Hour supervision,

(2) Conformance with safety and emergency codes,

(3) Food service, and

(4) Availability of emergency medical care.

(f) Privilege of communication. The mandatory notification requirements of consular and diplomatic officers pursuant to § 236.1(e) of this chapter apply when an inadmissible alien is detained for removal proceedings, including for purpose of conducting the credible fear determination.

HISTORY:

[47 FR 30046, July 9, 1982, as amended at 47 FR 46494, Oct. 19, 1982; 54 FR 101, Jan. 4, 1989.; 54 FR 6365, Feb. 9, 1989; 60 FR 16043, Mar. 29, 1995; 62 FR 10312, 10355, Mar. 6, 1997; 64 FR 8478, 8494, Feb. 19, 1999; 65 FR 82254, 82256, Dec. 28, 2000; 66 FR 7863, Jan. 26, 2001; 69 FR 69480, 69490, Nov. 29, 2004; 76 FR 53764, 53790, Aug. 29, 2011; 82 FR 4769, 4771, Jan. 17, 2017; 87 FR 18078, 18220, Mar. 29, 2022]

§ 235.4 Withdrawal of application for admission.

The Attorney General may, in his or her discretion, permit any alien applicant for admission to withdraw his or her application for admission in lieu of removal proceedings under section 240 of the Act or expedited removal under section 235(b)(1) of the Act. The alien's decision to withdraw his or her application for admission must be made voluntarily, but nothing in this section shall be construed as to give an alien the right to withdraw his or her application for admission. Permission to withdraw an application for admission should not normally be granted unless the alien intends and is able to depart the United States immediately. An alien permitted to withdraw his or her application for admission shall normally remain in carrier or Service custody pending departure, unless the district director determines that parole of the alien is warranted in accordance with § 212.5(b) of this chapter.

HISTORY:

[48 FR 35349, Aug. 4, 1983; 62 FR 10312, 10358, March 6, 1997, as corrected at 62 FR 15362, 15363, April 1, 1997; 65 FR 82254, 82256, Dec. 28, 2000; 66 FR 7863, Jan. 26, 2001]

§ 235.5 Preinspection.

(a) In United States territories and possessions. In the case of any aircraft proceeding from Guam, the Commonwealth of the Northern Mariana Islands (beginning November 28, 2009), Puerto Rico, or the United States Virgin Islands destined directly and without touching at a foreign port or place, to any other of such places, or to one of the States of the United States or the District of Columbia, the examination of the passengers and crew required by the Act may be made prior to the departure of the aircraft, and in such event, final determination of admissibility will be made immediately prior to such departure. The examination will be conducted in accordance with sections 232, 235, and 240 of the Act and 8 CFR parts 235 and 240. If it appears to the immigration officer that any person in the United States being examined under this section is prima facie removable from the United States, further action with respect to his or her examination will be deferred and further proceedings regarding removability conducted as provided in section 240 of the Act and 8 CFR part 240. When the foregoing inspection procedure is applied to any aircraft, persons examined and found admissible will be placed aboard the aircraft, or kept at the airport separate and apart from the general public until they are permitted to board the aircraft. No other person will be permitted to depart on such aircraft until and unless he or she is found to be admissible as provided in this section.

(b) In foreign territory. In the case of any aircraft, vessel, or train proceeding directly, without stopping, from a port or place in foreign territory to a port-of-entry in the United States, the examination and inspection of passengers and crew required by the Act and final determination of admissibility may be made immediately prior to such departure at the port or place in the foreign territory and shall have the same effect under the Act as though made at the destined port-of-entry in the United States.

HISTORY:

[23 FR 3997, June 7, 1958, as amended at 24 FR 2583, Apr. 3, 1959; 50 FR 11842, Mar. 26, 1985; 54 FR 101, Jan. 4, 1989.; 62 FR 10312, 10358, Mar. 6, 1997; 74 FR 2824, 2836, Jan. 16, 2009; 74 FR 25387, 25388, May 28, 2009]

§ 235.6 Referral to immigration judge. [Effective until December 31, 2025]

(a) Notice —.

(1) Referral by Form I-862, Notice to Appear. An immigration officer or asylum officer will sign and deliver a Form I-862 to an alien in the following cases:

(i) If, in accordance with the provisions of section 235(b)(2)(A) of the Act, the examining immigration officer detains an alien for a proceeding before an immigration judge under section 240 of the Act; or

(ii) If an immigration officer verifies that an alien subject to expedited removal under section 235(b)(1) of the Act has been admitted as a lawful permanent resident or refugee, or granted asylum, or, upon review pursuant to §235.3(b)(5)(iv) of chapter I, an immigration judge determines that the alien was once so admitted or granted asylum, provided that such status has not been terminated by final administrative action, and the DHS initiates removal proceedings against the alien under section 240 of the Act.

(iii) [Removed and reserved.]

(iv) [Removed and reserved.]

(2) Referral by Form I-863, Notice of Referral to Immigration Judge. An immigration officer will sign and deliver a Form I-863 to an alien in the following cases:

(i) If an asylum officer determines that the alien does not have a credible fear of persecution or torture, and the alien requests a review of that determination by an immigration judge;

(ii) If, in accordance with section 235(b)(1)(C) of the Act, an immigration officer refers an expedited removal order entered on an alien claiming to be a lawful permanent resident, refugee, asylee, or U.S. citizen for whom the officer could not verify such status to an immigration judge for review of the order; or

(iii) If an immigration officer refers an applicant in accordance with the provisions of § 208.2(c)(1) or (2) of this chapter to an immigration judge for an asylum- or withholding-only hearing.

(b) Certification for mental condition; medical appeal. An alien certified under sections 212(a)(1) and 232(b) of the Act shall be advised by the examining immigration officer that he or she may appeal to a board of medical examiners of the United States Public Health Service pursuant to section 232 of the Act. If such appeal is taken, the district director shall arrange for the convening of the medical board.

(c) The provisions of part 235 are separate and severable from one another. In the event that any provision in part 235 is stayed, enjoined, not implemented, or otherwise held invalid, the remaining provisions shall nevertheless be implemented as an independent rule and continue in effect.

HISTORY:

[24 FR 6477, Aug. 12, 1959, as amended at 44 FR 4653, Jan. 23, 1979; 56 FR 50812, Oct. 9, 1991; 62 FR 9071, 9074, Feb. 28, 1997; 62 FR 10312, 10358, Mar. 6, 1997; 64 FR 8478, 8494, Feb. 19, 1999; 74 FR 55726, 55739, Oct. 28, 2009; 85 FR 29264, 29316, May 14, 2020; 85 FR 80274, 80393, Dec. 11, 2020; 85 FR 84160, 84196, Dec. 23, 2020; 86 FR 6847, Jan. 25, 2021; 86 FR 15069, Mar. 22, 2021; 86

FR 73615, Dec. 28, 2021; 87 FR 18078, 18220, Mar. 29, 2022; 87 FR 79789, Dec. 28, 2022; 89 FR 105386, Dec. 27, 2024]

§ 235.6 Referral to immigration judge. [Effective December 31, 2025]

(a) Notice —.

(1) Referral by Form I-862, Notice to Appear. An immigration officer or asylum officer will sign and deliver a Form I-862 to an alien in the following cases:

(i) If, in accordance with the provisions of section 235(b)(2)(A) of the Act, the examining immigration officer detains an alien for a proceeding before an immigration judge under section 240 of the Act; or

(ii) If an immigration officer verifies that an alien subject to expedited removal under section 235(b)(1) of the Act has been admitted as a lawful permanent resident or refugee, or granted asylum, or, upon review pursuant to §235.3(b)(5)(iv) of chapter I, an immigration judge determines that the alien was once so admitted or granted asylum, provided that such status has not been terminated by final administrative action, and the DHS initiates removal proceedings against the alien under section 240 of the Act.

(iii) [Removed and reserved.]

(iv) [Removed and reserved.]

(2) Referral by Form I-863, Notice of Referral to Immigration Judge. An immigration officer will sign and deliver a Form I-863 to an alien in the following cases:

(i) If an asylum officer determines that the alien has not established a credible fear of persecution, reasonable possibility of persecution, reasonable possibility of torture, or that it is more likely than not that the alien would be tortured in the prospective country of removal, and the alien requests a review of that determination by an immigration judge; or

(ii) If, in accordance with section 235(b)(1)(C) of the Act, an immigration officer refers an expedited removal order entered on an alien claiming to be a lawful permanent resident, refugee, asylee, or U.S. citizen for whom the officer could not verify such status to an immigration judge for review of the order; or

(iii) If an immigration officer refers an applicant in accordance with the provisions of § 208.2(c)(1) or (2) of this chapter to an immigration judge for an asylum- or withholding-only hearing.

(b) Certification for mental condition; medical appeal. An alien certified under sections 212(a)(1) and 232(b) of the Act shall be advised by the examining immigration officer that he or she may appeal to a board of medical examiners of the United States Public Health Service pursuant to section 232 of the Act. If such appeal is taken, the district director shall arrange for the convening of the medical board.

(c) The provisions of part 235 are separate and severable from one another. In the event that any provision in part 235 is stayed, enjoined, not implemented, or otherwise held invalid, the remaining provisions shall nevertheless be implemented as an independent rule and continue in effect.

HISTORY:

[24 FR 6477, Aug. 12, 1959, as amended at 44 FR 4653, Jan. 23, 1979; 56 FR 50812, Oct. 9, 1991; 62 FR 9071, 9074, Feb. 28, 1997; 62 FR 10312, 10358, Mar. 6, 1997; 64 FR 8478, 8494, Feb. 19, 1999; 74 FR 55726, 55739, Oct. 28, 2009; 85 FR 29264, 29316, May 14, 2020; 85 FR 80274, 80393, Dec. 11, 2020; 85 FR 84160, 84196, Dec. 23, 2020; 86 FR 6847, Jan. 25, 2021; 86 FR 15069, Mar. 22, 2021; 86 FR 73615, Dec. 28, 2021; 87 FR 18078, 18220, Mar. 29, 2022; 87 FR 79789, Dec. 28, 2022; 89 FR 105386, Dec. 27, 2024]

§ 235.7 Automated inspection services (PORTPASS).

(a) PORTPASS Program —

(1) Definitions —

(i) Port Passenger Accelerated Service System (PORTPASS). A system in which certain ports-of-entry (POEs) are identified and designated by the Service as providing access to the United States for a group of identified, low-risk, border crossers. Alien participants in the PORTPASS program are personally inspected, identified, and screened in advance of approval for participation in the program by an immigration officer, and may apply to enter the United States through a dedicated commuter lane (DCL) or through an automated permit port (APP). Such advance inspection and identification, when the enrolled participant satisfies the conditions and requirements set fourth in this section, satisfies the reporting requirements of § 235.1(a). Each successful use of PORTPASS constitutes a separate and completed inspection and application for entry by the alien program participants on the date PORTPASS is used. United States citizens who meet the eligibility requirements for participation are subject to all rules, procedures, and conditions for use set forth in this section.

(ii) SENTRI program. Although the SENTRI program is a PORTPASS program, all the parameters of the SENTRI program, including the eligibility requirements, application procedures, redress procedures, registration of vehicles, use of dedicated commuter lanes, and fee requirements are specified in § 235.14. For purposes of the SENTRI program, § 235.14 supersedes the provisions of this section.

(iii) Automated Permit Port (APP). A POE designated by the Service to provide access to the United States by an identified, low-risk, border crosser through the use of automation when the POE is not staffed. An APP has limited hours of operation and is located at a remote location on a land border. This program is limited to the northern border of the United States.

(iv) Dedicated commuter lane (DCL). A special lane set apart from the normal flow of traffic at a land border POE which allows an accelerated inspection for identified, low-risk travelers. This program is limited to the northern border of the United States and the California-Mexico border.

(v) DCL system costs fee. A fee charged to a participant to cover the cost of the implementation and operation of the PORTPASS system. If a participant wishes to enroll more than one vehicle for use in the PORTPASS system, he or she will be assessed an additional vehicle fee for each additional vehicle enrolled. Regardless of when the additional vehicle is enrolled, the expiration date for use of that vehicle in the DCL will be the same date that the respective participant's authorized use of the lane expires, or is otherwise revoked.

(2) Designation of POEs for PORTPASS access. The following criteria shall be used by the Service in the selection of a POE when classifying the POE as having PORTPASS access:

(i) The location has an identifiable group of low-risk border crossers;

(ii) The institution of PORTPASS access will not significantly inhibit normal traffic flow;

(iii) The POE selected for access via a DCL has a sufficient number of Service personnel to perform primary and secondary inspection functions.

(3) General eligibility requirements for PORTPASS program applicants. Applicants to PORTPASS must be citizens or lawful permanent residents of the United States, or nonimmigrants determined to be eligible by the Commissioner of the Service. Non-United States citizens must meet all applicable documentary and entry eligibility requirements of the Act. Applicants must agree to furnish all information requested on the application, and must agree to terms set forth for use of the PORTPASS program. Use of the PORTPASS program constitutes application for entry into the United States. Criminal justice information databases will be checked to assist in determining the applicant's eligibility for the PORTPASS program at the time the Form I-823, Application-Alternative Inspection Services, is submitted. Criminal justice information on PORTPASS participants will be updated regularly, and the results will be checked electronically at the time of each approved participant's use of PORTPASS. Notwithstanding the provisions of 8 CFR part 264, fingerprints on Form FD-258 or in the manner prescribed by the Service may be required.

(4) Application.

(i) Application for PORTPASS access shall be made on Form I-823, Application-Alternative Inspection Services. Applications may be submitted during regular working hours at the principal Port-of-Entry having jurisdiction over the Port-of-Entry for which the applicant requests access. Applications may also be submitted by mail.

(ii) Each person seeking PORTPASS access must file a separate application.

(iii) The number of persons and vehicles which can use a DCL is limited numerically by the technology of the system. For this reason, distribution of applications at each POE may be limited.

(iv) Applications must be supported by evidence of citizenship, and, in the case of lawful permanent residents of the United States, evidence of lawful permanent resident status in the United States. Alien applicants required to possess a valid visa must present documentation establishing such possession and any other documentation as required by the Act at the time of the application, and must be in possession of such documentation at the time of each entry, and at all times while present in the United States. Evidence of residency must be submitted by all applicants. Evidence of employment may be required to be furnished by the applicant. A current valid driver's license, and evidence of vehicle registration and insurance for the vehicle which will be occupied by the applicant as a driver or passenger when he or she uses the DCL or APP must be presented to the Service prior to approval of the application.

(v) A completed Form I-823 must be accompanied by the fee as prescribed in 8 CFR 103.7(d)(7). Each PORTPASS applicant 14 years-of-age or older must complete the application and pay the application fee. Applicants under the age of 14 will be required to complete the application, but will not be required to pay the application fee. An application for a replacement PORTPASS card must be made on the Form I-823, and filed with the fee prescribed in 8 CFR 103.7(d)(7). The district director having jurisdiction over the POE where the applicant requests access may, in his or her discretion, waive the application or replacement fee.

(vi) If fingerprints are required to assist in a determination of eligibility at that POE, the applicant will be so advised by the Service prior to submitting his or her application. The applicant shall also be informed at that time of the current Federal Bureau of Investigation fee for conducting a fingerprint check. This fee must be paid by the applicant to the Service before any processing of the application shall occur. The fingerprint fee may be not be waived.

(vii) Each applicant must present himself or herself for an inspection and/or positive identification at a time designated by the Service prior to approval of the application.

(viii) Each vehicle that a PORTPASS participant desires to register in PORTPASS must be inspected and approved by the Service prior to use in the PORTPASS system. Evidence of valid, current registration and vehicle insurance must be presented to the Service at the time the vehicle is inspected. If the vehicle is not owned by the participant, the participant may be required to present written permission from the registered owner authorizing use of the vehicle in the PORTPASS program throughout the PORTPASS registration period.

(ix) An applicant, whether an occupant or driver, may apply to use more than one vehicle in the DCL. The first vehicle listed on the Form I-823 will be designated as the applicant's primary vehicle. The second vehicle, if not designated by another applicant as his or her primary vehicle, is subject to the additional vehicle charge as prescribed by the Service.

(x) An application may be denied in the discretion of the district director having jurisdiction over the POE where the applicant requests access. Notice of such denial shall be given to the applicant. There is no appeal from the denial, but denial is without prejudice to reapplying for this or any other Service benefit. Re-applications, or applications following revocation of permission to use the lane, will not be considered by the Service until 90 days have passed following the date of denial or revocation. Criteria which will be considered in the decision to approve or deny the application include the following: admissibility to the United States and documentation so evidencing, criminal history and/or evidence of criminality, purpose of travel, employment, residency, prior immigration history, possession of current driver's license, vehicle insurance and registration, and vehicle inspection.

(xi) Applications approved by the Service will entitle the applicant to seek entry via a designated PORTPASS Program POE for a period of 2 years from the date of approval of the application unless approval is otherwise withdrawn. An application for a replacement card will not extend the initial period of approval.

(5) By applying for and participating in the PORTPASS program, each approved participant acknowledges and agrees to all of the following:

(i) The installation and/or use of, in the vehicle approved for use in the PORTPASS program, any and all decals, devices, technology or other methodology deemed necessary by the Service to ensure inspection of the person(s) seeking entry through a DCL, in addition to any fee and/or monetary deposit assessed by the Service pending return of any and all such decals, devices, technology, and other methodology in undamaged condition.

(ii) That all devices, decals, or other equipment, methodology, or technology used to identify or inspect persons or vehicles seeking entry via any PORTPASS program remains the property of the United States Government at all times, and must be surrendered upon request by the Service. Each participant agrees to abide by the terms set forth by the Service for use of any device, decal, or other equipment, method or technology.

(iii) The payment of a system costs fee as determined by the Service to be necessary to cover the costs of implementing, maintaining, and operating the PORTPASS program.

(iv) That each occupant of a vehicle applying for entry through PORTPASS must have current approval from the Service to apply for entry through the PORTPASS program in that vehicle.

(v) That a participant must be in possession of any authorization document(s) issued for PORTPASS access and any other entry document(s) as required by the Act or by regulation at the time of each entry to the United States.

(vi) That a participant must positively identify himself or herself in the manner prescribed by the Service at the time of each application for entry via the PORTPASS.

(vii) That each use of PORTPASS constitutes a separate application for entry to the United States by the alien participant.

(viii) That each participant agrees to be responsible for all contents of the vehicle that he or she occupies when using PORTPASS.

(ix) That a participant may not import merchandise or transport controlled or restricted items using PORTPASS. The entry of any merchandise or goods must be in accordance with the laws and regulations of all other Federal inspection agencies.

(x) That a participant must abide by all Federal, state and local laws regarding the importation of alcohol or agricultural products or the importation or possession of controlled substances as defined in section 101 of the Controlled Substance Act (21 U.S.C. § 802).

(xi) That a participant will be subject to random checks or inspections that may be conducted by the Service at any time and at any location, to ensure compliance.

(xii) That current vehicle registration and, if applicable, current permission to use the vehicle in PORTPASS, and evidence of current vehicle insurance, shall be in the vehicle at all times during use of PORTPASS.

(xiii) Participant agrees to notify the Service if a vehicle approved for use in a PORTPASS program is sold, stolen, damaged, or disposed of otherwise. If a vehicle is sold, it is the responsibility of the participant to remove or obliterate any identifying device or other authorization for participation in the program or at the time of sale unless otherwise notified by the Service. If any license plates are replaced on an enrolled vehicle, the participant must submit a properly executed Form I-823, without fee, prior to use of the vehicle in the PORTPASS program.

(xiv) That APP-approved participants who wish to enter the United States through a POE other than one designated as an APP through which they may pass must present themselves for inspection or examination by an immigration officer during normal business hours. Entry to the United States during hours when a Port of Entry is not staffed may be made only through a POE designated as an APP.

(b) Violation of condition of the PORTPASS program. A PORTPASS program participant who violates any condition of the PORTPASS program, or who has violated any immigration law or regulation, or a law or regulation of the United States Customs Service or other Federal Inspection Service, or who is otherwise determined by an immigration officer to be inadmissible to the United States or ineligible to participate in PORTPASS, may have the PORTPASS access revoked at the discretion of the district director or the chief patrol agent and may be subject to other applicable sanctions, such as criminal and/or administrative prosecution or deportation, as well as possible seizure of goods and/or vehicles.

(c) Judicial review. Nothing in this section is intended to create any right or benefit, substantive or procedural, enforceable in law or equity by a party against the Department of Justice, the Immigration and Naturalization Service, their officers or any employees of the Department of Justice.

HISTORY:

[60 FR 50386, 50389, Sept. 29, 1995, as confirmed and revised at 61 FR 53830, 53831, Oct. 16, 1996, redesignated at 62 FR 10312, 10358, March 6, 1997; 68 FR 10143, 10145, Mar. 4, 2003; 85 FR 46788, 46926, Aug. 3, 2020; 89 FR 22607, 22628, Apr. 2, 2024]

§ 235.8 Inadmissibility on security and related grounds.

(a) Report. When an immigration officer or an immigration judge suspects that an arriving alien appears to be inadmissible under section 212(a)(3)(A) (other than clause (ii)), (B), or (C) of the Act, the immigration officer or immigration judge shall order the alien removed and report the action promptly to the district director who has administrative jurisdiction over the place where the alien has arrived or where the hearing is being held. The immigration officer shall, if possible, take a brief sworn question-and-answer statement from the alien, and the alien shall be notified by personal service of Form I-147, Notice of Temporary Inadmissibility, of the action taken and the right to submit a written statement and additional information for consideration by the Attorney General. The district director shall forward the report to the regional director for further action as provided in paragraph (b) of this section.

(b) **Action by regional director.**

(1) In accordance with section 235(c)(2)(B) of the Act, the regional director may deny any further inquiry or hearing by an immigration judge and order the alien removed by personal service of Form I-148, Notice of Permanent Inadmissibility, or issue any other order disposing of the case that the regional director considers appropriate.

(2) If the regional director concludes that the case does not meet the criteria contained in section 235(c)(2)(B) of the Act, the regional director may direct that:

(i) An immigration officer shall conduct a further examination of the alien, concerning the alien's admissibility; or,

(ii) The alien's case be referred to an immigration judge for a hearing, or for the continuation of any prior hearing.

(3) The regional director's decision shall be in writing and shall be signed by the regional director. Unless the written decision contains confidential information, the disclosure of which would be prejudicial to the public interest, safety, or security of the United States, the written decision shall be served on the alien. If the written decision contains such confidential information, the alien shall be served with a separate written order showing the disposition of the case, but with the confidential information deleted.

(4) The Service shall not execute a removal order under this section under circumstances that violate section 241(b)(3) of the Act or Article 3 of the Convention Against Torture. The provisions of part 208 of this chapter relating to consideration or review by an immigration judge, the Board of Immigration Appeals, or an asylum officer shall not apply.

(c) Finality of decision. The regional director's decision under this section is final when it is served upon the alien in accordance with paragraph (b)(3) of this section. There is no administrative appeal from the regional director's decision.

(d) Hearing by immigration judge. If the regional director directs that an alien subject to removal under this section be given a hearing or further hearing before an immigration judge, the hearing and all further proceedings in the matter shall be conducted in accordance with the provisions of section 240 of the Act and other applicable sections of the Act to the same extent as though the alien had been referred to an immigration judge by the examining immigration officer. In a case where the immigration judge ordered the alien removed pursuant to paragraph (a) of this section, the Service shall refer the case back to the immigration judge and proceedings shall be automatically reopened upon receipt of the notice of referral. If confidential information, not previously considered in the matter, is presented supporting the inadmissibility of the alien under section 212(a)(3)(A) (other than clause (ii)), (B) or (C) of the Act, the disclosure of which, in the discretion of the immigration judge, may be prejudicial to the public interest, safety, or security, the immigration judge may again order the alien removed under the authority of section 235(c) of the Act and further action shall be taken as provided in this section.

(e) Nonapplicability. The provisions of this section shall apply only to arriving aliens, as defined in 8 CFR 1.2. Aliens present in the United States who have not been admitted or paroled may be subject to proceedings under Title V of the Act.

HISTORY:

[22 FR 9791, Dec. 6, 1957; 22 FR 9519, Nov. 28, 1957, as amended at 48 FR 8, Jan. 3, 1983; 48 FR 30350, July 1, 1983; 62 FR 10312, 10358, Mar. 6, 1997; 64 FR 8478, 8494, Feb. 19, 1999; 76 FR 53764, 53790, Aug. 29, 2011]

§ 235.9 Northern Mariana identification card.

During the two-year period that ended July 1, 1990, the Service issued Northern Marianas Identification Cards to aliens who acquired United States citizenship when the Covenant to Establish a Commonwealth of the Northern Mariana Islands in Political Union with the United States entered into force on November 3, 1986. These cards remain valid as evidence of United States citizenship. Although the Service no longer issues these cards, a United States citizen to whom a card was issued may file Form I-777, Application for Issuance or Replacement of Northern Marianas Card, to obtain replacement of a lost, stolen, or mutilated Northern Marianas Identification Card.

HISTORY:

[53 FR 23380, June 22, 1988, redesignated and revised at 62 FR 10312, 10359, March 6, 1997]

§ 235.10 U.S. Citizen Identification Card.

(a) General. Form I-197, U.S. Citizen Identification Card, is no longer issued by the Service but valid existing cards will continue to be acceptable documentation of U.S. citizenship. Possession of the identification card is not mandatory for any purpose. A U.S. Citizen Identification Card remains the property of the United States. Because the identification card is no longer issued, there are no provisions for replacement cards.

(b) **Surrender and voidance.**

(1) Institution of proceeding under section 240 or 342 of the Act. A U.S. Citizen Identification Card must be surrendered provisionally to a Service office upon noti-

fication by the district director that a proceeding under section 240 or 342 of the Act is being instituted against the person to whom the card was issued. The card shall be returned to the person if the final order in the proceeding does not result in voiding the card under this paragraph. A U.S. Citizen Identification Card is automatically void if the person to whom it was issued is determined to be an alien in a proceeding conducted under section 240 of the Act, or if a certificate, document, or record relating to that person is canceled under section 342 of the Act.

(2) Investigation of validity of identification card. A U.S. Citizen Identification Card must be surrendered provisionally upon notification by a district director that the validity of the card is being investigated. The card shall be returned to the person who surrendered it if the investigation does not result in a determination adverse to his or her claim to be a United States citizen. When an investigation results in a tentative determination adverse to the applicant's claim to be a United States citizen, the applicant shall be notified by certified mail directed to his or her last known address. The notification shall inform the applicant of the basis for the determination and of the intention of the district director to declare the card void unless within 30 days the applicant objects and demands an opportunity to see and rebut the adverse evidence. Any rebuttal, explanation, or evidence presented by the applicant must be included in the record of proceeding. The determination whether the applicant is a United States citizen must be based on the entire record and the applicant shall be notified of the determination. If it is determined that the applicant is not a United States citizen, the applicant shall be notified of the reasons, and the card deemed void. There is no appeal from the district director's decision.

(3) Admission of alienage. A U.S. Citizen Identification Card is void if the person to whom it was issued admits in a statement signed before an immigration officer that he or she is an alien and consents to the voidance of the card. Upon signing the statement the card must be surrendered to the immigration officer.

(4) Surrender of void card. A void U.S. Citizen Identification Card which has not been returned to the Service must be surrendered without delay to an immigration officer or to the issuing office of the Service.

(c) U.S. Citizen Identification Card previously issued on Form I-179. A valid Form I-179, U.S. Citizen Identification Card, continues to be valid subject to the provisions of this section.

HISTORY:

[48 FR 9504, Mar. 7, 1983; 62 FR 10312, 10359, March 6, 1997]

§ 235.11 Admission of conditional permanent residents.

(a) **General.**

(1) Conditional residence based on family relationship. An alien seeking admission to the United States with an immigrant visa as the spouse or son or daughter of a United States citizen or lawful permanent resident shall be examined to determine whether the conditions of section 216 of the Act apply. If so, the alien shall be admitted conditionally for a period of 2 years. At the time of admission, the alien shall be notified that the alien and his or her petitioning spouse must file a Form I-751, Petition to Remove the Conditions on Residence, within the 90-day period immediately preceding the second anniversary of the alien's admission for permanent residence.

(2) Conditional residence based on entrepreneurship. An alien seeking admission to the United States with an immigrant visa as an alien entrepreneur (as defined in section 216A(f)(1) of the Act) or the spouse or unmarried minor child of an alien entrepreneur shall be admitted conditionally for a period of 2 years. At the time of admission, the alien shall be notified that the principal alien (entrepreneur) must file a Form I-829, Petition by Entrepreneur to Remove Conditions, within the 90-day period immediately preceding the second anniversary of the alien's admission for permanent residence.

(b) Correction of endorsement on immigrant visa. If the alien is subject to the provisions of section 216 of the Act, but the classification endorsed on the immigrant visa does not so indicate, the endorsement shall be corrected and the alien shall be admitted as a lawful permanent resident on a conditional basis, if otherwise admissible. Conversely, if the alien is not subject to the provisions of section 216 of the Act, but the visa classification endorsed on the immigrant visa indicates that the alien is subject thereto (e.g., if the second anniversary of the marriage upon which the immigrant visa is based occurred after the issuance of the visa and prior to the alien's application for admission) the endorsement on the visa shall be corrected and the alien shall be admitted as a lawful permanent resident without conditions, if otherwise admissible.

(c) Expired conditional permanent resident status. The lawful permanent resident alien status of a conditional resident automatically terminates if the conditional basis of such status is not removed by the Service through approval of a Form I-751, Petition to Remove the Conditions on Residence or, in the case of an alien entrepreneur (as defined in section 216A(f)(1) of the Act), Form I-829, Petition by Entrepreneur to Remove Conditions. Therefore, an alien who is seeking admission as a returning resident subsequent to the second anniversary of the date on which conditional residence was obtained (except as provided in § 211.1(b)(1) of this chapter) and whose conditional basis of such residence has not been removed pursuant to section 216(c) or 216A(c) of the Act, whichever is applicable, shall be placed under removal proceedings. However, in a case where conditional residence was based on a marriage, removal proceedings may be terminated and the alien may be admitted as a returning resident if the required Form I-751 is filed jointly, or by the alien alone (if appropriate), and approved by the Service. In the case of an alien entrepreneur, removal proceedings may be terminated and the alien admitted as a returning resident if the required Form I-829 is filed by the alien entrepreneur and approved by the Service.

HISTORY:

[53 FR 30021, Aug. 10, 1988; 59 FR 26592, May 23, 1994; 62 FR 10312, 10360, March 6, 1997.]

§ 235.12 Global Entry program.

(a) Program description. The Global Entry program is a voluntary international trusted traveler program consisting of an integrated passenger processing system that facilitates the movement of pre-approved, low-risk, air travelers by providing dedicated CBP processing at specified airports. In order to participate, a person must meet the eligibility requirements specified in this section, apply in advance, undergo vetting by CBP, and be accepted into the program. The Global Entry program allows participants dedicated CBP processing at selected airports identified by CBP at https://www.cbp.gov/. Participants in the Global Entry program may also take advantage of certain benefits of the Secure Electronic Network for Travelers Rapid Inspection (SENTRI) and NEXUS programs. Please see http://www.cbp.gov for additional information. Participants will be processed through the use of CBP-approved technology that will include the use of biometrics to validate identity and to perform enforcement queries.

(b) Program eligibility criteria.

(1) Eligible individuals. The following individuals, who hold a valid, machine-readable passport, a valid, machine-readable U.S. Lawful Permanent Resident Card (Form I-551), or other appropriate travel document as determined by CBP, may apply to participate in Global Entry:

(i) U.S. citizens, U.S. nationals, and U.S. lawful permanent residents absent any of the disqualifying factors described in paragraph (b)(2) of this section.

(ii) Certain nonimmigrant aliens from countries that have entered into arrangements with CBP concerning international trusted traveler programs absent any of the disqualifying factors described in paragraph (b)(2) of this section, and subject to the conditions set forth in the particular arrangement. Individuals from a country that has entered into such an arrangement with CBP may be eligible to apply for participation in Global Entry only after CBP announces the arrangement by publication of a notice in the Federal Register The notice will include the country, the scope of eligibility of nonimmigrant aliens from that country (e.g., whether only citizens of the foreign country or citizens and non-citizens are eligible) and other conditions that may apply based on the terms of the arrangement. CBP may change or terminate these arrangements without prior notice to the public, but will announce such actions as soon as practicable on Federal Register

(iii) Persons under the age of 18 who meet the eligibility criteria of paragraph (b)(1)(i) or (ii) of this section must have the consent of a parent or legal guardian to participate in Global Entry and provide proof of such consent in accordance with CBP instructions.

(2) Disqualifying factors. An individual is ineligible to participate in Global Entry if CBP, at its sole discretion, determines that the individual presents a potential risk for terrorism, criminality (such as smuggling), or is otherwise not a low-risk traveler. This risk determination will be based in part upon an applicant's ability to demonstrate past compliance with laws, regulations, and policies. Reasons why an applicant may not qualify for participation include:

(i) The applicant provides false or incomplete information on the application;

(ii) The applicant has been arrested for, or convicted of, any criminal offense or has pending criminal charges or outstanding warrants in any country;

(iii) The applicant has been found in violation of any customs, immigration, or agriculture regulations, procedures, or laws in any country;

(iv) The applicant is the subject of an investigation by any federal, state, or local law enforcement agency in any country;

(v) The applicant is inadmissible to the United States under applicable immigration laws or has, at any time, been granted a waiver of inadmissibility or parole;

(vi) The applicant is known or suspected of being or having been engaged in conduct constituting, in preparation for, in aid of, or related to terrorism; or

(vii) The applicant cannot satisfy CBP of his or her low-risk status or meet other program requirements.

(c) Participating airports. The Global Entry program allows participants dedicated CBP processing at the locations identified at https://www.cbp.gov/. Expansions of the Global Entry program to new airports will be announced by publication in the Federal Register and at https://www.cbp.gov/.

(d) Program application.

(1) Each applicant must complete and submit the program application electronically through an approved application process as determined by CBP. The application and application instructions for the Global Entry program are available at https://www.globalentry.gov/.

(2) Except for certain minors, all applicants must pay the non-refundable fee in the amount set forth at 8 CFR 103.7(d)(13) for "Global Entry." Minors under the age of 18 who apply to the Global Entry program concurrently with a parent or legal guardian, or whose parent or legal guardian is already a participant of Global Entry, are exempt from payment of the applicable fee. The fee is to be paid to CBP at the time of application through the online TTP System, which can be found through https://www.cbp.gov/, or other CBP-approved process.

(3) Every applicant accepted into Global Entry is accepted for a period of 5 years provided participation is not terminated by CBP prior to the end of the 5-year period. Each applicant may apply to renew participation up to one year prior to the close of the participation period.

(4) Each applicant may check the status of his or her application through his or her account with the application system in use for Global Entry.

(e) Interview and enrollment.

(1) After submitting the application, conditionally approved applicants will be notified by CBP that they need to undergo a personal interview.

(2) Each applicant must bring to the interview with CBP the original of the identification document specified in his or her application. During the interview, CBP will collect biometric information from the applicant (e.g., a set of ten fingerprints and/or digital photograph) to conduct background checks or as otherwise required for participation in the program.

(3) CBP may provide for alternative enrollment procedures, as necessary, to facilitate enrollment and ensure an applicant's eligibility for the program.

(f) Valid machine-readable passport or valid lawful permanent resident card. Each participant must possess a valid, machine-readable passport, a valid, machine-readable U.S. Lawful Permanent Resident Card (Form I-551), or other appropriate travel document as determined by CBP.

(g) Arrival procedures. In order to utilize the Global Entry program, each participant must:

(1) Proceed to Global Entry Processing and follow all CBP instructions; and

(2) Proceed to the nearest open primary inspection station if CBP determines it is appropriate.

(h) Application for entry, examination, and inspection. Each successful use of Global Entry constitutes a separate and completed inspection and application for entry by the participant on the date that Global Entry is used. Global Entry participants may be subject to further CBP examination and inspection at any time during the arrival process.

(i) Pilot participant enrollment. Upon implementation of the Global Entry Program, participants in the Global Entry pilot will be automatically enrolled in the Global Entry Program for 5 years from the date of enrollment in the pilot.

(j) Denial and removal.

(1) If an applicant is denied participation in Global Entry, CBP will notify the applicant of the denial, and the reasons for the denial. CBP will also provide instructions regarding how to proceed if the applicant wishes to seek additional information as to the reason for the denial.

(2) A Global Entry participant may be removed from the program for any of the following reasons:

(i) CBP, at its sole discretion, determines that the participant has engaged in any disqualifying activities under the Global Entry program as outlined in § 235.12(b)(2);

(ii) CBP, at its sole discretion, determines that the participant provided false information in the application and/or during the application process;

(iii) CBP, at its sole discretion, determines that the participant failed to follow the terms, conditions and requirements of the program;

(iv) CBP, at its sole discretion, determines that the participant has been arrested or convicted of a crime or otherwise no longer meets the program eligibility criteria; or

(v) CBP, at its sole discretion, determines that such action is otherwise necessary.

(3) CBP will notify the participant of his or her suspension or removal in writing. Such suspension or removal is effective immediately.

(4) An applicant or participant denied or removed will not receive a refund, in whole or in part, of his or her application processing fee.

(k) Redress. An individual whose application is denied or who is removed from the program has two possible methods of redress. These processes do not create or confer any legal right, privilege or benefit on the applicant or participant, and are wholly discretionary on the part of CBP. The methods of redress are:

(1) DHS Traveler Redress Inquiry Program (DHS TRIP). The applicant/participant may choose to initiate the redress process through DHS Traveler Redress Program (DHS TRIP). An applicant/participant seeking redress may obtain the necessary forms and information to initiate the process on the DHS TRIP website, or by contacting DHS TRIP by mail at the address on the DHS TRIP website.

(2) Ombudsman. Applicants (including applicants who were not scheduled for an interview at an enrollment center) and participants may contest a denial or removal by submitting a reconsideration request to the CBP Trusted Traveler Ombudsman through the online TTP System or other CBP-approved process.

HISTORY:

[77 FR 5681, 5690, Feb. 6, 2012; 85 FR 46788, 46926, Aug. 3, 2020; 89 FR 22607, 22628, Apr. 2, 2024]

§ 235.13 U.S. Asia-Pacific Economic Cooperation Business Travel Card Program.

(a) Description. The U.S. Asia-Pacific Economic Cooperation (APEC) Business Travel Card Program is a voluntary program designed to facilitate travel for bona fide U.S. business persons engaged in business in the APEC region and U.S. government officials actively engaged in APEC business within the APEC region. Participants will receive a U.S. APEC Business Travel Card that will enable them access to fast-track immigration lanes at participating airports in foreign APEC member economies. In order to obtain a U.S. APEC Business Travel Card, an individual must meet the eligibility requirements specified in this section, apply in advance, pay any requisite fee and be approved as a card holder. The APEC member economies are identified at http://www.apec.org.

(b) Program eligibility criteria —

(1) Eligible individuals. An individual is eligible for the U.S. APEC Business Travel Card if he or she is:

(i) A U.S. citizen;

(ii) An existing member in good standing of a CBP trusted traveler program or approved for membership in a CBP trusted traveler program during the application process described in paragraph (c) of this section. For the purpose of this section only, "trusted traveler program" is defined as a voluntary program of the Department that allows U.S. Customs and Border Protection to expedite clearance of pre-approved, low-risk travelers arriving in the United States; and

(iii) A bona fide U.S. business person engaged in business in the APEC region or U.S. Government official actively engaged in APEC business.

(A) "APEC business" means U.S. government activities that support the work of APEC.

(B) A "bona fide business person engaged in business in the APEC region" means a person engaged in the trade of goods, the provision of services, or the conduct of investment activities in the APEC region. Professional athletes, news correspondents, entertainers, musicians, artists or persons engaged in similar occupations are not considered to be bona fide business persons engaged in business in the APEC region.

(2) Conditions regarding the use of the U.S. APEC Business Travel Card

(i) The U.S. APEC Business Travel Card is not transferable and may be used only by the U.S. APEC Business Travel Card holder and not by anyone else including the card holder's spouse or child.

(ii) The U.S. APEC Business Travel Card can be used only if the card holder is traveling solely for business purposes to a foreign APEC member economy and is not engaging in paid employment in the foreign APEC member economy.

(c) Application process.

(1) Each applicant must complete and submit an application electronically through the Global Entry Enrollment System (GOES) or other applicable process as determined by CBP. The application and application instructions for the card are available as an add-on to the CBP trusted traveler application at www.globalentry.gov.

(2) Each applicant must certify that he or she is an existing member in good standing in a CBP trusted traveler program or that he or she has submitted an application to a CBP trusted traveler program; that he or she is a bona fide U.S. business person engaged in business in the APEC region or U.S. Government official actively engaged in APEC business; and, that he or she is not a professional athlete, news correspondent, entertainer, musician, artist or person engaged in a similar occupation.

(3) Each applicant must provide his or her signature so that the signature will appear on the face of the card.

(4) If the applicant is not a member of a CBP trusted traveler program, the applicant must concurrently apply for membership in a CBP trusted traveler program and be approved for such membership. Applicants for a CBP trusted traveler program must have an in-person interview, undergo a vetting process and pay the relevant CBP trusted traveler fee. Active membership in a CBP trusted traveler program is necessary for the entire duration of the U.S. APEC Business Travel Card. If membership in the CBP trusted traveler program is set to lapse before the U.S. APEC Business Travel Card expires, the individual must renew his or her CBP trusted traveler membership prior to its expiration date in order to retain membership in the U.S. APEC Business Travel Card Program.

(5) Each applicant must pay a non-refundable fee in the amount set forth at 8 CFR 103.7(d)(14) for "U.S. Asia-Pacific Economic Cooperation (APEC) Business Travel Card" at the time of application. The fee is to be paid to CBP at the time of application through the Federal Government's on-line payment system, Pay.gov or other CBP-approved process.

(6) The U.S. APEC Business Travel Card is valid for a period of five years or until the expiration date of the card holder's passport if that is earlier, provided that membership is not terminated by CBP prior to the end of this period. CBP can terminate use of the U.S. APEC Business Travel Card if the card holder is no longer a member of a CBP trusted traveler program or if the individual is not compliant with the program requirements. Each applicant may apply to renew the card prior to its expiration.

(d) Expedited entry privileges. The U.S. APEC Business Travel Card will enable card holders access to a dedicated fast-track lane for expedited immigration processing at participating airports in foreign APEC member economies.

(e) Entry requirements. U.S. APEC Business Travel Card holders must present any travel or identity documentation, such as a passport and visa, required by the foreign APEC member economies.

(f) Denial and removal.

(1) If an applicant is denied a U.S. APEC Business Travel Card, CBP will notify the applicant of the denial, and the reasons for the denial. CBP will also provide instructions regarding how to proceed if the applicant wishes to seek additional information as to the reason for the denial.

(2) A U.S. APEC Business Travel Card holder may be removed from the U.S. APEC Business Travel Card Program if CBP determines at its sole discretion that:

(i) The U.S. APEC Business Travel Card holder provided false information in the application and/or during the application process;

(ii) The U.S. APEC Business Travel Card holder failed to follow the terms, conditions and requirements of the program (including continued active membership in a CBP trusted traveler program);

(iii) The U.S. APEC Business Travel Card holder has been arrested or convicted of a crime or otherwise no longer meets the program eligibility criteria; or

(iv) Such action is otherwise necessary.

(3) CBP will notify the U.S. APEC Business Travel Card holder of his or her removal in writing. Such removal is effective immediately.

(4) A U.S. APEC Business Travel Card applicant or a U.S. APEC Business Travel Card holder who is denied or removed will not receive a refund, in whole or in part, of the application fee.

(g) Redress. An individual whose application is denied or whose participation is terminated has two possible methods of redress. These processes do not create or confer any legal right, privilege, or benefit on the applicant or participant, and are wholly discretionary on the part of CBP. The methods of redress are:

(1) Enrollment center. If the applicant or participant applied concurrently for the U.S. APEC Business Travel Card and a CBP trusted traveler program, the applicant or participant may contest his or her denial or removal by writing to the enrollment center where that individual's CBP trusted traveler program interview was conducted. If the applicant or participant was

already a member of a CBP trusted traveler program, the applicant or participant may contest his or her denial or removal by writing to the enrollment center where that individual's signature was collected for the U.S. APEC Business Travel Card. The enrollment center addresses are available at www.globalentry.gov, http://www.globalentry.gov/exus.html and http://www-.globalentry.gov/sentri.html. The letter must be received by CBP within 30 calendar days of the date provided as the date of removal. The individual should write on the envelope "Redress Request RE: U.S. APEC Business Travel Card." The letter should address any facts or conduct listed in the notification from CBP as contributing to the denial or removal and why the applicant or participant believes the reason for the action is invalid. If the applicant or participant believes that the denial or removal was based upon inaccurate information, the individual should also include any reasonably available supporting documentation with the letter. After review, CBP will inform the individual of its redress decision. If the individual's request for redress is successful, the individual's eligibility to be a U.S. APEC Business Travel Card holder will continue immediately.

(2) Ombudsman. Applicants and participants may contest a denial or removal by writing to the CBP Trusted Traveler Ombudsman at the address listed on the Web site www.globalentry.gov.

HISTORY:

[79 FR 27161, 27174, May 13, 2014, as confirmed and amended at 81 FR 84403, 84415, Nov. 23, 2016; 84 FR 27704, 27707, June 14, 2019; 85 FR 46788, 46926, Aug. 3, 2020]

§ 235.14 SENTRI program.

(a) Program description. The Secure Electronic Network for Travelers Rapid Inspection (SENTRI) trusted traveler program is a voluntary program that allows certain pre-approved, low-risk travelers dedicated processing at specified land border ports along the U.S.-Mexico border. In order to participate, a person must meet the eligibility requirements specified in this section, apply in advance, undergo vetting by CBP, and be accepted into the program. A SENTRI participant will be issued a Radio Frequency Identification (RFID) card or other CBP-approved document that grants the individual access to specific, dedicated primary lanes (SENTRI lanes). These lanes are identified at http://www.cbp.gov. A SENTRI participant may utilize a vehicle in the dedicated SENTRI lanes into the United States from Mexico only if the vehicle is approved by CBP for such purpose. Participants in the SENTRI program may also be able to take advantage of certain benefits of the Global Entry and NEXUS programs. Please see http://www.cbp.gov for additional information.

(b) Program eligibility criteria —

(1) Eligible individuals. Any individual may apply to participate in the SENTRI program absent any of the disqualifying factors described in paragraph (b)(2) of this section. Persons under the age of 18 must have the consent of a parent or legal guardian to participate in the SENTRI program and provide proof of such consent in accordance with CBP instructions.

(2) Disqualifying factors. An individual is ineligible to participate in the SENTRI program if CBP, at its sole discretion, determines that the individual presents a potential risk for terrorism, criminality (such as smuggling), or CBP is unable to establish that the applicant can be considered low-risk. This risk determination will be based in part upon an applicant's ability to demonstrate past compliance with laws, regulations, and policies. Reasons why an applicant may not qualify for participation include:

(i) The applicant provides false or incomplete information on his or her application;

(ii) The applicant has been arrested for, or convicted of, any criminal offense or has pending criminal charges or outstanding warrants in any country;

(iii) The applicant has been found in violation of any customs, immigration, or agriculture regulations, procedures, or laws in any country;

(iv) The applicant is the subject of an investigation by any Federal, State or local law enforcement agency in any country;

(v) The applicant is inadmissible to the United States under applicable immigration laws or has, at any time, been granted a waiver of inadmissibility or parole;

(vi) The applicant is known or suspected of being or having been engaged in conduct constituting, in preparation for, in aid of, or related to terrorism; or

(vii) The applicant cannot satisfy CBP of his or her low-risk status or meet other program requirements.

(c) Program application.

(1) Each applicant must complete and submit the program application electronically through an approved application process as determined by CBP. The application and application instructions for the SENTRI program are available at http://www.cbp.gov.

(2) During the application process, an applicant must provide information on any vehicle that will utilize the SENTRI lanes. The vehicle must be approved by CBP to utilize the dedicated SENTRI lanes. Registration of one vehicle for use in the SENTRI lanes is included in the application fee provided the vehicle is registered at the time of initial application or at renewal. If any vehicle is registered after the initial application or renewal is filed, or if an applicant or participant wishes to register more than one vehicle for use in the SENTRI lanes, they will be assessed an additional fee in the amount set forth at 8 CFR 103.7(d)(16). The fee is to be paid to CBP at the time the vehicle is registered through the online TTP System, which can be found at http://www.cbp.gov, or other CBP-approved process.

(3) Except for certain minors, all other applicants must pay the non-refundable fee in the amount set forth at 8 CFR 103.7(d)(16) for the "SENTRI program". Minors under the age of 18 who apply concurrently with a parent or legal guardian, or whose parent or legal guardian is already a participant of SENTRI, are exempt from payment of the applicable fee. The fee is to

be paid to CBP at the time of application through the TTP System or other CBP-approved process.

(4) Every applicant accepted into the SENTRI program is accepted for a period of 5 years provided participation is not terminated by CBP prior to the end of the 5-year period. Each applicant may apply to renew participation up to one year prior to the close of the participation period.

(5) Each applicant may check the status of his or her application through his or her account with the application system in use for the SENTRI program.

(d) Interview and enrollment.

(1) After submitting the application, conditionally approved applicants will be notified by CBP to schedule a personal interview.

(2) Each applicant must provide CBP the original of the identification document specified in his or her application. During the interview, CBP will collect biometric information from the applicant (e.g., a set of fingerprints and/or digital photograph) to conduct background checks or as otherwise required for participation in the program.

(3) CBP may provide for alternative enrollment procedures, as necessary, to facilitate enrollment and ensure an applicant's eligibility for the program.

(e) SENTRI lanes. A SENTRI participant is issued a Radio Frequency Identification (RFID) card or other CBP-approved document. This RFID card or other CBP-approved document will grant the participant access to specific, dedicated primary lanes into the United States from Mexico (SENTRI lanes). These lanes are identified at http://www.cbp.gov. A SENTRI participant may utilize a vehicle in the dedicated SENTRI lanes into the United States from Mexico only if the vehicle is approved by CBP for such purpose.

(f) Denial and removal.

(1) If an applicant is denied participation in the SENTRI program, or an applicant's or participant's vehicle is not approved for use in the SENTRI lanes, CBP will notify the applicant of the denial, and the reasons for the denial. CBP will also provide instructions regarding how to proceed if the applicant wishes to seek additional information as to the reason for the denial.

(2) A SENTRI participant may be removed from the program for any of the following reasons:

(i) CBP, at its sole discretion, determines that the participant has engaged in any disqualifying activities as outlined in paragraph (b)(2) of this section;

(ii) CBP, at its sole discretion, determines that the participant provided false information in the application and/or during the application process;

(iii) CBP, at its sole discretion, determines that the participant failed to follow the terms, conditions and requirements of the program;

(iv) CBP determines that the participant has been arrested or convicted of a crime or otherwise determines, at its sole discretion, that the participant no longer meets the program eligibility criteria; or

(v) CBP, at its sole discretion, determines that such action is otherwise necessary.

(3) CBP will notify the participant of their removal from the program in writing. Such removal is effective immediately.

(4) An applicant or participant denied or removed will not receive a refund, in whole or in part, of his or her application fee.

(g) Redress. An individual whose application is denied or who is removed from the program or whose vehicle is not approved for use in the program has two possible methods for redress. These processes do not create or confer any legal right, privilege, or benefit on the applicant or participant, and are wholly discretionary on the part of CBP. The methods of redress are:

(1) DHS Traveler Redress Inquiry Program (DHS TRIP). The applicant/participant may choose to initiate the redress process through DHS TRIP. An applicant/participant seeking redress may obtain the necessary forms and information to initiate the process on the DHS TRIP website, or by contacting DHS TRIP by mail at the address on this website.

(2) Ombudsman. Applicants and participants may contest a denial or removal from the program by submitting a reconsideration request to the CBP Trusted Traveler Ombudsman through the TTP System or other CBP-approved process.

HISTORY:

[89 FR 22607, 22629, Apr. 2, 2024]

§ 235.15 Inadmissible aliens and expedited removal during emergency border circumstances.

(a) Applicability. Notwithstanding §§ 235.3(b)(2)(i) and 235.3(b)(4)(i) (but not § 235.3(b)(4)(ii)), the provisions of this section apply to any alien described in § 235.3(b)(1)(i) through (ii) if the alien is described in § 208.13(g) and is not described in section 3(b) of the Presidential Proclamation of June 3, 2024, as defined in 8 CFR 208.13(h).

(b) Expedited removal.

(1) [Reserved]

(2) Determination of inadmissibility —

(i) Record of proceeding.

(A) A noncitizen who is arriving in the United States, or other alien as designated pursuant to § 235.3(b)(1)(ii), who is determined to be inadmissible under section 212(a)(6)(C) or 212(a)(7) of the Act (except an alien for whom documentary requirements are waived under § 211.1(b)(3) or § 212.1 of this chapter) shall be ordered removed from the United States in accordance with section 235(b)(1) of the Act. In every case in which the expedited removal provisions will be applied and before removing an alien from the United States pursuant to this section, the examining immigration officer shall create a record of the facts of the case and statements made by the alien.

(B) The examining immigration officer shall advise the alien of the charges against him or her on Form I-860, Notice and Order of Expedited Removal, and the alien shall be given an opportunity to respond to those charges. After obtaining supervisory concurrence in accordance with § 235.3(b)(7), the examining immigration official shall serve the alien with Form I-860 and the alien shall sign the form acknowledging receipt. Interpretative assistance shall be used if necessary to communicate with the alien.

(ii) [Reserved]

(iii) [Reserved]

(3) [Reserved]

(4) Claim of asylum or fear of persecution or torture.

(i) If an alien subject to the expedited removal provisions manifests a fear of return, or expresses an intention to apply for asylum or protection, expresses a fear of persecution or torture, or expresses a fear of return to his or her country or the country of removal, the inspecting officer shall not proceed further with removal of the alien until the alien has been referred for an interview by an asylum officer in accordance with part 208 of this chapter.

(A) The inspecting immigration officer shall document whether the alien has manifested or affirmatively expressed such intention, fear, or concern.

(B) The referring officer shall provide the alien with a written disclosure describing the purpose of the referral and the credible fear interview process; the right to consult with other persons prior to the interview and any review thereof at no expense to the United States Government; the right to request a review by an immigration judge of the asylum officer's credible fear determination; and the consequences of failure to establish a credible fear of persecution or torture.

(ii) [Reserved]

(c)-(f) [Reserved]

(g) Severability. The Department intends that in the event that any provision of paragraphs (a), (b)(2)(i), and (b)(4) of this section, § 208.35, or the Presidential Proclamation of June 3, 2024, as defined in 8 CFR 208.13(h), is held to be invalid or unenforceable by its terms, or as applied to any person or circumstance, the provisions of this section and § 208.35 should be construed so as to continue to give the maximum effect to those provisions permitted by law, unless such holding is that a provision is wholly invalid and unenforceable, in which event the provision should be severed from the remainder of this section and the holding should not affect the remainder of this section or the application of the provision to persons not similarly situated or to dissimilar circumstances.

HISTORY:

[89 FR 48710, 48770, June 7, 2024, as confirmed at 89 FR 81156, Oct. 7, 2024; 89 FR 81156, 81285, Oct. 7, 2024]

PART 236

APPREHENSION AND DETENTION OF INADMISSIBLE AND DEPORTABLE ALIENS; REMOVAL OF ALIENS ORDERED REMOVED

Subpart A. Detention of Aliens Prior to Order of Removal

Rule

Subpart B. Family Unity Program

Subpart C. Deferred Action for Childhood Arrivals

AUTHORITY NOTE APPLICABLE TO ENTIRE PART:

AUTHORITY:

5 U.S.C. 301, 552, 552a; 6 U.S.C. 112(a)(2), 112(a)(3), 112(b)(1), 112(e), 202, 251, 279, 291; 8 U.S.C. 1103, 1182, 1224, 1225, 1226, 1227, 1231, 1232, 1324a, 1357, 1362, 1611; 18 U.S.C. 4002, 4013(c)(4); 8 CFR part 2.

Subpart A

Detention of Aliens Prior to Order of Removal

§ 236.1 Apprehension, custody, and detention.

(a) Detainers. The issuance of a detainer under this section shall be governed by the provisions of § 287.7 of this chapter.

(b) Warrant of arrest.

(1) In general. At the time of issuance of the notice to appear, or at any time thereafter and up to the time removal proceedings are completed, the respondent may be arrested and taken into custody under the authority of Form I-200, Warrant of Arrest. A warrant of arrest may be issued only by those immigration officers listed in § 287.5(e)(2) of this chapter and may be served only by those immigration officers listed in § 287.5(e)(3) of this chapter.

(2) If, after the issuance of a warrant of arrest, a determination is made not to serve it, any officer authorized to issue such warrant may authorize its cancellation.

(c) Custody issues and release procedures.

(1) In general.

(i) After the expiration of the Transition Period Custody Rules (TPCR) set forth in section 303(b)(3) of Div. C of Pub. L. 104-208, no alien described in section

236(c)(1) of the Act may be released from custody during removal proceedings except pursuant to section 236(c)(2) of the Act.

(ii) Paragraph (c)(2) through (c)(8) of this section shall govern custody determinations for aliens subject to the TPCR while they remain in effect. For purposes of this section, an alien "subject to the TPCR" is an alien described in section 303(b)(3)(A) of Div. C of Pub. L. 104-208 who is in deportation proceedings, subject to a final order of deportation, or in removal proceedings. The TPCR do not apply to aliens in exclusion proceedings under former section 236 of the Act, aliens in expedited removal proceedings under section 235(b)(1) of the Act, or aliens subject to a final order of removal.

(2) Aliens not lawfully admitted. Subject to paragraph (c)(6)(i) of this section, but notwithstanding any other provision within this section, an alien subject to the TPCR who is not lawfully admitted is not eligible to be considered for release from custody.

(i) An alien who remains in status as an alien lawfully admitted for permanent residence, conditionally admitted for permanent residence, or lawfully admitted for temporary residence is "lawfully admitted" for purposes of this section.

(ii) An alien in removal proceedings, in deportation proceedings, or subject to a final order of deportation, and not described in paragraph (c)(2)(i) of this section, is not "lawfully admitted" for purposes of this section unless the alien last entered the United States lawfully and is not presently an applicant for admission to the United States.

(3) Criminal aliens eligible to be considered for release. Except as provided in this section, or otherwise provided by law, an alien subject to the TPCR may be considered for release from custody if lawfully admitted. Such an alien must first demonstrate, by clear and convincing evidence, that release would not pose a danger to the safety of other persons or of property. If an alien meets this burden, the alien must further demonstrate, by clear and convincing evidence, that the alien is likely to appear for any scheduled proceeding (including any appearance required by the Service or EOIR) in order to be considered for release in the exercise of discretion.

(4) Criminal aliens ineligible to be considered for release except in certain special circumstances. An alien, other than an alien lawfully admitted for permanent residence, subject to section 303(b)(3)(A) (ii) or (iii) of Div. C. of Pub. L. 104-208 is ineligible to be considered for release if the alien:

(i) Is described in section 241(a)(2)(C) of the Act (as in effect prior to April 1, 1997), or has been convicted of a crime described in section 101(a)(43)(B), (E)(ii) or (F) of the Act (as in effect on April 1, 1997);

(ii) Has been convicted of a crime described in section 101(a)(43)(G) of the Act (as in effect on April 1, 1997) or a crime or crimes involving moral turpitude related to property, and sentenced therefor (including in the aggregate) to at least 3 years' imprisonment;

(iii) Has failed to appear for an immigration proceeding without reasonable cause or has been subject to a bench warrant or similar legal process (unless quashed, withdrawn, or cancelled as improvidently issued);

(iv) Has been convicted of a crime described in section 101(a)(43)(Q) or (T) of the Act (as in effect on April 1, 1997);

(v) Has been convicted in a criminal proceeding of a violation of section 273, 274, 274C, 276, or 277 of the Act, or has admitted the factual elements of such a violation;

(vi) Has overstayed a period granted for voluntary departure;

(vii) Has failed to surrender or report for removal pursuant to an order of exclusion, deportation, or removal;

(viii) Does not wish to pursue, or is statutorily ineligible for, any form of relief from exclusion, deportation, or removal under this chapter or the Act; or

(ix) Is described in paragraphs (c)(5)(i)(A), (B), or (C) of this section but has not been sentenced, including in the aggregate but not including any portions suspended, to at least 2 years' imprisonment, unless the alien was lawfully admitted and has not, since the commencement of proceedings and within the 10 years prior thereto, been convicted of a crime, failed to comply with an order to surrender or a period of voluntary departure, or been subject to a bench warrant or similar legal process (unless quashed, withdrawn, or cancelled as improvidently issued). An alien eligible to be considered for release under this paragraph must meet the burdens described in paragraph (c)(3) of this section in order to be released from custody in the exercise of discretion.

(5) Criminal aliens ineligible to be considered for release

(i) A criminal alien subject to section 303(b)(3)(A)(ii) or (iii) of Div. C of Pub. L. 104-208 is ineligible to be considered for release if the alien has been sentenced, including in the aggregate but not including any portions suspended, to at least 2 years' imprisonment, and the alien

(A) Is described in section 237(a)(2)(D)(i) or (ii) of the Act (as in effect on April 1, 1997), or has been convicted of a crime described in section 101(a)(43)(A), (C), (E)(i), (H), (I), (K)(iii), or (L) of the Act (as in effect on April 1, 1997);

(B) Is described in section 237(a)(2)(A)(iv) of the Act; or

(C) Has escaped or attempted to escape from the lawful custody of a local, State, or Federal prison, agency, or officer within the United States.

(ii) Notwithstanding paragraph (c)(5)(i) of this section, a permanent resident alien who has not, since the commencement of proceedings and within the 15 years prior thereto, been convicted of a crime, failed to comply with an order to surrender or a period of voluntary departure, or been subject to a bench warrant or similar legal process (unless quashed, withdrawn, or cancelled as improvidently issued), may be considered for release under paragraph (c)(3) of this section.

(6) Unremovable aliens and certain long-term detainees.

(i) If the district director determines that an alien subject to section 303(b)(3)(A)(ii) or (iii) of Div. C of Pub. L. 104-208 cannot be removed from the United States because the designated country of removal or deportation will not accept the alien's return, the district director may, in the exercise of discretion, consider release of the alien from custody upon such terms and conditions as the district director may prescribe, without regard to paragraphs (c)(2), (c)(4), and (c)(5) of this section.

(ii) The district director may also, notwithstanding paragraph (c)(5) of this section, consider release from custody, upon such terms and conditions as the district director may prescribe, of any alien described in paragraph (c)(2)(ii) of this section who has been in the Service's custody for six months pursuant to a final order of deportation terminating the alien's status as a lawful permanent resident.

(iii) The district director may release an alien from custody under this paragraph only in accordance with the standards set forth in paragraph (c)(3) of this section and any other applicable provisions of law.

(iv) The district director's custody decision under this paragraph shall not be subject to redetermination by an immigration judge, but, in the case of a custody decision under paragraph (c)(6)(ii) of this section, may be appealed to the Board of Immigration Appeals pursuant to paragraph (d)(3)(iii) of this section.

(7) Construction. A reference in this section to a provision in section 241 of the Act as in effect prior to April 1, 1997, shall be deemed to include a reference to the corresponding provision in section 237 of the Act as in effect on April 1, 1997. A reference in this section to a "crime" shall be considered to include a reference to a conspiracy or attempt to commit such a crime. In calculating the 10-year period specified in paragraph (c)(4) of this section and the 15-year period specified in paragraph (c)(5) of this section, no period during which the alien was detained or incarcerated shall count toward the total. References in paragraph (c)(6)(i) of this section to the "district director" shall be deemed to include a reference to any official designated by the Assistant Secretary/Director of ICE to exercise custody authority over aliens covered by that paragraph. Nothing in this part shall be construed as prohibiting an alien from seeking reconsideration of the Service's determination that the alien is within a category barred from release under this part.

(8) Any officer authorized to issue a warrant of arrest may, in the officer's discretion, release an alien not described in section 236(c)(1) of the Act, under the conditions at section 236(a)(2) and (3) of the Act; provided that the alien must demonstrate to the satisfaction of the officer that such release would not pose a danger to property or persons, and that the alien is likely to appear for any future proceeding. Such an officer may also, in the exercise of discretion, release an alien in deportation proceedings pursuant to the authority in section 242 of the Act (as designated prior to April 1, 1997), except as otherwise provided by law.

(9) When an alien who, having been arrested and taken into custody, has been released, such release may be revoked at any time in the discretion of the district director, acting district director, deputy district director, assistant district director for investigations, assistant district director for detention and deportation, or officer in charge (except foreign), in which event the alien may be taken into physical custody and detained. If detained, unless a breach has occurred, any outstanding bond shall be revoked and canceled.

(10) The provisions of § 103.6 of this chapter shall apply to any bonds authorized. Subject to the provisions of this section, the provisions of § 1003.19 of this chapter shall govern availability to the respondent of recourse to other administrative authority for release from custody.

(11) An immigration judge may not exercise the authority provided in this section, and the review process described in paragraph (d) of this section shall not apply, with respect to any alien beyond the custody jurisdiction of the immigration judge as provided in § 1003.19(h) of this chapter.

(d) Appeals from custody decisions.

(1) Application to immigration judge. After an initial custody determination by the district director, including the setting of a bond, the respondent may, at any time before an order under 8 CFR part 240 becomes final, request amelioration of the conditions under which he or she may be released. Prior to such final order, and except as otherwise provided in this chapter, the immigration judge is authorized to exercise the authority in section 236 of the Act (or section 242(a)(1) of the Act as designated prior to April 1, 1997 in the case of an alien in deportation proceedings) to detain the alien in custody, release the alien, and determine the amount of bond, if any, under which the respondent may be released, as provided in § 1003.19 of this chapter. If the alien has been released from custody, an application for amelioration of the terms of release must be filed within 7 days of release.

(2) Application to the district director. After expiration of the 7-day period in paragraph (d)(1) of this section, the respondent may request review by the district director of the conditions of his or her release.

(3) Appeal to the Board of Immigration Appeals. An appeal relating to bond and custody determinations may be filed to the Board of Immigration Appeals in the following circumstances:

(i) In accordance with § 1003.38 of this chapter, the alien or the Service may appeal the decision of an immigration judge pursuant to paragraph (d)(1) of this section.

(ii) The alien, within 10 days, may appeal from the district director's decision under paragraph (d)(2)(i) of this section.

(4) Effect of filing an appeal. The filing of an appeal from a determination of an immigration judge or district director under this paragraph shall not operate to delay compliance with the order (except as provided in § 1003.19(i)), nor stay the administrative proceedings or removal.

(e) Privilege of communication. Every detained alien shall be notified that he or she may communicate with the consular or diplomatic officers of the country of his or her nationality in the United States. Existing treaties with the following countries require immediate communication with appropriate consular or diplomatic officers whenever nationals of the following countries are detained in removal proceedings, whether or not requested by the alien and even if the alien requests that no communication be undertaken in his or her behalf. When notifying consular or diplomatic officials, Service officers shall not reveal the fact that any detained alien has applied for asylum or withholding of removal.

Algeria[1]
Antigua and Barbuda
Armenia
Azerbaijan
Bahamas, The
Barbados
Belarus
Belize
Brunei
Bulgaria
China (People's Republic of)[2]
Costa Rica
Cyprus
Czech Republic
Dominica
Fiji
Gambia, The
Georgia
Ghana
Grenada
Guyana
Hong Kong[3]
Hungary
Jamaica
Kazakhstan
Kiribati
Kuwait
Kyrgyzstan
Malaysia
Malta
Mauritius
Moldova
Mongolia
Nigeria
Philippines
Poland[4]
Romania
Russian Federation
St. Kitts and Nevis
St. Lucia
St. Vincent/Grenadines
Seychelles
Sierra Leone
Singapore
Slovak Republic
Tajikistan
Tanzania
Tonga
Trinidad and Tobago
Tunisia
Turkmenistan
Tuvalu
Ukraine
United Kingdom[5]
U.S.S.R.[6]
Uzbekistan
Zambia
Zimbabwe

(f) Notification to Executive Office for Immigration Review of change in custody status. The Service shall notify the Immigration Court having administrative control over the Record of Proceeding of any change in custody location or of release from, or subsequent taking into, Service custody of a respondent/applicant pursuant to § 1003.19(g) of this chapter.

(g) Notice of custody determination.

(1) In general. At the time of issuance of the notice to appear, or at any time thereafter and up to the time removal proceedings are completed, an immigration official may issue a Form I-286, Notice of Custody Determination. A notice of custody determination may be issued by those immigration officials listed in 8 CFR 287.5(e)(2) and may be served by those immigration officials listed in 8 CFR 287.5(e)(3), or other officers or employees of the Department or the United States who are delegated the authority to do so pursuant to 8 CFR 2.1.

(2) Cancellation. If after the issuance of a notice of custody determination, a determination is made not to

[1]Arrangements with the countries listed in 8 CFR 236.1(e) provide that U.S. authorities shall notify responsible representatives within 72 hours of the arrest or detention of one of their nationals.

[2]Notification is not mandatory in the case of any person who carries a "Republic of China" passport issued by Taiwan. Such persons should be informed without delay that the nearest office of the Taipei Economic and Cultural Representative Office ("TECRO"), the unofficial entity representing Taiwan's interests in the United States, can be notified at their request.

[3]Hong Kong reverted to Chinese sovereignty on July 1, 1997, and is now officially referred to as the Hong Kong Special Administrative Region, or "S.A.R." Under paragraph 3(f)(2) of the March 25, 1997, U.S.-China Agreement on the Maintenance of the U.S. Consulate General in the Hong Kong Special Administrative Region, U.S. officials are required to notify Chinese officials of the arrest or detention of the bearers of Hong Kong passports in the same manner as is required for bearers of Chinese passports—i.e., immediately, and in any event, within four days of the arrest or detention.

[4]Consular communication is not mandatory for any Polish national who has been admitted for permanent residence in the United States. Such notification should only be provided upon request by a Polish national with permanent residency in the United States.

[5]United Kingdom includes England, Scotland, Wales, Northern Ireland and Islands and the British dependencies of Anguilla, British Virgin Islands, Bermuda, Montserrat, and the Turks and Caicos Islands. Their residents carry British passports.

[6]All U.S.S.R. successor states are covered by this agreement. They are: Armenia, Azerbaijan, Belarus, Georgia, Kazakhstan, Kyrgyzstan, Moldova, Russian Federation, Tajikistan, Turkmenistan, Ukraine, and Uzbekistan. Although the U.S.S.R. no longer exists, the U.S.S.R is listed here, because some nationals of its successor states may still be traveling on a U.S.S.R. passport. Mandatory consular notification applies to any national of such a state, including one traveling on a U.S.S.R. passport.

serve it, any official authorized to issue such notice may authorize its cancellation.

HISTORY:

[42 FR 46045, Sept. 14, 1977; 62 FR 10312, 10360, March 6, 1997, as corrected and amended at 62 FR 15362, 15363, April 1, 1997; 63 FR 27441, 27449, May 19, 1998; 65 FR 80281, 80294, Dec. 21, 2000; 70 FR 67087, 67088, Nov. 4, 2005; 72 FR 1923, 1924, Jan. 17, 2007; 81 FR 62353, 62355, Sept. 9, 2016]

§ 236.2 Confined aliens, incompetents, and minors.

(a) Service. If the respondent is confined, or if he or she is an incompetent, or a minor under the age of 14, the notice to appear, and the warrant of arrest, if issued, shall be served in the manner prescribed in § 239.1 of this chapter upon the person or persons specified by 8 CFR 103.8(c).

(b) Service custody and cost of maintenance. An alien confined because of physical or mental disability in an institution or hospital shall not be accepted into physical custody by the Service until an order of removal has been entered and the Service is ready to remove the alien. When such an alien is an inmate of a public or private institution at the time of the commencement of the removal proceedings, expenses for the maintenance of the alien shall not be incurred by the Government until he or she is taken into physical custody by the Service.

HISTORY:

[42 FR 46045, Sept. 14, 1977, as amended at 44 FR 4653, Jan. 23, 1979; 46 FR 43956, Sept. 2, 1981; 62 FR 9071, 9074, Feb. 28, 1997; 62 FR 10312, 10361, March 6, 1997; 76 FR 53764, 53790, Aug. 29, 2011]

§ 236.3 Processing, detention, and release of alien minors.

(a) Generally.

(1) DHS treats all minors and unaccompanied alien children (UACs) in its custody with dignity, respect and special concern for their particular vulnerability.

(2) The provisions of this section apply to all minors in the legal custody of DHS, including minors who are subject to the mandatory detention provisions of the INA and applicable regulations, to the extent authorized by law.

(b) Definitions. For the purposes of this section:

(1) Minor means any alien who has not attained eighteen (18) years of age and has not been:

(i) Emancipated in an appropriate state judicial proceeding; or

(ii) Incarcerated due to a conviction for a criminal offense in which he or she was tried as an adult.

(2) Special needs minor means a minor whose mental and/or physical condition requires special services and treatment as identified during an individualized needs assessment as referenced in paragraph (i)(4)(iii) of this section. A minor may have special needs due to drug or alcohol abuse, serious emotional disturbance, mental illness or intellectual disability, or a physical condition or chronic illness that requires special services or treatment. A minor who has suffered serious neglect or abuse may be considered a minor with special needs if the minor requires special services or treatment as a result of the neglect or abuse.

(3) Unaccompanied alien child (UAC) has the meaning provided in 6 U.S.C. 279(g)(2), that is, a child who has no lawful immigration status in the United States and who has not attained 18 years of age; and with respect to whom: There is no parent or legal guardian present in the United States; or no parent or legal guardian in the United States is available to provide care and physical custody. An individual may meet the definition of UAC without meeting the definition of minor.

(4) Custody means within the physical and legal control of an institution or person.

(5) Emergency means an act or event (including, but not limited to, a natural disaster, facility fire, civil disturbance, or medical or public health concerns at one or more facilities) that prevents timely transport or placement of minors, or impacts other conditions provided by this section.

(6) Escape-risk means that there is a serious risk that the minor will attempt to escape from custody. Factors to consider when determining whether a minor is an escape-risk include, but are not limited to, whether:

(i) The minor is currently subject to a final order of removal;

(ii) The minor's immigration history includes: A prior breach of bond, a failure to appear before DHS or the immigration courts, evidence that the minor is indebted to organized smugglers for his transport, or a voluntary departure or previous removal from the United States pursuant to a final order of removal; or

(iii) The minor has previously absconded or attempted to abscond from state or Federal custody.

(7) Family unit means a group of two or more aliens consisting of a minor or minors accompanied by his/her/their adult parent(s) or legal guardian(s). In determining the existence of a parental relationship or a legal guardianship for purposes of this definition, DHS will consider all available reliable evidence. If DHS determines that there is insufficient reliable evidence available that confirms the relationship, the minor will be treated as a UAC.

(8) Family Residential Center (FRC) means a facility used by ICE for the detention of family units.

(9) Licensed facility means an ICE detention facility that is licensed by the state, county, or municipality in which it is located, if such a licensing process exists. Licensed facilities shall comply with all applicable state child welfare laws and regulations and all state and local building, fire, health, and safety codes. If a licensing process for the detention of minors accompanied by a parent or legal guardian is not available in the state, county, or municipality in which an ICE detention facility is located, DHS shall employ an entity outside of DHS that has relevant audit experience to ensure compliance with the family residential standards established by ICE. Such audits will take place at the opening of a facility and on a regular, ongoing basis

thereafter. DHS will make the results of these audits publicly available.

(10) Influx means a situation in which there are, at any given time, more than 130 minors or UACs eligible for placement in a licensed facility under this section or corresponding provisions of ORR regulations, including those who have been so placed or are awaiting such placement.

(11) Non-secure facility means a facility that meets the definition of non-secure under state law in the state in which the facility is located. If no such definition of non-secure exists under state law, a DHS facility shall be deemed non-secure if egress from a portion of the facility's building is not prohibited through internal locks within the building or exterior locks and egress from the facility's premises is not prohibited through secure fencing around the perimeter of the building.

(12) Office of Refugee Resettlement (ORR) means the U.S. Department of Health and Human Services, Administration for Children and Families, Office of Refugee Resettlement.

(c) Age determination.

(1) For purposes of exercising the authorities described in this part, DHS shall determine the age of an alien in accordance with 8 U.S.C. 1232(b)(4). Age determination decisions shall be based upon the totality of the evidence and circumstances.

(2) If a reasonable person would conclude that an individual is an adult, despite his or her claim to be under the age of 18, DHS may treat such person as an adult for all purposes, including confinement and release on bond, recognizance, or other conditions of release. In making this determination, an immigration officer may require such an individual to submit to a medical or dental examination conducted by a medical professional or other appropriate procedures to verify his or her age.

(3) If an individual previously considered to have been an adult is subsequently determined to be under the age of 18, DHS will then treat such individual as a minor or UAC as prescribed by this section.

(d) Determining whether an alien is a UAC.

(1) Time of determination. Immigration officers will make a determination as to whether an alien under the age of 18 is a UAC at the time of encounter or apprehension and prior to the detention or release of such alien.

(2) Aliens who are no longer UACs. When an alien previously determined to have been a UAC has reached the age of 18, when a parent or legal guardian in the United States is available to provide care and physical custody for such an alien, or when such alien has obtained lawful immigration status, the alien is no longer a UAC. An alien who is no longer a UAC is not eligible to receive legal protections limited to UACs under the relevant sections of the Act. Nothing in this paragraph affects USCIS' independent determination of its initial jurisdiction over asylum applications filed by UACs pursuant to section 208(b)(3)(C) of the Act.

(3) Age-out procedures. When an alien previously determined to have been a UAC is no longer a UAC because he or she turns 18 years old, relevant ORR and ICE procedures shall apply.

(e) Transfer of minors who are not UACs from one facility to another.

(1) In the case of an influx or emergency, as defined in paragraph (b) of this section, DHS will transfer a minor who is not a UAC, and who does not meet the criteria for secure detention pursuant to paragraph (i)(1) of this section, to a licensed facility as defined in paragraph (b)(9) of this section, which is non-secure, as expeditiously as possible. Otherwise, to the extent consistent with law or court order, DHS will transfer such minor within three (3) days, if the minor was apprehended in a district in which a licensed program is located, or within five (5) days in all other cases.

(2) In the case of an emergency or influx, DHS will abide by written guidance detailing all reasonable efforts that it will take to transfer all minors who are not UACs as expeditiously as possible.

(f) Transfer of UACs from DHS to HHS.

(1) All UACs apprehended by DHS, except those who are processed in accordance with 8 U.S.C. 1232(a)(2), will be transferred to ORR for care, custody, and placement in accordance with 6 U.S.C. 279 and 8 U.S.C. 1232.

(2) DHS will notify ORR within 48 hours upon the apprehension or discovery of a UAC or any claim or suspicion that an unaccompanied alien detained in DHS custody is under 18 years of age.

(3) Unless exceptional circumstances are present, DHS will transfer custody of a UAC as soon as practicable after receiving notification of an ORR placement, but no later than 72 hours after determining that the minor is a UAC per paragraph (d) of this section. In the case of exceptional circumstances, DHS will abide by written guidance detailing the efforts that it will take to transfer all UACs as required by law.

(4) The following relate to the conditions of transfer of UACs with unrelated detained adults:

(i) UACs will not generally be transported with unrelated detained adults. A UAC will not be transported with an unrelated detained adult(s) unless the UAC is being transported from the place of apprehension to a DHS facility or if separate transportation is otherwise impractical or unavailable.

(ii) When separate transportation is impractical or unavailable, necessary precautions will be taken to ensure the UAC's safety, security, and well-being. If a UAC is transported with any unrelated detained adult(s), DHS will separate the UAC from the unrelated adult(s) to the extent operationally feasible and take necessary precautions for protection of the UAC's safety, security, and well-being.

(g) DHS procedures in the apprehension and processing of minors or UACs—

(1) Processing—

(i) Notice of rights and request for disposition. Every minor or UAC who enters DHS custody, including minors and UACs who request voluntary departure or request to withdraw their application for admission, will be issued a Form I-770, Notice of Rights and Request for Disposition, which will include a statement that the minor or UAC may make a telephone call to a parent, close relative, or friend. The notice shall be provided, read, or explained to the minor or UAC in a language and manner that he or she understands. In the event that a minor or UAC is no longer amenable to voluntary departure or to a withdrawal of an application for admission, the minor or UAC will be issued a new Form I-770 or the Form I-770 will be updated, as needed.

(ii) Notice of Right to Judicial Review. Every minor who is not a UAC who is transferred to or remains in a DHS detention facility will be provided with a Notice of Right to Judicial Review, which informs the minor of his or her right to seek judicial review in United States District Court with jurisdiction and venue over the matter if the minor believes that his or her detention does not comply with the terms of paragraph (i) of this section. The Notice shall be read and explained to the minor in a language and manner that he or she understands.

(iii) Current list of counsel. Every minor who is not a UAC who is transferred to or remains in a DHS detention facility will be provided the free legal service provider list, prepared pursuant to section 239(b)(2) of the Act.

(2) DHS custodial care immediately following apprehension.

(i) Following the apprehension of a minor or UAC, DHS will process the minor or UAC as expeditiously as possible. Consistent with 6 CFR 115.114, minors and UACs shall be held in the least restrictive setting appropriate to the minor or UAC's age and special needs, provided that such setting is consistent with the need to protect the minor or UAC's well-being and that of others, as well as with any other laws, regulations, or legal requirements. DHS will hold minors and UACs in facilities that are safe and sanitary and that are consistent with DHS's concern for their particular vulnerability. Facilities will provide access to toilets and sinks, drinking water and food as appropriate, access to emergency medical assistance as needed, and adequate temperature and ventilation. DHS will provide adequate supervision and will provide contact with family members arrested with the minor or UAC in consideration of the safety and well-being of the minor or UAC, and operational feasibility. UACs generally will be held separately from unrelated adult detainees in accordance with 6 CFR 115.14(b) and 115.114(b). In the event that such separation is not immediately possible, UACs in facilities covered by 6 CFR 115.114 may be housed with an unrelated adult for no more than 24 hours except in the case of an emergency.

(ii) Consistent with the statutory requirements, DHS will transfer UACs to HHS in accordance with the procedures described in paragraph (f) of this section.

(h) Detention of family units. DHS's policy is to maintain family unity, including by detaining families together where appropriate and consistent with law and available resources. If DHS determines that detention of a family unit is required by law, or is otherwise appropriate, the family unit may be transferred to an FRC which is a licensed facility and non-secure.

(i) Detention of minors who are not UACs in DHS custody. In any case in which DHS does not release a minor who is not a UAC, said minor shall remain in DHS detention. Consistent with 6 CFR 115.14, minors shall be detained in the least restrictive setting appropriate to the minor's age and special needs, provided that such setting is consistent with the need to protect the minor's well-being and that of others, as well as with any other laws, regulations, or legal requirements. The minor shall be placed temporarily in a licensed facility, which will be non-secure, until such time as release can be effected or until the minor's immigration proceedings are concluded, whichever occurs earlier. If immigration proceedings are concluded and result in a final order of removal, DHS will detain the minor for the purpose of removal. If immigration proceedings result in a grant of relief or protection from removal where both parties have waived appeal or the appeal period defined in 8 CFR 1003.38(b) has expired, DHS will release the minor.

(1) A minor who is not a UAC referenced under this paragraph (i)(1) may be held in or transferred to a suitable state or county juvenile detention facility, or a secure DHS detention facility, or DHS contracted facility having separate accommodations for minors, whenever the Field Office Director and the ICE supervisory or management personnel have probable cause to believe that the minor:

(i) Has been charged with, is chargeable with, or has been convicted of a crime or crimes, or is the subject of delinquency proceedings, has been adjudicated delinquent, or is chargeable with a delinquent act or acts, that fit within a pattern or practice of criminal activity;

(ii) Has been charged with, is chargeable with, or has been convicted of a crime or crimes, or is the subject of delinquency proceedings, has been adjudicated delinquent, or is chargeable with a delinquent act or acts, that involve violence against a person or the use or carrying of a weapon;

(iii) Has committed, or has made credible threats to commit, a violent or malicious act (whether directed at himself or others) while in Federal or state government custody or while in the presence of an immigration officer;

(iv) Has engaged, while in the licensed facility, in conduct that has proven to be unacceptably disruptive of the normal functioning of the licensed facility in which the minor has been placed and transfer to another facility is necessary to ensure the welfare of the minor or others, as determined by the staff of the licensed facility;

(v) Is determined to be an escape-risk pursuant to paragraph (b)(6) of this section; or

(vi) Must be held in a secure facility for his or her own safety.

(2) DHS will not place a minor who is not a UAC in a secure facility pursuant to paragraph (i)(1) if there are less restrictive alternatives that are available and appropriate in the circumstances, such as transfer to a facility which would provide intensive staff supervision and counseling services or another licensed facility. All determinations to place a minor in a secure facility will

be reviewed and approved by the ICE Juvenile Coordinator referenced in paragraph (o) of this section. Secure facilities shall permit attorney-client visits in accordance with applicable facility rules and regulations.

(3) Unless a secure facility is otherwise authorized pursuant to this section, ICE facilities used for the detention of minors who are not UACs shall be non-secure facilities.

(4) Non-secure, licensed ICE facilities to which minors who are not UACs are transferred pursuant to the procedures in paragraph (e) of this section shall abide by applicable family residential standards established by ICE. At a minimum, such standards shall include provisions or arrangements for the following services for each minor who is not a UAC in its care:

(i) Proper physical care and maintenance, including suitable living, accommodations, food and snacks, appropriate clothing, and personal grooming items;

(ii) Appropriate routine medical, mental health and dental care, family planning services, and emergency health care services, including a complete medical examination (including screening for infectious disease) within 48 hours of admission, excluding weekends and holidays, unless the minor was recently examined at another facility; appropriate immunizations in accordance with the U.S. Public Health Service (PHS), Centers for Disease Control and Prevention; administration of prescribed medication and special diets; appropriate mental health interventions when necessary;

(iii) An individualized needs assessment which includes:

(A) Various initial intake forms;

(B) Essential data relating to the identification and history of the minor and family;

(C) Identification of the minor's special needs including any specific problem(s) which appear to require immediate intervention;

(D) An educational assessment and plan;

(E) An assessment of family relationships and interaction with adults, peers and authority figures;

(F) A statement of religious preference and practice;

(G) An assessment of the minor's personal goals, strengths and weaknesses; and

(H) Identifying information regarding immediate family members, other relatives, godparents, or friends who may be residing in the United States and may be able to assist in family reunification;

(iv) Educational services appropriate to the minor's level of development and communication skills in a structured classroom setting, Monday through Friday, which concentrates primarily on the development of basic academic competencies and secondarily on English Language Training (ELT). The educational program should include subjects similar to those found in U.S. programs and include science, social studies, math, reading, writing, and physical education. The program design should be appropriate for the minor's estimated length of stay and can include the necessary skills appropriate for transition into a U.S. school district. The program should also include acculturation and adaptation services which include information regarding the development of social and inter-personal skills that contribute to those abilities as age appropriate;

(v) Appropriate reading materials in languages other than English for use during the minor's leisure time;

(vi) Activities according to a recreation and leisure time plan which shall include daily outdoor activity, weather permitting, at least one hour per day of large muscle activity and one hour per day of structured leisure time activities (this should not include time spent watching television). Activities should be increased to a total of three hours on days when school is not in session;

(vii) At least one individual counseling session or mental health wellness interaction (if the minor does not want to participate in a counseling session) per week conducted by trained social work staff with the specific objectives of reviewing the minor's progress, establishing new short-term objectives, and addressing both the developmental and crisis-related needs of each minor;

(viii) Group counseling sessions at least twice a week. This is usually an informal process and takes place with all the minors present and can be held in conjunction with other structured activities. It is a time when new minors present in the facility are given the opportunity to get acquainted with the staff, other children, and the rules of the program. It is an open forum where everyone gets a chance to speak. Daily program management is discussed and decisions are made about recreational activities, etc. It is a time for staff and minors to discuss whatever is on their minds and to resolve problems;

(ix) Upon admission, a comprehensive orientation regarding program intent, services, rules (written and verbal), expectations and the availability of legal assistance;

(x) Whenever possible, access to religious services of the minor's choice;

(xi) Visitation and contact with family members (regardless of their immigration status) which is structured to encourage such visitation. The staff shall respect the minor's privacy while reasonably preventing the unauthorized release of the minor and preventing the transfer of contraband;

(xii) A reasonable right to privacy, which shall include the right to:

(A) Wear his or her own clothes, when available;

(B) Retain a private space in the residential facility for the storage of personal belongings;

(C) Talk privately on the phone, as permitted by applicable facility rules and regulations;

(D) Visit privately with guests, as permitted by applicable facility rules and regulations; and

(E) Receive and send uncensored mail unless there is a reasonable belief that the mail contains contraband;

(xiii) When necessary, communication with adult relatives living in the United States and in foreign countries regarding legal issues related to the release and/or removal of the minor;

(xiv) Legal services information regarding the availability of free legal assistance, the right to be represented by counsel at no expense to the Government, the right to apply for asylum or to request voluntary departure;

(xv) Attorney-client visits in accordance with applicable facility rules and regulations;

(xvi) Service delivery is to be accomplished in a manner which is sensitive to the age, culture, native language, and the complex needs of each minor;

(xvii) Parents/legal guardians will be responsible for supervising their children and providing parental support in managing their children's behavior. Licensed facility rules and discipline standards shall be formulated with consideration for the range of ages and maturity in the program and shall be culturally sensitive to the needs of alien minors. DHS shall not subject minors to corporal punishment, humiliation, mental abuse, or punitive interference with the daily functions of living, such as eating or sleeping. Any sanctions employed shall not adversely affect a minor's health, or physical or psychological well-being; or deny minors regular meals, sufficient sleep, exercise, medical care, correspondence privileges, or legal assistance;

(xviii) Licensed facilities will maintain and safeguard individual case records. Agencies and organizations will maintain a system of accountability which preserves the confidentiality of client information and protects the records from unauthorized use or disclosure;

(xix) Licensed facilities will maintain adequate records and make regular reports as required by DHS that permit DHS to monitor and enforce the regulations in this part and other requirements and standards as DHS may determine are in the best interests of the minors; and

(xx) Licensed facilities will maintain a grievance and complaint filing process for aliens housed therein and post information about the process in a common area of the facility. Aliens will be required to follow the proscribed process for filing formal and informal grievances against facility staff that comports with the ICE Family Residential Standards Grievance Procedures. Complaints regarding conditions of detention shall be filed under the procedures required by the DHS Office of the Inspector General or the DHS Office of Civil Rights and Civil Liberties. Staff is prohibited from retaliating against anyone who files, or on whose behalf is filed, a grievance or complaint. In the event of an emergency, a licensed, non-secure facility described in this paragraph (i) may transfer temporary physical custody of a minor prior to securing permission from DHS, but shall notify DHS of the transfer as soon as is practicable thereafter, but in all cases within 8 hours.

(j) Release of minors who are not UACs from DHS custody.

(1) DHS will make and record prompt and continuous efforts on its part toward the release of the minor who is not a UAC.

(2) If a minor who is not a UAC is in expedited removal proceedings (including if he or she is awaiting a credible fear determination), or is subject to a final expedited removal order, custody is governed by § 235.3(b)(2)(iii) or (b)(4)(ii) of this chapter, as applicable.

(3) If a minor who is not a UAC is subject to pending removal proceedings under section 240 of the Act, DHS will consider whether to release the minor pursuant to section 212(d)(5) or section 236(a), and the implementing regulations in 8 CFR 212.5 and § 235.3, as applicable.

(4) The parole of minors who are not UACs who are detained pursuant to section 235(b)(1)(B)(ii) of the Act or § 235.3(c) of this chapter will generally serve an urgent humanitarian reason warranting release on parole if DHS determines that detention is not required to secure the minor's timely appearance before DHS or the immigration court, or to ensure the minor's safety and well-being or the safety of others. In making this determination, DHS may consider aggregate and historical data, officer experience, statistical information, or any other probative information. The determination whether to parole a minor who is not a UAC is in the unreviewable discretion of DHS.

(5) If DHS determines to release a minor who is not a UAC during removal proceedings under section 240 of the Act, the following procedures shall apply:

(i) If a parent or legal guardian is available to provide care and physical custody, DHS will make prompt and continuous efforts to release the minor to that parent or legal guardian. Nothing in this paragraph (j)(5)(i) precludes the release of a minor who is not a UAC to an adult relative (brother, sister, aunt, uncle, or grandparent) who is not in detention and is available to provide care and physical custody. Release of a minor who is not a UAC to an adult relative other than a parent or legal guardian is within the unreviewable discretion of DHS.

(ii) Prior to releasing a minor who is not a UAC to an adult relative pursuant to paragraph (j)(5)(i) of this section, DHS will use all available reliable evidence to determine whether the relationship is bona fide. If no reliable evidence is available that confirms the relationship, DHS may continue to keep the minor who is not a UAC in custody or treat the minor as a UAC and transfer the UAC to HHS custody, as outlined in paragraph (f) of this section.

(iii) DHS shall assist without undue delay in making transportation arrangements to the DHS office nearest the location of the relative to whom a minor is to be released. DHS may, in its discretion, provide transportation to minors.

(iv) Nothing herein shall require DHS to release a minor to any person or agency whom DHS has reason to believe may harm or neglect the minor or fail to present him or her before DHS or the immigration courts when requested to do so.

(k) Procedures upon transfer—

(1) Possessions. Whenever a minor or UAC is transferred from one ICE placement to another, or from an ICE placement to an ORR placement, he or she will be transferred with all possessions and legal papers; provided, however, that if the minor or UAC's possessions exceed the amount normally permitted by the carrier in use, the possessions shall be shipped to the minor or UAC in a timely manner.

(2) Notice to counsel. A minor or UAC who is represented will not be transferred from one ICE placement to another, or from an ICE placement to an ORR placement, until notice is provided to his or her counsel, except in unusual and compelling circumstances, such as where the safety of the minor or UAC or others is threatened or the minor or UAC has been determined to be an escape-risk, or where counsel has waived such notice. In unusual and compelling circumstances, notice will be sent to counsel within 24 hours following the transfer.

(*l*) Notice to parent of refusal of release or application for relief.

(1) A parent shall be notified of any of the following requests if the parent is present in the United States and can reasonably be contacted, unless such notification is otherwise prohibited by law or DHS determines that notification of the parent would pose a risk to the minor's safety or well-being:

(i) A minor or UAC in DHS custody refuses to be released to his or her parent; or

(ii) A minor or a UAC seeks release from DHS custody or seeks voluntary departure or a withdrawal of an application for admission, parole, or any form of relief from removal before DHS, and that the grant of such request or relief may effectively terminate some interest inherent in the parent-child relationship and/or the minor or UAC's rights and interests are adverse with those of the parent.

(2) Upon notification, the parent will be afforded an opportunity to present his or her views and assert his or her interest to DHS before a determination is made as to the merits of the request for relief.

(m) Bond hearings. Bond determinations made by DHS for minors who are in removal proceedings pursuant to section 240 of the Act and who are also in DHS custody may be reviewed by an immigration judge pursuant to 8 CFR part 1236 to the extent permitted by 8 CFR 1003.19. Minors in DHS custody who are not in section 240 proceedings are ineligible to seek review by an immigration judge of their DHS custody determinations.

(n) Retaking custody of a previously released minor.

(1) In addition to the ability to make a UAC determination upon each encounter as set forth in paragraph (c) of this section, DHS may take a minor back into custody if there is a material change in circumstances indicating the minor is an escape-risk, a danger to the community, or has a final order of removal. If the minor is accompanied, DHS shall place the minor in accordance with paragraphs (e) and (i) of this section. If the minor is a UAC, DHS shall transfer the minor into HHS custody in accordance with paragraph (e) of this section.

(2) DHS may take a minor back into custody if there is no longer a parent, legal guardian, or other adult relative (brother, sister, aunt, uncle, or grandparent) available to care for the minor. If the minor is a UAC, DHS will transfer custody to HHS as outlined in paragraph (e) of this section.

(3) Minors who are not UACs and who are taken back into DHS custody may request a custody redetermination hearing in accordance with paragraph (m) of this section and to the extent permitted by 8 CFR 1003.19.

(o) Monitoring.

(1) CBP and ICE each shall identify a Juvenile Coordinator for the purpose of monitoring compliance with the terms of this section.

(2) In addition to the monitoring required by paragraph (o)(1) of this section, the Juvenile Coordinators shall collect and periodically examine relevant statistical information about UACs and minors who remain in CBP or ICE custody for longer than 72 hours. Such statistical information may include but not necessarily be limited to:

(i) Biographical information;

(ii) Dates of custody; and

(iii) Placements, transfers, removals, or releases from custody, including the reasons for a particular placement.

HISTORY:

[55 FR 30686, July 27, 1990; 59 FR 62302, Dec. 5, 1994; 60 FR 34090, June 30, 1995; 62 FR 10312, 10362, March 6, 1997; 67 FR 39255, 39258, June 7, 2002; 84 FR 44392, 44525, Aug. 23, 2019]

§ 236.4 Removal of S-5, S-6, and S-7 nonimmigrants.

(a) Condition of classification. As a condition of classification and continued stay in classification pursuant to section 101(a)(15)(S) of the Act, nonimmigrants in S classification must have executed Form I-854, Part B, Inter-agency Alien Witness and Informant Record, certifying that they have knowingly waived their right to a removal hearing and right to contest, other than on the basis of an application for withholding of deportation or removal, any removal action, including detention pending deportation or removal, instituted before lawful permanent resident status is obtained.

(b) **Determination of deportability.**

(1) A determination to remove a deportable alien classified pursuant to section 101(a)(15)(S) of the Act shall be made by the district director having jurisdiction over the place where the alien is located.

(2) A determination to remove such a deportable alien shall be based on one or more of the grounds of deportability listed in section 237 of the Act based on conduct committed after, or conduct or a condition not disclosed to the Service prior to, the alien's classification as an S nonimmigrant under section 101(a)(15)(S) of the Act, or for a violation of, or failure to adhere to, the particular terms and conditions of status in S nonimmigrant classification.

(c) **Removal procedures.**

(1) A district director who determines to remove an alien witness or informant in S nonimmigrant classification shall notify the Commissioner, the Assistant Attorney General, Criminal Division, and the relevant law enforcement agency in writing to that effect. The Assistant Attorney General, Criminal Division, shall concur in or object to that decision. Unless the Assistant Attorney General, Criminal Division, objects within 7 days, he or she shall be deemed to have concurred in the

decision. In the event of an objection by the Assistant Attorney General, Criminal Division, the matter will be expeditiously referred to the Deputy Attorney General for a final resolution. In no circumstances shall the alien or the relevant law enforcement agency have a right of appeal from any decision to remove.

(2) A district director who has provided notice as set forth in paragraph (c)(1) of this section and who has been advised by the Commissioner that the Assistant Attorney General, Criminal Division, has not objected shall issue a Warrant of Removal. The alien shall immediately be arrested and taken into custody by the district director initiating the removal. An alien classified under the provisions of section 101(a)(15)(S) of the Act who is determined, pursuant to a warrant issued by a district director, to be deportable from the United States shall be removed from the United States to his or her country of nationality or last residence. The agency that requested the alien's presence in the United States shall ensure departure from the United States and so inform the district director in whose jurisdiction the alien has last resided. The district director, if necessary, shall oversee the alien's departure from the United States and, in any event, shall notify the Commissioner of the alien's departure.

(d) Withholding of removal. An alien classified pursuant to section 101(a)(15)(S) of the Act who applies for withholding of removal shall have 10 days from the date the Warrant of Removal is served upon the alien to file an application for such relief with the district director initiating the removal order. The procedures contained in §§ 208.2 and 208.16 of this chapter shall apply to such an alien who applies for withholding of removal.

(e) Inadmissibility. An alien who applies for admission under the provisions of section 101(a)(15)(S) of the Act who is determined by an immigration officer not to be eligible for admission under that section or to be inadmissible to the United States under one or more of the grounds of inadmissibility listed in section 212 of the Act and which have not been previously waived by the Commissioner will be taken into custody. The district director having jurisdiction over the port-of-entry shall follow the notification procedures specified in paragraph (c)(1) of this section. A district director who has provided such notice and who has been advised by the Commissioner that the Assistant Attorney General, Criminal Division, has not objected shall remove the alien without further hearing. An alien may not contest such removal, other than by applying for withholding of removal.

HISTORY:

[43 FR 16445, Apr. 19, 1978; 62 FR 10312, 10362, March 6, 1997]

§ 236.5 Fingerprints and photographs.

Every alien 14 years of age or older against whom proceedings based on deportability under section 237 of the Act are commenced under this part by service of a notice to appear shall be fingerprinted and photographed. Such fingerprints and photographs shall be made available to Federal, State, and local law enforcement agencies upon request to the district director or chief patrol agent having jurisdiction over the alien's record. Any such alien, regardless of his or her age, shall be photographed and/or fingerprinted if required by any immigration officer authorized to issue a notice to appear. Every alien 14 years of age or older who is found to be inadmissible to the United States and ordered removed by an immigration judge shall be fingerprinted, unless during the preceding year he or she has been fingerprinted at an American consular office.

HISTORY:

[42 FR 46045, Sept. 14, 1977. Redesignated at 43 FR 16445, Apr. 19, 1978, and amended at 52 FR 2939, Jan. 29, 1987; 62 FR 10312, 10363, March 6, 1997]

§ 236.6 Information regarding detainees.

No person, including any state or local government entity or any privately operated detention facility, that houses, maintains, provides services to, or otherwise holds any detainee on behalf of the Service (whether by contract or otherwise), and no other person who by virtue of any official or contractual relationship with such person obtains information relating to any detainee, shall disclose or otherwise permit to be made public the name of, or other information relating to, such detainee. Such information shall be under the control of the Service and shall be subject to public disclosure only pursuant to the provisions of applicable federal laws, regulations and executive orders. Insofar as any documents or other records contain such information, such documents shall not be public records. This section applies to all persons and information identified or described in it, regardless of when such persons obtained such information, and applies to all requests for public disclosure of such information, including requests that are the subject of proceedings pending as of April 17, 2002.

HISTORY:

[67 FR 19508, 19511, Apr. 22, 2002, as confirmed at 68 FR 4364, 4367, Jan. 29, 2003]

§§ 236.7 — 236.9 [Reserved]

[NO TEXT IN ORIGINAL]

Subpart B

Family Unity Program

§ 236.10 Description of program.

The family unity program implements the provisions of section 301 of the Immigration Act of 1990, Public Law 101-649. This Act is referred to in this subpart as "IMMACT 90".

HISTORY:

[60 FR 44260, 44268, Aug. 25, 1995; 62 FR 10312, 10363, March 6, 1997]

§ 236.11 Definitions.

In this subpart, the term:

Eligible immigrant means a qualified immigrant who is the spouse or unmarried child of a legalized alien.

For purposes of §§ 236.10 to 236.18 only, Legalized alien means an alien who:

(1) Is a temporary or permanent resident under section 210 or 245A of the Act;

(2) Is a permanent resident under section 202 of the Immigration Reform and Control Act of 1986 (Cuban/ Haitian Adjustment); or

(3) Is a naturalized U.S. citizen who was a permanent resident under section 210 or 245A of the Act or section 202 of the Immigrant Reform and Control Act of 1986 (IRCA) (Cuban/Haitian Adjustment), and maintained such a status until his or her naturalization.

HISTORY:

[62 FR 10312, 10363, March 6, 1997; 65 FR 43677, 43679, July 14, 2000]

§ 236.12 Eligibility.

(a) General. An alien who is not a lawful permanent resident is eligible to apply for benefits under the Family Unity Program if he or she establishes:

(1) That he or she entered the United States before May 5, 1988 (in the case of a relationship to a legalized alien described in subsection (b)(2)(B) or (b)(2)(C) of section 301 of IMMACT 90), or as of December 1, 1988 (in the case of a relationship to a legalized alien described in subsection (b)(2)(A) of section 301 of IMMACT 90), and has been continuously residing in the United States since that date; and

(2) That as of May 5, 1988, (in the case of a relationship to a legalized alien described in subsection (b)(2)(B) or (b)(2) (C) of section 301 of IMMACT 90) or as of December 1, 1988, (in the case of a relationship to a legalized alien described in subsection (b)(2) (A) of section 301 of IMMACT 90), he or she was the spouse or unmarried child of a legalized alien, and that he or she has been eligible continuously since that time for family-sponsored immigrant status under section 203(a) (1), (2), or (3) or as an immediate relative under section 201 (b)(2) of the Act based on the same relationship.

(b) Legalization application pending as of May 5, 1988 or December 1, 1988. An alien whose legalization application was filed on or before May 5, 1988 (in the case of a relationship to a legalized alien described in subsection (b)(2)(B) or (b)(2)(C) of section 301 of IMMACT 90), or as of December 1, 1988 (in the case of a relationship to a legalized alien described in subsection (b)(2)(A) of section 301 of IMMACT 90), but not approved until after that date will be treated as having been a legalized alien as of May 5, 1988 (in the case of a relationship to a legalized alien described in subsection (b)(2)(B) or (b)(2)(C) of section 301 of IMMACT 90), or as of December 1, 1988 (in the case of a relationship to a legalized alien described in subsection (b)(2)(A) of section 301 of IMMACT 90), for purposes of the Family Unity Program.

HISTORY:

[2 FR 10312, 10363, March 6, 1997; 65 FR 43677, 43679, July 14, 2000]

§ 236.13 Ineligible aliens.

The following categories of aliens are ineligible for benefits under the Family Unity Program:

(a) An alien who is deportable under any paragraph in section 237(a) of the Act, except paragraphs (1)(A), (1)(B), (1)(C), and (3)(A); provided that an alien who is deportable under section 237(a)(1)(A) of such Act is also ineligible for benefits under the Family Unity Program if deportability is based upon a ground of inadmissibility described in section 212(a)(2) or (3) of the Act;

(b) An alien who has been convicted of a felony or three or more misdemeanors in the United States;

(c) An alien described in section 241(b)(3)(B) of the Act; or

(d) An alien who has committed an act of juvenile delinquency (as defined in 18 U.S.C. 5031) which if committed by an adult would be classified as:

(1) A felony crime of violence that has an element the use or attempted use of physical force against another individual; or

(2) A felony offense that by its nature involves a substantial risk that physical force against another individual may be used in the course of committing the offense.

HISTORY:

[62 FR 10312, 10363, March 6, 1997; 65 FR 43677, 43680, July 14, 2000]

§ 236.14 Filing.

(a) General. A Form I-817, Application for Family Unity Benefits, must be filed with the correct fee required in 8 CFR 106.2 and the required supporting documentation. A separate application with appropriate fee and documentation must be filed for each person claiming eligibility.

(b) Decision. The service center director has sole jurisdiction to adjudicate an application for benefits under the Family Unity Program. The director will provide the applicant with specific reasons for any decision to deny an application. Denial of an application may not be appealed. An applicant who believes that the grounds for denial have been overcome may submit another application with the appropriate fee and documentation.

(c) Referral of denied cases for consideration of issuance of notice to appear. If an application is denied, the case will be referred to the district director with jurisdiction over the alien's place of residence for consideration of whether to issue a notice to appear. After an initial denial, an applicant's case will not be referred for issuance of a notice to appear until 90 days from the date of the initial denial, to allow the alien the opportunity to file a new Form I-817 application in order to attempt to overcome the basis of the denial. However, if the applicant is found not to be eligible for benefits under § 236.13(b), the Service reserves the right to issue a notice to appear at any time after the initial denial.

HISTORY:

[62 FR 10312, 10364, March 6, 1997; 65 FR 43677, 43680, July 14, 2000; 66 FR 29661, 29672, June 1, 2001, as confirmed at 67 FR 38341, 38350, June 4, 2002; 74 FR 26933, 26939, June 5, 2009; 85 FR 46788, 46926, Aug. 3, 2020]

§ 236.15 Voluntary departure and eligibility for employment.

(a) Authority. Voluntary departure under this section implements the provisions of section 301 of IMMACT 90, and authority to grant voluntary departure under the family unity program derives solely from that section. Voluntary departure under the family unity program shall be governed solely by this section, notwithstanding the provisions of section 240B of the Act and 8 CFR part 240.

(b) Children of legalized aliens. Children of legalized aliens residing in the United States, who were born during an authorized absence from the United States of mothers who are currently residing in the United States under voluntary departure pursuant to the Family Unity Program, may be granted voluntary departure under section 301 of IMMACT 90 for a period of 2 years.

(c) Duration of voluntary departure. An alien whose application for benefits under the Family Unity Program is approved will receive voluntary departure for 2 years, commencing with the date of approval of the application. Voluntary departure under this section shall be considered effective from the date on which the application was properly filed.

(d) Employment authorization. An alien granted benefits under the Family Unity Program is authorized to be employed in the United States and will receive an employment authorization document. The validity period of the employment authorization document will coincide with the period of voluntary departure.

(e) Extension of voluntary departure. An application for an extension of voluntary departure under the Family Unity Program must be filed by the alien on Form I-817 along with the correct fee required in 8 CFR 106.2 and the required supporting documentation. The submission of a copy of the previous approval notice will assist in shortening the processing time. An extension may be granted if the alien continues to be eligible for benefits under the Family Unity Program. However, an extension may not be approved if the legalized alien is a lawful permanent resident, or a naturalized U.S. citizen who was a lawful permanent resident under section 210 or 245A of the Act or section 202 of the Immigration Reform and Control Act of 1986 (IRCA), Pub. L. 66-903, and maintained such status until his or her naturalization, and a petition for family-sponsored immigrant status has not been filed on behalf of the applicant. In such case, the Service will notify the alien of the reason for the denial and afford him or her the opportunity to file another Form I-817 once the petition, Form I-130, has been filed on his or her behalf. No charging document will be issued for a period of 90 days from the date of the denial.

(f) Supporting documentation for extension application. Supporting documentation need not include documentation provided with the previous application(s). The extension application shoud only include changes to previous applications and evidence of continuing eligibility since the date of prior approval.

HISTORY:

[62 FR 10312, 10364, March 6, 1997; 65 FR 43677, 43680, July 14, 2000; 85 FR 46788, 46926, Aug. 3, 2020]

§ 236.16 Travel outside the United States.

An alien granted Family Unity Program benefits who intends to travel outside the United States temporarily must apply for advance authorization in accordance with 8 CFR .2(a). The authority to grant an application for advance authorization for an alien granted Family Unity Program benefits rests solely with USCIS. An alien who is granted advance authorization and returns to the United States in accordance with such authorization, and who is found not to be inadmissible under section 212(a)(2) or (3) of the Act, shall be inspected and admitted in the same immigration status as the alien had at the time of departure, and shall be provided the remainder of the voluntary departure period previously granted under the Family Unity Program.

HISTORY:

[62 FR 10312, 10364, March 6, 1997; 76 FR 53764, 53790, Aug. 29, 2011]

§ 236.17 Eligibility for Federal financial assistance programs.

An alien granted Family Unity Program benefits based on a relationship to a legalized alien as defined in § 236.11 is ineligible for public welfare assistance in the same manner and for the same period as the legalized alien who is ineligible for such assistance under section 245A(h) or 210(f) of the Act, respectively.

HISTORY:

[62 FR 10312, 10364, March 6, 1997]

§ 236.18 Termination of Family Unity Program benefits.

(a) Grounds for termination. The Service may terminate benefits under the Family Unity Program whenever the necessity for the termination comes to the attention of the Service. Such grounds will exist in situations including, but not limited to, those in which:

(1) A determination is made that Family Unity Program benefits were acquired as the result of fraud or willful misrepresentation of a material fact;

(2) The beneficiary commits an act or acts which render him or her inadmissible as an immigrant ineligible for benefits under the Family Unity Program;

(3) The legalized alien upon whose status benefits under the Family Unity Program were based loses his or her legalized status;

(4) The beneficiary is the subject of a final order of exclusion, deportation, or removal issued subsequent to the grant of Family Unity benefits unless such final order is based on entry without inspection; violation of status; or failure to comply with section 265 of the Act; or inadmissibility at the time of entry other than inadmissibility pursuant to section 212(a)(2) or 212(a)(3) of the Act, regardless of whether the facts giving rise to such ground occurred before or after the benefits were granted; or

(5) A qualifying relationship to a legalized alien no longer exists.

(b) Notice procedure. Notice of intent to terminate and of the grounds thereof shall be served pursuant to the provisions of § 103.5a of this chapter. The alien shall be given 30 days to respond to the notice and may submit to the Service additional evidence in rebuttal. Any final decision of termination shall also be served pursuant to the provisions of § 103.5a of this chapter. Nothing in this section shall preclude the Service from commencing exclusion or deportation proceedings prior to termination of Family Unity Program benefits.

(c) Effect of termination. Termination of benefits under the Family Unity Program, other than as a result of a final order of removal, shall render the alien amenable to removal proceedings under section 240 of the Act. If benefits are terminated, the period of voluntary departure under this section is also terminated.

HISTORY:

[62 FR 10312, 10364, March 6, 1997; 65 FR 43677, 43680, July 14, 2000]

Subpart C

Deferred Action for Childhood Arrivals

§ 236.21 Applicability.

(a) This subpart applies to requests for deferred action under the enforcement discretion policy set forth in this subpart, which will be described as Deferred Action for Childhood Arrivals (DACA). This subpart does not apply to or govern any other request for or grant of deferred action or any other DHS deferred action policy.

(b) Except as specifically provided in this subpart, the provisions of 8 CFR part 103 do not apply to requests filed under this subpart.

(c)(1) Deferred action is an exercise of the Secretary's broad authority to establish national immigration enforcement policies and priorities under 6 U.S.C. 202(5) and section 103 of the Act. It is a form of enforcement discretion not to pursue the removal of certain aliens for a limited period in the interest of ordering enforcement priorities in light of limitations on available resources, taking into account humanitarian considerations and administrative convenience. It furthers the administrability of the complex immigration system by permitting the Secretary to focus enforcement on higher priority targets. This temporary forbearance from removal does not confer any right or entitlement to remain in or reenter the United States. A grant of deferred action under this section does not preclude DHS from commencing removal proceedings at any time or prohibit DHS or any other Federal agency from initiating any criminal or other enforcement action at any time.

(2) During this period of forbearance, on the basis of this subpart only, USCIS may grant employment authorization pursuant to 8 CFR 274a.13 and 274a.12(c)(33) to DACA recipients who have demonstrated an economic need.

(3) During this period of forbearance, on the basis of this subpart only, a DACA recipient is considered "lawfully present" under the provisions of 8 CFR 1.3(a)(4)(vi).

(4) During this period of forbearance, on the basis of this subpart only, a DACA recipient is not considered "unlawfully present" for the purpose of inadmissibility under section 212(a)(9) of the Act.

(d) This subpart rescinds and replaces the DACA guidance set forth in the Memorandum issued by the Secretary of Homeland Security on June 15, 2012. All current grants of deferred action and any ancillary features previously issued pursuant to the Memorandum remain in effect and will expire according to their existing terms. All such current grants of deferred action and any ancillary features, as well as any requests for renewals of those grants and new requests, are hereafter governed by this subpart and not the Memorandum.

HISTORY:

[87 FR 53152, 53297, Aug. 30, 2022]

§ 236.22 Discretionary determination.

(a) Deferred Action for Childhood Arrivals; in general.

(1) USCIS may consider requests for Deferred Action for Childhood Arrivals submitted by aliens described in paragraph (b) of this section.

(2) A pending request for deferred action under this section does not authorize or confer any interim immigration benefits such as employment authorization or advance parole.

(3) Subject to paragraph (c) of this section, the requestor bears the burden of demonstrating by a preponderance of the evidence that he or she meets the threshold criteria described in paragraph (b) of this section.

(b) Threshold criteria. Subject to paragraph (c) of this section, a request for deferred action under this section may be granted only if USCIS determines in its sole discretion that the requestor meets each of the following threshold criteria and merits a favorable exercise of discretion:

(1) Came to the United States under the age of 16. The requestor must demonstrate that he or she first resided in the United States before his or her sixteenth birthday.

(2) Continuous residence in the United States from June 15, 2007, to the time of filing of the request. The requestor also must demonstrate that he or she has been residing in the United States continuously from June 15, 2007, to the time of filing of the request. As used in this section, "residence" means the principal, actual dwelling place in fact, without regard to intent, and specifically the country of the actual dwelling place. Brief, casual, and innocent absences from the United States will not break the continuity of one's residence. However, unauthorized travel outside of the United States on or after August 15, 2012, will interrupt continuous residence, regardless of whether it was otherwise brief, casual, and innocent. An absence will be considered brief, casual, and innocent if it occurred before August 15, 2012, and—

(i) The absence was short and reasonably calculated to accomplish the purpose for the absence;

(ii) The absence was not because of a post-June 15, 2007 order of exclusion, deportation, or removal;

(iii) The absence was not because of a post-June 15, 2007 order of voluntary departure, or an administrative grant of voluntary departure before the requestor was placed in exclusion, deportation, or removal proceedings; and

(iv) The purpose of the trip, and the requestor's actions while outside the United States, were not contrary to law.

(3) Physical presence in the United States. The requestor must demonstrate that he or she was physically present in the United States both on June 15, 2012, and at the time of filing of the request for Deferred Action for Childhood Arrivals under this section.

(4) Lack of lawful immigration status. Both on June 15, 2012, and at the time of filing of the request for Deferred Action for Childhood Arrivals under this section, the requestor must not have been in a lawful immigration status. If the requestor was in lawful immigration status at any time before June 15, 2012, or at any time after June 15, 2012, and before the submission date of the request, he or she must submit evidence that that lawful status had expired or otherwise terminated prior to those dates.

(5) Education or veteran status. The requestor must currently be enrolled in school, have graduated or obtained a certificate of completion from high school, have obtained a General Educational Development certificate, or be an honorably discharged veteran of the United States Coast Guard or Armed Forces of the United States.

(6) Criminal history, public safety, and national security. The requestor must not have been convicted (as defined in section 101(a)(48) of the Act and as demonstrated by any of the documents or records listed in § 1003.41 of this chapter) of a felony, a misdemeanor described in this paragraph (b)(6), or three or more other misdemeanors not occurring on the same date and not arising out of the same act, omission, or scheme of misconduct, or otherwise pose a threat to national security or public safety. For purposes of this paragraph (b)(6) only, expunged convictions, juvenile delinquency adjudications, and convictions under State (including U.S. territory) laws for immigration-related offenses are not considered disqualifying convictions. For purposes of this paragraph (b)(6) only, a single misdemeanor is disqualifying if it is a misdemeanor as defined by Federal law (specifically, one for which the maximum term of imprisonment authorized is 1 year or less but greater than 5 days) and that meets the following criteria:

(i) Regardless of the sentence imposed, is an offense of domestic violence, sexual abuse or exploitation, burglary, unlawful possession or use of a firearm, drug distribution or trafficking, or driving under the influence; or

(ii) If not an offense listed above, is one for which the individual was sentenced to time in custody of more than 90 days. The sentence must involve time to be served in custody and, therefore, does not include a suspended sentence.

(7) Age at time of request. The requestor must have been born on or after June 16, 1981. Additionally, the requestor must be at least 15 years of age at the time of filing his or her request, unless, at the time of his or her request, he or she is in removal proceedings, has a final order of removal, or has a voluntary departure order.

(c) Final discretionary determination. Deferred action requests submitted under this section are determined on a case-by-case basis. Even if the threshold criteria in paragraph (b) are all found to have been met, USCIS retains the discretion to assess the individual's circumstances and to determine that any factor specific to that individual makes deferred action inappropriate.

HISTORY:

[87 FR 53152, 53297, Aug. 30, 2022]

§ 236.23 Procedures for request, terminations, and restrictions on information use.

(a) General.

(1) A request for Deferred Action for Childhood Arrivals must be filed in the manner and on the form designated by USCIS, with the required fee, including any biometrics required by 8 CFR 103.16. A request for Deferred Action for Childhood Arrivals must also contain a request for employment authorization filed pursuant to 8 CFR 274a.12(c)(33) and 274a.13.

(2) All requests for Deferred Action for Childhood Arrivals, including any requests made by aliens in removal proceedings before EOIR, must be filed with USCIS. USCIS has exclusive jurisdiction to consider requests for Deferred Action for Childhood Arrivals. EOIR shall have no jurisdiction to consider requests for Deferred Action for Childhood Arrivals or to review USCIS approvals or denials of such requests. A voluntary departure order or a final order of exclusion, deportation, or removal is not a bar to requesting Deferred Action for Childhood Arrivals. An alien who is in removal proceedings may request Deferred Action for Childhood Arrivals regardless of whether those proceedings have been administratively closed. An alien who is in immigration detention may request Deferred

Action for Childhood Arrivals but may not be approved for Deferred Action for Childhood Arrivals unless the alien is released from detention by ICE prior to USCIS' decision on the Deferred Action for Childhood Arrivals request.

(3) USCIS may request additional evidence from the requestor, including, but not limited to, by notice, interview, or other appearance of the requestor. USCIS may deny a request for Deferred Action for Childhood Arrivals without prior issuance of a request for evidence or notice of intent to deny.

(4) A grant of Deferred Action for Childhood Arrivals will be provided for an initial or renewal period of 2 years, subject to DHS's discretion. Related work authorization granted pursuant to 8 CFR 274a.12(c)(33), if approved in DHS's discretion, will be issued, subject to DHS's discretion, for the period of the associated grant of Deferred Action for Childhood Arrivals.

(b) Consideration of a request for Deferred Action for Childhood Arrivals. In considering requests for Deferred Action for Childhood Arrivals, USCIS may consult, as it deems appropriate in its discretion and without notice to the requestor, with any other component or office of DHS, including ICE and CBP, any other Federal agency, or any State or local law enforcement agency, in accordance with paragraph (e) of this section.

(c) Notice of decision.

(1) USCIS will notify the requestor and, if applicable, the requestor's attorney of record or accredited representative of the decision in writing. Denial of a request for Deferred Action for Childhood Arrivals does not bar a requestor from applying for any benefit or form of relief under the immigration laws or requesting any other form of prosecutorial discretion, including another request for Deferred Action for Childhood Arrivals.

(2) If USCIS denies a request for Deferred Action for Childhood Arrivals under this section, USCIS will not issue a Notice to Appear or refer a requestor's case to U.S. Immigration and Customs Enforcement for possible enforcement action based on such denial unless USCIS determines that the case involves denial for fraud, a threat to national security, or public safety concerns.

(3) There is no administrative appeal from a denial of a request for Deferred Action for Childhood Arrivals. The alien may not file, pursuant to 8 CFR 103.5 or otherwise, a motion to reopen or reconsider a denial of a request for Deferred Action for Childhood Arrivals.

(d) Termination.

(1) Discretionary termination. USCIS may terminate a grant of Deferred Action for Childhood Arrivals at any time in its discretion. USCIS will provide a Notice of Intent to Terminate and an opportunity to respond prior to terminating a grant of Deferred Action for Childhood Arrivals, except USCIS may terminate a grant of Deferred Action for Childhood Arrivals without a Notice of Intent to Terminate and an opportunity to respond if the Deferred Action for Childhood Arrivals recipient is convicted of a national security-related offense involving conduct described in 8 U.S.C. 1182(a)(3)(B)(iii), (iv), or 1227(a)(4)(A)(i), or an egregious public safety offense. If USCIS terminates a grant of Deferred Action for Childhood Arrivals without a Notice of Intent to Terminate and an opportunity to respond, USCIS will provide the individual with notice of the termination.

(2) Departure without advance parole and reentry without inspection. USCIS may terminate a grant of Deferred Action for Childhood Arrivals, in its discretion and following issuance of a Notice of Intent to Terminate with an opportunity to respond, for DACA recipients who depart from the United States without first obtaining an advance parole document and subsequently enter the United States without inspection.

(3) Automatic termination of employment authorization. Any grant of employment authorization pursuant to § 274a.12(c)(33) of this chapter will automatically terminate upon termination of a grant of Deferred Action for Childhood Arrivals, rather than in accordance with § 274a.14(a)(1)(ii) of this chapter. Notice of intent to revoke employment authorization is not required pursuant to § 274a.14(a)(2) of this chapter.

(e) Restrictions on information use.

(1) Information contained in a request for Deferred Action for Childhood Arrivals related to the requestor will not be used by DHS for the purpose of initiating immigration enforcement proceedings against such requestor, unless DHS is initiating immigration enforcement proceedings against the requestor due to a criminal offense, fraud, a threat to national security, or public safety concerns.

(2) Information contained in a request for Deferred Action for Childhood Arrivals related to the requestor's family members or guardians will not be used for immigration enforcement purposes against such family members or guardians.

HISTORY:

[87 FR 53152, 53297, Aug. 30, 2022]

§ 236.24 Severability.

(a) Any provision of this subpart held to be invalid or unenforceable as applied to any person or circumstance shall be construed so as to continue to give the maximum effect to the provision permitted by law, including as applied to persons not similarly situated or to dissimilar circumstances, unless such holding is that the provision of this subpart is invalid and unenforceable in all circumstances, in which event the provision shall be severable from the remainder of this subpart and shall not affect the remainder thereof.

(b) The provisions in § 236.21(c)(2) through (4) and § 274a.12(c)(14) and 274a.12(c)(33) are intended to be severable from one another, from this subpart and any grant of forbearance from removal resulting from this subpart, and from any provision referenced in those paragraphs, including such referenced provision's application to persons with deferred action generally.

HISTORY:

[87 FR 53152, 53297, Aug. 30, 2022]

§ 236.25 No private rights.

This subpart is an exercise of the Secretary's enforcement discretion. This subpart—

(a) Is not intended to and does not supplant or limit otherwise lawful activities of the Department or the Secretary; and

(b) Is not intended to and does not create any rights, substantive or procedural, enforceable at law by any party in any matter, civil or criminal.

HISTORY:

[87 FR 53152, 53297, Aug. 30, 2022]

PART 238

EXPEDITED REMOVAL OF AGGRAVATED FELONS

AUTHORITY NOTE APPLICABLE TO ENTIRE PART:

AUTHORITY:

8 U.S.C. 1228; 8 CFR part 2.

§ 238.1 Proceedings under section 238(b) of the Act.

(a) Definitions. As used in this part the term:

Deciding Service officer means a district director, chief patrol agent, or another immigration officer designated by a district director, chief patrol agent, the Deputy Executive Associate Commissioner for Detention and Removal, or the Director of the Office of Juvenile Affairs, so long as that person is not the same person as the Issuing Service Officer.

Issuing Service officer means any Service officer listed in § 239.1 of this chapter as authorized to issue notices to appear.

(b) Preliminary consideration and Notice of Intent to Issue a Final Administrative Deportation Order; commencement of proceedings —

(1) Basis of Service charge. An issuing Service officer shall cause to be served upon an alien a Form I-851, Notice of Intent to Issue a Final Administrative Deportation Order (Notice of Intent), if the officer is satisfied that there is sufficient evidence, based upon questioning of the alien by an immigration officer and upon any other evidence obtained, to support a finding that the individual:

(i) Is an alien;

(ii) Has not been lawfully admitted for permanent residence, or has conditional permanent resident status under section 216 of the Act;

(iii) Has been convicted (as defined in section 101(a)(48) of the Act and as demonstrated by any of the documents or records listed in § 1003.41 of this chapter) of an aggravated felony and such conviction has become final; and

(iv) Is deportable under section 237(a)(2)(A)(iii) of the Act, including an alien who has neither been admitted nor paroled, but who is conclusively presumed deportable under section 237(a)(2)(A)(iii) by operation of section 238(c) of the Act ("Presumption of Deportability").

(2) Notice.

(i) Removal proceedings under section 238(b) of the Act shall commence upon personal service of the Notice of Intent upon the alien, as prescribed by 8 CFR 103.8. The Notice of Intent shall set forth the preliminary determinations and inform the alien of the Service's intent to issue a Form I-851A, Final Administrative Removal Order, without a hearing before an immigration judge. The Notice of Intent shall constitute the charging document. The Notice of Intent shall include allegations of fact and conclusions of law. It shall advise that the alien: has the privilege of being represented, at no expense to the government, by counsel of the alien's choosing, as long as counsel is authorized to practice in removal proceedings; may request withholding of removal to a particular country if he or she fears persecution or torture in that country; may inspect the evidence supporting the Notice of Intent; may rebut the charges within 10 calendar days after service of such Notice (or 13 calendar days if service of the Notice was by mail).

(ii) The Notice of Intent also shall advise the alien that he or she may designate in writing, within the rebuttal period, the country to which he or she chooses to be deported in accordance with section 241 of the Act, in the event that a Final Administrative Removal Order is issued, and that the Service will honor such designation only to the extent permitted under the terms, limitations, and conditions of section 241 of the Act.

(iii) The Service must determine that the person served with the Notice of Intent is the person named on the notice.

(iv) The Service shall provide the alien with a list of available free legal services programs qualified under 8 CFR part 3 and organizations recognized pursuant to 8 CFR part 292, located within the district or sector where the Notice of Intent is issued.

(v) The Service must either provide the alien with a written translation of the Notice of Intent or explain the contents of the Notice of Intent to the alien in the alien's native language or in a language that the alien understands.

(c) Alien's response —

(1) Time for response. The alien will have 10 calendar days from service of the Notice of Intent or 13 calendar days if service is by mail, to file a response to the Notice of Intent. In the response, the alien may: designate his or her choice of country for removal; submit a written response rebutting the allegations supporting the charge and/or requesting the opportunity to review the Government's evidence; and/or submit a statement indicating an intention to request withholding of removal under 8 CFR 208.16 of this chapter, and/or request in writing an extension of time for response, stating the specific reasons why such an extension is necessary.

(2) Nature of rebuttal or request to review evidence.

(i) If an alien chooses to rebut the allegations contained in the Notice of Intent, the alien's written response must indicate which finding(s) are being challenged and should be accompanied by affidavit(s), documentary information, or other specific evidence supporting the challenge.

(ii) If an alien's written response requests the opportunity to review the Government's evidence, the Service shall serve the alien with a copy of the evidence in the record of proceeding upon which the Service is relying to support the charge. The alien may, within 10 calendar days following service of the Government's evidence (13 calendar days if service is by mail), furnish a final response in accordance with paragraph (c)(1) of this section. If the alien's final response is a rebuttal of the allegations, such a final response should be accompanied by affidavit(s), documentary information, or other specific evidence supporting the challenge.

(d) Determination by deciding Service officer —

(1) No response submitted or concession of deportability. If the deciding Service officer does not receive a timely response and the evidence in the record of proceeding establishes deportability by clear, convincing, and unequivocal evidence, or if the alien concedes deportability, then the deciding Service officer shall issue and cause to be served upon the alien a Final Administrative Removal Order that states the reasons for the deportation decision. The alien may, in writing, waive the 14-day waiting period before execution of the final order of removal provided in a paragraph (f) of this section.

(2) Response submitted —

(i) Insufficient rebuttal; no genuine issue of material fact. If the alien timely submits a rebuttal to the allegations, but the deciding Service officer finds that deportability is established by clear, convincing, and unequivocal evidence in the record of proceeding, the deciding Service officer shall issue and cause to be served upon the alien a Final Administrative Removal Order that states the reasons for the decision of deportability.

(ii) Additional evidence required.

(A) If the deciding Service officer finds that the record of proceeding, including the alien's timely rebuttal, raises a genuine issue of material fact regarding the preliminary findings, the deciding Service officer may either obtain additional evidence from any source, including the alien, or cause to be issued a notice to appear to initiate removal proceedings under section 240 of the Act. The deciding Service officer may also obtain additional evidence from any source, including the alien, if the deciding Service officer deems that such additional evidence may aid the officer in the rendering of a decision.

(B) If the deciding Service officer considers additional evidence from a source other than the alien, that evidence shall be made a part of the record of proceeding, and shall be provided to the alien. If the alien elects to submit a response to such additional evidence, such response must be filed with the Service within 10 calendar days of service of the additional evidence (or 13 calendar days if service is by mail). If the deciding Service officer finds, after considering all additional evidence, that deportability is established by clear, convincing, and unequivocal evidence in the record of proceeding, the deciding Service officer shall issue and cause to be served upon the alien a Final Administrative Removal Order that states the reasons for the decision of deportability.

(iii) Conversion to proceedings under section 240 of the Act. If the deciding Service officer finds that the alien is not amenable to removal under section 238 of the Act, the deciding Service officer shall terminate the expedited proceedings under section 238 of the Act and shall, where appropriate, cause to be issued a notice to appear for the purpose of initiating removal proceedings before an immigration judge under section 240 of the Act.

(3) Termination of proceedings by deciding Service officer. Only the deciding Service officer may terminate proceedings under section 238 of the Act, in accordance with this section.

(e) Proceedings commenced under section 240 of the Act. In any proceeding commenced under section 240 of the Act which is based on deportability under section 237 of the Act, if it appears that the respondent alien is subject to removal pursuant to section 238 of the Act, the immigration judge may, upon the Service's request, terminate the case and, upon such termination, the Service may commence administrative proceedings under section 238 of the Act. However, in the absence of any such request, the immigration judge shall complete the proceeding commenced under section 240 of the Act.

(f) Executing final removal order of deciding Service officer —

(1) Time of execution. Upon the issuance of a Final Administrative Removal Order, the Service shall issue a Warrant of Removal in accordance with § 241.2 of this chapter; such warrant shall be executed no sooner than 14 calendar days after the date the Final Administrative Removal Order is issued, unless the alien knowingly, voluntarily, and in writing waives the 14-day period.

(2) Country to which alien is to be removed. The deciding Service officer shall designate the country of removal in the manner prescribed by section 241 of the Act.

(3) Withholding of removal. If the alien has requested withholding of removal under § 208.16 of this chapter, the deciding officer shall, upon issuance of a Final Administrative Removal Order, immediately refer the alien's case to an asylum officer to conduct a reasonable fear determination in accordance with § 208.31 of this chapter.

(g) Arrest and detention. At the time of issuance of a Notice of Intent or at any time thereafter and up to the time the alien becomes the subject of a Warrant of Removal, the alien may be arrested and taken into custody under the authority of a Warrant of Arrest issued by an officer listed in § 287.5(e)(2) of this chapter. The decision of the Service concerning custody or bond shall not be administratively appealable during proceedings initiated under section 238 of the Act and this part.

(h) Record of proceeding. The Service shall maintain a record of proceeding for judicial review of the Final Administrative Removal Order sought by any petition for review. The record of proceeding shall include, but not necessarily be limited to: the charging document (Notice of Intent); the Final Administrative Removal Order (including any supplemental memorandum of decision); the alien's response, if any; all evidence in support of the charge; and any admissible evidence, briefs, or documents submitted by either party respecting deportability. The executed duplicate of the Notice of Intent in the record of proceedings shall be retained as evidence that the individual upon whom the notice for the proceeding was served was, in fact, the alien named in the notice.

HISTORY:

[62 FR 10312, 10365, Mar. 6, 1997; 64 FR 8478, 8494, Feb. 19, 1999; 67 FR 39255, 39258, June 7, 2002; 76 FR 53764, 53791, Aug. 29, 2011; 81 FR 62353, 62355, Sept. 9, 2016]

PART 239

INITIATION OF REMOVAL PROCEEDINGS

Rule

AUTHORITY NOTE APPLICABLE TO ENTIRE PART:

AUTHORITY:

8 U.S.C. 1103, 1221, 1229; Homeland Security Act of 2002, Public Law 107-296; 8 CFR part 2.

§ 239.1 Notice to appear.

(a) Issuance of notice to appear. Any immigration officer, or supervisor thereof, performing an inspection of an arriving alien at a port-of-entry may issue a notice to appear to such alien. In addition, the following officers, or officers acting in such capacity, may issue a notice to appear:

(1) District directors (except foreign);

(2) Deputy district directors (except foreign);

(3) Chief patrol agents;

(4) Deputy chief patrol agents;

(5) Division chiefs;

(6) Assistant chief patrol agents;

(7) Patrol agents in charge;

(8) Deputy patrol agents in charge;

(9) Border patrol watch commanders;

(10) Special operations supervisors;

(11) Supervisory border patrol agents;

(12) Directors of air operations;

(13) Directors of marine operations;

(14) Supervisory air and marine interdiction agents;

(15) Service center directors;

(16) Deputy service center directors;

(17) Assistant service center directors for examinations;

(18) Supervisory immigration services officers;

(19) Supervisory immigration officers;

(20) Supervisory asylum officers;

(21) Officers in charge (except foreign);

(22) Assistant officers in charge (except foreign);

(23) Special agents in charge;

(24) Deputy special agents in charge;

(25) Associate special agents in charge;

(26) Assistant special agents in charge;

(27) Resident agents in charge;

(28) Supervisory special agents;

(29) Directors of investigations;

(30) District directors for interior enforcement;

(31) Deputy or assistant district directors for interior enforcement;

(32) Director of enforcement and removal operations;

(33) Field office directors;

(34) Deputy field office directors;

(35) Supervisory deportation officers;

(36) Supervisory detention and deportation officers;

(37) Directors or officers in charge of detention facilities;

(38) Directors of field operations;

(39) Assistant directors of field operations;

(40) Port directors;

(41) Assistant port directors;

(42) Field operations watch commanders;

(43) Field operations chiefs;

(44) Unit Chief, Law Enforcement Support Center;

(45) Section Chief, Law Enforcement Support Center; or

(46) Other duly authorized officers or employees of the Department of Homeland Security or of the United States who are delegated the authority as provided by 8 CFR 2.1 to issue notices to appear, and who have successfully completed any required immigration law enforcement training.

(b) Service of notice to appear. Service of the notice to appear shall be in accordance with section 239 of the Act.

HISTORY:

[62 FR 10312, 10366, March 6, 1997; 67 FR 39255, 39258, June 7, 2002; 68 FR 10922, 10924, Mar. 6, 2003; 68 FR 35273, 35275, June 13, 2003; 70 FR 67087, 67089, Nov. 4, 2005; 81 FR 62353, 62355, Sept. 9, 2016]

§ 239.2 Cancellation of notice to appear.

(a) Any officer authorized by § 239.1(a) to issue a notice to appear may cancel such notice prior to jurisdiction vesting with the immigration judge pursuant to § 3.14 of this chapter provided the officer is satisfied that:

(1) The respondent is a national of the United States;

(2) The respondent is not deportable or inadmissible under immigration laws;

(3) The respondent is deceased;

(4) The respondent is not in the United States;

(5) The notice was issued for the respondent's failure to file a timely petition as required by section 216(c) of the Act, but his or her failure to file a timely petition

was excused in accordance with section 216(d)(2)(B) of the Act;

(6) The notice to appear was improvidently issued, or

(7) Circumstances of the case have changed after the notice to appear was issued to such an extent that continuation is no longer in the best interest of the government.

(b) A notice to appear issued pursuant to section 235(b)(3) of the Act may be canceled under provisions in paragraphs (a)(2) and (a)(6) of this section only by the issuing officer, unless it is impracticable for the issuing officer to cancel the notice.

(c) Motion to dismiss. After commencement of proceedings pursuant to 8 CFR 1003.14, ICE counsel, or any officer enumerated in paragraph (a) of this section, may move for dismissal of the matter on the grounds set out under paragraph (a) of this section.

(d) Motion for remand. After commencement of the hearing, ICE counsel, or any officer enumerated in paragraph (a) of this section may move for remand of the matter to district jurisdiction on the ground that the foreign relations of the United States are involved and require further consideration.

(e) Warrant of arrest. When a notice to appear is canceled or proceedings are terminated under this section any outstanding warrant of arrest is canceled.

HISTORY:

[62 FR 10312, 10367, March 6, 1997; 68 FR 35273, 35276, June 13, 2003]

§ 239.3 Effect of filing notice to appear.

The filing of a notice to appear shall have no effect in determining periods of unlawful presence as defined in section 212(a)(9)(B) of the Act.

HISTORY:

[62 FR 10312, 10367, March 6, 1997]

PART 240

VOLUNTARY DEPARTURE, SUSPENSION OF DEPORTATION AND SPECIAL RULE CANCELLATION OF REMOVAL

AUTHORITY NOTE APPLICABLE TO ENTIRE PART:

AUTHORITY:

8 U.S.C. 1103; 1182, 1186a, 1224, 1225, 1226, 1227, 1251, 1252 note, 1252a, 1252b, 1362; secs. 202 and 203, Pub. L. 105-100 (111 Stat. 2160, 2193); sec. 902, Pub. L. 105-277 (112 Stat. 2681); 8 CFR part 2.

Subpart B

Cancellation of Removal

§ 240.21 Suspension of Deportation and Adjustment of Status Under Section 244(a) of the Act (as in effect before April 1, 1997) and Cancellation of Removal and Adjustment of Status Under Section 240A(b) of the Act for Certain Nonpermanent Residents.

(a) **Applicability of annual cap on suspension of deportation or cancellation of removal.**

(1) As used in this section, the term cap means the numerical limitation of 4,000 grants of suspension of deportation or cancellation of removal in any fiscal year (except fiscal year 1998, which has a limitation of 8,000 grants) pursuant to section 240A(e) of the Act.

(2) The provisions of this section apply to grants of suspension of deportation pursuant to section 244(a) of the Act (as in effect before April 1, 1997) or cancellation of removal pursuant to section 240A(b) of the Act that are subject to a numerical limitation in section 240A(e) of the Act for any fiscal year. This section does not apply to grants of suspension of deportation or cancellation of removal to aliens described in section 309(c)(5)(C)(i) of the Illegal Immigration Reform and Immigrant Responsibility Act (IIRIRA), as amended by section 203(a)(1) of the Nicaraguan Adjustment and Central American Relief Act (NACARA), or aliens in deportation proceedings prior to April 1, 1997, who apply for suspension of deportation pursuant to section 244(a)(3) of the Act (as in effect prior to April 1, 1997). The Immigration Court and the Board shall no longer issue conditional grants of suspension of deportation or cancellation of removal as provided in 8 CFR 240.21 (as in effect prior to September 30, 1998).

(b) **Conditional grants of suspension of deportation or cancellation of removal in fiscal year 1998 cases.**

(1) Conversion to grants. Except with respect to cases described in paragraphs (b)(2) and (b)(3) of this section, EOIR shall grant suspension of deportation or

cancellation of removal without condition prior to October 1, 1998, to the first 8,000 aliens given conditional grants of suspension of deportation or cancellation of removal (as determined by the date of the immigration judge's order or, if the order was appealed to the Board, the date such order was entered by the Board.)

(2) Treatment of certain nationals of Nicaragua and Cuba who received conditional grants of suspension of deportation or cancellation of removal on or before September 30, 1998.

(i) NACARA adjustment request. An application for suspension of deportation or cancellation of removal filed by a national of Nicaragua or Cuba that was granted on a conditional basis on or before September 30, 1998, shall be deemed to be a request for adjustment of status pursuant to section 202 of NACARA ("NACARA adjustment") for the period starting September 30, 1998 and ending December 31, 1998. The Service shall provide the applicant with notice of the date, time, and place at which the applicant must appear before a Service officer to perfect the request for NACARA adjustment. Such notice shall include an attestation form, Attestation of Alien and Memorandum of Creation of Record of Lawful Permanent Residence, Form I-895, regarding the applicant's eligibility for NACARA adjustment.

(ii) Submission of documentation. To perfect the request for NACARA adjustment, the applicant must appear before a Service officer on the date scheduled with the following documentation:

(A) The order granting suspension of deportation or cancellation of removal on a conditional basis issued on or before September 30, 1998;

(B) A completed, but unsigned Form I-895, which the applicant shall be required to sign and to attest to the veracity of the information contained therein in the presence of a Service officer;

(C) Any applicable applications for waiver of inadmissibility; and

(D) Two "ADIT-style" photographs; meeting the specifications in the instructions attached to Form I-895.

(iii) Waiver of documentation and fees. The provisions of § 245.13(e) and (f) of this chapter relating to documentary requirements for NACARA adjustment are waived with respect to an alien seeking to perfect a request for adjustment of status pursuant to paragraph (b)(2) of this section. In addition, the fees for the NACARA adjustment and for any applications for waivers of inadmissibility submitted in conjunction with perfecting a request for NACARA adjustment shall be waived.

(iv) NACARA adjustment determination. In determining an applicant's eligibility for NACARA adjustment under the provisions of paragraph (b)(2) of this section, unless the Service officer before whom the applicant appears is not satisfied that the applicant is admissible to the United States in accordance with section 202(a)(1)(B) of NACARA, and has continuously resided in the United States from December 1, 1995, through the date of appearance before the Service officer (not counting an absence or absences from the United States totaling 180 days or less or any absences that occurred pursuant to advance authorization for parole (Form I-512 issued by the Service)), the Service officer shall accept an alien's attestation of admissibility and/or continuous physical presence as sufficient evidence that the applicant has met the admissibility and/or continuous physical presence requirement for NACARA adjustment. If the Service officer grants NACARA adjustment, then the Service officer shall create a record of lawful permanent residence and the prior order granting suspension of deportation or cancellation of removal on a conditional basis shall be automatically vacated and the deportation or removal proceedings shall be automatically terminated. The Service officer (whose decision in this regard is not subject to appeal) shall not adjust the applicant to lawful permanent resident status pursuant to section 202 of NACARA if:

(A) The Service officer is not satisfied that the applicant is eligible for NACARA adjustment and so indicates on the attestation form; or

(B) The applicant indicates on the attestation form that he or she does not wish to receive NACARA adjustment.

(v) Automatic conversion. If the Service officer does not adjust the applicant to lawful permanent resident status pursuant to section 202 of NACARA, the applicant's conditional grant of suspension of deportation or cancellation of removal shall be automatically converted to a grant of suspension of deportation or cancellation of removal. Upon such a conversion, the Service shall create a record of lawful permanent residence based upon the grant of suspension of deportation or cancellation of removal.

(vi) Failure to appear. An alien who fails to appear to perfect his or her request for NACARA adjustment shall have his or her conditional grant of suspension of deportation or cancellation of removal automatically converted by the Immigration Court or the Board to a grant of suspension of deportation or cancellation of removal effective December 31, 1998.

(3) Conditional grants not converted in fiscal year 1998. The provisions of paragraphs (b)(1) and (b)(2) of this section for granting relief shall not apply with respect to:

(i) Any case in which a conditional grant of suspension of deportation or cancellation of removal is pending on appeal before the Board as of September 30, 1998 or, if the right to appeal to the Board has not been waived, the time for an appeal has not expired. After the Board issues its decision or the time for appeal has expired, the conditional grant shall be converted to a grant when a grant is available.

(ii) Any other conditional grant not described in paragraphs (b)(1), (b)(2) or (b)(3)(i) of this section, which was not converted to a grant in fiscal year 1998. Such a conditional grant shall be converted to a grant when a grant is available.

(4) Motion to reopen. The Service may file a motion to reopen within 90 days after the alien is issued a grant of suspension of deportation or cancellation of removal pursuant to paragraphs (b)(1), (b)(2), or (b)(3)

of this section, if after the issuance of a conditional grant by the Immigration Court or the Board the applicant committed an act that would have rendered him or her ineligible for suspension of deportation or cancellation or removal at the time of the conversion.

(5) Travel for aliens conditionally granted suspension of deportation or cancellation of removal. If the Immigration Court or the Board granted suspension of deportation or cancellation of removal on a conditional basis or, if the conditional grant by the Immigration Court was appealed to the Board and the Board issued such a conditional grant, the alien shall retain the conditional grant of suspension of deportation or cancellation of removal upon return to the United States following a temporary absence abroad and be permitted to resume completion of his or her case, provided that:

(i) The alien departed on or before September 30, 1998 with or without a grant of advance parole from the District Director; or

(ii) The alien, prior to his or her departure from the United States after September 30, 1998, obtained a grant of advance parole from the District Director in accordance with section 212(d)(5) of the Act and § 212.5 of this chapter and complied with the terms and conditions of the advance parole.

(c) Grants of suspension of deportation or cancellation of removal in fiscal years subsequent to fiscal year 1998. On and after October 1, 1998, the Immigration Court and the Board may grant applications for suspension of deportation and adjustment of status under section 244(a) of the Act (as in effect prior to April 1, 1997) or cancellation of removal and adjustment of status under section 240A(b) of the Act that meet the statutory requirements for such relief and warrant a favorable exercise of discretion until the annual numerical limitation has been reached in that fiscal year. The awarding of such relief shall be determined according to the date the order granting such relief becomes final as defined in §§ 3.1(d)(3) and 3.39 of this chapter.

(1) Applicability of the annual cap. When grants are no longer available in a fiscal year, further decisions to grant or deny such relief shall be reserved until such time as a grant becomes available under the annual limitation in a subsequent fiscal year. Immigration judges and the Board may deny without reserving decision or may pretermit those suspension of deportation or cancellation of removal applications in which the applicant has failed to establish statutory eligibility for relief. The basis of such denial or pretermission may not be based on an unfavorable exercise of discretion, a finding of no good moral character on a ground not specifically noted in section 101(f) of the Act, a failure to establish exceptional or extremely unusual hardship to a qualifying relative in cancellation cases, or a failure to establish extreme hardship to the applicant and/or qualifying relative in suspension cases.

(2) Aliens applying for additional forms of relief. Whether or not the cap has been reached, the Immigration Court or the Board shall adjudicate concurrently all other forms of relief for which the alien has applied. Applications for suspension of deportation or cancellation of removal shall be denied in the exercise of discretion if the alien is granted asylum or adjustment of status, including pursuant to section 202 of NACARA, while the suspension of deportation or cancellation of removal application is pending. Where an appeal of a decision granting asylum or adjustment is sustained by the Board, a decision to deny as a matter of discretion an application for suspension of deportation or cancellation of removal on this basis shall be reconsidered.

HISTORY:

[62 FR 51760, 51762, Oct. 3, 1997; 63 FR 52134, 52138, Sept. 30, 1998; 66 FR 6436, 6446, Jan. 22, 2001]

Subpart C

Voluntary Departure

§ 240.25 Voluntary departure — authority of the Service.

(a) Authorized officers. The authority contained in section 240B(a) of the Act to permit aliens to depart voluntarily from the United States may be exercised in lieu of being subject to proceedings under section 240 of the Act by district directors, assistant district directors for investigations, assistant district directors for examinations, officers in charge, chief patrol agents, the Deputy Executive Associate Director for Enforcement and Removal Operations, the Director of the Office of Juvenile Affairs, service center directors, and assistant service center directors for examinations.

(b) Conditions. The Service may attach to the granting of voluntary departure any conditions it deems necessary to ensure the alien's timely departure from the United States, including the posting of a bond, continued detention pending departure, and removal under safeguards. The alien shall be required to present to the Service, for inspection and photocopying, his or her passport or other travel documentation sufficient to assure lawful entry into the country to which the alien is departing. The Service may hold the passport or documentation for sufficient time to investigate its authenticity. A voluntary departure order permitting an alien to depart voluntarily shall inform the alien of the penalties under section 240B(d) of the Act.

(c) Decision. The authorized officer, in his or her discretion, shall specify the period of time permitted for voluntary departure, and may grant extensions thereof, except that the total period allowed, including any extensions, shall not exceed 120 days. Every decision regarding voluntary departure shall be communicated in writing on Form I-210, Notice of Action — Voluntary Departure. Voluntary departure may not be granted unless the alien requests such voluntary departure and agrees to its terms and conditions.

(d) Application. Any alien who believes himself or herself to be eligible for voluntary departure under this section may apply therefor at any office of the Service. After the commencement of removal proceedings, the application may be communicated through the Service counsel. If the Service agrees to voluntary departure after proceedings have commenced, it may either:

(1) Join in a motion to terminate the proceedings, and if the proceedings are terminated, grant voluntary departure; or

(2) Join in a motion asking the immigration judge to permit voluntary departure in accordance with § 240.26.

(e) Appeals. An appeal shall not lie from a denial of an application for voluntary departure under this section, but the denial shall be without prejudice to the alien's right to apply to the immigration judge for voluntary departure in accordance with § 240.26 or for relief from removal under any provision of law.

(f) Revocation. If, subsequent to the granting of an application for voluntary departure under this section, it is ascertained that the application should not have been granted, that grant may be revoked without advance notice by any officer authorized to grant voluntary departure under § 240.25(a). Such revocation shall be communicated in writing, citing the statutory basis for revocation. No appeal shall lie from revocation.

HISTORY:

[62 FR 10312, 10371, March 6, 1997; 67 FR 39255, 39258, June 7, 2002; 81 FR 62353, 62355, Sept. 9, 2016]

Subpart H

Applications for Suspension of Deportation or Special Rule Cancellation of Removal Under Section 203 of Pub. L. 105-100

§ 240.60 Definitions.

As used in this subpart the term:

ABC means American Baptist Churches v. Thornburgh, 760 F. Supp. 796 (N.D. Cal. 1991).

ABC class member refers to:

(1) Any Guatemalan national who first entered the United States on or before October 1, 1990; and

(2) Any Salvadoran national who first entered the United States on or before September 19, 1990.

Asylum application pending adjudication by the Service means any asylum application for which the Service has not served the applicant with a final decision or which has not been referred to the Immigration Court.

Filed an application for asylum means the proper filing of a principal asylum application or filing a derivative asylum application by being properly included as a dependent spouse or child in an asylum application pursuant to the regulations and procedures in effect at the time of filing the principal or derivative asylum application.

IIRIRA means the Illegal Immigration Reform and Immigrant Responsibility Act of 1996, enacted as Pub. L. 104-208 (110 Stat. 3009-625).

NACARA means the Nicaraguan Adjustment and Central American Relief Act (NACARA), enacted as title II of Pub. L. 105-100 (111 Stat. 2160, 2193), as amended by the Technical Corrections to the Nicaraguan Adjustment and Central American Relief Act, Pub. L. 105-139 (111 Stat. 2644).

Registered ABC class member means an ABC class member who:

(1) In the case of an ABC class member who is a national of El Salvador, properly submitted an ABC registration form to the Service on or before October 31, 1991, or applied for temporary protected status on or before October 31, 1991; or

(2) In the case of an ABC class member who is a national of Guatemala, properly submitted an ABC registration form to the Service on or before December 31, 1991.

HISTORY:

[64 FR 27856, 27876, May 21, 1999]

§ 240.61 Applicability.

(a) Except as provided in paragraph (b) of this section, this subpart H applies to the following aliens:

(1) A registered ABC class member who has not been apprehended at the time of entry after December 19, 1990;

(2) A Guatemalan or Salvadoran national who filed an application for asylum with the Service on or before April 1, 1990, either by filing an application with the Service or filing the application with the Immigration Court and serving a copy of that application on the Service.

(3) An alien who entered the United States on or before December 31, 1990, filed an application for asylum on or before December 31, 1991, and, at the time of filing the application, was a national of the Soviet Union, Russia, any republic of the former Soviet Union, Latvia, Estonia, Lithuania, Poland, Czechoslovakia, Romania, Hungary, Bulgaria, Albania, East Germany, Yugoslavia, or any state of the former Yugoslavia;

(4) An alien who is the spouse or child of an individual described in paragraph (a)(1), (a)(2), or (a)(3) of this section at the time a decision is made to suspend the deportation, or cancel the removal, of the individual described in paragraph (a)(1), (a)(2), or (a)(3) of this section;

(5) An alien who is:

(i) The unmarried son or unmarried daughter of an individual described in paragraph (a)(1), (a)(2), or (a)(3) of this section and is 21 years of age or older at the time a decision is made to suspend the deportation, or cancel the removal, of the parent described in paragraph (a)(1), (a)(2), or (a)(3) of this section; and

(ii) Entered the United States on or before October 1, 1990.

(b) This subpart H does not apply to any alien who has been convicted at any time of an aggravated felony, as defined in section 101(a)(43) of the Act.

HISTORY:

[64 FR 27856, 27876, May 21, 1999]

§ 240.62 Jurisdiction.

(a) Office of International Affairs. Except as provided in paragraph (b) of this section, the Office of International Affairs shall have initial jurisdiction to grant or refer to the Immigration Court or Board an application for suspension of deportation or special rule cancellation of removal filed by an alien described in § 240.61, provided:

(1) In the case of a national of El Salvador described in § 240.61(a)(1), the alien filed a complete asylum application on or before January 31, 1996 (with an administrative grace period extending to February 16, 1996), or otherwise met the asylum application filing deadline pursuant to the ABC settlement agreement, and the application is still pending adjudication by the Service;

(2) In the case of a national of Guatemala described in § 240.61(a)(1), the alien filed a complete asylum application on or before January 3, 1995, or otherwise met the asylum application filing deadline pursuant to the ABC settlement agreement, and the application is still pending adjudication by the Service;

(3) In the case of an individual described in § 240.61(a)(2) or (3), the individual's asylum application is pending adjudication by the Service;

(4) In the case of an individual described in § 240.61(a)(4) or (5), the individual's parent or spouse has an application pending with the Service under this subpart H or has been granted relief by the Service under this subpart.

(b) Immigration Court. The Immigration Court shall have exclusive jurisdiction over an application for suspension of deportation or special rule cancellation of removal filed pursuant to section 309(f)(1)(A) or (B) of IIRIRA, as amended by NACARA, by an alien who has been served Form I-221, Order to Show Cause, or Form I-862, Notice to Appear, after a copy of the charging document has been filed with the Immigration Court, unless the alien is covered by one of the following exceptions:

(1) Certain ABC class members.

(i) The alien is a registered ABC class member for whom proceedings before the Immigration Court or the Board have been administratively closed or continued (including those aliens who had final orders of deportation or removal who have filed and been granted a motion to reopen as required under 8 CFR 3.43);

(ii) The alien is eligible for benefits of the ABC settlement agreement and has not had a de novo asylum adjudication pursuant to the settlement agreement; and

(iii) The alien has not moved for and been granted a motion to recalendar proceedings before the Immigration Court or the Board to request suspension of deportation.

(2) Spouses, children, unmarried sons, and unmarried daughters.

(i) The alien is described in § 240.61(a) (4) or (5);

(ii) The alien's spouse or parent is described in § 240.61(a)(1), (a)(2), or (a)(3) and has a Form I-881 pending with the Service; and

(iii) The alien's proceedings before the Immigration Court have been administratively closed, or the alien's proceedings before the Board have been continued, to permit the alien to file an application for suspension of deportation or special rule cancellation of removal with the Service.

HISTORY:

[64 FR 27856, 27877, May 21, 1999]

§ 240.63 Application process.

(a) Form and fees. Except as provided in paragraph (b) of this section, the application must be made on the form prescribed by USCIS for this program and filed in accordance with the instructions for that form. An applicant who submitted to EOIR a completed, Application for Suspension of Deportation, before the effective date of the form prescribed by USCIS may apply with USCIS by submitting the completed Application for Suspension of Deportation attached to a completed first page of the application. Each application must be filed with the required fees as provided in 8 CFR 106.2.

(b) Applications filed with EOIR. If jurisdiction rests with the Immigration Court under § 260.62(b), the application must be made on the Form I-881, if filed subsequent to June 21, 1999. The application form, along with any supporting documents, must be filed with the Immigration Court and served on the Service's district counsel in accordance with the instructions on or accompanying the form. Applications for suspension of deportation or special rule cancellation of removal filed prior to June 21, 1999 shall be filed on Form EOIR-40.

(c) Applications filed with the Service. If jurisdiction rests with the Service under § 240.62(a), the Form I-881 and supporting documents must be filed in accordance with the instructions on or accompanying the form.

(d) Conditions and consequences of filing. Applications filed under this section shall be filed under the following conditions and shall have the following consequences:

(1) The information provided in the application may be used as a basis for the initiation of removal proceedings, or to satisfy any burden of proof in exclusion, deportation, or removal proceedings;

(2) The applicant and anyone other than a spouse, parent, son, or daughter of the applicant who assists the applicant in preparing the application must sign the application under penalty of perjury. The applicant's signature establishes a presumption that the applicant is aware of the contents of the application. A person other than a relative specified in this paragraph who assists the applicant in preparing the application also must provide his or her full mailing address;

(3) An application that does not include a response to each of the questions contained in the application, is unsigned, or is unaccompanied by the required materials specified in the instructions to the application is incomplete and shall be returned by mail to the applicant within 30 days of receipt of the application by the Service; and

(4) Knowing placement of false information on the application may subject the person supplying that information to criminal penalties under title 18 of the United States Code and to civil penalties under section 274C of the Act.

HISTORY:

[64 FR 27856, 27877, May 21, 1999; 74 FR 26933, 26939, June 5, 2009; 85 FR 46788, 46926, Aug. 3, 2020; 89 FR 6194, 6398, Jan. 31, 2024]

§ 240.64 Eligibility — general.

(a) Burden and standard of proof. The burden of proof is on the applicant to establish by a preponderance of the evidence that he or she is eligible for suspension of deportation or special rule cancellation of removal and that discretion should be exercised to grant relief.

(b) Calculation of continuous physical presence and certain breaks in presence. For purposes of calculating continuous physical presence under this section, section 309(c)(5)(A) of IIRIRA and section 240A(d)(1) of the Act shall not apply to persons described in § 240.61. For purposes of this subpart H, a single absence of 90 days or less or absences which in the aggregate total no more than 180 days shall be considered brief.

(1) For applications for suspension of deportation made under former section 244 of the Act, as in effect prior to April 1, 1997, the burden of proof is on the applicant to establish that any breaks in continuous physical presence were brief, casual, and innocent and did not meaningfully interrupt the period of continuous physical presence in the United States. For purposes of evaluating whether an absence is brief, single absences in excess of 90 days, or absences that total more than 180 days in the aggregate will be evaluated on a case-by-case basis. An applicant must establish that any absence from the United States was casual and innocent and did not meaningfully interrupt the period of continuous physical presence.

(2) For applications for special rule cancellation of removal made under section 309(f)(1) of IIRIRA, as amended by NACARA, the applicant shall be considered to have failed to maintain continuous physical presence in the United States if he or she has departed from the United States for any period in excess of 90 days or for any periods in the aggregate exceeding 180 days. The applicant must establish that any period of absence less than 90 days was casual and innocent and did not meaningfully interrupt the period of continuous physical presence in the United States.

(3) For all applications made under this subpart, a period of continuous physical presence is terminated whenever an alien is removed from the United States under an order issued pursuant to any provision of the Act or the alien has voluntarily departed under the threat of deportation or when the departure is made for purposes of committing an unlawful act.

(4) The requirements of continuous physical presence in the United States under this subpart shall not apply to an alien who:

(i) Has served for a minimum period of 24 months in an active-duty status in the Armed Forces of the United States and, if separated from such service, was separated under honorable conditions, and

(ii) At the time of the alien's enlistment or induction, was in the United States.

(c) Factors relevant to extreme hardship. Except as described in paragraph (d) of this section, extreme hardship shall be determined as set forth in § 240.58.

(d) **Rebuttable presumption of extreme hardship for certain classes of aliens.**

(1) Presumption of extreme hardship. An applicant described in paragraphs (a)(1) or (a)(2) of § 240.61 who has submitted a completed Form I-881 or Form EOIR-40 to either the Service or the Immigration Court, in accordance with § 240.63 shall be presumed to have established that deportation or removal from the United States would result in extreme hardship to the applicant or to his or her spouse, parent, or child, who is a citizen of the United States or an alien lawfully admitted for permanent residence.

(2) Rebuttal of presumption. A presumption of extreme hardship as described in paragraph (d)(1) of this section shall be rebutted if the evidence in the record establishes that it is more likely than not that neither the applicant nor a qualified relative would suffer extreme hardship if the applicant were deported or removed from the United States. In making such a determination, the adjudicator shall consider relevant factors, including those listed in § 240.58.

(3) Burden of proof. In those cases where a presumption of extreme hardship applies, the burden of proof shall be on the Service to establish that it is more likely than not that neither the applicant nor a qualified relative would suffer extreme hardship if the applicant were deported or removed from the United States.

(4) Effect of rebuttal.

(i) A determination that it is more likely than not that neither the applicant nor a qualified relative would suffer extreme hardship if the applicant were deported or removed from the United States shall be grounds for referral to the Immigration Court or dismissal of an application submitted initially to the Service. The applicant is entitled to a de novo adjudication and will again be considered to have a presumption of extreme hardship before the Immigration Court.

(ii) If the Immigration Court determines that extreme hardship will not result from deportation or removal from the United States, the application will be denied.

HISTORY:

[64 FR 27856, 27877, May 21, 1999, as corrected at 64 FR 33386, June 23, 1999]

§ 240.65 Eligibility for suspension of deportation.

(a) Applicable statutory provisions. To establish eligibility for suspension of deportation under this section, the applicant must be an individual described in § 240.61; must establish that he or she is eligible under former section 244 of the Act, as in effect prior to April 1, 1997; must not be subject to any bars to eligibility in former section 242B(e) of the Act, as in effect prior to April 1, 1997, or any other provisions of law; and must not have been convicted of an aggravated felony or be an alien described in former section 241(a)(4)(D) of the Act, as in effect prior to April 1, 1997 (relating to Nazi persecution and genocide).

(b) General rule. To establish eligibility for suspension of deportation under former section 244(a)(1) of the Act, as in effect prior to April 1, 1997, an alien must be deportable under any law of the United States, except the provisions specified in paragraph (c) of this section, and must establish:

(1) The alien has been physically present in the United States for a continuous period of not less than 7 years immediately preceding the date the application was filed;

(2) During all of such period the alien was and is a person of good moral character; and

(3) The alien's deportation would, in the opinion of the Attorney General, result in extreme hardship to the alien or to the alien's spouse, parent, or child, who is a citizen of the United States or an alien lawfully admitted for permanent residence.

(c) Aliens deportable on criminal or certain other grounds. To establish eligibility for suspension of deportation under former section 244(a)(2) of the Act, as in effect prior to April 1, 1997, an alien who is deportable under former section 241(a) (2), (3), or (4) of the Act, as in effect prior to April 1, 1997 (relating to criminal activity, document fraud, failure to register, and security threats), must establish that:

(1) The alien has been physically present in the United States for a continuous period of not less than 10 years immediately following the commission of an act, or the assumption of a status constituting a ground for deportation;

(2) The alien has been and is a person of good moral character during all of such period; and

(3) The alien's deportation would, in the opinion of the Attorney General, result in exceptional and extremely unusual hardship to the alien, or to the alien's spouse, parent, or child, who is a citizen of the United States or an alien lawfully admitted for permanent residence.

(d) Battered spouses and children. To establish eligibility for suspension of deportation under former section 244(a)(3) of the Act, as in effect prior to April 1, 1997, an alien must be deportable under any law of the United States, except under former section 241(a)(1)(G) of the Act, as in effect prior to April 1, 1997 (relating to marriage fraud), and except under the provisions specified in paragraph (c) of this section, and must establish that:

(1) The alien has been physically present in the United States for a continuous period of not less than 3 years immediately preceding the date the application was filed;

(2) The alien has been battered or subjected to extreme cruelty in the United States by a spouse or parent who is a United States citizen or lawful permanent resident (or is the parent of a child of a United States citizen or lawful permanent resident and the child has been battered or subjected to extreme cruelty in the United States by such citizen or permanent resident parent); and

(3) During all of such time in the United States the alien was and is a person of good moral character; and

(4) The alien's deportation would, in the opinion of the Attorney General, result in extreme hardship to the alien or the alien's parent or child.

HISTORY:

[64 FR 27856, 27878, May 21, 1999]

§ 240.66 Eligibility for special rule cancellation of removal.

(a) Applicable statutory provisions. To establish eligibility for special rule cancellation of removal, the applicant must show he or she is eligible under section 309(f)(1) of IIRIRA, as amended by section 203 of NACARA. The applicant must be described in § 240.61, must be inadmissible or deportable, must not be subject to any bars to eligibility in sections 240(b)(7), 240A(c), or 240B(d) of the Act, or any other provisions of law, and must not have been convicted of an aggravated felony or be an alien described in section 241(b)(3)(B)(I) of the Act (relating to persecution of others).

(b) General rule. To establish eligibility for special rule cancellation of removal under section 309(f)(1)(A) of IIRIRA, as amended by section 203 of NACARA, the alien must establish that:

(1) The alien is not inadmissible under section 212(a)(2) or (3) or deportable under section 237(a)(2), (3) or (4) of the Act (relating to criminal activity, document fraud, failure to register, and security threats);

(2) The alien has been physically present in the United States for a continuous period of 7 years immediately preceding the date the application was filed;

(3) The alien has been a person of good moral character during the required period of continuous physical presence; and

(4) The alien's removal from the United States would result in extreme hardship to the alien, or to the alien's spouse, parent or child who is a United States citizen or an alien lawfully admitted for permanent residence.

(c) Aliens inadmissible or deportable on criminal or certain other grounds. To establish eligibility for special rule cancellation of removal under section 309(f)(1)(B) of IIRIRA, as amended by section 203 of NACARA, the alien must be described in § 240.61 and establish that:

(1) The alien is inadmissible under section 212(a)(2) of the Act (relating to criminal activity), or deportable under paragraphs (a)(2) (other than section 237(a)(2)(A)(iii), relating to aggravated felony convictions), or (a)(3) of section 237 of the Act (relating to criminal activity, document fraud, and failure to register);

(2) The alien has been physically present in the United States for a continuous period of not less than 10 years immediately following the commission of an

act, or the assumption of a status constituting a ground for removal;

(3) The alien has been a person of good moral character during the required period of continuous physical presence; and

(4) The alien's removal from the United States would result in exceptional and extremely unusual hardship to the alien or to the alien's spouse, parent, or child, who is a United States citizen or an alien lawfully admitted for permanent residence.

HISTORY:

[64 FR 27856, 27879, May 21, 1999]

§ 240.67 Procedure for interview before an asylum officer.

(a) Fingerprinting requirements. USCIS will notify each applicant 14 years of age or older to appear for an interview only after the applicant has complied with fingerprinting requirements pursuant to 8 CFR 103.16, and USCIS has received a definitive response from the FBI that a full criminal background check has been completed. A definitive response that a full criminal background check on an applicant has been completed includes:

(1) Confirmation from the FBI that an applicant does not have an administrative or criminal record;

(2) Confirmation from the FBI that an applicant has an administrative or a criminal record; or

(3) Confirmation from the FBI that two properly prepared fingerprint cards (Form FD-258) have been determined unclassifiable for the purpose of conducting a criminal background check and have been rejected.

(b) **Interview.**

(1) The asylum officer shall conduct the interview in a non-adversarial manner and, except at the request of the applicant, separate and apart from the general public. The purpose of the interview shall be to elicit all relevant and useful information bearing on the applicant's eligibility for suspension of deportation or special rule cancellation of removal. If the applicant has an asylum application pending with the Service, the asylum officer may also elicit information relating to the application for asylum in accordance with § 208.9 of this chapter. At the time of the interview, the applicant must provide complete information regarding the applicant's identity, including name, date and place of birth, and nationality, and may be required to register this identity electronically or through any other means designated by the Attorney General.

(2) The applicant may have counsel or a representative present, may present witnesses, and may submit affidavits of witnesses and other evidence.

(3) An applicant unable to proceed with the interview in English must provide, at no expense to the Service, a competent interpreter fluent in both English and a language in which the applicant is fluent. The interpreter must be at least 18 years of age. The following individuals may not serve as the applicant's interpreter: the applicant's attorney or representative of record; a witness testifying on the applicant's behalf; or, if the applicant also has an asylum application pending with the Service, a representative or employee of the applicant's country of nationality, or, if stateless, country of last habitual residence. Failure without good cause to comply with this paragraph may be considered a failure to appear for the interview for purposes of § 240.68.

(4) The asylum officer shall have authority to administer oaths, verify the identity of the applicant (including through the use of electronic means), verify the identity of any interpreter, present and receive evidence, and question the applicant and any witnesses.

(5) Upon completion of the interview, the applicant or the applicant's representative shall have an opportunity to make a statement or comment on the evidence presented. The asylum officer may, in the officer's discretion, limit the length of such statement or comment and may require its submission in writing. Upon completion of the interview, and except as otherwise provided by the asylum officer, the applicant shall be informed of the requirement to appear in person to receive and to acknowledge receipt of the decision and any other accompanying material at a time and place designated by the asylum officer.

(6) The asylum officer shall consider evidence submitted by the applicant with the application, as well as any evidence submitted by the applicant before or at the interview. As a matter of discretion, the asylum officer may grant the applicant a brief extension of time following an interview, during which the applicant may submit additional evidence.

HISTORY:

[64 FR 27856, 27879, May 21, 1999; 76 FR 53764, 53791, Aug. 29, 2011]

§ 240.68 Failure to appear at an interview before an asylum officer or failure to follow requirements for fingerprinting.

(a) Failure to appear for a scheduled interview without prior authorization may result in dismissal of the application or waiver of the right to an adjudication by an asylum officer. A written request to reschedule will be granted if it is an initial request and is received by the Asylum Office at least 2 days before the scheduled interview date. All other requests to reschedule the interview, including those submitted after the interview date, will be granted only if the applicant has a reasonable excuse for not appearing, and the excuse was received by the Asylum Office in writing within a reasonable time after the scheduled interview date.

(b) Failure to comply with fingerprint processing requirements without reasonable excuse may result in dismissal of the application or waiver of the right to an adjudication by an asylum officer.

(c) Failure to appear shall be excused if the notice of the interview or fingerprint appointment was not mailed to the applicant's current address and such address had been provided to the Office of International Affairs by the applicant prior to the date of mailing in accordance with section 265 of the Act and Service regulations, unless the asylum officer determines that the applicant received reasonable notice of the interview or fingerprinting appointment.

HISTORY:

[64 FR 27856, 27880, May 21, 1999]

§ 240.69 Reliance on information compiled by other sources.

In determining whether an applicant is eligible for suspension of deportation or special rule cancellation of removal, the asylum officer may rely on material described in § 208.12 of this chapter. Nothing in this subpart shall be construed to entitle the applicant to conduct discovery directed toward records, officers, agents, or employees of the Service, the Department of Justice, or the Department of State.

HISTORY:

[64 FR 27856, 27880, May 21, 1999]

§ 240.70 Decision by the Service.

(a) Service of decision. Unless the asylum officer has granted the application for suspension of deportation or special rule cancellation of removal at the time of the interview or as otherwise provided by an Asylum Office, the applicant will be required to return to the Asylum Office to receive service of the decision on the applicant's application. If the applicant does not speak English fluently, the applicant shall bring an interpreter when returning to the office to receive service of the decision.

(b) Grant of suspension of deportation. An asylum officer may grant suspension of deportation to an applicant eligible to apply for this relief with the Service who qualifies for suspension of deportation under former section 244(a)(1) of the Act, as in effect prior to April 1, 1997, who is not an alien described in former section 241(a)(4)(D) of the Act, as in effect prior to April 1, 1997, and who admits deportability under any law of the United States, excluding former section 241(a)(2), (3), or (4) of the Act, as in effect prior to April 1, 1997. If the Service has made a preliminary decision to grant the applicant suspension of deportation under this subpart, the applicant shall be notified of that decision and will be asked to sign an admission of deportability or inadmissibility. The applicant must sign the admission before the Service may grant the relief sought. If suspension of deportation is granted, the Service shall adjust the status of the alien to lawful permanent resident, effective as of the date that suspension of deportation is granted.

(c) Grant of cancellation of removal. An asylum officer may grant cancellation of removal to an applicant who is eligible to apply for this relief with the Service, and who qualifies for cancellation of removal under section 309(f)(1)(A) of IIRIRA, as amended by section 203 of NACARA, and who admits deportability under section 237(a), excluding paragraphs (2), (3), and (4), of the Act, or inadmissibility under section 212(a), excluding paragraphs (2) or (3), of the Act. If the Service has made a preliminary decision to grant the applicant cancellation of removal under this subpart, the applicant shall be notified of that decision and asked to sign an admission of deportability or inadmissibility. The applicant must sign the concession before the Service may grant the relief sought. If the Service grants cancellation of removal, the Service shall adjust the status of the alien to lawful permanent resident, effective as of the date that cancellation of removal is granted.

(d) Referral of the application. Except as provided in paragraphs (e) and (f) of this section, and unless the applicant is granted asylum or is in lawful immigrant or non-immigrant status, an asylum officer shall refer the application for suspension of deportation or special rule cancellation of removal to the Immigration Court for adjudication in deportation or removal proceedings, and will provide the applicant with written notice of the statutory or regulatory basis for the referral, if:

(1) The applicant is not clearly eligible for suspension of deportation under former section 244(a)(1) of the Act as in effect prior to April 1, 1997, or for cancellation of removal under section 309(f)(1)(A) of IIRIRA, as amended by NACARA;

(2) The applicant does not appear to merit relief as a matter of discretion;

(3) The applicant appears to be eligible for suspension of deportation or special rule cancellation of removal under this subpart, but does not admit deportability or inadmissibility; or

(4) The applicant failed to appear for a scheduled interview with an asylum officer or failed to comply with fingerprinting processing requirements and such failure was not excused by the Service, unless the application is dismissed.

(e) Dismissal of the application. An asylum officer shall dismiss without prejudice an application for suspension of deportation or special rule cancellation of removal submitted by an applicant who has been granted asylum, or who is in lawful immigrant or non-immigrant status. An asylum officer may also dismiss an application for failure to appear, pursuant to § 240.68. The asylum officer will provide the applicant written notice of the statutory or regulatory basis for the dismissal.

(f) Special provisions for certain ABC class members whose proceedings before EOIR were administratively closed or continued. The following provisions shall apply with respect to an ABC class member who was in proceedings before the Immigration Court or the Board, and those proceedings were closed or continued pursuant to the ABC settlement agreement:

(1) Suspension of deportation or asylum granted. If an asylum officer grants asylum or suspension of deportation, the previous proceedings before the Immigration Court or Board shall be terminated as a matter of law on the date relief is granted.

(2) Asylum denied and application for suspension of deportation not approved. If an asylum officer denies asylum and does not grant the applicant suspension of deportation, the Service shall move to recalendar proceedings before the Immigration Court or resume pro-

ceedings before the Board, whichever is appropriate. The Service shall refer to the Immigration Court or the Board the application for suspension of deportation. In the case where jurisdiction rests with the Board, an application for suspension of deportation that is referred to the Board will be remanded to the Immigration Court for adjudication.

(g) Special provisions for dependents whose proceedings before EOIR were administratively closed or continued. If an asylum officer grants suspension of deportation or special rule cancellation of removal to an applicant described in § 240.61(a)(4) or (a)(5), whose proceedings before EOIR were administratively closed or continued, those proceedings shall terminate as of the date the relief is granted. If suspension of deportation or special rule cancellation of removal is not granted, the Service shall move to recalendar proceedings before the Immigration Court or resume proceedings before the Board, whichever is appropriate. The Service shall refer to the Immigration Court or the Board the application for suspension of deportation or special rule cancellation of removal. In the case where jurisdiction rests with the Board, an application for suspension of deportation or special rule cancellation of removal that is referred to the Board will be remanded to the Immigration Court for adjudication.

(h) Special provisions for applicants who depart the United States and return under a grant of advance parole while in deportation proceedings. Notwithstanding paragraphs (f) and (g) of this section, for purposes of adjudicating an application for suspension of deportation or special rule cancellation of removal under this subpart, if an applicant departs and returns to the United States pursuant to a grant of advance parole while in deportation proceedings, including deportation proceedings administratively closed or continued pursuant to the ABC settlement agreement, the deportation proceedings will be considered terminated as of the date of applicant's departure from the United States. A decision on the NACARA application shall be issued in accordance with paragraph (a), and paragraphs (c) through (e) of this section.

HISTORY:

[64 FR 27856, 27880, May 21, 1999]

PART 241

APPREHENSION AND DETENTION OF ALIENS ORDERED REMOVED

Subpart A. Post-Hearing Detention and Removal

Subpart B. Deportation of Excluded Aliens (For Hearings Commenced Prior to April 1, 1997)

Subpart C. Deportation of Aliens in the United States (For Hearings Commenced Prior to April 1, 1997)

AUTHORITY NOTE APPLICABLE TO ENTIRE PART:

AUTHORITY:

5 U.S.C. 301, 552, 552a; 8 U.S.C. 1103, 1182, 1223, 1224, 1225, 1226, 1227, 1228, 1231, 1251, 1253, 1255, 1330, 1362; 18 U.S.C. 4002, 4013(c)(4); Pub. L. 107-296, 116 Stat. 2135 (6 U.S.C. 101, et seq.); 8 CFR part 2.

Subpart A

Post-Hearing Detention and Removal

§ 241.1 Final order of removal.

An order of removal becomes final in accordance with 8 CFR 1241.1.

HISTORY:

[53 FR 9282, Mar. 22, 1988. Redesignated at 56 FR 8906, Mar. 4, 1991, and amended at 56 FR 38333, Aug. 13, 1991; 62 FR 10312, 10378, March 6, 1997; 70 FR 661, 673, Jan. 5, 2005]

§ 241.2 Warrant of removal.

(a) Issuance of a warrant of removal —

(1) In general. A Form I-205, Warrant of Removal, based on the final administrative removal order in the alien's case will be issued by any of the following immigration officials:

(i) Director, Enforcement and Removal Operations;
(ii) Deputy Assistant Director, Field Operations;
(iii) Field Office Directors;
(iv) Deputy Field Office Directors;
(v) Assistant Field Office Directors;
(vi) Officers in Charge;
(vii) Special Agents in Charge;

(viii) Deputy Special Agents in Charge;
(ix) Associate Special Agents in Charge;
(x) Assistant Special Agents in Charge;
(xi) Group Supervisors;
(xii) Resident Agents in Charge;
(xiii) District Field Officers;
(xiv) Chief Patrol Agents;
(xv) Deputy Chief Patrol Agents;
(xvi) Division Chiefs;
(xvii) Assistant Chief Patrol Agents;
(xviii) Patrol Agents in Charge;
(xix) Deputy Patrol Agents in Charge;
(xx) Watch Commanders, Border Patrol;
(xxi) Director of Air Operations;
(xxii) Director of Marine Operations;
(xxiii) Supervisory Air and Marine Interdiction Agents;
(xxiv) Unit Chief, Law Enforcement Support Center;
(xxv) Section Chief, Law Enforcement Support Center;
(xxvi) Port Directors;
(xxvii) Assistant Port Directors;
(xxviii) Directors, Field Operations;
(xxix) Assistant Directors, Field Operations;
(xxx) Watch Commanders, Field Operations;
(xxxi) Chiefs, Field Operations; and
(xxxii) Other duly authorized officers or employees of the Department of Homeland Security or the United States who are delegated the authority as provided in 8 CFR 2.1 to issue Warrants of Removal, and who have successfully completed any required immigration law enforcement training.

(2) Costs and care during removal. The immigration officials listed in paragraphs (a)(1)(i) through (xxxi) of this section, and other officers or employees of the Department or the United States who are delegated the authority as provided in 8 CFR 2.1, shall exercise the authority contained in section 241 of the Act to determine at whose expense the alien shall be removed and whether his or her mental or physical condition requires personal care and attention en route to his or her destination.

(b) Execution of the warrant of removal. Any officer authorized by 8 CFR 287.5(e)(3) to execute administrative warrants of arrest may execute a warrant of removal.

HISTORY:

[62 FR 10312, 10378, March 6, 1997; 67 FR 39255, 39258, June 7, 2002; 70 FR 67087, 67089, Nov. 4, 2005; 81 FR 62353, 62355, Sept. 9, 2016]

§ 241.3 Detention of aliens during removal period.

(a) Assumption of custody. Once the removal period defined in section 241(a)(1) of the Act begins, an alien in the United States will be taken into custody pursuant to the warrant of removal.

(b) Cancellation of bond. Any bond previously posted will be canceled unless it has been breached or is subject to being breached.

(c) Judicial stays. The filing of (or intention to file) a petition or action in a Federal court seeking review of the issuance or execution of an order of removal shall not delay execution of the Warrant of Removal except upon an affirmative order of the court.

(d) Information regarding detainees. Disclosure of information relating to detainees shall be governed by the provisions of 8 CFR 236.3.

HISTORY:

[62 FR 10312, 10378, March 6, 1997; 70 FR 661, 673, Jan. 5, 2005]

§ 241.4 Continued detention of inadmissible, criminal, and other aliens beyond the removal period.

(a) Scope. The authority to continue an alien in custody or grant release or parole under sections 241(a)(6) and 212(d)(5)(A) of the Act shall be exercised by the Commissioner or Deputy Commissioner, as follows: Except as otherwise directed by the Commissioner or his or her designee, the Executive Associate Commissioner for Field Operations (Executive Associate Commissioner), the Deputy Executive Associate Commissioner for Detention and Removal, the Director of the Detention and Removal Field Office or the district director may continue an alien in custody beyond the removal period described in section 241(a)(1) of the Act pursuant to the procedures described in this section. Except as provided for in paragraph (b)(2) of this section, the provisions of this section apply to the custody determinations for the following group of aliens:

(1) An alien ordered removed who is inadmissible under section 212 of the Act, including an excludable alien convicted of one or more aggravated felony offenses and subject to the provisions of section 501(b) of the Immigration Act of 1990, Public Law 101-649, 104 Stat. 4978, 5048 (codified at 8 U.S.C. 1226(e)(1) through (e)(3)(1994));

(2) An alien ordered removed who is removable under section 237(a)(1)(C) of the Act;

(3) An alien ordered removed who is removable under sections 237(a)(2) or 237(a)(4) of the Act, including deportable criminal aliens whose cases are governed by former section 242 of the Act prior to amendment by the Illegal Immigration Reform and Immigrant Responsibility Act of 1996, Div. C of Public Law 104-208, 110 Stat. 3009-546; and

(4) An alien ordered removed who the decision-maker determines is unlikely to comply with the removal order or is a risk to the community.

(b) **Applicability to particular aliens. —**

(1) Motions to reopen. An alien who has filed a motion to reopen immigration proceedings for consideration of relief from removal, including withholding or deferral of removal pursuant to 8 CFR 208.16 or 208.17, shall remain subject to the provisions of this section unless the motion to reopen is granted. Section 236 of the Act and 8 CFR 236.1 govern custody determinations for aliens who are in pending immigration proceedings before the Executive Office for Immigration Review.

(2) Parole for certain Cuban nationals. The review procedures in this section do not apply to any inadmissible Mariel Cuban who is being detained by the Service pending an exclusion or removal proceeding, or following entry of a final exclusion or pending his or her return to Cuba or removal to another country. Instead, the determination whether to release on parole, or to revoke such parole, or to detain, shall in the case of a Mariel Cuban be governed by the procedures in 8 CFR 212.12.

(3) Individuals granted withholding or deferral of removal. Aliens granted withholding of removal under section 241(b)(3) of the Act or withholding or deferral of removal under the Convention Against Torture who are otherwise subject to detention are subject to the provisions of this part 241. Individuals subject to a termination of deferral hearing under 8 CFR 208.17(d) remain subject to the provisions of this part 241 throughout the termination process.

(4) Service determination under 8 CFR 241.13. The custody review procedures in this section do not apply after the Service has made a determination, pursuant to the procedures provided in 8 CFR 241.13, that there is no significant likelihood that an alien under a final order of removal can be removed in the reasonably foreseeable future. However, if the Service subsequently determines, because of a change of circumstances, that there is a significant likelihood that the alien may be removed in the reasonably foreseeable future to the country to which the alien was ordered removed or to a third country, the alien shall again be subject to the custody review procedures under this section.

(c) Delegation of authority. The Attorney General's statutory authority to make custody determinations under sections 241(a)(6) and 212(d)(5)(A) of the Act when there is a final order of removal is delegated as follows:

(1) District Directors and Directors of Detention and Removal Field Offices. The initial custody determination described in paragraph (h) of this section and any further custody determination concluded in the 3 month period immediately following the expiration of the 90-day removal period, subject to the provisions of paragraph (c)(2) of this section, will be made by the district director or the Director of the Detention and Removal Field Office having jurisdiction over the alien. The district director or the Director of the Detention and Removal Field Office shall maintain appropriate files respecting each detained alien reviewed for possible release, and shall have authority to determine the order in which the cases shall be reviewed, and to coordinate activities associated with these reviews in his or her respective jurisdictional area.

(2) Headquarters Post-Order Detention Unit (HQPDU). For any alien the district director refers for further review after the removal period, or any alien who has not been released or removed by the expiration of the three-month period after the review, all further custody determinations will be made by the Executive Associate Commissioner, acting through the HQPDU.

(3) The HQPDU review plan. The Executive Associate Commissioner shall appoint a Director of the HQPDU. The Director of the HQPDU shall have authority to establish and maintain appropriate files respecting each detained alien to be reviewed for possible release, to determine the order in which the cases shall be reviewed, and to coordinate activities associated with these reviews.

(4) Additional delegation of authority. All references to the Executive Associate Commissioner, the Director of the Detention and Removal Field Office, and the district director in this section shall be deemed to include any person or persons (including a committee) designated in writing by the Executive Associate Commissioner, the Director of the Detention and Removal Field Office, or the district director to exercise powers under this section.

(d) Custody determinations. A copy of any decision by the district director, Director of the Detention and Removal Field Office, or Executive Associate Commissioner to release or to detain an alien shall be provided to the detained alien. A decision to retain custody shall briefly set forth the reasons for the continued detention. A decision to release may contain such special conditions as are considered appropriate in the opinion of the Service. Notwithstanding any other provisions of this section, there is no appeal from the district director's or the Executive Associate Commissioner's decision.

(1) Showing by the alien. The district director, Director of the Detention and Removal Field Office, or Executive Associate Commissioner may release an alien if the alien demonstrates to the satisfaction of the Attorney General or her designee that his or her release will not pose a danger to the community or to the safety of other persons or to property or a significant risk of flight pending such alien's removal from the United States. The district director or the Executive Associate Commissioner may also, in accordance with the procedures and consideration of the factors set forth in this section, continue in custody any alien described in paragraphs (a) and (b)(1) of this section.

(2) Service of decision and other documents. All notices, decisions, or other documents in connection with the custody reviews conducted under this section by the district director, Director of the Detention and Removal Field Office, or Executive Associate Commissioner shall be served on the alien, in accordance with 8 CFR 103.8, by the Service district office having jurisdiction over the alien. Release documentation (including employment authorization if appropriate) shall be issued by the district office having jurisdiction over the alien in accordance with the custody determination made by the district director or by the Executive Associate Commissioner. Copies of all such documents will be retained in the alien's record and forwarded to the HQPDU.

(3) Alien's representative. The alien's representative is required to complete Form G-28, Notice of Entry of Appearance as Attorney or Representative, at the time of the interview or prior to reviewing the detainee's records. The Service will forward by regular mail a copy of any notice or decision that is being served on the

alien only to the attorney or representative of record. The alien remains responsible for notification to any other individual providing assistance to him or her.

(e) Criteria for release. Before making any recommendation or decision to release a detainee, a majority of the Review Panel members, or the Director of the HQPDU in the case of a record review, must conclude that:

(1) Travel documents for the alien are not available or, in the opinion of the Service, immediate removal, while proper, is otherwise not practicable or not in the public interest;

(2) The detainee is presently a non-violent person;

(3) The detainee is likely to remain nonviolent if released;

(4) The detainee is not likely to pose a threat to the community following release;

(5) The detainee is not likely to violate the conditions of release; and

(6) The detainee does not pose a significant flight risk if released.

(f) Factors for consideration. The following factors should be weighed in considering whether to recommend further detention or release of a detainee:

(1) The nature and number of disciplinary infractions or incident reports received when incarcerated or while in Service custody;

(2) The detainee's criminal conduct and criminal convictions, including consideration of the nature and severity of the alien's convictions, sentences imposed and time actually served, probation and criminal parole history, evidence of recidivism, and other criminal history;

(3) Any available psychiatric and psychological reports pertaining to the detainee's mental health;

(4) Evidence of rehabilitation including institutional progress relating to participation in work, educational, and vocational programs, where available;

(5) Favorable factors, including ties to the United States such as the number of close relatives residing here lawfully;

(6) Prior immigration violations and history;

(7) The likelihood that the alien is a significant flight risk or may abscond to avoid removal, including history of escapes, failures to appear for immigration or other proceedings, absence without leave from any halfway house or sponsorship program, and other defaults; and

(8) Any other information that is probative of whether the alien is likely to —

(i) Adjust to life in a community,

(ii) Engage in future acts of violence,

(iii) Engage in future criminal activity,

(iv) Pose a danger to the safety of himself or herself or to other persons or to property, or

(v) Violate the conditions of his or her release from immigration custody pending removal from the United States.

(g) Travel documents and docket control for aliens continued in detention —

(1) Removal period

(i) The removal period for an alien subject to a final order of removal shall begin on the latest of the following dates:

(A) the date the order becomes administratively final;

(B) If the removal order is subject to judicial review (including review by habeas corpus) and if the court has ordered a stay of the alien's removal, the date on which, consistent with the court's order, the removal order can be executed and the alien removed; or

(C) If the alien was detained or confined, except in connection with a proceeding under this chapter relating to removability, the date the alien is released from the detention or confinement.

(ii) The removal period shall run for a period of 90 days. However, the removal period is extended under section 241(a)(1)(C) of the Act if the alien fails or refuses to make timely application in good faith for travel or other documents necessary to the alien's departure or conspires or acts to prevent the alien's removal subject to an order of removal. The Service will provide such an alien with a Notice of Failure to Comply, as provided in paragraph (g)(5) of this section, before the expiration of the removal period. The removal period shall be extended until the alien demonstrates to the Service that he or she has complied with the statutory obligations. Once the alien has complied with his or her obligations under the law, the Service shall have a reasonable period of time in order to effect the alien's removal.

(2) In general. The district director shall continue to undertake appropriate steps to secure travel documents for the alien both before and after the expiration of the removal period. If the district director is unable to secure travel documents within the removal period, he or she shall apply for assistance from Headquarters Detention and Deportation, Office of Field Operations. The district director shall promptly advise the HQPDU Director when travel documents are obtained for an alien whose custody is subject to review by the HQPDU. The Service's determination that receipt of a travel document is likely may by itself warrant continuation of detention pending the removal of the alien from the United States.

(3) Availability of travel document. In making a custody determination, the district director and the Director of the HQPDU shall consider the ability to obtain a travel document for the alien. If it is established at any stage of a custody review that, in the judgment of the Service, travel documents can be obtained, or such document is forthcoming, the alien will not be released unless immediate removal is not practicable or in the public interest.

(4) Removal. The Service will not conduct a custody review under these procedures when the Service notifies the alien that it is ready to execute an order of removal.

(5) Alien's compliance and cooperation.

(i) Release will be denied and the alien may remain in detention if the alien fails or refuses to make timely application in good faith for travel documents necessary to the alien's departure or conspires or acts to prevent the alien's removal. The detention provisions of section 241(a)(2) of the Act will continue to apply, including provisions that mandate detention of certain criminal and terrorist aliens.

(ii) The Service shall serve the alien with a Notice of Failure to Comply, which shall advise the alien of the following: the provisions of sections 241(a)(1)(C) (extension of removal period) and 243(a) of the Act (criminal penalties related to removal); the circumstances demonstrating his or her failure to comply with the requirements of section 241(a)(1)(C) of the Act; and an explanation of the necessary steps that the alien must take in order to comply with the statutory requirements.

(iii) The Service shall advise the alien that the Notice of Failure to Comply shall have the effect of extending the removal period as provided by law, if the removal period has not yet expired, and that the Service is not obligated to complete its scheduled custody reviews under this section until the alien has demonstrated compliance with the statutory obligations.

(iv) The fact that the Service does not provide a Notice of Failure to Comply, within the 90-day removal period, to an alien who has failed to comply with the requirements of section 241(a)(1)(C) of the Act, shall not have the effect of excusing the alien's conduct.

(h) District director's or Director of the Detention and Removal Field Office's custody review procedures. The district director's or Director of the Detention and Removal Field Office's custody determination will be developed in accordance with the following procedures:

(1) Records review. The district director or Director of the Detention and Removal Field Office will conduct the initial custody review. For aliens described in paragraphs (a) and (b)(1) of this section, the district director or Director of the Detention and Removal Field Office will conduct a records review prior to the expiration of the removal period. This initial post-order custody review will consist of a review of the alien's records and any written information submitted in English to the district director or Director of the Detention and Removal Field Office by or on behalf of the alien. However, the district director or Director of the Detention and Removal Field Office may in his or her discretion schedule a personal or telephonic interview with the alien as part of this custody determination. The district director or Director of the Detention and Removal Field Office may also consider any other relevant information relating to the alien or his or her circumstances and custody status.

(2) Notice to alien. The district director or Director of the Detention and Removal Field Office will provide written notice to the detainee approximately 30 days in advance of the pending records review so that the alien may submit information in writing in support of his or her release. The alien may be assisted by a person of his or her choice, subject to reasonable security concerns at the institution and panel's discretion, in preparing or submitting information in response to the district director's notice. Such assistance shall be at no expense to the Government. If the alien or his or her representative requests additional time to prepare materials beyond the time when the district director or Director of the Detention and Removal Field Office expects to conduct the records review, such a request will constitute a waiver of the requirement that the review occur prior to the expiration of the removal period.

(3) Factors for consideration. The district director's or Director of the Detention and Removal Field Office's review will include but is not limited to consideration of the factors described in paragraph (f) of this section. Before making any decision to release a detainee, the district director must be able to reach the conclusions set forth in paragraph (e) of this section.

(4) District director's or Director of the Detention and Removal Field Office's decision. The district director or Director of the Detention and Removal Field Office will notify the alien in writing that he or she is to be released from custody, or that he or she will be continued in detention pending removal or further review of his or her custody status.

(5) District office or Detention and Removal Field office staff. The district director or the Director of the Detention and Removal Field Office may delegate the authority to conduct the custody review, develop recommendations, or render the custody or release decisions to those persons directly responsible for detention within his or her geographical areas of responsibility. This includes the deputy district director, the assistant director for detention and deportation, the officer-in-charge of a detention center, the assistant director of the detention and removal field office, the director of the detention and removal resident office, the assistant director of the detention and removal resident office, officers in charge of service processing centers, or such other persons as the district director or the Director of the Detention and Removal Field Office may designate from the professional staff of the Service.

(i) Determinations by the Executive Associate Commissioner. Determinations by the Executive Associate Commissioner to release or retain custody of aliens shall be developed in accordance with the following procedures.

(1) Review panels. The HQPDU Director shall designate a panel or panels to make recommendations to the Executive Associate Commissioner. A Review Panel shall, except as otherwise provided, consist of two persons. Members of a Review Panel shall be selected from the professional staff of the Service. All recommendations by the two-member Review Panel shall be unanimous. If the vote of the two-member Review Panel is split, it shall adjourn its deliberations concerning that particular detainee until a third Review Panel member is added. The third member of any Review Panel shall be the Director of the HQPDU or his or her designee. A recommendation by a three-member Review Panel shall be by majority vote.

(2) Records review. Initially, and at the beginning of each subsequent review, the HQPDU Director or a Review Panel shall review the alien's records. Upon completion of this records review, the HQPDU Director or the Review Panel may issue a written recommendation that the alien be released and reasons therefore.

(3) Personal interview.

(i) If the HQPDU Director does not accept a panel's recommendation to grant release after a records review, or if the alien is not recommended for release, a Review Panel shall personally interview the detainee. The scheduling of such interviews shall be at the discretion of the HQPDU Director. The HQPDU Director will provide a translator if he or she determines that such assistance is appropriate.

(ii) The alien may be accompanied during the interview by a person of his or her choice, subject to reasonable security concerns at the institution's and panel's discretion, who is able to attend at the time of the scheduled interview. Such assistance shall be at no expense to the Government. The alien may submit to the Review Panel any information, in English, that he or she believes presents a basis for his or her release.

(4) Alien's participation. Every alien shall respond to questions or provide other information when requested to do so by Service officials for the purpose of carrying out the provisions of this section.

(5) Panel recommendation. Following completion of the interview and its deliberations, the Review Panel shall issue a written recommendation that the alien be released or remain in custody pending removal or further review. This written recommendation shall include a brief statement of the factors that the Review Panel deems material to its recommendation.

(6) Determination. The Executive Associate Commissioner shall consider the recommendation and appropriate custody review materials and issue a custody determination, in the exercise of discretion under the standards of this section. The Executive Associate Commissioner's review will include but is not limited to consideration of the factors described in paragraph (f) of this section. Before making any decision to release a detainee, the Executive Associate Commissioner must be able to reach the conclusions set forth in paragraph (e) of this section. The Executive Associate Commissioner is not bound by the panel's recommendation.

(7) No significant likelihood or removal. During the custody review process as provided in this paragraph (i), or at the conclusion of that review, if the alien submits, or the record contains, information providing a substantial reason to believe that the removal of a detained alien is not significantly likely in the reasonably foreseeable future, the HQPDU shall treat that as a request for review and initiate the review procedures under § 241.13. To the extent relevant, the HQPDU may consider any information developed during the custody review process under this section in connection with the determinations to be made by the Service under § 241.13. The Service shall complete the custody review under this section unless the HQPDU is able to make a prompt determination to release the alien under an order of supervision under § 241.13 because there is no significant likelihood that the alien will be removed in the reasonably foreseeable future.

(j) **Conditions of release. —**

(1) In general. The district director, Director of the Detention and Removal Field Office, or Executive Associate Commissioner shall impose such conditions or special conditions on release as the Service considers appropriate in an individual case or cases, including but not limited to the conditions of release noted in 8 CFR 212.5(c) and § 241.5. An alien released under this section must abide by the release conditions specified by the Service in relation to his or her release or sponsorship.

(2) Sponsorship. The district director, Director of the Detention and Removal Field Office, or Executive Associate Commissioner may, in the exercise of discretion, condition release on placement with a close relative who agrees to act as a sponsor, such as a parent, spouse, child, or sibling who is a lawful permanent resident or a citizen of the United States, or may condition release on the alien's placement or participation in an approved halfway house, mental health project, or community project when, in the opinion of the Service, such condition is warranted. No detainee may be released until sponsorship, housing, or other placement has been found for the detainee, if ordered, including but not limited to, evidence of financial support.

(3) Employment authorization. The district director, Director of the Detention and Removal Field Office, and the Executive Associate Commissioner, may, in the exercise of discretion, grant employment authorization under the same conditions set forth in § 241.5(c) for aliens released under an order of supervision.

(4) Withdrawal of release approval. The district director, Director of the Detention and Removal Field Office, or Executive Associate Commissioner may, in the exercise of discretion, withdraw approval for release of any detained alien prior to release when, in the decision-maker's opinion, the conduct of the detainee, or any other circumstance, indicates that release would no longer be appropriate.

(k) Timing of reviews. The timing of reviews shall be in accordance with the following guidelines:

(1) District director or Director of the Detention and Removal Field Office.

(i) Prior to the expiration of the removal period, the district director or Director of the Detention and Removal Field Office shall conduct a custody review for an alien described in paragraphs (a) and (b)(1) of this section where the alien's removal, while proper, cannot be accomplished during the period or is impracticable or contrary to the public interest. As provided in paragraph (h)(4) of this section, the district director or Director of the Detention and Removal Field Office will notify the alien in writing that he or she is to be released from custody, or that he or she will be continued in detention pending removal or further review of his or her custody status.

(ii) When release is denied pending the alien's removal, the district director or Director of the Detention and Removal Field Office in his or her discretion may retain responsibility for custody determinations for up to three months after expiration of the removal period, during which time the district director or Director of the Detention and Removal Field Office may conduct such additional review of the case as he or she deems appropriate. The district director or Director of the Detention and Removal Field Office may release the alien if he or she is not removed within the three-month period following the expiration of the removal period, in accordance with paragraphs (e), (f), and (j) of this section, or the district director or Director of the Detention and Removal Field Office may refer the alien to the HQPDU for further custody review.

(2) HQPDU reviews.

(i) District director or Director of the Detention and Removal Field Office referral for further review. When the district director or Director of the Detention and Removal Field Office refers a case to the HQPDU for further review, as provided in paragraph (c)(2) of this section, authority over the custody determination transfers to the Executive Associate Commissioner, according to procedures established by the HQPDU. The Service will provide the alien with approximately 30 days notice of this further review, which will ordinarily be conducted by the expiration of the removal period or as soon thereafter as practicable.

(ii) District director or Director of the Detention and Removal Field Office retains jurisdiction. When the district director or Director of the Detention and Removal Field Office has advised the alien at the 90-day review as provided in paragraph (h)(4) of this section that he or she will remain in custody pending removal or further custody review, and the alien is not removed within three months of the district director or Director of the Detention and Removal Field Office's decision, authority over the custody determination transfers from the district director or Director of the Detention and Removal Field Office to the Executive Associate Commissioner. The initial HQPDU review will ordinarily be conducted at the expiration of the three-month period after the 90-day review or as soon thereafter as practicable. The Service will provide the alien with approximately 30 days notice of that review.

(iii) Continued detention cases. A subsequent review shall ordinarily be commenced for any detainee within approximately one year of a decision by the Executive Associate Commissioner declining to grant release. Not more than once every three months in the interim between annual reviews, the alien may submit a written request to the HQPDU for release consideration based on a proper showing of a material change in circumstances since the last annual review. The HQPDU shall respond to the alien's request in writing within approximately 90 days.

(iv) Review scheduling. Reviews will be conducted within the time periods specified in paragraphs (k)(1)(i), (k)(2)(i), (k)(2)(ii), and (k)(2)(iii) of this section or as soon as possible thereafter, allowing for any unforeseen circumstances or emergent situation.

(v) Discretionary reviews. The HQPDU Director, in his or her discretion, may schedule a review of a detainee at shorter intervals when he or she deems such review to be warranted.

(3) Postponement of review. In the case of an alien who is in the custody of the Service, the district director or the HQPDU Director may, in his or her discretion, suspend or postpone the custody review process if such detainee's prompt removal is practicable and proper, or for other good cause. The decision and reasons for the delay shall be documented in the alien's custody review file or A file, as appropriate. Reasonable care will be exercised to ensure that the alien's case is reviewed once the reason for delay is remedied or if the alien is not removed from the United States as anticipated at the time review was suspended or postponed.

(4) Transition provisions.

(i) The provisions of this section apply to cases that have already received the 90-day review. If the alien's last review under the procedures set out in the Executive Associate Commissioner memoranda entitled Detention Procedures for Aliens Whose Immediate Repatriation is Not Possible or Practicable, February 3, 1999; Supplemental Detention Procedures, April 30, 1999; Interim Changes and Instructions for Conduct of Post-order Custody Reviews, August 6, 1999; Review of Long-term Detainees, October 22, 1999, was a records review and the alien remains in custody, the HQPDU will conduct a custody review within six months of that review (Memoranda available at http://www.ins.usdoj.gov). If the alien's last review included an interview, the HQPDU review will be scheduled one year from the last review. These reviews will be conducted pursuant to the procedures in paragraph (i) of this section, within the time periods specified in this paragraph or as soon as possible thereafter, allowing for resource limitations, unforeseen circumstances, or an emergent situation.

(ii) Any case pending before the Board on December 21, 2000 will be completed by the Board. If the Board affirms the district director's decision to continue the alien in detention, the next scheduled custody review will be conducted one year after the Board's decision in accordance with the procedures in paragraph (i) of this section.

(l) **Revocation of release —**

(1) Violation of conditions of release. Any alien described in paragraph (a) or (b)(1) of this section who has been released under an order of supervision or other conditions of release who violates the conditions of release may be returned to custody. Any such alien who violates the conditions of an order of supervision is subject to the penalties described in section 243(b) of the Act. Upon revocation, the alien will be notified of the reasons for revocation of his or her release or parole. The alien will be afforded an initial informal interview promptly after his or her return to Service custody to afford the alien an opportunity to respond to the reasons for revocation stated in the notification.

(2) Determination by the Service. The Executive Associate Commissioner shall have authority, in the exercise of discretion, to revoke release and return to Service custody an alien previously approved for release under the procedures in this section. A district director may also revoke release of an alien when, in the district director's opinion, revocation is in the public interest and circumstances do not reasonably permit referral of the case to the Executive Associate Commissioner. Release may be revoked in the exercise of discretion when, in the opinion of the revoking official:

(i) The purposes of release have been served;

(ii) The alien violates any condition of release;

(iii) It is appropriate to enforce a removal order or to commence removal proceedings against an alien; or

(iv) The conduct of the alien, or any other circumstance, indicates that release would no longer be appropriate.

(3) Timing of review when release is revoked. If the alien is not released from custody following the informal interview provided for in paragraph (l)(1) of this section, the HQPDU Director shall schedule the review process in the case of an alien whose previous release or parole from immigration custody pursuant to a decision of either the district director, Director of the Detention and Removal Field Office, or Executive Associate Commissioner under the procedures in this section has been or is subject to being revoked. The normal review process will commence with notification to the alien of a records review and scheduling of an interview, which will ordinarily be expected to occur within approximately three months after release is revoked. That custody review will include a final evaluation of any contested facts relevant to the revocation and a determination whether the facts as determined warrant revocation and further denial of release. Thereafter, custody reviews will be conducted annually under the provisions of paragraphs (i), (j), and (k) of this section.

HISTORY:

[62 FR 10312, 10378, March 6, 1997; 65 FR 80281, 80294, Dec. 21, 2000; 66 FR 56967, 56976, Nov. 14, 2001; 66 FR 56967, 56977, Nov. 14, 2001; 67 FR 39255, 39259, June 7, 2002; 70 FR 661, 673, Jan. 5, 2005; 76 FR 53764, 53791, Aug. 29, 2011]

§ 241.5 Conditions of release after removal period.

(a) Order of supervision. An alien released pursuant to Sec. 241.4 shall be released pursuant to an order of supervision. The Commissioner, Deputy Commissioner, Executive Associate Commissioner Field Operations, regional director, district director, acting district director, deputy district director, assistant district director for investigations, assistant district director for detention and deportation, or officer-in-charge may issue Form I-220B, Order of Supervision. The order shall specify conditions of supervision including, but not limited to, the following:

(1) A requirement that the alien report to a specified officer periodically and provide relevant information under oath as directed;

(2) A requirement that the alien continue efforts to obtain a travel document and assist the Service in obtaining a travel document;

(3) A requirement that the alien report as directed for a mental or physical examination or examinations as directed by the Service;

(4) A requirement that the alien obtain advance approval of travel beyond previously specified times and distances; and

(5) A requirement that the alien provide DHS with written notice of any change of address in the prescribed manner.

(b) Posting of bond. An officer authorized to issue an order of supervision may require the posting of a bond in an amount determined by the officer to be sufficient to ensure compliance with the conditions of the order, including surrender for removal.

(c) Employment authorization. An officer authorized to issue an order of supervision may, in his or her discretion, grant employment authorization to an alien released under an order of supervision if the officer specifically finds that:

(1) The alien cannot be removed in a timely manner; or

(2) The removal of the alien is impracticable or contrary to public interest.

HISTORY:

[62 FR 10312, 10378, March 6, 1997; 65 FR 80281, 80298, Dec. 21, 2000; 70 FR 661, 673, Jan. 5, 2005; 76 FR 53764, 53791, Aug. 29, 2011]

§ 241.6 Administrative stay of removal.

(a) Any request of an alien under a final order of deportation or removal for a stay of deportation or removal shall be filed on Form I-246, Stay of Removal, with the district director having jurisdiction over the place where the alien is at the time of filing. The Commissioner, Deputy Commissioner, Executive Associate Commissioner for Field Operations, Deputy Executive Associate Commissioner for Detention and Removal, the Director of the Office of Juvenile Affairs, regional directors, or district director, in his or her discretion and in consideration of factors listed in 8 CFR 212.5 and section 241(c) of the Act, may grant a stay of removal or deportation for such time and under such conditions as he or she may deem appropriate. Neither the request nor failure to receive notice of disposition of the request shall delay removal or relieve the alien from strict compliance with any outstanding notice to surrender for deportation or removal.

(b) Denial by the Commissioner, Deputy Commissioner, Executive Associate Commissioner for Field Operations, Deputy Executive Associate Commissioner for Detention and Removal, Director of the Office of Juvenile Affairs, regional director, or district director of a request for a stay is not appealable, but such denial shall not preclude an immigration judge or the Board from granting a stay in connection with a previously filed motion to reopen or a motion to reconsider as provided in 8 CFR part 3.

(c) The Service shall take all reasonable steps to comply with a stay granted by an immigration judge or the Board. However, such a stay shall cease to have effect if granted (or communicated) after the alien has been placed aboard an aircraft or other conveyance for removal and the normal boarding has been completed.

HISTORY:

[62 FR 10312, 10379, March 6, 1997; 65 FR 80281, 80298, Dec. 21, 2000; 67 FR 39255, 39259, June 7, 2002]

§ 241.7 Self-removal.

A district director, the Deputy Executive Associate Commissioner for Detention and Removal, or the Director of the Office of Juvenile Affairs may permit an alien ordered removed (including an alien ordered excluded or deported in proceedings prior to April 1, 1997) to depart at his or her own expense to a destination of his or her own choice. Any alien who has departed from the United States while an order of deportation or removal is outstanding shall be considered to have been deported, excluded and deported, or removed, except that an alien who departed before the expiration of the voluntary departure period granted in connection with an alternate order of deportation or removal shall not be considered to be so deported or removed.

HISTORY:

[62 FR 10312, 10379, March 6, 1997; 67 FR 39255, 39260, June 7, 2002]

§ 241.8 Reinstatement of removal orders.

(a) Applicability. An alien who illegally reenters the United States after having been removed, or having departed voluntarily, while under an order of exclusion, deportation, or removal shall be removed from the United States by reinstating the prior order. The alien has no right to a hearing before an immigration judge in such circumstances. In establishing whether an alien is subject to this section, the immigration officer shall determine the following:

(1) Whether the alien has been subject to a prior order of removal. The immigration officer must obtain the prior order of exclusion, deportation, or removal relating to the alien.

(2) The identity of the alien, i.e., whether the alien is in fact an alien who was previously removed, or who departed voluntarily while under an order of exclusion, deportation, or removal. In disputed cases, verification of identity shall be accomplished by a comparison of fingerprints between those of the previously excluded, deported, or removed alien contained in Service records and those of the subject alien. In the absence of fingerprints in a disputed case the alien shall not be removed pursuant to this paragraph.

(3) Whether the alien unlawfully reentered the United States. In making this determination, the officer shall consider all relevant evidence, including statements made by the alien and any evidence in the alien's possession. The immigration officer shall attempt to verify an alien's claim, if any, that he or she was lawfully admitted, which shall include a check of Service data systems available to the officer.

(b) Notice. If an officer determines that an alien is subject to removal under this section, he or she shall provide the alien with written notice of his or her determination. The officer shall advise the alien that he or she may make a written or oral statement contesting the determination. If the alien wishes to make such a statement, the officer shall allow the alien to do so and shall consider whether the alien's statement warrants reconsideration of the determination.

(c) Order. If the requirements of paragraph (a) of this section are met, the alien shall be removed under the previous order of exclusion, deportation, or removal in accordance with section 241(a)(5) of the Act.

(d) Exception for applicants for benefits under section 902 of HRIFA or sections 202 or 203 of NACARA. If an alien who is otherwise subject to this section has applied for adjustment of status under either section 902 of Division A of Public Law 105-277, the Haitian Refugee Immigrant Fairness Act of 1998 (HRIFA), or section 202 of Pubic Law 105-100, the Nicaraguan Adjustment and Central American Relief Act (NACARA), the provisions of section 241(a)(5) of the Immigration and Nationality Act shall not apply. The immigration officer may not reinstate the prior order in accordance with this section unless and until a final decision to deny the application for adjustment has been made. If the application for adjustment of status is granted, the prior order shall be rendered moot.

(e) Exception for withholding of removal. If an alien whose prior order of removal has been reinstated under this section expresses a fear of returning to the country designated in that order, the alien shall be immediately referred to an asylum officer for an interview to determine whether the alien has a reasonable fear of persecution or torture pursuant to § 208.31 of this chapter.

(f) Execution of reinstated order. Execution of the reinstated order of removal and detention of the alien shall be administered in accordance with this part.

HISTORY:

[62 FR 10312, 10379, March 6, 1997; 64 FR 8478, 8495, Feb. 19, 1999; 66 FR 29449, 29451, May 31, 2001]

§ 241.9 Notice to transportation line of alien's removal.

(a) An alien who has been ordered removed shall, immediately or as promptly as the circumstances permit, be offered for removal to the owner, agent, master, commanding officer, person in charge, purser, or consignee of the vessel or aircraft on which the alien is to be removed, as determined by the district director, with a written notice specifying the cause of inadmissibility or deportability, the class of travel in which such alien arrived and is to be removed, and with the return of any documentation that will assist in effecting his or her removal. If special care and attention are required, the provisions of § 241.10 shall apply.

(b) Failure of the carrier to accept for removal an alien who has been ordered removed shall result in the carrier being assessed any costs incurred by the Service for detention after the carrier's failure to accept the alien for removal, including the cost of any transportation as required under section 241(e) of the Act. The User Fee Account shall not be assessed for expenses incurred because of the carrier's violation of the provisions of section 241 of the Act and this paragraph. The Service will, at the carrier's option, retain custody of the alien for an additional 7 days beyond the date of the removal order. If, after the third day of this additional 7-day period, the carrier has not made all the necessary transportation arrangements for the alien to be returned to his or her point of embarkation by the end of the additional 7-day period, the Service will make the arrangements and bill the carrier for its costs.

HISTORY:

[62 FR 10312, 10379, March 6, 1997]

§ 241.10 Special care and attention of removable aliens.

When, in accordance with section 241(c)(3) of the Act, a transportation line is responsible for the expenses of an inadmissible or deportable alien's removal, and the alien requires special care and attention, the alien shall be delivered to the owner, agent, master, commanding officer, person in charge, purser, or consignee of the vessel or aircraft on which the alien will be removed, who shall be given Forms I-287, I-287A, and I-287B. The reverse of Form I-287A shall be signed by the officer of the vessel or aircraft to whom the alien has been delivered and immediately returned to the immigration officer effecting delivery. Form I-287B shall be retained by the receiving officer and subsequently filled out by the agents or persons therein designated and returned by mail to the district director named on the form. The transportation line shall at its own expense forward the alien from the foreign port of disembarkation to the final destination specified on Form I-287. The special care and attention shall be continued to such final destination, except when the foreign public officers decline to allow such attendant to proceed and they take charge of the alien, in which case this fact shall be recorded by the transportation line on the reverse of Form I-287B. If the transportation line fails, refuses, or neglects to provide the necessary special care and attention or comply with the directions of Form I-287, the district director shall thereafter and without notice employ suitable persons, at the expense of the transportation line, and effect such removal.

HISTORY:

[62 FR 10312, 10380, March 6, 1997]

§ 241.11 Detention and removal of stowaways.

(a) Presentation of stowaways. The owner, agent, master, commanding officer, charterer, or consignee of a vessel or aircraft (referred to in this section as the carrier) bringing any alien stowaway to the United States is required to detain the stowaway on board the vessel or aircraft, at the expense of the owner of the vessel or aircraft, until completion of the inspection of the alien by an immigration officer. If detention on board the vessel or aircraft pending inspection is not possible, the carrier shall advise the Service of this fact without delay, and the Service may authorize that the carrier detain the stowaway at another designated location, at the expense of the owner, until the immigration officer arrives. No notice to detain the alien shall be required. Failure to detain an alien stowaway pending inspection shall result in a civil penalty under section 243(c)(1)(A) of the Act. The owner, agent, master, commanding officer, charterer, or consignee of a vessel or aircraft must present the stowaway for inspection, along with any documents or evidence of identity or nationality in the possession of the alien or obtained by the carrier relating to the alien stowaway, and must provide any available information concerning the alien's boarding or apprehension.

(b) Removal of stowaways from vessel or aircraft for medical treatment. The district director may parole an alien stowaway into the United States for medical treatment, but the costs of detention and treatment of the alien stowaway shall be at the expense of the owner of the vessel or aircraft, and such removal of the stowaway from the vessel or aircraft does not relieve the carrier of the requirement to remove the stowaway from the United States once such medical treatment has been completed.

(c) **Repatriation of stowaways —**

(1) Requirements of carrier. Following inspection, an immigration officer may order the owner, agent, master, commanding officer, charterer, or consignee of a vessel or aircraft bringing any alien stowaway to the United States to remove the stowaway on the vessel or aircraft of arrival, unless it is impracticable to do so or other factors exist which would preclude removal on the same vessel or aircraft. Such factors may include, but are not limited to, sanitation, health, and safety concerns for the crew and/or stowaway, whether the stowaway is a female or a juvenile, loss of insurance coverage on account of the stowaway remaining aboard, need for repairs to the vessel, and other similar circumstances. If the owner, agent, master, commanding officer, charterer, or consignee requests that he or she be allowed to remove the stowaway by other means, the Service shall favorably consider any such request, provided the carrier has obtained, or will obtain in a timely manner, any necessary travel documents and has made or will make all transportation arrangements. The owner, agent, master, commanding officer, charterer, or consignee shall transport the stowaway or arrange for secure escort of the stowaway to the vessel or aircraft of departure to ensure that the stowaway departs the United States. All expenses relating to removal shall be borne by the owner. Other than requiring compliance with the detention and removal requirements contained in section 241(d)(2) of the Act, the Service shall not impose additional conditions on the carrier regarding security arrangements. Failure to comply with an order to remove an alien stowaway shall result in a civil penalty under section 243(c)(1)(A) of the Act.

(2) Detention of stowaways ordered removed. If detention of the stowaway is required pending removal on other than the vessel or aircraft of arrival, or if the stowaway is to be removed on the vessel or aircraft of arrival but departure of the vessel or aircraft is not imminent and circumstances preclude keeping the stowaway on board the vessel or aircraft, the Service shall take the stowaway into Service custody. The owner is responsible for all costs of maintaining and detaining the stowaway pending removal, including costs for stowaways seeking asylum as described in paragraph (d) of this section. Such costs will be limited to those normally incurred in the detention of an alien by the Service, including, but not limited to, housing, food, transportation, medical expenses, and other reasonable costs incident to the detention of the stowaway.

The Service may require the posting of a bond or other surety to ensure payment of costs of detention.

(d) **Stowaways claiming asylum —**

(1) Referral for credible fear determination. A stowaway who indicates an intention to apply for asylum or a fear of persecution or torture upon return to his or her native country or country of last habitual residence (if not a national of any country) shall be removed from the vessel or aircraft of arrival in accordance with § 208.5(b) of this chapter. The immigration officer shall refer the alien to an asylum officer for a determination of credible fear in accordance with section 235(b)(1)(B) of the Act and § 208.30 of this chapter. The stowaway shall be detained in the custody of the Service pending the credible fear determination and any review thereof. Parole of such alien, in accordance with section 212(d)(5) of the Act, may be permitted only when the Attorney General determines, in the exercise of discretion, that parole is required to meet a medical emergency or is necessary for a legitimate law enforcement objective. A stowaway who has established a credible fear of persecution or torture in accordance with § 208.30 of this chapter may be detained or paroled pursuant to § 212.5 of this chapter during any consideration of the asylum application. In determining whether to detain or parole the alien, the Service shall consider the likelihood that the alien will abscond or pose a security risk.

(2) Costs of detention of asylum-seeking stowaways. The owner of the vessel or aircraft that brought the stowaway to the United States shall reimburse the Service for the costs of maintaining and detaining the stowaway pending a determination of credible fear under section 235(b)(1)(B) of the Act, up to a maximum period of 72 hours. The owner is also responsible for the costs of maintaining and detaining the stowaway during the period in which the stowaway is pursuing his or her asylum application, for a maximum period of 15 working days, excluding Saturdays, Sundays, and holidays. The 15-day period shall begin on the day following the day in which the alien is determined to have a credible fear of persecution by the asylum officer, or by the immigration judge if such review was requested by the alien pursuant to section 235(b)(1)(B)(iii)(III) of the Act, but not later than 72 hours after the stowaway was initially presented to the Service for inspection. Following the determination of credible fear, if the stowaway's application for asylum is not adjudicated within 15 working days, the Service shall pay the costs of detention beyond this time period. If the stowaway is determined not to have a credible fear of persecution, or if the stowaway's application for asylum is denied, including any appeals, the carrier shall be notified and shall arrange for repatriation of the stowaway at the expense of the owner of the vessel or aircraft on which the stowaway arrived.

HISTORY:

[62 FR 10312, 10380, March 6, 1997; 64 FR 8478, 8495, Feb. 19, 1999]

§ 241.12 Nonapplication of costs of detention and maintenance.

The owner of a vessel or aircraft bringing an alien to the United States who claims to be exempt from payment of the costs of detention and maintenance of the alien pursuant to section 241(c)(3)(B) of the Act shall establish to the satisfaction of the district director in charge of the port of arrival that such costs should not be applied. The district director shall afford the owner a reasonable time within which to submit affidavits and briefs to support the claim. There is no appeal from the decision of the district director.

HISTORY:

[62 FR 10312, 10381, March 6, 1997]

§ 241.13 Determination of whether there is a significant likelihood of removing a detained alien in the reasonably foreseeable future.

(a) Scope. This section establishes special review procedures for those aliens who are subject to a final order of removal and are detained under the custody review procedures provided at § 241.4 after the expiration of the removal period, where the alien has provided good reason to believe there is no significant likelihood of removal to the country to which he or she was ordered removed, or to a third country, in the reasonably foreseeable future.

(b) **Applicability to particular aliens.**

(1) Relationship to § 241.4. Section 241.4 shall continue to govern the detention of aliens under a final order of removal, including aliens who have requested a review of the likelihood of their removal under this section, unless the Service makes a determination under this section that there is no significant likelihood of removal in the reasonably foreseeable future. The Service may release an alien under an order of supervision under § 241.4 if it determines that the alien would not pose a danger to the public or a risk of flight, without regard to the likelihood of the alien's removal in the reasonably foreseeable future.

(2) Continued detention pending determinations.

(i) The Service's Headquarters Post-order Detention Unit (HQPDU) shall continue in custody any alien described in paragraph (a) of this section during the time the Service is pursuing the procedures of this section to determine whether there is no significant likelihood the alien can be removed in the reasonably foreseeable future. The HQPDU shall continue in custody any alien described in paragraph (a) of this section for whom it has determined that special circumstances exist and custody procedures under § 241.14 have been initiated.

(ii) The HQPDU has no obligation to release an alien under this section until the HQPDU has had the opportunity during a six-month period, dating from the beginning of the removal period (whenever that period begins and unless that period is extended as provided in section 241(a)(1) of the Act), to make its determination as to whether there is a significant likelihood of removal in the reasonably foreseeable future.

(3) Limitations. This section does not apply to:

(i) Arriving aliens, including those who have not entered the United States, those who have been granted immigration parole into the United States, and Mariel Cubans whose parole is governed by § 212.12 of this chapter;

(ii) Aliens subject to a final order of removal who are still within the removal period, including aliens whose removal period has been extended for failure to comply with the requirements of section 241(a)(1)(C) of the Act; or

(iii) Aliens who are ordered removed by the Alien Terrorist Removal Court pursuant to title 5 of the Act.

(c) Delegation of authority. The HQPDU shall conduct a review under this section, in response to a request from a detained alien, in order to determine whether there is no significant likelihood that the alien will be removed in the reasonably foreseeable future. If so, the HQPDU shall determine whether the alien should be released from custody under appropriate conditions of supervision or should be referred for a determination under § 241.14 as to whether the alien's continued detention may be justified by special circumstances.

(d) **Showing by the alien.**

(1) Written request. An eligible alien may submit a written request for release to the HQPDU asserting the basis for the alien's belief that there is no significant likelihood that the alien will be removed in the reasonably foreseeable future. The alien may submit whatever documentation to the HQPDU he or she wishes in support of the assertion that there is no significant likelihood of removal in the reasonably foreseeable future.

(2) Compliance and cooperation with removal efforts. The alien shall include with the written request information sufficient to establish his or her compliance with the obligation to effect his or her removal and to cooperate in the process of obtaining necessary travel documents.

(3) Timing of request. An eligible alien subject to a final order of removal may submit, at any time after the removal order becomes final, a written request under this section asserting that his or her removal is not significantly likely in the reasonably foreseeable future. However, the Service may, in the exercise of its discretion, postpone its consideration of such a request until after expiration of the removal period.

(e) **Review by HQPDU.**

(1) Initial response. Within 10 business days after the HQPDU receives the request (or, if later, the expiration of the removal period), the HQPDU shall respond in writing to the alien, with a copy to counsel of record, by regular mail, acknowledging receipt of the request for a review under this section and explaining the procedures that will be used to evaluate the request. The notice shall advise the alien that the Service may continue to detain the alien until it has made a determination under this section whether there is a significant likelihood the alien can be removed in the reasonably foreseeable future.

(2) Lack of compliance, failure to cooperate. The HQPDU shall first determine if the alien has failed to make reasonable efforts to comply with the removal order, has failed to cooperate fully in effecting removal, or has obstructed or hampered the removal process. If so, the HQPDU shall so advise the alien in writing, with a copy to counsel of record by regular mail. The HQPDU shall advise the alien of the efforts he or she needs to make in order to assist in securing travel documents for return to his or her country of origin or a third country, as well as the consequences of failure to make such efforts or to cooperate, including the provisions of section 243(a) of the Act. The Service shall not be obligated to conduct a further consideration of the alien's request for release until the alien has responded to the HQPDU and has established his or her compliance with the statutory requirements.

(3) Referral to the State Department. If the HQPDU believes that the alien's request provides grounds for further review, the Service may, in the exercise of its discretion, forward a copy of the alien's release request to the Department of State for information and assistance. The Department of State may provide detailed country conditions information or any other information that may be relevant to whether a travel document is obtainable from the country at issue. The Department of State may also provide an assessment of the accuracy of the alien's assertion that he or she cannot be returned to the country at issue or to a third country. When the Service bases its decision, in whole or in part, on information provided by the Department of State, that information shall be made part of the record.

(4) Response by alien. The Service shall permit the alien an opportunity to respond to the evidence on which the Service intends to rely, including the Department of State's submission, if any, and other evidence of record presented by the Service prior to any HQPDU decision. The alien may provide any additional relevant information to the Service, including reasons why his or her removal would not be significantly likely in the reasonably foreseeable future even though the Service has generally been able to accomplish the removal of other aliens to the particular country.

(5) Interview. The HQPDU may grant the alien an interview, whether telephonically or in person, if the HQPDU determines that an interview would provide assistance in reaching a decision. If an interview is scheduled, the HQPDU will provide an interpreter upon its determination that such assistance is appropriate.

(6) Special circumstances. If the Service determines that there are special circumstances justifying the alien's continued detention nowithstanding the determination that removal is not significantly likely in the reasonably foreseeable future, the Service shall initiate the review procedures in § 241.14, and provide written notice to the alien. In appropriate cases, the Service may initiate review proceedings under § 241.14 before completing the HQPDU review under this section.

(f) Factors for consideration. The HQPDU shall consider all the facts of the case including, but not limited to, the history of the alien's efforts to comply with the order of removal, the history of the Service's efforts to remove aliens to the country in question or to third countries, including the ongoing nature of the Service's efforts to remove this alien and the alien's assistance with those efforts, the reasonably foreseeable results of those efforts, and the views of the Department of State regarding the prospects for removal of aliens to the country or countries in question. Where the Service is continuing its efforts to remove the alien, there is no presumptive period of time within which the alien's removal must be accomplished, but the prospects for the timeliness of removal must be reasonable under the circumstances.

(g) Decision. The HQPDU shall issue a written decision based on the administrative record, including any documentation provided by the alien, regarding the likelihood of removal and whether there is a significant likelihood that the alien will be removed in the reasonably foreseeable future under the circumstances. The HQPDU shall provide the decision to the alien, with a copy to counsel of record, by regular mail.

(1) Finding of no significant likelihood of removal. If the HQPDU determines at the conclusion of the review that there is no significant likelihood that the alien will be removed in the reasonably foreseeable future, despite the Service's and the alien's efforts to effect removal, then the HQPDU shall so advise the alien. Unless there are special circumstances justifying continued detention, the Service shall promptly make arrangements for the release of the alien subject to appropriate conditions, as provided in paragraph (h) of this section. The Service may require that the alien submit to a medical or psychiatric examination prior to establishing appropriate conditions for release or determining whether to refer the alien for further proceedings under § 214.14 because of special circumstances justifying continued detention. The Service is not required to release an alien if the alien refuses to submit to a medical or psychiatric examination as ordered.

(2) Denial. If the HQPDU determines at the conclusion of the review that there is a significant likelihood that the alien will be removed in the reasonably foreseeable future, the HQPDU shall deny the alien's request under this section. The denial shall advise the alien that his or her detention will continue to be governed under the established standards in § 214.4. There is no administrative appeal from the HQPDU decision denying a request from an alien under this section.

(h) **Conditions of release.**

(1) In general. An alien's release pursuant to an HQPDU determination that the alien's removal is not significantly likely in the reasonably foreseeable future shall be upon appropriate conditions specified in this paragraph and in the order of supervision, in order to protect the public safety and to promote the ability of the Service to effect the alien's removal as ordered, or removal to a third country, should circumstances change in the future. The order of supervision shall include all of the conditions provided in section 241(a)(3) of the Act, and § 241.5, and shall also include the conditions that the alien obey all laws, including any applicable prohibitions on the possession or use of firearms (see, e.g., 18 U.S.C. 922(g)); and that the alien continue to seek to obtain travel documents and provide the Service with all correspondence to Embassies/Consulates requesting the issuance of travel documents and any reply from the Embassy/Consulate. The order of supervision may also include any other conditions that the HQPDU considers necessary to ensure public safety and guarantee the alien's compliance with the order of removal, including, but not limited to, attendance at any rehabilitative/sponsorship program or submission for medical or psychiatric examination, as ordered.

(2) Advice of consequences for violating conditions of release. The order of supervision shall advise an alien released under this section that he or she must abide by the conditions of release specified by the Service. The order of supervision shall also advise the alien of the consequences of violation of the conditions of release, including the authority to return the alien to custody and the sanctions provided in section 243(b) of the Act.

(3) Employment authorization. The Service may, in the exercise of its discretion, grant employment authorization under the same conditions set forth in § 241.5(c) for aliens released under an order of supervision.

(4) Withdrawal of release approval. The Service may, in the exercise of its discretion, withdraw approval for release of any alien under this section prior to release in order to effect removal in the reasonably foreseeable future or where the alien refuses to comply with the conditions of release.

(i) Revocation of release.

(1) Violation of conditions of release. Any alien who has been released under an order of supervision under this section who violates any of the conditions of release may be returned to custody and is subject to the penalties described in section 243(b) of the Act. In suitable cases, the HQPDU shall refer the case to the appropriate U.S. Attorney for criminal prosecution. The alien may be continued in detention for an additional six months in order to effect the alien's removal, if possible, and to effect the conditions under which the alien had been released.

(2) Revocation for removal. The Service may revoke an alien's release under this section and return the alien to custody if, on account of changed circumstances, the Service determines that there is a significant likelihood that the alien may be removed in the reasonably foreseeable future. Thereafter, if the alien is not released from custody following the informal interview provided for in paragraph (h)(3) of this section, the provisions of § 241.4 shall govern the alien's continued detention pending removal.

(3) Revocation procedures. Upon revocation, the alien will be notified of the reasons for revocation of his or her release. The Service will conduct an initial informal interview promptly after his or her return to Service custody to afford the alien an opportunity to respond to the reasons for revocation stated in the notification. The alien may submit any evidence or information that he or she believes shows there is no significant likelihood he or she be removed in the reasonably foreseeable future, or that he or she has not violated the order of supervision. The revocation custody review will include an evaluation of any contested

facts relevant to the revocation and a determination whether the facts as determined warrant revocation and further denial of release.

(j) Subsequent requests for review. If the Service has denied an alien's request for release under this section, the alien may submit a request for review of his or her detention under this section, six months after the Service's last denial of release under this section. After applying the procedures in this section, the HQPDU shall consider any additional evidence provided by the alien or available to the Service as well as the evidence in the prior proceedings but the HQPDC shall render a de novo decision on the likelihood of removing the alien in the reasonably foreseeable future under the circumstances.

HISTORY:

[66 FR 56967, 56977, Nov. 14, 2001; 70 FR 661, 673, Jan. 5, 2005]

§ 241.14 Continued detention of removable aliens on account of special circumstances.

(a) Scope. The Service may invoke the procedures of this section in order to continue detention of particular removable aliens on account of special circumstances even though there is no significant likelihood that the alien will be removed in the reasonably foreseeable future.

(1) Applicability. This section applies to removable aliens as to whom the Service has made a determination under § 241.13 that there is no significant likelihood of removal in the reasonably foreseeable future. This section does not apply to aliens who are not subject to the special review provisions under § 241.13.

(2) Jurisdiction. The immigration judges and the Board have jurisdiction with respect to determinations as to whether release of an alien would pose a special danger to the public, as provided in paragraphs (f) through (k) of this section, but do not have jurisdiction with respect to aliens described in paragraphs (b), (c), or (d) of this section.

(b) Aliens with a highly contagious disease that is a threat to public safety. If, after a medical examination of the alien, the Service determines that a removable alien presents a threat to public safety initiate efforts with the Public Health Service or proper State and local government officials to secure appropriate arrangements for the alien's continued medical care or treatment.

(1) Recommendation. The Service shall not invoke authority to continue detention of an alien under this paragraph except upon the express recommendation of the Public Health Service. The Service will provide every reasonably available form of treatment while the alien remains in the custody of the Service.

(2) Conditions of release. If the Service, in consultation with the Public Health Service and the alien, identifies an appropriate medical facility that will treat the alien, then the alien may be released on condition that he or she continue with appropriate medical treatment until he or she no longer poses a threat to public safety because of a highly contagious disease.

(c) Aliens detained on account of serious adverse foreign policy consequences of release.

(1) Certification. The Service shall continue to detain a removable alien where the Attorney General or Deputy Attorney General has certified in writing that:

(i) Without regard to the grounds upon which the alien has been found inadmissible or removable, the alien is a person described in section 212(a)(3)(C) or section 237(a)(4)(C) of the Act;

(ii) The alien's release is likely to have serious adverse foreign policy consequences for the United States; and

(iii) No conditions of release can reasonably be expected to avoid those serious adverse foreign policy consequences,

(2) Foreign policy consequences. A certification by the Attorney General or Deputy Attorney General that an alien should not be released from custody on account of serious adverse foreign policy consequences shall be made only after consultation with the Department of State and upon the recommendation of the Secretary of State.

(3) Ongoing review. The certification is subject to ongoing review on a semi-annual basis but is not subject to further administrative review.

(d) Aliens detained on account of security or terrorism concerns.

(1) (1) Standard for continued detention. Subject to the review procedures under this paragraph (d), the Service shall continue to detain a removable alien based on a determination in writing that:

(i) The alien is a person described in section 212(a)(3)(A) or (B) or section 237(a)(4)(A) of (B) of the Act or the alien has engaged or will likely engage in any other activity that endangers the national security;

(ii) The alien's release presents a significant threat to the national security or a significant risk of terrorism; and

(iii) No conditions of release can reasonably be expected to avoid the threat to the national security or the risk of terrorism, as the case may be.

(2) Procedure. Prior to the Commissioner's recommendation to the Attorney General under paragraph (d)(5) of this section, the alien shall be notified of the Service's intention to continue the alien in detention and of the alien's right to submit a written statement and additional information for consideration by the Commissioner. The Service shall continue to detain the alien pending the decision of the Attorney General under this paragraph. To the greatest extent consistent with protection of the national security and classified information:

(i) The Service shall provide a description of the factual basis for the alien's continued detention; and

(ii) The alien shall have a reasonable opportunity to examine evidence against him or her, and to present information on his or her own behalf.

(3) Aliens ordered removed on grounds other than national security or terrorism. If the alien's final order of removal was based on grounds of inadmissibility other than any of those stated in section 212(a)(3)(A)(i), (A)(iii), or (B) of the Act, or on grounds of deportability

other than any of those stated in section 237(a)(4)(A) or (B) of the Act:

(i) An immigration officer shall, if possible, conduct an interview in person and take a sworn question-and-answer statement from the alien, and the Service shall provide an interpreter for such interview, if such assistance is determined to be appropriate; and

(ii) The alien may be accompanied at the interview by an attorney or other representative of his or her choice in accordance with 8 CFR part 292, at no expense to the government.

(4) Factors for consideration. In making a recommendation to the Attorney General that an alien should not be released from custody on account of security or terrorism concerns, the Commissioner shall take into account all relevant information, including but not limited to:

(i) The recommendations of appropriate enforcement officials of the Service, including the director of the Headquarters Post-order Detention Unit (HQPDU), and of the Federal Bureau of Investigation or other federal law enforcement or national security agencies;

(ii) The statements and information submitted by the alien, if any;

(iii) The extent to which the alien's previous conduct (including but not limited to the commission of national security or terrorism-related offenses, engaging in terrorist activity or other activity that poses a danger to the national security and any prior convictions in a federal, state or foreign court) indicates a likelihood that the alien's release would present a significant threat to the national security or a significant risk of terrorism; and

(iv) Other special circumstances of the alien's case indicating that release from detention would present a significant threat to the national security or a significant risk of terrorism.

(5) Recommendation to the Attorney General. The Commissioner shall submit a written recommendation and make the record available to the Attorney General. If the continued detention is based on a significant risk of terrorism, the recommendation shall state in as much detail as practicable the factual basis for this determination.

(6) Attorney General certification. Based on the record developed by the Service, and upon this recommendation of the Commissioner and the Director of the Federal Bureau of Investigation, the Attorney General may certify that an alien should continue to be detained on account of security or terrorism grounds as provided in this paragraph (d). Before making such a certification, the Attorney General shall order any further procedures or reviews as may be necessary under the circumstances to ensure the development of a complete record, consistent with the obligations to protect national security and classified information and to comply with the requirements of due process.

(7) Ongoing review. The detention decision under this paragraph (d) is subject to ongoing review on a semi-annual basis as provided in this paragraph (d), but is not subject to further administrative review. After the initial certification by the Attorney General, further certifications under paragraph (d)(6) of this section may be made by the Deputy Attorney General.

(e) [Reserved]

(f) Detention of aliens determined to be specially dangerous.

(1) Standard for continued detention. Subject to the review procedures provided in this section, the Service shall continue to detain an alien if the release of the alien would pose a special danger to the public, because:

(i) The alien has previously committed one or more crimes of violence as defined in 18 U.S.C. 16;

(ii) Due to a mental condition or personality disorder and behavior associated with that condition or disorder, the alien is likely to engage in acts of violence in the future; and

(iii) No conditions of release can reasonably be expected to ensure the safety of the public.

(2) Determination by the Commissioner. The Service shall promptly initiate review proceedings under paragraph (g) of this section if the Commissioner has determined in writing that the alien's release would pose a special danger to the public, according to the standards of paragraph (f)(1) of this section.

(3) Medical or mental health examination. Before making such a determination, the Commissioner shall arrange for a report by a physician employed or designated by the Public Health Service based on a full medical and psychiatric examination of the alien. The report shall include recommendations pertaining to whether, due to a mental condition or personality disorder and behavior associated with that condition or disorder, the alien is likely to engage in acts of violence in the future.

(4) Detention pending review. After the Commissioner or Deputy Commissioner has made a determination under this paragraph, the Service shall continue to detain the alien, unless an immigration judge or the Board issues an administratively final decision dismissing the review proceedings under this section.

(g) Referral to Immigration Judge. Jurisdiction for an immigration judge to review a determination by the Service pursuant to paragraph (f) of this section that an alien is specially dangerous shall commence with the filing by the Service of a Notice of Referral to the Immigration Judge (Form I-863) with the Immigration Court having jurisdiction over the place of the alien's custody. The Service shall promptly provide to the alien by personal service a copy of the Notice of Referral to the Immigration Judge and all accompanying documents.

(1) Factual basis. The Service shall attach a written statement that contains a summary of the basis for the Commissioner's determination to continue to detain the alien, including a description of the evidence relied upon to reach the determination regarding the alien's special dangerousness. The Service shall attach copies of all relevant documents used to reach its decision to continue to detain the alien.

(2) Notice of reasonable cause hearing. The Service shall attach a written notice advising the alien that the Service is initiating proceedings for the continued de-

tention of the alien and informing the alien of the procedures governing the reasonable cause hearing, as set forth at paragraph (h) of this section.

(3) Notice of alien's rights. The Service shall also provide written notice advising the alien of his or her rights during the reasonable cause hearing and the merits hearing before the Immigration Court, as follows:

(i) The alien shall be provided with a list of free legal services providers, and may be represented by an attorney or other representative of his or her choice in accordance with 8 CFR part 292, at no expense to the Government;

(ii) The Immigration Court shall provide an interpreter for the alien, if necessary, for the reasonable cause hearing and the merits hearing.

(iii) The alien shall have a reasonable opportunity to examine evidence against the alien, to present evidence in the alien's own behalf, and to cross-examine witnesses presented by the Service; and

(iv) The alien shall have the right, at the merits hearing, to cross-examine the author of any medical or mental health reports used as a basis for the determination under paragraph (f) of this section that the alien is specially dangerous.

(4) Record. All proceedings before the immigration judge under this section shall be recorded. The Immigration Court shall create a record of proceeding that shall include all testimony and documents related to the proceedings.

(h) Reasonable cause hearing. The immigration judge shall hold a preliminary hearing to determine whether the evidence supporting the Service's determination is sufficient to establish reasonable cause to go forward with a merits hearing under paragraph (i) of this section. A finding of reasonable cause under this section will be sufficient to warrant the alien's continued detention pending the completion of the review proceedings under this section.

(1) Scheduling of hearing. The reasonable cause hearing shall be commenced not later than 10 business days after the filing of the Form I-863. The Immigration Court shall provide prompt notice to the alien and to the Service of the time and place of the hearing. The hearing may be continued at the request of the alien or his or her representative.

(2) Evidence. The Service must show that there is reasonable cause to conduct a merits hearing under a merits hearing under paragraph (i) of this section. The Service may offer any evidence that is material and relevant to the proceeding. Testimony of witnesses, if any, shall be under oath or affirmation. The alien may, but is not required to, offer evidence on his or her own behalf.

(3) Decision. The immigration judge shall render a decision, which should be in summary form, within 5 business days after the close of the record, unless that time is extended by agreement of both parties, by a determination from the Chief Immigration Judge that exceptional circumstances make it impractical to render the decision on a highly expedited basis, or because of delay caused by the alien. If the immigration judge determines that the Service has met its burden of establishing reasonable cause, the immigration judge shall advise the alien and the Service, and shall schedule a merits hearing under paragraph (i) of this section to review the Service's determination that the alien is specially dangerous. If the immigration judge determines that the Service has not met its burden, the immigration judge shall order that the review proceedings under this section be dismissed. The order and any documents offered shall be included in the record of proceedings, and may be relied upon in a subsequent merits hearing.

(4) Appeal. If the immigration judge dismisses the review proceedings, the Service may appeal to the Board of Immigration Appeals in accordance with § 3.38 of this chapter, except that the Service must file the Notice of Appeal (Form EOIR-26) with the Board within 2 business days after the immigration judge's order. The Notice of Appeal should state clearly and conspicuously that it is an appeal of a reasonable cause decision under this section.

(i) If the Service reserves appeal of a dismissal of the reasonable cause hearing, the immigration judge's order shall be stayed until the expiration of the time to appeal. Upon the Service's filing of a timely Notice of Appeal, the immigration judge's order shall remain in abeyance pending a final decision of the appeal. The stay shall expire if the Service fails to file a timely Notice of Appeal.

(ii) The Board will decide the Service's appeal, by single Board Member review, based on the record of proceedings before the immigration judge. The Board shall expedite its review as far as practicable, as the highest priority among the appeals filed by detained aliens, and shall determine the issue within 20 business days of the filing of the notice of appeal, unless that time is extended by agreement of both parties, by a determination from the Chairman of the Board that exceptional circumstances make it impractical to render the decision on a highly expedited basis, or because of delay caused by the alien.

(iii) If the Board determines that the Service has met its burden of showing reasonable cause under this paragraph (h), the Board shall remand the case to the immigration judge for the scheduling of a merits hearing under paragraph (i) of this section. If the Board determines that the Service has not met its burden, the Board shall dismiss the review proceedings under this section.

(i) Merits hearing. If there is reasonable cause to conduct a merits hearing under this section, the immigration judge shall promptly schedule the hearing and shall expedite the proceedings as far as practicable. The immigration judge shall allow adequate time for the parties to prepare for the merits hearing, but, if requested by the alien, the hearing shall commence within 30 days. The hearing may be continued at the request of the alien or his or her representative, or at the request of the Service upon a showing of exceptional circumstances by the Service.

(1) Evidence. The Service shall have the burden of proving, by clear and convincing evidence, that the

alien should remain in custody because the alien's release would pose a special danger to the public, under the standards of paragraph (f)(1) of this section. The immigration judge may receive into evidence any oral or written statement that is material and relevant to this determination. Testimony of witnesses shall be under oath or affirmation. The alien may, but is not required to, offer evidence on his or her own behalf.

(2) Factors for consideration. In making any determination in a merits hearing under this section, the immigration judge shall consider the following non-exclusive list of factors:

(i) The alien's prior criminal history, particularly the nature and seriousness of any prior crimes involving violence or threats of violence;

(ii) The alien's previous history of recidivism, if any, upon release from either Service or criminal custody;

(iii) The substantiality of the Service's evidence regarding the alien's current mental condition or personality disorder;

(iv) The likelihood that the alien will engage in acts of violence in the future; and

(v) The nature and seriousness of the danger to the public posed by the alien's release.

(3) Decision. After the closing of the record, the immigration judge shall render a decision as soon as practicable. The decision may be oral or written. The decision shall state whether or not the Service has met its burden of establishing that the alien should remain in custody because the alien's release would pose a special danger to the public, under the standards of paragraph (f)(1) of this section. The decision shall also include the reasons for the decision under each of the standards of paragraph (f)(1) of this section, although a formal enumeration of findings is not required. Notice of the decision shall be served in accordance with § 240.13(a) or (b).

(i) If the immigration judge determines that the Service has met its burden, the immigration judge shall enter an order providing for the continued detention of the alien.

(ii) If the immigration judge determines that the Service has failed to meet its burden, the immigration judge shall order that the review proceedings under this section be dismissed.

(4) Appeal. Either party may appeal an adverse decision to the Board of Immigration Appeals in accordance with § 3.38 of this chapter, except that, if the immigration judge orders dismissal of the proceedings, the Service shall have only 5 business days to file a Notice of Appeal with the Board. The Notice of Appeal should state clearly and conspicuously that this is an appeal of a merits decision under this section.

(i) If the Service reserves appeal of a dismissal, the immigration judge's order shall be stayed until the expiration of the time to appeal. Upon the Service's filing of a timely Notice of Appeal, the immigration judge's order shall remain in abeyance pending a final decision of the appeal. The stay shall expire if the Service fails to file a timely Notice of Appeal.

(ii) The Board shall conduct its review of the appeal as provided in 8 CFR part 3, but shall expedite its review as far as practicable, as the highest priority among the appeals filed by detained aliens. The decision of the Board shall be final as provided in § 3.1(d)(3) of this chapter.

(j) Release of alien upon dismissal of proceedings. If there is an administratively final decision by the immigration judge or the Board dismissing the review proceedings under this section upon conclusion of the reasonable cause hearing or the merits hearing, the Service shall promptly release the alien on conditions of supervision, as determined by the Service, pursuant to § 241.13. The conditions of supervision shall not be subject to review by the immigration judge or the Board.

(k) **Subsequent review for aliens whose release would pose a special danger to the public.**

(1) Periodic review. In any case where the immigration judge or the Board has entered an order providing for the alien to remain in custody after a merits hearing pursuant to paragraph (i) of this section, the Service shall continue to provide an ongoing, periodic review of the alien's continued detention, according to § 241.4 and paragraphs (f)(1)(ii) and (f)(1)(iii) of this section.

(2) Alien's request for review. The alien may also request a review of his or her custody status because of changed circumstances, as provided in this paragraph (k). The request shall be in writing and directed to the HQPDU.

(3) Time for review. An alien may only request a review of his or her custody status under this paragraph (k) no earlier than six months after the last decision of the immigration judge under this section or, if the decision was appealed, the decision of the Board.

(4) Showing of changed circumstances. The alien shall bear the initial burden to establish a material change in circumstances such that the release of the alien would no longer pose a special danger to the public under the standards of paragraph (f)(1) of this section.

(5) Review by the Service. If the Service determines, upon consideration of the evidence submitted by the alien and other relevant evidence, that the alien is not likely to commit future acts of violence or that the Service will be able to impose adequate conditions of release so that the alien will not pose a special danger to the public, the Service shall release the alien from custody pursuant to the procedures in § 241.13. If the Service determines that continued detention is needed in order to protect the public, the Service shall provide a written notice to the alien stating the basis for the Service's determination, and provide a copy of the evidence relied upon by the Service. The notice shall also advise the alien of the right to move to set aside the prior review proceedings under this section.

(6) Motion to set aside determination in prior review proceedings. If the Service denies the alien's request for release from custody, the alien may file a motion with the Immigration Court that had jurisdiction over the merits hearing to set aside the determination in the prior review proceedings under this section. The immigration judge shall consider any evidence submitted by

the alien or relied upon by the Service and shall provide an opportunity for the Service to respond to the motion.

(i) If the immigration judge determines that the alien has provided good reason to believe that, because of a material change in circumstances, releasing the alien would no longer pose a special danger to the public under the standards of paragraph (f)(1) of this section, the immigration judge shall set aside the determination in the prior review proceedings under this section and schedule a new merits hearing as provided in paragraph (i) of this section.

(ii) Unless the immigration judge determines that the alien has satisfied the requirements under paragraph (k)(6)(i) of this section, the immigration judge shall deny the motion. Neither the immigration judge nor the Board may sua sponte set aside a determination in prior review proceedings. Notwithstanding 8 CFR 3.23 or 3.2 (motions to reopen), the provisions set forth in this paragraph (k) shall be the only vehicle for seeking review based on material changed circumstances.

(iii) The alien may appeal an adverse decision to the Board in accordance with § 3.38 of this chapter. The Notice of Appeal should state clearly and conspicuously that this is an appeal of a denial of a motion to set aside a prior determination in review proceedings under this section.

HISTORY:

[66 FR 56967, 56979, Nov. 14, 2001]

§ 241.15 Countries to which aliens may be removed.

(a) Country. For the purposes of section 241(b) of the Act (8 U.S.C. 1231(b)), the Secretary retains discretion to remove an alien to any country described in section 241(b) of the Act (8 U.S.C. 1231(b)), without regard to the nature or existence of a government.

(b) Acceptance. For the purposes of section 241(b) of the Act (8 U.S.C. 1231(b)), the Secretary retains discretion to determine the effect, if any, of acceptance or lack thereof, when an acceptance by a country is required, and what constitutes sufficient acceptance.

(c) Absence or lack of response. The absence of or lack of response from a de jure or functioning government (whether recognized by the United States, or otherwise) or a body acting as a de jure or functioning government in the receiving country does not preclude the removal of an alien to a receiving country.

(d) Prior commitment. No commitment of acceptance by the receiving country is required prior to designation of the receiving country, before travel arrangements are made, or before the alien is transported to the receiving country.

(e) Specific provisions regarding acceptance. Where the Department cannot remove an alien under section 241(b)(2)(A)-(D) of the Act, acceptance is not required to remove an alien to a receiving country pursuant to section 241(b)(2)(E)(i)-(vi) of the Act. Where the Department cannot remove an arriving alien under section 241(b)(1)(A) or (B) of the Act, acceptance is not required to remove an alien to a receiving country pursuant to section 241(b)(1)(C)(i)-(iii) of the Act.

(f) Interest of the United States controlling. The Secretary or his designee may designate a country previously identified in section 241(b)(2)(A)-(D) of the Act when selecting a removal country under section 241(b)(2)(E) of the Act (and may designate a country previously identified in section 241(b)(1)(A) or (B) of the Act when selecting an alternative removal country under subsection 241(b)(1)(C) of the Act) if the Secretary or his designee determines that such designation is in the best interests of the United States.

(g) Limitation on construction. Nothing in this section shall be construed to create any substantive or procedural right or benefit that is legally enforceable by any party against the United States or its agencies or officers or any other person.

HISTORY:

[67 FR 19508, 19511, Apr. 22, 2002, as confirmed at 68 FR 4364, 4367, Jan. 29, 2003; 70 FR 661, 673, Jan. 5, 2005]

§§ 241.16 — 241.19 [Reserved]

[NO TEXT IN ORIGINAL]

HISTORY:

[62 FR 10312, 10378, March 6, 1997]

Subpart B

Deportation of Excluded Aliens (For Hearings Commenced Prior to April 1, 1997)

§ 241.20 Proceedings commenced prior to April 1, 1997.

Subpart B of 8 CFR part 241 applies to exclusion proceedings commenced prior to April 1, 1997. All references to the Act contained in this subpart are references to the Act in effect prior to April 1, 1997.

HISTORY:

[62 FR 10312, 10381, March 6, 1997]

§ 241.21 Stay of deportation of excluded alien.

The district director in charge of the port of arrival may stay the immediate deportation of an excluded alien pursuant to sections 237 (a) and (d) of the Act under such conditions as he or she may prescribe.

HISTORY:

[62 FR 10312, 10381, March 6, 1997]

§ 241.22 Notice to surrender for deportation.

An alien who has been finally excluded pursuant to 8 CFR part 240, subpart D may at any time surrender himself or herself to the custody of the Service and shall surrender to such custody upon notice in writing of the time and place for his or her surrender. The Service may take the alien into custody at any time. An alien taken into custody either upon notice to surrender or by arrest shall not be deported less than 72 hours thereafter without his or her consent thereto filed in writing with the district director in charge of the place of his or her detention. An alien in foreign contiguous territory shall be informed that he or she may remain there in lieu of surrendering to the Service, but that he or she will be deemed to have acknowledged the execution of the order of exclusion and deportation in his or her case upon his or her failure to surrender at the time and place prescribed.

HISTORY:
[62 FR 10312, 10381, March 6, 1997]

§ 241.23 Cost of maintenance not assessed.

A claim pursuant to section 237(a)(1) of the Act shall be established to the satisfaction of the district director in charge of the port of arrival, from whose adverse decision no appeal shall lie. The district director shall afford the line a reasonable time within which to submit affidavits and briefs to support its claim.

HISTORY:
[62 FR 10312, 10381, March 6, 1997]

§ 241.24 Notice to transportation line of alien's exclusion.

(a) An excluded alien shall, immediately or as promptly as the circumstances permit, be offered for deportation to the master, commanding officer, purser, person in charge, agent, owner, or consignee of the vessel or aircraft on which the alien is to be deported, as determined by the district director, with a written notice specifying the cause of exclusion, the class of travel in which such alien arrived and is to be deported, and with the return of any documentation that will assist in effecting his or her deportation. If special care and attention are required, the provisions of § 241.10 shall apply.

(b) Failure of the carrier to accept for removal an alien who has been ordered excluded and deported shall result in the carrier being assessed any costs incurred by the Service for detention after the carrier's failure to accept the alien for removal including the cost of any transportation. The User Fee Account shall not be assessed for expenses incurred because of the carrier's violation of the provisions of section 237 of the Act and this paragraph. The Service will, at the carrier's option, retain custody of the excluded alien for an additional 7 days beyond the date of the deportation/exclusion order. If, after the third day of this additional 7-day period, the carrier has not made all the necessary transportation arrangements for the excluded alien to be returned to his or her point of embarkation by the end of the additional 7-day period, the Service will make the arrangements and bill the carrier for its costs.

HISTORY:
[62 FR 10312, 10381, March 6, 1997]

§ 241.25 Deportation.

(a) Definitions of terms. For the purposes of this section, the following terms mean:

(1) Adjacent island — as defined in section 101(b)(5) of the Act.

(2) Foreign contiguous territory — any country sharing a common boundary with the United States.

(3) Residence in foreign contiguous territory or adjacent island — any physical presence, regardless of intent, in a foreign contiguous territory or an adjacent island if the government of such territory or island agrees to accept the alien.

(4) Aircraft or vessel — any conveyance and other mode of travel by which arrival is effected.

(5) Next available flight — the carrier's next regularly scheduled departure to the excluded alien's point of embarkation regardless of seat availability. If the carrier's next regularly scheduled departure to the excluded aliens point of embarkation is full, the carrier has the option of arranging for return transportation on other carriers which service the excluded aliens point of embarkation.

(b) Place to which deported. Any alien (other than an alien crewmember or an alien who boarded an aircraft or vessel in foreign contiguous territory or an adjacent island) who is ordered excluded shall be deported to the country where the alien boarded the vessel or aircraft on which the alien arrived in the United States. Otherwise, the Secretary may, as a matter of discretion, deport the alien to the country of which the alien is a subject, citizen, or national; the country where the alien was born; the country where the alien has a residence; or any other country.

(c) Contiguous territory and adjacent islands. Any alien ordered excluded who boarded an aircraft or vessel in foreign contiguous territory or in any adjacent island shall be deported to such foreign contiguous territory or adjacent island if the alien is a native, citizen, subject, or national of such foreign contiguous territory or adjacent island, or if the alien has a residence in such foreign contiguous territory or adjacent island. Otherwise, the alien shall be deported, in the first instance, to the country in which is located the port at which the alien embarked for such foreign contiguous territory or adjacent island.

(d) Land border pedestrian arrivals. Any alien ordered excluded who arrived at a land border on foot shall be deported in the same manner as if the alien had boarded a vessel or aircraft in foreign contiguous territory.

HISTORY:
[62 FR 10312, 10381, March 6, 1997; 70 FR 661, 673, Jan. 5, 2005]

§§ 241.26 — 241.29 [Reserved]

[NO TEXT IN ORIGINAL]

Subpart C

Deportation of Aliens in the United States (For Hearings Commenced Prior to April 1, 1997)

§ 241.30 Proceedings commenced prior to April 1, 1997.

Subpart C of 8 CFR part 241 applies to deportation proceedings commenced prior to April 1, 1997. All references to the Act contained in this subpart are references to the Act in effect prior to April 1, 1997.

HISTORY:
[62 FR 10312, 10382, March 6, 1997]

§ 241.31 Final order of deportation.

An order of deportation becomes final in accordance with 8 CFR 1241.31.

HISTORY:
[62 FR 10312, 10382, March 6, 1997; 70 FR 661, 674, Jan. 5, 2005]

§ 241.32 Warrant of deportation.

A Form I-205, Warrant of Deportation, based upon the final administrative order of deportation in the alien's case shall be issued by a district director. The district director shall exercise the authority contained in section 243 of the Act to determine at whose expense the alien shall be deported and whether his or her mental or physical condition requires personal care and attention en route to his or her destination.

HISTORY:
[62 FR 10312, 10382, March 6, 1997]

§ 241.33 Expulsion.

(a) Execution of order. Except in the exercise of discretion by the district director, and for such reasons as are set forth in § 212.5(b) of this chapter, once an order of deportation becomes final, an alien shall be taken into custody and the order shall be executed. An order of deportation becomes final in accordance with 8 CFR 1241.31.

(b) Service of decision. In the case of an order entered by any of the authorities enumerated above, the order shall be executed no sooner than 72 hours after service of the decision, regardless of whether the alien is in Service custody, provided that such period may be waived on the knowing and voluntary request of the alien. Nothing in this paragraph shall be construed, however, to preclude assumption of custody by the Service at the time of issuance of the final order.

HISTORY:
[62 FR 10312, 10382, March 6, 1997; 65 FR 82254, 82256, Dec. 28, 2000; 66 FR 7863, Jan. 26, 2001; 70 FR 661, 674, Jan. 5, 2005]

PART 244

TEMPORARY PROTECTED STATUS FOR NATIONALS OF DESIGNATED STATES

Rule

AUTHORITY NOTE APPLICABLE TO ENTIRE PART:

AUTHORITY:
8 U.S.C. 1103, 1254, 1254a note, 8 CFR part 2.

§ 244.1 Definitions.

As used in this part:

Brief, casual, and innocent absence means a departure from the United States that satisfies the following criteria:

(1) Each such absence was of short duration and reasonably calculated to accomplish the purpose(s) for the absence;

(2) The absence was not the result of an order of deportation, an order of voluntary departure, or an administrative grant of voluntary departure without the institution of deportation proceedings; and

(3) The purposes for the absence from the United States or actions while outside of the United States were not contrary to law.

Charging document means the written instrument which initiates a proceeding before an Immigration Judge. For proceedings initiated prior to April 1, 1997, these documents include an Order to Show Cause, a Notice to Applicant for Admission Detained for Hearing before Immigration Judge, and a Notice of Intention to Rescind and Request for Hearing by Alien. For proceedings initiated after April 1, 1997, these documents include a Notice to Appear, a Notice of Referral to Immigration Judge, and a Notice of Intention to Rescind and Request for Hearing by Alien.

Continuously physically present means actual physical presence in the United States for the entire period specified in the regulations. An alien shall not be considered to have failed to maintain continuous physical presence in the United States by virtue of brief, casual, and innocent absences as defined within this section.

Continuously resided means residing in the United States for the entire period specified in the regulations. An alien shall not be considered to have failed to maintain continuous residence in the United States by reason of a brief, casual and innocent absence as defined within this section or due merely to a brief temporary trip abroad required by emergency or extenuating circumstances outside the control of the alien.

Felony means a crime committed in the United States, punishable by imprisonment for a term of more than one year, regardless of the term such alien actually served, if any, except: When the offense is defined by the State as a misdemeanor and the sentence actually imposed is one year or less regardless of the term such alien actually served. Under this exception for purposes of section 244 of the Act, the crime shall be treated as a misdemeanor.

Foreign state means any foreign country or part thereof as designated by the Attorney General pursuant to section 244 of the Act.

Misdemeanor means a crime committed in the United States, either:

(1) Punishable by imprisonment for a term of one year or less, regardless of the term such alien actually served, if any, or

(2) A crime treated as a misdemeanor under the term "felony" of this section.

For purposes of this definition, any crime punishable by imprisonment for a maximum term of five days or less shall not be considered a felony or misdemeanor.

Prima facie means eligibility established with the filing of a completed application for Temporary Protected Status containing factual information that if unrebutted will establish a claim of eligibility under section 244 of the Act.

Register means to properly file, with the director, a completed application, with proper fee, for Temporary Protected Status during the registration period designated under section 244(b) of the Act.

HISTORY:

[46 FR 25598, May 8, 1981, as amended at 55 FR 24859, June 19, 1990; 60 FR 37328, July 20, 1995; redesignated at 62 FR 10312, 10367, 10382, March 6, 1997; 63 FR 63593, 63595, Nov. 16, 1998; 64 FR 4780, 4781, Feb. 1, 1999, as confirmed at 65 FR 82256, 82257, Dec. 28, 2000; 66 FR 7863, Jan. 26, 2001]

§ 244.2 Eligibility.

Except as provided in §§ 244.3 and 244.4, an alien may in the discretion of the director be granted Temporary Protected Status if the alien establishes that he or she:

(a) Is a national, as defined in section 101(a)(21) of the Act, of a foreign state designated under section 244(b) of the Act;

(b) Has been continuously physically present in the United States since the effective date of the most recent designation of that foreign state;

(c) Has continuously resided in the United States since such date as the Attorney General may designate;

(d) Is admissible as an immigrant except as provided under § 244.3;

(e) Is not ineligible under § 244.4; and

(f)(1) Registers for Temporary Protected Status during the initial registration period announced by public notice in the Federal Register, or

(2) During any subsequent extension of such designation if at the time of the initial registration period:

(i) The applicant is a nonimmigrant or has been granted voluntary departure status or any relief from removal;

(ii) The applicant has an application for change of status, adjustment of status, asylum, voluntary departure, or any relief from removal which is pending or subject to further review or appeal;

(iii) The applicant is a parolee or has a pending request for reparole; or

(iv) The applicant is a spouse or child of an alien currently eligible to be a TPS registrant.

(3) Eligibility for late initial registration in a currently designated foreign state shall also continue until January 15, 1999, for any applicant who would have been eligible to apply previously if paragraph (f)(2) of this section as revised had been in effect before November 16, 1998.

(g) Has filed an application for late registration with the appropriate Service director within a 60-day period immediately following the expiration or termination of conditions described in paragraph (f)(2) of this section.

HISTORY:

[52 FR 24982, July 2, 1987; redesignated at 62 FR 10312, 10367, 10382, March 6, 1997; 63 FR 63593, 63595, Nov. 16, 1998]

§ 244.3 Applicability of grounds of inadmissibility.

(a) Grounds of inadmissibility not to be applied. Paragraphs (4), (5)(A) and (B), and (7)(A)(i) of section 212(a) of the Act shall not render an alien ineligible for Temporary Protected Status.

(b) Waiver of grounds of inadmissibility. Except as provided in paragraph (c) of this section, USCIS may waive any other provision of section 212(a) of the Act in the case of individual aliens for humanitarian purposes, to assure family unity, or when the granting of such a waiver is in the public interest. If an alien is inadmissible on grounds which may be waived as set forth in this paragraph, he or she shall be advised of the procedures for applying for a waiver.

(c) Grounds of inadmissibility that may not be waived. USCIS may not waive the following provisions of section 212(a) of the Act:

(1) Paragraphs (2)(A)(i), (2)(B), and (2)(C) (relating to criminals and drug offenses);

(2) Paragraphs (3)(A), (3)(B), (3)(C), and (3)(D) (relating to national security); or

(3) Paragraph (3)(E) (relating to those who assisted in the Nazi persecution).

HISTORY:

[56 FR 619, Jan. 7, 1991.; 58 FR 58937, Nov. 5, 1993; redesignated at 62 FR 10312, 10367, 10382, March 6, 1997; 76 FR 53764, 53791, Aug. 29, 2011]

§ 244.4 Ineligible aliens.

An alien is ineligible for Temporary Protected Status if the alien:

(a) Has been convicted of any felony or two or more misdemeanors, as defined in § 244.1, committed in the United States, or

(b) Is an alien described in section 208(b)(2)(A) of the Act.

HISTORY:

[56 FR 619, Jan. 7, 1991, as amended at 56 FR 23497, May 22, 1991; redesignated at 62 FR 10312, 10367, 10382, March 6, 1997; 63 FR 63593, 63596, Nov. 16, 1998; 76 FR 53764, 53791, Aug. 29, 2011]

§ 244.5 Temporary treatment benefits for eligible aliens.

(a) Prior to the registration period. Prior to the registration period established by DHS, a national of a foreign state designated by DHS shall be afforded temporary treatment benefits upon the filing, after the effective date of such designation, of a completed application for Temporary Protected Status which establishes the alien's prima facie eligibility for benefits under section 244 of the Act. This application may be filed without fee. Temporary treatment benefits, if granted, shall terminate unless the registration fee is paid or a waiver is sought within the first thirty days of the registration period designated by DHS. If the registration fee is paid or a waiver is sought within such thirty day period, temporary treatment benefits shall continue until terminated under § 244.13. The denial of temporary treatment benefits prior to the registration period designated by DHS shall be without prejudice to the filing of an application for Temporary Protected Status during such registration period.

(b) During the registration period. Upon the filing of an application for Temporary Protected Status, the alien shall be afforded temporary treatment benefits, if the application establishes the alien's prima facie eligibility for Temporary Protected Status. Such temporary treatment benefits shall continue until terminated under § 244.13.

(c) Denied benefits. There shall be no appeal from the denial of temporary treatment benefits.

HISTORY:

[56 FR 619, May 22, 1991, as amended at 56 FR 23497, May 22, 1991; redesignated at 62 FR 10312, 10367, 10382, March 6, 1997; 63 FR 63593, 63596, Nov. 16, 1998; 76 FR 53764, 53791, Aug. 29, 2011]

§ 244.6 Application.

(a) An application for Temporary Protected Status (TPS) must be submitted in accordance with the form instructions, the applicable country-specific Federal Register notice that announces the procedures for TPS registration or re-registration and, except as otherwise provided in this section, with the appropriate fees as described in 8 CFR part 106.

(b) An applicant for TPS may also request an employment authorization document under 8 CFR part 274a by filing an Application for Employment Authorization in accordance with the form instructions and in accordance with 8 CFR 106.2 and 106.3.

HISTORY:

[56 FR 619, Jan. 7, 1991, as amended at 56 FR 23497, May 22, 1991; 58 FR 58937, Nov. 5, 1993; redesignated at 62 FR 10312, 10367, 10382, March 6, 1997; 63 FR 12979, 12987, March 17, 1998; 63 FR 63593, 63596, Nov. 16, 1998; 64 FR 4780, 4781, Feb. 1, 1999, as confirmed at 65 FR 82256, 82257, Dec. 28, 2000; 66 FR 7863, Jan. 26, 2001; 76 FR 53764, 53791, Aug. 29, 2011; 85 FR 46788, 46926, Aug. 3, 2020; 89 FR 6194, 6399, Jan. 31, 2024]

§ 244.7 Filing the application.

(a) An application for Temporary Protected Status must be filed on the form designated by USCIS with any prescribed fees and in accordance with the form instructions.

(b) An application for Temporary Protected Status must be filed during the registration period established by DHS, except in the case of an alien described in § 244.2(f)(2).

(c) Each applicant must pay a fee, as determined at the time of the designation of the foreign state, except as provided in § 244.5(a).

(d) If the alien has a pending deportation or exclusion proceeding before the immigration judge or Board of Immigration Appeals at the time a foreign state is designated under section 244(b) of the Act, the alien shall be given written notice concerning Temporary Protected Status. Such alien shall have the opportunity to submit an application for Temporary Protected Status to the director under paragraph (a) of this section during the published registration period unless the basis of the charging document, if established, would render the alien ineligible for Temporary Protected Status under § 244.3(c) or § 244.4. Eligibility for Temporary Protected Status in the latter instance shall be decided by the Executive Office for Immigration Review during such proceedings.

HISTORY:

[56 FR 619, Jan. 7, 1991, as amended at 56 FR 23497, May 22, 1991; 58 FR 58937, Nov. 5, 1993; redesignated at 62 FR 10312, 10367, 10382, March 6, 1997; 63 FR 63593, 63596, Nov. 16, 1998; 74 FR 26933, 26940, June 5, 2009; 76 FR 53764, 53791, Aug. 29, 2011, as corrected at 76 FR 73475, Nov. 29, 2011]

§ 244.8 Appearance.

The applicant may be required to appear in person before an immigration officer. The applicant may be required to present documentary evidence to establish his or her eligibility. The applicant may have a representative as defined in § 292.1 of this chapter present during any examination. Such representative shall not directly participate in the examination; however, such representative may consult with and provide advice to the applicant. The record of examination shall consist of the application, documents relating to the application, and the decision of the director.

HISTORY:

[56 FR 619, Jan. 7, 1991, as amended at 56 FR 23497, May 22, 1991; redesignated at 62 FR 10312, 10367, 10382, March 6, 1997; 63 FR 63593, 63596, Nov. 16, 1998]

§ 244.9 Evidence.

(a) Documentation. Applicants shall submit all documentation as required in the instructions or requested by the Service. The Service may require proof of unsuccessful efforts to obtain documents claimed to be unavailable. If any required document is unavailable, an affidavit or other credible evidence may be submitted.

(1) Evidence of identity and nationality. Each application must be accompanied by evidence of the applicant's identity and nationality, if available. If these documents are unavailable, the applicant shall file an affidavit showing proof of unsuccessful efforts to obtain such identity documents, explaining why the consular process is unavailable, and affirming that he or she is a national of the designated foreign state. A personal interview before an immigration officer shall be required for each applicant who fails to provide documentary proof of identity or nationality. During this interview, the applicant may present any secondary evidence that he or she feels would be helpful in showing nationality. Acceptable evidence in descending order of preference may consist of:

(i) Passport;

(ii) Birth certificate accompanied by photo identification; and/or

(iii) Any national identity document from the alien's country of origin bearing photo and/or fingerprint.

(2) Proof of residence. Evidence to establish proof of continuous residence in the United States during the requisite period of time may consist of any of the following:

(i) Employment records, which may consist of pay stubs, W-2 Forms, certification of the filing of Federal, State, or local income tax returns; letters from employer(s) or, if the applicant has been self employed, letters from banks, and other firms with whom he or she has done business. In all of the above, the name of the alien and the name of the employer or other interested organization must appear on the form or letter, as well as relevant dates. Letters from employers must be in affidavit form, and shall be signed and attested to by the employer under penalty of perjury. Such letters from employers must include:

(A) Alien's address(es) at the time of employment;

(B) Exact period(s) of employment;

(C) Period(s) of layoff; and

(D) Duties with the company.

(ii) Rent receipts, utility bills (gas, electric, telephone, etc.), receipts, or letters from companies showing the dates during which the applicant received service;

(iii) School records (letters, report cards, etc.) from the schools that the applicant or his or her children have attended in the United States showing name of school and period(s) of school attendance;

(iv) Hospital or medical records showing medical treatment or hospitalization of the applicant or his or her children, showing the name of the medical facility or physician as well as the date(s) of the treatment or hospitalization;

(v) Attestations by churches, unions, or other organizations of the applicant's residence by letter which:

(A) Identifies applicant by name;

(B) Is signed by an official whose title is also shown;

(C) Shows inclusive dates of membership;

(D) States the address where applicant resided during the membership period;

(E) Includes the seal of the organization impressed on the letter or is on the letterhead of the organization, if the organization has letterhead stationery;

(F) Establishes how the attestor knows the applicant; and

(G) Establishes the origin of the information being attested to.

(vi) Additional documents to support the applicant's claim, which may include:

(A) Money order receipts for money sent in or out of the country;

(B) Passport entries;

(C) Birth certificates of children born in the United States;

(D) Bank books with dated transactions;

(E) Correspondence between the applicant and other persons or organizations;

(F) Social Security card;

(G) Selective Service card;

(H) Automobile license receipts, title, vehicle registration, etc;

(I) Deeds, mortgages, contracts to which applicant has been a party;

(J) Tax receipts;

(K) Insurance policies, receipts, or letters; and/or

(L) Any other relevant document.

(3) Evidence of eligibility under section 244(c)(2) of the Act. An applicant has the burden of showing that he or she is eligible for benefits under this part.

(4) Evidence of valid immigrant or nonimmigrant status. In the case of an alien described in § 244.2(f)(2), evidence of admission for lawful permanent residence or nonimmigrant status must be submitted by the applicant.

(b) Sufficiency of evidence. The sufficiency of all evidence will be judged according to its relevancy, consistency, credibility, and probative value. To meet his or her burden of proof the applicant must provide supporting documentary evidence of eligibility apart from his or her own statements.

(c) Failure to timely respond. Failure to timely respond to a request for information, or to appear for a scheduled interview, without good cause, will be deemed an abandonment of the application and will result in a denial of the application for lack of prosecution. Such failure shall be excused if the request for information, or the notice of the interview was not mailed to the applicant's most recent address provided to the Service.

HISTORY:

[56 FR 619, Jan. 7, 1991, as amended at 56 FR 23497, May 22, 1991; 58 FR 58937, Nov. 5, 1993; redesignated at 62 FR 10312, 10367, 10382, March 6, 1997; 63 FR 63593, 63596, Nov. 16, 1998; 76 FR 53764, 53791, Aug. 29, 2011]

§ 244.10 Decision and appeal.

(a) Temporary treatment benefits. USCIS will grant temporary treatment benefits to the applicant if the applicant establishes prima facie eligibility for Temporary Protected Status in accordance with 8 CFR 244.5.

(b) Temporary Protected Status. Upon review of the evidence presented, USCIS may approve or deny the application for Temporary Protected Status in the exercise of discretion, consistent with the standards for eligibility in 8 CFR 244.2, 244.3, and 244.4.

(c) Denial. The initial decision to deny Temporary Protected Status, a waiver of inadmissibility, or temporary treatment benefits shall be in writing served in person or by mail to the alien's most recent address provided to the Service and shall state the reason(s) for the denial. Except as otherwise provided in this section, the alien will be given written notice of his or her right to appeal. If an appeal is filed, the administrative record shall be forwarded to the USCIS AAO for review and decision, except as otherwise provided in this section.

(1) If the basis for the denial of the Temporary Protected Status constitutes a ground for deportability or inadmissibility which renders the alien ineligible for Temporary Protected Status under § 244.4 or inadmissible under § 244.3(c), the decision shall include a charging document which sets forth such ground(s).

(2) If such a charging document is issued, the alien shall not have the right to appeal the USCIS decision denying Temporary Protected Status as provided in 8 CFR 103.3. However, the decision will also apprise the alien of his or her right to a de novo determination of his or her eligibility for Temporary Protected Status in removal proceedings pursuant to section 240 of the Act and 8 CFR 1244.18.

(d) Administrative appeal. The appellate decision will be served in accordance with 8 CFR 103.8. If the appeal is dismissed, the decision must state the reasons for dismissal.

(1) If the appeal is dismissed on appeal under 8 CFR 244.18(b), the decision shall also apprise the alien of his or her right to a de novo determination of eligibility for Temporary Protected Status in removal proceedings pursuant to section 240 of the Act and 8 CFR 1244.18.

(2) If the appeal is dismissed, USCIS may issue a charging document if no charging document is presently filed with the Immigration Court.

(3) If a charging document has previously been filed or is pending before the Immigration Court, either party may move to re-calendar the case after the administrative appeal is dismissed.

(e) Grant of temporary treatment benefits.

(1) Temporary treatment benefits shall be evidenced by the issuance of an employment authorization document. The alien shall be given, in English and in the language of the designated foreign state or a language that the alien understands, a notice of the registration requirements for Temporary Protected Status and a notice of the following benefits:

(i) Temporary stay of deportation; and

(ii) Temporary employment authorization.

(2) Unless terminated under § 244.13, temporary treatment benefits shall remain in effect until a final decision has been made on the application for Temporary Protected Status.

(f) **Grant of temporary protected status.**

(1) The decision to grant Temporary Protected Status shall be evidenced by the issuance of an alien registration document. For those aliens requesting employment authorization, the employment authorization document will act as alien registration.

(2) The alien shall be provided with a notice, in English and in the language of the designated foreign state or a language that the alien understands, of the following benefits:

(i) The alien shall not be deported while maintaining Temporary Protected Status;

(ii) Employment authorization;

(iii) The privilege to travel abroad with the prior consent of the director as provided in § 244.15;

(iv) For the purposes of adjustment of status under section 245 of the Act and change of status under section 248 of the Act, the alien is considered as being in, and maintaining, lawful status as a nonimmigrant while the alien maintains Temporary Protected Status.

(v) An alien eligible to apply for Temporary Protected Status under § 244.2(f)(2), who was prevented from filing a late application for registration because the regulations failed to provide him or her with this opportunity, will be considered to have been maintaining lawful status as a nonimmigrant until the benefit is granted.

(3) The benefits contained in the notice are the only benefits the alien is entitled to under Temporary Protected Status.

(4) Such notice shall also advise the alien of the following:

(i) The alien must remain eligible for Temporary Protected Status;

(ii) The alien must register annually with the district office or service center having jurisdiction over the alien's place of residence; and

(iii) The alien's failure to comply with paragraphs (f)(4) (i) or (ii) of this section will result in the withdrawal of Temporary Protected Status, including work authorization granted under this Program, and may result in the alien's deportation from the United States.

HISTORY:

[56 FR 619, Jan. 7, 1991, as amended at 56 FR 23497, May 22, 1991; 58 FR 58937, Nov. 5, 1993; 60 FR 34090, June 30, 1995; redesignated at 62 FR 10312, 10367, 10382, March 6, 1997; 63 FR 63593, 63596, Nov. 16, 1998; 64 FR 4780, 4782, Feb. 1, 1999, as confirmed at 65 FR 82256, 82257, Dec. 28, 2000; 66 FR 7863, Jan. 26, 2001; 76 FR 53764, 53791, Aug. 29, 2011]

§ 244.11 Renewal of application; appeal to the Board of Immigration Appeals.

If a charging document is served on the alien with a notice of denial or withdrawal of Temporary Protected Status, an alien may renew the application for Temporary Protected Status in deportation or exclusion proceedings. The decision of the immigration judge as to eligibility for Temporary Protected Status may be appealed to the Board of Immigration Appeals pursuant to 8 CFR 1003. The provisions of this section do not extend the benefits of Temporary Protected Status beyond the termination of a foreign state's designation pursuant to § 244.19.

HISTORY:

[56 FR 619, Jan. 7, 1991, as amended at 56 FR 23497, May 22, 1991; redesignated at 62 FR 10312, 10367, 10382, March 6, 1997; 63 FR 63593, 63596, Nov. 16, 1998; 76 FR 53764, 53792, Aug. 29, 2011]

§ 244.12 Employment authorization.

(a) Upon approval of an application for Temporary Protected Status, USCIS shall grant an employment authorization document valid during the initial period of the foreign state's designation (and any extensions of such period).

(b) If the alien's Temporary Protected Status is withdrawn under § 244.14, employment authorization expires upon notice of withdrawal or on the date stated on the employment authorization document, whichever occurs later.

(c) If Temporary Protected Status is denied by USCIS, employment authorization shall terminate upon notice of denial or at the expiration of the employment authorization document, whichever occurs later.

(d) If the application is renewed or appealed in deportation or exclusion proceedings, or pending administrative appeal pursuant to § 244.18(b), employment authorization will be extended during the pendency of the renewal and/or appeal.

HISTORY:

[56 FR 619, Jan. 7, 1991, as amended at 56 FR 23498, May 22, 1991; 60 FR 21975, May 4, 1995; redesignated at 62 FR 10312, 10367, 10382, March 6, 1997; 63 FR 63593, 63596, Nov. 16, 1998; 64 FR 4780, 4782, Feb. 1, 1999, as confirmed at 65 FR 82256, 82257, Dec. 28, 2000; 66 FR 7863, Jan. 26, 2001; 76 FR 53764, 53792, Aug. 29, 2011]

§ 244.13 Termination of temporary treatment benefits.

(a) Temporary treatment benefits terminate upon a final determination with respect to the alien's eligibility for Temporary Protected Status.

(b) Temporary treatment benefits terminate, in any case, sixty (60) days after the date that notice is published of the termination of a foreign state's designation under section 244(b)(3) of the Act.

HISTORY:

[56 FR 619, Jan. 7, 1991.; redesignated at 62 FR 10312, 10367, 10382, March 6, 1997; 63 FR 63593, 63596, Nov. 16, 1998]

§ 244.14 Withdrawal of Temporary Protected Status.

(a) Authority of USCIS. USCIS may withdraw the status of an alien granted Temporary Protected Status under section 244 of the Act at any time upon the occurrence of any of the following:

(1) The alien was not in fact eligible at the time such status was granted, or at any time thereafter becomes ineligible for such status;

(2) The alien has not remained continuously physically present in the United States from the date the alien was first granted Temporary Protected Status under this part. For the purpose of this provision, an alien granted Temporary Protected Status under this part shall be deemed not to have failed to maintain continuous physical presence in the United States if the alien departs the United States after first obtaining permission from USCIS to travel pursuant to § 244.15;

(3) The alien fails without good cause to register with DHS annually within thirty (30) days before the end of each 12-month period after the granting of Temporary Protected Status.

(b) **Decision by USCIS.**

(1) Withdrawal of an alien's status under paragraph (a) of this section shall be in writing and served by personal service pursuant to 8 CFR 103.8(a)(2). If the ground for withdrawal is 8 CFR 244.14(a)(3), the notice shall provide that the alien has thirty (30) days within which to provide evidence of good cause for failure to register. If the alien fails to respond within thirty (30) days, Temporary Protected Status shall be withdrawn without further notice.

(2) Withdrawal of the alien's Temporary Protected Status under paragraph (b)(1) of this section may subject the applicant to exclusion or deportation proceedings under sections 235, 236, 237, 238, 240, or 241 of the Act as appropriate.

(3) If the basis for the withdrawal of Temporary Protected Status constitutes a ground of deportability or excludability which renders an alien ineligible for Temporary Protected Status under § 244.4 or inadmissible under § 244.3(c), the decision shall include a charging document which sets forth such ground(s) with notice of the right of a de novo determination of eligibility for Temporary Protected Status in deportation or exclusion proceedings. If the basis for withdrawal does not constitute such a ground, the alien shall be given written notice of his or her right to appeal to the AAU. Upon receipt of an appeal, the administrative record will be forwarded to the AAU for review and decision pursuant to the authority delegated under § 103.1(f)(2). Temporary Protected Status benefits will be extended during the pendency of an appeal.

(c) Decision by AAU. If a decision to withdraw Temporary Protected Status is entered by the AAU, the AAU shall notify the alien of the decision and the right to a de novo determination of eligibility for Temporary Protected Status in deportation or exclusion proceedings, if the alien is then deportable or excludable, as provided by § 244.10(d).

HISTORY:

[56 FR 619, Jan. 7, 1991, as amended at 56 FR 23498, May 22,

1991; redesignated at 62 FR 10312, 10367, 10382, March 6, 1997; 63 FR 63593, 63596, Nov. 16, 1998; 76 FR 53764, 53792, Aug. 29, 2011, as corrected at 76 FR 73475, Nov. 29, 2011]

§ 244.15 Travel abroad.

(a) After the grant of Temporary Protected Status, the alien must remain continuously physically present in the United States under the provisions of section 244(c)(3)(B) of the Act. The grant of Temporary Protected Status shall not constitute permission to travel abroad. Permission to travel may be granted by the director pursuant to the Service's advance parole provisions. There is no appeal from a denial of advance parole.

(b) Failure to obtain advance parole prior to the alien's departure from the United States may result in the withdrawal of Temporary Protected Status and/or the institution or recalendering of deportation or exclusion proceedings against the alien.

HISTORY:

[56 FR 619, Jan. 7, 1991, as amended at 56 FR 23498, May 22, 1991; redesignated at 62 FR 10312, 10367, 10382, March 6, 1997; 63 FR 63593, 63597, Nov. 16, 1998; 64 FR 4780, 4782, Feb. 1, 1999, as confirmed at 65 FR 82256, 82257, Dec. 28, 2000; 66 FR 7863, Jan. 26, 2001]

§ 244.16 Confidentiality.

The information contained in the application and supporting documents submitted by an alien shall not be released in any form whatsoever to a third party requester without a court order, or the written consent of the alien. For the purpose of this provision, a third party requester means any requester other than the alien, his or her authorized representative, an officer of DHS, or any federal or State law enforcement agency. Any information provided under this part may be used for purposes of enforcement of the Act or in any criminal proceeding.

HISTORY:

[56 FR 619, Jan. 7, 1991.; redesignated at 62 FR 10312, 10367, 10382, March 6, 1997; 76 FR 53764, 53792, Aug. 29, 2011]

§ 244.17 Periodic registration.

(a) Aliens granted Temporary Protected Status must re-register periodically in accordance with USCIS instructions. Such registration applies to nationals of those foreign states designated for more than one year by DHS or where a designation has been extended for a year or more. Applicants for re-registration must apply during the period provided by USCIS. Re-registration applicants do not need to pay the fee that was required for initial registration except the biometric services fee, unless that fee is waived in the applicable form instructions, and if requesting an employment authorization document, the application fee for an Application for Employment Authorization. By completing the application, applicants attest to their continuing eligibility. Such applicants do not need to submit additional supporting documents unless USCIS requests that they do so.

(b) If an alien fails to register without good cause, USCIS will withdraw Temporary Protected Status. USCIS may, for good cause, accept and approve an untimely registration request.

HISTORY:

[56 FR 619, Jan. 7, 1991, as amended at 56 FR 23498, May 22, 1991; 60 FR 21975, May 4, 1995; redesignated at 62 FR 10312, 10367, 10382, March 6, 1997; 63 FR 63593, 63597, Nov. 16, 1998; 76 FR 53764, 53792, Aug. 29, 2011; 5 FR 46788, 46926, Aug. 3, 2020; 89 FR 6194, 6399, Jan. 31, 2024]

§ 244.18 Issuance of charging documents; detention.

(a) A charging document may be issued against an alien granted Temporary Protected Status on grounds of deportability or excludability which would have rendered the alien statutorily ineligible for such status pursuant to §§ 244.3(c) and 244.4. Aliens shall not be deported for a particular offense for which the Service has expressly granted a waiver. If the alien is deportable on a waivable ground, and no such waiver for the charged offense has been previously granted, then the alien may seek such a waiver in deportation or exclusion proceedings. The charging document shall constitute notice to the alien that his or her status in the United States is subject to withdrawal. A final order of deportation or exclusion against an alien granted Temporary Protected Status shall constitute a withdrawal of such status.

(b) The filing of the charging document by DHS with the Immigration Court renders inapplicable any other administrative, adjudication or review of eligibility for Temporary Protected Status. The alien shall have the right to a de novo determination of his or her eligibility for Temporary Protected Status in removal proceedings pursuant to section 240 of the Act and 8 CFR 1244.18. Review by the Board of Immigration Appeals shall be the exclusive administrative appellate review procedure. If an appeal is already pending before the Administrative Appeals Office (AAO), USCIS will notify the AAO of the filing of the charging document, in which case the pending appeal shall be dismissed and the record of proceeding returned to the jurisdiction where the charging document was filed.

(c) Upon denial of Temporary Protected Status by the Administrative Appeals Unit, the Administrative Appeals Unit shall immediately forward the record of proceeding to the director having jurisdiction over the alien's place of residence. The director shall, as soon as practicable, file a charging document with the Immigration Court if the alien is then deportable or excludable under section 241(a) or section 212(a) of the Act, respectively.

(d) An alien who is determined by USCIS deportable or inadmissible upon grounds which would have rendered the alien ineligible for such status as provided in 8 CFR 244.3(c) and 8 CFR 244.4 may be detained under the provisions of this chapter pending removal proceedings. Such alien may be removed from the United States upon entry of a final order of removal.

HISTORY:

[56 FR 619, Jan. 7, 1991, as amended at 56 FR 23498, May 22, 1991; 60 FR 34090, June 30, 1995; redesignated at 62 FR 10312, 10367, 10382, March 6, 1997; 63 FR 63593, 63597, Nov. 16, 1998; 64 FR 4780, 4782, Feb. 1, 1999, as confirmed at 65 FR 82256, 82257, Dec. 28, 2000; 66 FR 7863, Jan. 26, 2001; 76 FR 53764, 53792, Aug. 29, 2011]

§ 244.19 Termination of designation.

Upon the termination of designation of a foreign state, those nationals afforded temporary Protected Status shall, upon the sixtieth (60th) day after the date notice of termination is published in the Federal Register, or on the last day of the most recent extension of designation by the Attorney General, automatically and without further notice or right of appeal, lose Temporary Protected Status in the United States. Such termination of a foreign state's designation is not subject to appeal.

HISTORY:

[56 FR 619, Jan. 7, 1991.; redesignated at 62 FR 10312, 10367, 10382, March 6, 1997; 63 FR 63593, 63597, Nov. 16, 1998]

§ 244.20 [This section was removed. See 75 FR 58962, 58990, Sept. 24, 2010.]

[NO TEXT IN ORIGINAL]

HISTORY:

[57 FR 34507, Aug. 5, 1992; redesignated at 62 FR 10312, 10367, 10382, March 6 1997]

AUTHORITY:

(8 U.S.C. 1103, 1254, 1254a note, 8 CFR part 2.)

PART 245

ADJUSTMENT OF STATUS TO THAT OF PERSON ADMITTED FOR PERMANENT RESIDENCE

Rule

Rule

AUTHORITY NOTE APPLICABLE TO ENTIRE PART:

AUTHORITY:

8 U.S.C. 1101, 1103, 1182, 1252, 1255; Pub. L. 105-100, section 202, 111 Stat. 2160, 2193; Pub. L. 105-277, section 902, 112 Stat. 2681; Pub. L. 110-229, tit. VII, 122 Stat. 754; 8 CFR part 2.

§ 245.1 Eligibility.

(a) General. Any alien who is physically present in the United States, except for an alien who is ineligible to apply for adjustment of status under paragraph (b) or (c) of this section, may apply for adjustment of status to that of a lawful permanent resident of the United States if the applicant is eligible to receive an immigrant visa and an immigrant visa is immediately available at the time of filing of the application. A special immigrant described under section 101(a)(27)(J) of the Act shall be deemed, for the purpose of applying the adjustment to status provisions of section 245(a) of the Act, tohave been paroled into the United States, regardless of the actual method of entry into the United States.

(b) Restricted aliens. The following categories of aliens are ineligible to apply for adjustment of status to that of a lawful permanent resident alien under section 245 of the Act, unless the alien establishes eligibility under the provisions of section 245(i) of the Act and § 245.10, is not included in the categories of aliens prohibited from applying for adjustment of status listed in § 245.1(c), is eligible to receive an immigrant visa, and has an immigrant visa immediately available at the time of filing the application for adjustment of status:

(1) Any alien who entered the United States in transit without a visa;

(2) Any alien who, on arrival in the United States, was serving in any capacity on board a vessel or aircraft or was destined to join a vessel or aircraft in the United States to serve in any capacity thereon;

(3) Any alien who was not admitted or paroled following inspection by an immigration officer;

(4) Any alien who, on or after January 1, 1977, was employed in the United States without authorization prior to filing an application for adjustment of status. This restriction shall not apply to an alien who is:

(i) An immediate relative as defined in section 201(b) of the Act;

(ii) A special immigrant as defined in section 101(a)(27)(H) or (J) of the Act;

(iii) Eligible for the benefits of Public Law 101-238 (the Immigration Nursing Relief Act of 1989) and files an application for adjustment of status on or before October 17, 1991; or

(iv) Eligible for the benefits of Public Law 101-238 (the Immigration Nursing Relief Act of 1989), and has not entered into or continued in unauthorized employment on or after November 29, 1990.

(5) Any alien who on or after November 6, 1986 is not in lawful immigration status on the date of filing his or her application for adjustment of status, except an applicant who is an immediate relative as defined in section 201(b) or a special immigrant as defined in section 101(a)(27)(H), (I), or (J);

(6) Any alien who files an application for adjustment of status on or after November 6, 1986, who has failed (other than through no fault of his or her own or for technical reasons) to maintain continuously a lawful status since entry into the United States, except an applicant who is an immediate relative as defined in section 201(b) of the Act or a special immigrant as defined in section 101(a)(27)(H), (I), or (J) of the Act;

(7) Any alien admitted as a visitor under the visa waiver provisions of 8 CFR 212.1(e) or (q), other than an immediate relative as defined in section 201(b) of the Act;

(8) Any alien admitted as a Visa Waiver Pilot Program visitor under the provisions of section 217 of the Act and part 217 of this chapter other than an immediate relative as defined in section 201(b) of the Act;

(9) Any alien who seeks adjustment of status pursuant to an employment-based immigrant visa petition under section 203(b) of the Act and who is not maintaining a lawful nonimmigrant status at the time he or she files an application for adjustment of status; and

(10) Any alien who was ever employed in the United States without the authorization of the Service or who has otherwise at any time violated the terms of his or her admission to the United States as a nonimmigrant, except an alien who is an immediate relative as defined in section 201(b) of the Act or a special immigrant as defined in section 101(a)(27)(H), (I), (J), or (K) of the Act. For purposes of this paragraph, an alien who meets the requirements of § 274a.12(c)(9) of this chapter shall not be deemed to have engaged in unauthorized employment during the pendency of his or her adjustment application.

(c) Ineligible aliens. The following categories of aliens are ineligible to apply for adjustment of status to that of a lawful permanent resident alien under section 245 of the Act:

(1) Any nonpreference alien who is seeking or engaging in gainful employment in the United States who is not the beneficiary of a valid individual or blanket labor certification issued by the Secretary of Labor or who is not exempt from certification requirements under § 212.8(b) of this chapter;

(2) Except for an alien who is applying for residence under the provisions of section 133 of the Immigration Act of 1990, any alien who has or had the status of an exchange visitor under section 101(a)(15)(J) of the Act and who is subject to the foreign residence requirement of section 212(e) of the Act, unless the alien has complied with the foreign residence requirement or has been granted a waiver of that requirement, under that section. An alien who has been granted a waiver under section 212(e)(iii) of the Act based on a request by a State Department of Health (or its equivalent) under Pub. L. 103-416 shall be ineligible to apply for adjustment of status under section 245 of the Act if the terms and conditions specified in section 214(l) of the Act and § 212.7(c)(9) of this chapter have not been met;

(3) Any alien who has nonimmigrant status under paragraph (15)(A), (15)(E), or (15)(G) of section 101(a) of the Act, or has an occupational status which would, if the alien were seeking admission to the United States, entitle the alien to nonimmigrant status under those paragraphs, unless the alien first executes and submits the written waiver required by section 247(b) of the Act and part 247 of this chapter;

(4) Any alien who claims immediate relative status under section 201(b) or preference status under sections 203(a) or 203(b) of the Act, unless the applicant is the beneficiary of a valid unexpired visa petition filed in accordance with part 204 of this chapter;

(5) Any alien who is already an alien lawfully admitted to the United States for permanent residence on a conditional basis pursuant to section 216 or 216A of the Act, regardless of any other quota or non-quota immigrant visa classification for which the alien may otherwise be eligible;

(6) Any alien admitted to the United States as a nonimmigrant defined in section 101(a)(15)(K) of the Act, unless:

(i) In the case of a K-1 fiance(e) under section 101(a)(15)(K)(i) of the Act or the K-2 child of a fiance(e) under section 101(a)(15)(K)(iii) of the Act, the alien is applying for adjustment of status based upon the marriage of the K-1 fiance(e) which was contracted within 90 days of entry with the United States citizen who filed a petition on behalf of the K-1 fiance(e) pursuant to § 214.2(k) of this chapter;

(ii) In the case of a K-3 spouse under section 101(a)(15)(K)(ii) of the Act or the K-4 child of a spouse under section 101(a)(15)(K)(iii) of the Act, the alien is applying for adjustment of status based upon the marriage of the K-3 spouse to the United States citizen who filed a petition on behalf of the K-3 spouse pursuant to § 214.2(k) of this chapter;

(7) A nonimmigrant classified pursuant to section 101(a)(15)(S) of the Act, unless the nonimmigrant is applying for adjustment of status pursuant to the

request of a law enforcement authority, the provisions of section 101(a)(15)(S) of the Act, and 8 CFR 245.11;

(8) Any alien who seeks to adjust status based upon a marriage which occurred on or after November 10, 1986, and while the alien was in exclusion, deportation, or removal proceedings, or judicial proceedings relating thereto.

(i) Commencement of proceedings. The period during which the alien is in deportation, exclusion, or removal proceedings or judicial proceedings relating thereto, commences:

(A) With the issuance of the Form I-221, Order to Show Cause and Notice of Hearing prior to June 20, 1991;

(B) With the filing of a Form I-221, Order to Show Cause and Notice of Hearing, issued on or after June 20, 1991, with the Immigration Court;

(C) With the issuance of Form I-122, Notice to Applicant for Admission Detained for Hearing Before Immigration Judge, prior to April 1, 1997,

(D) With the filing of a Form I-862, Notice to Appear, with the Immigration Court, or

(E) With the issuance and service of Form I-860, Notice and Order of Expedited Removal.

(ii) Termination of proceedings. The period during which the alien is in exclusion, deportation, or removal proceedings, or judicial proceedings relating thereto, terminates:

(A) When the alien departs from the United States while an order of exclusion, deportation, or removal is outstanding or before the expiration of the voluntary departure time granted in connection with an alternate order of deportation or removal;

(B) When the alien is found not to be inadmissible or deportable from the United States;

(C) When the Form I-122, I-221, I-860, or I-862 is canceled;

(D) When proceedings are terminated by the immigration judge or the Board of Immigration Appeals; or

(E) When a petition for review or an action for habeas corpus is granted by a Federal court on judicial review.

(iii) Exemptions. This prohibition shall no longer apply if:

(A) The alien is found not to be inadmissible or deportable from the United States;

(B) Form I-122, I-221, I-860, or I-862, is canceled;

(C) Proceedings are terminated by the immigration judge or the Board of Immigration Appeals;

(D) A petition for review or an action for habeas corpus is granted by a Federal court on judicial review;

(E) The alien has resided outside the United States for 2 or more years following the marriage; or

(F) The alien establishes the marriage is bona fide by providing clear and convincing evidence that the marriage was entered into in good faith and in accordance with the laws of the place where the marriage took place, was not entered into for the purpose of procuring the alien's entry as an immigrant, and no fee or other consideration was given (other than to an attorney for assistance in preparation of a lawful petition) for the filing of a petition.

(iv) Request for exemption. No application or fee is required to request the exemption under section 245(e) of the Act. The request must be made in writing and submitted with the Form I-485. Application for Permanent Residence. The request must state the basis for requesting consideration for the exemption and must be supported by documentary evidence establishing eligibility for the exemption.

(v) Evidence to establish eligibility for the bona fide marriage exemption. Section 204(g) of the Act provides that certain visa petitions based upon marriages entered into during deportation, exclusion or related judicial proceedings may be approved only if the petitioner provides clear and convincing evidence that the marriage is bona fide. Evidence that a visa petition based upon the same marriage was approved under the bona fide marriage exemption to section 204(g) of the Act will be considered primary evidence of eligibility for the bona fide marriage exemption provided in this part. The applicant will not be required to submit additional evidence to qualify for the bona fide marriage exemption provided in this part, unless the district director determines that such additional evidence is needed. In cases where the district director notifies the applicant that additional evidence is required, the applicant must submit documentary evidence which clearly and convincingly establishes that the marriage was entered into in good faith and not entered into for the purpose of procuring the alien's entry as an immigrant. Such evidence may include:

(A) Documentation showing joint ownership of property;

(B) Lease showing joint tenancy of a common residence;

(C) Documentation showing commingling of financial resources;

(D) Birth certificates of children born to the applicant and his or her spouse;

(E) Affidavits of third parties having knowledge of the bona fides of the marital relationship, or

(F) Other documentation establishing that the marriage was not entered into in order to evade the immigration laws of the United States.

(vi) Decision. An application for adjustment of status filed during the prohibited period shall be denied, unless the applicant establishes eligibility for an exemption from the general prohibition.

(vii) Denials. The denial of an application for adjustment of status because the marriage took place during the prohibited period shall be without prejudice to the consideration of a new application or a motion to reopen a previously denied application, if deportation or exclusion proceedings are terminated while the alien is in the United States. The denial shall also be without prejudice to the consideration of a new application or motion to reopen the adjustment of status application, if the applicant presents clear and convincing evidence establishing eligibility for the bona fide marriage exemption contained in this part.

(viii) Appeals. An application for adjustment of status to lawful permanent resident which is denied by the district director solely because the applicant failed to establish eligibility for the bona fide marriage exemption contained in this part may be appealed to the Associate Commissioner, Examinations, in accordance with 8 CFR part 103. The appeal to the Associate Commissioner, Examinations, shall be the single level of appellate review established by statute.

(d) Definitions —

(1) Lawful Immigration Status. For purposes of section 245(c)(2) of the Act, the term "lawful immigration status" will only describe the immigration status of an individual who is:

(i) In lawful permanent resident status;

(ii) An alien admitted to the United States in nonimmigrant status as defined in section 101(a)(15) of the Act, whose initial period of admission has not expired or whose nonimmigrant status has been extended in accordance with part 214 of this chapter;

(iii) In refugee status under section 207 of the Act, such status not having been revoked;

(iv) In asylee status under section 208 of the Act, such status not having been revoked;

(v) In parole status which has not expired, been revoked or terminated; or

(vi) Eligible for the benefits of Public Law 101-238 (the Immigration Nursing Relief Act of 1989) and files an application for adjustment of status on or before October 17, 1991.

(2) No fault of the applicant or for technical reasons. The parenthetical phrase other than through no fault of his or her own or for technical reasons shall be limited to:

(i) Inaction of another individual or organization designated by regulation to act on behalf of an individual and over whose actions the individual has no control, if the inaction is acknowledged by that individual or organization (as, for example, where a designated school official certified under § 214.2(f) of this chapter or an exchange propram sponsor under § 214.2(j) of this chapter did not provide required notification to the Service of continuation of status, or did not forward a request for continuation of status to the Service); or

(ii) A technical violation resulting from inaction of the Service (as for example, where an applicant establishes that he or she properly filed a timely request to maintain status and the Service has not yet acted on that request). An individual whose refugee or asylum status has expired through passage of time, but whose status has not been revoked, will be considered to have gone out of status for a technical reason.

(iii) A technical violation caused by the physical inability of the applicant to request an extension of nonimmigrant stay from the Service either in person or by mail (as, for example, an individual who is hospitalized with an illness at the time nonimmigrant stay expires). The explanation of such a technical violation shall be accompanied by a letter explaining the circumstances from the hospital or attending physician.

(iv) A technical violation resulting from the Service's application of the maximum five/six year period of stay for certain H-1 nurses only if the applicant was subsequently reinstated to H-1 status in accordance with the terms of Public Law 101-656 (Immigration Amendments of 1988).

(3) Effect of departure. The departure and subsequent reentry of an individual who was employed without authorization in the United States after January 1, 1977 does not erase the bar to adjustment of status in section 245(c)(2) of the Act. Similarly, the departure and subsequent reentry of an individual who has not maintained a lawful immigration status on any previous entry into the United States does not erase the bar to adjustment of status in section 245(c)(2) of the Act for any application filed on or after November 6, 1986.

(e) Special categories —

(1) Alien medical graduates. Any alien who is a medical graduate qualified for special immigrant classification under section 101(a)(27)(H) of the Act and is the beneficiary of an approved petition as required under section 204(a)(1)(E)(i) of the Act is eligible for adjustment of status. An accompanying spouse and children also may apply for adjustment of status under this section. Temporary absences from the United States for 30 days or less, during which the applicant was practicing or studying medicine, do not interrupt the continuous presence requirement. Temporary absences authorized under the Service's advance parole procedures will not be considered interruptive of continuous presence when the alien applies for adjustment of status.

(2) [Reserved]

(3) Special immigrant juveniles.

(i) Eligibility for adjustment of status. For the limited purpose of meeting one of the eligibility requirements for adjustment of status under section 245(a) of the Act, which requires that an individual be inspected and admitted or paroled, an applicant classified as a special immigrant juvenile under section 101(a)(27)(J) of the Act will be deemed to have been paroled into the United States as provided in § 245.1(a) and section 245(h) of the Act.

(ii) Bars to adjustment. An applicant classified as a special immigrant juvenile is subject only to the adjustment bar described in section 245(c)(6) of the Act. Therefore, an applicant classified as a special immigrant juvenile is barred from adjustment if deportable due to engagement in terrorist activity or association with terrorist organizations (section 237(a)(4)(B) of the Act). There is no waiver of or exemption to this adjustment bar if it applies.

(iii) Inadmissibility provisions that do not apply. The following inadmissibility provisions of section 212(a) of the Act do not apply to an applicant classified as a special immigrant juvenile and do not render the applicant ineligible for the benefit:

(A) Public charge (section 212(a)(4) of the Act);

(B) Labor certification (section 212(a)(5)(A) of the Act);

(C) Aliens present without admission or parole (section 212(a)(6)(A) of the Act);

(D) Misrepresentation (section 212(a)(6)(C) of the Act);

(E) Stowaways (section 212(a)(6)(D) of the Act);

(F) Documentation requirements for immigrants (section 212(a)(7)(A) of the Act);

(G) Aliens unlawfully present (section 212(a)(9)(B) of the Act);

(iv) Inadmissibility provisions that do apply. Except as provided for in paragraph (e)(3)(iii) of this section, all inadmissibility provisions in section 212(a) of the Act apply to an applicant classified as a special immigrant juvenile.

(v) Waivers.

(A) Pursuant to section 245(h)(2)(B) of the Act, USCIS may grant a waiver for humanitarian purposes, to assure family unity, or in the public interest for any applicable provision of section 212(a) of the Act to an applicant seeking to adjust status based upon their classification as a special immigrant juvenile, except for the following provisions:

(1) Conviction of certain crimes (section 212(a)(2)(A) of the Act) (except for a single offense of simple possession of 30 grams or less of marijuana);

(2) Multiple criminal convictions (section 212(a)(2)(B) of the Act) (except for a single offense of simple possession of 30 grams or less of marijuana);

(3) Controlled substance traffickers (section 212(a)(2)(C) of the Act) (except for a single offense of simple possession of 30 grams or less of marijuana);

(4) Security and related grounds (section 212(a)(3)(A) of the Act);

(5) Terrorist activities (section 212(a)(3)(B) of the Act);

(6) Foreign policy (section 212(a)(3)(C) of the Act); or

(7) Participants in Nazi persecution, genocide, or the commission of any act of torture or extrajudicial killing (section 212(a)(3)(E) of the Act).

(B) The relationship between an applicant classified as a special immigrant juvenile and the applicant's natural or prior adoptive parents cannot be considered a factor in issuing a waiver based on family unity under paragraph (v) of this section.

(vi) No parental immigration rights based on special immigrant juvenile classification. The natural or prior adoptive parent(s) of an applicant classified as a special immigrant juvenile will not be accorded any right, privilege, or status under the Act by virtue of their parentage. This prohibition applies to all of the applicant's natural and prior adoptive parent(s) and remains in effect even after the special immigrant juvenile becomes a lawful permanent resident or a United States citizen.

(vii) No contact. During the application or interview process, USCIS will take no action that requires an applicant classified as a special immigrant juvenile to contact the person who allegedly battered, abused, neglected, or abandoned the applicant (or the family member of such person(s)).

(f) Concurrent applications to overcome grounds of inadmissibility. Except as provided in 8 CFR parts 235 and 249, an application under this part shall be the sole method of requesting the exercise of discretion under sections 212(g), (h), (i), and (k) of the Act, as they relate to the inadmissibility of an alien in the United States.

(g) Availability of immigrant visas under section 245 and priority dates —

(1) Availability of immigrant visas under section 245. An alien is ineligible for the benefits of section 245 of the Act unless an immigrant visa is immediately available to him or her at the time the application is filed. If the applicant is a preference alien, the current Department of State Bureau of Consular Affairs Visa Bulletin will be consulted to determine whether an immigrant visa is immediately available. A preference immigrant visa is considered available for accepting and processing if the applicant has a priority date on the waiting list which is earlier than the date shown in the Bulletin (or the Bulletin shows that numbers for visa applicants in his or her category are current). Information concerning the immediate availability of an immigrant visa may be obtained at any Service office.

(2) Priority dates. The priority date of an applicant who is seeking the allotment of an immigrant visa number under one of the preference classes specified in section 203(a) or 203(b) of the Act by virtue of a valid visa petition approved in his or her behalf shall be fixed by the date on which such approved petition was filed.

(h) Conditional basis of status. Whenever an alien spouse (as defined in section 216(g)(1) of the Act), an alien son or daughter (as defined in section 216(g)(2) of the Act), an alien entrepreneur (as defined in section 216A(f)(1) of the Act), or an alien spouse or child (as defined in section 216A(f)(2) of the Act) is granted adjustment of status to that of lawful permanent residence, the alien shall be considered to have obtained such status on a conditional basis subject to the provisions of section 216 or 216A of the Act, as appropriate.

(i) Adjustment of status from K-3/K-4 status. An alien admitted to the United States as a K-3 under section 101(a)(15)(K)(ii) of the Act may apply for adjustment of status to that of a permanent resident pursuant to section 245 of the Act at any time following the approval of the Form I-130 petition filed on the alien's behalf, by the same citizen who petitioned for the alien's K-3 status. An alien admitted to the United States as a K-4 under section 101(a)(15)(K)(iii) of the Act may apply for adjustment of status to that of permanent residence pursuant to section 245 of the Act at any time following the approval of the Form I-130 petition filed on the alien's behalf, by the same citizen who petitioned for the alien's parent's K-3 status. Upon approval of the application, the director shall record his or her lawful admission for permanent residence in accordance with that section and subject to the conditions prescribed in section 216 of the Act. An alien admitted to the U.S. as a K-3/K-4 alien may not adjust to that of permanent resident status in any way other than as a spouse or child of the U.S. citizen who originally filed the petition for that alien's K-3/K-4 status.

HISTORY:

[30 FR 14778, Nov. 30, 1965; 52 FR 6321, 48084, 1987; 53 FR 24903, 30022, 1988; 54 FR 29441, 47676, (1989); 55 FR 10397, 1990; 56 FR 28040, 28313, 49840, 1991; 57 FR 56812, 56813, 1992; 58 FR 42851, Aug. 12, 1993; 59 FR 51095, Oct. 7, 1994; 60 FR 26683, May 18, 1995, as confirmed at 62 FR 18506, 18508, April 16,

1997; 60 FR 34090, June 30, 1995; 60 FR 44260, 44269, Aug. 25, 1995; 62 FR 10312, 10382, March 6, 1997; 62 FR 39417, 39424, July 23, 1997; 66 FR 42587, 42594, Aug. 14, 2001; 67 FR 49561, 49563, July 31, 2002; 71 FR 27585, 27591, May 12, 2006; 74 FR 55726, 55739, Oct. 28, 2009; 76 FR 53764, 53792, Aug. 29, 2011; 87 FR 13066, 13112, Mar. 8, 2022; 89 FR 6194, 6399, Jan. 31, 2024]

§ 245.2 Application.

(a) **General —**

(1) Jurisdiction. USCIS has jurisdiction to adjudicate an application for adjustment of status filed by any alien, unless the immigration judge has jurisdiction to adjudicate the application under 8 CFR 1245.2(a)(1).

(2) Proper filing of application —

(i) Under section 245.

(A) An immigrant visa must be immediately available in order for an alien to properly file an adjustment application under section 245 of the Act See § 245.1(g)(1) to determine whether an immigrant visa is immediately available.

(B) If, at the time of filing, approval of a visa petition filed for classification under section 201(b)(2)(A)(i), section 203(a) or section 203(b)(1), (2) or (3) of the Act would make a visa immediately available to the alien beneficiary, the alien beneficiary's adjustment application will be considered properly filed whether submitted concurrently with or subsequent to the visa petition, provided that it meets the filing requirements contained in parts 103 and 245. For any other classification, the alien beneficiary may file the adjustment application only after the Service has approved the visa petition.

(C) A visa petition and an adjustment application are concurrently filed only if:

(1) The visa petitioner and adjustment applicant each file their respective form at the same time, bundled together within a single mailer or delivery packet, with the proper filing fees on the same day and at the same Service office, or;

(2) the visa petitioner filed the visa petition, for which a visa number has become immediately available, on, before or after July 31, 2002, and the adjustment applicant files the adjustment application, together with the proper filing fee and a copy of the Form I-797, Notice of Action, establishing the receipt and acceptance by the Service of the underlying Form I-140 visa petition, at the same Service office at which the visa petitioner filed the visa petition, or;

(3) The visa petitioner filed the visa petition, for which a visa number has become immediately available, on, before, or after July 31, 2002, and the adjustment applicant files the adjustment application, together with proof of payment of the filing fee with the Service and a copy of the Form I-797 Notice of Action establishing the receipt and acceptance by the Service of the underlying Form I-140 visa petition, with the Immigration Court or the Board of Immigration Appeals when jurisdiction lies under paragraph (a)(1) of this section.

(ii) Under the Act of November 2, 1966. An application for the benefits of section 1 of the Act of November 2, 1966 is not properly filed unless the applicant was inspected and admitted or paroled into the United States subsequent to January 1, 1959. An applicant is ineligible for the benefits of the Act of November 2, 1966 unless he or she has been physically present in the United States for one year (amended from two years by the Refugee Act of 1980).

(3) Submission of documents —

(i) General. A separate application shall be filed by each applicant for benefits under section 245, or the Act of November 2, 1966. Each application shall be accompanied by an executed Form G-325A, if the applicant has reached his or her 14th birthday. Form G-325A shall be considered part of the application. An application under this part shall be accompanied by the document specified in the instructions which are attached to the application.

(ii) Under section 245. An application for adjustment of status is submitted on Form I-485, Application for Permanent Residence. The application must be accompanied by the appropriate fee as explained in the instructions to the application.

(iii) Under section 245(i). An alien who seeks adjustment of status under the provisions of section 245(i) of the Act must file Form I-485, with the required fee. The alien must also file Supplement A to Form I-485, with any required additional sum.

(iv) Under the Act of November 2, 1966. An application for adjustment of status is made on Form I-485A. The application must be accompanied by Form I-643, Health and Human Services Statistical Data Sheet. The application must include a clearance from the local police jurisdiction for any area in the United States when the applicant has lived for six months or more since his or her 14th birthday.

(4) Effect of departure —

(i) General. The effect of a departure from the United States is dependent upon the law under which the applicant is applying for adjustment.

(ii) Under section 245 of the Act.

(A) The departure from the United States of an applicant who is under exclusion, deportation, or removal proceedings shall be deemed an abandonment of the application constituting grounds for termination of the proceeding by reason of the departure. Except as provided in paragraph (a)(4)(ii)(B) and (C) of this section, the departure of an applicant who is not under exclusion, deportation, or removal proceedings shall be deemed an abandonment of the application constituting grounds for termination of any pending application for adjustment of status, unless the applicant was previously granted advance parole by the Service for such absences, and was inspected upon returning to the United States. If the adjustment application of an individual granted advance parole is subsequently denied the individual will be treated as an applicant for admission, and subject to the provisions of section 212 and 235 of the Act.

(B) The travel outside of the United States by an applicant for adjustment who is not under exclusion, deportation, or removal proceedings shall not be deemed an abandonment of the application if he or she was previously granted advance parole by the Service for such absences, and was inspected and paroled upon returning to the United States. If the adjustment of status application of such individual is subsequently denied, he or she will be treated as an applicant for admission, and subject to the provisions of section 212 and 235 of the Act.

(C) The travel outside of the United States by an applicant for adjustment of status who is not under exclusion, deportation, or removal proceeding and who is in lawful H-1 or L-1 status shall not be deemed an abandonment of the application if, upon returning to this country, the alien remains eligible for H or L status, is coming to resume employment with the same employer for whom he or she had previously been authorized to work as an H-1 or L-1 nonimmigrant, and, is in possession of a valid H or L visa (if required). The travel outside of the United States by an applicant for adjustment of status who is not under exclusion, deportation, or removal proceeding and who is in lawful H-4 or L-2 status shall not be deemed an abandonment of the application if the spouse or parent of such alien through whom the H-4 or L-2 status was obtained is maintaining H-1 or L-1 status and the alien remains otherwise eligible for H-4 or L-2 status, and, the alien is in possession of a valid H-4 or L-2 visa (if required). The travel outside of the United States by an applicant for adjustment of status, who is not under exclusion, deportation, or removal proceeding and who is in lawful K-3 or K-4 status shall not be deemed an abandonment of the application if, upon returning to this country, the alien is in possession of a valid K-3 or K-4 visa and remains eligible for K-3 or K-4 status.

(D) The travel outside of the United States by an applicant for adjustment of status who is not under exclusion, deportation, or removal proceeding and who is in lawful V status shall not be deemed an abandonment of the application if, upon returning to this country, the alien is admissible as a V nonimmigrant.

(iii) Under the Act of November 2, 1966. If an applicant who was admitted or paroled subsequent to January 1, 1959, later departs from the United States temporarily with no intention of abandoning his or her residence, and is readmitted or paroled upon return, the temporary absence shall be disregarded for purposes of the applicant's "last arrival" into the United States in regard to cases filed under section 1 of the Act of November 2, 1966.

(5) Decision —

(i) General. The applicant shall be notified of the decision of the director and, if the application is denied, the reasons for the denial.

(ii) Under section 245 of the Act. If the application is approved, the applicant's permanent residence shall be recorded as of the date of the order approving the adjustment of status. An application for adjustment of status, as a preference alien, shall not be approved until an immigrant visa number has been allocated by the Department of State. No appeal lies from the denial of an application by the director, but the applicant, if not an arriving alien, retains the right to renew his or her application in proceedings under 8 CFR part 240. Also, an applicant who is a parolee and meets the two conditions described in § 245.2(a)(1) may renew a denied application in proceedings under 8 CFR part 240 to determine admissibility. At the time of renewal of the application, an applicant does not need to meet the statutory requirement of section 245(c) of the Act, or § 245.1(g), if, in fact, those requirements were met at the time the renewed application was initially filed with the director. Nothing in this section shall entitle an alien to proceedings under section 240 of the Act who is not otherwise so entitled.

(iii) Under the Act of November 2, 1966. If the application is approved, the applicant's permanent residence shall be recorded in accordance with the provisions of section 1. No appeal lies from the denial of an application by the director, but the applicant, if not an arriving alien, retains the right to renew his or her application in proceedings under 8 CFR part 240. Also, an applicant who is a parolee and meets the two conditions described in § 245.2(a)(1) may renew a denied application in proceedings under 8 CFR part 240 to determine admissibility.

(b) Application under section 2 of the Act of November 2, 1966. An application by a native or citizen of Cuba or by his spouse or child residing in the United States with him, who was lawfully admitted to the United States for permanent residence prior to November 2, 1966, and who desires such admission to be recorded as of an earlier date pursuant to section 2 of the Act of November 2, 1966, shall be made on Form I-485A. The application shall be accompanied by the Permanent Resident Card, Form I-151 or I-551, issued to the applicant in connection with his lawful admission for permanent residence. No appeal shall lie from the decision. If the application is approved, the applicant will be furnished with a replacement of his Form I-151 or I-551 bearing the new date as of which the lawful admission for permanent residence has been recorded.

(c) Application under section 214(d) of the Act. An application for permanent resident status pursuant to section 214(d) of the Act shall be filed on Form I-485. A separate application shall be filed by each applicant. If the application is approved, USCIS shall record the lawful admission of the applicant as of the date of approval. The applicant shall be notified of the decision and, if the application is denied, of the reasons therefor. No appeal shall lie from the denial of an application but such denial shall be without prejudice to the alien's right to renew his or her application in proceedings under 8 CFR part 240.

HISTORY:

[30 FR 14778, Nov. 30, 1965; 51 FR 7432, 25357, 1986; 52 FR 34764, 1987; 54 FR 29441, 47348, 47676, 1989; 55 FR 10397, 1990; 56 FR 28042, 49841, 1991; 57 FR 56813, 1992; 58 FR 35838, July 1, 1993; 59 FR 33905, July 1, 1994; 59 FR 51095, Oct. 7, 1994; 62 FR 10312, 10383, March 6, 1997; 63 FR 70313, 70315, Dec. 21, 1998; 64 FR 29208, 29211, June 1, 1999; 66 FR 42587, 42594, Aug. 14, 2001; 66 FR 46697, 46704, Sept. 7, 2001; 67 FR 49561, 49563, July 31, 2002; 71 FR 27585, 27591, May 12, 2006; 72 FR 61791, 61792, Nov. 1, 2007; 74 FR 26933, 26940, June 5, 2009; 76 FR 53764, 53792, Aug. 29, 2011]

§ 245.3 Adjustment of status under section 13 of the Act of September 11, 1957, as amended.

Any application for benefits under section 13 of the

Act of September 11, 1957, as amended, must be filed on Form I-485 with the director having jurisdiction over the applicant's place of residence. The benefits under section 13 are limited to aliens who were admitted into the United States under section 101, paragraphs (a)(15)(A)(i), (a)(15)(A)(ii), (a)(15)(G)(i), or (a)(15)(G)(ii) of the Immigration and Nationality Act who performed diplomatic or semi-diplomatic duties and to their immediate families, and who establish that there are compelling reasons why the applicant or the member of the applicant's immediate family is unable to return to the country represented by the government which accredited the applicant and that adjustment of the applicant's status to that of an alien lawfully admitted for permanent residence would be in the national interest. Aliens whose duties were of a custodial, clerical, or menial nature, and members of their immediate families, are not eligible for benefits under section 13. In view of the annual limitation of 50 on the number of aliens whose status may be adjusted under section 13, any alien who is prima facie eligible for adjustment of status to that of a lawful permanent resident under another provision of law shall be advised to apply for adjustment pursuant to such other provision of law. An applicant for the benefits of section 13 shall not be subject to the labor certification requirement of section 212(a)(14) of the Immigration and Nationality Act. The applicant shall be notified of the decision and, if the application is denied, of the reasons for the denial and of the right to appeal under the provisions of part 103 of this chapter. Any applications pending with the Service before December 29, 1981 must be resubmitted to comply with the requirements of this section.

HISTORY:

[47 FR 44238, Oct. 7, 1982; 59 FR 33905, July 1, 1994]

AUTHORITY:

(Secs. 103, 245, of the Immigration and Nationality Act, as amended; 71 Stat. 642, as amended, sec. 17, Pub. L. 97-116, 95 Stat. 1619 (8 U.S.C. 1103, 1255, 1255b))

§ 245.4 Documentary requirements.

The provisions of part 211 of this chapter relating to the documentary requirements for immigrants shall not apply to an applicant under this part.

HISTORY:

[30 FR 14779, Nov. 30, 1965. Redesignated at 48 FR 4770, Feb. 3, 1983, and further redesignated at 52 FR 6322, Mar. 3, 1982, and further redesignated at 56 FR 49481, Oct. 2, 1991; 84 FR 41292, 41507, Aug. 14, 2019; 86 FR 14221, 14228, Mar. 15, 2021]

AUTHORITY:

(Secs. 103, 214, 245 Immigration and Nationality Act, as amended; (8 U.S.C. 1103, 1184, 8 U.S.C. 1255, Sec. 2, 96 Stat. 1157, 8 U.S.C. 1255 note))

§ 245.5 Medical examination.

Pursuant to section 232(b) of the Act, an applicant for adjustment of status shall be required to have a medical examination by a designated civil surgeon, whose report setting forth the findings of the mental and physical condition of the applicant, including compliance with section 212(a)(1)(A)(ii) of the Act, shall be incorporated into the record. A medical examination shall not be required of an applicant for adjustment of status who entered the United States as a nonimmigrant spouse, fiance, or fiancee of a United States citizen or the child of such an alien as defined in section 101(a)(15)(K) of the Act and § 214.2(k) of this chapter if the applicant was medically examined prior to, and as a condition of, the issuance of the nonimmigrant visa; provided that the medical examination must have occurred not more than 1 year prior the date of application for adjustment of status. Any applicant certified under paragraphs (1)(A)(ii) or (1)(A)(iii) of section 212(a) of the Act may appeal to a Board of Medical Officers of the U.S. Public Health Service as provided in section 234 of the Act and part 235 of this chapter.

HISTORY:

[56 FR 49841, Oct. 2, 1991; 62 FR 10312, 10384, March 6, 1997; 66 FR 42587, 42595, Aug. 14, 2001]

§ 245.6 Interview.

Each applicant for adjustment of status under this part shall be interviewed by an immigration officer. This interview may be waived in the case of a child under the age of 14; when the applicant is clearly ineligible under section 245(c) of the Act or § 245.1 of this chapter; or when it is determined by the Service that an interview is unnecessary.

HISTORY:

[57 FR 49375, Nov. 2, 1992, as confirmed at 61 FR 59825, 59827, Nov. 25, 1996]

§ 245.7 Adjustment of status of certain Soviet and Indochinese parolees under the Foreign Operations Appropriations Act for Fiscal Year 1990 (Pub. L. 101-167).

(a) Application. Each person applying for benefits under section 599E of Public Law 101-167, 103 Stat. 1195, 1263, must file an application on the form prescribed by USCIS with the fee prescribed in 8 CFR 106.2 and in accordance with the form instructions.

(b) Aliens eligible to apply for adjustment. The benefits of this section shall only apply to an alien who:

(1) Was a national of the Soviet Union, Vietnam, Laos, or Cambodia, and

(2) Was inspected and granted parole into the United States during the period beginning on August 15, 1988, and ending on September 30, 1990, after being denied refugee status.

(c) Eligibility. Benefits under Section 599E of Public Law 101-167 are limited to any alien described in paragraph (b) of this section who:

(1) Applies for such adjustment,

(2) Has been physically present in the United States for at least one year and is physically present in the United States on the date the application for such adjustment is filed,

(3) Is admissible to the United States as an immigrant, except as provided in paragraph (d) of this section, and

(4) Pays a fee for the processing of such application.

(d) Waiver of certain grounds for inadmissibility. The provisions of paragraphs (14), (15), (20), (21), (25), (28) (other than subparagraph (F), and (32) of section 212(a) of the Act shall not apply to adjustment under this section. The Attorney General may waive any other provision of section 212(a) (other than paragraph (23)(B), (27), (29), or (33)) with respect to such an adjustment for humanitarian purposes, to assure family unity, or when it is otherwise in the public interest.

(e) Date of approval. Upon approval of such an application for adjustment of status, the Attorney General shall create a record of the alien's admission as a lawful permanent resident as of the date of the alien's inspection and parole described in paragraph (b)(2) of this section.

(f) No offset in number of visas available. When an alien is granted the status of having been lawfully admitted for permanent residence under this section, the Secretary of State shall not be required to reduce the number of immigrant visas authorized to be issued under the Immigration and Nationality Act.

HISTORY:

[55 FR 24800, July 19, 1990. Redesignated at 56 FR 49841, Oct. 2, 1991; 59 FR 33905, July 1, 1994; 63 FR 12979, 12987, March 17, 1998; 74 FR 26933, 26940, June 5, 2009; 76 FR 53764, 53792, Aug. 29, 2011; 85 FR 46788, 46926, Aug. 3, 2020]

§ 245.8 Adjustment of status as a special immigrant under section 101(a)(27)(K) of the Act.

(a) Application. Each person applying for adjustment of status as a special immigrant under section 101(a)(27)(K) of the Act must file a Form I-485, Application to Register Permanent Residence or Adjust Status. Benefits under this section are limited to aliens who have served honorably (or are enlisted to serve) in the Armed Forces of the United States for at least 12 years, and their spouses and children. For purposes of this section, special immigrants described in section 101(a)(27)(K) of the Act and his or her spouse and children shall be deemed to have been paroled into the United States pursuant to section 245(g) of the Act. Each applicant must file a separate application with the appropriate fee.

(b) Eligibility. The benefits of this section shall apply only to an alien described in section 101(a)(27)(K) of the Act who applies for such adjustment. The accompanying spouse or child of an applicant for adjustment of status who benefits from Public Law 102-110 may also apply for adjustment of status. The provisions of section 245(c) of the Act do not apply to the principal Armed Forces special immigrant or to his or her spouse or child.

(c) Interview of the applicant. Upon completion of the adjustment of status interview for a special immigrant under section 101(a)(27)(K) of the Act, the director shall make a prima facie determination regarding eligibility for naturalization benefits if the applicant is to be granted status as an alien lawfully admitted for permanent residence. If the director determines that the applicant is immediately eligible for naturalization under section 328 or 329 of the Act, the director shall advise the applicant that he or she is eligible to apply for naturalization on Form N-400, Application to File Petition for Naturalization. If the applicant wishes to apply for naturalization, the director shall instruct the applicant concerning the requirements for naturalization and provide him or her with the necessary forms.

(d) Spouse or child outside the United States. When a spouse or child of an alien granted special immigrant status under section 101(a)(27)(K) of the Act is outside the United States, the principal alien may file Form I-824, Application for Action on an Approved Application or Petition, with the office which approved the original application.

(e) Removal provisions of section 237 of the Act. If the Service is made aware by notification from the appropriate executive department or by any other means that a section 101(a)(27)(K) special immigrant who has already been granted permanent residence fails to complete his or her total active duty service obligation for reasons other than an honorable discharge, the alien may become subject to the removal provisions of section 237 of the Act, provided the alien is in one or more of the classes of deportable aliens specified in section 237 of the Act. The Service shall obtain a current Form DD-214, Certificate of Release or Discharge from Active Duty, from the appropriate executive department for verification of the alien's failure to maintain eligibility.

(f) Rescission proceedings under section 246 of the Act. If the Service determines that a military special immigrant under section 101(a)(27)(K) of the Act was not in fact eligible for adjustment of status, the Service may pursue rescission proceedings under section 246 of the Act.

HISTORY:

[57 FR 33862, July 31, 1992; 58 FR 50836, Sept. 29, 1993; 62 FR 10312, 10384, March 6, 1997; 74 FR 26933, 26940, June 5, 2009]

§ 245.9 [This section was removed and reserved. See 76 FR 53764, 53793, Aug. 29, 2011.]

[NO TEXT IN ORIGINAL]

HISTORY:

[58 FR 35838, July 1, 1993; 62 FR 10312, 10384, March 6, 1997; 62 FR 63249, 63254, Nov. 28, 1997; 76 FR 53764, 53793, Aug. 29, 2011]

AUTHORITY:

(8 U.S.C. 1101, 1103, 1182, 1255; section 202, Public Law 105-100, 111 Stat. 2160, 2193; section 902, Public Law 105-277, 112 Stat. 2681; Title VII of Public Law 110-229; 8 CFR part 2.)

§ 245.10 Adjustment of status upon payment of additional sum under section 245(i).

(a) Definitions. As used in this section the term:

(1)(i) Grandfathered alien means an alien who is the beneficiary (including a spouse or child of the alien beneficiary if eligible to receive a visa under section 203(d) of the Act) of:

(A) A petition for classification under section 204 of the Act which was properly filed with the Attorney General on or before April 30, 2001, and which was approvable when filed; or

(B) An application for labor certification under section 212(a)(5)(A) of the Act that was properly filed pursuant to the regulations of the Secretary of Labor on or before April 30, 2001, and which was approvable when filed.

(ii) If the qualifying visa petition or application for labor certification was filed after January 14, 1998, the alien must have been physically present in the United States on December 21, 2000. This requirement does not apply with respect to a spouse or child accompanying or following to join a principal alien who is a grandfathered alien as described in this section.

(2) Properly filed means:

(i) With respect to a qualifying immigrant visa petition, that the application was physically received by the Service on or before April 30, 2001, or if mailed, was postmarked on or before April 30, 2001, and accepted for filing as provided in § 103.2(a)(1) and (a)(2) of this chapter; and

(ii) With respect to a qualifying application for labor certification, that the application was properly filed and accepted pursuant to the regulations of the Secretary of Labor, 20 CFR 656.21.

(3) Approvable when filed means that, as of the date of the filing of the qualifying immigrant visa petition under section 204 of the Act or qualifying application for labor certification, the qualifying petition or application was properly filed, meritorious in fact, and non-frivolous ("frivolous" being defined herein as patently without substance). This determination will be made based on the circumstances that existed at the time the qualifying petition or application was filed. A visa petition that was properly filed on or before April 30, 2001, and was approvable when filed, but was later withdrawn, denied, or revoked due to circumstances that have arisen after the time of filing, will preserve the alien beneficiary's grandfathered status if the alien is otherwise eligible to file an application for adjustment of status under section 245(i) of the Act.

(4) Circumstances that have arisen after the time of filing means circumstances similar to those outlined in § 205.1(a)(3)(i) or (a)(3)(ii) of this chapter.

(b) Eligibility. An alien who is included in the categories of restricted aliens under § 245.1(b) and meets the definition of a "grandfathered alien" may apply for adjustment of status under section 245 of the Act if the alien meets the requirements of paragraphs (b)(1) through (b)(7) of this section:

(1) Is physically present in the United States;

(2) Is eligible for immigrant classification and has an immigrant visa number immediately available at the time of filing for adjustment of status;

(3) Is not inadmissible from the United States under any provision of section 212 of the Act, or all grounds for inadmissibility have been waived;

(4) Properly files Form I-485, Application to Register Permanent Residence or Adjust Status on or after October 1, 1994, with the required fee for that application;

(5) Properly files Supplement A to Form I-485 on or after October 1, 1994;

(6) Pays an additional sum of $ 1,000, unless payment of the additional sum is not required under section 245(i) of the Act; and

(7) Will adjust status under section 245 of the Act to that of lawful permanent resident of the United States on or after October 1, 1994.

(c) Payment of additional sum. An adjustment applicant filing under the provisions of section 245(i) of the Act must pay the standard adjustment application filing fee as specified in 8 CFR 106.2. Each application submitted under the provisions of section 245(i) of the Act must be submitted with an additional sum of $ 1,000. An applicant must submit the additional sum of $ 1,000 only once per application for adjustment of status submitted under the provisions of section 245(i) of the Act. However, an applicant filing under the provisions of section 245(i) of the Act is not required to pay the additional sum if, at the time the application for adjustment of status is filed, the alien is:

(1) Unmarried and less than 17 years of age;

(2) The spouse of a legalized alien, qualifies for and has properly filed Form I-817, Application for Voluntary Departure under the Family Unity Program, and submits a copy of his or her receipt or approval notice for filing Form I-817; or

(3) The child of a legalized alien, is unmarried and less than 21 years of age, qualifies for and has filed Form I-817, and submits a copy of his or her receipt or approval notice for filing Form I-817. Such an alien must pay the additional sum if he or she has reached the age of 21 years at the time of filing for adjustment of status. Such an alien must meet all other conditions for adjustment of status contained in the Act and in this chapter.

(d) Pending adjustment application with the Service or Executive Office for Immigration Review filed without Supplement A to Form I-485 and additional sum. An alien who filed an adjustment of status application with the Service in accordance with § 103.2 of this chapter will be allowed the opportunity to amend such an application to request consideration under the provisions of section 245(i) of the Act, if it appears that the alien is not otherwise ineligible for adjustment of status. The Service shall notify the applicant in writing of the Service's intent to deny the adjustment of status application, and any other requests for benefits that derive from the adjustment application, unless Supplement A to Form I-485 and any required additional sum is filed within 30 days of the date of the notice. If the application for adjustment of status is pending before the Executive Office for Immigration Review (EOIR), EOIR will allow the respondent an opportunity to amend an adjustment of status application filed in accordance with § 103.2 of this chapter (to include Supplement A to Form I-485 and proof of remittance to the INS of the required additional sum) in order to request consideration under the provisions of section 245(i) of the Act.

(e) Applications for Adjustment of Status filed before October 1, 1994. The provisions of section 245(i) of the Act shall not apply to an application for adjustment of status that was filed before October 1, 1994. The provisions of section 245(i) of the Act also shall not apply to a motion to reopen or reconsider an application for adjustment of status if the application for adjustment of status was filed before October 1, 1994. An applicant whose pre-October 1, 1994, application for adjustment of status has been denied may file a new application for adjustment of status pursuant to section 245(i) of the Act on or after October 1, 1994, provided that such new application is accompanied by: the required fee; Supplement A to Form I-485; the additional sum required by section 245(i) of the Act; and all other required initial and additional evidence.

(f) **Effect of section 245(i) on completed adjustment applications before the Service.**

(1) Any motion to reopen or reconsider before the Service alleging availability of section 245(i) of the Act must be filed in accordance with § 103.5 of this chapter. If said motion to reopen with the Service is granted, the alien must remit to the Service Supplement A to Form I-485 and the additional sum required by section 245(i) of the Act. If the alien had previously remitted Supplement A to Form I-485 and the additional sum with the application which is the subject of the motion to reopen, then no additional sum need be remitted upon such reopening.

(2) An alien whose adjustment application was adjudicated and denied by the Service because of ineligibility under section 245(a) or (c) of the Act and now alleges eligibility due to the availability of section 245(i) of the Act may file a new application for adjustment of status pursuant to section 245(i) of the Act, provided that such new application is accompanied by the required fee for the application, Supplement A to Form I-485, additional sum required by section 245(i) of the Act and all other required and additional evidence.

(g) Aliens deportable under section 237(a)(4)(B) of the Act are ineligible to adjust status. Section 237(a)(4)(B) of the Act renders any alien who has engaged, is engaged, or at any time after admission engages in any terrorist activity, as defined in section 212(a)(3)(B)(iii) of the Act, deportable. Under section 245(c)(6) of the Act, persons who are deportable under section 237(a)(4)(B) of the Act are ineligible to adjust status under section 245(a) of the Act. Any person who is deportable under section 237(a)(4)(B) of the Act is also ineligible to adjust status under section 245(i) of the Act.

(h) Asylum or diversity immigrant visa applications. An asylum application, diversity visa lottery application, or diversity visa lottery-winning letter does not serve to grandfather the alien for purposes of section 245(i) of the Act. However, an otherwise grandfathered alien may use winning a diversity visa as a basis for adjustment.

(i) Denial, withdrawal, or revocation of the approval of a visa petition or application for labor certification. The denial, withdrawal, or revocation of the approval of a qualifying immigrant visa petition, or application for labor certification, that was properly filed on or before April 30, 2001, and that was approvable when filed, will not preclude its grandfathered alien (including the grandfathered alien's family members) from seeking adjustment of status under section 245(i) of the Act on the basis of another approved visa petition, a diversity visa, or any other ground for adjustment of status under the Act, as appropriate.

(j) Substitution of a beneficiary on an application for a labor certification. Only the alien who was the beneficiary of the application for the labor certification on or before April 30, 2001, will be considered to have been grandfathered for purposes of filing an application for adjustment of status under section 245(i) of the Act. An alien who was previously the beneficiary of the application for the labor certification but was subsequently replaced by another alien on or before April 30, 2001, will not be considered to be a grandfathered alien. An alien who was substituted for the previous beneficiary of the application for the labor certification after April 30, 2001, will not be considered to be a grandfathered alien.

(k) Changes in employment. An applicant for adjustment under section 245(i) of the Act who is adjusting status through an employment-based category is not required to work for the petitioner who filed the petition that grandfathered the alien, unless he or she is seeking adjustment based on employment for that same petitioner.

(*l*) Effects of grandfathering on an alien's nonimmigrant status. An alien's nonimmigrant status is not affected by the fact that he or she is a grandfathered alien. Lawful immigration status for a nonimmigrant is defined in § 245.1(d)(1)(ii).

(m) Effect of grandfathering on unlawful presence under section (a)(9)(B) and (c) of the Act. If the alien is not in a period of stay authorized by the Attorney General, the fact that he or she is a grandfathered alien does not prevent the alien from accruing unlawful presence under section 212(a)(9)(B) and (C) of the Act.

(n) **Evidentiary requirement to demonstrate physical presence on December 21, 2000.**

(1) Unless the qualifying immigrant visa petition or application for labor certification was filed on or before January 14, 1998, a principal grandfathered alien must establish that he or she was physically present in the United States on December 21, 2000, to be eligible to apply to adjust status under section 245(i) of the Act. If no one document establishes the alien's physical presence on December 21, 2000, he or she may submit several documents establishing his or her physical presence in the United States prior to, and after December 21, 2000.

(2) To demonstrate physical presence on December 21, 2000, the alien may submit copies of documents issued by the former INS or EOIR such as arrival-departure forms or notices to appear in immigration court.

(3) To demonstrate physical presence on December 21, 2000, the alien may submit other government

documentation. Other government documentation issued by a Federal, state, or local authority must bear the signature, seal, or other authenticating instrument of such authority (if the document normally bears such instrument), be dated at the time of issuance, and bear a date of issuance not later than December 21, 2000. For this purpose, the term Federal, state, or local authority includes any governmental, educational, or administrative function operated by Federal, state, county, or municipal officials. Examples of such other documentation include, but are not limited to:

(i) A state driver's license;

(ii) A state identification card;

(iii) A county or municipal hospital record;

(iv) A public college or public school transcript;

(v) Income tax records;

(vi) A certified copy of a Federal, state, or local governmental record which was created on or prior to December 21, 2000, shows that the applicant was present in the United States at the time, and establishes that the applicant sought on his or her own behalf, or some other party sought on the applicant's behalf, a benefit from the Federal, state, or local governmental agency keeping such record;

(vii) A certified copy of a Federal, state, or local governmental record which was created on or prior to December 21, 2000, that shows that the applicant was present in the United States at the time, and establishes that the applicant submitted an income tax return, property tax payment, or similar submission or payment to the Federal, state, or local governmental agency keeping such record;

(viii) A transcript from a private or religious school that is registered with, or approved or licensed by, appropriate State or local authorities, accredited by the State or regional accrediting body, or by the appropriate private school association, or maintains enrollment records in accordance with State or local requirements or standards.

(4) To demonstrate physical presence on December 21, 2000, the alien may submit non-government documentation. Examples of documentation establishing physical presence on December 21, 2000, may include, but are not limited to:

(i) School records;

(ii) Rental receipts;

(iii) Utility bill receipts;

(iv) Any other dated receipts;

(v) Personal checks written by the applicant bearing a bank cancellation stamp;

(vi) Employment records, including pay stubs;

(vii) Credit card statements showing the dates of purchase, payment, or other transaction;

(viii) Certified copies of records maintained by organizations chartered by the Federal or State government, such as public utilities, accredited private and religious schools, and banks;

(ix) If the applicant established that a family unit was in existence and cohabiting in the United States, documents evidencing the presence of another member of the same family unit; and

(x) For applicants who have ongoing correspondence or other interaction with the Service, a list of the types and dates of such correspondence or other contact that the applicant knows to be contained or reflected in Service records.

(5)(i) The adjudicator will evaluate all evidence on a case-by-case basis and will not accept a personal affidavit attesting to physical presence on December 21, 2000, without requiring an interview or additional evidence to validate the affidavit.

(ii) In all cases, any doubts as to the existence, authenticity, veracity, or accuracy of the documentation shall be resolved by the official government record, with records of the Service and the Executive Office for Immigration Review (EOIR) having precedence over the records of other agencies. Furthermore, determinations as to the weight to be given any particular document or item of evidence shall be solely within the discretion of the adjudicating authority (i.e., the Service or EOIR). It shall be the responsibility of the applicant to obtain and submit copies of the records of any other government agency that the applicant desires to be considered in support of his or her application.

HISTORY:

[59 FR 51095, Oct. 7, 1994, as corrected at 59 FR 53020, Oct. 20, 1994; 62 FR 10312, 10384, March 6, 1997; 62 FR 39417, 39424, July 23, 1997; 62 FR 50999, 51000, Sept. 30, 1997; 62 FR 55152, 55153, Oct. 23, 1997; 66 FR 16383, 16388, Mar. 26, 2001; 76 FR 53764, 53793, Aug. 29, 2011; 85 FR 46788, 46926, Aug. 3, 2020]

§ 245.11 Adjustment of aliens in S nonimmigrant classification.

(a) Eligibility. An application on Form I-854, requesting that an alien witness or informant in S nonimmigrant classification be allowed to adjust status to that of lawful permanent resident, may only be filed by the federal or state law enforcement authority ("LEA") (which shall include a federal or state court or a United States Attorney's Office) that originally requested S classification for the alien. The completed application shall be filed with the Assistant Attorney General, Criminal Division, Department of Justice, who will forward only properly certified applications to the Commissioner, Immigration and Naturalization Service, for approval. Upon receipt of an approved Form I-854 allowing the S nonimmigrant to adjust status to that of lawful permanent resident, the alien may proceed to file with that Form, Form I-485, Application to Register Permanent Residence or Adjust Status, pursuant to the following process.

(1) Request to allow S nonimmigrant to apply for adjustment of status to that of lawful permanent resident. The LEA that requested S nonimmigrant classification for an S nonimmigrant witness or informant pursuant to section 101(a)(15)(S) of the Act may request that the principal S nonimmigrant be allowed to apply for adjustment of status by filing Form I-854 with the Assistant Attorney General, Criminal Division, in accordance with the instructions on, or attached to, that form and certifying that the alien has fulfilled the terms of his or her admission and classification. The

same Form I-854 may be used by the LEA to request that the principals nonimmigrant's spouse, married and unmarried sons and daughters, regardless of age, and parents who are in derivative S nonimmigrant classification and who are qualified family members as described in paragraph (b) of this section similarly be allowed to apply for adjustment of status pursuant to section 101(a)(15)(S) of the Act.

(2) Certification. Upon receipt of an LEA's request for the adjustment of an alien in S nonimmigrant classification on Form I-854, the Assistant Attorney General, Criminal Division, shall review the information and determine whether to certify the request to the Commissioner in accordance with the instructions on the form.

(3) Submission of requests for adjustment of status to the Commissioner. No application by an LEA on Form I-854 requesting the adjustment to lawful permanent resident status of an S nonimmigrant shall be forwarded to the Commissioner unless first certified by the Assistant Attorney General, Criminal Division.

(4) Decision on request to allow adjustment of S nonimmigrant. The Commissioner shall make the final decision on a request to allow an S nonimmigrant to apply for adjustment of status to lawful permanent resident.

(i) In the event the Commissioner decides to deny an application on Form I-854 to allow an S nonimmigrant to apply for adjustment of status, the Assistant Attorney General, Criminal Division, and the relevant LEA shall be notified in writing to that effect. The Assistant Attorney General, Criminal Division, shall concur in or object to that decision. Unless the Assistant Attorney General, Criminal Division, objects within 7 days, he or she shall be deemed to have concurred in the decision. In the event of an objection by the Assistant Attorney General, Criminal Division, the matter will be expeditiously referred to the Deputy Attorney General for a final resolution. In no circumstances shall be alien or the relevant LEA have a right of appeal from any decision to deny.

(ii) Upon approval of the request on Form I-854, the Commissioner shall forward a copy of the approved form to the Assistant Attorney General and the S nonimmigrant, notifying them that the S nonimmigrant may proceed to file Form I-485 and request adjustment of status to that of lawful permanent resident, and that, to be eligible for adjustment of status, the nonimmigrant must otherwise:

(A) Meet the requirements of paragraph (b) of this section, if requesting adjustment as a qualified family member of the certified principal S nonimmigrant witness or informant;

(B) Be admissible to the United States as an immigrant, unless the ground of inadmissibility has been waived;

(C) Establish eligibility for adjustment of status under all provisions of section 245 of the Act, unless the basis for ineligibility has been waived; and

(D) Properly file with his or her Form I-485, Application to Register Permanent Residence or Adjust Status, the approved Form I-854.

(b) Family members —

(1) Qualified family members. A qualified family member of an S nonimmigrant includes the spouse, married or unmarried son or daughter, or parent of a principal S nonimmigrant who meets the requirements of paragraph (a) of this section, provided that:

(i) The family member qualified as the spouse, married or unmarried son or daughter, or parent (as defined in section 101(b) of the Act) of the principal S nonimmigrant when the family member was admitted as or granted a change of status to that of a nonimmigrant under section 101(a)(15)(S) of the Act;

(ii) The family member was admitted in S nonimmigrant classification to accompany, or follow to join, the principal S-5 or S-6 alien pursuant to the LEA's request;

(iii) The family member is not inadmissible from the United States as a participant in Nazi persecution or genocide as described in section 212(a)(3)(E) of the Act;

(iv) The qualifying relationship continues to exist; and

(v) The principal alien has adjusted status, has a pending application for adjustment of status or is concurrently filing an application for adjustment of status under section 101(a)(15)(S) of the Act.

(vi) Paragraphs (b)(1)(iv) and (v) of this section do not apply if the alien witness or informant has died and, in the opinion of the Attorney General, was in compliance with the terms of his or her S classification under section 245(i) (1) and (2) of the Act.

(2) Other family member. The adjustment provisions in this section do not apply to a family member who has not been classified as an S nonimmigrant pursuant to a request on Form I-854 or who does not otherwise meet the requirements of paragraph (b) of this section. However, a spouse or an unmarried child who is less than 21 years old, and whose relationship to the principal S nonimmigrant or qualified family member was established prior to the approval of the principal S nonimmigrant's adjustment of status application, may be accorded the priority date and preference category of the principal S nonimmigrant or qualified family member, in accordance with the provisions of section 203(d) of the Act. Such a spouse or child:

(i) May use the principal S nonimmigrant or qualified member's priority date and category when it becomes current, in accordance with the limitations set forth in sections 201 and 202 of the Act;

(ii) May seek immigrant visa issuance abroad or adjustment of status to that of a lawful permanent resident of the United States when the priority date becomes current for the spouse's or child's country of chargeability under the fourth employment-based preference classification;

(iii) Must meet all the requirements for immigrant visa issuance or adjustment of status, unless those requirements have been waived;

(iv) Is not applying for adjustment of status under 101(a)(15)(S) of the Act, is not required to file Form I-854, and is not required to obtain LEA certification; and

(v) Will lose eligibility for benefits if the child marries or has his or her twenty-first birthday before being admitted with an immigrant visa or granted adjustment of status.

(c) Waivers of inadmissibility. An alien seeking to adjust status pursuant to the provisions of section 101(a)(15)(S) of the Act may not be denied adjustment of status for conduct or a condition that:

(1) Was disclosed to the Attorney General prior to admission; and

(2) Was specifically waived pursuant to the waiver provisions set forth at section 212(d)(1) and 212(d)(3) of the Act.

(d) Application. Each S nonimmigrant requesting adjustment of status under section 101(a)(15)(S) of the Act must:

(1) File Form I-485, with the prescribed fee, accompanied by the approved Form I-854, and the supporting documents specified in the instructions to Form I-485 and described in 8 CFR 245.2. Secondary evidence may be submitted if the nonimmigrant is unable to obtain the required primary evidence as provided in 8 CFR 103.2(b)(2). The S nonimmigrant applying to adjust must complete Part 2 of Form I-485 by checking box "h-other" and writing "S" or "S-Qualified Family Member." Qualified family members must submit documentary evidence of the relationship to the principal S nonimmigrant witness or informant.

(2) Submit detailed and inclusive evidence of eligibility for the adjustment of status benefits of S classification, which shall include:

(i) A photocopy of all pages of the alien's most recent passport or an explanation of why the alien does not have a passport; or

(ii) An attachment on a plain piece of paper showing the dates of all arrivals and departures from the United States in S nonimmigrant classification and the reason for each departure; and

(iii) Primary evidence of a qualifying relationship to the principal S nonimmigrant, such as birth or marriage certificate. If any required primary evidence is unavailable, church or school records, or other secondary evidence may be submitted. If such documents are unavailable, affidavits may be submitted as provided in 8 CFR 103.2(b)(2).

(e) Priority date. The S nonimmigrant's priority date shall be the date his or her application for adjustment of status as an S nonimmigrant is properly filed with the Service.

(f) Visa number limitation. An adjustment of status application under section 101(a)(15)(S) of the Act may be filed regardless of the availability of immigrant visa numbers. The adjustment of status application may not, however, be approved and the alien's adjustment of status to that of lawful permanent resident of the United States may not be granted until a visa number becomes available for the alien under the worldwide allocation for employment-based immigrants under section 201(d) and section 203(b)(4) of the Act. The applicant may request employment authorization or permission to travel outside the United States while the application is pending by filing an application pursuant to 8 CFR 274a.13 or 8 CFR 223.2.

(g) Filing and decision. An application for adjustment of status filed by an S nonimmigrant under section 101(a)(15)(S) of the Act shall be filed with the district director having jurisdiction over the alien's place of residence. Upon approval of adjustment of status under this section, the district director shall record the alien's lawful admission for permanent residence as of the date of such approval. The district director shall notify the Commissioner and the Assistant Attorney General, Criminal Division, of the adjustment.

(h) Removal under section 237 of the Act. Nothing in this section shall prevent an alien adjusted pursuant to the terms of these provisions from being removed for conviction of a crime of moral turpitude committed within 10 years after being provided lawful permanent residence under this section or for any other ground under section 237 of the Act.

(i) Denial of application. In the event the district director decides to deny an application on Form I-485 and an approved Form I-854 to allow an S nonimmigrant to adjust status, the Assistant Attorney General, Criminal Division, and the relevant LEA shall be notified in writing to that effect. The Assistant Attorney General, Criminal Division, shall concur in or object to that decision. Unless the Assistant Attorney General, Criminal Division, objects within 7 days, he or she shall be deemed to have concurred in the decision. In the event of an objection by the Assistant Attorney General, Criminal Division, the matter will be expeditiously referred to the Deputy Attorney General for a final resolution. In no circumstances shall the alien or the relevant LEA have a right of appeal from any decision to deny. A denial of an adjustment application under this paragraph may not be renewed in subsequent removal proceedings.

HISTORY:

[60 FR 44260, 44269, Aug. 25, 1995; 62 FR 10312, 10384, March 6, 1997; 76 FR 53764, 53793, Aug. 29, 2011]

§ 245.12 [This section was removed and reserved. See 76 FR 53764, 53793, Aug. 29, 2011.]

[NO TEXT IN ORIGINAL]

HISTORY:

[62 FR 28314, 28315, May 23, 1997, as confirmed and revised at 65 FR 20069, 20070, Apr. 14, 2000; 74 FR 26933, 26940, June 5, 2009; 76 FR 53764, 53793, Aug. 29, 2011]

AUTHORITY:

(8 U.S.C. 1101, 1103, 1182, 1255; section 202, Public Law 105-100, 111 Stat. 2160, 2193; section 902, Public Law 105-277, 112 Stat. 2681; Title VII of Public Law 110-229; 8 CFR part 2.)

§ 245.13 [This section was removed and reserved. See 76 FR 53764, 53793, Aug. 29, 2011.]

[NO TEXT IN ORIGINAL]

HISTORY:

[63 FR 27823, 27829, May 21, 1998, as confirmed and amended at

65 FR 15846, 15854, Mar. 24, 2000; 66 FR 29449, 29451, May 31, 2001; 76 FR 53764, 53793, Aug. 29, 2011]

AUTHORITY:

(8 U.S.C. 1101, 1103, 1182, 1255; section 202, Public Law 105-100, 111 Stat. 2160, 2193; section 902, Public Law 105-277, 112 Stat. 2681; Title VII of Public Law 110-229; 8 CFR part 2.)

§ 245.14 [Reserved]

[NO TEXT IN ORIGINAL]

HISTORY:

[63 FR 55007, 55012, Oct. 14, 1998; 68 FR 43901, 43921, July 25, 2003]

AUTHORITY:

(8 U.S.C. 1101, 1103, 1182, 1255; sec. 202, Pub. L. 105-100, 111 Stat. 2160, 2193; sec. 902, Pub. L. 105-277, 112 Stat. 2681; 8 CFR part 2.)

§ 245.15 Adjustment of Status of Certain Haitian Nationals under the Haitian Refugee Immigrant Fairness Act of 1998 (HRIFA).

(a) Definitions. As used in this section, the terms:

Abandoned and abandonment mean that both parents have, or the sole or surviving parent has, or in the case of a child who has been placed into a guardianship, the child's guardian or guardians have, willfully forsaken all parental or guardianship rights, obligations, and claims to the child, as well as all control over and possession of the child, without intending to transfer these rights to any specific person(s).

Guardian means a person lawfully invested (by order of a competent Federal, State, or local authority) with the power, and charged with the duty, of taking care of, including managing the property, rights, and affairs of, a child.

Orphan and orphaned refer to the involuntary detachment or severance of a child from his or her parents due to any of the following:

(1) The death or disappearance of, desertion by, or separation or loss from both parents, as those terms are defined in § 204.3(b) of this chapter;

(2) The irrevocable and written release of all parental rights by the sole parent, as that term is defined in § 204.3(b) of this chapter, based upon the inability of that parent to provide proper care (within the meaning of that phrase in § 204.3(b) of this chapter) for the child, provided that at the time of such irrevocable release such parent is legally obligated to provide such care; or

(3) The death or disappearance, as that term is defined in § 204.3(b) of this chapter, of one parent and the irrevocable and written release of all parental rights by the sole remaining parent based upon the inability of that parent to provide proper care (within the meaning of that phrase in § 204.3(b) of this chapter) for the child, provided that at the time of such irrevocable release such parent is legally obligated to provide such care.

Parent, father, or mother means a parent, father, or mother only where the relationship exists by reason of any of the circumstances set forth in paragraphs (A) through (E) of section 101(b)(1) of the Act.

Sole remaining parent means a person who is the child's only parent because:

(1) The child's other parent has died; or

(2) The child's other parent has been certified by competent Haitian authorities to be presumed dead as a result of his or her disappearance, within the meaning of that term as set forth in § 204.3(b) of this chapter.

(b) Applicability of provisions of section 902 of HRIFA in general. Section 902 of Division A of Public Law 105-277, the Haitian Refugee Immigrant Fairness Act of 1998 (HRIFA), provides special rules for adjustment of status for certain nationals of Haiti, and without regard to section 241(a)(5) of the Act, if they meet the other requirements of HRIFA.

(1) Principal applicants. Section 902(b)(1) of HRIFA defines five categories of principal applicants who may apply for adjustment of status, if the alien was physically present in the United States on December 31, 1995:

(i) An alien who filed for asylum before December 31, 1995;

(ii) An alien who was paroled into the United States prior to December 31, 1995, after having been identified as having a credible fear of persecution, or paroled for emergent reasons or reasons deemed strictly in the public interest; or

(iii) An alien who at the time of arrival in the United States and on December 31, 1995, was unmarried and under 21 years of age and who:

(A) Arrived in the United States without parents in the United States and has remained, without parents, in the United States since his or her arrival;

(B) Became orphaned subsequent to arrival in the United States; or

(C) Was abandoned by parents or guardians prior to April 1, 1998, and has remained abandoned since such abandonment.

(2) Dependents. Section 902(d) of HRIFA provides for certain Haitian nationals to apply for adjustment of status as the spouse, child, or unmarried son or daughter of a principal HRIFA beneficiary, even if the individual would not otherwise be eligible for adjustment under section 902. The eligibility requirements for dependents are described further in paragraph (d) of this section.

(c) Eligibility of principal HRIFA applicants. A Haitian national who is described in paragraph (b)(1) of this section is eligible to apply for adjustment of status under the provisions of section 902 of HRIFA if the alien meets the following requirements:

(1) Physical presence. The alien is physically present in the United States at the time the application is filed;

(2) Proper application. The alien properly files an application for adjustment of status in accordance with this section, including the evidence described in paragraphs (h), (i), (j), and (k) of this section. For purposes of § 245.15 of this chapter only, an Application to Register Permanent Residence or Adjust Status (Form I-485) submitted by a principal applicant for benefits under HRIFA may be considered to have been properly filed if it:

(i) Is received not later than March 31, 2000, at the Nebraska Service Center, the Board, or the Immigration Court having jurisdiction;

(ii) Has been properly completed and signed by the applicant;

(iii) Identifies the provision of HRIFA under which the applicant is seeking adjustment of status; and

(iv) Is accompanied by either:

(A) The correct fee as specified in 8 CFR 106.2; or

(B) [Removed and Reserved]

(3) Admissibility. The alien is not inadmissible to the United States for permanent residence under any provisions of section 212(a) of the Act, except as provided in paragraph (e) of this section; and

(4) Continuous physical presence. The alien has been physically present in the United States for a continuous period beginning on December 31, 1995, and ending on the date the application for adjustment is granted, except for the following periods of time:

(i) Any period or periods of absence from the United States not exceeding 180 days in the aggregate; and

(ii) Any periods of absence for which the applicant received an advance parole authorization prior to his or her departure from the United States, provided the applicant returned to the United States in accordance with the conditions of such authorization.

(iii) Any periods of absence from the United States occurring after October 21, 1998, and before July 12, 1999, provided the applicant departed the United States prior to December 31, 1998.

(d) Eligibility of dependents of a principal HRIFA beneficiary. A Haitian national who is the spouse, child, or unmarried son or daughter of a principal beneficiary eligible for adjustment of status under the provisions of HRIFA is eligible to apply for benefits as a dependent, if the dependent alien meets the following requirements:

(1) Physical presence. The alien is physically present in the United States at the time the application is filed;

(2) Proper application. The alien properly files an application for adjustment of status as a dependent in accordance with this section, including the evidence described in paragraphs (h) and (l) of this section;

(3) Admissibility. The alien is not inadmissible to the United States for permanent residence under any provisions of section 212(a) of the Act, except as provided in paragraph (e) of this section;

(4) Relationship. The qualifying relationship to the principal alien must have existed at the time the principal was granted adjustment of status and must continue to exist at the time the dependent alien is granted adjustment of status. To establish the qualifying relationship to the principal alien, evidence must be submitted in accordance with § 204.2 of this chapter. Such evidence should consist of the documents specified in § 204.2(a)(1)(i)(B), (a)(1)(iii)(B), (a)(2), (d)(2), and (d)(5) of this chapter;

(5) Continuous physical presence. If the alien is applying as the unmarried son or unmarried daughter of a principal HRIFA beneficiary, he or she must have been physically present in the United States for a continuous period beginning not later than December 31, 1995, and ending on the date the application for adjustment is granted, as provided in paragraphs (c)(4) and (j) of this section.

(e) **Applicability of grounds of inadmissibility contained in section 212(a).**

(1) Certain grounds of inadmissibility inapplicable to HRIFA applicants. Paragraphs (4), (5), (6)(A), (7)(A) and (9)(B) of section 212(a) of the Act are inapplicable to HRIFA principal applicants and their dependents. Accordingly, an applicant for adjustment of status under section 902 of HRIFA need not establish admissibility under those provisions in order to be able to adjust his or her status to that of permanent resident.

(2) Availability of individual waivers. If a HRIFA applicant is inadmissible under any of the other provisions of section 212(a) of the Act for which an immigrant waiver is available, the applicant may apply for one or more of the immigrant waivers of inadmissibility under section 212 of the Act, in accordance with § 212.7 of this chapter. In considering an application for waiver under section 212(g) of the Act by an otherwise statutorily eligible applicant for adjustment of status under HRIFA who was paroled into the United States from the U.S. Naval Base at Guantanamo Bay, for the purpose of receiving treatment of an HIV or AIDS condition, the fact that his or her arrival in the United States was the direct result of a government decision to provide such treatment should be viewed as a significant positive factor when weighing discretionary factors. In considering an application for waiver under section 212(i) of the Act by an otherwise statutorily eligible applicant for adjustment of status under HRIFA who used counterfeit documents to travel from Haiti to the United States, the adjudicator shall, when weighing discretionary factors, take into consideration the general lawlessness and corruption which was widespread in Haiti at the time of the alien's departure, the difficulties in obtaining legitimate departure documents at that time, and other factors unique to Haiti at that time which may have induced the alien to commit fraud or make willful misrepresentations.

(3) Special rule for waiver of inadmissibility grounds for HRIFA applicants under section 212(a)(9)(A) and 212(a)(9)(C) of the Act. An applicant for adjustment of status under HRIFA who is inadmissible under section 212(a)(9)(A) or 212(a)(9)(C) of the Act, may apply for a waiver of these grounds of inadmissibility while present in the United States. Such an alien must file Form I-601, Application for Waiver of Grounds of Excludability. If the application for adjustment is pending at the Nebraska Service Center, Form I-601 must be filed with the director of that office. If the application for adjustment is pending at a district office, Form I-601 must be filed with the district director having jurisdiction over the application. If the application for adjustment is pending before the immigration court, Form I-601 must be filed with the immigration judge having jurisdiction, or with the Board of Immigration Appeals if the appeal is pending before the Board.

(f) **Time for filing of applications.**

(1) Applications for HRIFA benefits by a principal HRIFA applicant. The application period begins on June 11, 1999. To benefit from the provisions of section

902 of HRIFA, an alien who is applying for adjustment as a principal applicant must properly file an application for adjustment of status before April 1, 2000.

(2) Applications by dependent aliens. The spouse, minor child, or unmarried son or daughter of an alien who is eligible for adjustment of status as a principal beneficiary under HRIFA may file an application for adjustment of status under this section concurrently with or subsequent to the filing of the application of the principal HRIFA beneficiary. An application filed by a dependent may not be approved prior to approval of the principal's application.

(g) **Jurisdiction for filing of applications —**

(1) Filing of applications with USCIS. USCIS has jurisdiction over all applications for the benefits of section 902 of HRIFA as a principal applicant or as a dependent under this section, except for applications filed by aliens who are in pending immigration proceedings as provided in paragraph (g)(2) of this section. All applications filed with USCIS for the benefits of section 902 of HRIFA must be submitted on the form designated by USCIS with the fees prescribed in 8 CFR 106.2 and in accordance with the form instructions. After proper filing of the application, USCIS will instruct the applicant to appear for biometrics collection as prescribed in 8 CFR 103.16.

(2) Filing of applications by aliens in pending exclusion, deportation, or removal proceedings. An alien who is in exclusion, deportation, or removal proceedings pending before the Immigration Court or the Board, or who has a pending motion to reopen or motion to reconsider filed with the Immigration Court or the Board on or before May 12, 1999, must apply for HRIFA benefits to the Immigration Court or the Board, as provided in paragraph (p)(1) of this section, rather than to the Service. However, an alien whose proceeding has been administratively closed (see paragraph (p)(4) of this section) may only apply for HRIFA benefits with the Service as provided in paragraph (g)(1) of this section.

(3)(i) Filing of applications with the Service by aliens who are subject to a final order of exclusion, deportation, or removal. An alien who is subject to a final order of exclusion, deportation, or removal, and who has not been denied adjustment of status under section 902 of HRIFA by the Immigration Court or the Board, may only apply for HRIFA benefits with the Service as provided in paragraph (g)(1) of this section. This includes applications for HRIFA benefits filed by aliens who have filed a motion to reopen or motion to reconsider a final order after May 12, 1999.

(ii) An alien present in the United States who is subject to a final order of exclusion, deportation, or removal and has been denied adjustment of status under section 902 of HRIFA by the Immigration Court or the Board, or who never applied for adjustment of status with the Service, an Immigration Court, or the Board on or before March 31, 2000, and who was made eligible for HRIFA benefits under the Legal Immigration Family Equity Act of 2000 (LIFE Act) and LIFE amendments, Public Law 106-553 and Public Law 106-554, respectively, may file a motion to reopen with either the Immigration Court or the Board, whichever had jurisdiction last. As provided by the LIFE Act, motions to reopen must be filed on or before June 19, 2001.

(iii) Stay of final order of exclusion, deportation, or removal. The filing of an application for adjustment under section 902 of HRIFA with the Service shall not stay the execution of such final order unless the applicant has requested and been granted a stay in connection with the HRIFA application. An alien who has filed a HRIFA application with the Service may file an Application for Stay of Removal (Form I-246) in accordance with section 241(c)(2) of the Act and § 241.6 of this chapter.

(iv) Grant of stay. Absent evidence of the applicant's statutory ineligibility for adjustment of status under section 902 of HRIFA or significant negative discretionary factors, a Form I-246 filed by a bona fide applicant for adjustment under section 902 of HRIFA shall be approved and the removal of the applicant shall be stayed until such time as the Service has adjudicated the application for adjustment in accordance with this section.

(h) Application and supporting documents. Each applicant for adjustment of status must file an Application to Register Permanent Residence or Adjust Status (Form I-485). An applicant should complete Part 2 of Form I-485 by checking box "h — other" and writing "HRIFA — Principal" or "HRIFA — Dependent" next to that block. Each application must be accompanied by:

(1) Application fee. The fee for Form I-485 prescribed in 8 CFR 106.2;

(2) [Removed and Reserved]

(3) Identifying information.

(i) A copy of the applicant's birth certificate or other record of birth as provided in paragraph (m) of this section;

(ii) A completed Biographic Information Sheet (Form G-325A), if the applicant is between 14 and 79 years of age;

(iii) A report of medical examination, as specified in § 245.5 of this chapter; and

(iv) Two photographs, as described in the instructions to Form I-485;

(4) Arrival-Departure Record. A copy of the Form I-94 (see § 1.4), Arrival-Departure Record, issued at the time of the applicant's arrival in the United States, if the alien was inspected and admitted or paroled;

(5) Police clearances. If the applicant is 14 years old or older, a police clearance from each municipality where the alien has resided for 6 months or longer since arriving in the United States. If there are multiple local law enforcement agencies (e.g., city police and county sheriff) with jurisdiction over the alien's residence, the applicant may obtain a clearance from either agency. If the applicant resides or resided in a State where the State police maintain a compilation of all local arrests and convictions, a statewide clearance is sufficient. If the applicant presents a letter from the local police agencies involved, or other evidence, to the effect that the applicant attempted to obtain such clearance but was unable to do so because of local or State policy, the

director or immigration judge having jurisdiction over the application may waive the local police clearance. Furthermore, if such local police agency has provided the Service or the Immigration Court with a blanket statement that issuance of such police clearance is against local or State policy, the director or immigration judge having jurisdiction over the case may waive the local police clearance requirement regardless of whether the applicant individually submits a letter from that local police agency;

(6) Proof of Haitian nationality. If the applicant acquired Haitian nationality other than through birth in Haiti, a copy of the certificate of naturalization or certificate of citizenship issued by the Haitian government; and

(7) Additional supporting evidence. Additional supporting evidence pertaining to the applicant as provided in paragraphs (i) through (l) of this section.

(i) Evidence of presence in the United States on December 31, 1995. An alien seeking HRIFA benefits as a principal applicant must provide with the application evidence establishing the alien's presence in the United States on December 31, 1995. Such evidence may consist of the evidence listed in § 245.22.

(j) Evidence of continuity of presence in the United States since December 31, 1995. An alien seeking HRIFA benefits as a principal applicant, or as the unmarried son or daughter of a principal applicant, must provide with the application evidence establishing continuity of the alien's physical presence in the United States since December 31, 1995. (This requirement does not apply to a dependent seeking HRIFA benefits as the spouse or minor child of a principal applicant.)

(1) Evidence establishing presence. Evidence establishing the continuity of the alien's physical presence in the United States since December 31, 1995, may consist of any documentation issued by any governmental or nongovernmental authority, provided such evidence bears the name of the applicant, was dated at the time it was issued, and bears the signature, seal, or other authenticating instrument of the authorized representative of the issuing authority, if the document would normally contain such authenticating instrument.

(2) Examples. Documentation establishing continuity of physical presence may include, but is not limited to:

(i) School records;

(ii) Rental receipts;

(iii) Utility bill receipts;

(iv) Any other dated receipts;

(v) Personal checks written by the applicant bearing a dated bank cancellation stamp;

(vi) Employment records, including pay stubs;

(vii) Credit card statements showing the dates of purchase, payment, or other transaction;

(viii) Certified copies of records maintained by organizations chartered by the Federal or State government, such as public utilities, accredited private and religious schools, and banks;

(ix) If the applicant establishes that a family unit was in existence and cohabiting in the United States, documents evidencing presence of another member of that same family unit; and

(x) For applicants who have had ongoing correspondence or other interaction with the Service, a list of the types and dates of such correspondence or other contact that the applicant knows to be contained or reflected in Service records.

(3) Evidence relating to absences from the United States since December 31, 1995. If the alien is applying as a principal applicant, or as the unmarried son or daughter of a principal applicant, and has departed from and returned to the United States since December 31, 1995, the alien must provide with the application an attachment on a plain piece of paper showing:

(i) The date of the applicant's last arrival in the United States before December 31, 1995;

(ii) The date of each departure (if any) from the United States since that arrival;

(iii) The reason for each departure; and

(iv) The date, manner, and place of each return to the United States.

(k) Evidence establishing the alien's eligibility under section 902(b) of HRIFA. An alien seeking HRIFA benefits as a principal applicant must provide with the application evidence establishing that the alien satisfies one of the eligibility standards described in paragraph (b)(1) of this section.

(1) Applicant for asylum. If the alien is a principal applicant who filed for asylum before December 31, 1995, the applicant must provide with the application either:

(i) A photocopy of the first page of the Application for Asylum and Withholding of Removal (Form I-589); or

(ii) If the alien is not in possession of a photocopy of the first page of the Form I-589, a statement to that effect giving the date of filing and the location of the Service office or Immigration Court at which it was filed;

(2) Parolee. If the alien is a principal applicant who was paroled into the United States prior to December 31, 1995, after having been identified as having a credible fear of persecution, or paroled for emergent reasons or reasons deemed strictly in the public interest, the applicant must provide with the application either:

(i) A photocopy of the Arrival-Departure Record (Form I-94) issued when he or she was granted parole; or

(ii) If the alien is not in possession of the original Form I-94, a statement to that effect giving the date of parole and the location of the Service port-of-entry at which parole was authorized.

(3) Child without parents. If the alien is a principal applicant who arrived in the United States as a child without parents in the United States, the applicant must provide with the application:

(i) Evidence, showing the date, location, and manner of his or her arrival in the United States, such as:

(A) A photocopy of the Form I-94 issued at the time of the alien's arrival in the United States;

(B) A copy of the airline or vessel records showing transportation to the United States;

(C) Other similar documentation; or

(D) If none of the documents in paragraphs (k)(3)(i)(A)-(C) of this section are available, a statement from the applicant, accompanied by whatever evidence the applicant is able to submit in support of that statement; and

(ii) Evidence establishing the absence of the child's parents, which may include either:

(A) Evidence showing the deaths of, or disappearance or desertion by, the applicant's parents; or

(B) Evidence showing that the applicant's parents did not live in the United States with the applicant. Such evidence may include, but is not limited to, documentation or affidavits showing that the applicant's parents have been continuously employed outside the United States, are deceased, disappeared, or abandoned the applicant prior to the applicant's arrival, or were otherwise engaged in activities showing that they were not in the United States, or (if they have been in the United States) that the applicant and his or her parents did not reside together.

(4) Orphaned child. If the alien is a principal applicant who is or was a child who became orphaned subsequent to arrival in the United States, the applicant must provide with the application:

(i) Evidence, showing the date, location, and manner of his or her arrival in the United States, such as:

(A) A photocopy of the Form I-94 issued at the time of the alien's arrival in the United States;

(B) A copy of the airline or vessel records showing transportation to the United States;

(C) Other similar documentation; or

(D) If none of the documents in paragraphs (k)(4)(i)(A)-(C) of this section are available, a statement from the applicant, accompanied by whatever evidence the applicant is able to submit in support of that statement; and

(ii) Either:

(A) The death certificates of both parents (or in the case of a child having only one parent, the death certificate of the sole parent) showing that the death or deaths occurred after the date of the applicant's arrival in the United States;

(B) Evidence from a State, local, or other court or governmental authority having jurisdiction and authority to make decisions in matters of child welfare establishing the disappearance of, the separation or loss from, or desertion by, both parents (or, in the case of a child born out of wedlock who has not been legitimated, the sole parent); or

(C) Evidence of:

(1) Either:

(i) The child having only a sole parent, as that term is defined in § 204.3(b) of this chapter;

(ii) The death of one parent; or

(iii) Certification by competent Haitian authorities that one parent is presumed dead as a result of his or her disappearance, within the meaning of that term as set forth in § 204.3(b) of this chapter; and

(2) A copy of a written statement executed by the sole parent, or the sole remaining parent, irrevocably releasing all parental rights based upon the inability of that parent to provide proper care for the child.

(5) Abandoned child. If the alien is a principal applicant who was abandoned by parents or guardians prior to April 1, 1998, and has remained abandoned since such abandonment, the applicant must provide with the application:

(i) Evidence, showing the date, location, and manner of his or her arrival in the United States, such as:

(A) A photocopy of the Form I-94 issued at the time of the alien's arrival in the United States;

(B) A copy of the airline or vessel records showing transportation to the United States;

(C) Other similar documentation; or

(D) If none of the documents in paragraphs (k)(5)(i)(A)-(C) of this section are available, a statement from the applicant, accompanied by whatever evidence the applicant is able to submit in support of that statement; and

(ii) Either:

(A) Evidence from a State, local, or other court or governmental authority having jurisdiction and authority to make decisions in matters of child welfare establishing such abandonment; or

(B) Evidence to establish that the applicant would have been considered to be abandoned according to the laws of the State where he or she resides, or where he or she resided at the time of the abandonment, had the issue been presented to the proper authorities.

(*l*) **Evidence relating to applications by dependents under section 902(d) of HRIFA —**

(1) Evidence of spousal relationship. If the alien is applying as the spouse of a principal HRIFA beneficiary, the applicant must provide with the application a copy of their certificate of marriage and copies of documents showing the legal termination of all other marriages by the applicant or the other beneficiary.

(2) Evidence of parent-child relationship. If the applicant is applying as the child, unmarried son, or unmarried daughter of a principal HRIFA beneficiary, and the principal beneficiary is not the applicant's biological mother, the applicant must provide with the application evidence to demonstrate the parent-child relationship between the principal beneficiary and the applicant. Such evidence may include copies of the applicant's parent's marriage certificate and documents showing the legal termination of all other marriages, an adoption decree, or other relevant evidence.

(m) Secondary evidence. Except as otherwise provided in this paragraph, if the primary evidence required in this section is unavailable, church or school records, or other secondary evidence pertinent to the facts in issue, may be submitted. If such documents are unavailable, affidavits may be submitted. The applicant may submit as many types of secondary evidence as necessary to establish birth, marriage, or other relevant events. Documentary evidence establishing that primary evidence is unavailable must accompany secondary evidence of birth or marriage in the home country. The unavailability of such documents may be shown by submission of a copy of the written request for a copy of such documents which was sent to the official keeper of the records. In adjudicating the application for adjustment of status under section 902 of HRIFA, the Service or immigration judge shall determine the weight to be given such secondary evidence. Secondary evidence may not be submitted in lieu of the documentation specified in paragraphs (i) or (j) of this section. However, subject to verification by the Service, if the documentation specified in this paragraph or in paragraphs (h)(3)(i), (i), (j), (l)(1), and (l)(2) of this section is already contained in the Service's file relating to the applicant, the applicant may submit an affidavit to that effect in lieu of the actual documentation.

(n) **Authorization to be employed in the United States while the application is pending —**

(1) Application for employment authorization. An applicant for adjustment of status under section 902 of HRIFA who wishes to obtain initial or continued employment authorization during the pendency of the adjustment application must file an application on the form designated by USCIS with the fee prescribed in 8 CFR 106.2 and in accordance with the form instructions. The applicant may submit the application either concurrently with or subsequent to the filing of the application for HRIFA benefits.

(2) Adjudication and issuance. Employment authorization may not be issued to an applicant for adjustment of status under section 902 of HRIFA until the adjustment application has been pending for 180 days, unless USCIS verifies that DHS records contain evidence that the applicant meets the criteria set forth in section 902(b) or 902(d) of HRIFA, and determines that there is no indication that the applicant is clearly ineligible for adjustment of status under section 902 of HRIFA, in which case USCIS may approve the application for employment authorization, and issue the resulting document, immediately upon such verification. If USCIS fails to adjudicate the application for employment authorization upon the expiration of the 180-day waiting period, or within 90 days of the filing of application for employment authorization, whichever comes later, the applicant shall be eligible for an employment authorization document. Nothing in this section shall preclude an applicant for adjustment of status under HRIFA from being granted an initial employment authorization or an extension of employment authorization under any other provision of law or regulation for which the applicant may be eligible.

(o) **Adjudication of HRIFA applications filed with the Service —**

(1) Referral for interview. Except as provided in paragraphs (o)(2) and (o)(3) of this section, all aliens filing applications for adjustment of status with the Service under this section must be personally interviewed by an immigration officer at a local office of the Service. If the Director of the Nebraska Service Center determines that an interview of the applicant is necessary, the Director shall forward the case to the appropriate local Service office for interview and adjudication.

(2) Approval without interview. Upon examination of the application, including all other evidence submitted in support of the application, all relevant Service records and all other relevant law enforcement indices, the Director may approve the application without an interview if the Director determines that:

(i) The alien's claim to eligibility for adjustment of status under section 902 of HRIFA is verified through existing Service records; and

(ii) The alien is clearly eligible for adjustment of status.

(3) Denial without interview. If, upon examination of the application, all supporting documentation, all relevant Service records, and all other relevant law enforcement indices, the Director determines that the alien is clearly ineligible for adjustment of status under HRIFA and that an interview of the applicant is not necessary, the Director may deny the application.

(p) **Adjudication of HRIFA applications filed in pending exclusion, deportation, or removal proceedings —**

(1) Proceedings pending before an Immigration Court. Except as provided in paragraph (p)(4) of this section, the Immigration Court shall have sole jurisdiction over an application for adjustment of status under this section filed by an alien who is in exclusion, deportation, or removal proceedings pending before an immigration judge or the Board, or who has a pending motion to reopen or motion to reconsider filed with an immigration judge or the Board on or before May 12, 1999. The immigration judge having jurisdiction over the exclusion, deportation, or removal proceedings shall have jurisdiction to accept and adjudicate any application for adjustment of status under section 902 of HRIFA during the course of such proceedings. All applications for adjustment of status under section 902 of HRIFA filed with an Immigration Court shall be subject to the requirements of §§ 3.11 and 3.31 of this chapter.

(2) Motion to reopen or motion to reconsider. If an alien who has a pending motion to reopen or motion to reconsider timely filed with an immigration judge on or before May 12, 1999, files an application for adjustment of status under section 902 of HRIFA, the immigration judge shall reopen the alien's proceedings for consideration of the adjustment application, unless the alien is clearly ineligible for adjustment of status under section 902 of HRIFA.

(3) Proceedings pending before the Board. Except as provided in paragraph (d)(4) of this section, in the case of an alien who either has a pending appeal with the Board or has a pending motion to reopen or motion to reconsider timely filed with the Board on or before May 12, 1999, the Board shall remand, or reopen and remand, the proceedings to the Immigration Court for the sole purpose of adjudicating an application for adjustment of status under section 902 of HRIFA, unless the alien is clearly ineligible for adjustment of status under section 902 of HRIFA. If the immigration judge denies, or the alien fails to file, the application for adjustment of status under section 902 of HRIFA, the immigration judge shall certify the decision to the Board for consideration in conjunction with the applicant's previously pending appeal or motion.

(4) Administrative closure of exclusion, deportation, or removal proceedings.

(i) An alien who is in exclusion, deportation, or removal proceedings, or who has a pending motion to reopen or a motion to reconsider such proceedings filed on or before May 12, 1999, may request that the proceedings be administratively closed, or that the motion be indefinitely continued, in order to allow the alien to file such application with the Service as prescribed in paragraph (g) of this section. If the alien appears to be eligible to file an application for adjustment of status under this section, the Immigration Court or the Board (whichever has jurisdiction) shall, with the concurrence of the Service, administratively close the proceedings or continue indefinitely the motion.

(ii) In the case of an otherwise-eligible alien whose exclusion, deportation, or removal proceedings have been administratively closed for reasons not specified in this section, the alien may only apply before the Service for adjustment of status under this section.

(q) **Approval of HRIFA applications —**

(1) Applications approved by the Service. If the Service approves the application for adjustment of status under the provisions of section 902 of HRIFA, the director shall record the alien's lawful admission for permanent residence as of the date of such approval and notify the applicant accordingly. The director shall also advise the alien regarding the delivery of his or her Permanent Resident Card and of the process for obtaining temporary evidence of alien registration. If the alien had previously been issued a final order of exclusion, deportation, or removal, such order shall be deemed canceled as of the date of the director's approval of the application for adjustment of status. If the alien had been in exclusion, deportation, or removal proceedings that were administratively closed, such proceedings shall be deemed terminated as of the date of approval of the application for adjustment of status by the director.

(2) Applications approved by an immigration judge or the Board. If an immigration judge or (upon appeal) the Board grants an application for adjustment under the provisions of section 902 of HRIFA, the date of the alien's lawful admission for permanent residence shall be the date of such grant.

(r) Review of decisions by the Service denying HRIFA applications —

(1)(i) Denial notification. If the Service denies the application for adjustment of status under the provisions of section 902 of HRIFA, the director shall notify the applicant of the decision and of any right to renew the application in proceedings before the Immigration Court.

(ii) An alien made eligible for adjustment of status under HRIFA by the LIFE Act amendments and whose case has not been referred to EOIR under paragraphs (r)(2) or (r)(3) of this section, may file a motion to reopen with the Service.

(2) Renewal of application for HRIFA benefits in removal, deportation, or exclusion proceedings. An alien who is not the subject of a final order of removal, deportation, or exclusion may renew his or her application for adjustment under section 902 of HRIFA during the course of such removal, deportation, or exclusion proceedings.

(i) Initiation of removal proceedings. In the case of an alien who is not maintaining valid nonimmigrant status and who had not previously been placed in exclusion, deportation, or removal proceedings, the director shall initiate removal proceedings in accordance with § 239.1 of this chapter.

(ii) Recalendaring or reinstatement of prior proceedings. In the case of an alien whose previously initiated exclusion, deportation, or removal proceeding had been administratively closed or continued indefinitely under paragraph (p)(4) of this section, the director shall make a request for recalendaring or reinstatement to the Immigration Court that had administratively closed the proceeding, or the Board, as appropriate, when the application has been denied. The Immigration Court or the Board will then recalendar or reinstate the prior exclusion, deportation, or removal proceeding.

(iii) Filing of renewed application. A principal alien may file a renewed application for HRIFA benefits with the Immigration Court either before or after March 31, 2000, if he or she had filed his or her initial application for such benefits with the Service on or before March 31, 2000. A dependent of a principal applicant may file such renewed application with the Immigration Court either before or after March 31, 2000, regardless of when he or she filed his or her initial application for HRIFA benefits with the Service.

(3) Aliens with final orders. In the case of an alien who is the subject of an outstanding final order of exclusion, deportation, or removal, the Service shall refer the decision to deny the application by filing a Notice of Certification (Form I-290C) with the Immigration Court that issued the final order for consideration in accordance with paragraph (s) of this section.

(4)(i) An alien whose case has been referred to the Immigration Court under paragraphs (r)(2) or (r)(3) of this section, or who filed an appeal with the Board after his or her application for adjustment of status under section 902 of HRIFA was denied, and whose proceedings are pending, and who is now eligible for adjustment of status under HRIFA as amended by section 1505(b) of the LIFE Act and its amendments, may renew the application for adjustment of status with either the Immigration Court or the Board, whichever has jurisdiction. The application will be adjudicated in accordance with section 1505(b) of the LIFE Act and its amendments.

(ii) An alien present in the United States who is subject to a final order of exclusion, deportation or removal after his or her HRIFA adjustment application was denied by an Immigration Court or the Board, but who was made eligible for HRIFA adjustment as a result of section 1505(b) of the LIFE Act and its amendments, may file a motion to reopen with either the Immigration Court or the Board, whichever had jurisdiction last. Such motion to reopen must be filed on or before June 19, 2001.

(s) **Action of immigration judge upon referral of decision by a notice of certification.**

(1) General. Upon the referral by a notice of certification of a decision to deny the application, in accordance with paragraph (r)(3) of this section, the immigration judge will conduct a hearing to determine whether the alien is eligible for adjustment of status under section 902 of HRIFA in accordance with this paragraph (s)(1).

(2) Stay pending review. When the Service refers a decision to the Immigration Court on a Notice of Certification (Form I-290C) in accordance with paragraph (r)(3) of this section, the referral shall not stay the execution of the final order. Execution of such final order shall proceed unless a stay of execution is specifically granted by the immigration judge, the Board, or an authorized Service officer.

(3) Appeal of Immigration Court decision. Once the immigration judge issues his or her decision on the application, either the alien or the Service may appeal the decision to the Board. Such appeal must be filed pursuant to the requirements for appeals to the Board from an Immigration Court decision set forth in §§ 3.3 and 3.8 of this chapter.

(4) Rescission or reopening of the decision of an Immigration Court. The decision of an Immigration Court under paragraph (s)(1) of this section denying an application for adjustment under section 902 of HRIFA for failure to appear may be rescinded or reopened only:

(i) Upon a motion to reopen filed within 180 days after the date of the denial if the alien demonstrates that the failure to appear was because of exceptional circumstances as defined in section 240(e)(1) of the Act;

(ii) Upon a motion to reopen filed at any time if the alien demonstrates that he or she did not receive notice of the hearing in person (or, if personal service was not practicable, through service by mail to the alien or to the alien's counsel of record, if any) or the alien demonstrates that he or she was in Federal or State custody and the failure to appear was through no fault of the alien; or

(iii) Upon a motion to reopen filed not later than June 19, 2001, by an alien present in the United States who became eligible for adjustment of status under HRIFA, as amended by section 1505, of Public Law 106-554.

(t) **Parole authorization for purposes of travel —**

(1) Travel from and return to the United States while the application for adjustment of status is pending. If an applicant for benefits under section 902 of HRIFA desires to travel outside, and return to, the United States while the application for adjustment of status is pending, he or she must file a request for advance parole authorization on the form designated by USCIS with the fee prescribed in 8 CFR 106.2 and in accordance with the form instructions. Unless the applicant files an advance parole request prior to departing from the United States and USCIS approves such request, his or her application for adjustment of status under section 902 of HRIFA is deemed to be abandoned as of the moment of departure. Parole may only be authorized pursuant to the authority contained in, and the standards prescribed in, section 212(d)(5) of the Act.

(2) Parole authorization for the purpose of filing an application for adjustment of status under section 902 of HRIFA.

(i) An otherwise eligible applicant who is outside the United States and wishes to come to the United States in order to apply for benefits under section 902 of HRIFA may request parole authorization for such purpose by filing a request on the form designated by USCIS with the fee prescribed in 8 CFR 106.2 and in accordance with the form instructions. Such application must be supported by a photocopy of the application for adjustment of status that the alien will file once he or she has been paroled into the United States. The applicant must include photocopies of all the supporting documentation listed in paragraph (h) of this section, except the filing fee, the medical report, the fingerprint card, and the local police clearances.

(ii) If the Director of the Nebraska Service Center is satisfied that the alien will be eligible for adjustment of status once the alien has been paroled into the United States and files the application, he or she may issue an Authorization for Parole of an Alien into the United States (Form I-512) to allow the alien to travel to, and be paroled into, the United States for a period of 60 days.

(iii) The applicant shall have 60 days from the date of parole to file the application for adjustment of status. If the alien files the application for adjustment of status within that 60-day period, the Service may re-parole the alien for such time as is necessary for adjudication of the application. Failure to file such application for adjustment of status within 60 days shall result in the alien being returned to the custody of the Service and being examined as an arriving alien applying for admission. Such examination will be conducted in accordance with the provisions of section 235(b)(1) of the Act if the alien is inadmissible under section 212(a)(6)(C) or 212(a)(7) of the Act, or section 240 of the Act if the alien is inadmissible under any other grounds.

(iv) Parole may only be authorized pursuant to the authority contained in, and the standards prescribed in, section 212(d)(5) of the Act. The authority of the Director of the Nebraska Service Center to authorize parole from outside the United States under this provision shall expire on March 31, 2000.

(3) Effect of departure on an outstanding warrant of exclusion, deportation, or removal. If an alien who is the subject of an outstanding final order of exclusion, deportation, or removal departs from the United States, with or without an advance parole authorization, such final order shall be executed by the alien's departure. The execution of such final order shall not preclude the applicant from filing an Application for Permission to Reapply for Admission Into the United States After Deportation or Removal (Form I-212) in accordance with § 212.2 of this chapter.

(u) **Tolling the physical presence in the United States provision for certain individuals.**

(1) Departure with advance authorization for parole. In the case of an alien who departed the United States

after having been issued an Authorization for Parole of an Alien into the United States (Form I-512), and who returns to the United States in accordance with the conditions of that document, the physical presence in the United States requirement of section 902(b)(1) of HRIFA is tolled while the alien is outside the United States pursuant to the issuance of the Form I-512.

(2) Request for parole authorization from outside the United States. In the case of an alien who is outside the United States and submits an application for parole authorization in accordance with paragraph (t)(2) of this section, and such application for parole authorization is granted by the Service, the physical presence requirement contained in section 902(b)(1) of HRIFA is tolled from the date the application is received at the Nebraska Service Center until the alien is paroled into the United States pursuant to the issuance of the Form I-512.

(3) Departure without advance authorization for parole. In the case of an otherwise-eligible applicant who departed the United States on or before December 31, 1998, the physical presence in the United States provision of section 902(b)(1) of HRIFA is tolled as of October 21, 1998, and until July 12, 1999.

(v) Judicial review of HRIFA adjustment of status determinations. Pursuant to the provisions of section 902(f) of HRIFA, there shall be no judicial appeal or review of any administrative determination as to whether the status of an alien should be adjusted under the provisions of section 902 of HRIFA.

HISTORY:

[64 FR 25756, 25767, May 12, 1999, as confirmed and amended at 65 FR 15835, 15844, Mar. 24, 2000; 66 FR 29449, 29452, May 31, 2001; 67 FR 78667, 78673, Dec. 26, 2002; 76 FR 53764, 53793, Aug. 29, 2011; 78 FR 18457, 18472, Mar. 27, 2013, as confirmed at 81 FR 91646, 91670, Dec. 19, 2016; 81 FR 82398, 82490, Nov. 18, 2016; 85 FR 46788, 46926, Aug. 3, 2020]

§ 245.18 Physicians with approved employment-based petitions serving in a medically underserved area or a Veterans Affairs facility.

(a) Which physicians are eligible for this benefit? Any alien physician who has been granted a national interest waiver under § 204.12 of this chapter may submit Form I-485 during the 6-year period following Service approval of a second preference employment-based immigrant visa petition.

(b) Do alien physicians have special time-related requirements for adjustment?

(1) Alien physicians who have been granted a national interest waiver under § 204.12 of this chapter must meet all the adjustment of status requirements of this part.

(2) The Service shall not approve an adjustment application filed by an alien physician who obtained a waiver under section 203(b)(2)(B)(ii) of the Act until the alien physician has completed the period of required service established in § 204.12 of this chapter.

(c) Are the filing procedures and documentary requirements different for these particular alien physicians? Alien physicians submitting adjustment applications upon approval of an immigrant petition are required to follow the procedures outlined within this part with the following modifications.

(1) Delayed fingerprinting. Fingerprinting, as noted in the Form I-485 instructions, will not be scheduled at the time of filing. Fingerprinting will be scheduled upon the physician's completion of the required years of service.

(2) Delayed medical examination. The required medical examination, as specified in § 245.5, shall not be submitted with Form I-485. The medical examination report shall be submitted with the documentary evidence noting the physician's completion of the required years of service.

(d) **Employment authorization.**

(1) Once USCIS has approved a petition described in paragraph (a) of this section, the alien physician may apply for permanent residence and employment authorization on the forms designated by USCIS with the fee prescribed in 8 CFR 106.2 and in accordance with the form instructions.

(2) Since section 203(b)(2)(B)(ii) of the Act requires the alien physician to complete the required employment before USCIS can approve the alien physician's adjustment application, an alien physician who was in lawful nonimmigrant status when he or she filed the adjustment application is not required to maintain a nonimmigrant status while the adjustment application remains pending. Even if the alien physician's nonimmigrant status expires, the alien physician shall not be considered to be unlawfully present, so long as the alien physician is practicing medicine in accordance with § 204.5(k)(4)(iii) of this chapter.

(e) When does the Service begin counting the physician's 5-year or 3-year medical practice requirement? Except as provided in this paragraph, the 6-year period during which a physician must provide the required 5 years of service begins on the date of the notice approving the Form I-140 and the national interest waiver. Alien physicians who have a 3-year medical practice requirement must complete their service within the 4-year period beginning on that date.

(1) If the physician does not already have employment authorization and so must obtain employment authorization before the physician can begin working, then the period begins on the date the Service issues the employment authorization document.

(2) If the physician formerly held status as a J-1 nonimmigrant, but obtained a waiver of the foreign residence requirement and a change of status to that of an H-1B nonimmigrant, pursuant to section 214(1) of the Act, as amended by section 220 of Public Law 103-416, and § 212.7(c)(9) of this chapter, the period begins on the date of the alien's change from J-1 to H-1B status. The Service will include the alien's compliance with the 3-year period of service required under section 214(l) in calculating the alien's compliance with the period of service required under section 203(b)(2)(B)(ii)(II) of the Act and this section.

(3) An alien may not include any time employed as a J-1 nonimmigrant physician in calculating the alien's compliance with the 5 or 3-year medical practice re-

quirement. If an alien is still in J-1 nonimmigrant status when the Service approves a Form I-140 petition with a national interest job offer waiver, the aggregate period during which the medical practice requirement period must be completed will begin on the date the Service issues an employment authorization document.

(f) Will the Service provide information to the physician about evidence and supplemental filings? The Service shall provide the physician with the information and the projected timetables for completing the adjustment process, as described in this paragraph. If the physician either files the Form I-485 concurrently with or waits to subsequently file the Form I-485 while the previously filed Form I-140 is still pending, then the Service will given this information upon approval of the Form I-140. If the physician does not file the adjustment application until after approval of the Form I-140 visa petition, the Service shall provide this information upon receipt of the Form I-485 adjustment application.

(1) The Service shall note the date that the medical service begins (provided the physician already had work authorization at the time the Form I-140 was filed) or the date that an employment authorization document was issued.

(2) A list of the evidence necessary to satisfy the requirements of paragraphs (g) and (h) of this section.

(3) A projected timeline noting the dates that the physician will need to submit preliminary evidence two years and 120 days into his or her medical service in an underserved area or VA facility, and a projected date six years and 120 days in the future on which the physician's final evidence of completed medical service will be due.

(g) Will physicians be required to file evidence prior to the end of the 5 or 3-year period?

(1) For physicians with a 5-year service requirement, no later than 120 days after the second anniversary of the approval of Petition for Immigrant Worker, Form I-140, the alien physician must submit to the Service Center having jurisdiction over his or her place of employment documentary evidence that proves the physician has in fact fulfilled at least 12 months of qualifying employment. This may be accomplished by submitting the following.

(i) Evidence noted in paragraph (h) of this section that is available at the second anniversary of the I-140 approval.

(ii) Documentation from the employer attesting to the fill-time medical practice and the date on which the physician began his or her medical service.

(2) Physicians with a 3-year service requirement are not required to make a supplemental filing, and must only comply with the requirements of paragraph (h) of this section.

(h) What evidence is needed to prove final compliance with the service requirement? No later than 120 days after completion of the service requirement established under § 204.12(a) of this section, an alien physician must submit to the Service Center having jurisdiction over his or her place of employment documentary evidence that proves the physician has in fact satisfied the service requirement. Such evidence must include, but is not limited to:

(1) Individual Federal income tax returns, including copies of the alien'sW-2 forms, for the entire 3-year period or the balance years of the 5-year period that follow the submission of the evidence required in paragraph (e) of this section;

(2) Documentation from the employer attesting to the full-time medical service rendered during the required aggregate period. The documentation shall address instances of breaks in employment, other than routine breaks such as paid vacations;

(3) If the physician established his or her own practice, documents noting the actual establishment of the practice, including incorporation of the medical practice (if incorporated), the business license, and the business tax returns and tax withholding documents submitted for the entire 3 year period, or the balance years of the 5-year period that follow the submission of the evidence required in paragraph (e) of this section.

(i) What if the physician does not comply with the requirements of paragraphs (f) and (g) of this section? If an alien physician does not submit (in accordance with paragraphs (f) and (g) of this section) proof that he or she has completed the service required under 8 CFR 204.12(a), USCIS shall serve the alien physician with a written notice of intent to deny the alien physician's application for adjustment of status and, after the denial is finalized, to revoke approval of the Form I-140 and national interest waiver. The written notice shall require the alien physician to provide the evidence required by paragraph (f) or (g) of this section. If the alien physician fails to submit the evidence within the allotted time, USCIS shall deny the alien physician's application for adjustment of status and shall revoke approval of the Form I-140 and of the national interest waiver.

(j) Will a Service officer interview the physician?

(1) Upon submission of the evidence noted in paragraph (h) of this section, the Service shall match the documentary evidence with the pending form I-485 and schedule the alien physician for fingerprinting at an Application Support Center.

(2) The local Service office shall schedule the alien for an adjustment interview with a Service officer, unless the Service waives the interview as provided in § 245.6. The local Service office shall also notify the alien if supplemental documentation should either be mailed to the office, or brought to the adjustment interview.

(k) Are alien physicians allowed to travel outside the United States during the mandatory 3 or 5-year service period? An alien physician who has been granted a national interest waiver under § 204.12 of this chapter and has a pending application for adjustment of status may travel outside of the United States during the required 3 or 5-year service period by obtaining advanced parole prior to traveling. Such physicians may apply for advance parole on the form designated by USCIS with the fee prescribed in 8 CFR 106.2 and in accordance with the form instructions.

(*l*) What if the Service denies the adjustment application? If the Service denies the adjustment application, the alien physician may renew the application in removal proceedings.

HISTORY:

[65 FR 53889, 53895, Sept. 6, 2000, as corrected at 65 FR 57861, Sept. 26, 2000, as corrected at 65 FR 63118, Oct. 20, 2000; 65 FR 53889, 53895, Sept. 6, 2000, as corrected at 65 FR 57943, 57944, Sept. 27, 2000; 67 FR 49561, 49563, July 31, 2002; 72 FR 19100, 19107, Apr. 17, 2007; 76 FR 53764, 53793, Aug. 29, 2011; 85 FR 46788, 46927, Aug. 3, 2020]

§ 245.20 [This section was removed and reserved See 76 FR 53764, 53793, Aug. 29, 2011.]

[NO TEXT IN ORIGINAL]

HISTORY:

[66 FR 27445, 27448, May 17, 2001, as confirmed and removed 76 FR 53764, 53778, 53793, Aug. 29, 2011]

AUTHORITY:

(8 U.S.C. 1101, 1103, 1182, 1255; section 202, Public Law 105-100, 111 Stat. 2160, 2193; section 902, Public Law 105-277, 112 Stat. 2681; Title VII of Public Law 110-229; 8 CFR part 2.)

§ 245.21 Adjustment of status of certain nationals of Vietnam, Cambodia, and Laos (section 586 of Public Law 106-429).

(a) Eligibility. USCIS may adjust the status to that of a lawful permanent resident, a native or citizen of Vietnam, Cambodia, or Laos who:

(1) Was inspected and paroled into the United States before October 1, 1997;

(2) Was paroled into the United States from Vietnam under the auspices of the Orderly Departure Program (ODP), a refugee camp in East Asia, or a displaced person camp administered by the United Nations High Commissioner for Refugees (UNHCR) in Thailand;

(3) Was physically present in the United States prior to and on October 1, 1997; and

(4) Is otherwise eligible to receive an immigrant visa and is otherwise admissible as an immigrant to the United States except as provided in paragraphs (e) and (f) of this section.

(b) Application. An applicant must submit an application on the form designated by USCIS with the fee specified in 8 CFR 106.2 and in accordance with the form instructions.

(c) Applications from aliens in immigration proceedings. An alien in pending immigration proceedings who believes he or she is eligible for adjustment of status under section 586 of Public Law 106-429 must apply directly to USCIS in accordance with paragraph (b) of this section. An immigration judge or the Board of Immigration Appeals may not adjudicate applications for adjustment of status under this section. An alien who is currently in immigration proceedings who alleges eligibility for adjustment of status under section 586 of Public Law 106-429 may contact Service counsel after filing an application to request the consent of USCIS to the filing of a joint motion for administrative closure. Unless USCIS consents to such a motion, the immigration judge or the Board may not defer or dismiss the proceeding in connection with section 586 of Public Law 106-429.

(d) Applications from aliens with final orders of removal, deportation, or exclusion. An alien with a final order of removal, deportation, or exclusion who believes he or she is eligible for adjustment of status under section 586 of Public Law 106-429 must apply directly to USCIS in accordance with paragraph (b) of this section.

(1) An application under this section does not automatically stay the order of removal, deportation, or exclusion. An alien who is eligible for adjustment of status under section 586 of Public Law 106-429 may request a stay of removal during the pendency of the application. The regulations governing such a request are found at 8 CFR 241.6.

(2) DHS will exercise its discretion not to grant a stay of removal, deportation, or exclusion with respect to an alien who is inadmissible on any of the grounds specified in paragraph (m)(3) of this section, unless there is substantial reason to believe that USCIS will grant the necessary waivers of inadmissibility.

(3) An immigration judge or the Board may not grant a motion to re-open or stay in connection with an application under this section.

(4) If USCIS approves the application, the approval will constitute the automatic re-opening of the alien's immigration proceedings, vacating of the final order of removal, deportation, or exclusion, and termination of the reopened proceedings.

(e) Grounds of inadmissibility that do not apply. In making a determination of whether an applicant is otherwise eligible for admission to the United States for lawful permanent residence under the provisions of section 586 of Public Law 106-429, the grounds of inadmissibility under sections 212(a)(4), (a)(5), (a)(7)(A), and (a)(9) of the Act shall not apply.

(f) Waiver of grounds of inadmissibility. In connection with an application for adjustment of status under this section, the alien may apply for a waiver of the grounds of inadmissibility under sections 212(a)(1), (a)(6)(B), (a)(6)(C), (a)(6)(F), (a)(8)(A), (a)(10)(B), and (a)(10)(D) of the Act as provided in section 586(c) of Public Law 106-429, if the alien demonstrates that a waiver is necessary to prevent extreme hardship to the alien, or to the alien's spouse, parent, son or daughter who is a U.S. citizen or an alien lawfully admitted for permanent residence. In addition, the alien may apply for any other waiver of inadmissibility under section 212 of the Act, if eligible. In order to obtain a waiver for any of these grounds, the applicant must submit an application on the form designated by USCIS with the fee prescribed in 8 CFR 106.2 and in accordance with the form instructions.

(g) Evidence. Applicants must submit evidence that demonstrates they are eligible for adjustment of status under section 586 of Public Law 106-429. Such evidence shall include the following:

(1) A birth certificate or other record of birth;

(2) Documentation to establish that the applicant was physically present in the United States on October

1, 1997, under the standards set forth in § 245.22 of this chapter.

(3) A copy of the applicant's Arrival-Departure Record (Form I-94 (see § 1.4)) or other evidence that the alien was inspected or paroled into the United States prior to October 1, 1997, from one of the three programs listed in paragraph (a)(2) of this section. Subject to verification, documentation pertaining to paragraph (a)(2) of this section is already contained in USCIS files and the applicant may submit an affidavit to that effect in lieu of actual documentation.

(h) Employment authorization. Applicants who want to obtain employment authorization based on a pending application for adjustment of status under this section may apply on the form specified by USCIS with the fee prescribed in 8 CFR 106.2 and in accordance with the form instructions.

(i) Travel while an application to adjust status is pending. An applicant who wishes to travel outside the United States while the application is pending must obtain advance permission by filing the application specified by USCIS with the fee prescribed in 8 CFR 106.2 and in accordance with the form instructions.

(j) Approval and date of admission as a lawful permanent resident. When the USCIS approves an application to adjust status to that of lawful permanent resident based on section 586 of Public Law 106-429, the applicant will be notified in writing of the USCIS's decision. In addition, the record of the alien's admission as a lawful permanent resident will be recorded as of the date of the alien's inspection and parole into the United States, as described in paragraph (a)(1) of this section.

(k) Notice of denial. When USCIS denies an application to adjust status to that of lawful permanent resident based on section 586 of Public Law 106-429, the applicant will be notified of the decision in writing.

(*l*) Administrative review. An alien whose application for adjustment of status under section 586 of Public Law 106-429 is denied by USCIS may appeal the decision to the Administrative Appeals Office in accordance with 8 CFR 103.3(a)(2).

HISTORY:

[67 FR 78667, 78673, Dec. 26, 2002; 76 FR 53764, 53793, Aug. 29, 2011, as corrected at 76 FR 73475, Nov. 29, 2011; 78 FR 18457, 18472, Mar. 27, 2013, as confirmed at 81 FR 91646, 91670, Dec. 19, 2016; 85 FR 46788, 46927, Aug. 3, 2020]

§ 245.22 Evidence to demonstrate an alien's physical presence in the United States on a specific date.

(a) Evidence. Generally, an alien who is required to demonstrate his or her physical presence in the United States on a specific date in connection with an application to adjust status to that of an alien lawfully admitted for permanent residence should submit evidence according to this section. In cases where a more specific regulation relating to a particular adjustment of status provision has been issued in the 8 CFR, such regulation is controlling to the extent that it conflicts with this section.

(b) The number of documents. If no one document establishes the alien's physical presence on the required date, he or she may submit several documents establishing his or her physical presence in the United States prior to and after that date.

(c) DHS-issued documentation. An applicant for permanent residence may demonstrate physical presence by submitting DHS-issued (or predecessor agency-issued) documentation such as an arrival-departure form or notice to appear in immigration proceedings.

(d) Government-issued documentation. To demonstrate physical presence on the required date, the alien may submit other government documentation. Other government documentation issued by a Federal, State, or local authority must bear the signature, seal, or other authenticating instrument of such authority (if the document normally bears such instrument), be dated at the time of issuance, and bear a date of issuance not later than the required date. For this purpose, the term Federal, State, or local authority includes any governmental, educational, or administrative function operated by Federal, State, county, or municipal officials. Examples of such other documentation include, but are not limited to:

(1) A state driver's license;

(2) A state identification card;

(3) A county or municipal hospital record;

(4) A public college or public school transcript;

(5) Income tax records;

(6) A certified copy of a Federal, State, or local governmental record that was created on or prior to the required date, shows that the applicant was present in the United States at the time, and establishes that the applicant sought in his or her own behalf, or some other party sought in the applicant's behalf, a benefit from the Federal, State, or local governmental agency keeping such record;

(7) A certified copy of a Federal, State, or local governmental record that was created on or prior to the required date, that shows that the applicant was present in the United States at the time, and establishes that the applicant submitted an income tax return, property tax payment, or similar submission or payment to the Federal, State, or local governmental agency keeping such record; or

(8) A transcript from a private or religious school that is registered with, or approved or licensed by, appropriate State or local authorities, accredited by the State or regional accrediting body, or by the appropriate private school association, or maintains enrollment records in accordance with State or local requirements or standards. Such evidence will only be accepted to document the physical presence of an alien who was in attendance and under the age of 21 on the specific date that physical presence in the United States is required.

(e) Copies of records. It shall be the responsibility of the applicant to obtain and submit copies of the records of any other government agency that the applicant desires to be considered in support of his or her application. If the alien is not in possession of such a document or documents, but believes that a copy is already contained in the Service file relating to him or her, he or she may submit a statement as to the name and location of the issuing Federal, State, or local government agency, the type of document and the date on which it was issued.

(f) Other relevant document(s) and evaluation of evidence. The adjudicator will consider any other relevant document(s) as well as evaluate all evidence submitted, on a case-by-case basis. The Service may require an interview when necessary.

(g) Accuracy of documentation. In all cases, any doubts as to the existence, authenticity, veracity, or accuracy of the documentation shall be resolved by the official government record, with records of the Service having precedence over the records of other agencies. Furthermore, determinations as to the weight to be given any particular document or item of evidence shall be solely within the discretion of the adjudicating authority.

HISTORY:

[67 FR 78667, 78674, Dec. 26, 2002; 76 FR 53764, 53794, Aug. 29, 2011]

§ 245.23 Adjustment of noncitizens in T nonimmigrant classification.

(a) Eligibility of principal T-1 applicants. Except as described in paragraph (c) of this section, a noncitizen may be granted adjustment of status to that of a noncitizen lawfully admitted for permanent residence, provided the noncitizen:

(1) Applies for such adjustment.

(2) Was lawfully admitted to the United States as a T-1 nonimmigrant, as defined in 8 CFR 214.201.

(3) Continues to hold T-1 nonimmigrant status at the time of application.

(4) Has been physically present in the United States for a continuous period of at least 3 years since the date of lawful admission as a T-1 nonimmigrant, or has been physically present in the United States for a continuous period during the investigation or prosecution of acts of trafficking and the Attorney General has determined that the investigation or prosecution is complete, whichever period is less; except

(i) If the applicant has departed from the United States for any single period in excess of 90 days or for any periods in the aggregate exceeding 180 days, the applicant shall be considered to have failed to maintain continuous physical presence in the United States for purposes of section 245(l)(1)(A) of the Act; and

(ii) If the noncitizen was granted T nonimmigrant status, such noncitizen's physical presence in the CNMI before, on, or after November 28, 2009, and subsequent to the grant of T nonimmigrant status, is considered as equivalent to presence in the United States pursuant to an admission in T nonimmigrant status.

(5) Is admissible to the United States under the Act, or otherwise has been granted a waiver by USCIS of any applicable ground of inadmissibility, at the time of examination for adjustment.

(6) Has been a person of good moral character since first being lawfully admitted as a T-1 nonimmigrant and until USCIS completes the adjudication of the application for adjustment of status.

(7)(i) Has, since first being lawfully admitted as a T-1 nonimmigrant, and until the conclusion of adjudication of the application, complied with any reasonable request for assistance in the detection, investigation or prosecution of acts of trafficking, as defined in § 8 CFR 214.201; or

(ii) Would suffer extreme hardship involving unusual and severe harm upon removal from the United States, as provided in 8 CFR 214.209; or

(iii) Was younger than 18 years of age at the time of the victimization that qualified the T nonimmigrant for relief under section 101(a)(15)(T) of the Act, 8 U.S.C. 1101(a)(15)(T); or

(iv) Established an inability to cooperate with a reasonable request for assistance at the time their Application for T Nonimmigrant Status was approved, as defined in 8 CFR 214.202(c)(1) and (2).

(b) Eligibility of derivative family members. A derivative family member of a T-1 nonimmigrant status holder may be granted adjustment of status to that of a noncitizen lawfully admitted for permanent residence, provided:

(1) The T-1 nonimmigrant has applied for adjustment of status under this section and meets the eligibility requirements described under paragraph (a) of this section;

(2) The derivative family member was lawfully admitted to the United States in derivative T nonimmigrant status under section 101(a)(15)(T)(ii) of the Act, and continues to hold such status at the time of application;

(3) The derivative family member has applied for such adjustment; and

(4) The derivative family member is admissible to the United States under the Act, or otherwise has been granted a waiver by USCIS of any applicable ground of inadmissibility, at the time of examination for adjustment.

(5) The derivative family member does not automatically lose T nonimmigrant status when the T-1 nonimmigrant adjusts status.

(c) Exceptions. A noncitizen is not eligible for adjustment of status under paragraph (a) or (b) of this section if:

(1) Their T nonimmigrant status has been revoked pursuant to 8 CFR 214.213;

(2) They are described in section 212(a)(3), 212(a)(10)(C), or 212(a)(10)(E) of the Act; or

(3) They are inadmissible under any other provisions of section 212(a) of the Act and have not obtained a waiver of inadmissibility in accordance with 8 CFR 212.18 or 214.210.

(4) Where the applicant establishes that the victimization was a central reason for their unlawful presence in the United States, section 212(a)(9)(B)(iii) of the Act is not applicable, and the applicant need not obtain a waiver of that ground of inadmissibility. The applicant, however, must submit with their application for adjustment of status evidence sufficient to demonstrate that the victimization suffered was a central reason for the

unlawful presence in the United States. To qualify for this exception, the victimization need not be the sole reason for the unlawful presence but the nexus between the victimization and the unlawful presence must be more than tangential, incidental, or superficial.

(d) Jurisdiction.

(1) USCIS shall determine whether a T-1 applicant for adjustment of status under this section was lawfully admitted as a T-1 nonimmigrant and continues to hold such status, has been physically present in the United States during the requisite period, is admissible to the United States or has otherwise been granted a waiver of any applicable ground of inadmissibility, and has been a person of good moral character during the requisite period.

(2) USCIS shall determine whether the applicant received a reasonable request for assistance in the investigation or prosecution of acts of trafficking as defined in 8 CFR 214.201 and 214.208(c), and, if so, whether the applicant complied in such request.

(3) If USCIS determines that the applicant failed to comply with any reasonable request for assistance, USCIS shall deny the application for adjustment of status unless USCIS finds that the applicant would suffer extreme hardship involving unusual and severe harm upon removal from the United States.

(e) Application —

(1) Filing requirements. Each T-1 principal applicant and each derivative family member who is applying for adjustment of status must file an Application to Register Permanent Residence or Adjust Status; and

(i) Accompanying documents, in accordance with the form instructions;

(ii) A photocopy of the applicant's Notice of Action, granting T nonimmigrant status;

(iii) A photocopy of all pages of their most recent passport or an explanation of why they do not have a passport;

(iv) A copy of the applicant's Arrival-Departure Record; and

(v) Evidence that the applicant was lawfully admitted in T nonimmigrant status and continues to hold such status at the time of application. For T nonimmigrants who traveled outside the United States and returned to the United States after presenting an Advance Parole Document issued while the adjustment of status application was pending, the date that the applicant was first admitted in lawful T status will be the date of admission for purposes of this section, regardless of how the applicant's Arrival-Departure Record is annotated.

(2) T-1 principal applicants. In addition to the items in paragraph (e)(1) of this section, T-1 principal applicants must submit:

(i) Evidence, including an affidavit from the applicant and a photocopy of all pages of all of the applicant's passports valid during the required period (or equivalent travel document or a valid explanation of why the applicant does not have a passport), that they have been continuously physically present in the United States for the requisite period as described in paragraph (a)(2) of this section. Applicants should submit evidence described in § 245.22. A signed statement from the applicant attesting to the applicant's continuous physical presence alone will not be sufficient to establish this eligibility requirement. If additional documentation is not available, the applicant must explain why in an affidavit and provide additional affidavits from others with first-hand knowledge who can attest to the applicant's continuous physical presence by specific facts.

(A) If the applicant has departed from and returned to the United States while in T-1 nonimmigrant status, the applicant must submit supporting evidence showing the dates of each departure from the United States and the date, manner, and place of each return to the United States.

(B) Applicants applying for adjustment of status under this section who have less than 3 years of continuous physical presence while in T-1 nonimmigrant status must submit a document signed by the Attorney General or their designee, attesting that the investigation or prosecution is complete.

(ii) Evidence of good moral character in accordance with paragraph (g) of this section; and

(A) Evidence that the applicant has complied with any reasonable request for assistance in the investigation or prosecution of the trafficking as described in paragraph (f)(1) of this section since having first been lawfully admitted in T-1 nonimmigrant status and until the adjudication of the application; or

(B) Evidence that the applicant would suffer extreme hardship involving unusual and severe harm if removed from the United States as described in paragraph (f)(2) of this section.

(3) Evidence relating to discretion. Each applicant seeking adjustment under section 245(l) of the Act bears the burden of showing that discretion should be exercised in their favor. Where adverse factors are present, an applicant may offset these by submitting supporting documentation establishing mitigating equities that the applicant wants USCIS to consider. Depending on the nature of adverse factors, the applicant may be required to clearly demonstrate that the denial of adjustment of status would result in exceptional and extremely unusual hardship. Moreover, depending on the gravity of the adverse factors, such a showing might still be insufficient. For example, only the most compelling positive factors would justify a favorable exercise of discretion in cases where the applicant has committed or been convicted of a serious violent crime, a crime involving sexual abuse committed upon a child, or multiple drug-related crimes, or where there are security- or terrorism-related concerns.

(f) Assistance in the investigation or prosecution or a showing of extreme hardship. Each T-1 principal applicant must establish that since having been lawfully admitted as a T-1 nonimmigrant and up until the adjudication of the application, they complied with any reasonable request for assistance in the investigation or prosecution of the acts of trafficking, as defined in 8 CFR 214.201, or establish that they would suffer extreme hardship involving unusual and severe harm upon removal from the United States.

(1) Each T-1 applicant for adjustment of status under section 245(l) of the Act must submit evidence demonstrating that the applicant has complied with any reasonable requests for assistance in the investigation or prosecution of the human trafficking offenses during the requisite period; or

(2) In lieu of showing continued compliance with requests for assistance, an applicant may establish that they would suffer extreme hardship involving unusual and severe harm upon removal from the United States.

(i) The hardship determination will be evaluated on a case-by-case basis, in accordance with the factors described in 8 CFR 214.209.

(ii) Where the basis for the hardship claim represents a continuation of the hardship claimed in the Application for T Nonimmigrant Status, the applicant need not re-document the entire claim, but rather may submit evidence to establish that the previously established hardship is ongoing. However, in reaching its decision regarding hardship under this section, USCIS is not bound by its previous hardship determination made under 8 CFR 214.209.

(g) Good moral character. A T-1 nonimmigrant applicant for adjustment of status under this section must demonstrate that they have been a person of good moral character since first being lawfully admitted as a T-1 nonimmigrant and until USCIS completes the adjudication of their applications for adjustment of status. Claims of good moral character will be evaluated on a case-by-case basis, taking into account section 101(f) of the Act and the standards of the community. The applicant must submit evidence of good moral character as follows:

(1) An affidavit from the applicant attesting to their good moral character, accompanied by a local police clearance or a state-issued criminal background check from each locality or state in the United States in which the applicant has resided for 6 or more months during the requisite period in continued presence or T-1 nonimmigrant status.

(2) If police clearances, criminal background checks, or similar reports are not available for some or all locations, the applicant may include an explanation and submit other evidence with their affidavit.

(3) USCIS will consider other credible evidence of good moral character, such as affidavits from responsible persons who can knowledgeably attest to the applicant's good moral character.

(4) An applicant who is under 14 years of age is generally presumed to be a person of good moral character and is not required to submit evidence of good moral character. However, if there is reason to believe that an applicant who is under 14 years of age may lack good moral character, USCIS may require evidence of good moral character.

(h) Filing and decision. An application for adjustment of status from a T nonimmigrant under section 245(l) of the Act shall be filed with the USCIS office identified in the instructions to the Application to Register Permanent Residence or Adjust Status. Upon approval of adjustment of status under this section, USCIS will record the noncitizen's lawful admission for permanent residence as of the date of such approval and will notify the applicant in writing. Derivative family members' applications may not be approved before the principal applicant's application is approved.

(i) Denial. If the application for adjustment of status or the application for a waiver of inadmissibility is denied, USCIS will notify the applicant in writing of the reasons for the denial and of the right to appeal the decision to the Administrative Appeals Office (AAO) pursuant to the AAO appeal procedures found at 8 CFR 103.3. Denial of the T-1 principal applicant's application will result in the automatic denial of a derivative family member's application.

(j) Effect of Departure.

(1) If an applicant for adjustment of status under this section departs the United States, they shall be deemed to have abandoned the application, and it will be denied.

(2) If, however, the applicant is not under exclusion, deportation, or removal proceedings, and they filed an Application for Travel Document, in accordance with the instructions on the form, or any other appropriate form, and was granted advance parole by USCIS for such absences, and was inspected and paroled upon returning to the United States, they will not be deemed to have abandoned the application.

(3) If the adjustment of status application of such an individual is subsequently denied, they will be treated as an applicant for admission subject to sections 212 and 235 of the Act. If an applicant for adjustment of status under this section is under exclusion, deportation, or removal proceedings, USCIS will deem the application for adjustment of status abandoned as of the moment of the applicant's departure from the United States.

(k) Inapplicability. Sections 245.1 and 245.2 do not apply to noncitizens seeking adjustment of status under this section.

(*l*) Annual limit of T-1 principal applicant adjustments —

(1) General. The total number of T-1 principal applicants whose status is adjusted to that of lawful permanent residents under this section may not exceed the statutory limit in any fiscal year.

(2) Waiting list.

(i) All eligible applicants who, due solely to the limit imposed in section 245(l)(4) of the Act and paragraph (l)(1) of this section, are not granted adjustment of status will be placed on a waiting list. USCIS will send the applicant written notice of such placement.

(ii) Priority on the waiting list will be determined by the date the application was properly filed, with the oldest applications receiving the highest priority.

(iii) In the following fiscal year, USCIS will proceed with granting adjustment of status to applicants on the waiting list who remain admissible and eligible for adjustment of status in order of highest priority until the available numbers are exhausted for the given fiscal year.

(iv) After the status of qualifying applicants on the waiting list has been adjusted, any remaining numbers for that fiscal year will be issued to new qualifying applicants in the order that the applications were properly filed.

HISTORY:

[73 FR 75540, 75558, Dec. 12, 2008; 78 FR 18457, 18472, Mar. 27, 2013, as confirmed at 81 FR 91646, 91670, Dec. 19, 2016; 81 FR 92266, 92312, Dec. 19, 2016; 84 FR 41292, 41507, Aug. 14, 2019; 85 FR 46788, 46927, Aug. 3, 2020; 86 FR 14221, 14228, Mar. 15, 2021; 87 FR 55472, 55639, Sept. 9, 2022; 89 FR 34864, 34941, Apr. 30, 2024]

§ 245.24 Adjustment of aliens in U nonimmigrant status.

(a) Definitions. As used in this section, the term:

(1) Continuous Physical Presence means the period of time that the alien has been physically present in the United States and must be a continuous period of at least 3 years since the date of admission as a U nonimmigrant continuing through the date of the conclusion of adjudication of the application for adjustment of status. If the alien has departed from the United States for any single period in excess of 90 days or for any periods in the aggregate exceeding 180 days, the applicant must include a certification from the agency that signed the Form I-918, Supplement B, in support of the alien's U nonimmigrant status that the absences were necessary to assist in the criminal investigation or prosecution or were otherwise justified.

(2) Qualifying Family Member means a U-1 principal applicant's spouse, child, or, in the case of an alien child, a parent who has never been admitted to the United States as a nonimmigrant under sections 101(a)(15)(U) and 214(p) of the Act.

(3) U Interim Relief means deferred action and work authorization benefits provided by USCIS or the Immigration and Naturalization Service to applicants for U nonimmigrant status deemed prima facie eligible for U nonimmigrant status prior to publication of the U nonimmigrant status regulations.

(4) U Nonimmigrant means an alien who is in lawful U-1, U-2, U-3, U-4, or U-5 status.

(5) Refusal to Provide Assistance in a Criminal Investigation or Prosecution is the refusal by the alien to provide assistance to a law enforcement agency or official that had responsibility for the investigation or prosecution of persons in connection with the qualifying criminal activity after the alien was granted U nonimmigrant status. The Attorney General will determine whether the alien's refusal was unreasonable under the totality of the circumstances based on all available affirmative evidence. The Attorney General may take into account such factors as general law enforcement, prosecutorial, and judicial practices; the kinds of assistance asked of other victims of crimes involving an element of force, coercion, or fraud; the nature of the request to the alien for assistance; the nature of the victimization; the applicable guidelines for victim and witness assistance; and the specific circumstances of the applicant, including fear, severe traumatization (both mental and physical), and the age and maturity of the applicant.

(b) Eligibility of U Nonimmigrants. Except as described in paragraph (c) of this section, an alien may be granted adjustment of status to that of an alien lawfully admitted for permanent residence, provided the alien:

(1) Applies for such adjustment;

(2)(i) Was lawfully admitted to the United States as either a U-1, U-2, U-3, U-4 or U-5 nonimmigrant, as defined in 8 CFR 214.1(a)(2), and

(ii) Continues to hold such status at the time of application; or accrued at least 4 years in U interim relief status and files a complete adjustment application within 120 days of the date of approval of the Form I-918, Petition for U Nonimmigrant Status;

(3) Has continuous physical presence for 3 years as defined in paragraph (a)(1) of this section;

(4) Is not inadmissible under section 212(a)(3)(E) of the Act;

(5) Has not unreasonably refused to provide assistance to an official or law enforcement agency that had responsibility in an investigation or prosecution of persons in connection with the qualifying criminal activity after the alien was granted U nonimmigrant status, as determined by the Attorney General, based on affirmative evidence; and

(6) Establishes to the satisfaction of the Secretary that the alien's presence in the United States is justified on humanitarian grounds, to ensure family unity, or is in the public interest.

(c) Exception. An alien is not eligible for adjustment of status under paragraph (b) of this section if the alien's U nonimmigrant status has been revoked pursuant to 8 CFR 214.14(h).

(d) Application Procedures for U nonimmigrants. Each U nonimmigrant who is requesting adjustment of status must submit:

(1) Form I-485, Application to Register Permanent Residence or Adjust Status, in accordance with the form instructions;

(2) The fee prescribed in 8 CFR 106.2 or an application for a fee waiver;

(3) [Removed and Reserved]

(4) A photocopy of the alien's Form I-797, Notice of Action, granting U nonimmigrant status;

(5) A photocopy of all pages of all of the applicant's passports valid during the required period (or equivalent travel document or a valid explanation of why the applicant does not have a passport) and documentation showing the following:

(i) The date of any departure from the United States during the period that the applicant was in U nonimmigrant status;

(ii) The date, manner, and place of each return to the United States during the period that the applicant was in U nonimmigrant status; and

(iii) If the applicant has been absent from the United States for any period in excess of 90 days or for any periods in the aggregate of 180 days or more, a certification from the investigating or prosecuting agency that the absences were necessary to assist in the investigation or prosecution of the criminal activity or were otherwise justified;

(6) A copy of the alien's Form I-94 (see § 1.4), Arrival-Departure Record;

(7) Evidence that the applicant was lawfully admitted in U nonimmigrant status and continues to hold such status at the time of application;

(8) Evidence pertaining to any request made to the alien by an official or law enforcement agency for assistance in an investigation or prosecution of persons in connection with the qualifying criminal activity, and the alien's response to such request;

(9) Evidence, including an affidavit from the applicant, that he or she has continuous physical presence for at least 3 years as defined in paragraph (a)(1) of this section. Applicants should submit evidence described in 8 CFR 245.22. A signed statement from the applicant attesting to continuous physical presence alone will not be sufficient to establish this eligibility requirement. If additional documentation is not available, the applicant must explain why in an affidavit and provide additional affidavits from others with first-hand knowledge who can attest to the applicant's continuous physical presence by specific facts;

(10) Evidence establishing that approval is warranted. Any other information required by the instructions to Form I-485, including whether adjustment of status is warranted as a matter of discretion on humanitarian grounds, to ensure family unity, or is otherwise in the public interest; and

(11) Evidence relating to discretion. An applicant has the burden of showing that discretion should be exercised in his or her favor. Although U adjustment applicants are not required to establish that they are admissible, USCIS may take into account all factors, including acts that would otherwise render the applicant inadmissible, in making its discretionary decision on the application. Where adverse factors are present, an applicant may offset these by submitting supporting documentation establishing mitigating equities that the applicant wants USCIS to consider when determining whether or not a favorable exercise of discretion is appropriate. Depending on the nature of the adverse factors, the applicant may be required to clearly demonstrate that the denial of adjustment of status would result in exceptional and extremely unusual hardship. Moreover, depending on the gravity of the adverse factors, such a showing might still be insufficient. For example, USCIS will generally not exercise its discretion favorably in cases where the applicant has committed or been convicted of a serious violent crime, a crime involving sexual abuse committed upon a child, or multiple drug-related crimes, or where there are security- or terrorism-related concerns.

(e) Continued assistance in the investigation or prosecution. Each applicant for adjustment of status under section 245(m) of the Act must provide evidence of whether or not any request was made to the alien to provide assistance, after having been lawfully admitted as a U nonimmigrant, in an investigation or prosecution of persons in connection with the qualifying criminal activity, and his or her response to any such requests.

(1) An applicant for adjustment of status under section 245(m) of the Act may submit a document signed by an official or law enforcement agency that had responsibility for the investigation or prosecution of persons in connection with the qualifying criminal activity, affirming that the applicant complied with (or did not unreasonably refuse to comply with) reasonable requests for assistance in the investigation or prosecution during the requisite period. To meet this evidentiary requirement, applicants may submit a newly executed Form I-918, Supplement B, "U Nonimmigrant Status Certification."

(2) If the applicant does not submit a document described in paragraph (e)(1) of this section, the applicant may submit an affidavit describing the applicant's efforts, if any, to obtain a newly executed Form I-918, Supplement B, or other evidence describing whether or not the alien received any request to provide assistance in a criminal investigation or prosecution, and the alien's response to any such request.

(i) The applicant should also include, when possible, identifying information about the law enforcement personnel involved in the case and any information, of which the applicant is aware, about the status of the criminal investigation or prosecution, including any charges filed and the outcome of any criminal proceedings, or whether the investigation or prosecution was dropped and the reasons.

(ii) If applicable, an applicant may also provide a more detailed description of situations where the applicant refused to comply with requests for assistance because the applicant believed that the requests for assistance were unreasonable.

(3) In determining whether the applicant has satisfied the continued assistance requirement, USCIS or the Department of Justice may at its discretion contact the certifying agency that executed the applicant's original Form I-918, Supplement B, "U Nonimmigrant Status Certification" or any other law enforcement agency.

(4) In accordance with procedures determined by the Department of Justice and the Department of Homeland Security, USCIS will refer certain applications for adjustment of status to the Department of Justice for determination of whether the applicant unreasonably refused to provide assistance in a criminal investigation or prosecution. If the applicant submits a document described in paragraph (e)(1) of this section, USCIS will not refer the application for consideration by the Department of Justice absent extraordinary circumstances. In other cases, USCIS will only refer an application to the Department of Justice if an official or law enforcement agency has provided evidence that the alien has refused to comply with requests to provide assistance in an investigation or prosecution of persons in connection with the qualifying criminal activity or if there are other affirmative evidence in the record suggesting that the applicant may have unreasonably refused to provide such assistance. In these instances, USCIS will request that the Department of Justice determine, based on all available affirmative evidence, whether the applicant unreasonably refused to provide

assistance in a criminal investigation or prosecution. The Department of Justice will have 90 days to provide a written determination to USCIS, or where appropriate, request an extension of time to provide such a determination. After such time, USCIS may adjudicate the application whether or not the Department of Justice has provided a response.

(f) Decision. The decision to approve or deny a Form I-485 filed under section 245(m) of the Act is a discretionary determination that lies solely within USCIS's jurisdiction. After completing its review of the application and evidence, USCIS will issue a written decision approving or denying Form I-485 and notify the applicant of this decision.

(1) Approvals. If USCIS determines that the applicant has met the requirements for adjustment of status and merits a favorable exercise of discretion, USCIS will approve the Form I-485. Upon approval of adjustment of status under this section, USCIS will record the alien's lawful admission for permanent residence as of the date of such approval.

(2) Denials. Upon the denial of an application for adjustment of status under section 245(m) of the Act, the applicant will be notified in writing of the decision and the reason for the denial in accordance with 8 CFR part 103. If an applicant chooses to appeal the denial to the Administrative Appeals Office pursuant to the provisions of 8 CFR 103.3, the denial will not become final until the appeal is adjudicated.

(g) Filing petitions for qualifying family members. A principal U-1 applicant may file an immigrant petition under section 245(m)(3) of the Act on behalf of a qualifying family member as defined in paragraph (a)(2) of this section, provided that:

(1) The qualifying family member has never held U nonimmigrant status;

(2) The qualifying family relationship, as defined in paragraph (a)(2) of this section, exists at the time of the U-1 principal's adjustment and continues to exist through the adjudication of the adjustment or issuance of the immigrant visa for the qualifying family member;

(3) The qualifying family member or the principal U-1 alien, would suffer extreme hardship as described in 8 CFR 245.24(g) (to the extent the factors listed are applicable) if the qualifying family member is not allowed to remain in or enter the United States; and

(4) The principal U-1 alien has adjusted status to that of a lawful permanent resident, has a pending application for adjustment of status, or is concurrently filing an application for adjustment of status.

(h) Procedures for filing petitions for qualifying family members.

(1) Required documents. For each qualifying family member who plans to seek an immigrant visa or adjustment of status under section 245(m)(3) of the Act, the U-1 principal applicant must submit, either concurrently with, or after he or she has filed, his or her Form I-485:

(i) Form I-929 in accordance with the form instructions;

(ii) The fee prescribed in 8 CFR 106.2 or an application for a fee waiver;

(iii) Evidence of the relationship listed in paragraph (a)(2) of this section, such as a birth or marriage certificate. If primary evidence is unavailable, secondary evidence or affidavits may be submitted in accordance with 8 CFR 103.2(b)(2);

(iv) Evidence establishing that either the qualifying family member or the U-1 principal alien would suffer extreme hardship if the qualifying family member is not allowed to remain in or join the principal in the United States. Extreme hardship is evaluated on a case-by-case basis, taking into account the particular facts and circumstances of each case. Applicants are encouraged to document all applicable factors in their applications, as the presence or absence of any one factor may not be determinative in evaluating extreme hardship. To establish extreme hardship to a qualifying family member who is physically present in the United States, an applicant must demonstrate that removal of the qualifying family member would result in a degree of hardship beyond that typically associated with removal. Factors that may be considered in evaluating whether removal would result in extreme hardship to the alien or to the alien's qualifying family member include, but are not limited to:

(A) The nature and extent of the physical or mental abuse suffered as a result of having been a victim of criminal activity;

(B) The impact of loss of access to the United States courts and criminal justice system, including but not limited to, participation in the criminal investigation or prosecution of the criminal activity of which the alien was a victim, and any civil proceedings related to family law, child custody, or other court proceeding stemming from the criminal activity;

(C) The likelihood that the perpetrator's family, friends, or others acting on behalf of the perpetrator in the home country would harm the applicant or the applicant's children;

(D) The applicant's needs for social, medical, mental health, or other supportive services for victims of crime that are unavailable or not reasonably accessible in the home country;

(E) Where the criminal activity involved arose in a domestic violence context, the existence of laws and social practices in the home country that punish the applicant or the applicant's child(ren) because they have been victims of domestic violence or have taken steps to leave an abusive household;

(F) The perpetrator's ability to travel to the home country and the ability and willingness of authorities in the home country to protect the applicant or the applicant's children; and

(G) The age of the applicant, both at the time of entry to the United States and at the time of application for adjustment of status; and

(v) Evidence, including a signed statement from the qualifying family member and other supporting documentation, to establish that discretion should be exercised in his or her favor. Although qualifying family members are not required to establish that they are admissible on any of the grounds set forth in section 212(a) of the Act other than on section 212(a)(3)(E) of the Act, USCIS may take into account all factors, including acts that would otherwise render the applicant inadmissible, in making its discretionary decision on the application. Where adverse factors are present, an applicant may offset these by submitting supporting documentation establishing mitigating equities that the applicant wants USCIS to consider when determining whether or not a favorable exercise of discretion is appropriate. Depending on the nature of the adverse factors, the applicant may be required to clearly demonstrate that the denial of adjustment of status would result in exceptional and extremely unusual hardship. Moreover, depending on the gravity of the adverse factors, such a showing might still be insufficient. For example, USCIS will generally not exercise its discretion favorably in cases where the applicant has committed or been convicted of a serious violent crime, a crime involving sexual abuse committed upon a child, or multiple drug-related crimes, or where there are security- or terrorism-related concerns.

(2) Decision. The decision to approve or deny a Form I-929 is a discretionary determination that lies solely within USCIS's jurisdiction. The Form I-929 for a qualifying family member may not be approved, however, until such time as the principal U-1 applicant's application for adjustment of status has been approved. After completing its review of the application and evidence, USCIS will issue a written decision and notify the applicant of that decision in writing.

(i) Approvals.

(A) For qualifying family members who are outside of the United States, if the Form I-929 is approved, USCIS will forward notice of the approval either to the Department of State's National Visa Center so the applicant can apply to the consular post for an immigrant visa, or to the appropriate port of entry for a visa exempt alien.

(B) For qualifying family members who are physically present in the United States, if the Form I-929 is approved, USCIS will forward notice of the approval to the U-1 principal applicant.

(ii) Denials. If the Form I-929 is denied, the applicant will be notified in writing of the reason(s) for the denial in accordance with 8 CFR part 103. If an applicant chooses to appeal the denial to the Administrative Appeals Office pursuant to 8 CFR 103.3, the denial will not become final until the appeal is adjudicated. Denial of the U-1 principal applicant's application will result in the automatic denial of a qualifying family member's Form I-929. There shall be no appeal of such an automatic denial.

(i) Application procedures for qualifying family members who are physically present in the United States to request adjustment of status.

(1) Required documents. Qualifying family members in the United States may request adjustment of status by submitting:

(i) Form I-485, Application to Register Permanent Residence or Adjust Status, in accordance with the form instructions;

(ii) An approved Form I-929, Petition for Qualifying Family Member of a U-1 Nonimmigrant;

(iii) The fee prescribed in 8 CFR 106.2 or an application for a fee waiver; and

(2) Decision. The decision to approve or deny Form I-485 is a discretionary determination that lies solely within USCIS's jurisdiction. After completing its review of the application and evidence, USCIS will issue a written decision approving or denying Form I-485 and notify the applicant of this decision in writing.

(i) Approvals. Upon approval of a Form I-485 under this section, USCIS shall record the alien's lawful admission for permanent residence as of the date of such approval.

(ii) Denial. Upon the denial of any application for adjustment of status, the applicant will be notified in writing of the decision and the reason for the denial in accordance with 8 CFR part 103. If an applicant chooses to appeal the denial to the Administrative Appeals Office pursuant to the provisions of 8 CFR 103.3, the denial will not become final until the appeal is adjudicated. During the appeal period, the applicant may not obtain or renew employment authorization under 8 CFR 274a.12(c)(9). Denial of the U-1 principal applicant's application will result in the automatic denial of a qualifying family member's Form I-485; such an automatic denial is not appealable.

(j) Effect of departure. If an applicant for adjustment of status under this section departs the United States, he or she shall be deemed to have abandoned the application, and it will be denied. If, however, the applicant is not under exclusion, deportation, or removal proceedings, and he or she filed a Form I-131, Application for Travel Document, in accordance with the instructions on the form, or any other appropriate form, and was granted advance parole by USCIS for such absences, and was inspected and paroled upon returning to the United States, he or she will not be deemed to have abandoned the application. If the adjustment of status application of such an individual is subsequently denied, he or she will be treated as an applicant for admission subject to sections 212 and 235 of the Act. If an applicant for adjustment of status under this section is under exclusion, deportation, or removal proceedings, USCIS will deem the application for adjustment of status abandoned as of the moment of the applicant's departure from the United States.

(k) Exclusive jurisdiction. USCIS shall have exclusive jurisdiction over adjustment applications filed under section 245(m) of the Act.

(*l*) Inapplicability of 8 CFR 245.1 and 245.2. The provisions of 8 CFR 245.1 and 245.2 do not apply to aliens seeking adjustment of status under section 245(m) of the Act.

HISTORY:

[73 FR 75540, 75560, Dec. 12, 2008, as corrected at 74 FR 395, Jan. 6, 2009.; 78 FR 18457, 18472, Mar. 27, 2013, as confirmed at 81 FR 91646, 91670, Dec. 19, 2016; 85 FR 46788, 46927, Aug. 3, 2020]

§ 245.25 Adjustment of status of aliens with approved employment-based immigrant visa petitions; validity of petition and offer of employment.

(a) Validity of petition for continued eligibility for

adjustment of status. An alien who has a pending application to adjust status to that of a lawful permanent resident based on an approved employment-based immigrant visa petition filed under section 204(a)(1)(F) of the Act on the applicant's behalf must have a valid offer of employment based on a valid petition at the time the application to adjust status is filed and at the time the alien's application to adjust status is adjudicated, and the applicant must intend to accept such offer of employment. Prior to a final administrative decision on an application to adjust status, USCIS may require that the applicant demonstrate, or the applicant may affirmatively demonstrate to USCIS, on Form I-485 Supplement J, with any supporting material and credible documentary evidence, in accordance with the form instructions that:

(1) The employment offer by the petitioning employer is continuing; or

(2) Under section 204(j) of the Act, the applicant has a new offer of employment from the petitioning employer or a different U.S. employer, or a new offer based on self-employment, in the same or a similar occupational classification as the employment offered under the qualifying petition, provided that:

(i) The alien's application to adjust status based on a qualifying petition has been pending for 180 days or more; and

(ii) The qualifying immigrant visa petition:

(A) Has already been approved; or

(B) Is pending when the beneficiary notifies USCIS of a new job offer 180 days or more after the date the alien's adjustment of status application was filed, and the petition is subsequently approved:

(1) Adjudication of the pending petition shall be without regard to the requirement in 8 CFR 204.5(g)(2) to continuously establish the ability to pay the proffered wage after filing and until the beneficiary obtains lawful permanent residence; and

(2) The pending petition will be approved if it was eligible for approval at the time of filing and until the alien's adjustment of status application has been pending for 180 days, unless approval of the qualifying immigrant visa petition at the time of adjudication is inconsistent with a requirement of the Act or another applicable statute; and

(iii) The approval of the qualifying petition has not been revoked.

(3) In all cases, the applicant and his or her intended employer must demonstrate the intention for the applicant to be employed under the continuing or new employment offer (including self-employment) described in paragraphs (a)(1) and (2) of this section, as applicable, within a reasonable period upon the applicant's grant of lawful permanent resident status.

(b) Definition of same or similar occupational classification. The term "same occupational classification" means an occupation that resembles in every relevant respect the occupation for which the underlying employment-based immigrant visa petition was approved. The term "similar occupational classification" means an occupation that shares essential qualities or has a marked resemblance or likeness with the occupation for which the underlying employment- based immigrant visa petition was approved.

HISTORY:
[81 FR 82398, 82490, Nov. 18, 2016]

PART 245A—

ADJUSTMENT OF STATUS TO THAT OF PERSONS ADMITTED FOR TEMPORARY OR PERMANENT RESIDENT STATUS UNDER SECTION 245A OF THE IMMIGRATION AND NATIONALITY ACT

Subpart A. Immigration Reform and Control Act of 1986 (Irca) Legalization Provisions

Rule

Subpart B. Legal Immigration Family Equity (Life) Act Legalization Provisions

Subpart C. Life Act Amendments Family Unity Provisions

AUTHORITY NOTE APPLICABLE TO ENTIRE PART:

AUTHORITY:
8 U.S.C. 1101, 1103, 1255a and 1255a note.

Subpart A

Immigration Reform and Control Act of 1986 (Irca) Legalization Provisions

§ 245a.1 Definitions.

As used in this chapter:

(a) Act means the Immigration and Nationality Act, as amended by The Immigration Reform and Control Act of 1986.

(b) Service means the Immigration and Naturalization Service (INS).

(c)(1) Resided continuously as used in section 245A(a)(2) of the Act, means that the alien shall be regarded as having resided continuously in the United States if, at the time of filing of the application for temporary resident status:

An alien who after appearing for a scheduled interview to obtain an immigrant visa at a Consulate or Embassy in Canada or Mexico but who subsequently is not issued an immigrant visa and who is paroled back into the United States, pursuant to the statewide criteria program, shall be regarded as having been granted advance parole by the Service.

(i) No single absence from the United States has exceeded forty-five (45) days, and the aggregate of all absences has not exceeded one hundred and eighty (180) days between January 1, 1982 through the date the application for temporary resident status is filed, unless the alien can establish that due to emergent reasons, his or her return to the United States could not be accomplished within the time period allowed;

(ii) The alien was maintaining residence in the United States; and

(iii) The alien's departure from the United States was not based on an order of deportation.

An alien who has been absent from the United States in accordance with the Service's advance parole procedures shall not be considered as having interrupted his or her continuous residence as required at the time of filing an application.

(2) Continuous residence, as used in section 245A(b)(1)(B) of the Act, means that the alien shall be regarded as having resided continuously in the United States if, at the time of applying for adjustment from temporary residence to permanent resident status: No single absence from the United States has exceeded thirty (30) days, and the aggregate of all absences has not exceeded ninety (90) days between the date of granting of lawful temporary resident status and of applying for permanent resident status, unless the alien can establish that due to emergent reasons the return to the United States could not be accomplished within the time period(s) allowed.

(d) In the term alien's unlawful status was known to the government, the term government means the Immigration and Naturalization Service. An alien's unlawful status was known to the government only if:

(1) The Service received factual information constituting a violation of the alien's nonimmigrant status from any agency, bureau or department, or subdivision thereof, of the Federal government, and such information was stored or otherwise recorded in the official Service alien file, whether or not the Service took follow-up action on the information received. In order to meet the standard of information constituting a violation of the alien's nonimmigrant status, the alien must have made a clear statement or declaration to the other federal agency, bureau or department that he or she was in violation of nonimmigrant status; or

(2) An affirmative determination was made by the Service prior to January 1, 1982 that the alien was subject to deportation proceedings. Evidence that may be presented by an alien to support an assertion that such a determination was made may include, but is not limited to, official Service documents issued prior to January 1, 1982, i.e., Forms I-94 (see § 1.4), Arrival-Departure Records granting a period of time in which to depart the United States without imposition of proceedings; Forms I-210, Voluntary Departure Notice letter; and Forms I-221, Order to Show Cause and Notice of Hearing. Evidence from Service records that may be used to support a finding that such a determination was made may include, but is not limited to, record copies of the aforementioned forms and other documents contained in alien files, i.e., Forms I-213, Record of Deportable Alien;

Unexecuted Forms I-205, Warrant of Deportation; Forms I-265, Application for Order to Show Cause and Processing Sheet; Forms I-541, Order of Denial of Application for Extension of Stay granting a period of time in which to depart the United States without imposition of proceedings, or any other Service record reflecting that the alien's nonimmigrant status was considered by the Service to have terminated or the alien was otherwise determined to be subject to deportation proceedings prior to January 1, 1982, whether or not deportation proceedings were instituted; or

(3) A copy of a response by the Service to any other agency which advised that agency that a particular alien had no legal status in the United States or for whom no record could be found.

(4) The applicant produces documentation from a school approved to enroll foreign students under § 214.3 which establishes that the said school forwarded to the Service a report that clearly indicated the applicant had violated his or her nonimmigrant student status prior to January 1, 1982. A school may submit an affirmation that the school did forward to the Service the aforementioned report and that the school no longer has available copies of the actual documentation sent. In order to be eligible under this part, the applicant must not have been reinstated to nonimmigrant student status.

(e) The term to make a determination as used in § 245a.2(t)(3) of this part means obtaining and reviewing all information required to adjudicate an application for the benefit sought and making a decision thereon. If fraud, willful misrepresentation or concealment of a material fact, knowingly providing a false writing or document, knowingly making a false statement or representation, or any other activity prohibited by section 245A(c)(6) of the Act is established during the process of making the determination on the application, the Service shall refer to the United States Attorney for prosecution of the alien or of any person who created or supplied a false writing or document for use in an application for adjustment of status under this part.

(f) The term continuous physical presence as used in section 245A(a)(3)(A) of the Act means actual continuous presence in the United States since November 6, 1986 until filing of any application for adjustment of status. Aliens who were outside of the United States on the date of enactment or departed the United States after enactment may apply for legalization if they reentered prior to May 1, 1987, provided they meet the continuous residence requirements, and are otherwise eligible for legalization.

(g) Brief, casual, and innocent means a departure authorized by the Service (advance parole) subsequent to May 1, 1987 of not more than thirty (30) days for legitimate emergency or humanitarian purposes unless a further period of authorized departure has been granted in the discretion of the district director or a departure was beyond the alien's control.

(h) The term brief and casual absences as used in section 245a(b)(3)(A) of the Act permits temporary trips abroad as long as the alien establishes a continuing intention to adjust to lawful permanent resident status. However, such absences must comply with § 245a.3(b)(2) of this chapter in order for the alien to maintain continuous residence as specified in the Act.

(i) Public cash assistance means income or needs-based monetary assistance to include, but not limited to, supplemental security income received by the alien through federal, state, or local programs designed to meet subsistence levels. It does not include assistance in kind, such as food stamps, public housing, or other non-cash benefits, nor does it include work-related compensation or certain types of medical assistance (Medicare, Medicaid, emergency treatment, services to pregnant women or children under 18 years of age, or treatment in the interest of public health).

(j) Legalization Office means local offices of the Immigration and Naturalization Service which accept and process applications for Legalization or Special Agricultural Worker status, under the authority of the INS district directors in whose districts such offices are located.

(k) Regional Processing Facility means Service offices established in each of the four Service regions to adjudicate, under the authority of the INS Directors of the Regional Processing Facilities, applications for adjustment of status under section 210, 245A(a) or 245A(b)(1) of the Act.

(l) Designated entity means any state, local, church, community, farm labor organization, voluntary organization, association of agricultural employers or individual determined by the Service to be qualified to assist aliens in the preparation of applications for Legalization status.

(m) The term family unity as used in section 245(d)(2)(B)(i) of the Act means maintaining the family group without deviation or change. The family group shall include the spouse, unmarried minor children under 18 years of age who are not members of some other household, and parents who reside regularly in the household of the family group.

(n) The term prima facie as used in section 245(e)(1) and (2) of the Act means eligibility is established if the applicant presents a completed I-687 and specific factual information which in the absence of rebuttal will establish a claim of eligibility under this part.

(o) Misdemeanor means a crime committed in the United States, either (1) punishable by imprisonment for a term of one year or less, regardless of the term such alien actually served, if any, or (2) a crime treated as a misdemeanor under 8 CFR 245a.1(p). For purposes of this definition, any crime punishable by imprisonment for a maximum term of five days or less shall not be considered a misdemeanor.

(p) Felony means a crime committed in the United States, punishable by imprisonment for a term of more than one year, regardless of the term such alien actually served, if any, except: When the offense is defined by the State as a misdemeanor and the sentence actually imposed is one year or less regardless of the term such alien actually served. Under this exception, for purposes of 8 CFR part 245a, the crime shall be treated as a misdemeanor.

(q) Subject of an Order to Show Cause means actual service of the Order to Show Cause upon the alien through the mail or by personal service.

(r) A qualified designated entity in good-standing with the Service means those designated entities whose cooperative agreements were not suspended or terminated by the Service or those whose agreements were not allowed to lapse by the Service prior to January 30, 1989 (the expiration date of the INS cooperative agreements for all designated entities), or those whose agreements were not terminated for cause by the Service subsequent to January 30, 1989.

Subsequent to January 30, 1989, and throughout the period ending on November 6, 1990, a QDE in good-standing may: (1) Serve as an authorized course provider under § 245a.3(b)(5)(i)(C) of this chapter; (2) Administer the IRCA Test for Permanent Residency (proficiency test), provided an agreement has been entered into with and authorization has been given by INS under § 245a.1(s)(5) of this chapter; and, (3) Certify as true and complete copies of original documents submitted in support of Form I-698 in the format prescribed in § 245a.3(d)(2) of this chapter.

(s) Satisfactorily pursuing, as used in section 245A(b)(1)(D)(i)(II) of the Act, means:

(1) An applicant for permanent resident status has attended a recognized program for at least 40 hours of a minimum 60-hour course as appropriate for his or her ability level, and is demonstrating progress according to the performance standards of the English/citizenship course prescribed by the recognized program in which

he or she is enrolled (as long as enrollment occurred on or after May 1, 1987, course standards include attainment of particular functional skills related to communicative ability, subject matter knowledge, and English language competency, and attainment of these skills is measured either by successful completion of learning objectives appropriate to the applicant's ability level, or attainment of a determined score on a test or tests, or both of these); or

(2) An applicant presents a high school diploma or general educational development diploma (GED) from a school in the United States. A GED gained in a language other than English is acceptable only if a GED English proficiency test has been passed. (The curriculum for both the high school diploma and the GED must have included at least 40 hours of instruction in English and U.S. history and government); or

(3) An applicant has attended for a period of one academic year (or the equivalent thereof according to the standards of the learning institution), a state recognized, accredited learning institution in the United States and that institution certifies such attendance (as long as the curriculum included at least 40 hours of instruction in English and U.S. history and government); or

(4) An applicant has attended courses conducted by employers, social, community, or private groups certified (retroactively, if necessary, as long as enrollment occurred on or after May 1, 1987, and the curriculum included at least 40 hours of instruction in English and U.S. history and government) by the district director or the Director of the Outreach Program under § 245a.3(b)(5)(i)(D) of this chapter; or

(5) An applicant attests to having completed at least 40 hours of individual study in English and U.S. history and government and passes the proficiency test for legalization, called the IRCA Test for Permanent Residency, indicating that the applicant is able to read and understand minimal functional English within the context of the history and government of the United States. Such test may be given by INS, as well as, State Departments of Education (SDEs) (and their accredited educational agencies) and Qualified Designated Entities in good-standing (QDEs) upon agreement with and authorization by INS. Those SDEs and QDEs wishing to participate in this effort should write to the Director of the INS Outreach Program at 425 "I" Street, NW., Washington, DC 20536, for further information.

(t) Minimal understanding of ordinary English as used in section 245A(b)(1)(D)(i) of the Act means an applicant can satisfy basic survival needs and routine social demands. The person can handle jobs that involve following simple oral and very basic written communication.

(u) Curriculum means a defined course for an instructional program. Minimally, the curriculum prescribes what is to be taught, how the course is to be taught, with what materials, and when and where. The curriculum must:

(1) Teach words and phrases in ordinary, everyday usage;

(2) Include the content of the Federal Citizenship Text series as the basis for curriculum development (other texts with similar content may be used in addition to, but not in lieu of, the Federal Citizenship Text series);

(3) Be designed to provide at least 60 hours of instruction per class level;

(4) Be relevant and educationally appropriate for the program focus and the intended audience; and

(5) Be available for examination and review by INS as requested.

(v) The term developmentally disabled means the same as the term developmental disability defined in section 102(5) of the Developmental Disabilities Assistance and Bill of Rights Act of 1987, Public Law 100-146. As a convenience to the public, that definition is printed here in its entirety:

The term developmental disability means a severe, chronic disability of a person which:

(1) Is attributable to a mental or physical impairment or combination of mental and physical impairments;

(2) Is manifested before the person attains age twenty-two;

(3) Is likely to continue indefinitely;

(4) Results in substantial functional limitations in three or more of the following areas of major life activity: (i) Self-care, (ii) receptive and expressive language, (iii) learning, (iv) mobility, (v) self direction, (vi) capacity for independent living, and (vii) economic self-sufficiency; and

(5) Reflects the person's need for a combination and sequence of special, interdisciplinary, or generic care, treatment, or other services which are of lifelong or extended duration and are individually planned and coordinated.

HISTORY:

[52 FR 16208, May 1, 1987, as amended at 52 FR 43845, Nov. 17, 1987; 53 FR 9863, Mar. 28, 1988; 53 FR 23382, June 22, 1988; 53 FR 43992, Oct. 31, 1988; 54 FR 29448, July 12, 1989; 56 FR 31061, July 9, 1991; 78 FR 18457, 18472, Mar. 27, 2013, as confirmed at 81 FR 91646, 91670, Dec. 19, 2016]

§ 245a.2 Application for temporary residence.

(a) Application period for temporary residence.

(1) An alien who has resided unlawfully in the United States since January 1, 1982, who believes that he or she meets the eligibility requirements of section 245A of the Act must make application within the twelve month period beginning on May 5, 1987 and ending on May 4, 1988, except as provided in the following paragraphs.

(2)(i) [Reserved]

(ii) An alien who is the subject of an Order to Show Cause issued under section 242 of the Act during the period beginning on May 5, 1987 and ending on April 4, 1988 must file an application for adjustment of status to that of a temporary resident prior to the thirty-first day after the issuance of the Order to Show Cause.

(iii) An alien who is the subject of an Order to Show Cause issued under section 242 of the Act during the period beginning on April 5, 1988 and ending on May 4, 1988 must file an application for adjustment of status to that of a temporary resident not later than May 4, 1988.

(iv) An alien, described in paragraphs (a)(2)(i) through (iii) of this section, who fails to file an application for adjustment of status to that of a temporary resident under section 245A(a) of the Act during the respective time period(s), will be statutorily ineligible for such adjustment of status.

(b) Eligibility. The following categories of aliens, who are otherwise eligible to apply for legalization, may file for adjustment to temporary residence status:

(1) An alien (other than an alien who entered as a nonimmigrant) who establishes that he or she entered the United States prior to January 1, 1982, and who has thereafter resided continuously in the United States in an unlawful status, and who has been physically present in the United States from November 6, 1986, until the date of filing the application.

(2) An alien who establishes that he or she entered the United States as a nonimmigrant prior to January 1, 1982, and whose period of authorized admission expired through the passage of time prior to January 1, 1982, and who has thereafter resided continuously in the United States in an unlawful status, and who has been physically present in the United States from November 6, 1986, until the date of filing the application.

(3) An alien who establishes that he or she entered the United States as a nonimmigrant prior to January 1, 1982, and whose unlawful status was known to the Government as of January 1, 1982, and who has thereafter resided continuously in the United States in an unlawful status, and who has been physically present in the United States from November 6, 1986, until the date of filing the application.

(4) An alien described in paragraphs (b) (1) through (3) of this section who was at any time a nonimmigrant exchange visitor (as defined in section 101(a)(15)(J) of the Act), must establish that he or she was not subject to the two-year foreign residence requirements of section 212(e) or has fulfilled that requirement or has received a waiver of such requirements and has resided continuously in the United States in unlawful status since January 1, 1982.

(5) An alien who establishes that he or she was granted voluntary departure, voluntary return, extended voluntary departure or placed in deferred action category by the Service prior to January 1, 1982 and who has thereafter resided continuously in such status in the United States and who has been physically present in the United States from November 6, 1986 until the date of filing the application.

(6) An alien who establishes that he or she was paroled into the United States prior to January 1, 1982, and whose parole status terminated prior to January 1, 1982, and who has thereafter resided continuously in such status in the United States, and who has been physically present in the United States from November 6, 1986, until the date of filing the application.

(7) An alien who establishes that he or she is a Cuban or Haitian Entrant who was physically present in the United States prior to January 1, 1982, and who has thereafter resided continuously in the United States, and who has been physically present in the United States from November 6, 1986, until the date of filing the application, without regard to whether such alien has applied for adjustment of status pursuant to section 202 of the Act.

(8) An alien's eligibility under the categories described in section 245(a)(2)(b) (1) through (7) and (9) through (15) shall not be affected by entries to the United States subsequent to January 1, 1982 that were not documented on Service Form I-94 (see § 1.4), Arrival-Departure Record.

(9) An alien who would be otherwise eligible for legalization and who was present in the United States in an unlawful status prior to January 1, 1982, and reentered the United States as a nonimmigrant, such entry being documented on Service Form I-94, Arrival-Departure Record, in order to return to an unrelinquished unlawful residence.

(10) An alien described in paragraph (b)(9) of this section must receive a waiver of the excludable charge 212(a)(19) as an alien who entered the United States by fraud.

(11) A nonimmigrant who entered the United States for duration of status ("D/S") is one of the following classes, A, A-1, A-2, G, G-1, G-2, G-3 or G-4, whose qualifying employment terminated or who ceased to be recognized by the Department of State as being entitled to such classification prior to January 1, 1982, and who has thereafter continued to reside in the United States in an unlawful status. An alien who was a dependent family member and who may be otherwise eligible for legalization may be considered a member of this class of eligible aliens if the dependent family member was also in A and G status when the principal A or G alien's status terminated or ceased to be recognized by the Department of State.

(12) A nonimmigrant who entered the United States for duration of status ("D/S") in one of the following classes, F, F-1, or F-2, who completed a full course of study, including practical training and whose time period if any to depart the United States after completion of study expired prior to January 1, 1982 and who has remained in the United States in an unlawful status since that time. A dependent F-2 alien otherwise eligible who was admitted into the United States with a specific time period, as opposed to duration of status, documented on Service Form I-94, Arrival-Departure Record that extended beyond January 1, 1982 is considered eligible if the principal F-1 alien is found eligible.

(13) An alien who establishes that he or she is a member of the class in the Silva-Levi lawsuit (No. 76-C-4268 (N.D. ILL. March 22, 1977)); that is, an alien from an independent country of the Western Hemisphere who was present in the United States prior to March 11, 1977, and was known by the Immigration and Naturalization Service (INS) to have a priority date for the issuance of an immigrant visa between July

1, 1968 and December 31, 1976, inclusive, and who was clearly eligible for an immigrant visa.

(14) An alien who filed an asylum application prior to January 1, 1982 and whose application was subsequently denied or whose application has not yet been decided is considered an alien in an unlawful status known to the government.

(15) An alien, otherwise eligible who departed the United States and was paroled into the United States on or before May 1, 1987 in order to return to an unrelinquished unlawful residence.

(c) Ineligible aliens.

(1) An alien who has been convicted of a felony, or three or more misdemeanors.

(2) An alien who has assisted in the persecution of any person or persons on account of race, religion, nationality, membership in a particular social group or political opinion.

(3) An alien excludable under the provisions of section 212(a) of the Act whose grounds of excludability may not be waived, pursuant to section 245A(d)(2)(B)(ii) of this Act.

(4) An alien who at any time was a nonimmigrant exchange visitor who is subject to the two-year foreign residence requirement unless the requirement has been satisfied or waived pursuant to the provisions of section 212(e) of the Act who has resided continuously in the United States in an unlawful status since January 1, 1982.

(5) [Reserved]

(6) An alien who is the subject of an Order to Show Cause issued under section 242 of the Act during the period beginning on May 5, 1987 and ending on April 4, 1988 who does not file an application for adjustment of status to that of temporary resident under section 245A(a) of the Act prior to the thirty-first day after issuance of the order.

(7) An alien who is the subject of an Order to Show Cause issued under section 242 of the Act during the period beginning on April 5, 1988 and ending on May 4, 1988 who does not file an application for adjustment of status to that of a temporary resident under section 245A(a) of the Act prior to May 5, 1988.

(8) An alien who was paroled into the United States prior to January 1, 1982 and whose parole status terminated or expired subsequent to January 1, 1982, except an alien who was granted advance parole.

(d) Documentation. Evidence to support an alien's eligibility for the legalization program shall include documents establishing proof of identity, proof of residence, and proof of financial responsibility, as well as photographs, a completed fingerprint card (Form FD-258), and a completed medical report of examination (Form I-693). All documentation submitted will be subject to Service verification. Applications submitted with unverifiable documentation may be denied. Failure by an applicant to authorize release to INS of information protected by the Privacy Act and/or related laws in order for INS to adjudicate a claim may result in denial of the benefit sought. Acceptable supporting documents for these three categories are discussed below.

(1) Proof of identity. Evidence to establish identity is listed below in descending order of preference:

(i) Passport;

(ii) Birth certificate;

(iii) Any national identity document from the alien's country of origin bearing photo and fingerprint (e.g., a "cedula" or "cartilla");

(iv) Driver's license or similar document issued by a state if it contains a photo;

(v) Baptismal Record/Marriage Certificate; or

(vi) Affidavits.

(2) Assumed names —

(i) General. In cases where an applicant claims to have met any of the eligibility criteria under an assumed name, the applicant has the burden of proving that the applicant was in fact the person who used that name. The applicant's true identity is established pursuant to the requirements of paragraph (d)(1) of this section. The assumed name must appear in the documentation provided by the applicant to establish eligibility. To meet the requirements of this paragraph documentation must be submitted to prove the common identity, i.e., that the assumed name was in fact used by the applicant.

(ii) Proof of common identity. The most persuasive evidence is a document issued in the assumed name which identifies the applicant by photograph, fingerprint or detailed physical description. Other evidence which will be considered are affidavit(s) by a person or persons other than the applicant, made under oath, which identify the affiant by name and address, state the affiant's relationship to the applicant and the basis of the affiant's knowledge of the applicant's use of the assumed name. Affidavits accompanied by a photograph which has been identified by the affiant as the individual known to affiant under the assumed name in question will carry greater weight.

(3) Proof of residence. Evidence to establish proof of continuous residence in the United States during the requisite period of time may consist of any combination of the following:

(i) Past employment records, which may consist of pay stubs, W-2 Forms, certification of the filing of Federal income tax returns on IRS Form 6166, state verification of the filing of state income tax returns, letters from employer(s) or, if the applicant has been in business for himself or herself, letters from banks and other firms with whom he or she has done business. In all of the above, the name of the alien and the name of the employer or other interested organization must appear on the form or letter, as well as relevant dates. Letters from employers should be on employer letterhead stationery, if the employer has such stationery, and must include:

(A) Alien's address at the time of employment;

(B) Exact period of employment;

(C) Periods of layoff;

(D) Duties with the company;

(E) Whether or not the information was taken from official company records; and

(F) Where records are located and whether the Service may have access to the records.

If the records are unavailable, an affidavit form-letter stating that the alien's employment records are unavailable and why such records are unavailable may be accepted in lieu of (3)(i)(E) and (3)(i)(F) of this paragraph. This affidavit form-letter shall be signed, attested to by the employer under penalty of perjury, and shall state the employer's willingness to come forward and give testimony if requested.

(ii) Utility bills (gas, electric, phone, etc.), receipts, or letters from companies showing the dates during which the applicant received service are acceptable documentation.

(iii) School records (letters, report cards, etc.) from the schools that the applicant or their children have attended in the United States must show name of school and periods of school attendance.

(iv) Hospital or medical records showing treatment or hospitalization of the applicant or his or her children must show the name of the medical facility or physician and the date(s) of the treatment or hospitalization.

(v) Attestations by churches, unions, or other organizations to the applicant's residence by letter which:

(A) Identifies applicant by name;

(B) Is signed by an official (whose title is shown);

(C) Shows inclusive dates of membership;

(D) States the address where applicant resided during membership period;

(E) Includes the seal of the organization impressed on the letter or the letterhead of the organization, if the organization has letterhead stationery;

(F) Establishes how the author knows the applicant; and

(G) Establishes the origin of the information being attested to.

(vi) Additional documents to support the applicant's claim may include:

(A) Money order receipts for money sent in or out of the country;

(B) Passport entries;

(C) Birth certificates of children born in the United States;

(D) Bank books with dated transactions;

(E) Letters or correspondence between applicant and another person or organization;

(F) Social Security card;

(G) Selective Service card;

(H) Automobile license receipts, title, vehicle registration, etc.;

(I) Deeds, mortgages, contracts to which applicant has been a party;

(J) Tax receipts;

(K) Insurance policies, receipts, or letters; and

(L) Any other relevant document.

(4) Proof of financial responsibility. An applicant for adjustment of status under this part is subject to the provisions of section 212(a)(15) of the Act relating to excludability of aliens likely to become public charges. Generally, the evidence of employment submitted under paragraph (d)(3)(i) of this section will serve to demonstrate the alien's financial responsibility during the documented period(s) of employment. If the alien's period(s) of residence in the United States include significant gaps in employment or if there is reason to believe that the alien may have received public assistance while employed, the alien may be required to provide proof that he or she has not received public cash assistance. An applicant for residence who is determined likely to become a public charge and is unable to overcome this determination after application of the special rule will be denied adjustment. The burden of proof to demonstrate the inapplicability of this provision of law lies with the applicant who may provide:

(i) Evidence of a history of employment (i.e., employment letter, W-2 Forms, income tax returns, etc.);

(ii) Evidence that he/she is self-supporting (i.e., bank statements, stocks, other assets, etc.); or

(iii) Form I-134, Affidavit of Support, completed by a spouse in behalf of the applicant and/or children of the applicant or a parent in behalf of children which guarantees complete or partial financial support. Acceptance of the affidavit of support shall be extended to other family members where family circumstances warrant.

(5) Burden of proof. An alien applying for adjustment of status under this part has the burden of proving by a preponderance of the evidence that he or she has resided in the United States for the requisite periods, is admissible to the United States under the provisions of section 245a of the Act, and is otherwise eligible for adjustment of status under this section. The inference to be drawn from the documentation provided shall depend on the extent of the documentation, its credibility and amenability to verification as set forth in paragraph (d) of this section.

(6) Evidence. The sufficiency of all evidence produced by the applicant will be judged according to its probative value and credibility. To meet his or her burden of proof, an applicant must provide evidence of eligibility apart from his or her own testimony. In judging the probative value and credibility of the evidence submitted, greater weight will be given to the submission of original documentation.

(e) Filing of application.

(1) The application must be filed on Form I-687 at an office of a designated entity or at a Service Legalization Office within the jurisdiction of the District wherein the applicant resides. If the application is filed with a designated entity, the alien must have consented to having the designated entity forward the application to the legalization office. In the case of applications filed at a legalization office, the district director may, at his or her discretion:

(i) Require the applicant to file the application in person; or

(ii) Require the applicant to file the application by mail; or

(iii) Permit the filing of applications either by mail or in person.

The applicant must appear for a personal interview at the legalization office as scheduled. If the applicant is 14 years of age or older, the application must be accompanied by a completed Form FD-258 (Applicant Card).

(2) At the time of the interview, wherever possible, original documents must be submitted except the following: Official government records; employment or employment-related records maintained by employers, unions, or collective bargaining organizations; medical records; school records maintained by a school or school board; or other records maintained by a party other than the applicant. Copies of records maintained by parties other than the applicant which are submitted in evidence must be certified as true and correct by such parties and must bear their seal or signature or the signature and title of persons authorized to act in their behalf. If at the time of the interview the return of original documents is desired by the applicant, they must be accompanied by notarized copies or copies certified true and correct by a qualified designated entity or by the alien's representative in the format prescribed in § 204.2(j)(1) or (2) of this chapter. At the discretion of the district director, original documents, even if accompanied by certified copies, may be temporarily retained for forensic examination by the Document Analysis Unit at the Regional Processing Facility having jurisdiction over the legalization office to which the documents were submitted.

(3) A separate application must be filed by each applicant with the fees required by 8 CFR 106.2.

(f) Filing date of application. The date the alien submits a completed application to a Service Legalization Office or designated entity shall be considered the filing date of the application, provided that in the case of an application filed at a designated entity the alien has consented to having the designated entity forward the application to the Service Legalization Office having jurisdiction over the location of the alien's residence. The designated entities are required to forward completed applications to the appropriate Service Legalization Office within sixty days of receipt.

(g) Selective Service registration. At the time of filing an application under this section, male applicants over the age of 17 and under the age of 26 are required to be registered under the Military Selective Service Act. An applicant shall present evidence that he has previously registered under that Act in the form of a letter of acknowledgement from the Selective Service System, or such alien shall present a completed and signed Form SSS-1 at the time of filing Form I-687 with the Immigration and Naturalization Service or a designated entity. Form SSS-1 will be forwarded to the Selective Service System by the Service.

(h) Continuous residence.

(1) For the purpose of this Act, an applicant for temporary resident status shall be regarded as having resided continuously in the United States if, at the time of filing of the application:

(i) No single absence from the United States has exceeded forty-five (45) days, and the aggregate of all absences has not exceeded one hundred and eighty (180) days between January 1, 1982 through the date the application for temporary resident status is filed, unless the alien can establish that due to emergent reasons, his or her return to the United States could not be accomplished within the time period allowed;

(ii) The alien was maintaining a residence in the United States; and

(iii) The alien's departure from the United States was not based on an order of deportation.

(2) An alien who has been absent from the United States in accordance with the Service's advance parole procedures shall not be considered as having interrupted his or her continuous residence as required at the time of filing an application under this section.

(i) Medical examination. An applicant under this part shall be required to submit to an examination by a designated civil surgeon at no expense to the government. The designated civil surgeon shall report on the findings of the mental and physical condition of the applicant and the determination of the alien's immunization status. Results of the medical examinaton must be presented to the Service at the time of interview and shall be incorporated into the record. Any applicant certified under paragraphs (1), (2), (3), (4), or (5) of section 212(a) of the Act may appeal to a Board of Medical Officers of the U.S. Public Health Service as provided in section 234 of the Act and part 235 of this chapter.

(j) Interview. Each applicant, regardless of age, must appear at the appropriate Service Office and must be fingerprinted for the purpose of issuance of an employment authorization document and Form I-688. Each applicant shall be interviewed by an immigration officer, except that the interview may be waived for a child under 14, or when it is impractical because of the health or advanced age of the applicant.

(k) Applicability of exclusion grounds —

(1) Grounds of exclusion not to be applied. The following paragraphs of section 212(a) of the Act shall not apply to applicants for temporary resident status: (14) Workers entering without Labor Certification; (20) immigrants not in possession of a valid entry document; (21) visas issued without compliance with section 203; (25) illiterates; and (32) graduates of non-accredited medical schools.

(2) Waiver of grounds of exclusion. Except as provided in paragraph (k)(3) of this section, the Attorney General may waive any other provision of section 212(a) of the Act only in the case of individual aliens for humanitarian purposes, to assure family unity, or when the granting of such a waiver is in the public interest. If an alien is excludable on grounds which may be waived as set forth in this paragraph, he or she shall be advised of the procedures for applying for a waiver of grounds of excludability on Form I-690. When an application for waiver of grounds of excludability is filed jointly with an application for temporary residence under this section, it shall be accepted for processing at the legalization office. If an application for waiver of grounds of excludability is submitted after the alien's preliminary interview at the legalization office, it shall be forwarded to the appropriate Regional Processing Facility. All applications for waivers of grounds of excludability must be accompanied by the correct fee in the exact amount. All fees for applications filed in the United States must be in the form of a money order, cashier's check, or bank check. No personal checks or currency

will be accepted. Fees will not be waived or refunded under any circumstances. An application for waiver of grounds of excludability under this part shall be approved or denied by the director of the Regional Processing Facility in whose jurisdiction the applicant's application for adjustment of status was filed except that in cases involving clear statutory ineligibility or admitted fraud, such application may be denied by the district director in whose jurisdiction the application is filed, and in cases returned to a Service Legalization Office for re-interview, such application may be approved at the discretion of the district director. The applicant shall be notified of the decision and, if the application is denied, of the reason therefor. Appeal from an adverse decision under this part may be taken by the applicant on Form I-694 within 30 days after the service of the notice only to the Service's Administrative Appeals Unit pursuant to the provisions of § 103.3(a) of this chapter.

(3) Grounds of exclusion that may not be waived. Notwithstanding any other provision of the Act, the following provisions of section 212(a) may not be waived by the Attorney General under paragraph (k)(2) of this section:

(i) Paragraphs (9) and (10) (criminals);

(ii) Paragraph (23) (narcotics) except for a single offense of simple possession of thirty grams or less of marijuana;

(iii) Paragraphs (27) (prejudicial to the public interest), (28) (communist), and (29) (subversive);

(iv) Paragraph (33) (participated in Nazi persecution).

(4) Special rule for determination of public charge. An alien who has a consistent employment history which shows the ability to support himself or herself even though his or her income may be below the poverty level, may be admissible. The alien's employment history need not be continuous in that it is uninterrupted. It should be continuous in the sense that the alien shall be regularly attached to the workforce, has an income over a substantial period of the applicable time, and has demonstrated the capacity to exist on his or her income without recourse to public cash assistance. This regulation is prospective in that the Service shall determine, based on the alien's history, whether he or she is likely to become a public charge. Past acceptance of public cash assistance within a history of consistent employment will enter into this decision. The weight given in considering applicability of the public charge provisions will depend on many factors, but the length of time an applicant has received public cash assistance will constitute a significant factor.

(5) Public assistance and criminal history verification. Declarations by an applicant that he or she has not been the recipient of public cash assistance and/or has not had a criminal record are subject to a verification of facts by the Service. The applicant must agree to fully cooperate in the verification process. Failure to assist the Service in verifying information necessary for the adjudication of the application may result in a denial of the application.

(*l*) Continous physical presence since November 6, 1986.

(1) An alien applying for adjustment to temporary resident status must establish that he or she has been continuously physically present in the United States since November 6, 1986. Aliens who were outside of the United States on the date of enactment or departed the United States after enactment may apply for legalization if they reentered prior to May 1, 1987, and meet the continuous residence requirements and are otherwise eligible for legalization.

(2) A brief, casual and innocent absence means a departure authorized by the Service (advance parole) subsequent to May 1, 1987 of not more than thirty (30) days for legitimate emergency or humanitarian purposes unless a further period of authorized departure has been granted in the discretion of the district director or a departure was beyond the alien's control.

(m) Departure.

(1) During the time period from the date that an alien's application establishing prima facie eligibility for temporary resident status is reviewed at a Service Legalization Office and the date status as a temporary resident is granted, the alien applicant can only be readmitted to the United States provided his or her departure was authorized under the Service's advance parole provisions contained in § 212.5(f) of this chapter.

(2) An alien whose application for temporary resident status has been approved may be admitted to the United States upon return as a returning temporary resident provided he or she:

(i) Is not under deportation proceedings, such proceedings having been instituted subsequent to the approval of temporary resident status. A temporary resident alien will not be considered deported if that alien departs the United States while under an outstanding order of deportation issued prior to the approval of temporary resident status;

(ii) Has not been absent from the United States more than thirty (30) days on the date application for admission is made;

(iii) Has not been absent from the United States for an aggregate period of more than 90 days since the date the alien was granted lawful temporary resident status;

(iv) Presents Form I-688;

(v) Presents himself or herself for inspection; and

(vi) Is otherwise admissible.

(3) The periods of time in paragraph (m)(2)(ii) and (m)(2)(iii) of this section may be waived at the discretion of the Attorney General in cases where the absence from the United States was due merely to a brief temporary trip abroad due to emergent or extenuating circumstances beyond the alien's control.

(n)(1) Employment and travel authorization; general. Authorization for employment and travel abroad for temporary resident status applicants under section 245A(a) of the Act may only be granted by a Service Office. INS district directors will determine the Service location for the completion of processing of travel documentation. In the case of an application which has been filed with a designated entity, employment authorization may only be granted by the Service after the application has been properly received at the Service Office.

(2) Employment authorization prior to the granting of temporary resident status.

(i) Permission to travel abroad and accept employment may be granted to the applicant after an interview has been conducted in connection with an application establishing prima facie eligibility for temporary resident status. Permission to travel abroad may be granted in emergent circumstances in accordance with the Service's advance parole provisions contained in § 212.5(f) of this chapter after an interview has been conducted in connection with an application establishing prima facie eligiblity for temporary resident status.

(ii) If an interview appointment cannot be scheduled within 30 days from the date an application is filed at a Service office, authorization to accept employment will be granted, valid until the scheduled appointment date. Employment authorization, both prior and subsequent to an interview, will be restricted to increments of 1 year, pending final determination on the application for temporary resident status. If a final determination has not been made prior to the expiration date on the Employment Authorization Document (Form I-766, Form I-688A or Form I-688B), that date may be extended upon return of the employment authorization document by the applicant to the appropriate Service office.

(3) Employment and travel authorization upon grant of temporary resident status. Upon the granting of an application for adjustment to temporary resident status, the service center will forward a notice of approval to the applicant at his or her last known address and to his or her qualified designated entity or representative. The applicant may appear at any Service office and, upon surrender of the previously issued Employment Authorization Document, will be issued Form I-688, Temporary Resident Card, authorizing employment and travel abroad.

(4) Revocation of employment authorization upon denial of temporary resident status. Upon denial of an application for adjustment to temporary resident status the alien will be notified that if a timely appeal is not submitted, employment authorization shall be automatically revoked on the final day of the appeal period.

(o) Decision. The applicant shall be notified in writing of the decision, and, if the application is denied, of the reason therefor. An appeal from an adverse decision under this part may be taken by the applicant on Form I-694.

(p) Appeal process. An adverse decision under this part may be appealed to the Associate Commissioner, Examinations (Administrative Appeals Unit). Any appeal with the required fee shall be filed with the Regional Processing Facility within thirty (30) days after service of the notice of denial in accordance with the procedures of § 103.3(a) of this chapter. An appeal received after the thirty (30) day period has tolled will not be accepted. The thirty (30) day period includes any time required for service or receipt by mail.

(q) Motions. The Regional Processing Facility director may sua sponte reopen and reconsider any adverse decision. When an appeal to the Associate Commissioner, Examinations (Administrative Appeals Unit) has been filed, the INS director of the Regional Processing Facility may issue a new decision that will grant the benefit which has been requested. The director's new decision must be served on the appealing party within 45 days of receipt of any briefs and/or new evidence, or upon expiration of the time allowed for the submission of any briefs. Motions to reopen a proceeding or reconsider a decision shall not be considered under this part.

(r) Certifications. The Regional Processing Facility director may, in accordance with § 103.4 of this chapter, certify a decision to the Associate Commissioner, Examinations (Administrative Appeals Unit) when the case involves an unusually complex or novel question of law or fact. The party affected shall be given notice of such certification and of the right to submit a brief within thirty (30) days from service of the notice.

(s) Date of adjustment to temporary residence. The status of an alien whose application for temporary resident status is approved shall be adjusted to that of a lawful temporary resident as of the date indicated on the application fee receipt issued at Service Legalization Office.

(t) Limitation on access to information and confidentiality.

(1) No person other than a sworn officer or employee of the Justice Department or bureau of agency thereof, will be permitted to examine individual applications, except employees of designated entities where applications are filed with the same designated entity. For purposes of this part, any individual employed under contract by the Service to work in connection with the legalization program shall be considered an "employee of the Justice Department or bureau or agency thereof."

(2) Files and records prepared by designated entites under this section are confidential. The Attorney General and the Service shall not have access to these files and records without the consent of the alien.

(3) No information furnished pursuant to an application for legalization under this section shall be used for any purpose except: (i) To make a determination on the application; or, (ii) for the enforcement of the provisions encompassed in section 245A(c)(6) of the Act, except as provided in paragraph (t)(4) of this section.

(4) If a determination is made by the Service that the alien has, in connection with his or her application, engaged in fraud or willful misrepresentation or concealment of a material fact, knowingly provided a false writing or document in making his or her application, knowingly made a false statement or representation, or engaged in any other activity prohibited by section 245A(c)(6) of the Act, the Service shall refer the matter to the United States Attorney for prosecution of the alien or of any person who created or supplied a false writing or document for use in an application for adjustment of status under this part.

(5) Information obtained in a granted legalization application and contained in the applicant's file is subject to subsequent review in reference to future

benefits applied for (including petitions for naturalization and permanent resident status for relatives).

(u) Termination of temporary resident status —

(1) Termination of temporary resident status; General. The status of an alien lawfully admitted for temporary residence under section 245A(a)(1) of the Act may be terminated at any time in accordance with section 245A(b)(2) of the Act. It is not necessary that a final order of deportation be entered in order to terminate temporary resident status. The temporary resident status may be terminated upon the occurrence of any of the following:

(i) It is determined that the alien was ineligible for temporary residence under section 245A of this Act;

(ii) The alien commits an act which renders him or her inadmissible as an immigrant, unless a waiver is secured pursuant to § 245a.2(k)(2).

(iii) The alien is convicted of any felony, or three or more misdemeanors;

(iv) The alien fails to file for adjustment of status from temporary resident to permanent resident on Form I-698 within forty-three (43) months of the date he/she was granted status as a temporary resident under § 245a.1 of this part.

(2) Procedure—

(i) Termination by the Service. Except as provided in paragraph (u)(2)(ii) of this section, termination of an alien's temporary resident status under paragraph (u)(1) of this section will be made before instituting deportation proceedings against a temporary resident alien and only on notice sent to the alien by certified mail directed to his or her last known address, and to his or her representative, if any. The alien must be given an opportunity to offer evidence in opposition to the grounds alleged for termination of his or her status. Evidence in opposition must be submitted within thirty (30) days after the service of the Notice of Intent to Terminate. If the alien's status is terminated, the director of the regional processing facility shall notify the alien of the decision and the reasons for the termination, and further notify the alien that any Service Form I-94, Arrival-Departure Record or other official Service document issued to the alien authorizing employment and/or travel abroad, or any Form I-688, Temporary Resident Card previously issued to the alien will be declared void by the director of the regional processing facility within thirty (30) days if no appeal of the termination decision is filed within that period. The alien may appeal the decision to the Associate Commissioner, Examinations (Administrative Appeals Unit). Any appeal with the required fee shall be filed with the regional processing facility within thirty (30) days after the service of the notice of termination. If no appeal is filed within that period, the I-94, I-688 or other official Service document shall be deemed void, and must be surrendered without delay to an immigration officer or to the issuing office of the Service.

(ii) Termination upon entry of final order of deportation or exclusion.

(A) The Service may institute deportation or exclusion proceedings against a temporary resident alien without regard to the procedures set forth in paragraph (u)(2)(i) of this section:

(1) If the ground for deportation arises under section 241(a)(2)(A)(iii) of the Act (8 U.S.C. 1251(a)(2)(A)(iii));

(2) If the ground for deportation arises after the acquisition of temporary resident status, and the basis of such ground of deportation is not waivable pursuant to section 245A(d)(2)(B)(ii) of the Act (8 U.S.C. 1255a(d)(2)(B)(ii)); or

(3) If the ground for exclusion arises after the acquisition of temporary resident status and is not waivable pursuant to section 245A(d)(2)(B)(ii) of the Act (8 U.S.C. 1255a(d)(2)(B)(ii)).

(B) In such cases, the entry of a final order of deportation or exclusion will automatically terminate an alien's temporary resident status acquired under section 245A(a)(1) of the Act.

(3) Termination not construed as rescission under section 246. For the purposes of this part the phrase termination of status of an alien granted lawful temporary residence under section 245A(a) of the Act shall not be construed to necessitate a rescission of status as described in section 246 of the Act, and the proceedings required by the regulations issued thereunder shall not apply.

(4) Return to unlawful status after termination. Termination of the status of any alien previously adjusted to lawful temporary residence under section 245A(a) of the Act shall act to return such alien to the unlawful status held prior to the adjustment, and render him or her amenable to exclusion or deportation proceedings under section 236 or 242 of the Act, as appropriate.

(v) Ineligibility for immigration benefits. An alien whose status is adjusted to that of a lawful temporary resident under section 245A of the Act is not entitled to submit a petition pursuant to section 203(a)(2) or to any other benefit or consideration accorded under the Act to aliens lawfuly admitted for permanent residence.

(w) Declaration of Intending Citizen. An alien who has been granted the status of temporary resident under section 245A(a)(1) of this Act may assert a claim of discrimination on the basis of citizenship status under section 274B of the Act only if he or she has previously filed Form I-772 (Declaration of Intending Citizen) after being granted such status. The Declaration of Intending Citizen is not required as a basis for filing a petition for naturalization; nor shall it be regarded as a right to United States citizenship; nor shall it be regarded as evidence of a person's status as a resident.

HISTORY:

[52 FR 16208, May 1, 1987, as amended at 52 FR 43845, 43846, Nov. 17, 1987; 53 FR 23382, June 22, 1988; 54 FR 29449, July 12, 1989; 56 FR 31061, July 9, 1991; 58 FR 45236, Aug. 27, 1993, as confirmed at 59 FR 1470, Jan. 11, 1994; 60 FR 21039, May 1, 1995; 60 FR 21975, May 4, 1995; 61 FR 46534, 46536, Sept. 4, 1996; 65 FR 82254, 82256, Dec. 28, 2000; 66 FR 7863, Jan. 26, 2001; 78 FR 18457, 18472, Mar. 27, 2013, as confirmed at 81 FR 91646, 91670, Dec. 19, 2016; 85 FR 46788, 46927, Aug. 3, 2020; 89 FR 6194, 6399, Jan. 31, 2024]

§ 245a.3 Application for adjustment from temporary to permanent resident status.

(a) Application period for permanent residence.

(1) An alien may submit an application for lawful permanent resident status, with fee, immediately subsequent to the granting of lawful temporary resident status. Any application received prior to the alien's becoming eligible for adjustment to permanent resident status will be administratively processed and held by the INS, but will not be considered filed until the beginning of the nineteenth month after the date the alien was granted temporary resident status as defined in § 245a.2(s) of this chapter.

(2) No application shall be denied for failure to timely apply before the end of 43 months from the date of actual approval of the temporary resident application.

(3) The Service Center Director shall sua sponte reopen and reconsider without fee any application which was previously denied for late filing. No additional fee will be required for those applications which are filed during the twelve month extension period but prior to July 9, 1991.

(b) Eligibility. Any alien who has been lawfully admitted for temporary resident status under section 245A(a) of the Act, such status not having been terminated, may apply for adjustment of status of that of an alien lawfully admitted for permanent residence if the alien:

(1) Applies for such adjustment anytime subsequent to the granting of temporary resident status but on or before the end of 43 months from the date of actual approval of the termporary resident application. The alien need not be physically present in the United States at the time of application; however, the alien must establish continuous residence in the United States in accordance with the provisions of paragraph (b)(2) of this section and must be physically present in the United States at the time of interview and/or processing for permanent resident status (ADIT processing);

(2) Establishes continuous residence in the United States since the date the alien was granted such temporary residence status. An alien shall be regarded as having resided continuously in the United States for the purpose of this part if, at the time of applying for adjustment from temporary to permanent resident status, or as of the date of eligibility for permanent residence, whichever is later, no single absence from the United States has exceeded thirty (30) days, and the aggregate of all absences has not exceeded ninety (90) days between the date of approval of the temporary resident application, Form I-687 (not the "roll-back" date) and the date the alien applied or became eligible for permanent resident status, whichever is later, unless the alien can establish that due to emergent reasons or circumstances beyond his or her control, the return to the United States could not be accomplished within the time period(s) allowed. A single absence from the United States of more than 30 days, and aggregate absences of more than 90 days during the period for which continuous residence is required for adjustment to permanent residence, shall break the continuity of such residence, unless the temporary resident can establish to the satisfaction of the district director or the Director of the Regional Processing Facility that he or she did not, in fact, abandon his or her residence in the United States during such period;

(3) Is admissible to the United States as an immigrant, except as otherwise provided in paragraph (g) of this section; and has not been convicted of any felony, or three or more misdemeanors; and

(4)(i)(A) Can demonstrate that the alien meets the requirements of section 312 of the Immigration and Nationality Act, as amended (relating to minimal understanding of ordinary English and a knowledge and understanding of the history and government of the United States); or

(B) Is satisfactorily pursuing a course of study recognized by the Attorney General to achieve such an understanding of English and such a knowledge and understanding of the history and government of the United States.

(ii) The requirements of paragraph (b)(4)(i) of this section must be met by each applicant. However, these requirements shall be waived without formal application for persons who, as of the date of application or the date of eligibility for permanent residence under this part, whichever date is later, are:

(A) Under 16 years of age; or

(B) 65 years of age or older; or

(C) Over 50 years of age who have resided in the United States for at least 20 years and submit evidence establishing the 20-year qualification requirement. Such evidence must be submitted pursuant to the requirements contained in Section 245a.2(d)(3) of this chapter; or

(D) Developmentally disabled as defined at § 245a.1(v) of this chapter. Such persons must submit medical evidence concerning their developmental disability; or

(E) Physically unable to comply. The physical disability must be of a nature which renders the applicant unable to acquire the four language skills of speaking, understanding, reading, and writing English in accordance with the criteria and precedence established in OI 312.1(a)(2)(iii) (Interpretations). Such persons must submit medical evidence concerning their physical disability.

(iii)(A) Literacy and basic citizenship skills may be demonstrated for purposes of complying with paragraph (b)(4)(i)(A) of this section by:

(1) Speaking and understanding English during the course of the interview for permanent resident status. An applicant's ability to read and write English shall be tested by excerpts from one or more parts of the Federal Textbooks on Citizenship at the elementary literacy level. The test of an applicant's knowledge and understanding of the history and form of government of the United States shall be given in the English language. The scope of the testing shall be limited to subject matter covered in the revised (1987) Federal Textbooks on Citizenship or other approved training material. The test questions shall be selected from a list of 100 standardized questions developed by the Service. In choosing the subject matter and in phrasing questions, due consideration shall be given to the extent of the

applicant's education, background, age, length of residence in the United States, opportunities available and efforts made to acquire the requisite knowledge, and any other elements or factors relevant to an appraisal of the adequacy of his or her knowledge and understanding; or

(2) By passing a standardized section 312 test (effective retroactively as of November 7, 1988) such test being given in the English language by the Legalization Assistance Board with the Educational Testing Service (ETS) or the California State Department of Education with the Comprehensive Adult Student Assessment System (CASAS). The scope of the test is based on the 1987 edition of the Federal Textbooks on Citizenship series written at the elementary literacy level. An applicant may evidence passing of the standardized section 312 test by submitting the approved testing organization's standard notice of passing test results at the time of filing Form I-698, subsequent to filing the application but prior to the interview, or at the time of the interview. The test results may be independently verified by INS, if necessary.

(B) An applicant who fails to pass the English literacy and/or the U.S. history and government tests at the time of the interview, shall be afforded a second opportunity after six (6) months (or earlier, at the request of the applicant) to pass the tests, submit evidence of passing an INS approved section 312 standardized examination or submit evidence of fulfillment of any one of the "satisfactorily pursuing" alternatives listed at § 245a.1(s) of this chapter. The second interview shall be conducted prior to the denial of the application for permanent residence and may be based solely on the failure to pass the basic citizenship skills requirements. An applicant whose period of eligibility expires prior to the end of the six-month re-test period, shall still be accorded the entire six months within which to be re-tested.

(iv) To satisfy the English language and basic citizenship skills requirements under the "satisfactorily pursuing" standard as defined at § 245a.1(s) of this chapter the applicant must submit evidence of such satisfactory pursuit in the form of a "Certificate of Satisfactory Pursuit" (Form I-699) issued by the designated school or program official attesting to the applicant's satisfactory pursuit of the course of study as defined at § 245a.1(s)(1) and (4) of this chapter; or a high school diploma or general educational development diploma (GED) under § 245a.1(s)(2) of this chapter; or certification on letterhead stationery from a state recognized, accredited learning institution under § 245a.1(s)(3) of this chapter; or evidence of having passed the IRCA Test for Permanent Residency under § 245a.1(s)(5) of this chapter. Such applicants shall not then be required to demonstrate that they meet the requirements of § 245a.3(b)(4)(i)(A) of this chapter in order to be granted lawful permanent residence provided they are otherwise eligible. Evidence of "Satisfactory Pursuit" may be submitted at the time of filing Form I-698, subsequent to filing the application but prior to the interview, or at the time of the interview (the applicant's name and A90M number must appear on any such evidence submitted). An applicant need not necessarily be enrolled in a recognized course of study at the time of application for permanent residency.

(v) Enrollment in a recognized course of study as defined in § 245a.3(b)(5) and issuance of a "Certificate of Satisfactory Pursuit" must occur subsequent to May 1, 1987.

(5) A course of study in the English language and in the history and government of the United States shall satisfy the requirement of paragraph (b)(4)(i) of this section if the course materials for such instruction include textbooks published under the authority of section 346 of the Act, and it is

(i) Sponsored or conducted by: (A) An established public or private institution of learning recognized as such by a qualified state certifying agency; (B) An institution of learning approved to issue Forms I-20 in accordance with § 214.3 of this chapter; (C) A qualified designated entity within the meaning of section 245A(c)(2) of the Act, in good-standing with the Service; or (D) Is certified by the district director in whose jurisdiction the program is conducted, or is certified by the Director of the Outreach Program nationally.

(ii) A program seeking certification as a course of study recognized by the Attorney General under paragraph (b)(5)(i)(D) of this section shall file Form I-803, Petition for Attorney General Recognition to Provide Course of Study for Legalization: Phase II, with the Director of Outreach for national level programs or with the district director having jurisdiction over the area in which the school or program is located. In the case of local programs, a separate petition must be filed with each district director when a parent organization has schools or programs in more than one INS district. A petition must identify by name and address those schools or programs included in the petition. No fee shall be required to file Form I-803;

(A) The Director of Outreach and the district directors may approve a petition where they have determined that (1) a need exists for a course of study in addition to those already certified under § 245a.3(b)(5)(i) (A), (B), or (C); and/or (2) of this chapter the petitioner has historically provided educational services in English and U.S. history and government but is not already certified under § 245a.3(b)(5)(i)(A), (B), or (C); and (3) of this chapter the petitioner is otherwise qualified to provide such course of study;

(B) Upon approval of the petition the Director of Outreach and district directors shall issue a Certificate of Attorney General Recognition on Form I-804 to the petitioner. If the petition is denied, the petitioner shall be notified in writing of the decision therefor. No appeal shall lie from a denial of Form I-803, except that in such case where the petitions of a local, cross-district program are approved in one district and denied in another within the same State, the petitioner may request review of the denied petition by the appropriate Regional Commissioner. The Regional Commissioner shall then make a determination in this case;

(C) Each district director shall compile and maintain lists of programs approved under paragraph (b)(5)(i)(D) of this section within his or her jurisdiction. The Director of Outreach shall compile and maintain lists of approved national level programs.

(6) Notice of participation. All courses of study recognized under § 245a.3(b)(5)(i)(A) through (C) of this chapter which are already conducting or will conduct English and U.S. history and government courses for temporary residents must submit a Notice of Participation to the district director in whose jurisdiction the program is conducted. Acceptance of "Certificates of Satisfactory Pursuit" (Form I-699) shall be delayed until such time as the course provider submits the Notice of Participation, which notice shall be in the form of a letter typed on the letterhead of the course provider (if available) and include the following:

(i) The name(s) of the school(s)/program(s).

(ii) The complete addresses and telephone numbers of sites where courses will be offered, and class schedules.

(iii) The complete names of persons who are in charge of conducting English and U.S. history and government courses of study.

(iv) A statement that the course of study will issue "Certificates of Satisfactory Pursuit" to temporary resident enrollees according to INS regulations.

(v) A list of designated officials of the recognized course of study authorized to sign "Certificates of Satisfactory Pursuit", and samples of their original signatures.

(vi) A statement that if a course provider charges a fee to temporary resident enrollees, the fee will not be excessive.

(vii) Evidence of recognition under 8 CFR 245a.3(b)(5)(i)(A), (B), or (C) (e.g., certification from a qualified state certifying agency; evidence of INS approval for attendance by nonimmigrant students, such as the school code number, or the INS identification number from the QDE cooperative agreement).

The course provider shall notify the district director, in writing, of any changes to the information contained in the Notice of Participation subsequent to its submission within ten (10) days of such change.

A Certificate of Attorney General Recognition to Provide Course of Study for Legalization (Phase II), Form I-804, shall be issued to course providers who have submitted a Notice of Participation in accordance with the provisions of this section by the distict director. A Notice of Participation deficient in any way shall be returned to the course provider to correct the deficiency. Upon the satisfaction of the district director that the deficiency has been corrected, the course provider shall be issued Form I-804. Each district director shall compile and maintain lists of recognized courses within his or her district.

(7) Fee structure. No maximum fee standard will be imposed by the Attorney General. However, if it is believed that a fee charged is excessive, this factor alone will justify non-certification of the course provider by INS as provided in § 245a.3(b)(10) and/or (12) of this section. Once fees are established, any change in fee without prior approval of the district director or the Director of Outreach may justify de-certification. In determining whether or not a fee is excessive, district directors and the Director of Outreach shall consider such factors as the means of instruction, class size, prevailing wages of instructors in the area of the program, and additional costs such as rent, materials, utilities, insurance, and taxes. District directors and the Director of Outreach may also seek the assistance of various Federal, State and local entities as the need arises (e.g., State Departments of Education) to determine the appropriateness of course fees.

(8) The Citizenship textbooks to be used by applicants for lawful permanent residence under section 245A of the Act shall be distributed by the Service to appropriate representatives of public schools. These textbooks may otherwise be purchased from the Superintendent of Documents, Government Printing Office, Washington, DC 20402, and are also available at certain public institutions.

(9) Maintenance of Student Records. Course providers conducting courses of study recognized under § 245a.3(b)(5) of this chapter shall maintain for each student, for a period of three years from the student's enrollment, the following information and documents:

(i) Name (as copied exactly from the I-688A or I-688);

(ii) A-number (90 million series);

(iii) Date of enrollment;

(iv) Attendance records;

(v) Assessment records;

(vi) Photocopy of signed "Certificate of Satisfactory Pursuit" issued to the student.

(10) Issuance of "Certificate of Satisfactory Pursuit" (I-699).

(i) Each recognized course of study shall prepare a standardized certificate that is signed by the designated official. The Certificate shall be issued to an applicant who has attended a recognized course of study for at least 40 hours of a minimum of 60-hour course as appropriate for his or her ability level, and is demonstrating progress according to the performance standards of the English and U.S. history and government course prescribed. Such standards shall conform with the provisions of § 245a.1(s) of this chapter.

(ii) The district director shall reject a certificate if it is determined that the certificate is fraudulent or was fraudulently issued.

(iii) The district director shall reject a Certificate if it is determined that the course provider is not complying with INS regulations. In the case of non-compliance, the district director will advise the course provider in writing of the specific deficiencies and give the provider thirty (30) days within which to correct such deficiencies.

(iv) District directors will accept Certificates from course providers once it is determined that the deficiencies have been satisfactorily corrected.

(v) Course providers which engage in fraudulent activities or fail to conform with INS regulations will be removed from the list of INS approved programs. INS will not accept Certificates from these providers.

(vi) Certificates may be accepted if a program is cited for deficiencies or decertified at a later date and no fraud was involved.

(vii) Certificates shall not be accepted from a course provider that has been decertified unless the alien enrolled in and had been issued a certificate prior to the decertification, provided that no fraud was involved.

(viii) The appropriate State agency responsbile for SLIAG funding shall be notified of all decertifications by the district director.

(11) Designated official.

(i) The designated official is the authorized person from each recognized course of study whose signature appears on all "Certificates of Satisfactory Pursuit" issued by that course;

(ii) The designated official must be a regularly employed member of the school administration whose office is located at the school and whose compensation does not come from commissions for recruitment of foreign students;

(iii)(A) The head of the school system or school, the director of the Qualified Designated Entity, the head of a program approved by the Attorney General, or the president or owner of other institutions recognized by the Attorney General must specify a designated official. Such designated official may not delegate this designation to any other person. Each school or institution may have up to three (3) designated officials at any one time. In a multi-campus institution, each campus may have up to three (3) designated officials at any one time;

(B) Each designated official shall have read and otherwise be familiar with the "Requirements and Guidelines for Courses of Study Recognized by the Attorney General". The signature of a designated official shall affirm the official's compliance with INS regulations;

(C) The name, title, and sample signature of each designated official for each recognized course of study shall be on file with the district director in whose jurisdiction the program is conducted.

(12) Monitoring by INS

(i) INS Outreach personnel in conjunction with the district director shall monitor the course providers in each district in order to:

(A) Assure that the program is a course of study recognized by the Attorney General under the provisions of § 245a.3(b)(5).

(B) Verify the existence of curriculm as defined in § 245a.1(u) on file for each level of instruction provided in English language and U.S. history and government classes.

(C) Assure that "Certificates of Satisfactory Pursuit" are being issued in accordance with § 245a.3(b)(10).

(D) Assure that records are maintained on each temporary resident enrollee in accordance with § 245a.3(b)(9).

(E) Assure that fees (if any) assessed by the course provider are in compliance in accordance with § 245a.3(b)(7).

(ii) If INS has reason to believe that the service is not being provided to the applicant, INS will issue a 24-hour minimum notice to the service provider before any site visit is conducted.

(iii) If it is determined that a course provider is not performing according to the standards established in either § 245a.3(b)(10) or (12) of this chapter, the district director shall institute decertification proceedings. Notice of Intent to Decertify shall be provided to the course provider. The course provider has 30 days within which to correct performance according to standards established. If after the 30 days, the district director is not satisfied that the basis for decertification has been overcome, the course provider will be decertified. The appropriate State agency shall be notified in accordance with § 245a.3(b)(10)(viii) of this chapter. A copy of the notice of decertification shall be sent to the State agency.

(13) Courses of study recognized by the Attorney General as defined at § 245a.3(b)(5) of this chapter shall provide certain standards for the selection of teachers. Since some programs may be in locations where selection of qualified staff is limited, or where budget constraints restrict options, the following list of qualities for teacher selection is provided as guidance. Teacher selections should include as many of the following qualities as possible:

(i) Specific training in Teaching English to Speakers of Other Languages (TESOL);

(ii) Experience as a classroom teacher with adults;

(iii) Cultural sensitivity and openness;

(iv) Familiarity with compentency-based education;

(v) Knowledge of curriculum and materials adaptation;

(vi) Knowledge of a second language.

(c) Ineligible aliens.

(1) An alien who has been convicted of a felony, or three or more misdemeanors in the United States.

(2) An alien who is inadmissible to the United States as an immigrant, except as provided in § 245a.3(g)(1).

(3) An alien who was previously granted temporary resident status pursuant to section 245A(a) of the Act who has not filed an application for permanent resident status under section 245A(b)(1) of the Act by the end of 43 months from the date of actual approval of the temporary resident application.

(4) An alien who was not previously granted temporary resident status under section 245A(a) of the Act.

(5) An alien whose temporary resident status has been terminated under § 245a.2(u) of this chapter

(d) Filing the application. The provisions of part 211 of this chapter relating to the documentary requirements for immigrants shall not apply to an applicant under this part.

(1) The application must be filed on Form I-698. Form I-698 must be accompanied by the correct fee and documents specified in the instructions. The application will be mailed to the director having jurisdiction over the applicant's place of residence.

(2) Certification of documents. The submission of original documents is not required at the time of filing Form I-698. A copy of a document submitted in support of Form I-698 filed pursuant to section 245A(b) of the Act and this part may be accepted, though unaccompanied by the original, if the copy is certified as true and complete by

(i) An attorney in the format prescribed in § 204.2(j)(1) of this chapter; or

(ii) An alien's representative in the format prescribed in § 204.2(j)(2) of this chapter; or

(iii) A qualified designated entity (QDE) in good standing as defined in § 245a.1(r) of this chapter, if the copy bears a certification by the QDE in good-standing, typed or rubber-stamped in the following language:

I certify that I have compared this copy with its original and it is a true and complete copy.

Signed:

Date:

Name: --QDE in good-standing representative

Name of QDE in good-standing: --

Address of QDE in good-standing: --

INS-QDE Cooperative Agreement Number: --

(iv) Authentication. Certification of documents must be authenticated by an original signature. A facsimile signature on a rubber stamp will not be acceptable.

(v) Original documents. Original documents must be presented when requested by the Service. Official government records, employment or employment-related records maintained by employers, unions, or collective bargaining organizations, medical records, school records maintained by a school or school board or other records maintained by a party other than the applicant which are submitted in evidence must be certified as true and complete by such parties and must bear their seal or signature or the signature and title of persons authorized to act in their behalf. At the discretion of the district director and/or the Regional Processing Facility director, original documents may be kept for forensic examination.

(3) A separate application must be filed by each applicant with the fees required by 8 CFR 106.2.

(4) Applicants who filed for temporary resident status prior to December 1, 1987, are required to submit the results of a serologic test for HIV virus on Form I-693, "Medical Examination of Aliens Seeking Adjustment of Status", completed by a designated civil surgeon, unless the serologic test for HIV was performed and the results were submitted on Form I-693 when the applicant filed for temporary resident status. Applicants who did submit an I-693 reflecting a serologic test for HIV was performed prior to December 1, 1987, must submit evidence of this fact when filing the I-698 application in order to be relieved from the requirement of submitting another I-693. If such evidence is not available, applicants may note on their I-698 application their prior submission of the results of the serologic test for HIV. This information shall then be verified at the Regional Processing Facility. Applicants having to submit an I-693 pursuant to this section are not required to have a complete medical examination. All HIV-positive applicants shall be advised that a waiver of the ground of excludability under section 212(a)(6) of the Act is available and shall be provided the opportunity to apply for the waiver. To be eligible for the waiver, the applicant must establish that:

(i) The danger to the public health of the United States created by the alien's admission to the United States is minimal,

(ii) The possibility of the spread of the infection created by the alien's admission to the United States is minimal, and

(iii) There will be no cost incurred by any government agency without prior consent of that agency. Provided these criteria are met, the waiver may be granted only for humanitarian purposes, to assure family unity, or when the granting of such a waiver is in the public interest in accordance with § 245a.3(g)(2) of this chapter.

(5) If necessary, the validity of an alien's temporary resident card (I-688) will be extended in increments of one (1) year until such time as the decision on an alien's properly filed application for permanent residence becomes final.

(6) An application lacking the proper fee or incomplete in any way shall be returned to the applicant with request for the proper fee, correction, additional information, and/or documentation. Once an application has been accepted by the Service and additional information and/or documentation is required, the applicant shall be sent a notice to submit such information and/or documentation. In such case the application Form I-698 shall be retained at the RPF. If a response to this request is not received within 60 days, a second request for correction, additional information, and/or documentation shall be made. If the second request is not complied with by the end of 43 months from the date the application for temporary residence, Form I-687, was approved the application for permanent residence will be adjudicated on the basis of the existing record.

(e) Interview. Each applicant regardless of age, must appear at the appropriate Service office and must be fingerprinted for the purpose of issuance of Form I-551. Each applicant shall be interviewed by an immigration officer, except that the adjudicative interview may be waived for a child under 14, or when it is impractical because of the health or advanced age of the applicant. An applicant failing to appear for the scheduled interview may, for good cause, be afforded another interview. Where an applicant fails to appear for two scheduled interviews, his or her application shall be held in abeyance until the end of 43 months from the date the application for temporary residence was approved and adjudicated on the basis of the existing record.

(f) Numerical limitations. The numerical limitations of sections 201 and 202 of the Act do not apply to the adjustment of aliens to lawful permanent resident status under section 245A(b) of the Act.

(g) Applicability of exclusion grounds.—

(1) Grounds of exclusion not to be applied. The following paragraphs of section 212(a) of the Act shall not apply to applicants for adjustment of status from temporary resident to permanent resident status: (14) workers entering without labor certification; (20) immigrants not in possession of valid entry documents; (21) visas issued without compliance of section 203; (25)

illiterates; and (32) graduates of non-accredited medical schools.

(2) Waiver of grounds of excludability. Except as provided in paragraph (g)(3) of this section, the Service may waive any provision of section 212(a) of the Act only in the case of individual aliens for humanitarian purposes, to assure family unity, or when the granting of such a waiver is otherwise in the public interest. In any case where a provision of section 212(a) of the Act has been waived in connection with an alien's application for lawful temporary resident status under section 245A(a) of the Act, no additional waiver of the same ground of excludability will be required when the alien applies for permanent resident status under section 245A(b)(1) of the Act. In the event that the alien was excludable under any provision of section 212(a) of the Act at the time of temporary residency and failed to apply for a waiver in connection with the application for temporary resident status, or becomes excludable subsequent to the date temporary residence was granted, a waiver of the ground of excludability, if available, will be required before permanent resident status may be granted.

(3) Grounds of exclusion that may not be waived. Notwithstanding any other provisions of the Act the following provisions of section 212(a) of the Act may not be waived by the Attorney General under paragraph (g)(2) of this section:

(i) Paragraphs (9) and (10) (criminals);

(ii) Paragraph (15) (public charge) except for an alien who is or was an aged, blind, or disabled individual (as defined in section 1614(a)(1) of the Social Security Act);

(iii) Paragraph (23) (narcotics), except for a single offense of simple possession of thirty grams or less of marijuana;

(iv) Paragraphs (27) (prejudicial to the public interest), (28) (communists), and (29) (subversives);

(v) Paragraph (33) (participated in Nazi persecution).

(4) Determination of Likely to become a public charge and Special Rule. Prior to use of the special rule for determination of public charge, paragraph (g)(4)(iii) of this section, an alien must first be determined to be excludable under section 212(a)(15) of the Act. If the applicant is determined to be likely to become a public charge, he or she may still be admissible under the terms of the Special Rule.

(i) In determining whether an alien is likely to become a public charge financial responsibility of the alien is to be established by examining the totality of the alien's circumstances at the time of his or her application for legalization. The existence or absence of a particular factor should never be the sole criteria for determining if an alien is likely to become a public charge. The determination of financial responsibility should be a prospective evaluation based on the alien's age, health, income, and vocation.

(ii) The Special Rule for determination of public charge, paragraph (g)(4)(iii) of this section, is to be applied only after an initial determination that the alien is inadmissible under the provisions of section 212(a)(15) of the act.

(iii) Special Rule. An alien who has a consistent employment history which shows the ability to support himself or herself even though his or her income may be below the poverty level is not excludable under paragraph (g)(3)(ii) of this section. The alien's employment history need not be continuous in that it is uninterrupted. It should be continuous in the sense that the alien shall be regularly attached to the workforce, has an income over a substantial period of the applicable time, and has demonstrated the capacity to exist on his or her income without recourse to public cash assistance. The Special Rule is prospective in that the Service shall determine, based on the alien's history, whether he or she is likely to become a public charge. Past acceptance of public cash assistance within a history of consistent employment will enter into this decision. The weight given in considering applicability of the public charge provisions will depend on many factors, but the length of time an applicant has received public cash assistance will constitute a significant factor. It is not necessary to file a waiver in order to apply the Special Rule for Determination of Public Charge.

(5) Public cash assistance and criminal history verification. Declarations by an applicant that he or she has not been the recipient of public cash assistance and/or has not had a criminal record are subject to a verification of facts by the Service. The applicant must agree to fully cooperate in the verification process. Failure to assist the Service in verifying information necessary for proper adjudication may result in denial of the application.

(h) Departure. An applicant for adjustment to lawful permanent resident status under section 245A(b)(1) of the Act who was granted lawful temporary resident status under section 245A(a) of the Act, shall be permitted to return to the United States after such brief and casual trips abroad, as long as the alien reflects a continuing intention to adjust to lawful permanent resident status. However, such absences from the United States must not exceed the periods of time specified in § 245a.3(b)(2) of this chapter in order for the alien to maintain continuous residence as specified in the Act.

(i) Decision. The applicant shall be notified in writing of the decision, and, if the application is denied, of the reason therefor. Applications for permanent residence under this chapter will not be denied at local INS offices (districts, suboffices, and legalization offices) until the entire record of proceeding has been reviewed. An application will not be denied if the denial is based on adverse information not previously furnished to the Service by the alien without providing the alien an opportunity to rebut the adverse information and to present evidence in his or her behalf. If inconsistencies are found between information submitted with the adjustment application and information previously furnished to the Service, the applicant shall be afforded the opportunity to explain discrepancies or rebut any adverse information. A party affected under this part by an adverse decision is entitled to file an appeal on Form I-694. If an application is denied, work authorization will be granted until a final decision has been rendered on an appeal or until the end of the appeal period if no appeal is filed. An applicant whose appeal period has ended is no longer considered to be an Eligible Legalized Alien for the purposes of the administration of State Legalization Impact Assistance Grants (SLIAG) funding. An alien whose application is denied will not be required to surrender his or her temporary resident card (I-688) until such time as the appeal period has tolled, or until expiration date of the I-688, whichever date is later. After exhaustion of an appeal, an applicant who believes that the grounds for denial have been overcome may submit another application with fee, provided that the application is submitted within his or her eligibility period.

(j) Appeal process. An adverse decision under this part may be appealed to the Associate Commissioner, Examinations (Administrative Appeals Unit) the appellate authority designated in § 103.1(f)(2). Any appeal shall be submitted to the Regional Processing Facility with the required fee within thirty (30) days after service of the Notice of Denial in accordance with the procedures of § 103.3(a) of this chapter. An appeal received after the thirty (30) day period has tolled will not be accepted. The thirty (30) day period for submitting an appeal begins three days after the notice of denial is mailed. If a review of the Record of Proceeding (ROP) is requested by the alien or his or her legal representative and an appeal has been properly filed, an additional thirty (30) days will be allowed for this review from the time the Record of Proceeding is photocopied and mailed. A brief may be submitted with the appeal form or submitted up to thirty (30) calendar days from the date of receipt of the appeal form at the Regional Processing Facility. Briefs filed after submission of the appeal should be mailed directly to the Regional Processing Facility. For good cause shown, the time within which a brief supporting an appeal may be submitted may be extended by the Director of the Regional Processing Facility.

(k) Motions. The Regional Processing Facility director may reopen and reconsider any adverse decision sua sponte. When an appeal to the Associate Commissioner, Examinations (Administrative Appeals Unit) has been filed, the INS director of the Regional Processing Facility may issue a new decision that will grant the benefit which has been requested. The director's new decision must be served on the appealing party within forty-five (45) days of receipt of any briefs and/or new evidence, or upon expiration of the time allowed for the submission of any briefs.

(*l*) Certifications. The Regional Processing Facility director or district director may, in accordance with § 103.4 of this chapter, certify a decision to the Associate Commissioner, Examinations (Administrative Appeals Unit) when the case involves an unusually complex or novel question of law or fact. The decision on an appealed case subsequently remanded back to either the Regional Processing Facility director or the district director will be certified to the Administrative Appeals Unit.

(m) Date of adjustment to permanent residence. The status of an alien whose application for permanent resident status is approved shall be adjusted to that of a lawful permanent resident as of the date of filing of the application for permanent residence or the eligibility date, whichever is later. For purposes of making application to petition for naturalization, the continuous residence requirements for naturalization shall begin as of the date the alien's status is adjusted to that of a person lawfully admitted for permanent residence under this part.

(n) Limitation on access to information and confidentiality.

(1) No person other than a sworn officer or employee of the Department of Justice or bureau of agency thereof, will be permitted to examine individual applications. For purposes of this part, any individual employed under contract by the Service to work in connection with the Legalization Program shall be considered an employee of the Department of Justice or bureau or agency thereof.

(2) No information furnished pursuant to an application for permanent resident status under this section shall be used for any purpose except: (i) To make a determination on the application; or (ii) for the enforcement of the provisions encompassed in section 245A(c)(6) of the Act, except as provided in paragraph (n)(3) of this section.

(3) If a determination is made by the Service that the alien has, in connection with his or her application, engaged in fraud or willful misrepresentation or concealment of a material fact, knowingly provided a false writing or document in making his or her application, knowingly made a false statement or representation, or engaged in any other activity prohibited by section 245A(c)(6) of the Act, the Service shall refer the matter to the United States Attorney for prosecution of the alien and/or of any person who created or supplied a false writing or document for use in an application for adjustment of status under this part.

(4) Information contained in granted legalization files may be used by the Service at a later date to make a decision (i) On an immigrant visa petition or other status filed by the applicant under section 204(a) of the Act; (ii) On a naturalization application submitted by the applicant; (iii) For the preparation of reports to Congress under section 404 of IRCA, or; (iv) For the furnishing of information, at the discretion of the Attorney General, in the same manner and circumstances as census information may be disclosed by the Secretary of Commerce under section 8 of title 13, Unites States Code.

(o) Rescission. Rescission of adjustment of status under 245a shall occur under the guidelines established in section 246 of the Act.

HISTORY:

[54 FR 29449, July 12, 1989; 54 FR 43384, Oct. 24, 1989; as amended at 56 FR 31061, July 9, 1991; 57 FR 3926, Feb. 3, 1992; 59 FR 33905, July 1, 1994; 85 FR 46788, 46927, Aug. 3, 2020; 89 FR 6194, 6399, Jan. 31, 2024]

§ 245a.4 Adjustment to lawful resident status of certain nationals of countries for which extended voluntary departure has been made available.

(a) Definitions. As used in this section:

(1) Act means the Immigration and Nationality Act, as amended by the Immigration Reform and Control Act of 1986.

(2) Service means the Immigration and Naturalization Service (INS).

(3) Resided continuously means that the alien shall be regarded as having resided continuously in the United States if, at the time of filing of the application for temporary resident status:

(i) No single absence from the United States has exceeded 45 days, and the aggregate of all absences has not exceeded 180 days between July 21, 1984, through the date the application for temporary resident status is filed, unless the alien can establish that due to emergent reasons, his or her return to the United States could not be accomplished within the time period allowed;

(ii) The alien was maintaining residence in the United States; and

(iii) The alien's departure from the United States was not based on an order of deportation.

An alien who has been absent from the United States in accordance with the Service's advance parole procedures shall not be considered as having interrupted his or her continuous residence as required at the time of filing an application. An alien who, after appearing for a scheduled interview to obtain an immigrant visa at a Consulate or Embassy in Canada or Mexico but who subsequently is not issued an immigrant visa and who is paroled back into the United States pursuant to the stateside criteria program, shall be considered as having resided continuously.

(4) Continous residence means that the alien shall be regarded as having resided continously in the United States if, at the time of applying for adjustment from temporary residence to permanent resident status: No single absence from the United States has exceeded 30 days, and the aggregate of all absences has not exceeded 90 days between the date on which lawful temporary resident status was granted and the date permanent resident status was applied for, unless the alien can establish that due to emergent reasons or extenuating circumstances beyond his or her control, the return to the United States could not be accomplished within the time period(s) allowed. A single absence from the United States of more than 30 days, and aggregate absences of more than 90 days during the period for which continuous residence is required for adjustment to permanent resident status, shall break the continuity of such residence unless the temporary resident can establish to the satisfaction of the district director that he or she did not, in fact, abandon his or her residence in the United States during such period.

(5) To make a determination means obtaining and reviewing all information required to adjudicate an application for the benefit sought and making a decision thereon. If fraud, willful misrepresentation or concealment of a material fact, knowingly providing a false writing or document, knowingly making a false statement or representation, or any other activity prohibited by the Act is established during the process of making the determination on the application, the Service shall refer the matter to the United States Attorney for prosecution of the alien or of any person who created or supplied a false writing or document for use in an application for adjustment of status under this part.

(6) Continuous physical presence means actual continuous presence in the United States since December 22, 1987, until filing of any application for adjustment of status. Aliens who were outside of the United States after enactment may apply for temporary residence if they reentered prior to March 21, 1988, provided they meet the continuous residence requirements, and are otherwise eligible for legalization.

(7) Brief, casual, and innocent means a departure authorized by the Service (advance parole) subsequent to March 21, 1988, for not more than 30 days for legitimate emergency or humanitarian purposes unless a further period of authorized departure has been granted in the discretion of the district director or a departure was beyond the alien's control.

(8) Brief and casual means temporary trips abroad as long as the alien establishes a continuing intention to adjust to lawful permanent resident status. However, such absences must not exceed the specific periods of time required in order to maintain continuous residence.

(9) Certain nationals of countries for which extended voluntary departure has been made available on the basis of a nationality group determination at any time during the 5-year period ending on November 1, 1987 is limited to nationals of Poland, Afghanistan, Ethiopia, and Uganda.

(10) Public cash assistance means income or need-based monetary assistance to include, but not limited to, supplemental security income received by the alien through federal, state, or local programs designed to meet subsistence levels. It does not include assistance in kind, such as food stamps, public housing, or other non-cash benefits, nor does it include work related compensation or certain types of medical assistance (Medicare, Medicaid, emergency treatment, services to pregnant women or children under 18 years of age, or treatment in the interest of public health).

(11) Designated entity means any state, local, church, community, farm labor organization, voluntary organization, association of agricultural employers or individual determined by the Service to be qualified to assist aliens in the preparation of applications for legalization status.

(12) Through the passage of time means through the expiration date of the nonimmigrant permission to remain in the United States, including any extensions and/or change of status.

(13) Prima facie eligibility means eligibility is established if the applicant presents a completed I-687 and

specific factual information which in the absence of rebuttal will establish a claim of eligibility under this part.

(b) Application for temporary residence —

(1) Application for temporary residence

(i) An alien who is a national of Poland, Uganda, Ethiopia, or Afghanistan who has resided continuously in the United States since prior to July 2l, 1984, and who believes that he or she meets the eligibility requirements of section 245A of the Act must make application within the 21-month period beginning on March 21, 1988, and ending on December 22, 1989.

(ii) An alien who fails to file an application for adjustment of status to that of a temporary resident under § 245A.4 of this part during the time period, will be statutorily ineligible for such adjustment of status.

(2) Eligibility

(i) The following categories of aliens who are not otherwise excludable under section 212(a) of the Act are eligible to apply for status to that of a person admitted for temporary residence:

(A) An alien who is a national of Poland, Uganda, Ethiopia, or Afghanistan, (other than an alien who entered as a nonimmigrant) who establishes that he or she entered the United States prior to July 21, 1984, and who has thereafter resided continuously in the United States, and who has been physically present in the United States from December 22, 1987, until the date of filing the application.

(B) An alien who is a national of Poland, Uganda, Ethiopia, or Afghanistan, and establishes that he or she entered the United States as a nonimmigrant prior to July 21, 1984, and whose period of authorized admission expired through the passage of time prior to January 21, 1985, and who has thereafter resided continuously in the United States, and who has been physically present in the United States from December 22, 1987, until the date of filing the application.

(C) An alien who is a national of Poland, Uganda, Ethiopia, or Afghanistan, and establishes that he or she entered the United States as a nonimmigrant prior to July 21, 1984, and who applied for asylum prior to July 21, 1984, and who has thereafter resided continuously in the United States, and who has been physically present in the United States from December 22, 1987, until the date of filing the application.

(D) An alien who is a national of Poland, Uganda, Ethiopia, or Afghanistan, who would otherwise be eligible for temporary resident status and who establishes that he or she resided continuously in the United States prior to July 21, 1984, and who subsequently reentered the United States as a nonimmigrant in order to return to an unrelinquished residence. An alien described in this paragraph must have received a waiver of 212(a)(19) as an alien who entered the United States by fraud.

(E) An alien who is a national of Poland, Uganda, Ethiopia, or Afghanistan, and was a nonimmigrant who entered the United States in the classification A, A-1, A-2, G, G-1, G-2, G-3, or G-4, for Duration of Status (D/S), and whose qualifying employment terminated or who ceased to be recognized by the Department of State as being entitled to such classification prior to January 21, 1985, and who thereafter continued to reside in the United States.

(F) An alien who is a national of Poland, Uganda, Ethiopia, or Afghanistan, and who was a nonimmigrant who entered the United States as an F, F-1, or F-2 for Duration of Status (D/S), and who completed a full course of studies, including practical training (if any), and whose time period to depart the United States after completion of studies expired prior to January 21, 1985, and who has thereafter continued to reside in the United States. Those students placed in a nunc pro tunc retroactive student status which would otherwise preclude their eligibility for legalization under this section, must present evidence that they had otherwise terminated their status during the requisite time period. A dependent F-2 alien otherwise eligible who was admitted into the United States with a specific time period, as opposed to duration of status, documented on Service Form I-94 (see § 1.4), Arrival-Departure Record that extended beyond July 21, 1984 is considered eligible if the principal F-1 alien is found eligible.

(3) Ineligible aliens.

(i) An alien who has been convicted of a felony, or three or more misdemeanors.

(ii) An alien who has assisted in the persecution of any person or persons on account of race, religion, nationality, membership in a particular social group, or political opinion.

(iii) An alien excludable under the provisions of section 212(a) of the Act whose grounds of excludability may not be waived.

(4) Documentation. Evidence to support an alien's eligibility for temporary residence status shall include documents establishing proof of identity, proof of nationality, proof of residence, and proof of financial responsibility, as well as photographs, a completed fingerprint card (Form FD-258), and a completed medical report of examination (Form I-693). All documentation submitted will be subject to Service verification. Applications submitted with unverifiable documentation may be denied. Failure by an applicant to authorize release to INS of information protected by the Privacy Act and/or related laws in order for INS to adjudicate a claim may result in denial of the benefit sought. Acceptable supporting documents for the four categories of documentation are discussed as follows:

(i) Proof of identity. Evidence to establish identity is listed below in descending order of preference:

(A) Passport;

(B) Birth certificate;

(C) Any national identity document from the alien's country of origin bearing photo and fingerprint;

(D) Driver's license or similar document issued by a state if it contains a photo;

(E) Baptismal Record/Marriage Certificate; or

(F) Affidavits.

(ii) Proof of nationality. Evidence to establish nationality is listed as follows:

(A) Passport;

(B) Birth certificate;

(C) Any national identity document from the alien's country of origin bearing photo and fingerprint;

(D) Other credible documents, including those created by, or in the possession of the INS, or any other documents (excluding affidavits) that, when taken singly, or together as a whole, establish the alien's nationality.

(iii) Assumed names —

(A) General. In cases where an applicant claims to have met any of the eligibility criteria under an assumed name, the applicant has the burden of proving that the applicant was in fact the person who used that name. The applicant's true identity is established pursuant to the requirements of paragraph (b)(4)(i) and (ii) of this section. The assumed name must appear in the documentation provided by the applicant to establish eligibility. To meet the requirement of this paragraph, documentation must be submitted to prove the common identity, i.e., that the assumed name was in fact used by the applicant.

(B) Proof of common identity. The most persuasive evidence is a document issued in the assumed name which identifies the applicant by photograph, fingerprint, or detailed physical description. Other evidence which will be considered are affidavit(s) by a person or persons other than the applicant, made under oath, which identify the affiant by name and address, state the affiant's relationship to the applicant and the basis of the affiant's knowledge of the applicant's use of the assumed name. Affidavits accompanied by a photograph which has been identified by the affiant as the individual known to the affiant under the assumed name in question will carry greater weight.

(iv) Proof of residence. — Evidence to establish proof of continuous residence in the United States during the requisite period of time may consist of any combination of the following:

(A) Past employment records, which may consist of pay stubs, W-2 Forms, certification of the filing of Federal income tax returns on IRS Form 6166, a state verification of the filing of state income tax returns, letters from employer(s) or, if the applicant has been in business for himself or herself, letters from banks and other firms with whom he or she has done business. In all of the above, the name of the alien and the name of the employer or other interested organizations must appear on the form or letter, as well as relevant dates. Letters from employers should be on employer letterhead stationery, if the employer has such stationery, and must include:

(1) Alien's address at the time of employment;

(2) Exact period of employment;

(3) Periods of layoff;

(4) Duties with the company;

(5) Whether or not the information was taken from official company records; and

(6) Where records are located, whether the Service may have access to the records.

If the records are unavailable, an affidavit form letter stating that the alien's employment records are unavailable and why such records are unavailable may be accepted in lieu of paragraphs (b)(4)(iv)(A)(5) and (6) of this section. This affidavit form letter shall be signed, attested to by the employer under penalty of perjury, and shall state the employer's willingness to come forward and give testimony if requested.

(B) Utility bills (gas, electric, phone, etc.) receipts, or letters from companies showing the dates during which the applicant received service are acceptable documentation.

(C) School records (letters, report cards, etc.) from the schools that the applicant or his or her children have attended in the United States must show the name of school and periods of school attendance.

(D) Hospital or medical records showing treatment or hospitalization of the applicant or his or her children must show the name of the medical facility or physician and the date(s) of the treatment or hospitalization.

(E) Attestations by churches, unions, or other organizations as to the applicant's residence by letter which:

(1) Identify applicant by name;

(2) Are signed by an official (whose title is shown);

(3) Show inclusive dates of membership;

(4) State the address where applicant resided during membership period;

(5) Include the seal of the organization impressed on the letter or the letterhead of the organization, if the organization has letterhead stationery;

(6) Establish how the author knows the applicant; and

(7) Establish the origin of the information being attested to.

(F) Additional documents to support the applicant's claim may include:

(1) Money order receipts for money sent into or out of the country;

(2) Passport entries;

(3) Birth certificates of children born in the United States;

(4) Bank books with dated transactions;

(5) Letters or correspondence between applicant and other person or organization;

(6) Social Security card;

(7) Selective Service card;

(8) Automobile license receipts, title, vehicle registration, etc.;

(9) Deeds, mortgages, contracts to which applicant has been a party;

(10) Tax receipts;

(11) Insurance policies, receipts, or letters; and

(12) Any other relevant document.

(v) Proof of financial responsibility. An applicant for adjustment of status under this part is subject to the provisions of section 212(a)(15) of the Act relating to excludability of aliens likely to become public charges. Generally, the evidence of employment submitted under paragraph (b)(4)(iv)(A) of this section will serve to demonstrate the alien's financial responsibility during the documented period(s) of employment. If the alien's period(s) of residence in the United States include significant gaps in employment or if there is reason to believe that the alien may have received public assistance while employed, the alien may be required to provide proof that he or she has not received public cash assistance. An applicant for residence who is determined likely to become a public charge and is unable to overcome this determination after application of the Special Rule under paragraph (b)(11)(iv)(C) of this section will be denied adjustment. The burden of proof to demonstrate the inapplicability of this provision of law lies with the applicant who may provide:

(A) Evidence of a history of employment (i.e., employment letter, W-2 forms, income tax returns, etc.);

(B) Evidence that he/she is self-supporting (i.e., bank statements, stocks, other assets, etc.); or

(C) Form I-134. Affidavit of Support, completed by a spouse on behalf of the applicant and/or children of the applicant or a parent in behalf of children which guarantees complete or partial financial support. Acceptance of the Affidavit of Support shall be extended to other family members in unusual family circumstances.

Generally, the evidence of employment submitted under paragraph (b)(4)(iv)(A) of this section will serve to demonstrate the alien's financial responsibility during the documented period(s) of employment. If the alien's period(s) of residence in the United States include significant gaps in employment or if there is reason to believe that the alien may have received public assistance while employed, the alien may be required to provide proof that he or she has not received public cash assistance. An applicant for residence who is likely to become a public charge will be denied adjustment.

(vi) Burden of proof. An alien applying for adjustment of status under this part has the burden of proving by a preponderance of the evidence that he or she has resided in the United States for the requisite periods, is admissible to the United States under the provisions of section 245A of the Act, and is otherwise eligible for adjustment of status under this section. The inference to be drawn from the documentation provided shall depend on the extent of the documentation, its credibility and amenability to verification.

(vii) Evidence. The sufficiency of all evidence produced by the applicant will be judged according to its probative value and credibility. To meet his or her burden of proof, an applicant must provide evidence of eligibility apart from his or her own testimony. In judging the probative value and credibility of the evidence submitted, greater weight will be given to the submission of original documentation.

(5) Filing of application

(i) The application must be filed on Form I-687 at an office of a designated entity or at a Service office within the jurisdiction of the district where the applicant resides. If the application is filed with a designated entity, the alien must have consented to having the designated entity forward the application to the Service office. In the case of applications filed at a Service office, the district director may, at his or her discretion:

(A) Require the applicant to file the application in person; or

(B) Require the applicant to file the application by mail; or

(C) Permit the filing of applications whether by mail or in person.

The applicant must appear for a personal interview at the Service office as scheduled. If the applicant is 14 years of age or older, the application must be accompanied by a completed Form FD-258 (Applicant Card).

(ii) At the time of the interview, whenever possible, original documents must be submitted except the following: Official government records; employment or employment-related records maintained by employers, union, or collective bargaining organizations; medical records; school records maintained by a school or school board; or other records maintained by a party other than the applicant. Copies of records maintained by parties other than the applicant which are submitted in evidence must be certified as true and correct by such parties and must bear their seal or signature or the signature and title of persons authorized to act in their behalf. If at the time of the interview the return of the original document is desired by the applicant, the document must be accompanied by notarized copies or copies certified true and correct by a qualified designated entity or by the alien's representative in the format prescribed in § 204.2(j)(1) or (2) of this chapter. At the discretion of the district director, original documents, even if accompanied by certified copies, may be temporarily retained for forensic examination by the Document Analysis Unit at the Regional Processing Facility having jurisdiction over the Service office to which the documents were submitted.

(iii) A separate application must be filed by each applicant with the fees required by 8 CFR 106.2.

(6) Filing date of application. The date the alien submits a completed application to a Service office or designated entity shall be considered the filing date of the application, provided that in the case of an application filed at a designated entity the alien has consented to having the designated entity forward the application to the Service office having jurisdiction over the location of the alien's residence. Designated entities are required to forward completed applications to the appropriate Service office within 60 days of receipt.

(7) Selective Service registration. At the time of filing an application under this section, male applicants over the age of 17 and under the age of 26, are required to be registered under the Military Selective Service Act. An applicant shall present evidence that he has previously registered under that Act in the form of a letter of acknowledgement from the Selective Service System, or such alien shall present a completed and signed Form SSS-1 at the time of filing Form I-687 with the Immigration and Naturalization Service or a designated entity. Form SSS-1 will be forwarded to the Selective Service System by the Service.

(8) Continuous residence

(i) For the purpose of this Act, an applicant for temporary residence status shall be regarded as having resided continuously in the United States if, at the time of filing of the application:

(A) No single absence from the United States has exceeded 45 days, and the aggregate of all absences has not exceeded 180 days between July 2l, 1984, through the date the application for temporary resident status is filed, unless the alien can establish that due to emergent reasons, his or her return to the United States could not be accomplished within the time period allowed;

(B) The alien was maintaining a residence in the United States; and

(C) The alien's departure from the United States was not based on an order of deportation.

(ii) An alien who has been absent from the United States in accordance with the Service's advance parole procedures shall not be considered as having interrupted his or her continuous residence as required at the time of filing an application under this section.

(9) Medical examination.

(i) An applicant under this part shall be required to submit to an examination by a designated civil surgeon at no expense to the government. The designated civil surgeon shall report on the findings of the mental and physical condition of the applicant and the determination of the alien's immunization status on Form I-693, "Medical Examination of Aliens Seeking Adjustment of Status, (Pub. L. 99-603)". Results of the medical examination must be presented to the Service at the time of interview and shall be incorporated into the record. Any applicant certified under paragraphs (1), (2), (3), (4) or (5) of section 212(a) of the Act may appeal to a Board of Medical Officers of the U.S. Public Health Service as provided in section 234 of the Act and part 235 of this chapter.

(ii) All applicants who file for temporary resident status are required to include the results of a serological test for the HIV virus on the I-693. All HIV-positive applicants shall be advised that a waiver is available and shall be provided with the opportunity to apply for a waiver.

(10) Interview. Each applicant, regardless of age, must appear at the appropriate Service office and must be fingerprinted for the purpose of issuance of an employment authorization document and Form I-688. Each applicant shall be interviewed by an immigration officer, except that the interview may be waived for a child under 14 years of age, or when it is impractical because of the health or advanced age of the applicant.

(11) Applicability of exclusion grounds.

(i) Grounds of exclusion not to be applied. Paragraphs (14), (workers entering without labor certification); (20), (immigrants not in possession of a valid entry document); (21), (visas issued without compliance with section 203); (25), (illiterates); and (32) (graduates of non-accredited medical schools) of section 212(a) of the Act shall not apply to applicants for temporary resident status.

(ii) Waiver of grounds of exclusion. Except as provided in paragraph (b)(11)(iii) of this section, the Attorney General may waive any other provision of section 212(a) of the Act only in the case of individual aliens for humanitarian purposes, to assure family unity, or when the granting of such a waiver is in the public interest. If an alien is excludable on grounds which may be waived as set forth in this paragraph, he or she shall be advised of the procedures for applying for a waiver of grounds of excludability on Form I-690. When an application for waiver of grounds of excludability is filed jointly with an application for temporary residence under this section, it shall be accepted for processing at the Service office. If an application for waiver of grounds of excludability is submitted after the alien's preliminary interview at the Service office, it shall be forwarded to the appropriate Regional Processing Facility. All applications for waivers of grounds of excludability must be accompanied by the correct fee in the exact amount. All fees for applications filed in the United States must be in the form of a money order, cashier's check, or bank check. No personal checks or currency will be accepted. Fees will not be waived or refunded under any circumstances. An application for waiver of grounds of excludability under this part shall be approved or denied by the director of the Regional Processing Facility in whose jurisdiction the alien's application for adjustment of status was filed except that in cases involving clear statutory ineligibility or fraud, such application may be denied by the district director in whose jurisdiction the application is filed, and in cases returned to a Service office for re-interview, such application may be approved at the discretion of the district director. The applicant shall be notified of the decision and, if the application is denied, of the reason therefore. Appeal from an adverse decision under this part may be taken by the applicant on Form I-694 within 30 days after the service of the notice only to the Service's Administrative Appeals Unit pursuant to the provisions of section 103.3(a) of this chapter.

(iii) Grounds of exclusion that may not be waived. Notwithstanding any other provision of the Act, the following provisions of section 212(a) may not be waived by the Attorney General under paragraph (b)(11)(ii) of this section:

(A) Paragraphs (9) and (10) (criminals);

(B) Paragraph (23) (narcotics) except for a single offense of simple possession of thirty grams or less of marijuana;

(C) Paragraphs (27) (prejudicial to the public interest), (28) (communist), and (29) (subversive);

(D) Paragraph (33) (participated in Nazi persecution).

(iv) Determination of Likely to become a public charge and the special rule.

(A) Prior to use of the special rule for determination of public charge, an alien must first be determined to be excludable under section 212(a)(15) of the Act. If the applicant is determined to be likely to become a public charge, he or she may still be admissible under the terms of the Special Rule.

(B) In determining whether an alien is likely to become a public charge, financial responsibility of the alien is to be established by examining the totality of the alien's circumstances at the time of his or her application for legalization. The existence or absence of a particular factor should never be the sole criterion for determining if an alien is likely to become a public charge. The determination of financial responsibility should be a prospective evaluation based on the alien's age, health, income and vocation.

(C) An alien who has a consistent employment history which shows the ability to support himself or herself even though his or her income may be below the poverty level may be admissible under this section. The alien's employment history need not be continuous in that it is uninterrupted. It should be continuous in the sense that the alien shall be regularly attached to the workforce, has an income over a substantial period of the applicable time, and has demonstrated the capacity to exist on his or her income without recourse to public cash assistance. The Special Rule is prospective in that the Service shall determine, based on the alien's history, whether he or she is likely to become a public charge. Past acceptance of public cash assistance within a history of consistent employment will enter into this decision. The weight given in considering applicability of the public charge provisions will depend on many factors, but the length of time an applicant has received public cash assistance will constitute a significant factor. It is not necessary to file a waiver in order to apply the Special Rule for Determination of Public Charge.

(v) Public assistance and criminal history verification. Declarations by an applicant that he or she has not been the recipient of public cash assistance and/or has not had a criminal record are subject to a verification of facts by the Service. The applicant must agree to fully cooperate in the verification process. Failure to assist the Service in verifying information necessary for the adjudication of the application may result in a denial of the application.

(12) Continuous physical presence since December 22, 1987.

(i) An alien applying for adjustment to temporary resident status must establish that he or she has been continuously physically present in the United States since December 22, 1987. Aliens who were outside of the United States on the date of enactment or departed the United States after enactment may apply for legalization if they reentered prior to March 21, 1988, and meet the continuous residence requirements and are otherwise eligible for legalization.

(ii) A brief, casual and innocent absence means a departure authorized by the Service (advance parole) subsequent to March 21, 1988, of not more than thirty (30) days for legitimate emergency or humanitarian purposes unless a further period of authorized departure has been granted in the discretion of the district director or a departure was beyond the alien's control.

(13) Departure.

(i) During the time period from the date that an alien's application establishing prima facie eligibility for temporary resident status is reviewed at a Service office and the date status as a temporary resident is granted, the alien applicant can be readmitted to the United States provided his or her departure was authorized under the Service's advance parole provisions contained in § 212.5(f) of this chapter.

(ii) An alien whose application for temporary resident status has been approved may be admitted to the United States upon return as a returning temporary resident provided he or she:

(A) Is not under deportation proceedings, such proceedings having been instituted subsequent to the approval of temporary resident status. A temporary resident alien will not be considered deported if that alien departs the United States while under an outstanding order of deportation issued prior to the approval of temporary resident status;

(B) Has not been absent from the United States for more than 30 days on the date application for admission is made;

(C) Has not been absent from the United States for an aggregate period of more than 90 days since the date the alien was granted lawful temporary resident status;

(D) Presents Form I-688;

(E) Presents himself or herself for inspection; and

(F) Is otherwise admissible.

(iii) The periods of time in paragraphs (b)(13)(ii)(B) and (C) of this section may be waived at the discretion of the Attorney General in cases where the absence from the United States was due merely to a brief and casual trip abroad due to emergent or extenuating circumstances beyond the alien's control.

(14) Employment and travel authorization. —

(i) General. Authorization for employment and travel abroad for temporary resident status applicants under this section may be granted only by a Service office. INS district directors will determine the Service location for the completion of processing travel documentation. In the case of an application which has been filed with a designated entity, employment authorization may be granted by the Service only after the application has been properly received at the Service office.

(ii) Employment and travel authorization prior to the granting of temporary resident status.

(A) Permission to travel abroad and accept employment may be granted to the applicant after an interview has been conducted in connection with an application establishing prima facie eligibility for temporary resident status. Permission to travel abroad may be granted in emergent circumstances in accordance with the Service's advance parole provisions contained in § 212.5(f) of this chapter after an interview has been conducted in connection with an application establishing prima facie eligibility for temporary resident status.

(B) If an appointment cannot be scheduled within 30 days, authorization to accept employment will be granted, valid until the scheduled appointment date. The appointment letter will be endorsed with the temporary employment authorization. An employment authorization document will be given to the applicant after an interview has been completed by an immigration officer unless a formal denial is issued by a Service office. This temporary employment authorization will be restricted to six-months duration, pending final determination on the application for temporary resident status.

(iii) Employment and travel authorization upon grant of temporary resident status. Upon grant of an application for adjustment to temporary resident status by a Regional Processing Facility, the processing facility will forward a notice of approval to the alien at his or her last known address, or to his or her legal representative. The alien will be required to return to the appropriate INS office, surrender the I-688A or employment authorization document previously issued, and obtain Form I-688, Temporary Resident Card, authorizing employment and travel abroad.

(iv) Revocation of employment authorization upon denial of temporary resident status. Upon denial of an application for adjustment to temporary resident status, the alien will be notified that if a timely appeal is not submitted, employment authorization shall be automatically revoked on the final day of the appeal period. An applicant whose appeal period has ended is no longer considered to be an Eligible Legalized Alien for the purposes of the administration of State Legalization Impact Assistance Grants (SLIAG) funding.

(15) Decision. The applicant shall be notified in writing of the decision. If the application is denied, the reason(s) for the decision shall be provided to the applicant. An appeal from an adverse decision under this part may be taken by the applicant on Form I-694.

(16) Appeal process. An adverse decision under this part may be appealed to the Associate Commissioner, Examinations (Administrative Appeals Unit), the appellate authority designated in § 103.1(f)(2). Any appeal shall be submitted to the Regional Processing Facility (RPF) with the required fee within 30 days after service of the Notice of Denial in accordance with the procedures of § 103.3(a) of this chapter. An appeal received after the 30-day period will not be accepted. The 30-day period for submission of an appeal begins three days after the Notice of Denial is mailed as provided in 8 CFR 103.8(b). If a review of the Record of Proceeding (ROP) is requested by the alien or his or her legal representative and an appeal has been properly filed, an additional 30 days will be allowed for this review beginning at the time the ROP is mailed. A brief may be submitted with the appeal form or submitted up to 30 calendar days from the date of receipt of the appeal form at the RPF. Briefs filed after submission of the appeal should be mailed directly to the RPF. For good cause shown, the time within which a brief supporting an appeal may be submitted may be extended by the Director of the Regional Processing Facility.

(17) Motions. The Regional Processing Facility director may sua sponte reopen and reconsider any adverse decision. When an appeal to the Associate Commissioner, Examinations (Administrative Appeals Unit) has been filed, the INS director of the Regional Processing Facility may issue a new decision granting the benefit which has been requested. The director's new decision must be served on the appealing party within 45 days of receipt of any briefs and/or new evidence, or upon expiration of the time allowed for the submission of any briefs. Motions to reopen a proceeding or reconsider a decision shall not be considered under this part.

(18) Certifications. The Regional Processing Facility director may, in accordance with § 103.4 of this chapter, certify a decision to the Associate Commissioner, Examinations (Administrative Appeals Unit) when the case involves an unusually complex or novel question of law or fact. The decision on an appealed case subsequently remanded to the Regional Processing Facility director will be certified to the Administrative Appeals Unit.

(19) Date of adjustment to temporary residence. The status of an alien whose application for temporary resident status is approved shall be adjusted to that of a lawful temporary resident as of the date indicated on the application fee receipt issued at the Service office.

(20) Termination of temporary resident status. —

(i) Termination of temporary resident status (General). The status of an alien lawfully admitted for temporary residence under § 245a.4 of this part may be terminated at any time. It is not necessary that a final order of deportation be entered in order to terminate temporary resident status. The temporary resident status may be terminated upon the occurrence of any of the following:

(A) It is determined that the alien was ineligible for temporary residence under § 245a.4 of this part;

(B) The alien commits an act which renders him or her inadmissible as an immigrant unless a waiver is obtained, as provided in this part;

(C) The alien is convicted of any felony, or three or more misdemeanors;

(D) The alien fails to file for adjustment of status from temporary resident to permanent resident within 31 months of the date he or she was granted status as a temporary resident.

(ii) Procedure. Termination of an alien's status will be made only on notice to the alien sent by certified mail directed to his or her last known address, and, if applicable, to his or her representative. The alien must be given an opportunity to offer evidence in opposition to the grounds alleged for termination of his or her status. Evidence in opposition must be submitted within 30 days after the service of the Notice of Intent to Terminate. If the alien's status is terminated, the director of the Regional Processing Facility shall notify the alien of the decision and the reason for the termination, and further notify the alien that any Service Form issued to the alien authorizing employment and/or travel abroad, or any Form I-688, Temporary Resident Card previously issued to the alien will be declared void by the director of the Regional Processing Facility within 30 days if no appeal of the termination decision is filed within that period. The alien may appeal the decision to the Associate Commissioner, Examinations (Administrative Appeals Unit). Any appeal along with the required fee, shall be filed with the Regional Processing Facility within 30 days after the service of the notice of termination. If no appeal is filed within that period, the official Service document shall be deemed void, and must be surrendered without delay to an immigration officer or to the issuing office of the Service.

(iii) Termination not construed as rescission under section 246. For the purposes of this part the phrase termination of status of an alien granted lawful temporary residence under this section shall not be construed to necessitate a rescission of status as described in section 246 of the Act, and the proceedings required by the regulations issued thereunder shall not apply.

(iv) Return to unlawful status after termination. Termination of the status of any alien previously adjusted to lawful temporary residence shall act to return such alien to the status held prior to the adjustment, and render him or her amenable to exclusion or deportation proceedings under sections 236 or 242 of the Act, as appropriate.

(21) Ineligibility for immigration benefits. An alien whose status is adjusted to that of a lawful temporary resident under § 245a.4 of this part is not entitled to submit a petition pursuant to section 203(a)(2), nor is such alien entitled to any other benefit or consideration accorded under the Act to aliens lawfully admitted for permanent residence.

(22) Declaration of intending citizen. An alien who has been granted the status of temporary resident under § 245a.4 of this part may assert a claim of discrimination on the basis of citizenship status under section 274B of the Act only if he or she has previously filed Form I-772 (Declaration of Intending Citizen) after being granted such status. The Declaration of Intending Citizen is not required as a basis for filing a petition for naturalization; nor shall it be regarded as a right to United States citizenship; nor shall it be regarded as evidence of a person's status as a resident.

(23) Limitation on access to information and confidentiality.

(i) No person other than a sworn officer or employee of the Department of Justice or bureau or agency thereof, will be permitted to examine individual applications. For purposes of this part, any individual employed under contract by the Service to work in connection with the Legalization Program shall be considered an employee of the Department of Justice or bureau or agency thereof.

(ii) No information furnished pursuant to an application for temporary or permanent resident status under this section shall be used for any purpose except:

(A) To make a determination on the application; or,

(B) for the enforcement of the provisions encompassed in section 245A(c)(6) of the Act, except as provided in paragraph (b)(23)(iii) of this section.

(iii) If a determination is made by the Service that the alien has, in connection with his or her application, engaged in fraud or willful misrepresentation or concealment of a material fact, knowingly provided a false writing or document in making his or her application, knowingly made a false statement or representation, or engaged in any other activity prohibited by section 245A(c)(6) of the Act, the Service shall refer the matter to the United States Attorney for prosecution of the alien or of any person who created or supplied a false writing or document for use in an application for adjustment of status under this part.

(iv) Information contained in granted legalization files may be used by the Service at a later date to make a decision on an immigrant visa petition (or other status petition) filed by the applicant under section 204(a), or for naturalization applications submitted by the applicant.

(c) Adjustment from temporary to permanent resident status. The provisions of § 245a.3 of this part shall be applied to aliens adjusting to permanent residence under this part.

HISTORY:

[54 FR 6505, Feb. 13, 1989, as amended at 54 FR 29455, July 12, 1989; 54 FR 47676, Nov. 16, 1989; 60 FR 21976, May 4, 1995; 65 FR 82254, 82256, Dec. 28, 2000; 66 FR 7863, Jan. 26, 2001; 76 FR 53764, 53794, Aug. 29, 2011; 78 FR 18457, 18472, Mar. 27, 2013, as confirmed at 81 FR 91646, 91670, Dec. 19, 2016; 85 FR 46788, 46927, Aug. 3, 2020; 89 FR 6194, 6399, Jan. 31, 2024]

§ 245a.5 Temporary disqualification of certain newly legalized aliens from receiving benefits from programs of financial assistance furnished under federal law.

(a) Except as provided in § 245a.5(b), any alien who has obtained the status of an alien lawfully admitted for temporary residence pursuant to section 245A of the Act (Adjustment of Status of Certain Entrants Before January 1, 1982, to that of Person Admitted for Lawful Residence) or 210A of the Act (Determinations of Agricultural Labor Shortages and Admission of Additional Special Agricultural Workers) is ineligible, for a period of five years from the date such status was obtained, for benefits financed directly or indirectly, in whole or in part, through the programs identified in § 245a.5(c) of this chapter.

(b)(1) Section 245a.5(a) shall not apply to a Cuban or Haitian entrant (as defined in paragraph (1) or (2)(A) of section 501(e) of Public Law 96-422, as in effect on April 1, 1983), or in the case of assistance (other than aid to families with dependent children) which is furnished to an alien who is an aged, blind, or disabled individual (as defined in section 1614(a)(1) of the Social Security Act).

(2) With respect to any alien who has obtained the status of an alien lawfully admitted for temporary residence pursuant to section 210A of the Act only, assistance furnished under the Legal Services Corporation Act (42 U.S.C. 2996, et seq.) or title V of the Housing Act of 1949 (42 U.S.C. 1471 et seq.) shall not be construed to be financial assistance referred to in § 245a.5(a).

(3) Section 245a.5(a) shall not apply to benefits financed through the programs identified in § 245a.5(c), which are marked with an asterisk (*), except to the extent that such benefits:

(i) Consist of, or are financed by, financial assistance in the form of grants, wages, loan, loan guarantees, or otherwise, which is furnished by the Federal Government directly, or indirectly through a State or local government or a private entity, to eligible individuals or to private suppliers of goods or services to such individuals, or is furnished to a State or local government that provides to such individuals goods or services of a kind that is offered by private suppliers, and

(ii) Are targeted to individuals in financial need; either (A) in order to be eligible, individuals must establish that their income or wealth is below some maximum level, or, with respect to certain loan or loan guarantee programs, that they are unable to obtain financing from alternative sources, or at prevailing interest rates, or at rates that would permit the achievement of program goals, or (B) distribution of assistance is directed, geographically or otherwise, in a way that is intended to primarily benefit persons in financial need, as evidenced by references to such intent in the authorizing legislation.

(c) The programs of Federal financial assistance referred to in § 245a.5(a) are those identified in the list set forth below. The General Services Administration (GSA) Program Numbers set forth in the right column of the program list refer to the program identification numbers used in the Catalog of Federal Domestic Assistance, published by the United States General Services Administration, as updated through December, 1986.

	GSA Program Numbers
Department of Agriculture:	
Farm Operating Loans	10.406
Farm Ownership Loans	10.407
Department of Health and Human Services:	
Assistance Payments — Maintenance Assistance (Maintenance Assistance; Emergency Assistance; State Aid; Aid to Families with Dependent Children)	13.780
Low-Income Home Energy Assistance	13.789
* Community Services Block Grant	13.792
* Community Services Block Grant — Discretionary Awards	13.793
Department of Housing and Urban Development:	
Mortgage Insurance — Housing in Older, Declining Areas (223(e))	14.123
Mortgage Insurance — Special Credit Risks (237)	14.140
* Community Development Block Grants/Entitlement Grants	14.218
* Community Development Block Grants/Small Cities Program (Small Cities)	14.219
Section 312 Rehabilitation Loans (312)	14.220
* Urban development action grants	14.221
*Community Development Block Grants/State's Program	14.228
Section 221(d)(3) Mortgage Insurance for Multifamily Rental Housing for Low and Moderate Income Families (Below Market Interest Rate)	14.136
Department of Labor:	
Senior Community Service Employment Program (SCSEP)	17.235
Office of Personnel Management:	
Federal Employment for Disadvantaged Youth — Part-Time (Stay-in-School Program)	27.003
Federal Employment for Disadvantaged Youth — Summer (Summer Aides)	27.004
Small Business Administration:	
Small Business Loans (7(a) Loans)	59.012
Department of Energy:	
Weatherization Assistance for Low-Income Persons	81.042
Department of Education:	
Patricia Roberts Harris Fellowships (Graduate and Professional Study; Graduate and Professional Study Opportunity Fellowships; Public Service Education Fellowships)	84.094
Legal Training for the Disadvantaged (The American Bar Association Fund for Public Education)	84.136
Allen J. Ellender Fellowship Program (Ellender Fellowship)	84.148
Legal Services Corporation:	
Payments to Legal Services Corporation	

HISTORY:

[54 FR 29437, July 12, 1989, as amended at 54 FR 49964, Dec. 4, 1989]

§ 245a.6 Treatment of denied application under part 245a, Subpart B.

If the district director finds that an eligible alien as defined at § 245a.10 has not established eligibility under section 1104 of the LIFE Act (part 245a, Subpart B), the district director shall consider whether the eligible alien has established eligibility for adjustment to temporary resident status under section 245A of the Act, as in effect before enactment of section 1104 of the LIFE Act (part 245a, Subpart A). In such an adjudication using this Subpart A, the district director will deem the "date of filing the application" to be the date the eligible alien establishes that he or she was "front-desked" or that, though he or she took concrete steps to apply, the front-desking policy was a substantial cause of his or her failure to apply. If the eligible alien has established eligibility for adjustment to temporary resident status, the LIFE Legalization application shall be deemed converted to an application for temporary residence under this Subpart A.

HISTORY:

[67 FR 38341, 38350, June 4, 2002]

Subpart B

Legal Immigration Family Equity (Life) Act Legalization Provisions

§ 245a.10 Definitions.

In this Subpart B, the terms:

Eligible alien means an alien (including a spouse or child as defined at section 101(b)(1) of the Act of the alien who was such as of the date the alien alleges that he or she attempted to file or was discouraged from filing an application for legalization during the original application period) who, before October 1, 2000, filed with the Attorney General a written claim for class membership, with or without filing fee, pursuant to a court order issued in the case of:

(1) Catholic Social Services, Inc. v. Meese, vacated sub nom. Reno v. Catholic Social Services, Inc., 509 U.S. 43 (1993) (CSS);

(2) League of United Latin American Citizens v. INS, vacated sub nom. Reno v. Catholic Social Services, Inc., 509 U.S. 43 (1993) (LULAC); or

(3) Zambrano v. INS, vacated, 509 U.S. 918 (1993) (Zambrano).

Lawful Permanent Resident (LPR) means the status of having been lawfully accorded the privilege of residing permanently in the United States as an immigrant in accordance with the immigration laws, such status not having changed.

LIFE Act means the Legal Immigration Family Equity Act and the LIFE Act Amendments of 2000.

LIFE Legalization means the provisions of section 1104 of the LIFE Act and section 1503 of the LIFE Act Amendments.

Prima facie means eligibility is established if an "eligible alien" presents a properly filed and completed Form I-485 and specific factual information which in the absence of rebuttal will establish a claim of eligibility under this Subpart B.

Written claim for class membership means a filing, in writing, in one of the forms listed in § 245a.14 that provides the Attorney General with notice that the applicant meets the class definition in the cases of CSS, LULAC or Zambrano.

HISTORY:

[66 FR 29661, 29673, June 1, 2001, as confirmed and amended at 67 FR 38341, 38350, June 4, 2002, as corrected at 67 FR 66532, Nov. 1, 2002]

§ 245a.11 Eligibility to adjust to LPR status.

An eligible alien, as defined in § 245a.10, may adjust status to LPR status under LIFE Legalization if:

(a) He or she properly files, with fee, Form I-485, Application to Register Permanent Residence or Adjust Status, with the Service during the application period beginning June 1, 2001, and ending June 4, 2003.

(b) He or she entered the United States before January 1, 1982, and resided continuously in the United States in an unlawful status since that date through May 4, 1988;

(c) He or she was continuously physically present in the United States during the period beginning on November 6, 1986, and ending on May 4, 1988;

(d) He or she is not inadmissible to the United States for permanent residence under any provisions of section 212(a) of the Act, except as provided in § 245a.18, and that he or she:

(1) Has not been convicted of any felony or of three or more misdemeanors committed in the United States;

(2) Has not assisted in the persecution of any person or persons on account of race, religion, nationality, membership in a particular social group, or political opinion; and

(3) Is registered or registering under the Military Selective Service Act, if the alien is required to be so registered; and

(e) He or she can demonstrate basic citizenship skills.

HISTORY:

[66 FR 29661, 29673, June 1, 2001, as confirmed and amended at 67 FR 38341, 38350, June 4, 2002]

§ 245a.12 Filing and applications.

(a) When to file. The application period began on June 1, 2001, and ends on June 4, 2003. To benefit from the provisions of LIFE Legalization, an alien must properly file an application for adjustment of status, Form I-485, with appropriate fee, to the Service during the application period as described in this section. All applications, whether filed in the United States or filed from abroad, must be postmarked on or before June 4, 2003, to be considered timely filed.

(1) If the postmark is illegible or missing, and the application was mailed from within the United States, the Service will consider the application to be timely filed if it is received on or before June 9, 2003.

(2) If the postmark is illegible or missing, and the application was mailed from outside the United States, the Service will consider the application to be timely filed if it is received on or before June 18, 2003.

(3) If the postmark is made by other than the United States Post Office, and is filed from within the United States, the application must bear a date on or before June 4, 2003, and must be received on or before June 9, 2003.

(4) If an application filed from within the United States bears a postmark that was made by other than the United States Post Office, bears a date on or before June 4, 2003, and is received after June 9, 2003, the alien must establish:

(i) That the application was actually deposited in the mail before the last collection of the mail from the place of deposit that was postmarked by the United States Post Office June 4, 2003; and

(ii) That the delay in receiving the application was due to a delay in the transmission of the mail; and

(iii) The cause of such delay.

(5) If an application filed from within the United States bears both a postmark that was made by other

than the United States Post Office and a postmark that was made by the United States Post Office, the Service shall disregard the postmark that was made by other than the United States Post Office.

(6) If an application filed from abroad bears both a foreign postmark and a postmark that was subsequently made by the United States Post Office, the Service shall disregard the postmark that was made by the United States Post Office.

(7) In all instances, the burden of proof is on the applicant to establish timely filing of an application for LIFE Legalization.

(b) Filing of applications in the United States. The Service has jurisdiction over all applications for the benefits of LIFE Legalization under this Subpart B. All applications filed with the Service for the benefits of LIFE Legalization must be submitted by mail to the Service. After proper filing of the application, the Service will instruct the applicant to appear for fingerprinting as prescribed in 8 CFR 103.16. The Director of the National Benefit Center shall have jurisdiction over all applications filed with the Service for LIFE Legalization adjustment of status, unless the Director refers the applicant for a personal interview at a local Service office as provided in § 245a.19.

(1) Aliens in exclusion, deportation, or removal proceedings, or who have a pending motion to reopen or motion to reconsider. An alien who is prima facie eligible for adjustment of status under LIFE Legalization who is in exclusion, deportation, or removal proceedings before the Immigration Court or the Board of Immigration Appeals (Board), or who is awaiting adjudication of a motion to reopen or motion to reconsider filed with the Immigration Court of the Board, may request that the proceedings be administratively closed or that the motion filed be indefinitely continued, in order to allow the alien to pursue a LIFE Legalization application with the Service. In the request to administratively close the matter or indefinitely continue the motion, the alien must include documents demonstrating prima facie eligibility for the relief, and proof that the application for relief had been properly filed with the Service as prescribed in this section. With the concurrence of Service counsel, if the alien appears eligible to file for relief under LIFE Legalization, the Immigration Court or the Board, whichever has jurisdiction, shall administratively close the proceeding or continue the motion indefinitely.

(2) If an alien has a matter before the Immigration Court or the Board that has been administratively closed for reasons unrelated to this Subpart B, the alien may apply before the Service for LIFE Legalization adjustment of status.

(3) Aliens with final orders of exclusion, deportation, or removal. An alien, who is prima facie eligible for adjustment of status under LIFE Legalization, and who is subject to a final order of exclusion, deportation, or removal, may apply to the Service for LIFE Legalization adjustment.

(c) Filing of applications from outside the United States. An applicant for LIFE Legalization may file an application for LIFE Legalization from abroad. An application for LIFE Legalization filed from outside the United States shall be submitted by mail to the Service according to the instructions on the application. The National Benefit Center Director shall have jurisdiction over all applications filed with the Service for LIFE Legalization adjustment of status. After reviewing the application and all evidence with the application, the Service shall notify the applicant of any further requests for evidence regarding the application and, if eligible, how an interview will be conducted.

(d) Application and supporting documentation. Each applicant for LIFE Legalization adjustment of status must submit the form prescribed by USCIS completed in accordance with the form instructions accompanied by the required evidence.

(1) The Form I-485 application fee as contained in 8 CFR 103.7(b)(1).

(2) [Removed and Reserved]

(3) Evidence to establish identity, such as a passport, birth certificate, any national identity document from the alien's country of origin bearing photo and fingerprint, driver's license or similar document issued by a state if it contains a photo, or baptismal record/marriage certificate.

(4) [Removed and Reserved]

(5) A report of medical examination, as specified in § 245.5 of this chapter.

(6) [Removed and Reserved]

(7) Proof of application for class membership in CSS, LULAC, or Zambrano class action lawsuits as described in § 245a.14.

(8) Proof of continuous residence in an unlawful status since prior to January 1, 1982, through May 4, 1988, as described in § 245a.15.

(9) Proof of continuous physical presence from November 6, 1986, through May 4, 1988, as described in § 245a.16.

(10) Proof of citizenship skills as described in § 245a.17. This proof may be submitted either at the time of filing the application, subsequent to filing the application but prior to the interview, or at the time of the interview.

(e) Burden of proof. An alien applying for adjustment of status under this part has the burden of proving by a preponderance of the evidence that he or she has resided in the United States for the requisite periods, is admissible to the United States under the provisions of section 212(a) of the Act, and is otherwise eligible for adjustment of status under this Subpart B. The inference to be drawn from the documentation provided shall depend on the extent of the documentation, its credibility and amenability to verification as set forth in paragraph (f) of this section.

(f) Evidence. The sufficiency of all evidence produced by the applicant will be judged according to its probative value and credibility. To meet his or her burden of proof, an applicant must provide evidence of eligibility apart from his or her own testimony. In judging the probative value and credibility of the evidence submitted, greater weight will be given to the submission of original documentation. Subject to verification by the Service, if the evidence required to be submitted by the applicant is already contained in the Service's file or databases relating to the applicant, the applicant may submit a statement to that effect in lieu of the actual documentation.

HISTORY:

[66 FR 29661, 29673, June 1, 2001, as confirmed and amended at 67 FR 38341, 38350, June 4, 2002; 76 FR 53764, 53794, Aug. 29, 2011; 85 FR 46788, 46927, Aug. 3, 2020; 89 FR 6194, 6399, Jan. 31, 2024]

§ 245a.13 During pendency of application.

(a) In general. When an eligible alien in the United States submits a prima facie application for adjustment of status under LIFE Legalization during the application period, until a final determination on his or her application has been made, the applicant:

(1) May not be deported or removed from the United States;

(2) Is authorized to engage in employment in the United States and is provided with an "employment authorized" endorsement or other appropriate work permit; and

(3) Is allowed to travel and return to the United States as described at paragraph (e) of this section. Any domestic LIFE Legalization applicant who departs the United States while his or her application is pending without advance parole may be denied re admission to the United States as described at paragraph (e) of this section.

(b) Determination of filing of claim for class membership. With respect to each LIFE Legalization application for adjustment of status that is properly filed under this Subpart B during the application period, the Service will first determine whether or not the applicant is an "eligible alien" as defined under § 245a.10 of this Subpart B by virtue of having filed with the Service a claim of class membership in the CSS, LULAC, or Zambrano lawsuit before October 1, 2000. If the Service's records indicate, or if the evidence submitted by the applicant with the application establishes, that the alien had filed the requisite claim of class membership before October 1, 2000, then the Service will proceed to adjudicate the application under the remaining standards of eligibility.

(c) Prima facie eligibility. Unless the Service has evidence indicating ineligibility due to criminal grounds of inadmissibility, an application for adjustment of status shall be treated as a prima facie application during the pendency of application, until the Service has made a final determination on the application, if:

(1) The application was properly filed under this Subpart B during the application period; and

(2) The applicant establishes that he or she filed the requisite claim for class membership in the CSS, LULAC, or Zambrano lawsuit.

(d) Authorization to be employed in the United States while the application is pending.

(1) Application for employment authorization. An applicant for adjustment of status under LIFE Legalization who wishes to obtain initial or continued employment authorization during the pendency of the adjustment application must file a Form I-765, Application for Employment Authorization, with the Service, including the fee as set forth in 8 CFR 106.2. The applicant may submit Form I-765 either concurrently with or subsequent to the filing of the application for adjustment of status benefits on Form I-485.

(2) Adjudication and issuance. Until a final determination on the application has been made, an eligible alien who submits a prima facie application for adjustment of status under this Subpart B shall be authorized to engage in employment in the United States and be provided with an "employment authorized" endorsement or other appropriate work permit in accordance with § 274a.12(c)(24) of this chapter. An alien shall not be granted employment authorization pursuant to LIFE Legalization until he or she has submitted a prima facie application for adjustment of status under this Subpart B. If the Service finds that additional evidence is required from the alien in order to establish prima facie eligibility for LIFE Legalization, the Service shall request such evidence from the alien in writing. Nothing in this section shall preclude an applicant for adjustment of status under LIFE Legalization from being granted an initial employment authorization or an extension of employment authorization under any other provision of law or regulation for which the alien may be eligible.

(e) Travel while the application is pending. This paragraph is authorized by section 1104(c)(3) of the LIFE Act relating to the ability of an alien to travel abroad and return to the United States while his or her LIFE Legalization adjustment application is pending. Parole authority is granted to the National Benefit Center Director for the purposes described in this section. Nothing in this section shall preclude an applicant for adjustment of status under LIFE Legalization from being granted advance parole or admission into the United States under any other provision of law or regulation for which the alien may be eligible.

(1) An applicant for LIFE Legalization benefits who wishes to travel during the pendency of the application and who is applying from within the United States should file, with his or her application for adjustment, at the National Benefit Center, a Form I-131, Application for Travel Document, with fee as set forth in 8 CFR 106.2. The Service shall approve the Form I-131 and issue an advance parole document, unless the Service finds that the alien's application does not establish a prima facie claim to adjustment of status under LIFE Legalization.

(2) An eligible alien who has properly filed a Form I-485 pursuant to this Subpart B, and who needs to travel abroad pursuant to the standards prescribed in section 212(d)(5) of the Act, may file a Form I-131 with the district director having jurisdiction over his or her place of residence.

(3) If an alien travels abroad and returns to the United States with a grant of advance parole, the Service shall presume that the alien is entitled to return under section 1104(c)(3)(B) of the LIFE Act, unless, in a removal or expedited removal proceeding,

the Service shows by a preponderance of the evidence, that one or more of the provisions of § 245a.11(d) makes the alien ineligible for adjustment of status under LIFE Legalization.

(4) If an alien travels abroad and returns without a grant of advance parole, he or she shall be denied admission and shall be subject to removal or expedited removal unless the alien establishes, clearly and beyond doubt, that:

(i) He or she filed an application for adjustment pursuant to LIFE Legalization during the application period that presented a prima facie claim to adjustment of status under LIFE Legalization; and,

(ii) His or her absence was either a brief and casual trip consistent with an intention on the alien's part to pursue his or her LIFE Legalization adjustment application, or was a brief temporary trip that occurred because of the alien's need to tend to family obligations relating to a close relative's death or illness or similar family need.

(5) An applicant for LIFE Legalization benefits who applies for admission into the United States shall not be subject to the provisions of section 212(a)(9)(B) of the Act.

(6) Denial of admission under this section is not a denial of the alien's application for adjustment. The alien may continue to pursue his or her application for adjustment from abroad, and may also appeal any denial of such application from abroad. Such application shall be adjudicated in the same manner as other applications filed from abroad.

(f) Stay of final order of exclusion, deportation, or removal. The filing of a LIFE Legalization adjustment application on or after June 1, 2001, and on or before June 4, 2003, stays the execution of any final order of exclusion, deportation, or removal. This stay shall remain in effect until there is a final decision on the LIFE Legalization application, unless the district director who intends to execute the order makes a formal determination that the applicant does not present a prima facie claim to LIFE Legalization eligibility pursuant to §§ 245a.18(a)(1) or (a)(2), or §§ 245a.18(c)(2)(i), (c)(2)(ii), (c)(2)(iii), (c)(2)(iv), (c)(2)(v), or (c)(2)(vi), and serves the applicant with a written decision explaining the reason for this determination. Any such stay determination by the district director is not appealable. Neither an Immigration Judge nor the Board has jurisdiction to adjudicate an application for stay of execution of an exclusion, deportation, or removal order, on the basis of the alien's having filed a LIFE Legalization adjustment application.

HISTORY:

[66 FR 29661, 29674, June 1, 2001, as confirmed and amended at 67 FR 38341, 38350, 38351, June 4, 2002; 85 FR 46788, 46927, Aug. 3, 2020]

§ 245a.14 Application for class membership in the CSS, LULAC, or Zambrano lawsuit.

The Service will first determine whether an alien filed a written claim for class membership in the CSS, LULAC, or Zambrano lawsuit as reflected in the Service's indices, a review of the alien's administrative file with the Service, and by all evidence provided by the alien. An alien must provide with the application for LIFE Legalization evidence establishing that, before October 1, 2000, he or she was a class member applicant in the CSS, LULAC, or Zambrano lawsuit. An alien should include as many forms of evidence as the alien has available to him or her. Such forms of evidence include, but are not limited to:

(a) An Employment Authorization Document (EAD) or other employment document issued by the Service pursuant to the alien's class membership in the CSS, LULAC, or Zambrano lawsuit (if a photocopy of the EAD is submitted, the alien's name, A-number, issuance date, and expiration date should be clearly visible);

(b) Service document(s) addressed to the alien, or his or her representative, granting or denying the class membership, which includes date, alien's name and A-number;

(c) The questionnaire for class member applicant under CSS, LULAC, or Zambrano submitted with the class membership application, which includes date, alien's full name and date of birth;

(d) Service document(s) addressed to the alien, or his or her representative, discussing matters pursuant to the class membership application, which includes date, alien's name and A-number. These include, but are not limited to the following:

(1) Form I-512, Parole authorization, or denial of such;

(2) Form I-221, Order to Show Cause;

(3) Form I-862, Notice to Appear;

(4) Final order of removal or deportation;

(5) Request for evidence letter (RFE); or

(6) Form I-687 submitted with the class membership application.

(e) Form I-765, Application for Employment Authorization, submitted pursuant to a court order granting interim relief.

(f) An application for a stay of deportation, exclusion, or removal pursuant to a court's order granting interim relief.

(g) Any other relevant document(s).

HISTORY:

[66 FR 29661, 29676, June 1, 2001, as confirmed and amended at 67 FR 38341, 38350, 38351, June 4, 2002]

§ 245a.15 Continuous residence in an unlawful status since prior to January 1, 1982, through May 4, 1988.

(a) General. The Service will determine whether an alien entered the United States before January 1, 1982, and resided in continuous unlawful status since such date through May 4, 1988, based on the evidence provided by the alien. An alien must provide with the application for LIFE Legalization evidence establishing that he or she entered the United States before January 1, 1982, and resided in continuous unlawful status since that date through May 4, 1988.

(b) Evidence.

(1) A list of evidence that may establish an alien's continuous residence in the United States can be found at § 245a.2(d)(3).

(2) The following evidence may establish an alien's unlawful status in the United States:

(i) Form I-94 (see § 1.4), Arrival-Departure Record;

(ii) Form I-20A-B, Certificate of Eligibility for Nonimmigrant (F-1) Student Status — For Academic and Language Students;

(iii) Form IAP-66, Certificate of Eligibility for Exchange Visitor Status;

(iv) A passport; or

(v) Nonimmigrant visa(s) issued to the alien.

(c) Continuous residence. An alien shall be regarded as having resided continuously in the United States if:

(1) No single absence from the United States has exceeded forty-five (45) days, and the aggregate of all absences has not exceeded one hundred and eighty (180) days between January 1, 1982, and May 4, 1988, unless the alien can establish that due to emergent reasons, his or her return to the United States could not be accomplished within the time period allowed;

(2) The alien was maintaining residence in the United States; and

(3) The alien's departure from the United States was not based on an order of deportation.

(d) Unlawful status. The following categories of aliens, who are otherwise eligible to adjust to LPR status pursuant to LIFE Legalization, may file for adjustment of status provided they resided continuously in the United States in an unlawful status since prior to January 1, 1982, through May 4, 1988:

(1) An eligible alien who entered the United States without inspection prior to January 1, 1982.

(2) Nonimmigrants. An eligible alien who entered the United States as a nonimmigrant before January 1, 1982, whose authorized period of admission as a nonimmigrant expired before January 1, 1982, through the passage of time, or whose unlawful status was known to the Government before January 1, 1982. Known to the Government means documentation existing in one or more Federal Government agencies' files such that when such document is taken as a whole, it warrants a finding that the alien's status in the United States was unlawful. Any absence of mandatory annual and/or quarterly registration reports from Federal Government files does not warrant a finding that the alien's unlawful status was known to the Government.

(i) A or G nonimmigrants. An eligible alien who entered the United States for duration of status (D/S) in one of the following nonimmigrant classes, A-1, A-2, G-1, G-2, G-3 or G-4, whose qualifying employment terminated or who ceased to be recognized by the Department of State as being entitled to such classification prior to January 1, 1982. A dependent family member may be considered a member of this class if the dependent family member was also in A or G status when the principal A or G alien's status terminated or ceased to be recognized by the Department of State.

(ii) F nonimmigrants. An eligible alien who entered the United States for D/S in one of the following nonimmigrant classes, F-1 or F-2, who completed a full course of study, including practical training, and whose time period, if any, to depart the United States after completion of study expired prior to January 1, 1982. A dependent F-2 alien otherwise eligible who was admitted into the United States with a specific time period, as opposed to duration of status, documented on Form I-94, Arrival-Departure Record, that extended beyond January 1, 1982, is considered eligible if the principal F-1 alien is found eligible.

(iii) Nonimmigrant exchange visitors. An eligible alien who was at any time a nonimmigrant exchange alien (as defined in section 101(a)(15)(J) of the Act), who entered the United States before January 1, 1982, and who:

(A) Was not subject to the 2-year foreign residence requirement of section 212(e) of the Act; or

(B) Has fulfilled the 2-year foreign residence requirement of section 212(e) of the Act; or

(C) Has received a waiver for the 2-year foreign residence requirement of section 212(e) of the Act.

(3) Asylum applicants. An eligible alien who filed an asylum application prior to January 1, 1982, and whose application was subsequently denied or whose application was not decided by May 4, 1988.

(4) Aliens considered to be in unlawful status. Aliens who were present in the United States in one of the following categories were considered to be in unlawful status:

(i) An eligible alien who was granted voluntary departure, voluntary return, extended voluntary departure, or placed in deferred action category by the Service prior to January 1, 1982.

(ii) An eligible alien who is a Cuban or Haitian entrant (as described in paragraph (1) or (2)(A) of section 501(e) of Public Law 96-422 and at § 212.5(g) of this chapter), who entered the United States before January 1, 1982. Pursuant to section 1104(c)(2)(B)(iv) of the LIFE Act, such alien is considered to be in an unlawful status in the United States.

(iii) An eligible alien who was paroled into the United States prior to January 1, 1982, and whose parole status terminated prior to January 1, 1982.

(iv) An eligible alien who entered the United States before January 1, 1982, and whose entries to the United States subsequent to January 1, 1982, were not documented on Form I-94.

HISTORY:

[66 FR 29661, 29676, June 1, 2001, as confirmed at 67 FR 38341, 38350, June 4, 2002; 78 FR 18457, 18472, Mar. 27, 2013, as confirmed at 81 FR 91646, 91670, Dec. 19, 2016]

§ 245a.16 Continuous physical presence from November 6, 1986, through May 4, 1988.

(a) The Service will determine whether an alien was continuously physically present in the United States from November 6, 1986, through May 4, 1988, based on the evidence provided by the alien. An alien must provide with the application evidence establishing his or her continuous physical presence in the United States from November 6, 1986, through May 4, 1988.

Evidence establishing the alien's continuous physical presence in the United States from November 6, 1986, to May 4, 1988, may consist of any documentation issued by any governmental or nongovernmental authority, provided such evidence bears the name of the applicant, was dated at the time it was issued, and bears the signature, seal, or other authenticating instrument of the authorized representative of the issuing authority, if the document would normally contain such authenticating instrument.

(b) For purposes of this section, an alien shall not be considered to have failed to maintain continuous physical presence in the United States by virtue of brief, casual, and innocent absences from the United States. Also, brief, casual, and innocent absences from the United States are not limited to absences with advance parole. Brief, casual, and innocent absence(s) as used in this paragraph means temporary, occasional trips abroad as long as the purpose of the absence from the United States was consistent with the policies reflected in the immigration laws of the United States.

(c) An alien who has been absent from the United States in accordance with the Service's advance parole procedures shall not be considered as having interrupted his or her continuous physical presence as required at the time of filing an application under this section.

HISTORY:

[66 FR 29661, 29677, June 1, 2001, as confirmed and amended at 67 FR 38341, 38350, 38351, June 4, 2002]

§ 245a.17 Citizenship skills.

(a) Requirements. Applicants for adjustment under LIFE Legalization must meet the requirements of section 312(a) of the Act (8 U.S.C. 1423(a)) (relating to minimal understanding of ordinary English and a knowledge and understanding of the history and government of the United States). Unless an exception under paragraph (c) of this section applies to the applicant, LIFE Legalization applicants must establish that:

(1) He or she has complied with the same requirements as those listed for naturalization applicants under §§ 312.1 and 312.2 of this chapter; or

(2) He or she has a high school diploma or general educational development diploma (GED) from a school in the United States. A GED gained in a language other than English is acceptable only if a GED English proficiency test has been passed. (The curriculum for both the high school diploma and the GED must have included at least 40 hours of instruction in English and United States history and government). The applicant may submit a high school diploma or GED either at the time of filing Form I-485, subsequent to filing the application but prior to the interview, or at the time of the interview (the applicant's name and A-number must appear on any such evidence submitted); or

(3) He or she has attended, or is attending, a state recognized, accredited learning institution in the United States, and that institution certifies such attendance. The course of study at such learning institution must be for a period of one academic year (or the equivalent thereof according to the standards of the learning institution) and the curriculum must include at least 40 hours of instruction in English and United States history and government. The applicant may submit certification on letterhead stationery from a state recognized, accredited learning institution either at the time of filing Form I-485, subsequent to filing the application but prior to the interview, or at the time of the interview (the applicant's name and A-number must appear on any such evidence submitted).

(b) Second interview. An applicant who fails to pass the English literacy and/or the United States history and government tests at the time of the interview, shall be afforded a second opportunity after 6 months (or earlier, at the request of the applicant) to pass the tests or submit evidence as described in paragraphs (a)(2) or (a)(3) of this section. The second interview shall be conducted prior to the denial of the application for permanent residence and may be based solely on the failure to pass the basic citizenship skills requirements.

(c) Exceptions. LIFE Legalization applicants are exempt from the requirements listed under paragraph (a)(1) of this section if he or she has qualified for the same exceptions as those listed for naturalization applicants under §§ 312.1(b)(3) and 312.2(b) of this chapter. Further, at the discretion of the Attorney General, the requirements listed under paragraph (a) of this section may be waived if the LIFE Legalization applicant:

(1) Is 65 years of age or older on the date of filing; or

(2) Is developmentally disabled as defined under § 245a.1(v).

HISTORY:

[66 FR 29661, 29677, June 1, 2001, as confirmed and amended at 67 FR 38341, 38350, 38351, June 4, 2002]

§ 245a.18 Ineligibility and applicability of grounds of inadmissibility.

(a) Ineligible aliens.

(1) An alien who has been convicted of a felony or of three or misdemeanors committed in the United States is ineligible for adjustment to LPR status under this Subpart B; or

(2) An alien who has assisted in the persecution of any person or persons on account of race, religion, nationality, membership in a particular social group, or political opinion is ineligible for adjustment of status under this Subpart B.

(b) Grounds of inadmissibility not to be applied. Section 212(a)(5) of the Act (labor certification requirements) and section 212(a)(7)(A) of the Act (immigrants not in possession of valid visa and/or travel documents) shall not apply to applicants for adjustment to LPR status under this Subpart B.

(c) Waiver of grounds of inadmissibility. Except as provided in paragraph (c)(2) of this section, the Service may waive any provision of section 212(a) of the Act only in the case of individual aliens for humanitarian purposes, to ensure family unity, or when the granting of such a waiver is otherwise in the public interest. If available, an applicant may apply for an individual waiver as provided in paragraph (c)(1) of this section without regard to section 241(a)(5) of the Act.

(1) Special rule for waiver of inadmissibility grounds for LIFE Legalization applicants under sections 212(a)(9)(A) and 212(a)(9)(C) of the Act. An applicant for adjustment of status under LIFE Legalization who is inadmissible under section 212(a)(9)(A) or 212(a)(9)(C) of the Act, may apply for a waiver of these grounds of inadmissibility while present in the United States, without regard to the normal requirement that a Form I-212, Application for Permission to Reapply for Admission into the United States After Deportation or Removal, be filed prior to embarking or re-embarking for travel to the United States, and without regard to the length of time since the alien's removal or deportation from the United States. Such an alien shall file Form I-690, Application for Waiver of Grounds of Excludability Under Sections 245A or 210 of the Immigration and Nationality Act, with the district director having jurisdiction over the applicant's case if the application for adjustment of status is pending at a local office, or with the Director of the National Benefit Center. Approval of a waiver of inadmissibility under section 212(a)(9)(A) or section 212(a)(9)(C) of the Act does not cure a break in continuous residence resulting from a departure from the United States at any time during the period from January 1, 1982, and May 4, 1988, if the alien was subject to a final exclusion or deportation order at the time of the departure.

(2) Grounds of inadmissibility that may not be waived. Notwithstanding any other provisions of the Act, the following provisions of section 212(a) of the Act may not be waived by the Attorney General under paragraph (c) of this section:

(i) Section 212(a)(2)(A)(i)(I) (crimes involving moral turpitude);

(ii) Section 212(a)(2)(A)(i)(II) (controlled substance, except for so much of such paragraph as relates to a single offense of simple possession of 30 grams or less of marijuana);

(iii) Section 212(a)(2)(B) (multiple criminal convictions);

(iv) Section 212(a)(2)(C) (controlled substance traffickers);

(v) Section 212(a)(3) (security and related grounds); and

(vi) Section 212(a)(4) (public charge) except for an alien who is or was an aged, blind, or disabled individual (as defined in section 1614(a)(1) of the Social Security Act). If a LIFE Legalization applicant is determined to be inadmissible under section 212(a)(4) of the Act, he or she may still be admissible under the Special Rule described under paragraph (d)(3) of this section.

(d)(1) In determining whether an alien is "likely to become a public charge", financial responsibility of the alien is to be established by examining the totality of the alien's circumstance at the time of his or her application for adjustment. The existence or absence of a particular factor should never be the sole criteria for determining if an alien is likely to become a public charge. The determination of financial responsibility should be a prospective evaluation based on the alien's age, health, family status, assets, resources, education and skills.

(2) An alien who has a consistent employment history that shows the ability to support himself or herself even though his or her income may be below the poverty level is not excludable under paragraph (c)(2)(vi) of this section. The alien's employment history need not be continuous in that it is uninterrupted. In applying the Special Rule, the Service will take into account an alien's employment history in the United States to include, but not be limited to, employment prior to and immediately following the enactment of IRCA on November 6, 1986. However, the Service will take into account that an alien may not have consistent employment history due to the fact that an eligible alien was in an unlawful status and was not authorized to work. Past acceptance of public cash assistance within a history of consistent employment will enter into this decision. The weight given in considering applicability of the public charge provisions will depend on many factors, but the length of time an applicant has received public cash assistance will constitute a significant factor. It is not necessary to file a waiver in order to apply the Special Rule for determination of public charge.

(3) In order to establish that an alien is not inadmissible under paragraph (c)(2)(vi) of this section, an alien may file as much evidence available to him or her establishing that the alien is not likely to become a public charge. An alien may have filed on his or her behalf a Form I-134, Affidavit of Support. The failure to submit Form I-134 shall not constitute an adverse factor.

(e) Public cash assistance and criminal history verification. Declarations by an alien that he or she has not been the recipient of public cash assistance and/or has not had a criminal record are subject to a verification by the Service. The alien must agree to fully cooperate in the verification process. Failure to assist the Service in verifying information necessary for proper adjudication may result in denial of the application.

HISTORY:

[66 FR 29661, 29677, June 1, 2001, as confirmed and amended at 67 FR 38341, 38350, 38351, June 4, 2002; 85 FR 46788, 46927, Aug. 3, 2020]

§ 245a.19 Interviews.

(a) All aliens filing applications for adjustment of status with the Service under this section must be personally interviewed, except that the adjudicative interview may be waived for a child under the age of 14, or when it is impractical because of the health or advanced age of the applicant. Applicants will be interviewed by an immigration officer as determined by the Director of the National Benefit Center. An applicant failing to appear for the scheduled interview may, for good cause, be afforded another interview. Where an applicant fails to appear for two scheduled interviews, his or her application shall be denied for lack of prosecution. Applications for LIFE Legalization adjustment may be denied without interview if the applicant is determined to be statutorily ineligible.

(b) At the time of the interview, wherever possible, original documents must be submitted except the following: official government records; employment or employment-related records maintained by employers, unions, or collective bargaining organizations; medical records; school records maintained by a school or school board; or other records maintained by a party other than the applicant. Copies of records maintained by parties other than the applicant which are submitted in evidence must be certified as true and correct by such parties and must bear their seal or signature or the signature and title of persons authorized to act in their behalf.

(c) If at the time of the interview the return of original documents is desired by the applicant, they must be accompanied by notarized copies or copies certified true and correct by the alien's representative. At the discretion of the district director, original documents, even if accompanied by certified copies, may be temporarily retained for forensic examination by the Service.

HISTORY:

[66 FR 29661, 29678, June 1, 2001, as confirmed at 67 FR 38341, 38350, June 4, 2002; 85 FR 46788, 46927, Aug. 3, 2020]

§ 245a.20 Decisions, appeals, motions, and certifications.

(a) Decisions.

(1) Approval of applications. If the Service approves the application for adjustment of status under LIFE Legalization, the district director shall record the alien's lawful admission for permanent residence as of the date of such approval and notify the alien accordingly. The district director shall also advise the alien regarding the delivery of his or her Form I-551, Permanent Resident Card, and of the process for obtaining temporary evidence of alien registration. If the alien has previously been issued a final order of exclusion, deportation, or removal, such order shall be deemed canceled as of the date of the district director's approval of the application for adjustment of status. If the alien had been in exclusion, deportation, or removal proceedings that were administratively closed, such proceedings shall be deemed terminated as of the date of approval of the application for adjustment of status by the district director.

(2) Denials. The alien shall be notified in writing of the decision of denial and of the reason(s) therefore. An applicant affected under this part by an adverse decision is entitled to file an appeal on Form I-290B Notice of Appeal to the Administrative Appeals Office (AAO), with the required fee specified in 8 CFR 106.2. Renewal of employment authorization issued pursuant to 8 CFR 245a.13 will be granted until a final decision has been rendered on appeal or until the end of the appeal period if no appeal is filed. After exhaustion of an appeal, an alien who believes that the grounds for denial have been overcome may submit another application with fee, provided that the application is submitted on or before June 4, 2003.

(b) Appeals process. An adverse decision under this part may be appealed to the Associate Commissioner, Examinations, Administrative Appeals Office (AAO), who is the appellate authority designated in § 103.1(f)(3) of this chapter. Any appeal shall be submitted to the Service office that rendered the decision with the required fee.

(1) If an appeal is filed from within the United States, it must be received by the Service within 30 calendar days after service of the Notice of Denial (NOD) in accordance with the procedures of § 103.3(a) of this chapter. An appeal received after the 30 day period has tolled will not be accepted. The 30 day period for submitting an appeal begins 3 days after the NOD is mailed. If a review of the Record of Proceeding (ROP) is requested by the alien or his or her legal representative, and an appeal has been properly filed, an additional 30 days will be allowed for this review from the time the ROP is photocopied and mailed.

(2) If an applicant's last known address of record was outside the United States, and the NOD was mailed to that foreign address, the appeal must be received by the Service within 60 calendar days after service of the NOD in accordance with the procedures of § 103.3(a) of this chapter. An appeal received after the 60 day period has tolled will not be accepted. The 60-day period for submitting an appeal begins 3 days after the NOD is mailed.

(c) Motions. The Service director who denied the application may reopen and reconsider any adverse decision sua sponte. When an appeal to the AAO has been filed, the director may issue a new decision that will grant the benefit that has been requested. Motions to reopen a proceeding or reconsider a decision shall not be considered under this Subpart B.

(d) Certifications. The Service director who adjudicates the application may, in accordance with § 103.4 of this chapter, certify a decision to the AAO when the case involves an unusually complex or novel question of law or fact.

(e) Effect of final adjudication of application on aliens previously in proceedings.

(1) Upon the granting of an application. If the application for LIFE Legalization is granted, proceedings shall be deemed terminated or a final order of exclusion, deportation, or removal shall be deemed canceled as of the date of the approval of the LIFE Legalization application for adjustment of status.

(2) Upon the denial of an application.

(i) Where proceedings were administratively closed. In the case of an alien whose previously initiated exclusion, deportation or removal proceeding had been administratively closed or continued indefinitely under § 245a.12(b)(1), the director shall make a request for recalendaring to the Immigration Court that had administratively closed the proceeding, or the Board, as appropriate, when there is a final decision denying the

LIFE Legalization application. The Immigration Court or the Board will then recalendar the prior proceeding.

(ii) Where final order was stayed. If the application for LIFE Legalization is denied, the stay of a final order of exclusion, deportation, or removal afforded in § 245a.13(f) shall be deemed lifted as of the date of such denial.

HISTORY:

[66 FR 29661, 29678, June 1, 2001, as confirmed and amended at 67 FR 38341, 38350, 38352, June 4, 2002; 72 FR 19100, 19107, Apr. 17, 2007; 85 FR 46788, 46927, Aug. 3, 2020]

§ 245a.21 Confidentiality.

(a) No person other than a sworn officer or employee of the Department of Justice or bureau or agency thereof, will be permitted to examine individual applications. For purposes of this part, any individual employed under contract by the Service to work in connection with the LIFE Legalization provisions shall be considered an employee of the Department of Justice or bureau or agency thereof.

(b) No information furnished pursuant to an application for permanent resident status under this Subpart B shall be used for any purpose except:

(1) To make a determination on the application;

(2) For the enforcement of the provisions encompassed in section 245A(c)(6) of the Act, except as provided in paragraphs (c) of this section; or

(3) For the purposes of rescinding, pursuant to section 246(a) of the Act (8 U.S.C. 1256(a)), any adjustment of status obtained by the alien.

(c) If a determination is made by the Service that the alien has, in connection with his or her application, engaged in fraud or willful misrepresentation or concealment of a material fact, knowingly provided a false statement or document in making his or her application, knowingly made a false statement or representation, or engaged in any other activity prohibited by section 245A(c)(6) of the Act, the Service shall refer the matter to the United States Attorney for prosecution of the alien and/or of any person who created or supplied a false statement or document for use in an application for adjustment of status under this Subpart B.

(d) Information contained in granted files may be used by the Service at a later date to make a decision:

(1) On an immigrant visa petition or other status filed by the applicant under section 204(a) of the Act;

(2) On a naturalization application submitted by the applicant;

(3) For the preparation of reports to Congress under section 404 of the Immigration Reform and Control Act of 1986; or

(4) For the furnishing of information, at the discretion of the Attorney General, in the same manner and circumstances as census information may be disclosed by the Secretary of Commerce under 13 U.S.C. 8.

(e) Information concerning whether the applicant has at any time been convicted of a crime may be used or released for immigration enforcement or law enforcement purposes.

HISTORY:

[66 FR 29661, 29679, June 1, 2001, as confirmed at 67 FR 38341, 38350, June 4, 2002]

§ 245a.22 Rescission.

(a) Rescission of adjustment of status under LIFE Legalization shall occur only under the procedures of 8 CFR part 246.

(b) Information furnished by an eligible alien pursuant to any application filed under LIFE Legalization may be used by the Attorney General, and other officials and employees of the Department of Justice and any bureau or agency thereof, for purposes of rescinding, pursuant to 8 CFR part 246, any adjustment of status obtained by the alien.

HISTORY:

[66 FR 29661, 29680, June 1, 2001, as confirmed at 67 FR 38341, 38350, June 4, 2002]

§§ 245a.23 — 245a.29 [Reserved]

[NO TEXT IN ORIGINAL]

HISTORY:

[66 FR 29661, 29680, June 1, 2001, as confirmed at 67 FR 38341, 38350, June 4, 2002]

AUTHORITY:

(8 U.S.C. 1101, 1103, 1255a and 1255a note.)

Subpart C

Life Act Amendments Family Unity Provisions

§ 245a.30 Description of program.

This Subpart C implements the Family Unity provisions of section 1504 of the LIFE Act Amendments, Public Law 106-554.

HISTORY:

[66 FR 29661, 29680, June 1, 2001, as confirmed at 67 FR 38341, 38350, June 4, 2002]

§ 245a.31 Eligibility.

An alien who is currently in the United States may obtain Family Unity benefits under section 1504 of the LIFE Act Amendments if he or she establishes that:

(a) He or she is the spouse or unmarried child under the age of 21 of an eligible alien (as defined under § 245a.10) at the time the alien's application for Family Unity benefits is adjudicated and thereafter;

(b) He or she entered the United States before December 1, 1988, and resided in the United States on such date; and

(c) If applying for Family Unity benefits on or after June 5, 2003, he or she is the spouse or unmarried child under the age of 21 of an alien who has filed a Form I-485 pursuant to this Subpart B.

HISTORY:

[66 FR 29661, 29680, June 1, 2001, as confirmed and amended at 67 FR 38341, 38350, 38352, June 4, 2002]

§ 245a.32 Ineligible aliens.

The following categories of aliens are ineligible for Family Unity benefits under the LIFE Act Amendments:

(a) An alien who has been convicted of a felony or of three or more misdemeanors in the United States; or

(b) An alien who has ordered, incited, assisted, or otherwise participated in the persecution of an individual because of the individual's race, religion, nationality, membership in a particular social group, or political opinion; or

(c) An alien who has been convicted by a final judgment of a particularly serious crime and who is a danger to the community of the United States; or

(d) An alien who the Attorney General has serious reasons to believe has committed a serious nonpolitical crime outside the United States before the alien arrived in the United States; or

(e) An alien who the Attorney General has reasonable grounds to believe is a danger to the security of the United States.

HISTORY:

[66 FR 29661, 29680, June 1, 2001, as confirmed at 67 FR 38341, 38350, June 4, 2002]

§ 245a.33 Filing.

(a) General. An application for Family Unity benefits under section 1504 of the LIFE Act Amendments must be filed on a Form I-817, Application for Family Unity Benefits, with the National Benefit Center. A Form I-817 must be filed with the correct fee required in 8 CFR 106.2 and the required supporting documentation. A separate application with appropriate fee and documentation must be filed for each person claiming eligibility.

(b) Decision. The National Benefit Center Director has sole jurisdiction to adjudicate an application for Family Unity benefits under the LIFE Act Amendments. The Director will provide the applicant with specific reasons for any decision to deny an application. Denial of an application may not be appealed. An applicant who believes that the grounds for denial have been overcome may submit another application with the appropriate fee and documentation.

(c) Referral of denied cases for consideration of issuance of notice to appear. If an application is denied, the case will be referred to the district director with jurisdiction over the alien's place of residence for consideration of whether to issue a notice to appear. After an initial denial, an applicant's case will not be referred for issuance of a notice to appear until 90 days from the date of the initial denial, to allow the alien the opportunity to file a new Form I-817 application in order to attempt to overcome the basis of the denial. However, if the applicant is found not to be eligible for benefits under § 245a.32(a), the Service reserves the right to issue a notice to appear at any time after the initial denial.

HISTORY:

[66 FR 29661, 29680, June 1, 2001, as confirmed at 67 FR 38341, 38350, June 4, 2002; 72 FR 19100, 19107, Apr. 17, 2007; 85 FR 46788, 46927, Aug. 3, 2020]

§ 245a.34 Protection from removal, eligibility for employment, and period of authorized stay.

(a) Scope of protection. Nothing in this Subpart C shall be construed to limit the authority of the Service to commence removal proceedings against an applicant for or beneficiary of Family Unity benefit under this Subpart C on any ground of removal. Also, nothing in this Subpart C shall be construed to limit the authority of the Service to take any other enforcement action against such an applicant or beneficiary with respect to any ground of removal not specified in paragraphs (a)(1) through (a)(4) of this section. Protection from removal under this Subpart C is limited to the grounds of removal specified in:

(1) Section 237(a)(1)(A) of the Act (aliens who were inadmissible at the time of entry or adjustment of status), except that the alien may be removed if he or she is inadmissible because of a ground listed in section 212(a)(2) (criminal and related grounds) or in section 212(a)(3) (security and related grounds) of the Act; or

(2) Section 237(a)(1)(B) of the Act (aliens present in the United States in violation of the Act or any other law of the United States);

(3) Section 237(a)(1)(C) of the Act (aliens who violated their nonimmigrant status or violated the conditions of entry); or

(4) Section 237(a)(3)(A) of the Act (aliens who failed to comply with the change of address notification requirements).

(b) Duration of protection from removal. When an alien whose application for Family Unity benefits under the LIFE Act Amendments is approved, he or she will receive protection from removal, commencing with the date of approval of the application. A grant of protection from removal under this section shall be considered effective from the date on which the application was properly filed.

(1) In the case of an alien who has been granted Family Unity benefits under the LIFE Act Amendments based on the principal alien's application for LIFE Legalization, any evidence of protection from removal shall be dated to expire 1 year after the date of approval, or the day before the alien's 21st birthday, whichever comes first.

(2) In the case of an alien who has been granted Family Unity benefits under the LIFE Act Amendments based on the principal alien's adjustment to LPR status pursuant to his or her LIFE Legalization application, any evidence of protection from removal shall be dated to expire 2 years after the date of approval, or the day before the alien's 21st birthday, whichever comes first.

(c) Employment authorization. An alien granted Family Unity benefits under the LIFE Act Amendments is authorized to be employed in the United States.

(1) In the case of an alien who has been granted Family Unity benefits based on the principal alien's application for LIFE Legalization, the validity period of the employment authorization document shall be dated to expire 1 year after the date of approval of the Form I-817, or the day before the alien's 21st birthday, whichever comes first.

(2) In the case of an alien who has been granted Family Unity benefits based on the principal alien's adjustment to LPR status pursuant to his or her LIFE Legalization application, the validity period of the employment authorization document shall be dated to expire 2 years after the date of approval of the Form I-817, or the day before the alien's 21st birthday, whichever comes first.

(d) Period of authorized stay. An alien granted Family Unity benefits under the LIFE Act Amendments is deemed to have received an authorized period of stay approved by the Attorney General within the scope of section 212(a)(9)(B) of the Act.

HISTORY:

[66 FR 29661, 29680, June 1, 2001, as confirmed and amended at 67 FR 38341, 38350, 38352, June 4, 2002]

§ 245a.35 Travel outside the United States.

(a) An alien who departs the United States while his or her application for Family Unity benefits is pending will be deemed to have abandoned the application and the application will be denied.

(b) An alien granted Family Unity benefits under the LIFE Act Amendments who intends to travel outside the United States temporarily must apply for advance authorization using Form I-131. The authority to grant an application for advance authorization for an alien granted Family Unity benefits under the LIFE Act Amendments rests solely with the Service. An alien who is granted advance authorization and returns to the United States in accordance with such authorization, and who is found not to be inadmissible under section 212(a)(2) or (3) of the Act, shall be paroled into the United States. He or she shall be provided the remainder of the protection from removal period previously granted under the Family Unity provisions of the LIFE Act Amendments.

HISTORY:

[66 FR 29661, 29681, June 1, 2001, as confirmed at 67 FR 38341, 38350, June 4, 2002]

§ 245a.36 [Reserved]

[NO TEXT IN ORIGINAL]

HISTORY:

[66 FR 29661, 29681, June 1, 2001, as confirmed at 67 FR 38341, 38350, June 4, 2002]

AUTHORITY:

(8 U.S.C. 1101, 1103, 1255a and 1255a note.)

§ 245a.37 Termination of Family Unity Program benefits.

(a) Grounds for termination. The Service may terminate Family Unity benefits under the LIFE Act Amendments whenever the necessity for the termination comes to the attention of the Service. Such grounds will exist in situations including, but not limited to, those in which:

(1) A determination is made that Family Unity benefits were acquired as the result of fraud or willful misrepresentation of a material fact;

(2) The beneficiary commits an act or acts which render him or her ineligible for Family Unity benefits under the LIFE Act Amendments;

(3) The alien, upon whose status Family Unity benefits under the LIFE Act were based, fails to apply for LIFE Legalization by June 4, 2003, has his or her LIFE Legalization application denied, or loses his or her LPR status; or

(4) A qualifying relationship to the alien, upon whose status Family Unity benefits under the LIFE Act Amendments were based, no longer exists.

(b) Notice procedure. Notice of intent to terminate and of the grounds thereof shall be served pursuant to the provisions of 8 CFR 103.8. The alien shall be given 30 days to respond to the notice and may submit to the Service additional evidence in rebuttal. Any final decision of termination shall also be served pursuant to the provisions of 8 CFR 103.8. Nothing in this section shall preclude the Service from commencing removal proceedings prior to termination of Family Unity benefits.

(c) Effect of termination. Termination of Family Unity benefits under the LIFE Act Amendments shall render the alien amenable to removal under any ground specified in section 237 of the Act (including those grounds described in § 245a.34(a)). In addition, the alien will no longer be considered to be in a period of stay authorized by the Attorney General as of the date of such termination.

HISTORY:

[66 FR 29661, 29681, June 1, 2001, as confirmed and amended at 67 FR 38341, 38350, 38352, June 4, 2002; 76 FR 53764, 53794, Aug. 29, 2011]

PART 246

RESCISSION OF ADJUSTMENT OF STATUS

Rule

AUTHORITY NOTE APPLICABLE TO ENTIRE PART:

AUTHORITY:

8 U.S.C. 1103, 1254, 1255, 1256, 1259; 8 CFR part 2.

§ 246.1 Notice.

If it appears to a district director that a person residing in his or her district was not in fact eligible for the adjustment of status made in his or her case, or it appears to an asylum office director that a person granted adjustment of status by an asylum officer pursuant to 8 CFR 240.70 was not in fact eligible for adjustment of status, a proceeding shall be commenced by the personal service upon such person of a notice of intent to rescind, which shall inform him or her of the allegations upon which it is intended to rescind the adjustment of his or her status. In such a proceeding the person shall be known as the respondent. The notice shall also inform the respondent that he or she may submit, within thirty days from the date of service of the notice, an answer in writing under oath setting forth reasons why such rescission shall not be made, and that he or she may, within such period, request a hearing before an immigration judge in support of, or in lieu of, his or her written answer. The respondent shall further be informed that he or she may have the assistance of or be represented by counsel or representative of his or her choice qualified under part 292 of this chapter, at no expense to the Government, in the preparation of his or her answer or in connection with his or her hearing, and that he or she may present such evidence in his or her behalf as may be relevant to the rescission.

HISTORY:

[28 FR 6737, June 29, 1963, as amended at 37 FR 11471, June 8, 1972; 62 FR 10312, 10385, March 6, 1997; 64 FR 27856, 27881, May 21, 1999]

§ 246.2 Allegations admitted; no answer filed; no hearing requested.

If the answer admits the allegations in the notice, or if no answer is filed within the thirty-day period, or if no hearing is requested within such period, the district director or asylum office director shall rescind the adjustment of status previously granted, and no appeal shall lie from his decision.

HISTORY:

[27 FR 10789, Nov. 6, 1962; 62 FR 10312, 10385, March 6, 1997; 64 FR 27856, 27881, May 21, 1999]

§ 246.3 Allegations contested or denied; hearing requested.

If, within the prescribed time following service of the notice pursuant to § 246.1, the respondent has filed an answer which contests or denies any allegation in the notice, or a hearing is requested, a hearing pursuant to § 246.5 shall be conducted by an immigration judge, and the requirements contained in §§ 240.3, 240.4, 240.5, 240.6, 240.7, and 240.9 of this chapter shall be followed.

HISTORY:

[29 FR 13243, Sept. 24, 1964; 62 FR 10312, 10385, March 6, 1997]

§ 246.4 Immigration judge's authority; withdrawal and substitution.

In any proceeding conducted under this part, the immigration judge shall have authority to interrogate, examine, and cross-examine the respondent and other witnesses, to present and receive evidence, to determine whether adjustment of status shall be rescinded, to make decisions thereon, including an appropriate order, and to take any other action consistent with applicable provisions of law and regulations as may be appropriate to the disposition of the case. Nothing contained in this part shall be construed to diminish the authority conferred on immigration judges by the Act. The immigration judge assigned to conduct a hearing shall, at any time, withdraw if he or she deems himself or herself disqualified. If a hearing has begun but no evidence has been adduced other than the notice and answer, if any, pursuant to §§ 246.1 and 246.2, or if an immigration judge becomes unavailable to complete his or her duties within a reasonable time, or if at any time the respondent consents to a substitution, another immigration judge may be assigned to complete the case. The new immigration judge shall familiarize himself or herself with the record in the case and shall state for the record that he or she is familiar with the record in the case.

HISTORY:

[27 FR 10789, Nov. 6, 1962; 62 FR 10312, 10385, March 6, 1997]

§ 246.5 Hearing.

(a) Service counsel. The Government shall be represented at the hearing by a Service counsel who shall have authority to present evidence, and to interrogate, examine, and cross-examine the respondent and other witnesses. The Service counsel is authorized to appeal from a decision of the immigration judge pursuant to § 246.7 and to move for reopening or reconsideration pursuant to § 3.23 of this chapter.

(b) Opening. The immigration judge shall advise the respondent of the nature of the proceeding and the legal authority under which it is conducted; advise the respondent of his or her right to representation, at no expense to the Government, by counsel or representative of his or her own choice qualified under part 292 of this chapter and require him or her to state then and there whether he or she desires representation; advise the respondent that he or she will have a reasonable opportunity to examine and object to the evidence against him or her, to present evidence in his or her own behalf, and to cross-examine witnesses presented by the Government; place the respondent under oath; read the allegations in the notice to the respondent and explain them in nontechnical language, and enter the notice and respondent's answer, if any, as exhibits in the record.

(c) Pleading by respondent. The immigration judge shall require the respondent to state for the record whether he or she admits or denies the allegations contained in the notice, or any of them, and whether he or she concedes that his or her adjustment of status should be rescinded. If the respondent admits all of the allegations and concedes that the adjustment of status in his or her case should be rescinded under the allegations set forth in the notice, and the immigration judge is satisfied that no issues of law or fact remain, he or she may determine that rescission as alleged has been established by the respondent's admissions. The allegations contained in the notice shall be taken as admitted when the respondent, without reasonable cause, fails or refuses to attend or remain in attendance at the hearing.

HISTORY:
[27 FR 10789, Nov. 6, 1962; 62 FR 10312, 10385, March 6, 1997]

§ 246.6 Decision and order.

The decision of the immigration judge may be oral or written. The formal enumeration of findings is not required. The order shall direct either that the proceeding be terminated or that the adjustment of status be rescinded. Service of the decision and finality of the order of the immigration judge shall be in accordance with, and as stated in §§ 240.13 (a) and (b) and 240.14 of this chapter.

HISTORY:
[27 FR 10789, Nov. 6, 1962; 62 FR 10312, 10385, March 6, 1997]

§ 246.7 Appeals.

Pursuant to 8 CFR part 3, an appeal shall lie from a decision of an immigration judge under this part to the Board of Immigration Appeals. An appeal shall be taken within 30 days after the mailing of a written decision or the stating of an oral decision. The reasons for the appeal shall be specifically identified in the Notice of Appeal (Form EOIR 26); failure to do so may constitute a ground for dismissal of the appeal by the Board.

HISTORY:
[29 FR 7236, June 3, 1964; 61 FR 18900, 18910, April 29, 1996, as corrected at 61 FR 32924, June 26, 1996; 62 FR 10312, 10386, March 6, 1997]

§ 246.8 [Reserved]

[NO TEXT IN ORIGINAL]

HISTORY:
[27 FR 10789, Nov. 6, 1962; 62 FR 10312, 10386, March 6, 1997]

AUTHORITY:
(Secs. 103, 244, 245, 246, 249, 66 Stat. 173, 214, 217, 219; 8 U.S.C. 1103, 1254, as amended, 1255, as amended, 1256, 1259, as amended.)

§ 246.9 Surrender of Form I-551.

A respondent whose status as a permanent resident has been rescinded in accordance with section 246 of the Act and this part, shall, upon demand, promptly surrender to the district director having administrative jurisdiction over the office in which the action under this part was taken, the Form I-551 issued to him or her at the time of the grant of permanent resident status.

HISTORY:
[27 FR 10789, Nov. 6, 1962, as amended at 45 FR 32657, May 19, 1980; 62 FR 10312, 10386, March 6, 1997]

PART 247

ADJUSTMENT OF STATUS OF CERTAIN RESIDENT ALIENS

Rule

AUTHORITY NOTE APPLICABLE TO ENTIRE PART:

AUTHORITY:
8 U.S.C. 1101, 1103, and 1257.

§ 247.1 Scope of part.

The provisions of this part apply to an alien who is lawfully admitted for permanent residence and has an occupational status which, if he were seeking admission to the United States, would entitle him to a nonimmigrant status under paragraph (15)(A) or (15)(G) of section 101(a) of the Act, and to his immediate family; also, an alien who was lawfully admitted for permanent residence and has an occupational status which, if he were seeking admission to the United States, would entitle him to a nonimmigrant status under paragraph (15)(E) of section 101(a) of the Act, and to his spouse and children.

HISTORY:
[22 FR 9801, Dec. 6, 1957]

§ 247.11 Notice.

If it appears to a district director that an alien residing in his district, who was lawfully admitted for permanent residence, has an occupational status described in section 247 of the Act, he shall cause a notice on Form I-509 to be served on such alien by personal service informing him that it is proposed to adjust his status, unless the alien requests that he be permitted to retain his status as a resident alien and executes and files with such district director a Form I-508 (Waiver of Rights, Privileges, Exemptions and Immunities) and, if a French national receiving salary from the French Republic, Form I-508F (election as to tax exemption under the Convention between the United States and the French Republic), within 10 days after service of the notice, or the alien, within such 10-day period, files with the district director a written answer under oath setting forth reasons why his status should not be adjusted. The notice shall also advise the person that he may, within such period and upon his request have an opportunity to appear in person, in support or in lieu of his written answer, before an immigration officer designated for that purpose. The person shall further be advised that he may have the assistance of counsel without expense to the Government of the United States in the preparation of his answer or in connection with such personal appearance, and may examine the evidence upon which it is proposed to base such adjustment.

HISTORY:

[22 FR 9801, Dec. 6, 1957, as amended at 37 FR 11471, June 8, 1972]

§ 247.12 Disposition of case.

(a) Allegations admitted or no answer filed. If the waiver Form I-508 and, if applicable, Form I-508F is not filed by the alien within the time prescribed, and the answer admits the allegations in the notice, or no answer is filed, the district director shall place a notation on the notice describing the alien's adjusted nonimmigrant status and shall cause a set of Forms I-94 (see § 1.4) to be prepared evidencing the nonimmigrant classification to which the alien has been adjusted and no appeal shall lie from such decision. Form I-94A shall be delivered to the alien and shall constitute notice to him of such adjustment. The alien's nonimmigrant status shall be for such time, under such conditions, and subject to such regulations as are applicable to the particular nonimmigrant status granted and shall be subject to such other terms and conditions, including the exaction of bond as the district director may deem appropriate.

(b) Answer filed; personal appearance. Upon receipt of an answer asserting a defense to the allegations made in the notice without requesting a personal appearance, or if a personal appearance is requested or directed, the case shall be assigned to an immigration officer. Pertinent evidence, including testimony of witnesses, shall be incorporated in the record. The immigration officer shall prepare a report summarizing the evidence and containing his findings and recommendation. The record, including the report and recommendation of the immigration officer, shall be forwarded to the district director who caused the notice to be served. The district director shall note on the report of the immigration officer whether he approves or disapproves the recommendation of the immigration officer. If the decision of the district director is that the matter be terminated, the alien shall be informed of such decision. If the decision of the district director is that the status of the alien should be adjusted to that of a nonimmigrant, his decision shall provide that unless the alien, within 10 days of receipt of notification of such decision, requests permission to retain his status as an immigrant and files with the district director Form I-508 and, if applicable, Form I-508F, the alien's immigrant status be adjusted to that of a nonimmigrant. The alien shall be informed of such decision and of the reasons therefor, and of his right to appeal in accordance with the provisions of part 103 of this chapter. If the alien does not request that he be permitted to retain status and file the Form I-508 and, if applicable, Form I-508F within the period provided therefor, the district director, without further notice to the alien, shall cause a set of Forms I-94 to be prepared evidencing the nonimmigrant classification to which the alien has been adjusted. Form I-94A shall be delivered to the alien. The alien's nonimmigrant status shall be for such time, under such conditions, and subject to such regulations as are applicable to the particular nonimmigrant status created and shall be subject to such other terms and conditions, including the exaction of bond, as the district director may deem appropriate.

HISTORY:

[22 FR 9801, Dec. 6, 1957, as amended at 23 FR 9124, Nov. 26, 1958; 35 FR 13829, Sept. 1, 1970; 78 FR 18457, 18472, Mar. 27, 2013, as confirmed at 81 FR 91646, 91670, Dec. 19, 2016]

§ 247.13 Disposition of Form I-508.

If Form I-508 is executed and filed, the duplicate copy thereof (noted to show the election made on Form I-508F, if applicable) shall be filed in the office of the Assistant Commissioner, Administrative Division, and may be made available for inspection by any interested officer or agency of the United States.

HISTORY:

[35 FR 13829, Sept. 1, 1970]

§ 247.14 Surrender of documents.

An alien whose status as a permanent resident has been adjusted to that of a nonimmigrant in accordance with section 247 of the Act and this part, shall, upon demand, promptly surrender to the district director having administrative jurisdiction over the office in which the action under this part was taken any documents (such as Form I-151 or I-551 or any other form of Permanent Resident Card, immigrant identification card, resident alien's border-crossing identification card (Form I-187), certificate of registry, or certificate of lawful entry) in his possession evidencing his former permanent resident status.

HISTORY:

[22 FR 9802, Dec. 6, 1957, as amended at 45 FR 32657, May 19, 1980; 63 FR 70313, 70316, Dec. 21, 1998]

PART 248

CHANGE OF NONIMMIGRANT CLASSIFICATION

Rule

AUTHORITY NOTE APPLICABLE TO ENTIRE PART:

AUTHORITY:

8 U.S.C. 1101, 1103, 1184, 1258; 8 CFR part 2.

§ 248.1 Eligibility.

(a) General. Except for those classes enumerated in § 248.2, any alien lawfully admitted to the United States as a nonimmigrant, including an alien who acquired such status pursuant to section 247 of the Act, 8 U.S.C. 1257, who is continuing to maintain his or her nonimmigrant status, may apply to have his or her nonimmigrant classification changed to any nonimmigrant classification other than that of a spouse or fianc(e), or the child of such alien, under section 101(a)(15)(K) of the Act, 8 U.S.C. 1101(a)(15)(K), or as an alien in transit under section 101(a)(15)(C) of the Act, 8 U.S.C. 1101(a)(15)(C). An alien defined by section 101(a)(15)(V), or 101(a)(15)(U) of the Act, 8 U.S.C. 1101(a)(15)(V) or 8 U.S.C. 1101(a)(15)(U), may be accorded nonimmigrant status in the United States by following the procedures set forth respectively in § 214.15(f) or § 214.14 of this chapter.

(b) Except in the case of an alien applying to obtain V nonimmigrant status in the United States under § 214.15(f) of this chapter, a change of status may not be approved for an alien who failed to maintain the previously accorded status or whose status expired before the application or petition was filed, except that failure to file before the period of previously authorized status expired may be excused in the discretion of USCIS, and without separate application, where it is demonstrated at the time of filing that:

(1) The failure to file a timely application was due to extraordinary circumstances beyond the control of the applicant or petitioner, and USCIS finds the delay commensurate with the circumstances;

(2) The alien has not otherwise violated his or her nonimmigrant status;

(3) The alien remains a bona fide nonimmigrant; and

(4) The alien is not the subject of removal proceedings under 8 CFR part 240.

(c) Change of nonimmigrant classification to that of a nonimmigrant student.

(1) Except as provided in paragraph (c)(3) of this section, a nonimmigrant applying for a change of classification as an F-1 or M-1 student is not considered ineligible for such a change solely because the applicant may have started attendance at school before the application was submitted. USCIS will deny an application for a change to classification as an M-1 student if the applicant intends to pursue the course of study solely in order to qualify for a subsequent change of nonimmigrant classification to that of an alien temporary worker under section 101(a)(15)(H) of the Act. Furthermore, an alien may not change from classification as an M-1 student to that of an F-1 student.

(2) [Reserved]

(3) A nonimmigrant who is admitted as, or changes status to, a B-1 or B-2 nonimmigrant on or after April 12, 2002, or who files a request to extend the period of authorized stay as a B-1 or B-2 nonimmigrant on or after such date, may not pursue a course of study at an approved school unless the Service has approved his or her application for change of status to a classification as an F-1 or M-1 student. USCIS will deny the change of status if the B-1 or B-2 nonimmigrant enrolled in a course of study before filing the application for change of status or while the application is pending.

(d) Application for change of nonimmigrant classification from that of a student under section 101(a)(15)(M)(i) to that described in section 101(a)(15)(H). A district director shall deny an application for change of nonimmigrant classification from that of an M-1 student to that of an alien temporary worker under section 101(a)(15)(H) of the Act if the education or training which the student received while an M-1 student enables the student to meet the qualifications for temporary worker classification under section 101(a)(15)(H) of the Act.

(e) Change of nonimmigrant classification to that as described in section 101(a)(15)(N). An application for change to N status shall not be denied on the grounds the applicant is an intending immigrant. Change of status shall be granted for three years not to exceed termination of eligibility under section 101(a)(15)(N) of the Act. Employment authorization pursuant to section 274(A) of the Act may be granted to an alien accorded nonimmigrant status under section 101(a)(15)(N) of the Act. Employment authorization is automatically terminated when the alien changes status or is no longer eligible for classification under section 101(a)(15)(N) of the Act.

HISTORY:

[36 FR 9001, May 18, 1971, as amended at 48 FR 14592, Apr. 5, 1983; 52 FR 11621, Apr. 10, 1987; 59 FR 1465, Jan. 12, 1994; 62 FR 10312, 10386, March 6, 1997; 66 FR 42587, 42595, Aug. 14, 2001; 66 FR 46697, 46704, Sept. 7, 2001; 67 FR 18062, 18064, Apr. 12, 2002; 72 FR 53014, 53041, Sept. 17, 2007; 76 FR 53764, 53794, Aug. 29, 2011; 84 FR 41292, 41508, Aug. 14, 2019, as corrected at 84 FR 52357, 52363, Oct. 1, 2019; 86 FR 14221, 14228, Mar. 15, 2021]

§ 248.2 Ineligible classes.

(a) Except as described in paragraph (b) of this section, the following categories of aliens are not eligible to change their nonimmigrant status under section 248 of the Act, 8 U.S.C. 1258:

(1) Any alien in immediate and continuous transit through the United States without a visa;

(2) Any alien classified as a nonimmigrant under section 101(a)(15) (C), (D), (K), or (S) of the Act;

(3) Any alien admitted as a nonimmigrant under section 101(a)(15)(J) of the Act, or who acquired such status after admission in order to receive graduate medical education or training, whether or not the alien was subject to, received a waiver of, or fulfilled the two-year foreign residence requirement of section 212(e) of the Act. This restriction shall not apply when the alien is a foreign medical graduate who was granted a waiver under section 212(e)(iii) of the Act pursuant to a request made by a State Department of Public Health (or its equivalent) under Pub. L. 103-416, and the alien complies with the terms and conditions imposed on the waiver under section 214(k) of the Act and the implementing regulations at § 212.7(c)(9) of this chapter. A foreign medical graduate who was granted a waiver under Pub. L. 103-416 and who does not fulfill the

requisite 3-year employment contract or otherwise comply with the terms and conditions imposed on the waiver is ineligible to apply for change of status to any other nonimmigrant classification; and

(4) Any alien classified as a nonimmigrant under section 101(a)(15)(J) of the Act (other than an alien described in paragraph (c) of this section) who is subject to the foreign residence requirement of section 212(e) of the Act and who has not received a waiver of the residence requirement, except when the alien applies to change to a classification under section 101(a)(15)(A) or (G) of the Act.

(5) Any alien admitted as a visitor under the visa waiver provisions of § 212.1(e) of this chapter.

(6) Any alien admitted as a Visa Waiver Pilot Program visitor under the provisions of section 217 of the Act and part 217 of this chapter.

(b) The prohibition against a change of nonimmigrant status for the categories of aliens described in paragraphs (a)(1) through (6) of this section is inapplicable to aliens applying for a change of nonimmigrant status to that of a nonimmigrant under section 101(a)(15)(U) of the Act, 8 U.S.C. 1101(a)(15)(U).

HISTORY:

[47 FR 44238, Oct. 7, 1982, as amended at 48 FR 41017, Sept. 13, 1983; 52 FR 48084, Dec. 18, 1987; 53 FR 24903, June 30, 1988; 60 FR 26683, May 18, 1995, as confirmed at 62 FR 18506, 18508, April 16, 1997; 60 FR 44260, 44271, Aug. 25, 1995; 72 FR 53014, 53041, Sept. 17, 2007]

AUTHORITY:

8 U.S.C. 1101, 1103, 1184, 1187, 1258.

§ 248.3 Petition and application.

Requests for a change of status must be filed on the form designated by USCIS with the fee prescribed in 8 CFR 106.2 and in accordance with the form instructions.

(a) Requests by petitioners. A petitioner must submit a request for a change of status to E-1, E-2, E-3, H-1C, H-1B, H-1B1, H-2A, H-2B, H-3, L-1, O-1, O-2, P-1, P-2, P-3, Q-1, R-1, or TN nonimmigrant.

(b) Application by nonimmigrant.

(1) Individual applicant. Any nonimmigrant who seeks to change status to:

(i) A dependent nonimmigrant classification as the spouse or child of a principal whose nonimmigrant classification is listed in paragraph (a) of this section, or

(ii) Any other nonimmigrant classification not listed in paragraph (a) of this section must apply for a change of status on his or her own behalf.

(2) Multiple applicants. More than one person may be included in an application where the co-applicants are all members of a single family group and either all hold the same nonimmigrant status or one holds a nonimmigrant status and the co-applicants are his or her spouse and/or children who hold derivative nonimmigrant status based on the principal's nonimmigrant status.

(c) Special provisions for change of nonimmigrant classification to, or from, a position classified under section 101(a)(15) (A) or (G) of the Act. Each application for change of nonimmigrant classification to, or from, a position classified under section 101(a)(15)(A) or (G) must be filed on the prescribed application accompanied by the appropriate endorsement from the Department of State recommending the change of status. If the Department of State recommends against the change, the application shall be denied. An application for a change of classification by a principal alien in a position classified A-1, A-2, G-1, G-2, G-3, or G-4 shall be processed without fee. Members of the principal alien's immediate family who are included on the principal alien's application shall also be processed without fee.

(d) [Reserved]

(e) Change of classification not required. The following do not need to request a change of classification:

(1) An alien classified as a visitor for business under section 101(a)(15)(B) of the Act who intends to remain in the United States temporarily as a visitor for pleasure during the period of authorized admission; or

(2) An alien classified under sections 101(a)(15)(A) or 101(a)(15)(G) of the Act as a member of the immediate family of a principal alien classified under the same section, or an alien classified under sections 101(a)(15)(E), (H), (I), (J), or (L) of the Act as the spouse or child who accompanied or followed-to-join a principal alien who is classified under the same section, may attend school in the United States, provided that the principal alien or spouse or child maintain their nonimmigrant status.

(f) Approval of application. If the application is granted, the applicant shall be notified of the decision and granted a new period of time to remain in the United States without the requirement of filing a separate application and paying a separate fee for an extension of stay. The applicant's nonimmigrant status under his new classification shall be subject to the terms and conditions applicable generally to such classification and to such other additional terms and conditions, including exaction of bond, which USCIS deems appropriate to the case.

(g) Denial of application. When the application is denied, the applicant shall be notified of the decision and the reasons for the denial. There is no appeal from the denial of the application under this chapter.

(h) Change to S nonimmigrant classification. An eligible state or federal law enforcement agency ("LEA"), which shall include a state or federal court or a United States Attorney's Office, may seek to change the nonimmigrant classification of a nonimmigrant lawfully admitted to the United States, except those enumerated in § 248.2 of this chapter, to that of an alien witness or informant pursuant to section 101(a)(15)(S) of the Act by filing with the Assistant Attorney General, Criminal Division, the forms designated by USCIS with the fee prescribed in 8 CFR 106.2 and in accordance with the form instructions establishing eligibility for the change of nonimmigrant classification.

(1) If the Assistant Attorney General, Criminal Division, certifies the request for S nonimmigrant classification in accordance with the procedures set forth in 8 CFR 214.2(t), the Assistant Attorney General shall

forward the LEA's request on Form I-854 with Form I-539 to the Commissioner. No request for change of nonimmigrant classification to S classification may proceed to the Commissioner unless it has first been certified by the Assistant Attorney General, Criminal Division.

(2) In the event the Commissioner decides to deny an application to change nonimmigrant classification to S nonimmigrant classification, the Assistant Attorney General, Criminal Division, and the relevant LEA shall be notified in writing to that effect. The Assistant Attorney General, Criminal Division, shall concur in or object to that decision. Unless the Assistant Attorney General, Criminal Division, objects within 7 days, he or she shall be deemed to have concurred in the decision. In the event of an objection by the Assistant Attorney General, Criminal Division, the matter will be expeditiously referred to the Deputy Attorney General for a final resolution. In no circumstances shall the alien or the relevant LEA have a right of appeal from any decision to deny.

(i) Change of nonimmigrant status to perform labor in a health care occupation. A request for a change of nonimmigrant status filed by, or on behalf of, an alien seeking to perform labor in a health care occupation as provided in 8 CFR 212.15(c), must be accompanied by a certificate as described in 8 CFR 212.15(f), or if the alien is eligible, a certified statement as described in 8 CFR 212.15(h). See 8 CFR 214.1(j) for a special rule concerning applications for change of status for aliens admitted temporarily under section 212(d)(3) of the Act and 8 CFR 212.15(n).

HISTORY:

[36 FR 9001, May 18, 1971, as amended at 48 FR 14593, Apr. 5, 1983; 48 FR 41017, Sept. 13, 1983; 48 FR 44763, Sept. 30, 1983; 50 FR 25697, June 21, 1985; 59 FR 1466, Jan. 12, 1994; 60 FR 44260, 44271, Aug. 25, 1995; 65 FR 14774, 14779, 14780, Mar. 17, 2000, as corrected at 65 FR 18432, Apr. 7, 2000; 66 FR 31107, 31114, June 11, 2001; 67 FR 76256, 76280, Dec. 11, 2002; 68 FR 43901, 43921, July 25, 2003; 73 FR 61332, 61336, Oct. 16, 2008; 74 FR 26933, 26940, June 5, 2009; 81 FR 2068, 2083, Jan. 15, 2016; 85 FR 46788, 46927, Aug. 3, 2020]

PART 249

CREATION OF RECORDS OF LAWFUL ADMISSION FOR PERMANENT RESIDENCE

AUTHORITY NOTE APPLICABLE TO ENTIRE PART:

AUTHORITY:

8 U.S.C. 1103, 1182, 1259; 8 CFR part 2.

§ 249.1 Waiver of inadmissibility.

In conjunction with an application under section 249 of the Act, an otherwise eligible alien who is inadmissible under paragraph (9), (10), or (12) of section 212(a) of the Act or so much of paragraph (23) of section 212(a) of the Act as relates to a single offense of simple possession of 30 grams or less of marihuana may request a waiver of such ground of inadmissibility under section 212(h) of the Act. Any alien within the classes described in subparagraphs (B) through (H) of section 212(a)(28) of the Act may apply for the benefits of section 212(a)(28)(I)(ii) in conjunction with an application under section 249 of the Act.

HISTORY:

[47 FR 44238, Oct. 7, 1982]

§ 249.2 Application.

(a) Jurisdiction. An application by an alien, other than an arriving alien, who has been served with a notice to appear or warrant of arrest shall be considered only in proceedings under 8 CFR part 240. In any other case, an alien who believes he or she meets the eligibility requirements of section 249 of the Act shall apply to the district director having jurisdiction over his or her place of residence. The application shall be made on Form I-485 and shall be accompanied by Form G-325A, which shall be considered part of the application. The application shall also be accompanied by documentary evidence establishing continuous residence in the United States since prior to January 1, 1972, or since entry and prior to July 1, 1924. All documents must be submitted in accordance with § 103.2(b) of this chapter. Documentary evidence may include any records of official or personal transactions or recordings of events occurring during the period of claimed residence. Affidavits of credible witnesses may also be accepted. Persons unemployed and unable to furnish evidence in their own names may furnish evidence in the names of parents or other persons with whom they have been living, if affidavits of the parents or other persons are submitted attesting to the residence. The numerical limitations of sections 201 and 202 of the Act shall not apply.

(b) Decision. The applicant shall be notified of the decision and, if the application is denied, of the reasons therefor. If the application is granted, a Form I-551, showing that the applicant has acquired the status of an alien lawfully admitted for permanent residence, shall not be issued until the applicant surrenders any other document in his or her possession evidencing compliance with the alien registration requirements of former or existing law. No appeal shall lie from the denial of an application by the district director. However, an alien, other than an arriving alien, may renew the denied application in proceedings under 8 CFR part 240.

HISTORY:

[52 FR 6322, Mar. 3, 1987; 62 FR 10312, 10386, March 6, 1997]

§ 249.3 Reopening and reconsideration.

An applicant who alleged entry and residence since prior to July 1, 1924, but in whose case a record was created as of the date of approval of the application because evidence of continuous residence prior to July 1, 1924, was not submitted, may have his case reopened and reconsidered pursuant to § 103.5 of this chapter. Upon the submission of satisfactory evidence, a record of admission as of the date of alleged entry may be created.

HISTORY:
[29 FR 11494, Aug. 11, 1964]

PART 250

REMOVAL OF ALIENS WHO HAVE FALLEN INTO DISTRESS

Rule

§ 250.1 Application.

Application for removal shall be made on Form I-243. No appeal shall lie from the decision of the district director.

HISTORY:
[22 FR 9802, Dec. 6, 1957]

AUTHORITY:
Secs. 103, 250, 66 Stat. 173, 219; 8 U.S.C. 1103, 1260.

§ 250.2 Removal authorization.

If the district director grants the application he shall issue an authorization for the alien's removal on Form I-202. Upon issuance of the authorization, or as soon thereafter as practicable, the alien may be removed from the United States at government expense.

HISTORY:
[22 FR 9802, Dec. 6, 1957]

AUTHORITY:
Secs. 103, 250, 66 Stat. 173, 219; 8 U.S.C. 1103, 1260.

PART 251

ARRIVAL AND DEPARTURE MANIFESTS AND LISTS: SUPPORTING DOCUMENTS

Rule

AUTHORITY NOTE APPLICABLE TO ENTIRE PART:

AUTHORITY:
8 U.S.C. 1103, 1182, 1221, 1281, 1282, 8 CFR part 2.

§ 251.1 Arrival manifests and lists.

(a) **Vessels —**

(1) General. Except as provided in paragraph (a)(6) of this section, the master or agent of every vessel arriving in the United States from a foreign place or an outlying possession of the United States must submit a manifest of all crewmen on board by electronically submitting the data elements required on CBP Form I–418, Passenger List—Crew List, via an electronic data interchange system approved by CBP.

(2) Longshore work information. Except as provided in paragraph (a)(6) of this section, the master or agent of the vessel must electronically submit via an electronic data interchange system approved by CBP an affirmation as to whether crewmen aboard the vessel will be used to perform longshore work at any United States port before the vessel departs the United States.

(i) If no longshore work will be performed, no further information regarding longshore work is required.

(ii) If longshore work will be performed, the master or agent must indicate which exception listed in section 258 of the Act permits the work. The exceptions are:

(A) The hazardous cargo exception;

(B) The prevailing practice exception in accordance with a port's collective bargaining agreements;

(C) The prevailing practice exception at a port where there is no collective bargaining agreement, but for which the vessel files an attestation;

(D) The prevailing practice exception for automated vessels; and

(E) The reciprocity exception.

(iii) If longshore work will be performed under the hazardous cargo exception, the vessel must either be a tanker or be transporting dry bulk cargo that qualifies as hazardous. All tankers qualify for the hazardous cargo exception, except for a tanker that has been gas-freed to load non-hazardous dry bulk commodities.

(A) To invoke the exception for tankers, the master or agent must indicate in the manifest that the vessel is a qualifying tanker.

(B) If the vessel is transporting dry bulk hazardous cargo, the master or agent must indicate in the manifest that the vessel's dry bulk cargo is hazardous and must show the immigration officer the dangerous cargo manifest that is signed by the master or an authorized representative of the owner, and that under 46 CFR 148.02 must be kept in a conspicuous place near the bridge house.

(iv) If longshore work will be performed under the prevailing practice exception, the master or agent must indicate in the manifest each port at which longshore work will be performed under this exception. Additionally, for each port the master or agent must indicate either that:

(A) The practice of nonimmigrant crewmen doing longshore work is in accordance with all collective bargaining agreements covering 30 percent or more of the longshore workers in the port;

(B) The port has no collective bargaining agreement covering 30 percent or more of the longshore workers in the port and an attestation has been filed with the Secretary of Labor;

(C) An attestation that was previously filed is still valid and the vessel continues to comply with the conditions stated in that attestation; or

(D) The longshore work consists of operating an automated, self-unloading conveyor belt or a vacuum-actuated system.

(v) If longshore work will be performed under the reciprocity exception, the master or agent must indicate in the manifest that the work will be done under the reciprocity exception, and will indicate the nationality of the vessel's registry and the nationality or nationalities of the holders of a majority of the ownership interest in the vessel.

(3) Exception for certain Great Lakes vessels

(i) A manifest is not required for a vessel of United States, Canadian, or British registry engaged solely in traffic on the Great Lakes or the St. Lawrence River and connecting waterways, herein designated as a Great Lakes vessel, unless:

(A) The vessel employs nonimmigrant crewmen who will do longshore work at a port in the United States; or

(B) The vessel employs crewmen of other than United States, Canadian, or British citizenship.

(ii) In either situation, the master must follow the instructions prescribed in paragraph (a)(2) of this section.

(iii) After submission of a manifest on the first voyage of a calendar year, a manifest is not required on subsequent arrivals unless a nonimmigrant crewman of other than Canadian or British citizenship is employed on the vessel who was not aboard and listed on the last prior manifest, or a change has occurred regarding the performance of longshore work in the United States by nonimmigrant crewmen, or a change has occurred in the exception that the master or agent of the vessel wishes to invoke which was not indicated in the last prior manifest.

(4) The master or agent of a vessel that only bunkers at a United States port en route to another United States port must electronically submit via an electronic data interchange system approved by CBP the time, date, and place of bunkering.

(5) If documentation is required to support an exception, as described in § 258.2 of this chapter, it must be sent to CBP electronically or be presented to CBP upon arrival at the port of immigration inspection.

(6) Exception to the requirement to submit Form I–418 data elements and longshore work information electronically. The master or agent of any vessel that is arriving in the United States from a foreign place or an outlying possession of the United States, and is required to submit a manifest, may submit a paper Form I–418 to CBP upon arrival at the port where immigration inspection is performed when:

(i) The master or agent of the vessel is unable to electronically submit the data elements required on Form I–418 via an electronic data interchange system approved by CBP because there is no internet access in that location or onboard computers are experiencing technical difficulties, and there is no shore-side support available; or

(ii) CBP is experiencing technical difficulties affecting its receipt or processing of electronically submitted information, or, in its discretion, CBP determines that a paper Form I–418 is acceptable under the circumstances presented by the master or agent of a vessel.

(b) Aircraft. The captain or agent of every aircraft arriving in the United States from a foreign place or from an outlying possession of the United States, except an aircraft arriving in the United States directly from Canada on a flight originating in that country, shall present to the immigration officer at the port where the inspection is performed a manifest on United States Customs Service Form 7507 or on the International Civil Aviation Organization's General Declaration of all the alien crewmembers on board, including alien crewmembers who are returning to the United States after taking an aircraft of the same line from the United States to a foreign place or alien crewmembers who are entering the United States as passengers solely for the purpose of taking an aircraft of the same line from the United States to a foreign port. The captain or agent of an aircraft that only refuels at the United States en route to another United States port must annotate the manifest presented at the onward port to indicate the time, date, and place of refueling. The surname, given name, and middle initial of each alien crewman listed also shall be shown on the manifest. In addition, the captain or agent of the aircraft shall indicate the total number of United States' citizen crewmembers and total number of alien crewmembers.

(c) Additional documents. The master, captain, or agent shall prepare as a part of the manifest, when one is required for presentation to an immigration officer, a completely executed set of Forms I-95, Conditional Landing Permit, for each nonimmigrant alien crewman on board, except:

(1) A Canadian or British citizen crewman serving on a vessel plying solely between Canada and the United States; or

(2) A nonimmigrant crewman who is in possession of an unmutilated Form I-184, Alien Crewman Landing Permit and Identification Card, or an unmutilated Form I-95 with space for additional endorsements previously issued to him or her as a member of the crew of the same vessel or an aircraft of the same line on his or her last prior arrival in the United States, following which he or she departed from the United States as a member of the crew of the same vessel or an aircraft of the same line.

HISTORY:

[30 FR 6777, May 19, 1965, as amended at 32 FR 9632, July 4, 1967; 34 FR 12560, Aug. 1, 1969; 34 FR 19799, Dec. 18, 1969; 45 FR 32658, May 19, 1980; 46 FR 43827, Sept. 1, 1981; 56 FR 26017, June 6, 1991; 57 FR 40833, Sept. 8, 1992; 58 FR 48779, Sept. 20, 1993; 59 FR 47063, Sept. 14, 1994; 60 FR 14353, Mar. 17, 1995; 62 FR 10312, 10386, March 6, 1997; 86 FR 73618, 73629, Dec. 28, 2021]

§ 251.2 Notification of illegal landings.

As soon as discovered, the master or agent of any vessel from which an alien crewman has illegally landed or deserted in the United States shall inform the immigration officer in charge of the port where the illegal landing or desertion occurred, in writing, of the name, nationality, passport number and, if known, the personal description, circumstances and time of such illegal landing or desertion of such alien crewman, and furnish any other information and documents that might aid in his or her apprehension, including any passport surrendered pursuant to § 252.1(d) of this chapter. Failure to file notice of illegal landing or desertion and to furnish any surrendered passport within 24 hours of the time of such landing or desertion becomes known shall be regarded as lack of compliance with section 251(d) of the Act.

HISTORY:

[28 FR 209, Jan. 9, 1963.; 62 FR 10312, 10387, March 6, 1997]

§ 251.3 Departure manifests and lists for vessels.

(a) Form I–418, Passenger List-Crew List. Except as provided in paragraphs (b) and (c) of this section, the master or agent of every vessel departing from the United States directly to some foreign place or outlying possession of the United States must electronically submit the data elements required on Form I–418 via an electronic data interchange system approved by CBP, except when a manifest is not required pursuant to section 251.1(a). Submission of inaccurate or incomplete data will be regarded as lack of compliance with section 251(c) of the Act.

(b) Exception for certain Great Lakes vessels. The required list need not be submitted for Canadian or British crewmembers of Great Lakes vessels described in § 251.1(a)(3).

(c) Exception to the requirement to submit Form I–418 data elements electronically. The master or agent of any vessel that is departing from the United States directly to some foreign place or outlying possession of the United States, and is required to submit a manifest, may submit a paper Form I– 418 to CBP at the port from which such vessel is to depart when:

(1) The master or agent of the vessel is unable to submit the data elements required on Form I–418 electronically via an electronic data interchange system approved by CBP because there is no internet access in that location or onboard computers are experiencing technical difficulties, and there is no shore-side support available; or

(2) CBP is experiencing technical difficulties affecting its receipt or processing of electronically submitted information, or, in its discretion, CBP determines that a paper Form I–418 is acceptable under the circumstances presented by the master or agent of a vessel.

HISTORY:

[30 FR 6777, May 19, 1965, as amended at 33 FR 17137, Nov. 19, 1968; 62 FR 10312, 10387, March 6, 1997; 86 FR 73618, 73630, Dec. 28, 2021]

§ 251.4 Departure manifests and lists for aircraft.

(a) United States Customs Service Form 7507 or International Civil Aviation Organization's General Declaration. The captain or agent of every aircraft departing from the United States for a foreign place or an outlying possession of the United States, except on a flight departing for and terminating in Canada, shall submit to the immigration officer at the port from which such aircraft is to depart a completed United States Customs Service Form 7507 or the International Civil Aviation Organization's General Declaration. The form shall contain a list of all alien crewmen on board, including alien crewmen who arrived in the United States as crewmen on an aircraft of the same line and who are departing as passengers. The surname, given name, and middle initial of each such alien crewman listed shall be shown. In addition, the captain or agent of the aircraft shall indicate the total number of alien crewmembers and the total number of United States citizen crewmembers.

(b) Notification of changes in employment for aircraft. The agent of the air transportation line shall immediately notify in writing the nearest immigration office of the termination of employment in the United States of each alien employee of the line furnishing the name, birth date, birthplace, nationality, passport number, and other available information concerning such alien. The procedure to follow in obtaining permission to pay off or discharge an alien crewman in the United States after initial immigration inspection, other than an alien lawfully admitted for permanent residence, is set forth in § 252.1(f) of this chapter.

HISTORY:

[30 FR 6777, May 19, 1965, as amended at 33 FR 17137, Nov. 19, 1968; 34 FR 12561, Aug. 1, 1969; 62 FR 10312, 10387, March 6, 1997]

§ 251.5 Arrival and departure manifests for crew.

In addition to the electronic manifest transmission requirement applicable to crew members specified in §§ 231.1 and 231.2 of this chapter, the master or commanding officer, or authorized agent, owner, or consignee, of a commercial vessel or commercial aircraft arriving in or departing from the United States must submit arrival and departure manifests in accordance with §§ 251.1, 251.3, and 251.4.

HISTORY:

[70 FR 17820, 17849, Apr. 7, 2005; 86 FR 73618, 73630, Dec. 28, 2021]

§ 251.6 Exemptions for private vessels and aircraft.

The provisions of this part relating to the presentation of arrival and departure manifests do not apply to a private vessel or private aircraft not engaged directly or indirectly in the carrying of persons or cargo for hire.

HISTORY:

[32 FR 9632, July 4, 1967; 62 FR 10312, 10387, March 6, 1997; redesignated and revised at 70 FR 17820, 17849, Apr. 7, 2005]

PART 252

LANDING OF ALIEN CREWMEN

AUTHORITY NOTE APPLICABLE TO ENTIRE PART:

AUTHORITY:
8 U.S.C. 1103, 1184, 1185 (pursuant to E.O. 13323 published on January 2, 2004), 1258, 1281, 1282; 8 CFR part 2.

§ 252.1 Examination of crewmen.

(a) Detention prior to examination. All persons employed in any capacity on board any vessel or aircraft arriving in the United States shall be detained on board the vessel or at the airport of arrival by the master or agent of such vessel or aircraft until admitted or otherwise permitted to land by an officer of the Service.

(b) Classes of aliens subject to examination under this part. The examination of every nonimmigrant alien crewman arriving in the United States shall be in accordance with this part except that the following classes of persons employed on vessels or aircraft shall be examined in accordance with the provisions of 8 CFR parts 235 and 240:

(1) Canadian or British citizen crewmen serving on vessels plying solely between Canada and the United States; or

(2) Canadian or British citizen crewmen of aircraft arriving in a State of the United States directly from Canada on flights originating in that country. The crew of a vessel arriving at a United States port that may not require inspection by or clearance from the United States Customs Service is, nevertheless, subject to examination under this part; however, the master of such a vessel is not required to present Form I-95 for any crewman who is not an applicant for a conditional landing permit.

(c) Requirements for landing permits.

Every alien crewman applying for landing privileges in the United States is subject to the provisions of 8 CFR 235.1(d)(1)(ii) and (iii), and must make his or her application in person before a Customs and Border Protection (CBP) officer, present whatever documents are required, establish to the satisfaction of the inspecting officer that he or she is not inadmissible under any provision of the law, and is entitled clearly and beyond doubt to landing privileges in the United States.

(d) Authorization to land. The immigration officer in his discretion may grant an alien crewman authorization to land temporarily in the United States for: (1) Shore leave purposes during the period of time the vessel or aircraft is in the port of arrival or other ports in the United States to which it proceeds directly without touching at a foreign port or place, not exceeding 29 days in the aggregate, if the immigration officer is satisfied that the crewman intends to depart on the vessel on which he arrived or on another aircraft of the same transportation line, and the crewman's passport is surrendered for safe keeping to the master of the arriving vessel, or (2) the purpose of departing from the United States as a crewman on a vessel other than the one on which he arrived, or departing as a passenger by means of other transportation, within a period of 29 days, if the immigration officer is satisfied that the crewman intends to depart in that manner, that definite arrangements for such departure have been made, and the immigration officer has consented to the pay off or discharge of the crewman from the vessel on which he arrived. A crewman granted a conditional permit to land under section 252(a)(1) of the Act and paragraph (d)(1) of this section is required to depart with his vessel from its port of arrival and from each other port in the United States to which it thereafter proceeds coastwise without touching at a foreign port or place; however, he may rejoin his vessel at another port in the United States before it touches at a foreign port or place if he has advance written permission from the master or agent to do so.

(e) Conditional permits to land. Unless the crewman is in possession of Form I-184 and is landed under paragraph (d)(1) of this section, the immigration officer shall give to each alien nonimmigrant crewman permitted to land a copy of the Form I-95 presented by the crewman, endorsed to show the date and place of admission and the type of conditional landing permit.

(f) Change of status. An alien nonimmigrant crewman landed pursuant to the provisions of this part shall be ineligible for any extension of stay or for a change of nonimmigrant classification under part 248 of this chapter. A crewman admitted under paragraph (d)(1) of this section may, if still maintaining status, apply for a conditional landing permit under paragraph (d)(2) of this section. The application shall not be approved unless an application on Form I-408, filed pursuant to paragraph (h) of this section, has been approved authorizing the master or agent of the vessel on which the crewman arrived to pay off or discharge the crewman and unless evidence is presented by the master or agent of the vessel to which the crewman will be transferred that a specified position on that vessel has been authorized for him or that satisfactory arrangements have been completed for the repatriation of the alien crewman. If the application is approved, the crewman shall be given a new Form I-95 endorsed to show landing authorized under paragraph (d)(2) of this section for the period necessary to accomplish his scheduled reshipment, which shall not exceed 29 days from the date of his landing, upon surrendering any conditional landing permit previously issued to him on Form I-95.

(g) Refusal of conditional landing permit. When an alien crewman is refused a conditional landing permit for any reason, the Form I-95 presented by him at time of examination shall be endorsed "Permission to land temporarily at all U.S. ports is refused" and the Form I-95 shall be given to the master or agent of the vessel or aircraft and, in the case of vessels, the alien crewman's name shall be listed on the Form I-410 delivered to the master of the vessel upon completion of the examination of the crew. If an alien crewman who has been refused a conditional landing permit is in possession of Form I-184, the Form I-184 shall be lifted by the examining immigration officer and, except in the case of an alien crewman who is refused a conditional landing permit solely because he is not in possession of a valid passport or visa, the Form I-184 shall be voided. In the case of an alien crewman refused a conditional landing permit because he is not in possession of a valid passport or visa, the Form I-184 shall be delivered to the master or agent of the vessel with instructions to return it to the alien crewman after the vessel has departed from the United States.

(h) Authorization to pay off or discharge an alien crewman. Application to pay off or discharge an alien crewman, except an alien lawfully admitted for permanent residence, shall be made by the owner, agent, consignee, charterer, master, or commanding officer of the vessel or aircraft on which the alien crewman arrived on Form I-408 filed with the immigration officer having jurisdiction over the area in which the vessel or aircraft is located at the time of application. The applicant shall be notified of the decision, and, if the application is denied, of the reasons therefor. There shall be no appeal from the denial of an application on Form I-408.

HISTORY:

[23 FR 2788, Apr. 26, 1958, as amended at 27 FR 11875, Dec. 1, 1962; 29 FR 13243, Sept. 24, 1964; 29 FR 14432, Oct. 21, 1964; 32 FR 9633, July 4, 1967; 33 FR 9332, June 26, 1968; 33 FR 17137, Nov. 19, 1968; 58 FR 48779, Sept. 20, 1993; 59 FR 47063, Sept. 14, 1994; 60 FR 14353, Mar. 17, 1995; 62 FR 10312, 10388, March 6, 1997; 69 FR 53318, 53333, Aug. 31, 2004]

§ 252.2 Revocation of conditional landing permits; removal.

(a) Revocation and removal while vessel is in the United States. A crewman whose landing permit is subject to revocation pursuant to section 252(b) of the Act may be taken into custody by any immigration officer without a warrant of arrest and be transferred to the vessel of arrival, if the vessel is in any port in the United States and has not departed foreign since the crewman was issued his or her conditional landing permit. Detention and removal of the crewman shall be at the expense of the transportation line on which the crewman arrived. Removal may be effected on the vessel of arrival or, if the master of the vessel has requested in writing, by alternate means if removal on the vessel of arrival is impractical.

(b) Revocation and removal after vessel has departed the United States. A crewman who was granted landing privileges prior to April 1, 1997, and who has not departed foreign on the vessel of arrival, or on another vessel or aircraft if such permission was granted pursuant to § 252.1(f), is subject to removal proceedings under section 240 of the Act as an alien deportable pursuant to section 237(a)(1)(C)(i) of the Act. A crewman who was granted landing privileges on or after April 1, 1997, and who has not departed foreign on the vessel of arrival, or on another vessel or aircraft if such permission was granted pursuant to § 252.1(f), shall be removed from the United States without a hearing, except as provided in § 208.2(b)(1) of this chapter. In either case, if the alien is removed within 5 years of the date of landing, removal of the crewman shall be at the expense of the owner of the vessel. In the case of a crewman ordered removed more than 5 years after the date of landing, removal shall be at the expense of the appropriation for the enforcement of the Act.

HISTORY:

[29 FR 15253, Nov. 13, 1964; 62 FR 10312, 10388, March 6, 1997]

§ 252.3 Great Lakes vessels and tugboats arriving in the United States from Canada; special procedures.

(a) United States vessels and tugboats. An immigration examination shall not be required of any crewman aboard a Great Lakes vessel of United States registry or a tugboat of United States registry arriving from Canada at a port of the United States who has been examined and admitted by an immigration officer as a member of the crew of the same vessel or tugboat or of any other vessel or tugboat of the same company during the current calendar year.

(b) Canadian or British vessels or tugboats. An alien crewman need not be presented for inspection if the alien crewman:

(1) Serves aboard a Great Lakes vessel of Canadian or British registry or aboard a tugboat of Canadian or British registry arriving at a United States port-of-entry from Canada;

(2) Seeks admission for a period of less than 29 days;

(3) Has, during the current calendar year, been inspected and admitted by an immigration officer as a member of the crew of the same vessel or tugboat, or of any other vessel or tugboat of the same company;

(4) Is either a British or Canadian citizen or is in possession of a valid Form I-95 previously issued to him or her as a member of the crew of the same vessel or tugboat, or of any other vessel or tugboat of the same company;

(5) Does not request or require landing privileges in the United States beyond the time the vessel or tugboat will be in port; and,

(6) Will depart to Canada with the vessel or tugboat.

HISTORY:

[41 FR 24700, June 18, 1976; 62 FR 10312, 10388, March 6, 1997]

§ 252.4 Permanent landing permit and identification card.

A Form I-184 is valid until revoked. It shall be revoked when an immigration officer finds that the crewman is in the United States in willful violation of the terms and conditions of his or her permission to land, or that he or she is inadmissible to the United States. On revocation, the Form I-184 shall be surrendered to an immigration officer. No appeal shall lie from the revocation of Form I-184.

HISTORY:

[43 FR 37174, Aug. 22, 1978; 62 FR 10312, 10388, March 6, 1997]

§ 252.5 Special procedures for deserters from Spanish or Greek ships of war.

(a) General. Under E.O. 11267 of January 19, 1966 (31 FR 807) and 28 CFR 0.109, and E.O. 11300 of August 17, 1966, (31 FR 11009), and 28 CFR 0.110, the Commissioner and immigration officers (as defined in § 103.1(j) of this chapter) are designated as "competent national authorities" on the part of the United States within the meaning of Article XXIV of the 1903 Treaty of Friendship and General Relations between the United States and Spain (33 Stat. 2105, 2117), and "local authorities" and "competent officers" on the part of the United States within the meaning of Article XIII of the Convention between the United States and Greece (33 Stat. 2122, 2131).

(b) Application for restoration. On application of a Consul General, Consul, Vice-Consul, or Consular-Agent of the Spanish or Greek Government, made in writing pursuant to Article XXIV of the treaty, or Article XIII of the Convention, respectively, stipulating for the restoration of crewmen deserting, stating that the person named therein has deserted from a ship of war of that government, while in any port of the United States, and on proof by the exhibition of the register, crew list, or official documents of the vessel, or a copy or extract therefrom, duly certified, that the person named belonged, at the time of desertion, to the crew of such vessel, such person shall be taken into custody by any immigration officer without a warrant of arrest. Written notification of charges shall be served on the alien when he or she is taken into custody or as soon as practical thereafter.

(c) Examination. Within a reasonable period of time after the arrest, the alien shall be accorded an examination by the district director, acting district director, or the deputy district director having jurisdiction over the place of arrest. The alien shall be informed that he or she may have the assistance of or be represented by a counsel or representative of his or her choice qualified under 8 CFR part 292 without expense to the Government, and that he or she may present such evidence in his or her behalf as may be relevant to this proceeding. If, upon the completion of such examination, it is determined that:

(1) The individual sought by the Spanish or Greek authorities had deserted from a Spanish or Greek ship of war in a United States port;

(2) The individual actually arrested and detained is the person sought;

(3) The individual is not a citizen of the United States; and

(4) The individual had not previously been arrested for the same cause and set at liberty because he or she had been detained for more than 3 months, or more than 2 months in the case of a deserter from a Greek ship of war, from the day of his or her arrest without the Spanish or Greek authorities having found an opportunity to send him or her home, the individual shall be served with a copy of the findings, from which no appeal shall lie, and be surrendered forthwith to the Spanish or Greek authorities if they are prepared to remove him or her from the United States. On written request of the Spanish or Greek authorities, the individual shall be detained, at their expense, for a period not exceeding 3 months or 2 months, respectively, from the day of arrest to afford opportunity to arrange for his or her departure from the United States.

(d) Timely departure not effected. If the Spanish authorities delay in sending the individual home for more than 3 months, or if the Greek authorities delay in sending the individual home for more than 2 months, from the day of his or her arrest, the individual shall be dealt with as any other alien unlawfully in the United States under the removal provisions of the Act, as amended.

(e) Commission of crime. If the individual has committed any crime or offense in the United States, he or she shall not be placed at the disposal of the consul until after the proper tribunal having jurisdiction in his or her case shall have pronounced sentence, and such sentence shall have been executed.

HISTORY:

[31 FR 12774, Sept. 30, 1966; 62 FR 10312, 10388, March 6, 1997]

PART 253

PAROLE OF ALIEN CREWMEN

Rule

AUTHORITY NOTE APPLICABLE TO ENTIRE PART:

AUTHORITY:

8 U.S.C. 1103, 1182, 1282, 1283, 1285; 8 CFR part 2.

§ 253.1 Parole.

(a) General. When a crewman is paroled into the United States pursuant to the provisions of this part under the provisions of section 212(d)(5) of the Act, he shall be given Form I-94 (see § 1.4), reflecting the terms of parole. A notice on Form I-259 shall be served upon the agent, and, if available, upon the owner and master or commanding officer of the vessel or aircraft, which shall specify the purpose of the parole and the conditions under which the alien crewman is paroled into the United States. The Form I-259 shall also specify the Service office to which the alien crewman is to be presented for inspection upon termination of the parole. The guarantee of payment for medical and other related expenses required by section 253 of the Act shall be executed by the owner, agent, consignee, commanding officer or master on Form I-510.

(b) Afflicted crewman. Any alien crewman afflicted with feeblemindedness, insanity, epilepsy, tuberculosis in any form, leprosy, or any dangerous contagious disease, or an alien crewman suspected of being so afflicted shall upon arrival at the first port of call in the United States, be paroled to the medical institution designated by the district director in whose district the port is located, in the custody (other than during the period of time he is in such medical institution) of the agent of the vessel or aircraft on which such alien arrived in the United States and at the expense of the transportation line for a period initially not to exceed thirty days, for treatment and observation, under the provisions of section 212(d)(5) of the Act. Unless the Public Health Surgeon at the first port certifies that such parole be effected immediately for emergent reasons, the district director may defer execution of parole to a subsequent port of the United States to which the vessel or aircraft will proceed, if facilities not readily available at the first port are readily available at such subsequent port of call. Notice to remove an afflicted alien crewman shall be served by the examining immigration officer upon the master or agent of the vessel or aircraft on Form I-259 and shall specify the date when and the place to which such alien crewman shall be removed and the reasons therefor.

(c) Disabled crewman. Any alien crewman who becomes disabled in any port of the United States, whom the master or agent of the vessel or aircraft is obliged under foreign law to return to another country, may be paroled into the United States under the provisions of section 212(d)(5) of the Act for the period of time and under the conditions set by the district director in whose district the port is located, in the custody of the agent of the vessel or aircraft for the purpose of passing through the United States and transferring to another vessel or aircraft for departure to such foreign country, by the most direct and expeditious route.

(d) Shipwrecked or castaway seamen or airmen. A shipwrecked or castaway alien seaman or airman who is rescued by or transferred at sea to a vessel or aircraft destined directly for the United States and who is brought to the United States on such vessel or aircraft other than as a member of its crew shall be paroled into the United States under the provisions of section 212(d)(5) of the Act for the period of time and under the conditions set by the district director in whose district the port is located, in the custody of the appropriate foreign consul or the agent of the aircraft or vessel which was wrecked or from which such seaman or airman was removed, for the purpose of treatment or observation in a hospital, if such is required, and for departure to the appropriate foreign country by the most direct and expeditious route.

(e) Medical treatment or observation. Any alien crewman denied a conditional landing permit or whose conditional landing permit issued under § 252.1(d)(1) of this chapter is revoked may, upon the request of the master or agent, be paroled into the United States under the provisions of section 212(d)(5) of the Act in the custody of the agent of the vessel or aircraft and at the expense of the transportation line for medical treatment or observation.

(f) Crewman, stowaway, or alien removable under section 235(c) alleging persecution or torture. Any alien crewman, stowaway, or alien removable under section 235(c) of the Act who alleges that he or she cannot return to his or her country of nationality or last habitual residence (if not a national of any country) because of fear of persecution in that country on account of race, religion, nationality, membership in a particular social group, or political opinion, or because of fear of torture is eligible to apply for asylum or withholding of removal under 8 CFR part 208. Service officers shall take particular care to ensure that the provisions of § 208.5(b) of this chapter regarding special duties toward aliens aboard certain vessels are closely followed.

(g) Other crewmen. In the discretion of the district director, any alien crewman not within the purview of paragraphs (b) through (f) of this section may for other emergent reasons or for reasons deemed strictly in the public interest be paroled into the United States under the provisions of section 212(d)(5) of the Act for the period of time and under the conditions set by the district director having jurisdiction over the area where the alien crewman is located.

HISTORY:

[22 FR 9804, Dec. 6, 1957, as amended at 26 FR 11797, Dec. 8, 1961; 32 FR 4341, Mar. 22, 1967; 32 FR 9633, July 4, 1967; 55 FR 30687, July 27, 1990; 62 FR 10312, 10389, Mar. 6, 1997; 64 FR 8478, 8495, Feb. 19, 1999; 78 FR 18457, 18472, Mar. 27, 2013, as confirmed at 81 FR 91646, 91670, Dec. 19, 2016]

§ 253.2 Termination of parole.

(a) General. At the expiration of the period of parole authorized by the district director, or when the purpose of the parole has been served, whichever is earlier, the agent upon whom the relating Form I-259 was served as provided in § 253.1, shall present the alien crewman for inspection to an immigration officer at the Service office specified in the Form I-259. If the agent cannot present the alien crewman, the agent shall immediately submit a report of the reasons therefor to the district director. The district director shall take such further action as the circumstances may require. If the vessel or aircraft on which the alien crewman arrived in the United States is still in the United States when he is presented for inspection, he shall be treated as an applicant for a conditional landing permit and his case shall be dealt with in the same manner as any other applicant for a conditional landing permit. If the vessel or aircraft on which the alien crewman arrived in the United States departed before he was presented for inspection, the agent shall be directed by means of written notice on Form I-259 to arrange for the removal of the alien crewman from the United States, and if such alien crewman thereafter departs voluntarily from the United States within the time specified by the district director, such departure shall not be considered a deportation within the meaning of this section.

(b) Revocation of parole. When an immigration officer has reason to believe that an alien crewman paroled into the United States pursuant to the provisions of §

253.1 has violated the conditions of parole, the immigration officer may take such alien crewman into custody without a warrant of arrest. Following such action, the alien crewman shall be accorded, without undue delay, an examination by another immigration officer. If it is determined on the basis of such examination that the individual detained is an alien crewman who was paroled into the United States pursuant to the provisions of § 253.1 and that he has violated the conditions of the parole or has remained in the United States beyond the period authorized by the district director, the district director shall cause to be served upon the alien crewman a written notice that his parole has been revoked, setting forth the reasons for such action. If the vessel or aircraft upon which the alien crewman arrived in the United States is still in the United States, the alien crewman shall be delivered to that vessel or aircraft and Form I-259 shall be served upon the master or commanding officer of the vessel or aircraft directing that the alien crewman be detained on board the vessel or aircraft and deported from the United States. A copy of Form I-259 shall also be served on the agent for the vessel or aircraft. If the vessel or aircraft upon which the alien crewman arrived in the United States has departed from the United States, the agent or owner of the vessel or aircraft shall be directed by means of a notice on Form I-259 to effect the deportation of the alien crewman from the United States. Pending deportation, the alien crewman shall be continued in custody, unless the district director authorizes his release on parole under such conditions, including the posting of a suitable bond, as the district director may prescribe.

HISTORY:
[32 FR 4342, Mar. 22, 1967]

PART 258

LIMITATIONS ON PERFORMANCE OF LONGSHORE WORK BY ALIEN CREWMEN

§ 258.1 Limitations — General.

(a) Longshore work defined. Longshore work means any activity relating to the loading and unloading of cargo, the operation of cargo-related equipment [whether or not integral to the vessel], and the handling of mooring lines on the dock when the vessel is made fast or let go, in the United States or the coastal waters thereof.

(1) Longshore work is not included in the term "normal operation and service on board a vessel" for the purposes of section 101(a)(15)(D)(i) of the Act except as provided in sections 258 (c) or (d) of the Act.

(2) A vessel that uses nonimmigrant crewmen to perform longshore work, other than the activities allowed in particular circumstances under § 258.2 (a)(2), (b), or (c) of this part, shall be subject to a fine under section 251(d) of the Act.

(b) Port defined. For purposes of this section, the term port means a geographic area, either on a seacoast, lake, river, or other navigable body of water, which contains one or more publicly or privately owned terminals, piers, docks, or maritime facilities, which is commonly regarded as a port by other government maritime related agencies, such as the Maritime Administration.

HISTORY:
57 FR 30384, Sept. 8, 1992.

AUTHORITY:
8 U.S.C. 1101, 1103, 1281; 8 CFR part 2.

§ 258.2 Exceptions.

Any master or agent who uses nonimmigrant crewmen to perform longshore work at any United States port under the exceptions provided for in paragraphs (a)(2), (b), or (c) of this section must so indicate on the crew manifest and must indicate under which exception the work will be performed.

(a) Hazardous cargo.

(1) The term longshore work does not include the loading and unloading of any cargo for which the Secretary of Transportation has prescribed regulations under authority contained in chapter 37 of title 46, United States Code, section 311 of the Federal Water Pollution Control Act, section 4106 of the Oil Pollution Act of 1990, or section 105 or 106 of the Hazardous Materials Transportation Act.

(2) In order to invoke the hazardous cargo exception for safety and environmental protection, the master or agent must indicate in the manifest that the vessel is a qualifying tanker or carries hazardous dry bulk cargo.

(i) All tankers qualify for the hazardous cargo exception, including parcel tankers, except for a tanker that has been gas-freed to transport non-hazardous dry bulk commodities.

(ii) In order for a vessel to qualify for the hazardous cargo exception as a dry bulk hazardous cargo carrier, the master or agent must show the immigration officer the dangerous cargo manifest that is required by Coast Guard regulation 46 CFR 148.02-3(a) to be kept near the bridge house.

(b) Prevailing practice exception.

(1) Nonimmigrant crewmen may perform longshore work under this exception if:

(i) There is in effect in the local port one or more collective bargaining agreements, each covering at least 30 percent of the persons performing longshore work at the port, and each of which permits the longshore activity to be performed by the nonimmigrant crewman, or

(ii) There is no collective bargaining agreement in effect in the local port covering at least 30 percent of the persons performing longshore work at the port, and the employer of the crewmen has filed an attestation with the Secretary of Labor that the Secretary of Labor has accepted.

(2) Documentation to be presented under the prevailing practice exception.

(i) If the master or agent indicates in the manifest, or on Form I–418 if submitting the paper version, that nonimmigrant crewmen will perform longshore work at a port under the prevailing practice exception as permitted by all collective bargaining agreements covering 30 percent or more of the persons performing longshore work at the port, then the master or agent must present to the examining immigration officer an affidavit from the local stevedore. The stevedore or a union representative of the employees' association must state on the affidavit that all bargaining agreements covering 30 percent or more of the longshore workers at the port allow nonimmigrant crewmen either to perform all longshore work or to perform those specified longshore activities that crewmen on the vessel intend to perform.

(ii) Where there is no collective bargaining agreement in effect at a port covering at least 30 percent of the persons who do longshore work, and the master or agent indicates in the manifest that nonimmigrant crewmen will perform such work under the prevailing practice exception, then the master or agent must present a copy of the notification received from the Secretary of Labor that the attestation required for this exception has been accepted.

(iii) When an unanticipated emergency occurs, the master or agent of a vessel may file an attestation with the Secretary of Labor up to the date on which crewmen perform longshore work.

(A) If, because of an unanticipated emergency, crewmen on a vessel perform longshore work under the prevailing practice exception at a port, a revised manifest must be submitted together with complete documentation, as specified in paragraph (b)(2)(ii) of this section, within 14 days of the longshore work having been done. Failure to present the required documentation may result in a fine under section 251 of the Act.

(B) All documents submitted after inspection must be sent to the CBP seaport office that inspected the vessel.

(iv) Attestations are valid for one year from the date of filing and cover nonimmigrant crewmen landing during that period if the master or agent indicates in the manifest that the vessel's crew continue to comply with the conditions in the attestation. When the vessel's master or agent intends to use a previously accepted attestation that is still valid, the master or agent must submit a copy of the notification from the Secretary of Labor that the attestation was accepted and must indicate in the manifest that the vessel continues to comply with the conditions of the attestation.

(3) Use of automated self-unloading conveyor belt or vacuum-actuated system on a vessel. An automated self-unloading conveyor belt or a vacuum-actuated system may be operated by a nonimmigrant crewman under the prevailing practice exception when no collective bargaining agreement at the local port prevents it. The master or agent is not required to file an attestation for nonimmigrant crewmen to perform such activity in such a circumstance unless the Secretary of Labor has determined that such activity is not the prevailing practice at that port, and has publicized this finding. When invoking this exception, the master or agent of the vessel must indicate in the manifest that the longshore work consists of operating a self-unloading conveyor belt or a vacuum-actuated system on the vessel under the prevailing practice exception.

(4) Sanctions upon notification by the Secretary of Labor. If CBP is notified by the Secretary of Labor that an entity has either misrepresented facts in its attestation or has failed to meet a condition attested to, then the CBP will take the necessary steps to prevent the landing of vessels owned or chartered by the offending entity in accordance with section 258(c)(4)(E)(i) of the Act. CBP may also impose a sanction as provided in that section, including the prohibition of any vessel owned or chartered by the violating entity from landing at any United States port for up to one year.

(5) The three variations of the prevailing practice exception — collective bargaining agreement, attestation process, and automated equipment — are port specific. If a vessel is to use nonimmigrant crewmen to perform longshore work under the prevailing practice exception, the appropriate documentation required under paragraph (b)(2) of this section must be presented for each port at which the longshore work will be performed.

(c) Reciprocity exception. Nonimmigrant crewmen may perform longshore work in a United States port under this exception if:

(1) The vessel on which the crewmen serve is registered in a country that does not prohibit crewmen aboard United States vessels from performing longshore work, or a specified longshore activity, when United States vessels land in that country, as determined by the Secretary of State; and

(2) The master or agent presents an affidavit from the crewmen's employer or the vessel's owner that a majority of the ownership interest in the vessel is held by nationals of a country or countries that do not prohibit such longshore activity by crewmen aboard United States vessels when they land in those countries.

(d) Vessels that qualify for multiple exceptions. A vessel that qualifies for more than one exception under this section may invoke the exception that the master or agent chooses.

(e) Lack of documentation required by an exception. If a vessel invokes an exception to the prohibition against nonimmigrant crewmen performing longshore work, but lacks any documentation required to accompany the manifest when invoking the exception, then the vessel's crewmen must not perform longshore work. If the longshore work is performed despite the lack of documentation that the immigration officer has indicated on the electronically populated, or in the circumstances specified in section 251.1 of this chapter, paper, Form I–418, then the vessel is subject to fine under section 251(d) of the Act.

HISTORY:

57 FR 30384, Sept. 8, 1992; 86 FR 73618, 73630, Dec. 28, 2021]

§ 258.3 Action upon arrival.

(a) The master or agent of the vessel shall state on the manifest at the first port of entry:

(1) Whether or not nonimmigrant crewmen aboard the vessel will perform longshore work at any port before departing the United States; and

(2) If nonimmigrant crewmen will perform longshore work, which exception in section 258 of the Act permits them to do so.

(b) If nonimmigrant crewmen will perform longshore work, the master or agent of the vessel shall present with the manifest any documentation required by 8 CFR 258.2 for the exception invoked.

(c) If, at the time of inspection, the master or agent fails to present the documentation required for the exception invoked, then the vessel is prohibited from using nonimmigrant crewmen to perform longshore work. If crewmen aboard the vessel perform longshore work despite the prohibition, the vessel is subject to fine under section 251(d) of the Act.

(d) The examining immigration officer shall give the master or agent a Receipt for Crew List, Form I-410, on which the officer shall note whether or not nonimmigrant crewmen will do longshore work at any port of call and, if so, under which exception. The officer shall also note which documentation supporting the exception accompanied the manifest, and any failure to present documentation which failure would prohibit crewmen from performing longshore work under the exception that the vessel invoked.

(e) If a vessel's crewmen perform longshore activity not sanctioned by an exception but performed to prevent the imminent destruction of goods or property; severe damage to vessels, docks, or real estate; possible environmental contamination; or possible injury or death to a person, a concise report of the incident shall be made within 14 days of the incident to the Immigration and Naturalization Service seaport office that performed the inspection. If the Service agrees that the situation was one of imminent danger requiring immediate action, no fine will be imposed for the performance of a longshore activity in this isolated instance.

(f) Failure to deliver true and complete information on the manifest or any documentation required to support an exception may result in a fine against the owner, agent, consignee, master, or commanding officer under section 251(d) of the Act.

HISTORY:

57 FR 30384, Sept. 8, 1992.

AUTHORITY:

8 U.S.C. 1101, 1103, 1281; 8 CFR part 2.

§ 258.4 Debarment of vessels.

(a) Definitions. The following definitions apply throughout this section:

Good cause, for purposes of extending the deadline for filing an answer, includes: technical difficulties or natural disasters that affect the violating entity's ability to receive, process, or transmit relevant information or data; or other instances in which CBP, in its discretion, determines that an undue hardship on the violating entity warrants an extension of the deadline for filing an answer.

Mitigation in a debarment proceeding means determining the length of the debarment, the ports covered by the debarment, and the vessels subject to the debarment. It does not include revocation of the requirement to debar.

Mitigation meeting is a personal appearance before a designated CBP official in which representatives of the violating entity can provide information and explain why CBP should mitigate the debarment.

(b) Notice of intent to debar.

(1) Issuance of notice. Upon receipt of a notice of violation from the Secretary of Labor pursuant to section 258 of the Immigration and Nationality Act (8 U.S.C. 1288(c)(4)(E)(i)), CBP will serve a notice of intent to debar on the entity subject to the notice of violation, as provided in paragraph (b)(3) of this section.

(2) Contents of notice. The notice of intent to debar will include the following:

(i) The proposed period of debarment, not to exceed one year;

(ii) The ports covered by the proposed debarment;

(iii) A brief explanation of the reasons for the proposed debarment;

(iv) The statutory and regulatory authority for the proposed debarment;

(v) A statement that the entity subject to the debarment may file an answer and request a mitigation meeting pursuant to paragraph (c) of this section;

(vi) The procedures for filing an answer and requesting a mitigation meeting, including the date by which the answer must be received and the address to which it may be submitted; and

(vii) A statement that in the absence of a timely filed answer, the proposed debarment will become final 30 days after service of the notice of intent to debar.

(3) Service. The notice of intent to debar will be served by a method that demonstrates receipt, such as certified mail with return receipt or express courier delivery, by the entity identified in the notice of violation received from the Secretary of Labor. The date of service is the date of receipt.

(c) Answer; request for mitigation meeting.

(1) General. Any entity upon which the notice has been served, or its authorized representative, may file with CBP an answer that indicates the specific reasons why the proposed debarment should be mitigated and whether a mitigation meeting is requested. CBP must receive the answer within 30 days from the date of service of the notice of intent to debar.

(2) Procedures.

(i) Form. The answer must be dated, typewritten or legibly written, signed under oath, and include the address at which the entity or its authorized representative desires to receive further communications. CBP may require that the answer and any supporting documentation be in English or be accompanied by an English translation certified by a competent translator.

(ii) Supporting documentation required. In addition to an answer, any entity responding to a notice of intent to debar must submit documentary evidence in support of any request for mitigation and may file a brief in support of any arguments made. The entity may present evidence in support of any request for mitigation at a mitigation meeting.

(iii) Mitigation meeting. A mitigation meeting will be conducted if requested by the entity subject to the proposed debarment in accordance with the requirements of this section, or if directed at any time by CBP.

(iv) Good cause extension. CBP, in its discretion, may extend the deadline for filing an answer up to an additional 30 days from the original receipt of CBP's notice upon a showing of good cause. Upon receipt of a request to extend the deadline for filing an answer, CBP will respond to the request for an extension within 5 business days by certified mail or express courier.

(d) Disposition of case.

(1) No response filed or allegations not contested. If no answer is timely filed or the answer admits the allegations in the notice of intent to debar and does not request mitigation or a mitigation meeting, the proposed debarment specified in the notice of intent to debar automatically will become a final order of debarment 30 days after service of the notice of intent to debar. If CBP grants a good cause extension pursuant to paragraph (c)(2)(iv) of this section, and no answer is timely filed, the proposed debarment automatically will become a final order of debarment when the time for filing an answer expires.

(2) Answer filed; mitigation meeting requested. If an answer is timely filed that requests mitigation and/or a mitigation meeting, CBP will determine a final debarment in accordance with paragraph (e) of this section.

(3) Unavailability of appeal. The final order of debarment is not subject to appeal.

(4) Notice of final order of debarment.

(i) CBP will issue to the entity subject to the debarment a final order of debarment in writing.

(ii) CBP will send notice, by certified mail or express courier, to all interested parties, including the relevant U.S. ports of entry, that the entity subject to the debarment is debarred and stating the terms of the debarment.

(e) Debarment.

(1) Generally. In determining a proposed debarment and a final debarment, CBP will consider the information received from the Secretary of Labor, any evidence or arguments timely presented by the entity subject to the debarment, and any other relevant factors.

(2) Other relevant factors. Other relevant factors include, but are not limited to, the following:

(i) The previous history of violations of any provision of the INA by the entity subject to the debarment;

(ii) The number of U.S. workers adversely affected by the violation;

(iii) The gravity of the violation;

(iv) The efforts made by the entity subject to the debarment to comply in good faith with the regulatory and statutory requirements governing performance of longshore work by nonimmigrant crewmen;

(v) The remedial efforts by the entity subject to the debarment;

(vi) The commitment to future compliance by the entity subject to the debarment;

(vii) The extent of cooperation with the investigation by the entity subject to the debarment;

(viii) The extent of financial gain/loss to the entity subject to the debarment due to the violation; and

(ix) The potential financial loss, injury, or adverse effect to other parties, including U.S. workers, likely to result from the debarment.

(f) Notice of completion of debarment. Upon completion of any debarment, CBP will send notice, by certified mail or express courier, to all interested parties, including the entity subject to the debarment, and the relevant U.S. ports of entry, that the entity subject to the debarment has completed the debarment and is once again permitted to enter U.S. ports.

(g) Record. CBP will keep a record of the debarment proceedings which includes, but is not limited to, the materials exchanged between CBP and the parties. Records will be retained in accordance with CBP's Records Retention Schedule and the Freedom of Information Act.

HISTORY:

[89 FR 23501, 23503, Apr. 4, 2024]

PART 264

REGISTRATION AND FINGERPRINTING OF ALIENS IN THE UNITED STATES

Rule

AUTHORITY NOTE APPLICABLE TO ENTIRE PART:

AUTHORITY:

8 U.S.C. 1103, 1201, 1302-1305; 8 CFR part 2.

§ 264.1 Registration and fingerprinting.

(a) Prescribed registration forms. The following forms are prescribed as registration forms:

Form No. and Class

G-325R, Biographic Information (Registration), or its successor form.

I-67, Inspection Record—Hungarian refugees (Act of July 25, 1958).

I-94, Arrival-Departure Record—Aliens admitted as nonimmigrants; aliens paroled into the United States under section 212(d)(5) of the Immigration and Nationality Act; aliens whose claimed entry prior to July 1, 1924, cannot be verified, they having satisfactorily established residence in the United States since prior to July 1, 1924; aliens lawfully admitted to the United States for permanent residence who have not been registered previously; aliens who are granted permission to depart without the institution of deportation proceedings or against whom deportation proceedings are being instituted.

I-95, Crewmen's Landing Permit—Crewmen arriving by vessel or aircraft.

I-181, Memorandum of Creation of Record of Lawful Permanent Residence—Aliens presumed to be lawfully admitted to the United States under 8 CFR 101.1.

I-485, Application for Status as Permanent Resident—Applicants under sections 245 and 249 of the Immigration and Nationality Act as amended, and section 13 of the Act of September 11, 1957.

I-590, Registration for Classification as Refugee—Escapee—Refugee-escapees paroled pursuant to section 1 of the Act of July 14, 1960.

I-687, Application for Status as a Temporary Resident—Applicants under section 245A of the Immigration and Nationality Act, as amended.

I-691, Notice of Approval for Status as a Temporary Resident—Aliens adjusted to lawful temporary residence under 8 CFR 210.2 and 245A.2.

I-698, Application to Adjust Status from Temporary to Permanent Resident—Applicants under section 245A of the Immigration and Nationality Act, as amended.

I-700, Application for Status as a Temporary Resident—Applicants under section 210 of the Immigration and Nationality Act, as amended.

I-817, Application for Voluntary Departure under the Family Unity Program.

(b) Evidence of registration. The following forms constitute evidence of registration:

Form No. and Class

I-94, Arrival-Departure Record—Aliens admitted as nonimmigrants; aliens paroled into the United States under section 212(d)(5) of the Immigration and Nationality Act; aliens whose claimed entry prior to July 1, 1924, cannot be verified, they having satisfactorily established residence in the United States since prior to July 1, 1924; and aliens granted permission to depart without the institution of deportation proceedings.

I-95, Crewmen's Landing Permit—Crewmen arriving by vessel or aircraft.

I-184, Alien Crewman Landing Permit and Identification Card—Crewmen arriving by vessel.

I-185, Nonresident Alien Canadian Border Crossing Card—Citizens of Canada or British subjects residing in Canada.

I-186, Nonresident Alien Mexican Border Crossing Card—Citizens of Mexico residing in Mexico.

I-221, Order to Show Cause and Notice of Hearing—Aliens against whom deportation proceedings are being instituted.

I-221S, Order to Show Cause, Notice of Hearing, and Warrant for Arrest of Alien—Aliens against whom deportation proceedings are being instituted.

I-551, Permanent Resident Card—Lawful permanent resident of the United States.

I-766, Employment Authorization Document.

Form I-862, Notice to Appear—Aliens against whom removal proceedings are being instituted.

Form I-863, Notice of Referral to Immigration Judge—Aliens against whom removal proceedings are being instituted.

USCIS Proof of Alien G-325R Registration, or its successor form.

Note to paragraph (b): In addition to the forms noted in this paragraph (b), a valid, unexpired nonimmigrant DHS admission or parole stamp in a foreign passport constitutes evidence of registration.

(c) Replacement of alien registration. Any alien whose registration document is not available for any reason must immediately apply for a replacement document in the manner prescribed by USCIS.

(d) Surrender of registration. If an alien is naturalized, dies, permanently departs, or is deported from the United States, or evidence of registration is found by a person other than the one to whom such evidence was issued, the person in possession of the document shall forward it to a USCIS office.

(e) Fingerprinting waiver.

(1) Fingerprinting is waived for nonimmigrant aliens admitted as foreign government officials and employees; international organization representatives, officers and employees; NATO representatives, officers and employees, and holders of diplomatic visas while they maintain such nonimmigrant status. Fingerprinting is also waived for other nonimmigrant aliens, while they maintain nonimmigrant status, who are nationals of countries which do not require fingerprinting of United States citizens temporarily residing therein.

(2) Fingerprinting is waived for every nonimmigrant alien not included in paragraph (e)(1) of this section who departs from the United States within one year of his admission, provided he maintains his nonimmigrant status during that time; each such alien not previously fingerprinted shall apply therefor at once if he remains in the United States in excess of one year.

(3) Every nonimmigrant alien not previously fingerprinted shall apply therefor at once upon his failure to maintain his nonimmigrant status.

(f) [Reserved]

(g) Registration and fingerprinting of children who reach age 14. Within 30 days after reaching the age of 14, any alien in the United States not exempt from alien registration under the Act and this chapter must apply for registration and fingerprinting, unless fingerprinting is waived under paragraph (e) of this section, in accordance with applicable form instructions.

(1) Permanent residents. If such alien is a lawful permanent resident of the United States and is temporarily absent from the United States when he reaches the age of 14, he must apply for registration and provide a photograph within 30 days of his or her return to the United States in accordance with appli-

cable form instructions. The alien, if a lawful permanent resident of the United States, must surrender any prior evidence of alien registration. USCIS will issue the alien new evidence of alien registration.

(2) Others. In the case of an alien who is not a lawful permanent resident, the alien's previously issued registration document will be noted to show that he or she has been registered and the date of registration.

HISTORY:

[25 FR 10495, Nov. 2, 1960; 52 FR 16194, 1987; 53 FR 43986, 1988; 54 FR 50340, 51816, 1989; 55 FR 20262, 1990; 56 FR 483, 1991.; 57 FR 6462, Feb. 25, 1992, as confirmed at 60 FR 66062, 66066, Dec. 21, 1995; 57 FR 14627, 1992; 58 FR 48779, Sept. 20, 1993; 58 FR 68024, Dec. 23, 1993, as confirmed at 61 FR 47668, 47669, Sept. 10, 1996; 59 FR 1466, Jan. 11, 1994; 61 FR 37673, 37675, July 19, 1996; 61 FR 46534, 46537, Sept. 4, 1996; 63 FR 70313, 70316, Dec. 21, 1998; 67 FR 52584, 52591, Aug. 12, 2002; 67 FR 71443, 71450, Dec. 2, 2002; 68 FR 67578, 67583, Dec. 2, 2003; 76 FR 53764, 53795, Aug. 29, 2011; 78 FR 18457, 18473, Mar. 27, 2013, as confirmed at 81 FR 91646, 91670, Dec. 19, 2016; 81 FR 94231, 94234, Dec. 23, 2016; 90 FR 11793, 11800, Mar. 12, 2025]

§ 264.2 Application for creation of record of permanent residence.

(a) Jurisdiction. An applicant who believes that he/she is eligible for presumption of lawful admission for permanent residence under § 101.1 or § 101.2 of this chapter or for lawful permanent residence as a person born in the United States to a foreign diplomatic officer under § 101.3 of this chapter shall submit his/her application for creation of a record of lawful permanent residence on Form I-485 in accordance with the instructions on the form and paragraph (c) of this section. The applicant must be physically present in the United States at the time of submission of his/her application.

(b) Applicant under eighteen years old. If the applicant is under eighteen years old, the applicant's parent or legal guardian shall prepare and sign the application in the applicant's behalf.

(c) Filing application —

(1) Presumption of lawful admission for permanent residence. An applicant who believes that he/she is eligible for presumption of lawful admission for permanent residence under § 101.1 or § 101.2 of this chapter shall submit the following:

(i) A completed Form I-485, with the fee required in 8 CFR 106.2 and any initial evidence required on the application form and in this section.

(ii) Form G-325A, Biographic Information.

(iii) [Reserved]

(iv) A list of all the applicant's arrivals in and departures from the United States.

(v) A statement signed by the applicant indicating the basis of the applicant's claim to presumption of lawful admission for permanent residence.

(vi) Documentary evidence substantiating the applicant's claim to presumption of lawful admission for permanent residence, including proof of continuous residence in the United States.

(vii) Two photographs prepared in accordance with the specifications outlined in the instructions on the application form. The immigration officer to whom the application is submitted, however, may waive the photographs for just cause.

(2) Lawful permanent residence as a person born in the United States under diplomatic status. An applicant who believes that he/she is eligible for lawful permanent residence as a person born in the United States to a foreign diplomatic officer under § 101.3 of this chapter shall submit the following:

(i) A completed Form I-485, with the fee required in 8 CFR 106.2 and any initial evidence required on the application form and in this section.

(ii) Form G-325A, Biographic Information.

(iii) [Reserved]

(iv) The applicant's birth certificate.

(v) An executed Form I-508, Waiver of Rights, Privileges, Exemptions, and Immunities.

(vi) Official confirmation of the diplomatic classification and occupational title of the applicant's parent(s) at the time of the applicant's birth.

(vii) A list of all the applicant's arrivals in and departures from the United States.

(viii) Proof of continuous residence in the United States.

(ix) Two photographs prepared in accordance with the specifications outlined in the instructions on the application form. The immigration officer to whom the application is submitted, however, may waive the photographs for just cause.

(3) Applicant under fourteen years old. An applicant under fourteen years old shall not submit Form G-325A, Biographic Information.

(d) Fingerprinting. After filing an application, each applicant 14 years of age or older shall be fingerprinted as prescribed in 8 CFR 103.16.

(e) Personal appearance. Each applicant, including an applicant under eighteen years of age, must submit his/her application in person. This requirement may be waived at the discretion of the immigration officer to whom the application is submitted because of confinement of age, physical infirmity, illiteracy, or other compelling reason.

(f) Interview. The applicant may be required to appear in person before an immigration officer prior to adjudication of the application to be interviewed under oath concerning his/her eligibility for creation of a record of lawful permanent residence.

(g) Decision. The decision regarding creation of a record of lawful permanent residence for an alien eligible for presumption of lawful admission for permanent residence or for a person born in the United States to a foreign diplomatic officer will be made by the district director having jurisdiction over the applicant's place of residence.

(h) **Date of record of lawful permanent residence —**

(1) Presumption of lawful admission for permanent residence. If the application is granted, the applicant's permanent residence will be recorded as of the date of the applicant's arrival in the United States under the conditions which caused him/her to be eligible for presumption of lawful admission for permanent residence.

(2) Lawful permanent residence as a person born in the United States under diplomatic status. If the application is granted, the applicant's permanent residence will be recorded as of his/her date of birth.

(i) Denied application. If the application is denied, the decision may not be appealed.

HISTORY:

[47 FR 941, Jan. 8, 1982.; 58 FR 48779, Sept. 20, 1993; 63 FR 12979, 12987, March 17, 1998; 74 FR 26933, 26940, June 5, 2009; 76 FR 53764, 53795, Aug. 29, 2011; 85 FR 46788, 46927, Aug. 3, 2020]

AUTHORITY:

(Secs. 101(a)(20), 103, 262, 264 of the Immigration and Nationality Act, as amended; 8 U.S.C. 1101(a)(20), 1103, 1302, 1304)

§ 264.4 [Reserved]

[NO TEXT IN ORIGINAL]

HISTORY:

[59 FR 1466, Jan. 11, 1994; 60 FR 40069, Aug. 7, 1995]

AUTHORITY:

(8 U.S.C. 1103, 1182, 1184, 1201, 1301-1305.)

§ 264.5 Application for a replacement Permanent Resident Card.

(a) Filing instructions. A request to replace a Permanent Resident Card must be filed in accordance with the appropriate form instructions and with the fee specified in 8 CFR 106.2.

(b) Permanent residents required to file. A permanent resident shall apply for a replacement Permanent Resident Card:

(1) When the previous card has been lost, stolen, or destroyed;

(2) When the existing card will be expiring within six months;

(3) When the existing card has been mutilated;

(4) When the bearer's name or other biographic information has been legally changed since issuance of the existing card;

(5) When the applicant is taking up actual residence in the United States after having been a commuter, or is a permanent resident taking up commuter status;

(6) When the applicant has been automatically converted to permanent resident status;

(7) When the previous card was issued but never received;

(8) When the bearer of the card reaches the age of 14 years, unless the existing card will expire prior to the bearer's 16th birthday; or

(9) If the existing card bears incorrect data on account of Service error.

(c) Other filings by a permanent resident.

(1) A permanent resident shall apply on the designated form to replace a prior edition of the alien registration card issued on Form AR-3, AR-103, or I-151.

(2) A permanent resident may apply on the designated form to replace any edition of the Permanent Resident Card for any other reason not specified in paragraphs (b) and (c)(1) of this section.

(d) Conditional permanent residents required to file. A conditional permanent resident whose card is expiring may apply to have the conditions on residence removed in accordance with 8 CFR 216.4 or 8 CFR 216.6. A conditional resident who seeks to replace a permanent resident card that is not expiring within 90 days may apply for a replacement card on the form prescribed by USCIS:

(1) To replace a card that was lost, stolen, or destroyed;

(2) To replace a card that was issued but never received;

(3) Where the prior card has been mutilated;

(4) Where the prior card is incorrect on account of Service error; or

(5) Where his or her name or other biographic data has changed since the card was issued.

(e) Supporting documentation.

(1) The prior Permanent Resident Card must be surrendered to USCIS if a new card is being requested in accordance with paragraphs (b)(2) through (5) and (b)(8) and (9) of this section.

(2) A request to replace a Permanent Resident Card filed pursuant to paragraph (b)(4) of this section must include evidence of the name change such as a court order or marriage certificate.

(3) A request to replace a Permanent Resident Card in order to change any other biographic data on the card must include documentary evidence verifying the new data.

(f) Decision. If an application is denied, the applicant shall be notified of the reasons for denial. No appeal shall lie from this decision.

(g) Eligibility for evidence of permanent residence while in deportation, exclusion, or removal proceedings. A person in deportation, exclusion, or removal proceedings is entitled to evidence of permanent resident status until ordered excluded, deported, or removed. USCIS will issue such evidence in the form of a temporary permanent resident document that will remain valid until the proceedings are concluded. Issuance of evidence of permanent residence to an alien who had permanent resident status when the proceedings commenced shall not affect those proceedings.

(h) Temporary evidence of registration. USCIS may issue temporary evidence of registration and lawful permanent resident status to a lawful permanent resident alien who is departing temporarily from the United States and has applied for issuance of a replacement permanent resident card if USCIS is unable to issue and deliver such card prior to the alien's contemplated return to the United States. The alien must surrender such temporary evidence upon receipt of his or her permanent resident card.

(i) Waiver of requirements. USCIS may waive the photograph, in person filing, and fingerprinting requirements of this section in cases of confinement due to advanced age or physical infirmity.

HISTORY:

[58 FR 48779, Sept. 20, 1993; 59 FR 1466, Jan. 11, 1994; 59 FR

33905, July 1, 1994; 63 FR 12979, 12987, Mar. 17, 1998, as corrected at 63 FR 17489, Apr. 9, 1998; 63 FR 70313, 70316, Dec. 21, 1998; 65 FR 57723, 57724, Sept. 26, 2000; 74 FR 26933, 26940, June 5, 2009; 76 FR 53764, 53795, Aug. 29, 2011; 85 FR 46788, 46927, Aug. 3, 2020; 89 FR 6194, 6399, Jan. 31, 2024]

§ 264.6 Application for a nonimmigrant arrival-departure record.

(a) Eligibility. USCIS may issue a new or replacement arrival-departure record to a nonimmigrant who seeks:

(1) To replace a lost or stolen record;

(2) To replace a mutilated record; or

(3) Was not issued an arrival-departure record pursuant to 8 CFR 235.1(h)(1)(i), (iii), (iv), (v), or (vi) when last admitted as a nonimmigrant, and has not since been issued such record but now requires one.

(b) Application. A nonimmigrant may request issuance or replacement of a nonimmigrant arrival-departure record by applying on the form designated by USCIS with the fee prescribed in 8 CFR 106.2 and in accordance with the form instructions.

(c) Processing. A pending application filed under paragraph (a) of this section is temporary evidence of registration. If the application is approved, USCIS will issue an arrival-departure document. There is no appeal from the denial of this application.

HISTORY:

[59 FR 1466, Jan. 11, 1994; 76 FR 53764, 53795, Aug. 29, 2011; 85 FR 46788, 46927, Aug. 3, 2020]

PART 265
NOTICES OF ADDRESS

Rule

AUTHORITY NOTE APPLICABLE TO ENTIRE PART:

AUTHORITY:

8 U.S.C. 1103 and 1305.

§ 265.1 Reporting change of address.

Except for those exempted by section 263(b) of the Act, all aliens in the United States required to register under section 262 of the Act must report each change of address and new address within 10 days of such change in accordance with instructions provided by USCIS.

HISTORY:

[47 FR 44239, Oct. 7, 1982; 76 FR 53764, 53796, Aug. 29, 2011]

PART 270
PENALTIES FOR DOCUMENT FRAUD

Rule

AUTHORITY NOTE APPLICABLE TO ENTIRE PART:

AUTHORITY:

8 U.S.C. 1101, 1103, and 1324c; Pub. L. 101-410, 104 Stat. 890, as amended by Pub. L. 104-134, 110 Stat. 1321 and Pub. L. 114-74, 129 Stat. 599.

§ 270.1 Definitions.

For the purpose of this part—

Document means an instrument on which is recorded, by means of letters, figures, or marks, matters which may be used to fulfill any requirement of the Act. The term "document" includes, but is not limited to, an application required to be filed under the Act and any other accompanying document or material;

Entity means any legal entity, including, but not limited to, a corporation, partnership, joint venture, governmental body, agency, proprietorship, or association, including an agent or anyone acting directly or indirectly in the interest thereof.

HISTORY:

[57 FR 33866, July 31, 1992]

§ 270.2 Enforcement procedures.

(a) Procedures for the filing of complaints. Any person or entity having knowledge of a violation or potential violation of section 274C of the Act may submit a signed, written complaint to the Service office having jurisdiction over the business or residence of the potential violator or the location where the violation occurred. The signed, written complaint must contain sufficient information to identify both the complainant and the alleged violator, including their names and addresses. The complaint should also contain detailed factual allegations relating to the potential violation including the date, time and place of the alleged violation and the specific act or conduct alleged to constitute a violation of the Act. Written complaints may be delivered either by mail to the appropriate Service office or by personally appearing before any immigration officer at a Service office.

(b) Investigation. When the Service receives complaints from a third party in accordance with paragraph (a) of this section, it shall investigate only those complaints which, on their face, have a substantial probability of validity. The Service may also conduct investigations for violations on its own initiative, and without having received a written complaint. If it is determined after investigation that the person or entity has violated section 274C of the Act, the Service may issue and serve upon the alleged violator a Notice of Intent to Fine.

(c) Issuance of a subpoena. Service officers shall have reasonable access to examine any relevant evidence of any person or entity being investigated. The Service may issue subpoenas pursuant to its authority under sections 235(a) and 287 of the Act, in accordance with the procedures set forth in § 287.4 of this chapter.

(d) Notice of Intent to Fine. The proceeding to assess administrative penalties under section 274C of the Act is commenced when the Service issues a Notice of

Intent to Fine. Service of this notice shall be accomplished by personal service pursuant to 8 CFR 103.8(a)(2). Service is effective upon receipt, as evidenced by the certificate of service or the certified mail return receipt. The person or entity identified in the Notice of Intent to Fine shall be known as the respondent. The Notice of Intent to Fine may be issued by an officer defined in § 242.1 of this chapter or by an INS port director designated by his or her district director.

(e) Contents of the Notice of Intent to Fine.

(1) The Notice of Intent to Fine shall contain the basis for the charge(s) against the respondent, the statutory provisions alleged to have been violated, and the monetary amount of the penalty the Service intends to impose.

(2) The Notice of Intent to Fine shall provide the following advisals to the respondent:

(i) That the person or entity has the right to representation by counsel of his or her own choice at no expense to the government;

(ii) That any statement given may be used against the person or entity;

(iii) That the person or entity has the right to request a hearing before an administrative law judge pursuant to 5 U.S.C. 554-557, and that such request must be filed with INS within 60 days from the service of the Notice of Intent to Fine; and

(iv) That if a written request for a hearing is not timely filed, the Service will issue a final order from which there is no appeal.

(f) Request for hearing before an administrative law judge. If a respondent contests the issuance of a Notice of Intent to Fine, the respondent must file with the INS, within 60 days of the Notice of Intent to Fine, a written request for a hearing before an administrative law judge. Any written request for a hearing submitted in a foreign language must be accompanied by an English language translation. A request for hearing is deemed filed when it is either received by the Service office designated in the Notice of Intent to Fine, or addressed to such office, stamped with the proper postage, and postmarked within the 60-day period. In computing the 60-day period prescribed by this section, the day of service of the Notice of Intent to Fine shall not be included. In the request for a hearing, the respondent may, but is not required to, respond to each allegation listed in the Notice of Intent to Fine. A respondent may waive the 60-day period in which to request a hearing before an administrative law judge and ask that the INS issue a final order from which there is no appeal. Prior to execution of the waiver, a respondent who is not a United States citizen will be advised that a waiver of a section 274C hearing will result in the issuance of a final order and that the respondent will be excludable and/or deportable from the United States pursuant to the Act.

(g) Failure to file a request for hearing. If the respondent does not file a written request for a hearing within 60 days of service of the Notice of Intent to Fine, the INS shall issue a final order from which there shall be no appeal.

(h) Issuance of the final order. A final order may be issued by an officer defined in § 242.1 of this chapter, by an INS port director designated by his or her district director, or by the Director of the INS National Fines Office.

(i) Service of the final order—

(1) Generally. Service of the final order shall be accomplished by personal service pursuant to 8 CFR 103.8(a)(2). Service is effective upon receipt, as evidenced by the certificate of service or the certified mail return receipt.

(2) Alternative provisions for service in a foreign country. When service is to be effected upon a party in a foreign country, it is sufficient if service of the final order is made: (i) In the manner prescribed by the law of the foreign country for service in that country in an action in any of its courts of general jurisdiction; or

(ii) As directed by the foreign authority in response to a letter rogatory, when service in either case is reasonably calculated to give actual notice; or

(iii) When applicable, pursuant to 8 CFR 103.8(a)(2).

Service is effective upon receipt of the final order. Proof of service may be made as prescribed by the law of the foreign country, or, when service is pursuant to 8 CFR 103.8(a)(2), as evidenced by the certificate of service or the certified mail return receipt.

(j) Declination to file charges for document fraud committed by refugees at the time of entry. The Service shall not issue a Notice of Intent to Fine for acts of document fraud committed by an alien pursuant to direct departure from a country in which the alien has a well-founded fear of persecution or from which there is a significant danger that the alien would be returned to a country in which the alien would have a well-founded fear of persecution, provided that the alien has presented himself or herself without delay to an INS officer and shown good cause for his or her illegal entry or presence. Other acts of document fraud committed by such an alien may result in the issuance of a Notice of Intent to Fine and the imposition of civil money penalties.

HISTORY:

[57 FR 33866, July 31, 1992; 76 FR 53764, 53796, Aug. 29, 2011]

§ 270.3 Penalties.

(a) Criminal penalties. Nothing in section 274C of the Act shall be construed to diminish or qualify any of the penalties available for activities prohibited by this section but proscribed as well in title 18, United States Code.

(b) Civil penalties. A person or entity may face civil penalties for a violation of section 274C of the Act. Civil penalties may be imposed by the Service or by an administrative law judge for violations under section 274C of the Act. The Service may charge multiple violations of section 274C of the Act in a single Notice of Intent to Fine, and may impose separate penalties for each such unlawful act in a single proceeding or determination. However, in determining whether an offense is a first offense or a subsequent offense, a finding of more than one violation in the course of a single proceeding or determination will be counted as a single offense.

(1) A respondent found by the Service or an administrative law judge to have violated section 274C of the Act shall be subject to an order:

(i) To cease and desist from such behavior; and

(ii) To pay a civil penalty as follows:

(A) First offense under section 274C(a)(1) through (4). Not less than $275 and not exceeding $2,200 for each fraudulent document or each proscribed activity described in section 274C(a)(1) through (4) of the Act before March 27, 2008; not less than $375 and not exceeding $3,200 for each fraudulent document or each proscribed activity described in section 274C(a)(1) through (4) of the Act on or after March 27, 2008, and on or before November 2, 2015; and not less than $590 and not exceeding $4,730 for each fraudulent document or each proscribed activity described in section 274C(a)(1) through (4) of the Act after November 2, 2015.

(B) First offense under section 274C(a)(5) or (6). Not less than $250 and not exceeding $2,000 for each fraudulent document or each proscribed activity described in section 274C(a)(5) or (6) of the Act before March 27, 2008; not less than $275 and not exceeding $2,200 for each fraudulent document or each proscribed activity described in section 274C(a)(5) or (6) of the Act on or after March 27, 2008, and on or before November 2, 2015; and not less than $500 and not exceeding $3,988 for each fraudulent document or each proscribed activity described in section 274C(a)(5) or (6) of the Act after November 2, 2015.

(C) Subsequent offenses under section 274C(a)(1) through (4). Not less than $2,200 and not more than $5,500 for each fraudulent document or each proscribed activity described in section 274C(a)(1) through (4) of the Act before March 27, 2008; not less than $3,200 and not exceeding $6,500 for each fraudulent document or each proscribed activity described in section 274C(a)(1) through (4) of the Act occurring on or after March 27, 2008 and on or before November 2, 2015; and not less than $4,730 and not more than $11,823 for each fraudulent document or each proscribed activity described in section 274C(a)(1) through (4) of the Act after November 2, 2015.

(D) Subsequent offenses under section 274C(a)(5) or (6). Not less than $2,000 and not more than $5,000 for each fraudulent document or each proscribed activity described in section 274C(a)(5) or (6) of the Act before March 27, 2008; not less than $2,200 and not exceeding $5,500 for each fraudulent document or each proscribed activity described in section 274C(a)(5) or (6) of the Act occurring on or after March 27, 2008, and on or before November 2, 2015; and not less than $3,988 and not more than $9,970 for each fraudulent document or each proscribed activity described in section 274C(a)(5) or (6) of the Act after November 2, 2015.

(2) Where an order is issued to a respondent composed of distinct, physically separate subdivisions each of which provides separately for the hiring, recruiting, or referring for a fee for employment (without reference to the practices of, and not under the common control of or common control with, another subdivision), each subdivision shall be considered a separate person or entity.

HISTORY:

[57 FR 33866, July 31, 1992; 64 FR 47099, 47101, Aug. 30, 1999; 73 FR 10130, 10135, Feb. 26, 2008; 81 FR 42987, 43001, July 1, 2016, as confirmed and amended at 82 FR 8571, 8579, Jan. 27, 2017; 83 FR 13826, 13834, Apr. 2, 2018; 84 FR 13499, 13508, Apr. 5, 2019; 85 FR 36469, 36478, June 17, 2020; 86 FR 57532, 57539, Oct. 18, 2021; 87 FR 1317, 1326, Jan. 11, 2022; 88 FR 2175, 2182, Jan. 13, 2023; 89 FR 53849, 53858, June 28, 2024; 90 FR 1, 9, Jan. 2, 2025]

PART 271

DILIGENT AND REASONABLE EFFORTS TO PREVENT THE UNAUTHORIZED ENTRY OF ALIENS BY THE OWNERS OF RAILROAD LINES, INTERNATIONAL BRIDGES OR TOLL ROADS

Rule

§ 271.1 Procedures for inspections.

(a) Applicability. The following terms and conditions apply to those owners or operators of railroad lines, international bridges, or toll roads, which provide a means for an alien to come to the United States.

(b) Inspection of facility. Based upon a written request by the owners or operators, the INS district director or his designee shall inspect the facility or method utilized in order to ensure that owners and operators have acted diligently in taking adequate steps to prevent the unlawful entry of aliens into the United States. Such measures may include but are not necessarily limited to fencing, barricades, lighting, or security guards. If the district director determines that preventive measures are inadequate, he or she shall advise the owners or operators in writing, citing the reasons for such determination. If the owners or operators believe the requirements of the district director to be excessive or unnecessary, they may request that the Regional Commissioner having jurisdiction over the location where the facility is located, review the district director's requirements. The Regional Commissioner shall advise the owners or operators in writing of the results of his or her review.

(c) Preventive measures and certification. Upon a determination by the district director that reasonable and adequate preventive measures have been taken by the owners and operators, he or she shall certify that the owners and operators shall not be liable for the penalty described in section 271(a), so long as the facility or method utilized is maintained in the condition in which approved and certified.

(d) Revocation of certification. The District Director having jurisdiction over the location where the facility is located, in his or her discretion, may at any time, conduct an inspection of said facility to determine if any violation is occurring. If the facility is found to be not in compliance, said certification will be revoked.

HISTORY:

[53 FR 26036, July 11, 1988]

AUTHORITY:

8 U.S.C. 1103 and 1321.

PART 273

CARRIER RESPONSIBILITIES AT FOREIGN PORTS OF EMBARKATION; REDUCING, REFUNDING, OR WAIVING FINES UNDER SECTION 273 OF THE ACT

Rule

AUTHORITY NOTE APPLICABLE TO ENTIRE PART:

AUTHORITY:

8 U.S.C. 1103, 1323; 8 CFR part 2.

§ 273.1 General.

In any fines case in which a fine is imposed under section 273 of the Act involving an alien brought to the United States after December 24, 1994, the carrier may seek a reduction, refund, or waiver of fine, as provided for by section 273(e) of the Act, in accordance with this part. The provisions of section 273(e) of the Act and of this part do not apply to any fine imposed under any provision other than section 273 (a)(1) and (b) of the Act.

HISTORY:

[63 FR 23643, 23655, Apr. 30, 1998]

§ 273.2 Definition.

As used in this part, the term Carrier means an individual or organization engaged in transporting passengers or goods for hire to the United States.

HISTORY:

[63 FR 23643, 23655, Apr. 30, 1998]

§ 273.3 Screening procedures.

(a) Applicability. The terms and conditions contained in paragraph (b) of this section apply to those owners, operators, or agents of carriers which transport passengers to the United States.

(b) Procedures at ports of embarkation. At each port of embarkation carriers shall take reasonable steps to prevent the boarding of improperly documented aliens destined to the United States by taking the following steps:

(1) Screening of passengers by carrier personnel prior to boarding and examination of their travel documents to ensure that:

(i) The passport or travel document presented is not expired and is valid for entry into the United States;

(ii) The passenger is the rightful holder;

(iii) If the passenger requires a visa, the visa is valid for the holder and any other accompanying passengers named in the passport; and

(iv) Passengers described in part 215, subpart B, of this chapter have complied with EVUS requirements as appropriate.

(2) Refusing to board any passenger determined to be improperly documented. Failure to refuse boarding when advised to do so by a Service or Consular Officer may be considered by the Service as a factor in its evaluation of applications under § 273.5.

(3) Implementing additional safeguards such as, but not necessarily limited to, the following:

(i) For instances in which the carrier suspects fraud, assessing the adequacy of the documents presented by asking additional, pertinent questions or by taking other appropriate steps to corroborate the identity of passengers, such as requesting secondary information.

(ii) Conducting a second check of passenger documents, when necessary at high-risk ports of embarkation, at the time of boarding to verify that all passengers are properly documented consistent with paragraph (b)(1) of this section. This includes a recheck of documents at the final foreign port of embarkation for all passengers, including those originally boarded at a prior stop or who are being transported to the United States under the Transit Without Visa (TWOV) or International-to-International (ITI) Programs.

(iii) Providing a reasonable level of security during the boarding process so that passengers are unable to circumvent any carrier document checks.

(4) Transmitting visa numbers. Carriers must transmit to U.S. Customs and Border Protection the visa number for any passenger who requires a visa. The visa number must be transmitted using the Advance Passenger Information System, consistent with the procedural requirements for transmission of electronic passenger manifests in 19 CFR parts 4 (vessel) and 122 (aircraft).

HISTORY:

[63 FR 23643, 23655, Apr. 30, 1998; 81 FR 72481, 72493, Oct. 20, 2016]

§ 273.4 Demonstration by carrier that screening requirements were met.

(a) To be eligible to apply for reduction, refund, or waiver of a fine, the carrier shall provide evidence that it screened all passengers on the conveyance for the instant flight or voyage in accordance with the procedures listed in § 273.3.

(b) The Service may, at any time, conduct an inspection of a carrier's document screening procedures at ports of embarkation to determine compliance with the procedures listed in § 273.3, to the extent permitted by the local competent authority responsible for port access or security. If necessary, the carrier shall use its good offices to obtain this permission from the local authority. If the carrier's port of embarkation operation is found not to be in compliance, the carrier will be notified by the Service that it will not be eligible for refund, reduction, or waiver of fines under section 273(e) of the Act unless the carrier can establish that lack of compliance was beyond the carrier's control.

HISTORY:
[63 FR 23643, 23655, Apr. 30, 1998]

§ 273.5 General criteria used for reduction, refund, or waiver of fines.

(a) Upon application by the carrier, the Service shall determine whether circumstances exist which would justify a reduction, refund, or waiver of fines pursuant to section 273(e) of the Act.

(b) Applications for reduction, refund, or waiver of fine under section 273(e) of the Act shall be made in accordance with the procedures outlined in 8 CFR 280.12 and 8 CFR 280.51.

(c) In determining the amount of the fine reduction, refund, or waiver, the Service shall consider:

(1) The effectiveness of the carrier's screening procedures;

(2) The carrier's history of fines violations, including fines, liquidated damages, and user fee payment records; and,

(3) The existence of any extenuating circumstances.

HISTORY:
[63 FR 23643, 23655, Apr. 30, 1998]

§ 273.6 Memorandum of Understanding.

(a) Carriers may apply to enter into a Memorandum of Understanding (MOU) with the Service for an automatic reduction, refund, or waiver of fines imposed under section 273 of the Act.

(b) Carriers signatory to an MOU will not be required to apply for reduction, refund, or waiver of fines in accordance with the procedures outlined in 8 CFR 280.12 and 8 CFR 280.51, but will follow procedures as set forth in the MOU.

(c) Carriers signatory to an MOU will have fines reduced, refunded, or waived according to performance standards enumerated in the MOU or as determined by the Service.

(d) Carriers signatory to an MOU are not precluded from seeking additional reduction, refund, or waiver of fines in accordance with the procedures outlined in 8 CFR 280.12 and 8 CFR 280.51.

HISTORY:
[63 FR 23643, 23655, Apr. 30, 1998]

PART 274
SEIZURE AND FORFEITURE OF CONVEYANCES

Rule

AUTHORITY NOTE APPLICABLE TO ENTIRE PART:

AUTHORITY:
8 U.S.C. 1103, 1324(b); 18 U.S.C. 983, 19 U.S.C. 66, 1600, 1618, 1619, 1624; 22 U.S.C. 401; 31 U.S.C. 5321; 49 U.S.C. 80304.

§ 274.1 Seizure and forfeiture authority.

Any officer of Customs and Border Protection or Immigration and Customs Enforcement may seize and forfeit any property that has been or is being used in the commission of a violation of any statutory authority involving the unlawful introduction of aliens, contraband or proceeds of such introduction, pursuant to, but not limited to, section 274(a) of the Act (8 U.S.C. 1324(a)). All seizures and forfeitures in such cases will be administered in accordance with 19 CFR parts 162 and 171.

HISTORY:
[53 FR 43187, Oct. 26, 1988; 73 FR 9010, 9011, Feb. 19, 2008, as confirmed at 75 FR 37707, 37708, June 30, 2010]

§ 274.2 Delegation of authority.

All powers provided to Fines, Penalties and Forfeitures Officers in 19 CFR parts 162 and 171 are provided to the Chief, Office of Border Patrol or his designees, for purposes of administering seizures and forfeitures made by Border Patrol Officers.

HISTORY:
[53 FR 43187, Oct. 26, 1988; 73 FR 9010, 9011, Feb. 19, 2008, as confirmed at 75 FR 37707, 37708, June 30, 2010]

§ 274.3 [This section was removed. See 73 FR 9010, 9011, Feb. 19, 2008, as confirmed at 75 FR 37707, 37708, June 30, 2010.]

[NO TEXT IN ORIGINAL]

HISTORY:
[53 FR 43187, Oct. 26, 1988]

AUTHORITY:
(8 U.S.C. 1103, 1324(b).)

§ 274.4 [This section was removed. See 73 FR 9010, 9011, Feb. 19, 2008, as confirmed at 75 FR 37707, 37708, June 30, 2010.]

[NO TEXT IN ORIGINAL]

HISTORY:
[53 FR 43187, Oct. 26, 1988]

AUTHORITY:
(8 U.S.C. 1103, 1324(b).)

§ 274.5 [This section was removed. See 73 FR 9010, 9011, Feb. 19, 2008, as confirmed at 75 FR 37707, 37708, June 30, 2010.]

[NO TEXT IN ORIGINAL]

HISTORY:
[53 FR 43187, Oct. 26, 1988]

AUTHORITY:
(8 U.S.C. 1103, 1324(b).)

§ 274.6 [This section was removed. See 73 FR 9010, 9011, Feb. 19, 2008, as confirmed at 75 FR 37707, 37708, June 30, 2010.]

[NO TEXT IN ORIGINAL]

HISTORY:
[53 FR 43187, Oct. 26, 1988]

AUTHORITY:
(8 U.S.C. 1103, 1324(b).)

§ 274.7 [This section was removed. See 73 FR 9010, 9011, Feb. 19, 2008, as confirmed at 75 FR 37707, 37708, June 30, 2010.]

[NO TEXT IN ORIGINAL]

HISTORY:
[53 FR 43187, Oct. 26, 1988]

AUTHORITY:
(8 U.S.C. 1103, 1324(b).)

§ 274.8 [This section was removed. See 73 FR 9010, 9011, Feb. 19, 2008, as confirmed at 75 FR 37707, 37708, June 30, 2010.]

[NO TEXT IN ORIGINAL]

HISTORY:
[53 FR 43187, Oct. 26, 1988]

AUTHORITY:
(8 U.S.C. 1103, 1324(b).)

§ 274.9 [This section was removed. See 73 FR 9010, 9011, Feb. 19, 2008, as confirmed at 75 FR 37707, 37708, June 30, 2010.]

[NO TEXT IN ORIGINAL]

HISTORY:
[53 FR 43187, Oct. 26, 1988, as amended at 56 FR 8686, Mar. 1, 1991]

AUTHORITY:
(8 U.S.C. 1103, 1324(b).)

§ 274.10 [This section was removed. See 73 FR 9010, 9011, Feb. 19, 2008, as confirmed at 75 FR 37707, 37708, June 30, 2010.]

[NO TEXT IN ORIGINAL]

HISTORY:
[53 FR 43187, Oct. 26, 1988, as amended at 56 FR 8686, Mar. 1, 1991]

AUTHORITY:
(8 U.S.C. 1103, 1324(b).)

§ 274.11 [This section was removed. See 73 FR 9010, 9011, Feb. 19, 2008, as confirmed at 75 FR 37707, 37708, June 30, 2010.]

[NO TEXT IN ORIGINAL]

HISTORY:
[53 FR 43187, Oct. 26, 1988, as amended at 56 FR 8686, Mar. 1, 1991]

AUTHORITY:
(8 U.S.C. 1103, 1324(b).)

§ 274.12 [This section was removed. See 73 FR 9010, 9011, Feb. 19, 2008, as confirmed at 75 FR 37707, 37708, June 30, 2010.]

[NO TEXT IN ORIGINAL]

HISTORY:
[53 FR 43187, Oct. 26, 1988, as amended at 56 FR 8686, Mar. 1, 1991]

AUTHORITY:
(8 U.S.C. 1103, 1324(b).)

§ 274.13 [This section was removed. See 73 FR 9010, 9011, Feb. 19, 2008, as confirmed at 75 FR 37707, 37708, June 30, 2010.]

[NO TEXT IN ORIGINAL]

HISTORY:
[53 FR 43187, Oct. 26, 1988]

AUTHORITY:
(8 U.S.C. 1103, 1324(b).)

§ 274.14 [This section was removed. See 73 FR 9010, 9011, Feb. 19, 2008, as confirmed at 75 FR 37707, 37708, June 30, 2010.]

[NO TEXT IN ORIGINAL]

HISTORY:
[53 FR 43187, Oct. 26, 1988]

AUTHORITY:
(8 U.S.C. 1103, 1324(b).)

§ 274.15 [This section was removed. See 73 FR 9010, 9011, Feb. 19, 2008, as confirmed at 75 FR 37707, 37708, June 30, 2010.]

[NO TEXT IN ORIGINAL]

HISTORY:
[53 FR 43187, Oct. 26, 1988]

AUTHORITY:
(8 U.S.C. 1103, 1324(b).)

§ 274.16 [This section was removed. See 73 FR 9010, 9011, Feb. 19, 2008, as confirmed at 75 FR 37707, 37708, June 30, 2010.]

[NO TEXT IN ORIGINAL]

HISTORY:
[53 FR 43187, Oct. 26, 1988]

AUTHORITY:
(8 U.S.C. 1103, 1324(b).)

§ 274.17 [This section was removed. See 73 FR 9010, 9011, Feb. 19, 2008, as confirmed at 75 FR 37707, 37708, June 30, 2010.]

[NO TEXT IN ORIGINAL]

HISTORY:
[53 FR 43187, Oct. 26, 1988]

AUTHORITY:
(8 U.S.C. 1103, 1324(b).)

§ 274.18 [This section was removed. See 73 FR 9010, 9011, Feb. 19, 2008, as confirmed at 75 FR 37707, 37708, June 30, 2010.]

[NO TEXT IN ORIGINAL]

HISTORY:
[53 FR 43187, Oct. 26, 1988]

AUTHORITY:
(8 U.S.C. 1103, 1324(b).)

§ 274.19 [This section was removed. See 73 FR 9010, 9011, Feb. 19, 2008, as confirmed at 75 FR 37707, 37708, June 30, 2010.]

[NO TEXT IN ORIGINAL]

HISTORY:
[53 FR 43187, Oct. 26, 1988]

AUTHORITY:
(8 U.S.C. 1103, 1324(b).)

§ 274.20 [This section was removed. See 73 FR 9010, 9011, Feb. 19, 2008, as confirmed at 75 FR 37707, 37708, June 30, 2010.]

[NO TEXT IN ORIGINAL]

HISTORY:
[53 FR 43187, Oct. 26, 1988]

AUTHORITY:
(8 U.S.C. 1103, 1324(b).)

PART 274A —

CONTROL OF EMPLOYMENT OF ALIENS

Subpart A. Employer Requirements

Rule

AUTHORITY NOTE APPLICABLE TO ENTIRE PART:

AUTHORITY:
8 U.S.C. 1101, 1103, 1105a, 1324a; 48 U.S.C. 1806; Pub. L. 101–410, 104 Stat. 890, as amended by Pub. L. 114–74, 129 Stat. 599; Title VII of Pub. L. 110–229, 122 Stat. 754; Pub. L. 115–218, 132 Stat. 1547; 8 CFR part 2.

Subpart A

Employer Requirements

§ 274a.1 Definitions.

For the purpose of this part —

(a) The term unauthorized alien means, with respect to employment of an alien at a particular time, that the alien is not at that time either: (1) Lawfully admitted for permanent residence, or (2) authorized to be so employed by this Act or by the Attorney General;

(b) The term entity means any legal entity, including but not limited to, a corporation, partnership, joint venture, governmental body, agency, proprietorship, or association;

(c) The term hire means the actual commencement of employment of an employee for wages or other remuneration. For purposes of section 274A(a)(4) of the Act and 8 CFR 274a.5, a hire occurs when a person or entity uses a contract, subcontract, or exchange entered into, renegotiated, or extended after November 6, 1986 (or, with respect to the Commonwealth of the Northern Mariana Islands, after the transition program effective date as defined in 8 CFR 1.1), to obtain the labor of an alien in the United States, knowing that the alien is an unauthorized alien;

(d) The term refer for a fee means the act of sending or directing a person or transmitting documentation or information to another, directly or indirectly, with the intent of obtaining employment in the United States for such person, for remuneration whether on a retainer or contingency basis; however, this term does not include union hiring halls that refer union members or non-union individuals who pay union membership dues;

(e) The term recruit for a fee means the act of soliciting a person, directly or indirectly, and referring that person to another with the intent of obtaining employment for that person, for remuneration whether on a retainer or contingency basis; however, this term does not include union hiring halls that refer union members or non-union individuals who pay union membership dues;

(f) The term employee means an individual who provides services or labor for an employer for wages or other remuneration but does not mean independent contractors as defined in paragraph (j) of this section or those engaged in casual domestic employment as stated in paragraph (h) of this section;

(g) The term employer means a person or entity, including an agent or anyone acting directly or indirectly in the interest thereof, who engages the services or labor of an employee to be performed in the United States for wages or other remuneration. In the case of an independent contractor or contract labor or services, the term employer shall mean the independent contractor or contractor and not the person or entity using the contract labor;

(h) The term employment means any service or labor performed by an employee for an employer within the United States, including service or labor performed on a vessel or aircraft that has arrived in the United States and has been inspected, or otherwise included within the provisions of the Anti-Reflagging Act codified at 46 U.S.C. 8704, but not including duties performed by nonimmigrant crewmen defined in sections 101 (a)(10) and (a)(15)(D) of the Act. However, employment does not include casual employment by individuals who provide domestic service in a private home that is sporadic, irregular or intermittent;

(i) The term State employment agency means any State government unit designated to cooperate with the United States Employment Service in the operation of the public employment service system;

(j) The term independent contractor includes individuals or entities who carry on independent business, contract to do a piece of work according to their own means and methods, and are subject to control only as to results. Whether an individual or entity is an independent contractor, regardless of what the individual or entity calls itself, will be determined on a case-by-case basis. Factors to be considered in that determination include, but are not limited to, whether the individual or entity: supplies the tools or materials; makes services available to the general public; works for a number of clients at the same time; has an opportunity for profit or loss as a result of labor or services provided; invests in the facilities for work; directs the order or sequence in which the work is to be done and determines the hours during which the work is to be done. The use of labor or services of an independent contractor are subject to the restrictions in section 274A(a)(4) of the Act and § 274a.5 of this part;

(k) The term pattern or practice means regular, repeated, and intentional activities, but does not include isolated, sporadic, or accidental acts;

(l)(1) The term knowing includes not only actual knowledge but also knowledge which may fairly be inferred through notice of certain facts and circumstances which would lead a person, through the exercise of reasonable care, to know about a certain condition. Constructive knowledge may include, but is not limited to, situations where an employer:

(i) Fails to complete or improperly completes the Employment Eligibility Verification Form, I-9;

(ii) Has information available to it that would indicate that the alien is not authorized to work, such as Labor Certification and/or an Application for Prospective Employer; or

(iii) Acts with reckless and wanton disregard for the legal consequences of permitting another individual to introduce an unauthorized alien into its work force or to act on its behalf.

(2) Knowledge that an employee is unauthorized may not be inferred from an employee's foreign appearance or accent. Nothing in this definition should be interpreted as permitting an employer to request more or different documents than are required under section 274(b) of the Act or to refuse to honor documents tendered that on their face reasonably appear to be genuine and to relate to the individual.

HISTORY:

[52 FR 16221, May 1, 1987, as amended at 53 FR 8612, Mar. 16, 1988; 55 FR 25931, June 25, 1990; 56 FR 41783, Aug. 23, 1991; 72 FR 45611, 45623, Aug. 15, 2007, as confirmed and amended at 73 FR 63843, 63867, Oct. 28, 2008; 74 FR 51447, 51452, Oct. 7, 2009; 74 FR 55726, 55739, Oct. 28, 2009]

§ 274a.2 Verification of identity and employment authorization.

(a) General. This section establishes requirements and procedures for compliance by persons or entities when hiring, or when recruiting or referring for a fee, or when continuing to employ individuals in the United States.

(1) Recruiters and referrers for a fee. For purposes of complying with section 274A(b) of the Act and this section, all references to recruiters and referrers for a fee are limited to a person or entity who is either an agricultural association, agricultural employer, or farm labor contractor (as defined in section 3 of the Migrant and Seasonal Agricultural Worker Protection Act, Pub. L. 97-470 (29 U.S.C. 1802)).

(2) Verification form. Form I–9, Employment Eligibility Verification Form, is used in complying with the requirements of this 8 CFR 274a.1– 274a.11. Form I–9 can be in paper or electronic format. A fillable electronic Form I–9 as well as a paper format Form I–9 may be obtained and downloaded from http://www.uscis.gov. Paper forms may also be ordered at https:// www.uscis-.gov/forms/forms-by-mail or by contacting the USCIS Contact Center at 1–800–375–5283 or 1–800–767–1833 (TTY). Alternatively, Form I–9 can be electronically generated or retained, provided that the resulting form is legible; there is no change to the name, content, or sequence of the data elements and instructions; no additional data elements or language are inserted; and the standards specified under 8 CFR 274a.2(e), (f), (g), (h), and (i), as applicable, are met. When copying or printing the paper Form I–9, the text of the two-sided form may be reproduced by making either double-sided or singlesided copies.

(3) Attestation Under Penalty and Perjury. In conjunction with completing the Form I-9, an employer or recruiter or referrer for a fee must examine documents that evidence the identity and employment authorization of the individual. The employer or recruiter or referrer for a fee and the individual must each complete an attestation on the Form I-9 under penalty of perjury.

(b) Employment verification requirements —

(1) Examination of documents and completion of Form I-9

(i) A person or entity that hires or recruits or refers for a fee an individual for employment must ensure that the individual properly:

(A) Completes section 1 — "Employee Information and Verification" — on the Form I-9 at the time of hire and signs the attestation with a handwritten or electronic signature in accordance with paragraph (h) of this section; or if an individual is unable to complete the Form I-9 or needs it translated, someone may assist him or her. The preparer or translator must read the Form I-9 to the individual, assist him or her in completing Section 1 — "Employee Information and Verification," and have the individual sign or mark the Form I-9 by a handwritten signature, or an electronic signature in accordance with paragraph (h) of this section, in the appropriate place; and

(B) Present to the employer or the recruiter or referrer for a fee documentation as set forth in paragraph (b)(1)(v) of this section establishing his or her identity and employment authorization within the time limits set forth in paragraphs (b)(1)(ii) through (b)(1)(v) of this section.

(ii) Except as provided in paragraph (b)(1)(viii) of this section, an employer, his or her agent, or anyone acting directly or indirectly in the interest thereof, must within three business days of the hire:

(A) Physically examine (or otherwise examine pursuant to an alternative procedure authorized by the Secretary under paragraph (b)(1)(ix) of this section) the documentation presented by the individual establishing identity and employment authorization as set forth in paragraph (b)(1)(v) of this section and ensure that the documents presented appear to be genuine and to relate to the individual; and

(B) Complete section 2 — "Employer Review and Verification" — on the Form I-9 within three business days of the hire and sign the attestation with a handwritten signature or electronic signature in accordance with paragraph (i) of this section.

(iii) An employer who hires an individual for employment for a duration of less than three business days must comply with paragraphs (b)(1)(ii)(A) and (b)(1)(ii)(B) of this section at the time of the hire. An employer may not accept a receipt, as described in paragraph (b)(1)(vi) of this section, in lieu of the required document if the employment is for less than three business days.

(iv) A recruiter or referrer for a fee for employment must comply with paragraphs (b)(1)(ii)(A) and (b)(1)(ii)(B) of this section within three business days of the date the referred individual is hired by the employer. Recruiters and referrers may designate agents to complete the employment verification procedures on their behalf including but not limited to notaries, national associations, or employers. If a recruiter or referrer designates an employer to complete the employment verification procedures, the employer need only provide the recruiter or referrer with a photocopy or printed electronic image of the Form I-9, electronic Form I-9, or a Form I-9 on microfilm or microfiche.

(v) The individual may present either an original document which establishes both employment authorization and identity, or an original document which establishes employment authorization and a separate original document which establishes identity. Only unexpired documents are acceptable. The identification number and expiration date (if any) of all documents must be noted in the appropriate space provided on the Form I-9.

(A) The following documents, so long as they appear to relate to the individual presenting the document, are acceptable to evidence both identity and employment authorization:

(1) A United States passport;

(2) An Alien Registration Receipt Card or Permanent Resident Card (Form I-551);

(3) A foreign passport that contains a temporary I-551 stamp, or temporary I-551 printed notation on a machine-readable immigrant visa;

(4) An Employment Authorization Document which contains a photograph (Form I-766);

(5) In the case of an individual who is employment-authorized incident to status or parole with a specific employer, a foreign passport with an Arrival/Departure Record, Form I-94 (as defined in 8 CFR 1.4) or Form I-94A, bearing the same name as the passport and containing an endorsement by DHS indicating such employment-authorized status or parole, as long as the period of endorsement has not yet expired and the employment is not in conflict with the individual's employment-authorized status or parole;

(6) A passport from the Federated States of Micronesia (FSM) or the Republic of the Marshall Islands (RMI) with Form I-94 or Form I-94A indicating nonimmigrant admission under the Compact of Free Association Between the United States and the FSM or RMI;

(7) In the case of an individual lawfully enlisted for military service in the Armed Forces under 10 U.S.C. 504, a military identification card issued to such individual may be accepted only by the Armed Forces.

(B) The following documents are acceptable to establish identity only:

(1) For individuals 16 years of age or older:

(i) A driver's license or identification card containing a photograph, issued by a state (as defined in section 101(a)(36) of the Act) or an outlying possession of the United States (as defined by section 101(a)(29) of the Act). If the driver's license or identification card does not contain a photograph, identifying information shall be included such as: name, date of birth, sex, height, color of eyes, and address;

(ii) School identification card with a photograph;

(iii) Voter's registration card;

(vi) U.S. military card or draft record;

(v) Identification card issued by federal, state, or local government agencies or entities. If the identification card does not contain a photograph, identifying information shall be included such as: name, date of birth, sex, height, color of eyes, and address;

(vi) Military dependent's identification card;

(vii) Native American tribal documents;

(viii) United States Coast Guard Merchant Mariner Card;

(ix) Driver's license issued by a Canadian government authority;

(2) For individuals under age 18 who are unable to produce a document listed in paragraph (b)(1)(v)(B)(1) of this section, the following documents are acceptable to establish identity only:

(i) School record or report card;

(ii) Clinic doctor or hospital record;

(iii) Daycare or nursery school record.

(3) Minors under the age of 18 who are unable to produce one of the identity documents listed in paragraph (b)(1)(v)(B) (1) or (2) of this section are exempt from producing one of the enumerated identity documents if:

(i) The minor's parent or legal guardian completes on the Form I-9 Section 1 — "Employee Information and Verification" and in the space for the minor's signature, the parent or legal guardian writes the words, "minor under age 18."

(ii) The minor's parent or legal guardian completes on the Form I-9 the "Preparer/Translator certification."

(iii) The employer or the recruiter or referrer for a fee writes in Section 2 — "Employer Review and Verification" under List B in the space after the words "Document Identification X #" the words, "minor under age 18."

(4) Individuals with handicaps, who are unable to produce one of the identity documents listed in paragraph (b)(1)(v)(B) (1) or (2) of this section, who are being placed into employment by a nonprofit organization, association or as part of a rehabilitation program, may follow the procedures for establishing identity provided in this section for minors under the age of 18, substituting where appropriate, the term "special placement" for "minor under age 18", and permitting, in addition to a parent or legal guardian, a representative from the nonprofit organization, association or rehabilitation program placing the individual into a position of employment, to fill out and sign in the appropriate section, the Form I-9. For purposes of this section the term individual with handicaps means any person who

(i) Has a physical or mental impairment which substantially limits one or more of such person's major life activities,

(ii) Has a record of such impairment, or

(iii) Is regarded as having such impairment.

(C) The following are acceptable documents to establish employment authorization only:

(1) A Social Security account number card other than one that specifies on the face that the issuance of the card does not authorize employment in the United States;

(2) Certification or report of birth issued by the Department of State, including Forms FS-545, DS-1350, FS-240;

(3) An original or certified copy of a birth certificate issued by a State, county, municipal authority or outlying possession of the United States bearing an official seal;

(4) Native American tribal document;

(5) United States Citizen Identification Card, Form I-197;

(6) Identification card for use of resident citizen in the United States, Form I-179;

(7) An employment authorization document issued by the Department of Homeland Security.

(D) The following are acceptable documents to establish both identity and employment authorization in the Commonwealth of the Northern Mariana Islands only, for a two-year period starting from the transition program effective date (as defined in 8 CFR 1.1), in addition to those documents listed in paragraph (b)(1)(v)(A) of this section:

(1) In the case of an alien with employment authorization in the Commonwealth of the Northern Mariana Islands incident to status for a period of up to two years following the transition program effective date that is unrestricted or otherwise authorizes a change of employer:

(i) The unexpired foreign passport and an Alien Entry Permit with red band issued to the alien by the Office of the Attorney General, Division of Immigration of the Commonwealth of the Northern Mariana Islands before the transition program effective date, as long as the period of employment authorization has not yet expired, or

(ii) An unexpired foreign passport and temporary work authorization letter issued by the Department of Labor of the Commonwealth of the Northern Mariana Islands before the transition program effective date, and containing the name and photograph of the individual, as long as the period of employment authorization has not yet expired and the proposed employment is not in conflict with any restrictions or limitations identified on the Temporary Work Authorization letter;

(iii) An unexpired foreign passport and a permanent resident card issued by the Commonwealth of the Northern Mariana Islands.

(2) [Reserved]

(vi) Special rules for receipts. Except as provided in paragraph (b)(1)(iii) of this section, unless the individual indicates or the employer or recruiter or referrer for a fee has actual or constructive knowledge that the individual is not authorized to work, an employer or recruiter or referrer for a fee must accept a receipt for the application for a replacement document or a document described in paragraphs (b)(1)(vi)(B)((1) and (b)(1)(vi)(C)((1) of this section in lieu of the required document in order to comply with any requirement to examine documentation imposed by this section, in the following circumstances:

(A) Application for a replacement document. The individual:

(1) Is unable to provide the required document within the time specified in this section because the document was lost, stolen, or damaged;

(2) Presents a receipt for the application for the replacement document within the time specified in this section; and

(3) Presents the replacement document within 90 days of the hire or, in the case of reverification, the date employment authorization expires; or

(B) Form I-94 or I-94A indicating temporary evidence of permanent resident status. The individual indicates in section 1 of the Form I-9 that he or she is a lawful permanent resident and the individual:

(1) Presents the arrival portion of Form I-94 or Form I-94A containing an unexpired "Temporary I-551" stamp and a photograph of the individual, which is designated for purposes of this section as a receipt for Form I-551; and

(2) Presents the Form I-551 by the expiration date of the "Temporary I-551" stamp or, if the stamp has no expiration date, within one year from the issuance date of the arrival portion of the Form I-94 or Form I-94A; or

(C) Form I-94 or I-94A indicating refugee status. The individual indicates in section 1 of the Form I-9 that he or she is an alien authorized to work and the individual:

(1) Presents the departure portion of Form I-94 or I-94A containing an unexpired refugee admission stamp, which is designated for purposes of this section as a receipt for the Form I-766, or a social security account number card that contains no employment restrictions; and

(2) Presents, within 90 days of the hire or, in the case of reverification, the date employment authorization expires, either an unexpired Form I-766, or a social security account number card that contains no employment restrictions and a document described under paragraph (b)(1)(v)(B) of this section.

(vii) If an individual's employment authorization expires, the employer, recruiter or referrer for a fee must reverify on the Form I-9 to reflect that the individual is still authorized to work in the United States; otherwise, the individual may no longer be employed, recruited, or referred. Reverification on the Form I-9 must occur not later than the date work authorization expires and must comply with the applicable document presentation and examination procedures in paragraphs (b)(1)(ii)(A) and (b)(1)(ix) of this section, and form instructions. If an Employment Authorization Document (Form I-766) as described in 8 CFR 274a.13(d) was presented for completion of the Form I-9 in combination with a Notice of Action (Form I-797C), stating that the original Employment Authorization Document has been automatically extended, reverification applies upon the expiration of the automatically extended validity period under 8 CFR 274a.13(d) and not upon the expiration date indicated on the face of the individual's Employment Authorization Document. In order to reverify on the Form I-9, the employee or referred individual must present a document that either shows continuing employment eligibility or is a new grant of work authorization. The employer or the recruiter or referrer for a fee must review this document, and if it appears to be genuine and relate to the individual, reverify by noting the document's identification number and expiration date, if any, on the Form I-9 and signing the attestation by a handwritten signature or electronic signature in accordance with paragraph (i) of this section.

(viii) An employer will not be deemed to have hired an individual for employment if the individual is continuing in his or her employment and has a reasonable expectation of employment at all times.

(A) An individual is continuing in his or her employment in one of the following situations:

(1) An individual takes approved paid or unpaid leave on account of study, illness or disability of a family member, illness or pregnancy, maternity or paternity leave, vacation, union business, or other temporary leave approved by the employer;

(2) An individual is promoted, demoted, or gets a pay raise;

(3) An individual is temporarily laid off for lack of work;

(4) An individual is on strike or in a labor dispute;

(5) An individual is reinstated after disciplinary suspension for wrongful termination, found unjustified by any court, arbitrator, or administrative body, or otherwise resolved through reinstatement or settlement;

(6) An individual transfers from one distinct unit of an employer to another distinct unit of the same employer; the employer may transfer the individual's Form I-9 to the receiving unit;

(7) An individual continues his or her employment with a related, successor, or reorganized employer, provided that the employer obtains and maintains from the previous employer records and Forms I-9 where applicable. For this purpose, a related, successor, or reorganized employer includes:

(i) The same employer at another location;

(ii) An employer who continues to employ some or all of a previous employer's workforce in cases involving a corporate reorganization, merger, or sale of stock or assets;

(iii) An employer who continues to employ any employee of another employer's workforce where both employers belong to the same multi-employer association and the employee continues to work in the same bargaining unit under the same collective bargaining agreement. For purposes of this subsection, any agent designated to complete and maintain the Form I-9 must record the employee's date of hire and/or termination each time the employee is hired and/or terminated by an employer of the multi-employer association; or

(8) An individual is engaged in seasonal employment.

(B) The employer who is claiming that an individual is continuing in his or her employment must also establish that the individual expected to resume employment at all times and that the individual's expectation is reasonable. Whether an individual's expectation is reasonable will be determined on a case-by-case basis taking into consideration several factors. Factors which would indicate that an individual has a reasonable expectation of employment include, but are not limited to, the following:

(1) The individual in question was employed by the employer on a regular and substantial basis. A determination of a regular and substantial basis is established by a comparison of other workers who are similarly employed by the employer;

(2) The individual in question complied with the employer's established and published policy regarding his or her absence;

(3) The employer's past history of recalling absent employees for employment indicates a likelihood that the individual in question will resume employment with the employer within a reasonable time in the future;

(4) The former position held by the individual in question has not been taken permanently by another worker;

(5) The individual in question has not sought or obtained benefits during his or her absence from employment with the employer that are inconsistent with an expectation of resuming employment with the employer within a reasonable time in the future. Such benefits include, but are not limited to, severance and retirement benefits;

(6) The financial condition of the employer indicates the ability of the employer to permit the individual in question to resume employment within a reasonable time in the future; or

(7) The oral and/or written communication between employer, the employer's supervisory employees and the individual in question indicates that it is reasonably likely that the individual in question will resume employment with the employer within a reasonable time in the future.

(ix) As an optional alternative to the physical examination procedure described in paragraph (b)(1)(ii)(A) of this section, the Secretary may, consistent with applicable law and via notice published in the Federal Register, authorize alternative documentation examination procedures with respect to some or all employers. The Secretary may adopt such procedures:

(A) As part of a pilot program;

(B) Upon the Secretary's determination that such procedures offer an equivalent level of security to that of physical examination as indicated by, for instance, observed measures of system integrity (such as error or fraud rates) or the procedure's capacity for confirming certain documents or information; or

(C) As a temporary measure to address a public health emergency declared by the Secretary of Health and Human Services pursuant to Section 319 of the Public Health Service Act, or a national emergency declared by the President pursuant to Sections 201 and 301 of the National Emergencies Act.

(2) Retention and Inspection of Form I-9

(i) A paper (with original handwritten signatures), electronic (with acceptable electronic signatures that meet the requirements of paragraphs (h) and (i) of this section or original paper scanned into an electronic format, or a combination of paper and electronic formats that meet the requirements of paragraphs (e), (f), and (g) of this section), or microfilm or microfiche copy of the original signed version of Form I-9 must be retained by an employer or a recruiter or referrer for a fee for the following time periods:

(A) In the case of an employer, three years after the date of the hire or one year after the date the individual's employment is terminated, whichever is later; or

(B) In the case of a recruiter or referrer for a fee, three years after the date of the hire.

(ii) Any person or entity required to retain Forms I-9 in accordance with this section shall be provided with at least three business days notice prior to an inspection of Forms I-9 by officers of an authorized agency of the United States. At the time of inspection, Forms I-9 must be made available in their original paper, electronic form, a paper copy of the electronic form, or on microfilm or microfiche at the location where the request for production was made. If Forms I-9 are kept at another location, the person or entity must inform the officer of the authorized agency of the United States of the location where the forms are kept and make arrangements for the inspection. Inspections may be performed at an office of an authorized agency of the United States. A recruiter or referrer for a fee who has designated an employer to complete the employment verification procedures may present a photocopy or printed electronic image of the Form I-9 in lieu of presenting the Form I-9 in its original paper or electronic form or on microfilm or microfiche, as set forth in paragraph (b)(1)(iv) of this section. Any refusal or delay in presentation of the Forms I-9 for inspection is a violation of the retention requirements as set forth in section 274A(b)(3) of the Act. No Subpoena or warrant shall be required for such inspection, but the use of such enforcement tools is not precluded. In addition, if the person or entity has not complied with a request to present the Forms I-9, any officer listed in 8 CFR 287.4 may compel production of the Forms I-9 and any other relevant documents by issuing a subpoena. Nothing in this section is intended to limit the subpoena power under section 235(d)(4) of the Act.

(iii) The following standards shall apply to Forms I-9 presented on microfilm or microfiche submitted to an officer of the Service, the Special Counsel for Immigration-Related Unfair Employment Practices, or the Department of Labor: Microfilm, when displayed on a microfilm reader (viewer) or reproduced on paper must exhibit a high degree of legibility and readability. For this purpose, legibility is defined as the quality of a letter or numeral which enables the observer to positively and quickly identify it to the exclusion of all other letters or numerals. Readability is defined as the quality of a group of letters or numerals being recognizable as words or whole numbers. A detailed index of all microfilmed data shall be maintained and arranged in such a manner as to permit the immediate location of any particular record. It is the responsibility of the employer, recruiter or referrer for a fee:

(A) To provide for the processing, storage and maintenace of all microfilm, and

(B) To be able to make the contents thereof available as required by law. The person or entity presenting the microfilm will make available a reader-printer at the examination site for the ready reading, location and reproduction of any record or records being maintained on microfilm. Reader-printers made available to an officer of the Service, the Special Counsel for Immigration-Related Unfair Employment Practices, or the Department of Labor shall provide safety features and be in clean condition, properly maintained and in good working order. The reader-printers must have the capacity to display and print a complete page of information. A person or entity who is determined to have failed to comply with the criteria established by this regulation for the presentation of microfilm or microfiche to the Service, the Special Counsel for Immigration-Related Unfair Employment Practices, or the Department of Labor, and at the time of the inspection does not present a properly completed Form I-9 for the employee, is in violation of section 274A(a)(1)(B) of the Act and § 274a.2(b)(2).

(iv) Paragraphs (e), (f), (g), (h), and (i) of this section specify the standards for electronic Forms I-9.

(3) Copying of documentation. An employer, or a recruiter or referrer for a fee may, but is not required to, copy or make an electronic image of a document presented by an individual solely for the purpose of complying with the verification requirements of this section. If such a copy or electronic image is made, it must either be retained with the Form I-9 or stored with the employee's records and be retrievable consistent with paragraphs (e), (f), (g), (h), and (i) of this section. The copying or electronic imaging of any such document and retention of the copy or electronic image does not relieve the employer from the requirement to fully complete section 2 of the Form I-9. An employer, recruiter or referrer for a fee should not, however, copy or electronically image only the documents of individuals of certain national origins or citizenship statuses. To do so may violate section 274B of the Act.

(4) Limitation on use of Form I-9. Any information contained in or appended to the Form I-9, including copies or electronic images of documents listed in paragraph (c) of this section used to verify an individual's identity or employment eligibility, may be used only for enforcement of the Act and sections 1001, 1028, 1546, or 1621 of title 18, United States Code.

(c) Employment verification requirements in the case of hiring an individual who was previously employed.

(1) When an employer hires an individual whom that person or entity has previously employed, if the employer has previously completed the Form I-9 and complied with the verification requirements set forth in paragraph (b) of this section with regard to the individual, the employer may (in lieu of completing a new Form I-9) inspect the previously completed Form I-9 and:

(i) If upon inspection of the Form I-9, the employer determines that the Form I-9 relates to the individual and that the individual is still eligible to work, that previously executed Form I-9 is sufficient for purposes of section 274A(b) of the Act if the individual is hired within three years of the date of the initial execution of the Form I-9 and the employer updates the Form I-9 to reflect the date of rehire; or

(ii) If upon inspection of the Form I-9, the employer determines that the individual's employment authorization has expired, the employer must reverify such employment authorization on the Form I-9 in accordance with paragraph (b)(1)(vii) of this section, including complying with the applicable document presentation and examination procedures in paragraphs (b)(1)(ii)(A) and (b)(1)(ix) of this section, and form instructions; otherwise the individual may no longer be employed.

(2) For purposes of retention of the Form I-9 by an employer for a previously employed individual hired pursuant to paragraph (c)(1) of this section, the employer shall retain the Form I-9 for a period of three years commencing from the date of the initial execution of the Form I-9 or one year after the individual's employment is terminated, whichever is later.

(d) Employment verification requirements in the case of recruiting or referring for a fee an individual who was previously recruited or referred.

(1) When a recruiter or referrer for a fee refers an individual for whom that recruiter or referrer for a fee has previously completed a Form I-9 and complied with the verification requirements set forth in paragraph (b) of this section with regard to the individual, the recruiter or referrer may (in lieu of completing a new Form I-9) inspect the previously completed Form I-9 and:

(i) If upon inspection of the Form I-9, the recruiter or referrer for a fee determines that the Form I-9 relates to the individual and that the individual is still eligible to work, that previously executed Form I-9 is sufficient for purposes of section 274A(b) of the Act if the individual is referred within three years of the date of the initial execution of the Form I-9 and the recruiter or referrer for a fee updates the Form I-9 to reflect the date of rehire; or

(ii) If upon inspection of the Form I-9, the recruiter or referrer determines that the individual's employment authorization has expired, the recruiter or referrer for a fee must reverify on the Form I-9 in accordance with paragraph (b)(1)(vii) of this section; otherwise the individual may no longer be recruited or referred.

(2) For purposes of retention of the Form I-9 by a recruiter or referrer for a previously recruited or referred individual pursuant to paragraph (d)(1) of this section, the recruiter or referrer shall retain the Form I-9 for a period of three years from the date of the rehire.

(e) Standards for electronic retention of Form I-9.

(1) Any person or entity who is required by this section to complete and retain Forms I-9 may complete or retain electronically only those pages of the Form I-9 on which employers and employees enter data in an electronic generation or storage system that includes:

(i) Reasonable controls to ensure the integrity, accuracy and reliability of the electronic generation or storage system;

(ii) Reasonable controls designed to prevent and detect the unauthorized or accidental creation of, addition to, alteration of, deletion of, or deterioration of an electronically completed or stored Form I-9, including the electronic signature if used;

(iii) An inspection and quality assurance program evidenced by regular evaluations of the electronic generation or storage system, including periodic checks of the electronically stored Form I-9, including the electronic signature if used;

(iv) In the case of electronically retained Forms I-9, a retrieval system that includes an indexing system that permits searches consistent with the requirements of paragraph (e)(6) of this section; and

(v) The ability to reproduce legible and readable hardcopies.

(2) All documents reproduced by the electronic retention system must exhibit a high degree of legibility and readability when displayed on a video display terminal or when printed on paper, microfilm, or microfiche. The term "legibility" means the observer must be able to identify all letters and numerals positively and quickly, to the exclusion of all other letters or numerals. The term "readability" means that the observer must be able to recognize any group of letters or numerals that form words or numbers as those words or complete numbers. The employer, or recruiter or referrer for a fee, must ensure that the reproduction process maintains the legibility and readability of the electronically stored document.

(3) An electronic generation or storage system must not be subject, in whole or in part, to any agreement (such as a contract or license) that would limit or restrict access to and use of the electronic generation or storage system by an agency of the United States, on the premises of the employer, recruiter or referrer for a fee (or at any other place where the electronic generation or storage system is maintained), including personnel, hardware, software, files, indexes, and software documentation.

(4) A person or entity who chooses to complete or retain Forms I-9 electronically may use one or more electronic generation or storage systems. Each electronic generation or storage system must meet the requirements of this paragraph, and remain available as long as required by the Act and these regulations. Employers may implement new electronic storage systems provided:

(i) All systems meet the requirements of paragraphs (e), (f), (g), (h) and (i) of this section; and

(ii) Existing Forms I-9 are retained in a system that remains fully accessible.

(5) For each electronic generation or storage system used, the person or entity retaining the Form I-9 must maintain, and make available upon request, complete descriptions of:

(i) The electronic generation and storage system, including all procedures relating to its use; and

(ii) The indexing system.

(6) An "indexing system" for the purposes of paragraphs (e)(1)(iv) and (e)(5) of this section is a system that permits the identification and retrieval for viewing or reproducing of relevant documents and records maintained in an electronic storage system. For example, an indexing system might consist of assigning each electronically stored document a unique identification number and maintaining a separate database

that contains descriptions of all electronically stored books and records along with their identification numbers. In addition, any system used to maintain, organize, or coordinate multiple electronic storage systems is treated as an indexing system. The requirement to maintain an indexing system will be satisfied if the indexing system is functionally comparable to a reasonable hardcopy filing system. The requirement to maintain an indexing system does not require that a separate electronically stored documents and records description database be maintained if comparable results can be achieved without a separate description database.

(7) Any person or entity choosing to retain completed Forms I-9 electronically may use reasonable data compression or formatting technologies as part of the electronic storage system as long as the requirements of 8 CFR 274a.2 are satisfied.

(8) At the time of an inspection, the person or entity required to retain completed Forms I-9 must:

(i) Retrieve and reproduce (including printing copies on paper, if requested) only the Forms I-9 electronically retained in the electronic storage system and supporting documentation specifically requested by an agency of the United States, along with associated audit trails. Generally, an audit trail is a record showing who has accessed a computer system and the actions performed within or on the computer system during a given period of time;

(ii) Provide a requesting agency of the United States with the resources (e.g., appropriate hardware and software, personnel and documentation) necessary to locate, retrieve, read, and reproduce (including paper copies) any electronically stored Forms I-9, any supporting documents, and their associated audit trails, reports, and other data used to maintain the authenticity, integrity, and reliability of the records; and

(iii) Provide, if requested, any reasonably available or obtainable electronic summary file(s), such as a spreadsheet, containing all of the information fields on all of the electronically stored Forms I-9 requested by a requesting agency of the United States.

(f) Documentation.

(1) A person or entity who chooses to complete and/or retain Forms I-9 electronically must maintain and make available to an agency of the United States upon request documentation of the business processes that:

(i) Create the retained Forms I-9;

(ii) Modify and maintain the retained Forms I-9; and

(iii) Establish the authenticity and integrity of the Forms I-9, such as audit trails.

(2) Insufficient or incomplete documentation is a violation of section 274A(a)(1)(B) of the Act.

(3) Any officer listed in 8 CFR 287.4 may issue a subpoena to compel production of any documentation required by 8 CFR 274a.2. Nothing in this section is intended to limit the subpoena power of an agency of the United States under section 235(d)(4) of the Act.

(g) Security.

(1) Any person or entity who elects to complete or retain Forms I-9 electronically must implement an effective records security program that:

(i) Ensures that only authorized personnel have access to electronic records;

(ii) Provides for backup and recovery of records to protect against information loss, such as power interruptions;

(iii) Ensures that employees are trained to minimize the risk of unauthorized or accidental alteration or erasure of electronic records; and

(iv) Ensure that whenever the electronic record is created, completed, updated, modified, altered, or corrected, a secure and permanent record is created that establishes the date of access, the identity of the individual who accessed the electronic record, and the particular action taken.

(2) An action or inaction resulting in the unauthorized alteration, loss, or erasure of electronic records, if it is known, or reasonably should be known, to be likely to have that effect, is a violation of section 274A(b)(3) of the Act.

(h) Electronic signatures for employee.

(1) If a Form I-9 is completed electronically, the attestations in Form I-9 must be completed using a system for capturing an electronic signature that meets the standards set forth in this paragraph. The system used to capture the electronic signature must include a method to acknowledge that the attestation to be signed has been read by the signatory. The electronic signature must be attached to, or logically associated with, an electronically completed Form I-9. In addition, the system must:

(i) Affix the electronic signature at the time of the transaction;

(ii) Create and preserve a record verifying the identity of the person producing the signature; and

(iii) Upon request of the employee, provide a printed confirmation of the transaction to the person providing the signature.

(2) Any person or entity who is required to ensure proper completion of a Form I-9 and who chooses electronic signature for a required attestation, but who has failed to comply with the standards set forth in this paragraph, is deemed to have not properly completed the Form I-9, in violation of section 274A(a)(1)(B) of the Act and 8 CFR 274a.2(b)(2).

(i) Electronic signatures for employer, recruiter or referrer, or representative. If a Form I-9 is completed electronically, the employer, the recruiter or referrer for a fee, or the representative of the employer or the recruiter or referrer, must attest to the required information in Form I-9. The system used to capture the electronic signature should include a method to acknowledge that the attestation to be signed has been read by the signatory. Any person or entity who has failed to comply with the criteria established by this regulation for electronic signatures, if used, and at the time of inspection does not present a properly completed Form I-9 for the employee, is in violation of section 274A(a)(1)(B) of the Act and 8 CFR 274a.2(b)(2).

HISTORY:

[52 FR 16221, May 1, 1987, as amended at 53 FR 8612, Mar. 16, 1988; 55 FR 25932, June 25, 1990; 56 FR 41784-41786, Aug. 23,

1991; 58 FR 48780, Sept. 20, 1993; 59 FR 47063, Sept. 14, 1994; 60 FR 14353, Mar. 17, 1995; 61 FR 46534, 46537, Sept. 4, 1996; 61 FR 52235, 52236, Oct. 7, 1996; 62 FR 51001, 51005, Sept. 30, 1997, as corrected at 62 FR 52620, Oct. 8, 1997; 64 FR 6187, 6189, Feb. 9, 1999, as corrected at 64 FR 11533, Mar. 9, 1999; 71 FR 34510, 34514, June 15, 2006; 73 FR 76505, 76511, Dec. 17, 2008, as corrected at 74 FR 2838, Jan. 16, 2009, and 74 FR 10455, Mar. 11, 2009, and as confirmed at 76 FR 21225, 21232, Apr. 15, 2011; 74 FR 5899, Feb. 3, 2009; 74 FR 7993, 7995, Feb. 23, 2009; 74 FR 55726, 55739, Oct. 28, 2009, as corrected at 74 FR 62207, Nov. 27, 2009; 75 FR 42575, 42578, July 22, 2010; 78 FR 18457, 18472, Mar. 27, 2013, as confirmed at 81 FR 91646, 91670, Dec. 19, 2016; 81 FR 82398, 82491, Nov. 18, 2016; 82 FR 5238, 5289, Jan. 17, 2017; 82 FR 31887, July 11, 2017; 85 FR 29264, 29317, May 14, 2020; 88 FR 47990, 48022, July 25, 2023; 89 FR 101208, 101267, Dec. 13, 2024]

§ 274a.3 Continuing employment of unauthorized aliens.

An employer who continues the employment of an employee hired after November 6, 1986, knowing that the employee is or has become an unauthorized alien with respect to that employment, is in violation of section 274A(a)(2) of the Act.

HISTORY:

[52 FR 16221, May 1, 1987, as amended at 53 FR 8613, Mar. 16, 1988]

§ 274a.4 Good faith defense.

An employer or a recruiter or referrer for a fee for employment who shows good faith compliance with the employment verification requirements of § 274a.2(b) of this part shall have established a rebuttable affirmative defense that the person or entity has not violated section 274A(a)(1)(A) of the Act with respect to such hiring, recruiting, or referral.

HISTORY:

52 FR 16221, May 1, 1987.

§ 274a.5 Use of labor through contract.

Any person or entity who uses a contract, subcontract, or exchange entered into, renegotiated, or extended after November 6, 1986 (or, with respect to the Commonwealth of the Northern Mariana Islands, after the transition program effective date as defined in 8 CFR 1.1), to obtain the labor or services of an alien in the United States knowing that the alien is an unauthorized alien with respect to performing such labor or services, shall be considered to have hired the alien for employment in the United States in violation of section 274A(a)(1)(A) of the Act.

HISTORY:

[55 FR 25934, June 25, 1990; 74 FR 55726, 55739, Oct. 28, 2009]

§ 274a.6 State employment agencies.

(a) General. Pursuant to sections 274A(a)(5) and 274A(b) of the Act, a state employment agency as defined in § 274a.1 of this part may, but is not required to, verify identity and employment eligibility of individuals referred for employment by the agency. However, should a state employment agency choose to do so, it must:

(1) Complete the verification process in accordance with the requirements of § 274a.2(b) of this part provided that the individual may not present receipts in lieu of documents in order to complete the verification process as otherwise permitted by § 274a.2(b)(1)(vi) of this part; and

(2) Complete the verification process prior to referral for all individuals for whom a certification is required to be issued pursuant to paragraph (c) of this section.

(b) Compliance with the provisions of section 274A of the Act. A state employment agency which chooses to verify employment eligibility of individuals pursuant to § 274a.2(b) of this part shall comply with all provisions of section 274A of the Act and the regulations issued thereunder.

(c) State employment agency certification.

(1) A state employment agency which chooses to verify employment eligibility pursuant to paragraph (a) of this section shall issue to an employer who hires an individual referred for employment by the agency, a certification as set forth in paragraph (d) of this section. The certification shall be transmitted by the state employment agency directly to the employer, personally by an agency official, or by mail, so that it will be received by the employer within 21 business days of the date that the referred individual is hired. In no case shall the certification be transmitted to the employer from the state employment agency by the individual referred. During this period:

(i) The job order or other appropriate referral form issued by the state employment agency to the employer, on behalf of the individual who is referred and hired, shall serve as evidence, with respect to that individual, of the employer's compliance with the provisions of section 274A(a)(1)(B) of the Act and the regulations issued thereunder.

(ii) In the case of a telephonically authorized job referral by the state employment agency to the employer, an appropriate annotation by the employer shall be made and shall serve as evidence of the job order. The employer should retain the document containing the annotation where the employer retains Forms I-9.

(2) Job orders or other referrals, including telephonic authorizations, which are used as evidence of compliance pursuant to paragraph (c)(1)(i) of this section shall contain:

(i) The name of the referred individual;

(ii) The date of the referral;

(iii) The job order number or other applicable identifying number relating to the referral;

(iv) The name and title of the referring state employment agency official; and

(v) The telephone number and address of the state employment agency.

(3) A state employment agency shall not be required to verify employment eligibility or to issue a certification to an employer to whom the agency referred an individual if the individual is hired for a period of employment not to exceed 3 days in duration. Should a state agency choose to verify employment eligibility

and to issue a certification to an employer relating to an individual who is hired for a period of employment not to exceed 3 days in duration, it must verify employment eligibility and issue certifications relating to all such individuals. Should a state employment agency choose not to verify employment eligibility or issue certifications to employers who hire, for a period not to exceed 3 days in duration, agency-referred individuals, the agency shall notify employers that, as a matter of policy, it does not perform verifications for individuals hired for that length of time, and that the employers must complete the identity and employment eligibility requirements pursuant to § 274a.2(b) of this part. Such notification may be incorporated into the job order or other referral form utilized by the state employment agency as appropriate.

(4) An employer to whom a state employment agency issues a certification relating to an individual referred by the agency and hired by the employer, shall be deemed to have complied with the verification requirements of § 274a.2(b) of this part provided that the employer:

(i) Reviews the identifying information contained in the certification to ensure that it pertains to the individual hired;

(ii) Observes the signing of the certification by the individual at the time of its receipt by the employer as provided for in paragraph (d)(13) of this section;

(iii) Complies with the provisions of § 274a.2(b)(1)(vii) of this part by either:

(A) Updating the state employment agency certification in lieu of Form I-9, upon expiration of the employment authorization date, if any, which was noted on the certification issued by the state employment agency pursuant to paragraph (d)(11) of this section; or

(B) By no longer employing an individual upon expiration of his or her employment authorization date noted on the certification;

(iv) Retains the certification in the same manner prescribed for Form I-9 in § 274a.2(b)(2) of this part, to wit, three years after the date of the hire or one year after the date the individual's employment is terminated, whichever is later; and

(v) Makes it available for inspection to officers of the Service or the Department of Labor, pursuant to the provisions of section 274A(b)(3) of the Act, and § 274a.2(b)(2) of this part.

(5) Failure by an employer to comply with the provisions of paragraph (c)(4)(iii) of this section shall constitute a violation of section 274A(a)(2) of the Act and shall subject the employer to the penalties contained in section 274A(e)(4) of the Act, and § 274a.10 of this part.

(d) Standards for state employment agency certifications. All certifications issued by a state employment agency pursuant to paragraph (c) of this section shall conform to the following standards. They must:

(1) Be issued on official agency letterhead;

(2) Be signed by an appropriately designated official of the agency;

(3) Bear a date of issuance;

(4) Contain the employer's name and address;

(5) State the name and date of birth of the individual referred;

(6) Identify the position or type of employment for which the individual is referred;

(7) Bear a job order number relating to the position or type of employment for which the individual is referred;

(8) Identify the document or documents presented by the individual to the state employment agency for the purposes of identity and employment eligibility verification;

(9) State the identifying number or numbers of the document or documents described in paragraph (d)(8) of this section;

(10) Certify that the agency has complied with the requirements of section 274A(b) of the Act concerning verification of the identity and employment eligibility of the individual referred, and has determined that, to the best of the agency's knowledge, the individual is authorized to work in the United States;

(11) Clearly state any restrictions, conditions, expiration dates or other limitations which relate to the individual's employment eligibility in the United States, or contain an affirmative statement that the employment authorization of the referred individual is not restricted;

(12) State that the employer is not required to verify the individual's identity or employment eligibility, but must retain the certification in lieu of Form I-9;

(13) Contain a space or a line for the signature of the referred individual, requiring the individual under penalty of perjury to sign his or her name before the employer at the time of receipt of the certification by the employer; and

(14) State that counterfeiting, falsification, unauthorized issuance or alteration of the certification constitutes a violation of federal law pursuant to title 18, U.S.C. 1546.

(e) Retention of Form I-9 by state employment agencies. A Form I-9 utilized by a state employment agency in verifying the identity and employment eligibility of an individual pursuant to § 274a.2(b) of this part must be retained by a state employment agency for a period of three years from the date that the individual was last referred by the agency and hired by an employer. A state employment agency may retain a Form I-9 either in its original form, or on microfilm or microfiche.

(f) Retention of state employment agency certifications. A certification issued by a state employment agency pursuant to this section shall be retained:

(1) By a state employment agency, for a period of three years from the date that the individual was last referred by the agency and hired by an employer, and in a manner to be determined by the agency which will enable the prompt retrieval of the information contained on the original certification for comparison with the relating Form I-9;

(2) By the employer, in the original form, and in the same manner and location as the employer has designated for retention of Forms I-9, and for the period of time provided in paragraph (c)(4)(iv) of this section.

(g) State employment agency verification requirements in the case of an individual who was previously referred and certified. When a state employment agency refers an individual for whom the verification requirements have been previously complied with and a Form I-9 completed, the agency shall inspect the previously completed Form I-9:

(1) If, upon inspection of the Form, the agency determines that the Form I-9 pertains to the individual and that the individual remains authorized to be employed in the United States, no additional verification need be conducted and no new Form I-9 need be completed prior to issuance of a new certification provided that the individual is referred by the agency within 3 years of the execution of the initial Form I-9.

(2) If, upon inspection of the Form, the agency determines that the Form I-9 pertains to the individual but that the individual does not appear to be authorized to be employed in the United States based on restrictions, expiration dates or other conditions annotated on the Form I-9, the agency shall not issue a certification unless the agency follows the updating procedures pursuant to § 274a.2(b)(1)(vii) of this part; otherwise the individual may no longer be referred for employment by the state employment agency.

(3) For the purposes of retention of the Form I-9 by a state employment agency pursuant to paragraph (e) of this section, for an individual previously referred and certified, the state employment agency shall retain the Form for a period of 3 years from the date that the individual is last referred and hired.

(h) Employer verification requirements in the case of an individual who was previously referred and certified. When an employer rehires an individual for whom the verification and certification requirements have been previously complied with by a state employment agency, the employer shall inspect the previously issued certification.

(1) If, upon inspection of the certification, the employer determines that the certification pertains to the individual and that the individual remains authorized to be employed in the United States, no additional verification need be conducted and no new Form I-9 or certification need be completed provided that the individual is rehired by the employer within 3 years of the issuance of the initial certification, and that the employer follows the same procedures for the certification which pertain to Form I-9, as specified in § 274a.2(c)(1)(i) of this part.

(2) If, upon inspection of the certification, the employer determines that the certification pertains to the individual but that the certification reflects restrictions, expiration dates or other conditions which indicate that the individual no longer appears authorized to be employed in the United States, the employer shall verify that the individual remains authorized to be employed and shall follow the updating procedures for the certification which pertain to Form I-9, as specified in § 274a.2(c)(1)(ii) of this part; otherwise the individual may no longer be employed.

(3) For the purposes of retention of the certification by an employer pursuant to this paragraph for an individual previously referred and certified by a state employment agency and rehired by the employer, the employer shall retain the certification for a period of 3 years after the date that the individual is last hired, or one year after the date the individual's employment is terminated, whichever is later.

HISTORY:

[52 FR 43053, Nov. 9, 1987]

§ 274a.7 Pre-enactment provisions for employees hired prior to November 7, 1986 or in the CNMI prior to the transition program effective date.

(a) For employees who are continuing in their employment and have a reasonable expectation of employment at all times (as set forth in 8 CFR 274a.2(b)(1)(viii)), except those individuals described in 8 CFR 274a.2(b)(1)(viii)(A)(7)(iii) and (b)(1)(viii)(A)(8):

(1) The penalty provisions set forth in section 274A(e) and (f) of the Act for violations of sections 274A(a)(1)(B) and 274A(a)(2) of the Act shall not apply to employees who were hired prior to November 7, 1986.

(2) The penalty provisions set forth in section 274A(e) and (f) of the Act for violations of section 274A(a)(1)(B) of the Act shall not apply to employees who were hired in the CNMI prior to the transition program effective date as defined in 8 CFR 1.1.

(b) For purposes of this section, an employee who was hired prior to November 7, 1986 (or if hired in the CNMI, prior to the transition program effective date) shall lose his or her pre-enactment status if the employee:

(1) Quits; or

(2) Is terminated by the employer; the term termination shall include, but is not limited to, situations in which an employee is subject to seasonal employment; or

(3) Is excluded or deported from the United States or departs the United States under a grant of voluntary departure; or

(4) Is no longer continuing his or her employment (or does not have a reasonable expectation of employment at all times) as set forth in § 274a.2(b)(1)(viii).

HISTORY:

[52 FR 16221, May 1, 1987, as amended at 53 FR 8613, Mar. 16, 1988; 55 FR 25935, June 25, 1990; 56 FR 41786, Aug. 23, 1991; 74 FR 55726, 55740, Oct. 28, 2009]

§ 274a.8 Prohibition of indemnity bonds.

(a) General. It is unlawful for a person or other entity, in hiring or recruiting or referring for a fee for employment of an individual, to require the individual to post a bond or security, to pay or agree to pay an amount, or otherwise to provide a financial guarantee or indemnity, against any potential liability arising under this part relating to such hiring, recruiting, or referring of the individual. However, this prohibition does not apply to performance clauses which are stipulated by agreement between contracting parties.

(b) Penalty. Any person or other entity who requires any individual to post a bond or security as stated in this section shall, after notice and opportunity for an administrative hearing in accordance with section 274A(e)(3)(B) of the Act, be subject to a civil monetary penalty of $1,000 for each violation before September 29, 1999, of $1,100 for each violation occurring on or after September 29, 1999, but on or before November 2, 2015, and of $2,861 for each violation occurring after November 2, 2015, and to an administrative order requiring the return to the individual of any amounts received in violation of this section or, if the individual cannot be located, to the general fund of the Treasury.

HISTORY:

[52 FR 16221, May 1, 1987; 64 FR 47099, 47101, Aug. 30, 1999; 81 FR 42987, 43002, July 1, 2016, as confirmed and amended at 82 FR 8571, 8579, 8580, Jan. 27, 2017; 83 FR 13826, 13835, Apr. 2, 2018; 84 FR 13499, 13508, Apr. 5, 2019; 85 FR 36469, 36478, June 17, 2020; 86 FR 57532, 57540, Oct. 18, 2021; 87 FR 1317, 1326, Jan. 11, 2022; 88 FR 2175, 2183, Jan. 13, 2023; 89 FR 53849, 53859, June 28, 2024; 90 FR 1, 9, Jan. 2, 2025]

§ 274a.9 Enforcement procedures.

(a) Procedures for the filing of complaints. Any person or entity having knowledge of a violation or potential violation of section 274A of the Act may submit a signed, written complaint in person or by mail to the Service office having jurisdiction over the business or residence of the potential violator. The signed, written complaint must contain sufficient information to identify both the complainant and the potential violator, including their names and addresses. The complaint should also contain detailed factual allegations relating to the potential violation including the date, time and place of the alleged violation and the specific act or conduct alleged to constitute a violation of the Act. Written complaints may be delivered either by mail to the appropriate Service office or by personally appearing before any immigration officer at a Service office.

(b) Investigation. The Service may conduct investigations for violations on its own initiative and without having received a written complaint. When the Service receives a complaint from a third party, it shall investigate only those complaints that have a reasonable probability of validity. If it is determined after investigation that the person or entity has violated section 274A of the Act, the Service may issue and serve a Notice of Intent to Fine or a Warning Notice upon the alleged violator. Service officers shall have reasonable access to examine any relevant evidence of any person or entity being investigated.

(c) Warning notice. The Service and/or the Department of Labor may in their discretion issue a Warning Notice to a person or entity alleged to have violated section 274A of the Act. This Warning Notice will contain a statement of the basis for the violations and the statutory provisions alleged to have been violated.

(d) Notice of Intent to Fine. The proceeding to assess administrative penalties under section 274A of the Act is commenced when the Service issues a Notice of Intent to Fine on Form I-763. Service of this Notice shall be accomplished pursuant to part 103 of this chapter. The person or entity identified in the Notice of Intent to Fine shall be known as the respondent. The Notice of Intent to Fine may be issued by an officer defined in § 242.1 of this chapter with concurrence of a Service attorney.

(1) Contents of the Notice of Intent to Fine.

(i) The Notice of Intent to Fine will contain the basis for the charge(s) against the respondent, the statutory provisions alleged to have been violated, and the penalty that will be imposed.

(ii) The Notice of Intent to Fine will provide the following advisals to the respondent:

(A) That the person or entity has the right to representation by counsel of his or her own choice at no expense to the government;

(B) That any statement given may be used against the person or entity;

(C) That the person or entity has the right to request a hearing before an Administrative Law Judge pursuant to 5 U.S.C. 554-557, and that such request must be made within 30 days from the service of the Notice of Intent to Fine;

(D) That the Service will issue a final order in 45 days if a written request for a hearing is not timely received and that there will be no appeal of the final order.

(e) Request for Hearing Before an Administrative Law Judge. If a respondent contests the issuance of a Notice of Intent to Fine, the respondent must file with the INS, within thirty days of the service of the Notice of Intent to Fine, a written request for a hearing before an Administrative Law Judge. Any written request for a hearing submitted in a foreign language must be accompanied by an English language translation. A request for a hearing is not deemed to be filed until received by the Service office designated in the Notice of Intent to Fine. In computing the thirty day period prescribed by this section, the day of service of the Notice of Intent to Fine shall not be included. If the Notice of Intent to Fine was served by ordinary mail, five days shall be added to the prescribed thirty day period. In the request for a hearing, the respondent may, but is not required to, respond to each allegation listed in the Notice of Intent to Fine.

(f) Failure to file a request for hearing. If the respondent does not file a request for a hearing in writing within thirty days of the day of service of the Notice of Intent to Fine (thirty-five days if served by ordinary mail), the INS shall issue a final order from which there is no appeal.

HISTORY:

[52 FR 16221, May 1, 1987, as amended at 53 FR 8613, Mar. 16, 1988; 55 FR 25935, June 25, 1990; 56 FR 41786, Aug. 23, 1991; 61 FR 52235, 52236, Oct. 7, 1996]

§ 274a.10 Penalties.

(a) Criminal penalties. Any person or entity which engages in a pattern or practice of violations of subsection (a)(1)(A) or (a)(2) of the Act shall be fined not more than $ 3,000 for each unauthorized alien, imprisoned for not more than six months for the entire pattern or practice, or both, notwithstanding the provisions of any other Federal law relating to fine levels.

(b) Civil penalties. A person or entity may face civil penalties for a violation of section 274A of the Act. Civil penalties may be imposed by the Service or an administrative law judge for violations under section 274A of the Act. In determining the level of the penalties that will be imposed, a finding of more than one violation in the course of a single proceeding or determination will be counted as a single offense. However, a single offense will include penalties for each unauthorized alien who is determined to have been knowingly hired or recruited or referred for a fee.

(1) A respondent found by the Service or an administrative law judge to have knowingly hired, or to have knowingly recruited or referred for a fee, an unauthorized alien for employment in the United States or to have knowingly continued to employ an unauthorized alien in the United States, shall be subject to the following order:

(i) To cease and desist from such behavior;

(ii) To pay a civil fine according to the following schedule:

(A) First offense—not less than $275 and not more than $2,200 for each unauthorized alien with respect to whom the offense occurred before March 27, 2008; not less than $375 and not exceeding $3,200, for each unauthorized alien with respect to whom the offense occurred occurring on or after March 27, 2008, and on or before November 2, 2015; and not less than $716 and not more than $5,724 for each unauthorized alien with respect to whom the offense occurred occurring after November 2, 2015;

(B) Second offense—not less than $2,200 and not more than $5,500 for each unauthorized alien with respect to whom the second offense occurred before March 27, 2008; not less than $3,200 and not more than $6,500, for each unauthorized alien with respect to whom the second offense occurred on or after March 27, 2008, and on or before November 2, 2015; and not less than $5,724 and not more than $14,308 for each unauthorized alien with respect to whom the second offense occurred after November 2, 2015; or

(C) More than two offenses—not less than $3,300 and not more than $11,000 for each unauthorized alien with respect to whom the third or subsequent offense occurred before March 27, 2008; not less than $4,300 and not exceeding $16,000, for each unauthorized alien with respect to whom the third or subsequent offense occurred on or after March 27, 2008, and on or before November 2, 2015; and not less than $8,586 and not more than $28,619 for each unauthorized alien with respect to whom the third or subsequent offense occurred after November 2, 2015; and

(iii) To comply with the requirements of section 274a.2(b) of this part, and to take such other remedial action as is appropriate.

(2) A respondent determined by the Service (if a respondent fails to request a hearing) or by an administrative law judge, to have failed to comply with the employment verification requirements as set forth in § 274a.2(b), shall be subject to a civil penalty in an amount of not less than $100 and not more than $1,000 for each individual with respect to whom such violation occurred before September 29, 1999; not less than $110 and not more than $1,100 for each individual with respect to whom such violation occurred on or after September 29, 1999, and on or before November 2, 2015; and not less than $288 and not more than $2,861 for each individual with respect to whom such violation occurred after November 2, 2015. In determining the amount of the penalty, consideration shall be given to:

(i) The size of the business of the employer being charged;

(ii) The good faith of the employer;

(iii) The seriousness of the violation;

(iv) Whether or not the individual was an unauthorized alien; and

(v) The history of previous violations of the employer.

(3) Where an order is issued with respect to a respondent composed of distinct, physically separate subdivisions which do their own hiring, or their own recruiting or referring for a fee for employment (without reference to the practices of, and under the control of, or common control with another subdivision) the subdivision shall be considered a separate person or entity.

(c) Enjoining pattern or practice violations. If the Attorney General has reasonable cause to believe that a person or entity is engaged in a pattern or practice of employment, recruitment or referral in violation of section 274A(a)(1)(A) or (2) of the Act, the Attorney General may bring civil action in the appropriate United States District Court requesting relief, including a permanent or temporary injunction, restraining order, or other order against the person or entity, as the Attorney General deems necessary.

HISTORY:

[52 FR 16221, May 1, 1987, as amended at 55 FR 25935, June 25, 1990; 56 FR 41786, Aug. 23, 1991; 64 FR 47099, 47101, Aug. 30, 1999; 73 FR 10130, 10136, Feb. 26, 2008; 81 FR 42987, 43002, July 1, 2016, as corrected at 81 FR 57442, Aug. 23, 2016, as confirmed and amended at 82 FR 8571, 8579, 8580, Jan. 27, 2017; 83 FR 13826, 13835, Apr. 2, 2018; 84 FR 13499, 13508, Apr. 5, 2019; 85 FR 36469, 36479, June 17, 2020; 86 FR 57532, 57540, Oct. 18, 2021; 87 FR 1317, 1326, Jan. 11, 2022; 88 FR 2175, 2183, Jan. 13, 2023; 89 FR 53849, 53859, June 28, 2024; 90 FR 1, 9, Jan. 2, 2025]

§ 274a.11 [Reserved]

[NO TEXT IN ORIGINAL]

HISTORY:

[52 FR 16221, May 1, 1987]

Subpart B

Employment Authorization

§ 274a.12 Classes of aliens authorized to accept employment.

(a) Aliens authorized employment incident to status. Pursuant to the statutory or regulatory reference cited, the following classes of aliens are authorized to be employed in the United States without restrictions as to location or type of employment as a condition of their admission or subsequent change to one of the indicated classes. Any alien who is within a class of aliens described in paragraphs (a)(3), (a)(4), (a)(6)-(a)(8), (a)(10)-(a)(15), or (a)(20) of this section, and who seeks to be employed in the United States, must apply to U.S. Citizenship and Immigration Services (USCIS) for a document evidencing such employment authorization. USCIS may, in its discretion, determine the validity period assigned to any document issued evidencing an alien's authorization to work in the United States.

(1) An alien who is a lawful permanent resident (with or without conditions pursuant to section 216 of the Act), as evidenced by Form I-551 issued by the Service. An expiration date on the Form I-551 reflects only that the card must be renewed, not that the bearer's work authorization has expired;

(2) An alien admitted to the United States as a lawful temporary resident pursuant to sections 245A or 210 of the Act, as evidenced by an employment authorization document issued by the Service;

(3) An alien admitted to the United States as a refugee pursuant to section 207 of the Act for the period of time in that status, as evidenced by an employment authorization document issued by the Service;

(4) An alien paroled into the United States as a refugee for the period of time in that status, as evidenced by an employment authorization document issued by the Service;

(5) An alien granted asylum under section 208 of the Act for the period of time in that status, as evidenced by an employment authorization document, issued by USCIS to the alien. An expiration date on the employment authorization document issued by USCIS reflects only that the document must be renewed, and not that the bearer's work authorization has expired. Evidence of employment authorization shall be granted in increments not exceeding 5 years for the period of time the alien remains in that status.

(6) An alien admitted to the United States as a nonimmigrant fiance or fiancee pursuant to section 101(a)(15)(K)(i) of the Act, or an alien admitted as a child of such alien, for the period of admission in that status, as evidenced by an employment authorization document issued by the Service;

(7) An alien admitted as a parent (N-8) or dependent child (N-9) of an alien granted permanent residence under section 101(a)(27)(I) of the Act, as evidenced by an employment authorization document issued by the Service;

(8) An alien admitted to the United States as a nonimmigrant pursuant to the Compact of Free Association between the United States and of the Federated States of Micronesia, the Republic of the Marshall Islands, or the Republic of Palau;

(9) Any alien admitted as a nonimmigrant spouse pursuant to section 101(a)(15)(K)(ii) of the Act, or an alien admitted as a child of such alien, for the period of admission in that status, as evidenced by an employment authorization document, with an expiration date issued by the Service;

(10) An alien granted withholding of deportation or removal for the period of time in that status, as evidenced by an employment authorization document issued by the Service;

(11) An alien whose enforced departure from the United States has been deferred in accordance with a directive from the President of the United States to the Secretary. Employment is authorized for the period of time and under the conditions established by the Secretary pursuant to the Presidential directive;

(12) An alien granted Temporary Protected Status under section 244 of the Act for the period of time in that status, as evidenced by an employment authorization document issued by the Service;

(13) An alien granted voluntary departure by the Attorney General under the Family Unity Program established by section 301 of the Immigration Act of 1990, as evidenced by an employment authorization document issued by the Service;

(14) An alien granted Family Unity benefits under section 1504 of the Legal Immigrant Family Equity (LIFE) Act Amendments, Public Law 106-554, and the provisions of 8 CFR part 245a, Subpart C of this chapter, as evidenced by an employment authorization document issued by the Service;

(15) Any alien in V nonimmigrant status as defined in section 101(a)(15)(V) of the Act and 8 CFR 214.15;

(16) Any alien in T-1 nonimmigrant status, pursuant to 8 CFR 214.11, for the period in that status, as evidenced by an employment authorization document issued by USCIS to the alien.

(17) [Reserved]

(18) [Reserved]

(19) Any alien in U-1 nonimmigrant status, pursuant to 8 CFR 214.14, for the period of time in that status, as evidenced by an employment authorization document issued by USCIS to the alien.

(20) Any alien in U-2, U-3, U-4, or U-5 nonimmigrant status, pursuant to 8 CFR 214.14, for the period of time in that status, as evidenced by an employment authorization document issued by USCIS to the alien.

(b) Aliens authorized for employment with a specific employer incident to status or parole. The following classes of aliens are authorized to be employed in the United States by the specific employer and subject to any restrictions described in the section(s) of this chapter indicated as a condition of their parole or of their admission in, or subsequent change to, the designated nonimmigrant classification. An alien in one of these classes is not issued an employment authorization document by DHS:

(1) A foreign government official (A-1 or A-2), pursuant to § 214.2(a) of this chapter. An alien in this status may be employed only by the foreign government entity;

(2) An employee of a foreign government official (A-3), pursuant to § 214.2(a) of this chapter. An alien in this status may be employed only by the foreign government official;

(3) A foreign government official in transit (C-2 or C-3), pursuant to § 214.2(c) of this chapter. An alien in this status may be employed only by the foreign government entity;

(4) [Reserved]

(5) A nonimmigrant treaty trader (E-1) or treaty investor (E-2), pursuant to § 214.2(e) of this chapter. An alien in this status may be employed only by the treaty-qualifying company through which the alien attained the status. Employment authorization does not extend to the dependents of the principal treaty trader or treaty investor (also designated "E'1" or "E-2"), other than those specified in paragraph (c)(2) of this section;

(6) A nonimmigrant (F-1) student who is in valid nonimmigrant student status and pursuant to 8 CFR 214.2(f) is seeking:

(i) On-campus employment for not more than twenty hours per week when school is in session or full-time employment when school is not in session if the student intends and is eligible to register for the next term or session. Part-time on-campus employment is authorized by the school and no specific endorsement by a school official or Service officer is necessary;

(ii) [Reserved]

(iii) Curricular practical training (internships, cooperative training programs, or work-study programs which are part of an established curriculum) after having been enrolled full-time in a Service approved institution for one full academic year. Curricular practical training (part-time or full-time) is authorized by the Designated School Official on the student's Form I-20. No Service endorsement is necessary.

(iv) An Employment Authorization Document, Form I-766 or successor form, under paragraph (c)(3)(i)(C) of this section based on a STEM Optional Practical Training extension, and whose timely filed Form I-765 or successor form is pending and employment authorization and accompanying Form I-766 or successor form issued under paragraph (c)(3)(i)(B) of this section have expired. Employment is authorized beginning on the expiration date of the Form I-766 or successor form issued under paragraph (c)(3)(i)(B) of this section and ending on the date of USCIS' written decision on the current Form I-765 or successor form, but not to exceed 180 days. For this same period, such Form I-766 or successor form is automatically extended and is considered unexpired when combined with a Certificate of Eligibility for Nonimmigrant (F-1/M-1) Students, Form I-20 or successor form, endorsed by the Designated School Official recommending such an extension; or

(v) Pursuant to 8 CFR 214.2(h) is seeking H-1B nonimmigrant status and whose duration of status and employment authorization have been extended pursuant to 8 CFR 214.2(f)(5)(vi).

(7) A representative of an international organization (G-1, G-2, G-3, or G-4), pursuant to § 214.2(g) of this chapter. An alien in this status may be employed only by the foreign government entity or the international organization;

(8) A personal employee of an official or representative of an international organization (G-5), pursuant to § 214.2(g) of this chapter. An alien in this status may be employed only by the official or representative of the international organization;

(9) A temporary worker or trainee (H-1, H-2A, H-2B, or H-3), under 8 CFR 214.2(h), or a nonimmigrant specialty occupation worker under section 101(a)(15)(H)(i)(b)(1) of the Act. An alien in this status may be employed only by the petitioner through whom the status was obtained. In the case of a professional H-2B athlete who is traded from one organization to another organization, employment authorization for the player will automatically continue for a period of 30 days after acquisition by the new organization, within which time the new organization is expected to file a new petition for H-2B classification. If a new petition is not filed within 30 days, employment authorization will cease. If a new petition is filed within 30 days, the professional athlete's employment authorization will continue until the petition is adjudicated. If the new petition is denied, employment authorization will cease. In the case of a nonimmigrant with H-1B status, employment authorization will automatically continue upon the filing of a qualifying petition under 8 CFR 214.2(h)(2)(i)(H) until such petition is adjudicated, in accordance with section 214(n) of the Act and 8 CFR 214.2(h)(2)(i)(H).

(10) An information media representative (I), pursuant to § 214.2(i) of this chapter. An alien in this status may be employed only for the sponsoring foreign news agency or bureau. Employment authorization does not extend to the dependents of an information media representative (also designated "I");

(11) An exchange visitor (J-1), pursuant to § 214.2(j) of this chapter and 22 CFR part 62. An alien in this status may be employed only by the exchange visitor program sponsor or appropriate designee and within the guidelines of the program approved by the Department of State as set forth in the Form DS-2019, Certificate of Eligibility, issued by the program sponsor;

(12) An intra-company transferee (L-1), pursuant to § 214.2(1) of this chapter. An alien in this status may be employed only by the petitioner through whom the status was obtained;

(13) An alien having extraordinary ability in the sciences, arts, education, business, or athletics (O-1), and an accompanying alien (O-2), under 8 CFR 214.2(o). An alien in this status may be employed only by the petitioner through whom the status was obtained. In the case of a professional O-1 athlete who is traded from one organization to another organization, employment authorization for the player will automatically continue for a period of 30 days after the acquisition by the new organization, within which time the new organization is expected to file a new petition for O nonimmigrant classification. If a new petition is not filed within 30 days, employment authorization will cease. If a new petition is filed within 30 days, the professional athlete's employment authorization will continue until the petition is adjudicated. If the new petition is denied, employment authorization will cease.

(14) An athlete, artist, or entertainer (P-1, P-2, or P-3), under 8 CFR 214.2(p). An alien in this status may be employed only by the petitioner through whom the status was obtained. In the case of a professional P-1 athlete who is traded from one organization to another organization, employment authorization for the player will automatically continue for a period of 30 days after the acquisition by the new organization, within which time the new organization is expected to file a new petition for P-1 nonimmigrant classification. If a new petition is not filed within 30 days, employment authorization will cease. If a new petition is filed within 30 days, the professional athlete's employment authorization will continue until the petition is adjudicated. If the new petition is denied, employment authorization will cease.

(15) An international cultural exchange visitor (Q-1), according to § 214.2(q)(1) of this chapter. An alien may only be employed by the petitioner through whom the status was obtained;

(16) An alien having a religious occupation, pursuant to § 214.2(r) of this chapter. An alien in this status may be employed only by the religious organization through whom the status was obtained;

(17) Officers and personnel of the armed services of nations of the North Atlantic Treaty Organization, and representatives, officials, and staff employees of NATO (NATO-1, NATO-2, NATO-3, NATO-4, NATO-5 and NATO-6), pursuant to § 214.2(o) of this chapter. An alien in this status may be employed only by NATO;

(18) An attendant, servant or personal employee (NATO-7) of an alien admitted as a NATO-1, NATO-2, NATO-3, NATO-4, NATO-5, or NATO-6, pursuant to § 214.2(o) of this chapter. An alien admitted under this classification may be employed only by the NATO alien through whom the status was obtained;

(19) A nonimmigrant pursuant to section 214(e) of the Act. An alien in this status must be engaged in business activities at a professional level in accordance with the provisions of Chapter 16 of the Agreement Between the United States of America, the United Mexican States, and Canada (USMCA);

(20) A nonimmigrant alien within the class of aliens described in paragraphs (b)(2), (b)(5), (b)(8), (b)(9), (b)(10), (b)(11), (b)(12), (b)(13), (b)(14), (b)(16), (b)(19), (b)(23) and (b)(25) of this section whose status has expired but on whose behalf an application for an extension of stay was timely filed pursuant to § 214.2 or § 214.6 of this chapter. These aliens are authorized to continue employment with the same employer for a period not to exceed 240 days beginning on the date of the expiration of the authorized period of stay. Such authorization shall be subject to any conditions and limitations noted on the initial authorization. However, if the district director or service center director adjudicates the application prior to the expiration of this 240 day period and denies the application for extension of stay, the employment authorization under this paragraph shall automatically terminate upon notification of the denial decision;

(21) A nonimmigrant alien within the class of aliens described in 8 CFR 214.2(h)(1)(ii)(C) or 8 CFR 214.2(h)(1)(ii)(D) for whom a nonfrivolous petition requesting an extension of stay is properly filed pursuant to 8 CFR 214.2 and 8 CFR 103.2(a) requesting the same classification that the nonimmigrant alien currently holds. Pursuant to 8 CFR 214.2(h)(2)(i)(I), such alien is authorized to start new employment upon the proper filing of the nonfrivolous petition requesting an extension of stay in the same classification, or as of the requested start date, whichever is later. The employment authorization under this paragraph (b)(21) automatically ceases upon the adjudication or withdrawal of the H–2A or H–2B petition;

(22) An alien in E-2 CNMI Investor nonimmigrant status pursuant to 8 CFR 214.2(e)(23). An alien in this status may be employed only by the qualifying company through which the alien attained the status. An alien in E-2 CNMI Investor nonimmigrant status may be employed only in the Commonwealth of the Northern Mariana Islands for a qualifying entity. An alien who attained E-2 CNMI Investor nonimmigrant status based upon a Foreign Retiree Investment Certificate or Certification is not employment-authorized. Employment authorization does not extend to the dependents of the principal investor (also designated E-2 CNMI Investor nonimmigrants) other than those specified in paragraph (c)(12) of this section;

(23) A Commonwealth of the Northern Mariana Islands transitional worker (CW–1) pursuant to 8 CFR 214.2(w). An alien in this status may be employed only in the CNMI during the transition period, and only by the petitioner through whom the status was obtained, or as otherwise authorized by 8 CFR 214.2(w).

(24) [Reserved]

(25) A nonimmigrant treaty alien in a specialty occupation (E-3) pursuant to section 101(a)(15)(E)(iii) of the Act; or

(26)-(30) [Reserved]

(31) [Effective Jan. 28, 2022 through Jan. 28, 2025.]

(i) Pursuant to 8 CFR 214.2(h)(27) and notwithstanding 8 CFR 214.2(h)(2)(i)(D), an alien is authorized to be employed no earlier than the start date of employment indicated in the H-2B petition and no earlier than January 28, 2022, by a new employer that has filed an H-2B petition naming the alien as a beneficiary and requesting an extension of stay for the alien, for a period not to exceed 60 days beginning on:

(A) The later of the "Received Date" on Form I-797 (Notice of Action) acknowledging receipt of the petition, or the start date of employment indicated on the new H-2B petition, for petitions filed on or after January 28, 2022; or

(B) The later of January 28, 2022 or the start date of employment indicated on the new H-2B petition, for petitions that are pending as of January 28, 2022

(ii) If USCIS adjudicates the new petition prior to the expiration of the 60-day period in paragraph (b)(31)(i) of this section and denies the new petition for extension of stay, or if the petitioner withdraws the new petition before the expiration of the 60-day period, the employment authorization under this paragraph (b)(31) will automatically terminate upon 15 days after the date of the denial decision or the date on which the new petition is withdrawn. Nothing in this section is intended to alter the availability of employment authorization related to professional H-2B athletes who are traded between organizations pursuant to paragraph (b)(9) of this section and 8 CFR 214.2(h)(6)(vii).

(iii) Authorization to initiate employment changes pursuant to 8 CFR 214.2(h)(27) and paragraph (b)(31)(i) of this section begins at 12 a.m. on January 28, 2022, and ends at the end of July 27, 2022.

(32) [Effective May 18, 2022 through May 18, 2025]

(i) Pursuant to 8 CFR 214.2(h)(28) and notwithstanding 8 CFR 214.2(h)(2)(i)(D), an alien is authorized to be employed no earlier than the start date of employment indicated in the H-2B petition and no earlier than July 28, 2022, by a new employer that has filed an H-2B petition naming the alien as a beneficiary and requesting an extension of stay for the alien, for a period not to exceed 60 days beginning on:

(A) The later of the "Received Date" on Form I-797 (Notice of Action) acknowledging receipt of the petition, or the start date of employment indicated on the new H-2B petition, for petitions filed on or after July 28, 2022; or

(B) The later of July 28, 2022 or the start date of employment indicated on the new H-2B petition, for petitions that are pending as of July 28, 2022.

(ii) If USCIS adjudicates the new petition prior to the expiration of the 60-day period in paragraph (b)(32)(i) of this section and denies the new petition for extension of stay, or if the petitioner withdraws the new petition before the expiration of the 60-day period, the employment authorization under this paragraph (b)(32) will automatically terminate upon 15 days after the date of the denial decision or the date on which the new petition is withdrawn. Nothing in this section is intended to alter the availability of employment authorization related to professional H-2B athletes who are traded between organizations pursuant to paragraph (b)(9) of this section and 8 CFR 214.2(h)(6)(vii).

(iii) Authorization to initiate employment changes pursuant to 8 CFR 214.2(h)(28) and paragraph (b)(32)(i) of this section begins at 12 a.m. on July 28, 2022, and ends at the end of January 24, 2023.

(33) [Effective Dec. 15, 2022 through Dec. 15, 2025]

(i) Pursuant to 8 CFR 214.2(h)(29) and notwithstanding 8 CFR 214.2(h)(2)(i)(D), an alien is authorized to be employed no earlier than the start date of employment indicated in the H-2B petition and no earlier than January 25, 2023, by a new employer that has filed an H-2B petition naming the alien as a beneficiary and requesting an extension of stay for the alien, for a period not to exceed 60 days beginning on:

(A) The later of the "Received Date" on Form I-797 (Notice of Action) acknowledging receipt of the petition, or the start date of employment indicated on the new H-2B petition, for petitions filed on or after January 25, 2023; or

(B) The later of January 25, 2023 or the start date of employment indicated on the new H-2B petition, for petitions that are pending as of January 25, 2023.

(ii) If USCIS adjudicates the new petition prior to the expiration of the 60-day period in paragraph (b)(33)(i) of this section and denies the new petition for extension of stay, or if the petitioner withdraws the new petition before the expiration of the 60-day period, the employment authorization under this paragraph (b)(33) will automatically terminate upon 15 days after the date of the denial decision or the date on which the new petition is withdrawn. Nothing in this section is intended to alter the availability of employment authorization related to professional H-2B athletes who are traded between organizations pursuant to paragraph (b)(9) of this section and 8 CFR 214.2(h)(6)(vii).

(iii) Authorization to initiate employment changes pursuant to 8 CFR 214.2(h)(29) and paragraph (b)(33)(i) of this section begins at 12 a.m. on January 25, 2023, and ends at the end of January 24, 2024.

(34) [Effective Nov. 17, 2023 through Nov. 17, 2026]

(i) Pursuant to 8 CFR 214.2(h)(31) and notwithstanding 8 CFR 214.2(h)(2)(i)(D), an alien is authorized to be employed no earlier than the start date of employment indicated in the H-2B petition and no earlier than January 25, 2024, by a new employer that has filed an H-2B petition naming the alien as a beneficiary and requesting an extension of stay for the alien, for a period not to exceed 60 days beginning on:

(A) The later of the "Received Date" on Form I-797 (Notice of Action) acknowledging receipt of the petition, or the start date of employment indicated on the new H-2B petition, for petitions filed on or after January 25, 2024; or

(B) The later of January 25, 2024, or the start date of employment indicated on the new H-2B petition, for petitions that are pending as of January 25, 2024.

(ii) If USCIS adjudicates the new petition prior to the expiration of the 60-day period in paragraph (b)(34)(i) of this section and denies the new petition for extension of stay, or if the petitioner withdraws the new petition before the expiration of the 60-day period, the employment authorization under this paragraph (b)(34) will automatically terminate upon 15 days after the date of the denial decision or the date on which the new petition is withdrawn. Nothing in this section is intended to alter the availability of employment authorization related to professional H-2B athletes who are traded between organizations pursuant to paragraph (b)(9) of this section and 8 CFR 214.2(h)(6)(vii).

(iii) Authorization to initiate employment changes pursuant to 8 CFR 214.2(h)(31) and paragraph (b)(34)(i) of this section begins at 12 a.m. on January 25, 2024, and ends at the end of January 24, 2025.

(35) [Effective Dec. 2, 2024 through Dec. 2, 2027]

(i) Pursuant to 8 CFR 214.2(h)(32) and notwithstanding 8 CFR 214.2(h)(2)(i)(D), an alien is authorized to be employed no earlier than the start date of employment indicated in the H-2B petition and no earlier than January 25, 2025, by a new employer that has filed an H-2B petition naming the alien as a beneficiary and requesting an extension of stay for the alien, for a period not to exceed 60 days beginning on:

(A) The later of the "Received Date" on Form I-797 (Notice of Action) acknowledging receipt of the petition, or the start date of employment indicated on the new

H-2B petition, for petitions filed on or after January 25, 2025; or

(B) The later of January 25, 2025, or the start date of employment indicated on the new H-2B petition, for petitions that are pending as of January 25, 2025.

(ii) If USCIS adjudicates the new petition prior to the expiration of the 60-day period in paragraph (b)(35)(i) of this section and denies the new petition for extension of stay, or if the petitioner withdraws the new petition before the expiration of the 60-day period, the employment authorization under this paragraph (b)(35) will automatically terminate upon 15 days after the date of the denial decision or the date on which the new petition is withdrawn. Nothing in this section is intended to alter the availability of employment authorization related to professional H-2B athletes who are traded between organizations pursuant to paragraph (b)(9) of this section and 8 CFR 214.2(h)(6)(vii).

(iii) Authorization to initiate employment changes pursuant to 8 CFR 214.2(h)(32) and paragraph (b)(35)(i) of this section begins at 12 a.m. on January 25, 2025, and ends at the end of January 24, 2026.

(36) [Reserved]

(37) An alien paroled into the United States as an entrepreneur pursuant to 8 CFR 212.19 for the period of authorized parole. An entrepreneur who has timely filed a non-frivolous application requesting re-parole with respect to the same start-up entity in accordance with 8 CFR 212.19 prior to the expiration of his or her parole, but whose authorized parole period expires during the pendency of such application, is authorized to continue employment with the same start-up entity for a period not to exceed 240 days beginning on the date of expiration of parole. Such authorization shall be subject to any conditions and limitations on such expired parole. If DHS adjudicates the application prior to the expiration of this 240-day period and denies the application for re-parole, the employment authorization under this paragraph shall automatically terminate upon notification to the alien of the denial decision.

(c) Aliens who must apply for employment authorization. An alien within a class of aliens described in this section must apply for work authorization. If authorized, such an alien may accept employment subject to any restrictions stated in the regulations or cited on the employment authorization document. USCIS, in its discretion, may establish a specific validity period for an employment authorization document, which may include any period when an administrative appeal or judicial review of an application or petition is pending.

(1) An alien spouse or unmarried dependent child; son or daughter of a foreign government official (A-1 or A-2) pursuant to 8 CFR 214.2(a)(2) and who presents an endorsement from an authorized representative of the Department of State;

(2) An alien spouse or unmarried dependent son or daughter of an alien employee of the Coordination Council for North American Affairs (E-1) pursuant to § 214.2(e) of this chapter;

(3) A nonimmigrant (F-1) student who:

(i)(A) Is seeking pre-completion practical training pursuant to 8 CFR 214.2(f)(10)(ii)(A)(1) and (2);

(B) Is seeking authorization to engage in up to 12 months of post-completion Optional Practical Training (OPT) pursuant to 8 CFR 214.2(f)(10)(ii)(A)(3); or

(C) Is seeking a 24-month OPT extension pursuant to 8 CFR 214.2(f)(10)(ii)(C);

(ii) Has been offered employment under the sponsorship of an international organization within the meaning of the International Organization Immunities Act (59 Stat. 669) and who presents a written certification from the international organization that the proposed employment is within the scope of the organization's sponsorship. The F-1 student must also present a Form I-20 ID or SEVIS Form I-20 with employment page completed by DSO certifying eligibility for employment; or

(iii) Is seeking employment because of severe economic hardship pursuant to 8 CFR 214.2(f)(9)(ii)(C) and has filed the Form I-20 ID and Form I-538 (for non-SEVIS schools), or SEVIS Form I-20 with employment page completed by the DSO certifying eligibility, and any other supporting materials such as affidavits which further detail the unforeseen economic circumstances that require the student to seek employment authorization.

(4) An alien spouse or unmarried dependent child; son or daughter of a foreign government official (G-1, G-3 or G-4) pursuant to 8 CFR 214.2(g) and who presents an endorsement from an authorized representative of the Department of State;

(5) An alien spouse or minor child of an exchange visitor (J-2) pursuant to § 214.2(j) of this chapter;

(6) A nonimmigrant (M-1) student seeking employment for practical training pursuant to 8 CFR 214.2(m) following completion of studies. The alien may be employed only in an occupation or vocation directly related to his or her course of study as recommended by the endorsement of the designated school official on the I-20 ID;

(7) A dependent of an alien classified as NATO-1 through NATO-7 pursuant to § 214.2(n) of this chapter;

(8) An alien who has filed a complete application for asylum or withholding of deportation or removal pursuant to 8 CFR part 208, whose application:

(i) Has not been decided, and who is eligible to apply for employment authorization under § 208.7 of this chapter because the 150-day period set forth in that section has expired. Employment authorization may be granted according to the provisions of § 208.7 of this chapter in increments to be determined by the Commissioner and shall expire on a specified date; or

(ii) Has been recommended for approval, but who has not yet received a grant of asylum or withholding or deportation or removal;

(9) An alien who has filed an application for adjustment of status to lawful permanent resident pursuant to part 245 of this chapter. For purposes of section 245(c)(8) of the Act, an alien will not be deemed to be an "unauthorized alien" as defined in section 274A(h)(3) of the Act while his or her properly filed Form I-485 application is pending final adjudication, if the alien

has otherwise obtained permission from the Service pursuant to 8 CFR 274a.12 to engage in employment, or if the alien had been granted employment authorization prior to the filing of the adjustment application and such authorization does not expire during the pendency of the adjustment application. Upon meeting these conditions, the adjustment applicant need not file an application for employment authorization to continue employment during the period described in the preceding sentence;

(10) An alien who has filed an application for suspension of deportation under section 244 of the Act (as it existed prior to April 1, 1997), cancellation of removal pursuant to section 240A of the Act, or special rule cancellation of removal under section 309(f)(1) of the Illegal Immigration Reform and Immigrant Responsibility Act of 1996, enacted as Pub. L. 104-208 (110 Stat. 3009-625) (as amended by the Nicaraguan Adjustment and Central American Relief Act (NACARA)), title II of Pub. L. 105-100 (111 Stat. 2160, 2193) and whose properly filed application has been accepted by the Service or EOIR;

(11) Except as provided in paragraphs (b)(37) and (c)(34) of this section and § 212.19(h)(4) of this chapter, an alien paroled into the United States temporarily for urgent humanitarian reasons or significant public benefit pursuant to section 212(d)(5) of the Act.

(12) An alien spouse of a long-term investor in the Commonwealth of the Northern Mariana Islands (E-2 CNMI Investor) other than an E-2 CNMI investor who obtained such status based upon a Foreign Retiree Investment Certificate, pursuant to 8 CFR 214.2(e)(23). An alien spouse of an E-2 CNMI Investor is eligible for employment in the CNMI only;

(13) [Reserved]

(14) Except as provided for in paragraph (c)(33) of this section, an alien who has been granted deferred action, an act of administrative convenience to the government that gives some cases lower priority, if the alien establishes an economic necessity for employment.

(15) [Reserved]

(16) Any alien who has filed an application for creation of record of lawful admission for permanent residence pursuant to part 249 of this chapter;

(17) A nonimmigrant visitor for business (B-1) who:

(i) Is a personal or domestic servant who is accompanying or following to join an employer who seeks admission into, or is already in, the United States as a nonimmigrant defined under sections 101(a)(15) (B), (E), (F), (H), (I), (J), (L) or section 214(e) of the Act. The personal or domestic servant shall have a residence abroad which he or she has no intention of abandoning and shall demonstrate at least one year's experience as a personal or domestic servant. The nonimmigrant's employer shall demonstrate that the employer/employee relationship has existed for at least one year prior to the employer's admission to the United States; or, if the employer/employee relationship existed for less than one year, that the employer has regularly employed (either year-round or seasonally) personal or domestic servants over a period of several years preceding the employer's admission to the United States;

(ii) Is a domestic servant of a United States citizen accompanying or following to join his or her United States citizen employer who has a permanent home or is stationed in a foreign country, and who is visiting temporarily in the United States. The employer/employee relationship shall have existed prior to the commencement of the employer's visit to the United States; or

(iii) Is an employee of a foreign airline engaged in international transportation of passengers freight, whose position with the foreign airline would otherwise entitle the employee to classification under section 101(a)(15)(E)(i) of the Immigration and Nationality Act, and who is precluded from such classification solely because the employee is not a national of the country of the airline's nationality or because there is no treaty of commerce and navigation in effect between the United States and the country of the airline's nationality.

(18) An alien against whom a final order of deportation or removal exists and who is released on an order of supervision under the authority contained in section 241(a)(3) of the Act may be granted employment authorization in the discretion of the district director only if the alien cannot be removed due to the refusal of all countries designated by the alien or under section 241 of the Act to receive the alien, or because the removal of the alien is otherwise impracticable or contrary to the public interest. Additional factors which may be considered by the district director in adjudicating the application for employment authorization include, but are not limited to, the following:

(i) The existence of economic necessity to be employed;

(ii) The existence of a dependent spouse and/or children in the United States who rely on the alien for support; and

(iii) The anticipated length of time before the alien can be removed from the United States.

(19) An alien applying for Temporary Protected Status pursuant to section 244 of the Act shall apply for employment authorization only in accordance with the procedures set forth in part 244 of this chapter.

(20) Any alien who has filed a completed legalization application pursuant to section 210 of the Act (and part 210 of this chapter).

(21) A principal nonimmigrant witness or informant in S classification, and qualified dependent family members.

(22) Any alien who has filed a completed legalization application pursuant to section 245A of the Act (and part 245a of this chapter). Employment authorization shall be granted in increments not exceeding 1 year during the period the application is pending (including any period when an administrative appeal is pending) and shall expire on a specified date.

(23) [Reserved]

(24) An alien who has filed an application for adjustment pursuant to section 1104 of the LIFE Act, Public Law 106-553, and the provisions of 8 CFR part 245a, Subpart B of this chapter.

(25) Any alien in T-2, T-3, T-4, T-5, or T-6 nonimmigrant status, pursuant to 8 CFR 214.11, for the period in that status, as evidenced by an employment authorization document issued by USCIS to the alien.

(26) An H-4 nonimmigrant spouse of an H-1B nonimmigrant described as eligible for employment authorization in 8 CFR 214.2(h)(9)(iv).

(27) — (32) [Reserved]

(33) An alien who has been granted deferred action pursuant to 8 CFR 236.21 through 236.23, Deferred Action for Childhood Arrivals, if the alien establishes an economic necessity for employment.

(34) A spouse of an entrepreneur parolee described as eligible for employment authorization in § 212.19(h)(3) of this chapter.

(35) An alien who is the principal beneficiary of a valid immigrant petition under section 203(b)(1), 203(b)(2) or 203(b)(3) of the Act described as eligible for employment authorization in 8 CFR 204.5(p).

(36) A spouse or child of a principal beneficiary of a valid immigrant petition under section 203(b)(1), 203(b)(2) or 203(b)(3) of the Act described as eligible for employment authorization in 8 CFR 204.5(p).

(37) [Reserved.]

(38) [Reserved.]

(39) [Reserved.]

(40) A noncitizen applicant for T nonimmigrant status, and eligible family members, who have pending, bona fide applications, and who merit a favorable exercise of discretion.

(d) An alien lawfully enlisted in one of the Armed Forces, or whose enlistment the Secretary with jurisdiction over such Armed Force has determined would be vital to the national interest under 10 U.S.C. 504(b)(2), is authorized to be employed by that Armed Force in military service, if such employment is not otherwise authorized under this section and the immigration laws. An alien described in this section is not issued an employment authorization document.

(e) Basic criteria to establish economic necessity. Title 45 — Public Welfare, Poverty Guidelines, 45 CFR 1060.2 should be used as the basic criteria to establish eligibility for employment authorization when the alien's economic necessity is identified as a factor. The alien shall submit an application for employment authorization listing his or her assets, income, and expenses as evidence of his or her economic need to work. Permission to work granted on the basis of the alien's application for employment authorization may be revoked under § 274a.14 of this chapter upon a showing that the information contained in the statement was not true and correct.

HISTORY:

[52 FR 16221, May 1, 1987, as amended at 53 FR 8614, Mar. 16, 1988; 53 FR 46855, Nov. 21, 1988; 54 FR 16, Jan. 3, 1989.; 55 FR 25936, June 25, 1990; 56 FR 624, Jan. 7, 1991.; 56 FR 23499, May 22, 1991; 56 FR 41787, Aug. 23, 1991; 56 FR 55616, Oct. 29, 1991; 57 FR 6462, Feb. 25, 1992, as confirmed and amended at 60 FR 66062, 66069, Dec. 21, 1995; 57 FR 14627, Apr. 21, 1992; 57 FR 31956, July 20, 1992; 57 FR 42885, Sept. 17, 1992; 58 FR 48780, Sept. 20, 1993; 58 FR 69217, Dec. 30, 1993, as corrected at 59 FR 52894, Oct. 20, 1994, and confirmed at 63 FR 1331, 1334, Jan. 9, 1998; 59 FR 47063, Sept. 14, 1994; 59 FR 62302, Dec. 5, 1994; 60 FR 14353, Mar. 17. 1995; 60 FR 21976, May 4, 1995; 60 FR 44260, 44271, Aug. 25, 1995; 61 FR 46534, 46537, Sept. 4, 1996; 62 FR 10312, 10389, Mar. 6, 1997; 62 FR 18508, 18514, Apr. 16, 1997, as corrected at 62 FR 46553, Sept. 3, 1997; 62 FR 39417, 39425, July 23, 1997; 63 FR 27823, 27833, May 21, 1998; 63 FR 63593, 63597, Nov. 16, 1998, as comfirmed and amended at 65 FR 15846, 15854, Mar. 24, 2000; 64 FR 25756, 25773, May 12, 1999, as confirmed and amended at 65 FR 15835, 15846, Mar. 24, 2000; 64 FR 27856, 27881, May 21, 1999; 65 FR 14774, 14780, Mar. 17, 2000; 65 FR 43677, 439680, July 14, 2000; 66 FR 29661, 29681, June 1, 2001, as confirmed at 67 FR 38341, 38350, June 4, 2002; 66 FR 42587, 42595, Aug. 14, 2001; 66 FR 46697, 46704, Sept. 7, 2001; 67 FR 4784, 4803, Jan. 31, 2002; 67 FR 76256, 76280, Dec. 11, 2002; 69 FR 34913, June 23, 2004; 69 FR 45555, 45557, July 30, 2004, as corrected at 69 FR 47763, Aug. 6, 2004; 72 FR 53014, 53041, Sept. 17, 2007; 73 FR 18944, 18956, Apr. 8, 2008; 73 FR 76891, 76914, Dec. 18, 2008; 74 FR 7993, 7995, Feb. 23, 2009; 74 FR 26514, 26515, June 3, 2009; 74 FR 55094, 55111, Oct. 27, 2009, as confirmed and amended at 76 FR 55502, Sept. 7, 2011; 74 FR 55726, 55740, Oct. 28, 2009; 75 FR 47699, 47701, Aug. 9, 2010; 75 FR 58962, 58990, Sept. 24, 2010; 75 FR 79264, 79277, Dec. 20, 2010; 76 FR 53764, 53796, Aug. 29, 2011; 80 FR 10284, 10311, Feb. 25, 2015; 81 FR 2068, 2084, Jan. 15, 2016; 81 FR 13040, 13117, Mar. 11, 2016; 81 FR 82398, 82491, Nov. 18, 2016; 81 FR 92266, 92312, Dec. 19, 2016; 82 FR 5238, 5289, Jan. 17, 2017; 82 FR 31887, July 11, 2017; 85 FR 21739, 21745, Apr. 20, 2020; 85 FR 28843, 28851, May 14, 2020; 85 FR 29264, 29317, May 14, 2020; 85 FR 38532, 38628, June 26, 2020; 85 FR 46788, 46928, Aug. 3, 2020; 85 FR 51304, 51311, Aug. 20, 2020; 85 FR 82291, 82298, Dec. 18, 2020; 86 FR 28198, 28232, May 25, 2021; 87 FR 4722, 4760, Jan. 28, 2022; 87 FR 30334, 30377, May 18, 2022, as corrected at 87 FR 31095, May 23, 2022; 87 FR 41027, 41031, July 11, 2022; 87 FR 53152, 53300, Aug. 30, 2022; 87 FR 57795, 57798, Sept. 22, 2022; 87 FR 76816, 76876, Dec. 15, 2022; 88 FR 80394, 80458, Nov. 17, 2023; 89 FR 6194, 6399, Jan. 31, 2024; 89 FR 34864, 34943, Apr. 30, 2024; 89 FR 95626, 95683, Dec. 2, 2024; 89 FR 103202, 103334, Dec. 18, 2024]

§ 274a.13 Application for employment authorization. [Effective until October 15, 2025]

(a) Application. An alien requesting employment authorization or an Employment Authorization Document (Form I-766), or both, may be required to apply on a form designated by USCIS with any prescribed fee(s) in accordance with the form instructions. An alien may file such request concurrently with a related benefit request that, if granted, would form the basis for eligibility for employment authorization, only to the extent permitted by the form instructions or as announced by USCIS on its Web site.

(1) The approval of applications filed under 8 CFR 274a.12(c), except for 8 CFR 274a.12(c)(8), are within the discretion of USCIS. Where economic necessity has been identified as a factor, the alien must provide information regarding his or her assets, income, and expenses.

(2) An initial employment authorization request for asylum applicants under 8 CFR 274a.12(c)(8) must be filed on the form designated by USCIS in accordance with the form instructions. The applicant also must submit a copy of the underlying application for asylum or withholding of deportation, together with evidence that the application has been filed in accordance with 8 CFR 208.3 and 208.4. An application for an initial employment authorization or for a renewal of employment authorization filed in relation to a pending claim for asylum shall be adjudicated in accordance with 8 CFR 208.7. An application for renewal or replacement

of employment authorization submitted in relation to a pending claim for asylum, as provided in 8 CFR 208.7, must be filed, with fee or application for waiver of such fee.

(b) Approval of application. If the application is granted, the alien shall be notified of the decision and issued an employment authorization document valid for a specific period and subject to any terms and conditions as noted.

(c) Denial of application. If the application is denied, the applicant shall be notified in writing of the decision and the reasons for the denial. There shall be no appeal from the denial of the application.

(d) Renewal application —

(1) Automatic extension of Employment Authorization Documents. Except as otherwise provided in this chapter or by law, notwithstanding § 274a.14(a)(1)(i), the validity period of an expired or expiring Employment Authorization Document (Form I-766) and, for aliens who are not employment authorized incident to status, also the attendant employment authorization, will be automatically extended for an additional period not to exceed 540 days if the request for renewal meets all of the criteria listed in paragraphs (d)(1)(i) through (iii) of this section and was pending on May 4, 2022, or was properly filed on or after May 4, 2022. For renewal applications properly filed and adjudicated before May 4, 2022, the validity period of such an expired or expiring Employment Authorization Document (Form I-766) and, for aliens who were not employment authorized incident to status, also the attendant employment authorization, was automatically extended for an additional period not to exceed 180 days if the request for renewal met all of the criteria listed in paragraphs (d)(1)(i) through (iii) of this section. The first day of the automatic extension under this paragraph is the day after the expiration date shown on the face of the expired or expiring Employment Authorization Document (Form I-766). To be eligible for the automatic extension under this paragraph, the request must be:

(i) Properly filed on a form designated by USCIS and as provided by form instructions before the expiration date shown on the face of the Employment Authorization Document, or, for Temporary Protected Status-related Employment Authorization Documents (EADs), during the re-registration filing period described in the applicable Federal Register notice;

(ii) Based on the same employment authorization category as shown on the face of the expiring Employment Authorization Document or is for an individual approved for Temporary Protected Status whose EAD was issued pursuant to 8 CFR 274a.12(c)(19); and

(iii) Based on a class of aliens whose eligibility to apply for employment authorization continues notwithstanding expiration of the Employment Authorization Document and is based on an employment authorization category that does not require adjudication of an underlying application or petition before adjudication of the renewal application, including aliens described in 8 CFR 274a.12(a)(12) granted Temporary Protected Status and pending applicants for Temporary Protected Status who are issued an EAD under 8 CFR 274a.12(c)(19), as may be announced on the USCIS Web site.

(2) Terms and conditions. Any extension authorized under this paragraph (d) shall be subject to any conditions and limitations noted in the immediately preceding employment authorization.

(3) Termination. For renewal requests pending on May 4, 2022, or properly filed on or after May 4, 2022, the period authorized by paragraph (d)(1) of this section automatically terminates the earlier of up to 540 days after the expiration date of the Employment Authorization Document (Form I-766), or upon issuance of notification of a decision denying the renewal request. For renewal applications that were properly filed and adjudicated before May 4, 2022, the period authorized by paragraph (d)(1) of this section automatically terminated upon the earlier of up to 180 days after the expiration date of the Employment Authorization Document (Form I-766) or issuance of notification of a decision denying the renewal request. Nothing in paragraph (d) of this section will affect DHS's ability to otherwise terminate any employment authorization or Employment Authorization Document, or extension period for such employment or document, by written notice to the applicant, by notice to a class of aliens published in the Federal Register, or as provided by statute or regulation including 8 CFR 274a.14.

(4) Unexpired Employment Authorization Documents. An Employment Authorization Document (Form I-766) that has expired on its face is considered unexpired when combined with a Notice of Action (Form I-797C), which demonstrates that the requirements of paragraph (d)(1) of this section have been met.

HISTORY:

[52 FR 16221, May 1, 1987, as amended at 53 FR 8614, Mar. 16, 1988; 55 FR 25937, June 25, 1990; 56 FR 41787, Aug. 23, 1991; 57 FR 6462, Feb. 25, 1992, as confirmed at 60 FR 66062, 66067, Dec. 21, 1995; 57 FR 14627, Apr. 21, 1992; 58 FR 12149, Mar. 3, 1993, as corrected at 58 FR 14145, Mar. 13, 1993; 59 FR 33905, July 1, 1994; 59 FR 62303, Dec. 5, 1994; 60 FR 21976, May 4, 1995; 63 FR 27823, 27833, May 21, 1998, as corrected at 63 FR 39121, July 21, 1998, as confirmed and amended at 65 FR 15846, 15854, Mar. 24, 2000; 64 FR 25756, 25773, May 12, 1999, as confirmed and amended at 65 FR 15835, 15846, Mar. 24, 2000; 72 FR 53014, 53042, Sept. 17, 2007; 74 FR 26933, 26940, June 5, 2009; 76 FR 53764, 53796, Aug. 29, 2011; 80 FR 10284, 10312, Feb. 25, 2015; 81 FR 82398, 82491, Nov. 18, 2016; 85 FR 38532, 38628, June 26, 2020; 87 FR 26614, 26651, May 4, 2022; 87 FR 57795, 57799, Sept. 22, 2022; 89 FR 24628, 24676, Apr. 8, 2024; 89 FR 101208, 101267, Dec. 13, 2024]

§ 274a.13 Application for employment authorization. [Effective October 15, 2025; Effective until September 20, 2027]

(a) Application. An alien requesting employment authorization or an Employment Authorization Document (Form I-766), or both, may be required to apply on a form designated by USCIS with any prescribed fee(s) in accordance with the form instructions. An alien may file such request concurrently with a related benefit request that, if granted, would form the basis for eligibility for employment authorization, only to the extent permitted by the form instructions or as announced by USCIS on its Web site.

(1) The approval of applications filed under 8 CFR 274a.12(c), except for 8 CFR 274a.12(c)(8), are within the discretion of USCIS. Where economic necessity has been identified as a factor, the alien must provide information regarding his or her assets, income, and expenses.

(2) An initial employment authorization request for asylum applicants under 8 CFR 274a.12(c)(8) must be filed on the form designated by USCIS in accordance with the form instructions. The applicant also must submit a copy of the underlying application for asylum or withholding of deportation, together with evidence that the application has been filed in accordance with 8 CFR 208.3 and 208.4. An application for an initial employment authorization or for a renewal of employment authorization filed in relation to a pending claim for asylum shall be adjudicated in accordance with 8 CFR 208.7. An application for renewal or replacement of employment authorization submitted in relation to a pending claim for asylum, as provided in 8 CFR 208.7, must be filed, with fee or application for waiver of such fee.

(b) Approval of application. If the application is granted, the alien shall be notified of the decision and issued an employment authorization document valid for a specific period and subject to any terms and conditions as noted.

(c) Denial of application. If the application is denied, the applicant shall be notified in writing of the decision and the reasons for the denial. There shall be no appeal from the denial of the application.

(d) Renewal application —

(1) Automatic extension of Employment Authorization Documents. Except as otherwise provided in this chapter or by law, notwithstanding § 274a.14(a)(1)(i), the validity period of an expired or expiring Employment Authorization Document (Form I-766) and, for aliens who are not employment authorized incident to status, also the attendant employment authorization, will be automatically extended for an additional period not to exceed 540 days if the request for renewal meets all of the criteria listed in paragraphs (d)(1)(i) through (iii) of this section and was pending on May 4, 2022, or was properly filed on or after May 4, 2022. For renewal applications properly filed and adjudicated before May 4, 2022, the validity period of such an expired or expiring Employment Authorization Document (Form I-766) and, for aliens who were not employment authorized incident to status, also the attendant employment authorization, was automatically extended for an additional period not to exceed 180 days if the request for renewal met all of the criteria listed in paragraphs (d)(1)(i) through (iii) of this section. The first day of the automatic extension under this paragraph is the day after the expiration date shown on the face of the expired or expiring Employment Authorization Document (Form I-766). To be eligible for the automatic extension under this paragraph, the request must be:

(i) Properly filed on a form designated by USCIS and as provided by form instructions before the expiration date shown on the face of the Employment Authorization Document, or, for Temporary Protected Status-related Employment Authorization Documents (EADs), during the re-registration filing period described in the applicable Federal Register notice;

(ii) Based on the same employment authorization category as shown on the face of the expiring Employment Authorization Document or is for an individual approved for Temporary Protected Status whose EAD was issued pursuant to 8 CFR 274a.12(c)(19); and

(iii) Based on a class of aliens whose eligibility to apply for employment authorization continues notwithstanding expiration of the Employment Authorization Document and is based on an employment authorization category that does not require adjudication of an underlying application or petition before adjudication of the renewal application, including aliens described in 8 CFR 274a.12(a)(12) granted Temporary Protected Status and pending applicants for Temporary Protected Status who are issued an EAD under 8 CFR 274a.12(c)(19), as may be announced on the USCIS Web site.

(2) Terms and conditions. Any extension authorized under this paragraph (d) shall be subject to any conditions and limitations noted in the immediately preceding employment authorization.

(3) Termination. For renewal requests pending on May 4, 2022, or properly filed on or after May 4, 2022, the period authorized by paragraph (d)(1) of this section automatically terminates the earlier of up to 540 days after the expiration date of the Employment Authorization Document (Form I-766), or upon issuance of notification of a decision denying the renewal request. For renewal applications that were properly filed and adjudicated before May 4, 2022, the period authorized by paragraph (d)(1) of this section automatically terminated upon the earlier of up to 180 days after the expiration date of the Employment Authorization Document (Form I-766) or issuance of notification of a decision denying the renewal request. Nothing in paragraph (d) of this section will affect DHS's ability to otherwise terminate any employment authorization or Employment Authorization Document, or extension period for such employment or document, by written notice to the applicant, by notice to a class of aliens published in the Federal Register , or as provided by statute or regulation including 8 CFR 274a.14.

(4) Unexpired Employment Authorization Documents. An Employment Authorization Document (Form I-766) that has expired on its face is considered unexpired when combined with a Notice of Action (Form I-797C), which demonstrates that the requirements of paragraph (d)(1) of this section have been met.

HISTORY:

[52 FR 16221, May 1, 1987, as amended at 53 FR 8614, Mar. 16, 1988; 55 FR 25937, June 25, 1990; 56 FR 41787, Aug. 23, 1991; 57 FR 6462, Feb. 25, 1992, as confirmed at 60 FR 66062, 66067, Dec. 21, 1995; 57 FR 14627, Apr. 21, 1992; 58 FR 12149, Mar. 3, 1993, as corrected at 58 FR 14145, Mar. 13, 1993; 59 FR 33905, July 1, 1994; 59 FR 62303, Dec. 5, 1994; 60 FR 21976, May 4, 1995; 63 FR 27823, 27833, May 21, 1998, as corrected at 63 FR 39121, July 21, 1998, as confirmed and amended at 65 FR 15846, 15854, Mar. 24, 2000; 64 FR 25756, 25773, May 12, 1999, as confirmed and amended at 65 FR 15835, 15846, Mar. 24, 2000; 72 FR 53014, 53042, Sept. 17, 2007; 74 FR 26933, 26940, June 5, 2009; 76 FR 53764, 53796, Aug.

29, 2011; 80 FR 10284, 10312, Feb. 25, 2015; 81 FR 82398, 82491, Nov. 18, 2016; 85 FR 38532, 38628, June 26, 2020; 87 FR 26614, 26651, May 4, 2022; 87 FR 57795, 57799, Sept. 22, 2022; 89 FR 24628, 24676, Apr. 8, 2024; 89 FR 101208, 101267, Dec. 13, 2024]

§ 274a.13 Application for employment authorization. [Effective September 20, 2027]

(a) Application. An alien requesting employment authorization or an Employment Authorization Document (Form I-766), or both, may be required to apply on a form designated by USCIS with any prescribed fee(s) in accordance with the form instructions. An alien may file such request concurrently with a related benefit request that, if granted, would form the basis for eligibility for employment authorization, only to the extent permitted by the form instructions or as announced by USCIS on its Web site.

(1) The approval of applications filed under 8 CFR 274a.12(c), except for 8 CFR 274a.12(c)(8), are within the discretion of USCIS. Where economic necessity has been identified as a factor, the alien must provide information regarding his or her assets, income, and expenses.

(2) An initial employment authorization request for asylum applicants under 8 CFR 274a.12(c)(8) must be filed on the form designated by USCIS in accordance with the form instructions. The applicant also must submit a copy of the underlying application for asylum or withholding of deportation, together with evidence that the application has been filed in accordance with 8 CFR 208.3 and 208.4. An application for an initial employment authorization or for a renewal of employment authorization filed in relation to a pending claim for asylum shall be adjudicated in accordance with 8 CFR 208.7. An application for renewal or replacement of employment authorization submitted in relation to a pending claim for asylum, as provided in 8 CFR 208.7, must be filed, with fee or application for waiver of such fee.

(b) Approval of application. If the application is granted, the alien shall be notified of the decision and issued an employment authorization document valid for a specific period and subject to any terms and conditions as noted.

(c) Denial of application. If the application is denied, the applicant shall be notified in writing of the decision and the reasons for the denial. There shall be no appeal from the denial of the application.

(d) Renewal application —

(1) Automatic extension of Employment Authorization Documents. Except as otherwise provided in this chapter or by law, notwithstanding § 274a.14(a)(1)(i), the validity period of an expired or expiring Employment Authorization Document (Form I-766) and, for aliens who are not employment authorized incident to status, also the attendant employment authorization, will be automatically extended for an additional period not to exceed 540 days if the request for renewal meets all of the criteria listed in paragraphs (d)(1)(i) through (iii) of this section and was pending on May 4, 2022, or was properly filed on or after May 4, 2022. For renewal applications properly filed and adjudicated before May 4, 2022, the validity period of such an expired or expiring Employment Authorization Document (Form I-766) and, for aliens who were not employment authorized incident to status, also the attendant employment authorization, was automatically extended for an additional period not to exceed 180 days if the request for renewal met all of the criteria listed in paragraphs (d)(1)(i) through (iii) of this section. The first day of the automatic extension under this paragraph is the day after the expiration date shown on the face of the expired or expiring Employment Authorization Document (Form I-766). To be eligible for the automatic extension under this paragraph, the request must be:

(i) Properly filed on a form designated by USCIS and as provided by form instructions before the expiration date shown on the face of the Employment Authorization Document, or, for Temporary Protected Status-related Employment Authorization Documents (EADs), during the re-registration filing period described in the applicable Federal Register notice;

(ii) Based on the same employment authorization category as shown on the face of the expiring Employment Authorization Document or is for an individual approved for Temporary Protected Status whose EAD was issued pursuant to 8 CFR 274a.12(c)(19); and

(iii) Based on a class of aliens whose eligibility to apply for employment authorization continues notwithstanding expiration of the Employment Authorization Document and is based on an employment authorization category that does not require adjudication of an underlying application or petition before adjudication of the renewal application, including aliens described in 8 CFR 274a.12(a)(12) granted Temporary Protected Status and pending applicants for Temporary Protected Status who are issued an EAD under 8 CFR 274a.12(c)(19), as may be announced on the USCIS Web site.

(2) Terms and conditions. Any extension authorized under this paragraph (d) shall be subject to any conditions and limitations noted in the immediately preceding employment authorization.

(3) Termination. For renewal requests pending on May 4, 2022, or properly filed on or after May 4, 2022, the period authorized by paragraph (d)(1) of this section automatically terminates the earlier of up to 540 days after the expiration date of the Employment Authorization Document (Form I-766), or upon issuance of notification of a decision denying the renewal request. For renewal applications that were properly filed and adjudicated before May 4, 2022, the period authorized by paragraph (d)(1) of this section automatically terminated upon the earlier of up to 180 days after the expiration date of the Employment Authorization Document (Form I-766) or issuance of notification of a decision denying the renewal request. Nothing in paragraph (d) of this section will affect DHS's ability to otherwise terminate any employment authorization or Employment Authorization Document, or extension period for such employment or document, by written notice to the applicant, by notice to a class of aliens published in the Federal Register , or as provided by statute or regulation including 8 CFR 274a.14.

(4) Unexpired Employment Authorization Documents. An Employment Authorization Document (Form I-766) that has expired on its face is considered unexpired when combined with a Notice of Action (Form I-797C), which demonstrates that the requirements of paragraph (d)(1) of this section have been met.

HISTORY:

[52 FR 16221, May 1, 1987, as amended at 53 FR 8614, Mar. 16, 1988; 55 FR 25937, June 25, 1990; 56 FR 41787, Aug. 23, 1991; 57 FR 6462, Feb. 25, 1992, as confirmed at 60 FR 66062, 66067, Dec. 21, 1995; 57 FR 14627, Apr. 21, 1992; 58 FR 12149, Mar. 3, 1993, as corrected at 58 FR 14145, Mar. 13, 1993; 59 FR 33905, July 1, 1994; 59 FR 62303, Dec. 5, 1994; 60 FR 21976, May 4, 1995; 63 FR 27823, 27833, May 21, 1998, as corrected at 63 FR 39121, July 21, 1998, as confirmed and amended at 65 FR 15846, 15854, Mar. 24, 2000; 64 FR 25756, 25773, May 12, 1999, as confirmed and amended at 65 FR 15835, 15846, Mar. 24, 2000; 72 FR 53014, 53042, Sept. 17, 2007; 74 FR 26933, 26940, June 5, 2009; 76 FR 53764, 53796, Aug. 29, 2011; 80 FR 10284, 10312, Feb. 25, 2015; 81 FR 82398, 82491, Nov. 18, 2016; 85 FR 38532, 38628, June 26, 2020; 87 FR 26614, 26651, May 4, 2022; 87 FR 57795, 57799, Sept. 22, 2022; 89 FR 24628, 24676, Apr. 8, 2024; 89 FR 101208, 101267, Dec. 13, 2024]

§ 274a.14 Termination of employment authorization.

(a) Automatic termination of employment authorization —

(1) Employment authorization granted under § 274a.12(c) of this chapter shall automatically terminate upon the occurrence of one of the following events:

(i) The expiration date specified by the Service on the employment authorization document is reached;

(ii) Exclusion or deportation proceedings are instituted (however, this shall not preclude the authorization of employment pursuant to § 274a.12(c) of this part where appropriate); or

(iii) The alien is granted voluntary departure.

(2) Termination of employment authorization pursuant to this paragraph does not require the service of a notice of intent to revoke; employment authorization terminates upon the occurrence of any event enumerated in paragraph (a)(1) of this section.

However, automatic revocation under this section does not preclude reapplication for employment authorization under § 274.12(c) of this part.

(b) Revocation of employment authorization —

(1) Basis for revocation of employment authorization. Employment authorization granted under § 274a.12(c) of this chapter may be revoked by the district director:

(i) Prior to the expiration date, when it appears that any condition upon which it was granted has not been met or no longer exists, or for good cause shown; or

(ii) Upon a showing that the information contained in the application is not true and correct.

(2) Notice of intent to revoke employment authorization. When a district director determines that employment authorization should be revoked prior to the expiration date specified by the Service, he or she shall serve written notice of intent to revoke the employment authorization. The notice will cite the reasons indicating that revocation is warranted. The alien will be granted a period of fifteen days from the date of service of the notice within which to submit countervailing evidence. The decision by the district director shall be final and no appeal shall lie from the decision to revoke the authorization.

(c) Automatic termination of temporary employment authorization granted prior to June 1, 1987 —

(1) Temporary employment authorization granted prior to June 1, 1987, pursuant to 8 CFR 274a.12(c) (§ 109.1(b) contained in the 8 CFR edition revised as of January 1, 1987), shall automatically terminate on the date specified by the Service on the document issued to the alien, or on December 31, 1996, whichever is earlier. Automatic termination of temporary employment authorization does not preclude a subsequent application for temporary employment authorization.

(2) A document issued by the Service prior to June 1, 1987, that authorized temporary employment authorization for any period beyond December 31, 1996, is null and void pursuant to paragraph (c)(1) of this section. The alien shall be issued a new employment authorization document upon application to the Service if the alien is eligible for temporary employment authorization pursuant to 274A.12(c).

(3) No notice of intent to revoke is necessary for the automatic termination of temporary employment authorization pursuant to this part.

HISTORY:

[52 FR 16221, May 1, 1987, as amended at 53 FR 8614, Mar. 16, 1988; 53 FR 20087, June 1, 1988; 61 FR 46534, 46537, Sept. 4, 1996; 85 FR 38532, 38628, June 26, 2020; 87 FR 57795, 57799, Sept. 22, 2022]

PART 280

IMPOSITION AND COLLECTION OF FINES

Rule

AUTHORITY NOTE APPLICABLE TO ENTIRE PART:

AUTHORITY:

8 U.S.C. 1103, 1221, 1223, 1227, 1229, 1253, 1281, 1283, 1284, 1285, 1286, 1322, 1323, 1330; 66 Stat. 173, 195, 197, 201, 203, 212,

219, 221-223, 226, 227, 230; Pub. L. 101-410, 104 Stat. 890, as amended by Pub. L. 114-74, 129 Stat. 599.

§ 280.1 Notice of intention to fine; administrative proceedings not exclusive.

Whenever a district director or the Associate Commissioner for Examinations, or the Director for the National Fines Office has reason to believe that any person has violated any of the provisions of the Immigration and Nationality Act and has thereby become liable to the imposition of an administrative fine under the Immigration and Nationality Act, he shall cause a Notice of Intention to Fine, Form I-79, to be served as provided in this part. Nothing in this subchapter shall affect, restrict, or prevent the institution of a civil suit, in the discretion of the Attorney General, under the authority contained in section 280 of the Immigration and Nationality Act.

HISTORY:

[22 FR 9807, Dec. 6, 1957, as amended at 54 FR 18649, May 2, 1989]

§ 280.2 Special provisions relating to aircraft.

In any case in which the imposition of a fine is predicated upon an alleged violation of a regulation promulgated under authority of section 239 of the Immigration and Nationality Act, the procedure prescribed in this part shall be followed and the aircraft involved shall not be granted clearance pending determination of the question of liability to the payment of any fine, or while the fine remains unpaid; but clearance may be granted prior to the determination of such question upon the deposit of a sum sufficient to cover such fine or of a bond with sufficient surety to secure the payment thereof, approved by the Commisioner. If the alleged violation was by the owner or person in command of the aircraft, the penalty provided for shall be a lien against the aircraft, which, except as provided in § 280.21, shall be seized by the district director or by an immigration officer designated by the district director, and placed in the custody of the customs officer who is in charge of the port of entry or customs station nearest the place of seizure. If the owner or owners of the airport at which such aircraft is located are the owners of the seized aircraft, the aircraft shall be removed to another suitable place for storage if practicable.

HISTORY:

[22 FR 9807, Dec. 6, 1957, as amended at 32 FR 17651, Dec. 12, 1967; 56 FR 26020, June 6, 1991]

§ 280.3 Departure of vessel or aircraft prior to denial of clearance.

If any vessel or aircraft which is subject to the imposition of a fine shall have departed from the United States prior to the denial of clearance by the district director of customs and such vessel or aircraft is subsequently found in the United States, a Notice of Intention to Fine, Form I-79, shall be served as provided in this part, if such form has not been previously served for the same violation. Clearance of such vessel or aircraft shall be withheld by the district director of customs, and the procedure prescribed in this part shall be followed to the same extent and in the same manner as though the vessel or aircraft had not departed from the United States. Aircraft subject to the provisions of § 280.2, which shall have departed from the United States prior to the time of seizure could be effected, shall be subject to all of the provisions of this part, if subsequently found in the United States, to the same extent as though it had not departed from the United States.

HISTORY:

[22 FR 9807, Dec. 6, 1957, as amended at 32 FR 17651, Dec. 12, 1967]

§ 280.4 Data concerning cost of transportation.

Within five days after request therefor, transportation companies shall furnish to the district director or the Associate Commissioner for Examinations, or the Director for the National Fines Office pertinent information contained in the original transportation contract of all rejected aliens whose cases are within the purview of any of the provisions of the Immigration and Nationality Act relating to refund of passage monies, and shall specify the exact amounts paid for transportation from the initial point of departure (which point shall be indicated) to the foreign port of embarkation, from the latter to the port of arrival in the United States and from the port of arrival to the inland point of destination, respectively, and also the amount paid for headtax, if any.

HISTORY:

[22 FR 9807, Dec. 6, 1957, as amended at 54 FR 18649, May 2, 1989]

§ 280.5 Mitigation or remission of fines.

In any case in which mitigation or remission of a fine is authorized by the Immigration and Nationality Act, the party served with Notice of Intention to Fine may apply in writing to the district director or the Associate Commissioner for Examinations, or the Director for the National Fines Office for such mitigation or remission.

HISTORY:

[22 FR 9807, Dec. 6, 1957, as amended at 54 FR 18649, May 2, 1989]

§ 280.6 Bond to obtain clearance; form.

A bond to obtain clearance of a vessel or aircraft under section 231, 237, 239, 243, 251, 253, 254, 255, 256, 272, or 273 of the Immigration and Nationality Act shall be filed on Form I-310.

HISTORY:

[22 FR 9807, Dec. 6, 1957, as amended at 54 FR 102, Jan. 4, 1989]

§ 280.7 Approval of bonds or acceptance of cash deposit to obtain clearance.

The district director of customs is authorized to approve the bond, or accept the sum of money which is being offered for deposit under any provision of the Immigration and Nationality Act or by this chapter for the purpose of obtaining clearance of a vessel or aircraft with the exception of sections 239, 251(d), 255, 256, 272, and 273(d) in which the Commissioner of the Immigration and Naturalization Service is authorized to approve the bond or accept the sum of money which is being offered for deposit.

HISTORY:

[22 FR 9807, Dec. 6, 1957, as amended at 32 FR 17651, Dec. 12, 1967; 56 FR 26020, June 6, 1991]

§ 280.11 Notice of intention to fine; procedure.

Notice of Intention to Fine, Form I-79, shall be prepared in triplicate, with one additional copy for each additional person on whom the service of such notice is contemplated. The notice shall be addressed to any or all of the available persons subject to fine. A copy of the notice shall be served by personal service on each such person. If the notice is delivered personally, the person upon whom it is served shall be requested to acknowledge such service by signing his name to the duplicate and triplicate copies. The officer effecting such service shall attest to the service by signing his name thereon and shall indicate thereon the date and place of service. If the person so served refuses to acknowledge service, or if service is made by leaving it at an office or mailing it, the person making such service shall indicate the method and date on the duplicate and triplicate copies of Form I-79, and shall sign his name upon such copies. The duplicate copy shall be retained by the district director of immigration and naturalization or the Associate Commissioner for Examinations, or the Director for the National Fines Office and the triplicate copy shall be delivered directly to the district director of customs for the district in which the vessel or aircraft is located, and the district director of customs shall withhold clearance until deposit is made or bond furnished as provided in the Immigration and Nationality Act. If the vessel or aircraft is located in a customs district which is outside the jurisdiction of the office of the Service having jurisdiction over the matter, the triplicate copy shall be forwarded to the office of the Service nearest such customs district for delivery to the district director of customs.

HISTORY:

[22 FR 9807, Dec. 6, 1957, as amended at 32 FR 17651, Dec. 12, 1967; 37 FR 11471, June 8, 1972; 54 FR 18649, May 2, 1989]

§ 280.12 Answer and request or order for interview.

Within 30 days following the service of the Notice of Intention to Fine (which period the district director or the Associate Commissioner for Examinations, or the Director for the National Fines Office may extend for an additional period of 30 days upon good cause being shown), any person upon whom a notice under this part has been served may file with the district director or the Associate Commissioner for Examinations, or the Director for the National Fines Office a written defense, in duplicate, under oath setting forth the reasons why a fine should not be imposed, or if imposed, why it should be mitigated or remitted if permitted by the Immigration and Nationality Act, and stating whether a personal appearance is desired. Documentary evidence shall be submitted in support of such defense and a brief may be submitted in support of any argument made. If a personal interview is requested, the evidence in opposition to the imposition of the fine and in support of the request for mitigation or remission may be presented at such interview. An interview shall be conducted if requested by the party as provided hereinabove or, if directed at any time by the Board, the Commissioner, or the district director or the Associate Commissioner for Examinations, or the Director for the National Fines Office.

HISTORY:

[22 FR 9807, Dec. 6, 1957, as amended at 54 FR 18649, May 2, 1989]

§ 280.13 Disposition of case.

(a) Allegations admitted or no answer filed. If a request for personal appearance is not filed and (1) the answer admits the allegations in the notice, or (2) no answer is filed, the district director or the Associate Commissioner for Examinations, or the Director for the National Fines Office shall enter such order in the case as he deems appropriate and no appeal from his decision may be taken.

(b) Answer filed; personal appearance. Upon receipt of an answer asserting a defense to the allegations in the notice without requesting a personal appearance, or if a personal appearance is requested or directed, the case shall be assigned to an immigration officer. The immigration officer shall prepare a report summarizing the evidence and containing his findings and recommendation. The record, including the report and recommendation of the immigration officer, shall be forwarded to the district director or the Associate Commissioner for Examinations, or the Director for the National Fines Office. The district director or the Associate Commissioner for Examinations, or the Director for the National Fines Office shall note on the report of the immigration officer whether he approves or disapproves the recommendation of the immigration officer. The person shall be informed in writing of the decision of the district director or the Associate Commissioner for Examinations, or the Director for the National Fines Office and, if his decision is that a fine shall be imposed or that the requested mitigation or remission shall not be granted, of the reasons for such decision. From the decision of the district director or the Associate Commissioner for Examinations, or the Director for the National Fines Office an appeal may be taken to the Board as provided in 8 CFR part 1003.

HISTORY:

[22 FR 9808, Dec. 6, 1957, as amended at 23 FR 9124, Nov. 26, 1958; 54 FR 18649, May 2, 1989; 76 FR 74625, 74629, Dec. 1, 2011]

§ 280.14 Record.

The record made under § 280.13 shall include the request for the interview or a reference to the order directing the interview; the medical certificate, if any; a copy of any record of hearing before a Board of Special Inquiry, Hearing Examiner, Hearing Officer, or Special Inquiry Officer which is relevant to the fine proceedings; the duplicate copy of the Notice of Intention to Fine; the evidence upon which such Notice was based; the duplicate of any notices to detain, deport, deliver, or remove aliens; notice to pay expenses; evidence as to whether any deposit was made or bond furnished in accordance with the Immigration and Nationality Act; reports of investigations conducted; documentary evidence and testimony adduced at the interview; the original of any affidavit or brief filed in opposition to the imposition of fine; the application for mitigation or remission; and any other relevant matter.

HISTORY:

[22 FR 9807, Dec. 6, 1957]

§ 280.15 Notice of final decision to district director of customs.

At such time as the decision under this part is final, the regional administrative officer shall be furnished a copy of the decision by the district director of immigration and naturalization or the Associate Commissioner for Examinations, or the Director for the National Fines Office. The regional administrative officer shall notify the district director of customs who was furnished a copy of the Notice of Intention to Fine of the final decision made in the case. Such notification need not be made if the regional administrative officer has been previously furnished with a notice of collection of the amount of the penalty by the district director of customs.

HISTORY:

[32 FR 17651, Dec. 12, 1967, as amended at 54 FR 18649, May 2, 1989]

§ 280.21 Seizure of aircraft.

Seizure of an aircraft under the authority of section 239 of the Act and § 280.2 will not be made if such aircraft is damaged to an extent that its value is less than the amount of the fine which may be imposed. If seizure of an aircraft for violation of section 239 of the Act is to be made, Form G-297 (Order to Seize Aircraft) and Form G-298 (Public Notice of Seizure) shall be prepared in septuple and the originals furnished to the immigration officer who will effect the seizure. The original of Form G-297, properly endorsed as to date and place of seizure, shall be returned for retention in the relating file after seizure is effected. The original of Form G-298 shall be placed on the seized aircraft and a copy retained in the file. Copies of both forms shall be served upon the owner of the aircraft and the pilot if other than the owner. Copies shall also be furnished the district director of customs and the United States Attorney for the district in which the seizure was made. In addition, immediately upon the seizure of an aircraft, or prior thereto, if circumstances permit, a full report of the facts in the case shall be submitted by the district director to the United States Attorney for the district in which the seizure was made, together with copies of Form G-296 (Report of Violation) and Form I-79 (Notice of Intention to Fine). The report shall include the cost incurred in seizing and guarding the aircraft and an estimate of the further additional cost likely to be incurred.

HISTORY:

[29 FR 14433, Oct. 21, 1964, as amended at 32 FR 17651, Dec. 12, 1967]

§ 280.51 Application for mitigation or remission.

(a) When application may be filed. An application for mitigation or remission of a fine may be filed as provided under § 280.12 of this part; or, within 30 days after the date of receipt of the district director's or the Associate Commissioner for Examinations, or the Director for the National Fines Office's decision to impose a fine whether or not the applicant responded to the Notice of Intention to Fine.

(b) Form and contents of application. An application for mitigation or remission shall be filed in duplicate under oath and shall include information, supported by documentary evidence, as to the basis of the claim to mitigation or remission, and as to the action, if any, which may have been taken by the applicant, or as to the circumstances present in the case which, in the opinion of the applicant, justified the granting of his application.

(c) Disposition of application. The application, if filed with the answer, shall be disposed of as provided in § 280.13. In any other case the application shall be considered and decided by the district director or the Associate Commissioner for Examinations, or the Director for the National Fines Office from whose decision an appeal may be taken to the Board as provided in 8 CFR part 1003.

HISTORY:

[22 FR 9808, Dec. 6, 1957, as amended at 23 FR 9124, Nov. 26, 1958; 46 FR 28624, May 28, 1981; 54 FR 18649, May 2, 1989; FR 76 74625, 74629, Dec. 1, 2011]

§ 280.52 Payment of fines.

(a) All fines assessed pursuant to sections 231(d); 237(b); 239; 251(d); 254(a); 255; 256; 271(a); 272, 273 and 274(c) of the Act shall be made payable to and collected by the Service.

(b) All fines collected pursuant to sections 271(a) and 273 of the Act shall be deposited in the Immigration User Fee Account established in accordance with the provisions of section 286 of the Act.

(c) From the amounts collected under paragraphs (a) and (b) of this section, the increase in penalties collected resulting from the amendments made by sections 203(b), 543(a), and 544 of the Immigration Act of 1990, shall be credited to the appropriation for activities authorized under section 280(b) of the Act.

HISTORY:

[56 FR 26020, June 6, 1991]

§ 280.53 Civil monetary penalties inflation adjustment.

(a) Statutory authority. In accordance with the requirements of the Federal Civil Penalties Inflation Adjustment Act of 1990, Public Law 101-410, 104 Stat. 890, as amended by the Federal Civil Penalties Inflation Adjustment Act Improvements Act of 2015, Public Law 114-74, Sec. 701, 129 Stat. 599, the civil monetary penalties listed in paragraph (b) of this section are adjusted as provided in paragraph (b).

(b) Adjustment of penalties. For violations occurring on or before November 2, 2015, the penalty amount prior to adjustment applies. For violations occurring after November 2, 2015, the listed penalties are adjusted as follows:

(1) Section 231(g) of the Act, penalties for non-compliance with arrival and departure manifest requirements for passengers, crewmembers, or occupants transported on commercial vessels or aircraft arriving to or departing from the United States: From $1,696 to $1,740.

(2) Section 234 of the Act, penalties for non-compliance with landing requirements at designated ports of entry for aircraft transporting aliens: From $4,610 to $4,730.

(3) Section 240B(d) of the Act, penalties for failure to depart voluntarily: From $1,942 minimum/$9,718 maximum to $1,992 minimum/$9,970 maximum.

(4) Section 243(c)(1)(A) of the Act, penalties for violations of removal orders relating to aliens transported on vessels or aircraft, under section 241(d) of the Act, or for costs associated with removal under section 241(e) of the Act: From $3,887 to $3,988.

(5) Penalties for failure to remove alien stowaways under section 241(d)(2) of the Act: From $9,718 to $9,970.

(6) Section 251(d) of the Act, penalties for failure to report an illegal landing or desertion of alien crewmen, and for each alien not reported on arrival or departure manifest or lists required in accordance with section 251 of the Act: From $460 to $472; and penalties for use of alien crewmen for longshore work in violation of section 251(d) of the Act: From $11,524 to $11,823.

(7) Section 254(a) of the Act, penalties for failure to control, detain, or remove alien crewmen: From $1,152 minimum/$6,913 maximum to $1,182 minimum/$7,093 maximum.

(8) Section 255 of the Act, penalties for employment on passenger vessels of aliens afflicted with certain disabilities: From $2,304 to $2,364.

(9) Section 256 of the Act, penalties for discharge of alien crewmen: From $3,457 minimum/$6,913 maximum to $3,547 minimum/$7,093 maximum.

(10) Section 257 of the Act, penalties for bringing into the United States alien crewmen with intent to evade immigration laws: From $23,048 maximum to $23,647 maximum.

(11) Section 271(a) of the Act, penalties for failure to prevent the unauthorized landing of aliens: From $6,913 to $7,093.

(12) Section 272(a) of the Act, penalties for bringing to the United States aliens subject to denial of admission on a health-related ground: From $6,913 to $7,093.

(13) Section 273(b) of the Act, penalties for bringing to the United States aliens without required documentation: From $6,913 to $7,093.

(14) Section 274D of the Act, penalties for failure to depart: From $973 maximum to $998 maximum, for each day the alien is in violation.

(15) Section 275(b) of the Act, penalties for improper entry: From $97 minimum/$487 maximum to $100 minimum/$500 maximum, for each entry or attempted entry.

HISTORY:

[64 FR 47099, 47102, Aug. 30, 1999; 73 FR 10130, 10136, Feb. 26, 2008; 76 FR 74625, 74629, Dec. 1, 2011; 81 FR 42987, 43002, July 1, 2016, as confirmed and revised at 82 FR 8571, 8579, 8580, Jan. 27, 2017; 83 FR 13826, 13835, Apr. 2, 2018; 84 FR 13499, 13509, Apr. 5, 2019; 85 FR 36469, 36479, June 17, 2020; 86 FR 57532, 57540, Oct. 18, 2021; 87 FR 1317, 1327, Jan. 11, 2022; 88 FR 2175, 2183, Jan. 13, 2023; 89 FR 53849, 53859, June 28, 2024; 90 FR 1, 10, Jan. 2, 2025]

PART 286

IMMIGRATION USER FEE

Rule

AUTHORITY NOTE APPLICABLE TO ENTIRE PART:

AUTHORITY:

8 U.S.C. 1101, 1103, 1356; Title VII of Public Law 110-229; 8 CFR part 2.

§ 286.1 Definitions.

The following definitions apply to the following terms in this part:

(a) The term adjacent islands means Anguilla, Antigua, Aruba, Bahamas, Barbados, Barbuda, Bermuda, Bonaire, British Virgin Islands, Cayman Islands, Cuba,

Curacao, Dominica, the Dominican Republic, Grenada, Guadeloupe, Haiti, Jamaica, Marie-Galante, Martinique, Miquelon, Montserrat, Saba, Saint Barthellemy, Saint Christopher, Saint Eustatius, Saint Kitts-Nevis, Saint Lucia, Saint Maarten, Saint Martin, Saint Pierre, Saint Vincent and Grenadines, Trinidad and Tobago, Turks and Caicos Islands, and other British, French and Netherlands territory or possessions bordering on the Caribbean Sea.

(b) The term collector means an air or sea carrier, travel agent, tour wholesaler, or other entity which collects, but may or may not be required to remit, fees pursuant to this part.

(c) The term commercial aircraft means any civilian aircraft being used to transport persons or property for compensation or hire.

(d) The term commercial vessel means any civilian vessel being used to transport persons or property for compensation or hire.

(e) The term Assistant Commissioner, Office of Financial Management means the Office of the Assistant Commissioner, Financial Management, Immigration and Naturalization Service, Room 6307, 425 I Street NW., Washington, DC 20536.

(f) The term fee means the immigration user fee.

(g) The term port of entry means a port or place designated by the Commissioner at which a person may apply for admission into the United States.

(h) The term remitter means an air or sea carrier, travel agent, tour wholesaler, or other entity which collects, including receipt of fees collected by collectors which are not required to remit fees, and remits fees pursuant to this part.

(i) Territories or possessions of the United States means American Samoa, Baker Island, Howland Island, Jarvis Island, Johnston Atoll, Kingman Reef, Midway, Swains Island, Palmyra Island, and Wake Island.

(j) The term document for transportation means any document accepted by a carrier in return for transportation.

(k) United States, when used in a geographical sense, means the continental United States, Alaska, Hawaii, Puerto Rico, Guam, the Virgin Islands of the United States, and the Commonwealth of the Northern Mariana Islands.

HISTORY:

[53 FR 5757, Feb. 26, 1988; 59 FR 49349, Sept. 28, 1994; 63 FR 51271, 51272, Sept. 25, 1998; 74 FR 55726, 55740, Oct. 28, 2009]

§ 286.2 Fee for arrival of passengers aboard commercial aircraft or commercial vessels.

(a) A fee, in the amount prescribed in section 286(d) of the Act, per individual is charged and collected by the Commissioner for the immigration inspection of each passenger aboard a commercial aircraft or commercial vessel, arriving at a port-of-entry in the United States, or for the preinspection of a passenger in a place outside the United States prior to such arrival, except as provided in § 286.3.

(b) A fee, in the amount prescribed in section 286(e)(3) of the Act, per individual, is charged and collected by the Commissioner for the immigration inspection at a port-of-entry in the United States, or for the preinspection in a place outside the United States of each commercial vessel passenger whose journey originated in the United States, Canada, Mexico, territories or possessions of the United States, or adjacent islands, except as provided in § 286.3. All tickets or documents for transportation on voyages that are booked on or after February 27, 2003, will be subject to this immigration user fee.

(c) Each commercial aircraft and vessel carrier or ticket-selling agent whose monthly collections in any month exceed $ 50,000 shall submit a summary statement showing the amount of user fees collected that month. The summary statement is due on the last business day of the following month. This information shall be forwarded to the Immigration and Naturalization Service, Chief, Analysis and Formulation Branch, 425 I Street, NW., Room 6307, Washington, DC 20536. For the months of December, March, June, and August, the quarterly remittance and statement required by § 286.5 will serve as the monthly report for those months. Therefore, a monthly report is required for all other months in which monthly collections exceed $ 50,000.

HISTORY:

[53 FR 5757, Feb. 26, 1988; 59 FR 49348, Sept. 28, 1994; 63 FR 51271, 51272, Sept. 25, 1998; 67 FR 15333, 15334, Apr. 1, 2002; 68 FR 4090, 4092, Jan. 28, 2003]

§ 286.3 Exceptions.

The fees set forth in §§ 286.2(a) and 286.2(b) shall not be charged or collected from passengers who fall within any one of the following categories:

(a) Persons arriving at designated ports-of-entry by the following vessels, when operating on a regular schedule: Great Lakes international ferries or Great Lakes vessels on the Great Lakes and connecting waterways;

(b) Persons directly connected with the operation, navigation, or business of the commercial aircraft or commercial vessel including working crew, deadheading crew, U.S. Federal Aviation Administration inspectors, sky marshals, and commercial airline or commercial vessel employees on official business;

(c) Persons who are listed as foreign diplomats on the accreditation list maintained by the U.S. Department of State or who are in possession of a diplomatic visa (A-1 and 2, G-1 thru 4) valid for entry into the United States;

(d) Persons who are passengers on any commercial aircraft or commercial vessel owned or operated exclusively by the Government of the United States or a foreign government, including any agency or political subdivision thereof, so long as that aircraft or vessel is not transporting any persons or property for commercial purposes.

(e) Persons who are passengers on commercial aircraft or commercial vessels under contract to the U.S. Department of Defense, if they have been preinspected outside of the United States under a joint Service and U.S. Department of Defense military inspection program;

(f) Persons arriving on an aircraft or vessel due to an emergency or forced landing when the original destination of the aircraft or vessel was not the United States; and

(g) Persons transiting the United States who are not inspected by the Service. Transit without visa passengers who are inspected by the Service are not excepted from payment of the fee under this section.

HISTORY:

[53 FR 5757, Feb. 26, 1988; 59 FR 49348, Sept. 28, 1994; 68 FR 4090, 4092, Jan. 28, 2003]

§ 286.4 Fee collection responsibility.

(a) It is the responsibility of the air or sea carriers, travel agents, tour wholesalers, or other parties, which issue tickets or documents for transportation on or after December 1, 1986, to collect the fee set forth in § 286.2 of this part from all passengers transported to the United States who are not excepted under § 286.3 of this part.

(b) Tickets and documents for transportation shall be marked by the collector of the fee to indicate that the required fee has been collected. Such markings shall be in accordance with the procedures set forth in the ARC Industry Agents Handbook, the SATO Ticketing Handbook, or compatible procedures set forth in the operations manual of individual collectors.

(c) It is the responsibility of the carrier transporting a passenger from the United States to collect the fee upon departure, if the passenger was not excepted under § 286.3 of this part and tickets or documents for transportation of the passenger do not reflect collection of the fee at the time of issuance. If at the time of departure such a passenger refuses to pay the fee, the carrier shall record the full name, complete address, nationality, passport number, and alien file number, if any, of the passenger and immediately notify the Associate Commissioner, Finance.

HISTORY:

[53 FR 5757, Feb. 26, 1988; 59 FR 49349, Sept. 28,1994]

§ 286.5 Remittance and statement procedures.

(a) The air or sea carrier whose ticket stock or document for transportation reflects collection of the fee is responsible for remittance of the fee to the Service. The travel agent, tour wholesaler, or other entity, which issues their own non-carrier related ticket or document for transportation to an air or sea passenger who is not excepted from the fee pursuant to § 286.3 of this part, is responsible for remittance of the fee to the Service, unless by contract the carrier will remit the fee.

(b)(1) Fee remittances shall be sent to the Immigration and Naturalization Service, at a designated Treasury depository, for receipt no later than 31 days after the close of the calendar quarter in which the fees are collected, except the fourth quarter payment for fees collected shall be made on the date that is 10 days before the end of the U.S. Government's fiscal year, and the first quarter payment shall include any collections made in the preceding quarter that were not remitted with the previous payment. The fourth quarter payment shall include collections for the months of July and August. The fiscal year referenced is the U.S. Government's fiscal year which begins on October 1 and ends on September 30.

(2) Late payments will be subject to interest, penalty, and handling charges as provided in the Debt Collection Act of 1982 (31 U.S.C. 3717). Refunds by a remitter of fees collected in conjunction with unused tickets or documents for transportation shall be netted against the next subsequent remittance.

(c) Along with the remittance, as set forth in paragraph (b) of this section, each remitter making such remittance shall attach a statement which sets forth the following:

(1) Name and address;

(2) Taxpayer identification number;

(3) Calendar quarter covered by the payment;

(4) Interest and penalty charges; and

(5) Total amount collected and remitted.

(d) Remittances shall be made in U.S. dollars by check or money order through a U.S. bank, to Assistant Commissioner, Office of Financial Management, INS.

(e) Annually, each U.S. based remitter, which retains an independent accountant and which remits $ 10,000 or more in fees in any one calendar quarter, shall submit to the Assistant Commissioner, Financial Management a report from the independent accountant in accordance with the Statement on Standards for Attestation Engagements on the application of Passenger User Fee Collection and Remittance Procedures established by the American Institute of Certified Public Accountants and the Service, to the Assistant Commissioner, Financial Management. Each foreign-based remitter, which retains an independent accountant and which remits $ 10,000 or more in fees in any one calendar quarter, shall submit a similar report to the Assistant Commissioner, Financial Management from the independent accountant in accordance with generally accepted accounting principles of their respective countries. These reports from the independent accountants are to be submitted for receipt by the Assistant Commissioner, Financial Management no later than ninety (90) days after the close of the fiscal year of each remitter. Each remitter, which does not retain an independent accountant or which does not remit $ 10,000 or more in any one calendar quarter, shall certify under oath on each statement submitted pursuant to paragraph (c) of this section that they have complied with the applicable statutes and regulations.

(f) The Commissioner reserves the right to conduct an independent audit of any collector or remitter not providing the report or certification required pursuant to paragraph (e) of this section or based upon other information indicating non-compliance in order to assure the accuracy of the remittances of fees collected and remitted and compliance with the applicable statutes and regulations.

(g) In order to enforce compliance with the provisions of this part, the Commissioner may issue a subpoena requiring the production of records, evidence, and witnesses pursuant to the procedures set forth in § 287.4 of this chapter. The authority to issue a subpoena pursuant to this section is limited to the Commissioner, Deputy Commissioner, Associate Commissioner for Management, Director for Program Inspection, all Regional Commissioners; and all District Directors.

HISTORY:

[53 FR 5757, Feb. 26, 1988, as amended at 55 FR 729, Jan. 9, 1990.; 59 FR 49348, 49349, Sept. 28, 1994; 63 FR 51271, 51272, Sept. 25, 1998]

§ 286.6 Maintenance of records.

Each collector and remitter shall maintain records necessary for the Service to verify the accuracy of fees collected and remitted and to otherwise determine compliance with the applicable statutes and regulations. Such records shall be maintained for a period of two years from the date of fee collection. Each remitter shall advise the Assistant Commissioner, Office of Financial Management of the name, address, and telephone number of a responsible officer who shall have the authority to verify and produce any records required to be maintained under this part. The Assistant Commissioner, Office of Financial Management shall be promptly notified of any changes of the responsible officer.

HISTORY:

[53 FR 5757, Feb. 26, 1988; 59 FR 49349, Sept. 28, 1994; 63 FR 51271, 51272, Sept. 25, 1998]

§ 286.7 Penalties.

Failure of any air or sea carrier to comply with the provisions of section 286 of the Act and this part shall subject it to one or more of the following:

(a) Termination of existing agreements under the provisions of section 238 of the Act; and

(b) Suspension of enroute inspections or preinspections.

HISTORY:

[53 FR 5757, Feb. 26, 1988]

§ 286.8 Establishment of pilot programs for the charging of a land border fee for inspection services.

Under the provisions of section 286(q) of the Act, the Service may establish pilot programs at one or more land border ports-of-entry to charge fees for immigration inspection services to be collected by the Commissioner. Individual ports-of-entry selected by the Commissioner to participate in such pilot programs may charge a fee to enhance inspection services and to recover the cost of:

(a) Hiring additional immigration inspectors, including all associated personnel costs such as salary, benefits, and overtime;

(b) Expansion, operation, and maintenance of information systems for nonimmigrant control;

(c) Construction costs, including those associated with adding new primary traffic lanes (with the concurrence of the General Services Administration);

(d) Procuring detection devices and conducting training to identify fraudulent documents used by applicants for entry to the United States; and

(e) Other administrative costs associated with the PORTPASS Program.

(f) Costs associated with the administration of the Land Border Inspection Fee account.

HISTORY:

[56 FR 21919, May 13, 1991; 60 FR 16041, Mar. 29, 1995; 60 FR 50386, 50390, Sept. 29, 1995, as confirmed and amended at 61 FR 53830, 53831, 53833, Oct. 16, 1996]

§ 286.9 Fee for processing applications and issuing documentation at land border Ports-of-Entry.

(a) General. A fee may be charged and collected by the Commissioner for the processing and issuance of specified Service documents at land border Ports-of-Entry. These fees, as specified in 8 CFR 103.7(d), shall be dedicated to funding the cost of providing application-processing services at land border ports.

(b) **Forms for which a fee may be charged.**

(1) A nonimmigrant alien who is required to be issued, or requests to be issued, Form I-94 (see § 1.4), Arrival/Departure Record, for admission at a land border Port-of-Entry must remit the required fee for issuance of Form I-94 upon determination of admissibility.

(2) A nonimmigrant alien applying for admission at a land border Port-of-Entry as a Visa Waiver Program applicant pursuant to § 217.2(c) or § 217.3(c) of this chapter must remit the required fee for issuance of Form I-94W, as prescribed in § 103.7(d)(5) of this chapter, upon determination of admissibility.

(3) A Mexican national in possession of a valid Form DSP-150, B-1/B-2 Visa and Border Crossing Card, issued by the DOS, or a passport and combined B-1/B-2 visa and non-biometric BCC (or similar stamp in a passport) issued by the DOS, who is required to be issued Form I-94, Arrival/Departure Record, pursuant to § 235.1(f) of this chapter, must remit the required fee for issuance of Form I-94 upon determination of admissibility.

(4) A citizen or lawful permanent resident alien of the United States or a Canadian citizen or permanent resident of Canada who is a national of a designated Visa Waiver Program country listed in § 217.2(a) of this chapter who requests Form I-68, Canadian Border Boat Landing Permit, pursuant to § 235.1(e) of this chapter, for entry to the United States from Canada as an eligible pleasure boater on a designated body of water, must remit the required fee at the time of application for Form I-68.

HISTORY:

[60 FR 40069, Aug. 7, 1995; 62 FR 10312, 10390, March 6, 1997; 67 FR 71443, 71450, Dec. 2, 2002; 68 FR 5190, 5194, Jan. 31, 2003; 78 FR 18457, 18472, Mar. 27, 2013, as confirmed at 81 FR 91646, 91670, Dec. 19, 2016; 85 FR 46788, 46928, Aug. 3, 2020, as corrected at 85 FR 53645, August 31, 2020; 87 FR 18967, 18981, Apr. 1, 2022]

PART 287

FIELD OFFICERS; POWERS AND DUTIES

Rule

AUTHORITY NOTE APPLICABLE TO ENTIRE PART:

AUTHORITY:

8 U.S.C. 1103, 1182, 1225, 1226, 1251, 1252, 1357; Homeland Security Act of 2002, Pub. L. 107-296 (6 U.S.C. 1, et seq.); 8 CFR part 2.

§ 287.1 Definitions.

(a)(1) External boundary. The term external boundary, as used in section 287(a)(3) of the Act, means the land boundaries and the territorial sea of the United States extending 12 nautical miles from the baselines of the United States determined in accordance with international law.

(2) Reasonable distance. The term reasonable distance, as used in section 287(a) (3) of the Act, means within 100 air miles from any external boundary of the United States or any shorter distance which may be fixed by the chief patrol agent for CBP, or the special agent in charge for ICE, or, so far as the power to board and search aircraft is concerned any distance fixed pursuant to paragraph (b) of this section.

(b) Reasonable distance; fixing by chief patrol agents and special agents in charge. In fixing distances not exceeding 100 air miles pursuant to paragraph (a) of this section, chief patrol agents and special agents in charge shall take into consideration topography, confluence of arteries of transportation leading from external boundaries, density of population, possible inconvenience to the traveling public, types of conveyances used, and reliable information as to movements of persons effecting illegal entry into the United States: Provided, That whenever in the opinion of a chief patrol agent or special agent in charge a distance in his or her sector or district of more than 100 air miles from any external boundary of the United States would because of unusual circumstances be reasonable, such chief patrol agent or special agent in charge shall forward a complete report with respect to the matter to the Commissioner of CBP, or the Assistant Secretary for ICE, as appropriate, who may, if he determines that such action is justified, declare such distance to be reasonable.

(c) Patrolling the border. The phrase patrolling the border to prevent the illegal entry of aliens into the United States as used in section 287 of the Immigration and Nationality Act means conducting such activities as are customary, or reasonable and necessary, to prevent the illegal entry of aliens into the United States.

(d) Arrested by federal, state, or local law enforcement official. The term arrested, as used in section 287(d) of the Act (as amended by section 1701 (Subtitle M) of the Anti-Drug Abuse Act of 1986, Pub. L. 99-509), means that an alien has been —

(1) Physically taken into custody for a criminal violation of the controlled substance laws; and

(2) Subsequently booked, charged or otherwise officially processed; or

(3) Provided an initial appearance before a judicial officer where the alien has been informed of the charges and the right to counsel.

(e) Law enforcement or other official. The phrase law enforcement official (or other official), as used in section 287(d) of the Act, means an officer or employee of an agency engaged in the administration of criminal justice pursuant to statute or executive order, including (1) courts; (2) a government agency or component which performs the administration of criminal justice as defined in 28 CFR part 20 including performance of any of the following activities: detection, apprehension, detention, pretrial release, post-trial release, prosecution, adjudication, correctional supervision, or rehabilitation of accused persons or criminal offenders.

(f) Controlled substance. The term controlled substance, as used in section 287(d)(3) of the Act, shall mean the same as that referenced in the Controlled Substances Act, 21 U.S.C. 801 et seq., and shall include any substance contained in Schedules I through V of 21 CFR 1308.1 et seq. For the purposes of this chapter, the term controlled substance includes controlled substance analogues as defined in 21 U.S.C. 802(23) and 813.

(g) Basic immigration law enforcement training. The phrase basic immigration law enforcement training, as used in §§ 287.5 and 287.8, means the successful completion of one of the following courses of training provided at the Immigration Officer Academy or Border Patrol Academy: Immigration Officer Basic Training Course after 1971; Border Patrol Basic Training Course after 1950; Immigration Detention Enforcement Officer Basic Training Course after 1977; and Immigration Customs Enforcement Special Agent Training, after 2002; or training substantially equivalent thereto as determined by the Commissioner of CBP or the Assistant Secretary for ICE with respect to personnel in their respective bureaus. The phrase basic immigration law enforcement training also means the successful completion of the Other than Permanent Full-Time

(OTP) Immigration Inspector Basic Training Course after 1991 in the case of individuals who are OTP immigration inspectors. Conversion by OTP immigration to any other status requires training applicable to that position.

(h) References to specific titles of officers mean all individuals holding such positions and any individual acting in such position.

(i) Nothing in this part limits the authority of any DHS officers to act pursuant to any authorities that they may otherwise possess.

HISTORY:

[22 FR 9808, Dec. 6, 1957, as amended at 29 FR 13244, Sept. 24, 1964; 53 FR 9283, Mar. 22, 1988; 57 FR 47258, Oct. 15, 1992; 59 FR 42415, Aug. 17, 1994; 68 FR 35273, 35276, June 13, 2003]

§ 287.2 Disposition of criminal cases.

Whenever a special agent in charge, port director, or chief patrol agent has reason to believe that there has been a violation punishable under any criminal provision of the immigration and nationality laws administered or enforced by the Department, he or she shall immediately initiate an investigation to determine all the pertinent facts and circumstances and shall take such further action as he or she deems necessary. In no case shall this investigation prejudice the right of an arrested person to be taken without unnecessary delay before a United States magistrate judge, a United States district judge, or, if necessary, a judicial officer empowered in accordance with 18 U.S.C. 3041 to commit persons charged with offenses against the laws of the United States.

HISTORY:

[35 FR 16362, Oct. 20, 1970; 59 FR 42415, Aug. 17, 1994; 68 FR 35273, 35276, June 13, 2003]

§ 287.3 Disposition of cases of aliens arrested without warrant.

(a) Examination. An alien arrested without a warrant of arrest under the authority contained in section 287(a)(2) of the Act will be examined by an officer other than the arresting officer. If no other qualified officer is readily available and the taking of the alien before another officer would entail unnecessary delay, the arresting officer, if the conduct of such examination is a part of the duties assigned to him or her, may examine the alien.

(b) Determination of proceedings. If the examining officer is satisfied that there is prima facie evidence that the arrested alien was entering, attempting to enter, or is present in the United States in violation of the immigration laws, the examining officer will refer the case to an immigration judge for further inquiry in accordance with 8 CFR parts 235, 239, or 240, order the alien removed as provided for in section 235(b)(1) of the Act and § 235.3(b) of this chapter, or take whatever other action may be appropriate or required under the laws or regulations applicable to the particular case.

(c) Notifications and information. Except in the case of an alien subject to the expedited removal provisions of section 235(b)(1)(A) of the Act, an alien arrested without warrant and placed in formal proceedings under section 238 or 240 of the Act will be advised of the reasons for his or her arrest and the right to be represented at no expense to the Government. The examining officer will provide the alien with a list of the available free legal services provided by organizations and attorneys qualified under 8 CFR part 1003 and organizations recognized under § 292.2 of this chapter or 8 CFR 1292.2 that are located in the district where the hearing will be held. The examining officer shall note on Form I-862 that such a list was provided to the alien. The officer will also advise the alien that any statement made may be used against him or her in a subsequent proceeding.

(d) Custody procedures. Unless voluntary departure has been granted pursuant to subpart C of 8 CFR part 240, a determination will be made within 48 hours of the arrest, except in the event of an emergency or other extraordinary circumstance in which case a determination will be made within an additional reasonable period of time, whether the alien will be continued in custody or released on bond or recognizance and whether a notice to appear and warrant of arrest as prescribed in 8 CFR parts 236 and 239 will be issued.

HISTORY:

[51 FR 34082, Sept. 25, 1986; 62 FR 9071, 9074, Feb. 28, 1997; 62 FR 10312, 10390, March 6, 1997; 66 FR 48334, 48335, Sept. 20, 2001; 68 FR 35273, 35276, June 13, 2003]

§ 287.4 Subpoena.

(a) Who may issue —

(1) Criminal or civil investigations. All District Directors; Deputy District Directors; Chief Patrol Agents; Deputy Chief Patrol Agents; Assistant Chief Patrol Agents; Officers in Charge; Patrol Agents in Charge; Assistant Patrol Agents in Charge; Field Operations Supervisors; Special Operations Supervisors; Supervisory Border Patrol Agents; Assistant District Directors, Investigations; Supervisory Criminal Investigators, Anti-Smuggling; Regional Directors; Service Center Directors; Assistant District Directors, Examinations; Director, Detention and Removal; Special Agents in Charge; all Special Agents in supervisory positions; Field Office Directors; Deputy Field Office Directors; and any other immigration officer who has been expressly delegated such authority as provided by 8 CFR 2.1 may issue a subpoena requiring the production of records and evidence for use in criminal or civil investigations.

(2) Proceedings other than naturalization proceedings -

(i) Prior to commencement of proceedings. All District Directors; Deputy District Directors; Chief Patrol Agents; Deputy Chief Patrol Agents; Officers in Charge; Director, Detention and Removal; Special Agents in Charge; Deputy Special Agents in Charge; Resident Agents in Charge; District Field Officers; Field Office Directors; Deputy Field Office Directors; and Port Directors may issue a subpoena requiring the attendance of witnesses or the production of documentary evidence, or both, for use in any proceeding under this chapter I, other than under 8 CFR part 335, or any application made ancillary to the proceeding.

(ii) Subsequent to commencement of any immigration court proceeding. Procedures for the issuance of a subpoena after the commencement of proceedings, in cases other than those arising under part 335 of this chapter, are set forth at 8 CFR 1003.35(b) and 1287.4.

(b) Form of subpoena. All subpoenas shall be issued on Form I-138.

(1) Criminal or civil investigations. The subpoena shall command the person or entity to which it is addressed to attend and to give testimony at a time or place specified. A subpoena shall also command the person or entity to which it is addressed to produce the books, papers, or documents specified in the subpoena. A subpoena may direct the taking of a deposition before an immigration officer of the Department.

(2) Proceedings other than naturalization proceedings. Every subpoena issued under the provisions of this section shall state the title of the proceeding and shall command the person to whom it is directed to attend and to give testimony at a time and place specified. A subpoena shall also command the person to whom it is directed to produce the books, papers, or documents specified in the subpoena. A subpoena may direct the taking of a deposition before an immigration officer of the Department.

(c) Service. A subpoena issued under this section may be served by any person, over 18 years of age not a party to the case, designated to make such service by the District Director; Deputy District Director; Chief Patrol Agent; Deputy Chief Patrol Agent; Assistant Chief Patrol Agent; Patrol Agent in Charge; Officer in Charge; Assistant District Director, Investigations; Supervisory Criminal Investigator, Anti-Smuggling; Regional Director; Special Agent in Charge; Deputy Special Agent in Charge; Resident Agent in Charge; District Field Officer; Field Office Director; Deputy Field Office Director; Supervisory Deportation Officer; Supervisory Detention and Deportation Officer; and Port Director having administrative jurisdiction over the office in which the subpoena is issued. The Director, Detention and Removal, shall also have the authority to make such designation. Service of the subpoena shall be made by delivering a copy thereof to the person named therein and by tendering to him/her the fee for one day's attendance and the mileage allowed by law by the United States District Court for the district in which the testimony is to be taken. When the subpoena is issued on behalf of the Department, fee and mileage need not be tendered at the time of service. A record of such service shall be made and attached to the original copy of the subpoena.

(d) Invoking aid of court. If a witness neglects or refuses to appear and testify as directed by the subpoena served upon him or her in accordance with the provisions of this section, the officer or immigration judge issuing the subpoena shall request the United States Attorney for the district in which the subpoena was issued to report such neglect or refusal to the United States District Court and to request such court to issue an order requiring the witness to appear and testify and to produce the books, papers, or documents designated in the subpoena.

HISTORY:

[50 FR 30134, July 24, 1985; 50 FR 47205, Nov. 15, 1985, as amended at 55 FR 12628, Apr. 5, 1990; 60 FR 56936, 56937, Nov. 13, 1995; 62 FR 10312, 10390, March 6, 1997; 67 FR 39255, 39260, June 7, 2002; 68 FR 35273, 35276, June 13, 2003]

§ 287.5 Exercise of power by immigration officers.

(a) Power and authority to interrogate and administer oaths. Any immigration officer is hereby authorized and designated to exercise anywhere in or outside the United States the power conferred by:

(1) Section 287(a)(1) of the Act to interrogate, without warrant, any alien or person believed to be an alien concerning his or her right to be, or to remain, in the United States, and

(2) Section 287(b) of the Act to administer oaths and to take and consider evidence concerning the privilege of any person to enter, reenter, pass through, or reside in the United States; or concerning any matter which is material or relevant to the enforcement of the Act and the administration of the immigration and naturalization functions of the Department.

(b) Power and authority to patrol the border. The following immigration officers who have successfully completed basic immigration law enforcement training are hereby authorized and designated to exercise the power to patrol the border conferred by section 287(a)(3) of the Act:

(1) Border patrol agents;

(2) Air and marine agents;

(3) Special agents;

(4) CBP officers;

(5) Supervisory and managerial personnel who are responsible for supervising the activities of those officers listed in this paragraph; and

(6) Immigration officers who need the authority to patrol the border under section 287(a)(3) of the Act in order to effectively accomplish their individual missions and who are designated, individually or as a class, by the Commissioner of CBP, or the Assistant Secretary/Director of ICE.

(c) Power and authority to arrest —

(1) Arrests of aliens under section 287(a)(2) of the Act for immigration violations. The following immigration officers who have successfully completed basic immigration law enforcement training are hereby authorized and designated to exercise the arrest power conferred by section 287(a)(2) of the Act and in accordance with 8 CFR 287.8(c):

(i) Border patrol agents;

(ii) Air and marine agents;

(iii) Special agents;

(iv) Deportation officers;

(v) CBP officers;

(vi) Immigration enforcement agents;

(vii) Supervisory and managerial personnel who are responsible for supervising the activities of those officers listed in this paragraph; and

(viii) Immigration officers who need the authority to arrest aliens under section 287(a)(2) of the Act in order to effectively accomplish their individual missions and who are designated, individually or as a class, by the Commissioner of CBP, the Assistant Secretary/Director of ICE, or the Director of the USCIS.

(2) Arrests of persons under section 287(a)(4) of the Act for felonies regulating the admission or removal of aliens. The following immigration officers who have successfully completed basic immigration law enforcement training are hereby authorized and designated to exercise the arrest power conferred by section 287(a)(4) of the Act and in accordance with 8 CFR 287.8(c):

(i) Border patrol agents;

(ii) Air and marine agents;

(iii) Special agents;

(iv) Deportation officers;

(v) CBP officers;

(vi) Immigration enforcement agents;

(vii) Supervisory and managerial personnel who are responsible for supervising the activities of those officers listed in this paragraph; and

(viii) Immigration officers who need the authority to arrest persons under section 287(a)(4) of the Act in order to effectively accomplish their individual missions and who are designated, individually or as a class, by the Commissioner of CBP, the Assistant Secretary/ Director of ICE, or the Director of the USCIS.

(3) Arrests of persons under section 287(a)(5)(A) of the Act for any offense against the United States. The following immigration officers who have successfully completed basic immigration law enforcement training are hereby authorized and designated to exercise the arrest power conferred by section 287(a)(5)(A) of the Act and in accordance with 8 CFR 287.8(c):

(i) Border patrol agents;

(ii) Air and marine agents;

(iii) Special agents;

(iv) Deportation officers;

(v) CBP officers;

(vi) Supervisory and managerial personnel who are responsible for supervising the activities of those officers listed in this paragraph; and

(vii) Immigration officers who need the authority to arrest persons under section 287(a)(5)(A) of the Act in order to effectively accomplish their individual missions and who are designated, individually or as a class, by the Commissioner of CBP, or the Assistant Secretary/Director of ICE.

(4) Arrests of persons under section 287(a)(5)(B) of the Act for any felony

(i) Section 287(a)(5)(B) of the Act authorizes designated immigration officers, as listed in paragraph (c)(4)(iii) of this section, to arrest persons, without warrant, for any felony cognizable under the laws of the United States if:

(A) The immigration officer has reasonable grounds to believe that the person to be arrested has committed or is committing such a felony;

(B) The immigration officer is performing duties relating to the enforcement of the immigration laws at the time of the arrest;

(C) There is a likelihood of the person escaping before a warrant can be obtained for his or her arrest; and

(D) The immigration officer has been certified as successfully completing a training program that covers such arrests and the standards with respect to the immigration enforcement activities of the Department as defined in 8 CFR 287.8.

(ii) The following immigration officers who have successfully completed basic immigration law enforcement training are hereby authorized and designated to exercise the arrest power conferred by section 287(a)(5)(B) of the Act and in accordance with 8 CFR 287.8(c):

(A) Border patrol agents;

(B) Air and marine agents;

(C) Special agents;

(D) Deportation officers;

(E) CBP officers;

(F) Supervisory and managerial personnel who are responsible for supervising the activities of those officers listed in this paragraph; and

(G) Immigration officers who need the authority to arrest persons under section 287(a)(5)(B) of the Act in order to effectively accomplish their individual missions and who are designated, individually or as a class, by the Commissioner of CBP or the Assistant Secretary/ Director of ICE.

(iii) Notwithstanding the authorization and designation set forth in paragraph (c)(4)(ii) of this section, no immigration officer is authorized to make an arrest for any felony under the authority of section 287(a)(5)(B) of the Act until such time as he or she has been certified as successfully completing a training course encompassing such arrests and the standards for enforcement activities are defined in 8 CFR 287.8. Such certification will be valid for the duration of the immigration officer's continuous employment, unless it is suspended or revoked by the Commissioner of CBP or the Assistant Secretary/Director of ICE, or their respective designees, for just cause.

(5) Arrests of persons under section 274(a) of the Act who bring in, transport, or harbor certain aliens, or induce them to enter.

(i) Section 274(a) of the Act authorizes designated immigration officers, as listed in paragraph (c)(5)(ii) of this section, to arrest persons who bring in, transport, or harbor aliens, or induce them to enter the United States in violation of law. When making an arrest, the designated immigration officer shall adhere to the provisions of the enforcement standard governing the conduct of arrests in 8 CFR 287.8(c).

(ii) The following immigration officers who have successfully completed basic immigration law enforcement training are authorized and designated to exercise the arrest power conferred by section 274(a) of the Act:

(A) Border patrol agents;

(B) Air and marine agents;

(C) Special agents;

(D) Deportation officers;

(E) CBP officers;

(F) Supervisory and managerial personnel who are responsible for supervising the activities of those officers listed in this paragraph; and

(G) Immigration officers who need the authority to arrest persons under section 274(a) of the Act in order to effectively accomplish their individual missions and who are designated, individually or as a class, by the Commissioner of CBP or the Assistant Secretary/Director of ICE.

(6) Custody and transportation of previously arrested persons. In addition to the authority to arrest pursuant to a warrant of arrest in paragraph (e)(3)(iv) of this section, detention enforcement officers and immigration enforcement agents who have successfully completed basic immigration law enforcement training are hereby authorized and designated to take and maintain custody of and transport any person who has been arrested by an immigration officer pursuant to paragraphs (c)(1) through (c)(5) of this section.

(d) Power and authority to conduct searches. The following immigration officers who have successfully completed basic immigration law enforcement training are hereby authorized and designated to exercise the power to conduct searches conferred by section 287(c) of the Act:

(1) Border patrol agents;

(2) Air and marine agents;

(3) Special agents;

(4) Deportation officers;

(5) CBP officers;

(6) Immigration enforcement agents;

(7) Supervisory and managerial personnel who are responsible for supervising the activities of those officers listed in this paragraph; and

(8) Immigration officers who need the authority to conduct searches under section 287(c) of the Act in order to effectively accomplish their individual missions and who are designated, individually or as a class, by the Commissioner of CBP, the Assistant Secretary/Director of ICE, or the Director of USCIS.

(e) Power and authority to execute warrants —

(1) Search warrants. The following immigration officers who have successfully completed basic immigration law enforcement training are hereby authorized and designated to exercise the power conferred by section 287(a) of the Act to execute a search warrant:

(i) Border patrol agents;

(ii) Air and marine agents;

(iii) CBP officers;

(iv) Special agents;

(v) Deportation officers;

(vi) Immigration enforcement agents;

(vii) Supervisory and managerial personnel who are responsible for supervising the activities of those officers listed in this paragraph; and

(viii) Immigration officers who need the authority to execute search warrants under section 287(a) of the Act in order to effectively accomplish their individual missions and who are designated, individually or as a class, by the Commissioner of CBP or the Assistant Secretary/Director of ICE.

(2) Issuance of arrest warrants for immigration violations. A warrant of arrest may be issued by any of the following immigration officials who have been authorized or delegated such authority:

(i) District directors (except foreign);

(ii) Deputy district directors (except foreign);

(iii) Assistant district directors for investigations;

(iv) Deputy assistant district directors for investigations;

(v) Assistant district directors for deportation;

(vi) Deputy assistant district directors for deportation;

(vii) Assistant district directors for examinations;

(viii) Deputy assistant district directors for examinations;

(ix) Officers in charge (except foreign);

(x) Assistant officers in charge (except foreign);

(xi) Chief patrol agents;

(xii) Deputy chief patrol agents;

(xiii) Division chiefs;

(xiv) Assistant chief patrol agents;

(xv) Patrol agents in charge;

(xvi) Deputy patrol agents in charge;

(xvii) Border Patrol watch commanders;

(xviii) Special operations supervisors;

(xix) Supervisory border patrol agents;

(xx) Directors of air operations;

(xxi) Directors of marine operations;

(xxii) Supervisory air and marine interdiction agents;

(xxiii) Executive Associate Director of Homeland Security Investigations;

(xxiv) Institutional Hearing Program directors;

(xxv) Director, Field Operations;

(xxvi) Assistant Director, Field Operations;

(xxvii) Port directors;

(xxviii) Assistant port directors;

(xxix) Field operations watch commanders;

(xxx) Field operations chiefs;

(xxxi) Supervisory deportation officers;

(xxxii) Supervisory detention and deportation officers;

(xxxiii) Group Supervisors;

(xxxiv) Director, Office of Detention and Removal Operations;

(xxxv) Special Agents in Charge;

(xxxvi) Deputy Special Agents in Charge;

(xxxvii) Associate Special Agents in Charge;

(xxxviii) Assistant Special Agents in Charge;

(xxxix) Field Office Directors;

(xl) Deputy Field Office Directors;

(xli) District Field Officers;

(xlii) Supervisory immigration services officers;

(xliii) Supervisory immigration officers;

(xliv) Supervisory asylum officers;

(xlv) Supervisory special agents;

(xlvi) Director of investigations;

(xlvii) Directors or officers in charge of detention facilities;

(xlviii) Directors of field operations;

(xlix) Deputy or assistant directors of field operations;

(l) Unit Chief, Law Enforcement Support Center;

(li) Section Chief, Law Enforcement Support Center;

(lii) Immigration Enforcement Agents; or

(liii) Other duly authorized officers or employees of the Department of Homeland Security or the United States who are delegated the authority as provided in 8 CFR 2.1 to issue warrants of arrest, and who have successfully completed any required immigration law enforcement training.

(3) Service of warrant of arrests for immigration violations. The following immigration officers who have successfully completed basic immigration law enforcement training are hereby authorized and designated to exercise the power pursuant to section 287(a) of the Act to execute warrants of arrest for administrative immigration violations issued under section 236 of the Act or to execute warrants of criminal arrest issued under the authority of the United States:

(i) Border patrol agents;

(ii) Air and marine agents;

(iii) Special agents;

(iv) Deportation officers;

(v) Detention enforcement officers or immigration enforcement agents (warrants of arrest for administrative immigration violations only);

(vi) CBP officers;

(vii) Supervisory and managerial personnel who are responsible for supervising the activities of those officers listed in this paragraph; and

(viii) Immigration officers who need the authority to execute arrest warrants for immigration violations under section 287(a) of the Act in order to effectively accomplish their individual missions and who are designated, individually or as a class, by the Commissioner of CBP or the Assistant Secretary/Director of ICE.

(4) Service of warrant of arrests for non-immigration violations. The following immigration officers who have successfully completed basic immigration law enforcement training are hereby authorized and designated to exercise the power to execute warrants of criminal arrest for non-immigration violations issued under the authority of the United States:

(i) Border patrol agents;

(ii) Air and marine agents;

(iii) CBP officers

(iv) Special agents;

(v) Deportation officers;

(vi) Immigration enforcement agents;

(vii) Supervisory and managerial personnel who are responsible for supervising the activities of those officers listed in this paragraph; and

(viii) Immigration officers who need the authority to execute warrants of arrest for non-immigration violations under section 287(a) of the Act in order to effectively accomplish their individual missions and who are designated, individually or as a class, by the Commissioner of CBP or the Assistant Secretary/Director of ICE.

(f) Power and authority to carry firearms. The following immigration officers who have successfully completed basic immigration enforcement training are hereby authorized and designated to exercise the power conferred by section 287(a) of the Act to carry firearms provided that they are individually qualified by training and experience to handle and safely operate the firearms they are permitted to carry, maintain proficiency in the use of such firearms, and adhere to the provisions of the enforcement standard governing the use of force in 8 CFR 287.8(a):

(1) Border patrol agents;

(2) Air and marine agents;

(3) Special agents;

(4) Deportation officers;

(5) Detention enforcement officers or immigration enforcement agents;

(6) CBP officers;

(7) Supervisory and managerial personnel who are responsible for supervising the activities of those officers listed in this paragraph; and

(8) Immigration officers who need the authority to carry firearms under section 287(a) of the Act in order to effectively accomplish their individual missions and who are designated, individually or as a class, by the Commissioner of CBP or the Assistant Secretary/Director of ICE.

HISTORY:

[29 FR 12584, Sept. 4, 1964; 59 FR 42415, Aug. 17, 1994; 62 FR 10312, 10390, March 6, 1997; 67 FR 39255, 39260, June 7, 2002; 68 FR 35273, 35277, June 13, 2003; 70 FR 67087, 67089, Nov. 4, 2005; 76 FR 53764, 53797, Aug. 29, 2011; 81 FR 62353, 62356, Sept. 9, 2016]

§ 287.6 Proof of official records.

(a) Domestic. In any proceeding under this chapter, an official record or entry therein, when admissible for any purpose, shall be evidenced by an official publication thereof, or by a copy attested by the official having legal custody of the record or by an authorized deputy.

(b) Foreign: Countries not Signatories to Convention.

(1) In any proceeding under this chapter, an official record or entry therein, when admissible for any purpose, shall be evidenced by an official publication thereof, or by a copy attested by an officer so authorized. This attested copy in turn may but need not be certified by any authorized foreign officer both as to the genuineness of the signature of the attesting officer and as to his/her official position. The signature and official position of this certifying foreign officer may then likewise be certified by any other foreign officer so authorized, thereby creating a chain of certificates.

(2) The attested copy, with the additional foreign certificates if any, must be certified by an officer in the Foreign Service of the United States, stationed in the foreign country where the record is kept. This officer must certify the genuineness of the signature and the official position either of (i) the attesting officer; or (ii) any foreign officer whose certification of genuineness of signature and official position relates directly to the attestation or is in a chain of certificates of genuineness of signature and official position relating to the attestation.

(c) Foreign: Countries Signatory to Convention Abolishing the Requirement of Legislation for Foreign Public Document.

(1) In any proceeding under this chapter, a public document or entry therein, when admissible for any purpose, may be evidenced by an official publication, or by a copy properly certified under the Convention. To be properly certified, the copy must be accompanied by a certificate in the form dictated by the Convention. This certificate must be signed by a foreign officer so authorized by the signatory country, and it must certify (i) the authenticity of the signature of the person signing the document; (ii) the capacity in which that person acted, and (iii) where appropriate, the identity of the seal or stamp which the document bears.

(2) No certification is needed from an officer in the Foreign Service of public documents.

(3) In accordance with the Convention, the following are deemed to be public documents:

(i) Documents emanating from an authority or an official connected with the courts of tribunals of the state, including those emanating from a public prosecutor, a clerk of a court or a process server;

(ii) Administrative documents;

(iii) Notarial acts; and

(iv) Official certificates which are placed on documents signed by persons in their private capacity, such as official certificates recording the registration of a document or the fact that it was in existence on a certain date, and official and notarial authentication of signatures.

(4) In accordance with the Convention, the following are deemed not to be public documents, and thus are subject to the more stringent requirements of § 287.6(b) above:

(i) Documents executed by diplomatic or consular agents; and

(ii) Administrative documents dealing directly with commercial or customs operations.

(d) Canada. In any proceedings under this chapter, an official record or entry therein, issued by a Canadian governmental entity within the geographical boundaries of Canada, when admissible for any purpose, shall be evidenced by a certified copy of the original record attested by the official having legal custody of the record or by an authorized deputy.

HISTORY:

[50 FR 37834, Sept. 18, 1985, as amended at 54 FR 39337, Sept. 26, 1989; 54 FR 48851, Nov. 28, 1989]

§ 287.7 Detainer provisions under section 287(d)(3) of the Act.

(a) Detainers in general. Detainers are issued pursuant to sections 236 and 287 of the Act and this chapter 1. Any authorized immigration officer may at any time issue a Form I-247, Immigration Detainer-Notice of Action, to any other Federal, State, or local law enforcement agency. A detainer serves to advise another law enforcement agency that the Department seeks custody of an alien presently in the custody of that agency, for the purpose of arresting and removing the alien. The detainer is a request that such agency advise the Department, prior to release of the alien, in order for the Department to arrange to assume custody, in situations when gaining immediate physical custody is either impracticable or impossible.

(b) Authority to issue detainers. The following officers are authorized to issue detainers:

(1) Border patrol agents, including aircraft pilots;

(2) Special agents;

(3) Deportation officers;

(4) Immigration inspectors;

(5) Adjudications officers;

(6) Immigration enforcement agents;

(7) Supervisory and managerial personnel who are responsible for supervising the activities of those officers listed in this paragraph; and

(8) Immigration officers who need the authority to issue detainers under section 287(d)(3) of the Act in order to effectively accomplish their individual missions and who are designated individually or as a class, by the Commissioner of CBP, the Assistant Secretary for ICE, or the Director of USCIS.

(c) Availability of records. In order for the Department to accurately determine the propriety of issuing a detainer, serving a notice to appear, or taking custody of an alien in accordance with this section, the criminal justice agency requesting such action or informing the Department of a conviction or act that renders an alien inadmissible or removable under any provision of law shall provide the Department with all documentary records and information available from the agency that reasonably relates to the alien's status in the United States, or that may have an impact on conditions of release.

(d) Temporary detention at Department request. Upon a determination by the Department to issue a detainer for an alien not otherwise detained by a criminal justice agency, such agency shall maintain custody of the alien for a period not to exceed 48 hours, excluding Saturdays, Sundays, and holidays in order to permit assumption of custody by the Department.

(e) Financial responsibility for detention. No detainer issued as a result of a determination made under this chapter I shall incur any fiscal obligation on the part of the Department, until actual assumption of custody by the Department, except as provided in paragraph (d) of this section.

HISTORY:

[53 FR 9283, Mar. 22, 1988, as amended at 55 FR 43327, Oct. 29, 1990; 59 FR 42418, Aug. 17, 1994; 62 FR 10312, 10392, March 6, 1997; 68 FR 35273, 35279, June 13, 2003; 76 FR 53764, 53797, Aug. 29, 2011]

§ 287.8 Standards for enforcement activities.

The following standards for enforcement activities contained in this section must be adhered to by every immigration officer involved in enforcement activities. Any violation of this section shall be reported to the Office of the Inspector General or such other entity as may be provided for in 8 CFR 287.10.

(a) Use of force —

(1) Non-deadly force

(i) Non-deadly force is any use of force other than that which is considered deadly force as defined in paragraph (a)(2) of this section.

(ii) Non-deadly force may be used only when a designated immigration officer, as listed in paragraph (a)(1)(iv) of this section, has reasonable grounds to believe that such force is necessary.

(iii) A designated immigration officer shall always use the minimum non-deadly force necessary to accomplish the officer's mission and shall escalate to a higher level of non-deadly force only when such higher level of force is warranted by the actions, apparent intentions, and apparent capabilities of the suspect, prisoner, or assailant.

(iv) The following immigration officers who have successfully completed basic immigration law enforcement training are hereby authorized and designated to exercise the power conferred by section 287(a) of the Act to use non-deadly force should circumstances warrant it:

(A) Border patrol agents;

(B) Air and marine agents;

(C) Special agents;

(D) Deportation officers;

(E) Detention enforcement officers or immigration enforcement agents;

(F) CBP officers;

(G) Supervisory and managerial personnel who are responsible for supervising the activities of those officers listed in this paragraph; and

(H) Immigration officers who need the authority to use non-deadly force under section 287(a) of the Act in order to effectively accomplish their individual missions and who are designated, individually or as a class, by the Commissioner of CBP or the Assistant Secretary/Director of ICE.

(2) Deadly force.

(i) Deadly force is any use of force that is likely to cause death or serious physical injury.

(ii) Deadly force may be used only when a designated immigration officer, as listed in paragraph (a)(2)(iii) of this section, has reasonable grounds to believe that such force is necessary to protect the designated immigration officer or other persons from the imminent danger of death or serious physical injury.

(iii) The following immigration officers who have successfully completed basic immigration law enforcement training are hereby authorized and designated to exercise the power conferred by section 287(a) of the Act to use deadly force should circumstances warrant it:

(A) Border patrol agents;

(B) Air and marine agents;

(C) Special agents

(D) Deportation officers;

(E) Detention enforcement officers or immigration enforcement agents;

(F) CBP officers;

(G) Supervisory and managerial personnel who are responsible for supervising the activities of those officers listed above; and

(H) Immigration officers who need the authority to use deadly force under section 287(a) of the Act in order to effectively accomplish their individual missions and who are designated, individually or as a class, by the Commissioner of CBP or the Assistant Secretary/Director of ICE.

(b) Interrogation and detention not amounting to arrest.

(1) Interrogation is questioning designed to elicit specific information. An immigration officer, like any other person, has the right to ask questions of anyone as long as the immigration officer does not restrain the freedom of an individual, not under arrest, to walk away.

(2) If the immigration officer has a reasonable suspicion, based on specific articulable facts, that the person being questioned is, or is attempting to be, engaged in an offense against the United States or is an alien illegally in the United States, the immigration officer may briefly detain the person for questioning.

(3) Information obtained from this questioning may provide the basis for a subsequent arrest, which must be effected only by a designated immigration officer, as listed in 8 CFR 287.5(c). The conduct of arrests is specified in paragraph (c) of this section.

(c) Conduct of arrests —

(1) Authority. Only designated immigration officers are authorized to make an arrest. The list of designated immigration officers may vary depending on the type of arrest as listed in § 287.5(c)(1) through (c)(5).

(2) General procedures.

(i) An arrest shall be made only when the designated immigration officer has reason to believe that the person to be arrested has committed an offense against the United States or is an alien illegally in the United States.

(ii) A warrant of arrest shall be obtained except when the designated immigration officer has reason to believe that the person is likely to escape before a warrant can be obtained.

(iii) At the time of the arrest, the designated immigration officer shall, as soon as it is practical and safe to do so:

(A) Identify himself or herself as an immigration officer who is authorized to execute an arrest; and

(B) State that the person is under arrest and the reason for the arrest.

(iv) With respect to an alien arrested and administratively charged with being in the United States in violation of law, the arresting officer shall adhere to the procedures set forth in 8 CFR 287.3 if the arrest is made without a warrant.

(v) With respect to a person arrested and charged with a criminal violation of the laws of the United States, the arresting officer shall advise the person of the appropriate rights as required by law at the time of the arrest, or as soon thereafter as practicable. It is the duty of the immigration officer to assure that the warnings are given in a language the subject understands, and that the subject acknowledges that the warnings are understood. The fact that a person has been advised of his or her rights shall be documented on appropriate Department forms and made a part of the arrest record.

(vi) Every person arrested and charged with a criminal violation of the laws of the United States shall be brought without unnecessary delay before a United States magistrate judge, a United States district judge or, if necessary, a judicial officer empowered in accordance with 18 U.S.C. 3041 to commit persons charged with such crimes. Accordingly, the immigration officer shall contact an Assistant United States Attorney to arrange for an initial appearance.

(vii) The use of threats, coercion, or physical abuse by the designated immigration officer to induce a suspect to waive his or her rights or to make a statement is prohibited.

(d) Transportation —

(1) Vehicle transportation. All persons will be transported in a manner that ensures the safety of the persons being transported. When persons arrested or detained are being transported by vehicle, each person will be searched as thoroughly as circumstances permit before being placed in the vehicle. The person being transported shall not be handcuffed to the frame or any part of the moving vehicle or an object in the moving vehicle. The person being transported shall not be left unattended during transport unless the immigration officer needs to perform a law enforcement function.

(2) Airline transportation. Escorting officers must abide by all Federal Aviation Administration, Transportation Security Administration, and airline carrier rules and regulations pertaining to weapons and the transportation of prisoners.

(e) Vehicular pursuit.

(1) A vehicular pursuit is an active attempt by a designated immigration officer, as listed in paragraph (e)(2) of this section, in a designated pursuit vehicle to apprehend fleeing suspects who are attempting to avoid apprehension. A designated pursuit vehicle is defined as a vehicle equipped with emergency lights and siren, placed in or on the vehicle, that emit audible and visual signals in order to warn others that emergency law enforcement activities are in progress.

(2) The following immigration officers who have successfully completed basic immigration law enforcement training are hereby authorized and designated to initiate a vehicular pursuit:

(i) Border patrol agents;

(ii) Air and marine agents;

(iii) CBP officers;

(iv) Supervisory personnel who are responsible for supervising the activities of those officers listed in this paragraph; and

(v) Immigration officers who need the authority to initiate a vehicular pursuit in order to effectively accomplish their individual mission and who are designated, individually or as a class, by the Commissioner of CBP or the Assistant Secretary/Director of ICE.

(f) Site inspections.

(1) Site inspections are Border and Transportation Security Directorate enforcement activities undertaken to locate and identify aliens illegally in the United States, or aliens engaged in unauthorized employment, at locations where there is a reasonable suspicion, based on articulable facts, that such aliens are present.

(2) An immigration officer may not enter into the non-public areas of a business, a residence including the curtilage of such residence, or a farm or other outdoor agricultural operation, except as provided in section 287(a)(3) of the Act, for the purpose of questioning the occupants or employees concerning their right to be or remain in the United States unless the officer has either a warrant or the consent of the owner or other person in control of the site to be inspected. When consent to enter is given, the immigration officer must note on the officer's report that consent was given and, if possible, by whom consent was given. If the immigration officer is denied access to conduct a site inspection, a warrant may be obtained.

(3) Adequate records must be maintained noting the results of every site inspection, including those where no illegal aliens are located.

(4) Nothing in this section prohibits an immigration officer from entering into any area of a business or other activity to which the general public has access or onto open fields that are not farms or other outdoor agricultural operations without a warrant, consent, or any particularized suspicion in order to question any person whom the officer believes to be an alien concerning his or her right to be or remain in the United States.

(g) Guidelines. The criminal law enforcement authorities authorized under this part will be exercised in a manner consistent with all applicable guidelines and policies of the Department of Justice and the Department of Homeland Security.

HISTORY:

[59 FR 42418, Aug. 17, 1994; 68 FR 35273, 35280, June 13, 2003; 81 FR 62353, 62357, Sept. 9, 2016]

§ 287.9 Criminal search warrant and firearms policies.

(a) A search warrant should be obtained prior to conducting a search in a criminal investigation unless a specific exception to the warrant requirement is authorized by statute or recognized by the courts. Such exceptions may include, for example, the consent of the person to be searched, exigent circumstances, searches incident to a lawful arrest, and border searches. The Commissioner of CBP and the Assistant Secretary for ICE shall promulgate guidelines governing officers' conduct relating to search and seizure.

(b) In using a firearm, an immigration officer shall adhere to the standard of conduct set forth in 8 CFR 287.8(a)(2). An immigration officer may carry only firearms (whether Department issued or personally owned) that have been approved pursuant to guidelines promulgated by the Commissioner of CBP or the Assistant Secretary for ICE. These officials shall promulgate guidelines with respect to:

(1) Investigative procedures to be followed after a shooting incident involving an officer;

(2) Loss or theft of an approved firearm;

(3) Maintenance of records with respect to the issuance of firearms and ammunition; and

(4) Procedures for the proper care, storage, and maintenance of firearms, ammunition, and related equipment.

HISTORY:

[59 FR 42420, Aug. 17, 1994; 68 FR 35273, 35281, June 13, 2003]

§ 287.10 Expedited internal review process.

(a) Violations of standards for enforcement activities. Alleged violations of the standards for enforcement activities established in accordance with the provisions of § 287.8 shall be investigated expeditiously consistent with the policies and procedures of the Department of Homeland Security and pursuant to any guidelines issued by the Secretary.

(b) Complaints. Any persons wishing to lodge a complaint pertaining to violations of enforcement standards contained in § 287.8 may contact the Department of Homeland Security, Office of the Inspector General, 245 Murray Drive — Building 410, Washington, DC, 20548, or telephone 1-800-323-8603. With respect to employees of the former INS, persons may contact the Office of Internal Audit, Bureau of Immigration and Customs Enforcement, 425 I Street NW., Washington, DC, 20536.

(c) Expedited processing of complaints. When an allegation or complaint of violation of § 287.8 is lodged against an employee or officer of the Department, the allegation or complaint shall be referred promptly for investigation in accordance with the policies and procedures of the Department. At the conclusion of an investigation of an allegation or complaint of violation of § 287.8, the investigative report shall be referred promptly for appropriate action in accordance with the policies and procedures of the Department.

(d) Unsubstantiated complaints. When an investigative report does not support the allegation, the employee or officer against whom the allegation was made shall be informed in writing that the matter has been closed as soon as practicable. No reference to the allegation shall be filed in the official's or employee's official personnel file.

(e) Jurisdiction of Department of Justice organizations. Nothing in this section alters or limits, is intended to alter or limit, or shall be construed to alter or limit, the jurisdiction or authority conferred upon the Federal Bureau of Investigation, the United States Attorneys, the Criminal Division or the Civil Rights Division, or any other component of the Department of Justice that may have jurisdiction regarding criminal violations of law.

HISTORY:

[59 FR 42420, Aug. 17, 1994; 68 FR 35273, 35281, June 13, 2003]

§ 287.11 Pre-enrolled Access Lane.

(a) Pre-enrolled Access Lane (PAL). A PAL is a designated traffic lane located at a Service checkpoint, which, when in operation, may be used exclusively by enrolled participants and their passengers in vehicles authorized by the Service to pass through the checkpoint.

(b) **General requirements for Pre-enrolled Access Lane Program.**

(1) Participation in the Pre-enrolled Access Lane program is wholly voluntary and failure to apply or denial of an application does not prevent any person from passing through the checkpoint in the regular traffic lanes.

(2) Only United States citizens and members of the classes of aliens which the Commissioner of the Service or her delegates determine to be eligible may enroll in the PAL program. To participate in the PAL program, an applicant must have a permanent or temporary residence in the United States, and must agree to furnish all information requested on the application.

(3) The applicant must agree to all terms and conditions required for use of a Pre-enrolled Access Lane. Immigration, criminal justice information, and law enforcement records and databases will be checked to assist in determining the applicant's eligibility. The Service may require applicants to submit fingerprints, and the Service may provide those fingerprints to Federal, State, and local government agencies for the purpose of determining eligibility to participate in the PAL program.

(4) Any vehicle used in a Pre-enrolled Access Lane must have current approval from the Service for use in the PAL program.

(5) Enrolled participants may be issued an identification document showing authorization to participate in the PAL program, and, if such a document is issued, participants must have it in their possession whenever using the PAL. In addition, alien participants must be in possession of a valid form constituting evidence of alien registration pursuant to § 264.1(b) of this chapter at all times while using the PAL.

(6) The Service will install any and all equipment, decals, devices, technology, or methodology it deems necessary on registered vehicles to ensure that only authorized persons and vehicles use the PAL.

(7) All devices, decals, or other equipment, methodology, or technology used to identify persons or vehicles using a Pre-enrolled Access Lane remain the property of the United States Government at all times and must be surrendered upon request of the Service. Enrolled participants must abide by the terms set forth by the Service for use of any device, decal, or other equipment, methodology, or technology. If a vehicle is sold or otherwise disposed of, it is the responsibility of the enrolled participant to remove or obliterate any identifying decal or other authorization for participation in the PAL program before or at the time of sale or disposal unless otherwise notified by the Service. If the Service installs an electronic transmitter or similar device on the vehicle, the enrolled participant must have that device removed by the Service at the PAL enrollment center prior to sale or disposal of an authorized vehicle.

(8) Enrolled participants in the PAL program may carry passengers who are not enrolled in the program in their authorized vehicles in the PAL as long as all

passengers are United States citizens, lawful permanent residents of the United States, or rightful holders of valid nonimmigrant United States visas.

(c) **Application.**

(1) Application for Pre-enrolled Access Lane participation shall be made on Form I-866, Application — Checkpoint Pre-enrolled Access Lane.

(2) Each person wishing to enroll in the Pre-enrolled Access Lane program must submit a separate application.

(3) Applications must be supported by documents establishing identity, United States citizenship or lawful immigration status in the United States, a valid driver's license, and vehicle registration for all vehicles being registered. The Service may require additional documentation where appropriate to substantiate information provided on the application, as well as written permission from the vehicle owner to use any vehicle not owned by the applicant in the PAL.

(4) Each person filing an application may be required to present himself or herself for an interview at a time and place designated by the Service prior to approval of the application.

(5) The Service may inspect any vehicle that a PAL applicant desires to register for use in the PAL to ensure that it does not present evidence of having been used or prepared to be used to smuggle aliens or controlled substances, and the Service must approve all vehicles prior to use in the PAL. The Service may prohibit the use of certain types of vehicles in the PAL for reasons of safety and law enforcement.

(6) An application may be denied by the Chief Patrol Agent having jurisdiction over the PAL enrollment center where the application is filed. Written notice of the decision on the application shall be given to the applicant or mailed by ordinary mail to the applicant's last known address. There is no appeal from a denial, but denial is without prejudice to reapplying for this program. Re-applications following denial or revocation of the privilege to participate in the PAL program will not be considered by the Service until 90 days after the date of denial or revocation.

(7) Registration in the PAL program is limited to individuals who the Service has determined present a low risk of using the PAL for unlawful purposes. Criteria that will be considered in the decision to approve or deny the application include the following: lawful presence in the United States, criminal history and/or evidence of criminality, employment, residency, prior immigration history, possession of a valid driver's license, vehicle type, registration, and inspection.

(8) Applications approved by the Service will entitle the authorized person and the authorized vehicle to use the PAL for 2 years from the date of approval of the application or until authorization is revoked, whichever occurs first.

(d) Acknowledgments and agreements. By signing and submitting the Form I-866 each applicant acknowledges and agrees to all of the conditions for participation in the PAL program and the statements on the Form I-866.

(e) Violation of conditions of a Pre-enrolled Access Lane and Revocation. An enrolled participant who violates any condition of the PAL program, or any applicable law or regulation, or who is otherwise determined by an immigration officer to be ineligible to participate in the PAL program, may have his or her authorization and the authorization of his or her vehicle(s) revoked by the Chief Patrol Agent with jurisdiction over the PAL enrollment center where the application is filed and may be subject to other applicable sanctions, such as criminal and/or civil penalties, removal, and/or possible seizure of goods and/or vehicles. If an authorized vehicle is sold, stolen, or otherwise disposed of, authorization to use that vehicle in the PAL is automatically revoked. Within 24 hours of when an authorized vehicle is stolen, or within 7 days of when such vehicle is sold, or otherwise disposed of or the license plates are changed, enrolled participants must give, in person or by facsimile transmission, written notice of such occurrence to the PAL enrollment center at which their application was filed. Failure to do so will result in the automatic revocation of the authorization to use the PAL of the person who registered such vehicle in the PAL program. Unless revocation is automatic, the Service will give notice of revocation to the enrolled PAL participant or mail it by ordinary mail to his or her last known address. However, written notification is not necessary prior to revocation of the privilege to participate in the PAL program. There is no appeal from the revocation of an authorization to participate in the PAL program.

(f) No benefits or rights conferred. This section does not, is not intended to, shall not be construed to, and may not be relied upon to confer any immigration benefit or status to any alien or create any rights, substantive or procedural, enforceable in law or equity by any party in any matter.

HISTORY:

[59 FR 42420, Aug. 17, 1994; 62 FR 19024, 19025, April 18, 1997]

§ 287.12 Scope.

With regard to this part, these regulations provide internal guidance on specific areas of law enforcement authority. These regulations do not, are not intended to, and shall not be construed to exclude, supplant, or limit otherwise lawful activities of the Department or the Secretary. These regulations do not, are not intended to, shall not be construed to, and may not be relied upon to create any rights, substantive or procedural, enforceable at law by any party in any matter, civil or criminal. The Secretary shall have exclusive authority to enforce these regulations through such administrative and other means as he may deem appropriate.

HISTORY:

[59 FR 42420, Aug. 17, 1994; redesignated at 62 FR 19024, 19025, April 18, 1997; 68 FR 35273, 35282, June 13, 2003]

PART 289

AMERICAN INDIANS BORN IN CANADA

Rule

§ 289.1 Definition.

The term American Indian born in Canada as used in section 289 of the Act includes only persons possessing 50 per centum or more of the blood of the American Indian race. It does not include a person who is the spouse or child of such an Indian or a person whose membership in an Indian tribe or family is created by adoption, unless such person possesses at least 50 per centum or more of such blood.

HISTORY:
[29 FR 11494, Aug. 11, 1964]

AUTHORITY:
Secs. 103, 262, 289, 66 Stat. 173, 224, 234; 8 U.S.C. 1103, 1302, 1359; 45 Stat. 401, 54 Stat. 670; 8 U.S.C. 226a, 451.

§ 289.2 Lawful admission for permanent residence.

Any American Indian born in Canada who at the time of entry was entitled to the exemption provided for such person by the Act of April 2, 1928 (45 Stat. 401), or section 289 of the Act, and has maintained residence in the United States since his entry, shall be regarded as having been lawfully admitted for permanent residence. A person who does not possess 50 per centum of the blood of the American Indian race, but who entered the United States prior to December 24, 1952, under the exemption provided by the Act of April 2, 1928, and has maintained his residence in the United States since such entry shall also be regarded as having been lawfully admitted for permanent residence. In the absence of a Service record of arrival in the United States, the record of registration under the Alien Registration Act, of 1940 (54 Stat. 670; 8 U.S.C. 451), or section 262 of the Act, or other satisfactory evidence may be accepted to establish the date of entry.

HISTORY:
[29 FR 11494, Aug. 11, 1964]

AUTHORITY:
Secs. 103, 262, 289, 66 Stat. 173, 224, 234; 8 U.S.C. 1103, 1302, 1359; 45 Stat. 401, 54 Stat. 670; 8 U.S.C. 226a, 451.

§ 289.3 Recording the entry of certain American Indians born in Canada.

The lawful admission for permanent residence of an American Indian born in Canada shall be recorded on Form I-181.

HISTORY:
[33 FR 7485, May 21, 1968]

AUTHORITY:
Secs. 103, 262, 289, 66 Stat. 173, 224, 234; 8 U.S.C. 1103, 1302, 1359; 45 Stat. 401, 54 Stat. 670; 8 U.S.C. 226a, 451.

PART 292

REPRESENTATION AND APPEARANCES

Rule

AUTHORITY NOTE APPLICABLE TO ENTIRE PART:

AUTHORITY:
6 U.S.C. 112; 8 U.S.C. 1103, 1252b, 1362.

§ 292.1 Representation of others.

(a) A person entitled to representation may be represented by any of the following, subject to the limitations in 8 CFR 103.2(a)(3):

(1) Attorneys in the United States. Any attorney as defined in 8 CFR 1.2.

(2) Law students and law graduates not yet admitted to the bar. A law student who is enrolled in an accredited U.S. law school, or a graduate of an accredited U.S. law school who is not yet admitted to the bar, provided that:

(i) He or she is appearing at the request of the person entitled to representation;

(ii) In the case of a law student, he or she has filed a statement that he or she is participating, under the direct supervision of a faculty member, licensed attorney, or accredited representative, in a legal aid program or clinic conducted by a law school or non-profit organization, and that he or she is appearing without direct or indirect remuneration from the alien he or she represents;

(iii) In the case of a law graduate, he or she has filed a statement that he or she is appearing under the supervision of a licensed attorney or accredited representative and that he or she is appearing without direct or indirect remuneration from the alien he or she represents; and

(iv) The law student's or law graduate's appearance is permitted by the DHS official before whom he or she wishes to appear. The DHS official may require that a law student be accompanied by the supervising faculty member, attorney, or accredited representative.

(3) Reputable individuals. Any reputable individual of good moral character, provided that:

(i) He is appearing on an individual case basis, at the request of the person entitled to representation;

(ii) He is appearing without direct or indirect renumeration and files a written declaration to that effect;

(iii) He has a pre-existing relationship or connection with the person entitled to representation (e.g., as a relative, neighbor, clergyman, business associate or personal friend), provided that such requirement may be waived, as a matter of administrative discretion, in cases where adequate representation would not otherwise be available; and

(iv) His or her appearance is permitted by the DHS official before whom he or she seeks to appear, provided that such permission will not be granted with respect to any individual who regularly engages in immigration and naturalization practice or preparation, or holds himself or herself out to the public as qualified to do so.

(4) Accredited representatives. A person representing an organization described in § 292.2 of this chapter who has been accredited by the Board.

(5) Accredited officials. An accredited official, in the United States, of the government to which an alien owes allegiance, if the official appears solely in his official capacity and with the alien's consent.

(6) Attorneys outside the United States. An attorney, other than one described in 8 CFR 1.2, who is licensed to practice law and is in good standing in a court of general jurisdiction of the country in which he or she resides and who is engaged in such practice, may represent parties in matters before DHS, provided that he or she represents persons only in matters outside the geographical confines of the United States as defined in section 101(a)(38) of the Act, and that the DHS official before whom he or she wishes to appear allows such representation as a matter of discretion.

(b) Persons formerly authorized to practice. A person, other than a representative of an organization described in § 292.2 of this chapter, who on December 23, 1952, was authorized to practice before the Board and the Service may continue to act as a representative, subject to the provisions of § 292.3 of this chapter.

(c) Former employees. No person previously employed by the Department of Justice shall be permitted to act as a representative in any case in violation of the provisions of 28 CFR 45.735-7.

(d) Amicus curiae. The Board may grant permission to appear, on a case-by-case basis, as amicus curiae, to an attorney or to an organization represented by an attorney, if the public interest will be served thereby.

(e) Except as set forth in this section, no other person or persons shall represent others in any case.

HISTORY:

[40 FR 23271, May 29. 1975, as amended at 53 FR 7728, Mar. 10, 1988; 55 FR 49251, Nov. 27, 1990; 61 FR 53609, 53610, Oct. 15, 1996; 62 FR 23634, 23635, May 1, 1997; 75 FR 5225, 5227, Feb. 2, 2010; 76 FR 53764, 53797, Aug. 29, 2011]

§ 292.2 Organizations qualified for recognition; requests for recognition; withdrawal of recognition; accreditation of representatives; roster.

(a) Qualifications of organizations. A non-profit religious, charitable, social service, or similar organization established in the United States and recognized as such by the Board may designate a representative or representatives to practice before the Service alone or the Service and the Board (including practice before the Immigration Court). Such organization must establish to the satisfaction of the Board that:

(1) It makes only nominal charges and assesses no excessive membership dues for persons given assistance; and

(2) It has at its disposal adequate knowledge, information and experience.

(b) Requests for recognition. An organization having the qualifications prescribed in paragraph (a) of this section may file an application for recognition on a Form G-27 directly with the Board, along with proof of service of a copy of the application on the district director having jurisdiction over the area in which the organization is located. The district director, within 30 days from the date of service, shall forward to the Board a recommendation for approval or disapproval of the application and the reasons therefor, or request a specified period of time in which to conduct an investigation or otherwise obtain relevant information regarding the applicant. The district director shall include proof of service of a copy of such recommendation or request on the organization. The organization shall have 30 days in which to file a response with the Board to a recommendation by a district director that is other than favorable, along with proof of service of a copy of such response on the district director. If the Board approves a request for time to conduct an investigation, or in its discretion remands the application to the district director for further information, the organization shall be advised of the time granted for such purpose. The Service shall promptly forward the results of any investigation or inquiry to the Board, along with its recommendations for approval or disapproval and the reasons therefor, and proof of service of a copy of the submission on the organization. The organization shall have 30 days from the date of such service to file a response with the Board to any matters raised therein, with proof of service of a copy of the response on the district director. Requests for extensions of filing times must be submitted in writing with the reasons therefor and may be granted by the Board in its discretion. Oral argument may be heard before the Board in its discretion at such date and time as the Board may direct. The organization and Service shall be informed by the Board of the action taken regarding an application. Any recognized organization shall promptly notify the Board of any changes in its name, address, or public telephone number.

(c) Withdrawal of recognition. The Board may withdraw the recognition of any organization which has failed to maintain the qualifications required by § 292.2(a). Withdrawal of recognition may be accomplished in accordance with the following procedure:

(1) The Service, by the district director within whose jurisdiction the organization is located, may conduct an investigation into any organization it believes no longer meets the standards for recognition.

(2) If the investigation establishes to the satisfaction of the district director that withdrawal proceedings should be instituted, he shall cause a written statement of the grounds upon which withdrawal is sought to be served upon the organization, with notice to show cause why its recognition should not be withdrawn. The notice will call upon the organization to appear before a special inquiry officer for a hearing at a time and place stated, not less than 30 days after service of the notice.

(3) The special inquiry officer shall hold a hearing, receive evidence, make findings of fact, state his recommendations, and forward the complete record to the Board.

(4) The organization and the Service shall have the opportunity of appearing at oral argument before the Board at a time specified by the Board.

(5) The Board shall consider the entire record and render its decision. The order of the Board shall constitute the final disposition of the proceedings.

(d) Accreditation of representatives. An organization recognized by the Board under paragraph (b) of this section may apply for accreditation of persons of good moral character as its representatives. An organization may apply to have a representative accredited to practice before the Service alone or the Service and the Board (including practice before immigration judges). An application for accreditation shall fully set forth the nature and extent of the proposed representative's experience and knowledge of immigration and naturalization law and procedure and the category of accreditation sought. No individual may submit an application on his or her own behalf. An application shall be filed directly with the Board, along with proof of service of a copy of the application on the district director having jurisdiction over the area in which the requesting organization is located. The district director, within 30 days from the date of service, shall forward to the Board a recommendation for approval or disapproval of the application and the reasons therefor, or request a specified period of time in which to conduct an investigation or otherwise obtain relevant information regarding the applicant. The district director shall include proof of service of a copy of such recommendation or request on the organization. The organization shall have 30 days in which to file a response with the Board to a recommendation by a distrct director that is other than favorable, with proof of service of a copy of such response on the district director. If the Board approves a request for time to conduct an investigation, or in its discretion remands the application to the district director for further information, the organization shall be advised of the time granted for such purpose. The district director shall promptly forward the results of any investigation or inquiry to the Board, along with a recommendation for approval or disapproval and the reasons therefor, and proof of service of a copy of the submission on the organization. The organization shall have 30 days from the date of service to file a response with the Board to any matters raised therein, with proof or service of a copy of the response on the district director. Requests for extensions of filing times must be submitted in writing with the reasons therefor and may be granted by the Board in its discretion. Oral argument may be heard before the Board in its discretion at such date and time as the Board may direct. The Board may approve or disapprove an application in whole or in part and shall inform the organization and the district director of the action taken with regard to an application. The accreditation of a representative shall be valid for a period of three years only; however, the accreditation shall remain valid pending Board consideration of an application for renewal of accreditation if the application is filed at least 60 days before the third anniversary of the date of the Board's prior accreditation of the representative. Accreditation terminates when the Board's recognition of the organization ceases for any reason or when the representative's employment or other connection with the organization ceases. The organization shall promptly notify the Board of such changes.

(e) Roster. The Board shall maintain an alphabetical roster of recognized organizations and their accredited representatives. A copy of the roster shall be furnished to the Commissioner and he shall be advised from time to time of changes therein.

HISTORY:

[40 FR 23272, May 29, 1975, as amended at 49 FR 44086, Nov. 2, 1984; 62 FR 9071, 9075, Feb. 28, 1997]

§ 292.3 Professional conduct for practitioners — Rules and procedures.

(a) General provisions.

(1) Authority to sanction. An adjudicating official or the Board of Immigration Appeals (Board) may impose disciplinary sanctions against any practitioner if it finds it to be in the public interest to do so. It will be in the public interest to impose disciplinary sanctions against a practitioner who is authorized to practice before DHS when such person has engaged in criminal, unethical, or unprofessional conduct, or in frivolous behavior, as set forth in 8 CFR 1003.102. In accordance with the disciplinary proceedings set forth in 8 CFR part 1003, an adjudicating official or the Board may impose any of the following disciplinary sanctions:

(i) Expulsion which is permanent, from practice before the Board and the Immigration Courts, or DHS, or before all three authorities;

(ii) Suspension, including immediate suspension, from practice before the Board and the Immigration Courts, or DHS, or before all three authorities;

(iii) Public or private censure; or

(iv) Such other disciplinary sanctions as the adjudicating official or the Board deems appropriate.

(2) Persons subject to sanctions. Persons subject to sanctions include any practitioner. A practitioner is any attorney as defined in 8 CFR 1.2 who does not represent the federal government, or any representative as defined in 8 CFR 1.2. Attorneys employed by DHS will be subject to discipline pursuant to paragraph (i) of this section.

(b) Grounds of discipline. It is deemed to be in the public interest for the adjudicating official or the Board to impose disciplinary sanctions as described in paragraph (a)(1) of this section against any practitioner who falls within one or more of the categories enumerated in 8 CFR 1003.102. These categories do not constitute the exclusive grounds for which disciplinary sanctions may be imposed in the public interest. Nothing in this regulation should be read to denigrate the practitioner's duty to represent zealously his or her client within the bounds of the law.

(c) **Immediate suspension and summary disciplinary proceedings; duty of practitioner to notify DHS of conviction or discipline.**

(1) Immediate suspension proceedings. Immediate suspension proceedings will be conducted in accordance with the provisions set forth in 8 CFR 1003.103. DHS shall file a petition with the Board to suspend immediately from practice before DHS any practitioner who has been found guilty of, or pleaded guilty or nolo contendere to, a serious crime, as defined in 8 CFR 1003.102(h), any practitioner who has been suspended or disbarred by, or while a disciplinary investigation or proceeding is pending has resigned from, the highest court of any State, possession, territory, or Commonwealth of the United States, or the District of Columbia, or any Federal court; or who has been placed on an interim suspension pending a final resolution of the underlying disciplinary matter.

(2) Copies and proof of service. A copy of the petition will be forwarded to EOIR, which may submit a written request to the Board that entry of any order immediately suspending a practitioner before DHS also apply to the practitioner's authority to practice before the Board and the Immigration Courts. Proof of service on the practitioner of EOIR's request to broaden the scope of any immediate suspension must be filed with the Board.

(3) Summary disciplinary proceedings. Summary disciplinary proceedings will be conducted in accordance with the provisions set forth in 8 CFR 1003.103. DHS shall promptly initiate summary disciplinary proceedings against any practitioner described in paragraph (c)(1) of this section by the issuance of a Notice of Intent to Discipline, upon receipt of a certified copy of the order, judgment, and/or record evidencing the underlying criminal conviction, discipline, or resignation, and accompanied by a certified copy of such document. Delays in initiation of summary disciplinary proceedings under this section will not impact an immediate suspension imposed pursuant to paragraph (c)(1) of this section. Any such proceeding will not be concluded until all direct appeals from an underlying criminal conviction have been completed.

(4) Duty of practitioner to notify DHS of conviction or discipline. Within 30 days of the issuance of the initial order, even if an appeal of the conviction or discipline is pending, of any conviction or discipline for professional misconduct entered on or after July 27, 2000, a practitioner must notify DHS disciplinary counsel if the practitioner has been: Found guilty of, or pleaded guilty or nolo contendere to, a serious crime, as defined in 8 CFR 1003.102(h); suspended or disbarred by, or while a disciplinary investigation or proceeding is pending has resigned from, the highest court of any State, possession, territory, or Commonwealth of the United States, or the District of Columbia, or any Federal court; or placed on an interim suspension pending a final resolution of the underlying disciplinary matter. Failure to notify DHS disciplinary counsel as required may result in immediate suspension as set forth in paragraph (c)(1) of this section.

(d) **Filing of complaints of misconduct occurring before DHS; preliminary inquiry; resolutions; referral of complaints.**

(1) Filing of complaints of misconduct occurring before DHS. Complaints of criminal, unethical, or unprofessional conduct, or of frivolous behavior by a practitioner before DHS must be filed with the DHS disciplinary counsel. Disciplinary complaints must be submitted in writing and must state in detail the information that supports the basis for the complaint, including, but not limited to, the names and addresses of the complainant and the practitioner, the date(s) of the conduct or behavior, the nature of the conduct or behavior, the individuals involved, the harm or damages sustained by the complainant, and any other relevant information. The DHS disciplinary counsel will notify EOIR disciplinary counsel of any disciplinary complaint that pertains, in whole or in part, to a matter before the Board or the Immigration Courts.

(2) Preliminary inquiry. Upon receipt of a disciplinary complaint or on its own initiative, the DHS disciplinary counsel will initiate a preliminary inquiry. If a complaint is filed by a client or former client, the complainant thereby waives the attorney-client privilege and any other applicable privilege, to the extent necessary to conduct a preliminary inquiry and any subsequent proceeding based thereon. If the DHS disciplinary counsel determines that a complaint is without merit, no further action will be taken. The DHS disciplinary counsel may, in his or her discretion, close a preliminary inquiry if the complainant fails to comply with reasonable requests for assistance, information, or documentation. The complainant and the practitioner will be notified of any such determination in writing.

(3) Resolutions reached prior to the issuance of a Notice of Intent to Discipline. The DHS disciplinary counsel may, in his or her discretion, issue warning letters and admonitions, and may enter into agreements in lieu of discipline, prior to the issuance of a Notice of Intent to Discipline.

(e) **Notice of Intent to Discipline.**

(1) Issuance of Notice to Practitioner. If, upon completion of the preliminary inquiry, the DHS disciplinary counsel determines that sufficient prima facie evidence exists to warrant charging a practitioner with professional misconduct as set forth in 8 CFR 1003.102, it will file with the Board and issue to the practitioner who was the subject of the preliminary inquiry a Notice of Intent to Discipline. Service of this notice will be made upon the practitioner by either certified mail to his or her last known address, as defined in paragraph (e)(2) of this section, or by personal delivery. Such notice shall contain a statement of the charge(s), a copy of the preliminary inquiry report, the proposed disci-

plinary sanctions to be imposed, the procedure for filing an answer or requesting a hearing, and the mailing address and telephone number of the Board. In summary disciplinary proceedings brought pursuant to § 292.3(c), a preliminary inquiry report is not required to be filed with the Notice of Intent to Discipline. Notice of Intent to Discipline proceedings will be conducted in accordance with the provisions set forth in 8 CFR 1003.105 and 1003.106.

(2) Practitioner's address. For the purposes of this section, the last known address of a practitioner is the practitioner's address as it appears in DHS records if the practitioner is actively representing an applicant or petitioner before DHS on the date the DHS disciplinary counsel issues the Notice of Intent to Discipline. If the practitioner does not have a matter pending before DHS on the date of the issuance of a Notice of Intent to Discipline, then the last known address for a practitioner will be as follows:

(i) Attorneys in the United States: The attorney's address that is on record with a state jurisdiction that licensed the attorney to practice law.

(ii) Accredited representatives: The address of a recognized organization with which the accredited representative is affiliated.

(iii) Accredited officials: The address of the embassy of the foreign government that employs the accredited official.

(iv) All other practitioners: The address for the practitioner that appears in DHS records for the application or petition proceeding in which the DHS official permitted the practitioner to appear.

(3) Copy of Notice to EOIR; reciprocity of disciplinary sanctions. A copy of the Notice of Intent to Discipline shall be forwarded to the EOIR disciplinary counsel. Under Department of Justice regulations in 8 CFR chapter V, the EOIR disciplinary counsel may submit a written request to the Board or the adjudicating official requesting that any discipline imposed upon a practitioner which restricts his or her authority to practice before DHS also apply to the practitioner's authority to practice before the Board and the Immigration Courts. Proof of service on the practitioner of any request to broaden the scope of the proposed discipline must be filed with the Board or the adjudicating official.

(4) Answer. The practitioner shall file a written answer or a written request for a hearing to the Notice of Intent to Discipline in accordance with 8 CFR 1003.105. If a practitioner fails to file a timely answer, proceedings will be conducted according to 8 CFR 1003.105.

(f) Right to be heard and disposition; decision; appeal; and reinstatement after expulsion or suspension. Upon the filing of an answer, the matter shall be heard, decided, and appeals filed according to the procedures set forth in 8 CFR 1003.106. Reinstatement proceedings after expulsion or suspension shall be conducted according to the procedures set forth in 8 CFR 1003.107.

(g) Referral. In addition to, or in lieu of, initiating disciplinary proceedings against a practitioner, the DHS disciplinary counsel may notify any appropriate Federal and/or state disciplinary or regulatory authority of any complaint filed against a practitioner. Any final administrative decision imposing sanctions against a practitioner (other than a private censure) will be reported to any such disciplinary or regulatory authority in every jurisdiction where the disciplined practitioner is admitted or otherwise authorized to practice.

(h) Confidentiality.

(1) Complaints and preliminary inquiries. Except as otherwise provided by law or regulation or as authorized by this regulation, information concerning complaints or preliminary inquiries is confidential. A practitioner whose conduct is the subject of a complaint or preliminary inquiry, however, may waive confidentiality, except that the DHS disciplinary counsel may decline to permit a waiver of confidentiality if it is determined that an ongoing preliminary inquiry may be substantially prejudiced by a public disclosure before the filing of a Notice of Intent to Discipline.

(i) Disclosure of information for the purpose of protecting the public. The DHS disciplinary counsel may disclose information concerning a complaint or preliminary inquiry for the protection of the public when the necessity for disclosing information outweighs the necessity for preserving confidentiality in circumstances including, but not limited to, the following:

(A) A practitioner has caused, or is likely to cause, harm to client(s), the public, or the administration of justice, such that the public or specific individuals should be advised of the nature of the allegations. If disclosure of information is made pursuant to this paragraph, the DHS disciplinary counsel may define the scope of information disseminated and may limit the disclosure of information to specified individuals or entities;

(B) A practitioner has committed criminal acts or is under investigation by law enforcement authorities;

(C) A practitioner is under investigation by a disciplinary or regulatory authority, or has committed acts or made omissions that may reasonably result in investigation by such an authority;

(D) A practitioner is the subject of multiple disciplinary complaints and the DHS disciplinary counsel has determined not to pursue all of the complaints. The DHS disciplinary counsel may inform complainants whose allegations have not been pursued of the status of any other preliminary inquiries or the manner in which any other complaint(s) against the practitioner have been resolved.

(ii) Disclosure of information for the purpose of conducting a preliminary inquiry. The DHS disciplinary counsel may, in his or her discretion, disclose documents and information concerning complaints and preliminary inquiries to the following individuals or entities:

(A) To witnesses or potential witnesses in conjunction with a complaint or preliminary inquiry;

(B) To other governmental agencies responsible for the enforcement of civil or criminal laws;

(C) To agencies and other jurisdictions responsible for conducting disciplinary investigations or proceedings;

(D) To the complainant or a lawful designee; and

(E) To the practitioner who is the subject of the complaint or preliminary inquiry or the practitioner's counsel of record.

(2) Resolutions reached prior to the issuance of a Notice of Intent to Discipline. Resolutions, such as warning letters, admonitions, and agreements in lieu of discipline, reached prior to the issuance of a Notice of Intent to Discipline, will remain confidential. However, such resolutions may become part of the public record if the practitioner becomes subject to a subsequent Notice of Intent to Discipline.

(3) Notices of Intent to Discipline and action subsequent thereto. Notices of Intent to Discipline and any action that takes place subsequent to their issuance, except for the imposition of private censures, may be disclosed to the public, except that private censures may become part of the public record if introduced as evidence of a prior record of discipline in any subsequent disciplinary proceeding. Settlement agreements reached after the issuance of a Notice of Intent to Discipline may be disclosed to the public upon final approval by the adjudicating official or the Board. Disciplinary hearings are open to the public, except as noted in 8 CFR 1003.106(a)(v).

(i) Discipline of government attorneys. Complaints regarding the conduct or behavior of DHS attorneys shall be directed to the Office of the Inspector General, DHS. If disciplinary action is warranted, it will be administered pursuant to the Department's attorney discipline procedures.

HISTORY:

[23 FR 2672, Apr. 23, 1958, as amended at 23 FR 9124, Nov. 26, 1958; 34 FR 12213, July 24, 1969; 36 FR 11903, June 23, 1971; 52 FR 24981, July 2, 1987; 57 FR 11574, Apr. 6, 1992; 60 FR 34090, June 30, 1995; 65 FR 39513, 39531, June 27, 2000; 75 FR 5225, 5228, Feb. 2, 2010; 76 FR 53764, 53797, Aug. 29, 2011]

§ 292.4 Appearances.

(a) Authority to appear and act. An appearance must be filed on the appropriate form as prescribed by DHS by the attorney or accredited representative appearing in each case. The form must be properly completed and signed by the petitioner, applicant, or respondent to authorize representation in order for the appearance to be recognized by DHS. The appearance will be recognized by the specific immigration component of DHS in which it was filed until the conclusion of the matter for which it was entered. This does not change the requirement that a new form must be filed with an appeal filed with the Administrative Appeals Office of USCIS. Substitution may be permitted upon the written withdrawal of the attorney or accredited representative of record or upon the filing of a new form by a new attorney or accredited representative. When an appearance is made by a person acting in a representative capacity, his or her personal appearance or signature will constitute a representation that under the provisions of this chapter he or she is authorized and qualified to appear as a representative as provided in 8 CFR 103.2(a)(3) and 292.1. Further proof of authority to act in a representative capacity may be required.

(b) A party to a proceeding and his or her attorney or representative will be permitted to examine the record of proceeding in accordance with 6 CFR part 5.

HISTORY:

[23 FR 2673, Apr. 23, 1958, as amended at 32 FR 9633, July 4, 1967; 52 FR 2941, Jan. 29, 1987; 59 FR 1466, Jan. 1, 1994; 75 FR 5225, 5230, Feb. 2, 2010; 76 FR 53764, 53797, Aug. 29, 2011]

§ 292.5 Service upon and action by attorney or representative of record.

(a) Representative capacity. Whenever a person is required by any of the provisions of this chapter to give or be given notice; to serve or be served with any paper other than a warrant of arrest or a subpoena; to make a motion; to file or submit an application or other document; or to perform or waive the performance of any act, such notice, service, motion, filing, submission, performance, or waiver shall be given by or to, served by or upon, made by, or requested of the attorney or representative of record, or the person himself if unrepresented.

(b) Right to representation. Whenever an examination is provided for in this chapter, the person involved shall have the right to be represented by an attorney or representative who shall be permitted to examine or cross-examine such person and witnesses, to introduce evidence, to make objections which shall be stated succinctly and entered on the record, and to submit briefs. Provided, that nothing in this paragraph shall be construed to provide any applicant for admission in either primary or secondary inspection the right to representation, unless the applicant for admission has become the focus of a criminal investigation and has been taken into custody.

HISTORY:

[37 FR 11471, June 8, 1972 and 45 FR 81733, Dec. 12, 1980; 46 FR 2025, Jan. 8, 1981; 58 FR 49911, Sept. 24, 1993, as confirmed at 60 FR 6650]

§ 292.6 Interpretation.

Interpretations of this part will be made by the Board of Immigration Appeals, subject to the provisions of 8 CFR part 1003.

HISTORY:

[32 FR 9633, July 4, 1967; 75 FR 5225, 5230, Feb. 2, 2010]

PART 293
DEPOSIT OF AND INTEREST ON CASH RECEIVED TO SECURE IMMIGRATION BONDS

Rule

AUTHORITY NOTE APPLICABLE TO ENTIRE PART:

AUTHORITY:
8 U.S.C. 1363.

§ 293.1 Computation of interest.

The Secretary of the Treasury determines the rate at which an immigration bond secured by cash shall bear interest, consistent with 8 CFR 293.2. Interest shall be computed from the deposit date to and including the refund date or breach date of the immigration bond. For purposes of this part, the deposit date shall be the date shown on the receipt for the cash received as security on an immigration bond. The refund date shall be the date upon which the interest is certified to the Treasury Department for payment. The breach date shall be the date the immigration bond was breached as shown on Form I-323 — "Notice — Immigration Bond Breached." In counting the number of days for which interest shall be computed, the day on which the cash was deposited shall not be counted; however, the refund date or the breach date shall be counted.

HISTORY:
[36 FR 13677, July 23, 1971; 80 FR 34239, 34242, June 16, 2015]

§ 293.2 Interest rate.

Interest on cash deposited to secure immigration bonds will be at the rate as determined by the Secretary of the Treasury, but in no case will exceed 3 per centum per annum or be less than zero. The rate will be published by Treasury on the Treasury Web site or through another mechanism.

HISTORY:
[36 FR 13677, July 23, 1971; 80 FR 34239, 34242, June 16, 2015]

§ 293.3 Time of payment.

Interest shall be paid only at time of disposition of principal cash when the immigration bond has been cancelled or declared breached.

HISTORY:
[36 FR 13677, July 23, 1971; 80 FR 34239, 34242, June 16, 2015]

§ 293.4 [This section was removed. See 80 FR 34239, 34242, June 16, 2015.]

[NO TEXT IN ORIGINAL]

HISTORY:
[36 FR 13677, July 23, 1971]

AUTHORITY:
(Sec. 103, 66 Stat. 173; 8 U.S.C. 1103. Interprets and applies sec. 293, 84 Stat. 413.)

PART 299
IMMIGRATION FORMS

AUTHORITY NOTE APPLICABLE TO ENTIRE PART:

AUTHORITY:
8 U.S.C. 1101 and note, 1103; 8 CFR part 2.

§ 299.1 Prescribed forms.

A listing of USCIS, ICE, and CBP approved forms referenced in chapter I can be viewed on the Office of Management and Budget Web site at http://www.reginfo.gov. A listing of approved USCIS forms can also be viewed on its Internet Web site.

HISTORY:
[53 FR 33444, Aug. 31, 1988, as amended at 54 FR 102, Jan. 4, 1989.; 54 FR 7174, Feb. 17, 1989; 54 FR 29440, July 12, 1989; 54 FR 30370, July 20, 1989; 54 FR 39337, Sept. 26, 1989; 54 FR 48231, Nov. 22, 1989; 55 FR 12629, Apr. 5, 1990; 56 FR 624, Jan. 7, 1991.; 56 FR 21920, May 13, 1991; 57 FR 6183, Feb. 21, 1992: 57 FR 6462, Feb. 25, 1992, as confirmed at 60 FR 66062, 66067, Dec. 21, 1995; 57 FR 14627, Apr. 21, 1992; 58 FR 48780, Sept. 20, 1993; 58 FR 58937, Nov. 5, 1993; 59 FR 25556, May 17, 1994, as corrected at 59 FR 35978, July 14, 1994, and confirmed and amended at 61 FR 47799, 47800, Sept. 11, 1996; 59 FR 47063, Sept. 14, 1994; 60 FR 9774, Feb. 22, 1995; 60 FR 14353, Mar. 17, 1995; 60 FR 37328, July 20, 1995; 60 FR 43954, 43962, Aug. 24, 1995; 60 FR 44260, 44271, Aug. 25, 1995; 60 FR 50386, 50390, Sept. 29, 1995, as confirmed at 61 FR 53830, 53831, Oct. 16, 1996; 61 FR 28003, 28013, June 4, 1996; 61 FR 46534, 46537, Sept. 4, 1996; 61 FR 53830, 53833, Oct. 16, 1996; 62 FR 10312, 10393, Mar. 6, 1997; 62 FR 19024, 19026, Apr. 18, 1997; 62 FR 54346, 54356, Oct. 20, 1997, as confirmed and amended at 71 FR 35732, 35749, 35756, June 21, 2006; 63 FR 3792, 3797, Jan. 27, 1998; 63 FR 12979, 12987, Mar. 17, 1998; 63 FR 27823, 27833, May 21, 1998; 63 FR 32113, 32117, June 12, 1998; 63 FR 65657, 65660, Nov. 30, 1998; 63 FR 70313, 70316, Dec. 21, 1998; 64 FR 25756, 25773, May 12, 1999, as confirmed and amended at 65 FR 15835, 15846, 15847, 15856, Mar. 24, 2000; 64 FR 27856, 27881, May 21, 1999; 65 FR 10678, 10684, Feb. 29, 2000; 65 FR 43677, 43680, July 14, 2000; 66 FR 29661, 29681, June 1, 2001, as confirmed and amended at 67 FR 38341, 38350, 38352, June 4, 2002, as corrected at 67 FR 66532, Nov. 1, 2002; 66 FR 29682, 29686, June 1, 2001; 66 FR 31107, 31114, June 11, 2001; 66 FR 46697, 46704, Sept. 7, 2001; 67 FR 4784, 4803, Jan. 31, 2002; 67 FR 49561, 49564, July 31, 2002; 67 FR 71443, 71450, Dec. 2, 2002; 68 FR 43901, 43921, July 25, 2003; 69 FR 39814, 39826, July 1, 2004; 71 FR 35732, 35756, June 21, 2006; 72 FR 53014, 53042, Sept. 17, 2007; 72 FR 56832, 56867, Oct. 4, 2007; 73 FR 28026, 28031, May 15, 2008; 73 FR 72276, 72296, Nov. 26, 2008; 73 FR 74605, Dec. 9, 2008; 73 FR 75540, 75563, Dec. 12, 2008; 74 FR 55094, 55111, Oct. 27, 2009, as confirmed at 76 FR 55502, Sept. 7, 2011; 74 FR 55726, 55740, Oct. 28, 2009; 74 FR 67969, Dec. 22, 2009; 76 FR 53764, 53797, Aug. 29, 2011]

§ 299.2 Distribution of Service forms.

The distribution of official Immigration and Naturalization applications, petitions, and related forms is as follows:

(a) Any officer or employee of the Service may issue official application or petition and related forms to the person for whose use the form is intended or to a person identified as a representative of the intended user in the quantity required for filing the application or petition and related forms.

(b) A small quantity, twenty-five (25) copies, may be issued to organizations an practitioners who make written request to the Regional Commissioner for the geographic location of the requester if such forms have not been made available for purchase from the Superintendent of Documents, Washington, DC 20402.

(c) Voluntary agencies (VOLAGS) participating in the Outreach Program of the Service who make written request to the Regional Commissioner for the geographic location of the requester may be furnished Service forms gratis in the volumes requested.

HISTORY:

[43 FR 14304, Apr. 5, 1978, as amended at 45 FR 6777, Jan. 30, 1980; 45 FR 21611, Apr. 2, 1980]

§ 299.3 [This section was removed and reserved. See 76 FR 53764, 53797, Aug. 29, 2011.]

[NO TEXT IN ORIGINAL]

HISTORY:

[49 FR 7104, Feb. 27, 1984, as amended at 52 FR 16195, May 1, 1987; 55 FR 12629, Apr. 5, 1990; 59 FR 25558, May 17, 1994; as confirmed and amended at 61 FR 47799, 47800, Sept. 11, 1996; 76 FR 53764, 53797, Aug. 29, 2011]

AUTHORITY:

(8 U.S.C. 1101 and note, 1103; 8 CFR part 2.)

§ 299.4 Reproduction of Public Use Forms by public and private entities.

(a) Duplication requirements. All forms required for applying for a specific benefit in compliance with the immigration and naturalization regulations, including those which have been made available for purchase by the Superintendent of Documents as listed in § 299.3, may be printed or otherwise reproduced. Such reproduction must be by an appropriate duplicating process and at the expense of the public or private entity. Forms printed or reproduced by public or private entities shall be:

(1) In black ink or dye that will not fade or "feather" within 20 years, and

(2) Conform to the officially printed forms currently in use with respect to:

(i) Size,

(ii) Wording and language,

(iii) Arrangement, style and size of type, and

(iv) Paper specifications (White, standard copier or typing paper).

(b) Requirements for electronic generation. Public or private entities may electronically generate forms required for applying for a specific benefit, in compliance with the immigration and naturalization regulations, at their own expense. This includes forms that have been made available for purchase by the Superintendent of Documents, as listed in § 299.3 provided that each form satisfies the following requirements:

(1) An electronic reproduction must be complete, containing all questions which appear on the official form. The wording and punctuation of all data elements and identifying information must match exactly. No data elements may be added or deleted. The sequence and format for each item on the form must be replicated to mirror the authorized agency form. Each item must be printed on the same page in the same location. Likewise, multiple-part sets may be printed as single sheets provided that the destination of the carbon copy is clearly identified on the bottom of the form. An electronic reproduction of a multi page form does not need to match the head-to-head or head-to-foot printing configuration of the official form. In the case of the Form I-20 A-B/I-20ID, Certificate of Eligibility for Nonimmigrant (F-1) Student Status-For Academic and Language Students, private entities may generate this form in single-page format rather than double-sided format, provided that the student's name, school, and date of birth is printed in a shaded box on the top of page 4 of the form, using the same type size and font style as the body of the form.

(2) The final form must match the design, format, and dimensions of the official form. All blocks must remain the same size and lines must remain the same length. No variations will be permissible.

(c) The accuracy of electronically generated forms is the responsibility of the private entities. Changes to existing forms, as announced by the Service, must be promptly incorporated into the private entity software program application. Deviations from the aforementioned standards may result in the return or denial of the applicant's application/petition for a particular benefit.

(d) Electronic printers that provide for near-letter-quality documents should be used to generate electronic forms. Dot matrix printers that are only capable of producing draft quality documents should not be used for form generation, but may be used for the entry of data in a preprinted form where appropriate.

(e) Any form with poor print quality or other defect which renders it illegible, difficult to read, or displays added or missing data elements, will be rejected by the Service. Any problems regarding the acceptability of a specific electronic version of a particular Service form may be brought to the attention of the Director, Policy Directives and Instructions Branch, 425 "I" Street, NW., Room 4034, Washington, DC 20536, telephone number (202) 514-3048.

HISTORY:

[45 FR 6777, Jan. 30, 1980; 59 FR 25558, May 17, 1994, as confirmed and amended at 61 FR 47799, 47801, Sept. 11, 1996; 65 FR 61259, 61260, Oct. 17, 2000]

§ 299.5 [This section was removed and reserved. See 76 FR 53764, 53797, Aug. 29, 2011.]

[NO TEXT IN ORIGINAL]

HISTORY:

[53 FR 33442, Aug. 31, 1988, as amended at 53 FR 43986, Oct. 31,

1988; 54 FR 7174, Feb. 17, 1989; 54 FR 29440, July 12, 1989; 54 FR 30370, July 20, 1989; 54 FR 48231, Nov. 22, 1989; 55 FR 12629, Apr. 5, 1990; 56 FR 624, Jan. 7, 1991.; 56 FR 21920, May 13, 1991; 56 FR 22822, May 17, 1991; 56 FR 50480, Oct. 7, 1991, as confirmed at 60 FR 6650, Feb. 3, 1995; 57 FR 6183, Feb. 21, 1992; 57 FR 6462, Feb. 25, 1992, as confirmed at 60 FR 66062, 66067, Dec. 21, 1995; 58 FR 49911, Sept. 24, 1993, as confirmed at 60 FR 6650, Feb. 3, 1995; 58 FR 58937, Nov. 5, 1993; 59 FR 25559, May 17, 1994, 59 FR 35978, July 14, 1994, as amended at 59 FR 62303, Dec. 5, 1994; 60 FR 44260, 44271, Aug. 25, 1995; 60 FR 50386, 50390, Sept. 29, 1995, as confirmed at 61 FR 53830, 53831, Oct. 16, 1996; 61 FR 28003, 28013, June 4, 1996; 61 FR 47799, 47801, Sept. 11, 1996; 61 FR 53830, 53833, Oct. 16, 1996; 62 FR 10312, 10394, Mar. 6, 1997; 62 FR 12915, 12923, Mar. 19, 1997; 62 FR 19024, 19026, Apr. 18, 1997; 62 FR 54346, 54356, Oct. 20, 1997, as confirmed and amended at 71 FR 35732, 35749, 35757, June 21, 2006; 63 FR 3792, 3797, Jan. 27, 1998; 63 FR 12979, 12987, Mar. 17, 1998; 63 FR 27823, 27834, May 21, 1998, as confirmed at 65 FR 15846, 15854, Mar. 24, 2000; 63 FR 65657, 65660, Nov. 30, 1998; 64 FR 25756, 25773, May 12, 1999, as confirmed at 65 FR 15835, 15844, Mar. 24, 2000; 64 FR 27856, 27881, May 21, 1999; 65 FR 10678, 10684, Feb. 29, 2000; 66 FR 29661, 29682, June 1, 2001, as confirmed at 67 FR 38341, 38350, June 4, 2002; 66 FR 29682, 29686, June 1, 2001; 66 FR 46697, 46705, Sept. 7, 2001; 67 FR 4784, 4803, Jan. 31, 2002; 67 FR 71443, 71450, Dec. 2, 2002; 68 FR 43901, 43921, July 25, 2003; 69 FR 39814, 39827, July 1, 2004; 71 FR 35732, 35757, June 21, 2006; 72 FR 53014, 53042, Sept. 17, 2007; 73 FR 28026, 28032, May 15, 2008; 73 FR 72276, 72297, Nov. 26, 2008; 73 FR 75540, 75564, Dec. 12, 2008; 74 FR 55094, 55112, Oct. 27, 2009, as confirmed at 76 FR 55502, Sept. 7, 2011; 74 FR 55726, 55740, Oct. 28, 2009; 74 FR 67969, Dec. 22, 2009; 76 FR 53764, 53797, Aug. 29, 2011]

AUTHORITY:

(8 U.S.C. 1101 and note, 1103; 8 CFR part 2.)

SUBCHAPTER C

NATIONALITY REGULATIONS

Rule
320.3. How, where, and what forms and other documents should be filed?
320.4. Who must appear for an interview on the application for citizenship?
320.5. Decision.

Part 322. Child Born Outside the United States; Requirements for Application for Certificate of Citizenship

322.1. What are the definitions used in this part?
322.2. Eligibility.
322.3. Application and supporting documents.
322.4. Interview.
322.5. Decision.

Part 324. Special Classes of Persons Who May Be Naturallzed: Women Who Have Lost United States Citizenship by Marriage and Former Citizens Whose Naturalization Is Authorized by Prlvate Law

324.1. Definitions.
324.2. Former citizen at birth or by naturalization.
324.3. Women, citizens of the United States at birth, who lost or are believed to have lost citizenship by marriage and whose marriage has terminated.
324.4. Women restored to United States citizenship by the act of June 25, 1936, as amended by the act of July 2, 1940.
324.5. Former citizen of the United States whose naturalization by taking the oath is authorized by a private law.

Part 325. Nationals but Not Citizens of the United States; Residence Within Outlying Possessions

325.1. [Reserved]
325.2. Eligibility.
325.3. Residence.
325.4. Application; Documents.

Part 327. Special Classes of Persons Who May Be Naturalized: Persons Who Lost United States Citizenship Through Service in Armed Forces of Foreign Country During World War II

327.1. Eligibility.
327.2. Procedure for naturalization.

Part 328. Special Classes of Persons Who May Be Naturalized: Persons with 1 Year of Service in the United States Armed Forces

328.1. Definitions.
328.2. Eligibility.
328.3. [This section was removed and reserved. See 74 FR 26933, 26941, June 5, 2009.]
328.4. Application and evidence.

Part 329. Special Classes of Persons Who May Be Naturalized: Persons with Active Duty or Certain Ready Reserve Service in the United States Armed Forces During Specified Periods of Hostilities

329.1. Definitions.
329.2. Eligibility.
329.3. [This section was removed and reserved. See 74 FR 26933, 26941, June 5, 2009.]
329.4. Application and evidence.
329.5. [This section was removed. See 76 FR 53764, 53800, Aug. 29, 2011.]

Part 330. Special Classes of Persons Who May Be Naturalized: Seamen

Rule
330.1. Eligibility.
330.2. Application.

Part 331. Alien Enemies; Naturalization Under Specified Conditions and Procedures

331.1. Definitions.
331.2. Eligibility.
331.3. Investigation.
331.4. Procedures.

Part 332. Naturalization Administration

332.1. Designation of USCIS employees to administer oaths and conduct examinations and hearings.
332.2. [This section was removed and reserved. See 76 FR 53764, 53801, Aug. 29, 2011.]
332.3. [This section was removed and reserved. See 76 FR 53764, 53801, Aug. 29, 2011.]
332.4. [This section was removed and reserved. See 76 FR 53764, 53801, Aug. 29, 2011.]
332.5. Official forms for use by clerks of court.

Part 333. Photographs

333.1. Description of required photographs.
333.2. Attachment of photographs to documents.

Part 334. Application for Naturalization

334.1. Filing of application for naturalization.
334.2. Application for naturalization.
334.3. [Reserved]
334.4. Investigation and report if applicant is sick or disabled.
334.5. Amendment of application for naturalization; reopening proceedings.
334.6 — 334.10. [Reserved]
334.11. Declaration of intention.
334.12 — 334.15. [Reserved]
334.16. [This section was removed. See 76 FR 53764, 53801, Aug. 29, 2011.]
334.17. [This section was removed. See 76 FR 53764, 53801, Aug. 29, 2011.]
334.18. [This section was removed. See 76 FR 53764, 53801, Aug. 29, 2011.]

Part 335. Examination on Application for Naturalization

335.1. Investigation of applicant.
335.2. Examination of applicant.
335.3. Determination on application; continuance of examination.
335.4. Use of record of examination.
335.5. Receipt of derogatory information after grant.
335.6. Failure to appear for examination.
335.7. Failure to prosecute application after initial examination.
335.8. [Reserved]
335.9. Transfer of application.
335.10. Withdrawal of application.
335.11. [This section was removed. See 76 FR 53764, 53802, Aug. 29, 2011.]
335.12. [This section was removed. See 76 FR 53764, 53802, Aug. 29, 2011.]
335.13. [This section was removed. See 76 FR 53764, 53802, Aug. 29, 2011.]

Part 336. Hearings on Denials of Applications for Naturalization

336.1. Denial after section 335 examination.

PART 301

NATIONALS AND CITIZENS OF THE UNITED STATES AT BIRTH

AUTHORITY NOTE APPLICABLE TO ENTIRE PART:

AUTHORITY:
8 U.S.C. 1103, 1401; 8 CFR part 2.

§ 301.1 Procedures.

(a) **Application.**

(1) As provided in 8 CFR part 341, a person residing in the United States who desires to be documented as a United States citizen pursuant to section 301(h) of the Act may apply for a passport at a United States passport agency or may submit an application on the form specified by USCIS in accordance with the form instructions and with the fee prescribed by 8 CFR 106.2. The applicant will be notified when and where to appear before a USCIS officer for examination on his or her application.

(2) A person residing outside of the United States who desires to be documented as a United States citizen under section 301(h) of the Act shall make his or her claim at a United States embassy or consulate, in accordance with such regulations as may be prescribed in the Secretary of State.

(b) Oath of allegiance; issuance of certificate. Upon determination by the district director that a person is a United States citizen pursuant to section 301(h) of the Act, the person shall take the oath of allegiance, prescribed in 8 CFR part 337, before an officer of the Service designated to administer the oath of allegiance within the United States, and a certificate of citizenship shall be issued. The person shall be considered a United States citizen as of the date of his or her birth.

HISTORY:

[61 FR 35111, 35112, July 5, 1996, as corrected at 61 FR 43948, Aug. 27, 1996, as confirmed and revised at 62 FR 39926, 39927, July 25, 1997; 74 FR 26933, 26940, June 5, 2009; 76 FR 53764, 53797, Aug. 29, 2011; 85 FR 46788, 46928, Aug. 3, 2020]

PART 306

SPECIAL CLASSES OF PERSONS WHO MAY BE NATURALIZED: VIRGIN ISLANDERS

§ 306.1 Persons eligible.

Any Danish citizen who resided in the Virgin Islands of the United States on January 17, 1917, and in those Islands, Puerto Rico, or the United States on February 25, 1927, and who had preserved his Danish citizenship by making the declaration prescribed by Article VI of the treaty entered into between the United States and Denmark on August 4, 1916, and proclaimed January 25, 1917, may renounce his Danish citizenship before any court of record in the United States irrespective of his place of residence, in accordance with the provisions of this part.

HISTORY:

22 FR 9812, Dec. 6, 1957.

AUTHORITY:

Secs. 103, 306, 332, 66 Stat. 173, 237, 252; 8 U.S.C. 1103, 1406, 1443.

§ 306.2 United States citizenship; when acquired.

Immediately upon making the declaration of renunciation as described in § 306.12 the declarant shall be deemed to be a citizen of the United States. No certificate of naturalization or of citizenship shall be issued by the clerk of court to any person obtaining, or who has obtained citizenship solely under section 306(a)(1) of the Immigration and Nationality Act or under section 1 of the act of February 25, 1927.

HISTORY:

22 FR 9812, Dec. 6, 1957.

AUTHORITY:

Secs. 103, 306, 332, 66 Stat. 173, 237, 252; 8 U.S.C. 1103, 1406, 1443.

§ 306.11 Preliminary application form; filing; examination.

A person of the class described in § 306.1 shall submit to the Service on Form N-350 preliminary application to renounce Danish citizenship, in accordance with the instructions contained therein. The applicant shall be notified in writing when and where to appear before a representative of the Service for examination as to his eligibility to renounce Danish citizenship and for assistance in filing the renunciation.

HISTORY:

22 FR 9812, Dec. 6, 1957.

AUTHORITY:

Secs. 103, 306, 332, 66 Stat. 173, 237, 252; 8 U.S.C. 1103, 1406, 1443.

§ 306.12 Renunciation forms; disposition.

The renunciation shall be made and executed by the applicant under oath, in duplicate, on Form N-351 and filed in the office of the clerk of court. The usual procedural requirements of the Immigration and Nationality Act shall not apply to proceedings under this part. The fee shall be fixed by the court or the clerk thereof in accordance with the law and rules of the court, and no accounting therefor shall be required to be made to the Service. The clerk shall retain the original of Form N-351 as the court record and forward the duplicate to the district director exercising administrative naturalization jurisdiction over the area in which the court is located.

HISTORY:

22 FR 9812, Dec. 6, 1957.

AUTHORITY:

Secs. 103, 306, 332, 66 Stat. 173, 237, 252; 8 U.S.C. 1103, 1406, 1443.

PART 310

NATURALIZATION AUTHORITY

AUTHORITY NOTE APPLICABLE TO ENTIRE PART:

AUTHORITY:

8 U.S.C. 1103, 1421, 1443, 1447, 1448; 8 CFR part 2.

§ 310.1 Administrative naturalization authority.

(a) Attorney General. Commencing October 1, 1991, section 310 of the Act confers the sole authority to naturalize persons as citizens of the United States upon the Attorney General.

(b) Commissioner of the Immigration and Naturalization Service. Pursuant to § 2.1 of this chapter, the Commissioner of the Immigration and Naturalization Service is authorized to perform such acts as are necessary and proper to implement the Attorney General's authority under the provisions of section 310 of the Act.

HISTORY:

[56 FR 50480, Oct. 7, 1991, as confirmed at 60 FR 6650, Feb. 3, 1995]

§ 310.2 Jurisdiction to accept applications for naturalization.

USCIS shall accept an application for naturalization from an applicant who is subject to a continuous residence requirement under section 316(a) or 319(a) of the Act as much as three months before the date upon which the applicant would otherwise satisfy such continuous residence requirement in the State or Service district, as defined in 8 CFR 316.1, where residence is to be established for naturalization purposes. At the time of examination on the application, the applicant will be required to prove that he or she satisfies the residence requirements for the residence reflected in the application.

HISTORY:

[56 FR 50480, Oct. 7, 1991, as confirmed at 60 FR 6650, Feb. 3, 1995; 76 FR 53764, 53797, Aug. 29, 2011]

§ 310.3 Administration of the oath of allegiance.

(a) An applicant for naturalization may elect, at the time of filing of, or at the examination on, the application, to have the oath of allegiance and renunciation under section 337(a) of the Act administered in a public ceremony conducted by the Service or by any court described in section 310(b) of the Act, subject to section 310(b)(1)(B) of the Act.

(b) The jurisdiction of all such courts specified to administer the oath of allegiance shall extend only to those persons who are resident within the respective jurisdictional limits of such courts, except as otherwise provided in section 316(f)(2) of the Act. Persons who temporarily reside within the jurisdictional limits of a court in order to pursue an application properly filed pursuant to section 319(b), 328(a), or 329 of the Act or section 405 of the Immigration Act of 1990 are not subject to the exclusive jurisdiction provisions of section 310(b)(1)(B) of the Act.

(c)(1) A court that wishes to exercise exclusive jurisdiction to administer the oath of allegiance for the 45-day period specified in section 310(b)(1)(B) of the Act shall notify, in writing, the district director of the Service office having jurisdiction over the place in which the court is located, of the court's intent to exercise such exclusive jurisdiction.

(2) At least 60 days prior to the holding of any oath administration ceremony referred to in § 337.8 of this chapter, the clerk of court shall give written notice to the appropriate district director of the time, date, and place of such ceremony and of the number of persons who may be accommodated.

(d) A court that has notified the Service pursuant to paragraph (c)(1) of this section shall have exclusive authority to administer the oath of allegiance to persons residing within its jurisdiction for a period of 45 days beginning on the date that the Service notifies the clerk of court of the applicant's eligibility for naturalization. Such exclusive authority shall be effective only if on the date the Service notifies the clerk of court of the applicant's eligibility, the court has notified the Service of the day or days during such 45-day period on which the court has scheduled oath administration ceremonies available to the applicant. The Service must submit the notification of the applicant's eligibility to the clerk of court within 10 days of the approval of the application pursuant to § 337.8 of this chapter.

(e) Waiver of exclusive authority. A court exercising exclusive authority to administer the oath of allegiance pursuant to paragraph (c) of this section may waive such exclusive authority when it is determined by the court that the Service failed to notify the court within a reasonable time prior to a scheduled oath ceremony of the applicant's eligibility such that it is impractical for the applicant to appear at that ceremony. The court shall notify the district director in writing of the waiver of exclusive authority as it relates to a specific applicant, and the Service shall promptly notify the applicant. The Service shall then arrange for the administration of the oath of allegiance pursuant to § 337.2 of this chapter.

HISTORY:

[56 FR 50480, Oct. 7, 1991, as confirmed at 60 FR 6650, Feb. 3, 1995; 58 FR 49911, Sept. 24, 1993, as confirmed at 60 FR 6650, Feb. 3, 1995; 66 FR 32138, 32144, June 13, 2001]

§ 310.4 Judicial naturalization authority and withdrawal of petitions.

(a) Jurisdiction. No court shall have jurisdiction under section 310(a) of the Act, to naturalize a person unless a petition for naturalization with respect to that person was filed with the naturalization court before October 1, 1991.

(b) **Withdrawal of petitions.**

(1) In the case of any petition for naturalization which was pending in any court as of November 29, 1990, the petitioner may elect to withdraw such petition, and have the application for naturalization considered under the administrative naturalization process. Such petition must be withdrawn after October 1, 1991, but not later than December 31, 1991.

(2) Except as provided in paragraph (b)(1) of this section, the petitioner shall not be permitted to withdraw his or her petition for naturalization, unless the Attorney General consents to the withdrawal.

(c) **Judicial proceedings.**

(1) All pending petitions not withdrawn in the manner and terms described in paragraph (b) of this section, shall be decided, on the merits, by the naturalization court, in conformity with the applicable provisions of the judicial naturalization authority of the prior statute. The reviewing court shall enter a final order.

(2) In cases where the petitioner fails to prosecute his or her petition, the court shall decide the petition upon its merits unless the Attorney General moves that the petition be dismissed for lack of prosecution.

HISTORY:

[56 FR 50480, Oct. 7, 1991, as confirmed at 60 FR 6650, Feb. 3, 1995]

§ 310.5 Judicial review.

(a) After 120 davs following examination. An applicant for naturalization may seek judicial review of a pending application for naturalization in those instances where the Service fails to make a determination under section 335 of the Act within 120 days after an examination is conducted under part 335 of this chapter. An applicant shall make a proper application for relief to the United States District Court having jurisdiction over the district in which the applicant resides. The court may either determine the issues brought before it on their merits, or remand the matter to the Service with appropriate instructions.

(b) After denial of an application. After an application for naturalization is denied following a hearing before a Service officer pursuant to section 336(a) of the Act, the applicant may seek judicial review of the decision pursuant to section 310 of the Act.

HISTORY:

[56 FR 50480, Oct. 7, 1991, as confirmed at 60 FR 6650, Feb. 3, 1995]

PART 312

EDUCATIONAL REQUIREMENTS FOR NATURALIZATION

§ 312.1 Literacy requirements.

(a) General. Except as otherwise provided in paragraph (b) of this section, no person shall be naturalized as a citizen of the United States upon his or her own application unless that person can demonstrate an understanding of the English language, including an ability to read, write, and speak words in ordinary usage in the English language.

(b) Exceptions. The following persons need not demonstrate an ability to read, write and speak words in ordinary usage in the English language:

(1) A person who, on the date of filing of his or her application for naturalization, is over 50 years of age and has been living in the United States for periods totalling at least 20 years subsequent to a lawful admission for permanent residence;

(2) A person who, on the date of filing his or her application for naturalization, is over 55 years of age and has been living in the United States for periods totalling at least 15 years subsequent to a lawful admission for permanent residence; or

(3) The requirements of paragraph (a) of this section shall not apply to any person who is unable, because of a medically determinable physical or mental impairment or combination of impairments which has lasted or is expected to last at least 12 months, to demonstrate an understanding of the English language as noted in paragraph (a) of this section. The loss of any cognitive abilities based on the direct effects of the illegal use of drugs will not be considered in determining whether a person is unable to demonstrate an understanding of the English language. For purposes of this paragraph, the term medically determinable means an impairment that results from anatomical, physiological, or psychological abnormalities which can be shown by medically acceptable clinical or laboratory diagnostic techniques to have resulted in functioning so impaired as to render an individual unable to demonstrate an understanding of the English language as required by this section, or that renders the individual unable to fulfill the requirements for English proficiency, even with reasonable modifications to the methods of determining English proficiency as outlined in paragraph (c) of this section.

(c) **Literacy examination.**

(1) Verbal skills. The ability of an applicant to speak English will be determined by a designated immigration officer from the applicant's answers to questions normally asked in the course of the examination.

(2) Reading and writing skills. Except as noted in 8 CFR 312.3, an applicant's ability to read and write English must be tested in a manner prescribed by USCIS. USCIS will provide a description of test study materials and testing procedures on the USCIS Internet Web site.

HISTORY:

[56 FR 50481, Oct. 7, 1991, as confirmed at 60 FR 6650, Feb. 3, 1995; 62 FR 12915, 12923, March 19, 1997, as corrected at 62 FR 15751, April 2, 1997; 64 FR 7990, 7993, Feb. 18, 1999; 76 FR 53764, 53797, Aug. 29, 2011]

AUTHORITY:

8 U.S.C. 1103, 1423, 1443, 1447, 1448.

§ 312.2 Knowledge of history and government of the United States.

(a) General. No person shall be naturalized as a citizen of the United States upon his or her own application unless that person can demonstrate a knowledge and understanding of the fundamentals of the history, and of the principles and form of government, of the United States. A person who is exempt from the literacy requirement under § 312.1(b) (1) and (2) must still satisfy this requirement.

(b) Exceptions.

(1) The requirements of paragraph(a) of this section shall not apply to any person who is unable to demonstrate a knowledge and understanding of the funda-

mentals of the history, and of the principles and form of government of the Untied States because of a medically determinable physical or mental impairment, that already has or is expected to last at least 12 months. The loss of any cognitive skills based on the direct effects of the illegal use of drugs will not be considered in determining whether an individual may be exempted. For the purposes of this paragraph the term medically determinable means an impairment that results from anatomical, physiological, or psychological abnormalities which can be shown by medically acceptable clinical or laboratory diagnosis techniques to have resulted in functioning so impaired as to render an individual to be unable to demonstrate the knowledge required by this section or that renders the individuals unable to participate in the testing procedures for naturalization, even with reasonable modifications.

(2) Medical certification. All persons applying for naturalization and seeking an exception from the requirements of § 312.1(a) and paragraph (a) of this section based on the disability exceptions must submit Form N-648, Medical Certification for Disability Exceptions, to be completed by a medical or osteopathic doctor licensed to practice medicine in the United States or a clinical psychologist licensed to practice psychology in the United States (including the United States territories of Guam, Puerto Rico, and the Virgin Islands). Form N-648 must be submitted as an attachment to the applicant's Form N-400, Application for Naturalization. These medical professionals shall be experienced in diagnosing those with physical or mental medically determinable impairments and shall be able to attest to the origin, nature, and extent of the medical condition as it relates to the disability exceptions noted under § 312.1(b)(3) and paragraph (b)(1) of this section. In addition, the medical professionals making the disability determination must sign a statement on the Form N-648 that they have answered all the questions in a complete and truthful manner, that they (and the applicant) agree to the release of all medical records relating to the applicant that may be requested by the Service and that they attest that any knowingly false or misleading statements may subject the medical professional to the penalties for perjury pursuant to title 18, United Stated Code, Section 1546 and to civil penalties under section 274C of the Act. The Service also reserves the right to refer the applicant to another authorized medical source for a supplemental disability determination. This option shall be invoked when the Service has credible doubts about the veracity of a medical certification that has been presented by the applicant. An affidavit or attestation by the applicant, his or her relatives, or guardian on his or her medical condition is not a a sufficient medical attestation for purposes of satisfying this requirement.

(c) History and government examination.

(1) Procedure. The examination of an applicant's knowledge of the history and form of government of the United States must be given orally in English by a designated immigration officer, except:

(i) If the applicant is exempt from the English literacy requirement under 8 CFR 312.1(b), the examination may be conducted in the applicant's native language with the assistance of an interpreter selected in accordance with 8 CFR 312.4 but only if the applicant's command of spoken English is insufficient to conduct a valid examination in English;

(ii) The examination may be conducted in the applicant's native language, with the assistance of an interpreter selected in accordance with 8 CFR 312.4, if the applicant is required to satisfy and has satisfied the English literacy requirement under 8 CFR 312.1(a), but the officer conducting the examination determines that an inaccurate or incomplete record of the examination would result if the examination on technical or complex issues were conducted in English, or

(iii) The applicant has met the requirements of 8 CFR 312.3.

(2) Scope and substance. The scope of the examination will be limited to subject matters prescribed by USCIS. In choosing the subject matters, in phrasing questions and in evaluating responses, due consideration must be given to the applicant's:

(i) Education,

(ii) Background,

(iii) Age,

(iv) Length of residence in the United States,

(v) Opportunities available and efforts made to acquire the requisite knowledge, and

(vi) Any other elements or factors relevant to an appraisal of the adequacy of the applicant's knowledge and understanding.

(Approved by the Office of Management and Budget under control number 1115-0208)

HISTORY:

[56 FR 50481, Oct. 7, 1991, as confirmed at 60 FR 6650, Feb. 3, 1995; 58 FR 49912, Sept. 24, 1993, as confirmed at 60 FR 6650, Feb. 3, 1995; 62 FR 12915, 12923, March 19, 1997, as corrected at 62 FR 15751, April 2, 1997; 64 FR 7990, 7993, Feb. 18, 1999; 76 FR 53764, 53797, Aug. 29, 2011]

AUTHORITY:

8 U.S.C. 1103, 1423, 1443, 1447, 1448.

§ 312.3 Testing of applicants who obtained permanent residence pursuant to section 245A of the Act.

An applicant who has obtained lawful permanent resident alien status pursuant to section 245A of the Act, and who, at that time, demonstrated English language proficiency in reading and writing, and knowledge of the government and history of the United States through either an examination administered by USCIS or the INS or a standardized section 312 test authorized by the USCIS or the INS for use with Legalization applicants as provided in section 245A(b)(1)(D)(iii) of the Act, will not be reexamined on those skills at the time of the naturalization interview. However, such applicant, unless otherwise exempt, must still demonstrate his or her ability to speak and understand English in accordance with 8 CFR 312.1(c)(1) and establish eligibility for naturalization through testimony in the English language.

HISTORY:

[56 FR 50481, Oct. 7, 1991, as confirmed at 60 FR 6650, Feb. 3, 1995; 58 FR 49912, Sept. 24, 1993, as confirmed and revised at 60 FR 6650, 6651, Feb. 3, 1995; 76 FR 53764, 53798, Aug. 29, 2011]

AUTHORITY:

8 U.S.C. 1103, 1423, 1443, 1447, 1448.

§ 312.4 Selection of interpreter.

An interpreter to be used under § 312.2 may be selected either by the applicant or by the Service. However, the Service reserves the right to disqualify an interpreter provided by the applicant in order to ensure the integrity of the examination. Where the Service disqualifies an interpreter, the Service must provide another interpreter for the applicant in a timely manner. If rescheduling of the interview is required, then a new date shall be set as soon as practicable so as not to delay unduly the adjudication of the application. The officer who disqualifies an interpreter shall make a written record of the reason(s) for disqualification as part of the record of the application.

HISTORY:

[56 FR 50481, Oct. 7, 1991, as confirmed and revised at 60 FR 6650, 6651, Feb. 3, 1995; 58 FR 49912, Sept. 24, 1993, as confirmed and revised at 60 FR 6650, 6651, Feb. 3, 1995]

AUTHORITY:

8 U.S.C. 1103, 1423, 1443, 1447, 1448.

§ 312.5 Failure to meet educational and literacy requirements.

(a) An applicant for naturalization who fails the English literacy or history and government test at the first examination will be afforded a second opportunity to pass the test(s) within 90 days after the first examination during the pendency of the application.

(b) If an applicant who receives notice of the second scheduled examination date fails to appear without good cause for that second examination without prior notification to the Service, the applicant will be deemed to have failed this second examination. Before an applicant may request a postponement of the second examination to a date that is more than 90 days after the initial examination, the applicant must agree in writing to waive the requirement under section 336 of the Act that the Service must render a determination on the application within 120 days from the initial interview, and instead to permit the Service to render a decision within 120 days from the second interview.

HISTORY:

[56 FR 50481, Oct. 7, 1991, as confirmed at 60 FR 6650, Feb. 3, 1995; 58 FR 49912, Sept. 24, 1993, as confirmed at 60 FR 6650, Feb. 3, 1995]

AUTHORITY:

8 U.S.C. 1103, 1423, 1443, 1447, 1448.

PART 313
MEMBERSHIP IN THE COMMUNIST PARTY OR ANY OTHER TOTALITARIAN ORGANIZATIONS

§ 313.1 Definitions.

For purposes of this part:

Advocate includes, but is not limited to, advising, recommending, furthering by overt act, or admitting a belief in a doctrine, and may include the giving, lending, or promising of support or of money or any thing of value to be used for advocating such doctrine.

Advocating Communism means advocating the establishment of a totalitarian communist dictatorship, including the economic, international, and governmental doctrines of world communism, in all countries of the world through the medium of an internationally coordinated communist revolutionary movement.

Affiliation with an organization includes, but is not limited to, the giving, lending, or promising of support or of money or any thing of value, to that organization to be used for any purpose.

Circulate includes circulating, distributing, or displaying a work.

Communist Party includes:

(1) The Communist Party of the United States;

(2) The Communist Political Association;

(3) The Communist Party of any state of the United States, of any foreign state, or of any political or geographical subdivision of any foreign state;

(4) Any section, subsidiary, branch, affiliate, or subdivision of any such association or party;

(5) The direct predecessors or successors of any such association or party, regardless of what name such group or organization may have used, may now bear, or may hereafter adopt; and

(6) Any communist-action or communist-front organization that is registered or required to be registered under section 786 of title 50 of the United States Code, provided that the applicant knew or had reason to believe, while he or she was a member, that such organization was a communist-front organization.

Organization includes, but is not limited to, an organization, corporation, company, partnership, association, trust, foundation, or fund, and any group of persons, whether incorporated or not, permanently or temporarily associated together for joint action on any subject or subjects.

Publication or publishing of a work includes writing or printing a work; permitting, authorizing, or consenting to the writing or printing of a work; and paying for the writing or printing of a work.

Subversive is any individual who advocates or teaches:

(1) Opposition to all organized government;

(2) The overthrow, by force or violence or other unconstitutional means, of the Government of the United States or of all forms of law;

(3) The duty, necessity, or propriety of the unlawful assaulting or killing, either individually or by position, of any officer or officers of the United States or of any other organized government, because of his, her, or their official character;

(4) The unlawful damage, injury, or destruction of property; or

(5) Sabotage.

Totalitarian dictatorship and totalitarianism refer to systems of government not representative in fact and characterized by:

(1) The existence of a single political party, organized on a dictatorial basis, with so close an identity between the policies of such party and the government policies of the country in which the party exists that the government and the party constitute an indistinguishable unit; and

(2) The forcible suppression of all opposition to such a party.

Totalitarian party includes:

(1) Any party in the United States which advocates totalitarianism;

(2) Any party in any State of the United States, in any foreign state, or in any political or geographical subdivision of any foreign state which advocates or practices totalitarianism;

(3) Any section, subsidiary, branch, affiliate, or subdivision of any such association or party; and

(4) The direct predecessors or successors of any such association or party, regardless of what name such group or organization may have used, may now bear, or may hereafter adopt.

HISTORY:

[56 FR 50482, Oct. 7, 1991, as confirmed at 60 FR 6650, Feb. 3, 1995; 58 FR 49912, Sept. 20, 1993, as confirmed at 60 FR 6650, Feb. 3, 1995]

AUTHORITY:

8 U.S.C. 1103, 1424, 1443

§ 313.2 Prohibitions.

Except as provided in § 313.3, no applicant for naturalization shall be naturalized as a citizen of the United States if, within ten years immediately preceding the filing of an application for naturalization or after such filing but before taking the oath of citizenship, such applicant:

(a) Is or has been a member of or affiliated with the Communist Party or any other totalitarian party; or

(b) Is or has advocated communism or the establishment in the United States of a totalitarian dictatorship; or

(c) Is or has been a member of or affiliated with an organization that advocates communism or the establishment in the United States of a totalitarian dictatorship, either through its own utterance or through any written or printed matter published by such organization; or

(d) Is or has been a subversive, or a member of, or affiliated with, a subversive organization; or

(e) Knowingly is publishing or has published any subversive written or printed matter, or written or printed matter advocating communism; or

(f) Knowingly circulates or has circulated, or knowingly possesses or has possessed for the purpose of circulating, subversive written or printed matter, or written or printed matter advocating communism; or

(g) Is or has been a member of, or affiliated with, any organization that publishes or circulates, or that possesses for the purpose of publishing or circulating, any subversive written or printed matter, or any written or printed matter advocating communism.

HISTORY:

[56 FR 50482, Oct. 7, 1991, as confirmed at 60 FR 6650, Feb. 3, 1995]

AUTHORITY:

8 U.S.C. 1103, 1424, 1443.

§ 313.3 Statutory exemptions.

(a) General. An applicant shall bear the burden of establishing that classification in one of the categories listed under § 313.2 is not a bar to naturalization.

(b) Exemptions. Despite membership in or affiliation with an organization covered by § 313.2, an applicant may be naturalized if the applicant establishes that such membership or affiliation is or was:

(1) Involuntary;

(2) Without awareness of the nature or the aims of the organization, and was discontinued if the applicant became aware of the nature or aims of the organization;

(3) Terminated prior to the attainment of age sixteen by the applicant, or more than ten years prior to the filing of the application for naturalization;

(4) By operation of law; or

(5) Necessary for purposes of obtaining employment, food rations, or other essentials of living.

(c) Awareness and participation —

(1) Exemption applicable. The exemption under paragraph (b)(2) of this section may be found to apply only to an applicant whose participation in the activities of an organization covered under § 313.2 was minimal in nature, and who establishes that he or she was unaware of the nature of the organization while a member of the organization.

(2) Exemptions inapplicable. The exemptions under paragraphs (b)(4) and (b)(5) of this section will not apply to any applicant who served as a functionary of an organization covered under § 313.2, or who was aware of and believed in the organization's doctrines.

(d) Essentials of living —

(1) Exemption applicable. The exemption under paragraph (b)(5) of this section may be found to apply only to an applicant who can demonstrate:

(i) That membership in the covered organization was necessary to obtain the essentials of living like food, shelter, clothing, employment, and an education, which were routinely available to the rest of the population — for purposes of this exemption, higher education will qualify as an essential of living only if the applicant can establish the existence of special circumstances which convert the need for higher education into a need as basic as the need for food or employment: and,

(ii) That he or she participated only to the minimal extent necessary to receive the essential of living.

(2) Exemption inapplicable. The exemption under paragraph (b)(5) of this section will not be applicable to an applicant who became a member of an organization covered under 313.2 to receive certain benefits:

(i) Without compulsion from the governing body of the relevant country; or

(ii) Which did not qualify as essentials of living.

HISTORY:

[56 FR 50482, Oct. 7, 1991, as confirmed at 60 FR 6650, Feb. 3, 1995]

AUTHORITY:

8 U.S.C. 1103, 1424, 1443.

§ 313.4 Procedure.

In all cases in which the applicant claims membership or affiliation in any of the organizations covered by § 313.2, the applicant shall attach to the application a detailed written statement describing such membership or affiliation, including the periods of membership or affiliation, whether the applicant held any office in the organization, and whether membership or affiliation was voluntary or involuntary. If the applicant alleges that membership or affiliation was involuntary, or that one of the other exemptions in § 313.3 applies, the applicant's statement shall set forth the basis of that allegation.

HISTORY:

[56 FR 50482, Oct. 7, 1991, as confirmed at 60 FR 6650, Feb. 3, 1995]

AUTHORITY:

8 U.S.C. 1103, 1424, 1443.

PART 315

PERSONS INELIGIBLE TO CITIZENSHIP: EXEMPTION FROM MILITARY SERVICE

§ 315.1 Definitions.

As used in this part:

Exemption from military service means either:

(1) A permanent exemption from induction into the Armed Forces or the National Security Training Corps of the United States for military training or military service; or

(2) The release or discharge from military training or military service in the Armed Forces or in the National Security Training Corps of the United States.

Induction means compulsory entrance into military service of the United States whether by conscription or, after being notified of a pending conscription, by enlistment.

Treaty national means an alien who is a national of a country with which the United States has a treaty relating to the reciprocal exemption of aliens from military training or military service.

HISTORY:

[56 FR 50483, Oct. 7, 1991, as confirmed at 60 FR 6650, Feb. 3, 1995]

AUTHORITY:

8 U.S.C. 1103, 1443.

§ 315.2 Ineligibility and exceptions.

(a) Ineligibility. Except as provided in paragraph (b) of this section, any alien who has requested, applied for, and obtained an exemption from military service on the ground that he or she is an alien shall be ineligible for approval of his or her application for naturalization as a citizen of the United States.

(b) Exceptions. The prohibition in paragraph (a) of this section does not apply to an alien who establishes by clear and convincing evidence that:

(1) At the time that he or she requested an exemption from military service, the applicant had no liability for such service even in the absence of an exemption;

(2) The applicant did not request or apply for the exemption from military service, but such exemption was automatically granted by the United States government;

(3) The exemption from military service was based upon a ground other than the applicant's alienage;

(4) In claiming an exemption from military service, the applicant did not knowingly and intentionally waive his or her eligibility for naturalization because he or she was misled by advice from a competent United States government authority, or from a competent authority of the government of his or her country of nationality, of the consequences of applying for an exemption from military service and was, therefore, unable to make an intelligent choice between exemption and citizenship;

(5) The applicant applied for and received an exemption from military service on the basis of alienage, but was subsequently inducted into the Armed Forces, or the National Security Training Corps, of the United States; however, an applicant who voluntarily enlists in and serves in the Armed Forces of the United States, after applying for and receiving an exemption from military service on the basis of alienage, does not satisfy this exception to paragraph (a) of this section;

(6) Prior to requesting the exemption from military service:

(i) The applicant was a treaty national who had served in the armed forces of the country of which he or she was a national; however, a treaty national who did not serve in the armed forces of the country of nationality prior to requesting the exemption from military service does not satisfy this exception to paragraph (a) of this section;

(ii) The applicant served a minimum of eighteen months in the armed forces of a nation that was a member of the North Atlantic Treaty Organization at the time of the applicant's service; or

(iii) The applicant served a minimum of twelve months in the armed forces of a nation that was a member of the North Atlantic Treaty Organization at the time of the applicant's service, provided that the applicant applied for registration with the Selective Service Administration after September 28, 1971; or

(7) The applicant is applying for naturalization pursuant to section 329 of the Act.

HISTORY:

[56 FR 50483, Oct. 7, 1991, as confirmed at 60 FR 6650, Feb. 3, 1995]

AUTHORITY:

8 U.S.C. 1103, 1443.

§ 315.3 Evidence.

(a) The records of the Selective Service System and the military department under which the alien served shall be conclusive evidence of whether the alien was relieved or discharged from liability for military service because he or she was an alien.

(b) The regulations of the Selective Service Administration and its predecessors will be controlling with respect to the requirement to register for, and liability for, service in the Armed Forces of the United States.

HISTORY:

[56 FR 50483, Oct. 7, 1991, as confirmed at 60 FR 6650, Feb. 3, 1995]

AUTHORITY:

8 U.S.C. 1103, 1443.

§ 315.4 Exemption treaties.

(a) The following countries currently have effective treaties providing reciprocal exemption of aliens from military service:

Argentina (Art. X, 10 Stat. 1005, 1009, effective 1853)

Austria (Art. VI, 47 Stat. 1876, 1880, effective 1928)

China (Art. XIV, 63 Stat. 1299, 1311, effective 1946)

Costa Rica (Art. IX, 10 Stat. 916, 921, effective 1851)

Estonia (Art. VI, 44 Stat. 2379, 2381, effective 1925)

Honduras (Art. VI, 45 Stat. 2618, 2622, effective 1927)

Ireland (Art. III, 1 US 785, 789, effective 1950)

Italy (Art. XIII, 63 Stat. 2255, 2272, effective 1948)

Latvia (Art. VI, 45 Stat. 2641, 2643, effective 1928)

Liberia (Art. VI, 54 Stat. 1739, 1742, effective 1938)

Norway (Art. VI, 47 Stat. 2135, 2139, effective 1928)

Paraguay (Art. XI, 12 Stat. 1091, 1096, effective 1859)

Spain (Art. V, 33 Stat. 2105, 2108, effective 1902)

Switzerland (Art. II, 11 Stat. 587, 589, effective 1850)

Yugoslavia (Serbia) (Art. IV, 22 Stat. 963, 964, effective 1881)

(b) The following countries previously had treaties providing for reciprocal exemption of aliens from military service:

El Salvador (Art. VI, 46 Stat. 2817, 2821, effective 1926 to February 8, 1958)

Germany (Art. VI, 44 Stat. 2132, 2136, effective 1923 to June 2, 1954)

Hungary (Art. VI, 44 Stat, 2441, 2445, effective 1925 to July 5, 1952)

Thailand (Siam) (Art. 1, 53 Stat. 1731, 1732, effective 1937 to June 8, 1968)

HISTORY:

[56 FR 50483, Oct. 7, 1991, as confirmed at 60 FR 6650, Feb. 3, 1995]

AUTHORITY:

8 U.S.C. 1103, 1443.

PART 316

GENERAL REQUIREMENTS FOR NATURALIZATION

AUTHORITY NOTE APPLICABLE TO ENTIRE PART:

AUTHORITY:

8 U.S.C. 1103, 1181, 1182, 1443, 1447; 8 CFR part 2.

§ 316.1 Definitions.

As used in this part, the term:

Application means any form, as defined in 8 CFR part 1, on which an applicant requests a benefit relating to naturalization.

Residence in the Service district where the application is filed means residence in the geographical area over which a particular local field office of USCIS ordinarily has jurisdiction for purposes of naturalization, regardless of where or how USCIS may require such benefit request to be submitted, or whether jurisdiction for the purpose of adjudication is relocated or internally reassigned to another USCIS office.

Service district means the geographical area over which a particular local field office of USCIS ordinarily has jurisdiction for purposes of naturalization.

HISTORY:

[56 FR 50484, Oct. 7, 1991, as confirmed at 60 FR 6650, Feb. 3, 1995; 76 FR 53764, 53798, Aug. 29, 2011]

§ 316.2 Eligibility.

(a) General. Except as otherwise provided in this chapter, to be eligible for naturalization, an alien must establish that he or she:

(1) Is at least 18 years of age;

(2) Has been lawfully admitted as a permanent resident of the United States;

(3) Has resided continuously within the United States, as defined under § 316.5, for a period of at least five years after having been lawfully admitted for permanent residence;

(4) Has been physically present in the United States for at least 30 months of the five years preceding the date of filing the application;

(5) Immediately preceding the filing of an application, or immediately preceding the examination on the application if the application was filed early pursuant to section 334(a) of the Act and the three month period falls within the required period of residence under section 316(a) or 319(a) of the Act, has resided, as defined under § 316.5, for at least three months in a State or Service district having jurisdiction over the applicant's actual place of residence;

(6) Has resided continuously within the United States from the date of application for naturalization up to the time of admission to citizenship;

(7) For all relevant time periods under this paragraph, has been and continues to be a person of good moral character, attached to the principles of the Constitution of the United States, and favorably disposed toward the good order and happiness of the United States; and

(8) Is not a person described in Section 314 of the Act relating to deserters of the United States Armed Forces or those persons who departed from the United States to evade military service in the United States Armed Forces.

(b) Burden of proof. The applicant shall bear the burden of establishing by a preponderance of the evidence that he or she meets all of the requirements for naturalization, including that the applicant was lawfully admitted as a permanent resident to the United States, in accordance with the immigration laws in effect at the time of the applicant's initial entry or any subsequent reentry.

HISTORY:

[56 FR 50484, Oct. 7, 1991, as confirmed and revised at 60 FR 6650, 6651, Feb. 3, 1995; 58 FR 49912, Sept. 24, 1993, as confirmed at 60 FR 6650, Feb. 3, 1995; 76 FR 53764, 53798, Aug. 29, 2011]

§ 316.3 [This section was removed and reserved. See 74 FR 26933, 26940, June 5, 2009.]

[NO TEXT IN ORIGINAL]

HISTORY:

[56 FR 50484, Oct. 7, 1991, as confirmed at 60 FR 6650, Feb. 3, 1995]

AUTHORITY:

(8 U.S.C. 1103, 1181, 1182, 1443, 1447; 8 CFR part 2.)

§ 316.4 Application; documents.

(a) The applicant will apply for naturalization in accordance with instructions provided on the form prescribed by USCIS for that purpose.

(b) At the time of the examination on the application for naturalization, the applicant may be required to establish the status of lawful permanent resident by submitting the original evidence, issued by the Service, of lawful permanent residence in the United States. The applicant may be also required to submit any passports, or any other documents that have been used to enter the United States at any time after the original admission for permanent residence.

HISTORY:

[56 FR 50484, Oct. 7, 1991, as confirmed at 60 FR 6650, Feb. 3, 1995; 58 FR 48780, Sept. 20, 1993; 59 FR 47063, Sept. 14, 1994; 60 FR 14353, Mar. 17, 1995; 63 FR 12979, 12987, March 17, 1998; 63 FR 70313, 70316, Dec, 21, 1998; 76 FR 53764, 53798, Aug. 29, 2011]

§ 316.5 Residence in the United States.

(a) General. Unless otherwise specified, for purposes of this chapter, including § 316.2 (a)(3), (a)(5), and (a)(6), an alien's residence is the same as that alien's domicile, or principal actual dwelling place, without regard to the alien's intent, and the duration of an alien's residence in a particular location is measured from the moment the alien first establishes residence in that location.

(b) Residences in specific cases —

(1) Military personnel. For applicants who are serving in the Armed Forces of the United States but who do not qualify for naturalization under part 328 of this chapter, the applicant's residence shall be:

(i) The State or Service District where the applicant is physically present for at least three months, immediately preceding the filing of an application for naturalization, or immediately preceding the examination on the application if the application was filed early pursuant to section 334(a) of the Act and the three month period falls within the required period of residence under section 316(a) or 319(a) of the Act;

(ii) The location of the residence of the applicant's spouse and/or minor child(ren); or

(iii) The applicant's home of record as declared to the Armed Forces at the time of enlistment and as currently reflected in the applicant's military personnel file.

(2) Students. An applicant who is attending an educational institution in a State or Service District other than the applicant's home residence may apply for naturalization:

(i) Where that institution is located; or

(ii) In the State of the applicant's home residence if the applicant can establish that he or she is financially dependent upon his or her parents at the time that the application is filed and during the naturalization process.

(3) Commuter aliens. An applicant who is a commuter alien, as described in § 211.5 of this chapter, must establish a principal dwelling place in the United States with the intention of permanently residing there, and must thereafter acquire the requisite period of residence before eligibility for naturalization may be established. Accordingly, a commuter resident alien may not apply for naturalization until he or she has actually taken up permanent residence in the United States and until such residence has continued for the required statutory period. Such an applicant bears the burden of providing evidence to that effect.

(4) Residence in multiple states. If an applicant claims residence in more than one State, the residence for purposes of this part shall be determined by reference to the location from which the annual federal income tax returns have been and are being filed.

(5) Residence during absences of less than one year.

(i) An applicant's residence during any absence of less than one year shall continue to be the State or Service district where the applicant last resided at the time of the applicant's departure abroad.

(ii) Return to the United States. If, upon returning to the United States, an applicant returns to the State or Service district where the applicant last resided, the applicant will have complied with the continuous residence requirement specified in § 316.2(a)(5) when at least three months have elapsed, including any part of the applicant's absence, from the date on which the applicant first established that residence. If the applicant establishes residence in a State or Service district other than the one in which he or she last resided, the applicant must complete three months at that new residence to be eligible for naturalization.

(6) Spouse of military personnel. Pursuant to section 319(e) of the Act, any period of time the spouse of a United States citizen resides abroad will be treated as residence in any State or district of the United States for purposes of naturalization under section 316(a) or 319(a) of the Act if, during the period of time abroad, the applicant establishes that he or she was:

(i) The spouse of a member of the Armed Forces;

(ii) Authorized to accompany and reside abroad with that member of the Armed Forces pursuant to the member's official orders; and

(iii) Accompanying and residing abroad with that member of the Armed Forces in marital union in accordance with 8 CFR 319.1(b).

(c) Disruption of continuity of residence —

(1) Absence from the United States

(i) For continuous periods of between six (6) months and one (1) year. Absences from the United States for continuous periods of between six (6) months and one (1) year during the periods for which continuous residence is required under § 316.2 (a)(3) and (a)(6) shall disrupt the continuity of such residence for purposes of this part unless the applicant can establish otherwise to the satisfaction of the Service. This finding remains valid even if the applicant did not apply for or otherwise request a nonresident classification for tax purposes, did not document an abandonment of lawful permanent resident status, and is still considered a lawful permanent resident under immigration laws. The types of documentation which may establish that the applicant did not disrupt the continuity of his or her residence in the United States during an extended absence include, but are not limited to, evidence that during the absence:

(A) The applicant did not terminate his or her employment in the United States;

(B) The applicant's immediate family remained in the United States;

(C) The applicant retained full access to his or her United States abode; or

(D) The applicant did not obtain employment while abroad.

(ii) For period in excess of one (1) year. Unless an applicant applies for benefits in accordance with § 316.5(d), absences from the United States for a continuous period of one (1) year or more during the period for which continuous residence is required under § 316.2 (a)(3) and (a)(5) shall disrupt the continuity of the applicant's residence. An applicant described in this paragraph who must satisfy a five-year statutory residence period may file an application for naturalization four years and one day following the date of the applicant's return to the United States to resume permanent residence. An applicant described in this paragraph who must satisfy a three-year statutory residence period may file an application for naturalization two years and one day following the date of the applicant's return to the United States to resume permanent residence.

(2) Claim of nonresident alien status for income tax purposes after lawful admission as a permanent resident. An applicant who is a lawfully admitted permanent resident of the United States, but who voluntarily claims nonresident alien status to qualify for special exemptions from income tax liability, or fails to file either federal or state income tax returns because he or she considers himself or herself to be a nonresident alien, raises a rebuttable presumption that the applicant has relinquished the privileges of permanent resident status in the United States.

(3) Removal and return. Any departure from the United States while under an order of removal (including previously issued orders of exclusion or deportation) terminates the applicant's status as a lawful permanent resident and, therefore, disrupts the continuity of residence for purposes of this part.

(4) Readmission after a deferred inspection or exclusion proceeding. An applicant who has been readmitted as a lawful permanent resident after a deferred inspection or by the immigration judge during exclusion proceedings shall satisfy the residence and physical presence requirements under § 316.2 (a)(3), (a)(4), (a)(5), and (a)(6) in the same manner as any other applicant for naturalization.

(d) Application for benefits with respect to absences; appeal —

(1) Preservation of residence under section 316(b) of the Act

(i) An application for the residence benefits under section 316(b) of the Act to cover an absence from the United States for a continuous period of one year or more shall be submitted to the Service on Form N-470 with the required fee, in accordance with the form's instructions. The application may be filed either before or after the applicant's employment commences, but must be filed before the applicant has been absent from the United States for a continuous period of one year.

(ii) An approval of Form N-470 under section 316(b) of the Act shall cover the spouse and dependent unmarried sons and daughters of the applicant who are residing abroad as members of the applicant's household during the period covered by the application. The notice of approval, Form N-472, shall identify the family members so covered.

(iii) An applicant whose Form N-470 application under section 316(b) of the Act has been approved, but who voluntarily claims nonresident alien status to qualify for special exemptions from income tax liability, raises a rebuttable presumption that the applicant has relinquished a claim of having retained lawful permanent resident status while abroad. The applicant's family members who were covered under section 316(b) of the Act and who were listed on the applicant's Form N-472 will also be subject to the rebuttable presumption that they have relinquished their claims to lawful permanent resident status.

(2) Preservation of residence under section 317 of the Act. An application for the residence and physical presence benefits of section 317 of the Act to cover any absences from the United States, whether before or after December 24, 1952, shall be submitted to the Service on Form N-470 with the required fee, in accordance with the form's instructions. The application may be filed either before or after the applicant's absence from the United States or the performance of the functions or services described in section 317 of the Act.

(3) Approval, denial, and appeal. The applicant under paragraphs (d)(1) or (d)(2) of this section shall be notified of the Service's disposition of the application on Form N-472. If the application is denied, the Service shall specify the reasons for the denial, and shall inform the applicant of the right to appeal in accordance with the provisions of part 103 of this chapter.

HISTORY:

[56 FR 50484, Oct. 7, 1991, as amended at 56 FR 50487, Oct. 7, 1991, as confirmed and revised at 60 FR 6650, 6651, Feb. 3, 1995; 58 FR 49912, Sept. 24, 1993, as confirmed at 60 FR 6650, Feb. 3, 1995; 62 FR 10312, 10394, March 6, 1997; 76 FR 53764, 53798, Aug. 29, 2011]

§ 316.6 Physical presence for certain spouses of military personnel.

Pursuant to section 319(e) of the Act, any period of time the spouse of a United States citizen resides abroad will be treated as physical presence in any State or district of the United States for purposes of naturalization under section 316(a) or 319(a) of the Act if, during the period of time abroad, the applicant establishes that he or she was:

(a) The spouse of a member of the Armed Forces;

(b) Authorized to accompany and reside abroad with that member of the Armed Forces pursuant to the member's official orders; and

(c) Accompanying and residing abroad with that member of the Armed Forces in marital union in accordance with 8 CFR 319.1(b).

HISTORY:

[76 FR 53764, 53798, Aug. 29, 2011]

§§ 316.7 — 316.9 [Reserved]

[NO TEXT IN ORIGINAL]

HISTORY:

56 FR 50484, Oct. 7, 1991.

§ 316.10 Good moral character.

(a) Requirement of good moral character during the statutory period.

(1) An applicant for naturalization bears the burden of demonstrating that, during the statutorily prescribed period, he or she has been and continues to be a person of good moral character. This includes the period between the examination and the administration of the oath of allegiance.

(2) In accordance with section 101(f) of the Act, the Service shall evaluate claims of good moral character on a case-by-case basis taking into account the elements enumerated in this section and the standards of the average citizen in the community of residence. The Service is not limited to reviewing the applicant's conduct during the five years immediately preceding the filing of the application, but may take into consideration, as a basis for its determination, the applicant's conduct and acts at any time prior to that period, if the conduct of the applicant during the statutory period does not reflect that there has been reform of character from an earlier period or if the earlier conduct and acts appear relevant to a determination of the applicant's present moral character.

(b) Finding of a lack of good moral character.

(1) An applicant shall be found to lack good moral character, if the applicant has been:

(i) Convicted of murder at any time; or

(ii) Convicted of an aggravated felony as defined in section 101(a)(43) of the Act on or after November 29, 1990.

(2) An applicant shall be found to lack good moral character if during the statutory period the applicant:

(i) Committed one or more crimes involving moral turpitude, other than a purely political offense, for which the applicant was convicted, except as specified in section 212(a)(2)(A)(ii)(II) of the Act;

(ii) Committed two or more offenses for which the applicant was convicted and the aggregate sentence actually imposed was five years or more, provided that, if the offense was committed outside the United States, it was not a purely political offense;

(iii) Violated any law of the United States, any State, or any foreign country relating to a controlled substance, provided that the violation was not a single offense for simple possession of 30 grams or less of marijuana;

(iv) Admits committing any criminal act covered by paragraphs (b)(2) (i), (ii), or (iii) of this section for which there was never a formal charge, indictment, arrest, or conviction, whether committed in the United States or any other country;

(v) Is or was confined to a penal institution for an aggregate of 180 days pursuant to a conviction or convictions (provided that such confinement was not outside the United States due to a conviction outside the United States for a purely political offense);

(vi) Has given false testimony to obtain any benefit from the Act, if the testimony was made under oath or affirmation and with an intent to obtain an immigration benefit; this prohibition applies regardless of whether the information provided in the false testimony was material, in the sense that if given truthfully it would have rendered ineligible for benefits either the applicant or the person on whose behalf the applicant sought the benefit;

(vii) Is or was involved in prostitution or commercialized vice as described in section 212(a)(2)(D) of the Act;

(viii) Is or was involved in the smuggling of a person or persons into the United States as described in section 212(a)(6)(E) of the Act;

(ix) Has practiced or is practicing polygamy;

(x) Committed two or more gambling offenses for which the applicant was convicted;

(xi) Earns his or her income principally from illegal gambling activities; or

(xii) Is or was a habitual drunkard.

(3) Unless the applicant establishes extenuating circumstances, the applicant shall be found to lack good moral character if, during the statutory period, the applicant:

(i) Willfully failed or refused to support dependents;

(ii) Had an extramarital affair which tended to destroy an existing marriage; or

(iii) Committed unlawful acts that adversely reflect upon the applicant's moral character, or was convicted or imprisoned for such acts, although the acts do not fall within the purview of § 316.10(b) (1) or (2).

(c) Proof of good moral character in certain cases —

(1) Effect of probation or parole. An applicant who has been on probation, parole, or suspended sentence during all or part of the statutory period is not thereby precluded from establishing good moral character, but such probation, parole, or suspended sentence may be considered by the Service in determining good moral character. An application will not be approved until after the probation, parole, or suspended sentence has been completed.

(2) Full and unconditional executive pardon —

(i) Before the statutory period. An applicant who has received a full and unconditional executive pardon prior to the beginning of the statutory period is not precluded by § 316.10(b)(1) from establishing good moral character provided the applicant demonstrates that reformation and rehabilitation occurred prior to the beginning of the statutory period.

(ii) During the statutory period. An applicant who receives a full and unconditional executive pardon during the statutory period is not precluded by § 316.10(b)(2) (i) and (ii) from establishing good moral character, provided the applicant can demonstrate that extenuating and/or exonerating circumstances exist that would establish his or her good moral character.

(3) Record expungement —

(i) Drug offenses. Where an applicant has had his or her record expunged relating to one of the narcotics offenses under section 212(a)(2)(A)(i)(II) and section 241(a)(2)(B) of the Act, that applicant shall be considered as having been "convicted" within the meaning of § 316.10(b)(2)(ii), or, if confined, as having been confined as a result of "conviction" for purposes of § 316.10(b)(2)(iv).

(ii) Moral turpitude. An applicant who has committed or admits the commission of two or more crimes involving moral turpitude during the statutory period is precluded from establishing good moral character, even though the conviction record of one such offense has been expunged.

HISTORY:

[56 FR 50484, Oct. 7, 1991, as confirmed at 60 FR 6650, Feb. 3, 1995; 58 FR 49913, Sept. 24, 1993, as confirmed at 60 FR 6650, Feb. 3, 1995]

§ 316.11 Attachment to the Constitution; favorable disposition towards the good order and happiness.

(a) General. An applicant for naturalization must establish that during the statutorily prescribed period, he or she has been and continues to be attached to the principles of the Constitution of the United States and favorably disposed toward the good order and happiness of the United States. Attachment implies a depth of conviction which would lead to active support of the Constitution. Attachment and favorable disposition relate to mental attitude, and contemplate the exclusion from citizenship of applicants who are hostile to the basic form of government of the United States, or who disbelieve in the principles of the Constitution.

(b) Advocacy of peaceful change. At a minimum, the applicant shall satisfy the general standard of paragraph (a) of this section by demonstrating an acceptance of the democratic, representational process established by the Constitution, a willingness to obey the laws which may result from that process, and an understanding of the means for change which are prescribed by the Constitution. The right to work for political change shall be consistent with the standards in paragraph (a) of this section only if the changes advocated would not abrogate the current Government and establish an entirely different form of government.

(c) Membership in the Communist Party or any other totalitarian organization. An applicant who is or has been a member of or affiliated with the Communist Party or any other totalitarian organization shall be ineligible for naturalization, unless the applicant's membership meets the exceptions in sections 313 and 335 of the Act and § 313.4 of this chapter.

HISTORY:

[56 FR 50484, Oct. 7, 1991, as confirmed at 60 FR 6650, Feb. 3, 1995]

§ 316.12 Applicant's legal incompetency during statutory period.

(a) General. An applicant who is legally competent at the time of the examination on the naturalization application and of the administration of the oath of allegiance may be admitted to citizenship, provided that the applicant fully understands the purpose and responsibilities of the naturalization procedures.

(b) Legal incompetence. Naturalization is not precluded if, during part of the statutory period, the applicant was legally incompetent or confined to a mental institution.

(1) There is a presumption that the applicant's good moral character, attachment, and favorable disposition

which existed prior to the period of legal incompetency continued through that period. The Service may, however, consider an applicant's actions during a period of legal incompetence, as evidence tending to rebut this presumption.

(2) If the applicant has been declared legally incompetent, the applicant has the burden of establishing that legal competency has been restored. The applicant shall submit legal and medical evidence to determine and establish the claim of legal competency.

(3) The applicant shall bear the burden of establishing that any crimes committed, regardless of whether the applicant was convicted, occurred while the applicant was declared legally incompetent.

HISTORY:

[56 FR 50484, Oct. 7, 1991, as confirmed at 60 FR 6650, Feb. 3, 1995]

§ 316.13 [Reserved]

[NO TEXT IN ORIGINAL]

HISTORY:

56 FR 50484, Oct. 7, 1991.

§ 316.14 Adjudication — examination, grant, denial.

(a) Examination. The examination on an application for naturalization shall be conducted in accordance with Section 335 of the Act.

(b) **Determination —**

(1) Grant or denial. Subject to supervisory review, the employee of the Service who conducts the examination under paragraph (a) of this section shall determine whether to grant or deny the application, and shall provide reasons for the determination, as required under section 335(d) of the Act.

(2) Appeal. An applicant whose application for naturalization has been denied may request a hearing, which shall be carried out in accordance with section 336 of the Act.

HISTORY:

[56 FR 50484, Oct. 7, 1991, as confirmed at 60 FR 6650, Feb. 3, 1995]

§§ 316.15 — 316.19 [Reserved]

[NO TEXT IN ORIGINAL]

HISTORY:

56 FR 50484, Oct. 7, 1991.

§ 316.20 American institutions of research, public international organizations, and designations under the International Immunities Act.

(a) American institutions of research. The following-listed organizations have been determined to be American Institutions of research recognized by the Attorney General:

African Medical and Research Foundation (AMREF-USA).

Albert Einstein College of Medicine of Yeshiva University (only in relationship to its research programs).

American Friends of the Middle East, Inc.

American Institutes of Research in the Behavioral Sciences (only in relationship to research projects abroad).

American Universities Field Staff, Inc.

American University, The, Cairo, Egypt.

American University of Beirut (Near East College Associations).

Arctic Institute of North America, Inc.

Armour Research Foundation of Illinois Institute of Technology.

Asia Foundation, The (formerly Committee for a Free Asia, Inc.).

Association of Universities for Research in Astronomy (AURA, Inc.), Tucson, AZ.

Atomic Bomb Casualty Commission.

Beirut University College.

Bermuda Biological Station for Research, Inc.

Bernice P. Biship Museum of Polynesian Antiquities, Ethnology and Natural History at Honolulu, HI.

Brookhaven National Laboratory, Associated Universities, Inc.

Brown University (Department of Engineering), Providence, RI.

Buffalo Eye Bank and Research Society, Inc.

Burma Office of Robert N. Nathan Associates, Inc.

California State University at Long Beach, Department of Geological Sciences.

Carleton College (Department of Sociology and Anthropology), Northfield, MN.

Center of Alcohol Studies, Laboratory of Applied Biodynamics of Yale University.

Central Registry of Jewish Losses in Egypt.

College of Engineering, University of Wisconsin.

College of Medicine, State University of New York.

Colorado State University (Research Foundation), Fort Collins, CO.

Colorado University (International Economic Studies Center), Boulder, CO.

Columbia University (Parker School of Foreign and Comparative Law) and (Faculty of Pure Science), New York, NY.

Cornell University (International Agricultural Development, University of the Philippines-Cornell University Graduate Education Program).

Dartmouth Medical School.

Department of French, Department of Scandinavian Languages, and Department of Near Eastern Languages of the University of California, Berkeley, CA.

Duke University.

Environmental Research Laboratory of the University of Arizona.

Fletcher School of Law and Diplomacy, Medford, MA.

Ford Foundation, 477 Madison Avenue, New York, NY.

Free Europe, Inc. (formerly Free Europe Committee, Inc.; National Committee for a Free Europe (including Radio Free Europe)).

Georgetown University.

George Williams Hooper Foundation, San Francisco Medical Center, University of California, San Francisco, CA.

Gorgas Memorial Institute of Tropical and Preventive Medicine, Inc., and its operating unit, the Gorgas Memorial Laboratory.

Graduate Faculty of Political and Social Science Division of the New School for Social Research, New York, NY.

Harvard University (research and educational programs only)

Harvard-Yenching Institute.

Humboldt State University, School of Natural Resources, Wildlife Management Department.

Indiana University at Bloomington, Indianapolis, South Bend, Northwest, Kokomo, Southeast, East, and Fort Wayne

Institute for Development Anthropology, Inc.

Institute of International Education, Inc.

Institute of International Studies, University of California, Berkeley, CA.

International Center for Social Research, New York, NY.

International Development Foundation, Inc.

International Development Services, Inc.

International Research Associates, Inc.

Inter University Program for Chinese Language Studies (formerly Stanford Center for Chinese Studies) in Taipei, Taiwan.

Iowa State University.

Iran Foundation, Inc., The.

Kossuth Foundation, Inc., The, New York, NY.

Louisiana State University.

Massachusetts Institute of Technology.

Michigan State University, East Lansing, MI.

Missouri Botanical Garden (research and educational programs only)

Natural Science Foundation, Philadelphia, PA.

New York Zoological Society.

Paderewski Foundation, Inc.

Peabody Museum of Natural History of Yale University.

People to People Health Foundation, Inc., The (only in relationship to the scientific research activities that will be carried on abroad by the medical staff of the SS "Hope").

Pierce College (in relationship to research by an instructor, Department of Psychology), Athens, Greece.

Population Council, The, New York, NY.

Radio Liberty Committee, Inc. (formerly American Committee for Liberation, Inc.; American Committee for Liberation of the Peoples of Russia, Inc.; American Committee for Liberation from Bolshevism, Inc.).

Rockefeller Foundation.

Rutgers University, the State University of New Jersey

School of International Relations of the University of Southern California.

SIRIMAR (Societa Internazionale Recerche Marine) Division, Office of the Vice President for Research, Pennsylvania State University.

Social Science Research Council.

Solar Energy Research Institute (SERI).

Stanford Electronic Laboratories, Department of Electrical Engineering, School of Engineering, Stanford University, Stanford, CA.

Stanford Research Institute, Menlo Park, CA.

Stanford University (the George Vanderbilt Foundation), Stanford, CA.

Syracuse University.

Tulane University Graduate School.

Tulane University Medical School.

University of Alabama.

University of Alabama Medical Center.

University of Chicago (as a participant in the International Cooperation Administration Program No. W-74 only).

University of Colorado (Department of History), Boulder, CO.

University of Connecticut, College of Liberal Arts and Science (Department of Germanic and Slavic Languages).

University of Hawaii, Honolulu, HI.

University of Ilinois at Urbana-Champaign, Austria-Illinois Exchange Program.

University of Kansas, Office of International Programs.

University of La Verne (La Verne College of Athens)

University of Michigan (School of Natural Resources), Ann Arbor, MI.

University of Minnesota, Department of Plant Pathology (in relationship to research project abroad).

University of Nebraska Mission in Columbia, South America.

University of North Carolina at Chapel Hill.

University of Notre Dame, Notre Dame, IN.

University of Puerto Rico.

University of Washington (Department of Marketing, Transportation, and International Business) and (The School of Public Health and Community Medicine), Seattle, WA.

Wayne State University, Detroit, MI.

Wenner-Gren Foundation for Anthropological Research, Inc.

Williams College, Economic Department, Williamstown, MA.

(b) Public international organizations of which the United States is a member by treaty or statute. The following-listed organizations have been determined to be public international organizations of which the United States is a member by treaty or statute:

The North Atlantic Treaty Organization.

United Nations and all agencies and organizations which are a part thereof.

(c) International Organizations Immunities Act designations. The following public international organizations are entitled to enjoy the privileges, exemptions, and immunities provided for in the International Organizations Immunities Act, and are considered as public international organizations of which the United States is a member by treaty or statute within the meaning of section 316(b) of the Act and as public international organizations in which the United States participates by treaty or statute within the meaning of section 319(b) of the Act:

African Development Bank (E.O. 12403, Feb. 8, 1983).

African Development Fund (E.O. 11977, Mar. 14, 1977).

Asian Development Bank (E.O. 11334, Mar. 7, 1967).

Caribbean Organization (E.O. 10983, Dec. 30, 1961).

Criminal Police Organization (E.O. 12425, June 16, 1983).

Customs Cooperation Council (E.O. 11596, June 5, 1971).

European Space Research Organization (ESRO) (E.O. 11760, Jan. 17, 1974).

Food and Agriculture Organization, The (E.O. 9698, Feb 19, 1946).

Great Lakes Fishery Commission (E.O. 11059, Oct. 23, 1962).

Inter-American Defense Board (E.O. 10228, Mar. 26, 1951).

Inter-American Development Bank (E.O. 10873, Apr. 8, 1960).

Inter-American Institute for Cooperation on Agriculture (E.O. 9751, July 11, 1946).

Inter-American Statistical Institute (E.O. 9751, July 11, 1946).

Inter-American Tropical Tuna Commission (E.O. 11059, Oct. 23, 1962).

Intergovernmental Committee for European Migration (formerly the Provisional Intergovernmental Committee for the Movement of Migrants from Europe) (E.O. 10335, Mar. 28, 1952).

Intergovernmental Maritime Consultative Organization (E.O. 10795, Dec. 13, 1958).

International Atomic Energy Agency (E.O. 10727, Aug. 31, 1957).

International Bank for Reconstruction and Development (E.O. 9751, July 11, 1946).

International Centre for Settlement of Investment Disputes (E.O. 11966, Jan. 19, 1977).

International Civil Aviation Organization (E.O. 9863, May 31, 1947).

International Coffee Organization (E.O. 11225, May 22, 1965).

International Cotton Advisory Committee (E.O. 9911, Dec. 19, 1947).

International Development Association (E.O. 11966, Jan. 19, 1977).

International Fertilizer Development Center (E.O. 11977, Mar. 14, 1977).

International Finance Corporation (E.O. 10680, Oct. 2, 1956).

International Food Policy Research Institute (E.O. 12359, Apr. 22, 1982).

International Hydrographic Bureau (E.O. 10769, May 29, 1958).

International Institute for Cotton (E.O. 11283, May 27, 1966).

International Joint Commission—United States and Canada (E.O. 9972, June 25, 1948).

International Labor Organization, The (functions through staff known as The International Labor Office) (E.O. 9698, Feb. 19, 1946).

International Maritime Satellite Organization (E.O. 12238, Sept. 12, 1980).

International Monetary Fund (E.O. 9751, July 11, 1946).

International Pacific Halibut Commission (E.O. 11059, Oct. 23, 1962).

International Secretariat for Volunteer Service (E.O. 11363, July 20, 1967).

International Telecommunication Union (E.O. 9863, May 31, 1947).

International Telecommunications Satellite Organization (INTELSAT) (E.O. 11718, May 14, 1973).

International Wheat Advisory Committee (E.O. 9823, Jan. 24, 1947).

Multinational Force and Observers (E.O. 12359, Apr. 22, 1982).

Organization for European Economic Cooperation (E.O. 10133, June 27, 1950) (Now known as Organization for Economic Cooperation and Development; 28 FR 2959, Mar. 26, 1963).

Organization of African Unity (OAU) (E.O. 11767, Feb. 19, 1974).

Organization of American States (includes Pan American Union) (E.O. 10533, June 3, 1954).

Pan American Health Organization (includes Pan American Sanitary Bureau) (E.O. 10864, Feb. 18, 1960).

Preparatory Commission of the International Atomic Energy Agency (E.O. 10727, Aug. 31, 1957).

Preparatory Commission for the International Refugee Organization and its successor, the International Refugee Organization (E.O. 9887, Aug. 22, 1947).

South Pacific Commission (E.O. 10086, Nov. 25, 1949).

United International Bureau for the Protection of Intellectual Property (BIRPI) (E.O. 11484, Sept. 29, 1969).

United Nations, The (E.O. 9698, Feb. 19, 1946).

United Nations Educational, Scientific, and Cultural Organizations (E.O. 9863, May 31, 1947).

Universal Postal Union (E.O. 10727, Aug. 31, 1957).

World Health Organization (E.O. 10025, Dec. 30, 1948).

World Intellectual Property Organization (E.O. 11866, June 18, 1975).

World Meteorological Organization (E.O. 10676, Sept. 1, 1956).

HISTORY:

[32 FR 9634, July 4, 1967; Redesignated and amended at 56 FR 50487, Oct. 7, 1991, as confirmed at 60 FR 6650, Feb. 3, 1995; 62 FR 36447, 36448, July 8, 1997; 62 FR 49131, 49132, Sept. 19, 1997; 68 FR 61333, 61334, Oct. 28, 2003]

PART 318

PENDING REMOVAL PROCEEDINGS

AUTHORITY NOTE APPLICABLE TO ENTIRE PART:

AUTHORITY:

8 U.S.C. 1103, 1252, 1429, 1443; 8 CFR part 2.

§ 318.1 Warrant of arrest.

For the purposes of section 318 of the Act, a notice to appear issued under 8 CFR part 239 (including a charging document issued to commence proceedings under sections 236 or 242 of the Act prior to April 1, 1997) shall be regarded as a warrant of arrest.

HISTORY:

[22 FR 9813, Dec. 6, 1957; 62 FR 10312, 10394, March 6, 1997]

PART 319

SPECIAL CLASSES OF PERSONS WHO MAY BE NATURALIZED: SPOUSES OF UNITED STATES CITIZENS

§ 319.1 Persons living in marital union with United States citizen spouse.

(a) Eligibility. To be eligible for naturalization under section 319(a) of the Act, the spouse of a United States citizen must establish that he or she:

(1) Has been lawfully admitted for permanent residence to the United States;

(2) Has resided continuously within the United States, as defined under § 316.5 of this chapter, for a period of at least three years after having been lawfully admitted for permanent residence;

(3) Has been living in marital union with the citizen spouse for the three years preceding the date of examination on the application, and the spouse has been a United States citizen for the duration of that three year period;

(4) Has been physically present in the United States for periods totaling at least 18 months;

(5) Has resided, as defined in § 316.5 of this chapter, for at least 3 months immediately preceding the filing of the application, or immediately preceding the examination on the application if the application was filed early pursuant to section 334(a) of the Act and the three month period falls within the required period of residence under section 316(a) or 319(a) of the Act, in the State or Service district having jurisdiction over the alien's actual place of residence;

(6) Has resided continuously within the United States from the date of application for naturalization until the time of admission to citizenship;

(7) For all relevant periods under this paragraph, has been and continues to be a person of good moral character, attached to the principles of the Constitution of the United States, and favorably disposed toward the good order and happiness of the United States; and

(8) Has complied with all other requirements for naturalization as provided in part 316 of this chapter, except for those contained in § 316.2 (a)(3) through (a)(5) of this chapter.

(b) **Marital union —**

(1) General. An applicant lives in marital union with a citizen spouse if the applicant actually resides with his or her current spouse. The burden is on the applicant to establish, in each individual case, that a particular marital union satisfies the requirements of this part.

(2) Loss of Marital Union —

(i) Divorce, death or expatriation. A person is ineligible for naturalization as the spouse of a United States citizen under section 319(a) of the Act if, before or after the filing of the application, the marital union ceases to exist due to death or divorce, or the citizen spouse has expatriated. Eligibility is not restored to an applicant whose relationship to the citizen spouse terminates before the applicant's admission to citizenship, even though the applicant subsequently marries another United States citizen.

(ii) Separation —

(A) Legal separation. Any legal separation will break the continuity of the marital union required for purposes of this part.

(B) Informal separation. Any informal separation that suggests the possibility of marital disunity will be evaluated on a case-by-case basis to determine whether it is sufficient enough to signify the dissolution of the marital union.

(C) Involuntary separation. In the event that the applicant and spouse live apart because of circumstances beyond their control, such as military service in the Armed Forces of the United States or essential business or occupational demands, rather than because of voluntary legal or informal separation, the resulting separation, even if prolonged, will not preclude naturalization under this part.

(c) Physical presence in the United States. In the event that the alien spouse has never been in the United States, eligibility under this section is not established even though the alien spouse resided abroad in marital union with the citizen spouse during the three year period.

HISTORY:

[56 FR 50488, Oct. 7, 1991, as confirmed at 60 FR 6650, Feb. 3, 1995; 76 FR 53764, 53798, Aug. 29, 2011]

AUTHORITY:

8 U.S.C. 1103, 1430, 1443.

§ 319.2 Person whose United States citizen spouse is employed abroad.

(a) Eligibility. To be eligible for naturalization under section 319(b) of the Act, the alien spouse of a United States citizen must:

(1) Establish that his or her citizen spouse satisfies the requirements under section 319(b)(1) of the Act, including that he or she is regularly stationed abroad. For purposes of this section, a citizen spouse is regularly stationed abroad if he or she proceeds abroad, for a period of not less than one year, pursuant to an employment contract or orders, and assumes the duties of employment;

(2) At the time of examination on the application for naturalization, be present in the United States pursuant to a lawful admission for permanent residence;

(3) At the time of naturalization, be present in the United States;

(4) Declare in good faith, upon naturalization before the Service, an intention:

(i) To reside abroad with the citizen spouse; and

(ii) To take up residence within the United States immediately upon the termination of the citizen spouse's employment abroad;

(5) Be a person of good moral character, attached to the principles of the Constitution of the United States, and favorably disposed toward the good order and happiness of the United States; and

(6) Comply with all other requirements for naturalization as provided in part 316 of this chapter, except for those contained in § 316.2(a)(3) through (a)(6) of this chapter.

(b) Alien spouse's requirement to depart abroad immediately after naturalization. An alien spouse seeking naturalization under section 319(b) of the Act must:

(1) Establish that he or she will depart to join the citizen spouse within 30 to 45 days after the date of naturalization;

(2) Notify the Service immediately of any delay or cancellation of the citizen spouse's assignment abroad; and

(3) Notify the Service immediately if he or she is unable to reside with the citizen spouse because the citizen spouse is employed abroad in an area of hostilities where dependents may not reside.

(c) Loss of marital union due to death, divorce, or expatriation of the citizen spouse. A person is ineligible for naturalization as the spouse of a United States citizen under section 319(b) of the Act if, before or after the filing of the application, the marital union ceases to exist due to death or divorce, or the citizen spouse has expatriated. Eligibility is not restored to an applicant whose relationship to the citizen spouse terminates before the applicant's admission into citizenship, even though the applicant subsequently marries another United States citizen.

HISTORY:

[56 FR 50488, Oct. 7, 1991, as confirmed at 60 FR 6650, Feb. 3, 1995]

AUTHORITY:

8 U.S.C. 1103, 1430, 1443.

§ 319.3 Surviving spouses of United States citizens who died during a period of honorable service in an active duty status in the Armed Forces of the United States.

(a) Eligibility. To be eligible for naturalization under section 319(d) of the Act, the surviving spouse, child, or parent of a United States citizen must:

(1) Establish that his or her citizen spouse, child, or parent died during a period of honorable service in an active duty status in the Armed Forces of the United States and, in the case of a surviving spouse, establish that he or she was living in marital union with the citizen spouse, in accordance with 8 CFR 319.1(b), at the time of the citizen spouse's death;

(2) At the time of examination on the application for naturalization, reside in the United States pursuant to a lawful admission for permanent residence;

(3) Be a person of good moral character, attached to the principles of the Constitution of the United States, and favorably disposed toward the good order and happiness of the United States; and

(4) Comply with all other requirements for naturalization as provided in 8 CFR 316, except for those contained in 8 CFR 316.2(a)(3) through (6).

(b) Remarriage of the surviving spouse. The surviving spouse of a United States citizen described under paragraph (a)(1) of this section remains eligible for naturalization under section 319(d) of the Act, even if the surviving spouse remarries.

HISTORY:

[56 FR 50488, Oct. 7, 1991, as confirmed at 60 FR 6650, Feb. 3, 1995; 76 FR 53764, 53798, Aug. 29, 2011]

AUTHORITY:

8 U.S.C. 1103, 1430, 1443.

§ 319.4 Persons continuously employed for 5 years by United States organizations engaged in disseminating information.

To be eligible for naturalization under section 319(c) of the Act, an applicant must:

(a) Establish that he or she is employed as required under section 319(c)(1) of the Act;

(b) Reside in the United States pursuant to a lawful admission for permanent residence;

(c) Establish that he or she has been employed as required under paragraph (a) of this section continuously for a period of not less than five years after a lawful admission for permanent residence;

(d) File his or her application for naturalization while employed as required under paragraph (a) of this section, or within six months following the termination of such employment;

(e) Be present in the United States at the time of naturalization;

(f) Declare in good faith, upon naturalization before the Service, an intention to take up residence within the United States immediately upon his or her termination of employment;

(g) Be a person of good moral character, attached to the principles of the Constitution of the United States, and favorably disposed toward the good order and happiness of the United States; and

(h) Comply with all other requirements for naturalization as provided in part 316 of this chapter, except for those contained in § 316.2(a)(3) through (a)(6) of this chapter.

HISTORY:

[56 FR 50489, Oct. 7, 1991, as confirmed at 60 FR 6650, Feb. 3, 1995]

AUTHORITY:

8 U.S.C. 1103, 1430, 1443.

§ 319.5 Public international organizations in which the U.S. participates by treaty or statute.

Organizations designated by the President as international organizations pursuant to the International Organizations Immunities Act are considered as public international organizations in which the United States participates by treaty or statute within the meaning of section 319(b) or the Act. For a list of such organizations see § 316.20(b) of this chapter. In addition, the following have been determined to be public international organizations within the purview of section 319(b) of the Act:

The North Atlantic Treaty Organization.

The United Nations and all agencies and organizations which are a part thereof.

The regional commissioner shall forward a copy of each decision regarding a public international organization to the Assistant Commissioner, Naturalization.

HISTORY:

[32 FR 9635, July 4, 1967; Further redesignated at 33 FR 255, Jan. 9, 1968.; Redesignated and amended at 56 FR 50489, Oct. 7, 1991, as confirmed at 60 FR 6650, Feb. 3, 1995]

AUTHORITY:

8 U.S.C. 1103, 1430, 1443.

§ 319.6 United States nonprofit organizations engaged abroad in disseminating information which significantly promotes U.S. interests.

The following have been determined to be U.S. incorporated nonprofit organizations principally engaged in conducting abroad through communications media the dissemination of information which significantly promotes U.S. interests abroad within the purview of section 319(c) of the Act:

Free Europe, Inc.; formerly Free Europe Committee, Inc.; National Committee for a Free Europe (including Radio Free Europe)).

Radio Liberty Committee, Inc. (formerly American Committee for Liberation, Inc.; American Committee for Liberation of the Peoples of Russia, Inc.; American Committee for Liberation from Bolshevism, Inc.).

HISTORY:

[33 FR 255, Jan. 9, 1968.; Redesignated and amended at 56 FR 50489, Oct. 7, 1991, as confirmed at 60 FR 6650, Feb. 3, 1995]

AUTHORITY:

8 U.S.C. 1103, 1430, 1443.

§§ 319.7 — 319.10 [Reserved]

[NO TEXT IN ORIGINAL]

HISTORY:

[NO SOURCE IN ORIGINAL]

AUTHORITY:

8 U.S.C. 1103, 1430, 1443.

§ 319.11 Filing of application.

(a) General. An applicant under this part must submit an application for naturalization in accordance with the form instructions with the fee required by 8 CFR 106.2. An alien spouse applying for naturalization under section 319(b) of the Act who is described in 8 CFR 319.2 must also submit a statement of intent containing the following information about the citizen spouse's employment and future intent:

(1) The name of the employer and:

(i) The nature of the employer's business; or

(ii) The ministerial, religious, or missionary activity in which the employer is engaged;

(2) Whether the employing entity is owned in whole or in part by United States interests;

(3) Whether the employing entity is engaged in whole or in part in the development of the foreign trade and commerce of the United States;

(4) The nature of the activity in which the citizen spouse is engaged;

(5) The anticipated period of employment abroad;

(6) Whether the alien spouse intends to reside abroad with the citizen spouse; and,

(7) Whether the alien spouse intends to take up residence within the United States immediately upon the termination of such employment abroad of the citizen spouse.

(b) **Applications by military spouses —**

(1) General. The alien spouses of United States military personnel being assigned abroad must satisfy the basic requirements of section 319(b) of the Act and of paragraph (a) of this section.

(2) Government expense. In the event that transportation expenses abroad for the alien spouse are to be paid by military authorities, a properly executed Certificate of Overseas Assignment to Support Application to File Petition for Naturalization, DD Form 1278 will be submitted in lieu of the statement of intent required by paragraph (a) of this section. Any DD Form 1278 issued more than 90 days in advance of departure is unacceptable for purposes of this section.

(3) Private expense. In the event that the alien spouse is not authorized to travel abroad at military expense, the alien spouse must submit in lieu of the statement of intent required by paragraph (a) of this section:

(i) A copy of the citizen spouse's military travel orders,

(ii) A letter from the citizen spouse's commanding officer indicating that the military has no objection to the applicant traveling to and residing in the vicinity of the citizen spouse's new duty station; and

(iii) Evidence of transportation arrangements to the new duty station.

HISTORY:

[56 FR 50489, Oct. 7, 1991, as confirmed at 60 FR 6650, Feb. 3, 1995; 76 FR 53764, 53798, Aug. 29, 2011; 85 FR 46788, 46928, Aug. 3, 2020]

AUTHORITY:
8 U.S.C. 1103, 1430, 1443.

PART 320

CHILD BORN OUTSIDE THE UNITED STATES AND RESIDING PERMANENTLY IN THE UNITED STATES; REQUIREMENTS FOR AUTOMATIC ACQUISITION OF CITIZENSHIP

AUTHORITY NOTE APPLICABLE TO ENTIRE PART:

AUTHORITY:
8 U.S.C. 1103, 1443; 8 CFR part 2.

§ 320.1 What definitions are used in this part?

As used in this part, the term:

Adopted means adopted pursuant to a full, final and complete adoption. If a foreign adoption of an orphan was not full and final, was defective, or the unmarried U.S. citizen parent or U.S. citizen parent and spouse jointly did not see and observe the child in person prior to or during the foreign adoption proceedings, the child is not considered to have been fully, finally and completely adopted and must be readopted in the United States. Readoption requirements may be waived if the state of residence of the United States citizen parent(s) recognizes the foreign adoption as full and final under that state's adoption laws.

Adopted child means a person who has been adopted as defined above and who meets the requirements of section 101(b)(1)(E) or (F) of the Act.

Child means a person who meets the requirements of section 101(c)(1) of the Act.

Joint custody, in the case of a child of divorced or legally separated parents, means the award of equal responsibility for and authority over the care, education, religion, medical treatment, and general welfare of a child to both parents by a court of law or other appropriate government entity pursuant to the laws of the state or country of residence.

Legal custody refers to the responsibility for and authority over a child.

(1) For the purpose of the CCA, the Service will presume that a U.S. citizen parent has legal custody of a child, and will recognize that U.S. citizen parent as having lawful authority over the child, absent evidence to the contrary, in the case of:

(i) A biological child who currently resides with both natural parents (who are married to each other, living in marital union, and not separated),

(ii) A biological child who currently resides with a surviving natural parent (if the other parent is deceased), or

(iii) In the case of a biological child born out of wedlock who has been legitimated and currently resides with the natural parent.

(2) In the case of an adopted child, a determination that a U.S. citizen parent has legal custody will be based on the existence of a final adoption decree. In the case of a child of divorced or legally separated parents, the Service will find a U.S. citizen parent to have legal custody of a child, for the purpose of the CCA, where there has been an award of primary care, control, and maintenance of a minor child to a parent by a court of law or other appropriate government entity pursuant to the laws of the state or country of residence. The Service will consider a U.S. citizen parent who has been awarded "joint custody," to have legal custody of a child. There may be other factual circumstances under which the Service will find the U.S. citizen parent to have legal custody for purposes of the CCA.

HISTORY:
[66 FR 32138, 32144, June 13, 2001]

§ 320.2 Who is eligible for citizenship?

(a) General. To be eligible for citizenship under section 320 of the Act, a person must establish that the following conditions have been met after February 26, 2001:

(1) The child has at least one United States citizen parent (by birth or naturalization);

(2) The child is under 18 years of age; and

(3) The child is residing in the United States in the legal and physical custody of the United States citizen parent, pursuant to a lawful admission for permanent residence.

(b) Additional requirements if child is adopted. If adopted, the child must meet all of the requirements in paragraph (a) of this section as well as satisfy the requirements applicable to adopted children under section 101(b)(1) of the Act.

HISTORY:
[66 FR 32138, 32144, June 13, 2001]

§ 320.3 How, where, and what forms and other documents should be filed?

(a) Application. Individuals who are applying for a certificate of citizenship on their own behalf should submit the request in accordance with the form instructions on the form prescribed by USCIS for that purpose. An application for a certificate of citizenship under this section on behalf of a child who has not reached the age of 18 years must be submitted by that child's U.S. citizen biological or adoptive parent(s), or legal guardian.

(b) Evidence.

(1) An applicant under this section must establish eligibility as described in 8 CFR 320.2. An applicant must submit the following supporting evidence unless such evidence is already contained in USCIS administrative file(s):

(i) The child's birth certificate or record;

(ii) Marriage certificate of child's parents (if applicable);

(iii) If the child's parents were married before their marriage to each other, proof of termination of any previous marriage of each parent (e.g., death certificate or divorce decree);

(iv) Evidence of U.S. citizenship of parent, (i.e., birth certificate; naturalization certificate; FS-240, Report of Birth Abroad; a valid unexpired U.S. passport; or certificate of citizenship);

(v) If the child was born out of wedlock, documents verifying legitimation according to the laws of the child's residence or domicile or father's residence or domicile (if applicable);

(vi) In case of divorce, legal separation, or adoption, documentation of legal custody;

(vii) Copy of Permanent Resident Card/Alien Registration Receipt Card or other evidence of lawful permanent resident status (e.g. I-551 stamp in a valid foreign passport or Service-issued travel document);

(viii) If adopted, a copy of the full, final adoption decree and, if the adoption was outside of the United States and the child immigrated as an IR-4 (orphans coming to the United States to be adopted by U.S. citizen parent(s)), evidence that the foreign adoption is recognized by the state where the child is permanently residing; and

(ix) Evidence of all legal name changes, if applicable, for the child and U.S. citizen parent.

(2) If the Service requires any additional documentation to make a decision on the application for certificate of citizenship, applicants may be asked to provide that documentation under separate cover or at the time of interview. Applicants do not need to submit documents that were submitted in connection with: An application for immigrant visa and retained by the American Consulate for inclusion in the immigrant visa package, or an immigrant petition or application and included in a Service administrative file. Applicants should indicate that they wish to rely on such documents and identify the administrative file(s) by name and alien number. The Service will only request the required documentation again if necessary.

HISTORY:

[66 FR 32138, 32144, June 13, 2001; 74 FR 26933, 26940, June 5, 2009; 76 FR 53764, 53799, Aug. 29, 2011]

§ 320.4 Who must appear for an interview on the application for citizenship?

All applicants (and U.S. citizen parent(s) if application filed on behalf of a minor biological or adopted child) must appear for examination unless such examination is waived under the guidelines expressed in § 341.2 of this chapter.

HISTORY:

[66 FR 32138, 32144, June 13, 2001]

§ 320.5 Decision.

(a) Approval of application. If the application for the certificate of citizenship is approved, after the applicant takes the oath of allegiance prescribed in 8 CFR 337.1 (unless the oath is waived), USCIS will issue a certificate of citizenship.

(b) Denial of application. If the decision of USCIS is to deny the application for a certificate of citizenship under this section, the applicant will be advised in writing of the reasons for denial and of the right to appeal in accordance with 8 CFR 103.3(a). An applicant may file an appeal within 30 days of service of the decision in accordance with the instructions on the form prescribed by USCIS for that purpose, and with the fee required by 8 CFR 106.2.

(c) Subsequent application. After an application for a certificate of citizenship has been denied and the time for appeal has expired, USCIS will reject a subsequent application submitted by the same individual and the applicant will be instructed to submit a motion for reopening or reconsideration in accordance with 8 CFR 103.5. The motion must be accompanied by the rejected application and the fee specified in 8 CFR 106.2.

HISTORY:

[66 FR 32138, 32145 June 13, 2001; 76 FR 53764, 53799, Aug. 29, 2011; 85 FR 46788, 46928, Aug. 3, 2020]

PART 322

CHILD BORN OUTSIDE THE UNITED STATES; REQUIREMENTS FOR APPLICATION FOR CERTIFICATE OF CITIZENSHIP

AUTHORITY NOTE APPLICABLE TO ENTIRE PART:

AUTHORITY:

8 U.S.C. 1103, 1443; 8 CFR part 2.

§ 322.1 What are the definitions used in this part?

As used in this part the term:

Adopted means adopted pursuant to a full, final and complete adoption. In the case of an orphan adoption, if a foreign adoption was not full and final, was defective, or the unmarried U.S. citizen parent or U.S. citizen parent and spouse jointly did not see and observe the child in person prior to or during the foreign adoption proceedings, an orphan is not considered to have been adopted and must be readopted in the United States or satisfy the requirements of section 101(b)(1)(E) of the Act.

Adopted child means a person who has been adopted as defined above and who meets the requirements of section 101(b)(1)(E), (F) or (G) of the Act.

Child means a person who meets the requirements of section 101(c)(1) of the Act.

Lawful admission shall have the same meaning as provided in section 101(a)(13) of the Act.

Joint custody, in the case of a child of divorced or legally separated parents, means the award of equal responsibility for and authority over the care, education, religion, medical treatment and general welfare of a child to both parents by a court of law or other appropriate government entity pursuant to the laws of the state or country of residence.

Legal custody refers to the responsibility for and authority over a child.

(1) For the purpose of the CCA, the Service will presume that a U.S. citizen parent has legal custody of a child, and will recognize that U.S. citizen parent as having lawful authority over the child, absent evidence to the contrary, in the case of:

(i) A biological child who currently resides with both natural parents (who are married to each other, living in marital union, and not separated),

(ii) A biological child who currently resides with a surviving natural parent (if the other parent is deceased), or

(iii) In the case of a biological child born out of wedlock who has been legitimated and currently resides with the natural parent.

(2) In the case of an adopted child, a determination that a U.S. citizen parent has legal custody will be based on the existence of a final adoption decree. In the case of a child of divorced or legally separated parents, the Service will find a U.S. citizen parent to have legal custody of a child, for the purpose of the CCA, where there has been an award of primary care, control, and maintenance of a minor child to a parent by a court of law or other appropriate government entity pursuant to the laws of the state or country of residence. The Service will consider a U.S. citizen parent who has been awarded "joint custody," to have legal custody of a child. There may be other factual circumstances under which the Service will find the U.S. citizen parent to have legal custody for purposes of the CCA.

HISTORY:

[56 FR 50489, Oct. 7, 1991; 66 FR 32138, 32145, June 13, 2001; 76 FR 53764, 53799, Aug. 29, 2011]

§ 322.2 Eligibility.

(a) General. A child will be eligible for citizenship under section 322 of the Act, if the following conditions have been fulfilled:

(1) The child has at least one United States citizen parent (by birth or naturalization);

(2) The United States citizen parent has been physically present in the United States or its outlying possessions for at least 5 years, at least 2 of which were after the age of 14, or the United States citizen parent has a United States citizen parent who has been physically present in the United States or its outlying possessions for at least 5 years, at least 2 of which were after the age of 14;

(3) The child currently is under 18 years of age;

(4) The child currently is residing outside the United States in the legal and physical custody of the United States citizen parent; and

(5) The child is temporarily present in the United States pursuant to a lawful admission and is maintaining such lawful status in the United States.

(b) Additional requirements if child is adopted. If an adopted child, all of the requirements in paragraph (a) of this section must be fulfilled and the child must satisfy the requirements applicable to adopted children under section 101(b)(1) of the Act.

(c) Exceptions for children of military personnel. Pursuant to section 322(d) of the Act, a child of a member of the Armed Forces of the United States residing abroad is exempt from the temporary physical presence, lawful admission, and maintenance of lawful status requirements under 8 CFR 322.2(a)(5), if the child:

(1) Is authorized to accompany and reside abroad with the member of the Armed Forces pursuant to the member's official orders; and

(2) Is accompanying and residing abroad with the member of the Armed Forces.

HISTORY:

[56 FR 50489, Oct. 7, 1991, as confirmed at 60 FR 6650, Feb. 3, 1995; 58 FR 49913, Sept. 24, 1993, as confirmed at 60 FR 6650, Feb. 3, 1995; 66 FR 32138, 32145, June 13, 2001; 76 FR 53764, 53799, Aug. 29, 2011]

§ 322.3 Application and supporting documents.

(a) Application. A U.S. citizen parent of an alien child (including an adopted child) may file an application for the child to become a citizen and obtain a certificate of citizenship under section 322 of the Act by submitting an application on the form prescribed by USCIS in accordance with the form instructions and with the fee prescribed by 8 CFR 106.2. If the U.S. citizen parent has died, the child's U.S. citizen grandparent or U.S. citizen legal guardian may submit the application, provided the application is filed not more than 5 years after the death of the U.S. citizen parent.

(b) Evidence.

(1) An applicant under this section shall establish eligibility under § 322.2. In addition to the forms and the appropriate fee as required in 8 CFR 106.2, an applicant must submit the following required documents unless such documents are already contained in the Service administrative file(s):

(i) The child's birth certificate or record;

(ii) Marriage certificate of child's parents (if applicable);

(iii) If the child's parents were married before their marriage to each other, proof of termination of any previous marriage of each parent (e.g., death certificate or divorce decree);

(iv) Evidence of U.S. citizenship of parent (i.e., birth certificate; naturalization certificate; FS-240, Report of Birth Abroad; a valid unexpired U.S. passport; or certificate of citizenship);

(v) If the child was born out of wedlock, documents verifying legitimation according to the laws of the child's residence or domicile or father's residence or domicile (if applicable);

(vi) In case of divorce, legal separation, or adoption, documentation of legal custody (if applicable);

(vii) Documentation establishing that the U.S. citizen parent or U.S. citizen grandparent meets the required physical presence requirements (e.g., school records, military records, utility bills, medical records, deeds, mortgages, contracts, insurance policies, receipts, or attestations by churches, unions, or other organizations);

(viii) Evidence that the child is present in the United States pursuant to a lawful admission and is maintaining such lawful status, or evidence establishing that the child qualifies for an exception to these requirements as provided in 8 CFR 322.2(c) pursuant to section 322(d) of the Act. Such evidence may be presented at the time of interview when appropriate;

(ix) If adopted, a copy of a full, final adoption decree;

(x) For adopted children (not orphans) applying under section 322 of the Act, evidence that they satisfy the requirements of section 101(b)(1)(E);

(xi) For adopted orphans applying under section 322 of the Act, a copy of notice of approval of the orphan petition and supporting documentation for such petition (except the home study) or evidence that the child has been admitted for lawful permanent residence in the United States with the immigrant classification of IR-3 (Orphan adopted abroad by a U.S. citizen) or IR-4 (Orphan to be adopted by a U.S. citizen);

(xii) For a Hague Convention adoptee applying under section 322 of the Act, a copy of the notice of approval of the Convention adoptee petition and its supporting documentation, or evidence that the child has been admitted for lawful permanent residence in the United States with the immigrant classification of IH-3 (Hague Convention Orphan adopted abroad by a U.S. citizen) or IH-4 (Hague Convention Orphan to be adopted by a U.S. citizen); and

(xiii) Evidence of all legal name changes, if applicable, for the child, U.S. citizen parent, U.S. citizen grandparent, or U.S. citizen legal guardian.

(2) If USCIS requires any additional documentation to make a decision on the application, the parents may be asked to provide that documentation under separate cover or at the time of interview. Parents do not need to submit documents that were submitted in connection with: An application for immigrant visa and retained by the American Consulate for inclusion in the immigrant visa package, or another immigrant petition or application and included in a Service administrative file. Parents should indicate that they wish to rely on such documents and identify the administrative file(s) by name and alien number. The Service will only request the required documentation again if necessary.

HISTORY:

[56 FR 50489, Oct. 7, 1991, as confirmed at 60 FR 6650, Feb. 3, 1995; 66 FR 32138, 32146, June 13, 2001; 72 FR 56832, 56867, Oct. 4, 2007; 74 FR 26933, 26940, June 5, 2009; 76 FR 53764, 53799, Aug. 29, 2011; 85 FR 46788, 46928, Aug. 3, 2020]

§ 322.4 Interview.

The U.S. citizen parent and the child must appear in person before a USCIS officer for examination on the application under this section. If the U.S. citizen parent is deceased, the child's U.S. citizen grandparent or U.S. citizen legal guardian who filed the application on the child's behalf must appear.

HISTORY:

[56 FR 50489, Oct. 7, 1991, as confirmed at 60 FR 6650, Feb. 3, 1995; 66 FR 32138, 32146, June 13, 2001; 76 FR 53764, 53799, Aug. 29, 2011]

§ 322.5 Decision.

(a) Approval of application. If the application for certificate of citizenship is approved, after the applicant takes the oath of allegiance prescribed in 8 CFR 337.1 (unless the oath is waived), USCIS will issue a certificate of citizenship. The child is a citizen as of the date of approval and administration of the oath of allegiance.

(b) Denial of application. If the USCIS decision is to deny the application for a certificate of citizenship under this section, the applicant will be furnished with the reasons for denial and advised of the right to appeal in accordance with the provisions of 8 CFR 103.3(a). An applicant may file an appeal within 30 days of service of the decision in accordance with the instructions on the form prescribed by USCIS for that purpose, and with the fee required by 8 CFR 106.2.

(c) Subsequent application. After an application for a certificate of citizenship has been denied and the time for appeal has expired, USCIS will reject a subsequent application submitted by the same individual and the applicant will be instructed to submit a motion for reopening or reconsideration in accordance with 8 CFR 103.5. The motion must be accompanied by the rejected application and the fee specified in 8 CFR 106.2.

HISTORY:

[56 FR 50489, Oct. 7, 1991, as confirmed at 60 FR 6650, Feb. 3, 1995; 66 FR 32138, 32146, June 13, 2001; 76 FR 53764, 53800, Aug. 29, 2011; 85 FR 46788, 46928, Aug. 3, 2020]

PART 324

SPECIAL CLASSES OF PERSONS WHO MAY BE NATURALLZED: WOMEN WHO HAVE LOST UNITED STATES CITIZENSHIP BY MARRIAGE AND FORMER CITIZENS WHOSE NATURALIZATION IS AUTHORIZED BY PRLVATE LAW

§ 324.1 Definitions.

As used in this part:

Oath means the Oath of Allegiance as prescribed in section 337 of the Act.

HISTORY:

[56 FR 50490, Oct. 7, 1991, as confirmed at 60 FR 6650, Feb. 3, 1995]

AUTHORITY:

8 U.S.C. 1103, 1435, 1443, 1448, 1101 note.

§ 324.2 Former citizen at birth or by naturalization.

(a) Eligibility. To be eligible for naturalization under section 324(a) of the Act, an applicant must establish that she:

(1) Was formerly a United States citizen;

(2) Lost or may have lost United States citizenship:

(i) Prior to September 22, 1922, by marriage to an alien, or by the loss of United States citizenship of the applicant's spouse; or

(ii) On or after September 22, 1922, by marriage before March 3, 1931 to an alien ineligible to citizenship;

(3) Did not acquire any other nationality by affirmative act other than by marriage;

(4) Either:

(i) Has resided in the United States continuously since the date of the marriage referred to in paragraph (a)(2) of this section; or

(ii) Has been lawfully admitted for permanent residence prior to filing an application for naturalization;

(5) Has been and is a person of good moral character, attached to the principles of the Constitution of the United States, and favorably disposed toward the good order and happiness of the United States, for the period of not less than five years immediately preceding the examination on the application for naturalization up to the time of admission to citizenship; and

(6) Complies with all other requirements for naturalization as provided in part 316 of this chapter, except that:

(i) The applicant is not required to satisfy the residence requirements under § 316.2(a)(3) through (a)(6) of this chapter; and,

(ii) The applicant need not set forth an intention to reside permanently within the United States.

(b) Application. An applicant for naturalization under this section must submit an application on the form designated by USCIS in accordance with the form instructions and with the fee prescribed in 8 CFR 106.2 as required by 8 CFR 316.4. The application must be accompanied by a statement describing the applicant's eligibility as provided in paragraph (a) of this section as well as any available documentation to establish those facts.

HISTORY:

[56 FR 50490, Oct. 7, 1991, as confirmed at 60 FR 6650, Feb. 3, 1995; 74 FR 26933, 26941, June 5, 2009; 76 FR 53764, 53800, Aug. 29, 2011, as corrected at 76 FR 73475, Nov. 29, 2011; 85 FR 46788, 46928, Aug. 3, 2020]

AUTHORITY:

8 U.S.C. 1103, 1435, 1443, 1448, 1101 note.

§ 324.3 Women, citizens of the United States at birth, who lost or are believed to have lost citizenship by marriage and whose marriage has terminated.

(a) Eligibility. To be eligible for naturalization under section 324(c) of the Act, an applicant must establish:

(1) That she was formerly a United States citizen by birth;

(2) That she lost or may have lost her United States citizenship:

(i) Prior to September 22, 1922, by marriage to an alien; or

(ii) On or after September 22, 1922, by marriage to an alien ineligible to citizenship before March 3, 1931;

(3) That the marriage specified in paragraph (a)(2) of this section terminated subsequent to January 12, 1941;

(4) That she did not acquire any other nationality by affirmative act other than by marriage; and

(5) That she is not proscribed from naturalization under section 313 of the Act.

(b) **Procedures —**

(1) Application. An applicant eligible for naturalization pursuant to paragraph (a) of this section, who desires to regain citizenship pursuant to section 324(c) of the Act, shall submit, without fee, an application for naturalization on the form prescribed by USCIS in accordance with the instructions on the form.

(2) Oath of Allegiance. USCIS shall review the applicant's submission, and shall inform the applicant of her eligibility under section 324(c) of the Act to take the oath in conformity with part 337 of this chapter. After the applicant has taken the oath, the applicant will be furnished with a copy of the oath by the clerk of the Court or USCIS, as appropriate, properly certified, for which a fee not exceeding $ 5 may be charged. The oath may also be taken abroad before any diplomatic or consular officer of the United States, in accordance with such regulations as may be prescribed by the Secretary of State.

HISTORY:

[56 FR 50490, 50491, Oct. 7, 1991, as confirmed at 60 FR 6650, Feb. 3, 1995; 74 FR 26933, 26941, June 5, 2009; 76 FR 53764, 53800, Aug. 29, 2011]

AUTHORITY:

8 U.S.C. 1103, 1435, 1443, 1448, 1101 note.

§ 324.4 Women restored to United States citizenship by the act of June 25, 1936, as amended by the act of July 2, 1940.

A woman who was restored to citizenship by the act of June 25, 1936, as amended by the act of July 2, 1940, but who failed to take the oath of allegiance prescribed by the naturalization laws prior to December 24, 1952, may take the oath before any naturalization court or USCIS office within the United States. Such woman shall comply with the procedural requirements of § 324.4(b) and (c) except that a fee not exceeding $ 1.00 may be charged if the woman requests a copy of the oath.

HISTORY:

[22 FR 9814, Dec. 6, 1957; Redesignated and amended at 56 FR 50490, 50491, Oct. 7, 1991, as confirmed at 60 FR 6650, Feb. 3, 1995; 74 FR 26933, 26941, June 5, 2009]

AUTHORITY:

8 U.S.C. 1103, 1435, 1443, 1448, 1101 note.

§ 324.5 Former citizen of the United States whose naturalization by taking the oath is authorized by a private law.

A former citizen of the United States whose naturalization by taking the oath before any naturalization court or office of USCIS within the United States is authorized by a private law must submit an application on the form specified by USCIS, without fee, in accordance with the form instructions.

HISTORY:
[23 FR 2673, Apr. 23, 1958; Redesignated and amended at 56 FR 50490, 50491, Oct. 7, 1991, as confirmed at 60 FR 6650, Feb. 3, 1995; 74 FR 26933, 26941, June 5, 2009; 76 FR 53764, 53800, Aug. 29, 2011]

AUTHORITY:
8 U.S.C. 1103, 1435, 1443, 1448, 1101 note.

PART 325

NATIONALS BUT NOT CITIZENS OF THE UNITED STATES; RESIDENCE WITHIN OUTLYING POSSESSIONS

§ 325.1 [Reserved]

[NO TEXT IN ORIGINAL]

HISTORY:
56 FR 50491, Oct. 7, 1991.

AUTHORITY:
8 U.S.C. 1103, 1436, 1443.

§ 325.2 Eligibility.

An applicant for naturalization under section 325 of the Act who owes permanent allegiance to the United States, and who is otherwise qualified may be naturalized if:

(a) The applicant becomes a resident of any State; and

(b) The applicant complies with all of the applicable requirements in parts 316 or 319 of this chapter, as appropriate, except as modified in this part.

HISTORY:
[56 FR 50491, Oct. 7, 1991, as confirmed at 60 FR 6650, Feb. 3, 1995]

AUTHORITY:
8 U.S.C. 1103, 1436, 1443.

§ 325.3 Residence.

(a) For purposes of applying the residence and physical presence requirements in parts 316 and 319 of this chapter, except as they relate to the required three months' residence in a State or Service district, residence and physical presence in an outlying possession of the United States will count as residence and physical presence in the United States.

(b) An applicant who intends to resume residence in an outlying possession after naturalization will be regarded as having established that he or she intends to reside permanently in the United States.

HISTORY:
[56 FR 50491, Oct. 7, 1991, as confirmed at 60 FR 6650, Feb. 3, 1995]

AUTHORITY:
8 U.S.C. 1103, 1436, 1443.

§ 325.4 Application; Documents.

(a) An application for naturalization under this part shall be submitted in compliance with § 316.4(a) of this chapter.

(b) The applicant shall submit with the application:

(1) A birth certificate or other evidence of national status;

(2) Proof of identity; and

(3) Evidence of actual residence in the State or Service district, as defined in 8 CFR 316.1, for three months immediately preceding the filing of the application, or immediately preceding the examination on the application if the application was filed early pursuant to section 334(a) of the Act and the three month period falls within the required period of residence under section 316(a) or 319(a) of the Act.

HISTORY:
[56 FR 50491, Oct. 7, 1991, as confirmed at 60 FR 6650, Feb. 3, 1995; 76 FR 53764, 53800, Aug. 29, 2011]

AUTHORITY:
8 U.S.C. 1103, 1436, 1443.

PART 327

SPECIAL CLASSES OF PERSONS WHO MAY BE NATURALIZED: PERSONS WHO LOST UNITED STATES CITIZENSHIP THROUGH SERVICE IN ARMED FORCES OF FOREIGN COUNTRY DURING WORLD WAR II

§ 327.1 Eligibility.

To be eligible for naturalization under section 327 of the Act, an applicant must establish that:

(a) The applicant, on or after September 1, 1939 and on or before September 2, 1945:

(1) Served in the military, air or naval forces of any country at war with a country with which the United States was at war after December 7, 1941 and before September 2, 1945; or

(2) Took an oath of allegiance or obligation for purposes of entering or serving in the military, air, or, naval forces of any country at war with a country with which the United States was at war after December 7, 1941 and before September 2, 1945;

(b) The applicant was a United States citizen at the time of the service or oath specified in paragraph (a) of this section;

(c) The applicant lost United States citizenship as a result of the service or oath specified in paragraph (a) of this section;

(d) The applicant has been lawfully admitted for permanent residence and intends to reside permanently in the United States;

(e) The applicant is, and has been for a period of at least five years immediately preceding taking the oath required in § 327.2(c), a person of good moral character, attached to the principles of the Constitution of the United States, and favorably disposed toward the good order and happiness of the United States; and

(f) The applicant has complied with all other requirements for naturalization as provided in part 316 of this chapter, except for those contained in § 316.2 (a)(3) through (a)(6) of this chapter.

HISTORY:

[56 FR 50492, Oct. 7, 1991, as confirmed at 60 FR 6650, Feb. 3, 1995]

AUTHORITY:

8 U.S.C. 1103, 1438, 1443.

§ 327.2 Procedure for naturalization.

(a) Application. An applicant who is eligible for naturalization pursuant to section 327 of the Act and § 327.1 shall submit an Application for Naturalization, Form N-400, in accordance with § 316.4 of this chapter. Such application must be accompanied by a statement describing the applicant's eligibility under § 327.1 (a), (b), and (c) and any available documentation to establish those facts.

(b) Oath of Allegiance. Upon naturalization of the applicant, the district director shall transmit a copy of the oath of allegiance taken by the applicant to the Department of State.

HISTORY:

[56 FR 50492, Oct. 7, 1991, as confirmed at 60 FR 6650, Feb. 3, 1995; 74 FR 26933, 26941, June 5, 2009]

AUTHORITY:

8 U.S.C. 1103, 1438, 1443.

PART 328

SPECIAL CLASSES OF PERSONS WHO MAY BE NATURALIZED: PERSONS WITH 1 YEAR OF SERVICE IN THE UNITED STATES ARMED FORCES

§ 328.1 Definitions.

As used in this part:

Honorable service means only that military service which is designated as honorable service by the executive department under which the applicant performed that military service. Any service that is designated to be other than honorable will not qualify under this section.

Service in the Armed Forces of the United States means:

(1) Active or reserve service in the United States Army, United States Navy, United States Marines, United States Air Force, or United States Coast Guard; or

(2) Service in a National Guard unit during such time as the unit is Federally recognized as a reserve component of the Armed Forces of the United States.

HISTORY:

[56 FR 50492, Oct. 7, 1991, as confirmed at 60 FR 6650, Feb. 3, 1995]

AUTHORITY:

8 U.S.C. 1103, 1439, 1443.

§ 328.2 Eligibility.

To be eligible for naturalization under section 328(a) of the Act, an applicant must establish that the applicant:

(a) Has served honorably in and, if separated, has been separated honorably from, the Armed Forces of the United States;

(b) Has served under paragraph (a) of this section for a period of 1 or more years, whether that service is continuous or discontinuous;

(c) Is a lawful permanent resident of the United States at the time of the examination on the application;

(d) Has been, during any period within five years preceding the filing of the application for naturalization, or the examination on the application if eligible for early filing under section 334(a) of the Act, and continues to be, of good moral character, attached to the principles of the Constitution of the United States, and favorably disposed toward the good order and happiness of the United States.

(1) An applicant is presumed to satisfy the requirements of this paragraph during periods of honorable service under paragraph (a) of this section.

(2) An applicant must establish that he or she satisfies the requirements of this paragraph from the date of discharge from military until the date of admission to citizenship.

(3) An applicant whose honorable service is discontinuous must also demonstrate that he or she satisfies the requirements of this paragraph for those periods of time when that applicant is not in honorable service.

(e) Has complied with all other requirements for naturalization as provided in part 316 of this chapter, except that:

(1) An applicant who files an application for naturalization while still in honorable service, or within six months after termination of such service, is generally not required to satisfy the residence requirements under § 316.2(a)(3) through (a)(6) of this chapter; however, if the applicant's military service is discontinuous, that applicant must establish, for periods between

honorable service during the five years immediately preceding the date of filing the application, or the examination on the application if eligible for early filing under section 334(a) of the Act, that he or she resided in the United States and in the State or Service district in the United States in which the application is filed.

(2) An applicant who files an application for naturalization more than six months after terminating honorable service must satisfy the residence requirements under § 316.2(a)(3) through (a)(6) of this chapter. However, any honorable service by the applicant within the five years immediately preceding the date of filing of the application shall be considered as residence within the United States for purposes of § 316.2(a)(3) of this chapter.

HISTORY:

[56 FR 50492, Oct. 7, 1991, as confirmed at 60 FR 6650, Feb. 3, 1995; 75 FR 2785, 2787, Jan. 19, 2010]

AUTHORITY:

8 U.S.C. 1103, 1439, 1443.

§ 328.3 [This section was removed and reserved. See 74 FR 26933, 26941, June 5, 2009.]

[NO TEXT IN ORIGINAL]

HISTORY:

[56 FR 50492, Oct. 7, 1991, as confirmed at 60 FR 6650, Feb. 3, 1995]

AUTHORITY:

(8 U.S.C. 1103, 1439, 1443.)

§ 328.4 Application and evidence.

(a) Application. An applicant for naturalization under section 328 of the Act must submit an application on the form prescribed by USCIS in accordance with the form instructions and as provided in 8 CFR 316.4.

(b) Evidence. The applicant's eligibility for naturalization under 8 CFR 328.2(a) or (b) will be established only by the certification of honorable service by the executive department under which the applicant served or is serving.

HISTORY:

[56 FR 50492, Oct. 7, 1991, as confirmed at 60 FR 6650, Feb. 3, 1995; 75 FR 2785, 2787, Jan. 19, 2010; 76 FR 53764, 53800, Aug. 29, 2011]

AUTHORITY:

8 U.S.C. 1103, 1439, 1443.

PART 329

SPECIAL CLASSES OF PERSONS WHO MAY BE NATURALIZED: PERSONS WITH ACTIVE DUTY OR CERTAIN READY RESERVE SERVICE IN THE UNITED STATES ARMED FORCES DURING SPECIFIED PERIODS OF HOSTILITIES

AUTHORITY NOTE APPLICABLE TO ENTIRE PART:

AUTHORITY:

8 U.S.C. 1103, 1440, 1443; 8 CFR part 2.

§ 329.1 Definitions.

As used in this part:

Honorable service and separation means service and separation from service which the executive department under which the applicant served determines to be honorable, including:

(1) That such applicant had not been separated from service on account of alienage;

(2) That such applicant was not a conscientious objector who performed no military, air or naval duty; and

(3) That such applicant did not refuse to wear a military uniform.

Service in an active duty status in the Armed Forces of the United States means active service in the following organizations:

(1) United States Army, United States Navy, United States Marines, United States Air Force, United States Coast Guard; or

(2) A National Guard unit during such time as the unit is Federally recognized as a reserve component of the Armed Forces of the United States and that unit is called for active duty.

World War I means the period beginning on April 6, 1917, and ending on November 11, 1918.

HISTORY:

[56 FR 50493, Oct. 7, 1991, as confirmed at 60 FR 6650, Feb. 3, 1995]

§ 329.2 Eligibility.

To be eligible for naturalization under section 329(a) of the Act, an applicant must establish that he or she:

(a) Has served honorably in the Armed Forces of the United States as a member of the Selected Reserve of the Ready Reserve or in an active duty status in the Armed Forces of the United States during:

(1) World War I;

(2) The period beginning on September 1, 1939 and ending on December 31, 1946;

(3) The period beginning on June 25, 1950 and ending on July 1, 1955;

(4) The period beginning on February 28, 1961 and ending on October 15, 1978; or

(5) Any other period as may be designated by the President in an Executive Order pursuant to section 329(a) of the Act;

(6) [Redesignated as (a)(5). See 58 FR 49913, Sept. 24, 1993.]

(b) If separated, has been separated honorably from service in the Armed Forces of the United States under paragraph (a) of this section;

(c) Satisfies the permanent residence requirement in one of the following ways:

(1) Any time after enlistment or induction into the Armed Forces of the United States, the applicant was lawfully admitted to the United States as a permanent resident; or

(2) At the time of enlistment or induction, the applicant was physically present in the geographical territory of the United States, the Canal Zone, American Samoa, Midway Island (prior to August 21, 1959), or Swain's Island, or in the ports, harbors, bays, enclosed sea areas, or the three-mile territorial sea along the coasts of these land areas, whether or not the applicant has been lawfully admitted to the United States as a permanent resident;

(d) Has been, for at least one year prior to filing the application for naturalization, and continues to be, of good moral character, attached to the principles of the Constitution of the United States, and favorably disposed toward the good order and happiness of the United States; and

(e) Has complied with all other requirements for naturalization as provided in part 316 of this chapter, except that:

(1) The applicant may be of any age;

(2) The applicant is not required to satisfy the residence requirements under § 316.2 (a)(3) through (a)(6) of this chapter; and

(3) The applicant may be naturalized even if an outstanding notice to appear pursuant to 8 CFR part 239 (including a charging document issued to commence proceedings under sections 236 or 242 of the Act prior to April 1, 1997) exists.

HISTORY:

[56 FR 50493, Oct. 7, 1991, as confirmed at 60 FR 6650, Feb. 3, 1995; 58 FR 49913, Sept. 24, 1993, as confirmed at 60 FR 6650, Feb. 3, 1995; 62 FR 10312, 10395, March 6, 1997; 75 FR 2785, 2787, Jan. 19, 2010]

§ 329.3 [This section was removed and reserved. See 74 FR 26933, 26941, June 5, 2009.]

[NO TEXT IN ORIGINAL]

HISTORY:

[56 FR 50493, Oct. 7, 1991, as confirmed at 60 FR 6650, Feb. 3, 1995]

AUTHORITY:

(8 U.S.C. 1103, 1440, 1443; 8 CFR part 2.)

§ 329.4 Application and evidence.

(a) Application. An applicant for naturalization under section 329 of the Act must submit an application on the form prescribed by USCIS in accordance with the form instructions and as provided in 8 CFR 316.4.

(b) Evidence. The applicant's eligibility for naturalization under 8 CFR 329.2(a), (b), or (c)(2) will be established only by a certification of honorable service by the executive department under which the applicant served or is serving.

HISTORY:

[56 FR 50493, Oct. 7, 1991, as confirmed and revised at 60 FR 6650, 6651, Feb. 3, 1995; 75 FR 2785, 2787, Jan. 19, 2010; 76 FR 53764, 53800, Aug. 29, 2011]

§ 329.5 [This section was removed. See 76 FR 53764, 53800, Aug. 29, 2011.]

[NO TEXT IN ORIGINAL]

HISTORY:

[56 FR 11061, Mar. 15, 1991; 58 FR 45421, Aug. 30, 1993; 60 FR 45658, 45659, Sept. 1, 1995; 74 FR 26933, 26941, June 5, 2009; 76 FR 53764, 53800, Aug. 29, 2011]

AUTHORITY:

(8 U.S.C. 1103, 1440, 1443; 8 CFR part 2.)

PART 330

SPECIAL CLASSES OF PERSONS WHO MAY BE NATURALIZED: SEAMEN

§ 330.1 Eligibility.

To be eligible for naturalization under section 330 of the Act, an applicant must establish that he or she:

(a) Has been lawfully admitted as a permanent resident of the United States;

(b) Has served honorably or with good conduct, during such periods of lawful residence, in a capacity other than as a member of the Armed Forces of the United States, on board:

(1) A vessel operated by the United States, or an agency thereof, the full legal and equitable title to which is in the United States; or

(2) A vessel, whose home port is the United States, and

(i) Which is registered under the laws of the United States; or

(ii) The full legal and equitable title to which is in a citizen of the United States, or a corporation organized under the laws of any of the several States of the United States;

(c) Served in the capacity specified in paragraph (b) of this section within five years immediately preceding the date on which the applicant filed the application for naturalization, or on which the alien is examined, if the application was filed early pursuant to section 334(a) of the Act.

(d) Has been, during the five years preceding the filing of the application for naturalization, or the examination on the application if the application was filed early under section 334(a) of the Act, and continues to be, of good moral character, attached to the principles of the Constitution of the United States, and favorably disposed toward the good order and happiness of the United States.

(1) An applicant is presumed to satisfy the requirements of this paragraph during periods of service in accordance with paragraphs (b) and (c) of this section, as reflected by the records and certificates submitted by the applicant under § 330.2(b).

(2) An applicant must demonstrate that he or she satisfies the requirements of this paragraph for those required periods when that applicant did not perform service in accordance with paragraphs (b) and (c) of this section; and

(e) Has complied with all other requirements for naturalization as provided in part 316 of this chapter, except that, for purposes of the residence requirements under paragraphs § 316.2 (a)(3) and (a)(4) of this chapter, service satisfying the conditions of this section shall be considered as residence and physical presence within the United States.

HISTORY:

[56 FR 50493, Oct. 7, 1991, as confirmed at 60 FR 6650, Feb. 3, 1995]

AUTHORITY:

8 U.S.C. 1103, 1443.

§ 330.2 Application.

(a) An applicant for naturalization under section 330 of the Act must submit an application on the form designated by USCIS.

(b) An applicant under this part must submit authenticated copies of the records and certificates of either:

(1) The Executive Department or Agencies having custody of records reflecting the applicant's service on a vessel in United States Government Service, if the applicant provided service under § 330.1(b)(1); or

(2) The masters of those vessels maintaining a home port in the United States, and either registered under the laws of the United States or owned by United States citizens or corporations, if the applicant provided service under § 330.1(b)(2).

HISTORY:

[56 FR 50493, Oct. 7, 1991, as confirmed at 60 FR 6650, Feb. 3, 1995; 74 FR 26933, 26941, June 5, 2009; 76 FR 53764, 53800, Aug. 29, 2011]

AUTHORITY:

8 U.S.C. 1103, 1443.

PART 331

ALIEN ENEMIES; NATURALIZATION UNDER SPECIFIED CONDITIONS AND PROCEDURES

§ 331.1 Definitions.

As used in this part:

Alien enemy means any person who is a native, citizen, subject or denizen of any country, state or sovereignty with which the United States is at war, for as long as the United States remains at war, as determined by proclamation of the President or resolution of Congress.

Denizen includes, but is not limited to, any person who has been admitted to residence and is entitled to certain rights in a country other than the one of the person's nationality. A person holding a status in another country equivalent to that of a lawful permanent resident in the United States would be considered to be a denizen.

HISTORY:

[56 FR 50494, Oct. 7, 1991, as confirmed at 60 FR 6650, Feb. 3, 1995]

AUTHORITY:

8 U.S.C. 1103, 1443.

§ 331.2 Eligibility.

An alien enemy may be naturalized as a citizen of the United States under section 331 of the Act if:

(a) The alien's application for naturalization is pending at the beginning of the state of war, or the Service has granted the alien an exception from the classification as an alien enemy after conducting an investigation in accordance with § 331.3;

(b) The alien's loyalty to the United States is fully established upon investigation by the Service in accordance with § 331.3; and

(c) The alien is otherwise entitled to admission to citizenship.

HISTORY:

[56 FR 50494, Oct. 7, 1991, as confirmed at 60 FR 6650, Feb. 3, 1995]

AUTHORITY:

8 U.S.C. 1103, 1443.

§ 331.3 Investigation.

The Service shall conduct a full investigation of any alien enemy whose application for naturalization is pending upon declaration of war or at any time thereafter. This investigation may take place either prior to or after the examination on the application. This investigation shall encompass, but not be limited to, the applicant's loyalty to the United States and attachment to the country, state, or sovereignty with which the United States is at war.

HISTORY:

[56 FR 50494, Oct. 7, 1991, as confirmed at 60 FR 6650, Feb. 3, 1995]

AUTHORITY:

8 U.S.C. 1103, 1443.

§ 331.4 Procedures.

(a) Upon determining that an applicant for naturalization is an alien enemy, the Service shall notify the applicant in writing of its determination. Upon service of this notice to the applicant, the provisions of section 336(b) of the Act will no longer apply to such applicant, until that applicant is no longer classifiable as an alien enemy.

(b) Upon completion of the investigation described in § 331.3, if the Service concludes that the applicant's loyalty and attachment to the United States have been fully established, the application may be granted.

HISTORY:

[56 FR 50494, Oct. 7, 1991, as confirmed at 60 FR 6650, Feb. 3, 1995]

AUTHORITY:

8 U.S.C. 1103, 1443.

PART 332

NATURALIZATION ADMINISTRATION

§ 332.1 Designation of USCIS employees to administer oaths and conduct examinations and hearings.

(a) Examinations. All USCIS officers are hereby designated to conduct the examination for naturalization required under section 335 of the Act, provided that each officer so designated has received appropriate training.

(b) Hearings. Section 336 of the Act authorizes USCIS officers who are designated under paragraph (a) of this section to conduct hearings under that section.

(c) Depositions. All USCIS officers who are designated under paragraph (a) of this section are hereby designated to take depositions in matters relating to the administration of naturalization and citizenship laws.

(d) Oaths and affirmations. All USCIS officers who are designated under paragraph (a) of this section are hereby designated to administer oaths or affirmations except for the oath of allegiance as provided in 8 CFR 337.2.

HISTORY:
[56 FR 50494, Oct. 7, 1991, as confirmed at 60 FR 6650, Feb. 3, 1995; 76 FR 53764, 53800, Aug. 29, 2011]

AUTHORITY:
8 U.S.C. 1103, 1443, 1447.

§ 332.2 [This section was removed and reserved. See 76 FR 53764, 53801, Aug. 29, 2011.]

[NO TEXT IN ORIGINAL]

HISTORY:
[51 FR 35628, Oct. 7, 1986; Redesignated and amended at 56 FR 50494, Oct. 7, 1991, as confirmed at 60 FR 6650, Feb. 3, 1995; 63 FR 12979, 12987, March 17, 1998; 76 FR 53764, 53801, Aug. 29, 2011]

AUTHORITY:
(8 U.S.C. 1103, 1443, 1447.)

§ 332.3 [This section was removed and reserved. See 76 FR 53764, 53801, Aug. 29, 2011.]

[NO TEXT IN ORIGINAL]

HISTORY:
[56 FR 50495, Oct. 7, 1991, as confirmed at 60 FR 6650, Feb. 3, 1995; 76 FR 53764, 53801, Aug. 29, 2011]

AUTHORITY:
(8 U.S.C. 1103, 1443, 1447.)

§ 332.4 [This section was removed and reserved. See 76 FR 53764, 53801, Aug. 29, 2011.]

[NO TEXT IN ORIGINAL]

HISTORY:
[22 FR 9818, Dec. 6, 1957; Redesignated at 56 FR 50495, Oct. 7, 1991, as confirmed at 60 FR 6650, Feb. 3, 1995; 76 FR 53764, 53801, Aug. 29, 2011]

AUTHORITY:
(8 U.S.C. 1103, 1443, 1447.)

§ 332.5 Official forms for use by clerks of court.

(a) Official forms essential to exercise of jurisdiction. Before exercising jurisdiction in naturalization proceedings, the naturalization court shall direct the clerk of such court upon written application to obtain from the Service, in accordance with section 310(c) of the Immigration and Nationality Act, proper forms, records, booked, and supplies required in naturalization proceedings. Such jurisdiction may not be exercised until such official forms, records, and books have been supplied to such court. Only such forms as are supplied shall be used in naturalization proceedings. Where sessions of the court are held at different places, the judge of such court may require the clerk to obtain a separate supply of official forms, records and books for each such place.

(b) Official forms prescribed for use of clerks of naturalization courts. Clerks of courts shall use only the forms listed in § 499.1 of this chapter in the exercise of naturalization jurisdiction.

(c) Initial application for official forms. Whenever the initial application for forms, records, books and supplies is made by a State court of record, it shall be accompanied by a certificate of the Attorney General of the State, certifying that the said court is a court of record, having a seal, a clerk, and jurisdiction in actions at law or in equity, or at law and in equity, in which the amount in controversy is unlimited.

(d) Subsequent application for use of official forms. Included with the initial supply of official forms, records, and books furnished to the various courts by the Service shall be Form N-3 entitled "Requisition for Forms and Binders," and thereafter such forms shall be used by clerks of courts in making requisition for forms, records, books, and supplies for use in naturalization proceedings in their respective courts.

HISTORY:
[22 FR 9817, Dec. 6, 1957; Redesignated and amended at 56 FR 50495, Oct. 7, 1991, as confirmed at 60 FR 6650, Feb. 3, 1995]

AUTHORITY:
8 U.S.C. 1103, 1443, 1447.

PART 333

PHOTOGRAPHS

§ 333.1 Description of required photographs.

(a) Every applicant who is required to provide photographs under section 333 of the Act must do so as prescribed by USCIS in its form instructions.

(b) The applicant, except in the case of a child or other person physically incapable of signing his or her name, shall sign each copy of the photograph on the front of the photograph with his or her full true name, in such manner as not to obscure the features. An applicant unable to write may make the signature by a mark. An applicant for naturalization must sign the photographs in the English language, unless the applicant is exempt from the English language requirement of part 312 of this chapter and is unable to sign in English, in which case the photographs may be signed in any language.

(c)(1) If a child is unable to sign his or her name, the photographs must be signed by a parent or guardian, the signature reading "(name of child) by (name of parent or guardian)."

(2) If an adult is physically unable to sign or make a mark, a guardian or the Service employee conducting the interview will sign the photographs as provided in paragraph (c)(1) of this section.

(d) The photographs must be signed when submitted with an application if the instructions accompanying the application so require. If signature is not required by the instructions, the photographs are to be submitted without being signed and shall be signed at such later time during the processing of the application as may be appropriate.

HISTORY:

[56 FR 50495, Oct. 7, 1991; 76 FR 53764, 53801, Aug. 29, 2011]

AUTHORITY:

8 U.S.C. 1103, 1443.

§ 333.2 Attachment of photographs to documents.

A photograph of the applicant must be securely and permanently attached to each certificate of naturalization or citizenship, or to any other document that requires a photograph, in a manner prescribed by USCIS.

HISTORY:

[56 FR 50495, Oct. 7, 1991; 76 FR 53764, 53801, Aug. 29, 2011]

AUTHORITY:

8 U.S.C. 1103, 1443.

PART 334

APPLICATION FOR NATURALIZATION

AUTHORITY NOTE APPLICABLE TO ENTIRE PART:

AUTHORITY:

8 U.S.C. 1103, 1443; 8 CFR part 2.

§ 334.1 Filing of application for naturalization.

Any person who is an applicant under sections 316, 319, 324, 325, 327, 328, 329, or 330 of the Act and the corresponding parts of this chapter, may apply for naturalization in accordance with the procedures prescribed in this chapter in accordance with the instructions on the form.

HISTORY:

[56 FR 50496, Oct. 7, 1991, as confirmed at 60 FR 6650, Feb. 3, 1995; 66 FR 32138, 32147, June 13, 2001; 74 FR 26933, 26941, June 5, 2009]

§ 334.2 Application for naturalization.

(a) An applicant may file an application for naturalization with required initial evidence in accordance with the general form instructions for naturalization. The applicant must include the fee as required in 8 CFR 106.2.

(b) An application for naturalization may be filed up to 90 days prior to the completion of the required period of residence, which may include the three-month period of residence required to establish jurisdiction under section 316(a) or 319(a) of the Act.

HISTORY:

[56 FR 50496, Oct. 7, 1991, as confirmed at 60 FR 6650, Feb. 3, 1995; 58 FR 48780, Sept. 20, 1993; 59 FR 47063, Sept. 14, 1994; 60 FR 14353, Mar. 17, 1995; 66 FR 32138, 32147, June 13, 2001; 76 FR 53764, 53801, Aug. 29, 2011; 85 FR 46788, 46929, Aug. 3, 2020]

§ 334.3 [Reserved]

[NO TEXT IN ORIGINAL]

§ 334.4 Investigation and report if applicant is sick or disabled.

Whenever it appears that an applicant for naturalization may be unable, because of sickness or other disability, to appear for the initial examination on the application or for any subsequent interview, the district director shall cause an investigation to be conducted to determine the circumstances surrounding the sickness or disability. The district director shall determine, based on available medical evidence, whether the sickness or disability is of a nature which so incapacitates the applicant as to prevent the applicant's appearance at a Service office having jurisdiction over the applicant's place of residence. If so, the district director shall designate another place where the applicant may appear for the requisite naturalization proceedings.

HISTORY:

[56 FR 50496, Oct. 7, 1991, as confirmed at 60 FR 6650, Feb. 3, 1995; 58 FR 49913, Sept. 24, 1993, as confirmed at 60 FR 6650, Feb. 3, 1995]

§ 334.5 Amendment of application for naturalization; reopening proceedings.

(a) **Clerical amendments —**

(1) By applicant. An applicant may request that the application for naturalization be amended either prior to or subsequent to the administration of the oath of allegiance.

(2) By Service. The Service may amend, at any time, an application for naturalization when in receipt of

information that clearly indicates that a clerical error has occurred.

(3) Amendment procedure. Any amendment will be limited to the correction of clerical errors arising from oversight or omission. If the amendment is approved, the amended application shall be filed with the original application for naturalization.

(b) Substantive amendments. Any substantive amendments which affect the jurisdiction or the decision on the merits of the application will not be authorized. When the Service is in receipt of any information that would indicate that an application for naturalization should not have been granted on the merits, the Service may institute proceedings to reopen the application before admission to citizenship, or to revoke the naturalization of a person who has been admitted to citizenship, in accordance with section 340 of the Act and § 335.5 of this chapter.

HISTORY:

[56 FR 50496, Oct. 7, 1991, as confirmed at 60 FR 6650, Feb. 3, 1995]

§§ 334.6 — 334.10 [Reserved]

[NO TEXT IN ORIGINAL]

HISTORY:

[NO SOURCE IN ORIGINAL]

§ 334.11 Declaration of intention.

(a) Application. Any person who is a lawful permanent resident over 18 years of age may file an application for a declaration of intention to become a citizen of the United States while present in the United States. Such application, with the requisite fee, shall be filed on the form specified by USCIS, in accordance with the form instructions.

(b) Approval. If approved, USCIS will retain the application in the file and advise the applicant of the action taken.

(c) Denial. If an application is denied, the applicant shall be notified in writing of the reasons for denial. No appeal shall lie from this decision.

HISTORY:

[56 FR 50496, Oct. 7, 1991, as confirmed at 60 FR 6650, Feb. 3, 1995; 58 FR 49913, Sept. 24, 1993, as confirmed at 60 FR 6650, Feb. 3, 1995; 74 FR 26933, 26941, June 5, 2009; 76 FR 53764, 53801, Aug. 29, 2011]

§§ 334.12 — 334.15 [Reserved]

[NO TEXT IN ORIGINAL]

HISTORY:

[NO SOURCE IN ORIGINAL]

§ 334.16 [This section was removed. See 76 FR 53764, 53801, Aug. 29, 2011.]

[NO TEXT IN ORIGINAL]

HISTORY:

[22 FR 9819, Dec. 6, 1957, as amended at 32 FR 9635, July 4, 1967; 45 FR 10313, Feb. 15, 1980; 56 FR 50496, Oct. 7, 1991; 76 FR 53764, 53801, Aug. 29, 2011]

AUTHORITY:

(8 U.S.C. 1103, 1443; 8 CFR part 2.)

§ 334.17 [This section was removed. See 76 FR 53764, 53801, Aug. 29, 2011.]

[NO TEXT IN ORIGINAL]

HISTORY:

[22 FR 9820, Dec. 6, 1957; 22 FR 9520, Nov. 28, 1957, as amended at 23 FR 5820, Aug. 1, 1958; 56 FR 50496, Oct. 7, 1991; 76 FR 53764, 53801, Aug. 29, 2011]

AUTHORITY:

(8 U.S.C. 1103, 1443; 8 CFR part 2.)

§ 334.18 [This section was removed. See 76 FR 53764, 53801, Aug. 29, 2011.]

[NO TEXT IN ORIGINAL]

HISTORY:

[22 FR 9819, Dec. 6, 1957, as amended at 56 FR 50496, Oct. 7, 1991; 76 FR 53764, 53801, Aug. 29, 2011]

AUTHORITY:

(8 U.S.C. 1103, 1443; 8 CFR part 2.)

PART 335

EXAMINATION ON APPLICATION FOR NATURALIZATION

§ 335.1 Investigation of applicant.

Subsequent to the filing of an application for naturalization, the Service shall conduct an investigation of the applicant. The investigation shall consist, at a minimum, of a review of all pertinent records, police department checks, and a neighborhood investigation in the vicinities where the applicant has resided and has been employed, or engaged in business, for at least the five years immediately preceding the filing of the application. The district director may waive the neighborhood investigation of the applicant provided for in this paragraph.

HISTORY:

[56 FR 50497, Oct. 7, 1991, as confirmed at 60 FR 6650, Feb 3, 1995]

AUTHORITY:

8 U.S.C. 1103, 1443, 1447.

§ 335.2 Examination of applicant.

(a) General. Subsequent to the filing of an application for naturalization, each applicant shall appear in person before a USCIS officer designated to conduct examinations pursuant to 8 CFR 332.1. The examination shall be uniform throughout the United States and shall encompass all factors relating to the applicant's eligibility for naturalization. The applicant may request the presence of an attorney or representative who has filed an appearance in accordance with part 292 of this chapter.

(b) Completion of criminal background checks before examination. USCIS will notify applicants for naturalization to appear before a USCIS officer for initial examination on the naturalization application only after USCIS has received a definitive response from the Federal Bureau of Investigation that a full criminal background check of an applicant has been completed. A definitive response that a full criminal background check on an applicant has been completed includes:

(1) Confirmation from the Federal Bureau of Investigation that an applicant does not have an administrative or a criminal record;

(2) Confirmation from the Federal Bureau of Investigation that an applicant has an administrative or a criminal record; or

(3) Confirmation from the Federal Bureau of Investigation that the fingerprint data submitted for the criminal background check has been rejected.

(c) Procedure. Prior to the beginning of the examination, USCIS shall make known to the applicant the official capacity in which the officer is conducting the examination. The applicant shall be questioned, under oath or affirmation, in a setting apart from the public. Whenever necessary, the examining officer shall correct written answers in the application for naturalization to conform to the oral statements made under oath or affirmation. USCIS shall maintain, for the record, brief notations of the examination for naturalization. At a minimum, the notations shall include a record of the test administered to the applicant on English literacy and basic knowledge of the history and government of the United States. USCIS may have a stenographic, mechanical, electronic, or videotaped transcript made, or may prepare an affidavit covering the testimony of the applicant. The questions to the applicant shall be repeated in different form and elaborated, if necessary, until the officer conducting the examination is satisfied that the applicant either fully understands the questions or is unable to understand English. The applicant and USCIS shall have the right to present such oral or documentary evidence and to conduct such cross-examination as may be required for a full and true disclosure of the facts.

(d) Witnesses. Witnesses, if called, shall be questioned under oath or affirmation to discover their own credibility and competency, as well as the extent of their personal knowledge of the applicant and his or her qualifications to become a naturalized citizen.

(1) Issuance of subpoenas. Subpoenas requiring the attendance of witnesses or the production of documentary evidence, or both, may be issued by the examining officer upon his or her own volition, or upon written request of the applicant or his or her attorney or representative. Such written request shall specify, as nearly as possible, the relevance, materiality, and scope of the testimony or documentary evidence sought and must show affirmatively that the testimony or documentary evidence cannot otherwise be produced. The examining officer shall document in the record his or her refusal to issue a subpoena at the request of the applicant.

(2) Service of subpoenas. Subpoenas will be issued on the form designated by USCIS and a record will be made of service. The subpoena may be served by any person over 18 years of age, not a party to the case, designated to make such service by USCIS.

(3) Witness fees. Mileage and fees for witnesses subpoenaed under this section shall be paid by the party at whose instance the subpoena is issued, at rates allowed and under conditions prescribed by the Service. Before issuing a subpoena, the officer may require the deposit of an amount adequate to cover the fees and mileage involved.

(4) Failure to appear. If the witness subpoenaed neglects or refuses to testify or to produce documentary evidence as directed by the subpoena, the district director shall request that the United States Attorney for the proper district report such neglect or refusal to any District Court of the United States, and file a motion in such court for an order directing the witness to appear and to testify and produce the documentary evidence described in the subpoena.

(5) Extraterritorial testimony. The testimony of a witness may be taken outside the United States. The witness's name and address shall be sent to the Service office abroad which has jurisdiction over the witness's residence. The officer taking the statement shall be given express instructions regarding any aspect of the case which may require special development or emphasis during the interrogation of the witness.

(e) Record of examination. At the conclusion of the examination, all corrections made on the application form and all supplemental material shall be consecutively numbered and listed in the space provided on the applicant's affidavit contained in the application form. The affidavit shall be executed under the following oath (or affirmation): "I swear (affirm) and certify under penalty of perjury under the laws of the United States of America that I know that the contents of this application for naturalization subscribed by me, and the evidence submitted with it, are true and correct to the best of my knowledge and belief." The affidavit must then be subscribed and sworn to, or affirmed, by the applicant and signed by the USCIS officer. Evidence received by the officer shall be placed into the record for determination of the case. All documentary or written evidence shall be properly identified and introduced into the record as exhibits by number, unless read into the record. A deposition or statement taken by a USCIS officer during the initial examination or any subsequent examination shall be included as part of the record on the application.

(f) Use of interpreter. If the use of an interpreter is authorized pursuant to 8 CFR 312.4, the examining officer shall note on the application the use and identity of any interpreter. If the USCIS officer is proficient in the applicant's native language, the USCIS officer may conduct the examination in that language with the consent of the applicant.

HISTORY:

[56 FR 50497, Oct. 7, 1991, as confirmed at 60 FR 6650, Feb. 3, 1995; 58 FR 49913, Sept. 24, 1993, as confirmed at 60 FR 6650, Feb. 3, 1995; 63 FR 12979, 12987, March 17, 1998; 76 FR 53764, 53801, Aug. 29, 2011]

AUTHORITY:

8 U.S.C. 1103, 1443, 1447.

§ 335.3 Determination on application; continuance of examination.

(a) USCIS shall grant the application if the applicant has complied with all requirements for naturalization under this chapter. A decision to grant or deny the application shall be made at the time of the initial examination or within 120-days after the date of the initial examination of the applicant for naturalization under § 335.2. The applicant shall be notified that the application has been granted or denied and, if the application has been granted, of the procedures to be followed for the administration of the oath of allegiance pursuant to part 337 of this chapter.

(b) Rather than make a determination on the application, USCIS may continue the initial examination on an application for one reexamination, to afford the applicant an opportunity to overcome deficiencies on the application that may arise during the examination. The officer must inform the applicant in writing of the grounds to be overcome or the evidence to be submitted. The applicant shall not be required to appear for a reexamination earlier than 60 days after the first examination. However, the reexamination on the continued case shall be scheduled within the 120-day period after the initial examination, except as otherwise provided under § 312.5(b) of this chapter. If the applicant is unable to overcome the deficiencies in the application, the application shall be denied pursuant to § 336.1 of this chapter.

HISTORY:

[56 FR 50497, Oct. 7, 1991, as confirmed at 60 FR 6650, Feb. 3, 1995; 58 FR 49914, Sept. 24, 1993, as confirmed at 60 FR 6650, Feb. 3, 1995; 76 FR 53764, 53801, Aug. 29, 2011]

AUTHORITY:

8 U.S.C. 1103, 1443, 1447.

§ 335.4 Use of record of examination.

In the event that an application is denied, the record of the examination on the application for naturalization, including the executed and corrected application form and supplements, affidavits, transcripts of testimony, documents, and other evidence, shall be submitted to the USCIS officer described in 8 CFR 332.1 to conduct hearings on denials of applications for naturalization in accordance with part 336 of this chapter. The record of the examination shall be used for examining the petitioner and witnesses, if required to properly dispose of issues raised in the matter.

HISTORY:

[56 FR 50498, Oct. 7, 1991, as confirmed at 60 FR 6650, Feb. 3, 1995; 76 FR 53764, 53801, Aug. 29, 2011]

AUTHORITY:

8 U.S.C. 1103, 1443, 1447.

§ 335.5 Receipt of derogatory information after grant.

In the event that USCIS receives derogatory information concerning an applicant whose application has already been granted as provided in § 335.3(a) of this chapter, but who has not yet taken the oath of allegiance as provided in part 337 of this chapter, USCIS shall remove the applicant's name from any list of granted applications or of applicants scheduled for administration of the oath of allegiance, until such time as the matter can be resolved. USCIS shall notify the applicant in writing of the receipt of the specific derogatory information, with a motion to reopen the previously adjudicated application, giving the applicant 15 days to respond. If the applicant overcomes the derogatory information, the application will be granted and the applicant will be scheduled for administration of the oath of allegiance. Otherwise the motion to reopen will be granted and the application will be denied pursuant to § 336.1 of this chapter.

HISTORY:

[56 FR 50498, Oct. 7, 1991, as confirmed at 60 FR 6650, Feb. 3, 1995; 58 FR 49914, Sept. 24, 1993, as confirmed at 60 FR 6650, Feb. 3, 1995; 76 FR 53764, 53801, Aug. 29, 2011]

AUTHORITY:

8 U.S.C. 1103, 1443, 1447.

§ 335.6 Failure to appear for examination.

(a) An applicant for naturalization shall be deemed to have abandoned his or her application if he or she fails to appear for the examination pursuant to § 335.3 and fails to notify USCIS of the reason for non-appearance within 30 days of the scheduled examination. Such notification shall be in writing and contain a request for rescheduling of the examination. In the absence of a timely notification, USCIS may administratively close the application without making a decision on the merits.

(b) An applicant may reopen an administratively closed application by submitting a written request to USCIS within one (1) year from the date the application was closed. Such reopening shall be without additional fee. The date of the request for reopening shall be the date of filing of the application for purposes of determining eligibility for naturalization.

(c) If the applicant does not request reopening of an administratively closed application within one year from the date the application was closed, USCIS will consider that application to have been abandoned, and shall dismiss the application without further notice to the applicant.

HISTORY:

[58 FR 49914, Sept. 24, 1993, as confirmed and revised at 60 FR 6650, 6651, Feb. 2, 1995; 76 FR 53764, 53801, Aug. 29, 2011]

AUTHORITY:

8 U.S.C. 1103, 1443, 1447.

§ 335.7 Failure to prosecute application after initial examination.

An applicant for naturalization who has appeared for the examination on his or her application as provided in 8 CFR 335.2 will be considered as failing to prosecute such application if he or she, without good cause being shown, either failed to excuse an absence from a subsequently required appearance, or fails to provide within a reasonable period of time such documents, information, or testimony deemed by USCIS to be necessary to establish his or her eligibility for naturalization. USCIS will deliver notice of requests for appearance or evidence as provided in 8 CFR 103.8. In the event that the applicant fails to respond within 30 days of the date of notification, USCIS will adjudicate the application on the merits pursuant to 8 CFR 336.1.

HISTORY:

[58 FR 49914, Sept. 24, 1993, as confirmed and revised at 60 FR 6650, 6651, Feb. 3, 1995; 76 FR 53764, 53801, Aug. 29, 2011]

AUTHORITY:

8 U.S.C. 1103, 1443, 1447.

§ 335.8 [Reserved]

[NO TEXT IN ORIGINAL]

§ 335.9 Transfer of application.

(a) Request for transfer of application. An applicant who, after filing an application for naturalization, changes residence, or plans to change residence within three months, may request, in writing, that a pending application be transferred from the current USCIS office to the USCIS office having jurisdiction over the applicant's new place of residence. The request shall be submitted to the office where the application was originally filed. The request shall include the applicant's name, alien registration number, date of birth, complete current address including name of the county, complete address at the time of filing the application, reason for the request to transfer the application, and the date the applicant moved or intends to move to the new jurisdiction.

(b) Discretion to authorize transfer. USCIS may authorize the transfer of an application for naturalization after such application has been filed. In the event that USCIS does not consent to the transfer of the application, the application shall be adjudicated on its merits by USCIS office retaining jurisdiction. If upon such adjudication the application is denied, the written decision pursuant to § 336.1 of this chapter shall also address the reason(s) for USCIS's decision not to consent to the transfer request.

HISTORY:

[56 FR 50498, Oct. 7, 1991, as confirmed at 60 FR 6650, Feb. 3, 1995; 58 FR 49914, Sept. 24, 1993, as confirmed at 60 FR 6650, Feb. 3, 1995; 76 FR 53764, 53801, Aug. 29, 2011, as corrected at 76 FR 73475, Nov. 29, 2011]

AUTHORITY:

8 U.S.C. 1103, 1443, 1447.

§ 335.10 Withdrawal of application.

An applicant may request, in writing, that his or her application, filed with USCIS, be withdrawn. If USCIS consents to the withdrawal, the application will be denied without further notice to the applicant and without prejudice to any future application. The withdrawal by the applicant will constitute a waiver of any review pursuant to part 336 of this chapter. If USCIS does not consent to the withdrawal, the application for naturalization shall be adjudicated on its merits.

HISTORY:

[56 FR 50498, Oct. 7, 1991, as confirmed at 60 FR 6650, Feb. 3, 1995; 76 FR 53764, 53801, Aug. 29, 2011]

AUTHORITY:

8 U.S.C. 1103, 1443, 1447.

§ 335.11 [This section was removed. See 76 FR 53764, 53802, Aug. 29, 2011.]

[NO TEXT IN ORIGINAL]

HISTORY:

[22 FR 9821, Dec. 6, 1957, as amended at 23 FR 2673, Apr. 23, 1958; 45 FR 83195, Dec. 18, 1980; 46 FR 5861, Jan. 21, 1981; 47 FR 10778, Mar. 12, 1982; 56 FR 50498, Oct. 7, 1991, as confirmed at 60 FR 6650, Feb. 3, 1995; 76 FR 53764, 53802, Aug. 29, 2011]

AUTHORITY:

(8 U.S.C. 1103, 1443, 1447.)

§ 335.12 [This section was removed. See 76 FR 53764, 53802, Aug. 29, 2011.]

[NO TEXT IN ORIGINAL]

HISTORY:

[38 FR 29878, Oct. 30, 1973, as amended at 56 FR 50498, Oct. 7, 1991, as confirmed at 60 FR 6650, Feb. 3, 1995; 76 FR 53764, 53802, Aug. 29, 2011]

AUTHORITY:

(8 U.S.C. 1103, 1443, 1447.)

§ 335.13 [This section was removed. See 76 FR 53764, 53802, Aug. 29, 2011.]

[NO TEXT IN ORIGINAL]

HISTORY:

[22 FR 9822, Dec. 6, 1957, as amended at 35 FR 17530, Nov. 14, 1970; 56 FR 50498, Oct. 7, 1991, as confirmed at 60 FR 6650, Feb. 3, 1995; 76 FR 53764, 53802, Aug. 29, 2011]

AUTHORITY:

(8 U.S.C. 1103, 1443, 1447.)

PART 336

HEARINGS ON DENIALS OF APPLICATIONS FOR NATURALIZATION

§ 336.1 Denial after section 335 examination.

(a) After completing all examination procedures contained in part 335 of this chapter and determining to deny an application for naturalization, USCIS will serve a written notice of denial upon an applicant for naturalization no later than 120 days after the date of the applicant's first examination on the application.

(b) A notice of denial shall be prepared in a written, narrative format, and shall recite, in clear concise language, the pertinent facts upon which the determination was based, the specific legal section or sections applicable to the finding of ineligibility, and the conclusions of law reached by the examining officer in rendering the decision. Such notice of denial shall also contain a specific statement of the applicant's right either to accept the determination of the examining officer, or request a hearing before an immigration officer.

(c) Service of the notice of denial must be by personal service as described in 8 CFR 103.8, or upon the attorney or representative of record as provided in part 292 of this chapter.

HISTORY:
[56 FR 50499, Oct. 7, 1991, as confirmed at 60 FR 6650, Feb. 3, 1995; 76 FR 53764, 53802, Aug. 29, 2011]

AUTHORITY:
8 U.S.C. 1103, 1443, 1447, 1448.

§ 336.2 USCIS hearing.

(a) The applicant, or his or her authorized representative, may request a hearing on the denial of the applicant's application for naturalization by filing a request with USCIS within thirty days after the applicant receives the notice of denial.

(b) Upon receipt of a timely request for a hearing, USCIS will schedule a review hearing, within a reasonable period of time not to exceed 180 days from the date upon which the appeal is filed. The review will be with an officer other than the officer who conducted the original examination or who rendered determination upon which the hearing is based, and who is classified at a grade level equal to or higher than the grade of the examining officer. The reviewing officer will have the authority and discretion to review the application for naturalization, to examine the applicant, and either to affirm the findings and determination of the original examining officer or to re-determine the original decision in whole or in part. The reviewing officer will also have the discretion to review any administrative record which was created as part of the examination procedures as well USCIS files and reports. He or she may receive new evidence or take such additional testimony as may be deemed relevant to the applicant's eligibility for naturalization or which the applicant seeks to provide. Based upon the complexity of the issues to be reviewed or determined, and upon the necessity of conducting further examinations with respect to essential naturalization requirements, such as literacy or civics knowledge, the reviewing immigration officer may, in his or her discretion, conduct a full de novo hearing or may utilize a less formal review procedure, as he or she deems reasonable and in the interest of justice.

(c) Improperly filed request for hearing.

(1) Request for hearing filed by a person or entity not entitled to file

(i) Rejection without refund of filing fee. A request for hearing filed by a person or entity who is not entitled to file such a request must be rejected as improperly filed. In such a case, any filing fee will not be refunded.

(ii) Request for hearing by attorney or representative without proper Form G-28. If a request for hearing is filed by an attorney or representative who has not properly filed a notice of entry of appearance as attorney or representative entitling that person to file the request for hearing, the appeal will be considered as improperly filed. In such a case, any filing fee will not be refunded regardless of the action taken. The reviewing official will ask the attorney or representative to submit a proper notice of entry within 15 days of the request. If such notice is not submitted within the time allowed, the official may, on his or her own motion, under 8 CFR 103.5(a)(5)(i), make a new decision favorable to the affected party without notifying the attorney or representative. The request for hearing may be considered properly filed as of its original filing date if the attorney or representative submits a properly executed notice entitling that person to file the request for hearing.

(2) Untimely request for hearing.

(i) Rejection without refund of filing fee. A request for hearing which is not filed within the time period allowed must be rejected as improperly filed. In such a case, any filing fee will not be refunded.

(ii) Untimely request for hearing treated as motion. If an untimely request for hearing meets the requirements of a motion to reopen as described in 8 CFR 103.5(a)(2) or a motion to reconsider as described in 8 CFR 103.5(a)(3), the request for hearing must be treated as a motion and a decision must be made on the merits of the case.

HISTORY:
[56 FR 50499, Oct. 7, 1991, as confirmed at 60 FR 6650, Feb. 3, 1995 58 FR 49914, Sept. 24, 1993, as confirmed at 60 FR 6650, Feb. 3, 1995; 76 FR 53764, 53802, Aug. 29, 2011]

AUTHORITY:
8 U.S.C. 1103, 1443, 1447, 1448.

§§ 336.3 — 336.8 [Reserved]

[NO TEXT IN ORIGINAL]

HISTORY:
56 FR 50499, Oct. 7, 1991.

AUTHORITY:
8 U.S.C. 1103, 1443, 1447, 1448.

§ 336.9 Judicial review of denial determinations on applications for naturalization.

(a) General. The provisions in part 310 of this chapter shall provide the sole and exclusive procedures for requesting judicial review of final determinations on applications for naturalization made pursuant to section 336(a) of the Act and the provisions of this chapter by USCIS on or after October 1, 1991.

(b) Filing a petition. Under these procedures, an applicant must file a petition for review in the United States District Court having jurisdiction over his or her place of residence, in accordance with Chapter 7 of Title 5, United States Code, within a period of not more than 120 days after the USCIS final determination. The petition for review must be brought against USCIS, and service of the petition for review must be made upon DHS and upon the USCIS office where the hearing was held pursuant to 8 CFR 336.2.

(c) Standard of review. The review will be de novo, and the court will make its own findings of fact and conclusions of law. The court may also conduct, at the request of the petitioner, a hearing de novo on the application for naturalization.

(d) Exhaustion of remedies. A USCIS determination denying an application for naturalization under section 335(a) of the Act shall not be subject to judicial review until the applicant has exhausted those administrative remedies available to the applicant under section 336 of the Act. Every petition for judicial review shall state whether the validity of the final determination to deny an application for naturalization has been upheld in any prior administrative proceeding and, if so, the nature and date of such proceeding and the forum in which such proceeding took place.

HISTORY:

[56 FR 50499, Oct. 7, 1991; 76 FR 53764, 53802, Aug. 29, 2011]

AUTHORITY:

8 U.S.C. 1103, 1443, 1447, 1448.

PART 337

OATH OF ALLEGIANCE

AUTHORITY NOTE APPLICABLE TO ENTIRE PART:

AUTHORITY:

8 U.S.C. 1103, 1443, 1448; 8 CFR part 2.

§ 337.1 Oath of allegiance.

(a) Form of oath. Except as otherwise provided in the Act and after receiving notice from the district director that such applicant is eligible for naturalization pursuant to § 335.3 of this chapter, an applicant for naturalization shall, before being admitted to citizenship, take in a public ceremony held within the United States the following oath of allegiance, to a copy of which the applicant shall affix his or her signature:

I hereby declare, on oath, that I absolutely and entirely renounce and abjure all allegiance and fidelity to any foreign prince, potentate, state, or sovereignty, of whom or which I have heretofore been a subject or citizen; that I will support and defend the Constitution and laws of the United States of America against all enemies, foreign and domestic; that I will bear true faith and allegiance to the same; that I will bear arms on behalf of the United States when required by the law; that I will perform noncombatant service in the Armed Forces of the United States when required by the law; that I will perform work of national importance under civilian direction when required by the law; and that I take this obligation freely, without any mental reservation or purpose of evasion; so help me God.

(b) Alteration of form of oath; affirmation in lieu of oath. In those cases in which a petitioner or applicant for naturalization is exempt from taking the oath prescribed in paragraph (a) of this section in its entirety, the inapplicable clauses shall be deleted and the oath shall be taken in such altered form. When a petitioner or applicant for naturalization, by reason of religious training and belief (or individual interpretation thereof), or for other reasons of good conscience, cannot take the oath prescribed in paragraph (a) of this section with the words "on oath" and "so help me God" included, the words "and solemnly affirm" shall be substituted for the words "on oath," the words "so help me God" shall be deleted, and the oath shall be taken in such modified form. Any reference to 'oath of allegiance' in this chapter is understood to mean equally 'affirmation of allegiance' as described in this paragraph.

(c) Obligations of oath. A petitioner or applicant for naturalization shall, before being naturalized, establish that it is his or her intention, in good faith, to assume and discharge the obligations of the oath of allegiance, and that his or her attitude toward the Constitution and laws of the United States renders him or her capable of fulfilling the obligations of such oath.

(d) Renunciation of title or order of nobility. A petitioner or applicant for naturalization who has borne any hereditary title or has been of any of the orders of nobility in any foreign state shall, in addition to taking the oath of allegiance prescribed in paragraph (a) of this section, make under oath or affirmation in public an express renunciation of such title or order of nobility, in the following form:

(1) I further renounce the title of (give title or titles) which I have heretofore held; or

(2) I further renounce the order of nobility (give the order of nobility) to which I have heretofore belonged.

HISTORY:

[22 FR 9824, Dec. 6, 1957, as amended at 24 FR 2584, Apr. 3, 1959; 32 FR 13756, Oct. 3, 1967; 56 FR 50499, Oct. 7, 1991, as confirmed at 60 FR 6650, Feb. 3, 1995]

§ 337.2 Oath administered by USCIS or EOIR.

(a) Public ceremony. An applicant for naturalization who has elected to have his or her oath of allegiance administered by USCIS or an immigration judge and is not subject to the exclusive oath administration authority of an eligible court pursuant to section 310(b) of the Act must appear in person in a public ceremony, unless such appearance is specifically excused under the terms and conditions set forth in this part. Such ceremony will be held at a time and place designated by USCIS or EOIR within the United States (or abroad as permitted for certain applicants in accordance with 8 U.S.C. 1443a) and within the jurisdiction where the application for naturalization was filed, or into which the application for naturalization was transferred pursuant to 8 CFR 335.9. Naturalization ceremonies will be conducted at regular intervals as frequently as necessary to ensure timely naturalization, but in all events at least once monthly where it is required to minimize unreasonable delays. Naturalization ceremonies will be presented in such a manner as to preserve the dignity and significance of the occasion.

(b) Authority to administer oath of allegiance. The Secretary may delegate authority to administer the oath of allegiance prescribed in section 337 of the Act to such officials of DHS and to immigration judges or officials designated by the Attorney General as may be necessary for the efficient administration of the naturalization program.

(c) Execution of questionnaire. Immediately prior to being administered the oath of allegiance, each applicant must complete the questionnaire on the form designated by USCIS. USCIS will review each completed questionnaire and may further question the applicant regarding the responses provided. If derogatory information is revealed, USCIS will remove the applicant's name from the list of eligible persons as provided in 8 CFR 335.5 and he or she will not be administered the oath.

HISTORY:

[56 FR 50500, Oct. 7, 1993, as confirmed at 60 FR 6650, Feb. 3, 1995; 58 FR 49915, Sept. 24, 1993, as confirmed at 60 FR 6650, Feb. 3, 1995; 60 FR 37803, July 24, 1995; 76 FR 53764, 53802, Aug. 29, 2011]

§ 337.3 Expedited administration of oath of allegiance.

(a) An applicant may be granted an expedited oath administration ceremony by either the court or USCIS upon demonstrating sufficient cause. In determining whether to grant an expedited oath administration ceremony, the court or USCIS shall consider special circumstances of a compelling or humanitarian nature. Special circumstances may include but are not limited to:

(1) The serious illness of the applicant or a member of the applicant's family;

(2) Permanent disability of the applicant sufficiently incapacitating as to prevent the applicant's personal appearance at a scheduled ceremony;

(3) The developmental disability or advanced age of the applicant which would make appearance at a scheduled ceremony inapproriate; or

(4) Urgent or compelling circumstances relating to travel or employment determined by the court or USCIS to be sufficiently meritorious to warrant special consideration.

(b) Courts exercising exclusive authority may either hold an expedited oath administration ceremony or refer the applicant to USCIS in order for either the Immigration Judge or USCIS to conduct an oath administration ceremony, if an expedited judicial oath administration ceremony is impractical. The court shall inform USCIS in writing of its decision to grant the applicant an expedited oath administration ceremony and that the court has relinquished exclusive jurisdiction as to that applicant.

(c) All requests for expedited administration of the oath of allegiance shall be made in writing to either the court or USCIS. Such requests shall contain sufficient information to substantiate the claim of special circumstances to permit either the court or USCIS to properly exercise the discretionary authority to grant the relief sought. The court or USCIS may seek verification of the validity of the information provided in the request. If the applicant submits a written request to USCIS, but is awaiting an oath administration ceremony by a court pursuant to § 337.8, USCIS promptly shall provide the court with a copy of the request without reaching a decision on whether to grant or deny the request.

HISTORY:

[56 FR 50500, Oct. 7, 1991, as confirmed and revised at 60 FR 6650, 6651, Feb. 3, 1995; 58 FR 49915, Sept. 24, 1993, as confirmed and revised at 60 FR 6650, 6651, Feb. 3, 1995; 60 FR 37804, July 24, 1995; 76 FR 53764, 53803, Aug. 29, 2011]

§ 337.4 When requests for change of name granted.

When the court has granted the petitioner's change of name request, the petitioner shall subscribe his or her new name to the written oath of allegiance.

HISTORY:

[56 FR 50500, Oct. 7, 1991, as confirmed at 60 FR 6650, Feb. 3, 1995]

§§ 337.5 — 337.6 [Reserved]

[NO TEXT IN ORIGINAL]

HISTORY:

[NO SOURCE IN ORIGINAL]

§ 337.7 Information and assignment of individuals under exclusive jurisdiction.

(a) No later than at the time of the examination on the application pursuant to § 335.2 of this chapter, an employee of USCIS shall advise the applicant of his or her right to elect the site for the administration of the oath of allegiance, subject to the exclusive jurisdiction provision of § 310.3(d) of this chapter. In order to assist the applicant in making an informed decision, USCIS shall advise the applicant of the upcoming Immigration Judge or USCIS conducted and judicial ceremonies at which the applicant may appear, if found eligible for naturalization.

(b) An applicant whose application has been approved by USCIS who is subject to the exclusive jurisdiction of a court pursuant to § 310.2(d) of this chapter, shall be advised of the next available court ceremony and provided with a written notice to appear at that ceremony. If the applicant is subject to the exclusive jurisdiction of more than one court exercising exclusive jurisdiction, the applicant will be informed of the upcoming ceremonies in each affected court. The applicant shall decide which court he or she wishes to administer the oath of allegiance.

HISTORY:

[58 FR 49915, Sept. 24, 1993, as confirmed at 60 FR 6650, Feb. 3, 1995; 60 FR 37804, July 24, 1995; 76 FR 53764, 53803, Aug. 29, 2011]

§ 337.8 Oath administered by the courts.

(a) Notification of election. An applicant for naturalization not subject to the exclusive jurisdiction of 8 CFR 310.2(d) must notify USCIS at the time of the filing of, or no later than at the examination on, the application of his or her election to have the oath of allegiance administered in an appropriate court having jurisdiction over the applicant's place of residence.

(b) **Certificate of eligibility.**

(1) Exclusive jurisdiction. In those instances falling within the exclusive jurisdiction provision of section 310(b)(1)(B) of the Act, USCIS will notify the court of the applicant's eligibility for admission to United States citizenship by notifying the clerk of the court within 10 days of the approval of the application.

(2) Non-exclusive jurisdiction. In those instances in which the applicant has elected to have the oath administered in a court ceremony, USCIS will notify the clerk of the court in writing that the applicant has been determined by the USCIS to be eligible for admission to United States citizenship upon taking the requisite oath of allegiance and renunciation in a public ceremony. If a scheduled hearing date is not available at the time of notification, USCIS will notify the applicant in writing that the applicant has been approved but no ceremony date is yet available.

(c) **Preparation of lists.**

(1) At or prior to the oath administration ceremony, the representative attending the ceremony will submit to the court, in duplicate, lists of persons to be administered the oath of allegiance and renunciation. After the ceremony, and after any required amendments and notations have been made to the lists, the clerk of the court will sign the lists.

(2) The originals of all court lists specified in this section will be filed permanently in the court, and the duplicates returned by the clerk of the court to USCIS. The same disposition will be made of any list presented to, but not approved by, the court.

(d) Personal representation of the government at oath administration ceremonies. An oath administration ceremony must be attended by a representative of USCIS who will review each completed questionnaire and may further question the applicant regarding the responses provided. If derogatory information is revealed, the USCIS representative will remove the applicant's name from the list of eligible persons as provided in 8 CFR 335.5 and the court will not administer the oath to such applicant.

(e) Written report in lieu of personal representation. If it is impractical for a USCIS representative to be present at a judicial oath administration ceremony, written notice of that fact will be given by the USCIS to the court. The list of persons to be administered the oath of allegiance and renunciation, forms, memoranda, and certificates will be transmitted to the clerk of the court, who will submit the appropriate lists to the court.

(f) Withdrawal from court. An applicant for naturalization not subject to the exclusive jurisdiction of 8 CFR 310.3(d) who has elected to have the oath administered in a court oath ceremony may, for good cause shown, request that his or her name be removed from the list of persons eligible to be administered the oath at a court oath ceremony and request that the oath be administered by an immigration judge or USCIS. Such request must be in writing to the USCIS office which granted the application and must cite the reasons for the request. USCIS will consider the good cause shown and the best interests of the applicant in making a decision. If it is determined that the applicant will be permitted to withdraw his or her name from the court ceremony, USCIS will give written notice to the court of the applicant's withdrawal, and the applicant will be scheduled for the next available oath ceremony, conducted by an Immigration Judge or USCIS, as if he or she had never elected the court ceremony.

HISTORY:

[56 FR 50500, Oct. 7, 1991, as confirmed at 60 FR 6650, Feb. 3, 1995; 58 FR 49914, Sept. 24, 1993, as confirmed at 60 FR 6650, Feb. 3, 1995; 60 FR 37804, July 24, 1995; 76 FR 53764, 53803, Aug. 29, 2011]

§ 337.9 Effective date of naturalization.

(a) An applicant for naturalization shall be deemed a citizen of the United States as of the date on which the applicant takes the prescribed oath of allegiance in an administrative ceremony or in a ceremony conducted by an appropriate court under § 337.8 of this chapter.

(b) [Reserved]

HISTORY:

[56 FR 50500, Oct. 7, 1991, as confirmed at 60 FR 6650, Feb. 3, 1995; 60 FR 37804, July 24, 1995, 66 FR 32138, 32147, June 13, 2001; 76 FR 53764, 53803, Aug. 29, 2011]

§ 337.10 Failure to appear for oath administration ceremony.

An applicant who fails to appear without good cause for more than one oath administration ceremony for which he or she was duly notified shall be presumed to have abandoned his or her intent to be naturalized. Such presumption shall be regarded as the receipt of derogatory information, and the procedures contained in § 335.5 of this chapter shall be followed.

HISTORY:

[58 FR 49916, Sept. 24, 1993, as confirmed at 60 FR 6650, Feb. 3, 1995]

PART 338

CERTIFICATE OF NATURALIZATION

AUTHORITY NOTE APPLICABLE TO ENTIRE PART:

AUTHORITY:
8 U.S.C. 1103, 1443; 8 CFR part 2.

§ 338.1 Execution and issuance of certificate.

(a) Issuance. When an applicant for naturalization has taken and subscribed to the oath of allegiance in accordance with 8 CFR part 337, USCIS will issue a Certificate of Naturalization at the conclusion of the oath administration ceremony.

(b) Contents of certificate. The certificate must be issued to the applicant in accordance with section 338 of the Act in his or her true, full, and correct name as it exists at the time of the administration of the oath of allegiance. The certificate must show, under "country of former nationality," the name of the applicant's last country of citizenship, as shown in the application and USCIS records, even though the applicant may be stateless at the time of admission to citizenship.

HISTORY:
[56 FR 50501, Oct. 7, 1991, as confirmed at 60 FR 6650, Feb. 3, 1995; 58 FR 49916, Sept. 24, 1993, as confirmed at 60 FR 6650, Feb. 3, 1995; 76 FR 53764, 53803, Aug. 29, 2011]

§ 338.2 Execution in case name is changed.

Whenever the name of an applicant has been changed by order of a court as a part of a naturalization, the clerk of court, or his or her authorized deputy, shall forward a copy of the order changing the applicant's name with the notifications required by part 339 of this chapter. The Certificate of Naturalization will be issued to the applicant in the name as changed.

HISTORY:
[56 FR 50501, Oct. 7, 1991, as confirmed at 60 FR 6650, Feb. 3, 1995]

§ 338.3 Delivery of certificates.

No Certificate of Naturalization will be delivered in any case in which the naturalized person has not surrendered his or her Permanent Resident Card to USCIS. Upon a finding that the card is destroyed or otherwise unavailable, USCIS may waive the surrender of the card and the Certificate of Naturalization shall then be delivered to the naturalized person.

HISTORY:
[56 FR 50501, Oct. 7, 1991, as confirmed at 60 FR 6650, Feb. 3, 1995; 63 FR 70313, 70316, Dec. 21, 1998; 76 FR 53764, 53803, Aug. 29, 2011]

§ 338.4 [Reserved]

[NO TEXT IN THE ORIGINAL]

§ 338.5 Correction of certificates.

(a) Application. Whenever a Certificate of Naturalization has been delivered which does not conform to the facts shown on the application for naturalization, or a clerical error was made in preparing the certificate, an application for issuance of a corrected certificate may be filed, without fee, in accordance with the form instructions.

(b) Court-issued certificates. If the certificate was originally issued by a clerk of court under a prior statute and USCIS finds that a correction is justified and can be made without mutilating the certificate, USCIS will authorize the issuing court to make the necessary correction and to place a dated endorsement of the court on the reverse of the certificate explaining the correction. The authorization will be filed with the naturalization record of the court, the corrected certificate will be returned to the naturalized person, and the duplicate will be endorsed to show the date and nature of the correction and endorsement made, and then returned to USCIS. No fee will be charged the naturalized person for the correction.

(c) USCIS-issued certificates. If the certificate was originally issued by USCIS (or its predecessor agency), and USCIS finds that a correction was justified, the correction shall be made to the certificate and a dated endorsement made on the reverse of the certificate.

(d) Administrative actions. When a correction made pursuant to paragraphs (b) or (c) of this section would or does result in mutilation of a certificate, USCIS will issue a replacement Certificate of Naturalization and destroy the surrendered certificate.

(e) Data change. The correction will not be deemed to be justified where the naturalized person later alleges that the name or date of birth which the applicant stated to be his or her correct name or date of birth at the time of naturalization was not in fact his or her name or date of birth at the time of the naturalization.

HISTORY:
[56 FR 50501, Oct. 7, 1991, as confirmed at 60 FR 6650, Feb. 3, 1995; 76 FR 53764, 53803, Aug. 29, 2011]

§§ 338.6 — 338.10 [Reserved]

[NO TEXT IN ORIGINAL]

HISTORY:
[NO SOURCE IN ORIGINAL]

§ 338.11 [This section was removed and reserved. See 76 FR 53764, 53804, Aug. 29, 2011.]

[NO TEXT IN ORIGINAL]

HISTORY:
[56 FR 30679, July 5, 1991, as amended at 56 FR 50501, Oct. 7, 1991, as confirmed at 60 FR 6650, Feb. 3, 1995; 76 FR 53764, 53804, Aug. 29, 2011]

AUTHORITY:
(8 U.S.C. 1103, 1443; 8 CFR part 2.)

§ 338.12 [This section was removed and reserved. See 76 FR 53764, 53804, Aug. 29, 2011.]

[NO TEXT IN ORIGINAL]

HISTORY:
[56 FR 30680, July 5, 1991; 56 FR 38485, Aug. 13, 1991, as

amended at 56 FR 50501, Oct. 7, 1991, as confirmed at 60 FR 6650, Feb. 3, 1995; 76 FR 53764, 53804, Aug. 29, 2011]

AUTHORITY:
(8 U.S.C. 1103, 1443; 8 CFR part 2.)

§ 338.13 [This section was removed and reserved. See 76 FR 53764, 53804, Aug. 29, 2011.]

[NO TEXT IN ORIGINAL]

HISTORY:
[22 FR 9824, Dec. 6, 1957, as amended at 56 FR 50502, Oct. 7, 1991, as confirmed at 60 FR 6650, Feb. 3, 1995; 76 FR 53764, 53804, Aug. 29, 2011]

AUTHORITY:
(8 U.S.C. 1103, 1443; 8 CFR part 2.)

PART 339

FUNCTIONS AND DUTIES OF CLERKS OF COURT REGARDING NATURALIZATION PROCEEDINGS

§ 339.1 Administration of oath of allegiance to applicants for naturalization.

It shall be the duty of a judge of a court that administers an oath of allegiance to ensure that such oath is administered to each applicant for naturalization who has chosen to appear before the court. The clerk of court shall issue to each person to whom such oath is administered the Certificate of Naturalization provided by USCIS in accordance with 8 CFR 338.1. The clerk of court shall provide to each person whose name was changed as part of the naturalization proceedings, pursuant to section 336(e) of the Act, certified evidence of such name change.

HISTORY:
[56 FR 50502, Oct. 7, 1991, as confirmed at 60 FR 6650, Feb. 3, 1995; 58 FR 49916, Sept. 24, 1993, as confirmed at 60 FR 6650, Feb. 3, 1995; 76 FR 53764, 53804, Aug. 29, 2011]

AUTHORITY:
8 U.S.C. 1103, 1443, 1448.

§ 339.2 Monthly reports.

(a) Oath administration ceremonies. Clerks of court will on the first day of each month or immediately following each oath ceremony submit to USCIS a report listing all oath administration ceremonies held and the total number of persons issued the oath at each ceremony, in accordance with USCIS instructions. The report will include a list of persons attending naturalization oath ceremonies during the month, and certified copies of any court orders granting changes of name.

(b) Petitions filed for de novo hearings. The clerk of court must submit to USCIS a monthly report of all persons who have filed de novo review petitions before the court. The report shall include each petitioner's name, alien registration number, date of filing of the petition for a de novo review, and, once an order has been entered, the disposition.

(c) Other proceedings and orders. The clerk of court must forward to USCIS copies of the records of such other proceedings and other orders instituted on or issued by the court affecting or relating to the naturalization of any person as may be required from time to time.

(d) Use of reports for accounting purposes. State and federal courts may use the reports as a monthly billing document, submitted to USCIS for reimbursement in accordance with section 344(f)(1) of the Act. USCIS will use the information submitted to calculate costs incurred by courts in performing their naturalization functions. State and federal courts will be reimbursed pursuant to terms set forth in annual agreements entered into between DHS and the Administrative Office of United States Courts.

HISTORY:
[56 FR 50502, Oct. 7, 1991, as confirmed at 60 FR 6650, Feb. 3, 1995; 58 FR 49916, Sept. 24, 1993, as confirmed and revised at 60 FR 6650, 6652, Feb. 3, 1995; 76 FR 53764, 53804, Aug. 29, 2011]

AUTHORITY:
8 U.S.C. 1103, 1443, 1448.

§ 339.3 Relinquishment of naturalization jurisdiction.

Whenever a court relinquishes naturalization jurisdiction, the clerk of court shall, within ten days following the date of relinquishment, furnish the district director having administrative jurisdiction over the place in which the court is located, a certified copy of the order of court relinquishing jurisdiction. A representative of the Service shall thereafter examine the naturalization records in the office of the clerk of court and shall bind and lock them. The clerk of court shall return all unused forms and blank certificates of naturalization to the district director with his monthly report on Form N-4.

HISTORY:
[22 FR 9825, Dec. 6, 1957]

AUTHORITY:
8 U.S.C. 1103, 1443, 1448.

§ 339.4 Binding of naturalization records.

Whenever a volume of petitions for naturalization, applications to take the oath of allegiance, declarations of intention, orders of court, or other documents affecting or relating to the naturalization of persons is completed, it shall be bound and locked by the clerk of court.

HISTORY:
[22 FR 9825, Dec. 6, 1957]

AUTHORITY:
8 U.S.C. 1103, 1443, 1448.

§ 339.5 Recordkeeping.

The maintenance of records and submission of reports under this chapter may be accomplished by either electronic or paper means.

HISTORY:
[56 FR 50502, Oct. 7, 1991, as confirmed at 60 FR 6650, Feb. 3, 1995]

AUTHORITY:
8 U.S.C. 1103, 1443, 1448.

PART 340

REVOCATION OF NATURALIZATION

AUTHORITY NOTE APPLICABLE TO ENTIRE PART:

AUTHORITY:
8 U.S.C. 1103, 1443

§ 340.1 [This section was removed and reserved. See 76 FR 53764, 53804, Aug. 29, 2011.]

[NO TEXT IN ORIGINAL]

HISTORY:
[61 FR 55550, 55553, Oct. 28, 1996; 65 FR 17127, 17128, Mar. 31, 2000, as confirmed and removed at 76 FR 53764, 53778, 53804, Aug. 29, 2011]

AUTHORITY:
(8 U.S.C. 1103, 1443)

§ 340.2 Revocation proceedings pursuant to section 340(a) of the Act.

(a) Recommendations for institution of revocation proceedings. Whenever it appears that any grant of naturalization may have been illegally procured or procured by concealment of a material fact or by willful misrepresentation, and a prima facie case exists for revocation pursuant to section 340(a) of the Act, USCIS will make a recommendation regarding revocation.

(b) Recommendation for criminal prosecution. If it appears to USCIS that a case described in paragraph (a) of this section is amenable to criminal penalties under 18 U.S.C. 1425 for unlawful procurement of citizenship or naturalization, the facts will be reported to the appropriate United States Attorney for possible criminal prosecution.

HISTORY:
[29 FR 2740, Feb. 27, 1964, as amended at 56 FR 50502, Oct. 7, 1991, as confirmed at 60 FR 6650, Feb. 3, 1995; redesignated and revised at 61 FR 55550, 55554, Oct. 28, 1996; 76 FR 53764, 53804, Aug. 29, 2011]

PART 341

CERTIFICATES OF CITIZENSHIP

AUTHORITY NOTE APPLICABLE TO ENTIRE PART:

AUTHORITY:
Pub. L. 82-414, 66 Stat. 173, 238, 254, 264, as amended; 8 U.S.C. 1103, 1409(c), 1443, 1444, 1448, 1452, 1455; 8 CFR part 2.

§ 341.1 Application.

An application for a certificate of citizenship by or in behalf of a person who claims to have acquired United States citizenship under section 309(c) of the Act or to have acquired or derived United States citizenship as specified in section 341 of the Act must be submitted on the form designated by USCIS with the fee specified in 8 CFR 106.2 and in accordance with the instructions on the form.

HISTORY:
[52 FR 19719, May 27, 1987; 76 FR 53764, 53804, Aug. 29, 2011; 85 FR 46788, 46929, Aug. 3, 2020]

§ 341.2 Examination upon application.

(a) Personal appearance of applicant and parent or guardian —

(1) When testimony may be omitted. An application may be processed without interview if the USCIS officer adjudicating the case has in the administrative file(s) all the required documentation necessary to establish the applicant's eligibility for U.S. citizenship, or if the application is accompanied by one of the following:

(i) A Department of State Form FS-240 (Report of Birth Abroad of a Citizen of the United States);

(ii) An unexpired United States passport issued initially for a full five/ten-year period to the applicant as a citizen of the United States, or

(iii) The applicant's parent(s)' naturalization certificate(s).

(2) Testimony required. Each applicant, when notified to do so, shall appear in person before an officer for examination under oath or affirmation upon the application. A person under 18 years of age must have a parent or guardian apply, appear, and testify for the applicant, unless one is unavailable and the district director is satisfied that the applicant is old enough to provide reliable testimony. The same rule will apply for incompetent applicants. At the examination the applicant and the acting parent or guardian, if necessary, shall present testimony and evidence pertinent to the claim to citizenship and shall have the right to review and rebut any adverse evidence on file, and to cross-examine witnesses called by the Government.

(b) Witness —

(1) Personal appearance. A witness shall be called to testify under oath or affirmation at the discretion of USCIS only if that person's testimony is needed to prove a particular point, and only if alternative proof is unavailable or more difficult to produce than is the witness.

(2) Substitution and waiver. When testimony is deemed necessary by the district director and the presentation of the person or persons through whom citizenship is claimed is precluded by reason of death, refusal to testify, unknown whereabouts, advanced age, mental or physical incapacity, or severe illness or infirmity, another witness or witnesses shall be produced. A substitute witness also may be produced in lieu of such person if such person is a member of the United States Armed Forces serving outside the United States in an

area where his testimony could not be taken without imposing extreme hardship upon him, or without unduly delaying action on the application, and no issue is present which can be resolved only by this testimony.

(c) Proof. The burden of proof shall be upon the claimant, or his parent or guardian if one is acting in his behalf, to establish the claimed citizenship by a preponderance of the evidence.

(d) Assignment and authority of officer. USCIS will conduct the examination provided for in paragraphs (a) and (b) of this section. The assigned officer shall have authority to administer oaths or affirmations; to present and receive evidence; to rule upon offers of proof; to take or cause to be taken depositions or interrogatories; to regulate the course of the examination; to examine and cross-examine all witnesses appearing in the proceedings; to grant or order continuances; to consider and rule upon objections to the introduction of evidence; to make a report and recommendation as to whether the application shall be granted or denied, and to take such other action as may be appropriate to the conduct of the examination and the disposition of the application.

(e) Conduct of examination. The assigned officer shall, at the commencement of the examination of the claimant or the acting parent or guardian, advise them of their rights as set forth in paragraphs (a) and (f) of this section, and shall interrogate them under oath or affirmation with regard to each assertion made in the application and any other matter pertinent to the claim to citizenship; in addition, when a witness is deemed necessary, he shall interrogate each witness with regard to pertinent matters within the personal knowledge of the witness, such as the relationship between the claimant and the citizen source or sources; the citizenship of the latter, and any possible expatriatory acts performed by the claimant and the citizen source or sources. He may, in his discretion, have a transcript made of the testimony. At the conclusion of the examination of the claimant or the action parent or guardian, all corrections made on the applications form shall be consecutively numbered and recorded in the space provided therefor in the form. The affidavit shall then be signed and sworn to or affirmed by the claimant or the acting parent or guardian; and the remainder of the affidavit completed and signed by the assigned officer.

(f) Representation during proceedings. The claimant shall have the right to representation during the proceedings, as provided in part 292 of this chapter, and such representative shall have the right to examine and cross-examine witnesses appearing in the proceedings; to introduce evidence; to object to the introduction of evidence, which objections shall be stated succinctly and entered on the record, and to submit briefs. If the claimant is not represented by an attorney or representative, the assigned officer shall assist him in the introduction of all evidence available in his behalf.

HISTORY:

[30 FR 5472, Apr. 16, 1965; 30 FR 5621, Apr. 21, 1965, as amended at 32 FR 6260, Apr. 21, 1967; 45 FR 84011, Dec. 22, 1980; 51 FR 35629, Oct. 7, 1986; 66 FR 32138, 32147, June 13, 2001; 76 FR 53764, 53804, Aug. 29, 2011]

§ 341.3 Depositions.

If satisfied that a witness whose testimony is essential is not available for examination in the United States, the assigned officer may authorize the taking of a deposition abroad by written interrogatories before a DHS or Department of State official.

HISTORY:

[30 FR 5472, Apr. 16, 1965; 76 FR 53764, 53804, Aug. 29, 2011]

§ 341.4 Surrender of immigration documents.

Each claimant shall surrender any immigration identification and permanent resident cards in his or her possession.

HISTORY:

[30 FR 5472, Apr. 16, 1965; 63 FR 70313, 70316, Dec. 21, 1998]

§ 341.5 Decision.

(a) Adjudication. USCIS may adjudicate the application only after the appropriate approving official has reviewed the report, findings, recommendation, and endorsement of the USCIS officer assigned to adjudicate the application.

(b) Approval. If the application is granted, USCIS will prepare a certificate of citizenship and, unless the claimant is unable by reason of mental incapacity or young age to understand the meaning of the oath, he or she must take and subscribe to the oath of renunciation and allegiance prescribed by 8 CFR 337 before USCIS within the United States. Except as provided in paragraph (c), delivery of the certificate in accordance with 8 CFR 103.2(b)(19) and 8 CFR 103.8 must be made in the United States to the claimant or the acting parent or guardian.

(c) Approval pursuant to section 322(d) of the Act. Persons eligible for naturalization pursuant to section 322(d) of the Act may subscribe to the oath of renunciation and allegiance and may be issued a certificate of citizenship outside of the United States, in accordance with 8 U.S.C. 1443a.

(d) Denial. If USCIS denies the application, the applicant will be furnished the reasons for denial and advised of the right to appeal in accordance with 8 CFR 103.3.

(e) Subsequent application. After an application for a certificate of citizenship has been denied and the time for appeal has expired, USCIS will reject a subsequent application submitted by the same individual and the applicant will be instructed to submit a motion to reopen or reconsider in accordance with 8 CFR 103.5. The motion must be accompanied by the rejected application and the fee specified in 8 CFR 106.2.

HISTORY:

[50 FR 39649, Sept. 30, 1985; 50 FR 41480, Oct. 11, 1985; 76 FR 53764, 53804, Aug. 29, 2011; 85 FR 46788, 46929, Aug. 3, 2020]

§ 341.6 [This section was removed. See 76 FR 53764, 53805, Aug. 29, 2011.]

[NO TEXT IN ORIGINAL]

HISTORY:
[50 FR 39649, Sept. 30, 1985; 76 FR 53764, 53805, Aug. 29, 2011]

§ 341.7 [This section was removed. See 76 FR 53764, 53805, Aug. 29, 2011.]

[NO TEXT IN ORIGINAL]

HISTORY:
[55 FR 31037, July 31, 1990; 66 FR 32138, 32147, June 13, 2001; 76 FR 53764, 53805, Aug. 29, 2011]

PART 342

ADMINISTRATIVE CANCELLATION OF CERTIFICATES, DOCUMENTS, OR RECORDS

AUTHORITY NOTE APPLICABLE TO ENTIRE PART:

AUTHORITY:
8 U.S.C. 1103, 1453.

§ 342.1 Notice.

If it shall appear to a district director that a person has illegally or fraudulently obtained or caused to be created a certificate, document, or record described in section 342 of the Act, a notice shall be served upon the person of intention to cancel the certificate, document, or record. The notice shall contain allegations of the reasons for the proposed action and shall advise the person that he may submit, within 60 days of service of the notice, an answer in writing under oath or affirmation showing cause why the certificate, document, or record should not be canceled, that he may appear in person before a naturalization examiner in support of, or in lieu of his written answer, and that he may have present at that time, without expense to the Government, an attorney or representative qualified under part 292 of this chapter. In such proceedings the person shall be known as the respondent.

HISTORY:
[29 FR 5511, Apr. 24, 1964, as amended at 37 FR 2767, Feb. 5, 1972]

§ 342.2 Service of notice.

The notice required by 8 CFR 342.1 must be by personal service as described in 8 CFR 103.8(a)(2).

HISTORY:
[29 FR 5511, Apr. 24, 1964; 76 FR 53764, 53805, Aug. 29, 2011]

§ 342.3 Allegations admitted; no answer filed; no personal appearance requested.

If the answer admits all material allegations in the notice, or if no answer is filed within the 60-day period or any extension thereof and no personal appearance is requested within such period or periods, it shall be deemed to authorize the district director, without further notice to respondent, to find the facts to be as alleged in the notice and to cancel the certificate, document, or record. No appeal shall lie from such decision. Written notice of the decision shall be served upon the respondent with demand for surrender of the certificate, document, or record forthwith.

HISTORY:
28 FR 209, Jan. 9, 1963.

§ 342.4 Answer asserting defense; personal appearance requested.

If the respondent files an answer within the prescribed period asserting a defense to the allegations in the notice, or requests a personal appearance, with or without an answer, the district director shall designate a naturalization examiner to consider the case. The respondent shall be notified that he may appear in person or through counsel with any witnesses and evidence in defense of the allegations, and shall be informed of the date, time, and place for such appearance.

HISTORY:
28 FR 209, Jan. 9, 1963.

§ 342.5 Conduct of examination.

(a) Authority of naturalization examiner. The naturalization examiner assigned to consider the case shall have authority to administer oaths or affirmations to respondent and witnesses, issue subpoenas, present and receive evidence, rule upon offers of proof, take or cause depositions or interrogatories to be taken, regulate the course of the examination, take testimony of respondent and witnesses, grant continuances, consider and rule upon objections to the introduction of evidence, make recommendations to the district director as to whether cancellation shall be ordered or the proceedings terminated, and to take any other action as may be appropriate to the conduct and disposition of the case.

(b) Assignment of additional officer. The district director may, in his discretion, assign an officer of the Service to examine and cross-examine the respondent and witnesses and to present evidence pertinent to the case. The naturalization examiner designated under § 342.4 may take such part in the proceedings as he may deem necessary.

(c) Examination. The naturalization examiner designated under § 342.4 shall, prior to commencement of the examination, make known to the respondent his official capacity and that of any officer assigned pursuant to paragraph (b) of this section, the nature of the proceedings, his right to representation by counsel, to examine or object to evidence against him, to present evidence in his own behalf, to cross-examine witnesses presented by the Government, and shall read the allegations in the notice to respondent and, if necessary, explain them to him. The respondent shall be asked whether he admits or denies the material allegations in the notice, or any of them, and whether he concedes illegality or fraud. If respondent admits all the material allegations and that the certificate, document, or record was procured by fraud or illegality, and no issue of law or fact remains, the naturalization examiner may determine that fraud or illegality has been established on the basis of the respondent's admissions. The allegations in the notice shall be taken as admitted if respondent, without reasonable cause, fails or refuses to attend or remain in attendance at the examination. The examination shall be recorded verbatim except for statements made off the record with the permission of the naturalization examiner.

(d) Prior statements. The naturalization examiner assigned to consider the case may receive in evidence any oral or written statement which is material and relevant to any issue in the case previously made by the respondent or by any other person during any investigation, examination, hearing, trial, proceeding, or interrogation.

HISTORY:
[28 FR 209, Jan. 9, 1963, as amended at 32 FR 3340, Feb. 28, 1967]

§ 342.6 Depositions.

Upon good cause shown, the testimony of any witness may be taken by depositions, either orally or upon written interrogatories before a person having authority to administer oaths (affirmations), as may be designated by the naturalization examiner.

HISTORY:
[37 FR 2767, Feb. 5, 1972]

§ 342.7 Report and recommendation.

The naturalization examiner shall prepare a report summarizing the evidence, discussing the applicable law, and containing his findings and recommendations. The record, including the report and recommendation, shall be forwarded to the district director, who shall sign the report, either approving or disapproving the recommendation. If the decision of the district director is that the proceedings be terminated, the respondent shall be so informed.

HISTORY:
28 FR 209, Jan. 9, 1963.

§ 342.8 Appeals.

Should the district director find that the certificate, document, or record was fraudulently or illegally obtained, he shall enter an order that it be cancelled and the certificate or document surrendered to the Service forthwith. Written notification of such action shall be given the respondent, with a copy of the decision, findings and decision of the district director, and he shall be informed of his right of appeal in accordance with the provisions of part 103 of this chapter.

HISTORY:
28 FR 209, Jan. 9, 1963.

§ 342.9 Notice re 18 U.S.C. 1428.

The notice to surrender a cancelled certificate of citizenship or copy thereof, prescribed by section 1428 of Title 18 of the United States Code, shall be given by the district director in whose district the person who has possession or control of such document resides.

HISTORY:
[28 FR 9282, Aug. 23, 1963]

PART 343

CERTIFICATE OF NATURALIZATION OR REPATRIATION; PERSONS WHO RESUMED CITIZENSHIP UNDER SECTION 323 OF THE NATIONALITY ACT OF 1940, AS AMENDED, OR SECTION 4 OF THE ACT OF JUNE 29, 1906

AUTHORITY NOTE APPLICABLE TO ENTIRE PART:

AUTHORITY:
8 U.S.C. 1101, 1103, 1443, 1454, and 1455.

§ 343.1 Application.

A person who lost citizenship of the United States incidental to service in one of the allied armies during World War I or II, or by voting in a political election in a country not at war with the United States during World War II, and who was naturalized under the provisions of section 323 of the Nationality Act of 1940, as amended, or a person who, before January 13, 1941, resumed United States citizenship under the twelfth subdivision of section 4 of the act of June 29, 1906, may obtain a certificate evidencing such citizenship by making application in accordance with USCIS instructions. The applicant shall be required to appear in person before an assigned officer for interrogation under oath or affirmation upon the application. When the application is approved, a certificate of naturalization or repatriation shall be issued and delivered in person, in the United States only, upon the applicant's signed receipt therefor. If the application is denied, the applicant shall be notified of the reasons therefor and his right to appeal in accordance with the provisions of part 103 of this chapter.

HISTORY:

[23 FR 9125, Nov. 26, 1958, as amended at 32 FR 9635, July 4, 1967; 76 FR 53764, 53805, Aug. 29, 2011]

PART 343A

NATURALIZATION AND CITIZENSHIP PAPERS LOST, MUTILATED, OR DESTROYED; NEW CERTIFICATE IN CHANGED NAME; CERTIFIED COPY OF REPATRIATION PROCEEDINGS

AUTHORITY NOTE APPLICABLE TO ENTIRE PART:

AUTHORITY:

8 U.S.C. 1101 note, 1103, 1435, 1443, 1454, and 1455.

§ 343a.1 Application for replacement of or new papers relating to naturalization, citizenship, or repatriation.

(a) Lost, mutilated, or destroyed naturalization papers. A person whose declaration of intention, certificate of naturalization, citizenship, or repatriation, or whose certified copy of proceedings under the act of June 25, 1936, as amended, or under section 317(b) of the Nationality Act of 1940, or under section 324(c) of the Immigration and Nationality Act, or under the provisions of any private law, has been lost, mutilated, or destroyed, must apply on the form designated by USCIS with the fee specified in 8 CFR part 106 and in accordance with the form instructions.

(b) New certificate in changed name. A naturalized citizen whose name has been changed after naturalization by order of court or by marriage must apply for a new certificate of naturalization, or of citizenship, in the changed name.

(c) **Adjudication and disposition.**

(1) Interview. The applicant shall only be required to appear in person for interview under oath or affirmation in specific cases. Those cases which necessitate an interview enabling an officer to properly adjudicate the application at the office having jurisdiction will be determined by USCIS.

(2) Approval. If an application for a new certificate of naturalization, citizenship, or repatriation or a new declaration of intention is approved, the new certificate or declaration will be issued and delivered by personal service in accordance with 8 CFR 103.8(a)(2). If an application for a new certified copy of the proceedings under the Act of June 25, 1936, as amended, or under section 317(b) of the Nationality Act of 1940, or under section 324(c) of the Immigration and Nationality Act, or under the provisions of any private law is approved, a certified photocopy of the record of the proceedings will be issued. If, subsequent to naturalization or repatriation, the applicant's name was changed by marriage, the certification of the photocopy will show both the name in which the proceedings were conducted and the changed name. The new certified copy will be delivered to the applicant in accordance with 8 CFR 103.8(a)(2).

(3) Denial. If the application is denied, the applicant shall be notified of the reasons for the denial and of the right to appeal in accordance with 8 CFR 103.3.

HISTORY:

[23 FR 9125, Nov. 26, 1958, as amended at 32 FR 9635, July 7, 1967; 51 FR 35629, Oct. 7, 1986; 76 FR 53764, 53805, Aug. 29, 2011; 85 FR 46788, 46929, Aug. 3, 2020]

§ 343a.2 Return or replacement of surrendered certificate of naturalization or citizenship.

A certificate of naturalization or citizenship which is contained in a USCIS file, and which was surrendered on a finding that loss of nationality occurred directly or through a parent as a result of the application of any of the following sections of law may, upon request, be returned to the person to whom it was originally issued, notwithstanding the fact that he or she has since been naturalized or repatriated in the United States or abroad:

(a) Section 404 (b) or (c) of the Nationality Act of 1940;

(b) Section 352 of the Immigration and Nationality Act, which was invalidated by Schneider v. Rusk, 377 U.S. 163;

(c) Section 401(e) of the Nationality Act of 1940;

(d) Section 349(a)(5) of the Immigration and Nationality Act, which was invalidated by Afroyim v. Rusk, 387 U.S. 253;

(e) Section 301(b) of the Immigration and Nationality Act

(f) Section 301(c) of the Immigration and Nationality Act relative to persons born after May 24, 1934, which was invalidated by amendment to section 301(b) on October 27, 1972, Public Law 92-584.

If, after having been surrendered to the Department of State or to USCIS, the certificate was lost, mutilated, or destroyed as a result of action by USCIS or that Department, a replacement certificate may be issued in the name shown in the surrendered certificate without fee and without requiring the submission of an application. A surrendered certificate shall not be regarded as mutilated and a replacement shall not be issued solely because of holes made in it to accommodate a fastener, unless the citizen declines to accept the return of the surrendered certificate in that condition and insists upon issuance of a replacement. When it is desired that the replacement certificate be furnished in a name other than the one shown in the surrendered certificate, the regular application procedure with payment of fee must be followed.

HISTORY:

[51 FR 35629, Oct. 7, 1986]

PART 343B

SPECIAL CERTIFICATE OF NATURALIZATION FOR RECOGNITION BY A FOREIGN STATE

§ 343b.1 Application.

A naturalized citizen who desires to obtain recognition as a citizen of the United States by a foreign state shall submit an application on the form designated by USCIS with the fee specified in 8 CFR 106.2 and in accordance with the form instructions. He shall not be furnished with verification of his naturalization for such purpose in any other way. An applicant who is a claimant against a foreign government for property damage pursuant to the provisions of a peace treaty shall not be requested to furnish the name, official title, and address of a foreign official unless such information is available when the investigation of the applicant is conducted. The applicant shall be required to appear in person before an assigned officer for interrogation under oath or affirmation upon the application.

HISTORY:

[32 FR 9636, July 4, 1967, as amended at 56 FR 50502, Oct. 7, 1991, as confirmed at 60 FR 6650, Feb. 3, 1995; 76 FR 53764, 53805, Aug. 29, 2011; 85 FR 46788, 46929, Aug. 3, 2020]

AUTHORITY:

8 U.S.C. 1103, 1443, 1454, 1455.

§ 343b.2 Number of applications required.

A special certificate of naturalization is delivered to one foreign government official only. An applicant who desires recognition as a U.S. citizen by more than one foreign official, whether in the same country or not, must file a separate application for each certificate required.

HISTORY:

[32 FR 9636, July 4, 1967]

AUTHORITY:

8 U.S.C. 1103, 1443, 1454, 1455.

§ 343b.3 Interview.

When the application presents a prima facie case, USCIS may issue a certificate without first interviewing the applicant. In all other cases, the applicant must be interviewed. The interviewing officer must provide a complete written report of the interview before forwarding the application for issuance of the certificate.

HISTORY:

[32 FR 9636, July 4, 1967; 58 FR 49917, Sept. 24, 1993, as confirmed at 60 FR 6650, Feb. 3, 1995; 76 FR 53764, 53805, Aug. 29, 2011]

AUTHORITY:

8 U.S.C. 1103, 1443, 1454, 1455.

§ 343b.4 Applicant outside of United States.

If the application is received by a DHS office outside the United States, an officer will, when practicable, interview the applicant before the application is forwarded to USCIS for issuance of the certificate. When an interview is not practicable, or is not conducted because the application is submitted directly to USCIS in the United States, the certificate may nevertheless be issued and the recommendation conditioned upon satisfactory interview by the Department of State. When forwarding the certificate in such a case, USCIS will inform the Secretary of State that the applicant has not been interviewed, and request to have the applicant interviewed regarding identity and possible expatriation. If identity is not established or if expatriation has occurred, the Department of State will return the certificate to USCIS for disposition.

HISTORY:

[37 FR 7584, Apr. 18, 1972; 76 FR 53764, 53805, Aug. 29, 2011]

AUTHORITY:

8 U.S.C. 1103, 1443, 1454, 1455.

§ 343b.5 Verification of naturalization.

The application shall not be granted without first obtaining verification of the applicant's naturalization.

HISTORY:

[32 FR 9636, July 4, 1967]

AUTHORITY:

8 U.S.C. 1103, 1443, 1454, 1455.

§ 343b.11 Disposition of application.

(a) Approval. If the application is granted, USCIS will prepare a special certificate of naturalization and forward it to the Secretary of State for transmission to the proper authority of the foreign state in accordance with procedures agreed to between DHS and the Department of State, retain the application and a record of the disposition in the DHS file, and notify the applicant of the actions taken.

(b) Denial. If the application is denied, the applicant will be notified of the reasons for denial and of the right to appeal in accordance with 8 CFR 103.3.

HISTORY:

[23 FR 9126, Nov. 26, 1958 and 32 FR 9636, July 4, 1967, as amended at 36 FR 11636, June 17, 1971; 45 FR 38340, June 9, 1980; 76 FR 53764, 53806, Aug. 29, 2011]

AUTHORITY:

8 U.S.C. 1103, 1443, 1454, 1455.

PART 343C

CERTIFICATIONS FROM RECORDS

AUTHORITY NOTE APPLICABLE TO ENTIRE PART:

AUTHORITY:

5 U.S.C. 552; 8 U.S.C. 1103.

§ 343c.1 Application for certification of naturalization record of court or certificate of naturalization or citizenship.

An application for certification of a naturalization record of any court, or of any part thereof, or of any certificate of naturalization, repatriation, or citizenship, under section 343(e) of the Act for use in complying with any statute, Federal or State, or in any judicial proceeding, shall be made on the form designated by USCIS in accordance with the form instructions.

HISTORY:
[40 FR 50703, Oct. 31, 1975; 76 FR 53764, 53806, Aug. 29, 2011]

PART 349
LOSS OF NATIONALITY

§ 349.1 Japanese renunciation of nationality.

A Japanese who renounced United States nationality pursuant to the provisions of section 401(i), Nationality Act of 1940, who claims that his renunciation is void, shall complete Form N-576, Supplemental Affidavit to be Submitted with Applications of Japanese Renunciants. The affidavit shall be submitted to the Assistant Attorney General, Civil Division, Department of Justice, Washington, DC 20530, with a covering letter requesting a determination of the validity of the renunciation.

HISTORY:
[32 FR 9636, July 4, 1967]

AUTHORITY:
Sec. 103, 66 Stat. 173; 8 U.S.C. 1103. Interprets or applies 401(i), 54 Stat. 1169; 8 U.S.C. 801, 1946 ed.

PART 392
SPECIAL CLASSES OF PERSONS WHO MAY BE NATURALIZED: PERSONS WHO DIE WHILE SERVING ON ACTIVE DUTY WITH THE UNITED STATES ARMED FORCES DURING CERTAIN PERIODS OF HOSTILITIES

§ 392.1 Definitions.

As used in this part:

Active-duty status means full-time duty in the active military service of the United States, and includes full-time training duty, which constitutes qualifying service under section 329(a) of the Act. Active service in the United States Coast Guard during one of the periods of hostilities specified herein shall constitute service in the military, air, or naval forces of the United States. Active-duty status also includes annual training duty and attendance, while in the active military service, at a service school designated by the military authorities under 10 U.S.C. 101(22). The order of a national guardsman into active duty for training under 10 U.S.C. 672 constitutes service in active-duty status in the military forces of the United States. Active duty in a noncombatant capacity is qualifying service.

Decedent means the person on whose behalf an application for a certificate of posthumous citizenship is made.

Induction, enlistment, and reenlistment, refer to the decedent's place of entry into active duty military service.

Korean Hostilities relates to the period from June 25, 1950, to July 1, 1955, inclusive.

Lodge Act means the Act of June 30, 1950, which qualified for naturalization nonresident aliens who served honorably for 5 years in the United States Army during specified periods, notwithstanding that they never formally became lawful permanent residents of the United States.

Next-of-kin means the closest surviving blood or legal relative of the decedent in the following order of succession:

(1) The surviving spouse;

(2) The decedent's surviving son or daughter, if the decedent has no surviving spouse;

(3) The decedent's surviving parent, if the decedent has no surviving spouse or sons or daughters; or,

(4) The decedent's surviving brother or sister, if none of the persons described in paragraphs (1) through (3) of this definition survive the decedent.

Other periods of military hostilities means any period designated by the President under Executive Order as a period in which Armed Forces of the United States are or were engaged in military operations involving armed conflict with a hostile foreign force.

Representative means:

(1) The duly appointed executor or administrator of the decedent's estate, including a special administrator appointed for the purpose of seeking the decedent's naturalization; or,

(2) The duly appointed guardian, conservator, or committee of the decedent's next-of-kin; or,

(3) A service organization listed in 38 U.S.C. 3402, or chartered by Congress, or State, or other service organization recognized by the Department of Veterans Affairs.

Vietnam Hostilities relates to the period from February 28, 1961, to October 15, 1978, inclusive.

World War I relates to the period from April 6, 1917, to November 11, 1918, inclusive.

World War II relates to the period from September 1, 1939, to December 31, 1946, inclusive.

HISTORY:
56 FR 22822, May 17, 1991.

AUTHORITY:
8 U.S.C. 1103, 1440 and note, and 1440-1; 8 CFR part 2.

§ 392.2 Eligibility for posthumous citizenship.

(a) General. Any alien or noncitizen national of the United States is eligible for posthumous United States citizenship who:

(1) Served honorably in an active-duty status with the military, air, or naval forces of the United States during World War I, World War II, the Korean Hostilities, the Vietnam Hostilities, or in other periods of military hostilities designated by the President under Executive Order; and,

(2) Died as a result of injury or disease incurred in or aggravated by service in the United States Armed Forces during a period of military hostilities listed in paragraph (a)(1) of this section. Where the person died subsequent to separation from military service, the death must have resulted from an injury or disease that was sustained, acquired, or exacerbated during active-duty service in a qualifying period of military hostilities as specified in this part.

(b) Qualifying enlistment. In conjunction with the qualifying service as described in paragraph (a)(1) of this section, the decedent must have:

(1) Enlisted, reenlisted, or been inducted in the United States, the Canal Zone, American Samoa, or Swains Island;

(2) Been lawfully admitted to the United States for permanent residence, at any time; or,

(3) Enlisted or reenlisted in the United States Army pursuant to the provisions of the Lodge Act. In such case, the decedent shall be considered to have been lawfully admitted to the United States as a permanent resident for purposes of this section, provided he or she:

(i) Entered the United States, its outlying possessions, or the Canal Zone, at some time during the period of army service, pursuant to military orders; and

(ii) Was honorably discharged following completion of at least 5 full years of active duty service, even though the active-duty service may not have occurred during a qualifying period of hostilities specified in section 329(a) of the Act.

(c) Character of military service. Where the character of military service is not certified as honorable by the executive department under which the person served, or where the person was dishonorably discharged or discharged under conditions other than honorable, such service shall not satisfy the requirement of paragraph (a)(1) of this section.

(d) Certification of eligibility.

(1) The executive department under which the decedent served shall determine whether:

(i) The decedent served honorably in an active-duty status;

(ii) The separation from such service was under honorable conditions; and,

(iii) The decedent died as a result of injury or disease incurred in, or aggravated by active duty service during a qualifying period of military hostilities.

(2) The certification required by section 329A(c)(2) of the Act to prove military service and service-connected death must be requested by the applicant on the form designated by USCIS in accordance with the form instructions. The form will also be used to verify the decedent's place of induction, enlistment, or reenlistment.

HISTORY:

[56 FR 22822, May 17, 1991; 76 FR 53764, 53806, Aug. 29, 2011]

AUTHORITY:

8 U.S.C. 1103, 1440 and note, and 1440-1; 8 CFR part 2.

§ 392.3 Application for posthumous citizenship.

(a) **Persons who may apply.**

(1) Only one person who is either the next-of-kin or another representative of the decedent shall be permitted to apply for posthumous citizenship on the decedent's behalf. A person who is a next-of-kin who wishes to apply for posthumous citizenship on behalf of the decedent, shall, if there is a surviving next-of-kin in the line of succession above him or her, be required to obtain authorization to make the application from all surviving next-of-kin in the line of succession above him or her. The authorization shall be in the form of an affidavit stating that the affiant authorizes the requester to apply for posthumous citizenship on behalf of the decedent. The affidavit must include the name and address of the affiant, and the relationship of the affiant to the decedent.

(2) When there is a surviving next-of-kin, an application for posthumous citizenship shall only be accepted from a representative provided authorization has been obtained from all surviving next-of-kin. However, this requirement shall not apply to the executor or administrator of the decedent's estate. In the case of a service organization acting as a representative, authorization must also have been obtained from any appointed representative. A veterans service organization must submit evidence of recognition by the Department of Veterans Affairs.

Once USCIS has granted posthumous citizenship to a person, no subsequent applications on his or her behalf shall be approved, nor shall any additional original certificates be issued, except in the case of an application for issuance of a replacement certificate for one lost, mutilated, or destroyed.

(b) Application. An application for posthumous citizenship must be submitted on the form designated by USCIS in accordance with the form instructions.

(c) Application period. An application for posthumous citizenship must be filed no later than two years after the date of the decedent's death.

(d) Denial of application. When the application is denied, the applicant shall be notified of the decision and the reason(s) for denial. There is no appeal from the denial of an application under this part.

HISTORY:

[56 FR 22822, May 17, 1991; 74 FR 26933, 26941, June 5, 2009; 76 FR 53764, 53806, Aug. 29, 2011]

AUTHORITY:

8 U.S.C. 1103, 1440 and note, and 1440-1; 8 CFR part 2.

§ 392.4 Issuance of a certificate of citizenship.

(a) Approval of application. When an application for posthumous citizenship under this part has been approved, USCIS will issue a Certificate of Citizenship to the applicant in the name of the decedent.

(b) Delivery of certificate. Delivery of the Certificate of Citizenship shall be made by registered mail to the address designated by the applicant. If the applicant resides outside the United States, the certificate shall be sent by registered mail to the Service office abroad, if one is located where delivery is to be made; otherwise, it shall be forwarded to the nearest American Embassy or Consulate.

(c) Effective date of citizenship. Where the Service has approved an Application for Posthumous Citizenship (Form N-644), the decedent shall be considered a United States citizen as of the date of his or her death.

(d) Ineligibility for immigration benefits. The granting of posthumous citizenship under section 329A of the Immigration and Naturalization Act, as amended, and issuance of a certificate under paragraph (a) of this section, shall not entitle the surviving spouse, parent, son, daughter, or other relative of the decedent to any benefit under any provision of the Act. Nor shall such grant make applicable the provisions of section 319(d) of the Act to the surviving spouse.

(e) Replacement certificate. An application for a replacement Certificate of Citizenship must be submitted on the form designated by USCIS with the fee specified in 8 CFR 106.2 and in accordance with the form instructions.

HISTORY:

[56 FR 22822, May 17, 1991; 76 FR 53764, 53806, Aug. 29, 2011; 85 FR 46788, 46929, Aug. 3, 2020]

AUTHORITY:

8 U.S.C. 1103, 1440 and note, and 1440-1; 8 CFR part 2.

PART 499

[PART 499 WAS REMOVED. SEE 76 FR 53764, 53806, AUG. 29, 2011.]

PART 499 [PART 499 WAS REMOVED. SEE 76 FR 53764, 53806, AUG. 29, 2011.]

[NO TEXT IN ORIGINAL]

§ 499.1 [This section was removed. See 76 FR 53764, 53806, Aug. 29, 2011.]

[NO TEXT IN ORIGINAL]

HISTORY:

[49 FR 7104, Feb. 27, 1984, as amended at 53 FR 33445, Aug. 31, 1988; 54 FR 7174, Feb. 17, 1989; 55 FR 12629, Apr. 5, 1990; 56 FR 22824, May 17, 1991; 56 FR 50502, 50503, Oct. 7, 1991, as confirmed at 60 FR 6650, Feb. 3, 1995; 58 FR 49917, Sept. 24, 1993, as confirmed at 60 FR 6650, Feb. 3, 1995; 59 FR 25561, May 17, 1994, as confirmed and amended at 61 FR 47799, 47801, Sept. 11, 1996; 62 FR 12915, 12924, March 19, 1997; 64 FR 7990, 7993, Feb. 18, 1999; 76 FR 53764, 53806, Aug. 29, 2011]

AUTHORITY:

(8 U.S.C. 1103; 8 CFR part 2.)

CHAPTER V

EXECUTIVE OFFICE FOR IMMIGRATION REVIEW, DEPARTMENT OF JUSTICE

Subchapter

SUBCHAPTER A

GENERAL PROVISIONS

Part 1001. Definitions

Rule

PART 1001

DEFINITIONS

AUTHORITY NOTE APPLICABLE TO ENTIRE PART:

AUTHORITY:

5 U.S.C. 301; 8 U.S.C. 1101, 1103; Pub. L. 107-296, 116 Stat. 2135; Title VII of Pub. L. 110-229.

§ 1001.1 Definitions.

As used in this chapter:

(a) The terms defined in section 101 of the Immigration and Nationality Act (66 Stat. 163) shall have the meanings ascribed to them in that section and as supplemented, explained, and further defined in this chapter.

(b) The term Act means the Immigration and Nationality Act, as amended.

(c) The term Service means the Immigration and Naturalization Service, as it existed prior to March 1, 2003. Unless otherwise specified, references to the Service on or after that date mean the offices of the Department of Homeland Security to which the functions of the former Service were transferred pursuant to the Homeland Security Act, Public Law 107-296 (Nov. 25, 2002), as provided in 8 CFR chapter I.

(d) The term Commissioner means the Commissioner of the Immigration and Naturalization Service prior to March 1, 2003. Unless otherwise specified, references to the Commissioner on or after that date mean those officials of the Department of Homeland Security who have succeeded to the functions of the Commissioner of the former Service, as provided in 8 CFR chapter I.

(e) The term Board means the Board of Immigration Appeals.

(f) The term attorney means any person who is eligible to practice law in and is a member in good standing of the bar of the highest court of any State, possession, territory, or Commonwealth of the United States, or of the District of Columbia, and is not under any order suspending, enjoining, restraining, disbarring, or otherwise restricting him in the practice of law.

(g) Unless the context otherwise requires, the term case means any proceeding arising under any immigration or naturalization law, Executive order, or Presidential proclamation, or preparation for or incident to such proceeding, including preliminary steps by any private person or corporation preliminary to the filing of the application or petition by which any proceeding under the jurisdiction of the Service or the Board is initiated.

(h) The term day when computing the period of time for taking any action provided in this chapter including the taking of an appeal, shall include Saturdays, Sundays, and legal holidays, except that when the last day of the period so computed falls on a Saturday, Sunday or a legal holiday, the period shall run until the end of the next day which is not a Saturday, Sunday, nor a legal holiday.

(i) The term practice means exercising professional judgment to provide legal advice or legal services related to any matter before EOIR. Practice includes, but is not limited to, determining available forms of relief from removal or protection; providing advice regarding legal strategies; drafting or filing any document on behalf of another person appearing before EOIR based on an analysis of applicable facts and law; or appearing on behalf of another person in any matter before EOIR.

(j) The term representative refers to a person who is entitled to represent others as provided in §§ 1292.1(a)(2), (3), (4), (5), (6), and 1292.1(b) of this chapter.

(k) The term preparation means the act or acts consisting solely of filling in blank spaces on printed forms with information provided by the applicant or petitioner that are to be filed with or submitted to EOIR, where such acts do not include the exercise of professional judgment to provide legal advice or legal services. When this act is performed by someone other than a practitioner, the fee for filling in blank spaces on printed forms, if any, must be nominal, and the individual may not hold himself or herself out as qualified in legal matters or in immigration and naturalization procedure.

(l) The term immigration judge means an attorney whom the Attorney General appoints as an administrative judge within the Executive Office for Immigration Review, qualified to conduct specified classes of proceedings, including a hearing under section 240 of the Act. An immigration judge shall be subject to such supervision and shall perform such duties as the Attorney General shall prescribe, but shall not be employed by the Immigration and Naturalization Service.

(m) The term representation before the Board and the Service includes practice and preparation as defined in paragraphs (i) and (k) of this section.

(n) The term Executive Office means Executive Office for Immigration Review.

(o) The term Director, unless otherwise specified, means the Director of the Executive Office for Immigration Review. For a definition of the term Director when used in the context of an official with the Department of Homeland Security, see 8 CFR 1.1(o).

(p) The term lawfully admitted for permanent residence means the status of having been lawfully accorded the privilege of residing permanently in the United States as an immigrant in accordance with the immigration laws, such status not having changed. Such status terminates upon entry of a final administrative order of exclusion, deportation, removal, or rescission.

(q) The term arriving alien means an applicant for admission coming or attempting to come into the United States at a port-of-entry, or an alien seeking transit through the United States at a port-of-entry, or an alien interdicted in international or United States waters and brought into the United States by any means, whether or not to a designated port-of-entry, and regardless of the means of transport. An arriving alien remains an arriving alien even if paroled pursuant to section 212(d)(5) of the Act, and even after any such parole is terminated or revoked. However, an arriving alien who was paroled into the United States before April 1, 1997, or who was paroled into the United States on or after April 1, 1997, pursuant to a grant of advance parole which the alien applied for and obtained in the United States prior to the alien's departure from and return to the United States, will not be treated, solely by reason of that grant of parole, as an arriving alien under section 235(b)(1)(A)(i) of the Act.

(r) The term respondent means a person named in a Notice to Appear issued in accordance with section 239(a) of the Act, or in an Order to Show Cause issued in accordance with § 242.1 of 8 CFR chapter I as it existed prior to April 1, 1997.

(s) The terms government counsel or DHS counsel, in the context of proceedings in which DHS has appeared, mean any officer assigned to represent DHS in any proceeding before an immigration judge or the Board of Immigration Appeals.

(t) The term aggravated felony means a crime (or a conspiracy or attempt to commit a crime) described in section 101(a)(43) of the Act. This definition is applicable to any proceeding, application, custody determination, or adjudication pending on or after September 30, 1996, but shall apply under section 276(b) of the Act only to violations of section 276(a) of the Act occurring on or after that date.

(u) The term Department, unless otherwise specified, means the Department of Justice.

(v) The term Secretary, unless otherwise specified, means the Secretary of Homeland Security.

(w) The term DHS means the Department of Homeland Security. These rules incorporate by reference the organizational definitions for components of DHS as provided in 8 CFR 1.1.

(x) [Reserved]

(y) [Reserved]

(z) [Reserved]

(aa) [Reserved]

(bb) The term transition program effective date as used with respect to extending the immigration laws to the Commonwealth of the Northern Mariana Islands means November 28, 2009.

(cc) The term case eligible for electronic filing means any case that DHS seeks to bring before an immigration court after EOIR has formally established an electronic filing system for that court, or any case before an immigration court or the Board of Immigration Appeals that has an electronic record of proceeding. Any reference to a record of proceeding in this chapter shall include an electronic record of proceeding.

(dd) The term filing means the actual receipt of a document by the appropriate immigration court or the Board of Immigration Appeals. An electronic filing that is accepted by the Board or an immigration court will be deemed filed on the date it was submitted. A paper filing that is accepted by the Board or an immigration court will be deemed filed on the date it was received by the Board or the immigration court. A filing that is rejected by the Board or the immigration court as an improper filing will not be deemed filed on the date it was submitted or received.

(ee) The term service means physically presenting, mailing, or electronically providing a document to the appropriate party or parties; except that an Order to Show Cause or Notice of Deportation Hearing shall be served in person to the alien, or by certified mail to the alien or the alien's attorney, and a Notice to Appear shall be served to the alien in person, or if personal service is not practicable, shall be served by regular mail to the alien or the alien's attorney of record.

(ff) The term practitioner means an attorney as defined in paragraph (f) of this section who does not represent the Federal Government, or a representative as defined in paragraph (j) of this section.

(gg) The term noncitizen means "alien," as defined in section 101(a)(3) of the Act.

(hh) The term unaccompanied child means "unaccompanied alien child," as defined in 6 U.S.C. 279(g)(2).

HISTORY:

[23 FR 9115, Nov. 26, 1958, as amended at 30 FR 14772, Nov. 30, 1965; 34 FR 12213, July 24, 1969; 38 FR 8590, April 4, 1973; 40 FR 23271, May 29, 1975; 48 FR 8039, Feb. 25, 1983, 52 FR 2936, Jan. 29, 1987; 53 FR 30016, Aug. 10, 1988; 61 FR 18900, 18904, Apr. 29, 1996; 62 FR 10312, 10330, Mar. 6, 1997; 63 FR 19382, 19383, Apr. 20, 1998; 68 FR 9824, 9830, Feb. 28, 2003; 68 FR 10349, 10350, Mar. 5, 2003; 69 FR 44903, 44905, July 28, 2004; 71 FR 27585, 27591, May 12, 2006; 73 FR 76914, 76922, Dec. 18, 2008; 74 FR 55726, 55741, Oct. 28, 2009; 81 FR 92346, 92361, Dec. 19, 2016; 84 FR 44537, 44541, Aug. 26, 2019; as confirmed at 85 FR 69465, Nov. 3, 2020; 86 FR 70708, 70719, Dec. 13, 2021; 87 FR 56204, 56217, Sept. 14, 2022; 89 FR 46742, 46787, May 29, 2024]

PART 1003

EXECUTIVE OFFICE FOR IMMIGRATION REVIEW

AUTHORITY NOTE APPLICABLE TO ENTIRE PART:

AUTHORITY:

5 U.S.C. 301; 6 U.S.C. 521; 8 U.S.C. 1101, 1103, 1154, 1155, 1158, 1182, 1226, 1229, 1229a, 1229b, 1229c, 1231, 1254a, 1255, 1324d, 1330, 1361, 1362; 28 U.S.C. 509, 510, 1746; sec. 2 Reorg. Plan No. 2 of 1950; 3 CFR, 1949-1953 Comp., p. 1002; section 203 of Pub. L. 105-100, 111 Stat. 2196-200; sections 1506 and 1510 of Pub. L. 106-386, 114 Stat. 1527-29, 1531-32; section 1505 of Pub. L. 106-554, 114 Stat. 2763A-326 to -328.

§ 1003.0 Executive Office for Immigration Review.

(a) Organization. Within the Department of Justice, there shall be an Executive Office for Immigration Review (EOIR), headed by a Director who is appointed by the Attorney General. The Director shall be assisted by a Deputy Director and the heads of EOIR's other components, who shall report to the Director and Deputy Director. EOIR shall include the Board of Immigration Appeals, the Office of the Chief Immigration Judge, the Office of the Chief Administrative Hearing Officer, the Office of Policy, the Office of the General Counsel, and such other components and staff as the Attorney General or the Director may provide.

(b) Powers of the Director. —

(1) In general. The Director shall manage EOIR and its employees and shall be responsible for the direction and supervision of each EOIR component in the execution of its respective duties pursuant to the Act and the provisions of this chapter. Unless otherwise provided by the Attorney General, the Director shall report to the Deputy Attorney General and the Attorney General. The Director shall have the authority to:

(i) Issue operational instructions and policy, including procedural instructions regarding the implementation of new statutory or regulatory authorities;

(ii) Direct the conduct of all EOIR employees to ensure the efficient disposition of all pending cases, including the power, in his discretion, to set priorities or time frames for the resolution of cases; to direct that the adjudication of certain cases be deferred; to regulate the assignment of adjudicators to cases; and otherwise to manage the docket of matters to be decided by the Board, the immigration judges, the Chief Administrative Hearing Officer, or the administrative law judges;

(iii) Provide for appropriate administrative coordination with the other components of the Department of Justice, with the Department of Homeland Security, with the Department of Health and Human Services, and with the Department of State;

(iv) Evaluate the performance of the Board of Immigration Appeals, the Office of the Chief Immigration Judge, the Office of the Chief Administrative Hearing Officer, and other EOIR activities, make appropriate reports and inspections, and take corrective action where needed;

(v) Provide for performance appraisals for immigration judges and Board members while fully respecting their roles as adjudicators, including a process for reporting adjudications that reflect temperament problems or poor decisional quality;

(vi) Administer an examination for newly-appointed immigration judges and Board members with respect to their familiarity with key principles of immigration law before they begin to adjudicate matters, and evaluate the temperament and skills of each new immigration judge or Board member within 2 years of appointment;

(vii) Provide for comprehensive, continuing training and support for Board members, immigration judges, and EOIR staff in order to promote the quality and consistency of adjudications;

(viii) Implement a process for receiving, evaluating, and responding to complaints of inappropriate conduct by EOIR adjudicators; and

(ix) Exercise such other authorities as the Attorney General may provide.

(2) Delegations.

(i) Except as provided in paragraph (b)(2)(ii) of this section, the Director may delegate the authority given to him by this part or otherwise by the Attorney General to the Deputy Director, the Chairman of the Board of Immigration Appeals, the Chief Immigration Judge, the Chief Administrative Hearing Officer, the Assistant Director for Policy, the General Counsel, or any other EOIR employee.

(ii) The Director may not delegate the authority assigned to the Director in § 1292.18 of this chapter and may not delegate any other authority to adjudicate cases arising under the Act or regulations of this chapter unless expressly authorized to do so.

(c) Limit on the authority of the Director. Except as provided by statute, regulation, or delegation of authority from the Attorney General, or when acting as a designee of the Attorney General, the Director shall have no authority to adjudicate cases arising under the Act or regulations or to direct the result of an adjudication assigned to the Board, an immigration judge, the Chief Administrative Hearing Officer, or an Administrative Law Judge. When acting under authority described in this paragraph (c), the Director shall exercise independent judgment and discretion in considering and determining the cases and may take any action consistent with the Director's authority as is appropriate and necessary for the disposition of the case. Nothing in this part, however, shall be construed to limit the authority of the Director under paragraph (a) or (b) of this section.

(d) Deputy Director. The Deputy Director shall advise and assist the Director in the supervision and management of EOIR and the formulation of policy and guidelines. Unless otherwise limited by law or by order of the Director, the Deputy Director shall exercise the full authority of the Director in the discharge of his or her duties.

(e) Office of Policy. Within EOIR, there shall be an Office of Policy consisting of an Assistant Director for Policy and other such staff as the Director deems necessary. Subject to the supervision of the Director, the Office of Policy shall provide assistance to the Director and heads of the other components within EOIR.

(1) In general. In coordination with the Director and subject to the Director's supervision, the Assistant Director for Policy shall supervise all policy activities of EOIR. Subject to the supervision of the Director and in coordination with other components as appropriate, the Assistant Director for Policy shall also oversee EOIR's regulatory development and implementation process, shall supervise and coordinate EOIR's internal development, dissemination, and implementation of policy guidance, shall supervise and administer EOIR's pro bono and legal orientation program activities, shall supervise the provision of legal and policy training to all components within EOIR on all relevant matters under its supervision, and shall perform other such duties or exercise other such authorities as the Director may provide.

(2) Limit on the Authority of the Assistant Director for Policy. The Assistant Director for Policy shall have no authority to adjudicate cases arising under the Act or regulations, except under paragraph (e)(3) of this section, and shall not direct the result of an adjudication assigned to the Board, an immigration judge, the Chief Administrative Hearing Officer, or an Administrative Law Judge; provided, however, that nothing in this part shall be construed to limit the authority of the Assistant Director for Policy under paragraph (e)(1) of this section.

(3) Recognition and accreditation. The Assistant Director for Policy, in consultation with the Director, shall maintain a division within the Office of Policy to develop and administer a program to recognize organizations and accredit representatives to provide representation before the Immigration Courts, the Board, and DHS, or DHS alone. The Assistant Director for Policy shall determine whether an organization and its representatives meet the eligibility requirements for recognition and accreditation in accordance with this chapter. The Assistant Director for Policy shall also have the authority to administratively terminate the recognition of an organization and the accreditation of a representative and to maintain the roster of recognized organizations and their accredited representatives. The Assistant Director for Policy, in consultation with the Director, may also delegate authority established in 8 CFR 1292.6 and 8 CFR 1292.11 through 1292.20 within the Office of Policy.

(f) General Counsel. Subject to the supervision of the Director, the General Counsel shall serve as the chief legal counsel of EOIR on matters of ethics, records management, release of information pursuant to the Freedom of Information Act, employee performance and discipline (except in matters related to the discipline of adjudicators for decisions made in the adjudication of cases under the Act), practitioner discipline, and other related areas not inconsistent with the law. Subject to the supervision of the Director, the General Counsel shall supervise all legal activities and provide legal advice and assistance to the Director, Deputy Director, and other component heads in accordance with this section. In consultation with other EOIR components as appropriate, the General Counsel may also advise the Director or Deputy Director on other legal matters, including matters related to immigration law or policy and related to adjudicator discipline, provided that the General Counsel shall have no authority, directly or indirectly, to direct or influence the adjudication of any cases under the Act.

(1) Professional standards. The General Counsel shall administer programs to protect the integrity of legal representation in immigration proceedings before EOIR, including administering the disciplinary program for practitioners and recognized organizations under subpart G of this part.

(2) Fraud issues. The General Counsel shall designate an anti-fraud officer who shall—

(i) Serve as a point of contact relating to concerns about possible fraud upon EOIR, particularly with respect to matters relating to fraudulent applications or documents affecting multiple removal proceedings, applications for relief from removal, appeals, or other proceedings before EOIR;

(ii) Coordinate with investigative authorities of the Department of Homeland Security, the Department of Justice, and other appropriate agencies with respect to the identification of and response to such fraud; and

(iii) Notify the EOIR disciplinary counsel and other appropriate authorities with respect to instances of fraud, misrepresentation, or abuse pertaining to an attorney or accredited representative.

(g) Citizenship Requirement for Employment.

(1) An application to work at EOIR, either as an employee or a volunteer, must include a signed affirmation from the applicant that he or she is a citizen of the United States of America. If requested, the applicant must document United States citizenship.

(2) The Director of EOIR may, by explicit written determination and to the extent permitted by law, authorize the appointment of an alien to an EOIR position when necessary to accomplish the work of EOIR.

HISTORY:

[48 FR 8039, Feb. 25, 1983; 60 FR 29468, June 5, 1995; 63 FR 51518, 51519, Sept. 28, 1998; redesignated at 68 FR 9824, 9830, Feb. 28, 2003; 72 FR 53673, 53676, Sept. 20, 2007; 81 FR 92346, 92361, Dec. 19, 2016; 84 FR 44537, 44541, Aug. 26, 2019; as confirmed at 85 FR 69465, Nov. 3, 2020; 85 FR 69465, 69482, Nov. 3, 2020; 89 FR 46742, 46787, May 29, 2024]

Subpart A

Board of Immigration Appeals

§ 1003.1 Organization, jurisdiction, and powers of the Board of Immigration Appeals.

(a)(1) Organization. There shall be in the Department of Justice a Board of Immigration Appeals, subject to the general supervision of the Director, Executive Office for Immigration Review (EOIR). The Board shall consist of 15 members.. The Board shall consist of 28 members. A vacancy, or the absence or unavailability of a Board member, shall not impair the right of the remaining members to exercise all the powers of the Board. The Board members shall also be known as Appellate Immigration Judges.

(2) Chairman. The Attorney General shall designate one of the Board members to serve as Chairman. The Attorney General may designate one or two Vice Chairmen to assist the Chairman in the performance of his duties and to exercise all of the powers and duties of the Chairman in the absence or unavailability of the Chairman. The Chairman of the Board of Immigration Appeals shall also be known as the Chief Appellate Immigration Judge, and a Vice Chairman of the Board of Immigration Appeals shall also be known as a Deputy Chief Appellate Immigration Judge.

(i) The Chairman, subject to the supervision of the Director, shall direct, supervise, and establish internal operating procedures and policies of the Board. The Chairman shall have authority to:

(A) Issue operational instructions and policy, including procedural instructions regarding the implementation of new statutory or regulatory authorities;

(B) Provide for appropriate training of Board members and staff on the conduct of their powers and duties;

(C) Direct the conduct of all employees assigned to the Board to ensure the efficient disposition of all pending cases, including the power, in his discretion, to set priorities or time frames for the resolution of cases; to direct that the adjudication of certain cases be deferred, to regulate the assignment of Board members to cases, and otherwise to manage the docket of matters to be decided by the Board;

(D) Evaluate the performance of the Board by making appropriate reports and inspections, and take corrective action where needed;

(E) Adjudicate cases as a Board member, including the authorities described in paragraph (d)(1)(ii) of this section; and

(F) Exercise such other authorities as the Director may provide.

(ii) The Chairman shall have no authority to direct the result of an adjudication assigned to another Board member or to a panel; provided, however, that nothing in this section shall be construed to limit the management authority of the Chairman under paragraph (a)(2)(i) of this section.

(3) Panels. The Chairman shall divide the Board into three-member panels and designate a presiding member of each panel if the Chairman or Vice Chairman is not assigned to the panel. The Chairman may from time to time make changes in the composition of such panels and of presiding members. Each three-member panel shall be empowered to decide cases by majority vote, and a majority of the Board members assigned to the panel shall constitute a quorum for such panel. In addition, the Chairman shall assign any number of Board members, as needed, to serve on the screening panel to implement the case management process as provided in paragraph (e) of this section.

(4) Temporary Board members. Upon the recommendation of the Director, the Attorney General may in his discretion appoint immigration judges, retired Board members, retired immigration judges, and administrative law judges employed within, or retired from, EOIR to serve as temporary Board members for renewable terms not to exceed six months. In addition, upon the recommendation of the Director and with the approval of the Deputy Attorney General, the Attorney General may in his discretion appoint one or more senior EOIR attorneys with at least ten years of experience in the field of immigration law to serve as temporary Board members for renewable terms not to exceed six months. A temporary Board member shall have the authority of a Board member to adjudicate assigned cases, except that temporary Board members shall not have the authority to vote on any matter decided by the Board en banc. Temporary Board members shall also be known as temporary Appellate Immigration Judges.

(5) En banc process. A majority of the permanent Board members shall constitute a quorum for purposes of convening the Board en banc. The Board may on its own motion by a majority vote of the permanent Board members, or by direction of the Chairman, consider any case en banc, or reconsider as the Board en banc any case that has been considered or decided by a three-member panel. En banc proceedings are not favored, and shall ordinarily be ordered only where necessary to address an issue of particular importance or to secure or maintain consistency of the Board's decisions.

(6) Board staff. There shall also be attached to the Board such number of attorneys and other employees as the Deputy Attorney General, upon recommendation of the Director, shall from time to time direct.

(7) [Reserved]

(b) Appellate jurisdiction. Appeals may be filed with the Board of Immigration Appeals from the following:

(1) Decisions of Immigration Judges in exclusion cases, as provided in 8 CFR part 240, subpart D.

(2) Decisions of Immigration Judges in deportation cases, as provided in 8 CFR part 1240, Subpart E, except that no appeal shall lie seeking review of a length of a period of voluntary departure granted by an Immigration Judge under section 244E of the Act as it existed prior to April 1, 1997.

(3) Decisions of Immigration Judges in removal proceedings, as provided in 8 CFR part 1240, except that no appeal shall lie seeking review of the length of a period of voluntary departure granted by an immigration judge under section 240B of the Act or part 1240 of this chapter.

(4) Decisions involving administrative fines and penalties, including mitigation thereof, as provided in part 280 of this chapter.

(5) Decisions on petitions filed in accordance with section 204 of the act (except petitions to accord preference classifications under section 203(a)(3) or section 203(a)(6) of the act, or a petition on behalf of a child described in section 101(b)(1)(F) of the act), and decisions on requests for revalidation and decisions revoking the approval of such petitions, in accordance with section 205 of the act, as provided in parts 204 and 205, respectively, of 8 CFR chapter I or parts 1204 and 1205, respectively, of this chapter.

(6) Decisions on applications for the exercise of the discretionary authority contained in section 212(d)(3) of the act as provided in part 1212 of this chapter.

(7) Determinations relating to bond, parole, or detention of an alien as provided in 8 CFR part 1236, subpart A.

(8) Decisions of Immigration Judges in rescission of adjustment of status cases, as provided in part 1246 of this chapter.

(9) Decisions of Immigration Judges in asylum proceedings pursuant to § 1208.2(b) and (c) of this chapter.

(10) Decisions of Immigration Judges relating to Temporary Protected Status as provided in 8 CFR part 1244.

(11) [Reserved]

(12) Decisions of Immigration Judges on applications for adjustment of status referred on a Notice of Certification (Form I-290C) to the Immigration Court in accordance with §§ 1245.13(n)(2) and 1245.15(n)(3) of this chapter or remanded to the Immigration Court in accordance with §§ 1245.13(d)(2) and 1245.15(e)(2) of this chapter.

(13) Decisions of adjudicating officials in disciplinary proceedings involving practitioners or recognized organizations as provided in subpart G of this part.

(14) Decisions of immigration judges regarding custody of aliens subject to a final order of removal made pursuant to § 1241.14 of this chapter.

(c) Jurisdiction by certification. The Secretary, or any other duly authorized officer of DHS, an immigration judge, or the Board may in any case arising under paragraph (b) of this section certify such case to the Board for adjudication. The Board, in its discretion, may review any such case by certification without regard to the provisions of § 1003.7 if it determines that the parties have already been given a fair opportunity to make representations before the Board regarding the case, including the opportunity to request oral argument and to submit a brief.

(d) Powers of the Board —

(1) Generally. The Board shall function as an appellate body charged with the review of those administrative adjudications under the Act that the Attorney General may by regulation assign to it. The Board shall resolve the questions before it in a manner that is timely, impartial, and consistent with the Act and regulations. In addition, the Board, through precedent decisions, shall provide clear and uniform guidance to DHS, the immigration judges, and the general public on the proper interpretation and administration of the Act and its implementing regulations.

(i) The Board shall be governed by the provisions and limitations prescribed by applicable law, regulations, and procedures, and by decisions of the Attorney General (through review of a decision of the Board, by written order, or by determination and ruling pursuant to section 103 of the Act).

(ii) Subject to the governing standards set forth in paragraph (d)(1)(i) of this section, Board members shall exercise their independent judgment and discretion in considering and determining the cases coming before the Board, and a panel or Board member to whom a case is assigned may take any action consistent with their authorities under the Act and the regulations as necessary or appropriate for the disposition or alternative resolution of the case. Such actions include administrative closure, termination of proceedings, and dismissal of proceedings. The standards for the administrative closure, dismissal, and termination of cases are set forth in paragraph (l) of this section, 8 CFR 1239.2(c), and paragraph (m) of this section, respectively.

(2) Summary dismissal of appeals —

(i) Standards. A single Board member or panel may summarily dismiss any appeal or portion of any appeal in any case in which:

(A) The party concerned fails to specify the reasons for the appeal on Form EOIR-26 or Form EOIR-29 (Notices of Appeal) or other document filed therewith;

(B) The only reason for the appeal specified by the party concerned involves a finding of fact or a conclusion of law that was conceded by that party at a prior proceeding;

(C) The appeal is from an order that granted the party concerned the relief that had been requested;

(D) The Board is satisfied, from a review of the record, that the appeal is filed for an improper purpose, such as to cause unnecessary delay, or that the appeal lacks an arguable basis in fact or in law unless the Board determines that it is supported by a good faith argument for extension, modification, or reversal of existing law;

(E) The party concerned indicates on Form EOIR-26 or Form EOIR-29 that he or she will file a brief or statement in support of the appeal and, thereafter, does not file such brief or statement, or reasonably explain his or her failure to do so, within the time set for filing;

(F) The appeal does not fall within the Board's jurisdiction, or lies with the Immigration Judge rather than the Board;

(G) The appeal is untimely, or barred by an affirmative waiver of the right of appeal that is clear on the record; or

(H) The appeal fails to meet essential statutory or regulatory requirements or is expressly excluded by statute or regulation.

(ii) Action by the Board. The Board's case management screening plan shall promptly identify cases that are subject to summary dismissal pursuant to this paragraph. An order dismissing any appeal pursuant to this paragraph (d)(2) shall constitute the final decision of the Board.

(iii) Disciplinary consequences. The filing by a practitioner, as defined in § 1003.101(b), of an appeal that is summarily dismissed under paragraph (d)(2)(i) of this section, may constitute frivolous behavior under § 1003.102(j). Summary dismissal of an appeal under paragraph (d)(2)(i) of this section does not limit the other grounds and procedures for disciplinary action against attorneys or representatives.

(3) Scope of review.

(i) The Board will not engage in de novo review of findings of fact determined by an immigration judge. Facts determined by the immigration judge, including findings as to the credibility of testimony, shall be reviewed only to determine whether the findings of the immigration judge are clearly erroneous.

(ii) The Board may review questions of law, discretion, and judgment and all other issues in appeals from decisions of immigration judges de novo.

(iii) The Board may review de novo all questions arising in appeals from decisions issued by DHS officers.

(iv) Except for taking administrative notice of commonly known facts such as current events or the contents of official documents, the Board will not engage in factfinding in the course of deciding cases. A party asserting that the Board cannot properly resolve an appeal without further factfinding must file a motion for remand. If new evidence is submitted on appeal, that submission may be deemed a motion to remand and considered accordingly. If further factfinding is needed in a particular case, the Board may remand the proceeding to the immigration judge or, as appropriate, to DHS.

(4) Rules of practice. The Board shall have authority, with the approval of the Director, EOIR, to prescribe procedures governing proceedings before it.

(5) Discipline of practitioners and recognized organizations. The Board shall have the authority pursuant to § 1003.101 et seq. to impose sanctions upon practitioners who appear in a representative capacity before the Board, the Immigration Courts, or DHS, and upon recognized organizations. The Board shall also have the authority pursuant to § 1003.107 to reinstate disciplined practitioners to appear in a representative capacity before the Board and the Immigration Courts, or DHS, or all three authorities.

(6) Identity, law enforcement, or security investigations or examinations

(i) The Board shall not issue a decision affirming or granting to an alien an immigration status, relief or protection from removal, or other immigration benefit, as provided in 8 CFR 1003.47(b), that requires completion of identity, law enforcement, or security investigations or examinations if:

(A) Identity, law enforcement, or security investigations or examinations have not been completed during the proceedings;

(B) DHS reports to the Board that the results of prior identity, law enforcement, or security investigations or examinations are no longer current under the standards established by DHS and must be updated; or

(C) Identity, law enforcement, or security investigations or examinations have uncovered new information bearing on the merits of the alien's application for relief.

(ii) Except as provided in paragraph (d)(6)(iv) of this section, if identity, law enforcement, or security investigations or examinations are necessary in order to adjudicate the appeal or motion, the Board will provide notice to both parties that the case is being placed on hold until such time as all identity, law enforcement, or security investigations or examinations are completed or updated and the results have been reported to the Board. The Board's notice will notify the noncitizen that DHS will contact the noncitizen with instructions, consistent with § 1003.47(d), to take any additional steps necessary to complete or update the identity, law enforcement, or security investigations or examinations only if DHS is unable to independently update the necessary identity, law enforcement, or security investigations or examinations. The Board's notice will also advise the noncitizen of the consequences for failing to comply with the requirements of this section. DHS is responsible for obtaining biometrics and other biographical information to complete or update the identity, law enforcement, or security investigations or examinations with respect to any noncitizen in detention.

(iii) In any case placed on hold under paragraph (d)(6)(ii) of this section, DHS shall report to the Board promptly when the identity, law enforcement, or security investigations or examinations have been completed or updated. If DHS obtains relevant information as a result of the identity, law enforcement, or security investigations or examinations, or if the noncitizen fails to comply with the necessary procedures for collecting biometrics or other biographical information after receiving instructions from DHS under paragraph (d)(6)(ii) of this section, DHS may move the Board to remand the record to the immigration judge for consideration of whether, in view of the new information, or the noncitizen's failure to comply with the necessary procedures for collecting biometrics or other biographical information after receiving instructions from DHS under paragraph (d)(6)(ii) of this section, immigration relief or protection should be denied, either on grounds of ineligibility as a matter of law or as a matter of discretion. If DHS fails to report the results of timely completed or updated identity, law enforcement or security investigations or examinations within 180 days from the date of the Board's notice under paragraph (d)(6)(ii) of this section, the Board may continue to hold the case under paragraph (d)(6)(ii) of this section, as needed, or remand the case to the immigration judge for further proceedings under § 1003.47(h).

(iv) The Board is not required to hold a case pursuant to paragraph (d)(6)(ii) of this section if the Board decides to dismiss the respondent's appeal or deny the relief or protection sought.

(v) The immigration relief or protection described in § 1003.47(b) and granted by the Board shall take effect as provided in § 1003.47(i).

(7) Finality of decision.

(i) The decision of the Board shall be final except in those cases reviewed by the Attorney General in accordance with paragraph (h) of this section. The Board may return a case to DHS or an immigration judge for such further action as may be appropriate without entering a final decision on the merits of the case.

(ii) In cases involving voluntary departure, the Board may issue an order of voluntary departure under section 240B of the Act, with an alternate order of removal, if the noncitizen requested voluntary departure before an immigration judge, the noncitizen's notice of appeal specified that the noncitizen is appealing the immigration judge's denial of voluntary departure and identified the specific factual and legal findings that the noncitizen is challenging, and the Board finds that the noncitizen is otherwise eligible for voluntary departure, as provided in 8 CFR 1240.26(k). In order to grant voluntary departure, the Board must find that all applicable statutory and regulatory criteria have been met, based on the record and within the scope of its review authority on appeal, and that the noncitizen merits voluntary departure as a matter of discretion. If the record does not contain sufficient factual findings regarding eligibility for voluntary departure, the Board may remand the decision to the immigration judge for further factfinding.

(e) Case management system. The Chairman shall establish a case management system to screen all cases and to manage the Board's caseload. Unless a case meets the standards for assignment to a three-member panel under paragraph (e)(6) of this section, all cases shall be assigned to a single Board member for disposition. The Chairman, under the supervision of the Director, shall be responsible for the success of the case management system. The Chairman shall designate, from time to time, a screening panel comprising a sufficient number of Board members who are authorized, acting alone, to adjudicate appeals as provided in this paragraph (e). The provisions of this paragraph (e) shall apply to all cases before the Board, regardless of whether they were initiated by filing a Notice of Appeal, filing a motion, or receipt of a remand from Federal court or the Attorney General.

(1) Initial screening. All cases shall be referred to the screening panel for review. Appeals subject to summary dismissal as provided in paragraph (d)(2) of this section should be promptly dismissed.

(2) Miscellaneous dispositions. A single Board member may grant an unopposed motion or a motion to withdraw an appeal pending before the Board. In addition, a single Board member may adjudicate a DHS motion to remand any appeal from the decision of a DHS officer where DHS requests that the matter be remanded to DHS for further consideration of the appellant's arguments or evidence raised on appeal; a case where remand is required because of a defective or missing transcript; and other procedural or ministerial issues as provided by the case management plan.

(3) Merits review. In any case that has not been summarily dismissed, the case management system shall arrange for the prompt completion of the record of proceeding and transcript, and the issuance of a briefing schedule, as appropriate. A single Board member assigned under the case management system shall determine the appeal on the merits as provided in paragraph (e)(4) or (5) of this section, unless the Board member determines that the case is appropriate for review and decision by a three-member panel under the standards of paragraph (e)(6) of this section. The Board member may summarily dismiss an appeal after completion of the record of proceeding.

(4) Affirmance without opinion

(i) The Board member to whom a case is assigned shall affirm the decision of the DHS officer or the immigration judge without opinion if the Board member determines that the result reached in the decision under review was correct; that any errors in the decision under review were harmless or nonmaterial; and that

(A) The issues on appeal are squarely controlled by existing Board or federal court precedent and do not involve the application of precedent to a novel factual situation; or

(B) The factual and legal issues raised on appeal are not so substantial that the case warrants the issuance of a written opinion in the case.

(ii) If the Board member determines that the decision should be affirmed without opinion, the Board shall issue an order that reads as follows: "The Board affirms, without opinion, the result of the decision below. The decision below is, therefore, the final agency determination. See 8 CFR 1003.1(e)(4)." An order affirming without opinion issued under authority of this provision shall not include further explanation or reasoning. Such an order approves the result reached in the decision below; it does not necessarily imply approval of all of the reasoning of that decision but does signify the Board's conclusion that any errors in the decision of the immigration judge or DHS were harmless or nonmaterial.

(5) Other decisions on the merits by single Board member. If the Board member to whom an appeal is assigned determines, upon consideration of the merits, that the decision is not appropriate for affirmance without opinion, the Board member shall issue a brief order affirming, modifying, or remanding the decision under review, unless the Board member designates the case for decision by a three-member panel under paragraph (e)(6) of this section under the standards of the case management plan. A single Board member may reverse the decision under review if such reversal is plainly consistent with and required by intervening Board or judicial precedent, by an intervening Act of Congress, or by an intervening final regulation. A motion to reconsider or to reopen a decision that was rendered by a single Board member may be adjudicated by that Board member unless the case is reassigned to a three-member panel as provided under the standards of the case management plan.

(6) Panel decisions. Cases may only be assigned for review by a three-member panel if the case presents one of these circumstances:

(i) The need to settle inconsistencies among the rulings of different immigration judges;

(ii) The need to establish a precedent construing the meaning of laws, regulations, or procedures;

(iii) The need to review a decision by an immigration judge or DHS that is not in conformity with the law or with applicable precedents;

(iv) The need to resolve a case or controversy of major national import;

(v) The need to review a clearly erroneous factual determination by an immigration judge;

(vi) The need to reverse the decision of an immigration judge or DHS, other than a reversal under § 1003.1(e)(5) or

(vii) The need to resolve a complex, novel, unusual, or recurring issue of law or fact.

(7) Oral argument. When an appeal has been taken, a request for oral argument if desired shall be included in the Notice of Appeal. A three-member panel or the Board en banc may hear oral argument, as a matter of discretion, at such date and time as is established under the Board's case management plan. Oral argument shall be held at the offices of the Board unless the Deputy Attorney General or the Deputy Attorney General's designee authorizes oral argument to be held elsewhere. DHS may be represented before the Board by an officer or counsel of DHS designated by DHS. No oral argument will be allowed in a case that is assigned for disposition by a single Board member.

(8) Timeliness. As provided under the case management system, the Board shall promptly enter orders of summary dismissal, or other miscellaneous dispositions, in appropriate cases consistent with paragraph (e)(1) of this section. In all other cases, after completion of the record on appeal, including any briefs, motions, or other submissions on appeal, the Board member or panel to which the case is assigned shall issue a decision on the merits as soon as practicable, with a priority for cases or custody appeals involving detained noncitizens.

(i) Except in exigent circumstances as determined by the Chairman, or as provided in paragraph (d)(6) of this section, the Board shall dispose of all cases assigned to a single Board member within 90 days of completion of the record, or within 180 days after a case is assigned to a three-member panel (including any additional opinion by a member of the panel).

(ii) In exigent circumstances, the Chairman may grant an extension in particular cases of up to 60 days as a matter of discretion. Except as provided in paragraph (e)(8)(iii) or (iv) of this section, in those cases where the panel is unable to issue a decision within the established time limits, as extended, the Chairman shall either self-assign the case or assign the case to a Vice Chairman for final decision within 14 days or shall refer the case to the Attorney General for decision. If a dissenting or concurring panel member fails to complete the member's opinion by the end of the extension period, the decision of the majority will be issued without the separate opinion.

(iii) In rare circumstances, such as when an impending decision by the United States Supreme Court or a United States Court of Appeals, or impending Department regulatory amendments, or an impending en banc Board decision may substantially determine the outcome of a case or group of cases pending before the Board, the Chairman may hold the case or cases until such decision is rendered, temporarily suspending the time limits described in this paragraph (e)(8).

(iv) [Reserved]

(v) The Chairman shall notify the Director of EOIR and the Attorney General if a Board member consistently fails to meet the assigned deadlines for the disposition of appeals, or otherwise fails to adhere to the standards of the case management system. The Chairman shall also prepare a report assessing the timeliness of the disposition of cases by each Board member on an annual basis.

(vi) The provisions of this paragraph (e)(8) establishing time limits for the adjudication of appeals reflect an internal management directive in favor of timely dispositions, but do not affect the validity of any decision issued by the Board and do not, and shall not be interpreted to, create any substantive or procedural rights enforceable before any immigration judge or the Board, or in any court of law or equity.

(9) The provisions of paragraphs (e)(4)(i) and (e)(5) and (6) of this section are internal agency directives for the purpose of efficient management and disposition of cases pending before the Board and are not intended to create any substantive or procedural rights to a particular form of Board decision. A decision by the Board under paragraph (e)(4), (5), or (6) of this section carries the presumption that the Board properly and thoroughly considered all issues, arguments, and claims raised or presented by the parties on appeal or in a motion that were deemed appropriate to the disposition of the appeal or motion, whether or not specifically mentioned in the decision. A decision by the Board under paragraph (e)(4), (5), or (6) also carries the presumption that the Board did not need to consider any issue, argument, or claim not raised or presented by the parties on appeal or in a motion to the Board. In any decision under paragraph (e)(5) or (6) of this section, the Board may rule, in the exercise of its discretion as provided under this part, on any issue, argument, or claim not raised by the parties, and the Board may solicit supplemental briefing from the parties on the issues to be considered before rendering a decision.

(f) Service of Board decisions. The decision of the Board shall be in writing. The Board shall transmit a copy to DHS and serve a copy upon the noncitizen or the noncitizen's representative, as provided in 8 CFR part 1292.

(g) Decisions as precedents—

(1) In general. Except as Board decisions may be modified or overruled by the Board or the Attorney General, decisions of the Board and decisions of the Attorney General are binding on all officers and employees of DHS or immigration judges in the administration of the immigration laws of the United States.

(2) Precedent decisions. Selected decisions designated by the Board, decisions of the Attorney General,

and decisions of the Secretary of Homeland Security as provided in paragraph (h)(2)(i) of this section will be published and serve as precedents in all proceedings involving the same issue or issues.

(3) Designation of precedents. By majority vote of the permanent Board members, or as directed by the Attorney General or his designee, selected decisions of the Board issued by a three-member panel or by the Board en banc may be designated to be published and to serve as precedents in all proceedings involving the same issue or issues. In determining whether to publish a precedent decision, the Board may take into account relevant considerations, in the exercise of discretion, including among other matters:

(i) Whether the case involves a substantial issue of first impression;

(ii) Whether the case involves a legal, factual, procedural, or discretionary issue that can be expected to arise frequently in immigration cases;

(iii) Whether the issuance of a precedent decision is needed because the decision announces a new rule of law, or modifies, clarifies, or distinguishes a rule of law or prior precedent;

(iv) Whether the case involves a conflict in decisions by immigration judges, the Board, or the federal courts;

(v) Whether there is a need to achieve, maintain, or restore national uniformity of interpretation of issues under the immigration laws or regulations; and

(vi) Whether the case warrants publication in light of other factors that give it general public interest.

(h) Referral of cases to the Attorney General.

(1) The Board shall refer to the Attorney General for review of its decision all cases that:

(i) The Attorney General directs the Board to refer to him.

(ii) The Chairman or a majority of the Board believes should be referred to the Attorney General for review.

(iii) The Secretary of Homeland Security, or specific officials of the Department of Homeland Security designated by the Secretary with the concurrence of the Attorney General, refers to the Attorney General for review.

(2) In any case the Attorney General decides, the Attorney General's decision shall be stated in writing and shall be transmitted to the Board or Secretary, as appropriate, for transmittal and service as provided in paragraph (f) of this section.

(i) Publication of Secretary's precedent decisions. The Secretary of Homeland Security, or specific officials of the Department of Homeland Security designated by the Secretary with the concurrence of the Attorney General, may file with the Attorney General decisions relating to the administration of the immigration laws of the United States for publication as precedent in future proceedings, and, upon approval of the Attorney General as to the lawfulness of such decision, the Director of the Executive Office for Immigration Review shall cause such decisions to be published in the same manner as decisions of the Board and the Attorney General.

(j) Continuation of jurisdiction and procedure. The jurisdiction of, and procedures before, the Board of Immigration Appeals in exclusion, deportation, removal, rescission, asylum-only, and any other proceedings, shall remain in effect as in effect on February 28, 2003, until the regulations in this chapter are further modified by the Attorney General. Where a decision of an officer of the Immigration and Naturalization Service was, before March 1, 2003, appealable to the Board or to an immigration judge, or an application denied could be renewed in proceedings before an immigration judge, the same authority and procedures shall be followed until further modified by the Attorney General.

(k) [Reserved.]

(l) Administrative closure and recalendaring. Administrative closure is the temporary suspension of a case. Administrative closure removes a case from the Board's docket until the case is recalendared. Recalendaring places a case back on the Board's docket.

(1) Administrative closure before the Board. Board Members may, in the exercise of discretion, administratively close a case upon the motion of a party, after applying the standard set forth at paragraph (l)(3) of this section. The administrative closure authority described in this section is not limited by the authority provided in any other provisions in this title that separately authorize or require administrative closure in certain circumstances, including 8 CFR 214.15(l), 245.15(p)(4), 1214.2(a), 1214.3, 1240.62(b), 1240.70(f) through (h), 1245.13, 1245.15(p)(4)(i), and 1245.21(c).

(2) Recalendaring before the Board. At any time after a case has been administratively closed under paragraph (l)(1) of this section, the Board may, in the exercise of discretion, recalendar the case pursuant to a party's motion to recalendar. In deciding whether to grant such a motion, the Board shall apply the standard set forth at paragraph (l)(3) of this section.

(3) Standard for administrative closure and recalendaring. The Board shall grant a motion to administratively close or recalendar filed jointly by both parties, or filed by one party where the other party has affirmatively indicated its non-opposition, unless the Board articulates unusual, clearly identified, and supported reasons for denying the motion. In all other cases, in deciding whether to administratively close or to recalendar a case, the Board shall consider the totality of the circumstances, including as many of the factors listed under paragraphs (l)(3)(i) and (ii) of this section as are relevant to the particular case. The Board may also consider other factors where appropriate. No single factor is dispositive. The Board, having considered the totality of the circumstances, may grant a motion to administratively close or to recalendar a particular case over the objection of a party. Although administrative closure may be appropriate where a petition, application, or other action is pending outside of proceedings before the Board, such a pending petition, application, or other action is not required for a case to be administratively closed.

(i) As the circumstances of the case warrant, the factors relevant to a decision to administratively close a case include:

(A) The reason administrative closure is sought;

(B) The basis for any opposition to administrative closure;

(C) Any requirement that a case be administratively closed in order for a petition, application, or other action to be filed with, or granted by, DHS;

(D) The likelihood the noncitizen will succeed on any petition, application, or other action that the noncitizen is pursuing, or that the noncitizen states in writing or on the record at a hearing that they plan to pursue, outside of proceedings before the Board;

(E) The anticipated duration of the administrative closure;

(F) The responsibility of either party, if any, in contributing to any current or anticipated delay;

(G) The ultimate anticipated outcome of the case pending before the Board; and

(H) The ICE detention status of the noncitizen.

(ii) As the circumstances of the case warrant, the factors relevant to a decision to recalendar a case include:

(A) The reason recalendaring is sought;

(B) The basis for any opposition to recalendaring;

(C) The length of time elapsed since the case was administratively closed;

(D) If the case was administratively closed to allow the noncitizen to file a petition, application, or other action outside of proceedings before the Board, whether the noncitizen filed the petition, application, or other action and, if so, the length of time that elapsed between when the case was administratively closed and when the noncitizen filed the petition, application, or other action;

(E) If a petition, application, or other action that was pending outside of proceedings before the Board has been adjudicated, the result of that adjudication;

(F) If a petition, application, or other action remains pending outside of proceedings before the Board, the likelihood the noncitizen will succeed on that petition, application, or other action;

(G) The ultimate anticipated outcome if the case is recalendared; and

(H) The ICE detention status of the noncitizen.

(m) Termination. The Board shall have the authority to terminate cases before it as set forth in paragraphs (m)(1) and (2) of this section. A motion to dismiss a case in removal proceedings before the Board for a reason other than authorized by 8 CFR 1239.2(c) shall be deemed a motion to terminate under paragraph (m)(1) of this section.

(1) Removal, deportation, and exclusion proceedings —

(i) Mandatory termination. In removal, deportation, and exclusion proceedings, the Board shall terminate the case where at least one of the requirements in paragraphs (m)(1)(i)(A) through (G) of this section is met.

(A) No charge of deportability, inadmissibility, or excludability can be sustained.

(B) Fundamentally fair proceedings are not possible because the noncitizen is mentally incompetent and adequate safeguards are unavailable.

(C) The noncitizen has, since the initiation of proceedings, obtained United States citizenship.

(D) The noncitizen has, since the initiation of proceedings, obtained at least one status listed in paragraphs (m)(1)(i)(D)(1) through (4) of this section, provided that the status has not been revoked or terminated, and the noncitizen would not have been deportable, inadmissible, or excludable as charged if the noncitizen had obtained such status before the initiation of proceedings.

(1) Lawful permanent resident status.

(2) Refugee status.

(3) Asylee status.

(4) Nonimmigrant status as defined in section 101(a)(15)(S), (T), or (U) of the Act.

(E) Termination is required under 8 CFR 1245.13(l).

(F) Termination is otherwise required by law.

(G) The parties jointly filed a motion to terminate, or one party filed a motion to terminate and the other party affirmatively indicated its non-opposition, unless the Board articulates unusual, clearly identified, and supported reasons for denying the motion.

(ii) Discretionary termination. In removal, deportation, or exclusion proceedings, the Board may, in the exercise of discretion, terminate the case upon the motion of a party where at least one of the requirements listed in paragraphs (m)(1)(ii)(A) through (F) of this section is met. The Board shall consider the reason termination is sought and the basis for any opposition to termination when adjudicating the motion to terminate.

(A) The noncitizen has filed an asylum application with USCIS pursuant to section 208(b)(3)(C) of the Act pertaining to unaccompanied children, as defined in 8 CFR 1001.1(hh).

(B) The noncitizen is prima facie eligible for naturalization, relief from removal, or a lawful status; USCIS has jurisdiction to adjudicate the associated petition, application, or other action if the noncitizen were not in proceedings; and the noncitizen has filed the petition, application, or other action with USCIS. However, no filing is required where the noncitizen is prima facie eligible for adjustment of status or naturalization. Where the basis of a noncitizen's motion for termination is that the noncitizen is prima facie eligible for naturalization, the Board shall not grant the motion if it is opposed by DHS. The Board shall not terminate a case for the noncitizen to pursue an asylum application before USCIS, except as provided for in paragraph (m)(1)(ii)(A) of this section.

(C) The noncitizen is a beneficiary of Temporary Protected Status, deferred action, or Deferred Enforced Departure.

(D) USCIS has granted the noncitizen's application for a provisional unlawful presence waiver pursuant to 8 CFR 212.7(e).

(E) Termination is authorized by 8 CFR 1216.4(a)(6) or 1238.1(e).

(F) Due to circumstances comparable to those described in paragraphs (m)(1)(ii)(A) through (E) of this section, termination is similarly necessary or appropriate for the disposition or alternative resolution of the case. However, the Board may not terminate a case for purely humanitarian reasons, unless DHS expressly consents to such termination, joins in a motion to terminate, or affirmatively indicates its non-opposition to a noncitizen's motion.

(2) Other proceedings —

(i) Mandatory termination. In proceedings other than removal, deportation, or exclusion proceedings, the Board shall terminate the case where the parties have jointly filed a motion to terminate, or one party has filed a motion to terminate and the other party has affirmatively indicated its non-opposition, unless the Board articulates unusual, clearly identified, and supported reasons for denying the motion. In addition, the Board shall terminate such a case where required by law.

(ii) Discretionary termination. In proceedings other than removal, deportation, or exclusion proceedings, the Board may, in the exercise of discretion, terminate the case upon the motion of a party where terminating the case is necessary or appropriate for the disposition or alternative resolution of the case. However, the Board may not terminate a case for purely humanitarian reasons, unless DHS expressly consents to such termination, joins in a motion to terminate, or affirmatively indicates its non-opposition to a noncitizen's motion.

(iii) Limitation on termination. Nothing in paragraphs (m)(2)(i) and (ii) of this section authorizes the Board to terminate a case where prohibited by another regulatory provision. Further, nothing in paragraphs (m)(2)(i) and (ii) of this section authorizes the Board to terminate a case for the noncitizen to pursue an asylum application before USCIS, unless the noncitizen has filed an asylum application with USCIS pursuant to section 208(b)(3)(C) of the Act pertaining to unaccompanied children, as defined in 8 CFR 1001.1(hh).

HISTORY:

[23 FR 9117, Nov. 26, 1958, as amended at 27 FR 96, Jan. 5, 1962.; 27 FR 10789, Nov. 6, 1962; 30 FR 14772, Nov. 30, 1965; 36 FR 316, Jan. 9, 1971.; 40 FR 37207, Aug. 26, 1975; 44 FR 67960, Nov. 28, 1979; 47 FR 16772, Apr. 20, 1982; 48 FR 8039, Feb. 25, 1983; 52 FR 2943, Jan. 29, 1987; 52 FR 24981, July 2, 1987; 53 FR 15659, May 3, 1988; 55 FR 30680, July 27, 1990; 56 FR 624, Jan. 7, 1991.; 57 FR 11570, Apr. 6, 1992; 59 FR 1899, Jan. 13, 1994; 59 FR 47231, Sept. 15, 1994; 60 FR 29469, June 5, 1995; 60 FR 57313, Nov. 15, 1995; 61 FR 18900, 18904, Apr. 29, 1996; 61 FR 59305, Nov. 22, 1996; 62 FR 9071, 9072, Feb. 28, 1997; 62 FR 10312, 10330, Mar. 6, 1997, as corrected at 62 FR 15362, Apr. 1, 1997; 63 FR 27823, 27829, May 21, 1998, as confirmed at 65 FR 15846, 15854, Mar. 24, 2000; 63 FR 31889, 31890, June 11, 1998; 63 FR 51518, 51519, Sept. 28, 1998; 64 FR 25756, 25766, May 12, 1999, as confirmed at 65 FR 15835, 15844, Mar. 24, 2000; 64 FR 56135, 56141, Oct. 18, 1999; 65 FR 20068, Apr. 14, 2000; 65 FR 39513, 39526, June 27, 2000; 66 FR 6436, 6445, Jan. 22, 2001; 66 FR 47379, 47380, Sept. 12, 2001; 66 FR 56967, 56976, Nov. 14, 2001; 67 FR 54878, 54901, Aug. 26, 2002; redesignated and amended at 68 FR 9824, 9830, 9831, 9846, Feb. 28, 2003; 68 FR 10349, 10350, Mar. 5, 2003; 69 FR 44903, 44906, July 28, 2004; 70 FR 4743, 4752, Jan. 31, 2005; 71 FR 70855, 70857, Dec. 7, 2006, as confirmed at 73 FR 33875, 33876, June 16, 2008; 73 FR 76914, 76923, Dec. 18, 2008; 80 FR 31461, 31463, June 3, 2015; 80 FR 59053, 59510, Oct. 1, 2015; 81 FR 92346, 92361, Dec. 19, 2016; 83 FR 8321, 8323, Feb. 27, 2018; 84 FR 31463, 31470, July 2, 2019; 84 FR 44537, 44542, Aug. 26, 2019; as confirmed at 85 FR 69465, Nov. 3, 2020; 85 FR 18105, 18107, Apr. 1, 2020; 85 FR 80274, 80393, Dec. 11, 2020; 85 FR 81588, 81651, Dec. 16, 2020; 86 FR 70708, 70719, Dec. 13, 2021; 89 FR 22630, 22636, Apr. 2, 2024; 89 FR 46742, 46787, May 29, 2024; 90 FR 15525, 15408, Apr. 14, 2025]

§ 1003.2 Reopening or reconsideration before the Board of Immigration Appeals.

(a) General. The Board may at any time reopen or reconsider on its own motion any case in which it has rendered a decision. A request by DHS or by the party affected by the decision to reopen or reconsider a case the Board has decided must be in the form of a written motion to the Board. The decision to grant or deny a motion to reopen or reconsider is within the discretion of the Board, subject to the restrictions of this section. The Board has discretion to deny a motion to reopen even if the moving party has made out a prima facie case for relief.

(b) Motion to reconsider.

(1) A motion to reconsider shall state the reasons for the motion by specifying the errors of fact or law in the prior Board decision and shall be supported by pertinent authority. When a motion to reconsider the decision of an immigration judge or of a DHS officer is pending at the time an appeal is filed with the Board, or when such motion is filed subsequent to the filing with the Board of an appeal from the decision sought to be reconsidered, the motion may be deemed a motion to remand the decision for further proceedings before the immigration judge or the DHS officer from whose decision the appeal was taken. Such motion may be consolidated with and considered by the Board in connection with the appeal to the Board.

(2) A motion to reconsider a decision must be filed with the Board within 30 days after the mailing of the Board decision or on or before July 31, 1996, whichever is later. A party may file only one motion to reconsider any given decision and may not seek reconsideration of a decision denying a previous motion to reconsider. In removal proceedings pursuant to section 240 of the Act, an alien may file only one motion to reconsider a decision that the noncitizen is removable from the United States.

(3) A motion to reconsider based solely on an argument that the case should not have been affirmed without opinion by a single Board Member, or by a three-Member panel, is barred.

(c) Motion to reopen.

(1) A motion to reopen proceedings shall state the new facts that will be proven at a hearing to be held if the motion is granted and shall be supported by affidavits or other evidentiary material. A motion to reopen proceedings for the purpose of submitting an application for relief must be accompanied by the appropriate application for relief and all supporting documentation. A motion to reopen proceedings shall not be granted unless it appears to the Board that evidence sought to be offered is material and was not available and could not have been discovered or presented at the former hearing; nor shall any motion to reopen for the purpose of affording the noncitizen an opportunity to apply for any form of discretionary relief be granted if it appears

that the noncitizen's right to apply for such relief was fully explained to him or her and an opportunity to apply therefore was afforded at the former hearing, unless the relief is sought on the basis of circumstances that have arisen subsequent to the hearing. Subject to the other requirements and restrictions of this section, and notwithstanding the provisions in § 1001.1(p) of this chapter, a motion to reopen proceedings for consideration or further consideration of an application for relief under section 212(c) of the Act (8 U.S.C. 1182(c)) may be granted if the noncitizen demonstrates that he or she was statutorily eligible for such relief prior to the entry of the administratively final order of deportation.

(2) Except as provided in paragraph (c)(3) of this section, a party may file only one motion to reopen deportation or exclusion proceedings (whether before the Board or the immigration judge) and that motion must be filed no later than 90 days after the date on which the final administrative decision was rendered in the proceeding sought to be reopened, or on or before September 30, 1996, whichever is later. Except as provided in paragraph (c)(3) of this section, a noncitizen may file only one motion to reopen removal proceedings (whether before the Board or the immigration judge) and that motion must be filed no later than 90 days after the date on which the final administrative decision was rendered in the proceeding sought to be reopened.

(3) In removal proceedings pursuant to section 240 of the Act, the time limitation set forth in paragraph (c)(2) of this section shall not apply to a motion to reopen filed pursuant to the provisions of § 1003.23(b)(4)(ii). The time and numerical limitations set forth in paragraph (c)(2) of this section shall not apply to a motion to reopen proceedings:

(i) Filed pursuant to the provisions of § 1003.23(b)(4)(iii)(A)(1) or § 1003.23(b)(4)(iii)(A)(2);

(ii) To apply or reapply for asylum or withholding of deportation based on changed circumstances arising in the country of nationality or in the country to which deportation has been ordered, if such evidence is material and was not available and could not have been discovered or presented at the previous hearing;

(iii) Agreed upon by all parties and jointly filed. Notwithstanding such agreement, the parties may contest the issues in a reopened proceeding; or

(iv) Filed by DHS in exclusion or deportation proceedings when the basis of the motion is fraud in the original proceeding or a crime that would support termination of asylum in accordance with 8 CFR 1208.24.

(4) A motion to reopen a decision rendered by an immigration judge or DHS officer that is pending when an appeal is filed, or that is filed while an appeal is pending before the Board, may be deemed a motion to remand for further proceedings before the immigration judge or the DHS officer from whose decision the appeal was taken. Such motion may be consolidated with, and considered by the Board in connection with, the appeal to the Board.

(d) Departure, deportation, or removal. A motion to reopen or a motion to reconsider shall not be made by or on behalf of a person who is the subject of exclusion, deportation, or removal proceedings subsequent to his or her departure from the United States. Any departure from the United States, including the deportation or removal of a person who is the subject of exclusion, deportation, or removal proceedings, occurring after the filing of a motion to reopen or a motion to reconsider, shall constitute a withdrawal of such motion.

(e) Judicial proceedings. Motions to reopen or reconsider shall state whether the validity of the exclusion, deportation, or removal order has been or is the subject of any judicial proceeding and, if so, the nature and date thereof, the court in which such proceeding took place or is pending, and its result or status. In any case in which an exclusion, deportation, or removal order is in effect, any motion to reopen or reconsider such order shall include a statement by or on behalf of the moving party declaring whether the subject of the order is also the subject of any pending criminal proceeding under the Act, and, if so, the current status of that proceeding. If a motion to reopen or reconsider seeks discretionary relief, the motion shall include a statement by or on behalf of the moving party declaring whether the noncitizen for whose relief the motion is being filed is subject to any pending criminal prosecution and, if so, the nature and current status of that prosecution.

(f) Stay of deportation. Except where a motion is filed pursuant to the provisions of § 1003.23(b)(4)(ii) and (b)(4)(iii)(A), the filing of a motion to reopen or a motion to reconsider shall not stay the execution of any decision made in the case. Execution of such decision shall proceed unless a stay of execution is specifically granted by the Board, the immigration judge, or an authorized DHS officer.

(g) Filing procedures. This paragraph applies to the filing of documents related to reopening and reconsideration before the Board.

(1) English language, entry of appearance, and proof of service requirements. A motion and any submission made in conjunction with a motion must be in English or accompanied by a certified English translation. If a party other than DHS is represented, any motion or related filing by that party must be accompanied by a Form EOIR–27, Notice of Entry of Appearance as Attorney or Representative Before the Board, pursuant to 8 CFR 1003.38(g)(1). If a party other than DHS is pro se and receives document assistance from a practitioner with a motion or related filing pursuant to 8 CFR 1003.38(g)(2), a Form EOIR–60 must be filed with the motion or related filing. In all cases, the motion must include proof of service on the opposing party of the motion and all attachments. If the moving party is not DHS, service of the motion must be made upon the DHS office in which the case was completed before the immigration judge.

(2) Distribution of motion papers.

(i) A motion to reopen or motion to reconsider a decision of the Board pertaining to proceedings before an immigration judge shall be filed directly with the Board. Such motion must be accompanied by a payment in a manner authorized by EOIR or fee waiver request in satisfaction of the fee requirements of § 1003.8. The record of proceeding pertaining to such a motion shall be forwarded to the Board upon the request or order of the Board.

(ii) A motion to reopen or a motion to reconsider a decision of the Board pertaining to a matter initially adjudicated by an officer of DHS shall be filed with the officer of DHS having administrative control over the record of proceeding.

(iii) If the motion is made by DHS in proceedings in which DHS has administrative control over the record of proceedings, the record of proceedings in the case and the motion shall be filed directly with the Board. If such motion is filed directly with an office of DHS, the entire record of proceeding shall be forwarded to the Board by the DHS officer promptly upon receipt of the briefs of the parties, or upon expiration of the time allowed for the submission of such briefs.

(3) Briefs and response. The moving party may file a brief if it is included with the motion. If the motion is filed directly with the Board pursuant to paragraph (g)(2)(i) of this section, the opposing party shall have 21 days from the date of service of the motion to file a brief in opposition to the motion directly with the Board. If the motion is filed with a DHS office pursuant to paragraph (g)(2)(ii) of this section, the opposing party shall have 21 days from the date of filing of the motion to file a brief in opposition to the motion directly with DHS. In all cases, briefs and any other filings made in conjunction with a motion shall include proof of service on the opposing party. The Board, in its discretion, may extend the time within which such brief is to be submitted and may authorize the filing of a brief directly with the Board. A motion shall be deemed unopposed unless a timely response is made. The Board may, in its discretion, consider a brief filed out of time.

(4) Filing parties. DHS and all attorneys and accredited representatives of record for respondents, applicants, or petitioners are required to electronically file all documents with the Board through EOIR's electronic filing application in all cases eligible for electronic filing. Although not required, unrepresented respondents, applicants, or petitioners; reputable individuals and accredited officials who are the representatives of record; other authorized individuals; and practitioners filing an EOIR-60, may electronically file documents with the Board through EOIR's electronic filing application in cases eligible for electronic filing. An unrepresented respondent, applicant, or petitioner; reputable individual; accredited official; other authorized individual; or practitioner filing an EOIR-60, who elects to use EOIR's electronic filing application shall be required to register with EOIR as a condition of using that application. If a party not required to file electronically opts to use EOIR's electronic filing application for a case, the individual must electronically file all documents with the Board for that case unless the Board, only upon a motion filed by the individual with good cause shown, grants leave to opt out of using the electronic filing application. Such an indvidual who has been granted leave to opt out of using EOIR's electronic filing application for a case may not subsequently opt in again to use that application for the same case.

(5) Filing requirements. Parties must make the originals of all filed documents available upon request to the Board or the opposing party for review. If EOIR's electronic filing application is unavailable due to an unplanned system outage on the last day for filing in a specific case, then the filing deadline will be extended to the first day that the electronic filing application becomes accessible that is not a Saturday, Sunday, or legal holiday. For planned system outages, parties must electronically file documents during system availability within the applicable filing deadline or paper file documents within the applicable filing deadline. EOIR will issue public communications for planned system outages ahead of the scheduled outage. Any planned system outage announced five or fewer business days prior to the start of the outage will be treated as an unplanned outage. The Board retains discretion to accept paper filings in all cases.

(6) Classified information. Notwithstanding any other provision of this chapter, classified information is never allowed to be electronically filed.

(7) Sealed medical documents. Notwithstanding any other provision of this chapter, parties are not permitted to file electronically any sealed medical documents.

(8) Signatures. All documents filed with the Board that require a signature must have an original, handwritten ink signature, an encrypted digital signature, or an electronic signature. Electronic filings submitted through EOIR's electronic filing application that require the user's signature may have a conformed signature. This paragraph (g)(8) is subject to the requirements of the application or document being submitted.

(9) Service. The service of filings with the Board depends on whether the documents are filed through EOIR's electronic filing application or in paper.

(i) Service of electronic filings. If all parties are using EOIR's electronic filing application in a specific case, the parties do not need to serve a document that is filed through EOIR's electronic filing application on the opposing party. EOIR's electronic filing application will effectuate service by providing a notification of all electronically filed documents on all parties by email. Upon successful upload by one of the parties, EOIR will email a notification to the email addresses provided in paragraph (g)(9)(ii) of this section. If one or more parties are not filing through EOIR's electronic filing application in a specific case, the parties must follow the service procedures in paragraph (g)(9)(iii) of this section.

(ii) Valid email address. Use of EOIR's electronic filing application requires a valid email address for electronic service. The Board will use the email address provided through eRegistry for electronic service on participating parties. Users must immediately update their eRegistry account if their email address changes. Representatives must additionally file a new Form EOIR-27 with the Board if their email address changes. EOIR will consider service completed when the electronic notification is delivered to the last email address on file provided by the user.

(iii) Service of paper filings. If electronic filing is not being used in a particular case, the party filing with the

Board must serve a copy of the filing on the opposing party and include a certificate of service showing service on the opposing party with their filing. If the moving party is not DHS, service of the motion shall be made upon the ICE Office of the Principal Legal Advisor for the field location in which the case was completed before the immigration judge.

(h) Oral argument. A request for oral argument, if desired, shall be incorporated in the motion to reopen or reconsider. The Board, in its discretion, may grant or deny requests for oral argument.

(i) Ruling on motion. Rulings upon motions to reopen or motions to reconsider shall be by written order. Any motion for reconsideration or reopening of a decision issued by a single Board member will be referred to the screening panel for disposition by a single Board member, unless the screening panel member determines, in the exercise of judgment, that the motion for reconsideration or reopening should be assigned to a three-member panel under the standards of § 1003.1(e)(6). If the order directs a reopening and further proceedings are necessary, the record shall be returned to the immigration court or the DHS officer having administrative control over the place where the reopened proceedings are to be conducted. If the motion to reconsider is granted, the decision upon such reconsideration shall affirm, modify, or reverse the original decision made in the case.

HISTORY:

[27 FR 96, Jan. 5, 1962.; 61 FR 18900, 18904, April 29, 1996, as corrected at 61 FR 32924, June 26, 1996; 62 FR 10312, 10330, March 6, 1997; 64 FR 56135, 56142, Oct. 18, 1999; 67 FR 54878, 54904, Aug. 26, 2002; redesignated and amended at 68 FR 9824, 9830, 9846, Feb. 28, 2003; 68 FR 10349, 10350, Mar. 5, 2003; 85 FR 81588, 81654, Dec. 16, 2020; 86 FR 70708, 70719, Dec. 13, 2021; 87 FR 56204, 56217, Sept. 14, 2022; 89 FR 46742, 46790, May 29, 2024]

§ 1003.3 Notice of appeal.

(a) Filing —

(1) Appeal from decision of an immigration judge. A party affected by a decision of an immigration judge which may be appealed to the Board under this chapter shall be given notice of the opportunity for filing an appeal. An appeal from a decision of an immigration judge shall be taken by filing a Notice of Appeal from a Decision of an Immigration Judge (Form EOIR-26) directly with the Board, within the time specified in § 1003.38. The appealing parties are only those parties who are covered by the decision of an immigration judge and who are specifically named on the Notice of Appeal. The appeal must reflect proof of service of a copy of the appeal and all attachments on the opposing party. An appeal is not properly filed unless it is received at the Board, along with all required documents, fees or fee waiver requests, and proof of service, within the time specified in the governing sections of this chapter. A Notice of Appeal may not be filed by any party who has waived appeal pursuant to § 1003.39.

(2) Appeal from decision of a DHS officer. A party affected by a decision of a DHS officer that may be appealed to the Board under this chapter shall be given notice of the opportunity to file an appeal. An appeal from a decision of a DHS officer shall be taken by filing a Notice of Appeal to the Board of Immigration Appeals from a Decision of a DHS Officer (Form EOIR-29) directly with the DHS office having administrative control over the record of proceeding within 30 days of the service of the decision being appealed. An appeal is not properly filed until it is received at the appropriate DHS office, together with all required documents, and the fee provisions of § 1003.8 are satisfied.

(3) General requirements for all appeals. The appeal must be accompanied by a check, money order, or fee waiver request in satisfaction of the fee requirements of § 1003.8. If the respondent or applicant is represented, pursuant to 8 CFR 1003.38(g)(1), a Form EOIR–27, Notice of Entry of Appearance as Attorney or Representative Before the Board, must be filed with the Notice of Appeal. If the respondent or applicant receives document assistance from a practitioner with the appeal, pursuant to 8 CFR 1003.38(g)(2), a Form EOIR–60 must be filed with the Notice of Appeal. The appeal and all attachments must be in English or accompanied by a certified English translation..

(b) Statement of the basis of appeal. The party taking the appeal must identify the reasons for the appeal in the Notice of Appeal (Form EOIR-26 or Form EOIR-29) or in any attachments thereto, in order to avoid summary dismissal pursuant to § 1003.1(d)(2)(i). The statement must specifically identify the findings of fact, the conclusions of law, or both, that are being challenged. If a question of law is presented, supporting authority must be cited. If the dispute is over the findings of fact, the specific facts contested must be identified. Where the appeal concerns discretionary relief, the appellant must state whether the alleged error relates to statutory grounds of eligibility or to the exercise of discretion and must identify the specific factual and legal finding or findings that are being challenged. The appellant must also indicate in the Notice of Appeal (Form EOIR-26 or Form EOIR-29) whether he or she desires oral argument before the Board and whether he or she will be filing a separate written brief or statement in support of the appeal. An appellant who asserts that the appeal may warrant review by a three-member panel under the standards of § 1003.1(e)(6) may identify in the Notice of Appeal the specific factual or legal basis for that contention.

(c) Briefs —

(1) Appeal from decision of an immigration judge. Briefs in support of or in opposition to an appeal from a decision of an immigration judge shall be filed directly with the Board. In those cases that are transcribed, the briefing schedule shall be set by the Board after the transcript is available. In cases involving noncitizens in custody, the parties shall be provided 21 days in which to file simultaneous briefs unless a shorter period is specified by the Board. Reply briefs shall be permitted only by leave of the Board and only if filed within 21 days of the deadline for the initial briefs. In cases involving noncitizens who are not in custody, the appellant shall be provided 21 days in which to file a brief,

unless a shorter period is specified by the Board. The appellee shall have the same period of time in which to file a reply brief that was initially granted to the appellant to file their brief. The time to file a reply brief commences from the date upon which the appellant's brief was due, as originally set or extended by the Board. The Board, upon written motion, may extend the period for filing a brief or a reply brief for up to 90 days for good cause shown. In its discretion, the Board may consider a brief that has been filed out of time. In its discretion, the Board may request supplemental briefing from the parties after the expiration of the briefing deadline. All briefs, filings, and motions filed in conjunction with an appeal shall include proof of service on the opposing party.

(2) Appeal from decision of a DHS officer. Briefs in support of or in opposition to an appeal from a decision of a DHS officer shall be filed directly with DHS in accordance with the instructions in the decision of the DHS officer. The applicant or petitioner and DHS shall be provided 21 days in which to file a brief, unless a shorter period is specified by the DHS officer from whose decision the appeal is taken, and reply briefs shall be permitted only by leave of the Board. Upon written request of the noncitizen, the DHS officer from whose decision the appeal is taken or the Board may extend the period for filing a brief for good cause shown. The Board may authorize the filing of briefs directly with the Board. In its discretion, the Board may consider a brief that has been filed out of time. All briefs and other documents filed in conjunction with an appeal, unless filed by a noncitizen directly with a DHS office, shall include proof of service on the opposing party.

(d) Effect of certification. The certification of a case, as provided in this part, shall not relieve the party affected from compliance with the provisions of this section in the event that he or she is entitled and desires to appeal from an initial decision, nor shallit serve to extend the time specified in the applicable parts of this chapter for the taking of an appeal.

(e) Effect of departure from the United States. Departure from the United States of a person who is the subject of deportation proceedings, prior to the taking of an appeal from a decision in his or her case, shall constitute a waiver of his or her right to appeal.

(f) Application on effective date. All cases and motions pending on September 25, 2002, shall be adjudicated according to the rules in effect on or after that date, except that § 1003.1(d)(3)(i) shall not apply to appeals filed before September 25, 2002. A party to an appeal or motion pending on August 26, 2002, may, until September 25, 2002, or the expiration of any briefing schedule set by the Board, whichever is later, submit a brief or statement limited to explaining why the appeal or motion does or does not meet the criteria for three-member review under § 1003.1(e)(6).

(g) Filing. This paragraph applies to the filing of documents related to appeals before the Board.

(1) Filing parties. DHS and all attorneys and accredited representatives of record for respondents, applicants, or petitioners are required to electronically file all documents with the Board through EOIR's electronic filing application in all cases eligible for electronic filing. Although not required, unrepresented respondents, applicants, or petitioners; reputable individuals and accredited officials, who are the representatives of record; other authorized individuals; and practitioners filing an EOIR-60, may electronically file documents with the Board through EOIR's electronic filing application in cases eligible for electronic filing. An unrepresented respondent, applicant, or petitioner; reputable individual; accredited official; other authorized individual; or practitioner filing an EOIR-60, who elects to use EOIR's electronic filing application shall be required to register with EOIR as a condition of using that application. If a party not required to file electronically opts to use EOIR's electronic filing application for a case, the individual must electronically file all documents with the Board for that case unless the Board, only upon a motion filed by the individual with good cause shown, grants leave to opt out of using the electronic filing application. Such an individual who has been granted leave to opt out of using EOIR's electronic filing application for a case may not subsequently opt in to use that application for the same case.

(2) Filing requirements. Parties must make the originals of all filed documents available upon request to the Board or to the opposing party for review. If EOIR's electronic filing application is unavailable due to an unplanned system outage on the last day for filing in a specific case, then the filing deadline will be extended to the first day that the electronic filing application becomes accessible that is not a Saturday, Sunday, or legal holiday. For planned system outages, parties must electronically file documents during system availability within the applicable filing deadline or paper file documents within the applicable filing deadline. EOIR will issue public communications for planned system outages ahead of the scheduled outage. Any planned system outage announced five or fewer business days prior to the start of the outage will be treated as an unplanned outage. The Board retains discretion to accept paper filings in all cases.

(3) Classified information. Notwithstanding any other provision of this chapter, classified information is never allowed to be electronically filed.

(4) Sealed medical documents. Notwithstanding any other provision of this chapter, parties are not permitted to file electronically any sealed medical documents.

(5) Signatures. All documents filed with the Board that require a signature must have an original, handwritten ink signature, an encrypted digital signature, or an electronic signature. Electronic filings submitted through EOIR's electronic filing application that require the user's signature may have a conformed signature. This paragraph is subject to the requirements of the application or document being submitted.

(6) Service. The service of filings with the Board depends on whether the documents are filed through EOIR's electronic filing application or in paper.

(i) Service of electronic filings. If all parties are using EOIR's electronic filing application in a specific case, the parties do not need to serve a document that is filed through EOIR's electronic filing application on the opposing party. EOIR's electronic filing application will effectuate service by providing a notification of all electronically filed documents on all parties by email. Upon successful upload by one of the parties, EOIR will email a notification to the email addresses provided in paragraph (g)(6)(ii) of this section. If one or more parties are not filing through EOIR's electronic filing application in a specific case, the parties must follow the service procedures in paragraph (g)(6)(iii) of this section.

(ii) Valid email address. Use of EOIR's electronic filing application requires a valid email address for electronic service. The Board will use the email address provided through eRegistry for electronic service on participating parties. Users must immediately update their eRegistry account if their email address changes. Representatives must additionally file a new Form EOIR-27 with the Board if their email address changes. EOIR will consider service completed when the electronic notification is delivered to the last email address on file provided by the user.

(iii) Service of paper filings. If electronic filing is not being used in a particular case, the party filing with the Board must serve a copy of the filing on the opposing party and include a certificate of service showing service on the opposing party with their filing.

HISTORY:

[23 FR 9118, Nov. 26, 1958, as amended by Order No. 325-64, 29 FR 14717, Oct. 29, 1964; 48 FR 8040, Feb. 25, 1983; 52 FR 2936, Jan. 29, 1987; 60 FR 34089, June 30, 1995; 61 FR 18900, 18906, Apr. 29, 1996; 66 FR 6436, 6445, Jan. 22, 2001; 67 FR 54878, 54904, Aug. 26, 2002; redesignated and amended at 68 FR 9824, 9830, 9846, Feb. 28, 2003; 85 FR 81588, 81654, Dec. 16, 2020; 86 FR 70708, 70720, Dec. 13, 2021; 87 FR 56204, 56217, Sept. 14, 2022; 89 FR 46742, 46791, May 29, 2024]

§ 1003.4 Withdrawal of appeal.

In any case in which an appeal has been taken, the party taking the appeal may file a written withdrawal thereof with the office at which the notice of appeal was filed. If the record in the case has not been forwarded to the Board on appeal in accordance with § 1003.5, the decision made in the case shall be final to the same extent as if no appeal had been taken. If the record has been forwarded on appeal, the withdrawal of the appeal shall be forwarded to the Board and, if no decision in the case has been made on the appeal, the record shall be returned and the initial decision shall be final to the same extent as if no appeal had been taken. If a decision on the appeal has been made by the Board in the case, further action shall be taken in accordance therewith. Departure from the United States of a person who is the subject of deportation proceedings subsequent to the taking of an appeal, but prior to a decision thereon, shall constitute a withdrawal of the appeal, and the initial decision in the case shall be final to the same extent as though no appeal had been taken. Departure from the United States of a person who is the subject of deportation or removal proceedings, except for arriving aliens as defined in § 1001.1(q) of this chapter, subsequent to the taking of an appeal, but prior to a decision thereon, shall constitute a withdrawal of the appeal, and the initial decision in the case shall be final to the same extent as though no appeal had been taken.

HISTORY:

[29 FR 2692, Feb. 26, 1964, as amended at 52 FR 2936, Jan. 29, 1987; 61 FR 18900, 18906, Apr. 29, 1996; 62 FR 10312, 10331, Mar. 6, 1997; redesignated and amended at 68 FR 9824, 9830, 9846, Feb. 28, 2003; 68 FR 10349, 10350, Mar. 5, 2003]

§ 1003.5 Forwarding of record on appeal.

(a) *Appeal from decision of an immigration judge.* If an appeal is taken from a decision of an immigration judge, the record of proceeding shall be promptly forwarded to the Board upon the request or the order of the Board. Where transcription of an oral decision is required, the immigration judge shall review the transcript and approve the decision within 14 days of receipt, or within 7 days after the immigration judge returns to their duty station if the immigration judge was on leave or detailed to another location. The Chairman and the Chief Immigration Judge shall determine the most effective and expeditious way to transcribe proceedings before the immigration judges, and shall take such steps as necessary to reduce the time required to produce transcripts of those proceedings and to ensure their quality.

(b) *Appeal from decision of a DHS officer.* If an appeal is taken from a decision of a DHS officer, the record of proceeding shall be forwarded to the Board by the DHS officer promptly upon receipt of the briefs of the parties, or upon expiration of the time allowed for the submission of such briefs. A DHS officer need not forward such an appeal to the Board, but may reopen and reconsider any decision made by the officer if the new decision will grant the benefit that has been requested in the appeal. The new decision must be served on the appealing party within 45 days of receipt of any briefs or upon expiration of the time allowed for the submission of any briefs. If the new decision is not served within these time limits or the appealing party does not agree that the new decision disposes of the matter, the record of proceeding shall be immediately forwarded to the Board.

HISTORY:

[48 FR 52432, Nov. 18, 1983; 61 FR 18900, 18907, Apr. 29, 1996; 67 FR 54878, 54904, Aug. 26, 2002; redesignated at 68 FR 9824, 9830, Feb. 28, 2003; 85 FR 81588, 81654, Dec. 16, 2020; 89 FR 46742, 46791, May 29, 2024]

§ 1003.6 Stay of execution of decision.

(a) Except as provided under § 236.1 of this chapter, § 1003.19(i), and paragraph (b) of this section, the decision in any proceeding under this chapter from which an appeal to the Board may be taken shall not be executed during the time allowed for the filing of an appeal unless a waiver of the right to appeal is filed, nor shall such decision be executed while an appeal is pending or while a case is before the Board by way of certification.

(b) The provisions of paragraph (a) of this section shall not apply to an order of an Immigration Judge under § 1003.23 or § 242.22 of 8 CFR chapter I denying a motion to reopen or reconsider or to stay deportation, except where such order expressly grants a stay or where the motion was filed pursuant to the provisions of § 1003.23(b)(4)(iii). The Board may, in its discretion, stay deportation while an appeal is pending from any such order if no stay has been granted by the Immigration Judge or a Service officer.

(c) The following procedures shall be applicable with respect to custody appeals in which DHS has invoked an automatic stay pursuant to 8 CFR 1003.19(i)(2).

(1) The stay shall lapse if DHS fails to file a notice of appeal with the Board within ten business days of the issuance of the order of the immigration judge. DHS should identify the appeal as an automatic stay case. To preserve the automatic stay, the attorney for DHS shall file with the notice of appeal a certification by a senior legal official that—

(i) The official has approved the filing of the notice of appeal according to review procedures established by DHS; and

(ii) The official is satisfied that the contentions justifying the continued detention of the alien have evidentiary support, and the legal arguments are warranted by existing law or by a non-frivolous argument for the extension, modification, or reversal of existing precedent or the establishment of new precedent.

(2) The immigration judge shall prepare a written decision explaining the custody determination within five business days after the immigration judge is advised that DHS has filed a notice of appeal, or, with the approval of the Board in exigent circumstances, as soon as practicable thereafter (not to exceed five additional business days). The immigration court shall prepare and submit the record of proceedings without delay.

(3) The Board will track the progress of each custody appeal which is subject to an automatic stay in order to avoid unnecessary delays in completing the record for decision. Each order issued by the Board should identify the appeal as an automatic stay case. The Board shall notify the parties in a timely manner of the date the automatic stay is scheduled to expire.

(4) If the Board has not acted on the custody appeal, the automatic stay shall lapse 90 days after the filing of the notice of appeal. However, if the Board grants a motion by the alien for an enlargement of the 21-day briefing schedule provided in § 1003.3(c), the Board's order shall also toll the 90-day period of the automatic stay for the same number of days.

(5) DHS may seek a discretionary stay pursuant to 8 CFR 1003.19(i)(1) to stay the immigration judge's order in the event the Board does not issue a decision on the custody appeal within the period of the automatic stay. DHS may submit a motion for discretionary stay at any time after the filing of its notice of appeal of the custody decision, and at a reasonable time before the expiration of the period of the automatic stay, and the motion may incorporate by reference the arguments presented in its brief in support of the need for continued detention of the alien during the pendency of the removal proceedings. If DHS has submitted such a motion and the Board is unable to resolve the custody appeal within the period of the automatic stay, the Board will issue an order granting or denying a motion for discretionary stay pending its decision on the custody appeal. The Board shall issue guidance to ensure prompt adjudication of motions for discretionary stays. If the Board fails to adjudicate a previously-filed stay motion by the end of the 90-day period, the stay will remain in effect (but not more than 30 days) during the time it takes for the Board to decide whether or not to grant a discretionary stay.

(d) If the Board authorizes an alien's release (on bond or otherwise), denies a motion for discretionary stay, or fails to act on such a motion before the automatic stay period expires, the alien's release shall be automatically stayed for five business days. If, within that five-day period, the Secretary of Homeland Security or other designated official refers the custody case to the Attorney General pursuant to 8 CFR 1003.1(h)(1), the alien's release shall continue to be stayed pending the Attorney General's consideration of the case. The automatic stay will expire 15 business days after the case is referred to the Attorney General. DHS may submit a motion and proposed order for a discretionary stay in connection with referring the case to the Attorney General. For purposes of this paragraph and 8 CFR 1003.1(h)(1), decisions of the Board shall include those cases where the Board fails to act on a motion for discretionary stay. The Attorney General may order a discretionary stay pending the disposition of any custody case by the Attorney General or by the Board.

HISTORY:

[36 FR 316, Jan. 9, 1971.; 61 FR 18900, 18907, April 29, 1996, as corrected at 61 FR 21065, May 9, 1996; 63 FR 27441, 27448, May 19, 1998; redesignated and amended at 68 FR 9824, 9830, 9846, Feb. 28, 2003; 68 FR 10349, 10350, Mar. 5, 2003; 71 FR 57873, 57884, Oct. 2, 2006]

§ 1003.7 Notice of certification.

Whenever, in accordance with the provisions of § 1003.1(c), a case is certified to the Board, the noncitizen or other party affected shall be given notice of certification. An immigration judge or DHS officer may certify a case only after an initial decision has been made and before an appeal has been taken. If it is known at the time the initial decision is rendered that the case will be certified, the notice of certification shall be included in such decision and no further notice of certification shall be required. If it is not known until after the initial decision is rendered that the case will be certified, the office of DHS or the Immigration Court having administrative control over the record of proceeding shall cause a Notice of Certification to be served upon the parties. In either case, the notice shall inform the parties that the case is required to be certified to the Board and that they have the right to make representations before the Board, including the making of a request for oral argument and the submission of a brief. If either party desires to submit a brief, it shall be submitted to the office of DHS or the Immigration Court having administrative control over the record of proceeding for transmittal to the Board within the time prescribed in § 1003.3(c). The case shall be certified and forwarded to the Board by the office of DHS or Immigration Court having administrative jurisdiction over the case upon receipt of the brief, or upon the expiration of the time within which the brief may be submitted, or upon receipt of a written waiver of the right to submit a brief. The Board in its discretion may elect to accept for review or not accept for review any such certified case. If the Board declines to accept a certified case for review, the underlying decision shall become final on the date the Board declined to accept the case.

HISTORY:

[52 FR 2936, Jan 29, 1987; 52 FR 7369, Mar. 10, 1987; 60 FR 34089, June 30, 1995; 61 FR 18900, 18907, Apr. 29, 1996; redesignated and amended at 68 FR 9824, 9830, 9846, Feb. 28, 2003; 85 FR 81588, 81655, Dec. 16, 2020; 89 FR 46742, 46791, May 29, 2024]

§ 1003.8 Fees before the Board.

(a) Appeals and motions before the Board —

(1) When a fee is required. Except as provided in paragraph (a)(2) of this section and 8 CFR 1208.4(d)(3), a filing fee prescribed in 8 CFR 1103.7, or a fee waiver request pursuant to paragraph (a)(3) of this section, is required in connection with the filing of an appeal, a motion to reopen, or a motion to reconsider before the Board.

(2) When a fee is not required. A filing fee is not required in the following instances:

(i) A custody bond appeal filed pursuant to § 1003.1(b)(7);

(ii) A motion to reopen that is based exclusively on an application for relief that does not require a fee;

(iii) A motion to reconsider that is based exclusively on a prior application for relief that did not require a fee;

(iv) A motion filed while an appeal, a motion to reopen, or a motion to reconsider is already pending before the Board;

(v) A motion requesting only a stay of removal, deportation, or exclusion;

(vi) Any appeal or motion filed by the Department of Homeland Security;

(vii) A motion that is agreed upon by all parties and is jointly filed; or

(viii) An appeal or motion filed under a law, regulation, or directive that specifically does not require a filing fee.

(3) When a fee may be waived. The Board has the discretion to waive a fee for an appeal, motion to reconsider, or motion to reopen upon a showing that the filing party is unable to pay the fee. Fee waivers shall be requested through the filing of a Fee Waiver Request (Form EOIR-26A), including the declaration to be signed under penalty of perjury substantiating the filing party's inability to pay the fee. The fee waiver request shall be filed along with the Notice of Appeal or the motion. If the fee waiver request does not establish the inability to pay the required fee, the appeal or motion will not be deemed properly filed, provided the Board grants 15 days to re-file the rejected document with the filing fee or new fee waiver request and tolls any applicable filing deadline during the 15-day cure period.

(4) Method of payment. When a fee is required for an appeal or motion, the fee shall accompany the appeal or motion.

(i) In general. Except as provided in paragraph (a)(4)(ii) of this section, the fee for filing an appeal or motion with the Board shall be paid by check, money order, or electronic payment in a manner and form authorized by the Executive Office for Immigration Review. When paid by check or money order, the fee shall be payable to the "United States Department of Justice," drawn on a bank or other institution that is located within the United States, and payable in United States currency. The check or money order shall bear the full name and alien registration number of the alien. A payment that is uncollectible does not satisfy a fee requirement.

(ii) Appeals from Department of Homeland Security decisions. The fee for filing an appeal, within the jurisdiction of the Board, from the decision of a Department of Homeland Security officer shall be paid to the Department of Homeland Security in accordance with § 1103.7(b).

(b) Applications for relief. Fees for applications for relief are not collected by the Board, but instead are paid to the Department of Homeland Security in accordance with 8 CFR 103.7. When a motion before the Board is based upon an application for relief, only the fee for the motion to reopen shall be paid to the Board, and payment of the fee for the application for relief shall not accompany the motion. If the motion is granted and proceedings are remanded to the immigration judge, the application fee shall be paid in the manner specified in 8 CFR 1003.24(c)(1).

HISTORY:

[23 FR 9118, Nov. 26, 1958, as amended at 27 FR 7488, July 31, 1962; 48 FR 8040, Feb. 25, 1983; 61 FR 18900, 18907, Apr. 29, 1996; redesignated and amended at 68 FR 9824, 9830, 9846, Feb. 28, 2003; 68 FR 10349, 10350, Mar. 5, 2003; 69 FR 44903, 44906, July 28, 2004; 85 FR 81698, 81750, Dec. 16, 2020; 85 FR 82750, 82793, Dec. 18, 2020; 86 FR 70708, 70721, Dec. 13, 2021]

Subpart B

Office of the Chief Immigration Judge

§ 1003.9 Office of the Chief Immigration Judge.

(a) Organization. Within the Executive Office for Immigration Review, there shall be an Office of the Chief Immigration Judge (OCIJ), consisting of the Chief Immigration Judge, the immigration judges, and such other staff as the Director deems necessary. The Attorney General shall appoint the Chief Immigration

Judge. The Director may designate immigration judges to serve as Deputy and Assistant Chief Immigration Judges as may be necessary to assist the Chief Immigration Judge in the management of the OCIJ.

(b) Powers of the Chief Immigration Judge. Subject to the supervision of the Director, the Chief Immigration Judge shall be responsible for the supervision, direction, and scheduling of the immigration judges in the conduct of the hearings and duties assigned to them. The Chief Immigration Judge shall have the authority to:

(1) Issue operational instructions and policy, including procedural instructions regarding the implementation of new statutory or regulatory authorities;

(2) Provide for appropriate training of the immigration judges and other OCIJ staff on the conduct of their powers and duties;

(3) Direct the conduct of all employees assigned to OCIJ to ensure the efficient disposition of all pending cases, including the power, in his discretion, to set priorities or time frames for the resolution of cases, to direct that the adjudication of certain cases be deferred, to regulate the assignment of immigration judges to cases, and otherwise to manage the docket of matters to be decided by the immigration judges;

(4) Evaluate the performance of the Immigration Courts and other OCIJ activities by making appropriate reports and inspections, and take corrective action where needed;

(5) Adjudicate cases as an immigration judge, including the authorities described in § 1003.10(b); and

(6) Exercise such other authorities as the Director may provide.

(c) Limit on the Authority of the Chief Immigration Judge. The Chief Immigration Judge shall have no authority to direct the result of an adjudication assigned to another immigration judge, provided, however, that nothing in this part shall be construed to limit the authority of the Chief Immigration Judge in paragraph (b) of this section.

(d) Immigration Court. The term Immigration Court shall refer to the local sites of the OCIJ where proceedings are held before immigration judges and where the records of those proceedings are created and maintained.

HISTORY:

[48 FR 8040, Feb. 25, 1983; 62 FR 10312, 10331, Mar. 6, 1997; redesignated at 68 FR 9824, 9830, Feb. 28, 2003; 72 FR 53673, 53677, Sept. 20, 2007; 89 FR 46742, 46792, May 29, 2024]

§ 1003.10 Immigration judges.

(a) Appointment. The immigration judges are attorneys whom the Attorney General appoints as administrative judges within the Office of the Chief Immigration Judge to conduct specified classes of proceedings, including hearings under section 240 of the Act. Immigration judges shall act as the Attorney General's delegates in the cases that come before them.

(b) Powers and duties. In conducting hearings under section 240 of the Act and such other proceedings the Attorney General may assign to them, immigration judges shall exercise the powers and duties delegated to them by the Act and by the Attorney General through regulation. In deciding the individual cases before them, and subject to the applicable governing standards set forth in paragraph (d) of this section, immigration judges shall exercise their independent judgment and discretion and may take any action consistent with their authorities under the Act and regulations that is necessary or appropriate for the disposition or alternative resolution of such cases. Such actions include administrative closure, termination of proceedings, and dismissal of proceedings. The standards for the administrative closure, dismissal, and termination of cases are set forth in § 1003.18(c), 8 CFR 1239.2(c), and § 1003.18(d), respectively. Immigration judges shall administer oaths, receive evidence, and interrogate, examine, and cross-examine noncitizens and any witnesses. Subject to §§ 1003.35 and 1287.4 of this chapter, they may issue administrative subpoenas for the attendance of witnesses and the presentation of evidence. In all cases, immigration judges shall seek to resolve the questions before them in a timely and impartial manner consistent with the Act and regulations. In the absence of exceptional circumstances, an immigration judge shall complete administrative adjudication of an asylum application within 180 days after the date an application is filed. For purposes of this paragraph (b) and of §§ 1003.29 and 1240.6 of this chapter, the term exceptional circumstances refers to exceptional circumstances (such as battery or extreme cruelty to the alien or any child or parent of the alien, serious illness of the party or immigration judge, or serious illness or death of the spouse, child, or parent of the alien, but not including less compelling circumstances) beyond the control of the parties or the immigration court. A finding of good cause does not necessarily mean that an exceptional circumstance has also been established.

(c) Review. Decisions of immigration judges are subject to review by the Board of Immigration Appeals in any case in which the Board has jurisdiction as provided in 8 CFR 1003.1.

(d) Governing standards set forth in paragraph (d) of this section. Immigration judges shall be governed by the provisions and limitations prescribed by the Act and this chapter, by the decisions of the Board, and by the Attorney General (through review of a decision of the Board, by written order, or by determination and ruling pursuant to section 103 of the Act).

(e) Temporary immigration judges. (1) Designation. The Director is authorized to designate or select temporary immigration judges as provided in this paragraph (e).

(i) The Director may designate or select, with the approval of the Attorney General, former Board members, former immigration judges, administrative law judges employed within or retired from EOIR, and administrative law judges from other Executive Branch agencies to serve as temporary immigration judges for renewable terms not to exceed six months. Administrative law judges from other Executive Branch agencies must have the consent of their agencies to be designated as temporary immigration judges.

(ii) In addition, the Director may designate, with the approval of the Attorney General, Department of Justice attorneys with at least 10 years of legal experience in the field of immigration law to serve as temporary immigration judges for renewable terms not to exceed six months.

(2) Authority. A temporary immigration judge shall have the authority of an immigration judge to adjudicate assigned cases and administer immigration court matters, as provided in the immigration laws and regulations, subject to paragraph (e)(3) of this section.

(3) Assignment of temporary immigration judges. The Chief Immigration Judge is responsible for the overall oversight and management of the utilization of temporary immigration judges and for evaluating the results of the process. The Chief Immigration Judge shall ensure that each temporary immigration judge has received a suitable level of training to enable the temporary immigration judge to carry out the duties assigned.

HISTORY:

[48 FR 8040, Feb. 25, 1983; 62 FR 10312, 10331, Mar. 6, 1997; redesignated at 68 FR 9824, 9830, Feb. 28, 2003; 72 FR 53673, 53677, Sept. 20, 2007; 79 FR 39953, 39956, July 11, 2014; 85 FR 81588, 81655, Dec. 16, 2020; 85 FR 81698, 81750, Dec. 16, 2020; 89 FR 46742, 46792, May 29, 2024]

§ 1003.11 Administrative control Immigration Courts.

An administrative control Immigration Court is one that creates and maintains Records of Proceedings for Immigration Courts within an assigned geographical area. All documents and correspondence pertaining to a Record of Proceeding shall be filed with the Immigration Court having administrative control over that Record of Proceeding and shall not be filed with any other Immigration Court. A list of the administrative control Immigration Courts with their assigned geographical areas will be made available to the public at any Immigration Court.

HISTORY:

[52 FR 2942, Jan. 29, 1987; 60 FR 34090, June 30, 1995; 62 FR 10312, 10331, Mar. 6, 1997; redesignated at 68 FR 9824, 9830, Feb. 28, 2003]

Subpart C

Immigration Court — Rules of Procedure

§ 1003.12 Scope of rules.

These rules are promulgated to assist in the expeditious, fair, and proper resolution of matters coming before Immigration Judges. Except where specifically stated, the rules in this subpart apply to matters before Immigration Judges, including, but not limited to, deportation, exclusion, removal, bond, rescission, departure control, asylum proceedings, and disciplinary proceedings under this part 1003. The sole procedures for review of credible fear determinations by Immigration Judges are provided for in § 1003.42.

HISTORY:

[57 FR 11571, Apr. 6, 1992; 62 FR 10312, 10331, Mar. 6, 1997; 65 FR 39513, 39526, June 27, 2000; redesignated and amended at 68 FR 9824, 9830, 9846, Feb. 28, 2003]

§ 1003.13 Definitions.

As used in this subpart:

Administrative control means custodial responsibility for the Record of Proceeding as specified in § 1003.11.

Charging document means the written instrument which initiates a proceeding before an Immigration Judge. For proceedings initiated prior to April 1, 1997, these documents include an Order to Show Cause, a Notice to Applicant for Admission Detained for Hearing before Immigration Judge, and a Notice of Intention to Rescind and Request for Hearing by Alien. For proceedings initiated after April 1, 1997, these documents include a Notice to Appear, a Notice of Referral to Immigration Judge, and a Notice of Intention to Rescind and Request for Hearing by Alien.

HISTORY:

[57 FR 11571, Apr. 6, 1992; 59 FR 1899, Jan. 13, 1994; 60 FR 34089, June 30, 1995; 62 FR 10312, 10332, Mar. 6, 1997; redesignated and amended at 68 FR 9824, 9830, 9846, Feb. 28, 2003; 86 FR 70708, 70722, Dec. 13, 2021]

§ 1003.14 Jurisdiction and commencement of proceedings.

(a) Jurisdiction vests, and proceedings before an Immigration Judge commence, when a charging document is filed with the Immigration Court by the Service. The charging document must include a certificate showing service on the opposing party pursuant to § 1003.32 which indicates the Immigration Court in which the charging document is filed. However, no charging document is required to be filed with the Immigration Court to commence bond proceedings pursuant to §§ 1003.19, 1236.1(d) and 1240.2(b) of this chapter.

(b) When an Immigration Judge has jurisdiction over an underlying proceeding, sole jurisdiction over applications for asylum shall lie with the Immigration Judge.

(c) Immigration Judges have jurisdiction to administer the oath of allegiance in administrative naturalization ceremonies conducted by the Service in accordance with § 1337.2(b) of this chapter.

(d) The jurisdiction of, and procedures before, immigration judges in exclusion, deportation and removal, rescission, asylum-only, and any other proceedings shall remain in effect as it was in effect on February 28, 2003, until the regulations in this chapter are further modified by the Attorney General. Where a decision of an officer of the Immigration and Naturalization Service was, before March 1, 2003, appealable to the Board or an immigration judge, or an application denied could be renewed in proceedings before an immigration judge, the same authority and procedures shall be followed until further modified by the Attorney General.

HISTORY:

[57 FR 11571, Apr. 6, 1992; 60 FR 34089, June 30, 1995; 62 FR 10312, 10332, Mar. 6, 1997; redesignated and amended at 68 FR 9824, 9830, 9832, 9846, Feb. 28, 2003; 68 FR 10349, 10350, Mar. 5, 2003]

§ 1003.15 Contents of the order to show cause and notice to appear and notification of change of address.

(a) In the Order to Show Cause, the Service shall provide the following administrative information to the Executive Office for Immigration Review. Omission of any of these items shall not provide the alien with any substantive or procedural rights:

(1) The alien's names and any known aliases;

(2) The alien's address;

(3) The alien's registration number, with any lead alien registration number with which the alien is associated;

(4) The alien's alleged nationality and citizenship;

(5) The language that the alien understands;

(b) The Order to Show Cause and Notice to Appear must also include the following information:

(1) The nature of the proceedings against the alien;

(2) The legal authority under which the proceedings are conducted;

(3) The acts or conduct alleged to be in violation of law;

(4) The charges against the alien and the statutory provisions alleged to have been violated;

(5) Notice that the alien may be represented, at no cost to the government, by counsel or other representative authorized to appear pursuant to 8 CFR 1292.1;

(6) The address of the Immigration Court where the Service will file the Order to Show Cause and Notice to Appear; and

(7) A statement that the alien must advise the Immigration Court having administrative control over the Record of Proceeding of his or her current address and telephone number and a statement that failure to provide such information may result in an in absentia hearing in accordance with § 1003.26.

(c) Contents of the Notice to Appear for Removal Proceedings. In the Notice to Appear for removal proceedings, the Service shall provide the following administrative information to the Immigration Court. Failure to provide any of these items shall not be construed as affording the alien any substantive or procedural rights.

(1) The alien's names and any known aliases;

(2) The alien's address;

(3) The alien's registration number, with any lead alien registration number with which the alien is associated;

(4) The alien's alleged nationality and citizenship; and

(5) The language that the alien understands.

(d) **Address and telephone number.**

(1) If the alien's address is not provided on the Order to Show Cause or Notice to Appear, or if the address on the Order to Show Cause or Notice to Appear is incorrect, the alien must provide to the Immigration Court where the charging document has been filed, within five days of service of that document, a written notice of an address and telephone number at which the alien can be contacted. The alien may satisfy this requirement by completing and filing Form EOIR-33.

(2) Within five days of any change of address, the alien must provide written notice of the change of address on Form EOIR-33 to the Immigration Court where the charging document has been filed, or if venue has been changed, to the Immigration Court to which venue has been changed.

HISTORY:

[57 FR 11571, Apr. 6, 1992; 60 FR 34089, June 30, 1995; 62 FR 10312, 10332, Mar. 6, 1997; redesignated and amended at 68 FR 9824, 9830, 9846, Feb. 28, 2003; 68 FR 10349, 10350, Mar. 5, 2003]

§ 1003.16 Representation.

(a) The government may be represented in proceedings before an Immigration Judge.

(b) The alien may be represented in proceedings before an Immigration Judge by an attorney or other representative of his or her choice in accordance with 8 CFR part 1292, at no expense to the government.

HISTORY:

[52 FR 2936, Jan. 29, 1987. Redesignated at 57 FR 11571, Apr. 6, 1992; 62 FR 10312, 10332, Mar. 6, 1997; redesignated at 68 FR 9824, 9830, Feb. 28, 2003; 68 FR 10349, 10350, Mar. 5, 2003]

§ 1003.17 Entry of appearance.

(a) Entering an appearance using Form EOIR–28. A practitioner must enter an appearance in proceedings before an immigration court using Form EOIR–28 to perform the functions of and become the practitioner of record. The practitioner of record is authorized and required to appear in immigration court on behalf of the respondent, file all documents on behalf of the respondent, and accept service of process of all documents filed in the proceedings. The practitioner may enter an appearance to be the practitioner of record for all proceedings before the immigration court, or for custody and bond proceedings only, or for all proceedings other than custody and bond proceedings. A practitioner's entry of appearance in only a custody or bond proceeding shall be separate and apart from an entry of appearance in any proceeding other than custody or bond before the immigration court. The Form EOIR–28 must indicate whether the practitioner's entry of appearance is for all proceedings, for custody and bond proceedings only, or for all proceedings other than custody and bond proceedings.

(1) Filing Form EOIR–28. The practitioner must file a copy of the Form EOIR–28 with the immigration court and serve a copy on DHS as required by 8 CFR

1003.32. The practitioner must file and serve a Form EOIR–28 even if the practitioner has previously filed a separate Notice of Entry of Appearance with DHS for appearances before DHS or previously entered a limited appearance using Form EOIR–61 in connection with document assistance under paragraph (b) of this section.

(2) Effect of Filing Form EOIR–28. A practitioner who enters an appearance using Form EOIR–28 is the practitioner of record and must appear in immigration court on behalf of the respondent, file all documents on behalf of the respondent, and accept service of process of all documents filed in the proceedings, consistent with 8 CFR 1292.5. Filing a Form EOIR–28 provides the practitioner with access to the record of proceedings during the course of proceedings. A respondent shall be considered represented for the proceedings in which an EOIR–28 has been filed.

(3) Withdrawal or substitution. A practitioner who enters an appearance on behalf of a respondent before the immigration court by filing a Form EOIR–28 remains the practitioner of record unless an immigration judge permits withdrawal or substitution during proceedings upon oral or written motion submitted without fee.

(b) Entering a limited appearance for document assistance using Form EOIR– 61. A practitioner who provides assistance to a pro se respondent with the drafting, completion, or filling in of blank spaces of a specific motion, brief, form, or other document or set of documents intended to be filed with the immigration court, regardless of whether such assistance is considered "practice" or "preparation" as defined in 8 CFR 1001.1, must disclose such limited assistance to the immigration court using Form EOIR–61, unless pursuant to paragraph (a) the practitioner has filed a Form EOIR–28 to become the practitioner of record.

(1) Filing Form EOIR–61. A Form EOIR–61 must not be filed as a standalone document. The single Form EOIR–61 must be filed with the immigration court at the same time as the document or set of documents with which the practitioner assisted. Any subsequent filing of a document or set of documents with which a practitioner assisted must be accompanied by a new Form EOIR–61.

(2) Effect of Filing Form EOIR–61. A practitioner who enters a limited appearance using Form EOIR–61 is not the practitioner of record, is not required to appear on behalf of respondent before the immigration court, and is not required to submit a motion to withdraw or substitute. The submission of a Form EOIR–61 does not create additional ongoing obligations between the practitioner, the respondent, and EOIR. An appearance through Form EOIR–61 does not provide the practitioner with access to the record of proceedings. A respondent who received assistance pursuant to this paragraph is not represented, remains pro se, and is subject to service of process of all documents filed in the proceedings, consistent with 8 CFR 1292.5.

(c) Completing an appearance form, proof of qualification, disclosure requirements, and identification. The practitioner must properly complete and sign any Form EOIR–28 or Form EOIR– 61, as required by the form instructions. A practitioner's personal appearance or signature on the Form EOIR–28 or Form EOIR–61 constitutes an attestation that the person is authorized and qualified to appear as a practitioner in accordance with § 1292.1. Further proof that the practitioner meets the qualifications of a practitioner as defined in § 1292.1 may be required. The completion of a Form EOIR–28 or Form EOIR–61 in connection with an application or form that requires disclosure of the preparer does not relieve a practitioner from complying with the particular disclosure requirements of the application or form. Notwithstanding the completion of a Form EOIR–28 or Form EOIR–61, the practitioner must identify themselves by name, accompanied by their signature, on any document filed or intended to be filed with the immigration court pursuant to an appearance under paragraph (a) or (b).

HISTORY:

[57 FR 11571, Apr. 6, 1992; 60 FR 34089, June 30, 1995; 62 FR 10312, 10332, Mar. 6, 1997; redesignated and amended at 68 FR 9824, 9830, 9846, Feb. 28, 2003; 80 FR 59500, 59502, Oct. 1, 2015; 86 FR 70708, 70722, Dec. 13, 2021; 87 FR 56204, 56258, Sept. 14, 2022]

§ 1003.18 Docket management.

(a) Scheduling. The Immigration Court shall be responsible for scheduling cases and providing notice to the government and the alien of the time, place, and date of hearings.

(b) Notice. In removal proceedings pursuant to section 240 of the Act, the Service shall provide in the Notice to Appear, the time, place and date of the initial removal hearing, where practicable. If that information is not contained in the Notice to Appear, the Immigration Court shall be responsible for scheduling the initial removal hearing and providing notice to the government and the alien of the time, place, and date of hearing. In the case of any change or postponement in the time and place of such proceeding, the Immigration Court shall provide written notice to the alien specifying the new time and place of the proceeding and the consequences under section 240(b)(5) of the Act of failing, except under exceptional circumstances as defined in section 240(e)(1) of the Act, to attend such proceeding. No such notice shall be required for an alien not in detention if the alien has failed to provide the address required in section 239(a)(1)(F) of the Act.

(c) Administrative closure and recalendaring. Administrative closure is the temporary suspension of a case. Administrative closure removes a case from the immigration court's active calendar until the case is recalendared. Recalendaring places a case back on the immigration court's active calendar.

(1) Administrative closure before immigration judges. An immigration judge may, in the exercise of discretion, administratively close a case upon the motion of a party, after applying the standard set forth at paragraph (c)(3) of this section. The administrative closure authority described in this section is not limited by the authority provided in any other provisions in

this title that separately authorize or require administrative closure in certain circumstances, including 8 CFR 214.15(l), 245.15(p)(4), 1214.2(a), 1214.3, 1240.62(b), 1240.70(f) through (h), 1245.13, 1245.15(p)(4)(i), and 1245.21(c).

(2) Recalendaring before immigration judges. At any time after a case has been administratively closed under paragraph (c)(1) of this section, an immigration judge may, in the exercise of discretion, recalendar the case pursuant to a party's motion to recalendar. In deciding whether to grant such a motion, the immigration judge shall apply the standard set forth at paragraph (c)(3) of this section.

(3) Standard for administrative closure and recalendaring. An immigration judge shall grant a motion to administratively close or recalendar filed jointly by both parties, or filed by one party where the other party has affirmatively indicated its non-opposition, unless the immigration judge articulates unusual, clearly identified, and supported reasons for denying the motion. In all other cases, in deciding whether to administratively close or to recalendar a case, an immigration judge shall consider the totality of the circumstances, including as many of the factors listed under paragraphs (c)(3)(i) and (ii) of this section as are relevant to the particular case. The immigration judge may also consider other factors where appropriate. No single factor is dispositive. The immigration judge, having considered the totality of the circumstances, may grant a motion to administratively close or to recalendar a particular case over the objection of a party. Although administrative closure may be appropriate where a petition, application, or other action is pending outside of proceedings before the immigration judge, such a pending petition, application, or other action is not required for a case to be administratively closed.

(i) As the circumstances of the case warrant, the factors relevant to a decision to administratively close a case include:

(A) The reason administrative closure is sought;

(B) The basis for any opposition to administrative closure;

(C) Any requirement that a case be administratively closed in order for a petition, application, or other action to be filed with, or granted by, DHS;

(D) The likelihood the noncitizen will succeed on any petition, application, or other action that the noncitizen is pursuing, or that the noncitizen states in writing or on the record at a hearing that they plan to pursue, outside of proceedings before the immigration judge;

(E) The anticipated duration of the administrative closure;

(F) The responsibility of either party, if any, in contributing to any current or anticipated delay;

(G) The ultimate anticipated outcome of the case pending before the immigration judge; and

(H) The ICE detention status of the noncitizen.

(ii) As the circumstances of the case warrant, the factors relevant to a decision to recalendar a case include:

(A) The reason recalendaring is sought;

(B) The basis for any opposition to recalendaring;

(C) The length of time elapsed since the case was administratively closed;

(D) If the case was administratively closed to allow the noncitizen to file a petition, application, or other action outside of proceedings before the immigration judge, whether the noncitizen filed the petition, application, or other action and, if so, the length of time that elapsed between when the case was administratively closed and when the noncitizen filed the petition, application, or other action;

(E) If a petition, application, or other action that was pending outside of proceedings before the immigration judge has been adjudicated, the result of that adjudication;

(F) If a petition, application, or other action remains pending outside of proceedings before the immigration judge, the likelihood the noncitizen will succeed on that petition, application, or other action;

(G) The ultimate anticipated outcome if the case is recalendared; and

(H) The ICE detention status of the noncitizen.

(d) Termination. Immigration judges shall have the authority to terminate cases before them as set forth in paragraphs (d)(1) and (2) of this section. A motion to dismiss a case in removal proceedings before an immigration judge for a reason other than authorized by 8 CFR 1239.2(c) shall be deemed a motion to terminate under paragraph (d)(1) of this section.

(1) Removal, deportation, and exclusion proceedings —

(i) Mandatory termination. In removal, deportation, and exclusion proceedings, immigration judges shall terminate the case where at least one of the requirements in paragraphs (d)(1)(i)(A) through (G) of this section is met.

(A) No charge of deportability, inadmissibility, or excludability can be sustained.

(B) Fundamentally fair proceedings are not possible because the noncitizen is mentally incompetent and adequate safeguards are unavailable.

(C) The noncitizen has, since the initiation of proceedings, obtained United States citizenship.

(D) The noncitizen has, since the initiation of proceedings, obtained at least one status listed in paragraphs (d)(1)(i)(D)(1) through (4) of this section, provided that the status has not been revoked or terminated, and the noncitizen would not have been deportable, inadmissible, or excludable as charged if the noncitizen had obtained such status before the initiation of proceedings.

(1) Lawful permanent resident status.

(2) Refugee status.

(3) Asylee status.

(4) Nonimmigrant status as defined in section 101(a)(15)(S), (T), or (U) of the Act.

(E) Termination is required under 8 CFR 1245.13(l).

(F) Termination is otherwise required by law.

(G) The parties jointly filed a motion to terminate, or one party filed a motion to terminate and the other party affirmatively indicated its non-opposition, unless the immigration judge articulates unusual, clearly identified, and supported reasons for denying the motion.

(ii) Discretionary termination. In removal, deportation, or exclusion proceedings, immigration judges may, in the exercise of discretion, terminate the case upon the motion of a party where at least one of the requirements listed in paragraphs (d)(1)(ii)(A) through (F) of this section is met. The immigration judge shall consider the reason termination is sought and the basis for any opposition to termination when adjudicating the motion to terminate.

(A) The noncitizen has filed an asylum application with USCIS pursuant to section 208(b)(3)(C) of the Act pertaining to unaccompanied children, as defined in 8 CFR 1001.1(hh).

(B) The noncitizen is prima facie eligible for naturalization, relief from removal, or lawful status; USCIS has jurisdiction to adjudicate the associated petition, application, or other action if the noncitizen were not in proceedings; and the noncitizen has filed the petition, application, or other action with USCIS. However, no filing is required where the noncitizen is prima facie eligible for adjustment of status or naturalization. Where the basis of a noncitizen's motion for termination is that the noncitizen is prima facie eligible for naturalization, the immigration judge shall not grant the motion if it is opposed by DHS. Immigration judges shall not terminate a case for the noncitizen to pursue an asylum application before USCIS, except as provided for in paragraph (d)(1)(ii)(A) of this section.

(C) The noncitizen is a beneficiary of Temporary Protected Status, deferred action, or Deferred Enforced Departure.

(D) USCIS has granted the noncitizen's application for a provisional unlawful presence waiver pursuant to 8 CFR 212.7(e).

(E) Termination is authorized by 8 CFR 1216.4(a)(6) or 1238.1(e).

(F) Due to circumstances comparable to those described in paragraphs (d)(1)(ii)(A) through (E) of this section, termination is similarly necessary or appropriate for the disposition or alternative resolution of the case. However, immigration judges may not terminate a case for purely humanitarian reasons, unless DHS expressly consents to such termination, joins in a motion to terminate, or affirmatively indicates its non-opposition to a noncitizen's motion.

(2) Other proceedings —

(i) Mandatory termination. In proceedings other than removal, deportation, or exclusion proceedings, immigration judges shall terminate the case where the parties have jointly filed a motion to terminate, or one party has filed a motion to terminate and the other party has affirmatively indicated its non-opposition, unless the immigration judge articulates unusual, clearly identified, and supported reasons for denying the motion. In addition, immigration judges shall terminate such a case where required by law.

(ii) Discretionary termination. In proceedings other than removal, deportation, or exclusion proceedings, immigration judges may, in the exercise of discretion, terminate the case upon the motion of a party where terminating the case is necessary or appropriate for the disposition or alternative resolution of the case. However, immigration judges may not terminate a case for purely humanitarian reasons, unless DHS expressly consents to such termination, joins in a motion to terminate, or affirmatively indicates its non-opposition to a noncitizen's motion.

(iii) Limitation on termination. Nothing in paragraphs (d)(2)(i) and (ii) of this section authorizes immigration judges to terminate a case where prohibited by another regulatory provision. Further, nothing in paragraphs (d)(2)(i) and (ii) of this section authorizes the immigration judge to terminate a case for the noncitizen to pursue an asylum application before USCIS, unless the noncitizen has filed an asylum application with USCIS pursuant to section 208(b)(3)(C) of the Act pertaining to unaccompanied children, as defined in 8 CFR 1001.1(hh).

HISTORY:

[52 FR 2936, Jan. 29, 1987. Redesignated at 57 FR 11571, Apr. 6, 1992; 60 FR 34089, June 30, 1995; 62 FR 10312, 10332, Mar. 6, 1997; redesignated at 68 FR 9824, 9830, Feb. 28, 2003; 89 FR 46742, 46792, May 29, 2024]

§ 1003.19 Custody/bond.

(a) Custody and bond determinations made by the service pursuant to 8 CFR part 1236 may be reviewed by an Immigration Judge pursuant to 8 CFR part 1236.

(b) Application for an initial bond redetermination by a respondent, or his or her attorney or representative, may be made orally, in writing, or, at the discretion of the Immigration Judge, by telephone.

(c) Applications for the exercise of authority to review bond determinations shall be made to one of the following offices, in the designated order:

(1) If the respondent is detained, to the Immigration Court having jurisdiction over the place of detention;

(2) To the Immigration Court having administrative control over the case; or

(3) To the Office of the Chief Immigration Judge for designation of an appropriate Immigration Court.

(d) Consideration by the Immigration Judge of an application or request of a respondent regarding custody or bond under this section shall be separate and apart from, and shall form no part of, any deportation or removal hearing or proceeding. The determination of the Immigration Judge as to custody status or bond may be based upon any information that is available to the Immigration Judge or that is presented to him or her by the alien or the Service.

(e) After an initial bond redetermination, an alien's request for a subsequent bond redetermination shall be made in writing and shall be considered only upon a showing that the alien's circumstances have changed materially since the prior bond redetermination.

(f) The determination of an Immigration Judge with respect to custody status or bond redetermination shall be entered on the appropriate form at the time such decision is made and the parties shall be informed orally or in writing of the reasons for the decision. An appeal from the determination by an Immigration

Judge may be taken to the Board of Immigration Appeals pursuant to § 1003.38.

(g) While any proceeding is pending before the Executive Office for Immigration Review, the Service shall immediately advise the Immigration Court having administrative control over the Record of Proceeding of a change in the respondent/applicant's custody location or of release from Service custody, or subsequent taking into Service custody, of a respondent/applicant. This notification shall be in writing and shall state the effective date of the change in custody location or status, and the respondent/applicant's current fixed street address, including zip code.

(h)(1)(i) While the Transition Period Custody Rules (TPCR) set forth in section 303(b)(3) of Div. C of Pub. L. 104-208 remain in effect, an immigration judge may not redetermine conditions of custody imposed by the Service with respect to the following classes of aliens:

(A) Aliens in exclusion proceedings;

(B) Arriving aliens in removal proceedings, including persons paroled after arrival pursuant to section 212(d)(5) of the Act;

(C) Aliens described in section 237(a)(4) of the Act;

(D) Aliens subject to section 303(b)(3)(A) of Pub. L. 104-208 who are not "lawfully admitted" (as defined in § 1236.1(c)(2) of this chapter); or

(E) Aliens designated in § 1236.1(c) of this chapter as ineligible to be considered for release.

(ii) Nothing in this paragraph shall be construed as prohibiting an alien from seeking a redetermination of custody conditions by the Service in accordance with part 1235 or 1236 of this chapter. In addition, with respect to paragraphs (h)(1)(i)(C), (D), and (E) of this section, nothing in this paragraph shall be construed as prohibiting an alien from seeking a determination by an immigration judge that the alien is not properly included within any of those paragraphs.

(2)(i) Upon expiration of the Transition Period Custody Rules set forth in section 303(b)(3) of Div. C. of Pub. L. 104-208, an immigration judge may not redetermine conditions of custody imposed by the Service with respect to the following classes of aliens:

(A) Aliens in exclusion proceedings;

(B) Arriving aliens in removal proceedings, including aliens paroled after arrival pursuant to section 212(d)(5) of the Act;

(C) Aliens described in section 237(a)(4) of the Act;

(D) Aliens in removal proceedings subject to section 236(c)(1) of the Act (as in effect after expiration of the Transition Period Custody Rules); and

(E) Aliens in deportation proceedings subject to section 242(a)(2) of the Act (as in effect prior to April 1, 1997, and as amended by section 440(c) of Pub. L. 104-132).

(ii) Nothing in this paragraph shall be construed as prohibiting an alien from seeking a redetermination of custody conditions by the Service in accordance with part 1235 or 1236 of this chapter. In addition, with respect to paragraphs (h)(2)(i)(C), (D), and (E) of this section, nothing in this paragraph shall be construed as prohibiting an alien from seeking a determination by an immigration judge that the alien is not properly included within any of those paragraphs.

(3) Except as otherwise provided in paragraph (h)(1) of this section, an alien subject to section 303(b)(3)(A) of Div. C of Pub. L. 104-208 may apply to the Immigration Court, in a manner consistent with paragraphs (c)(1) through (c)(3) of this section, for a redetermination of custody conditions set by the Service. Such an alien must first demonstrate, by clear and convincing evidence, that release would not pose a danger to other persons or to property. If an alien meets this burden, the alien must further demonstrate, by clear and convincing evidence, that the alien is likely to appear for any scheduled proceeding or interview.

(4) Unremovable aliens. A determination of a district director (or other official designated by the Commissioner) regarding the exercise of authority under section 303(b)(3)(B)(ii) of Div. C. of Pub. L. 104-208 (concerning release of aliens who cannot be removed because the designated country of removal will not accept their return) is final, and shall not be subject to redetermination by an immigration judge.

(i) Stay of custody order pending appeal by the government —

(1) General discretionary stay authority. The Board of Immigration Appeals (Board) has the authority to stay the order of an immigration judge redetermining the conditions of custody of an alien when the Department of Homeland Security appeals the custody decision or on its own motion. DHS is entitled to seek a discretionary stay (whether or not on an emergency basis) from the Board in connection with such an appeal at any time.

(2) Automatic stay in certain cases. In any case in which DHS has determined that an alien should not be released or has set a bond of $ 10,000 or more, any order of the immigration judge authorizing release (on bond or otherwise) shall be stayed upon DHS's filing of a notice of intent to appeal the custody redetermination (Form EOIR-43) with the immigration court within one business day of the order, and, except as otherwise provided in 8 CFR 1003.6(c), shall remain in abeyance pending decision of the appeal by the Board. The decision whether or not to file Form EOIR-43 is subject to the discretion of the Secretary.

HISTORY:

[57 FR 11571, Apr. 6, 1992; 60 FR 34089, June 30, 1995; 62 FR 10312, 10332, Mar. 6, 1997; 63 FR 27441, 27448, May 19, 1998; 66 FR 54909, 54911, Oct. 31, 2001; redesignated and amended at 68 FR 9824, 9830, 9846, Feb. 28, 2003; 68 FR 10349, 10350, Mar. 5, 2003; 70 FR 4743, 4753, Jan. 31, 2005; 71 FR 57873, 57884, Oct. 2, 2006]

§ 1003.20 Change of venue.

(a) Venue shall lie at the Immigration Court where jurisdiction vests pursuant to § 1003.14.

(b) The Immigration Judge, for good cause, may change venue only upon motion by one of the parties, after the charging document has been filed with the Immigration Court. The Immigration Judge may grant a change of venue only after the other party has been given notice and an opportunity to respond to the motion to change venue.

(c) No change of venue shall be granted without identification of a fixed street address, including city, state and ZIP code, where the respondent/applicant may be reached for further hearing notification.

HISTORY:

[57 FR 11572, Apr. 6, 1992, as confirmed at 59 FR 1899, Jan. 13, 1994; 60 FR 34089, June 30, 1995; 62 FR 10312, 10332, Mar. 6, 1997; redesignated and amended at 68 FR 9824, 9830, 9846, Feb. 28, 2003]

§ 1003.21 Pre-hearing conferences and statement.

(a) Pre-hearing conferences may be scheduled at the discretion of the Immigration Judge. The conference may be held to narrow issues, to obtain stipulations between the parties, to exchange information voluntarily, and otherwise to simplify and organize the proceeding.

(b) The Immigration Judge may order any party to file a pre-hearing statement of position that may include, but is not limited to: A statement of facts to which both parties have stipulated, together with a statement that the parties have communicated in good faith to stipulate to the fullest extent possible; a list of proposed witnesses and what they will establish; a list of exhibits, copies of exhibits to be introduced, and a statement of the reason for their introduction; the estimated time required to present the case; and, a statement of unresolved issues involved in the proceedings.

(c) If submission of a pre-hearing statement is ordered under paragraph (b) of this section, an Immigration Judge also may require both parties, in writing prior to the hearing, to make any evidentiary objections regarding matters contained in the pre-hearing statement. If objections in writing are required but not received by the date for receipt set by the Immigration Judge, admission of all evidence described in the pre-hearing statement shall be deemed unopposed.

HISTORY:

[57 FR 11572, Apr. 6, 1992, as confirmed at 59 FR 1899, Jan. 13, 1994; redesignated at 68 FR 9824, 9830, Feb. 28, 2003]

§ 1003.22 Interpreters.

Any person acting as an interpreter in a hearing shall swear or affirm to interpret and translate accurately, unless the interpreter is an employee of the United States Government, in which event no such oath or affirmation shall be required.

HISTORY:

[52 FR 2936, Jan. 29, 1987. Redesignated at 57 FR 11571, Apr. 6, 1992; redesignated at 68 FR 9824, 9830, Feb. 28, 2003]

§ 1003.23 Reopening or reconsideration before the immigration court.

(a) Pre-decision motions. Unless otherwise permitted by the immigration judge, motions submitted prior to the final order of an immigration judge shall be in writing and shall state, with particularity the grounds therefor, the relief sought, and the jurisdiction. The immigration judge may set and extend time limits for the making and replying to of motions and replies thereto. A motion shall be deemed unopposed unless timely response is made.

(b) Before the Immigration Court —

(1) In general. An immigration judge may upon the immigration judge's own motion at any time, or upon motion of DHS or the noncitizen, reopen or reconsider any case in which the judge has rendered a decision, unless jurisdiction is vested with the Board of Immigration Appeals. Subject to the exceptions in this paragraph (b)(1) and paragraph (b)(4), a party may file only one motion to reconsider and one motion to reopen proceedings. A motion to reconsider must be filed within 30 days of the date of entry of a final administrative order of removal, deportation, or exclusion, or on or before July 31, 1996, whichever is later. A motion to reopen must be filed within 90 days of the date of entry of a final administrative order of removal, deportation, or exclusion, or on or before September 30, 1996, whichever is later. A motion to reopen or to reconsider shall not be made by or on behalf of a person who is the subject of removal, deportation, or exclusion proceedings subsequent to his or her departure from the United States. Any departure from the United States, including the deportation or removal of a person who is the subject of exclusion, deportation, or removal proceedings, occurring after the filing of a motion to reopen or a motion to reconsider shall constitute a withdrawal of such motion. The time and numerical limitations set forth in this paragraph (b)(1) do not apply to motions by the Service in removal proceedings pursuant to section 240 of the Act. Nor shall such limitations apply to motions by the Service in exclusion or deportation proceedings, when the basis of the motion is fraud in the original proceeding or a crime that would support termination of asylum in accordance with § 1208.22(e) of this chapter.

(i) Form and contents of the motion. The motion shall be in writing and signed by the affected party or the attorney or representative of record, if any. The motion and any submission made in conjunction with it must be in English or accompanied by a certified English translation. Motions to reopen or reconsider shall state whether the validity of the exclusion, deportation, or removal order has been or is the subject of any judicial proceeding and, if so, the nature and date thereof, the court in which such proceeding took place or is pending, and its result or status. In any case in which an exclusion, deportation, or removal order is in effect, any motion to reopen or reconsider such order shall include a statement by or on behalf of the moving party declaring whether the subject of the order is also the subject of any pending criminal proceeding under the Act, and, if so, the current status of that proceeding.

(ii) Filing. Motions to reopen or reconsider a decision of an immigration judge must be filed with the immigration court having administrative control over the Record of Proceeding. If necessary under § 1003.32, a motion to reopen or a motion to reconsider shall include a certificate showing service on the opposing party of the motion and all attachments. If the moving party is not DHS, service of the motion shall be made upon the ICE Office of the Principal Legal Advisor for the field location in which the case was completed. If the moving party, other than DHS, is represented, a Form EOIR-28, Notice of Appearance as Attorney or Representative Before an Immigration Judge must be filed with the motion. For any motion requiring a fee, that motion must be accompanied by a fee receipt, an alternate proof of payment consistent with § 1103.7(a)(3), or a fee waiver request pursuant to § 1103.7(c). If filed in paper, the motion must be filed in duplicate with the immigration court.

(iii) Assignment to an immigration judge. If the immigration judge is unavailable or unable to adjudicate the motion to reopen or reconsider, the Chief Immigration Judge or a delegate of the Chief Immigration Judge shall reassign such motion to another immigration judge.

(iv) Replies to motions; decision. The immigration judge may set and extend time limits for replies to motions to reopen or reconsider. A motion shall be deemed unopposed unless timely response is made. The decision to grant or deny a motion to reopen or a motion to reconsider is within the discretion of the immigration judge.

(v) Stays. Except in cases involving in absentia orders, the filing of a motion to reopen or a motion to reconsider shall not stay the execution of any decision made in the case. Execution of such decision shall proceed unless a stay of execution is specifically granted by the immigration judge, the Board, or an authorized DHS officer.

(2) Motion to reconsider. A motion to reconsider shall state the reasons for the motion by specifying the errors of fact or law in the Immigration Judge's prior decision and shall be supported by pertinent authority. Such motion may not seek reconsideration of a decision denying previous motion to reconsider.

(3) Motion to reopen. A motion to reopen proceedings shall state the new facts that will be proven at a hearing to be held if the motion is granted and shall be supported by affidavits and other evidentiary material. Any motion to reopen for the purpose of acting on an application for relief must be accompanied by the appropriate application for relief and all supporting documents. A motion to reopen will not be granted unless the Immigration Judge is satisfied that evidence sought to be offered is material and was not available and could not have been discovered or presented at the former hearing. A motion to reopen for the purpose of providing the alien an opportunity to apply for any form of discretionary relief will not be granted if it appears that the alien's right to apply for such relief was fully explained to him or her by the Immigration Judge and an opportunity to apply therefore was afforded at the hearing, unless the relief is sought on the basis of circumstances that have arisen subsequent to the hearing. Pursuant to section 240A(d)(1) of the Act, a motion to reopen proceedings for consideration or further consideration of an application for relief under section 240A(a) (cancellation of removal for certain permanent residents) or 240A(b) (cancellation of removal and adjustment of status for certain nonpermanent residents) may be granted only if the alien demonstrates that he or she was statutorily eligible for such relief prior to the service of a notice to appear, or prior to the commission of an offense referred to in section 212(a)(2) of the Act that renders the alien inadmissible or removable under sections 237(a)(2) of the Act or (a)(4), whichever is earliest. The Immigration Judge has discretion to deny a motion to reopen even if the moving party has established a prima facie case for relief.

(4) Exceptions to filing deadlines —

(i) Asylum and withholding of removal. The time and numerical limitations set forth in paragraph (b)(1) of this section shall not apply if the basis of the motion is to apply for asylum under section 208 of the Act or withholding of removal under section 241(b)(3) of the Act or withholding of removal under the Convention Against Torture, and is based on changed country conditions arising in the country of nationality or the country to which removal has been ordered, if such evidence is material and was not available and could not have been discovered or presented at the previous proceeding. The filing of a motion to reopen under this section shall not automatically stay the removal of the alien. However, the alien may request a stay and, if granted by the Immigration Judge, the alien shall not be removed pending disposition of the motion by the Immigration Judge. If the original asylum application was denied based upon a finding that it was frivolous, then the alien is ineligible to file either a motion to reopen or reconsider, or for a stay of removal.

(ii) Order entered in absentia removal proceedings. An order of removal entered in absentia in removal proceedings pursuant to section 240(b)(5) of the Act may be rescinded only upon a motion to reopen filed within 180 days after the date of the order of removal, if the alien demonstrates that the failure to appear was because of exceptional circumstances as defined in section 240(e)(1) of the Act. An order entered in absentia pursuant to section 240(b)(5) may be rescinded upon a motion to reopen filed at any time if the alien demonstrates that he or she did not receive notice in accordance with sections 239(a)(1) or (2) of the Act, or the alien demonstrates that he or she was in Federal or state custody and the failure to appear was through no fault of the alien. However, in accordance with section 240(b)(5)(B) of the Act, no written notice of a change in time or place of proceeding shall be required if the alien has failed to provide the address required under section 239(a)(1)(F) of the Act. The filing of a motion under this paragraph shall stay the removal of the alien pending disposition of the motion by the Immigration Judge. An alien may file only one motion pursuant to this paragraph.

(iii) Order entered in absentia in deportation or exclusion proceedings.

(A) An order entered in absentia in deportation proceedings may be rescinded only upon a motion to reopen filed:

(1) Within 180 days after the date of the order of deportation if the alien demonstrates that the failure to appear was because of exceptional circumstances beyond the control of the alien (e.g., serious illness of the alien or serious illness or death of an immediate relative of the alien, but not including less compelling circumstances); or

(2) At any time if the alien demonstrates that he or she did not receive notice or if the alien demonstrates that he or she was in federal or state custody and the failure to appear was through no fault of the alien.

(B) A motion to reopen exclusion hearings on the basis that the immigration judge improperly entered an order of exclusion in absentia must be supported by evidence that the noncitizen had reasonable cause for his failure to appear.

(C) The filing of a motion to reopen under paragraph (b)(4)(iii)(A) of this section shall stay the deportation of the alien pending decision on the motion and the adjudication of any properly filed administrative appeal.

(D) The time and numerical limitations set forth in paragraph (b)(1) of this section shall not apply to a motion to reopen filed pursuant to the provisions of paragraph (b)(4)(iii)(A) of this section.

(iv) Jointly filed motions. The time and numerical limitations set forth in paragraph (b)(1) of this section shall not apply to a motion to reopen agreed upon by all parties and jointly filed.

HISTORY:

[52 FR 2936, Jan. 29, 1987, as amended at 55 FR 30680, July 27, 1990; redesignated at 57 FR 11571, Apr. 6, 1992; 60 FR 34089, June 30, 1995; 61 FR 18900, 18907, Apr. 29, 1996, as corrected at 61 FR 19976, May 3, 1996, as corrected at 61 FR 21228, May 9, 1996; 62 FR 10312, 10332, Mar. 6, 1997, as corrected at 62 FR 15362, Apr. 1, 1997, and 62 FR 17048, Apr. 9, 1997; 64 FR 8478, 8487, Feb. 19, 1999; redesignated at 68 FR 9824, 9830, Feb. 28, 2003; 68 FR 10349, 10350, Mar. 5, 2003; 85 FR 81588, 81655, Dec. 16, 2020; 86 FR 70708, 70722, Dec. 13, 2021; 89 FR 46742, 46793, May 29, 2024]

§ 1003.24 Fees pertaining to matters within the jurisdiction of an immigration judge.

(a) Generally. All fees for the filing of motions and applications in connection with proceedings before the immigration judges are paid to the Department of Homeland Security in accordance with 8 CFR 103.7 and 8 CFR part 106, including fees for applications published by the Executive Office for Immigration Review. The immigration court does not collect fees.

(b) Motions to reopen or reconsider —

(1) When a fee is required. Except as provided in paragraph (b)(2) of this section, a filing fee prescribed in 8 CFR 1103.7, or a fee waiver request pursuant to paragraph (d) of this section, is required in connection with the filing of a motion to reopen or a motion to reconsider.

(2) When a fee is not required. A filing fee is not required in the following instances:

(i) A motion to reopen that is based exclusively on an application for relief that does not require a fee;

(ii) A motion to reconsider that is based exclusively on a prior application for relief that did not require a fee;

(iii) A motion filed while proceedings are already pending before the immigration court;

(iv) A motion requesting only a stay of removal, deportation, or exclusion;

(v) A motion to reopen a deportation or removal order entered in absentia if the motion is filed pursuant to section 242B(c)(3)(B) of the Act (8 U.S.C. 1252b(c)(3)(B)), as it existed prior to April 1, 1997, or section 240(b)(5)(C)(ii) of the Act (8 U.S.C. 1229a(b)(5)(C)(ii)), as amended;

(vi) Any motion filed by the Department of Homeland Security;

(vii) A motion that is agreed upon by all parties and is jointly filed; or

(viii) A motion filed under a law, regulation, or directive that specifically does not require a filing fee.

(c) Applications for relief —

(1) When filed during proceedings. When an application for relief is filed during the course of proceedings, the fee for that application must be paid in advance to the Department of Homeland Security in accordance with 8 CFR 103.7 and 8 CFR part 106. The fee receipt must accompany the application when it is filed with the immigration court except as provided by 8 CFR 1208.4(d)(3).

(2) When submitted with a motion to reopen. When a motion to reopen is based upon an application for relief, the fee for the motion to reopen shall be paid to the Department of Homeland Security and the fee receipt shall accompany the motion. Payment of the fee for the application for relief must be paid to the Department of Homeland Security within the time specified by the immigration judge.

(d) Fee waivers. The immigration judge has the discretion to waive a fee for a motion or application for relief upon a showing that the filing party is unable to pay the fee. The request for a fee waiver must be accompanied by a properly executed affidavit or unsworn declaration made pursuant to 28 U.S.C. 1746 substantiating the filing party's inability to pay the fee. If the request for a fee waiver is denied, the application or motion will not be deemed properly filed, provided the immigration judge grants 15 days to re-file the rejected document with the filing fee or new fee waiver request and tolls any applicable filing deadline during the 15-day cure period.

HISTORY:

[52 FR 2936, Jan. 29, 1987; redesignated at 57 FR 11571, Apr. 6, 1992; 61 FR 18900, 18908, Apr. 29, 1996; redesignated at 68 FR 9824, 9830, Feb. 28, 2003; 68 FR 10349, 10350, Mar. 5, 2003; 69 FR 44903, 44906, July 28, 2004; 85 FR 81698, 81750, Dec. 16, 2020; 85 FR 82750, 82793, Dec. 18, 2020; 86 FR 70708, 70722, Dec. 13, 2021]

§ 1003.25 Form of the proceeding.

(a) Waiver of presence of the parties. The Immigration Judge may, for good cause, and consistent with section 240(b) of the Act, waive the presence of the alien at a hearing when the alien is represented or when the alien is a minor child at least one of whose parents or whose legal guardian is present. When it is impracticable by reason of an alien's mental incompetency for the alien to be present, the presence of the alien may be waived provided that the alien is represented at the hearing by an attorney or legal representative, a near relative, legal guardian, or friend.

(b) Stipulated request for order; waiver of hearing. An Immigration Judge may enter an order of deportation, exclusion or removal stipulated to by the alien (or the alien's representative) and the Service. The Immigration Judge may enter such an order without a hearing and in the absence of the parties based on a review of the charging document, the written stipulation, and supporting documents, if any. If the alien is unrepresented, the Immigration Judge must determine that the alien's waiver is voluntary, knowing, and intelligent. The stipulated request and required waivers shall be signed on behalf of the government and by the alien and his or her attorney or representative, if any. The attorney or representative shall file a Notice of Appearance in accordance with § 1003.16(b). A stipulated order shall constitute a conclusive determination of the alien's deportability or removability from the United States. The stipulation shall include:

(1) An admission that all factual allegations contained in the charging document are true and correct as written;

(2) A concession of deportability or inadmissibility as charged;

(3) A statement that the alien makes no application for relief under the Act;

(4) A designation of a country for deportation or removal under section 241(b)(2)(A)(i) of the Act;

(5) A concession to the introduction of the written stipulation of the alien as an exhibit to the Record of Proceeding;

(6) A statement that the alien understands the consequences of the stipulated request and that the alien enters the request voluntarily, knowingly, and intelligently;

(7) A statement that the alien will accept a written order for his or her deportation, exclusion or removal as a final disposition of the proceedings; and

(8) A waiver of appeal of the written order of deportation or removal.

(c) Telephonic or video hearings. An Immigration Judge may conduct hearings through video conference to the same extent as he or she may conduct hearings in person. An Immigration Judge may also conduct a hearing through a telephone conference, but an evidentiary hearing on the merits may only be conducted through a telephone conference with the consent of the alien involved after the alien has been advised of the right to proceed in person or, where available, through a video conference, except that credible fear determinations may be reviewed by the Immigration Judge through a telephone conference without the consent of the alien.

HISTORY:

[52 FR 2936, Jan. 29, 1987. Redesignated at 57 FR 11571, Apr. 6, 1992; 60 FR 26353, May 17, 1995; 62 FR 10312, 10334, Mar. 6, 1997; redesignated and amended at 68 FR 9824, 9830, 9846, Feb. 28, 2003]

§ 1003.26 In absentia hearings.

(a) In any exclusion proceeding before an Immigration Judge in which the applicant fails to appear, the Immigration Judge shall conduct an in absentia hearing if the Immigration Judge is satisfied that notice of the time and place of the proceeding was provided to the applicant on the record at a prior hearing or by written notice to the applicant or to the applicant's counsel of record on the charging document or at the most recent address in the Record of Proceeding.

(b) In any deportation proceeding before an Immigration Judge in which the respondent fails to appear, the Immigration Judge shall order the respondent deported in absentia if: (1) The Service establishes by clear, unequivocal and convincing evidence that the respondent is deportable; and (2) the Immigration Judge is satisfied that written notice of the time and place of the proceedings and written notice of the consequences of failure to appear, as set forth in section 242B(c) of the Act (8 U.S.C. 1252b(c)), were provided to the respondent in person or were provided to the respondent or the respondent's counsel of record, if any, by certified mail.

(c) In any removal proceeding before an Immigration Judge in which the alien fails to appear, the Immigration Judge shall order the alien removed in absentia if:

(1) The Service establishes by clear, unequivocal, and convincing evidence that the alien is removable; and

(2) The Service establishes by clear, unequivocal, and convincing evidence that written notice of the time and place of proceedings and written notice of the consequences of failure to appear were provided to the alien or the alien's counsel of record.

(d) Written notice to the alien shall be considered sufficient for purposes of this section if it was provided at the most recent address provided by the alien. If the respondent fails to provide his or her address as required under § 1003.15(d), no written notice shall be required for an Immigration Judge to proceed with an in absentia hearing. This paragraph shall not apply in the event that the Immigration Judge waives the appearance of an alien under § 1003.25.

HISTORY:

[57 FR 11572, Apr. 6, 1992, as confirmed and amended at 59 FR 1899, Jan. 13, 1994; 62 FR 10312, 10334, Mar. 6, 1997, as corrected at 62 FR 15362, Apr. 1, 1997; redesignated and amended at 68 FR 9824, 9830, 9846, Feb. 28, 2003]

§ 1003.27 Public access to hearings.

All hearings, other than exclusion hearings, shall be open to the public except that:

(a) Depending upon physical facilities, the Immigration Judge may place reasonable limitations upon the number in attendance at any one time with priority being given to the press over the general public;

(b) For the purpose of protecting witnesses, parties, or the public interest, the Immigration Judge may limit attendance or hold a closed hearing.

(c) In any proceeding before an Immigration Judge concerning an abused alien spouse, the hearing and the Record of Proceeding shall be closed to the public unless the abused spouse agrees that the hearing and the Record of Proceeding shall be open to the public. In any proceeding before an Immigration Judge concerning an abused alien child, the hearing and the Record of Proceeding shall be closed to the public.

(d) Proceedings before an Immigration Judge shall be closed to the public if information subject to a protective order under § 1003.46, which has been filed under seal pursuant to § 1003.31(d), may be considered.

HISTORY:

[52 FR 2936, Jan. 29, 1987. Redesignated and amended at 57 FR 11571, 11572, Apr. 6, 1992, as confirmed at 59 FR 1899, Jan. 13, 1994; 62 FR 10312, 10334, Mar. 6, 1997; 67 FR 36799, 36802, May 28, 2002; redesignated and amended at 68 FR 9824, 9830, 9846, Feb. 28, 2003]

§ 1003.28 Recording equipment.

The only recording equipment permitted in the proceeding will be the equipment used by the Immigration Judge to create the official record. No other photographic, video, electronic, or similar recording device will be permitted to record any part of the proceeding.

HISTORY:

[52 FR 2936, Jan. 29, 1987. Redesignated at 57 FR 11571, Apr. 6, 1992; redesignated at 68 FR 9824, 9830, Feb. 28, 2003]

§ 1003.29 Continuances.

The immigration judge may grant a motion for continuance for good cause shown, provided that nothing in this section shall authorize a continuance that causes the adjudication of an asylum application to exceed 180 days in the absence of exceptional circumstances, consistent with section 208(d)(5)(A)(iii) of the Act and §1003.10(b).

HISTORY:

[52 FR 2936, Jan. 29, 1987. Redesignated at 57 FR 11571, Apr. 6, 1992; redesignated at 68 FR 9824, 9830, Feb. 28, 2003; 85 FR 81698, 81750, Dec. 16, 2020]

§ 1003.30 Additional charges in deportation or removal hearings.

At any time during deportation or removal proceedings, additional or substituted charges of deportability and/or factual allegations may be lodged by the Service in writing. The alien shall be served with a copy of these additional charges and/or allegations and the Immigration Judge shall read them to the alien. The Immigration Judge shall advise the alien, if he or she is not represented by counsel, that the alien may be so represented. The alien may be given a reasonable continuance to respond to the additional factual allegations and charges. Thereafter, the provision of § 1240.10(b) of this chapter relating to pleading shall apply to the additional factual allegations and charges.

HISTORY:

[52 FR 2936, Jan. 29, 1987. Redesignated at 57 FR 11571, Apr. 6, 1992; 62 FR 10312, 10335, Mar. 6, 1997; redesignated at 68 FR 9824, 9830, Feb. 28, 2003; 68 FR 10349, 10350, Mar. 5, 2003]

§ 1003.31 Filing documents and applications.

This section applies to the filing of all documents, including motions and applications, before the immigration courts.

(a) Filing parties. DHS and all attorneys and accredited representatives of record for persons appearing before the immigration courts are required to electronically file all documents, including charging documents, with the immigration courts through EOIR's electronic filing application in all cases eligible for electronic filing. Although not required, unrepresented respondents or applicants; reputable individuals and accredited officials who are representatives of record; other authorized individuals; and practitioners filing an EOIR-61, may electronically file documents with the immigration courts through EOIR's electronic filing application in cases eligible for electronic filing. An unrepresented respondent or applicant; reputable individual; accredited official; other authorized individual; or practitioner filing an EOIR-61, who elects to use EOIR's electronic filing application shall be required to register with EOIR as a condition of using that application. If a party not required to file electronically opts to use EOIR's electronic filing application for a case, the individual must electronically file all documents with the immigration courts for that case unless an immigration judge, only upon a motion filed by the individual with good cause shown, grants leave to opt out of using the electronic filing application. Such an individual who has been granted leave to opt out of using EOIR's electronic filing application for a case may not subsequently opt in to use that application for the same case.

(b) Filing requirements. If EOIR's electronic filing application is unavailable due to an unplanned system outage on the last day for filing in a specific case, then the filing deadline will be extended to the first day that the electronic filing application becomes accessible that is not a Saturday, Sunday, or legal holiday. For planned system outages, parties must electronically file documents during system availability within the applicable filing deadline or paper file documents within the applicable filing deadline. EOIR will issue public communications for planned system outages ahead of the scheduled outage. Any planned system outage announced five or fewer business days prior to the start of the outage will be treated as an unplanned outage. In all other situations in cases eligible for electronic filing, an immigration judge retains the discretion to accept paper filings in all cases.

(c) Originals. Parties must make the originals of all filed documents available upon request to the immigration court or the opposing party for review.

(d) Classified information. Notwithstanding any other provision of this chapter, classified information is never allowed to be electronically filed.

(e) Sealed medical documents. Notwithstanding any other provision of this chapter, parties are not permitted to file electronically any sealed medical documents.

(f) Where to file. All documents that are to be considered in a proceeding before an immigration judge must be filed with the immigration court having administrative control over the Record of Proceeding.

(g) Fees. Except as provided in § 1240.11(f) of this chapter, all documents or applications filed with the immigration courts requiring the payment of a fee must be accompanied by a fee receipt from DHS, alternate proof of payment consistent with § 1103.7(a)(3) of this chapter, or a fee waiver request pursuant to § 1103.7(c). Except as provided in § 1003.8, any fee relating to immigration judge proceedings shall be paid to, and accepted by, any DHS office authorized to accept fees for other purposes pursuant to § 1103.7(a).

(h) Filing deadlines. The immigration judge may set and extend time limits for the filing of applications and related documents and responses thereto, if any. If an application or document is not filed within the time set by the immigration judge, the opportunity to file that application or document shall be deemed waived.

(i) Filing under seal. DHS may file documents under seal by including a cover sheet identifying the contents of the submission as containing information which is being filed under seal. Documents filed under seal shall only be examined by persons with authorized access to the administrative record.

(j) Signatures. All documents filed with the immigration courts that require a signature must have an original, handwritten ink signature, an encrypted digital signature, or an electronic signature. Electronic filings submitted through EOIR's electronic filing application that require the user's signature may have a conformed signature. This paragraph is subject to the requirements of the application or document being submitted.

HISTORY:

[57 FR 11572, Apr. 6, 1992, as confirmed at 59 FR 1899, Jan. 13, 1994; 60 FR 34089, June 30, 1995; 61 FR 18900, 18908, Apr. 29, 1996, as corrected at 61 FR 19976, May 3, 1996, as corrected at 61 FR 21228, May 9, 1996; 61 FR 46373, 46374, Sept. 3, 1996; 62 FR 45148, 45149, Aug. 26, 1997; 67 FR 36799, 36802, May 28, 2002; redesignated and amended at 68 FR 9824, 9830, 9846, Feb. 28, 2003; 68 FR 10349, 10350, Mar. 5, 2003]; 85 FR 81698, 81750, Dec. 16, 2020; 86 FR 70708, 70722, Dec. 13, 2021]

§ 1003.32 Service and size of documents.

The service of filings with the immigration courts depends on whether the documents are filed through EOIR's electronic filing application or in paper.

(a) Service of electronic filings. If all parties are using EOIR's electronic filing application in a specific case, the parties do not need to serve a document that is filed through EOIR's electronic filing application on the opposing party. If all parties are using EOIR's electronic filing application in a specific case, EOIR's electronic filing application will effectuate service by providing a notification of all electronically filed documents on all parties. Upon successful upload by one of the parties, EOIR will email a notification to the email addresses provided in paragraph (b) of this section. If one or more parties are not filing through EOIR's electronic filing application in a specific case, the parties must follow the service procedures in paragraph (c) of this section.

(b) Valid email address. Use of EOIR's electronic filing application requires a valid email address for electronic service. The immigration courts will use the email address provided through eRegistry for electronic service on participating parties. Users must immediately update their eRegistry account if their email address changes. Representatives must additionally file a new Form EOIR-28 with the immigration court if their email address changes. EOIR will consider service completed when the electronic notification is delivered to the last email address on file provided by the user.

(c) Service of paper filings. If electronic filing is not being used in a particular case, the party filing with the immigration court must serve a copy of the filing on the opposing party and include a certificate of service showing service on the opposing party with their filing. The immigration judge will not consider any documents or applications that do not contain a certificate of service unless service is made on the record during a hearing.

(d) Size and format of documents. Unless otherwise permitted by the immigration judge, all written material presented to immigration judges including offers of evidence, correspondence, briefs, memoranda, or other documents must be submitted on 8 1/2 ″ x 11″ size pages, whether filed electronically or in paper. The immigration judge may require that exhibits and other written material presented be indexed, paginated, and that a table of contents be provided.

HISTORY:

[52 FR 2936, Jan. 29, 1987. Redesignated and amended at 57 FR 11571, 11572, Apr. 6, 1992, as confirmed at 59 FR 1899, Jan. 13, 1994; redesignated at 68 FR 9824, 9830, Feb. 28, 2003; 86 FR 70708, 70723, Dec. 13, 2021]

§ 1003.33 Translation of documents.

Any foreign language document offered by a party in a proceeding shall be accompanied by an English language translation and a certification signed by the translator that must be printed legibly or typed. Such certification must include a statement that the translator is competent to translate the document, and that the translation is true and accurate to the best of the translator's abilities.

HISTORY:

[57 FR 11573, Apr. 6, 1992, as confirmed and amended at 59 FR 1899, 1900, Jan. 13, 1994; redesignated at 68 FR 9824, 9830, Feb. 28, 2003]

§ 1003.34 Testimony.

Testimony of witnesses appearing at the hearing shall be under oath or affirmation.

HISTORY:

[52 FR 2936, Jan. 29, 1987. Redesignated at 57 FR 11571, Apr. 6, 1992; redesignated at 68 FR 9824, 9830, Feb. 28, 2003]

§ 1003.35 Depositions and subpoenas.

(a) Depositions. If an Immigration Judge is satisfied that a witness is not reasonably available at the place of hearing and that said witness' testimony or other evidence is essential, the Immigration Judge may order the taking of deposition either at his or her own instance or upon application of a party. Such order shall designate the official by whom the deposition shall be taken, may prescribe and limit the content, scope, or manner of taking the deposition, and may direct the production of documentary evidence.

(b) **Subpoenas issued subsequent to commencement of proceedings.**

(1) General. In any proceeding before an Immigration Judge, other than under 8 CFR part 335, the Immigration Judge shall have exclusive jurisdiction to issue subpoenas requiring the attendance of witnesses or for the production of books, papers and other documentary evidence, or both. An Immigration Judge may issue a subpoena upon his or her own volition or upon application of the Service or the alien.

(2) Application for subpoena. A party applying for a subpoena shall be required, as a condition precedent to its issuance, to state in writing or at the proceeding, what he or she expects to prove by such witnesses or documentary evidence, and to show affirmatively that he or she has made diligent effort, without success, to produce the same.

(3) Issuance of subpoena. Upon being satisfied that a witness will not appear and testify or produce documentary evidence and that the witness' evidence is essential, the Immigration Judge shall issue a subpoena. The subpoena shall state the title of the proceeding and shall command the person to whom it is directed to attend and to give testimony at a time and place specified. The subpoena may also command the person to whom it is directed to produce the books, papers, or documents specified in the subpoena.

(4) Appearance of witness. If the witness is at a distance of more than 100 miles from the place of the proceeding, the subpoena shall provide for the witness' appearance at the Immigration Court nearest to the witness to respond to oral or written interrogatories, unless there is no objection by any party to the witness' appearance at the proceeding.

(5) Service. A subpoena issued under this section may be served by any person over 18 years of age not a party to the case.

(6) Invoking aid of court. If a witness neglects or refuses to appear and testify as directed by the subpoena served upon him or her in accordance with the provisions of this section, the Immigration Judge issuing the subpoena shall request the United States Attorney for the district in which the subpoena was issued to report such neglect or refusal to the United States District Court and to request such court to issue an order requiring the witness to appear and testify and to produce the books, papers or documents designated in the subpoena.

HISTORY:

[52 FR 2936, Jan. 29, 1987. Redesignated at 57 FR 11571, Apr. 6, 1992; 62 FR 10312, 10335, Mar. 6, 1997; redesignated at 68 FR 9824, 9830, Feb. 28, 2003]

§ 1003.36 Record of proceeding.

The Immigration Court shall create and control the Record of Proceeding.

HISTORY:

[52 FR 2936, Jan. 29, 1987. Redesignated at 57 FR 11571, Apr. 6, 1992; 60 FR 34089, June 30, 1995; redesignated at 68 FR 9824, 9830, Feb. 28, 2003]

§ 1003.37 Decisions.

(a) A decision of the immigration judge may be rendered orally or in writing. If the decision is oral, it shall be stated by the immigration judge in the presence of the parties and a memorandum summarizing the oral decision shall be served on the parties. If the decision is in writing, it shall be served on the parties by personal service, mail, or electronic notification.

(b) A written copy of the decision will not be sent to an alien who has failed to provide a written record of an address.

HISTORY:

[57 FR 11573, Apr. 6, 1992, as confirmed and amended at 59 FR 1899, 1900, Jan. 13, 1994; redesignated at 68 FR 9824, 9830, Feb. 28, 2003; 86 FR 70708, 70723, Dec. 13, 2021]

§ 1003.38 Appeals.

(a) Decisions of Immigration Judges may be appealed to the Board of Immigration Appeals as authorized by 8 CFR 1003.1(b).

(b) The Notice of Appeal from a Decision of an Immigration Judge (Form EOIR-26) shall be filed directly with the Board of Immigration Appeals within 30 calendar days after the stating of an immigration judge's oral decision or the mailing or electronic notification of an immigration judge's written decision. If the final date for filing falls on a Saturday, Sunday, or legal holiday, this appeal time shall be extended to the next business day. A Notice of Appeal (Form EOIR-26) may not be filed by any party who has waived appeal.

(c) The date of filing of the Notice of Appeal (Form EOIR-26) shall be the date the Notice is received by the Board.

(d) A Notice of Appeal (Form EOIR-26) must be accompanied by the appropriate fee or by an Appeal Fee Waiver Request (Form EOIR-26A). If the fee is not paid or the Appeal Fee Waiver Request (Form EOIR-26A) is not filed within the specified time period indicated in paragraph(b) of this section, the appeal will not be deemed properly filed and the decision of the Immigration Judge shall be final to the same extent as though no appeal had been taken.

(e) Within five working days of any change of address, an alien must provide written notice of the change of address on Form EOIR-33 to the Board. Where a party is represented, the representative should also provide to the Board written notice of any change in the representative's business mailing address.

(f) Briefs may be filed by both parties pursuant to 8 CFR 1003.3(c).

(g) In proceedings before the Board on behalf of a respondent, a practitioner must enter an appearance using Form EOIR–27 or Form EOIR–60.

(1) Entering an appearance using Form EOIR–27. In proceedings before the Board, in order to become the practitioner of record, which authorizes and requires the practitioner to appear before the Board on behalf of the respondent, file all documents on behalf of the respondent, and accept service of process of all documents filed in the proceedings, a practitioner must enter an appearance using Form EOIR–27.

(i) Filing Form EOIR–27. The practitioner must file a copy of the Form EOIR–27 with the Board and serve a copy on DHS as required by 8 CFR 1003.32. The practitioner must file and serve a Form EOIR–27 even if the practitioner has previously filed a separate Notice of Entry of Appearance with DHS for appearances before DHS or a Form EOIR–28 with the immigration court, or has previously entered a limited appearance using a Form EOIR–60 in connection with document assistance under paragraph (g)(2) of this section.

(ii) Effect of filing Form EOIR–27. A practitioner who enters an appearance using Form EOIR–27 is the practitioner of record and must appear before the Board on behalf of the respondent, file all documents on behalf of the respondent, and accept service of process of all documents filed in the proceedings, consistent with 8 CFR 1292.5. Filing a Form EOIR–27 provides the practitioner with access to the record of proceedings during the course of proceedings. A respondent shall be considered represented for the proceedings in which a Form EOIR–27 has been filed.

(iii) Withdrawal or substitution. A practitioner who enters an appearance on behalf of a respondent before the Board by filing a Form EOIR–27 remains the practitioner of record unless the Board permits withdrawal or substitution during proceedings only upon written motion submitted without fee.

(2) Entering a limited appearance for document assistance using Form EOIR– 60. A practitioner who provides assistance to a pro se respondent with the drafting, completion, or filling in of blank spaces of a motion, brief, form, or other specific document or set of documents intended to be filed with the Board, regardless of whether such assistance is considered "practice" or "preparation" as defined in § 1001.1, must disclose such limited assistance to the Board using Form EOIR–60, unless pursuant to paragraph (g)(1) the practitioner has filed a Form EOIR–27 to become the practitioner of record.

(i) Filing Form EOIR–60. A Form EOIR–60 must not be filed as a standalone document. The single Form EOIR–60 must be filed with the Board at the same time as the document or set of documents with which the practitioner assisted. Any subsequent filing of a document or set of documents with which a practitioner assisted must be accompanied by a new Form EOIR–60.

(ii) Effect of Filing Form EOIR–60. A practitioner who enters a limited appearance using Form EOIR–60 is not the practitioner of record, is not required to appear before the Board, and is not required to submit a motion to withdraw or substitute. The submission of a Form EOIR–60 does not create additional ongoing obligations between the practitioner, the respondent, and EOIR. An appearance through Form EOIR–60 does not provide the practitioner with access to the record of proceedings. A respondent who received assistance pursuant to this paragraph is not represented, remains pro se, and is subject to service of process of all documents filed in the proceedings, consistent with 8 CFR 1292.5.

(3) Completing an appearance form, proof of qualification, disclosure requirements, and identification. The practitioner must properly complete and sign any Form EOIR–27 or Form EOIR– 60, as required by the form instructions. A practitioner's personal appearance or signature on the Form EOIR–27 or Form EOIR–60 constitutes a representation that the person is authorized and qualified to appear as a practitioner in accordance with 8 CFR 1292.1. Further proof that the practitioner meets the qualifications of a practitioner as defined in 8 CFR 1292.1 may be required. The completion of a Form EOIR–27 or Form EOIR–60 in connection with an application or form that requires disclosure of the preparer does not relieve a practitioner from complying with the particular disclosure requirements of the application or form.

Notwithstanding the filing of a Form EOIR–27 or Form EOIR–60, the practitioner must identify themselves by name, accompanied by their signature, on any document filed or intended to be filed with the Board pursuant to an appearance under paragraph (g)(1) or (2) of this section.

HISTORY:

[52 FR 2936, Jan. 29, 1987; redesignated at 57 FR 11571, Apr. 6, 1992; 60 FR 34089, June 30, 1995; 61 FR 18900, 18908, Apr. 29, 1996; redesignated and amended at 68 FR 9824, 9830, 9846, Feb. 28, 2003; 86 FR 70708, 70723, Dec. 13, 2021; 87 FR 56204, 56258, Sept. 14, 2022]

§ 1003.39 Finality of decision.

Except when certified to the Board, the decision of the Immigration Judge becomes final upon waiver of appeal or upon expiration of the time to appeal if no appeal is taken whichever occurs first.

HISTORY:

[52 FR 2936, Jan. 29, 1987. Redesignated and amended at 57 FR 11571, 11573, Apr. 6, 1992; redesignated at 68 FR 9824, 9830, Feb. 28, 2003]

§ 1003.40 Local operating procedures.

An Immigration Court having administrative control over Records of Proceedings may establish local operating procedures, provided that:

(a) Such operating procedure(s) shall not be inconsistent with any provision of this chapter;

(b) A majority of the judges of the local Immigration Court shall concur in writing therein; and

(c) The Chief Immigration Judge has approved the proposed operating procedure(s) in writing.

HISTORY:

[52 FR 2936, Jan. 29, 1987. Redesignated at 57 FR 11571, Apr. 6, 1992; 60 FR 34090, June 30, 1995; redesignated at 68 FR 9824, 9830, Feb. 28, 2003]

§ 1003.41 Evidence of criminal conviction.

In any proceeding before an Immigration Judge,

(a) Any of the following documents or records shall be admissible as evidence in proving a criminal conviction:

(1) A record of judgment and conviction;

(2) A record of plea, verdict and sentence;

(3) A docket entry from court records that indicates the existence of a conviction;

(4) Minutes of a court proceeding or a transcript of a hearing that indicates the existence of a conviction;

(5) An abstract of a record of conviction prepared by the court in which the conviction was entered, or by a state official associated with the state's repository of criminal justice records, that indicates the following: The charge or section of law violated, the disposition of the case, the existence and date of conviction, and the sentence;

(6) Any document or record prepared by, or under the direction of, the court in which the conviction was entered that indicates the existence of a conviction.

(b) Any document or record of the types specified in paragraph (a) of this section may be submitted if it complies with the requirement of § 287.6(a) of this chapter, or a copy of any such document or record may be submitted if it is attested in writing by an immigration officer to be a true and correct copy of the original.

(c) Any record of conviction or abstract that has been submitted by electronic means to the Service from a state or court shall be admissible as evidence to prove a criminal conviction if it:

(1) Is certified by a state official associated with the state's repository of criminal justice records as an official record from its repository or by a court official from the court in which conviction was entered as an official record from its repository. Such certification may be by means of a computer-generated signature and statement of authenticity; and,

(2) Is certified in writing by a Service official as having been received electronically from the state's record repository or the court's record repository.

(d) Any other evidence that reasonably indicates the existence of a criminal conviction may be admissible as evidence thereof.

HISTORY:

[58 FR 38953, July 21, 1993; redesignated at 68 FR 9824, 9830, Feb. 28, 2003]

§ 1003.42 Review of credible fear determinations. [Effective until December 27, 2025]

(a) Referral. Jurisdiction for an immigration judge to review a negative fear determination by an asylum officer pursuant to section 235(b)(1)(B) of the Act shall commence with the filing by DHS of the Notice of Referral to Immigration Judge. DHS shall also file with the notice of referral a copy of the written record of determination as defined in section 235(b)(1)(B)(iii)(II) of the Act, including a copy of the alien's written request for review, if any.

(b) Record of proceeding. The Immigration Court shall create a Record of Proceeding for a review of a negative fear determination. This record shall not be merged with any later proceeding involving the same alien.

(c) Procedures and evidence. The Immigration Judge may receive into evidence any oral or written statement which is material and relevant to any issue in the review. The testimony of the alien shall be under oath or affirmation administered by the Immigration Judge. If an interpreter is necessary, one will be provided by the Immigration Court. The Immigration Judge shall determine whether the review shall be in person, or through telephonic or video connection (where available). The alien may consult with a person or persons of the alien's choosing prior to the review.

(d) The immigration judge shall make a de novo determination as to whether there is a significant possibility, taking into account the credibility of the statements made by the alien in support of the alien's claim, and such other facts as are known to the immigration judge, that the alien could establish eligibility for asylum under section 208 of the Act or withholding of removal under section 241(b)(3)(B) of the Act or deferral of removal under the Convention Against Torture.

(e) Timing. The immigration judge shall conclude the review to the maximum extent practicable within 24 hours, but in no case later than 7 days after the date the supervisory asylum officer has approved the asylum officer's negative credible fear determination issued on the Record of Negative Credible Fear Finding and Request for Review.

(f) Decision.

(1) The decision of the immigration judge shall be rendered in accordance with the provisions of 8 CFR 1208.30(g)(2). In reviewing the negative fear determination by DHS, the immigration judge shall apply relevant precedent issued by the Board of Immigration Appeals, the Attorney General, the Federal circuit court of appeals having jurisdiction over the immigration court where the Request for Review is filed, and the Supreme Court.

(2) No appeal shall lie from a review of a negative fear determination made by an Immigration Judge, but the Attorney General, in the Attorney General's sole and unreviewable discretion, may direct that the Immigration Judge refer a case for the Attorney General's review following the Immigration Judge's review of a negative fear determination.

(3) In any case the Attorney General decides, the Attorney General's decision shall be stated in writing and shall be transmitted to the Board for transmittal and service as provided in 8 CFR 1003.1(f). Such decision by the Attorney General may be designated as precedent as provided in 8 CFR 1003.1(g).

(g) Custody. An immigration judge shall have no authority to review an alien's custody status in the course of a review of a negative fear determination made by DHS.

(h) Safe Third Country Agreement—

(1) Applicants for admission, 2002 U.S.-Canada Agreement, which includes the Additional Protocol of 2022. An immigration judge has no jurisdiction to review a determination by an asylum officer that an applicant for admission is not eligible to apply for asylum pursuant to the 2002 U.S.-Canada Agreement, which includes the Additional Protocol of 2022, formed under section 208(a)(2)(A) of the Act and should be returned to Canada to pursue their claims for asylum or other protection under the laws of Canada. See 8 CFR 208.30(e)(6). However, in any case where an asylum officer has found that an applicant for admission qualifies for an exception to that Agreement, which includes the Additional Protocol of 2022, or that the Agreement, which includes the Additional Protocol of 2022, does not apply, an immigration judge does have jurisdiction to review a negative credible fear finding made thereafter by the asylum officer as provided in this section.

(2) Aliens in transit. An immigration judge has no jurisdiction to review any determination by DHS that an alien being removed from Canada in transit through the United States should be returned to Canada to pursue asylum claims under Canadian law, under the terms of the 2002 U.S.-Canada Agreement, which includes the Additional Protocol of 2022.

(3) Applicants for admission. An immigration judge has no jurisdiction to review a determination by an asylum officer that an alien is not eligible to apply for asylum pursuant to a bilateral or multilateral agreement with a third country under section 208(a)(2)(A) of the Act and should be removed to the third country to pursue his or her claims for asylum or other protection under the laws of that country. See 8 CFR 208.30(e)(7). However, if the asylum officer has determined that the alien may not or should not be removed to a third country under section 208(a)(2)(A) of the Act and subsequently makes a negative fear determination, an immigration judge has jurisdiction to review the negative fear finding as provided in this section.

(4) Aliens in transit through the United States from countries other than Canada. An immigration judge has no jurisdiction to review any determination by DHS that an alien being removed from a receiving country in transit through the United States should be returned to pursue asylum claims under the receiving country's law, under the terms of the applicable cooperative agreement. See 8 CFR 208.30(e)(7).

(i) Severability. The provisions of part 1003 are separate and severable from one another. In the event that any provision in part 1003 is stayed, enjoined, not implemented, or otherwise held invalid, the remaining provisions shall nevertheless be implemented as an independent rule and continue in effect.

HISTORY:

[62 FR 10312, 10335, March 6, 1997; 64 FR 8478, 8487, Feb. 19, 1999; redesignated at 68 FR 9824, 9830, Feb. 28, 2003; 69 FR 69490, 69496, Nov. 29, 2004; 83 FR 55934, 55952, Nov. 9, 2018; 84 FR 33829, 33844, July 16, 2019; 84 FR 63994, 64009, Nov. 19, 2019; 85 FR 80274, 80393, Dec. 11, 2020; 85 FR 84160, 84196, Dec. 23, 2020; 86 FR 6847, Jan. 25, 2021; 86 FR 15069, Mar. 22, 2021; 86 FR 73615, Dec. 28, 2021; 87 FR 18078, 18220, Mar. 29, 2022; 87 FR 79789, Dec. 28, 2022; 88 FR 18227, 18240, Mar. 28, 2023; 88 FR 31314, 31451, May 16, 2023; 89 FR 105392, 105401, Dec. 27, 2024; 89 FR 105386, Dec. 27, 2024]

§ 1003.42 Review of credible fear determinations. [Effective December 27, 2025; Effective until December 31, 2025]

(a) Referral. Jurisdiction for an immigration judge to review a negative credible fear determination by an asylum officer pursuant to section 235(b)(1)(B) of the Act shall commence with the filing by DHS of Form I-863, Notice of Referral to Immigration Judge, and a complete copy of the record of determination as defined in section 235(b)(1)(B)(iii)(II) of the Act with the immigration court.

(b) Record of proceeding. The immigration court shall create a Record of Proceeding for a review of a negative fear determination. This record shall not be merged with any later proceeding involving the same noncitizen.

(c) Procedures and evidence. The immigration judge may receive into evidence any oral or written statement which is material and relevant to any issue in the review. The testimony of the noncitizen shall be under oath or affirmation administered by the immigration judge. If an interpreter is necessary, one will be provided by the immigration court. The immigration judge shall determine whether the review shall be in person, or through telephonic or video connection (where available). The noncitizen may consult with a person or persons of the noncitizen's choosing prior to the review.

(d) Standard of review. The immigration judge shall make a de novo determination as to whether there is a significant possibility, taking into account the credibility of the statements made by the noncitizen in support of the noncitizen's claim, and such other facts as are known to the immigration judge, that the noncitizen could establish eligibility for asylum under section 208 of the Act, or could establish eligibility for withholding of removal under section 241(b)(3)(B) of the Act, or withholding or deferral of removal under the Convention Against Torture with respect to the country or countries of removal identified pursuant to section 241(b) of the Act. This determination shall, where relevant, include review of the asylum officer's application of any bars to asylum and withholding of removal pursuant to 8 CFR 208.30(e)(5).

(e) Timing. The immigration judge shall conclude the review to the maximum extent practicable within 24 hours, but in no case later than 7 days after the date the supervisory asylum officer has concurred with the asylum officer's negative credible fear determination issued on the Form I-869, Record of Negative Credible Fear Finding and Request for Review.

(f) Decision.

(1) The decision of the immigration judge shall be rendered in accordance with the provisions of 8 CFR 1208.30(g)(2). In reviewing the negative fear determination by DHS, the immigration judge shall apply relevant precedent issued by the Board of Immigration Appeals, the Attorney General, the Federal circuit court of appeals having jurisdiction over the immigration court where the Request for Review is filed, and the Supreme Court.

(2) No appeal shall lie from a review of a negative fear determination made by an immigration judge, but the Attorney General, in the Attorney General's sole and unreviewable discretion, may direct that the immigration judge refer a case for the Attorney General's review following the immigration judge's review of a negative fear determination.

(3) In any case the Attorney General decides, the Attorney General's decision shall be stated in writing and shall be transmitted to the Board for transmittal and service as provided in 8 CFR 1003.1(f). Such decision by the Attorney General may be designated as precedent as provided in 8 CFR 1003.1(g).

(g) Custody. An immigration judge shall have no authority to review a noncitizen's custody status in the course of a review of a negative fear determination made by DHS.

(h) Asylum cooperative agreement —

(1) Applicants for admission, 2002 U.S.-Canada Agreement, which includes the Additional Protocol of 2022. An immigration judge has no jurisdiction to review a determination by an asylum officer that an applicant for admission is not eligible to apply for asylum pursuant to the 2002 U.S.-Canada Agreement, which includes the Additional Protocol of 2022, formed under section 208(a)(2)(A) of the Act and should be returned to Canada to pursue their claims for asylum or other protection under the laws of Canada. See 8 CFR 208.30(e)(6). However, in any case where an asylum officer has found that an applicant for admission qualifies for an exception to that Agreement, which includes the Additional Protocol of 2022, or that the Agreement, which includes the Additional Protocol of 2022, does not apply, an immigration judge does have jurisdiction to review a negative credible fear finding made thereafter by the asylum officer as provided in this section.

(2) Noncitizens in transit. An immigration judge has no jurisdiction to review any determination by DHS that a noncitizen being removed from Canada in transit through the United States should be returned to Canada to pursue asylum claims under Canadian law, under the terms of the 2002 U.S.-Canada Agreement, which includes the Additional Protocol of 2022.

(3) Applicants for admission. An immigration judge has no jurisdiction to review a determination by an asylum officer that a noncitizen is not eligible to apply for asylum pursuant to a bilateral or multilateral agreement with a third country under section 208(a)(2)(A) of the Act and should be removed to the third country to pursue his or her claims for asylum or other protection under the laws of that country. See 8 CFR 208.30(e)(7). However, if the asylum officer has determined that the noncitizen may not or should not be removed to a third country under section 208(a)(2)(A) of the Act and subsequently makes a negative fear determination, an immigration judge has jurisdiction to review the negative fear finding as provided in this section.

(4) Noncitizens in transit through the United States from countries other than Canada. An immigration judge has no jurisdiction to review any determination by DHS that a noncitizen being removed from a receiving country in transit through the United States should be returned to pursue asylum claims under the receiving country's law, under the terms of the applicable cooperative agreement. See 8 CFR 208.30(e)(7).

(i) Severability. The provisions of part 1003 are separate and severable from one another. In the event that any provision in part 1003 is stayed, enjoined, not implemented, or otherwise held invalid, the remaining provisions shall nevertheless be implemented as an independent rule and continue in effect.

HISTORY:

[62 FR 10312, 10335, March 6, 1997; 64 FR 8478, 8487, Feb. 19, 1999; redesignated at 68 FR 9824, 9830, Feb. 28, 2003; 69 FR 69490, 69496, Nov. 29, 2004; 83 FR 55934, 55952, Nov. 9, 2018; 84 FR 33829, 33844, July 16, 2019; 84 FR 63994, 64009, Nov. 19, 2019; 85 FR 80274, 80393, Dec. 11, 2020; 85 FR 84160, 84196, Dec. 23, 2020; 86 FR 6847, Jan. 25, 2021; 86 FR 15069, Mar. 22, 2021; 86 FR 73615, Dec. 28, 2021; 87 FR 18078, 18220, Mar. 29, 2022; 87 FR 79789, Dec. 28, 2022; 88 FR 18227, 18240, Mar. 28, 2023; 88 FR 31314, 31451, May 16, 2023; 89 FR 105392, 105401, Dec. 27, 2024; 89 FR 105386, Dec. 27, 2024]

§ 1003.42 Review of credible fear determinations. [Effective December 31, 2025]

(a) Referral. Jurisdiction for an immigration judge to review a negative credible fear determination by an asylum officer pursuant to section 235(b)(1)(B) of the Act shall commence with the filing by DHS of Form I-863, Notice of Referral to Immigration Judge, and a complete copy of the record of determination as defined in section 235(b)(1)(B)(iii)(II) of the Act with the immigration court.

(b) Record of proceeding. The immigration court shall create a Record of Proceeding for a review of a negative fear determination. This record shall not be merged with any later proceeding involving the same noncitizen.

(c) Procedures and evidence. The immigration judge may receive into evidence any oral or written statement which is material and relevant to any issue in the review. The testimony of the noncitizen shall be under oath or affirmation administered by the immigration judge. If an interpreter is necessary, one will be provided by the immigration court. The immigration judge shall determine whether the review shall be in person, or through telephonic or video connection (where available). The noncitizen may consult with a person or persons of the noncitizen's choosing prior to the review.

(d) The immigration judge shall make a de novo determination as to whether there is a significant possibility, taking into account the credibility of the statements made by the noncitizen in support of the noncitizen's claim, whether the noncitizen is subject to any mandatory bars to applying for asylum or being eligible for asylum under section 208(a)(2)(B)-(D) and (b)(2) of the Act, including any bars established by regulation under section 208(b)(2)(C) of the Act, and such other facts as are known to the immigration judge, that the noncitizen could establish his or her ability to apply for or be granted asylum under section 208 of the Act. The immigration judge shall make a de novo determination as to whether there is a reasonable possibility, taking into account the credibility of the statements made by the noncitizen in support of the noncitizen's claim, whether the noncitizen is subject to any mandatory bars to eligibility for withholding of removal under section 241(b)(3)(B) of the Act, and such other facts as are known to the immigration judge, that the noncitizen would be persecuted on account of his or her race, religion, nationality, membership in a particular social group, or political opinion in the country of removal, consistent with the criteria in 8 CFR 1208.16(b). The immigration judge shall also make de novo determinations as to whether there is a reasonable possibility that the noncitizen would be tortured in the country of removal and whether it is more likely than not that the noncitizen would be tortured in the country of removal, in both instances taking into account the credibility of the statements made by the noncitizen in support of the noncitizen's claim and such other facts as are known to the immigration judge, consistent with the criteria in 8 CFR 1208.16(c), 8 CFR 1208.17, and 8 CFR 1208.18.

(e) Timing. The immigration judge shall conclude the review to the maximum extent practicable within 24 hours, but in no case later than 7 days after the date the supervisory asylum officer has concurred with the asylum officer's negative credible fear determination issued on the Form I-869, Record of Negative Credible Fear Finding and Request for Review.

(f) Decision.

(1) The decision of the immigration judge shall be rendered in accordance with the provisions of 8 CFR 1208.30(g)(2). In reviewing the negative fear determination by DHS, the immigration judge shall apply relevant precedent issued by the Board of Immigration Appeals, the Attorney General, the Federal circuit court of appeals having jurisdiction over the immigration court where the Request for Review is filed, and the Supreme Court.

(2) No appeal shall lie from a review of a negative fear determination made by an immigration judge, but the Attorney General, in the Attorney General's sole and unreviewable discretion, may direct that the immigration judge refer a case for the Attorney General's review following the immigration judge's review of a negative fear determination.

(3) In any case the Attorney General decides, the Attorney General's decision shall be stated in writing and shall be transmitted to the Board for transmittal and service as provided in 8 CFR 1003.1(f). Such decision by the Attorney General may be designated as precedent as provided in 8 CFR 1003.1(g).

(g) Custody. An immigration judge shall have no authority to review a noncitizen's custody status in the course of a review of a negative fear determination made by DHS.

(h) Asylum cooperative agreement —

(1) Applicants for admission, 2002 U.S.-Canada Agreement, which includes the Additional Protocol of 2022. An immigration judge has no jurisdiction to review a determination by an asylum officer that an applicant for admission is not eligible to apply for asylum pursuant to the 2002 U.S.-Canada Agreement, which includes the Additional Protocol of 2022, formed under section 208(a)(2)(A) of the Act and should be returned to Canada to pursue their claims for asylum or other protection under the laws of Canada. See 8 CFR 208.30(e)(6). However, in any case where an asylum officer has found that an applicant for admission qualifies for an exception to that Agreement, which includes the Additional Protocol of 2022, or that the Agreement, which includes the Additional Protocol of 2022, does not apply, an immigration judge does have jurisdiction to review a negative credible fear finding made thereafter by the asylum officer as provided in this section.

(2) Noncitizens in transit. An immigration judge has no jurisdiction to review any determination by DHS that a noncitizen being removed from Canada in transit through the United States should be returned to Canada to pursue asylum claims under Canadian law, under the terms of the 2002 U.S.-Canada Agreement, which includes the Additional Protocol of 2022.

(3) Applicants for admission. An immigration judge has no jurisdiction to review a determination by an asylum officer that a noncitizen is not eligible to apply for asylum pursuant to a bilateral or multilateral agreement with a third country under section 208(a)(2)(A) of the Act and should be removed to the third country to pursue his or her claims for asylum or other protection under the laws of that country. See 8 CFR 208.30(e)(7). However, if the asylum officer has determined that the noncitizen may not or should not be removed to a third country under section 208(a)(2)(A) of the Act and subsequently makes a negative fear determination, an immigration judge has jurisdiction to review the negative fear finding as provided in this section.

(4) Noncitizens in transit through the United States from countries other than Canada. An immigration judge has no jurisdiction to review any determination by DHS that a noncitizen being removed from a receiving country in transit through the United States should be returned to pursue asylum claims under the receiving country's law, under the terms of the applicable cooperative agreement. See 8 CFR 208.30(e)(7).

(i) Severability. The provisions of part 1003 are separate and severable from one another. In the event that any provision in part 1003 is stayed, enjoined, not implemented, or otherwise held invalid, the remaining provisions shall nevertheless be implemented as an independent rule and continue in effect.

HISTORY:

[62 FR 10312, 10335, March 6, 1997; 64 FR 8478, 8487, Feb. 19, 1999; redesignated at 68 FR 9824, 9830, Feb. 28, 2003; 69 FR 69490, 69496, Nov. 29, 2004; 83 FR 55934, 55952, Nov. 9, 2018; 84 FR 33829, 33844, July 16, 2019; 84 FR 63994, 64009, Nov. 19, 2019; 85 FR 80274, 80393, Dec. 11, 2020; 85 FR 84160, 84196, Dec. 23, 2020; 86 FR 6847, Jan. 25, 2021; 86 FR 15069, Mar. 22, 2021; 86 FR 73615, Dec. 28, 2021; 87 FR 18078, 18220, Mar. 29, 2022; 87 FR 79789, Dec. 28, 2022; 88 FR 18227, 18240, Mar. 28, 2023; 88 FR 31314, 31451, May 16, 2023; 89 FR 105392, 105401, Dec. 27, 2024; 89 FR 105386, Dec. 27, 2024]

§ 1003.43 Motions to reopen for suspension of deportation and cancellation of removal pursuant to section 203(c) of NACARA and section 1505(c) of the LIFE Act Amendments.

(a) Standard for Adjudication. Except as provided in this section, a motion to reopen proceedings under section 309(g) or (h) of the Illegal Immigration Reform and Immigrant Responsibility Act (Pub. L. 104-208) (IIRIRA), as amended by section 203(c) of the Nicaraguan Adjustment and Central American Relief Act (Pub. L. 105-100) (NACARA) and by section 1505(c) of the Legal Immigration Family Equity Act Amendments (Pub. L. 106-554) (LIFE Act Amendments), respectively, will be adjudicated under applicable statutes and regulations governing motions to reopen.

(b) Aliens eligible to reopen proceedings under section 203 of NACARA. A motion to reopen proceedings to apply for suspension of deportation or cancellation of removal under the special rules of section 309(g) of IIRIRA, as amended by section 203(c) of NACARA, must establish that the alien:

(1) Is prima facie eligible for suspension of deportation pursuant to former section 244(a) of the Act (as in effect prior to April 1, 1997) or the special rule for cancellation of removal pursuant to section 309(f) of IIRIRA, as amended by section 203(b) of NACARA;

(2) Was or would be ineligible:

(i) For suspension of deportation by operation of section 309(c)(5) of IIRIRA (as in effect prior to November 19, 1997); or

(ii) For cancellation of removal pursuant to section 240A of the Act, but for operation of section 309(f) of IIRIRA, as amended by section 203(b) of NACARA;

(3) Has not been convicted at any time of an aggravated felony; and

(4) Is within one of the six classes of aliens described in paragraphs (d)(1) through (d)(6) of this section.

(c) Aliens eligible to reopen proceedings under section 1505(c) of the LIFE Act Amendments. A motion to reopen proceedings to apply for suspension of deportation or cancellation of removal under the special rules of section 309(h) of IIRIRA, as amended by section 1505(c) of the LIFE Act Amendments, must establish that the alien:

(1) Is prima facie eligible for suspension of deportation pursuant to former section 244(a) of the Act (as in effect prior to April 1, 1997) or cancellation of removal pursuant to section 240A(b) of the Act and section 309(f) of IIRIRA, as amended by section 203(b) of NACARA;

(2) Was or would be ineligible, by operation of section 241(a)(5) of the Act, for suspension of deportation pursuant to former section 244(a) of the Act (as in effect prior to April 1, 1997) or cancellation of removal pursuant to section 240A(b) of the Act and section 309(f) of IIRIRA, as amended by section 203(b) of NACARA, but for enactment of section 1505(c) of the LIFE Act Amendments;

(3) Has not been convicted at any time of an aggravated felony; and

(4) Is within one of the eight classes of aliens described in paragraph (d) of this section.

(d) Classes of Eligible Aliens.

(1) Class 1. A national of El Salvador who:

(i) First entered the United States on or before September 19, 1990;

(ii) Registered for benefits pursuant to the settlement agreement in American Baptist Churches, et al. v. Thornburgh, 760 F. Supp. 796 (N.D. Cal. 1991) (ABC) on or before October 31, 1991, or applied for Temporary Protected Status (TPS) on or before October 31, 1991; and

(iii) Was not apprehended after December 19, 1990, at time of entry.

(2) Class 2. A national of Guatemala who:

(i) First entered the United States on or before October 1, 1990;

(ii) Registered for ABC benefits on or before December 31, 1991; and

(iii) Was not apprehended after December 19, 1990, at time of entry.

(3) Class 3. A national of Guatemala or El Salvador who applied for asylum with the Service on or before April 1, 1990.

(4) Class 4. An alien who:

(i) Entered the United States on or before December 31, 1990;

(ii) Applied for asylum on or before December 31, 1991; and

(iii) At the time of filing such application for asylum was a national of the Soviet Union, Russia, any republic of the former Soviet Union, Latvia, Estonia, Lithuania, Poland, Czechoslovakia, Romania, Hungary, Bulgaria, Albania, East Germany, Yugoslavia, or any state of the former Yugoslavia.

(5) Class 5. The spouse or child of a person who is described in paragraphs (d)(1) through (d)(4) of this section and such person is prima facie eligible for and has applied for suspension of deportation or special rule cancellation of removal under section 203 of NACARA.

(6) Class 6. An unmarried son or daughter of a person who is described in paragraphs (d)(1) through (d)(4) of this section and such person is prima facie eligible for and has applied for suspension of deportation or special rule cancellation of removal under section 203 of NACARA. If the son or daughter is 21 years of age or older, the son or daughter must have entered the United States on or before October 1, 1990.

(7) Class 7. An alien who was issued an Order to Show Cause or was in deportation proceedings before

April 1, 1997, and who applied for suspension of deportation as a battered alien under former section 244(a)(3) of the Act (as in effect before September 30, 1996).

(8) Class 8. An alien:

(i) Who is or was the spouse or child of a person described in paragraphs (d)(1) through (d)(4) of this section:

(A) At the time a decision is rendered to suspend deportation or cancel removal of that person;

(B) At the time that person filed an application for suspension of deportation or cancellation of removal; or

(C) At the time that person registered for ABC benefits, applied for TPS, or applied for asylum; and

(ii) Who has been battered or subjected to extreme cruelty (or the spouse described in paragraph (d)(8)(i) of this section has a child who has been battered or subjected to extreme cruelty) by the person described in paragraphs (d)(1) through (d)(4) of this section.

(e) Motion to reopen under section 203 of NACARA.

(1) An alien filing a motion to reopen proceedings pursuant to section 309(g) of IIRIRA, as amended by section 203(c) of NACARA, may initially file a motion to reopen without an application for suspension of deportation or cancellation of removal and supporting documents, but the motion must be filed no later than September 11, 1998. An alien may file only one motion to reopen pursuant to section 309(g) of IIRIRA. In such motion to reopen, the alien must address each of the four requirements for eligibility described in paragraph (b) of this section and establish that the alien satisfies each requirement.

(2) A motion to reopen filed pursuant to paragraph (b) of this section shall be considered complete at the time of submission of an application for suspension of deportation or special rule cancellation of removal and accompanying documents. Such application must be submitted no later than November 18, 1999. Aliens described in paragraphs (d)(5) or (d)(6) of this section must include, as part of their submission, proof that their parent or spouse is prima facie eligible and has applied for relief under section 203 of NACARA.

(3) The Service shall have 45 days from the date the alien serves the Immigration Court with either the Form EOIR-40 or the Form I-881 application for suspension of deportation or special rule cancellation of removal to respond to that completed motion. If the alien fails to submit the required application on or before November 18, 1999, the motion will be denied as abandoned.

(f) **Motion to reopen under section 1505(c) of the LIFE Act Amendments.**

(1) An alien filing a motion to reopen proceedings pursuant to section 309(h) of IIRIRA, as amended by section 1505(c) of the LIFE Act Amendments, must file a motion to reopen with an application for suspension of deportation or cancellation of removal and supporting documents, on or before October 16, 2001. An alien may file only one motion to reopen proceedings pursuant to section 309(h) of IIRIRA. In such motion to reopen, the alien must address each of the four requirements for eligibility described in paragraph (c) of this section and establish that the alien satisfies each requirement.

(2) A motion to reopen and the accompanying application and supporting documents filed pursuant to paragraph (c) of this section must be submitted on or before October 16, 2001. Aliens described in paragraphs (d)(5) and (d)(6) of this section must include, as part of their submission, proof that their parent or spouse is prima facie eligible and has applied for relief under section 203 of NACARA.

(3) The Service shall have 45 days from the date the alien serves the Immigration Court to respond to that motion to reopen.

(g) Fee for motion to reopen waived. No filing fee is required for a motion to reopen to apply for suspension of deportation or cancellation of removal under the special rules of section 309(g) or (h) of IIRIRA, as amended by section 203(c) of NACARA and by section 1505(c) of the LIFE Act Amendments, respectively.

(h) **Jurisdiction over motions to reopen under section 203 of NACARA and remand of appeals.**

(1) Notwithstanding any other provisions, any motion to reopen filed pursuant to the special rules of section 309(g) of IIRIRA, as amended by section 203(c) of NACARA, shall be filed with the Immigration Court, even if the Board of Immigration Appeals (Board) issued an order in the case. The Immigration Court that last had jurisdiction over the proceedings will adjudicate the motion.

(2) The Board will remand to the Immigration Court any presently pending appeal in which the alien appears eligible to apply for suspension of deportation or cancellation of removal under the special rules of section 309(g) of IIRIRA, as amended by section 203 of NACARA, and appears prima facie eligible for that relief. The alien will then have the opportunity to apply for suspension or cancellation under the special rules of NACARA before the Immigration Court.

(i) **Jurisdiction over motions to reopen under section 1505(c) of the LIFE Act Amendments and remand of appeals.**

(1) Notwithstanding any other provisions, any motion to reopen filed pursuant to paragraph (f) of this section to apply for suspension of deportation or cancellation of removal under section 1505(c) of the LIFE Act Amendments shall be filed with the Immigration Court or the Board, whichever last held jurisdiction over the case. Only an alien with a reinstated final order, or an alien with a newly issued final order that was issued based on the alien having reentered the United States illegally after having been removed or having departed voluntarily under a prior order of removal that was subject to reinstatement under section 241(a)(5) of the Act, may file a motion to reopen with the Immigration Court or the Board pursuant to this section. An alien whose final order has not been reinstated and as to whom a newly issued final order, as described in this section, has not been issued may apply for suspension of deportation or special rule cancellation of removal before the Service pursuant to section 309(h)(1) of IIRIRA, as amended by section 1505(c) of the LIFE Act Amendments, according to the jurisdic-

tional provisions for applications before the Service set forth in 8 CFR 240.62(a) or before the Immigration Court as set forth in 8 CFR 240.62(b).

(2) If the Immigration Court has jurisdiction and grants only the motion to reopen filed pursuant to paragraph (f) of this section, the scope of the reopened proceeding shall be limited to a determination of the alien's eligibility for suspension of deportation or cancellation of removal pursuant to section 309(h)(1) of IIRIRA, as amended by section 1505(c) of the LIFE Act Amendments.

(3) If the Board has jurisdiction and grants only the motion to reopen filed pursuant to paragraph (f) of this section, it shall remand the case to the Immigration Court solely for adjudication of the application for suspension of deportation or cancellation of removal pursuant to section 309(h)(1) of IIRIRA, as amended by section 1505(c) of the LIFE Act Amendments.

(4) Nothing in this section shall be interpreted to preclude or restrict the applicability of any other exceptions regarding motions to reopen that are provided for in 8 CFR 1003.2(c)(3) and 1003.23(b).

HISTORY:

[63 FR 31890, 31894, June 11, 1998, as corrected at 63 FR 35117, June 29, 1998, and 63 FR 36992, July 8, 1998; 64 FR 13663, 13666, Mar. 22, 1999; 66 FR 37119, 37123, July 17, 2001; redesignated and amended at 68 FR 9824, 9830, 9846, Feb. 28, 2003]

§ 1003.44 Special motion to seek section 212(c) relief for aliens who pleaded guilty or nolo contendere to certain crimes before April 1, 1997.

(a) Standard for adjudication. This section applies to certain aliens who formerly were lawful permanent residents, who are subject to an administratively final order of deportation or removal, and who are eligible to apply for relief under former section 212(c) of the Act and 8 CFR 1212.3 with respect to convictions obtained by plea agreements reached prior to a verdict at trial prior to April 1, 1997. A special motion to seek relief under section 212(c) of the Act will be adjudicated under the standards of this section and 8 CFR 1212.3. This section is not applicable with respect to any conviction entered after trial.

(b) General eligibility. The alien has the burden of establishing eligibility for relief, including the date on which the alien and the prosecution agreed on the plea of guilt or nolo contendere. Generally, a special motion under this section to seek section 212(c) relief must establish that the alien:

(1) Was a lawful permanent resident and is now subject to a final order of deportation or removal;

(2) Agreed to plead guilty or nolo contendere to an offense rendering the alien deportable or removable, pursuant to a plea agreement made before April 1, 1997;

(3) Had seven consecutive years of lawful unrelinquished domicile in the United States prior to the date of the final administrative order of deportation or removal; and

(4) Is otherwise eligible to apply for section 212(c) relief under the standards that were in effect at the time the alien's plea was made, regardless of when the plea was entered by the court.

(c) Aggravated felony definition. For purposes of eligibility to apply for section 212(c) relief under this section and 8 CFR 1212.3, the definition of aggravated felony in section 101(a)(43) of the Act is that in effect at the time the special motion or the application for section 212(c) relief is adjudicated under this section. An alien shall be deemed to be ineligible for section 212(c) relief if he or she has been charged and found deportable or removable on the basis of a crime that is an aggravated felony, except as provided in 8 CFR 1212.3(f)(4).

(d) Effect of prior denial of section 212(c) relief. A motion under this section will not be granted with respect to any conviction where an alien has previously been denied section 212(c) relief by an immigration judge or by the Board on discretionary grounds.

(e) Scope of proceedings. Proceedings shall be reopened under this section solely for the purpose of adjudicating the application for section 212(c) relief, but if the immigration judge or the Board grants a motion by the alien to reopen the proceedings on other applicable grounds under 8 CFR 1003.2 or 1003.23 of this chapter, all issues encompassed within the reopened proceedings may be considered together, as appropriate.

(f) Procedure for filing a special motion to seek section 212(c) relief. An eligible alien shall file a special motion to seek section 212(c) relief with the immigration judge or the Board, whichever last held jurisdiction over the case. An eligible alien must submit a copy of the Form I-191 application, and supporting documents, with the special motion. The motion must contain the notation "special motion to seek section 212(c) relief." The Department of Homeland Security (DHS) shall have 45 days from the date of filing of the special motion to respond. In the event the DHS does not respond to the motion, the DHS retains the right in the proceedings to contest any and all issues raised.

(g) **Relationship to motions to reopen or reconsider on other grounds.**

(1) Other pending motions to reopen or reconsider. An alien who has previously filed a motion to reopen or reconsider that is still pending before an immigration judge or the Board, other than a motion for section 212(c) relief, must file a separate special motion to seek section 212(c) relief pursuant to this section. The new motion shall specify any other motions currently pending before an immigration judge or the Board. An alien who has previously filed a motion to reopen under 8 CFR 1003.2 or 1003.23 based on INS v. St. Cyr is not required to file a new special motion under this section, but he or she may supplement the previous motion if it is still pending. Any motion for section 212(c) relief described in this section pending before the Board or an immigration judge on the effective date of this rule that would be barred by the time or number limitations on motions shall be deemed to be a motion filed pursuant to this section, and shall not count against the number restrictions for other motions to reopen.

(2) Motions previously filed pursuant to prior provision. If an alien previously filed a motion to apply for section 212(c) relief with an immigration judge or the Board pursuant to the prior provisions of this section, as in effect before October 28, 2004, and the motion is still pending, the motion will be adjudicated pursuant to the standards of this section, both as revised and as previously in effect, and the alien does not need to file a new special motion pursuant to paragraph (g)(1) of this section. However, if a motion filed under the prior provisions of this section was denied because the alien did not satisfy the requirements contained therein, the alien must file a new special motion pursuant to this section, if eligible, in order to apply for section 212(c) relief based on the requirements established in this section.

(3) Effect of a prior denial of a motion to reopen or motion to reconsider filed after the St. Cyr decision. A motion under this section will not be granted where an alien has previously submitted a motion to reopen or motion to reconsider based on the St. Cyr decision and that motion was denied by an immigration judge or the Board (except on account of time or number limitations for such motions).

(4) Limitations for motions. The filing of a special motion under this section has no effect on the time and number limitations for motions to reopen or reconsider that may be filed on grounds unrelated to section 212(c).

(h) Deadline to file a special motion to seek section 212(c) relief under this section. An alien subject to a final administrative order of deportation or removal must file a special motion to seek section 212(c) relief on or before April 26, 2005. An eligible alien may file one special motion to seek section 212(c) relief under this section.

(i) Fees. No filing fee is required at the time the alien files a special motion to seek section 212(c) relief under this section. However, if the special motion is granted, and the alien has not previously filed an application for section 212(c) relief, the alien will be required to submit the appropriate fee receipt at the time the alien files the Form I-191 with the immigration court.

(j) Remands of appeals. If the Board has jurisdiction and grants the motion to apply for section 212(c) relief pursuant to this section, it shall remand the case to the immigration judge solely for adjudication of the section 212(c) application.

(k) Limitations on eligibility under this section. This section does not apply to:

(1) Aliens who have departed the United States and are currently outside the United States;

(2) Aliens issued a final order of deportation or removal who then illegally returned to the United States; or

(3) Aliens who have not been admitted or paroled.

HISTORY:

[66 FR 6436, 6445, Jan. 22, 2001, as corrected at 66 FR 8149, Jan. 29, 2001; redesignated and amended at 68 FR 9824, 9830, 9846, Feb. 28, 2003; 69 FR 57826, 57833, Sept. 28, 2004]

§ 1003.46 Protective orders, sealed submissions in Immigration Courts.

(a) Authority. In any immigration or bond proceeding, Immigration Judges may, upon a showing by the Service of a substantial likelihood that specific information submitted under seal or to be submitted under seal will, if disclosed, harm the national security (as defined in section 219(c)(2) of the Act) or law enforcement interests of the United States, issue a protective order barring disclosure of such information.

(b) Motion by the service. The Service may at any time after filing a Notice to Appear, or other charging document, file with the Immigration Judge, and serve upon the respondent, a motion for an order to protect specific information it intends to submit or is submitting under seal. The motion shall describe, to the extent practical, the information that the Service seeks to protect from disclosure. The motion shall specify the relief requested in the protective order. The respondent may file a response to the motion within ten days after the motion is served.

(c) Sealed annex to motion. In the Service's discretion, the Service may file the specific information as a sealed annex to the motion, which shall not be served upon the respondent. If the Service files a sealed annex, or the Immigration Judge, in his or her discretion, instructs that the information be filed as a sealed annex in order to determine whether to grant or deny the motion, the Immigration Judge shall consider the information only for the purpose of determining whether to grant or deny the motion.

(d) Due deference. The Immigration Judge shall give appropriate deference to the expertise of senior officials in law enforcement and national security agencies in any averments in any submitted affidavit in determining whether the disclosure of information will harm the national security or law enforcement interests of the United States.

(e) Denied motions. If the motion is denied, any sealed annex shall be returned to the Service, and the Immigration Judge shall give no weight to such information. The Service may immediately appeal denial of the motion to the Board, which shall have jurisdiction to hear the appeal, by filing a Notice of Appeal and the sealed annex with the Board. The Immigration Judge shall hold any further proceedings in abeyance pending resolution of the appeal by the Board.

(f) Granted motions. If the motion is granted, the Immigration Judge shall issue an appropriate protective order.

(1) The Immigration Judge shall ensure that the protective order encompasses such witnesses as the respondent demonstrates are reasonably necessary to the presentation of his case. If necessary, the Immigration Judge may impose the requirements of the protective order on any witness before the Immigration Judge to whom such information may be disclosed.

(2) The protective order may require that the respondent, and his or her attorney or accredited representative, if any:

(i) Not divulge any of the information submitted under the protective order, or any information derived therefrom, to any person or entity, other than authorized personnel of the Executive Office for Immigration Review, the Service, or such other persons approved by the Service or the Immigration Judge;

(ii) When transmitting any information under a protective order, or any information derived therefrom, to the Executive Office for Immigration Review or the Service, include a cover sheet identifying the contents of the submission as containing information subject to a protective order under this section;

(iii) Store any information under a protective order, or any information derived therefrom, in a reasonably secure manner, and return all copies of such information to the Service upon completion of proceedings, including judicial review; and

(iv) Such other requirements as the Immigration Judge finds necessary to protect the information from disclosure.

(3) Upon issuance of such protective order, the Service shall serve the respondent with the protective order and the sealed information. A protective order issued under this section shall remain in effect until vacated by the Immigration Judge.

(4) Further review of the protective order before the Board shall only be had pursuant to review of an order of the Immigration Judge resolving all issues of removability and any applications for relief pending in the matter pursuant to 8 CFR 1003.1(b). Notwithstanding any other provision of this section, the Immigration Judge shall retain jurisdiction to modify or vacate a protective order upon motion of the Service or the respondent. An Immigration Judge may not grant a motion by the respondent to modify or vacate a protective order until either: the Service files a response to such motion or 10 days after service of such motion on the Service.

(g) Admissibility as Evidence. The issuance of a protective order shall not prejudice the respondent's right to challenge the admissibility of the information subject to a protective order. The Immigration Judge may not find the information inadmissible solely because it is subject to a protective order.

(h) Seal. Any submission to the Immigration Judge, including any briefs, referring to information subject to a protective order shall be filed under seal. Any information submitted subject to a protective order under this paragraph shall remain under seal as part of the administrative record.

(i) Administrative enforcement. If the Service establishes that a respondent, or the respondent's attorney or accredited representative, has disclosed information subject to a protective order, the Immigration Judge shall deny all forms of discretionary relief, except bond, unless the respondent fully cooperates with the Service or other law enforcement agencies in any investigation relating to the noncompliance with the protective order and disclosure of the information; and establishes by clear and convincing evidence either that extraordinary and extremely unusual circumstances exist or that failure to comply with the protective order was beyond the control of the respondent and his or her attorney or accredited representative. Failure to comply with a protective order may also result in the suspension of an attorney's or an accredited representative's privilege of appearing before the Executive Office for Immigration Review or before the Service pursuant to 8 CFR part 1003, subpart G.

HISTORY:

[67 FR 36799, 36802, May 28, 2002; redesignated and amended at 68 FR 9824, 9830, 9846, Feb. 28, 2003]

§ 1003.47 Identity, law enforcement, or security investigations or examinations relating to applications for immigration relief, protection, or restriction on removal.

(a) In general. The procedures of this section are applicable to any application for immigration relief, protection, or restriction on removal that is subject to the conduct of identity, law enforcement, or security investigations or examinations as described in paragraph (b) of this section, in order to ensure that DHS has completed the appropriate identity, law enforcement, or security investigations or examinations before the adjudication of the application.

(b) Covered applications. The requirements of this section apply to the granting of any form of immigration relief in immigration proceedings which permits the alien to reside in the United States, including but not limited to the following forms of relief, protection, or restriction on removal to the extent they are within the authority of an immigration judge or the Board to grant:

(1) Asylum under section 208 of the Act.

(2) Adjustment of status to that of a lawful permanent resident under sections 209 or 245 of the Act, or any other provision of law.

(3) Waiver of inadmissibility or deportability under sections 209(c), 212, or 237 of the Act, or any provision of law.

(4) Permanent resident status on a conditional basis or removal of the conditional basis of permanent resident status under sections 216 or 216A of the Act, or any other provision of law.

(5) Cancellation of removal or suspension of deportation under section 240A or former section 244 of the Act, or any other provision of law.

(6) Relief from removal under former section 212(c) of the Act.

(7) Withholding of removal under section 241(b)(3) of the Act or under the Convention Against Torture.

(8) Registry under section 249 of the Act.

(9) Conditional grants relating to the above, such as for applications seeking asylum pursuant to section 207(a)(5) of the Act or cancellation of removal in light of section 240A(e) of the Act.

(c) Completion of applications for immigration relief, protection, or restriction on removal. Failure to file necessary documentation and comply with the requirements to provide biometrics and other biographical information in conformity with the applicable regulations, the instructions to the applications, the biometrics notice, and instructions provided by DHS, within the time allowed by the immigration judge's order, constitutes abandonment of the application and the immigration judge may enter an appropriate order dismissing the application unless the applicant demonstrates that such failure was the result of good cause. Nothing in this section shall be construed to affect the provisions in 8 CFR 1208.4 regarding the timely filing of asylum applications or the determination of a respondent's compliance with any other deadline for initial filing of an application, including the consequences of filing under the Child Status Protection Act.

(d) Biometrics and other biographical information. At any hearing at which a respondent expresses an intention to file or files an application for relief for which identity, law enforcement, or security investigations or examinations are required under this section, unless DHS advises the immigration judge that such information is unnecessary in the particular case, DHS shall notify the respondent of the need to provide biometrics and other biographical information and shall provide a biometrics notice and instructions to the respondent for such procedures. The immigration judge shall specify for the record when the respondent receives the biometrics notice and instructions and the consequences for failing to comply with the requirements of this section. Whenever required by DHS, the applicant shall make arrangements with an office of DHS to provide biometrics and other biographical information (including for any other person covered by the same application who is required to provide biometrics and other biographical information) before or as soon as practicable after the filing of the application for relief in the immigration proceedings. Failure to provide biometrics or other biographical information of the applicant or any other covered individual within the time allowed will constitute abandonment of the application or of the other covered individual's participation unless the applicant demonstrates that such failure was the result of good cause. DHS is responsible for obtaining biometrics and other biographical information with respect to any alien in detention.

(e) Conduct of investigations or examinations. DHS shall endeavor to initiate all relevant identity, law enforcement, or security investigations or examinations concerning the alien or beneficiaries promptly, to complete those investigations or examinations as promptly as is practicable (considering, among other things, increased demands placed upon such investigations), and to advise the immigration judge of the results in a timely manner, on or before the date of a scheduled hearing on any application for immigration relief filed in the proceedings. The immigration judges, in scheduling hearings, shall allow a period of time for DHS to undertake the necessary identity, law enforcement, or security investigations or examinations prior to the date that an application is scheduled for hearing and disposition, with a view to minimizing the number of cases in which hearings must be continued.

(f) Continuance for completion of investigations or examinations. If DHS has not reported on the completion and results of all relevant identity, law enforcement, or security investigations or examinations for an applicant and his or her beneficiaries by the date that the application is scheduled for hearing and disposition, after the time allowed by the immigration judge pursuant to paragraph (e) of this section, the immigration judge may continue proceedings for the purpose of completing the investigations or examinations, or hear the case on the merits. DHS shall attempt to give reasonable notice to the immigration judge of the fact that all relevant identity, law enforcement, or security investigations or examinations have not been completed and the amount of time DHS anticipates is required to complete those investigations or examinations.

(g) Adjudication after completion of investigations or examinations. In no case shall an immigration judge grant an application for immigration relief that is subject to the conduct of identity, law enforcement, or security investigations or examinations under this section until after DHS has reported to the immigration judge that the appropriate investigations or examinations have been completed and are current as provided in this section and DHS has reported any relevant information from the investigations or examinations to the immigration judge.

(h) Adjudication upon remand from the Board. In any case remanded pursuant to 8 CFR 1003.1(d)(6), the immigration judge shall consider the results of the identity, law enforcement, or security investigations or examinations subject to the provisions of this section. If new information is presented, the immigration judge may hold a further hearing if necessary to consider any legal or factual issues, including issues relating to credibility, if relevant. The immigration judge shall then enter an order granting or denying the immigration relief sought.

(i) Procedures when immigration relief granted. At the time that the immigration judge or the Board grants any relief under this section that would entitle the respondent to a new document evidencing such relief, the decision granting such relief shall include advice that the respondent will need to contact an appropriate office of DHS. Information concerning DHS locations and local procedures for document preparation shall be routinely provided to EOIR and updated by DHS. Upon respondent's presentation of a final order from the immigration judge or the Board granting such relief and submission of any biometric and other information necessary, DHS shall prepare such documents in keeping with section 264 of the Act and regulations thereunder and other relevant law.

(j) Voluntary departure. The procedures of this section do not apply to the granting of voluntary departure prior to the conclusion of proceedings pursuant to 8 CFR 1240.26(b) or at the conclusion of proceedings pursuant to 8 CFR 1240.26(c). If DHS seeks a continuance in order to complete pending identity, law enforcement, or security investigations or examinations, the immigration judge may grant additional time in the exercise of discretion, and the 30-day period for the immigration judge to grant voluntary departure, as provided in § 1240.26(b)(1)(ii), shall be extended accordingly.

(k) Custody hearings. The foregoing provisions of this section do not apply to proceedings seeking the redetermination of conditions of custody of an alien during the pendency of immigration proceedings under section 236 of the Act. In scheduling an initial custody redetermination hearing, the immigration judge shall, to the extent practicable consistent with the expedited nature of such cases, take account of the brief initial period of time needed for DHS to conduct the automated portions of its identity, law enforcement, or security investigations or examinations with respect to aliens detained in connection with immigration proceedings. If at the time of the custody hearing DHS seeks a brief continuance in an appropriate case based on unresolved identity, law enforcement, or security investigations or examinations, the immigration judge in the exercise of discretion may grant one or more continuances for a limited period of time which is reasonable under the circumstances.

HISTORY:

[70 FR 4743, 4753, Jan. 31, 2005]

Subpart D

Special Provisions

§ 1003.55 Treatment of post-conviction orders.

(a) Applicability of Matter of Thomas & Thompson, 27 I&N Dec. 674 (A.G. 2019).

(1) Matter of Thomas & Thompson shall not apply to a criminal sentence:

(i) Where a court at any time granted a request to modify, clarify, vacate, or otherwise alter the sentence and the request was filed on or before October 25, 2019; or

(ii) Where the noncitizen demonstrates that the noncitizen reasonably and detrimentally relied on the availability of an order modifying, clarifying, vacating, or otherwise altering the sentence entered in connection with a guilty plea, conviction, or sentence on or before October 25, 2019.

(2) Where paragraph (a)(1) of this section applies, the adjudicator shall assess the relevant order under Matter of Cota-Vargas, 23 I7N Dec. 849 (BIA 2005), Matter of Song, 23 I&N Dec. 173 (BIA 2001), and Matter of Estrada, 26 I&N Dec. 749 (BIA 2016), as applicable.

(b) Post-conviction orders correcting errors. Adjudicators shall give effect to an order that corrects a genuine ambiguity, mistake, or typographical error on the face of the original conviction or sentencing order and that was entered to give effect to the intent of the original order.

HISTORY:

[89 FR 46742, 46794, May 29, 2024]

Subpart E

List of Pro Bono Legal Service Providers

§ 1003.61 General provisions.

(a) Definitions —

(1) Director. Director means the Director of the Executive Office for Immigration Review (EOIR), pursuant to 8 CFR 1001.1(o), and shall also include any office or official within EOIR to whom the Director delegates authority with respect to subpart E of this part.

(2) Pro bono legal services. Pro bono legal services are those uncompensated legal services performed for indigent individuals or the public good without any expectation of either direct or indirect remuneration, including referral fees (other than filing fees or photocopying and mailing expenses), although a representative may be regularly compensated by the firm, organization, or pro bono referral service with which he or she is associated.

(3) Organization. A non-profit religious, charitable, social service, or similar group established in the United States.

(4) Pro bono referral service. A referral service, offered by a non-profit group, association, or similar organization established in the United States that assists persons in locating pro bono representation by making case referrals to attorneys or organizations that are available to provide pro bono representation.

(5) Provider. Any organization, pro bono referral service, or attorney whose name is included on the List of Pro Bono Legal Service Providers.

(b) Authority. The Director shall maintain a list, known as the List of Pro Bono Legal Service Providers (List), of organizations, pro bono referral services, and attorneys qualified under this subpart to provide pro bono legal services in immigration proceedings. The List, which shall be updated not less than quarterly, shall be provided to individuals in removal and other proceedings before an immigration court.

(c) Qualification. An organization, pro bono referral service, or attorney qualifies to be included on the List if the eligibility requirements under § 1003.62 and the application procedures under § 1003.63 are met.

(d) Organizations. Approval of an organization's application to be included on the List under this subpart is not equivalent to recognition under part 1292 of this chapter. Recognition under part 1292 of this chapter does not constitute a successful application for purposes of the List.

HISTORY:

[62 FR 9071, 9073, Feb. 28, 1997; redesignated and amended at 68 FR 9824, 9830, 9846, Feb. 28, 2003; 68 FR 10349, 10350, Mar. 5, 2003; 80 FR 59503, 59510, Oct. 1, 2015]

§ 1003.62 Eligibility.

(a) Organizations recognized under part 1292. An organization that is recognized under part 1292 of this chapter is eligible to apply to have its name included on the List if the organization meets the requirements in paragraphs (a)(1) through (3) of this section.

(1) The organization will provide a minimum of 50 hours per year of pro bono legal services to individuals at each immigration court location where the organization intends to be included on the List, in cases where an attorney or representative of the organization, or an attorney or representative to whom the organization has referred the case for pro bono representation, files a Form EOIR-28 Notice of Entry of Appearance as Attorney or Representative before the Immigration Court (EOIR-28 Notice of Entry of Appearance). When an attorney or representative of the organization represents the individual pro bono before the immigration court location, the organization may count, toward the 50-hour requirement, the attorney's or representative's out-of-court preparation time and in-court time. When the organization refers the case for pro bono legal services outside the organization, the organization may count, toward the 50-hour requirement, time the organization's attorneys and representatives spent providing pro bono legal services, for example conducting an intake interview or mentoring the attorney or representative to whom the case is referred. However, the organization is not permitted to count the time of the attorney or representative to whom the case was referred.

(2) The organization has on its staff at least one attorney, as defined in § 1292.1(a)(1) of this chapter, or at least one representative accredited under part 1292 of this chapter, to practice before the immigration courts and the Board of Immigration Appeals.

(3) No attorney or representative who will provide pro bono legal services on the organization's behalf in cases pending before EOIR is the subject of an order of disbarment under § 1003.101(a)(1) or suspension under § 1003.101(a)(2).

(b) Organizations not recognized under part 1292. An organization that is not recognized under part 1292 of this chapter is eligible to apply to have its name included on the List if the organization meets the requirements in paragraphs (b)(1) through (3) of this section.

(1) The organization will provide a minimum of 50 hours per year of pro bono legal services to individuals at each immigration court location where the organization intends to be included on the List, in cases where an attorney or representative of the organization, or an attorney or representative to whom the organization has referred the case for pro bono representation, files a Form EOIR-28 Notice of Entry of Appearance. When an attorney or representative of the organization represents the individual pro bono before the immigration court location, the organization may count, toward the 50-hour requirement, the attorney's or representative's out-of-court preparation time and in-court time. When the organization refers the case for pro bono legal services outside the organization, the organization may count, toward the 50-hour requirement, time the organization's attorneys or representatives spent providing pro bono legal services, for example conducting an intake interview or mentoring the attorney or representative to whom the case is referred. However, the organization is not permitted to count the time of the attorney or representative to whom the case was referred.

(2) The organization has on its staff at least one attorney, as defined in § 1292.1(a)(1) of this chapter.

(3) No attorney or representative who will provide pro bono legal services on the organization's behalf in cases pending before EOIR is the subject of an order of disbarment under § 1003.101(a)(1) or suspension under § 1003.101(a)(2).

(c) Pro bono referral services. A referral service is eligible to apply to have its name included on the List at each immigration court location where the referral service either refers or plans to refer cases to attorneys or organizations that will provide pro bono legal services to individuals in proceedings before an immigration judge.

(d) Attorneys. An attorney, as defined in § 1292.1(a)(1) of this chapter, is eligible to apply to have his or her name included on the List if the attorney meets the requirements in paragraphs (d)(1) through (3) of this section.

(1) The attorney is not the subject of an order of disbarment under § 1003.101(a)(1) or suspension under § 1003.101(a)(2);

(2) The attorney will provide a minimum of 50 hours per year of pro bono legal services to individuals at each immigration court location where the attorney intends to be included on the List, in cases where he or she files a Form EOIR-28 Notice of Entry of Appearance. The attorney may count, toward the requirement, both out-of-court preparation time and in-court time.

(3) The attorney cannot provide pro bono legal services through or in association with an organization or pro bono referral service described in paragraph (a), (b), or (c) of this section because:

(i) Such an organization or referral service is unavailable; or

(ii) The range of services provided by an available organization(s) or referral service(s) is insufficient to address the needs of the community.

HISTORY:

[62 FR 9071, 9073, Feb. 28, 1997; redesignated at 68 FR 9824, 9830, Feb. 28, 2003; 68 FR 10349, 10350, Mar. 5, 2003; 80 FR 59503, 59510, Oct. 1, 2015]

§ 1003.63 Applications.

(a) Generally. To be included on the List, any organization, pro bono referral service, or attorney that is eligible under § 1003.62 to apply to be included on the List must file an application with the Director. Applications must be received by the Director at least 60 days in advance of the quarterly update in order to be considered. The application must:

(1) Establish by clear and convincing evidence that the applicant qualifies to be on the List pursuant to § 1003.61(c);

(2) Specify how the organization, pro bono referral service, or attorney wants its name and contact information to be set forth on the List; and

(3) Identify each immigration court location where the organization, pro bono referral service, or attorney provides, or plans to provide, pro bono legal services.

(b) Organizations. An organization, whether recognized or not under part 1292, must submit with its application a declaration signed by an authorized officer of the organization that states under penalty of perjury:

(1) That it will provide annually at least 50 hours of pro bono legal services to individuals in removal or other proceedings before each immigration court location identified in its application;

(2) That every attorney and accredited representative who will represent clients pro bono before EOIR on behalf of the organization is registered to practice before EOIR under § 1292.1(f);

(3) That no attorney or representative who will provide pro bono legal services on behalf of the organization in cases pending before EOIR:

(i) Is under any order suspending, enjoining, restraining, disbarring, or otherwise restricting him or her in the practice of law; or

(ii) Is the subject of an order of disbarment under § 1003.101(a)(1) or suspension under § 1003.101(a)(2); and

(4) Any specific limitations it has in providing pro bono legal services (e.g., not available to assist detained individuals or those with criminal convictions, or available for asylum cases only).

(c) Pro bono referral services. A pro bono referral service must submit with its application a declaration signed by an authorized officer of the referral service that states under penalty of perjury:

(1) That it will offer its referral services to individuals in removal or other proceedings before each immigration court location identified in its application; and

(2) Any specific limitations it has in providing its pro bono referral services (e.g., not available to assist detained individuals or those with criminal convictions, or available only for asylum cases).

(d) Attorneys. An attorney must submit with his or her application a declaration that states under penalty of perjury:

(1) That he or she will provide annually at least 50 hours of pro bono legal services to individuals in removal or other proceedings before each immigration court location identified in his or her application;

(2) Any specific limitations the attorney has in providing pro bono legal services (e.g., not available to assist detained individuals or those with criminal convictions, or available for asylum cases only);

(3) A description of the good-faith efforts he or she made to provide pro bono legal services through an organization or pro bono referral service described in § 1003.62(a), (b), or (c) to individuals appearing before each immigration court location listed in the application;

(4) An explanation that any such organization or referral service is unavailable or that the range of services provided by available organization(s) or referral service(s) is insufficient to address the needs of the community;

(5) His or her EOIR registration number;

(6) That he or she is not under any order suspending, enjoining, restraining, disbarring, or otherwise restricting him or her in the practice of law; and

(7) That he or she is not the subject of an order of disbarment under § 1003.101(a)(1) or suspension under § 1003.101(a)(2).

(e) Applications approved before November 30, 2015. Providers whose applications to be included on the List were approved before November 30, 2015 must file an application under this section as follows: Organizations and pro bono referral services, within one year of November 30, 2015; attorneys, within six months of November 30, 2015. The names of providers who do not file an application as required by this paragraph shall be removed from the List following expiration of the application time period, the removal of which will be reflected no later than in the next quarterly update.

(f) Notice and comments —

(1) Public notice and comment. The names of the applicants, whether organizations, pro bono referral services, or individuals, meeting the regulatory requirements to be included on the List shall be publicly posted for 15 days after review of the applications by the Director, and upon request a copy of each application shall be made available for public review. Any individual may forward to the Director comments or a recommendation for approval or disapproval of an application within 30 days from the first date the name of the applicant is publicly posted. The commenting party shall include his or her name and address. A comment or recommendation may be sent to the Director electronically, in which case the Director shall transmit the comment or recommendation to the applicant. A comment or recommendation not sent to the Director electronically must include proof of service on the applicant.

(2) Response. The applicant has 15 days to respond from the date the applicant was served with, or notified by the Director of, the comment. All responses must be filed with the Director and include proof of service of a copy of such response on the commenting party.

HISTORY:

[62 FR 9071, 9073, Feb. 28, 1997; redesignated and amended at 68 FR 9824, 9830, 9846, Feb. 28, 2003; 80 FR 59503, 59511, Oct. 1, 2015; 86 FR 70708, 70723, Dec. 13, 2021]

§ 1003.64 Approval and denial of applications.

(a) Authority. The Director in his discretion shall have the authority to approve or deny an application to be included on the List of Pro Bono Legal Service Providers. The Director may request additional information from the applicant to determine whether the applicant qualifies to be included on the List.

(b) Decision. The applicant shall be notified of the decision in writing. The written notice shall be served at the address provided on the application unless the applicant subsequently provides a change of address pursuant to § 1003.66, or shall be transmitted to the applicant electronically..

(1) Denials. If the application is denied, the applicant shall be given a written explanation of the grounds for such denial, and the decision shall be final. Such denial shall be without prejudice to file another application at any time after the next quarterly publication of the List.

(2) Approval and continuing qualification. If the application is approved, the applicant's name will be included on the List at the next quarterly update. Every three years from the date of approval, a provider must file with the Director a declaration, under penalty of perjury, stating that the provider remains qualified to be included on the List under § 1003.62(a), (b), (c), or (d). For organizations and attorneys, the declaration must include alien registration numbers of clients in whose cases the provider rendered pro bono legal services under § 1003.62(a)(1), (b)(1), or (d)(2), representing at least 50 hours of pro bono legal services each year since the provider's most recent such declaration, or since the provider was included on the List, whichever was more recent. Organizations must provide, for each case listed, the name of the organization's attorneys or representatives who provided representation or other pro bono legal services, or the name of the attorney, representative, or organization the case was referred to for pro bono legal services. If a provider fails to timely file the declaration or declares that it is no longer qualified to be included on the List, the provider's name will be removed from the List at the next quarterly update. Failure to file a declaration within the applicable time period does not prohibit the filing of a new application to be included on the List.

HISTORY:

[62 FR 9071, 9073, Feb. 28, 1997; redesignated and amended at 68 FR 9824, 9830, 9846, Feb. 28, 2003; 68 FR 10349, 10350, Mar. 5, 2003; 80 FR 59503, 59512, Oct. 1, 2015; 86 FR 70708, 70723, Dec. 13, 2021]

§ 1003.65 Removal of a provider from the List.

(a) Automatic removal. If the Director determines that an attorney on the List is the subject of a final order of disbarment under § 1003.101(a)(1), or an order of suspension under § 1003.101(a)(2), then the Director shall:

(1) Remove the name of the attorney from the List no later than at the next quarterly update; and

(2) Notify the attorney of such removal in writing, at the last known address given by the provider or electronically.

(b) Requests for removal.

(1) Any provider may, at any time, submit a written request to have the provider's name removed from the List. The written request may include an explanation for the voluntary removal. Upon such written request, the name of the provider shall be removed from the List, and such removal will be reflected no later than in the next quarterly update.

(2) Any provider removed from the List at the provider's request may seek reinstatement to the List upon written notice to the Director. Any request for reinstatement must include a new declaration of eligibility, as set forth under § 1003.63(b), (c), or (d). Reinstatement to the List is at the sole discretion of the Director. Upon the Director's approval of reinstatement, the provider's name shall be included on the List no later than in the next quarterly update. Reinstatement to the List does not affect the requirement under § 1003.64(b)(2) that a provider submit a new declaration of eligibility every three years from the date of the approval of the original application to be included on the List.

(c) EOIR inquiry in response to complaints. If EOIR receives complaints that a particular provider on the List may no longer be accepting new pro bono clients, the Director may send a written inquiry to the provider noting that EOIR has received complaints with regard to the provider's acceptance of pro bono clients and allowing an opportunity for the provider to state whether the provider is continuing to comply with the regulations in this subpart or, if appropriate, whether the provider wishes to request voluntary removal from the List as provided in paragraph (b) of this section. The Director may remove a provider from the List for failure to respond to a written inquiry issued under this paragraph within 30 days or such additional time period stated by the Director in the written inquiry.

(d) Procedures for removing providers from the List. The following provisions apply in cases not covered by paragraphs (a), (b), or (c) of this section.

(1) Grounds. A provider shall be removed from the List if it, he, or she:

(i) Fails to comply with § 1003.66;

(ii) Has filed a false declaration in connection with an application filed pursuant to § 1003.63;

(iii) Improperly uses the List primarily to advertise or solicit clients for compensated legal services; or

(iv) Fails to comply with any and all other requirements of this subpart.

(2) Notice. If the Director determines that a provider falls within one or more of the enumerated grounds under paragraph (d)(1) of this section, the Director shall promptly notify the provider in writing, at the address last provided to the Director by the provider or electronically, of the Director's intention to remove the name of the provider from the List.

(3) Response. The provider may submit a written answer within 30 days from the date the notice is served or is sent to the provider electronically. The provider must establish by clear and convincing evidence that the provider continues to meet the qualifications for inclusion on the List, by declaration under penalty of perjury as to the provider's continued compliance with eligibility requirements under this subchapter, which must include alien registration numbers of clients in whose cases the provider rendered pro bono legal services under § 1003.62(a)(1), (b)(2), or (d)(2), representing at least 50 hours of pro bono legal services each year since the provider's most recent declaration under § 1003.64(b)(2), or since the provider was included on the List, whichever was more recent.

(4) Decision. If, after consideration of any response submitted by the provider, the Director determines that the provider is no longer qualified to remain on the List, the Director shall:

(i) Remove the name of the provider from the List no later than in the next quarterly update; and

(ii) Notify the provider of such removal in writing, at the address last provided to the Director by the provider or electronically.

(5) Disciplinary Action. Removal from the List pursuant to § 1003.65(a), (b), (c), or (d) shall be without prejudice to the authority to discipline a practitioner under EOIR's rules and procedures for professional conduct for practitioners listed in 8 CFR part 1003, subpart G.

HISTORY:

[62 FR 9071, 9074, Feb. 28, 1997; redesignated and amended at 68 FR 9824, 9830, 9846, Feb. 28, 2003; 68 FR 10349, 10350, Mar. 5, 2003; 80 FR 59503, 59512, Oct. 1, 2015; 86 FR 70708, 70723, Dec. 13, 2021]

§ 1003.66 Changes in information or status.

All providers with a pending application or currently on the List must notify the Director in writing within ten business days if:

(a) The provider's contact information has changed;

(b) Any specific limitations in providing pro bono legal services under § 1003.63(b)(4), (c)(2), or (d)(2) have changed; or

(c) The provider is no longer eligible under § 1003.62.

HISTORY:

[80 FR 59503, 59513, Oct. 1, 2015]

Subpart G

Professional Conduct for Practitioners — Rules and Procedures

§ 1003.101 General provisions.

(a) Authority to sanction. An adjudicating official or the Board of Immigration Appeals (the Board) may impose disciplinary sanctions against any practitioner if it finds it to be in the public interest to do so. It will be in the public interest to impose disciplinary sanctions against a practitioner who is authorized to practice before the Board and the Immigration Courts when such person has engaged in criminal, unethical, or unprofessional conduct, or in frivolous behavior, as set forth in § 1003.102. In accordance with the disciplinary proceedings set forth in this subpart and outlined below, an adjudicating official or the Board may impose any of the following disciplinary sanctions:

(1) Disbarment, which is permanent, from practice before the Board and the Immigration Courts or the DHS, or before all three authorities;

(2) Suspension, including immediate suspension, from practice before the Board and the Immigration Courts or DHS, or before all three authorities;

(3) Public or private censure; or

(4) Such other disciplinary sanctions as the adjudicating official or the Board deems appropriate.

(b) Persons subject to sanctions. Persons subject to sanctions include any practitioner. Attorneys employed by the Department of Justice shall be subject to discipline pursuant to § 1003.109. Nothing in this regulation shall be construed as authorizing persons who do not meet the definition of practitioner to represent individuals before the Board and the immigration courts or the DHS.

(c) The administrative termination of a representative's accreditation under 8 CFR 1292.17 after the issuance of a Notice of Intent to Discipline pursuant to § 1003.105(a)(1) shall not preclude the continuation of disciplinary proceedings and the imposition of sanctions, unless counsel for the government moves to withdraw the Notice of Intent to Discipline and the adjudicating official or the Board grants the motion.

HISTORY:

[65 FR 39513, 39526, June 27, 2000; redesignated and amended at 68 FR 9824, 9830, 9846, Feb. 28, 2003; 68 FR 10349, 10350, Mar. 5, 2003; 73 FR 76914, 76923, Dec. 18, 2008; 77 FR 2011, 2014, Jan. 13, 2012, as confirmed at 78 FR 24669, 24670, Apr. 26, 2013; 81 FR 92346, 92362, Dec. 19, 2016; 87 FR 56204, 56258, Sept. 14, 2022]

§ 1003.102 Grounds.

[PUBLISHER'S NOTE: This section was amended at 73 FR 76914, 76923, Dec. 18, 2008, effective Jan. 20, 2009. The amendatory instruction omitted a reference to adding paragraph (u), however, text for paragraph (u) was set out. Paragraph (u) has been added in accordance with the apparent intent of the agency. It is expected that the agency will publish a correction in the Federal Register.]

It is deemed to be in the public interest for an adjudicating official or the Board to impose disciplinary sanctions against any practitioner who falls within one or more of the categories enumerated in this section, but these categories do not constitute the exclusive grounds for which disciplinary sanctions may be imposed in the public interest. Nothing in this regulation should be read to denigrate the practitioner's duty to represent zealously his or her client within the bounds of the law. A practitioner who falls within one of the following categories shall be subject to disciplinary sanctions in the public interest if he or she:

(a) Charges or receives, either directly or indirectly:

(1) In the case of an attorney, any fee or compensation for specific services rendered for any person that shall be deemed to be grossly excessive. The factors to be considered in determining whether a fee or compensation is grossly excessive include the following: The time and labor required, the novelty and difficulty of the questions involved, and the skill requisite to perform the legal service properly; the likelihood, if apparent to the client, that the acceptance of the particular employment will preclude other employment by the attorney; the fee customarily charged in the locality for similar legal services; the amount involved and the results obtained; the time limitations imposed by the client or by the circumstances; the nature and length of the professional relationship with the client; and the

experience, reputation, and ability of the attorney or attorneys performing the services,

(2) In the case of an accredited representative as defined in § 1292.1(a)(4) of this chapter, any fee or compensation for specific services rendered for any person, except that an accredited representative may be regularly compensated by the organization of which he or she is an accredited representative, or

(3) In the case of a law student or law graduate as defined in § 1292.1(a)(2) of this chapter, any fee or compensation for specific services rendered for any person, except that a law student or law graduate may be regularly compensated by the organization or firm with which he or she is associated as long as he or she is appearing without direct or indirect remuneration from the client he or she represents;

(b) Bribes, attempts to bribe, coerces, or attempts to coerce, by any means whatsoever, any person (including a party to a case or an officer or employee of the Department of Justice) to commit any act or to refrain from performing any act in connection with any case;

(c) Knowingly or with reckless disregard makes a false statement of material fact or law, or willfully misleads, misinforms, threatens, or deceives any person (including a party to a case or an officer or employee of the Department of Justice), concerning any material and relevant matter relating to a case, including knowingly or with reckless disregard offering false evidence. If a practitioner has offered material evidence and comes to know of its falsity, the practitioner shall take appropriate remedial measures;

(d) Solicits professional employment, through in-person or live telephone contact or through the use of runners, from a prospective client with whom the practitioner has no family or prior professional relationship, when a significant motive for the practitioner's doing so is the practitioner's pecuniary gain. If the practitioner has no family or prior professional relationship with the prospective client known to be in need of legal services in a particular matter, the practitioner must include the words "Advertising Material" on the outside of the envelope of any written communication and at the beginning and ending of any recorded communication. Such advertising material or similar solicitation documents may not be distributed by any person in or around the premises of any building in which a immigration court is located;

(e) Is subject to a final order of disbarment or suspension, or has resigned while a disciplinary investigation or proceeding is pending;

(f) Knowingly or with reckless disregard makes a false or misleading communication about his or her qualifications or services. A communication is false or misleading if it:

(1) Contains a material misrepresentation of fact or law, or omits a fact necessary to make the statement considered as a whole not materially misleading, or,

(2) Contains an assertion about the practitioner or the practitioner's qualifications or services that cannot be substantiated. A practitioner shall not state or imply that the practitioner has been recognized or certified as a specialist in immigration or nationality law unless such certification is granted by the appropriate State regulatory authority or by an organization that has been approved by the appropriate State regulatory authority to grant such certification. An accredited representative shall not state or imply that the accredited representative:

(i) Is approved to practice before the immigration courts or the Board, if the representative is only approved as an accredited representative before DHS;

(ii) Is an accredited representative for an organization other than a recognized organization through which the representative acquired accreditation; or

(iii) Is an attorney.

(g) Engages in contumelious or otherwise obnoxious conduct, with regard to a case in which he or she acts in a representative capacity, which would constitute contempt of court in a judicial proceeding;

(h) Has been found guilty of, or pleaded guilty or nolo contendere to, a serious crime, in any court of the United States, or of any state, possession, territory, commonwealth, or the District of Columbia. A serious crime includes any felony and also includes any lesser crime, a necessary element of which, as determined by the statutory or common law definition of such crime in the jurisdiction where the judgment was entered, involves interference with the administration of justice, false swearing, misrepresentation, fraud, willful failure to file income tax returns, deceit, dishonesty, bribery, extortion, misappropriation, theft, or an attempt, or a conspiracy or solicitation of another, to commit a serious crime. A plea or verdict of guilty or a conviction after a plea of nolo contendere is deemed to be a conviction within the meaning of this section;

(i) Knowingly or with reckless disregard falsely certifies a copy of a document as being a true and complete copy of an original;

(j) Engages in frivolous behavior in a proceeding before an Immigration Court, the Board, or any other administrative appellate body under title II of the immigration court Act, provided:

(1) A practitioner engages in frivolous behavior when he or she knows or reasonably should have known that his or her actions lack an arguable basis in law or in fact, or are taken for an improper purpose, such as to harass or to cause unnecessary delay. Actions that, if taken improperly, may be subject to disciplinary sanctions include, but are not limited to, the making of an argument on any factual or legal question, the submission of an application for discretionary relief, the filing of a motion, or the filing of an appeal. The signature of a practitioner on any filing, application, motion, appeal, brief, or other document constitutes certification by the signer that the signer has read the filing, application, motion, appeal, brief, or other document and that, to the best of the signer's knowledge, information, and belief, formed after inquiry reasonable under the circumstances, the document is well-grounded in fact and is warranted by existing law or by a good faith argument for the extension, modification, or reversal of existing law or the establishment of new law, and is not interposed for any improper purpose.

(2) The imposition of disciplinary sanctions for frivolous behavior under this section in no way limits the authority of the Board to dismiss an appeal summarily pursuant to § 1003.1(d);

(k) Engages in conduct that constitutes ineffective assistance of counsel, as previously determined in a finding by the Board, an immigration judge in an immigration proceeding, or a Federal court judge or panel, and a disciplinary complaint is filed within one year of the finding;

(l) Repeatedly fails to appear for pre-hearing conferences, scheduled hearings, or case-related meetings in a timely manner without good cause;

(m) Assists any person, other than a practitioner as defined in § 1003.101(b), in the performance of activity that constitutes the unauthorized practice of law. The practice of law before EOIR means engaging in practice or preparation as those terms are defined in §§ 1001.1(i) and (k);

(n) Engages in conduct that is prejudicial to the administration of justice or undermines the integrity of the adjudicative process. Conduct that will generally be subject to sanctions under this ground includes any action or inaction that seriously impairs or interferes with the adjudicative process when the practitioner should have reasonably known to avoid such conduct;

(o) Fails to provide competent representation to a client. Competent representation requires the legal knowledge, skill, thoroughness, and preparation reasonably necessary for the representation. Competent handling of a particular matter includes inquiry into and analysis of the factual and legal elements of the problem, and use of methods and procedures meeting the standards of competent practitioners;

(p) Fails to abide by a client's decisions concerning the objectives of representation and fails to consult with the client as to the means by which they are to be pursued, in accordance with paragraph (r) of this section. A practitioner may take such action on behalf of the client as is impliedly authorized to carry out the representation;

(q) Fails to act with reasonable diligence and promptness in representing a client.

(1) A practitioner's workload must be controlled and managed so that each matter can be handled competently.

(2) A practitioner has the duty to act with reasonable promptness. This duty includes, but shall not be limited to, complying with all time and filing limitations. This duty, however, does not preclude the practitioner from agreeing to a reasonable request for a postponement that will not prejudice the practitioner's client.

(3) A practitioner should carry through to conclusion all matters undertaken for a client, consistent with the scope of representation as previously determined by the client and practitioner, unless the client terminates the relationship or the practitioner obtains permission to withdraw in compliance with applicable rules and regulations. If a practitioner has handled a proceeding that produced a result adverse to the client and the practitioner and the client have not agreed that the practitioner will handle the matter on appeal, the practitioner must consult with the client about the client's appeal rights and the terms and conditions of possible representation on appeal;

(r) Fails to maintain communication with the client throughout the duration of the client-practitioner relationship. It is the obligation of the practitioner to take reasonable steps to communicate with the client in a language that the client understands. A practitioner is only under the obligation to attempt to communicate with his or her client using addresses or phone numbers known to the practitioner. In order to properly maintain communication, the practitioner should:

(1) Promptly inform and consult with the client concerning any decision or circumstance with respect to which the client's informed consent is reasonably required;

(2) Reasonably consult with the client about the means by which the client's objectives are to be accomplished. Reasonable consultation with the client includes the duty to meet with the client sufficiently in advance of a hearing or other matter to ensure adequate preparation of the client's case and compliance with applicable deadlines;

(3) Keep the client reasonably informed about the status of the matter, such as significant developments affecting the timing or the substance of the representation; and

(4) Promptly comply with reasonable requests for information, except that when a prompt response is not feasible, the practitioner, or a member of the practitioner's staff, should acknowledge receipt of the request and advise the client when a response may be expected;

(s) Fails to disclose to the adjudicator legal authority in the controlling jurisdiction known to the practitioner to be directly adverse to the position of the client and not disclosed by opposing counsel;

(t) Repeatedly fails to submit a signed and completed entry of appearance using the appropriate form in compliance with applicable rules and regulations, including 8 CFR 292.4(a), 1003.17, and 1003.38;

(1) Has engaged in practice or preparation as those terms are defined in §§ 1001.1(i) and (k), and

(2) Has been deemed to have engaged in a pattern or practice of failing to submit such forms, in compliance with applicable rules and regulations. Notwithstanding the foregoing, in each case where the respondent is represented, every pleading, application, motion, or other filing shall be signed by the practitioner of record in his or her individual name;

(u) Repeatedly drafts notices, motions, briefs, or claims that are filed with DHS or EOIR that reflect little or no attention to the specific factual or legal issues applicable to a client's case, but rather rely on boilerplate language indicative of a substantial failure to competently and diligently represent the client;

(v) Acts outside the scope of the representative's approved authority as an accredited representative.

(w) Repeatedly fails to sign any pleading, application, motion, petition, brief, or other document prepared, drafted, or filed with DHS or EOIR. The practitioner's signature must be in the practitioner's individual name and must be handwritten or electronically in conformity with the rules and instructions of the applicable system.

HISTORY:

[65 FR 39513, 39526, June 27, 2000; redesignated and amended at 68 FR 9824, 9830, 9846, Feb. 28, 2003; 68 FR 10349, 10350, Mar. 5, 2003; 73 FR 76914, 76923, Dec. 18, 2008; 81 FR 92346, 92362, Dec. 19, 2016; 87 FR 56204, 56259, Sept. 14, 2022]

§ 1003.103 Immediate suspension and summary disciplinary proceedings; duty of practitioner to notify EOIR of conviction or discipline.

(a) Immediate Suspension —

(1) Petition. The EOIR disciplinary counsel shall file a petition with the Board to suspend immediately from practice before the Board and the Immigration Courts any practitioner who has been found guilty of, or pleaded guilty or nolo contendere to, a serious crime, as defined in § 1003.102(h), or any practitioner who has been suspended or disbarred by, or while a disciplinary investigation or proceeding is pending has resigned from, the highest court of any State, possession, territory, or Commonwealth of the United States, or the District of Columbia, or any Federal court, or who has been placed on an interim suspension pending a final resolution of the underlying disciplinary matter.

(2) DHS petition. DHS may file a petition with the Board to suspend immediately from practice before DHS any practitioner described in paragraph (a)(1) of this section. See 8 CFR 292.3(c).

(3) Copy of petition. A copy of a petition filed by the EOIR disciplinary counsel shall be forwarded to DHS, which may submit a written request to the Board that entry of any order immediately suspending a practitioner before the Board or the Immigration Courts also apply to the practitioner's authority to practice before DHS. A copy of a petition filed by DHS shall be forwarded to the EOIR disciplinary counsel, who may submit a written request to the Board that entry of any order immediately suspending a practitioner before DHS also apply to the practitioner's authority to practice before the Board and Immigration Courts. Proof of service on the practitioner of any request to broaden the scope of an immediate suspension or proposed discipline must be filed with the Board or the adjudicating official.

(4) Immediate suspension. Upon the filing of a petition for immediate suspension pursuant to §§ 1003.103(a)(1) or 1003.103(a)(2), together with a certified copy of a court record finding that a practitioner has been found guilty of, or pleaded guilty or nolo contendere to, a serious crime, or has been disciplined or has resigned, as described in paragraph (a)(1) of this section, the Board shall forthwith enter an order immediately suspending the practitioner from practice before the Board, the Immigration Courts, and/or DHS, notwithstanding the pendency of an appeal, if any, of the underlying disciplinary proceeding, pending final disposition of a summary disciplinary proceeding as provided in paragraph (b) of this section. Such immediate suspension will continue until imposition of a final administrative decision. If an immediate suspension is imposed upon a practitioner, the Board may require that notice of such suspension be posted at the Board, the Immigration Courts, or DHS. Upon good cause shown, the Board may set aside such order of immediate suspension when it appears in the interest of justice to do so. If a final administrative decision includes the imposition of a period of suspension, time spent by the practitioner under immediate suspension pursuant to this paragraph may be credited toward the period of suspension imposed under the final administrative decision.

(b) Summary disciplinary proceedings. The EOIR disciplinary counsel (or DHS pursuant to 8 CFR 292.3(c)(3)) shall promptly initiate summary disciplinary proceedings against any practitioner described in paragraph (a) of this section by the issuance of a Notice of Intent to Discipline, upon receipt of a certified copy of the order, judgment, or record evidencing the underlying criminal conviction, discipline, or resignation, and accompanied by a certified copy of such document. However, delays in initiation of summary disciplinary proceedings under this section will not impact an immediate suspension imposed pursuant to paragraph (a) of this section. Summary proceedings shall be conducted in accordance with the provisions set forth in §§ 1003.105 and 1003.106. Any such summary proceeding shall not be concluded until all direct appeals from an underlying criminal conviction shall have been completed.

(1) In matters concerning criminal convictions, a certified copy of the court record, docket entry, or plea shall be conclusive evidence of the commission of the crime in any summary disciplinary proceeding based thereon.

(2) In the case of a summary proceeding based upon a final order of disbarment or suspension, or a resignation while a disciplinary investigation or proceeding is pending (i.e., reciprocal discipline), a certified copy of a judgment or order of discipline shall establish a rebuttable presumption of the professional misconduct. Disciplinary sanctions shall follow in such a proceeding unless the attorney can rebut the presumption by demonstrating clear and convincing evidence that:

(i) The underlying disciplinary proceeding was so lacking in notice or opportunity to be heard as to constitute a deprivation of due process;

(ii) There was such an infirmity of proof establishing the attorney's professional misconduct as to give rise to the clear conviction that the adjudicating official could not, consistent with his or her duty, accept as final the conclusion on that subject; or

(iii) The imposition of discipline by the adjudicating official would result in grave injustice.

(c) Duty of practitioner and recognized organizations to notify EOIR of conviction or discipline. A practitioner and if applicable, the authorized officer of each recognized organization with which a practitioner is affiliated must notify the EOIR disciplinary counsel within 30 days of the issuance of the initial order, even if an appeal of the conviction or discipline is pending, when the practitioner has been found guilty of, or pleaded guilty or nolo contendere to, a serious crime, as defined in § 1003.102(h), or has been disbarred or suspended by, or while a disciplinary investigation or proceeding is pending has resigned from, the highest court of any State, possession, territory or Commonwealth of the United States, or the District of Columbia, or any Federal court. A practitioner's failure to do so may result in an immediate suspension as set forth in paragraph (a) of this section and other final discipline. An organization's failure to do so may result in the administrative termination of its recognition for violating the reporting requirement under 8 CFR 1292.14. This duty to notify applies only to convictions for serious crimes and to orders imposing discipline for professional misconduct entered on or after August 28, 2000.

HISTORY:

[65 FR 39513, 39527, June 27, 2000; redesignated and amended at 68 FR 9824, 9830, 9846, Feb. 28, 2003; 73 FR 76914, 76923, Dec. 18, 2008, as corrected at 74 FR 201, Jan. 5, 2009.; 77 FR 2011, 2014, Jan. 13, 2012, as confirmed at 78 FR 24669, 24670, Apr. 26, 2013; 81 FR 92346, 92362, Dec. 19, 2016]

§ 1003.104 Filing of complaints; preliminary inquiries; resolutions; referral of complaints.

(a) **Filing complaints —**

(1) Practitioners authorized to practice before the Board and the Immigration Courts. Complaints of criminal, unethical, or unprofessional conduct, or of frivolous behavior by a practitioner who is authorized to practice before the Board and the Immigration Courts shall be filed with the EOIR disciplinary counsel. Disciplinary complaints must be submitted in writing and must state in detail the information that supports the basis for the complaint, including, but not limited to, the names and addresses of the complainant and the practitioner, the date(s) of the conduct or behavior, the nature of the conduct or behavior, the individuals involved, the harm or damages sustained by the complainant, and any other relevant information. Any individual may file a complaint with the EOIR disciplinary counsel using the Form EOIR-44. The EOIR disciplinary counsel shall notify DHS of any disciplinary complaint that pertains, in whole or part, to a matter before DHS.

(2) Practitioners authorized to practice before DHS. Complaints of criminal, unethical, or unprofessional conduct, or frivolous behavior by a practitioner who is authorized to practice before DHS shall be filed with DHS pursuant to the procedures set forth in § 292.3(d) of this chapter.

(b) Preliminary inquiry. Upon receipt of a disciplinary complaint or on its own initiative, the EOIR disciplinary counsel will initiate a preliminary inquiry. If a complaint is filed by a client or former client, the complainant thereby waives the attorney-client privilege and any other privilege relating to the representation to the extent necessary to conduct a preliminary inquiry and any subsequent proceedings based thereon. If the EOIR disciplinary counsel determines that a complaint is without merit, no further action will be taken. The EOIR disciplinary counsel may, in the disciplinary counsel's discretion, close a preliminary inquiry if the complainant fails to comply with reasonable requests for assistance, information, or documentation. The complainant and the practitioner shall be notified of any such determination in writing.

(c) Resolution reached prior to the issuance of a Notice of Intent to Discipline. The EOIR disciplinary counsel, in its discretion, may issue warning letters and admonitions, and may enter into agreements in lieu of discipline, prior to the issuance of a Notice of Intent to Discipline.

(d) Referral of complaints of criminal conduct. If the EOIR disciplinary counsel receives credible information or allegations that a practitioner has engaged in criminal conduct, the EOIR disciplinary counsel shall refer the matter to DHS or the appropriate United States Attorney and, if appropriate, to the Inspector General, the Federal Bureau of Investigation, or other law enforcement agency. In such cases, in making the decision to pursue disciplinary sanctions, the EOIR disciplinary counsel shall coordinate in advance with the appropriate investigative and prosecutorial authorities within the Department to ensure that neither the disciplinary process nor criminal prosecutions are jeopardized.

HISTORY:

[65 FR 39513, 39528, June 27, 2000; redesignated at 68 FR 9824, 9830, Feb. 28, 2003; 73 FR 76914, 76924, Dec. 18, 2008; 81 FR 92346, 92362, Dec. 19, 2016]

§ 1003.105 Notice of Intent to Discipline.

(a) **Issuance of Notice.**

(1) If, upon completion of the preliminary inquiry, the EOIR disciplinary counsel determines that sufficient prima facie evidence exists to warrant charging a practitioner with professional misconduct as set forth in § 1003.102 or a recognized organization with misconduct as set forth in § 1003.110, the EOIR disciplinary counsel will file with the Board and issue to the practitioner or organization that was the subject of the preliminary inquiry a Notice of Intent to Discipline. In cases involving practitioners, service of the notice will be made upon the practitioner either by certified mail to the practitioner's last known address, as defined in paragraph (a)(2) of this section, or by personal delivery. In cases involving recognized organizations, service of the notice will be made upon the authorized officer of the organization either by certified mail at the address of the organization or by personal delivery. The notice shall contain a statement of the charge(s), a copy of the preliminary inquiry report, the proposed disciplinary sanctions to be imposed, the procedure for filing an answer or requesting a hearing, and the mailing address and telephone number of the Board. In summary disciplinary proceedings brought pursuant to § 1003.103(b), a preliminary inquiry report is not required to be filed with the Notice of Intent to Discipline. If a Notice of Intent to Discipline is filed against an accredited representative, the EOIR disciplinary counsel shall send a copy of the notice to the authorized officer of the recognized organization through which the

representative is accredited at the address of the organization.

(2) For the purposes of this section, the last known address of a practitioner is the practitioner's address as it appears in EOIR's case management system if the practitioner is actively representing a party before EOIR on the date that the EOIR disciplinary counsel issues the Notice of Intent to Discipline. If the practitioner does not have a matter pending before EOIR on the date of the issuance of a Notice of Intent to Discipline, then the last known address for a practitioner will be as follows:

(i) Attorneys in the United States: the attorney's address that is on record with a state jurisdiction that licensed the attorney to practice law.

(ii) Accredited representatives: the address of a recognized organization with which the accredited representative is affiliated.

(iii) Accredited officials: the address of the embassy of the foreign government that employs the accredited official.

(iv) All other practitioners: the address for the practitioner that appears in EOIR's case management system for the most recent matter on which the practitioner represented a party.

(3) DHS Issuance of Notice to practitioner. DHS may file a Notice of Intent to Discipline with the Board in accordance with 8 CFR 292.3(e).

(b) Copy of notice; reciprocity of discipline. A copy of the Notice of Intent to Discipline filed by the EOIR disciplinary counsel shall be forwarded to DHS, which may submit a written request to the Board or the adjudicating official requesting that any discipline imposed upon a practitioner which restricts his or her authority to practice before the Board and the Immigration Courts also apply to the practitioner's authority to practice before DHS. A copy of the Notice of Intent to Discipline filed by DHS shall be forwarded to the EOIR disciplinary counsel, who may submit a written request to the Board or the adjudicating official requesting that any discipline imposed upon a practitioner that restricts his or her authority to practice before DHS also apply to the practitioner's authority to practice before the Board and the Immigration Courts. Proof of service on the practitioner of any request to broaden the scope of the proposed discipline must be filed with the adjudicating official.

(c) Answer —

(1) Filing. The practitioner or, in cases involving a recognized organization, the organization, shall file a written answer to the Notice of Intent to Discipline with the Board within 30 days of the date of service of the Notice of Intent to Discipline unless, on motion to the Board, an extension of time to answer is granted for good cause. A motion for an extension of time to answer must be received by the Board no later than three (3) working days before the time to answer has expired. A copy of the answer and any such motion shall be served by the practitioner on the counsel for the government.

(2) Contents. The answer shall contain a statement of facts which constitute the grounds of defense and shall specifically admit or deny each allegation set forth in the Notice of Intent to Discipline. Every allegation in the Notice of Intent to Discipline which is not denied in the answer shall be deemed to be admitted and may be considered as proved, and no further evidence in respect of such allegation need be adduced. The practitioner or, in cases involving a recognized organization, the organization, may also state affirmatively special matters of defense and may submit supporting documents, including affidavits or statements, along with the answer.

(3) Request for hearing. The practitioner or, in cases involving a recognized organization, the organization, shall also state in the answer whether a hearing on the matter is requested. If no such request is made, the opportunity for a hearing will be deemed waived.

(d) **Failure to file an answer.**

(1) Failure to file an answer within the time period prescribed in the Notice of Intent to Discipline, except where the time to answer is extended by the Board, shall constitute an admission of the allegations in the Notice of Intent to Discipline and no further evidence with respect to such allegations need be adduced.

(2) Upon such a default by the practitioner or, in cases involving a recognized organization, the organization, the counsel for the government shall submit to the Board proof of service of the Notice of Intent to Discipline. The practitioner or the organization shall be precluded thereafter from requesting a hearing on the matter. The Board shall issue a final order adopting the proposed disciplinary sanctions in the Notice of Intent to Discipline unless to do so would foster a tendency toward inconsistent dispositions for comparable conduct or would otherwise be unwarranted or not in the interests of justice. With the exception of cases in which the Board has already imposed an immediate suspension pursuant to § 1003.103 or that otherwise involve an accredited representative or recognized organization, any final order imposing discipline shall not become effective sooner than 15 days from the date of the order to provide the practitioner opportunity to comply with the terms of such order, including, but not limited to, withdrawing from any pending immigration matters and notifying immigration clients of the imposition of any sanction. Any final order imposing discipline against an accredited representative or recognized organization shall become effective immediately. A practitioner or a recognized organization may file a motion to set aside a final order of discipline issued pursuant to this paragraph, with service of such motion on counsel for the government, provided:

(i) Such a motion is filed within 15 days of the date of service of the final order; and

(ii) The practitioner's or the recognized organization's failure to file an answer was due to exceptional circumstances (such as serious illness of the practitioner or death of an immediate relative of the practitioner, but not including less compelling circumstances) beyond the control of the practitioner or the recognized organization.

HISTORY:

[65 FR 39513, 39528, June 27, 2000; redesignated and amended at 68 FR 9824, 9830, 9846, Feb. 28, 2003; 68 FR 10349, 10350, Mar. 5, 2003; 73 FR 76914, 76925, Dec. 18, 2008; 77 FR 2011, 2014, Jan. 13, 2012, as confirmed at 78 FR 24669, 24670, Apr. 26, 2013; 81 FR 92346, 92362, Dec. 19, 2016]

§ 1003.106 Right to be heard and disposition.

(a) Right to be heard—

(1) Summary disciplinary proceedings. A practitioner who is subject to summary disciplinary proceedings pursuant to § 1003.103(b) must make a prima facie showing to the Board in his or her answer that there is a material issue of fact in dispute with regard to the basis for summary disciplinary proceedings, or with one or more of the exceptions set forth in § 1003.103(b)(2)(i) through (iii). If the practitioner files a timely answer and the Board determines that there is a material issue of fact in dispute with regard to the basis for summary disciplinary proceedings, or with one or more of the exceptions set forth in § 1003.103(b)(2)(i) through (iii), then the Board shall refer the case to the Chief Immigration Judge for the appointment of an adjudicating official. If the practitioner fails to make such a prima facie showing, the Board shall retain jurisdiction over the case and issue a final order. Notwithstanding the foregoing, the Board shall refer any case to the Chief Immigration Judge for the appointment of an adjudicating official in which the practitioner has filed a timely answer and the case involves a charge or charges that cannot be adjudicated under the summary disciplinary proceedings provisions in § 1003.103(b). The Board shall refer such a case regardless of whether the practitioner has requested a hearing.

(2) [Procedure.] The procedures set forth in paragraphs (b) through (d) of this section apply to cases in which the practitioner or recognized organization files a timely answer to the Notice of Intent to Discipline, with the exception of cases in which the Board issues a final order pursuant to § 1003.105(d)(2) or § 1003.106(a)(1).

(i) The Chief Immigration Judge shall, upon the filing of an answer, appoint an Immigration Judge as an adjudicating official. At the request of the Chief Immigration Judge, the Chief Administrative Hearing Officer may appoint an Administrative Law Judge as an adjudicating official. The Director may appoint either an Immigration Judge or Administrative Law Judge as an adjudicating official if the Chief Immigration Judge or the Chief Administrative Hearing Officer does not appoint an adjudicating official or if the Director determines it is in the interest of efficiency to do so. An Immigration Judge or Administrative Law Judge shall not serve as the adjudicating official in any case in which the Judge is the complainant, in any case involving a practitioner who regularly appears before the Judge, or in any case involving a recognized organization whose representatives regularly appear before the Judge.

(ii) Upon the practitioner's or, in cases involving a recognized organization, the organization's, request for a hearing, the adjudicating official may designate the time and place of the hearing with due regard to the location of the practitioner's practice or residence or of the recognized organization, the convenience of witnesses, and any other relevant factors. When designating the time and place of a hearing, the adjudicating official shall provide for the service of a notice of hearing on the practitioner or the authorized officer of the recognized organization and the counsel for the government. The practitioner or the recognized organization shall be afforded adequate time to prepare a case in advance of the hearing. Pre-hearing conferences may be scheduled at the discretion of the adjudicating official in order to narrow issues, to obtain stipulations between the parties, to exchange information voluntarily, and otherwise to simplify and organize the proceeding. Settlement agreements reached after the issuance of a Notice of Intent to Discipline are subject to final approval by the adjudicating official or, if the practitioner or organization has not filed an answer, subject to final approval by the Board.

(iii) The practitioner or, in cases involving a recognized organization, the organization, may be represented by counsel at no expense to the government. Counsel for the practitioner or the organization shall file the appropriate Notice of Entry of Appearance (Form EOIR-27 or EOIR-28) in accordance with the procedures set forth in this part. Each party shall have a reasonable opportunity to examine and object to evidence presented by the other party, to present evidence, and to cross-examine witnesses presented by the other party. If the practitioner or the recognized organization files an answer but does not request a hearing, then the adjudicating official shall provide the parties an opportunity to submit briefs and evidence to support or refute any of the charges or affirmative defenses.

(iv) In rendering a decision, the adjudicating official shall consider the following: The complaint, the preliminary inquiry report, the Notice of Intent to Discipline, the answer, any supporting documents, and any other evidence, including pleadings, briefs, and other materials. Counsel for the government shall bear the burden of proving the grounds for disciplinary sanctions enumerated in the Notice of Intent to Discipline by clear and convincing evidence.

(v) The record of proceedings, regardless of whether an immigration judge or an administrative law judge is the adjudicating official, shall conform to the requirements of 8 CFR part 1003, subpart C and 8 CFR 1240.9. Disciplinary hearings shall be conducted in the same manner as Immigration Court proceedings as is appropriate, and shall be open to the public, except that:

(A) Depending upon physical facilities, the adjudicating official may place reasonable limitations upon the number of individuals in attendance at any one time, with priority being given to the press over the general public, and

(B) For the purposes of protecting witnesses, parties, or the public interest, the adjudicating official may limit attendance or hold a closed hearing.

(3) Failure to appear in proceedings. If the practitioner or, in cases involving a recognized organization, the organization, requests a hearing as provided in § 1003.105(c)(3) but fails to appear, the adjudicating official shall then proceed and decide the case in the absence of the practitioner or the recognized organiza-

tion in accordance with paragraph (b) of this section, based on the available record, including any additional evidence or arguments presented by the counsel for the government at the hearing. In such a proceeding the counsel for the government shall submit to the adjudicating official proof of service of the Notice of Intent to Discipline as well as the Notice of the Hearing. The practitioner or the recognized organization shall be precluded thereafter from participating further in the proceedings. A final order imposing discipline issued pursuant to this paragraph shall not be subject to further review, except that the practitioner or the recognized organization may file a motion to set aside the order, with service of such motion on counsel for the government, provided:

(i) Such a motion is filed within 15 days of the date of issuance of the final order; and

(ii) The practitioner's or the recognized organization's failure to appear was due to exceptional circumstances (such as serious illness of the practitioner or death of an immediate relative of the practitioner, but not including less compelling circumstances) beyond the control of the practitioner or the recognized organization.

(b) Decision. The adjudicating official shall consider the entire record and, as soon as practicable, render a decision. If the adjudicating official finds that one or more grounds for disciplinary sanctions enumerated in the Notice of Intent to Discipline have been established by clear and convincing evidence, the official shall rule that the disciplinary sanctions set forth in the Notice of Intent to Discipline be adopted, modified, or otherwise amended. If the adjudicating official determines that the practitioner should be suspended, the time period for such suspension shall be specified. If the adjudicating official determines that the organization's recognition should be revoked, the official may also identify the persons affiliated with the organization who were directly involved in the conduct that constituted the grounds for revocation. If the adjudicating official determines that the organization's recognition should be terminated, the official shall specify the time restriction, if any, before the organization may submit a new request for recognition. Any grounds for disciplinary sanctions enumerated in the Notice of Intent to Discipline that have not been established by clear and convincing evidence shall be dismissed. The adjudicating official shall provide for service of a written decision or memorandum summarizing an oral decision on the practitioner or, in cases involving a recognized organization, on the authorized officer of the organization and on the counsel for the government. Except as provided in paragraph (a)(2) of this section, the adjudicating official's decision becomes final only upon waiver of appeal or expiration of the time for appeal to the Board, whichever comes first, and does not take effect during the pendency of an appeal to the Board as provided in § 1003.6. A final order imposing discipline against an accredited representative or recognized organization shall take effect immediately.

(c) Appeal. Upon issuance of a decision by the adjudicating official, either party or both parties may appeal to the Board to conduct a review pursuant to § 1003.1(d)(3). Parties must comply with all pertinent provisions for appeals to the Board, including provisions relating to forms and fees, as set forth in Part 1003, and must use Form EOIR-45. The decision of the Board is the final administrative order as provided in § 1003.1(d)(7), and shall be served upon the practitioner or, in cases involving a recognized organization, the organization, as provided in § 1003.1(f). With the exception of cases in which the Board has already imposed an immediate suspension pursuant to § 1003.103 or cases involving accredited representatives or recognized organizations, any final order imposing discipline shall not become effective sooner than 15 days from the date of the order to provide the practitioner opportunity to comply with the terms of such order, including, but not limited to, withdrawing from any pending immigration matters and notifying immigration clients of the imposition of any sanction. A final order imposing discipline against an accredited representative or recognized organization shall take effect immediately. A copy of the final administrative order of the Board shall be served upon the counsel for the government. If disciplinary sanctions are imposed against a practitioner or a recognized organization (other than a private censure), the Board may require that notice of such sanctions be posted at the Board, the Immigration Courts, or DHS for the period of time during which the sanctions are in effect, or for any other period of time as determined by the Board.

(d) Referral. In addition to, or in lieu of, initiating disciplinary proceedings against a practitioner, the EOIR disciplinary counsel may notify an appropriate Federal or state disciplinary or regulatory authority of any complaint filed against a practitioner. Any final administrative decision imposing sanctions against a practitioner (other than a private censure) shall be reported to any such disciplinary or regulatory authority in every jurisdiction where the disciplined practitioner is admitted or otherwise authorized to practice. In addition, the EOIR disciplinary counsel shall transmit notice of all public discipline imposed under this rule to the National Lawyer Regulatory Data Bank maintained by the American Bar Association.

HISTORY:

[65 FR 39513, 39529, June 27, 2000; redesignated and amended at 68 FR 9824, 9830, 9846, Feb. 28, 2003; 68 FR 10349, 10350, Mar. 5, 2003; 73 FR 76914, 76925, Dec. 18, 2008; 77 FR 2011, 2015, Jan. 13, 2012, as confirmed at 78 FR 24669, 24670, Apr. 26, 2013; 81 FR 92346, 92363, Dec. 19, 2016; 86 FR 70708, 70723, Dec. 13, 2021]

§ 1003.107 Reinstatement after disbarment or suspension.

(a) **Reinstatement upon expiration of suspension.**

(1) Except as provided in paragraph (c)(1) of this section, after the period of suspension has expired, a practitioner who has been suspended and wishes to be reinstated must file a motion to the Board requesting reinstatement to practice before the Board and the Immigration Courts, or DHS, or before all three au-

thorities. The practitioner must demonstrate by clear and convincing evidence that notwithstanding the suspension, the practitioner otherwise meets the definition of attorney or representative as set forth in § 1001.1(f) and (j), respectively, of this chapter. The practitioner must serve a copy of such motion on the EOIR disciplinary counsel. In matters in which the practitioner was ordered suspended from practice before DHS, the practitioner must serve a copy of such motion on the DHS disciplinary counsel.

(2) The EOIR disciplinary counsel and, in matters in which the practitioner was ordered suspended from practice before DHS, the DHS disciplinary counsel, may reply within 13 days of service of the motion in the form of a written response objecting to the reinstatement on the ground that the practitioner failed to comply with the terms of the suspension. The response must include supporting documentation or evidence of the petitioner's failure to comply with the terms of the suspension. The Board, in its discretion, may afford the parties additional time to file briefs or hold a hearing to determine if the practitioner meets all the requirements for reinstatement.

(3) If a practitioner does not meet the definition of attorney or representative, the Board shall deny the motion for reinstatement without further consideration. If the practitioner failed to comply with the terms of the suspension, the Board shall deny the motion and indicate the circumstances under which the practitioner may apply for reinstatement. If the practitioner meets the definition of attorney or representative and the practitioner otherwise has complied with the terms of the suspension, the Board shall grant the motion and reinstate the practitioner.

(b) **Early reinstatement.**

(1) Except as provided in paragraph (c) of this section, a practitioner who has been disbarred or who has been suspended for one year or more may file a petition for reinstatement directly with the Board after one-half of the suspension period has expired or one year has passed, whichever is greater, provided that notwithstanding the suspension, the practitioner otherwise meets the definition of attorney or representative as set forth in § 1001.1(f) and (j), respectively, of this chapter. A copy of such a petition shall be served on the EOIR disciplinary counsel. In matters in which the practitioner was ordered disbarred or suspended from practice before DHS, a copy of such petition shall be served on the DHS disciplinary counsel.

(2) A practitioner seeking early reinstatement must demonstrate by clear and convincing evidence that the practitioner possesses the moral and professional qualifications required to appear before the Board, the Immigration Courts, or DHS, and that the practitioner's reinstatement will not be detrimental to the administration of justice. The EOIR disciplinary counsel and, in matters in which the practitioner was ordered disbarred or suspended from practice before DHS, the DHS disciplinary counsel, may reply within 30 days of service of the petition in the form of a written response to the Board, which may include, but is not limited to, documentation or evidence of the practitioner's failure to comply with the terms of the disbarment or suspension or of any complaints filed against the disbarred or suspended practitioner subsequent to the practitioner's disbarment or suspension.

(3) If a practitioner cannot meet the definition of attorney or representative, the Board shall deny the petition for reinstatement without further consideration. If the petition for reinstatement is found to be otherwise inappropriate or unwarranted, the petition shall be denied. Any subsequent petitions for reinstatement may not be filed before the end of one year from the date of the Board's previous denial of reinstatement, unless the practitioner is otherwise eligible for reinstatement under paragraph (a). If the petition for reinstatement is determined to be timely, the practitioner meets the definition of attorney or representative, and the petitioner has otherwise established by the requisite standard of proof that the practitioner possesses the qualifications set forth herein, and that reinstatement will not be detrimental to the administration of justice, the Board shall grant the petition and reinstate the practitioner. The Board, in its discretion, may hold a hearing to determine if the practitioner meets all of the requirements for reinstatement.

(c) **Accredited representatives.**

(1) An accredited representative who has been suspended for a period of time greater than the remaining period of validity of the representative's accreditation at the time of the suspension is not eligible to be reinstated under § 1003.107(a) or (b). In such circumstances, after the period of suspension has expired, an organization may submit a new request for accreditation pursuant to 8 CFR 1292.13 on behalf of such an individual.

(2) Disbarment. An accredited representative who has been disbarred is permanently barred from appearing before the Board, the Immigration Courts, or DHS as an accredited representative and cannot seek reinstatement.

(d) Appearance after reinstatement. A practitioner who has been reinstated to practice by the Board must file a new Notice of Entry of Appearance of Attorney or Representative in each case on the form required by applicable rules and regulations, even if the reinstated practitioner previously filed such a form in a proceeding before the practitioner was disciplined.

HISTORY:

[65 FR 39513, 39530, June 27, 2000; redesignated at 68 FR 9824, 9830, Feb. 28, 2003; 68 FR 10349, 10350, Mar. 5, 2003; 73 FR 76914, 76926, Dec. 18, 2008; 77 FR 2011, 2015, Jan. 13, 2012, as confirmed at 78 FR 24669, 24670, Apr. 26, 2013; 81 FR 92346, 92364, Dec. 19, 2016]

§ 1003.108 Confidentiality.

(a) Complaints and preliminary inquiries. Except as otherwise provided by law or regulation, information concerning complaints or preliminary inquiries is confidential. A practitioner or recognized organization whose conduct is the subject of a complaint or preliminary inquiry, however, may waive confidentiality, except that the EOIR disciplinary counsel may decline to permit a waiver of confidentiality if it is determined that an ongoing preliminary inquiry may be substantially prejudiced by public disclosure before the filing of a Notice of Intent to Discipline.

(1) Disclosure of information for the purpose of protecting the public. The EOIR disciplinary counsel may disclose information concerning a complaint or preliminary inquiry for the protection of the public when the necessity for disclosing information outweighs the necessity for preserving confidentiality in circumstances including, but not limited to, the following:

(i) A practitioner or recognized organization has caused, or is likely to cause, harm to client(s), the public, or the administration of justice, such that the public or specific individuals should be advised of the nature of the allegations. If disclosure of information is made pursuant to this paragraph, the EOIR disciplinary counsel may define the scope of information disseminated and may limit the disclosure of information to specified individuals and entities;

(ii) A practitioner or recognized organization has committed criminal acts or is under investigation by law enforcement authorities;

(iii) A practitioner or recognized organization is under investigation by a disciplinary or regulatory authority, or has committed acts or made omissions that may reasonably result in investigation by such authorities;

(iv) A practitioner or recognized organization is the subject of multiple disciplinary complaints and the EOIR disciplinary counsel has determined not to pursue all of the complaints. The EOIR disciplinary counsel may inform complainants whose allegations have not been pursued of the status of any other preliminary inquiries or the manner in which any other complaint(s) against the practitioner or recognized organization have been resolved.

(2) Disclosure of information for the purpose of conducting a preliminary inquiry. The EOIR disciplinary counsel, in the exercise of discretion, may disclose documents and information concerning complaints and preliminary inquiries to the following individuals and entities:

(i) To witnesses or potential witnesses in conjunction with a complaint or preliminary inquiry;

(ii) To other governmental agencies responsible for the enforcement of civil or criminal laws;

(iii) To agencies and other jurisdictions responsible for disciplinary or regulatory investigations and proceedings;

(iv) To the complainant or a lawful designee;

(v) To the practitioner or recognized organization who is the subject of the complaint or preliminary inquiry or the practitioner's or recognized organization's counsel of record.

(3) Disclosure of information for the purpose of recognition of organizations and accreditation of representatives. The EOIR disciplinary counsel, in the exercise of discretion, may disclose information concerning complaints or preliminary inquiries regarding applicants for recognition and accreditation, recognized organizations or their authorized officers, or accredited representatives to the Assistant Director for Policy (or the Assistant Director for Policy's delegate) for any purpose related to the recognition of organizations and accreditation of representatives.

(b) Resolutions reached prior to the issuance of a Notice of Intent to Discipline. Resolutions reached prior to the issuance of a Notice of Intent to Discipline, such as warning letters, admonitions, and agreements in lieu of discipline are confidential, except that resolutions that pertain to an accredited representative may be disclosed to the accredited representative's organization and the Assistant Director for Policy (or the Assistant Director for Policy's delegate). However, all such resolutions may become part of the public record if the practitioner becomes subject to a subsequent Notice of Intent to Discipline.

(c) Notices of Intent to Discipline and action subsequent thereto. Notices of Intent to Discipline and any action that takes place subsequent to their issuance, except for the imposition of private censures, may be disclosed to the public, except that private censures may become part of the public record if introduced as evidence of a prior record of discipline in any subsequent disciplinary proceeding. Settlement agreements reached after the issuance of a Notice of Intent to Discipline may be disclosed to the public upon final approval by the adjudicating official or the Board. Disciplinary hearings are open to the public, except as noted in § 1003.106(a)(1)(v).

HISTORY:

[65 FR 39513, 39530, June 27, 2000; redesignated and amended at 68 FR 9824, 9830, 9846, Feb. 28, 2003; 73 FR 76914, 76927, Dec. 18, 2008; 81 FR 92346, 92365, Dec. 19, 2016; 84 FR 44537, 44542, Aug. 26, 2019; as confirmed at 85 FR 69465, Nov. 3, 2020]

§ 1003.109 Discipline of government attorneys.

Complaints regarding the conduct or behavior of Department attorneys, Immigration Judges, or Board Members shall be directed to the Office of Professional Responsibility, United States Department of Justice. If disciplinary action is warranted, it shall be administered pursuant to the Department's attorney discipline procedures.

HISTORY:

[65 FR 39513, 39531, June 27, 2000; redesignated at 68 FR 9824, 9830, Feb. 28, 2003]

§ 1003.110 Sanction of recognized organizations.

(a) Authority to sanction.

(1) An adjudicating official or the Board may impose disciplinary sanctions against a recognized organization if it is in the public interest to do so. It will be in the public interest to impose disciplinary sanctions if a recognized organization has engaged in the conduct described in paragraph (b) of this section. In accordance with the disciplinary proceedings set forth in this subpart, an adjudicating official or the Board may impose the following sanctions:

(i) Revocation, which removes the organization and its accredited representatives from the recognition and accreditation roster and permanently bars the organization from future recognition;

(ii) Termination, which removes the organization and its accredited representatives from the recognition and accreditation roster but does not bar the organization from future recognition. In terminating recognition under this section, the adjudicating official or the Board may preclude the organization from submitting a new request for recognition under 8 CFR 1292.13 before a specified date; or

(iii) Such other disciplinary sanctions, except a suspension, as the adjudicating official or the Board deems appropriate.

(2) The administrative termination of an organization's recognition under 8 CFR 1292.17 after the issuance of Notice of Intent to Discipline pursuant to § 1003.105(a)(1) shall not preclude the continuation of disciplinary proceedings and the imposition of sanctions, unless counsel for the government moves to dismiss the Notice of Intent to Discipline and the adjudicating official or the Board grants the motion.

(3) The imposition of disciplinary sanctions against a recognized organization does not result in disciplinary sanctions against that organization's accredited representatives; disciplinary sanctions, if any, against an organization's accredited representatives must be imposed separately from disciplinary sanctions against the organization. Termination or revocation of an organization's recognition has the effect of terminating the accreditation of representatives of that organization, but such individuals may retain or seek accreditation through another recognized organization.

(b) Grounds. It shall be deemed to be in the public interest for an adjudicating official or the Board to impose disciplinary sanctions against any recognized organization that violates one or more of the grounds specified in this paragraph, except that these grounds do not constitute the exclusive grounds for which disciplinary sanctions may be imposed in the public interest. A recognized organization may be subject to disciplinary sanctions if it:

(1) Knowingly or with reckless disregard provides a false statement or misleading information in applying for recognition or accreditation of its representatives;

(2) Knowingly or with reckless disregard provides false or misleading information to clients or prospective clients regarding the scope of authority of, or the services provided by, the organization or its accredited representatives;

(3) Fails to adequately supervise accredited representatives;

(4) Employs, receives services from, or affiliates with an individual who performs an activity that constitutes the unauthorized practice of law or immigration fraud; or

(5) Engages in the practice of law through staff when it does not have an attorney or accredited representative.

(c) Joint disciplinary proceedings. The EOIR disciplinary counsel or DHS disciplinary counsel may file a Notice of Intent to Discipline against a recognized organization and one or more of its accredited representatives pursuant to § 1003.101 et seq. Disciplinary proceedings conducted on such notices, if they are filed jointly with the Board, shall be joined and referred to the same adjudicating official pursuant to § 1003.106. An adjudicating official may join related disciplinary proceedings after the filing of a Notice of Intent to Discipline.

HISTORY:

[81 FR 92346, 92365, Dec. 19, 2016]

§ 1003.111 Interim suspension.

(a) Petition for interim suspension —

(1) EOIR Petition. In conjunction with the filing of a Notice of Intent to Discipline or at any time thereafter during disciplinary proceedings before an adjudicating official, the EOIR disciplinary counsel may file a petition for an interim suspension of an accredited representative. Such suspension, if issued, precludes the representative from practicing before the Board and the Immigration Courts during the pendency of disciplinary proceedings and continues until the issuance of a final order in the disciplinary proceedings.

(2) DHS Petition. In conjunction with the filing of a Notice of Intent to Discipline or at any time thereafter during disciplinary proceedings before an adjudicating official, the DHS disciplinary counsel may file a petition for an interim suspension of an accredited representative. Such suspension, if issued, precludes the representative from practicing before DHS during the pendency of disciplinary proceedings and continues until the issuance of a final order in the disciplinary proceedings.

(3) Contents of the petition. In the petition, counsel for the government must demonstrate by a preponderance of the evidence that the accredited representative poses a substantial threat of irreparable harm to clients or prospective clients. An accredited representative poses a substantial threat of irreparable harm to clients or prospective clients if the representative committed three or more acts in violation of the grounds of discipline described at § 1003.102, when actual harm or threatened harm is demonstrated, or engages in any other conduct that, if continued, will likely cause irreparable harm to clients or prospective clients. Counsel for the government must serve the petition on the accredited representative, as provided in § 1003.105, and send a copy of the petition to the authorized officer of the recognized organization at the address of the organization through which the representative is accredited.

(4) Requests to broaden scope. The EOIR disciplinary counsel or DHS disciplinary counsel may submit a request to broaden the scope of any interim suspension order such that an accredited representative would be precluded from practice before the Board, the Immigration Courts, and DHS.

(b) Response. The accredited representative may file a written response to the petition for interim suspension within 30 days of service of the petition.

(c) Adjudication. Upon the expiration of the time to respond to the petition for an interim suspension, the adjudicating official will consider the petition for an interim suspension, the accredited representative's response, if any, and any other evidence presented by the parties before determining whether to issue an interim suspension. If the adjudicating official imposes an interim suspension on the representative, the adjudicating official may require that notice of the interim suspension be posted at the Board and the Immigration Courts, or DHS, or all three authorities. Upon good cause shown, the adjudicating official may set aside an order of interim suspension when it appears in the interest of justice to do so. If a final order in the disciplinary proceedings includes the imposition of a period of suspension against an accredited representative, time spent by the representative under an interim suspension pursuant to this section may be credited toward the period of suspension imposed under the final order.

HISTORY:
[81 FR 92346, 92365, Dec. 19, 2016]

SUBCHAPTER B

IMMIGRATION REGULATIONS

Part

PART 1101

PRESUMPTION OF LAWFUL ADMISSION

Rule

AUTHORITY NOTE APPLICABLE TO ENTIRE PART:

AUTHORITY:
8 U.S.C. 1103, 8 CFR part 2.

§ 1101.1 Presumption of lawful admission.

A member of the following classes shall be presumed to have been lawfully admitted for permanent residence even though a record of his admission cannot be found, except as otherwise provided in this section, unless he abandoned his lawful permanent resident status or subsequently lost that status by operation of law:

(a) Prior to June 30, 1906. An alien who establishes that he entered the United States prior to June 30, 1906.

(b) United States land borders. An alien who establishes that, while a citizen of Canada or Newfoundland, he entered the United States across the Canadian border prior to October 1, 1906; an alien who establishes that while a citizen of Mexico he entered the United States across the Mexican border prior to July 1, 1908; an alien who establishes that, while a citizen of Mexico, he entered the United States at the port of Presidio, Texas, prior to October 21, 1918, and an alien for whom a record of his actual admission to the United States does not exist but who establishes that he gained admission to the United States prior to July 1, 1924, pursuant to preexamination at a United States immigration station in Canada and that a record of such preexamination exists.

(c) Virgin Islands. An alien who establishes that he entered the Virgin Islands of the United States prior to July 1, 1938, even though a record of his admission prior to that date exists as a non-immigrant under the Immigration Act of 1924.

(d) Asiatic barred zone. An alien who establishes that he is of a race indigenous to, and a native of a country within, the Asiatic zone defined in section 3 of the Act of February 5, 1917, as amended, that he was a member of a class of aliens exempted from exclusion by the provisions of that section, and that he entered the United States prior to July 1, 1924, provided that a record of his admission exists.

(e) Chinese and Japanese aliens —

(1) Prior to July 1, 1924. A Chinese alien for whom there exists a record of his admission to the United

States prior to July 1, 1924, under the laws and regulations formerly applicable to Chinese and who establishes that at the time of his admission he was a merchant, teacher, or student, and his son or daughter under 21 or wife accompanying or following to join him; a traveler for curiosity or pleasure and his accompanying son or daughter under 21 or accompanying wife; a wife of a United States citizen; a returning laborer; and a person erroneously admitted as a United States citizen under section 1993 of the Revised Statutes of the United States, as amended, his father not having resided in the United States prior to his birth.

(2) On or after July 1, 1924. A Chinese alien for whom there exists a record of his admission to the United States as a member of one of the following classes; an alien who establishes that he was readmitted between July 1, 1924, and December 16, 1943, inclusive, as a returning Chinese laborer who acquired lawful permanent residence prior to July 1, 1924; a person erroneously admitted between July 1, 1924, and June 6, 1927, inclusive, as a United States citizen under section 1993 of the Revised Statutes of the United States, as amended, his father not having resided in the United States prior to his birth; an alien admitted at any time after June 30, 1924, under section 4 (b) or (d) of the Immigration Act of 1924; an alien wife of a United States citizen admitted between June 13, 1930, and December 16, 1943, inclusive, under section 4(a) of the Immigration Act of 1924; an alien admitted on or after December 17, 1943, under section 4(f) of the Immigration Act of 1924; an alien admitted on or after December 17, 1943, under section 317(c) of the Nationality Act of 1940, as amended; an alien admitted on or after December 17, 1943, as a preference or nonpreference quota immigrant pursuant to section 2 of that act; and a Chinese or Japanese alien admitted to the United States between July 1, 1924, and December 23, 1952, both dates inclusive, as the wife or minor son or daughter of a treaty merchant admitted before July 1, 1924, if the husband-father was lawfully admitted to the United States as a treaty merchant before July 1, 1924, or, while maintaining another status under which he was admitted before that date, and his status changed to that of a treaty merchant or treaty trader after that date, and was maintaining the changed status at the time his wife or minor son or daughter entered the United States.

(f) Citizens of the Philippine Islands —

(1) Entry prior to May 1, 1934. An alien who establishes that he entered the United States prior to May 1, 1934, and that he was on the date of his entry a citizen of the Philippine Islands, provided that for the purpose of petitioning for naturalization he shall not be regarded as having been lawfully admitted for permanent residence unless he was a citizen of the Commonwealth of the Philippines on July 2, 1946.

(2) Entry between May 1, 1934, and July 3, 1946. An alien who establishes that he entered Hawaii between May 1, 1934, and July 3, 1946, inclusive, under the provisions of the last sentence of section 8(a)(1) of the Act of March 24, 1934, as amended, that he was a citizen of the Philippine Islands when he entered, and that a record of such entry exists.

(g) Temporarily admitted aliens. The following aliens who when admitted expressed an intention to remain in the United States temporarily or to pass in transit through the United States, for whom records of admission exist, but who remained in the United States: An alien admitted prior to June 3, 1921, except if admitted temporarily under the 9th proviso to section 3 of the Immigration Act of 1917, or as an accredited official of a foreign government, his suite, family, or guest, or as a seaman in pursuit of his calling; an alien admitted under the Act of May 19, 1921, as amended, who was admissible for permanent residence under that Act notwithstanding the quota limitation's thereof and his accompanying wife or unmarried son or daughter under 21 who was admissible for permanent residence under that Act notwithstanding the quota limitations thereof; and an alien admitted under the Act of May 19, 1921, as amended, who was charged under that Act to the proper quota at the time of his admission or subsequently and who remained so charged.

(h) Citizens of the Trust Territory of the Pacific Islands who entered Guam prior to December 24, 1952. An alien who establishes that while a citizen of the Trust Territory of the Pacific Islands he entered Guam prior to December 24, 1952, by records, such as Service records subsequent to June 15, 1952, records of the Guamanian Immigration Service, records of the Navy or Air Force, or records of contractors of those agencies, and was residing in Guam on December 24, 1952.

(i) Aliens admitted to Guam. An alien who establishes that he was admitted to Guam prior to December 24, 1952, by records such as Service records subsequent to June 15, 1952, records of the Guamanian Immigration Service, records of the Navy or Air Force, or records of contractors of those agencies; that he was not excludable under the Act of February 5, 1917, as amended; and that he continued to reside in Guam until December 24, 1952, and thereafter was not admitted or readmitted into Guam as a nonimmigrant, provided that the provisions of this paragraph shall not apply to an alien who was exempted from the contract laborer provisions of section 3 of the Immigration Act of February 5, 1917, as amended, through the exercise, expressly or impliedly, of the 4th or 9th provisos to section 3 of that act.

(j) Erroneous admission as United States citizens or as children of citizens.

(1)(i) An alien for whom there exists a record of admission prior to September 11, 1957, as a United States citizen who establishes that at the time of such admission he was the child of a United States citizen parent; he was erroneously issued a United States passport or included in the United States passport of his citizen parent accompanying him or to whom he was destined; no fraud or misrepresentation was practiced by him in the issuance of the passport or in gaining admission; he was otherwise admissible at the time of entry except for failure to meet visa or passport requirements; and he has maintained a residence in the United States since the date of admission, or (ii) an alien who meets all of the foregoing requirements except that if he were, in fact, a citizen of the United States a passport would not have been required, or it had been individually waived, and was erroneously admitted as a United States citizen by a Service officer. For the purposes of all of the foregoing, the terms child and parent shall be defined as in section 101(b) of the Immigration and Nationality Act, as amended.

(2) An alien admitted to the United States before July 1, 1948, in possession of a section 4(a) 1924 Act nonquota immigration visa issued in accordance with State Department regulations, including a child of a United States citizen after he reached the age of 21, in the absence of fraud or misrepresentation; a member of a naturalized person's family who was admitted to the United States as a United States citizen or as a section 4(a) 1924 Act nonquota immigrant on the basis of that naturalization, unless he knowingly participated in the unlawful naturalization of the parent or spouse rendered void by cancellation, or knew at any time prior to his admission to the United States of the cancellation; and a member of a naturalized person's family who knew at any time prior to his admission to the United States of the cancellation of the naturalization of his parent or spouse but was admitted to the United States as a United States citizen pursuant to a State Department or Service determination based upon a then prevailing administrative view, provided the State Department or Service knew of the cancellation.

HISTORY:

[23 FR 9119, Nov. 26, 1958, as amended at 24 FR 2583, Apr. 3, 1959; 24 FR 6476, Aug. 12, 1959; 25 FR 581, Jan. 23, 1960.; 31 FR 535, Jan. 15, 1966.; 68 FR 9824, 9832, Feb. 28, 2003]

§ 1101.2 Presumption of lawful admission; entry under erroneous name or other errors.

An alien who entered the United States as either an immigrant or nonimmigrant under any of the following circumstances shall be regarded as having been lawfully admitted in such status, except as otherwise provided in this part: An alien otherwise admissible whose entry was made and recorded under other than his full true and correct name or whose entry record contains errors in recording sex, names of relatives, or names of foreign places of birth or residence, provided that he establishes by clear, unequivocal, and convincing evidence that the record of the claimed admission relates to him, and, if entry occurred on or after May 22, 1918, if under other than his full, true and correct name that he also establishes that the name was not adopted for the purpose of concealing his identity when obtaining a passport or visa, or for the purpose of using the passport or visa of another person or otherwise evading any provision of the immigration laws, and that the name used at the time of entry was one by which he had been known for a sufficient length of time prior to making application for a passport or visa to have permitted the issuing authority or authorities to have made any necessary investigation concerning him or that his true identity was known to such officials.

HISTORY:

[32 FR 9622, July 4, 1967; 68 FR 9824, 9832, Feb. 28, 2003]

§ 1101.3 Creation of record of lawful permanent resident status for person born under diplomatic status in the United States.

(a) **Person born to foreign diplomat.**

(1) Status of person. A person born in the United States to a foreign diplomatic officer accredited to the United States, as a matter of international law, is not subject to the jurisdiction of the United States. That person is not a United States citizen under the Fourteenth Amendment to the Constitution. Such a person may be considered a lawful permanent resident at birth.

(2) Definition of foreign diplomatic officer. Foreign diplomatic officer means a person listed in the State Department Diplomatic List, also known as the Blue List. It includes ambassadors, ministers, charge1s d'affaires, counselors, secretaries and attache1s of embassies and legations as well as members of the Delegation of the Commission of the European Communities. The term also includes individuals with comparable diplomatic status and immunities who are accredited to the United Nations or to the Organization of American States, and other individuals who are also accorded comparable diplomatic status.

(b) Child born subject to the jurisdiction of the United States. A child born in the United States is born subject to the jurisdiction of the United States and is a United States citizen if the parent is not a "foreign diplomatic officer" as defined in paragraph (a)(2) of this section. This includes, for example, a child born in the United States to one of the following foreign government officials or employees:

(1) Employees of foreign diplomatic missions whose names appear in the State Department list entitled "Employees of Diplomatic Missions Not Printed in the Diplomatic List," also known as the White List; employees of foreign diplomatic missions accredited to the United Nations or the Organization of American States; or foreign diplomats accredited to other foreign states. The majority of these individuals enjoy certain diplomatic immunities, but they are not "foreign diplomatic officers" as defined in paragraph (a)(2) of this section. The immunities, if any, of their family members are derived from the status of the employees or diplomats.

(2) Foreign government employees with limited or no diplomatic immunity such as consular officials named on the State Department list entitled "Foreign Consular Officers in the United States" and their staffs.

(c) Voluntary registration as lawful permanent resident of person born to foreign diplomat. Since a person born in the United States to a foreign diplomatic officer is not subject to the jurisdiction of the United States, his/her registration as a lawful permanent resident of the United States is voluntary. The provisions of section 262 of the Act do not apply to such a person unless and until that person ceases to have the rights, privileges, exemptions, or immunities which may be claimed by a foreign diplomatic officer.

(d) Retention of lawful permanent residence. To be eligible for lawful permanent resident status under paragraph (a) of this section, an alien must establish that he/she has not abandoned his/her residence in the United States. One of the tests for retention of lawful permanent resident status is continuous residence, not continuous physical presence, in the United States. Such a person will not be considered to have abandoned his/her residence in the United States solely by having been admitted to the United States in a nonimmigrant classification under paragraph (15)(A) or (15)(G) of section 101(a) of the Act after a temporary stay in a foreign country or countries on one or several occasions.

HISTORY:

[47 FR 940, Jan. 8, 1982.; 68 FR 9824, 9832, Feb. 28, 2003]

AUTHORITY:

(Secs. 101(a)(20), 103, 262, 264 of the Immigration and Nationality Act, as amended; 8 U.S.C. 1101(a)(20), 1103, 1302, 1304)

§ 1101.4 Registration procedure.

The procedure for an application for creation of a record of lawful permanent residence and a Permanent Resident Card, Form I-551, for a person eligible for presumption of lawful admission for permanent residence under § 1101.1 or § 1101.2 or for lawful permanent residence as a person born in the United States to a foreign diplomatic officer under § 1101.3 is described in § 264.2 of 8 CFR chapter I.

HISTORY:

[47 FR 941, Jan. 8, 1982.; 63 FR 70313, 70315, Dec. 21, 1998; 68 FR 9824, 9832, 9846, Feb. 28, 2003; 68 FR 10349, 10351, Mar. 5, 2003]

AUTHORITY:

(Secs. 101(a)(20), 103, 262, 264 of the Immigration and Nationality Act, as amended; 8 U.S.C. 1101(a)(20), 1103, 1302, 1304)

§ 1101.5 Special immigrant status for certain G-4 nonimmigrants.

(a) Application. An application for adjustment to special immigrant status under section 101(a)(27)(I) of the INA shall be made on Form I-485. The application date of the I-485 shall be the date of acceptance by the Service as properly filed. If the application date is other than the fee receipt date it must be noted and initialed by a Service officer. The date of application for adjustment of status is the closing date for computing the residence and physical presence requirement. The applicant must have complied with all requirements as of the date of application.

(b) Documentation. All documents must be submitted in accordance with § 103.2(b) of this chapter. The application shall be accompanied by documentary evidence establishing the aggregate residence and physical presence required. Documentary evidence may include official employment verification, records of official or personnel transactions or recordings of events occurring during the period of claimed residence and physical presence. Affidavits of credible witnesses may also be accepted. Persons unable to furnish evidence in their own names may furnish evidence in the names of parents or other persons with whom they have been living, if affidavits of the parents or other persons are submitted attesting to the claimed residence and physical presence. The claimed family relationship to the principle G-4 international organization officer or employee must be substantiated by the submission of verifiable civil documents.

(c) Residence and physical presence requirements. All applicants applying under sections 101(a)(27)(I) (i), (ii), and (iii) of the INA must have resided and been physically present in the United States for a designated period of time.

For purposes of this section only, an absence from the United States to conduct official business on behalf of the employing organization, or approved customary leave shall not be subtracted from the aggregated period of required residence or physical presence for the current or former G-4 officer or employee or the accompanying spouse and unmarried sons or daughters of such officer or employee, provided residence in the United States is maintained during such absences, and the duty station of the principle G-4 nonimmigrant continues to be in the United States. Absence from the United States by the G-4 spouse or unmarried son or daughter without the principle G-4 shall not be subtracted from the aggregate period of residence and physical presence if on customary leave as recognized by the international organization employer. Absence by the unmarried son or daughter while enrolled in a school outside the United States will not be counted toward the physical presence requirement.

(d) Maintenance of nonimmigrant status. Section 101(a)(27)(I) (i), and (ii) requires the applicant to accrue the required period of residence and physical presence in the United States while maintaining status as a G-4 or N nonimmigrant. Section 101(a)(27)(I)(iii) requires such time accrued only in G-4 nonimmigrant status.

Maintaining G-4 status for this purpose is defined as maintaining qualified employment with a "G" international organization or maintaining the qualifying family relationship with the G-4 international organization officer or employee. Maintaining status as an N nonimmigrant for this purpose requires the qualifying family relationship to remain in effect. Unauthorized employment will not remove an otherwise eligible alien from G-4 status for residence and physical presence requirements, provided the qualifying G-4 status is maintained.

HISTORY:

[54 FR 5927, Feb. 7, 1989; 68 FR 9824, 9832, Feb. 28, 2003]

PART 1103

APPEALS, RECORDS, AND FEES

Rule

AUTHORITY NOTE APPLICABLE TO ENTIRE PART:

AUTHORITY:

8 U.S.C. 1101, 1103, 1304, 1356; 31 U.S.C. 9701; 28 U.S.C. 509, 510.

§ 1103.3 Denials, appeals, and precedent decisions.

(a) DHS regulations. The regulations pertaining to denials, appeals, and precedent decisions of the Department of Homeland Security are contained in 8 CFR Chapter I.

(b) [Removed and Reserved]

(c) DHS precedent decisions. The Secretary of Homeland Security, or specific officials of the Department of Homeland Security designated by the Secretary with the concurrence of the Attorney General, may file with the Attorney General decisions relating to the administration of the immigration laws of the United States for publication as precedent in future proceedings, and upon approval of the Attorney General as to the lawfulness of such decision, the Director of the Executive Office for Immigration Review shall cause such decisions to be published in the same manner as decisions of the Board and the Attorney General.

HISTORY:

[31 FR 3062, Feb. 24, 1966, as amended at 37 FR 927, Jan. 21, 1972.; 48 FR 36441, Aug. 11, 1983; 49 FR 7355, Feb. 29, 1984; 52 FR 16192, May 1, 1987; 54 FR 29881, July 17, 1989; 55 FR 20769, 20775, May 21, 1990; 55 FR 23345, June 7, 1990; 57 FR 11573, Apr. 6, 1992, as confirmed at 1899, Jan. 13, 1994; 68 FR 9824, 9833, 9846, Feb. 28, 2003; 68 FR 10349, 10352, Mar. 5, 2003; 81 FR 92346, 92366, Dec. 19, 2016]

§ 1103.4 Certifications.

(a) **Certification of other than special agricultural worker and legalization cases —**

(1) General. The Commissioner or the Commissioner's delegate may direct that any case or class of cases be certified to another Service official for decision. In addition, regional commissioners, regional service center directors, district directors, officers in charge in districts 33 (Bangkok, Thailand), 35 (Mexico City, Mexico), and 37 (Rome, Italy), and the Director, National Fines Office, may certify their decisions to the appropriate appellate authority (as designated in this chapter) when the case involves an unusually complex or novel issue of law or fact.

(2) Notice to affected party. When a case is certified to a Service officer, the official certifying the case shall notify the affected party using a Notice of Certification (Form I-290C). The affected party may submit a brief to the officer to whom the case is certified within 30 days after service of the notice. If the affected party does not wish to submit a brief, the affected party may waive the 30-day period.

(3) Favorable action. The Service officer to whom a case is certified may suspend the 30-day period for submission of a brief if that officer takes action favorable to the affected party.

(4) Initial decision. A case within the appellate jurisdiction of the Associate Commissioner, Examinations, or for which there is no appeal procedure may be certified only after an initial decision is made.

(5) Certification to AAU. A case described in paragraph (a)(4) of this section may be certified to the AAU.

(6) Appeal to Board. In a case within the Board's appellate jurisdiction, an unfavorable decision of the Service official to whom the case is certified (whether made initially or upon review) is the decision which may be appealed to the Board under § 1003.1(b) of this chapter.

(7) Other applicable provisions. The provisions of § 1103.3(a)(2)(x) of this part also apply to decisions on certified cases. The provisions of § 1103.3(b) of this part also apply to requests for oral argument regarding certified cases considered by the AAU.

(b) Certification of denials of special agricultural worker and legalization applications. The Regional Processing Facility director or the district director may, in accordance with paragraph (a) of this section, certify a decision to the Associate Commissioner, Examinations (Administrative Appeals Unit) (the appellate authority designated in § 1103.1(f)(2)) of this part, when the case involves an unusually complex or novel question of law or fact.

HISTORY:

[52 FR 661, Jan. 8, 1987, as amended at 53 FR 43985, Oct. 31, 1988; 55 FR 20770, May 21, 1990; 68 FR 9824, 9833, 9846, Feb. 28, 2003; 68 FR 10349, 10352, Mar. 5, 2003]

§ 1103.7 Fees.

(a) Remittances

(1) In general. Fees shall be submitted in connection with any formal appeal, motion, or application prescribed in this chapter in the amount prescribed by law or regulation. Payment of any fee under this section does not constitute filing of the appeal, motion, or application with the Board of Immigration Appeals or with the immigration court.

(2) Board of Immigration Appeals. The fee for filing an appeal or a motion with the Board of Immigration Appeals shall be paid pursuant to the provisions of 8 CFR 1003.8 when a fee is required.

(3) All other fees payable in connection with immigration proceedings. Except as provided in 8 CFR 1003.8, the Executive Office for Immigration Review does not accept the payment of any fee relating to Executive Office for Immigration Review proceedings. Instead, such fees, when required, shall be paid to, and accepted by, an office of the Department of Homeland Security authorized to accept fees, as provided in 8 CFR 103.7(a)(1). The Department of Homeland Security shall return to the payer, at the time of payment, a receipt for any fee paid, and shall also return to the payer any documents, submitted with the fee, relating to any immigration proceeding. The fee receipt and the application or motion shall then be submitted to the Executive Office for Immigration Review. If the payer has paid any required fee but has not received the fee receipt from the Department of Homeland Security by the deadline set by the immigration judge, the payer must instead provide to the immigration court a copy of

proof of the payment to the Department of Homeland Security with the filing. The payer must then submit a copy of the fee receipt by a new deadline set by the immigration judge. If the immigration judge does not set a deadline, the alien must submit the fee receipt no later than 45 days after the date of filing of the application. Remittances to the Department of Homeland Security for applications, motions, or forms filed in connection with immigration proceedings shall be payable subject to the provisions of 8 CFR 103.7(a)(2).

(b) Amounts of fees —

(1) Appeals. For filing an appeal to the Board of Immigration Appeals, when a fee is required pursuant to 8 CFR 1003.8, as follows:

Form EOIR–26. For filing an appeal from a decision of an immigration judge—$975.

Form EOIR–29. For filing an appeal from a decision of an officer of the Department of Homeland Security—$705.

Form EOIR–45. For filing an appeal from a decision of an adjudicating official in a practitioner disciplinary case—$675.

(2) Motions. For filing a motion to reopen or a motion to reconsider, when a fee is required pursuant to 8 CFR 1003.8 or 1003.24, as follows:

Motion to reopen or motion to reconsider before the immigration court—$145.

Motion to reopen or motion to reconsider before the Board of Immigration Appeals—$895.

(3) Multiple parties. When an appeal or motion is filed on behalf of two or more aliens and the aliens are covered by one decision, only one fee is required.

(4) Applications for Relief —

(i) Forms published by the Executive Office for Immigration Review. Fees for applications for relief shall be paid in accordance with 8 CFR 1003.8(b) and 1003.24(c) as follows:

Form EOIR–40. Application for Suspension of Deportation—$305.

Form EOIR–42A. Application for Cancellation of Removal for Certain Permanent Residents—$305.

Form EOIR–42B. Application for Cancellation of Removal and Adjustment of Status for Certain Nonpermanent Residents—$360.

(ii) Forms published by the Department of Homeland Security. The fees for applications published by the Department of Homeland Security and used in immigration proceedings are governed by 8 CFR 103.7 and 8 CFR part 106. Consistent with 8 CFR 106.2, no fee shall apply to a Form I–589 filed with an immigration judge for the sole purpose of seeking withholding of removal under section 241(b)(3) of the Act or protection under the Convention Against Torture regulations.

(c) Fee waivers. For provisions relating to the authority of the Board or the immigration judges to waive any of the fees prescribed in paragraph (b) of this section, see 8 CFR 1003.8 and 1003.24. No waiver may be granted with respect to the fee prescribed for a Department of Homeland Security form or action that is identified as non-waivable in regulations of the Department of Homeland Security.

(d) Requests for records under the Freedom of Information Act. Fees for production or disclosure of records under 5 U.S.C. 552 may be waived or reduced in accordance with 28 CFR 16.10.

HISTORY:

[38 FR 35296, Dec. 27, 1973; 51 FR 8183, 39994, 1986; 52 FR 3, 2939, 16193, 19719, 1987.; 53 FR 43985, 1988; 54 FR 13, 29882, 48231, 13515, 47348, 48577, 51870, 1989.; 55 FR 12629, 20775, 29342, 1990; 56 FR 624, 21919, 22822, 31060, 12649, 23496, 23498, 32501, 49672, 50480, 1991.; 57 FR 39626, 5227, 6182, 34507, 1992; 57 FR 6460, as confirmed at 60 FR 66062, 66067, Dec. 21, 1995; 57 FR 11573, Apr. 16, 1992, as confirmed at 59 FR 1899, Jan. 13, 1994; 58 FR 30699, May 27, 1993, as confirmed at 60 FR 9774, Feb. 22, 1995; 58 FR 31148, June 1, 1993; 58 FR 58937, Nov. 5, 1993; 58 FR 69210, Dec. 30, 1993, as confirmed at 63 FR 1331, 1334, Jan. 9, 1998; 59 FR 26590, May 23, 1994; 59 FR 30518, June 14, 1994; 59 FR 51095, Oct. 7, 1994; 60 FR 21974, May 4, 1995; 60 FR 34090, June 30, 1995; 60 FR 37328, July 20, 1995; 60 FR 40068, Aug. 7, 1995; 60 FR 50386, 50388, Sept. 29, 1995, as confirmed at 61 FR 53830, 53831, Oct. 16, 1996; 61 FR 18900, 18909, Apr. 29, 1996; 61 FR 28003, 28013, June 4, 1996; 61 FR 35597, 35598, July 8, 1996; 61 FR 46373, 46374, Sept. 3, 1996, as corrected at 61 FR 47550, Sept. 9, 1996; 61 FR 53303, 53304, Oct. 11, 1996; 62 FR 10312, 10336, Mar. 6, 1997; 62 FR 39417, 39423, July 23, 1997; 62 FR 45148, 45149, Aug. 26, 1997; 63 FR 12979, 12985, 12986, Mar. 17, 1998; 63 FR 30105, 30108, June 3, 1998; 63 FR 43604, 43609, 43610, Aug. 14, 1998; 63 FR 63593, 63595, Nov. 16, 1998; 63 FR 65657, 65659, Nov. 30, 1998; 64 FR 27856, 27875, May 21, 1999; 64 FR 69883, 69888, Dec. 15, 1999; 65 FR 10678, 10684, Feb. 29, 2000; 65 FR 43528, 43531, July 13, 2000, withdrawn at 67 FR 61474, Oct. 1, 2002; 65 FR 67616, 67617, Nov. 13, 2000; 66 FR 29661, 29672, 29682, 29685, June 1, 2001, as confirmed at 67 FR 38341, 38350, June 4, 2002; 66 FR 49514, Sept. 28, 2001; 66 FR 65811, 65816, Dec. 21, 2001; 67 FR 4784, 4794, Jan. 31, 2002; 67 FR 60107, 60111, Sept. 25, 2002; 67 FR 71443, 71447, Dec. 2, 2002; 67 FR 76256, 76270, Dec. 11, 2002; 68 FR 3798, 3800, Jan. 24, 2003; 68 FR 9824, 9833, 9846, Feb. 28, 2003; 68 FR 10349, 10352, Mar. 5, 2003; 69 FR 44903, 44907, July 28, 2004; 85 FR 81698, 81750, Dec. 16, 2020; 85 FR 82750, 82793, Dec. 18, 2020; 86 FR 70708, 70723, Dec. 13, 2021]

PART 1204

IMMIGRANT PETITIONS

AUTHORITY NOTE APPLICABLE TO ENTIRE PART:

AUTHORITY:

8 U.S.C. 1101, 1103, 1151, 1153, 1154, 1182, 1186a, 1255, 1641; 8 CFR part 2.

§ 1204.1 Single level of appellate review.

The decision of the Board of Immigration Appeals concerning the denial of a relative visa petition under 8 CFR chapter I, part 204 because the petitioner failed to establish eligibility for the bona fide marriage exemption contained in that part will constitute the single level of appellate review established by statute.

HISTORY:

[68 FR 9824, 9833, Feb. 28, 2003]

PART 1205
REVOCATION OF APPROVAL OF PETITIONS

AUTHORITY NOTE APPLICABLE TO ENTIRE PART:

AUTHORITY:
8 U.S.C. 1101, 1103, 1151, 1153, 1154, 1155, 1182, and 1186a

§ 1205.1 Automatic revocation.

(a) Reasons for automatic revocation. The approval of a petition or self-petition made under section 204 of the Act and in accordance with part 204 of 8 CFR chapter I is revoked as of the date of approval:

(1) If the Secretary of State shall terminate the registration of the beneficiary pursuant to the provisions of section 203(e) of the Act before October 1, 1991, or section 203(g) of the Act on or after October 1, 1994;

(2) If the filing fee and associated service charge are not paid within 14 days of the notification to the remitter that his or her check or other financial instrument used to pay the filing fee has been returned as not payable; or

(3) If any of the following circumstances occur before the beneficiary's or self-petitioner's journey to the United States commences or, if the beneficiary or self-petitioner is an applicant for adjustment of status to that of a permanent resident, before the decision on his or her adjustment application becomes final:

(i) Immediate relative and family-sponsored petitions, other than Amerasian petitions.

(A) Upon written notice of withdrawal filed by the petitioner or self-petitioner with any officer of the Service who is authorized to grant or deny petitions.

(B) Upon the death of the beneficiary or the self-petitioner.

(C) Upon the death of the petitioner, except as provided for in 8 CFR 205.1(a)(3)(i)(C).

(D) Upon the legal termination of the marriage when a citizen or lawful permanent resident of the United States has petitioned to accord his or her spouse immediate relative or family-sponsored preference immigrant classification under section 201(b) or section 203(a)(2) of the Act. The approval of a spousal self-petition based on the relationship to an abusive citizen or lawful permanent resident of the United States filed under section 204(a)(1)(A)(iii) or 204(a)(1)(B)(ii) of the Act, however, will not be revoked solely because of the termination of the marriage to the abuser.

(E) Upon the remarriage of the spouse of an abusive citizen or lawful permanent resident of the United States when the spouse has self-petitioned under section 204(a)(1)(A)(iii) or 204(a)(1)(B)(ii) of the Act for immediate relative classification under section 201(b) of the Act or for preference classification under section 203(a)(2) of the Act.

(F) Upon a child reaching the age of 21, when he or she has been accorded immediate relative status under section 201(b) of the Act. A petition filed on behalf of a child under section 204(a)(1)(A)(i) of the Act or a self-petition filed by a child of an abusive United States citizen under section 204(a)(1)(A)(iv) of the Act, however, will remain valid for the duration of the relationship to accord preference status under section 203(a)(1) of the Act if the beneficiary remains unmarried, or to accord preference status under section 203(a)(3) of the Act if he or she marries.

(G) Upon the marriage of a child, when he or she has been accorded immediate relative status under section 201(b) of the Act. A petition filed on behalf of the child under section 204(a)(1)(A)(i) of the Act or a self-petition filed by a child of an abusive United States citizen under section 204(a)(1)(A)(iv) of the Act, however, will remain valid for the duration of the relationship to accord preference status under section 203(a)(3) of the Act if he or she marries.

(H) Upon the marriage of a person accorded preference status as a son or daughter of a United States citizen under section 203(a)(1) of the Act. A petition filed on behalf of the son or daughter, however, will remain valid for the duration of the relationship to accord preference status under section 203(a)(3) of the Act.

(I) Upon the marriage of a person accorded status as a son or daughter of a lawful permanent resident alien under section 203(a)(2) of the Act.

(J) Upon legal termination of the petitioner's status as an alien admitted for lawful permanent residence in the United States unless the petitioner became a United States citizen. The provisions of 8 CFR 204.2(i)(3) shall apply if the petitioner became a United States citizen.

(ii) Petition for Pub. L. 97-359 Amerasian.

(A) Upon formal notice of withdrawal filed by the petitioner with the officer who approved the petition.

(B) Upon the death of the beneficiary.

(C) Upon the death or bankruptcy of the sponsor who executed Form I-361, Affidavit of Financial Support and Intent to Petition for Legal Custody for Pub. L. 97-359 Amerasian. In that event, a new petition may be filed in the beneficiary's behalf with the documentary evidence relating to sponsorship and, in the case of a beneficiary under 18 years of age, placement. If the new petition is approved, it will be given the priority date of the previously approved petition.

(D) Upon the death or substitution of the petitioner if other than the beneficiary or sponsor. However, if the petitioner dies or no longer desires or is able to proceed with the petition, and another person 18 years of age or older, an emancipated minor, or a corporation incorporated in the United States desires to be substituted for the deceased or original petitioner, a written request may be submitted to the Service or American consular office where the petition is located to reinstate the petition and restore the original priority date.

(E) Upon the beneficiary's reaching the age of 21 when the beneficiary has been accorded classification under section 201(b) of the Act. Provided that all requirements of section 204(f) of the Act continue to be met, however, the petition is to be considered valid for purposes of according the beneficiary preference classification under section 203(a)(1) of the Act if the beneficiary remains unmarried or under section 203(a)(3) if the beneficiary marries.

(F) Upon the beneficiary's marriage when the beneficiary has been accorded classification under section 201(b) or section 203(a)(1) of the Act. Provided that all requirements of section 204(f) of the Act continue to be met, however, the petition is to be considered valid for purposes of according the beneficiary preference classification under section 203(a)(3) of the Act.

(iii) Petitions under section 203(b), other than special immigrant juvenile petitions.

(A) Upon invalidation pursuant to 20 CFR Part 656 of the labor certification in support of the petition.

(B) Upon the death of the petitioner or beneficiary.

(C) Upon written notice of withdrawal filed by the petitioner, in employment-based preference cases, with any officer of the Service who is authorized to grant or deny petitions.

(D) Upon termination of the employer's business in an employment-based preference case under section 203(b)(1)(B), 203(b)(1)(C), 203(b)(2), or 203(b)(3) of the Act.

(iv) Special immigrant juvenile petitions. Unless the beneficiary met all of the eligibility requirements as of November 29, 1990, and the petition requirements as of November 29, 1990, and the petition for classification as a special immigrant juvenile was filed before June 1, 1994, or unless the change in circumstances resulted from the beneficiary's adoption or placement in a guardianship situation:

(A) Upon the beneficiary reaching the age of 21;

(B) Upon the marriage of the beneficiary;

(C) Upon the termination of the beneficiary's dependency upon the juvenile court;

(D) Upon the termination of the beneficiary's eligibility for long-term foster care; or

(E) Upon the determination in administrative or judicial proceedings that it is in the beneficiary's best interest to be returned to the country of nationality or last habitual residence of the beneficiary or of his or her parent or parents.

(b) Notice. When it shall appear to the director that the approval of a petition has been automatically revoked, he or she shall cause a notice of such revocation to be sent promptly to the consular office having jurisdiction over the visa application and a copy of such notice to be mailed to the petitioner's last known address.

HISTORY:

[41 FR 55849, Dec. 23, 1976, as amended at 48 FR 19156, Apr. 28, 1983; 49 FR 29567, July 23, 1984; 49 FR 30679, Aug. 1, 1984; 53 FR 30017, Aug. 10, 1988; 58 FR 42850, Aug. 12, 1993; 61 FR 13061, 13077, March 26, 1996; 68 FR 9824, 9833, Feb. 28, 2003; 68 FR 10349, 10352, Mar. 5, 2003; 71 FR 35732, 35757, June 21, 2006]

§ 1205.2 Revocation on notice.

(a) General. Any Service officer authorized to approve a petition under section 204 of the Act may revoke the approval of that petition upon notice to the petitioner on any ground other than those specified in § 1205.1 when the necessity for the revocation comes to the attention of this Service.

(b) Notice of intent. Revocation of the approval of a petition of self-petition under paragraph (a) of this section will be made only on notice to the petitioner or self-petitioner. The petitioner or self-petitioner must be given the opportunity to offer evidence in support of the petition or self-petition and in opposition to the grounds alleged for revocation of the approval.

(c) Notification of revocation. If, upon reconsideration, the approval previously granted is revoked, the director shall provide the petitioner or the self-petitioner with a written notification of the decision that explains the specific reasons for the revocation. The director shall notify the consular officer having jurisdiction over the visa application, if applicable, of the revocation of an approval.

(d) Appeals. The petitioner or self-petitioner may appeal the decision to revoke the approval within 15 days after the service of notice of the revocation. The appeal must be filed as provided in part 1003 of this chapter, unless the Associate Commissioner for Examinations exercises appellate jurisdiction over the revocation under part 103 of 8 CFR chapter I. Appeals filed with the Associate Commissioner for Examinations must meet the requirements of part 103 of 8 CFR chapter I.

HISTORY:

[48 FR 19156, Apr. 28, 1983; 58 FR 42851, Aug. 12, 1993; 61 FR 13061, 13078, March 26, 1996; 68 FR 9824, 9833, 9846, Feb. 28, 2003; 68 FR 10349, 10352, Mar. 5, 2003]

PART 1207

ADMISSION OF REFUGEES

Rule

AUTHORITY NOTE APPLICABLE TO ENTIRE PART:

AUTHORITY:

8 U.S.C. 1101, 1103, 1151, 1157, 1159, 1182; 8 CFR part 2.

§ 1207.3 Waivers of inadmissibility.

(a) Authority. Section 207(c)(3) of the Act sets forth grounds of inadmissibility under section 212(a) of the Act which are not applicable and those which may be waived in the case of an otherwise qualified refugee and the conditions under which such waivers may be approved. Officers in charge of overseas offices are delegated authority to initiate the necessary investigations to establish the facts in each waiver application pending before them and to approve or deny such waivers.

(b) Filing requirements. The applicant for a waiver must submit Form I-602, Application by Refugee for Waiver of Grounds of Inadmissibility, with the Service office processing his or her case. The burden is on the applicant to show that the waiver should be granted based upon humanitarian grounds, family unity, or the public interest. The applicant shall be notified in writing of the decision, including the reasons for denial, if the application is denied. There is no appeal from such decision.

HISTORY:

[46 FR 45118, Sept. 10, 1981; 62 FR 10312, 10336, March 6, 1997; 68 FR 9824; 9833, Feb. 28, 2003]

PART 1208

PROCEDURES FOR ASYLUM AND WITHHOLDING OF REMOVAL

Subpart A. Asylum and Withholding of Removal

AUTHORITY NOTE APPLICABLE TO ENTIRE PART:

AUTHORITY:

8 U.S.C. 1101, 1103, 1158, 1226, 1252, 1282; Title VII of Pub. L. 110-229; Pub. L. 115-218.

Subpart A

Asylum and Withholding of Removal

§ 1208.1 General.

(a) **Applicability.**

(1) In general. Unless otherwise provided in this chapter V, this subpart A shall apply to all applications for asylum under section 208 of the Act or for withholding of deportation or withholding of removal under section 241(b)(3) of the Act, or under the Convention Against Torture, whether before an asylum officer or an immigration judge, regardless of the date of filing. For purposes of this chapter V, withholding of removal shall also mean withholding of deportation under section 243(h) of the Act, as it appeared prior to April 1, 1997, except as provided in § 1208.16(d). Such applications are hereinafter referred to as "asylum applications." The provisions of this part shall not affect the finality or validity of any decision made by a district director, an immigration judge, or the Board of Immigration Appeals in any such case prior to April 1, 1997. No asylum application that was filed with a district director, asylum officer, or immigration judge prior to April 1, 1997, may be reopened or otherwise reconsidered under the provisions of this part except by motion granted in the exercise of discretion by the Board of Immigration Appeals, an immigration judge, or an asylum officer for proper cause shown. Motions to reopen or reconsider must meet the requirements of sections 240(c)(6) and (c)(7) of the Act, and 8 CFR parts 1003 and 1103, where applicable.

(2) Commonwealth of the Northern Mariana Islands. The provisions of this subpart A shall not apply prior to January 1, 2030, to an alien physically present in or arriving in the Commonwealth of the Northern Mariana Islands seeking to apply for asylum. No application for asylum may be filed prior to January 1, 2030, pursuant to section 208 of the Act by an alien physically present in or arriving in the Commonwealth of the Northern Mariana Islands. Effective on the transition program effective date, the provisions of this subpart A shall apply to aliens physically present in or arriving in the CNMI with respect to withholding of removal under section 241(b)(3) of the Act and withholding and deferral of removal under the Convention Against Torture.

(b) Training of asylum officers. The Director of International Affairs shall ensure that asylum officers receive special training in international human rights law, nonadversarial interview techniques, and other relevant national and international refugee laws and principles. The Director of International Affairs shall also, in cooperation with the Department of State and other appropriate sources, compile and disseminate to asylum officers information concerning the persecution of persons in other countries on account of race, religion, nationality, membership in a particular social group, or political opinion, torture of persons in other countries, and other information relevant to asylum determinations, and shall maintain a documentation center with information on human rights conditions.

(c) Particular social group. For purposes of adjudicating an application for asylum under section 208 of the Act or an application for withholding of removal under section 241(b)(3) of the Act, a particular social group is one that is based on an immutable or fundamental characteristic, is defined with particularity, and is recognized as socially distinct in the society at question. Such a particular social group cannot be defined exclusively by the alleged persecutory acts or harm and must also have existed independently of the alleged persecutory acts or harm that forms the basis of the claim. The Attorney General, in general, will not favorably adjudicate claims of aliens who claim a fear of persecution on account of membership in a particular social group consisting of or defined by the following circumstances: past or present criminal activity or association (including gang membership); presence in a country with generalized violence or a high crime rate; being the subject of a recruitment effort by criminal, terrorist, or persecutory groups; the targeting of the applicant for criminal activity for financial gain based on perceptions of wealth or affluence; interpersonal disputes of which governmental authorities were unaware or uninvolved; private criminal acts of which governmental authorities were unaware or uninvolved; past or present terrorist activity or association; past or present persecutory activity or association; or, status as an alien returning from the United States. This list is nonexhaustive, and the substance of the alleged particular social group, rather than the precise form of its delineation, shall be considered in determining whether the group falls within one of the categories on the list. No alien shall be found to be a refugee or have it decided that the alien's life or freedom would be threatened based on membership in a particular social group in any case unless that person first articulates on the record, or provides a basis on the record for determining, the definition and boundaries of the alleged particular social group. A failure to define, or provide a basis for defining, a formulation of a particular social group before an immigration judge shall waive any such claim for all purposes under the Act, including on appeal. Any waived claim on this basis shall not serve as the basis for any motion to reopen or reconsider for any reason, including a claim of ineffective assistance of counsel unless the alien complies with the procedural requirements for such a motion and demonstrates that counsel's failure to define, or provide a basis for defining, a formulation of a particular social group was both not a strategic choice and constituted egregious conduct.

(d) Political opinion. For purposes of adjudicating an application for asylum under section 208 of the Act or an application for withholding of removal under section 241(b)(3) of the Act, a political opinion is one expressed by or imputed to an applicant in which the applicant possesses an ideal or conviction in support of the furtherance of a discrete cause related to political control of a State or a unit thereof. The Attorney General, in general, will not favorably adjudicate claims of aliens who claim a fear of persecution on account of a political opinion defined solely by generalized disapproval of, disagreement with, or opposition to criminal, terrorist, gang, guerilla, or other non-state organizations absent expressive behavior in furtherance of a cause against such organizations related to efforts by the State to control such organizations or behavior that is antithetical to or otherwise opposes the ruling legal entity of the State or a legal sub-unit of the State. A person who has been forced to abort a pregnancy or to undergo involuntary sterilization, or who has been persecuted for failure or refusal to undergo such a procedure or for other resistance to a coercive population control program, shall be deemed to have been persecuted on account of political opinion, and a person who has a well-founded fear that he or she will be forced to undergo such a procedure or subject to persecution for such failure, refusal, or resistance shall be deemed to have a well-founded fear of persecution on account of political opinion.

(e) Persecution. For purposes of adjudicating an application for asylum under section 208 of the Act or an application for withholding of removal under section 241(b)(3) of the Act, persecution requires an intent to target a belief or characteristic, a severe level of harm, and the infliction of a severe level of harm by the government of a country or by persons or an organization that the government was unable or unwilling to control. For purposes of evaluating the severity of the level of harm, persecution is an extreme concept involving a severe level of harm that includes actions so severe that they constitute an exigent threat. Persecution does not encompass the generalized harm that arises out of civil, criminal, or military strife in a country, nor does it encompass all treatment that the

United States regards as unfair, offensive, unjust, or even unlawful or unconstitutional. It does not include intermittent harassment, including brief detentions; threats with no actual effort to carry out the threats, except that particularized threats of a severe harm of immediate and menacing nature made by an identified entity may constitute persecution; or, non-severe economic harm or property damage, though this list is nonexhaustive. The existence of government laws or policies that are unenforced or infrequently enforced do not, by themselves, constitute persecution, unless there is credible evidence that those laws or policies have been or would be applied to an applicant personally.

(f) Nexus. For purposes of adjudicating an application for asylum under section 208 of the Act or an application for withholding of removal under section 241(b)(3) of the Act, the Attorney General, in general, will not favorably adjudicate the claims of aliens who claim persecution based on the following list of nonexhaustive circumstances:

(1) Interpersonal animus or retribution;

(2) Interpersonal animus in which the alleged persecutor has not targeted, or manifested an animus against, other members of an alleged particular social group in addition to the member who has raised the claim at issue;

(3) Generalized disapproval of, disagreement with, or opposition to criminal, terrorist, gang, guerilla, or other non-state organizations absent expressive behavior in furtherance of a discrete cause against such organizations related to control of a State or expressive behavior that is antithetical to the State or a legal unit of the State;

(4) Resistance to recruitment or coercion by guerilla, criminal, gang, terrorist or other non-state organizations;

(5) The targeting of the applicant for criminal activity for financial gain based on wealth or affluence or perceptions of wealth or affluence;

(6) Criminal activity;

(7) Perceived, past or present, gang affiliation; or,

(8) Gender.

(g) Evidence based on stereotypes. For purposes of adjudicating an application for asylum under section 208 of the Act or an application for withholding of removal under section 241(b)(3) of the Act, evidence offered in support of such an application which promotes cultural stereotypes about a country, its inhabitants, or an alleged persecutor, including stereotypes based on race, religion, nationality, or gender, shall not be admissible in adjudicating that application, provided that nothing in this paragraph shall be construed as prohibiting the submission of evidence that an alleged persecutor holds stereotypical views of the applicant.

HISTORY:

[55 FR 30680, July 27, 1990; 59 FR 62297, Dec. 5, 1994; 62 FR 10312, 10337, Mar. 6, 1997; 64 FR 8478, 8487, Feb. 19, 1999; 68 FR 9824, 9834, 9846, Feb. 28, 2003; 68 FR 10349, 10352, Mar. 5, 2003; 74 FR 55726, 55741, Oct. 28, 2009; 85 FR 23902, 23904, Apr. 30, 2020; 85 FR 80274, 80394, Dec. 11, 2020]

§ 1208.2 Jurisdiction.

(a) U.S. Citizenship and Immigration Services (USCIS).

(1) Except as provided in paragraph (b) or (c) of this section, USCIS shall have initial jurisdiction over:

(i) An asylum application filed by an alien physically present in the United States or seeking admission at a port-of-entry; and

(ii) Interviews provided in accordance with section 235(b)(1)(B)(ii) of the Act to further consider the application for asylum of an alien, other than a stowaway, found to have a credible fear of persecution or torture in accordance with 8 CFR 208.30(f) and retained by USCIS, or referred to USCIS by an immigration judge pursuant to §§ 1003.42 of this chapter and 1208.30, after the immigration judge has vacated a negative credible fear determination. Interviews to further consider applications for asylum under this paragraph (a)(1)(ii) are governed by the procedures provided for under 8 CFR 208.9. Further consideration of an asylum application filed by a stowaway who has received a positive credible fear determination will be under the jurisdiction of an immigration judge pursuant to paragraph (c) of this section.

(2) USCIS shall also have initial jurisdiction over credible fear determinations under 8 CFR 208.30 and reasonable fear determinations under 8 CFR 208.31.

(b) Jurisdiction of Immigration Court in general. Immigration judges shall have exclusive jurisdiction over asylum applications filed by an alien who has been served a Form I-221, Order to Show Cause; Form I-122, Notice to Applicant for Admission Detained for a Hearing before an Immigration Judge; or Form I-862, Notice to Appear, after the charging document has been filed with the Immigration Court. Immigration judges shall also have jurisdiction over any asylum applications filed prior to April 1, 1997, by alien crewmembers who have remained in the United States longer than authorized, by applicants for admission under the Visa Waiver Pilot Program, and by aliens who have been admitted to the United States under the Visa Waiver Pilot Program. Immigration judges shall also have the authority to review reasonable fear determinations referred to the Immigration Court under § 1208.31, and credible fear determinations referred to the Immigration Court under § 1208.30.

(c) Certain aliens not entitled to proceedings under section 240 of the Act.

(1) Asylum applications and withholding of removal applications only. After Form I-863, Notice of Referral to Immigration Judge, has been filed with the Immigration Court, an immigration judge shall have exclusive jurisdiction over any asylum application filed on or after April 1, 1997, by:

(i) An alien crewmember who:

(A) Is an applicant for a landing permit;

(B) Has been refused permission to land under section 252 of the Act; or

(C) On or after April 1, 1997, was granted permission to land under section 252 of the Act, regardless of whether the alien has remained in the United States longer than authorized;

(ii) An alien stowaway who has been found to have a credible fear of persecution or torture pursuant to the procedures set forth in subpart B of this part;

(iii) An alien who is an applicant for admission pursuant to the Visa Waiver Program under section 217 of the Act, except that if such an alien is an applicant for admission to the Commonwealth of the Northern Mariana Islands, then he or she shall not be eligible for asylum prior to January 1, 2030;

(iv) An alien who was admitted to the United States pursuant to the Visa Waiver Program under section 217 of the Act and has remained longer than authorized or has otherwise violated his or her immigration status, except that if such an alien was admitted to the Commonwealth of the Northern Mariana Islands, then he or she shall not be eligible for asylum in the Commonwealth of the Northern Mariana Islands prior to January 1, 2030;

(v) An alien who has been ordered removed under § 235(c) of the Act, as described in § 235.8(a) of this chapter (applicable only in the event that the alien is referred for proceedings under this paragraph by the Regional Director pursuant to section 235.8(b)(2)(ii) of this chapter);

(vi) An alien who is an applicant for admission, or has been admitted, as an alien classified under section 101(a)(15)(S) of the Act (applicable only in the event that the alien is referred for proceedings under this paragraph by the district director);

(vii) An alien who is an applicant for admission to Guam or the Commonwealth of the Northern Mariana Islands pursuant to the Guam-CNMI Visa Waiver Program under section 212(l) of the Act, except that if such an alien is an applicant for admission to the Commonwealth of the Northern Mariana Islands, then he or she shall not be eligible for asylum prior to January 1, 2030; or

(viii) An alien who was admitted to Guam or the Commonwealth of the Northern Mariana Islands pursuant to the Guam-CNMI Visa Waiver Program under section 212(l) of the Act and has remained longer than authorized or has otherwise violated his or her immigration status, except that if such an alien was admitted to the Commonwealth of the Northern Mariana Islands, then he or she shall not be eligible for asylum in the Commonwealth of the Northern Mariana Islands prior to January 1, 2030.

(ix) [Removed and Reserved]

(2) Withholding of removal applications only. After Form I-863, Notice of Referral to Immigration Judge, has been filed with the Immigration Court, an immigration judge shall have exclusive jurisdiction over any application for withholding of removal filed by:

(i) An alien who is the subject of a reinstated removal order pursuant to section 241(a)(5) of the Act; or

(ii) An alien who has been issued an administrative removal order pursuant to section 238 of the Act as an alien convicted of committing an aggravated felony.

(3) Rules of procedure.

(i) General. Except as provided in this section, proceedings falling under the jurisdiction of the immigration judge pursuant to paragraph (c)(1) or (2) of this section shall be conducted in accordance with the same rules of procedure as proceedings conducted under 8 CFR part 1240, subpart A. The scope of review in proceedings conducted pursuant to paragraph (c)(1) of this section shall be limited to a determination of whether the alien is eligible for asylum or withholding or deferral of removal, and whether asylum shall be granted in the exercise of discretion. The scope of review in proceedings conducted pursuant to paragraph (c)(2) of this section shall be limited to a determination of whether the alien is eligible for withholding or deferral of removal. During such proceedings, all parties are prohibited from raising or considering any other issues, including but not limited to issues of admissibility, deportability, eligibility for waivers, and eligibility for any other form of relief.

(ii) Notice of hearing procedures and in-absentia decisions. The alien will be provided with notice of the time and place of the proceeding. The request for asylum and withholding of removal submitted by an alien who fails to appear for the hearing shall be denied. The denial of asylum and withholding of removal for failure to appear may be reopened only upon a motion filed with the immigration judge with jurisdiction over the case. Only one motion to reopen may be filed, and it must be filed within 90 days, unless the alien establishes that he or she did not receive notice of the hearing date or was in Federal or State custody on the date directed to appear. The motion must include documentary evidence, which demonstrates that:

(A) The alien did not receive the notice;

(B) The alien was in Federal or State custody and the failure to appear was through no fault of the alien; or

(C) "Exceptional circumstances," as defined in section 240(e)(1) of the Act, caused the failure to appear.

(iii) Relief. The filing of a motion to reopen shall not stay removal of the alien unless the immigration judge issues an order granting a stay pending disposition of the motion. An alien who fails to appear for a proceeding under this section shall not be eligible for relief under section 240A, 240B, 245, 248, or 249 of the Act for a period of 10 years after the date of the denial, unless the applicant can show exceptional circumstances resulted in his or her failure to appear.

HISTORY:

[55 FR 30680, July 27, 1990; 59 FR 62298, Dec. 5, 1994; 60 FR 34090, June 30, 1995; 60 FR 44260, 44264, Aug. 25, 1995; 62 FR 10312, 10337, Mar. 6, 1997, as corrected at 62 FR 15362, Apr. 1, 1997; 64 FR 8478, 8487, Feb. 19, 1999; 65 FR 76121, 76130, Dec. 6, 2000; 68 FR 9824, 9834, 9846, Feb. 28, 2003; 68 FR 10349, 10352, Mar. 5, 2003; 74 FR 55726, 55741, Oct. 28, 2009; 85 FR 23902, 23904, Apr. 30, 2020; 85 FR 80274, 80395, Dec. 11, 2020; 87 FR 18078, 18221, Mar. 29, 2022]

§ 1208.3 Form of application.

(a)

(1) Except for applicants described in paragraph (a)(2) of this section, an asylum applicant must file Form I-589, Application for Asylum and for Withholding of Removal, together with any additional supporting evidence in accordance with the instructions on the

form. The applicant's spouse and children shall be listed on the application and may be included in the request for asylum if they are in the United States. One additional copy of the principal applicant's Form I-589 must be submitted for each dependent included in the principal's application.

(2) In proceedings under § 1240.17 of this chapter, the written record of a positive credible fear determination issued in accordance with 8 CFR 208.30(f), and §§ 1003.42 of this chapter and 1208.30, shall be construed as the asylum application and satisfies the application filing requirements and § 1208.4(b). The written record of the positive credible fear determination shall be considered a complete asylum application for purposes of § 1208.4(a), with the date of service of the positive credible fear determination on the alien considered the date of filing and receipt, and shall be subject to the conditions and consequences provided for in paragraph (c) of this section following the applicant's signature at the asylum merits interview before the USCIS asylum officer. The applicant's spouse and children may be included in the request for asylum only if they were included in the credible fear determination pursuant to 8 CFR 208.30(c), or also presently have an application for asylum pending adjudication with USCIS pursuant to 8 CFR 208.2(a)(1)(ii). If USCIS does not grant the applicant's asylum application after an interview conducted in accordance with 8 CFR 208.9 and if a spouse or child who was included in the request for asylum does not separately file an asylum application that is adjudicated by USCIS, the application will be deemed to satisfy the application filing requirements of § 1208.4(b) for a spouse or child who was included in the request for asylum. The asylum applicant may subsequently seek to amend, correct, or supplement the record of proceedings created before the asylum officer or during the credible fear review process as set forth in § 1240.17(g) of this chapter concerning the consideration of documentary evidence and witness testimony.

(b) An asylum application shall be deemed to constitute at the same time an application for withholding of removal, unless adjudicated in deportation or exclusion proceedings commenced prior to April 1, 1997. In such instances, the asylum application shall be deemed to constitute an application for withholding of deportation under section 243(h) of the Act, as that section existed prior to April 1, 1997. Where a determination is made that an applicant is ineligible to apply for asylum under section 208(a)(2) of the Act, an asylum application shall be construed as an application for withholding of removal.

(c) Form I-589 shall be filed under the following conditions and shall have the following consequences:

(1) If the application was filed on or after January 4, 1995, information provided in the application may be used as a basis for the initiation of removal proceedings, or to satisfy any burden of proof in exclusion, deportation, or removal proceedings;

(2) The applicant and anyone other than a spouse, parent, son, or daughter of the applicant who assists the applicant in preparing the application must sign the application under penalty of perjury. The applicant's signature establishes a presumption that the applicant is aware of the contents of the application. A person other than a relative specified in this paragraph who assists the applicant in preparing the application also must provide his or her full mailing address;

(3) An asylum application under paragraph (a)(1) of this section must be properly filed in accordance with the form instructions and with §§ 1003.24, 1003.31(b), and 1103.7(a)(3) of this chapter, including payment of a fee, if any, as explained in the instructions to the application. For purposes of filing with an immigration court, an asylum application under paragraph (a)(1) of this section is incomplete if it does not include a response to each of the required questions contained in the form, is unsigned, is unaccompanied by the required materials specified in paragraph (a) of this section, is not completed and submitted in accordance with the form instructions, or is unaccompanied by any required fee receipt or other proof of payment as provided in § 1208.4(d)(3). The filing of an incomplete application shall not commence the period after which the applicant may file an application for employment authorization. An application that is incomplete shall be rejected by the immigration court. If an applicant wishes to have his or her application for asylum considered, he or she shall correct the deficiencies in the incomplete application and refile it within 30 days of rejection. Failure to correct the deficiencies in an incomplete application or failure to timely refile the application with the deficiencies corrected, absent exceptional circumstances as defined in § 1003.10(b) of this chapter, shall result in a finding that the alien has abandoned that application and waived the opportunity to file such an application;

(4) Knowing placement of false information on the application may subject the person placing that information on the application to criminal penalties under title 18 of the United States Code and to civil or criminal penalties under section 274C of the Act; and

(5) Knowingly filing a frivolous application on or after April 1, 1997, so long as the applicant has received the notice required by section 208(d)(4) of the Act, shall render the applicant permanently ineligible for any benefits under the Act pursuant to § 1208.20.

HISTORY:

[55 FR 30680, July 27, 1990, as amended at 56 FR 50812, Oct. 9, 1991; 59 FR 62298, Dec. 5, 1994; 60 FR 34090, June 30, 1995; 62 FR 10312, 10338, March 6, 1997; 65 FR 76121, 76131, Dec. 6, 2000; 68 FR 9824, 9834, 9846, Feb. 28, 2003; 85 FR 81698, 81750, Dec. 16, 2020; 87 FR 18078, 18221, Mar. 29, 2022]

§ 1208.4 Filing the application.

Except as prohibited in paragraph (a) of this section, asylum applications shall be filed in accordance with paragraph (b) of this section.

(a) Prohibitions on filing. Section 208(a)(2) of the Act prohibits certain aliens from filing for asylum on or after April 1, 1997, unless the alien can demonstrate to the satisfaction of the Attorney General that one of the exceptions in section 208(a)(2)(D) of the Act applies. Such prohibition applies only to asylum applications under section 208 of the Act and not to applications for withholding of removal under § 1208.16. If an applicant files an asylum application and it appears that one or more of the prohibitions contained in section 208(a)(2) of the Act apply, an asylum officer, in an interview, or an immigration judge, in a hearing, shall review the application and give the applicant the opportunity to present any relevant and useful information bearing on any prohibitions on filing to determine if the application should be rejected. For the purpose of making determinations under section 208(a)(2) of the Act, the following rules shall apply:

(1) Authority. Only an asylum officer, an immigration judge, or the Board of Immigration Appeals is authorized to make determinations regarding the prohibitions contained in section 208(a)(2)(B) or (C) of the Act.

(2) One-year filing deadline.

(i) For purposes of section 208(a)(2)(B) of the Act, an applicant has the burden of proving:

(A) By clear and convincing evidence that the application has been filed within 1 year of the date of the alien's arrival in the United States, or

(B) To the satisfaction of the asylum officer, the immigration judge, or the Board that he or she qualifies for an exception to the 1-year deadline.

(ii) The 1-year period shall be calculated from the date of the alien's last arrival in the United States or April 1, 1997, whichever is later. When the last day of the period so computed falls on a Saturday, Sunday, or legal holiday, the period shall run until the end of the next day that is not a Saturday, Sunday, or legal holiday. For the purpose of making determinations under section 208(a)(2)(B) of the Act only, an application is considered to have been filed on the date it is received by the Service, pursuant to § 103.2(a)(7) of 8 CFR chapter I. In a case in which the application has not been received by the Service within 1 year from the applicant's date of entry into the United States, but the applicant provides clear and convincing documentary evidence of mailing the application within the 1-year period, the mailing date shall be considered the filing date. For cases before the immigration court, the application is considered to have been filed on the date it is received by the immigration court. For cases before the Board of Immigration Appeals, the application is considered to have been filed on the date it is received by the Board. In the case of an application that appears to have been filed more than a year after the applicant arrived in the United States, the asylum officer, the immigration judge, or the Board will determine whether the applicant qualifies for an exception to the deadline. The failure to have provided required biometrics and other biographical information does not prevent the "filing" of an asylum application for purposes of the one-year filing rule of section 208(a)(2)(B) of the Act. See 8 CFR 1003.47. For aliens present in or arriving in the Commonwealth of the Northern Mariana Islands, the 1-year period shall be calculated from January 1, 2030, or from the date of the alien's last arrival in the United States (including the Commonwealth of the Northern Mariana Islands), whichever is later. No period of physical presence in the Commonwealth of the Northern Mariana Islands prior to January 1, 2030, shall count toward the 1-year period. After November 28, 2009, any travel to the Commonwealth of the Northern Mariana Islands from any other State shall not re-start the calculation of the 1-year period.

(3) Prior denial of application. For purposes of section 208(a)(2)(C) of the Act, an asylum application has not been denied unless denied by an immigration judge or the Board of Immigration Appeals.

(4) Changed circumstances.

(i) The term "changed circumstances" in section 208(a)(2)(D) of the Act shall refer to circumstances materially affecting the applicant's eligibility for asylum. They may include, but are not limited to:

(A) Changes in conditions in the applicant's country of nationality or, if the applicant is stateless, country of last habitual residence;

(B) Changes in the applicant's circumstances that materially affect the applicant's eligibility for asylum, including changes in applicable U.S. law and activities the applicant becomes involved in outside the country of feared persecution that place the applicant at risk; or

(C) In the case of an alien who had previously been included as a dependent in another alien's pending asylum application, the loss of the spousal or parent-child relationship to the principal applicant through marriage, divorce, death, or attainment of age 21.

(ii) The applicant shall file an asylum application within a reasonable period given those "changed circumstances." If the applicant can establish that he or she did not become aware of the changed circumstances until after they occurred, such delayed awareness shall be taken into account in determining what constitutes a "reasonable period."

(5) The term "extraordinary circumstances" in section 208(a)(2)(D) of the Act shall refer to events or factors directly related to the failure to meet the 1-year deadline. Such circumstances may excuse the failure to file within the 1-year period as long as the alien filed the application within a reasonable period given those circumstances. The burden of proof is on the applicant to establish to the satisfaction of the asylum officer, the immigration judge, or the Board of Immigration Appeals that the circumstances were not intentionally created by the alien through his or her own action or inaction, that those circumstances were directly related to the alien's failure to file the application within the 1-year period, and that the delay was reasonable under the circumstances. Those circumstances may include but are not limited to:

(i) Serious illness or mental or physical disability, including any effects of persecution or violent harm suffered in the past, during the 1-year period after arrival;

(ii) Legal disability (e.g., the applicant was an unaccompanied minor or suffered from a mental impairment) during the 1-year period after arrival;

(iii) Ineffective assistance of counsel, provided that:

(A) The alien files an affidavit setting forth in detail the agreement that was entered into with counsel with respect to the actions to be taken and what representations counsel did or did not make to the respondent in this regard;

(B) The counsel whose integrity or competence is being impugned has been informed of the allegations leveled against him or her and given an opportunity to respond; and

(C) The alien indicates whether a complaint has been filed with appropriate disciplinary authorities with respect to any violation of counsel's ethical or legal responsibilities, and if not, why not;

(iv) The applicant maintained Temporary Protected Status, lawful immigrant or nonimmigrant status, or was given parole, until a reasonable period before the filing of the asylum application;

(v) The applicant filed an asylum application prior to the expiration of the 1-year deadline, but that application was rejected by the Service as not properly filed, was returned to the applicant for corrections, and was refiled within a reasonable period thereafter; and

(vi) The death or serious illness or incapacity of the applicant's legal representative or a member of the applicant's immediate family.

(6) Asylum cooperative agreements. Immigration judges have authority to consider issues under section 208(a)(2)(A) of the Act, relating to the determination of whether an alien is ineligible to apply for asylum and should be removed to a third country pursuant to a bilateral or multilateral agreement, only with respect to aliens whom DHS has chosen to place in removal proceedings under section 240 of the Act, as provided in 8 CFR 1240.11(g) and (h). For DHS regulations relating to determinations by immigration officers on this subject, see 8 CFR 208.30(e)(6) and (7).

(b) Filing location

(1) With the service center by mail. Except as provided in paragraphs (b)(2), (b)(3), (b)(4) and (b)(5) of this section, asylum applications shall be filed directly by mail with the service center servicing the asylum office with jurisdiction over the place of the applicant's residence or, in the case of an alien without a United States residence, the applicant's current lodging or the land border port-of-entry through which the alien seeks admission to the United States.

(2) With the asylum office. An asylum application shall be filed directly with the asylum office having jurisdiction over the matter in the case of an alien who:

(i) Has received the express consent of the asylum office director or the Director of Asylum to do so, or

(ii) Previously was included in a spouse's or parent's pending application but is no longer eligible to be included as a derivative. In such cases, the derivative should include a cover letter referencing the previous application and explaining that he or she is now independently filing for asylum.

(3) With the Immigration Court. Asylum applications shall be filed directly with the Immigration Court having jurisdiction over the case in the following circumstances:

(i) During exclusion, deportation, or removal proceedings, with the Immigration Court having jurisdiction over the underlying proceeding except that an alien in proceedings under § 1240.17 of this chapter is not required to file the Form I-589.

(ii) After completion of exclusion, deportation, or removal proceedings, and in conjunction with a motion to reopen pursuant to 8 CFR part 1003 where applicable, with the Immigration Court having jurisdiction over the prior proceeding. Any such motion must reasonably explain the failure to request asylum prior to the completion of the proceedings.

(iii) In asylum proceedings pursuant to § 1208.2(c)(1) and after the Form I-863, Notice of Referral to Immigration Judge, has been served on the alien and filed with the Immigration Court having jurisdiction over the case.

(4) With the Board of Immigration Appeals. In conjunction with a motion to remand or reopen pursuant to §§ 1003.2 and 1003.8 of this chapter where applicable, an initial asylum application shall be filed with the Board of Immigration Appeals if jurisdiction over the proceedings is vested in the Board of Immigration Appeals under 8 CFR part 1003. Any such motion must reasonably explain the failure to request asylum prior to the completion of the proceedings.

(5) With the district director. In the case of any alien described in § 1208.2(c)(1) and prior to the service on the alien of Form I-863, any asylum application shall be submitted to the district director having jurisdiction pursuant to 8 CFR part 103. If the district director elects to issue the Form I-863, the district director shall forward such asylum application to the appropriate Immigration Court with the Form I-863 being filed with that Immigration Court.

(c) Amending an application after filing. Upon request of the alien and as a matter of discretion, the asylum officer or immigration judge having jurisdiction may permit an asylum applicant to amend or supplement the application, but any delay caused by such request shall extend the period within which the applicant may not apply for employment authorization in accordance with § 1208.7(a).

(d) Filing deadline.

(1) For any alien in asylum-and-withholding-only proceedings pursuant to § 1208.2(c)(1) and paragraph (b)(3)(iii) of this section, the immigration judge shall comply with the requirements of § 1240.11(c)(1)(i) through (iii) of this chapter and shall set a deadline of fifteen days from the date of the alien's first hearing before an immigration judge by which the alien must file an asylum application, which includes an application for withholding of removal under section 241(b)(3) of the Act and protection under §§ 1208.16 through 1208.18. The immigration judge may extend the deadline for good cause. If the alien does not file an asylum application by the deadline set by the immigration judge, the immigration judge shall deem the opportunity to file such an application waived, and the case shall be returned to the Department of Homeland Security. For any alien in proceedings pursuant to § 1208.2(c)(2), the immigration judge shall comply with the requirements of § 1240.11(c)(1)(i) through (iii) and shall set a deadline of fifteen days from the date of the alien's first hearing before an immigration judge by

which the alien must file an application for withholding of removal under section 241(b)(3) of the Act, which includes an application for protection under §§ 1208.16 through 1208.18. The immigration judge may extend the deadline for good cause. If the alien does not file an application by the deadline set by the immigration judge, the immigration judge shall deem the opportunity to file such an application waived, and the case shall be returned to the Department of Homeland Security.

(2) If the alien must pay a fee for submission of the asylum application, the alien must submit the DHS-issued fee receipt together with the application by the deadline set by the immigration judge in paragraph (d)(1) of this section.

(3) If the alien has paid any required fee but has not received the fee receipt from DHS by the deadline set by the immigration judge, the alien must instead provide to the immigration court a copy of proof of the payment to DHS with the asylum application. The alien must then submit a copy of the fee receipt by a new deadline set by the immigration judge. If the immigration judge does not set a deadline, the alien must submit the fee receipt no later than 45 days after the date of filing of the application.

HISTORY:

[55 FR 30680, July 27, 1990, as amended at 56 FR 50812, Oct. 9, 1991; 59 FR 62298, Dec. 5, 1994; 60 FR 34090, June 30, 1995; 62 FR 10312, 10338, Mar. 6, 1997; 64 FR 8478, 8488, Feb. 19, 1999, as corrected at 64 FR 13881, Mar. 23, 1999; 65 FR 76121, 76131, Dec. 6, 2000; 68 FR 9824, 9834, 9846, Feb. 28, 2003; 68 FR 10349, 10352, Mar. 5, 2003; 69 FR 69490, 69497, Nov. 29, 2004; 70 FR 4743, 4754, Jan. 31, 2005; 74 FR 55726, 55741, Oct. 28, 2009; 84 FR 63994, 64010, Nov. 19, 2019; 85 FR 23902, 23904, Apr. 30, 2020]; 85 FR 81698, 81751, Dec. 16, 2020; 86 FR 70708, 70724, Dec. 13, 2021; 87 FR 18078, 18221, Mar. 29, 2022]

§ 1208.5 Special duties toward aliens in custody of DHS.

(a) *General*. When an alien in the custody of DHS requests asylum or withholding of removal, or expresses a fear of persecution or harm upon return to his or her country of origin or to agents thereof, DHS shall make available the appropriate application forms and shall provide the applicant with the information required by section 208(d)(4) of the Act, including in the case of an alien who is in custody with a positive credible fear determination under 8 CFR 208.30 or a reasonable fear determination pursuant to 8 CFR 208.31, and except in the case of an alien who is in custody pending a credible fear determination under 8 CFR 208.30 or a reasonable fear determination pursuant to 8 CFR 208.31.Although DHS does not have a duty in the case of an alien who is in custody pending a credible fear or reasonable fear determination under either 8 CFR 1208.30 or 8 CFR 1208.31, DHS may provide the appropriate forms, upon request. Where possible, expedited consideration shall be given to applications of detained aliens. Except as provided in paragraph (c) of this section, such alien shall not be excluded, deported, or removed before a decision is rendered on his or her asylum application. Furthermore, except as provided in paragraph (c) of this section, an alien physically present in or arriving in the Commonwealth of the Northern Mariana Islands shall not be excluded, deported, or removed before a decision is rendered on his or her application for withholding of removal pursuant to section 241(b)(3) of the Act and withholding of removal under the Convention Against Torture. No application for asylum may be filed prior to January 1, 2030, pursuant to section 208 of the Act by an alien physically present in or arriving in the Commonwealth of the Northern Mariana Islands.

(b) *Certain aliens aboard vessels*.

(1) (1) If an alien crewmember or alien stowaway on board a vessel or other conveyance alleges, claims, or otherwise makes known to an immigration inspector or other official making an examination on the conveyance that he or she is unable or unwilling to return to his or her country of nationality or last habitual residence (if not a national of any country) because of persecution or a fear of persecution in that country on account of race, religion, nationality, membership in a particular social group, or political opinion, or if the alien expresses a fear of torture upon return to that country, the alien shall be promptly removed from the conveyance. If the alien makes such fear known to an official while off such conveyance, the alien shall not be returned to the conveyance but shall be retained in or transferred to the custody of the Service.

(i) An alien stowaway will be referred to an asylum officer for a credible fear determination under § 1208.30.

(ii) An alien crewmember shall be provided the appropriate application forms and information required by section 208(d)(4) of the Act and may then have 10 days within which to submit an asylum application to the district director having jurisdiction over the port-of-entry. The district director may extend the 10-day filing period for good cause. Once the application has been filed, the district director, pursuant to § 1208.4(b), shall serve Form I-863 on the alien and immediately forward any such application to the appropriate Immigration Court with a copy of the Form I-863 being filed with that court.

(iii) An alien crewmember physically present in or arriving in the Commonwealth of the Northern Mariana Islands can request withholding of removal pursuant to section 241(b)(3) of the Act and withholding of removal under the Convention Against Torture. However, such an alien crewmember is not eligible to request asylum pursuant to section 208 of the Act prior to January 1, 2030.

(2) Pending adjudication of the application, and, in the case of a stowaway the credible fear determination and any review thereof, the alien may be detained by the Service or otherwise paroled in accordance with 8 CFR 212.5. However, pending the credible fear determination, parole of an alien stowaway may be permitted only when the Attorney General determines, in the exercise of discretion, that parole is required to meet a medical emergency or is necessary for a legitimate law enforcement objective.

(c) *Exception to prohibition on removal.* A motion to reopen or an order to remand accompanied by an asylum application pursuant to § 1208.4(b)(3)(iii) shall not stay execution of a final exclusion, deportation, or removal order unless such stay is specifically granted by the Board of Immigration Appeals or the immigration judge having jurisdiction over the motion.

HISTORY:

[55 FR 30680, July 27, 1990; 62 FR 10312, 10339, Mar. 6, 1997; 64 FR 8478, 8488, Feb. 19, 1999; 65 FR 76121, 76132, Dec. 6, 2000; 68 FR 9824, 9834, 9846, Feb. 28, 2003; 68 FR 10349, 10352, Mar. 5, 2003; 74 FR 55726, 55741, Oct. 28, 2009; 85 FR 23902, 23904, Apr. 30, 2020; 85 FR 80274, 80395, Dec. 11, 2020; 87 FR 18078, 18221, Mar. 29, 2022]

§ 1208.6 Disclosure to third parties.

(a) Information contained in or pertaining to any application for refugee admission, asylum, withholding of removal under section 241(b)(3) of the Act, or protection under regulations issued pursuant to the Convention Against Torture's implementing legislation, records pertaining to any credible fear determination conducted pursuant to § 208.30, and records pertaining to any reasonable fear determination conducted pursuant to § 208.31, shall not be disclosed without the written consent of the applicant, except as permitted by this section or at the discretion of the Attorney General.

(b) The confidentiality of other records kept by DHS and the Executive Office for Immigration Review that indicate that a specific alien has applied for refugee admission, asylum, withholding of removal under section 241(b)(3) of the Act, or protection under regulations issued pursuant to the Convention Against Torture's implementing legislation, or has received a credible fear or reasonable fear interview, or received a credible fear or reasonable fear review shall also be protected from disclosure, except as permitted in this section. DHS will coordinate with the Department of State to ensure that the confidentiality of those records is maintained if they are transmitted to Department of State offices in other countries.

(c) This section shall not apply to any disclosure to:

(1) Any United States Government official or contractor having a need to examine information in connection with:

(i) The adjudication of asylum applications;

(ii) The consideration of a request for a credible fear or reasonable fear interview, or a credible fear or reasonable fear review;

(iii) The defense of any legal action arising from the adjudication of, or failure to adjudicate, the asylum application, or from a credible fear determination or reasonable fear determination under § 1208.30 or § 1208.31;

(iv) The defense of any legal action of which the asylum application, credible fear determination, or reasonable fear determination is a part; or

(v) Any United States Government investigation concerning any criminal or civil matter; or

(2) Any Federal, State, or local court in the United States considering any legal action:

(i) Arising from the adjudication of, or failure to adjudicate, the asylum application, or from a credible fear or reasonable fear determination under § 1208.30 or § 1208.31; or

(ii) Arising from the proceedings of which the asylum application, credible fear determination, or reasonable fear determination is a part.

(d)(1) Any information contained in an application for refugee admission, asylum, withholding of removal under section 241(b)(3) the Act, or protection under regulations issued pursuant to the Convention Against Torture's implementing legislation, any relevant and applicable information supporting that application, any information regarding an alien who has filed such an application, and any relevant and applicable information regarding an alien who has been the subject of a reasonable fear or credible fear determination may be disclosed:

(i) As part of an investigation or adjudication of the merits of that application or of any other application under the immigration laws;

(ii) As part of any State or Federal criminal investigation, proceeding, or prosecution;

(iii) Pursuant to any State or Federal mandatory reporting requirement;

(iv) To deter, prevent, or ameliorate the effects of child abuse;

(v) As part of any proceeding arising under the immigration laws, including proceedings arising under the Act; and

(vi) As part of the Government's defense of any legal action relating to the alien's immigration or custody status, including petitions for review filed in accordance with 8 U.S.C. 1252.

(2) If information may be disclosed under paragraph (d)(1) of this section, the disclosure provisions in paragraphs (a), (b), and (c) of this section shall not apply.

(e) Nothing in this section shall be construed as prohibiting the disclosure of information contained in an application for refugee admission, asylum, withholding of removal under section 241(b)(3)(B) of the Act, or protection under the regulations issued pursuant to the Convention Against Torture's implementing legislation, any relevant and applicable information supporting that application, information regarding an alien who has filed such an application, or information regarding an alien who has been the subject of a reasonable fear or credible fear determination:

(1) Among employees of the Department of Justice, the Department of Homeland Security, the Department of State, the Department of Health and Human Services, the Department of Labor, or a U.S. national security agency having a need to examine the information for an official purpose; or

(2) Where a United States government employee or contractor has a good faith and reasonable belief that disclosure is necessary to prevent the commission of a crime, the furtherance of an ongoing crime, or to ameliorate the effects of a crime.

HISTORY:

[55 FR 30680, July 27, 1990; 62 FR 10312, 10340, March 6, 1997;

65 FR 76121, 76133, Dec. 6, 2000; 68 FR 9824, 9834, 9846, Feb. 28, 2003; 85 FR 80274, 80395, Dec. 11, 2020]

§ 1208.7 Employment authorization.

(a) **Application and approval.**

(1) Subject to the restrictions contained in sections 208(d) and 236(a) of the Act, an applicant for asylum who is not an aggravated felon shall be eligible pursuant to §§ 1274a.12(c)(8) and 1274a.13(a) of this chapter to submit a Form I-765, Application for Employment Authorization. Except in the case of an alien whose asylum application has been recommended for approval, or in the case of an alien who filed an asylum application prior to January 4, 1995, the application shall be submitted no earlier than 150 days after the date on which a complete asylum application submitted in accordance with §§ 1208.3 and 1208.4 has been received. In the case of an applicant whose asylum application has been recommended for approval, the applicant may apply for employment authorization when he or she receives notice of the recommended approval. If an asylum application has been returned as incomplete in accordance with § 1208.3(c)(3), the 150-day period will commence upon receipt by the Service of a complete asylum application. An applicant whose asylum application has been denied by an asylum officer or by an immigration judge within the 150-day period shall not be eligible to apply for employment authorization. If an asylum application is denied prior to a decision on the application for employment authorization, the application for employment authorization shall be denied. If the asylum application is not so denied, the Service shall have 30 days from the date of filing of the Form I-765 to grant or deny that application, except that no employment authorization shall be issued to an asylum applicant prior to the expiration of the 180-day period following the filing of the asylum application filed on or after April 1, 1997.

(2) The time periods within which the alien may not apply for employment authorization and within which the Service must respond to any such application and within which the asylum application must be adjudicated pursuant to section 208(d)(5)(A)(iii) of the Act shall begin when the alien has filed a complete asylum application in accordance with §§ 1208.3 and 1208.4. Any delay requested or caused by the applicant shall not be counted as part of these time periods, including delays caused by failure without good cause to follow the requirements for fingerprint processing. Such time periods shall also be extended by the equivalent of the time between issuance of a request for evidence pursuant to § 103.2(b)(8) of 8 CFR chapter I and the receipt of the applicant's response to such request.

(3) The provisions of paragraphs (a)(1) and (a)(2) of this section apply to applications for asylum filed on or after January 4, 1995.

(4) Employment authorization pursuant to § 1274a.12(c)(8) of this chapter may not be granted to an alien who fails to appear for a scheduled interview before an asylum officer or a hearing before an immigration judge, unless the applicant demonstrates that the failure to appear was the result of exceptional circumstances.

(b) Renewal and termination. Employment authorization shall be renewable, in increments to be determined by the Commissioner, for the continuous period of time necessary for the asylum officer or immigration judge to decide the asylum application and, if necessary, for completion of any administrative or judicial review.

(1) If the asylum application is denied by the asylum officer, the employment authorization shall terminate at the expiration of the employment authorization document or 60 days after the denial of asylum, whichever is longer.

(2) If the application is denied by the immigration judge, the Board of Immigration Appeals, or a Federal court, the employment authorization terminates upon the expiration of the employment authorization document, unless the applicant has filed an appropriate request for administrative or judicial review.

(c) Supporting evidence for renewal of employment authorization. In order for employment authorization to be renewed under this section, the alien must provide the Service (in accordance with the instructions on or attached to the employment authorization application) with a Form I-765, the required fee (unless waived in accordance with 8 CFR 103.7 and 8 CFR part 106), and (if applicable) proof that he or she has continued to pursue his or her asylum application before an immigration judge or sought administrative or judicial review. For purposes of employment authorization, pursuit of an asylum application is established by presenting to the Service one of the following, depending on the stage of the alien's immigration proceedings:

(1) If the alien's case is pending in proceedings before the immigration judge, and the alien wishes to continue to pursue his or her asylum application, a copy of any asylum denial, referral notice, or charging document placing the alien in such proceedings;

(2) If the immigration judge has denied asylum, a copy of the document issued by the Board of Immigration Appeals to show that a timely appeal has been filed from a denial of the asylum application by the immigration judge; or

(3) If the Board of Immigration Appeals has dismissed the alien's appeal of a denial of asylum, or sustained an appeal by the Service of a grant of asylum, a copy of the petition for judicial review or for habeas corpus pursuant to section 242 of the Act, date stamped by the appropriate court.

(d) In order for employment authorization to be renewed before its expiration, the application for renewal must be received by the Service 90 days prior to expiration of the employment authorization.

HISTORY:

[55 FR 30680, July 27, 1990; 58 FR 12148, Mar. 3, 1993, as corrected at 58 FR 14145, Mar. 16, 1993; 59 FR 62298, Dec. 5, 1994; 60 FR 21974, May 4, 1995; 60 FR 34090, June 30, 1995; 62 FR 10312, 10340, March 6, 1997; 63 FR 12979, 12986, March 17, 1998; 68 FR 9824, 9834, 9846, Feb. 28, 2003; 68 FR 10349, 10352, Mar. 5, 2003; 85 FR 81698, 81751, Dec. 16, 2020; 85 FR 82750, 82794, Dec. 18, 2020]

§ 1208.8 Limitations on travel outside the United States.

(a) An applicant who leaves the United States without first obtaining advance parole under § 212.5(f) of this chapter shall be presumed to have abandoned his or her application under this section.

(b) An applicant who leaves the United States pursuant to advance parole under § 1212.5(f) of this chapter and returns to the country of claimed persecution shall be presumed to have abandoned his or her application, unless the applicant is able to establish compelling reasons for such return.

HISTORY:

[55 FR 30680, July 27, 1990; 59 FR 62299, Dec. 5, 1994; 62 FR 10312, 10341, March 6, 1997; 65 FR 82254, 82255, Dec. 28, 2000; 66 FR 7863, Jan. 26, 2001; 68 FR 9824, 9834, Feb. 28, 2003; 68 FR 10349, 10352, Mar. 5, 2003]

§ 1208.9 Procedure for interview before an asylum officer. [This section was removed and reserved, effective January 15, 2021. 85 FR 81698, 81751, Dec. 16, 2020.]

§ 1208.10 Failure to appear at a scheduled hearing before an immigration judge; failure to follow requirements for biometrics and other biographical information processing.

Failure to appear for a scheduled immigration hearing without prior authorization may result in dismissal of the application and the entry of an order of deportation or removal in absentia. Failure to comply with processing requirements for biometrics and other biographical information within the time allowed will result in dismissal of the application, unless the applicant demonstrates that such failure was the result of good cause. DHS is responsible for obtaining biometrics and other biographical information with respect to any alien in custody.

HISTORY:

[55 FR 30680, July 27, 1990; 59 FR 62300, Dec. 5, 1994; 62 FR 10312, 10341, March 6, 1997; 63 FR 12979, 12986, March 17, 1998; 68 FR 9824, 9834, Feb. 28, 2003; 70 FR 4743, 4754, Jan. 31, 2005]

§ 1208.11 Comments from the Department of State.

(a) The immigration judge may request, in his or her discretion, specific comments from the Department of State regarding individual cases or types of claims under consideration, or other information the immigration judge deems appropriate.

(b) With respect to any asylum application, the Department of State may provide, at its discretion, to the Immigration Court:

(1) Detailed country conditions information relevant to eligibility for asylum, withholding of removal under section 241(b)(3) of the Act, and withholding of removal under the Convention Against Torture;

(2) An assessment of the accuracy of the applicant's assertions about conditions in the applicant's country of nationality or habitual residence and the applicant's particular situation;

(3) Information about whether persons who are similarly situated to the applicant are persecuted or tortured in the applicant's country of nationality or habitual residence and the frequency of such persecution or torture; or

(4) Such other information as it deems relevant.

(c) Any comments received pursuant to paragraph (b) of this section shall be made part of the record. Unless the comments are classified under an applicable Executive Order, the applicant shall be provided an opportunity to review and respond to such comments prior to the issuance of any decision to deny the application.

HISTORY:

[55 FR 30680, July 27, 1990; 59 FR 62300, Dec. 5, 1994; 62 FR 10312, 10341, Mar. 6, 1997; 64 FR 8478, 8488, Feb. 19, 1999; 68 FR 9824, 9834, Feb. 28, 2003; 78 FR 19077, 19079, Mar. 29, 2013]

§ 1208.12 Reliance on information compiled by other sources.

(a) In deciding an asylum application, which includes an application for withholding of removal under 241(b)(3) of the Act and protection under §§ 1208.16 through 1208.18, or in deciding whether the alien has a credible fear of persecution or torture pursuant to § 1208.30, or a reasonable fear of persecution or torture pursuant to § 1208.31, an immigration judge may rely on material provided by the Department of State, other Department of Justice offices, the Department of Homeland Security, or other U.S. Government agencies, and may rely on foreign government and nongovernmental sources if those sources are determined by the judge to be credible and the material is probative. On his or her own authority, an immigration judge may submit relevant evidence into the record, if the source is credible and the evidence is probative, and may consider it in deciding an asylum application, which includes an application for withholding of removal under section 241(b)(3) of the Act and protection under §§ 1208.16 through 1208.18, provided that a copy of the evidence has been provided to both parties and both parties have had an opportunity to comment on or object to the evidence prior to the issuance of the immigration judge's decision.

(b) Nothing in this part shall be construed to entitle the applicant to conduct discovery directed toward the records, officers, agents, or employees of the Service, the Department of Justice, or the Department of State. Persons may continue to seek documents available through a Freedom of Information Act (FOIA) request pursuant to 28 CFR part 16.

HISTORY:

[55 FR 30680, July 27, 1990; 59 FR 62300, Dec. 4, 1995; 62 FR 10312, 10342, Mar. 6, 1997; 64 FR 8478, 8488, Feb. 19, 1999; 65 FR 76121, 76133, Dec. 6, 2000; 68 FR 9824, 9834, 9846, Feb. 28, 2003; 68 FR 10349, 10352, Mar. 5, 2003]; 85 FR 81698, 81751, Dec. 16, 2020]

§ 1208.13 Establishing asylum eligibility. [Effective until December 31, 2025]

(a) Burden of proof. The burden of proof is on the applicant for asylum to establish that he or she is a refugee as defined in section 101(a)(42) of the Act. The testimony of the applicant, if credible, may be sufficient to sustain the burden of proof without corroboration. The fact that the applicant previously established a credible fear of persecution for purposes of section 235(b)(1)(B) of the Act does not relieve the alien of the additional burden of establishing eligibility for asylum.

(b) Eligibility. The applicant may qualify as a refugee either because he or she has suffered past persecution or because he or she has a well-founded fear of future persecution.

(1) Past persecution. An applicant shall be found to be a refugee on the basis of past persecution if the applicant can establish that he or she has suffered persecution in the past in the applicant's country of nationality or, if stateless, in his or her country of last habitual residence, on account of race, religion, nationality, membership in a particular social group, or political opinion, and is unable or unwilling to return to, or avail himself or herself of the protection of, that country owing to such persecution. An applicant who has been found to have established such past persecution shall also be presumed to have a well-founded fear of persecution on the basis of the original claim. That presumption may be rebutted if an asylum officer or immigration judge makes one of the findings described in paragraph (b)(1)(i) of this section. If the applicant's fear of future persecution is unrelated to the past persecution, the applicant bears the burden of establishing that the fear is well-founded.

(i) Discretionary referral or denial. Except as provided in paragraph (b)(1)(iii) of this section, an asylum officer shall, in the exercise of his or her discretion, refer or deny, or an immigration judge, in the exercise of his or her discretion, shall deny the asylum application of an alien found to be a refugee on the basis of past persecution if any of the following is found by a preponderance of the evidence:

(A) There has been a fundamental change in circumstances such that the applicant no longer has a well-founded fear of persecution in the applicant's country of nationality or, if stateless, in the applicant's country of last habitual residence, on account of race, religion, nationality, membership in a particular social group, or political opinion; or

(B) The applicant could avoid future persecution by relocating to another part of the applicant's country of nationality or, if stateless, another part of the applicant's country of last habitual residence, and under all the circumstances, it would be reasonable to expect the applicant to do so.

(ii) Burden of proof. In cases in which an applicant has demonstrated past persecution under paragraph (b)(1) of this section, the Service shall bear the burden of establishing by a preponderance of the evidence the requirements of paragraphs (b)(1)(i)(A) or (B) of this section.

(iii) Grant in the absence of well-founded fear of persecution. An applicant described in paragraph (b)(1)(i) of this section who is not barred from a grant of asylum under paragraph (c) of this section, may be granted asylum, in the exercise of the decision-maker's discretion, if:

(A) The applicant has demonstrated compelling reasons for being unwilling or unable to return to the country arising out of the severity of the past persecution; or

(B) The applicant has established that there is a reasonable possibility that he or she may suffer other serious harm upon removal to that country.

(2) Well-founded fear of persecution

(i) An applicant has a well-founded fear of persecution if:

(A) The applicant has a fear of persecution in his or her country of nationality or, if stateless, in his or her country of last habitual residence, on account of race, religion, nationality, membership in a particular social group, or political opinion;

(B) There is a reasonable possibility of suffering such persecution if he or she were to return to that country; and

(C) He or she is unable or unwilling to return to, or avail himself or herself of the protection of, that country because of such fear.

(ii) An applicant does not have a well-founded fear of persecution if the applicant could avoid persecution by relocating to another part of the applicant's country of nationality or, if stateless, another part of the applicant's country of last habitual residence, if under all the circumstances it would be reasonable to expect the applicant to do so.

(iii) In evaluating whether the applicant has sustained the burden of proving that he or she has a well-founded fear of persecution, the asylum officer or immigration judge shall not require the applicant to provide evidence that there is a reasonable possibility he or she would be singled out individually for persecution if:

(A) The applicant establishes that there is a pattern or practice in his or her country of nationality or, if stateless, in his or her country of last habitual residence, of persecution of a group of persons similarly situated to the applicant on account of race, religion, nationality, membership in a particular social group, or political opinion; and

(B) The applicant establishes his or her own inclusion in, and identification with, such group of persons such that his or her fear of persecution upon return is reasonable.

(3) Reasonableness of internal relocation. For purposes of determinations under paragraphs (b)(1)(i) and (ii) and (b)(2) of this section, adjudicators should consider the totality of the relevant circumstances regarding an applicant's prospects for relocation, including the size of the country of nationality or last habitual residence, the geographic locus of the alleged persecution, the size, numerosity, and reach of the alleged persecutor, and the applicant's demonstrated ability to

relocate to the United States in order to apply for asylum.

(i) In cases in which the applicant has not established past persecution, the applicant shall bear the burden of establishing that it would not be reasonable for him or her to relocate, unless the persecution is by a government or is government-sponsored.

(ii) In cases in which the persecutor is a government or is government-sponsored, it shall be presumed that internal relocation would not be reasonable, unless the Department of Homeland Security establishes by a preponderance of the evidence that, under all the circumstances, it would be reasonable for the applicant to relocate.

(iii) Regardless of whether an applicant has established persecution in the past, in cases in which the persecutor is not the government or a government-sponsored actor, or otherwise is a private actor, there shall be a presumption that internal relocation would be reasonable unless the applicant establishes, by a preponderance of the evidence, that it would be unreasonable to relocate.

(iv) For purposes of determinations under paragraphs (b)(3)(ii) and (iii) of this section, persecutors who are private actors—including persecutors who are gang members, officials acting outside their official capacity, family members who are not themselves government officials, or neighbors who are not themselves government officials—shall not be considered to be persecutors who are the government or government sponsored absent evidence that the government sponsored the persecution.

(c) Mandatory denials —

(1) Applications filed on or after April 1, 1997. For applications filed on or after April 1, 1997, an applicant shall not qualify for asylum if section 208(a)(2) or 208(b)(2) of the Act applies to the applicant. If the applicant is found to be ineligible for asylum under either section 208(a)(2) or 208(b)(2) of the Act, the applicant shall be considered for eligibility for withholding of removal under section 241(b)(3) of the Act. The applicant shall also be considered for eligibility for withholding of removal under the Convention Against Torture if the applicant requests such consideration or if the evidence presented by the alien indicates that the alien may be tortured in the country of removal.

(2) Applications filed before April 1, 1997

(i) An immigration judge or asylum officer shall not grant asylum to any applicant who filed his or her application before April 1, 1997, if the alien:

(A) Having been convicted by a final judgment of a particularly serious crime in the United States, constitutes a danger to the community;

(B) Has been firmly resettled within the meaning of § 1208.15;

(C) Can reasonably be regarded as a danger to the security of the United States;

(D) Has been convicted of an aggravated felony, as defined in section 101(a)(43) of the Act; or

(E) Ordered, incited, assisted, or otherwise participated in the persecution of any person on account of race, religion, nationality, membership in a particular social group, or political opinion.

(F) Is described within section 212(a)(3)(B)(i)(I),(II), and (III) of the Act as it existed prior to April 1, 1997, and as amended by the Anti-terrorist and Effective Death Penalty Act of 1996 (AEDPA), unless it is determined that there are no reasonable grounds to believe that the individual is a danger to the security of the United States.

(ii) If the evidence indicates that one of the above grounds apply to the applicant, he or she shall have the burden of proving by a preponderance of the evidence that he or she did not so act.

(3) [Removed and reserved.]

(4) [Removed and reserved.]

(5) [Removed and reserved.]

(6) Additional limitations on eligibility for asylum. For applications filed on or after November 20, 2020, an alien shall be found ineligible for asylum if:

(i) The alien has been convicted on or after such date of an offense arising under sections 274(a)(1)(A), 274(a)(2), or 276 of the Act;

(ii) The alien has been convicted on or after such date of a Federal, State, tribal, or local crime that the immigration judge knows or has reason to believe was committed in support, promotion, or furtherance of the activity of a criminal street gang as that term is defined either under the jurisdiction where the conviction occurred or in section 521(a) of title 18;

(iii) The alien has been convicted on or after such date of an offense for driving while intoxicated or impaired as those terms are defined under the jurisdiction where the conviction occurred (including a conviction for driving while under the influence of or impaired by alcohol or drugs) without regard to whether the conviction is classified as a misdemeanor or felony under Federal, State, tribal, or local law, in which such impaired driving was a cause of serious bodily injury or death of another person;

(iv)(A) The alien has been convicted on or after such date of a second or subsequent offense for driving while intoxicated or impaired as those terms are defined under the jurisdiction where the conviction occurred (including a conviction for driving while under the influence of or impaired by alcohol or drugs) without regard to whether the conviction is classified as a misdemeanor or felony under Federal, State, tribal, or local law;

(B) A finding under paragraph (c)(6)(iv)(A) of this section does not require the immigration judge to find the first conviction for driving while intoxicated or impaired (including a conviction for driving while under the influence of or impaired by alcohol or drugs) as a predicate offense. The immigration judge need only make a factual determination that the alien was previously convicted for driving while intoxicated or impaired as those terms are defined under the jurisdiction where the convictions occurred (including a conviction for driving while under the influence of or impaired by alcohol or drugs).

(v)(A) The alien has been convicted on or after such date of a crime that involves conduct amounting to a crime of stalking; or a crime of child abuse, child neglect, or child abandonment; or that involves conduct amounting to a domestic assault or battery offense, including a misdemeanor crime of domestic violence, as described in section 922(g)(9) of title 18, a misdemeanor crime of domestic violence as described in section 921(a)(33) of title 18, a crime of domestic violence as described in section 12291(a)(8) of title 34, or any crime based on conduct in which the alien harassed, coerced, intimidated, voluntarily or recklessly used (or threatened to use) force or violence against, or inflicted physical injury or physical pain, however slight, upon a person, and committed by:

(1) An alien who is a current or former spouse of the person;

(2) An alien with whom the person shares a child in common;

(3) An alien who is cohabiting with or has cohabited with the person as a spouse;

(4) An alien similarly situated to a spouse of the person under the domestic or family violence laws of the jurisdiction where the offense occurs; or

(5) Any other alien against a person who is protected from that alien's acts under the domestic or family violence laws of the United States or any State, tribal government, or unit of local government.

(B) In making a determination under paragraph (c)(6)(v)(A) of this section, including in determining the existence of a domestic relationship between the alien and the victim, the underlying conduct of the crime may be considered and the immigration judge is not limited to facts found by the criminal court or provided in the underlying record of conviction.

(C) An alien who was convicted of offenses described in paragraph (c)(6)(v)(A) of this section is not subject to ineligibility for asylum on that basis if the alien would be described in section 237(a)(7)(A) of the Act were the crimes or conduct considered grounds for deportability under section 237(a)(2)(E)(i) through (ii) of the Act.

(vi) The alien has been convicted on or after such date of—

(A) Any felony under Federal, State, tribal, or local law;

(B) Any misdemeanor offense under Federal, State, tribal, or local law involving:

(1) The possession or use of an identification document, authentication feature, or false identification document without lawful authority, unless the alien can establish that the conviction resulted from circumstances showing that the document was presented before boarding a common carrier, that the document related to the alien's eligibility to enter the United States, that the alien used the document to depart a country in which the alien has claimed a fear of persecution, and that the alien claimed a fear of persecution without delay upon presenting himself or herself to an immigration officer upon arrival at a United States port of entry;

(2) The receipt of Federal public benefits, as defined in 8 U.S.C. 1611(c), from a Federal entity, or the receipt of similar public benefits from a State, tribal, or local entity, without lawful authority; or

(3) Possession or trafficking of a controlled substance or controlled-substance paraphernalia, other than a single offense involving possession for one's own use of 30 grams or less of marijuana.

(vii) The immigration judge knows or has reason to believe that the alien has engaged on or after such date in acts of battery or extreme cruelty as defined in 8 CFR 204.2(c)(1)(vi), upon a person, and committed by:

(A) An alien who is a current or former spouse of the person;

(B) An alien with whom the person shares a child in common;

(C) An alien who is cohabiting with or has cohabited with the person as a spouse;

(D) An alien similarly situated to a spouse of the person under the domestic or family violence laws of the jurisdiction where the offense occurs; or

(E) Any other alien against a person who is protected from that alien's acts under the domestic or family violence laws of the United States or any State, tribal government, or unit of local government, even if the acts did not result in a criminal conviction;

(F) Except that an alien who was convicted of offenses or engaged in conduct described in paragraph (c)(6)(vii) of this section is not subject to ineligibility for asylum on that basis if the alien would be described in section 237(a)(7)(A) of the Act were the crimes or conduct considered grounds for deportability under section 237(a)(2)(E)(i)–(ii) of the Act.

(7) For purposes of paragraph (c)(6) of this section:

(i) The term "felony" means any crime defined as a felony by the relevant jurisdiction (Federal, State, tribal, or local) of conviction, or any crime punishable by more than one year of imprisonment.

(ii) The term "misdemeanor" means any crime defined as a misdemeanor by the relevant jurisdiction (Federal, State, tribal, or local) of conviction, or any crime not punishable by more than one year of imprisonment.

(iii) Whether any activity or conviction also may constitute a basis for removability under the Act is immaterial to a determination of asylum eligibility.

(iv) All references to a criminal offense or criminal conviction shall be deemed to include any attempt, conspiracy, or solicitation to commit the offense or any other inchoate form of the offense.

(v) No order vacating a conviction, modifying a sentence, clarifying a sentence, or otherwise altering a conviction or sentence, shall have any effect unless the immigration judge determines that—

(A) The court issuing the order had jurisdiction and authority to do so; and

(B) The order was not entered for rehabilitative purposes or for purposes of ameliorating the immigration consequences of the conviction or sentence.

(8) For purposes of paragraph (c)(7)(v)(B) of this section, the order shall be presumed to be for the purpose of ameliorating immigration consequences if:

(i) The order was entered after the initiation of any proceeding to remove the alien from the United States; or

(ii) The alien moved for the order more than one year after the date of the original order of conviction or sentencing.

(9) An immigration judge is authorized to look beyond the face of any order purporting to vacate a conviction, modify a sentence, or clarify a sentence to determine whether the requirements of paragraph (c)(7)(v) of this section have been met in order to determine whether such order should be given any effect under this section.

(d) Discretion. Factors that fall short of grounds of mandatory denial of an asylum application may constitute discretionary considerations.

(1) The following are significant adverse discretionary factors that a decision-maker shall consider, if applicable, in determining whether an alien merits a grant of asylum in the exercise of discretion:

(i) An alien's unlawful entry or unlawful attempted entry into the United States unless such entry or attempted entry was made in immediate flight from persecution in a contiguous country or unless such entry or attempted entry was made by an alien under the age of 18 at the time the entry or attempted entry was made;

(ii) The failure of an alien to apply for protection from persecution or torture in at least one country outside the alien's country of citizenship, nationality, or last lawful habitual residence through which the alien transited before entering the United States unless:

(A) The alien received a final judgment denying the alien protection in such country;

(B) The alien demonstrates that he or she satisfies the definition of "victim of a severe form of trafficking in persons" provided in 8 CFR 214.11; or

(C) Such country or countries were, at the time of the transit, not parties to the 1951 Convention relating to the Status of Refugees, the 1967 Protocol relating to the Status of Refugees, or the Convention Against Torture and Other Cruel, Inhuman or Degrading Treatment or Punishment; and

(iii) An alien's use of fraudulent documents to enter the United States, unless the alien arrived in the United States by air, sea, or land directly from the applicant's home country without transiting through any other country.

(2)(i) The Attorney General, except as provided in paragraph (d)(2)(ii) of this section, will not favorably exercise discretion under section 208 of the Act for an alien who:

(A) Immediately prior to his arrival in the United States or en route to the United States from the alien's country of citizenship, nationality, or last lawful habitual residence, spent more than 14 days in any one country unless:

(1) The alien demonstrates that he or she applied for protection from persecution or torture in such country and the alien received a final judgment denying the alien protection in such country;

(2) The alien demonstrates that he or she satisfies the definition of "victim of a severe form of trafficking in persons" provided in 8 CFR 214.11; or

(3) Such country was, at the time of the transit, not a party to the 1951 Convention relating to the Status of Refugees the 1967 Protocol relating to the Status of Refugees, or the Convention against Torture and Other Cruel, Inhuman or Degrading Treatment or Punishment;

(B) Transits through more than one country between his country of citizenship, nationality, or last habitual residence and the United States unless:

(1) The alien demonstrates that he or she applied for protection from persecution or torture in at least one such country and the alien received a final judgment denying the alien protection in such country;

(2) The alien demonstrates that he or she satisfies the definition of "victim of a severe form of trafficking in persons" provided in 8 CFR 214.11; or

(3) All such countries through which the alien transited en route to the United States were, at the time of the transit, not parties to the 1951 Convention relating to the Status of Refugees, the 1967 Protocol relating to the Status of Refugees, or the Convention against Torture and Other Cruel, Inhuman or Degrading Treatment or Punishment;

(C) Would otherwise be subject to § 1208.13(c) but for the reversal, vacatur, expungement, or modification of a conviction or sentence unless the alien was found not guilty;

(D) Accrued more than one year of unlawful presence in the United States, as defined in sections 212(a)(9)(B)(ii) and (iii) of the Act, prior to filing an application for asylum;

(E) At the time the asylum application is filed with the immigration court or is referred from DHS has:

(1) Failed to timely file (or timely file a request for an extension of time to file) any required Federal, State, or local income tax returns;

(2) Failed to satisfy any outstanding Federal, State, or local tax obligations; or

(3) Has income that would result in tax liability under section 1 of the Internal Revenue Code of 1986 and that was not reported to the Internal Revenue Service;

(F) Has had two or more prior asylum applications denied for any reason;

(G) Has withdrawn a prior asylum application with prejudice or been found to have abandoned a prior asylum application;

(H) Failed to attend an interview regarding his or her asylum application with DHS, unless the alien shows by a preponderance of the evidence that:

(1) Exceptional circumstances prevented the alien from attending the interview; or

(2) The interview notice was not mailed to the last address provided by the alien or the alien's representative and neither the alien nor the alien's representative received notice of the interview; or

(I) Was subject to a final order of removal, deportation, or exclusion and did not file a motion to reopen to seek asylum based on changed country conditions within one year of the changes in country conditions.

(ii) Where one or more of the adverse discretionary factors set forth in paragraph (d)(2)(i) of this section are present, the Attorney General, in extraordinary circumstances, such as those involving national security or foreign policy considerations, or cases in which an alien, by clear and convincing evidence, demonstrates that the denial of the application for asylum would result in exceptional and extremely unusual hardship to the alien, may favorably exercise discretion under section 208 of the Act, notwithstanding the applicability of paragraph (d)(2)(i). Depending on the gravity of the circumstances underlying the application of paragraph (d)(2)(i), a showing of extraordinary circumstances might still be insufficient to warrant a favorable exercise of discretion under section 208 of the Act.

(e) Prima facie eligibility.

(1) Notwithstanding any other provision of this part, upon oral or written motion by the Department of Homeland Security, an immigration judge shall, if warranted by the record, pretermit and deny any application for asylum, withholding of removal under section 241(b)(3) of the Act, or protection under the regulations issued pursuant to the Convention Against Torture's implementing legislation if the alien has not established a prima facie claim for relief or protection under applicable law. An immigration judge need not conduct a hearing prior to pretermitting and denying an application under this paragraph (e)(1) but must consider any response to the motion before making a decision.

(2) Notwithstanding any other provision of this part, upon his or her own authority, an immigration judge shall, if warranted by the record, pretermit and deny any application for asylum, withholding of removal under section 241(b)(3) of the Act, or protection under the regulations issued pursuant to the Convention Against Torture's implementing legislation if the alien has not established a prima facie claim for relief or protection under applicable law, provided that the immigration judge shall give the parties at least 10 days' notice prior to entering such an order. An immigration judge need not conduct a hearing prior to pretermitting and denying an application under this paragraph (e)(2) but must consider any filings by the parties within the 10-day period before making a decision.

(f) Lawful pathways condition. For applications filed by aliens who entered the United States between May 11, 2023, and May 11, 2025, also refer to the provisions on asylum eligibility described in § 1208.33.

(g) Entry during emergency border circumstances. For a noncitizen who entered the United States across the southern border (as that term is described in section 4(d) of the Presidential Proclamation of June 3, 2024, as defined in paragraph (h) of this section) between the dates described in section 1 and section 2(a) of such Proclamation (or the revocation of such Proclamation, whichever is earlier), or between the dates described in section 2(b) and section 2(a) of such Proclamation (or the revocation of such Proclamation, whichever is earlier), refer to the provisions on asylum eligibility described in § 1208.35.

(h) References to the Presidential Proclamation of June 3, 2024. For purposes of paragraph (g) of this section and § 1208.35, the Presidential Proclamation of June 3, 2024, refers to Proclamation 10773 of June 3, 2024, as amended by the Presidential Proclamation of September 27, 2024. The Department intends that in the event the Presidential Proclamation of September 27, 2024, or the portions of this chapter referring to it are rendered inoperative by court order, this chapter shall continue to operate as if the references to that Proclamation have been stricken.

HISTORY:

[55 FR 30680, July 27, 1990; 59 FR 62300, Dec. 5, 1994; 62 FR 10312, 10342, Mar. 6, 1997; 64 FR 8478, 8488, Feb. 19, 1999; 65 FR 76121, 76133, Dec. 6, 2000; 68 FR 9824, 9834, 9846, Feb. 28, 2003; 83 FR 55934, 55952, Nov. 9, 2018; 84 FR 33829, 33844, July 16, 2019; 85 FR 67202, 67259, Oct. 21, 2020; 85 FR 80274, 80396, Dec. 11, 2020; 85 FR 82260, 82289, Dec. 17, 2020; 85 FR 84160, 84196, Dec. 23, 2020; 86 FR 6847, Jan. 25, 2021; 86 FR 15069, Mar. 22, 2021; 86 FR 73615, Dec. 28, 2021; 87 FR 79789, Dec. 28, 2022; 88 FR 31314, 31451, May 16, 2023; 89 FR 48710, 48769, June 7, 2024, as confirmed at 89 FR 81156, Oct. 7, 2024; 89 FR 81156, 81285, Oct. 7, 2024; 89 FR 105386, Dec. 27, 2024]

§ 1208.13 Establishing asylum eligibility. [Effective December 31, 2025]

(a) Burden of proof. The burden of proof is on the applicant for asylum to establish that he or she is a refugee as defined in section 101(a)(42) of the Act. The testimony of the applicant, if credible, may be sufficient to sustain the burden of proof without corroboration. The fact that the applicant previously established a credible fear of persecution for purposes of section 235(b)(1)(B) of the Act does not relieve the alien of the additional burden of establishing eligibility for asylum.

(b) Eligibility. The applicant may qualify as a refugee either because he or she has suffered past persecution or because he or she has a well-founded fear of future persecution.

(1) Past persecution. An applicant shall be found to be a refugee on the basis of past persecution if the applicant can establish that he or she has suffered persecution in the past in the applicant's country of nationality or, if stateless, in his or her country of last habitual residence, on account of race, religion, nationality, membership in a particular social group, or political opinion, and is unable or unwilling to return to, or avail himself or herself of the protection of, that country owing to such persecution. An applicant who has been found to have established such past persecution shall also be presumed to have a well-founded fear of persecution on the basis of the original claim. That presumption may be rebutted if an asylum officer or immigration judge makes one of the findings described in paragraph (b)(1)(i) of this section. If the applicant's fear of future persecution is unrelated to the past persecution, the applicant bears the burden of establishing that the fear is well-founded.

(i) Discretionary referral or denial. Except as provided in paragraph (b)(1)(iii) of this section, an asylum officer shall, in the exercise of his or her discretion, refer or deny, or an immigration judge, in the exercise of his or her discretion, shall deny the asylum application of an alien found to be a refugee on the basis of past persecution if any of the following is found by a preponderance of the evidence:

(A) There has been a fundamental change in circumstances such that the applicant no longer has a well-founded fear of persecution in the applicant's country of nationality or, if stateless, in the applicant's country of last habitual residence, on account of race, religion, nationality, membership in a particular social group, or political opinion; or

(B) The applicant could avoid future persecution by relocating to another part of the applicant's country of nationality or, if stateless, another part of the applicant's country of last habitual residence, and under all the circumstances, it would be reasonable to expect the applicant to do so.

(ii) Burden of proof. In cases in which an applicant has demonstrated past persecution under paragraph (b)(1) of this section, the Service shall bear the burden of establishing by a preponderance of the evidence the requirements of paragraphs (b)(1)(i)(A) or (B) of this section.

(iii) Grant in the absence of well-founded fear of persecution. An applicant described in paragraph (b)(1)(i) of this section who is not barred from a grant of asylum under paragraph (c) of this section, may be granted asylum, in the exercise of the decision-maker's discretion, if:

(A) The applicant has demonstrated compelling reasons for being unwilling or unable to return to the country arising out of the severity of the past persecution; or

(B) The applicant has established that there is a reasonable possibility that he or she may suffer other serious harm upon removal to that country.

(2) Well-founded fear of persecution

(i) An applicant has a well-founded fear of persecution if:

(A) The applicant has a fear of persecution in his or her country of nationality or, if stateless, in his or her country of last habitual residence, on account of race, religion, nationality, membership in a particular social group, or political opinion;

(B) There is a reasonable possibility of suffering such persecution if he or she were to return to that country; and

(C) He or she is unable or unwilling to return to, or avail himself or herself of the protection of, that country because of such fear.

(ii) An applicant does not have a well-founded fear of persecution if the applicant could avoid persecution by relocating to another part of the applicant's country of nationality or, if stateless, another part of the applicant's country of last habitual residence, if under all the circumstances it would be reasonable to expect the applicant to do so.

(iii) In evaluating whether the applicant has sustained the burden of proving that he or she has a well-founded fear of persecution, the asylum officer or immigration judge shall not require the applicant to provide evidence that there is a reasonable possibility he or she would be singled out individually for persecution if:

(A) The applicant establishes that there is a pattern or practice in his or her country of nationality or, if stateless, in his or her country of last habitual residence, of persecution of a group of persons similarly situated to the applicant on account of race, religion, nationality, membership in a particular social group, or political opinion; and

(B) The applicant establishes his or her own inclusion in, and identification with, such group of persons such that his or her fear of persecution upon return is reasonable.

(3) Reasonableness of internal relocation. For purposes of determinations under paragraphs (b)(1)(i) and (ii) and (b)(2) of this section, adjudicators should consider the totality of the relevant circumstances regarding an applicant's prospects for relocation, including the size of the country of nationality or last habitual residence, the geographic locus of the alleged persecution, the size, numerosity, and reach of the alleged persecutor, and the applicant's demonstrated ability to relocate to the United States in order to apply for asylum.

(i) In cases in which the applicant has not established past persecution, the applicant shall bear the burden of establishing that it would not be reasonable for him or her to relocate, unless the persecution is by a government or is government-sponsored.

(ii) In cases in which the persecutor is a government or is governmentsponsored, it shall be presumed that internal relocation would not be reasonable, unless the Department of Homeland Security establishes by a preponderance of the evidence that, under all the circumstances, it would be reasonable for the applicant to relocate.

(iii) Regardless of whether an applicant has established persecution in the past, in cases in which the persecutor is not the government or a government-sponsored actor, or otherwise is a private actor, there shall be a presumption that internal relocation would be reasonable unless the applicant establishes, by a preponderance of the evidence, that it would be unreasonable to relocate.

(iv) For purposes of determinations under paragraphs (b)(3)(ii) and (iii) of this section, persecutors who are private actors—including persecutors who are gang members, officials acting outside their official capacity, family members who are not themselves government officials, or neighbors who are not themselves government officials—shall not be considered to be persecutors who are the government or governmentsponsored absent evidence that the government sponsored the persecution.

(c) Mandatory denials —

(1) Applications filed on or after April 1, 1997. For applications filed on or after April 1, 1997, an applicant shall not qualify for asylum if section 208(a)(2) or 208(b)(2) of the Act applies to the applicant. If the applicant is found to be ineligible for asylum under either section 208(a)(2) or 208(b)(2) of the Act, the applicant shall be considered for eligibility for withholding of removal under section 241(b)(3) of the Act. The applicant shall also be considered for eligibility for

withholding of removal under the Convention Against Torture if the applicant requests such consideration or if the evidence presented by the alien indicates that the alien may be tortured in the country of removal.

(2) Applications filed before April 1, 1997

(i) An immigration judge or asylum officer shall not grant asylum to any applicant who filed his or her application before April 1, 1997, if the alien:

(A) Having been convicted by a final judgment of a particularly serious crime in the United States, constitutes a danger to the community;

(B) Has been firmly resettled within the meaning of § 1208.15;

(C) Can reasonably be regarded as a danger to the security of the United States;

(D) Has been convicted of an aggravated felony, as defined in section 101(a)(43) of the Act; or

(E) Ordered, incited, assisted, or otherwise participated in the persecution of any person on account of race, religion, nationality, membership in a particular social group, or political opinion.

(F) Is described within section 212(a)(3)(B)(i)(I),(II), and (III) of the Act as it existed prior to April 1, 1997, and as amended by the Anti-terrorist and Effective Death Penalty Act of 1996 (AEDPA), unless it is determined that there are no reasonable grounds to believe that the individual is a danger to the security of the United States.

(ii) If the evidence indicates that one of the above grounds apply to the applicant, he or she shall have the burden of proving by a preponderance of the evidence that he or she did not so act.

(3) [Removed and reserved.]

(4) [Removed and reserved.]

(5) [Removed and reserved.]

(6) Additional limitations on eligibility for asylum. For applications filed on or after November 20, 2020, an alien shall be found ineligible for asylum if:

(i) The alien has been convicted on or after such date of an offense arising under sections 274(a)(1)(A), 274(a)(2), or 276 of the Act;

(ii) The alien has been convicted on or after such date of a Federal, State, tribal, or local crime that the immigration judge knows or has reason to believe was committed in support, promotion, or furtherance of the activity of a criminal street gang as that term is defined either under the jurisdiction where the conviction occurred or in section 521(a) of title 18;

(iii) The alien has been convicted on or after such date of an offense for driving while intoxicated or impaired as those terms are defined under the jurisdiction where the conviction occurred (including a conviction for driving while under the influence of or impaired by alcohol or drugs) without regard to whether the conviction is classified as a misdemeanor or felony under Federal, State, tribal, or local law, in which such impaired driving was a cause of serious bodily injury or death of another person;

(iv)(A) The alien has been convicted on or after such date of a second or subsequent offense for driving while intoxicated or impaired as those terms are defined under the jurisdiction where the conviction occurred (including a conviction for driving while under the influence of or impaired by alcohol or drugs) without regard to whether the conviction is classified as a misdemeanor or felony under Federal, State, tribal, or local law;

(B) A finding under paragraph (c)(6)(iv)(A) of this section does not require the immigration judge to find the first conviction for driving while intoxicated or impaired (including a conviction for driving while under the influence of or impaired by alcohol or drugs) as a predicate offense. The immigration judge need only make a factual determination that the alien was previously convicted for driving while intoxicated or impaired as those terms are defined under the jurisdiction where the convictions occurred (including a conviction for driving while under the influence of or impaired by alcohol or drugs).

(v)(A) The alien has been convicted on or after such date of a crime that involves conduct amounting to a crime of stalking; or a crime of child abuse, child neglect, or child abandonment; or that involves conduct amounting to a domestic assault or battery offense, including a misdemeanor crime of domestic violence, as described in section 922(g)(9) of title 18, a misdemeanor crime of domestic violence as described in section 921(a)(33) of title 18, a crime of domestic violence as described in section 12291(a)(8) of title 34, or any crime based on conduct in which the alien harassed, coerced, intimidated, voluntarily or recklessly used (or threatened to use) force or violence against, or inflicted physical injury or physical pain, however slight, upon a person, and committed by:

(1) An alien who is a current or former spouse of the person;

(2) An alien with whom the person shares a child in common;

(3) An alien who is cohabiting with or has cohabited with the person as a spouse;

(4) An alien similarly situated to a spouse of the person under the domestic or family violence laws of the jurisdiction where the offense occurs; or

(5) Any other alien against a person who is protected from that alien's acts under the domestic or family violence laws of the United States or any State, tribal government, or unit of local government.

(B) In making a determination under paragraph (c)(6)(v)(A) of this section, including in determining the existence of a domestic relationship between the alien and the victim, the underlying conduct of the crime may be considered and the immigration judge is not limited to facts found by the criminal court or provided in the underlying record of conviction.

(C) An alien who was convicted of offenses described in paragraph (c)(6)(v)(A) of this section is not subject to ineligibility for asylum on that basis if the alien would be described in section 237(a)(7)(A) of the Act were the crimes or conduct considered grounds for deportability under section 237(a)(2)(E)(i) through (ii) of the Act.

(vi) The alien has been convicted on or after such date of—

(A) Any felony under Federal, State, tribal, or local law;

(B) Any misdemeanor offense under Federal, State, tribal, or local law involving:

(1) The possession or use of an identification document, authentication feature, or false identification document without lawful authority, unless the alien can establish that the conviction resulted from circumstances showing that the document was presented before boarding a common carrier, that the document related to the alien's eligibility to enter the United States, that the alien used the document to depart a country in which the alien has claimed a fear of persecution, and that the alien claimed a fear of persecution without delay upon presenting himself or herself to an immigration officer upon arrival at a United States port of entry;

(2) The receipt of Federal public benefits, as defined in 8 U.S.C. 1611(c), from a Federal entity, or the receipt of similar public benefits from a State, tribal, or local entity, without lawful authority; or

(3) Possession or trafficking of a controlled substance or controlled-substance paraphernalia, other than a single offense involving possession for one's own use of 30 grams or less of marijuana.

(vii) The immigration judge knows or has reason to believe that the alien has engaged on or after such date in acts of battery or extreme cruelty as defined in 8 CFR 204.2(c)(1)(vi), upon a person, and committed by:

(A) An alien who is a current or former spouse of the person;

(B) An alien with whom the person shares a child in common;

(C) An alien who is cohabiting with or has cohabited with the person as a spouse;

(D) An alien similarly situated to a spouse of the person under the domestic or family violence laws of the jurisdiction where the offense occurs; or

(E) Any other alien against a person who is protected from that alien's acts under the domestic or family violence laws of the United States or any State, tribal government, or unit of local government, even if the acts did not result in a criminal conviction;

(F) Except that an alien who was convicted of offenses or engaged in conduct described in paragraph (c)(6)(vii) of this section is not subject to ineligibility for asylum on that basis if the alien would be described in section 237(a)(7)(A) of the Act were the crimes or conduct considered grounds for deportability under section 237(a)(2)(E)(i)–(ii) of the Act.

(7) For purposes of paragraph (c)(6) of this section:

(i) The term "felony" means any crime defined as a felony by the relevant jurisdiction (Federal, State, tribal, or local) of conviction, or any crime punishable by more than one year of imprisonment.

(ii) The term "misdemeanor" means any crime defined as a misdemeanor by the relevant jurisdiction (Federal, State, tribal, or local) of conviction, or any crime not punishable by more than one year of imprisonment.

(iii) Whether any activity or conviction also may constitute a basis for removability under the Act is immaterial to a determination of asylum eligibility.

(iv) All references to a criminal offense or criminal conviction shall be deemed to include any attempt, conspiracy, or solicitation to commit the offense or any other inchoate form of the offense.

(v) No order vacating a conviction, modifying a sentence, clarifying a sentence, or otherwise altering a conviction or sentence, shall have any effect unless the immigration judge determines that—

(A) The court issuing the order had jurisdiction and authority to do so; and

(B) The order was not entered for rehabilitative purposes or for purposes of ameliorating the immigration consequences of the conviction or sentence.

(8) For purposes of paragraph (c)(7)(v)(B) of this section, the order shall be presumed to be for the purpose of ameliorating immigration consequences if:

(i) The order was entered after the initiation of any proceeding to remove the alien from the United States; or

(ii) The alien moved for the order more than one year after the date of the original order of conviction or sentencing.

(9) An immigration judge is authorized to look beyond the face of any order purporting to vacate a conviction, modify a sentence, or clarify a sentence to determine whether the requirements of paragraph (c)(7)(v) of this section have been met in order to determine whether such order should be given any effect under this section.

(10)(i) Public health emergencies. If a communicable disease has triggered an ongoing declaration of a public health emergency under Federal law, such as under section 319 of the Public Health Service Act, 42 U.S.C. 247d, or section 564 of the Food, Drug, and Cosmetic Act, 21 U.S.C. 360bbb–3, then an alien is ineligible for asylum under section 208 of the Act on the basis of there being reasonable grounds for regarding the alien as a danger to the security of the United States under section 208(b)(2)(A)(iv) of the Act if the alien—

(A) Exhibits symptoms indicating that he or she is afflicted with the disease, per guidance issued by the Secretary or the Attorney General, as appropriate, or

(B) Has come into contact with the disease within the number of days equivalent to the longest known incubation and contagion period for the disease, per guidance issued by the Secretary or the Attorney General, as appropriate.

(ii) Danger to the public health caused by an epidemic outside of the United States. If, regarding a communicable disease of public health significance as defined at 42 CFR 34.2(b), the Secretary and the Attorney General, in consultation with the Secretary of Health and Human Services, have jointly—

(A) Determined that the physical presence in the United States of aliens who are coming from a country or countries (or one or more subdivisions or regions thereof), or have embarked at a place or places, where such disease is prevalent or epidemic (or had come from that country or countries (or one or more subdivisions or regions thereof), or had embarked at that place or places, during a period in which the disease was prevalent or epidemic there) would cause a danger to the public health in the United States, and

(B) Designated the foreign country or countries (or one or more subdivisions or regions thereof), or place or places, and the period of time or circumstances under which they jointly deem it necessary for the public health that aliens or classes of aliens described in paragraph (c)(1)(ii)(A) of this section who are still within the number of days equivalent to the longest known incubation and contagion period for the disease be regarded as a danger to the security of the United States under section 208(b)(2)(A)(iv) of the Act, including any relevant exceptions as appropriate, then—

(C) An alien or class of aliens are ineligible for asylum under section 208 of the Act on the basis of there being reasonable grounds for regarding the alien or class of aliens as a danger to the security of the United States under section 208(b)(2)(A)(iv) of the Act if the alien or class of aliens are described in paragraph (c)(10)(ii)(A) of this section and are regarded as a danger to the security of the United States as provided for in paragraph (c)(10)(ii)(B) of this section.

(iii) The grounds for mandatory denial described in paragraphs (c)(10)(i) and (ii) of this section shall not apply to an alien who is applying for asylum or withholding of removal in the United States upon return from Canada to the United States and pursuant to the Agreement Between the Government of the United States and the Government of Canada for Cooperation in the Examination of Refugee Status Claims from Nationals of Third Countries.

(d) Discretion. Factors that fall short of grounds of mandatory denial of an asylum application may constitute discretionary considerations.

(1) The following are significant adverse discretionary factors that a decision-maker shall consider, if applicable, in determining whether an alien merits a grant of asylum in the exercise of discretion:

(i) An alien's unlawful entry or unlawful attempted entry into the United States unless such entry or attempted entry was made in immediate flight from persecution in a contiguous country or unless such entry or attempted entry was made by an alien under the age of 18 at the time the entry or attempted entry was made;

(ii) The failure of an alien to apply for protection from persecution or torture in at least one country outside the alien's country of citizenship, nationality, or last lawful habitual residence through which the alien transited before entering the United States unless:

(A) The alien received a final judgment denying the alien protection in such country;

(B) The alien demonstrates that he or she satisfies the definition of "victim of a severe form of trafficking in persons" provided in 8 CFR 214.11; or

(C) Such country or countries were, at the time of the transit, not parties to the 1951 Convention relating to the Status of Refugees, the 1967 Protocol relating to the Status of Refugees, or the Convention Against Torture and Other Cruel, Inhuman or Degrading Treatment or Punishment; and

(iii) An alien's use of fraudulent documents to enter the United States, unless the alien arrived in the United States by air, sea, or land directly from the applicant's home country without transiting through any other country.

(2)(i) The Attorney General, except as provided in paragraph (d)(2)(ii) of this section, will not favorably exercise discretion under section 208 of the Act for an alien who:

(A) Immediately prior to his arrival in the United States or en route to the United States from the alien's country of citizenship, nationality, or last lawful habitual residence, spent more than 14 days in any one country unless:

(1) The alien demonstrates that he or she applied for protection from persecution or torture in such country and the alien received a final judgment denying the alien protection in such country;

(2) The alien demonstrates that he or she satisfies the definition of "victim of a severe form of trafficking in persons" provided in 8 CFR 214.11; or

(3) Such country was, at the time of the transit, not a party to the 1951 Convention relating to the Status of Refugees the 1967 Protocol relating to the Status of Refugees, or the Convention against Torture and Other Cruel, Inhuman or Degrading Treatment or Punishment;

(B) Transits through more than one country between his country of citizenship, nationality, or last habitual residence and the United States unless:

(1) The alien demonstrates that he or she applied for protection from persecution or torture in at least one such country and the alien received a final judgment denying the alien protection in such country;

(2) The alien demonstrates that he or she satisfies the definition of "victim of a severe form of trafficking in persons" provided in 8 CFR 214.11; or

(3) All such countries through which the alien transited en route to the United States were, at the time of the transit, not parties to the 1951 Convention relating to the Status of Refugees, the 1967 Protocol relating to the Status of Refugees, or the Convention against Torture and Other Cruel, Inhuman or Degrading Treatment or Punishment;

(C) Would otherwise be subject to § 1208.13(c) but for the reversal, vacatur, expungement, or modification of a conviction or sentence unless the alien was found not guilty;

(D) Accrued more than one year of unlawful presence in the United States, as defined in sections 212(a)(9)(B)(ii) and (iii) of the Act, prior to filing an application for asylum;

(E) At the time the asylum application is filed with the immigration court or is referred from DHS has:

(1) Failed to timely file (or timely file a request for an extension of time to file) any required Federal, State, or local income tax returns;

(2) Failed to satisfy any outstanding Federal, State, or local tax obligations; or

(3) Has income that would result in tax liability under section 1 of the Internal Revenue Code of 1986

and that was not reported to the Internal Revenue Service;

(F) Has had two or more prior asylum applications denied for any reason;

(G) Has withdrawn a prior asylum application with prejudice or been found to have abandoned a prior asylum application;

(H) Failed to attend an interview regarding his or her asylum application with DHS, unless the alien shows by a preponderance of the evidence that:

(1) Exceptional circumstances prevented the alien from attending the interview; or

(2) The interview notice was not mailed to the last address provided by the alien or the alien's representative and neither the alien nor the alien's representative received notice of the interview; or

(I) Was subject to a final order of removal, deportation, or exclusion and did not file a motion to reopen to seek asylum based on changed country conditions within one year of the changes in country conditions.

(ii) Where one or more of the adverse discretionary factors set forth in paragraph (d)(2)(i) of this section are present, the Attorney General, in extraordinary circumstances, such as those involving national security or foreign policy considerations, or cases in which an alien, by clear and convincing evidence, demonstrates that the denial of the application for asylum would result in exceptional and extremely unusual hardship to the alien, may favorably exercise discretion under section 208 of the Act, notwithstanding the applicability of paragraph (d)(2)(i). Depending on the gravity of the circumstances underlying the application of paragraph (d)(2)(i), a showing of extraordinary circumstances might still be insufficient to warrant a favorable exercise of discretion under section 208 of the Act.

(e) Prima facie eligibility.

(1) Notwithstanding any other provision of this part, upon oral or written motion by the Department of Homeland Security, an immigration judge shall, if warranted by the record, pretermit and deny any application for asylum, withholding of removal under section 241(b)(3) of the Act, or protection under the regulations issued pursuant to the Convention Against Torture's implementing legislation if the alien has not established a prima facie claim for relief or protection under applicable law. An immigration judge need not conduct a hearing prior to pretermitting and denying an application under this paragraph (e)(1) but must consider any response to the motion before making a decision.

(2) Notwithstanding any other provision of this part, upon his or her own authority, an immigration judge shall, if warranted by the record, pretermit and deny any application for asylum, withholding of removal under section 241(b)(3) of the Act, or protection under the regulations issued pursuant to the Convention Against Torture's implementing legislation if the alien has not established a prima facie claim for relief or protection under applicable law, provided that the immigration judge shall give the parties at least 10 days' notice prior to entering such an order. An immigration judge need not conduct a hearing prior to pretermitting and denying an application under this paragraph (e)(2) but must consider any filings by the parties within the 10-day period before making a decision.

(f) Lawful pathways condition. For applications filed by aliens who entered the United States between May 11, 2023, and May 11, 2025, also refer to the provisions on asylum eligibility described in § 1208.33.

(g) Entry during emergency border circumstances. For a noncitizen who entered the United States across the southern border (as that term is described in section 4(d) of the Presidential Proclamation of June 3, 2024, as defined in paragraph (h) of this section) between the dates described in section 1 and section 2(a) of such Proclamation (or the revocation of such Proclamation, whichever is earlier), or between the dates described in section 2(b) and section 2(a) of such Proclamation (or the revocation of such Proclamation, whichever is earlier), refer to the provisions on asylum eligibility described in § 1208.35.

(h) References to the Presidential Proclamation of June 3, 2024. For purposes of paragraph (g) of this section and § 1208.35, the Presidential Proclamation of June 3, 2024, refers to Proclamation 10773 of June 3, 2024, as amended by the Presidential Proclamation of September 27, 2024. The Department intends that in the event the Presidential Proclamation of September 27, 2024, or the portions of this chapter referring to it are rendered inoperative by court order, this chapter shall continue to operate as if the references to that Proclamation have been stricken.

HISTORY:

[55 FR 30680, July 27, 1990; 59 FR 62300, Dec. 5, 1994; 62 FR 10312, 10342, Mar. 6, 1997; 64 FR 8478, 8488, Feb. 19, 1999; 65 FR 76121, 76133, Dec. 6, 2000; 68 FR 9824, 9834, 9846, Feb. 28, 2003; 83 FR 55934, 55952, Nov. 9, 2018; 84 FR 33829, 33844, July 16, 2019; 85 FR 67202, 67259, Oct. 21, 2020; 85 FR 80274, 80396, Dec. 11, 2020; 85 FR 82260, 82289, Dec. 17, 2020; 85 FR 84160, 84196, Dec. 23, 2020; 86 FR 6847, Jan. 25, 2021; 86 FR 15069, Mar. 22, 2021; 86 FR 73615, Dec. 28, 2021; 87 FR 79789, Dec. 28, 2022; 88 FR 31314, 31451, May 16, 2023; 89 FR 48710, 48769, June 7, 2024, as confirmed at 89 FR 81156, Oct. 7, 2024; 89 FR 81156, 81285, Oct. 7, 2024; 89 FR 105386, Dec. 27, 2024]

§ 1208.14 Approval, denial, referral, or dismissal of application.

(a) By an immigration judge. Unless otherwise prohibited in § 1208.13(c), an immigration judge may grant or deny asylum in the exercise of discretion to an applicant who qualifies as a refugee under section 101(a)(42) of the Act. In no case shall an immigration judge grant asylum without compliance with the requirements of § 1003.47 concerning identity, law enforcement, or security investigations or examinations.

(b) Approval by an asylum officer. In any case within the jurisdiction of USCIS, unless otherwise prohibited in § 1208.13(c), an asylum officer, subject to review within USCIS, may grant, in the exercise of his or her distraction, asylum to an applicant who qualifies as a refugee under section 101(a)(42) of the Act, and whose identity has been checked pursuant to section 208(d)(5)(A)(i) of the Act.

(c) Denial, referral, or dismissal by an asylum officer. If the asylum officer, subject to review within USCIS, does not grant asylum to an applicant after an interview conducted in accordance with 8 CFR 208.9, or if, as provided in 8 CFR 208.10, the applicant is deemed to have waived the applicant's right to an interview or an adjudication by an asylum officer, the asylum officer shall deny, refer, or dismiss the application, as follows:

(1) Inadmissible or deportable aliens. Except for applicants described in paragraph (c)(4)(ii) of this section who have not already been subject to proceedings in accordance with 8 CFR 235.3, in the case of an applicant who appears to be inadmissible or deportable under section 212(a) or 237(a) of the Act, the asylum officer shall refer the application to an immigration judge, together with the appropriate charging document, for adjudication in removal proceedings (or, where charging documents may not be issued, shall dismiss the application).

(2) Alien in valid status. In the case of an applicant who is maintaining valid immigrant, nonimmigrant, or Temporary Protected Status at the time the application is decided, the asylum officer shall deny the application for asylum.

(3) Alien with valid parole. If an applicant has been paroled into the United States and the parole has not expired or been terminated by the Service, the asylum officer shall deny the application for asylum.

(4) Alien paroled into the United States whose parole has expired or is terminated.

(i) Alien paroled prior to April 1, 1997, or with advance authorization for parole. In the case of an applicant who was paroled into the United States prior to April 1, 1997, or who, prior to departure from the United States, had received an advance authorization for parole, the asylum officer shall refer the application, together with the appropriate charging documents, to an immigration judge for adjudication in removal proceedings if the parole has expired, the Service has terminated parole, or the Service is terminating parole through issuance of the charging documents, pursuant to § 1212.5(d)(2)(i) of this chapter.

(ii) Alien paroled on or after April 1, 1997, without advance authorization for parole. In the case of an applicant who is an arriving alien or is otherwise subject to removal under § 235.3(b) of chapter I, and was paroled into the United States on or after April 1, 1997, without advance authorization for parole prior to departure from the United States, the asylum officer will take the following actions, if the parole has expired or been terminated:

(A) Inadmissible under section 212(a)(6)(C) or 212(a)(7) of the Act. If the applicant appears inadmissible to the United States under section 212(a)(6)(C) or 212(a)(7) of the Act and the asylum officer does not intend to lodge any additional charges of inadmissibility, the asylum officer shall proceed in accordance with § 235.3(b) of chapter I. If such applicant is found to have a credible fear of persecution or torture based on information elicited from the asylum interview, an asylum officer may refer the applicant directly to an immigration judge in removal proceedings under section 240 of the Act, without conducting a separate credible fear interview pursuant to § 208.30 of chapter I. If such applicant is not found to have a credible fear based on information elicited at the asylum interview, an asylum officer will conduct a credible fear interview and the applicant will be subject to the credible fear process specified at § 208.30 of chapter I.

(B) Inadmissible on other grounds. In the case of an applicant who was paroled into the United States on or after April 1, 1997, and will be charged as inadmissible to the United States under provisions of the Act other than, or in addition to, sections 212(a)(6)(C) or 212(a)(7), the asylum officer shall refer the application to an immigration judge for adjudication in removal proceedings.

(d) Applicability of § 103.2(b) of this chapter. No application for asylum or withholding of deportation shall be subject to denial pursuant to § 103.2(b) of this chapter.

(e) Duration. If the applicant is granted asylum, the grant will be effective for an indefinite period, subject to termination as provided in § 1208.24.

(f) Effect of denial of principal's application on separate applications by dependents. The denial of an asylum application filed by a principal applicant for asylum shall also result in the denial of asylum status to any dependents of that principal applicant who are included in that same application. Such denial shall not preclude a grant of asylum for an otherwise eligible dependent who has filed a separate asylum application, nor shall such denial result in an otherwise eligible dependent becoming ineligible to apply for asylum due to the provisions of section 208(a)(2)(C) of the Act.

(g) Applicants granted lawful permanent residence status. If an asylum applicant is granted adjustment of status to lawful permanent resident, the Service may provide written notice to the applicant that his or her asylum application will be presumed abandoned and dismissed without prejudice, unless the applicant submits a written request within 30 days of the notice, that the asylum application be adjudicated. If an applicant does not respond within 30 days of the date the written notice was sent or served, the Service may presume the asylum application abandoned and dismiss it without prejudice.

HISTORY:

[55 FR 30680, July 27, 1990; 59 FR 62300, Dec. 5, 1994; 62 FR 10312, 10342, March 6, 1997; 63 FR 12979, 12986, March 17, 1998; 64 FR 27856, 27875, May 21, 1999; 65 FR 76121, 76134, Dec. 6, 2000; 68 FR 9824, 9834, 9846, Feb. 28, 2003; 68 FR 10349, 10352, Mar. 5, 2003; 70 FR 4743, 4754, Jan. 31, 2005; 85 FR 80274, 80397, Dec. 11, 2020; 87 FR 18078, 18221, Mar. 29, 2022]

§ 1208.15 Definition of "firm resettlement."

(a) An alien is considered to be firmly resettled if, after the events giving rise to the alien's asylum claim:

(1) The alien resided in a country through which the alien transited prior to arriving in or entering the United States and —

(i) Received or was eligible for any permanent legal immigration status in that country;

(ii) Resided in such a country with any non-permanent but indefinitely renewable legal immigration status (including asylee, refugee, or similar status but excluding status such as of a tourist); or

(iii) Resided in such a country and could have applied for and obtained any non-permanent but indefinitely renewable legal immigration status in that country;

(2) The alien physically resided voluntarily, and without continuing to suffer persecution in any one country for one year or more after departing his country of nationality or last habitual residence and prior to arrival in or entry into the United States, provided that time spent in Mexico by an alien who is not a native or citizen of Mexico solely as a direct result of being returned to Mexico pursuant to section 235(b)(2)(C) of the Act or of being subject to metering would not be counted for purposes of this paragraph; or

(3)(i) The alien is a citizen of a country other than the one where the alien alleges a fear of persecution and the alien was present in that country after departing his country of nationality or last habitual residence and prior to arrival in or entry into the United States, or

(ii) the alien was a citizen of a country other than the one where the alien alleges a fear of persecution, the alien was present in that country after departing his country of nationality or last habitual residence and prior to arrival in or entry into the United States, and the alien renounced that citizenship after arriving in the United States.

(b) The provisions of 8 CFR 1240.8(d) shall apply when the evidence of record indicates that the firm resettlement bar may apply. In such cases, the alien shall bear the burden of proving the bar does not apply. Either DHS or the immigration judge may raise the issue of the application of the firm resettlement bar based on the evidence of record. The firm resettlement of an alien's parent(s) shall be imputed to the alien if the resettlement occurred before the alien turned 18 and the alien resided with the alien's parents at the time of the firm resettlement unless he or she could not have derived any permanent legal immigration status or any nonpermanent but indefinitely renewable legal immigration status (including asylee, refugee, or similar status but excluding status such as of a tourist) from the alien's parent.

HISTORY:

[55 FR 30680, July 27, 1990; 62 FR 10312, 10343, March 6, 1997; 65 FR 76121, 76135, Dec. 6, 2000; 68 FR 9824, 9834, Feb. 28, 2003; 85 FR 80274, 80397, Dec. 11, 2020]

§ 1208.16 Withholding of removal under section 241(b)(3)(B) of the Act and withholding of removal under the Convention Against Torture. [Effective until December 31, 2025]

(a) Consideration of application for withholding of removal. Consideration of eligibility for statutory withholding of removal and protection under the Convention Against Torture by a DHS officer is as provided at 8 CFR 208.16. In exclusion, deportation, or removal proceedings, an immigration judge may adjudicate both an asylum claim and a request for withholding of removal whether or not asylum is granted.

(b) Eligibility for withholding of removal under section 241(b)(3) of the Act; burden of proof. The burden of proof is on the applicant for withholding of removal under section 241(b)(3) of the Act to establish that his or her life or freedom would be threatened in the proposed country of removal on account of race, religion, nationality, membership in a particular social group, or political opinion. The testimony of the applicant, if credible, may be sufficient to sustain the burden of proof without corroboration. The evidence shall be evaluated as follows:

(1) Past threat to life or freedom

(i) If the applicant is determined to have suffered past persecution in the proposed country of removal on account of race, religion, nationality, membership in a particular social group, or political opinion, it shall be presumed that the applicant's life or freedom would be threatened in the future in the country of removal on the basis of the original claim. This presumption may be rebutted if an asylum officer or immigration judge finds by a preponderance of the evidence:

(A) There has been a fundamental change in circumstances such that the applicant's life or freedom would not be threatened on account of any of the five grounds mentioned in this paragraph upon the applicant's removal to that country; or

(B) The applicant could avoid a future threat to his or her life or freedom by relocating to another part of the proposed country of removal and, under all the circumstances, it would be reasonable to expect the applicant to do so.

(ii) In cases in which the applicant has established past persecution, the Service shall bear the burden of establishing by a preponderance of the evidence the requirements of paragraphs (b)(1)(i)(A) or (b)(1)(i)(B) of this section.

(iii) If the applicant's fear of future threat to life or freedom is unrelated to the past persecution, the applicant bears the burden of establishing that it is more likely than not that he or she would suffer such harm.

(2) Future threat to life or freedom. An applicant who has not suffered past persecution may demonstrate that his or her life or freedom would be threatened in the future in a country if he or she can establish that it is more likely than not that he or she would be persecuted on account of race, religion, nationality, membership in a particular social group, or political opinion upon removal to that country. Such an applicant cannot demonstrate that his or her life or freedom would be threatened if the asylum officer or immigration judge finds that the applicant could avoid a future threat to his or her life or freedom by relocating to another part of the proposed country of removal and, under all the circumstances, it would be reasonable to expect the applicant to do so. In evaluating whether it is more likely than not that the applicant's life or freedom would be threatened in a particular country on account of race, religion, nationality, membership in a particular social group, or political opinion, the asylum officer or immigration judge shall not require the appli-

cant to provide evidence that he or she would be singled out individually for such persecution if:

(i) The applicant establishes that in that country there is a pattern or practice of persecution of a group of persons similarly situated to the applicant on account of race, religion, nationality, membership in a particular social group, or political opinion; and

(ii) The applicant establishes his or her own inclusion in and identification with such group of persons such that it is more likely than not that his or her life or freedom would be threatened upon return to that country.

(3) Reasonableness of internal relocation. For purposes of determinations under paragraphs (b)(1) and (2) of this section, adjudicators should consider the totality of the relevant circumstances regarding an applicant's prospects for relocation, including the size of the country of nationality or last habitual residence, the geographic locus of the alleged persecution, the size, reach, or numerosity of the alleged persecutor, and the applicant's demonstrated ability to relocate to the United States in order to apply for withholding of removal.

(i) In cases in which the applicant has not established past persecution, the applicant shall bear the burden of establishing that it would not be reasonable for him or her to relocate, unless the persecutor is a government or is government-sponsored.

(ii) In cases in which the persecutor is a government or is government-sponsored, it shall be presumed that internal relocation would not be reasonable, unless the DHS establishes by a preponderance of the evidence that, under all the circumstances, it would be reasonable for the applicant to relocate.

(iii) Regardless of whether an applicant has established persecution in the past, in cases in which the persecutor is not the government or a government-sponsored actor, or otherwise is a private actor, there shall be a presumption that internal relocation would be reasonable unless the applicant establishes, by a preponderance of the evidence, that it would be unreasonable to relocate.

(iv) For purposes of determinations under paragraphs (b)(3)(ii) and (iii) of this section, persecutors who are private actors, including persecutors who are gang members, public official who are not acting under color of law, or family members who are not themselves government officials or neighbors who are not themselves government officials, shall not be considered to be persecutors who are the government or government-sponsored absent evidence that the government sponsored the persecution.

(c) Eligibility for withholding of removal under the Convention Against Torture.

(1) For purposes of regulations under Title II of the Act, "Convention Against Torture" shall refer to the United Nations Convention Against Torture and Other Cruel, Inhuman or Degrading Treatment or Punishment, subject to any reservations, understandings, declarations, and provisos contained in the United States Senate resolution of ratification of the Convention, as implemented by section 2242 of the Foreign Affairs Reform and Restructuring Act of 1998 (Pub. L. 105-277, 112 Stat. 2681, 2681-821). The definition of torture contained in § 1208.18(a) of this part shall govern all decisions made under regulations under Title II of the Act about the applicability of Article 3 of the Convention Against Torture.

(2) The burden of proof is on the applicant for withholding of removal under this paragraph to establish that it is more likely than not that he or she would be tortured if removed to the proposed country of removal. The testimony of the applicant, if credible, may be sufficient to sustain the burden of proof without corroboration.

(3) In assessing whether it is more likely than not that an applicant would be tortured in the proposed country of removal, all evidence relevant to the possibility of future torture shall be considered, including, but not limited to:

(i) Evidence of past torture inflicted upon the applicant;

(ii) Evidence that the applicant could relocate to a part of the country of removal where he or she is not likely to be tortured;

(iii) Evidence of gross, flagrant or mass violations of human rights within the country of removal, where applicable; and

(iv) Other relevant information regarding conditions in the country of removal.

(4) In considering an application for withholding of removal under the Convention Against Torture, the immigration judge shall first determine whether the alien is more likely than not to be tortured in the country of removal. If the immigration judge determines that the alien is more likely than not to be tortured in the country of removal, the alien is entitled to protection under the Convention Against Torture. Protection under the Convention Against Torture will be granted either in the form of withholding of removal or in the form of deferral of removal. An alien entitled to such protection shall be granted withholding of removal unless the alien is subject to mandatory denial of withholding of removal under paragraphs (d)(2) or (d)(3) of this section. If an alien entitled to such protection is subject to mandatory denial of withholding of removal under paragraphs (d)(2) or (d)(3) of this section, the alien's removal shall be deferred under § 1208.17(a).

(d) Approval or denial of application.

(1) General. Subject to paragraphs (d)(2) and (d)(3) of this section, an application for withholding of deportation or removal to a country of proposed removal shall be granted if the applicant's eligibility for withholding is established pursuant to paragraphs (b) or (c) of this section.

(2) Mandatory denials—

(i) In general. Except as provided in paragraph (d)(3) of this section, an application for withholding of removal under section 241(b)(3) of the Act or under the regulations issued pursuant to the legislation implementing the Convention Against Torture shall be denied if the applicant falls within section 241(b)(3)(B) of the Act or, for applications for withholding of deportation adjudicated in proceedings commenced prior to

April 1, 1997, within section 243(h)(2) of the Act as it appeared prior to that date. For purposes of section 241(b)(3)(B)(ii) of the Act, or section 243(h)(2)(B) of the Act as it appeared prior to April 1, 1997, an alien who has been convicted of a particularly serious crime shall be considered to constitute a danger to the community. If the evidence indicates the applicability of one or more of the grounds for denial of withholding enumerated in the Act, the applicant shall have the burden of proving by a preponderance of the evidence that such grounds do not apply.

(ii) Public health emergencies. If a communicable disease has triggered an ongoing declaration of a public health emergency under Federal law, such as under section 319 of the Public Health Service Act, 42 U.S.C. 247d, or section 564 of the Food, Drug, and Cosmetic Act, 21 U.S.C. 360bbb–3, then an alien is ineligible for withholding of removal under section 241(b)(3) of the Act and under the regulations issued pursuant to the legislation implementing the Convention Against Torture on the basis of there being reasonable grounds for regarding the alien as a danger to the security of the United States under section 241(b)(3)(B)(iv) of the Act if the alien—

(A) Exhibits symptoms indicating that he or she is afflicted with the disease, per guidance issued by the Secretary or the Attorney General, as appropriate; or

(B) Has come into contact with the disease within the number of days equivalent to the longest known incubation and contagion period for the disease, per guidance issued by the Secretary or the Attorney General, as appropriate.

(iii) Danger to the public health caused by an epidemic outside of the United States. If, regarding a communicable disease of public health significance as defined at 42 CFR 34.2(b), the Secretary and the Attorney General, in consultation with the Secretary of Health and Human Services, have jointly—

(A) Determined that the physical presence in the United States of aliens who are coming from a country or countries (or one or more subdivisions or regions thereof), or have embarked at a place or places, where such disease is prevalent or epidemic (or had come from that country or countries (or one or more subdivisions or regions thereof), or had embarked at that place or places, during a period in which the disease was prevalent or epidemic there) would cause a danger to the public health in the United States; and

(B) Designated the foreign country or countries (or one or more subdivisions or regions thereof), or place or places, and the period of time or circumstances under which they jointly deem it necessary for the public health that aliens or classes of aliens described in paragraph (d)(2)(iii)(A) of this section who are still within the number of days equivalent to the longest known incubation and contagion period for the disease be regarded as a danger to the security of the United States under section 241(b)(3)(B)(iv) of the Act, including any relevant exceptions as appropriate, then—

(C) An alien or class of aliens are ineligible for withholding of removal under section 241(b)(3) of the Act and under the regulations issued pursuant to the legislation implementing the Convention Against Torture on the basis of there being reasonable grounds for regarding the alien or class of aliens as a danger to the security of the United States under section 241(b)(3)(B)(iv) of the Act if the alien or class of aliens are described in paragraph (d)(2)(iii)(A) of this section and are regarded as a danger to the security of the United States as provided for in paragraph (d)(2)(iii)(B) of this section.

(iv) The grounds for mandatory denial described in paragraphs (d)(2)(ii) and (iii) of this section shall not apply to an alien who is applying for asylum or withholding of removal in the United States upon return from Canada to the United States and pursuant to the Agreement Between the Government of the United States and the Government of Canada for Cooperation in the Examination of Refugee Status Claims from Nationals of Third Countries).

(3) Exception to the prohibition on withholding of deportation in certain cases. Section 243(h)(3) of the Act, as added by section 413 of Pub. L. 104-132 (110 Stat. 1214), shall apply only to applications adjudicated in proceedings commenced before April 1, 1997, and in which final action had not been taken before April 24, 1996. The discretion permitted by that section to override section 243(h)(2) of the Act shall be exercised only in the case of an applicant convicted of an aggravated felony (or felonies) where he or she was sentenced to an aggregate term of imprisonment of less than 5 years and the immigration judge determines on an individual basis that the crime (or crimes) of which the applicant was convicted does not constitute a particularly serious crime. Nevertheless, it shall be presumed that an alien convicted of an aggravated felony has been convicted of a particularly serious crime. Except in the cases specified in this paragraph, the grounds for denial of withholding of deportation in section 243(h)(2) of the Act as it appeared prior to April 1, 1997, shall be deemed to comply with the Protocol Relating to the Status of Refugees, Jan. 31, 1967, T.I.A.S. No. 6577.

(e) [Removed and reserved].

(f) Removal to third country.

(1) Nothing in this section or § 1208.17 shall prevent the Department of Homeland Security from removing an alien requesting protection to a third country other than a country to which removal is currently withheld or deferred.

(2) If an alien requests withholding or deferral of removal to the applicable home country or another specific country, nothing in this section or § 1208.17 precludes the Department of Homeland Security from removing the alien to a third country prior to a determination or adjudication of the alien's initial request for withholding or deferral of removal if, after being notified of the identity of the prospective third country of removal and provided an opportunity to demonstrate that he or she is more likely than not to be tortured in that third country, the alien fails to establish that they are more likely than not to be tortured there. However, such a removal shall be executed only if the alien was:

(i) Advised at the time of requesting withholding or deferral of removal of the possibility of being removed to a third country prior to a determination or adjudication of the same under the conditions set forth in this paragraph, and

(ii) Provided, but did not accept, an opportunity to withdraw the request for withholding or deferral of removal in order to prevent such removal and, instead, proceed to removal pursuant to section 241(b) of the Act, as appropriate.

HISTORY:

[55 FR 30680, July 27, 1990; 59 FR 62301, Dec. 5, 1994; 60 FR 44260, 44264, Aug. 25, 1995; 62 FR 10312, 10343, Mar. 6, 1997; 64 FR 8478, 8488, Feb. 19, 1999; 65 FR 76121, 76135, Dec. 6, 2000; 68 FR 9824, 9834, 9846, Feb. 28, 2003; 85 FR 67202, 67260, Oct. 21, 2020; 85 FR 80274, 80398, Dec. 11, 2020; 85 FR 84160, 84197, Dec. 23, 2020; 86 FR 6847, Jan. 25, 2021; 86 FR 15069, Mar. 22, 2021; 86 FR 73615, Dec. 28, 2021; 87 FR 18078, 18222, Mar. 29, 2022; 87 FR 79789, Dec. 28, 2022; 89 FR 105386, Dec. 27, 2024]

§ 1208.16 Withholding of removal under section 241(b)(3)(B) of the Act and withholding of removal under the Convention Against Torture. [Effective December 31, 2025]

(a) Consideration of application for withholding of removal. Consideration of eligibility for statutory withholding of removal and protection under the Convention Against Torture by a DHS officer is as provided at 8 CFR 208.16. In exclusion, deportation, or removal proceedings, an immigration judge may adjudicate both an asylum claim and a request for withholding of removal whether or not asylum is granted.

(b) Eligibility for withholding of removal under section 241(b)(3) of the Act; burden of proof. The burden of proof is on the applicant for withholding of removal under section 241(b)(3) of the Act to establish that his or her life or freedom would be threatened in the proposed country of removal on account of race, religion, nationality, membership in a particular social group, or political opinion. The testimony of the applicant, if credible, may be sufficient to sustain the burden of proof without corroboration. The evidence shall be evaluated as follows:

(1) Past threat to life or freedom

(i) If the applicant is determined to have suffered past persecution in the proposed country of removal on account of race, religion, nationality, membership in a particular social group, or political opinion, it shall be presumed that the applicant's life or freedom would be threatened in the future in the country of removal on the basis of the original claim. This presumption may be rebutted if an asylum officer or immigration judge finds by a preponderance of the evidence:

(A) There has been a fundamental change in circumstances such that the applicant's life or freedom would not be threatened on account of any of the five grounds mentioned in this paragraph upon the applicant's removal to that country; or

(B) The applicant could avoid a future threat to his or her life or freedom by relocating to another part of the proposed country of removal and, under all the circumstances, it would be reasonable to expect the applicant to do so.

(ii) In cases in which the applicant has established past persecution, the Service shall bear the burden of establishing by a preponderance of the evidence the requirements of paragraphs (b)(1)(i)(A) or (b)(1)(i)(B) of this section.

(iii) If the applicant's fear of future threat to life or freedom is unrelated to the past persecution, the applicant bears the burden of establishing that it is more likely than not that he or she would suffer such harm.

(2) Future threat to life or freedom. An applicant who has not suffered past persecution may demonstrate that his or her life or freedom would be threatened in the future in a country if he or she can establish that it is more likely than not that he or she would be persecuted on account of race, religion, nationality, membership in a particular social group, or political opinion upon removal to that country. Such an applicant cannot demonstrate that his or her life or freedom would be threatened if the asylum officer or immigration judge finds that the applicant could avoid a future threat to his or her life or freedom by relocating to another part of the proposed country of removal and, under all the circumstances, it would be reasonable to expect the applicant to do so. In evaluating whether it is more likely than not that the applicant's life or freedom would be threatened in a particular country on account of race, religion, nationality, membership in a particular social group, or political opinion, the asylum officer or immigration judge shall not require the applicant to provide evidence that he or she would be singled out individually for such persecution if:

(i) The applicant establishes that in that country there is a pattern or practice of persecution of a group of persons similarly situated to the applicant on account of race, religion, nationality, membership in a particular social group, or political opinion; and

(ii) The applicant establishes his or her own inclusion in and identification with such group of persons such that it is more likely than not that his or her life or freedom would be threatened upon return to that country.

(3) Reasonableness of internal relocation. For purposes of determinations under paragraphs (b)(1) and (2) of this section, adjudicators should consider the totality of the relevant circumstances regarding an applicant's prospects for relocation, including the size of the country of nationality or last habitual residence, the geographic locus of the alleged persecution, the size, reach, or numerosity of the alleged persecutor, and the applicant's demonstrated ability to relocate to the United States in order to apply for withholding of removal.

(i) In cases in which the applicant has not established past persecution, the applicant shall bear the burden of establishing that it would not be reasonable for him or her to relocate, unless the persecutor is a government or is government-sponsored.

(ii) In cases in which the persecutor is a government or is government-sponsored, it shall be presumed that internal relocation would not be reasonable, unless the DHS establishes by a preponderance of the evidence that, under all the circumstances, it would be reasonable for the applicant to relocate.

(iii) Regardless of whether an applicant has established persecution in the past, in cases in which the persecutor is not the government or a government-sponsored actor, or otherwise is a private actor, there shall be a presumption that internal relocation would be reasonable unless the applicant establishes, by a preponderance of the evidence, that it would be unreasonable to relocate.

(iv) For purposes of determinations under paragraphs (b)(3)(ii) and (iii) of this section, persecutors who are private actors, including persecutors who are gang members, public official who are not acting under color of law, or family members who are not themselves government officials or neighbors who are not themselves government officials, shall not be considered to be persecutors who are the government or government-sponsored absent evidence that the government sponsored the persecution.

(c) Eligibility for withholding of removal under the Convention Against Torture.

(1) For purposes of regulations under Title II of the Act, "Convention Against Torture" shall refer to the United Nations Convention Against Torture and Other Cruel, Inhuman or Degrading Treatment or Punishment, subject to any reservations, understandings, declarations, and provisos contained in the United States Senate resolution of ratification of the Convention, as implemented by section 2242 of the Foreign Affairs Reform and Restructuring Act of 1998 (Pub. L. 105-277, 112 Stat. 2681, 2681-821). The definition of torture contained in § 1208.18(a) of this part shall govern all decisions made under regulations under Title II of the Act about the applicability of Article 3 of the Convention Against Torture.

(2) The burden of proof is on the applicant for withholding of removal under this paragraph to establish that it is more likely than not that he or she would be tortured if removed to the proposed country of removal. The testimony of the applicant, if credible, may be sufficient to sustain the burden of proof without corroboration.

(3) In assessing whether it is more likely than not that an applicant would be tortured in the proposed country of removal, all evidence relevant to the possibility of future torture shall be considered, including, but not limited to:

(i) Evidence of past torture inflicted upon the applicant;

(ii) Evidence that the applicant could relocate to a part of the country of removal where he or she is not likely to be tortured;

(iii) Evidence of gross, flagrant or mass violations of human rights within the country of removal, where applicable; and

(iv) Other relevant information regarding conditions in the country of removal.

(4) In considering an application for withholding of removal under the Convention Against Torture, the immigration judge shall first determine whether the alien is more likely than not to be tortured in the country of removal. If the immigration judge determines that the alien is more likely than not to be tortured in the country of removal, the alien is entitled to protection under the Convention Against Torture. Protection under the Convention Against Torture will be granted either in the form of withholding of removal or in the form of deferral of removal. An alien entitled to such protection shall be granted withholding of removal unless the alien is subject to mandatory denial of withholding of removal under paragraphs (d)(2) or (d)(3) of this section. If an alien entitled to such protection is subject to mandatory denial of withholding of removal under paragraphs (d)(2) or (d)(3) of this section, the alien's removal shall be deferred under § 1208.17(a).

(d) Approval or denial of application.

(1) General. Subject to paragraphs (d)(2) and (d)(3) of this section, an application for withholding of deportation or removal to a country of proposed removal shall be granted if the applicant's eligibility for withholding is established pursuant to paragraphs (b) or (c) of this section.

(2) Mandatory denials—

(i) In general. Except as provided in paragraph (d)(3) of this section, an application for withholding of removal under section 241(b)(3) of the Act or under the regulations issued pursuant to the legislation implementing the Convention Against Torture shall be denied if the applicant falls within section 241(b)(3)(B) of the Act or, for applications for withholding of deportation adjudicated in proceedings commenced prior to April 1, 1997, within section 243(h)(2) of the Act as it appeared prior to that date. For purposes of section 241(b)(3)(B)(ii) of the Act, or section 243(h)(2)(B) of the Act as it appeared prior to April 1, 1997, an alien who has been convicted of a particularly serious crime shall be considered to constitute a danger to the community. If the evidence indicates the applicability of one or more of the grounds for denial of withholding enumerated in the Act, the applicant shall have the burden of proving by a preponderance of the evidence that such grounds do not apply.

(ii) Public health emergencies. If a communicable disease has triggered an ongoing declaration of a public health emergency under Federal law, such as under section 319 of the Public Health Service Act, 42 U.S.C. 247d, or section 564 of the Food, Drug, and Cosmetic Act, 21 U.S.C. 360bbb–3, then an alien is ineligible for withholding of removal under section 241(b)(3) of the Act and under the regulations issued pursuant to the legislation implementing the Convention Against Torture on the basis of there being reasonable grounds for regarding the alien as a danger to the security of the United States under section 241(b)(3)(B)(iv) of the Act if the alien—

(A) Exhibits symptoms indicating that he or she is afflicted with the disease, per guidance issued by the Secretary or the Attorney General, as appropriate; or

(B) Has come into contact with the disease within the number of days equivalent to the longest known incubation and contagion period for the disease, per guidance issued by the Secretary or the Attorney General, as appropriate.

(iii) Danger to the public health caused by an epidemic outside of the United States. If, regarding a communicable disease of public health significance as defined at 42 CFR 34.2(b), the Secretary and the Attorney General, in consultation with the Secretary of Health and Human Services, have jointly—

(A) Determined that the physical presence in the United States of aliens who are coming from a country or countries (or one or more subdivisions or regions thereof), or have embarked at a place or places, where such disease is prevalent or epidemic (or had come from that country or countries (or one or more subdivisions or regions thereof), or had embarked at that place or places, during a period in which the disease was prevalent or epidemic there) would cause a danger to the public health in the United States; and

(B) Designated the foreign country or countries (or one or more subdivisions or regions thereof), or place or places, and the period of time or circumstances under which they jointly deem it necessary for the public health that aliens or classes of aliens described in paragraph (d)(2)(iii)(A) of this section who are still within the number of days equivalent to the longest known incubation and contagion period for the disease be regarded as a danger to the security of the United States under section 241(b)(3)(B)(iv) of the Act, including any relevant exceptions as appropriate, then—

(C) An alien or class of aliens are ineligible for withholding of removal under section 241(b)(3) of the Act and under the regulations issued pursuant to the legislation implementing the Convention Against Torture on the basis of there being reasonable grounds for regarding the alien or class of aliens as a danger to the security of the United States under section 241(b)(3)(B)(iv) of the Act if the alien or class of aliens are described in paragraph (d)(2)(iii)(A) of this section and are regarded as a danger to the security of the United States as provided for in paragraph (d)(2)(iii)(B) of this section.

(iv) The grounds for mandatory denial described in paragraphs (d)(2)(ii) and (iii) of this section shall not apply to an alien who is applying for asylum or withholding of removal in the United States upon return from Canada to the United States and pursuant to the Agreement Between the Government of the United States and the Government of Canada for Cooperation in the Examination of Refugee Status Claims from Nationals of Third Countries).

(3) Exception to the prohibition on withholding of deportation in certain cases. Section 243(h)(3) of the Act, as added by section 413 of Pub. L. 104-132 (110 Stat. 1214), shall apply only to applications adjudicated in proceedings commenced before April 1, 1997, and in which final action had not been taken before April 24, 1996. The discretion permitted by that section to override section 243(h)(2) of the Act shall be exercised only in the case of an applicant convicted of an aggravated felony (or felonies) where he or she was sentenced to an aggregate term of imprisonment of less than 5 years and the immigration judge determines on an individual basis that the crime (or crimes) of which the applicant was convicted does not constitute a particularly serious crime. Nevertheless, it shall be presumed that an alien convicted of an aggravated felony has been convicted of a particularly serious crime. Except in the cases specified in this paragraph, the grounds for denial of withholding of deportation in section 243(h)(2) of the Act as it appeared prior to April 1, 1997, shall be deemed to comply with the Protocol Relating to the Status of Refugees, Jan. 31, 1967, T.I.A.S. No. 6577.

(e) [Removed and reserved].

(f) Removal to third country.

(1) Nothing in this section or § 1208.17 shall prevent the Department of Homeland Security from removing an alien requesting protection to a third country other than a country to which removal is currently withheld or deferred.

(2) If an alien requests withholding or deferral of removal to the applicable home country or another specific country, nothing in this section or § 1208.17 precludes the Department of Homeland Security from removing the alien to a third country prior to a determination or adjudication of the alien's initial request for withholding or deferral of removal if, after being notified of the identity of the prospective third country of removal and provided an opportunity to demonstrate that he or she is more likely than not to be tortured in that third country, the alien fails to establish that they are more likely than not to be tortured there. However, such a removal shall be executed only if the alien was:

(i) Advised at the time of requesting withholding or deferral of removal of the possibility of being removed to a third country prior to a determination or adjudication of the same under the conditions set forth in this paragraph, and

(ii) Provided, but did not accept, an opportunity to withdraw the request for withholding or deferral of removal in order to prevent such removal and, instead, proceed to removal pursuant to section 241(b) of the Act, as appropriate.

HISTORY:

[55 FR 30680, July 27, 1990; 59 FR 62301, Dec. 5, 1994; 60 FR 44260, 44264, Aug. 25, 1995; 62 FR 10312, 10343, Mar. 6, 1997; 64 FR 8478, 8488, Feb. 19, 1999; 65 FR 76121, 76135, Dec. 6, 2000; 68 FR 9824, 9834, 9846, Feb. 28, 2003; 85 FR 67202, 67260, Oct. 21, 2020; 85 FR 80274, 80398, Dec. 11, 2020; 85 FR 84160, 84197, Dec. 23, 2020; 86 FR 6847, Jan. 25, 2021; 86 FR 15069, Mar. 22, 2021; 86 FR 73615, Dec. 28, 2021; 87 FR 18078, 18222, Mar. 29, 2022; 87 FR 79789, Dec. 28, 2022; 89 FR 105386, Dec. 27, 2024]

§ 1208.17 Deferral of removal under the Convention Against Torture.

(a) Grant of deferral of removal. An alien who: has been ordered removed; has been found under § 1208.16(c)(3) to be entitled to protection under the Convention Against Torture; and is subject to the provisions for mandatory denial of withholding of removal under § 1208.16(d)(2) or (d)(3), shall be granted deferral of removal to the country where he or she is more likely than not to be tortured.

(b) Notice to Alien. (1) After an immigration judge orders an alien described in paragraph (a) of this section removed, the immigration judge shall inform the alien that his or her removal to the country where he or she is more likely than not to be tortured shall be deferred until such time as the deferral is terminated under this section. The immigration judge shall inform the alien that deferral of removal:

(1) Does not confer upon the alien any lawful or permanent immigration status in the United States;

(i) Does not confer upon the alien any lawful or permanent immigration status in the United States;

(ii) Will not necessarily result in the alien being released from the custody of the Service if the alien is subject to such custody;

(iii) Is effective only until terminated; and

(iv) Is subject to review and termination if the immigration judge determines that it is not likely that the alien would be tortured in the country to which removal has been deferred, or if the alien requests that deferral be terminated.

(2) The immigration judge shall also inform the alien that removal has been deferred only to the country in which it has been determined that the alien is likely to be tortured, and that the alien may be removed at any time to another country where he or she is not likely to be tortured.

(c) Detention of an alien granted deferral of removal under this section. Nothing in this section shall alter the authority of the Service to detain an alien whose removal has been deferred under this section and who is otherwise subject to detention. In the case of such an alien, decisions about the alien's release shall be made according to part 241 of this chapter.

(d) Termination of deferral of removal.

(1) At any time while deferral of removal is in effect, the INS District Counsel for the District with jurisdiction over an alien whose removal has been deferred under paragraph (a) of this section may file a motion with the Immigration Court having administrative control pursuant to § 1003.11 of this chapter to schedule a hearing to consider whether deferral of removal should be terminated. The Service motion shall be granted if it is accompanied by evidence that is relevant to the possibility that the alien would be tortured in the country to which removal has been deferred and that was not presented at the previous hearing. The Service motion shall not be subject to the requirements for reopening in §§ 3.2 and 3.23 of this chapter.

(2) The Immigration Court shall provide notice to the alien and the Service of the time, place, and date of the termination hearing. Such notice shall inform the alien that the alien may supplement the information in his or her initial application for withholding of removal under the Convention Against Torture and shall provide that the alien must submit any such supplemental information within 10 calendar days of service of such notice (or 13 calendar days if service of such notice was by mail). At the expiration of this 10 or 13 day period, the Immigration Court shall forward a copy of the original application, and any supplemental information the alien or the Service has submitted, to the Department of State, together with notice to the Department of State of the time, place and date of the termination hearing. At its option, the Department of State may provide comments on the case, according to the provisions of § 1208.11 of this part.

(3) The immigration judge shall conduct a hearing and make a de novo determination, based on the record of proceeding and initial application in addition to any new evidence submitted by the Service or the alien, as to whether the alien is more likely than not to be tortured in the country to which removal has been deferred. This determination shall be made under the standards for eligibility set out in § 1208.16(c). The burden is on the alien to establish that it is more likely than not that he or she would be tortured in the country to which removal has been deferred.

(4) If the immigration judge determines that the alien is more likely than not to be tortured in the country to which removal has been deferred, the order of deferral shall remain in place. If the immigration judge determines that the alien has not established that he or she is more likely than not to be tortured in the country to which removal has been deferred, the deferral of removal shall be terminated and the alien may be removed to that country. Appeal of the immigration judge's decision shall lie to the Board.

(e) Termination at the request of the alien.

(1) At any time while deferral of removal is in effect, the alien may make a written request to the Immigration Court having administrative control pursuant to § 1003.11 of this chapter to terminate the deferral order. If satisfied on the basis of the written submission that the alien's request is knowing and voluntary, the immigration judge shall terminate the order of deferral and the alien may be removed.

(2) If necessary the immigration judge may calendar a hearing for the sole purpose of determining whether the alien's request is knowing and voluntary. If the immigration judge determines that the alien's request is knowing and voluntary, the order of deferral shall be terminated. If the immigration judge determines that the alien's request is not knowing and voluntary, the alien's request shall not serve as the basis for terminating the order of deferral.

(f) Termination pursuant to § 1208.18(c). At any time while deferral of removal is in effect, the Attorney General may determine whether deferral should be terminated based on diplomatic assurances forwarded by the Secretary of State pursuant to the procedures in § 1208.18(c).

HISTORY:

[55 FR 30680, July 27, 1990; 59 FR 62301, Dec. 5, 1994; 62 FR 10312, 10344, Mar. 6, 1997; 64 FR 8478, 8489, Feb. 19, 1999; 68 FR 9824, 9834, 9846, Feb. 28, 2003; 68 FR 10349, 10352, Mar. 5, 2003]

§ 1208.18 Implementation of the Convention Against Torture.

(a) Definitions. The definitions in this subsection incorporate the definition of torture contained in Article 1 of the Convention Against Torture, subject to the reservations, understandings, declarations, and provisos contained in the United States Senate resolution of ratification of the Convention.

(1) Torture is defined as any act by which severe pain or suffering, whether physical or mental, is intentionally inflicted on a person for such purposes as obtaining from him or her or a third person information or a confession, punishing him or her for an act he or she or a third person has committed or is suspected of having committed, intimidating or coercing him or her or a third person, or for any reason based on discrimination of any kind, when such pain or suffering is inflicted by, or at the instigation of, or with the consent or acquiescence of, a public official acting in an official capacity or other person acting in an official capacity. Pain or suffering inflicted by a public official who is not acting under color of law shall not constitute pain or suffering inflicted by, or at the instigation of, or with the consent or acquiescence of, a public official acting in an official capacity or other person acting in an official capacity, although a different public official acting in an official capacity or other person acting in an official capacity could instigate, consent to, or acquiesce in the pain or suffering inflicted by the public official who is not acting under color of law.

(2) Torture is an extreme form of cruel and inhuman treatment and does not include lesser forms of cruel, inhuman or degrading treatment or punishment that do not amount to torture.

(3) Torture does not include pain or suffering arising only from, inherent in or incidental to lawful sanctions. Lawful sanctions include judicially imposed sanctions and other enforcement actions authorized by law, including the death penalty, but do not include sanctions that defeat the object and purpose of the Convention Against Torture to prohibit torture.

(4) In order to constitute torture, mental pain or suffering must be prolonged mental harm caused by or resulting from:

(i) The intentional infliction or threatened infliction of severe physical pain or suffering;

(ii) The administration or application, or threatened administration or application, of mind altering substances or other procedures calculated to disrupt profoundly the senses or the personality;

(iii) The threat of imminent death; or

(iv) The threat that another person will imminently be subjected to death, severe physical pain or suffering, or the administration or application of mind altering substances or other procedures calculated to disrupt profoundly the sense or personality.

(5) In order to constitute torture, an act must be specifically intended to inflict severe physical or mental pain or suffering. An act that results in unanticipated or unintended severity of pain and suffering is not torture.

(6) In order to constitute torture an act must be directed against a person in the offender's custody or physical control.

(7) Acquiescence of a public official requires that the public official, prior to the activity constituting torture, have awareness of such activity and thereafter breach his or her legal responsibility to intervene to prevent such activity. Such awareness requires a finding of either actual knowledge or willful blindness. Willful blindness means that the public official acting in an official capacity or other person acting in an official capacity was aware of a high probability of activity constituting torture and deliberately avoided learning the truth; it is not enough that such public official acting in an official capacity or other person acting in an official capacity was mistaken, recklessly disregarded the truth, or negligently failed to inquire. In order for a public official to breach his or her legal responsibility to intervene to prevent activity constituting torture, the official must have been charged with preventing the activity as part of his or her duties and have failed to intervene. No person will be deemed to have breached a legal responsibility to intervene if such person is unable to intervene, or if the person intervenes but is unable to prevent the activity that constitutes torture.

(8) Noncompliance with applicable legal procedural standards does not per se constitute torture.

(b) Applicability of §§ 1208.16(c) and 1208.17(a).

(1) Aliens in proceedings on or after March 22, 1999.

(i) An alien who is in exclusion, deportation, or removal proceedings on or after March 22, 1999, may apply for withholding of removal under § 1208.16(c), and, if applicable, may be considered for deferral of removal under § 1208.17(a).

(ii) In addition, an alien may apply for withholding of removal under 8 CFR 208.16(c), and, if applicable, may be considered for deferral of removal under 8 CFR 208.17(a), in the following situation: The alien is determined to be an applicant for admission under section 235(b)(1) of the Act, the alien is found to have a credible fear of persecution or torture, the alien's case is subsequently retained by or referred to USCIS pursuant to the jurisdiction provided at 8 CFR 208.2(a)(1)(ii) to consider the application for asylum, and that application for asylum is not granted.

(2) Aliens who were ordered removed, or whose removal orders became final, before March 22, 1999. An alien under a final order of deportation, exclusion, or removal that became final prior to March 22, 1999 may move to reopen proceedings for the sole purpose of seeking protection under § 1208.16(c). Such motions shall be governed by §§ 1003.23 and 1003.2 of this chapter, except that the time and numerical limitations on motions to reopen shall not apply and the alien shall not be required to demonstrate that the evidence sought to be offered was unavailable and could not have been discovered or presented at the former hearing. The motion to reopen shall not be granted unless:

(i) The motion is filed within June 21, 1999; and

(ii) The evidence sought to be offered establishes a prima facie case that the applicant's removal must be withheld or deferred under §§ 1208.16(c) or 1208.17(a).

(3) Aliens who, on March 22, 1999, have requests pending with the Service for protection under Article 3 of the Convention Against Torture.

(i) Except as otherwise provided, after March 22, 1999, the Service will not:

(A) Consider, under its pre-regulatory administrative policy to ensure compliance with the Convention Against Torture, whether Article 3 of that Convention prohibits the removal of an alien to a particular country, or

(B) Stay the removal of an alien based on a request filed with the Service for protection under Article 3 of that Convention.

(ii) For each alien who, on or before March 22, 1999, filed a request with the Service for protection under Article 3 of the Convention Against Torture, and whose request has not been finally decided by the Service, the Service shall provide written notice that, after March 22, 1999, consideration for protection under Article 3 can be obtained only through the provisions of this rule.

(A) The notice shall inform an alien who is under an order of removal issued by EOIR that, in order to seek consideration of a claim under §§ 1208.16(c) or 1208.17(a), such an alien must file a motion to reopen with the immigration court or the Board of Immigration Appeals. This notice shall be accompanied by a stay of removal, effective until 30 days after service of the notice on the alien. A motion to reopen filed under this paragraph for the limited purpose of asserting a claim under §§ 1208.16(c) or 1208.17(a) shall not be subject to the requirements for reopening in §§ 1003.2 and 1003.23 of this chapter. Such a motion shall be granted if it is accompanied by a copy of the notice described in paragraph (b)(3)(ii) or by other convincing evidence that the alien had a request pending with the Service for protection under Article 3 of the Convention Against Torture on March 22, 1999. The filing of such a motion shall extend the stay of removal during the pendency of the adjudication of this motion.

(B) The notice shall inform an alien who is under an administrative order of removal issued by the Service under section 238(b) of the Act or an exclusion, deportation, or removal order reinstated by the Service under section 241(a)(5) of the Act that the alien's claim to withholding of removal under § 1208.16(c) or deferral of removal under § 1208.17(a) will be considered under § 1208.31.

(C) The notice shall inform an alien who is under an administrative order of removal issued by the Service under section 235(c) of the Act that the alien's claim to protection under the Convention Against Torture will be decided by the Service as provided in § 1208.18(d) and 235.8(b)(4) and will not be considered under the provisions of this part relating to consideration or review by an immigration judge, the Board of Immigration Appeals, or an asylum officer.

(4) Aliens whose claims to protection under the Convention Against Torture were finally decided by the Service prior to March 22, 1999. Sections 1208.16(c) and 1208.17 (a) and paragraphs (b)(1) through (b)(3) of this section do not apply to cases in which, prior to March 22, 1999, the Service has made a final administrative determination about the applicability of Article 3 of the Convention Against Torture to the case of an alien who filed a request with the Service for protection under Article 3. If, prior to March 22, 1999, the Service determined that an applicant cannot be removed consistent with the Convention Against Torture, the alien shall be considered to have been granted withholding of removal under § 1208.16(c), unless the alien is subject to mandatory denial of withholding of removal under § 1208.16(d)(2) or (d)(3), in which case the alien will be considered to have been granted deferral of removal under 1208.17(a). If, prior to March 22, 1999, the Service determined that an alien can be removed consistent with the Convention Against Torture, the alien will be considered to have been finally denied withholding of removal under § 1208.16(c) and deferral of removal under § 1208.17(a).

(c) Diplomatic assurances against torture obtained by the Secretary of State.

(1) The Secretary of State may forward to the Attorney General assurances that the Secretary has obtained from the government of a specific country that an alien would not be tortured there if the alien were removed to that country.

(2) If the Secretary of State forwards assurances described in paragraph (c)(1) of this section to the Attorney General for consideration by the Attorney General or her delegates under this paragraph, the Attorney General shall determine, in consultation with the Secretary of State, whether the assurances are sufficiently reliable to allow the alien's removal to that country consistent with Article 3 of the Convention Against Torture. The Attorney General's authority under this paragraph may be exercised by the Deputy Attorney General or by the Commissioner, Immigration and Naturalization Service, but may not be further delegated.

(3) Once assurances are provided under paragraph (c)(2) of this section, the alien's claim for protection under the Convention Against Torture shall not be considered further by an immigration judge, the Board of Immigration Appeals, or an asylum officer.

(d) Cases involving aliens ordered removed under section 235(c) of the Act. With respect to an alien terrorist or other alien subject to administrative removal under section 235(c) of the Act who requests protection under Article 3 of the Convention Against Torture, the Service will assess the applicability of Article 3 through the removal process to ensure that a removal order will not be executed under circumstances that would violate the obligations of the United States under Article 3. In such cases, the provisions of Part 1208 relating to consideration or review by an immigration judge, the Board of Immigration Appeals, or an asylum officer shall not apply.

(e) Judicial review of claims for protection from removal under Article 3 of the Convention Against Torture.

(1) Pursuant to the provisions of section 2242(d) of the Foreign Affairs Reform and Restructuring Act of 1998, there shall be no judicial appeal or review of any action, decision, or claim raised under the Convention or that section, except as part of the review of a final order of removal pursuant to section 242 of the Act; provided however, that any appeal or petition regarding an action, decision, or claim under the Convention or under section 2242 of the Foreign Affairs Reform and Restructuring Act of 1998 shall not be deemed to include or authorize the consideration of any adminis-

trative order or decision, or portion thereof, the appeal or review of which is restricted or prohibited by the Act.

(2) Except as otherwise expressly provided, nothing in this paragraph shall be construed to create a private right of action or to authorize the consideration or issuance of administrative or judicial relief.

HISTORY:

[64 FR 8478, 8490, Feb. 19, 1999, as corrected at 64 FR 13881, Mar. 23, 1999; 68 FR 9824, 9834, 9846, Feb. 28, 2003; 68 FR 10349, 10352, Mar. 5, 2003; 85 FR 80274, 80398, Dec. 11, 2020; 87 FR 18078, 18222, Mar. 29, 2022]

§ 1208.19 Decisions. [This section was removed and reserved, effective May 31, 2022. See 87 FR 18078, 18222, Mar. 29, 2022.]

§ 1208.20 Determining if an asylum application is frivolous.

(a) For applications filed on or after April 1, 1997, and before January 11, 2021, an applicant is subject to the provisions of section 208(d)(6) of the Act only if the alien received the notice required by section 208(d)(4)(A) of the Act and a final order by an immigration judge or the Board of Immigration Appeals specifically finds that the alien knowingly filed a frivolous asylum application. An application is frivolous if:

(1) Any of the material elements in the asylum application is deliberately fabricated, and the immigration judge or the Board is satisfied that the applicant, during the course of the proceedings, has had sufficient opportunity to account for any discrepancies or implausible aspects of the claim.

(2) Paragraphs (b) through (f) shall only apply to applications filed on or after January 11, 2021.

(b) For applications filed on or after January 11, 2021, an asylum officer may determine that the applicant knowingly filed a frivolous asylum application and may refer the applicant to an immigration judge on that basis, so long as the applicant has received the notice required by section 208(d)(4)(A) of the Act. For applications referred to an immigration judge, an asylum officer's determination that an application is frivolous will not render an applicant permanently ineligible for immigration benefits unless an immigration judge or the Board makes a finding of frivolousness as described in paragraph (c) of this section.

(c) For applications filed on or after January 11, 2021, an asylum application is frivolous if it:

(1) Contains a fabricated material element;

(2) Is premised upon false or fabricated evidence unless the application would have been granted without the false or fabricated evidence;

(3) Is filed without regard to the merits of the claim; or

(4) Is clearly foreclosed by applicable law.

(d) If the alien has been provided the warning required by section 208(d)(4)(A) of the Act, he or she need not be given any additional or further opportunity to account for any issues with his or her claim prior to the entry of a frivolousness finding.

(e) An asylum application may be found frivolous even if it was untimely filed.

(f) A withdrawn asylum application may be found frivolous unless:

(1) The alien wholly disclaims the application and withdraws it with prejudice;

(2) The alien is eligible for and agrees to accept voluntary departure for a period of no more than 30 days pursuant to section 240B(a) of the Act;

(3) The alien withdraws any and all other applications for relief or protection with prejudice; and

(4) The alien waives his right to appeal and any rights to file, for any reason, a motion to reopen or reconsider.

(g) For purposes of this section, a finding that an alien filed a knowingly frivolous asylum application shall not preclude the alien from seeking withholding of removal under section 241(b)(3) of the Act or protection under the regulations issued pursuant to the Convention Against Torture's implementing legislation.

HISTORY:

[55 FR 30680, July 27, 1990; 60 FR 34090, June 30, 1995; 61 FR 18900, 18909, April 29, 1996; 62 FR 10312, 10344, Mar. 6, 1997; 63 FR 3792, 3796, Jan. 27, 1998; redesignated and revised at 64 FR 8478, 8490, 8492, Feb. 19, 1999; redesignated at 65 FR 76121, 76136, Dec. 6, 2000; 68 FR 9824, 9834, Feb. 28, 2003; 85 FR 80274, 80398, Dec. 11, 2020]

§ 1208.21 Admission of the asylee's spouse and children.

(a) Eligibility. In accordance with section 208(b)(3) of the Act, a spouse, as defined in section 101(a)(35) of the Act, 8 U.S.C. 1101(a)(35), or child, as defined in section 101(b)(1) of the Act, also may be granted asylum if accompanying, or following to join, the principal alien who was granted asylum, unless it is determined that the spouse or child is ineligible for asylum under section 208(b)(2)(A)(i), (ii), (iii), (iv) or (v) of the Act for applications filed on or after April 1, 1997, or under § 1208.13(c)(2)(i)(A), (C), (D), (E), or (F) for applications filed before April 1, 1997.

(1) The spouse or child ordered, incited, assisted, or otherwise participated in the persecution of any persons on account of race, religion, nationality, membership in a particular social group, or political opinion;

(2) The spouse or child, having been convicted by a final judgment of a particularly serious crime in the United States, constitutes a danger to the community of the United States;

(3) The spouse or child has been convicted of an aggravated felony, as defined in section 101(a)(43) of the Act; or

(4) There are reasonable grounds for regarding the spouse or child a danger to the security of the United States.

(b) Relationship. The relationship of spouse and child as defined in sections 101(a)(35) and 101(b)(1) of the Act must have existed at the time the principal alien's asylum application was approved and must continue to exist at the time of filing for accompanying or following-to-join benefits and at the time of the spouse or child's subsequent admission to the United States. If the asylee proves that the asylee is the parent of a child who was born after asylum was granted, but who was in utero on the date of the asylum grant, the child shall be eligible to accompany or follow-to-join the asylee. The child's mother, if not the principal asylee, shall not be eligible to accompany or follow-to-join the principal asylee unless the child's mother was the principal asylee's spouse on the date the principal asylee was granted asylum.

(c) Spouse or child in the United States. When a spouse or child of an alien granted asylum is in the United States, but was not included in the asylee's application, the asylee may request accompanying or following-to-join benefits for his/her spouse or child by filing for each qualifying family member a separate Form I-730, Refugee/Asylee Relative Petition, and supporting evidence, with the designated Service office, regardless of the status of that spouse or child in the United States. A recent photograph of each derivative must accompany the Form I-730. The photograph must clearly identify the derivative, and will be made part of the derivative's immigration record for identification purposes. Additionally, a separate Form I-730 must be filed by the asylee for each qualifying family member before February 28, 2000, or within 2 years of the date in which he/she was granted asylum status, whichever is later, unless it is determined by the Service that this period should be extended for humanitarian reasons. Upon approval of the Form I-730, the Service will notify the asylee of such approval on Form I-797, Notice of Action. Employment will be authorized incident to status. To demonstrate employment authorization, the Service will issue a Form I-94, Arrival-Departure Record, which also reflects the derivative's current status as an asylee, or the derivative may apply under § 274a.12(a) of this chapter, using Form I-765, Application for Employment Authorization, and a copy of the Form I-797. The approval of the Form I-730 shall remain valid for the duration of the relationship to the asylee and, in the case of a child, while the child is under 21 years of age and unmarried, provided also that the principal's status has not been revoked. However, the approved Form I-730 will cease to confer immigration benefits after it has been used by the beneficiary for admission to the United States as a derivative of an asylee.

(d) Spouse or child outside the United States. When a spouse or child of an alien granted asylum is outside the United States, the asylee may request accompanying or following-to-join benefits for his/her spouse or child(ren) by filing a separate Form I-730 for each qualifying family member with the designated Service office, setting forth the full name, relationship, date and place of birth, and current location of each such person. A recent photograph of each derivative must accompany the Form I-730. The photograph must clearly identify the derivative, and will be made part of the derivative's immigration record for identification purposes. A separate Form I-730 for each qualifying family member must be filed before February 28, 2000, or within 2 years of the date in which the asylee was granted asylum status, whichever is later, unless the Service determines that the filing period should be extended for humanitarian reasons. When the Form I-730 is approved, the Service will notify the asylee of such approval on Form I-797. The approved Form I-730 shall be forwarded by the Service to the Department of State for delivery to the American Embassy or Consulate having jurisdiction over the area in which the asylee's spouse or child is located. The approval of the Form I-730 shall remain valid for the duration of the relationship to the asylee and, in the case of a child, while the child is under 21 years of age and unmarried, provided also that the principal's status has not been revoked. However, the approved Form I-730 will cease to confer immigration benefits after it has been used by the beneficiary for admission to the United States as a derivative of an asylee.

(e) Denial. If the spouse or child is found to be ineligible for the status accorded under section 208(c) of the Act, a written notice stating the basis for denial shall be forwarded to the principal alien. No appeal shall lie from this decision.

(f) Burden of proof. To establish the claimed relationship of spouse or child as defined in sections 101(a)(35) and 101(b)(1) of the Act, evidence must be submitted with the request as set forth in part 204 of this chapter. Where possible this will consist of the documents specified in § 204.2 (a)(1)(i)(B), (a)(1)(iii)(B), (a)(2), (d)(2), and (d)(5) of 8 CFR chapter I. The burden of proof is on the principal alien to establish by a preponderance of the evidence that any person on whose behalf he or she is making a request under this section is an eligible spouse or child.

(g) Duration. The spouse or child qualifying under section 208(c) of the Act shall be granted asylum for an indefinite period unless the principal's status is revoked.

HISTORY:

[55 FR 30680, July 27, 1990; 60 FR 34090, June 30, 1995; 61 FR 18900, 18909, April 29, 1996; 62 FR 10312, 10344, Mar. 6, 1997; 63 FR 3792, 3796, Jan. 27, 1998; redesignated at 64 FR 8478, 8490, Feb. 19, 1999; redesignated and amended at 65 FR 76121, 76136, Dec. 6, 2000; 68 FR 9824, 9834, 9846, Feb. 28, 2003; 68 FR 10349, 10352, Mar. 5, 2003]

§ 1208.22 Effect on exclusion, deportation, and removal proceedings.

An alien who has been granted asylum may not be deported or removed unless asylum status is terminated pursuant to 8 CFR 208.24 or § 1208.24. An alien in exclusion, deportation, or removal proceedings who is granted withholding of removal or deportation, or deferral of removal, may not be deported or removed to the country to which his or her deportation or removal is ordered withheld or deferred unless the withholding order is terminated pursuant to 8 CFR 208.24 or § 1208.24 or deferral is terminated pursuant to 8 CFR 208.17 or § 1208.17(d) or (e).

HISTORY:

[55 FR 30680, July 27, 1990; 59 FR 62301, Dec. 5, 1994; 62 FR 10312, 10344, Mar. 6, 1997; redesignated and revised at 64 FR

8478, 8490, 8492, Feb. 19, 1999; redesignated and revised at 65 FR 76121, 76136, Dec. 6, 2000; 68 FR 9824, 9834, 9846, Feb. 28, 2003; 87 FR 18078, 18222, Mar. 29, 2022]

§ 1208.23 Restoration of status.

An alien who was maintaining his or her nonimmigrant status at the time of filing an asylum application and has such application denied may continue in or be restored to that status, if it has not expired.

HISTORY:

[55 FR 30680, July 27, 1990; 59 FR 62301, Dec. 5, 1994; 62 FR 10312, 10344, Mar. 6, 1997; redesignated at 64 FR 8478, 8490, Feb. 19, 1999; redesignated at 65 FR 76121, 76136, Dec. 6, 2000; 68 FR 9824, 9834, Feb. 28, 2003]

§ 1208.24 Termination of asylum or withholding of removal or deportation.

(a) Termination of asylum by the Service. Except as provided in paragraph (e) of this section, an asylum officer may terminate a grant of asylum made under the jurisdiction of an asylum officer or a district director if following an interview, the asylum officer determines that:

(1) There is a showing of fraud in the alien's application such that he or she was not eligible for asylum at the time it was granted;

(2) As to applications filed on or after April 1, 1997, one or more of the conditions described in section 208(c)(2) of the Act exist; or

(3) As to applications filed before April 1, 1997, the alien no longer has a well-founded fear of persecution upon return due to a change of country conditions in the alien's country of nationality or habitual residence or the alien has committed any act that would have been grounds for denial of asylum under § 1208.13(c)(2).

(b) Termination of withholding of deportation or removal by the Service. Except as provided in paragraph (e) of this section, an asylum officer may terminate a grant of withholding of deportation or removal made under the jurisdiction of an asylum officer or a district director if the asylum officer determines, following an interview, that:

(1) The alien is no longer entitled to withholding of deportation or removal because, owing to a fundamental change in circumstances relating to the original claim, the alien's life or freedom no longer would be threatened on account of race, religion, nationality, membership in a particular social group, or political opinion in the country from which deportation or removal was withheld.

(2) There is a showing of fraud in the alien's application such that the alien was not eligible for withholding of removal at the time it was granted;

(3) The alien has committed any other act that would have been grounds for denial of withholding of removal under section 241(b)(3)(B) of the Act had it occurred prior to the grant of withholding of removal; or

(4) For applications filed in proceedings commenced before April 1, 1997, the alien has committed any act that would have been grounds for denial of withholding of deportation under section 243(h)(2) of the Act.

(c) Procedure. Prior to the termination of a grant of asylum or withholding of deportation or removal, the alien shall be given notice of intent to terminate, with the reasons therefor, at least 30 days prior to the interview specified in paragraph (a) of this section before an asylum officer. The alien shall be provided the opportunity to present evidence showing that he or she is still eligible for asylum or withholding of deportation or removal. If the asylum officer determines that the alien is no longer eligible for asylum or withholding of deportation or removal, the alien shall be given written notice that asylum status or withholding of deportation or removal and any employment authorization issued pursuant thereto, are terminated.

(d) Termination of derivative status. The termination of asylum status for a person who was the principal applicant shall result in termination of the asylum status of a spouse or child whose status was based on the asylum application of the principal. Such termination shall not preclude the spouse or child of such alien from separately asserting an asylum or withholding of deportation or removal claim.

(e) Removal proceedings. When an alien's asylum status or withholding of removal or deportation is terminated under this section, the Service shall initiate removal proceedings, as appropriate, if the alien is not already in exclusion, deportation, or removal proceedings. Removal proceedings may take place in conjunction with a termination hearing scheduled under § 1208.24(f).

(f) Termination of asylum, or withholding of deportation or removal, by an immigration judge or the Board of Immigration Appeals. An immigration judge or the Board of Immigration Appeals may reopen a case pursuant to § 1003.2 or § 1003.23 of this chapter for the purpose of terminating a grant of asylum, or a withholding of deportation or removal. In such a reopened proceeding, the Service must establish, by a preponderance of evidence, one or more of the grounds set forth in paragraphs (a) or (b) of this section. In addition, an immigration judge may terminate a grant of asylum, or a withholding of deportation or removal, made under the jurisdiction of the Service at any time after the alien has been provided a notice of intent to terminate by the Service. Any termination under this paragraph may occur in conjunction with an exclusion, deportation, or removal proceeding.

(g) Termination of asylum for arriving aliens. If the Service determines that an applicant for admission who had previously been granted asylum in the United States falls within conditions set forth in § 1208.24 and is inadmissible, the Service shall issue a notice of intent to terminate asylum and initiate removal proceedings under section 240 of the Act. The alien shall present his or her response to the intent to terminate during proceedings before the immigration judge.

HISTORY:

[55 FR 30680, July 27, 1990; 62 FR 10312, 10344, Mar. 6, 1997; redesignated at 64 FR 8478, 8490, Feb. 19, 1999; redesignated and amended at 65 FR 76121, 76136, Dec. 6, 2000; 68 FR 9824, 9834, 9846, Feb. 28, 2003; 68 FR 10349, 10352, Mar. 5, 2003]

§ 1208.25 Severability.

The provisions of part 1208 are separate and severable from one another. In the event that any provision in part 1208 is stayed, enjoined, not implemented, or otherwise held invalid, the remaining provisions shall nevertheless be implemented as an independent rule and continue in effect.

HISTORY:
85 FR 80274, 80399, Dec. 11, 2020]

Subpart B

Credible Fear of Persecution

§ 1208.30 Credible fear determinations involving stowaways and applicants for admission who are found inadmissible pursuant to section 212(a)(6)(C) or 212(a)(7) of the Act. [Effective until December 31, 2025]

(a) Jurisdiction. The provisions of this subpart apply to aliens subject to sections 235(a)(2) and 235(b)(1) of the Act. Pursuant to section 235(b)(1)(B) of the Act, DHS has exclusive jurisdiction to make the determinations described in this subpart. Except as otherwise provided in this subpart, paragraphs (b) through (g) of this section are the exclusive procedures applicable to stowaways and applicants for admission who are found inadmissible pursuant to section 212(a)(6)(C) or 212(a)(7) of the Act and who receive fear interviews, determinations, and reviews under section 235(b)(1)(B) of the Act. Prior to January 1, 2030, an alien physically present in or arriving in the Commonwealth of the Northern Mariana Islands is ineligible to apply for asylum and may only establish eligibility for withholding of removal pursuant to section 241(b)(3) of the Act or withholding or deferral of removal under the regulations in §§ 1208.16(c) through (f), 1208.17, and 1208.18 issued pursuant to the Convention Against Torture's implementing legislation.

(b) Treatment of dependents. A spouse or child of an alien may be included in that alien's fear evaluation and determination, if such spouse or child:

(1) Arrived in the United States concurrently with the principal alien; and

(2) Desires to be included in the principal alien's determination. However, any alien may have his or her evaluation and determination made separately, if he or she expresses such a desire.

(c)-(d) [Reserved]

(e) Determination. For the standards and procedures for asylum officers in conducting credible fear interviews, and in making positive and negative credible fear determinations, see 8 CFR 208.30. The immigration judges will review such determinations as provided in paragraph (g) of this section and §§ 1003.42 and 1240.17 of this chapter.

(f) [Reserved]

(g) Procedures for negative fear determinations—

(1) [Removed and reserved.]

(2) Review by immigration judge of a negative credible fear finding.

(i) The asylum officer's negative decision regarding credible fear shall be subject to review by an immigration judge upon the applicant's request, or upon the applicant's refusal or failure either to request or to decline the review after being given such opportunity, in accordance with section 235(b)(1)(B)(iii)(III) of the Act. The immigration judge shall not have the authority to remand the case to the asylum officer.

(ii) The record of the negative credible fear determination, including copies of the Form I-863, Notice of Referral to Immigration Judge, the asylum officer's notes, the summary of the material facts, and other materials upon which the determination was based shall be provided to the immigration judge with the negative determination.

(iii) A credible fear hearing will be closed to the public unless the alien states for the record or submits a written statement that the alien is waiving that requirement; in that event the hearing shall be open to the public, subject to the immigration judge's discretion as provided in § 1003.27 of this chapter.

(iv) Upon review of the asylum officer's negative credible fear determination:

(A) If the immigration judge concurs with the determination of the asylum officer that the alien does not have a credible fear of persecution or torture, the case shall be returned to DHS for removal of the alien. The immigration judge's decision is final and may not be appealed. USCIS may nevertheless reconsider a negative credible fear finding as provided at 8 CFR 208.30(g)(1)(i).

(B) If the immigration judge finds that the alien, other than an alien stowaway, possesses a credible fear of persecution or torture, the immigration judge shall vacate the Notice and Order of Expedited Removal and refer the case back to DHS for further proceedings consistent with § 1208.2(a)(1)(ii). Alternatively, DHS may commence removal proceedings under section 240 of the Act, during which time the alien may file an application for asylum and withholding of removal in accordance with § 1208.4(b)(3)(i).

(C) If the immigration judge finds that an alien stowaway possesses a credible fear of persecution or torture, the alien shall be allowed to file an application for asylum and withholding of removal before the immigration judge in accordance with § 1208.4(b)(3)(iii). The immigration judge shall decide the application as provided in that section. Such decision may be appealed by either the stowaway or DHS to the Board of Immigration Appeals. If a denial of the application for asylum and for withholding of removal becomes final, the alien shall be removed from the United States in accordance with section 235(a)(2) of the Act. If an approval of the application for asylum or for withholding of removal becomes final, DHS shall terminate removal proceedings under section 235(a)(2) of the Act.

HISTORY:

[62 FR 10312, 10345, Mar. 6, 1997; 64 FR 8478, 8492, Feb. 19, 1999; 65 FR 76121, 76136, Dec. 6, 2000; 68 FR 9824, 9834, 9846, Feb. 28, 2003; 68 FR 10349, 10352, Mar. 5, 2003; 69 FR 69490, 69497, Nov. 29, 2004; 74 FR 55726, 55742, Oct. 28, 2009; 83 FR 55934, 55952, Nov. 9, 2018; 84 FR 33829, 33843, July 16, 2019; 85 FR 23902, 23904, Apr. 30, 2020; 85 FR 80274, 80399, Dec. 11, 2020; 85 FR 84160, 84198, Dec. 23, 2020; 86 FR 6847, Jan. 25, 2021; 86 FR 15069, Mar. 22, 2021; 86 FR 73615, Dec. 28, 2021; 87 FR 18078, 18222, Mar. 29, 2022; 87 FR 79789, Dec. 28, 2022; 88 FR 31314, 31451, May 16, 2023; 89 FR 105386, Dec. 27, 2024]

§ 1208.30 Credible fear determinations involving stowaways and applicants for admission who are found inadmissible pursuant to section 212(a)(6)(C) or 212(a)(7) of the Act. [Effective December 31, 2025]

(a) Jurisdiction. The provisions of this subpart apply to aliens subject to sections 235(a)(2) and 235(b)(1) of the Act. Pursuant to section 235(b)(1)(B) of the Act, DHS has exclusive jurisdiction to make the determinations described in this subpart. Except as otherwise provided in this subpart, paragraphs (b) through (g) of this section are the exclusive procedures applicable to stowaways and applicants for admission who are found inadmissible pursuant to section 212(a)(6)(C) or 212(a)(7) of the Act and who receive fear interviews, determinations, and reviews under section 235(b)(1)(B) of the Act. Prior to January 1, 2030, an alien physically present in or arriving in the Commonwealth of the Northern Mariana Islands is ineligible to apply for asylum and may only establish eligibility for withholding of removal pursuant to section 241(b)(3) of the Act or withholding or deferral of removal under the regulations in §§ 1208.16(c) through (f), 1208.17, and 1208.18 issued pursuant to the Convention Against Torture's implementing legislation.

(b) Treatment of dependents. A spouse or child of an alien may be included in that alien's fear evaluation and determination, if such spouse or child:

(1) Arrived in the United States concurrently with the principal alien; and

(2) Desires to be included in the principal alien's determination. However, any alien may have his or her evaluation and determination made separately, if he or she expresses such a desire.

(c)-(d) [Reserved]

(e) Determination. For the standards and procedures for asylum officers in conducting credible fear interviews, and in making positive and negative credible fear determinations, see 8 CFR 208.30. The immigration judges will review such determinations as provided in paragraph (g) of this section and §§ 1003.42 and 1240.17 of this chapter.

(f) [Reserved]

(g) Procedures for negative fear determinations—

(1) [Removed and reserved.]

(2) Review by immigration judge of a negative credible fear finding.

(i) The asylum officer's negative decision regarding credible fear shall be subject to review by an immigration judge upon the applicant's request, or upon the applicant's refusal or failure either to request or to decline the review after being given such opportunity, in accordance with section 235(b)(1)(B)(iii)(III) of the Act. The immigration judge shall not have the authority to remand the case to the asylum officer.

(ii) The record of the negative credible fear determination, including copies of the Form I-863, Notice of Referral to Immigration Judge, the asylum officer's notes, the summary of the material facts, and other materials upon which the determination was based shall be provided to the immigration judge with the negative determination.

(iii) A credible fear hearing will be closed to the public unless the alien states for the record or submits a written statement that the alien is waiving that requirement; in that event the hearing shall be open to the public, subject to the immigration judge's discretion as provided in § 1003.27 of this chapter.

(iv) Upon review of the asylum officer's negative credible fear determination:

(A) If the immigration judge concurs with the determination of the asylum officer that the alien does not have a credible fear of persecution or torture, the case shall be returned to DHS for removal of the alien. The immigration judge's decision is final and may not be appealed. USCIS may nevertheless reconsider a negative credible fear finding as provided at 8 CFR 208.30(g)(1)(i).

(B) If the immigration judge finds that the alien, other than an alien stowaway, possesses a credible fear of persecution or torture, the immigration judge shall vacate the Notice and Order of Expedited Removal and refer the case back to DHS for further proceedings consistent with § 1208.2(a)(1)(ii). Alternatively, DHS may commence removal proceedings under section 240 of the Act, during which time the alien may file an application for asylum and withholding of removal in accordance with § 1208.4(b)(3)(i).

(C) If the immigration judge finds that an alien stowaway possesses a credible fear of persecution or torture, the alien shall be allowed to file an application for asylum and withholding of removal before the immigration judge in accordance with § 1208.4(b)(3)(iii). The immigration judge shall decide the application as provided in that section. Such decision may be appealed by either the stowaway or DHS to the Board of Immigration Appeals. If a denial of the application for asylum and for withholding of removal becomes final, the alien shall be removed from the United States in accordance with section 235(a)(2) of the Act. If an approval of the application for asylum or for withholding of removal becomes final, DHS shall terminate removal proceedings under section 235(a)(2) of the Act.

HISTORY:

[62 FR 10312, 10345, Mar. 6, 1997; 64 FR 8478, 8492, Feb. 19, 1999; 65 FR 76121, 76136, Dec. 6, 2000; 68 FR 9824, 9834, 9846, Feb. 28, 2003; 68 FR 10349, 10352, Mar. 5, 2003; 69 FR 69490, 69497, Nov. 29, 2004; 74 FR 55726, 55742, Oct. 28, 2009; 83 FR 55934, 55952, Nov. 9, 2018; 84 FR 33829, 33843, July 16, 2019; 85 FR 23902, 23904, Apr. 30, 2020; 85 FR 80274, 80399, Dec. 11, 2020; 85 FR 84160, 84198, Dec. 23, 2020; 86 FR 6847, Jan. 25, 2021; 86 FR 15069, Mar. 22, 2021; 86 FR 73615, Dec. 28, 2021; 87 FR 18078,

18222, Mar. 29, 2022; 87 FR 79789, Dec. 28, 2022; 88 FR 31314, 31451, May 16, 2023; 89 FR 105386, Dec. 27, 2024]

§ 1208.31 Reasonable fear of persecution or torture determinations involving noncitizens ordered removed under section 238(b) of the Act and noncitizens whose removal is reinstated under section 241(a)(5) of the Act.

(a) Jurisdiction. This section shall apply to any noncitizen ordered removed under section 238(b) of the Act or whose deportation, exclusion, or removal order is reinstated under section 241(a)(5) of the Act who, in the course of the administrative removal or reinstatement process, expresses a fear of returning to the country of removal. DHS has exclusive jurisdiction to make reasonable fear determinations, and EOIR has exclusive jurisdiction to review such determinations.

(b) [Removed and reserved.]

(c) [Removed and reserved.]

(d) [Removed and reserved.]

(e) Referral to Immigration Judge. If an asylum officer determines that a noncitizen described in this section has a reasonable fear of persecution or torture, the officer shall so inform the noncitizen and issue a Form I-863, Notice of Referral to the Immigration Judge, for full consideration of the request for withholding of removal only. Such cases shall be adjudicated by the immigration judge in accordance with the provisions of § 1208.16. Appeal of the immigration judge's decision shall lie to the Board of Immigration Appeals.

(f) Removal of noncitizens with no reasonable fear of persecution or torture. If the asylum officer determines that the noncitizen has not established a reasonable fear of persecution or torture, the asylum officer shall inform the noncitizen in writing of the decision and shall inquire whether the noncitizen wishes to have an immigration judge review the negative decision, using the Record of Negative Reasonable Fear Finding and Request for Review by Immigration Judge, on which the noncitizen must indicate whether he or she desires such review. If the noncitizen refuses to make an indication, DHS shall consider such a response as a decision to decline review.

(g) Review by immigration judge. The asylum officer's negative decision regarding reasonable fear shall be subject to de novo review by an immigration judge upon the noncitizen's request. The immigration judge's review shall, where relevant, include review of the asylum officer's application of any bars to withholding of removal pursuant to 8 CFR 208.31(c). If the noncitizen requests review of the asylum officer's negative decision regarding reasonable fear, the asylum officer shall serve the noncitizen with a Form I-863, Notice of Referral to Immigration Judge. The record of determination, including copies of the Form I-863, Notice of Referral to Immigration Judge, the asylum officer's notes, the summary of the material facts, and other materials upon which the determination was based shall be provided to the immigration judge with the negative determination. In the absence of exceptional circumstances, such review shall be conducted by the immigration judge within 10 days of the filing of the Form I-863, Notice of Referral to Immigration Judge, and the complete record of determination with the immigration court. Upon review of the asylum officer's negative reasonable fear determination:

(1) If the immigration judge concurs with the asylum officer's determination that the noncitizen does not have a reasonable fear of persecution or torture, the case shall be returned to DHS for removal of the noncitizen. No appeal shall lie from the immigration judge's decision.

(2) If the immigration judge finds that the noncitizen has a reasonable fear of persecution or torture, the noncitizen may submit an Application for Asylum and for Withholding of Removal. Such application shall be considered de novo in all respects by an immigration judge regardless of any determination made under this paragraph.

(i) TThe immigration judge shall consider only the noncitizen's application for withholding of removal under 8 CFR 1208.16 and shall determine whether the noncitizen's removal to the country of removal must be withheld or deferred.

(ii) Appeal of the immigration judge's decision whether removal must be withheld or deferred lies with the Board of Immigration Appeals. If the noncitizen or DHS appeals the immigration judge's decision, the Board shall review only the immigration judge's decision regarding the noncitizen's eligibility for withholding or deferral of removal under 8 CFR 1208.16.

HISTORY:

[64 FR 8478, 8493, Feb. 19, 1999, as corrected at 64 FR 13881, Mar. 23, 1999; 68 FR 9824, 9834, 9846, Feb. 28, 2003; 68 FR 10349, 10352, Mar. 5, 2000; 85 FR 80274, 80400, Dec. 11, 2020; 89 FR 105392, 105402, Dec. 27, 2024]

Subpart C

Lawful Pathways and Asylum Eligibility for Certain Aliens Who Entered Between May 11, 2023, and May 11, 2025

§ 1208.33 Lawful pathways condition on asylum eligibility.

Notwithstanding any contrary section of this part, including §§ 1208.2, 1208.13, and 1208.30—

(a) Condition on eligibility.

(1) Applicability. A rebuttable presumption of ineligibility for asylum applies to a noncitizen who enters the United States from Mexico at the southwest land border or adjacent coastal borders without documents sufficient for lawful admission as described in section 212(a)(7) of the Act and whose entry was:

(i) Between May 11, 2023, and May 11, 2025,

(ii) Subsequent to the end of implementation of the Title 42 public health Order issued on August 2, 2021, and related prior orders issued pursuant to the authorities in sections 362 and 365 of the Public Health Service

Act (42 U.S.C. 265, 268) and the implementing regulation at 42 CFR 71.40, and

(iii) After the noncitizen traveled through a country other than the noncitizen's country of citizenship, nationality, or, if stateless, last habitual residence, that is a party to the 1951 United Nations Convention relating to the Status of Refugees or the 1967 Protocol relating to the Status of Refugees.

(2) Exceptions to applicability of the rebuttable presumption. The rebuttable presumption described in paragraph (a)(1) of this section does not apply if:

(i) The noncitizen was, at the time of entry, an unaccompanied child as defined in 8 CFR 1001.1(hh); or

(ii) The noncitizen, or a member of the noncitizen's family as described in § 208.30(c) with whom the noncitizen is traveling:

(A) Was provided appropriate authorization to travel to the United States to seek parole, pursuant to a DHS-approved parole process;

(B) Presented at a port of entry, pursuant to a pre-scheduled time and place, or presented at a port of entry without a pre-scheduled time and place, if the noncitizen demonstrates by a preponderance of the evidence that it was not possible to access or use the DHS scheduling system due to language barrier, illiteracy, significant technical failure, or other ongoing and serious obstacle; or

(C) Sought asylum or other protection in a country through which the noncitizen traveled and received a final decision denying that application. A final decision includes any denial by a foreign government of the applicant's claim for asylum or other protection through one or more of that government's pathways for that claim. A final decision does not include a determination by a foreign government that the noncitizen abandoned the claim.

(3) Rebuttal of the presumption.

(i) The presumption in paragraph (a)(1) of this section can be rebutted if a noncitizen demonstrates by a preponderance of the evidence that exceptionally compelling circumstances exist, including if the noncitizen demonstrates that, at the time of entry, the noncitizen or a member of the noncitizen's family as described in § 208.30(c) with whom the noncitizen is traveling:

(A) Faced an acute medical emergency;

(B) Faced an imminent and extreme threat to life or safety, such as an imminent threat of rape, kidnapping, torture, or murder; or

(C) Satisfied the definition of "victim of a severe form of trafficking in persons" provided in 8 CFR 214.201.

(ii) A noncitizen who demonstrates by a preponderance of the evidence any of the circumstances in paragraph (a)(3)(i) of this section shall necessarily rebut the presumption in paragraph (a)(1) of this section.

(b) Application in credible fear determinations.

(1) Where an asylum officer has issued a negative credible fear determination pursuant to 8 CFR 208.33(b), and the noncitizen has requested immigration judge review of that credible fear determination, the immigration judge shall evaluate the case de novo, as specified in paragraph (b)(2) of this section. In all cases under paragraph (b)(2), the immigration judge's review shall, where relevant, include review of the asylum officer's application of any bars to withholding of removal pursuant to 8 CFR 208.33(b)(2). In doing so, the immigration judge shall take into account the credibility of the statements made by the noncitizen in support of the noncitizen's claim and such other facts as are known to the immigration judge.

(2) The immigration judge shall first determine whether the noncitizen is covered by the presumption at 8 CFR 208.33(a)(1) and 1208.33(a)(1) and, if so, whether the noncitizen has rebutted the presumption in accordance with 8 CFR 208.33(a)(3) and 1208.33(a)(3).

(i) Where the immigration judge determines that the noncitizen is not covered by the presumption, or that the presumption has been rebutted, the immigration judge shall further determine, consistent with § 1208.30, whether the noncitizen has established a significant possibility of eligibility for asylum under section 208 of the Act, or has established a significant possibility of eligibility for withholding of removal under section 241(b)(3) of the Act or withholding or deferral of removal under the Convention Against Torture with respect to the country or countries of removal identified by DHS pursuant to section 241(b) of the Act. Where the immigration judge determines that the noncitizen has established a significant possibility of eligibility for one of those forms of relief or protection, the immigration judge shall issue a positive credible fear finding. Where the immigration judge determines that the noncitizen has not established a significant possibility of eligibility for any of those forms of relief or protection, the immigration judge shall issue a negative credible fear finding.

(ii) Where the immigration judge determines that the noncitizen is covered by the presumption and that the presumption has not been rebutted, the immigration judge shall further determine whether the noncitizen has established a reasonable possibility of persecution (meaning a reasonable possibility of being persecuted because of their race, religion, nationality, political opinion, or membership in a particular social group) or torture with respect to the country or countries of removal identified by DHS pursuant to section 241(b) of the Act. Where the immigration judge determines that the noncitizen has established a reasonable possibility of persecution or torture, the immigration judge shall issue a positive credible fear finding. Where the immigration judge determines that the noncitizen has not established a reasonable possibility of persecution or torture, the immigration judge shall issue a negative credible fear finding.

(3) Following the immigration judge's determination, the case will proceed as indicated in 8 CFR 208.33(b)(2)(v)(A) through (C).

(4) If, under 8 CFR 208.33(b)(2), DHS issues a Form I-862, Notice to Appear, to commence removal proceedings under section 240 of the Act, the noncitizen may apply for asylum, withholding of removal under section 241(b)(3) of the Act, withholding of removal under the Convention Against Torture, or any other form of relief

or protection for which the noncitizen is eligible during those removal proceedings.

(c) Family unity and removal proceedings. In removal proceedings under section 240 of the Act, where a principal asylum applicant is eligible for withholding of removal under section 241(b)(3) of the Act or withholding of removal under § 1208.16(c)(2) and would be granted asylum but for the presumption in paragraph (a)(1) of this section, and where an accompanying spouse or child as defined in section 208(b)(3)(A) of the Act does not independently qualify for asylum or other protection from removal or the principal asylum applicant has a spouse or child who would be eligible to follow to join that applicant as described in section 208(b)(3)(A) of the Act, the presumption shall be deemed rebutted as an exceptionally compelling circumstance in accordance with paragraph (a)(3) of this section.

(d) Continuing applicability of condition on eligibility.

(1) Subject to paragraph (d)(2) of this section, the condition on asylum eligibility in paragraph (a)(1) of this section shall apply to any asylum application filed by a noncitizen who entered the United States during the time and in the manner specified in paragraph (a)(1) of this section and who is not covered by an exception in paragraph (a)(2) of this section, regardless of when the application is filed and adjudicated.

(2) The conditions on asylum eligibility in paragraph (a)(1) of this section shall not apply to an asylum application filed by a noncitizen described in paragraph (d)(1) of this section if the asylum application is filed after May 11, 2025, the noncitizen was under the age of 18 at the time of the entry referenced in paragraph (d)(1) of this section, and the noncitizen is applying for asylum as a principal applicant.

(e) Severability. The Department intends that any provision of this section held to be invalid or unenforceable by its terms, or as applied to any person or circumstance, should be construed so as to continue to give the maximum effect to the provision permitted by law, unless such holding is that the provision is wholly invalid and unenforceable, in which event the provision should be severed from the remainder of this section and the holding should not affect the remainder of this section or the application of the provision to persons not similarly situated or to dissimilar circumstances.

HISTORY:

[88 FR 31314, 31451, May 16, 2023; 89 FR 81156, 81285, Oct. 7, 2024; 89 FR 105392, 105402, Dec. 27, 2024]

Subpart D

Eligibility for Aliens Who Enter the United States During Emergency Border Circumstances

1208.35 Limitation on asylum eligibility and credible fear procedures for those who enter the United States during emergency border circumstances.

Notwithstanding any contrary section of this chapter, including §§ 1003.42, 1208.2, 1208.13, 1208.30, and 1208.33—

(a) Limitation on eligibility.

(1) Applicability. An noncitizen who is described in § 1208.13(g) and who is not described in section 3(b) of the Presidential Proclamation of June 3, 2024, as defined in 8 CFR 1208.13(h), is ineligible for asylum.

(2) Exceptions.

(i) This limitation on eligibility does not apply if the noncitizen demonstrates by a preponderance of the evidence that exceptionally compelling circumstances exist, including if the noncitizen, or the noncitizen's family member as described in 8 CFR 208.30(c) with whom the noncitizen is traveling, demonstrates by a preponderance of the evidence that, at the time of entry, the noncitizen or a member of the noncitizen's family as described in § 208.30(c) with whom the noncitizen is traveling:

(A) Faced an acute medical emergency;

(B) Faced an imminent and extreme threat to life or safety, such as an imminent threat of rape, kidnapping, torture, or murder; or

(C) Satisfied the definition of "victim of a severe form of trafficking in persons" provided in § 214.201 of this title.

(ii) An noncitizen who demonstrates by a preponderance of the evidence any of the circumstances in paragraph (a)(2)(i) of this section shall necessarily establish exceptionally compelling circumstances.

(iii) An noncitizen described in section 3(b) of the Presidential Proclamation of June 3, 2024, as defined in 8 CFR 1208.13(h), or who establishes exceptionally compelling circumstances under paragraph (a)(2)(i) of this section has established exceptionally compelling circumstances under § 1208.33(a)(3).

(b) Application in credible fear determinations.

(1) Where an asylum officer has issued a negative credible fear determination pursuant to 8 CFR 208.35(b), and the noncitizen has requested immigration judge review of that credible fear determination, the immigration judge shall evaluate the case de novo, as specified in paragraph (b)(2) of this section. In doing so, the immigration judge shall take into account the credibility of the statements made by the noncitizen in support of the noncitizen's claim and such other facts as are known to the immigration judge.

(2) The immigration judge shall first determine whether the noncitizen is subject to the limitation on asylum eligibility under paragraph (a) of this section.

(i) Where the immigration judge determines that the noncitizen is not subject to the limitation on asylum eligibility under paragraph (a) of this section because the noncitizen is not described in § 1208.13(g), the immigration judge shall follow the procedures in § 1208.33(b).

(ii) Where the immigration judge determines that the noncitizen is not subject to the limitation on asylum eligibility under paragraph (a) of this section because the noncitizen is described in section 3(b) of the Presidential Proclamation of June 3, 2024, as defined in 8 CFR 1208.13(h), or is excepted from the limitation on asylum eligibility under paragraph (a)(2) of this section, the immigration judge shall follow the procedures in § 1208.30.

(iii) Where the immigration judge determines that the noncitizen is subject to the limitation on asylum eligibility under paragraph (a) of this section, the immigration judge shall assess the noncitizen under the procedures set forth in § 1208.33(b)(2)(ii) except that the immigration judge shall apply a reasonable probability standard. For purposes of this section, reasonable probability means substantially more than a reasonable possibility, but somewhat less than more likely than not.

(3) Following the immigration judge's determination, the case will proceed as indicated in 8 CFR 208.35(b)(2)(v)(A) and (B).

(4) If the limitation on asylum eligibility in paragraph (a) of this section is held to be invalid or unenforceable by its terms, or as applied to any person or circumstance, then during the period(s) described in § 1208.13(g), the immigration judge shall, as applicable, apply a reasonable probability screening standard for any protection screening under § 1208.33(b)(2)(ii).

(c) Family unity and removal proceedings. In removal proceedings under section 240 of the Act, where a principal asylum applicant is found eligible for withholding of removal under section 241(b)(3) of the Act or withholding of removal under § 1208.16(c)(2) and would be granted asylum but for the limitation on asylum eligibility in paragraph (a)(1) of this section or § 1208.33(a), or both, and where an accompanying spouse or child as defined in section 208(b)(3)(A) of the Act does not independently qualify for asylum or other protection from removal or the principal asylum applicant has a spouse or child who would be eligible to follow to join that applicant as described in section 208(b)(3)(A) of the Act, the noncitizen shall be deemed to have established exceptionally compelling circumstances under paragraph (a)(2)(i) of this section and § 1208.33(a)(3)(i).

(d) Continuing applicability of limitation on eligibility.

(1) Subject to paragraph (d)(2) of this section, the limitation on asylum eligibility in paragraph (a) of this section shall apply to any asylum application filed by an noncitizen who entered the United States during the time and in the manner described in § 1208.13(g) and who is not covered by an exception in paragraph (d)(2) of this section, regardless of when the application is filed and adjudicated.

(2) The limitation on asylum eligibility in paragraph (a) of this section shall not apply to an noncitizen who was under the age of 18 at the time of the noncitizen's entry, if—

(i) The noncitizen is applying for asylum as a principal applicant; and

(ii) The asylum application is filed after the period of time in 1208.13(g) during which the noncitizen entered.

(e) Severability. The Department intends that in the event that any provision of this section or the Presidential Proclamation of June 3, 2024, as defined in 8 CFR 1208.13(h), is held to be invalid or unenforceable by its terms, or as applied to any person or circumstance, the provisions of this section should be construed so as to continue to give the maximum effect to those provisions permitted by law, unless such holding is that a provision is wholly invalid and unenforceable, in which event the provision should be severed from the remainder of this section and the holding should not affect the remainder of this section or the application of the provision to persons not similarly situated or to dissimilar circumstances.

HISTORY:
[89 FR 48710, 48771, June 7, 2024, as confirmed at 89 FR 81156, Oct. 7, 2024; 89 FR 81156, 81285, Oct. 7, 2024; 89 FR 105392, 105403, Dec. 27, 2024]

PART 1209

ADJUSTMENT OF STATUS OF REFUGEES AND ALIENS GRANTED ASYLUM

Rule

AUTHORITY NOTE APPLICABLE TO ENTIRE PART:

AUTHORITY:
8 U.S.C. 1101, 1103, 1157, 1158, 1159, 1228, 1252, 1282; Title VII of Pub. L. 110-229; Pub. L. 115-218.

§ 1209.1 Adjustment of status of refugees.

The provisions of this section shall provide the sole and exclusive procedure for adjustment of status by a refugee admitted under section 207 of the Act whose application is based on his or her refugee status.

(a) **Eligibility.**

(1) Every alien in the United States who is classified as a refugee under part 207 of this chapter, whose status has not been terminated, is required to apply to the Service 1 year after entry in order for the Service to determine his or her admissibility under section 212 of the Act.

(2) Every alien processed by the Immigration and Naturalization Service abroad and paroled into the United States as a refugee after April 1, 1980, and before May 18, 1980, shall be considered as having entered the United States as a refugee under section 207(a) of the Act.

(b) Application. Upon admission to the United States, every refugee entrant shall be notified of the requirement to submit an application for permanent residence 1 year after entry. An application for the benefits of section 209(a) of the Act shall be filed on Form I-485, without fee, with the director of the appropriate Service office identified in the instructions which accompany the Form I-485. A separate application must be filed by each alien. Every applicant who is 14 years of age or older must submit a completed Form G-325A (Biographical Information) with the Form I-485 application. Following submission of the Form I-485 application, a refugee entrant who is 14 years of age or older will be required to execute a Form FD-258 (Applicant Fingerprint Card) at such time and place as the Service will designate.

(c) Medical examination. A refugee seeking adjustment of status under section 209(a) of the Act is not required to repeat the medical examination performed under § 207.2(c) of chapter I, unless there were medical grounds of inadmissibility applicable at the time of admission. The refugee is, however, required to establish compliance with the vaccination requirements described under section 212(a)(1)(A)(ii) of the Act, by submitting with the adjustment of status application a vaccination supplement, completed by a designated civil surgeon in the United States.

(d) Interview. The Service director having jurisdiction over the application will determine, on a case-by-case basis, whether an interview by an immigration officer is necessary to determine the applicant's admissibility for permanent resident status under this part.

(e) Decision. The director will notify the applicant in writing of the decision of his or her application for admission to permanent residence. If the applicant is determined to be inadmissible or no longer a refugee, the director will deny the application and notify the applicant of the reasons for the denial. The director will, in the same denial notice, inform the applicant of his or her right to renew the request for permanent residence in removal proceedings under section 240 of the Act. There is no appeal of the denial of an application by the director, but such denial will be without prejudice to the alien's right to renew the application in removal proceedings under part 240 of this chapter. If the applicant is found to be admissible for permanent residence under section 209(a) of the Act, the director will approve the application and admit the applicant for lawful permanent residence as of the date of the alien's arrival in the United States. An alien admitted for lawful permanent residence will be issued Form I-551, Alien Registration Receipt Card.

HISTORY:

[46 FR 45119, Sept. 10, 1981; 62 FR 10312, 10346, Mar. 6, 1997; 63 FR 12979, 12986, Mar. 17, 1998; 63 FR 30105, 30109, June 3, 1998; 68 FR 9824, 9835, Feb. 28, 2003; 68 FR 10349, 10353, Mar. 5, 2003]

§ 1209.2 Adjustment of status of alien granted asylum.

The provisions of this section shall be the sole and exclusive procedure for adjustment of status by an asylee admitted under section 208 of the Act whose application is based on his or her asylee status.

(a) Eligibility.

(1) Except as provided in paragraph (a)(2) or (a)(3) of this section, the status of any alien who has been granted asylum in the United States may be adjusted to that of an alien lawfully admitted for permanent residence, provided the alien:

(i) Applies for such adjustment;

(ii) Has been physically present in the United States for at least one year after having been granted asylum;

(iii) Continues to be a refugee within the meaning of section 101(a)(42) of the Act, or is the spouse or child of a refugee;

(iv) Has not been firmly resettled in any foreign country; and

(v) Is admissible to the United States as an immigrant under the Act at the time of examination for adjustment without regard to paragraphs (4), (5)(A), (5)(B), and (7)(A)(i) of section 212(a) of the Act, and (vi) has a refugee number available under section 207(a) of the Act.

If the application for adjustment filed under this part exceeds the refugee numbers available under section 207(a) of the Act for the fiscal year, a waiting list will be established on a priority basis by the date the application was properly filed.

(2) An alien, who was granted asylum in the United States prior to November 29, 1990 (regardless of whether or not such asylum has been terminated under section 208(b) of the Act), and is no longer a refugee due to a change in circumstances in the foreign state where he or she feared persecution, may also have his or her status adjusted by the director to that of an alien lawfully admitted for permanent residence even if he or she is no longer able to demonstrate that he or she continues to be a refugee within the meaning of section 101(a)(42) of the Act, or to be a spouse or child of such a refugee or to have been physically present in the United States for at least one year after being granted asylum, so long as he or she is able to meet the requirements noted in paragraphs (a)(1)(i), (iv), and (v) of this section. Such persons are exempt from the numerical limitations of section 209(b) of the Act. However, the number of aliens who are natives of any foreign state who may adjust status pursuant to this paragraph in any fiscal year shall not exceed the difference between the per country limitation established under section 202(a) of the Act and the number of aliens who are chargeable to that foreign state in the fiscal year under section 202 of the Act. Aliens who applied for adjustment of status under section 209(b) of the Act before June 1, 1990, are also exempt from its numerical limitation without any restrictions.

(3) No alien arriving in or physically present in the Commonwealth of the Northern Mariana Islands may apply to adjust status under section 209(b) of the Act in the Commonwealth of the Northern Mariana Islands prior to January 1, 2030.

(b) Inadmissible Alien. An applicant who is inadmissible to the United States under section 212(a) of the Act, may, under section 209(c) of the Act, have the grounds of inadmissibility waived by the director (except for those grounds under paragraphs (27), (29), (33), and so much of (23) as relates to trafficking in narcotics) for humanitarian purposes, to assure family unity, or when it is otherwise in the public interest. An application for the waiver may be filed on Form I-602 (Application by Refugee for Waiver of Grounds of Excludability) with the application for adjustment. An applicant for adjustment who has had the status of an exchange alien nonimmigrant under section 101(a)(15)(J) of the Act, and who is subject to the foreign resident requirement of section 212(e) of the Act, shall be eligible for adjustment without regard to the foreign residence requirement.

(c) Application. An application for the benefits of section 209(b) of the Act may be filed on Form I-485, with the correct fee, with the director of the appropriate Service office identified in the instructions to the Form I-485. A separate application must be filed by each alien. Every applicant who is 14 years of age or older must submit a completed Form G-325A (Biographic Information) with the Form I-485 application. Following submission of the Form I-485 application, every applicant who is 14 years of age or older will be required to execute a Form FD-258 (Applicant Fingerprint Card) at such time and place as the Service will designate. Except as provided in paragraph (a)(2) of this section, the application must also be supported by evidence that the applicant has been physically present in the United States for at least 1 year. If an alien has been placed in deportation or exclusion proceedings, the application can be filed and considered only in proceedings under section 240 of the Act.

(d) Medical examination. An alien seeking adjustment of status under section 209(b) of the Act 1 year following the grant of asylum under section 208 of the Act shall submit the results of a medical examination to determine whether any grounds of inadmissibility described under section 212(a)(1)(A) of the Act apply. Form I-693, Medical Examination of Aliens Seeking Adjustment of Status, and a vaccination supplement to determine compliance with the vaccination requirements described under section 212(a)(1)(A)(ii) of the Act must be completed by a designed civil surgeon in the United States and submitted at the time of application for adjustment of status.

(e) Interview. Each applicant for adjustment of status under this part shall be interviewed by an immigration officer. The interview may be waived for a child under 14 years of age. The Service director having jurisdiction over the application will determine, on a case-by-case basis, whether an interview by an immigration officer is necessary to determine the applicant's admissibility for permanent resident status under this part.

(f) Decision. The applicant shall be notified of the decision, and if the application is denied, of the reasons for denial. No appeal shall lie from the denial of an application by the director but such denial will be without prejudice to the alien's right to renew the application in proceedings under part 240 of this chapter. If the application is approved, the director shall record the alien's admission for lawful permanent residence as of the date one year before the date of the approval of the application, but not earlier than the date of the approval for asylum in the case of an applicant approved under paragraph (a)(2) of this section.

HISTORY:

[46 FR 45119, Sept. 10, 1981, as amended at 56 FR 26898, June 12, 1991; 57 FR 42883, 42884, Sept. 17, 1992; 58 FR 12149, Mar. 3, 1993, as corrected at 58 FR 14145, Mar. 16, 1993; 62 FR 10312, 10346, Mar. 6, 1997; 63 FR 12979, 12986, Mar. 17, 1998; 63 FR 30105, 30109, June 3, 1998; 68 FR 9824, 9835, Feb. 28, 2003; 74 FR 55726, 55742, Oct. 28, 2009; 85 FR 23902, 23904, Apr. 30, 2020]

PART 1211

DOCUMENTARY REQUIREMENTS: IMMIGRANTS; WAIVERS

Rule

AUTHORITY NOTE APPLICABLE TO ENTIRE PART:

AUTHORITY:

8 U.S.C. 1101, 1103, 1181, 1182, 1203, 1225, 1257; 8 CFR part 2.

§ 1211.4 Waiver of documents for returning residents.

(a) Pursuant to the authority contained in section 211(b) of the Act, an alien previously lawfully admitted to the United States for permanent residence who, upon return from a temporary absence was inadmissible because of failure to have or to present a valid passport, immigrant visa, reentry permit, border crossing card, or other document required at the time of entry, may be granted a waiver of such requirement in the discretion of the district director if the district director determines that such alien:

(1) Was not otherwise inadmissible at the time of entry, or having been otherwise inadmissible at the time of entry is with respect thereto qualified for an exemption from deportability under section 237(a)(1)(H) of the Act; and

(2) Is not otherwise subject to removal.

(b) Denial of a waiver by the district director is not appealable but shall be without prejudice to renewal of an application and reconsideration in proceedings before the immigration judge.

HISTORY:

[32 FR 9625, July 4, 1967. Redesignated at 41 FR 55849, Dec. 23, 1976; 62 FR 10312, 10347, Mar. 6, 1997; 68 FR 9824, 9835, Feb. 28, 2003]

PART 1212

DOCUMENTARY REQUIREMENTS: NONIMMIGRANTS; WAIVERS; ADMISSION OF CERTAIN INADMISSIBLE ALIENS; PAROLE

Rule

AUTHORITY NOTE APPLICABLE TO ENTIRE PART:

AUTHORITY:

8 U.S.C. 1101, 1103, 1157, 1158, 1159, 1228, 1252, 1282; Title VII of Pub. L. 110-229; Pub. L. 115-218.

§ 1212.1 Documentary requirements for nonimmigrants.

[PUBLISHER'S NOTE: 68 FR 10349, 10353, Mar. 5, 2003, purported to substitute "of 8 CFR chapter I" for "of this chapter" in paragraph (g)(3) of § 1212.1. However this could not implemented, since paragraph (g)(3) did not exist in § 1212.1. It was determined that paragraph (g)(3) of § 1212.2 should instead be amended. For the convenience of the user, the amendment has been implemented according to the apparent intent of the agency. A correction is anticipated.]

A valid unexpired visa and an unexpired passport, valid for the period set forth in section 212(a)(26) of the Act, shall be presented by each arriving nonimmigrant alien except that the passport validity period for an applicant for admission who is a member of a class described in section 102 of the Act is not required to extend beyond the date of his application for admission if so admitted, and except as otherwise provided in the Act, this chapter, and for the following classes:

(a) Citizens of Canada or Bermuda, Bahamian nationals or British subjects resident in certain islands.

(1) Canadian citizens. A passport is not required except after a visit outside of the Western Hemisphere. A visa is not required.

(2) Citizens of the British Overseas Territory of Bermuda. A passport is not required except after a visit outside of the Western Hemisphere. A visa is not required.

(3) Bahamian nationals or British subjects resident in the Bahamas. A passport is required. A visa required of such an alien unless, prior to or at the time of embarkation for the United States on a vessel or aircraft, the alien satisfied the examining U.S. immigration officer at the Bahamas, that he or she is clearly and beyond a doubt entitled to admission, under section 212(a) of the Immigration and Nationality Act, in all other respects.

(4) British subjects resident in the Cayman Islands or in the Turks and Caicos Islands. A passport is required. A visa is required of such an alien unless he or she arrives directly from the Cayman Islands or the Turks and Caicos Islands and presents a current certificate from the Clerk of Court of the Cayman Islands or the Turks and Caicos Islands indicating no criminal record.

(b) Certain Caribbean residents.

(1) British, French, and Netherlands nationals, and nationals of certain adjacent islands of the Caribbean which are independent countries. A visa is not required of a British, French, or Netherlands national, or of a national of Barbados, Grenada, Jamaica, or Trinidad and Tobago, who has his or her residence in British, French, or Netherlands territory located in the adjacent islands of the Caribbean area, or in Barbados, Grenada, Jamaica, or Trinidad and Tobago, who:

(i) Is proceeding to the United States as an agricultural worker;

(ii) Is the beneficiary of a valid, unexpired indefinite certification granted by the Department of Labor for employment in the Virgin Islands of the United States and is proceeding to the Virgin Islands of the United States for such purpose, or

(iii) Is the spouse or child of an alien described in paragraph (b)(1)(i) or (b)(1)(ii) of this section, and is accompanying or following to join him or her.

(2) Nationals of the British Virgin Islands. A visa is not required of a national of the British Virgin Islands who has his or her residence in the British Virgin Islands, if:

(i) The alien is seeking admission solely to visit the Virgin Islands of the United States; or

(ii) At the time of embarking on an aircraft at St. Thomas, U.S. Virgin Islands, the alien meets each of the following requirements:

(A) The alien is traveling to any other part of the United States by aircraft as a nonimmigrant visitor for business or pleasure (as described in section 101(a)(15)(B) of the Act);

(B) The alien satisfies the examining U.S. Immigration officer at the port-of-entry that he or she is clearly and beyond a doubt entitled to admission in all other respects; and

(C) The alien presents a current Certificate of Good Conduct issued by the Royal Virgin Islands Police Department indicating that he or she has no criminal record.

(c) Mexican nationals.

(1) A visa and a passport are not required of a Mexican national who:

(i) Is in possession of a Form DSP-150, B-1/B-2 Visa and Border Crossing Card, containing a machine-readable biometric identifier, issued by the DOS and is applying for admission as a temporary visitor for business or pleasure from contiguous territory.

(ii) Is a Mexican national entering solely for the purpose of applying for a Mexican passport or other official Mexican document at a Mexican consular office on the United States side of the border.

(2) A visa shall not be required of a Mexican national who:

(i) Is in possession of a Form DSP-150, with a biometric identifier, issued by the DOS, and a passport, and is applying for admission as a temporary visitor for business or pleasure from other than contiguous territory;

(ii) Is a crew member employed on an aircraft belonging to a Mexican company owned carrier authorized to engage in commercial transportation into the United States; or

(iii) Bears a Mexican diplomatic or official passport and who is a military or civilian official of the Federal Government of Mexico entering the United States for 6 months or less for a purpose other than on assignment as a permanent employee to an office of the Mexican Federal Government in the United States, and the official's spouse or any of the official's dependent family members under 19 years of age, bearing diplomatic or official passports, who are in the actual company of such official at the time of admission into the United States. This provision does not apply to the spouse or any of the official's family members classifiable under section 101(a)(15)(F) or (M) of the Act.

(3) A Mexican national who presents a BCC at a POE must present the DOS-issued DSP-150 containing a machine-readable biometric identifier. The alien will not be permitted to cross the border into the United States unless the biometric identifier contained on the card matches the appropriate biometric characteristic of the alien.

(4) Mexican nationals presenting a combination B-1/B-2 nonimmigrant visa and border crossing card (or similar stamp in a passport), issued by DOS prior to April 1, 1998, that does not contain a machine-readable biometric identifier, may be admitted on the basis of the nonimmigrant visa only, provided it has not expired and the alien remains admissible. A passport is also required.

(5) Aliens entering pursuant to International Boundary and Water Commission Treaty. A visa and a passport are not required of an alien employed either directly or indirectly on the construction, operation, or maintenance of works in the United States undertaken in accordance with the treaty concluded on February 3, 1944, between the United States and Mexico regarding the functions of the International Boundary and Water Commission, and entering the United States temporarily in connection with such employment.

(d) Citizens of the Freely Associated States, formerly Trust Territory of the Pacific Islands. Citizens of the Republic of the Marshall Islands and the Federated States of Micronesia may enter into, lawfully engage in employment, and establish residence in the United States and its territories and possessions without regard to paragraphs (14), (20) and (26) of section 212(a) of the Act pursuant to the terms of Pub. L. 99-239. Pending issuance by the aforementioned governments of travel documents to eligible citizens, travel documents previously issued by the Trust Territory of the Pacific Islands will continue to be accepted for purposes of identification and to establish eligibility for admission into the United States, its territories and possessions.

(e) Aliens entering Guam pursuant to section 14 of Public Law 99-396, "Omnibus Territories Act" and 8 CFR 212.1(e).

(1) As provided in 8 CFR 212.1(e), until November 28, 2009, a visa is not required of an alien who is a citizen of a country enumerated in 8 CFR 212.1(e)(3) who:

(i) Is classifiable as a visitor for business or pleasure;

(ii) Is solely entering and staying on Guam for a period not to exceed fifteen days;

(iii) Is in possession of a round-trip nonrefundable and nontransferable transportation ticket bearing a confirmed departure date not exceeding fifteen days from the date of admission to Guam;

(iv) Is in possession of a completed and signed Visa Waiver Information Form (Form I-736);

(v) Waives any right to review or appeal the immigration officer's determination of admissibility at the port of entry at Guam; and

(vi) Waives any right to contest any action for deportation, other than on the basis of a request for asylum.

(2) The DHS regulations for waiver of the visa requirement for aliens entering Guam pursuant to section 14 of Public Law 99-396, prior to November 28, 2009, are set forth at 8 CFR 212.1(e).

(3) [Reserved]

(4) Admission under 8 CFR 212.1(e) renders an alien ineligible for:

(i) Adjustment of status to that of a temporary resident or, except under the provisions of section 245(i) of the Act or as an immediate relative as defined in section 201(b), to that of a lawful permanent resident;

(ii) Change of nonimmigrant status; or

(iii) Extension of stay.

(f) Direct transits —

(1) Transit without visa. A passport and visa are not required of an alien who is being transported in immediate and continuous transit through the United States in accordance with the terms of an agreement entered into between the transportation line and the Service under the provisions of section 238(d) of the Act on Form I-426 to insure such immediate and continuous transit through, and departure from, the United States en route to a specifically designated foreign country: Provided, That such alien is in possession of a travel document or documents establishing his/her identity and nationality and ability to enter some country other than the United States.

(2) Unavailability to transit. This waiver of passport and visa requirement is not available to an alien who is a citizen of Afghanistan, Angola, Bangladesh, Belarus, Bosnia-Herzegovina, Burma, Burundi, Central African Republic, People's Republic of China, Columbia, Congo (Brazzaville), Cuba, India, Iran, Iraq, Libya, Nigeria, North Korea, Pakistan, Serbia, Seirra Leone, Somalia, Sri Lanka, and Sudan.

(3) Foreign government officials in transit. If an alien is of the class described in section 212(d)(8) of the Act, only a valid unexpired visa and a travel document valid for entry into a foreign country for at least 30 days from the date of admission to the United States are required.

(g) Unforeseen emergency. A nonimmigrant seeking admission to the United States must present an unexpired visa and a passport valid for the amount of time set forth in section 212(a)(7)(B) of the Act or a valid biometric border crossing card, issued by the DOS on Form DSP-150, at the time of application for admission, unless the nonimmigrant satisfies the requirements described in one or more of the paragraphs (a) through (f),(i) or (o) of this section. Upon a nonimmigrant's application on Form I-193, Application for Waiver of Passport and/or Visa, a district director may, in the exercise of his or her discretion, on a case-by-case basis, waive the documentary requirements if satisfied that the nonimmigrant cannot present the required documents because of an unforeseen emergency. The district director or the Deputy Commissioner may at any time revoke a waiver previously authorized pursuant to this paragraph and notify the nonimmigrant in writing to that effect.

(h) Nonimmigrant spouses, fiancees, fiances, and children of U.S. citizens. Notwithstanding any of the provisions of this part, an alien seeking admission as a spouse, fiancee, fiance, or child of a U.S. citizen, or as a child of the spouse, fiane, or finacee of a U.S. citizen, pursuant to section 101(a)(15)(K) of the Act shall be in possession of an unexpired nonimmigrant visa issued by an American consular officer classifying the alien under that section, or be inadmissible under section 212(a)(7)(B) of the Act.

(i) Visa Waiver Pilot Program. A visa is not required of any alien who is eligible to apply for admission to the United States as a Visa Waiver Pilot Program applicant pursuant to the provisions of section 217 of the Act and part 217 of this chapter if such alien is a national of a country designated under the Visa Waiver Pilot Program, who seeks admission to the United States for a period of 90 days or less as a visitor for business or pleasure.

(j) Officers authorized to act upon recommendations of United States consular officers for waiver of visa and passport requirements. All district directors, the officers in charge are authorized to act upon recommendations made by United States consular officers or by officers of the Visa Office, Department of State, pursuant to the provisions of 22 CFR 41.7 for waiver of visa and passport requirements under the provisions of section 212(d)(4)(A) of the Act. The District Director at Washington, DC, has jurisdiction in such cases recommended to the Service at the seat of Government level by the Department of State. Neither an application nor fee are required if the concurrence in a passport or visa waiver is requested by a U.S. consular officer or by an officer of the Visa Office. The district director or the Deputy Commissioner, may at any time revoke a waiver previously authorized pursuant to this paragraph and notify the nonimmigrant alien in writing to that effect.

(k) Cancellation of nonimmigrant visas by immigration officers. Upon receipt of advice from the Department of State that a nonimmigrant visa has been revoked or invalidated, and request by that Department for such action, immigration officers shall place an appropriate endorsement thereon.

(l) Treaty traders and investors. Notwithstanding any of the provisions of this part, an alien seeking admission as a treaty trader or investor under the provisions of Chapter 16 of the North American Free Trade Agreement (NAFTA) pursuant to section 101(a)(15)(E) of the Act, shall be in possession of a nonimmigrant visa issued by an American consular officer classifying the alien under that section.

(m) Aliens in S classification. Notwithstanding any of the provisions of this part, an alien seeking admission pursuant to section 101(a)(15)(S) of the Act must be in possession of appropriate documents issued by a United States consular officer classifying the alien under that section.

(n) Alien in Q-2 classification. Notwithstanding any of the provisions of this part, an alien seeking admission as a principal according to section 101(a)(15)(Q)(ii) of the Act must be in possession of a Certification Letter issued by the Department of State's Program Administrator documenting participation in the Irish peace process cultural and training programs.

(o) Alien in T-2 through T-4 classification. Individuals seeking T-2 through T-4 nonimmigrant status may avail themselves of the provisions of paragraph (g) of this section, except that the authority to waive documentary requirements resides with the Service Center.

(p) [Reserved]

(q) Aliens admissible under the Guam-CNMI Visa Waiver Program and 8 CFR 212.1(q).

(1) Eligibility for Program. As provided in 8 CFR 212.1(q), in accordance with Public Law 110-229, beginning November 28, 2009, the Secretary of Homeland Security, in consultation with the Secretaries of the Departments of Interior and State, may waive the visa requirement in the case of a nonimmigrant alien who seeks admission to Guam or to the Commonwealth of the Northern Mariana Islands (CNMI) under the Guam-CNMI Visa Waiver Program. To be admissible under the Guam-CNMI Visa Waiver Program, prior to embarking on a carrier for travel to Guam or the CNMI, each nonimmigrant alien must:

(i) Be a national of a country or geographic area listed in 8 CFR 212.1(q)(2);

(ii) Be classifiable as a visitor for business or pleasure;

(iii) Be solely entering and staying on Guam or the CNMI for a period not to exceed forty-five days;

(iv) Be in possession of a round trip ticket that is nonrefundable and nontransferable and bears a confirmed departure date not exceeding forty-five days from the date of admission to Guam or the CNMI. "Round trip ticket" includes any return trip transportation ticket issued by a participating carrier, electronic ticket record, airline employee passes indicating return passage, individual vouchers for return passage, group vouchers for return passage for charter flights, or military travel orders which include military dependents for return to duty stations outside the United States on U.S. military flights;

(v) Be in possession of a completed and signed Guam-CNMI Visa Waiver Information Form (CBP Form I-736);

(vi) Be in possession of a completed and signed I-94, Arrival-Departure Record (CBP Form I-94);

(vii) Be in possession of a valid unexpired ICAO compliant, machine readable passport issued by a country that meets the eligibility requirements of paragraph (q)(2) of this section;

(viii) Have not previously violated the terms of any prior admissions. Prior admissions include those under the Guam-CNMI Visa Waiver Program, the prior Guam Visa Waiver Program, the Visa Waiver Program as described in section 217(a) of the Act and admissions pursuant to any immigrant or nonimmigrant visa;

(ix) Waive any right to review or appeal an immigration officer's determination of admissibility at the port of entry into Guam or the CNMI;

(x) Waive any right to contest any action for deportation or removal, other than on the basis of: an application for withholding of removal under section 241(b)(3) of the INA; withholding of removal under the regulations implementing Article 3 of the United Nations Convention Against Torture and Other Cruel, Inhuman or Degrading Treatment or Punishment; or, an application for asylum if permitted under section 208 of the Act; and

(xi) If a resident of Taiwan, possess a Taiwan National Identity Card and a valid Taiwan passport with a valid re-entry permit issued by the Taiwan Ministry of Foreign Affairs.

(2) Implementing regulations. The DHS regulations for waiver of the visa requirement for aliens seeking admission to Guam or to the CNMI under the Guam-CNMI Visa Waiver Program are set forth at 8 CFR 212.1(q).

(3) [Reserved]

(4) Admission under 8 CFR 212.1(q). Admission under 8 CFR 212.1(q) renders an alien ineligible for:

(i) Adjustment of status to that of a temporary resident or, except as provided by section 245(i) of the Act, other than as an immediate relative as defined in section 201(b) of the Act, to that of a lawful permanent resident;

(ii) Change of nonimmigrant status; or

(iii) Extension of stay.

(5)-(7) [Reserved]

(8) Inadmissibility and Deportability

(i) Determinations of inadmissibility.

(A) An alien who applies for admission under the provisions of the Guam-CNMI Visa Waiver Program, who is determined by an immigration officer to be inadmissible to Guam or the CNMI under one or more of the grounds of inadmissibility listed in section 212 of the Act (other than for lack of a visa), or who is in possession of and presents fraudulent or counterfeit travel documents, will be refused admission into Guam or the CNMI and removed. Such refusal and removal shall be effected without referral of the alien to an immigration judge for further inquiry, examination, or hearing, except that an alien who presents himself or herself as an applicant for admission to Guam under the Guam-CNMI Visa Waiver Program, who applies for asylum, withholding of removal under section 241(b)(3) of the INA or withholding of removal under the regulations implementing Article 3 of the United Nations Convention Against Torture and Other Cruel, Inhuman or Degrading Treatment or Punishment must be issued a Form I-863, Notice of Referral to Immigration Judge, for a proceeding in accordance with 8 CFR 208.2(c)(1) and (2) and 1208.2(c)(1) and (2). The provisions of 8 CFR part 1208 subpart A shall not apply to an alien present or arriving in the CNMI seeking to apply for asylum prior to January 1, 2015. No application for asylum may be filed pursuant to section 208 of the Act by an alien present or arriving in the CNMI prior to January 1, 2030; however, aliens physically present in the CNMI during the transition period who express a fear of persecution or torture only may establish eligibility for withholding or deferral of removal pursuant to INA 241(b)(3) or pursuant to the regulations implementing Article 3 of the United Nations Convention Against Torture and Other Cruel, Inhuman or Degrading Treatment or Punishment.

(B) [Reserved]

(C) Refusal of admission under this paragraph or 8 CFR 212.1(q)(8)(i) shall not constitute removal for purposes of the Act.

(ii) Determination of deportability.

(A) An alien who has been admitted to either Guam or the CNMI under the provisions of this section who is determined by an immigration officer to be deportable from either Guam or the CNMI under one or more of the grounds of deportability listed in section 237 of the Act, shall be removed from either Guam or the CNMI to his or her country of nationality or last residence. Such removal will be determined by DHS authority that has jurisdiction over the place where the alien is found, and will be effected without referral of the alien to an immigration judge for a determination of deportability, except that an alien admitted to Guam under the Guam-CNMI Visa Waiver Program who applies for asylum or other form of protection from persecution or torture must be issued a Form I-863 for a proceeding in accordance with 8 CFR 208.2(c)(1) and (2) and 1208.2(c)(1) and (2). The provisions of 8 CFR part 1208 subpart A shall not apply to an alien present or arriving in the CNMI seeking to apply for asylum prior to January 1, 2015. No application for asylum may be filed pursuant to section 208 of the INA by an alien present or arriving in the CNMI prior to January 1, 2015; however, aliens physically present or arriving in the CNMI prior to January 1, 2030, may apply for withholding of removal under section 241(b)(3) of the Act and withholding of removal under the regulations implementing Article 3 of the United Nations Convention Against Torture, Inhuman or Degrading Treatment or Punishment.

(B) Removal by DHS under paragraph (b)(1) of this section or 8 CFR 212.1(q)(8)(ii) is equivalent in all respects and has the same consequences as removal after proceedings conducted under section 240 of the Act.

(iii) [Reserved]

HISTORY:

[26 FR 12066, Dec. 16, 1961; 51 FR 18769, 44783; 52 FR 48083, 1987; 53 FR 24900, 1988; 54 FR 13, 48577, 1989.; 55 FR 36259, 1990; 58 FR 4891, Jan. 19, 1993; 58 FR 38046, July 15, 1993, as confirmed at 59 FR 35615, July 13, 1994; 58 FR 43438, Aug. 16,

1993; 58 FR 69210, Dec. 30, 1993, as corrected at 59 FR 1992, Jan. 13, 1994, and confirmed at 63 FR 1331, 1334, Jan. 9, 1998; 59 FR 1467, Jan. 11, 1994; 59 FR 35615, July 13, 1994; 59 FR 51095, Oct. 7, 1994; 60 FR 44260, 44264, Aug. 25, 1995; 61 FR 11717, 11720, March 22, 1996; 64 FR 7989, 7990, Feb. 18, 1999; 65 FR 14774, 14777, Mar. 17, 2000; 66 FR 235, 236, Jan. 3, 2001, as confirmed at 66 FR 51821, 51822, Oct. 11, 2001; 66 FR 1017, 1018, Jan. 5, 2001; 66 FR 8743, Feb. 2, 2001; 66 FR 17321, 17322, Mar. 30, 2001; 66 FR 32529, 32530, June 15, 2001; 66 FR 42587, 42593, Aug. 14, 2001; 67 FR 4784, 4795, Jan. 31, 2002; 67 FR 71443, 71447, Dec. 2, 2002; 68 FR 5190, 5193, Jan. 31, 2003; 68 FR 9824, 9835, Feb. 28, 2003; 74 FR 55726, 55742, Oct. 28, 2009, as corrected at 74 FR 62207, 62208, Nov. 27, 2009; 85 FR 23902, 23904, Apr. 30, 2020]

AUTHORITY:

(Secs. 103, 104, 212 of the Immigration and Nationality Act, as amended (8 U.S.C. 1103, 1104, 1132))

§ 1212.2 Consent to reapply for admission after deportation, removal or departure at Government expense.

[PUBLISHER'S NOTE: 68 FR 10349, 10353, Mar. 5, 2003, purported to substitute "of 8 CFR chapter I" for "of this chapter" in paragraph (g)(3) of § 1212.1. However this could not implemented, since paragraph (g)(3) did not exist in § 1212.1. It was determined that paragraph (g)(3) of § 1212.2 should instead be amended. For the convenience of the user, the amendment has been implemented according to the apparent intent of the agency. A correction is anticipated.]

(a) Evidence. Any alien who has been deported or removed from the United States is inadmissible to the United States unless the alien has remained outside of the United States for five consecutive years since the date of deportation or removal. If the alien has been convicted of an aggravated felony, he or she must remain outside of the United States for twenty consecutive years from the deportation date before he or she is eligible to re-enter the United States. Any alien who has been deported or removed from the United States and is applying for a visa, admission to the United States, or adjustment of status, must present proof that he or she has remained outside of the United States for the time period required for re-entry after deportation or removal. The examining consular or immigration officer must be satisfied that since the alien's deportation or removal, the alien has remained outside the United States for more than five consecutive years, or twenty consecutive years in the case of an alien convicted of an aggravated felony as defined in section 101(a)(43) of the Act. Any alien who does not satisfactorily present proof of absence from the United States for more than five consecutive years, or twenty consecutive years in the case of an alien convicted of an aggravated felony, to the consular or immigration officer, and any alien who is seeking to enter the United States prior to the completion of the requisite five- or twenty-year absence, must apply for permission to reapply for admission to the United States as provided under this part. A temporary stay in the United States under section 212(d)(3) of the Act does not interrupt the five or twenty consecutive year absence requirement.

(b) Alien applying to consular officer for nonimmigrant visa or nonresident alien border crossing card.

(1) An alien who is applying to a consular officer for a nonimmigrant visa or a nonresident alien border crossing card, must request permission to reapply for admission to the United States if five years, or twenty years if the alien's deportation was based upon a conviction for an aggravated felony, have not elapsed since the date of deportation or removal. This permission shall be requested in the manner prescribed through the consular officer, and may be granted only in accordance with sections 212(a)(17) and 212(d)(3)(A) of the Act and § 1212.4 of this part. However, the alien may apply for such permission by submitting Form I-212, Application for Permission to Reapply for Admission into the United States after Deportation or Removal, to the consular officer if that officer is willing to accept the application, and recommends to the district director that the alien be permitted to apply.

(2) The consular officer shall forward the Form I-212 to the district director with jurisdiction over the place where the deportation or removal proceedings were held.

(c) Special provisions for an applicant for nonimmigrant visa under section 101(a)(15)(K) of the Act.

(1) An applicant for a nonimmigrant visa under section 101(a)(15)(K) must:

(i) Be the beneficiary of a valid visa petition approved by the Service; and

(ii) File an application on Form I-212 with the consular officer for permission to reapply for admission to the United States after deportation or removal.

(2) The consular officer must forward the Form I-212 to the Service office with jurisdiction over the area within which the consular officer is located. If the alien is ineligible on grounds which, upon the applicant's marriage to the United States citizen petitioner, may be waived under section 212 (g), (h), or (i) of the Act, the consular officer must also forward a recommendation as to whether the waiver should be granted.

(d) Applicant for immigrant visa. Except as provided in paragraph (g)(3) of this section, an applicant for an immigrant visa who is not physically present in the United States and who requires permission to reapply must file Form I-212 with the district director having jurisdiction over the place where the deportation or removal proceedings were held. Except as provided in paragraph (g)(3) of this section, if the applicant also requires a waiver under section 212 (g), (h), or (i) of the Act, Form I-601, Application for Waiver of Grounds of Excludability, must be filed simultaneously with the Form I-212 with the American consul having jurisdiction over the alien's place of residence. The consul must forward these forms to the appropriate Service office abroad with jurisdiction over the area within which the consul is located.

(e) Applicant for adjustment of status. An applicant for adjustment of status under section 245 of the Act and part 245 of this chapter must request permission to reapply for entry in conjunction with his or her application for adjustment of status. This request is made by filing an application for permission to reapply, Form I-212, with the district director having jurisdiction over the place where the alien resides. If the application under section 245 of the Act has been initiated, renewed, or is pending in a proceeding before an immigration judge, the district director must refer the Form I-212 to the immigration judge for adjudication.

(f) Applicant for admission at port of entry. Within five years of the deportation or removal, or twenty years in the case of an alien convicted of an aggravated felony, an alien may request permission at a port of entry to reapply for admission to the United States. The alien shall file the Form I-212 with the district director having jurisdiction over the port of entry.

(g) Other applicants.

(1) Any applicant for permission to reapply for admission under circumstances other than those described in paragraphs (b) through (f) of this section must file Form I-212. This form is filed with either:

(i) The district director having jurisdiction over the place where the deportation or removal proceedings were held; or

(ii) The district director who exercised or is exercising jurisdiction over the applicant's most recent proceeding.

(2) If the applicant is physically present in the United States but is ineligible to apply for adjustment of status, he or she must file the application with the district director having jurisdiction over his or her place of residence.

(3) If an alien who is an applicant for parole authorization under § 245.15(t)(2) of 8 CFR chapter I requires consent to reapply for admission after deportation, removal, or departure at Government expense, or a waiver under section 212(g), 212(h), or 212(i) of the Act, he or she may file the requisite Form I-212 or Form I-601 at the Nebraska Service Center concurrently with the Form I-131, Application for Travel Document. If an alien who is an applicant for parole authorization under § 245.13(k)(2) of 8 CFR chapter I requires consent to reapply for admission after deportation, removal, or departure at Government expense, or a waiver under section 212(g), 212(h), or 212(i) of the Act, he or she may file the requisite Form I-212 or Form I-601 at the Texas Service Center concurrently with the Form I-131, Application for Travel Document.

(h) Decision. An applicant who has submitted a request for consent to reapply for admission after deportation or removal must be notified of the decision. If the application is denied, the applicant must be notified of the reasons for the denial and of his or her right to appeal as provided in part 103 of this chapter. Except in the case of an applicant seeking to be granted advance permission to reapply for admission prior to his or her departure from the United States, the denial of the application shall be without prejudice to the renewal of the application in the course of proceedings before an immigration judge under section 242 of the Act and this chapter.

(i) Retroactive approval.

(1) If the alien filed Form I-212 when seeking admission at a port of entry, the approval of the Form I-212 shall be retroactive to either:

(i) The date on which the alien embarked or reembarked at a place outside the United States; or

(ii) The date on which the alien attempted to be admitted from foreign contiguous territory.

(2) If the alien filed Form I-212 in conjunction with an application for adjustment of status under section 245 of the Act, the approval of Form I-212 shall be retroactive to the date on which the alien embarked or reembarked at a place outside the United States.

(j) Advance approval. An alien whose departure will execute an order of deportation shall receive a conditional approval depending upon his or her satisfactory departure. However, the grant of permission to reapply does not waive inadmissibility under section 212(a) (16) or (17) of the Act resulting from exclusion, deportation, or removal proceedings which are instituted subsequent to the date permission to reapply is granted.

HISTORY:

[56 FR 23212, May 21, 1991; 64 FR 25756, 25766, May 12, 1999, as confirmed and amended at 65 FR 15846, 15854, Mar. 24, 2000; 68 FR 9824, 9835, 9846, Feb. 28, 2003; 68 FR 10349, 10353, Mar. 5, 2003]

§ 1212.3 Application for the exercise of discretion under former section 212(c).

(a) Jurisdiction. An application by an eligible alien for the exercise of discretion under former section 212(c) of the Act (as in effect prior to April 1, 1997), if made in the course of proceedings under section 240 of the Act, or under former sections 235, 236, or 242 of the Act (as in effect prior to April 1, 1997), shall be submitted to the immigration judge by filing Form I-191, Application for Advance Permission to Return to Unrelinquished Domicile.

(b) Filing of application. The application may be filed prior to, at the time of, or at any time after the applicant's departure from or arrival into the United States. All material facts or circumstances that the applicant knows or believes apply to the grounds of excludability, deportability, or removability must be described in the application. The applicant must also submit all available documentation relating to such grounds.

(c) [Reserved]

(d) Validity. Once an application is approved, that approval is valid indefinitely. However, the approval covers only those specific grounds of excludability, deportability, or removability that were described in the application. An applicant who failed to describe any other grounds of excludability, deportability, or removability, or failed to disclose material facts existing at the time of the approval of the application, remains excludable, deportable, or removable under the previously unidentified grounds. If the applicant is excludable, deportable, or removable based upon any previously unidentified grounds a new application must be filed.

(e) **Filing or renewal of applications before an immigration judge.**

(1) An eligible alien may renew or submit an application for the exercise of discretion under former section 212(c) of the Act in proceedings before an immigration judge under section 240 of the Act, or under former sections 235, 236, or 242 of the Act (as it existed prior to

April 1, 1997), and under this chapter. Such application shall be adjudicated by the immigration judge, without regard to whether the applicant previously has made application to the district director.

(2) The immigration judge may grant or deny an application for relief under section 212(c), in the exercise of discretion, unless such relief is prohibited by paragraph (f) of this section or as otherwise provided by law.

(3) An alien otherwise entitled to appeal to the Board of Immigration Appeals may appeal the denial by the immigration judge of this application in accordance with the provisions of § 1003.38 of this chapter.

(f) Limitations on discretion to grant an application under section 212(c) of the Act. An application for relief under former section 212(c) of the Act shall be denied if:

(1) The alien has not been lawfully admitted for permanent residence;

(2) The alien has not maintained lawful domicile in the United States, as either a lawful permanent resident or a lawful temporary resident pursuant to section 245A or section 210 of the Act, for at least seven consecutive years immediately preceding the filing of the application;

(3) The alien is subject to inadmissibility or exclusion from the United States under paragraphs (3)(A), (3)(B), (3)(C), (3)(E), or (10)(C) of section 212(a) of the Act;

(4) The alien has been charged and found to be deportable or removable on the basis of a crime that is an aggravated felony, as defined in section 101(a)(43) of the Act (as in effect at the time the application for section 212(c) relief is adjudicated), except as follows:

(i) An alien whose convictions for one or more aggravated felonies were entered pursuant to plea agreements made on or after November 29, 1990, but prior to April 24, 1996, is ineligible for section 212(c) relief only if he or she has served a term of imprisonment of five years or more for such aggravated felony or felonies, and

(ii) An alien is not ineligible for section 212(c) relief on account of an aggravated felony conviction entered pursuant to a plea agreement that was made before November 29, 1990; or

(5) The alien is deportable under former section 241 of the Act or removable under section 237 of the Act on a ground which does not have a statutory counterpart in section 212 of the Act.

(g) Relief for certain aliens who were in deportation proceedings before April 24, 1996. Section 440(d) of Antiterrorism and Effective Death Penalty Act of 1996 (AEDPA) shall not apply to any applicant for relief under this section whose deportation proceedings were commenced before the Immigration Court before April 24, 1996.

(h) Availability of section 212(c) relief for aliens who pleaded guilty or nolo contendere to certain crimes. For purposes of this section, the date of the plea agreement will be considered the date the plea agreement was agreed to by the parties. Aliens are not eligible to apply for section 212(c) relief under the provisions of this paragraph with respect to convictions entered after trial.

(1) Pleas before April 24, 1996. Regardless of whether an alien is in exclusion, deportation, or removal proceedings, an eligible alien may apply for relief under former section 212(c) of the Act, without regard to the amendment made by section 440(d) of the Antiterrorism and Effective Death Penalty Act of 1996, with respect to a conviction if the alien pleaded guilty or nolo contendere and the alien's plea agreement was made before April 24, 1996.

(2) Pleas between April 24, 1996 and April 1, 1997. Regardless of whether an alien is in exclusion, deportation, or removal proceedings, an eligible alien may apply for relief under former section 212(c) of the Act, as amended by section 440(d) of the Antiterrorism and Effective Death Penalty Act of 1996, with respect to a conviction if the alien pleaded guilty or nolo contendere and the alien's plea agreement was made on or after April 24, 1996, and before April 1, 1997.

(3) Please on or after April 1, 1997. Section 212(c) relief is not available with respect to convictions arising from plea agreements made on or after April 1, 1997.

HISTORY:

[56 FR 50034, Oct. 3, 1991; 60 FR 34090, June 30, 1995; 61 FR 59824, 59825, Nov. 25, 1996, as confirmed at 62 FR 43466, 43467, Aug. 14, 1997; 66 FR 6436, 6446, Jan. 22, 2001; 68 FR 9824, 9835, Feb. 28, 2003; 68 FR 10349, 10353, Mar. 5, 2003; 69 FR 57826, 57834, Sept. 28, 2004]

§ 1212.4 Applications for the exercise of discretion under section 212(d)(1) and 212(d)(3).

(a) Applications under section 212(d)(3)(A) —

(1) General. District directors and officers in charge outside the United States in the districts of Bangkok, Thailand; Mexico City, Mexico; and Rome, Italy are authorized to act upon recommendations made by consular officers for the exercise of discretion under section 212(d)(3)(A) of the Act. The District Director, Washington, DC, has jurisdiction in such cases recommended to the Service at the seat-of-government level by the Department of State. When a consular officer or other State Department official recommends that the benefits of section 212(d)(3)(A) of the Act be accorded an alien, neither an application nor fee shall be required. The recommendation shall specify:

(i) The reasons for inadmissibility and each section of law under which the alien is inadmissible;

(ii) Each intended date of arrival;

(iii) The length of each proposed stay in the United States;

(iv) The purpose of each stay;

(v) The number of entries which the alien intends to make; and

(vi) The justification for exercising the authority contained in section 212(d)(3) of the Act.

If the alien desires to make multiple entries and the consular officer or other State Department official believes that the circumstances justify the issuance of a visa valid for multiple entries rather than for a specified number of entries, and recommends that the alien be accorded an authorization valid for multiple entries, the information required by items (ii) and (iii) shall be furnished only with respect to the initial entry. Item (ii) does not apply to a bona fide crewman. The consular officer or other State Department official shall be notified of the decision on his recommendation. No appeal by the alien shall lie from an adverse decision made by a Service officer on the recommendation of a consular officer or other State Department official.

(2) Authority of consular officers to approve section 212(d)(3)(A) recommendations pertaining to aliens inadmissible under section 212(a)(28)(C). In certain categories of visa cases defined by the Secretary of State, United States consular officers assigned to visa-issuing posts abroad may, on behalf of the Attorney General pursuant to section 212(d)(3)(A) of the Act, approve a recommendation by another consular officer that an alien be admitted temporarily despite visa ineligibility solely because the alien is of the class of aliens defined at section 212(a)(28)(C) of the Act, as a result of presumed or actual membership in, or affiliation with, an organization described in that section. Authorizations for temporary admission granted by consular officers shall be subject to the terms specified in § 1212.4(c) of this chapter. Any recommendation which is not clearly approvable shall, and any recommendation may, be presented to the appropriate official of the Immigration and Naturalization Service for a determination.

(b) Applications under section 212(d)(3)(B). An application for the exercise of discretion under section 212(d)(3)(B) of the Act shall be submitted on Form I-192 to the district director in charge of the applicant's intended port of entry prior to the applicant's arrival in the United States. (For Department of State procedure when a visa is required, see 22 CFR 41.95 and paragraph (a) of this section.) If the application is made because the applicant may be inadmissible due to present or past membership in or affiliation with any Communist or other totalitarian party or organization, there shall be attached to the application a written statement of the history of the applicant's membership or affiliation, including the period of such membership or affiliation, whether the applicant held any office in the organization, and whether his membership or affiliation was voluntary or involuntary. If the applicant alleges that his membership or affiliation was involuntary, the statement shall include the basis for that allegation. When the application is made because the applicant may be inadmissible due to disease, mental or physical defect, or disability of any kind, the application shall describe the disease, defect, or disability. If the purpose of seeking admission to the United States is for treatment, there shall be attached to the application statements in writing to establish that satisfactory treatment cannot be obtained outside the United States; that arrangements have been completed for treatment, and where and from whom treatment will be received; what financial arrangements for payment of expenses incurred in connection with the treatment have been made, and that a bond will be available if required. When the application is made because the applicant may be inadmissible due to the conviction of one or more crimes, the designation of each crime, the date and place of its commission and of the conviction thereof, and the sentence or other judgment of the court shall be stated in the application; in such a case the application shall be supplemented by the official record of each conviction, and any other documents relating to commutation of sentence, parole, probation, or pardon. If the application is made at the time of the applicant's arrival to the district director at a port of entry, the applicant shall establish that he was not aware of the ground of inadmissibility and that it could not have been ascertained by the exercise of reasonable diligence, and he shall be in possession of a passport and visa, if required, or have been granted a waiver thereof. The applicant shall be notified of the decision and if the application is denied of the reasons therefor and of his right to appeal to the Board within 15 days after the mailing of the notification of decision in accordance with the Provisions of part 1003 of this chapter. If denied, the denial shall be without prejudice to renewal of the application in the course of proceedings before a special inquiry officer under sections 235 and 236 of the Act and this chapter. When an appeal may not be taken from a decision of a special inquiry officer excluding an alien but the alien has applied for the exercise of discretion under section 212(d)(3)(B) of the Act, the alien may appeal to the Board from a denial of such application in accordance with the provisions of § 236.5(b) of this chapter.

(c) Terms of authorization.

(1) General. Except as provided in paragraph (c)(2) of this section, each authorization under section 212(d)(3)(A) or (B) of the Act shall specify:

(i) Each section of law under which the alien is inadmissible;

(ii) The intended date of each arrival, unless the applicant is a bona fide crewman. However, if the authorization is valid for multiple entries rather than for a specified number of entries, this information shall be specified only with respect to the initial entry;

(iii) The length of each stay authorized in the United States, which shall not exceed the period justified and shall be subject to limitations specified in 8 CFR part 214. However, if the authorization is valid for multiple entries rather than for a specified number of entries, this information shall be specified only with respect to the initial entry;

(iv) The purpose of each stay;

(v) The number of entries for which the authorization is valid;

(vi) Subject to the conditions set forth in paragraph (c)(2) of this section, the dates on or between which each application for admission at POEs in the United States is valid;

(vii) The justification for exercising the authority contained in section 212(d)(3) of the Act; and

(viii) That the authorization is subject to revocation at any time.

(2) Conditions of admission.

(i) For aliens issued an authorization for temporary admission in accordance with this section, admissions pursuant to section 212(d)(3) of the Act shall be subject to the terms and conditions set forth in the authorization.

(ii) The period for which the alien's admission is authorized pursuant to this section shall not exceed the period justified, or the limitations specified, in 8 CFR part 214 for each class of nonimmigrant, whichever is less.

(3) Validity.

(i) Authorizations granted to crew members may be valid for a maximum period of 2 years for application for admission at U.S. POEs and may be valid for multiple entries.

(ii) An authorization issued in conjunction with an application for a Form DSP-150, B-1/B-2 Visa and Border Crossing Card, issued by the DOS shall be valid for a period not to exceed the validity of the biometric BCC for applications for admission at U.S. POEs and shall be valid for multiple entries.

(iii) A multiple entry authorization for a person other than a crew member or applicant for a Form DSP-150 may be made valid for a maximum period of 5 years for applications for admission at U.S. POEs.

(iv) An authorization that was previously issued in conjunction with Form I-185, Nonresident Alien Canadian Border Crossing Card, and that is noted on the card may remain valid. Although the waiver may remain valid, the non-biometric border crossing card portion of this document is not valid after that date. This waiver authorization shall cease if otherwise revoked or voided.

(v) A single-entry authorization to apply for admission at a U.S. POE shall not be valid for more than 6 months from the date the authorization is issued.

(vi) An authorization may not be revalidated. Upon expiration of the authorization, a new application and authorization are required.

(d) Admission of groups inadmissible under section 212(a)(28) for attendance at international conferences. When the Secretary of State recommends that a group of nonimmigrant aliens and their accompanying family members be admitted to attend international conferences notwithstanding their inadmissibility under section 212(a)(28) of the Act, the Deputy Commissioner, may enter an order pursuant to the authority contained in section 212(d)(3)(A) of the Act specifying the terms and conditions of their admission and stay.

(e) Inadmissibility under section 212(a)(1). Pursuant to the authority contained in section 212(d)(3) of the Act, the temporary admission of a nonimmigrant visitor is authorized notwithstanding inadmissibility under section 212(a)(1) of the Act, if such alien is accompanied by a member of his/her family, or a guardian who will be responsible for him/her during the period of admission authorized.

(f) Action upon alien's arrival. Upon admitting an alien who has been granted the benefits of section 212(d)(3)(A) of the Act, the immigration officer shall be guided by the conditions and limitations imposed in the authorization and noted by the consular officer in the alien's passport. When admitting any alien who has been granted the benefits of section 212(d)(3)(B) of the Act, the Immigration officer shall note on the arrival-departure record, Form I-94, or crewman's landing permit, Form I-95, issued to the alien, the conditions and limitations imposed in the authorization.

(g) Authorizations issued to crewmen without limitation as to period of validity. When a crewman who has a valid section 212(d)(3) authorization without any time limitation comes to the attention of the Service, his travel document shall be endorsed to show that the validity of his section 212(d)(3) authorization expires as of a date six months thereafter, and any previously-issued Form I-184 shall be lifted and Form I-95 shall be issued in its place and similarly endorsed.

(h) Revocation. The Deputy Commissioner or the district director may at any time revoke a waiver previously authorized under section 212(d)(3) of the Act and shall notify the nonimmigrant in writing to that effect.

(i) Alien witnesses and informants. —

(1) Waivers under section 212(d)(1) of the Act. Upon the application of a federal or state law enforcement authority ("LEA"), which shall include a state or federal court or United States Attorney's Office, pursuant to the filing of Form I-854, Inter-Agency Alien Witness and Informant Record, for nonimmigrant classification described in section 101(a)(15)(S) of the Act, the Commissioner shall determine whether a ground of exclusion exists with respect to the alien for whom classification is sought and, if so, whether it is in the national interest to exercise the discretion to waive the ground of excludability, other than section 212(a)(3)(E) of the Act. The Commissioner may at any time revoke a waiver previously authorized under section 212(d)(1) of the Act. In the event the Commissioner decides to revoke a previously authorized waiver for an S nonimmigrant, the Assistant Attorney General, Criminal Division, and the relevant LEA shall be notified in writing to that effect. The Assistant Attorney General, Criminal Division, shall concur in or object to the decision. Unless the Assistant Attorney General, Criminal Division, objects within 7 days, he or she shall be deemed to have concurred in the decision. In the event of an objection by the Assistant Attorney General, Criminal Division, the matter will be expeditiously referred to the Deputy Attorney General for a final resolution. In no circumstances shall the alien or the relevant LEA have a right of appeal from any decision to revoke.

(2) Grounds of removal. Nothing shall prohibit the Service from removing from the United States an alien classified pursuant to section 101(a)(15)(S) of the Act for conduct committed after the alien has been admitted to the United States as an S nonimmigrant, or after the alien's change to S classification, or for conduct or a condition undisclosed to the Attorney General prior to the alien's admission in, or change to, S classification, unless such conduct or condition is waived prior to admission and classification. In the event the Commissioner decides to remove an S nonimmigrant from the United States, the Assistant Attorney General, Criminal Division, and the relevant LEA shall be notified in writing to that effect. The Assistant Attorney General, Criminal Division, shall concur in or object to that

decision. Unless the Assistant Attorney General, Criminal Division, objects within 7 days, he or she shall be deemed to have concurred in the decision. In the event of an objection by the Assistant Attorney General, Criminal Division, the matter will be expeditiously referred to the Deputy Attorney General for a final resolution. In no circumstances shall the alien or the relevant LEA have a right of appeal from any decision to remove.

HISTORY:

[29 FR 15252, Nov. 13, 1964, as amended at 30 FR 12330, Sept. 28, 1965; 31 FR 10413, Aug. 3, 1966; 32 FR 15469, Nov. 7, 1967; 35 FR 3065, Feb. 17, 1970; 35 FR 7637, May 16, 1970; 40 FR 30470, July 21, 1975; 51 FR 32295, Sept. 10, 1986; 53 FR 40867, Oct. 19, 1988; 60 FR 44260, 44264, Aug. 25, 1995, as corrected at 60 FR 52248, Oct. 5, 1995; 67 FR 71443, 71448, Dec. 2, 2002; 68 FR 9824, 9835, 9846, Feb. 28, 2003; 68 FR 10349, 10353, Mar. 5, 2003]

§ 1212.5 Parole of aliens into the United States.

Procedures and standards for the granting of parole by the Department of Homeland Security can be found at 8 CFR 212.5.

HISTORY:

[47 FR 30045, July 9, 1982, as amended at 47 FR 46494, Oct. 19, 1982; 52 FR 16194, May 1, 1987; 52 FR 48802, Dec. 28, 1987; 53 FR 17450, May 17, 1988; 61 FR 36610, 36611, July 12, 1996, as confirmed at 63 FR 31895, 31896, June 11, 1998; 62 FR 10312, 10348, March 6, 1997; 65 FR 80281, 80294, Dec. 21, 2000; 65 FR 82254, 82255, Dec. 28, 2000; 66 FR 7863, Jan. 26, 2001; 67 FR 39255, 39257, June 7, 2002; 68 FR 9824, 9835, 9846, Feb. 28, 2003; 68 FR 10349, 10353, Mar. 5, 2003; 69 FR 69490, 69497, Nov. 29, 2004]

§ 1212.6 Border crossing identification cards.

The regulations of the Department of Homeland Security pertaining to border crossing identification cards can be found at 8 CFR 212.6.

HISTORY:

[30 FR 10184, Aug. 17, 1965, as amended at 34 FR 129, Jan. 4, 1969.; 35 FR 3065, Feb. 17, 1970; 37 FR 7584, Apr. 18, 1972; 37 FR 8061, Apr. 25, 1972; 45 FR 11114, Feb. 20, 1980; 46 FR 25082, May 5, 1981; 48 FR 35349, Aug. 4, 1983; 60 FR 40068, Aug. 7, 1995; 62 FR 9071, 9074, Feb. 28, 1997; 62 FR 10312, 10349, Mar. 6, 1997; 67 FR 71443, 71448, Dec. 2, 2002; 68 FR 9824, 9835, 9846, Feb. 28, 2003; 68 FR 10349, 10353, Mar. 5, 2003; 81 FR 92346, 92367, Dec. 19, 2016]

§ 1212.7 Waiver of certain grounds of inadmissibility.

(a) General —

(1) Filing procedure —

(i) Immigrant visa or K nonimmigrant visa applicant. An applicant for an immigrant visa or "K" nonimmigrant visa who is inadmissible and seeks a waiver of inadmissibility shall file an application on Form I-601 at the consular office considering the visa application. Upon determining that the alien is admissible except for the grounds for which a waiver is sought, the consular officer shall transmit the Form I-601 to the Service for decision.

(ii) Adjustment of status applicant. An applicant for adjustment of status who is excludable and seeks a waiver under section 212(h) or (i) of the Act shall file an application on Form I-601 with the director or immigration judge considering the application for adjustment of status.

(iii) Parole authorization applicant under § 1245.15(t). An applicant for parole authorization under § 1245.15(t) of this chapter who is inadmissible and seeks a waiver under section 212(h) or (i) of the Act must file an application on Form I-601 with the Director of the Nebraska Service Center considering the Form I-131.

(iv) Parole authorization applicant under § 1245.13(k)(2) of this chapter. An applicant for parole authorization under § 1245.13(k)(2) of this chapter who is inadmissible and seeks a waiver under section 212(h) or (i) of the Act must file an application on Form I-601 with the Director of the Texas Service Center adjudicating the Form I-131.

(2) Termination of application for lack of prosecution. An applicant may withdraw the application at any time prior to the final decision, whereupon the case will be closed and the consulate notified. If the applicant fails to prosecute the application within a reasonable time either before or after interview the applicant shall be notified that if he or she fails to prosecute the application within 30 days the case will be closed subject to being reopened at the applicant's request. If no action has been taken within the 30-day period immediately thereafter, the case will be closed and the appropriate consul notified.

(3) Decision. If the application is approved the director shall complete Form I-607 for inclusion in the alien's file and shall notify the alien of the decision. If the application is denied the applicant shall be notified of the decision, of the reasons therefor, and of the right to appeal in accordance with part 103 of this chapter.

(4) Validity. A waiver granted under section 212(h) or section 212(i) of the Act shall apply only to those grounds of excludability and to those crimes, events or incidents specified in the application for waiver. Once granted, the waiver shall be valid indefinitely, even if the recipient of the waiver later abandons or otherwise loses lawful permanent resident status, except that any waiver which is granted to an alien who obtains lawful permanent residence on a conditional basis under section 216 of the Act shall automatically terminate concurrently with the termination of such residence pursuant to the provisions of section 216. Separate notification of the termination of the waiver is not required when an alien is notified of the termination of residence under section 216 of the Act, and no appeal shall lie from the decision to terminate the waiver on this basis. However, if the respondent is found not to be deportable in a deportation proceeding based on the termination, the waiver shall again become effective. Nothing in this subsection shall preclude the director from reconsidering a decision to approve a waiver if the decision is determined to have been made in error.

(b) Section 212(g) (tuberculosis and certain mental conditions) —

(1) General. Any alien who is ineligible for a visa and is excluded from admission into the United States under section 212(a) (1), (3), or (6) of the Act may file an Application for Waiver of Grounds of Excludability (Form I-601) under section 212(g) of the Act at an office designated in paragraph (2). The family member specified in section 212(g) of the Act may file the waiver for the applicant if the applicant is incompetent to file the waiver personally.

(2) Locations for filing Form I-601. Form I-601 may be filed at any one of the following offices:

(i) The American consulate where the application for a visa is being considered if the alien is outside the United States;

(ii) The Service office having jurisdiction over the port of entry where the alien is applying for admission into the United States;

(iii) The Service office having jurisdiction over the alien if the alien is in the United States;

(iv) The Nebraska Service Center, if the alien is outside the United States and seeking parole authorization under § 1245.15(t)(2) of this chapter; or

(v) The Texas Service Center if the alien is outside the United States and is seeking parole authorization under § 1245.13(k)(2) of this chapter.

(3) Section 212(a)(6) (tuberculosis). If the alien is excludable under section 212(a)(6) of the Act because of tuberculosis, he shall execute Statement A on the reverse of page 1 of Form I-601. In addition, he or his sponsor in the United States is responsible for having Statement B executed by the physician or health facility which has agreed to supply treatment or observation; and, if required, Statement C shall be executed by the appropriate local or State health officer.

(4) Section 212(a) (1) or (3) (certain mental conditions) —

(i) Arrangements for submission of medical report. If the alien is excludable under section 212(a) (1) or (3) (because of mental retardation or because of a past history of mental illness) he or his sponsoring family member shall submit an executed Form I-601 to the consular or Service office with a statement that arrangements have been made for the submission to that office of a medical report. The medical report shall contain a complete medical history of the alien, including details of any hospitalization or institutional care or treatment for any physical or mental condition; findings as to the current physical condition of the alien, including reports of chest X-ray examination and of serologic test for syphilis if the alien is 15 years of age or over, and other pertinent diagnostic tests; and findings as to the current mental condition of the alien, with information as to prognosis and life expectancy and with a report of a psychiatric examination conducted by a psychiatrist who shall, in case of mental retardation, also provide an evaluation of the alien's intelligence. For an alien with a past history of mental illness, the medical report shall also contain available information on which the U.S. Public Health Service can base a finding as to whether the alien has been free of such mental illness for a period of time sufficient in the light of such history to demonstrate recovery. Upon receipt of the medical report, the consular or Service office shall refer it to the U.S. Public Health Service for review.

(ii) Submission of statement. Upon being notified that the medical report has been reviewed by the U.S. Public Health Service and determined to be acceptable, the alien or the alien's sponsoring family member shall submit a statement to the consular or Service office. The statement must be from a clinic, hospital, institution, specialized facility, or specialist in the United States approved by the U.S. Public Health Service. The alien or alien's sponsor may be referred to the mental retardation or mental health agency of the state of proposed residence for guidance in selecting a post-arrival medical examining authority who will complete the evaluation and provide an evaluation report to the Centers for Disease Control. The statement must specify the name and address of the specialized facility, or specialist, and must affirm that:

(A) The specified facility or specialist agrees to evaluate the alien's mental status and prepare a complete report of the findings of such evaluation.

(B) The alien, the alien's sponsoring family member, or another responsible person has made complete financial arrangements for payment of any charges that may be incurred after arrival for studies, care, training and service;

(C) The Director, Division of Quarantine, Center for Prevention Services, Centers for Disease Control, Atlanta, GA. 30333 shall be furnished:

(1) The report evaluating the alien's mental status within 30 days after the alien's arrival; and

(2) Prompt notification of the alien's failure to report to the facility or specialist within 30 days after being notified by the U.S. Public Health Service that the alien has arrived in the United States.

(D) The alien shall be in an outpatient, inpatient, study, or other specified status as determined by the responsible local physcian or specialist during the initial evaluation.

(5) Assurances: Bonds. In all cases under paragraph (b) of this section the alien or his or her sponsoring family member shall also submit an assurance that the alien will comply with any special travel requirements as may be specified by the U.S. Public Health Service and that, upon the admission of the alien into the United States, he or she will proceed directly to the facility or specialist specified for the initial evaluation, and will submit to such further examinations or treatment as may be required, whether in an outpatient, inpatient, or other status. The alien, his or her sponsoring family member, or other responsible person shall provide such assurances or bond as may be required to assure that the necessary expenses of the alien will be met and that he or she will not become a public charge. For procedures relating to cancellation or breaching of bonds, see part 103 of 8 CFR chapter I.

(c) Section 212(e).

(1) An alien who was admitted to the United States as an exchange visitor, or who acquired that status after admission, is subject to the foreign residence requirement of section 212(e) of the Act if his or her

participation in an exchange program was financed in whole or in part, directly or indirectly, by a United States government agency or by the government of the country of his or her nationality or last foreign residence.

(2) An alien is also subject to the foreign residence requirement of section 212(e) of the Act if at the time of admission to the United States as an exchange visitor or at the time of acquisition of exchange visitor status after admission to the United States, the alien was a national or lawful permanent resident of a country which the Director of the United States Information Agency had designated, through public notice in the Federal Register, as clearly requiring the services of persons engaged in the field of specialized knowledge or skill in which the alien was to engage in his or her exchange visitor program.

(3) An alien is also subject to the foreign residence requirement of section 212(e) of the Act if he or she was admitted to the United States as an exchange visitor on or after January 10, 1977 to receive graduate medical education or training, or following admission, acquired such status on or after that date for that purpose. However, an exchange visitor already participating in an exchange program of graduate medical education or training as of January 9, 1977 who was not then subject to the foreign residence requirement of section 212(e) and who proceeds or has proceeded abroad temporarily and is returning to the United States to participate in the same program, continues to be exempt from the foreign residence requirement.

(4) A spouse or child admitted to the United States or accorded status under section 101(a)(15)(J) of the Act to accompany or follow to join an exchange visitor who is subject to the foreign residence requirement of section 212(e) of the Act is also subject to that requirement.

(5) An alien who is subject to the foreign residence requirement and who believes that compliance therewith would impose exceptional hardship upon his/her spouse or child who is a citizen of the United States or a lawful permanent resident alien, or that he or she cannot return to the country of his or her nationality or last residence because he or she will be subject to persecution on account of race, religion, or political opinion, may apply for a waiver on Form I-612. The alien's spouse and minor children, if also subject to the foreign residence requirement, may be included in the application, provided the spouse has not been a participant in an exchange program.

(6) Each application based upon a claim to exceptional hardship must be accompanied by the certificate of marriage between the applicant and his or her spouse and proof of legal termination of all previous marriages of the applicant and spouse; the birth certificate of any child who is a United States citizen or lawful permanent resident alien, if the application is based upon a claim of exceptional hardship to a child, and evidence of the United States citizenship of the applicant's spouse or child, when the application is based upon a claim of exceptional hardship to a spouse or child who is a citizen of the United States.

(7) Evidence of United States citizenship and of status as a lawful permanent resident shall be in the form provided in part 204 of 8 CFR chapter I. An application based upon exceptional hardship shall be supported by a statement, dated and signed by the applicant, giving a detailed explanation of the basis for his or her belief that his or her compliance with the foreign residence requirement of section 212(e) of the Act, as amended, would impose exceptional hardship upon his or her spouse or child who is a citizen of the United States or a lawful permanent resident thereof. The statement shall include all pertinent information concerning the incomes and savings of the applicant and spouse. If exceptional hardship is claimed upon medical grounds, the applicant shall submit a medical certificate from a qualified physician setting forth in terms understandable to a layman the nature and effect of the illness and prognosis as to the period of time the spouse or child will require care or treatment.

(8) An application based upon the applicant's belief that he or she cannot return to the country of his or her nationality or last residence because the applicant would be subject to persecution on account of race, religion, or political opinion, must be supported by a statement, dated and signed by the applicant, setting forth in detail why the applicant believes he or she would be subject to persecution.

(9) Waivers under Pub. L. 103-416 based on a request by a State Department of Public Health (or equivalent). In accordance with section 220 of Pub. L. 103-416, an alien admitted to the United States as a nonimmigrant under section 101(a)(15)(J) of the Act, or who acquired status under section 101(a)(15)(J) of the Act after admission to the United States, to participate in an exchange program of graduate medical education or training (as of January 9, 1977), may apply for a waiver of the 2-year home country residence and physical presence requirement (the "2-year requirement") under section 212(e)(iii) of the Act based on a request by a State Department of Pubic Health, or its equivalent. To initiate the application for a waiver under Pub. L. 103-416, the Department of Public Health, or its equivalent, or the State in which the foreign medical graduate seeks to practice medicine, must request the Director of USIA to recommend a waiver to the Service. The waiver may be granted only if the Director of USIA provides the Service with a favorable waiver recommendation. Only the Service, however, may grant or deny the waiver application. If granted, such a waiver shall be subject to the terms and conditions imposed under section 214(l) of the Act (as redesignated by section 671(a)(3)(A) of Pub. L. 104-208). Although the alien is not required to submit a separate waiver application to the Service, the burden rests on the alien to establish eligibility for the waiver. If the Service approves a waiver request made under Pub. L. 103-416, the foreign medical graduate (and accompanying dependents) may apply for change of nonimmigrant status, from J-1 to H-1B and, in the case of dependents of such a foreign medical graduate, from J-2 to H-4. Aliens receiving waivers under section 220 of Pub. L. 103-416

are subject, in all cases, to the provisions of section 214(g)(1)(A) of the Act.

(i) Eligiblity criteria. J-1 foreign medical graduates (with accompanying J-2 dependents) are eligible to apply for a waiver of the 2-year requirement under Pub. L. 103-416 based on a request by a State Department of Public Health (or its equivalent) if:

(A) They were admitted to the United States under section 101(a)(15)(J) of the Act, or acquired J nonimmigrant status before June 1, 2002, to pursue graduate medical education or training in the United States.

(B) They have entered into a bona fide, full-time employment contract for 3 years to practice medicine at a health care facility located in an area or areas designated by the Secretary of Health and Human Services as having a shortage of health care professionals ("HHS-designated shortage area");

(C) They agree to commence employment within 90 days of receipt of the waiver under this section and agree to practice medicine for 3 years at the facility named in the waiver application and only in HHS-designated shortage areas. The health care facility named in the waiver application may be operated by:

(1) An agency of the Government of the United States or of the State in which it is located; or

(2) A charitable, educational, or other not-for-profit organization; or

(3) Private medical practitioners.

(D) The Department of Public Health, or its equivalent, in the State where the health care facility is located has requested the Director, USIA, to recommend the waiver, and the Director, USIA, submits a favorable waiver recommendation to the Service; and

(E) Approval of the waiver will not cause the number of waivers granted pursuant to Pub. L. 103-416 and this section to foreign medical graduates who will practice medicine in the same state to exceed 20 during the current fiscal year.

(ii) Decision on waivers under Pub. L. 103-416 and notification to the alien —

(A) Approval. If the Director of USIA submits a favorable waiver recommendation on behalf of a foreign medical graduate pursuant to Pub. L. 103-416, and the Service grants the waiver, the alien shall be notified of the approval on Form I-797 (or I-797A or I-797B, as appropriate). The approval notice shall clearly state the terms and conditions imposed on the waiver, and the Service's records shall be noted accordingly.

(B) Denial. If the Director of USIA issues a favorable waiver recommendation under Pub. L. 103-416 and the Service denies the waiver, the alien shall be notified of the decision and of the right to appeal under 8 CFR part 1103. However, no appeal shall lie where the basis for denial is that the number of waivers granted to the State in which the foreign medical graduate will be employed would exceed 20 for that fiscal year.

(iii) Conditions. The foreign medical graduate must agree to commence employment for the health care facility specified in the waiver application within 90 days of receipt of the waiver under Pub. L. 103-416. The foreign medical graduate may only fulfill the requisite 3-year employment contract as an H-1B nonimmigrant. A foreign medical graduate who receives a waiver under Pub. L. 103-416 based on a request by a State Department of Public Health (or equivalent), and changes his or her nonimmigrant classification from J-1 to H-1B, may not apply for permanent residence or for any other change of nonimmigrant classification unless he or she has fulfilled the 3-year employment contract with the health care facility and in the specified HHS-designated shortage area named in the waiver application.

(iv) Failure to fulfill the three-year employment contract due to extenuating circumstances. A foreign medical graduate who fails to meet the terms and conditions imposed on the waiver under section 214(l) of the Act and this paragraph will once again become subject to the 2-year requirement under section 212(e) of the Act.

Under section 214(l)(1)(B) of the Act, however, the Service, in the exercise of discretion, may excuse early termination of the foreign medical graduate's 3-year period of employment with the health care facility named in the waiver application due to extenuating circumstances. Extenuating circumstances may include, but are not limited to, closure of the health care facility or hardship to the alien. In determining whether to excuse such early termination of employment, the Service shall base its decision on the specific facts of each case. In all cases, the burden of establishing eligibility for a favorable exercise of discretion rests with the foreign medical graduate. Depending on the circumstances, closure of the health care facility named in the waiver application may, but need not, be considered an extenuating circumstance excusing early termination of employment. Under no circumstances will a foreign medical graduate be eligible to apply for change of status to another nonimmigrant category, for an immigrant visa or for status as a lawful permanent resident prior to completing the requisite 3-year period of employment for a health care facility located in an HHS-designated shortage area.

(v) Required evidence. A foreign medical graduate who seeks to have early termination of employment excused due to extenuating circumstances shall submit documentary evidence establishing such a claim. In all cases, the foreign medical graduate shall submit an employment contract with another health care facility located in an HHS-designated shortage area for the balance of the required 3-year period of employment. A foreign medical graduate claiming extenuating circumstances based on hardship shall also submit evidence establishing that such hardship was caused by unforeseen circumstances beyond his or her control. A foreign medical graduate claiming extenuating circumstances based on closure of the health care facility named in the waiver application shall also submit evidence that the facility has closed or is about to be closed.

(vi) Notification requirements. A J-1 foreign medical graduate who has been granted a waiver of the 2-year requirement pursuant to Pub. L. 103-416, is required to comply with the terms and conditions specified in section 214(l) of the Act and the implementing regulations in this section. If the foreign medical graduate subsequently applies for and receives H-1B status, he or she must also comply with the terms and conditions of that nonimmigrant status. Such compliance shall also include notifying the Service of any material change in the terms and conditions of the H-1B employment, by filing either an amended or a new H-1B petition, as required, under §§ 214.2(h)(2)(i)(D), 214.2(h)(2)(i)(E), and 214.2(h)(11) of 8 CFR chapter I.

(A) Amended H-1B petitions. The health care facility named in the waiver application and H-1B petition shall file an amended H-1B petition, as required under § 214.2(h)(2)(i)(E) of 8 CFR chapter I, if there are any material changes in the terms and conditions of the beneficiary's employment or eligibility as specified in the waiver application filed under Pub. L. 103-416 and in the subsequent H-1B petition. In such a case, an amended H-1B petition shall be accompanied by evidence that the alien will continue practicing medicine with the original employer in an HHS-designated shortage area.

(B) New H-1B petitions. A health care facility seeking to employ a foreign medical graduate who has been granted a waiver under Pub. L. 103-416 (prior to the time the alien has completed his or her 3-year contract with the facility named in the waiver application and original H-1B petition), shall file a new H-1B petition with the Service, as required under §§ 214.2(h)(2)(i) (D) and (E) of 8 CFR chapter I. Although a new waiver application need not be filed, the new H-1B petition shall be accompanied by the documentary evidence generally required under § 214.2(h) of 8 CFR chapter I, and the following additional documents:

(1) A copy of Form I-797 (and/or I-797A and I-797B) relating to the waiver and nonimmigrant H status granted under Pub. L. 103-416;

(2) An explanation from the foreign medical graduate, with supporting evidence, establishing that extenuating circumstances necessitate a change in employment;

(3) An employment contract establishing that the foreign medical graduate will practice medicine at the health care facility named in the new H-1B petition for the balance of the required 3-year period; and

(4) Evidence that the geographic area or areas of intended employment indicated in the new H-1B petition are in HHS-designated shortage areas.

(C) Review of amended and new H-1B petitions for foreign medical graduates granted waivers under Pub. L. 103-416 and who seek to have early termination of employment excused due to extenuating circumstances —

(1) Amended H-1B petitions. The waiver granted under Pub. L. 103-416 may be affirmed, and the amended H-1B petition may be approved, if the petitioning health care facility establishes that the foreign medical graduate otherwise remains eligible for H-1B classification and that he or she will continue practicing medicine in an HHS-designated shortage area.

(2) New H-1B petitions. The Service shall review a new H-1B petition filed on behalf of a foreign medical graduate who has not yet fulfilled the required 3-year period of employment with the health care facility named in the waiver application and in the original H-1B petition to determine whether extenuating circumstances exist which warrant a change in employment, and whether the waiver granted under Pub. L. 103-416 should be affirmed. In conducting such a review, the Service shall determine whether the foreign medical graduate will continue practicing medicine in an HHS-designated shortage area, and whether the new H-1B petitioner and the foreign medical graduate have satisfied the remaining H-1B eligibility criteria described under section 101(a)(15)(H) of the Act and § 214.2(h) of 8 CFR chapter I. If these criteria have been satisfied, the waiver granted to the foreign medical graduate under Pub. L. 103-416 may be affirmed, and the new H1-B petition may be approved in the exercise of discretion, thereby permitting the foreign medical graduate to serve the balance of the requisite 3-year employment period at the health care facility named in the new H-1B petition.

(D) Failure to notify the Service of any material changes in employment. Foreign medical graduates who have been granted a waiver of the 2-year requirement and who have obtained H-1B status under Pub. L. 103-416 but fail to: Properly notify the Service of any material change in the terms and conditions of their H-1B employment, by having their employer file an amended or a new H-1B petition in accordance with this section and § 214.2(h) of 8 CFR chapter I; or establish continued eligibility for the waiver and H-1B status, shall (together with their dependents) again become subject to the 2-year requirement. Such foreign medical graduates and their accompanying H-4 dependents also become subject to deportation under section 241(a)(1)(C)(i) of the Act.

(10) The applicant and his or her spouse may be interviewed by an immigration officer in connection with the application and consultation may be had with the Director, United States Information Agency and the sponsor of any exchange program in which the applicant has been a participant.

(11) The applicant shall be notified of the decision, and if the application is denied, of the reasons therefor and of the right of appeal in accordance with the provisions of part 103 of this chapter. However, no appeal shall lie from the denial of an application for lack of a favorable recommendation from the Secretary of State. When an interested United States Government agency requests a waiver of the two-year foreign-residence requirement and the Director, United States Information Agency had made a favorable recommendation, the interested agency shall be notified of the decision on its request and, if the request is denied, of the reasons thereof, and of the right of appeal. If the foreign country of the alien's nationality or last residence has furnished statement in writing that it has no objection to his/her being granted a waiver of the foreign residence requirement and the Director, United States Information Agency has made a favorable recommendation, the Director shall be notified of the decision and, if the foreign residence requirement is not waived, of the reasons therefor and of the foregoing right of appeal. However, this "no objection" provision is not applicable to the exchange visitor admitted to the

United States on or after January 10, 1977 to receive graduate medical education or training, or who acquired such status on or after that date for such purpose; except that the alien who commenced a program before January 10, 1977 and who was readmitted to the United States on or after that date to continue participation in the same program, is eligible for the "no objection" waiver.

(d) Criminal grounds of inadmissibility involving violent or dangerous crimes. The Attorney General, in general, will not favorably exercise discretion under section 212(h)(2) of the Act (8 U.S.C. 1182(h)(2)) to consent to an application or reapplication for a visa, or admission to the United States, or adjustment of status, with respect to immigrant aliens who are inadmissible under section 212(a)(2) of the Act in cases involving violent or dangerous crimes, except in extraordinary circumstances, such as those involving national security or foreign policy considerations, or cases in which an alien clearly demonstrates that the denial of the application for adjustment of status or an immigrant visa or admission as an immigrant would result in exceptional and extremely unusual hardship. Moreover, depending on the gravity of the alien's underlying criminal offense, a showing of extraordinary circumstances might still be insufficient to warrant a favorable exercise of discretion under section 212(h)(2) of the Act.

HISTORY:

[29 FR 12584, Sept. 4, 1964, and 29 FR 13242; Sept. 24, 1964, as amended at 30 FR 14776, Nov. 30, 1965; 32 FR 2500, Feb. 7, 1967; 37 FR 22725, Oct. 31, 1972; 46 FR 45327, Sept. 11, 1981; 47 FR 44235, Oct. 7, 1982; 48 FR 20684, May 9, 1983; 48 FR 23159, May 24, 1983; 48 FR 30610, July 5, 1983; 49 FR 48530, Dec. 13, 1984; 53 FR 30017, Aug. 10, 1988; 60 FR 26681, May 18, 1995, as confirmed and amended at 62 FR 18506, 18508, Apr. 16, 1997; 64 FR 25756, 25766, May 12, 1999, as confirmed and amended at 65 FR 15835, 15844, 15846, 15854, Mar. 24, 2000; 66 FR 42587, 42593, Aug. 14, 2001; 67 FR 78675, 78678, Dec. 26, 2002; 68 FR 9824, 9835, Feb. 28, 2003; 68 FR 10349, 10353, Mar. 5, 2003]

AUTHORITY:

(Secs. 103, 203, 212 of the Immigration and Nationality Act, as amended by secs. 4, 5, 18 of Pub. L. 97-116, 95 Stat. 1611, 1620, (8 U.S.C. 1103, 1153, 1182)

§ 1212.8 Certification requirement of section 212(a)(14).

(a) General. The certification requirement of section 212(a)(14) of the Act applies to aliens seeking admission to the United States or adjustment of status under section 245 of the Act for the purpose of performing skilled or unskilled labor, who are preference immigrants as described in section 203(a) (3) or (6) of the Act, or who are nonpreference immigrants as described in section 203(a)(8). The certification requirement shall not be applicable to a nonpreference applicant for admission to the United States or to a nonpreference applicant for adjustment of status under section 245 who establishes that he will not perform skilled or unskilled labor. A native of the Western Hemisphere who established a priority date with a consular officer prior to January 1, 1977 and who was found to be entitled to an exemption from the labor certification requirement of section 212(a)(14) of the Act under the law in effect prior to January 1, 1977 as the parent, spouse or child of a United States citizen or lawful permanent resident alien shall continue to be exempt from that requirement for so long as the relationship upon which the exemption is based continues to exist.

(b) Aliens not required to obtain labor certifications. The following persons are not considered to be within the purview of section 212(a)(14) of the Act and do not require a labor certification: (1) A member of the Armed Forces of the United States; (2) a spouse or child accompanying or following to join his spouse or parent who either has a labor certification or is a nondependent alien who does not require such a certification; (3) a female alien who intends to marry a citizen or alien lawful permanent resident of the United States, who establishes satisfactorily that she does not intend to seek employment in the United States and whose fiance has guaranteed her support; (4) an alien who establishes on Form I-526 that he has invested, or is actively in the process of investing, capital totaling at least $ 40,000 in an enterprise in the United States of which he will be a principal manager and that the enterprise will employ a person or persons in the United States of which he will be a principal manager and that the enterprise will employ a person or persons in the United States who are United States citizens or aliens lawfully admitted for permnanent residence, exclusive of the alien, his spouse and children. A copy of a document submitted in support of Form I-526 may be accepted though unaccompanied by the original, if the copy bears a certification by an attorney, typed or rubber-stamped in the language set forth in § 204.2(j) of 8 CFR chapter I. However, the original document shall be submitted, if submittal is requested by the Service.

HISTORY:

[31 FR 10021, July 23, 1966; 31 FR 10355, Aug. 22, 1966, as amended at 34 FR 5326, Mar. 18, 1969; 38 FR 31166, Nov. 12, 1973; 41 FR 37566, Sept. 7, 1976; 41 FR 55850, Dec. 23, 1976; 47 FR 44990, Oct. 13, 1982; 48 FR 19157, Apr. 28, 1983; 68 FR 9824, 9835, Feb. 28, 2003; 68 FR 10349, 10353, Mar. 5, 2003]

§ 1212.9 Applicability of section 212(a)(32) to certain derivative third and sixth preference and nonpreference immigrants.

A derivative beneficiary who is the spouse or child of a qualified third or sixth preference or nonpreference immigrant and who is also a graduate of a medical school as defined by section 101(a)(41) of the Act is not considered to be an alien who is coming to the United States principally to perform services as a member of the medical profession. Therefore, a derivative third or sixth preference or nonpreference immigrant under section 203(a)(8) of the Act, who is also a graduate of a medical school, is eligible for an immigrant visa or for adjustment of status under section 245 of the Act, whether or not such derivative immigrant has passed Parts I and II of the National Board of Medical Examiners Examination or equivalent examination.

HISTORY:

[45 FR 63836, Sept. 26, 1980; 68 FR 9824, 9835, Feb. 28, 2003]

AUTHORITY:

(Secs. 103, 203(a)(8), and 212(a)(32), 8 U.S.C 1103, 1153(a)(8), and 1182(a)(32))

§ 1212.10 Section 212(k) waiver.

Any applicant for admission who is in possession of an immigrant visa, and who is excludable under sections 212(a)(14), (20), or (21) of the Act, may apply to the district director at the port of entry for a waiver under section 212(k) of the Act. If the application for waiver is denied by the district director, the application may be renewed in exclusion proceedings before an immigration judge as provided in part 1236 of this chapter.

HISTORY:

[47 FR 44236, Oct. 7, 1982; 68 FR 9824, 9835, Feb. 28, 2003; 68 FR 10349, 10353, Mar. 5, 2003]

AUTHORITY:

(Secs. 103, 203, 212 of the Immigration and Nationality Act, as amended by secs. 4, 5, 18 of Pub. L. 97-116, 95 Stat. 1611, 1620, (8 U.S.C. 1103, 1153, 1182)

§ 1212.11 Controlled substance convictions.

In determining the admissibility of an alien who has been convicted of a violation of any law or regulation of a State, the United States, or a foreign country relating to a controlled substance, the term controlled substance as used in section 212(a)(23) of the Act, shall mean the same as that referenced in the Controlled Substances Act, 21 U.S.C. 801, et seq., and shall include any substance contained in Schedules I through V of 21 CFR 1308.1, T3et seq. For the purposes of this section, the term controlled substance includes controlled substance analogues as defined in 21 U.S.C. 802(23) and 813.

HISTORY:

[53 FR 9282, Mar. 22, 1988; 68 FR 9824, 9835, Feb. 28, 2003]

§ 1212.12 Parole determinations and revocations respecting Mariel Cubans.

(a) Scope. This section applies to any native of Cuba who last came to the United States between April 15, 1980, and October 20, 1980 (hereinafter referred to as Mariel Cuban) and who is being detained by the Immigration and Naturalization Service (hereinafter referred to as the Service) pending his or her exclusion hearing, or pending his or her return to Cuba or to another country. It covers Mariel Cubans who have never been paroled as well as those Mariel Cubans whose previous parole has been revoked by the Service. It also applies to any Mariel Cuban, detained under the authority of the Immigration and Nationality Act in any facility, who has not been approved for release or who is currently awaiting movement to a Service or Bureau Of Prisons (BOP) facility. In addition, it covers the revocation of parole for those Mariel Cubans who have been released on parole at any time.

(b) Parole authority and decision. The authority to grant parole under section 212(d)(5) of the Act to a detained Mariel Cuban shall be exercised by the Commissioner, acting through the Associate Commissioner for Enforcement, as follows:

(1) Parole decisions. The Associate Commissioner for Enforcement may, in the exercise of discretion, grant parole to a detained Mariel Cuban for emergent reasons or for reasons deemed strictly in the public interest. A decision to retain in custody shall briefly set forth the reasons for the continued detention. A decision to release on parole may contain such special conditions as are considered appropriate. A copy of any decision to parole or to detain, with an attached copy translated into Spanish, shall be provided to the detainee. Parole documentation for Mariel Cubans shall be issued by the district director having jurisdiction over the alien, in accordance with the parole determination made by the Associate Commissioner for Enforcement.

(2) Additional delegation of authority. All references to the Commissioner and Associate Commissioner for Enforcement in this section shall be deemed to include any person or persons (including a committee) designated in writing by the Commissioner or Associate Commissioner for Enforcement to exercise powers under this section.

(c) Review Plan Director. The Associate Commissioner for Enforcement shall appoint a Director of the Cuban Review Plan. The Director shall have authority to establish and maintain appropriate files respecting each Mariel Cuban to be reviewed for possible parole, to determine the order in which the cases shall be reviewed, and to coordinate activities associated with these reviews.

(d) Recommendations to the Associate Commissioner for Enforcement. Parole recommendations for detained Mariel Cubans shall be developed in accordance with the following procedures.

(1) Review Panels. The Director shall designate a panel or panels to make parole recommendations to the Associate Commissioner for Enforcement. A Cuban Review Panel shall, except as otherwise provided, consist of two persons. Members of a Review Panel shall be selected from the professional staff of the Service. All recommendations by a two-member Panel shall be unanimous. If the vote of a two-member Panel is split, it shall adjourn its deliberations concerning that particular detainee until a third Panel member is added. A recommendation by a three-member Panel shall be by majority vote. The third member of any Panel shall be the Director of the Cuban Review Plan or his designee.

(2) Criteria for Review. Before making any recommendation that a detainee be granted parole, a majority of the Cuban Review Panel members, or the Director in case of a record review, must conclude that:

(i) The detainee is presently a nonviolent person;

(ii) The detainee is likely to remain nonviolent;

(iii) The detainee is not likely to pose a threat to the community following his release; and

(iv) The detainee is not likely to violate the conditions of his parole.

(3) Factors for consideration. The following factors should be weighed in considering whether to recommend further detention or release on parole of a detainee:

(i) The nature and number of disciplinary infractions or incident reports received while in custody;

(ii) The detainee's past history of criminal behavior;

(iii) Any psychiatric and psychological reports pertaining to the detainee's mental health;

(iv) Institutional progress relating to participation in work, educational and vocational programs;

(v) His ties to the United States, such as the number of close relatives residing lawfully here;

(vi) The likelihood that he may abscond, such as from any sponsorship program; and

(vii) Any other information which is probative of whether the detainee is likely to adjust to life in a community, is likely to engage in future acts of violence, is likely to engage in future criminal activity, or is likely to violate the conditions of his parole.

(4) Procedure for review. The following procedures will govern the review process:

(i) Record review. Initially, the Director or a Panel shall review the detainee's file. Upon completion of this record review, the Director or the Panel shall issue a written recommendation that the detainee be released on parole or scheduled for a personal interview.

(ii) Personal interview. If a recommendation to grant parole after only a record review is not accepted or if the detainee is not recommended for release, a Panel shall personally interview the detainee. The scheduling of such interviews shall be at the discretion of the Director. The detainee may be accompanied during the interview by a person of his choice, who is able to attend at the time of the scheduled interview, to assist in answering any questions. The detainee may submit to the Panel any information, either orally or in writing, which he believes presents a basis for release on parole.

(iii) Panel recommendation. Following completion of the interview and its deliberations, the Panel shall issue a written recommendation that the detainee be released on parole or remain in custody pending deportation or pending further observation and subsequent review. This written recommendation shall include a brief statement of the factors which the Panel deems material to its recommendation. The recommendation and appropriate file material shall be forwarded to the Associate Commissioner for Enforcement, to be considered in the exercise of discretion pursuant to § 1212.12(b).

(e) Withdrawal of parole approval. The Associate Commissioner for Enforcement may, in his or her discretion, withdraw approval for parole of any detainee prior to release when, in his or her opinion, the conduct of the detainee, or any other circumstance, indicates that parole would no longer be appropriate.

(f) Sponsorship. No detainee may be released on parole until suitable sponsorship or placement has been found for the detainee. The paroled detainee must abide by the parole conditions specified by the Service in relation to his sponsorship or placement. The following sponsorships and placements are suitable:

(1) Placement by the Public Health Service in an approved halfway house or mental health project;

(2) Placement by the Community Relations Service in an approved halfway house or community project; and

(3) Placement with a close relative such as a parent, spouse, child, or sibling who is a lawful permanent resident or a citizen of the United States.

(g) Timing of reviews. The timing of review shall be in accordance with the following guidelines.

(1) Parole revocation cases. The Director shall schedule the review process in the case of a new or returning detainee whose previous immigration parole has been revoked. The review process will commence with a scheduling of a file review, which will ordinarily be expected to occur within approximately three months after parole is revoked. In the case of a Mariel Cuban who is in the custody of the Service, the Cuban Review Plan Director may, in his or her discretion, suspend or postpone the parole review process if such detainee's prompt deportation is practicable and proper.

(2) Continued detention cases. A subsequent review shall be commenced for any detainee within one year of a refusal to grant parole under § 1212.12(b), unless a shorter interval is specified by the Director.

(3) Discretionary reviews. The Cuban Review Plan Director, in his discretion, may schedule a review of a detainee at any time when the Director deems such a review to be warranted.

(h) Revocation of parole. The Associate Commissioner for Enforcement shall have authority, in the exercise of discretion, to revoke parole in respect to Mariel Cubans. A district director may also revoke parole when, in the district director's opinion, revocation is in the public interest and circumstances do not reasonably permit referral of the case to the Associate Commissioner. Parole may be revoked in the exercise of discretion when, in the opinion of the revoking official:

(1) The purposes of parole have been served;

(2) The Mariel Cuban violates any condition of parole;

(3) It is appropriate to enforce an order of exclusion or to commence proceedings against a Mariel Cuban; or

(4) The period of parole has expired without being renewed.

HISTORY:

[52 FR 48802, Dec. 28, 1987; 59 FR 13870, Mar. 24, 1994; 65 FR 80281, 80294, Dec. 21, 2000; 68 FR 9824, 9835, 9846, Feb. 28, 2003]

§ 1212.13 Severability.

The provisions of part 1212 are separate and severable from one another. In the event that any provision in part 1212 is stayed, enjoined, not implemented, or otherwise held invalid, the remaining provisions shall nevertheless be implemented as an independent rule and continue in effect.

HISTORY:

[68 FR 9824, 9835, Feb. 28, 2003; 85 FR 80274, 80399, Dec. 11, 2020]

§ 1212.14 Parole determinations for alien witnesses and informants for whom a law enforcement authority ("LEA") will request S classification.

(a) Parole authority. Parole authorization under section 212(d)(5) of the Act for aliens whom LEAs seek to bring to the United States as witnesses or informants in criminal/counter terrorism matters and to apply for S classification shall be exercised as follows:

(1) Grounds of eligibility. The Commissioner may, in the exercise of discretion, grant parole to an alien (and the alien's family members) needed for law enforcement purposes provided that a state or federal LEA:

(i) Establishes its intention to file, within 30 days after the alien's arrival in the United States, a completed Form I-854, Inter-Agency Alien Witness and Informant Record, with the Assistant Attorney General, Criminal Division, Department of Justice, in accordance with the instructions on or attached to the form, which will include the names of qualified family members for whom parole is sought;

(ii) Specifies the particular operational reasons and basis for the request, and agrees to assume responsibility for the alien during the period of the alien's temporary stay in the United States, including maintaining control and supervision of the alien and the alien's whereabouts and activities, and further specifies any other terms and conditions specified by the Service during the period for which the parole is authorized;

(iii) Agrees to advise the Service of the alien's failure to report quarterly any criminal conduct by the alien, or any other activity or behavior on the alien's part that may constitute a ground of excludability or deportability;

(iv) Assumes responsibility for ensuring the alien's departure on the date of termination of the authorized parole (unless the alien has been admitted in S nonimmigrant classification pursuant to the terms of paragraph (a)(2) of this section), provides any and all assistance needed by the Service, if necessary, to ensure departure, and verifies departure in a manner acceptable to the Service;

(v) Provide LEA seat-of-government certification that parole of the alien is essential to an investigation or prosecution, is in the national interest, and is requested pursuant to the terms and authority of section 212(d)(5) of the Act;

(vi) Agrees that no promises may be, have been, or will be made by the LEA to the alien that the alien will or may:

(A) Remain in the United States in parole status or any other nonimmigrant classification;

(B) Adjust status to that of lawful permanent resident; or

(C) Otherwise attempt to remain beyond the authorized parole. The alien (and any family member of the alien who is 18 years of age or older) shall sign a statement acknowledging an awareness that parole only authorizes a temporary stay in the United States and does not convey the benefits of S nonimmigrant classification, any other nonimmigrant classification, or any entitlement to further benefits under the Act; and

(vii) Provides, in the case of a request for the release of an alien from Service custody, certification that the alien is eligible for parole pursuant to § 235.3 of chapter I.

(2) Authorization.

(i) Upon approval of the request for parole, the Commissioner shall notify the Assistant Attorney General, Criminal Division, of the approval.

(ii) Upon notification of approval of a request for parole, the LEA will advise the Commissioner of the date, time, and place of the arrival of the alien. The Commissioner will coordinate the arrival of the alien in parole status with the port director prior to the time of arrival.

(iii) Parole will be authorized for a period of thirty (30) days to commence upon the alien's arrival in the United States in order for the LEA to submit a completed Form I-854 to the Assistant Attorney General, Criminal Division. Upon the submission to the Assistant Attorney General of the Form I-854 requesting S classification, the period of parole will be automatically extended while the request is being reviewed. The Assistant Attorney General, Criminal Division, will notify the Commissioner of the submission of a Form I-854.

(b) **Termination of parole —**

(1) General. The Commissioner may terminate parole for any alien (including a member of the alien's family) in parole status under this section where termination is in the public interest. A district director may also terminate parole when, in the district director's opinion, termination is in the public interest and circumstances do not reasonably permit referral of the case to the Commissioner. In such a case, the Commissioner shall be notified immediately. In the event the Commissioner, or in the appropriate case, a district director, decides to terminate the parole of a alien witness or informant authorized under the terms of this paragraph, the Assistant Attorney General, Criminal Division, and the relevant LEA shall be notified in writing to that effect. The Assistant Attorney General, Criminal Division, shall concur in or object to that decision. Unless the Assistant Attorney General, Criminal Division, objects within 7 days, he or she shall be deemed to have concurred in the decision. In the event of an objection by the Assistant Attorney General, Criminal Division, the matter will be expeditiously referred to the Deputy Attorney General for a final resolution. In no circumstances shall the alien or the relevant LEA have a right of appeal from any decision to terminate parole.

(2) Termination of parole and admission in S classification. When an LEA has filed a request for an alien in authorized parole status to be admitted in S nonimmigrant classification and that request has been approved by the Commissioner pursuant to the procedures outlines in 8 CFR 214.2(t), the Commissioner may, in the exercise of discretion:

(i) Terminate the alien's parole status;

(ii) Determine eligibility for waivers; and

(iii) Admit the alien in S nonimmigrant classification pursuant to the terms and conditions of section 101(a)(15(S) of the Act and 8 CFR 214.2(t).

(c) Departure. If the alien's parole has been terminated and the alien has been ordered excluded from the United States, the LEA shall ensure departure from the United States and so inform the district director in whose jurisdiction the alien has last resided. The district director, if necessary, shall oversee the alien's departure from the United States and, in any event, shall notify the Commissioner of the alien's departure. The Commissioner shall be notified in writing of the failure of any alien authorized parole under this paragraph to depart in accordance with an order of exclusion and deportation entered after parole authorized under this paragraph has been terminated.

(d) Failure to comply with procedures. Any failure to adhere to the parole procedures contained in this section shall immediately be brought to the attention of the Commissioner, who will notify the Attorney General.

HISTORY:

[60 FR 44260, 44265, Aug. 25, 1995; 68 FR 9824, 9835, Feb. 28, 2003; 68 FR 10349, 10353, Mar. 5, 2003; 85 FR 80274, 80400, Dec. 11, 2020]

§ 1212.15 Certificates for foreign health care workers.

(a) Inadmissible aliens. With the exception of the aliens described in paragraph (b) of this section, any alien coming to the United States for the primary purpose of performing labor in a health care occupation listed in paragraph (c) of this section is inadmissible to the United States unless the alien presents a certificate as described in paragraph (f) of this section.

(b) Inapplicability of the ground of inadmissibility. The following aliens are not subject to this ground of inadmissibility:

(1) Aliens seeking admission to the United States to perform services in a non-clinical health care occupation. A non-clinical health-care occupation is one where the alien is not required to perform direct or indirect patient care. Occupations which are considered to be non-clinical include, but are not limited to, medical teachers, medical researchers, managers of health care facilities, and medical consultants to the insurance industry;

(2) The spouse and dependent children of any immigrant alien who is seeking to immigrate in order to accompany or follow to join the principal alien; and

(3) Any alien applying for adjustment of status to that of a permanent resident under any provision of law other than an alien who is seeking to immigrate on the basis of an employment-based immigrant visa petition which was filed for the purpose of obtaining the alien's services in a health care occupation described in paragraph (c) of this section.

(c) Occupations affected by this provision. With the exception of the aliens described in paragraph (b) of this section, any alien seeking admission to the United States as an immigrant or any alien applying for adjustment of status to a permanent resident to perform labor in one of the following health care occupations, regardless of where he or she received his or her education or training, is subject to this provision:

(1) Licensed Practical Nurses, Licensed Vocational Nurses, and Registered Nurses.

(2) Occupational Therapists.

(3) Physical Therapists.

(4) Speech-Language Pathologists and Audiologists.

(5) Medical Technologists (Clinical Laboratory Scientists).

(6) Physician Assistants.

(7) Medical Technicians (Clinical Laboratory Technicians).

(d) Presentation of the certificate. An alien described in paragraph (a) of this section who is applying for admission as an immigrant seeking to perform labor in a health care occupation as described in this section must present a certificate to a consular officer at the time of visa issuance and to the Service at the time of admission or adjustment of status. The certificate must be valid at the time of visa issuance and admission at a port-of-entry, or, if applicable, at the time of adjustment of status.

(e) Organizations approved by the Service to issue certificates for health care workers.

(1) The Commission on Graduates of Foreign Nursing Schools may issue certificates pursuant to 8 U.S.C. 1182(a)(5)(C), and section 212(a)(5)(C) of the Act for the occupations of nurse (licensed practical nurse, licensed vocational nurse, and registered nurse), physical therapist, occupational therapist, speech-language pathologist and audiologist, medical technologist (clinical laboratory scientist), physician assistant, and medical technician (clinical laboratory technician).

(2) The National Board for Certification in Occupational Therapy is authorized by the Service to issue certificates under section 343 for the occupation of occupational therapist.

(3) The Foreign Credentialing Commission on Physical Therapy is authorized by the Service to issue certificates under section 343 for the occupation of physical therapist.

(f) Contents of the certificate. A certificate must contain the following information:

(1) The name and address of the certifying organization;

(2) A point of contact where the organization may be contacted in order to verify the validity of the certificate;

(3) The date of the certificate was issued;

(4) The occupation for which the certificate was issued;

(5) The alien's name, and date and place of birth;

(6) Verification that the alien's education, training, license, and experience are comparable with that required for an American health care worker of the same type;

(7) Verification that the alien's education, training, license, and experience are authentic and, in the case of a license, unencumbered;

(8) Verification that the alien's education, training, license, and experience meet all applicable statutory and regulatory requirements for admission into the

United States as an immigrant under section 203(b) of the Act. This verification is not binding on the Service; and

(9) Verification either that the alien has passed a test predicting success on the occupation's licensing or certification examination, provided such a test is recognized by a majority of States licensing the occupation for which the certificate is issued, or that the alien has passed the occupation's licensing or certification examination.

(g) **English testing requirement.**

(1) With the exception of those aliens described in paragraph (g)(2) of this section, every alien must meet certain English language requirements in order to obtain a certificate. The Secretary of Health and Human Services has determined that an alien must have a passing score on one of the two tests listed in paragraph (g)(3) of this section before he or she can be granted a certificate.

(2) Aliens exempt form the English language requirement. Aliens who have graduated from a college, university, or professional training school located in Australia, Canada (except Quebec), Ireland, New Zealand, the United Kingdom, and the United States are exempt from the English language requirement.

(3) Approved testing services.

(i) Michigan English Language Assessment Battery (MELAB). Effective June 30, 2000, the MELAB Oral Interview Speaking Test is no longer being given overseas and is only being administered in the United States and Canada. Applicants may take MELAB Parts 1, 2, and 3, plus the Test of Spoken English offered by the Educational Testing Service.

(ii) Test of English as a Foreign Language, Educational Testing Service (ETS).

(4) Passing scores for various occupations.

(i) Occupational and physical therapists. An alien seeking to perform labor in the United States as an occupational therapist or physical therapist must obtain the following scores on the English tests administered by ETS: Test Of English as a Foreign Language (TOEFL), Paper-Based 560, Computer-Based 220; Test of Written English (TWE): 4.5; Test of Spoken English (TSE): 50. Certifying organizations shall not accept the results of the MELAB for the occupation of occupational therapist or physical therapist. Aliens seeking to obtain a certificate to work as an occupational or physical therapist must take the test offered by the ETS. The MELAB scores are not acceptable for these occupations.

(ii) Registered nurses. An alien coming to the United States to perform labor as a registered nurse must obtain the following scores to obtain a certificate: ETS: TOEFL: Paper-Based 540, Computer-Based 207; TWE: 4.0; TSE: 50; MELAB: Final Score 79; Oral Interview: 3+.

(iii) Licensed practical nurses and licensed vocational nurses. An alien coming to the United States to perform labor as a licensed practical nurse or licensed vocational nurse must have the following scores to be issued a certificate: ETS: TOEFL: Paper-Based 530, Computer-Based 197; TWE: 4.0; TSE: 50; MELAB: Final Score 77; Oral Interview: 3+.

(iv) Speech-language pathologists and Audiologists, medical technologists (clinical laboratory scientists), and physician assistants. An alien coming to the United States to perform labor as a speech-language pathologist and audiologist, a medical technologist (clinical laboratory scientist), or a physician assistant must have the following scores to be issued a certificate: ETS: TOEFL: Paper-Based 540, Computer-Based 207; TWE: 4.0; TSE: 50; MELAB: Final Score 79; Oral Interview: 3+.

(v) Medical technicians (clinical laboratory technicians). An alien coming to the United States to perform labor as a medical technician (clinical laboratory technician) must have the following scores to be issued a certificate: ETS: TOEFL: Paper-Based 530, Computer-Based 197; TWE: 4.0; TSE: 50; MELAB: Final Score 77; Oral Interview: 3+.

HISTORY:

[63 FR 55007, 55011, Oct. 14, 1998; 64 FR 23174, 23177, Apr. 30, 1999; 66 FR 3440, 3444, Jan. 16, 2001; 68 FR 9824, 9835, Feb. 28, 2003]

§ 1212.16 Applications for exercise of discretion relating to T nonimmigrant status.

(a) Filing the waiver application. An alien applying for the exercise of discretion under section 212(d)(13) or (d)(3)(B) of the Act (waivers of inadmissibility) in connection with an application for T nonimmigrant status shall submit Form I-192, with the appropriate fee in accordance with § 103.7(b)(1) of this chapter or an application for a fee waiver, to the Service with the completed Form I-914 application package for status under section 101(a)(15)(T)(i) of the Act.

(b) **Treatment of waiver application.**

(1) The Service shall determine whether a ground of inadmissibility exists with respect to the alien applying for T nonimmigrant status. If a ground of inadmissibility is found, the Service shall determine if it is in the national interest to exercise discretion to waive the ground of inadmissibility, except for grounds of inadmissibility based upon sections 212(a)(3), 212(a)(10)(C) and 212(a)(10)(E) of the Act, which the Commissioner may not waive. Special consideration will be given to the granting of a waiver of a ground of inadmissibility where the activities rendering the alien inadmissible were caused by or incident to the victimization described under section 101(a)(15)(T)(i) of the Act.

(2) In the case of applicants inadmissible on criminal and related grounds under section 212(a)(2) of the Act, the Service will only exercise its discretion in exceptional cases unless the criminal activities rendering the alien inadmissible were caused by or were incident to the victimization described under section 101(a)(15)(T)(i) of the Act.

(3) An application for waiver of a ground of inadmissibility for T nonimmigrant status (other than under section 212(a)(6) of the Act) will be granted only in exceptional cases when the ground of inadmissibility would prevent or limit the ability of the applicant to

adjust to permanent resident status after the conclusion of 3 years.

(4) The Service shall have sole discretion to grant or deny a waiver, and there shall be no appeal of a decision to deny a waiver. However, nothing in this paragraph (b) is intended to prevent an applicant from re-filing a request for a waiver of a ground of inadmissibility in appropriate cases.

(c) Incident to victimization. When an applicant for status under section 101(a)(15)(T) of the Act seeks a waiver of a ground of inadmissibility under section 212(d)(13) of the Act on grounds other than those described in sections 212(a)(1) and (a)(4) of the Act, the applicant must establish that the activities rendering him or her inadmissible were caused by, or were incident to, the victimization described in section 101(a)(15)(T)(i)(I) of the Act.

(d) Revocation. The Commissioner may at any time revoke a waiver previously authorized under section 212(d) of the Act. Under no circumstances shall the alien or any party acting on his or her behalf have a right to appeal from a decision to revoke a waiver.

HISTORY:

[67 FR 4784, 4795, Jan. 31, 2002; 68 FR 9824, 9835, Feb. 28, 2003]

PART 1214
REVIEW OF NONIMMIGRANT CLASSES

AUTHORITY NOTE APPLICABLE TO ENTIRE PART:

AUTHORITY:

8 U.S.C. 1101, 1102, 1103, 1182, 1184, 1186a, 1187, 1221, 1281, 1282, 1301-1305 and 1372; sec. 643, Pub. L. 104-208, 110 Stat. 3009-708; section 141 of the Compacts of Free Association with the Federated States of Micronesia and the Republic of the Marshall Islands, and with the Government of Palau, 48 U.S.C. 1901, note, and 1931 note, respectively; 8 CFR part 2.

§ 1214.1 Review of requirements for admission, extension, and maintenance of status.

Every nonimmigrant alien who applies for admission to, or an extension of stay in, the United States, shall establish that he or she is admissible to the United States, or that any ground of inadmissibility has been waived under section 212(d)(3) of the Act. Upon application for admission, the alien shall present a valid passport and valid visa unless either or both documents have been waived. However, an alien applying for extension of stay shall present a passport only if requested to do so by the Service. The passport of an alien applying for admission shall be valid for a minimum of six months from the expiration date of the contemplated period of stay, unless otherwise provided in this chapter, and the alien shall agree to abide by the terms and conditions of his or her admission. The passport of an alien applying for extension of stay shall be valid at the time of application for extension, unless otherwise provided in this chapter, and the alien shall agree to maintain the validity of his or her passport and to abide by all the terms and conditions of his extension. The alien shall also agree to depart the United States at the expiration of his or her authorized period of admission or extension, or upon abandonment of his or her authorized nonimmigrant status. At the time a nonimmigrant alien applies for admission or extension of stay he or she shall post a bond on Form I-352 in the sum of not less than $ 500, to insure the maintenance of his or her nonimmigrant status and departure from the United States, if required to do so by the director, immigration judge or Board of Immigration Appeals.

HISTORY:

[68 FR 9824, 9836, Feb. 28, 2003]

§ 1214.2 Review of alien victims of severe forms of trafficking in persons; aliens in pending immigration proceedings.

(a) Applications for T visas while in proceedings. Individuals who believe they are victims of severe forms of trafficking in persons and who are in pending immigration proceedings must inform DHS if they intend to apply for T nonimmigrant status under this section. With the concurrence of DHS counsel, a victim of a severe form of trafficking in persons in proceedings before an immigration judge or the Board of Immigration Appeals may request that the proceedings be administratively closed (or that a motion to reopen or motion to reconsider be indefinitely continued) in order to allow the alien to pursue an application for T nonimmigrant status with DHS. If the alien appears eligible for T nonimmigrant status, the immigration judge or the Board, whichever has jurisdiction, may grant such a request to administratively close the proceeding or continue a motion to reopen or motion to reconsider indefinitely. In the event DHS finds an alien ineligible for T-1 nonimmigrant status, DHS may recommence proceedings that have been administratively closed by filing a motion to re-calendar with the immigration court or a motion to reinstate with the Board. If the alien is in DHS custody pending the completion of immigration proceedings, DHS may continue to detain the alien until a decision has been rendered on the application. An alien who is in custody and requests bond or a bond redetermination will be governed by the provisions of part 236 of this chapter.

(b) Stay of final order of exclusion, deportation, or removal. A determination by DHS that an application for T-1 nonimmigrant status is bona fide automatically stays the execution of any final order of exclusion, deportation, or removal. This stay shall remain in effect until there is a final decision on the T application. The filing of an application for T nonimmigrant status does not stay the execution of a final order unless DHS has determined that the application is bona fide. Neither an immigration judge nor the Board of Immigration Appeals has jurisdiction to adjudicate an application for a stay of execution, deportation, or removal order, on the basis of the filing of an application for T nonimmigrant status.

HISTORY:

[68 FR 9824, 9836, Feb. 28, 2003; 86 FR 70708, 70724, Dec. 13, 2021]

§ 1214.3 Certain spouses and children of lawful permanent residents; aliens in proceedings; V visas.

An alien who is already in immigration proceedings and believes that he or she may have become eligible to apply for V nonimmigrant status should request before the immigration judge or the Board of Immigration Appeals, as appropriate, that the proceedings be administratively closed (or before the Board that a previously-filed motion for reopening or reconsideration be indefinitely continued) in order to allow the alien to pursue an application for V nonimmigrant status with the Service. If the alien appears eligible for V nonimmigrant status, the immigration judge or the Board, whichever has jurisdiction, shall administratively close the proceeding or continue the motion indefinitely. In the event that the Service finds an alien eligible for V nonimmigrant status, the Service can adjudicate the change of status under this section. In the event that the Service finds an alien ineligible for V nonimmigrant status, the Service shall recommence proceedings by filing a motion to re-calendar.

HISTORY:

[68 FR 9824, 9836, Feb. 28, 2003]

PART 1215

CONTROLS OF ALIENS DEPARTING FROM THE UNITED STATES

Rule

AUTHORITY NOTE APPLICABLE TO ENTIRE PART:

AUTHORITY:

Sec. 104, 66 Stat. 174, Proc. 3004, 18 FR 489; 8 U.S.C. 1104, 3 CFR, 1953 Supp. Interpret or apply sec. 215, 66 Stat. 190; (8 U.S.C. 1185).

§ 1215.1 Definitions.

For the purpose of this part:

(a) The term alien means any person who is not a citizen or national of the United States.

(b) The term Commissioner means the Commissioner of Immigration and Naturalization.

(c) The term regional commissioner means an officer of the Immigration and Naturalization Service duly appointed or designated as a regional commissioner, or an officer who has been designated to act as a regional commissioner.

(d) The term district director means an officer of the Immigration and Naturalization Service duly appointed or designated as a district director, or an officer who has been designated to act as a district director.

(e) The term United States means the several States, the District of Columbia, the Canal Zone, Puerto Rico, the Virgin Islands, Guam, American Samoa, Swains Island, the Trust Territory of the Pacific Islands, and all other territory and waters, continental and insular, subject to the jurisdiction of the United States.

(f) The term continental United States means the District of Columbia and the several States, except Alaska and Hawaii.

(g) The term geographical part of the United States means: (1) The continental United States, (2) Alaska, (3) Hawaii, (4) Puerto Rico, (5) the Virgin Islands, (6) Guam, (7) the Canal Zone, (8) American Samoa, (9) Swains Island, or (10) the Trust Teritory of the Pacific Islands.

(h) The term depart from the United States means depart by land, water, or air: (1) From the United States for any foreign place, or (2) from one geographical part of the United States for a separate geographical part of the United States: Provided, That a trip or journey upon a public ferry, passenger vessel sailing coastwise on a fixed schedule, excursion vessel, or aircraft, having both termini in the continental United States or in any one of the other geographical parts of the United States and not touching any territory or waters under the jurisdiction or control of a foreign power, shall not be deemed a departure from the United States.

(i) The term departure-control officer means any immigration officer as defined in the regulations of the Immigration and Naturalization Service who is designated to supervise the departure of aliens, or any officer or employee of the United States designated by the Governor of the Canal Zone, the High Commissioner of the Trust Territory of the Pacific Islands, or the governor of an outlying possession of the United States, to supervise the departure of aliens.

(j) The term port of departure means a port in the continental United States, Alaska, Guam, Hawaii, Puerto Rico or the Virgin Islands, designated as a port of entry by the Attorney General or by the Commissioner, or in exceptional circumstances such other place as the departure-control officer may, in his discretion, designate in an individual case, or a port in American Samoa, Swains Island, the Canal Zone, or the Trust Territory of the Pacific Islands, designated as a port of entry by the chief executive officer thereof.

(k) The term special inquiry officer shall have the meaning ascribed thereto in section 101(b)(4) of the Immigration and Nationality Act.

HISTORY:

[45 FR 65516, Oct. 3, 1980; 68 FR 9824, 9836, Feb. 28, 2003]

§ 1215.2 Authority of departure-control officer to prevent alien's departure from the United States.

(a) No alien shall depart, or attempt to depart, from the United States if his departure would be prejudicial to the interests of the United States under the provisions of § 1215.3. Any departure-control officer who knows or has reason to believe that the case of an alien in the United States comes within the provisions of § 1215.3 shall temporarily prevent the departure of such alien from the United States and shall serve him with a written temporary order directing him not to depart, or attempt to depart, from the United States until notified of the revocation of the order.

(b) The written order temporarily preventing an alien, other than an enemy alien, from departing from the United States shall become final 15 days after the date of service thereof upon the alien, unless prior thereto the alien requests a hearing as hereinafter provided. At such time as the alien is served with an order temporarily preventing his departure from the United States, he shall be notified in writing concerning the provisions of this paragraph, and shall be advised of his right to request a hearing if entitled thereto under § 1215.4. In the case of an enemy alien, the written order preventing departure shall become final on the date of its service upon the alien.

(c) Any alien who seeks to depart from the United States may be required, in the discretion of the departure-control officer, to be examined under oath and to submit for official inspection all documents, articles, and other property in his possession which are being removed from the United States upon, or in connection with, the alien's departure. The departure-control officer may permit certain other persons, including officials of the Department of State and interpreters, to participate in such examination or inspection and may exclude from presence at such examination or inspection any person whose presence would not further the objectives of such examination or inspection. The departure-control officer shall temporarily prevent the departure of any alien who refuses to submit to such examination or inspection, and may, if necessary to the enforcement of this requirement, take possession of the alien's passport or other travel document.

HISTORY:

[45 FR 65516, Oct. 3, 1980; 68 FR 9824, 9836, 9846, Feb. 28, 2003]

§ 1215.3 Aliens whose departure is deemed prejudicial to the interests of the United States.

The departure from the United States of any alien within one or more of the following categories shall be deemed prejudicial to the interests of the United States.

(a) Any alien who is in possession of, and who is believed likely to disclose to unauthorized persons, information concerning the plans, preparation, equipment, or establishments for the national defense and security of the United States.

(b) Any alien who seeks to depart from the United States to engage in, or who is likely to engage in, activities of any kind designed to obstruct, impede, retard, delay or counteract the effectiveness of the national defense of the United States or the measures adopted by the United States or the United Nations for the defense of any other country.

(c) Any alien who seeks to depart from the United States to engage in, or who is likely to engage in, activities which would obstruct, impede, retard, delay, or counteract the effectiveness of any plans made or action taken by any country cooperating with the United States in measures adopted to promote the peace, defense, or safety of the United States or such other country.

(d) Any alien who seeks to depart from the United States for the purpose of organizing, directing, or participating in any rebellion, insurrection, or violent uprising in or against the United States or a country allied with the United States, or of waging war against the United States or its allies, or of destroying, or depriving the United States of sources of supplies or materials vital to the national defense of the United States, or to the effectiveness of the measures adopted by the United States for its defense, or for the defense of any other country allied with the United States.

(e) Any alien who is subject to registration for training and service in the Armed Forces of the United States and who fails to present a Registration Certificate (SSS Form No. 2) showing that he has complied with his obligation to register under the Universal Military Training and Service Act, as amended.

(f) Any alien who is a fugitive from justice on account of an offense punishable in the United States.

(g) Any alien who is needed in the United States as a witness in, or as a party to, any criminal case under investigation or pending in a court in the United States: Provided, That any alien who is a witness in, or a party to, any criminal case pending in any criminal court proceeding may be permitted to depart from the United States with the consent of the appropriate prosecuting authority, unless such alien is otherwise prohibited from departing under the provisions of this part.

(h) Any alien who is needed in the United States in connection with any investigation or proceeding being, or soon to be, conducted by any official executive, legislative, or judicial agency in the United States or by any governmental committee, board, bureau, commission, or body in the United States, whether national, state, or local.

(i) Any alien whose technical or scientific training and knowledge might be utilized by an enemy or a potential enemy of the United States to undermine and defeat the military and defensive operations of the

United States or of any nation cooperating with the United States in the interests of collective security.

(j) Any alien, where doubt exists whether such alien is departing or seeking to depart from the United States voluntarily except an alien who is departing or seeking to depart subject to an order issued in extradition, exclusion, or deportation proceedings.

(k) Any alien whose case does not fall within any of the categories described in paragraphs (a) to (j), inclusive, of this section, but which involves circumstances of a similar character rendering the alien's departure prejudicial to the interests of the United States.

HISTORY:

[45 FR 65516, Oct. 3, 1980; 68 FR 9824, 9836, Feb. 28, 2003]

§ 1215.4 Procedure in case of alien prevented from departing from the United States.

(a) Any alien, other than an enemy alien, whose departure has been temporarily prevented under the provisions of § 1215.2, may, within 15 days of the service upon him of the written order temporarily preventing his departure, request a hearing before a special inquiry officer. The alien's request for a hearing shall be made in writing and shall be addressed to the district director having administrative jurisdiction over the alien's place of residence. If the alien's request for a hearing is timely made, the district director shall schedule a hearing before a special inquiry officer, and notice of such hearing shall be given to the alien. The notice of hearing shall, as specifically as security considerations permit, inform the alien of the nature of the case against him, shall fix the time and place of the hearing, and shall inform the alien of his right to be represented, at no expense to the Government, by counsel of his own choosing.

(b) Every alien for whom a hearing has been scheduled under paragraph (a) of this section shall be entitled: (1) To appear in person before the special inquiry officer, (2) to be represented by counsel of his own choice, (3) to have the opportunity to be heard and to present evidence, (4) to cross-examine the witnesses who appear at the hearing, except that if, in the course of the examination, it appears that further examination may divulge information of a confidential or security nature, the special inquiry officer may, in his discretion, preclude further examination of the witness with respect to such matters, (5) to examine any evidence in possession of the Government which is to be considered in the disposition of the case, provided that such evidence is not of a confidential or security nature the disclosure of which would be prejudicial to the interests of the United States, (6) to have the time and opportunity to produce evidence and witnesses on his own behalf, and (7) to reasonable continuances, upon request, for good cause shown.

(c) Any special inquiry officer who is assigned to conduct the hearing provided for in this section shall have the authority to: (1) Administer oaths and affirmations, (2) present and receive evidence, (3) interrogate, examine, and cross examine under oath or affirmation both the alien and witnesses, (4) rule upon all objections to the introduction of evidence or motions made during the course of the hearing, (5) take or cause depositions to be taken, (6) issue subpoenas, and (7) take any further action consistent with applicable provisions of law, Executive orders, proclamations, and regulations.

HISTORY:

[45 FR 65516, Oct. 3, 1980; 68 FR 9824, 9836, 9846, Feb. 28, 2003]

§ 1215.5 Hearing procedure before special inquiry officer.

(a) The hearing before the special inquiry officer shall be conducted in accordance with the following procedure:

(1) The special inquiry officer shall advise the alien of the rights and privileges accorded him under the provisions of § 1215.4.

(2) The special inquiry officer shall enter of record: (i) A copy of the order served upon the alien temporarily preventing his departure from the United States, and (ii) a copy of the notice of hearing furnished the alien.

(3) The alien shall be interrogated by the special inquiry officer as to the matters considered pertinent to the proceeding, with opportunity reserved to the alien to testify thereafter in his own behalf, if he so chooses.

(4) The special inquiry officer shall present on behalf of the Government such evidence, including the testimony of witnesses and the certificates or written statements of Government officials or other persons, as may be necessary and available. In the event such certificates or statements are received in evidence, the alien may request and, in the discretion of the special inquiry officer, be given an opportunity to interrogate such officials or persons, by deposition or otherwise, at a time and place and in a manner fixed by the special inquiry officer: Provided, That when in the judgment of the special inquiry officer any evidence relative to the disposition of the case is of a confidential or security nature the disclosure of which would be prejudicial to the interests of the United States, such evidence shall not be presented at the hearing but shall be taken into consideration in arriving at a decision in the case.

(5) The alien may present such additional evidence, including the testimony of witnesses, as is pertinent and available.

(b) A complete verbatim transcript of the hearing, except statements made off the record shall be recorded. The alien shall be entitled, upon request, to the loan of a copy of the transcript, without cost, subject to reasonable conditions governing its use.

(c) Following the completion of the hearing, the special inquiry officer shall make and render a recommended decision in the case, which shall be governed by and based upon the evidence presented at the hearing and any evidence of a confidential or security nature which the Government may have in its possession. The decision of the special inquiry officer shall recommend: (1) That the temporary order preventing the departure of the alien from the United States be made final, or (2) that the temporary order preventing the departure of the alien from the United States be revoked. This recommended decision of the special inquiry officer shall be made in writing and shall set forth the officer's reasons for such decision. The alien concerned shall at his request be furnished a copy of the recommended decision of the special inquiry officer, and shall be allowed a reasonable time, not to exceed 10 days, in which to submit representations with respect thereto in writing.

(d) As soon as practicable after the completion of the hearing and the rendering of a decision by the special inquiry officer, the district director shall forward the entire record of the case, including the recommended decision of the special inquiry officer and any written representations submitted by the alien, to the regional commissioner having jurisdiction over his district. After reviewing the record, the regional commissioner shall render a decision in the case, which shall be based upon the evidence in the record and on any evidence or information of a confidential or security nature which he deems pertinent. Whenever any decision is based in whole or in part on confidential or security information not included in the record, the decision shall state that such information was considered. A copy of the regional commissioner's decision shall be furnished the alien, or his attorney or representative. No administrative appeal shall lie from the regional commissioner's decision.

(e) Notwithstanding any other provision of this part, the Administrator of the Bureau of Security and Consular Affairs referred to in section 104(b) of the Immigration and Nationality Act, or such other officers of the Department of State as he may designate, after consultation with the Commissioner, or such other officers of the Immigration and Naturalization Service as he may designate, may at any time permit the departure of an individual alien or of a group of aliens from the United States if he determines that such action would be in the national interest. If the Administrator specifically requests the Commissioner to prevent the departure of a particular alien or of a group of aliens, the Commissioner shall not permit the departure of such alien or aliens until he has consulted with the Administrator.

(f) In any case arising under §§ 1215.1 to 1215.7, the Administrator shall, at his request, be kept advised, in as much detail as he may indicate is necessary, of the facts and of any action taken or proposed.

HISTORY:

[45 FR 65516, Oct. 3, 1980; 68 FR 9824, 9836, 9846, Feb. 28, 2003]

§ 1215.6 Departure from the Canal Zone, the Trust Territory of the Pacific Islands, or outlying possessions of the United States.

(a) In addition to the restrictions and prohibitions imposed by the provisions of this part upon the departure of aliens from the United States, any alien who seeks to depart from the Canal Zone, the Trust Territory of the Pacific Islands, or an outlying possession of the United States shall comply with such other restrictions and prohibitions as may be imposed by regulations prescribed, with the concurrence of the Administrator of the Bureau of Security and Consular Affairs and the Commissioner, by the Governor of the Canal Zone, the High Commissioner of the Trust Territory of the Pacific Islands, or by the governor of an outlying possession of the United States, respectively. No alien shall be prevented from departing from such zone, territory, or possession without first being accorded a hearing as provided in §§ 1215.4 and 1215.5.

(b) The Governor of the Canal Zone, the High Commissioner of the Trust Territory of the Pacific Islands, or the governor of any outlying possession of the United States shall have the authority to designate any employee or class of employees of the United States as hearing officers for the purpose of conducting the hearing referred to in paragraph (a) of this section. The hearing officer so designated shall exercise the same powers, duties, and functions as are conferred upon special inquiry officers under the provisions of this part. The chief executive officer of such zone, territory, or possession shall, in lieu of the regional commissioner, review the recommended decision of the hearing officer, and shall render a decision in any case referred to him, basing it on evidence in the record and on any evidence or information of a confidential or a security nature which he deems pertinent.

HISTORY:

[45 FR 65516, Oct. 3, 1980; 68 FR 9824, 9836, 9846, Feb. 28, 2003]

§ 1215.7 Instructions from the Administrator required in certain cases.

In the absence of appropriate instructions from the Administrator of the Bureau of Security and Consular Affairs, departure-control officers shall not exercise the authority conferred by § 1215.2 in the case of any alien who seeks to depart from the United States in the status of a nonimmigrant under section 101(a)(15) (A) or (G) of the Immigration and Nationality Act, or in the status of a nonimmigrant under section 11(3), 11(4), or 11(5) of the Agreement between the United Nations and the United States of America regarding the Headquarters of the United Nations (61 Stat. 756): Provided, That in cases of extreme urgency, where the national security so requires, a departure-control officer may preliminarily exercise the authority conferred by § 1215.2 pending the outcome of consultation with the Administrator, which shall be undertaken immediately. In all cases arising under this section, the decision of the Administrator shall be controlling: Provided, That any decision to prevent the departure of an alien shall be based upon a hearing and record as prescribed in this part.

HISTORY:

[45 FR 65516, Oct. 3, 1980; 68 FR 9824, 9836, 9846, Feb. 28, 2003]

PART 1216

CONDITIONAL BASIS OF LAWFUL PERMANENT RESIDENCE STATUS

Rule

AUTHORITY NOTE APPLICABLE TO ENTIRE PART:

AUTHORITY:

8 U.S.C. 1101, 1103, 1154, 1184, 1186a, 1186b, and 8 CFR part 2.

§ 1216.1 Definition of conditional permanent resident.

A conditional permanent resident is an alien who has been lawfully admitted for permanent residence within the meaning of section 101(a)(20) of the Act, except that a conditional permanent resident is also subject to the conditions and responsibilities set forth in section 216 or 216A of the Act, whichever is applicable, and part 1216 of this chapter. Unless otherwise specified, the rights, privileges, responsibilities and duties which apply to all other lawful permanent residents apply equally to conditional permanent residents, including but not limited to the right to apply for naturalization (if otherwise eligible), the right to file petitions on behalf of qualifying relatives, the privilege of residing permanently in the United States as an immigrant in accordance with the immigration laws, such status not having changed; the duty to register with the Selective Service System, when required; and the responsibility for complying with all laws and regulations of the United States. All references within this chapter to lawful permanent residents apply equally to conditional permanent residents, unless otherwise specified. The conditions of section 216 of the Act shall not apply to lawful permanent resident status based on a self-petitioning relationship under section 204(a)(1)(A)(iii), 204(a)(1)(A)(iv), 204(a)(1)(b)(ii), or 204(a)(1)(B)(iii) of the Act or based on eligibility as the derivative child of a self-petitioning spouse under section 204(a)(1)(A)(iii) or 204(a)(1)(B)(ii) of the Act, regardless of the date on which the marriage to the abusive citizen or lawful permanent resident occurred.

HISTORY:

[53 FR 30018, Aug. 10, 1988; 59 FR 26590, May 23, 1994; 61 FR 13061, 13079, Mar. 26, 1996; 68 FR 9824, 9837, 9846, Feb. 28, 2003]

§ 1216.2 Notification requirements.

(a) When alien acquires status of conditional permanent resident. At the time an alien acquires conditional permanent residence through admission to the United States with an immigrant visa or adjustment of status under section 245 of the Act, the Service shall notify the alien of the conditional basis of the alien's status, of the requirement that the alien apply for removal of the conditions within the ninety days immediately preceding the second anniversary of the alien's having been granted such status, and that failure to apply for removal of the conditions will result in automatic termination of the alien's lawful status in the United States.

(b) When alien is required to apply for removal of the conditional basis of lawful permanent resident status. Approximately 90 days before the second anniversary of the date on which the alien obtained conditional permanent residence, the Service should notify the alien a second time of the requirement that the alien and the petitioning spouse or the alien entrepreneur must file a petition to remove the conditional basis of the alien's lawful permanent residence. Such notification shall be mailed to the alien's last known address.

(c) Effect of failure to provide notification. Failure of the Service to provide notification as required by either paragraph (a) or (b) of this section does not relieve the alien and the petitioning spouse, or the alien entrepreneur of the requirement to file a petition to remove conditions within the 90 days immediately preceding the second anniversary of the date on which the alien obtained permanent residence.

HISTORY:

[53 FR 30018, Aug. 10, 1988; 59 FR 26590, May 23, 1994; 68 FR 9824, 9837, Feb. 28, 2003]

§ 1216.3 Termination of conditional resident status.

(a) During the two-year conditional period. The director shall send a formal written notice to the conditional permanent resident of the termination of the alien's conditional permanent resident status if the director determines that any of the conditions set forth in section 216(b)(1) or 216A(b)(1) of the Act, whichever is applicable, are true, or it becomes known to the government that an alien entrepreneur who was admitted pursuant to section 203(b)(5) of the Act obtained his or her investment capital through other than legal means (such as through the sale of illegal drugs). If the Service issues a notice of intent to terminate an alien's conditional resident status, the director shall not adjudicate Form I-751 or Form I-829 until it has been determined that the alien's status will not be terminated. During this time, the alien shall continue to be a lawful conditional permanent resident with all the rights, privileges, and responsibilities provided to persons possessing such status. Prior to issuing the notice of termination, the director shall provide the alien with an opportunity to review and rebut the evidence upon which the decision is to be based, in accordance with § 103.2(b)(2) of 8 CFR chapter I. The termination of status, and all of the rights and privileges concomitant thereto (including authorization to accept or continue in employment in this country), shall take effect as of the date of such determination by the director, although the alien may request a review of such determination in removal proceedings. In addition to the notice of termination, the director shall issue a notice to appear in accordance with 8 CFR part 1239. During the ensuing removal proceedings, the alien may submit evidence to rebut the determination of the director. The burden of proof shall be on the Service to establish, by a preponderance of the evidence, that one or more of the conditions in section 216(b)(1) or 216A(b)(1) of the Act, whichever is applicable, are true, or that an alien entrepreneur who was admitted pursuant to section 203(b)(5) of the Act obtained his or her investment capital through other than legal means (such as through the sale of illegal drugs).

(b) Determination of fraud after two years. If, subsequent to the removal of the conditional basis of an alien's permanent resident status, the director determines that an alien spouse obtained permanent resident status through a marriage which was entered into for the purpose of evading the immigration laws or an alien entrepreneur obtained permanent resident status through a commercial enterprise which was improper under section 216A(b)(1) of the Act, the director may institute rescission proceedings pursuant to section 246 of the Act (if otherwise appropriate) or removal proceedings under section 240 of the Act.

HISTORY:

[53 FR 30018, Aug. 10, 1988; 59 FR 26590, May 23, 1994; 62 FR 10312, 10349, Mar. 6, 1997; 68 FR 9824, 9837, Feb. 28, 2003; 68 FR 10349, 10353, Mar. 5, 2003]

§ 1216.4 Joint petition to remove conditional basis of lawful permanent resident status for alien spouse.

(a) **Filing the petition —**

(1) General procedures. Within the 90-day period immediately preceding the second anniversary of the date on which the alien obtained permanent residence, the alien and the alien's spouse who filed the original immigrant visa petition or fiance/fiancee petition through which the alien obtained permanent residence must file a Petition to Remove the Conditions on Residence (Form I-751) with the Service. The petition shall be filed within this time period regardless of the amount of physical presence which the alien has accumulated in the United States. Before Form I-751 may be considered as properly filed, it must be accompanied by the fee required under 8 CFR 103.7 and 8 CFR part 106 and by documentation as described in paragraph (a)(5) of this section, and it must be properly signed by the alien and the alien's spouse. If the joint petition cannot be filed due to the termination of the marriage through annulment, divorce, or the death of the petitioning spouse, or if the petitioning spouse refuses to join in the filing of the petition, the conditional permanent resident may apply for a waiver of the requirement to file the joint petition in accordance with the provisions of § 1216.5 of this part. Upon receipt of a properly filed Form I-751, the alien's conditional permanent resident status shall be extended automatically, if necessary, until such time as the director has adjudicated the petition.

(2) Dependent children. Dependent children of a conditional permanent resident who acquired conditional permanent resident status concurrently with the parent may be included in the joint petition filed by the parent and the parent's petitioning spouse. A child shall be deemed to have acquired conditional residence status concurrently with the parent if the child's residence was acquired on the same date or within 90 days thereafter. Children who cannot be included in a joint petition filed by the parent and parent's petitioning spouse due to the child's not having acquired conditional resident status concurrently with the parent, the death of the parent, or other reasons may file a separate Petition to Remove the Conditions on Residence (Form I-751).

(3) Jurisdiction. Form I-751 shall be filed with the director of the regional service center having jurisdiction over the alien's place of residence.

(4) Physical presence at time of filing. A petition may be filed regardless of whether the alien is physically present in the United States. However, if the alien is outside the United States at the time of filing, he or she must return to the United States, with his or her spouse and dependent children, to comply with the interview requirements contained in the Act. Furthermore, if the documentation submitted in support of the petition includes affidavits of third parties having knowledge of the bona fides of the marital relationship, the petitioner must arrange for the affiants to be present at the interview, at no expense to the government. Once the petition has been properly filed, the alien may travel outside the United States and return if in possession of documentation as set forth in § 1211.1(b)(1) of this chapter, provided the alien and the petitioning spouse comply with the interview requirements described in § 1216.4(b). An alien who is not physically present in the United States during the filing period but subsequently applies for admission to the United States shall be processed in accordance with § 1235.11 of this chapter.

(5) Documentation. Form I-751 shall be accompanied by evidence that the marriage was not entered into for the purpose of evading the immigration laws of the United States. Such evidence may include:

(i) Documentation showing joint ownership of property;

(ii) Lease showing joint tenancy of a common residence;

(iii) Documentation showing commingling of financial resources;

(iv) Birth certificates of children born to the marriage;

(v) Affidavits of third parties having knowledge of the bona fides of the marital relationship, or

(vi) Other documentation establishing that the marriage was not entered into in order to evade the immigration laws of the United States.

(6) Termination of status for failure to file petition. Failure to properly file Form I-751 within the 90-day period immediately preceding the second anniversary

of the date on which the alien obtained lawful permanent residence on a conditional basis shall result in the automatic termination of the alien's permanent residence status and the initiation of proceedings to remove the alien from the United States. In such proceedings the burden shall be on the alien to establish that he or she complied with the requirement to file the joint petition within the designated period. Form I-751 may be filed after the expiration of the 90-day period only if the alien establishes to the satisfaction of the director, in writing, that there was good cause for the failure to file Form I-751 within the required time period. If the joint petition is filed prior to the jurisdiction vesting with the immigration judge in removal proceedings and the director excuses the late filing and approves the petition, he or she shall restore the alien's permanent residence status, remove the conditional basis of such status and cancel any outstanding notice to appear in accordance with § 1239.2 of this chapter. If the joint petition is not filed until after jurisdiction vests with the immigration judge, the immigration judge may terminate the matter upon joint motion by the alien and the Service.

(b) **Interview —**

(1) Authority to waive interview. The director of the regional service center shall review the Form I-751 filed by the alien and the alien's spouse to determine whether to waive the interview required by the Act. If satisfied that the marriage was not for the purpose of evading the immigration laws, the regional service center director may waive the interview and approve the petition. If not so satisfied, then the regional service center director shall forward the petition to the district director having jurisdiction over the place of the alien's residence so that an interview of both the alien and the alien's spouse may be conducted. The director must either waive the requirement for an interview and adjudicate the petition or arrange for an interview within 90 days of the date on which the petition was properly filed.

(2) Location of interview. Unless waived, an interview on the Form I-751 shall be conducted by an immigration examiner or other officer so designated by the district director at the district office, files control office or suboffice having jurisdiction over the residence of the joint petitioners.

(3) Termination of status for failure to appear for interview. If the conditional resident alien and/or the petitioning spouse fail to appear for an interview in connection with the joint petition required by section 216(c) of the Act, the alien's permanent residence status will be automatically terminated as of the second anniversary of the date on which the alien obtained permanent residence. The alien shall be provided with written notification of the termination and the reasons therefor, and a notice to appear shall be issued placing the alien under removal proceedings. The alien may seek review of the decision to terminate his or her status in such proceedings, but the burden shall be on the alien to establish compliance with the interview requirements. If the alien submits a written request that the interview be rescheduled or that the interview be waived, and the director determines that there is good cause for granting the request, the interview may be rescheduled or waived, as appropriate. If the interview is rescheduled at the request of the petitioners, the Service shall not be required to conduct the interview within the 90-day period following the filing of the petition.

(c) Adjudication of petition. The director shall adjudicate the petition within 90 days of the date of the interview, unless the interview is waived in accordance with paragraph (b)(1) of this section. In adjudicating the petition the director shall determine whether —

(1) The qualifying marriage was entered into in accordance with the laws of the place where the marriage took place;

(2) The qualifying marriage has been judicially annulled or terminated, other than through the death of a spouse;

(3) The qualifying marriage was entered into for the purpose of procuring permanent residence status for the alien; or

(4) A fee or other consideration was given (other than a fee or other consideration to an attorney for assistance in preparation of a lawful petition) in connection with the filing of the petition through which the alien obtained conditional permanent residence. If derogatory information is determined regarding any of these issues, the director shall offer the petitioners the opportunity to rebut such information. If the petitioners fail to overcome such derogatory information the director may deny the joint petition, terminate the alien's permanent residence, and issue a notice to appear to initiate removal proceedings. If derogatory information not relating to any of these issues is determined during the course of the interview, such information shall be forwarded to the investigations unit for appropriate action. If no unresolved derogatory information is determined relating to these issues, the petition shall be approved and the conditional basis of the alien's permanent residence status removed, regardless of any action taken or contemplated regarding other possible grounds for removal.

(d) **Decision —**

(1) Approval. If the director approves the joint petition he or she shall provide written notice of the decision to the alien and shall require the alien to report to the appropriate office of the Service for processing for a new Permanent Resident Card (if necessary), at which time the alien shall surrender any Permanent Resident Card previously issued.

(2) Denial. If the director denies the joint petition, he or she shall provide written notice to the alien of the decision and the reason(s) therefor and shall issue a notice to appear under section 239 of the Act and 8 CFR part 1239. The alien's lawful permanent resident status shall be terminated as of the date of the director's written decision. The alien shall also be instructed to surrender any Permanent Resident Card previously issued by the Service. No appeal shall lie from the decision of the director; however, the alien may seek review of the decision in removal proceedings. In such proceedings the burden of proof shall be on the Service

to establish, by a preponderance of the evidence, that the facts and information set forth by the petitioners are not true or that the petition was properly denied.

HISTORY:

[53 FR 30018, Aug. 10, 1988, as amended at 54 FR 30369, July 20, 1989; 59 FR 26590, 26591, May 23, 1994; 62 FR 10312, 10349, Mar. 6, 1997; 63 FR 70313, 70315, Dec. 21, 1998; 68 FR 9824, 9837, 9846, Feb. 28, 2003; 68 FR 10349, 10353, Mar. 5, 2003; 85 FR 82750, 82794, Dec. 18, 2020]

§ 1216.5 Waiver of requirement to file joint petition to remove conditions by alien spouse.

(a) General.

(1) A conditional resident alien who is unable to meet the requirements under section 216 of the Act for a joint petition for removal of the conditional basis of his or her permanent resident status may file Form I-751, Petition to Remove the Conditions on Residence, if the alien requests a waiver, was not at fault in failing to meet the filing requirement, and the conditional resident alien is able to establish that:

(i) Deportation or removal from the United States would result in extreme hardship;

(ii) The marriage upon which his or her status was based was entered into in good faith by the conditional resident alien, but the marriage was terminated other than by death, and the conditional resident was not at fault in failing to file a timely petition; or

(iii) The qualifying marriage was entered into in good faith by the conditional resident but during the marriage the alien spouse or child was battered by or subjected to extreme cruelty committed by the citizen or permanent resident spouse or parent.

(2) A conditional resident who is in exclusion, deportation, or removal proceedings may apply for the waiver only until such time as there is a final order of exclusion, deportation or removal.

(b) Fee. Form I-751 shall be accompanied by the appropriate fee required under 8 CFR 103.7 and 8 CFR part 106.

(c) Jurisdiction. Form I-751 shall be filed with the regional service center director having jurisdiction over the alien's place of residence.

(d) Interview. The service center director may refer the application to the appropriate local office and require that the alien appear for an interview in connection with the application for a waiver. The director shall deny the application and initiate removal proceedings if the alien fails to appear for the interview as required, unless the alien establishes good cause for such failure and the interview is rescheduled.

(e) Adjudication of waiver application.

(1) Application based on claim of hardship. In considering an application for a waiver based upon an alien's claim that extreme hardship would result from the alien's removal from the United States, the director shall take into account only those factors that arose subsequent to the alien's entry as a conditional permanent resident. The director shall bear in mind that any removal from the United States is likely to result in a certain degree of hardship, and that only in those cases where the hardship is extreme should the application for a waiver be granted. The burden of establishing that extreme hardship exists rests solely with the applicant.

(2) Application for waiver based upon the alien's claim that the marriage was entered into in good faith. In considering whether an alien entered into a qualifying marriage in good faith, the director shall consider evidence relating to the amount of commitment by both parties to the marital relationship. Such evidence may include —

(i) Documentation relating to the degree to which the financial assets and liabilities of the parties were combined;

(ii) Documentation concerning the length of time during which the parties cohabited after the marriage and after the alien obtained permanent residence;

(iii) Birth certificates of children born to the marriage; and

(iv) Other evidence deemed pertinent by the director.

(3) Application for waiver based on alien's claim of having been battered or subjected to extreme mental cruelty. A conditional resident who entered into the qualifying marriage in good faith, and who was battered or was the subject of extreme cruelty or whose child was battered by or was the subject of extreme cruelty perpetrated by the United States citizen or permanent resident spouse during the marriage, may request a waiver of the joint filing requirement. The conditional resident parent of a battered or abused child may apply for the waiver regardless of the child's citizenship or immigration status.

(i) For the purpose of this chapter the phrase "was battered by or was the subject of extreme cruelty" includes, but is not limited to, being the victim of any act or threatened act of violence, including any forceful detention, which results or threatens to result in physical or mental injury. Psychological or sexual abuse or exploitation, including rape, molestation, incest (if the victim is a minor) or forced prostitution shall be considered acts of violence.

(ii) A conditional resident or former conditional resident who has not departed the United States after termination of resident status may apply for the waiver. The conditional resident may apply for the waiver regardless of his or her present marital status. The conditional resident may still be residing with the citizen or permanent resident spouse, or may be divorced or separated.

(iii) Evidence of physical abuse may include, but is not limited to, expert testimony in the form of reports and affidavits from police, judges, medical personnel, school officials and social service agency personnel. The Service must be satisfied with the credibility of the sources of documentation submitted in support of the application.

(iv) The Service is not in a position to evaluate testimony regarding a claim of extreme mental cruelty provided by unlicensed or untrained individuals. Therefore, all waiver applications based upon claims of extreme mental cruelty must be supported by the evaluation of a professional recognized by the Service as an expert in the field. An evaluation which was obtained in the course of the divorce proceedings may be submitted if it was provided by a professional recognized by the Service as an expert in the field.

(v) The evaluation must contain the professional's full name, professional address and license number. It must also identify the licensing, certifying, or registering authority. The Service retains the right to verify the professional's license.

(vi) The Service's decision on extreme mental cruelty waivers will be based upon the evaluation of the recognized professional. The Service reserves the right to request additional evaluations from expert witnesses chosen by the Service. Requests for additional evaluations must be authorized by the Assistant Regional Commissioner for Adjudications.

(vii) Licensed clinical social workers, psychologists, and psychiatrists are professionals recognized by the Service for the purpose of this section. A clinical social worker who is not licensed only because the state in which he or she practices does not provide for licensing will be considered a licensed professional recognized by the Service if he or she is included in the Register of Clinical Social Workers published by the National Association of Social Workers or is certified by the American Board of Examiners in Clinical Social Work.

(viii) As directed by the statute, the information contained in the application and supporting documents shall not be released without a court order or the written consent of the applicant; or, in the case of a child, the written consent of the parent or legal guardian who filed the waiver application on the child's behalf. Information may be released only to the applicant, his or her authorized representative, an officer of the Department of Justice, or any federal or State law enforcement agency. Any information provided under this part may be used for the purposes of enforcement of the Act or in any criminal proceeding.

(f) Decision. The director shall provide the alien with written notice of the decision on the application for waiver. If the decision is adverse, the director shall advise the alien of the reasons therefor, notify the alien of the termination of his or her permanent residence status, instruct the alien to surrender any Permanent Resident Card issued by the Service and issue a notice to appear placing the alien in removal proceedings. No appeal shall lie from the decision of the director; however, the alien may seek review of such decision in removal proceedings.

HISTORY:

[53 FR 30018, Aug. 10, 1988, as amended at 56 FR 22637, May 16, 1991; 59 FR 26591, May 23, 1994; 62 FR 10312, 10350, Mar. 6, 1997; 63 FR 70313, 70315, Dec. 21, 1998; 68 FR 9824, 9837, Feb. 28, 2003; 68 FR 10349, 10353, Mar. 5, 2003; 85 FR 82750, 82794, Dec. 18, 2020]

§ 1216.6 Petition by entrepreneur to remove conditional basis of lawful permanent resident status.

(a) Filing the petition —

(1) General procedures. A petition to remove the conditional basis of the permanent resident status of an alien accorded conditional permanent residence pursuant to section 203(b)(5) of the Act must be filed by the alien entrepreneur on Form I-829, Petition by Entrepreneur to Remove Conditions. The alien entrepreneur must file Form I-829 within the 90-day period preceding the second anniversary of his or her admission to the United States as a conditional permanent resident. Before Form I-829 may be considered as properly filed, it must be accompanied by the fee required under 8 CFR 103.7 and 8 CFR part 106, and by documentation as described in paragraph (a)(4) of this section, and it must be properly signed by the alien. Upon receipt of a properly filed Form I-829, the alien's conditional permanent resident status shall be extended automatically, if necessary, until such time as the director has adjudicated the petition. The entrepreneur's spouse and children should be included in the petition to remove conditions. Children who have reached the age of twenty-one or who have married during the period of conditional permanent residence and the former spouse of an entrepreneur, who was divorced from the entrepreneur during the period of conditional permanent residence, may be included in the alien entrepreneur's petition or may file a separate petition.

(2) Jurisdiction. Form I-829 must be filed with the regional service center having jurisdiction over the location of the alien entrepreneur's commercial enterprise in the United States.

(3) Physical presence at time of filing. A petition may be filed regardless of whether the alien is physically present in the United States. However, if the alien is outside the United States at the time of filing, he or she must return to the United States, with his or her spouse and children, if necessary, to comply with the interview requirements contained in the Act. Once the petition has been properly filed, the alien may travel outside the United States and return if in possession of documentation as set forth in § 1211.1(b)(1) of this chapter, provided the alien complies with the interview requirements described in paragraph (b) of this section. An alien who is not physically present in the United States during the filing period but subsequently applies for admission to the United States shall be processed in accordance with § 1235.11 of this chapter.

(4) Documentation. The petition for removal of conditions must be accompanied by the following evidence:

(i) Evidence that a commercial enterprise was established by the alien. Such evidence may include, but is not limited to, Federal income tax returns;

(ii) Evidence that the alien invested or was actively in the process of investing the requisite capital. Such evidence may include, but is not limited to, an audited financial statement or other probative evidence; and

(iii) Evidence that the alien sustained the actions described in paragraph (a)(4)(i) and (a)(4)(ii) of this section throughout the period of the alien's residence in the United States. The alien will be considered to have sustained the actions required for removal of conditions if he or she has, in good faith, substantially met the capital investment requirement of the statute and continuously maintained his or her capital investment over the two years of conditional residence. Such evidence may include, but is not limited to, bank statements, invoices, receipts, contracts, business licenses, Federal or State income tax returns, and Federal or State quarterly tax statements.

(iv) Evidence that the alien created or can be expected to create within a reasonable time ten full-time jobs for qualifying employees. In the case of a "troubled business" as defined in 8 CFR 204.6(j)(4)(ii), the alien entrepreneur must submit evidence that the commercial enterprise maintained the number of existing employees at no less than the pre-investment level for the period following his or her admission as a conditional permanent resident. Such evidence may include payroll records, relevant tax documents, and Forms I-9.

(5) Termination of status for failure to file petition. Failure to properly file Form I-829 within the 90-day period immediately preceding the second anniversary of the date on which the alien obtained lawful permanent residence on a conditional basis shall result in the automatic termination of the alien's permanent resident status and the initiation of deportation proceedings. The director shall send a written notice of termination and an order to show cause to an alien entrepreneur who fails to timely file a petition for removal of conditions. No appeal shall lie from this decision; however, the alien may request a review of the determination during deportation proceedings. In deportation proceedings, the burden of proof shall rest with the alien to show by a preponderance of the evidence that he or she complied with the requirement to file the petition within the designated period. The director may deem the petition to have been filed prior to the second anniversary of the alien's obtaining conditional permanent resident status and accept and consider a late petition if the alien demonstrates to the director's satisfaction that failure to file a timely petition was for good cause and due to extenuating circumstances. If the late petition is filed prior to jurisdiction vesting with the immigration judge in deportation proceedings and the director excuses the late filing and approves the petition, he or she shall restore the alien's permanent resident status, remove the conditional basis of such status, and cancel any outstanding order to show cause in accordance with § 242.7 of 8 CFR chapter I. If the petition is not filed until after jurisdiction vests with the immigration judge, the immigration judge may terminate the matter upon joint motion by the alien and the Service.

(6) Death of entrepreneur and effect on spouse and children. If an entrepreneur dies during the prescribed two-year period of conditional permanent residence, the spouse and children of the entrepreneur will be eligible for removal of conditions if it can be demonstrated that the conditions set forth in paragraph (a)(4) of this section have been met.

(b) Petition review —

(1) Authority to waive interview. The director of the service center shall review the Form I-829 and the supporting documents to determine whether to waive the interview required by the Act. If satisfied that the requirements set forth in paragraph (c)(1) of this section have been met, the service center director may waive the interview and approve the petition. If not so satisfied, then the service center director shall forward the petition to the district director having jurisdiction over the location of the alien entrepreneur's commercial enterprise in the United States so that an interview of the alien entrepreneur may be conducted. The director must either waive the requirement for an interview and adjudicate the petition or arrange for an interview within 90 days of the date on which the petition was properly filed.

(2) Location of interview. Unless waived, an interview relating to the Form I-829 shall be conducted by an immigration examiner or other officer so designated by the district director at the district office that has jurisdiction over the location of the alien entrepreneur's commercial enterprise in the United States.

(3) Termination of status for failure to appear for interview. If the alien fails to appear for an interview in connection with the petition when requested by the Service, the alien's permanent resident status will be automatically terminated as of the second anniversary of the date on which the alien obtained permanent residence. The alien will be provided with written notification of the termination and the reasons therefore, and an order to show cause shall be issued placing the alien under deportation proceedings. The alien may seek review of the decision to terminate his or her status in such proceedings, but the burden shall be on the alien to establish by a preponderance of the evidence that he or she complied with the interview requirements. If the alien has failed to appear for a scheduled interview, he or she may submit a written request to the district director asking that the interview be rescheduled or that the interview be waived. That request should explain his or her failure to appear for the scheduled interview, and if a request for waiver of the interview, the reasons such waiver should be granted. If the district director determines that there is good cause for granting the request, the interview may be rescheduled or waived, as appropriate. If the district director waives the interview, he or she shall restore the alien's conditional permanent resident status, cancel any outstanding order to show cause in accordance with § 1216.6(a)(5), and proceed to adjudicate the alien's petition. If the district director reschedules that alien's interview, he or she shall restore the alien's conditional permanent resident status, and cancel any outstanding order to show cause in accordance with § 1216.6(a)(5). If the interview is rescheduled at the request of the alien, the Service shall not be required to conduct the interview within the 90-day period following the filing of the petition.

(c) Adjudication of petition.

(1) The decision on the petition shall be made within 90 days of the date of filing or within 90 days of the interview, whichever is later. In adjudicating the petition, the director shall determine whether:

(i) A commercial enterprise was established by the alien;

(ii) The alien invested or was actively in the process of investing the requisite capital; and

(iii) The alien sustained the actions described in paragraphs (c)(1)(i) and (c)(1)(ii) of this section throughout the period of the alien's residence in the United States. The alien will be considered to have sustained the actions required for removal of conditions if he or she has, in good faith, substantially met the capital investment requirement of the statute and continuously maintained his or her capital investment over the two years of conditional residence.

(iv) The alien created or can be expected to create within a reasonable period of time ten full-time jobs to qualifying employees. In the case of a "troubled business" as defined in 8 CFR 204.6(j)(4)(ii), the alien maintained the number of existing employees at no less than the pre-investment level for the previous two years.

(2) If derogatory information is determined regarding any of these issues or it becomes known to the government that the entrepreneur obtained his or her investment funds through other than legal means (such as through the sale of illegal drugs), the director shall offer the alien entrepreneur the opportunity to rebut such information. If the alien entrepreneur fails to overcome such derogatory information or evidence the investment funds were obtained through other than legal means, the director may deny the petition, terminate the alien's permanent resident status, and issue an order to show cause. If derogatory information not relating to any of these issues is determined during the course of the interview, such information shall be forwarded to the investigations unit for appropriate action. If no unresolved derogatory information is determined relating to these issues, the petition shall be approved and the conditional basis of the alien's permanent resident status removed, regardless of any action taken or contemplated regarding other possible grounds for deportation.

(d) Decision —

(1) Approval. If, after initial review or after the interview, the director approves the petition, he or she will remove the conditional basis of the alien's permanent resident status as of the second anniversary of the alien's entry as a conditional permanent resident. He or she shall provide written notice of the decision to the alien and shall require the alien to report to the appropriate district office for processing for a new Permanent Resident Card, Form I-551, at which time the alien shall surrender any Permanent Resident Card previously issued.

(2) Denial. If, after initial review or after the interview, the director denies the petition, he or she shall provide written notice to the alien of the decision and the reason(s) therefor, and shall issue an order to show cause why the alien should not be deported from the United States. The alien's lawful permanent resident status and that of his or her spouse and any children shall be terminated as of the date of the director's written decision. The alien shall also be instructed to surrender any Permanent Resident Card previously issued by the Service. No appeal shall lie from this decision; however, the alien may seek review of the decision in deportation proceedings. In deportation proceedings, the burden shall rest with the Service to establish by a preponderance of the evidence that the facts and information in the alien's petition for removal of conditions are not true and that the petition was properly denied.

HISTORY:

[59 FR 26591, May 23, 1994; 63 FR 70313, 70315, Dec. 21, 1998; 68 FR 9824, 9837, Feb. 28, 2003; 68 FR 10349, 10353, Mar. 5, 2003; 85 FR 82750, 82794, Dec. 18, 2020]

PART 1235

INSPECTION OF PERSONS APPLYING FOR ADMISSION

Rule

AUTHORITY NOTE APPLICABLE TO ENTIRE PART:

AUTHORITY:

8 U.S.C. 1101 and note, 1102, 1103, 1182 and note, 1184, 1187, 1223, 1225, 1226, 1227, 1255; 8 U.S.C. 1185 note (section 7209 of Pub. L. 108-458); Title VII of Pub. L. 110-229; Pub. L. 115-218.

§ 1235.1 Scope of examination. [This section was removed and reserved, effective Jan. 11, 2021. See 85 FR 79779, 79802, Dec. 11, 2020.]

§ 1235.2 Parole for deferred inspection. [This section was removed and reserved, effective Jan. 11, 2021. See 85 FR 79779, 79802, Dec. 11, 2020.]

§ 1235.3 Inadmissible aliens and expedited removal. [This section was removed and reserved, effective Jan. 11, 2021. See 85 FR 79779, 79802, Dec. 11, 2020.]

§ 1235.4 Withdrawal of application for admission.

The Attorney General may, in his or her discretion, permit any alien applicant for admission to withdraw his or her application for admission in lieu of removal proceedings under section 240 of the Act or expedited removal under section 235(b)(1) of the Act. The alien's decision to withdraw his or her application for admission must be made voluntarily, but nothing in this section shall be construed as to give an alien the right to withdraw his or her application for admission. Permission to withdraw an application for admission should not normally be granted unless the alien intends and is able to depart the United States immediately. An alien permitted to withdraw his or her application for admission shall normally remain in carrier or Service custody pending departure, unless the district director determines that parole of the alien is warranted in accordance with § 1212.5(b) of this chapter.

HISTORY:

[48 FR 35349, Aug. 4, 1983; 62 FR 10312, 10358, Mar. 6, 1997, as corrected at 62 FR 15362, 15363, Apr. 1, 1997; 65 FR 82254, 82256, Dec. 28, 2000; 66 FR 7863, Jan. 26, 2001; 68 FR 9824, 9837, Feb. 28, 2003; 68 FR 10349, 10354, Mar. 5, 2003]

§ 1235.5 Preinspection.

(a) In United States territories and possessions. For provisions of the DHS regulations with respect to examinations of passengers and crew in the case of any aircraft proceeding from Guam, the Commonwealth of the Northern Mariana Islands (beginning November 28, 2009), Puerto Rico, or the United States Virgin Islands destined directly and without touching at a foreign port or place, to any other of such places, or to one of the States of the United States or the District of Columbia, See 8 CFR 235.5.

(b) In foreign territory. In the case of any aircraft, vessel, or train proceeding directly, without stopping, from a port or place in foreign territory to a port-of-entry in the United States, the examination and inspection of passengers and crew required by the Act and final determination of admissibility may be made immediately prior to such departure at the port or place in the foreign territory and shall have the same effect under the Act as though made at the destined port-of-entry in the United States.

§ 1235.5 Preinspection. [This section was removed and reserved, effective Jan. 11, 2021. See 85 FR 79779, 79802, Dec. 11, 2020.]

§ 1235.6 Referral to immigration judge. [Effective until December 31, 2025]

(a) Notice —.

(1) Referral by Form I-862, Notice to Appear. An immigration officer or asylum officer will sign and deliver a Form I-862 to an alien in the following cases:

(i) If, in accordance with the provisions of section 235(b)(2)(A) of the Act, the examining immigration officer detains an alien for a proceeding before an immigration judge under section 240 of the Act; or

(ii) If an immigration officer verifies that an alien subject to expedited removal under section 235(b)(1) of the Act has been admitted as a lawful permanent resident or refugee, or granted asylum, or, upon review pursuant to § 235.3(b)(5)(iv) of chapter I, an immigration judge determines that the alien was once so admitted or granted asylum, provided that such status has not been terminated by final administrative action, and DHS initiates removal proceedings against the alien under section 240 of the Act.

(2) Referral by Form I-863, Notice of Referral to Immigration Judge. An immigration officer will sign and deliver a Form I-863 to an alien in the following cases:

(i) If an asylum officer determines that an alien does not have a credible fear of persecution or torture, and the alien requests a review of that determination by an immigration judge;

(ii) If, in accordance with section 235(b)(1)(C) of the Act, an immigration officer refers an expedited removal order entered on an alien claiming to be a lawful permanent resident, refugee, asylee, or U.S. citizen for whom the officer could not verify such status to an immigration judge for review of the order; or

(iii) If an immigration officer refers an applicant in accordance with the provisions of 8 CFR 208.2(b) to an immigration judge.

(b) Certification for mental condition; medical appeal. An alien certified under sections 212(a)(1) and 232(b) of the Act shall be advised by the examining immigration officer that he or she may appeal to a board of medical examiners of the United States Public Health Service pursuant to section 232 of the Act. If such appeal is taken, the district director shall arrange for the convening of the medical board.

(c) The provisions of part 1235 are separate and severable from one another. In the event that any provision in part 1235 is stayed, enjoined, not implemented, or otherwise held invalid, the remaining provisions shall nevertheless be implemented as an independent rule and continue in effect.

HISTORY:

[24 FR 6477, Aug. 12, 1959, as amended at 44 FR 4653, Jan. 23, 1979; 56 FR 50812, Oct. 9, 1991; 62 FR 9071, 9074, Feb. 28, 1997; 62 FR 10312, 10358, Mar. 6, 1997; 64 FR 8478, 8494, Feb. 19, 1999; 68 FR 9824, 9837, 9846, Feb. 28, 2003; 68 FR 10349, 10354, Mar. 5, 2003; 74 FR 55726, 55744, Oct. 28, 2009; 85 FR 23902, 23904, Apr. 30, 2020; 85 FR 80274, 80401, Dec. 11, 2020, as corrected at 86 FR 1737, Jan. 11, 2021; 85 FR 84160, 84198, Dec. 23, 2020; 86 FR 6847, Jan. 25, 2021; 86 FR 15069, Mar. 22, 2021; 86 FR 73615, Dec. 28, 2021; 87 FR 18078, 18223, Mar. 29, 2022; 87 FR 79789, Dec. 28, 2022; 89 FR 105386, Dec. 27, 2024]

§ 1235.6 Referral to immigration judge. [Effective December 31, 2025]

(a) Notice —.

(1) Referral by Form I-862, Notice to Appear. An immigration officer or asylum officer will sign and deliver a Form I-862 to an alien in the following cases:

(i) If, in accordance with the provisions of section 235(b)(2)(A) of the Act, the examining immigration officer detains an alien for a proceeding before an immigration judge under section 240 of the Act; or

(ii) If an immigration officer verifies that an alien subject to expedited removal under section 235(b)(1) of the Act has been admitted as a lawful permanent resident or refugee, or granted asylum, or, upon review pursuant to § 235.3(b)(5)(iv) of chapter I, an immigration judge determines that the alien was once so admitted or granted asylum, provided that such status has not been terminated by final administrative action, and DHS initiates removal proceedings against the alien under section 240 of the Act.

(2) Referral by Form I-863, Notice of Referral to Immigration Judge. An immigration officer will sign and deliver a Form I-863 to an alien in the following cases:

(i) If an asylum officer determines that an alien does not have a credible fear of persecution or torture, and the alien requests a review of that determination by an immigration judge;

(ii) If, in accordance with section 235(b)(1)(C) of the Act, an immigration officer refers an expedited removal order entered on an alien claiming to be a lawful permanent resident, refugee, asylee, or U.S. citizen for whom the officer could not verify such status to an immigration judge for review of the order; or

(iii) If an immigration officer refers an applicant in accordance with the provisions of 8 CFR 208.2(b) to an immigration judge.

(b) Certification for mental condition; medical appeal. An alien certified under sections 212(a)(1) and 232(b) of the Act shall be advised by the examining immigration officer that he or she may appeal to a board of medical examiners of the United States Public Health Service pursuant to section 232 of the Act. If such appeal is taken, the district director shall arrange for the convening of the medical board.

(c) The provisions of part 1235 are separate and severable from one another. In the event that any provision in part 1235 is stayed, enjoined, not implemented, or otherwise held invalid, the remaining provisions shall nevertheless be implemented as an independent rule and continue in effect.

HISTORY:

[24 FR 6477, Aug. 12, 1959, as amended at 44 FR 4653, Jan. 23, 1979; 56 FR 50812, Oct. 9, 1991; 62 FR 9071, 9074, Feb. 28, 1997; 62 FR 10312, 10358, Mar. 6, 1997; 64 FR 8478, 8494, Feb. 19, 1999; 68 FR 9824, 9837, 9846, Feb. 28, 2003; 68 FR 10349, 10354, Mar. 5, 2003; 74 FR 55726, 55744, Oct. 28, 2009; 85 FR 23902, 23904, Apr. 30, 2020; 85 FR 80274, 80401, Dec. 11, 2020, as corrected at 86 FR 1737, Jan. 11, 2021; 85 FR 84160, 84198, Dec. 23, 2020; 86 FR 6847, Jan. 25, 2021; 86 FR 15069, Mar. 22, 2021; 86 FR 73615, Dec. 28, 2021; 87 FR 18078, 18223, Mar. 29, 2022; 87 FR 79789, Dec. 28, 2022; 89 FR 105386, Dec. 27, 2024]

§ 1235.8 Inadmissibility on security and related grounds.

(a) Report. When an immigration officer or an immigration judge suspects that an arriving alien appears to be inadmissible under section 212(a)(3)(A) (other than clause (ii)), (B), or (C) of the Act, the immigration officer or immigration judge shall order the alien removed and report the action promptly to the district director who has administrative jurisdiction over the place where the alien has arrived or where the hearing is being held. The immigration officer shall, if possible, take a brief sworn question-and-answer statement from the alien, and the alien shall be notified by personal service of Form I-147, Notice of Temporary Inadmissibility, of the action taken and the right to submit a written statement and additional information for consideration by the Attorney General. The district director shall forward the report to the regional director for further action as provided in paragraph (b) of this section.

(b) **Action by regional director.**

(1) In accordance with section 235(c)(2)(B) of the Act, the regional director may deny any further inquiry or hearing by an immigration judge and order the alien removed by personal service of Form I-148, Notice of Permanent Inadmissibility, or issue any other order disposing of the case that the regional director considers appropriate.

(2) If the regional director concludes that the case does not meet the criteria contained in section 235(c)(2)(B) of the Act, the regional director may direct that:

(i) An immigration officer shall conduct a further examination of the alien, concerning the alien's admissibility; or,

(ii) The alien's case be referred to an immigration judge for a hearing, or for the continuation of any prior hearing.

(3) The regional director's decision shall be in writing and shall be signed by the regional director. Unless the written decision contains confidential information, the disclosure of which would be prejudicial to the public interest, safety, or security of the United States, the written decision shall be served on the alien. If the written decision contains such confidential information, the alien shall be served with a separate written order showing the disposition of the case, but with the confidential information deleted.

(4) The Service shall not execute a removal order under this section under circumstances that violate section 241(b)(3) of the Act or Article 3 of the Convention Against Torture. The provisions of part 1208 of this chapter relating to consideration or review by an immigration judge, the Board of Immigration Appeals, or an asylum officer shall not apply.

(c) Finality of decision. The regional director's decision under this section is final when it is served upon the alien in accordance with paragraph (b)(3) of this section. There is no administrative appeal from the regional director's decision.

(d) Hearing by immigration judge. If the regional director directs that an alien subject to removal under this section be given a hearing or further hearing before an immigration judge, the hearing and all further proceedings in the matter shall be conducted in accordance with the provisions of section 240 of the Act and other applicable sections of the Act to the same extent as though the alien had been referred to an immigration judge by the examining immigration officer. In a case where the immigration judge ordered the alien removed pursuant to paragraph (a) of this section, the Service shall refer the case back to the immigration judge and proceedings shall be automatically reopened upon receipt of the notice of referral. If confidential information, not previously considered in the matter, is presented supporting the inadmissibility of the alien under section 212(a)(3)(A) (other than clause (ii)), (B) or (C) of the Act, the disclosure of which, in the discretion of the immigration judge, may be prejudicial to the public interest, safety, or security, the immigration judge may again order the alien removed under the authority of section 235(c) of the Act and further action shall be taken as provided in this section.

(e) Nonapplicability. The provisions of this section shall apply only to arriving aliens, as defined in § 1001.1(q) of this chapter. Aliens present in the United States who have not been admitted or paroled may be subject to proceedings under Title V of the Act.

HISTORY:

[22 FR 9791, Dec. 6, 1957; 22 FR 9519, Nov. 28, 1957, as amended at 48 FR 8, Jan. 3, 1983; 48 FR 30350, July 1, 1983; 62 FR 10312, 10358, Mar. 6, 1997; 64 FR 8478, 8494, Feb. 19, 1999; 68 FR 9824, 9837, Feb. 28, 2003; 68 FR 10349, 10354, Mar. 5, 2003]

§ 1235.9 Northern Mariana identification card.

During the two-year period that ended July 1, 1990, the Service issued Northern Marianas Identification Cards to aliens who acquired United States citizenship when the Covenant to Establish a Commonwealth of the Northern Mariana Islands in Political Union with the United States entered into force on November 3, 1986. These cards remain valid as evidence of United States citizenship. Although the Service no longer issues these cards, a United States citizen to whom a card was issued may file Form I-777, Application for Issuance or Replacement of Northern Marianas Card, to obtain replacement of a lost, stolen, or mutilated Northern Marianas Identification Card.

HISTORY:

[53 FR 23380, June 22, 1988, redesignated and revised at 62 FR 10312, 10359, Mar. 6, 1997; 68 FR 9824, 9837, Feb. 28, 2003]

§ 1235.10 U.S. Citizen Identification Card.

(a) General. Form I-197, U.S. Citizen Identification Card, is no longer issued by the Service but valid existing cards will continue to be acceptable documentation of U.S. citizenship. Possession of the identification card is not mandatory for any purpose. A U.S. Citizen Identification Card remains the property of the United States. Because the identification card is no longer issued, there are no provisions for replacement cards.

(b) **Surrender and voidance.**

(1) Institution of proceeding under section 240 or 342 of the Act. A U.S. Citizen Identification Card must be surrendered provisionally to a Service office upon notification by the district director that a proceeding under section 240 or 342 of the Act is being instituted against the person to whom the card was issued. The card shall be returned to the person if the final order in the proceeding does not result in voiding the card under this paragraph. A U.S. Citizen Identification Card is automatically void if the person to whom it was issued is determined to be an alien in a proceeding conducted under section 240 of the Act, or if a certificate, document, or record relating to that person is canceled under section 342 of the Act.

(2) Investigation of validity of identification card. A U.S. Citizen Identification Card must be surrendered provisionally upon notification by a district director that the validity of the card is being investigated. The card shall be returned to the person who surrendered it if the investigation does not result in a determination adverse to his or her claim to be a United States citizen. When an investigation results in a tentative determination adverse to the applicant's claim to be a United States citizen, the applicant shall be notified by certified mail directed to his or her last known address. The notification shall inform the applicant of the basis for the determination and of the intention of the district director to declare the card void unless within 30 days the applicant objects and demands an opportunity to see and rebut the adverse evidence. Any rebuttal, explanation, or evidence presented by the applicant must be included in the record of proceeding. The determination whether the applicant is a United States citizen must be based on the entire record and the applicant shall be notified of the determination. If it is determined that the applicant is not a United States citizen, the applicant shall be notified of the reasons, and the card deemed void. There is no appeal from the district director's decision.

(3) Admission of alienage. A U.S. Citizen Identification Card is void if the person to whom it was issued admits in a statement signed before an immigration officer that he or she is an alien and consents to the voidance of the card. Upon signing the statement the card must be surrendered to the immigration officer.

(4) Surrender of void card. A void U.S. Citizen Identification Card which has not been returned to the Service must be surrendered without delay to an immigration officer or to the issuing office of the Service.

(c) U.S. Citizen Identification Card previously issued on Form I-179. A valid Form I-179, U.S. Citizen Identification Card, continues to be valid subject to the provisions of this section.

HISTORY:

[48 FR 9504, Mar. 7, 1983; 62 FR 10312, 10359, Mar. 6, 1997; 68 FR 9824, 9837, Feb. 28, 2003]

§ 1235.11 Admission of conditional permanent residents.

(a) **General.**

(1) Conditional residence based on family relationship. An alien seeking admission to the United States with an immigrant visa as the spouse or son or daughter of a United States citizen or lawful permanent resident shall be examined to determine whether the conditions of section 216 of the Act apply. If so, the alien shall be admitted conditionally for a period of 2 years. At the time of admission, the alien shall be notified that the alien and his or her petitioning spouse must file a Form I-751, Petition to Remove the Conditions on

Residence, within the 90-day period immediately preceding the second anniversary of the alien's admission for permanent residence.

(2) Conditional residence based on entrepreneurship. An alien seeking admission to the United States with an immigrant visa as an alien entrepreneur (as defined in section 216A(f)(1) of the Act) or the spouse or unmarried minor child of an alien entrepreneur shall be admitted conditionally for a period of 2 years. At the time of admission, the alien shall be notified that the principal alien (entrepreneur) must file a Form I-829, Petition by Entrepreneur to Remove Conditions, within the 90-day period immediately preceding the second anniversary of the alien's admission for permanent residence.

(b) Correction of endorsement on immigrant visa. If the alien is subject to the provisions of section 216 of the Act, but the classification endorsed on the immigrant visa does not so indicate, the endorsement shall be corrected and the alien shall be admitted as a lawful permanent resident on a conditional basis, if otherwise admissible. Conversely, if the alien is not subject to the provisions of section 216 of the Act, but the visa classification endorsed on the immigrant visa indicates that the alien is subject thereto (e.g., if the second anniversary of the marriage upon which the immigrant visa is based occurred after the issuance of the visa and prior to the alien's application for admission) the endorsement on the visa shall be corrected and the alien shall be admitted as a lawful permanent resident without conditions, if otherwise admissible.

(c) Expired conditional permanent resident status. The lawful permanent resident alien status of a conditional resident automatically terminates if the conditional basis of such status is not removed by the Service through approval of a Form I-751, Petition to Remove the Conditions on Residence or, in the case of an alien entrepreneur (as defined in section 216A(f)(1) of the Act), Form I-829, Petition by Entrepreneur to Remove Conditions. Therefore, an alien who is seeking admission as a returning resident subsequent to the second anniversary of the date on which conditional residence was obtained (except as provided in § 1211.1(b)(1) of this chapter) and whose conditional basis of such residence has not been removed pursuant to section 216(c) or 216A(c) of the Act, whichever is applicable, shall be placed under removal proceedings. However, in a case where conditional residence was based on a marriage, removal proceedings may be terminated and the alien may be admitted as a returning resident if the required Form I-751 is filed jointly, or by the alien alone (if appropriate), and approved by the Service. In the case of an alien entrepreneur, removal proceedings may be terminated and the alien admitted as a returning resident if the required Form I-829 is filed by the alien entrepreneur and approved by the Service.

HISTORY:

[53 FR 30021, Aug. 10, 1988; 59 FR 26592, May 23, 1994; 62 FR 10312, 10360, Mar. 6, 1997; 68 FR 9824, 9837, Feb. 28, 2003; 68 FR 10349, 10354, Mar. 5, 2003]

PART 1236

APPREHENSION AND DETENTION OF INADMISSIBLE AND DEPORTABLE ALIENS; REMOVAL OF ALIENS ORDERED REMOVED

Subpart A. Detention of Aliens Prior to Order of Removal

Rule

AUTHORITY NOTE APPLICABLE TO ENTIRE PART:

AUTHORITY:

5 U.S.C. 301, 552, 552a; 8 U.S.C. 1103, 1182, 1224, 1225, 1226, 1227, 1231, 1362; 18 U.S.C. 4002, 4013(c)(4); 8 CFR part 2.

Subpart A

Detention of Aliens Prior to Order of Removal

§ 1236.1 Apprehension, custody, and detention.

(a) Detainers. The issuance of a detainer under this section shall be governed by the provisions of § 287.7 of 8 CFR chapter I.

(b) Warrant of arrest.

(1) In general. At the time of issuance of the notice to appear, or at any time thereafter and up to the time removal proceedings are completed, the respondent may be arrested and taken into custody under the authority of Form I-200, Warrant of Arrest. A warrant of arrest may be issued only by those immigration officers listed in § 287.5(e)(2) of 8 CFR chapter I and may be served only by those immigration officers listed in § 287.5(e)(3) of 8 CFR chapter I.

(2) If, after the issuance of a warrant of arrest, a determination is made not to serve it, any officer authorized to issue such warrant may authorize its cancellation.

(c) Custody issues and release procedures.

(1) In general.

(i) After the expiration of the Transition Period Custody Rules (TPCR) set forth in section 303(b)(3) of Div. C of Pub. L. 104-208, no alien described in section 236(c)(1) of the Act may be released from custody during removal proceedings except pursuant to section 236(c)(2) of the Act.

(ii) Paragraph (c)(2) through (c)(8) of this section shall govern custody determinations for aliens subject to the TPCR while they remain in effect. For purposes of this section, an alien "subject to the TPCR" is an alien described in section 303(b)(3)(A) of Div. C of Pub. L. 104-208 who is in deportation proceedings, subject to a final order of deportation, or in removal proceedings.

The TPCR do not apply to aliens in exclusion proceedings under former section 236 of the Act, aliens in expedited removal proceedings under section 235(b)(1) of the Act, or aliens subject to a final order of removal.

(2) Aliens not lawfully admitted. Subject to paragraph (c)(6)(i) of this section, but notwithstanding any other provision within this section, an alien subject to the TPCR who is not lawfully admitted is not eligible to be considered for release from custody.

(i) An alien who remains in status as an alien lawfully admitted for permanent residence, conditionally admitted for permanent residence, or lawfully admitted for temporary residence is "lawfully admitted" for purposes of this section.

(ii) An alien in removal proceedings, in deportation proceedings, or subject to a final order of deportation, and not described in paragraph (c)(2)(i) of this section, is not "lawfully admitted" for purposes of this section unless the alien last entered the United States lawfully and is not presently an applicant for admission to the United States.

(3) Criminal aliens eligible to be considered for release. Except as provided in this section, or otherwise provided by law, an alien subject to the TPCR may be considered for release from custody if lawfully admitted. Such an alien must first demonstrate, by clear and convincing evidence, that release would not pose a danger to the safety of other persons or of property. If an alien meets this burden, the alien must further demonstrate, by clear and convincing evidence, that the alien is likely to appear for any scheduled proceeding (including any appearance required by the Service or EOIR) in order to be considered for release in the exercise of discretion.

(4) Criminal aliens ineligible to be considered for release except in certain special circumstances. An alien, other than an alien lawfully admitted for permanent residence, subject to section 303(b)(3)(A) (ii) or (iii) of Div. C. of Pub. L. 104-208 is ineligible to be considered for release if the alien:

(i) Is described in section 241(a)(2)(C) of the Act (as in effect prior to April 1, 1997), or has been convicted of a crime described in section 101(a)(43)(B), (E)(ii) or (F) of the Act (as in effect on April 1, 1997);

(ii) Has been convicted of a crime described in section 101(a)(43)(G) of the Act (as in effect on April 1, 1997) or a crime or crimes involving moral turpitude related to property, and sentenced therefor (including in the aggregate) to at least 3 years' imprisonment;

(iii) Has failed to appear for an immigration proceeding without reasonable cause or has been subject to a bench warrant or similar legal process (unless quashed, withdrawn, or cancelled as improvidently issued);

(iv) Has been convicted of a crime described in section 101(a)(43)(Q) or (T) of the Act (as in effect on April 1, 1997);

(v) Has been convicted in a criminal proceeding of a violation of section 273, 274, 274C, 276, or 277 of the Act, or has admitted the factual elements of such a violation;

(vi) Has overstayed a period granted for voluntary departure;

(vii) Has failed to surrender or report for removal pursuant to an order of exclusion, deportation, or removal;

(viii) Does not wish to pursue, or is statutorily ineligible for, any form of relief from exclusion, deportation, or removal under this chapter or the Act; or

(ix) Is described in paragraphs (c)(5)(i)(A), (B), or (C) of this section but has not been sentenced, including in the aggregate but not including any portions suspended, to at least 2 years' imprisonment, unless the alien was lawfully admitted and has not, since the commencement of proceedings and within the 10 years prior thereto, been convicted of a crime, failed to comply with an order to surrender or a period of voluntary departure, or been subject to a bench warrant or similar legal process (unless quashed, withdrawn, or cancelled as improvidently issued). An alien eligible to be considered for release under this paragraph must meet the burdens described in paragraph (c)(3) of this section in order to be released from custody in the exercise of discretion.

(5) Criminal aliens ineligible to be considered for release

(i) A criminal alien subject to section 303(b)(3)(A)(ii) or (iii) of Div. C of Pub. L. 104-208 is ineligible to be considered for release if the alien has been sentenced, including in the aggregate but not including any portions suspended, to at least 2 years' imprisonment, and the alien

(A) Is described in section 237(a)(2)(D)(i) or (ii) of the Act (as in effect on April 1, 1997), or has been convicted of a crime described in section 101(a)(43)(A), (C), (E)(i), (H), (I), (K)(iii), or (L) of the Act (as in effect on April 1, 1997);

(B) Is described in section 237(a)(2)(A)(iv) of the Act; or

(C) Has escaped or attempted to escape from the lawful custody of a local, State, or Federal prison, agency, or officer within the United States.

(ii) Notwithstanding paragraph (c)(5)(i) of this section, a permanent resident alien who has not, since the commencement of proceedings and within the 15 years prior thereto, been convicted of a crime, failed to comply with an order to surrender or a period of voluntary departure, or been subject to a bench warrant or similar legal process (unless quashed, withdrawn, or cancelled as improvidently issued), may be considered for release under paragraph (c)(3) of this section.

(6) Unremovable aliens and certain long-term detainees.

(i) If the district director determines that an alien subject to section 303(b)(3)(A)(ii) or (iii) of Div. C of Pub. L. 104-208 cannot be removed from the United States because the designated country of removal or deportation will not accept the alien's return, the district director may, in the exercise of discretion, consider release of the alien from custody upon such terms and conditions as the district director may prescribe, without regard to paragraphs (c)(2), (c)(4), and (c)(5) of this section.

(ii) The district director may also, notwithstanding paragraph (c)(5) of this section, consider release from custody, upon such terms and conditions as the district director may prescribe, of any alien described in paragraph (c)(2)(ii) of this section who has been in the Service's custody for six months pursuant to a final order of deportation terminating the alien's status as a lawful permanent resident.

(iii) The district director may release an alien from custody under this paragraph only in accordance with the standards set forth in paragraph (c)(3) of this section and any other applicable provisions of law.

(iv) The district director's custody decision under this paragraph shall not be subject to redetermination by an immigration judge, but, in the case of a custody decision under paragraph (c)(6)(ii) of this section, may be appealed to the Board of Immigration Appeals pursuant to paragraph (d)(3)(iii) of this section.

(7) Construction. A reference in this section to a provision in section 241 of the Act as in effect prior to April 1, 1997, shall be deemed to include a reference to the corresponding provision in section 237 of the Act as in effect on April 1, 1997. A reference in this section to a "crime" shall be considered to include a reference to a conspiracy or attempt to commit such a crime. In calculating the 10-year period specified in paragraph (c)(4) of this section and the 15-year period specified in paragraph (c)(5) of this section, no period during which the alien was detained or incarcerated shall count toward the total. References in paragraph (c)(6)(i) of this section to the "district director" shall be deemed to include a reference to any official designated by the Commissioner to exercise custody authority over aliens covered by that paragraph. Nothing in this part shall be construed as prohibiting an alien from seeking reconsideration of the Service's determination that the alien is within a category barred from release under this part.

(8) Any officer authorized to issue a warrant of arrest may, in the officer's discretion, release an alien not described in section 236(c)(1) of the Act, under the conditions at section 236(a)(2) and (3) of the Act; provided that the alien must demonstrate to the satisfaction of the officer that such release would not pose a danger to property or persons, and that the alien is likely to appear for any future proceeding. Such an officer may also, in the exercise of discretion, release an alien in deportation proceedings pursuant to the authority in section 242 of the Act (as designated prior to April 1, 1997), except as otherwise provided by law.

(9) When an alien who, having been arrested and taken into custody, has been released, such release may be revoked at any time in the discretion of the district director, acting district director, deputy district director, assistant district director for investigations, assistant district director for detention and deportation, or officer in charge (except foreign), in which event the alien may be taken into physical custody and detained. If detained, unless a breach has occurred, any outstanding bond shall be revoked and canceled.

(10) The provisions of § 103.6 of 8 CFR chapter I shall apply to any bonds authorized. Subject to the provisions of this section, the provisions of § 1003.19 of this chapter shall govern availability to the respondent of recourse to other administrative authority for release from custody.

(11) An immigration judge may not exercise the authority provided in this section, and the review process described in paragraph (d) of this section shall not apply, with respect to any alien beyond the custody jurisdiction of the immigration judge as provided in § 1003.19(h) of this chapter.

(d) Appeals from custody decisions.

(1) Application to immigration judge. After an initial custody determination by the district director, including the setting of a bond, the respondent may, at any time before an order under 8 CFR part 1240 becomes final, request amelioration of the conditions under which he or she may be released. Prior to such final order, and except as otherwise provided in this chapter, the immigration judge is authorized to exercise the authority in section 236 of the Act (or section 242(a)(1) of the Act as designated prior to April 1, 1997 in the case of an alien in deportation proceedings) to detain the alien in custody, release the alien, and determine the amount of bond, if any, under which the respondent may be released, as provided in § 1003.19 of this chapter. If the alien has been released from custody, an application for amelioration of the terms of release must be filed within 7 days of release.

(2) Application to the district director. After expiration of the 7-day period in paragraph (d)(1) of this section, the respondent may request review by the district director of the conditions of his or her release.

(3) Appeal to the Board of Immigration Appeals. An appeal relating to bond and custody determinations may be filed to the Board of Immigration Appeals in the following circumstances:

(i) In accordance with § 1003.38 of this chapter, the alien or the Service may appeal the decision of an immigration judge pursuant to paragraph (d)(1) of this section.

(ii) The alien, within 10 days, may appeal from the district director's decision under paragraph (d)(2)(i) of this section.

(4) Effect of filing an appeal. The filing of an appeal from a determination of an immigration judge or district director under this paragraph shall not operate to delay compliance with the order (except as provided in § 1003.19(i)), nor stay the administrative proceedings or removal.

(e) Privilege of communication. Every detained alien shall be notified that he or she may communicate with the consular or diplomatic officers of the country of his or her nationality in the United States. Existing treaties with the following countries require immediate communication with appropriate consular or diplomatic officers whenever nationals of the following countries are detained in removal proceedings, whether or not requested by the alien and even if the alien requests that no communication be undertaken in his or her behalf. When notifying consular or diplomatic officials, Service officers shall not reveal the fact that any detained alien has applied for asylum or withholding of removal.

Albania [1]
Antigua
Armenia
Azerbaijan
Bahamas
Barbados
Belarus
Belize
Brunei
Bulgaria
China (People's Republic of) [2]
Costa Rica
Cyprus
Czech Republic
Dominica
Fiji
Gambia, The
Georgia
Ghana
Grenada
Guyana
Hungary
Jamaica
Kazakhstan
Kiribati
Kuwait
Kyrgyzstan
Malaysia
Malta
Mauritius
Moldova
Mongolia
Nigeria
Philippines
Poland
Romania
Russian Federation
St. Kitts/Nevis
St. Lucia
St. Vincent/Grenadines
Seychelles
Sierra Leone
Singapore
Slovak Republic
South Korea
Tajikistan
Tanzania
Tonga
Trinidad/Tobago
Turkmenistan
Tuvalu
Ukraine
United Kingdom [3]
U.S.S.R. [4]
Uzbekistan
Zambia

(f) Notification to Executive Office for Immigration Review of change in custody status. The Service shall notify the Immigration Court having administrative control over the Record of Proceeding of any change in custody location or of release from, or subsequent taking into, Service custody of a respondent/applicant pursuant to § 1003.19(g) of this chapter.

HISTORY:

[42 FR 46045, Sept. 14, 1977; 62 FR 10312, 10360, March 6, 1997, as corrected and amended at 62 FR 15362, 15363, April 1, 1997; 63 FR 27441, 27449, May 19, 1998; 65 FR 80281, 80294, Dec. 21, 2000; 68 FR 9824, 9838, Feb. 28, 2003; 68 FR 10349, 10354, Mar. 5, 2003]

§ 1236.2 Confined aliens, incompetents, and minors.

(a) Service. If the respondent is confined, or if he or she is an incompetent, or a minor under the age of 14, the notice to appear, and the warrant of arrest, if issued, shall be served in the manner prescribed in § 1239.1 of this chapter upon the person or persons specified by § 103.5a(c) of 8 CFR chapter I.

(b) Service custody and cost of maintenance. An alien confined because of physical or mental disability in an institution or hospital shall not be accepted into physical custody by the Service until an order of removal has been entered and the Service is ready to remove the alien. When such an alien is an inmate of a public or private institution at the time of the commencement of the removal proceedings, expenses for the maintenance of the alien shall not be incurred by the Government until he or she is taken into physical custody by the Service.

HISTORY:

[42 FR 46045, Sept. 14, 1977, as amended at 44 FR 4653, Jan. 23, 1979; 46 FR 43956, Sept. 2, 1981; 62 FR 9071, 9074, Feb. 28, 1997; 62 FR 10312, 10361, March 6, 1997; 68 FR 9824, 9838, Feb. 28, 2003; 68 FR 10349, 10354, Mar. 5, 2003]

§ 1236.3 Detention and release of juveniles.

(a) Juveniles. A juvenile is defined as an alien under the age of 18 years.

(b) Release. Juveniles for whom bond has been posted, for whom parole has been authorized, or who have been ordered released on recognizance, shall be released pursuant to the following guidelines:

(1) Juveniles shall be released, in order of preference, to:

(i) A parent;

(ii) Legal guardian; or

[1]Arrangements with these countries provide that U.S. authorities shall notify responsible representatives within 72 hours of the arrest or detention of one of their nationals.

[2]When Taiwan nationals (who carry "Republic of China" passports) are detained, notification should be made to the nearest office of the Taiwan Economic and Cultural Representative's Office, the unofficial entity representing Taiwan's interests in the United States.

[3]British dependencies are also covered by this agreement. They are: Anguilla, British Virgin Islands, Hong Kong, Bermuda, Montserrat, and the Turks and Caicos Islands. Their residents carry British passports.

[4]All U.S.S.R. successor states are covered by this agreement. They are: Armenia, Azerbaijan, Belarus, Georgia, Kazakhstan, Kyrgyzstan, Moldova, Russian Federation, Tajikistan, Turkmenistan, Ukraine, and Uzbekistan.

(iii) An adult relative (brother, sister, aunt, uncle, grandparent) who is not presently in Service detention, unless a determination is made that the detention of such juvenile is required to secure his or her timely appearance before the Service or the Immigration Court or to ensure the juvenile's safety or that of others. In cases where the parent, legal guardian, or adult relative resides at a location distant from where the juvenile is detained, he or she may secure release at a Service office located near the parent, legal guardian, or adult relative.

(2) If an individual specified in paragraphs (b)(1)(i) through (iii) of this section cannot be located to accept custody of a juvenile, and the juvenile has identified a parent, legal guardian, or adult relative in Service detention, simultaneous release of the juvenile and the parent, legal guardian, or adult relative shall be evaluated on a discretionary case-by-case basis.

(3) In cases where the parent or legal guardian is in Service detention or outside the United States, the juvenile may be released to such person as is designated by the parent or legal guardian in a sworn affidavit, executed before an immigration officer or consular officer, as capable and willing to care for the juvenile's well-being. Such person must execute an agreement to care for the juvenile and to ensure the juvenile's presence at all future proceedings before the Service or an immigration judge.

(4) In unusual and compelling circumstances and in the discretion of the Director of the Office of Juvenile Affairs, a juvenile may be released to an adult, other than those identified in paragraphs (b)(1)(i) through (b)(1)(iii) of this section, who executes an agreement to care for the juvenile's well-being and to ensure the juvenile's presence at all future proceedings before the Service or an immigration judge.

(c) Juvenile coordinator. The case of a juvenile for whom detention is determined to be necessary should be referred to the "Juvenile Coordinator," whose responsibilities should include, but not be limited to, finding suitable placement of the juvenile in a facility designated for the occupancy of juveniles. These may include juvenile facilities contracted by the Service, state or local juvenile facilities, or other appropriate agencies authorized to accommodate juveniles by the laws of the state or locality.

(d) Detention. In the case of a juvenile for whom detention is determined to be necessary, for such interim period of time as is required to locate suitable placement for the juvenile, whether such placement is under paragraph (b) or (c) of this section, the juvenile may be temporarily held by Service authorities or placed in any Service detention facility having separate accommodations for juveniles.

(e) Refusal of release. If a parent of a juvenile detained by the Service can be located, and is otherwise suitable to receive custody of the juvenile, and the juvenile indicates a refusal to be released to his or her parent, the parent(s) shall be notified of the juvenile's refusal to be released to the parent(s), and they shall be afforded the opportunity to present their views to the district director, chief patrol agent, Director of the Office of Juvenile Affairs or immigration judge before a custody determination is made.

(f) Notice to parent of application for relief. If a juvenile seeks release from detention, voluntary departure, parole, or any form of relief from removal, where it appears that the grant of such relief may effectively terminate some interest inherent in the parent-child relationship and/or the juvenile's rights and interests are adverse with those of the parent, and the parent is presently residing in the United States, the parent shall be given notice of the juvenile's application for relief, and shall be afforded an opportunity to present his or her views and assert his or her interest to the district director, Director of the Office of Juvenile Affairs or immigration judge before a determination is made as to the merits of the request for relief.

(g) Voluntary departure. Each juvenile, apprehended in the immediate vicinity of the border, who resides permanently in Mexico or Canada, shall be informed, prior to presentation of the voluntary departure form or being allowed to withdraw his or her application for admission, that he or she may make a telephone call to a parent, close relative, a friend, or to an organization found on the free legal services list. A juvenile who does not reside in Mexico or Canada who is apprehended shall be provided access to a telephone and must in fact communicate either with a parent, adult relative, friend, or with an organization found on the free legal services list prior to presentation of the voluntary departure form. If such juvenile, of his or her own volition, asks to contact a consular officer, and does in fact make such contact, the requirements of this section are satisfied.

(h) Notice and request for disposition. When a juvenile alien is apprehended, he or she must be given a Form I-770, Notice of Rights and Disposition. If the juvenile is less than 14 years of age or unable to understand the notice, the notice shall be read and explained to the juvenile in a language he or she understands. In the event a juvenile who has requested a hearing pursuant to the notice subsequently decides to accept voluntary departure or is allowed to withdraw his or her application for admission, a new Form I-770 shall be given to, and signed by the juvenile.

HISTORY:

[55 FR 30686, July 27, 1990; 59 FR 62302, Dec. 5, 1994; 60 FR 34090, June 30, 1995; 62 FR 10312, 10362, March 6, 1997; 67 FR 39255, 39258, June 7, 2002; 68 FR 9824, 9838, Feb. 28, 2003]

§ 1236.4 Removal of S-5, S-6, and S-7 nonimmigrants.

[PUBLISHER'S NOTE: 68 FR 10349, 10354, Mar. 5, 2003, purported to substitute "1208.2 and 1208.16" for "208.2 and 208.16" in paragraph (d) of § 1236.5. However this could not implemented, since paragraph (d) did not exist in § 1236.5. It was determined that paragraph (d) of § 1236.4 should instead be amended. For the convenience of the user, the amendment has been implemented according to the apparent intent of the agency. A correction is anticipated.]

(a) Condition of classification. As a condition of classification and continued stay in classification pursuant to section 101(a)(15)(S) of the Act, nonimmigrants in S classification must have executed Form I-854, Part B, Inter-agency Alien Witness and Informant Record, certifying that they have knowingly waived their right to a removal hearing and right to contest, other than on the basis of an application for withholding of deportation or removal, any removal action, including detention pending deportation or removal, instituted before lawful permanent resident status is obtained.

(b) Determination of deportability.

(1) A determination to remove a deportable alien classified pursuant to section 101(a)(15)(S) of the Act shall be made by the district director having jurisdiction over the place where the alien is located.

(2) A determination to remove such a deportable alien shall be based on one or more of the grounds of deportability listed in section 237 of the Act based on conduct committed after, or conduct or a condition not disclosed to the Service prior to, the alien's classification as an S nonimmigrant under section 101(a)(15)(S) of the Act, or for a violation of, or failure to adhere to, the particular terms and conditions of status in S nonimmigrant classification.

(c) Removal procedures.

(1) A district director who determines to remove an alien witness or informant in S nonimmigrant classification shall notify the Commissioner, the Assistant Attorney General, Criminal Division, and the relevant law enforcement agency in writing to that effect. The Assistant Attorney General, Criminal Division, shall concur in or object to that decision. Unless the Assistant Attorney General, Criminal Division, objects within 7 days, he or she shall be deemed to have concurred in the decision. In the event of an objection by the Assistant Attorney General, Criminal Division, the matter will be expeditiously referred to the Deputy Attorney General for a final resolution. In no circumstances shall the alien or the relevant law enforcement agency have a right of appeal from any decision to remove.

(2) A district director who has provided notice as set forth in paragraph (c)(1) of this section and who has been advised by the Commissioner that the Assistant Attorney General, Criminal Division, has not objected shall issue a Warrant of Removal. The alien shall immediately be arrested and taken into custody by the district director initiating the removal. An alien classified under the provisions of section 101(a)(15)(S) of the Act who is determined, pursuant to a warrant issued by a district director, to be deportable from the United States shall be removed from the United States to his or her country of nationality or last residence. The agency that requested the alien's presence in the United States shall ensure departure from the United States and so inform the district director in whose jurisdiction the alien has last resided. The district director, if necessary, shall oversee the alien's departure from the United States and, in any event, shall notify the Commissioner of the alien's departure.

(d) Withholding of removal. An alien classified pursuant to section 101(a)(15)(S) of the Act who applies for withholding of removal shall have 10 days from the date the Warrant of Removal is served upon the alien to file an application for such relief with the district director initiating the removal order. The procedures contained in §§ 1208.2 and 1208.16 of this chapter shall apply to such an alien who applies for withholding of removal.

(e) Inadmissibility. An alien who applies for admission under the provisions of section 101(a)(15)(S) of the Act who is determined by an immigration officer not to be eligible for admission under that section or to be inadmissible to the United States under one or more of the grounds of inadmissibility listed in section 212 of the Act and which have not been previously waived by the Commissioner will be taken into custody. The district director having jurisdiction over the port-of-entry shall follow the notification procedures specified in paragraph (c)(1) of this section. A district director who has provided such notice and who has been advised by the Commissioner that the Assistant Attorney General, Criminal Division, has not objected shall remove the alien without further hearing. An alien may not contest such removal, other than by applying for withholding of removal.

HISTORY:

[43 FR 16445, Apr. 19, 1978; 62 FR 10312, 10362, March 6, 1997; 68 FR 9824, 9838, Feb. 28, 2003; 68 FR 10349, 10354, Mar. 5, 2003]

§ 1236.5 Fingerprints and photographs.

[PUBLISHER'S NOTE: 68 FR 10349, 10354, Mar. 5, 2003, purported to substitute "1208.2 and 1208.16" for "208.2 and 208.16" in paragraph (d) of § 1236.5. However this could not implemented, since paragraph (d) did not exist in § 1236.5. It was determined that paragraph (d) of § 1236.4 should instead be amended. For the convenience of the user, the amendment has been implemented according to the apparent intent of the agency. A correction is anticipated.]

Every alien 14 years of age or older against whom proceedings based on deportability under section 237 of the Act are commenced under this part by service of a notice to appear shall be fingerprinted and photographed. Such fingerprints and photographs shall be made available to Federal, State, and local law enforcement agencies upon request to the district director or chief patrol agent having jurisdiction over the alien's record. Any such alien, regardless of his or her age, shall be photographed and/or fingerprinted if required by any immigration officer authorized to issue a notice to appear. Every alien 14 years of age or older who is found to be inadmissible to the United States and ordered removed by an immigration judge shall be fingerprinted, unless during the preceding year he or she has been fingerprinted at an American consular office.

HISTORY:

[42 FR 46045, Sept. 14, 1977. Redesignated at 43 FR 16445, Apr. 19, 1978, and amended at 52 FR 2939, Jan. 29, 1987; 62 FR 10312, 10363, March 6, 1997; 68 FR 9824, 9838, Feb. 28, 2003]

§ 1236.6 Information regarding detainees.

No person, including any state or local government entity or any privately operated detention facility, that houses, maintains, provides services to, or otherwise holds any detainee on behalf of the Service (whether by contract or otherwise), and no other person who by virtue of any official or contractual relationship with such person obtains information relating to any detainee, shall disclose or otherwise permit to be made public the name of, or other information relating to, such detainee. Such information shall be under the control of the Service and shall be subject to public disclosure only pursuant to the provisions of applicable federal laws, regulations and executive orders. Insofar as any documents or other records contain such information, such documents shall not be public records. This section applies to all persons and information identified or described in it, regardless of when such persons obtained such information, and applies to all requests for public disclosure of such information, including requests that are the subject of proceedings pending as of April 17, 2002.

HISTORY:

[67 FR 19508, 19511, Apr. 22, 2002, as confirmed at 68 FR 4364, 4367, Jan. 29, 2003; 68 FR 9824, 9838, Feb. 28, 2003]

§§ 1236.7 — 1236.9 [Reserved]

[NO TEXT IN ORIGINAL]

HISTORY:

[62 FR 10360, Mar. 6, 1997; 68 FR 9824, 9838, Feb. 28, 2003]

AUTHORITY:

(5 U.S.C. 301, 552, 552a; 8 U.S.C. 1103, 1182, 1224, 1225, 1226, 1227, 1231, 1362; 18 U.S.C. 4002, 4013(c)(4); 8 CFR part 2.)

PART 1238

EXPEDITED REMOVAL OF AGGRAVATED FELONS

AUTHORITY NOTE APPLICABLE TO ENTIRE PART:

AUTHORITY:

8 U.S.C. 1228; 8 CFR part 2.

§ 1238.1 Proceedings under section 238(b) of the Act.

(a) Definitions. As used in this part the term:

Deciding Service officer means a district director, chief patrol agent, or another immigration officer designated by a district director, chief patrol agent, the Deputy Executive Associate Commissioner for Detention and Removal, or the Director of the Office of Juvenile Affairs, so long as that person is not the same person as the Issuing Service Officer.

Issuing Service officer means any Service officer listed in § 1239.1 of this chapter as authorized to issue notices to appear.

(b) Preliminary consideration and Notice of Intent to Issue a Final Administrative Deportation Order; commencement of proceedings —

(1) Basis of Service charge. An issuing Service officer shall cause to be served upon an alien a Form I-851, Notice of Intent to Issue a Final Administrative Deportation Order (Notice of Intent), if the officer is satisfied that there is sufficient evidence, based upon questioning of the alien by an immigration officer and upon any other evidence obtained, to support a finding that the individual:

(i) Is an alien;

(ii) Has not been lawfully admitted for permanent residence, or has conditional permanent resident status under section 216 of the Act;

(iii) Has been convicted (as defined in section 101(a)(48) of the Act and as demonstrated by any of the documents or records listed in § 1003.41 of this chapter) of an aggravated felony and such conviction has become final; and

(iv) Is deportable under section 237(a)(2)(A)(iii) of the Act, including an alien who has neither been admitted nor paroled, but who is conclusively presumed deportable under section 237(a)(2)(A)(iii) by operation of section 238(c) of the Act ("Presumption of Deportability").

(2) Notice.

(i) Removal proceedings under section 238(b) of the Act shall commence upon personal service of the Notice of Intent upon the alien, as prescribed by §§ 103.5a(a)(2) and 103.5a(c)(2) of 8 CFR chapter I. The Notice of Intent shall set forth the preliminary determinations and inform the alien of the Service's intent to issue a Form I-851A, Final Administrative Removal Order, without a hearing before an immigration judge. The Notice of Intent shall constitute the charging document. The Notice of Intent shall include allegations of fact and conclusions of law. It shall advise that the alien: has the privilege of being represented, at no expense to the government, by counsel of the alien's choosing, as long as counsel is authorized to practice in removal proceedings; may request withholding of removal to a particular country if he or she fears persecution or torture in that country; may inspect the evidence supporting the Notice of Intent; may rebut the charges within 10 calendar days after service of such Notice (or 13 calendar days if service of the Notice was by mail).

(ii) The Notice of Intent also shall advise the alien that he or she may designate in writing, within the rebuttal period, the country to which he or she chooses to be deported in accordance with section 241 of the Act, in the event that a Final Administrative Removal Order is issued, and that the Service will honor such designation only to the extent permitted under the terms, limitations, and conditions of section 241 of the Act.

(iii) The Service must determine that the person served with the Notice of Intent is the person named on the notice.

(iv) The Service shall provide the alien with a list of available free legal services programs qualified under 8 CFR part 1003 and organizations recognized pursuant to 8 CFR part 1292, located within the district or sector where the Notice of Intent is issued.

(v) The Service must either provide the alien with a written translation of the Notice of Intent or explain the contents of the Notice of Intent to the alien in the alien's native language or in a language that the alien understands.

(c) Alien's response —

(1) Time for response. The alien will have 10 calendar days from service of the Notice of Intent or 13 calendar days if service is by mail, to file a response to the Notice of Intent. In the response, the alien may: designate his or her choice of country for removal; submit a written response rebutting the allegations supporting the charge and/or requesting the opportunity to review the Government's evidence; and/or submit a statement indicating an intention to request withholding of removal under 8 CFR 1208.16 of this chapter, and/or request in writing an extension of time for response, stating the specific reasons why such an extension is necessary.

(2) Nature of rebuttal or request to review evidence.

(i) If an alien chooses to rebut the allegations contained in the Notice of Intent, the alien's written response must indicate which finding(s) are being challenged and should be accompanied by affidavit(s), documentary information, or other specific evidence supporting the challenge.

(ii) If an alien's written response requests the opportunity to review the Government's evidence, the Service shall serve the alien with a copy of the evidence in the record of proceeding upon which the Service is relying to support the charge. The alien may, within 10 calendar days following service of the Government's evidence (13 calendar days if service is by mail), furnish a final response in accordance with paragraph (c)(1) of this section. If the alien's final response is a rebuttal of the allegations, such a final response should be accompanied by affidavit(s), documentary information, or other specific evidence supporting the challenge.

(d) Determination by deciding Service officer —

(1) No response submitted or concession of deportability. If the deciding Service officer does not receive a timely response and the evidence in the record of proceeding establishes deportability by clear, convincing, and unequivocal evidence, or if the alien concedes deportability, then the deciding Service officer shall issue and cause to be served upon the alien a Final Administrative Removal Order that states the reasons for the deportation decision. The alien may, in writing, waive the 14-day waiting period before execution of the final order of removal provided in a paragraph (f) of this section.

(2) Response submitted —

(i) Insufficient rebuttal; no genuine issue of material fact. If the alien timely submits a rebuttal to the allegations, but the deciding Service officer finds that deportability is established by clear, convincing, and unequivocal evidence in the record of proceeding, the deciding Service officer shall issue and cause to be served upon the alien a Final Administrative Removal Order that states the reasons for the decision of deportability.

(ii) Additional evidence required.

(A) If the deciding Service officer finds that the record of proceeding, including the alien's timely rebuttal, raises a genuine issue of material fact regarding the preliminary findings, the deciding Service officer may either obtain additional evidence from any source, including the alien, or cause to be issued a notice to appear to initiate removal proceedings under section 240 of the Act. The deciding Service officer may also obtain additional evidence from any source, including the alien, if the deciding Service officer deems that such additional evidence may aid the officer in the rendering of a decision.

(B) If the deciding Service officer considers additional evidence from a source other than the alien, that evidence shall be made a part of the record of proceeding, and shall be provided to the alien. If the alien elects to submit a response to such additional evidence, such response must be filed with the Service within 10 calendar days of service of the additional evidence (or 13 calendar days if service is by mail). If the deciding Service officer finds, after considering all additional evidence, that deportability is established by clear, convincing, and unequivocal evidence in the record of proceeding, the deciding Service officer shall issue and cause to be served upon the alien a Final Administrative Removal Order that states the reasons for the decision of deportability.

(iii) Conversion to proceedings under section 240 of the Act. If the deciding Service officer finds that the alien is not amenable to removal under section 238 of the Act, the deciding Service officer shall terminate the expedited proceedings under section 238 of the Act and shall, where appropriate, cause to be issued a notice to appear for the purpose of initiating removal proceedings before an immigration judge under section 240 of the Act.

(3) Termination of proceedings by deciding Service officer. Only the deciding Service officer may terminate proceedings under section 238 of the Act, in accordance with this section.

(e) Proceedings commenced under section 240 of the Act. In any proceeding commenced under section 240 of the Act which is based on deportability under section 237 of the Act, if it appears that the respondent alien is subject to removal pursuant to section 238 of the Act, the immigration judge may, upon the Service's request, terminate the case and, upon such termination, the Service may commence administrative proceedings under section 238 of the Act. However, in the absence of any such request, the immigration judge shall complete the proceeding commenced under section 240 of the Act.

(f) Executing final removal order of deciding Service officer —

(1) Time of execution. Upon the issuance of a Final Administrative Removal Order, the Service shall issue a Warrant of Removal in accordance with § 1241.2 of this chapter; such warrant shall be executed no sooner

than 14 calendar days after the date the Final Administrative Removal Order is issued, unless the alien knowingly, voluntarily, and in writing waives the 14-day period.

(2) Country to which alien is to be removed. The deciding Service officer shall designate the country of removal in the manner prescribed by section 241 of the Act.

(3) Withholding of removal. If the alien has requested withholding of removal under § 1208.16 of this chapter, the deciding officer shall, upon issuance of a Final Administrative Removal Order, immediately refer the alien's case to an asylum officer to conduct a reasonable fear determination in accordance with § 1208.31 of this chapter.

(g) Arrest and detention. At the time of issuance of a Notice of Intent or at any time thereafter and up to the time the alien becomes the subject of a Warrant of Removal, the alien may be arrested and taken into custody under the authority of a Warrant of Arrest issued by an officer listed in § 287.5(e)(2) of 8 CFR chapter I. The decision of the Service concerning custody or bond shall not be administratively appealable during proceedings initiated under section 238 of the Act and this part.

(h) Record of proceeding. The Service shall maintain a record of proceeding for judicial review of the Final Administrative Removal Order sought by any petition for review. The record of proceeding shall include, but not necessarily be limited to: the charging document (Notice of Intent); the Final Administrative Removal Order (including any supplemental memorandum of decision); the alien's response, if any; all evidence in support of the charge; and any admissible evidence, briefs, or documents submitted by either party respecting deportability. The executed duplicate of the Notice of Intent in the record of proceedings shall be retained as evidence that the individual upon whom the notice for the proceeding was served was, in fact, the alien named in the notice.

HISTORY:

[62 FR 10312, 10365, Mar. 6, 1997; 64 FR 8478, 8494, Feb. 19, 1999; 67 FR 39255, 39258, June 7, 2002; 68 FR 9824, 9838, Feb. 28, 2003; 68 FR 10349, 10355, Mar. 5, 2003]

PART 1239

INITIATION OF REMOVAL PROCEEDINGS

Rule

AUTHORITY NOTE APPLICABLE TO ENTIRE PART:

AUTHORITY:

8 U.S.C. 1103, 1221, 1229.

§ 1239.1 Notice to appear.

(a) Commencement. Every removal proceeding conducted under section 240 of the Act (8 U.S.C. 1229a) to determine the deportability or inadmissibility of an alien is commenced by the filing of a notice to appear with the immigration court. For provisions relating to the issuance of a notice to appear by an immigration officer, or supervisor thereof, see 8 CFR 239.1(a).

(b) Service of notice to appear. Service of the notice to appear shall be in accordance with section 239 of the Act.

HISTORY:

[62 FR 10312, 10366, Mar. 6, 1997; 67 FR 39255, 39258, June 7, 2002; 68 FR 9824, 9838, Feb. 28, 2003; 69 FR 44903, 44907, July 28, 2004]

§ 1239.2 Cancellation of notice to appear.

(a) Prior to commencement of proceedings. For provisions relating to the authority of an immigration officer to cancel a notice to appear prior to the vesting of jurisdiction with the immigration judge, see 8 CFR 239.2(a) and (b).

(b) Ordering termination or dismissal. After commencement of proceedings, an immigration judge or Board member shall have authority to resolve or dispose of a case through an order of dismissal or an order of termination. An immigration judge or Board member may enter an order of dismissal in cases where DHS moves for dismissal pursuant to paragraph (c) of this section. A motion to dismiss removal proceedings for a reason other than those authorized by paragraph (c) of this section shall be deemed a motion to terminate and adjudicated pursuant to 8 CFR 1003.1(m), pertaining to cases before the Board, or 8 CFR 1003.18(d), pertaining to cases before the immigration court, as applicable.

(c) Motion to dismiss. After commencement of proceedings pursuant to 8 CFR 1003.14, government counsel or an officer enumerated in 8 CFR 239.1(a) may move for dismissal of the matter on the grounds set out under 8 CFR 239.2(a). Dismissal of the matter shall be without prejudice to the alien or the Department of Homeland Security.

(d) Motion for remand. After commencement of the hearing, government counsel or an officer enumerated in 8 CFR 239.1(a) may move for remand of the matter to the Department of Homeland Security on the ground that the foreign relations of the United States are involved and require further consideration. Remand of the matter shall be without prejudice to the alien or the Department of Homeland Security.

(e) Warrant of arrest. When a notice to appear is canceled or proceedings are terminated under this section any outstanding warrant of arrest is canceled.

(f) [Reserved.]

HISTORY:

[62 FR 10312, 10367, March 6, 1997; 68 FR 9824, 9838, 9846, Feb. 28, 2003; 68 FR 10349, 10355, Mar. 5, 2003; 69 FR 44903, 44907, July 28, 2004; 89 FR 46742, 46794, May 29, 2024]

§ 1239.3 Effect of filing notice to appear.

The filing of a notice to appear shall have no effect in determining periods of unlawful presence as defined in section 212(a)(9)(B) of the Act.

HISTORY:

[62 FR 10312, 10367, March 6, 1997; 68 FR 9824, 9838, Feb. 28, 2003]

PART 1240

PROCEEDINGS TO DETERMINE REMOVABILITY OF NONCITIZENS IN THE UNITED STATES

AUTHORITY NOTE APPLICABLE TO ENTIRE PART:

AUTHORITY:

8 U.S.C. 1103, 1158, 1182, 1186a, 1186b, 1225, 1226, 1227, 1228, 1229a, 1229b, 1229c, 1252 note, 1361, 1362; secs. 202 and 203, Pub. L. 105-100 (111 Stat. 2160, 2193); sec. 902, Pub. L. 105-277 (112 Stat. 2681).

Subpart A

Removal Proceedings

§ 1240.1 Immigration judges.

(a) Authority.

(1) In any removal proceeding pursuant to section 240 of the Act, the immigration judge shall have the authority to:

(i) Determine removability pursuant to section 240(a)(1) of the Act; to make decisions, including orders of removal as provided by section 240(c)(1)(A) of the Act;

(ii) To determine applications under sections 208, 212(a)(2)(F), 212(a)(6)(F)(ii), 212(a)(9)(B)(v), 212(d)(11), 212(d)(12), 212(g), 212(h), 212(i), 212(k), 237(a)(1)(E)(iii), 237(a)(1)(H), 237(a)(3)(C)(ii), 240A(a) and (b), 240B, 245, and 249 of the Act, section 202 of Pub. L. 105-100, section 902 of Pub. L. 105-277, and former section 212(c) of the Act (as it existed prior to April 1, 1997);

(iii) To order withholding of removal pursuant to section 241(b)(3) of the Act and pursuant to the Convention Against Torture; and

(iv) To take any other action consistent with applicable law and regulations as may be appropriate.

(2) An immigration judge may certify his or her decision in any case under section 240 of the Act to the Board of Immigration Appeals when it involves an unusually complex or novel question of law or fact. Nothing contained in this part shall be construed to diminish the authority conferred on immigration judges under sections 101(b)(4) and 103 of the Act.

(b) Withdrawal and substitution of immigration judges. The immigration judge assigned to conduct the hearing shall at any time withdraw if he or she deems himself or herself disqualified. If an immigration judge becomes unavailable to complete his or her duties, another immigration judge may be assigned to complete the case. The new immigration judge shall familiarize himself or herself with the record in the case and shall state for the record that he or she has done so.

(c) Conduct of hearing. The immigration judge shall receive and consider material and relevant evidence, rule upon objections, and otherwise regulate the course of the hearing.

(d) Withdrawal of application for admission. An immigration judge may allow only an arriving alien to withdraw an application for admission. Once the issue of inadmissibility has been resolved, permission to withdraw an application for admission should ordinarily be granted only with the concurrence of the Service. An immigration judge shall not allow an alien to withdraw an application for admission unless the alien, in addition to demonstrating that he or she possesses both the intent and the means to depart immediately from the United States, establishes that factors directly relating to the issue of inadmissibility indicate that the granting of the withdrawal would be in the interest of justice. During the pendency of an appeal from the order of removal, permission to withdraw an application for admission must be obtained from the immigration judge or the Board.

HISTORY:

[62 FR 10312, 10367, Mar. 6, 1997; 62 FR 15362, 15363, Apr. 1, 1997; 63 FR 27823, 27829, May 21, 1998, as confirmed at 65 FR 15846, 15854, Mar. 24, 2000; 64 FR 8478, 8495, Feb. 19, 1999; 64 FR 25756, 25766, May 12, 1999, as confirmed at 65 FR 15835, 15844, Mar. 24, 2000; redesignated at 68 FR 9824, 9838, Feb. 28, 2003; 69 FR 57826, 57835, Sept. 28, 2004; 72 FR 53673, 53678, Sept. 20, 2007]

§ 1240.2 DHS Counsel.

(a) Authority. DHS counsel shall present on behalf of the government evidence material to the issues of deportability or inadmissibility and any other issues that may require disposition by the immigration judge. The duties of the DHS counsel include, but are not limited to, the presentation of evidence and the interrogation, examination, and cross-examination of the respondent or other witnesses. Nothing contained in this subpart diminishes the authority of an immigration judge to conduct proceedings under this part. The DHS counsel is authorized to appeal from a decision of the immigration judge pursuant to § 1003.38 of this chapter and to move for reopening or reconsideration pursuant to § 1003.23 of this chapter.

(b) Assignment. In a removal proceeding, DHS shall assign an attorney to each case within the provisions of § 1240.10(d), and to each case in which an unrepresented respondent is incompetent or is under 18 years of age, and is not accompanied by a guardian, relative, or friend. In a case in which the removal proceeding would result in an order of removal, DHS shall assign an attorney to each case in which a respondent's nationality is in issue. A DHS counsel shall be assigned in every case in which the Commissioner approves the submission of non-record information under § 1240.11(a)(3). In his or her discretion, whenever he or she deems such assignment necessary or advantageous, the General Counsel may assign a DHS counsel to any other case at any stage of the proceeding.

HISTORY:

[62 FR 10312, 10368, March 6, 1997; redesignated at 68 FR 9824, 9838, 9846, Feb. 28, 2003; 68 FR 10349, 10355, Mar. 5, 2003; 86 FR 70708, 70724, Dec. 13, 2021]

§ 1240.3 Representation by counsel.

The respondent may be represented at the hearing by an attorney or other representative qualified under 8 CFR part 1292.

HISTORY:

[62 FR 10312, 10368, March 6, 1997; redesignated at 68 FR 9824, 9838, Feb. 28, 2003; 68 FR 10349, 10355, Mar. 5, 2003]

§ 1240.4 Incompetent respondents.

When it is impracticable for the respondent to be present at the hearing because of mental incompetency, the attorney, legal representative, legal guardian, near relative, or friend who was served with a copy of the notice to appear shall be permitted to appear on behalf of the respondent. If such a person cannot reasonably be found or fails or refuses to appear, the custodian of the respondent shall be requested to appear on behalf of the respondent.

HISTORY:

[62 FR 10312, 10368, March 6, 1997; redesignated at 68 FR 9824, 9838, Feb. 28, 2003]

§ 1240.5 Interpreter.

Any person acting as an interpreter in a hearing before an immigration judge under this part shall be sworn to interpret and translate accurately, unless the interpreter is an employee of the United States Government, in which event no such oath shall be required.

HISTORY:

[62 FR 10312, 10368, March 6, 1997; redesignated at 68 FR 9824, 9838, Feb. 28, 2003]

§ 1240.6 Postponement and adjournment of hearing.

After the commencement of the hearing, the immigration judge may grant a reasonable adjournment either at his or her own instance or, for good cause shown, upon application by the respondent or the Department of Homeland Security, provided that nothing in this section shall authorize an adjournment that causes the adjudication of an asylum application to exceed 180 days in the absence of exceptional circumstances, consistent with section 208(d)(5)(A)(iii) of the Act and § 1003.10(b) of this chapter.

HISTORY:

[62 FR 10312, 10368, March 6, 1997; redesignated at 68 FR 9824, 9838, Feb. 28, 2003; 85 FR 81698, 81751, Dec. 16, 2020]

§ 1240.7 Evidence in removal proceedings under section 240 of the Act.

(a) Use of prior statements. The immigration judge may receive in evidence any oral or written statement that is material and relevant to any issue in the case previously made by the respondent or any other person during any investigation, examination, hearing, or trial.

(b) Testimony. Testimony of witnesses appearing at the hearing shall be under oath or affirmation administered by the immigration judge.

(c) Depositions. The immigration judge may order the taking of depositions pursuant to § 1003.35 of this chapter.

HISTORY:

[62 FR 10312, 10368, March 6, 1997; redesignated at 68 FR 9824, 9838, Feb. 28, 2003; 68 FR 10349, 10355, Mar. 5, 2003]

§ 1240.8 Burdens of proof in removal proceedings.

(a) Deportable aliens. A respondent charged with deportability shall be found to be removable if the Service proves by clear and convincing evidence that the respondent is deportable as charged.

(b) Arriving aliens. In proceedings commenced upon a respondent's arrival in the Untied States or after the revocation or expiration of parole, the respondent must prove that he or she is clearly and beyond a doubt entitled to be admitted to the United States and is not inadmissible as charged.

(c) Aliens present in the United States without being admitted or paroled. In the case of a respondent charged as being in the United States without being admitted or paroled, the Service must first establish the alienage of the respondent. Once alienage has been established, unless the respondent demonstrates by clear and convincing evidence that he or she is lawfully in the United States pursuant to a prior admission, the respondent must prove that he or she is clearly and beyond a doubt entitled to be admitted to the United States and is not inadmissible as charged.

(d) Relief from removal. The respondent shall have the burden of establishing that he or she is eligible for any requested benefit or privilege and that it should be granted in the exercise of discretion. If the evidence indicates that one or more of the grounds for mandatory denial of the application for relief may apply, the alien shall have the burden of proving by a preponderance of the evidence that such grounds do not apply.

HISTORY:

[62 FR 10312, 10368, March 6, 1997; redesignated at 68 FR 9824, 9838, Feb. 28, 2003]

§ 1240.9 Contents of record.

The hearing before the immigration judge, including the testimony, exhibits, applications, proffers, and requests, the immigration judge's decision, and all written orders, motions, appeals, briefs, and other papers filed in the proceedings shall constitute the record in the case. The hearing shall be recorded verbatim except for statements made off the record with the permission of the immigration judge. In his or her discretion, the immigration judge may exclude from the record any arguments made in connection with motions, applications, requests, or objections, but in such event the person affected may submit a brief.

HISTORY:

[62 FR 10312, 10368, March 6, 1997; redesignated at 68 FR 9824, 9838, Feb. 28, 2003]

§ 1240.10 Hearing.

(a) Opening. In a removal proceeding, the immigration judge shall:

(1) Advise the respondent of his or her right to representation, at no expense to the government, by counsel of his or her own choice authorized to practice in the proceedings and require the respondent to state then and there whether he or she desires representation;

(2) Advise the respondent of the availability of pro bono legal services for the immigration court location at which the hearing will take place, and ascertain that the respondent has received a list of such pro bono legal service providers.

(3) Ascertain that the respondent has received a copy of appeal rights.

(4) Advise the respondent that he or she will have a reasonable opportunity to examine and object to the evidence against him or her, to present evidence in his or her own behalf and to cross-examine witnesses presented by the government (but the respondent shall not be entitled to examine such national security information as the government may proffer in opposition to the respondent's admission to the United States or to

an application by the respondent for discretionary relief);

(5) Place the respondent under oath;

(6) Read the factual allegations and the charges in the notice to appear to the respondent and explain them in non-technical language; and

(7) Enter the notice to appear as an exhibit in the Record of Proceeding.

(b) Public access to hearings. Removal hearings shall be open to the public, except that the immigration judge may, in his or her discretion, close proceedings as provided in § 1003.27 of this chapter.

(c) Pleading by respondent. The immigration judge shall require the respondent to plead to the notice to appear by stating whether he or she admits or denies the factual allegations and his or her removability under the charges contained therein. If the respondent admits the factual allegations and admits his or her removability under the charges and the immigration judge is satisfied that no issues of law or fact remain, the immigration judge may determine that removability as charged has been established by the admissions of the respondent. The immigration judge shall not accept an admission of removability from an unrepresented respondent who is incompetent or under the age of 18 and is not accompanied by an attorney or legal representative, a near relative, legal guardian, or friend; nor from an officer of an institution in which a respondent is an inmate or patient. When, pursuant to this paragraph, the immigration judge does not accept an admission of removability, he or she shall direct a hearing on the issues.

(d) Issues of removability. When removability is not determined under the provisions of paragraph (c) of this section, the immigration judge shall request the assignment of DHS counsel, and shall receive evidence as to any unresolved issues, except that no further evidence need be received as to any facts admitted during the pleading. The alien shall provide a court certified copy of a Judicial Recommendation Against Deportation (JRAD) to the immigration judge when such recommendation will be the basis of denying any charge(s) brought by DHS in the proceedings against the alien. No JRAD is effective against a charge of deportability under former section 241(a)(11) of the Act or if the JRAD was granted on or after November 29, 1990.

(e) Additional charges in removal hearings. At any time during the proceeding, additional or substituted charges of inadmissibility and/or deportability and/or factual allegations may be lodged by DHS in writing. The alien in removal proceedings shall be served with a copy of these additional charges and allegations. The immigration judge shall read the additional factual allegations and charges to the alien and explain them to him or her. The immigration judge shall advise the alien, if he or she is not represented by counsel, that the alien may be so represented, and that he or she may be given a reasonable continuance to respond to the additional factual allegations and charges. Thereafter, the provision of § 1240.6(b) relating to pleading shall apply to the additional factual allegations and charges.

(f) Country of removal. With respect to an arriving alien covered by section 241(b)(1) of the Act, the country, or countries in the alternative, to which the alien may be removed will be determined pursuant to section 241(b)(1) of the Act. In any other case, the immigration judge shall notify the respondent that if he or she is finally ordered removed, the country of removal will in the first instance be the country designated by the respondent, except as otherwise provided under section 241(b)(2) of the Act, and shall afford him or her an opportunity then and there to make such designation. The immigration judge shall also identify for the record a country, or countries in the alternative, to which the alien's removal may be made pursuant to section 241(b)(2) of the Act if the country of the alien's designation will not accept him or her into its territory, or fails to furnish timely notice of acceptance, or if the alien declines to designate a country. In considering alternative countries of removal, acceptance or the existence of a functioning government is not required with respect to an alternative country described in section 241(b)(1)(C)(i)-(iii) of the Act or a removal country described in section 241(b)(2)(E)(i)-(iv) of the Act. See 8 CFR 241.15.

HISTORY:

[62 FR 10312, 10369, March 6, 1997; redesignated and amended at 68 FR 9824, 9838, 9846, Feb. 28, 2003; 68 FR 10349, 10355, Mar. 5, 2003; 70 FR 661, 674, Jan. 5, 2005; 80 FR 59503, 59513, Oct. 1, 2015; 86 FR 70708, 70724, Dec. 13, 2021]

§ 1240.11 Ancillary matters, applications.

(a) Creation of the status of an alien lawfully admitted for permanent residence.

(1) In a removal proceeding, an alien may apply to the immigration judge for cancellation of removal under section 240A of the Act, adjustment of status under section 245 of the Act, adjustment of status under section 1 of the Act of November 2, 1966 (as modified by section 606 of Pub. L. 104-208), section 101 or 104 of the Act of October 28, 1977, section 202 of Pub. L. 105-100, or section 902 of Pub. L. 105-277, or for the creation of a record of lawful admission for permanent residence under section 249 of the Act. The application shall be subject to the requirements of § 1240.20, and 8 CFR parts 1245 and 1249. The approval of any application made to the immigration judge under section 245 of the Act by an alien spouse (as defined in section 216(g)(1) of the Act) or by an alien entrepreneur (as defined in section 216A(f)(1) of the Act) shall result in the alien's obtaining the status of lawful permanent resident on a conditional basis in accordance with the provisions of section 216 or 216A of the Act, whichever is applicable. However, the Petition to Remove the Conditions on Residence required by section 216(c) of the Act, or the Petition by Entrepreneur to Remove Conditions required by section 216A(c) of the Act shall be made to the director in accordance with 8 CFR part 1216.

(2) In conjunction with any application for creation of status of an alien lawfully admitted for permanent residence made to an immigration judge, if the alien is inadmissible under any provision of section 212(a) of

the Act, and believes that he or she meets the eligibility requirements for a waiver of the ground of inadmissibility, he or she may apply to the immigration judge for such waiver. The immigration judge shall inform the alien of his or her apparent eligibility to apply for any of the benefits enumerated in this chapter and shall afford the alien an opportunity to make application during the hearing, in accordance with the provisions of § 1240.8(d). In a relevant case, the immigration judge may adjudicate the sufficiency of an Affidavit of Support Under Section 213A (Form I-864), executed on behalf of an applicant for admission or for adjustment of status, in accordance with the provisions of section 213A of the Act and 8 CFR part 213a.

(3) In exercising discretionary power when considering an application for status as a permanent resident under this chapter, the immigration judge may consider and base the decision on information not contained in the record and not made available for inspection by the alien, provided the Commissioner has determined that such information is relevant and is classified under the applicable Executive Order as requiring protection from unauthorized disclosure in the interest of national security. Whenever the immigration judge believes that he or she can do so while safeguarding both the information and its source, the immigration judge should inform the alien of the general nature of the information in order that the alien may have an opportunity to offer opposing evidence. A decision based in whole or in part on such classified information shall state that the information is material to the decision.

(b) Voluntary departure. The alien may apply to the immigration judge for voluntary departure in lieu of removal pursuant to section 240B of the Act and subpart C of this part. The immigration judge shall advise the alien of the consequences of filing a post-decision motion to reopen or reconsider prior to the expiration of the time specified by the immigration judge for the alien to depart voluntarily.

(c) Applications for asylum and withholding of removal.

(1) If the alien expresses fear of persecution or harm upon return to any of the countries to which the alien might be removed pursuant to § 1240.10(f), and the alien has not previously filed an application for asylum or withholding of removal that has been referred to the immigration judge by an asylum officer in accordance with § 1208.14 of this chapter, the immigration judge shall:

(i) Advise the alien that he or she may apply for asylum in the United States or withholding of removal to those countries;

(ii) Make available the appropriate application forms; and

(iii) Advise the alien of the privilege of being represented by counsel at no expense to the government and of the consequences, pursuant to section 208(d)(6) of the Act, of knowingly filing a frivolous application for asylum. The immigration judge shall provide to the alien a list of persons who have indicated their availability to represent aliens in asylum proceedings on a pro bono basis.

(2) An application for asylum or withholding of removal must be filed with the Immigration Court, pursuant to § 1208.4(b) of this chapter. Upon receipt of an application, the Immigration Court may forward a copy to the Department of State pursuant to § 1208.11 of this chapter and shall calendar the case for a hearing. The reply, if any, from the Department of State, unless classified under an applicable Executive Order, shall be given to both the alien and to DHS counsel and shall be included in the record.

(3) Applications for asylum and withholding of removal so filed will be decided by the immigration judge pursuant to the requirements and standards established in 8 CFR part 1208 of this chapter after an evidentiary hearing to resolve factual issues in dispute. An evidentiary hearing extending beyond issues related to the basis for a mandatory denial of the application pursuant to § 1208.14 or § 1208.16 of this chapter is not necessary once the immigration judge has determined that such a denial is required.

(i) Evidentiary hearings on applications for asylum or withholding of removal will be open to the public unless the alien expressly requests that the hearing be closed pursuant to § 3.27 of this chapter. The immigration judge shall inquire whether the alien requests such closure.

(ii) Nothing in this section is intended to limit the authority of the immigration judge to properly control the scope of any evidentiary hearing.

(iii) During the removal hearing, the alien shall be examined under oath on his or her application and may present evidence and witnesses in his or her own behalf. The alien has the burden of establishing that he or she is a refugee as defined in section 101(a)(42) of the Act pursuant to the standards set forth in § 1208.13 of this chapter.

(iv) DHS counsel may call witnesses and present evidence for the record, including information classified under the applicable Executive Order, provided the immigration judge or the Board has determined that such information is relevant to the hearing. When the immigration judge receives such classified information, he or she shall inform the alien. The agency that provides the classified information to the immigration judge may provide an unclassified summary of the information for release to the alien, whenever it determines it can do so consistently with safeguarding both the classified nature of the information and its sources. The summary should be as detailed as possible, in order that the alien may have an opportunity to offer opposing evidence. A decision based in whole or in part on such classified information shall state whether such information is material to the decision.

(4) The decision of an immigration judge to grant or deny asylum or withholding of removal shall be communicated to the alien and to the DHS counsel. An adverse decision shall state why asylum or withholding of removal was denied.

(d) Application for relief under sections 237(a)(1)(H) and 237(a)(1)(E)(iii) of the Act. The respondent may apply to the immigration judge for relief from removal under sections 237(a)(1)(H) and 237(a)(1)(E)(iii) of the Act.

(e) General. An application under this section shall be made only during the hearing and shall not be held to constitute a concession of alienage or deportability in any case in which the respondent does not admit his or her alienage or deportability. However, nothing in this section shall prohibit DHS from using information supplied in an application for asylum or withholding of deportation or removal submitted to DHS on or after January 4, 1995, as the basis for issuance of a charging document or to establish alienage or deportability in a case referred to an immigration judge under § 1208.14(b) of this chapter. The alien shall have the burden of establishing that he or she is eligible for any requested benefit or privilege and that it should be granted in the exercise of discretion. Nothing contained in this section is intended to foreclose the respondent from applying for any benefit or privilege that he or she believes himself or herself eligible to receive in proceedings under this part. Nothing in this section is intended to limit the Attorney General's authority to remove an alien to any country permitted by section 241(b) of the Act.

(f) Fees. The alien shall not be required to pay a fee on more than one application within paragraphs (a) and (c) of this section, provided that the minimum fee imposed when more than one application is made shall be determined by the cost of the application with the highest fee. When a motion to reopen or reconsider is made concurrently with an application for relief seeking one of the immigration benefits set forth in paragraphs (a) and (c) of this section, only the fee set forth in § 1103.7(b)(1) of this chapter for the motion must accompany the motion and application for relief. If such a motion is granted, the appropriate fee for the application for relief, if any, set forth in § 1103.7(b)(4) of this chapter, must be paid within the time specified in order to complete the application.

(g) U.S.-Canada safe third country agreement, which includes the Additional Protocol of 2022.

(1) The immigration judge has authority to apply section 208(a)(2)(A) of the Act, relating to a determination that an alien may be removed to Canada pursuant to the 2002 U.S.-Canada Agreement ("Agreement"), in the case of an alien who is subject to the terms of the Agreement, which includes the Additional Protocol of 2022, and is placed in proceedings pursuant to section 240 of the Act. In an appropriate case, the immigration judge shall determine whether under that Agreement, which includes the Additional Protocol of 2022, the alien should be returned to Canada, or whether the alien should be permitted to pursue asylum or other protection in the United States.

(2) An alien described in paragraph (g)(1) of this section is ineligible to apply for asylum, pursuant to section 208(a)(2)(A) of the Act, unless the immigration judge determines, by preponderance of the evidence, that:

(i) The Agreement, which includes the Additional Protocol of 2022, does not apply to the alien or does not preclude the alien from applying for asylum in the United States; or

(ii) The alien qualifies for an exception to the Agreement, which includes the Additional Protocol of 2022, as set forth in paragraph (g)(3) of this section.

(3) The immigration judge shall apply the applicable regulations in deciding whether the alien qualifies for any exception under the Agreement, which includes the Additional Protocol of 2022, that would permit the United States to exercise authority over the alien's asylum claim. The exceptions under the Agreement, which includes the Additional Protocol of 2022, are codified at 8 CFR 208.30(e)(6)(iii). The immigration judge shall not review, consider, or decide any issues pertaining to any discretionary determination on whether the alien should be permitted to pursue an asylum claim in the United States notwithstanding the general terms of the Agreement, which includes the Additional Protocol of 2022, as such discretionary public interest determinations are reserved to DHS. However, an alien in removal proceedings who is otherwise ineligible to apply for asylum under the Agreement, which includes the Additional Protocol of 2022, may apply for asylum if DHS files a written notice in the proceedings before the immigration judge that it has decided in the public interest to allow the alien to pursue claims for asylum or withholding of removal.

(4) An alien who is found to be ineligible to apply for asylum under section 208(a)(2)(A) of the Act is ineligible to apply for withholding of removal pursuant to section 241(b)(3) of the Act and the Convention Against Torture. However, the alien may apply for any other relief from removal for which the alien may be eligible. If an alien who is subject to the Agreement, which includes the Additional Protocol of 2022, and section 208(a)(2)(A) of the Act is ordered removed, the alien shall be ordered removed to Canada, in which the alien will be able to pursue his or her claims for asylum or protection against persecution or torture under the laws of Canada

(h) Other asylum cooperative agreements.

(1) The immigration judge has authority to apply section 208(a)(2)(A) of the Act, relating to a determination that an alien may be removed to a third country pursuant to a bilateral or multilateral agreement—other than the 2002 U.S.-Canada Agreement, which includes the Additional Protocol of 2022—in the case of an alien who is subject to the terms of the relevant agreement and is placed in proceedings pursuant to section 240 of the Act. In an appropriate case, the immigration judge shall determine whether under the relevant agreement the alien should be removed to the third country, or whether the alien should be permitted to pursue asylum or other protection claims in the United States. If more than one agreement applies to the alien and the alien is ordered removed, the immigration judge shall enter alternate orders of removal to each relevant country.

(2) An alien described in paragraph (h)(1) of this section is ineligible to apply for asylum pursuant to section 208(a)(2)(A) of the Act, or for withholding of removal or CAT protection in the United States, unless

the immigration judge determines, by a preponderance of the evidence, that:

(i) The relevant agreement does not apply to the alien or does not preclude the alien from applying for asylum in the United States;

(ii) The alien qualifies for an exception to the relevant agreement as set forth in paragraph (h)(3) of this section and the Federal Register document specifying the exceptions particular to the relevant agreement; or

(iii) The alien has demonstrated that it is more likely than not that he or she would be persecuted on account of a protected ground or tortured in the third country.

(3) The immigration judge shall apply the applicable regulations in deciding whether an alien described in paragraph (h)(1) of this section qualifies for an exception under the relevant agreement that would permit the United States to exercise authority over the alien's asylum claim. The exceptions for agreements with countries other than Canada are further explained by the applicable published Federal Register document setting out each Agreement and its exceptions. The immigration judge shall not review, consider, or decide any issues pertaining to any discretionary determination on whether an alien described in paragraph (h)(1) of this section should be allowed to pursue an application for asylum in the United States notwithstanding the general terms of an agreement, as section 208(a)(2)(A) of the Act reserves to the Secretary or his delegates the determination whether it is in the public interest for the alien to receive asylum in the United States. However, an alien in removal proceedings who is otherwise ineligible to apply for asylum under an agreement may apply for asylum if DHS files a written notice in the proceedings before the immigration judge that DHS has decided in the public interest that the alien may pursue an application for asylum or withholding of removal in the United States.

(4) If the immigration judge determines that an alien described in paragraph (h)(1) of this section is subject to the terms of agreements formed pursuant to section 208(a)(2)(A) of the Act, and that the alien has failed to demonstrate that it is more likely than not that the alien would be persecuted on account of a protected ground or tortured in those third countries, then the alien is ineligible to apply for withholding of removal pursuant to section 241(b)(3) of the Act and the Convention Against Torture notwithstanding any other provision in this chapter. However, the alien may apply for any other relief from removal for which the alien may be eligible. If an alien who is subject to section 208(a)(2)(A) of the Act is ordered removed, the alien shall be ordered removed to the relevant third country in which the alien will be able to pursue his or her claims for asylum or protection against persecution or torture under the laws of that country.

HISTORY:

[62 FR 10312, 10369, Mar. 6, 1997; 62 FR 45148, 45150, Aug. 26, 1997; 63 FR 27823, 27829, May 21, 1998, as confirmed at 65 FR 15846, 15854, Mar. 24, 2000; 64 FR 25756, 25766, May 12, 1999, as confirmed at 65 FR 15835, 15844, Mar. 24, 2000; redesignated and amended at 68 FR 9824, 9838, 9846, Feb. 28, 2003; 68 FR 10349, 10355, Mar. 5, 2003; 69 FR 69490, 69497, Nov. 29, 2004; 71 FR 35732, 35757, June 21, 2006; 73 FR 76927, 76937, Dec. 18, 2008; 78 FR 19077, 19080, Mar. 29, 2013; 84 FR 63994, 64010, Nov. 19, 2019; 85 FR 82750, 82794, Dec. 18, 2020; 86 FR 70708, 70724, Dec. 13, 2021; 88 FR 18227, 18240, Mar. 28, 2023]

§ 1240.12 Decision of the immigration judge.

(a) Contents. The decision of the immigration judge may be oral or written. The decision of the immigration judge shall include a finding as to inadmissibility or deportability. The formal enumeration of findings is not required. The decision shall also contain reasons for granting or denying the request. The decision shall be concluded with the order of the immigration judge.

(b) Summary decision. Notwithstanding the provisions of paragraph (a) of this section, in any case where inadmissibility or deportability is determined on the pleadings pursuant to § 1240.10(b) and the respondent does not make an application under § 1240.11, the alien is statutorily ineligible for relief, or the respondent applies for voluntary departure only and the immigration judge grants the application, the immigration judge may enter a summary decision or, if voluntary departure is granted, a summary decision with an alternate order of removal.

(c) Order of the immigration judge. The order of the immigration judge shall direct the respondent's removal from the United States, or the termination of the proceedings, or other such disposition of the case as may be appropriate. The immigration judge is authorized to issue orders in the alternative or in combination as he or she may deem necessary.

(d) Removal. When a respondent is ordered removed from the United States, the immigration judge shall identify a country, or countries in the alternative, to which the alien's removal may in the first instance be made, pursuant to the provisions of section 241(b) of the Act. In the event that the Department of Homeland Security is unable to remove the alien to the specified or alternative country or countries, the order of the immigration judge does not limit the authority of the Department of Homeland Security to remove the alien to any other country as permitted by section 241(b) of the Act.

HISTORY:

[62 FR 10312, 10370, March 6, 1997; redesignated and amended at 68 FR 9824, 9838, 9846, Feb. 28, 2003; 70 FR 661, 674, Jan. 5, 2005]

§ 1240.13 Notice of decision.

(a) Written decision. A written decision shall be served upon the respondent and the DHS counsel, together with the notice referred to in § 1003.3 of this chapter. Service by mail is complete upon mailing.

(b) Oral decision. An oral decision shall be stated by the immigration judge in the presence of the respondent and the DHS counsel, if any, at the conclusion of the hearing. A copy of the summary written order shall be furnished at the request of the respondent or the DHS counsel.

(c) Summary decision. When the immigration judge renders a summary decision as provided in §

1240.12(b), he or she shall serve a copy thereof upon the respondent and the DHS counsel at the conclusion of the hearing.

(d) Decision to remove. If the immigration judge decides that the respondent is removable and orders the respondent to be removed, the immigration judge shall advise the respondent of such decision, and of the consequences for failure to depart under the order of removal, including civil and criminal penalties described at sections 274D and 243 of the Act. Unless appeal from the decision is waived, the respondent shall be furnished with Form EOIR-26, Notice of Appeal, and advised of the provisions of § 1240.15.

HISTORY:

[62 FR 10312, 10371, March 6, 1997; redesignated and amended at 68 FR 9824, 9838, 9846, Feb. 28, 2003; 68 FR 10349, 10355, Mar. 5, 2003; 86 FR 70708, 70724, Dec. 13, 2021]

§ 1240.14 Finality of order.

The order of the immigration judge shall become final in accordance with § 1003.39 of this chapter.

HISTORY:

[62 FR 10312, 10371, March 6, 1997; redesignated at 68 FR 9824, 9838, Feb. 28, 2003; 68 FR 10349, 10355, Mar. 5, 2003]

§ 1240.15 Appeals.

Pursuant to 8 CFR part 1003, an appeal shall lie from a decision of an immigration judge to the Board of Immigration Appeals, except that no appeal shall lie from an order of removal entered in absentia. The procedures regarding the filing of a Form EOIR 26, Notice of Appeal, fees, and briefs are set forth in §§ 1003.3, 1003.31, and 1003.38 of this chapter. An appeal shall be filed within 30 calendar days after the mailing of a written decision, the stating of an oral decision, or the service of a summary decision. The filing date is defined as the date of receipt of the Notice of Appeal by the Board of Immigration Appeals. The reasons for the appeal shall be stated in the Notice of Appeal in accordance with the provisions of § 1003.3(b) of this chapter. Failure to do so may constitute a ground for dismissal of the appeal by the Board pursuant to § 1003.1(d)(2) of this chapter.

HISTORY:

[62 FR 10312, 10371, March 6, 1997; 66 FR 6436, 6446, Jan. 22, 2001; redesignated at 68 FR 9824, 9838, Feb. 28, 2003; 68 FR 10349, 10355, Mar. 5, 2003]

§ 1240.16 Application of new procedures or termination of proceedings in old proceeedings pursuant to section 309(c) of Public Law 104-208.

The Attorney General shall have the sole discretion to apply the provisions of section 309(c) of Public Law 104-208, which provides for the application of new removal procedures to certain cases in exclusion or deportation proceedings and for the termination of certain cases in exclusion or deportation proceedings and initiation of new removal proceedings. The Attorney General's application of the provisions of section 309(c) shall become effective upon publication of a notice in the Federal Register. However, if the Attorney General determines, in the exercise of his or her discretion, that the delay caused by publication would adversely affect the interests of the United States or the effective enforcement of the immigration laws, the Attorney General's application shall become effective immediately upon issuance, and shall be published in the Federal Register as soon as practicable thereafter.

HISTORY:

[62 FR 10312, 10371, March 6, 1997; redesignated at 68 FR 9824, 9838, Feb. 28, 2003]

§ 1240.17 Removal proceedings where the respondent has a credible fear of persecution or torture.

(a) Scope. This section applies in cases referred to the immigration court under 8 CFR 208.14(c)(1) where the respondent has been found to have a credible fear of persecution or torture, and U.S. Citizenship and Immigration Services (USCIS) subsequently adjudicated but did not grant the respondent's application for asylum under section 208 of the Act; or the respondent was included in a spouse's or parent's application under 8 CFR 208.2(a)(1)(ii) that USCIS subsequently adjudicated but did not grant under section 208 of the Act. Except as otherwise provided in this section, removal proceedings for such respondents shall be governed by the same rules and procedures that apply to proceedings conducted under this subpart. In all cases, such proceedings shall be conducted in accordance with section 208 of the Act. Should any part of the USCIS process governing cases covered by 8 CFR 208.2(a)(1)(ii) be enjoined or vacated, the Executive Office for Immigration Review (EOIR) shall have the discretion to adjudicate any case referred to EOIR under 8 CFR 208.14(c)(1) using the rules and procedures that apply to proceedings conducted under this subpart without regard to this section.

(b) Commencement of proceedings. Removal proceedings conducted under this section shall commence when DHS files a Notice to Appear (NTA) pursuant to 8 CFR part 1239 and schedules the master calendar hearing to take place 30 days after the date the NTA is served or, if a hearing cannot be held on that date, on the next available date no later than 35 days after the date of service. Where the NTA is served by mail, the date of service shall be construed as the date the NTA is mailed. The DHS component issuing the NTA shall also identify for the respondent and the immigration court that the case is subject to the provisions of this section. DHS shall personally serve the NTA on the respondent whenever practicable and by mail when personal service is not effectuated, and shall inform the respondent of the right to be represented by counsel.

(c) Service of the record. No later than the date of the master calendar hearing, DHS shall serve on the respondent and on the immigration court where the NTA is filed the record initiating proceedings as defined in this paragraph (c). The record initiating proceedings shall include the record of proceedings for the asylum merits interview, as outlined in 8 CFR 208.9(f), the Form I-213, Record of Deportable/Inadmissible Alien, pertaining to the respondent, and the asylum officer's written decision issued pursuant to 8 CFR 208.19. If service is not effectuated as provided in this paragraph (c), the schedule of proceedings pursuant to paragraph (f) of this section shall be delayed until service is effectuated.

(d) Failure to appear. An immigration judge shall issue an in absentia removal order where the respondent fails to appear at the master calendar hearing scheduled under paragraph (b) of this section, or at a later status conference or hearing under this section, if the requirements under section 240(b)(5) of the Act and § 1003.26 of this chapter are met, unless the immigration judge waives the respondent's presence under § 1003.25(a) of this chapter. If the asylum officer determined the respondent eligible for withholding of removal under the Act or withholding or deferral of removal under the Convention Against Torture, the immigration judge shall give effect to the protection for which the asylum officer determined the respondent eligible, unless DHS makes a prima facie showing, through evidence that specifically pertains to the respondent and was not in the record of proceedings for the USCIS asylum merits interview, that the respondent is not eligible for such protection(s). Where DHS makes such a showing at the master calendar hearing or status conference, the immigration judge shall allow the respondent a reasonable opportunity of at least 10, but no more than 30, days to respond before issuing an order.

(e) Form of application. In removal proceedings under this section, the written record of the positive credible fear determination issued in accordance with 8 CFR 208.30(f) satisfies the respondent's filing requirement for the application for asylum, withholding of removal under the Act, and withholding or deferral of removal under the Convention Against Torture. The record of the proceedings for the hearing before the asylum officer, as outlined in 8 CFR 208.9(f), and the asylum officer's decision, together with any amendment, correction, or supplementation made before the immigration judge as described in § 1208.3(a)(2) of this chapter, shall be admitted as evidence and considered by the immigration judge, in addition to any further documentation and testimony provided by the parties under the procedures in this section.

(f) Schedule of proceedings —

(1) Master calendar hearing. At the master calendar hearing, the immigration judge shall perform the functions required by § 1240.10(a), including advising the respondent of the right to be represented, at no expense to the Government, by counsel of the respondent's own choice. In addition, the immigration judge shall advise the respondent as to the nature of removal proceedings under this section, including: That the respondent has pending applications for asylum, withholding of removal under the Act and withholding or deferral of removal under the Convention Against Torture, as appropriate; that the respondent has the right to present evidence in support of the applications; that the respondent has the right to call witnesses and to testify at any merits hearing; and that the respondent must comply with the deadlines that govern the submission of evidence. Except where the respondent is ordered removed in absentia, at the conclusion of the master calendar hearing, the immigration judge shall schedule a status conference 30 days after the master calendar hearing or, if a status conference cannot be held on that date, on the next available date no later than 35 days after the master calendar hearing. The immigration judge shall inform the respondent of the requirements for the status conference. The adjournment of the case until the status conference shall not constitute a continuance for the purposes of paragraph (h)(2) of this section.

(2) Status conference. The purpose of the status conference shall be to take pleadings, identify and narrow the issues, determine whether the case can be decided on the documentary record, and, if necessary, ready the case for a merits hearing. At the status conference, the immigration judge shall advise the respondent that: The respondent has the right to present evidence in support of the applications; the respondent has the right to call witnesses and to testify at any merits hearing; and the respondent must comply with the deadlines that govern the submission of evidence. Based on the parties' representations at the status conference and an independent evaluation of the record, the immigration judge shall decide whether further proceedings are warranted or whether the case will be decided on the documentary record in accordance with paragraph (f)(4) of this section. If the immigration judge determines that further proceedings are warranted, the immigration judge shall schedule the merits hearing to take place 60 days after the master calendar hearing or, if the merits hearing cannot be held on that date, on the next available date no later than 65 days after the master calendar hearing. The immigration judge may schedule additional status conferences prior to the merits hearing if the immigration judge determines that such conferences are warranted and would contribute to the efficient resolution of the case.

(i) The respondent. At the status conference, the respondent shall plead to the NTA under § 1240.10(c), and indicate orally or in writing whether the respondent intends to seek any protection(s) for which the asylum officer did not find the respondent eligible.

(A)

(1) If the respondent indicates that the respondent intends to contest removal or seek any protection(s) for which the asylum officer did not determine the respondent eligible, the respondent shall, either orally or in writing:

(i) Indicate whether the respondent intends to testify before the immigration court;

(ii) Identify any witnesses the respondent intends to call in support of the applications at the merits hearing;

(iii) Provide any additional documentation in support of the applications;

(iv) Describe any alleged errors or omissions in the asylum officer's decision or the record of proceedings before the asylum officer;

(v) Articulate or confirm any additional bases for asylum and related protection, whether or not they were presented to or developed before the asylum officer; and

(vi) State any additional requested forms of relief or protection.

(2) If the respondent is unrepresented, the respondent shall not be required to provide items set forth in paragraphs (f)(2)(i)(A)(1)(iv), (v), and (vi) of this section.

(B) If the respondent indicates that the respondent does not intend to contest removal or seek any protection(s) for which the asylum officer did not find the respondent eligible, the immigration judge shall order the respondent removed, and no further proceedings shall be held by the immigration judge. If the asylum officer determined the respondent eligible for withholding of removal under the Act or withholding or deferral of removal under the Convention Against Torture, the immigration judge shall give effect to the protection(s) for which the asylum officer determined the respondent eligible, unless DHS makes a prima facie showing, through evidence that specifically pertains to the respondent and was not in the record of proceedings for the USCIS asylum merits interview, that the respondent is not eligible for such protection(s).

(ii) DHS.

(A) At the status conference, DHS shall indicate orally or in writing whether it intends to:

(1) Rest on the record;

(2) Waive cross examination of the respondent;

(3) Otherwise participate in the case; or

(4) Waive appeal if the immigration judge decides that the respondent's application should be granted.

(B) If DHS indicates that it will participate in the case, it shall, either orally or in writing at the status conference, or in a written submission pursuant to paragraph (f)(3)(i) of this section:

(1) State its position on each of the respondent's claimed grounds for asylum or related protection;

(2) State which elements of the respondent's claim for asylum or related protection it is contesting and which facts it is disputing, if any, and provide an explanation of its position;

(3) Identify any witnesses it intends to call at any merits hearing;

(4) Provide any additional non-rebuttal or non-impeachment evidence; and

(5) State whether the appropriate identity, law enforcement, or security investigations or examinations required by section 208(d)(5)(A)(i) of the Act and § 1003.47 of this chapter have been completed.

(C) Any position DHS expresses pursuant to paragraph (f)(2)(ii)(A) of this section may be retracted, orally or in writing, prior to the issuance of the immigration judge's decision, if DHS seeks consideration of evidence pursuant to the standard laid out in paragraph (g)(2) of this section. Where the immigration judge holds a merits hearing or hearings, any position DHS expressed pursuant to paragraph (f)(2)(ii)(A) may only be retracted prior to the final hearing; if no such hearing is held, the retraction must take place prior to the immigration judge's decision.

(3) Written submissions.

(i) If DHS intends to participate in the case, DHS shall file a written statement that provides any information required under paragraph (f)(2)(ii) of this section that DHS did not provide at the status conference, as well as any other relevant information or argument in response to the respondent's submissions. DHS's written statement, if any, shall be filed no later than 15 days prior to the scheduled merits hearing or, if the immigration judge determines that no such hearing is warranted, no later than 15 days following the status conference. Where DHS intends to participate in the case but does not timely provide its position as required under paragraph (f)(2)(ii) of this section, either at the status conference or in its written statement, to one or more of the respondent's claimed grounds for asylum or related protection, including which arguments raised by the respondent it is disputing and which facts it is contesting, the immigration judge shall have authority to deem those arguments or claims unopposed; provided, however, that DHS may respond at the merits hearing to any arguments or claimed bases for asylum first advanced by the respondent after the status conference.

(ii) The respondent may submit a filing no later than 5 days prior to the scheduled merits hearing or, if the immigration judge determines that no such hearing is warranted, no later than 25 days following the status conference, that supplements the respondent's oral statement or written submission under paragraph (f)(2)(i) of this section. In the respondent's supplemental filing, if any, the respondent shall reply to any statement submitted by DHS, identify any additional witnesses, and provide any additional documentation in support of respondent's applications.

(4) Merits hearings.

(i) If DHS has indicated that it waives cross examination and neither the respondent nor DHS has requested to present testimony under the pre-hearing procedures in paragraph (f)(2) and (3) of this section, the immigration judge shall decide the case on the documentary record, without holding a merits hearing, unless the immigration judge, after consideration of the record, determines that a merits hearing is necessary to fulfill the immigration judge's duty to fully develop the record.

(ii) If the respondent has timely requested to present testimony and DHS has indicated that it waives cross examination and does not intend to present testimony or produce evidence, and the immigration judge concludes, consistent with the immigration judge's duty to fully develop the record, that the respondent's application can be granted without further testimony, the immigration judge shall grant the application without holding a merits hearing.

(iii) In all other situations, the immigration judge shall proceed as follows:

(A) If the immigration judge determines that proceedings can be completed at the merits hearing scheduled under paragraph (f)(1) of this section, the immigration judge shall hold the scheduled merits hearing, at which the immigration judge shall swear the respondent to the truth and accuracy of any information or statements submitted pursuant to paragraphs (f)(2) and (3) of this section, hear all live testimony requested by the parties, consider the parties' submissions, and, whenever practicable, issue an oral decision in the case.

(B) If the immigration judge determines that proceedings cannot be completed at the merits hearing scheduled under paragraph (f)(1) of this section, the immigration judge may conduct a portion of the scheduled hearing, hold a status conference in lieu of the scheduled hearing, and take any other steps the immigration judge deems necessary and efficient to expeditiously resolve the case. The immigration judge shall schedule any and all subsequent merits hearings to occur no later than 30 days after the initial merits hearing.

(5) Decision. Whenever practicable, the immigration judge shall issue an oral decision on the date of the final merits hearing or, if the immigration judge determines that no merits hearing is warranted, no more than 30 days after the status conference. The immigration judge may not, however, issue a decision in a case where DHS has made a prima facie showing, through evidence that specifically pertains to the respondent and was not in the record of proceedings for the USCIS asylum merits interview, that the respondent is not eligible for withholding of removal or protection under the Convention Against Torture unless the respondent was first provided a reasonable opportunity of at least 10, but no more than 30, days to respond to the evidence submitted by DHS. Where issuance of an oral decision on the date specified under the first sentence of this paragraph (f)(5) is not practicable, the immigration judge shall issue an oral or written decision as soon as practicable, and in no case more than 45 days after the date specified under the first sentence of this paragraph (f)(5).

(g) Consideration of evidence and testimony.

(1) The immigration judge shall exclude documentary evidence or witness testimony only if it is not relevant or probative; if its use is fundamentally unfair; or if the documentary evidence is not submitted or the testimony is not requested by the applicable deadline, absent a timely request for a continuance or filing extension that is granted.

(2) The immigration judge may consider documentary evidence or witness testimony submitted after the applicable deadline, taking into account any timely requests for continuances or filing extensions that are granted, but before the immigration judge has issued a decision, only if the evidence could not reasonably have been obtained and presented before the applicable deadline through the exercise of due diligence or if the exclusion of such evidence would violate a statute or the Constitution. The admission of such evidence shall not automatically entitle either party to a continuance or filing extension; such a continuance or extension is governed by paragraph (h) of this section.

(h) Continuances, adjournments, and filing extensions —

(1) In general. For cases governed by this section, an immigration judge may grant a continuance of a hearing date or extension of a filing deadline only as set forth in this paragraph (h).

(2) Respondent-requested continuances and filings extensions.

(i) The immigration judge may, for good cause shown, grant the respondent continuances and extend the respondent's filing deadlines. Each such continuance or extension shall not exceed 10 calendar days, unless the immigration judge determines that a longer period is more efficient. The immigration judge may not grant the respondent continuances or extensions for good cause that cause a merits hearing to occur more than 90 days after the master calendar hearing.

(ii) The immigration judge may grant the respondent continuances or extensions that cause a merits hearing to occur more than 90 days after the master calendar hearing only if the respondent demonstrates that the continuance or extension is necessary to ensure a fair proceeding and the need for the continuance or extension exists despite the respondent's exercise of due diligence. The length of any such continuance or extension shall be limited to the time necessary to ensure a fair proceeding. The immigration judge may not grant the respondent continuances or extensions pursuant to this paragraph (h)(2)(ii) that cause a merits hearing to occur more than 135 days after the master calendar hearing.

(iii) The immigration judge may grant the respondent continuances or extensions notwithstanding the requirements of paragraphs (h)(2)(i) and (ii) of this section if the respondent demonstrates that failure to grant the continuance or extension would be contrary to statute or the Constitution.

(iv) In calculating the delay to a merits hearing for purposes of applying paragraphs (h)(2)(i) and (ii) of this section, the immigration judge shall exclude any continuances, hearing delays, or filing extensions issued pursuant to paragraphs (h)(3) and (4) of this section.

(3) DHS-requested continuances and filings extensions. The immigration judge may, based on significant Government need, grant DHS continuances and extend DHS's filing deadlines. Significant Government need may include, but is not limited to, confirming domestic or foreign law-enforcement interest in the respondent, conducting forensic analysis of documents submitted in support of a relief application or other fraud-related investigations, and securing criminal history information, translations of foreign language documents, witness testimony or affidavits, or evidence suggesting that the respondent is described in sections 208(a)(2)(A)(C), 208(b)(2), or 241(b)(3)(B) of the Act or has filed a frivolous asylum application as defined in 8 CFR 208.20.

(4) Continuances, adjournments, and filing extensions due to exigent circumstances. The immigration judge may continue a status conference or a hearing, or

extend a filing deadline, and a status conference or a hearing set forth in this section may be adjourned, where necessary due to exigent circumstances, such as the unavailability of an immigration judge, the respondent, or either party's counsel assigned to the case due to illness; or the closure of the immigration court or a relevant DHS office. Any such continuance, extension, or adjournment shall be limited to the shortest period feasible and shall not be counted against the time limits set forth in paragraphs (h)(2)(i) and (ii) of this section. A new finding of exigent circumstances must be made to justify any and every subsequent continuance, extension, or adjournment under this paragraph (h)(4).

(i) Decision.

(1) Where the asylum officer did not grant asylum and did not determine that the respondent was eligible for withholding of removal under the Act or for withholding or deferral of removal under the Convention Against Torture based on the record before USCIS, the immigration judge shall adjudicate, de novo, the respondent's applications for asylum and, if necessary, for withholding of removal under the Act, and withholding or deferral of removal under the Convention Against Torture.

(2) Except as provided in paragraph (f)(2)(i)(B) of this section, where the asylum officer did not grant asylum but determined the respondent eligible for withholding of removal under the Act, or for withholding or deferral of removal under the Convention Against Torture, the immigration judge shall adjudicate, de novo, the respondent's application for asylum. If the immigration judge subsequently denies asylum and enters a removal order, the immigration judge shall give effect to the protection(s) for which the asylum officer determined the applicant eligible, unless DHS has demonstrated, through evidence or testimony that specifically pertains to the respondent and was not in the record of proceedings for the USCIS asylum merits interview, that the respondent is not eligible for such protection(s). The immigration judge shall also grant any additional protection(s) for which the immigration judge finds the applicant eligible. DHS shall not be permitted to appeal to the Board the grant of any protection(s) for which the asylum officer determined the respondent eligible, except to argue that the immigration judge should have denied the application(s) based on the evidence allowed under this paragraph (i)(2).

(3) Where the respondent has requested voluntary departure in the alternative to, or in lieu of, asylum and related protection, the immigration judge shall adjudicate this application where necessary.

(j) Changes of venue. Where an immigration judge grants a motion to change venue under § 1003.20 of this chapter, the schedule of proceedings pursuant to paragraph (f) of this section commences again with the master calendar hearing at the court to which venue has been changed.

(k) Exceptions. The provisions in paragraphs (f) through (h) of this section shall not apply in any of the following circumstances:

(1) The respondent was under the age of 18 on the date the NTA was issued, except where the respondent is in removal proceedings with one or more adult family members.

(2) The respondent has produced evidence of prima facie eligibility for relief or protection other than asylum, withholding of removal under the Act, withholding or deferral of removal under the Convention Against Torture, or voluntary departure, and the respondent is seeking to apply for, or has applied for, such relief or protection.

(3) The respondent has produced evidence that supports a prima facie showing that the respondent is not subject to removal as charged (including under any additional or substitute charges of removal brought by DHS pursuant to § 1240.10(e)), and the immigration judge determines, under § 1240.10(d), that the issue of whether the respondent is subject to removal cannot be resolved simultaneously with the adjudication of the respondent's applications for asylum, withholding of removal under the Act, or withholding or deferral of removal under the Convention Against Torture.

(4) The immigration judge, pursuant to § 1240.10(f), finds the respondent subject to removal to a country other than the country or countries in which the respondent claimed a fear of persecution, torture, or both before the asylum officer and the respondent claims a fear of persecution, torture, or both in that alternative country or countries.

(5) The case has been reopened or remanded following the immigration judge's order.

(6) The respondent has exhibited indicia of mental incompetency.

(l) Termination of protection. Nothing in this section shall preclude DHS from seeking termination of asylum, withholding of removal under the Act, or withholding or deferral of removal under the Convention Against Torture pursuant to 8 CFR 208.17(d) and 208.24(f).

HISTORY:

[62 FR 10367, Mar.6, 1997; redesignated at 68 FR 9824, 9838, Feb. 28, 2003; 87 FR 18078, 18223, Mar. 29, 2022]

AUTHORITY:

(8 U.S.C. 1103; 1182, 1186a, 1224, 1225, 1226, 1227, 1251, 1252 note, 1252a, 1252b, 1362; secs. 202 and 203, Pub. L. 105-100 (111 Stat. 2160, 2193); sec. 902, Pub. L. 105-277 (112 Stat. 2681); 8 CFR part 2.)

§ 1240.18 [Reserved]

[NO TEXT IN ORIGINAL]

HISTORY:

[62 FR 10367, Mar.6, 1997; redesignated at 68 FR 9824, 9838, Feb. 28, 2003]

AUTHORITY:

(8 U.S.C. 1103; 1182, 1186a, 1224, 1225, 1226, 1227, 1251, 1252 note, 1252a, 1252b, 1362; secs. 202 and 203, Pub. L. 105-100 (111 Stat. 2160, 2193); sec. 902, Pub. L. 105-277 (112 Stat. 2681); 8 CFR part 2.)

Subpart B
Cancellation of Removal

§ 1240.19 [Reserved]

[NO TEXT IN ORIGINAL]

HISTORY:
[68 FR 9824, 9838, Feb. 28, 2003]

AUTHORITY:
(8 U.S.C. 1103; 1182, 1186a, 1224, 1225, 1226, 1227, 1251, 1252 note, 1252a, 1252b, 1362; secs. 202 and 203, Pub. L. 105-100 (111 Stat. 2160, 2193); sec. 902, Pub. L. 105-277 (112 Stat. 2681); 8 CFR part 2.)

§ 1240.20 Cancellation of removal and adjustment of status under section 240A of the Act.

(a) Jurisdiction. An application for the exercise of discretion under section 240A of the Act shall be submitted on Form EOIR-42, Application for Cancellation of Removal, to the Immigration Court having administrative control over the Record of Proceeding of the underlying removal proceeding under section 240 of the Act. The application must be accompanied by payment of the filing fee as set forth in § 1103.7(b) of this chapter or a request for a fee waiver.

(b) Filing the application. The application may be filed only with the Immigration Court after jurisdiction has vested pursuant to § 1003.14 of this chapter.

(c) For cases raised under section 240A(b)(2) of the Act, extreme hardship shall be determined as set forth in § 1240.58 of this part.

HISTORY:
[62 FR 10312, 10371, March 6, 1997; 64 FR 27856, 27875, May 21, 1999; redesignated and amended at 68 FR 9824, 9838, 9846, Feb. 28, 2003; 68 FR 10349, 10355, Mar. 5, 2003; 85 FR 82750, 82794, Dec. 18, 2020]

§ 1240.21 Suspension of Deportation and Adjustment of Status Under Section 244(a) of the Act (as in effect before April 1, 1997) and Cancellation of Removal and Adjustment of Status Under Section 240A(b) of the Act for Certain Nonpermanent Residents.

(a) **Applicability of annual cap on suspension of deportation or cancellation of removal.**

(1) As used in this section, the term cap means the numerical limitation of 4,000 grants of suspension of deportation or cancellation of removal in any fiscal year (except fiscal year 1998, which has a limitation of 8,000 grants) pursuant to section 240A(e) of the Act.

(2) The provisions of this section apply to grants of suspension of deportation pursuant to section 244(a) of the Act (as in effect before April 1, 1997) or cancellation of removal pursuant to section 240A(b) of the Act that are subject to a numerical limitation in section 240A(e) of the Act for any fiscal year. This section does not apply to grants of suspension of deportation or cancellation of removal to aliens described in section 309(c)(5)(C)(i) of the Illegal Immigration Reform and Immigrant Responsibility Act (IIRIRA), as amended by section 203(a)(1) of the Nicaraguan Adjustment and Central American Relief Act (NACARA), or aliens in deportation proceedings prior to April 1, 1997, who apply for suspension of deportation pursuant to section 244(a)(3) of the Act (as in effect prior to April 1, 1997). The Immigration Court and the Board shall no longer issue conditional grants of suspension of deportation or cancellation of removal as provided in 8 CFR 1240.21 (as in effect prior to September 30, 1998).

(b) [Reserved]

(c) Grants of suspension of deportation or cancellation of removal in fiscal years subsequent to fiscal year 1998. On and after October 1, 1998, the Immigration Court and the Board may grant applications for suspension of deportation and adjustment of status under section 244(a) of the Act (as in effect prior to April 1, 1997) or cancellation of removal and adjustment of status under section 240A(b) of the Act that meet the statutory requirements for such relief and warrant a favorable exercise of discretion until the annual numerical limitation has been reached in that fiscal year. The awarding of such relief shall be determined according to the date the order granting such relief becomes final as defined in §§ 1003.1(d)(7) and 1003.39 of this chapter.

(1) Applicability of the annual limitation. When grants are no longer available in a fiscal year, further decisions to grant such relief must be reserved until such time as a grant becomes available under the annual limitation in a subsequent fiscal year.

(2) Aliens applying for additional forms of relief. Whether or not the cap has been reached, the Immigration Court or the Board shall adjudicate concurrently all other forms of relief for which the alien has applied. Applications for suspension of deportation or cancellation of removal shall be denied in the exercise of discretion if the alien is granted asylum or adjustment of status, including pursuant to section 202 of NACARA, while the suspension of deportation or cancellation of removal application is pending. Where an appeal of a decision granting asylum or adjustment is sustained by the Board, a decision to deny as a matter of discretion an application for suspension of deportation or cancellation of removal on this basis shall be reconsidered.

HISTORY:
[62 FR 51760, 51762, Oct. 3, 1997; 63 FR 52134, 52138, Sept. 30, 1998; 66 FR 6436, 6446, Jan. 22, 2001; 68 FR 9824, 9839, 9846, Feb. 28, 2003; 68 FR 10349, 10355, Mar. 5, 2003; 82 FR 57336, 57339, Dec. 5, 2017]

§§ 1240.22 — 1240.24 [Reserved]

[NO TEXT IN ORIGINAL]

HISTORY:
[68 FR 9824, 9838, Feb. 28, 2003]

AUTHORITY:
(8 U.S.C. 1103; 1182, 1186a, 1224, 1225, 1226, 1227, 1251, 1252 note, 1252a, 1252b, 1362; secs. 202 and 203, Pub. L. 105-100 (111

Stat. 2160, 2193); sec. 902, Pub. L. 105-277 (112 Stat. 2681); 8 CFR part 2.)

Subpart C

Voluntary Departure

§ 1240.26 Voluntary departure—authority of the Executive Office for Immigration Review.

(a) Eligibility: general. An noncitizen previously granted voluntary departure under section 240B of the Act, including by DHS under § 240.25, and who fails to depart voluntarily within the time specified, shall thereafter be ineligible, for a period of ten years, for voluntary departure or for relief under sections 240A, 245, 248, and 249 of the Act.

(b) Prior to completion of removal proceedings. —

(1) Grant by the immigration judge

(i) An noncitizen may be granted voluntary departure by an immigration judge pursuant to section 240B(a) of the Act only if the noncitizen:

(A) Makes such request prior to or at the master calendar hearing at which the case is initially calendared for a merits hearing;

(B) Makes no additional requests for relief (or if such requests have been made, such requests are withdrawn prior to any grant of voluntary departure pursuant to this section);

(C) Concedes removability;

(D) Waives appeal of all issues; and

(E) Has not been convicted of a crime described in section 101(a)(43) of the Act and is not deportable under section 237(a)(4).

(ii) The judge may not grant voluntary departure under section 240B(a) of the Act beyond 30 days after the master calendar hearing at which the case is initially calendared for a merits hearing, except pursuant to a stipulation under paragraph (b)(2) of this section.

(2) Stipulation. At any time prior to the completion of removal proceedings, the DHS counsel may stipulate to a grant of voluntary departure under section 240B(a) of the Act.

(3) Conditions

(i) The judge may impose such conditions as he or she deems necessary to ensure the noncitizen's timely departure from the United States, including the posting of a voluntary departure bond to be canceled upon proof that the noncitizen has departed the United States within the time specified. The noncitizen shall be required to present to DHS, for inspection and photocopying, the noncitizen's passport or other travel documentation sufficient to assure lawful entry into the country to which the noncitizen is departing, unless:

(A) A travel document is not necessary to return to the noncitizen's native country or to which country the noncitizen is departing; or

(B) The document is already in the possession of DHS.

(ii) DHS may hold the passport or documentation for sufficient time to investigate its authenticity. If such documentation is not immediately available to the noncitizen, but the immigration judge is satisfied that the noncitizen is making diligent efforts to secure it, voluntary departure may be granted for a period not to exceed 120 days, subject to the condition that the noncitizen within 60 days must secure such documentation and present it to DHS. DHS in its discretion may extend the period within which the noncitizen must provide such documentation. If the documentation is not presented within the 60-day period or any extension thereof, the voluntary departure order shall vacate automatically and the alternate order of removal will take effect, as if in effect on the date of issuance of the immigration judge order.

(iii) If the noncitizen files a post-decision motion to reopen or reconsider during the period allowed for voluntary departure, the grant of voluntary departure shall be terminated automatically, and the alternate order of removal will take effect immediately. The penalties for failure to depart voluntarily under section 240B(d) of the Act shall not apply if the noncitizen has filed a post-decision motion to reopen or reconsider during the period allowed for voluntary departure. Upon the granting of voluntary departure, the immigration judge shall advise the noncitizen of the provisions of this paragraph (b)(3)(iii).

(iv) The automatic termination of a grant of voluntary departure and the effectiveness of the alternative order of removal shall not affect, in any way, the date that the order of the immigration judge or the Board became administratively final, as determined under the provisions of the applicable regulations in this chapter.

(c) At the conclusion of the removal proceedings. —

(1) Required findings. An immigration judge may grant voluntary departure at the conclusion of the removal proceedings under section 240B(b) of the Act, if he or she finds that:

(i) The noncitizen has been physically present in the United States for period of at least one year preceding the date the Notice to Appear was served under section 239(a) of the Act;

(ii) The noncitizen is, and has been, a person of good moral character for at least five years immediately preceding the application;

(iii) The noncitizen has not been convicted of a crime described in section 101(a)(43) of the Act and is not deportable under section 237(a)(4); and

(iv) The noncitizen has established by clear and convincing evidence that the noncitizen has the means to depart the United States and has the intention to do so.

(2) Travel documentation. Except as otherwise provided in paragraph (b)(3) of this section, the clear and convincing evidence of the means to depart shall include in all cases presentation by the noncitizen of a passport or other travel documentation sufficient to assure lawful entry into the country to which the noncitizen is departing. DHS shall have full opportunity to inspect and photocopy the documentation, and to challenge its authenticity or sufficiency before voluntary departure is granted.

(3) Conditions. The immigration judge may impose such conditions as he or she deems necessary to ensure the noncitizen's timely departure from the United States. The immigration judge shall advise the noncitizen of the conditions set forth in this paragraph (c)(3)(i)-(iii). If the immigration judge imposes conditions beyond those specifically enumerated below, the immigration judge shall advise the noncitizen of such conditions before granting voluntary departure. Upon the conditions being set forth, the noncitizen shall be provided the opportunity to accept the grant of voluntary departure or decline voluntary departure if he or she is unwilling to accept the amount of the bond or other conditions. In all cases under section 240B(b) of the Act:

(i) The noncitizen shall be required to post a voluntary departure bond, in an amount necessary to ensure that the noncitizen departs within the time specified, but in no case less than $ 500. Before granting voluntary departure, the immigration judge shall advise the noncitizen of the specific amount of the bond to be set and the duty to post the bond with the ICE Field Office Director within 5 business days of the immigration judge's order granting voluntary departure.

(ii) An noncitizen who has been granted voluntary departure shall, within 30 days of filing of an appeal with the Board, submit sufficient proof of having posted the required voluntary departure bond. If the noncitizen does not provide timely proof to the Board that the required voluntary departure bond has been posted with DHS, the Board will not reinstate the period of voluntary departure in its final order.

(iii) Upon granting voluntary departure, the immigration judge shall advise the noncitizen that if the noncitizen files a post-order motion to reopen or reconsider during the period allowed for voluntary departure, the grant of voluntary departure shall terminate automatically and the alternate order of removal will take effect immediately.

(iv) The automatic termination of an order of voluntary departure and the effectiveness of the alternative order of removal shall not impact, in any way, the date that the order of the immigration judge or the Board became administratively final, as determined under the provisions of the applicable regulations in this chapter.

(v) If, after posting the voluntary departure bond the noncitizen satisfies the condition of the bond by departing the United States prior to the expiration of the period granted for voluntary departure, the noncitizen may apply to the ICE Field Office Director for the bond to be canceled, upon submission of proof of the noncitizen's timely departure by such methods as the ICE Field Office Director may prescribe.

(vi) The voluntary departure bond may be canceled by such methods as the ICE Field Office Director may prescribe if the noncitizen is subsequently successful in overturning or remanding the immigration judge's decision regarding removability.

(4) Provisions relating to bond. The voluntary departure bond shall be posted with the ICE Field Office Director within 5 business days of the immigration judge's order granting voluntary departure, and the ICE Field Office Director may, at the ICE Field Office Director's discretion, hold the noncitizen in custody until the bond is posted. Because the purpose of the voluntary departure bond is to ensure that the noncitizen does depart from the United States, as promised, the failure to post the bond, when required, within 5 business days may be considered in evaluating whether the noncitizen should be detained based on risk of flight, and also may be considered as a negative discretionary factor with respect to any discretionary form of relief. The noncitizen's failure to post the required voluntary departure bond within the time required does not terminate the noncitizen's obligation to depart within the period allowed or exempt the noncitizen from the consequences for failure to depart voluntarily during the period allowed. However, if the noncitizen had waived appeal of the immigration judge's decision, the noncitizen's failure to post the required voluntary departure bond within the period allowed means that the alternate order of removal takes effect immediately pursuant to 8 CFR 1241.1(f), except that an noncitizen granted the privilege of voluntary departure under 8 CFR 1240.26(c) will not be deemed to have departed under an order of removal if the noncitizen:

(i) Departs the United States no later than 25 days following the failure to post bond;

(ii) Provides to DHS such evidence of the noncitizen's departure as the ICE Field Office Director may require; and

(iii) Provides evidence DHS deems sufficient that he or she remains outside of the United States.

(d) Alternate order of removal. Upon granting a request made for voluntary departure either prior to the completion of proceedings or at the conclusion of proceedings, the immigration judge shall also enter an alternate order or removal.

(e) Periods of time. If voluntary departure is granted prior to the completion of removal proceedings, the immigration judge may grant a period not to exceed 120 days. If voluntary departure is granted at the conclusion of proceedings, the immigration judge may grant a period not to exceed 60 days.

(1) Motion to reopen or reconsider filed during the voluntary departure period. The filing of a motion to reopen or reconsider prior to the expiration of the period allowed for voluntary departure has the effect of automatically terminating the grant of voluntary departure, and accordingly does not toll, stay, or extend the period allowed for voluntary departure under this section. See paragraphs (b)(3)(iii) and (c)(3)(ii) of this section. If the noncitizen files a post-order motion to reopen or reconsider during the period allowed for voluntary departure, the penalties for failure to depart voluntarily under section 240B(d) of the Act shall not apply. The Board shall advise the noncitizen of the condition provided in this paragraph in writing if it reinstates the immigration judge's grant of voluntary departure.

(2) Motion to reopen or reconsider filed after the expiration of the period allowed for voluntary departure. The filing of a motion to reopen or a motion to reconsider after the time allowed for voluntary depar-

ture has already expired does not in any way impact the period of time allowed for voluntary departure under this section. The granting of a motion to reopen or reconsider that was filed after the penalties under section 240B(d) of the Act had already taken effect, as a consequence of the noncitizen's prior failure voluntarily to depart within the time allowed, does not have the effect of vitiating or vacating those penalties, except as provided in section 240B(d)(2) of the Act.

(f) Extension of time to depart. Authority to extend the time within which to depart voluntarily specified initially by an immigration judge or the Board is only within the jurisdiction of the district director, the Deputy Executive Associate Commissioner for Detention and Removal, or the Director of the Office of Juvenile Affairs. An immigration judge or the Board may reinstate voluntary departure in a removal proceeding that has been reopened for a purpose other than solely making an application for voluntarily departure if reopening was granted prior to the expiration of the original period of voluntary departure. In no event can the total period of time, including any extension, exceed 120 days or 60 days as set forth in section 240B of the Act. The filing of a motion to reopen or reconsider does not toll, stay, or extend the period allowed for voluntary departure. The filing of a petition for review has the effect of automatically terminating the grant of voluntary departure, and accordingly also does not toll, stay, or extend the period allowed for voluntary departure.

(g) Administrative Appeals. No appeal shall lie regarding the length of a period of voluntary departure (as distinguished from issues of whether to grant voluntary departure).

(h) Reinstatement of voluntary departure. An immigration judge or the Board may reinstate voluntary departure in a removal proceeding that has been reopened for a purpose other than solely making application for voluntary departure, if reopening was granted prior to the expiration of the original period of voluntary departure. In no event can the total period of time, including any extension, exceed 120 days or 60 days as set forth in section 240B of the Act and paragraph (a) of this section.

(i) Effect of filing a petition for review. If, prior to departing the United States, the noncitizen files a petition for review pursuant to section 242 of the Act (8 U.S.C. 1252) or any other judicial challenge to the administratively final order, any grant of voluntary departure shall terminate automatically upon the filing of the petition or other judicial challenge and the alternate order of removal entered pursuant to paragraph (d) of this section shall immediately take effect, except that an noncitizen granted the privilege of voluntary departure under 8 CFR 1240.26(c) will not be deemed to have departed under an order of removal if the noncitizen departs the United States no later than 30 days following the filing of a petition for review, provides to DHS such evidence of the noncitizen's departure as the ICE Field Office Director may require, and provides evidence DHS deems sufficient that he or she remains outside of the United States. The Board shall advise the noncitizen of the condition provided in this paragraph in writing if it reinstates the immigration judge's grant of voluntary departure. The automatic termination of a grant of voluntary departure and the effectiveness of the alternative order of removal shall not affect, in any way, the date that the order of the immigration judge or the Board became administratively final, as determined under the provisions of the applicable regulations in this chapter. Since the grant of voluntary departure is terminated by the filing of the petition for review, the noncitizen will be subject to the alternate order of removal, but the penalties for failure to depart voluntarily under section 240B(d) of the Act shall not apply to an noncitizen who files a petition for review, and who remains in the United States while the petition for review is pending.

(j) [Reserved].

(k) Authority of the Board to grant voluntary departure in the first instance. The following procedures apply to any request for voluntary departure reviewed by the Board:

(1) If the Board finds that an immigration judge incorrectly denied a noncitizen's request for voluntary departure or failed to provide appropriate advisals, the Board may consider the noncitizen's request for voluntary departure de novo and, if warranted, may enter its own order of voluntary departure with an alternate order of removal.

(2) In cases in which a noncitizen has appealed an immigration judge's decision or in which DHS and the noncitizen have both appealed an immigration judge's decision, the Board shall not grant voluntary departure under section 240B(a) of the Act unless:

(i) The noncitizen requested voluntary departure under that section before the immigration judge, the immigration judge denied the request, and the noncitizen timely appealed;

(ii) The noncitizen's notice of appeal specified that the noncitizen is appealing the immigration judge's denial of voluntary departure and identified the specific factual and legal findings that the noncitizen is challenging;

(iii) The Board finds that the immigration judge's decision was in error; and

(iv) The Board finds that the noncitizen meets all applicable statutory and regulatory criteria for voluntary departure under that section.

(3) In cases in which DHS has appealed an immigration judge's decision, the Board shall not grant voluntary departure under section 240B(b) of the Act unless:

(i) The noncitizen requested voluntary departure under that section before the immigration judge and provided evidence or a proffer of evidence in support of the noncitizen's request;

(ii) The immigration judge either granted the request or did not rule on it; and,

(iii) The Board finds that the noncitizen meets all applicable statutory and regulatory criteria for voluntary departure under that section.

(4) The Board may impose such conditions as it deems necessary to ensure the noncitizen's timely departure from the United States, if supported by the

record on appeal and within the scope of the Board's authority on appeal. Unless otherwise indicated in this section, the Board shall advise the noncitizen in writing of the conditions set by the Board, consistent with the conditions set forth in paragraphs (b) through (e), (h), and (i) of this section (other than paragraph (c)(3)(ii) of this section), except that the Board shall advise the noncitizen of the duty to post the bond with the ICE Field Office Director within 30 business days of the Board's order granting voluntary departure. If documentation sufficient to assure lawful entry into the country to which the noncitizen is departing is not contained in the record, but the noncitizen continues to assert a request for voluntary departure under section 240B of the Act and the Board finds that the noncitizen is otherwise eligible for voluntary departure under the Act, the Board may grant voluntary departure for a period not to exceed 120 days, subject to the condition that the noncitizen within 60 days must secure such documentation and present it to DHS and the Board. If the Board imposes conditions beyond those specifically enumerated, the Board shall advise the noncitizen in writing of such conditions. The noncitizen may accept or decline the grant of voluntary departure and may manifest a declination either by written notice to the Board, by failing to timely post any required bond, or by otherwise failing to comply with the Board's order. The grant of voluntary departure shall automatically terminate upon a filing by the noncitizen of a motion to reopen or reconsider the Board's decision, or by filing a timely petition for review of the Board's decision. The noncitizen may decline voluntary departure when unwilling to accept the amount of the bond or other conditions.

(*l*) Penalty for failure to depart. There shall be a rebuttable presumption that the civil penalty for failure to depart, pursuant to section 240B(d)(1)(A) of the Act, shall be set at $3,000 unless the immigration judge or the Board specifically orders a higher or lower amount at the time of granting voluntary departure within the permissible range allowed by law. The immigration judge or the Board shall advise the noncitizen of the amount of this civil penalty at the time of granting voluntary departure.

HISTORY:

[62 FR 10312, 10372, March 6, 1997; 67 FR 39255, 39258, June 7, 2002; redesignated and amended at 68 FR 9824, 9838, 9846, Feb. 28, 2003; 68 FR 10349, 10355, Mar. 5, 2003; 85 FR 81588, 81655, Dec. 16, 2020; 73 FR 76927, 76937, Dec. 18, 2008, as corrected at 83 FR 65485, Dec. 21, 2018; 86 FR 70708, 70724, Dec. 13, 2021; 89 FR 46742, 46795, May 29, 2024]

§§ 1240.27 — 1240.29 [Reserved]

[NO TEXT IN ORIGINAL]

HISTORY:

[68 FR 9824, 9838, Feb. 28, 2003]

AUTHORITY:

(8 U.S.C. 1103; 1182, 1186a, 1224, 1225, 1226, 1227, 1251, 1252 note, 1252a, 1252b, 1362; secs. 202 and 203, Pub. L. 105-100 (111 Stat. 2160, 2193); sec. 902, Pub. L. 105-277 (112 Stat. 2681); 8 CFR part 2.)

Subpart D

Exclusion of Aliens (For Proceedings Commenced Prior to April 1, 1997)

§ 1240.30 Proceedings prior to April 1, 1997.

Subpart D of 8 CFR part 1240 applies to exclusion proceedings commenced prior to April 1, 1997, pursuant to the former section 236 of the Act. An exclusion proceeding is commenced by the filing of Form I-122 with the Immigration Court, and an alien is considered to be in exclusion proceedings only upon such filing. All references to the Act contained in this subpart are references to the Act in effect prior to April 1, 1997.

HISTORY:

[62 FR 10312, 10373, March 6, 1997; redesignated and amended at 68 FR 9824, 9838, 9846, Feb. 28, 2003]

§ 1240.31 Authority of immigration judges.

In determining cases referred for further inquiry as provided in section 235 of the Act, immigration judges shall have the powers and authority conferred upon them by the Act and this chapter, including the adjudication of applications for adjustment of status pursuant to section 202 of Pub. L. 105-100, or section 902 of Pub. L. 105-277. Subject to any specific limitation prescribed by the Act and this chapter, immigration judges shall also exercise the discretion and authority conferred upon the Attorney General by the Act as is appropriate and necessary for the disposition of such cases.

HISTORY:

[62 FR 10312, 10373, Mar. 6, 1997; 63 FR 27823, 27829, May 21, 1998, as confirmed at 65 FR 15846, 15854, Mar. 24, 2000; 64 FR 25756, 25766, May 12, 1999, as confirmed at 65 FR 15835, 15844, Mar. 24, 2000; redesignated at 68 FR 9824, 9838, Feb. 28, 2003]

§ 1240.32 Hearing.

(a) Opening. Exclusion hearings shall be closed to the public, unless the alien at his or her own instance requests that the public, including the press, be permitted to attend; in that event, the hearing shall be open, provided that the alien states for the record that he or she is waiving the requirement in section 236 of the Act that the inquiry shall be kept separate and apart from the public. When the hearing is to be open, depending upon physical facilities, reasonable limitation may be placed upon the number in attendance at any one time, with priority being given to the press over the general public. The immigration judge shall ascertain whether the applicant for admission is the person to whom Form I-122 was previously delivered by the examining immigration officer as provided in 8 CFR part 1235; enter a copy of such form in evidence as an exhibit in the case; inform the applicant of the nature and purpose of the hearing; advise him or her of the privilege of being represented by an attorney of his or her own choice at no expense to the Government; advise him or her of the availability of pro bono legal services for the immigration court location at which the hearing will take place, and ascertain that he or she has received a list of such pro bono legal service providers; and request him or her to ascertain then and there whether he or she desires representation; advise him or her that he or she will have a reasonable opportunity to present evidence in his or her own behalf, to examine and object to evidence against him or her, and to cross-examine witnesses presented by the Government; and place the applicant under oath.

(b) Procedure. The immigration judge shall receive and adduce material and relevant evidence, rule upon objections, and otherwise regulate the course of the hearing.

(c) Attorney for DHS. DHS shall assign an attorney to each case in which an applicant's nationality is in issue and may assign an attorney to any case in which such assignment is deemed necessary or advantageous. The duties of the DHS counsel include, but are not limited to, the presentation of evidence and the interrogation, examination, and cross-examination of the applicant and other witnesses. Nothing contained in this section diminishes the authority of an immigration judge to conduct proceedings under this part.

(d) Depositions. The procedures specified in § 1240.48(e) shall apply.

(e) Record. The hearing before the immigration judge, including the testimony, exhibits, applications, proffers, and requests, the immigration judge's decision, and all written orders, motions, appeals, and other papers filed in the proceeding shall constitute the record in the case. The hearing shall be recorded verbatim except for statements made off the record with the permission of the immigration judge.

HISTORY:

[62 FR 10312, 10373, March 6, 1997; redesignated and amended at 68 FR 9824, 9838, 9846, Feb. 28, 2003; 68 FR 10349, 10355, Mar. 5, 2003; 80 FR 59503, 59513, Oct. 1, 2015; 86 FR 70708, 70724, Dec. 13, 2021]

§ 1240.33 Applications for asylum or withholding of deportation.

(a) If the alien expresses fear of persecution or harm upon return to his or her country of origin or to a country to which the alien may be deported after a determination of excludability from the United States pursuant to this subpart, and the alien has not been referred to the immigration judge by an asylum officer in accordance with § 1208.14(b) of this chapter, the immigration judge shall:

(1) Advise the alien that he or she may apply for asylum in the United States or withholding of deportation to that other country; and

(2) Make available the appropriate application forms.

(b) An application for asylum or withholding of deportation must be filed with the Immigration Court, pursuant to § 1208.4(b) of this chapter. Upon receipt of an application, the Immigration Court may forward a copy to the Department of State pursuant to § 1208.11 of this chapter and shall calendar the case for a hearing. The reply, if any, from the Department of State, unless classified under an applicable Executive Order, shall be given to both the applicant and to DHS counsel and shall be included in the record.

(c) Applications for asylum or withholding of deportation so filed will be decided by the immigration judge pursuant to the requirements and standards established in 8 CFR part 1208 after an evidentiary hearing that is necessary to resolve material factual issues in dispute. An evidentiary hearing extending beyond issues related to the basis for a mandatory denial of the application pursuant to § 1208.13(c) of this chapter is not necessary once the immigration judge has determined that such denial is required.

(1) Evidentiary hearings on applications for asylum or withholding of deportation will be closed to the public unless the applicant expressly requests that it be open pursuant to § 1236.3 of this chapter.

(2) Nothing in this section is intended to limit the authority of the immigration judge properly to control the scope of any evidentiary hearing.

(3) During the exclusion hearing, the applicant shall be examined under oath on his or her application and may present evidence and witnesses on his or her own behalf. The applicant has the burden of establishing that he or she is a refugee as defined in section 101(a)(42) of the Act pursuant to the standard set forth in § 1208.13 of this chapter.

(4) The DHS counsel for the government may call witnesses and present evidence for the record, including information classified under the applicable Executive Order, provided the immigration judge or the Board has determined that such information is relevant to the hearing. The applicant shall be informed when the immigration judge receives such classified information. The agency that provides the classified information to the immigration judge may provide an unclassified summary of the information for release to the applicant whenever it determines it can do so consistently with safeguarding both the classified nature of the information and its source. The summary should be as detailed as possible, in order that the applicant may have an opportunity to offer opposing evidence. A decision based in whole or in part on such classified information shall state that such information is material to the decision.

(d) The decision of an immigration judge to grant or deny asylum or withholding of deportation shall be communicated to the applicant and to the DHS counsel for the government. An adverse decision will state why asylum or withholding of deportation was denied.

HISTORY:

[62 FR 10312, 10373, March 6, 1997; redesignated at 68 FR 9824, 9838, Feb. 28, 2003; 68 FR 10349, 10355, Mar. 5, 2003; 78 FR 19077, 19080, Mar. 29, 2013; 86 FR 70708, 70724, Dec. 13, 2021]

§ 1240.34 Renewal of application for adjustment of status under section 245 of the Act.

An adjustment application by an alien paroled under section 212(d)(5) of the Act, which has been denied by the district director, may be renewed in exclusion proceedings under section 236 of the Act (as in effect prior to April 1, 1997) before an immigration judge under the following two conditions: first, the denied application must have been properly filed subsequent to the applicant's earlier inspection and admission to the United States; and second, the applicant's later absence from and return to the United States must have been under the terms of an advance parole authorization on Form I-512 granted to permit the applicant's absence and return to pursue the previously filed adjustment application. In a relevant case, the immigration judge may adjudicate the sufficiency of an Affidavit of Support Under Section 213A (Form I-864), executed on behalf of an applicant for admission or for adjustment of status, in accordance with the provisions of section 213A of the Act and 8 CFR part 213a.

HISTORY:

[62 FR 10312, 10374, March 6, 1997; redesignated at 68 FR 9824, 9838, Feb. 28, 2003; 71 FR 35732, 35757, June 21, 2006]

§ 1240.35 Decision of the immigration judge; notice to the applicant.

(a) Decision. The immigration judge shall inform the applicant of his or her decision in accordance with § 1003.37 of this chapter.

(b) Advice to alien ordered excluded. An alien ordered excluded shall be furnished with Form I-296, Notice to Alien Ordered Excluded by Immigration Judge, at the time of an oral decision by the immigration judge or upon service of a written decision.

(c) Holders of refugee travel documents. Aliens who are the holders of valid unexpired refugee travel documents may be ordered excluded only if they are found to be inadmissible under section 212(a)(2), 212(a)(3), or 212(a)(6)(E) of the Act, and it is determined that on the basis of the acts for which they are inadmissible there are compelling reasons of national security or public order for their exclusion. If the immigration judge finds that the alien is inadmissible but determines that there are no compelling reasons of national security or public order for exclusion, the immigration judge shall remand the case to the district director for parole.

HISTORY:

[62 FR 10312, 10374, March 6, 1997; redesignated at 68 FR 9824, 9838, Feb. 28, 2003; 68 FR 10349, 10355, Mar. 5, 2003]

§ 1240.36 Finality of order.

The decision of the immigration judge shall become final in accordance with § 1003.37 of this chapter.

HISTORY:

[62 FR 10312, 10374, March 6, 1997; redesignated at 68 FR 9824, 9838, Feb. 28, 2003; 68 FR 10349, 10355, Mar. 5, 2003]

§ 1240.37 Appeals.

Except for temporary exclusions under section 235(c) of the Act, an appeal from a decision of an Immigration Judge under this part may be taken by either party pursuant to § 1003.38 of this chapter.

HISTORY:

[62 FR 10312, 10374, March 6, 1997; redesignated at 68 FR 9824, 9838, Feb. 28, 2003; 68 FR 10349, 10355, Mar. 5, 2003]

§ 1240.38 Fingerprinting of excluded aliens.

Every alien 14 years of age or older who is excluded from admission to the United States by an immigration judge shall be fingerprinted, unless during the preceding year he or she has been fingerprinted at an American consular office.

HISTORY:

[62 FR 10312, 10374, March 6, 1997; redesignated at 68 FR 9824, 9838, Feb. 28, 2003]

§ 1240.39 [Reserved]

[NO TEXT IN ORIGINAL]

HISTORY:

[62 FR 10312, 10374, March 6, 1997; redesignated at 68 FR 9824, 9838, Feb. 28, 2003]

AUTHORITY:

(8 U.S.C. 1103; 1182, 1186a, 1224, 1225, 1226, 1227, 1251, 1252 note, 1252a, 1252b, 1362; secs. 202 and 203, Pub. L. 105-100 (111 Stat. 2160, 2193); sec. 902, Pub. L. 105-277 (112 Stat. 2681); 8 CFR part 2.)

Subpart E

Proceedings to Determine Deportability of Aliens in the United States: Hearing and Appeal (For Proceedings Commenced Prior to April 1, 1997)

§ 1240.40 Proceedings commenced prior to April 1, 1997.

Subpart E of 8 CFR part 1240 applies only to deportation proceedings commenced prior to April 1, 1997. A deportation proceeding is commenced by the filing of Form I-221 (Order to Show Cause) with the Immigration Court, and an alien is considered to be in deportation proceedings only upon such filing, except in the case of an alien admitted to the United States under the provisions of section 217 of the Act. All references to the Act contained in this subpart pertain to the Act as in effect prior to April 1, 1997.

HISTORY:

[62 FR 10312, 10374, March 6, 1997; redesignated and amended at 68 FR 9824, 9838, 9846, Feb. 28, 2003; 68 FR 10349, 10355, Mar. 5, 2003]

§ 1240.41 Immigration judges.

(a) Authority. In any proceeding conducted under this part the immigration judge shall have the authority to determine deportability and to make decisions, including orders of deportation, as provided by section 242(b) and 242B of the Act; to reinstate orders of deportation as provided by section 242(f) of the Act; to determine applications under sections 208, 212(k), 241(a)(1)(E)(iii), 241(a)(1)(H), 244, 245 and 249 of the Act section 202 of Pub. L. 105-100, and section 902 of Pub. L. 105-277; to determine the country to which an alien's deportation will be directed in accordance with section 243(a) of the Act; to order temporary withholding of deportation pursuant to section 243(h) of the Act; and to take any other action consistent with applicable law and regulations as may be appropriate. An immigration judge may certify his or her decision in any case to the Board of Immigration Appeals when it involves an unusually complex or novel question of law or fact. Nothing contained in this part shall be construed to diminish the authority conferred on immigration judges under section 103 of the Act.

(b) Withdrawal and substitution of immigration judges. The immigration judge assigned to conduct the hearing shall at any time withdraw if he or she deems himself or herself disqualified. If an immigration judge becomes unavailable to complete his or her duties within a reasonable time, or if at any time the respondent consents to a substitution, another immigration judge may be assigned to complete the case. The new immigration judge shall familiarize himself or herself with the record in the case and shall state for the record that he or she has done so.

HISTORY:

[62 FR 10312, 10374, Mar. 6, 1997; 63 FR 27823, 27829, May 21, 1998, as corrected at 63 FR 39121, July 21, 1998 and confirmed at 65 FR 15846, 15854, Mar. 24, 2000; 64 FR 25756, 25767, May 12, 1999, as confirmed at 65 FR 15835, 15844, Mar. 24, 2000; redesignated at 68 FR 9824, 9838, Feb. 28, 2003]

§ 1240.42 Representation by counsel.

The respondent may be represented at the hearing by an attorney or other representative qualified under 8 CFR part 1292.

HISTORY:

[62 FR 10312, 10374, March 6, 1997; redesignated at 68 FR 9824, 9838, Feb. 28, 2003; 68 FR 10349, 10355, Mar. 5, 2003]

§ 1240.43 Incompetent respondents.

When it is impracticable for the respondent to be present at the hearing because of mental incompetency, the guardian, near relative, or friend who was served with a copy of the order to show cause shall be permitted to appear on behalf of the respondent. If such a person cannot reasonably be found or fails or refuses to appear, the custodian of the respondent shall be requested to appear on behalf of the respondent.

HISTORY:

[62 FR 10312, 10374, March 6, 1997; redesignated at 68 FR 9824, 9838, Feb. 28, 2003]

§ 1240.44 Interpreter.

Any person acting as interpreter in a hearing before an immigration judge under this part shall be sworn to interpret and translate accurately, unless the interpreter is an employee of the United States Government, in which event no such oath shall be required.

HISTORY:

[62 FR 10312, 10375, March 6, 1997; redesignated at 68 FR 9824, 9838, Feb. 28, 2003]

§ 1240.45 Postponement and adjournment of hearing.

After the commencement of the hearing, the immigration judge may grant a reasonable adjournment either at his or her own instance or, for good cause shown, upon application by the respondent or the Service.

HISTORY:

[62 FR 10312, 10375, March 6, 1997; redesignated at 68 FR 9824, 9838, Feb. 28, 2003]

§ 1240.46 Evidence.

(a) Sufficiency. A determination of deportability shall not be valid unless it is found by clear, unequivocal, and convincing evidence that the facts alleged as grounds for deportation are true.

(b) Use of prior statements. The immigration judge may receive in evidence any oral or written statement that is material and relevant to any issue in the case previously made by the respondent or any other person during any investigation, examination, hearing, or trial.

(c) Testimony. Testimony of witnesses appearing at the hearing shall be under oath or affirmation administered by the immigration judge.

(d) Depositions. The immigration judge may order the taking of depositions pursuant to § 1003.35 of this chapter.

HISTORY:

[62 FR 10312, 10375, March 6, 1997; redesignated at 68 FR 9824, 9838, Feb. 28, 2003; 68 FR 10349, 10355, Mar. 5, 2003]

§ 1240.47 Contents of record.

The hearing before the immigration judge, including the testimony, exhibits, applications, proffers, and requests, the immigration judge's decision, and all written orders, motions, appeals, briefs, and other papers filed in the proceedings shall constitute the record in the case. The hearing shall be recorded verbatim except for statements made off the record with the permission of the immigration judge. In his or her discretion, the immigration judge may exclude from the record any arguments made in connection with motions, applications, requests, or objections, but in such event the person affected may submit a brief.

HISTORY:

[62 FR 10312, 10375, March 6, 1997; redesignated at 68 FR 9824, 9838, Feb. 28, 2003]

§ 1240.48 Hearing.

(a) Opening. The immigration judge shall advise the

respondent of his or her right to representation, at no expense to the Government, by counsel of his or her own choice authorized to practice in the proceedings and require him or her to state then and there whether he or she desires representation; advise the respondent of the availability of pro bono legal services for the immigration court location at which the hearing will take place; ascertain that the respondent has received a list of such pro bono legal service providers, and a copy of Form I-618, Written Notice of Appeal Rights; advise the respondent that he or she will have a reasonable opportunity to examine and object to the evidence against him or her, to present evidence in his or her own behalf and to cross-examine witnesses presented by the Government; place the respondent under oath; read the factual allegations and the charges in the order to show cause to the respondent and explain them in nontechnical language, and enter the order to show cause as an exhibit in the record. Deportation hearings shall be open to the public, except that the immigration judge may, in his or her discretion and for the purpose of protecting witnesses, respondents, or the public interest, direct that the general public or particular individuals shall be excluded from the hearing in any specific case. Depending upon physical facilities, reasonable limitation may be placed upon the number in attendance at any one time, with priority being given to the press over the general public.

(b) Pleading by respondent. The immigration judge shall require the respondent to plead to the order to show cause by stating whether he or she admits or denies the factual allegations and his or her deportability under the charges contained therein. If the respondent admits the factual allegations and admits his or her deportability under the charges and the immigration judge is satisfied that no issues of law or fact remain, the immigration judge may determine that deportability as charged has been established by the admissions of the respondent. The immigration judge shall not accept an admission of deportability from an unrepresented respondent who is incompetent or under age 16 and is not accompanied by a guardian, relative, or friend; nor from an officer of an institution in which a respondent is an inmate or patient. When, pursuant to this paragraph, the immigration judge may not accept an admission of deportability, he or she shall direct a hearing on the issues.

(c) Issues of deportability. When deportability is not determined under the provisions of paragraph (b) of this section, the immigration judge shall request the assignment of a DHS counsel, and shall receive evidence as to any unresolved issues, except that no further evidence need be received as to any facts admitted during the pleading. The respondent shall provide a court certified copy of a Judicial Recommendation Against Deportation (JRAD) to the immigration judge when such recommendation will be the basis of denying any charge(s) brought by DHS in the proceedings against the respondent. No JRAD is effective against a charge of deportability under section 241(a)(11) of the Act or if the JRAD was granted on or after November 29, 1990.

(d) Additional charges. DHS may at any time during a hearing lodge additional charges of deportability, including factual allegations, against the respondent. Copies of the additional factual allegations and charges shall be submitted in writing for service on the respondent and entry as an exhibit in the record. The immigration judge shall read the additional factual allegations and charges to the respondent and explain them to him or her. The immigration judge shall advise the respondent if he or she is not represented by counsel that he or she may be so represented and also that he or she may have a reasonable time within which to meet the additional factual allegations and charges. The respondent shall be required to state then and there whether he or she desires a continuance for either of these reasons. Thereafter, the provisions of paragraph (b) of this section shall apply to the additional factual allegations and lodged charges.

HISTORY:

[62 FR 10312, 10375, March 6, 1997; redesignated at 68 FR 9824, 9838, Feb. 28, 2003; 68 FR 10349, 10355, Mar. 5, 2003; 80 FR 59503, 59513, Oct. 1, 2015; 86 FR 70708, 70724, Dec. 13, 2021]

§ 1240.49 Ancillary matters, applications.

(a) Creation of the status of an alien lawfully admitted for permanent residence. The respondent may apply to the immigration judge for suspension of deportation under section 244(a) of the Act; for adjustment of status under section 245 of the Act, or under section 1 of the Act of November 2, 1966, or under section 101 or 104 of the Act of October 28, 1977; or for the creation of a record of lawful admission for permanent residence under section 249 of the Act. The application shall be subject to the requirements of 8 CFR parts 1240, 1245, and 1249. The approval of any application made to the immigration judge under section 245 of the Act by an alien spouse (as defined in section 216(g)(1) of the Act) or by an alien entrepreneur (as defined in section 216A(f)(1) of the Act), shall result in the alien's obtaining the status of lawful permanent resident on a conditional basis in accordance with the provisions of section 216 or 216A of the Act, whichever is applicable. However, the Petition to Remove the Conditions on Residence required by section 216(c) of the Act or the Petition by Entrepreneur to Remove Conditions required by section 216A(c) of the Act shall be made to the director in accordance with 8 CFR part 1216. In conjunction with any application for creation of status of an alien lawfully admitted for permanent residence made to an immigration judge, if the respondent is inadmissible under any provision of section 212(a) of the Act and believes that he or she meets the eligibility requirements for a waiver of the ground of inadmissibility, he or she may apply to the immigration judge for such waiver. The immigration judge shall inform the respondent of his or her apparent eligibility to apply for any of the benefits enumerated in this paragraph and shall afford the respondent an opportunity to make application therefor during the hearing. In a relevant case, the immigration judge may adjudicate the sufficiency of an Affidavit of Support Under Section 213A

(Form I-864), executed on behalf of an applicant for admission or for adjustment of status, in accordance with the provisions of section 213A of the Act and 8 CFR part 213a. In exercising discretionary power when considering an application under this paragraph, the immigration judge may consider and base the decision on information not contained in the record and not made available for inspection by the respondent, provided the Commissioner has determined that such information is relevant and is classified under the applicable Executive Order as requiring protection from unauthorized disclosure in the interest of national security. Whenever the immigration judge believes that he or she can do so while safeguarding both the information and its source, the immigration judge should inform the respondent of the general nature of the information in order that the respondent may have an opportunity to offer opposing evidence. A decision based in whole or in part on such classified information shall state that the information is material to the decision.

(b) Voluntary departure. The respondent may apply to the immigration judge for voluntary departure in lieu of deportation pursuant to section 244(e) of the Act and § 1240.56.

(c) Applications for asylum or withholding of deportation.

(1) The immigration judge shall notify the respondent that if he or she is finally ordered deported, his or her deportation will in the first instance be directed pursuant to section 243(a) of the Act to the country designated by the respondent and shall afford him or her an opportunity then and there to make such designation. The immigration judge shall then specify and state for the record the country, or countries in the alternative, to which respondent's deportation will be directed pursuant to section 243(a) of the Act if the country of his or her designation will not accept him or her into its territory, or fails to furnish timely notice of acceptance, or if the respondent declines to designate a country.

(2) If the alien expresses fear of persecution or harm upon return to any of the countries to which the alien might be deported pursuant to paragraph (c)(1) of this section, and the alien has not previously filed an application for asylum or withholding of deportation that has been referred to the immigration judge by an asylum officer in accordance with § 1208.14(b) of this chapter, the immigration judge shall:

(i) Advise the alien that he or she may apply for asylum in the United States or withholding of deportation to those countries; and

(ii) Make available the appropriate application forms.

(3) An application for asylum or withholding of deportation must be filed with the Immigration Court, pursuant to § 1208.4(b) of this chapter. Upon receipt of an application, the Immigration Court may forward a copy to the Department of State pursuant to § 1208.11 of this chapter and shall calendar the case for a hearing. The reply, if any, of the Department of State, unless classified under an applicable Executive Order, shall be given to both the applicant and to DHS counsel and shall be included in the record.

(4) Applications for asylum or withholding of deportation so filed will be decided by the immigration judge pursuant to the requirements and standards established in 8 CFR part 1208 after an evidentiary hearing that is necessary to resolve factual issues in dispute. An evidentiary hearing extending beyond issues related to the basis for a mandatory denial of the application pursuant to § 1208.13 or § 1208.16 of this chapter is not necessary once the immigration judge has determined that such a denial is required.

(i) Evidentiary hearings on applications for asylum or withholding of deportation will be open to the public unless the applicant expressly requests that it be closed.

(ii) Nothing in this section is intended to limit the authority of the immigration judge properly to control the scope of any evidentiary hearing.

(iii) During the deportation hearing, the applicant shall be examined under oath on his or her application and may present evidence and witnesses in his or her own behalf. The applicant has the burden of establishing that he or she is a refugee as defined in section 101(a)(42) of the Act pursuant to the standard set forth in § 1208.13 of this chapter.

(iv) The DHS counsel for the government may call witnesses and present evidence for the record, including information classified under the applicable Executive Order, provided the immigration judge or the Board has determined that such information is relevant to the hearing. When the immigration judge receives such classified information he or she shall inform the applicant. The agency that provides the classified information to the immigration judge may provide an unclassified summary of the information for release to the applicant, whenever it determines it can do so consistently with safeguarding both the classified nature of the information and its source. The summary should be as detailed as possible, in order that the applicant may have an opportunity to offer opposing evidence. A decision based in whole or in part on such classified information shall state whether such information is material to the decision.

(5) The decision of an immigration judge to grant or deny asylum or withholding of deportation shall be communicated to the applicant and to the DHS counsel for the government. An adverse decision will state why asylum or withholding of deportation was denied.

(d) Application for relief under sections 241(a)(1)(H) and 241(a)(1)(E)(iii) of the Act. The respondent may apply to the immigration judge for relief from deportation under sections 241(a)(1)(H) and 241(a)(1)(E)(iii) of the Act.

(e) General. An application under this section shall be made only during the hearing and shall not be held to constitute a concession of alienage or deportability in any case in which the respondent does not admit his alienage or deportability. However, nothing in this section shall prohibit DHS from using information supplied in an application for asylum or withholding of deportation submitted to an asylum officer pursuant to

§ 1208.2 of this chapter on or after January 4, 1995, as the basis for issuance of an order to show cause or a notice to appear to establish alienage or deportability in a case referred to an immigration judge under § 1208.14(b) of this chapter. The respondent shall have the burden of establishing that he or she is eligible for any requested benefit or privilege and that it should be granted in the exercise of discretion. The respondent shall not be required to pay a fee on more than one application within paragraphs (a) and (c) of this section, provided that the minimum fee imposed when more than one application is made shall be determined by the cost of the application with the highest fee. Nothing contained in this section is intended to foreclose the respondent from applying for any benefit or privilege which he or she believes himself or herself eligible to receive in proceedings under this part.

HISTORY:

[62 FR 10312, 10375, March 6, 1997; redesignated and amended at 68 FR 9824, 9838, 9846, Feb. 28, 2003; 68 FR 10349, 10355, Mar. 5, 2003; 71 FR 35732, 35757, June 21, 2006; 78 FR 19077, 19080, Mar. 29, 2013; 86 FR 70708, 70724, Dec. 13, 2021]

§ 1240.50 Decision of the immigration judge.

(a) Contents. The decision of the immigration judge may be oral or written. Except when deportability is determined on the pleadings pursuant to § 1240.48(b), the decision of the immigration judge shall include a finding as to deportability. The formal enumeration of findings is not required. The decision shall also contain the reasons for granting or denying the request. The decision shall be concluded with the order of the immigration judge.

(b) Summary decision. Notwithstanding the provisions of paragraph (a) of this section, in any case where deportability is determined on the pleadings pursuant to § 1240.48(b) and the respondent does not make an application under § 1240.49, or the respondent applies for voluntary departure only and the immigration judge grants the application, the immigration judge may enter a summary decision on Form EOIR-7, Summary Order of Deportation, if deportation is ordered, or on Form EOIR-6, Summary Order of Voluntary Departure, if voluntary departure is granted with an alternate order of deportation.

(c) Order of the immigration judge. The order of the immigration judge shall direct the respondent's deportation, or the termination of the proceedings, or such other disposition of the case as may be appropriate. When deportation is ordered, the immigration judge shall specify the country, or countries in the alternate, to which respondent's deportation shall be directed. The immigration judge is authorized to issue orders in the alternative or in combination as he or she may deem necessary.

HISTORY:

[62 FR 10312, 10377, March 6, 1997; redesignated and amended at 68 FR 9824, 9838, 9846, Feb. 28, 2003]

§ 1240.51 Notice of decision.

(a) Written decision. A written decision shall be served upon the respondent and the DHS counsel, together with the notice referred to in § 1003.3 of this chapter. Service by mail is complete upon mailing.

(b) Oral decision. An oral decision shall be stated by the immigration judge in the presence of the respondent and the trail attorney, if any, at the conclusion of the hearing. Unless appeal from the decision is waived, the respondent shall be furnished with Form EOIR-26, Notice of Appeal, and advised of the provisions of § 1240.53. A printed copy of the oral decision shall be furnished at the request of the respondent or the DHS counsel.

(c) Summary decision. When the immigration judge renders a summary decision as provided in § 1240.51(b), he or she shall serve a copy thereof upon the respondent at the conclusion of the hearing. Unless appeal from the decision is waived, the respondent shall be furnished with Form EOIR-26, Notice of Appeal, and advised of the provisions of § 1240.54.

HISTORY:

[62 FR 10312, 10377, March 6, 1997; redesignated and amended at 68 FR 9824, 9838, 9846, Feb. 28, 2003; 68 FR 10349, 10355, Mar. 5, 2003; 86 FR 70708, 70725, Dec. 13, 2021]

§ 1240.52 Finality of order.

The decision of the immigration judge shall become final in accordance with § 1003.39 of this chapter.

HISTORY:

[62 FR 10312, 10377, March 6, 1997; redesignated at 68 FR 9824, 9838, Feb. 28, 2003; 68 FR 10349, 10355, Mar. 5, 2003]

§ 1240.53 Appeals.

(a) Appeal to the Board. Pursuant to 8 CFR part 1003, an appeal shall lie from a decision of an immigration judge to the Board, except that no appeal shall lie from an order of deportation entered in absentia. The procedures regarding the filing of a Form EOIR-26, Notice of Appeal, fees, and briefs are set forth in §§ 1003.3, 1003.31, and 1003.38 of this chapter. An appeal shall be filed within 30 calendar days after the mailing or electronic notification of a written decision, the stating of an oral decision, or the service of a summary decision. The filing date is defined as the date of receipt of the Notice of Appeal by the Board. The reasons for the appeal shall be stated in the Form EOIR-26, Notice of Appeal, in accordance with the provisions of § 1003.3(b) of this chapter. Failure to do so may constitute a ground for dismissal of the appeal by the Board pursuant to § 1003.1(d)(2) of this chapter.

(b) Prohibited appeals; legalization or applications. An alien respondent defined in § 245a.2(c)(6) or (7) of this chapter who fails to file an application for adjustment of status to that of a temporary resident within the prescribed period(s), and who is thereafter found to be deportable by decision of an immigration judge, shall not be permitted to appeal the finding of deportability based solely on refusal by the immigration judge to entertain such an application in deportation proceedings.

HISTORY:

[62 FR 10312, 10377, March 6, 1997; 66 FR 6436, 6446, Jan. 22, 2001; redesignated at 68 FR 9824, 9838, Feb. 28, 2003; 68 FR 10349, 10355, Mar. 5, 2003; 86 FR 70708, 70725, Dec. 13, 2021]

§ 1240.54 [Reserved]

[NO TEXT IN ORIGINAL]

HISTORY:

[62 FR 10312, 10377, March 6, 1997; redesignated at 68 FR 9824, 9838, Feb. 28, 2003]

AUTHORITY:

(5 U.S.C. 301; 8 U.S.C. 1101 note, 1103, 1252 note, 1252b, 1324b, 1362; 28 U.S.C. 509, 510, 1746; sec. 2 Reorg. Plan No. 2 of 1950; 3 CFR, 1949-1953 Comp., p. 1002; section 203 of Pub. L. 105-100, 111 Stat. 2196-200; sections 1506 and 1510 of Pub. L. 106-386, 114 Stat. 1527-29, 1531-32; section 1505 of Pub. L. 106-554, 114 Stat. 2763A-326 to-328.)

Subpart F

Suspension of Deportation and Voluntary Departure (For Proceedings Commenced Prior to April 1, 1997)

§ 1240.55 Proceedings commenced prior to April 1, 1997.

Subpart F of 8 CFR part 1240 applies to deportation proceedings commenced prior to April 1, 1997. A deportation proceeding is commenced by the filing of Form I-221 (Order to Show Cause) with the Immigration Court, and an alien is considered to be in deportation proceedings only upon such filing, except in the case of an alien admitted to the United States under the provisions of section 217 of the Act. All references to the Act contained in this subpart are references to the Act in effect prior to April 1, 1997.

HISTORY:

[62 FR 10312, 10377, March 6, 1997; redesignated and amended at 68 FR 9824, 9838, 9846, Feb. 28, 2003; 68 FR 10349, 10355, Mar. 5, 2003]

§ 1240.56 Application.

Notwithstanding any other provision of this chapter, an alien who is deportable because of a conviction on or after November 18, 1988, for an aggravated felony as defined in section 101(a)(43) of the Act, shall not be eligible for voluntary departure as prescribed in 8 CFR part 1240 and section 244 of the Act. Pursuant to subpart F of this part and section 244 of the Act, an immigration judge may authorize the suspension of an alien's deportation; or, if the alien establishes that he or she is willing and has the immediate means with which to depart promptly from the United States, an immigration judge may authorize the alien to depart voluntarily from the United States in lieu of deportation within such time as may be specified by the immigration judge when first authorizing voluntary departure, and under such conditions as the district director shall direct. An application for suspension of deportation shall be made on Form EOIR-40.

HISTORY:

[62 FR 10312, 10377, March 6, 1997; redesignated and amended at 68 FR 9824, 9838, 9846, Feb. 28, 2003; 68 FR 10349, 10355, Mar. 5, 2003]

§ 1240.57 Extension of time to depart.

Authority to reinstate or extend the time within which to depart voluntarily specified initially by an immigration judge or the Board is within the sole jurisdiction of the district director, except that an immigration judge or the Board may reinstate voluntary departure in a deportation proceeding that has been reopened for a purpose other than solely making an application for voluntary departure. A request by an alien for reinstatement or an extension of time within which to depart voluntarily shall be filed with the district director having jurisdiction over the alien's place of residence. Written notice of the district director's decision shall be served upon the alien and no appeal may be taken therefrom.

HISTORY:

[62 FR 10312, 10377, March 6, 1997; redesignated at 68 FR 9824, 9838, Feb. 28, 2003]

§ 1240.58 Extreme hardship.

(a) To be eligible for suspension of deportation under former section 244(a)(1) of the Act, as in effect prior to April 1, 1997, the alien must meet the requirements set forth in the Act, which include a showing that deportation would result in extreme hardship to the alien or to the alien's spouse, parent, or child, who is a citizen of the United States, or an alien lawfully admitted for permanent residence. Extreme hardship is evaluated on a case-by-case basis, taking into account the particular facts and circumstances of each case. Applicants are encouraged to cite and document all applicable factors in their applications, as the presence or absence of any one factor may not be determinative in evaluating extreme hardship. Adjudicators should weigh all relevant factors presented and consider them in light of the totality of the circumstances, but are not required to offer an independent analysis of each listed factor when rendering a decision. Evidence of an extended stay in the United States without fear of deportation and with the benefit of work authorization, when present in a particular case, shall be considered relevant to the determination of whether deportation will result in extreme hardship.

(b) To establish extreme hardship, an applicant must demonstrate that deportation would result in a degree of hardship beyond that typically associated with deportation. Factors that may be considered in evaluating whether deportation would result in extreme hardship to the alien or to the alien's qualified relative include, but are not limited to, the following:

(1) The age of the alien, both at the time of entry to the United States and at the time of application for suspension of deportation;

(2) The age, number, and immigration status of the alien's children and their ability to speak the native language and to adjust to life in the country of return;

(3) The health condition of the alien or the alien's children, spouse, or parents and the availability of any required medical treatment in the country to which the alien would be returned;

(4) The alien's ability to obtain employment in the country to which the alien would be returned;

(5) The length of residence in the United States;

(6) The existence of other family members who are or will be legally residing in the United States;

(7) The financial impact of the alien's departure;

(8) The impact of a disruption of educational opportunities;

(9) The psychological impact of the alien's deportation;

(10) The current political and economic conditions in the country to which the alien would be returned;

(11) Family and other ties to the country to which the alien would be returned;

(12) Contributions to and ties to a community in the United States, including the degree of integration into society;

(13) Immigration history, including authorized residence in the United States; and

(14) The availability of other means of adjusting to permanent resident status.

(c) For cases raised under section 244(a)(3) of the Act, the following factors should be considered in addition to, or in lieu of, the factors listed in paragraph (b) of this section.

(1) The nature and extent of the physical or psychological consequences of abuse;

(2) The impact of loss of access to the United States courts and criminal justice system (including, but not limited to, the ability to obtain and enforce orders of protection, criminal investigations and prosecutions, and family law proceedings or court orders regarding child support, maintenance, child custody, and visitation);

(3) The likelihood that the batterer's family, friends, or others acting on behalf of the batterer in the home country would physically or psychologically harm the applicant or the applicant's child(ren);

(4) The applicant's needs and/or needs of the applicant's child(ren) for social, medical, mental health or other supportive services for victims of domestic violence that are unavailable or not reasonably accessible in the home country;

(5) The existence of laws and social practices in the home country that punish the applicant or the applicant's child(ren) because they have been victims of domestic violence or have taken steps to leave an abusive household; and

(6) The abuser's ability to travel to the home country and the ability and willingness of authorities in the home country to protect the applicant and/or the applicant's children from future abuse.

(d) Nothing in § 1240.58 shall be construed as creating any right, interest, or entitlement that is legally enforceable by or on behalf of any party against the United States or its agencies, officers, or any other person.

HISTORY:

[64 FR 27856, 27875, May 21, 1999; redesignated and amended at 68 FR 9824, 9838, 9846, Feb. 28, 2003]

Subpart H

Applications for Suspension of Deportation or Special Rule Cancellation of Removal Under Section 203 of Pub. L. 105-100

§ 1240.60 Definitions.

As used in this subpart the term:

ABC means American Baptist Churches v. Thornburgh, 760 F. Supp. 796 (N.D. Cal. 1991).

ABC class member refers to:

(1) Any Guatemalan national who first entered the United States on or before October 1, 1990; and

(2) Any Salvadoran national who first entered the United States on or before September 19, 1990.

Asylum application pending adjudication by the Service means any asylum application for which the Service has not served the applicant with a final decision or which has not been referred to the Immigration Court.

Filed an application for asylum means the proper filing of a principal asylum application or filing a derivative asylum application by being properly included as a dependent spouse or child in an asylum application pursuant to the regulations and procedures in effect at the time of filing the principal or derivative asylum application.

IIRIRA means the Illegal Immigration Reform and Immigrant Responsibility Act of 1996, enacted as Pub. L. 104-208 (110 Stat. 3009-625).

NACARA means the Nicaraguan Adjustment and Central American Relief Act (NACARA), enacted as title II of Pub. L. 105-100 (111 Stat. 2160, 2193), as amended by the Technical Corrections to the Nicaraguan Adjustment and Central American Relief Act, Pub. L. 105-139 (111 Stat. 2644).

Registered ABC class member means an ABC class member who:

(1) In the case of an ABC class member who is a national of El Salvador, properly submitted an ABC registration form to the Service on or before October 31, 1991, or applied for temporary protected status on or before October 31, 1991; or

(2) In the case of an ABC class member who is a national of Guatemala, properly submitted an ABC registration form to the Service on or before December 31, 1991.

HISTORY:

[64 FR 27856, 27876, May 21, 1999; 68 FR 9824, 9840, Feb. 28, 2003]

§ 1240.61 Applicability.

(a) Except as provided in paragraph (b) of this section, this subpart H applies to the following aliens:

(1) A registered ABC class member who has not been apprehended at the time of entry after December 19, 1990;

(2) A Guatemalan or Salvadoran national who filed an application for asylum with the Service on or before April 1, 1990, either by filing an application with the Service or filing the application with the Immigration Court and serving a copy of that application on the Service.

(3) An alien who entered the United States on or before December 31, 1990, filed an application for asylum on or before December 31, 1991, and, at the time of filing the application, was a national of the Soviet Union, Russia, any republic of the former Soviet Union, Latvia, Estonia, Lithuania, Poland, Czechoslovakia, Romania, Hungary, Bulgaria, Albania, East Germany, Yugoslavia, or any state of the former Yugoslavia;

(4) An alien who is the spouse or child of an individual described in paragraph (a)(1), (a)(2), or (a)(3) of this section at the time a decision is made to suspend the deportation, or cancel the removal, of the individual described in paragraph (a)(1), (a)(2), or (a)(3) of this section;

(5) An alien who is:

(i) The unmarried son or unmarried daughter of an individual described in paragraph (a)(1), (a)(2), or (a)(3) of this section and is 21 years of age or older at the time a decision is made to suspend the deportation, or cancel the removal, of the parent described in paragraph (a)(1), (a)(2), or (a)(3) of this section; and

(ii) Entered the United States on or before October 1, 1990.

(b) This subpart H does not apply to any alien who has been convicted at any time of an aggravated felony, as defined in section 101(a)(43) of the Act.

HISTORY:

[64 FR 27856, 27876, May 21, 1999; 68 FR 9824, 9840, Feb. 28, 2003]

§ 1240.62 Jurisdiction.

(a) Office of International Affairs. Except as provided in paragraph (b) of this section, the Office of International Affairs shall have initial jurisdiction to grant or refer to the Immigration Court or Board an application for suspension of deportation or special rule cancellation of removal filed by an alien described in § 1240.61, provided:

(1) In the case of a national of El Salvador described in § 1240.61(a)(1), the alien filed a complete asylum application on or before January 31, 1996 (with an administrative grace period extending to February 16, 1996), or otherwise met the asylum application filing deadline pursuant to the ABC settlement agreement, and the application is still pending adjudication by the Service;

(2) In the case of a national of Guatemala described in § 1240.61(a)(1), the alien filed a complete asylum application on or before January 3, 1995, or otherwise met the asylum application filing deadline pursuant to the ABC settlement agreement, and the application is still pending adjudication by the Service;

(3) In the case of an individual described in § 1240.61(a)(2) or (3), the individual's asylum application is pending adjudication by the Service;

(4) In the case of an individual described in § 1240.61(a)(4) or (5), the individual's parent or spouse has an application pending with the Service under this subpart H or has been granted relief by the Service under this subpart.

(b) Immigration Court. The Immigration Court shall have exclusive jurisdiction over an application for suspension of deportation or special rule cancellation of removal filed pursuant to section 309(f)(1)(A) or (B) of IIRIRA, as amended by NACARA, by an alien who has been served Form I-221, Order to Show Cause, or Form I-862, Notice to Appear, after a copy of the charging document has been filed with the Immigration Court, unless the alien is covered by one of the following exceptions:

(1) Certain ABC class members.

(i) The alien is a registered ABC class member for whom proceedings before the Immigration Court or the Board have been administratively closed or continued (including those aliens who had final orders of deportation or removal who have filed and been granted a motion to reopen as required under 8 CFR 1003.43);

(ii) The alien is eligible for benefits of the ABC settlement agreement and has not had a de novo asylum adjudication pursuant to the settlement agreement; and

(iii) The alien has not moved for and been granted a motion to recalendar proceedings before the Immigration Court or the Board to request suspension of deportation.

(2) Spouses, children, unmarried sons, and unmarried daughters.

(i) The alien is described in § 1240.61(a) (4) or (5);

(ii) The alien's spouse or parent is described in § 1240.61(a)(1), (a)(2), or (a)(3) and has a Form I-881 pending with the Service; and

(iii) The alien's proceedings before the Immigration Court have been administratively closed, or the alien's proceedings before the Board have been continued, to permit the alien to file an application for suspension of deportation or special rule cancellation of removal with the Service.

HISTORY:

[64 FR 27856, 27877, May 21, 1999; 68 FR 9824, 9840, 9846, Feb. 28, 2003; 68 FR 10349, 10355, Mar. 5, 2003]

§ 1240.63 Application process.

(a) Form and Fees. Except as provided in paragraph (b) of this section, the application must be made on a Form I-881, Application for Suspension of Deportation or Special Rule Cancellation of Removal (pursuant to section 203 of Public Law 105-100 (NACARA)), and filed in accordance with the instructions for that form.

An applicant who submitted to EOIR a completed Form EOIR-40, Application for Suspension of Deportation, before the effective date of the Form I-881 may apply with the Service by submitting the completed Form EOIR-40 attached to a completed first page of the Form I-881. Each application must be filed with the filing and fingerprint fees as provided in § 1103.7(b)(1) of this chapter, or a request for fee waiver, as provided in § 1103.7(c) of this chapter. The fact that an applicant has also applied for asylum does not exempt the applicant from the fingerprinting fees associated with the Form I-881.

(b) Applications filed with EOIR. If jurisdiction rests with the Immigration Court under § 1240.62(b), the application must be made on the Form I-881, if filed subsequent to June 21, 1999. The application form, along with any supporting documents, must be filed with the Immigration Court and served on the Service's district counsel in accordance with the instructions on or accompanying the form. Applications for suspension of deportation or special rule cancellation of removal filed prior to June 21, 1999 shall be filed on Form EOIR-40.

(c) Applications filed with the Service. If jurisdiction rests with the Service under § 1240.62(a), the Form I-881 and supporting documents must be filed at the appropriate Service Center in accordance with the instructions on or accompanying the form.

(d) Conditions and consequences of filing. Applications filed under this section shall be filed under the following conditions and shall have the following consequences:

(1) The information provided in the application may be used as a basis for the initiation of removal proceedings, or to satisfy any burden of proof in exclusion, deportation, or removal proceedings;

(2) The applicant and anyone other than a spouse, parent, son, or daughter of the applicant who assists the applicant in preparing the application must sign the application under penalty of perjury. The applicant's signature establishes a presumption that the applicant is aware of the contents of the application. A person other than a relative specified in this paragraph who assists the applicant in preparing the application also must provide his or her full mailing address;

(3) An application that does not include a response to each of the questions contained in the application, is unsigned, or is unaccompanied by the required materials specified in the instructions to the application is incomplete and shall be returned by mail to the applicant within 30 days of receipt of the application by the Service; and

(4) Knowing placement of false information on the application may subject the person supplying that information to criminal penalties under title 18 of the United States Code and to civil penalties under section 274C of the Act.

HISTORY:

[64 FR 27856, 27877, May 21, 1999; 68 FR 9824, 9840, 9846, Feb. 28, 2003; 68 FR 10349, 10355, Mar. 5, 2003]

§ 1240.64 Eligibility — general.

(a) Burden and standard of proof. The burden of proof is on the applicant to establish by a preponderance of the evidence that he or she is eligible for suspension of deportation or special rule cancellation of removal and that discretion should be exercised to grant relief.

(b) Calculation of continuous physical presence and certain breaks in presence. For purposes of calculating continuous physical presence under this section, section 309(c)(5)(A) of IIRIRA and section 240A(d)(1) of the Act shall not apply to persons described in § 1240.61. For purposes of this subpart H, a single absence of 90 days or less or absences which in the aggregate total no more than 180 days shall be considered brief.

(1) For applications for suspension of deportation made under former section 244 of the Act, as in effect prior to April 1, 1997, the burden of proof is on the applicant to establish that any breaks in continuous physical presence were brief, casual, and innocent and did not meaningfully interrupt the period of continuous physical presence in the United States. For purposes of evaluating whether an absence is brief, single absences in excess of 90 days, or absences that total more than 180 days in the aggregate will be evaluated on a case-by-case basis. An applicant must establish that any absence from the United States was casual and innocent and did not meaningfully interrupt the period of continuous physical presence.

(2) For applications for special rule cancellation of removal made under section 309(f)(1) of IIRIRA, as amended by NACARA, the applicant shall be considered to have failed to maintain continuous physical presence in the United States if he or she has departed from the United States for any period in excess of 90 days or for any periods in the aggregate exceeding 180 days. The applicant must establish that any period of absence less than 90 days was casual and innocent and did not meaningfully interrupt the period of continuous physical presence in the United States.

(3) For all applications made under this subpart, a period of continuous physical presence is terminated whenever an alien is removed from the United States under an order issued pursuant to any provision of the Act or the alien has voluntarily departed under the threat of deportation or when the departure is made for purposes of committing an unlawful act.

(4) The requirements of continuous physical presence in the United States under this subpart shall not apply to an alien who:

(i) Has served for a minimum period of 24 months in an active-duty status in the Armed Forces of the United States and, if separated from such service, was separated under honorable conditions, and

(ii) At the time of the alien's enlistment or induction, was in the United States.

(c) Factors relevant to extreme hardship. Except as described in paragraph (d) of this section, extreme hardship shall be determined as set forth in § 1240.58.

(d) **Rebuttable presumption of extreme hardship for certain classes of aliens.**

(1) Presumption of extreme hardship. An applicant described in paragraphs (a)(1) or (a)(2) of § 1240.61 who has submitted a completed Form I-881 or Form EOIR-40 to either the Service or the Immigration Court, in accordance with § 1240.63 shall be presumed to have established that deportation or removal from the United States would result in extreme hardship to the applicant or to his or her spouse, parent, or child, who is a citizen of the United States or an alien lawfully admitted for permanent residence.

(2) Rebuttal of presumption. A presumption of extreme hardship as described in paragraph (d)(1) of this section shall be rebutted if the evidence in the record establishes that it is more likely than not that neither the applicant nor a qualified relative would suffer extreme hardship if the applicant were deported or removed from the United States. In making such a determination, the adjudicator shall consider relevant factors, including those listed in § 1240.58.

(3) Burden of proof. In those cases where a presumption of extreme hardship applies, the burden of proof shall be on the Service to establish that it is more likely than not that neither the applicant nor a qualified relative would suffer extreme hardship if the applicant were deported or removed from the United States.

(4) Effect of rebuttal.

(i) A determination that it is more likely than not that neither the applicant nor a qualified relative would suffer extreme hardship if the applicant were deported or removed from the United States shall be grounds for referral to the Immigration Court or dismissal of an application submitted initially to the Service. The applicant is entitled to a de novo adjudication and will again be considered to have a presumption of extreme hardship before the Immigration Court.

(ii) If the Immigration Court determines that extreme hardship will not result from deportation or removal from the United States, the application will be denied.

HISTORY:

[64 FR 27856, 27877, May 21, 1999, as corrected at 64 FR 33386, June 23, 1999; 68 FR 9824, 9840, 9846, Feb. 28, 2003]

§ 1240.65 Eligibility for suspension of deportation.

(a) Applicable statutory provisions. To establish eligibility for suspension of deportation under this section, the applicant must be an individual described in § 1240.61; must establish that he or she is eligible under former section 244 of the Act, as in effect prior to April 1, 1997; must not be subject to any bars to eligibility in former section 242B(e) of the Act, as in effect prior to April 1, 1997, or any other provisions of law; and must not have been convicted of an aggravated felony or be an alien described in former section 241(a)(4)(D) of the Act, as in effect prior to April 1, 1997 (relating to Nazi persecution and genocide).

(b) General rule. To establish eligibility for suspension of deportation under former section 244(a)(1) of the Act, as in effect prior to April 1, 1997, an alien must be deportable under any law of the United States, except the provisions specified in paragraph (c) of this section, and must establish:

(1) The alien has been physically present in the United States for a continuous period of not less than 7 years immediately preceding the date the application was filed;

(2) During all of such period the alien was and is a person of good moral character; and

(3) The alien's deportation would, in the opinion of the Attorney General, result in extreme hardship to the alien or to the alien's spouse, parent, or child, who is a citizen of the United States or an alien lawfully admitted for permanent residence.

(c) Aliens deportable on criminal or certain other grounds. To establish eligibility for suspension of deportation under former section 244(a)(2) of the Act, as in effect prior to April 1, 1997, an alien who is deportable under former section 241(a) (2), (3), or (4) of the Act, as in effect prior to April 1, 1997 (relating to criminal activity, document fraud, failure to register, and security threats), must establish that:

(1) The alien has been physically present in the United States for a continuous period of not less than 10 years immediately following the commission of an act, or the assumption of a status constituting a ground for deportation;

(2) The alien has been and is a person of good moral character during all of such period; and

(3) The alien's deportation would, in the opinion of the Attorney General, result in exceptional and extremely unusual hardship to the alien, or to the alien's spouse, parent, or child, who is a citizen of the United States or an alien lawfully admitted for permanent residence.

(d) Battered spouses and children. To establish eligibility for suspension of deportation under former section 244(a)(3) of the Act, as in effect prior to April 1, 1997, an alien must be deportable under any law of the United States, except under former section 241(a)(1)(G) of the Act, as in effect prior to April 1, 1997 (relating to marriage fraud), and except under the provisions specified in paragraph (c) of this section, and must establish that:

(1) The alien has been physically present in the United States for a continuous period of not less than 3 years immediately preceding the date the application was filed;

(2) The alien has been battered or subjected to extreme cruelty in the United States by a spouse or parent who is a United States citizen or lawful permanent resident (or is the parent of a child of a United States citizen or lawful permanent resident and the child has been battered or subjected to extreme cruelty in the United States by such citizen or permanent resident parent); and

(3) During all of such time in the United States the alien was and is a person of good moral character; and

(4) The alien's deportation would, in the opinion of the Attorney General, result in extreme hardship to the alien or the alien's parent or child.

HISTORY:

[64 FR 27856, 27878, May 21, 1999; 68 FR 9824, 9840, 9846, Feb. 28, 2003]

§ 1240.66 Eligibility for special rule cancellation of removal.

(a) Applicable statutory provisions. To establish eligibility for special rule cancellation of removal, the applicant must show he or she is eligible under section 309(f)(1) of IIRIRA, as amended by section 203 of NACARA. The applicant must be described in § 1240.61, must be inadmissible or deportable, must not be subject to any bars to eligibility in sections 240(b)(7), 240A(c), or 240B(d) of the Act, or any other provisions of law, and must not have been convicted of an aggravated felony or be an alien described in section 241(b)(3)(B)(I) of the Act (relating to persecution of others).

(b) General rule. To establish eligibility for special rule cancellation of removal under section 309(f)(1)(A) of IIRIRA, as amended by section 203 of NACARA, the alien must establish that:

(1) The alien is not inadmissible under section 212(a)(2) or (3) or deportable under section 237(a)(2), (3) or (4) of the Act (relating to criminal activity, document fraud, failure to register, and security threats);

(2) The alien has been physically present in the United States for a continuous period of 7 years immediately preceding the date the application was filed;

(3) The alien has been a person of good moral character during the required period of continuous physical presence; and

(4) The alien's removal from the United States would result in extreme hardship to the alien, or to the alien's spouse, parent or child who is a United States citizen or an alien lawfully admitted for permanent residence.

(c) Aliens inadmissible or deportable on criminal or certain other grounds. To establish eligibility for special rule cancellation of removal under section 309(f)(1)(B) of IIRIRA, as amended by section 203 of NACARA, the alien must be described in § 1240.61 and establish that:

(1) The alien is inadmissible under section 212(a)(2) of the Act (relating to criminal activity), or deportable under paragraphs (a)(2) (other than section 237(a)(2)(A)(iii), relating to aggravated felony convictions), or (a)(3) of section 237 of the Act (relating to criminal activity, document fraud, and failure to register);

(2) The alien has been physically present in the United States for a continuous period of not less than 10 years immediately following the commission of an act, or the assumption of a status constituting a ground for removal;

(3) The alien has been a person of good moral character during the required period of continuous physical presence; and

(4) The alien's removal from the United States would result in exceptional and extremely unusual hardship to the alien or to the alien's spouse, parent, or child, who is a United States citizen or an alien lawfully admitted for permanent residence.

HISTORY:

[64 FR 27856, 27879, May 21, 1999; 68 FR 9824, 9840, 9846, Feb. 28, 2003]

§ 1240.67 Procedure for interview before an asylum officer.

(a) Fingerprinting requirements. The Service will notify each applicant 14 years of age or older to appear for an interview only after the applicant has complied with fingerprinting requirements pursuant to § 103.2(e) of 8 CFR chapter I, and the Service has received a definitive response from the FBI that a full criminal background check has been completed. A definitive response that a full criminal background check on an applicant has been completed includes:

(1) Confirmation from the FBI that an applicant does not have an administrative or criminal record;

(2) Confirmation from the FBI that an applicant has an administrative or a criminal record; or

(3) Confirmation from the FBI that two properly prepared fingerprint cards (Form FD-258) have been determined unclassifiable for the purpose of conducting a criminal background check and have been rejected.

(b) **Interview.**

(1) The asylum officer shall conduct the interview in a non-adversarial manner and, except at the request of the applicant, separate and apart from the general public. The purpose of the interview shall be to elicit all relevant and useful information bearing on the applicant's eligibility for suspension of deportation or special rule cancellation of removal. If the applicant has an asylum application pending with the Service, the asylum officer may also elicit information relating to the application for asylum in accordance with § 1208.9 of this chapter. At the time of the interview, the applicant must provide complete information regarding the applicant's identity, including name, date and place of birth, and nationality, and may be required to register this identity electronically or through any other means designated by the Attorney General.

(2) The applicant may have counsel or a representative present, may present witnesses, and may submit affidavits of witnesses and other evidence.

(3) An applicant unable to proceed with the interview in English must provide, at no expense to the Service, a competent interpreter fluent in both English and a language in which the applicant is fluent. The interpreter must be at least 18 years of age. The following individuals may not serve as the applicant's interpreter: the applicant's attorney or representative of record; a witness testifying on the applicant's behalf; or, if the applicant also has an asylum application pending with the Service, a representative or employee of the applicant's country of nationality, or, if stateless, country of last habitual residence. Failure without good cause to comply with this paragraph may be considered a failure to appear for the interview for purposes of § 1240.68.

(4) The asylum officer shall have authority to administer oaths, verify the identity of the applicant (including through the use of electronic means), verify the

identity of any interpreter, present and receive evidence, and question the applicant and any witnesses.

(5) Upon completion of the interview, the applicant or the applicant's representative shall have an opportunity to make a statement or comment on the evidence presented. The asylum officer may, in the officer's discretion, limit the length of such statement or comment and may require its submission in writing. Upon completion of the interview, and except as otherwise provided by the asylum officer, the applicant shall be informed of the requirement to appear in person to receive and to acknowledge receipt of the decision and any other accompanying material at a time and place designated by the asylum officer.

(6) The asylum officer shall consider evidence submitted by the applicant with the application, as well as any evidence submitted by the applicant before or at the interview. As a matter of discretion, the asylum officer may grant the applicant a brief extension of time following an interview, during which the applicant may submit additional evidence.

HISTORY:

[64 FR 27856, 27879, May 21, 1999; 68 FR 9824, 9840, 9846, Feb. 28, 2003; 68 FR 10349, 10355, Mar. 5, 2003]

§ 1240.68 Failure to appear at an interview before an asylum officer or failure to follow requirements for fingerprinting.

(a) Failure to appear for a scheduled interview without prior authorization may result in dismissal of the application or waiver of the right to an adjudication by an asylum officer. A written request to reschedule will be granted if it is an initial request and is received by the Asylum Office at least 2 days before the scheduled interview date. All other requests to reschedule the interview, including those submitted after the interview date, will be granted only if the applicant has a reasonable excuse for not appearing, and the excuse was received by the Asylum Office in writing within a reasonable time after the scheduled interview date.

(b) Failure to comply with fingerprint processing requirements without reasonable excuse may result in dismissal of the application or waiver of the right to an adjudication by an asylum officer.

(c) Failure to appear shall be excused if the notice of the interview or fingerprint appointment was not mailed to the applicant's current address and such address had been provided to the Office of International Affairs by the applicant prior to the date of mailing in accordance with section 265 of the Act and Service regulations, unless the asylum officer determines that the applicant received reasonable notice of the interview or fingerprinting appointment.

HISTORY:

[64 FR 27856, 27880, May 21, 1999; 68 FR 9824, 9840, Feb. 28, 2003]

§ 1240.69 Reliance on information compiled by other sources.

In determining whether an applicant is eligible for suspension of deportation or special rule cancellation of removal, the asylum officer may rely on material described in § 1208.12 of this chapter. Nothing in this subpart shall be construed to entitle the applicant to conduct discovery directed toward records, officers, agents, or employees of the Service, the Department of Justice, or the Department of State.

HISTORY:

[64 FR 27856, 27880, May 21, 1999; 68 FR 9824, 9840, Feb. 28, 2003; 68 FR 10349, 10355, Mar. 5, 2003]

§ 1240.70 Decision by the Service.

(a) Service of decision. Unless the asylum officer has granted the application for suspension of deportation or special rule cancellation of removal at the time of the interview or as otherwise provided by an Asylum Office, the applicant will be required to return to the Asylum Office to receive service of the decision on the applicant's application. If the applicant does not speak English fluently, the applicant shall bring an interpreter when returning to the office to receive service of the decision.

(b) Grant of suspension of deportation. An asylum officer may grant suspension of deportation to an applicant eligible to apply for this relief with the Service who qualifies for suspension of deportation under former section 244(a)(1) of the Act, as in effect prior to April 1, 1997, who is not an alien described in former section 241(a)(4)(D) of the Act, as in effect prior to April 1, 1997, and who admits deportability under any law of the United States, excluding former section 241(a)(2), (3), or (4) of the Act, as in effect prior to April 1, 1997. If the Service has made a preliminary decision to grant the applicant suspension of deportation under this subpart, the applicant shall be notified of that decision and will be asked to sign an admission of deportability or inadmissibility. The applicant must sign the admission before the Service may grant the relief sought. If suspension of deportation is granted, the Service shall adjust the status of the alien to lawful permanent resident, effective as of the date that suspension of deportation is granted.

(c) Grant of cancellation of removal. An asylum officer may grant cancellation of removal to an applicant who is eligible to apply for this relief with the Service, and who qualifies for cancellation of removal under section 309(f)(1)(A) of IIRIRA, as amended by section 203 of NACARA, and who admits deportability under section 237(a), excluding paragraphs (2), (3), and (4), of the Act, or inadmissibility under section 212(a), excluding paragraphs (2) or (3), of the Act. If the Service has made a preliminary decision to grant the applicant cancellation of removal under this subpart, the applicant shall be notified of that decision and asked to sign an admission of deportability or inadmissibility. The applicant must sign the concession before the Service may grant the relief sought. If the Service grants cancellation of removal, the Service shall adjust the status of the alien to lawful permanent resident, effective as of the date that cancellation of removal is granted.

(d) Referral of the application. Except as provided in paragraphs (e) and (f) of this section, and unless the applicant is granted asylum or is in lawful immigrant or non-immigrant status, an asylum officer shall refer the application for suspension of deportation or special rule cancellation of removal to the Immigration Court for adjudication in deportation or removal proceedings, and will provide the applicant with written notice of the statutory or regulatory basis for the referral, if:

(1) The applicant is not clearly eligible for suspension of deportation under former section 244(a)(1) of the Act as in effect prior to April 1, 1997, or for cancellation of removal under section 309(f)(1)(A) of IIRIRA, as amended by NACARA;

(2) The applicant does not appear to merit relief as a matter of discretion;

(3) The applicant appears to be eligible for suspension of deportation or special rule cancellation of removal under this subpart, but does not admit deportability or inadmissibility; or

(4) The applicant failed to appear for a scheduled interview with an asylum officer or failed to comply with fingerprinting processing requirements and such failure was not excused by the Service, unless the application is dismissed.

(e) Dismissal of the application. An asylum officer shall dismiss without prejudice an application for suspension of deportation or special rule cancellation of removal submitted by an applicant who has been granted asylum, or who is in lawful immigrant or non-immigrant status. An asylum officer may also dismiss an application for failure to appear, pursuant to § 1240.68. The asylum officer will provide the applicant written notice of the statutory or regulatory basis for the dismissal.

(f) Special provisions for certain ABC class members whose proceedings before EOIR were administratively closed or continued. The following provisions shall apply with respect to an ABC class member who was in proceedings before the Immigration Court or the Board, and those proceedings were closed or continued pursuant to the ABC settlement agreement:

(1) Suspension of deportation or asylum granted. If an asylum officer grants asylum or suspension of deportation, the previous proceedings before the Immigration Court or Board shall be terminated as a matter of law on the date relief is granted.

(2) Asylum denied and application for suspension of deportation not approved. If an asylum officer denies asylum and does not grant the applicant suspension of deportation, the Service shall move to recalendar proceedings before the Immigration Court or resume proceedings before the Board, whichever is appropriate. The Service shall refer to the Immigration Court or the Board the application for suspension of deportation. In the case where jurisdiction rests with the Board, an application for suspension of deportation that is referred to the Board will be remanded to the Immigration Court for adjudication.

(g) Special provisions for dependents whose proceedings before EOIR were administratively closed or continued. If an asylum officer grants suspension of deportation or special rule cancellation of removal to an applicant described in § 1240.61(a)(4) or (a)(5), whose proceedings before EOIR were administratively closed or continued, those proceedings shall terminate as of the date the relief is granted. If suspension of deportation or special rule cancellation of removal is not granted, the Service shall move to recalendar proceedings before the Immigration Court or resume proceedings before the Board, whichever is appropriate. The Service shall refer to the Immigration Court or the Board the application for suspension of deportation or special rule cancellation of removal. In the case where jurisdiction rests with the Board, an application for suspension of deportation or special rule cancellation of removal that is referred to the Board will be remanded to the Immigration Court for adjudication.

(h) Special provisions for applicants who depart the United States and return under a grant of advance parole while in deportation proceedings. Notwithstanding paragraphs (f) and (g) of this section, for purposes of adjudicating an application for suspension of deportation or special rule cancellation of removal under this subpart, if an applicant departs and returns to the United States pursuant to a grant of advance parole while in deportation proceedings, including deportation proceedings administratively closed or continued pursuant to the ABC settlement agreement, the deportation proceedings will be considered terminated as of the date of applicant's departure from the United States. A decision on the NACARA application shall be issued in accordance with paragraph (a), and paragraphs (c) through (e) of this section.

HISTORY:

[64 FR 27856, 27880, May 21, 1999; 68 FR 9824, 9840, 9846, Feb. 28, 2003]

PART 1241

APPREHENSION AND DETENTION OF ALIENS ORDERED REMOVED

Subpart A. Post-Hearing Detention and Removal

Subpart B. Deportation of Excluded Aliens (For Hearings Commenced Prior to April 1, 1997)

Subpart C. Deportation of Aliens in the United States (For Hearings Commenced Prior to April 1, 1997)

AUTHORITY NOTE APPLICABLE TO ENTIRE PART:

AUTHORITY:
5 U.S.C. 301, 552, 552a; 8 U.S.C. 1103, 1182, 1223, 1224, 1225, 1226, 1227, 1231, 1251, 1253, 1255, 1330, 1362; 18 U.S.C. 4002, 4013(c)(4).

Subpart A

Post-Hearing Detention and Removal

§ 1241.1 Final order of removal.

An order of removal made by the immigration judge at the conclusion of proceedings under section 240 of the Act shall become final:

(a) Upon dismissal of an appeal by the Board of Immigration Appeals;

(b) Upon waiver of appeal by the respondent;

(c) Upon expiration of the time allotted for an appeal if the respondent does not file an appeal within that time;

(d) If certified to the Board or Attorney General, upon the date of the subsequent decision ordering removal;

(e) If an immigration judge orders an alien removed in the alien's absence, immediately upon entry of such order; or

(f) If an immigration judge issues an alternate order of removal in connection with a grant of voluntary departure, upon overstay of the voluntary departure period, or upon the failure to post a required voluntary departure bond within 5 business days. If the respondent has filed a timely appeal with the Board, the order shall become final upon an order of removal by the Board or the Attorney General, or upon overstay of the voluntary departure period granted or reinstated by the Board or the Attorney General.

HISTORY:
[53 FR 9282, Mar. 22, 1988. Redesignated at 56 FR 8906, Mar. 4, 1991, and amended at 56 FR 38333, Aug. 13, 1991; 62 FR 10312, 10378, March 6, 1997; 68 FR 9824, 9840, Feb. 28, 2003; 73 FR 76927, 76938, Dec. 18, 2008]

§ 1241.2 Warrant of removal; detention of aliens during removal period.

For the regulations of the Department of Homeland Security with respect to the detention and removal of aliens who are subject to a final order of removal, see 8 CFR part 241.

HISTORY:
[62 FR 10312, 10378, March 6, 1997; 67 FR 39255, 39258, June 7, 2002; 68 FR 9824, 9840, Feb. 28, 2003; 68 FR 10349, 10357, Mar. 5, 2003; 70 FR 661, 674, Jan. 5, 2005]

§ 1241.6 Administrative stay of removal.

(a) An alien under a final order of deportation or removal may seek a stay of deportation or removal from the Department of Homeland Security as provided in 8 CFR 241.6.

(b) A denial of a stay by the Department of Homeland Security shall not preclude an immigration judge or the Board from granting a stay in connection with a previously filed motion to reopen or a motion to reconsider as provided in 8 CFR part 1003.

(c) The Service shall take all reasonable steps to comply with a stay granted by an immigration judge or the Board. However, such a stay shall cease to have effect if granted (or communicated) after the alien has been placed aboard an aircraft or other conveyance for removal and the normal boarding has been completed.

HISTORY:
[62 FR 10312, 10379, March 6, 1997; 65 FR 80281, 80298, Dec. 21, 2000; 67 FR 39255, 39259, June 7, 2002; 68 FR 9824, 9840, Feb. 28, 2003; 68 FR 10349, 10357, Mar. 5, 2003; 70 FR 661, 674, Jan. 5, 2005]

§ 1241.7 Self-removal.

Any alien who has departed from the United States while an order of deportation or removal is outstanding shall be considered to have been deported, excluded and deported, or removed, except that an alien who departed before the expiration of the voluntary departure period granted in connection with an alternate order of deportation or removal shall not be considered to be so deported or removed.

HISTORY:
[62 FR 10312, 10379, March 6, 1997; 67 FR 39255, 39260, June 7, 2002; 68 FR 9824, 9840, Feb. 28, 2003; 70 FR 661, 674, Jan. 5, 2005]

§ 1241.8 Reinstatement of removal orders.

(a) Applicability. An alien who illegally reenters the United States after having been removed, or having departed voluntarily, while under an order of exclusion, deportation, or removal shall be removed from the United States by reinstating the prior order. The alien has no right to a hearing before an immigration judge in such circumstances. In establishing whether an alien is subject to this section, the immigration officer shall determine the following:

(1) Whether the alien has been subject to a prior order of removal. The immigration officer must obtain the prior order of exclusion, deportation, or removal relating to the alien.

(2) The identity of the alien, i.e., whether the alien is in fact an alien who was previously removed, or who departed voluntarily while under an order of exclusion, deportation, or removal. In disputed cases, verification of identity shall be accomplished by a comparison of fingerprints between those of the previously excluded, deported, or removed alien contained in Service records and those of the subject alien. In the absence of fingerprints in a disputed case the alien shall not be removed pursuant to this paragraph.

(3) Whether the alien unlawfully reentered the United States. In making this determination, the officer shall consider all relevant evidence, including state-

ments made by the alien and any evidence in the alien's possession. The immigration officer shall attempt to verify an alien's claim, if any, that he or she was lawfully admitted, which shall include a check of Service data systems available to the officer.

(b) Notice. If an officer determines that an alien is subject to removal under this section, he or she shall provide the alien with written notice of his or her determination. The officer shall advise the alien that he or she may make a written or oral statement contesting the determination. If the alien wishes to make such a statement, the officer shall allow the alien to do so and shall consider whether the alien's statement warrants reconsideration of the determination.

(c) Order. If the requirements of paragraph (a) of this section are met, the alien shall be removed under the previous order of exclusion, deportation, or removal in accordance with section 241(a)(5) of the Act.

(d) Exception for applicants for benefits under section 902 of HRIFA or sections 202 or 203 of NACARA. If an alien who is otherwise subject to this section has applied for adjustment of status under either section 902 of Division A of Public Law 105-277, the Haitian Refugee Immigrant Fairness Act of 1998 (HRIFA), or section 202 of Pubic Law 105-100, the Nicaraguan Adjustment and Central American Relief Act (NACARA), the provisions of section 241(a)(5) of the Immigration and Nationality Act shall not apply. The immigration officer may not reinstate the prior order in accordance with this section unless and until a final decision to deny the application for adjustment has been made. If the application for adjustment of status is granted, the prior order shall be rendered moot.

(e) Exception for withholding of removal. If an alien whose prior order of removal has been reinstated under this section expresses a fear of returning to the country designated in that order, the alien shall be immediately referred to an asylum officer for an interview to determine whether the alien has a reasonable fear of persecution or torture pursuant to § 1208.31 of this chapter.

(f) Execution of reinstated order. Execution of the reinstated order of removal and detention of the alien shall be administered in accordance with this part.

HISTORY:

[62 FR 10312, 10379, March 6, 1997; 64 FR 8478, 8495, Feb. 19, 1999; 66 FR 29449, 29451, May 31, 2001; 68 FR 9824, 9840, Feb. 28, 2003; 68 FR 10349, 10357, Mar. 5, 2003]

§ 1241.14 Continued detention of removable aliens on account of special circumstances.

(a) Scope. This section provides for the review of determinations by the Department of Homeland Security to continue the detention of particular removable aliens found to be specially dangerous. See 8 CFR 241.14.

(1) Applicability. This section applies to the review of the continued detention of removable aliens because the Department of Homeland Security has determined that release of the alien would pose a special danger to the public, where there is no significant likelihood of removal in the reasonably foreseeable future. This section does not apply to aliens who are not subject to the special review provisions under 8 CFR 241.13.

(2) Jurisdiction. The immigration judges and the Board have jurisdiction with respect to determinations as to whether release of an alien would pose a special danger to the public, as provided in paragraphs (f) through (k) of this section.

(b)-(e) [Reserved]

(f) Detention of aliens determined to be specially dangerous.

(1) Standard for continued detention. Subject to the review procedures provided in this section, the Service shall continue to detain an alien if the release of the alien would pose a special danger to the public, because:

(i) The alien has previously committed one or more crimes of violence as defined in 18 U.S.C. 16;

(ii) Due to a mental condition or personality disorder and behavior associated with that condition or disorder, the alien is likely to engage in acts of violence in the future; and

(iii) No conditions of release can reasonably be expected to ensure the safety of the public.

(2) Determination by the Commissioner. The Service shall promptly initiate review proceedings under paragraph (g) of this section if the Commissioner has determined in writing that the alien's release would pose a special danger to the public, according to the standards of paragraph (f)(1) of this section.

(3) Medical or mental health examination. Before making such a determination, the Commissioner shall arrange for a report by a physician employed or designated by the Public Health Service based on a full medical and psychiatric examination of the alien. The report shall include recommendations pertaining to whether, due to a mental condition or personality disorder and behavior associated with that condition or disorder, the alien is likely to engage in acts of violence in the future.

(4) Detention pending review. After the Commissioner or Deputy Commissioner has made a determination under this paragraph, the Service shall continue to detain the alien, unless an immigration judge or the Board issues an administratively final decision dismissing the review proceedings under this section.

(g) Referral to Immigration Judge. Jurisdiction for an immigration judge to review a determination by the Service pursuant to paragraph (f) of this section that an alien is specially dangerous shall commence with the filing by the Service of a Notice of Referral to the Immigration Judge (Form I-863) with the Immigration Court having jurisdiction over the place of the alien's custody. The Service shall promptly provide to the alien by personal service a copy of the Notice of Referral to the Immigration Judge and all accompanying documents.

(1) Factual basis. The Service shall attach a written statement that contains a summary of the basis for the Commissioner's determination to continue to detain the alien, including a description of the evidence relied upon to reach the determination regarding the alien's special dangerousness. The Service shall attach copies

of all relevant documents used to reach its decision to continue to detain the alien.

(2) Notice of reasonable cause hearing. The Service shall attach a written notice advising the alien that the Service is initiating proceedings for the continued detention of the alien and informing the alien of the procedures governing the reasonable cause hearing, as set forth at paragraph (h) of this section.

(3) Notice of alien's rights. The Service shall also provide written notice advising the alien of his or her rights during the reasonable cause hearing and the merits hearing before the Immigration Court, as follows:

(i) The alien shall be provided with the List of Pro Bono Legal Service Providers for the immigration court at which the hearing is being held and may be represented by an attorney or other representative of his or her choice in accordance with 8 CFR part 1292, at no expense to the Government;

(ii) The Immigration Court shall provide an interpreter for the alien, if necessary, for the reasonable cause hearing and the merits hearing.

(iii) The alien shall have a reasonable opportunity to examine evidence against the alien, to present evidence in the alien's own behalf, and to cross-examine witnesses presented by the Service; and

(iv) The alien shall have the right, at the merits hearing, to cross-examine the author of any medical or mental health reports used as a basis for the determination under paragraph (f) of this section that the alien is specially dangerous.

(4) Record. All proceedings before the immigration judge under this section shall be recorded. The Immigration Court shall create a record of proceeding that shall include all testimony and documents related to the proceedings.

(h) Reasonable cause hearing. The immigration judge shall hold a preliminary hearing to determine whether the evidence supporting the Service's determination is sufficient to establish reasonable cause to go forward with a merits hearing under paragraph (i) of this section. A finding of reasonable cause under this section will be sufficient to warrant the alien's continued detention pending the completion of the review proceedings under this section.

(1) Scheduling of hearing. The reasonable cause hearing shall be commenced not later than 10 business days after the filing of the Form I-863. The Immigration Court shall provide prompt notice to the alien and to the Service of the time and place of the hearing. The hearing may be continued at the request of the alien or his or her representative.

(2) Evidence. The Service must show that there is reasonable cause to conduct a merits hearing under a merits hearing under paragraph (i) of this section. The Service may offer any evidence that is material and relevant to the proceeding. Testimony of witnesses, if any, shall be under oath or affirmation. The alien may, but is not required to, offer evidence on his or her own behalf.

(3) Decision. The immigration judge shall render a decision, which should be in summary form, within 5 business days after the close of the record, unless that time is extended by agreement of both parties, by a determination from the Chief Immigration Judge that exceptional circumstances make it impractical to render the decision on a highly expedited basis, or because of delay caused by the alien. If the immigration judge determines that the Service has met its burden of establishing reasonable cause, the immigration judge shall advise the alien and the Service, and shall schedule a merits hearing under paragraph (i) of this section to review the Service's determination that the alien is specially dangerous. If the immigration judge determines that the Service has not met its burden, the immigration judge shall order that the review proceedings under this section be dismissed. The order and any documents offered shall be included in the record of proceedings, and may be relied upon in a subsequent merits hearing.

(4) Appeal. If the immigration judge dismisses the review proceedings, the Service may appeal to the Board of Immigration Appeals in accordance with § 1003.38 of this chapter, except that the Service must file the Notice of Appeal (Form EOIR-26) with the Board within 2 business days after the immigration judge's order. The Notice of Appeal should state clearly and conspicuously that it is an appeal of a reasonable cause decision under this section.

(i) If the Service reserves appeal of a dismissal of the reasonable cause hearing, the immigration judge's order shall be stayed until the expiration of the time to appeal. Upon the Service's filing of a timely Notice of Appeal, the immigration judge's order shall remain in abeyance pending a final decision of the appeal. The stay shall expire if the Service fails to file a timely Notice of Appeal.

(ii) The Board will decide the Service's appeal, by single Board Member review, based on the record of proceedings before the immigration judge. The Board shall expedite its review as far as practicable, as the highest priority among the appeals filed by detained aliens, and shall determine the issue within 20 business days of the filing of the notice of appeal, unless that time is extended by agreement of both parties, by a determination from the Chairman of the Board that exceptional circumstances make it impractical to render the decision on a highly expedited basis, or because of delay caused by the alien.

(iii) If the Board determines that the Service has met its burden of showing reasonable cause under this paragraph (h), the Board shall remand the case to the immigration judge for the scheduling of a merits hearing under paragraph (i) of this section. If the Board determines that the Service has not met its burden, the Board shall dismiss the review proceedings under this section.

(i) Merits hearing. If there is reasonable cause to conduct a merits hearing under this section, the immigration judge shall promptly schedule the hearing and shall expedite the proceedings as far as practicable. The immigration judge shall allow adequate time for the parties to prepare for the merits hearing, but, if requested by the alien, the hearing shall commence within 30 days. The hearing may be continued at the request of the alien or his or her representative, or at the request of the Service upon a showing of exceptional circumstances by the Service.

(1) Evidence. The Service shall have the burden of proving, by clear and convincing evidence, that the alien should remain in custody because the alien's release would pose a special danger to the public, under the standards of paragraph (f)(1) of this section. The immigration judge may receive into evidence any oral or written statement that is material and relevant to this determination. Testimony of witnesses shall be under oath or affirmation. The alien may, but is not required to, offer evidence on his or her own behalf.

(2) Factors for consideration. In making any determination in a merits hearing under this section, the immigration judge shall consider the following non-exclusive list of factors:

(i) The alien's prior criminal history, particularly the nature and seriousness of any prior crimes involving violence or threats of violence;

(ii) The alien's previous history of recidivism, if any, upon release from either Service or criminal custody;

(iii) The substantiality of the Service's evidence regarding the alien's current mental condition or personality disorder;

(iv) The likelihood that the alien will engage in acts of violence in the future; and

(v) The nature and seriousness of the danger to the public posed by the alien's release.

(3) Decision. After the closing of the record, the immigration judge shall render a decision as soon as practicable. The decision may be oral or written. The decision shall state whether or not the Service has met its burden of establishing that the alien should remain in custody because the alien's release would pose a special danger to the public, under the standards of paragraph (f)(1) of this section. The decision shall also include the reasons for the decision under each of the standards of paragraph (f)(1) of this section, although a formal enumeration of findings is not required. Notice of the decision shall be served in accordance with § 1240.13(a) or (b).

(i) If the immigration judge determines that the Service has met its burden, the immigration judge shall enter an order providing for the continued detention of the alien.

(ii) If the immigration judge determines that the Service has failed to meet its burden, the immigration judge shall order that the review proceedings under this section be dismissed.

(4) Appeal. Either party may appeal an adverse decision to the Board of Immigration Appeals in accordance with § 1003.38 of this chapter, except that, if the immigration judge orders dismissal of the proceedings, the Service shall have only 5 business days to file a Notice of Appeal with the Board. The Notice of Appeal should state clearly and conspicuously that this is an appeal of a merits decision under this section.

(i) If the Service reserves appeal of a dismissal, the immigration judge's order shall be stayed until the expiration of the time to appeal. Upon the Service's filing of a timely Notice of Appeal, the immigration judge's order shall remain in abeyance pending a final decision of the appeal. The stay shall expire if the Service fails to file a timely Notice of Appeal.

(ii) The Board shall conduct its review of the appeal as provided in 8 CFR part 3, but shall expedite its review as far as practicable, as the highest priority among the appeals filed by detained aliens. The decision of the Board shall be final as provided in § 1003.1(d)(3) of this chapter.

(j) Release of alien upon dismissal of proceedings. If there is an administratively final decision by the immigration judge or the Board dismissing the review proceedings under this section upon conclusion of the reasonable cause hearing or the merits hearing, the Service shall promptly release the alien on conditions of supervision, as determined by the Service, pursuant to § 1241.13. The conditions of supervision shall not be subject to review by the immigration judge or the Board.

(k) Subsequent review for aliens whose release would pose a special danger to the public.

(1) Periodic review. In any case where the immigration judge or the Board has entered an order providing for the alien to remain in custody after a merits hearing pursuant to paragraph (i) of this section, the Service shall continue to provide an ongoing, periodic review of the alien's continued detention, according to § 1241.4 and paragraphs (f)(1)(ii) and (f)(1)(iii) of this section.

(2) Alien's request for review. The alien may also request a review of his or her custody status because of changed circumstances, as provided in this paragraph (k). The request shall be in writing and directed to the HQPDU.

(3) Time for review. An alien may only request a review of his or her custody status under this paragraph (k) no earlier than six months after the last decision of the immigration judge under this section or, if the decision was appealed, the decision of the Board.

(4) Showing of changed circumstances. The alien shall bear the initial burden to establish a material change in circumstances such that the release of the alien would no longer pose a special danger to the public under the standards of paragraph (f)(1) of this section.

(5) Review by the Service. If the Service determines, upon consideration of the evidence submitted by the alien and other relevant evidence, that the alien is not likely to commit future acts of violence or that the Service will be able to impose adequate conditions of release so that the alien will not pose a special danger to the public, the Service shall release the alien from custody pursuant to the procedures in § 1241.13. If the Service determines that continued detention is needed in order to protect the public, the Service shall provide a written notice to the alien stating the basis for the Service's determination, and provide a copy of the evidence relied upon by the Service. The notice shall also advise the alien of the right to move to set aside the prior review proceedings under this section.

(6) Motion to set aside determination in prior review proceedings. If the Service denies the alien's request for

release from custody, the alien may file a motion with the Immigration Court that had jurisdiction over the merits hearing to set aside the determination in the prior review proceedings under this section. The immigration judge shall consider any evidence submitted by the alien or relied upon by the Service and shall provide an opportunity for the Service to respond to the motion.

(i) If the immigration judge determines that the alien has provided good reason to believe that, because of a material change in circumstances, releasing the alien would no longer pose a special danger to the public under the standards of paragraph (f)(1) of this section, the immigration judge shall set aside the determination in the prior review proceedings under this section and schedule a new merits hearing as provided in paragraph (i) of this section.

(ii) Unless the immigration judge determines that the alien has satisfied the requirements under paragraph (k)(6)(i) of this section, the immigration judge shall deny the motion. Neither the immigration judge nor the Board may sua sponte set aside a determination in prior review proceedings. Notwithstanding 8 CFR 1003.23 or 1003.2 (motions to reopen), the provisions set forth in this paragraph (k) shall be the only vehicle for seeking review based on material changed circumstances.

(iii) The alien may appeal an adverse decision to the Board in accordance with § 1003.38 of this chapter. The Notice of Appeal should state clearly and conspicuously that this is an appeal of a denial of a motion to set aside a prior determination in review proceedings under this section.

HISTORY:

[66 FR 56967, 56979, Nov. 14, 2001; 68 FR 9824, 9840, 9846, Feb. 28, 2003; 68 FR 10349, 10357, Mar. 5, 2003; 70 FR 661, 674, Jan. 5, 2005; 80 FR 59503, 59513, Oct. 1, 2015]

§ 1241.15 Lack of jurisdiction to review other country of removal.

The immigration judges and the Board of Immigration Appeals have no jurisdiction to review any determination by officers of the Department of Homeland Security under 8 CFR 241.15.

HISTORY:

[67 FR 19508, 19511, Apr. 22, 2002, as confirmed at 68 FR 4364, 4367, Jan. 29, 2003; 68 FR 9824, 9840, Feb. 28, 2003; 68 FR 10349, 10357, Mar. 5, 2003; 70 FR 661, 675, Jan. 5, 2005]

§§ 1241.16 — 1241.19 [Reserved]

[NO TEXT IN ORIGINAL]

AUTHORITY:

(5 U.S.C. 301, 552, 552a; 8 U.S.C. 1103, 1182, 1223, 1224, 1225, 1226, 1227, 1231, 1251, 1253, 1255, 1330, 1362; 18 U.S.C. 4002, 4013(c)(4); 8 CFR part 2.)

Subpart B

Deportation of Excluded Aliens (For Hearings Commenced Prior to April 1, 1997)

§ 1241.20 Aliens ordered excluded.

For the regulations of the Department of Homeland Security pertaining to the detention and deportation of excluded aliens, see 8 CFR 241.20 through 241.25.

HISTORY:

[62 FR 10312, 10381, March 6, 1997; 68 FR 9824, 9840, 9846, Feb. 28, 2003; 70 FR 661, 675, Jan. 5, 2005]

§§ 1241.26 — 1241.29 [Reserved]

[NO TEXT IN ORIGINAL]

AUTHORITY:

(5 U.S.C. 301, 552, 552a; 8 U.S.C. 1103, 1182, 1223, 1224, 1225, 1226, 1227, 1231, 1251, 1253, 1255, 1330, 1362; 18 U.S.C. 4002, 4013(c)(4); 8 CFR part 2.)

Subpart C

Deportation of Aliens in the United States (For Hearings Commenced Prior to April 1, 1997)

§ 1241.30 Aliens ordered deported.

For the regulations of the Department of Homeland Security pertaining to the detention and deportation of aliens ordered deported, see 8 CFR 241.30 through 241.33.

HISTORY:

[62 FR 10312, 10382, March 6, 1997; 68 FR 9824, 9840, 9846, Feb. 28, 2003; 68 FR 10349, 10357, Mar. 5, 2003; 70 FR 661, 675, Jan. 5, 2005]

§ 1241.31 Final order of deportation.

Except as otherwise required by section 242(c) of the Act for the specific purposes of that section, an order of deportation, including an alternate order of deportation coupled with an order of voluntary departure, made by the immigration judge in proceedings under 8 CFR part 1240 shall become final upon dismissal of an appeal by the Board of Immigration Appeals, upon waiver of appeal, or upon expiration of the time allotted for an appeal when no appeal is taken; or, if such an order is issued by the Board or approved by the Board upon certification, it shall be final as of the date of the Board's decision.

HISTORY:

[62 FR 10312, 10382, March 6, 1997; 68 FR 9824, 9840, Feb. 28, 2003; 68 FR 10349, 10357, Mar. 5, 2003]

§ 1241.32 Warrant of deportation.

A Form I-205, Warrant of Deportation, based upon the final administrative order of deportation in the alien's case shall be issued by a district director. The district director shall exercise the authority contained in section 243 of the Act to determine at whose expense the alien shall be deported and whether his or her mental or physical condition requires personal care and attention en route to his or her destination.

HISTORY:

[62 FR 10312, 10382, March 6, 1997; 68 FR 9824, 9840, Feb. 28, 2003]

§ 1241.33 Expulsion.

(a) Execution of order. Except in the exercise of discretion by the district director, and for such reasons as are set forth in § 1212.5(b) of this chapter, once an order of deportation becomes final, an alien shall be taken into custody and the order shall be executed. For the purposes of this part, an order of deportation is final and subject to execution upon the date when any of the following occurs:

(1) A grant of voluntary departure expires;

(2) An immigration judge enters an order of deportation without granting voluntary departure or other relief, and the alien respondent waives his or her right to appeal;

(3) The Board of Immigration Appeals enters an order of deportation on appeal, without granting voluntary departure or other relief; or

(4) A Federal district or appellate court affirms an administrative order of deportation in a petition for review or habeas corpus action.

(b) Service of decision. In the case of an order entered by any of the authorities enumerated above, the order shall be executed no sooner than 72 hours after service of the decision, regardless of whether the alien is in Service custody, provided that such period may be waived on the knowing and voluntary request of the alien. Nothing in this paragraph shall be construed, however, to preclude assumption of custody by the Service at the time of issuance of the final order.

HISTORY:

[62 FR 10312, 10382, March 6, 1997; 65 FR 82254, 82256, Dec. 28, 2000; 66 FR 7863, Jan. 26, 2001; 68 FR 9824, 9840, Feb. 28, 2003; 68 FR 10349, 10357, Mar. 5, 2003]

PART 1244

TEMPORARY PROTECTED STATUS FOR NATIONALS OF DESIGNATED STATES

Rule

AUTHORITY NOTE APPLICABLE TO ENTIRE PART:

AUTHORITY:

8 U.S.C. 1103, 1254, 1254a note, 8 CFR part 2.

§ 1244.1 Definitions.

As used in this part:

Brief, casual, and innocent absence means a departure from the United States that satisfies the following criteria:

(1) Each such absence was of short duration and reasonably calculated to accomplish the purpose(s) for the absence;

(2) The absence was not the result of an order of deportation, an order of voluntary departure, or an administrative grant of voluntary departure without the institution of deportation proceedings; and

(3) The purposes for the absence from the United States or actions while outside of the United States were not contrary to law.

Charging document means the written instrument which initiates a proceeding before an Immigration Judge. For proceedings initiated prior to April 1, 1997, these documents include an Order to Show Cause, a Notice to Applicant for Admission Detained for Hearing before Immigration Judge, and a Notice of Intention to Rescind and Request for Hearing by Alien. For proceedings initiated after April 1, 1997, these documents include a Notice to Appear, a Notice of Referral to Immigration Judge, and a Notice of Intention to Rescind and Request for Hearing by Alien.

Continuously physically present means actual physical presence in the United States for the entire period specified in the regulations. An alien shall not be considered to have failed to maintain continuous physical presence in the United States by virtue of brief, casual, and innocent absences as defined within this section.

Continuously resided means residing in the United States for the entire period specified in the regulations. An alien shall not be considered to have failed to maintain continuous residence in the United States by reason of a brief, casual and innocent absence as defined within this section or due merely to a brief temporary trip abroad required by emergency or extenuating circumstances outside the control of the alien.

Felony means a crime committed in the United States, punishable by imprisonment for a term of more than one year, regardless of the term such alien actually served, if any, except: When the offense is defined by the State as a misdemeanor and the sentence actually imposed is one year or less regardless of the term such alien actually served. Under this exception for purposes of section 244 of the Act, the crime shall be treated as a misdemeanor.

Foreign state means any foreign country or part thereof as designated by the Attorney General pursuant to section 244 of the Act.

Misdemeanor means a crime committed in the United States, either:

(1) Punishable by imprisonment for a term of one year or less, regardless of the term such alien actually served, if any, or

(2) A crime treated as a misdemeanor under the term "felony" of this section.

For purposes of this definition, any crime punishable by imprisonment for a maximum term of five days or less shall not be considered a felony or misdemeanor.

Prima facie means eligibility established with the filing of a completed application for Temporary Protected Status containing factual information that if unrebutted will establish a claim of eligibility under section 244 of the Act.

Register means to properly file, with the director, a completed application, with proper fee, for Temporary Protected Status during the registration period designated under section 244(b) of the Act.

HISTORY:

[46 FR 25598, May 8, 1981, as amended at 55 FR 24859, June 19, 1990; 60 FR 37328, July 20, 1995; redesignated at 62 FR 10312, 10367, 10382, March 6, 1997; 63 FR 63593, 63595, Nov. 16, 1998; 64 FR 4780, 4781, Feb. 1, 1999, as confirmed at 65 FR 82256, 82257, Dec. 28, 2000; 66 FR 7863, Jan. 26, 2001; 68 FR 9824, 9841, Feb. 28, 2003]

§ 1244.2 Eligibility.

Except as provided in §§ 1244.3 and 1244.4, an alien may in the discretion of the director be granted Temporary Protected Status if the alien establishes that he or she:

(a) Is a national, as defined in section 101(a)(21) of the Act, of a foreign state designated under section 244(b) of the Act;

(b) Has been continuously physically present in the United States since the effective date of the most recent designation of that foreign state;

(c) Has continuously resided in the United States since such date as the Attorney General may designate;

(d) Is admissible as an immigrant except as provided under § 1244.3;

(e) Is not ineligible under § 1244.4; and

(f)(1) Registers for Temporary Protected Status during the initial registration period announced by public notice in the Federal Register, or

(2) During any subsequent extension of such designation if at the time of the initial registration period:

(i) The applicant is a nonimmigrant or has been granted voluntary departure status or any relief from removal;

(ii) The applicant has an application for change of status, adjustment of status, asylum, voluntary departure, or any relief from removal which is pending or subject to further review or appeal;

(iii) The applicant is a parolee or has a pending request for reparole; or

(iv) The applicant is a spouse or child of an alien currently eligible to be a TPS registrant.

(3) Eligibility for late initial registration in a currently designated foreign state shall also continue until January 15, 1999, for any applicant who would have been eligible to apply previously if paragraph (f)(2) of this section as revised had been in effect before November 16, 1998.

(g) Has filed an application for late registration with the appropriate Service director within a 60-day period immediately following the expiration or termination of conditions described in paragraph (f)(2) of this section.

HISTORY:

[52 FR 24982, July 2, 1987; redesignated at 62 FR 10312, 10367, 10382, March 6, 1997; 63 FR 63593, 63595, Nov. 16, 1998; 68 FR 9824, 9841, 9846, Feb. 28, 2003]

§ 1244.3 Applicability of grounds of inadmissibility.

(a) Grounds of inadmissibility not to be applied. Paragraphs (4), (5) (A) and (B), and (7)(A)(i) of section 212(a) of the Act shall not render an alien ineligible for Temporary Protected Status.

(b) Waiver of grounds of inadmissibility. Except as provided in paragraph (c) of this section, the Service may waive any other provision of section 212(a) of the Act in the case of individual aliens for humanitarian purposes, to assure family unity, or when the granting of such a waiver is in the public interest. If an alien is inadmissible on grounds which may be waived as set forth in this paragraph, he or she shall be advised of the procedures for applying for a waiver of grounds of inadmissibility on Form I-601 (Application for waiver of grounds of excludability).

(c) Grounds of inadmissibility that may not be waived. The Service may not waive the following provisions of section 212(a) of the Act:

(1) Paragraphs (2)(A)(i), (2)(B), and (2)(C) (relating to criminals and drug offenses);

(2) Paragraphs (3)(A), (3)(B), (3)(C), and (3)(D) (relating to national security); or

(3) Paragraph (3)(E) (relating to those who assisted in the Nazi persecution).

HISTORY:

[56 FR 619, Jan. 7, 1991.; 58 FR 58937, Nov. 5, 1993; redesignated at 62 FR 10312, 10367, 10382, March 6, 1997; 68 FR 9824, 9841, Feb. 28, 2003]

§ 1244.4 Ineligible aliens.

An alien is ineligible for Temporary Protected Status if the alien:

(a) Has been convicted of any felony or two or more misdemeanors, as defined in § 1244.1, committed in the United States, or

(b) Is an alien described in section 208(b)(2)(A) of the Act.

HISTORY:

[56 FR 619, Jan. 7, 1991, as amended at 56 FR 23497, May 22, 1991; redesignated at 62 FR 10312, 10367, 10382, March 6, 1997; 63 FR 63593, 63596, Nov. 16, 1998; 68 FR 9824, 9841, 9846, Feb. 28, 200385 FR 80274, 80401, Dec. 11, 2020]

§ 1244.5 Temporary treatment benefits for eligible aliens.

(a) Prior to the registration period. Prior to the registration period established by the Attorney General, a national of a foreign state designated by the Attorney General shall be afforded temporary treatment benefits upon the filing, after the effective date of such designation, of a completed application for Temporary Protected Status which establishes the alien's prima facie eligibility for benefits under section 244 of the Act. This application may be filed without fee. Temporary treatment benefits, if granted, shall terminate unless the registration fee is paid or a waiver is sought within the first thirty days of the registration period designated by the Attorney General. If the registration fee is paid or a waiver is sought within such thirty day period, temporary treatment benefits shall continue until terminated under § 1244.13. The denial of temporary treatment benefits prior to the registration period designated by the Attorney General shall be without prejudice to the filing of an application for Temporary Protected Status during such registration period.

(b) During the registration period. Upon the filing of an application for Temporary Protected Status, the alien shall be afforded temporary treatment benefits, if the application establishes the alien's prima facie eligibility for Temporary Protected Status. Such temporary treatment benefits shall continue until terminated under § 1244.13.

(c) Denied benefits. There shall be no appeal from the denial of temporary treatment benefits.

HISTORY:

[56 FR 619, May 22, 1991, as amended at 56 FR 23497, May 22, 1991; redesignated at 62 FR 10312, 10367, 10382, March 6, 1997; 63 FR 63593, 63596, Nov. 16, 1998; 68 FR 9824, 9841, 9846, Feb. 28, 2003]

§ 1244.6 Application.

An application for Temporary Protected Status must be made in accordance with § 103.2 of this chapter except as provided in this section. Each application must be filed with the fee, as provided in 8 CFR 103.7 and 8 CFR part 106 by each individual seeking temporary protected status, except that the filing fee for the Form I-765 will be charged only for those applicants between the ages of 14 and 65 (inclusive) who are requesting employment authorization. Each application must include a completed Form I-821, Application for Temporary Protected Status, Form I-765, Application for Employment Authorization, two identification photographs (1 ½" x 1 ½"), and supporting evidence as provided in § 1244.9. Every applicant who is 14 years of age or older must be fingerprinted on Form FD-258, Applicant Card, as prescribed in § 103.2(e) of this chapter.

HISTORY:

[56 FR 619, Jan. 7, 1991, as amended at 56 FR 23497, May 22, 1991; 58 FR 58937, Nov. 5, 1993; redesignated at 62 FR 10312, 10367, 10382, March 6, 1997; 63 FR 12979, 12987, March 17, 1998; 63 FR 63593, 63596, Nov. 16, 1998; 64 FR 4780, 4781, Feb. 1, 1999, as confirmed at 65 FR 82256, 82257, Dec. 28, 2000; 66 FR 7863, Jan. 26, 2001; 68 FR 9824, 9841, 9846, Feb. 28, 2003; 85 FR 82750, 82794, Dec. 18, 2020]

§ 1244.7 Filing the application.

(a) An application for Temporary Protected Status shall be filed with the director having jurisdiction over the applicant's place of residence.

(b) An application for Temporary Protected Status must be filed during the registration period established by the Attorney General, except in the case of an alien described in § 1244.2(f)(2).

(c) Each applicant must pay a fee, as determined at the time of the designation of the foreign state, except as provided in § 1244.5(a).

(d) If the alien has a pending deportation or exclusion proceeding before the immigration judge or Board of Immigration Appeals at the time a foreign state is designated under section 244(b) of the Act, the alien shall be given written notice concerning Temporary Protected Status. Such alien shall have the opportunity to submit an application for Temporary Protected Status to the director under paragraph (a) of this section during the published registration period unless the basis of the charging document, if established, would render the alien ineligible for Temporary Protected Status under § 1244.3(c) or § 1244.4. Eligibility for Temporary Protected Status in the latter instance shall be decided by the Executive Office for Immigration Review during such proceedings.

HISTORY:

[56 FR 619, Jan. 7, 1991, as amended at 56 FR 23497, May 22, 1991; 58 FR 58937, Nov. 5, 1993; redesignated at 62 FR 10312, 10367, 10382, March 6, 1997; 63 FR 63593, 63596, Nov. 16, 1998; 68 FR 9824, 9841, 9846, Feb. 28, 2003]

§ 1244.8 Appearance.

The applicant may be required to appear in person before an immigration officer. The applicant may be required to present documentary evidence to establish his or her eligibility. The applicant may have a representative as defined in § 1292.1 of this chapter present during any examination. Such representative shall not directly participate in the examination; however, such representative may consult with and provide advice to the applicant. The record of examination shall consist of the application, documents relating to the application, and the decision of the director.

HISTORY:

[56 FR 619, Jan. 7, 1991, as amended at 56 FR 23497, May 22, 1991; redesignated at 62 FR 10312, 10367, 10382, March 6, 1997; 63 FR 63593, 63596, Nov. 16, 1998; 68 FR 9824, 9841, Feb. 28, 2003; 68 FR 10349, 10357, Mar. 5, 2003]

§ 1244.9 Evidence.

(a) Documentation. Applicants shall submit all documentation as required in the instructions or requested by the Service. The Service may require proof of unsuccessful efforts to obtain documents claimed to be unavailable. If any required document is unavailable, an affidavit or other credible evidence may be submitted.

(1) Evidence of identity and nationality. Each application must be accompanied by evidence of the applicant's identity and nationality, if available. If these documents are unavailable, the applicant shall file an affidavit showing proof of unsuccessful efforts to obtain such identity documents, explaining why the consular process is unavailable, and affirming that he or she is a national of the designated foreign state. A personal interview before an immigration officer shall be required for each applicant who fails to provide documentary proof of identity or nationality. During this interview, the applicant may present any secondary evidence that he or she feels would be helpful in showing nationality. Acceptable evidence in descending order of preference may consist of:

(i) Passport;

(ii) Birth certificate accompanied by photo identification; and/or

(iii) Any national identity document from the alien's country of origin bearing photo and/or fingerprint.

(2) Proof of residence. Evidence to establish proof of continuous residence in the United States during the requisite period of time may consist of any of the following:

(i) Employment records, which may consist of pay stubs, W-2 Forms, certification of the filing of Federal, State, or local income tax returns; letters from employer(s) or, if the applicant has been self employed, letters from banks, and other firms with whom he or she has done business. In all of the above, the name of the alien and the name of the employer or other interested organization must appear on the form or letter, as well as relevant dates. Letters from employers must be in affidavit form, and shall be signed and attested to by the employer under penalty of perjury. Such letters from employers must include:

(A) Alien's address(es) at the time of employment;

(B) Exact period(s) of employment;

(C) Period(s) of layoff; and

(D) Duties with the company.

(ii) Rent receipts, utility bills (gas, electric, telephone, etc.), receipts, or letters from companies showing the dates during which the applicant received service;

(iii) School records (letters, report cards, etc.) from the schools that the applicant or his or her children have attended in the United States showing name of school and period(s) of school attendance;

(iv) Hospital or medical records showing medical treatment or hospitalization of the applicant or his or her children, showing the name of the medical facility or physician as well as the date(s) of the treatment or hospitalization;

(v) Attestations by churches, unions, or other organizations of the applicant's residence by letter which:

(A) Identifies applicant by name;

(B) Is signed by an official whose title is also shown;

(C) Shows inclusive dates of membership;

(D) States the address where applicant resided during the membership period;

(E) Includes the seal of the organization impressed on the letter or is on the letterhead of the organization, if the organization has letterhead stationery;

(F) Establishes how the attestor knows the applicant; and

(G) Establishes the origin of the information being attested to.

(vi) Additional documents to support the applicant's claim, which may include:

(A) Money order receipts for money sent in or out of the country;

(B) Passport entries;

(C) Birth certificates of children born in the United States;

(D) Bank books with dated transactions;

(E) Correspondence between the applicant and other persons or organizations;

(F) Social Security card;

(G) Selective Service card;

(H) Automobile license receipts, title, vehicle registration, etc;

(I) Deeds, mortgages, contracts to which applicant has been a party;

(J) Tax receipts;

(K) Insurance policies, receipts, or letters; and/or

(L) Any other relevant document.

(3) Evidence of eligibility under section 244(c)(2) of the Act. An applicant has the burden of showing that he or she is eligible for benefits under this part.

(4) Evidence of valid immigrant or nonimmigrant status. In the case of an alien described in § 1244.2(f)(2), Form I-551 or Form I-94 must be submitted by the applicant.

(b) Sufficiency of evidence. The sufficiency of all evidence will be judged according to its relevancy, consistency, credibility, and probative value. To meet his or her burden of proof the applicant must provide supporting documentary evidence of eligibility apart from his or her own statements.

(c) Failure to timely respond. Failure to timely respond to a request for information, or to appear for a scheduled interview, without good cause, will be deemed an abandonment of the application and will result in a denial of the application for lack of prosecution. Such failure shall be excused if the request for information, or the notice of the interview was not mailed to the applicant's most recent address provided to the Service.

HISTORY:

[56 FR 619, Jan. 7, 1991, as amended at 56 FR 23497, May 22, 1991; 58 FR 58937, Nov. 5, 1993; redesignated at 62 FR 10312, 10367, 10382, March 6, 1997; 63 FR 63593, 63596, Nov. 16, 1998; 68 FR 9824, 9841, 9846, Feb. 28, 2003]

§ 1244.10 Decision by the director or Administrative Appeals Unit (AAU).

(a) Temporary treatment benefits. The director shall grant temporary treatment benefits to the applicant if the applicant establishes prima facie eligibility for Temporary Protected Status in accordance with § 1244.5.

(b) Temporary Protected Status. Upon review of the evidence presented, the director may approve or deny the application for Temporary Protected Status in the exercise of discretion, consistent with the standards for eligibility in §§ 1244.2, 1244.3, and 1244.4.

(c) Denial by director. The decision of the director to deny Temporary Protected Status, a waiver of grounds of inadmissibility, or temporary treatment benefits shall be in writing served in person or by mail to the alien's most recent address provided to the Service and shall state the reason(s) for the denial. Except as otherwise provided in this section, the alien shall be given written notice of his or her right to appeal a decision denying Temporary Protected Status. To exercise such right, the alien shall file a notice of appeal, Form I-290B, with the director who issued the denial. If an appeal is filed, the administrative record shall be forwarded to the AAU for review and decision, pursuant to authority delegated in § 103.1(f)(2), except as otherwise provided in this section.

(1) If the basis for the denial of the Temporary Protected Status constitutes a ground for deportability or excludability which renders the alien ineligible for Temporary Protected Status under § 1244.4 or inadmissible under § 1244.3(c), the decision shall include a charging document which sets forth such ground(s).

(2) If such a charging document is issued, the alien shall not have the right to appeal the director's decision denying Temporary Protected Status as provided in this subsection. The decision shall also apprise the alien of his or her right to a de novo determination of his or her eligibility for Temporary Protected Status in deportation or exclusion proceedings pursuant to §§ 1240.11 and 1244.18.

(d) Decision by AAU. The decision of the AAU shall be in writing served in person, or by mail to the alien's most recent address provided to the Service, and, if the appeal is dismissed, the decision shall state the reason(s) for the denial.

(1) If the appeal is dismissed by the AAU under § 1240.18(b), the decision shall also apprise the alien of his or her right to a de novo determination of eligibility for Temporary Protected Status in deportation or exclusion proceedings.

(2) If the appeal is dismissed by the AAU, the director may issue a charging document if no charging document is presently filed with the Immigration Court.

(3) If a charging document has previously been filed or is pending before the Immigration Court, either party may move to recalendar the case after the decision by the AAU.

(e) Grant of temporary treatment benefits.

(1) Temporary treatment benefits shall be evidenced by the issuance of an employment authorization document. The alien shall be given, in English and in the language of the designated foreign state or a language that the alien understands, a notice of the registration requirements for Temporary Protected Status and a notice of the following benefits:

(i) Temporary stay of deportation; and

(ii) Temporary employment authorization.

(2) Unless terminated under § 1244.13, temporary treatment benefits shall remain in effect until a final decision has been made on the application for Temporary Protected Status.

(f) Grant of temporary protected status.

(1) The decision to grant Temporary Protected Status shall be evidenced by the issuance of an alien registration document. For those aliens requesting employment authorization, the employment authorization document will act as alien registration.

(2) The alien shall be provided with a notice, in English and in the language of the designated foreign state or a language that the alien understands, of the following benefits:

(i) The alien shall not be deported while maintaining Temporary Protected Status;

(ii) Employment authorization;

(iii) The privilege to travel abroad with the prior consent of the director as provided in § 1244.15;

(iv) For the purposes of adjustment of status under section 245 of the Act and change of status under section 248 of the Act, the alien is considered as being in, and maintaining, lawful status as a nonimmigrant while the alien maintains Temporary Protected Status.

(v) An alien eligible to apply for Temporary Protected Status under § 1244.2(f)(2), who was prevented from filing a late application for registration because the regulations failed to provide him or her with this opportunity, will be considered to have been maintaining lawful status as a nonimmigrant until the benefit is granted.

(3) The benefits contained in the notice are the only benefits the alien is entitled to under Temporary Protected Status.

(4) Such notice shall also advise the alien of the following:

(i) The alien must remain eligible for Temporary Protected Status;

(ii) The alien must register annually with the district office or service center having jurisdiction over the alien's place of residence; and

(iii) The alien's failure to comply with paragraphs (f)(4) (i) or (ii) of this section will result in the withdrawal of Temporary Protected Status, including work authorization granted under this Program, and may result in the alien's deportation from the United States.

HISTORY:

[56 FR 619, Jan. 7, 1991, as amended at 56 FR 23497, May 22, 1991; 58 FR 58937, Nov. 5, 1993; 60 FR 34090, June 30, 1995; redesignated at 62 FR 10312, 10367, 10382, March 6, 1997; 63 FR 63593, 63596, Nov. 16, 1998; 64 FR 4780, 4782, Feb. 1, 1999, as confirmed at 65 FR 82256, 82257, Dec. 28, 2000; 66 FR 7863, Jan. 26, 2001; 68 FR 9824, 9841, 9846, Feb. 28, 2003; 68 FR 10349, 10357, Mar. 5, 2003]

§ 1244.11 Renewal of application; appeal to the Board of Immigration Appeals.

If a charging document is served on the alien with a notice of denial or withdrawal of Temporary Protected Status, an alien may renew the application for Temporary Protected Status in deportation or exclusion proceedings. The decision of the immigration judge as to eligibility for Temporary Protected Status may be appealed to the Board of Immigration Appeals pursuant to § 1003.3 of this chapter. The provisions of this section do not extend the benefits of Temporary Protected Status beyond the termination of a foreign state's designation pursuant to § 1244.19.

HISTORY:

[56 FR 619, Jan. 7, 1991, as amended at 56 FR 23497, May 22, 1991; redesignated at 62 FR 10312, 10367, 10382, March 6, 1997; 63 FR 63593, 63596, Nov. 16, 1998; 68 FR 9824, 9841, 9846, Feb. 28, 2003; 68 FR 10349, 10357, Mar. 5, 2003]

§ 1244.12 Employment authorization.

(a) Upon approval of an application for Temporary Protected Status, the INS shall grant an employment authorization document valid during the initial period of the foreign state's designation (and any extensions of such period).

(b) If the alien's Temporary Protected Status is withdrawn under § 1244.14, employment authorization expires upon notice of withdrawal or on the date stated on the employment authorization document, whichever occurs later.

(c) If Temporary Protected Status is denied by the INS, employment authorization shall terminate upon notice of denial or at the expiration of the employment authorization document, whichever occurs later.

(d) If the application is renewed or appealed in deportation or exclusion proceedings, or appealed to the Administrative Appeals Unit pursuant to § 1244.18(b), employment authorization will be extended during the pendency of the renewal and/or appeal.

HISTORY:

[56 FR 619, Jan. 7, 1991, as amended at 56 FR 23498, May 22, 1991; 60 FR 21975, May 4, 1995; redesignated at 62 FR 10312, 10367, 10382, March 6, 1997; 63 FR 63593, 63596, Nov. 16, 1998; 64 FR 4780, 4782, Feb. 1, 1999, as confirmed at 65 FR 82256, 82257, Dec. 28, 2000; 66 FR 7863, Jan. 26, 2001; 68 FR 9824, 9841, 9846, Feb. 28, 2003]

§ 1244.13 Termination of temporary treatment benefits.

[PUBLISHER'S NOTE: 68 FR 10349, 10357, Mar. 5, 2003, purported to substitute "1244.14(a)(3)" for "240.14(a)(3)" in § 1244.13. However this could not implemented, since the text did not exist in § 1244.13. It was determined § 1244.14 should instead be amended. For the convenience of the user, the amendment has been implemented according to the apparent intent of the agency. A correction is anticipated.]

(a) Temporary treatment benefits terminate upon a final determination with respect to the alien's eligibility for Temporary Protected Status.

(b) Temporary treatment benefits terminate, in any case, sixty (60) days after the date that notice is published of the termination of a foreign state's designation under section 244(b)(3) of the Act.

HISTORY:

[56 FR 619, Jan. 7, 1991.; redesignated at 62 FR 10312, 10367, 10382, March 6, 1997; 63 FR 63593, 63596, Nov. 16, 1998; 68 FR 9824, 9841, Feb. 28, 2003]

§ 1244.14 Withdrawal of Temporary Protected Status.

[PUBLISHER'S NOTE: 68 FR 10349, 10357, Mar. 5, 2003, purported to substitute "1244.14(a)(3)" for "240.14(a)(3)" in § 1244.13. However this could not implemented, since the text did not exist in § 1244.13. It was determined § 1244.14 should instead be amended. For the convenience of the user, the amendment has been implemented according to the apparent intent of the agency. A correction is anticipated.]

(a) Authority of director. The director may withdraw the status of an alien granted Temporary Protected Status under section 244 of the Act at any time upon the occurrence of any of the following:

(1) The alien was not in fact eligible at the time such status was granted, or at any time thereafter becomes ineligible for such status;

(2) The alien has not remained continuously physically present in the United States from the date the alien was first granted Temporary Protected Status under this part. For the purpose of this provision, an alien granted Temporary Protected Status under this part shall be deemed not to have failed to maintain continuous physical presence in the United States if the alien departs the United States after first obtaining permission from the district director to travel pursuant to § 1244.15;

(3) The alien fails without good cause to register with the Attorney General annually within thirty (30) days before the end of each 12-month period after the granting of Temporary Protected Status.

(b) Decision by director.

(1) Withdrawal of an alien's status under paragraph (a) of this section shall be in writing and served by personal service pursuant to § 103.5(a) of this chapter. If the ground for withdrawal is § 1244.14(a)(3), the notice shall provide that the alien has thirty (30) days within which to provide evidence of good cause for

failure to register. If the alien fails to respond within thirty (30) days, Temporary Protected Status shall be withdrawn without further notice.

(2) Withdrawal of the alien's Temporary Protected Status under paragraph (b)(1) of this section may subject the applicant to exclusion or deportation proceedings under sections 235, 236, 237, 238, 240, or 241 of the Act as appropriate.

(3) If the basis for the withdrawal of Temporary Protected Status constitutes a ground of deportability or excludability which renders an alien ineligible for Temporary Protected Status under § 1244.4 or inadmissible under § 1244.3(c), the decision shall include a charging document which sets forth such ground(s) with notice of the right of a de novo determination of eligibility for Temporary Protected Status in deportation or exclusion proceedings. If the basis for withdrawal does not constitute such a ground, the alien shall be given written notice of his or her right to appeal to the AAU. Upon receipt of an appeal, the administrative record will be forwarded to the AAU for review and decision pursuant to the authority delegated under § 103.1(f)(2). Temporary Protected Status benefits will be extended during the pendency of an appeal.

(c) Decision by AAU. If a decision to withdraw Temporary Protected Status is entered by the AAU, the AAU shall notify the alien of the decision and the right to a de novo determination of eligibility for Temporary Protected Status in deportation or exclusion proceedings, if the alien is then deportable or excludable, as provided by § 1244.10(d).

HISTORY:

[56 FR 619, Jan. 7, 1991, as amended at 56 FR 23498, May 22, 1991; redesignated at 62 FR 10312, 10367, 10382, March 6, 1997; 63 FR 63593, 63596, Nov. 16, 1998; 68 FR 9824, 9841, 9846, Feb. 28, 2003; 68 FR 10349, 10357, Mar. 5, 2003]

§ 1244.15 Travel abroad.

(a) After the grant of Temporary Protected Status, the alien must remain continuously physically present in the United States under the provisions of section 244(c)(3)(B) of the Act. The grant of Temporary Protected Status shall not constitute permission to travel abroad. Permission to travel may be granted by the director pursuant to the Service's advance parole provisions. There is no appeal from a denial of advance parole.

(b) Failure to obtain advance parole prior to the alien's departure from the United States may result in the withdrawal of Temporary Protected Status and/or the institution or recalendering of deportation or exclusion proceedings against the alien.

HISTORY:

[56 FR 619, Jan. 7, 1991, as amended at 56 FR 23498, May 22, 1991; redesignated at 62 FR 10312, 10367, 10382, March 6, 1997; 63 FR 63593, 63597, Nov. 16, 1998; 64 FR 4780, 4782, Feb. 1, 1999, as confirmed at 65 FR 82256, 82257, Dec. 28, 2000; 66 FR 7863, Jan. 26, 2001; 68 FR 9824, 9841, Feb. 28, 2003]

§ 1244.16 Confidentiality.

The information contained in the application and supporting documents submitted by an alien shall not be released in any form whatsoever to a third party requester without a court order, or the written consent of the alien. For the purpose of this provision, a third party requester means any requester other than the alien, his or her authorized representative, an officer of the Department of Justice, or any federal or State law enforcement agency. Any information provided under this part may be used for purposes of enforcement of the Act or in any criminal proceeding.

HISTORY:

[56 FR 619, Jan. 7, 1991.; redesignated at 62 FR 10312, 10367, 10382, March 6, 1997; 68 FR 9824, 9841, Feb. 28, 2003]

§ 1244.17 Annual registration.

(a) Aliens granted Temporary Protected Status must register annually with the INS having jurisdiction over their place of residence. Such registration will apply to nationals of those foreign states designated or redesignated for more than one year by the Attorney General pursuant to section 244(b) of the Act. Registration may be accomplished by mailing or submitting in person, depending on the practice in place at the INS, completed Forms I-821 and I-765 within the thirty (30) day period prior to the anniversary of the grant of Temporary Protected Status (inclusive of such anniversary date). Form I-821 will be filed without fee. Form I-765 will be filed with fee only if the alien is requesting employment authorization. Completing the block on the I-821 attesting to the continued maintenance of the conditions of eligibility will generally preclude the need for supporting documents or evidence. The Service, however, reserves the right to request additional information and/or documentation on a case-by-case basis.

(b) Unless the Service determines otherwise, registration by mail shall suffice to meet the alien's registration requirements. However, as part of the registration process, an alien will generally have to appear in person in order to secure a renewal of employment authorization unless the Service determines that employment authorization will be extended in another fashion due to operational need. The Service may also request that an alien appear in person as part of the registration process. In such cases, failure to appear without good cause shall be deemed a failure to register under this chapter.

(c) Failure to register without good cause will result in the withdrawal of the alien's Temporary Protected Status.

HISTORY:

[56 FR 619, Jan. 7, 1991, as amended at 56 FR 23498, May 22, 1991; 60 FR 21975, May 4, 1995; redesignated at 62 FR 10312, 10367, 10382, March 6, 1997; 63 FR 63593, 63597, Nov. 16, 1998; 68 FR 9824, 9841, Feb. 28, 2003]

§ 1244.18 Issuance of charging documents; detention.

(a) A charging document may be issued against an alien granted Temporary Protected Status on grounds of deportability or excludability which would have rendered the alien statutorily ineligible for such status pursuant to §§ 1244.3(c) and 1244.4. Aliens shall not be deported for a particular offense for which the Service has expressly granted a waiver. If the alien is deportable on a waivable ground, and no such waiver for the charged offense has been previously granted, then the alien may seek such a waiver in deportation or exclusion proceedings. The charging document shall constitute notice to the alien that his or her status in the United States is subject to withdrawal. A final order of deportation or exclusion against an alien granted Temporary Protected Status shall constitute a withdrawal of such status.

(b) The filing of the charging document by the Service with the Immigration Court renders inapplicable any other administrative, adjudication or review of eligibility for Temporary Protected Status. The alien shall have the right to a de novo determination of his or her eligibility for Temporary Protected Status in the deportation or exclusion proceedings. Review by the Board of Immigration Appeals shall be the exclusive administrative appellate review procedure. If an appeal is already pending before the Administrative Appeals Unit, the director shall notify the Administrative Appeals Unit of the filing of the charging document, in which case the pending appeal shall be dismissed and the record of proceeding returned to the jurisdiction where the charging document was filed.

(c) Upon denial of Temporary Protected Status by the Administrative Appeals Unit, the Administrative Appeals Unit shall immediately forward the record of proceeding to the director having jurisdiction over the alien's place of residence. The director shall, as soon as practicable, file a charging document with the Immigration Court if the alien is then deportable or excludable under section 241(a) or section 212(a) of the Act, respectively.

(d) An alien who is determined by the Service to be deportable or excludable upon grounds which would have rendered the alien ineligible for such status as provided in §§ 1244.3(c) and 1244.4 may be detained under the provisions of this chapter pending deportation or exclusion proceedings. Such alien may be removed from the United States upon entry of a final order of deportation or exclusion.

HISTORY:

[56 FR 619, Jan. 7, 1991, as amended at 56 FR 23498, May 22, 1991; 60 FR 34090, June 30, 1995; redesignated at 62 FR 10312, 10367, 10382, March 6, 1997; 63 FR 63593, 63597, Nov. 16, 1998; 64 FR 4780, 4782, Feb. 1, 1999, as confirmed at 65 FR 82256, 82257, Dec. 28, 2000; 66 FR 7863, Jan. 26, 2001; 68 FR 9824, 9841, 9846, Feb. 28, 2003; 68 FR 10349, 10357, Mar. 5, 2003]

§ 1244.19 Termination of designation.

Upon the termination of designation of a foreign state, those nationals afforded temporary Protected Status shall, upon the sixtieth (60th) day after the date notice of termination is published in the Federal Register, or on the last day of the most recent extension of designation by the Attorney General, automatically and without further notice or right of appeal, lose Temporary Protected Status in the United States. Such termination of a foreign state's designation is not subject to appeal.

HISTORY:

[56 FR 619, Jan. 7, 1991.; redesignated at 62 FR 10312, 10367, 10382, March 6, 1997; 63 FR 63593, 63597, Nov. 16, 1998; 68 FR 9824, 9841, Feb. 28, 2003]

§ 1244.20 Waiver of fees.

(a) Any of the fees prescribed in 8 CFR 103.7 and 8 CFR part 106 which relate to applications to the district director or service center director for Temporary Protected Status may be waived if the applicant establishes that he or she is unable to pay the prescribed fee. The applicant will have established his or her inability to pay when the adjudicating officer concludes, on the basis of the requisite affidavit and of any other information submitted, that it is more probable than not that:

(1) The applicant's gross income from all sources for the three-month period prior to the filing of the fee waiver request, including income received or earned by any dependent in the United States, was equaled or exceeded by essential expenditures for such three-month period; and

(2) The applicant does not own, possess, or control assets sufficient to pay the fee without substantial hardship.

(b) For purposes of this section, essential expenditures are limited to reasonable expenditures for rent, utilities, food, transportation to and from employment, and any essential extraordinary expenditures, such as essential medical expenses, or expenses for clothing, laundry, and child care, to the extent that the applicant can show that those expenditures made during the three-month period prior to the filing of the fee waiver request were reasonable and essential to his or her physical well-being or to earning a livelihood.

(c) For purposes of this section, the TPS registration fee (including the fee for employment authorization, if applicable) shall be considered an essential expenditure. A fee waiver will be granted if the sum of the fees for TPS registration and employment authorization equals or exceeds income and assets that remain after deducting other essential expenditures.

(d) If an adjudicating officer is satisfied that an applicant has established inability to pay, he or she shall not deny a fee waiver due to the cost of administering the TPS program.

(e) For purposes of this section, the following documentation shall be required:

(1) The applicant seeking a fee waiver must submit an affidavit, under penalty of perjury, setting forth information to establish that he or she satisfies the requirements of this section. The affidavit shall individually list:

(i) The applicant's monthly gross income from each source for each of the three months prior to the filing of the fee waiver request;

(ii) All assets owned, possessed, or controlled by the applicant or by his or her dependents;

(iii) The applicant's essential monthly expenditures, itemized for each of the three months prior to the filing of the fee waiver request, including essential extraordinary expenditures; and

(iv) The applicant's dependents in the United States, his or her relationship to those dependents, the dependents' ages, any income earned or received by those dependents, and the street address of each dependent's place of residence.

(2) The applicant may also submit other documentation tending to substantiate his or her inability to pay.

(f) If the adjudicating officer concludes based upon the totality of their circumstances that the information presented in the affidavit and in any other additional documentation is inaccurate or insufficient, the adjudicating officer may require that the applicant submit the following additional documents prior to the adjudication of a fee waiver:

(1) The applicant's employment records, pay stubs, W-2 forms, letter(s) from employer(s), and proof of filing of a local, state, or federal income tax return. The same documents may also be required from the applicant's dependents in the United States.

(2) The applicant's rent receipts, bills for essential utilities (for example, gas, electricity, telephone, water), food, medical expenses, and receipts for other essential expenditures.

(3) Documentation to show all assets owned, possessed, or controlled by the applicant or by dependents of the applicant.

(4) Evidence of the applicant's living arrangements in the United States (living with relative, living in his or her own house or apartment, etc.), and evidence of whether his or her spouse, children, or other dependents are residing in his or her household in the United States.

(5) Evidence of the applicant's essential extraordinary expenditures or those of his or her dependents residing in the United States.

(g) The adjudicating officer must consider the totality of the information submitted in each case before requiring additional information or rendering a final decision.

(h) All documents submitted by the applicant or required by the adjudicating officer in support of a fee waiver request are subject to verification by the Service.

(i) In requiring additional information, the adjudicating officer should consider that some applicants may have little or no documentation to substantiate their claims. An adjudicating officer may accept other evidence, such as an affidavit from a member of the community of good moral character, but only if the applicant provides an affidavit stating that more direct documentary evidence in unavailable.

HISTORY:

[57 FR 34507, Aug. 5, 1992; redesignated at 62 FR 10312, 10367, 10382, March 6, 1997; 68 FR 9824, 9841, Feb. 28, 2003; 85 FR 82750, 82794, Dec. 18, 2020]

PART 1245

ADJUSTMENT OF STATUS TO THAT OF PERSON ADMITTED FOR PERMANENT RESIDENCE

Rule

AUTHORITY NOTE APPLICABLE TO ENTIRE PART:

AUTHORITY:

8 U.S.C. 1101, 1103, 1182, 1255; section 202, Public Law 105-100, 111 Stat. 2160, 2193; section 902, Public Law 105-277, 112 Stat. 2681; Title VII of Public Law 110-229.

§ 1245.1 Eligibility.

(a) General. Any alien who is physically present in the United States, except for an alien who is ineligible to apply for adjustment of status under paragraph (b) or (c) of this section, may apply for adjustment of status to that of a lawful permanent resident of the United States if the applicant is eligible to receive an immigrant visa and an immigrant visa is immediately available at the time of filing of the application. A special immigrant described under section 101(a)(27)(J) of the Act shall be deemed, for the purpose of applying the adjustment to status provisions of section 245(a) of the Act, tohave been paroled into the United States, regardless of the actual method of entry into the United States.

(b) Restricted aliens. The following categories of aliens are ineligible to apply for adjustment of status to that of a lawful permanent resident alien under section 245 of the Act, unless the alien establishes eligibility under the provisions of section 245(i) of the Act and § 1245.10, is not included in the categories of aliens prohibited from applying for adjustment of status listed in § 1245.1(c), is eligible to receive an immigrant visa, and has an immigrant visa immediately available at the time of filing the application for adjustment of status:

(1) Any alien who entered the United States in transit without a visa;

(2) Any alien who, on arrival in the United States, was serving in any capacity on board a vessel or aircraft or was destined to join a vessel or aircraft in the United States to serve in any capacity thereon;

(3) Any alien who was not admitted or paroled following inspection by an immigration officer;

(4) Any alien who, on or after January 1, 1977, was employed in the United States without authorization prior to filing an application for adjustment of status. This restriction shall not apply to an alien who is:

(i) An immediate relative as defined in section 201(b) of the Act;

(ii) A special immigrant as defined in section 101(a)(27)(H) or (J) of the Act;

(iii) Eligible for the benefits of Public Law 101-238 (the Immigration Nursing Relief Act of 1989) and files an application for adjustment of status on or before October 17, 1991; or

(iv) Eligible for the benefits of Public Law 101-238 (the Immigration Nursing Relief Act of 1989), and has not entered into or continued in unauthorized employment on or after November 29, 1990.

(5) Any alien who on or after November 6, 1986 is not in lawful immigration status on the date of filing his or her application for adjustment of status, except an applicant who is an immediate relative as defined in section 201(b) or a special immigrant as defined in section 101(a)(27)(H), (I), or (J);

(6) Any alien who files an application for adjustment of status on or after November 6, 1986, who has failed (other than through no fault of his or her own or for technical reasons) to maintain continuously a lawful status since entry into the United States, except an applicant who is an immediate relative as defined in section 201(b) of the Act or a special immigrant as defined in section 101(a)(27)(H), (I), or (J) of the Act;

(7) Any alien admitted as a visitor under the visa waiver provisions of 8 CFR 212.1(e) or (q), other than an immediate relative as defined in section 201(b) of the Act;

(8) Any alien admitted as a Visa Waiver Pilot Program visitor under the provisions of section 217 of the Act and part 217 of 8 CFR chapter I other than an immediate relative as defined in section 201(b) of the Act;

(9) Any alien who seeks adjustment of status pursuant to an employment-based immigrant visa petition under section 203(b) of the Act and who is not maintaining a lawful nonimmigrant status at the time he or she files an application for adjustment of status; and

(10) Any alien who was ever employed in the United States without the authorization of the Service or who has otherwise at any time violated the terms of his or her admission to the United States as a nonimmigrant, except an alien who is an immediate relative as defined in section 201(b) of the Act or a special immigrant as defined in section 101(a)(27)(H), (I), (J), or (K) of the Act. For purposes of this paragraph, an alien who meets the requirements of § 1274a.12(c)(9) of this chapter shall not be deemed to have engaged in unauthorized employment during the pendency of his or her adjustment application.

(c) Ineligible aliens. The following categories of aliens are ineligible to apply for adjustment of status to that of a lawful permanent resident alien under section 245 of the Act:

(1) Any nonpreference alien who is seeking or engaging in gainful employment in the United States who is not the beneficiary of a valid individual or blanket labor certification issued by the Secretary of Labor or who is not exempt from certification requirements under § 1212.8(b) of this chapter;

(2) Except for an alien who is applying for residence under the provisions of section 133 of the Immigration Act of 1990, any alien who has or had the status of an exchange visitor under section 101(a)(15)(J) of the Act and who is subject to the foreign residence requirement of section 212(e) of the Act, unless the alien has complied with the foreign residence requirement or has been granted a waiver of that requirement, under that section. An alien who has been granted a waiver under section 212(e)(iii) of the Act based on a request by a State Department of Health (or its equivalent) under Pub. L. 103-416 shall be ineligible to apply for adjustment of status under section 245 of the Act if the terms and conditions specified in section 214(k) of the Act and § 1212.7(c)(9) of this chapter have not been met;

(3) Any alien who has nonimmigrant status under paragraph (15)(A), (15)(E), or (15)(G) of section 101(a) of the Act, or has an occupational status which would, if the alien were seeking admission to the United States, entitle the alien to nonimmigrant status under those paragraphs, unless the alien first executes and submits the written waiver required by section 247(b) of the Act and part 247 of 8 CFR chapter I;

(4) Any alien who claims immediate relative status under section 201(b) or preference status under sections 203(a) or 203(b) of the Act, unless the applicant is the beneficiary of a valid unexpired visa petition filed in accordance with part 204 of 8 CFR chapter I;

(5) Any alien who is already an alien lawfully admitted to the United States for permanent residence on a conditional basis pursuant to section 216 or 216A of the Act, regardless of any other quota or non-quota immi-

grant visa classification for which the alien may otherwise be eligible;

(6) Any alien admitted to the United States as a nonimmigrant defined in section 101(a)(15)(K) of the Act, unless:

(i) In the case of a K-1 fiance(e) under section 101(a)(15)(K)(i) of the Act or the K-2 child of a fiance(e) under section 101(a)(15)(K)(iii) of the Act, the alien is applying for adjustment of status based upon the marriage of the K-1 fiance(e) which was contracted within 90 days of entry with the United States citizen who filed a petition on behalf of the K-1 fiance(e) pursuant to § 214.2(k) of 8 CFR chapter I;

(ii) In the case of a K-3 spouse under section 101(a)(15)(K)(ii) of the Act or the K-4 child of a spouse under section 101(a)(15)(K)(iii) of the Act, the alien is applying for adjustment of status based upon the marriage of the K-3 spouse to the United States citizen who filed a petition on behalf of the K-3 spouse pursuant to § 214.2(k) of 8 CFR chapter I;

(7) A nonimmigrant classified pursuant to section 101(a)(15)(S) of the Act, unless the nonimmigrant is applying for adjustment of status pursuant to the request of a law enforcement authority, the provisions of section 101(a)(15)(S) of the Act, and 8 CFR 1245.11;

(8) Any alien who seeks to adjust status based upon a marriage which occurred on or after November 10, 1986, and while the alien was in exclusion, deportation, or removal proceedings, or judicial proceedings relating thereto.

(i) Commencement of proceedings. The period during which the alien is in deportation, exclusion, or removal proceedings or judicial proceedings relating thereto, commences:

(A) With the issuance of the Form I-221, Order to Show Cause and Notice of Hearing prior to June 20, 1991;

(B) With the filing of a Form I-221, Order to Show Cause and Notice of Hearing, issued on or after June 20, 1991, with the Immigration Court;

(C) With the issuance of Form I-122, Notice to Applicant for Admission Detained for Hearing Before Immigration Judge, prior to April 1, 1997,

(D) With the filing of a Form I-862, Notice to Appear, with the Immigration Court, or

(E) With the issuance and service of Form I-860, Notice and Order of Expedited Removal.

(ii) Termination of proceedings. The period during which the alien is in exclusion, deportation, or removal proceedings, or judicial proceedings relating thereto, terminates:

(A) When the alien departs from the United States while an order of exclusion, deportation, or removal is outstanding or before the expiration of the voluntary departure time granted in connection with an alternate order of deportation or removal;

(B) When the alien is found not to be inadmissible or deportable from the United States;

(C) When the Form I-122, I-221, I-860, or I-862 is canceled;

(D) When proceedings are terminated by the immigration judge or the Board of Immigration Appeals; or

(E) When a petition for review or an action for habeas corpus is granted by a Federal court on judicial review.

(iii) Exemptions. This prohibition shall no longer apply if:

(A) The alien is found not to be inadmissible or deportable from the United States;

(B) Form I-122, I-221, I-860, or I-862, is canceled;

(C) Proceedings are terminated by the immigration judge or the Board of Immigration Appeals;

(D) A petition for review or an action for habeas corpus is granted by a Federal court on judicial review;

(E) The alien has resided outside the United States for 2 or more years following the marriage; or

(F) The alien establishes the marriage is bona fide by providing clear and convincing evidence that the marriage was entered into in good faith and in accordance with the laws of the place where the marriage took place, was not entered into for the purpose of procuring the alien's entry as an immigrant, and no fee or other consideration was given (other than to an attorney for assistance in preparation of a lawful petition) for the filing of a petition.

(iv) Request for exemption. No application or fee is required to request the exemption under section 245(e) of the Act. The request must be made in writing and submitted with the Form I-485. Application for Permanent Residence. The request must state the basis for requesting consideration for the exemption and must be supported by documentary evidence establishing eligibility for the exemption.

(v) Evidence to establish eligibility for the bona fide marriage exemption. Section 204(g) of the Act provides that certain visa petitions based upon marriages entered into during deportation, exclusion or related judicial proceedings may be approved only if the petitioner provides clear and convincing evidence that the marriage is bona fide. Evidence that a visa petition based upon the same marriage was approved under the bona fide marriage exemption to section 204(g) of the Act will be considered primary evidence of eligibility for the bona fide marriage exemption provided in this part. The applicant will not be required to submit additional evidence to qualify for the bona fide marriage exemption provided in this part, unless the district director determines that such additional evidence is needed. In cases where the district director notifies the applicant that additional evidence is required, the applicant must submit documentary evidence which clearly and convincingly establishes that the marriage was entered into in good faith and not entered into for the purpose of procuring the alien's entry as an immigrant. Such evidence may include:

(A) Documentation showing joint ownership of property;

(B) Lease showing joint tenancy of a common residence;

(C) Documentation showing commingling of financial resources;

(D) Birth certificates of children born to the applicant and his or her spouse;

(E) Affidavits of third parties having knowledge of the bona fides of the marital relationship, or

(F) Other documentation establishing that the marriage was not entered into in order to evade the immigration laws of the United States.

(vi) Decision. An application for adjustment of status filed during the prohibited period shall be denied, unless the applicant establishes eligibility for an exemption from the general prohibition.

(vii) Denials. The denial of an application for adjustment of status because the marriage took place during the prohibited period shall be without prejudice to the consideration of a new application or a motion to reopen a previously denied application, if deportation or exclusion proceedings are terminated while the alien is in the United States. The denial shall also be without prejudice to the consideration of a new application or motion to reopen the adjustment of status application, if the applicant presents clear and convincing evidence establishing eligibility for the bona fide marriage exemption contained in this part.

(viii) Appeals. An application for adjustment of status to lawful permanent resident which is denied by the district director solely because the applicant failed to establish eligibility for the bona fide marriage exemption contained in this part may be appealed to the Associate Commissioner, Examinations, in accordance with 8 CFR part 103. The appeal to the Associate Commissioner, Examinations, shall be the single level of appellate review established by statute.

(d) Definitions —

(1) Lawful Immigration Status. For purposes of section 245(c)(2) of the Act, the term "lawful immigration status" will only describe the immigration status of an individual who is:

(i) In lawful permanent resident status;

(ii) An alien admitted to the United States in nonimmigrant status as defined in section 101(a)(15) of the Act, whose initial period of admission has not expired or whose nonimmigrant status has been extended in accordance with part 214 of 8 CFR chapter I;

(iii) In refugee status under section 207 of the Act, such status not having been revoked;

(iv) In asylee status under section 208 of the Act, such status not having been revoked;

(v) In parole status which has not expired, been revoked or terminated; or

(vi) Eligible for the benefits of Public Law 101-238 (the Immigration Nursing Relief Act of 1989) and files an application for adjustment of status on or before October 17, 1991.

(2) No fault of the applicant or for technical reasons. The parenthetical phrase other than through no fault of his or her own or for technical reasons shall be limited to:

(i) Inaction of another individual or organization designated by regulation to act on behalf of an individual and over whose actions the individual has no control, if the inaction is acknowledged by that individual or organization (as, for example, where a designated school official certified under § 214.2(f) of 8 CFR chapter I or an exchange propram sponsor under § 214.2(j) of 8 CFR chapter I did not provide required notification to the Service of continuation of status, or did not forward a request for continuation of status to the Service); or

(ii) A technical violation resulting from inaction of the Service (as for example, where an applicant establishes that he or she properly filed a timely request to maintain status and the Service has not yet acted on that request). An individual whose refugee or asylum status has expired through passage of time, but whose status has not been revoked, will be considered to have gone out of status for a technical reason.

(iii) A technical violation caused by the physical inability of the applicant to request an extension of nonimmigrant stay from the Service either in person or by mail (as, for example, an individual who is hospitalized with an illness at the time nonimmigrant stay expires). The explanation of such a technical violation shall be accompanied by a letter explaining the circumstances from the hospital or attending physician.

(iv) A technical violation resulting from the Service's application of the maximum five/six year period of stay for certain H-1 nurses only if the applicant was subsequently reinstated to H-1 status in accordance with the terms of Public Law 101-656 (Immigration Amendments of 1988).

(3) Effect of departure. The departure and subsequent reentry of an individual who was employed without authorization in the United States after January 1, 1977 does not erase the bar to adjustment of status in section 245(c)(2) of the Act. Similarly, the departure and subsequent reentry of an individual who has not maintained a lawful immigration status on any previous entry into the United States does not erase the bar to adjustment of status in section 245(c)(2) of the Act for any application filed on or after November 6, 1986.

(e) Special categories —

(1) Alien medical graduates. Any alien who is a medical graduate qualified for special immigrant classification under section 101(a)(27)(H) of the Act and is the beneficiary of an approved petition as required under section 204(a)(1)(E)(i) of the Act is eligible for adjustment of status. An accompanying spouse and children also may apply for adjustment of status under this section. Temporary absences from the United States for 30 days or less, during which the applicant was practicing or studying medicine, do not interrupt the continuous presence requirement. Temporary absences authorized under the Service's advance parole procedures will not be considered interruptive of continuous presence when the alien applies for adjustment of status.

(2) Adjustment of certain nurses who were in H-1 nonimmigrant status on September 1, 1989 (Pub. L. 101-238) —

(i) Eligibility. An alien is eligible to apply for adjustment of status without regard to the numerical limitations of sections 201 and 202 of the Act if:

(A) The applicant was admitted to the United States in, or had been granted a change of status to, nonimmigrant status under section 101(a)(15)(H)(i) of the Act on or before September 1, 1989, to perform services as a registered nurse (regardless of the date upon which the applicant's authorization to remain in the United States expired or will expire), and the applicant had not thereafter been granted a change to status to any other nonimmigrant classification prior to September 1, 1989,

(B) The applicant has been employed in the United States as a registered nurse for an aggregate of three years prior to the date of application for adjustment of status,

(C) The applicant's continued employment as a registered nurse meets the standards established for certification described in section 212(a)(5)(A)(i) of the Act,

(D) The applicant is the beneficiary of:

(1) A valid, unexpired visa petition filed prior to October 1, 1991, which has been approved to grant the applicant preference status under section 202(a) (3) or (6) of the Act (as in effect prior to October 1, 1991), and is deemed by operation of the automatic conversion provisions of section 4 of Public Law 102-110 (the Armed Forces Immigration Adjustment Act of 1991), to be effective to grant the applicant preference status under section 203(b) (2) or (3) of the Act (as in effect on and after October 1, 1991) because of his or here occupation as a registered nurse, provided the application for adjustment of status is approved no later than October 1, 1993, or

(2) A valid, unexpired visa petition filed on or after October 1, 1991, which has been approved to grant the applicant preference, status under section 203(b) (1), (2), or (3) of this Act (as in effect on and after October 1, 1991) because of his or her occupation as a registered nurse, and

(E) The applicant properly files an application for adjustment of status under the provisions of section 245 of the Act.

(ii) Application period. To benefit from the provisions of Public Law 101-238, an alien must properly file an application for adjustments of status under section 245 of the Act on or before March 20, 1995.

(iii) Application. An applicant for the benefits of Public Law 101-238 must file an application for adjustment of status on Form I-485, accompanied by the fee and supporting documents described in § 1245.2 of this part. Beneficiaries of Public Law 101-238 must also submit:

(A) Evidence that the applicant is the beneficiary of:

(1) A valid, unexpired visa petition filed prior to October 1, 1991, which has been approved to grant the applicant preference status under section 203(a) (3) or (6) of the Act (as in effect prior to October 1, 1991) and is deemed by operation of the automatic conversion provisions of section 4 of Public Law 101-110 to be effective to grant the applicant preference status under section 203(b) (2) or (3) of the Act (as in effect on and after October 1, 1991) because of his or her occupation as a registered nurse, provided the application for adjustment of status is approved no later than October 1, 1993, or

(2) A valid, unexpired visa petition filed on or after October 1, 1991, which has been approved to grant the applicant preference status under section 203(b) (1), (2), or (3) of the Act (as in effect on and after October 1, 1991) because of his or her occupation as a registered nurse, and

(B) A request, made on Form ETA 750 submitted in duplicate, for a determination by the district director that the alien is qualified for and will engage in the occupation of registered nurse, as currently listed on Schedule A (20 CFR part 656),

(C) Evidence showing that the applicant has been employed in the United States as a registered nurse for an aggregate of three years prior to the date the application for adjustment of status is filed, in the form of:

(1) Letters from employers stating the beginning and ending dates of employment as a registered nurse, or

(2) Other evidence of employment as a registered nurse, such as pay receipts supported by affidavits of co-workers, which is accompanied by evidence that the nurse has made reasonable efforts to obtain employment letter(s), but has been unable to do so because the current or former employer refuses to issue the letter or has gone out of business,

(D) Evidence that the applicant was licensed, either temporarily or permanently, as a registered nurse during all periods of qualifying employment, and

(E) Evidence which establishes that the applicant was in the United States in H-1 nonimmigrant status for the purpose of performing services as a registered nurse on September 1, 1989.

(iv) Effect of section 245(c)(2). An applicant for the benefits of the adjustment of status provisions of Public Law 101-238 must establish eligibility for adjustment of status under all provisions of section 245 unless those provisions have specifically been waived.

(A) Application for adjustment of status filed on or before October 17, 1991. An applicant who qualifies for the benefits of Public Law 101-238, who properly files an application for adjustment of status on or before October 17, 1991, may be granted adjustment of status even though the alien has engaged or is engaging in unauthorized employment. For purposes of adjustment of status, the applicant will be considered to have continuously maintained a lawful nonimmigrant status throughout his or her stay in the United States as a nonimmigrant and to be in lawful nonimmigrant status at the time the application is filed.

(B) Application for adjustment of status filed after October 17, 1991. An alien who files an application for adjustment of status after October 17, 1991, will not automatically be considered as having maintained lawful nonimmigrant status. An alien who files for adjustment after this date will be subject to the statutory bar of section 245(c)(2) of the Act and will be ineligible to apply for adjustment of status if he or she has failed to continuously maintain lawful nonimmigrant status (other than through no fault of his or her own or for technical reasons); if he or she was not in lawful nonimmigrant status at the time the application was filed; or if he or she was employed without authorization on or after November 29, 1990. Unauthorized employment which has been waived as a basis for ineligibility for adjustment of status may not be used as the basis of a determination that the applicant is ineligible for adjustment of status due to failure to continuously maintain lawful nonimmigrant status.

(C) Motions to reopen. Public Law 101-649 (the Immigration Act of 1990), which became law on November 29, 1990, retroactively amended Public Law 101-238 (the Immigration Nursing Relief Act of 1989). An alien whose application for adjustment of status under the provisions of Public Law 101-238 was denied by the district director before November 29, 1990, because of unauthorized employment, failure to continuously maintain a lawful nonimmigrant status, or not being in lawful immigration status at the time of filing, may file a motion to reopen the adjustment application. The motion to reopen must be made in accordance with the provisions of 8 CFR 103.5. The district director will reopen the application for adjustment of status and enter a new decision based upon the provisions of Public Law 101-238, as amended by Public Law 101-649. Any other alien whose application for adjustment of status was denied may file a motion to reopen or reconsider in accordance with normal statutory and regulatory provisions.

(v) Description of qualifying employment. Qualifying employment as a registered nurse may have taken place at any time before the alien files the application for adjustment of status. It may have occurred before, on, or after the enactment of Public Law 101-238. All qualifying employment must have occurred in the United States. The qualifying employment as a registered nurse may have occurred while the alien was in any immigration status, provided that the alien had been admitted in or changed to H-1 status for the purpose of performing services as a registered nurse on or before September 1, 1989, and had not thereafter changed from H-1 status to any other status before September 1, 1989. The employment need not have been continuous, provided the applicant can establish that he or she engaged in qualifying employment for a total of three or more years. Qualifying employment may include periods when the applicant possessed a provisional, temporary, interim, or other permit or license authorizing the applicant to perform services as a registered nurse; provided the license or permit was issued or recognized by the State Board of Nursing of the state in which the employment was performed. Qualifying employment may not include periods when the applicant performed duties as a registered nurse in violation of any state law regulating the employment of registered nurses in that state.

(vi) Effect of enactment on spouse or child —

(A) Spouse or child accompanying principal alien. The accompanying spouse or child of an applicant for adjustment of status who benefits from Public Law 101-238, may also apply for adjustment of status. All benefits and limitations of this section, including those resulting from the implementation of the adjustment of status provisions of section 162(f) of Public Law 101-649, apply equally to the principal applicant and his or her accompanying spouse or child.

(B) Spouse or child residing outside the United States or ineligible for adjustment of status. A spouse or child who is ineligible to apply for adjustment of status as an accompanying spouse or child is not immediately eligible for issuance of an immigrant visa under the provisions of Public Law 101-238. However, the spouse or child may be eligible for visa issuance under other provisions of the Act.

(1) Existing relationship. A spouse or child acquired by the principal alien prior to the approval of the principal's adjustment of status application may be accorded the derivative priority date and preference category of the principal alien. The spouse or child may use the priority date and category when it becomes current, in accordance with existing limitations outlined in sections 201 and 202 of the Act. The priority date is not considered immediately available for these family members under Public Law 101-238.

(2) Relationship entered into after adjustment of status is approved. An alien who acquires lawful permanent residence under the provisions of Public Law 101-238 may file a petition under section 204 of the Act for an alien spouse, unmarried son or unmarried daughter in accordance with existing laws and regulations. The priority date is not considered immediately available for these family members under Public Law 101-238.

(3) Special immigrant juveniles. Any alien qualified for special immigrant classification under section 101(a)(27)(J) of the Act shall be deemed, for the purpose of section 245(a) of the Act, to have been paroled into the United States, regardless of the alien's actual method of entry into the United States. Neither the provisions of section 245(c)(2) nor the exclusion provisions of sections 212(a)(4), (5)(A), or(7)(A) of the Act shall apply to a qualified special immigrant under section 101(a)(27)(J) of the Act. The exclusion provisions of sections 212(a)(2)(A), (2)(B), (2)(C) (except for so much of such paragraph as related to a single offense of simple possession of 30 grams or less of marijuana), (3)(A), (3)(B), (3)(C), or (3)(E) of the Act may not be waived. Any other exclusion provision may be waived on an individual basis for humanitarian purposes, family unity, or when it isotherwise in the public interest; however, the relationship between the alien and the alien's natural parents or prior adoptive parents shall not be considered a factor in a discretionary waiver determination.

(f) Concurrent applications to overcome grounds of inadmissibility. Except as provided in 8 CFR parts 1235 and 1249, an application under this part shall be the sole method of requesting the exercise of discretion under sections 212(g), (h), (i), and (k) of the Act, as they relate to the inadmissibility of an alien in the United States. No fee is required for filing an application to overcome the grounds of inadmissibility of the Act if filed concurrently with an application for adjustment of status under the provisions of the Act of October 28, 1977, and of this part.

(g) Availability of immigrant visas under section 245 and priority dates —

(1) Availability of immigrant visas under section 245. An alien is ineligible for the benefits of section 245 of the Act unless an immigrant visa is immediately available to him or her at the time the application is filed. If the applicant is a preference alien, the current Department of State Bureau of Consular Affairs Visa Bulletin will be consulted to determine whether an immigrant visa is immediately available. An immigrant visa is considered available for accepting and processing the application Form I-485 is the preference category applicant has a priority date on the waiting list which is earlier than the date shown in the Bulletin (or the Bulletin shows that numbers for visa applicants in his or her category are current). An immigrant visa is also considered immediately available if the applicant establishes eligibility for the benefits of Public Law 101-238. Information concerning the immediate availability of an immigrant visa may be obtained at any Service office.

(2) Priority dates. The priority date of an applicant who is seeking the allotment of an immigrant visa number under one of the preference classes specified in section 203(a) or 203(b) of the Act by virtue of a valid visa petition approved in his or her behalf shall be fixed by the date on which such approved petition was filed.

(h) Conditional basis of status. Whenever an alien spouse (as defined in section 216(g)(1) of the Act), an alien son or daughter (as defined in section 216(g)(2) of the Act), an alien entrepreneur (as defined in section 216A(f)(1) of the Act), or an alien spouse or child (as defined in section 216A(f)(2) of the Act) is granted adjustment of status to that of lawful permanent residence, the alien shall be considered to have obtained such status on a conditional basis subject to the provisions of section 216 or 216A of the Act, as appropriate.

(i) Adjustment of status from K-3/K-4 status. An alien admitted to the United States as a K-3 under section 101(a)(15)(K)(ii) of the Act may apply for adjustment of status to that of a permanent resident pursuant to section 245 of the Act at any time following the approval of the Form I-130 petition filed on the alien's behalf, by the same citizen who petitioned for the alien's K-3 status. An alien admitted to the United States as a K-4 under section 101(a)(15)(K)(iii) of the Act may apply for adjustment of status to that of permanent residence pursuant to section 245 of the Act at any time following the approval of the Form I-130 petition filed on the alien's behalf, by the same citizen who petitioned for the alien's parent's K-3 status. Upon approval of the application, the director shall record his or her lawful admission for permanent residence in accordance with that section and subject to the conditions prescribed in section 216 of the Act. An alien admitted to the U.S. as a K-3/K-4 alien may not adjust to that of permanent resident status in any way other than as a spouse or child of the U.S. citizen who originally filed the petition for that alien's K-3/K-4 status.

HISTORY:

[30 FR 14778, Nov. 30, 1965; 52 FR 6321, 48084, 1987; 53 FR 24903, 30022, 1988; 54 29441, 47676, 1989.; 55 FR 10397, 1990; 56 FR 28040, 28313, 49840, 1991; 57 FR 56812, 56813, 1992; 58 FR 42851, Aug. 12, 1993; 59 FR 51095, Oct. 7, 1994; 60 FR 26683, May 18, 1995, as confirmed at 62 FR 18506, 18508, April 16, 1997; 60 FR 34090, June 30, 1995; 60 FR 44260, 44269, Aug. 25, 1995; 62 FR 10312, 10382, March 6, 1997; 62 FR 39417, 39424, July 23, 1997; 66 FR 42587, 42594, Aug. 14, 2001; 67 FR 49561, 49563, July 31, 2002; 68 FR 9824, 9842, 9846, Feb. 28, 2003; 68 FR 10349, 10357, Mar. 5, 2003; 71 FR 27585, 27591, May 12, 2006; 74 FR 55726, 55744, Oct. 28, 2009]

AUTHORITY:

(Title I of Pub. L. 95-145 enacted Oct. 28, 1977 (91 Stat. 1223), sec. 103 of the Immigration and Nationality Act (8 U.S.C. 1103). Interpret or apply secs. 101, 212, 242 and 245 (8 U.S.C. 1101, 1182, 1252 and 1255))

§ 1245.2 Application.

(a) General —

(1) Jurisdiction

(i) In General. In the case of any alien who has been placed in deportation proceedings or in removal proceedings (other than as an arriving alien), the immigration judge hearing the proceeding has exclusive jurisdiction to adjudicate any application for adjustment of status the alien may file.

(ii) Arriving Aliens. In the case of an arriving alien who is placed in removal proceedings, the immigration judge does not have jurisdiction to adjudicate any application for adjustment of status filed by the arriving alien unless:

(A) The alien properly filed the application for adjustment of status with USCIS while the arriving alien was in the United States;

(B) The alien departed from and returned to the United States pursuant to the terms of a grant of advance parole to pursue the previously filed application for adjustment of status;

(C) The application for adjustment of status was denied by USCIS; and

(D) DHS placed the arriving alien in removal proceedings either upon the arriving alien's return to the United States pursuant to the grant of advance parole or after USCIS denied the application.

(2) Proper filing of application —

(i) Under section 245.

(A) An immigrant visa must be immediately available in order for an alien to properly file an adjustment application under section 245 of the Act See § 1245.1(g)(1) to determine whether an immigrant visa is immediately available.

(B) If, at the time of filing, approval of a visa petition filed for classification under section 201(b)(2)(A)(i), section 203(a) or section 203(b)(1), (2) or (3) of the Act would make a visa immediately available to the alien beneficiary, the alien beneficiary's adjustment application will be considered properly filed whether submitted concurrently with or subsequent to the visa petition, provided that it meets the filing requirements contained in parts 103 of 8 CFR chapter I and 1245 of this chapter. For any other classification, the alien beneficiary may file the adjustment application only after the Service has approved the visa petition.

(C) A visa petition and an adjustment application are concurrently filed only if:

(1) The visa petitioner and adjustment applicant each file their respective form at the same time, bundled together within a single mailer or delivery packet, with the proper filing fees on the same day and at the same Service office, or;

(2) the visa petitioner filed the visa petition, for which a visa number has become immediately available, on, before or after July 31, 2002, and the adjustment applicant files the adjustment application, together with the proper filing fee and a copy of the Form I-797, Notice of Action, establishing the receipt and acceptance by the Service of the underlying Form I-140 visa petition, at the same Service office at which the visa petitioner filed the visa petition, or;

(3) The visa petitioner filed the visa petition, for which a visa number has become immediately available, on, before, or after July 31, 2002, and the adjustment applicant files the adjustment application, together with proof of payment of the filing fee with the Service and a copy of the Form I-797 Notice of Action establishing the receipt and acceptance by the Service of the underlying Form I-140 visa petition, with the Immigration Court or the Board of Immigration Appeals when jurisdiction lies under paragraph (a)(1) of this section.

(ii) Under the Act of November 2, 1966. An application for the benefits of section 1 of the Act of November 2, 1966 is not properly filed unless the applicant was inspected and admitted or paroled into the United States subsequent to January 1, 1959. An applicant is ineligible for the benefits of the Act of November 2, 1966 unless he or she has been physically present in the United States for one year (amended from two years by the Refugee Act of 1980).

(3) Submission of documents —

(i) General. A separate application shall be filed by each applicant for benefits under section 245, or the Act of November 2, 1966. Each application shall be accompanied by an executed Form G-325A, if the applicant has reached his or her 14th birthday. Form G-325A shall be considered part of the application. An application under this part shall be accompanied by the document specified in the instructions which are attached to the application.

(ii) Under section 245. An application for adjustment of status is submitted on Form I-485, Application for Permanent Residence. The application must be accompanied by the appropriate fee as explained in the instructions to the application.

(iii) Under section 245(i). An alien who seeks adjustment of status under the provisions of section 245(i) of the Act must file Form I-485, with the required fee. The alien must also file Supplement A to Form I-485, with any required additional sum.

(iv) Under the Act of November 2, 1966. An application for adjustment of status is made on Form I-485A. The application must be accompanied by Form I-643, Health and Human Services Statistical Data Sheet. The application must include a clearance from the local police jurisdiction for any area in the United States when the applicant has lived for six months or more since his or her 14th birthday.

(4) Effect of departure —

(i) General. The effect of a departure from the United States is dependent upon the law under which the applicant is applying for adjustment.

(ii) Under section 245 of the Act.

(A) The departure from the United States of an applicant who is under exclusion, deportation, or removal proceedings shall be deemed an abandonment of the application constituting grounds for termination of the proceeding by reason of the departure. Except as provided in paragraph (a)(4)(ii)(B) and (C) of this section, the departure of an applicant who is not under exclusion, deportation, or removal proceedings shall be deemed an abandonment of the application constituting grounds for termination of any pending application for adjustment of status, unless the applicant was previously granted advance parole by the Service for such absences, and was inspected upon returning to the United States. If the adjustment application of an individual granted advance parole is subsequently denied the individual will be treated as an applicant for admission, and subject to the provisions of section 212 and 235 of the Act.

(B) The travel outside of the United States by an applicant for adjustment who is not under exclusion, deportation, or removal proceedings shall not be deemed an abandonment of the application if he or she was previously granted advance parole by the Service for such absences, and was inspected and paroled upon returning to the United States. If the adjustment of status application of such individual is subsequently denied, he or she will be treated as an applicant for admission, and subject to the provisions of section 212 and 235 of the Act.

(C) The travel outside of the United States by an applicant for adjustment of status who is not under exclusion, deportation, or removal proceeding and who is in lawful H-1 or L-1 status shall not be deemed an abandonment of the application if, upon returning to this country, the alien remains eligible for H or L status, is coming to resume employment with the same employer for whom he or she had previously been authorized to work as an H-1 or L-1 nonimmigrant, and, is in possession of a valid H or L visa (if required) and the original I-797 receipt notice for the application for adjustment of status. The travel outside of the United States by an applicant for adjustment of status who is not under exclusion, deportation, or removal proceeding and who is in lawful H-4 or L-2 status shall not be deemed an abandonment of the application if the spouse or parent of such alien through whom the H-4 or L-2 status was obtained is maintaining H-1 or L-1 status and the alien remains otherwise eligible for H-4 or L-2 status, and, the alien is in possession of a valid H-4 or L-2 visa (if required) and the original copy of the I-797 receipt notice for the application for adjustment of status. The travel outside of the United States by an applicant for adjustment of status, who is not under exclusion, deportation, or removal proceeding and who is in lawful K-3 or K-4 status shall not be deemed an abandonment of the application if, upon returning to this country, the alien is in possession of a valid K-3 or K-4 visa and remains eligible for K-3 or K-4 status.

(D) The travel outside of the United States by an applicant for adjustment of status who is not under exclusion, deportation, or removal proceeding and who is in lawful V status shall not be deemed an abandonment of the application if, upon returning to this country, the alien is admissible as a V nonimmigrant.

(iii) Under the Act of November 2, 1966. If an applicant who was admitted or paroled subsequent to January 1, 1959, later departs from the United States temporarily with no intention of abandoning his or her residence, and is readmitted or paroled upon return, the temporary absence shall be disregarded for purposes of the applicant's "last arrival" into the United States in regard to cases filed under section 1 of the Act of November 2, 1966.

(5) Decision —

(i) General. The applicant shall be notified of the decision of the director and, if the application is denied, the reasons for the denial.

(ii) Under section 245 of the Act. If the application is approved, the applicant's permanent residence shall be recorded as of the date of the order approving the adjustment of status. An application for adjustment of status, as a preference alien, shall not be approved until an immigrant visa number has been allocated by the Department of State, except when the applicant has established eligibility for the benefits of Public Law 101-238. No appeal lies from the denial of an application by the director, but the applicant, if not an arriving alien, retains the right to renew his or her application in proceedings under 8 CFR part 1240. Also, an applicant who is a parolee and meets the two conditions described in § 1245.2(a)(1) may renew a denied application in proceedings under 8 CFR part 1240 to determine admissibility. At the time of renewal of the application, an applicant does not need to meet the statutory requirement of section 245(c) of the Act, or § 1245.1(g), if, in fact, those requirements were met at the time the renewed application was initially filed with the director. Nothing in this section shall entitle an alien to proceedings under section 240 of the Act who is not otherwise so entitled.

(iii) Under the Act of November 2, 1966. If the application is approved, the applicant's permanent residence shall be recorded in accordance with the provisions of section 1. No appeal lies from the denial of an application by the director, but the applicant, if not an arriving alien, retains the right to renew his or her application in proceedings under 8 CFR part 1240. Also, an applicant who is a parolee and meets the two conditions described in § 1245.2(a)(1) may renew a denied application in proceedings under 8 CFR part 1240 to determine admissibility.

(b) Application under section 2 of the Act of November 2, 1966. An application by a native or citizen of Cuba or by his spouse or child residing in the United States with him, who was lawfully admitted to the United States for permanent residence prior to November 2, 1966, and who desires such admission to be recorded as of an earlier date pursuant to section 2 of the Act of November 2, 1966, shall be made on Form I-485A. The application shall be accompanied by the Permanent Resident Card, Form I-151 or I-551, issued to the applicant in connection with his lawful admission for permanent residence, and shall be submitted to the director having jurisdiction over the applicant's place of residence in the United States. The decision on the application shall be made by the director. No appeal shall lie from his decision. If the application is approved, the applicant will be furnished with a replacement of his Form I-151 or I-551 bearing the new date as of which the lawful admission for permanent residence has been recorded.

(c) Application under section 214(d) of the Act. An application for permanent resident status pursuant to section 214(d) of the Act shall be filed on Form I-485 with the director having jurisdiction over the applicant's place of residence. A separate application shall be filed by each applicant. If the application is approved, the director shall record the lawful admission of the applicant as of the date of approval. The applicant shall be notified of the decision and, if the application is denied, of the reasons therefor. No appeal shall lie from the denial of an application by the director but such denial shall be without prejudice to the alien's right to renew his or her application in proceedings under 8 CFR part 240.

HISTORY:

[30 FR 14778, Nov. 30, 1965; 51 FR 7432, 25357, 1986; 52 FR 34764, 1987; 54 FR 29441, 47348, 47676, 1989; 55 FR 10397, 1990; 56 FR 28042, 49841, 1991; 57 FR 56813, 1992; 58 FR 35838, July 1, 1993; 59 FR 33905, July 1, 1994; 59 FR 51095, Oct. 7, 1994; 62 FR 10312, 10383, March 6, 1997; 63 FR 70313, 70315, Dec. 21, 1998; 64 FR 29208, 29211, June 1, 1999; 66 FR 42587, 42594, Aug. 14, 2001; 66 FR 46697, 46704, Sept. 7, 2001; 67 FR 49561, 49563, July 31, 2002; 68 FR 9824, 9842, 9846, Feb. 28, 2003; 68 FR 10349, 10357, Mar. 5, 2003; 71 FR 27585, 27591, May 12, 2006]

§ 1245.3 Adjustment of status under section 13 of the Act of September 11, 1957, as amended.

Any application for benefits under section 13 of the Act of September 11, 1957, as amended, must be filed on Form I-485 with the director having jurisdiction over the applicant's place of residence. The benefits under section 13 are limited to aliens who were admitted into the United States under section 101, paragraphs (a)(15)(A)(i), (a)(15)(A)(ii), (a)(15)(G)(i), or (a)(15)(G)(ii) of the Immigration and Nationality Act who performed diplomatic or semi-diplomatic duties and to their immediate families, and who establish that there are compelling reasons why the applicant or the member of the applicant's immediate family is unable to return to the country represented by the government which accredited the applicant and that adjustment of the applicant's status to that of an alien lawfully admitted for permanent residence would be in the national interest. Aliens whose duties were of a custodial, clerical, or menial nature, and members of their immediate families, are not eligible for benefits under section 13. In view of the annual limitation of 50 on the number of aliens whose status may be adjusted under section 13, any alien who is prima facie eligible for adjustment of status to that of a lawful permanent resident under another provision of law shall be advised to apply for adjustment pursuant to such other provision of law. An applicant for the benefits of section 13 shall not be subject to the labor certification requirement of section 212(a)(14) of the Immigration and Nationality Act. The applicant shall be notified of the decision and, if the application is denied, of the reasons for the denial and of the right to appeal under the provisions of part 103 of this chapter. Any applications pending with the Service before December 29, 1981 must be resubmitted to comply with the requirements of this section.

HISTORY:

[47 FR 44238, Oct. 7, 1982; 59 FR 33905, July 1, 1994; 68 FR 9824, 9842, Feb. 28, 2003]

AUTHORITY:

(Secs. 103, 245, of the Immigration and Nationality Act, as amended; 71 Stat. 642, as amended, sec. 17, Pub. L. 97-116, 95 Stat. 1619 (8 U.S.C. 1103, 1255, 1255b))

§ 1245.4 Documentary requirements.

The provisions of part 1211 of this chapter relating to the documentary requirements for immigrants shall not apply to an applicant under this part.

HISTORY:

[30 FR 14779, Nov. 30, 1965. Redesignated at 48 FR 4770, Feb. 3, 1983, and further redesignated at 52 FR 6322, Mar. 3, 1982, and further redesignated at 56 FR 49481, Oct. 2, 1991; 68 FR 9824, 9842, Feb. 28, 2003; 68 FR 10349, 10357, Mar. 5, 2003]

AUTHORITY:

(Secs. 103, 214, 245 Immigration and Nationality Act, as amended; (8 U.S.C. 1103, 1184, 8 U.S.C. 1255, Sec. 2, 96 Stat. 1157, 8 U.S.C. 1255 note))

§ 1245.5 Medical examination.

Pursuant to section 232(b) of the Act, an applicant for adjustment of status shall be required to have a medical examination by a designated civil surgeon, whose report setting forth the findings of the mental and physical condition of the applicant, including compliance with section 212(a)(1)(A)(ii) of the Act, shall be incorporated into the record. A medical examination shall not be required of an applicant for adjustment of status who entered the United States as a nonimmigrant spouse, fiance, or fiancee of a United States citizen or the child of such an alien as defined in section 101(a)(15)(K) of the Act and § 214.2(k) of 8 CFR chapter I if the applicant was medically examined prior to, and as a condition of, the issuance of the nonimmigrant visa; provided that the medical examination must have occurred not more than 1 year prior the date of application for adjustment of status. Any applicant certified under paragraphs (1)(A)(ii) or (1)(A)(iii) of section 212(a) of the Act may appeal to a Board of Medical Officers of the U.S. Public Health Service as provided in section 234 of the Act and part 1235 of this chapter.

HISTORY:

[56 FR 49841, Oct. 2, 1991; 62 FR 10312, 10384, March 6, 1997; 66 FR 42587, 42595, Aug. 14, 2001; 68 FR 9824, 9842, Feb. 28, 2003; 68 FR 10349, 10357, Mar. 5, 2003]

§ 1245.6 Interview.

Each applicant for adjustment of status under this part shall be interviewed by an immigration officer. This interview may be waived in the case of a child under the age of 14; when the applicant is clearly ineligible under section 245(c) of the Act or § 1245.1 of this chapter; or when it is determined by the Service that an interview is unnecessary.

HISTORY:

[57 FR 49375, Nov. 2, 1992, as confirmed at 61 FR 59825, 59827, Nov. 25, 1996; 68 FR 9824, 9842, 9846, Feb. 28, 2003]

§ 1245.7 Adjustment of status of certain Soviet and Indochinese parolees under the Foreign Operations Appropriations Act for Fiscal Year 1990 (Pub. L. 101-167).

(a) Application. Each person applying for benefits under section 599E of Public Law 101-167 (103 Stat. 1195, 1263) must file Form I-485, Application to Register Permanent Residence or Adjust Status, with the director having jurisdiction over the applicant's place of residence and must pay the appropriate filing and fingerprinting fee, as prescribed in 8 CFR 103.7 and 8 CFR 103.17. Each application shall be accompanied by Form I-643, Health and Human Services Statistical Data for Refugee/Asylee Adjusting Status, and the results of a medical examination given in accordance with § 1245.8. In addition, if the applicant has reached his or her 14th birthday but is not over 79 years of age, the application shall be accompanied by a completed Form G-325A, Biographic Information, and the applicant shall be fingerprinted on Form FD-258, Applicant Card, as prescribed in § 103.2(e) of this chapter.

(b) Aliens eligible to apply for adjustment. The benefits of this section shall only apply to an alien who:

(1) Was a national of the Soviet Union, Vietnam, Laos, or Cambodia, and

(2) Was inspected and granted parole into the United States during the period beginning on August 15, 1988, and ending on September 30, 1990, after being denied refugee status.

(c) Eligibility. Benefits under Section 599E of Public Law 101-167 are limited to any alien described in paragraph (b) of this section who:

(1) Applies for such adjustment,

(2) Has been physically present in the United States for at least one year and is physically present in the United States on the date the application for such adjustment is filed,

(3) Is admissible to the United States as an immigrant, except as provided in paragraph (d) of this section, and

(4) Pays a fee for the processing of such application.

(d) Waiver of certain grounds for inadmissibility. The provisions of paragraphs (14), (15), (20), (21), (25), (28) (other than subparagraph (F), and (32) of section 212(a) of the Act shall not apply to adjustment under this section. The Attorney General may waive any other provision of section 212(a) (other than paragraph (23)(B), (27), (29), or (33)) with respect to such an adjustment for humanitarian purposes, to assure family unity, or when it is otherwise in the public interest.

(e) Date of approval. Upon approval of such an application for adjustment of status, the Attorney General shall create a record of the alien's admission as a lawful permanent resident as of the date of the alien's inspection and parole described in paragraph (b)(2) of this section.

(f) No offset in number of visas available. When an alien is granted the status of having been lawfully admitted for permanent residence under this section, the Secretary of State shall not be required to reduce the number of immigrant visas authorized to be issued under the Immigration and Nationality Act.

HISTORY:

[55 FR 24860, July 19, 1990. Redesignated at 56 FR 49841, Oct. 2, 1991; 59 FR 33905, July 1, 1994; 63 FR 12979, 12987, March 17, 1998; 68 FR 9824, 9842, 9846, Feb. 28, 2003; 85 FR 82750, 82794, Dec. 18, 2020]

§ 1245.8 Adjustment of status as a special immigrant under section 101(a)(27)(K) of the Act.

(a) Application. Each person applying for adjustment of status as a special immigrant under section 101(a)(27)(K) of the Act must file a Form I-485, Application to Register Permanent Residence or Adjust Status, with the director having jurisdiction over the applicant's place of residence. Benefits under this section are limited to aliens who have served honorably (or are enlisted to serve) in the Armed Forces of the United States for at least 12 years, and their spouses and children. For purposes of this section, special immigrants described in section 101(a)(27)(K) of the Act and his or her spouse and children shall be deemed to have been paroled into the United States pursuant to section 245(g) of the Act. Each applicant must file a separate application with the appropriate fee.

(b) Eligibility. The benefits of this section shall apply only to an alien described in section 101(a)(27)(K) of the Act who applies for such adjustment. The accompanying spouse or child of an applicant for adjustment of status who benefits from Public Law 102-110 may also apply for adjustment of status. The provisions of section 245(c) of the Act do not apply to the principal Armed Forces special immigrant or to his or her spouse or child.

(c) Interview of the applicant. Upon completion of the adjustment of status interview for a special immigrant under section 101(a)(27)(K) of the Act, the director shall make a prima facie determination regarding eligibility for naturalization benefits if the applicant is to be granted status as an alien lawfully admitted for permanent residence. If the director determines that the applicant is immediately eligible for naturalization under section 328 or 329 of the Act, the director shall advise the applicant that he or she is eligible to apply for naturalization on Form N-400, Application to File Petition for Naturalization. If the applicant wishes to apply for naturalization, the director shall instruct the applicant concerning the requirements for naturalization and provide him or her with the necessary forms.

(d) Spouse or child outside the United States. When a spouse or child of an alien granted special immigrant status under section 101(a)(27)(K) of the Act is outside the United States, the principal alien may file Form I-824, Application for Action on an Approved Application or Petition, with the office which approved the original application.

(e) Removal provisions of section 237 of the Act. If the Service is made aware by notification from the appropriate executive department or by any other means that a section 101(a)(27)(K) special immigrant who has already been granted permanent residence fails to complete his or her total active duty service obligation for reasons other than an honorable discharge, the alien may become subject to the removal provisions of section 237 of the Act, provided the alien is in one or more of the classes of deportable aliens specified in section 237 of the Act. The Service shall obtain a current Form DD-214, Certificate of Release or Discharge from Active Duty, from the appropriate executive department for verification of the alien's failure to maintain eligibility.

(f) Rescission proceedings under section 246 of the Act. If the Service determines that a military special immigrant under section 101(a)(27)(K) of the Act was not in fact eligible for adjustment of status, the Service may pursue rescission proceedings under section 246 of the Act.

HISTORY:

[57 FR 33862, July 31, 1992; 58 FR 50836, Sept. 29, 1993; 62 FR 10312, 10384, March 6, 1997; 68 FR 9824, 9842, Feb. 28, 2003]

§ 1245.9 Adjustment of Status of Certain Nationals of the People's Republic of China under Public Law 102-404.

(a) Principal applicant status. All nationals of the People's Republic of China who qualify under the provisions of paragraph (b) of this section may apply for adjustment of status as principals in their own right, regardless of age or marital status. Nationals of other countries who meet the requirements of paragraphs (b) and (c) of this section may apply for adjustment of status as qualified family members.

(b) Aliens eligible to apply for adjustment. An alien is eligible to apply for adjustment of status under the provisions of Public Law 102-404, if the alien:

(1) Is a national of the People's Republic of China or a qualified family member of an eligible national of the People's Republic of China;

(2) Was in the United States at some time between June 5, 1989, and April 11, 1990, inclusive, or would have been in the United States during this time period except for a brief, casual, and innocent departure from this country;

(3) Has resided continuously in the United States since April 11, 1990, except for brief, casual, and innocent absences;

(4) Was not physically present in the People's Republic of China for more than a cumulative total of 90 days between April 11, 1990, and October 9, 1992;

(5) Is admissible to the United States as an immigrant, unless the basis for excludability has been waived;

(6) Establishes eligibility for adjustment of status under all provisions of section 245 of the Act, unless the basis for ineligibility has been waived; and

(7) Properly files an application for adjustment of status under section 245 of the Act.

(c) Qualified family member who is not a national of the People's Republic of China. A qualified family member within the meaning of this section includes the spouse, child, son, or daughter of a national of the People's Republic of China who is eligible for benefits under the provisions of paragraph (b) of this section, provided that:

(1) He or she qualified as the spouse or child (as defined in section 101(b)(1) of the Act) of an eligible national of the People's Republic of China as of April 11, 1990; and

(2) The qualifying relationship continues to exist, or the family member is a son or daughter of an eligible national of the People's Republic of China and the family member was unmarried and under the age of 21 on April 11, 1990.

(d) Waivers of inadmissibility under section 212(a) of the Act. An applicant for the benefits of the adjustment of status provisions of Pub. L. 102-404 is automatically exempted from compliance with the requirements of sections 212(a)(5) and 212(a)(7)(A) of the Act. A Pub. L. 102-404 applicant may also apply for one or more waivers of inadmissibility under section 212(a) of the Act, except for inadmissibility under section 212(a)(2)(C), 212(a)(3)(A), 212(a)(3)(B), 212(a)(3)(C) or 212(a)(3)(E) of the Act.

(e) Waiver of the two-year foreign residence requirement of section 212(e). An applicant for the benefits of the adjustment of status provisions of Public Law 102-404 is automatically exempted from compliance with the two-year foreign residence requirement of section 212(e) of the Act.

(f) Waiver of section 245(c) of the Act. Public Law 102-404 provides that the provisions of section 245(c) of the Act shall not apply to persons applying for the adjustment of status benefits of Public Law 102-404.

(g) Application. Each applicant must file an application for adjustment of status on Form I-485, Application to Register Permanent Residence or Adjust Status, accompanied by the prescribed fee, and the supporting documents specified on the instructions to Form I-485 and described in § 1245.2. Secondary evidence may be submitted if the applicant is unable to obtain the required primary evidence. Applicants who are nationals of the People's Republic of China should complete Part 2 of Form I-485 by checking box "h — other" and writing "CSPA — Principal" next to that block. Applicants who are not nationals of the People's Republic of China should complete Part 2 of Form I-485 by checking box "h — other" and writing "CSPA — Qualified Family Member" next to that block. Each applicant for the benefits of Public Law 102-404 must also submit evidence of eligibility for the adjustment of status benefits of Public Law 102-404:

(1) A photocopy of all pages of the applicant's most recent passport or an explanation of why the applicant does not have a passport;

(2) An attachment on a plain piece of paper showing:

(i) The date of the applicant's last arrival in the United States before or on April 11, 1990;

(ii) The date of each departure the applicant made from the United States since that arrival (if the applicant did not depart the United States after the initial date of arrival, the applicant should write "I was in the United States on April 11, 1990, and I have not departed the United States since April 11, 1990");

(iii) The reason for each departure; and

(iv) The date of each return to the United States.

(3) An attachment on a plain piece of paper showing:

(i) The date the applicant arrived in the People's Republic of China; and

(ii) The date the applicant left the People's Republic of China for each trip the applicant made to the People's Republic of China between April 11, 1990, and October 9, 1992 (if the applicant did not travel to the People's Republic of China, the applicant should write "I was not in the People's Republic of China between April 11, 1990, and October 9, 1992");

(4) A copy of evidence showing that the applicant was found eligible for benefits under E.O. 12711, such as deferred enforced departure (DED), employment authorization, and/or waiver of the two-year foreign residence requirement, if the applicant previously applied for benefits under E.O. 12711; and

(5) Primary or secondary evidence of a qualifying family relationship to an eligible national of the People's Republic of China, such as a birth or marriage certificate, if the applicant is a qualified family member who is not a national of the People's Republic of China.

(h) Secondary evidence. If any required primary evidence is unavailable, church or school records, or other secondary evidence pertinent to the facts in issue, may be submitted. If such documents are unavailable, affidavits may be submitted. The applicant may submit as many types of secondary evidence as necessary to establish the birth, marriage, or other event. Documentary evidence establishing that primary evidence is unavailable need not accompany secondary evidence of birth or marriage in the People's Republic of China.

(i) Filing. The application period begins on July 1, 1993. To benefit from the provisions of Public Law 102-404 (the Chinese Student Protection Act of 1992), an alien must properly file an application for adjustment of status under section 245 of the Act on or before June 30, 1994. All applications for the benefits of Public Law 102-404 must be submitted by mail to the Service Center having jurisdiction over the applicant's place of residence in the United States. Pursuant to the deactivation clause of Public Law 102-404, if the President of the United States determines and certifies to Congress before July 1, 1993, that conditions in the People's Republic of China permit persons covered by Public Law 102-404 to safely return to the People's Republic of

China, no applications for lawful permanent resident status under Public Law 102-404 will be processed or granted.

(j) Immigrant classification and assignment of priority date. Public Law 102-404 provides eligible applicants with automatic classifications as immigrants under section 203(b)(3)(A)(i) of the Act. No immigrant visa petition is required and applicants need not meet the usual requirements for classification as skilled workers. The applicant's priority date shall be the date his or her application for adjustment of status under Public Law 102-404 is properly filed with the Service.

(k) Effect of immigrant visa number limitations. Eligible Public Law 102-404 applicants are exempt from the per-country immigrant visa number limitations of section 202(a)(2) of the Act. Eligible Public Law 102-404 applicants may file an application for adjustment of status under Public Law 102-404 without regard to immigrant visa number limitations of sections 202(a)(2) and 203(b)(3)(A)(i) of the Act. However, the adjustment of status application may not be approved and adjustment of status to that of a lawful permanent resident of the United States may not be granted until a visa number becomes available for the applicant under the worldwide allocation of immigrant visa numbers for employment-based aliens under section 203(b)(3)(A)(i) of the Act. The applicant may request initial or continued employment authorization during this period by filing Form I-765, Application for Employment Authorization. If the applicant needs to travel outside the United States during this period, he or she may file a request for advance parole on Form I-131, Application for Travel Document.

(l) Decision. In the case of an application for adjustment of status filed pursuant to the provisions of Public Law 102-404, the authority conferred upon district directors in 8 CFR part 1245 to accept and adjudicate an application for adjustment of status under section 245 of the Act is delegated exclusively to the service center director having jurisdiction over the applicant's place of residence in the United States. If the service center director transfers the application to the district director, authority to adjudicate an application for adjustment of status filed pursuant to the provisions of Public Law 102-404 lies with the district director having jurisdiction over the applicant's place of residence.

(m) Effect of enactment on family members other than qualified family members. The adjustment of status benefits and waivers provided by Public Law 102-404 do not apply to a spouse or child who is not a qualified family member as defined in paragraph (c) of this section. However, a spouse or child whose relationship to the principal alien was established prior to the approval of the principal's adjustment-of-status application may be accorded the derivative priority date and preference category of the principal alien, in accordance with the provisions of section 203(d) of the Act. The spouse or child may use the priority date and category when it becomes current, in accordance with the limitations set forth in sections 201 and 202 of the Act.

HISTORY:

[58 FR 35838, July 1, 1993; 62 FR 10312, 10384, March 6, 1997; 62 FR 63249, 63254, Nov. 28, 1997; 68 FR 9824, 9842, 9846, Feb. 28, 2003; 68 FR 10349, 10357, Mar. 5, 2003]

§ 1245.10 Adjustment of status upon payment of additional sum under section 245(i).

(a) Definitions. As used in this section the term:

(1)(i) Grandfathered alien means an alien who is the beneficiary (including a spouse or child of the alien beneficiary if eligible to receive a visa under section 203(d) of the Act) of:

(A) A petition for classification under section 204 of the Act which was properly filed with the Attorney General on or before April 30, 2001, and which was approvable when filed; or

(B) An application for labor certification under section 212(a)(5)(A) of the Act that was properly filed pursuant to the regulations of the Secretary of Labor on or before April 30, 2001, and which was approvable when filed.

(ii) If the qualifying visa petition or application for labor certification was filed after January 14, 1998, the alien must have been physically present in the United States on December 21, 2000. This requirement does not apply with respect to a spouse or child accompanying or following to join a principal alien who is a grandfathered alien as described in this section.

(2) Properly filed means:

(i) With respect to a qualifying immigrant visa petition, that the application was physically received by the Service on or before April 30, 2001, or if mailed, was postmarked on or before April 30, 2001, and accepted for filing as provided in § 103.2(a)(1) and (a)(2) of 8 CFR chapter I; and

(ii) With respect to a qualifying application for labor certification, that the application was properly filed and accepted pursuant to the regulations of the Secretary of Labor, 20 CFR 656.21.

(3) Approvable when filed means that, as of the date of the filing of the qualifying immigrant visa petition under section 204 of the Act or qualifying application for labor certification, the qualifying petition or application was properly filed, meritorious in fact, and non-frivolous ("frivolous" being defined herein as patently without substance). This determination will be made based on the circumstances that existed at the time the qualifying petition or application was filed. A visa petition that was properly filed on or before April 30, 2001, and was approvable when filed, but was later withdrawn, denied, or revoked due to circumstances that have arisen after the time of filing, will preserve the alien beneficiary's grandfathered status if the alien is otherwise eligible to file an application for adjustment of status under section 245(i) of the Act.

(4) Circumstances that have arisen after the time of filing means circumstances similar to those outlined in § 1205.1(a)(3)(i) or (a)(3)(ii) of this chapter.

(b) Eligibility. An alien who is included in the categories of restricted aliens under § 1245.1(b) and meets the definition of a "grandfathered alien" may apply for adjustment of status under section 245 of the Act if the alien meets the requirements of paragraphs (b)(1) through (b)(7) of this section:

(1) Is physically present in the United States;

(2) Is eligible for immigrant classification and has an immigrant visa number immediately available at the time of filing for adjustment of status;

(3) Is not inadmissible from the United States under any provision of section 212 of the Act, or all grounds for inadmissibility have been waived;

(4) Properly files Form I-485, Application to Register Permanent Residence or Adjust Status on or after October 1, 1994, with the required fee for that application;

(5) Properly files Supplement A to Form I-485 on or after October 1, 1994;

(6) Pays an additional sum of $ 1,000, unless payment of the additional sum is not required under section 245(i) of the Act; and

(7) Will adjust status under section 245 of the Act to that of lawful permanent resident of the United States on or after October 1, 1994.

(c) Payment of additional sum. An adjustment applicant filing under the provisions of section 245(i) of the Act must pay the standard adjustment application filing fee as specified in 8 CFR 103.7 and 8 CFR part 106. Each application submitted under the provisions of section 245(i) of the Act must be submitted with an additional sum of $ 1,000. An applicant must submit the additional sum of $ 1,000 only once per application for adjustment of status submitted under the provisions of section 245(i) of the Act. However, an applicant filing under the provisions of section 245(i) of the Act is not required to pay the additional sum if, at the time the application for adjustment of status is filed, the alien is:

(1) Unmarried and less than 17 years of age;

(2) The spouse of a legalized alien, qualifies for and has properly filed Form I-817, Application for Voluntary Departure under the Family Unity Program, and submits a copy of his or her receipt or approval notice for filing Form I-817; or

(3) The child of a legalized alien, is unmarried and less than 21 years of age, qualifies for and has filed Form I-817, and submits a copy of his or her receipt or approval notice for filing Form I-817. Such an alien must pay the additional sum if he or she has reached the age of 21 years at the time of filing for adjustment of status. Such an alien must meet all other conditions for adjustment of status contained in the Act and in this chapter.

(d) Pending adjustment application with the Service or Executive Office for Immigration Review filed without Supplement A to Form I-485 and additional sum. An alien who filed an adjustment of status application with the Service in accordance with § 103.2 of 8 CFR chapter I will be allowed the opportunity to amend such an application to request consideration under the provisions of section 245(i) of the Act, if it appears that the alien is not otherwise ineligible for adjustment of status. The Service shall notify the applicant in writing of the Service's intent to deny the adjustment of status application, and any other requests for benefits that derive from the adjustment application, unless Supplement A to Form I-485 and any required additional sum is filed within 30 days of the date of the notice. If the application for adjustment of status is pending before the Executive Office for Immigration Review (EOIR), EOIR will allow the respondent an opportunity to amend an adjustment of status application filed in accordance with § 103.2 of 8 CFR chapter I (to include Supplement A to Form I-485 and proof of remittance to the INS of the required additional sum) in order to request consideration under the provisions of section 245(i) of the Act.

(e) Applications for Adjustment of Status filed before October 1, 1994. The provisions of section 245(i) of the Act shall not apply to an application for adjustment of status that was filed before October 1, 1994. The provisions of section 245(i) of the Act also shall not apply to a motion to reopen or reconsider an application for adjustment of status if the application for adjustment of status was filed before October 1, 1994. An applicant whose pre-October 1, 1994, application for adjustment of status has been denied may file a new application for adjustment of status pursuant to section 245(i) of the Act on or after October 1, 1994, provided that such new application is accompanied by: the required fee; Supplement A to Form I-485; the additional sum required by section 245(i) of the Act; and all other required initial and additional evidence.

(f) **Effect of section 245(i) on completed adjustment applications before the Service.**

(1) Any motion to reopen or reconsider before the Service alleging availability of section 245(i) of the Act must be filed in accordance with § 103.5 of 8 CFR chapter I. If said motion to reopen with the Service is granted, the alien must remit to the Service Supplement A to Form I-485 and the additional sum required by section 245(i) of the Act. If the alien had previously remitted Supplement A to Form I-485 and the additional sum with the application which is the subject of the motion to reopen, then no additional sum need be remitted upon such reopening.

(2) An alien whose adjustment application was adjudicated and denied by the Service because of ineligibility under section 245(a) or (c) of the Act and now alleges eligibility due to the availability of section 245(i) of the Act may file a new application for adjustment of status pursuant to section 245(i) of the Act, provided that such new application is accompanied by the required fee for the application, Supplement A to Form I-485, additional sum required by section 245(i) of the Act and all other required and additional evidence.

(g) Aliens deportable under section 237(a)(4)(B) of the Act are ineligible to adjust status. Section 237(a)(4)(B) of the Act renders any alien who has engaged, is engaged, or at any time after admission engages in any terrorist activity, as defined in section 212(a)(3)(B)(iii) of the Act, deportable. Under section 245(c)(6) of the Act, persons who are deportable under section 237(a)(4)(B) of the Act are ineligible to adjust status under section 245(a) of the Act. Any person who is deportable under section 237(a)(4)(B) of the Act is also ineligible to adjust status under section 245(i) of the Act.

(h) Asylum or diversity immigrant visa applications. An asylum application, diversity visa lottery application, or diversity visa lottery-winning letter does not serve to grandfather the alien for purposes of section 245(i) of the Act. However, an otherwise grandfathered alien may use winning a diversity visa as a basis for adjustment.

(i) Denial, withdrawal, or revocation of the approval of a visa petition or application for labor certification. The denial, withdrawal, or revocation of the approval of a qualifying immigrant visa petition, or application for labor certification, that was properly filed on or before April 30, 2001, and that was approvable when filed, will not preclude its grandfathered alien (including the grandfathered alien's family members) from seeking adjustment of status under section 245(i) of the Act on the basis of another approved visa petition, a diversity visa, or any other ground for adjustment of status under the Act, as appropriate.

(j) Substitution of a beneficiary on an application for a labor certification. Only the alien who was the beneficiary of the application for the labor certification on or before April 30, 2001, will be considered to have been grandfathered for purposes of filing an application for adjustment of status under section 245(i) of the Act. An alien who was previously the beneficiary of the application for the labor certification but was subsequently replaced by another alien on or before April 30, 2001, will not be considered to be a grandfathered alien. An alien who was substituted for the previous beneficiary of the application for the labor certification after April 30, 2001, will not be considered to be a grandfathered alien.

(k) Changes in employment. An applicant for adjustment under section 245(i) of the Act who is adjusting status through an employment-based category is not required to work for the petitioner who filed the petition that grandfathered the alien, unless he or she is seeking adjustment based on employment for that same petitioner.

(l) Effects of grandfathering on an alien's nonimmigrant status. An alien's nonimmigrant status is not affected by the fact that he or she is a grandfathered alien. Lawful immigration status for a nonimmigrant is defined in § 1245.1(d)(1)(ii).

(m) Effect of grandfathering on unlawful presence under section (a)(9)(B) and (c) of the Act. If the alien is not in a period of stay authorized by the Attorney General, the fact that he or she is a grandfathered alien does not prevent the alien from accruing unlawful presence under section 212(a)(9)(B) and (C) of the Act.

(n) **Evidentiary requirement to demonstrate physical presence on December 21, 2000.**

(1) Unless the qualifying immigrant visa petition or application for labor certification was filed on or before January 14, 1998, a principal grandfathered alien must establish that he or she was physically present in the United States on December 21, 2000, to be eligible to apply to adjust status under section 245(i) of the Act. If no one document establishes the alien's physical presence on December 21, 2000, he or she may submit several documents establishing his or her physical presence in the United States prior to, and after December 21, 2000.

(2) To demonstrate physical presence on December 21, 2000, the alien may submit Service documentation. Examples of acceptable Service documentation include, but are not limited to:

(i) A photocopy of the Form I-94, Arrival-Departure Record, issued upon the alien's arrival in the United States;

(ii) A photocopy of the Form I-862, Notice to Appear;

(iii) A photocopy of the Form I-122, Notice to Applicant for Admission Detained for Hearing before Immigration Judge, issued by the Service on or prior to December 21, 2000, placing the applicant in exclusion proceedings under section 236 of the Act (as in effect prior to April 1, 1997);

(iv) A photocopy of the Form I-221, Order to Show Cause, issued by the Service on or prior to December 21, 2000, placing the applicant in deportation proceedings under section 242 or 242A of the Act (as in effect prior to April 1, 1997);

(v) A photocopy of any application or petition for a benefit under the Act filed by or on behalf of the applicant on or prior to December 21, 2000, which establishes his or her presence in the United States, or a fee receipt issued by the Service for such application or petition.

(3) To demonstrate physical presence on December 21, 2000, the alien may submit other government documentation. Other government documentation issued by a Federal, state, or local authority must bear the signature, seal, or other authenticating instrument of such authority (if the document normally bears such instrument), be dated at the time of issuance, and bear a date of issuance not later than December 21, 2000. For this purpose, the term Federal, state, or local authority includes any governmental, educational, or administrative function operated by Federal, state, county, or municipal officials. Examples of such other documentation include, but are not limited to:

(i) A state driver's license;

(ii) A state identification card;

(iii) A county or municipal hospital record;

(iv) A public college or public school transcript;

(v) Income tax records;

(vi) A certified copy of a Federal, state, or local governmental record which was created on or prior to December 21, 2000, shows that the applicant was present in the United States at the time, and establishes that the applicant sought on his or her own behalf, or some other party sought on the applicant's behalf, a benefit from the Federal, state, or local governmental agency keeping such record;

(vii) A certified copy of a Federal, state, or local governmental record which was created on or prior to December 21, 2000, that shows that the applicant was present in the United States at the time, and establishes that the applicant submitted an income tax return, property tax payment, or similar submission or payment to the Federal, state, or local governmental agency keeping such record;

(viii) A transcript from a private or religious school that is registered with, or approved or licensed by, appropriate State or local authorities, accredited by the State or regional accrediting body, or by the appropriate private school association, or maintains enrollment records in accordance with State or local requirements or standards.

(4) To demonstrate physical presence on December 21, 2000, the alien may submit non-government documentation. Examples of documentation establishing physical presence on December 21, 2000, may include, but are not limited to:

(i) School records;

(ii) Rental receipts;

(iii) Utility bill receipts;

(iv) Any other dated receipts;

(v) Personal checks written by the applicant bearing a bank cancellation stamp;

(vi) Employment records, including pay stubs;

(vii) Credit card statements showing the dates of purchase, payment, or other transaction;

(viii) Certified copies of records maintained by organizations chartered by the Federal or State government, such as public utilities, accredited private and religious schools, and banks;

(ix) If the applicant established that a family unit was in existence and cohabiting in the United States, documents evidencing the presence of another member of the same family unit; and

(x) For applicants who have ongoing correspondence or other interaction with the Service, a list of the types and dates of such correspondence or other contact that the applicant knows to be contained or reflected in Service records.

(5)(i) The adjudicator will evaluate all evidence on a case-by-case basis and will not accept a personal affidavit attesting to physical presence on December 21, 2000, without requiring an interview or additional evidence to validate the affidavit.

(ii) In all cases, any doubts as to the existence, authenticity, veracity, or accuracy of the documentation shall be resolved by the official government record, with records of the Service and the Executive Office for Immigration Review (EOIR) having precedence over the records of other agencies. Furthermore, determinations as to the weight to be given any particular document or item of evidence shall be solely within the discretion of the adjudicating authority (i.e., the Service or EOIR). It shall be the responsibility of the applicant to obtain and submit copies of the records of any other government agency that the applicant desires to be considered in support of his or her application.

HISTORY:

[59 FR 51095, Oct. 7, 1994, as corrected at 59 FR 53020, Oct. 20, 1994; 62 FR 10312, 10384, March 6, 1997; 62 FR 39417, 39424, July 23, 1997; 62 FR 50999, 51000, Sept. 30, 1997; 62 FR 55152, 55153, Oct. 23, 1997; 66 FR 16383, 16388, Mar. 26, 2001; 68 FR 9824, 9842, 9846, Feb. 28, 2003; 68 FR 10349, 10357, Mar. 5, 2003; 85 FR 82750, 82794, Dec. 18, 2020]

§ 1245.11 Adjustment of aliens in S nonimmigrant classification.

(a) Eligibility. An application on Form I-854, requesting that an alien witness or informant in S nonimmigrant classification be allowed to adjust status to that of lawful permanent resident, may only be filed by the federal or state law enforcement authority ("LEA") (which shall include a federal or state court or a United States Attorney's Office) that originally requested S classification for the alien. The completed application shall be filed with the Assistant Attorney General, Criminal Division, Department of Justice, who will forward only properly certified applications to the Commissioner, Immigration and Naturalization Service, for approval. Upon receipt of an approved Form I-854 allowing the S nonimmigrant to adjust status to that of lawful permanent resident, the alien may proceed to file with that Form, Form I-485, Application to Register Permanent Residence or Adjust Status, pursuant to the following process.

(1) Request to allow S nonimmigrant to apply for adjustment of status to that of lawful permanent resident. The LEA that requested S nonimmigrant classification for an S nonimmigrant witness or informant pursuant to section 101(a)(15)(S) of the Act may request that the principal S nonimmigrant be allowed to apply for adjustment of status by filing Form I-854 with the Assistant Attorney General, Criminal Division, in accordance with the instructions on, or attached to, that form and certifying that the alien has fulfilled the terms of his or her admission and classification. The same Form I-854 may be used by the LEA to request that the principals nonimmigrant's spouse, married and unmarried sons and daughters, regardless of age, and parents who are in derivative S nonimmigrant classification and who are qualified family members as described in paragraph (b) of this section similarly be allowed to apply for adjustment of status pursuant to section 101(a)(15)(S) of the Act.

(2) Certification. Upon receipt of an LEA's request for the adjustment of an alien in S nonimmigrant classification on Form I-854, the Assistant Attorney General, Criminal Division, shall review the information and determine whether to certify the request to the Commissioner in accordance with the instructions on the form.

(3) Submission of requests for adjustment of status to the Commissioner. No application by an LEA on Form I-854 requesting the adjustment to lawful permanent resident status of an S nonimmigrant shall be forwarded to the Commissioner unless first certified by the Assistant Attorney General, Criminal Division.

(4) Decision on request to allow adjustment of S nonimmigrant. The Commissioner shall make the final decision on a request to allow an S nonimmigrant to apply for adjustment of status to lawful permanent resident.

(i) In the event the Commissioner decides to deny an application on Form I-854 to allow an S nonimmigrant to apply for adjustment of status, the Assistant Attorney General, Criminal Division, and the relevant LEA shall be notified in writing to that effect. The Assistant Attorney General, Criminal Division, shall concur in or object to that decision. Unless the Assistant Attorney General, Criminal Division, objects within 7 days, he or she shall be deemed to have concurred in the decision. In the event of an objection by the Assistant Attorney General, Criminal Division, the matter will be expeditiously referred to the Deputy Attorney General for a final resolution. In no circumstances shall be alien or the relevant LEA have a right of appeal from any decision to deny.

(ii) Upon approval of the request on Form I-854, the Commissioner shall forward a copy of the approved form to the Assistant Attorney General and the S nonimmigrant, notifying them that the S nonimmigrant may proceed to file Form I-485 and request adjustment of status to that of lawful permanent resident, and that, to be eligible for adjustment of status, the nonimmigrant must otherwise:

(A) Meet the requirements of paragraph (b) of this section, if requesting adjustment as a qualified family member of the certified principal S nonimmigrant witness or informant;

(B) Be admissible to the United States as an immigrant, unless the ground of inadmissibility has been waived;

(C) Establish eligibility for adjustment of status under all provisions of section 245 of the Act, unless the basis for ineligibility has been waived; and

(D) Properly file with his or her Form I-485, Application to Register Permanent Residence or Adjust Status, the approved Form I-854.

(b) Family members —

(1) Qualified family members. A qualified family member of an S nonimmigrant includes the spouse, married or unmarried son or daughter, or parent of a principal S nonimmigrant who meets the requirements of paragraph (a) of this section, provided that:

(i) The family member qualified as the spouse, married or unmarried son or daughter, or parent (as defined in section 101(b) of the Act) of the principal S nonimmigrant when the family member was admitted as or granted a change of status to that of a nonimmigrant under section 101(a)(15)(S) of the Act;

(ii) The family member was admitted in S nonimmigrant classification to accompany, or follow to join, the principal S-5 or S-6 alien pursuant to the LEA's request;

(iii) The family member is not inadmissible from the United States as a participant in Nazi persecution or genocide as described in section 212(a)(3)(E) of the Act;

(iv) The qualifying relationship continues to exist; and

(v) The principal alien has adjusted status, has a pending application for adjustment of status or is concurrently filing an application for adjustment of status under section 101(a)(15)(S) of the Act.

(vi) Paragraphs (b)(1)(iv) and (v) of this section do not apply if the alien witness or informant has died and, in the opinion of the Attorney General, was in compliance with the terms of his or her S classification under section 245(i) (1) and (2) of the Act.

(2) Other family member. The adjustment provisions in this section do not apply to a family member who has not been classified as an S nonimmigrant pursuant to a request on Form I-854 or who does not otherwise meet the requirements of paragraph (b) of this section. However, a spouse or an unmarried child who is less than 21 years old, and whose relationship to the principal S nonimmigrant or qualified family member was established prior to the approval of the principal S nonimmigrant's adjustment of status application, may be accorded the priority date and preference category of the principal S nonimmigrant or qualified family member, in accordance with the provisions of section 203(d) of the Act. Such a spouse or child:

(i) May use the principal S nonimmigrant or qualified member's priority date and category when it becomes current, in accordance with the limitations set forth in sections 201 and 202 of the Act;

(ii) May seek immigrant visa issuance abroad or adjustment of status to that of a lawful permanent resident of the United States when the priority date becomes current for the spouse's or child's country of chargeability under the fourth employment-based preference classification;

(iii) Must meet all the requirements for immigrant visa issuance or adjustment of status, unless those requirements have been waived;

(iv) Is not applying for adjustment of status under 101(a)(15)(S) of the Act, is not required to file Form I-854, and is not required to obtain LEA certification; and

(v) Will lose eligibility for benefits if the child marries or has his or her twenty-first birthday before being admitted with an immigrant visa or granted adjustment of status.

(c) Waivers of inadmissibility. An alien seeking to adjust status pursuant to the provisions of section 101(a)(15)(S) of the Act may not be denied adjustment of status for conduct or a condition that:

(1) Was disclosed to the Attorney General prior to admission; and

(2) Was specifically waived pursuant to the waiver provisions set forth at section 212(d)(1) and 212(d)(3) of the Act.

(d) Application. Each S nonimmigrant requesting adjustment of status under section 101(a)(15)(S) of the Act must:

(1) File Form I-485, with the prescribed fee, accompanied by the approved Form I-854, and the supporting documents specified in the instructions to Form I-485 and described in 8 CFR 1245.2. Secondary evidence may be submitted if the nonimmigrant is unable to obtain the required primary evidence as provided in 8 CFR 103.2(b)(2). The S nonimmigrant applying to adjust must complete Part 2 of Form I-485 by checking box "h-other" and writing "S" or "S-Qualified Family Member." Qualified family members must submit documentary evidence of the relationship to the principal S nonimmigrant witness or informant.

(2) Submit detailed and inclusive evidence of eligibility for the adjustment of status benefits of S classification, which shall include:

(i) A photocopy of all pages of the alien's most recent passport or an explanation of why the alien does not have a passport; or

(ii) An attachment on a plain piece of paper showing the dates of all arrivals and departures from the United States in S nonimmigrant classification and the reason for each departure; and

(iii) Primary evidence of a qualifying relationship to the principal S nonimmigrant, such as birth or marriage certificate. If any required primary evidence is unavailable, church or school records, or other secondary evidence may be submitted. If such documents are unavailable, affidavits may be submitted as provided in 8 CFR 103.2(b)(2).

(e) Priority date. The S nonimmigrant's priority date shall be the date his or her application for adjustment of status as an S nonimmigrant is properly filed with the Service.

(f) Visa number limitation. An adjustment of status application under section 101(a)(15)(S) of the Act may be filed regardless of the availability of immigrant visa numbers. The adjustment of status application may not, however, be approved and the alien's adjustment of status to that of lawful permanent resident of the United States may not be granted until a visa number becomes available for the alien under the worldwide allocation for employment-based immigrants under section 201(d) and section 203(b)(4) of the Act. The alien may request initial or continued employment authorization while the adjustment application is pending by filing Form I-765, Application for Employment Authorization. If the alien needs to travel outside the United States during this period, he or she may file a request for advance parole on Form I-131, Application for Travel Document.

(g) Filing and decision. An application for adjustment of status filed by an S nonimmigrant under section 101(a)(15)(S) of the Act shall be filed with the district director having jurisdiction over the alien's place of residence. Upon approval of adjustment of status under this section, the district director shall record the alien's lawful admission for permanent residence as of the date of such approval. The district director shall notify the Commissioner and the Assistant Attorney General, Criminal Division, of the adjustment.

(h) Removal under section 237 of the Act. Nothing in this section shall prevent an alien adjusted pursuant to the terms of these provisions from being removed for conviction of a crime of moral turpitude committed within 10 years after being provided lawful permanent residence under this section or for any other ground under section 237 of the Act.

(i) Denial of application. In the event the district director decides to deny an application on Form I-485 and an approved Form I-854 to allow an S nonimmigrant to adjust status, the Assistant Attorney General, Criminal Division, and the relevant LEA shall be notified in writing to that effect. The Assistant Attorney General, Criminal Division, shall concur in or object to that decision. Unless the Assistant Attorney General, Criminal Division, objects within 7 days, he or she shall be deemed to have concurred in the decision. In the event of an objection by the Assistant Attorney General, Criminal Division, the matter will be expeditiously referred to the Deputy Attorney General for a final resolution. In no circumstances shall the alien or the relevant LEA have a right of appeal from any decision to deny. A denial of an adjustment application under this paragraph may not be renewed in subsequent removal proceedings.

HISTORY:

[60 FR 44260, 44269, Aug. 25, 1995; 62 FR 10312, 10384, March 6, 1997; 68 FR 9824, 9842, 9846, Feb. 28, 2003; 68 FR 10349, 10357, Mar. 5, 2003]

§ 1245.12 What are the procedures for certain Polish and Hungarian parolees who are adjusting status to that of permanent resident under the Illegal Immigration Reform and Immigrant Responsibility Act of 1996?

(a) **How do I apply for adjustment of status under this section?**

(1) Each person applying for adjustment of status, under section 646(b) of Public Law 104-208, must file a completed Form I-485, Application to Register Permanent Residence or Adjust Status, with the correct filing fee, with the Service director having jurisdiction over the applicant's place of residence.

(2) The application must include Form G-325A, Biographic Information and the results of the medical examination made according to § 232.1 of 8 CFR chapter I and § 1245.5.

(3) The application must include evidence to show the applicant was a national of Poland or Hungary who, after being denied refugee status, was inspected and granted parole into the United States between November 1, 1989, and December 31, 1991.

(4) The applicant must have been physically present in the United States for at least 1 year before filing a Form I-485.

(5) After receiving the Form I-485, the adjudicating Service office will notify each applicant who is 14 years old or older of the time and location for the required fingerprinting.

(b) How is my application for adjustment of status affected if I leave the United States while my application is still pending? The departure from the United States by an applicant for adjustment of status must be considered an abandonment of the application, as provided in § 1245.2(a)(4)(ii), unless the applicant was previously granted advance parole for such absence, and was reinspected on returning to the United States.

(c) Which grounds for inadmissibility do not apply or can be waived? The provisions of section 212(a) (4), (5), and (7)(A) of the Act will not apply to adjustment of status under § 1245.12. In addition, the director may waive any other ground of inadmissibility except section 212(a)(2)(C) or 212(a)(3)(A), (B), (C), or (E) of the Act, for humanitarian purposes, to ensure family unity, or when it is otherwise in the public interest.

(d) If my application for adjustment of status is approved under § 1245.12, what date will be recorded as my admission to permanent residence? On approval of the application for adjustment of status, the date of the applicant's admission to permanent resident status will be the date of the applicant's inspection and parole, as described in paragraph (a) of this section.

HISTORY:

[62 FR 28314, 28315, May 23, 1997, as confirmed and revised at 65 FR 20069, 20070, Apr. 14, 2000; 68 FR 9824, 9842, 9846, Feb. 28, 2003; 68 FR 10349, 10357, Mar. 5, 2003]

§ 1245.13 Adjustment of Status of Certain Nationals of Nicaragua and Cuba under Public Law 105-100.

(a) Aliens eligible to apply for adjustment. An alien is eligible to apply for adjustment of status under the provisions of section 202 of Pub. L. 105-100, as amended and without regard to section 241(a)(5) of the Act, if the alien:

(1) Is a national of Nicaragua or Cuba;

(2) Except as provided in paragraph (o) of this section, has been physically present in the United States for a continuous period beginning not later than December 1, 1995, and ending not earlier that the date the application for adjustment is granted, excluding:

(i) Any periods of absence from the United States not exceeding 180 days in the aggregate; and

(ii) Any periods of absence for which the applicant received an Advance Authorization for Parole (Form I-512) prior to his or her departure from the United States, provided the applicant returned to the United States in accordance with the conditions of such Advance Authorization for Parole;

(3) Is not inadmissible to the United States for permanent residence under any provisions of section 212(a) of the Act, with the exception of paragraphs (4), (5), (6)(A), (7)(A) and (9)(B). If available, an applicant may apply for an individual waiver as provided in paragraph (c) of this section;

(4) Is physically present in the United States at the time the application is filed; and

(5) Properly files an application for adjustment of status in accordance with this section.

(b) Qualified family members —

(1) Existence of relationship at time of adjustment. The spouse, child, or unmarried son or daughter of an alien eligible for adjustment of status under the provisions of Pub. L. 105-100 is eligible to apply for benefits as a dependent provided the qualifying relationship existed when the principal beneficiary was granted adjustment of status and the dependent meets all applicable requirements of sections 202(a) and (d) of Pub. L. 105-100.

(2) Spouse and minor children. If physically present in the United States, the spouse or minor child of an alien who is eligible for permanent residence under the provisions of Pub. L. 105-100 may also apply for and receive adjustment of status under this section, provided such spouse or child meets the criteria established in paragraph (a) of this section, except for the requirement of continuous physical presence in the United States since December 1, 1995. Such application may be filed concurrently with or subsequent to the filing of the principal's application but may not be approved prior to approval of the principal's application.

(3) Unmarried adult sons and daughters. An unmarried son or daughter of an alien who is eligible for permanent residence under the provisions of Pub. L. 105-100 may apply for and receive adjustment under this section, provided such son or daughter meets the criteria established in paragraph (a) of this section.

(c) General.

(1) Applicability of inadmissibility grounds contained in section 212(a). An applicant for the benefits of the adjustment of status provisions of section 202 of Pub. L. 105-100 need not establish admissibility under paragraphs (4), (5), (6)(A), (7)(A), and (9)(B) of section 212(a) of the Act in order to be able to adjust his or her status to that of permanent resident. An applicant under section 202 of Pub. L. 105-100 may also apply for one or more of the immigrant waivers of inadmissibility under section 212 of the Act, if applicable, in accordance with § 1212.7 of this chapter.

(2) Special rule for waiver of inadmissibility grounds for NACARA applicants under section 212(a)(9)(A) and 212(a)(9)(C) of the Act. An applicant for adjustment of status under section 202 of Public Law 105-100 who is inadmissible under section 212(a)(9)(A) or 212(a)(9)(C) of the Act, may apply for a waiver of these grounds of inadmissibility while present in the United States. Such an alien must file a Form I-601, Application for Waiver of Grounds of Excludability, with the director of the Texas Service Center if the application for adjustment is pending at that office, with the district director having jurisdiction over the application if the application for adjustment is pending at a district office, with the Immigration Judge having jurisdiction if the application for adjustment is pending before the Immigration Court, or with the Board of Immigration Appeals if the appeal is pending before the Board.

(d) General. Aliens in exclusion, deportation, or removal proceedings, and aliens subject to a final order of exclusion, deportation, or removal —

(1) Proceedings pending before an Immigration Court. Except as provided in paragraph (d)(3) of this section, while an alien is in exclusion, deportation, or removal proceedings pending before an immigration judge, or has a pending motion to reopen or motion to reconsider filed with an immigration judge on or before May 21, 1998, sole jurisdiction over an application for adjustment of status under section 202 of Public Law 105-100 shall lie with the immigration judge. If an alien who has a pending motion to reopen or motion to reconsider filed with an immigration judge on or before May 21, 1998 files an application for adjustment of status under section 202 of Pub. L. 105-100, the immigration judge shall reopen the alien's proceedings for consideration of the adjustment application, unless the alien is clearly ineligible for adjustment of status under section 202 of Pub. L. 105-100. All applications for adjustment of status under section 202 of Pub. L. 105-100 filed with an Immigration Court shall be

subject to the requirements of §§ 3.11 and 3.31 of this chapter.

(2) Proceedings pending before the Board of Immigration Appeals. Except as provided in paragraph (d)(3) of this section, in cases where a motion to reopen or motion to reconsider filed with the Board on or before May 21, 1998, or an appeal, is pending, the Board shall remand, or reopen and remand, the proceedings to the Immigration Court for the sole purpose of adjudicating an application for adjustment of status under section 202 of Public Law 105-100, unless the alien is clearly ineligible for adjustment of status under section 202 of Public Law 105-100. If the immigration judge denies, or the alien fails to file, the application for adjustment of status under section 202 of Public Law 105-100, the immigration judge shall certify the decision to the Board for consideration in conjunction with the previously pending appeal or motion.

(3) Administrative closure of pending exclusion, deportation, or removal proceedings.

(i) In the case of an alien who is in exclusion, deportation, or removal proceedings, or has a pending motion to reopen or a motion to reconsider such proceedings filed on or before May 21, 1998, and who appears to be eligible to file an application for adjustment of status under section 202 of Pub. L. 105-100, the Immigration Court having jurisdiction over such proceedings or motion, or if the matter is before the Board on appeal or by motion, the Board, shall, upon request of the alien and with the concurrence of the Service, administratively close the proceedings, or continue indefinitely the motion, to allow the alien to file such application with the Service as prescribed in paragraph (g) of this section.

(ii) In any case not administratively closed in accordance with paragraph (d)(3)(i) of this section, the immigration judge having jurisdiction over the exclusion, deportation, or removal proceedings shall have jurisdiction to accept and adjudicate any application for adjustment of status under section 202 of Pub. L. 105-100 during the course of such proceedings.

(4)(i) Aliens with final orders of exclusion, deportation, or removal. An alien who is subject to a final order of exclusion, deportation, or removal, and who has not been denied adjustment of status under section 202 of Public Law 105-100 by the immigration judge or the Board of Immigration Appeals, may apply to the Service for adjustment of status under section 202 of Pub. L. 105-100.

(ii) An alien may file a motion to reopen with the Immigration Court or the Board of Immigration Appeals, whichever had jurisdiction last, if the alien is present in the United States and subject to a final order of exclusion, deportation, or removal and has been denied adjustment of status under section 202 of NACARA by an Immigration Court or the Board or who never applied for adjustment of status on or before March 31, 2000, with either the Service, the Immigration Court or the Board, and who is now eligible for adjustment as a result of section 1505(a)(1) of the Legal Immigration Family Equity Act of 2000 (LIFE) and the LIFE amendments, Public Law 106-553 and Public Law 106-554, respectively. As provided by § 1505(a)(2) of the LIFE Act and its amendments, such a motion to reopen must be filed on or before June 19, 2001.

(5) Stay of final order of exclusion, deportation, or removal —

(i) With the Service. The filing of an application for adjustment under section 202 of Public Law 105-100 with the Service shall not stay the execution of such final order unless the applicant has filed, and the Service has approved an Application for Stay of Removal (Form I-246) in accordance with section 241(c)(2) of the Act and § 241.6 of this chapter. Absent evidence of the applicant's statutory ineligibility for adjustment of status under section 202 of Public Law 105-100 or significant negative discretionary factors, a Form I-246 filed by a bona fide applicant for adjustment under section 202 of Public Law 105-100 shall be approved, and the removal of the applicant shall be stayed until such time as the application for adjustment has been adjudicated in accordance with this section.

(ii) With EOIR. When the Service refers a decision to an immigration judge on a Notice of Certification (Form I-290C) in accordance with paragraph (m)(3) of this section, the referral shall not stay the execution of the final order. Execution of such final order shall proceed unless a stay of execution is specifically granted by the immigration judge, the Board, or an authorized Service officer.

(6) Effect on applications for adjustment under other provisions of the law. Nothing in this section shall be deemed to allow any alien who is in either exclusion proceedings that commenced prior to April 1, 1997, or removal proceedings as an inadmissible arriving alien that commenced on or after April 1, 1997, and who has not been paroled into the United States, to apply for adjustment of status under any provision of law other than section 202 of Pub. L. 105-100.

(e) Application and supporting documents. Each applicant for adjustment of status must file a Form I-485, Application to Register Permanent Residence or Adjust Status. An applicant should complete Part 2 of Form I-485 by checking box "h — other" and writing "NACARA — Principal" or "NACARA — Dependent" next to that block. Each application must be accompanied by:

(1) The fee prescribed in 8 CFR 103.7 and 8 CFR part 106;

(2) If the applicant is 14 years of age or older, the fee for fingerprinting prescribed in 8 CFR 103.7;

(3) Evidence of commencement of physical presence in the United States at any time on or before December 1, 1995. Such evidence may relate to any time at or after entry and may consist of either:

(i) Documentation evidencing one or more of the activities specified in section 202(b)(2)(A) of Public Law 105-100;

(ii) A copy of the Form I-94, Record of Arrival and Departure, issued to the applicant at the time of his or her inspection and admission or parole;

(iii) Other documentation issued by a Federal, State, or local authority provided such other documentation bears the signature, seal, or other authenticating instrument of such authority (if the document normally bears such instrument), was dated at the time of issuance, and bears a date of issuance not later than December 1, 1995. Examples of such other documentation include, but are not limited to:

(A) A State driver's license;

(B) A State identification card issued in lieu of a driver's license to a nondriver;

(C) A county or municipal hospital record;

(D) A public college or public school transcript; and

(E) Income tax records;

(iv) A copy of a petition on behalf of the applicant that was submitted to the Service on or before December 1, 1995, and that lists the applicant as being physically present in the United States;

(v) A certified copy of a Federal, State, or local governmental record that was created on or prior to December 1, 1995, shows that the applicant was present in the United States at the time, and establishes that the applicant sought on his or her own behalf, or some other party sought on the applicant's behalf, a benefit from the Federal, State, or local governmental agency keeping such record;

(vi) A certified copy of a Federal, State, or local governmental record that was created on or prior to December 1, 1995, shows that the applicant was present in the United States at the time, and establishes that the applicant submitted an income tax return, property tax payment, or similar submission or payment to the Federal, State, or local governmental agency keeping such record; or

(vii) In the case of an applicant who, while under the age of 21, attended a private or religious school in the United States on or prior to December 1, 1995, a transcript from such private or religious school, provided that the school:

(A) Is registered with, approved by, or licensed by, appropriate State or local authorities;

(B) Is accredited by the State or regional accrediting body, or by the appropriate private school association; or

(C) Maintains enrollment records in accordance with State or local requirements or standards;

(4) Evidence of continuity of physical presence in the United States since the last date on or prior to December 1, 1995, on which the applicant established commencement of physical presence in the United States. Such documentation may have been issued by any governmental or nongovernmental authority, provided such evidence bears the name of the applicant, was dated at the time it was issued, and bears the signature, seal, or other authenticating instrument of the issuing authority or its authorized representative, if the document would normally contain such authenticating instrument. Such documentation may include, but is not limited to:

(i) School records;

(ii) Rental receipts;

(iii) Utility bill receipts;

(iv) Any other dated receipts;

(v) Personal checks written by the applicant bearing a dated bank cancellation stamp;

(vi) Employment records, including pay stubs;

(vii) Credit card statements showing the dates of purchase, payment, or other transaction;

(viii) Certified copies of records maintained by organizations chartered by the government, such as public utilities, accredited private and parochial schools, and banks;

(ix) If the applicant establishes that a family unit was in existence and cohabiting in the United States, documents evidencing the physical presence in the United States of another member of that same family unit; and

(x) If the applicant has had correspondence or other interaction with the Service, a list of the types and dates of such correspondence or other contact that the applicant knows to be contained or reflected in Service records;

(5) A copy of the applicant's birth certificate;

(6) If the applicant is between 14 and 79 years of age, a completed Biographic Information Sheet (Form G-325A);

(7) A report of medical examination, as specified in § 1245.5;

(8) Two photographs, as described in the instructions to Form I-485;

(9) If the applicant is 14 years of age or older, a police clearance from each municipality where the alien has resided for 6 months or longer since arriving in the United States. If there are multiple local law enforcement agencies (e.g., city police and county sheriff) with jurisdiction over the alien's residence, the applicant may obtain a clearance from either agency. If the applicant resides or resided in a State where the State Police maintain a compilation of all local arrests and convictions, a statewide clearance is sufficient. If the applicant presents a letter from the local police agencies involved, or other evidence, to the effect that the applicant attempted to obtain such clearance but was unable to do so because of local or State policy, the director or immigration judge having jurisdiction over the application may waive the local police clearance. Furthermore, if such local police agency has provided the Service or the Immigration Court with a blanket statement that issuance of such police clearance is against local or state policy, the director or immigration judge having jurisdiction over the case may waive the local police clearance requirement regardless of whether the applicant individually submits a letter from that local police agency;

(10) If the applicant is applying as the spouse of another Public Law 105-100 beneficiary, a copy of their certificate of marriage and copies of documents showing the legal termination of all other marriages by the applicant or the other beneficiary;

(11) If the applicant is applying as the child, unmarried son, or unmarried daughter of another (principal) beneficiary under section 202 of Public Law 105-100 who is not the applicant's biological mother, copies of evidence (such as the applicant's parent's marriage certificate and documents showing the legal termination of all other marriages, an adoption decree, or other relevant evidence) to demonstrate the relationship between the applicant and the other beneficiary;

(12) A copy of the Form I-94, Arrival-Departure Record, issued at the time of the applicant's arrival in the United States, if the alien was inspected and admitted or paroled; and

(13) If the applicant has departed from and returned to the United States since December 1, 1995, an attachment on a plain piece of paper showing:

(i) The date of the applicant's last arrival in the United States before or on December 1, 1995;

(ii) The date of each departure from the United States since that arrival;

(iii) The reason for each departure; and

(iv) The date, manner, and place of each return to the United States.

(f) Secondary evidence. If the primary evidence required in paragraph (e)(4), (e)(9) or (e)(10 of this section is unavailable, church or school records, or other secondary evidence pertinent to the facts in issue, may be submitted. If such documents are unavailable, affidavits may be submitted. The applicant may submit as many types of secondary evidence as necessary to establish the birth, marriage, or other event. Documentary evidence establishing that primary evidence is unavailable must accompany secondary evidence of birth or marriage in the home country. In adjudicating the application for adjustment of status under section 202 of Public Law 105-100, the Service or immigration judge shall determine the weight to be given such secondary evidence. Secondary evidence may not be submitted in lieu of the documentation specified in paragraphs (e)(2) and (e)(3) of this section. However, subject to verification by the Service, if the documentation specified in paragraphs (e)(2) and (e)(3) is already contained in the Service's file relating to the applicant, the applicant may submit an affidavit to that effect in lieu of the actual documentation.

(g) Filing. The application period begins on June 22, 1998. To benefit from the provisions of section 202 of Public Law 105-100, an alien must properly file an application for adjustment of status before April 1, 2000. Except as provided in paragraph (d) of this section, all applications for the benefits of section 202 of Pub. L. 105-100 must be submitted by mail to: USINS Texas Service Center, P.O. Box 851804, Mesquite, TX 75185-1804. All applications must be accompanied by either the correct fee as specified in 8 CFR 103.7 and 8 CFR part 106; or a request for a fee waiver in accordance with 8 CFR 103.7 and 8 CFR part 106. An application received by the Service or Immigration Court before April 1, 2000, that has been properly signed and executed and for which a waiver of the filing fee has been requested shall be regarded as having been filed before the statutory deadline regardless of whether the fee waiver request is denied provided that the applicant submits the required fee within 30 days of the date of any notice that the fee waiver request has been denied. In a case over which the Board has jurisdiction, an application received by the Board before April 1, 2000, that has been properly signed and executed shall be considered filed before the statutory deadline without payment of the fee or submission of a fee waiver request. Upon demand by the Board, the payment of the fee or a request for a fee waiver shall be made upon submission of the application to the Immigration Court in accordance with 8 CFR 1240.11(f). If a request for a fee waiver is denied, the applicaion shall be considered as having been properly filed with the Immigration Court before the statutory deadline provided that the applicant submits the required fee within 30 days of the date of any notice that the fee waiver request has been denied. After proper filing of the application, the Service will notify the applicant to appear for fingerprinting as prescribed in § 103.2(c) of 8 CFR chapter I.

(h) Jurisdiction. Except as provide din paragraphs (d) and (i) of this section, the director of the Texas Service Center shall have jurisdiction over all applications for adjustment of status under section 202 of Public Law 105-100.

(i) Interview.

(1) Except as provided in paragraphs (d), (i)(2), and (i)(3) of this section, all applicants for adjustment of status under section 202 of Pub. L. 105-100 must be personally interviewed by an immigration officer at a local office of the Service. In any case in which the director of the Texas Service Center determines that an interview of the applicant is necessary, that director shall forward the case to the appropriate local Service office for interview and adjudication.

(2) In the case of an applicant who has submitted evidence of commencement of physical presence in the United States consisting of one or more of the documents specified in section 202(b)(2)(A)(i) through (v) or section (b)(2)(A)(vii) of Pub. L. 105-100 and upon examination of the application, including all other evidence submitted in support of the application, all relevant Service records and all other relevant law enforcement indices, if the director of the Texas Service Center determines that the alien is clearly eligible for adjustment of status under Pub. L. 105-100 and that an interview of the applicant is not necessary, the director may approve the application.

(3) Upon examination of the application, all supporting documentation, all relevant Service records, and all other relevant law enforcement indices, if the director of the Texas Service Center determines that the alien is clearly ineligible for adjustment of status under Pub. L. 105-100 and that an interview of the applicant is not necessary, the director may deny the application.

(j) Authorization to be employed in the United States while the application is pending.

(1) Application. An applicant for adjustment of status under section 202 of Pub. L. 105-100 who wishes to obtain initial or continued employment authorization during the pendency of the adjustment application must file an Application for Employment authorization (Form I-765), with fee as set forth in 8 CFR 103.7 and 8 CFR part 106. The applicant may submit Form I-765 concurrently with, or subsequent to, the filing of the Form I-485.

(2) Adjudication and issuance. In general, employment authorization may not be issued to an applicant for adjustment of status under section 202 of Pub. L. 105-100 until the adjustment application has been

pending for 180 days. However, if Service records contain one or more of the documents specified in section 202(b)(2)(A)(i) through (v) and (vii) of Pub. L. 105-100, evidence of the applicant's Nicaraguan or Cuban nationality, and no indication that the applicant is clearly ineligible for adjustment of status under section 202 of Pub. L. 105-100, the application for employment authorization may be approved, and the resulting document issued immediately upon verification that the Service record contains such information. If the Service fails to adjudicate the application for employment authorization upon expiration of the 180-day waiting period or within 90 days of the filing of application for employment authorization, whichever comes later, the alien shall be eligible for interim employment authorization in accordance with § 1274a.13(d) of this chapter. Nothing in this section shall preclude an applicant for adjustment of status under Pub. L. 105-100 from being granted an initial employment authorization or an extension of employment authorization under any other provision of law or regulation for which the alien may be eligible.

(k) Parole authorization for purposes of travel —

(1) Travel from and return to the United States while the application for adjustment of status is pending. If an applicant for benefits under section 202 of Pub. L. 105-100 desires to travel outside, and return to, the United States while the application for adjustment of status is pending, he or she must file a request for advance parole authorization on an Application for Travel Document (Form I-131), with fee as set forth in 8 CFR 103.7 and 8 CFR part 106 and in accordance with the instructions on the form. If the alien is either in deportation or removal proceedings, or subject to a final order of deportation or removal, the Form I-131 must be submitted to the Assistant Commissioner for International Affairs; otherwise the Form I-131 must be submitted to the director of the Texas Service Center, who shall have jurisdiction over such applications. Unless the applicant files an advance parole request prior to departing from the United States, and the Service approves such request, his or her application for adjustment of status under section 202 of Public Law 105-100 is deemed to be abandoned as of the moment of his or her departure. Parole may only be authorized pursuant to the authority contained in, and the standards prescribed in, section 212(d)(5) of the Act.

(2) Parole authorization for the purpose of filing an application for adjustment of status under section 202 of Pub. L. 105-100. An otherwise eligible applicant who is outside the United States and wishes to come to the United States in order to apply for benefits under section 202 of Pub. L. 105-100 may request parole authorization for such purpose by filing an Application for Travel Document (Form I-131) with the Texas Service Center, at P.O. Box 851804, Mesquite, TX 75185-1804. Such application must be supported by a photocopy of the Form I-485 that the alien will file once he or she has been paroled into the United States. The applicant must include photocopies of all the supporting documentation listed in paragraph (e) of this section, except the filing fee, the medical report, the fingerprint card, and the local police clearances. If the director of the Texas Service Center is satisfied that the alien will be eligible for adjustment of status once the alien has been paroled into the United States and files the application, he or she may issue an Authorization for Parole of an Alien into the United States (Form I-512) to allow the alien to travel to, and be paroled into, the United States for a period of 60 days. The applicant shall have 60 days from the date of parole to file the application for adjustment of status. If the alien files the application for adjustment of status within that 60-day period, the Service may re-parole the alien for such time as is necessary for adjudication of the application. Failure to file such application for adjustment of status within 60 days shall result in the alien being returned to the custody of the Service and being examined as an arriving alien applying for admission. Such examination will be conducted in accordance with the provisions of section 235(b)(1) of the Act if the alien is inadmissible under section 212(a)(6)(C) or 212(a)(7) of the Act, or section 240 of the Act if the alien is inadmissible under any other grounds. Parole may only be authorized pursuant to the authority contained in, and the standards prescribed in, section 212(d)(5) of the Act.

(3) Effect of departure on an outstanding warrant of exclusion, deportation, or removal. If an alien who is the subject of an outstanding final order of exclusion, deportation, or removal departs from the United States, with or without an advance parole authorization, such final order shall be executed by the alien's departure. The execution of such final order shall not preclude the applicant from filing an Application for Permission to Reapply for Admission Into the United States After Deportation or Removal (Form I-212) in accordance with § 1212.2 of this chapter.

(l) Approval. If the director approves the application for adjustment of status under the provisions of section 202 of Pub. L. 105-100, the director shall record the alien's lawful admission for permanent resident as of the date of such approval and notify the applicant accordingly. The director shall also advise the alien regarding the delivery of his or her Permanent Resident Card and of the process for obtaining temporary evidence of alien registration. If the alien had previously been issued a final order of exclusion, deportation, or removal, such order shall be deemed canceled as of the date of the director's approval of the application for adjustment of status. If the alien had been in exclusion, deportation, or removal proceedings that were administratively closed, such proceedings shall be deemed terminated as of the date of approval of the application for adjustment of status by the director. If an immigration judge grants or if the Board, upon appeal, grants an application for adjustment under the provisions of section 202 of Pub. L. 105-100, the alien's lawful admission for permanent residence shall be as of the date of such grant.

(m) Denial and review of decision.

(1) If the director denies the application for adjustment of status under the provisions of section 202 of

Public Law 105-100, the director shall notify the applicant of the decision. The director shall also:

(i) In the case of an alien who is not maintaining valid nonimmigrant status and who had not previously been placed in exclusion, deportation or removal proceedings, initiate removal proceedings in accordance with § 1239.1 of this chapter during which the alien may renew his or her application for adjustment of status under section 202 of Public Law 105-100; or

(ii) In the case of an alien whose previously initiated exclusion, deportation, or removal proceedings had been administratively closed or continued indefinitely under paragraph (d)(3) of this section, advise the Immigration Court that had administratively closed the proceedings, or the Board, as appropriate, of the denial of the application. Upon a motion to recalendar filed by the Service, the Immigration Court or the Board will then recalendar or reinstate the prior exclusion, deportation or removal proceedings, during which the alien may renew his or her application for adjustment under section 202 of Public Law 105-100; or

(iii) In the case of an alien who is the subject of an outstanding final order of exclusion, deportation, or removal, refer the decision to deny the application by filing a Form I-290C, Notice of Certification, with the Immigration Court that issued the final order for consideration in accordance with paragraph (n) of this section.

(2) Aliens who were denied adjustment of status by the director, but who are now eligible for such adjustment of status pursuant to section 1505(a)(1) of the LIFE Act and amendments, and have not been referred to immigration proceedings as specified in paragraph (m)(1) of this section may file a motion to reopen with the Service. If an alien has been referred to the Immigration Court or has filed an appeal with the Board after an Immigration Court has denied the application for adjustment under NACARA section 202, and proceedings are pending, then the application for adjustment of status will be adjudicated in accordance with section 1505(a) of the LIFE Act and its amendments. An alien present in the United States subject to a final order of removal after his or her application was denied by an Immigration Court or the Board, but who was made eligible for adjustment pursuant to section 1505(a) of the LIFE Act and its amendments may file a motion to reopen with the Immigration Court or the Board, whichever had jurisdiction last. Pursuant to section 1505(a)(2) of the LIFE Act and its amendments, motions to reopen proceedings before the Immigration Court or the Board must be filed on or before June 19, 2001.

(n) Action of immigration judge upon referral of decision by a Notice of Certification (Form I-290C) —

(1) General. Upon the referral by a Notice of Certification (Form I-290C) of a decision to deny the application, in accordance with paragraph (m)(3) of this section, and under the authority contained in § 1003.10 of this chapter, the immigration judge shall conduct a hearing to determine whether the alien is eligible for adjustment of status under section 202 of Public Law 105-100. Such hearing shall be conducted under the same rules of procedure as proceedings conducted under part 1240 of this chapter, except the scope of review shall be limited to a determination on the alien's eligibility for adjustment of status under section 202 of Public Law 105-100. During such proceedings all parties are prohibited from raising or considering any other issues, including but not limited to issues of admissibility, deportability, removability, and eligibility for any form of relief other than adjustment of status under section 202 of Public Law 105-100. Should the alien fail to appear for such hearing, the immigration judge shall deny the application for adjustment under section 202 of Public Law 105-100.

(2) Appeal of immigration judge decision. Once the immigration judge issues his or her decision on the application, either the alien or the Service may appeal the decision to the Board. Such appeal must be filed pursuant to the requirements for appeals to the Board from an immigration judge decision set forth in §§ 1003.3 and 1003.8 of this chapter.

(3) Rescission of the decision of an immigration judge. The decision of an immigration judge under paragraph (n)(1) of this section denying an application for adjustment under section 202 of Public Law 105-100 for failure to appear may be rescinded only:

(i) Upon a motion to reopen filed within 180 days after the date of the denial if the alien demonstrates that the failure to appear was because of exceptional circumstances as defined in section 240(e)(1) of the Act;

(ii) Upon a motion to reopen filed at any time if the alien demonstrates that the alien did not receive notice of the hearing in person (or, if personal service was not practicable, through service by mail to the alien or to the alien's counsel of record, if any) or the alien demonstrates that the alien was in Federal or State custody and the failure to appear was through no fault of the alien; or

(iii) Upon a motion to reopen filed not later than June 19, 2001, by an alien present in the United States who became eligible for adjustment of status under section 202 of Public Law 105-100, as amended by section 1505, Public Law 106-554.

(o) Transition period provisions for tolling the physical presence in the United States provision for certain individuals.

(1) Departure without advance authorization for parole. In the case of an otherwise eligible applicant who departed the United States on or before December 31, 1997, the physical presence in the United States provision of section 202(b)(1) of Pub. L. 105-100 is tolled as of November 19, 1997, and until July 20, 1998.

(2) Departure with advance authorization for parole. In the case of an alien who departed the United States after having been issued an Authorization for parole of an Alien into the United States (Form I-512), and who returns to the United States in accordance with the conditions of that document, the physical presence in the United States requirement of section 202(b)(1) of Pub. L. 105-100 is tolled while the alien is outside the United States pursuant to the issuance of the Form I-512.

(3) Request for parole authorization from outside the United States. In the case of an alien who is outside the United States and submits an application for parole authorization in accordance with paragraph (k)(2) of this section, and such application for parole authorization is granted by the Service, the physical presence in the United States provisions of section 202(b)(1) of Pub. L. 105-100 is tilled from the date the application is received at the Texas Service Center until the alien is paroled into the United States pursuant to the issuance of the Form I-512.

(Approved by the Office of Management and Budget Under Control Number 1115-0221.)

HISTORY:

[63 FR 27823, 27829, May 21, 1998, as confirmed and amended at 65 FR 15846, 15854, Mar. 24, 2000; 66 FR 29449, 29451, May 31, 2001; 68 FR 9824, 9842, 9846, Feb. 28, 2003; 68 FR 10349, 10357, Mar. 5, 2003; 85 FR 82750, 82794, Dec. 18, 2020]

§ 1245.14 Adjustment of status of certain health care workers.

An alien applying for adjustment of status to perform labor in a health care occupation as described in 8 CFR 1212.15(c) must present evidence at the time he or she applies for adjustment of status, and, if applicable, at the time of the interview on the application, that he or she has a valid certificate issued by the Commission on Graduates of Foreign Nursing Schools or the National Board of Certification in Occupational Therapy.

HISTORY:

[63 FR 55007, 55012, Oct. 14, 1998; 68 FR 9824, 9842, Feb. 28, 2003; 68 FR 10349, 10357, Mar. 5, 2003]

§ 1245.15 Adjustment of Status of Certain Haitian Nationals under the Haitian Refugee Immigrant Fairness Act of 1998 (HRIFA).

(a) Definitions. As used in this section, the terms:

Abandoned and abandonment mean that both parents have, or the sole or surviving parent has, or in the case of a child who has been placed into a guardianship, the child's guardian or guardians have, willfully forsaken all parental or guardianship rights, obligations, and claims to the child, as well as all control over and possession of the child, without intending to transfer these rights to any specific person(s).

Guardian means a person lawfully invested (by order of a competent Federal, State, or local authority) with the power, and charged with the duty, of taking care of, including managing the property, rights, and affairs of, a child.

Orphan and orphaned refer to the involuntary detachment or severance of a child from his or her parents due to any of the following:

(1) The death or disappearance of, desertion by, or separation or loss from both parents, as those terms are defined in § 204.3(b) of 8 CFR chapter I;

(2) The irrevocable and written release of all parental rights by the sole parent, as that term is defined in § 204.3(b) of 8 CFR chapter I, based upon the inability of that parent to provide proper care (within the meaning of that phrase in § 204.3(b) of 8 CFR chapter I) for the child, provided that at the time of such irrevocable release such parent is legally obligated to provide such care; or

(3) The death or disappearance, as that term is defined in § 204.3(b) of 8 CFR chapter I, of one parent and the irrevocable and written release of all parental rights by the sole remaining parent based upon the inability of that parent to provide proper care (within the meaning of that phrase in § 204.3(b) of 8 CFR chapter I) for the child, provided that at the time of such irrevocable release such parent is legally obligated to provide such care.

Parent, father, or mother means a parent, father, or mother only where the relationship exists by reason of any of the circumstances set forth in paragraphs (A) through (E) of section 101(b)(1) of the Act.

Sole remaining parent means a person who is the child's only parent because:

(1) The child's other parent has died; or

(2) The child's other parent has been certified by competent Haitian authorities to be presumed dead as a result of his or her disappearance, within the meaning of that term as set forth in § 204.3(b) of 8 CFR chapter I.

(b) Applicability of provisions of section 902 of HRIFA in general. Section 902 of Division A of Public Law 105-277, the Haitian Refugee Immigrant Fairness Act of 1998 (HRIFA), provides special rules for adjustment of status for certain nationals of Haiti, and without regard to section 241(a)(5) of the Act, if they meet the other requirements of HRIFA.

(1) Principal applicants. Section 902(b)(1) of HRIFA defines five categories of principal applicants who may apply for adjustment of status, if the alien was physically present in the United States on December 31, 1995:

(i) An alien who filed for asylum before December 31, 1995;

(ii) An alien who was paroled into the United States prior to December 31, 1995, after having been identified as having a credible fear of persecution, or paroled for emergent reasons or reasons deemed strictly in the public interest; or

(iii) An alien who at the time of arrival in the United States and on December 31, 1995, was unmarried and under 21 years of age and who:

(A) Arrived in the United States without parents in the United States and has remained, without parents, in the United States since his or her arrival;

(B) Became orphaned subsequent to arrival in the United States; or

(C) Was abandoned by parents or guardians prior to April 1, 1998, and has remained abandoned since such abandonment.

(2) Dependents. Section 902(d) of HRIFA provides for certain Haitian nationals to apply for adjustment of status as the spouse, child, or unmarried son or daughter of a principal HRIFA beneficiary, even if the individual would not otherwise be eligible for adjustment under section 902. The eligibility requirements for

dependents are described further in paragraph (d) of this section.

(c) Eligibility of principal HRIFA applicants. A Haitian national who is described in paragraph (b)(1) of this section is eligible to apply for adjustment of status under the provisions of section 902 of HRIFA if the alien meets the following requirements:

(1) Physical presence. The alien is physically present in the United States at the time the application is filed;

(2) Proper application. The alien properly files an application for adjustment of status in accordance with this section, including the evidence described in paragraphs (h), (i), (j), and (k) of this section. For purposes of § 1245.15 of this chapter only, an Application to Register Permanent Residence or Adjust Status (Form I-485) submitted by a principal applicant for benefits under HRIFA may be considered to have been properly filed if it:

(i) Is received not later than March 31, 2000, at the Nebraska Service Center, the Board, or the Immigration Court having jurisdiction;

(ii) Has been properly completed and signed by the applicant;

(iii) Identifies the provision of HRIFA under which the applicant is seeking adjustment of status; and

(iv) Is accompanied by either:

(A) The correct fee as specified in 8 CFR 103.7 and 8 CFR part 106; or

(B) A request for a fee waiver in accordance with 8 CFR 103.7 and 8 CFR part 106", provided such fee waiver request is subsequently granted; however, if such a fee waiver request is subsequently denied and the applicant submits the require fee within 30 days of the date of any notice that the fee waiver request had been denied, the application shall be regarded as having been filed before the statutory deadline. In addition, in a case over which the Board has jurisdiction, an application received by the Board before April 1, 2000, that has been properly signed and executed shall be considered filed before the statutory deadline without payment of the fee or submission of a fee waiver request. Upon remand by the Board, the payment of the fee or a request for a fee waiver shall be made upon submission of the application to the Immigration Court in accordance with 8 CFR 1240.11(f). If a request for a fee waiver is denied, the application shall be considered as having been properly filed with the Immigration Court before the statutory deadline provided that the applicant submits the required fee within 30 days of the date of any notice that the fee waiver request has been denied.

(3) Admissibility. The alien is not inadmissible to the United States for permanent residence under any provisions of section 212(a) of the Act, except as provided in paragraph (e) of this section; and

(4) Continuous physical presence. The alien has been physically present in the United States for a continuous period beginning on December 31, 1995, and ending on the date the application for adjustment is granted, except for the following periods of time:

(i) Any period or periods of absence from the United States not exceeding 180 days in the aggregate; and

(ii) Any periods of absence for which the applicant received an Advance Authorization for Parole (Form I-512) prior to his or her departure from the United States, provided the applicant returned to the United States in accordance with the conditions of such Advance Authorization for Parole.

(iii) Any periods of absence from the United States occurring after October 21, 1998, and before July 12, 1999, provided the applicant departed the United States prior to December 31, 1998.

(d) Eligibility of dependents of a principal HRIFA beneficiary. A Haitian national who is the spouse, child, or unmarried son or daughter of a principal beneficiary eligible for adjustment of status under the provisions of HRIFA is eligible to apply for benefits as a dependent, if the dependent alien meets the following requirements:

(1) Physical presence. The alien is physically present in the United States at the time the application is filed;

(2) Proper application. The alien properly files an application for adjustment of status as a dependent in accordance with this section, including the evidence described in paragraphs (h) and (l) of this section;

(3) Admissibility. The alien is not inadmissible to the United States for permanent residence under any provisions of section 212(a) of the Act, except as provided in paragraph (e) of this section;

(4) Relationship. The qualifying relationship to the principal alien must have existed at the time the principal was granted adjustment of status and must continue to exist at the time the dependent alien is granted adjustment of status. To establish the qualifying relationship to the principal alien, evidence must be submitted in accordance with § 204.2 of this chapter. Such evidence should consist of the documents specified in § 204.2(a)(1)(i)(B), (a)(1)(iii)(B), (a)(2), (d)(2), and (d)(5) of 8 CFR chapter I;

(5) Continuous physical presence. If the alien is applying as the unmarried son or unmarried daughter of a principal HRIFA beneficiary, he or she must have been physically present in the United States for a continuous period beginning not later than December 31, 1995, and ending on the date the application for adjustment is granted, as provided in paragraphs (c)(4) and (j) of this section.

(e) Applicability of grounds of inadmissibility contained in section 212(a).

(1) Certain grounds of inadmissibility inapplicable to HRIFA applicants. Paragraphs (4), (5), (6)(A), (7)(A) and (9)(B) of section 212(a) of the Act are inapplicable to HRIFA principal applicants and their dependents. Accordingly, an applicant for adjustment of status under section 902 of HRIFA need not establish admissibility under those provisions in order to be able to adjust his or her status to that of permanent resident.

(2) Availability of individual waivers. If a HRIFA applicant is inadmissible under any of the other provisions of section 212(a) of the Act for which an immigrant waiver is available, the applicant may apply for one or more of the immigrant waivers of inadmissibility under section 212 of the Act, in accordance with § 1212.7 of this chapter. In considering an application for waiver under section 212(g) of the Act by an otherwise

statutorily eligible applicant for adjustment of status under HRIFA who was paroled into the United States from the U.S. Naval Base at Guantanamo Bay, for the purpose of receiving treatment of an HIV or AIDS condition, the fact that his or her arrival in the United States was the direct result of a government decision to provide such treatment should be viewed as a significant positive factor when weighing discretionary factors. In considering an application for waiver under section 212(i) of the Act by an otherwise statutorily eligible applicant for adjustment of status under HRIFA who used counterfeit documents to travel from Haiti to the United States, the adjudicator shall, when weighing discretionary factors, take into consideration the general lawlessness and corruption which was widespread in Haiti at the time of the alien's departure, the difficulties in obtaining legitimate departure documents at that time, and other factors unique to Haiti at that time which may have induced the alien to commit fraud or make willful misrepresentations.

(3) Special rule for waiver of inadmissibility grounds for HRIFA applicants under section 212(a)(9)(A) and 212(a)(9)(C) of the Act. An applicant for adjustment of status under HRIFA who is inadmissible under section 212(a)(9)(A) or 212(a)(9)(C) of the Act, may apply for a waiver of these grounds of inadmissibility while present in the United States. Such an alien must file Form I-601, Application for Waiver of Grounds of Excludability. If the application for adjustment is pending at the Nebraska Service Center, Form I-601 must be filed with the director of that office. If the application for adjustment is pending at a district office, Form I-601 must be filed with the district director having jurisdiction over the application. If the application for adjustment is pending before the immigration court, Form I-601 must be filed with the immigration judge having jurisdiction, or with the Board of Immigration Appeals if the appeal is pending before the Board.

(f) Time for filing of applications.

(1) Applications for HRIFA benefits by a principal HRIFA applicant. The application period begins on June 11, 1999. To benefit from the provisions of section 902 of HRIFA, an alien who is applying for adjustment as a principal applicant must properly file an application for adjustment of status before April 1, 2000.

(2) Applications by dependent aliens. The spouse, minor child, or unmarried son or daughter of an alien who is eligible for adjustment of status as a principal beneficiary under HRIFA may file an application for adjustment of status under this section concurrently with or subsequent to the filing of the application of the principal HRIFA beneficiary. An application filed by a dependent may not be approved prior to approval of the principal's application.

(g) Jurisdiction for filing of applications —

(1) Filing of applications with the Service. The Service has jurisdiction over all applications for the benefits of section 902 of HRIFA as a principal applicant or as a dependent under this section, except for applications filed by aliens who are in pending immigration proceedings as provided in paragraph (g)(2) of this section. All applications filed with the Service for the benefits of section 902 of HRIFA must be submitted by mail to: USINS Nebraska Service Center, PO Box 87245, Lincoln, NE 68501-7245. After proper filing of the application, the Service will instruct the applicant to appear for fingerprinting as prescribed in § 103.2(e) of this chapter. The Director of the Nebraska Service Center shall have jurisdiction over all applications filed with the Service for adjustment of status under section 902 of HRIFA, unless the Director refers the applicant for a personal interview at a local Service office as provided in paragraph (o)(1) of this section.

(2) Filing of applications by aliens in pending exclusion, deportation, or removal proceedings. An alien who is in exclusion, deportation, or removal proceedings pending before the Immigration Court or the Board, or who has a pending motion to reopen or motion to reconsider filed with the Immigration Court or the Board on or before May 12, 1999, must apply for HRIFA benefits to the Immigration Court or the Board, as provided in paragraph (p)(1) of this section, rather than to the Service. However, an alien whose proceeding has been administratively closed (see paragraph (p)(4) of this section) may only apply for HRIFA benefits with the Service as provided in paragraph (g)(1) of this section.

(3)(i) Filing of applications with the Service by aliens who are subject to a final order of exclusion, deportation, or removal. An alien who is subject to a final order of exclusion, deportation, or removal, and who has not been denied adjustment of status under section 902 of HRIFA by the Immigration Court or the Board, may only apply for HRIFA benefits with the Service as provided in paragraph (g)(1) of this section. This includes applications for HRIFA benefits filed by aliens who have filed a motion to reopen or motion to reconsider a final order after May 12, 1999.

(ii) An alien present in the United States who is subject to a final order of exclusion, deportation, or removal and has been denied adjustment of status under section 902 of HRIFA by the Immigration Court or the Board, or who never applied for adjustment of status with the Service, an Immigration Court, or the Board on or before March 31, 2000, and who was made eligible for HRIFA benefits under the Legal Immigration Family Equity Act of 2000 (LIFE Act) and LIFE amendments, Public Law 106-553 and Public Law 106-554, respectively, may file a motion to reopen with either the Immigration Court or the Board, whichever had jurisdiction last. As provided by the LIFE Act, motions to reopen must be filed on or before June 19, 2001.

(iii) Stay of final order of exclusion, deportation, or removal. The filing of an application for adjustment under section 902 of HRIFA with the Service shall not stay the execution of such final order unless the applicant has requested and been granted a stay in connection with the HRIFA application. An alien who has filed a HRIFA application with the Service may file an Application for Stay of Removal (Form I-246) in accordance with section 241(c)(2) of the Act and § 1241.6 of this chapter.

(iv) Grant of stay. Absent evidence of the applicant's statutory ineligibility for adjustment of status under section 902 of HRIFA or significant negative discretionary factors, a Form I-246 filed by a bona fide applicant for adjustment under section 902 of HRIFA shall be approved and the removal of the applicant shall be stayed until such time as the Service has adjudicated the application for adjustment in accordance with this section.

(h) Application and supporting documents. Each applicant for adjustment of status must file an Application to Register Permanent Residence or Adjust Status (Form I-485). An applicant should complete Part 2 of Form I-485 by checking box "h — other" and writing "HRIFA — Principal" or "HRIFA — Dependent" next to that block. Each application must be accompanied by:

(1) Application fee. The fee for Form I-485 prescribed in 8 CFR 103.7 and 8 CFR part 106;

(2) Fingerprinting fee. If the applicant is 14 years of age or older, the fee for fingerprinting prescribed in 8 CFR 103.7 and 8 CFR part 106;

(3) Identifying information.

(i) A copy of the applicant's birth certificate or other record of birth as provided in paragraph (m) of this section;

(ii) A completed Biographic Information Sheet (Form G-325A), if the applicant is between 14 and 79 years of age;

(iii) A report of medical examination, as specified in § 1245.5 of this chapter; and

(iv) Two photographs, as described in the instructions to Form I-485;

(4) Arrival-Departure Record. A copy of the Form I-94, Arrival-Departure Record, issued at the time of the applicant's arrival in the United States, if the alien was inspected and admitted or paroled;

(5) Police clearances. If the applicant is 14 years old or older, a police clearance from each municipality where the alien has resided for 6 months or longer since arriving in the United States. If there are multiple local law enforcement agencies (e.g., city police and county sheriff) with jurisdiction over the alien's residence, the applicant may obtain a clearance from either agency. If the applicant resides or resided in a State where the State police maintain a compilation of all local arrests and convictions, a statewide clearance is sufficient. If the applicant presents a letter from the local police agencies involved, or other evidence, to the effect that the applicant attempted to obtain such clearance but was unable to do so because of local or State policy, the director or immigration judge having jurisdiction over the application may waive the local police clearance. Furthermore, if such local police agency has provided the Service or the Immigration Court with a blanket statement that issuance of such police clearance is against local or State policy, the director or immigration judge having jurisdiction over the case may waive the local police clearance requirement regardless of whether the applicant individually submits a letter from that local police agency;

(6) Proof of Haitian nationality. If the applicant acquired Haitian nationality other than through birth in Haiti, a copy of the certificate of naturalization or certificate of citizenship issued by the Haitian government; and

(7) Additional supporting evidence. Additional supporting evidence pertaining to the applicant as provided in paragraphs (i) through (l) of this section.

(i) Evidence of presence in the United States on December 31, 1995. An alien seeking HRIFA benefits as a principal applicant must provide with the application evidence establishing the alien's presence in the United States on December 31, 1995. Such evidence may consist of the evidence listed in § 1245.22.

(j) Evidence of continuity of presence in the United States since December 31, 1995. An alien seeking HRIFA benefits as a principal applicant, or as the unmarried son or daughter of a principal applicant, must provide with the application evidence establishing continuity of the alien's physical presence in the United States since December 31, 1995. (This requirement does not apply to a dependent seeking HRIFA benefits as the spouse or minor child of a principal applicant.)

(1) Evidence establishing presence. Evidence establishing the continuity of the alien's physical presence in the United States since December 31, 1995, may consist of any documentation issued by any governmental or nongovernmental authority, provided such evidence bears the name of the applicant, was dated at the time it was issued, and bears the signature, seal, or other authenticating instrument of the authorized representative of the issuing authority, if the document would normally contain such authenticating instrument.

(2) Examples. Documentation establishing continuity of physical presence may include, but is not limited to:

(i) School records;

(ii) Rental receipts;

(iii) Utility bill receipts;

(iv) Any other dated receipts;

(v) Personal checks written by the applicant bearing a dated bank cancellation stamp;

(vi) Employment records, including pay stubs;

(vii) Credit card statements showing the dates of purchase, payment, or other transaction;

(viii) Certified copies of records maintained by organizations chartered by the Federal or State government, such as public utilities, accredited private and religious schools, and banks;

(ix) If the applicant establishes that a family unit was in existence and cohabiting in the United States, documents evidencing presence of another member of that same family unit; and

(x) For applicants who have had ongoing correspondence or other interaction with the Service, a list of the types and dates of such correspondence or other contact that the applicant knows to be contained or reflected in Service records.

(3) Evidence relating to absences from the United States since December 31, 1995. If the alien is applying as a principal applicant, or as the unmarried son or daughter of a principal applicant, and has departed from and returned to the United States since December

31, 1995, the alien must provide with the application an attachment on a plain piece of paper showing:

(i) The date of the applicant's last arrival in the United States before December 31, 1995;

(ii) The date of each departure (if any) from the United States since that arrival;

(iii) The reason for each departure; and

(iv) The date, manner, and place of each return to the United States.

(k) Evidence establishing the alien's eligibility under section 902(b) of HRIFA. An alien seeking HRIFA benefits as a principal applicant must provide with the application evidence establishing that the alien satisfies one of the eligibility standards described in paragraph (b)(1) of this section.

(1) Applicant for asylum. If the alien is a principal applicant who filed for asylum before December 31, 1995, the applicant must provide with the application either:

(i) A photocopy of the first page of the Application for Asylum and Withholding of Removal (Form I-589); or

(ii) If the alien is not in possession of a photocopy of the first page of the Form I-589, a statement to that effect giving the date of filing and the location of the Service office or Immigration Court at which it was filed;

(2) Parolee. If the alien is a principal applicant who was paroled into the United States prior to December 31, 1995, after having been identified as having a credible fear of persecution, or paroled for emergent reasons or reasons deemed strictly in the public interest, the applicant must provide with the application either:

(i) A photocopy of the Arrival-Departure Record (Form I-94) issued when he or she was granted parole; or

(ii) If the alien is not in possession of the original Form I-94, a statement to that effect giving the date of parole and the location of the Service port-of-entry at which parole was authorized.

(3) Child without parents. If the alien is a principal applicant who arrived in the United States as a child without parents in the United States, the applicant must provide with the application:

(i) Evidence, showing the date, location, and manner of his or her arrival in the United States, such as:

(A) A photocopy of the Form I-94 issued at the time of the alien's arrival in the United States;

(B) A copy of the airline or vessel records showing transportation to the United States;

(C) Other similar documentation; or

(D) If none of the documents in paragraphs (k)(3)(i)(A)-(C) of this section are available, a statement from the applicant, accompanied by whatever evidence the applicant is able to submit in support of that statement; and

(ii) Evidence establishing the absence of the child's parents, which may include either:

(A) Evidence showing the deaths of, or disappearance or desertion by, the applicant's parents; or

(B) Evidence showing that the applicant's parents did not live in the United States with the applicant. Such evidence may include, but is not limited to, documentation or affidavits showing that the applicant's parents have been continuously employed outside the United States, are deceased, disappeared, or abandoned the applicant prior to the applicant's arrival, or were otherwise engaged in activities showing that they were not in the United States, or (if they have been in the United States) that the applicant and his or her parents did not reside together.

(4) Orphaned child. If the alien is a principal applicant who is or was a child who became orphaned subsequent to arrival in the United States, the applicant must provide with the application:

(i) Evidence, showing the date, location, and manner of his or her arrival in the United States, such as:

(A) A photocopy of the Form I-94 issued at the time of the alien's arrival in the United States;

(B) A copy of the airline or vessel records showing transportation to the United States;

(C) Other similar documentation; or

(D) If none of the documents in paragraphs (k)(4)(i)(A)-(C) of this section are available, a statement from the applicant, accompanied by whatever evidence the applicant is able to submit in support of that statement; and

(ii) Either:

(A) The death certificates of both parents (or in the case of a child having only one parent, the death certificate of the sole parent) showing that the death or deaths occurred after the date of the applicant's arrival in the United States;

(B) Evidence from a State, local, or other court or governmental authority having jurisdiction and authority to make decisions in matters of child welfare establishing the disappearance of, the separation or loss from, or desertion by, both parents (or, in the case of a child born out of wedlock who has not been legitimated, the sole parent); or

(C) Evidence of:

(1) Either:

(i) The child having only a sole parent, as that term is defined in § 204.3(b) of 8 CFR chapter I;

(ii) The death of one parent; or

(iii) Certification by competent Haitian authorities that one parent is presumed dead as a result of his or her disappearance, within the meaning of that term as set forth in § 204.3(b) of 8 CFR chapter I; and

(2) A copy of a written statement executed by the sole parent, or the sole remaining parent, irrevocably releasing all parental rights based upon the inability of that parent to provide proper care for the child.

(5) Abandoned child. If the alien is a principal applicant who was abandoned by parents or guardians prior to April 1, 1998, and has remained abandoned since such abandonment, the applicant must provide with the application:

(i) Evidence, showing the date, location, and manner of his or her arrival in the United States, such as:

(A) A photocopy of the Form I-94 issued at the time of the alien's arrival in the United States;

(B) A copy of the airline or vessel records showing transportation to the United States;

(C) Other similar documentation; or

(D) If none of the documents in paragraphs (k)(5)(i)(A)-(C) of this section are available, a statement from the applicant, accompanied by whatever evidence the applicant is able to submit in support of that statement; and

(ii) Either:

(A) Evidence from a State, local, or other court or governmental authority having jurisdiction and authority to make decisions in matters of child welfare establishing such abandonment; or

(B) Evidence to establish that the applicant would have been considered to be abandoned according to the laws of the State where he or she resides, or where he or she resided at the time of the abandonment, had the issue been presented to the proper authorities.

(l) Evidence relating to applications by dependents under section 902(d) of HRIFA —

(1) Evidence of spousal relationship. If the alien is applying as the spouse of a principal HRIFA beneficiary, the applicant must provide with the application a copy of their certificate of marriage and copies of documents showing the legal termination of all other marriages by the applicant or the other beneficiary.

(2) Evidence of parent-child relationship. If the applicant is applying as the child, unmarried son, or unmarried daughter of a principal HRIFA beneficiary, and the principal beneficiary is not the applicant's biological mother, the applicant must provide with the application evidence to demonstrate the parent-child relationship between the principal beneficiary and the applicant. Such evidence may include copies of the applicant's parent's marriage certificate and documents showing the legal termination of all other marriages, an adoption decree, or other relevant evidence.

(m) Secondary evidence. Except as otherwise provided in this paragraph, if the primary evidence required in this section is unavailable, church or school records, or other secondary evidence pertinent to the facts in issue, may be submitted. If such documents are unavailable, affidavits may be submitted. The applicant may submit as many types of secondary evidence as necessary to establish birth, marriage, or other relevant events. Documentary evidence establishing that primary evidence is unavailable must accompany secondary evidence of birth or marriage in the home country. The unavailability of such documents may be shown by submission of a copy of the written request for a copy of such documents which was sent to the official keeper of the records. In adjudicating the application for adjustment of status under section 902 of HRIFA, the Service or immigration judge shall determine the weight to be given such secondary evidence. Secondary evidence may not be submitted in lieu of the documentation specified in paragraphs (i) or (j) of this section. However, subject to verification by the Service, if the documentation specified in this paragraph or in paragraphs (h)(3)(i), (i), (j), (l)(1), and (l)(2) of this section is already contained in the Service's file relating to the applicant, the applicant may submit an affidavit to that effect in lieu of the actual documentation.

(n) Authorization to be employed in the United States while the application is pending —

(1) Application for employment authorization. An applicant for adjustment of status under section 902 of HRIFA who wishes to obtain initial or continued employment authorization during the pendency of the adjustment application must file an Application for Employment Authorization (Form I-765) with the Service, including the fee as set forth in 8 CFR 103.7 and 8 CFR part 106. The applicant may submit Form I-765 either concurrently with or subsequent to the filing of the application for HRIFA benefits on Form I-485.

(2) Adjudication and issuance. Employment authorization may not be issued to an applicant for adjustment of status under section 902 of HRIFA until the adjustment application has been pending for 180 days, unless the Director of the Nebraska Service Center verifies that Service records contain evidence that the applicant meets the criteria set forth in section 902(b) or 902(d) of HRIFA, and determines that there is no indication that the applicant is clearly ineligible for adjustment of status under section 902 of HRIFA, in which case the Director may approve the application for employment authorization, and issue the resulting document, immediately upon such verification. If the Service fails to adjudicate the application for employment authorization upon expiration of the 180-day waiting period, or within 90 days of the filing of application for employment authorization, whichever comes later, the alien shall be eligible for interim employment authorization in accordance with § 1274a.13(d) of this chapter. Nothing in this section shall preclude an applicant for adjustment of status under HRIFA from being granted an initial employment authorization or an extension of employment authorization under any other provision of law or regulation for which the alien may be eligible.

(o) Adjudication of HRIFA applications filed with the Service —

(1) Referral for interview. Except as provided in paragraphs (o)(2) and (o)(3) of this section, all aliens filing applications for adjustment of status with the Service under this section must be personally interviewed by an immigration officer at a local office of the Service. If the Director of the Nebraska Service Center determines that an interview of the applicant is necessary, the Director shall forward the case to the appropriate local Service office for interview and adjudication.

(2) Approval without interview. Upon examination of the application, including all other evidence submitted in support of the application, all relevant Service records and all other relevant law enforcement indices, the Director may approve the application without an interview if the Director determines that:

(i) The alien's claim to eligibility for adjustment of status under section 902 of HRIFA is verified through existing Service records; and

(ii) The alien is clearly eligible for adjustment of status.

(3) Denial without interview. If, upon examination of the application, all supporting documentation, all relevant Service records, and all other relevant law en-

forcement indices, the Director determines that the alien is clearly ineligible for adjustment of status under HRIFA and that an interview of the applicant is not necessary, the Director may deny the application.

(p) Adjudication of HRIFA applications filed in pending exclusion, deportation, or removal proceedings —

(1) Proceedings pending before an Immigration Court. Except as provided in paragraph (p)(4) of this section, the Immigration Court shall have sole jurisdiction over an application for adjustment of status under this section filed by an alien who is in exclusion, deportation, or removal proceedings pending before an immigration judge or the Board, or who has a pending motion to reopen or motion to reconsider filed with an immigration judge or the Board on or before May 12, 1999. The immigration judge having jurisdiction over the exclusion, deportation, or removal proceedings shall have jurisdiction to accept and adjudicate any application for adjustment of status under section 902 of HRIFA during the course of such proceedings. All applications for adjustment of status under section 902 of HRIFA filed with an Immigration Court shall be subject to the requirements of §§ 1003.11 and 1003.31 of this chapter.

(2) Motion to reopen or motion to reconsider. If an alien who has a pending motion to reopen or motion to reconsider timely filed with an immigration judge on or before May 12, 1999, files an application for adjustment of status under section 902 of HRIFA, the immigration judge shall reopen the alien's proceedings for consideration of the adjustment application, unless the alien is clearly ineligible for adjustment of status under section 902 of HRIFA.

(3) Proceedings pending before the Board. Except as provided in paragraph (d)(4) of this section, in the case of an alien who either has a pending appeal with the Board or has a pending motion to reopen or motion to reconsider timely filed with the Board on or before May 12, 1999, the Board shall remand, or reopen and remand, the proceedings to the Immigration Court for the sole purpose of adjudicating an application for adjustment of status under section 902 of HRIFA, unless the alien is clearly ineligible for adjustment of status under section 902 of HRIFA. If the immigration judge denies, or the alien fails to file, the application for adjustment of status under section 902 of HRIFA, the immigration judge shall certify the decision to the Board for consideration in conjunction with the applicant's previously pending appeal or motion.

(4) Administrative closure of exclusion, deportation, or removal proceedings.

(i) An alien who is in exclusion, deportation, or removal proceedings, or who has a pending motion to reopen or a motion to reconsider such proceedings filed on or before May 12, 1999, may request that the proceedings be administratively closed, or that the motion be indefinitely continued, in order to allow the alien to file such application with the Service as prescribed in paragraph (g) of this section. If the alien appears to be eligible to file an application for adjustment of status under this section, the Immigration Court or the Board (whichever has jurisdiction) shall, with the concurrence of the Service, administratively close the proceedings or continue indefinitely the motion.

(ii) In the case of an otherwise-eligible alien whose exclusion, deportation, or removal proceedings have been administratively closed for reasons not specified in this section, the alien may only apply before the Service for adjustment of status under this section.

(q) Approval of HRIFA applications —

(1) Applications approved by the Service. If the Service approves the application for adjustment of status under the provisions of section 902 of HRIFA, the director shall record the alien's lawful admission for permanent residence as of the date of such approval and notify the applicant accordingly. The director shall also advise the alien regarding the delivery of his or her Permanent Resident Card and of the process for obtaining temporary evidence of alien registration. If the alien had previously been issued a final order of exclusion, deportation, or removal, such order shall be deemed canceled as of the date of the director's approval of the application for adjustment of status. If the alien had been in exclusion, deportation, or removal proceedings that were administratively closed, such proceedings shall be deemed terminated as of the date of approval of the application for adjustment of status by the director.

(2) Applications approved by an immigration judge or the Board. If an immigration judge or (upon appeal) the Board grants an application for adjustment under the provisions of section 902 of HRIFA, the date of the alien's lawful admission for permanent residence shall be the date of such grant.

(r) Review of decisions by the Service denying HRIFA applications —

(1)(i) Denial notification. If the Service denies the application for adjustment of status under the provisions of section 902 of HRIFA, the director shall notify the applicant of the decision and of any right to renew the application in proceedings before the Immigration Court.

(ii) An alien made eligible for adjustment of status under HRIFA by the LIFE Act amendments and whose case has not been referred to EOIR under paragraphs (r)(2) or (r)(3) of this section, may file a motion to reopen with the Service.

(2) Renewal of application for HRIFA benefits in removal, deportation, or exclusion proceedings. An alien who is not the subject of a final order of removal, deportation, or exclusion may renew his or her application for adjustment under section 902 of HRIFA during the course of such removal, deportation, or exclusion proceedings.

(i) Initiation of removal proceedings. In the case of an alien who is not maintaining valid nonimmigrant status and who had not previously been placed in exclusion, deportation, or removal proceedings, the director shall initiate removal proceedings in accordance with § 1239.1 of this chapter.

(ii) Recalendaring or reinstatement of prior proceedings. In the case of an alien whose previously initiated exclusion, deportation, or removal proceeding had been administratively closed or continued indefinitely under paragraph (p)(4) of this section, the director shall make a request for recalendaring or reinstatement to the Immigration Court that had administratively closed the proceeding, or the Board, as appropriate, when the application has been denied. The Immigration Court or the Board will then recalendar or reinstate the prior exclusion, deportation, or removal proceeding.

(iii) Filing of renewed application. A principal alien may file a renewed application for HRIFA benefits with the Immigration Court either before or after March 31, 2000, if he or she had filed his or her initial application for such benefits with the Service on or before March 31, 2000. A dependent of a principal applicant may file such renewed application with the Immigration Court either before or after March 31, 2000, regardless of when he or she filed his or her initial application for HRIFA benefits with the Service.

(3) Aliens with final orders. In the case of an alien who is the subject of an outstanding final order of exclusion, deportation, or removal, the Service shall refer the decision to deny the application by filing a Notice of Certification (Form I-290C) with the Immigration Court that issued the final order for consideration in accordance with paragraph (s) of this section.

(4)(i) An alien whose case has been referred to the Immigration Court under paragraphs (r)(2) or (r)(3) of this section, or who filed an appeal with the Board after his or her application for adjustment of status under section 902 of HRIFA was denied, and whose proceedings are pending, and who is now eligible for adjustment of status under HRIFA as amended by section 1505(b) of the LIFE Act and its amendments, may renew the application for adjustment of status with either the Immigration Court or the Board, whichever has jurisdiction. The application will be adjudicated in accordance with section 1505(b) of the LIFE Act and its amendments.

(ii) An alien present in the United States who is subject to a final order of exclusion, deportation or removal after his or her HRIFA adjustment application was denied by an Immigration Court or the Board, but who was made eligible for HRIFA adjustment as a result of section 1505(b) of the LIFE Act and its amendments, may file a motion to reopen with either the Immigration Court or the Board, whichever had jurisdiction last. Such motion to reopen must be filed on or before June 19, 2001.

(s) Action on decisions referred to the Immigration Court by a Notice of Certification (Form I-290C) —

(1) General. Upon the referral by a Notice of Certification (Form I-290C) of a decision to deny the application, in accordance with paragraph (r)(3) of this section, the immigration judge shall conduct a hearing, under the authority contained in § 3.10 of this chapter, to determine whether the alien is eligible for adjustment of status under section 902 of HRIFA. Such hearing shall be conducted under the same rules of procedure as proceedings conducted under part 240 of this chapter, except the scope of review shall be limited to a determination of the alien's eligibility for adjustment of status under section 902 of HRIFA. During such proceedings, all parties are prohibited from raising or considering any unrelated issues, including, but not limited to, issues of admissibility, deportability, removability, and eligibility for any remedy other than adjustment of status under section 902 of HRIFA. Should the alien fail to appear for such hearing, the immigration judge shall deny the application for adjustment under section 902 of HRIFA.

(2) Stay pending review. When the Service refers a decision to the Immigration Court on a Notice of Certification (Form I-290C) in accordance with paragraph (r)(3) of this section, the referral shall not stay the execution of the final order. Execution of such final order shall proceed unless a stay of execution is specifically granted by the immigration judge, the Board, or an authorized Service officer.

(3) Appeal of Immigration Court decision. Once the immigration judge issues his or her decision on the application, either the alien or the Service may appeal the decision to the Board. Such appeal must be filed pursuant to the requirements for appeals to the Board from an Immigration Court decision set forth in §§ 1003.3 and 1003.8 of this chapter.

(4) Rescission or reopening of the decision of an Immigration Court. The decision of an Immigration Court under paragraph (s)(1) of this section denying an application for adjustment under section 902 of HRIFA for failure to appear may be rescinded or reopened only:

(i) Upon a motion to reopen filed within 180 days after the date of the denial if the alien demonstrates that the failure to appear was because of exceptional circumstances as defined in section 240(e)(1) of the Act;

(ii) Upon a motion to reopen filed at any time if the alien demonstrates that he or she did not receive notice of the hearing in person (or, if personal service was not practicable, through service by mail to the alien or to the alien's counsel of record, if any) or the alien demonstrates that he or she was in Federal or State custody and the failure to appear was through no fault of the alien; or

(iii) Upon a motion to reopen filed not later than June 19, 2001, by an alien present in the United States who became eligible for adjustment of status under HRIFA, as amended by section 1505, of Public Law 106-554.

(t) Parole authorization for purposes of travel —

(1) Travel from and return to the United States while the application for adjustment of status is pending. If an applicant for benefits under section 902 of HRIFA desires to travel outside, and return to, the United States while the application for adjustment of status is pending, he or she must file a request for advance parole authorization on an Application for Travel Document (Form I-131), with fee as set forth in 8 CFR 103.7 and 8 CFR part 106 and in accordance with the instructions on the form. If the alien is either in deportation or removal proceedings, or subject to a final order of deportation or removal, the Form I-131 must be submitted to the Director, Office of International Affairs; otherwise the Form I-131 must be submitted to the Director of the Nebraska Service Center, who shall have jurisdiction over such applications. Unless the

applicant files an advance parole request prior to departing from the United States, and the Service approves such request, his or her application for adjustment of status under section 902 of HRIFA is deemed to be abandoned as of the moment of his or her departure. Parole may only be authorized pursuant to the authority contained in, and the standards prescribed in, section 212(d)(5) of the Act.

(2) Parole authorization for the purpose of filing an application for adjustment of status under section 902 of HRIFA.

(i) An otherwise eligible applicant who is outside the United States and wishes to come to the United States in order to apply for benefits under section 902 of HRIFA may request parole authorization for such purpose by filing an Application for Travel Document (Form I-131) with the Nebraska Service Center, at P.O. Box 87245, Lincoln, NE 68501-7245. Such application must be supported by a photocopy of the Form I-485 that the alien will file once he or she has been paroled into the United States. The applicant must include photocopies of all the supporting documentation listed in paragraph (h) of this section, except the filing fee, the medical report, the fingerprint card, and the local police clearances.

(ii) If the Director of the Nebraska Service Center is satisfied that the alien will be eligible for adjustment of status once the alien has been paroled into the United States and files the application, he or she may issue an Authorization for Parole of an Alien into the United States (Form I-512) to allow the alien to travel to, and be paroled into, the United States for a period of 60 days.

(iii) The applicant shall have 60 days from the date of parole to file the application for adjustment of status. If the alien files the application for adjustment of status within that 60-day period, the Service may re-parole the alien for such time as is necessary for adjudication of the application. Failure to file such application for adjustment of status within 60 days shall result in the alien being returned to the custody of the Service and being examined as an arriving alien applying for admission. Such examination will be conducted in accordance with the provisions of section 235(b)(1) of the Act if the alien is inadmissible under section 212(a)(6)(C) or 212(a)(7) of the Act, or section 240 of the Act if the alien is inadmissible under any other grounds.

(iv) Parole may only be authorized pursuant to the authority contained in, and the standards prescribed in, section 212(d)(5) of the Act. The authority of the Director of the Nebraska Service Center to authorize parole from outside the United States under this provision shall expire on March 31, 2000.

(3) Effect of departure on an outstanding warrant of exclusion, deportation, or removal. If an alien who is the subject of an outstanding final order of exclusion, deportation, or removal departs from the United States, with or without an advance parole authorization, such final order shall be executed by the alien's departure. The execution of such final order shall not preclude the applicant from filing an Application for Permission to Reapply for Admission Into the United States After Deportation or Removal (Form I-212) in accordance with § 1212.2 of this chapter.

(u) Tolling the physical presence in the United States provision for certain individuals.

(1) Departure with advance authorization for parole. In the case of an alien who departed the United States after having been issued an Authorization for Parole of an Alien into the United States (Form I-512), and who returns to the United States in accordance with the conditions of that document, the physical presence in the United States requirement of section 902(b)(1) of HRIFA is tolled while the alien is outside the United States pursuant to the issuance of the Form I-512.

(2) Request for parole authorization from outside the United States. In the case of an alien who is outside the United States and submits an application for parole authorization in accordance with paragraph (t)(2) of this section, and such application for parole authorization is granted by the Service, the physical presence requirement contained in section 902(b)(1) of HRIFA is tolled from the date the application is received at the Nebraska Service Center until the alien is paroled into the United States pursuant to the issuance of the Form I-512.

(3) Departure without advance authorization for parole. In the case of an otherwise-eligible applicant who departed the United States on or before December 31, 1998, the physical presence in the United States provision of section 902(b)(1) of HRIFA is tolled as of October 21, 1998, and until July 12, 1999.

(v) Judicial review of HRIFA adjustment of status determinations. Pursuant to the provisions of section 902(f) of HRIFA, there shall be no judicial appeal or review of any administrative determination as to whether the status of an alien should be adjusted under the provisions of section 902 of HRIFA.

HISTORY:

[64 FR 25756, 25767, May 12, 1999, as confirmed and amended at 65 FR 15835, 15844, Mar. 24, 2000; 66 FR 29449, 29452, May 31, 2001; 67 FR 78667, 78673, Dec. 26, 2002; 68 FR 9824, 9842, 9846, Feb. 28, 2003; 68 FR 10349, 10357, Mar. 5, 2003; 85 FR 82750, 82794, Dec. 18, 2020]

§ 1245.18 How can physicians (with approved Forms I-140) that are serving in medically underserved areas or at a Veterans Affairs facility adjust status?

(a) Which physicians are eligible for this benefit? Any alien physician who has been granted a national interest waiver under § 204.12 of 8 CFR chapter I may submit Form I-485 during the 6-year period following Service approval of a second preference employment-based immigrant visa petition.

(b) Do alien physicians have special time-related requirements for adjustment?

(1) Alien physicians who have been granted a national interest waiver under § 204.12 of 8 CFR chapter I must meet all the adjustment of status requirements of this part.

(2) The Service shall not approve an adjustment application filed by an alien physician who obtained a

waiver under section 203(b)(2)(B)(ii) of the Act until the alien physician has completed the period of required service established in § 204.12 of 8 CFR chapter I.

(c) Are the filing procedures and documentary requirements different for these particular alien physicians? Alien physicians submitting adjustment applications upon approval of an immigrant petition are required to follow the procedures outlined within this part with the following modifications.

(1) Delayed fingerprinting. Fingerprinting, as noted in the Form I-485 instructions, will not be scheduled at the time of filing. Fingerprinting will be scheduled upon the physician's completion of the required years of service.

(2) Delayed medical examination. The required medical examination, as specified in § 1245.5, shall not be submitted with Form I-485. The medical examination report shall be submitted with the documentary evidence noting the physician's completion of the required years of service.

(d) Are alien physicians eligible for Form I-766, Employment Authorization Document?

(1) Once the Service has approved an alien physician's Form I-140 with a national interest waiver based upon full-time clinical practice in an underserved area or at a Veterans Affairs facility, the alien physician should apply for adjustment of status to that of lawful permanent resident on Form I-485, accompanied by an application for an Employment Authorization Document (EAD), Form I-765, as specified in § 274a.12(c)(9) of 8 CFR chapter I.

(2) Since section 203(b)(2)(B)(ii) of the Act requires the alien physician to complete the required employment before the Service can approve the alien physician's adjustment application, an alien physician who was in lawful nonimmigrant status when he or she filed the adjustment application is not required to maintain a nonimmigrant status while the adjustment application remains pending. Even if the alien physician's nonimmigrant status expires, the alien physician shall not be considered to be unlawfully present, so long as the alien physician is practicing medicine in accordance with § 204.5(k)(4)(iii) of 8 CFR chapter I.

(e) When does the Service begin counting the physician's 5-year or 3-year medical practice requirement? Except as provided in this paragraph, the 6-year period during which a physician must provide the required 5 years of service begins on the date of the notice approving the Form I-140 and the national interest waiver. Alien physicians who have a 3-year medical practice requirement must complete their service within the 4-year period beginning on that date.

(1) If the physician does not already have employment authorization and so must obtain employment authorization before the physician can begin working, then the period begins on the date the Service issues the employment authorization document.

(2) If the physician formerly held status as a J-1 nonimmigrant, but obtained a waiver of the foreign residence requirement and a change of status to that of an H-1B nonimmigrant, pursuant to section 214(1) of the Act, as amended by section 220 of Public Law 103-416, and § 212.7(c)(9) of 8 CFR chapter I, the period begins on the date of the alien's change from J-1 to H-1B status. The Service will include the alien's compliance with the 3-year period of service required under section 214(l) in calculating the alien's compliance with the period of service required under section 203(b)(2)(B)(ii)(II) of the Act and this section.

(3) An alien may not include any time employed as a J-1 nonimmigrant physician in calculating the alien's compliance with the 5 or 3-year medical practice requirement. If an alien is still in J-1 nonimmigrant status when the Service approves a Form I-140 petition with a national interest job offer waiver, the aggregate period during which the medical practice requirement period must be completed will begin on the date the Service issues an employment authorization document.

(f) Will the Service provide information to the physician about evidence and supplemental filings? The Service shall provide the physician with the information and the projected timetables for completing the adjustment process, as described in this paragraph. If the physician either files the Form I-485 concurrently with or waits to subsequently file the Form I-485 while the previously filed Form I-140 is still pending, then the Service will given this information upon approval of the Form I-140. If the physician does not file the adjustment application until after approval of the Form I-140 visa petition, the Service shall provide this information upon receipt of the Form I-485 adjustment application.

(1) The Service shall note the date that the medical service begins (provided the physician already had work authorization at the time the Form I-140 was filed) or the date that an employment authorization document was issued.

(2) A list of the evidence necessary to satisfy the requirements of paragraphs (g) and (h) of this section.

(3) A projected timeline noting the dates that the physician will need to submit preliminary evidence two years and 120 days into his or her medical service in an underserved area or VA facility, and a projected date six years and 120 days in the future on which the physician's final evidence of completed medical service will be due.

(g) Will physicians be required to file evidence prior to the end of the 5 or 3-year period?

(1) For physicians with a 5-year service requirement, no later than 120 days after the second anniversary of the approval of Petition for Immigrant Worker, Form I-140, the alien physician must submit to the Service Center having jurisdiction over his or her place of employment documentary evidence that proves the physician has in fact fulfilled at least 12 months of qualifying employment. This may be accomplished by submitting the following.

(i) Evidence noted in paragraph (h) of this section that is available at the second anniversary of the I-140 approval.

(ii) Documentation from the employer attesting to the fill-time medical practice and the date on which the physician began his or her medical service.

(2) Physicians with a 3-year service requirement are not required to make a supplemental filing, and must

only comply with the requirements of paragraph (h) of this section.

(h) What evidence is needed to prove final compliance with the service requirement? No later than 120 days after completion of the service requirement established under § 204.12(a) of this section, an alien physician must submit to the Service Center having jurisdiction over his or her place of employment documentary evidence that proves the physician has in fact satisfied the service requirement. Such evidence must include, but is not limited to:

(1) Individual Federal income tax returns, including copies of the alien's W-2 forms, for the entire 3-year period or the balance years of the 5-year period that follow the submission of the evidence required in paragraph (e) of this section;

(2) Documentation from the employer attesting to the full-time medical service rendered during the required aggregate period. The documentation shall address instances of breaks in employment, other than routine breaks such as paid vacations;

(3) If the physician established his or her own practice, documents noting the actual establishment of the practice, including incorporation of the medical practice (if incorporated), the business license, and the business tax returns and tax withholding documents submitted for the entire 3 year period, or the balance years of the 5-year period that follow the submission of the evidence required in paragraph (e) of this section.

(i) What if the physician does not comply with the requirements of paragraphs (f) and (g) of this section? If an alien physician does not submit (in accordance with paragraphs (f) and (g) of this section) proof that he or she has completed the service required under § 204.12(a) of 8 CFR chapter I, the Service shall serve the alien physician with a written notice of intent to deny the alien physician's application for adjustment of status and, after the denial is finalized, to revoke approval of the Form I-140 and national interest waiver. The written notice shall require the alien physician to provide the evidence required by paragraph (f) or (g) of this section within 30 days of the date of the written notice. The Service shall not extend this 30-day period. If the alien physician fails to submit the evidence within the 30-day period established by the written notice, the Service shall deny the alien physician's application for adjustment of status and shall revoke approval of the Form I-140 and of the national interest waiver.

(j) Will a Service officer interview the physician?

(1) Upon submission of the evidence noted in paragraph (h) of this section, the Service shall match the documentary evidence with the pending form I-485 and schedule the alien physician for fingerprinting at an Application Support Center.

(2) The local Service office shall schedule the alien for an adjustment interview with a Service officer, unless the Service waives the interview as provided in § 1245.6. The local Service office shall also notify the alien if supplemental documentation should either be mailed to the office, or brought to the adjustment interview.

(k) Are alien physicians allowed to travel outside the United States during the mandatory 3 or 5-year service period? An alien physician who has been granted a national interest waiver under § 204.12 of 8 CFR chapter I and has a pending application for adjustment of status may travel outside of the United States during the required 3 or 5-year service period by obtaining advanced parole prior to traveling. Alien physicians may apply for advanced parole by submitting form I-131, Application for Travel Document, to the Service office having jurisdiction over the alien physician's place of business.

(l) What if the Service denies the adjustment application? If the Service denies the adjustment application, the alien physician may renew the application in removal proceedings.

HISTORY:

[65 FR 53889, 53895, Sept. 6, 2000, as corrected at 65 FR 57861, Sept. 26, 2000, as corrected at 65 FR 63118, Oct. 20, 2000; 65 FR 53889, 53895, Sept. 6, 2000, as corrected at 65 FR 57943, 57944, Sept. 27, 2000; 67 FR 49561, 49563, July 31, 2002; 68 FR 9824, 9842, 9846, Feb. 28, 2003; 68 FR 10349, 10357, Mar. 5, 2003]

§ 1245.20 Adjustment of status of Syrian asylees under Public Law 106-378.

(a) Eligibility. An alien is eligible to apply to adjust status under Public Law 106-378 if the alien is:

(1) A Jewish national of Syria;

(2) Arrived in the United States after December 31, 1991, after being permitted by the Syrian Government to depart from Syria;

(3) Is physically present in the United States at the time of filing the application to adjust status;

(4) Applies for adjustment of status no later than October 26, 2001, or has a pending application for adjustment of status under the Act that was filed with the Service before October 27, 2000;

(5) Has been physically present in the United States for at least 1 year after being granted asylum;

(6) Has not firmly resettled in any foreign country; and

(7) Is admissible as an immigrant under the Act at the time of examination for adjustment.

(b) Qualified family members. The spouse, child, or unmarried son or daughter of an alien eligible for adjustment under Public Law 106-378 is eligible to apply for adjustment of status under this section if the alien meets the criteria set forth in paragraphs (a)(4) through (a)(7) of this section.

(c) Grounds not to be applied and waivers. The grounds of inadmissibility found at section 212(a)(4) of the Act, relating to public charge, and at section 212(a)(7)(A) of the Act, relating to documentation, do not apply to applicants for adjustment of status under Public Law 106-378. Applicants may also request the waivers found at sections 212(h), (i), and (k) of the Act, to the extent they are eligible.

(d) **Application.—**

(1) New applications. An applicant must submit From I-485, Application to Register Permanent Residence or Adjust Status, along with the appropriate

application fee as stated in 8 CFR 103.7 and 8 CFR part 106, to the Nebraska Service Center. The application must physically be received by the Nebraska Service Center no later than close of business on October 26, 2001. Applicants 14 years of age or older must also submit the fingerprinting service fee provided for in 8 CFR 103.7 and 8 CFR part 106. Each application filed must be accompanied by two photographs as described in the Form I-485 instructions; a completed Biographic Information Sheet (Form G-325A) if the applicant is between 14 and 79 years of age; and a report of medical examination (Form I-693 and vaccination supplement) as specified in 8 CFR 1245.5. On Form I-485, Part 2, question "h", applicants must write "SYRIAN ASYLEE-P.L. 106-378" to indicate that they are applying based on this provision.

(2) Filing of requests to change the basis of a pending Form I-485. —

(i) Request. An eligible Syrian national with a Form I-485 that is currently pending with the Service may request that the basis of his or her Form I-485 be changed to Public Law 106-378. The alien must submit this request in writing to the Nebraska Service Center. The request may only be granted if the 2,000 adjustment limit specified in paragraph (i) of this section has not yet been reached. The 2,000 adjustment limit includes both new and pending Form I-485 petitions. The applicant should clearly annotate "SYRIAN ASYLEE P.L. 106-378" on the envelope to identify the correspondence.

(ii) Time limit. If the Form I-485 was filed before October 27, 2000, there is no time limit for requesting a change of basis for adjustment of status. However, if the Form I-485 was filed on or after October 27, 2001, then the Service must receive the request for change of basis no later than October 27, 2001.

(e) Evidence. Applicants must submit evidence that demonstrates they are eligible for adjustment of status under Public Law 106-378. Required evidence includes the following:

(1) A copy of the alien's passport;

(2) A copy of the applicant's Arrival-Departure Record (Form I-94) or other evidence of inspection and admission or parole into the United States after December 31, 1991;

(3) Documentation including, but not limited to, those listed at § 1245.15(j)(2) to establish physical presence in the United States for at least 1 year after being granted asylum;

(4) If the applicant is the spouse of a principal alien applying for adjustment, he or she must submit a marriage certificate, if available, or other evidence to demonstrate the marriage; and

(5) If the applicant is the child of a principal alien applying for adjustment of status, he or she must submit a birth certificate, if available, or other evidence to demonstrate the relationship.

(f) Employment authorization. Applicants who want to obtain employment authorization based on a pending application for adjustment of status under Public Law 106-378 may submit Form I-765, Application for Employment Authorization, along with the application fee listed in 8 CFR 103.7 and 8 CFR part 106. If the Service approves the application for employment authorization, the applicant will be issued an employment authorization document.

(g) Travel while an application to adjust status is pending. Applicants who wish to travel abroad and re-enter the United States while an application for adjustment of status is pending without being considered to have abandoned that application must obtain advance parole prior to departing the United States. To obtain advance parole, applicants must file Form I-131, Application for a Travel Document, along with the application fee listed in 8 CFR 103.7 and 8 CFR part 106. If the Service approves Form I-131, the alien will be issued Form I-512, Authorization for the Parole of an Alien into the United States.

(h) Approval and date of admission as a lawful permanent resident. When the Service approves an application to adjust status to that of lawful permanent resident based on Public Law 106-378, the applicant will be notified in writing of the Service's decision. In addition, the record of the alien's admission as a lawful permanent resident will be recorded as of the date 1 year before the approval of the application.

(i) Number of adjustments under Public Law 106-378. No more than 2,000 aliens may have their status adjusted to that of lawful permanent resident under Public Law 106-378.

(j) **Notice of Denial. —**

(1) General. When the Service denies an application to adjust status to that of lawful permanent resident based on Public Law 106-378, the applicant will be notified of the decision and the reason for the denial in writing.

(2) Cases involving requests to change the basis of a pending Form I-485. If an applicant who requested that a pending Form I-485, be considered under Public Law 106-378, is found to be ineligible under Public Law 106-378, but he or she appears eligible for adjustment under the original section of the Act under which the Form I-485 was filed, the Service will provide the applicant with notice of this fact. Processing the Form I-485 under the original provision of law will resume as appropriate.

(k) Administrative review. An alien whose application for adjustment of status under Public Law 106-378 is denied by the Service may not appeal the decision. However, the denial will be without prejudice to the alien's right to renew the application in proceedings under 8 CFR part 1240 provided that the 2,000 statutory limit on such adjustments has not yet been reached.

HISTORY:

[66 FR 27445, 27448, May 17, 2001; 68 FR 9824, 9842, 9846, Feb. 28, 2003; 68 FR 10349, 10357, Mar. 5, 2003; 85 FR 82750, 82795, Dec. 18, 2020]

§ 1245.21 Adjustment of status of certain nationals of Vietnam, Cambodia, and Laos (section 586 of Public Law 106-429).

(a) Eligibility. DHS may adjust the status to that of a

lawful permanent resident, a native or citizen of Vietnam, Cambodia, or Laos who:

(1) Was inspected and paroled into the United States before October 1, 1997;

(2) Was paroled into the United States from Vietnam under the auspices of the Orderly Departure Program (ODP), a refugee camp in East Asia, or a displaced person camp administered by the United Nations High Commissioner for Refugees (UNHCR) in Thailand;

(3) Was physically present in the United States prior to and on October 1, 1997;

(4) Files an application for adjustment of status in accordance with paragraph (b) of this section during the 3-year application period; and

(5) Is otherwise eligible to receive an immigrant visa and is otherwise admissible as an immigrant to the United States except as provided in paragraphs (e) and (f) of this section.

(b) Applying for benefits under section 586 of Public Law 106-429.

(1) Application period. The application period lasts from January 27, 2003 until January 25, 2006. DHS will accept applications received after the end of the application period, but only if the 5,000 limit on adjustments has not been reached prior to the end of the three-year application period, and the application bears an official postmark dated on or before the final day of the application period. Postmarks will be evaluated in the following manner:

(i) If the postmark is illegible or missing, DHS will consider the application to be timely filed if it is received on or before 3 business days after the end of the application period.

(ii) In all instances, the burden of proof is on the applicant to establish timely filing of an application.

(2) Application. An alien must be physically present in the United States to apply for adjustment of status under section 586 of Public Law 106-429. An applicant must submit Form I-485, Application to Register Permanent Residence or Adjust Status, along with the appropriate application fee contained in 8 CFR 103.7 and 8 CFR part 106. Applicants who are 14 through 79 years of age must also submit the fingerprinting service fee provided for in 8 CFR 103.7 and 8 CFR part 106. Each application filed must be accompanied by evidence establishing eligibility as provided in paragraph (g) of this section; two photographs as described in the Form I-485 instructions; a completed Biographic Information Sheet (Form G-325A) if the applicant is between 14 and 79 years of age; a report of medical examination (Form I-693 and vaccination supplement) specified in § 1245.5; and, if needed, an application for waiver of inadmissibility. Under Part 2, question h of Form I-485, applicants must write "INDOCHINESE PAROLEE P.L. 106-429". Applications must be sent to: INS Nebraska Service Center, P.O. Box 87485, Lincoln NE 68501-7485.

(c) Applications from aliens in immigration proceedings. An alien in pending immigration proceedings who believes he or she is eligible for adjustment of status under section 586 of Public Law 106-429 must apply directly to DHS in accordance with paragraph (b) of this section. An immigration judge or the Board of Immigration Appeals may not adjudicate applications for adjustment of status under this section. An alien who is currently in immigration proceedings who alleges eligibility for adjustment of status under section 586 of Public Law 106-429 may contact DHS counsel after filing an application to request the consent of DHS to the filing of a joint motion for administrative closure. Unless DHS consents to such a motion, the immigration judge or the Board may not defer or dismiss the proceeding in connection with section 586 of Public Law 106-429.

(d) Applications from aliens with final orders of removal, deportation, or exclusion. An alien with a final order of removal, deportation, or exclusion who believes he or she is eligible for adjustment of status under section 586 of Public Law 106-429 must apply directly to DHS in accordance with paragraph (b) of this section.

(1) An application under this section does not automatically stay the order of removal, deportation, or exclusion. An alien who is eligible for adjustment of status under section 586 of Public Law 106-429 may request that the district director with jurisdiction over the alien grant a stay of removal during the pendency of the application. The regulations governing such a request are found at 8 CFR 241.6.

(2) DHS in general will exercise its discretion not to grant a stay of removal, deportation, or exclusion with respect to an alien who is inadmissible on any of the grounds specified in paragraph (m)(3) of this section, unless there is substantial reason to believe that DHS will grant the necessary waivers of inadmissibility.

(3) An immigration judge or the Board may not grant a motion to re-open or stay in connection with an application under this section.

(4) If DHS approves the application, the approval will constitute the automatic re-opening of the alien's immigration proceedings, vacating of the final order of removal, deportation, or exclusion, and termination of the reopened proceedings.

(e) Grounds of inadmissibility that do not apply. In making a determination of whether an applicant is otherwise eligible for admission to the United States for lawful permanent residence under the provisions of section 586 of Public Law 106-429, the grounds of inadmissibility under sections 212(a)(4), (a)(5), (a)(7)(A), and (a)(9) of the Act shall not apply.

(f) Waiver of grounds of inadmissibility. In connection with an application for adjustment of status under this section, the alien may apply for a waiver of the grounds of inadmissibility under sections 212(a)(1), (a)(6)(B), (a)(6)(C), (a)(6)(F), (a)(8)(A), (a)(10)(B), and (a)(10)(D) of the Act as provided in section 586(c) of Public Law 106-429, if the alien demonstrates that a waiver is necessary to prevent extreme hardship to the alien, or to the alien's spouse, parent, son or daughter who is a U.S. citizen or an alien lawfully admitted for permanent residence. In addition, the alien may apply for any other waiver of inadmissibility under section 212 of the Act, if eligible. In order to obtain a waiver for any of these grounds, an applicant must submit Form

I-601, Application for Waiver of Grounds of Excludability, with the application for adjustment.

(g) Evidence. Applicants must submit evidence that demonstrates they are eligible for adjustment of status under section 586 of Public Law 106-429. Such evidence shall include the following:

(1) A birth certificate or other record of birth;

(2) Documentation to establish that the applicant was physically present in the United States on October 1, 1997, under the standards set forth in § 1245.22 of this chapter.

(3) A copy of the applicant's Arrival-Departure Record (Form I-94) or other evidence that the alien was inspected or paroled into the United States prior to October 1, 1997, from one of the three programs listed in paragraph (a)(2) of this section. Subject to verification, documentation pertaining to paragraph (a)(2) of this section is already contained in DHS files and the applicant may submit an affidavit to that effect in lieu of actual documentation.

(h) Employment authorization. Applicants who want to obtain employment authorization based on a pending application for adjustment of status under this section may submit Form I-765, Application for Employment Authorization, along with the application fee listed in 8 CFR 103.7 and 8 CFR part 106. If DHS approves the application for employment authorization, the applicant will be issued an employment authorization document.

(i) Travel while an application to adjust status is pending. An alien may travel abroad while an application to adjust status is pending. Applicants must obtain advance parole in order to avoid the abandonment of their application to adjust status. An applicant may obtain advance parole by filing Form I-131, Application for a Travel Document, along with the application fee listed in 8 CFR 103.7 and 8 CFR part 106. If DHS approves Form I-131, the alien will be issued Form I-512, Authorization for the Parole of an Alien into the United States. Aliens granted advance parole will still be subject to inspection at a port-of-entry.

(j) Approval and date of admission as a lawful permanent resident. When DHS approves an application to adjust status to that of lawful permanent resident based on section 586 of Public Law 106-429, the applicant will be notified in writing of DHS's decision. In addition, the record of the alien's admission as a lawful permanent resident will be recorded as of the date of the alien's inspection and parole into the United States, as described in paragraph (a)(1) of this section.

(k) Notice of denial. When DHS denies an application to adjust status to that of lawful permanent resident based on section 586 of Public Law 106-429, the applicant will be notified of the decision in writing.

(l) Administrative review. An alien whose application for adjustment of status under section 586 of Public Law 106-429 is denied by DHS may appeal the decision to the Administrative Appeals Office in accordance with 8 CFR 103.3(a)(2).

(m) Number of adjustments permitted under this section.

(1) Limit. No more than 5,000 aliens may have their status adjusted to that of a lawful permanent resident under section 586 of Public Law 106-429.

(2) Counting procedures. Each alien granted adjustment of status under this section will count towards the 5,000 limit. DHS will assign a tracking number, ascending chronologically by filing date, to all applications properly filed in accordance with paragraphs (b) and (g) of this section. Except as described in paragraph (m)(3) of this section, DHS will adjudicate applications in that order until it reaches 5,000 approvals under this part. Applications initially denied but pending on administrative appeal will retain their place in the queue by virtue of their tracking number, pending DHS's adjudication of the appeal.

(3) Applications submitted with a request for the waiver of a ground of inadmissibility. In the discretion of DHS, applications that do not require adjudication of a waiver of inadmissibility under section 212(a)(2), (a)(6)(B), (a)(6)(F), (a)(8)(A), or (a)(10)(D) of the Act may be approved and assigned numbers within the 5,000 limit before those applications that do require a waiver of inadmissibility under any of those provisions. Applications requiring a waiver of any of those provisions will be assigned a tracking number chronologically by the date of approval of the necessary waivers rather than the date of filing of the application.

(4) Procedures when the 5,000 limit is reached. DHS will track the total number of adjustments and stop processing applications after the 5,000 limit has been reached. When the limit is reached, DHS will return any additional applications to applicants with a dated notice encouraging applicants to retain their application package and the notice in the event the 5,000 limit is expanded or eliminated and the alien wishes to apply again. DHS will keep an identifying chronological record of the application for purposes of processing applications under this section if the 5,000 limit subsequently is expanded or eliminated. If at the time the 5,000 limit is reached, it appears that Congress is about to pass legislation to expand or eliminate the cap, DHS retains the discretion to retain such applications and the related fees.

HISTORY:

[67 FR 78667, 78673, Dec. 26, 2002; 68 FR 9824, 9842, 9846, Feb. 28, 2003; 85 FR 82750, 82795, Dec. 18, 2020; 86 FR 70708, 70725, Dec. 13, 2021]

§ 1245.22 Evidence to demonstrate an alien's physical presence in the United States on a specific date.

(a) Evidence. Generally, an alien who is required to demonstrate his or her physical presence in the United States on a specific date in connection with an application to adjust status to that of an alien lawfully admitted for permanent residence should submit evidence according to this section. In cases where a more specific regulation relating to a particular adjustment of status provision has been issued in the 8 CFR, such regulation is controlling to the extent that it conflicts with this section.

(b) The number of documents. If no one document establishes the alien's physical presence on the required date, he or she may submit several documents establishing his or her physical presence in the United States prior to and after that date.

(c) Service-issued documentation. To demonstrate physical presence on a specific date, the alien may submit Service-issued documentation. Examples of acceptable Service documentation include, but are not limited to, photocopies of:

(1) Form I-94, Arrival-Departure Record, issued upon the alien's arrival in the United States;

(2) Form I-862, Notice to Appear, issued by the Service on or before the required date;

(3) Form I-122, Notice to Applicant for Admission Detained for Hearing before Immigration Judge, issued by the Service on or prior to the required date, placing the applicant in exclusion proceedings under section 236 of the Act (as in effect prior to April 1, 1997);

(4) Form I-221, Order to Show Cause, issued by the Service on or prior to the required date, placing the applicant in deportation proceedings under section 242 or 242A (redesignated as section 238) of the Act (as in effect prior to April 1, 1997); or

(5) Any application or petition for a benefit under the Act filed by or on behalf of the applicant on or prior to the required date that establishes his or her presence in the United States, or a fee receipt issued by the Service for such application or petition.

(d) Government-issued documentation. To demonstrate physical presence on the required date, the alien may submit other government documentation. Other government documentation issued by a Federal, State, or local authority must bear the signature, seal, or other authenticating instrument of such authority (if the document normally bears such instrument), be dated at the time of issuance, and bear a date of issuance not later than the required date. For this purpose, the term Federal, State, or local authority includes any governmental, educational, or administrative function operated by Federal, State, county, or municipal officials. Examples of such other documentation include, but are not limited to:

(1) A state driver's license;

(2) A state identification card;

(3) A county or municipal hospital record;

(4) A public college or public school transcript;

(5) Income tax records;

(6) A certified copy of a Federal, State, or local governmental record that was created on or prior to the required date, shows that the applicant was present in the United States at the time, and establishes that the applicant sought in his or her own behalf, or some other party sought in the applicant's behalf, a benefit from the Federal, State, or local governmental agency keeping such record;

(7) A certified copy of a Federal, State, or local governmental record that was created on or prior to the required date, that shows that the applicant was present in the United States at the time, and establishes that the applicant submitted an income tax return, property tax payment, or similar submission or payment to the Federal, State, or local governmental agency keeping such record; or

(8) A transcript from a private or religious school that is registered with, or approved or licensed by, appropriate State or local authorities, accredited by the State or regional accrediting body, or by the appropriate private school association, or maintains enrollment records in accordance with State or local requirements or standards. Such evidence will only be accepted to document the physical presence of an alien who was in attendance and under the age of 21 on the specific date that physical presence in the United States is required.

(e) Copies of records. It shall be the responsibility of the applicant to obtain and submit copies of the records of any other government agency that the applicant desires to be considered in support of his or her application. If the alien is not in possession of such a document or documents, but believes that a copy is already contained in the Service file relating to him or her, he or she may submit a statement as to the name and location of the issuing Federal, State, or local government agency, the type of document and the date on which it was issued.

(f) Other relevant document(s) and evaluation of evidence. The adjudicator will consider any other relevant document(s) as well as evaluate all evidence submitted, on a case-by-case basis. The Service may require an interview when necessary.

(g) Accuracy of documentation. In all cases, any doubts as to the existence, authenticity, veracity, or accuracy of the documentation shall be resolved by the official government record, with records of the Service having precedence over the records of other agencies. Furthermore, determinations as to the weight to be given any particular document or item of evidence shall be solely within the discretion of the adjudicating authority.

HISTORY:

[67 FR 78667, 78674, Dec. 26, 2002; 68 FR 9824, 9842, Feb. 28, 2003]

PART 1246

RESCISSION OF ADJUSTMENT OF STATUS

Rule

AUTHORITY NOTE APPLICABLE TO ENTIRE PART:

AUTHORITY:

8 U.S.C. 1103, 1254, 1255, 1256, 1259; 8 CFR part 2.

§ 1246.1 Notice.

If it appears to a district director that a person residing in his or her district was not in fact eligible for the adjustment of status made in his or her case, or it appears to an asylum office director that a person granted adjustment of status by an asylum officer pursuant to 8 CFR 1240.70 was not in fact eligible for adjustment of status, a proceeding shall be commenced by the personal service upon such person of a notice of intent to rescind, which shall inform him or her of the allegations upon which it is intended to rescind the adjustment of his or her status. In such a proceeding the person shall be known as the respondent. The notice shall also inform the respondent that he or she may submit, within thirty days from the date of service of the notice, an answer in writing under oath setting forth reasons why such rescission shall not be made, and that he or she may, within such period, request a hearing before an immigration judge in support of, or in lieu of, his or her written answer. The respondent shall further be informed that he or she may have the assistance of or be represented by counsel or representative of his or her choice qualified under part 292 of this chapter, at no expense to the Government, in the preparation of his or her answer or in connection with his or her hearing, and that he or she may present such evidence in his or her behalf as may be relevant to the rescission.

HISTORY:

[28 FR 6737, June 29, 1963, as amended at 37 FR 11471, June 8, 1972; 62 FR 10312, 10385, March 6, 1997; 64 FR 27856, 27881, May 21, 1999; 68 FR 9824, 9842, Feb. 28, 2003; 68 FR 10349, 10359, Mar. 5, 2003]

§ 1246.2 Allegations admitted; no answer filed; no hearing requested.

If the answer admits the allegations in the notice, or if no answer is filed within the thirty-day period, or if no hearing is requested within such period, the district director or asylum office director shall rescind the adjustment of status previously granted, and no appeal shall lie from his decision.

HISTORY:

[27 FR 10789, Nov. 6, 1962; 62 FR 10312, 10385, March 6, 1997; 64 FR 27856, 27881, May 21, 1999; 68 FR 9824, 9842, Feb. 28, 2003]

§ 1246.3 Allegations contested or denied; hearing requested.

If, within the prescribed time following service of the notice pursuant to § 1246.1, the respondent has filed an answer which contests or denies any allegation in the notice, or a hearing is requested, a hearing pursuant to § 1246.5 shall be conducted by an immigration judge, and the requirements contained in §§ 1240.3, 1240.4, 1240.5, 1240.6, 1240.7, and 1240.9 of this chapter shall be followed.

HISTORY:

[29 FR 13243, Sept. 24, 1964; 62 FR 10312, 10385, March 6, 1997; 68 FR 9824, 9842, 9846, Feb. 28, 2003; 68 FR 10349, 10359, Mar. 5, 2003]

§ 1246.4 Immigration judge's authority; withdrawal and substitution.

In any proceeding conducted under this part, the immigration judge shall have authority to interrogate, examine, and cross-examine the respondent and other witnesses, to present and receive evidence, to determine whether adjustment of status shall be rescinded, to make decisions thereon, including an appropriate order, and to take any other action consistent with applicable provisions of law and regulations as may be appropriate to the disposition of the case. Nothing contained in this part shall be construed to diminish the authority conferred on immigration judges by the Act. The immigration judge assigned to conduct a hearing shall, at any time, withdraw if he or she deems himself or herself disqualified. If a hearing has begun but no evidence has been adduced other than the notice and answer, if any, pursuant to §§ 1246.1 and 1246.2, or if an immigration judge becomes unavailable to complete his or her duties within a reasonable time, or if at any time the respondent consents to a substitution, another immigration judge may be assigned to complete the case. The new immigration judge shall familiarize himself or herself with the record in the case and shall state for the record that he or she is familiar with the record in the case.

HISTORY:

[27 FR 10789, Nov. 6, 1962; 62 FR 10312, 10385, March 6, 1997; 68 FR 9824, 9842, 9846, Feb. 28, 2003]

§ 1246.5 Hearing.

(a) DHS counsel. The Government shall be represented at the hearing by a DHS counsel who shall have authority to present evidence, and to interrogate, examine, and cross-examine the respondent and other witnesses. The DHS counsel is authorized to appeal from a decision of the immigration judge pursuant to § 1246.7 and to move for reopening or reconsideration pursuant to § 1003.23 of this chapter.

(b) Opening. The immigration judge shall advise the respondent of the nature of the proceeding and the legal authority under which it is conducted; advise the respondent of his or her right to representation, at no expense to the Government, by counsel or representative of his or her own choice qualified under part 1292 of this chapter and require him or her to state then and there whether he or she desires representation; advise the respondent that he or she will have a reasonable opportunity to examine and object to the evidence against him or her, to present evidence in his or her own behalf, and to cross-examine witnesses presented by the Government; place the respondent under oath; read the allegations in the notice to the respondent and explain them in nontechnical language, and enter the notice and respondent's answer, if any, as exhibits in the record.

(c) Pleading by respondent. The immigration judge shall require the respondent to state for the record whether he or she admits or denies the allegations contained in the notice, or any of them, and whether he or she concedes that his or her adjustment of status should be rescinded. If the respondent admits all of the allegations and concedes that the adjustment of status in his or her case should be rescinded under the allegations set forth in the notice, and the immigration judge is satisfied that no issues of law or fact remain, he or she may determine that rescission as alleged has been established by the respondent's admissions. The allegations contained in the notice shall be taken as admitted when the respondent, without reasonable cause, fails or refuses to attend or remain in attendance at the hearing.

HISTORY:

[27 FR 10789, Nov. 6, 1962; 62 FR 10312, 10385, March 6, 1997; 68 FR 9824, 9842, 9846, Feb. 28, 2003; 68 FR 10349, 10359, Mar. 5, 2003; 86 FR 70708, 70725, Dec. 13, 2021]

§ 1246.6 Decision and order.

The decision of the immigration judge may be oral or written. The formal enumeration of findings is not required. The order shall direct either that the proceeding be terminated or that the adjustment of status be rescinded. Service of the decision and finality of the order of the immigration judge shall be in accordance with, and as stated in §§ 1240.13 (a) and (b) and 1240.14 of this chapter.

HISTORY:

[27 FR 10789, Nov. 6, 1962; 62 FR 10312, 10385, March 6, 1997; 68 FR 9824, 9842, Feb. 28, 2003; 68 FR 10349, 10359, Mar. 5, 2003]

§ 1246.7 Appeals.

Pursuant to 8 CFR Part 1003, an appeal shall lie from a decision of an immigration judge under this part to the Board of Immigration Appeals. An appeal shall be taken within 30 days after the mailing of a written decision or the stating of an oral decision. The reasons for the appeal shall be specifically identified in the Notice of Appeal (Form EOIR 26); failure to do so may constitute a ground for dismissal of the appeal by the Board.

HISTORY:

[29 FR 7236, June 3, 1964; 61 FR 18900, 18910, April 29, 1996, as corrected at 61 FR 32924, June 26, 1996; 62 FR 10312, 10386, March 6, 1997; 68 FR 9824, 9842, Feb. 28, 2003; 68 FR 10349, 10359, Mar. 5, 2003]

§ 1246.8 [Reserved]

[NO TEXT IN ORIGINAL]

HISTORY:

[27 FR 10789, Nov. 6, 1962; 62 FR 10312, 10386, March 6, 1997; 68 FR 9824, 9842, Feb. 28, 2003]

AUTHORITY:

(Secs. 103, 244, 245, 246, 249, 66 Stat. 173, 214, 217, 219; 8 U.S.C. 1103, 1254, as amended, 1255, as amended, 1256, 1259, as amended.)

§ 1246.9 Surrender of Form I-551.

A respondent whose status as a permanent resident has been rescinded in accordance with section 246 of the Act and this part, shall, upon demand, promptly surrender to the district director having administrative jurisdiction over the office in which the action under this part was taken, the Form I-551 issued to him or her at the time of the grant of permanent resident status.

HISTORY:

[27 FR 10789, Nov. 6, 1962, as amended at 45 FR 32657, May 19, 1980; 62 FR 10312, 10386, March 6, 1997; 68 FR 9824, 9842, Feb. 28, 2003]

PART 1249

CREATION OF RECORDS OF LAWFUL ADMISSION FOR PERMANENT RESIDENCE

Rule

AUTHORITY NOTE APPLICABLE TO ENTIRE PART:

AUTHORITY:

8 U.S.C. 1103, 1182, 1259; 8 CFR part 2.

§ 1249.1 Waiver of inadmissibility.

In conjunction with an application under section 249 of the Act, an otherwise eligible alien who is inadmissible under paragraph (9), (10), or (12) of section 212(a) of the Act or so much of paragraph (23) of section 212(a) of the Act as relates to a single offense of simple possession of 30 grams or less of marihuana may request a waiver of such ground of inadmissibility under section 212(h) of the Act. Any alien within the classes described in subparagraphs (B) through (H) of section 212(a)(28) of the Act may apply for the benefits of section 212(a)(28)(I)(ii) in conjunction with an application under section 249 of the Act.

HISTORY:

[47 FR 44238, Oct. 7, 1982; 68 FR 9824, 9843, Feb. 28, 2003]

§ 1249.2 Application.

(a) Jurisdiction. An application by an alien, other than an arriving alien, who has been served with a notice to appear or warrant of arrest shall be considered only in proceedings under 8 CFR Part 1240. In any other case, an alien who believes he or she meets the eligibility requirements of section 249 of the Act shall apply to the district director having jurisdiction over his or her place of residence. The application shall be made on Form I-485 and shall be accompanied by Form G-325A, which shall be considered part of the application. The application shall also be accompanied by documentary evidence establishing continuous residence in the United States since prior to January 1,

1972, or since entry and prior to July 1, 1924. All documents must be submitted in accordance with § 103.2(b) of this chapter. Documentary evidence may include any records of official or personal transactions or recordings of events occurring during the period of claimed residence. Affidavits of credible witnesses may also be accepted. Persons unemployed and unable to furnish evidence in their own names may furnish evidence in the names of parents or other persons with whom they have been living, if affidavits of the parents or other persons are submitted attesting to the residence. The numerical limitations of sections 201 and 202 of the Act shall not apply.

(b) Decision. The applicant shall be notified of the decision and, if the application is denied, of the reasons therefor. If the application is granted, a Form I-551, showing that the applicant has acquired the status of an alien lawfully admitted for permanent residence, shall not be issued until the applicant surrenders any other document in his or her possession evidencing compliance with the alien registration requirements of former or existing law. No appeal shall lie from the denial of an application by the district director. However, an alien, other than an arriving alien, may renew the denied application in proceedings under 8 CFR Part 1240.

HISTORY:

[52 FR 6322, Mar. 3, 1987; 62 FR 10312, 10386, March 6, 1997; 68 FR 9824, 9843, Feb. 28, 2003; 68 FR 10349, 10359, Mar. 5, 2003]

§ 1249.3 Reopening and reconsideration.

An applicant who alleged entry and residence since prior to July 1, 1924, but in whose case a record was created as of the date of approval of the application because evidence of continuous residence prior to July 1, 1924, was not submitted, may have his case reopened and reconsidered pursuant to § 103.5 of 8 CFR chapter I. Upon the submission of satisfactory evidence, a record of admission as of the date of alleged entry may be created.

HISTORY:

[29 FR 11494, Aug. 11, 1964; 68 FR 9824, 9843, Feb. 28, 2003; 68 FR 10349, 10359, Mar. 5, 2003]

PART 1270

PENALTIES FOR DOCUMENT FRAUD

Rule

AUTHORITY NOTE APPLICABLE TO ENTIRE PART:

AUTHORITY:

8 U.S.C. 1101, 1103, and 1324c; Pub. L. 101-410, 104 Stat. 890, as amended by Pub. L. 104-134, 110 Stat. 1321.

§ 1270.1 Definitions.

[PUBLISHER'S NOTE: 68 FR 10349, 10359, Mar. 5, 2003, purported to amend paragraphs (c), (d), (h), and (i) of § 1270.1. However this could not implemented, since these paragraphs did not exist. It was determined that paragraphs (c), (d), (h), and (i) of § 1270.2 should instead be amended. For the convenience of the user, the amendment has been implemented in § 1270.2 according to the apparent intent of the agency. A correction is anticipated.]

For the purpose of this part —

Document means an instrument on which is recorded, by means of letters, figures, or marks, matters which may be used to fulfill any requirement of the Act. The term "document" includes, but is not limited to, an application required to be filed under the Act and any other accompanying document or material;

Entity means any legal entity, including, but not limited to, a corporation, partnership, joint venture, governmental body, agency, proprietorship, or association, including an agent or anyone acting directly or indirectly in the interest thereof.

HISTORY:

[57 FR 33866, July 31, 1992; 68 FR 9824, 9843, Feb. 28, 2003]

§ 1270.2 Enforcement procedures.

[PUBLISHER'S NOTE: 68 FR 10349, 10359, Mar. 5, 2003, purported to amend paragraphs (c), (d), (h), and (i) of § 1270.1. However this could not implemented, since these paragraphs did not exist. It was determined that paragraphs (c), (d), (h), and (i) of § 1270.2 should instead be amended. For the convenience of the user, the amendment has been implemented according to the apparent intent of the agency. A correction is anticipated.]

(a) Procedures for the filing of complaints. Any person or entity having knowledge of a violation or potential violation of section 274C of the Act may submit a signed, written complaint to the Service office having jurisdiction over the business or residence of the potential violator or the location where the violation occurred. The signed, written complaint must contain sufficient information to identify both the complainant and the alleged violator, including their names and addresses. The complaint should also contain detailed factual allegations relating to the potential violation including the date, time and place of the alleged violation and the specific act or conduct alleged to constitute a violation of the Act. Written complaints may be delivered either by mail to the appropriate Service office or by personally appearing before any immigration officer at a Service office.

(b) Investigation. When the Service receives complaints from a third party in accordance with paragraph (a) of this section, it shall investigate only those complaints which, on their face, have a substantial probability of validity. The Service may also conduct investigations for violations on its own initiative, and without having received a written complaint. If it is determined after investigation that the person or entity has violated section 274C of the Act, the Service may issue and serve upon the alleged violator a Notice of Intent to Fine.

(c) Issuance of a subpoena. Service officers shall have reasonable access to examine any relevant evidence of any person or entity being investigated. The Service may issue subpoenas pursuant to its authority under sections 235(a) and 287 of the Act, in accordance with the procedures set forth in § 1287.4 of this chapter.

(d) Notice of Intent to Fine. The proceeding to assess administrative penalties under section 274C of the Act is commenced when the Service issues a Notice of Intent to Fine. Service of this notice shall be accomplished by personal service pursuant to § 103.5a(a)(2) of 8 CFR chapter I. Service is effective upon receipt, as evidenced by the certificate of service or the certified mail return receipt. The person or entity identified in the Notice of Intent to Fine shall be known as the respondent. The Notice of Intent to Fine may be issued by an officer defined in § 242.1 of this chapter or by an INS port director designated by his or her district director.

(e) Contents of the Notice of Intent to Fine.

(1) The Notice of Intent to Fine shall contain the basis for the charge(s) against the respondent, the statutory provisions alleged to have been violated, and the monetary amount of the penalty the Service intends to impose.

(2) The Notice of Intent to Fine shall provide the following advisals to the respondent:

(i) That the person or entity has the right to representation by counsel of his or her own choice at no expense to the government;

(ii) That any statement given may be used against the person or entity;

(iii) That the person or entity has the right to request a hearing before an administrative law judge pursuant to 5 U.S.C. 554-557, and that such request must be filed with INS within 60 days from the service of the Notice of Intent to Fine; and

(iv) That if a written request for a hearing is not timely filed, the Service will issue a final order from which there is no appeal.

(f) Request for hearing before an administrative law judge. If a respondent contests the issuance of a Notice of Intent to Fine, the respondent must file with the INS, within 60 days of the Notice of Intent to Fine, a written request for a hearing before an administrative law judge. Any written request for a hearing submitted in a foreign language must be accompanied by an English language translation. A request for hearing is deemed filed when it is either received by the Service office designated in the Notice of Intent to Fine, or addressed to such office, stamped with the proper postage, and postmarked within the 60-day period. In computing the 60-day period prescribed by this section, the day of service of the Notice of Intent to Fine shall not be included. In the request for a hearing, the respondent may, but is not required to, respond to each allegation listed in the Notice of Intent to Fine. A respondent may waive the 60-day period in which to request a hearing before an administrative law judge and ask that the INS issue a final order from which there is no appeal. Prior to execution of the waiver, a respondent who is not a United States citizen will be advised that a waiver of a section 274C hearing will result in the issuance of a final order and that the respondent will be excludable and/or deportable from the United States pursuant to the Act.

(g) Failure to file a request for hearing. If the respondent does not file a written request for a hearing within 60 days of service of the Notice of Intent to Fine, the INS shall issue a final order from which there shall be no appeal.

(h) Issuance of the final order. A final order may be issued by an officer defined in § 242.1 of 8 CFR chapter I, by an INS port director designated by his or her district director, or by the Director of the INS National Fines Office.

(i) Service of the final order —

(1) Generally. Service of the final order shall be accomplished by personal service pursuant to § 103.5a(a)(2) of 8 CFR chapter I. Service is effective upon receipt, as evidenced by the certificate of service or the certified mail return receipt.

(2) Alternative provisions for service in a foreign country. When service is to be effected upon a party in a foreign country, it is sufficient if service of the final order is made: (i) In the manner prescribed by the law of the foreign country for service in that country in an action in any of its courts of general jurisdiction; or

(ii) As directed by the foreign authority in response to a letter rogatory, when service in either case is reasonably calculated to give actual notice; or

(iii) When applicable, pursuant to § 103.5a(a)(2) of 8 CFR chapter I.

Service is effective upon receipt of the final order. Proof of service may be made as prescribed by the law of the foreign country, or, when service is pursuant to § 103.5a(a)(2) of 8 CFR chapter I, as evidenced by the certificate of service or the certified mail return receipt.

(j) Declination to file charges for document fraud committed by refugees at the time of entry. The Service shall not issue a Notice of Intent to Fine for acts of document fraud committed by an alien pursuant to direct departure from a country in which the alien has a well-founded fear of persecution or from which there is a significant danger that the alien would be returned to a country in which the alien would have a well-founded fear of persecution, provided that the alien has presented himself or herself without delay to an INS officer and shown good cause for his or her illegal entry or presence. Other acts of document fraud committed by such an alien may result in the issuance of a Notice of Intent to Fine and the imposition of civil money penalties.

HISTORY:

[57 FR 33866, July 31, 1992; 68 FR 9824, 9843, Feb. 28, 2003; 68 FR 10349, 10359, Mar. 5, 2003]

§ 1270.3 Penalties.

(a) Criminal penalties. Nothing in section 274C of the Act shall be construed to diminish or qualify any of the penalties available for activities prohibited by this section but proscribed as well in title 18, United States Code.

(b) Civil penalties. A person or entity may face civil penalties for a violation of section 274C of the Act. Civil penalties may be imposed by the Service or by an administrative law judge for violations under section 274C of the Act. The Service may charge multiple violations of section 274C of the Act in a single Notice of Intent to Fine, and may impose separate penalties for each such unlawful act in a single proceeding or determination. However, in determining whether an offense is a first offense or a subsequent offense, a finding of more than one violation in the course of a single proceeding or determination will be counted as a single offense.

(1) A respondent found by the Service or an administrative law judge to have violated section 274C of the Act shall be subject to an order:

(i) To cease and desist from such behavior; and

(ii) To pay a civil penalty as follows:

(A) First offense. Not less than $ 250 and not exceeding $ 2,000 for each fraudulent document or each proscribed activity described in section 274C(a)(1) through (a)(4) of the Act before September 29, 1999, and not less than $ 275 and not exceeding $ 2,200, for each fraudulent document or each proscribed activity on or after September 29, 1999.

(B) Subsequent offenses. Not less than $ 2,000 and not more than $ 5,000 for each fraudulent document or each proscribed activity described in section 274C(a)(1) through (a)(4) of the Act before September 29, 1999, and not less than $ 2,200 and not exceeding $ 5,500, for each fraudulent document or each proscribed activity occurring on or after September 29, 1999.

(2) Where an order is issued to a respondent composed of distinct, physically separate subdivisions each of which provides separately for the hiring, recruiting, or referring for a fee for employment (without reference to the practices of, and not under the common control of or common control with, another subdivision), each subdivision shall be considered a separate person or entity.

HISTORY:

[57 FR 33866, July 31, 1992; 64 FR 47099, 47101, Aug. 30, 1991; 68 FR 9824, 9843, Feb. 28, 2003]

PART 1274A

CONTROL OF EMPLOYMENT OF ALIENS

Subpart A. Employer Requirements

AUTHORITY NOTE APPLICABLE TO ENTIRE PART:

AUTHORITY:

8 U.S.C. 1101, 1103, 1324a.

Subpart A

Employer Requirements

§ 1274a.1 Employer requirements.

(a) Applicable regulations. The regulations of the Department of Homeland Security (DHS) relating to the implementation of the employment eligibility and verification provisions of section 274A of the Immigration and Nationality Act (Act) are contained in 8 CFR part 274a.

(b) Adjudication of civil penalty proceedings. The procedures for hearings before an administrative law judge relating to civil penalties sought by DHS under section 274A of the Act are contained in 28 CFR part 68. The regulations governing employment eligibility and verification in 8 CFR part 274a are applicable to hearings before an administrative law judge and, to the extent relevant, to cases before an immigration judge or the Board of Immigration Appeals.

HISTORY:

[52 FR 16221, May 1, 1987, as amended at 53 FR 8612, Mar. 16, 1988; 55 FR 25931, June 25, 1990; 56 FR 41783, Aug. 23, 1991; 68

FR 9824, 9844, 9846, Feb. 28, 2003; 74 FR 2337, 2340, Jan. 15, 2009, as confirmed at 76 FR 16525, 16526, Mar. 24, 2011]

§ 1274a.2 [This section was removed. See 74 FR 2337, 2340, Jan. 15, 2009, as confirmed at 76 FR 16525, 16526, Mar. 24, 2011.]

[NO TEXT IN ORIGINAL]

HISTORY:

[52 FR 16221, May 1, 1987, as amended at 53 FR 8612, Mar. 16, 1988; 55 FR 25932, June 25, 1990; 56 FR 41784-41786, Aug. 23, 1991; 58 FR 48780, Sept. 20, 1993; 59 FR 47063, Sept. 14, 1994; 60 FR 14353, Mar. 17, 1995; 61 FR 46534, 46537, Sept. 4, 1996; 61 FR 52235, 52236, Oct. 7, 1996; 62 FR 51001, 51005, Sept. 30, 1997, as corrected at 62 FR 52620, Oct. 8, 1997; 64 FR 6187, 6189, Feb. 9, 1999, as corrected at 64 FR 11533, Mar. 9, 1999; 68 FR 9824, 9844, 9846, Feb. 28, 2003]

AUTHORITY:

(8 U.S.C. 1101, 1103, 1324a.)

§ 1274a.3 [This section was removed. See 74 FR 2337, 2340, Jan. 15, 2009, as confirmed at 76 FR 16525, 16526, Mar. 24, 2011.]

[NO TEXT IN ORIGINAL]

HISTORY:

[52 FR 16221, May 1, 1987, as amended at 53 FR 8613, Mar. 16, 1988; 68 FR 9824, 9844, Feb. 28, 2003]

AUTHORITY:

(8 U.S.C. 1101, 1103, 1324a.)

§ 1274a.4 [This section was removed. See 74 FR 2337, 2340, Jan. 15, 2009, as confirmed at 76 FR 16525, 16526, Mar. 24, 2011.]

[NO TEXT IN ORIGINAL]

HISTORY:

[52 FR 16221, May 1, 1987; 68 FR 9824, 9844, 9846, Feb. 28, 2003]

AUTHORITY:

(8 U.S.C. 1101, 1103, 1324a.)

§ 1274a.5 [This section was removed. See 74 FR 2337, 2340, Jan. 15, 2009, as confirmed at 76 FR 16525, 16526, Mar. 24, 2011.]

[NO TEXT IN ORIGINAL]

HISTORY:

[55 FR 25934, June 25, 1990; 68 FR 9824, 9844, Feb. 28, 2003]

AUTHORITY:

(8 U.S.C. 1101, 1103, 1324a.)

§ 1274a.6 [This section was removed. See 74 FR 2337, 2340, Jan. 15, 2009, as confirmed at 76 FR 16525, 16526, Mar. 24, 2011.]

[NO TEXT IN ORIGINAL]

HISTORY:

[52 FR 43053, Nov. 9, 1987; 68 FR 9824, 9844, 9846, Feb. 28, 2003]

AUTHORITY:

(8 U.S.C. 1101, 1103, 1324a.)

§ 1274a.7 [This section was removed. See 74 FR 2337, 2340, Jan. 15, 2009, as confirmed at 76 FR 16525, 16526, Mar. 24, 2011.]

[NO TEXT IN ORIGINAL]

HISTORY:

[52 FR 16221, May 1, 1987, as amended at 53 FR 8613, Mar. 16, 1988; 55 FR 25935, June 25, 1990; 56 FR 41786, Aug. 23, 1991; 68 FR 9824, 9844, 9846, Feb. 28, 2003]

AUTHORITY:

(8 U.S.C. 1101, 1103, 1324a.)

§ 1274a.8 [This section was removed. See 74 FR 2337, 2340, Jan. 15, 2009, as confirmed at 76 FR 16525, 16526, Mar. 24, 2011.]

[NO TEXT IN ORIGINAL]

HISTORY:

[52 FR 16221, May 1, 1987; 64 FR 47099, 47101, Aug. 30, 1999; 68 FR 9824, 9844, Feb. 28, 2003]

AUTHORITY:

(8 U.S.C. 1101, 1103, 1324a.)

§ 1274a.9 Enforcement procedures.

(a)-(d) [Reserved]

(e) Request for Hearing Before an Administrative Law Judge. If a respondent contests the issuance of a Notice of Intent to Fine, the respondent must file with DHS, within thirty days of DHS of the Notice of Intent to Fine, a written request for a hearing before an Administrative Law Judge. Any written request for a hearing submitted in a foreign language must be accompanied by an English language translation. A request for a hearing is not deemed to be filed until received by DHS office designated in the Notice of Intent to Fine. In computing the thirty day period prescribed by this section, the day of service of the Notice of Intent to Fine shall not be included. If the Notice of Intent to Fine was served by ordinary mail, five days shall be added to the prescribed thirty day period. In the request for a hearing, the respondent may, but is not required to, respond to each allegation listed in the Notice of Intent to Fine.

(f) Failure to file a request for a hearing. If the respondent does not file a request for a hearing in writing within thirty days of the date of service of a Notice of Intent to Fine (thirty-five days if served by ordinary mail), the final order issued by DHS shall not be subject to a hearing before an administrative law judge under 28 CFR part 68.

HISTORY:

[52 FR 16221, May 1, 1987, as amended at 53 FR 8613, Mar. 16, 1988; 55 FR 25935, June 25, 1990; 56 FR 41786, Aug. 23, 1991; 61 FR 52235, 52236, Oct. 7, 1996; 68 FR 9824, 9844, Feb. 28, 2003; 74 FR 2337, 2340, Jan. 15, 2009, as confirmed at 76 FR 16525, 16526, Mar. 24, 2011]

§ 1274a.10 Penalties.

The regulations pertaining to the imposition of penalties for violations of the provisions of section 274A of the Immigration and Nationality Act are contained in 8 CFR part 274a and 28 CFR part 68.

HISTORY:
[52 FR 16221, May 1, 1987, as amended at 55 FR 25935, June 25, 1990; 56 FR 41786, Aug. 23, 1991; 64 FR 47099, 47101, Aug. 30, 1999; 68 FR 9824, 9844, 9846, Feb. 28, 2003; 73 FR 10130, 10136, Feb. 26, 2008]

§ 1274a.11 [Reserved]

[NO TEXT IN ORIGINAL]

HISTORY:
[52 FR 16221, May 1, 1987; 68 FR 9824, 9844, Feb. 28, 2003]

AUTHORITY:
(8 U.S.C. 1101, 1103, 1324a; 8 CFR part 2.)

Subpart B

[Subpart B was Removed and Reserved. See 74 FR 2337, 2340, Jan. 15, 2009, as Confirmed at 76 FR 16525, 16526, Mar. 24, 2011.]

SUBPART B — [SUBPART B WAS REMOVED AND RESERVED. SEE 74 FR 2337, 2340, JAN. 15, 2009, AS CONFIRMED AT 76 FR 16525, 16526, MAR. 24, 2011.]

[NO TEXT IN ORIGINAL]

§ 1274a.12 [This section was removed and reserved. See 74 FR 2337, 2340, Jan. 15, 2009, as confirmed at 76 FR 16525, 16526, Mar. 24, 2011.]

[NO TEXT IN ORIGINAL]

HISTORY:
[52 FR 16221, May 1, 1987, as amended at 53 FR 8614, Mar. 16, 1988; 53 FR 46855, Nov. 21, 1988; 54 FR 16, Jan. 3, 1989.; 55 FR 25936, June 25, 1990; 56 FR 624, Jan. 7, 1991.; 56 FR 23499, May 22, 1991; 56 FR 41787, Aug. 23, 1991; 56 FR 55616, Oct. 29, 1991; 57 FR 6462, Feb. 25, 1992, as confirmed and amended at 60 FR 66062, 66069, Dec. 21, 1995; 57 FR 14627, Apr. 21, 1992; 57 FR 31956, July 20, 1992; 57 FR 42885, Sept. 17, 1992; 58 FR 48780, Sept. 20, 1993; 58 FR 69217, Dec. 30, 1993, as corrected at 59 FR 52894, Oct. 20, 1994, and confirmed at 63 FR 1331, 1334, Jan. 9, 1998; 59 FR 47063, Sept. 14, 1994; 59 FR 62302, Dec. 5, 1994; 60 FR 14353, Mar. 17. 1995; 60 FR 21976, May 4, 1995; 60 FR 44260, 44271, Aug. 25, 1995; 61 FR 46534, 46537, Sept. 4, 1996; 62 FR 10312, 10389, Mar. 6, 1997; 62 FR 18508, 18514, Apr. 16, 1997, as corrected at 62 FR 46553, Sept. 3, 1997; 62 FR 39417, 39425, July 23, 1997; 63 FR 27823, 27833, May 21, 1998; 63 FR 63593, 63597, Nov. 16, 1998, as comfirmed and amended at 65 FR 15846, 15854, Mar. 24, 2000; 64 FR 25756, 25773, May 12, 1999, as confirmed and amended at 65 FR 15835, 15846, Mar. 24, 2000; 64 FR 27856, 27881, May 21, 1999; 65 FR 14774, 14780, Mar. 17, 2000; 65 FR 43677, 439680, July 14, 2000; 66 FR 29661, 29681, June 1, 2001, as confirmed at 67 FR 38341, 38350, June 4, 2002; 66 FR 42587, 42595, Aug. 14, 2001; 66 FR 46697, 46704, Sept. 7, 2001; 67 FR 4784, 4803, Jan. 31, 2002; 67 FR 76256, 76280, Dec. 11, 2002; 68 FR 9824, 9844, 9846, Feb. 28, 2003; 68 FR 10349, 10359, Mar. 5, 2003]

AUTHORITY:
(8 U.S.C. 1101, 1103, 1324a.)

§ 1274a.13 [This section was removed and reserved. See 74 FR 2337, 2340, Jan. 15, 2009, as confirmed at 76 FR 16525, 16526, Mar. 24, 2011.]

[NO TEXT IN ORIGINAL]

HISTORY:
[52 FR 16221, May 1, 1987, as amended at 53 FR 8614, Mar. 16, 1988; 55 FR 25937, June 25, 1990; 56 FR 41787, Aug. 23, 1991; 57 FR 6462, Feb. 25, 1992, as confirmed at 60 FR 66062, 66067, Dec. 21, 1995; 57 FR 14627, Apr. 21, 1992; 58 FR 12149, Mar. 3, 1993, as corrected at 58 FR 14145, Mar. 13, 1993; 59 FR 33905, July 1, 1994; 59 FR 62303, Dec. 5, 1994; 60 FR 21976, May 4, 1995; 63 FR 27823, 27833, May 21, 1998, as corrected at 63 FR 39121, July 21, 1998, as confirmed and amended at 65 FR 15846, 15854, Mar. 24, 2000; 64 FR 25756, 25773, May 12, 1999, as confirmed and amended at 65 FR 15835, 15846, Mar. 24, 2000; 68 FR 9824, 9844, 9846, Feb. 28, 2003]

AUTHORITY:
(8 U.S.C. 1101, 1103, 1324a.)

§ 1274a.14 [This section was removed and reserved. See 74 FR 2337, 2340, Jan. 15, 2009, as confirmed at 76 FR 16525, 16526, Mar. 24, 2011.]

[NO TEXT IN ORIGINAL]

HISTORY:
[52 FR 16221, May 1, 1987, as amended at 53 FR 8614, Mar. 16, 1988; 53 FR 20087, June 1, 1988; 61 FR 46534, 46537, Sept. 4, 1996; 68 FR 9824, 9844, 9846, Feb. 28, 2003]

AUTHORITY:
(8 U.S.C. 1101, 1103, 1324a.)

PART 1280

IMPOSITION AND COLLECTION OF FINES

AUTHORITY NOTE APPLICABLE TO ENTIRE PART:

AUTHORITY:
8 U.S.C. 1103, 1221, 1223, 1227, 1229, 1253, 1281, 1283, 1284, 1285, 1286, 1322, 1323, 1330; 66 Stat. 173, 195, 197, 201, 203, 212, 219, 221-223, 226, 227, 230; Pub. L. 101-410, 104 Stat. 890, as amended by Pub. L. 104-134, 110 Stat. 1321.

§ 1280.1 Review of fines and civil monetary penalties imposed by DHS.

(a) Applicable regulations. The regulations of the Department of Homeland Security (DHS) relating to the imposition of certain fines and civil monetary penalties under provisions of the Immigration and Nationality Act, including sections 231(g), 234, 240B(d), 241(d) and (e), 243(c)(1), 251(d), 254(a), 255, 256, 257, 271(a), 272(a), 273(b), 274D, and 275(b), are contained in 8 CFR part 280.

(b) Adjudication of civil monetary penalty proceedings. The Board of Immigration Appeals (Board) has appellate authority to review DHS decisions involving fines and civil monetary penalties imposed under 8 CFR part 280, as provided under 8 CFR part 1003. The regulations in 8 CFR part 280 governing the imposition of certain fines and civil monetary penalties are applicable in such proceedings before the Board.

(c) Civil monetary penalties under sections 274A, 274B, or 274C. For regulations relating to civil monetary penalties imposed under sections 274A, 274B, or 274C of the Act, See 8 CFR parts 274a and 1274a and 28 CFR part 68.

HISTORY:
[22 FR 9807, Dec. 6, 1957, as amended at 54 FR 18649, May 2, 1989; 68 FR 9824, 9844, Feb. 28, 2003; 76 FR 74625, 74630, Dec. 1, 2011]

§ 1280.2 [This section was removed. See 76 FR 74625, 74630, Dec. 1, 2011.]

[NO TEXT IN ORIGINAL]

HISTORY:
[22 FR 9807, Dec. 6, 1957, as amended at 32 FR 17651, Dec. 12, 1967; 56 FR 26020, June 6, 1991; 68 FR 9824, 9844, 9846, Feb. 28, 2003]

AUTHORITY:
(8 U.S.C. 1103, 1221, 1223, 1227, 1229, 1253, 1281, 1283, 1284, 1285, 1286, 1322, 1323, and 1330; 66 Stat. 173, 195, 197, 201, 203, 212, 219, 221-223, 226, 227, 230; Pub. L. 101-410, 104 Stat. 890, as amended by Pub. L. 104-134, 110 Stat. 1321.)

§ 1280.3 [This section was removed. See 76 FR 74625, 74630, Dec. 1, 2011.]

[NO TEXT IN ORIGINAL]

HISTORY:
[22 FR 9807, Dec. 6, 1957, as amended at 32 FR 17651, Dec. 12, 1967; 68 FR 9824, 9844, 9846, Feb. 28, 2003]

AUTHORITY:
(8 U.S.C. 1103, 1221, 1223, 1227, 1229, 1253, 1281, 1283, 1284, 1285, 1286, 1322, 1323, and 1330; 66 Stat. 173, 195, 197, 201, 203, 212, 219, 221-223, 226, 227, 230; Pub. L. 101-410, 104 Stat. 890, as amended by Pub. L. 104-134, 110 Stat. 1321.)

§ 1280.4 [This section was removed. See 76 FR 74625, 74630, Dec. 1, 2011.]

[NO TEXT IN ORIGINAL]

HISTORY:
[22 FR 9807, Dec. 6, 1957, as amended at 54 FR 18649, May 2, 1989; 68 FR 9824, 9844, Feb. 28, 2003]

AUTHORITY:
(8 U.S.C. 1103, 1221, 1223, 1227, 1229, 1253, 1281, 1283, 1284, 1285, 1286, 1322, 1323, and 1330; 66 Stat. 173, 195, 197, 201, 203, 212, 219, 221-223, 226, 227, 230; Pub. L. 101-410, 104 Stat. 890, as amended by Pub. L. 104-134, 110 Stat. 1321.)

§ 1280.5 [This section was removed. See 76 FR 74625, 74630, Dec. 1, 2011.]

[NO TEXT IN ORIGINAL]

HISTORY:
[22 FR 9807, Dec. 6, 1957, as amended at 54 FR 18649, May 2, 1989; 68 FR 9824, 9844, Feb. 28, 2003]

AUTHORITY:
(8 U.S.C. 1103, 1221, 1223, 1227, 1229, 1253, 1281, 1283, 1284, 1285, 1286, 1322, 1323, and 1330; 66 Stat. 173, 195, 197, 201, 203, 212, 219, 221-223, 226, 227, 230; Pub. L. 101-410, 104 Stat. 890, as amended by Pub. L. 104-134, 110 Stat. 1321.)

§ 1280.6 [This section was removed. See 76 FR 74625, 74630, Dec. 1, 2011.]

[NO TEXT IN ORIGINAL]

HISTORY:
[22 FR 9807, Dec. 6, 1957, as amended at 54 FR 102, Jan. 4, 1989.; 68 FR 9824, 9844, Feb. 28, 2003]

AUTHORITY:
(8 U.S.C. 1103, 1221, 1223, 1227, 1229, 1253, 1281, 1283, 1284, 1285, 1286, 1322, 1323, and 1330; 66 Stat. 173, 195, 197, 201, 203, 212, 219, 221-223, 226, 227, 230; Pub. L. 101-410, 104 Stat. 890, as amended by Pub. L. 104-134, 110 Stat. 1321.)

§ 1280.7 [This section was removed. See 76 FR 74625, 74630, Dec. 1, 2011.]

[NO TEXT IN ORIGINAL]

HISTORY:
[22 FR 9807, Dec. 6, 1957, as amended at 32 FR 17651, Dec. 12, 1967; 56 FR 26020, June 6, 1991; 68 FR 9824, 9844, Feb. 28, 2003]

AUTHORITY:

(8 U.S.C. 1103, 1221, 1223, 1227, 1229, 1253, 1281, 1283, 1284, 1285, 1286, 1322, 1323, and 1330; 66 Stat. 173, 195, 197, 201, 203, 212, 219, 221-223, 226, 227, 230; Pub. L. 101-410, 104 Stat. 890, as amended by Pub. L. 104-134, 110 Stat. 1321.)

§ 1280.11 [This section was removed. See 76 FR 74625, 74630, Dec. 1, 2011.]

[NO TEXT IN ORIGINAL]

HISTORY:

[22 FR 9807, Dec. 6, 1957, as amended at 32 FR 17651, Dec. 12, 1967; 37 FR 11471, June 8, 1972; 54 FR 18649, May 2, 1989; 68 FR 9824, 9844, Feb. 28, 2003]

AUTHORITY:

(8 U.S.C. 1103, 1221, 1223, 1227, 1229, 1253, 1281, 1283, 1284, 1285, 1286, 1322, 1323, and 1330; 66 Stat. 173, 195, 197, 201, 203, 212, 219, 221-223, 226, 227, 230; Pub. L. 101-410, 104 Stat. 890, as amended by Pub. L. 104-134, 110 Stat. 1321.)

§ 1280.12 [This section was removed. See 76 FR 74625, 74630, Dec. 1, 2011.]

[NO TEXT IN ORIGINAL]

HISTORY:

[22 FR 9807, Dec. 6, 1957, as amended at 54 FR 18649, May 2, 1989; 68 FR 9824, 9844, Feb. 28, 2003]

AUTHORITY:

(8 U.S.C. 1103, 1221, 1223, 1227, 1229, 1253, 1281, 1283, 1284, 1285, 1286, 1322, 1323, and 1330; 66 Stat. 173, 195, 197, 201, 203, 212, 219, 221-223, 226, 227, 230; Pub. L. 101-410, 104 Stat. 890, as amended by Pub. L. 104-134, 110 Stat. 1321.)

§ 1280.13 [This section was removed. See 76 FR 74625, 74630, Dec. 1, 2011.]

[NO TEXT IN ORIGINAL]

HISTORY:

[22 FR 9808, Dec. 6, 1957, as amended at 23 FR 9124, Nov. 26, 1958; 54 FR 18649, May 2, 1989; 68 FR 9824, 9844, Feb. 28, 2003]

AUTHORITY:

(8 U.S.C. 1103, 1221, 1223, 1227, 1229, 1253, 1281, 1283, 1284, 1285, 1286, 1322, 1323, and 1330; 66 Stat. 173, 195, 197, 201, 203, 212, 219, 221-223, 226, 227, 230; Pub. L. 101-410, 104 Stat. 890, as amended by Pub. L. 104-134, 110 Stat. 1321.)

§ 1280.14 [This section was removed. See 76 FR 74625, 74630, Dec. 1, 2011.]

[NO TEXT IN ORIGINAL]

HISTORY:

[22 FR 9807, Dec. 6, 1957; 68 FR 9824, 9844, 9846, Feb. 28, 2003]

AUTHORITY:

(8 U.S.C. 1103, 1221, 1223, 1227, 1229, 1253, 1281, 1283, 1284, 1285, 1286, 1322, 1323, and 1330; 66 Stat. 173, 195, 197, 201, 203, 212, 219, 221-223, 226, 227, 230; Pub. L. 101-410, 104 Stat. 890, as amended by Pub. L. 104-134, 110 Stat. 1321.)

§ 1280.15 [This section was removed. See 76 FR 74625, 74630, Dec. 1, 2011.]

[NO TEXT IN ORIGINAL]

HISTORY:

[32 FR 17651, Dec. 12, 1967, as amended at 54 FR 18649, May 2, 1989; 68 FR 9824, 9844, Feb. 28, 2003]

AUTHORITY:

(8 U.S.C. 1103, 1221, 1223, 1227, 1229, 1253, 1281, 1283, 1284, 1285, 1286, 1322, 1323, and 1330; 66 Stat. 173, 195, 197, 201, 203, 212, 219, 221-223, 226, 227, 230; Pub. L. 101-410, 104 Stat. 890, as amended by Pub. L. 104-134, 110 Stat. 1321.)

§ 1280.21 [This section was removed. See 76 FR 74625, 74630, Dec. 1, 2011.]

[NO TEXT IN ORIGINAL]

HISTORY:

[29 FR 14433, Oct. 21, 1964, as amended at 32 FR 17651, Dec. 12, 1967; 68 FR 9824, 9844, 9846, Feb. 28, 2003]

AUTHORITY:

(8 U.S.C. 1103, 1221, 1223, 1227, 1229, 1253, 1281, 1283, 1284, 1285, 1286, 1322, 1323, and 1330; 66 Stat. 173, 195, 197, 201, 203, 212, 219, 221-223, 226, 227, 230; Pub. L. 101-410, 104 Stat. 890, as amended by Pub. L. 104-134, 110 Stat. 1321.)

§ 1280.51 [This section was removed. See 76 FR 74625, 74630, Dec. 1, 2011.]

[NO TEXT IN ORIGINAL]

HISTORY:

[22 FR 9808, Dec. 6, 1957, as amended at 23 FR 9124, Nov. 26, 1958; 46 FR 28624, May 28, 1981; 54 FR 18649, May 2, 1989; 68 FR 9824, 9844, 9846, Feb. 28, 2003]

AUTHORITY:

(8 U.S.C. 1103, 1221, 1223, 1227, 1229, 1253, 1281, 1283, 1284, 1285, 1286, 1322, 1323, and 1330; 66 Stat. 173, 195, 197, 201, 203, 212, 219, 221-223, 226, 227, 230; Pub. L. 101-410, 104 Stat. 890, as amended by Pub. L. 104-134, 110 Stat. 1321.)

§ 1280.52 [This section was removed. See 76 FR 74625, 74630, Dec. 1, 2011.]

[NO TEXT IN ORIGINAL]

HISTORY:

[56 FR 26020, June 6, 1991; 68 FR 9824, 9844, Feb. 28, 2003]

AUTHORITY:

(8 U.S.C. 1103, 1221, 1223, 1227, 1229, 1253, 1281, 1283, 1284, 1285, 1286, 1322, 1323, and 1330; 66 Stat. 173, 195, 197, 201, 203, 212, 219, 221-223, 226, 227, 230; Pub. L. 101-410, 104 Stat. 890, as amended by Pub. L. 104-134, 110 Stat. 1321.)

§ 1280.53 [This section was removed. See 76 FR 74625, 74630, Dec. 1, 2011.]

[NO TEXT IN ORIGINAL]

HISTORY:

[64 FR 47099, 47102, Aug. 30, 1999; 68 FR 9824, 9844, Feb. 28, 2003]

AUTHORITY:

(8 U.S.C. 1103, 1221, 1223, 1227, 1229, 1253, 1281, 1283, 1284, 1285, 1286, 1322, 1323, and 1330; 66 Stat. 173, 195, 197, 201, 203, 212, 219, 221-223, 226, 227, 230; Pub. L. 101-410, 104 Stat. 890, as amended by Pub. L. 104-134, 110 Stat. 1321.)

PART 1287
FIELD OFFICERS; POWERS AND DUTIES

AUTHORITY NOTE APPLICABLE TO ENTIRE PART:

AUTHORITY:
8 U.S.C. 1103, 1182, 1225, 1226, 1251, 1252, 1357.

§ 1287.4 Subpoena.

(a) **Who may issue —**

(1) Criminal or civil investigations. For provisions relating to the authority of immigration officers to issue a subpoena requiring the production of records and evidence for use in criminal or civil investigations, see 8 CFR 287.4(a)(1).

(2) Proceedings other than naturalization proceedings —

(i) Prior to commencement of proceedings. For provisions relating to who may issue a subpoena requiring the attendance of witnesses or the production of documentary evidence, or both, for use in any proceeding under this title, other than under 8 CFR part 335, or any application made ancillary to the proceeding, see 8 CFR 287.4(a)(2)(i).

(ii) Subsequent to commencement of any proceeding.

(A) In any proceeding under this chapter and in any proceeding ancillary thereto, an immigration judge having jurisdiction over the matter may, upon his/her own volition or upon application of government counsel, the alien, or other party affected, issue subpoenas requiring the attendance of witnesses or for the production of books, papers and other documentary evidence, or both.

(B) Application for subpoena. A party applying for a subpoena shall be required, as a condition precedent to its issuance, to state in writing or at the proceeding, what he/she expects to prove by such witnesses or documentary evidence, and to show affirmatively that he/she has made diligent effort, without success, to produce the same.

(C) Issuance of subpoena. Upon being satisfied that a witness will not appear and testify or produce documentary evidence and that the witness' evidence is essential, the immigration judge shall issue a subpoena.

(D) Appearance of witness. If the witness is at a distance of more than 100 miles from the place of the proceeding, the subpoena shall provide for the witnesses' appearance at the Service office nearest to the witness to respond to oral or written interrogatories, unless the Service indicates that there is no objection to bringing the witness the distance required to enable him/her to testify in person.

(b) Form of subpoena. All subpoenas shall be issued on Form I-138.

(1) Criminal or civil investigations. The subpoena shall command the person or entity to which it is addressed to attend and to give testimony at a time or place specified. A subpoena shall also command the person or entity to which it is addressed to produce the books, papers, or documents specified in the subpoena. A subpoena may direct the taking of a deposition before an officer of the Service.

(2) Proceedings other than naturalization proceedings. Every subpoena issued under the provisions of this section shall state the title of the proceeding and shall command the person to whom it is directed to attend and to give testimony at a time and place specified. A subpoena shall also command the person to whom it is directed to produce the books, papers, or documents specified in the subpoena. A subpoena may direct the making of a deposition before an officer of the Service.

(c) Service. For provisions relating to who may serve a subpoena issued under this section, see 8 CFR 287.4(c).

(d) Invoking aid of court. If a witness neglects or refuses to appear and testify as directed by the subpoena served upon him or her in accordance with the provisions of this section, the immigration judge issuing the subpoena shall request the United States Attorney for the district in which the subpoena was issued to report such neglect or refusal to the United States District Court and to request such court to issue an order requiring the witness to appear and testify and to produce the books, papers, or documents designated in the subpoena.

HISTORY:
[50 FR 30134, July 24, 1985; 50 FR 47205, Nov. 15, 1985, as amended at 55 FR 12628, Apr. 5, 1990; 60 FR 56936, 56937, Nov. 13, 1995; 62 FR 10312, 10390, March 6, 1997; 67 FR 39255, 39260, June 7, 2002; 68 FR 9824, 9845, Feb. 28, 2003; 69 FR 44903, 44907, July 28, 2004]

§ 1287.6 Proof of official records.

(a) Domestic. In any proceeding under this chapter, an official record or entry therein, when admissible for any purpose, shall be evidenced by an official publication thereof, or by a copy attested by the official having legal custody of the record or by an authorized deputy.

(b) Foreign: Countries not Signatories to Convention.

(1) In any proceeding under this chapter, an official record or entry therein, when admissible for any purpose, shall be evidenced by an official publication thereof, or by a copy attested by an officer so authorized. This attested copy in turn may but need not be certified by any authorized foreign officer both as to the genuineness of the signature of the attesting officer and as to his/her official position. The signature and official position of this certifying foreign officer may then likewise be certified by any other foreign officer so authorized, thereby creating a chain of certificates.

(2) The attested copy, with the additional foreign certificates if any, must be certified by an officer in the Foreign Service of the United States, stationed in the

foreign country where the record is kept. This officer must certify the genuineness of the signature and the official position either of (i) the attesting officer; or (ii) any foreign officer whose certification of genuineness of signature and official position relates directly to the attestation or is in a chain of certificates of genuineness of signature and official position relating to the attestation.

(c) Foreign: Countries Signatory to Convention Abolishing the Requirement of Legislation for Foreign Public Document.

(1) In any proceeding under this chapter, a public document or entry therein, when admissible for any purpose, may be evidenced by an official publication, or by a copy properly certified under the Convention. To be properly certified, the copy must be accompanied by a certificate in the form dictated by the Convention. This certificate must be signed by a foreign officer so authorized by the signatory country, and it must certify (i) the authenticity of the signature of the person signing the document; (ii) the capacity in which that person acted, and (iii) where appropriate, the identity of the seal or stamp which the document bears.

(2) No certification is needed from an officer in the Foreign Service of public documents.

(3) In accordance with the Convention, the following are deemed to be public documents:

(i) Documents emanating from an authority or an official connected with the courts of tribunals of the state, including those emanating from a public prosecutor, a clerk of a court or a process server;

(ii) Administrative documents;

(iii) Notarial acts; and

(iv) Official certificates which are placed on documents signed by persons in their private capacity, such as official certificates recording the registration of a document or the fact that it was in existence on a certain date, and official and notarial authentication of signatures.

(4) In accordance with the Convention, the following are deemed not to be public documents, and thus are subject to the more stringent requirements of § 1287.6(b) above:

(i) Documents executed by diplomatic or consular agents; and

(ii) Administrative documents dealing directly with commercial or customs operations.

(d) Canada. In any proceedings under this chapter, an official record or entry therein, issued by a Canadian governmental entity within the geographical boundaries of Canada, when admissible for any purpose, shall be evidenced by a certified copy of the original record attested by the official having legal custody of the record or by an authorized deputy.

HISTORY:

[50 FR 37834, Sept. 18, 1985, as amended at 54 FR 39337, Sept. 26, 1989; 54 FR 48851, Nov. 28, 1989; 68 FR 9824, 9845, 9846, Feb. 28, 2003]

PART 1292

REPRESENTATION AND APPEARANCES

In General

AUTHORITY NOTE APPLICABLE TO ENTIRE PART:

AUTHORITY:

8 U.S.C. 1103, 1362.

IN GENERAL

§ 1292.1 Representation of others.

(a) A person entitled to representation may be represented by any of the following:

(1) Attorneys in the United States. Any attorney as defined in § 1001.1(f) of this chapter and who, once the registration requirements in paragraph (f) of this section have taken effect, is registered to practice with the Executive Office for Immigration Review.

(2) Law students and law graduates not yet admitted to the bar. A law student who is enrolled in an accredited U.S. law school, or a graduate of an accredited U.S. law school who is not yet admitted to the bar, provided that:

(i) He or she is appearing at the request of the person entitled to representation;

(ii) In the case of a law student, he or she has filed a statement that he or she is participating, under the direct supervision of an EOIR-registered licensed attorney or accredited representative, in a legal aid program or clinic conducted by a law school or non-profit organization, and that he or she is without direct or indirect remuneration from the alien he or she represents;

(iii) In the case of a law graduate, he or she has filed a statement that he or she is appearing under the supervision of an EOIR-registered licensed attorney or accredited representative and that he or she is appearing without direct or indirect remuneration from the alien he or she represents;

(iv) When the law student or law graduate appears before the immigration court or the Board of Immigration Appeals, the law student or law graduate is supervised by an attorney or accredited representative who must appear simultaneously at the same hearing. The accompanying attorney or accredited representative must be authorized to practice before EOIR and be prepared to proceed with the case at all times; and

(v) All filings by law students and law graduates are made through an EOIR-registered attorney or accredited representative.

(3) Reputable individuals. Any reputable individual of good moral character, provided that:

(i) He is appearing on an individual case basis, at the request of the person entitled to representation;

(ii) He is appearing without direct or indirect remuneration and files a written declaration to that effect;

(iii) He has a pre-existing relationship or connection with the person entitled to representation (e.g., as a relative, neighbor, clergyman, business associate or personal friend), provided that such requirement may be waived, as a matter of administrative discretion, in cases where adequate representation would not otherwise be available; and

(iv) His appearance is permitted by the official before whom he wished to appear (namely, a special inquiry officer, district director, officer-in-charge, regional commissioner, the Commissioner, or the Board), provided that such permission shall not be granted with respect to any individual who regularly engages in immigration and naturalization practice or preparation, or holds himself out to the public as qualified to do so.

(4) Accredited representative. An individual whom EOIR has authorized to represent immigration clients on behalf of a recognized organization, and whose period of accreditation is current and has not expired. A partially accredited representative is authorized to practice solely before DHS. A fully accredited representative is authorized to practice before DHS, and upon registration, to practice before the Immigration Courts and the Board.

(5) Accredited officials. An accredited official, in the United States, of the government to which an alien owes allegiance, if the official appears solely in his official capacity and with the alien's consent.

(b) Persons formerly authorized to practice. A person, other than a representative of an organization described in § 1292.2 of this chapter, who on December 23, 1952, was authorized to practice before the Board and the Service may continue to act as a representative, subject to the provisions of § 1292.3 of this chapter.

(c) Former employees. No person previously employed by the Department of Justice shall be permitted to act as a representative in any case in violation of the provisions of 28 CFR 45.735-7.

(d) Amicus curiae. The Board may grant permission to appear, on a case-by-case basis, as amicus curiae, to an attorney or to an organization represented by an attorney, if the public interest will be served thereby.

(e) Except as set forth in this section, no other person or persons shall represent others in any case.

(f) Registration requirement for attorneys and accredited representatives. The Director or his designee is authorized to register, and establish procedures for registering, attorneys and accredited representatives, specified in paragraph (a) of this section, as a condition of practice before immigration judges or the Board of Immigration Appeals. Such registration procedures will include a requirement for electronic registration and that each registrant validate his or her identity by presenting photo identification. The Director or his designee may administratively suspend from practice before the immigration judges and the Board any attorney or accredited representative who fails to provide the following required registration information: name, business address(es), business telephone number(s), date of birth, email address, bar admission information (if applicable), and recognized organization (if applicable), or who, after having provided that information, fails to present photo identification or comply with any other validation requirements implemented by the Director. After such a system has been established, an immigration judge may, under extraordinary and rare circumstances, permit an unregistered attorney or accredited representative to appear at one hearing if the immigration judge first acquires from the attorney or accredited representative, on the record, the required registration information. An unregistered attorney or accredited representative who is permitted to appear at a hearing in such circumstances must complete the electronic registration process without delay after the hearing at which he or she is permitted to appear.

HISTORY:

[40 FR 23271, May 29. 1975, as amended at 53 FR 7728, Mar. 10, 1988; 55 FR 49251, Nov. 27, 1990; 61 FR 53609, 53610, Oct. 15, 1996; 62 FR 23634, 23635, May 1, 1997; 68 FR 9824, 9845, 9846, Feb. 28, 2003; 68 FR 10349, 10360, Mar. 5, 2003; 73 FR 76914, 76927, Dec. 18, 2008; 78 FR 19400, 19408, Apr. 1, 2013; 81 FR 92346, 92367, Dec. 19, 2016; 86 FR 70708, 70725, Dec. 13, 2021]

§ 1292.2 [This section was removed and reserved. See 81 FR 92346, 92367, Dec. 19, 2016.]

[NO TEXT IN ORIGINAL]

HISTORY:

[40 FR 23272, May 29, 1975, as amended at 49 FR 44086, Nov. 2, 1984; 62 FR 9071, 9075, Feb. 28, 1997; 68 FR 9824, 9845, 9846, Feb. 28, 2003]

AUTHORITY:

(8 U.S.C. 1103, 1252b, 1362; 6 U.S.C. 521, 522.)

§ 1292.3 Conduct for practitioners and recognized organizations — rules and procedures.

Practitioners, as defined in § 1003.101(b) of this chapter, and recognized organizations are subject to the imposition of sanctions as provided in 8 CFR part 1003, subpart G, § 1003.101 et seq., and 8 CFR 292.3 (pertaining to practice before DHS).

HISTORY:

[23 FR 2672, Apr. 23, 1958, as amended at 23 FR 9124, Nov. 26, 1958; 34 FR 12213, July 24, 1969; 36 FR 11903, June 23, 1971; 52 FR 24981, July 2, 1987; 57 FR 11574, Apr. 6, 1992; 60 FR 34090, June 30, 1995; 65 FR 39513, 39531, June 27, 2000; 68 FR 9824, 9845, Feb. 28, 2003; 68 FR 10349, 10360, Mar. 5, 2003; 77 FR 2011, 2015, Jan. 13, 2012, as confirmed at 78 FR 24669, 24670, Apr. 26, 2013; 81 FR 92346, 92367, Dec. 19, 2016]

§ 1292.4 Appearances.

(a) An appearance shall be filed on the appropriate form by the attorney or representative appearing in each case. During Immigration Judge or Board proceedings, withdrawal and/or substitution of counsel is permitted only in accordance with §§ 1003.16 and 1003.36 respectively. During proceedings before the Service, substitution may be permitted upon the written withdrawal of the attorney or representative of record, or upon notification of the new attorney or representative. When an appearance is made by a person acting in a representative capacity, his or her personal appearance or signature shall constitute a representation that under the provisions of this chapter he or she is authorized and qualified to represent. Further proof of authority to act in a representative capacity may be required. A notice of appearance entered in application or petition proceedings must be signed by the applicant or petitioner to authorize representation in order for the appearance to be recognized by the Service.

(b) Availability of records. During the time a case is pending, and except as otherwise provided in § 103.2(b) of 8 CFR chapter I, a party to a proceeding or his attorney or representative shall be permitted to examine the record of proceeding in a Service office. He may, in conformity with § 103.10 of 8 CFR chapter I, obtain copies of Service records or information therefrom and copies of documents or transcripts of evidence furnished by him. Upon request, he may in addition, be loaned a copy of the testimony and exhibits contained in the record of proceeding upon giving his receipt for such copies and pledging that it will be surrendered upon final disposition of the case or upon demand. If extra copies of exhibits do not exist, they shall not be furnished free on loan; however, they shall be made available for copying or purchase of copies as provided in § 103.10 of 8 CFR chapter I.

HISTORY:

[23 FR 2673, Apr. 23, 1958, as amended at 32 FR 9633, July 4, 1967; 52 FR 2941, Jan. 29, 1987; 59 FR 1466, Jan. 1, 1994; 68 FR 9824, 9845, Feb. 28, 2003; 68 FR 10349, 10360, Mar. 5, 2003]

§ 1292.5 Service upon and action by attorney or representative of record.

(a) Representative capacity. Whenever a person is required by any of the provisions of this chapter to give or be given notice; to serve or be served with any paper other than a warrant of arrest or a subpoena; to make a motion; to file or submit an application or other document; or to perform or waive the performance of any act, such notice, service, motion, filing, submission, performance, or waiver shall be given by or to, served by or upon, made by, or requested of the attorney or representative of record, or the person himself if unrepresented.

(b) Right to representation. Whenever an examination is provided for in this chapter, the person involved shall have the right to be represented by an attorney or representative who shall be permitted to examine or cross-examine such person and witnesses, to introduce evidence, to make objections which shall be stated succinctly and entered on the record, and to submit briefs. Provided, that nothing in this paragraph shall be construed to provide any applicant for admission in either primary or secondary inspection the right to representation, unless the applicant for admission has become the focus of a criminal investigation and has been taken into custody.

HISTORY:

[37 FR 11471, June 8, 1972 and 45 FR 81733, Dec. 12, 1980; 46 FR 2025, Jan. 8, 1981; 58 FR 49911, Sept. 24, 1993, as confirmed at 60 FR 6650; 68 FR 9824, 9845, Feb. 28, 2003]

§ 1292.6 Interpretation.

Interpretations of §§ 1292.1 through 1292.6 will be made by the Board, subject to the provisions of part 1003 of this chapter. Interpretations of §§ 1292.11 through 1292.20 will be made by the Assistant Director for Policy (or the Assistant Director for Policy's delegate) or the Director.

HISTORY:

[32 FR 9633, July 4, 1967; 68 FR 9824, 9845, Feb. 28, 2003; 68 FR 10349, 10360, Mar. 5, 2003; 81 FR 92346, 92367, Dec. 19, 2016; 84 FR 44537, 44542, Aug. 26, 2019; as confirmed at 85 FR 69465, Nov. 3, 2020; 85 FR 69465, 69482, Nov. 3, 2020]

RECOGNITION OF ORGANIZATIONS AND ACCREDITATION OF NON-ATTORNEY REPRESENTATIVES

§ 1292.11 Recognition of an organization.

(a) In general. The Assistant Director for Policy (or the Assistant Director for Policy's delegate), in the exercise of discretion, may recognize an eligible organization to provide representation through accredited representatives who appear on behalf of clients before the Immigration Courts, the Board, and DHS, or DHS alone. The Assistant Director for Policy (or the Assistant Director for Policy's delegate) will determine whether an organization is eligible for recognition. To be eligible for recognition, the organization must establish that:

(1) The organization is a non-profit religious, charitable, social service, or similar organization that provides immigration legal services primarily to low-income and indigent clients within the United States, and, if the organization charges fees, has a written policy for accommodating clients unable to pay fees for immigration legal services;

(2) The organization is a Federal tax-exempt organization established in the United States;

(3) The organization is simultaneously applying to have at least one employee or volunteer of the organization approved as an accredited representative by the Assistant Director for Policy (or the Assistant Director for Policy's delegate) and at least one application for accreditation is concurrently approved, unless the organization is seeking renewal of recognition and has an accredited representative or is seeking renewal of recognition on inactive status as described in § 1292.16(i);

(4) The organization has access to adequate knowledge, information, and experience in all aspects of immigration law and procedure; and

(5) The organization has designated an authorized officer to act on behalf of the organization.

(b) Proof of status as non-profit religious, charitable, social service, or similar organization established in the United States and service to low-income and indigent clients. The organization must submit: A copy of its organizing documents, including a statement of its mission or purpose; a declaration from its authorized officer attesting that it serves primarily low-income and indigent clients; a summary of the legal services to be provided; if it charges fees for legal services, fee schedules and organizational policies or guidance regarding fee waivers or reduced fees based on financial need; and its annual budget. The organization may also submit additional documentation to demonstrate non-profit status and service to primarily low-income and indigent individuals, such as reports prepared for funders or information about other free or low-cost immigration-related services that it provides (e.g., educational or outreach events).

(c) Annual budget. The organization must submit its annual budget for providing immigration legal services for the current year and, if available, its annual budget for providing immigration legal services for the prior year. If the annual budgets for both the current and prior years are unavailable, the organization must submit its projected annual budget for the upcoming year. The annual budget should describe how the organization is funded and include information about the organization's operating expenses and sources of revenue for providing immigration legal services. Sources of revenue may include, but are not limited to, grants, fees, donations, or dues.

(d) Proof of tax-exempt status. The organization must submit a copy of its currently valid IRS tax-exemption determination letter, alternative documentation to establish Federal tax-exempt status, or proof that is has applied for Federal tax-exempt status.

(e) Proof of knowledge, information, and experience. The organization must submit: A description of the immigration legal services that the organization seeks to offer; a description of the legal resources to which the organization has access; an organizational chart showing names, titles, and supervisors of immigration legal staff members; a description of the qualifications, experience, and breadth of immigration knowledge of these staff members, including, but not limited to resumes, letters of recommendation, certifications, and a list of all relevant, formal immigration-related trainings attended by staff members; and any agreement or proof of a formal arrangement entered into with non-staff immigration practitioners and recognized organizations for consultations or technical legal assistance.

(f) Validity period of recognition. Recognition is valid for a period of six years from the date of the Assistant Director for Policy's (or the Assistant Director for Policy's delegate's) approval of recognition, unless the organization has been granted conditional recognition. Conditional recognition is granted to an organization that has not been recognized previously, that has Federal tax-exempt status pending, or that has been approved for recognition after recognition was previously terminated pursuant to § 1292.17 or 8 CFR 1003.101 et seq. Conditional recognition is valid for two years from the date of the Assistant Director for Policy's (or the Assistant Director for Policy's delegate's) approval of conditional recognition. Any organization's recognition is subject to being terminated pursuant to § 1292.17 or upon the issuance of disciplinary sanctions (termination or revocation) under 8 CFR 1003.101 et seq.

HISTORY:

[81 FR 92346, 92367, Dec. 19, 2016; 84 FR 44537, 44542, Aug. 26, 2019; as confirmed at 85 FR 69465, Nov. 3, 2020]

§ 1292.12 Accreditation of representatives.

(a) In general. Only recognized organizations, or organizations simultaneously applying for recognition, may request accreditation of individuals. The Assistant Director for Policy (or the Assistant Director for Policy's delegate), in the exercise of discretion, may approve accreditation of an eligible individual as a representative of a recognized organization for either full or partial accreditation. An individual who receives full accreditation may represent clients before the Immigration Courts, the Board, and DHS. An individual who receives partial accreditation may represent clients only before DHS. In the request for accreditation, the organization must specify whether it seeks full or partial accreditation and establish eligibility for accreditation for the individual. To establish eligibility for accreditation, an organization must demonstrate that the individual for whom the organization seeks accreditation:

(1) Has the character and fitness to represent clients before the Immigration Courts and the Board, or DHS, or before all three authorities. Character and fitness includes, but is not limited to, an examination of factors such as: Criminal background; prior acts involving

dishonesty, fraud, deceit, or misrepresentation; past history of neglecting professional, financial, or legal obligations; and current immigration status that presents an actual or perceived conflict of interest;

(2) Is employed by or is a volunteer of the organization;

(3) Is not an attorney as defined in 8 CFR 1001.1(f);

(4) Has not resigned while a disciplinary investigation or proceeding is pending and is not subject to any order disbarring, suspending, enjoining, restraining, or otherwise restricting the individual in the practice of law or representation before a court or any administrative agency;

(5) Has not been found guilty of, or pleaded guilty or nolo contendere to, a serious crime, as defined in 8 CFR 1003.102(h), in any court of the United States, or of any State, possession, territory, commonwealth, or the District of Columbia, or of a jurisdiction outside of the United States; and

(6) Possesses broad knowledge and adequate experience in immigration law and procedure. If an organization seeks full accreditation for an individual, it must establish that the individual also possesses skills essential for effective litigation.

(b) Request for accreditation. To establish that an individual satisfies the requirements of paragraph (a) of this section, the organization must submit a request for accreditation (Form EOIR-31A and supporting documents). The request for accreditation must be signed by the authorized officer and the individual to be accredited, both attesting that the individual satisfies these requirements.

(c) Proof of knowledge and experience. To establish that the individual satisfies the requirement in paragraph (a)(6) of this section, the organization must submit with its request for accreditation, at minimum: A description of the individual's qualifications, including education and immigration law experience; letters of recommendation from at least two persons familiar with the individual's qualifications; and documentation of all relevant, formal immigration-related training, including a course on the fundamentals of immigration law, procedure, and practice. An organization must also submit documentation that an individual for whom the organization seeks full accreditation has formal training, education, or experience related to trial and appellate advocacy.

(d) Validity period of accreditation. Accreditation is valid for a period of three years from the date of the Assistant Director for Policy's (or the Assistant Director for Policy's delegate's) approval of accreditation, unless the organization's recognition or the representative's accreditation is terminated pursuant to § 1292.17 or the organization or the representative is subject to disciplinary sanctions (termination, revocation, suspension, or disbarment) under 8 CFR 1003.101 et seq.

(e) Change in accreditation. An organization may request to change the accreditation of a representative from partial to full accreditation at any time during the validity period of accreditation or at renewal. Such a request will be treated as a new, initial request for full accreditation and must comply with this section.

HISTORY:

[81 FR 92346, 92367, Dec. 19, 2016; 84 FR 44537, 44542, Aug. 26, 2019; as confirmed at 85 FR 69465, Nov. 3, 2020]

§ 1292.13 Applying for recognition of organizations or accreditation of representatives.

(a) In general. An organization applying for recognition or accreditation of a representative must submit a request for recognition (Form EOIR-31) or a request for accreditation (Form EOIR-31A) to the Assistant Director for Policy (or the Assistant Director for Policy's delegate) with proof of service of a copy of the request on the appropriate USCIS office(s) in the jurisdictions where the organization offers or intends to offer immigration legal services. An organization must submit a separate request for accreditation (Form EOIR-31A) for each individual for whom it seeks accreditation. To determine whether an organization has established eligibility for recognition or accreditation of a representative, the Assistant Director for Policy (or the Assistant Director for Policy's delegate) shall review all information contained in the request for recognition or accreditation and may review any publicly available information or any other information that OLAP may obtain or possess about the organization, its authorized officer, or the proposed representative or may have received pursuant to paragraphs (b), (c), and (d) of this section. Unfavorable information obtained by the Assistant Director for Policy (or the Assistant Director for Policy's delegate) that may be relied upon to disapprove a recognition or accreditation request, if not previously served on the organization, shall be disclosed to the organization, and the organization shall be given a reasonable opportunity to respond. Prior to determining whether to approve or disapprove a request for recognition or accreditation, the Assistant Director for Policy (or the Assistant Director for Policy's delegate) may request additional information from the organization pertaining to the eligibility requirements for recognition or accreditation. The Assistant Director for Policy (or the Assistant Director for Policy's delegate), in writing, shall inform the organization and each USCIS office in the jurisdictions where the organization offers or intends to offer immigration legal services of the determination approving or disapproving the organization's request for recognition or accreditation of a representative. The Assistant Director for Policy (or the Assistant Director for Policy's delegate) may, in the exercise of discretion, extend the deadlines provided in this section. The Assistant Director for Policy (or the Assistant Director for Policy's delegate) is authorized to allow requests, notifications, recommendations, and determinations described in this section to be made electronically.

(b) USCIS recommendation and investigation. Within 30 days from the date of service of the request for recognition or accreditation, the USCIS office served with the request may submit to the Assistant Director for Policy (or the Assistant Director for Policy's delegate) a recommendation for approval or disapproval of the request for recognition or accreditation, including an explanation for the recommendation, or may request from the Assistant Director for Policy (or the Assistant Director for Policy's delegate) a specified period of additional time, generally no more than 30 days, in which to conduct an investigation or otherwise obtain relevant information regarding the organization, its authorized officer, or any individual for whom the organization seeks accreditation. The Assistant Director for Policy (or the Assistant Director for Policy's delegate) shall inform the organization if the Assistant Director for Policy (or the Assistant Director for Policy's delegate) grants a request from USCIS for additional time to conduct an investigation, or if, in the exercise of discretion, the Assistant Director for Policy (or the Assistant Director for Policy's delegate) has requested that USCIS conduct an investigation of the organization, its authorized officer, or any individual for whom the organization seeks accreditation. USCIS must submit any recommendation with proof of service of a copy of the recommendation on the organization. Within 30 days of service of an unfavorable recommendation, the organization may file with the Assistant Director for Policy (or the Assistant Director for Policy's delegate) a response to the unfavorable recommendation, along with proof of service of a copy of such response on the USCIS office that provided the recommendation.

(c) ICE recommendation. Upon receipt of a request for recognition or accreditation, the Assistant Director for Policy (or the Assistant Director for Policy's delegate) may request a recommendation or information from ICE in the jurisdictions where the organization offers or intends to offer immigration legal services regarding the organization, its authorized officer, or any individual for whom the organization seeks accreditation. Within 30 days from the date of receipt of the Assistant Director for Policy (or the Assistant Director for Policy's delegate's) request, ICE may make a recommendation or disclose information regarding the organization, its authorized officer, or individuals for whom the organization seeks accreditation. ICE must submit any recommendation with proof of service of a copy of the recommendation on the organization. Within 30 days of service of an unfavorable recommendation, the organization may file with the Assistant Director for Policy (or the Assistant Director for Policy's delegate) a response to the unfavorable recommendation, along with proof of service of a copy of such response on the ICE office that provided the recommendation. The Assistant Director for Policy (or the Assistant Director for Policy's delegate), in writing, shall inform ICE of the determination approving or disapproving the organization's request for recognition or accreditation of a representative.

(d) EOIR investigation. Upon receipt of a request for recognition or accreditation, the Assistant Director for Policy (or the Assistant Director for Policy's delegate) may request that the EOIR disciplinary counsel or anti-fraud officer conduct an investigation into the organization, its authorized officer, or any individual for whom the organization seeks accreditation. Within 30 days from the date of receipt of the Assistant Director for Policy (or the Assistant Director for Policy's delegate's) request, the EOIR disciplinary counsel or anti-fraud officer may disclose to the Assistant Director for Policy (or the Assistant Director for Policy's delegate) information, including complaints, preliminary inquiries, warning letters, and admonitions, relating to the organization, its authorized officer, or any individual for whom the organization seeks accreditation.

(e) Finality of decision. The Assistant Director for Policy (or the Assistant Director for Policy's delegate's) determination to approve a request for recognition or accreditation is final. An organization whose request for recognition or accreditation was disapproved may make one request for reconsideration of the disapproval within 30 days of the determination. An organization whose request for recognition or accreditation was disapproved, or whose request for reconsideration after disapproval and, if applicable, request for administrative review pursuant to § 1292.18 was denied, may submit a new request for recognition or accreditation at any time unless otherwise prohibited.

HISTORY:

[81 FR 92346, 92367, Dec. 19, 2016; 84 FR 44537, 44542, Aug. 26, 2019; as confirmed at 85 FR 69465, Nov. 3, 2020]

§ 1292.14 Reporting, recordkeeping, and posting requirements for recognized organizations.

(a) Duty to report changes. A recognized organization has a duty to promptly notify the Assistant Director for Policy (or the Assistant Director for Policy's delegate) in writing or electronically of changes in the organization's contact information, changes to any material information the organization provided in Form EOIR-31, Form EOIR-31A, or the documents submitted in support thereof, or changes that otherwise materially relate to the organization's eligibility for recognition or the eligibility for accreditation of any of the organization's accredited representatives. These changes may include alterations to: The organization's name, address, telephone number, Web site address, email address, or the designation of the authorized officer of the organization; an accredited representative's name or employment or volunteer status with the organization; and the organization's structure, including a merger of organizations that have already been individually accorded recognition, or a change in nonprofit or Federal tax-exempt status.

(b) Recordkeeping. A recognized organization must compile each of the following records in a timely manner, and retain them for a period of six years from the date the record is created, as long as the organization remains recognized:

(1) The organization's immigration legal services fee schedule, if the organization charges any fees for immigration legal services, for each office or location where such services are provided; and

(2) An annual summary of immigration legal services provided by the organization, which includes: The total number of clients served (whether through client intakes, applications prepared and filed with DHS, cases in which its attorneys or accredited representa-

tives appeared before the Immigration Courts or, if applicable, the Board, or referrals to attorneys or other organizations) and clients to whom it provided services at no cost; a general description of the immigration legal services and other immigration-related services (e.g., educational or outreach events) provided; a statement regarding whether services were provided pro bono or clients were charged in accordance with a fee schedule and organizational policies or guidance regarding fee waivers and reduced fees; and a list of the offices or locations where the immigration legal services were provided. The summary should not include any client-specific or client-identifying information. OLAP may require the organization to submit such records to it or DHS upon request.

(c) Posting. The Assistant Director for Policy (or the Assistant Director for Policy's delegate) shall have the authority to issue public notices regarding recognition and accreditation and to require recognized organizations and accredited representatives to post such public notices. Information contained in the public notices shall be limited to: The names and validity periods of a recognized organization and its accredited representatives, the requirements for recognition and accreditation, and the means to complain about a recognized organization or accredited representative.

HISTORY:

[81 FR 92346, 92367, Dec. 19, 2016; 84 FR 44537, 44542, Aug. 26, 2019; as confirmed at 85 FR 69465, Nov. 3, 2020]

§ 1292.15 Extension of recognition and accreditation to multiple offices or locations of an organization.

Upon approving an initial request for recognition or a request for renewal of recognition, or at any other time, the Assistant Director for Policy (or the Assistant Director for Policy's delegate), in the Assistant Director for Policy (or the Assistant Director for Policy's delegate's) discretion, may extend the recognition of an organization to any office or location where the organization offers services. To request extension of recognition, an organization that is seeking or has received recognition must submit a Form EOIR-31 that identifies the name and address of the organization's headquarters or designated office and the name and address of each other office or location for which the organization seeks extension of recognition. The organization must also provide a declaration from its authorized officer attesting that it periodically conducts inspections of each such office or location, exercises supervision and control over its accredited representatives at those offices and locations, and provides access to adequate legal resources at each such office or location. OLAP may require an organization to seek separate recognition for an office or location of the organization, for example, when a subordinate office or location has distinct operations, management structure, or funding sources from the organization's headquarters. The Assistant Director for Policy (or the Assistant Director for Policy's delegate's) determination to extend recognition to the offices or locations identified in Form EOIR-31 permits the organization's accredited representatives to provide immigration legal services out of those offices or locations. OLAP will post the address of each office or location to which recognition has been extended on the roster of recognized organizations and accredited representatives. The Assistant Director for Policy (or the Assistant Director for Policy's delegate) is authorized to allow requests and determinations described in this section to be made electronically.

HISTORY:

[81 FR 92346, 92367, Dec. 19, 2016; 84 FR 44537, 44542, Aug. 26, 2019; as confirmed at 85 FR 69465, Nov. 3, 2020]

§ 1292.16 Renewal of recognition and accreditation.

(a) In general. To retain its recognition and the accreditation of its representatives after the conclusion of the validity period specified in § 1292.11(f) or § 1292.12(d), an organization must submit a request for renewal of its recognition or the accreditation of its representatives (Form EOIR-31, Form EOIR-31A, and supporting documents). In the exercise of discretion, as provided in paragraph (i) of this section, the Assistant Director for Policy (or the Assistant Director for Policy's delegate) may approve an organization's request for renewal of recognition without a currently approved accredited representative.

(b) Timing of renewal —

(1) Recognition. An organization requesting renewal of recognition must submit the request on or before the sixth anniversary date of the organization's last approval or renewal of recognition or, for a conditionally recognized organization, on or before the second anniversary of the approval date of the conditional recognition. Any request must include proof of service of a copy of the request on the appropriate USCIS office(s) in the jurisdictions where the organization offers or intends to offer immigration legal services.

(2) Accreditation. An organization requesting renewal of accreditation of its representative must submit the request on or before the third anniversary date of the representative's last approval or renewal of accreditation, with proof of service of a copy of the request on the appropriate USCIS office(s) in the jurisdictions where the organization offers or intends to offer immigration legal services.

(3) The Assistant Director for Policy (or the Assistant Director for Policy's delegate), in the Assistant Director for Policy (or the Assistant Director for Policy's delegate's) discretion, may grant additional time to submit a request for renewal or accept a request for renewal filed out of time. The recognition of the organization and the accreditation of any representatives for whom the organization timely requests renewal shall remain valid pending the Assistant Director for Policy (or the Assistant Director for Policy's delegate's) consideration of the renewal requests, except in the case of an interim suspension pursuant to 8 CFR 1003.111.

(c) Renewal requirements —

(1) Recognition. The request for renewal of recognition must establish that the organization remains eligible for recognition under § 1292.11(a), include the records specified in § 1292.14(b) regarding fee schedules and the summary of immigration legal services provided that the organization compiled since the last approval of recognition, and describe any unreported changes that impact eligibility for recognition from the date of the last approval of recognition.

(2) Accreditation. Each request for renewal of accreditation must establish that the individual remains eligible for accreditation under § 1292.12(a) and has continued to receive formal training in immigration law and procedure commensurate with the services the organization provides and the duration of the representative's accreditation.

(d) Recommendations and investigations. Each USCIS office served with a request for renewal of recognition or a request for renewal of accreditation may submit to the Assistant Director for Policy (or the Assistant Director for Policy's delegate) a recommendation for approval or disapproval of that request pursuant to § 1292.13(b). The Assistant Director for Policy (or the Assistant Director for Policy's delegate) may request a recommendation from ICE or an investigation from the EOIR disciplinary counsel or anti-fraud officer, pursuant to § 1292.13(c) and (d).

(e) Renewal process. The Assistant Director for Policy (or the Assistant Director for Policy's delegate) shall review all information contained in the requests and may review any publicly available information or any other information that OLAP may possess about the organization, its authorized officer, or any individual for whom the organization seeks accreditation or renewal of accreditation or that OLAP may have received pursuant to § 1292.13(b) through (d). Unfavorable information obtained by the Assistant Director for Policy (or the Assistant Director for Policy's delegate) that may be relied upon to disapprove a recognition or accreditation request, if not previously served on the organization, shall be disclosed to the organization, and the organization shall be given a reasonable opportunity to respond. Prior to determining whether to approve or disapprove a request for renewal of recognition or accreditation, the Assistant Director for Policy (or the Assistant Director for Policy's delegate) may request additional information from the organization pertaining to the eligibility requirements for recognition or accreditation. The Assistant Director for Policy (or the Assistant Director for Policy's delegate), in writing, shall inform the organization and the appropriate DHS office(s) in the jurisdictions where the organization offers or intends to offer immigration legal services of the determination to approve or disapprove a request for renewal of recognition. If the Assistant Director for Policy (or the Assistant Director for Policy's delegate) renews recognition, the Assistant Director for Policy (or the Assistant Director for Policy's delegate) shall issue a written determination approving or disapproving each request for accreditation or renewal of accreditation. The Assistant Director for Policy (or the Assistant Director for Policy's delegate) is authorized to allow requests, notifications, recommendations, and determinations described in this section to be made electronically.

(f) Finality of decision. The Assistant Director for Policy (or the Assistant Director for Policy's delegate's) determination to approve a request to renew recognition or accreditation is final. An organization whose request for renewal of recognition or accreditation of its representatives has been disapproved may make one request for reconsideration of the disapproval within 30 days of the determination. The recognition of the organization and the accreditation of any representatives for whom the organization timely requests reconsideration shall remain valid pending the Assistant Director for Policy (or the Assistant Director for Policy's delegate's) consideration of the reconsideration request, except in the case of an interim suspension pursuant to 8 CFR 1003.111. An organization whose recognition or accreditation of its representatives is terminated because the organization's request to renew recognition or accreditation is disapproved or whose request for reconsideration after disapproval and, if applicable, request for administrative review pursuant to § 1292.18 was denied, may submit a new request for recognition and accreditation at any time unless otherwise prohibited.

(g) Validity period of recognition and accreditation after renewal. After renewal of recognition, the recognition of the organization is valid for a period of six years from the date of the Assistant Director for Policy (or the Assistant Director for Policy's delegate's) determination to renew recognition, unless the organization's recognition is terminated pursuant to § 1292.17 or the organization is subject to disciplinary sanctions (i.e., termination or revocation) under 8 CFR 1003.101 et seq. After renewal of accreditation, the accreditation of a representative is valid for a period of three years from the date of the Assistant Director for Policy (or the Assistant Director for Policy's delegate's) determination to renew accreditation, unless the organization's recognition or the representative's accreditation is terminated pursuant to § 1292.17 or the organization or the representative is subject to disciplinary sanctions (termination, revocation, suspension, or disbarment) under 8 CFR 1003.101 et seq.

(h) Organizations and representatives recognized and accredited prior to January 18, 2017 —

(1) Applicability. An organization or representative that received recognition or accreditation prior to January 18, 2017, through the Board under former § 1292.2 is subject to the provisions of this part. Such an organization or representative shall continue to be recognized or accredited until the organization is required to request renewal of its recognition and accreditation of its representatives as required by paragraphs (h)(2) and (3) of this section and pending the OLAP Director's determination on the organization's request for renewal if such a request is timely made, unless the organization's recognition or the representative's accreditation is terminated pursuant to § 1292.17 or the organization or the representative is subject to disciplinary sanctions (termination, revocation, suspension, or disbarment) under 8 CFR 1003.101 et seq.

(2) Renewal of recognition. To retain its recognition, an organization that received recognition prior to January 18, 2017, must request renewal of its recognition pursuant to this section on or before the following dates:

(i) Within 1 year of January 18, 2017, if the organization does not have an accredited representative on the effective date of this regulation;

(ii) Within 2 years of January 18, 2017, if the organization is not required to submit a request for renewal at an earlier date under paragraph (h)(2)(i) of this section, and the organization has been recognized for more than 10 years as of the effective date of this regulation; or

(iii) Within 3 years of January 18, 2017, if the organization is not required to submit a request for renewal at an earlier date under paragraph (h)(2)(i) or (ii) of this section.

(3) Renewal of accreditation. To retain the accreditation of its representatives who were accredited prior to January 18, 2017, an organization must request renewal of accreditation of its representatives on or before the date that the representative's accreditation would have expired under the prior rule.

(i) Inactive status. An organization shall be placed on inactive status if it has no currently approved accredited representative, and it promptly notified OLAP that it no longer has an accredited representative, as required by § 1292.14(a). An organization on inactive status is precluded from providing immigration legal services unless it has an attorney on staff. An organization shall be on inactive status for two years from the date the organization is placed on inactive status in order for the organization to apply for and have approved the accreditation of one or more representatives. If an organization on inactive status is subject to renewal while on inactive status, the organization must request renewal of recognition at the time required for renewal. The Assistant Director for Policy (or the Assistant Director for Policy's delegate), in the Assistant Director for Policy (or the Assistant Director for Policy's delegate's) discretion, may approve a request to renew an organization's recognition without a currently approved accredited representative, provided that the organization satisfies the renewal requirements under § 1292.16(c)(1) and attests that it intends to apply for and have approved the accreditation of one or more representatives within two years from the date of renewal. An organization renewed under such circumstances shall be on inactive status for two years from the date of renewal in order for the organization to apply for and have approved the accreditation of one or more representatives. The Assistant Director for Policy (or the Assistant Director for Policy's delegate), in the Assistant Director for Policy (or the Assistant Director for Policy's delegate's) discretion, may grant an organization additional time on inactive status beyond the time limits provided in this paragraph.

HISTORY:

[81 FR 92346, 92367, Dec. 19, 2016; 84 FR 44537, 44542, Aug. 26, 2019; as confirmed at 85 FR 69465, Nov. 3, 2020]

§ 1292.17 Administrative termination of recognition and accreditation.

(a) In general. The Assistant Director for Policy (or the Assistant Director for Policy's delegate) may administratively terminate an organization's recognition or a representative's accreditation and remove the organization or representative from the recognition and accreditation roster. Prior to issuing a determination to administratively terminate recognition or accreditation, the Assistant Director for Policy (or the Assistant Director for Policy's delegate) may request, in writing or electronically, information from the organization, representative, DHS, or EOIR, regarding the bases for termination. The Assistant Director for Policy (or the Assistant Director for Policy's delegate), in writing or electronically, shall inform the organization or the representative, as applicable, of the determination to terminate the organization's recognition or the representative's accreditation, and the reasons for the determination.

(b) Bases for administrative termination of recognition. The bases for termination of recognition under this section are:

(1) An organization did not submit a request to renew its recognition at the time required for renewal;

(2) An organization's request for renewal of recognition is disapproved or request for reconsideration after disapproval and if applicable, request for administrative review pursuant to § 1292.18 is denied;

(3) All of the organization's accredited representatives have been terminated pursuant to this section or suspended or disbarred pursuant to 8 CFR 1003.101 et seq., and the organization is not on inactive status as described in § 1292.16(i);

(4) An organization submits a written request to the Assistant Director for Policy (or the Assistant Director for Policy's delegate) for termination of its recognition;

(5) An organization fails to comply with its reporting, recordkeeping, or posting requirements under § 1292.14, after being notified of the deficiencies and having an opportunity to respond;

(6) An organization fails to maintain eligibility for recognition under § 1292.11, after being notified of the deficiencies and having an opportunity to respond; or

(7) An organization on inactive status fails to have an individual approved as an accredited representative within the time provided under § 1292.16(i).

(c) Bases for administrative termination of accreditation. The bases for termination of accreditation under this section are:

(1) An individual's organization has had its recognition terminated pursuant to this section or terminated or revoked pursuant to 8 CFR 1003.101 et seq.;

(2) An organization does not submit a request for renewal of the individual's accreditation at the time required for renewal;

(3) An organization's request for renewal of an individual's accreditation is disapproved or request for reconsideration after disapproval and, if applicable, request for administrative review pursuant to § 1292.18, is denied;

(4) An accredited representative submits a written request to the Assistant Director for Policy (or the Assistant Director for Policy's delegate) for termination of the representative's accreditation;

(5) An organization submits a written request to the Assistant Director for Policy (or the Assistant Director for Policy's delegate) for termination of the accreditation of one or more of its representatives; or

(6) An individual fails to maintain eligibility for accreditation under § 1292.12, after the individual's organization has been notified of the deficiencies and has had an opportunity to respond.

(d) Request for reconsideration. An organization whose recognition is terminated pursuant to paragraph (b)(5) or (6) of this section or the accreditation of its representative(s) is terminated pursuant to paragraph (c)(6) of this section may make one request for reconsideration of the disapproval within 30 days of the determination. The recognition of the organization and the accreditation of any representatives for whom the organization timely requests reconsideration shall remain valid pending the Assistant Director for Policy (or the Assistant Director for Policy's delegate's) consideration of the reconsideration request. The Assistant Director for Policy (or the Assistant Director for Policy's delegate) is authorized to allow requests and determinations described in this paragraph to be made electronically.

(e) Effect of administrative termination of recognition. The Assistant Director for Policy (or the Assistant Director for Policy's delegate's) determination to terminate recognition is final as of the date of service of the administrative termination notice. Upon service or electronic delivery of an administrative termination of recognition notice to the organization's accredited representatives by OLAP, the organization's representatives shall no longer be authorized to represent clients before the Immigration Courts, the Board, or DHS on behalf of that organization, but the notice shall not affect an individual's accreditation through another recognized organization unless otherwise specified. An organization whose recognition is terminated may submit a new request for recognition at any time after its termination unless otherwise prohibited.

(f) Effect of administrative termination of accreditation. The Assistant Director for Policy (or the Assistant Director for Policy's delegate's) determination to terminate accreditation is final as of the date of service of the administrative termination notice. Upon service or electronic delivery of an administrative termination of accreditation notice to an accredited representative by OLAP, the individual shall no longer be authorized to represent clients before the Immigration Courts, the Board, or DHS on behalf of that organization, but the notice does not affect the individual's accreditation through another organization unless specified in the determination. An organization may submit a request for accreditation on behalf of any individual whose accreditation has been terminated unless otherwise prohibited.

HISTORY:

[81 FR 92346, 92367, Dec. 19, 2016; 84 FR 44537, 44542, Aug. 26, 2019; as confirmed at 85 FR 69465, Nov. 3, 2020]

§ 1292.18 Administrative review of denied requests for reconsideration.

(a) Authority of the Director. The Director has the discretionary authority to review a request for reconsideration pursuant to § 1292.13(e), § 1292.16(f), or § 1292.17(d) that has been denied.

(1) An organization whose request for reconsideration pursuant to § 1292.13(e), § 1292.16(f), or § 1292.17(d) has been denied may request administrative review from the Director within ten (10) days of the denial, identifying the alleged factual or legal errors in the underlying determination. The request for administrative review shall be submitted to the Assistant Director for Policy (or the Assistant Director for Policy's delegate), who will forward the request to the Director.

(2) The Director may review a request for reconsideration pursuant to § 1292.13(e), § 1292.16(f), or § 1292.17(d) that has been denied on the Director's own initiative by issuing a notification of administrative review within ten (10) days of the denial. This notification shall state the issues to be reviewed.

(3) The recognition of the organization and the accreditation of any representatives that are subject to administrative review as described in this section shall remain valid pending the Director's consideration of the request, except in the case of an interim suspension pursuant to 8 CFR 1003.111.

(b) Review. The Director shall review the record before OLAP and the organization's request for administrative review, and, in the Director's discretion, may request additional filings from the organization. The Director may affirm the denial of the request for reconsideration or vacate the denial and return the matter to the Assistant Director for Policy (or the Assistant Director for Policy's delegate) for further action consistent with the Director's determination. The Director may not approve a request for recognition or accreditation or renewal thereof.

(c) Referral of cases to the Attorney General. The Director will refer to the Attorney General for review of decisions pursuant to this section in all cases that the Attorney General directs the Director to refer to him or that the Director believes should be referred to him.

(d) Decisions as precedents. The Director, in his discretion, may cause reconsideration decisions by the Assistant Director for Policy (or the Assistant Director for Policy's delegate) pursuant to § 1292.13(e), § 1292.16(f), or § 1292.17(d), or decisions by the Director pursuant to this section to be published as precedents in the same manner as decisions of the Board and the Attorney General. Such decisions by the Assistant Director for Policy (or the Assistant Director for Policy's delegate), except as overruled by the Director, and such decisions by the Director, except as overruled by the Attorney General, will serve as precedents in all proceedings under part 1292 involving the same issue or issues.

HISTORY:

[81 FR 92346, 92367, Dec. 19, 2016; 84 FR 31463, 31470, July 2, 2019; 84 FR 44537, 44542, Aug. 26, 2019; as confirmed at 85 FR 69465, Nov. 3, 2020; 85 FR 69465, 69482, Nov. 3, 2020]

§ 1292.19 Complaints against recognized organizations and accredited representatives.

(a) Filing complaints. Any individual may submit a complaint to EOIR or DHS that a recognized organization or accredited representative has engaged in behavior that is a ground of termination or otherwise contrary to the public interest. Complaints must be submitted in writing or on Form EOIR-44 to the EOIR disciplinary counsel or DHS disciplinary counsel and must state in detail the information that supports the basis for the complaint, including, but not limited to: The name and address of each complainant; the name and address of each recognized organization and accredited representative that is a subject of the complaint; the nature of the conduct or behavior; the individuals involved; and any other relevant information. EOIR disciplinary counsel and DHS disciplinary counsel shall notify each other of any complaint that pertains, in whole or in part, to a matter involving the other agency. EOIR may authorize that complaints submitted to the EOIR disciplinary counsel may be made electronically.

(b) Preliminary inquiry. Upon receipt of the complaint, the EOIR disciplinary counsel shall initiate a preliminary inquiry. If a complaint is filed by a client or former client of a recognized organization or any of its accredited representatives, the complainant waives the attorney-client privilege and any other privilege relating to the representation to the extent necessary to conduct a preliminary inquiry and any subsequent proceedings based thereon. If the EOIR disciplinary counsel determines that a complaint is without merit, no further action will be taken. The EOIR disciplinary counsel may also, in the disciplinary counsel's discretion, dismiss a complaint if the complainant fails to comply with reasonable requests for information or documentation. If the EOIR disciplinary counsel determines that a complaint has merit, the EOIR disciplinary counsel may disclose information concerning the complaint or the preliminary inquiry to the Assistant Director for Policy (or the Assistant Director for Policy's delegate) pursuant to 8 CFR 1003.108(a)(3) or initiate disciplinary proceedings through the filing of a Notice of Intent to Discipline pursuant to 8 CFR 1003.105. If a complaint involves allegations that a recognized organization or accredited representative engaged in criminal conduct, the EOIR disciplinary counsel shall refer the matter to DHS or the appropriate United States Attorney, and if appropriate, to the Inspector General, the Federal Bureau of Investigation, or other law enforcement agency.

HISTORY:

[81 FR 92346, 92367, Dec. 19, 2016; 84 FR 44537, 44542, Aug. 26, 2019; as confirmed at 85 FR 69465, Nov. 3, 2020]

§ 1292.20 Roster of recognized organizations and accredited representatives.

The Assistant Director for Policy (or the Assistant Director for Policy's delegate) shall maintain a roster of recognized organizations and their accredited representatives. An electronic copy of the roster shall be made available to the public and updated periodically.

HISTORY:

[81 FR 92346, 92367, Dec. 19, 2016; 84 FR 44537, 44542, Aug. 26, 2019; as confirmed at 85 FR 69465, Nov. 3, 2020]

SUBCHAPTER C

NATIONALITY REGULATIONS

PART 1299

IMMIGRATION REVIEW FORMS

AUTHORITY NOTE APPLICABLE TO ENTIRE PART:

AUTHORITY:

8 U.S.C. 1103, 1252, 1429, 1443; Homeland Security Act of 2002, Pub. L. 107-296.

§ 1299.1 Use of immigration forms.

In addition to forms prepared by the Executive Office for Immigration Review, the Executive Office for Immigration Review, immigration judges, the Board of Immigration Appeals, and administrative law judges use forms listed under 8 CFR chapter I, part 299.

HISTORY:

[68 FR 9824, 9845, Feb. 28, 2003]

§ 1299.2 Specific immigration review forms.

The Director of the Executive Office for Immigration Review may designate the specific version of a form listed in 8 CFR chapter I, part 299, which shall be utilized in filings before the immigration judges, the Board of Immigration Appeals, and administrative law judges.

HISTORY:

[68 FR 9824, 9845, Feb. 28, 2003]

PART 1337
OATH OF ALLEGIANCE

AUTHORITY NOTE APPLICABLE TO ENTIRE PART:

AUTHORITY:
8 U.S.C. 1103, 1443, 1448; 8 CFR part 2.

§ 1337.1 Oath of allegiance.

(a) Form of oath. Except as otherwise provided in the Act and after receiving notice from the district director that such applicant is eligible for naturalization pursuant to § 335.3 of 8 CFR chapter I, an applicant for naturalization shall, before being admitted to citizenship, take in a public ceremony held within the United States the following oath of allegiance, to a copy of which the applicant shall affix his or her signature:

I hereby declare, on oath, that I absolutely and entirely renounce and abjure all allegiance and fidelity to any foreign prince, potentate, state, or sovereignty, of whom or which I have heretofore been a subject or citizen; that I will support and defend the Constitution and laws of the United States of America against all enemies, foreign and domestic; that I will bear true faith and allegiance to the same; that I will bear arms on behalf of the United States when required by the law; that I will perform noncombatant service in the Armed Forces of the United States when required by the law; that I will perform work of national importance under civilian direction when required by the law; and that I take this obligation freely, without any mental reservation or purpose of evasion; so help me God.

(b) Alteration of form of oath; affirmation in lieu of oath. In those cases in which a petitioner or applicant for naturalization is exempt from taking the oath prescribed in paragraph (a) of this section in its entirety, the inapplicable clauses shall be deleted and the oath shall be taken in such altered form. When a petitioner or applicant for naturalization, by reason of religious training and belief (or individual interpretation thereof), or for other reasons of good conscience, cannot take the oath prescribed in paragraph (a) of this section with the words "on oath" and "so help me God" included, the words "and solemnly affirm" shall be substituted for the words "on oath," the words "so help me God" shall be deleted, and the oath shall be taken in such modified form. Any reference to 'oath of allegiance' in 8 CFR chapter I is understood to mean equally 'affirmation of allegiance' as described in this paragraph.

(c) Obligations of oath. A petitioner or applicant for naturalization shall, before being naturalized, establish that it is his or her intention, in good faith, to assume and discharge the obligations of the oath of allegiance, and that his or her attitude toward the Constitution and laws of the United States renders him or her capable of fulfilling the obligations of such oath.

(d) Renunciation of title or order of nobility. A petitioner or applicant for naturalization who has borne any hereditary title or has been of any of the orders of nobility in any foreign state shall, in addition to taking the oath of allegiance prescribed in paragraph (a) of this section, make under oath or affirmation in public an express renunciation of such title or order of nobility, in the following form:

(1) I further renounce the title of (give title or titles) which I have heretofore held; or

(2) I further renounce the order of nobility (give the order of nobility) to which I have heretofore belonged.

HISTORY:
[22 FR 9824, Dec. 6, 1957, as amended at 24 FR 2584, Apr. 3, 1959; 32 FR 13756, Oct. 3, 1967; 56 FR 50499, Oct. 7, 1991, as confirmed at 60 FR 6650, Feb. 3, 1995; 68 FR 9824, 9845, Feb. 28, 2003; 68 FR 10349, 10360, Mar. 5, 2003]

§ 1337.2 Oath administered by the Immigration and Naturalization Service or an Immigration Judge.

(a) Public ceremony. An applicant for naturalization who has elected to have his or her oath of allegiance administered by the Service or an Immigration Judge and is not subject to the exclusive oath administration authority of an eligible court pursuant to section 310(b) of the Act shall appear in person in a public ceremony, unless such appearance is specifically excused under the terms and conditions set forth in this part. Such ceremony shall be held at a time and place designated by the Service or the Executive Office for Immigration Review within the United States and within the jurisdiction where the application for naturalization was filed, or into which the application for naturalization was transferred pursuant to § 335.9 of 8 CFR chapter I. Such ceremonies shall be conducted at regular intervals as frequently as necessary to ensure timely naturalization, but in all events at least once monthly where it is required to minimize unreasonable delays. Such ceremonies shall be presented in such a manner as to preserve the dignity and significance of the occasion. District directors shall ensure that ceremonies conducted by the Service in their districts, inclusive of those held by suboffice managers, are in keeping with the Model Plan for Naturalization Ceremonies. Organizations traditionally involved in activities surrounding the ceremony should be encouraged to participate in Service-administered ceremonies by local arrangement.

(b) Authority to administer oath of allegiance. The authority of the Attorney General to administer the oath of allegiance shall be delegated to Immigration Judges and to the following officers of the Service: The Commissioner; district directors; deputy district directors; officers-in-charge; assistant officers-in-charge; or persons acting in behalf of such officers due to their absence or because their positions are vacant. In exceptional cases where the district director or officer-in-charge determines that it is appropriate for employees of a different rank to conduct ceremonies, the district director or officer-in-charge may make a request through the Commissioner to the Assistant Commissioner, Adjudications, for permission to delegate such authority. The request shall furnish the reasons for seeking exemption from the requirements of this paragraph. The Commissioner may delegate such authority to such other officers of the Service or the Department of Justice as he or she may deem appropriate.

(c) Execution of questionnaire. Immediately prior to being administered the oath of allegiance, each applicant shall complete the questionnaire on Form N-445. Each completed Form N-445 shall be reviewed by an officer of the Service who may question the applicant regarding the information thereon. If derogatory information is revealed, the applicant's name shall be removed from the list of eligible persons as provided in § 335.5 of 8 CFR chapter I and he or she shall not be administered the oath.

HISTORY:

[56 FR 50500, Oct. 7, 1993, as confirmed at 60 FR 6650, Feb. 3, 1995; 58 FR 49915, Sept. 24, 1993, as confirmed at 60 FR 6650, Feb. 3, 1995; 60 FR 37803, July 24, 1995; 68 FR 9824, 9845, Feb. 28, 2003; 68 FR 10349, 10360, Mar. 5, 2003]

§ 1337.3 Expedited administration of oath of allegiance.

(a) An applicant may be granted an expedited oath administration ceremony by either the court or the Service upon demonstrating sufficient cause. In determining whether to grant an expedited oath administration ceremony, the court or the district director shall consider special circumstances of a compelling or humanitarian nature. Special circumstances may include but are not limited to:

(1) The serious illness of the applicant or a member of the applicant's family;

(2) Permanent disability of the applicant sufficiently incapacitating as to prevent the applicant's personal appearance at a scheduled ceremony;

(3) The developmental disability or advanced age of the applicant which would make appearance at a scheduled ceremony inapproriate; or

(4) Urgent or compelling circumstances relating to travel or employment determined by the court or the Service to be sufficiently meritorious to warrant special consideration.

(b) Courts exercising exclusive authority may either hold an expedited oath administration ceremony or refer the applicant to the Service in order for either the Immigration Judge or the Service to conduct an oath administration ceremony, if an expedited judicial oath administration ceremony is impractical. The court shall inform the district director in writing of its decision to grant the applicant an expedited oath administration ceremony and that the court has relinquished exclusive jurisdiction as to that applicant.

(c) All requests for expedited administration of the oath of allegiance shall be made in writing to either the court or the Service. Such requests shall contain sufficient information to substantiate the claim of special circumstances to permit either the court or the Service to properly exercise the discretionary authority to grant the relief sought. The court or the Service may seek verification of the validity of the information provided in the request. If the applicant submits a written request to the Service, but is awaiting an oath administration ceremony by a court pursuant to § 1337.8, the Service promptly shall provide the court with a copy of the request without reaching a decision on whether to grant or deny the request.

HISTORY:

[56 FR 50500, Oct. 7, 1991, as confirmed and revised at 60 FR 6650, 6651, Feb. 3, 1995; 58 FR 49915, Sept. 24, 1993, as confirmed and revised at 60 FR 6650, 6651, Feb. 3, 1995; 60 FR 37804, July 24, 1995; 68 FR 9824, 9845, 9846, Feb. 28, 2003]

§ 1337.4 When requests for change of name granted.

When the court has granted the petitioner's change of name request, the petitioner shall subscribe his or her new name to the written oath of allegiance.

HISTORY:

[56 FR 50500, Oct. 7, 1991, as confirmed at 60 FR 6650, Feb. 3, 1995; 68 FR 9824, 9845, Feb. 28, 2003]

§§ 1337.5 — 1337.6 [Reserved]

[NO TEXT IN ORIGINAL]

HISTORY:

[NO SOURCE IN ORIGINAL]

AUTHORITY:

(8 U.S.C. 1103, 1443, 1448; 8 CFR part 2.)

§ 1337.7 Information and assignment of individuals under exclusive jurisdiction.

(a) No later than at the time of the examination on the application pursuant to § 335.2 of 8 CFR chapter I, an employee of the Service shall advise the applicant of his or her right to elect the site for the administration of the oath of allegiance, subject to the exclusive jurisdiction provision of § 310.3(d) of 8 CFR chapter I. In order to assist the applicant in making an informed decision, the Service shall advise the applicant of the upcoming Immigration Judge or Service conducted and judicial ceremonies at which the applicant may appear, if found eligible for naturalization.

(b) An applicant whose application has been approved by the Service who is subject to the exclusive jurisdiction of a court pursuant to § 310.2(d) of 8 CFR chapter I, shall be advised of the next available court ceremony and provided with a written notice to appear at that ceremony. If the applicant is subject to the exclusive jurisdiction of more than one court exercising exclusive jurisdiction, the applicant will be informed of the upcoming ceremonies in each affected court. The applicant shall decide which court he or she wishes to administer the oath of allegiance.

HISTORY:

[58 FR 49915, Sept. 24, 1993, as confirmed at 60 FR 6650, Feb. 3, 1995; 60 FR 37804, July 24, 1995; 68 FR 9824, 9845, Feb. 28, 2003; 68 FR 10349, 10360, Mar. 5, 2003]

§ 1337.8 Oath administered by the courts.

(a) Notification of election. An applicant for naturalization not subject to the exclusive jurisdiction of § 310.2(d) of 8 CFR chapter I shall notify the Service at the time of the filing of, or no later than at the examination on, the application of his or her election to have the oath of allegiance administered in an appropriate court having jurisdiction over the applicant's place of residence.

(b) **Certification of eligibility —**

(1) Exclusive jurisdiction. In those instances falling within the exclusive jurisdiction provision of section 310(b)(1)(B) of the Act, the Service shall notify the court of the applicant's eligibility for admission to United States citizenship by submitting to the clerk of court Form N-646 within ten (10) days of the approval of the application.

(2) Non-exclusive jurisdiction. In those instances in which the applicant has elected to have the oath administered in a court ceremony, the Service shall notify the clerk of court, in writing, using Form N-646, that the applicant has been determined by the Attorney General to be eligible for admission to United States citizenship upon taking the requisite oath of allegiance and renunciation in a public ceremony. If a scheduled hearing date is not available at the time of the notification, Form N-646 shall indicate that the applicant has not been scheduled for a ceremony and the applicant shall be informed in writing that the application has been approved but no ceremony date is yet available.

(c) **Preparation of lists.**

(1) At or prior to the oath administration ceremony the representative attending the ceremony shall submit to the court on Form N-647, in duplicate, lists of persons to be administered the oath of allegiance and renunciation. After the ceremony, and after any required amendments and notations have been made therein, the clerk of court shall sign the lists.

(2) The originals of all court lists specified in this section shall be filed permanently in the court, and the duplicates returned by the clerk of court to the appropriate Service office for retention by such office. The same disposition shall be made of any list presented to, but not approved by, the court.

(d) Personal representation of the government at oath administration ceremonies. An oath administration ceremony shall be attended by a representative of the Service, who shall review each applicant's completed questionnaire Form N-445. If necessary, the Service representative shall question the applicant regarding the information thereon. If the questioning reveals derogatory information, the applicant's name shall be removed from the list of eligible persons as provided in § 335.5 of 8 CFR chapter I and the court shall not administer the oath to such applicant.

(e) Written report in lieu of personal representation. If it is impracticable for a Service representative to be present at a judicial oath administration ceremony, written notice of that fact shall be given by the Service to the court. The applicants to be administered the oath shall be listed on the appropriate forms prescribed in paragraph (d) of this section. The forms, memoranda, and certificates of naturalization shall be transmitted to the clerk of court, who shall submit the appropriate lists to the court.

(f) Withdrawal from court. An applicant for naturalization not subject to the exclusive jurisdiction of § 310.3(d) of 8 CFR chapter I, who has elected to have the oath administered in a court oath ceremony, may, for good cause shown, request that his or her name be removed from the list of persons eligible to be administered the oath at a court oath ceremony and request that the oath be administered in a ceremony conducted by an Immigration Judge or the Service. Such request shall be in writing to the Service office which granted the application and shall cite the reasons for the request. The district director or officer-in-charge shall consider the good cause shown and the best interests of the applicant in making a decision. If it is determined that the applicant shall be permitted to withdraw his or her name from the court ceremony, the Service shall give written notice to the court of the applicant's withdrawal, and the applicant shall be scheduled for the next available oath ceremony, conducted by an Immigration Judge or the Service, as if he or she had never elected the court ceremony.

HISTORY:

[56 FR 50500, Oct. 7, 1991, as confirmed at 60 FR 6650, Feb. 3, 1995; 58 FR 49914, Sept. 24, 1993, as confirmed at 60 FR 6650, Feb. 3, 1995; 60 FR 37804, July 24, 1995; 68 FR 9824, 9845, Feb. 28, 2003; 68 FR 10349, 10360, Mar. 5, 2003]

§ 1337.9 Effective date of naturalization.

(a) An applicant for naturalization shall be deemed a citizen of the United States as of the date on which the applicant takes the prescribed oath of allegiance, administered either by the Service or an Immigration Judge in an administrative ceremony or in a ceremony conducted by an appropriate court under § 1337.8 of 8 CFR chapter I.

(b) [Reserved]

HISTORY:

[56 FR 50500, Oct. 7, 1991, as confirmed at 60 FR 6650, Feb. 3, 1995; 60 FR 37804, July 24, 1995, 66 FR 32138, 32147, June 13, 2001; 68 FR 9824, 9845, 9846, Feb. 28, 2003; 68 FR 10349, 10360, Mar. 5, 2003]

§ 1337.10 Failure to appear for oath administration ceremony.

An applicant who fails to appear without good cause for more than one oath administration ceremony for which he or she was duly notified shall be presumed to have abandoned his or her intent to be naturalized. Such presumption shall be regarded as the receipt of derogatory information, and the procedures contained in § 335.5 of 8 CFR chapter I shall be followed.

HISTORY:

[58 FR 49916, Sept. 24, 1993, as confirmed at 60 FR 6650, Feb. 3, 1995; 68 FR 9824, 9845, Feb. 28, 2003; 68 FR 10349, 10360, Mar. 5, 2003]

TITLE 22

FOREIGN RELATIONS

(Selected Chapter)

CHAPTER I

DEPARTMENT OF STATE

SUBCHAPTER E

VISAS

PART 40

REGULATIONS PERTAINING TO BOTH NONIMMIGRANTS AND IMMIGRANTS UNDER THE IMMIGRATION AND NATIONALITY ACT, AS AMENDED

AUTHORITY NOTE APPLICABLE TO ENTIRE PART:

AUTHORITY:
8 U.S.C. 1104, 1182, 1183a, 1641

Subpart A
General Provisions

§ 40.1 Definitions.

The following definitions supplement definitions contained in the Immigration and Nationality Act (INA). As used in the regulations in parts 40, 41, 42, 43 and 45 of this subchapter, the term:

(a)(1) Accompanying or accompanied by means not only an alien in the physical company of a principal alien but also an alien who is issued an immigrant visa within 6 months of:

(i) The date of issuance of a visa to the principal alien;

(ii) The date of adjustment of status in the United States of the principal alien; or

(iii) The date on which the principal alien personally appears and registers before a consular officer abroad to confer alternate foreign state chargeability or immigrant status upon a spouse or child.

(2) An "accompanying" relative may not precede the principal alien to the United States.

(b) Act means the Immigration and Nationality Act (or INA), as amended.

(c) Competent officer, as used in INA 101(a)(26), means a "consular officer" as defined in INA 101(a)(9).

(d) Consular officer, as defined in INA 101(a)(9) includes commissioned consular officers and the Deputy Assistant Secretary for Visa Services, and such other officers as the Deputy Assistant Secretary may designate for the purpose of issuing nonimmigrant and immigrant visas, but does not include a consular agent, an attache or an assistant attache. For purposes of this regulation, the term "other officers" includes civil service visa examiners employed by the Department of State for duty at visa-issuing offices abroad, upon certification by the chief of the consular section under whose direction such examiners are employed that the examiners are qualified by knowledge and experience to perform the functions of a consular officer in the issuance or refusal of visas. The designation of visa examiners shall expire upon termination of the examiners' employment for such duty and may be terminated at any time for cause by the Deputy Assistant Secretary. The assignment by the Department of any foreign service officer to a diplomatic or consular office abroad in a position administratively designated as requiring, solely, partially, or principally, the performance of consular functions, and the initiation of a request for a consular commission, constitutes designation of the officer as a "consular officer" within the meaning of INA 101(a)(9).

(e) Department means the Department of State of the United States of America.

(f) Dependent area means a colony or other component or dependent area overseas from the governing foreign state.

(g) DHS means the Department of Homeland Security.

(h) Documentarily qualified means that the alien has reported that all the documents specified by the consular officer as sufficient to meet the requirements of INA 222(b) have been obtained, and the consular office has completed the necessary clearance procedures. This term is used only with respect to the alien's qualification to apply formally for an immigrant visa; it bears no connotation that the alien is eligible to receive a visa.

(i) Entitled to immigrant classification means that the alien:

(1) Is the beneficiary of an approved petition granting immediate relative or preference status;

(2) Has satisfied the consular officer as to entitlement to special immigrant status under INA 101(a)(27)(A) or (B);

(3) Has been selected by the annual selection system to apply under INA 203(c); or

(4) Is an alien described in § 40.51(c).

(j) Foreign state, for the purposes of alternate chargeability pursuant to INA 202(b), is not restricted to those areas to which the numerical limitation prescribed by INA 202(a) applies but includes dependent areas, as defined in this section.

(k) INA means the Immigration and Nationality Act, as amended.

(l) Make or file an application for a visa means:

(1) For a nonimmigrant visa applicant, submitting for formal adjudication by a consular officer of an electronic application, Form DS-160, signed electronically by clicking the box designated "Sign Application" in the certification section of the application or, as directed by a consular officer, a completed Form DS-156, with any required supporting documents and biometric data, as well as the requisite processing fee or evidence of the prior payment of the processing fee when such documents are received and accepted for adjudication by the consular officer.

(2) For an immigrant visa applicant, personally appearing before a consular officer and verifying by oath or affirmation the statements contained on Form DS-230 or Form DS-260 and in all supporting documents, having previously submitted all forms and documents required in advance of the appearance and paid the visa application processing fee.

(m) Native means born within the territory of a foreign state, or entitled to be charged for immigration purposes to that foreign state pursuant to INA section 202(b).

(n) Not subject to numerical limitation means that the alien is entitled to immigrant status as an immediate relative within the meaning of INA 201(b)(2)(i), or as a special immigrant within the meaning of INA 101(a)(27) (A) and (B), unless specifically subject to a limitation other than under INA 201(a), (b), or (c).

(o) Parent, father, and mother, as defined in INA 101(b)(2), are terms which are not changed in meaning if the child becomes 21 years of age or marries.

(p) Port of entry means a port or place designated by the DHS at which an alien may apply to DHS for admission into the United States.

(q) Principal alien means an alien from whom another alien derives a privilege or status under the law or regulations.

(r) Regulation means a rule which is established under the provisions of INA 104(a) and is duly published in the FEDERAL REGISTER.

(s) Son or daughter includes only a person who would have qualified as a "child" under INA 101(b)(1) if the person were under 21 and unmarried.

(t) Western Hemisphere means North America (including Central America), South America and the islands immediately adjacent thereto including the places named in INA 101(b)(5).

HISTORY:

[56 FR 30422, July 2, 1991, as amended by 56 FR 43552, Sept. 3, 1991; 59 FR 15300, Mar. 31, 1994; 61 FR 1834, 1835, Jan. 24, 1996; 64 FR 55417, 55418, Oct. 13, 1999; 65 FR 54412, 54413, Sept. 8, 2000; 71 FR 34519, 34520, June 15, 2006; 73 FR 23067, 23068, Apr. 29, 2008; 75 FR 45475, 45476, Aug. 3, 2010]

§ 40.2 Documentation of nationals.

(a) Nationals of the United States. A national of the United States shall not be issued a visa or other documentation as an alien for entry into the United States.

(b) Former Nationals of the United States. A former national of the United States who seeks to enter the United States must comply with the documentary requirements applicable to aliens under the INA.

HISTORY:

56 FR 30422, July 2, 1991.

§ 40.3 Entry into areas under U.S. administration.

An immigrant or nonimmigrant seeking to enter an area which is under U.S. administration but which is not within the "United States", as defined in INA 101(a)(38), is not required by the INA to be documented with a visa unless the authority contained in INA 215 has been invoked.

HISTORY:

56 FR 30422, July 2, 1991.

§ 40.4 Furnishing records and information from visa files for court proceedings.

Upon receipt of a request for information from a visa file or record for use in court proceedings, as contemplated in INA 222(f), the consular officer must, prior to the release of the information, submit the request together with a full report to the Department.

HISTORY:

56 FR 30422, July 2, 1991.

§ 40.5 Limitations on the use of National Crime Information Center (NCIC) criminal history information.

(a) Authorized access. The FBI's National Crime Information Center (NCIC) criminal history records are law enforcement sensitive and can only be accessed by authorized consular personnel with visa processing responsibilities.

(b) Use of information. NCIC criminal history record information shall be used solely to determine whether or not to issue a visa to an alien or to admit an alien to the United States. All third party requests for access to NCIC criminal history record information shall be referred to the FBI.

(c) Confidentiality and protection of records. To protect applicants' privacy, authorized Department personnel must secure all NCIC criminal history records, automated or otherwise, to prevent access by unauthorized persons. Such criminal history records must be destroyed, deleted or overwritten upon receipt of updated versions.

HISTORY:

[67 FR 8477, 8478, Feb. 25, 2002]

§ 40.6 Basis for refusal.

A visa can be refused only upon a ground specifically set out in the law or implementing regulations. The term "reason to believe", as used in INA 221(g), shall be considered to require a determination based upon facts or circumstances which would lead a reasonable person to conclude that the applicant is ineligible to receive a visa as provided in the INA and as implemented by the regulations. Consideration shall be given to any evidence submitted indicating that the ground for a prior refusal of a visa may no longer exist. The burden of proof is upon the applicant to establish eligibility to receive a visa under INA 212 or any other provision of law or regulation.

HISTORY:

56 FR 30422, July 2, 1991.

§§ 40.7 — 40.8 [Reserved]

[NO TEXT IN ORIGINAL]

HISTORY:

56 FR 30422, July 2, 1991.

§ 40.9 Classes of inadmissible aliens.

Subparts B through L describe classes of inadmissible aliens who are ineligible to receive visas and who shall be ineligible for admission into the United States, except as otherwise provided in the Immigration and Nationality Act, as amended.

HISTORY:

[61 FR 59182, 59184, Nov. 21, 1996]

Subpart B

Medical Grounds of Ineligibility

§ 40.11 Medical grounds of ineligibility.

(a) Decision on eligibility based on findings of medical doctor. A finding of a panel physician designated by the post in whose jurisdiction the examination is performed pursuant to INA 212(a)(1) shall be binding on the consular officer, except that the officer may refer a panel physician finding in an individual case to USPHS for review.

(b) Waiver of ineligibility — INA 212(g). If an immigrant visa applicant is inadmissible under INA 212(a)(1)(A)(i), (ii), or (iii) but is qualified to seek the benefits of INA 212(g)(1)(A) or (B), 212(g)(2)(C), or 212(g)(3), the consular officer shall inform the alien of the procedure for applying to DHS for relief under the applicable provision of law. A visa may not be issued to the alien until the consular officer has received notification from DHS of the approval of the alien's application under INA 212(g), unless the consular officer has been delegated authority by the Secretary of Homeland Security to grant the particular waiver under INA 212(g).

(c) Waiver authority — INA 212(g)(2)(A) and (B). The consular officer may waive section 212(a)(1)(A)(ii) visa ineligibility if the alien qualifies for such waiver under the provisions of INA 212(g)(2)(A) or (B).

HISTORY:

[56 FR 30422, July 2, 1991; 62 FR 67564, 67567, Dec. 29, 1997, as confirmed at 63 FR 64626, 64628, Nov. 23, 1998; 71 FR 34519, 34520, June 15, 2006]

§§ 40.12—40.19 [Reserved]

[NO TEXT IN ORIGINAL]

Subpart C

Criminal and Related Grounds — Conviction of Certain Crimes

§ 40.21 Crimes involving moral turpitude and controlled substance violators.

(a) **Crimes involving moral turpitude —**

(1) Acts must constitute a crime under criminal law of jurisdiction where they occurred. A Consular Officer may make a finding of ineligibility under INA 212(a)(2)(A)(i)(I) based upon an alien's admission of the commission of acts which constitute the essential elements of a crime involving moral turpitude, only if the acts constitute a crime under the criminal law of the jurisdiction where they occurred. However, a Consular Officer must base a determination that a crime involves moral turpitude upon the moral standards generally prevailing in the United States.

(2) Conviction for crime committed under age 18

(i) An alien will not be ineligible to receive a visa under INA 212(a)(2)(A)(i)(I) by reason of any offense committed:

(A) Prior to the alien's fifteenth birthday, or

(B) Between the alien's fifteenth and eighteenth birthdays unless such alien was tried and convicted as an adult for a felony involving violence as defined in section 1(1) and section 16 of Title 18 of the United States Code.

(ii) An alien tried and convicted as an adult for a violent felony offense, as so defined, committed after having attained the age of fifteen years, will be subject to the provisions of INA 212(a)(2)(A)(i)(I) regardless of whether at the time of conviction juvenile courts existed within the convicting jurisdiction.

(3) Two or more crimes committed under age 18. An alien convicted of a crime involving moral turpitude or admitting the commission of acts which constitute the essential elements of such a crime and who has committed an additional crime involving moral turpitude shall be ineligible under INA 212(a)(2)(A)(i)(I), even though the crimes were committed while the alien was under the age of 18 years.

(4) Conviction in absentia. A conviction in absentia of a crime involving moral turpitude does not constitute a conviction within the meaning of INA 212(a)(2)(A)(i)(I).

(5) Effect of pardon by appropriate U.S. authorities/foreign states. An alien shall not be considered ineligible under INA 212(a)(2)(A)(i)(I) by reason of a conviction of a crime involving moral turpitude for which a full and unconditional pardon has been granted by the President of the United States. A legislative pardon, a pardon by the Governor of a State of the United States, or a pardon, amnesty, expungement of penal record or any other act of clemency granted by a foreign state shall not serve to remove a ground of ineligibility under INA 212(a)(2)(A)(i)(I).

(6) Political offenses. The term "purely political offense", as used in INA 212(a)(2)(A)(i)(I), includes offenses that resulted in convictions obviously based on fabricated charges or predicated upon repressive measures against racial, religious, or political minorities.

(7) Waiver of ineligibility — INA 212(h). If an immigrant visa applicant is ineligible under INA 212(a)(2)(A)(i)(I) but is qualified to seek the benefits of INA 212(h), the consular officer shall inform the alien of the procedure for applying to DHS for relief under that provision of law. A visa may not be issued to the alien until the consular officer has received notification from DHS of the approval of the alien's application under INA 212(h).

(b) **Controlled substance violators.**

(1) Date of conviction not pertinent. An alien shall be ineligible under INA 212(a)(2)(A)(i)(II) irrespective of whether the conviction for a violation of or for conspiracy to violate any law or regulation relating to a

controlled substance, as defined in the Controlled Substance Act (21 U.S.C. 802), occurred before, on, or after October 27, 1986.

(2) Waiver of ineligibility — INA 212(h). If an immigrant visa applicant is ineligible under INA 212(a)(2)(A)(i)(II) but is qualified to seek the benefits of INA 212(h), the consular officer shall inform the alien of the procedure for applying to DHS for relief under that provision of law. A visa may not be issued to the alien until the consular officer has received notification from DHS of the approval of the alien's application under INA 212(h).

HISTORY:

[56 FR 30422, July 2, 1991; 64 FR 55417, 55418, Oct. 13, 1999; 71 FR 34519, 34520, June 15, 2006; 89 FR 67857, 67859, Aug. 22, 2024]

§ 40.22 Multiple criminal convictions.

(a) Conviction(s) for crime(s) committed under age 18. An alien shall not be ineligible to receive a visa under INA 212(a)(2)(B) by reason of any offense committed prior to the alien's fifteenth birthday. Nor shall an alien be ineligible under INA 212(a)(2)(B) by reason of any offense committed between the alien's fifteenth and eighteenth birthdays unless such alien was tried and convicted as an adult for a felony involving violence as defined in section 1(l) and section 16 of Title 18 of the United States Code. An alien, tried and convicted as an adult for a violent felony offense, as so defined, committed after having attained the age of fifteen years, and who has also been convicted of at least one other such offense or any other offense committed as an adult, shall be subject to the provisions of INA 212(a)(2)(B) regardless of whether at that time juvenile courts existed within the jurisdiction of the conviction.

(b) Conviction in absentia. A conviction in absentia shall not constitute a conviction within the meaning of INA 212(a)(2)(B).

(c) Effect of pardon by appropriate U.S. authorities/foreign states. An alien shall not be considered ineligible under INA 212(a)(2)(B) by reason in part of having been convicted of an offense for which a full and unconditional pardon has been granted by the President of the United States. A legislative pardon, a pardon by the Governor of a State of the United States, or a pardon, amnesty, expungement of penal record or any other act of clemency granted by a foreign state shall not serve to remove a ground of ineligibility under INA 212(a)(2)(B).

(d) Political offense. The term "purely political offense", as used in INA 212(a)(2)(B), includes offenses that resulted in convictions obviously based on fabricated charges or predicated upon repressive measures against racial, religious, or political minorities.

(e) Waiver of ineligibility — INA 212(h). If an immigrant visa applicant is ineligible under INA 212(a)(2)(B) but is qualified to seek the benefits of INA 212(h), the consular officer shall inform the alien of the procedure for applying to DHS for relief under that provision of law. A visa may not be issued to the alien until the consular officer has received notification from DHS of the approval of the alien's application under INA 212(h).

HISTORY:

[56 FR 30422, July 2, 1991; 62 FR 67564, 67567, Dec. 29, 1997, as confirmed at 63 FR 64626, 64628, Nov. 23, 1998; 71 FR 34519, 34520, June 15, 2006; 89 FR 67857, 67859, Aug. 22, 2024]

§ 40.23 Controlled substance traffickers. [Reserved]

[NO TEXT IN ORIGINAL]

HISTORY:

56 FR 30422, July 2, 1991.

§ 40.24 Prostitution and commercialized vice.

(a) Activities within 10 years preceding visa application. An alien shall be ineligible under INA 212(a)(2)(D) only if —

(1) The alien is coming to the United States solely, principally, or incidentally to engage in prostitution, or has engaged in prostitution, or the alien directly or indirectly procures or attempts to procure, or procured or attempted to procure or to import prostitutes or persons for the purposes of prostitution, or receives or received, in whole or in part, the proceeds of prostitution; and

(2) The alien has performed one of the activities listed in § 40.24(a)(1) within the last ten years.

(b) Prostitution defined. The term "prostitution" means engaging in promiscuous sexual intercourse for hire. A finding that an alien has "engaged" in prostitution must be based on elements of continuity and regularity, indicating a pattern of behavior or deliberate course of conduct entered into primarily for financial gain or for other considerations of material value as distinguished from the commission of casual or isolated acts.

(c) Where prostitution not illegal. An alien who is within one or more of the classes described in INA 212(a)(2)(D) is ineligible to receive a visa under that section even if the acts engaged in are not prohibited under the laws of the foreign country where the acts occurred.

(d) Waiver of ineligibility — INA 212(h). If an immigrant visa applicant is ineligible under INA 212(a)(2)(D) but is qualified to seek the benefits of INA 212(h), the consular officer shall inform the alien of the procedure for applying to DHS for relief under that provision of law. A visa may not be issued to the alien until the consular officer has received notification from DHS of the approval of the alien's application under INA 212(h).

HISTORY:

[56 FR 30422, July 2, 1991; 71 FR 34519, 34520, June 15, 2006]

§ 40.25 Certain aliens involved in serious criminal activity who have asserted immunity from prosecution. [Reserved]

[NO TEXT IN ORIGINAL]

HISTORY:
56 FR 30422, July 2, 1991.

§§ 40.26—40.29 [Reserved]

[NO TEXT IN ORIGINAL]

Subpart D

Security and Related Grounds

§ 40.31 General. [Reserved]

[NO TEXT IN ORIGINAL]

HISTORY:
56 FR 30422, July 2, 1991.

§ 40.32 Terrorist activities. [Reserved]

[NO TEXT IN ORIGINAL]

HISTORY:
56 FR 30422, July 2, 1991.

§ 40.33 Foreign policy. [Reserved]

[NO TEXT IN ORIGINAL]

HISTORY:
56 FR 30422, July 2, 1991.

§ 40.34 Immigrant membership in totalitarian party.

(a) Definition of affiliate. The term affiliate, as used in INA 212(a)(3)(D), means an oganization which is related to, or identified with, a proscribed association or party, including any section, subsidiary, branch, or subdivision thereof, in such close association as to evidence an adherence to or a furtherance of the purposes and objectives of such association or party, or as to indicate a working alliance to bring to fruition the purposes and objectives of the proscribed association or party. An organization which gives, loans, or promises support, money, or other thing of value for any purpose to any proscribed association or party is presumed to be an affiliate of such association or party, but nothing contained in this paragraph shall be construed as an exclusive definition of the term affiliate.

(b) Service in Armed Forces. Service, whether voluntary or not, in the armed forces of any country shall not be regarded, of itself, as constituting or establishing an alien's membership in, or affiliation with, any proscribed party or organization, and shall not, of itself, constitute a ground of ineligibility to receive a visa.

(c) Voluntary Service in a Political Capacity. Voluntary service in a political capacity shall constitute affiliation with the political party or organization in power at the time of such service.

(d) Voluntary Membership After Age 16. If an alien continues or continued membership in or affiliation with a proscribed organization on or after reaching 16 years of age, only the alien's activities after reaching that age shall be pertinent to a determination of whether the continuation of membership or affiliation is or was voluntary.

(e) Operation of Law Defined. The term operation of law, as used in INA 212(a)(3)(D), includes any case wherein the alien automatically, and without personal acquiescence, became a member of or affiliated with a proscribed party or organization by official act, proclamation, order, edict, or decree.

(f) Membership in Organization Advocating Totalitarian Dictatorship in the United States. In accordance with the definition of totalitarian party contained in INA 101(a)(37), a former or present voluntary member of, or an alien who was, or is, voluntarily affiliated with a noncommunist party, organization, or group, or of any section, subsidiary, branch, affiliate or subdivision thereof, which during the time of its existence did not or does not advocate the establishment in the United States of a totalitarian dictatorship, is not considered ineligible under INA 212(a)(3)(D) to receive a visa.

(g) Waiver of ineligibility — 212(a)(3)(D)(iv). If an immigrant visa applicant is ineligible under INA 212(a)(3)(D) but is qualified to seek the benefits of INA 212(a)(3)(D)(iv), the consular officer shall inform the alien of the procedure for applying to DHS for relief under that provision of law. A visa may not be issued to the alien until the consular officer has received notification from DHS of the approval of the alien's application under INA 212(a)(3)(D)(iv).

HISTORY:
[56 FR 30422, July 2, 1991; 71 FR 34519, 34520, June 15, 2006]

§ 40.35 Participants in Nazi persecutions or genocide.

(a) Participation in Nazi persecutions. [Reserved]
(b) Participation in genocide. [Reserved]

HISTORY:
56 FR 30422, July 2, 1991.

§§ 40.36—40.39 [Reserved]

[NO TEXT IN ORIGINAL]

Subpart E

Evaluation of Applicants for Accreditation and Approval

§ 40.41 Public charge.

(a) Basis for determination of ineligibility. Any determination that an alien is ineligible under INA 212(a)(4) must be predicated upon circumstances indicating that, notwithstanding any affidavit of support that may have been filed on the alien's behalf, the alien is likely to become a public charge after admission, or, if applicable, that the alien has failed to fulfill the affidavit of support requirement of INA 212(a)(4)(C).

(b) Affidavit of support. Any alien seeking an immigrant visa under INA 201(b)(2), 203(a), or 203(b), based upon a petition filed by a relative of the alien (or in the case of a petition filed under INA 203(b) by an entity in which a relative has a significant ownership interest), shall be required to present to the consular officer an affidavit of support (AOS) on a form that complies with terms and conditions established by the Secretary of Homeland Security. Petitioners for applicants at a post designated by the Deputy Assistant Secretary for Visa Services for initial review of and assistance with such an AOS will be charged a fee for such review and assistance pursuant to the Schedule of Fees for Consular Services (22 CFR 22.1).

(c) Joint sponsors. Submission of one or more additional affidavits of support by a joint sponsor/sponsors is required whenever the relative sponsor's household income and significant assets, and the immigrant's assets, do not meet the Federal poverty line requirements of INA 213A.

(d) Posting of bond. A consular officer may issue a visa to an alien who is within the purview of INA 212(a)(4) (subject to the affidavit of support requirement and attribution of sponsor's income and resources under section 213A), upon receipt of a notice from DHS of the giving of a bond or undertaking in accordance with INA 213 and INA 221(g), and provided further that the officer is satisfied that the giving of such bond or undertaking removes the likelihood that the alien will become a public charge within the meaning of this section of the law and that the alien is otherwise eligible in all respects.

(e) Prearranged employment. An immigrant visa applicant relying on an offer of prearranged employment to establish eligibility under INA 212(a)(4), other than an offer of employment certified by the Department of Labor pursuant to INA 212(a)(5)(A), must provide written confirmation of the relevant information sworn and subscribed to before a notary public by the employer or an authorized employee or agent of the employer. The signer's printed name and position or other relationship with the employer must accompany the signature.

(f) Use of Federal poverty line Where INA 213A not applicable. An immigrant visa applicant, not subject to the requirements of INA 213A, and relying solely on personal income to establish eligibility under INA 212(a)(4), who does not demonstrate an annual income above the Federal poverty line, as defined in INA 213A(h), and who is without other adequate financial resources, shall be presumed ineligible under INA 212(a)(4).

HISTORY:

[56 FR 30422, July 2, 1991; 62 FR 67563, 67564, Dec. 29, 1997, as confirmed at 64 FR 50751, 50752, Sept. 20, 1999; 65 FR 78094, Dec. 14, 2000; 71 FR 34519, 34520, June 15, 2006; 84 FR 54996, 55012, Oct. 11, 2019; 88 FR 60574, 60582, Sept. 5, 2023]

§§ 40.42—40.49 [Reserved]

[NO TEXT IN ORIGINAL]

Subpart F

Standards for Intercountry Adoption Accreditation and Approval

§ 40.51 Labor certification.

(a) INA 212(a)(5) applicable only to certain immigrant aliens. INA 212(a)(5)(A) applies only to immigrant aliens described in INA 203(b)(2) or (3) who are seeking to enter the United States for the purpose of engaging in gainful employment.

(b) Determination of need for alien's labor skills. An alien within one of the classes to which INA 212(a)(5) applies as described in § 40.51(a) who seeks to enter the United States for the purpose of engaging in gainful employment, shall be ineligible under INA 212(a)(5)(A) to receive a visa unless the Secretary of Labor has certified to the Secretary of Homeland Security and the Secretary of State, that

(1) There are not sufficient workers in the United States who are able, willing, qualified, (or equally qualified in the case of aliens who are members of the teaching profession or who have exceptional ability in the sciences or the arts) and available at the time of application for a visa and at the place to which the alien is destined to perform such skilled or unskilled labor, and

(2) The employment of such alien will not adversely affect the wages and working conditions of the workers in the United States similarly employed.

(c) Labor certification not required in certain cases. A spouse or child accompanying or following to join an alien spouse or parent who is a beneficiary of a petition approved pursuant to INA 203(b)(2) or (3) is not considered to be within the purview of INA 212(a)(5).

HISTORY:

[56 FR 30422, July 2, 1991; 61 FR 1834, 1835, Jan. 24, 1996; 71 FR 34519, 34520, June 15, 2006]

§ 40.52 Unqualified physicians.

INA 212(a)(5)(B) applies only to immigrant aliens described in INA 203(b)(2) or (3).

HISTORY:

[56 FR 30422, July 2, 1991; 61 FR 1834, 1835, Jan. 24, 1996; 62 FR 67564, 67567, Dec. 29, 1997, as confirmed at 63 FR 64626, 64628, Nov. 23, 1998]

§ 40.53 Uncertified foreign health-care workers.

(a) Subject to paragraph (b) of this section, a consular officer must not issue a visa to any alien seeking admission to the United States for the purpose of performing services in a health care occupation, other than as a physician, unless, in addition to meeting all other requirements of law and regulation, the alien provides to the officer a certification issued by the Commission On Graduates of Foreign Nursing Schools (CGFNS) or another credentialing service that has been approved by the Secretary of Homeland Security for such purpose, which certificate complies with the provisions of sections 212(a)(5)(C) and 212(r) of the Act, 8 U.S.C. 1182(a)(5)(C) and 8 U.S.C. 1182(r), respectively, and the regulations found at 8 CFR 212.15.

(b) Paragraph (a) of this section does not apply to an alien:

(1) Seeking to enter the United States in order to perform services in a non-clinical health care occupation as described in 8 CFR 212.15(b)(1); or

(2) Who is the immigrant or nonimmigrant spouse or child of a foreign health care worker and who is seeking to accompany or follow to join as a derivative applicant the principal alien to whom this section applies; or

(3) Who is applying for an immigrant or a nonimmigrant visa for any purpose other than for the purpose of seeking entry into the United States in order to perform health care services as described in 8 CFR 212.15.

HISTORY:

[67 FR 77158, 77159, Dec. 17, 2002, as confirmed at 73 FR 62197, 62198, Oct. 20, 2008; 71 FR 34519, 34520, June 15, 2006]

§§ 40.54—40.59 [Reserved]

[NO TEXT IN ORIGINAL]

Subpart G

Illegal Entrants and Immigration Violators

§ 40.61 Aliens present without admission or parole.

INA 212(a)(6)(A)(i) does not apply at the time of visa issuance.

HISTORY:

[56 FR 30422, July 2, 1991; 62 FR 67564, 67567, Dec. 29, 1997, as confirmed at 63 FR 64626, 64628, Nov. 23, 1998]

§ 40.62 Failure to attend removal proceedings.

An alien who without reasonable cause failed to attend, or to remain in attendance at, a hearing initiated on or after April 1, 1997, under INA 240 to determine inadmissibility or deportability shall be ineligible for a visa under INA 212(a)(6)(B) for five years following the alien's subsequent departure or removal from the United States.

HISTORY:

[56 FR 30422, July 2, 1991; 61 FR 1832, 1833, Jan. 24, 1996; 62 FR 67564, 67567, Dec. 29, 1997, as confirmed at 63 FR 64626, 64628, Nov. 23, 1998]

§ 40.63 Misrepresentation; Falsely claiming citizenship

(a) Fraud and misrepresentation and INA 212(a)(6)(C) applicability to certain refugees. An alien who seeks to procure, or has sought to procure, or has procured a visa, other documentation, or entry into the United States or other benefit provided under the INA by fraud or by willfully misrepresenting a material fact at any time shall be ineligible under INA 212(a)(6)(C); Provided, That the provisions of this paragraph are not applicable if the fraud or misrepresentation was committed by an alien at the time the alien sought entry into a country other than the United States or obtained travel documents as a bona fide refugee and the refugee was in fear of being repatriated to a former homeland if the facts were disclosed in connection with an application for a visa to enter the United States: Provided further, That the fraud or misrepresentation was not committed by such refugee for the purpose of evading the quota or numerical restrictions of the U.S. immigration laws, or investigation of the alien's record at the place of former residence or elsewhere in connection with an application for a visa.

(b) Misrepresentation in application under Displaced Persons Act or Refugee Relief Act. Subject to the conditions stated in INA 212(a)(6)(c)(i), an alien who is found by the consular officer to have made a willful misrepresentation within the meaning of section 10 of the Displaced Persons Act of 1948, as amended, for the purpose of gaining admission into the United States as an eligible displaced person, or to have made a material misrepresentation within the meaning of section 11(e) of the Refugee Relief Act of 1953, as amended, for the purpose of gaining admission into the United States as an alien eligible thereunder, shall be considered ineligible under the provisions of INA 212(a)(6)(C).

(c) Waiver of ineligibility — INA 212(i). If an immigrant applicant is ineligible under INA 212(a)(6)(C) but is qualified to seek the benefits of INA 212(i), the consular officer shall inform the alien of the procedure for applying to DHS for relief under that provision of law. A visa may not be issued to the alien until the consular officer has received notification from DHS of the approval of the alien's application under INA 212(i).

HISTORY:

[56 FR 30422, July 2, 1991; 61 FR 1834, 1835, Jan. 24, 1996; 61 FR 59182, 59184, Nov. 21, 1996; 71 FR 34519, 34521, June 15, 2006]

§ 40.64 Stowaways.

INA 212(a)(6)(D) is not applicable at the time of visa application.

HISTORY:

56 FR 30422, July 2, 1991.

§ 40.65 Smugglers.

(a) General. A visa shall not be issued to an alien who at any time knowingly has encouraged, induced, assisted, abetted, or aided any other alien to enter or to try to enter the United States in violation of law.

(b) Waiver of ineligibility — INA 212(d)(11). If an immigrant applicant is ineligible under INA 212(a)(6)(E) but is qualified to seek the benefits of INA 212(d)(11), the consular officer shall inform the alien of the procedure for applying to DHS for relief under that provision of law. A visa may not be issued to the alien until the consular officer has received notification from DHS of the approval of the alien's application under INA 212(d)(11).

HISTORY:

[56 FR 30422, July 2, 1991; 71 FR 34519, 34521, June 15, 2006]

§ 40.66 Subject of civil penalty.

(a) General. An alien who is the subject of a final order imposing a civil penalty for a violation under INA 274C shall be ineligible for a visa under INA 212(a)(6)(F).

(b) Waiver of ineligibility. If an applicant is ineligible under paragraph (a) of this section but appears to the consular officer to meet the prerequisites for seeking the benefits of INA 212(d)(12), the consular officer shall inform the alien of the procedure for applying to DHS for relief under that provision of law. A visa may not be issued to the alien until the consular officer has received notification from DHS of the approval of the alien's application under INA 212(d)(12).

HISTORY:

[56 FR 30422, July 2, 1991; 62 FR 67564, 67567, Dec. 29, 1997, as confirmed at 63 FR 64626, 64628, Nov. 23, 1998; 71 FR 34519, 34521, June 15, 2006]

§ 40.67 Student visa abusers.

An alien ineligible under the provisions of INA 212(a)(6)(G) shall not be issued a visa unless the alien has complied with the time limitation set forth therein.

HISTORY:

[62 FR 67564, 67568, Dec. 29, 1997, as confirmed at 63 FR 64626, 64628, Nov. 23, 1998]

§ 40.68 Aliens subject to INA 222(g).

An alien who, under the provisions of INA 222(g), has voided a nonimmigrant visa by remaining in the United States beyond the period of authorized stay is ineligible for a new nonimmigrant visa unless the alien complies with the requirements in 22 CFR 41.101 (b) or (c) regarding the place of application.

HISTORY:

[63 FR 669, 670, Jan. 7, 1998, as confirmed at 63 FR 36365, 36366, July 6, 1998]

§ 40.69 [Reserved]

[NO TEXT IN ORIGINAL]

Subpart H

Documentation Requirements

§ 40.71 Documentation requirements for immigrants.

INA 212(a)(7)(A) is not applicable at the time of visa application. (For waiver of documentary requirements for immigrants see 22 CFR 42.1 and 42.2.)

HISTORY:

56 FR 30422, July 2, 1991.

§ 40.72 Documentation requirements for nonimmigrants.

A passport which is valid indefinitely for the return of the bearer to the country whose government issued such passport shall be deemed to have the required minimum period of validity as specified in INA 212(a)(7)(B).

HISTORY:

56 FR 30422, July 2, 1991.

§§ 40.73—40.79 [Reserved]

[NO TEXT IN ORIGINAL]

Subpart I

Ineligible for Citizenship.

§ 40.81 Ineligible for citizenship.

An alien will be ineligible to receive an immigrant visa under INA 212(a)(8)(A) if the alien is ineligible for citizenship, including as provided in INA 314 or 315.

HISTORY:

[56 FR 30422, July 2, 1991; 64 FR 55417, 55418, Oct. 13, 1999]

§ 40.82 Alien who departed the United States to avoid service in the armed forces.

(a) Applicability to immigrants. INA 212(a)(8)(A) applies to immigrant visa applicants who have departed from or remained outside the United States between September 8, 1939 and September 24, 1978, to avoid or evade training or service in the United States Armed Forces.

(b) Applicability to nonimmigrants. INA 212(a)(8)(B) applies to nonimmigrant visa applicants who have departed from or remained outside the United States between September 8, 1939 and September 24, 1978 to avoid or evade training or service in the U.S. Armed Forces except an alien who held nonimmigrant status at the time of such departure.

HISTORY:

56 FR 30422, July 2, 1991.

§§ 40.83—40.89 [Reserved]

[NO TEXT IN ORIGINAL]

Subpart J

Aliens Previously Removed

§ 40.91 Certain aliens previously removed.

(a) 5-year bar. An alien who has been found inadmissible, whether as a result of a summary determination of inadmissibility at the port of entry under INA 235(b)(1) or of a finding of inadmissibility resulting from proceedings under INA 240 initiated upon the alien's arrival in the United States, shall be ineligible for a visa under INA 212(a)(9)(A)(i) for 5 years following such alien's first removal from the United States.

(b) 10-year bar. An alien who has otherwise been removed from the United States under any provision of law, or who departed while an order of removal was in effect, is ineligible for a visa under INA 212(a)(9)(A)(ii) for 10 years following such removal or departure from the United States.

(c) 20-year bar. An alien who has been removed from the United States two or more times shall be ineligible for a visa under INA 212(a)(9)(A)(i) or INA 212(a)(9)(A)(ii), as appropriate, for 20 years following the most recent such removal or departure.

(d) Permanent bar. If an alien who has been removed has also been convicted of an aggravated felony, the alien is permanently ineligible for a visa under INA 212(a)(9)(A)(i) or 212(a)(9)(A)(ii), as appropriate.

(e) Exceptions. An alien shall not be ineligible for a visa under INA 212(a)(9)(A)(i) or (ii) if the Secretary of Homeland Security has consented to the alien's application for admission.

HISTORY:

[61 FR 59182, 59184, Nov. 21, 1996; 62 FR 67564, 67568, Dec. 29, 1997, as confirmed and amended at 63 FR 64626, 64628, Nov. 23, 1998; 71 FR 34519, 34521, June 15, 2006]

§ 40.92 Aliens unlawfully present.

(a) 3-year bar. An alien described in INA 212(a)(9)(B)(i)(I) shall be ineligible for a visa for 3 years following departure from the United States.

(b) 10-year bar. An alien described in INA 212(a)(9)(B)(i)(II) shall be ineligible for a visa for 10 years following departure from the United States.

(c) Waiver. If a visa applicant is inadmissible under paragraph (a) or (b) of this section but appears to the consular officer to meet the prerequisites for seeking the benefits of INA 212(a)(9)(B)(v), the alien shall be informed of the procedure for applying to DHS for relief under that provision of law.

HISTORY:

[61 FR 59182, 59184, Nov. 21, 1996; 62 FR 67564, 67568, Dec. 29, 1997, as confirmed at 63 FR 64626, 64628, Nov. 23, 1998; 71 FR 34519, 34521, June 15, 2006]

§ 40.93 Aliens unlawfully present after previous immigration violation.

An alien described in INA 212(a)(9)(C)(i) is permanently ineligible for a visa unless the Secretary of Homeland Security consents to the alien's application for readmission not less than 10 years following the alien's last departure from the United States. Such application for readmission shall be made prior to the alien's reembarkation at a place outside the United States.

HISTORY:

[61 FR 59182, 59184, Nov. 21, 1996; 62 FR 67564, 67568, Dec. 29, 1997, as confirmed at 63 FR 64626, 64628, Nov. 23, 1998; 71 FR 34519, 34521, June 15, 2006]

§§ 40.94—40.99 [Reserved]

[NO TEXT IN ORIGINAL]

Subpart K

Miscellaneous

§ 40.101 Practicing polygamists.

An immigrant alien shall be ineligible under INA 212(a)(9)(A) only if the alien is coming to the United States to practice polygamy.

HISTORY:

[56 FR 30422, July 2, 1991; redesignated at 61 FR 59182, 59184, Nov. 21, 1996]

§ 40.102 Guardian required to accompany excluded alien.

INA 212(a)(9)(B) is not applicable at the time of visa application.

HISTORY:

[56 FR 30422, July 2, 1991; redesignated at 61 FR 59182, 59184, Nov. 21, 1996]

§ 40.103 International child abduction.

An alien who would otherwise be ineligible under INA 212(a)(9)(C)(i) shall not be ineligible under such paragraph if the U.S. citizen child in question is physically located in a foreign state which is party to the Hague Convention on the Civil Aspects of International Child Abduction.

HISTORY:

[56 FR 30422, July 2, 1991; 61 FR 1832, 1833, Jan. 24, 1996; redesignated at 61 FR 59182, 59184, Nov. 21, 1996]

§ 40.104 Unlawful voters.

(a) Subject to paragraph (b) of this section, an alien is ineligible for a visa if the alien has voted in violation of any Federal, State, or local constitutional provision, statute, ordinance, or regulation.

(b) Such alien shall not be considered to be ineligible under paragraph (a) of this section if each natural parent of the alien (or, in the case of an adopted alien, each adoptive parent of the alien) is or was a citizen (whether by birth or naturalization), the alien permanently resided in the United States prior to attaining the age of 16, and the alien reasonably believed at the time of such violation that he or she was a citizen.

HISTORY:

[61 FR 59182, 59184, Nov. 21, 1996; 62 FR 67564, 67568, Dec. 29, 1997, as confirmed at 63 FR 64626, 64628, Nov. 23, 1998; 70 FR

35526, 35527, June 21, 2005, as confirmed at 73 FR 50194, Aug. 26, 2008]

§ 40.105 Former citizens who renounced citizenship to avoid taxation.

An alien who is a former citizen of the United States, who on or after September 30, 1996, has officially renounced United States citizenship and who has been determined by the Secretary of Homeland Security to have renounced citizenship to avoid United States taxation, is ineligible for a visa under INA 212(a)(10)(E).

HISTORY:

[61 FR 59182, 59184, Nov. 21, 1996; 62 FR 67564, 67568, Dec. 29, 1997, as confirmed at 63 FR 64626, 64628, Nov. 23, 1998; 71 FR 34519, 34521, June 15, 2006]

§§ 40.106—40.110 [Reserved]

[NO TEXT IN ORIGINAL]

Subpart L

Failure to Comply with Ina

§ 40.201 Failure of application to comply with INA.

(a) Refusal under INA 221(g). The consular officer shall refuse an alien's visa application under INA 221(g)(2) as failing to comply with the provisions of INA or the implementing regulations if:

(1) The applicant fails to furnish information as required by law or regulations;

(2) The application contains a false or incorrect statement other than one which would constitute a ground of ineligibility under INA 212(a)(6)(C);

(3) The application is not supported by the documents required by law or regulations;

(4) The applicant refuses to be fingerprinted as required by regulations;

(5) The necessary fee is not paid for the issuance of the visa or, in the case of an immigrant visa, for the application therefor;

(6) In the case of an immigrant visa application, the alien fails to swear to, or affirm, the application before the consular officer; or

(7) The application otherwise fails to meet specific requirements of law or regulations for reasons for which the alien is responsible.

(b) Reconsideration of refusals. A refusal of a visa application under paragraph (a)(1) of this section does not bar reconsideration of the application upon compliance by the applicant with the requirements of INA and the implementing regulations or consideration of a subsequent application submitted by the same applicant.

HISTORY:

[56 FR 30422, July 2, 1991; 61 FR 1834, 1835, Jan. 24, 1996; redesignated at 61 FR 59182, 59184, Nov. 21, 1996]

§ 40.202 Certain former exchange visitors.

An alien who was admitted into the United States as an exchange visitor, or who acquired such status after admission, and who is within the purview of INA 212(e) as amended by the Act of April 7, 1970, (84 Stat. 116) and by the Act of October 12, 1976, (90 Stat. 2301), is not eligible to apply for or receive an immigrant visa or a nonimmigrant visa under INA 101(a)(15) (H), (K), or (L), notwithstanding the approval of a petition on the alien's behalf, unless:

(a) It has been established that the alien has resided and has been physically present in the country of the alien's nationality or last residence for an aggregate of at least 2 years following the termination of the alien's exchange visitor status as required by INA 212(e), or

(b) The foreign residence requirement of INA 212(e) has been waived by the Secretary of Homeland Security in the alien's behalf.

HISTORY:

[56 FR 30422, July 2, 1991; redesignated at 61 FR 59182, 59184, Nov. 21, 1996; 71 FR 34519, 34521, June 15, 2006]

§ 40.203 Alien entitled to A, E, or G nonimmigrant classification.

An alien entitled to nonimmigrant classification under INA 101(a)(15) (A), (E), or (G) who is applying for an immigrant visa and who intends to continue the activities required for such nonimmigrant classification in the United States is not eligible to receive an immigrant visa until the alien executes a written waiver of all rights, privileges, exemptions and immunities which would accrue by reason of such occupational status.

HISTORY:

[56 FR 30422, July 2, 1991; redesignated at 61 FR 59182, 59184, Nov. 21, 1996]

§ 40.204 [Reserved]

[NO TEXT IN ORIGINAL]

§ 40.205 Applicant for immigrant visa under INA 203(c).

An alien shall be ineligible to receive a visa under INA 203(c) if the alien does not have a high school education or its equivalent, as defined in 22 CFR 42.33(a)(2), or does not have, within the five years preceding the date of application for such visa, at least two years of work experience in an occupation which requires at least two years of training or experience.

HISTORY:

[59 FR 55045, Nov. 3, 1994; redesignated at 61 FR 59182, 59184, Nov. 21, 1996]

§ 40.206 Frivolous applications [Reserved]

[NO TEXT IN ORIGINAL]

§§ 40.207—40.210 [Reserved]

[NO TEXT IN ORIGINAL]

Subpart M

Waiver of Ground of Ineligibility

§ 40.301 Waiver for ineligible nonimmigrants under INA 212(d)(3)(A).

(a) **Recommendations under INA 212(d)(3)(A)(i).**

(1) Consular officers, on their own initiative in cases they believe meet one of the criteria in paragraphs (a)(2)(i) through (v) of this section, may submit a report to the Department for possible transmission to the designated DHS office pursuant to INA 212(d)(3)(A)(i) (8 U.S.C. 1182(d)(3)(A)(i)), in the case of an alien who is classifiable as a nonimmigrant but who the consular officer knows or believes is ineligible to receive a nonimmigrant visa due to inadmissibility under the provisions of INA 212(a) (8 U.S.C. 1182(a)), other than INA 212(a)(3)(A)(i)(I), (3)(A)(ii), (3)(A)(iii), (3)(C), (3)(E)(i), or (3)(E)(ii).

(2) In response to a request from the Secretary of State, which shall be presumed to meet one of the criteria in paragraphs (a)(2)(i) through (v) of this section, or in response to a request from a visa applicant for a case that the consular officer has reason to believe meets one of the criteria in paragraphs (a)(2)(i) through (v), consular officers are required to submit a report to the Department for possible transmission to the designated DHS office pursuant to INA 212(d)(3)(A) in the case of an alien who is classifiable as a nonimmigrant but whom the consular officer knows or believes is ineligible to receive a nonimmigrant visa due to inadmissibility under the provisions of INA 212(a), other than INA 212(a)(3)(A)(i)(I), (3)(A)(ii), (3)(A)(iii), (3)(C), (3)(E)(i), or (3)(E)(ii).

(i) Foreign Relations: Refusal of the nonimmigrant visa application would become a bilateral irritant or be raised by a foreign government with a high ranking United States government official;

(ii) National security. The nonimmigrant visa applicant's admission to the United States would advance a U.S. national security interest;

(iii) Law enforcement. The nonimmigrant visa applicant's admission to the United States would advance an important U.S. law enforcement objective;

(iv) Significant public interest. The nonimmigrant visa applicant's admission to the United States would advance a significant U.S. public interest, or

(v) Urgent humanitarian or medical reasons. The nonimmigrant visa applicant's admission to the United States may be warranted due to urgent humanitarian or medical reasons.

(b) Recommendation to designated DHS office. Consular officers may recommend directly to the designated DHS office that the alien be admitted temporarily despite his or her inadmissibility in any case where a waiver may be available, unless the consular officer has reason to believe that the applicant is inadmissible under INA 212(a)(3)(A)(i), (3)(A)(ii), (3)(A)(iii), (3)(B), (3)(C), (3)(D), (3)(E)(i), (3)(E)(ii), (3)(E)(iii), (3)(F), or (3)(G). The Department may recommend that the Secretary of Homeland Security waive ineligibility under any ground in section 212(a) of the INA, except for sections 212(a)(3)(A)(i)(I), (3)(A)(ii), (3)(A)(iii), (3)(C), (3)(E)(i), and (3)(E)(ii).

(c) Secretary of Homeland Security may impose conditions. When the Secretary of Homeland Security authorizes the temporary admission of an inadmissible alien as a nonimmigrant and the consular officer is so informed, the consular officer may proceed with the issuance of a nonimmigrant visa to the alien, subject to the conditions, if any, imposed by the Secretary of Homeland Security.

HISTORY:

[56 FR 30422, July 2, 1991; redesignated at 61 FR 59182, 59184, Nov. 21, 1996; 71 FR 34519, 34521, June 15, 2006; 75 FR 82242, 82243, Dec. 30, 2010; 84 FR 19712, 19714, May 6, 2019]

PART 41

VISAS: DOCUMENTATION OF NONIMMIGRANTS UNDER THE IMMIGRATION AND NATIONALITY ACT, AS AMENDED

Subpart F. Business and Media Visas

Rule
41.51. Treaty trader, treaty investor, or treaty alien in a specialty occupation.
41.52. Information media representative.
41.53. Temporary workers and trainees.
41.54. Intracompany transferees (executives, managers, and specialized knowledge employees)
41.55. Aliens with extraordinary ability.
41.56. Athletes, artists and entertainers.
41.57. International cultural exchange visitors.
41.58. Aliens in religious occupations.
41.59. Professionals under the United States-Mexico-Canada Agreement (USMCA).

Subpart G. Students and Exchange Visitors

41.61. Students — academic and nonacademic.
41.62. Exchange visitors.
41.63. Two-year home-country physical presence requirement.

Subpart H. Transit Aliens

41.71. Transit aliens.

Subpart I. Fiance(e)s and Other Nonimmigrants

41.81. Fiance(e) or spouse of a U.S. citizen and derivative children.
41.82. Certain parents and children of section 101(a)(27)(I) special immigrants [Reserved]
41.83. Certain Witnesses and Informants.
41.84. Victims of trafficking in persons.
41.86. Certain spouses and children of lawful permanent resident aliens.

Subpart J. Application for Nonimmigrant Visa

41.101. Place of application.
41.102. Personal appearance of applicant.
41.103. Filing an application.
41.104. Passport requirements.
41.105. Supporting documents and fingerprinting.
41.106. Processing.
41.107. Visa fees.
41.108. Medical examination.

Subpart K. Issuance of Nonimmigrant Visa

41.111. Authority to issue visa.
41.112. Validity of visa.
41.113. Procedures in issuing visas.

Subpart L. Refusals and Revocations

41.121. Refusal of nonimmigrant visas.
41.122. Revocation of visas.
41.123. Discontinuance of Granting Nonimmigrant Visa Pursuant to INA 243(d).

AUTHORITY NOTE APPLICABLE TO ENTIRE PART:

AUTHORITY:
22 U.S.C. 2651a; 8 U.S.C. 1104, 1201, 1202, 1253; 6 U.S.C. 236; Public Law 105-277, 112 Stat. 2681-795 through 2681-801; 8 U.S.C. 1185 note (section 7209 of Pub. L. 108-458, as amended by section 546 of Pub. L. 109-295).

Subpart A

Passsport and Visas Not Required for Certain Nomimmigrants

§ 41.0 Definitions.

For purposes of this part and part 53:

Adjacent islands means Bermuda and the islands located in the Caribbean Sea, except Cuba.

Cruise ship means a passenger vessel over 100 gross tons, carrying more than 12 passengers for hire, making a voyage lasting more than 24 hours any part of which is on the high seas, and for which passengers are embarked or disembarked in the United States or its territories.

Ferry means any vessel operating on a pre-determined fixed schedule and route, which is being used solely to provide transportation between places that are no more than 300 miles apart and which is being used to transport passengers, vehicles, and/or railroad cars.

Pleasure vessel means a vessel that is used exclusively for recreational or personal purposes and not to transport passengers or property for hire.

United States means "United States" as defined in section 215(c) of the Immigration and Nationality Act of 1952, as amended (8 U.S.C. 1185(c)).

U.S. citizen means a United States citizen or a U.S. non-citizen national.

United States qualifying tribal entity means a tribe, band, or other group of Native Americans formally recognized by the United States Government which agrees to meet WHTI document standards.

HISTORY:
[73 FR 18384, 18418, Apr. 3, 2008]

§ 41.1 Exemption by law or treaty from passport and visa requirements.

Nonimmigrants in the following categories are exempt from the passport and visa requirements of INA 212(a)(7)(B)(i)(I), (i)(II):

(a) Alien members of the U.S. Armed Forces. An alien member of the U.S. Armed Forces in uniform or bearing proper military identification, who has not been lawfully admitted for permanent residence, coming to the United States under official orders or permit of such Armed Forces (Sec. 284, 86 Stat. 232; 8 U.S.C. 1354).

(b) [Reserved]

(c) Aliens entering from Guam, Puerto Rico, or the Virgin Islands. An alien departing from Guam, Puerto Rico, or the Virgin Islands of the United States, and seeking to enter the continental United States or any other place under the jurisdiction of the United States (Sec. 212, 66 Stat. 188; 8 U.S.C. 1182.)

(d) Armed Services personnel of a NATO member. Personnel belonging to the armed services of a government which is a Party to the North Atlantic Treaty and which has ratified the Agreement Between the Parties to the North Atlantic Treaty Regarding the Status of

Their Forces, signed at London on June 19, 1951, and entering the United States under Article III of that Agreement pursuant to an individual or collective movement order issued by an appropriate agency of the sending state or of NATO (TIAS 2846; 4 U.S.T. 1792.)

(e) Armed Services personnel attached to a NATO headquarters in the United States. Personnel attached to a NATO Headquarters in the United States set up pursuant to the North Atlantic Treaty, belonging to the armed services of a government which is a Party to the Treaty and entering the United States in connection with their official duties under the provisions of the Protocol on the Status of International Military Headquarters Set Up Pursuant to the North Atlantic Treaty (TIAS 2978; 5 U.S.T. 875.)

(f) Aliens entering pursuant to International Boundary and Water Commission Treaty. All personnel employed either directly or indirectly on the construction, operation, or maintenance of works in the United States undertaken in accordance with the treaty concluded on February 3, 1944, between the United States and Mexico regarding the functions of the International Boundary and Water Commission, and entering the United States temporarily in connection with such employment (59 Stat. 1252; TS 994.)

HISTORY:

[52 FR 42597, Nov. 5, 1987, as amended at 56 FR 30428, July 2, 1991; 61 FR 1834, 1835, Jan. 24, 1996; 71 FR 68412, 68430, Nov. 24, 2006; 73 FR 18384, 18418, Apr. 3, 2008]

§ 41.2 Exemption or Waiver by Secretary of State and Secretary of Homeland Security of passport and/or visa requirements for certain categories of nonimmigrants.

Pursuant to the authority of the Secretary of State and the Secretary of Homeland Security under the INA, as amended, a passport and/or visa is not required for the following categories of nonimmigrants:

(a) Canadian citizens. A visa is not required for an American Indian born in Canada having at least 50 percentum of blood of the American Indian race. A visa is not required for other Canadian citizens except for those who apply for admission in E, K, V, or S nonimmigrant classifications as provided in paragraphs (k) and (m) of this section and 8 CFR 212.1. A passport is required for Canadian citizens applying for admission to the United States, except when one of the following exceptions applies:

(1) NEXUS Program. A Canadian citizen who is traveling as a participant in the NEXUS program, and who is not otherwise required to present a passport and visa as provided in paragraphs (k) and (m) of this section and 8 CFR 212.1, may present a valid NEXUS program card when using a NEXUS Air kiosk or when entering the United States from contiguous territory or adjacent islands at a land or sea port-of-entry. A Canadian citizen who enters the United States by pleasure vessel from Canada under the remote inspection system may present a NEXUS program card.

(2) FAST Program. A Canadian citizen who is traveling as a participant in the FAST program, and who is not otherwise required to present a passport and visa as provided in paragraphs (k) and (m) of this section and 8 CFR 212.1, may present a valid FAST card at a land or sea port-of-entry prior to entering the United States from contiguous territory or adjacent islands.

(3) SENTRI Program. A Canadian citizen who is traveling as a participant in the SENTRI program, and who is not otherwise required to present a passport and visa as provided in paragraphs (k) and (m) of this section and 8 CFR 212.1, may present a valid SENTRI card at a land or sea port-of-entry prior to entering the United States from contiguous territory or adjacent islands.

(4) Canadian Indians. If designated by the Secretary of Homeland Security, a Canadian citizen holder of an Indian and Northern Affairs Canada ("INAC") card issued by the Canadian Department of Indian Affairs and North Development, Director of Land and Trust Services (LTS) in conformance with security standards agreed upon by the Governments of Canada and the United States, and containing a machine readable zone, and who is arriving from Canada, may present the card prior to entering the United States at a land port-of-entry.

(5) Children. A child who is a Canadian citizen who is seeking admission to the United States when arriving from contiguous territory at a sea or land port-of-entry, may present certain other documents if the arrival meets the requirements described in either paragraph (i) or (ii) of this section.

(i) Children Under Age 16. A Canadian citizen who is under the age of 16 is permitted to present an original or a copy of his or her birth certificate, a Canadian Citizenship Card, or a Canadian Naturalization Certificate when arriving in the United States from contiguous territory at land or sea ports-of-entry.

(ii) Groups of Children Under Age 19. A Canadian citizen who is under age 19 and who is traveling with a public or private school group, religious group, social or cultural organization, or team associated with a youth sport organization may present an original or a copy of his or her birth certificate, a Canadian Citizenship Card, or a Canadian Naturalization Certificate when applying for admission to the United States from contiguous territory at all land and sea ports-of-entry, when the group, organization or team is under the supervision of an adult affiliated with the organization and when the child has parental or legal guardian consent to travel. For purposes of this paragraph, an adult is considered to be a person who is age 19 or older. The following requirements will apply:

(A) The group, organization, or team must provide to CBP upon crossing the border, on organizational letterhead:

(1) The name of the group, organization or team, and the name of the supervising adult;

(2) A trip itinerary, including the stated purpose of the trip, the location of the destination, and the length of stay;

(3) A list of the children on the trip;

(4) For each child, the primary address, primary phone number, date of birth, place of birth, and the name of at least one parent or legal guardian.

(B) The adult leading the group, organization, or team must demonstrate parental or legal guardian consent by certifying in the writing submitted in paragraph (a)(5)(ii)(A) of this section that he or she has obtained for each child the consent of at least one parent or legal guardian.

(C) The procedure described in this paragraph is limited to members of the group, organization, or team that are under age 19. Other members of the group, organization, or team must comply with other applicable document and/or inspection requirements found in this part and 8 CFR parts 212 and 235.

(6) Enhanced Driver's License Programs. Upon the designation by the Secretary of Homeland Security of an enhanced driver's license as an acceptable document to denote identity and citizenship for purposes of entering the United States, Canadian citizens may be permitted to present these documents in lieu of a passport when seeking admission to the United States according to the terms of the agreements entered between the Secretary of Homeland Security and the entity. The Secretary of Homeland Security will announce, by publication of a notice in the Federal Register, documents designated under this paragraph. A list of the documents designated under this paragraph will also be made available to the public.

(b) Citizens of the British Overseas Territory of Bermuda. A visa is not required, except for Citizens of the British Overseas Territory of Bermuda who apply for admission in E, K, V, or S nonimmigrant visa classification as provided in paragraphs (k) and (m) of this section and 8 CFR 212.1. A passport is required for Citizens of the British Overseas Territory of Bermuda applying for admission to the United States.

(c) Bahamian nationals and British subjects resident in the Bahamas. A passport is required. A visa is not required if, prior to the embarkation of such an alien for the United States on a vessel or aircraft, the examining U.S. immigration officer at Freeport or Nassau determines that the individual is clearly and beyond a doubt entitled to admission.

(d) British subjects resident in the Cayman Islands or in the Turks and Caicos Islands. A passport is required. A visa is not required if the alien arrives directly from the Cayman Islands or the Turks and Caicos Islands and presents a current certificate from the Clerk of Court of the Cayman Islands or the Turks and Caicos Islands indicating no criminal record.

(e) Nationals and residents of the British Virgin Islands.

(1) A national of the British Virgin Islands and resident therein requires a passport but not a visa if proceeding to the United States Virgin Islands.

(2) A national of the British Virgin Islands and resident therein requires a passport but does not require a visa to apply for entry into the United States if such applicant:

(i) Is proceeding by aircraft directly from St. Thomas, U.S. Virgin Islands;

(ii) Is traveling to some other part of the United States solely for the purpose of business or pleasure as described in INA 101(a)(15)(B);

(iii) Satisfies the examining U.S. Immigration officer at that port of entry that he or she is admissible in all respects other than the absence of a visa; and

(iv) Presents a current certificate issued by the Royal Virgin Islands Police Force indicating that he or she has no criminal record.

(f) Mexican nationals.

(1) A visa and a passport are not required of a Mexican national who is applying for admission from Mexico as a temporary visitor for business or pleasure at a land port-of-entry, or arriving by pleasure vessel or ferry, if the national is in possession of a Form DSP-150, B-1/B-2 Visa and Border Crossing Card, containing a machine-readable biometric identifier, issued by the Department of State.

(2) A visa and a passport are not required of a Mexican national who is applying for admission from contiguous territory or adjacent islands at a land or sea port-of-entry, if the national is a member of the Texas Band of Kickapoo Indians or Kickapoo Tribe of Oklahoma who is in possession of a Form I-872 American Indian Card issued by U.S. Citizenship and Immigration Services (USCIS).

(3) A visa is not required of a Mexican national employed as a crew member on an aircraft belonging to a Mexican company authorized to engage in commercial transportation into the United States.

(4) A visa is not required of a Mexican national bearing a Mexican diplomatic or official passport who is a military or civilian official of the Federal Government of Mexico entering the United States for a stay of up to 6 months for any purpose other than on assignment as a permanent employee to an office of the Mexican Federal Government in the United States. A visa is also not required of the official's spouse or any of the official's dependent family members under 19 years of age who hold diplomatic or official passports and are in the actual company of the official at the time of entry. This waiver does not apply to the spouse or any of the official's family members classifiable under INA 101(a)(15) (F) or (M).

(g) Natives and residents of the Trust Territory of the Pacific Islands. A visa and a passport are not required of a native and resident of the Trust Territory of the Pacific Islands who has proceeded in direct and continuous transit from the Trust Territory to the United States.

(h) [Reserved]

(i) Individual cases of unforeseen emergencies. Except as provided in paragraphs (a) through (h) and (j) through (l) of this section, all nonimmigrants are required to present a valid, unexpired visa and passport upon arrival in the United States. A nonimmigrant may apply for a waiver of the visa and passport requirement if, either prior to the nonimmigrant's embarkation abroad or upon arrival at a port of entry, the Department of Homeland Security (DHS), U.S. Customs and Border Protection (CBP) district director concludes that the nonimmigrant is unable to present the required documents because of an unforeseen emergency. The CBP district director may grant a waiver of the visa or passport requirement pursuant to INA 212(d)(4)(A), without the prior concurrence of the Department of State, if the CBP district director concludes that the nonimmigrant's claim of emergency circumstances is legitimate and that approval of the waiver would be appropriate under all of the attendant facts and circumstances.

(j) Fiance(e) of a U.S. citizen. Notwithstanding the provisions of paragraphs (a) through (h) of this section, a visa is required of an alien described in such paragraphs who is classified, or who seeks classification, under INA 101(a)(15)(K).

(k) Visa waiver program.

(1) A visa is not required of any person who seeks admission to the United States for a period of 90 days or less as a visitor for business or pleasure and who is eligible to apply for admission to the United States as a Visa Waiver Program applicant. (For the list of countries whose nationals are eligible to apply for admission to the United States as Visa Waiver Program applicants, see 8 CFR 217.2(a)).

(2) An alien denied admission under the Visa Waiver Program by virtue of a ground of inadmissibility described in INA section 212(a) that is discovered at the time of the alien's application for admission at a port of entry or through use of an automated electronic database may apply for a visa as the only means of challenging such a determination. A consular officer must accept and adjudicate any such application if the alien otherwise fulfills all of the application requirements contained in part 41, § 41.2(l)(1).

(l) Treaty Trader and Treaty Investor. Notwithstanding the provisions of paragraph (a) of this section, a visa is required of a Canadian national who is classified, or who seeks classification, under INA 101(a)(15)(E).

CFR—T.22 § 41.3

HISTORY:

[52 FR 42597, Nov. 5, 1987, as amended at 53 FR 9110, Mar. 21, 1988; 53 FR 50162, Dec. 13, 1988; 53 FR 53375, Dec. 30, 1988; 54 FR 27121, June 27, 1989; 56 FR 30428, July 2, 1991; 56 FR 46717, Sept. 13, 1991, 58 FR 40586, July 29, 1993; 58 FR 43439, Aug. 16, 1993; 59 FR 1473, Jan. 11, 1994; 60 FR 15873, Mar. 28, 1995; 61 FR 35628, 35629, July 8, 1996; 61 FR 39318, 39319, July 29, 1996; 62 FR 51030, 51031, Sept. 30, 1997, as confirmed at 64 FR 35, Jan. 4, 1999.; 63 FR 16892, 16893, Apr. 7, 1998; 64 FR 7998, 7999, Feb. 18, 1999; 64 FR 28915, 28916, May 28, 1999; 64 FR 42032, 42033, Aug. 3, 1999; 66 FR 1033, 1034, Jan. 5, 2001; 66 FR 17361, 17362, Mar. 30, 2001; 66 FR 32540, 32541, June 15, 2001; 67 FR 30546, 30547, May 7, 2002, as corrected at 67 FR 50349, Aug. 2, 2002; 68 FR 5194, 5195, Jan. 31, 2003; 68 FR 46948, 46949, Aug. 7, 2003; 71 FR 34519, 34521, June 15, 2006; 71 FR 68412, 68430, Nov. 24, 2006; 73 FR 18384, 18418, Apr. 3, 2008; 81 FR 5906, 5908, Feb. 4, 2016, as confirmed at 83 FR 31451, July 6, 2018; 82 FR 41883, 41885, Sept. 5, 2017]

§ 41.3 Waiver by joint action of consular and immigration officers of passport and/or visa requirements.

Under the authority of INA 212(d)(4), the documentary requirements of INA 212(a)(7)(B)(i)(I), (i)(II) may be waived for any alien in whose case the consular officer serving the port or place of embarkation, or the Deputy Assistant Secretary of State for Visa Services or his or her designee, is satisfied after consultation with, and concurrence by, the appropriate immigration officer, that the case falls within any of the following categories:

(a) Residents of foreign contiguous territory; visa and passport waiver. An alien residing in foreign contiguous territory who does not qualify for any waiver provided in § 41.1 and is a member of a visiting group or excursion proceeding to the United States under circumstances which make it impractical to procure a passport and visa in a timely manner.

(b) Aliens for whom passport extension facilities are unavailable; passport waiver. As alien whose passport is not valid for the period prescribed in INA 212(a)(7)(B)(i)(I) and who is embarking for the United States at a port or place remote from any establishment at which the passport could be revalidated.

(c) Aliens precluded from obtaining passport extensions by foreign government restrictions; passport waiver. An alien whose passport is not valid for the period prescribed in INA 212(a)(7)(B)(i)(I) and whose government, as a matter of policy, does not revalidate passports more than 6 months prior to expiration or until the passport expires.

(d) Emergent circumstances; visa waiver. An alien well and favorably known at the consular office, who was previously issued a nonimmigrant visa which has expired, and who is proceeding directly to the United States under emergent circumstances which preclude the timely issuance of a visa.

(e) Members of armed forces and coast guards of foreign countries; visa and passport waiver. An alien on active duty in the armed forces or coast guard of a foreign country and a member of a group of such armed forces or coast guard traveling to the United States, on behalf of the alien's government or the United Nations, under arrangements made with the appropriate military authorities of the United States, coordinated within the U.S. Government by those U.S. military authorities, and approved by the Department of State and the Department of Homeland Security for such visit.

(f) Landed immigrants in Canada; passport waiver. An alien applying for a visa at a consular office in Canada:

(1) Who is a landed immigrant in Canada;

(2) Whose port and date of expected arrival in the United States are known; and

(3) Who is proceeding to the United States under emergent circumstances which preclude the timely procurement of a passport or Canadian certificate of identity.

(g) Authorization to individual consular office; visa and/or passport waiver. An alien within the district of a consular office which has been authorized by the Department, because of unusual circumstances prevailing in that district, to join with immigration officers abroad in waivers of documentary requirements in specific categories of cases, and whose case falls within one of those categories.

HISTORY:

[52 FR 42597, Nov. 5, 1987, as amended at 56 FR 30428, July 2,

1991; 60 FR 30188, June 8, 1995; 61 FR 1834, 1835, Jan. 24, 1996; 63 FR 48577, Sept. 11, 1998; 79 FR 19288, 19289, Apr. 8, 2014]

Subpart B

Classification of Nonimmigrants

§ 41.11 Entitlement to nonimmigrant status.

(a) Presumption of immigrant status and burden of proof. An applicant for a nonimmigrant visa, other than an alien applying for a visa under INA 101(a)(15) (H)(i) or (L), shall be presumed to be an immigrant until the consular officer is satisfied that the alien is entitled to a nonimmigrant status described in INA 101(a)(15) or otherwise established by law or treaty. The burden of proof is upon the applicant to establish entitlement for nonimmigrant status and the type of nonimmigrant visa for which application is made.

(b) Aliens unable to establish nonimmigrant status.

(1) A nonimmigrant visa shall not be issued to an alien who has failed to overcome the presumption of immigrant status established by INA 214(b).

(2) In a borderline case in which an alien appears to be otherwise entitled to receive a visa under INA 101(a)(15)(B) or (F) but the consular officer concludes that the maintenance of the alien's status or the departure of the alien from the United States as required is not fully assured, a visa may nevertheless be issued upon the posting of a bond with the Secretary of Homeland Security under terms and conditions prescribed by the consular officer.

HISTORY:

[52 FR 42597, Nov. 5, 1987, as amended at 57 FR 31448, July 16, 1992; 61 FR 1834, 1835, Jan. 24, 1996; 71 FR 34519, 34521, June 15, 2006; 85 FR 74875, 74882, Nov. 24, 2020]

§ 41.12 Classification symbols.

A nonimmigrant visa issued to an applicant within one of the classes described in this section shall bear an appropriate visa symbol to show its classification. The symbol shall be inserted in the space provided on the visa. The following visa symbols shall be used:

Table 1 to § 41.12

Symbol	Class	Section of law
A1	Ambassador, Public Minister, Career Diplomat or Consular Officer, or Immediate Family	INA 101(a)(15)(A)(i).
A2	Other Foreign Government Official or Employee, or Immediate Family	INA 101(a)(15)(A)(ii).
A3	Attendant, Servant, or Personal Employee of A1 or A2, or Immediate Family	INA 101(a)(15)(A)(iii).
B1	Temporary Visitor for Business	INA 101(a)(15)(B).
B2	Temporary Visitor for Pleasure	INA 101(a)(15)(B).
B1/B2	Temporary Visitor for Business & Pleasure	INA 101(a)(15)(B).
C1	Noncitizen in Transit	INA 101(a)(15)(C).
C1/D	Combined Transit and Crewmember Visa	INA 101(a)(15)(C) and (D).
C2	Noncitizen in Transit to United Nations Headquarters District Under Sec. 11.(3), (4), or (5) of the Headquarters Agreement	INA 101(a)(15)(C).
C3	Foreign Government Official, Immediate Family, Attendant, Servant, or Personal Employee, in Transit	INA 212(d)(8).
CW1	Commonwealth of the Northern Mariana Islands—Only Transitional Worker	Section 6(d) of Public Law 94-241, as added by Section 702(a) of Public Law 110-229; 48 U.S.C. 1806(d).
CW2	Spouse or Child of CW1	Section 6(d) of Public Law 94-241, as added by Section 702(a) of Public Law 110-229; 48 U.S.C. 1806(d).
D	Crewmember (Sea or Air)	INA 101(a)(15)(D).
E1	Treaty Trader, Spouse or Child	INA 101(a)(15)(E)(i).
E2	Treaty Investor, Spouse or Child	INA 101(a)(15)(E)(ii).
E2C	Commonwealth of the Northern Mariana Islands Investor, Spouse or Child	Section 6(c) of Public Law 94-241, as added by Section 702(a) of Public Law 110-229; 48 U.S.C. 1806(d).
E3	Australian National Coming to the United States Solely to Perform Services in a Specialty Occupation	INA 101(a)(15)(E)(iii).
E3D	Spouse or Child of E3	INA 101(a)(15)(E)(iii).
E3R	Returning E3	INA 101(a)(15)(E)(iii).
F1	Student in an Academic or Language Training Program	INA 101(a)(15)(F)(i).
F2	Spouse or Child of F1	INA 101(a)(15)(F)(ii).

Table 1 to § 41.12

Symbol	Class	Section of law
F3	Canadian or Mexican National Commuter Student in an Academic or Language Training Program	INA 101(a)(15)(F)(iii).
G1	Principal Resident Representative of Recognized Foreign Government to International Organization, Staff, or Immediate Family	INA 101(a)(15)(G)(i).
G2	Other Representative of Recognized Foreign Member Government to International Organization, or Immediate Family	INA 101(a)(15)(G)(ii).
G3	Representative of Non-recognized or Nonmember Foreign Government to International Organization, or Immediate Family	INA 101(a)(15)(G)(iii).
G4	International Organization Officer or Employee, or Immediate Family	INA 101(a)(15)(G)(iv).
G5	Attendant, Servant, or Personal Employee of G1 through G4, or Immediate Family	INA 101(a)(15)(G)(v).
H1B	Temporary Worker in a Specialty Occupation	INA 101(a)(15)(H)(i)(b).
H1B1	Chilean or Singaporean Temporary Worker in a Specialty Occupation	INA 101(a)(15)(H)(i)(b1).
H1C	Registered Nurse in Health Professional Shortage Area	INA 101(a)(15)(H)(i)(c).
H2A	Temporary Worker Performing Agricultural Services	INA 101(a)(15)(H)(ii)(a).
H2B	Temporary Non-Agricultural Worker	INA 101(a)(15)(H)(ii)(b).
H3	Trainee or Special Education Exchange Visitor	INA 101(a)(15)(H)(iii).
H4	Spouse or Child of H1B, H1B1, H1C, H2A, H2B, or H3	INA 101(a)(15)(H)(iv).
I	Representative of Foreign Information Media, Spouse and Child	INA 101(a)(15)(I).
J1	Exchange Visitor	INA 101(a)(15)(J).
J2	Spouse or Child of J1	INA 101(a)(15)(J).
K1	Fiancé(e) of United States Citizen	INA 101(a)(15)(K)(i).
K2	Child of Fiancé(e) of U.S. Citizen	INA 101(a)(15)(K)(iii).
K3	Spouse of U.S. citizen awaiting availability of immigrant visa	INA 101(a)(15)(K)(ii).
K4	Child of K3	INA 101(a)(15)(K)(iii).
L1	Intracompany Transferee (Executive, Managerial, and Specialized Knowledge Personnel Continuing Employment)	INA 101(a)(15)(L).
L2	Spouse or Child of L1	INA 101(a)(15)(L).
M1	Vocational Student or Other Nonacademic Student	INA 101(a)(15)(M)(i).
M2	Spouse or Child of M1	INA 101(a)(15)(M)(ii).
M3	Canadian or Mexican National Commuter Student (Vocational Student or Other Nonacademic Student)	INA 101(a)(15)(M)(iii).
N8	Parent of an Individual Classified by DHS as SK3 or SN3	INA 101(a)(15)(N)(i).
N9	Child of N8 or of Individual Classified by DHS as SK1, SK2, SK4, SN1, SN2 or SN4	INA 101(a)(15)(N)(ii).
NATO1	Principal Permanent Representative of Member State to NATO (including any of its Subsidiary Bodies) Resident in the U.S. and Resident Members of Official Staff; Secretary General, Assistant Secretaries General, and Executive Secretary of NATO; Other Permanent NATO Officials of Similar Rank, or Immediate Family	Art. 12, 5 UST 1094; Art. 20, 5 UST 1098.

Table 1 to § 41.12

Symbol	Class	Section of law
NATO2	Other Representative of Member State to NATO (including any of its Subsidiary Bodies) including Representatives, Advisers, and Technical Experts of Delegations, or Immediate Family; Dependents of Member of a Force Entering in Accordance with the Provisions of the NATO Status-of-Forces Agreement or in Accordance with the provisions of the "Protocol on the Status of International Military Headquarters"; Members of Such a Force if Issued Visas	Art. 13, 5 UST 1094; Art. 1, 4 UST 1794; Art. 3, 4 UST 1796.
NATO3	Official Clerical Staff Accompanying Representative of Member State to NATO (including any of its Subsidiary Bodies), or Immediate Family	Art. 14, 5 UST 1096.
NATO4	Official of NATO (Other Than Those Classifiable as NATO1), or Immediate Family	Art. 18, 5 UST 1098.
NATO5	Experts, Other Than NATO Officials Classifiable Under NATO4, Employed in Missions on Behalf of NATO, and their Dependents	Art. 21, 5 UST 1100.
NATO6	Member of a Civilian Component Accompanying a Force Entering in Accordance with the Provisions of the NATO Status-of-Forces Agreement; Member of a Civilian Component Attached to or Employed by an Allied Headquarters Under the "Protocol on the Status of International Military Headquarters" Set Up Pursuant to the North Atlantic Treaty; and their Dependents	Art. 1, 4 UST 1794; Art. 3, 5 UST 877.
NATO7	Attendant, Servant, or Personal Employee of NATO1, NATO2, NATO 3, NATO4, NATO5, and NATO6 Classes, or Immediate Family	Arts. 12-20, 5 UST 1094-1098.
O1	Worker with Extraordinary Ability or Achievement in Sciences, Arts, Education, Business, or Athletics	INA 101(a)(15)(O)(i).
O2	Person Accompanying and Assisting in the Artistic or Athletic Performance by O1	INA 101(a)(15)(O)(ii).
O3	Spouse or Child of O1 or O2	INA 101(a)(15)(O)(iii).
P1	Internationally Recognized Athlete or Member of Internationally Recognized Entertainment Group	INA 101(a)(15)(P)(i).
P2	Artist or Entertainer in a Reciprocal Exchange Program	INA 101(a)(15)(P)(ii).
P3	Artist or Entertainer in a Culturally Unique Program	INA 101(a)(15)(P)(iii).
P4	Spouse or Child of P1, P2, or P3	INA 101(a)(15)(P)(iv).
Q1	Participant in an International Cultural Exchange Program	INA 101(a)(15)(Q)(i).
R1	Member of a Religious Denomination Performing Religious Work	INA 101(a)(15)(R).
R2	Spouse or Child of R1	INA 101(a)(15)(R).
S5	Person Supplying Critical Information Relating to a Criminal Organization or Enterprise	INA 101(a)(15)(S)(i).
S6	Person Supplying Critical Information Relating to Terrorism	INA 101(a)(15)(S)(ii).
S7	Qualified Family Member of S5 or S6	INA 101(a)(15)(S).
T1	Victim of a Severe Form of Trafficking in Persons	INA 101(a)(15)(T)(i).
T2	Spouse of T1	INA 101(a)(15)(T)(ii).
T3	Child of T1	INA 101(a)(15)(T)(ii).
T4	Parent of a T1 under 21 years of age; or Parent of a T1 (Any Age) Who Faces Present Danger of Retaliation	INA 101(a)(15)(T)(ii).

Table 1 to § 41.12

Symbol	Class	Section of law
T5	Unmarried Sibling under 18 years of age of a T1 Under 21 Years of Age; or Unmarried Sibling Under 18 Years of Age of a T1 (Any Age), Who Faces Present Danger of Retaliation	INA 101(a)(15)(T)(ii).
T6	Adult or Minor Child of a Derivative Beneficiary of a T1 (Any Age) Who Faces Present Danger of Retaliation	INA 101(a)(15)(T)(ii).
TN	USMCA Professional	INA 214(e)(1).
TD	Spouse or Child of TN	INA 214(e)(1).
U1	Victim of Criminal Activity	INA 101(a)(15)(U)(i).
U2	Spouse of U1	INA 101(a)(15)(U)(ii).
U3	Child of U1	INA 101(a)(15)(U)(ii).
U4	Parent of U1 Under 21 Years of Age	INA 101(a)(15)(U)(ii).
U5	Unmarried Sibling Under Age 18 of U1 Under 21 Years of Age	INA 101(a)(15)(U)(ii).
V1	Spouse of a Lawful Permanent Resident Awaiting Availability of Immigrant Visa	INA 101(a)(15)(V)(i) or INA 101(a)(15)(V)(ii).
V2	Child of a Lawful Permanent Resident Awaiting Availability of Immigrant Visa	INA 101(a)(15)(V)(i) or INA 101(a)(15)(V)(ii).
V3	Child of a V1 or V2	INA 101(a)(15)(V)(i) or INA 101 (a)(15)(V)(ii) & INA 203(d).

HISTORY:

[57 FR 31448, July 16, 1992; 60 FR 10497, Feb. 27, 1995; 61 FR 1834, 1836, Jan. 24, 1996; 63 FR 48577, 48578, Sept. 11, 1998; 65 FR 14768, 14770, Mar. 17, 2000; 65 FR 20903, 20904, Apr. 19, 2000; 66 FR 32740, 32742, June 18, 2001; 66 FR 38153, 38154, July 23, 2001; 66 FR 53711, Oct. 24, 2001; 68 FR 47460, 47461, Aug. 11, 2003; 73 FR 14926, 14929, Mar. 20, 2008; 74 FR 61517, 61519, Nov. 25, 2009; 78 FR 68992, Nov. 18, 2013; 85 FR 38320, 38321, June 26, 2020; 86 FR 61064, 61065, Nov. 5, 2021; 88 FR 45068, 45070, July 14, 2023]

Subpart C

Foreign Government Officials

§ 41.21 Foreign Officials — General.

(a) Definitions. In addition to pertinent INA definitions, the following definitions are applicable:

(1) Accredited, as used in INA 101(a)(15)(A), 101(a)(15)(G), and 212(d)(8), means an alien holding an official position, other than an honorary official position, with a government or international organization and possessing a travel document or other evidence of intention to enter or transit the United States to transact official business for that government or international organization.

(2) Attendants, as used in INA 101(a)(15)(A)(iii), 101(a)(15)(G)(v), and 212(d)(8), and in the definition of the NATO-7 visa symbol, means aliens paid from the public funds of a foreign government or from the funds of an international organization, accompanying or following to join the principal alien to whom a duty or service is owed.

(3) Immediate family, as used in INA 101(a)(15)(A), 101(a)(15)(G), and 212(d)(8), and in classification under the NATO visa symbols, means:

(i) The spouse who resides regularly in the household of the principal alien and is not a member of some other household;

(ii) Unmarried sons and daughters, whether by blood or adoption, who reside regularly in the household of the principal alien and who are not members of some other household, and provided that such unmarried sons and daughters are:

(A) Under the age of 21, or

(B) Under the age of 23 and in full-time attendance as students at post-secondary educational institutions; and

(iii) Other individuals who:

(A) Reside regularly in the household of the principal alien;

(B) Are not members of some other household;

(C) Are recognized as dependents of the principal alien by the sending government or international organization, as demonstrated by eligibility for rights and benefits, such as the issuance of a diplomatic or official passport, or travel or other allowances; and

(D) Are individually authorized by the Department.

(4) Servants and personal employees, as used in INA 101(a)(15)(A)(iii), 101(a)(15)(G)(v), and 212(d)(8), and in classification under the NATO-7 visa symbol, means aliens employed in a domestic or personal capacity by a principal alien, who are paid from the private funds of the principal alien and seek to enter the United States solely for the purpose of such employment.

(b) Exception to passport validity requirement for aliens in certain A, G, and NATO classes. A nonimmigrant alien for whom the passport requirement of INA 212(a)(7)(B)(i)(I) has not been waived and who is within one of the classes:

(1) Described in INA 101(a)(15)(A)(i) and (ii); or

(2) Described in INA 101(a)(15)(G)(i), (ii), (iii), and (iv); or

(3) NATO-1, NATO-2, NATO-3, NATO-4, or NATO-6 may present a passport which is valid only for a sufficient period to enable the alien to apply for admission at a port of entry prior to its expiration.

(c) Exception to passport validity requirement for foreign government officials in transit. An alien classified C-3 under INA 212(d)(8) needs to present only a valid unexpired visa and a travel document which is valid for entry into a foreign country for at least 30 days from the date of application for admission into the United States.

(d) **Grounds for refusal of visas applicable to certain A, C, G, and NATO classes.**

(1) An A-1 or A-2 visa may not be issued to an alien the Department has determined to be persona non grata.

(2) Only the provisions of INA 212(a) cited below apply to the indicated classes of nonimmigrant visa applicants:

(i) Class A-1: INA 212(a) (3)(A), (3)(B), and (3)(C);

(ii) Class A-2: INA 212(a) (3)(A), (3)(B), and (3)(C);

(iii) Classes C-2 and C-3: INA 212(a) (3)(A), (3)(B), (3)(C), and (7)(B);

(iv) Classes G-1, G-2, G-3, and G-4: INA 212(a) (3)(A), (3)(B), and (3)(C);

(v) Classes NATO-1, NATO-2, NATO-3, NATO-4, and NATO-6: INA 212(a) (3)(A), (3)(B), and (3)(C);

(3) An alien within class A-3 or G-5 is subject to all grounds of refusal specified in INA 212 which are applicable to nonimmigrants in general.

(4) Notwithstanding the visa restrictions imposed by applicable laws and consistent with a provision in such laws providing for a regulatory exception to the visa restrictions contained therein, a visa may be issued to a visa applicant who is otherwise ineligible for a visa under such laws:

(i) To permit the United States to comply with the United Nations Headquarters Agreement and other applicable international obligations; and

(ii) To permit the United States and Burma to operate their diplomatic missions, and to permit the United States to conduct other official United States Government business in Burma.

HISTORY:

[52 FR 42597, Nov. 5, 1987; 53 FR 9111, Mar. 21, 1988, as amended at 56 FR 30428, July 2, 1991; 63 FR 48577, 48578, Sept. 11, 1998; 73 FR 56729, Sept. 30, 2008; 74 FR 36112, 36113, July 22, 2009; 78 FR 66814, 66815, Nov. 6, 2013; 81 FR 88101, 88102, Dec. 7, 2016]

§ 41.22 Officials of foreign governments.

(a) Criteria for classification of foreign government officials. (1) An alien is classifiable A-1 or A-2 under INA section 101(a)(15)(A) (i) or (ii) if the principal alien:

(i) Has been accredited by a foreign government recognized de jure by the United States;

(ii) Intends to engage solely in official activities for that foreign government while in the United States; and

(iii) Has been accepted by the President, the Secretary of State, or a consular officer acting on behalf of the Secretary of State.

(2) A member of the immediate family of a principal alien is classifiable A-1 or A-2 under INA section 101(a)(15)(A)(i) or (ii) if the principal alien is so classified.

(b) Classification under INA section 101(a)(15)(A). An alien entitled to classification under INA section 101(a)(15)(A) shall be classified under this section even if eligible for another nonimmigrant classification. An exception may be made where an immediate family member is classifiable as A-1 or A-2 under paragraph (a)(2) of this section is also independently classifiable as a principal under INA section 101(a)(15)(G)(i), (ii), (iii), (iv) or in NATO-1 through NATO-6 classification.

(c) Classification of attendants, servants, and personal employees. An alien is classifiable as a nonimmigrant under INA 101(a)(15)(A)(iii) if the consular officer is satisfied that the alien qualifies under those provisions.

(d) Referral to the Department of special cases concerning principal alien applicants. In any case in which there is uncertainty about the applicability of these regulations to a principal alien applicant requesting such nonimmigrant status, the matter shall be immediately referred to the Department for consideration as to whether acceptance of accreditation will be granted.

(e) Change of classification to that of a foreign government official. In the case of an alien in the United States seeking a change of nonimmigrant classification under INA 248 to a classification under INA 101(a)(15)(A) (i) or (ii), the question of acceptance of accreditation is determined by the Department.

(f) Termination of status. The Department may, in its discretion, cease to recognize as entitled to classification under INA 101(a)(15)(A) (i) or (ii) any alien who has nonimmigrant status under that provision.

(g) Classification of foreign government official. A foreign government official or employee seeking to enter the United States temporarily other than as a representative or employee of a foreign government is not classifiable under the provisions of INA 101(a)(15)(A).

(h) Courier and acting courier on official business—

(1) Courier of career. An alien regularly and professionally employed as a courier by the government of the country to which the alien owes allegiance is classifiable as a nonimmigrant under INA 101(a)(15)(A)(i), if the alien is proceeding to the United States on official business for that government.

(2) Official acting as courier. An alien not regularly and professionally employed as a courier by the government of the country to which the alien owes allegiance is classifiable as a nonimmigrant under INA 101(a)(15)(A)(ii), if the alien is holding an official position and is proceeding to the United States as a courier on official business for that government.

(3) Nonofficial serving as courier. An alien serving as a courier but not regularly and professionally employed as such who holds no official position with, or is not a national of, the country whose government the alien is serving, shall be classified as a nonimmigrant under INA 101(a)(15)(B).

(i) Official of foreign government not recognized by the United States. An official of a foreign government not recognized de jure by the United States, who is proceeding to or through the United States on an official mission or to an international organization shall be classified as a nonimmigrant under INA 101(a)(15)(B), (C), or (G)(iii).

HISTORY:

[52 FR 42597, Nov. 5, 1987; 78 FR 33699, 33700, June 5, 2013, 81 FR 88101, 88103, Dec. 7, 2016]

§ 41.23 Accredited officials in transit.

An accredited official of a foreign government intending to proceed in immediate and continuous transit through the United States on official business for that government is entitled to the benefits of INA 212(d)(8) if that government grants similar privileges to officials of the United States, and is classifiable C-3 under the provisions of INA 101(a)(15)(C). Members of the immediate family, attendants, servants, or personal employees of such an official receive the same classification as the principal alien.

HISTORY:

[52 FR 42597, Nov. 5, 1987.]

§ 41.24 International organization aliens.

(a) Definition of international organization. "International organization" means:

(1) Any public international organization which has been designated by the President by Executive Order as entitled to enjoy the privileges, exemptions, and immunities provided for in the International Organizations Immunities Act (59 Stat. 669, 22 U.S.C. 288); and

(2) For the purpose of special immigrant status under INA 101(a)(27)(I), INTELSAT or any successor or separated entity thereof.

(b) **Aliens coming to international organizations.**

(1) An alien is classifiable under INA 101(a)(15)(G) if the consular officer is satisfied that the alien is within one of the classes described in that section and seeks to enter or transit the United States in pursuance of official duties. If the purpose of the entry or transit is other than pursuance of official duties, the alien is not classifiable under INA section 101(a)(15)(G).

(2) An alien applying for a visa under the provisions of INA section 101(a)(15)(G) may not be refused solely on the grounds that the applicant is not a national of the country whose government the applicant represents.

(3) An alien seeking to enter the United States as a foreign government representative to an international organization, who is also proceeding to the United States on official business as a foreign government official within the meaning of INA section 101(a)(15)(A), shall be issued a visa under that section, if otherwise qualified.

(4) An alien not classifiable under INA section 101(a)(15)(A) or in NATO-1 through NATO-6 classification but entitled to classification under INA section 101(a)(15)(G) shall be classified under section 101(a)(15)(G), even if also eligible for another nonimmigrant classification. An alien classified under INA section 101(a)(15)(G) as an immediate family member of a principal alien classifiable G-1, G-2, G-3 or G-4, may continue to be so classified even if he or she obtains employment subsequent to his or her initial entry into the United States that would allow classification under INA section 101(a)(15)(A). Such alien shall not be classified in a category other than A or G, even if also eligible for another nonimmigrant classification.

(c) **Officers and employees of privatized INTELSAT, their family members and domestic servants.**

(1) Officers and employees of privatized INTELSAT who both were employed by INTELSAT, and held status under INA 101(a)(15)(G)(iv) for at least six months prior to privatization on July 17,2001, will continue to be so classifiable for so long as they are officers or employees of INTELSAT or a successor or separated entity thereof.

(2) Aliens who had had G — 4 status as officers and employees of INTELSAT but became officers or employees of a successor or separated entity of INTELSAT after at least six months of such employment, but prior to and in anticipation of privatization and subsequent to March 17, 2000, will also continue to be classifiable under INA 101(a)(15)(G)(iv) for so long as that employment continues.

(3) Family members of officers and employees described in paragraphs (c)(1) and (2) of this section who qualify as "immediate family" under § 41.21(a)(3) and who are accompanying or following to join the principal are also classifiable under INA 1010(a)(15)(G)(iv) for so long as the principal is so classified.

(4) Attendants, servants, and personal employees of officers and employees described in paragraphs (c)(1) and (2) of this section are not eligible for classification under INA 101(a)(15)(G)(v), given that the officers and employees described in paragraphs (c)(1) and (2) of this section are not officers or employees of an "international organization" for purposes of INA 101(a)(15)(G).

HISTORY:

[52 FR 42597, Nov. 5, 1987; 67 FR 1413, 1414, Jan. 11, 2002; 67 FR 18821, 18822, Apr. 17, 2002, as confirmed at 68 FR 32359, 32360, May 30, 2003; 78 FR 33699, 33700, June 5, 2013; 81 FR 88101, 88103, Dec. 7, 2016]

§ 41.25 NATO representatives, officials, and employees.

(a) Classification. An alien shall be classified under the symbol NATO-1, NATO-2, NATO-3, NATO-4, or NATO-5 if the consular officer is satisfied that the alien is seeking admission to the United States under the applicable provision of the Agreement on the Status of the North Atlantic Treaty Organization, National Representatives and International Staff, or is a member of the immediate family of an alien classified NATO-1 through NATO-5. (See § 41.12 for classes of aliens entitled to classification under each symbol.)

(b) Armed services personnel. Armed services personnel entering the United States in accordance with the provisions of the Agreement Between the Parties to the North Atlantic Treaty Regarding the Status of Their Forces or in accordance with the provisions of the Protocol on the Status of International Military Headquarters Set Up Pursuant to the North Atlantic Treaty may enter the United States under the appropriate treaty waiver of documentary requirements contained in § 41.1 (d) or (e). If a visa is issued it is classifiable under the NATO-2 symbol.

(c) Dependents of armed services personnel. Dependents of armed services personnel referred to in paragraph (b) of this section shall be classified under the symbol NATO-2.

(d) Members of civilian components and dependents. Alien members of a civilian component accompanying a force entering in accordance with the provisions of the NATO Status-of-Forces Agreement, and dependents, or alien members of a civilian component attached to or employed by an Allied Headquarters under the Protocol on the Status of International Military Headquarters, and dependents shall be classified under the symbol NATO-6.

(e) Attendant, servant, or personal employee of an alien classified NATO-1 through NATO-6. An alien attendant, servant, or personal employee of an alien classified NATO-1 through NATO-6, and any member of the immediate family of such attendant, servant, or personal employee, shall be classified under the symbol NATO-7.

HISTORY:

[52 FR 42597, Nov. 5, 1987.]

§ 41.26 Diplomatic visas.

(a) **Definitions.**

(1) “Diplomatic passport” means a national passport bearing that title and issued by a competent authority of a foreign government.

(2) “Diplomatic visa” means any nonimmigrant visa, regardless of classification, which bears that title and is issued in accordance with the regulations of this section.

(3) Equivalent of a diplomatic passport means a passport that:

(i) Is issued by a competent authority that does not issue diplomatic passports and

(ii) Has been designated by the Secretary as the equivalent of a diplomatic passport.

(b) Place of application. With the exception of certain aliens in the United States issued nonimmigrant visas by the Department under the provisions of § 41.111(b), application for a diplomatic visa shall be made at a diplomatic mission or at a consular office authorized to issue diplomatic visas, regardless of the nationality or residence of the applicant.

(c) Classes of aliens eligible to receive diplomatic visas. A nonimmigrant alien who presents a diplomatic passport or its equivalent shall, if otherwise qualified, be eligible to receive a diplomatic visa if:

(1) The nonimmigrant alien is within one of the following categories, irrespective of the classification of the visa under § 41.12:

(i) Heads of states and their alternates;

(ii) Members of a reigning royal family;

(iii) Governors-general, governors, high commissioners, and similar high administrative or executive officers of a territorial unit, and their alternates;

(iv) Cabinet ministers and their assistants holding executive or administrative positions not inferior to that of the head of a departmental division, and their alternates;

(v) Presiding officers of chambers of national legislative bodies;

(vi) Justices of the highest national court of a foreign country;

(vii) Ambassadors, public ministers, other officers of the diplomatic service and consular officers of career;

(viii) Military officers holding a rank not inferior to that of a brigadier general in the United States Army or Air Force and Naval officers holding a rank not inferior to that of a rear admiral in the United States Navy;

(ix) Military, naval, air and other attache and assistant attache assigned to a foreign diplomatic mission;

(x) Officers of foreign-government delegations to international organizations so designated by Executive Order;

(xi) Officers of foreign-government delegations to, and officers of, international bodies of an official nature, other than international organizations so designated by Executive Order;

(xii) Officers of a foreign government proceeding to the United States on a temporary basis or through the United States in the performance of their official duties;

(xiii) Officers of foreign-government delegations proceeding to or from a specific international conference of an official nature;

(xiv) Members of the immediate family of a principal alien who is within one of the classes described in paragraphs (c)(1)(i) through (xi) of this section;

(xv) Members of the immediate family accompanying or following to join the principal alien who is within one of the classes described in paragraphs (c)(1)(xii) and (c)(1)(xiii) of this section;

(xvi) Diplomatic couriers proceeding to or through the United States in the performance of their official duties; or

(2) The alien is classifiable as a G–4 and is accompanying any of these officers:

(i) The Secretary General of the United Nations;

(ii) An Under Secretary General of the United Nations;

(iii) An Assistant Secretary General of the United Nations;

(iv) The Administrator or the Deputy Administrator of the United Nations Development Program;

(v) An Assistant Administrator of the United Nations Development Program;

(vi) The Executive Director of the:

(A) United Nations Children’s Fund;

(B) United Nations Institute for Training and Research;

(C) United Nations Industrial Development Organization;

(vii) The Executive Secretary of the:

(A) United Nations Economic Commission for Africa;

(B) United Nations Economic Commission for Asia and the Far East;

(C) United Nations Economic Commission for Latin America;

(D) United Nations Economic Commission for Europe;

(viii) The Secretary General of the United Nations Conference on Trade and Development;

(ix) The Director General of the Latin American Institute for Economic and Social Planning;

(x) The United Nations High Commissioner for Refugees;

(xi) The United Nations Commissioner for Technical Cooperation;

(xii) The Commissioner General of the United Nations Relief and Works Agency for Palestine Refugees in the Near East;

(xiii) Members of the immediate family accompanying or following to join any principal nonimmigrant alien listed in paragraphs (c)(2)(i) through (xii) of this section.

(3) Other individual aliens or classes of aliens are eligible to receive diplomatic visas upon authorization of the Department, the Chief of a U.S. Diplomatic Mission, the Deputy Chief of Mission, the Counselor for Consular Affairs or the principal officer of a consular post not under the jurisdiction of a diplomatic mission.

HISTORY:

[52 FR 42597, Nov. 5, 1987; 53 FR 9111, Mar. 21, 1988; 86 FR 10453, 10456, Feb. 22, 2021]

§ 41.27 Official visas.

(a) Definition. "Official visa" means any nonimmigrant visa, regardless of classification, which bears that title and is issued in accordance with these regulations.

(b) Place of application. Official visas are ordinarily issued only when application is made in the consular district of the applicant's residence. When directed by the Department, or in the discretion of the consular officer, official visas may be issued when application is made in a consular district in which the alien is physically present but does not reside. Certain aliens in the United States may be issued official visas by the Department under the provisions of § 41.111(b).

(c) Classes of aliens eligible to receive official visas.

(1) A nonimmigrant within one of the following categories who is not eligible to receive a diplomatic visa shall, if otherwise qualified, be eligible to receive an official visa irrespective of classification of the visa under § 41.12:

(i) Aliens within a category described in § 41.26(c)(1) who are ineligible to receive a diplomatic visa because they are not in possession of a diplomatic passport or its equivalent;

(ii) Aliens classifiable under INA section 101(a)(15)(A)(i) or (ii), 8 U.S.C. 1101(a)(15)(A)(i) or (ii);

(iii) Aliens who are classifiable under INA section 101(a)(15)(G)(i), (ii), or (iv), 8 U.S.C. 1101(a)(15)(G)(i), (ii), or (iv);

(iv) Aliens who are classifiable under INA section 101(a)(15)(G)(iii), 8 U.S.C. 1101(a)(15)(G)(iii), as representatives of a foreign government traveling to an international organization so designated by Executive Order, where such foreign government is not a member of the international organization;

(v) Aliens classifiable under INA section 101(a)(15)(C), 8 U.S.C. 1101(a)(15)(C), as nonimmigrants described in INA section 212(d)(8), 8 U.S.C. 1182(d)(8);

(vi) Members and members-elect of national legislative bodies;

(vii) Justices of the lesser national and the highest state courts of a foreign country;

(viii) Officers and employees of national legislative bodies proceeding to or through the United States in the performance of their official duties;

(ix) Administrative, service, and similar employees attached to foreign-government delegations to, and employees of, international bodies of an official nature, other than international organizations so designated by Executive Order, proceeding to or through the United States in the performance of their official duties;

(x) Administrative, service, and similar employees of a foreign government proceeding to the United States on temporary duty or through the United States on a temporary basis in the performance of their official duties;

(xi) Administrative, service, and similar employees attached to foreign-government delegations proceeding to or from a specific international conference of an official nature;

(xii) Officers and employees of foreign governments recognized de jure by the United States who are stationed in foreign contiguous territories or adjacent islands;

(xiii) Members of the immediate family when accompanying or following to join a principal alien who is within one of the classes referred to or described in paragraphs (c)(1)(i) through (xii) of this section;

(2) Other individual aliens or classes of aliens are eligible to receive official visas upon the authorization of the Department, the Chief of a U.S. Diplomatic Mission, the Deputy Chief of Mission, the Counselor for Consular Affairs, or the principal officer of a consular post not under the jurisdiction of a diplomatic mission.

HISTORY:

[52 FR 42597, Nov. 5, 1987; 53 FR 9111, Mar. 21, 1988]; 86 FR 10453, 10456, Feb. 22, 2021]

Subpart D

Temporary Visitors

§ 41.31 Temporary visitors for business or pleasure.

(a) Classification. An alien is classifiable as a nonimmigrant visitor for business (B-1) or pleasure (B-2) if the consular officer is satisfied that the alien qualifies under the provisions of INA 101(a)(15)(B), and that:

(1) The alien intends to leave the United States at the end of the temporary stay (consular officers are authorized, if departure of the alien as required by law does not seem fully assured, to require the posting of a bond with the Secretary of Homeland Security in a sufficient sum to ensure that at the end of the temporary visit, or upon failure to maintain temporary visitor status, or any status subsequently acquired under INA 248, the alien will depart from the United States);

(2) The alien has permission to enter a foreign country at the end of the temporary stay; and

(3) Adequate financial arrangements have been made to enable the alien to carry out the purpose of the visit to and departure from the United States.

(b) **Definitions.**

(1) The term "business," as used in INA 101(a)(15)(B), refers to conventions, conferences, consultations and other legitimate activities of a commercial or professional nature. It does not include local employment or labor for hire. For the purposes of this section building or construction work, whether on-site or in plant, shall be deemed to constitute purely local employment or labor for hire; provided that the supervision or training of others engaged in building or construction work (but not the actual performance of any such building or construction work) shall not be deemed to constitute purely local employment or labor for hire if the alien is otherwise qualified as a B-1 nonimmigrant. An alien seeking to enter as a nonimmigrant for employment or labor pursuant to a contract or other prearrangement is required to qualify under the provisions of § 41.53. An alien of distinguished merit and ability seeking to enter the United States temporarily with the idea of performing temporary services of an exceptional nature requiring such merit and ability, but having no contract or other prearranged employment, may be classified as a nonimmigrant temporary visitor for business.

(2)(i) The term pleasure, as used in INA 101(a)(15)(B) for the purpose of visa issuance, refers to legitimate activities of a recreational character, including tourism, amusement, visits with friends or relatives, rest, medical treatment, and activities of a fraternal, social, or service nature, and does not include obtaining a visa for the primary purpose of obtaining U.S. citizenship for a child by giving birth in the United States.

(ii) Any visa applicant who seeks medical treatment in the United States under this provision shall be denied a visa under INA section 214(b) if unable to establish, to the satisfaction of a consular officer, a legitimate reason why he or she wishes to travel to the United States for medical treatment, that a medical practitioner or facility in the United States has agreed to provide treatment, and that the applicant has reasonably estimated the duration of the visit and all associated costs. The applicant also shall be denied a visa under INA section 214(b) if unable to establish to the satisfaction of the consular officer that he or she has the means derived from lawful sources and intent to pay for the medical treatment and all incidental expenses, including transportation and living expenses, either independently or with the pre-arranged assistance of others.

(iii) Any B nonimmigrant visa applicant who a consular officer has reason to believe will give birth during her stay in the United States is presumed to be traveling for the primary purpose of obtaining U.S. citizenship for the child.

HISTORY:

[52 FR 42597, Nov. 5, 1987; 53 FR 9172, Mar. 21, 1988; 71 FR 34519, 34521, June 15, 2006; 85 FR 4219, 4225, Jan. 24, 2020]

§ 41.32 Nonresident alien Mexican border crossing identification cards; combined border crossing identification cards and B-1/B-2 visitor visas.

(a) Combined B-1/B-2 visitor visa and border crossing identification card (B-1/B-2 Visa/BCC) —

(1) Authorization for issuance. Consular officers assigned to a consular office in Mexico designated by the Deputy Assistant Secretary for Visa Services for such purpose may issue a border crossing identification card, as that term is defined in INA 101(a)(6), in combination with a B-1/B-2 nonimmigrant visitor visa (B-1/B-2 Visa/BCC), to a nonimmigrant alien who:

(i) Is a citizen and resident of Mexico;

(ii) Seeks to enter the United States as a temporary visitor for business or pleasure as defined in INA 101(a)(15)(B) for periods of stay not exceeding six months;

(iii) Is otherwise eligible for a B-1 or a B-2 temporary visitor visa.

(2) Procedure for application. Mexican applicants shall apply for a B-1/B-2 Visa/BCC at any U.S. consular office in Mexico designated by the Deputy Assistant Secretary of State for Visa Services pursuant to paragraph (a) of this section to accept such applications. The application shall be submitted electronically on Form DS-160 or, as directed by a consular officer, on Form DS-156. If submitted electronically, it must be signed electronically by clicking the box designated "Sign Application" in the certification section of the application.

(3) Personal appearance. Each applicant shall appear in person before a consular officer to be interviewed regarding eligibility for a visitor visa, unless the consular officer waives personal appearance.

(4) Issuance and format. A B-1/B-2 Visa/BCC issued on or after April 1, 1998, shall consist of a card, Form DSP-150, containing a machine-readable biometric identifier. It shall contain the following data:

(i) Post symbol;

(ii) Number of the card;

(iii) Date of issuance;

(iv) Indicia "B-1/B-2 Visa and Border Crossing Card";

(v) Name, date of birth, and sex of the person to whom issued; and

(vi) Date of expiration.

(b) Validity. A BCC previously issued by a consular officer in Mexico on Form I-186, Nonresident Alien Mexican Border Crossing Card, or Form I-586, Nonresident Alien Border Crossing Card, is valid until the expiration date on the card (if any) unless previously revoked, but not later than the date, currently October 1, 2001, on which a machine-readable, biometric identifier in the card is required in order for the card to be usable for entry. The BCC portion of a B-1/B-2 Visa/BCC issued to a Mexican national pursuant to provisions of this section contained in the 22 CFR, parts 1 to 299, edition revised as of April 1, 1998 is valid until the date of expiration, unless previously revoked, but not later than the date, currently October 1, 2001, on which a machine-readable, biometric identifier in the card is required in order for the card to be usable for entry.

(c) Revocation. A consular or immigration officer may revoke a BCC issued on Form I-186 or Form I-586, or a B-1/B-2 Visa/BCC under the provisions of § 41.122, or if the consular or immigration officer determines that the alien to whom any such document was issued has ceased to be a resident and/or a citizen of Mexico. Upon revocation, the consular or immigration officer shall notify the issuing consular or immigration office. If the revoked document is a card, the consular or immigration officer shall take possession of the card and physically cancel it under standard security conditions. If the revoked document is a stamp in a passport the consular or immigration officer shall write or stamp "canceled" on the face of the document.

(d) **Voidance.**

(1) The voiding pursuant to INA 222(g) of the visa portion of a B-1/B-2 Visa/BCC issued at any time by a consular officer in Mexico under provisions of this section contained in the 22 CFR, parts 1 to 299, edition revised as of April 1, 1998, also voids the BCC portion of that document.

(2) A BCC issued at any time by a consular officer in Mexico under any provisions of this section contained in the 22 CFR, parts 1 to 299, edition revised as of April 1, 1998, is void if a consular or immigration officer determines that the alien has violated the conditions of the alien's admission into the United States, including the period of stay authorized by the Secretary of Homeland Security.

(3) A consular or immigration officer shall immediately take possession of a card determined to be void under paragraphs (d) (1) or (2) of this section and physically cancel it under standard security conditions. If the document voided in paragraphs (d) (1) or (2) is in the form of a stamp in a passport the officer shall write or stamp "canceled" across the face of the document.

(e) Replacement. When a B-1/B-2 Visa/BCC issued under the provisions of this section, or a BCC or B-1/B-2 Visa/BCC issued under any provisions of this section contained in the 22 CFR, parts 1 to 299, edition revised as of April 1, 1998, has been lost, mutilated, destroyed, or expired, the person to whom such card was issued may apply for a new B-1/B-2 Visa/BCC as provided in this section.

HISTORY:

[52 FR 42597, Nov. 5, 1987; 53 FR 9111, Mar. 21, 1988; 63 FR 16892, 16893, April 7, 1998; 64 FR 45162, 45163, Aug. 19, 1999; 71 FR 30589, 30591, May 30, 2006; 71 FR 34519, 34521, June 15, 2006; 73 FR 23067, 23068, Apr. 29, 2008]

§ 41.33 Nonresident alien Canadian border crossing identification card (BCC).

(a) Validity of Canadian BCC. A Canadian BCC or the BCC portion of a Canadian B-1/B-2 Visa/BCC issued to a permanent resident of Canada pursuant to provisions of this section contained in the 22 CFR, parts 1 to 299, edition revised as of April 1, 1998, is valid until the date of expiration, if any, unless previously revoked, but not later than the date, currently October 1, 2001, on which a machine readable biometric identifier is required in order for a BCC to be usable for entry.

(b) Revocation of Canadian BCC. A consular or immigration officer may revoke a BCC or a B-1/B-2 Visa/BCC issued in Canada at any time under the provisions of § 41.122, or if the consular or immigration officer determines that the alien to whom any such document was issued has ceased to be a permanent resident of Canada. Upon revocation, the consular or immigration officer shall notify the issuing consular office and if the revoked document is a card, the consular or immigration officer shall take possession of the card and physically cancel it under standard security conditions. If the revoked document is a stamp in a passport the consular or immigration officer shall write or stamp "canceled" on the face of the document.

(c) **Voidance.**

(1) The voiding pursuant to INA 222(g) of the visa portion of a B-1/B-2 Visa/BCC issued at any time by a consular officer in Canada under provisions of this section contained in the 22 CFR, parts 1 to 299, edition revised as of April 1, 1998, also voids the BCC portion of that document.

(2) A BCC issued at any time by a consular officer in Canada under any provisions of this section contained in the 22 CFR, parts 1 to 299, edition revised as of April 1, 1998, is void if a consular or immigration officer finds that the alien has violated the conditions of the alien's admission into the United States, including the period of stay authorized by the Secretary of Homeland Security.

(3) A consular or immigration officer shall immediately take possession of a card determined to be void under paragraphs (c) (1) or (2) of this section and physically cancel it under standard security conditions. If the document voided under paragraphs (c) (1) or (2) is in the form of a stamp in a passport the officer shall write or stamp "canceled" across the face of the document.

HISTORY:

[52 FR 42597, Nov. 5, 1987; 63 FR 16892, 16894, April 7, 1998; 64 FR 45162, 45164, Aug. 19, 1999; 71 FR 34519, 34521, June 15, 2006]

Subpart E

Crewman and Crew-List Visas

§ 41.41 Crewmen.

(a) Alien classifiable as crewman. An alien is classifiable as a nonimmigrant crewman upon establishing to the satisfaction of the consular officer the qualifications prescribed by INA 101(a)(15)(D), provided that the alien has permission to enter some foreign country after a temporary landing in the United States, unless the alien is barred from such classification under the provisions of INA 214(f).

(b) Alien not classifiable as crewman. An alien employed on board a vessel or aircraft in a capacity not required for normal operation and service, or an alien employed or listed as a regular member of the crew in excess of the number normally required, shall not be classified as a crewman.

HISTORY:

[66 FR 10363, 10364, Feb. 15, 2001]

§ 41.42 [Reserved]

[NO TEXT IN ORIGINAL]

HISTORY:

[52 FR 42597, Nov. 5, 1987, as amended at 56 FR 30428, July 2, 1991; 61 FR 1834, 1836, Jan. 24, 1996; 69 FR 12797, 12799, Mar. 18, 2004, as confirmed at 69 FR 43515, 43516, July 21, 2004]

AUTHORITY:

(8 U.S.C. 1104; Pub. L. 105-277, 112 Stat. 2681-795 through 2681-801.)

Subpart F

Business and Media Visas

§ 41.51 Treaty trader, treaty investor, or treaty alien in a specialty occupation.

(a) Treaty trader —

(1) Classification. An alien is classifiable as a nonimmigrant treaty trader (E-1) if the consular officer is satisfied that the alien qualifies under the provisions of INA 101(a)(15)(E)(i) and that the alien:

(i) Will be in the United States solely to carry on trade of a substantial nature, which is international in scope, either on the alien's behalf or as an employee of a foreign person or organization engaged in trade, principally between the United States and the foreign state of which the alien is a national, (consideration being given to any conditions in the country of which the alien is a national which may affect the alien's ability to carry on such substantial trade); and

(ii) Intends to depart from the United States upon the termination of E-1 status.

(2) Employee of treaty trader. An alien employee of a treaty trader may be classified E-1 if the employee is in or is coming to the United States to engage in duties of an executive or supervisory character, or, if employed in a lesser capacity, the employee has special qualifications that make the services to be rendered essential to the efficient operation of the enterprise. The employer must be:

(i) A person having the nationality of the treaty country, who is maintaining the status of treaty trader if in the United States or, if not in the United States, would be classifiable as a treaty trader; or

(ii) An organization at least 50% owned by persons having the nationality of the treaty country who are maintaining nonimmigrant treaty trader status if residing in the United States or, if not residing in the United States, who would be classifiable as treaty traders.

(3) Spouse and children of treaty trader. The spouse and children of a treaty trader accompanying or following to join the principal alien are entitled to the same classification as the principal alien. The nationality of a spouse or child of a treaty trader is not material to the classification of the spouse or child under the provisions of INA 101(a)(15)(E).

(4) Representative of foreign information media. Representatives of foreign information media shall first be considered for possible classification as nonimmigrants under the provisions of INA 101(a)(15)(I), before consideration is given to their possible classification as treaty traders under the provisions of INA 101(a)(15)(E) and of this section.

(5) Treaty country. A treaty country is for purposes of this section a foreign state with which a qualifying Treaty of Friendship, Commerce, and Navigation or its equivalent exists with the United States. A treaty country includes a foreign state that is accorded treaty visa privileges under INA 101(a)(15)(E) by specific legislation (other than the INA).

(6) Nationality of the treaty country. The authorities of the foreign state of which the alien claims nationality determine the nationality of an individual treaty trader. In the case of an organization, ownership must be traced as best as is practicable to the individuals who ultimately own the organization.

(7) Trade. The term "trade" as used in this section means the existing international exchange of items of trade for consideration between the United States and the treaty country. Existing trade includes successfully negotiated contracts binding upon the parties that call for the immediate exchange of items of trade. This exchange must be traceable and identifiable. Title to the trade item must pass from one treaty party to the other.

(8) Item of trade. Items that qualify for trade within these provisions include but are not limited to goods, services, technology, monies, international banking, insurance, transportation, tourism, communications, and some news gathering activities.

(9) Substantial trade. Substantial trade for the purposes of this section entails the quantum of trade sufficient to ensure a continuous flow of trade items between the United States and the treaty country. This continuous flow contemplates numerous exchanges over time rather than a single transaction, regardless of the monetary value. Although the monetary value of the trade item being exchanged is a relevant consideration, greater weight is given to more numerous exchanges of larger value. In the case of smaller businesses, an income derived from the value of numerous transactions that is sufficient to support the treaty

trader and his or her family constitutes a favorable factor in assessing the existence of substantial trade.

(10) Principal trade. Trade shall be considered to be principal trade between the United States and the treaty country when over 50% of the volume of international trade of the treaty trader is conducted between the United States and the treaty country of the treaty trader's nationality.

(11) Executive or supervisory character. The executive or supervisory element of the employee's position must be a principal and primary function of the position and not an incidental or collateral function. Executive and/or supervisory duties grant the employee ultimate control and responsibility for the enterprise's overall operation or a major component thereof.

(i) An executive position provides the employee great authority to determine policy of and direction for the enterprise.

(ii) A position primarily of supervisory character grants the employee supervisory responsibility for a significant proportion of an enterprise's operations and does not generally involve the direct supervision of low-level employees.

(12) Special qualifications. Special qualifications are those skills and/or aptitudes that an employee in a lesser capacity brings to a position or role that are essential to the successful or efficient operation of the enterprise.

(i) The essential nature of the alien's skills to the employing firm is determined by assessing the degree of proven expertise of the alien in the area of operations involved, the uniqueness of the specific skill or aptitude, the length of experience and/or training with the firm, the period of training or other experience necessary to perform effectively the projected duties, and the salary the special qualifications can command. The question of special skills and qualifications must be determined by assessing the circumstances on a case-by-case basis.

(ii) Whether the special qualifications are essential will be assessed in light of all circumstances at the time of each visa application on a case-by-case basis. A skill that is unique at one point may become commonplace at a later date. Skills required to start up an enterprise may no longer be essential after initial operations are complete and are running smoothly. Some skills are essential only in the short-term for the training of locally hired employees. Long-term essentiality might, however, be established in connection with continuous activities in such areas as product improvement, quality control, or the provision of a service not generally available in the United States.

(13) Labor disputes. Citizens of Canada or Mexico shall not be entitled to classification under this section if the Secretary of Homeland Security and the Secretary of Labor have certified that:

(i) There is in progress a strike or lockout in the course of a labor dispute in the occupational classification at the place or intended place of employment; and

(ii) The alien has failed to establish that the alien's entry will not affect adversely the settlement of the strike or lockout or the employment of any person who is involved in the strike or lockout.

(b) Treaty investor —

(1) Classification. An alien is classifiable as a nonimmigrant treaty investor (E'2) if the consular officer is satisfied that the alien qualifies under the provisions of INA 101(a)(15)(E)(ii) and that the alien:

(i) Has invested or is actively in the process of investing a substantial amount of capital in bona fide enterprise in the United States, as distinct from a relatively small amount of capital in a marginal enterprise solely for the purpose of earning a living; and

(ii) Is seeking entry solely to develop and direct the enterprise; and

(iii) Intends to depart from the United States upon the termination of E'2 status.

(2) Employee of treaty investor. An alien employee of a treaty investor may be classified E-2 if the employee is in or is coming to the United States to engage in duties of an executive or supervisory character, or, if employed in a lesser capacity, the employee has special qualifications that make the services to be rendered essential to the efficient operation of the enterprise. The employer must be:

(i) A person having the nationality of the treaty country, who is maintaining the status of treaty investor if in the United States or, if not in the United States, who would be classifiable as a treaty investor; or

(ii) An organization at least 50% owned by persons having the nationality of the treaty country who are maintaining nonimmigrant treaty investor status if residing in the United States or, if not residing in the United States, who would be classifiable as treaty investors.

(3) Spouse and children of treaty investor. The spouse and children of a treaty investor accompanying or following to join the principal alien are entitled to the same classification as the principal alien. The nationality of a spouse or child of a treaty investor is not material to the classification of the spouse or child under the provisions of INA 101(a)(15)(E).

(4) Representative of foreign information media. Representatives of foreign information media shall first be considered for possible classification as nonimmigrants under the provisions of INA 101(a)(15)(I), before consideration is given to their possible classification as nonimmigrants under the provisions of INA 101(a)(15)(E) and of this section.

(5) Treaty country. A treaty country is for purposes of this section a foreign state with which a qualifying Treaty of Friendship, Commerce, and Navigation or its equivalent exists with the United States. A treaty country includes a foreign state that is accorded treaty visa privileges under INA 101(a)(15)(E) by specific legislation (other than the INA).

(6) Nationality of the treaty country. The authorities of the foreign state of which the alien claims nationality determine the nationality of an individual treaty investor. In the case of an organization, ownership must be traced as best as is practicable to the individuals who ultimately own the organization.

(7) Investment. Investment means the treaty investor's placing of capital, including funds and other assets, at risk in the commercial sense with the objective of generating a profit. The treaty investor must be in possession of and have control over the capital invested or being invested. The capital must be subject to partial or total loss if investment fortunes reverse. Such investment capital must be the investor's unsecured personal business capital or capital secured by personal assets. Capital in the process of being invested or that has been invested must be irrevocably committed to the enterprise. The alien has the burden of establishing such irrevocable commitment given to the particular circumstances of each case. The alien may use any legal mechanism available, such as by placing invested funds in escrow pending visa issuance, that would not only irrevocably commit funds to the enterprise but that might also extend some personal liability protection to the treaty investor.

(8) Bona fide enterprise. The enterprise must be a real and active commercial or entrepreneurial undertaking, producing some service or commodity for profit and must meet applicable legal requirements for doing business in the particular jurisdiction in the United States.

(9) Substantial amount of capital. A substantial amount of capital constitutes that amount that is:

(i)(A) Substantial in the proportional sense, i.e., in relationship to the total cost of either purchasing an established enterprise or creating the type of enterprise under consideration;

(B) Sufficient to ensure the treaty investor's financial commitment to the successful operation of the enterprise; and

(C) Of a magnitude to support the likelihood that the treaty investor will successfully develop and direct the enterprise.

(ii) Whether an amount of capital is substantial in the proportionality sense is understood in terms of an inverted sliding scale; i.e., the lower the total cost of the enterprise, the higher, proportionately, the investment must be to meet these criteria.

(10) Marginal enterprise. A marginal enterprise is an enterprise that does not have the present or future capacity to generate more than enough income to provide a minimal living for the treaty investor and his or her family. An enterprise that does not have the capacity to generate such income but that has a present or future capacity to make a significant economic contribution is not a marginal enterprise. The projected future capacity should generally be realizable within five years from the date the alien commences normal business activity of the enterprise.

(11) Solely to develop and direct. The business or individual treaty investor does or will develop and direct the enterprise by controlling the enterprise through ownership of at least 50% of the business, by possessing operational control through a managerial position or other corporate device, or by other means.

(12) Executive or supervisory character. The executive or supervisory element of the employee's position must be a principal and primary function of the position and not an incidental or collateral function. Executive and/or supervisory duties grant the employee ultimate control and responsibility for the enterprise's overall operation or a major component thereof.

(i) An executive position provides the employee great authority to determine policy of and direction for the enterprise.

(ii) A position primarily of supervisory character grants the employee supervisory responsibility for a significant proportion of an enterprise's operations and does not generally involve the direct supervision of low-level employees.

(13) Special qualifications. Special qualifications are those skills and/or aptitudes that an employee in a lesser capacity brings to a position or role that are essential to the successful or efficient operation of the enterprise.

(i) The essential nature of the alien's skills to the employing firm is determined by assessing the degree of proven expertise of the alien in the area of operations involved, the uniqueness of the specific skill or aptitude, the length of experience and/or training with the firm, the period of training or other experience necessary to perform effectively the projected duties, and the salary the special qualifications can command. The question of special skills and qualifications must be determined by assessing the circumstances on a case by-case basis.

(ii) Whether the special qualifications are essential will be assessed in light of all circumstances at the time of each visa application on a case-by-case basis. A skill that is unique at one point may become commonplace at a later date. Skills required to start up an enterprise may no longer be essential after initial operations are complete and are running smoothly. Some skills are essential only in the short-term for the training of locally hired employees. Long-term essentiality might, however, be established in connection with continuous activities in such areas as product improvement, quality control, or the provision of a service not generally available in the United States.

(14) Labor disputes. Citizens of Canada or Mexico shall not be entitled to classification under this section if the Secretary of Homeland Security and the Secretary of Labor have certified that:

(i) There is in progress a strike or lockout in the course of a labor dispute in the occupational classification at the place or intended place of employment; and

(ii) The alien has failed to establish that the alien's entry will not affect adversely the settlement of the strike or lockout or the employment of any person who is involved in the strike or lockout.

(c) Nonimmigrant E-3 treaty aliens in specialty occupations —

(1) Classification. An alien is classifiable as a nonimmigrant treaty alien in a specialty occupation if the consular officer is satisfied that the alien qualifies under the provisions of INA 101(a)(15)(E)(iii) and that the alien:

(i) Possesses the nationality of the country statutorily designated for treaty aliens in specialty occupation status;

(ii) Satisfies the requirements of INA 214(i)(1) and the corresponding regulations defining specialty occupation promulgated by the Department of Homeland Security;

(iii) Presents to a consular officer a copy of the Labor Condition Application signed by the employer and approved by the Department of Labor, and meeting the attestation requirements of INA Section 212(t)(1);

(iv) Presents to a consular officer evidence of the alien's academic or other qualifying credentials as required under INA 214(i)(1), and a job offer letter or other documentation from the employer establishing that upon entry into the United States the applicant will be engaged in qualifying work in a specialty occupation, as defined in paragraph (c)(1)(ii) of this section, and that the alien will be paid the actual or prevailing wage referred to in INA 212(t)(1);

(v) Has a visa number allocated under INA 214(g)(11)(B); and,

(vi) Intends to depart upon the termination of E-3 status.

(2) Spouse and children of treaty alien in a specialty occupation. The spouse and children of a treaty alien in a specialty occupation accompanying or following to join the principal alien are, if otherwise admissible, entitled to the same classification as the principal alien. A spouse or child of a principal E-3 treaty alien need not have the same nationality as the principal in order to be classifiable under the provisions of INA 101(a)(15)(E). Spouses and children of E-3 principals are not subject to the numerical limitations of INA 214(g)(11)(B).

HISTORY:

[52 FR 42597, Nov. 5, 1987; 58 FR 68527, Dec. 28, 1993; 62 FR 48149, 48154, Sept. 12, 1997; 70 FR 52292, 52293, Sept. 2, 2005; 71 FR 34519, 34521, June 15, 2006]

§ 41.52 Information media representative.

(a) Representative of foreign press, radio, film, or other information media. An alien is classifiable as a nonimmigrant information media representative if the consular officer is satisfied that the alien qualifies under the provisions of INA 101(a)(15)(I) and is a representative of a foreign press, radio, film, or other information medium having its home office in a foreign country, the government of which grants reciprocity for similar privileges to representatives of such a medium having home offices in the United States.

(b) Classification when applicant eligible for both I visa and E visa. An alien who will be engaged in foreign information media activities in the United States and meets the criteria set forth in paragraph (a) of this section shall be classified as a nonimmigrant under INA 101(a)(15)(I) even if the alien may also be classifiable as a nonimmigrant under the provisions of INA 101(a)(15)(E).

(c) Spouse and children of information media representative. The spouse or child of an information media representative is classifiable under INA 101(a)(15)(I) if accompanying or following to join the principal alien.

HISTORY:

52 FR 42597, Nov. 5, 1987.

§ 41.53 Temporary workers and trainees.

(a) Requirements for H classification. An alien shall be classifiable under INA 101(a)(15)(H) if:

(1) The consular officer is satisfied that the alien qualifies under that section; and either

(2) With respect to the principal alien, the consular officer has received official evidence of the approval by DHS, or by the Department of Labor in the case of temporary agricultural workers of a petition to accord such classification or of the extension by DHS of the period of authorized entry in such classification; or

(3) The consular officer is satisfied the alien is the spouse or child of an alien so classified and is accompanying or following to join the principal alien.

(b) Petition approval. The approval of a petition by the Department of Homeland Security or by the Department of Labor does not establish that the alien is eligible to receive a nonimmigrant visa.

(c) Validity of visa. The period of validity of a visa issued on the basis of paragraph (a) to this section must not exceed the period indicated in the petition, notification, or confirmation required in paragraph (a)(2) of this section.

(d) Alien not entitled to H classification. The consular officer must suspend action on this alien's application and submit a report to the approving DHS office if the consular officer knows or has reason to believe that an alien applying for a visa under INA 101(a)(15)(H) is not entitled to the classification as approved.

(e) "Trainee" defined. The term Trainee, as used in INA 101(a)(15)(H)(iii), means a nonimmigrant alien who seeks to enter the United States temporarily at the invitation of an individual, organization, firm, or other trainer for the purpose of receiving instruction in any field of endeavor (other than graduate medical education or training), including agriculture, commerce, communication, finance, government, transportation, and the professions.

(f) Former exchange visitor. Former exchange visitors who are subject to the 2-year residence requirement of INA 212(e) are ineligible to apply for visas under INA 101(a)(15)(H) until they have fulfilled the residence requirement or obtained a waiver of the requirement.

HISTORY:

[57 FR 31449, July 16, 1992; 61 FR 1832, 1833, Jan. 24, 1996; 65 FR 52305, 52306, Aug. 29, 2000; 71 FR 34519, 34521, June 15, 2006]

§ 41.54 Intracompany transferees (executives, managers, and specialized knowledge employees)

(a) Requirements for L classification. An alien shall be classifiable under the provisions of INA section 101(a)(15)(L) if:

(1) The consular officer is satisfied that the alien qualifies under that section; and either

(2) In the case of an individual petition, the consular officer has received official evidence of the approval by

DHS of a petition to accord such classification or of the extension by DHS of the period of authorized stay in such classification; or

(3) In the case of a blanket petition,

(i) The alien has presented to the consular officer official evidence of the approval by DHS of a blanket petition listing only those intracompany relationships and positions found to qualify under INA section 101(a)(15)(L);

(ii) The alien is otherwise eligible for L-1 classification pursuant to the blanket petition; and,

(iii) The alien requests that he or she be accorded such classification for the purpose of being transferred to, or remaining in, qualifying positions identified in such blanket petition; or

(4) The consular officer is satisfied the alien is the spouse or child of an alien so classified and is accompanying or following to join the principal alien.

(b) Petition approval. The approval of a petition by DHS does not establish that the alien is eligible to receive a nonimmigrant visa.

(c) Alien not entitled to L-1 classification under individual petition. The consular officer must suspend action on the alien's application and submit a report to the approving DHS office if the consular officer knows or has reason to believe that an alien applying for a visa as the beneficiary of an approved individual petition under INA section 101(a)(15)(L) is not entitled to such classification as approved.

(d) Labor disputes. Citizens of Canada or Mexico shall not be entitled to classification under this section if the Secretary of Homeland Security and the Secretary of Labor have certified that:

(1) There is in progress a strike or lockout in the course of a labor dispute in the occupational classification at the place or intended place of employment; and,

(2) The alien has failed to establish that the alien's entry will not affect adversely the settlement of the strike or lockout or the employment of any person who is involved in the strike or lockout.

(e) Alien not entitled to L-1 classification under blanket petition. The consular officer shall deny L classification based on a blanket petition if the documentation presented by the alien claiming to be a beneficiary thereof does not establish to the satisfaction of the consular officer that

(1) The alien has been continuously employed by the same employer, an affiliate or a subsidiary thereof, for one year within the three years immediately preceding the application for the L visa;

(2) The alien was rendering services in a capacity that is managerial, executive, or involves specialized knowledge throughout that year; or

(3) The alien is destined to render services in such a capacity, as identified in the petition and in an organization listed in the petition.

(f) Former exchange visitor. Former exchange visitors who are subject to the two-year foreign residence requirement of INA section 212(e) are ineligible to apply for visas under INA section 101(a)(15)(L) until they have fulfilled the residence requirement or obtained a waiver of the requirement.

HISTORY:

[57 FR 31449, July 16, 1992; 58 FR 68527, Dec. 28, 1993; 61 FR 1832, 1833, Jan. 24, 1996; 71 FR 34519, 34521, June 15, 2006; 77 FR 8119, 8120, Feb. 14, 2012]

§ 41.55 Aliens with extraordinary ability.

(a) Requirements for O classification. An alien shall be classifiable under the provisions of INA 101(a)(15)(O) if:

(1) The consular officer is satisfied that the alien qualifies under the provisions of that section; and either

(2) With respect to the principal alien, the consular officer has received official evidence of the approval by DHS of a petition to accord such classification or of the extension by DHS of the period of authorized stay in such classification; or

(3) The consular officer is satisfied the alien is the spouse or child of an alien so classified and is accompanying or following to join the principal alien.

(b) Approval of visa. The approval of a petition by DHS does not establish that the alien is eligible to receive a nonimmigrant visa.

(c) Validity of visa. The period of validity of a visa issued on the basis of paragraph (a) to this section must not exceed the period indicated in the petition, notification, or confirmation required in paragraph (a)(2) of this section.

(d) Alien not entitled to O classification. The consular officer must suspend action on the alien's application and submit a report to the approving DHS office if the consular officer knows or has reason to believe that an alien applying for a visa under INA 101(a)(15)(O) is not entitled to the classification as approved.

HISTORY:

[57 FR 31450, July 16, 1992; 61 FR 1832, 1833, Jan. 24, 1996; 71 FR 34519, 34521, June 15, 2006]

§ 41.56 Athletes, artists and entertainers.

(a) Requirements for P classification. An alien shall be classifiable under the provisions of INA 101(a)(15)(P) if:

(1) The consular officer is satisfied that the alien qualifies under the provisions of that section; and either

(2) With respect to the principal alien, the consular officer has received official evidence of the approval by DHS of a petition to accord such classification or of the extension by DHS of the period of authorized stay in such classification; or

(3) The consular officer is satisfied the alien is the spouse or child of an alien so classified and is accompanying or following to join the principal alien.

(b) Approval of visa. The approval of a petition by DHS does not establish that the alien is eligible to receive a nonimmigrant visa.

(c) Validity of visa. The period of validity of a visa issued on the basis of paragraph (a) to this section must not exceed the period indicated in the petition, confirmation, or extension of stay required in paragraph (a)(2) of this section.

(d) Alien not entitled to P classification. The consular officer must suspend action on the alien's application and submit a report to the approving DHS office if the consular officer knows or has reason to believe that an alien applying for a visa under INA 101(a)(15)(P) is not entitled to the classification as approved.

HISTORY:

[57 FR 31450, July 16, 1992; 61 FR 1832, 1833, Jan. 24, 1996; 71 FR 34519, 34521, June 15, 2006]

§ 41.57 International cultural exchange visitors.

(a) International cultural exchange visitors —

(1) Requirements for classification under INA section 101(a)(15)(Q)(i). A consular officer may classify an alien under the provisions of INA 101(a)(15)(Q)(i) if:

(i) The consular officer is satisfied that the alien qualifies under the provisions of that section, and

(ii) The consular officer has received official evidence of the approval by DHS of a petition or the extension by DHS of the period of authorized stay in such classification.

(2) Approval of petition. DHS approval of a petition does not establish that the alien is eligible to receive a nonimmigrant visa.

(3) Validity of visa. The period of validity of a visa issued on the basis of this paragraph (a) must not exceed the period indicated in the petition, notification, or confirmation required in paragraph (a)(2) of this section.

(4) Alien not entitled to Q classification. The consular officer must suspend action on the alien's application and submit a report to the approving DHS office if the consular officer knows or has reason to believe that an alien does not qualify under INA section 101(a)(15)(Q)(i).

(b) [Reserved]

HISTORY:

[57 FR 31450, July 16, 1992; 61 FR 1832, 1833, Jan. 24, 1996; 65 FR 14768, 14770, Mar. 17, 2000; 66 FR 52500, 52502, Oct. 16, 2001; 71 FR 34519, 34521, June 15, 2006; 85 FR 38320, 38321, June 26, 2020]

§ 41.58 Aliens in religious occupations.

(a) Requirements for "R" classification. An alien shall be classifiable under the provisions of INA 101(a)(15)(R) if:

(1) The consular officer is satisfied that the alien qualifies under the provisions of that section; and

(2) With respect to the principal alien, the consular officer has received official evidence of the approval by USCIS of a petition to accord such classification or the extension by USCIS of the period of authorized stay in such classification; or

(3) The alien is the spouse or child of an alien so classified and is accompanying or following to join the principal alien.

(b) Petition approval. The approval of a petition by USCIS does not establish that the alien is eligible to receive a nonimmigrant visa.

(c) Validity of visa. The period of validity of a visa issued on the basis of paragraph (a) to this section must not precede or exceed the period indicated in the petition, notification, or confirmation required in paragraph (a)(2) of this section.

(d) Aliens not entitled to classification under INA 101(a)(15)(R). The consular officer must suspend action on the alien's application and submit a report to the approving USCIS office if the consular officer knows or has reason to believe that an alien applying for a visa under INA 101(a)(15)(R) is not entitled to the classification as approved.

HISTORY:

[57 FR 343, Jan. 6, 1992.; 60 FR 42036, Aug. 15, 1995; 74 FR 51236, 51237, Oct. 6, 2009]

§ 41.59 Professionals under the United States-Mexico-Canada Agreement (USMCA).

(a) Requirements for classification as a USMCA professional. An alien shall be classifiable under the provisions of INA 214(e) if:

(1) The consular officer is satisfied that the alien qualifies under the provisions of that section; and

(2) The alien shall have presented to the consular officer sufficient evidence of an offer of employment in the United States requiring employment of a person in a professional capacity consistent with Section D and Appendix 2 of Annex 16-A of Chapter 16 of the USMCA and sufficient evidence that the alien possesses the credentials of that profession as listed in said appendix; or

(3) The alien is the spouse or child of an alien so classified in accordance with paragraph (a)(2) of this section and is accompanying or following to join the principal alien.

(b) Visa validity. The period of validity of a visa issued pursuant to paragraph (a) of this section may not exceed the period established on a reciprocal basis.

(c) Temporary entry. Temporary entry means an entry into the United States without the intent to establish permanent residence. The alien must satisfy the consular officer that the proposed stay is temporary. A temporary period has a reasonable, finite end that does not equate to permanent residence. The circumstances surrounding an application should reasonably and convincingly indicate that the alien's temporary work assignment in the United States will end predictably and that the alien will depart upon completion of the assignment.

(d) Labor disputes. Citizens of Canada or Mexico shall not be entitled to classification under this section if the Secretary of Homeland Security and the Secretary of Labor have certified that:

(1) There is in progress a strike or lockout in the course of a labor dispute in the occupational classification at the place or intended place of employment; and

(2) The alien has failed to establish that the alien's entry will not affect adversely the settlement of the

strike or lockout or the employment of any person who is involved in the strike or lockout.

HISTORY:

[58 FR 68527, Dec. 28, 1993; 63 FR 10304, 10305, March 3, 1998; 71 FR 34519, 34521, June 15, 2006; 79 FR 7582, 7583, Feb. 10, 2014; 86 FR 61064, 61065, Nov. 5, 2021]

Subpart G

Students and Exchange Visitors

§ 41.61 Students — academic and nonacademic.

(a) **Definitions —**

(1) Academic, in INA 101(a)(15)(F), refers to an established college, university, seminary, conservatory, academic high school, elementary school, or other academic institution, or a language training program.

(2) Nonacademic, in INA 101(a)(15)(M), refers to an established vocational or other recognized nonacademic institution (other than a language training program).

(b) Classification. (1) An alien is classifiable under INA 101(a)(15)(F) (i) or (iii) or INA 101(a)(15)(M) (i) or (iii) if the consular officer is satisfied that the alien qualifies under one of those sections, and:

(i) The alien has been accepted for attendance for the purpose of pursuing a full course of study, or, for students classified under INA 101(a)(15) (F)(iii) and (M)(iii) Border Commuter Students, full or part-time course of study, in an academic institution approved by the Secretary of Homeland Security for foreign students under INA 101(a)(15)(F)(i) or a nonacademic institution approved under 101(a)(15)(M)(i). The alien has presented a SEVIS Form I-20, Form I-20A-B/I-20ID. Certificate of Eligibility For Nonimmigrant Student Status — For Academic and Language Students, or Form I-20M-N/I-20ID, Certificate of Eligibility for Nonimmigrant Student Status — For Vocational Students, properly completed and signed by the alien and a designated official as prescribed in regulations found at 8 CFR 214.2(F) and 214.2(M);

(ii) The alien possesses sufficient funds to cover expenses while in the United States or can satisfy the consular officer that other arrangements have been made to meet those expenses;

(iii) The alien, unless coming to participate exclusively in an English language training program, has sufficient knowledge of the English language to undertake the chosen course of study or training. If the alien's knowledge of English is inadequate, the consular officer may nevertheless find the alien so classifiable if the accepting institution offers English language training, and has accepted the alien expressly for a full course of study (or part-time course of study for Border Commuter Students) in a language with which the alien is familiar, or will enroll the alien in a combination of courses and English instruction which will constitute a full course of study if required; and

(iv) The alien intends, and will be able, to depart upon termination of student status.

(2) An alien otherwise qualified for classification as a student, who intends to study the English language exclusively, may be classified as a student under INA 101(a) (15) (F) (i) even though no credits are given by the accepting institution for such study. The accepting institution, however, must offer a full course of study in the English language and must accept the alien expressly for such study.

(3) The alien spouse and minor children of an alien who has been or will be issued a visa under INA 101(a) (15) (F) (i) or 101(a) (15) (M) (i) may receive nonimmigrant visas under INA 101(a) (15) (F) (ii) or 101(a) (15) (M) (ii) if the consular officer is satisfied that they will be accompanying or following to join the principal alien; that sufficient funds are available to cover their expenses in the United States; and, that they intend to leave the United States upon the termination of the status of the principal alien.

(c) Posting of bond. In borderline cases involving an alien otherwise qualified for classification under INA 101(a) (15) (F), the consular officer is authorized to require the posting of a bond with the Secretary of Homeland Security in a sum sufficient to ensure that the alien will depart upon the conclusion of studies or in the event of failure to maintain student status.

(d) Electronic verification and notification. A student's acceptance documentation must be verified by a consular official's review of the SEVIS data in the Consolidated Consular Database or via direct access to SEVIS or ISEAS prior to the issuance of an F-1, F-2, M-1 or M-3 visa. Evidence of the payment of any applicable fees, if not presented with other documentation, may also be verified through the Consolidated Consular Database or direct access to SEVIS. Upon issuance of an F or M visa, notification of such issuance must be entered into the SEVIS database.

HISTORY:

[52 FR 42597, Nov. 5, 1987; 67 FR 58693, 58695, Sept. 18, 2002; 68 FR 28129, 28131, May 23, 2003, as confirmed at 70 FR 7853, Feb. 16, 2005; 71 FR 34519, 34521, June 15, 2006]

§ 41.62 Exchange visitors.

(a) J-1 classification. An alien is classifiable as an exchange visitor if qualified under the provisions of INA 101(a) (15) (J) and the consular officer is satisfied that the alien:

(1) Has been accepted to participate, and intends to participate, in an exchange visitor program designated by the Bureau of Education and Cultural Affairs, Department of State, as evidenced by the presentation of a properly executed Form DS-2019, Certificate of Eligibility for Exchange Visitor (J-1) Status;

(2) Has sufficient funds to cover expenses or has made other arrangements to provide for expenses;

(3) Has sufficient knowledge of the English language to undertake the program for which selected, or, except for an alien coming to participate in a graduate medical education or training program, the sponsoring organization is aware of the language deficiency and has nevertheless indicated willingness to accept the alien; and

(4) Meets the requirements of INA 212(j) if coming to participate in a graduate medical education or training program.

(5) Electronic verification and notification. An exchange visitor's acceptance documentation and payment of any applicable fees must be verified by a consular official's review of the SEVIS database or via direct access to SEVIS or ISEAS prior to the issuance of a J-1 or J-2 visa. Evidence of the payment of any applicable fees, if not presented with other documentation, may also be verified through the Consolidated Consular Database or direct access to SEVIS. Upon issuance of a J-1 or J-2 visa, notification of such issuance must be entered into the SEVIS database.

(b) J-2 Classification. The spouse or minor child of an alien classified J-1 is classifiable J-2.

(c) Applicability of INA 212(e). (1) An alien is subject to the 2-year foreign residence requirement of INA 212(e) if:

(i) The alien's participation in one or more exchange programs was wholly or partially financed, directly or indirectly, by the U.S. Government or by the government of the alien's last legal permanent residence; or

(ii) At the time of the issuance of an exchange visitor visa and admission to the United States, or, if not required to obtain a nonimmigrant visa, at the time of admission as an exchange visitor, or at the time of acquisition of such status after admission, the alien is a national and resident or, if not a national, a legal permanent resident (or has status equivalent thereto) of a country which the Secretary of State has designated, through publication by public notice in the Federal Register, as clearly requiring the services of persons engaged in the field of specialized knowledge or skill in which the alien will engage during the exchange visitor program; or

(iii) The alien acquires exchange visitor status in order to receive graduate medical education or training in the United States.

(2) For the purposes of this paragraph the terms "financed directly" and "financed indirectly" are defined as set forth in section § 514.1 of Chapter V.

(3) The country in which 2 years' residence and physical presence will satisfy the requirements of INA 212(e) in the case of an alien determined to be subject to such requirements is the country of which the alien is a national and resident, or, if not a national, a legal permanent resident (or has status equivalent thereto).

(4) If an alien is subject to the 2-year foreign residence requirement of INA 212(e), the spouse or child of that alien, accompanying or following to join the alien, is also subject to that requirement if admitted to the United States pursuant to INA 101(a) (15) (J) or if status is acquired pursuant to that section after admission.

(d) Notification to alien concerning 2-year foreign residence requirement. Before the consular officer issues an exchange visitor visa, the consular officer must inform the alien whether the alien will be subject to the 2-year residence and physical presence requirement of INA 212(e) if admitted to the United States under INA 101(a) (15) (J) and, if so, the country in which 2 years' residence and physical presence will satisfy the requirement.

HISTORY:

[52 FR 42597, Nov. 5, 1987; 67 FR 58693, 58695, Sept. 18, 2002; 68 FR 28129, 28132, May 23, 2003, as confirmed at 70 FR 7853, Feb. 16, 2005; 72 FR 10060, 10061, Mar. 7, 2007]

§ 41.63 Two-year home-country physical presence requirement.

(a) Statutory basis for rule. Section 212(e) of the Immigration and Nationality Act, as amended, provides in substance as follows:

(1) No person admitted under Section 101(a) (15)(J) or acquiring such status after admission:

(i) Whose participation in the program for which he came to the United States was financed in whole or in part, directly or indirectly, by an agency of the United States Government or by the government of the country of his nationality or of his last legal permanent residence;

(ii) Who at the time of admission or acquisition of status under 101(a)(15)(J) was a national or legal permanent resident of a country which the Secretary of State, pursuant to regulations prescribed by him, had designated as clearly requiring the services of persons engaged in the field of specialized knowledge or skill in which the alien was engaged [See the most recent "Revised Exchange Visitor Skills List", at http://exchanges.state.gov/education/jexchanges/participation/skills]list.pdf]; or

(iii) Who came to the United States or acquired such status in order to receive graduate medical education or training, shall be eligible to apply for an immigrant visa, or for permanent residence, or for a nonimmigrant visa under section 101(a)(15)(H) or section 101(a)(15)(L) until is established that such person has resided and been physically present in the country of his nationality or his last legal permanent residence for an aggregate of at least two years following departure from the United States.

(2) Upon the favorable recommendation of the Secretary of State, pursuant to the request of an interested United States Government agency (or in the case of an alien who is a graduate of a foreign medical school pursuing a program in graduate medical education or training, pursuant to the request of a State Department of Public Health, or its equivalent), or of the Secretary of Homeland Security after the latter has determined that departure from the United States would impose exceptional hardship upon the alien's spouse or child (if such spouse or child is a citizen of the United States or a legal permanent resident alien), or that the alien cannot return to the country of his nationality or last legal permanent residence because he would be subject to persecution on account of race, religion, or political opinion, the Secretary of Homeland Security may waive the requirement of such two-year foreign residence abroad in the case of any alien whose admission to the United States is found by the Secretary of Homeland Security to be in the public interest except that in the case of a waiver requested by a State Department of

Public Health, or its equivalent, the waiver shall be subject to the requirements of section 214(l) of the Immigration and Nationality Act (8 U.S.C. 1184).

(3) Except in the case of an alien who is a graduate of a foreign medical school pursuing a program in graduate medical education or training, the Secretary of Homeland Security, upon the favorable recommendation of the Secretary of State, may also waive such two-year foreign residence requirement in any case in which the foreign country of the alien's nationality or last legal permanent residence has furnished the Secretary of State a statement in writing that it has no objection to such waiver in the case of such alien. Notwithstanding the foregoing, an alien who is a graduate of a foreign medical school pursuing a program in graduate medical education or training may obtain a waiver of such two-year foreign residence requirements if said alien meets the requirements of section 214(l) of the Immigration and Nationality Act (8 U.S.C. 1184) and paragraphs (a) (2) and (e) of this section.

(b) Request for waiver on the basis of exceptional hardship or probable persecution on account of race, religion, or political opinion.

(1) An exchange visitor who seeks a waiver of the two-year home-country residence and physical presence requirement on the grounds that such requirement would impose exceptional hardship upon the exchange visitor's spouse or child (if such spouse or child is a citizen of the United States or a legal permanent resident alien), or on the grounds that such requirement would subject the exchange visitor to persecution on account of race, religion, or political opinion, shall submit the application for waiver (DHS Form I-612) to the jurisdictional office of the Department of Homeland Security.

(2)(i) If the Secretary of Homeland Security (Secretary of DHS) determines that compliance with the two-year home-country residence and physical presence requirement would impose exceptional hardship upon the spouse or child of the exchange visitor, or would subject the exchange visitor to persecution on account of race, religion, or political opinion, the Secretary of DHS shall transmit a copy of his determination together with a summary of the details of the expected hardship or persecution, to the Waiver Review Division, in the Department of State's Bureau of Consular Affairs.

(ii) With respect to those cases in which the Secretary of DHS has determined that compliance with the two-year home-country residence and physical presence requirement would impose exceptional hardship upon the spouse or child of the exchange visitor, the Waiver Review Division shall review the program, policy, and foreign relations aspects of the case, make a recommendation, and forward it to the appropriate office at DHS. If it deems it appropriate, the Waiver Review Division may request the views of each of the exchange visitors' sponsors concerning the waiver application. Except as set forth in paragraph (g)(4) of this section, the recommendation of the Waiver Review Division shall constitute the recommendation of the Department of State.

(iii) With respect to those cases in which the Secretary of DHS has determined that compliance with the two-year home-country residence and physical presence requirement would subject the exchange visitor to persecution on account of race, religion, or political opinion, the Waiver Review Division shall review the program, policy, and foreign relations aspects of the case, including consultation if deemed appropriate with the Bureau of Human Rights and Humanitarian Affairs of the United States Department of State, make a recommendation, and forward such recommendation to the Secretary of DHS. Except as set forth in paragraph (g)(4) of this section, the recommendation of the Waiver Review Division shall constitute the recommendation of the Department of State and such recommendation shall be forwarded to DHS.

(c) Requests for waiver made by an interested United States Government Department of State.

(1) A United States Government agency may request a waiver of the two-year home-country residence and physical presence requirement on behalf of an exchange visitor if such exchange visitor is actively and substantially involved in a program or activity sponsored by or of interest to such agency.

(2) A United States Government agency requesting a waiver shall submit its request in writing and fully explain why the grant of such waiver request would be in the public interest and the detrimental effect that would result to the program or activity of interest to the requesting agency if the exchange visitor is unable to continue his or her involvement with the program or activity.

(3) A request by a United States Government agency shall be signed by the head of the agency, or his or her designee, and shall include copies of all IAP 66 or DS-2019 forms issued to the exchange visitor, his or her current address, and his or her country of nationality or last legal permanent residence.

(4) A request by a United States Government agency, excepting the Department of Veterans Affairs, on behalf of an exchange visitor who is a foreign medical graduate who entered the United States to pursue graduate medical education or training, and who is willing to provide primary care or specialty medicine in a designated primary care Health Professional shortage Area, or a Medically Underserved Area, or psychiatric care in a Mental Health Professional Shortage Area, shall, in additional to the requirement set forth in paragraphs (c)(2) and (3) of this section, include:

(i) A copy of the employment contract between the foreign medical graduate and the health care facility at which he or she will be employed. Such contract shall specify a term of employment of not less than three years and that the foreign medical graduate is to be employed by the facility for the purpose of providing not less than 40 hours per week of primary medical care, i.e. general or family practice, general internal medicine, pediatrics, or obstetrics and gynecology, in a designated primary care Health Professional Shortage Area or designated Medically Underserved Area ("MUA") or psychiatric care in a designated Mental Health Professional Shortage Area. Further, such employment contract shall not include a non-compete clause enforceable against the foreign medical graduate.

(ii) A statement, signed and dated by the head of the health care facility at which the foreign medical graduate will be employed, that the facility is located in an area designated by the Secretary of Health and Human Services as a Medically Underserved Area or Primary Medical Care Health Professional Shortage Area or Mental Health Professional Shortage Area and provides medical care to both Medicaid or Medicare eligible patients and indigent uninsured patients. The statement shall also list the primary care Health Professional Shortage Area, Mental Health Professional Shortage Area, or Medically Underserved Area/Population identifier number of the designation (assigned by the Secretary of Health and Human Services), and shall include the FIPS county code and census tract or block numbering area number (assigned by the Bureau of the Census) or the 9-digit zipcode of the area where the facility is located.

(iii) A statement, signed and dated by the foreign medical graduate exchange visitor that shall read as follows:

I, ———— (name of exchange visitor) hereby declare and certify, under penalty of the provisions of 18 U.S.C. 1001, that I do not now have pending nor am I submitting during the pendency of this request, another request to any United States Government department or agency or any State Department of Public Health, or equivalent, other than ———— (insert name of United States Government Agency requesting waiver) to act on my behalf in any matter relating to a waiver of my two-year home-country physical presence requirement.

(iv) Evidence that unsuccessful efforts have been made to recruit an American physician for the position to be filled.

(5) Except as set forth in paragraph (g)(4) of this section, the recommendation of the Waiver Review Division shall constitute the recommendation of the Department of State and such recommendation shall be forwarded to the Secretary of DHS.

(d) Requests for waiver made on the basis of a statement from the exchange visitor's home-country that it has no objection to the waiver.

(1) Applications for waiver of the two-year home-country residence and physical presence requirement may be supported by a statement of no objection by the exchange visitor's country of nationality or last legal permanent residence. The statement of no objection shall be directed to the Secretary of State through diplomatic channels; i.e., from the country's Foreign Office to the Department of State through the U.S. Mission in the foreign country concerned, or through the foreign country's head of mission or duly appointed designee in the United States to the Secretary of State in the form of a diplomatic note. This note shall include applicant's full name, date and place of birth, and present address. If deemed appropriate, the Department of State may request the views of each of the exchange visitor's sponsors concerning the waiver application.

(2) The Waiver Review Division shall review the program, policy, and foreign relations aspects of the case and forward its recommendation to the Secretary of DHS. Except as set forth in § 41.63(g)(4), infra, the recommendation of the Waiver Review Division shall constitute the recommendation of the Department of State.

(3) An exchange visitor who is a graduate of a foreign medical school and who is pursuing a program in graduate medical education or training in the United States is prohibited under section 212(e) of the Immigration and Nationality Act from applying for a waiver solely on the basis of no objection from his or her country of nationality or last legal permanent residence. However, an alien who is a graduate of a foreign medical school pursuing a program in graduate medical education or training may obtain a waiver of such two-year foreign residence requirements if said alien meets the requirements of section 214(l) of the Immigration and Nationality Act (8 U.S.C. 1184) and paragraphs (a)(2) and (e) of this section.

(e) Requests for waiver from a State Department of Public Health, or its equivalent, on the basis of Public Law 103-416.

(1) Pursuant to Public Law 103-416, in the case of an alien who is a graduate of a medical school pursuing a program in graduate medical education or training, a request for a waiver of the two-year home-country residence and physical presence requirement may be made by a State department of Public Health, or its equivalent. Such waiver shall be subject to the requirements of section 214(l) of the Immigration and Nationality Act (8 U.S.C. 1194(l)) and this § 41.63.

(2) With respect to such waiver under Public Law 104-416, if such alien is contractually obligated to return to his or her home country upon completion of the graduate medical education or training, the Secretary of State is to be furnished with a statement in writing that the country to which such alien is required to return has no objection to such waiver. The no objection statement shall be furnished to the Secretary of State in the manner and form set forth in paragraph (d) of this section and, additionally, shall bear a notation that it is being furnished pursuant to Public Law 103-416.

(3) The State Department of Public Health, or equivalent agency, shall include in the waiver application the following:

(i) A completed DS-3035. Copies of these forms may be obtained from the Visa Office or online at http://www.travel.state.gov.

(ii) A letter from the Director of the designated State Department of Public Health, or its equivalent, which identifies the foreign medical graduate by name, country of nationality or country of last legal permanent residence, and date of birth, and states that it is in the public interest that a waiver of the two-year home residence requirement be granted;

(iii) An employment contract between the foreign medical graduate and the health care facility named in the waiver application, to include the name and address of the health care facility, and the specific geographical area or areas in which the foreign medical graduate will practice medicine. The employment contract shall include a statement by the foreign medical graduate that he or she agrees to meet the requirements set forth in section 214(l) of the Immigration and Nationality Act. The term of the employment contract shall be at least three years and the geographical areas of employment shall only be in areas, within the respective state, designated by the Secretary of Health and Human Services as having a shortage of health care professionals, unless the waiver request is for an alien who will practice medicine in a facility that serves patients who reside in one or more geographic areas so designated by the Secretary of Health and Human Services without regard to whether such facility is located within such a designated geographic area. For the latter situation, which will be referred to as "non-designated requests", the contract should also state that the term of the employment contract shall be at least three years and employment shall only be in a facility that serves patients who reside in one or more geographic areas so designed by the Secretary of Health and Human Services as having a shortage of health care professionals.

(iv) Evidence establishing that the geographic area or areas in the state in which the foreign medical graduate will practice medicine or where patients who will be served by the foreign medical graduates reside, are areas which have been designated by the Secretary of Health and Human Services as having a shortage of health care professionals. For purposes of this paragraph, the geographic area or areas must be designated by the Department of Health and Human Services as a Health Professional Shortage Area ("HPSA") or as a Medically Underserved Area/Medically Underserved Population ("MUA/MUP").

(v) Copies of all forms IAP 66 or DS-2019 issued to the foreign medical graduate seeking the waiver;

(vi) A copy of the foreign medical graduate's curriculum vitae;

(vii) If the foreign medical graduate is otherwise contractually required to return to his or her home country at the conclusion of the graduate medical education or training, a copy of the statement of no objection from the foreign medical graduate's country of nationality or last residence; and,

(viii) Because of the numerical limitations on the approval of waivers under Public Law 103-416, i.e., no more than the maximum number of waivers for each State each fiscal year as mandated by law, each application from a State Department of Public Health, or its equivalent, shall be numbered sequentially, beginning on October 1 of each year. The "non-designated" requests will also be numbered sequentially with appropriate identifier.

(4) The Waiver Review Division shall review the program, policy, and foreign relations aspects of the case and forward its recommendation to the Secretary of DHS. Except as set forth in paragraph (g)(4) of this section, the recommendation of the Waiver Review Division shall constitute the recommendation of the Department of State.

(f) Changed Circumstances. An applicant for a waiver on the grounds of exceptional hardship or probable persecution on account of race, religion, or political opinion, has a continuing obligation to inform the Department of Homeland Security of changed circumstances material to his or her pending application.

(g) The Waiver Review Board.

(1) The Waiver Review Board ("Board") shall consist of the following persons or their designees:

(i) The Principal Deputy Assistant Secretary of the Bureau of Consular Affairs;

(ii) The Director of Office of Public Affairs for the Bureau of Consular Affairs;

(iii) The Legislative Management Officer for Consular Affairs, Bureau of Legislative Affairs;

(iv) The Director of the Office of Exchange Coordination and Designation in the Bureau of Educational and Cultural Affairs; and

(v) The Director of the Office of Policy and Evaluation in the Bureau of Educational and Cultural Affairs.

(2) A person who has had substantial prior involvement in a particular case referred to the Board may not be appointed to, or serve on, the Board for that particular case unless the Bureau of Consular Affairs determines that the individual's inclusion on the Board is otherwise necessary or practicably unavoidable.

(3) The Principal Deputy Assistant Secretary of Consular Affairs, or his or her designee, shall serve as Board Chairman. No designee under this paragraph (g)(3) shall serve for more than 2 years.

(4) Cases will be referred to the Board at the discretion of the Chief, Waiver Review Division, of the Visa Office. The Chief, Waiver Review Division, or his or her designee may, at the Chairman's discretion, appear and present facts related to the case but shall not participate in Board deliberations.

(5) The Chairman of the Board shall be responsible for convening the Board and distributing all necessary information to its members. Upon being convened, the Board shall review the case file and weigh the request against the program, policy, and foreign relations aspects of the case.

(6) The Bureau of Consular Affairs shall appoint, on a case-by-case basis, from among the attorneys in the State Department's Office of Legal Advisor one attorney to serve as legal advisor to the Board.

(7) At the conclusion of its review of the case, the Board shall make a written recommendation either to grant or to deny the waiver application. The written recommendation of a majority of the Board shall constitute the recommendation of the Board. Such recommendation shall be promptly transmitted by the Chairman to the Chief, Waiver Review Division.

(8) At the conclusion of its review of the case, the Board shall make a written recommendation either to grant or to deny the waiver application. The written recommendation of a majority of the Board shall constitute the recommendation of the Board. Such recommendation shall be promptly transmitted by the Chairman to the Chief, Waiver Review Division.

HISTORY:

[58 FR 15196, Mar. 19, 1993, as corrected at 58 FR 18305, Apr. 8, 1993, as corrected at 58 FR 48448, Sept. 16, 1993; 60 FR 16787, Apr. 3, 1995, as confirmed and revised at 60 FR 53124, Oct. 12, 1995; 62 FR 19221, 19222, Apr. 21, 1997; 62 FR 28801, 28803, May 28, 1997; redesignated and amended at 64 FR 54538, 54539, 54540, Oct. 7, 1999; 67 FR 77159, 77160, Dec. 17, 2002; 71 FR 34519, 34521, June 15, 2006; 72 FR 10060, 10061, Mar. 7, 2007]

Subpart H

Transit Aliens

§ 41.71 Transit aliens.

(a) Transit aliens — general. An alien is classifiable as a nonimmigrant transit alien under INA 101(a) (15) (C) if the consular officer is satisfied that the alien:

(1) Intends to pass in immediate and continuous transit through the United States;

(2) Is in possession of a common carrier ticket or other evidence of transportation arrangements to the alien's destination;

(3) Is in possession of sufficient funds to carry out the purpose of the transit journey, or has sufficient funds otherwise available for that purpose; and

(4) Has permission to enter some country other than the United States following the transit through the United States, unless the alien submits satisfactory evidence that such advance permission is not required.

(b) Certain aliens in transit to United Nations. An alien within the provisions of paragraph (3), (4), or (5) of section 11 of the Headquarters Agreement with the United Nations, to whom a visa is to be issued for the purpose of applying for admission solely in transit to the United Nations Headquarters District, may upon request or at the direction of the Secretary of State be issued a nonimmigrant visa bearing the symbol C-2. If such a visa is issued, the recipient shall be subject to such restrictions on travel within the United States as may be provided in regulations prescribed by the Secretary of Homeland Security.

HISTORY:

[52 FR 42597, Nov. 5, 1987; 71 FR 34519, 34521, June 15, 2006]

Subpart I

Fiance(e)s and Other Nonimmigrants

§ 41.81 Fiance(e) or spouse of a U.S. citizen and derivative children.

(a) Fiance(e). An alien is classifiable as a nonimmigrant fiance(e) under INA 101(a)(15)(K)(i) if:

(1) The consular officer is satisfied that the alien is qualified under that provision and the consular officer has received a petition filed by a U.S. citizen to confer nonimmigrant status as a fiance(e) on the alien, which has been approved by the DHS under INA 214(d), or a notification of such approval from that Service;

(2) The consular officer has received from the alien the alien's sworn statement of ability and intent to conclude a valid marriage with the petitioner within 90 days of arrival in the United States; and

(3) The alien has met all other qualifications in order to receive a nonimmigrant visa, including the requirements of paragraph (d) of this section.

(b) Spouse. An alien is classifiable as a nonimmigrant spouse under INA 101(a)(15)(K)(ii) when all of the following requirements are met:

(1) The consular officer is satisfied that the alien is qualified under that provision and the consular officer has received a petition approved by the DHS pursuant to INA 214(p)(1), that was filed by the U.S. citizen spouse of the alien in the United States.

(2) If the alien's marriage to the U.S. citizen was contracted outside of the United States, the alien is applying in the country in which the marriage took place, or if there is no consular post in that country, then at a consular post designated by the Deputy Assistant Secretary of State for Visa Services to accept immigrant visa applications for nationals of that country.

(3) If the marriage was contracted in the United States, the alien is applying in a country as provided in part 42, § 42.61 of this chapter.

(4) The alien otherwise has met all applicable requirements in order to receive a nonimmigrant visa, including the requirements of paragraph (d) of this section.

(c) Child. An alien is classifiable under INA 101(a)(15)(K)(iii) if:

(1) The consular officer is satisfied that the alien is the child of an alien classified under INA 101(a)(15)(K)(i) or (ii) and is accompanying or following to join the principal alien; and

(2) The alien otherwise has met all other applicable requirements in order to receive a nonimmigrant visa, including the requirements of paragraph (d) of this section.

(d) Eligibility as an immigrant required. The consular officer, insofar as is practicable, must determine the eligibility of an alien to receive a nonimmigrant visa under paragraphs (a), (b) or (c) of this section as if the alien were an applicant for an immigrant visa, except that the alien must be exempt from the vaccination requirement of INA 212(a)(1) and the labor certification requirement of INA 212(a)(5).

HISTORY:

[52 FR 42597, Nov. 5, 1987, as amended at 56 FR 30428, July 2, 1991; 66 FR 19390, 19393, Apr. 16, 2001; 71 FR 34519, 34521, June 15, 2006]

§ 41.82 Certain parents and children of section 101(a)(27)(I) special immigrants [Reserved]

[NO TEXT IN ORIGINAL]

HISTORY:

[61 FR 1837, 1838, Jan. 24, 1996, as confirmed at 67 FR 67108, Nov. 4, 2002.]

AUTHORITY:

(8 U.S.C. 1104.)

§ 41.83 Certain Witnesses and Informants.

(a) General. An alien shall be classifiable under the provisions of INA 101(a)(15)(S) if:

(1) The consular officer is satisfied that the alien qualifies under the provisions of that section; and

(2)(i) The consular officer has received verification from the Department of State, Visa Office, that:

(A) in the case of INA 101(a)(15)(S)(i) the DHS has certified that the alien is accorded such classification, or

(B) in the case of INA 101(a)(15)(S)(ii) the Assistant Secretary of State for Consular Affairs on behalf of the Secretary of State and the DHS have certified that the alien is accorded such classification;

(ii) and the alien is granted an INA 212(d)(1) waiver of any INA 212(a) ground of ineligibility known at the time of verification.

(b) Certification of S visa status. The certification of status under INA 101(a)(15)(S)(i) by the Secretary of Homeland Security or of status under INA 101(a)(15)(S)(ii) by the Secretary of State and the Secretary of Homeland Security acting jointly does not establish that the alien is eligible to receive a nonimmigrant visa.

(c) Validity of Visa. The period of validity of a visa authorized on the basis of paragraph (a) of this section shall not exceed the period indicated in the certification required in paragraph (b) and shall not in any case exceed the period of three years.

HISTORY:

[61 FR 1837, 1838, Jan. 24, 1996, as confirmed at 67 FR 67108, Nov. 4, 2002; 71 FR 34519, 34521, June 15, 2006]

§ 41.84 Victims of trafficking in persons.

(a) Eligibility. Under INA 101(a)(15)(T)(ii), an applicant accompanying, or following to join, may acquire derivative status as a parent, spouse, sibling or child (derivative family member) based on a relationship to an individual (the principal) who has applied for or who has been granted T-1 nonimmigrant status under INA 101(a)(15)(T)(i) or may acquire derivative status as an adult or minor child of the principal's derivative family member if the adult or minor child faces a present danger of retaliation as a result of the principal's escape from trafficking or cooperation with law enforcement. Such applicant will be eligible for a visa if:

(1) The consular officer is satisfied that the applicant has the required relationship to an individual who has been granted status by the Secretary for Homeland Security under INA 101(a)(15)(T)(i); or the consular officer is satisfied that the applicant has the required relationship with a derivative family member;

(2) The consular officer is satisfied that the applicant is otherwise admissible under the immigration laws of the United States; and

(3) The consular officer has received a DHS-approved I-914, Supplement A, evidencing that the applicant has been granted derivative status.

(b) Visa validity. A qualifying derivative family member may apply for a nonimmigrant visa under INA 101(a)(15)(T)(ii) only during the period in which the principal is in status under INA 101(a)(15)(T)(i). Any visa issued pursuant to such application shall be valid only for a period of three years or until the expiration of the principal's status as an individual classified under INA 101(a)(15)(T)(i), whichever is shorter.

HISTORY:

[68 FR 37963, 37964, June 26, 2003; 71 FR 34519, 34522, June 15, 2006; 88 FR 45068, 45072, July 14, 2023]

§ 41.86 Certain spouses and children of lawful permanent resident aliens.

(a) Definition of "remains pending". For the purposes of this section, a visa application "remains pending" if the applicant has applied for an immigrant visa in accordance with the definition in part 40, § 40.1(l)(2) and the visa has neither been issued, nor refused for any reason under applicable law and regulation.

(b) Entitlement to classification. A consular officer may classify an alien as a nonimmigrant under INA 101(a)(15)(V) if:

(1) The consular officer has received notification from the Department of State or the Department of Justice that a petition to accord status to the alien as a spouse or child pursuant to INA 203(a)(2)(A) was filed on or before December 21, 2000; or

(2) The alien is eligible to derive benefits pursuant to INA 203(d) as a child of an alien described in paragraph (b)(1) of this section and such alien has qualified for V classification; and

(3) It has been three years or more since the filing date of the petition described in paragraph (b)(1) of this section and applicable to paragraph (b)(2) of this section and either:

(i) The petition has not been approved; or

(ii) If it has been approved, either no immigrant visa number is immediately available or the alien's application for adjustment of status or the alien's application for a visa remains pending.

(c) Eligibility as an immigrant required. The consular officer, insofar as practicable, must determine the eligibility of an alien described in paragraph (b) of this section to receive a nonimmigrant visa under INA 101(a)(15)(V), other than an alien who previously has been granted V status in the United States by DHS, as if the alien were an applicant for an immigrant visa, except that the alien is exempt from the vaccination requirement of INA 212(a)(1), the labor certification requirement of INA 212(a)(5) and the unlawful presence ineligibility of INA 212(a)(9)(B).

(d) Place of application. Notwithstanding the requirements of § 41.101, in determining the place of application for an alien seeking a visa pursuant to INA 101(a)(15)(V) the requirements of part 42, §§ 42.61(a) and (b)(1) of this chapter will apply.

HISTORY:

[66 FR 19390, 19393, Apr. 16, 2001; 71 FR 34519, 34522, June 15, 2006]

Subpart J
Application for Nonimmigrant Visa

§ 41.101 Place of application.

(a) Application for regular visa made at jurisdictional consular office of alien's residence or physical presence.

(1) An alien applying for a nonimmigrant visa shall make application at a consular office having jurisdiction over the alien's place of residence, or if the alien is a resident of Taiwan, at the American Institute in Taiwan, unless —

(i) the alien is physically present in the United States and is entitled to apply for issuance or reissuance of a visa under the provisions of § 41.111(b); or

(ii) a consular office having jurisdiction over the area in which the alien is physically present but not resident has agreed, as a matter of discretion or at the direction of the Department, to accept the alien's application; or

(iii) The alien is subject to INA 222(g) and must apply as set forth in paragraph (b) or (c) of this section.

(2) The Deputy Assistant Secretary of State for Visa Services is authorized to designate the geographical area for which each consular office possesses jurisdiction to process nonimmigrant visa applications.

(b) Place of application for persons subject to INA 222(g). Notwithstanding the requirements of paragraph (a) of this section, an alien whose prior nonimmigrant visa has been voided pursuant to INA 222(g), who is applying for a new nonimmigrant visa, shall make application at a consular office which has jurisdiction in or for the country of the alien's nationality unless extraordinary circumstances have been determined to exist with respect to that alien as set forth in paragraph (c) of this section.

(c) Exceptions based on extraordinary circumstances.

(1) An alien physician serving in underserved areas of the United States under the provisions of INA 214(l) for whom an application for a waiver of the 2-year foreign residence requirement and/or a petition to accord H-1B status was filed prior to the end of the alien's authorized period of stay and was subsequently approved, but whose authorized stay expired during the adjudication of such application(s), shall make application in accordance with paragraph (a) of this section.

(2) Any other individual or group whose circumstances are determined to be extraordinary, in accordance with paragraph (d)(1) of this section, by the Deputy Assistant Secretary for Visa Services upon the favorable recommendation of an immigration or consular officer, shall make application in accordance with paragraph (a) of this section.

(3) An alien who has, or immediately prior to the alien's last entry into the United States had, a residence in a country other than the country of the alien's nationality shall apply at a consular office with jurisdiction in or for the country of residence.

(4) An alien who is a national and resident of a country in which there is no United States consular office shall apply at a consular office designated by the Deputy Assistant Secretary for Visa Services to accept immigrant visa applications from persons of that nationality.

(5) An alien who possesses more than one nationality and who has, or immediately prior to the alien's last entry into the United States had, a residence in one of the countries of the alien's nationality shall apply at a consular office in the country of such residence.

(d) Definitions relevant to INA 222(g).

(1) Extraordinary circumstances — Extraordinary circumstances may be found where compelling humanitarian or national interests exist or where necessary for the effective administration of the immigration laws. Extraordinary circumstances shall not be found upon the basis of convenience or financial burden to the alien, the alien's relative, or the alien's employer.

(2) Nationality — For purposes of paragraph (b) of this section, a stateless person shall be considered to be a national of the country which issued the alien's travel document.

(e) Regular visa defined. "Regular visa" means a nonimmigrant visa of any classification which does not bear the title "Diplomatic" or "Official." A nonimmigrant visa is issued as a regular visa unless the alien falls within one of the classes entitled to a diplomatic or an official visa as described in § 41.26(c) or § 41.27(c).

(f) [Reserved]

HISTORY:

[52 FR 42597, Nov. 5, 1987; 53 FR 9112, Mar. 21, 1988; 61 FR 1521, 1522, Jan. 22, 1996; 61 FR 53058, Oct. 10, 1996; 61 FR 56438, 56439, Nov. 1, 1996; 63 FR 669, 671, Jan. 7, 1998, as corrected and confirmed at 63 FR 36365, 36366, July 6, 1998; 65 FR 14768, 14771, Mar. 17, 2000; 66 FR 38539, 38542, July 25, 2001; 67 FR 66045, 66046, Oct. 30, 2002; 85 FR 38320, 38321, June 26, 2020]

§ 41.102 Personal appearance of applicant.

(a) Except when the requirement of personal appearance has been waived pursuant to paragraph (b), (c), or (d) of this section, each applicant for a nonimmigrant visa who is at least 14 years of age and not more than 79 years of age must personally appear before and be interviewed by a consular officer, who shall determine on the basis of the applicant's representations, the visa application and other relevant documentation:

(1) The proper nonimmigrant classification, if any, of the alien; and

(2) The alien's eligibility to receive a visa.

(b) Waivers of personal appearance by consular officers. Except as provided in paragraph (e) of this section or as otherwise instructed by the Deputy Assistant Secretary of State for Visa Services, a consular officer may waive the requirement of personal appearance if the consular officer concludes the alien presents no national security concerns requiring an interview and:

(1) Is within a class of nonimmigrants classifiable under the visa symbols A-1, A-2, C-2, C-3 (except attendants, servants, or personal employees of accredited officials), G-1, G-2, G-3, G-4, NATO-1, NATO-2, NATO-3, NATO-4, NATO-5, NATO-6, or is a Taipei Economic and Cultural Representative Office (TECRO)

nonimmigrant classifiable under visa symbol E-1, and is seeking a visa in such classification; or

(2) Is an applicant for a diplomatic or official visa as described in § 41.26 or § 41.27 of this chapter; or

(3) Is an applicant who is within 12 months of the expiration of the applicant's previously issued visa and:

(i) Is seeking re-issuance of a nonimmigrant visa in the same classification;

(ii) Is applying at the consular post of the applicant's usual residence; and

(iii) Is an applicant for whom the consular officer has no indication of visa ineligibility or of noncompliance with U.S. immigration laws and regulations.

(c) Waivers of personal appearance in the national interest. Except as provided in paragraph (e) of this section, the Secretary may waive the requirement of personal appearance of an individual applicant or a class of applicants if the Secretary determines that such waiver is in the national interest of the United States.

(d) Waivers of personal appearance in unusual or emergent circumstances. Except as provided in paragraph (e) of this section, the Deputy Assistant Secretary for Visa Services may waive the requirement of personal appearance of an individual applicant or a class of applicants if the Deputy Assistant Secretary determines that such waiver is necessary as a result of unusual or emergent circumstances.

(e) Cases in which personal appearance may not be waived. Except for a nonimmigrant applicant whose personal appearance is waived under paragraphs (b)(1), (b)(2), or (c) of this section, the personal appearance requirement may not be waived for:

(1) Any nonimmigrant applicant who is not a national or resident of the country in which he or she is applying.

(2) Any nonimmigrant applicant who was previously refused a visa, is listed in CLASS, or otherwise requires a Security Advisory Opinion, unless:

(i) The visa was refused and the refusal was subsequently overcome; or

(ii) The alien was found inadmissible, but the inadmissibility was waived.

(3) Any nonimmigrant applicant who is from a country designated by the Secretary of State as a state sponsor of terrorism, regardless of age, or who is a member of a group or sector designated by the Secretary of State under section 222(h)(2)(F) of the Immigration and Nationality Act.

HISTORY:

[52 FR 42597, Nov. 5, 1987; 53 FR 9112, Mar. 21, 1988; 66 FR 38539, 39542, July 25, 2001; 67 FR 66045, 66046, Oct. 30, 2002; 68 FR 40127, 40128, July 7, 2003; 71 FR 75662, 75663, Dec. 18, 2006; 80 FR 69588, 69589, Nov. 10, 2015]

§ 41.103 Filing an application.

(a) Filing an application—

(1) Filing of application required. Every alien seeking a nonimmigrant visa must make an electronic application on Form DS-160 or, as directed by a consular officer, an application on Form DS-156. The Form DS-160 must be signed electronically by clicking the box designated "Sign Application" in the certification section of the application.

(2) Filing of an electronic application (Form DS-160) or Form DS-156 by alien under 16 or physically incapable. The application for an alien under 16 years of age or one physically incapable of completing an application may be completed and executed by the alien's parent or guardian, or if the alien has no parent or guardian, by any person having legal custody of, or a legitimate interest in, the alien.

(3) Waiver of filing of application when personal appearance is waived. Even if personal appearance of a visa applicant is waived pursuant to 22 CFR 41.102, the requirement for filing an application is not waived.

(b) Application—

(1) Preparation of Electronic Nonimmigrant Visa Application (Form DS-160) or, alternatively, Form DS-156. The consular officer shall ensure that the application is fully and properly completed in accordance with the applicable regulations and instructions.

(2) Additional requirements and information as part of application. Applicants who are required to appear for a personal interview must provide a biometric, which will serve to authenticate identity and additionally verify the accuracy and truthfulness of the statements in the application at the time of interview. The consular officer may require the submission of additional necessary information or question an alien on any relevant matter whenever the consular officer believes that the information provided in the application is inadequate to permit a determination of the alien's eligibility to receive a nonimmigrant visa. Additional statements made by the alien become a part of the visa application. All documents required by the consular officer under the authority of § 41.105(a) are considered papers submitted with the alien's application within the meaning of INA 221(g)(1).

(3) Signature. The Form DS-160 shall be signed electronically by clicking the box designated "Sign Application" in the certification section of the application. This electronic signature attests to the applicant's familiarity with and intent to be bound by all statements in the NIV application under penalty of perjury. Alternatively, except as provided in paragraph (a)(2) of this section, the Form DS-156 shall be signed by the applicant, with intent to be bound by all statement in the NIV application under penalty of perjury.

(4) Registration. The Form DS-160 or the Form DS-156, when duly executed, constitutes the alien's registration for the purposes of INA 221(b).

HISTORY:

[52 FR 42597, Nov. 5, 1987; 66 FR 38539, 38542, July 25, 2001; 67 FR 66045, 66046, Oct. 30, 2002; 71 FR 34519, 34522, June 15, 2006; 73 FR 23067, 23068, Apr. 29, 2008]

§ 41.104 Passport requirements.

(a) Passports defined. "Passport" as defined in INA 101(a)(30) is not limited to a national passport or to a single document. A passport may consist of two or more documents which, when considered together, fulfill the requirements of a passport, provided that the documentary evidence of permission to enter a foreign country has been issued by a competent authority and clearly meets the requirements of INA 101(a)(30).

(b) Passport requirement. Except for certain persons in the A, C-3, G, and NATO classifications and persons for whom the passport requirement has been waived pursuant to the provisions of INA 212(d)(4), every applicant for a nonimmigrant visa is required to present a passport, as defined above and in INA 101(a)(30), which is valid for the period required by INA 212(a)(7)(B)(i)(I).

(c) A single passport including more than one person. The passport requirement for a nonimmigrant visa may be met by the presentation of a passport including more than one person, if such inclusion is authorized under the laws or regulations of the issuing authority and if a photograph of each visa applicant 16 years of age or over has been attached to the passport by the issuing authority.

(d) Applicants for diplomatic visas. Every applicant for a diplomatic visa must present a diplomatic passport, or the equivalent thereof, having the period of validity required by INA 212(a)(7)(B)(i)(I), unless such requirement has been waived pursuant to the authority contained in INA 212(d)(4) or unless the case falls within the provisions of § 41.21(b).

HISTORY:

[52 FR 42597, Nov. 5, 1987, as amended at 56 FR 30428, July 2, 1991; 61 FR 1521, 1522, Jan. 22, 1996; 61 FR 53058, Oct. 10, 1996; 66 FR 38539, 38543, July 25, 2001; 67 FR 66045, 66046, Oct. 30, 2002]

§ 41.105 Supporting documents and fingerprinting.

(a) **Supporting documents —**

(1) Authority to require documents. The consular officer is authorized to require documents considered necessary to establish the alien's eligibility to receive a nonimmigrant visa. All documents and other evidence presented by the alien, including briefs submitted by attorneys or other representatives, shall be considered by the consular officer.

(2) Unobtainable documents. If the consular officer is satisfied that a document or record required under the authority of this section is unobtainable, the consular officer may accept satisfactory alternative pertinent evidence. A document or other record shall be considered unobtainable if it cannot be procured without causing the applicant or a member of the applicant's family actual hardship as distinct from normal delay and inconvenience.

(3) Photographs required. Every applicant for a nonimmigrant visa must furnish photographs of the number and specification prescribed by the Department. The applicant must either upload a digital photograph electronically as part of submitting an online visa application or submit a paper photograph at the direction of the Department or consular officer. The photograph shall be considered signed when the applicant signs the appropriate application form pursuant to § 41.103(b)(3).

(4) Police certificates. A police certificate is a certification by the police or other appropriate authorities stating what, if anything, their records show concerning the alien. An applicant for a nonimmigrant visa is required to present a police certificate if the consular officer has reason to believe that a police or criminal record exists, except that no police certificate is required in the case of an alien who is within a class of nonimmigrants classifiable under visa symbols A-1, A-2, C-3, G-1 through G-4, NATO-1 through NATO-4 or NATO-6.

(b) Fingerprinting. Every applicant for a nonimmigrant visa must furnish fingerprints, as required by the consular officer.

HISTORY:

[52 FR 42597, Nov. 5, 1987; 53 FR 9112, 9172, Mar. 21, 1988; 61 FR 1521, 1522, Jan. 22, 1996; 61 FR 53058, Oct. 10, 1996; 64 FR 13510, Mar. 19, 1999; 67 FR 8477, 8478, Feb. 25, 2002; 72 FR 74174, 74175, Dec. 31, 2007; 73 FR 49091, 49092, Aug. 20, 2008; 88 FR 13694, 13696, Mar. 6, 2023]

§ 41.106 Processing.

Consular officers must ensure that the Form DS-160 or, alternatively, Form DS-156 is properly and promptly processed in accordance with the applicable regulations and instructions.

HISTORY:

[52 FR 42597, Nov. 5, 1987; 71 FR 34519, 34522, June 15, 2006; 73 FR 23067, 23069, Apr. 29, 2008]

§ 41.107 Visa fees.

(a) Fees based on reciprocity. The fees for the issuance of visas, including official visas, to nonimmigrant nationals or stateless residents of each foreign country shall be collected in the amounts prescribed by the Secretary of State unless, on the basis of reciprocity, no fee is chargeable. If practicable, fees will correspond to the total amount of all visa, entry, residence, or other similar fees, taxes or charges assessed or levied against nationals of the United States by the foreign countries of which such nonimmigrants are nationals or stateless residents.

(b) Fees when more than one alien included in visa. A single nonimmigrant visa may be issued to include all eligible family members if the spouse and unmarried minor children of a principal alien are included in one passport. Each alien must execute a separate application. The name of each family member shall be inserted in the space provided in the visa stamp. The visa fee to be collected shall equal the total of the fees prescribed by the Secretary of State for each alien included in the visa, unless upon a basis of reciprocity a lesser fee is chargeable.

(c) **Certain aliens exempted from fees.**

(1) Upon a basis of reciprocity, or as provided in section 13(a) of the Headquarters Agreement with the United Nations (61 Stat. 716; 22 U.S.C. 287, Note), no fee shall be collected for the application for or issuance

of a nonimmigrant visa to an alien who is within a class of nonimmigrants classifiable under the visa symbols A, G, C-2, C-3, or NATO, or B-1 issued for participation in an official observer mission to the United Nations, or who is issued a diplomatic visa as defined in § 41.26.

(2) The consular officer shall waive the nonimmigrant visa application and issuance fees for an alien who will be engaging in charitable activities for a charitable organization upon the written request of the charitable organization claiming that it will find the fees a financial burden, if the consular officer is satisfied that:

(i) The organization seeking relief from the fees is, if based in the United States, tax-exempt as a charitable organization under the provisions of section 501(c)(3) of the Internal Revenue Code (26 U.S.C. 501(c)(3)); if a foreign organization based outside the United States in a country having laws according recognition to charitable institutions, that it establishes that it is recognized as a charitable institution by that government; and if a foreign organization based in a country without such laws, that it is engaged in activities substantially similar to those underlying section 501(c)(3), and

(ii) The charitable activities in which the alien will engage are specified and will be a part of, or will be related to and in support of, the organization's provision of services, including but not limited to health care, food and housing, job training, and similar direct services and assistance to the poor and needy, and

(iii) The request includes the location of the proposed activities, the number and identifying data of each of the alien(s) who will be applying for visas, and

(iv) The proposed duration of the alien(s)'s temporary stay in the United States is reasonably consistent with the charitable purpose for which the alien(s) seek to enter the United States.

(3) Foreign national employees of the U. S. Government who are travelling to the United States on official business in connection with that employment.

(d) Refund of fees. A fee collected for the issuance of a nonimmigrant visa is refundable only if the principal officer at a post or the officer in charge of a consular section determines that the visa was issued in error or could not be used as a result of action taken by the U.S. Government for which the alien was not responsible and over which the alien had no control.

(e)(1) Visa processing surcharge. In addition to the collection of the fee prescribed in paragraph (a) of this section, a consular officer shall collect or ensure the collection of a surcharge for the processing of applications for machine readable nonimmigrant visas and for machine readable combined border crossing cards in the amount specified by the Secretary of State from such applicants as the Secretary of State shall designate. Such surcharge is refundable only if, as a result of action taken by the U.S. Goverment for which the alien was not responsible and over which the alien had no control, the alien's application is not processed.

(2) Notwithstanding paragraph (e)(1) of this section, a consular officer shall collect or insure the collection of a processing fee for a machine-readable combined border crossing card and nonimmigrant visa in an amount determined by the Secretary and set forth in 22 CFR 22.1 to be sufficient only to cover the cost for manufacturing the combined card and visa if:

(i) The alien is a Mexican citizen under the age of 15;

(ii) The alien is applying in Mexico; and

(iii) The alien has at least one parent or guardian who has a visa or is applying for a machine-readable combined border crossing card and visa.

HISTORY:

[52 FR 42597, Nov. 5, 1987; 59 FR 25325, May 16, 1994, as confirmed at 62 FR 24334, May 5, 1997; 63 FR 24107, 24108, May 1, 1998, as confirmed and amended at 63 FR 52969, 52970, Oct. 2, 1998; 65 FR 52306, 52307, Aug. 29, 2000, as confirmed at 68 FR 13627, Mar. 20, 2003; 66 FR 17510, 17511, Apr. 2, 2001; 66 FR 38539, 38543, July 25, 2001; 67 FR 38892, 38893, June 6, 2002, as corrected at 67 FR 40849, June 14, 2002; 67 FR 66045, 66046, Oct. 30, 2002]

§ 41.108 Medical examination.

(a) Requirements for medical examination. An applicant for a nonimmigrant visa shall be required to take a medical examination if:

(1) The alien is an applicant for a K nonimmigrant visa as a fiance(e) of a U.S. citizen or as the child of such an applicant; or,

(2) The alien is seeking admission for medical treatment and the consular officer considers a medical examination advisable; or,

(3) The consular officer has reason to believe that a medical examination might disclose that the alien is medically ineligible to receive a visa.

(b) Examination by panel physician. The required examination, which must be carried out in accordance with United States Public Health Service regulations, shall be conducted by a physician selected by the alien from a panel of physicians approved by the consular officer or, if the alien is in the United States, by a medical officer of the United States Public Health Service or by a contract physician from a list of physicians approved by the DHS for the examination of INA 245 adjustment of status applicants.

(c) Panel physician facility requirements. A consular officer may not include the name of a physician on the panel of physicians referred to in paragraph (b) of this section unless the physician has facilities to perform required serological and X-ray tests or is in a position to refer applicants to a qualified laboratory for such tests.

HISTORY:

[52 FR 42597, Nov. 5, 1987; 71 FR 34519, 34522, June 15, 2006]

Subpart K

Issuance of Nonimmigrant Visa

§ 41.111 Authority to issue visa.

(a) Issuance outside the United States. Any consular officer is authorized to issue regular and official visas. Diplomatic visas may be issued only by:

(1) A consular officer attached to a U.S. diplomatic mission, if authorized to do so by the Chief of Mission; or

(2) A consular officer assigned to a consular office under the jurisdiction of a diplomatic mission, if so authorized by the Department or the Chief, Deputy Chief, or Counselor for Consular Affairs of that mission, or, if assigned to a consular post not under the jurisdiction of a diplomatic mission, by the principal officer of that post.

(b) Issuance in the United States in certain cases. The Deputy Assistant Secretary for Visa Services and such officers of the Department as the former may designate are authorized, in their discretion, to issue nonimmigrant visas, including diplomatic visas, in the United States, to:

(1) Qualified applicants who are currently maintaining status and are properly classifiable in the A, C–2, C– 3, G or NATO category and intend to reenter the United States in that status after a temporary absence abroad and who also present evidence that:

(i) They have been lawfully admitted in that status or have, after admission, had their classification changed to that status; and

(ii) Their period of authorized stay in the United States in that status has not expired; and

(2) Children who are born in the United States, but who are not subject to the jurisdiction thereof because they are born to certain qualified individuals who are currently maintaining status and are properly classifiable in the A, C–2, C–3, G or NATO category.

(3) Other qualified applicants who:

(i) Are currently maintaining status in the E, H, I, L, O, or P nonimmigrant category;

(ii) Intend to reenter the United States in that status after a temporary absence abroad; and

(iii) Who also present evidence that:

(A) They were previously issued visas at a consular office abroad and admitted to the United States in the status which they are currently maintaining; and

(B) Their period of authorized admission in that status has not expired.

HISTORY:

[52 FR 42597, Nov. 5, 1987; 66 FR 12737, 12738, Feb. 28, 2001; 87 FR 53373, 53375, Aug. 31, 2022]

§ 41.112 Validity of visa.

(a) Significance of period of validity of visa. The period of validity of a nonimmigrant visa is the period during which the alien may use it in making application for admission. The period of visa validity has no relation to the period of time the immigration authorities at a port of entry may authorize the alien to stay in the United States.

(b) Validity of visa and number of applications for admission.

(1) Except as provided in paragraphs (c) and (d) of this section, a nonimmigrant visa shall have the validity prescribed in schedules provided to consular officers by the Department, reflecting insofar as practicable the reciprocal treatment accorded U.S. nationals, U.S. permanent residents, or aliens granted refugee status in the U.S. by the government of the country of which the alien is a national, permanent resident, refugee or stateless resident.

(2) Notwithstanding paragraph (b)(1) of this section, United States nonimmigrant visas shall have a maximum validity period of 10 years.

(3) An unexpired visa is valid for application for admission even if the passport in which the visa is stamped has expired, provided the alien is also in possession of a valid passport issued by the authorities of the country of which the alien is a national.

(c) Limitation on validity. If warranted in an individual case, a consular officer may issue a nonimmigrant visa for:

(1) A period of validity that is less than that prescribed on a basis of reciprocity,

(2) A number of applications for admission within the period of the validity of the visa that is less than that prescribed on a basis of reciprocity,

(3) Application for admission at a specified port or at specified ports of entry, or

(4) Use on and after a given date subsequent to the date of issuance.

(d) Automatic extension of validity at ports of entry.

(1) Provided that the requirements set out in paragraph (d)(2) of this section are fully met, the following provisions apply to nonimmigrant aliens seeking readmission at ports of entry:

(i) The validity of an expired nonimmigrant visa issued under INA 101(a)(15) may be considered to be automatically extended to the date of application for readmission; and

(ii) In cases where the original nonimmigrant classification of an alien has been changed by DHS to another nonimmigrant classification, the validity of an expired or unexpired nonimmigrant visa may be considered to be automatically extended to the date of application for readmission, and the visa may be converted as necessary to that changed classification.

(2) The provisions in paragraph (d)(1) of this section are applicable only in the case of a nonimmigrant alien who:

(i) Is in possession of a Form I-94, Arrival-Departure Record, endorsed by DHS to show an unexpired period of initial admission or extension of stay, provided that in the case of a qualified F student or the accompanying spouse or child of such student, is in possession of a current Form I-20, Certificate of Eligibility for Nonimmigrant Student Status, issued by the school that the student has been authorized to attend by DHS and endorsed by the issuing school official to indicate the period of initial admission or extension of stay authorized by DHS, and provided that in the case of a qualified J exchange visitor or the accompanying spouse or child of such exchange visitor, is in possession of a current Form DS-2019, Certificate of Eligibility for Exchange Visitor Status (J-NONIMMIGRANT), issued and endorsed by the Department of State-designated sponsor of the exchange program, to indicate the period of initial admission authorized by DHS or the extension of stay authorized by the Department of State;

(ii) Is applying for readmission after an absence not exceeding 30 days solely in contiguous territory, or, in the case of a student or exchange visitor or accompanying spouse or child meeting the stipulations of paragraph (d)(2)(i) of this section, after an absence not exceeding 30 days in contiguous territory or adjacent islands other than Cuba;

(iii) Has maintained and intends to resume nonimmigrant status;

(iv) Is applying for readmission within the authorized period of initial admission or extension of stay;

(v) Is in possession of a valid passport;

(vi) Does not require authorization for admission under INA 212(d)(3); and

(vii) Has not applied for a new visa while abroad.

(3) The provisions in paragraphs (d)(1) and (d)(2) of this section shall not apply to the nationals of countries identified as supporting terrorism in the Department's annual report to Congress entitled Patterns of Global Terrorism.

HISTORY:

[52 FR 42597, Nov. 5, 1987; 53 FR 9112, 9172, March 21, 1988, as amended at 55 FR 36028, Oct. 31, 1990; 62 FR 24331, 24332, May 5, 1997; 66 FR 38539, 38543, July 25, 2001; 67 FR 10322, 10323, Mar. 7, 2002, as confirmed at 68 FR 49351, 49353, Aug. 18, 2003; 67 FR 66045, 66046, Oct. 30, 2002; 71 FR 34519, 34522, June 15, 2006; 86 FR 55692, 55693, Oct. 7, 2021]

§ 41.113 Procedures in issuing visas.

(a) Evidence of visa. Except as provided in paragraph (b) of this section, a nonimmigrant visa shall be evidenced by a physical visa placed in the alien's passport or by an electronic visa located in the Department's records. The appropriate symbol as prescribed in § 41.12, showing the classification of the alien, shall be entered on the visa.

(b) Cases in which a physical visa is not placed in passport. In the following cases a physical visa shall be placed on the prescribed Form DS-232. In issuing such a visa, a notation shall be made on the Form DS-232 on which the visa is placed, specifying the pertinent subparagraph of this paragraph under which the action is taken.

(1) The alien's passport was issued by a government with which the United States does not have formal diplomatic relations, unless the Department has specifically authorized the placing of the visa in such passport;

(2) The passport requirement has been waived; or

(3) In other cases as authorized by the Department.

(c) Visa format. A machine-readable visa shall be in the format designated by the Department, and contain, at a minimum, the following data:

(1) Full name of the applicant;

(2) Visa type/class;

(3) Location of the visa issuing office;

(4) Passport number;

(5) Sex;

(6) Date of birth;

(7) Nationality;

(8) Number of applications for admission authorized, or the letter "M" for multiple applications for admission authorized;

(9) Date of issuance;

(10) Date of expiration;

(11) Visa control number.

(d) **Insertion of name, petition, and derivative status notation.**

(1) The surname and given name of the visa recipient shall be shown on the visa in the space provided.

(2) If the visa is being issued upon the basis of a petition approved by the Secretary of Homeland Security, the number of the petition, if any, the period for which the 'alien's admission has been authorized, and the name of the petitioner shall be reflected in the annotation field on the visa.

(3) In the case of an alien who derives status from a principal alien, the name of the principal alien and of the petitioner shall be reflected in the annotation field of the visa.

(e) Period of validity. If a nonimmigrant visa is issued for an unlimited number of applications for admission within the period of validity, the letter "M" shall be shown under the word "entries". Otherwise the number of permitted applications for admission shall be identified numerically. The date of issuance and the date of expiration of the visa shall be shown at the appropriate places in the visa by day, month, and year in that order. The standard three letter abbreviation for the month shall be used in all cases.

(f) Restriction to specified port(s) of entry. If a nonimmigrant visa is valid for admission only at one or more specified ports of entry, the names of those ports shall be entered in the annotation field. In cases where there is insufficient room to list the port(s) of entry, they shall be listed by hand on a clean passport page. Reference shall be made in the visa's annotation field citing the passport page upon which the port(s) of entry are listed.

(g) Delivery of visa. In issuing a nonimmigrant visa, the consular officer should deliver the passport containing the visa, or the prescribed Form DS-232 which bears the visa, to the alien or to the alien's authorized representative. Any relevant evidence furnished by the alien in accordance with § 41.103(b) should be retained, as required or necessary.

(h) Disposition of supporting documents. Original supporting documents furnished by the alien should be returned for presentation, if necessary, to the immigration authorities at the port of entry. Duplicate copies may be retained in the consular system, as required or necessary.

(i) Review of nonimmigrant visa issuances. Nonimmigrant visa issuances must be reviewed, in accordance with guidance by the Secretary of State, by consular supervisors, or a designated alternate, to ensure compliance with applicable laws and procedures.

HISTORY:

[52 FR 42597, Nov. 5, 1987, as amended at 56 FR 30428, July 2, 1991; 61 FR 1834, 1836, Jan. 24, 1996; 61 FR 53058, Oct. 10, 1996;

62 FR 24332, 24333, May 5, 1997; 66 FR 38539, 38543, July 25, 2001; 67 FR 66045, 66046, Oct. 30, 2002; 71 FR 34519, 34522, June 15, 2006; 71 FR 37494, 37495, June 30, 2006; 71 FR 50338, Aug. 25, 2006; 73 FR 23067, 23069, Apr. 29, 2008; 80 FR 67315, Nov. 2, 2015]

Subpart L

Refusals and Revocations

§ 41.121 Refusal of nonimmigrant visas.

(a) Grounds for refusal. Nonimmigrant visa refusals must be based on legal grounds, such as one or more provisions of INA 212(a), INA 212(e), INA 214(b) or (f) or (l) (as added by Section 625 of Pub. L. 104-208), INA 221(g), INA 222(g), or other applicable law. Certain classes of nonimmigrant aliens are exempted from specific provisions of INA 212(a) under INA 102 and, upon a basis of reciprocity, under INA 212(d)(8). When a visa application has been properly completed and executed in accordance with the provisions of the INA and the implementing regulations, the consular officer must issue the visa, refuse the visa, or, pursuant to an outstanding order under INA 243(d), discontinue granting the visa.

(b) **Refusal procedure.**

(1) When a consular officer knows or has reason to believe a visa applicant is ineligible and refuses the issuance of a visa, he or she must inform the alien of the ground(s) of ineligibility (unless disclosure is barred under INA 212(b)(2) or (3)) and whether there is, in law or regulations, a mechanism (such as a waiver) to overcome the refusal. The officer shall note the reason for the refusal on the application. Upon refusing the nonimmigrant visa, the consular officer shall retain the original of each document upon which the refusal was based, as well as each document indicating a possible ground of ineligibility, and should return all other supporting documents supplied by the applicant.

(2) If an alien, who has not yet filed a visa application, seeks advice from a consular officer, who knows or has reason to believe that the alien is ineligible to receive a visa on grounds which cannot be overcome by the presentation of additional evidence, the officer shall so inform the alien. The consular officer shall inform the applicant of the provision of law or regulations upon which a refusal of a visa, if applied for, would be based (subject to the exception in paragraph (b)(1) of this section). If practicable, the consular officer should request the alien to execute a nonimmigrant visa application in order to make a formal refusal. If the individual fails to execute a visa application in these circumstances, the consular officer shall treat the matter as if a visa had been refused and create a record of the presumed ineligibilty which shall be filed in the consular office.

(c) Nonimmigrant refusals must be reviewed, in accordance with guidance by the Secretary of State, by consular supervisors, or a designated alternate, to ensure compliance with laws and procedures. If the ground(s) of ineligibility upon which the visa was refused cannot be overcome by the presentation of additional evidence, the refusal must be reviewed without delay; that is, on the day of the refusal or as soon as it is administratively possible. If the ground(s) of ineligibility may be overcome by the presentation of additional evidence, and the applicant has indicated the intention to submit such evidence, a review of the refusal may be deferred for not more than 120 days. If the reviewing officer disagrees with the decision and he or she has a consular commission and title, the reviewing officer can assume responsibility and readjudicate the case. If the reviewing officer does not have a consular commission and title, he or she must consult with the adjudicating officer, or with the Visa Office, to resolve any disagreement.

(d) Review of refusal by Department. The Department may request a consular officer in a specific case or in specified classes of cases to submit a report if a visa has been refused. The Department will review each report and may furnish an advisory opinion to the consular officer for assistance in considering the case further. If the officer believes that action contrary to an advisory opinion should be taken, the case shall be resubmitted to the Department with an explanation of the proposed action. Rulings of the Department concerning an interpretation of law, as distinguished from an application of the law to the facts, shall be binding upon consular officers.

HISTORY:

[52 FR 42597, Nov. 5, 1987, as amended at 56 FR 30428, July 2, 1991; 63 FR 669, 671, Jan. 7, 1998, as confirmed at 63 FR 36365, 36366, July 6, 1998; 66 FR 10363, 10364, Feb. 15, 2001; 71 FR 37494, 37495, June 30, 2006; 71 FR 50338, 50339, Aug. 25, 2006; 84 FR 16610, 16612, Apr. 22, 2019]

§ 41.122 Revocation of visas.

(a) Grounds for revocation by consular officers. A consular officer, the Secretary, or a Department official to whom the Secretary has delegated this authority is authorized to revoke a nonimmigrant visa at any time, in his or her discretion.

(b) Provisional revocation—

(1) General. A provisional revocation is subject to reversal through internal procedures established by the Department of State. Upon reversal of the revocation, the visa immediately resumes the validity provided for on its face. Provisional revocation shall have the same force and effect as any other visa revocation under INA 221(i), unless and until the revocation has been reversed. Neither the provisional revocation of a visa nor the reversal of a provisional revocation limits, in any way, the revocation authority provided for under INA 221(i), with respect to the particular visa or any other visa.

(2) Pending visa eligibility determination. A consular officer, the Secretary, or any Department official to whom the Secretary has delegated this authority may provisionally revoke a nonimmigrant visa while considering information related to whether a visa holder is eligible for the visa.

(3) Automatic provisional revocation based on failure to comply with all EVUS requirements. Visas held by

individuals subject to the Electronic Visa Update System (EVUS) who have not complied with the conditions described in 8 CFR 215.24 or whose notification of compliance has expired or been rescinded are automatically provisionally revoked and are no longer valid for travel to the United States, without further notice to the visa holder. The automatic provisional revocation pursuant to this paragraph (b)(3) shall be automatically reversed upon compliance with EVUS requirements set out at 8 CFR part 215, subpart B, as confirmed by receipt of a notification of compliance. A visa revoked on grounds other than failure to comply with EVUS shall remain revoked, notwithstanding compliance with EVUS.

(c) Notice of revocation. Unless otherwise instructed by the Department, a consular officer shall, if practicable, notify the alien to whom the visa was issued that the visa was revoked or provisionally revoked. Regardless of delivery of such notice, once the revocation has been entered into the Department's Consular Lookout and Support System (CLASS), the visa is no longer to be considered valid for travel to the United States. The date of the revocation shall be indicated in CLASS and on any notice sent to the alien to whom the visa was issued. This paragraph (c) does not apply to provisional revocations under paragraph (b)(3) of this section.

(d) Procedure for physically canceling visas. Except for provisional revocations pursuant to paragraph (b)(3) of this section, a nonimmigrant visa that is revoked shall be canceled by writing or stamping the word "REVOKED" plainly across the face of the visa, if the visa is available to the consular officer. The failure or inability to physically cancel the visa does not affect the validity of the revocation.

(e) Revocation of visa by immigration officer. An immigration officer is authorized to revoke a valid visa by physically canceling it in accordance with the procedure described in paragraph (d) of this section if:

(1) The alien obtains an immigrant visa or an adjustment of status to that of permanent resident;

(2) The alien is ordered excluded from the United States under INA 236, as in effect prior to April 1, 1997, or removed from the United States pursuant to INA 235;

(3) The alien is notified pursuant to INA 235 by an immigration officer at a port of entry that the alien appears to be inadmissible to the United States, and the alien requests and is granted permission to withdraw the application for admission;

(4) A final order of deportation or removal or a final order granting voluntary departure with an alternate order of deportation or removal is entered against the alien;

(5) The alien has been permitted by DHS to depart voluntarily from the United States;

(6) DHS has revoked a waiver of inadmissibility granted pursuant to INA 212(d)(3)(A) in relation to the visa that was issued to the alien;

(7) The visa is presented in connection with an application for admission to the United States by a person other than the alien to whom the visa was issued;

(8) The visa has been physically removed from the passport in which it was issued; or

(9) The visa has been issued in a combined Mexican or Canadian B-1/B-2 visa and border crossing identification card, and the immigration officer makes the determination specified in § 41.32(c) with respect to the alien's Mexican citizenship and/or residence or the determination specified in § 41.33(b) with respect to the alien's status as a permanent resident of Canada.

HISTORY:

[52 FR 42597, Nov. 5, 1987; 63 FR 16892, 16895, April 7, 1998; 66 FR 10363, 10364, Feb. 15, 2001; 66 FR 38539, 38544, July 25, 2001; 67 FR 66045, 66046, Oct. 30, 2002; 71 FR 34519, 34522, June 15, 2006; 76 FR 23477, 23479, Apr. 27, 2011; 81 FR 72522, 72523, Oct. 20, 2016, as confirmed at 84 FR 22968, 22969, May 21, 2019]

§ 41.123 Discontinuance of Granting Nonimmigrant Visa Pursuant to INA 243(d).

(a) Grounds for discontinuance of granting a visa. Consular officers in a country subject to an order by the Secretary under INA 243(d) shall discontinue granting nonimmigrant visas for categories of nonimmigrant visas specified in the order of the Secretary (or his or her designee), and pursuant to procedures dictated by the Department.

(b) Discontinuance procedure—

(1) Applications refused or discontinued only. Starting on the day the Secretary's (or designee's) order to discontinue granting visas takes effect (effective date), no visas falling within the scope of the order, as described by the order, may be issued in the referenced country to an applicant who falls within the scope of the order, except as otherwise expressly provided in the order or related Department instructions. Beginning on the effective date, a consular officer must refuse the visa if the individual is not eligible for the visa under INA 212(a), INA 221(g), or other applicable law, but if the applicant is otherwise eligible, must process the application by discontinuing granting, regardless of when the application was filed, if the applicant falls within the scope of the order and no exception applies. The application processing fee will not be refunded. The requirement to discontinue issuance may not be waived, and continues until the sanction is terminated as described below.

(2) Geographic applicability. Visa sanctions under INA 243(d) only apply to visa issuance in the country that is sanctioned. If a consular officer has a reason to believe that a visa applicant potentially subject to INA 243(d) sanctions is applying at a post outside the sanctioned country to evade visa sanctions under INA 243(d) (e.g., the applicant provides no credible explanation for applying outside the country), the consular officer will transfer the case to the consular post in the consular district where INA 243(d) sanctions apply, review any other applicable Department instructions, and proceed accordingly. When cases are transferred to a consular district where INA 243(d) sanctions apply, the adjudication will be subject to the discontinuation of issuance under the sanctions.

(c) Termination of sanction. The Department shall notify consular officers in an affected country when the sanction under INA 243(d) has been lifted. After notification, normal consular operations may resume consistent with these regulations and guidance from the Department. Once the sanction under INA 243(d) is lifted, no new application processing fee is required in cases where issuance has been discontinued pursuant to an INA 243(d) order, and consular officers in the affected post must adjudicate the visa consistent with regulations and Department guidance. Consular officers may require applicants to update the visa application forms, must conduct any necessary adjudicatory steps, and may re-interview the applicant to determine eligibility.

HISTORY:
[84 FR 16610, 16612, Apr. 22, 2019]

PART 42

VISAS: DOCUMENTATION OF IMMIGRANTS UNDER THE IMMIGRATION AND NATIONALITY ACT, AS AMENDED

AUTHORITY NOTE APPLICABLE TO ENTIRE PART:

AUTHORITY:
8 U.S.C. 1104 and 1182; Pub. L. 105-277, 112 Stat. 2681; Pub. L. 108-449, 118 Stat. 3469; The Convention on Protection of Children and Co-operation in Respect of Intercountry Adoption (done at the Hague, May 29, 1993), S. Treaty Doc. 105-51 (1998), 1870 U.N.T.S. 167 (Reg. No. 31922 (1993)); 42 U.S.C. 14901-14954 (Pub. L. 106-279, 114 Stat. 825); 8 U.S.C. 1101 (Pub L. 117-31, 135 Stat. 309); 8 U.S.C. 1154 (Pub. L. 109-162, 119 Stat. 2960); 8 U.S.C. 1201 (Pub. L. 114-70, 129 Stat. 561).

Subpart A

Visa and Passport Not Required for Certain Immigrants

§ 42.1 Aliens not required to obtain immigrant visas.

An immigrant within any of the following categories is not required to obtain an immigrant visa:

(a) Aliens lawfully admitted for permanent residence. An alien who has previously been lawfully admitted for permanent residence and who is not required under the regulations of the Department of Homeland Security to present a valid immigrant visa upon returning to the United States.

(b) Alien members of U.S. Armed Forces. An alien member of the U.S. Armed Forces bearing military identification, who has previously been lawfully admitted for permanent residence and is coming to the United States under official orders or permit of those Armed Forces.

(c) Aliens entering from Guam, Puerto Rico, or the Virgin Islands. An alien who has previously been lawfully admitted for permanent residence who seeks to enter the continental United States or any other place under the jurisdiction of the United States directly from Guam, Puerto Rico, or the Virgin Islands of the United States.

(d) Child born after issuance of visa to accompanying parent. An alien child born after the issuance of an immigrant visa to an accompanying parent, who will arrive in the United States with the parent, and apply for admission during the period of validity of the visa issued to the parent.

(e) Child born of a national or lawful permanent resident mother during her temporary visit abroad. An alien child born during the temporary visit abroad of a mother who is a national or lawful permanent resident of the United States if applying for admission within 2 years of birth and accompanied by either parent applying and eligible for readmission as a permanent resident upon that parent's first return to the United States after the child's birth.

(f) American Indians born in Canada. An American Indian born in Canada and having at least 50 per centum of blood of the American Indian race.

HISTORY:

[52 FR 42613, Nov. 5, 1987; 71 FR 34519, 34522, June 15, 2006]

§ 42.2 Aliens not required to present passports.

An immigrant within any of the following categories is not required to present a passport in applying for an immigrant visa:

(a) Certain relatives of U.S. citizens. An alien who is the spouse, unmarried son or daughter, or parent, of a U.S. citizen, unless the alien is applying for a visa in the country of which the applicant is a national and the possession of a passport is required for departure.

(b) Returning aliens previously lawfully admitted for permanent residence. An alien previously lawfully admitted for permanent residence who is returning from a temporary visit abroad, unless the alien is applying for a visa in the country of which the applicant is a national and the possession of a passport is required for departure.

(c) Certain relatives of aliens lawfully admitted for permanent residence. An alien who is the spouse, unmarried son or daughter, or parent of an alien lawfully admitted for permanent residence, unless the alien is applying for a visa in the country of which the applicant is a national and the possession of a passport is required for departure.

(d) Stateless persons. An alien who is a stateless person, and accompanying spouse and unmarried son or daughter.

(e) Nationals of Communist-controlled countries. An alien who is a national of a Communist-controlled country and who is unable to obtain a passport from the government of that country, and accompanying spouse and unmarried son or daughter.

(f) Alien members of U.S. Armed Forces. An alien who is a member of the U.S. Armed Forces.

(g) **Beneficiaries of individual waivers.**

(1) An alien who would be within one of the categories described in paragraphs (a) through (d) of this section except that the alien is applying for a visa in a country of which the applicant is a national and possession of a passport is required for departure, in whose case the passport requirement has been waived by the Secretary of State, as evidence by a specific instruction from the Department.

(2) An alien unable to obtain a passport and not within any of the foregoing categories, in whose case the passport requirement imposed by § 42.64(b) or by DHS regulations has been waived by the Secretary of Homeland Security and the Secretary of State as evidenced by a specific instruction from the Department.

HISTORY:

[52 FR 42613, Nov. 5, 1987, as amended at 56 FR 49680, Oct. 1, 1991, as confirmed at 58 FR 48447, Sept. 16, 1993; 71 FR 34519, 34522, June 15, 2006]

Subpart B

Classification and Foreign State Chargeability

§ 42.11 Classification symbols.

An immigrant visa issued to an applicant who applies to one of the classes described below shall bear an appropriate visa symbol to show its classification.

Table 1 to § 42.11

Symbol	Class	Section of law
	Immediate Relatives	
IR1	Spouse of U.S. Citizen	INA 201(b).
IR2	Child of U.S. Citizen	INA 201(b).
IR3	Orphan Adopted Abroad by U.S. Citizen	INA 201(b) & INA 101(b)(1)(F).
IH3	Child from Hague Convention Country Adopted Abroad by U.S. Citizen	INA 201(b) & INA 101(b)(1)(F).
IR4	Orphan to be Adopted in U.S. by U.S. Citizen	INA 201(b) & INA 101(b)(1)(F).

Table 1 to § 42.11

Symbol	Class	Section of law
IH4	Child from Hague Convention Country to be Adopted in U.S. by U.S. Citizen	INA 201(b) & INA 101(b)(1)(G).
IR5	Parent of U.S. Citizen at Least 21 Years of Age	INA 201(b).
CR1	Spouse of U.S. Citizen (Conditional Status)	INA 201(b) & INA 216.
CR2	Child of U.S. Citizen (Conditional Status)	INA 201(b) & INA 216.
IW1	Certain Spouses of Deceased U.S. Citizens	INA 201(b).
IW2	Child of IW1	INA 201(b).
IB1	Self-petition Spouse of U.S. Citizen	INA 204(a)(1)(A)(iii).
IB2	Self-petition Child of U.S. Citizen	INA 204(a)(1)(A)(iv).
IB3	Child of IB1	INA 204(a)(1)(A)(iii).
IB5	Self-petition Parent of U.S. Citizen	INA 204(a)(1)(A)(vii).
VI5	Parent of U.S. Citizen Who Acquired Permanent Resident Status under the Virgin Islands Nonimmigrant Alien Adjustment Act	INA 201(b) & Section 2 of the Virgin Islands Nonimmigrant Alien Adjustment Act (Pub. L. 97-271).
	Vietnam Amerasian Immigrants	
AM1	Vietnam Amerasian Principal	Section 584(b)(1)(A) of the Foreign Operations, Export Financing, and Related Programs Appropriations Act, 1988 (as contained in section 101(e) of Pub. L. 100-102) as amended.
AM2	Spouse or Child of AM1	Section 584(b)(1)(A) and 584(b)(1)(B) of the Foreign Operations, Export Financing, and Related Programs Appropriations Act, 1988 (as contained in section 101(e) of Pub. L. 100-102) as amended.
AM3	Natural Mother of AM1 (and Spouse or Child of Such Mother) or Person Who has Acted in Effect as the Mother, Father, or Next-of-Kin of AM1 (and Spouse or Child of Such Person)	Section 584(b)(1)(A) and 584(b)(1)(C) of the Foreign Operations, Export Financing, and Related Programs Appropriations Act, 1988 (as contained in section 101(e) of Pub. L. 100-102) as amended.
	Special Immigrants	
SB1	Returning Resident	INA 101(a)(27)(A).
SC1	Person Who Lost U.S. Citizenship by Marriage	INA 101(a)(27)(B) & INA 324(a).
SC2	Person Who Lost U.S. Citizenship by Serving in Foreign Armed Forces	INA 101(a)(27)(B) & INA 327.
SI1	Certain Persons Employed by the U.S. Government in Iraq or Afghanistan as Translators or Interpreters	Section 1059 of Public Law 109-163, as amended.
SI2	Spouse of SI1	Section 1059 of Public Law 109-163, as amended.
SI3	Child of SI1	Section 1059 of Public Law 109-163, as amended.
SM1	Person Recruited Outside the United States Who Has Served or is Enlisted to Serve in the U.S. Armed Forces for 12 Years	INA 101(a)(27)(K).
SM2	Spouse of SM1	INA 101(a)(27)(K).
SM3	Child of SM1	INA 101(a)(27)(K).
SQ1	Certain Iraqis or Afghans Employed by or on Behalf of the U.S. Government	Section 602(b), Division F, Title VI, Omnibus Appropriations Act of 2009, Public Law 111-8, as amended and Section 1244 of Public Law 110-181, as amended.

Table 1 to § 42.11

Symbol	Class	Section of law
SQ2	Spouse of SQ1	Section 602(b), Division F, Title VI, Omnibus Appropriations Act of 2009, Public Law 111-8, as amended and Section 1244 of Public Law 110-181, as amended.
SQ3	Child of SQ1	Section 602(b), Division F, Title VI, Omnibus Appropriations Act of 2009, Public Law 111-8, as amended and Section 1244 of Public Law 110-181, as amended.
SU2	Spouse of U1	INA 245(m)(3) & INA 101(a)(15)(U)(ii).
SU3	Parent of U1	INA 245(m)(3) & INA 101(a)(15)(U)(ii).
SU5	Parent of U1	INA 245(m)(3) & INA 101(a)(15)(U)(ii).
	Family-Sponsored Preferences	
	Family 1st Preference	
F11	Unmarried Son or Daughter of U.S. Citizen	INA 203(a)(1).
F12	Child of F11	INA 203(b) & INA 203(a)(1).
B11	Self-petition Unmarried Son or Daughter of U.S. Citizen	INA 204(a)(1)(A)(iv) & INA 203(a)(1).
B12	Child of B11	INA 203(d), INA 204(a)(1)(A)(iv), & INA 203(a)(i).
	Family 2nd Preference (Subject to Per-Country Limitations)	
F21	Spouse of Lawful Permanent Resident	INA 203(a)(2)(A).
F22	Child of Lawful Permanent Resident	INA 203(a)(2)(A).
F23	Child of F21 or F22	INA 203(d) & INA 203(a)(2)(A).
F24	Unmarried Son or Daughter of Lawful Permanent Resident	INA 203(a)(2)(B).
F25	Child of F24	INA 203(d) & INA 203(a)(2)(B).
C21	Spouse of Lawful Permanent Resident (Conditional)	INA 203(a)(2)(A) & INA 216.
C22	Child of Lawful Permanent Resident (Conditional)	INA 203(a)(2)(A) & INA 216.
C23	Child of C21 or C22 (Conditional)	INA 203(a)(2)(A), INA 203(d) & INA 216.
C24	Unmarried Son or Daughter of Lawful Permanent Resident (Conditional)	INA 203(a)(2)(B) & INA 216.
C25	Child of C24 (Conditional)	INA 203(a)(2)(B), INA 203(d), & INA 216.
B21	Self-petition Spouse of Lawful Permanent Resident	INA 204(a)(1)(B)(ii).
B22	Self-petition Child of Lawful Permanent Resident	INA 204(a)(1)(B)(iii).
B23	Child of B21 or B22	INA 203(d) & INA 204(a)(1)(B)(ii).
B24	Self-petition Unmarried Son or Daughter of Lawful Permanent Resident	INA 204(a)(1)(B)(iii).
B25	Child of B24	INA 203(d) & INA 204(a)(1)(B)(iii).
	Family 2nd Preference (Exempt from Per-Country Limitations)	
FX1	Spouse of Lawful Permanent Resident	INA 202(a)(4)(A) & INA 203(a)(2)(A).
FX2	Child of Lawful Permanent Resident	INA 202(a)(4)(A) & INA 203(a)(2)(A).
FX3	Child of FX1 or FX2	INA 202(a)(4)(A), INA 203(a)(2)(A), & INA 203(d).
CX1	Spouse of Lawful Permanent Resident (Conditional)	INA 202(a)(4)(A), INA 203(a)(2)(A), & INA 216.
CX2	Child of Lawful Permanent Resident (Conditional)	INA 202(a)(4), INA 203(a)(2)(A), & INA 216.

Table 1 to § 42.11

Symbol	Class	Section of law
CX3	Child of CX1 or CX2 (Conditional)	INA 202(a)(4)(A), INA 203(a)(2)(A), INA 203(d), & INA 216.
BX1	Self-petition Spouse of Lawful Permanent Resident	INA 204(a)(1)(B)(ii).
BX2	Self-petition Child of Lawful Permanent Resident	INA 204(a)(1)(B)(iii).
BX3	Child of BX1 or BX2	INA 203(d) & INA 204(a)(1)(B)(ii).
	Family 3rd Preference	
F31	Married Son or Daughter of U.S. Citizen	INA 203(a)(3).
F32	Spouse of F31	INA 203(d) & INA 203(a)(3).
F33	Child of F31	INA 203(d) & INA 203(a)(3).
C31	Married Son or Daughter of U.S. Citizen (Conditional)	INA 203(a)(3) & INA 216.
C32	Spouse of C31 (Conditional)	INA 203(d), INA 203(a)(3), & INA 216.
C33	Child of C31 (Conditional)	INA 203(d), INA 203(a)(3), & INA 216.
B31	Self-petition Married Son or Daughter of U.S. Citizen	INA 204(a)(1)(A)(iv) & INA 203(a)(3).
B32	Spouse of B31	INA 203(d), INA 204(a)(1)(A)(iv) & INA 203(a)(3).
B33	Child of B31	INA 203(d), INA 204(a)(1)(A)(iv), & INA 203(a)(3).
	Family 4th Preference	
F41	Brother or Sister of U.S. Citizen at Least 21 Years of Age	INA 203(a)(4).
F42	Spouse of F41	INA 203(a)(4) & INA 203(d).
F43	Child of F41	INA 203(a)(4) & INA 203(d).
	Employment-Based Preferences	
	Employment 1st Preference (Priority Workers)	
E11	Person with Extraordinary Ability	INA 203(b)(1)(A).
E12	Outstanding Professor or Researcher	INA 203(b)(1)(B).
E13	Multinational Executive or Manager	INA 203(b)(1)(C).
E14	Spouse of E11, E12, or E13	INA 203(d), INA 203(b)(1)(A), INA 203(b)(1)(B), & INA 203(b)(1)(C).
E15	Child of E11, E12, or E13	INA 203(d), INA 203(b)(1)(A), INA 203(b)(1)(B), & INA 203(b)(1)(C).
	Employment 2nd Preference (Professionals Holding Advanced Degrees or Persons of Exceptional Ability)	
E21	Professional Holding Advanced Degree or Person of Exceptional Ability	INA 203(b)(2).
E22	Spouse of E21	INA 203(b)(2) & INA 203(d).
E23	Child of E21	INA 203(b)(2) & INA 203(d).
	Employment 3rd Preference (Skilled Workers, Professionals, or Other Workers)	
E31	Skilled Worker	INA 203(b)(3)(A)(i).
E32	Professional Holding Baccalaureate Degree	INA 203(b)(3)(A)(ii).
E34	Spouse of E31 or E32	INA 203(b)(3)(A)(i), INA 203(b)(3)(A)(ii), & INA 203(d).
E35	Child of E31 or E32	INA 203(b)(3)(A)(i), INA 203(B)(3)(A)(ii), & INA 203(d).
EW3	Other Worker (Subgroup Numerical Limit)	INA 203(b)(3)(A)(iii).
EW4	Spouse of EW3	INA 203(b)(3)(A)(iii) & INA 203(d).
EW5	Child of EW3	INA 203(b)(3)(A)(iii) & INA 203(d).

Table 1 to § 42.11

Symbol	Class	Section of law
	Employment 4th Preference (Certain Special Immigrants)	
BC1	Broadcaster in the U.S. Employed by the International Broadcasting Bureau of the Broadcasting Board of Governors or a Grantee of Such Organization	INA 101(a)(27)(M) & INA 203(b)(4).
BC2	Accompanying Spouse of BC1	INA 101(a)(27)(M) & INA 203(b)(4).
BC3	Accompanying Child of BC1	INA 101(a)(27)(M) & INA 203(b)(4).
SD1	Minister of Religion	INA 101(a)(27)(C)(ii)(I) & INA 203(b)(4).
SD2	Spouse of SD1	INA 101(a)(27)(C)(ii)(I) & INA 203(b)(4).
SD3	Child of SD1	INA 101(a)(27)(C)(ii)(I) & INA 203(b)(4).
SE1	Certain Employee or Former Employee of the U.S. Government Abroad	INA 101(a)(27)(D)(i) & INA 203(b)(4).
SE2	Spouse of SE1	INA 101(a)(27)(D)(i) & INA 203(b)(4).
SE3	Child of SE1	INA 101(a)(27)(D)(i) & INA 203(b)(4).
SF1	Former Employee of the Panama Canal Company or Canal Zone Government	INA 101(a)(27)(E) & INA 203 (b)(4).
SF2	Spouse or Child of SF1	INA 101(a)(27)(E) & INA 203 (b)(4).
SG1	Former Employee of the U.S. Government in the Panama Canal Zone (Panamanian National)	INA 101(a)(27)(E) & INA 203 (b)(4).
SG2	Spouse or Child of SG1	INA 101(a)(27)(E) & INA 203 (b)(4).
SH1	Former Employee of the Panama Canal Company or Canal Zone Government (Five Years of Service)	INA 101(a)(27)(E) & INA 203 (b)(4).
SH2	Spouse or Child of SH1	INA 101(a)(27)(E) & INA 203 (b)(4).
SJ1	Foreign Medical Graduate (Adjustment Only)	INA 101(a)(27)(H).
SJ2	Spouse or Child of SJ1	INA 101(a)(27)(H) & INA 203(b)(4).
SK1	Retired International Organization Employee	INA 101(a)(27)(I)(iii) & INA 203(b)(4).
SK2	Spouse of SK1	INA 101(a)(27)(I)(iv) & INA 203(b)(4).
SK3	Unmarried Son or Daughter of SK1	INA 101(a)(27)(I)(i) & INA 203(b)(4).
SK4	Surviving Spouse of a Deceased International Organization Employee	INA 101(a)(27)(I)(ii) & INA 203(b)(4).
SL1	Juvenile Court Dependent (Adjustment Only)	INA 101(a)(27)(J) & INA 203(b)(4).
SN1	Retired NATO6 Civilian Employee	INA 101(a)(27)(L) & INA 203(b)(4).
SN2	Spouse of SN1	INA 101(a)(27)(L) & INA 203(b)(4).
SN3	Unmarried Son or Daughter of SN1	INA 101(a)(27)(L) & INA 203(b)(4).
SN4	Surviving Spouse of Deceased NATO6 Civilian Employee	INA 101(a)(27)(L) & INA 203(b)(4).
SP	Beneficiary of a Petition or Labor Certification Application Filed Prior to September 11, 2001, if the Petition or Application was Rendered Void Due to the Terrorist Acts of September 11, 2001, or the Spouse, Child of such Beneficiary, or the Grandparent of a Child Orphaned by a Terrorist Act of September 11, 2001	Section 421 of Public Law 107-56.
SR1	Religious Worker	INA 101(a)(27)(C)(ii)(II) & (III), as amended & INA 203(b)(4).
SR2	Spouse of SR1	INA 101(a)(27)(C)(ii)(II) & (III), as amended & INA 203(b)(4).
SR3	Child of SR1	INA 101(a)(27)(C)(ii)(II) & (III), as amended & INA 203(b)(4).

Table 1 to § 42.11

Symbol	Class	Section of law
SS1	Surviving Spouse or Child of an Employee of the United States Government Abroad	INA 101(a)(27)(D)(ii) & INA 203(b)(4).
SS2	Current Spouse of SS1	INA 101(a)(27)(D)(ii), INA 203(b)(4) & INA 203(d).
SS3	Child of SS1 (Excludes Surviving Child of an Employee of the United States Government Abroad), provided the child meets the definition of 101(b)(1) of the INA	INA 101(a)(27)(D)(ii), INA 1101(b)(1), 203(b)(4), & INA 203(d).
Employment 5th Preference (Employment Creation Conditional Status) (Petitions Filed Before March 15, 2022)		
C51	Employment Creation, Outside Targeted Area	INA 203(b)(5)(A).
C52	Spouse of C51	INA 203(b)(5)(A) & INA 203(d).
C53	Child of C51	INA 203(b)(5)(A) & INA 203(d).
T51	Employment Creation in Targeted Rural/High Unemployment Area	INA 203(b)(5)(B).
T52	Spouse of T51	INA 203(b)(5)(B) & INA 203(d).
T53	Child of T51	INA 203(b)(5)(B) & INA 203(d).
R51	Regional Center Program, Not in Targeted Area	INA 203(b)(5) & Sec. 610 of the Departments of Commerce, Justice, and State, the Judiciary and Related Agencies Appropriations Act, 1993 (Pub. L. 102-395), as amended.
R52	Spouse of R51	INA 203(b)(5), INA 203(d), & Sec. 610 of the Departments of Commerce, Justice, and State, the Judiciary and Related Agencies Appropriations Act, 1993 (Pub. L. 102-395), as amended.
R53	Child of R51	INA 203(b)(5), INA 203(d), & Sec. 610 of the Departments of Commerce, Justice, and State, the Judiciary and Related Agencies Appropriations Act, 1993 (Pub. L. 102-395), as amended.
I51	Regional Center Program, Target Area	INA 203(b)(5) & Sec. 610 of the Departments of Commerce, Justice, and State, the Judiciary and Related Agencies Appropriations Act, 1993 (Pub. L. 102-395), as amended.
I52	Spouse of I51	INA 203(b)(5), INA 203(d), & Sec. 610 of the Departments of Commerce, Justice, and State, the Judiciary and Related Agencies Appropriations Act, 1993 (Pub. L. 102-395), as amended.
I53	Child of I51	INA 203(b)(5), INA 203(d), & Sec. 610 of the Departments of Commerce, Justice, and State, the Judiciary and Related Agencies Appropriations Act, 1993 (Pub. L. 102-395), as amended.
Employment 5th Preference (Employment Creation Conditional Status) (Petitions Filed On or After March 15, 2022)		
NU1	Investor in Non-Regional Center, Unreserved	INA 203(b)(5), Sec. 610 of the Departments of Commerce, Justice, and State, the Judiciary and Related Agencies Appropriations Act, 1993 (Pub. L. 102-395), as drafted, & Division BB of the Consolidated Appropriations Act, 2022 (Pub. L. 117-103).

Table 1 to § 42.11

Symbol	Class	Section of law
NU2	Spouse of NU1	INA 203(b)(5), INA 203(d), Sec. 610 of the Departments of Commerce, Justice, and State, the Judiciary and Related Agencies Appropriations Act, 1993 (Pub. L. 102-395), as drafted, & Division BB of the Consolidated Appropriations Act, 2022 (Pub. L. 117-103).
NU3	Child of NU1	INA 203(b)(5), INA 203(d), Sec. 610 of the Departments of Commerce, Justice, and State, the Judiciary and Related Agencies Appropriations Act, 1993 (Pub. L. 102-395), as drafted, & Division BB of the Consolidated Appropriations Act, 2022 (Pub. L. 117-103).
RU1	Investor in Regional Center, Unreserved	INA 203(b)(5), Sec. 610 of the Departments of Commerce, Justice, and State, the Judiciary and Related Agencies Appropriations Act, 1993 (Pub. L. 102-395), as drafted, & Division BB of the Consolidated Appropriations Act, 2022 (Pub. L. 117-103).
RU2	Spouse of RU1	INA 203(b)(5), INA 203(d), Sec. 610 of the Departments of Commerce, Justice, and State, the Judiciary and Related Agencies Appropriations Act, 1993 (Pub. L. 102-395), as drafted, & Division BB of the Consolidated Appropriations Act, 2022 (Pub. L. 117-103).
RU3	Child of RU1	INA 203(b)(5), INA 203(d), Sec. 610 of the Departments of Commerce, Justice, and State, the Judiciary and Related Agencies Appropriations Act, 1993 (Pub. L. 102-395), as drafted, & Division BB of the Consolidated Appropriations Act, 2022 (Pub. L. 117-103).
NR1	Investor in Non-Regional Center, Set Aside—Rural	INA 203(b)(5), Sec. 610 of the Departments of Commerce, Justice, and State, the Judiciary and Related Agencies Appropriations Act, 1993 (Pub. L. 102-395), as drafted, & Division BB of the Consolidated Appropriations Act, 2022 (Pub. L. 117-103).
NR2	Spouse of NR1	INA 203(b)(5), INA 203(d), Sec. 610 of the Departments of Commerce, Justice, and State, the Judiciary and Related Agencies Appropriations Act, 1993 (Pub. L. 102-395), as drafted, & Division BB of the Consolidated Appropriations Act, 2022 (Pub. L. 117-103).
NR3	Child of NR1	INA 203(b)(5), INA 203(d), Sec. 610 of the Departments of Commerce, Justice, and State, the Judiciary and Related Agencies Appropriations Act, 1993 (Pub. L. 102-395), as drafted, & Division BB of the Consolidated Appropriations Act, 2022 (Pub. L. 117-103).
NH1	Investor in Non-Regional Center, Set Aside—High Unemployment	INA 203(b)(5), Sec. 610 of the Departments of Commerce, Justice, and State, the Judiciary and Related Agencies Appropriations Act, 1993 (Pub. L. 102-395), as drafted, & Division BB of the Consolidated Appropriations Act, 2022 (Pub. L. 117-103).

Table 1 to § 42.11

Symbol	Class	Section of law
NH2	Spouse of NH1	INA 203(b)(5), INA 203(d), Sec. 610 of the Departments of Commerce, Justice, and State, the Judiciary and Related Agencies Appropriations Act, 1993 (Pub. L. 102-395), as drafted, & Division BB of the Consolidated Appropriations Act, 2022 (Pub. L. 117-103).
NH3	Child of NH1	INA 203(b)(5), Sec. 610 of the Departments of Commerce, Justice, and State, the Judiciary and Related Agencies Appropriations Act, 1993 (Pub. L. 102-395), as drafted, & Division BB of the Consolidated Appropriations Act, 2022 (Pub. L. 117-103).
RR1	Investor in Regional Center, Set Aside —Rural	INA 203(b)(5), INA 203(d), Sec. 610 of the Departments of Commerce, Justice, and State, the Judiciary and Related Agencies Appropriations Act, 1993 (Pub. L. 102-395), as drafted, & Division BB of the Consolidated Appropriations Act, 2022 (Pub. L. 117-103).
RR2	Spouse of RR1	INA 203(b)(5), INA 203(d), Sec. 610 of the Departments of Commerce, Justice, and State, the Judiciary and Related Agencies Appropriations Act, 1993 (Pub. L. 102-395), as drafted, & Division BB of the Consolidated Appropriations Act, 2022 (Pub. L. 117-103).
RR3	Child of RR1	INA 203(b)(5), Sec. 610 of the Departments of Commerce, Justice, and State, the Judiciary and Related Agencies Appropriations Act, 1993 (Pub. L. 102-395), as drafted, & Division BB of the Consolidated Appropriations Act, 2022 (Pub. L. 117-103).
RH1	Investor in Regional Center, Set Aside —High Unemployment	INA 203(b)(5), Sec. 610 of the Departments of Commerce, Justice, and State, the Judiciary and Related Agencies Appropriations Act, 1993 (Pub. L. 102-395), as drafted, & Division BB of the Consolidated Appropriations Act, 2022 (Pub. L. 117-103).
RH2	Spouse of RH1	INA 203(b)(5), INA 203(d), Sec. 610 of the Departments of Commerce, Justice, and State, the Judiciary and Related Agencies Appropriations Act, 1993 (Pub. L. 102-395), as drafted, & Division BB of the Consolidated Appropriations Act, 2022 (Pub. L. 117-103).
RH3	Child of RH1	INA 203(b)(5), INA 203(d), Sec. 610 of the Departments of Commerce, Justice, and State, the Judiciary and Related Agencies Appropriations Act, 1993 (Pub. L. 102-395), as drafted, & Division BB of the Consolidated Appropriations Act, 2022 (Pub. L. 117-103).
RI1	Investor in Regional Center, Set Aside —Infrastructure	INA 203(b)(5), Sec. 610 of the Departments of Commerce, Justice, and State, the Judiciary and Related Agencies Appropriations Act, 1993 (Pub. L. 102-395), as drafted, & Division BB of the Consolidated Appropriations Act, 2022 (Pub. L. 117-103).

Table 1 to § 42.11

Symbol	Class	Section of law
RI2	Spouse of RI1	INA 203(b)(5), INA 203(d), Sec. 610 of the Departments of Commerce, Justice, and State, the Judiciary and Related Agencies Appropriations Act, 1993 (Pub. L. 102-395), as drafted, & Division BB of the Consolidated Appropriations Act, 2022 (Pub. L. 117-103).
RI3	Child of RI1	INA 203(b)(5), INA 203(d), Sec. 610 of the Departments of Commerce, Justice, and State, the Judiciary and Related Agencies Appropriations Act, 1993 (Pub. L. 102-395), as drafted, & Division BB of the Consolidated Appropriations Act, 2022 (Pub. L. 117-103).
	Other Categories	
	Diversity Immigrants	
DV1	Diversity Immigrant	INA 203(c).
DV2	Spouse of DV1	INA 203(c) & 203(d).
DV3	Child of DV1	INA 203(c) & 203(d).

CFR—T.22 § 42.21

HISTORY:

[56 FR 49680, Oct. 1, 1991, as confirmed at 58 FR 48447, Sept. 16, 1993; 60 FR 10499, Feb. 27, 1995; 62 FR 613, 614, Jan. 6, 1997; 65 FR 20903, 20904, Apr. 19, 2000; 66 FR 32740, 32742, June 18, 2001; 66 FR 38153, 38154, July 23, 2001; 67 FR 55319, 55320, Aug. 29, 2002, as corrected at 67 FR 70839, Nov. 27, 2002; 73 FR 14926, 14931, Mar. 20, 2008; 74 FR 61517, 61521, Nov. 25, 2009; 79 FR 32481, 32482, June 5, 2014; 88 FR 45068, 45072, July 14, 2023; 89 FR 60565, 60566, July 26, 2024; 89 FR 99076, 99078, Dec. 10, 2024]

§ 42.12 Rules of chargeability.

(a) Applicability. An immigrant shall be charged to the numerical limitation for the foreign state or dependent area of birth, unless the case falls within one of the exceptions to the general rule of chargeability provided by INA 202(b) and paragraphs (b) through (e) of this section to prevent the separation of families or the alien is classifiable under:

(1) INA 201(b);

(2) INA 101(a)(27) (A) or (B);

(3) Section 112 of Public Law 101-649;

(4) Section 124 of Public Law 101-649;

(5) Section 132 of Public Law 101-649;

(6) Section 134 of Public Law 101-649; or

(7) Section 584(b)(1) as contained in section 101(e) of Public Law 100-202.

(b) Exception for child. If necessary to prevent the separation of a child from the alien parent or parents, an immigrant child, including a child born in a dependent area, may be charged to the same foreign state to which a parent is chargeable if the child is accompanying or following to join the parent, in accordance with INA 202(b)(1).

(c) Exception for spouse. If necessary to prevent the separation of husband and wife, an immigrant spouse, including a spouse born in a dependent area, may be charged to a foreign state to which a spouse is chargeable if accompanying or following to join the spouse, in accordance with INA 202(b)(2).

(d) Exception for alien born in the United States. An immigrant who was born in the United States shall be charged to the foreign state of which the immigrant is a citizen or subject. If not a citizen or subject of any country, the alien shall be charged to the foreign state of last residence as determined by the consular officer, in accordance with INA 202(b)(3).

(e) Exception for alien born in foreign state in which neither parent was born or had residence at time of alien's birth. An alien who was born in a foreign state, as defined in § 40.1, in which neither parent was born, and in which neither parent had a residence at the time of the applicant's birth, may be charged to the foreign state of either parent as provided in INA 202(b)(4). The parents of such an alien are not considered as having acquired a residence within the meaning of INA 202(b)(4), if, at the time of the alien's birth within the foreign state, the parents were visiting temporarily or were stationed there in connection with the business or profession and under orders or instructions of an employer, principal, or superior authority foreign to such foreign state.

HISTORY:

[52 FR 42613, Nov. 5, 1987, as amended at 56 FR 49681, Oct. 1, 1991, as confirmed at 58 FR 48447, Sept. 16, 1993]

Subpart C

Immigrants Not Subject to Numerical Limitations of Ina 201 and 202

§ 42.21 Immediate relatives.

(a) Entitlement to status. An alien who is a spouse or child of a United States citizen, or a parent of a U.S. citizen at least 21 years of age, shall be classified as an immediate relative under INA 201(b) if the consular officer has received from DHS an approved Petition to Classify Status of Alien Relative for Issuance of an Immigrant Visa, filed on the alien's behalf by the U.S. citizen and approved in accordance with INA 204, and the officer is satisfied that the alien has the relationship claimed in the petition. An immediate relative shall be documented as such unless the U.S. citizen refuses to file the required petition, or unless the immediate relative is also a special immigrant under INA 101(a)(27) (A) or (B) and not subject to any numerical limitation.

(b) Spouse of a deceased U.S. citizen. The spouse of a deceased U.S. citizen, and each child of the spouse, will be entitled to immediate relative status after the date of the citizen's death provided the spouse or child meets the criteria of INA 201(b)(2)(A)(i) or of section 423(a)(1) of Public Law 107-56 (USA Patriot Act) and the Consular Officer has received an approved petition from the DHS which accords such status, or official notification of such approval, and the Consular Officer is satisfied that the alien meets those criteria.

(c) Child of a U.S. citizen victim of terrorism. The child of a U.S. citizen slain in the terrorist actions of September 11, 2001, shall retain the status of an immediate relative child (regardless of changes in age or marital status) if the child files a petition for such status within two years of the citizen's death pursuant to section 423(a)(2) of Public Law 107-56, and the consular officer has received an approved petition according such status or official notification of such approval.

HISTORY:

[52 FR 49676, Oct. 1, 1991, as confirmed at 58 FR 48447, Sept. 16, 1993; 64 FR 55417, 55418, Oct. 13, 1999; 67 FR 1414, 1415, Jan. 11, 2002, as confirmed at 68 FR 13628, Mar. 20, 2003; 71 FR 34519, 34522, June 15, 2006]

§ 42.22 Returning resident aliens.

(a) Requirements for returning resident status. An alien shall be classifiable as a special immigrant under INA 101(a)(27)(A) if the consular officer is satisfied from the evidence presented that:

(1) The alien had the status of an alien lawfully admitted for permanent residence at the time of departure from the United States;

(2) The alien departed from the United States with the intention of returning and has not abandoned this intention; and

(3) The alien is returning to the United States from a temporary visit abroad and, if the stay abroad was protracted, this was caused by reasons beyond the alien's control and for which the alien was not responsible.

(b) Documentation needed. Unless the consular officer has reason to question the legality of the alien's previous admission for permanent residence or the alien's eligibility to receive an immigrant visa, only those records and documents required under INA 222(b) which relate to the period of residence in the United States and the period of the temporary visit abroad shall be required. If any required record or document is unobtainable, the provisions of § 42.65(d) shall apply.

(c) Returning resident alien originally admitted under the Act of December 28, 1945. An alien admitted into the United States under Section 1 of the Act of December 28, 1945 ("GI Brides Act") shall not be refused an immigrant visa after a temporary absence abroad solely because of a mental or physical defect or defects that existed at the time of the original admission.

HISTORY:

[52 FR 49676, Oct. 1, 1991, as confirmed at 58 FR 48447, Sept. 16, 1993; 63 FR 48577, 48578, Sept. 11, 1998]

§ 42.23 Certain former U.S. citizens.

(a) [Reserved]

(b) Military expatriates. An alien shall be classifiable as a special immigrant under INA 101(a)(27)(B) if the consular officer is satisfied by appropriate evidence that the alien was formerly a U.S. citizen and that the alien lost citizenship under the circumstances set forth in INA 327.

HISTORY:

[52 FR 49676, Oct. 1, 1991, as confirmed at 58 FR 48447, Sept. 16, 1993; 85 FR 38321, 38322, June 26, 2020]

§ 42.24 Adoption under the Hague Convention on Protection of Children and Co-operation in Respect of Intercountry Adoption and the Intercountry Adoption Act of 2000.

(a) Except as described in paragraph (n), for purposes of this section, the definitions in 22 CFR 96.2 apply.

(b) On or after the Convention effective date, as defined in 22 CFR 96.17, a child habitually resident in a Convention country who is adopted by a United States citizen deemed to be habitually resident in the United States in accordance with applicable DHS regulations must qualify for visa status under the provisions of INA section 101(b)(1)(G) as provided in this section. Such a child shall not be accorded status under INA section 101(b)(1)(F), provided that a child may be accorded status under INA section 101(b)(1)(F) if Form I-600A or I-600 was filed before the Convention effective date. Although this part 42 generally applies to the issuance of immigrant visas, this section 42.24 may also provide the basis for issuance of a nonimmigrant visa to permit a Convention adoptee to travel to the United States for purposes of naturalization under INA section 322.

(c) The provisions of this section govern the operations of consular officers in processing cases involving children for whom classification is sought under INA section 101(b)(1)(G), unless the Secretary of State has personally waived any requirement of the IAA or these regulations in a particular case in the interests of justice or to prevent grave physical harm to the child, to the extent consistent with the Convention.

(d) An alien child shall be classifiable under INA section 101(b)(1)(G) only if, before the child is adopted or legal custody for the purpose of adoption is granted, a petition for the child has been received and provisionally approved by a DHS officer or, where authorized by DHS, by a consular officer, and a visa application for the child has been received and annotated in accordance with paragraph (h) of this section by a consular officer. No alien child shall be issued a visa pursuant to INA section 101(b)(1)(G) unless the petition and visa application are finally approved.

(e) If a petition for a child under INA section 101(b)(1)(G) is properly filed with a consular officer, the consular officer will review the petition for the purpose of determining whether it can be provisionally approved in accordance with applicable DHS requirements. If a properly completed application for waiver of inadmissibility is received by a consular officer at the same time that a petition for a child under INA section 101(b)(1)(G) is received, provisional approval cannot take place unless the waiver is approved, and therefore the consular officer, pursuant to 8 CFR 204.313(i)(3) and 8 CFR 212.7, will forward the petition and the waiver application to DHS for decisions as to approval of the waiver and provisional approval of the petition. If a petition for a child under INA section 101(b)(1)(G) is received by a DHS officer, the consular officer will conduct any reviews, determinations or investigations requested by DHS with regard to the petition and classification determination in accordance with applicable DHS procedures.

(f) A petition shall be provisionally approved by the consular officer if, in accordance with applicable DHS requirements, it appears that the child will be classifiable under INA section 101(b)(1)(G) and that the proposed adoption or grant of legal custody will be in compliance with the Convention. If the consular officer knows or has reason to believe the petition is not provisionally approvable, the consular officer shall forward it to DHS pursuant to 8 CFR 204.313(i)(3).

(g) After a petition has been provisionally approved, a completed visa application form, any supporting documents required pursuant to § 42.63 and § 42.65, and any required fees must be submitted to the consular officer in accordance with § 42.61 for a provisional review of visa eligibility. The requirements in § 42.62, § 42.64, § 42.66 and § 42.67 shall also be satisfied to the extent practicable.

(h) A consular officer shall provisionally determine visa eligibility based on a review of the visa application, submitted supporting documents, and the provisionally approved petition. In so doing, the consular officer shall follow all procedures required to adjudicate the visa to the extent possible in light of the degree of compliance with §§ 42.62 through 42.67. If it appears, based on the available information, that the child would not be ineligible under INA section 212 or other applicable law to receive a visa, the consular officer shall so annotate the visa application. If evidence of an ineligibility is discovered during the review of the visa application, and the ineligibility was not waived in conjunction with provisional approval of the petition, the prospective adoptive parents shall be informed of the ineligibility and given an opportunity to establish that it will be overcome. If the visa application cannot be annotated as described above, the consular officer shall deny the visa in accordance with § 42.81, regardless of whether the application has yet been executed in accordance with § 42.67(a); provided however that, in cases in which a waiver may be available under the INA and the consular officer determines that the visa application appears otherwise approvable, the consular officer shall inform the prospective adoptive parents of the procedure for applying to DHS for a waiver. If in addition the consular officer comes to know or have reason to believe that the petition is not clearly approvable as provided in 8 CFR 204.313(i)(3), the consular officer shall forward the petition to DHS pursuant to that section.

(i) If the petition has been provisionally approved and the visa application has been annotated in accordance with subparagraph (h), the consular officer shall notify the country of origin that the steps required by Article 5 of the Convention have been taken.

(j) After the consular officer has received appropriate notification from the country of origin that the adoption or grant of legal custody has occurred and any remaining requirements established by DHS or §§ 42.61 through 42.67 have been fulfilled, the consular officer, if satisfied that the requirements of the IAA and the Convention have been met with respect to the adoption or grant of legal custody, shall affix to the adoption decree or grant of legal custody a certificate so indicating. This certificate shall constitute the certification required by IAA section 301(a) and INA section 204(d)(2). For purposes of determining whether to issue a certificate, the fact that a consular officer notified the country of origin pursuant to paragraph (i) of this section that the steps required by Article 5 of the Convention had been taken and the fact that the country of origin has provided appropriate notification that the adoption or grant of legal custody has occurred shall together constitute prima facie evidence of compliance with the Convention and the IAA.

(k) If the consular officer is unable to issue the certificate described in paragraph (j) of this section, the consular officer shall notify the country of origin of the consular officer's decision.

(l) After the consular officer determines whether to issue the certificate described in paragraph (j) of this section, the consular officer shall finally adjudicate the petition and visa application in accordance with standard procedures.

(m) If the consular officer is unable to give final approval to the visa application or the petition, then the consular officer shall forward the petition to DHS, pursuant to § 42.43 or 8 CFR 204.313(i)(3), as applicable, for appropriate action in accordance with applicable DHS procedures, and/or refuse the visa application in accordance with § 42.81. The consular officer shall notify the country of origin that the visa has been refused.

(n) Notwithstanding paragraphs (d) through (m) of this section, an alien described in paragraph (n)(1) of this section may qualify for visa status under INA section 101(b)(1)(G)(iii) without meeting the requirements set forth in paragraphs (d) through (m) of this section.

(1) Per Section 4(b) of the Intercountry Adoption Simplification Act, Public Law 111-287 (IASA), an alien otherwise described in INA section 101(b)(1)(G)(iii) who attained the age of 18 on or after April 1, 2008 shall be deemed to meet the age requirement imposed by INA section 101(b)(1)(G)(iii)(III), provided that a petition is filed for such child in accordance with DHS requirements not later than November 30, 2012.

(2) For any alien described in paragraph (n)(1) of this section, the competent authority" referred to in INA section 101(b)(1)(G)(i)(V)(aa) is a court or governmental agency of a foreign country of origin having jurisdiction and authority to make decisions in matters of child welfare, including adoption. If the competent authority over matters of child welfare no longer has jurisdiction or authority over the alien due to his or her age, then the passport issuing authority of the country of origin may be considered the competent authority for the purposes of INA section 101(b)(1)(G)(i)(V)(aa).

HISTORY:

[72 FR 61301, 61305, Oct. 30, 2007; 76 FR 67361, 67363, Nov. 1, 2011, as confirmed and amended at 78 FR 32989, 32990, June 3, 2013]

Subpart D

Immigrants Subject to Numerical Limitations

§ 42.31 Family-sponsored immigrants.

(a) Entitlement to status. An alien shall be classifiable as a family-sponsored immigrant under INA 203(a) (1), (2), (3) or (4) if the consular officer has received from DHS a Petition to Classify Status of Alien Relative for Issuance of Immigrant Visa approved in accordance with INA 204 to accord the alien such preference status, or official notification of such an approval, and the consular officer is satisfied that the alien has the relationship to the petitioner indicated in the petition. In the case of a petition according an alien status under INA 203(a) (1) or (3) or status as an unmarried son or daughter under INA 203(a)(2), the petitioner must be a "parent" as defined in INA 101(b)(2) and 22 CFR 40.1. In the case of a petition to accord an alien status under INA 203(a)(4) filed on or after January 1, 1977, the petitioner must be at least twenty-one years of age.

(b) Entitlement to derivative status. Pursuant to INA 203(d), and whether or not named in the petition, the child of a family-sponsored first, second, third or fourth preference immigrant or the spouse of a family-sponsored third or fourth preference immigrant, if not otherwise entitled to an immigrant status and the immediate issuance of a visa, is entitled to a derivative status corresponding to the classification and priority date of the beneficiary of the petition.

HISTORY:

[52 FR 49676, Oct. 1, 1991, as confirmed at 58 FR 48447, Sept. 16, 1993; 61 FR 1834, 1836, Jan. 24, 1996; 71 FR 34519, 34522, June 15, 2006]

§ 42.32 Employment-based preference immigrants.

Aliens subject to the worldwide level specified in section 201(d) for employment-based immigrants in a fiscal year shall be allotted visas as indicated below.

(a) First preference — Priority workers —

(1) Entitlement to status. An alien shall be classifiable as an employment-based first preference immigrant under INA 203(b)(1) if the consular office has received from DHS a Petition for Immigrant Worker approved in accordance with INA 204 to accord the alien such Preference status, or official notification of such an approval, and the consular officer is satisfied that the alien is within one of the classes described in INA 203(b)(1).

(2) Entitlement to derivative status. Pursuant to INA 203(d), and whether or not named in the petition, the child or spouse of an employment-based first preference immigrant, if not otherwise entitled to an immigrant status and the immediate issuance of a visa, is entitled to a derivative status corresponding to the classification and priority date of the beneficiary of the petition.

(b) Second preference — Professionals with advanced degrees or persons of exceptional ability —

(1) Entitlement to status. An alien shall be classifiable as an employment-based second preference immigrant under INA 203(b)(2) if the consular officer has received from DHS a Petition for Immigrant Worker approved in accordance with INA 204 to accord the alien such preference status, or official notification of such an approval, and the consular officer is satisfied that the alien is within one of the classes described in INA 203(b)(2).

(2) Entitlement to derivative status. Pursuant to INA 203(d), and whether or not named in the petition, the child or spouse of an employment-based second preference immigrant, if not otherwise entitled to an immigrant status and the immediate issuance of a visa, is entitled to a derivative status corresponding to the classification and priority date of the beneficiary of the petition.

(c) Third preference — Skilled workers, professionals, other workers —

(1) Entitlement to status. An alien shall be classifiable as an employment-based third preference immigrant under INA 203(b)(3) if the consular officer has received from DHS a Petition for Immigrant Worker approved in accordance with INA 204 to accord the alien such preference status, or official notification of such an approval, and the consular officer is satisfied that the alien is within one of the classes described in INA 203(b)(3).

(2) Entitlement to derivative status. Pursuant to INA 203(d), and whether or not named in the petition, the child or spouse of an employment-based third preference immigrant, if not otherwise entitled to an immigrant status and the immediate issuance of a visa,

is entitled to a derivative status corresponding to the classification and priority date of the beneficiary of the petition.

(d) Fourth preference — Special immigrants —

(1) Religious workers —

(i) Classification based on qualifications under INA 101(A)(27)(C). An alien shall be classifiable under INA 203(b)(4) as a special immigrant described in INA 101(a)(27)(C) if:

(A) The consular officer has received a petition approved by DHS to accord such classification, or an official notification of such approval; and

(B) The consular officer is satisfied from the evidence presented that the alien qualifies under that section; or

(C) The consular officer is satisfied the alien is the spouse or child of a religious worker so classified and is accompanying or following to join the principal alien.

(ii) Timeliness of application. An immigrant visa issued under INA 203(b)(4) to an alien described in INA 101(a)(27)(C), other than a minister of religion, who qualifies as a "religious worker" as defined in 8 CFR 204.5, shall bear the usual validity except that in no case shall it be valid later than September 30, 2003.

(2) See 22 CFR 42.34.

(3) Panama Canal employees —

(i) Entitlement to status. An alien who is subject to the numerical limitations specified in section 3201(c) of the Panama Canal Act of 1979, Public Law 96-70, is classifiable under INA 203(b)(4) as a special immigrant described in INA 101(a)(27) (E), (F) or (G) if the consular officer has received a petition approved by DHS to accord such classification, or official notification of such an approval, and the consular officer is satisfied that the alien is within one of the classes described in INA 101(a)(27) (E), (F), or (G).

(ii) Entitlement to derivative status. Pursuant to INA 203(d), and whether or not named in the petition, the spouse or child of any alien classified under INA 203(b)(4) as a special immigrant qualified under this section, if not otherwise entitled to an immigrant status and the immediate issuance of a visa, is entitled to a derivative status corresponding to the classification and priority date of the beneficiary of the petition.

(4) Spouse and children of certain Foreign Medical graduates. The accompanying spouse and children of a graduate of a foreign medical school or of a person qualified to practice medicine in a foreign state who has adjusted status as a special immigrant under the provisions of INA 101(a)(27)(H) are classifiable under INA 203(b)(4) as special immigrants defined in INA 101(a)(27)(H) if the consular officer has received an approved petition from DHS which accords such status and the consular officer is satisfied that the alien is within the class described in INA 101(a)(27)(H).

(5) Certain international organization and NATO civilian employees —

(i) Entitlement to status. An alien is classifiable under INA 203(b)(4) as a special immigrant defined in INA 101(a)(27)(I) or (L) if the consular officer has received a petition approved by the DHS to accord such classification, or official notification of such approval, and the consular officer is satisfied from the evidence presented that the alien is within one of the classes described therein.

(ii) Timeliness of application. An alien accorded status under INA 203(b)(4) because of qualification under INA 101(a)(27)(I) must appear for a final visa interview and issuance of the immigrant visa within six months of establishing entitlement to status.

(6) Certain juvenile court dependents. An alien shall be classifiable under INA 203(b)(4) as a special immigrant defined in INA 101(a)(27)(J) if the consular officer has received from DHS an approved petition to accord such status, or an official notification of such an approval, and the consular officer is satisfied the alien is within the class described in that section.

(7) Certain members of the United States Armed Forces recruited abroad —

(i) Entitlement to status. An alien is classifiable under INA 203(b)(4) as a special immigrant described in INA 101(a)(27)(K) if the consular office has received a petition approved by the DHS to accord such classification, or official notification of such an approval, and the consular officer is satisfied from the evidence presented that the alien is within the class described in INA 101(a)(27)(K).

(ii) Entitlement to derivative status. Pursuant to INA 203(d), and whether or not named in the petition, the spouse or child of any alien classified under INA 203(b)(4) as a special immigrant qualified under this section, if not otherwise entitled to an immigrant status and the immediate issuance of a visa, is entitled to a derivative status corresponding to the classification and priority date of the beneficiary of the petition.

(8) Certain United States international broadcasting employees —

(i) Entitlement to status. An alien is classifiable as a special immigrant under INA 203(b)(4) as described in INA 101(a)(27)(M), if the consular office has received a petition approved by the DHS to accord such classification, or official notification of such an approval, and the consular officer is satisfied from the evidence presented that the alien is within the class described in INA 101(a)(27)(M).

(ii) Entitlement to derivative status. Pursuant to INA 203(d), and whether or not named in the petition, the spouse or child of any alien classified under INA 203(b)(4) as a special immigrant qualified under this section, if not otherwise entitled to an immigrant status and the immediate issuance of a visa, is entitled to derivative status corresponding to the classification and priority date of the beneficiary of the petition.

(9) Certain Victims of the September 11, 2001 terrorist attacks

(i) Entitlement to status. An alien shall be classifiable as a special immigrant under INA 203(b)(4) as specified in section 421 of Public Law 107-56, if:

(A) The consular officer has received a petition approved by the DHS to accord such classification, or official notification of such an approval, and the consular officer is satisfied from the evidence presented that the alien is entitled to that classification; or

(B) The alien is the spouse or child of an alien so classified in paragraph (d)(9)(i) of this section and is accompanying or following to join the principal alien.

(ii) Ineligibility exemption. An alien classified under paragraph (d)(9)(i) of this section shall not be subject to the provisions of INA 212(a)(4).

(iii) Priority date. Aliens entitled to status under paragraph (d)(9)(i) of this section shall be assigned a priority date as of the date the petition was filed under INA 204 for classification under section INA 203(b)(4) and visas shall be issued in the chronological order of application submission. However, in the event that the annual limit for immigrants under INA 203 is reached, the alien may retain the earlier priority date of the petition that was revoked.

(e) Fifth preference — Employment-creation immigrants —

(1) Entitlement to status. An alien shall be classifiable as a fifth preference employment-creation immigrant if the consular officer has received from DHS an approved petition to accord such status, or official notification of such an approval, and the consular officer is satisfied that the alien is within the class described in INA 203(b)(5).

(2) Entitlement to derivative status. Pursuant to INA 203(d), and whether or not named in the petition, the spouse or child of an employment-based fifth preference immigrant, if not otherwise entitled to an immigrant status and the immediate issuance of a visa, is entitled to a derivative status corresponding to the classification and priority date of the beneficiary of the petition.

HISTORY:

[56 FR 49676, Oct. 1, 1991, as confirmed at 58 FR 48447, Sept. 16, 1993; as amended at 56 FR 51172, Oct. 10, 1991, as confirmed at 58 FR 48447, Sept. 16, 1993; 56 FR 55077, Oct. 24, 1991, as confirmed at 58 FR 48446, 48447, Sept. 16, 1993; 60 FR 35839, July 12, 1995; 63 FR 4394, Jan. 29, 1998; 63 FR 68393, Dec. 11, 1998; 65 FR 80744, 80745, Dec. 22, 2000; 66 FR 15349, 15350, Mar. 19, 2001, as confirmed at 67 FR 60562, Sept. 26, 2002; 68 FR 24638, 24639, May 8, 2003; 71 FR 34519, 34522, June 15, 2006; 85 FR 36323, 36326, June 16 2020]

§ 42.33 Diversity immigrants.

(a) **General.**

(1) Eligibility to compete for consideration under section 203(c). An alien will be eligible to compete for consideration for visa issuance under INA 203(c) during a fiscal year only if he or she is a native of a low-admission foreign state, as determined by the Secretary of Homeland Security pursuant to INA 203(c)(1)(E), with respect to the fiscal year in question; and if he or she has at least a high school education or its equivalent or, within the five years preceding the date of application for a visa, has two years of work experience in an occupation requiring at least two years training or experience. The eligibility for a visa under INA 203(c) ceases at the end of the fiscal year in question. Under no circumstances may a consular officer issue a visa or other documentation to an alien after the end of the fiscal year during which an alien possesses diversity visa eligibility.

(2) Definition of high school education or its equivalent. For the purposes of this section, the phrase high school education or its equivalent means the successful completion of a twelve-year course of elementary and secondary education in the United States or successful completion in another country of a formal course of elementary and secondary education comparable to completion of twelve years' elementary and secondary education in the United States.

(3) Determinations of work experience. For all cases registered for the 2003 Diversity Visa Program and Diversity Visa Programs occurring in subsequent fiscal years, consular officers must use the Department of Labor's O*Net On Line to determine qualifying work experience.

(4) Limitation on number of petitions per year. No more than one petition may be submitted by or on behalf of, any alien for consideration during any single fiscal year. If two or more petitions for any single fiscal year are submitted by, or on behalf of, any alien, all such petitions will be void pursuant to INA 204(a)(1)(I)(i) and the alien by or for whom the petition has been submitted will not be eligible for consideration for diversity visa issuance during the fiscal year in question.

(5) Northern Ireland. For purposes of determining eligibility to file a petition for consideration under INA 203(c) for a fiscal year, the districts comprising that portion of the United Kingdom of Great Britain and Northern Ireland, known as "Northern Ireland", will be treated as a separate foreign state. The districts comprising "Northern Ireland" are Antrim, Ards, Armagh, Ballymena, Ballymoney, Banbridge, Belfast, Carrickfergus, Castlereagh, Coleraine, Cookstown, Craigavon, Down, Dungannon, Fermanagh, Larne, Limavady, Lisburn, Londonderry, Magherafelt, Moyle, Newry and Mourne, Newtownabbey, North Down, Omagh, and Strabane.

(b) Petition requirement. An alien claiming to be entitled to compete for consideration under INA 203(c) must file a petition with the Department of State for such consideration. At the alien petitioner's request, another person may file a petition on behalf of the alien. The petition will consist of an electronic entry form that the alien petitioner or a person acting on the behalf of the alien petitioner must complete on-line and submit to the Department of State via a Web site established by the Department of State for the purpose of receiving such petitions. The Department will specify the address of the Web site prior to the commencement of the 30-day or greater period described in paragraph (b)(3) of this section using the notice procedure prescribed in that paragraph.

(1) Information to be provided in the petition. The website will include the electronic entry form mentioned in paragraph (b) of this section. The entry form will require the person completing the form to provide the following information, typed in the Roman alphabet, regarding the alien petitioner:

(i) The petitioner's full name;

(ii) The petitioner's date and place of birth (including city and country, province or other political subdivision of the country);

(iii) The petitioner's gender;

(iv) The country of which the petitioner claims to be a native, if other than the country of birth;

(v) The name[s], date[s] and place[s] of birth and gender of the petitioner's spouse and child[ren], if any, (including legally adopted and step-children), regardless of whether or not they are living with the petitioner or intend to accompany or follow to join the petitioner should the petitioner immigrate to the United States pursuant to INA 203(c), but excluding a spouse or a child[ren] who is already a U.S. citizen or U.S. lawful permanent resident;

(vi) A current mailing address for the petitioner;

(vii) The location of the consular office nearest to the petitioner's current residence or, if in the United States, nearest to the petitioner's last foreign residence prior to entry into the United States.

(2) Requirements for photographs. The petition will also require inclusion of a photograph of the petitioner and of his or her spouse and all unmarried children under the age of 21 years. The photographs must meet the following specifications:

(i) A digital image of the applicant from either a digital camera source or a scanned photograph via scanner. If scanned, the original photographic print must have been 2" by 2" (50mm x 50mm). Scanner hardware and digital image resolution requirements will be further specified in the public notice described in paragraph (b)(3) of this section.

(ii) The image must be in the Joint Photographic Experts Group (JPEG) File Interchange Format (JFIF) format.

(iii) The image must be in color.

(iv) The image must have been taken no more than six months prior to the date of the petition submission.

(v) The person being photographed must be directly facing the camera with the head neither tilted up, down, or to the side. The head must cover about 50% of the area of the photograph.

(vi) The photograph must be taken with the person in front of a neutral, light-colored background. Photos taken with very dark or patterned, busy backgrounds will not be accepted.

(vii) The person's face must be in focus.

(viii) The person in the photograph must not wear eyeglasses, sunglasses, or other paraphernalia that obstruct the view of the face.

(ix) A photograph with the person wearing a head covering or a hat is only acceptable if the covering or hat is worn specifically due to that person's religious beliefs, and even then, the hat or covering may not obscure any portion of the face. A photograph of a person wearing tribal, military, airline or other headgear not specifically religious in nature will not be accepted.

(3) Submission of petition. A petition for consideration for visa issuance under INA 203(c) must be submitted to the Department of State by electronic entry to an Internet website designated by the Department for that purpose. No fee will be collected at the time of submission of a petition, but a processing fee may be collected at a later date, as provided in paragraph (i) of this section. The Department will establish a period of not less than thirty days during each fiscal year within which aliens may submit petitions for approval of eligibility to apply for visa issuance during the following fiscal year. Each fiscal year the Department will give timely notice of both the website address and the exact dates of the petition submission period, as well as other pertinent information, through publication in the Federal Register and such other methods as will ensure the widest possible dissemination of the information, both abroad and within the United States.

(c) Processing of petitions. Entries received during the petition submission period established for the fiscal year in question and meeting all of the requirements of paragraph (b) of this section will be assigned a number in a separate numerical sequence established for each regional area specified in INA 203(c)(1)(F). Upon completion of the numbering of all petitions, all numbers assigned for each region will be separately rank-ordered at random by a computer using standard computer software for that purpose. The Department will then select in the rank orders determined by the computer program a quantity of petitions for each region estimated to be sufficient to ensure, to the extent possible, usage of all immigrant visas authorized under INA 203(c) for the fiscal year in question. The Department will consider petitions selected in this manner to have been approved tor the purposes of this section.

(d) Validity of approved petitions. A petition approved pursuant to paragraph (c) of this section will be valid for a period not to exceed Midnight of the last day of the fiscal year for which the petition was approved. At that time, the Department of State will consider approval of the petition to cease to be valid pursuant to INA 204(a)(1)(I)(ii)(II), which prohibits issuance of visas based upon petitions submitted and approved for a fiscal year after the last day of that fiscal year.

(e) Order of consideration. Consideration for visa issuance to aliens whose petitions have been approved pursuant to paragraph (c) of this section will be in the regional rank orders established pursuant that paragraph.

(f) Allocation of visa numbers. To the extent possible, diversity immigrant visa numbers will be allocated in accordance with INA 203(c)(1)(E) and will be allotted only during the fiscal year for which a petition to accord diversity immigrant status was submitted and approved. Under no circumstances will immigrant visa numbers be allotted after midnight of the last day of the fiscal year for which the petition was submitted and approved.

(g) Further processing. The Department will inform applicants whose petitions have been approved pursuant to paragraph (c) of this section of the steps necessary to meet the requirements of INA 222(b) in order to apply formally for an immigrant visa.

(h) Maintenance of certain information. (1) The Department will compile and maintain the following information concerning petitioners to whom immigrant visas are issued under INA 203(c):

(i) Age;

(ii) Country of birth;

(iii) Marital status;

(iv) Sex;

(v) Level of education; and

(vi) Occupation and level of occupational qualification.

(2) The Department will not maintain the names of visa recipients in connection with this information and the information will be compiled and maintained in such form that the identity of visa recipients cannot be determined therefrom.

(i) Diversity Visa Lottery fee. Consular officers shall collect, or ensure the collection of, the Diversity Visa Lottery fee from those persons who apply for a diversity immigrant visa, described in INA 203(c), after being selected by the diversity visa lottery program. The Diversity Visa Lottery fee, as prescribed by the Secretary of State, is set forth in the Schedule of Fees, 22 CFR 22.1.

HISTORY:

[56 FR 49676, Oct. 1, 1991, as confirmed at 58 FR 48447, Sept. 16, 1993; 59 FR 15301, Mar. 31, 1994; 61 FR 1523, 1524, Jan. 22, 1996, as corrected at 61 FR 6111, Feb. 16, 1996; 66 FR 39435, 39437, July 31, 2001; 66 FR 54135, 54136, Oct. 26, 2001; 67 FR 38892, 38893, June 6, 2002, as corrected at 67 FR 40849, June 14, 2002; 67 FR 51752, 51753, Aug. 9, 2002; 68 FR 49353, 49355, Aug. 18, 2003, as confirmed at 74 FR 2369, Jan. 15, 2009; 73 FR 7670, Feb. 11, 2008; 77 FR 18907, 18914, Mar. 29, 2012, as confirmed at 77 FR 57012, 57013, Sept. 17, 2012; 81 FR 63694, 63695, Sept. 16, 2016; 84 FR 25989, 25991, June 5, 2019; 87 FR 35414, 35415, June 10, 2022]

§ 42.34 Special immigrant visas-certain U.S. Government employees.

(a) General. An applicant is classifiable under INA 203(b)(4) as a special immigrant described in INA 101(a)(27)(D) provided:

(1)(i) The applicant has performed faithful service to the United States Government abroad, or the American Institute in Taiwan, for a total of fifteen years or more; or

(ii) The applicant is the surviving spouse or child of an employee of the United States Government abroad who performed faithful service for a total of not less than 15 years or was killed in the line of duty; and

(2) The principal officer of a Foreign Service establishment (or, in the case of the American Institute in Taiwan, the Director), recommends granting special immigrant status to such person in exceptional circumstances; and

(3) The Secretary of State, or designee, approves such recommendation and finds that it is in the national interest to grant such status.

(b) Petition requirement. An applicant who seeks classification as a special immigrant described in paragraph (a) of this section must file a Form DS-1884, Petition to Classify Special Immigrant under INA 203(b)(4) as an Employee or Former Employee of the U.S. Government Abroad, or the Surviving Spouse or Child of an Employee of the U.S. Government Abroad, with the Department of State. An applicant described in INA 101(a)(27)(D) may file such a petition only after, but within one year of, notification from the Department that the Secretary of State or designee has approved a recommendation from the principal officer that special immigrant status be accorded the applicant in exceptional circumstances and has found it in the national interest to do so.

(1) Petition fees. The Secretary of State shall establish a fee for the filing of a petition to accord status under INA 203(b)(4) which shall be collected following notification that the Secretary of State, or designee, has approved the recommendation that the applicant be granted status as a special immigrant under INA 101(a)(27)(D).

(2) Establishing priority date. The priority date of an applicant seeking status under INA 203(b)(4) as a special immigrant described in INA 101(a)(27)(D) shall be the date on which the petition to accord such classification, the DS-1884, is filed. The filing date of the petition is the date on which a properly completed form and the required fee are accepted by a Foreign Service post. Pursuant to INA 203(d), and whether named in the petition, the current spouse or child who meets the definition of "child" under INA 101(b)(1) of an applicant classified under INA 203(b)(4), if not otherwise entitled to an immigrant status and the immediate issuance of a visa, is entitled to the classification and priority date of the beneficiary of the petition.

(3) Delegation of authority to approve petitions. The authority to approve petitions to accord status under INA 203(b)(4) to an applicant described in INA 101(a)(27)(D) is hereby delegated to the chief consular officer at the post of recommendation or, in the absence of the consular officer, to any alternate approving officer designated by the principal officer. Such authority may not be exercised until the Foreign Service post has received formal notification of the Secretary of State or designee's approval of special immigrant status for the petitioning applicant.

(4) Petition validity. Except as noted in this paragraph, the validity of a petition approved for classification under INA 203(b)(4) shall be six months beyond the date of the Secretary of State's approval thereof or the availability of a visa number, whichever is later.

(5) Extension of special immigrant status and petition validity. If the principal officer of a post concludes that circumstances in a particular case are such that an extension of validity of the Secretary of State or designee's approval of the principal officer's recommendation or of the petition would be in the national interest, the principal officer shall recommend to the Secretary of State or designee that such validity be extended for not more than one additional year.

(c) Definitions —

(1) Full-time service. Where 15 years of service is the minimum time required for eligibility for a special immigrant visa, the employee must have been employed for a total of at least 15 full-time years, or the equivalent thereof, in the service of the U.S. Government abroad. The number of hours per week that qualify an employee as full-time is dependent on local law and prevailing practice in the country where the individual is or was employed, as reflected in the employment documentation submitted with the application for special immigrant status. The years of service may be met based on employment abroad with one,

or more than one, agency of the U.S. Government provided the total amount of full-time service with the U.S. Government is 15 years or more, or the equivalent thereof.

(2) Faithful service. Where faithful service is required for eligibility for a special immigrant visa, an employee must have performed faithfully in the position held. The principal officer has the primary responsibility for determining whether the employee's service meets this requirement. A record of disciplinary actions that have been taken against the employee does not automatically disqualify the applicant. The principal officer must assess the record of disciplinary actions considering the extent and gravity of the misconduct and when the incidents occurred, and determine whether the record as a whole, notwithstanding disciplinary actions, is one of faithful service.

(3) Continuity. Where 15 years of service is the minimum time required for eligibility for a special immigrant visa, the employee's period of service need not have been continuous but must have an aggregate total of 15 years of service to qualify.

(4) Abroad. The service must have occurred anywhere outside the United States, as the term "United States" is defined in INA 101(a)(38).

(5) Employment at the American Institute in Taiwan. INA 101(a)(27)(D) permits both present and former employees of the American Institute in Taiwan to apply for special immigrant status. An employee's service before and after the founding of the American Institute in Taiwan is counted toward the minimum 15 years of service requirement.

(6) Honorably retired. Separations within the meaning of "honorably retired" include, for example, those resulting from mandatory or voluntary retirement, reduction-in-force, or resignation for personal reasons. Separations not within the meaning of "honorably retired" would include a termination for cause or an involuntary termination or resignation in lieu of a termination for cause.

(7) Exceptional circumstances for employees of the United States Government abroad. For classification as a special immigrant under INA 101(a)(27)(D)(i), the principal officer must determine that an employee demonstrates at least one form of "exceptional circumstances" to support an application for special immigrant status.

(i) Prima facie indicators of exceptional circumstances. In the following situations, an employee's service with the U.S. Government generally will be deemed to have met exceptional circumstances.

(A) Diplomatic relations between the employee's country of nationality and the United States have been severed;

(B) Diplomatic relations between the country in which the employee was employed and the United States have been severed;

(C) The country in which the employee was employed and the United States have strained relations and the employee may be subjected to retribution by the local, State, Federal, or other official government body merely because of association with the U.S. Government, or the employee may be pressured to divulge information contrary to U.S. national interests; or

(D) The employee was hired at the Consulate General at Hong Kong on or before July 1, 1999.

(ii) Strong indicators of exceptional circumstances.

(A) It is believed that continued service to the U.S. Government might endanger the life of the employee;

(B) The employee has fulfilled responsibilities or given service in a manner that approaches the heroic;

(C) The employee has been awarded a global or a regional "Foreign Service National of the Year" Award;

(D) The employee has disclosed waste, fraud or abuse, a substantial and specific danger to public health or safety, or a violation of law, rule, or regulation within the Department or other U.S. Government agency, if such disclosure results in significant action by the Department or other U.S. Government agency against an offending party, such as termination or severance of a contractual relationship, or criminal charges against any person or entity.

(E) The employee has served the U.S. Government for a period of twenty years or more.

(8) Exceptional circumstances for surviving spouses and children. For classification as a special immigrant under INA 101(a)(27)(D)(ii), the principal officer must determine that the deceased employee:

(i) Was killed in the line of duty; or

(ii) Performed faithful service to the United States Government abroad for a total of not less than 15 years; and

(A) Was employed by the U.S. Government as of the date of their death or in the immediately preceding period as defined in paragraph (c)(9) of this section, or

(B) Was an honorably retired former employee who, prior to their death, demonstrated at least one form of "exceptional circumstances" as defined in paragraph (c)(7) of this section.

(9) Immediately preceding period.

(i) As provided in paragraph (c)(8)(ii)(A) of this section, a deceased employee is considered to have been employed by the U.S. Government in the period immediately preceding their death if such employment ceased due to circumstances that resulted in their death.

(ii) A deceased employee is presumed to not meet the criteria in paragraph (c)(8)(ii)(A) of this section if the employee's death occurred more than five years following cessation of employment. This presumption can be rebutted if the applicant establishes, to the satisfaction of the principal officer, that the employment ceased due to circumstances that resulted in the employee's death, and the Secretary or appropriate designee finds it in the national interest to grant such status. The principal officer has the primary responsibility for determining whether the applicant meets this criterion, taking into consideration as informed by the circumstances of the cessation of employment, the cause of the employee's death as documented by the applicant, and other relevant evidence the applicant presents that demonstrates that the cessation of employment was for reasons that ultimately resulted in the employee's death.

(10) Immediate intent to immigrate.

(i) The recommendation of the principal officer must certify that the applicant being recommended is prepared to file a petition within one year of the Department's notification to the post of approval of special immigrant status, and to pursue an immigrant visa application within six months of the Secretary of State's approval of the petition or of an immigrant visa becoming available, whichever is later. If the applicant is an employee who is not yet honorably retired, the recommendation must also certify that the employee intends permanent separation from U.S. Government employment abroad no later than the date of departure for the United States following issuance of an immigrant visa.

(ii) Employees of Hong Kong Consulate General hired on or before July 1, 1999, are not required to establish immediate intent to immigrate. Employees of the Hong Kong Consulate General who received or were approved for special immigrant status before July 1, 1999, also may continue employment with the U.S.

HISTORY:
85 FR 36323, 36326, June 16, 2020; 89 FR 99076, 99079, Dec. 10, 2024]

Subpart E

Petitions

§ 42.41 Effect of approved petition.

Consular officers are authorized to grant to an alien the immediate relative or preference status accorded in a petition approved in the alien's behalf upon receipt of the approved petition or official notification of its approval. The status shall be granted for the period authorized by law or regulation. The approval of a petition does not relieve the alien of the burden of establishing to the satisfaction of the consular officer that the alien is eligible in all respects to receive a visa.

HISTORY:
[56 FR 49682, Oct. 1, 1991, as confirmed at 58 FR 48447, Sept. 16, 1993]

§ 42.42 Petitions for immediate relative or preference status.

Petition for immediate relative or preference status. The consular officer may not issue a visa to an alien as an immediate relative entitled to status under 201(b), a family-sponsored immigrant entitled to preference status under 203(a)(1)-(4), or an employment-based preference immigrant entitled to status under INA 203(b)(1)-(5), unless the officer has received a petition filed and approved in accordance with INA 204 or official notification of such filing and approval.

HISTORY:
[56 FR 49682, Oct. 1, 1991, as confirmed at 58 FR 48447, Sept. 16, 1993]

§ 42.43 Suspension or termination of action in petition cases.

(a) Suspension of action. The consular officer shall suspend action in a petition case and return the petition, with a report of the facts, for reconsideration by DHS if the petitioner requests suspension of action, or if the officer knows or has reason to believe that approval of the petition was obtained by fraud, misrepresentation, or other unlawful means, or that the beneficiary is not entitled, for some other reason, to the status approved.

(b) **Termination of action.**

(1) The consular officer shall terminate action in a petition case upon receipt from DHS of notice of revocation of the petition in accordance with DHS regulations.

(2) The consular officer shall terminate action in a petition case subject to the provisions of INA 203(g) in accordance with the provisions of § 42.83.

HISTORY:
[56 FR 49682, Oct. 1, 1991, as confirmed at 58 FR 48447, Sept. 16, 1993; 71 FR 34519, 34522, June 15, 2006]

Subpart F

Numerical Controls and Priority Dates

§ 42.51 Department control of numerical limitations.

(a) Centralized control. Centralized control of the numerical limitations on immigration specified in INA 201, 202, and 203 is established in the Department. The Department shall limit the number of immigrant visas that may be issued and the number of adjustments of status that may be granted to aliens subject to these numerical limitations to a number:

(1) Not to exceed 27 percent of the world-wide total made available under INA 203 (a), (b) and (c) in any of the first three quarters of any fiscal year; and

(2) Not to exceed, in any month of a fiscal year, 10% of the world-wide total made available under INA 203 (a), (b) and (c) plus any balance remaining from authorizations for preceding months in the same fiscal year.

(b) Allocation of numbers. Within the foregoing limitations, the Department shall allocate immigrant visa numbers for use in connection with the issuance of immigrant visas and adjustments based on the chronological order of the priority dates of visa applicants classified under INA 203 (a) and (b) reported by consular officers pursuant to § 42.55(b) and of applicants for adjustment of status as reported by officers of the DHS, taking into account the requirements of INA 202(e) in such allocations. In the case of applicants under INA 203(c), visa numbers shall be allocated within the limitation for each specified geographical region in the random order determined in accordance with sec. 42.33(c) of this part.

(c) Recaptured visa numbers. An immigrant visa number shall be returned to the Department for reallocation within the fiscal year in which the visa was issued when:

(1) An immigrant having an immigrant visa is excluded from the United States and deported;

(2) An immigrant does not apply for admission to the United States before the expiration of the validity of the visa;

(3) An alien having a preference immigrant visa is found not to be a preference immigrant; or

(4) An immigrant visa is revoked pursuant to § 42.82.

HISTORY:

[56 FR 51174, Oct. 10, 1991, as confirmed at 58 FR 48446, Sept. 16, 1993; 59 FR 15302, Mar. 31, 1994; 63 FR 48577, 48578, Sept. 11, 1998; 71 FR 34519, 34522, June 15, 2006]

§ 42.52 Post records of visa applications.

(a) Waiting list. Records of individual visa applicants entitled to an immigrant classification and their priority dates shall be maintained at posts at which immigrant visas are issued. These records shall indicate the chronological and preferential order in which consideration may be given to immigrant visa applications within the several immigrant classifications subject to the numerical limitations specified in INA 201, 202, and 203. Similar records shall be kept for the classes specified in INA 201(b)(2) and 101(a)(27) (A) and (B) which are not subject to numerical limitations. The records which pertain to applicants subject to numerical limitations constitute "waiting lists" within the meaning of INA 203(e)(3) as redesignated by the Immigration Act of 1990.

(b) Entitlement to immigrant classification. An alien shall be entitled to immigrant classification if the alien:

(1) Is the beneficiary of an approved petition according immediate relative or preference status;

(2) Has satisfied the consular officer that the alien is entitled to special immigrant status under INA(101)(a)(27) (A) or (B);

(3) Is entitled to status as a Vietnam Amerasian under section 584(b)(1) of section 101(e) of Public Law 100-202 as amended by Public Law 101-167 and re-amended by Public Law 101-513; or

(4) Beginning in FY-95, is entitled to status as a diversity immigrant under INA 203(c).

(c) **Record made when entitlement to immigrant classification is established.**

(1) A record that an alien is entitled to an immigrant visa classification shall be made whenever the consular officer is satisfied-or receives evidence-that the alien is within the criteria set forth in paragraph (b) of this section.

(2) A separate record shall be made of family members entitled to derivative immigrant status whenever the consular officer determines that a spouse or child is chargeable to a different foreign state or other numerical limitation than the principal alien. The provisions of INA 202(b) are to be applied as appropriate when either the spouse or parent is reached on the waiting list.

(3) A separate record shall be made of a spouse or child entitled to derivative immigrant status whenever the consular officer determines that the principal alien intends to precede the family.

HISTORY:

[56 FR 51174, Oct. 10, 1991, as confirmed at 58 FR 48446, Sept. 16, 1993; 61 FR 1834, 1836, Jan. 24, 1996; 78 FR 31398, 31399, May 24, 2013]

§ 42.53 Priority date of individual applicants.

(a) Preference applicant. The priority date of a preference visa applicant under INA 203 (a) or (b) shall be the fiing date of the approved petition that accorded preference status.

(b) Former Western Hemisphere applicant with priority date prior to January 1, 1977. Notwithstanding the provisions of paragraph (a) of this section, an alien who, prior to January 1, 1977, was subject to the numerical limitation specified in section 21(e) of the Act of October 3, 1965, and who was registered as a Western Hemisphere immigrant with a priority date prior to January 1, 1977, shall retain that priority date as a preference immigrant upon approval of a petition according status under INA 203 (a) or (b).

(c) Derivative priority date for spouse or child of principal alien. A spouse or child of a principal alien acquired prior to the principal alien's admission shall be entitled to the priority date of the principal alien, whether or not named in the immigrant visa application of the principal alien. A child born of a marriage which existed at the time of a principal alien's admission to the United States is considered to have been acquired prior to the principal alien's admission.

HISTORY:

[56 FR 51174, Oct. 10, 1991, as confirmed at 58 FR 48446, Sept. 16, 1993]

§ 42.54 Order of consideration.

(a) General. Consular officers shall request applicants to take the steps necessary to meet the requirements of INA 222(b) in order to apply formally for a visa as follows:

(1) In the chronological order of the priority dates of all applicants within each of the immigrant classifications specified in INA 203 (a) and (b); and

(2) In the random order established by the Secretary of State for each region for the fiscal year for applicants entitled to status under INA 203(c).

HISTORY:

[56 FR 51174, Oct. 10, 1991, as confirmed at 58 FR 48446, Sept. 16, 1993; 59 FR 15302, Mar. 31, 1994; 61 FR 1834, 1836, Jan. 24, 1996; 63 FR 48577, 48578, Sept. 11, 1998]

§ 42.55 Reports on numbers and priority dates of applications on record.

(a) Consular officers shall report periodically, as the Department may direct, the number and priority dates of all applicants subject to the numerical limitations prescribed in INA 201, 202, and 203 whose immigrant visa applications have been recorded in accordance with § 42.52(c)

(b) Documentarily qualified applicants. Consular officers shall also report periodically, as the Department may direct, the number and priority dates of all applicants described in paragraph (a) of this section who have informed the consular office that they have obtained the documents required under INA 222(b), for whom the necessary clearance procedures have been completed.

HISTORY:

[56 FR 51174, Oct. 10, 1991; 61 FR 1834, 1836, Jan. 24, 1996]

Subpart G

Application for Immigrant Visas

§ 42.61 Place of application.

(a) Alien to apply in consular district of residence. Unless otherwise directed by the Department, an alien applying for an immigrant visa shall make application at the consular office having jurisdiction over the alien's place of residence; except that, unless otherwise directed by the Department, an alien physically present in an area but having no residence therein may make application at the consular office having jurisdiction over that area if the alien can establish that he or she will be able to remain in the area for the period required to process the application. Finally, a consular office may, as a matter of discretion, or shall, at the direction of the Department, accept an immigrant visa application from an alien who is neither a resident of, nor physically present in, the area designated for that office for such purpose. For the purposes of this section, an alien physically present in the United States shall be considered to be a resident of the area of his or her last residence prior to entry into the United States.

(b) **Transfer of immigrant visa cases.**

(1) All documents, papers, and other evidence relating to an applicant whose case is pending or has been refused at one post may be transferred to another post at the applicant's request and risk when there is reasonable justification for the transfer and the transferring post has no reason to believe that the alien will be unable to appear at the receiving post.

(2) Any approved petition granting immediate relative or preference status should be included among the documents when a case is transferred from one post to another.

(3) In no case may a visa number be transferred from one post to another. A visa number which cannot be used as a result of the transfer must be returned to the Department immediately.

HISTORY:

[56 FR 51174, Oct. 10, 1991; 59 FR 39955, Aug. 5, 1994]

§ 42.62 Personal appearance and interview of applicant.

(a) Personal appearance of applicant before consular officer. Every alien applying for an immigrant visa, including an alien whose application is executed by another person pursuant to § 42.63(a)(2) , shall be required to appear personally before a consular officer for the execution of the application or, if in Taiwan, before a designated officer of the American Institute in Taiwan, except that the personal appearance of any child under the age of 14 may be waived at the officer's discretion.

(b) Interview by consular officer.

(1) Every alien executing an immigrant visa application must be interviewed by a consular officer who shall determine on the basis of the applicant's representations and the visa application and other relevant documentation—

(i) The proper immigrant classification, if any, of the visa applicant, and

(ii) The applicant's eligibility to receive a visa.

(2) The officer has the authority to require that the alien answer any question deemed material to these determinations.

HISTORY:

[52 FR 42613, Nov. 5, 1987, as amended at 56 FR 49682, Oct. 1, 1991, as confirmed at 58 FR 48447, Sept. 16, 1993; 86 FR 70735, 70739, Dec. 13, 2021; 86 FR 70735, 70740, Dec. 13, 2021]

§ 42.63 Definitions.

(a) **Application Forms.**

(1) Application on Form DS-230 or Form DS-260 Required.—Every alien applying for an immigrant visa must make application, as directed by the consular officer, on Form DS-230, Application for Immigrant Visa and Alien Registration, or on Form DS-260, Electronic Application for Immigrant Visa and Alien Registration. This requirement may not be waived. Form DS-230 consists of parts I and II which, together, are meant in any reference to this Form.

(2) Application of alien under 14 or physically incapable. The application on Form DS-230 or on Form DS-260 for an alien under 14 years of age or one physically incapable of completing an application may be executed by the alien's parent or guardian, or, if the alien has no parent or guardian, by any person having legal custody of, or a legitimate interest in, the alien.

(b) Preparation of forms. The consular officer shall ensure that Form DS-230 or Form DS-260 and all other forms an alien is required to submit are fully and properly completed in accordance with the applicable regulations and instructions.

(c) Additional information as part of application. The officer may require the submission of additional information or question the alien on any relevant matter whenever the officer believes that the information provided in Form DS-230 or Form DS-260 is inadequate to determine the alien's eligibility to receive an immigrant visa. Additional statements made by the alien become a part of the visa application. All documents required under the authority of § 42.62 are considered papers submitted with the alien's application within the meaning of INA 221(g)(1).

HISTORY:

[52 FR 42613, Nov. 5, 1987, as amended at 56 FR 49682, Oct. 1, 1991, as confirmed at 58 FR 48447, Sept. 16, 1993; 61 FR 1834, 1836, Jan. 24, 1996; 71 FR 34519, 34522, June 15, 2006; 75 FR 45475, 45476, Aug. 3, 2010]

§ 42.64 Passport requirements.

(a) Passport defined. "Passport," as defined in INA 101(a)(30), is not limited to a national passport or to a single document. A passport may consist of two or more documents which, when considered together, fulfill the requirements of a passport, provided that documentary evidence of permission to enter a foreign country has been issued by a competent authority and clearly meets the requirements of INA 101(a)(30).

(b) Passport validity requirements. Except as provided in § 42.2, every applicant for an immigrant visa shall present a passport, as defined in INA 101(a)(30), that is valid for at least 60 days beyond the period of validity of the visa. The 60-day additional validity requirement does not apply to an applicant who would be excepted as provided in § 42.2 were it not for the fact that the applicant is applying in the country of which the applicant is a national and the possession of a passport is required for departure. Such an applicant may be issued a visa valid for 6 months or for such shorter period as will assure its expiration in unison with the passport.

(c) A single passport including more than one person. The passport requirement of this section may be met by the presentation of a passport including more than one person, if such inclusion is authorized under the laws or regulations of the issuing authority and if a photograph of each person 16 years of age or over is attached to the passport by the issuing authority.

HISTORY:

[52 FR 42613, Nov. 5, 1987; 53 FR 9112, Mar. 21, 1988; 63 FR 48577, 48578, Sept. 11, 1998]

§ 42.65 Supporting documents.

(a) Authority to require documents. The consular officer is authorized to require documents considered necessary to establish the alien's eligibility to receive an immigrant visa. All such documents submitted and other evidence presented by the alien, including briefs submitted by attorneys or other representatives, shall be considered by the officer.

(b) Basic documents required. An alien applying for an immigrant visa shall be required to furnish, if obtainable: A copy of a police certificate or certificates; a certified copy of any existing prison record, military record, and record of birth; and a certified copy of all other records or documents which the consular officer considers necessary.

(c) **Definitions.**

(1) Police certificate means a certification by the police or other appropriate authorities reporting information entered in their records relating to the alien. In the case of the country of an alien's nationality and the country of an alien's current residence (as of the time of visa application) the term "appropriate police authorities" means those of a country, area or locality in which the alien has resided for at least six months. In the case of all other countries, areas, or localities, the term "appropriate police authorities" means the authorities of any country, area, or locality in which the alien has resided for at least one year. A consular officer may require a police certificate regardless of length of residence in any country if he or she has reason to believe that a police record exists in the country, area, or locality concerned.

(2) Prison record means an official document containing a report of the applicant's record of confinement and conduct in a penal or correctional institution.

(3) Military record means an official document containing a complete record of the applicant's service and conduct while in military service, including any convictions of crime before military tribunals as distinguished from other criminal courts. A certificate of discharge from the military forces or an enrollment book belonging to the applicant shall not be acceptable in lieu of the official military record, unless it shows the alien's complete record while in military service. The applicant may, however, be required to present for inspection such a discharge certificate or enrollment book if deemed necessary by the consular officer to establish the applicant's eligibility to receive a visa.

(4) A certified copy of an alien's record of birth means a certificate issued by the official custodian of birth records in the country of birth showing the date and place of birth and the parentage of the alien, based upon the original registration of birth.

(5) Other records or documents include any records or documents establishing the applicant's relationship to a spouse or children, if any, and any records or documents pertinent to a determination of the applicant's identity, classification, or any other matter relating to the applicant's visa eligibility.

(d) **Unobtainable documents.**

(1) If the consular officer is satisfied, or the catalogue of available documents prepared by the Department indicates, that any document or record required under this section is unobtainable, the officer may permit the immigrant to submit other satisfactory evidence in lieu of such document or record. A document or other record shall be considered unobtainable if it cannot be procured without causing to the applicant or a family member actual hardship as opposed to normal delay and inconvenience.

(2) If the consular officer determines that a supporting document, as described in paragraph (b) of this section, is in fact unobtainable, although the catalogue of available documents shows it is available, the officer shall affix to the visa application a signed statement describing in detail the reasons for considering the record or document unobtainable and for accepting the particular secondary evidence attached to the visa.

(e) Authenticity of records and documents. If the consular officer has reason to believe that a required record or document submitted by an applicant is not authentic or has been altered or tampered with in any material manner, the officer shall take such action as may be necessary to determine its authenticity or to ascertain the facts to which the record or document purports to relate.

(f) Photographs. Every applicant shall furnish photographs of the number and specifications prescribed by the Department. The applicant must either upload a digital photograph electronically as part of submitting an online visa application, or a paper photograph at the direction of the Department. The photograph shall be considered signed when the applicant biometrically signs and executes the application under oath pursuant to § 42.67(a).

HISTORY:

[52 FR 42613, Nov. 5, 1987, as amended at 55 FR 29015, July 17, 1990; 56 FR 49682, Oct. 1, 1991, as confirmed at 58 FR 48447, Sept. 16, 1993; 88 FR 13694, 13696, Mar. 6, 2023]

§ 42.66 Medical examination.

(a) Medical examination required of all applicants. Before the issuance of an immigrant visa, the consular officer shall require every alien, regardless of age, to undergo a medical examination in order to determine eligibility to receive a visa.

(b) Examination by physician from approved panel. The required examination shall be conducted in accordance with requirements and procedures established by the United States Public Health Service and by a physician selected by the alien from a panel of physicians approved by the consular officer.

(c) Facilities required for panel physician. A consular officer shall not include the name of a physician on the panel of physicians referred to in paragraph (b) of this section unless the physician has facilities to perform required serological and X-ray tests or is in a position to refer applicants to a qualified laboratory for such tests.

HISTORY:

52 FR 42613, Nov. 5, 1987.

§ 42.67 Execution of application, registration, and fingerprinting.

(a) Execution of visa application:

(1) Application fee.— A fee is prescribed for each application for an immigrant visa. It shall be collected prior to the execution of the application and a receipt shall be issued.

(2) Oath and signature on Form DS-230. The applicant shall be required to read the Form DS-230, Application for Immigrant Visa and Alien Registration, when it is completed, or it shall be read to the applicant in the applicant's language, or the applicant shall otherwise be informed of its full contents. Applicants shall be asked whether they are willing to subscribe thereto. If the applicant is not willing to subscribe to the application unless changes are made in the information stated therein, the required changes shall be made. The application shall then be sworn to or affirmed and signed by or on behalf of the applicant before a consular officer, or a designated officer of the American Institute of Taiwan, who shall then sign the application over the officer's title.

(3) Oath and signature on Form DS-260. The applicant shall be required to read the Form DS-260, Electronic Application for Immigrant Visa and Alien Registration, when it has been completed, or it shall be read to the applicant in the applicant's language, or the applicant shall otherwise be informed of its full contents, before the applicant electronically signs and submits the application to the Department. At the time of the applicant's interview the applicant shall be asked whether they are willing to subscribe thereto to the information provided on Form DS-260. If the alien is not willing to subscribe to the application unless changes are made in the information stated therein, the required changes shall be made. The application shall then be sworn to or affirmed and signed, biometrically, by or on behalf of the applicant before a consular officer, or a designated officer who shall then electronically sign the application.

(b) Registration. The alien shall be considered to be registered for the purposes of INA 221(b) and 203(g) upon the filing of Form DS-230 or Form DS-260, when duly executed, or the transmission by the Department to the alien of a notification of the availability of an immigrant visa, whichever occurs first.

(c) Fingerprinting. Every applicant for an immigrant visa must furnish fingerprints prior to the execution of Form DS-230 or Form DS-260.

HISTORY:

[52 FR 42613, Nov. 5, 1987, as amended at 55 FR 29015, July 17, 1990; 56 FR 49682, Oct. 1, 1991, as confirmed at 58 FR 48447, Sept. 16, 1993; 67 FR 8477, 8478, Feb. 25, 2002; 67 FR 77160, 77161, Dec. 17, 2002; 71 FR 34519, 34522, June 15, 2006; 75 FR 45475, 45476, Aug. 3, 2010; 86 FR 70735, 70740, Dec. 13, 2021]

§ 42.68 Informal evaluation of family members if principal applicant precedes them. [This section was removed and reserved, effective Jan. 8, 2024. See 88 FR 85109, 85110, Dec. 7, 2023.]

Subpart H

Issuance of Immigrant Visas

§ 42.72 Validity of visas.

(a) Period of validity. With the exception indicated herein, the period of validity of an immigrant visa shall not exceed six months, beginning with the date of issuance. Any visa issued to a child lawfully adopted by a U.S. citizen and spouse while such citizen is serving abroad in the U.S. Armed Forces, is employed abroad by the U.S. Government, or is temporarily abroad on business, however, shall be valid until such time, for a period not to exceed 3 years, as the adoptive citizen parent returns to the United States in the course of that parent's military service, U.S. Government employment, or business.

(b) Extension of period of validity. If the visa was originally issued for a period of validity less than the maximum authorized by paragraph (a) of this section, the consular officer may extend the validity of the visa up to but not exceeding the maximum period permitted. If an immigrant applies for an extension at a consular office other than the issuing office, the consular officer shall, unless the officer is satisfied beyond doubt that the alien is eligible for the extension, communicate with the issuing office to determine if there is any objection to an extension. In extending the period of validity, the officer shall make an appropriate notation on the visa of the new expiration date, sign the document with title indicated, and impress the seal of the office thereon.

(c) [Reserved]

(d) Age and marital status in relation to validity of certain immigrant visas. In accordance with § 42.64(b), the validity of a visa may not extend beyond a date sixty days prior to the expiration of the passport. The period of validity of a visa issued to an immigrant as a child shall not extend beyond the day immediately proceding the date on which the alien becomes 21 years of age. The consular officer shall warn an alien, when appropriate, that the alien will be admissible as such an immigrant only if unmarried and under 21 years of age at the time of application for admission at a U.S. port of entry. The consular officer shall also warn an alien issued a visa as a first or second preference immigrant as an unmarried son or daughter of a citizen or lawful permanent resident of the United States that the alien will be admissible as such an immigrant only if unmarried at the time of application for admission at a U.S. port of entry.

HISTORY:

[52 FR 42613, Nov. 5, 1987, as amended at 56 FR 32323, July 16, 1991; 61 FR 1834, 1836, Jan. 24, 1996; 62 FR 27693, 27694, May 21, 1997, as corrected at 62 FR 32196, June 13, 1997; 64 FR 28915, 28916, May 28, 1999; 67 FR 38892, 38894, June 6, 2002, as corrected at 67 FR 40849, June 14, 2002; 68 FR 13627, 13628, Mar. 20, 2003]

§ 42.73 Procedure in issuing visas.

(a) Evidence of visa. An immigrant visa shall be evidenced by a physical visa or by an electronic visa located in the Department's records. The appropriate symbol as prescribed in § 42.11, showing the classification of the alien, shall be entered on the visa.

(b) Visa format. A machine-readable visa shall be in the format designated by the Department, and contain, at a minimum, the following data:

(1) Full name of the immigrant;

(2) Visa symbol;

(3) Location of the visa issuing office;

(4) Passport number;

(5) The registration number (A-number) assigned to the immigrant;

(6) Sex;

(7) Date of birth;

(8) Nationality;

(9) Date of issuance;

(10) Date of expiration;

(11) Visa control number;

(12) Any annotations entered to reflect waivers or other information useful to an immigration officer at a port of entry (POE) upon the immigrant's application for admission to the United States;

(13) A digitized photo of the immigrant; and

(14) Machine-readable data that can be processed by an immigration officer at a POE.

(c) Disposition of supporting documents. Post shall, wherever possible, return original supporting documents furnished by the alien. Duplicate copies may be retained in the consular system, as required or necessary.

HISTORY:

[52 FR 42613, Nov. 5, 1991, as amended at 56 FR 49682, Oct. 1, 1991, as confirmed at 58 FR 48447, Sept. 16, 1993; 71 FR 34519, 34522, June 15, 2006; 84 FR 35297, 35299, July 23, 2019]

§ 42.74 Issuance of new, replacement, or duplicate visas.

(a) New immigrant visa for a special immigrant under INA 101(a)(27)(A) and (B). The consular officer may issue a new immigrant visa to a qualified alien entitled to status under INA 101(a)(27)(A) or (B), provided that:

(1) The alien establishes that the original visa has been lost, mutilated, or has expired; or that the alien will be unable to use it during the period of its validity; and

(2) The alien pays anew the application processing fees prescribed in the Schedule of Fees (22 CFR 22.1); and

(3) The consular officer ascertains whether the original issuing office knows of any reason why a new visa should not be issued.

(b) Replacement immigrant visa for an immediate relative or for an alien subject to numerical limitation. A consular officer may issue a replacement visa under the original number of a qualified alien entitled to status as an immediate relative (INA 201(b)(2)), a family or employment preference immigrant (INA 203(a) or (b)), or a diversity immigrant (INA 203(c)), if—

(1) The alien is unable to use the visa during the period of its validity due to reasons beyond the alien's control;

(2) The visa is issued during the same fiscal year in which the original visa was issued, or in the following year in the case of an immediate relative only, if the original number had been reported as recaptured;

(3) The number has not been returned to the Department as a "recaptured visa number" in the case of a preference or diversity immigrant;

(4) The alien pays anew the application processing fees prescribed in the Schedule of Fees; and

(5) The consular officer ascertains whether the original issuing office knows of any reason why a new visa should not be issued.

(c) Replacement visa for adoptees. A consular officer may issue a replacement immigrant visa to a qualified alien, if the conditions in paragraphs (a)(1) and (3) of this section are met, and if the consular officer determines—

(1) A prior immigrant visa was issued on or after March 27, 2013, to a child who has been lawfully adopted, or who is coming to the United States to be adopted, by a United States citizen;

(2) The inability to use the visa was attributable to factors beyond the control of the adoptee or the adopting parent(s); and

(3) The application processing fee has been waived pursuant to § 42.71(b)(2) or has been paid anew.

(d) Duplicate visas issued within the validity period of the original visa. If the validity of a visa previously issued has not yet terminated and the original visa has been lost or mutilated, a duplicate visa may be issued containing all of the information appearing on the original visa, including the original issuance and expiration dates. The applicant shall execute a new application and provide copies of the supporting documents submitted in support of the original application. The alien must pay anew the application processing fees prescribed in the Schedule of Fees.

HISTORY:

[52 FR 42613, Nov. 5, 1987, as amended at 56 FR 49682, Oct. 1, 1991, as confirmed at 58 FR 48447, Sept. 16, 1993; 61 FR 1834, 1836, Jan. 24, 1996; 63 FR 4393, Jan. 29, 1998; 67 FR 1415, 1416, Jan. 11, 2002, as confirmed at 68 FR 13627, Mar. 20, 2003; 67 FR 38892, 38894, June 6, 2002, as corrected at 67 FR 40849, June 14, 2002; 71 FR 34519, 34522, June 15, 2006; 84 FR 35297, 35299, July 23, 2019; 87 FR 2703, 2705, Jan. 19, 2022]

Subpart I

Refusal, Revocation, and Termination of Registration

§ 42.81 Procedure in refusing immigrant visas.

(a) Grounds for refusal. When a visa application has been properly completed and executed before a consular officer in accordance with the provisions of the INA and the implementing regulations, the consular officer must issue the visa, refuse the visa under INA 212(a) or 221(g) or other applicable law or, pursuant to an outstanding order under INA 243(d), discontinue granting the visa.

(b) Refusal procedure. A consular officer may not refuse an immigrant visa until either Form DS-230, Application for Immigrant Visa and Alien Registration, or Form DS-260, Electronic Application for Immigrant Visa and Alien Registration, has been executed by the applicant. When an immigrant visa is refused, an appropriate record shall be made in duplicate on a form prescribed by the Department. The form shall be signed and dated by the consular officer. The consular officer shall inform the applicant of the provision of law or implementing regulation on which the refusal is based and of any statutory provision of law or implementing regulation under which administrative relief is available. Each document related to the refusal shall then be attached to Form DS-230 for retention in the refusal files. Alternatively, each document related to the refusal shall be electronically scanned and electronically attached to Form DS-260 for retention in the electronic refusal files. Any documents not related to the refusal shall be returned to the applicant. The original copy of a document that was scanned and attached to the DS-260 for the refusal file shall be returned to the applicant. If the ground of ineligibility may be overcome by the presentation of additional evidence and the applicant indicates an intention to submit such evidence, all documents may, with the consent of the alien, be retained in the consular files for a period not to exceed one year. If the refusal as not been overcome within one year, any documents not relating to the refusal shall be removed from the file and returned to the alien.

(c) Review of refusal at consular office. If the grounds of ineligibility upon which the visa was refused cannot be overcome by the presentation of additional evidence, the principal consular officer at a post, or a specifically designated alternate, shall review the case without delay, record the review decision, and sign and date the prescribed form. If the grounds of ineligibility may be overcome by the presentation of additional evidence and the applicant indicates the intention to submit such evidence, a review of the refusal may be deferred. If the principal consular officer or alternate does not concur in the refusal, that officer shall either (1) refer the case to the Department for an advisory opinion, or (2) assume responsibility for final action on the case.

(d) Review of refusal by Department. The Department may request a consular officer in an individual case or in specified classes of cases to submit a report if an immigrant visa has been refused. The Department will review each report and may furnish an advisory opinion to the consular officer for assistance in considering the case further. If the officer believes that action contrary to an advisory opinion should be taken, the case shall be resubmitted to the Department with an explanation of the proposed action. Rulings of the Department concerning an interpretation of law, as distinguished from an application of the law to the facts, are binding upon consular officers.

(e) Reconsideration of refusal. If a visa is refused, and the applicant within one year from the date of refusal adduces further evidence tending to overcome the ground of ineligibility on which the refusal was based, the case shall be reconsidered. In such circumstance, an additional application fee shall not be required.

HISTORY:

[52 FR 42613, Nov. 5, 1987; 53 FR 9112, Mar. 21, 1988; 66 FR 10363, 10364, Feb. 15, 2001; 71 FR 34519, 34522, June 15, 2006; 75 FR 45475, 45477, Aug. 3, 2010; 84 FR 16610, 16612, Apr. 22, 2019]

§ 42.82 Revocation of visas.

(a) Grounds for revocation by consular officers. A consular officer, the Secretary, or any Department official to whom the Secretary has delegated this authority is authorized to revoke an immigrant visa at any time, in his or her discretion.

(b) Provisional revocation. A consular officer, the Secretary, or any Department official to whom the Secretary has delegated this authority may provisionally revoke an immigrant visa while considering information related to whether a visa holder is eligible for the visa. Provisional revocation shall have the same force and effect as any other visa revocation under INA 221(i).

(c) Notice of revocation. Unless otherwise instructed by the Department, a consular officer shall, if practicable, notify the alien to whom the visa was issued that the visa was revoked or provisionally revoked. Regardless of delivery of such notice, once the revocation has been entered into the Department's Consular Lookout and Support System (CLASS), the visa is no longer to be considered valid for travel to the United States. The date of the revocation shall be indicated in CLASS and on any notice sent to the alien to whom the visa was issued.

(d) Procedure for physically canceling visas. An immigrant visa that is revoked shall be canceled by writing or stamping the word "REVOKED" plainly across the face of the visa, if the visa is available to the consular officer. The failure or inability to physically cancel the visa does not affect the validity of the revocation.

HISTORY:

[52 FR 42613, Nov. 5, 1987; 71 FR 34519, 34522, June 15, 2006; 76 FR 23477, 23479, Apr. 27, 2011]

§ 42.83 Termination of registration.

(a) Termination following failure of applicant to apply for visa. In accordance with INA 203(g), an alien's registration for an immigrant visa shall be terminated if, within one year after transmission of a notification of the availability of an immigrant visa, the applicant fails to apply for an immigrant visa.

(b) Termination following visa refusal. An alien's registration for an immigrant visa shall be terminated if, within one year following the refusal of the immigrant visa application under INA 221(g), the alien has failed to present to a consular officer evidence purporting to overcome the basis for refusal.

(c) Notice of termination. Upon the termination of registration under paragraph (a) of this section, the National Visa Center (NVC) shall notify the alien of the termination. The NVC shall also inform the alien of the right to have the registration reinstated if the alien, before the end of the second year after the missed appointment date if paragraph (a) applies, establishes to the satisfaction of the consular officer at the post where the alien is registered that the failure to apply for an immigrant visa was due to circumstances beyond the alien's control. If paragraph (b) applies, the consular officer at the post where the alien is registered shall, upon the termination of registration, notify the alien of the termination and the right to have the registration reinstated if the alien, before the end of the second year after the INA 221(g) refusal, establishes to the satisfaction of the consular officer at such post that the failure to present evidence purporting to overcome the ineligibility under INA 221(g) was due to circumstances beyond the alien's control.

(d) Reinstatement of registration. If the consular officer is satisfied that an alien, as provided for in paragraph (c) of this section, has established that failure to apply as scheduled for an immigrant visa or to present evidence purporting to overcome ineligibility under INA 221(g) was due to circumstances beyond the alien's control, the consular officer shall reinstate the alien's registration for an immigrant visa. Any petition approved under INA 204(b) which had been automatically revoked as a result of the termination of registration shall be considered to be automatically reinstated if the registration is reinstated.

(e) Interpretation of "circumstances beyond alien's control". For the purpose of this section, the term "circumstances beyond the alien's control" includes, but is not limited to, an illness or other physical disability preventing the alien from traveling, a refusal by the authorities of the country of an alien's residence to grant the alien permission to depart as an immigrant, and foreign military service.

HISTORY:

[52 FR 42613, Nov. 5, 1987, as amended at 56 FR 49682, Oct. 1, 1991, as confirmed at 58 FR 48447, Sept. 16, 1993; 73 FR 11027, 11028, Feb. 29, 2008]

§ 42.84 Discontinuance of Granting Immigrant Visa Pursuant to INA 243(d).

(a) Grounds for discontinuance of granting a visa. Consular officers in a country subject to an order by the Secretary under INA 243(d) shall discontinue granting immigrant visas for categories of immigrant visas specified in the order of the Secretary (or his or her designee), and pursuant to procedures dictated by the Department.

(b) Discontinuance procedure—

(1) Applications refused or discontinued only. Starting on the day the Secretary's (or designee's) order to discontinue granting visas takes effect (effective date), no visas falling within the scope of the order, as described by the order, may be issued in the referenced country to an applicant who falls within the scope of the order, except as otherwise expressly provided in the order or related Department instructions. Beginning on the effective date, a consular officer must refuse the visa if the individual is not eligible for the visa under INA 212(a), INA 221(g), or other applicable law, but if the applicant is otherwise eligible must process the application by discontinuing granting, regardless of when the application was filed, if the applicant falls within the scope of the order and no exception applies. The application processing fee will not be refunded. The requirement to discontinue issuance may not be waived, and continues until the sanction is terminated as described below. In the case of diversity immigrant selectees applying under INA 203(c), if the discontinuance of granting has not been lifted by the end of the fiscal year, the applicant will not be eligible for a diversity visa for that fiscal year, regardless of the

status of the diversity immigrant visa application at the time 243(d) sanctions were imposed.

(2) Geographic applicability. Visa sanctions under INA 243(d) only apply to visa issuance in the country that is sanctioned. If a consular officer has a reason to believe that a visa applicant potentially subject to INA 243(d) sanctions is applying at a post outside the sanctioned country to evade visa sanctions under INA 243(d), (e.g., the applicant provides no credible explanation for applying outside the country) the consular officer will transfer the case to the consular post in the consular district where INA 243(d) sanctions apply, review any other applicable Department instructions and proceed accordingly. When cases are transferred to a consular district where INA 243(d) sanctions apply, the adjudication will be subject to the discontinuation of issuance under the sanctions.

(b) Termination of sanction. The Department shall notify consular officers in an affected country the sanction under INA 243(d) has been lifted. After notification, normal consular operations may resume consistent with these regulations and guidance from the Department. Once the sanction under INA 243(d) is lifted, no new application processing fees are required in cases where issuance has been discontinued pursuant to an INA 243(d) order, and consular officers in the affected post must adjudicate the visa application consistent with regulations and Department guidance. Consular officers may require applicants to update the visa application forms, must conduct any necessary adjudicatory steps, and may re-interview to determine eligibility. In numerically controlled immigrant visa categories, an applicant's immigrant visa priority date may no longer be current once sanctions under INA 243(d) are lifted, in which case the applicant must await visa availability.

HISTORY:
[84 FR 16610, 16613, Apr. 22, 2019]

PART 46

CONTROL OF ALIENS DEPARTING FROM THE UNITED STATES

Rule

§ 46.1 Definitions.

For the purposes of this part:

(a) The term alien means any person who is not a citizen or national of the United States.

(b) The term Commissioner means the Commissioner of Immigration and Naturalization.

(c) The term regional commissioner means an officer of the Immigration and Naturalization Service duly appointed or designated as a regional commissioner, or an officer who has been designated to act as a regional commissioner.

(d) The term district director means an officer of the Immigration and Naturalization Service duly appointed or designated as a district director, or an officer who has been designated to act as a district director.

(e) The term United States means the several States, the District of Columbia, the Canal Zone, Puerto Rico, the Virgin Islands, Guam, American Samoa, Swains Island, the Trust Territory of the Pacific Islands, and all other territory and waters, continental and insular, subject to the jurisdiction of the United States.

(f) The term continental United States means the District of Columbia and the several States, except Alaska and Hawaii.

(g) The term geographical part of the United States means (1) the continental United States, (2) Alaska, (3) Hawaii, (4) Puerto Rico, (5) the Virgin Islands, (6) Guam, (7) the Canal Zone, (8) American Samoa, (9) Swains Island, or (10) the Trust Territory of the Pacific Islands.

(h) The term depart from the United States means depart by land, water, or air (1) from the United States for any foreign place, or (2) from one geographical part of the United States for a separate geographical part of the United States: Provided, That a trip or journey upon a public ferry, passenger vessel sailing coastwise on a fixed schedule, excursion vessel, or aircraft, having both termini in the continental United States or in any one of the other geographical parts of the United States and not touching any territory or waters under the jurisdiction or control of a foreign power, shall not be deemed a departure from the United States.

(i) The term departure-control officer means any immigration officer as defined in the regulations of the Immigration and Naturalization Service who is designated to supervise the departure of aliens, or any officer or employee of the United States designated by the Governor of the Canal Zone, the High Commissioner of the Trust Territory of the Pacific Islands, or the governor of an outlying possession of the United States, to supervise the departure of aliens.

(j) The term port of departure means a port in the continental United States, Alaska, Guam, Hawaii, Puerto Rico or the Virgin Islands, designated as a port of entry by the Attorney General or by the Commissioner, or in exceptional circumstances such other place as the departure-control officer may, in his discretion, designate in an individual case, or a port in American Samoa, Swains Island, the Canal Zone, or the Trust Territory of the Pacific Islands, designated as a port of entry by the chief executive officer thereof.

(k) The term special inquiry officer shall have the meaning ascribed thereto in section 101(b)(4) of the Immigration and Nationality Act.

HISTORY:
[22 FR 10827, Dec. 27, 1957, as amended at 25 FR 7022, July 23, 1960]

AUTHORITY:
Secs. 104, 215, 66 Stat. 174, 190; 8 U.S.C. 1104, 1185.

§ 46.2 Authority of departure-control officer to prevent alien's departure from the United States.

(a) No alien shall depart, or attempt to depart, from the United States if his departure would be prejudicial to the interests of the United States under the provisions of § 46.3. Any departure-control officer who knows or has reason to believe that the case of an alien in the United States comes within the provisions of § 46.3 shall temporarily prevent the departure of such alien from the United States and shall serve him with a written temporary order directing him not to depart, or attempt to depart, from the United States until notified of the revocation of the order.

(b) The written order temporarily preventing an alien, other than an enemy alien, from departing from the United States shall become final 15 days after the date of service thereof upon the alien, unless prior thereto the alien requests a hearing as hereinafter provided. At such time as the alien is served with an order temporarily preventing his departure from the United States, he shall be notified in writing concerning the provisions of this paragraph, and shall be advised of his right to request a hearing if entitled thereto under § 46.4. In the case of an enemy alien, the written order preventing departure shall become final on the date of its service upon the alien.

(c) Any alien who seeks to depart from the United States may be required, in the discretion of the departure-control officer, to be examined under oath and to submit for official inspection all documents, articles, and other property in his possession which are being removed from the United States upon, or in connection with, the alien's departure. The departure-control officer may permit such other persons, including officials of the Department of State and interpreters, to participate in such examination or inspection and may exclude from presence at such examination or inspection any person whose presence would not further the objectives of such examination or inspection. The departure-control officer shall temporarily prevent the departure of any alien who refuses to submit to such examination or inspection, and may, if necessary to cause the alien to submit to such examination or inspection, take possession of the alien's passport or other travel document or issue a subpoena requiring the alien to submit to such examination or inspection.

HISTORY:
[22 FR 10827, Dec. 27, 1957, as amended at 45 FR 64174, Sept. 29, 1980]

AUTHORITY:
Secs. 104, 215, 66 Stat. 174, 190; 8 U.S.C. 1104, 1185.

§ 46.3 Aliens whose departure is deemed prejudicial to the interests of the United States.

The departure from the United States of any alien within one or more of the following categories shall be deemed prejudicial to the interest of the United States:

(a) Any alien who is in possession of, and who is believed likely to disclose to unauthorized persons, information concerning the plans, preparations, equipment, or establishments for the national defense and security of the United States.

(b) Any alien who seeks to depart from the United States to engage in, or who is likely to engage in, activities of any kind designed to obstruct, impede, retard, delay or counteract the effectiveness of the national defense of the United States or the measures adopted by the United States or the United Nations for the defense of any other country.

(c) Any alien who seeks to depart from the United States to engage in, or who is likely to engage in, activities which would obstruct, impede, retard, delay, or counteract the effectiveness of any plans made or action taken by any country cooperating with the United States in measures adopted to promote the peace, defense, or safety of the United States or such other country.

(d) Any alien who seeks to depart from the United States for the purpose of organizing, directing, or participating in any rebellion, insurrection, or violent uprising in or against the United States or a country allied with the United States, or of waging war against the United States or its allies, or of destroying, or depriving the United States of sources of supplies or materials vital to the national defense of the United States, or to the effectiveness of the measures adopted by the United States for its defense, or for the defense of any other country allied with the United States.

(e) Any alien who is subject to registration for training and service in the Armed Forces of the United States and who fails to present a Registration Certificate (SSS Form No. 2) showing that he has complied with his obligation to register under the Universal Military Training and Service Act, as amended.

(f) Any alien who is a fugitive from justice on account of an offense punishable in the United States.

(g) Any alien who is needed in the United States as a witness in, or as a party to, any criminal case under investigation or pending in a court in the United States: Provided, That any alien who is a witness in, or a party to, any criminal case pending in any criminal court proceeding may be permitted to depart from the United States with the consent of the appropriate prosecuting authority, unless such alien is otherwise prohibited from departing under the provisions of this part.

(h) Any alien who is needed in the United States in connection with any investigation or proceeding being, or soon to be, conducted by any official executive, legislative, or judicial agency in the United States or by any governmental committee, board, bureau, commission, or body in the United States, whether national, state, or local.

(i) Any alien whose technical or scientific training and knowledge might be utilized by an enemy or a potential enemy of the United States to undermine and defeat the military and defensive operations of the

United States or of any nation cooperating with the United States in the interests of collective security.

(j) Any alien, where doubt exists whether such alien is departing or seeking to depart from the United States voluntarily except an alien who is departing or seeking to depart subject to an order issued in extradition, exclusion, or deportation proceedings.

(k) Any alien whose case does not fall within any of the categories described in paragraphs (a) to (j), inclusive, of this section, but which involves circumstances of a similar character rendering the alien's departure prejudicial to the interests of the United States.

HISTORY:

[22 FR 10828, Dec. 27, 1957, as amended at 42 FR 19479, Apr. 14, 1977; 45 FR 64174, Sept. 29, 1980]

AUTHORITY:

(Sec. 215, Immigration and Nationality Act, 66 Stat. 190, 8 U.S.C. 1185; Proc. No. 3004 of January 17, 1953)

§ 46.4 Procedure in case of alien prevented from departing from the United States.

(a) Any alien, other than an enemy alien, whose departure has been temporarily prevented under the provisions of § 46.2 may, within 15 days of the service upon him of the written order temporarily preventing his departure, request a hearing before a special inquiry officer. The alien's request for a hearing shall be made in writing and shall be addressed to the district director having administrative jurisdiction over the alien's place of residence. If the alien's request for a hearing is timely made, the district director shall schedule a hearing before a special inquiry officer, and notice of such hearing shall be given to the alien. The notice of hearing shall, as specifically as security considerations permit, inform the alien of the nature of the case against him, shall fix the time and place of the hearing, and shall inform the alien of his right to be represented, at no expense to the Government, by counsel of his own choosing.

(b) Every alien for whom a hearing has been scheduled under paragraph (a) of this section shall be entitled (1) to appear in person before the special inquiry officer, (2) to be represented by counsel of his own choice, (3) to have the opportunity to be heard and to present evidence, (4) to cross-examine the witnesses who appear at the hearing, except that if, in the course of the examination, it appears that further examination may divulge information of a confidential or security nature, the special inquiry officer may, in his discretion, preclude further examination of the witness with respect to such matters, (5) to examine any evidence in possession of the Government which is to be considered in the disposition of the case, provided that such evidence is not of a confidential or security nature the disclosure of which would be prejudicial to the interests of the United States, (6) to have the time and opportunity to produce evidence and witnesses on his own behalf, and (7) to reasonable continuances upon request, for good cause shown.

(c) Any special inquiry officer who is assigned to conduct the hearing provided for in this section shall have the authority to: (1) Administer oaths and affirmations, (2) present and receive evidence, (3) interrogate, examine, and cross-examine under oath or affirmation both the alien and witnesses, (4) rule upon all objections to the introduction of evidence or motions made during the course of the hearing, (5) take or cause depositions to be taken, (6) issue subpoenas, and (7) take any further action consistent with applicable provisions of law, executive orders, proclamations, and regulations.

HISTORY:

[22 FR 10828, Dec. 27, 1957, as amended at 27 FR 1358, Feb. 14, 1962]

AUTHORITY:

Secs. 104, 215, 66 Stat. 174, 190; 8 U.S.C. 1104, 1185.

§ 46.5 Hearing procedure before special inquiry officer.

(a) The hearing before the special inquiry officer shall be conducted in accordance with the following procedure:

(1) The special inquiry officer shall advise the alien of the rights and privileges accorded him under the provisions of § 46.4.

(2) The special inquiry officer shall enter of record (i) a copy of the order served upon the alien temporarily preventing his departure from the United States, and (ii) a copy of the notice of hearing furnished the alien.

(3) The alien shall be interrogated by the special inquiry officer as to the matters considered pertinent to the proceeding, with opportunity reserved to the alien to testify thereafter in his own behalf, if he so chooses.

(4) The special inquiry officer shall present on behalf of the Government such evidence, including the testimony of witnesses and the certificates or written statements of Government officials or other persons, as may be necessary and available. In the event such certificates or statements are recieved in evidence, the alien may request and, in the discretion of the special inquiry officer, be given an opportunity to interrogate such officials or persons, by deposition or otherwise, at a time and place and in a manner fixed by the special inquiry officer: Provided, That when in the judgment of the special inquiry officer any evidence relative to the disposition of the case is of a confidential or security nature the disclosure of which would be prejudicial to the interests of the United States, such evidence shall not be presented at the hearing but shall be taken into consideration in arriving at a decision in the case.

(5) The alien may present such additional evidence, including the testimony of witnesses, as is pertinent and available.

(b) A complete verbatim transcript of the hearing, except statements made off the record, shall be recorded. The alien shall be entitled, upon request, to the loan of a copy of the transcript, without cost, subject to reasonable conditions governing its use.

(c) Following the completion of the hearing, the special inquiry officer shall make and render a recommended decision in the case, which shall be governed by and based upon the evidence presented at the hearing and any evidence of a confidential or security nature which the Government may have in its possession. The decision of the special inquiry officer shall recommend (1) that the temporary order preventing the departure of the alien from the United States be made final, or (2) that the temporary order preventing the departure of the alien from the United States be revoked. This recommended decision of the special inquiry officer shall be made in writing and shall set forth the officer's reasons for such decision. The alien concerned shall at his request be furnished a copy of the recommended decision of the special inquiry officer, and shall be allowed a reasonable time, not to exceed 10 days, in which to submit representations with respect thereto in writing.

(d) As soon as practicable after the completion of the hearing and the rendering of a decision by the special inquiry officer, the district director shall forward the entire record of the case, including the recommended decision of the special inquiry officer and any written representations submitted by the alien, to the regional commissioner having jurisdiction over his district. After reviewing the record, the regional commissioner shall render a decision in the case, which shall be based upon the evidence in the record and on any evidence or information of a confidential or security nature which he deems pertinent. Whenever any decision is based in whole or in part on confidential or security information not included in the record, the decision shall state that such information was considered. A copy of the regional commissioner's decision shall be furnished the alien, or his attorney or representative. No administrative appeal shall lie from the regional commissioner's decision.

(e) Notwithstanding any other provision of this part, the Administrator of the Bureau of Security and Consular Affairs referred to in section 104(b) of the Immigration and Nationality Act, or such other officers of the Department of State as he may designate, after consultation with the Commissioner, or such other officers of the Immigration and Naturalization Service as he may designate, may at any time permit the departure of an individual alien or of a group of aliens from the United States if he determines that such action would be in the national interest. If the Administrator specifically requests the Commissioner to prevent the departure of a particular alien or of a group of aliens, the Commissioner shall not permit the departure of such alien or aliens until he has consulted with the Administrator.

(f) In any case arising under §§ 46.1 to 46.7, the Administrator shall, at his request, be kept advised, in as much detail as he may indicate is necessary, of the facts and of any action taken or proposed.

HISTORY:

[22 FR 10828, Dec. 27, 1957, as amended at 26 FR 3069, Apr. 11, 1961; 27 FR 1358, Feb. 14, 1962]

AUTHORITY:

Secs. 104, 215, 66 Stat. 174, 190; 8 U.S.C. 1104, 1185.

§ 46.6 Departure from the Canal Zone, the Trust Territory of the Pacific Islands, or outlying possessions of the United States.

(a) In addition to the restrictions and prohibitions imposed by the provisions of this part upon the departure of aliens from the United States, any alien who seeks to depart from the Canal Zone, the Trust Territory of the Pacific Islands, or an outlying possession of the United States shall comply with such other restrictions and prohibitions as may be imposed by regulations prescribed, with the concurrence of the Administrator of the Bureau of Security and Consular Affairs and the Commissioner, by the Governor of the Canal Zone, the High Commissioner of the Trust Territory of the Pacific Islands, or by the governor of an outlying possession of the United States, respectively. No alien shall be prevented from departing from such zone, territory, or possession without first being accorded a hearing as provided in §§ 46.4 and 46.5.

(b) The Governor of the Canal Zone, the High Commissioner of the Trust Territory of the Pacific Islands, or the governor of any outlying possession of the United States shall have the authority to designate any employee or class of employees of the United States as hearing officers for the purpose of conducting the hearing referred to in paragraph (a) of this section. The hearing officer so designated shall exercise the same powers, duties, and functions as are conferred upon special inquiry officers under the provisions of this part. The chief executive officer of such zone, territory, or possession shall, in lieu of the regional commissioner, review the recommended decision of the hearing officer, and shall render a decision in any case referred to him, basing it on evidence in the record and on any evidence or information of a confidential or a security nature which he deems pertinent.

HISTORY:

[22 FR 10829, Dec. 27, 1957, as amended at 26 FR 3069, Apr. 11, 1961]

AUTHORITY:

Secs. 104, 215, 66 Stat. 174, 190; 8 U.S.C. 1104, 1185.

§ 46.7 Instructions from the Administrator required in certain cases.

In the absence of appropriate instructions from the Administrator of the Bureau of Security and Consular Affairs, departure-control officers shall not exercise the authority conferred by § 46.2 in the case of any alien who seeks to depart from the United States in the status of a nonimmigrant under section 101(a)(15) (A) or (G) of the Immigration and Nationality Act, or in the status of a nonimmigrant under section 11(3), 11 (4), or 11(5) of the Agreement between the United Nations and the United States of America regarding the Headquarters of the United Nations (61 Stat. 756): Provided, That in cases of extreme urgency, where the national security so requires, a departure-control officer may preliminarily exercise the authority conferred by § 46.2 pending the outcome of consultation with the Administrator, which shall be undertaken immediately. In all cases arising under this section, the decision of the Administrator shall be controlling: Provided, That any decision to prevent the departure of an alien shall be based upon a hearing and record as prescribed in this part.

HISTORY:
[26 FR 3069, Apr. 11, 1961; 26 FR 3188, Apr. 14, 1961]

AUTHORITY:
Secs. 104, 215, 66 Stat. 174, 190; 8 U.S.C. 1104, 1185.

SUBCHAPTER F

NATIONALITY AND PASSPORTS

Part 50. Nationality Procedures

PART 50

NATIONALITY PROCEDURES

AUTHORITY NOTE APPLICABLE TO ENTIRE PART:

AUTHORITY:
22 U.S.C. 2651a; 8 U.S.C. 1104 and 1401 through 1504.

§ 50.1 Definitions.

The following definitions shall be applicable to this part:

(a) United States means the continental United States, the State of Hawaii, the Commonwealth of Puerto Rico, the Virgin Islands of the United States, the Canal Zone, American Samoa, Guam and any other islands or territory over which the United States exercises jurisdiction.

(b) Department means the Department of State of the United States of America.

(c) Secretary means the Secretary of State.

(d) National means a citizen of the United States or a noncitizen owing permanent allegiance to the United States.

(e) Passport means a travel document issued under the authority of the Secretary of State attesting to the identity and nationality of the bearer.

(f) Passport Agent means a person designated by the Department to accept passport applications.

(g) Designated nationality examiner means a United States citizen employee of the Department of State assigned or employed abroad (permanently or temporarily) and designated by the Deputy Assistant Secretary of State for Overseas Citizen Services, to grant, issue and verify U.S. passports. A designated nationality examiner may adjudicate claims of acquisition and loss of United States nationality and citizenship as required for the purpose of providing passport and related services. The authority of designated nationality examiners shall include the authority to examine, adjudicate, approve and deny passport applications and applications for related services. The authority of designated nationality examiners shall expire upon termination of the employee's assignment for such duty and may also be terminated at any time by the Deputy Assistant Secretary for Overseas Citizen Services.

HISTORY:
[31 FR 13537, Oct. 20, 1966, as amended at 31 FR 14521, Nov. 11, 1966; 61 FR 43310, 43311, Aug. 22, 1996]

Subpart A

Procedures for Determination of United States Nationality of a Person Abroad

§ 50.2 Determination of U.S. nationality of persons abroad.

The Department shall determine claims to United States nationality when made by persons abroad on the basis of an application for registration, for a passport, or for a Consular Report of Birth Abroad of a Citizen of the United States of America. Such determinations of nationality may be made abroad by a consular officer or a designated nationality examiner. A designated nationality examiner may accept and approve/disapprove applications for registration and accept and approve/disapprove applications for passports and issue passports. Under the supervision of a consular officer, designated nationality examiners shall accept, adjudicate, disapprove and provisionally approve applications for the Consular Report of Birth Abroad. A Consular Report of Birth Abroad may only be issued by a consular officer, who will review a designated nationality examiner's provisional approval of an application for such report and issue the report if satisfied that the claim to nationality has been established.

HISTORY:
[31 FR 13537, Oct. 20, 1966; 61 FR 43310, 43311, Aug. 22, 1996]

§ 50.3 Application for registration.

(a) A person abroad who claims U.S. nationality, or a representative on his behalf, may apply at a consular post for registration to establish his claim to U.S. nationality or to make his residence in the particular consular area a matter of record.

(b) The applicant shall execute the registration form prescribed by the Department and shall submit the supporting evidence required by subpart C of part 51 of this chapter. A diplomatic or consular officer or a designated nationality examiner shall determine the period of time for which the registration will be valid.

HISTORY:
[31 FR 13537, Oct. 20, 1966; 61 FR 43310, 43111, Aug. 22, 1996]

§ 50.4 Application for passport.

A claim to U.S. nationality in connection with an application for passport shall be determined by posts abroad in accordance with the regulations contained in part 51 of this chapter.

HISTORY:
[31 FR 13537, Oct. 20, 1966]

§ 50.5 Application for Consular Report of Birth Abroad of a Citizen of the United States of America.

Upon application by the parent(s) or the child's legal

guardian, a consular officer or designated nationality examiner may accept and adjudicate the application for a Consular Report of Birth Abroad of a Citizen of the United States of America for a child born in their consular district. In specific instances, the Department may authorize consular officers and other designated employees to adjudicate the application for a Consular Report of Birth Abroad of a child born outside his/her consular district. Under the supervision of a consular officer, designated nationality examiners shall accept, adjudicate, disapprove and provisionally approve applications for the Consular Report of Birth Abroad. The applicant shall be required to submit proof of the child's birth, identity and citizenship meeting the evidence requirements of subpart C of part 51 of this subchapter and shall include:

(a) Proof of child's birth. Proof of child's birth usually consists of, but is not limited to, an authentic copy of the record of the birth filed with local authorities, a baptismal certificate, a military hospital certificate of birth, or an affidavit of the doctor or the person attending the birth. If no proof of birth is available, the person seeking to register the birth shall submit his affidavit explaining why such proof is not available and setting forth the facts relating to the birth.

(b) Proof of child's citizenship. Evidence of parent's citizenship and, if pertinent, evidence of parent's physical presence in the United States as required for transmittal of claim of citizenship by the Immigration and Nationality Act of 1952 shall be submitted.

HISTORY:

[31 FR 13537, Oct. 20, 1966; 61 FR 43310, 43312, Aug. 22, 1996]

§ 50.6 Registration at the Department of birth abroad.

In the time of war or national emergency, passport agents may be designated to complete consular reports of birth for children born at military facilities which are not under the jurisdiction of a consular office. An officer of the Armed Forces having authority to administer oaths may take applications for registration under this section.

HISTORY:

[31 FR 13537, Oct. 20, 1966]

§ 50.7 Consular Report of Birth Abroad of a Citizen of the United States of America.

(a) Upon application and the submission of satisfactory proof of birth, identity and nationality, and at the time of the reporting of the birth, the consular officer may issue to the parent or legal guardian, when approved and upon payment of a prescribed fee, a Consular Report of Birth Abroad of a Citizen of the United States of America.

(b) Amended and replacement Consular Reports of Birth Abroad of a Citizen of the United States of America may be issued by the Department of State's Passport Office upon written request and payment of the required fee.

(c) When it reports a birth under § 50.6, the Department shall furnish the Consular Report of Birth Abroad of a Citizen of the United States of America to the parent or legal guardian upon application and payment of required fees.

(d) A Consular Report of Birth Abroad may be cancelled in accordance with applicable provisions in 22 CFR 51.60 through 51.74.

HISTORY:

[31 FR 13537, Oct. 20, 1966; 61 FR 43310, 43312, Aug. 22, 1996; 64 FR 19713, 19714, Apr. 22, 1999; 83 FR 21872, 21874, May 11, 2018; suspended in part at 83 FR 22848, 22849, May 17, 2018]

§ 50.8 Certification of Report of Birth Abroad of a United States Citizen.

At any time subsequent to the issuance of a Consular Report of Birth Abroad of a Citizen of the United States of America, when requested and upon payment of the required fee, the Department of State's Passport Office may issue to the citizen, the citizen's parent or legal guardian a certificate entitled "Certification of Report of Birth Abroad of a United States Citizen."

HISTORY:

[31 FR 13537, Oct. 20, 1966; 61 FR 43310, 43312, Aug. 22, 1996]

§ 50.9 Card of identity.

When authorized by the Department, consular offices or designated nationality examiners may issue a card of identity for travel to the United States to nationals of the United States being deported from a foreign country, to nationals/citizens of the United States involved in a common disaster abroad, or to a returning national of the United States to whom passport services have been denied or withdrawn under the provisions of this part or parts 51 or 53 of this subchapter.

HISTORY:

[37 FR 11459, June 8, 1972; 61 FR 43310, 43312, Aug. 22, 1996]

§ 50.10 Certificate of nationality.

(a) Any person who acquired the nationality of the United States at birth and who is involved in any judicial or administrative proceedings in a foreign state and needs to establish his U.S. nationality may apply for a certificate of nationality in the form prescribed by the Department.

(b) An applicant for a certificate of nationality must submit evidence of his nationality and documentary evidence establishing that he is involved in judicial or administrative proceedings in which proof of his U.S. nationality is required.

HISTORY:

[31 FR 13537, Oct. 20, 1966]

§ 50.11 Certificate of identity for travel to the United States to apply for admission.

(a) A person applying abroad for a certificate of identity under section 360(b) of the Immigration and

Nationality Act shall complete the application form prescribed by the Department and submit evidence to support his claim to U.S. nationality.

(b) When a diplomatic or consular officer denies an application for a certificate of identity under this section, the applicant may submit a written appeal to the Secretary through the U.S. embassy or consulate where the individual applied for the certificate of identity, stating the pertinent facts, the grounds upon which U.S. nationality is claimed, and his or her reasons for considering that the denial was not justified.

HISTORY:

[31 FR 14521, Nov. 11, 1966; 83 FR 21872, 21874, May 11, 2018; suspended in part at 83 FR 22848, 22849, May 17, 2018]

Subpart B

Retention and Resumption of Nationality

§ 50.20 Retention of nationality.

(a) **Section 351(b) of the Immigration and Nationality Act.**

(1) A person who desires to claim U.S. nationality under the provisions of section 351(b) of the Immigration and Nationality Act must, within the time period specified in the statute, assert a claim to U.S. nationality and subscribe to an oath of allegiance before a diplomatic or consular officer.

(2) In addition, the person shall submit to the Department a statement reciting the person's identity and acquisition or derivation of U.S. nationality, the facts pertaining to the performance of any act which would otherwise have been expatriative, and the person's desire to retain his U.S. nationality.

HISTORY:

[31 FR 13537, Oct. 20, 1966; 61 FR 29651, 29652, 29653, June 12, 1996]

§ 50.30 Resumption of nationality.

(a) **Section 324(c) of the Immigration and Nationality Act.**

(1) A woman formerly a citizen of the United States at birth who wishes to regain her citizenship under section 324(c) of the Immigration and Nationality Act may apply abroad to a diplomatic or consular officer on the form prescribed by the Department to take the oath of allegiance prescribed by section 337 of that Act.

(2) The applicant shall submit documentary evidence to establish her eligibility to take the oath of allegiance. If the diplomatic or consular officer or the Department determines, when the application is submitted to the Department for decision, that the applicant is ineligible for resumption of citizenship because of section 313 of the Immigration and Nationality Act, the oath shall not be administered.

(b) **The Act of June 25, 1936.**

(1) A woman who has been restored to citizenship by the Act of June 25, 1936, as amended by the Act of July 2, 1940, but who failed to take the oath of allegiance prior to December 24, 1952, as prescribed by the nationality laws, may apply abroad to any diplomatic or consular officer to take the oath of allegiance as prescribed by section 337 of the Immigration and Nationality Act.

(2) The applicant shall submit documentary evidence to establish her eligibility to take the oath of allegiance. If the diplomatic or consular officer or the Department determines, when the application is submitted to the Department, that the applicant is ineligible for resumption of citizenship under section 313 of the Immigration and Nationality Act, the oath shall not be administered.

(c) Certification of repatriation. Upon request and payment of the prescribed fee, a diplomatic or consular officer or the Department shall issue a certified copyof the application and oath administered to a woman repatriated under this section.

(d) **Section 324(d)(1) of the Immigration and Nationality Act.**

(1) A former citizen of the United States who did not retain U.S. citizenship by failure to fulfill residency requirements as set out in Section 201(g) of the 1940 Nationality Act or former 301(b) of the 1952 Immigration and Nationality Act, may regain his/her U.S. citizenship pursuant to Section 324(d) INA, by applying abroad at a diplomatic or consular post, or in the U.S. at any Immigration and Naturalization Service office in the form and manner prescribed by the Department of State and the Immigration and Naturalization Service (INS).

(2) The applicant shall submit documentary evidence to establish eligibility to take the oath of allegiance, which includes proof of birth abroad to a U.S. citizen parent between May 24, 1934 and December 24, 1952. If the diplomatic, consular, INS, or passport officer determines that the applicant is ineligible to regain citizenship under section 313 INA, the oath shall not be administered.

HISTORY:

[31 FR 13537, Oct. 20, 1966; 61 FR 29651, 29652, June 12, 1996]

Subpart C

Loss of Nationality

§ 50.40 Certification of loss of U.S. nationality.

(a) Administrative presumption. In adjudicating potentially expatriating acts pursuant to INA 349(a), the Department has adopted an administrative presumption regarding certain acts and the intent to commit them. U.S. citizens who naturalize in a foreign country; take a routine oath of allegiance; or accept non-policy level employment with a foreign government need not submit evidence of intent to retain U.S. nationality. In these three classes of cases, intent to retain U.S. citizenship will be presumed. A person who affirmatively asserts to a consular officer, after he or she has committed a potentially expatriating act, that it was his or her intent to relinquish U.S. citizenship will lose his or her U.S. citizenship. In other loss of nationality cases, the consular officer will ascertain whether or not there is evidence of intent to relinquish U.S. nationality.

(b) Whenever a person admits that he or she had the intent to relinquish citizenship by the voluntary and intentional performance of one of the acts specified in Section 349(a) of the Immigration and Nationality Act, and the person consents to the execution of an affidavit to that effect, the diplomatic or consular officer shall attach such affidavit to the certificate of loss of nationality.

(c) Whenever a diplomatic or consular officer has reason to believe that a person, while in a foreign country, has lost his U.S. nationality under any provision of chapter 3 of title III of the Immigration and Nationality Act of 1952, or under any provision of chapter IV of the Nationality Act of 1940, as amended, he shall prepare a certificate of loss of nationality containing the facts upon which such belief is based and shall forward the certificate to the Department.

(d) If the diplomatic or consular officer determines that any document containing information relevant to the statements in the certificate of loss of nationality should not be attached to the certificate, the person may summarize the pertinent information in the appropriate section of the certificate and send the documents together with the certificate to the Department.

(e) If the certificate of loss of nationality is approved by the Department, a copy shall be forwarded to the Immigration and Naturalization Service, Department of Justice. The diplomatic or consular office in which the certificate was prepared shall then forward a copy of the certificate to the person to whom it relates or his representative.

(f) Attorney or Other Third-Party Presence at In-Person CLN appointments. Individuals may, at their own expense, have a private attorney, interpreter, or other third party of their own choice physically present during any in-person appointment, including interview appointments, at a U.S. embassy or consulate abroad related to a request for a Certificate of Loss of Nationality (CLN); provided that:

(1) The individual and/or the attorney or other third party shall provide advance notice of the attorney's or other third party's intent to attend the CLN appointment in the manner specified by the Department of State and/or the specific U.S. embassy or consulate where the appointment is to take place;

(2) The individual requesting the CLN must appear in person for the mandatory in-person interview appointment(s); attendance by an attorney or other third party shall not be in lieu of the individual's in-person appearance;

(3) The diplomatic or consular officer will direct all interview questions to the individual requesting the CLN, and the individual must personally respond to the consular officer;

(4) The diplomatic or consular officer conducting the interview shall have the discretion to interview the individual alone, without an attorney or third-party present, when necessary to evaluate whether the individual has performed a potentially expatriating act independently, free from duress or coercion, and with intent to relinquish U.S. nationality;

(5) Nothing in this section abrogates any policies, security directives, and guidelines from the Department, Chief of Mission, or Diplomatic Security Service regarding admission to or conduct in the U.S. embassy or consulate. All persons entering a U.S. embassy or consulate shall comply with all policies, security directives, guidelines, and protocols including but not limited to those regarding security, identification, screening, electronic devices, recording, health, and conduct. Individuals may be refused entry or directed to leave the U.S. embassy or consulate for noncompliance with such policies, directives, guidelines, and protocols.

HISTORY:

[31 FR 13537, Oct. 20, 1966; redesignated and amended at 61 FR 29651, 29652, 29653, June 12, 1996, as corrected at 63 FR 20315, Apr. 24, 1998; 89 FR 41308, 41310, May 13, 2024]

§ 50.50 Renunciation of nationality.

(a) A person desiring to renounce U.S. nationality under section 349(a)(5) of the Immigration and Nationality Act shall appear before a diplomatic or consular officer of the United States in the manner and form prescribed by the Department. The renunciant must include on the form he signs a statement that he absolutely and entirely renounces his U.S. nationality together with all rights and privileges and all duties of allegiance and fidelity thereunto pertaining.

(b) The diplomatic or consular officer shall forward to the Department for approval the oath of renunciation together with a certificate of loss of nationality as provided by section 358 of the Immigration and Nationality Act. If the officer's report is approved by the Department, copies of the certificate shall be forwarded to the Immigration and Naturalization Service, Department of Justice, and to the person to whom it relates or his representative.

HISTORY:

[31 FR 13537, Oct. 20, 1966; 61 FR 29651, 29653, June 12, 1996]

§ 50.51 Review of finding of loss of nationality.

(a) There are no prescribed "procedures for administrative appeal" of issuance of a Certificate of Loss of Nationality for purposes of § 358 of the Immigration and Nationality Act (8 U.S.C. 1501) and no mandatory administrative review procedure prior to resort to judicial processes under § 360 of the Immigration and Nationality Act (8 U.S.C. 1503). Nevertheless, the Department may in its discretion review determinations of loss of nationality at any time after approval of issuance of the Certificate of Loss of Nationality to ensure consistency with governing law (see INA §§ 349 and 356, 8 U.S.C. 1481 and 1488). Such reconsideration may be initiated at the request of the person concerned or another person determined in accordance with guidance issued by the Department to have a legitimate interest.

(b) The primary grounds on which the Department will consider reversing a finding of loss of nationality and vacating a Certificate of Loss of Nationality are:

(1) The law under which the finding of loss was made has been held unconstitutional; or

(2) A major change in the interpretation of the law of expatriation is made as a result of a U.S. Supreme Court decision; or

(3) A major change in the interpretation of the law of expatriation is made by the Department, or is made by a court or another agency and adopted by the Department; and/or

(4) The person presents substantial new evidence, not previously considered, of involuntariness or absence of intent at the time of the expatriating act.

(c) When the Department reverses a finding of loss of nationality, the person concerned shall be considered not to have lost U.S. nationality as of the time the expatriating act was committed, and the Certificate of Loss of Nationality shall be vacated.

(d) Requesting the Department to reverse a finding of loss of nationality and vacate a Certificate of Loss of Nationality is not a prescribed "procedure for administrative appeal" for purposes of § 358 of the Immigration and Nationality Act (8 U.S.C. 1501). The Department's decision in response to such a request is not a prescribed "procedure for administrative appeal" for purposes of § 358 of the Immigration and Nationality Act (8 U.S.C. 1501). The issuance of a Certificate of Loss of Nationality by the Department is a "final administrative determination" and "final administrative denial" for purposes of §§ 358 and 360 of the Immigration and Nationality Act (8 U.S.C. 1501 and 1503), respectively.

HISTORY:

[44 FR 68827, Nov. 30, 1979; redesignated at 61 FR 29651, 29653, June 12, 1996; 73 FR 41256, 41258, July 18, 2008, as confirmed at 73 FR 62196, 62197, Oct. 20, 2008]

Subpart D

Third-Party Attendance at Appointments for Passport and Consular Report of Birth Abroad (CRBA) Appointments

§ 50.52 Attorney or other third-party assistance.

(a) A person appearing for a passport appointment at a passport agency or center domestically or a U.S. embassy or consulate overseas or for a Consular Report of Birth Abroad (CRBA) appointment overseas may be physically accompanied by a private attorney, interpreter, or other third party of their own choice at their own expense to provide assistance. All regulations related to passport and CRBA applications in this chapter continue to apply.

(1) An applicant and/or their third-party attendee or attorney may, at their own expense, bring their own interpreter to any passport and/or CRBA appointment, provided the applicant or their attorney or third-party attendee provides advance notice of such attendance pursuant to guidance issued by the Department.

(2) Attendance by an attorney or other third party at the appointment does not excuse the in-person appearance of the applicant as outlined by 22 CFR 51.21 and 51.28.

(3) Nothing in this section abrogates any policies, security directives, and guidelines from the Department, Chief of Mission, or Diplomatic Security Service regarding admission to or conduct in a domestic passport agency or center or at a U.S. embassy or consulate overseas. All persons entering a domestic passport agency or center or a U.S. embassy or consulate overseas shall comply with all policies, security directives, guidelines, and protocols, including but not limited to those regarding security, identification, screening, electronic devices, recording, health, and conduct. Individuals may be refused entry or directed to leave the U.S. embassy or consulate for noncompliance with such policies, directives, guidelines, and protocols.

HISTORY:

[89 FR 41308, 41310, May 13, 2024]

PART 51

PASSPORTS

AUTHORITY NOTE APPLICABLE TO ENTIRE PART:

AUTHORITY:

[8 U.S.C. 1104; 8 U.S.C. 1185; 8 U.S.C. 1185n (text of Pub. L. 108–458, 118 Stat. 3638, 3823 (Dec. 17, 2004)); 8 U.S.C. 1504; 8 U.S.C. 1714; 22 U.S.C. 211a, 212, 212a, 212b, 213, 213n (Pub. L. 106–113 Div. B, Sec. 1000(a)(7) [Div. A, Title II, Sec. 236], 113 Stat. 1536, 1501A–430); 214, 214a, 217a, 218, 2651a, 2671(d)(3), 2705, 2714, 2714a, 2721, and 3926; 26 U.S.C. 6039E; 26 CFR 301.6039E–1; 31 U.S.C. 9701; 34 U.S.C. 21501–21510; 42 U.S.C. 652(k); E.O. 11295, Aug. 5, 1966, 31 FR 10603, 3 CFR, 1966–1970 Comp., p. 570; Pub. L. 114–119, 130 Stat. 15.]

§ 51.1 Definitions.

The following definitions are applicable to this part:

Department means the United States Department of State.

Electronic passport means a passport containing an electronically readable device, an electronic chip encoded with the bearer's personal information printed on the data page, a digitized version of the bearer's photograph, a unique chip number, and a digital signature to protect the integrity of the stored information.

Minor means an unmarried, unemancipated person under 18 years of age.

Non-personal services contractor, for purposes of this part, is an individual working under a non-personal services contract as defined in 48 CFR 37.101.

Passport means a travel document regardless of format issued under the authority of the Secretary of

State attesting to the identity and nationality of the bearer.

Passport acceptance agent means a U.S. national designated by the Department to accept passport applications and to administer oaths and affirmations in connection with such applications.

Passport agent means a U.S. citizen employee of the Department of State, including consular officers, diplomatic officers and consular agents abroad, and such U.S. citizen Department of State employees or contractors as the Assistant Secretary for Consular Affairs may designate for the purpose of administering oaths and affirmations for passport applications.

Passport application means the application form for a United States passport, as prescribed by the Department pursuant to 22 U.S.C. 213 and all documents, photographs, and statements submitted with the form or thereafter in support of the application.

Passport authorizing officer means a U.S. citizen employee who is authorized by the Department to approve the issuance of passports.

Personal services contractor, for purposes of this part, means a contractor who is working under a personal services contract as described in 48 CFR 37.104.

Secretary means the Secretary of State.

Special issuance passport means a regular passport for which no passport fee is collected pursuant to § 51.52, and a service, official or diplomatic passport as defined in § 51.3.

United States when used in a geographical sense means the continental United States, Alaska, Hawaii, Puerto Rico, Guam, the Virgin Islands of the United States, and all other United States territories and possessions.

U.S. citizen means a person who acquired U.S. citizenship at birth or upon naturalization as provided by law and who has not subsequently lost such citizenship.

U.S. national means a U.S. citizen or a U.S. non-citizen national.

U.S. non-citizen national means a person on whom U.S. nationality, but not U.S. citizenship, has been conferred at birth under 8 U.S.C. 1408, or under other law or treaty, and who has not subsequently lost such non-citizen nationality.

HISTORY:

[31 FR 13540, Oct. 20, 1966, as amended at 31 FR 14522, Nov. 11, 1966; 61 FR 43310, 43312, Aug. 22, 1996; 66 FR 29904, 29906, June 4, 2001; 70 FR 61553, 61555, Oct. 25, 2005; 72 FR 64930, 64931, Nov. 19, 2007, as corrected at 73 FR 5435, Jan. 30, 2008; 81 FR 67156, 67157, Sept. 30, 2016, as confirmed at 83 FR 4143, Jan. 30, 2018]

Subpart A

General

§ 51.2 Passport issued to nationals only.

(a) A passport may be issued only to a U.S. national.

(b) Unless authorized by the Department, no person may bear more than one valid passport of the same type.

HISTORY:

[SD-165, 46 FR 2343, Jan. 9, 1981; 72 FR 64930, 64931, Nov. 19, 2007]

§ 51.3 Types of passports.

(a) Regular passport. A regular passport is issued to a national of the United States.

(b) Service passport. When authorized by the Department, a service passport may be issued to a non-personal services contractor traveling abroad to carry out duties in support of and pursuant to a contract with the U.S. government, when exceptional circumstances make a service passport necessary to enable the individual to carry out his or her contractual duties.

(c) Official passport. When authorized by the Department, an official passport may be issued to:

(1) An officer or employee of the U.S. government traveling abroad to carry out official duties, and family members of such persons;

(2) A U.S. government personal services contractor traveling abroad to carry out official duties on behalf of the U.S. government;

(3) A non-personal services contractor traveling abroad to carry out duties in support of and pursuant to a contract with the U.S. government when the contractor is unable to carry out such duties using a regular or service passport; or

(4) An official or employee of a state, local, tribal, or territorial government traveling abroad to carry out official duties in support of the U.S. government.

(d) Diplomatic passport. A diplomatic passport is issued to a Foreign Service Officer or to a person having diplomatic status or comparable status because he or she is traveling abroad to carry out diplomatic duties on behalf of the U.S. government. When authorized by the Department, spouses and family members of such persons may be issued diplomatic passports. When authorized by the Department, a diplomatic passport may be issued to a U.S. government contractor if the contractor meets the eligibility requirements for a diplomatic passport and the diplomatic passport is necessary to complete his or her contractual duties in support of the U.S. government.

(e) Passport card. A passport card is issued to a national of the United States on the same basis as a regular passport. It is valid only for departure from and entry to the United States through land and sea ports of entry between the United States and Mexico, Canada, the Caribbean and Bermuda. It is not a globally interoperable international travel document.

HISTORY:

[31 FR 13540, Oct. 20, 1966, as amended at 49 FR 16989, Apr. 23, 1984; 72 FR 64930, 64931, Nov. 19, 2007; 72 FR 74169, 74173, Dec. 31, 2007; 80 FR 27856, 27857, May 15, 2015, as confirmed at 81 FR 6757, Feb. 9, 2016; 81 FR 67156, 67157, Sept. 30, 2016, as confirmed at 83 FR 4143, Jan. 30, 2018]

§ 51.4 Validity of passports.

(a) Signature of bearer. A passport book is valid only when signed by the bearer in the space designated for signature, or, if the bearer is unable to sign, signed by a person with legal authority to sign on his or her behalf. A passport card is valid without the signature of the bearer.

(b) **Period of validity of a regular passport and a passport card.**

(1) A regular passport or passport card issued to an applicant 16 years of age or older is valid for ten years from date of issue unless the Department limits the validity period to a shorter period.

(2) A regular passport or passport card issued to an applicant under 16 years of age is valid for five years from date of issue unless the Department limits the validity period to a shorter period.

(3) A regular passport for which payment of the fee has been excused is valid for a period of five years from the date issued unless limited by the Department to a shorter period.

(c) Period of validity of a service passport. The period of validity of a service passport, unless limited by the Department to a shorter period, is five years from the date of issue, or so long as the bearer maintains the status pursuant to which the service passport is issued, whichever is shorter. A service passport which has not expired must be returned to the Department upon the termination of the bearer's status or at such other time as the Department may determine.

(d) Period of validity of an official passport. The period of validity of an official passport, unless limited by the Department to a shorter period, is five years from the date of issue, or so long as the bearer maintains his or her official status, whichever is shorter. An official passport which has not expired must be returned to the Department upon the termination of the bearer's official status or at such other time as the Department may determine.

(e) Period of validity of a diplomatic passport. The period of validity of a diplomatic passport, unless limited by the Department to a shorter period, is five years from the date of issue, or so long as the bearer maintains his or her diplomatic status, whichever is shorter. A diplomatic passport which has not expired must be returned to the Department upon the termination of the bearer's diplomatic status or at such other time as the Department may determine.

(f) Limitation of validity. The validity period of any passport may be limited by the Department to less than the normal validity period. The bearer of a limited passport may apply for a new passport, using the proper application and submitting the limited passport, applicable fees, photographs, and additional documentation, if required, to support the issuance of a new passport.

(g) Invalidity. A United States passport is invalid as soon as:

(1) The Department approves the revocation notification pursuant to § 51.65(a); or

(2) The passport has been reported as lost or stolen to the Department, a U.S. passport agency or a diplomatic or consular post abroad and the Department has recorded the reported loss or theft; or

(3) The passport is cancelled by the Department (physically, electronically, or otherwise) upon issuance of a new passport of the same type to the bearer; or

(4) The Department has sent a written notice to the bearer that the passport has been invalidated because the Department has not received the applicable fees; or

(5) The passport has been materially changed in physical appearance or composition, or contains a damaged, defective or otherwise nonfunctioning chip, or includes unauthorized changes, obliterations, entries or photographs, or has observable wear or tear that renders it unfit for use as a travel document, and the Department either takes possession of the passport or sends a written notice to the bearer); or

(6) The bearer of a special issuance passport no longer maintains the status pursuant to which the passport was issued; or

(7) The Department has sent a written notice to the bearer, directly or through the bearer's employing agency, stating that a special issuance passport has been cancelled by the Department.

(8) The Department approves a Certificate of Loss of Nationality for the passport holder pursuant to § 50.40 of this chapter and 8 U.S.C. 1481.

HISTORY:

[31 FR 13540, Oct. 20, 1966, as amended at 33 FR 12042, Aug. 24, 1968; 42 FR 17869, Apr. 4, 1977; 47 FR 56329, Dec. 16, 1982; 63 FR 7285, Feb. 13, 1998; 69 FR 15669, 15670, Mar. 26, 2004; 70 FR 53922, 53924, Sept. 13, 2005; 72 FR 64930, 64931, Nov. 19, 2007; 72 FR 74169, 74173, Dec. 31, 2007; 81 FR 67156, 67158, Sept. 30, 2016, as confirmed at 83 FR 4143, Jan. 30, 2018; 83 FR 21872, 21874, May 11, 2018; suspended in part at 83 FR 22848, 22849, May 17, 2018]

§ 51.5 Adjudication and issuance of passports.

(a) A passport authorizing officer may adjudicate applications and authorize the issuance of passports.

(b) A passport authorizing officer will examine the passport application and all documents, photographs and statements submitted in support of the application in accordance with guidance issued by the Department.

HISTORY:

[72 FR 64930, 64931, Nov. 19, 2007]

§ 51.6 Verification of passports and release of information from passport records.

(a) Verification. When required by a foreign government, a consular officer abroad may verify a U.S. passport.

(b) Release of information. Information in passport records is subject to the provisions of the Freedom of Information Act (FOIA) and the Privacy Act. Release of this information may be requested in accordance with Part 171 or Part 172 of this title.

HISTORY:

[31 FR 13540, Oct. 20, 1966; 70 FR 61553, 61555, Oct. 25, 2005; 72 FR 64930, 64931, Nov. 19, 2007]

§ 51.7 Passport property of the U.S. Government.

(a) A passport at all times remains the property of the United States and must be returned to the U.S. Government upon demand.

(b) Law enforcement authorities who take possession of a passport for use in an investigation or prosecution must return the passport to the Department on completion of the investigation and/or prosecution.

HISTORY:

[31 FR 13540, Oct. 20, 1966; 72 FR 64930, 64931, Nov. 19, 2007]

§ 51.8 Submission of currently valid passport.

(a) When applying for a new passport in person or by mail, an applicant must submit for cancellation any currently valid passport of the same type.

(b) When applying for a new passport on-line, an applicant must have the currently valid passport of the same type available for cancellation via the on-line process.

(c) If an applicant is unable to produce a passport under paragraph (a) or (b) of this section, they must submit a signed statement in the form prescribed by the Department setting forth the circumstances regarding the disposition of the passport.

(d) The Department may deny or limit a passport if the applicant has failed to provide a sufficient and credible explanation for lost, stolen, altered or mutilated passport(s) previously issued to the applicant, after being given a reasonable opportunity to do so.

HISTORY:

[31 FR 13540, Oct. 20, 1966, as amended at 31 FR 14521, Nov. 11, 1966; 49 FR 16989, Apr. 23, 1984; 72 FR 64930, 64931, Nov. 19, 2007; 86 FR 72520, 72523, Dec. 22, 2021]

§ 51.9 Amendment of passports.

Except for the convenience of the U.S. Government, no passport may be amended.

HISTORY:

[31 FR 13540, Oct. 20, 1966; 72 FR 64930, 64931, Nov. 19, 2007]

§ 51.10 Replacement passports.

A passport issuing office may issue a replacement passport without payment of applicable fees for the reasons specified in § 51.54.

HISTORY:

[72 FR 64930, 64931, Nov. 19, 2007]

Subpart B

Application

§ 51.20 General.

(a) An application for a passport, a replacement passport, or other passport related service must be completed using the forms the Department prescribes.

(b) The passport applicant must truthfully answer all questions and must state every material matter of fact pertaining to his or her eligibility for a passport. All information and evidence submitted in connection with an application is considered part of the application. A person providing false information as part of a passport application, whether contemporaneously with the form or at any other time, is subject to prosecution under applicable Federal criminal statutes.

HISTORY:

[33 FR 12043, Aug. 24, 1968, as amended at 49 FR 16989, Apr. 23, 1984; 70 FR 53922, 53924, Sept. 13, 2005; 72 FR 64930, 64931, Nov. 19, 2007; 80 FR 72591, 72592, Nov. 20, 2015]

§ 51.21 Execution of passport application.

(a) Application by personal appearance. Except as provided in § 51.28, to assist in establishing identity, a minor, a person who has never been issued a passport in his or her own name, a person who has not been issued a passport for the full validity period of 10 years in his or her own name within 15 years of the date of a new application, or a person who is otherwise not eligible to apply for a passport by mail under paragraphs (b) and (c) of this section, must apply for a passport by appearing in person before a passport agent or passport acceptance agent (see § 51.22). The applicant must verify the application by oath or affirmation before the passport agent or passport acceptance agent, sign the completed application, provide photographs as prescribed by the Department, provide any other information or documents requested and pay the applicable fees prescribed in the Schedule of Fees for Consular Services (see 22 CFR 22.1).

(b) Application by mail or on-line—persons in the United States.

(1) A person in the United States who previously has been issued a passport valid for 10 years in his or her own name may apply for a new passport by filling out, signing and mailing an application on the form prescribed by the Department if:

(i) The most recently issued previous passport was issued when the applicant was 16 years of age or older;

(ii) The application is made not more than 15 years following the issue date of the previous passport, except as provided in paragraph (e) of this section; and

(iii) The most recently issued previous passport of the same type is submitted with the new application.

(2) A person in the United States who previously has been issued a passport valid for 10 years in their own name may apply for a new passport by filling out, signing, and submitting an on-line application via the Department's official website if:

(i) The applicant's most recently issued passport was issued when the applicant was 16 years of age or older, and has one year or less of validity remaining;

(ii) The application is made not more than 15 years following the issue date of the most recently issued passport of the same type;

(iii) The most recently-issued passport of the same type is available for verification via the on-line process.

(3) The applicant must also provide photographs as prescribed by the Department and pay the applicable fees prescribed in the Schedule of Fees for Consular Services (22 CFR 22.1).

(c) Application by mail — persons abroad.

(1) A person in a foreign country where the Department has authorized a post to receive passport applications by mail who previously has been issued a passport valid for 10 years in his or her own name may apply for a new passport in that country by filling out, signing and mailing an application on the form prescribed by the Department if:

(i) The most recently issued previous passport was issued when the applicant was 16 years of age or older;

(ii) The application is made not more than 15 years following the issue date of the previous passport, except as provided in paragraph (e) of this section; and

(iii) The most recently issued previous passport of the same type is submitted with the new application.

(2) The applicant must also provide photographs as prescribed by the Department and pay the applicable fees prescribed in the Schedule of Fees for Consular Services (22 CFR 22.1).

(d) Nothing in this Part shall prohibit or limit the Department from authorizing an overseas post to accept a passport application or applications from persons outside the country or outside the person's country of residence in circumstances which prevent provision of these services to the person where they are located or in other unusual circumstances as determined by the Department.

(e) A senior passport authorizing officer may authorize acceptance of an application by mail where the application is made more than 15 years following the issue date of the previous passport as appropriate and in accordance with guidance issued by the Department.

HISTORY:

[44 FR 19393, Apr. 3, 1979, as amended at SD-165, 46 FR 2343, Jan. 9, 1981; 46 FR 16257, Mar. 12, 1981; 51 FR 20475, June 5, 1986; 55 FR 21538, May 25, 1990; 61 FR 43310, 43312, Aug. 22, 1996; 65 FR 39288, June 26, 2000; 66 FR 29904, 29906, June 4, 2001; 69 FR 15669, 15670, Mar. 26, 2004; 72 FR 64930, 64931, Nov. 19, 2007, as corrected at 73 FR 4077, 4078, Jan. 24, 2008; 86 FR 72520, 72523, Dec. 22, 2021]

§ 51.22 Passport agents and passport acceptance agents.

(a) U.S. citizen employees of the Department authorized to serve as passport agents. The following employees of the Department are authorized by virtue of their positions to serve as passport agents unless the Department in an individual case withdraws authorization:

(1) A passport authorizing officer;

(2) A consular officer, or a U.S. citizen consular agent abroad;

(3) A diplomatic officer specifically authorized by the Department to accept passport applications; and

(4) Such U.S. citizen Department of State employees and contractors as the Assistant Secretary for Consular Affairs may designate for the purpose of administering oaths and affirmations for passport applications.

(b) Persons designated by the Department to serve as passport acceptance agents. When designated by the Department, the following persons are authorized to serve as passport acceptance agents unless the Department in an individual case withdraws authorization.

(1) An employee of the clerk of any Federal court;

(2) An employee of the clerk of any state court of record;

(3) A postal employee at a United States post office that has been selected to accept passport applications;

(4) An employee of the Department of Defense at a military installation that has been authorized to accept passport applications;

(5) An employee of a federal agency that has been selected to accept passport applications; and

(6) Any other person specifically designated by the Department.

(c) Qualifications of persons designated by the Department to serve as passport acceptance agents. Before the Department will designate a person described in § 51.22(b) as a passport acceptance agent, his or her employer must certify that the person:

(1) Is a U.S. citizen or a U.S. non-citizen national;

(2) Is 18 years of age or older;

(3) Is a permanent employee, excluding ad hoc, contractual, and volunteer employees; and

(4) Does not have a record of either:

(i) A Federal or State felony conviction; or

(ii) A misdemeanor conviction for crimes involving moral turpitude or breach of trust, including but not limited to embezzlement, identity theft, misappropriation, document fraud, drug offenses, or dishonesty in carrying out a responsibility involving public trust.

(d) Training. A passport acceptance agent described in § 51.22(b) must be trained to apply procedures and practices as detailed in guidance provided by the Department. Training must be successfully completed before accepting passport applications.

(e) Responsibilities. The responsibilities of a passport acceptance agent described in § 51.22(b) include but are not limited to the following:

(1) Certifying the identity of each applicant. Passport acceptance agents must certify that they have personally witnessed the applicant signing his or her application, and that the applicant has:

(i) Personally appeared;

(ii) Presented proper identification, as documented on the application;

(iii) Submitted photographs that are a true likeness; and

(iv) Taken the oath administered by the acceptance agent.

(2) Safeguarding passport application information under the Privacy

Act of 1974. Passport acceptance agents described in § 51.22(b) must not retain copies of executed applications, nor release passport application information to anyone other than the applicant and the Department.

(3) Avoiding conflict of interest. Passport acceptance agents described in § 51.22(b) must not participate in any relationship that could be perceived as a conflict of

interest, including but not limited to providing commercial services related to the passport process.

(f) Documentation. Passport acceptance facilities within the United

States must maintain a current listing of all passport acceptance agents designated under § 51.22(b) working at its facility. This list must be updated at least annually and a copy provided to the officer specified by the Department at the appropriate passport issuing office.

(1) The current listing of all designated passport acceptance agents must include the passport acceptance agents':

(i) Names; and

(ii) Signatures.

(2) Any addition to or deletion from the current listing of designated passport acceptance agents is subject to prior approval by the Department.

HISTORY:

[31 FR 13540, Oct. 20, 1966; 72 FR 64930, 64931, Nov. 19, 2007]

§ 51.23 Identity of applicant.

(a) The applicant has the burden of establishing his or her identity.

(b) The applicant must establish his or her identity by the submission of a previous passport, other state, local, or federal government officially issued identification with photograph, or other identifying evidence which may include an affidavit of an identifying witness.

(c) The Department may require such additional evidence of identity as it deems necessary.

HISTORY:

[SD-165, 46 FR 2343, Jan. 9, 1981; 72 FR 64930, 64931, Nov. 19, 2007]

§ 51.24 Affidavit of identifying witness.

(a) An identifying witness must execute an affidavit in the form prescribed by the Department before the person who accepts the passport application.

(b) A person who has received or expects to receive a fee for his or her services in connection with executing the application or obtaining the passport may not serve as an identifying witness.

HISTORY:

[31 FR 13540, Oct. 20, 1966, as amended at 49 FR 16989, Apr. 23, 1984; 72 FR 64930, 64931, Nov. 19, 2007]

§ 51.25 Name of applicant to be used in passport.

(a) The passport shall be issued in the full name of the applicant, generally the name recorded in the evidence of nationality and identity.

(b) The applicant must explain any material discrepancies between the name on the application and the name recorded in the evidence of nationality and identity. The name provided by the applicant on the application may be used if the applicant submits the documentary evidence prescribed by the Department.

(c) A name change will be recognized for purposes of issuing a passport if the name change occurs in one of the following ways.

(1) Court order or decree. An applicant whose name has been changed by court order or decree must submit with his or her application a copy of the order or decree.

Acceptable types of court orders and decrees include but are not limited to:

(i) A name change order;

(ii) A divorce decree specifically declaring the return to a former name;

(2) Certificate of naturalization issued in a new name.

(3) Marriage. An applicant who has adopted a new name following marriage must present a copy of the marriage certificate.

(4) Operation of state law. An applicant must present operative government-issued legal documentation declaring the name change or issued in the new name.

(5) Customary usage. An applicant who has adopted a new name other than as prescribed in paragraphs (c)(1) through (4) of this section must submit evidence of public and exclusive use of the adopted name for a long period of time, in general five years, as prescribed in guidance issued by the Department. The evidence must include three or more public documents, including one government-issued identification with photograph and other acceptable public documents prescribed by the Department.

HISTORY:

[31 FR 13540, Oct. 20, 1966, as amended at 43 FR 1791, Jan. 12, 1978; 44 FR 19394, Apr. 3, 1979; 46 FR 2343, Jan. 9, 1981; 49 FR 16989, Apr. 23, 1984; 69 FR 15669, 15671, Mar. 26, 2004; 72 FR 64930, 64931, Nov. 19, 2007]

§ 51.26 Photographs.

The applicant must submit with his or her application photographs as prescribed by the Department that are a good likeness of and satisfactorily identify the applicant.

HISTORY:

[31 FR 13540, Oct. 20, 1966; 72 FR 64930, 64931, Nov. 19, 2007]

§ 51.27 Incompetents.

A legal guardian or other person with the legal capacity to act on behalf of a person declared incompetent may execute a passport application on the incompetent person's behalf.

HISTORY:

[31 FR 13540, Oct. 20, 1966, as amended at 43 FR 1791, Jan. 12, 1978; 44 FR 41777, July 18, 1979; 49 FR 16989, Apr. 23, 1984; 61 FR 6505, Feb. 21, 1996; 66 FR 29904, 29906, June 4, 2001; 69 FR 15669, 15671, Mar. 26, 2004; 69 FR 60811, 60813, Oct. 13, 2004, as corrected at 69 FR 61597, Oct. 20, 2004; 69 FR 67053, Nov. 16, 2004; 72 FR 64930, 64931, Nov. 19, 2007]

§ 51.28 Minors.

(a) Minors under age 16.

(1) Personal appearance. Minors under 16 years of age applying for a passport must appear in person, unless the personal appearance of the minor is specifically excused by a senior passport authorizing officer, pursuant to guidance issued by the Department. In cases where personal appearance is excused, the person(s) executing the passport application on behalf of the minor shall appear in person and verify the application by oath or affirmation before a person authorized by the Secretary to administer oaths or affirmations, unless these requirements are also excused by a senior passport authorizing officer pursuant to guidance issued by the Department.

(2) Execution of passport application by both parents or by each legal guardian. Except as specifically provided in this section, both parents or each of the minor's legal guardians, if any, whether applying for a passport for the first time or for a renewal, must execute the application on behalf of a minor under age 16 and provide documentary evidence of parentage or legal guardianship showing the minor's name, date and place of birth, and the names of the parent or parents or legal guardian.

(3) Execution of passport application by one parent or legal guardian. A passport application may be executed on behalf of a minor under age 16 by only one parent or legal guardian if such person provides:

(i) A written statement or affidavit from the non-applying parent or legal guardian, if applicable, consenting to the issuance of the passport, and signed before a notary public or, when authorized by the Department, a passport specialist at a public passport agency/center counter operated by the Department of State.

(ii) Documentary evidence that such person is the sole parent or has sole custody of the minor. Such evidence includes, but is not limited to, the following:

(A) A birth certificate providing the minor's name, date and place of birth and the name of only the applying parent;

(B) A copy of the death certificate for the non-applying parent or legal guardian;

(C) An adoption decree showing the name of only the applying parent;

(D) An order of a court of competent jurisdiction granting sole legal custody to the applying parent or legal guardian containing no travel restrictions inconsistent with issuance of the passport; or, specifically authorizing the applying parent or legal guardian to obtain a passport for the minor, regardless of custodial arrangements; or specifically authorizing the travel of the minor with the applying parent or legal guardian;

(E) An order of a court of competent jurisdiction terminating the parental rights of the non-applying parent or declaring the non-applying parent or legal guardian to be incompetent; and

(F) An order of a court of competent jurisdiction providing for joint legal custody or requiring the permission of both parents or the court for important decisions will be interpreted as requiring the permission of both parents or the court, as appropriate. Notwithstanding the existence of any such court order, a passport may be issued when compelling humanitarian or emergency reasons relating to the welfare of the minor exist.

(4) Execution of passport application by a person acting in loco parentis.

(i) A person may apply in loco parentis on behalf of a minor under age 16 by submitting a written statement or affidavit from all parents or each legal guardian, if any, specifically authorizing the application, and signed before a notary public or, when authorized by the Department, a passport specialist at a public passport agency/center counter operated by the Department of State.

(ii) If only one parent or legal guardian provides the written statement or affidavit, the applicant must provide documentary evidence that an application may be made by one parent or legal guardian, consistent with this regulation.

(5) Exigent or special family circumstances. A passport may be issued when only one parent, legal guardian or person acting in loco parentis executes the application, in cases of exigent or special family circumstances.

(i) "Exigent circumstances" are defined as time-sensitive circumstances in which the inability of the minor to obtain a passport would jeopardize the health and safety or welfare of the minor or would result in the minor being separated from the rest of his or her traveling party. "Time sensitive" generally means that there is not enough time before the minor's emergency travel to obtain either the required consent of both parents/legal guardians or documentation reflecting a sole parent's/legal guardian's custody rights.

(ii) "Special family circumstances" are defined as circumstances in which the minor's family situation makes it exceptionally difficult for one or both of the parents to execute the passport application; and/or compelling humanitarian circumstances where the minor's lack of a passport would jeopardize the health, safety, or welfare of the minor; or, pursuant to guidance issued by the Department, circumstances in which return of a minor to the jurisdiction of his or her home state or habitual residence is necessary to permit a court of competent jurisdiction to adjudicate or enforce a custody determination. A passport issued due to such special family circumstances may be limited for direct return to the United States in accordance with § 51.60(e).

(iii) A parent, legal guardian, or person acting in loco parentis who is applying for a passport for a minor under age 16 under this paragraph must submit a written statement with the application describing the exigent or special family circumstances he or she believes should be taken into consideration in applying an exception.

(iv) Determinations under § 51.28(a)(5) must be made by a senior passport authorizing officer pursuant to guidance issued by the Department.

(6) Nothing contained in this section shall prohibit any Department official adjudicating a passport application filed on behalf of a minor from requiring an applicant to submit other documentary evidence

deemed necessary to establish the applying adult's entitlement to obtain a passport on behalf of a minor under the age of 16 in accordance with the provisions of this regulation.

(b) Minors 16 years of age and above.

(1) A minor 16 years of age and above applying for a passport must appear in person and may execute the application for a passport on his or her own behalf unless the personal appearance of the minor is specifically excused by a senior passport authorizing officer pursuant to guidance issued by the Department, or unless, in the judgment of the person before whom the application is executed, it is not advisable for the minor to execute his or her own application. In such case, it must be executed by a parent or legal guardian of the minor, or by a person in loco parentis, unless the personal appearance of the parent, legal guardian or person in loco parentis is excused by the senior passport authorizing officer pursuant to guidance issued by the Department.

(2) The passport authorizing officer may at any time require a minor 16 years of age and above to submit the notarized consent of a parent, a legal guardian, or a person in loco parentis to the issuance of the passport.

(c) Rules applicable to all minors —

(1) Objections. At any time prior to the issuance of a passport to a minor, the application may be disapproved and a passport may be denied upon receipt of a written objection from a parent or legal guardian of the minor, or from another party claiming authority to object, so long as the objecting party provides sufficient documentation of his or her custodial rights or other authority to object.

(2) An order from a court of competent jurisdiction providing for joint legal custody or requiring the permission of both parents or the court for important decisions will be interpreted as requiring the permission of both parents or the court as appropriate.

(3) The Department will consider a court of competent jurisdiction to be a U.S. state or federal court or a foreign court located in the minor's home state or place of habitual residence.

(4) The Department may require that conflicts regarding custody orders, whether domestic or foreign, be settled by the appropriate court before a passport may be issued.

(5) Access by parents and legal guardians to passport records for minors. Either parent or any legal guardian of a minor may upon written request obtain information regarding the application for and issuance of a passport to a minor, unless the requesting parent's parental rights have been terminated by an order of a court of competent jurisdiction, a copy of which has been provided to the Department. The Department may deny such information to a parent or legal guardian if it determines that the minor objects to disclosure and the minor is 16 years of age or older or if the Department determines that the minor is of sufficient age and maturity to invoke his or her own privacy rights.

HISTORY:

[33 FR 12043, Aug. 24, 1968, as amended at SD-165, 46 FR 2343, Jan. 9, 1981; 49 FR 16989, Apr. 23, 1984; 72 FR 64930, 64931, Nov. 19, 2007; 88 FR 41024, 41025, June 23, 2023; 89 FR 60566, 60568, July 26, 2024]

§ 51.29 Attorney or other third-party assistance.

A person seeking passport services may be physically accompanied by an attorney, interpreter, or other third party of their own choice at their own expense in accordance with 22 CFR 50.52.

HISTORY:

[89 FR 41308, 41311, May 13, 2024]

Subpart C

Evidence of U.S. Citizenship or Nationality

§ 51.40 Burden of proof.

The applicant has the burden of proving that he or she is a U.S. citizen or non-citizen national.

HISTORY:

[31 FR 13540, Oct. 20, 1966, as amended at 49 FR 16989, Apr. 23, 1984; 66 FR 29904, 29907, June 4, 2001; 72 FR 64930, 64931, Nov. 19, 2007]

§ 51.41 Documentary evidence.

The applicant must provide documentary evidence that he or she is a U.S. citizen or non-citizen national.

HISTORY:

[31 FR 13540, Oct. 20, 1966; 66 FR 29904, 29907, June 4, 2001; 72 FR 64930, 64931, Nov. 19, 2007]

§ 51.42 Persons born in the United States applying for a passport for the first time.

(a) Primary evidence of birth in the United States. A person born in the United States generally must submit a birth certificate. The birth certificate must show the full name of the applicant, the applicant's place and date of birth, the full name of the parent(s), and must be signed by the official custodian of birth records, bear the seal of the issuing office, and show a filing date within one year of the date of birth.

(b) Secondary evidence of birth in the United States. If the applicant cannot submit a birth certificate that meets the requirement of paragraph (a) of this section, he or she must submit secondary evidence sufficient to establish to the satisfaction of the Department that he or she was born in the United States. Secondary evidence includes but is not limited to hospital birth certificates, baptismal certificates, medical and school records, certificates of circumcision, other documentary evidence created shortly after birth but generally not more than 5 years after birth, and/or affidavits of persons having personal knowledge of the facts of the birth.

HISTORY:

[72 FR 64930, 64931, Nov. 19, 2007]

§ 51.43 Persons born outside the United States applying for a passport for the first time.

(a) General. A person born outside the United States must submit documentary evidence that he or she meets all the statutory requirements for acquisition of U.S. citizenship or non-citizen nationality under the provision of law or treaty under which the person is claiming U.S. citizenship or non-citizen nationality.

(b) Documentary Evidence. (1) Types of documentary evidence of citizenship for a person born outside the United States include:

(i) A certificate of naturalization.

(ii) A certificate of citizenship.

(iii) A Consular Report of Birth Abroad.

(2) An applicant without one of these documents must produce supporting documents as required by the Department, showing acquisition of U.S. citizenship under the relevant provisions of law.

HISTORY:

[38 FR 4667, Feb. 20, 1973, as amended at 49 FR 16989, Apr. 23, 1984; 72 FR 64930, 64931, Nov. 19, 2007.

§ 51.44 Proof of resumption or retention of U.S. citizenship.

An applicant who claims to have resumed or retained U.S. citizenship must submit with the application a certificate of naturalization or evidence that he or she took the steps necessary to resume or retain U.S. citizenship in accordance with the applicable provision of law.

HISTORY:

[31 FR 13540, Oct. 20, 1966, as amended at 49 FR 16989, Apr. 23, 1984; 72 FR 64930, 64931, Nov. 19, 2007]

§ 51.45 Department discretion to require evidence of U.S. citizenship or non-citizen nationality.

The Department may require an applicant to provide any evidence that it deems necessary to establish that he or she is a U.S. citizen or non-citizen national, including evidence in addition to the evidence specified in 22 CFR 51.42 through 51.44.

HISTORY:

[31 FR 13540, Oct. 20, 1966; 72 FR 64930, 64931, Nov. 19, 2007]

§ 51.46 Return or retention of evidence of U.S. citizenship or non-citizen nationality.

The Department will generally return to the applicant evidence submitted in connection with an application for a passport. The Department may, however, retain evidence when it deems it necessary for anti-fraud or law enforcement or other similar purposes.

HISTORY:

[31 FR 13540, Oct. 20, 1966; 72 FR 64930, 64931, Nov. 19, 2007]

Subpart D

Fees

§ 51.50 Form of payment.

Passport fees must be paid in U.S. currency or in other forms of payments permitted by the Department.

HISTORY:

[31 FR 13540, Oct. 20, 1966; 72 FR 64930, 64931, Nov. 19, 2007]

§ 51.51 Passport fees.

The Department collects the following passport fees in the amounts prescribed in the Schedule of Fees for Consular Services (22 CFR 22.1):

(a) An application fee, which must be paid at the time of application, except as provided in § 51.52, and is not refundable, except as provided in § 51.53.

(b) An execution fee, except as provided in § 51.52, when the applicant is required to execute the application in person before a person authorized to administer oaths for passport purposes. The execution fee is collected at the time of application and is not refundable (see § 51.55). When execution services are provided by an official of a State or local government or of the United States Postal Service (USPS), the State or local government or USPS may retain the fee if authorized to do so by the Department.

(c) A fee for expedited passport processing, if applicable (see § 51.56).

(d) A surcharge in the amount of twenty-two dollars ($ 22) on the filing of each application for a passport book, in the amount of twenty-two dollars ($ 22) on the filing of each application for a passport card for an applicant age 16 or over, and in the amount of fifteen dollars ($ 15) on the filing of each application for a passport card for an applicant under age 16, in order to cover the costs of meeting the increased demand for passports as a result of actions taken to comply with section 7209(b) of the Intelligence Reform and Terrorism Prevention Act of 2004, Public Law 108-458 (8 U.S.C. 1185 note). The surcharge will be recovered by the Department of State from within the passport application fee reflected in the Schedule of Fees for Consular Services.

(e) An "enhanced border security" surcharge on the filing of each application for a regular passport in an amount set administratively by the Department and published in the Schedule of Fees for Consular Services.

(f) Any other fee that the Department is authorized or required by law to charge for passport services.

(g) The foregoing fees are applicable regardless of the validity period of the passport.

HISTORY:

[31 FR 13540, Oct. 20, 1966; 72 FR 64930, 64931, Nov. 19, 2007, as corrected at 73 FR 5435, Jan. 30, 2008; 75 FR 36522, 36535, June 28, 2010, as confirmed at 77 FR 5177, 5178, Feb. 2, 2012]

§ 51.52 Exemption from payment of passport fees.

(a) A person who is exempt from the payment of passport fees under this section may obtain a passport book only for no charge. A passport card will not be issued for no charge to the individuals exempt from the payment of passport fees under this section.

(b) The following persons are exempt from payment of passport fees except for the passport execution fee, unless their applications are executed before a federal official, in which case they are also exempt from payment of the passport execution fee:

(1) An officer or employee of the United States traveling on official business and the members of his or her immediate family. The applicant must submit evidence of the official purpose of the travel and, if applicable, authorization for the members of his or her immediate family to accompany or reside with him or her abroad.

(2) An American seaman who requires a passport in connection with his or her duties aboard a United States flag vessel.

(3) A widow, widower, child, parent, brother or sister of a deceased member of the United States Armed Forces proceeding abroad to visit the grave of such service member or to attend a funeral or memorial service for such member.

(4) Other persons whom the Department determines should be exempt from payment of passport fees for compelling circumstances, pursuant to guidance issued by the Department; or

(5) Other categories of persons exempted by law.

HISTORY:

[31 FR 13540, Oct. 20, 1966, as amended at 49 FR 16989, Apr. 23, 1984; 72 FR 64930, 64931, Nov. 19, 2007; 72 FR 74169, 74173, Dec. 31, 2007]

§ 51.53 Refunds.

(a) The Department will refund the passport application fee and the security surcharge to any person exempt from payment of passport fees under 22 CFR 51.52 from whom the fee was erroneously collected.

(b) The Department will refund an expedited passport processing fee if the Department fails to provide expedited passport processing as provided in 22 CFR 51.56.

(c) For procedures on refunds of $ 5.00 or less, see 22 CFR 22.6(b).

HISTORY:

[31 FR 13540, Oct. 20, 1966, as amended at 49 FR 16989, Apr. 23, 1984; 72 FR 64930, 64931, Nov. 19, 2007]

§ 51.54 Replacement passports without payment of applicable fees.

A passport issuing office may issue a replacement passport for the following reasons without payment of applicable fees:

(a) To correct an error or rectify a mistake of the Department;

(b) When the bearer has changed his or her name or other personal identifier listed on the data page of the passport, and applies for a replacement passport within one year of the date of the passport's original issuance.

(c) When the bearer of an emergency full fee passport issued for a limited validity period applies for a full validity passport within one year of the date of the passport's original issuance.

(d) When a passport is retained by U.S. law enforcement or judiciary for evidentiary purposes and the bearer is still eligible to have a passport.

(e) When a passport is issued to replace a passport with a failed electronic chip for the balance of the original validity period.

HISTORY:

[31 FR 13540, Oct. 20, 1966, as amended at 49 FR 16989, Apr. 23, 1984; 72 FR 64930, 64931, Nov. 19, 2007]

§ 51.55 Execution fee not refundable.

The fee for the execution of a passport application is not refundable.

HISTORY:

[31 FR 13540, Oct. 20, 1966; 72 FR 64930, 64931, Nov. 19, 2007]

§ 51.56 Expedited passport processing.

(a) Within the United States, an applicant for passport service (including issuance or replacement of a passport) may request expedited processing. The Department may decline the request.

(b) Expedited passport processing shall mean completing processing within the number of business days published on the Department's Web site, http://www.travel.state.gov, commencing when the application reaches a Passport Agency or, if the application is already with a Passport Agency, commencing when the request for expedited processing is approved. The processing will be considered completed when the passport is ready to be picked up by the applicant or is mailed to the applicant, or a letter of passport denial is transmitted to the applicant.

(c) A fee is charged for expedited passport processing (see 22 CFR 51.51(c)). The fee does not cover any costs of mailing above the normal level of service regularly provided by the Department. The cost of expedited mailing must be paid by the applicant.

(d) The Department will not charge the fee for expedited passport processing if the Department's error, mistake or delay caused the need for expedited processing.

HISTORY:

[72 FR 64930, 64931, Nov. 19, 2007; 74 FR 47726, 47727, Sept. 17, 2009; 80 FR 72591, 72592, Nov. 20, 2015]

Subpart E

Denial, Revocation, and Restriction of Passports and Cancellation of Consular Reports of Birth Abroad

§ 51.60 Denial and restriction of passports.

(a) The Department may not issue a passport, except a passport for direct return to the United States, in any case in which the Department determines or is informed by competent authority that:

(1) The applicant is in default on a loan received from the United States under 22 U.S.C. 2671(b)(2)(B) for the repatriation of the applicant and, where applicable, the applicant's spouse, minor child(ren), and/or other immediate family members, from a foreign country (see 22 U.S.C. 2671(d)); or

(2) The applicant has been certified by the Secretary of Health and Human Services as notified by a state agency under 42 U.S.C. 652(k) to be in arrears of child support in an amount determined by statute.

(3) [Reserved]

(4) The applicant is a covered sex offender as defined in 22 U.S.C. 212b(c)(1), unless the passport, no matter the type, contains the conspicuous identifier placed by the Department as required by 22 U.S.C. 212b.

(b) The Department may refuse to issue a passport in any case in which the Department determines or is informed by competent authority that:

(1) The applicant is the subject of an outstanding Federal warrant of arrest for a felony, including a warrant issued under the Federal Fugitive Felon Act (18 U.S.C. 1073); or

(2) The applicant is subject to a criminal court order, condition of probation, or condition of parole, any of which forbids departure from the United States and the violation of which could result in the issuance of a Federal warrant of arrest, including a warrant issued under the Federal Fugitive Felon Act; or

(3) The applicant is subject to a U.S. court order committing him or her to a mental institution; or

(4) The applicant has been legally declared incompetent by a court of competent jurisdiction in the United States; or

(5) The applicant is the subject of a request for extradition or provisional request for extradition which has been presented to the government of a foreign country; or

(6) The applicant is the subject of a subpoena received from the United States pursuant to 28 U.S.C. 1783, in a matter involving Federal prosecution for, or grand jury investigation of, a felony; or

(7) The applicant is a minor and the passport may be denied under 22 CFR 51.28; or

(8) The applicant is subject to an order of restraint or apprehension issued by an appropriate officer of the United States Armed Forces pursuant to chapter 47 of title 10 of the United States Code; or

(9) The applicant is the subject of an outstanding state or local warrant of arrest for a felony; or

(10) The applicant is the subject of a request for extradition or provisional arrest submitted to the United States by a foreign country.

(c) The Department may refuse to issue a passport in any case in which:

(1) The applicant has not repaid a loan received from the United States under 22 U.S.C. 2670(j) for emergency medical attention, dietary supplements, and other emergency assistance, including, if applicable, assistance provided to his or her child(ren), spouse, and/or other immediate family members in a foreign country; or

(2) The applicant has not repaid a loan received from the United States under 22 U.S.C. 2671(b)(2)(B) or 22 U.S.C. 2671(b)(2)(A) for the repatriation or evacuation of the applicant and, if applicable, the applicant's child(ren), spouse, and/or other immediate family members from a foreign country to the United States; or

(3) The applicant has previously been denied a passport under this section or 22 CFR 51.61, or the Department has revoked the applicant's passport or issued a limited passport for direct return to the United States under 22 CFR 51.62, and the applicant has not shown that there has been a change in circumstances since the denial, revocation or issuance of a limited passport that warrants issuance of a passport; or

(4) The Secretary determines that the applicant's activities abroad are causing or are likely to cause serious damage to the national security or the foreign policy of the United States.

(d) The Department may refuse to issue a passport in a case in which the Department is informed by an appropriate foreign government authority or international organization that the applicant is the subject of a warrant of arrest for a felony.

(e) The Department may refuse to issue a passport, except a passport for direct return to the United States, in any case in which the Department determines or is informed by a competent authority that the applicant is a minor who has been abducted, wrongfully removed or retained in violation of a court order or decree and return to his or her home state or habitual residence is necessary to permit a court of competent jurisdiction to determine custody matters.

(f) The Department may refuse to issue a passport to an applicant who fails to provide his or her Social Security account number on his or her passport application or who willfully, intentionally, negligently, or recklessly includes an incorrect or invalid Social Security account number.

(g) The Department shall not issue a passport card to an applicant who is a covered sex offender as defined in 22 U.S.C. 212b(c)(1).

(h) The Department may not issue a passport, except a limited validity passport for direct return to the United States or in instances where the Department finds that emergency circumstances or humanitarian reasons exist, in any case in which:

(1) The Department is notified by the Attorney General that, during the covered period as defined by 22 U.S.C. 212a:

(i) The applicant was convicted of a violation of 18 U.S.C. 2423, and

(ii) The individual used a passport or passport card or otherwise crossed an international border in committing the underlying offense.

(2) The applicant is certified by the Secretary of the Treasury as having a seriously delinquent tax debt as described in 26 U.S.C. 7345.

HISTORY:

[31 FR 14522, Nov. 11, 1966; 72 FR 64930, 64931, Nov. 19, 2007; 81 FR 60608, 60609, Sept. 2, 2016; 81 FR 66184, 66185, Sept. 27, 2016; 83 FR 21872, 21874, May 11, 2018; suspended in part at 83 FR 22848, 22849, May 17, 2018; 84 FR 67184, 67185, Dec. 9, 2019]

§ 51.61 Denial of passports to certain convicted drug traffickers.

(a) A passport may not be issued in any case in which the Department determines or is informed by competent authority that the applicant is subject to imprisonment or supervised release as the result of a felony conviction for a Federal or state drug offense, if the individual used a U.S. passport or otherwise crossed an international border in committing the offense, including a felony conviction arising under:

(1) The Controlled Substances Act (21 U.S.C. 801 et seq.) or the Controlled Substances Import and Export Act (21 U.S.C. 951 et seq.); or

(2) Any Federal law involving controlled substances as defined in section 802 of the Controlled Substances Act (21 U.S.C. 801 et seq.); or

(3) The Bank Secrecy Act (31 U.S.C. 5311 et seq.) or the Money Laundering Act (18 U.S.C. 1956 et seq.) if the Department is in receipt of information that supports the determination that the violation involved is related to illicit production of or trafficking in a controlled substance; or

(4) Any state law involving the manufacture, distribution, or possession of a controlled substance.

(b) A passport may be refused in any case in which the Department determines or is informed by competent authority that the applicant is subject to imprisonment or supervised release as the result of a misdemeanor conviction of a Federal or state drug offense if the individual used a U.S. passport or otherwise crossed an international border in committing the offense, other than a first conviction for possession of a controlled substance, including a misdemeanor conviction arising under:

(1) The Federal statutes described in § 51.61(a); or

(2) Any State law involving the manufacture, distribution, or possession of a controlled substance.

(c) Notwithstanding paragraph (a) of this section, the Department may issue a passport when the competent authority confirms, or the Department otherwise finds, that emergency circumstances or humanitarian reasons exist.

HISTORY:

[56 FR 55816, Oct. 30, 1991; 63 FR 5098, 5103, Jan. 30, 1998; 65 FR 14211, 14212, Mar. 16, 2000; 67 FR 34831, 34838, May 16, 2002; 71 FR 46396, 46398, Aug. 14, 2006; 72 FR 45636, 45637, Aug. 15, 2007; 72 FR 64930, 64931, Nov. 19, 2007]

§ 51.62 Revocation or limitation of passports and cancellation of Consular Reports of Birth Abroad.

(a) The Department may revoke or limit a passport when:

(1) The bearer of the passport may be denied a passport under 22 CFR 51.60 or 51.61 or any other applicable provision contained in this part;

(2) The passport was illegally, fraudulently or erroneously obtained from the Department; or was created through illegality or fraud practiced upon the Department; or

(3) The passport has been fraudulently altered or misused.

(b) The Department may revoke a passport when the Department has determined that the bearer of the passport is not a U.S. national, or the Department is on notice that the bearer's certificate of citizenship or certificate of naturalization has been cancelled.

(c) The Department may cancel a Consular Report of Birth Abroad when:

(1) The Consular Report of Birth Abroad was illegally, fraudulently or erroneously obtained from the Department, or was created through illegality or fraud practiced upon the Department;

(2) The Consular Report of Birth Abroad has been fraudulently altered or misused; or

(3) The Department has determined that the bearer of the Consular Report of Birth Abroad is not a U.S. national, or the Department is on notice that the bearer's certificate of citizenship has been cancelled.

(d) The Department shall revoke a U.S. passport in any case in which the Department is notified by the Attorney General, that during the covered period as defined by 22 U.S.C. 212a:

(1) The applicant was convicted of a violation of 18 U.S.C. 2423, and

(2) The individual used a passport or otherwise crossed an international border in committing the underlying offense.

(3) Notwithstanding paragraphs (d)(1) and (2) of this section, the Department may issue a limited validity passport for direct return to the United States.

HISTORY:

[33 FR 12043, Aug. 24, 1968, as amended at 37 FR 6053, Mar. 24, 1972; 49 FR 16989, Apr. 23, 1984; redesignated at 63 FR 5098, 5103, Jan. 30, 1998; 72 FR 64930, 64931, Nov. 19, 2007; 83 FR 21872, 21874, May 11, 2018; suspended at 83 FR 22848, 22849, May 17, 2018]

§ 51.63 Passports invalid for travel into or through restricted areas; prohibition on passports valid only for travel to Israel.

(a) The Secretary may restrict the use of a passport for travel to or use in a country or area which the Secretary has determined is:

(1) A country with which the United States is at war; or

(2) A country or area where armed hostilities are in progress; or

(3) A country or area in which there is imminent danger to the public health or physical safety of United States travelers.

(b) Any determination made and restriction imposed under paragraph (a) of this section, or any extension or revocation of the restriction, shall be published in the Federal Register .

(c) A passport may not be designated as valid only for travel to Israel.

HISTORY:

[33 FR 12043, Aug. 24, 1968, as amended at 52 FR 29515, Aug. 10, 1987; 59 FR 48999, Sept. 26, 1994; redesignated and amended at 63 FR 5098, 5103, Jan. 30, 1998; 65 FR 14211, 14212, Mar. 16, 2000; 72 FR 64930, 64931, Nov. 19, 2007]

§ 51.64 Special validation of passports for travel to restricted areas.

(a) A U.S. national may apply to the Department for a special validation of his or passport to permit its use for travel to, or use in, a restricted country or area. The application must be accompanied by evidence that the applicant falls within one of the categories in paragraph (c) of this section.

(b) The Department may grant a special validation if it determines that the validation is in the national interest of the United States.

(c) A special validation may be determined to be in the national interest if:

(1) The applicant is a professional reporter or journalist, the purpose of whose trip is to obtain, and make available to the public, information about the restricted area; or

(2) The applicant is a representative of the International Committee of the Red Cross or the American Red Cross traveling pursuant to an officially-sponsored Red Cross mission; or

(3) The applicant's trip is justified by compelling humanitarian considerations; or

(4) The applicant's request is otherwise in the national interest.

HISTORY:

[31 FR 13540, Oct. 20, 1966; redesignated at 63 FR 5098, 5103, Jan. 30, 1998; 70 FR 53922, 53924, Sept. 13, 2005; 70 FR 61553, 61555, Oct. 25, 2005; 72 FR 64930, 64931, Nov. 19, 2007]

§ 51.65 Notification of denial, revocation or cancellation of passports and Consular Reports of Birth Abroad.

(a) The Department will send notice in writing to any person whose application for issuance of a passport or Consular Report of Birth Abroad has been denied, whose passport has been revoked, or whose Consular Report of Birth Abroad has been cancelled. The notification will set forth the specific reasons for the denial, revocation or cancellation and, if applicable, the procedures for review available under 22 CFR 51.70 through 51.74.

(b) An application for a passport or Consular Report of Birth Abroad will be denied if an applicant fails to meet his or her burden of proof under the applicable regulations or otherwise does not provide documentation sufficient to establish entitlement to a passport or a Consular Report of Birth Abroad, or does not provide additional information as requested by the Department within the time provided in the notification by the Department that additional information is required. Thereafter, if an applicant wishes the Department to adjudicate his or her claim of entitlement to a passport or Consular Report of Birth Abroad, he or she must submit a new application, supporting documents, and photograph, along with all applicable fees.

(c) The Department may, in its sole discretion, administratively re-open a previously filed passport or Consular Report of Birth Abroad application in order to issue a passport or Consular Report of Birth Abroad.

HISTORY:

[31 FR 13540, Oct. 20, 1966; redesignated at 63 FR 5098, 5103, Jan. 30, 1998; 72 FR 64930, 64931, Nov. 19, 2007; 83 FR 21872, 21874, May 11, 2018; suspended at 83 FR 22848, 22849, May 17, 2018]

§ 51.66 Surrender of passport and/or Consular Report of Birth Abroad.

The bearer of a passport that is revoked or of a Consular Report of Birth Abroad that is cancelled must surrender it to the Department or its authorized representative upon demand.

HISTORY:

[59 FR 49000, Sept. 26, 1994; redesignated and amended at 63 FR 5098, 5103, Jan. 30, 1998; 70 FR 53922, 53925, Sept. 13, 2005; 72 FR 45888, 45890, Aug. 16, 2007; 72 FR 64930, 64931, Nov. 19, 2007; 83 FR 21872, 21875, May 11, 2018; suspended at 83 FR 22848, 22849, May 17, 2018]

Subpart F

Procedures for Review of Certain Denials and Revocations

§ 51.70 Request for hearing to review certain denials and revocations.

(a) A person whose passport has been denied or revoked under 22 CFR 51.60(b)(1) through (10), 51.60(c), 51.60(d), 51.61(b), 51.62(a)(1), or 51.62(a)(2), or whose Consular Report of Birth Abroad is cancelled under § 51.62(c)(1) or § 51.62(c)(2), may request a hearing to review the basis for the denial, revocation, or cancellation, provided that the Department receives such a request, in writing, from such person or his or her attorney within 60 days of his or her receipt of the notice of the denial, revocation, or cancellation. Failure to timely request a hearing means the denial, revocation, or cancellation is the Department's final action.

(b) The provisions of §§ 51.70 through 51.74 do not apply to any action of the Department denying, restricting, revoking, cancelling or invalidating a passport or Consular Report of Birth Abroad, or in any other way adversely affecting the ability of a person to receive or use a passport or Consular Report of Birth Abroad, for reasons not set forth in § 51.70(a), including, as applicable, those listed at:

(1) Section 51.60(a) (instances where the Department may not issue a passport, except for direct return to the United States);

(2) Section 51.60(f) (failure to provide a social security number, or purposefully providing an incorrect number);

(3) Section 51.60(g) (denial of passport cards to certain convicted sex offenders);

(4) Section 51.61(a) (denial of passports to certain convicted drug traffickers);

(5) Section 51.62(b) (revocation of passports for non-U.S. nationals or where a certificate of citizenship or naturalization has been cancelled);

(6) Section 51.62(c)(3) (cancellation of a Consular Report of Birth Abroad upon the Department's determination that the bearer is not a U.S. national or where a certificate of citizenship has been cancelled);

(7) Section 51.62(d) (revocation of passports issued to certain convicted sex offenders);

(8) Section 51.64 (specially validated passports);

(9) Any other provision not listed at § 51.70(a).

(c) If a timely request for a hearing is made by a person seeking a hearing in accordance with these regulations, the Department will make reasonable efforts to hold the hearing within 90 days of the date the Department receives the request.

(d) Within a reasonable period of time prior to the hearing, the Department will give the person requesting the hearing written notice of the date, time and place of the hearing and copies of the evidence relied on in denying, revoking, or cancelling the passport or Consular Report of Birth Abroad.

(e) The person requesting the hearing may obtain one continuance, not to exceed an additional 90 days, upon written request. The request for a continuance must be received by the Department as soon as practicable and in no case less than five business days prior to the scheduled hearing date. Any further continuances are within the sole discretion of the Department.

HISTORY:

[54 FR 8531, March 1, 1989; 62 FR 62694, 62695, Nov. 25, 1997, as confirmed at 63 FR 44777, Aug. 21, 1998; 71 FR 58496, Oct. 4, 2006; 72 FR 64930, 64931, Nov. 19, 2007; 83 FR 21872, 21874, May 11, 2018; suspended at 83 FR 22848, 22849, May 17, 2018]

§ 51.71 The hearing.

(a) The Department will name a hearing officer, who will generally be a Department employee from the Bureau of Consular Affairs. The hearing officer will make only preliminary findings of fact and submit recommendations based on the record of the hearing, as defined in 22 CFR 51.72, to the Deputy Assistant Secretary for Passport Services, or his or her designee, in the Bureau of Consular Affairs.

(b) The hearing shall take place in Washington, DC or, if the person requesting the hearing is overseas, at the appropriate U.S. diplomatic or consular post. The person requesting the hearing must appear in person or with or through his or her attorney. Failure to appear at the scheduled hearing will constitute an abandonment of the request for a hearing, and the Department's revocation, cancellation or denial will be considered the Department's final action.

(c) Any attorney appearing at a hearing must be admitted to practice in any state of the United States, the District of Columbia, or any territory or possession of the United States, or be admitted to practice before the courts of the country in which the hearing is to be held.

(d) There is no right to subpoena witnesses or to conduct discovery. However, the person requesting the hearing may testify in person, offer evidence in his or her own behalf, present witnesses, and make arguments at the hearing. The person requesting the hearing is responsible for all costs associated with the presentation of his or her case, including the cost of interpreters, who must be certified in accordance with standards established for federal courts under 28 U.S.C. 1827. The Department may present witnesses, offer evidence, and make arguments in its behalf. The Department is responsible for all costs associated with the presentation of its case.

(e) The hearing is informal and permissive. As such, the provisions of 5 U.S.C. 554 et seq. do not apply to the hearing. Formal rules of evidence also do not apply; however, the hearing officer may impose reasonable restrictions on relevancy, materiality, and competency of evidence presented. Testimony will be under oath or by affirmation under penalty of perjury. The hearing officer may not consider any information that is not also made available to the person requesting the hearing, the Department, and made a part of the record of the proceeding.

(f) If any witness is unable to appear, the hearing officer may, in his or her discretion, accept an affidavit or sworn deposition testimony of the witness, the cost for which will be the responsibility of the requesting party, subject to such limits as the hearing officer deems appropriate.

(g) The person requesting the hearing and the Department of State may submit written briefs or argument prior to the hearing, but it is not required. The hearing officer will specify the date and schedule for the parties to submit written briefs, should they choose to do so.

(h) The purpose of the hearing is to provide the person requesting the hearing an opportunity to challenge the basis for the Department's decision to deny or revoke the passport, or cancel the Consular Report of Birth Abroad. The burden of production is on the Department, and the Department shall provide the evidence it relied upon in revoking or denying the passport, or cancelling the Consular Report of Birth Abroad, prior to the hearing. The burden of persuasion is on the person requesting the hearing, to prove by a preponderance of the evidence that the Department improperly revoked the passport or denied the passport application, or cancelled the Consular Report of Birth Abroad, based on the facts and law in effect at the time such action was taken.

HISTORY:

[54 FR 8532, March 1, 1989; 72 FR 64930, 64931, Nov. 19, 2007; 83 FR 21872, 21875, May 11, 2018; suspended at 83 FR 22848, 22849, May 17, 2018]

SEE NOTE AS TO EXPIRATION OF THIS SECTION.

§ 51.72 Transcript and record of the hearing.

A qualified reporter, provided by the Department, will make a complete verbatim transcript of the hearing. The person requesting the hearing or his or her attorney may review and purchase a copy of the transcript directly from the reporter. The hearing transcript and all the information and documents received by the hearing officer, whether or not deemed relevant, will constitute the record of the hearing. The hearing officer's preliminary findings and recommendations are deliberative, and shall not be considered part of the record unless adopted by the Deputy Assistant Secretary for Passport Services, or his or her designee.

HISTORY:

[54 FR 8532, March 1, 1989; 64 FR 19713, 19714, Apr. 22, 1999; 72 FR 64930, 64931, Nov. 19, 2007; 83 FR 21872, 21876, May 11, 2018; suspended at 83 FR 22848, 22849, May 17, 2018]

§ 51.73 Privacy of hearing.

Only the person requesting the hearing, his or her attorney, an interpreter, the hearing officer, the reporter transcribing the hearing, and employees of the Department concerned with the presentation of the case may be present at the hearing. Witnesses may be present only while actually giving testimony or as otherwise directed by the hearing officer.

HISTORY:

[45 FR 11128, Feb. 20, 1980. Redesignated at 54 FR 8532, March 1, 1989; 72 FR 64930, 64931, Nov. 19, 2007; 83 FR 21872, 21876, May 11, 2018; suspended at 83 FR 22848, 22849, May 17, 2018]

§ 51.74 Final decision.

After reviewing the record of the hearing and the findings of fact and recommendations of the hearing officer, the Deputy Assistant Secretary for Passport Services will decide whether to uphold the denial or revocation of the passport. The Department will promptly notify the person requesting the hearing in writing of the decision. If the decision is to uphold the denial or revocation, the notice will contain the reason(s) for the decision. The decision is final and is not subject to further administrative review.

Dated: May 3, 2018.

HISTORY:

[45 FR 30619, May 9, 1980. Redesignated at 54 FR 8532, Mar. 1, 1989; 72 FR 64930, 64931, Nov. 19, 2007; 83 FR 21872, 21876, May 11, 2018; suspended at 83 FR 22848, 22849, May 17, 2018]

PART 52

[PART 52 WAS REMOVED. SEE 77 FR 65477, 65478, OCT. 29, 2012.]

PART 52 [PART 52 WAS REMOVED. SEE 77 FR 65477, 65478, OCT. 29, 2012.]

[NO TEXT IN ORIGINAL]

§ 52.1 [This section was removed. See 77 FR 65477, 65478, Oct. 29, 2012.]

[NO TEXT IN ORIGINAL]

HISTORY:

[31 FR 13546, Oct. 20, 1966]

AUTHORITY:

(Sec. 4, 63 Stat. 111, as amended; 22 U.S.C. 2658.)

§ 52.2 [This section was removed. See 77 FR 65477, 65478, Oct. 29, 2012.]

[NO TEXT IN ORIGINAL]

HISTORY:

[31 FR 13546, Oct. 20, 1966. Redesignated at 51 FR 26247, July 22, 1986]

AUTHORITY:

(Sec. 4, 63 Stat. 111, as amended; 22 U.S.C. 2658.)

§ 52.3 [This section was removed. See 77 FR 65477, 65478, Oct. 29, 2012.]

[NO TEXT IN ORIGINAL]

HISTORY:

[31 FR 13546, Oct. 20, 1966. Redesignated at 51 FR 26247, July 22, 1986]

AUTHORITY:

(Sec. 4, 63 Stat. 111, as amended; 22 U.S.C. 2658.)

PART 53

PASSPORT REQUIREMENT AND EXCEPTIONS

AUTHORITY NOTE APPLICABLE TO ENTIRE PART:

AUTHORITY:

8 U.S.C. 1185; 8 U.S.C. 1185 note (section 7209 of Pub. L. 108-458); E.O. 13323, 69 FR 241 (Dec. 30, 2003).

§ 53.1 Passport requirement; definitions.

(a) It is unlawful for a citizen of the United States, unless excepted under 22 CFR 53.2, to enter or depart, or attempt to enter or depart, the United States, without a valid U.S. passport.

(b) For purposes of this part "United States" means "United States" as defined in section 215(c) of the

Immigration and Nationality Act of 1952, as amended (8 U.S.C. 1185(c)).

HISTORY:

[31 FR 13546, Oct. 20, 1966; 71 FR 68412, 68430, Nov. 24, 2006]

§ 53.2 Exceptions.

(a) U.S. citizens, as defined in § 41.0 of this chapter, are not required to bear U.S. passports when traveling directly between parts of the United States as defined in § 51.1 of this chapter.

(b) A U.S. citizen is not required to bear a valid U.S. passport to enter or depart the United States:

(1) When traveling as a member of the Armed Forces of the United States on active duty and when he or she is in the uniform of, or bears documents identifying him or her as a member of, such Armed Forces, when under official orders or permit of such Armed Forces, and when carrying a military identification card; or

(2) When traveling entirely within the Western Hemisphere on a cruise ship, and when the U.S. citizen boards the cruise ship at a port or place within the United States and returns on the return voyage of the same cruise ship to the same United States port or place from where he or she originally departed. That U.S. citizen may present a government-issued photo identification document in combination with either an original or a copy of his or her birth certificate, a Consular Report of Birth Abroad issued by the Department, or a Certificate of Naturalization issued by U.S. Citizenship and Immigration Services before entering the United States; if the U.S. citizen is under the age of 16, he or she may present either an original or a copy of his or her birth certificate, a Consular Report of Birth Abroad issued by the Department, or a Certificate of Naturalization issued by U.S. Citizenship and Immigration Services; or

(3) When traveling as a U.S. citizen seaman, carrying an unexpired Merchant Marine Document (MMD) in conjunction with maritime business. The MMD is not sufficient to establish citizenship for purposes of issuance of a United States passport under part 51 of this chapter; or

(4) Trusted Traveler Programs.

(i) NEXUS Program. When traveling as a participant in the NEXUS program, he or she may present a valid NEXUS program card when using a NEXUS Air kiosk or when entering the United States from contiguous territory or adjacent islands at a land or sea port-of-entry. A U.S. citizen who enters the United States by pleasure vessel from Canada under the remote inspection system may also present a NEXUS program card;

(ii) FAST Program. A U.S. citizen who is traveling as a participant in the FAST program may present a valid FAST card when entering the United States from contiguous territory or adjacent islands at a land or sea port-of-entry;

(iii) SENTRI Program. A U.S. citizen who is traveling as a participant in the SENTRI program may present a valid SENTRI card when entering the United States from contiguous territory or adjacent islands at a land or sea port-of-entry; The NEXUS, FAST, and SENTRI cards are not sufficient to establish citizenship for purposes of issuance of a U.S. passport under part 51 of this chapter; or

(5) When arriving at land ports of entry and sea ports of entry from contiguous territory or adjacent islands, Native American holders of American Indian Cards (Form I-872) issued by U.S. Citizenship and Immigration Services (USCIS) may present those cards; or

(6) When arriving at land or sea ports of entry from contiguous territory or adjacent islands, U.S. citizen holders of a tribal document issued by a United States qualifying tribal entity or group of United States qualifying tribal entities as provided in 8 CFR 235.1(e) may present that document. Tribal documents are not sufficient to establish citizenship for purposes of issuance of a United States passport under part 51 of this chapter; or

(7) When bearing documents or combinations of documents the Secretary of Homeland Security has determined under Section 7209(b) of Public Law 108-458 (8 U.S.C. 1185 note) are sufficient to denote identity and citizenship. Such documents are not sufficient to establish citizenship for purposes of issuance of a U.S. passport under part 51 of this chapter; or

(8) When the U.S. citizen is employed directly or indirectly on the construction, operation, or maintenance of works undertaken in accordance with the treaty concluded on February 3, 1944, between the United States and Mexico regarding the functions of the International Boundary and Water Commission (IBWC), TS 994, 9 Bevans 1166, 59 Stat. 1219, or other related agreements, provided that the U.S. citizen bears an official identification card issued by the IBWC and is traveling in connection with such employment; or

(9) When the Department of State waives, pursuant to EO 13323 of December 30, 2003, Section 2, the requirement with respect to the U.S. citizen because there is an unforeseen emergency; or

(10) When the Department of State waives, pursuant to EO 13323 of December 30, 2003, Sec 2, the requirement with respect to the U.S. citizen for humanitarian or national interest reasons; or

(11) When the U.S. citizen is a child under the age of 19 arriving from contiguous territory in the following circumstances:

(i) Children Under Age 16. A United States citizen who is under the age of 16 is permitted to present either an original or a copy of his or her birth certificate, a Consular Report of Birth Abroad, or a Certificate of Naturalization issued by U.S. Citizenship and Immigration Services when entering the United States from contiguous territory at land or sea ports-of-entry; or

(ii) Groups of Children Under Age 19. A U.S. citizen who is under age 19 and who is traveling with a public or private school group, religious group, social or cultural organization, or team associated with a youth sport organization may present either an original or a copy of his or her birth certificate, a Consular Report of

Birth Abroad, or a Certificate of Naturalization issued by U.S. Citizenship and Immigration Services when arriving in the United States from contiguous territory at all land or sea ports of entry, when the group, organization or team is under the supervision of an adult affiliated with the organization and when the child has parental or legal guardian consent to travel. For purposes of this paragraph, an adult is considered to be a person who is age 19 or older.

The following requirements will apply:

(A) The group, organization, or team must provide to CBP upon crossing the border on organizational letterhead:

(1) The name of the group, organization or team, and the name of the supervising adult;

(2) A list of the children on the trip; and

(3) For each child, the primary address, primary phone number, date of birth, place of birth, and the name of at least one parent or legal guardian.

(B) The adult leading the group, organization, or team must demonstrate parental or legal guardian consent by certifying in the writing submitted in paragraph (b)(11)(ii)(A) of this section that he or she has obtained for each child the consent of at least one parent or legal guardian.

(C) The procedure described in this paragraph is limited to members of the group, organization, or team who are under age 19. Other members of the group, organization, or team must comply with other applicable document and/or inspection requirements found in 8 CFR parts 211, 212, or 235.

HISTORY:

[31 FR 13546, Oct. 20, 1966, as amended at 37 FR 11459, June 8, 1972; 51 FR 26247, July 22, 1986; 71 FR 68412, 68430, Nov. 24, 2006; 73 FR 18384, 18419, Apr. 3, 2008]

§ 53.3 Attempt of a citizen to enter without a valid passport.

The appropriate officer at the port of entry shall report to the Department of State any citizen of the United States who attempts to enter the United States contrary to the provisions of this part, so that the Department of State may apply the waiver provisions of § 53.2(h) and § 53.2(i) to such citizen, if appropriate.

HISTORY:

[31 FR 13546, Oct. 20, 1966; 71 FR 68412, 68430, Nov. 24, 2006]

§ 53.4 Optional use of a valid passport.

Nothing in this part shall be construed to prevent a citizen from using a valid U.S. passport in a case in which that passport is not required by this part 53, provided such travel is not otherwise prohibited.

HISTORY:

[31 FR 13546, Oct. 20, 1966; 71 FR 68412, 68430, Nov. 24, 2006]

FEDERAL RULES OF CRIMINAL PROCEDURE
(COMPLETE RULES)

HISTORY:

Amended April 24, 2023, eff. Dec. 1, 2023.

TITLE I. APPLICABILITY OF RULES

Rule 1. Scope; Definitions

(a) Scope.

(1) *In General.* These rules govern the procedure in all criminal proceedings in the United States district courts, the United States courts of appeals, and the Supreme Court of the United States.

(2) *State or Local Judicial Officer.* When a rule so states, it applies to a proceeding before a state or local judicial officer.

(3) *Territorial Courts.* These rules also govern the procedure in all criminal proceedings in the following courts:

(A) the district court of Guam;

(B) the district court for the Northern Mariana Islands, except as otherwise provided by law; and

(C) the district court of the Virgin Islands, except that the prosecution of offenses in that court must be by indictment or information as otherwise provided by law.

(4) *Removed Proceedings.* Although these rules govern all proceedings after removal from a state court, state law governs a dismissal by the prosecution.

(5) *Excluded Proceedings.* Proceedings not governed by these rules include:

(A) the extradition and rendition of a fugitive;

(B) a civil property forfeiture for violating a federal statute;

(C) the collection of a fine or penalty;

(D) a proceeding under a statute governing juvenile delinquency to the extent the procedure is inconsistent with the statute, unless Rule 20(d) provides otherwise;

(E) a dispute between seamen under 22 U.S.C. §§ 256–258; and

(F) a proceeding against a witness in a foreign country under 28 U.S.C. § 1784.

(b) Definitions. The following definitions apply to these rules:

(1) *"Attorney for the government"* means:

(A) the Attorney General or an authorized assistant;

(B) a United States attorney or an authorized assistant;

(C) when applicable to cases arising under Guam law, the Guam Attorney General or other person whom Guam law authorizes to act in the matter; and

(D) any other attorney authorized by law to conduct proceedings under these rules as a prosecutor.

(2) *"Court"* means a federal judge performing functions authorized by law.

(3) *"Federal judge"* means:

(A) a justice or judge of the United States as these terms are defined in 28 U.S.C. § 451;

(B) a magistrate judge; and

(C) a judge confirmed by the United States Senate and empowered by statute in any commonwealth, territory, or possession to perform a function to which a particular rule relates.

(4) *"Judge"* means a federal judge or a state or local judicial officer.

(5) *"Magistrate judge"* means a United States magistrate judge as defined in 28 U.S.C. §§ 631–639.

(6) *"Oath"* includes an affirmation.

(7) *"Organization"* is defined in 18 U.S.C. § 18.

(8) *"Petty offense"* is defined in 18 U.S.C. § 19.

(9) *"State"* includes the District of Columbia, and any commonwealth, territory, or possession of the United States.

(10) *"State or local judicial officer"* means:

(A) a state or local officer authorized to act under 18 U.S.C. § 3041; and

(B) a judicial officer empowered by statute in the District of Columbia or in any commonwealth, territory, or possession to perform a function to which a particular rule relates.

(11) *"Telephone"* means any technology for transmitting live electronic voice communication.

(12) *"Victim"* means a "crime victim" as defined in 18 U.S.C. § 3771(e).

(c) Authority of a Justice or Judge of the United States. When these rules authorize a magistrate judge to act, any other federal judge may also act.

HISTORY:

Amended April 24, 1972, eff. Oct. 1, 1972; April 28, 1982, eff. Aug. 1, 1982; April 22, 1993, eff. Dec. 1, 1993; April 26, 2002, eff. Dec. 1, 2002; April 23, 2008, eff. Dec. 1, 2008; April 26, 2011, eff. Dec. 1, 2011.

HISTORY; ANCILLARY LAWS AND DIRECTIVES

Other provisions:

Notes of Advisory Committee. 1. These rules are prescribed under the authority of two acts of Congress, namely: the act of June 29, 1940, ch 445, 18 U.S.C. [former] § 687 [see § 3771] (Proceedings in criminal cases prior to and including verdict; power of Supreme Court to prescribe rules), and the act of November 21, 1941, ch 492, 18 U.S.C. [former] § 689 [see §§ 3771, 3772] (Proceedings to punish for criminal contempt of court; application to sections 687 and 688).

2. The courts of the United States covered by the rules are enumerated in Rule 54(a). In addition to Federal courts in the continental United States they include district courts in Alaska, Hawaii, Puerto Rico and the Virgin Islands. In the Canal Zone only the rules governing proceedings after verdict, finding or plea of guilty are applicable.

3. While the rules apply to proceedings before commissioners when acting as committing magistrates, they do not govern when a commissioner acts as a trial magistrate for the trial of petty offenses committed on Federal reservations. That procedure is governed by rules adopted by order promulgated by the Supreme Court on January 6, 1941 (311 U.S. 733), pursuant to the Act of October 9, 1940, ch 785, secs 1– 5. See 18 U.S.C. [former] §§ 576– 576d [see §§ 3401, 3402] (relating to trial of petty offenses on Federal reservations by United States commissioners).

Notes of Advisory Committee on 1972 amendments. The rule is amended to make clear that the rules are applicable to courts of the United States and, where the rule so provides, to proceedings before United States magistrates and state or local judicial officers.

Primarily these rules are intended to govern proceedings in criminal cases triable in the United States District Court. Special rules have been promulgated, pursuant to the authority set forth in 28 U.S.C. § 636(c), for the trial of "minor offenses" before United States magistrates. (See Rules of Procedure for the Trial of Minor Offenses Before United States Magistrates (January 27, 1971).).

However, there is inevitably some overlap between the two sets of rules. The Rules of Criminal Procedure for the United States District Courts deal with preliminary, supplementary, and special proceedings which will often be conducted before United States magistrates. This is true, for example, with regard to rule 3—The Complaint; rule 4—Arrest Warrant or Summons Upon Complaint; rule 5—Initial Appearance Before the Magistrate; and rule 5.1—Preliminary Examination. It is also true, for example, of supplementary and special proceedings such as rule 40—Commitment to Another District, Removal; rule 41—Search and Seizure; and rule 46—Release from Custody. Other of these rules, where applicable, also apply to proceedings before United States magistrates. See Rules of Procedure for the Trial of Minor Offenses Before United States Magistrates, rule 1—Scope:

These rules govern the procedure and practice for the trial of minor offenses (including petty offenses) before United States magistrates under Title 18, U.S.C. § 3401, and for appeals in such cases to judges of the district courts. To the extent that pretrial and trial procedure and practice are not specifically covered by these rules, the Federal Rules of Criminal Procedure apply as to minor offenses other than petty offenses. All other proceedings in criminal matters, other than petty offenses, before United States magistrates are governed by the Federal Rules of Criminal Procedure.

State and local judicial officers are governed by these rules, but only when the rule specifically so provides. This is the case of rule 3—The Complaint; rule 4—Arrest Warrant or Summons Upon Complaint; and rule 5—Initial Appearance Before the Magistrate. These rules confer authority upon the "magistrate," a term which is defined in new rule 54 as follows:

"Magistrate" includes a United States magistrate as defined in 28 U.S.C. §§ 631– 639, a judge of the United States, another judge or judicial officer specifically empowered by statute in force in any territory or possession, the commonwealth of Puerto Rico, or the District of Columbia, to perform a function to which a particular rule relates, and a state or local judicial officer, authorized by 18 U.S.C. § 3041 to perform the functions prescribed in rules 3, 4, and 5.

Rule 41 provides that a search warrant may be issued by "a judge of a state court of record" and thus confers that authority upon appropriate state judicial officers.

The scope of rules 1 and 54 is discussed in C. Wright, Federal Practice and Procedure: Criminal §§ 21, 871– 874 (1969, Supp. 1971), and 8 and 8A J. Moore, Federal Practice chapters 1 and 54 (2d ed. Cipes 1970, Supp. 1971).

Notes of Advisory Committee on 1982 amendments. The amendment corrects an erroneous cross reference, from Rule 54(c) to Rule 54(a), and replaces the word "defined" with the more appropriate word "provided."

Notes of Advisory Committee on 1993 amendments. The Rule is amended to conform to the Judicial Improvements Act of 1990 [P.L. 101-650, Title III, Section 321] which provides that each United States magistrate appointed under section 631 of title 28, United States Code, shall be known as a United States magistrate judge.

Notes of Advisory Committee on 2002 amendments. Rule 1 is entirely revised and expanded to incorporate Rule 54, which deals with the application of the rules. Consistent with the title of the existing rule, the Committee believed that a statement of the scope of the rules should be placed at the beginning to show readers which proceedings are governed by these rules. The Committee also revised the rule to incorporate the definitions found in Rule 54(c) as a new Rule 1(b).

Rule 1(a) contains language from Rule 54(b). But language in current Rule 54(b)(2)–(4) has been deleted for several reasons: First, Rule 54(b)(2) refers to a venue statute that governs an offense committed on the high seas or somewhere outside the jurisdiction of a particular district; it is unnecessary and has been deleted because once venue has been established, the Rules of Criminal Procedure automatically apply. Second, Rule 54(b)(3) currently deals with peace bonds; that provision is inconsistent with the governing statute and has therefore been deleted. Finally, Rule 54(b)(4) references proceedings conducted before United States Magistrate Judges, a topic now covered in Rule 58.

Rule 1(a)(5) consists of material currently located in Rule 54(b)(5), with the exception of the references to the navigation laws and to fishery offenses. Those provisions were considered obsolete. But if those proceedings were to arise, they would be governed by the Rules of Criminal Procedure.

Rule 1(b) is composed of material currently located in Rule 54(c), with several exceptions. First, the reference to an "Act of Congress" has been deleted from the restyled rules; instead the rules use the self-explanatory term "federal statute." Second, the language concerning demurrers, pleas in abatement, etc., has been deleted as being anachronistic. Third, the definitions of "civil action" and "district court" have been deleted. Fourth, the term "attorney for the government" has been expanded to include reference to those attorneys who may serve as special or independent counsel under applicable federal statutes. The term "attorney for the government" contemplates an attorney of record in the case.

Fifth, the Committee added a definition for the term "court" in Rule 1(b)(2). Although that term originally was almost always synonymous with the term "district judge," the term might be misleading or unduly narrow because it may not cover the many functions performed by magistrate judges. See generally 28 U.S.C. §§ 132, 636. Additionally, the term does not cover circuit judges who may be authorized to hold a district court. See 28 U.S.C. § 291. The proposed definition continues the traditional view that "court" means district judge, but also reflects the current understanding that magistrate judges act as the "court" in many proceedings. Finally, the Committee intends that the term "court" be used principally to describe a judicial officer, except where a rule uses the term in a spatial sense, such as describing proceedings in "open court."

Sixth, the term "Judge of the United States" has been replaced with the term "Federal judge." That term includes Article III judges and magistrate judges and, as noted in Rule 1(b)(3)(C), federal judges other than Article III judges who may be authorized by statute to perform a particular act specified in the Rules of Criminal Procedure. The term does not include local judges in the District of Columbia. Seventh, the definition of "Law" has been deleted as being superfluous and possibly misleading because it suggests that administrative regulations are excluded.

Eighth, the current rules include three definitions of "magistrate judge." The term used in amended Rule 1(b)(5) is limited to United States magistrate judges. In the current rules the term magistrate judge includes not only United States magistrate judges, but also district court judges, court of appeals judges, Supreme Court justices, and where authorized, state and local officers. The Committee believed that the rules should reflect current practice, i.e., the wider and almost exclusive use of United States magistrate judges, especially in preliminary matters. The definition, however, is not intended to restrict the use of other federal judicial officers to perform those functions. Thus, Rule 1(c) has been added to make it clear that where the rules authorize a magistrate judge to act, any other federal judge or justice may act.

Finally, the term "organization" has been added to the list of definitions.

The remainder of the rule has been amended as part of the general restyling of the rules to make them more easily understood. In addition to changes made to improve the clarity, the Committee has changed language to make style and terminology consistent throughout the Criminal Rules. These changes are intended to be stylistic only.

Notes of Advisory Committee on 2008 amendments. *Note to Subdivision (b)(11).* This amendment incorporates the definition of the term "crime victim" found in the Crime Victims' Rights Act, codified as 18 U.S.C. § 3771(e). It provides that "the term 'crime victim' means a person directly and proximately harmed as a result of the commission of a Federal offense or an offense in the District of Columbia."

Upon occasion, disputes may arise over the question whether a particular person is a victim. Although the rule makes no special provision for such cases, the courts have the authority to do any necessary fact finding and make any necessary legal rulings.

Notes of Advisory Committee on 2011 amendments. *Note to Subdivisions (b)(11) and (12).* The added definition clarifies that the term "telephone" includes technologies enabling live voice conversations that have developed since the traditional "land line" telephone. Calls placed by cell phone or from a computer over the internet, for example, would be included. The definition is limited to live communication in order to ensure contemporaneous communication and excludes voice recordings. Live voice communication should include services for the hearing impaired, or other contemporaneous translation, where necessary.

Rule 2. Interpretation

These rules are to be interpreted to provide for the just determination of every criminal proceeding, to secure simplicity in procedure and fairness in administration, and to eliminate unjustifiable expense and delay.

HISTORY:

As amended April 29, 2002, eff. Dec. 1, 2002.

HISTORY; ANCILLARY LAWS AND DIRECTIVES

Other provisions:

Notes of Advisory Committee on Rules. Compare Federal Rules of Civil Procedure, Rule 1 (Scope of Rules), last sentence: "They [the Federal Rules of Civil Procedure] shall be construed to secure the just, speedy, and inexpensive determination of every action."

Notes of Advisory Committee on 2002 amendments. The language of Rule 2 has been amended as part of the general restyling of the Criminal Rules to make them more easily understood and to make style and terminology consistent throughout the rules. These changes are intended to be stylistic. No substantive change is intended.

In particular, Rule 2 has been amended to clarify the purpose of the Rules of Criminal Procedure. The words "are intended" have been changed to read "are to be interpreted." The Committee believed that that was the original intent of the drafters and more accurately reflects the purpose of the rules.

TITLE II. PRELIMINARY PROCEEDINGS

Rule

Rule 3. The Complaint

The complaint is a written statement of the essential facts constituting the offense charged. Except as provided in Rule 4.1, it must be made under oath before a magistrate judge or, if none is reasonably available, before a state or local judicial officer.

HISTORY:

As amended April 24, 1972, eff. Oct. 1, 1972; April 22, 1993, eff. Dec. 1, 1993; April 29, 2002, eff. Dec. 1, 2002; April 26, 2011, eff. Dec. 1, 2011.

HISTORY; ANCILLARY LAWS AND DIRECTIVES

Other provisions:

Notes of Advisory Committee. The rule generally states existing law and practice, 18 U.S.C. [former] § 591 [see § 3041] (Arrest and removal for trial); *United States v Simon* (D.C.Pa. 1916) 248 F. 980; *United States v Maresca* (D.C.N.Y. 1920) 266 F. 713. It eliminates, however, the requirement of conformity to State law as to the form and sufficiency of the complaint. See, also, Rule 57(b).

Notes of Advisory Committee on 1972 amendments. The amendment deletes the reference to "commissioner or other officer empowered to commit persons charged with offenses against the United States" and substitutes therefor "magistrate."

The change is editorial in nature to conform the language of the rule to the recently enacted Federal Magistrates Act. The term "magistrate" is defined in rule 54.

The Rule is amended to conform to the Judicial Improvements Act of 1990 [P.L. 101-650, Title III, Section 321] which provides that each United States magistrate appointed under section 631 of title 28, United States Code, shall be known as a United States magistrate judge.

Notes of Advisory Committee on 2002 amendments. The language of Rule 3 is amended as part of the general restyling of the Criminal Rules to make them more easily understood and to make style and terminology consistent throughout the rules. These changes are intended to be stylistic and no substantive change is intended, except as described below.

The amendment makes one change in practice. Currently, Rule 3 requires the complaint to be sworn before a "magistrate judge," which under current Rule 54 could include a state or local judicial officer. Revised Rule 1 no longer includes state and local officers in the definition of magistrate judges for the purposes of these rules. Instead, the definition includes only United States magistrate judges. Rule 3 requires that the complaint be made before a United States magistrate judge or before a state or local officer. The revised rule does, however, make a change to reflect prevailing practice and the outcome desired by the Committee — that the procedure take place before a federal judicial officer if one is reasonably available. As noted in Rule 1(c), where the rules, such as Rule 3, authorize a magistrate judge to act, any other federal judge may act.

Notes of Advisory Committee on 2011 amendments. Under the amended rule, the complaint and supporting material may be submitted by telephone or reliable electronic means; however, the rule requires that the judicial officer administer the oath or affirmation in person or by telephone. The Committee concluded that the benefits of making it easier to obtain judicial oversight of the arrest decision and the increasing reliability and accessibility to electronic communication warranted amendment of the rule. The amendment makes clear that the submission of a complaint to a judicial officer need not be done in person and may instead be made by telephone or other reliable electronic means. The successful experiences with electronic applications under Rule 41, which permits electronic applications for search warrants, support a comparable process for arrests. The provisions in Rule 41 have been transferred to new Rule 4.1, which governs applications by telephone or other electronic means under Rules 3, 4, 9, and 41.

Rule 4. Arrest Warrant or Summons on a Complaint

(a) Issuance. If the complaint or one or more affidavits filed with the complaint establish probable cause to believe that an offense has been committed and that the defendant committed it, the judge must issue an arrest warrant to an officer authorized to execute it. At the request of an attorney for the government, the judge must issue a summons, instead of a warrant, to a person authorized to serve it. A judge may issue more than one warrant or summons on the same complaint. If an individual defendant fails to appear in response to a summons, a judge may, and upon request of an attorney for the government must, issue a warrant. If an organizational defendant fails to appear in response to a summons, a judge may take any action authorized by United States law.

(b) Form.

(1) *Warrant.* A warrant must:

(A) contain the defendant's name or, if it is unknown, a name or description by which the defendant can be identified with reasonable certainty;

(B) describe the offense charged in the complaint;

(C) command that the defendant be arrested and brought without unnecessary delay before a magistrate judge or, if none is reasonably available, before a state or local judicial officer; and

(D) be signed by a judge.

(2) *Summons.* A summons must be in the same form as a warrant except that it must require the defendant to appear before a magistrate judge at a stated time and place.

(c) Execution or Service, and Return.

(1) *By whom.* Only a marshal or other authorized officer may execute a warrant. Any person authorized to serve a summons in a federal civil action may serve a summons.

(2) *Location.* A warrant may be executed, or a summons served, within the jurisdiction of the United States or anywhere else a federal statute authorizes an arrest. A summons to an organization under Rule 4(c)(3)(D) may also be served at a place not within a judicial district of the United States.

(3) *Manner.*

(A) A warrant is executed by arresting the defendant. Upon arrest, an officer possessing the original or a duplicate original warrant must show it to the defendant. If the officer does not possess the warrant, the officer must inform the defendant of the warrant's existence and of the offense charged and, at the defendant's request, must show the original or a duplicate original warrant to the defendant as soon as possible.

(B) A summons is served on an individual defendant:

(i) by delivering a copy to the defendant personally; or

(ii) by leaving a copy at the defendant's residence or usual place of abode with a person of suitable age and discretion residing at that location and by mailing a copy to the defendant's last known address.

(C) A summons is served on an organization in a judicial district of the United States by delivering a copy to an officer, to a managing or general agent, or to another agent appointed or legally authorized to receive service of process. If the agent is one authorized by statute and the statute so requires, a copy must also be mailed to the organization.

(D) A summons is served on an organization not within a judicial district of the United States:

(i) by delivering a copy, in a manner authorized by the foreign jurisdiction's law, to an officer, to a managing or general agent, or to an agent appointed or legally authorized to receive service of process; or

(ii) by any other means that gives notice, including one that is:

(a) stipulated by the parties;

(b) undertaken by a foreign authority in response to a letter rogatory, a letter of request, or a request submitted under an applicable international agreement; or

(c) permitted by an applicable international agreement.

(4) *Return.*

(A) After executing a warrant, the officer must return it to the judge before whom the defendant is brought in accordance with Rule 5. The officer may do so by reliable electronic means. At the request of an attorney for the government, an unexecuted warrant must be brought back to and canceled by a magistrate judge or, if none is reasonably available, by a state or local judicial officer.

(B) The person to whom a summons was delivered for service must return it on or before the return day.

(C) At the request of an attorney for the government, a judge may deliver an unexecuted warrant, an unserved summons, or a copy of the warrant or summons to the marshal or other authorized person for execution or service.

(d) Warrant by Telephone or Other Reliable Electronic Means. In accordance with Rule 4.1, a magistrate judge may issue a warrant or summons based on information communicated by telephone or other reliable electronic means.

HISTORY:

Amended Feb. 28, 1966, eff. July 1, 1966; April 24, 1972, eff. Oct. 1, 1972; April 22, 1974, eff. Dec. 1, 1975; July 31, 1975, P. L. 94-64, §§ 3(1)–(3), 89 Stat. 370; March 9, 1987, eff. Aug. 1, 1987; April 22, 1993, eff. Dec. 1, 1993; April 29, 2002, eff. Dec. 1, 2002; April 26, 2011, eff. Dec. 1, 2011; April 28, 2016, eff. Dec. 1, 2016.

HISTORY; ANCILLARY LAWS AND DIRECTIVES

Other provisions:

Notes of Advisory Committee.

Note to Subdivision (a). 1. The rule states the existing law relating to warrants issued by commissioner or other magistrate. United States Constitution, Amendment IV; 18 U.S.C. [former] § 591 [see § 3041] (Arrest and removal for trial).

2. The provision for summons is new, although a summons has been customarily used against corporate defendants, 28 U.S.C. [former] § 377 [see § 1651] (Power to issue writs); *United States v John Kelso Co.* 86 F. 304, (N.D. Cal., 1898). See also, *Albrecht v United States,* 273 U.S. 1, 8, 47 S.Ct. 250, 71 L.Ed. 505 (1927). The use of the summons in criminal cases is sanctioned by many States, among them Indiana, Maryland, Massachusetts, New York, New Jersey, Ohio, and others. See A.L.I. Code of Criminal Procedure (1931), Commentaries to secs. 12, 13, and 14. The use of the summons is permitted in England by 11 & 12 Vict., c. 42, sec. 1 (1848). More general use of a summons in place of a warrant was recommended by the National Commission on Law Observance and Enforcement, *Report on Criminal Procedure* (1931) 47. The Uniform Arrest Act, proposed by the Interstate Commission on Crime, provides for a summons. Warner, 28 Va.L.R. 315. See also, Medalie, 4 Lawyers Guild, R. 1, 6.

3. The provision for the issuance of additional warrants on the same complaint embodies the practice heretofore followed in some districts. It is desirable from a practical standpoint, since when a complaint names several defendants, it may be preferable to issue a separate warrant as to each in order to facilitate service and return, especially if the defendants are apprehended at different times and places. Berge, 42 Mich.L.R. 353, 356.

4. Failure to respond to a summons is not a contempt of court, but is ground for issuing a warrant.

Note to Subdivision (b). Compare Rule 9(b) and forms of warrant and summons, Appendix of Forms.

Note to Subdivision (c)(2). This rule and Rule 9(c)(1) modify the existing practice under which a warrant may be served only within the district in which it is issued. *Mitchell v Dexter,* 244 F. 926 (C.C.A. 1st, 1917); *Palmer v Thompson,* 20 App. D.C. 273 (1902); but see *In re Christian,* 82 F. 885 (C.C.W.D. Ark.), 1897; 2 Op.Atty.Gen. 564. When a defendant is apprehended in a district other than that in which the prosecution has been instituted, this change will eliminate some of the steps that are at present followed: the issuance of a warrant in the district where the prosecution is pending; the return of the warrant non est inventus; the filing of a complaint on the basis of the warrant and its return in the district in which the defendant is found; and the issuance of another warrant in the latter district. The warrant originally issued will have efficacy throughout the United States and will constitute authority for arresting the defendant wherever found. Waite, 27 Jour. of Am. Judicature Soc. 101, 103. The change will not modify or affect the rights of the defendant as to removal. See Rule 40. The authority of the marshal to serve process is not limited to the district for which he is appointed, 28 U.S.C. [former] § 503 [see § 547].

Note to Subdivision (c)(3). 1. The provision that the arresting officer need not have the warrant in his possession at the time of the arrest is rendered necessary by the fact that a fugitive may be discovered and apprehended by any one of many officers. It is obviously impossible for a warrant to be in the possession of every officer who is searching for a fugitive or who unexpectedly might find himself in a position to apprehend the fugitive. The rule sets forth the customary practice in such matters, which has the sanction of the courts. "It would be a strong proposition in an ordinary felony case to say that a fugitive from justice for whom a capias or warrant was outstanding could not be apprehended until the apprehending officer had physical possession of the capias or the warrant. If such were the law, criminals could circulate freely from one end of the land to the other, because they could always keep ahead of an officer with the warrant." *In re Kosopud,*

(N.D. Ohio), 272 F. 330, 336. Waite, 27 Jour. of Am. Judicature Soc. 101, 103. The rule, however, safeguards the defendant's rights in such case.

2. Service of summons under the rule is substantially the same as in civil actions under Federal Rules of Civil Procedure, Rule 4(d)(1) [28 U.S.C., Appendix].

Note to Subdivision (c)(4). Return of a warrant or summons to the commissioner or other officer is provided by 18 U.S.C. § 603 [see § 4084] (Writs; copy as jailer's authority). The return of all "copies of process" by the commissioner to the clerk of the court is provided by 18 U.S.C. [former] § 591 [see § 3041;] and see Rule 5(c), *infra*.

Notes of Advisory Committee on 1966 amendments. In *Giordenello v. United States,* 357 U.S. 480, 2 L.Ed.2d 1503, 78 S.Ct. 1245 (1958) it was held that to support the issuance of a warrant the complaint must contain in addition to a statement "of the essential facts constituting the offense" (Rule 3) a statement of the facts relied upon by the complainant to establish probable cause. The amendment permits the complainant to state the facts constituting probable cause in a separate affidavit in lieu of spelling them out in the complaint. See also *Jaben v. United States,* 381 U.S. 214, 14 L.Ed.2d 345, 85 S.Ct. 1365 (1965), reh den 382 U.S. 873, 15 L.Ed. 2d 114, 86 S.Ct. 19.

Notes of Advisory Committee on 1972 amendments. Throughout the rule the term "magistrate" is substituted for the term "commissioner." Magistrate is defined in Rule 54 to include a judge of the United States, a United States magistrate, and those state and local judicial officers specified in 18 U.S.C. § 3041.

Notes of Advisory Committee on 1974 amendments. The amendments are designed to achieve several objectives: (1) to make explicit the fact that the determination of probable cause may be based upon hearsay evidence; (2) to make clear that probable cause is a prerequisite to the issuance of a summons; and (3) to give priority to the issuance of a summons rather than a warrant.

Subdivision (a) makes clear that the normal situation is to issue a summons.

Subdivision (b) provides for the issuance of an arrest warrant in lieu of or in addition to the issuance of a summons.

Subdivision (b)(1) restates the provision of the old rule mandating the issuance of a warrant when a defendant fails to appear in response to a summons.

Subdivision (b)(2) provides for the issuance of an arrest warrant rather than a summons whenever "a valid reason is shown" for the issuance of a warrant. The reason may be apparent from the face of the complaint or may be provided by the federal law enforcement officer or attorney for the government. See comparable provision in rule 9.

Subdivision (b)(3) deals with the situation in which conditions change after a summons has issued. It affords the government an opportunity to demonstrate the need for an arrest warrant. This may be done in the district in which the defendant is located if this is the convenient place to do so.

Subdivision (c) provides that a warrant or summons may issue on the basis of hearsay evidence. What constitutes probable cause is left to be dealt with on a case-to-case basis, taking account of the unlimited variations in source of information and in the opportunity of the informant to perceive accurately the factual data which he furnishes. See *e.g., Giordenello v. United States,* 357 U.S. 480, 78 S.Ct. 1245, 2 L.Ed.2d 1503 (1958); *Aguilar v Texas,* 378 U.S. 108, 84 S.Ct. 1509, 12 L.Ed.2d 723 (1964); *United States v. Ventresca,* 380 U.S. 102, 85 S.Ct. 741, 13 L.Ed.2d 684 (1965); *Jaben v. United States,* 381 U.S. 214, 85 S.Ct. 1365, 14 L.Ed.2d 345 (1965); *McCray v. Illinois,* 386 U.S. 300, 87 S.Ct. 1056, 18 L.Ed.2d 62 (1967); *Spinelli v. United States,* 393 U.S. 410, 89 S.Ct. 584, 21 L.Ed.2d 637 (1969); *United States v. Harris,* 403 U.S. 573, 91 S.Ct. 2075, 29 L.Ed.2d 723 (1971); Note, The Informer's Tip as Probable Cause for Search or Arrest, 54 Cornell L.Rev. 958 (1969); C. Wright, Federal Practice and Procedure: Criminal § 52 (1969, Supp. 1971); 8 S.J. Moore, Federal Practice P 4.03 (2d ed. Cipes 1970, Supp. 1971).

Notes of Committee on the Judiciary on 1975 amendments (House Report No. 94-247). A. Amendments Proposed by the Supreme Court. Rule 4 of the Federal Rules of Criminal Procedure deals with arrest procedures when a criminal complaint has been filed. It provides in pertinent part: If it appears . . . that there is

> probable cause . . . a warrant for the arrest of the defendant shall issue to any officer authorized by law to execute it. Upon the *request* of the attorney for the government a summons instead of a warrant *shall* issue. [emphasis added].

The Supreme Court's amendments make a basic change in Rule 4. As proposed to be amended, Rule 4 gives priority to the issuance of a summons instead of an arrest warrant. In order for the magistrate to issue an arrest warrant, the attorney for the government must show a "valid reason."

B. Committee Action. The Committee agrees with and approves the basic change in Rule 4. The decision to take a citizen into custody is a very important one with far-reaching consequences. That decision ought to be made by a neutral official (a magistrate) rather than by an interested party (the prosecutor).

It has been argued that undesirable consequences will result if this change is adopted—including an increase in the number of fugitives and the introduction of substantial delays in our system of criminal justice. [See testimony of Assistant Attorney General W. Vincent Rakestraw in Hearings on Proposed Amendments to Federal Rules of Criminal Procedure Before the Subcommittee on Criminal Justice of the House Committee on the Judiciary, 93d Cong., 2d Sess., Serial No. 61, at 41–43 (1974) [hereinafter cited as "Hearing I"].] The Committee has carefully considered these arguments and finds them to be wanting. [The Advisory Committee on Criminal Rules has thoroughly analyzed the arguments raised by Mr. Rakestraw and convincingly demonstrated that the undesirable consequences predicted will not necessarily result. See Hearings on Proposed Amendments to Federal Rules on Proposed Amendments to Federal Rules of Criminal Procedure Before the Subcommittee on Criminal Justice of the House Committee on the Judiciary, 94th Congress, 1st Session, Serial No. 6, at 208–09 (1975) [hereinafter cited "Hearings II"].] The present rule permits the use of a summons in lieu of a warrant. The major difference between the present rule and the proposed rule is that the present rule vests the decision to issue a summons or a warrant in the prosecutor, while the proposed rule vests that decision in a judicial officer. Thus, the basic premise underlying the arguments against the proposed rule is the notion that only the prosecutor can be trusted to act responsibility in deciding whether a summons or a warrant shall issue.

The Committee rejects the notion that the federal judiciary cannot be trusted to exercise discretion wisely and in the public interest.

The Committee recast the language of Rule 4(b). No change in substance is intended. The phrase "valid reason" was changed to "good cause," a phrase with which lawyers are more familiar. [Rule 4, both as proposed by the Supreme Court and as changed by the Committee, does not in any way authorize a magistrate to issue a summons or a warrant sua sponte, nor does it enlarge, limit or change in any way the law governing warrantless arrests.]

The Committee deleted two sentences from Rule 4(c). These sentences permitted a magistrate to question the complainant and other witnesses under oath and required the magistrate to keep a record or summary of such a proceeding. The Committee does not intend this change to discontinue or discourage the practice of having the complainant appear personally or the practice of making a record or summary of such an appearance. Rather, the Committee intended to leave Rule 4(c) neutral on this matter, neither encouraging nor discouraging these practices.

The Committee added a new section that provides that the determination of good cause for the issuance of a warrant in lieu of a summons shall not be grounds for a motion to suppress evidence. This provision does not apply when the issue is whether there was probable cause to believe an offense has been committed. This provision does not in any way expand or limit the so-called "exclusionary rule."

Notes of Conference Committee on 1975 amendments (House Report No. 94-414). Rule 4(e)(3) deals with the manner in which warrants and summonses may be served. The House version provides two methods for serving a summons: (1) personal service upon the defendant, or (2) service by leaving it with someone of suitable age at the defendant's dwelling and by mailing it to the defendant's last known address. The Senate version provides three methods: (1) personal service, (2) service by leaving it with someone of suitable age at the defendant's dwelling, or (3) service by mailing it to defendant's last known address.

Approval of amendments by Act July 31, 1975; effective date. Act July 31, 1975, P. L. 94-64, § 2, 89 Stat. 370, provided that: "The amendments proposed by the United States Supreme Court to the Federal Rules of Criminal Procedure which are embraced in the order of that Court on April 22, 1974, are approved except as otherwise provided in this Act and shall take effect on December 1, 1975. Except with respect to the amendment to Rule 11, insofar as it adds Rule 11(e)(6), which shall take effect on August 1, 1975, the amendments made by section 3 of this Act shall also take effect on December 1, 1975.". For full classification of this Act, consult USCS Tables volumes.

Notes of Advisory Committee on 1987 amendments.

The amendments are technical. No substantive change is intended.

Notes of Advisory Committee on 1993 amendments.

The Rule is amended to conform to the Judicial Improvements Act of 1990 [P.L. 101-650, Title III, Section 321] which provides that each United States magistrate appointed under section 631 of title 28, United States Code, shall be known as a United States magistrate judge.

Notes of Advisory Committee on 2002 amendments.

The language of Rule 4 has been amended as part of the general restyling of the Criminal Rules to make them more easily understood and to make style and terminology consistent throughout the rules. These changes are intended to be stylistic, except as noted below.

The first non-stylistic change is in Rule 4(a), which has been amended to provide an element of discretion in those situations when the defendant fails to respond to a summons. Under the current rule, the judge must in all cases issue an arrest warrant. The revised rule provides discretion to the judge to issue an arrest warrant if the attorney for the government does not request that an arrest warrant be issued for a failure to appear.

Current Rule 4(b), which refers to the fact that hearsay evidence may be used to support probable cause, has been deleted. That language was added to the rule in 1974, apparently to reflect emerging federal case law. See Advisory Committee Note to 1974 Amendments to Rule 4 (citing cases). A similar amendment was made to Rule 41 in 1972. In the intervening years, however, the case law has become perfectly clear on that proposition. Thus, the Committee believed that the reference to hearsay was no longer necessary. Furthermore, the limited reference to hearsay evidence was misleading to the extent that it might have suggested that other forms of inadmissible evidence could not be considered. For example, the rule made no reference to considering a defendant's prior criminal record, which clearly may be considered in deciding whether probable cause exists. See, e.g., *Brinegar v. United States*, 338 U.S. 160 [93 L. Ed. 1879] (1949) (officer's knowledge of defendant's prior criminal activity). Rather than address that issue, or any other similar issues, the Committee believed that the matter was best addressed in Rule 1101(d)(3), Federal Rules of Evidence. That rule explicitly provides that the Federal Rules of Evidence do not apply to "preliminary examinations in criminal cases, . . . issuance of warrants for arrest, criminal summonses, and search warrants." The Advisory Committee Note accompanying that rule recognizes that: "The nature of the proceedings makes application of the formal rules of evidence inappropriate and impracticable." The Committee did not intend to make any substantive changes in practice by deleting the reference to hearsay evidence.

New Rule 4(b), which is currently Rule 4(c), addresses the form of an arrest warrant and a summons and includes two non-stylistic changes. First, Rule 4(b)(1)(C) mandates that the warrant require that the defendant be brought "without unnecessary delay" before a judge. The Committee believed that this was a more appropriate standard than the current requirement that the defendant be brought before the "nearest available" magistrate judge. This new language accurately reflects the thrust of the original rule, that time is of the essence and that the defendant should be brought with dispatch before a judicial officer in the district. Second, the revised rule states a preference that the defendant be brought before a federal judicial officer.

Rule 4(b)(2) has been amended to require that if a summons is issued, the defendant must appear before a magistrate judge. The current rule requires the appearance before a "magistrate," which could include a state or local judicial officer. This change is consistent with the preference for requiring defendants to appear before federal judicial officers stated in revised Rule 4(b)(1).

Rule 4(c) (currently Rule 4(d)) includes three changes. First, current Rule 4(d)(2) states the traditional rule recognizing the territorial limits for executing warrants. Rule 4(c)(2) includes new language that reflects the recent enactment of the Military Extraterritorial Jurisdiction Act (Pub. L. No. 106-523, 114 Stat. 2488) that permits arrests of certain military and Department of Defense personnel overseas. See also 14 U.S.C. § 89 (Coast Guard authority to effect arrests outside territorial limits of United States). Second, current Rule 4(d)(3) provides that the arresting officer is only required to inform the defendant of the offense charged and that a warrant exists if the officer does not have a copy of the warrant. As revised, Rule 4(c)(3)(A) explicitly requires the arresting officer in all instances to inform the defendant of the offense charged and of the fact that an arrest warrant exists. The new rule continues the current provision that the arresting officer need not have a copy of the warrant, but if the defendant requests to see it, the officer must show the warrant to the defendant as soon as possible. The rule does not attempt to define any particular time limits for showing the warrant to the defendant.

Third, Rule 4(c)(3)(C) is taken from former Rule 9(c)(1). That provision specifies the manner of serving a summons on an organization. The Committee believed that Rule 4 was the more appropriate location for general provisions addressing the mechanics of arrest warrants and summonses. Revised Rule 9 liberally cross-references the basic provisions appearing in Rule 4. Under the amended rule, in all cases in which a summons is being served on an organization, a copy of the summons must be mailed to the organization.

Fourth, a change is made in Rule 4(c)(4). Currently, Rule 4(d)(4) requires that an unexecuted warrant must be returned to the judicial officer or judge who issued it. As amended, Rule 4(c)(4)(A) provides that after a warrant is executed, the officer must return it to the judge before whom the defendant will appear under Rule 5. At the government's request, however, an unexecuted warrant must be canceled by a magistrate judge. The change recognizes the possibility that at the time the warrant is returned, the issuing judicial officer may not be available.

Notes of Advisory Committee on 2011 amendments.

Rule 4 is amended in three respects to make the arrest warrant process more efficient through the use of technology.

Note to Subdivision (c). First, Rule 4(c)(3)(A) authorizes a law enforcement officer to retain a duplicate original arrest warrant, consistent with the change to subdivision (d), which permits a court to issue an arrest warrant electronically rather than by physical delivery. The duplicate original warrant may be used in lieu of the original warrant signed by the magistrate judge to satisfy the requirement that the defendant be shown the warrant at or soon after an arrest. Cf. Rule 4.1(b)(5) (providing for a duplicate original search warrant).

Second, consistent with the amendment to Rule 41(f), Rule 4(c)(4)(A) permits an officer to make a return of the arrest warrant electronically. Requiring an in-person return can be burdensome on law enforcement, particularly in large districts when the return can require a great deal of time and travel. In contrast, no interest of the accused is affected by allowing what is normally a ministerial act to be done electronically.

Note to Subdivision (d). Rule 4(d) provides that a magistrate judge may issue an arrest warrant or summons based on information submitted electronically rather than in person. This change works in conjunction with the amendment to Rule 3, which permits a magistrate judge to consider a criminal complaint and accompanying documents that are submitted electronically. Subdivision (d) also incorporates the procedures for applying for and issuing electronic warrants set forth in Rule 4.1.

Notes of Advisory Committee on 2016 amendments.

Note to Subdivision (a). The amendment addresses a gap in the current rule, which makes no provision for organizational defendants who fail to appear in response to a criminal summons. The amendment explicitly limits the issuance of a warrant to individual defendants who fail to appear, and provides that the judge may take whatever action is authorized by law when an organizational defendant fails to appear. The rule does not attempt to specify the remedial actions a court may take when an organizational defendant fails to appear.

Subdivision (c)(2). The amendment authorizes service of a criminal summons on an organization outside a judicial district of the United States.

Subdivision (c)(3)(C). The amendment makes two changes to subdivision (c)(3)(C) governing service of a summons on an organization. First, like Civil Rule 4(h), the amended provision does not require a separate mailing to the organization when delivery has been made in the United States to an officer or to a managing or general agent. Service of process on an officer or a managing or general agent is in effect service on the principal. Mailing is required when delivery has been made on an agent authorized by statute, if the statute itself requires mailing to the entity.

Second, also like Civil Rule 4(h), the amendment recognizes that service outside the United States requires separate consideration, and it restricts Rule 4(c)(3)(C) and its modified mailing requirement to service on organizations within the United States. Service upon organizations outside the United States is governed by new subdivision (c)(3)(D).

These two modifications of the mailing requirement remove an unnecessary impediment to the initiation of criminal proceedings against organizations that commit domestic offenses but have no place of business or mailing address within the United States. Given the realities of today's global economy, electronic communication, and federal criminal practice, the mailing requirement should not shield a defendant organization when the Rule's core objective--notice of pending criminal proceedings--is accomplished.

Subdivision (c)(3)(D). This new subdivision states that a criminal summons may be served on an organizational defendant outside the United States and enumerates a non-exhaustive list of permissible means of service that provide notice to that defendant.

Although it is presumed that the enumerated means will provide notice, whether actual notice has been provided may be challenged in an individual case.

Subdivision (c)(3)(D)(i). Subdivision (i) notes that a foreign jurisdiction's law may authorize delivery of a copy of the criminal summons to an officer, or to a managing or general agent. This is a permissible means for serving an organization outside of the United States, just as it is for organizations within the United States. The subdivision also recognizes that a foreign jurisdiction's law may provide for service of a criminal summons by delivery to an appointed or legally authorized agent in a manner that provides notice to the entity, and states that this is an acceptable means of service.

Subdivision (c)(3)(D)(ii). Subdivision (ii) provides a non-exhaustive list illustrating other permissible means of giving service on organizations outside the United States, all of which must be carried out in a manner that "gives notice."

Paragraph (a) recognizes that service may be made by a means stipulated by the parties.

Paragraph (b) recognizes that service may be made by the diplomatic methods of letters rogatory and letters of request, and the last clause of the paragraph provides for service under international agreements that obligate the parties to provide broad measures of assistance, including the service of judicial documents. These include crime-specific multilateral agreements (e.g., the United Nations Convention Against Corruption (UNCAC), S. Treaty Doc. No. 109-6 (2003)), regional agreements (e.g., the Inter-American Convention on Mutual Assistance in Criminal Matters (OAS MLAT), S. Treaty Doc. No. 105-25 (1995)), and bilateral agreements.

Paragraph (c) recognizes that other means of service that provide notice and are permitted by an applicable international agreement are also acceptable when serving organizations outside the United States.

As used in this rule, the phrase "applicable international agreement" refers to an agreement that has been ratified by the United States and the foreign jurisdiction and is in force.

Amendments:

1975.

Act July 31, 1975, § 3(1)–(3) (effective 12/1/75, as provided by § 2 of such Act, which appears as a note to this section), substituted subsecs. (a) and (b), exclusive of subsequent amendment, for former subsecs. (a) and (b); struck out former subsec. (c); redesignated former subsec. (d) as subsec. (c); redesignated former subsec. (e) as subsec. (d), and in subsec. (d)(3), as so redesignated, substituted "and by mailing a copy of the summons to" for "or by mailing it to".

Rule 4.1. Complaint, Warrant, or Summons by Telephone or Other Reliable Electronic Means

(a) In General. A magistrate judge may consider information communicated by telephone or other reliable electronic means when reviewing a complaint or deciding whether to issue a warrant or summons.

(b) Procedures. If a magistrate judge decides to proceed under this rule, the following procedures apply:

(1) *Taking Testimony Under Oath.* The judge must place under oath—and may examine—the applicant and any person on whose testimony the application is based.

(2) *Creating a Record of the Testimony and Exhibits.*

(A) Testimony Limited to Attestation. If the applicant does no more than attest to the contents of a written affidavit submitted by reliable electronic means, the judge must acknowledge the attestation in writing on the affidavit.

(B) Additional Testimony or Exhibits. If the judge considers additional testimony or exhibits, the judge must:

(i) have the testimony recorded verbatim by an electronic recording device, by a court reporter, or in writing;

(ii) have any recording or reporter's notes transcribed, have the transcription certified as accurate, and file it;

(iii) sign any other written record, certify its accuracy, and file it; and

(iv) make sure that the exhibits are filed.

(3) *Preparing a Proposed Duplicate Original of a Complaint, Warrant, or Summons.* The applicant must prepare a proposed duplicate original of a complaint, warrant, or summons, and must read or otherwise transmit its contents verbatim to the judge.

(4) *Preparing an Original Complaint, Warrant, or Summons.* If the applicant reads the contents of the proposed duplicate original, the judge must enter those contents into an original complaint, warrant, or summons. If the applicant transmits the contents by reliable electronic means, the transmission received by the judge may serve as the original.

(5) *Modification.* The judge may modify the complaint, warrant, or summons. The judge must then:

(A) transmit the modified version to the applicant by reliable electronic means; or

(B) file the modified original and direct the applicant to modify the proposed duplicate original accordingly.

(6) *Issuance.* To issue the warrant or summons, the judge must:

(A) sign the original documents;

(B) enter the date and time of issuance on the warrant or summons; and

(C) transmit the warrant or summons by reliable electronic means to the applicant or direct the applicant to sign the judge's name and enter the date and time on the duplicate original.

(c) Suppression Limited. Absent a finding of bad faith, evidence obtained from a warrant issued under this rule is not subject to suppression on the ground that issuing the warrant in this manner was unreasonable under the circumstances.

HISTORY:

Added April 26, 2011, eff. Dec. 1, 2011.

HISTORY; ANCILLARY LAWS AND DIRECTIVES

Other provisions:

Notes of Advisory Committee. New Rule 4.1 brings together in one rule the procedures for using a telephone or other reliable electronic means for reviewing complaints and applying for and issuing warrants and summonses. In drafting Rule 4.1, the Committee recognized that modern technological developments have improved access to judicial officers, thereby reducing the necessity of government action without prior judicial approval. Rule 4.1 prescribes uniform procedures and ensures an accurate record.

The procedures that have governed search warrants "by telephonic or other means," formerly in Rule 41(d)(3) and (e)(3), have been relocated to this rule, reordered for easier application, and extended to arrest warrants, complaints, and summonses. Successful experience using electronic applications for search warrants under Rule 41, combined with increased access to reliable electronic communication, support the extension of these procedures to arrest warrants, complaints, and summonses.

With one exception noted in the next paragraph, the new rule preserves the procedures formerly in Rule 41 without change. By using the term "magistrate judge," the rule continues to require, as did former Rule 41(d)(3) and (e)(3), that a federal judge (and not a state judge) handle electronic applications, approvals, and issuances. The rule continues to require that the judge place an applicant under oath over the telephone, and permits the judge to examine the applicant, as Rule 41 had provided. Rule 4.1(b) continues to require that when electronic means are used to issue the warrant, the magistrate judge retain the original warrant. Minor changes in wording and reorganization of the language formerly in Rule 41 were made to aid in application of the rules, with no intended change in meaning.

The only substantive change to the procedures formerly in Rule 41(d)(3) and (e)(3) appears in new Rule 4.1(b)(2)(A). Former Rule 41(d)(3)(B)(ii) required the magistrate judge to make a verbatim record of the entire conversation with the applicant. New Rule 4.1(b)(2)(A) provides that when a warrant application and affidavit are sent electronically to the magistrate judge and the telephone conversation between the magistrate judge and affiant is limited to attesting to those written documents, a verbatim record of the entire conversation is no longer required. Rather, the magistrate judge should simply acknowledge in writing the attestation on the affidavit. This may be done, for example, by signing the jurat included on the Administrative Office of U.S. Courts form. Rule 4.1(b)(2)(B) carries forward the requirements formerly in Rule 41 to cases in which the magistrate judge considers testimony or exhibits in addition to the affidavit. In addition, Rule 4.1(b)(6) specifies that in order to issue a warrant or summons the magistrate judge must sign all of the original documents and enter the date and time of issuance on the warrant or summons. This procedure will create and maintain a complete record of the warrant application process.

Rule 5. Initial Appearance

(a) In general.

(1) *Appearance Upon an Arrest.*

(A) A person making an arrest within the United States must take the defendant without unnecessary delay before a magistrate judge, or before a state or local judicial officer as Rule 5(c) provides, unless a statute provides otherwise.

(B) A person making an arrest outside the United States must take the defendant without unnecessary delay before a magistrate judge, unless a statute provides otherwise.

(2) *Exceptions.*

(A) An officer making an arrest under a warrant issued upon a complaint charging solely a violation of 18 U.S.C. § 1073 need not comply with this rule if:

(i) the person arrested is transferred without unnecessary delay to the custody of appropriate state or local authorities in the district of arrest; and

(ii) an attorney for the government moves promptly, in the district where the warrant was issued, to dismiss the complaint.

(B) If a defendant is arrested for violating probation or supervised release, Rule 32.1 applies.

(C) If a defendant is arrested for failing to appear in another district, Rule 40 applies.

(3) *Appearance Upon a Summons.* When a defendant appears in response to a summons under Rule 4, a magistrate judge must proceed under Rule 5(d) or (e), as applicable.

(b) Arrest Without a Warrant. If a defendant is arrested without a warrant, a complaint meeting Rule 4(a)'s requirement of probable cause must be promptly filed in the district where the offense was allegedly committed.

(c) Place of Initial Appearance; Transfer to Another District.

(1) *Arrest in the District Where the Offense Was Allegedly Committed.* If the defendant is arrested in the district where the offense was allegedly committed:

(A) the initial appearance must be in that district; and

(B) if a magistrate judge is not reasonably available, the initial appearance may be before a state or local judicial officer.

(2) *Arrest in a District Other Than Where the Offense Was Allegedly Committed.* If the defendant was arrested in a district other than where the offense was allegedly committed, the initial appearance must be:

(A) in the district of arrest; or

(B) in an adjacent district if:

(i) the appearance can occur more promptly there; or

(ii) the offense was allegedly committed there and the initial appearance will occur on the day of arrest.

(3) *Procedures in a District Other Than Where the Offense Was Allegedly Committed.* If the initial appearance occurs in a district other than where the offense was allegedly committed, the following procedures apply:

(A) the magistrate judge must inform the defendant about the provisions of Rule 20;

(B) if the defendant was arrested without a warrant, the district court where the offense was allegedly committed must first issue a warrant before the magistrate judge transfers the defendant to that district;

(C) the magistrate judge must conduct a preliminary hearing if required by Rule 5.1;

(D) the magistrate judge must transfer the defendant to the district where the offense was allegedly committed if:

(i) the government produces the warrant, a certified copy of the warrant, or a reliable electronic form of either; and

(ii) the judge finds that the defendant is the same person named in the indictment, information, or warrant; and

(E) when a defendant is transferred and discharged, the clerk must promptly transmit the papers and any bail to the clerk in the district where the offense was allegedly committed.

(4) *Procedure for Persons Extradited to the United States.* If the defendant is surrendered to the United States in accordance with a request for the defendant's extradition, the initial appearance must be in the district (or one of the districts) where the offense is charged.

(d) Procedure in a Felony Case.

(1) *Advice.* If the defendant is charged with a felony, the judge must inform the defendant of the following:

(A) the complaint against the defendant, and any affidavit filed with it;

(B) the defendant's right to retain counsel or to request that counsel be appointed if the defendant cannot obtain counsel;

(C) the circumstances, if any, under which the defendant may secure pretrial release;

(D) any right to a preliminary hearing;

(E) the defendant's right not to make a statement, and that any statement made may be used against the defendant; and

(F) that a defendant who is not a United States citizen may request that an attorney for the government or a federal law enforcement official notify a consular officer from the defendant's country of nationality that the defendant has been arrested—but that even without the defendant's request, a treaty or other international agreement may require consular notification.

(2) *Consulting with Counsel.* The judge must allow the defendant reasonable opportunity to consult with counsel.

(3) *Detention or Release.* The judge must detain or release the defendant as provided by statute or these rules.

(4) *Plea.* A defendant may be asked to plead only under Rule 10.

(e) Procedure in a Misdemeanor Case. If the defendant is charged with a misdemeanor only, the judge must inform the defendant in accordance with Rule 58(b)(2).

(f) Reminder of Prosecutorial Obligation.

(1) *In General.* In all criminal proceedings, on the first scheduled court date when both prosecutor and defense counsel are present, the judge shall issue an oral and written order to prosecution and defense counsel that confirms the disclosure obligation of the prosecutor under Brady v. Maryland, 373 U.S. 83 (1963) and its progeny, and the possible consequences of violating such order under applicable law.

(2) *Formation of Order.* Each judicial council in which a district court is located shall promulgate a model order for the purpose of paragraph (1) that the court may use as it determines is appropriate.

(g) Video Teleconferencing. Video teleconferencing may be used to conduct an appearance under this rule if the defendant consents.

HISTORY:

Amended Feb. 28, 1966, eff. July 1, 1966; April 24, 1972, eff. Oct. 1, 1972; April 28, 1982, eff. Aug. 1, 1982; Oct. 12, 1984, P. L. 98-473, Title II, Ch I, § 209(a), 98 Stat. 1986; March 9, 1987, eff. Aug. 1, 1987; May 1, 1990, eff. Dec. 1, 1990; April 22, 1993, eff. Dec. 1, 1993; April 27, 1995, eff. Dec. 1, 1995; April 29, 2002, eff. Dec. 1, 2002; April 12, 2006, eff. Dec. 1, 2006; April 23, 2012, eff. Dec. 1, 2012; April 25, 2014, eff. Dec. 1, 2014; Oct. 21, 2020, P.L. 116-182, § 2, 134 Stat. 894.

HISTORY; ANCILLARY LAWS AND DIRECTIVES

Other provisions:

Notes of Advisory Committee.

Note to Subdivision (a). 1. The time within which a prisoner must be brought before a committing magistrate is defined differently in different statutes. The rule supersedes all statutory provisions on this point and fixes a single standard, i.e., "without unnecessary delay", 18 U.S.C. [former] § 593 (Operating illicit distillery; arrest; bail); 18 U.S.C. [former] § 595 (Persons arrested taken before nearest officer for hearing); 5 U.S.C. [former] § 300a [see 18 U.S.C. §§ 3052, 3107] (Division of Investigation; authority of officers to serve warrants and make arrests); 16 U.S.C. § 10 (Arrests by employees of park service for violations of laws and regulations); 16 U.S.C. § 706 (Migratory Bird Treaty Act; arrests; search warrants); D.C. Code (1940), Title 4, sec. 140 (Arrests without warrant); see, also, 33 U.S.C. §§ 436, 446, 452; 46 U.S.C. [former] § 708 [see 18 U.S.C. § 2279]. What constitutes "unnecessary delay", i.e., reasonable time within which the prisoner should be brought before a committing magistrate, must be determined in the light of all the facts and circumstances of the case. The following authorities discuss the question what constitutes reasonable time for this purpose in various situations: *Carroll v Parry,* 48 App.D.C. 453; *Janus v United States,* 38 F.2d 431 (C.C.A. 9th); *Commonwealth v Di Stasio,* 294 Mass. 273, 1 N.E.2d 189; *State v Freeman,* 86 N.C. 683; *Peloquin v Hibner,* 231 Wis. 77, 285 N.W. 380; see, also, Warner, 28 Va.L.R. 315, 339–341.

2. The rule also states the prevailing State practice, ALI Code of Criminal Procedure (1931), Commentaries to secs. 35, 36.

Note to Subdivisions (b) and (c). 1. These rules prescribe a uniform procedure to be followed at preliminary hearings before a commissioner. They supersede the general provisions of 18 U.S.C. [former] § 591 [see § 3041] (Arrest and removal for trial). The procedure prescribed by the rules is that generally prevailing. See *Wood v United States,* 128 F. 265, 271–272 (App. D.C.); A.L.I. Code of Criminal Procedure (1931), secs. 39–60 and Commentaries thereto; *Manual for United States Commissioners,* pp. 6–10, published by Administrative Office of the United States Courts.

2. Pleas before a commissioner are excluded, as a plea of guilty at this stage has no legal status or function except to serve as a waiver of preliminary examination. It has been held inadmissible in evidence at the trial, if the defendant was not represented by counsel when the plea was entered. *Wood v United States,* 128 F.2d 265 (App. D.C). The rule expressly provides for a waiver of examination, thereby eliminating any necessity for a provision as to plea.

Notes of Advisory Committee on 1966 amendments.

The first change is designed to insure that under the revision made in Rule 4(a) the defendant arrested on a warrant will receive the same information concerning the basis for the issuance of the warrant as would previously have been given him by the complaint itself.

The second change obligates the commissioner to inform the defendant of his right to request the assignment of counsel if he is unable to obtain counsel. Cf. the amendment to Rule 44, and the Advisory Committee's Note thereon.

Notes of Advisory Committee on 1972 amendments.

There are a number of changes made in rule 5 which are designed to improve the editorial clarity of the rule; to conform the rule to the Federal Magistrates Act; and to deal explicitly in the rule with issues as to which the rule is now silent and the law uncertain.

The principal editorial change is to deal separately with the initial appearance before the magistrate and the preliminary examination. They are dealt with together in old rule 5. They are separated in order to prevent confusion as to whether they constitute a single or two separate proceedings. Although the preliminary examination can be held at the time of the initial appearance, in practice this ordinarily does not occur. Usually counsel needs time to prepare for the preliminary examination, and as a consequence a separate date is typically set for the preliminary examination.

Because federal magistrates are reasonably available to conduct initial appearances, the rule is drafted on the assumption that the initial appearance is before a federal magistrate. If experience under the act indicates that there must be frequent appearances before state or local judicial officers it may be desirable to draft an additional rule, such as the following, detailing the procedure for an initial appearance before a state or local judicial officer:

Initial Appearance Before a State or Local Judicial Officer. If a United States magistrate is not reasonably available under rule 5(a), the arrested person shall be brought before a state or local judicial officer authorized by 18 U.S.C. § 3041, and such officer shall inform the person of the rights specified in rule 5(c) and shall authorize the release of the arrested person under the terms provided for by these rules and by 18 U.S.C. § 3146. The judicial officer shall immediately transmit any written order of release and any papers filed before him to the appropriate United States magistrate of the district and order the arrested person to appear before such United States magistrate within three days if not in custody or at the next regular hour of business of the United States magistrate if the arrested person is retained in custody. Upon his appearance before the United States magistrate, the procedure shall be that prescribed in rule 5.

Several changes are made to conform the language of the rule to the Federal Magistrates Act.

(1) The term "magistrate," which is defined in new rule 54, is substituted for the term "commissioner." As defined, "magistrate" includes those state and local judicial officers specified in 18 U.S.C. § 3041, and thus the initial appearance may be before a state or local judicial officer when a federal magistrate is not reasonably available. This is made explicit in subdivision (a).

(2) Subdivision (b) conforms the rule to the procedure prescribed in the Federal Magistrate Act when a defendant appears before a magistrate charged with a "minor offense" as defined in 18 U.S.C. § 3401(f):

"misdemeanors punishable under the laws of the United States, the penalty for which does not exceed imprisonment for a period of one year, or a fine of not more than $1,000, or both, except that such term does not include . . . [specified exceptions]."

If the "minor offense" is tried before a United States magistrate, the procedure must be in accordance with the Rules of Procedure for the Trial of Minor Offenses Before United States Magistrates (January 27, 1971).

(3) Subdivision (d) makes clear that a defendant is not entitled to a preliminary examination if he has been indicted by a grand jury prior to the date set for the preliminary examination or, in appropriate cases, if any information is filed in the district court prior to that date. See C. Wright, Federal Practice and Procedure: Criminal § 80, pp. 137–140 (1969, Supp. 1971). This is also provided in the Federal Magistrates Act, 18 U.S.C. § 3060(e).

Rule 5 is also amended to deal with several issues not dealt with in old rule 5:

Subdivision (a) is amended to make clear that a complaint, complying with the requirements of rule 4(a), must be filed whenever a person has been arrested without a warrant. This means that the complaint, or an affidavit or affidavits filed with the complaint, must show probable cause. As provided in rule 4(a) the showing of probable cause "may be based upon hearsay evidence in whole or in part."

Subdivision (c) provides that defendant should be notified of the general circumstances under which he is entitled to pretrial release under the Bail Reform Act of 1966 (18 U.S.C. §§ 3141– 3152). Defendants often do not in fact have counsel at the initial appearance and thus, unless told by the magistrate, may be unaware of their right to pretrial release. See C. Wright, Federal Practice and Procedure: Criminal § 78 N. 61 (1969).

Subdivision (c) makes clear that a defendant who does not waive his right to trial before a judge of the district court is entitled to a preliminary examination to determine probable cause for any offense except a petty offense. It also, by necessary implication, makes clear that a defendant is not entitled to a preliminary examination if he consents to be tried on the issue of guilt or innocence by the United States magistrate, even though the offense may be one not heretofore triable by the United States Commissioner and therefore one as to which the defendant had a right to a preliminary examination. The rationale is that the preliminary examination serves only to justify holding the defendant in custody or on bail during the period of time it takes to bind the defendant over to the district court for trial. See *State v Solomon* 158 Wis. 146, 147 N.W. 640 (1914). A similar conclusion is reached in the New York Proposed Criminal Procedure Law. See McKinney's Session Law News, April 10, 1969, at p. A-119.

Subdivision (c) also contains time limits within which the preliminary examination must be held. These are taken from 18 U.S.C. § 3060. The provisions for the extension of the prescribed time limits are the same as the provisions of 18 U.S.C. § 3060 with two exceptions: The new language allows delay consented to by the defendant only if there is "a showing of good cause, taking into account the public interest in the prompt disposition of criminal cases." This reflects the view of the Advisory Committee that delay, whether prosecution or defense induced, ought to be avoided whenever possible. The second difference between the new rule and 18 U.S.C. § 3060 is that the rule allows the decision to grant a continuance to be made by a United States magistrate as well as by a judge of the United

States. This reflects the view of the Advisory Committee that the United States magistrate should have sufficient judicial competence to make decisions such as that contemplated in subdivision (c).

Notes of Advisory Committee on 1982 amendments.

The amendment of subdivision (b) reflects the recent amendment of 18 U.S.C. § 3401(a), by the Federal Magistrate Act of 1979, to read: "When specially designated to exercise such jurisdiction by the district court or courts he serves, any United States magistrate shall have jurisdiction to try persons accused of, and sentence persons convicted of, misdemeanors committed within that judicial district.".

Notes of Advisory Committee on 1987 amendments.

The amendments are technical. No substantive change is intended.

Notes of Advisory Committee on 1990 amendments.

Rule 5(b) is amended to conform the rule to Rule 58.

Notes of Advisory Committee on 1993 amendments.

The Rule is amended to conform to the Judicial Improvements Act of 1990 [P.L. 101-650, Title III, Section 321] which provides that each United States magistrate appointed under section 631 of title 28, United States Code, shall be known as a United States magistrate judge.

Notes of Advisory Committee on 1995 amendments.

The amendment to Rule 5 is intended to address the interplay between the requirements for a prompt appearance before a magistrate judge and the processing of persons arrested for the offense of unlawfully fleeing to avoid prosecution under 18 U.S.C. § 1073, when no federal prosecution is intended. Title 18 U.S.C. § 1073 provides in part: Whoever moves or travels in interstate or foreign

> commerce with intent . . . to avoid prosecution, or custody or confinement after conviction, under the laws of the place from which he flees . . . shall be fined not more than $5,000 or imprisoned not more than five years, or both.
>
> Violations of this section may be prosecuted . . . only upon formal approval in writing by the Attorney General, the Deputy Attorney General, the Associate Attorney General, or an Assistant Attorney General of the United States, which function of approving prosecutions may not be delegated.

In enacting § 1073, Congress apparently intended to provide assistance to state criminal justice authorities in an effort to apprehend and prosecute state offenders. It also appears that by requiring permission of high ranking officials, Congress intended that prosecutions be limited in number. In fact, prosecutions under this section have been rare. The purpose of this statute is fulfilled when the person is apprehended and turned over to state or local authorities. In such cases the requirement of Rule 5 that any person arrested under a federal warrant must be brought before a federal magistrate judge becomes a largely meaningless exercise and a needless demand upon federal judicial resources.

In addressing this problem, several options are available to federal authorities when no federal prosecution is intended to ensue after the arrest. First, once federal authorities locate a fugitive, they may contact local law enforcement officials who make the arrest based upon the underlying out-of-state warrant. In that instance, Rule 5 is not implicated and the United States Attorney in the district issuing the § 1073 complaint and warrant can take action to dismiss both. In a second scenario, the fugitive is arrested by federal authorities who, in compliance with Rule 5, bring the person before a federal magistrate judge. If local law enforcement officers are present, they can take custody, once the United States Attorney informs the magistrate judge that there will be no prosecution under § 1073. Depending on the availability of state or local officers, there may be some delay in the Rule 5 proceedings; any delays following release to local officials, however, would not be a function of Rule 5. In a third situation, federal authorities arrest the fugitive but local law enforcement authorities are not present at the Rule 5 appearance. Depending on a variety of practices, the magistrate judge may calendar a removal hearing under Rule 40, or order that the person be held in federal custody pending further action by the local authorities.

Under the amendment, officers arresting a fugitive charged only with violating § 1073 need not bring the person before a magistrate judge under Rule 5(a) if there is no intent to actually prosecute the person under that charge. Two requirements, however, must be met. First, the arrested fugitive must be transferred without unnecessary delay to the custody of state officials. Second, steps must be taken in the appropriate district to dismiss the complaint alleging a violation of § 1073. The rule continues to contemplate that persons arrested by federal officials are entitled to prompt handling of federal charges, if prosecution is intended, and prompt transfer to state custody if federal prosecution is not contemplated.

Notes of Advisory Committee on 2002 amendments.

The language of Rule 5 has been amended as part of the general restyling of the Criminal Rules to make them more easily understood and to make style and terminology consistent throughout the rules. These changes are intended to be stylistic, except as noted below.

Rule 5 has been completely revised to more clearly set out the procedures for initial appearances and to recognize that such appearances may be required at various stages of a criminal proceeding, for example, where a defendant has been arrested for violating the terms of probation.

Rule 5(a), which governs initial appearances by an arrested defendant before a magistrate judge, includes several changes. The first is a clarifying change; revised Rule 5(a)(1) provides that a person making the arrest must bring the defendant "without unnecessary delay" before a magistrate judge, instead of the current reference to "nearest available" magistrate judge. This language parallels changes in Rule 4 and reflects the view that time is of the essence. The Committee intends no change in practice. In using the term, the Committee recognizes that on occasion there may be necessary delay in presenting the defendant, for example, due to weather conditions or other natural causes. A second change is non-stylistic, and reflects the stated preference (as in other provisions throughout the rules) that the defendant be brought before a federal judicial officer. Only if a magistrate judge is not available should the defendant be taken before a state or local officer.

The third sentence in current Rule 5(a), which states that a magistrate judge must proceed in accordance with the rule where a defendant is arrested without a warrant or given a summons, has been deleted because it is unnecessary.

Rule 5(a)(1)(B) codifies the caselaw reflecting that the right to an initial appearance applies not only when a person is arrested within the United States but also when an arrest occurs outside the United States. See, e.g., *United States v. Purvis*, 768 F.2d 1237 (11th Cir. 1985); *United States v. Yunis*, 859 F.2d 953 (D.C. Cir. 1988). In these circumstances, the Committee believes — and the rule so provides — that the initial appearance should be before a federal magistrate judge rather than a state or local judicial officer. Rule 5(a)(1)(B) has also been amended by adding the words, "unless a federal statute provides otherwise," to reflect recent enactment of the Military Extraterritorial Jurisdiction Act (Pub. L. No. 106-523, 114 Stat. 2488) that permits certain persons overseas to appear before a magistrate judge by telephonic communication.

Rule 5(a)(2)(A) consists of language currently located in Rule 5 that addresses the procedure to be followed where a defendant has been arrested under a warrant issued on a complaint charging solely a violation of 18 U.S.C. § 1073 (unlawful flight to avoid prosecution). Rule 5(a)(2)(B) and 5(a)(2)(C) are new provisions. They are intended to make it clear that when a defendant is arrested for violating probation or supervised release, or for failing to appear in another district, Rules 32.1 or 40 apply. No change in practice is intended.

Rule 5(a)(3) is new and fills a perceived gap in the rules. It recognizes that a defendant may be subjected to an initial appearance under this rule if a summons was issued under Rule 4, instead of an arrest warrant. If the defendant is appearing pursuant to a summons in a felony case, Rule 5(d) applies, and if the defendant is appearing in a misdemeanor case, Rule 5(e) applies.

Rule 5(b) carries forward the requirement in former Rule 5(a) that if the defendant is arrested without a warrant, a complaint must be promptly filed.

Rule 5(c) is a new provision and sets out where an initial appearance is to take place. If the defendant is arrested in the district where the offense was allegedly committed, under Rule 5(c)(1) the defendant must be taken to a magistrate judge in that district. If no magistrate judge is reasonably available, a state or local judicial officer may conduct the initial appearance. On the other hand, if the defendant is arrested in a district other than the district where the offense was allegedly committed, Rule 5(c)(2) governs. In those instances, the defendant must be taken to a magistrate judge within the district of arrest, unless the appearance can take place more promptly in an adjacent district. The Committee recognized that in some cases, the nearest magistrate judge may actually be across a district's lines. The remainder of Rule 5(c)(2) includes material formerly located in Rule 40.

Rule 5(d), derived from current Rule 5(c), has been retitled to more clearly reflect the subject of that subdivision and the procedure to be used if the defendant is charged with a felony. Rule 5(d)(4) has been added to make clear that a defendant may only be called upon to enter a plea under the provisions of Rule 10. That language is intended to reflect and reaffirm current practice.

The remaining portions of current Rule 5(c) have been moved to Rule 5.1, which deals with preliminary hearings in felony cases.

The major substantive change is in new Rule 5(f), which permits video teleconferencing for an appearance under this rule if the defendant consents. This change reflects the growing practice among state courts to use video teleconferencing to conduct initial proceedings. A similar amendment has been made to Rule 10 concerning arraignments.

In amending Rules 5, 10, and 43 (which generally requires the defendant's presence at all proceedings), the Committee carefully considered the argument that permitting a defendant to appear by video teleconferencing might be considered an erosion of an important element of the judicial process. Much can be lost when video teleconferencing occurs. First, the setting itself may not promote the public's confidence in the integrity and solemnity of a federal criminal proceeding; that is the view of some who have witnessed the use of such proceedings in some state jurisdictions. While it is difficult to quantify the intangible benefits and impact of requiring a defendant to be brought before a federal judicial officer in a federal courtroom, the Committee realizes that something is lost when a defendant is not required to make a personal appearance. A related consideration is that the defendant may be located in a room that bears no resemblance whatsoever to a judicial forum and the equipment may be inadequate for high quality transmissions. Second, using video teleconferencing can interfere with counsel's ability to meet personally with his or her client at what, at least in that jurisdiction, might be an important appearance before a magistrate judge. Third, the defendant may miss an opportunity to meet with family or friends, and others who might be able to assist the defendant, especially in any attempts to obtain bail. Finally, the magistrate judge may miss an opportunity to accurately assess the physical, emotional, and mental condition of a defendant — a factor that may weigh on pretrial decisions, such as release from detention.

On the other hand, the Committee considered that in some jurisdictions, the court systems face a high volume of criminal proceedings. In other jurisdictions, counsel may not be appointed until after the initial appearance and thus there is no real problem with a defendant being able to consult with counsel before or during that proceeding. The Committee was also persuaded to adopt the amendment because in some jurisdictions delays may occur in travel time from one location to another — in some cases requiring either the magistrate judge or the participants to travel long distances. In those instances, it is not unusual for a defense counsel to recognize the benefit of conducting a video teleconferenced proceeding, which will eliminate lengthy and sometimes expensive travel or permit the initial appearance to be conducted much sooner. Finally, the Committee was aware that in some jurisdictions, courtrooms now contain high quality technology for conducting such procedures, and that some courts are already using video teleconferencing — with the consent of the parties.

The Committee believed that, on balance and in appropriate circumstances, the court and the defendant should have the option of using video teleconferencing, as long as the defendant consents to that procedure. The question of when it would be appropriate for a defendant to consent is not spelled out in the rule. That is left to the defendant and the court in each case. Although the rule does not specify any particular technical requirements regarding the system to be used, if the equipment or technology is deficient, the public may lose confidence in the integrity and dignity of the proceedings.

The amendment does not require a court to adopt or use video teleconferencing. In deciding whether to use such procedures, a court may wish to consider establishing clearly articulated standards and procedures. For example, the court would normally want to insure that the location used for televising the video teleconferencing is conducive to the solemnity of a federal criminal proceeding. That might require additional coordination, for example, with the detention facility to insure that the room, furniture, and furnishings reflect the dignity associated with a federal courtroom. Provision should also be made to insure that the judge, or a surrogate, is in a position to carefully assess the defendant's condition. And the court should also consider establishing procedures for insuring that counsel and the defendant (and even the defendant's immediate family) are provided an ample opportunity to confer in private.

Notes of Advisory Committee on 2006 amendments.

Note to Subdivisions (c)(3)(C) and (D). The amendment to Rule 5(c)(3)(C) parallels an amendment to Rule 58(b)(2)(G), which in turn has been amended to remove a conflict between that rule and Rule 5.1(a), concerning the right to a preliminary hearing.

Rule 5(c)(3)(D) has been amended to permit the magistrate judge to accept a warrant by reliable electronic means. Currently, the rule requires the government to produce the original warrant, a certified copy of the warrant, or a facsimile copy of either of those documents. This amendment parallels similar changes to Rules 32.1(a)(5)(B)(i) and 41. The reference to a facsimile version of the warrant was removed because the Committee believed that the broader term "electronic form" includes facsimiles.

The amendment reflects a number of significant improvements in technology. First, more courts are now equipped to receive filings by electronic means, and indeed, some courts encourage or require that certain documents be filed by electronic means. Second, the technology has advanced to the state where such filings could be sent from, and received at, locations outside the courthouse. Third, electronic media can now provide improved quality of transmission and security measures. In short, in a particular case, using electronic media to transmit a document might be just as reliable and efficient as using a facsimile.

The term "electronic" is used to provide some flexibility to the rule and make allowance for further technological advances in transmitting data.

The rule requires that if electronic means are to be used to transmit a warrant to the magistrate judge, that the means used be "reliable." While the rule does not further define that term, the Committee envisions that a court or magistrate judge would make that determination as a local matter. In deciding whether a particular electronic means, or media, would be reliable, the court might consider first, the expected quality and clarity of the transmission. For example, is it possible to read the contents of the warrant in its entirety, as though it were the original or a clean photocopy? Second, the court may consider whether security measures are available to insure that the transmission is not compromised. In this regard, most courts are now equipped to require that certain documents contain a digital signature, or some other similar system for restricting access. Third, the court may consider whether there are reliable means of preserving the document for later use.

Notes of Advisory Committee on 2012 amendments.

Note to Subdivision (c)(4). The amendment codifies the longstanding practice that persons who are charged with criminal offenses in the United States and surrendered to the United States following extradition in a foreign country make their initial appearance in the jurisdiction that sought their extradition.

This rule is applicable even if the defendant arrives first in another district. The earlier stages of the extradition process have already fulfilled some of the functions of the initial appearance. During foreign extradition proceedings, the extradited person, assisted by counsel, is afforded an opportunity to review the charging document, U.S. arrest warrant, and supporting evidence. Rule 5(a)(1)(B) requires the person be taken before a magistrate judge without unnecessary delay. Consistent with this obligation, it is preferable not to delay an extradited person's transportation to hold an initial appearance in the district of arrival, even if the person will be present in that district for some time as a result of connecting flights or logistical difficulties. Interrupting an extradited defendant's transportation at this point can impair his or her ability to obtain and consult with trial counsel and to prepare his or her defense in the district where the charges are pending.

Notes of Advisory Committee on 2014 amendments.

Rule 5(d)(l)(F). Article 36 of the Vienna Convention on Consular Relations provides that detained foreign nationals shall be advised that they may have the consulate of their home country notified of their arrest and detention, and bilateral agreements with numerous countries require consular notification whether or not the detained foreign national requests it. Article 36 requires consular notification advice to be given "without delay," and arresting officers are primarily responsible for providing this advice.

Providing this advice at the initial appearance is designed, not to relieve law enforcement officers of that responsibility, but to provide additional assurance that U.S. treaty obligations are fulfilled, and to create a judicial record of that action. The Committee concluded that the most effective and efficient method of conveying this information is to provide it to every defendant, without attempting to determine the defendant's citizenship.

At the time of this amendment, many questions remain unresolved by the courts concerning Article 36, including whether it creates individual rights that may be invoked in a judicial proceeding and what, if any, remedy may exist for a violation of Article 36. *Sanchez-Llamas v. Oregon,* 548 U.S. 331 (2006). This amendment does not address those questions. More particularly, it does not create any such rights or remedies.

Amendments:

1984.

Act Oct. 12, 1984, § 209(a) (effective on enactment, as provided by § 235(a)(1)(B)(i) of such Act, which appears as 18 USCS § 3551 note), in subsec (c), substituted "shall detain or conditionally release the defendant" for "shall admit the defendant to bail".

2020.

The 2020 amendment by P.L. 116-182 added (f); and redesignated former (f) as (g).

Rule 5.1. Preliminary Hearing

(a) In general. If a defendant is charged with an offense other than a petty offense, a magistrate judge must conduct a preliminary hearing unless:

(1) the defendant waives the hearing;

(2) the defendant is indicted;

(3) the government files an information under Rule 7(b) charging the defendant with a felony;

(4) the government files an information charging the defendant with a misdemeanor; or

(5) the defendant is charged with a misdemeanor and consents to trial before a magistrate judge.

(b) Selecting a District. A defendant arrested in a district other than where the offense was allegedly committed may elect to have the preliminary hearing conducted in the district where the prosecution is pending.

(c) Scheduling. The magistrate judge must hold the preliminary hearing within a reasonable time, but no later than 14 days after the initial appearance if the defendant is in custody and no later than 21 days if not in custody.

(d) Extending the Time. With the defendant's consent and upon a showing of good cause—taking into account the public interest in the prompt disposition of criminal cases—a magistrate judge may extend the time limits in Rule 5.1(c) one or more times. If the defendant does not consent, the magistrate judge may extend the time limits only on a showing that extraordinary circumstances exist and justice requires the delay.

(e) Hearing and Finding. At the preliminary hearing, the defendant may cross-examine adverse witnesses and may introduce evidence but may not object to evidence on the ground that it was unlawfully acquired. If the magistrate judge finds probable cause to believe an offense has been committed and the defendant committed it, the magistrate judge must promptly require the defendant to appear for further proceedings.

(f) Discharging the Defendant. If the magistrate judge finds no probable cause to believe an offense has been committed or the defendant committed it, the magistrate judge must dismiss the complaint and discharge the defendant. A discharge does not preclude the government from later prosecuting the defendant for the same offense.

(g) Recording the Proceedings. The preliminary hearing must be recorded by a court reporter or by a suitable recording device. A recording of the proceeding may be made available to any party upon request. A copy of the recording and a transcript may be provided to any party upon request and upon any payment required by applicable Judicial Conference regulations.

(h) Producing a Statement.

(1) *In General.* Rule 26.2(a)–(d) and (f) applies at any hearing under this rule, unless the magistrate judge for good cause rules otherwise in a particular case.

(2) *Sanctions for Not Producing a Statement.* If a party disobeys a Rule 26.2 order to deliver a statement to the moving party, the magistrate judge must not consider the testimony of a witness whose statement is withheld.

HISTORY:

Added April 24, 1972, eff. Oct. 1, 1972; amended March 9, 1987, eff. Aug. 1, 1987; April 22, 1993, eff. Dec. 1, 1993; April 24, 1998, eff. Dec. 1, 1998; April 29, 2002, eff. Dec. 1, 2002; March 26, 2009, eff. Dec. 1, 2009.

HISTORY; ANCILLARY LAWS AND DIRECTIVES

Other provisions:

Notes of Advisory Committee. Rule 5.1 is, for the most part, a clarification of old rule 5(c).

Under the new rule, the preliminary examination must be conducted before a "federal magistrate" as defined in rule 54. Giving state or local judicial officers authority to conduct a preliminary examination does not seem necessary. There are not likely to be situations in which a "federal magistrate" is not "reasonably available" to conduct the preliminary examination, which is usually not held until several days after the initial appearance provided for in rule 5.

Subdivision (a) makes clear that a finding of probable cause may be based on "hearsay evidence in whole or in part." The propriety of relying upon hearsay at the preliminary examination has been a matter of some uncertainty in the federal system. See C. Wright, Federal Practice and Procedure: Criminal § 80 (1969, Supp. 1971); 8 J. Moore, Federal Practice P 504 [4] (2d ed. Cipes 1970, Supp. 1971); *Washington v Clemmer,* 339 F.2d 715, 719 (D.C. Cir. 1964); *Washington v Clemmer,* 339 F.2d 725, 728 (D.C. Cir. 1964); *Ross v Sirica,* 380 F.2d 557, 565 (D.C. Cir. 1967); *Howard v United States,* 389 F.2d 287, 292 (D.C. Cir. 1967); Weinberg and Weinberg, The Congressional Invitation to Avoid the Preliminary Hearing: An Analysis of Section 303 of the Federal Magistrates Act of 1968, 67 Mich.L.Rev. 1361, especially n. 92 at 1383 (1969); D. Wright, The Rules of Evidence Applicable to Hearings in Probable Cause, 37 Conn.B.J. 561 (1963); Comment, Preliminary Examination —Evidence and Due Process, 15 Kan.L.Rev. 374, 379–381 (1967).

A grand jury indictment may properly be based upon hearsay evidence. *Costello v United States,* 350 U.S. 359 (1956); 8 J. Moore, Federal Practice P 6.03 [2] (2d ed. Cipes 1970, Supp. 1971). This being so, there is practical advantage in making the evidentiary requirements for the preliminary examination as flexible as they are for the grand jury. Otherwise there will be increased pressure upon United States Attorneys to abandon the preliminary examination in favor of the grand jury indictment. See C. Wright, Federal Practice and Procedure: Criminal § 80 at p. 143 (1969). New York State, which also utilizes both the preliminary examination and the grand jury, has under consideration a new Code of Criminal Procedure which would allow the use of hearsay at the preliminary examination. See McKinney's Session Law News, April 10, 1969, pp. A119–A120.

For the same reason, subdivision (a) also provides that the preliminary examination is not the proper place to raise the issue of illegally obtained evidence. This is current law. In *Giordenello v United States,* 357 U.S. 480, 484 (1958), the Supreme Court said:

[T]he Commissioner here had no authority to adjudicate the admissibility at petitioner's later trial of the heroin taken from his person. That issue was for the trial court. This is specifically recognized by Rule 41(e) of the Criminal Rules, which provides that a defendant aggrieved by an unlawful search and seizure may ". . . move the district court . . . to suppress for use as evidence anything so obtained on the ground that . . ." the arrest warrant was defective on any of several grounds.

Dicta in *Costello v United States* 350 U.S. 359, 100 L.Ed. 397, 76 S.Ct. 406 (1956), and *United States v Blue* 384 U.S. 251, 16 L.Ed.2d 510, 86 S.Ct. 1416 (1966), also support the proposed rule. In *United States ex rel. Almeida v Rundle* 383 F.2d 421 (1967, 3d Cir.), the court, in considering the adequacy of an indictment, said:

On this score, it is settled law that (1) "[a]n indictment returned by a legally constituted nonbiased grand jury, . . . is enough to call for a trial of the charge on the merits and satisfies the requirements of the Fifth Amendment.", *Lawn v United States,* 355 U.S. 339, 349, 78 S.Ct. 311, 317, 2 L.Ed.2d 321 (1958); (2) an indictment cannot be challenged "on the ground that there was inadequate or incompetent evidence before the grand jury", *Costello v United States,* 350 U.S. 359, 363, 76 S.Ct. 406, 408, 100 L.Ed. 397 (1956); and (3) a prosecution is not abated, nor barred, even where "tainted evidence" has been submitted to a grand jury, *United States v Blue,* 384 U.S. 251, 86 S.Ct. 1416, 16 L.Ed.2d 510 (1966).

See also C. Wright, Federal Practice and Procedure: Criminal § 80 at 143 n. 5 (1969, Supp. 1971) 8 J. Moore, Federal Practice P 6.03 [3] (2d ed. Cipes 1970, Supp. 1971). The Manual for United States Commissioners (Administrative Office of United States Courts, 1948) provides at pp 24–25: "Motions for this purpose [to suppress illegally obtained evidence] may be made and heard only before a district judge. Commissioners are not empowered to consider or act upon such motions."

It has been urged that the rules of evidence at the preliminary examination should be those applicable at the trial because the purpose of the preliminary examination should be, not to review the propriety of the arrest or prior detention, but rather to determine whether there is evidence sufficient to justify subjecting the defendant to the expense and inconvenience of trial. See Weinberg and Weinberg, The Congressional Invitation to Avoid the Preliminary Hearing: An Analysis of Section 303 of the Federal Magistrates Act of 1968, 67 Mich.L.Rev. 1361, 1396–1399 (1969). The rule rejects this view for reasons largely of administrative necessity and the efficient administration of justice. The Congress has decided that a preliminary examination shall not be required when there is a grand jury indictment (18 U.S.C. § 3060). Increasing the procedural and evidentiary requirements applicable to the preliminary examination will therefore add to the administrative pressure to avoid the preliminary examination. Allowing objections to evidence on the ground that evidence has been illegally obtained would require two determinations of admissibility, one before the United States magistrate and one in the district court. The objective is to reduce, not increase, the number of preliminary motions.

To provide that a probable cause finding may be based upon hearsay does not preclude the magistrate from requiring a showing that admissible evidence will be available at the time of trial. See Comment, Criminal Procedure—Grand Jury—Validity of Indictment Based Solely on Hearsay Questioned When Direct Testimony Is Readily Available, 43 N.Y.U. L. Rev. 578 (1968); *United States v Umans,* 368 F.2d 725 (2d Cir. 1966), cert dismissed as improvidently granted 389 U.S. 80 (1967); *United States v Andrews,* 381 F.2d 377, 378 (2d Cir. 1967); *United States v Messina,* 388 F.2d 393, 394 n. 1 (2d Cir. 1968); *United States v Beltram,* 388 F.2d 449 (2d Cir. 1968); and *United States v Arcuri,* 282 F.Supp. 347 (E.D.N.Y. 1968). The fact that a defendant is not entitled to object to evidence alleged to have been illegally obtained does not deprive him of an opportunity for a pretrial determination of the admissibility of evidence. He can raise such an objection prior to trial in accordance with the provisions of rule 12.

Subdivision (b) makes it clear that the United States magistrate may not only discharge the defendant but may also dismiss the complaint. Current federal law authorizes the magistrate to discharge the defendant but he must await authorization from the United States Attorney before he can close his records on the case by dismissing the complaint. Making dismissal of the complaint a separate procedure accomplishes no worthwhile objective, and the new rule makes it clear that the magistrate can both discharge the defendant and file the record with the clerk.

Subdivision (b) also deals with the legal effect of a discharge of a defendant at a preliminary examination. This issue is not dealt with explicitly in the old rule. Existing federal case law is limited. What cases there are seem to support the right of the government to issue a new complaint and start over. See e.g., *Collins v Loisel,* 262 U.S. 426 (1923); *Morse v United States,* 267 U.S. 80 (1925). State law is similar. See *People v Dillon,* 197 N.Y. 254, 90 N.E. 820 (1910); *Tell v Wolke,* 21 Wis.2d 613, 124 N.W.2d 655 (1963). In the *Tell* case the Wisconsin court stated the common rationale for allowing the prosecutor to issue a new complaint and start over:

The state has no appeal from errors of law committed by a magistrate upon preliminary examination and the discharge on a preliminary would operate as an unchallengeable acquittal. . . . The only way an error of law committed on the preliminary examination prejudicial to the state may be challenged or corrected is by a preliminary examination on a second complaint. (21 Wis.2d at 619–620.).

Subdivision (c) is based upon old rule 5(c) and upon the Federal Magistrates Act, 18 U.S.C. § 3060(f). It provides methods for making available to counsel the record of the preliminary examination. See C. Wright, Federal Practice and Procedure: Criminal § 82 (1969, Supp. 1971). The new rule is designed to eliminate delay and expense occasioned by preparation of transcripts where listening to the tape recording would be sufficient. Ordinarily the recording should be made available pursuant to subdivision (c)(1). A written transcript may be provided under subdivision (c)(2) at the discretion of the court, a discretion which must be exercised in accordance with *Britt v North Carolina,* 404 U.S. 226, 30 L.Ed.2d 400, 405 (1971):

A defendant who claims the right to a free transcript does not, under our cases, bear the burden of proving inadequate such alternatives as may be suggested by the State or conjured up by a court in hindsight. In this case, however, petitioner has conceded that he had available an informal alternative which appears to be substantially equivalent to a transcript. Accordingly, we cannot conclude that the court below was in error in rejecting his claim.

The amendments are technical. No substantive change is intended.

Notes of Advisory Committee on 1993 amendments. The Rule is amended to conform to the Judicial Improvements Act of 1990 [P.L. 101-650, Title III, Section 321) which provides that each United States magistrate appointed under section 631 of title 28, United States Code, shall be known as a United States magistrate judge.

Notes of Advisory Committee on 1998 amendments. The addition of subdivision (d) mirrors similar amendments made in 1993 which extended the scope of Rule 26.2 to Rules 32, 32.1, 46 and Rule 8 of the Rules Governing Proceedings under 28 U.S.C. § 2255. As indicated in the Committee Notes accompanying those amendments, the primary reason for extending the coverage of Rule 26.2 rested heavily upon the compelling need for accurate information affecting a witness' credibility. That need, the Committee believes, extends to a preliminary examination under this rule where both the prosecution and the defense have high interests at stake.

A witness' statement must be produced only after the witness has personally testified.

Notes of Advisory Committee on 2002 amendments. The language of Rule 5.1 has been amended as part of the general restyling of the Criminal Rules to make them more easily understood and to make style and terminology consistent throughout the rules. These changes are intended to be stylistic, except as noted below.

First, the title of the rule has been changed. Although the underlying statute, 18 U.S.C. § 3060, uses the phrase *preliminary examination*, the Committee believes that the phrase *preliminary hearing* is more accurate. What happens at this proceeding is more than just an examination; it includes an evidentiary hearing, argument, and a judicial ruling. Further, the phrase *preliminary hearing* predominates in actual usage.

Rule 5.1(a) is composed of the first sentence of the second paragraph of current Rule 5(c). Rule 5.1(b) addresses the ability of a defendant to elect where a preliminary hearing will be held. That provision is taken from current Rule 40(a).

Rule 5.1(c) and (d) include material currently located in Rule 5(c): scheduling and extending the time limits for the hearing. The Committee is aware that in most districts, magistrate judges perform these functions. That point is also reflected in the definition of "court" in Rule 1(b), which in turn recognizes that magistrate judges may be authorized to act.

Rule 5.1(d) contains a significant change in practice. The revised rule includes language that expands the authority of a United States magistrate judge to grant a continuance for a preliminary hearing conducted under the rule. Currently, the rule authorizes a magistrate judge to grant a continuance only in those cases in which the defendant has consented to the continuance. If the defendant does not consent, then the government must present the matter to a district judge, usually on the same day. The proposed amendment conflicts with 18 U.S.C. § 3060, which tracks the original language of the rule and permits only district judges to grant continuances when the defendant objects. The Committee believes that this restriction is an anomaly and that it can lead to needless consumption of judicial and other resources. Magistrate judges are routinely required to make probable cause determinations and other difficult decisions regarding the defendant's liberty interests, reflecting that the magistrate judge's role has developed toward a higher level of responsibility for preindictment matters. The Committee believes that the change in the rule will provide greater judicial economy and that it is entirely appropriate to seek this change to the rule through the Rules Enabling Act procedures. See 28 U.S.C. § 2072(b). Under those procedures, approval by Congress of this rule change would supersede the parallel provisions in 18 U.S.C. § 3060.

Rule 5.1(e), addressing the issue of probable cause, contains the language currently located in Rule 5.1(a), with the exception of the sentence, "The finding of probable cause may be based upon hearsay evidence in whole or in part." That language was included in the original promulgation of the rule in 1972. Similar language was added to Rule 4 in 1974. In the Committee Note on the 1974 amendment, the Advisory Committee explained that the language was included to make it clear that a finding of probable cause may be based upon hearsay, noting that there had been some uncertainty in the federal system about the propriety of relying upon hearsay at the preliminary hearing. See Advisory Committee Note to Rule 5.1 (citing cases and commentary). Federal law is now clear on that proposition. Thus, the Committee believed that the reference to hearsay was no longer necessary. Further, the Committee believed that the matter was best addressed in Rule 1101(d)(3), Federal Rules of Evidence. That rule explicitly states that the Federal Rules of Evidence do not apply to "preliminary examinations in criminal cases, . . . issuance of warrants for arrest, criminal summonses, and search warrants." The Advisory Committee Note accompanying that rule recognizes that: "The nature of the proceedings makes application of the formal rules of evidence inappropriate and impracticable." The Committee did not intend to make any substantive changes in practice by deleting the reference to hearsay evidence.

Rule 5.1(f), which deals with the discharge of a defendant, consists of former Rule 5.1(b).

Rule 5.1(g) is a revised version of the material in current Rule 5.1(c). Instead of including detailed information in the rule itself concerning records of preliminary hearings, the Committee opted simply to direct the reader to the applicable Judicial Conference regulations governing records. The Committee did not intend to make any substantive changes in the way in which those records are currently made available.

Finally, although the rule speaks in terms of initial appearances being conducted before a magistrate judge, Rule 1(c) makes clear that a district judge may perform any function in these rules that a magistrate judge may perform.

Notes of Advisory Committee on 2009 amendments. The times set in the former rule at 10 or 20 days have been revised to 14 or 21 days. See the Committee Note to Rule 45(a).

TITLE III. THE GRAND JURY, THE INDICTMENT, AND THE INFORMATION

Rule

Rule 6. The Grand Jury

(a) Summoning a Grand Jury.

(1) *In General.* When the public interest so requires, the court must order that one or more grand juries be summoned. A grand jury must have 16 to 23 members, and the court must order that enough legally qualified persons be summoned to meet this requirement.

(2) *Alternate Jurors.* When a grand jury is selected, the court may also select alternate jurors. Alternate jurors must have the same qualifications and be selected in the same manner as any other juror. Alternate jurors replace jurors in the same sequence in which the alternates were selected. An alternate juror who replaces a juror is subject to the same challenges, takes the same oath, and has the same authority as the other jurors.

(b) Objection to the Grand Jury or to a Grand Juror.

(1) *Challenges.* Either the government or a defendant may challenge the grand jury on the ground that it was not lawfully drawn, summoned, or selected, and may challenge an individual juror on the ground that the juror is not legally qualified.

(2) *Motion to Dismiss an Indictment.* A party may move to dismiss the indictment based on an objection to the grand jury or on an individual juror's lack of legal qualification, unless the court has previously ruled on the same objection under Rule 6(b)(1). The motion to dismiss is governed by 28 U.S.C. § 1867(e). The court must not dismiss the indictment on the ground that a grand juror was not legally qualified if the record shows that at least 12 qualified jurors concurred in the indictment.

(c) Foreperson and Deputy Foreperson. The court will appoint one juror as the foreperson and another as the deputy foreperson. In the foreperson's absence, the deputy foreperson will act as the foreperson. The foreperson may administer oaths and affirmations and will sign all indictments. The foreperson—or another juror designated by the foreperson—will record the number of jurors concurring in every indictment and will file the record with the clerk, but the record may not be made public unless the court so orders.

(d) Who May Be Present.

(1) *While the Grand Jury Is in Session.* The following persons may be present while the grand jury is in session: attorneys for the government, the witness being questioned, interpreters when needed, and a court reporter or an operator of a recording device.

(2) *During Deliberations and Voting.* No person other than the jurors, and any interpreter needed to assist a hearing-impaired or speech-impaired juror, may be present while the grand jury is deliberating or voting.

(e) Recording and Disclosing the Proceedings.

(1) *Recording the Proceedings.* Except while the grand jury is deliberating or voting, all proceedings must be recorded by a court reporter or by a suitable recording device. But the validity of a prosecution is not affected by the unintentional failure to make a recording. Unless the court orders otherwise, an attorney for the government will retain control of the recording, the reporter's notes, and any transcript prepared from those notes.

(2) *Secrecy.*

(A) No obligation of secrecy may be imposed on any person except in accordance with Rule 6(e)(2)(B).

(B) Unless these rules provide otherwise, the following persons must not disclose a matter occurring before the grand jury:

(i) a grand juror;

(ii) an interpreter;

(iii) a court reporter;

(iv) an operator of a recording device;

(v) a person who transcribes recorded testimony;

(vi) an attorney for the government; or

(vii) a person to whom disclosure is made under Rule 6(e)(3)(A)(ii) or (iii);

(3) *Exceptions.*

(A) Disclosure of a grand-jury matter—other than the grand jury's deliberations or any grand juror's vote—may be made to:

(i) an attorney for the government for use in performing that attorney's duty;

(ii) any government personnel—including those of a state, state subdivision, Indian tribe, or foreign government—that an attorney for the government considers necessary to assist in performing that attorney's duty to enforce federal criminal law; or

(iii) a person authorized by 18 U.S.C. § 3322.

(B) A person to whom information is disclosed under Rule 6(e)(3)(A)(ii) may use that information only to assist an attorney for the government in performing that attorney's duty to enforce federal criminal law. An attorney for the government must promptly provide the court that impaneled the grand jury with the names of all persons to whom a disclosure has been made, and must certify that the attorney has advised those persons of their obligation of secrecy under this rule.

(C) An attorney for the government may disclose any grand-jury matter to another federal grand jury.

(D) An attorney for the government may disclose any grand-jury matter involving foreign intelligence, counterintelligence (as defined in 50 U.S.C. § 3003), or foreign intelligence information (as defined in Rule 6(e)(3)(D)(iii)) to any federal law enforcement, intelligence, protective, immigration, national defense, or national security official to assist the official receiving the information in the performance of that official's duties. An attorney for the government may also disclose any grand-jury matter involving, within the United States or elsewhere, a threat of attack or other grave hostile acts of a foreign power or its agent, a threat of domestic or international sabotage or terrorism, or clandestine intelligence gathering activities by an intelligence service or network of a foreign power or by its agent, to any appropriate federal, state, state subdivision, Indian tribal, or foreign government official, for the purpose of preventing or responding to such threat or activities.

(i) Any official who receives information under Rule 6(e)(3)(D) may use the information only as necessary in the conduct of that person's official duties subject to any limitations on the unauthorized disclosure of such information. Any state, state subdivision, Indian tribal, or foreign government official who receives information under Rule 6(e)(3)(D) may use the information only in a manner consistent with any guidelines issued by the Attorney General and the Director of National Intelligence.

(ii) Within a reasonable time after disclosure is made under Rule 6(e)(3)(D), an attorney for the government must file, under seal, a notice with the court in the district where the grand jury convened stating that such information was disclosed and the departments, agencies, or entities to which the disclosure was made.

(iii) As used in Rule 6(e)(3)(D), the term "foreign intelligence information" means:

(a) information, whether or not it concerns a United States person, that relates to the ability of the United States to protect against—

- actual or potential attack or other grave hostile acts of a foreign power or its agent;
- sabotage or international terrorism by a foreign power or its agent; or
- clandestine intelligence activities by an intelligence service or network of a foreign power or by its agent; or

(b) information, whether or not it concerns a United States person, with respect to a foreign power or foreign territory that relates to—

- the national defense or the security of the United States; or
- the conduct of the foreign affairs of the United States.

(E) The court may authorize disclosure—at a time, in a manner, and subject to any other conditions that it directs—of a grand-jury matter:

(i) preliminarily to or in connection with a judicial proceeding;

(ii) at the request of a defendant who shows that a ground may exist to dismiss the indictment because of a matter that occurred before the grand jury;

(iii) at the request of the government, when sought by a foreign court or prosecutor for use in an official criminal investigation;

(iv) at the request of the government if it shows that the matter may disclose a violation of State, Indian tribal, or foreign criminal law, as long as the disclosure is to an appropriate state, state subdivision, Indian tribal, or foreign government official for the purpose of enforcing that law; or

(v) at the request of the government if it shows that the matter may disclose a violation of military criminal law under the Uniform Code of Military Justice, as long as the disclosure is to an appropriate military official for the purpose of enforcing that law.

(F) A petition to disclose a grand-jury matter under Rule 6(e)(3)(E)(i) must be filed in the district where the grand jury convened. Unless the hearing is ex parte—as it may be when the government is the petitioner—the petitioner must serve the petition on, and the court must afford a reasonable opportunity to appear and be heard to:

(i) an attorney for the government;

(ii) the parties to the judicial proceeding; and

(iii) any other person whom the court may designate.

(G) If the petition to disclose arises out of a judicial proceeding in another district, the petitioned court must transfer the petition to the other court unless the petitioned court can reasonably determine whether disclosure is proper. If the petitioned court decides to transfer, it must send to the transferee court the material sought to be disclosed, if feasible, and a written evaluation of the need for continued grand jury secrecy. The transferee court must afford those persons identified in Rule 6(e)(3)(F) a reasonable opportunity to appear and be heard.

(4) *Sealed Indictment.* The magistrate judge to whom an indictment is returned may direct that the indictment be kept secret until the defendant is in custody or has been released pending trial. The clerk must then seal the indictment, and no person may disclose the indictment's existence except as necessary to issue or execute a warrant or summons.

(5) *Closed Hearing.* Subject to any right to an open hearing in a contempt proceeding, the court must close any hearing to the extent necessary to prevent disclosure of a matter occurring before a grand jury.

(6) *Sealed Records.* Records, orders, and subpoenas relating to grand-jury proceedings must be kept under seal to the extent and as long as necessary to prevent the unauthorized disclosure of a matter occurring before a grand jury.

(7) *Contempt.* A knowing violation of Rule 6, or of any guidelines jointly issued by the Attorney General and the Director of National Intelligence under Rule 6, may be punished as a contempt of court.

(f) Indictment and Return. A grand jury may indict only if at least 12 jurors concur. The grand jury—or its foreperson or deputy foreperson—must return the indictment to a magistrate judge in open court. To avoid unnecessary cost or delay, the magistrate judge may take the return by video teleconference from the court where the grand jury sits. If a complaint or information is pending against the defendant and 12 jurors do not concur in the indictment, the foreperson must promptly and in writing report the lack of concurrence to the magistrate judge.

(g) Discharging the Grand Jury. A grand jury must serve until the court discharges it, but it may serve more than 18 months only if the court, having determined that an extension is in the public interest, extends the grand jury's service. An extension may be granted for no more than 6 months, except as otherwise provided by statute.

(h) Excusing a Juror. At any time, for good cause, the court may excuse a juror either temporarily or permanently, and if permanently, the court may impanel an alternate juror in place of the excused juror.

(i) "Indian Tribe" Defined. "Indian tribe" means an Indian tribe recognized by the Secretary of the Interior on a list published in the Federal Register under 25 U.S.C. § 479a-1.

HISTORY:

Amended Feb. 28, 1966, eff. July 1, 1966; April 24, 1972, eff. Oct. 1, 1972; April 26 and July 8, 1976, eff. Aug. 1, 1976; July 30, 1977, P. L. 95-78, § 2(a), 91 Stat. 319; April 30, 1979, eff. Aug. 1, 1979; April 28, 1983, eff. Aug. 1, 1983; Oct. 12, 1984, P. L. 98-473, Title II, § 215(f), 98 Stat. 2016; April 29, 1985, eff. Aug. 1, 1985; March 9, 1987, eff. Aug. 1, 1987; April 22, 1993, eff. Dec. 1, 1993; April 26, 1999, eff. Dec. 1, 1999; Oct. 26, 2001, P. L. 107-56, Title II, § 203(a), 115 Stat. 278; April 29, 2002, eff. Dec. 1, 2002; Nov. 25, 2002, P. L. 107-296, Title VIII, Subtitle I, § 895, 116 Stat. 2256; Dec. 17, 2004, P. L. 108-458, Title VI, Subtitle F, § 6501(a), 118 Stat. 3760; April 12, 2006, eff. Dec. 1, 2006; April 26, 2011, eff. Dec. 1, 2011; April 25, 2014, eff. Dec. 1, 2014; Jan. 5, 2023, P.L. 117-347, Title III, Subtitle B, § 323(a)(1)(A), 136 Stat. 6206.

HISTORY; ANCILLARY LAWS AND DIRECTIVES

Other provisions:

Notes of Advisory Committee. *Note to Subdivision (a).* 1. The first sentence of this rule vests in the court full discretion as to the number of grand juries to be summoned and as to the times when they should be convened. This provision supersedes the existing law, which limits the authority of the court to summon more than one grand jury at the same time. At present two grand juries may be convened simultaneously only in a district which has a city or borough of at least 300,000 inhabitants, and three grand juries only in the Southern District of New York, 28 U.S.C. [former] § 421 (Grand juries; when, how and by whom summoned; length of service). This statute has been construed, however, as only limiting the authority of the court to summon more than one grand jury for a single place of holding court, and as not circumscribing the power to convene simultaneously several grand juries at different points within the same district. *Morris v United States* 128 F.2d 912, (C.C.A. 5th); *United States v Perlstein* 39 F.Supp. 965 (D.N.J.).

2. The provision that the grand jury shall consist of not less than 16 and not more than 23 members continues existing law, 28 U.S.C. § 419 [see 18 U.S.C. § 3321] (Grand jurors; number when less than required number).

3. The rule does not affect or deal with the method of summoning and selecting grand juries. Existing statutes on the subjects are not superseded. See 28 U.S.C. [former] §§ 411–426 [see §§ 1861–1870]. As these provisions of law relate to jurors for both criminal and civil cases, it seemed best not to deal with this subject.

Note to Subdivision (b)(1). Challenges to the array and to individual jurors, although rarely invoked in connection with the selection of grand juries, are nevertheless permitted in the Federal courts and are continued by this rule, *United States v Gale* 109 U.S. 65, 27 L.Ed. 857, 3 S.Ct. 1 (1883); *Clawson v United States* 114 U.S. 477, 29 L.Ed. 179, 5 S.Ct. 949 (1885); *Agnew v United States* 165 U.S. 36, 41 L.Ed. 624, 17 S.Ct. 235 (1897). It is not contemplated, however, that defendants held for action of the grand jury shall receive notice of the time and place of the impaneling of a grand jury, or that defendants in custody shall be brought to court to attend at the selection of the grand jury. Failure to challenge is not a waiver of any objection. The objection may still be interposed by motion under Rule 6(b)(2).

Note to Subdivision (b)(2). 1. The motion provided by this rule takes the place of a plea in abatement, or motion to quash. *Crowley v United States* 194 U.S. 461, 48 L.Ed. 1075, 24 S.Ct. 731 (1904); *United States v Gale, supra.*

2. The second sentence of the rule is a restatement of 18 U.S.C. [former] § 554(a) (Indictments and presentments; objection on ground of unqualified juror barred where twelve qualified jurors concurred; record of number concurring), and introduces no change in existing law.

Note to Subdivision (c). 1. This rule generally is a restatement of existing law, 18 U.S.C. [former] § 554(a) and 28 U.S.C. [former] § 420. Failure of the foreman to sign or endorse the indictment is an irregularity and is not fatal, *Frisbie v United States* 157 U.S. 160, 39 L.Ed. 657, 15 S.Ct. 586 (1895).

2. The provision for the appointment of a deputy foreman is new. Its purpose is to facilitate the transaction of business if the foreman is absent. Such a provision is found in the law of at least one State, N.Y. Code Criminal Procedure, sec. 244.

Note to Subdivision (d). This rule generally continues existing law. See 18 U.S.C. [former] § 556 (Indictments and presentments; defects of form); and 5 U.S.C. § 310 [see 28 U.S.C. § 515(a)] (Conduct of legal proceedings).

Note to Subdivision (e). 1. This rule continues the traditional practice of secrecy on the part of members of the grand jury, except when the court permits a disclosure, *Schmidt v United States* 115 F.2d 394, 21 Ohio Ops. 78 (C.C.A. 6th); *United States v American Medical Association* 26 F.Supp. 429 (D.C.); Cf. *Atwell v United States* 162 F. 97 (C.C.A. 4th); and see 18 U.S.C. [former] § 554(a) (Indictments and presentments; objection on ground of unqualified juror barred where twelve qualified jurors concurred; record of number concurring). Government attorneys are entitled to disclosure of grand jury proceedings, other than the deliberations and the votes of the jurors, inasmuch as they may be present in the grand jury room during the presentation of evidence. The rule continues this practice.

2. The rule does not impose any obligation of secrecy on witnesses. The existing practice on this point varies among the districts. The seal of secrecy on witnesses seems an unnecessary hardship and may lead to injustice if a witness is not permitted to make a disclosure to counsel or to an associate.

3. The last sentence authorizing the court to seal indictments continues present practice.

Note to Subdivision (f). This rule continues existing law, 18 U.S.C. [former] § 554 (Indictments and presentments; by twelve grand jurors). The purpose of the last sentence is to provide means for a prompt release of a defendant if in custody, or exoneration of bail if he is on bail, in the event that the grand jury considers the case of a defendant held for its action and finds no indictment.

Note to Subdivision (g). Under existing law a grand jury serves only during the term for which it is summoned, but the court may extend its period of service for as long as 18 months, 28 U.S.C. [former] § 421. During the extended period, however, a grand jury may conduct only investigations commenced during the original term. The rule continues the 18 months' maximum for the period of service of a grand jury, but provides for such service as a matter of course, unless the court terminates it at an earlier date. The matter is left in the discretion of the court, as it is under existing law. The expiration of a term of court as a time limitation is elsewhere entirely eliminated (Rule 45(c)) and specific time limitations are substituted therefor. This was previously done by the Federal Rules of Civil

Procedure for the civil side of the courts (Federal Rules of Civil Procedure, Rule 6(c), 28 U.S.C., Appendix). The elimination of the requirement that at an extended period the grand jury may continue only investigations previously commenced, will obviate such a controversy as was presented in *United States v Johnson* 319 U.S. 503, 87 L.Ed. 1546, 63 S.Ct. 1233 (1943).

Notes of Advisory Committee on 1966 amendments. Subdivision (d). The amendment makes it clear that recording devices may be used to take evidence at grand jury sessions.

Subdivision (e). The amendment makes it clear that the operator of a recording device and a typist who transcribes recorded testimony are bound to the obligation of secrecy.

Subdivision (f). A minor change conforms the language to what doubtless is the practice. The need for a report to the court that no indictment has been found may be present even though the defendant has not been "held to answer." If the defendant is in custody or has given bail, some official record should be made of the grand jury action so that the defendant can be released or his bail exonerated.

Notes of Advisory Committee on 1972 amendments. Subdivision (b)(2) is amended to incorporate by express reference the provisions of the Jury Selection and Service Act of 1968. That act provides in part:

The procedures prescribed by this section shall be the exclusive means by which a person accused of a Federal crime [or] the Attorney General of the United States . . . may challenge any jury on the ground that such jury was not selected in conformity with the provisions of this title. [28 U.S.C. § 1867(c)].

Under Rule 12(e) the judge shall decide the motion before trial or order it deferred until after verdict. The authority which the judge has to delay his ruling until after verdict gives him an option which can be exercised to prevent the unnecessary delay of a trial in the event that a motion attacking a grand jury is made on the eve of the trial. In addition, Rule 12(c) gives the judge authority to fix the time at which pretrial motions must be made. Failure to make a pretrial motion at the appropriate time may constitute a waiver under Rule 12(f).

Notes of Advisory Committee on 1976 amendments. Under the proposed amendment to rule 6(f), an indictment may be returned to a federal magistrate. ("Federal magistrate" is defined in rule 54(c) as including a United States magistrate as defined in 28 U.S.C. §§ 631–639 and a judge of the United States.) This change will foreclose the possibility of noncompliance with the Speedy Trial Act timetable because of the nonavailability of a judge. Upon the effective date of certain provisions of the Speedy Trial Act of 1974, the timely return of indictments will become a matter of critical importance; for the year commencing July 1, 1976, indictments must be returned within 60 days of arrest or summons, for the year following within 45 days, and thereafter within 30 days. 18 U.S.C. §§ 3161(b) and (f), 3163(a). The problem is acute in a one-judge district where, if the judge is holding court in another part of the district, or is otherwise absent, the return of the indictment must await the later reappearance of the judge at the place where the grand jury is sitting.

A corresponding change has been made to that part of subdivision (f) which concerns the reporting of a "no bill," and to that part of subdivision (e) which concerns keeping an indictment secret.

Criminal Procedure
Rule 6

The change in the third sentence of rule 6(f) is made so as to cover all situations in which by virtue of a pending complaint or information the defendant is in custody or released under some form of conditional release.

Effective date of amendments made by U.S. Supreme Court order of April 26, 1976. Act July 8, 1976, P. L. 94-349, § 1, 90 Stat. 822, provides: "That, notwithstanding the provisions of sections 3771 and 3772 of title 18 of the United States Code, the amendments to rules 6(e), 23, 24, 40.1 and 41(c)(2) of the Rules of Criminal Procedure for the United States district courts which are embraced by the order entered by the United States Supreme Court on April 26, 1976, and which were transmitted to the Congress on or about April 26, 1976, shall not take effect until August 1, 1977, or until and to the extent approved by Act of Congress, whichever is earlier. The remainder of the proposed amendments to the Federal Rules of Criminal Procedure shall become effective August 1, 1976, pursuant to law.".

Notes of Advisory Committee on 1977 amendments. The proposed definition of "attorneys for the government" in subdivision (e) is designed to facilitate an increasing need, on the part of government attorneys, to make use of outside expertise in complex litigation. The phrase "other government personnel" includes, but is not limited to, employees of administrative agencies and government departments.

Present subdivision (e) provides for disclosure "to the attorneys for the government for use in the performance of their duties." This limitation is designed to further "the long established policy that maintains the secrecy of the grand jury in federal courts." *United States v. Procter and Gamble Co.,* 356 U.S. 677 (1958).

As defined in rule 54(c), " 'Attorney for the government' means the Attorney General, an authorized assistant of the Attorney General, a United States Attorney, an authorized assistant of a United States Attorney and when applicable to cases arising under the laws of Guam . . ." The limited nature of this definition is pointed out in *In re Grand Jury Proceedings,* 309 F.2d 440 (3d Cir. 1962) at 443:

The term attorneys for the government is restrictive in its application. . . . If it had been intended that the attorneys for the administrative agencies were to have free access to matters occurring before a grand jury, the rule would have so provided.

The proposed amendment reflects the fact that there is often government personnel assisting the Justice Department in grand jury proceedings. In *In Re Grand Jury Investigation of William H. Pflaumer & Sons, Inc.,* 53 F.R.D. 464 (E.D. Pa. 1971), the opinion quoted the United States Attorney:

It is absolutely necessary in grand jury investigations involving analysis of books and records, for the government attorneys to rely upon investigative personnel (from the government agencies) for assistance.

See also 8 J. Moore, Federal Practice P6.05 at 6-28 (2d ed. Cipes, 1969):

The rule [6(e)] has presented a problem, however, with respect to attorneys and nonattorneys who are assisting in preparation of a case for the grand jury. . . . These assistants often cannot properly perform their work without having access to grand jury minutes.

Although case law is limited, the trend seems to be in the direction of allowing disclosure to government personnel who assist attorneys for the government in situations where their expertise is required. This is subject to the qualification that the matters disclosed be used only for the purposes of the grand jury investigation. The court may inquire as to the good faith of the assisting personnel, to ensure that access to material is not merely a subterfuge to gather evidence unattainable by means other than the grand jury. This approach was taken in *In re Grand Jury Investigation of William H. Pflaumer & Sons, Inc.,* 53 F.R.D. 464 (E.D. Pa. 1971); *In re April 1956 Term Grand Jury,* 239 F.2d 263 (7th Cir. 1956); *United States v. Anzelimo,* 319 F. Supp. 1106 (D.C. La. 1970). Another case, *Application of Kelly,* 19 F.R.D. 269 (S.D.N.Y. 1956), assumed, without deciding, that assistance given the attorney for the government by IRS and FBI agents was authorized.

The change at line 27 reflects the fact that under the Bail Reform Act of 1966 some persons will be released without requiring bail. See 18 U.S.C. §§ 3146, 3148.

Under the proposed amendment to rule 6(f), an indictment may be returned to a federal magistrate. ("Federal magistrate" is defined in rule 54(c) as including a United States magistrate as defined in 28 U.S.C. § 631–639 and a judge of the United States.) This change will foreclose the possibility of noncompliance with the Speedy Trial Act timetable because of the nonavailability of a judge. Upon the effective date of certain provisions of the Speedy Trial Act of 1974, the timely return of indictments will become a matter of critical importance; for the year commencing July 1, 1976, indictments must be returned within 60 days of arrest or summons, for the year following within 45 days, and thereafter within 30 days. 18 U.S.C. §§ 3161(b) and (f), 3163(a). The problem is acute in a one-judge district where, if the judge is holding court in another part of the district, or is otherwise absent, the return of the indictment must await the later reappearance of the judge at the place where the grand jury is sitting.

A corresponding change has been made to that part of subdivision (f) which concerns the reporting of a "no bill," and to that part of subdivision (e) which concerns keeping an indictment secret.

The change in the third sentence of rule 6(f) is made so as to cover all situations in which by virtue of a pending complaint or information the defendant is in custody or released under some form of conditional release.

Notes of Committee on the Judiciary on 1977 amendments to rules proposed by the Supreme Court (Senate Report No. 95-354). Rule 6(e) currently provides that "disclosure of matters occurring before the grand jury other than its deliberations and the vote of any juror may be made to the attorneys for the government for use in the performance of their duties." Rule 54(c) defines attorneys for the government to mean "the Attorney General, an authorized assistant to the Attorney General, a United States attorney, and an authorized assistant of the United States attorney, and when applicable to cases arising under the laws of Guam, means the Attorney General of Guam. . . ."

The Supreme Court proposal would change Rule 6(e) by adding the following new language:

For purposes of this subdivision, "attorneys for the government" includes those enumerated in Rule 54(c); it also includes such other government personnel as are necessary to assist the attorneys for the government in the performance of their duties.

It would also make a series of changes in the rule designed to make its provisions consistent with other provisions in the Rules and the Bail Reform Act of 1966.

The Advisory Committee note states that the proposed amendment is intended "to facilitate an increasing need, on the part of Government attorneys to make use of outside expertise in complex litigation". The note indicated that:

Although case law is limited, the trend seems to be in the direction of allowing disclosure to Government personnel who assist attorneys for the Government in situations where their expertise is required. This is subject to the qualification that the matter disclosed be used only for the purposes of the grand jury investigation.

It is past history at this point that the Supreme Court proposal attracted substantial criticism, which seemed to stem more from the lack of precision in defining, and consequent confusion and uncertainty concerning, the intended scope of the proposed change than from a fundamental disagreement with the objective.

Attorneys for the Government in the performance of their duties with a grand jury must possess the authority to utilize the services of other government employees. Federal crimes are "investigated" by the FBI, the IRS, or by Treasury agents and not by government prosecutors or the citizens who sit on grand juries. Federal agents gather and present information relating to criminal behavior to prosecutors who analyze and evaluate it and present it to grand juries. Often the prosecutors need the assistance of the agents in evaluating evidence. Also, if further investigation is required during or after grand jury proceedings, or even during the course of criminal trials, the Federal agents must do it. There is no reason for a barrier of secrecy to exist between the facets of the criminal justice system upon which we all depend to enforce the criminal laws.

The parameters of the authority of an attorney for the government to disclose grand jury information in the course of performing his own duties is not defined by Rule 6. However, a commonsense interpretation prevails, permitting "Representatives of other government agencies actively assisting United States attorneys in a grand jury investigation . . . access to grand jury material in the performance of their duties." [*United States v. Evans,* 526 F.2d 701 (5th Cir. 1976). See also *United States v. Hoffa,* 349 F.2d 20, 43 (6th Cir. 1965); *United States v. United States District Court,* 238 F.2d 713 (4th Cir. 1975), cert. denied, sub nom. *Valley Bell Dairy Co. v. United States,* 352 U.S. 981; *United States v. Culver,* 224 F. Supp. 419, 432 (D. Md. 1963); *United States v. Anzelmo,* 319 F. Supp. 1106, 1116 (E.D. La. 1970).] Yet projected against this current practice, and the weight of case law, is the anomalous language of Rule 6(e) itself, which, in its present state of uncertainty, is spawning some judicial decisions highly restrictive of the use of government experts that require the government to "show the necessity (to the Court) for each particular person's aid rather than showing merely a general necessity for assistance, expert or otherwise" [*J. R. Simplot Co. v. U.S. District Court of the District of Idaho,* Nos. 76-1893, 76-1995, slip opinion at 9 (9th Cir. filed Nov. 12, 1976)]; and that make Rule 6(e) orders subject to interlocutory appeal.

In this state of uncertainty, the Committee believes it is timely to redraft subdivision (e) of Rule 6 to make it clear.

Paragraph (1) as proposed by the Committee states the general rule that a grand jury, an interpreter, a stenographer, an operator of a recording device, a typist who transcribes recorded testimony, an attorney for the government, or government personnel to whom disclosure is made under paragraph (2)(A)(ii) shall not disclose matters occurring before the grand jury, except as otherwise provided in these rules. It also expressly provides that a knowing violation of Rule 6 may be punished as a contempt of court. In addition, it carries forward the current provision that no obligation of secrecy may be imposed on any person except in accordance with this Rule.

Having stated the general rule of nondisclosure, paragraph (2) sets forth exemptions from nondisclosure. Subparagraph (A) of paragraph (2) provides that disclosure otherwise prohibited, other than the grand jury deliberations and the vote of any grand juror, may be made to an attorney for the government for use in the performance of his duty and to such personnel as are deemed necessary by an attorney for the government to assist an attorney for the government in the performance of such attorney's duty to enforce Federal criminal law. In order to facilitate resolution of subsequent claims of improper disclosure, subparagraph (B) further provides that the names of government personnel designated to assist the attorney for the government shall be promptly provided to the district court and such personnel shall not utilize grand jury material for any purpose other than assisting the attorney for the government in the performance of such attorney's duty to enforce Federal criminal law. Although not expressly required by the rule, the Committee contemplates that the names of such personnel will generally be furnished to the court before disclosure is made to them. Subparagraph (C) permits disclosure as directed by a court preliminarily to or in connection with a judicial proceeding or, at the request of the defendant, upon a showing that grounds may exist for dismissing the indictment because of matters occurring before the grand jury. Paragraph (3) carries forward the last sentence of current Rule 6(e) with the technical changes recommended by the Supreme Court.

The Rule as redrafted is designed to accommodate the belief on the one hand that Federal prosecutors should be able, without the time consuming requirement of prior judicial interposition, to make such disclosures of grand jury information to other government personnel as they deem necessary to facilitate the performance of their duties relating to criminal law enforcement. On the other hand, the Rule seeks to allay the concerns of those who fear that such prosecutorial power will lead to misuse of the grand jury to enforce non-criminal Federal laws by (1) providing a clear prohibition, subject to the penalty of contempt and (2) requiring that a court order under paragraph (C) be obtained to authorize such a disclosure. There is, however, no intent to preclude the use of grand jury-developed evidence for civil law enforcement purposes. On the contrary, there is no reason why such use is improper, assuming that the grand jury was utilized for the legitimate purpose of a criminal investigation. Accordingly, the Committee believes and intends that the basis for a court's refusal to issue an order under paragraph (C) to enable the government to disclose grand jury information in a non-criminal proceeding should be no more restrictive than is the case today under prevailing court decisions. [*United States v. Procter & Gamble,* 356 U.S. 677, 683–684 (1958); Robert Hawthorne, Inc. v. Director of Internal Revenue Service] It is contemplated that the judicial hearing in connection with an application for a court order by the government under subparagraph (3)(C)(i) should be *ex parte* so as to preserve, to the maximum extent possible, grand jury secrecy.

Effective date of July 30, 1977 amendment. As to the effective date of the amendment made by § 2(a) of Act July 30, 1977, P. L. 95-78, see §§ 1 and 4 of such Act, which appear as 18 USCS § 3771 notes.

Notes of Advisory Committee on 1979 amendments. *Note to Subdivision (e)(1).* Proposed subdivision (e)(1) requires that all proceedings, except when the grand jury is deliberating or voting, be recorded. The existing rule does not require that grand jury proceedings be recorded. The provision in rule 6(d) that "a stenographer or operator of a recording device may be present while the grand jury is in session" has been taken to mean that recordation is permissive and not mandatory; see *United States v. Aloisio,* 440 F.2d 705 (7th Cir. 1971), collecting the cases. However, the cases rather frequently state that recordation of the proceedings is the better practice; see *United States v. Aloisio,* supra; *United States v. Cramer,* 447 F.2d 210 (2d Cir. 1971); *Schlinsky v. United States,* 379 F.2d 735 (1st Cir. 1967); and some cases require the district court, after a demand, to exercise discretion as to whether the proceedings should be recorded. *United States v. Price,* 474 F.2d 1223 (9th Cir. 1973); *United States v. Thoresen,* 428 F.2d 654 (9th Cir. 1970). Some district courts have adopted a recording requirement. See, e.g. *United States v. Aloisio,* supra; *United States v. Gramolini,* 301 F. Supp. 39 (D.R.I. 1969). Recording of grand jury proceedings is currently a requirement in a number of states. See, e.g., Cal. Pen. Code §§ 938–938.3; Iowa Code Ann. § 772.4; Ky. Rev. Stat. Ann. § 28.460; and Ky. R. Crim. P. § 5.16(2).

The assumption underlying the proposal is that the cost of such recording is justified by the contribution made to the improved administration of criminal justice. See *United States v. Gramolini,* supra, noting: "Nor can it be claimed that the cost of recordation is prohibitive; in an electronic age, the cost of recordation must be categorized as minuscule." For a discussion of the success of electronic recording in Alaska, see Reynolds, Alaska's Ten Years of Electronic Reporting, 56 A.B.A.J. 1080 (1970).

Among the benefits to be derived from a recordation requirement are the following:

(1) Ensuring that the defendant may impeach a prosecution witness on the basis of his prior inconsistent statements before the grand jury. As noted in the opinion of Oakes, J., in *United States v. Cramer*: "First, since *Dennis v. United States,* 384 U.S. 855, 86 S.Ct. 1840, 16 L.Ed.2d 973 (1966), a defendant has been entitled to examine the grand jury testimony of witnesses against him. On this point, the Court was unanimous, holding that there was 'no justification' for the District of Columbia Court of Appeals' 'relying upon [the] "assumption" ' that 'no inconsistencies would have come to light.' The Court's decision was based on the general proposition that ' [i]n our adversary system for determining guilt or innocence, it is rarely justifiable for the prosecution to have exclusive access to a storehouse of relevant facts.' In the case at bar the prosecution did have exclusive access to the grand jury testimony of the witness Sager, by virtue of being present, and the defense had none--to determine whether there were any inconsistencies with, say, his subsequent testimony as to damaging admissions by the defendant and his attorney Richard Thaler. The Government claims, and it is supported by the majority here, that there is no problem since

defendants were given the benefit of Sager's subsequent statements including these admissions as Jencks Act materials. But assuming this to be true, it does not cure the basic infirmity that the defense could not know whether the witness testified inconsistently before the grand jury."

(2) Ensuring that the testimony received by the grand jury is trustworthy. In *United States v. Cramer,* Oakes, J., also observed: "The recording of testimony is in a very real sense a circumstantial guaranty of trustworthiness. Without the restraint of being subject to prosecution for perjury, a restraint which is wholly meaningless or nonexistent if the testimony is unrecorded, a witness may make baseless accusations founded on hearsay or false accusations, all resulting in the indictment of a fellow citizen for a crime."

(3) Restraining prosecutorial abuses before the grand jury. As noted in *United States v. Gramolini:* "In no way does recordation inhibit the grand jury's investigation. True, recordation restrains certain prosecutorial practices which might, in its absence be used, but that is no reason not to record. Indeed, a sophisticated prosecutor must acknowledge that there develops between a grand jury and the prosecutor with whom the jury is closeted a rapport—a dependency relationship—which can easily be turned into an instrument of influence on grand jury deliberations. Recordation is the most effective restraint upon such potential abuses."

(4) Supporting the case made by the prosecution at trial. Oakes, J., observed in *United States v. Cramer*: "The benefits of having grand jury testimony recorded do not all inure to the defense. See, e.g., *United States v. DeSisto,* 329 F.2d 929, 934 (2d Cir.), cert. denied, 377 U.S. 979, 84 S.Ct. 1885, 12 L.Ed.2d 747 (1964) (conviction sustained in part on basis of witnesses's prior sworn testimony before grand jury)." Fed.R.Evid. 801(d)(1)(A) excludes from the category of hearsay the prior inconsistent testimony of a witness given before a grand jury. *United States v. Morgan,* 555 F.2d 238 (9th Cir. 1977). See also *United States v. Carlson,* 547 F.2d 1346 (8th Cir. 1976), admitting under Fed.R.Evid. 804(b)(5) the grand jury testimony of a witness who refused to testify at trial because of threats by the defendant.

Commentators have also supported a recording requirement. 8 Moore, Federal Practice par. 6.02 [2] [d] (2d ed. 1972) states: "Fairness to the defendant would seem to compel a change in the practice, particularly in view of the 1970 amendment to 18 U.S.C. § 3500 making grand jury testimony of government witnesses available at trial for purposes of impeachment. The requirement of a record may also prove salutary in controlling overreaching or improper examination of witnesses by the prosecutor." Similarly, 1 Wright, Federal Practice and Procedure—Criminal § 103 (1969), states that the present rule "ought to be changed, either by amendment or by judicial construction. The Supreme Court has emphasized the importance to the defense of access to the transcript of the grand jury proceedings [citing *Dennis*]. A defendant cannot have that advantage if the proceedings go unrecorded."American Bar Association, Report of the Special Committee on Federal Rules of Procedure, 52 F.R.D. 87, 94–95 (1971), renews the committee's 1965 recommendation "that all accusatorial grand jury proceedings either be transcribed by a reporter or recorded by electronic means."

Under proposed subdivision (e)(1), if the failure to record is unintentional, the failure to record would not invalidate subsequent judicial proceedings. Under present law, the failure to compel production of grand jury testimony where there is no record is not reversible error. See *Wyatt v. United States,* 388 F.2d 395 (10th Cir. 1968).

The provision that the recording or reporter's notes or any transcript prepared therefrom are to remain in the custody or control (as where the notes are in the immediate possession of a contract reporter employed by the Department of Justice) of the attorney for the government is in accord with present practice. It is specifically recognized, however, that the court in a particular case may have reason to order otherwise.

It must be emphasized that the proposed changes in rule 6(e) deal only with the recording requirement, and in no way expand the circumstances in which disclosure of the grand jury proceedings is permitted or required. "Secrecy of grand jury proceedings is not jeopardized by recordation. The making of a record cannot be equated with disclosure of its contents, and disclosure is controlled by other means." *United States v. Price,* 474 F.2d 1223 (9th Cir. 1973). Specifically, the proposed changes do not provide for copies of the grand jury minutes to defendants as a matter of right, as is the case in some states. See, e.g., Cal. Pen. Code § 938.1; Iowa Code Ann. § 772.4. The matter of disclosure continues to be governed by other provisions, such as rule 16(a) (recorded statements of the defendant), 18 U.S.C. § 3500 (statements of government witnesses), and the unchanged portions of rule 6(e), and the cases interpreting these provisions. See, e.g., *United States v. Howard,* 433 F.2d 1 (5th Cir. 1970), and *Beatrice Foods Co. v. United States,* 312 F.2d 29 (8th Cir. 1963), concerning the showing which must be made of improper matters occurring before the grand jury before disclosure is required.

Likewise, the proposed changes in rule 6(e) are not intended to make any change regarding whether a defendant may challenge a grand jury indictment. The Supreme Court has declined to hold that defendants may challenge indictments on the ground that they are not supported by sufficient or competent evidence. *Costello v. United States,* 350 U.S. 359 (1956); *Lawn v. United States,* 355 U.S. 339 (1958); *United States v. Blue,* 384 U.S. 251 (1966). Nor are the changes intended to permit the defendant to challenge the conduct of the attorney for the government before the grand jury absent a preliminary factual showing of serious misconduct.

Note to Subdivision (e)(3)(C). The sentence added to subdivision (e)(3)(C) gives express recognition to the fact that if the court orders disclosure, it may determine the circumstances of the disclosure. For example, if the proceedings are electronically recorded, the court would have discretion in an appropriate case to deny defendant the right to a transcript at government expense. While it takes special skills to make a stenographic record understandable, an electronic recording can be understood by merely listening to it, thus avoiding the expense of transcription.

Notes of Advisory Committee on 1983 amendments. *Note to Subdivision (e)(3)(C).* New subdivision (e)(3)(C)(iii) recognizes that it is permissible for the attorney for the government to make disclosure of matters occurring before one grand jury to another federal grand jury. Even absent a specific provision to that effect, the courts have permitted such disclosure in some circumstances. See, e.g., *United States v. Socony-Vacuum Oil Co.,* 310 U.S. 150 (1940); *United States v. Garcia,* 420 F.2d 309 (2d Cir. 1970). In this kind of situation, " [s]ecrecy of grand jury materials should be protected almost as well by the safeguards at the second grand jury proceeding, including the oath of the jurors, as by judicial supervision of the disclosure of such materials." *United States v. Malatesta,* 583 F.2d 748 (5th Cir.1978).

Note to Subdivision (e)(3)(D). In *Douglas Oil Co. v. Petrol Stops Northwest,* 441 U.S. 211 (1979), the Court held on the facts there presented that it was an abuse of discretion for the district judge to order disclosure of grand jury transcripts for use in civil proceedings in another district where that judge had insufficient knowledge of those proceedings to make a determination of the need for disclosure. The Court suggested a "better practice" on those facts, but declared that "procedures to deal with the many variations are best left to the rulemaking procedures established by Congress."

The first sentence of subdivision (e)(3)(D) makes it clear that when disclosure is sought under subdivision (e)(2)(C)(i), the petition is to be filed in the district where the grand jury was convened, whether or not it is the district of the "judicial proceeding" giving rise to the petition. Courts which have addressed the question have generally taken this view, e.g., *Illinois v. Sarbaugh,* 522 F.2d 768 (7th Cir. 1977). As stated in *Douglas Oil,*

those who seek grand jury transcripts have little choice other than to file a request with the court that supervised the grand jury, as it is the only court with control over the transcripts.

Quite apart from the practical necessity, the policies underlying Rule 6(e) dictate that the grand jury's supervisory court participate in reviewing such requests, as it is in the best position to determine the continuing need for grand jury secrecy. Ideally, the judge who supervised the grand jury should review the request for disclosure, as he will have firsthand knowledge of the grand jury's activities. But even other judges of the district where the grand jury sat may be able to discover facts affecting the need for secrecy more easily than would judges from elsewhere around the country. The records are in the custody of the District Court, and therefore are readily available for references. Moreover, the personnel of that court—particularly those of the United States Attorney's Office who worked with the grand jury—are more likely to be informed about the grand jury proceedings than those in a district that had no prior experience with the subject of the request.

The second sentence requires the petitioner to serve notice of his petition upon several persons who, by the third sentence, are recognized as entitled to appear and be heard on the matter. The notice requirement ensures that all interested parties, if they wish, may make a timely appearance. Absent such notice, these persons, who then might only learn of the order made in response to the motion after it was entered, have had to resort to the cumbersome and inefficient procedure of a motion to vacate the order. *In re Special February 1971 Grand Jury v. Conlisk,* 490 F.2d 894 (7th Cir. 1973).

Though some authority is to be found that parties to the judicial proceeding giving rise to the motion are not entitled to intervene, in that "the order to produce was not directed to" them, *United States v. American Oil Co.,* 456 F.2d 1043 (3d Cir. 1972), that position was rejected in *Douglas Oil,* where it was noted that such persons have standing "to object to the disclosure order, as release of the transcripts to their civil adversaries could result in substantial injury to them." As noted in *Illinois v. Sarbaugh,* supra, while present rule 6(e) "omits to state whether any one is entitled to object to disclosure,".

the rule seems to contemplate a proceeding of some kind, judicial proceedings are not normally ex parte, and persons in the situation of the intervenors [parties to the civil proceeding] are likely to be the only ones to object to an order for disclosure. If they are not allowed to appear, the advantages of an adversary proceeding are lost.

If the judicial proceeding is a class action, notice to the representative is sufficient.

The amendment also recognizes that the attorney for the government in the district where the grand jury convened also has an interest in the matter and should be allowed to be heard. It may sometimes be the case, as in *Douglas Oil,* that the prosecutor will have relatively little concern for secrecy, at least as compared with certain parties to the civil proceeding. Nonetheless, it is appropriate to recognize that generally the attorney for the government is entitled to be heard so that he may represent what *Douglas Oil* characterizes as "the public interest in secrecy," including the government's legitimate concern about "the possible effect upon the functioning of future grand juries" of unduly liberal disclosure.

The second sentence leaves it to the court to decide whether any other persons should receive notice and be allowed to intervene. This is appropriate, for the necessity for and feasibility of involving others may vary substantially from case to case. In *Douglas Oil,* it was noted that the individual who produced before the grand jury the information now sought has an interest in the matter:

Fear of future retribution or social stigma may act as powerful deterrents to those who would come forward and aid the grand jury in the performance of its duties. Concern as to the future consequences of frank and full testimony is heightened where the witness is an employee of a company under investigation.

Notice to such persons, however is by no means inevitably necessary, and in some cases the information sought may have reached the grand jury from such a variety of sources that it is not practicable to involve these sources in the disclosure proceeding. Similarly, while *Douglas Oil* notes that rule 6(e) secrecy affords "protection of the innocent accused from disclosure of the accusation made against him before the grand jury," it is appropriate to leave to the court whether that interest requires representation directly by the grand jury target at this time. When deemed necessary to protect the identity of such other persons, it would be a permissible alternative for the government or the court directly to give notice to these other persons, and thus the rule does not foreclose such action.

The notice requirement in the second sentence is inapplicable if the hearing is to be ex parte. The legislative history of rule 6(e) states: "It is contemplated that the judicial hearing in connection with an application for a court order by the government, under subparagraph (3)(C)(i) should be ex parte so as to preserve, to the maximum extent possible, grand jury secrecy." S.Rep. No. 95-354, 1977 U.S. Code Cong. & Admin. News p. 532. Although such cases are distinguishable from other cases arising under this subdivision because internal regulations limit further disclosure of information disclosed to the government, the rule provides only that the hearing "may" be ex parte when the petitioner is the government. This allows the court to decide that matter based upon the circumstances of the particular case. For example, an ex parte proceeding is much less likely to be appropriate if the government acts as petitioner as an accommodation to, e.g., a state agency.

Note to Subdivision (e)(3)(E). Under the first sentence in new subdivision (e)(3)(E), the petitioner or any intervenor might seek to have the matter transferred to the federal district court where the judicial proceeding giving rise to the petition is pending. Usually it will be the petitioner, who is seeking disclosure, who will desire the transfer, but this is not inevitably the case. An intervenor might seek transfer on the ground that the other court, with greater knowledge of the extent of the need, would be less likely to conclude "that the material . . . is needed to avoid a possible injustice" (the test under *Douglas Oil*). The court may transfer on its own motion, for as noted in *Douglas Oil,* if transfer is the better course of action it should not be foreclosed "merely because the parties have failed to specify the relief to which they are entitled."

It must be emphasized that transfer is proper only if the proceeding giving rise to the petition "is in federal district court in another district." If, for example, the proceeding is located in another district but is at the state level, a situation encompassed within rule 6(e)(3)(C)(i), *In re Special February 1971 Grand Jury v. Conlisk,* supra, there is no occasion to transfer. Ultimate resolution of the matter cannot be placed in the hands of the state court, and in such a case the federal court in that place would lack what *Douglas Oil* recognizes as the benefit to be derived from transfer: "first-hand knowledge of the litigation in which the transcripts allegedly are needed." Formal transfer is unnecessary in intradistrict cases, even when the grand jury court and judicial proceeding court are not in the same division.

As stated in the first sentence, transfer by the court is appropriate "unless it can reasonably obtain sufficient knowledge of the proceeding to determine whether disclosure is proper." (As reflected by the "whether disclosure is proper" language, the amendment makes no effort to define the disclosure standard; that matter is currently governed by *Douglas Oil* and the authorities cited therein, and is best left to elaboration by future case law.) The amendment expresses a preference for having the disclosure issue decided by the grand jury court. Yet, it must be recognized, as stated in *Douglas Oil,* that often this will not be possible because.

the judges of the court having custody of the grand jury transcripts will have no first-hand knowledge of the litigation in which the transcripts allegedly are needed, and no practical means by which such knowledge can be obtained. In such a case, a judge in the district of the grand jury cannot weigh in an informed manner the need for disclosure against the need for maintaining grand jury secrecy.

The penultimate sentence provides that upon transfer the transferring court shall order transmitted the material sought to be disclosed and also a written evaluation of the need for continuing grand jury secrecy. Because the transferring court is in the best position to assess the interest in continued grand jury secrecy in the particular instance, it is important that the court which will now have to balance that interest against the need for disclosure receive the benefit of the transferring court's assessment. Transmittal of the material sought to be disclosed will not only facilitate timely disclosure if it is thereafter ordered, but will also assist the other court in deciding how great the need for disclosure actually is. For example, with that material at hand the other court will be able to determine if there is any inconsistency between certain grand jury testimony and testimony received in the other judicial proceeding. The rule recognizes, however, that there may be instances in which transfer of everything sought to be disclosed is not feasible. See, e.g., *In re 1975-2 Grand Jury Investigation,* 566 F.2d 1293 (5th Cir. 1978) (court ordered transmittal of "an inventory of the grand jury subpoenas, transcripts, and documents," as the materials in question were "exceedingly voluminous, filling no less than 55 large file boxes and one metal filing cabinet").

The last sentence makes it clear that in a case in which the matter is transferred to another court, that court should permit the various interested parties specified in the rule to be heard. Even if those persons were previously heard before the court which ordered the transfer, this will not suffice. The order of transfer did not decide the ultimate issue of "whether a particularized need for disclosure outweighs the interest in continued grand jury secrecy," Douglas Oil, supra, which is what now remains to be resolved by the court to which transfer was made. Cf. *In re 1975-2 Grand Jury Investigation,* supra, holding that a transfer order is not appealable because it does not determine the ultimate question of disclosure, and thus " [n]o one has yet been aggrieved and no one will become aggrieved until [the court to which the matter was transferred] acts."

Note to Subdivision (e)(5). This addition to rule 6 would make it clear that certain hearings which would reveal matters which have previously occurred before a grand jury or are likely to occur before a grand jury with respect to a pending or ongoing investigation must be conducted in camera in whole or in part in order to prevent public disclosure of such secret information. One such hearing is that conducted under subdivision (e)(3)(D), for it will at least sometimes be necessary to consider and assess some of the "matters occurring before the grand jury" in order to decide the disclosure issue. Two other kinds of hearings at which information about a particular grand jury investigation might need to be discussed are those at which the question is whether to grant a grand jury witness immunity or whether to order a grand jury witness to comply fully with the terms of a subpoena directed to him.

A recent GAO study established that there is considerable variety in the practice as to whether such hearings are closed or open, and that open hearings often seriously jeopardize grand jury secrecy:

For judges to decide these matters, the witness' relationship to the case under investigation must be discussed. Accordingly, the identities of witnesses and targets, the nature of expected testimony, and the extent to which the witness is cooperating are often revealed during preindictment proceedings. Because the matters discussed can compromise the purposes of grand jury secrecy, some judges close the preindictment proceedings to the public and the press; others do not. When the proceeding is open, information that may otherwise be kept secret under rule 6(e) becomes available to the public and the press. . . .

Open preindictment proceedings are a major source of information which can compromise the purposes of grand jury secrecy. In 25 cases we were able to establish links between open proceedings and later newspaper articles containing information about the identities of witnesses and targets and the nature of grand jury investigations.

Comptroller General, More Guidance and Supervision Needed over Federal Grand Jury Proceedings 8–9 (Oct. 16, 1980).

The provisions of rule 6(e)(5) do not violate any constitutional right of the public or media to attend such pretrial hearings. There is no Sixth Amendment right in the public to attend pretrial proceedings, *Gannett Co., Inc. v. DePasquale,* 443 U.S. 368 (1979), and *Richmond Newspapers, Inc. v. Virginia,* 448 U.S. 555, (1980), only recognizes a First Amendment "right to attend criminal trials." *Richmond Newspapers* was based largely upon the "unbroken, uncontradicted history" of public trials, while in *Gannett* it was noted "there exists no persuasive evidence that at common law members of the public had any right to attend pretrial proceedings." Moreover, even assuming some public right to attend certain pretrial proceedings, see *United States v. Criden,* 675 F.2d 550 (3d Cir. 1982), that right is not absolute; it must give way, as stated in Richmond Newspapers, to "an overriding interest" in a particular case in favor of a closed proceeding. By permitting closure only "to the extent necessary to prevent disclosure of matters occurring before a grand jury," rule 6(e)(5) recognizes the longstanding interest in the secrecy of grand jury proceedings. Counsel or others allowed to be present at the closed hearing may be put under a protective order by the court.

Note to Subdivision (e)(5) is expressly made "subject to any right to an open hearing in contempt proceedings." This will accommodate any First Amendment right which might be deemed applicable in that context because of the proceedings' similarities to a criminal trial, cf. *United States v. Criden,* supra, and also any Fifth or Sixth Amendment right of the contemnor. The latter right clearly exists as to a criminal contempt proceeding, *In re Oliver,* 333 U.S. 257 (1948), and some authority is to be found recognizing such a right in civil contempt proceedings as well. *In re Rosahn,* 671 F.2d 690 (2d Cir. 1982). This right of the contemnor must be requested by him and, in any event, does not require that the entire contempt proceedings, including recitation of the substance of the questions he has refused to answer, be public. *Levine v. United States,* 362 U.S. 610 (1960).

Note to Subdivision (e)(6). Subdivision (e)(6) provides that records, orders and subpoenas relating to grand jury proceedings shall be kept under seal to the extent and for so long as is necessary to prevent disclosure of matters occurring before a grand jury. By permitting such documents as grand jury subpoenas and immunity orders to be kept under seal, this provision addresses a serious problem of grand jury secrecy and expressly authorizes a procedure now in use in many but not all districts. As reported in Comptroller General, More Guidance and Supervision Needed over Federal Grand Jury Proceedings 10, 14 (Oct. 16, 1980):

In 262 cases, documents presented at open preindictment proceedings and filed in public files revealed details of grand jury investigations. These documents are, of course, available to anyone who wants them, including targets of investigations. [There are] two documents commonly found in public files which usually reveal the identities of witnesses and targets. The first document is a Department of Justice authorization to a U.S. attorney to apply to the court for a grant of immunity for a witness. The second document is the court's order granting the witness immunity from prosecution and compelling him to testify and produce requested information. . . .

Subpoenas are the fundamental documents used during a grand jury's investigation because through subpoenas, grand juries can require witnesses to testify and produce documentary evidence for their consideration. Subpoenas can identify witnesses, potential targets, and the nature of an investigation. Rule 6(e) does not provide specific guidance on whether a grand jury's subpoena should be kept secret. Additionally, case law has not consistently stated whether the subpoenas are protected by rule 6(e).

District courts still have different opinions about whether grand jury subpoenas should be kept secret. Out of 40 Federal District Courts we contacted, 36 consider these documents to be secret. However, 4 districts do make them available to the public.

Note to Subdivision (g). In its present form, subdivision 6(g) permits a grand jury to serve no more than 18 months after its members have been sworn, and absolutely no exceptions are permitted. (By comparison, under the Organized Crime Control Act of 1970, Title I, 18 U.S.C. §§ 3331– 3334, special grand juries may be extended beyond their basic terms of 18 months if their business has not been completed.) The purpose of the amendment is to permit some degree of flexibility as to the discharge of grand juries where the public interest would be served by an extension.

As noted in *United States v. Fein,* 504 F.2d 1170 (2d Cir. 1974), upholding the dismissal of an indictment returned 9 days after the expiration of the 18-month period but during an attempted extension, under the present inflexible rule "it may well be that criminal proceedings which would be in the public interest will be frustrated and that those who might be found guilty will escape trial and conviction." The present inflexible rule can produce several undesirable consequences, especially when complex fraud, organized crime, tax or antitrust cases are under investigation: (i) wastage of a significant amount of time and resources by the necessity of presenting the case once again to a successor grand jury simply because the matter could not be concluded before the term of the first grand jury expired; (ii) precipitous action to conclude the investigation before the expiration date of the grand jury; and (iii) potential defendants may be kept under investigation for a longer time because of the necessity to present the matter again to another grand jury.

The amendment to subdivision 6(g) permits extension of a regular grand jury only "upon a determination that such extension is in the public interest." This permits some flexibility, but reflects the fact that extension of regular grand juries beyond 18 months is to be the exception and not the norm. The intention of the amendment is to make it possible for a grand jury to have sufficient extra time to wind up an investigation when, for example, such extension becomes necessary because of the unusual nature of the case or unforeseen developments.

Because terms of court have been abolished, 28 U.S.C. § 138, the second sentence of subdivision 6(g) has been deleted.

Notes of Advisory Committee on 1985 amendments.

Note to Subdivision (e)(3)(A)(ii). Rule 6(e)(3)(A)(ii) currently provides that an attorney for the government may disclose grand jury information, without prior judicial approval, to other government personnel whose assistance the attorney for the government deems necessary in conducting the grand jury investigation. Courts have differed over whether employees of state and local governments are "government personnel" within the meaning of the rule. Compare *In re Miami Federal Grand Jury No. 79-9,* 478 F.Supp. 490 (S.D. Fla. 1979), and *In re Grand Jury Proceedings,* 445 F.Supp. 349 (D.R.I. 1978) (state and local personnel not included); with *In re 1979 Grand Jury Proceedings,* 479 F.Supp. 93 (E.D.N.Y. 1979) (state and local personnel included). The amendment clarifies the rule to include state and local personnel.

It is clearly desirable that federal and state authorities cooperate, as they often do, in organized crime and racketeering investigations, in public corruption and major fraud cases, and in various other situations where federal and state criminal jurisdictions overlap. Because of such cooperation, government attorneys in complex grand jury investigations frequently find it necessary to enlist the help of a team of government agents. While the agents are usually federal personnel, it is not uncommon in certain types of investigations that federal prosecutors wish to obtain the assistance of state law enforcement personnel, which could be uniquely beneficial. The amendment permits disclosure to those personnel in the circumstances stated.

It must be emphasized that the disclosure permitted is limited. The disclosure under this subdivision is permissible only in connection with the attorney for the government's "duty to enforce federal criminal law" and only to those personnel "deemed necessary . . . to assist" in the performance of that duty. Under subdivision (e)(3)(B), the material disclosed may not be used for any other purpose, and the names of persons to whom disclosure is made must be promptly provided to the court.

Note to Subdivision (e)(3)(B). The amendment to subdivision (e)(3)(B) imposes upon the attorney for the government the responsibility to certify to the district court that he has advised those persons to whom disclosure was made under subdivision (e)(3)(A)(ii) of their obligation of secrecy under Rule 6. Especially with the amendment of subdivision (e)(3)(A)(ii) to include personnel of a state or subdivision of a state, who otherwise would likely be unaware of this obligation of secrecy, the giving of such advice is an important step in ensuring against inadvertent breach of grand jury secrecy. But because not all federal government personnel will otherwise know of this obligation, the giving of the advice and certification thereof is required as to *all* persons receiving disclosure under subdivision (e)(3)(A)(ii).

Note to Subdivision (e)(3)(C). It sometimes happens that during a federal grand jury investigation evidence will be developed tending to show a violation of state law. When this occurs, it is very frequently the case that this evidence cannot be communicated to the appropriate state officials for further investigation. For one thing, any state officials who might seek this information must show particularized need. *Illinois v. Abbott & Associates,* 103 S.Ct. 1356 [75 L.Ed.2d 281] (1983). For another, and more significant, it is often the case that the information relates to a state crime outside the context of any pending or even contemplated state judicial proceeding, so that the "preliminarily to or in connection with a judicial proceeding" requirement of subdivision (e)(3)(C)(i) cannot be met.

This inability lawfully to disclose evidence of a state criminal violation—evidence legitimately obtained by the grand jury—constitutes an unreasonable barrier to the effective enforcement of our two-tiered system of criminal laws. It would be removed by new subdivision (e)(3)(C)(iv), which would allow a court to permit disclosure to a state or local official for the purpose of enforcing state law when an attorney for the government so requests and makes the requisite showing.

The federal court has been given control over any disclosure which is authorized, for subdivision (e)(3)(C) presently states that "the disclosure shall be made in such manner, at such time, and under such conditions as the court may direct." The Committee is advised that it will be the policy of the Department of Justice under this amendment to seek such disclosure only upon approval of the Assistant Attorney General in charge of the Criminal Division. There is no intention, by virtue of this amendment, to have federal grand juries act as an arm of the state.

Notes of Advisory Committee on 1987 amendments. New subdivision (a)(2) gives express recognition to a practice now followed in some district courts, namely, that of designating alternate grand jurors at the time the grand jury is selected. (A person so designated does not attend court and is not paid the jury attendance fees and expenses authorized by 28 U.S.C. § 1871 unless subsequently impanelled pursuant to Rule 6(g).) Because such designation may be a more efficient procedure than election of additional grand jurors later as need arises under subdivision (g), the amendment makes it clear that it is a permissible step in the grand jury selection process.

This amendment [to (a)] is not intended to work any change in subdivision (g). In particular, the fact that one or more alternate jurors either have or have not been previously designated does not limit the district court's discretion under subdivision (g) to decide whether, if a juror is excused temporarily or permanently, another person should replace him to assure the continuity of the grand jury and its ability to obtain a quorum in order to complete its business.

The amendments [to (c) and (f)] are technical. No substantive change is intended.

Notes of Advisory Committee on 1993 amendments. The Rule is amended to conform to the Judicial Improvements Act of 1990 [P.L. 101-650, Title III, Section 321] which provides that each United States magistrate appointed under section 631 of title 28, United States Code, shall be known as a United States magistrate judge.

Notes of Advisory Committee on 1999 amendments. Subdivision 6(d). As currently written, Rule 6(d) absolutely bars any person, other than the jurors themselves, from being present during the jury's deliberations and voting. Accordingly, interpreters are barred from attending the deliberations and voting by the grand jury, even though they may have been present during the taking of testimony. The amendment is intended to permit interpreters to assist persons who are speech or hearing impaired and are serving on a grand jury. Although the Committee believes that the need for secrecy of grand jury deliberations and voting is paramount, permitting interpreters to assist hearing and speech impaired jurors in the process seems a reasonable accommodation. *See also United States v. Dempsey*, 830 F.2d 1084 (10th Cir. 1987) (constitutionally rooted prohibition of non-jurors being present during deliberations was not violated by interpreter for deaf petit jury member).

The subdivision has also been restyled and reorganized.

Subdivision 6(f). The amendment to Rule 6(f) is intended to avoid the problems associated with bringing the entire jury to the court for the purpose of returning an indictment. Although the practice is long-standing, in *Breese v.United States*, 226 U.S. 1 (1912) [57 L.Ed. 97], the Court rejected the argument that the requirement was rooted in the Constitution and observed that if there were ever any strong reasons for the requirement, "they have disappeared, at least in part." 226 U.S. at 9. The Court added that grand jury's presence at the time the indictment was presented was a defect, if at all, in form only. *Id.* at 11. Given the problems of space, in some jurisdictions the grand jury sits in a building completely separated from the courtrooms. In those cases, moving the entire jury to the courtroom for the simple process of presenting the indictment may prove difficult and time consuming. Even where the jury is in the same location, having all of the jurors present can be unnecessarily cumbersome in light of the fact that filing of the indictment requires a certification as to how the jurors voted.

The amendment provides that the indictment must be presented either by the jurors themselves, as currently provided for in the rule, or by the foreperson or the deputy foreperson, acting on behalf of the jurors. In an appropriate case, the court might require all of the jurors to be present if it had inquiries about the indictment.

Notes of Advisory Committee on 2002 amendments. The language of Rule 6 has been amended as part of the general restyling of the Criminal Rules to make them more easily understood and to make style and terminology consistent throughout the rules. These changes are intended to be stylistic, except as noted below.

The first change is in Rule 6(b)(1). The last sentence of current Rule 6(b)(1) provides that "Challenges shall be made before the administration of the oath to the jurors and shall be tried by the court." That language has been deleted from the amended rule. The remainder of this subdivision rests on the assumption that formal proceedings have begun against a person, i.e., an indictment has been returned. The Committee believed that although the first sentence reflects current practice of a defendant being able to challenge the composition or qualifications of the grand jurors after the indictment is returned, the second sentence does not comport with modern practice. That is, a defendant will normally not know the composition of the grand jury or identity of the grand jurors before they are administered their oath. Thus, there is no opportunity to challenge them and have the court decide the issue before the oath is given.

In Rule 6(d)(1), the term "court stenographer" has been changed to "court reporter." Similar changes have been made in Rule 6(e)(1) and (2).

Rule 6(e) continues to spell out the general rule of secrecy of grand-jury proceedings and the exceptions to that general rule. The last sentence in current Rule 6(e)(2), concerning contempt for violating Rule 6, now appears in Rule 6(e)(7). No change in substance is intended.

Rule 6(e)(3)(A)(ii) includes a new provision recognizing the sovereignty of Indian Tribes and the possibility that it would be necessary to disclose grand-jury information to appropriate tribal officials in order to enforce federal law. Similar language has been added to Rule 6(e)(3)(D)(iii).

Rule 6(e)(3)(A)(iii) is a new provision that recognizes that disclosure may be made to a person under 18 U.S.C. § 3322 (authorizing disclosures to an attorney for the government and banking regulators for enforcing civil forfeiture and civil banking laws). This reference was added to avoid the possibility of the amendments to Rule 6 superseding that particular statute.

Rule 6(e)(3)(C) consists of language located in current Rule 6(e)(3)(C)(iii). The Committee believed that this provision, which recognizes that prior court approval is not required for disclosure of a grand-jury matter to another grand jury, should be treated as a separate subdivision in revised Rule 6(e)(3). No change in practice is intended.

Rule 6(e)(3)(D)(iv) is a new provision that addresses disclosure of grand-jury information to armed forces personnel where the disclosure is for the purpose of enforcing military criminal law under the Uniform Code of Military Justice, 10 U.S.C. §§ 801–946. See, e.g., Department of Defense Directive 5525.7 (January 22, 1985); 1984 Memorandum of Understanding Between Department of Justice and the Department of Defense Relating to the Investigation and Prosecution of Certain Crimes; Memorandum of Understanding Between the Departments of Justice and Transportation (Coast Guard) Relating to the Investigations and Prosecution of Crimes Over Which the Two Departments Have Concurrent Jurisdiction (October 9, 1967).

In Rule 6(e)(3)(E)(ii), the Committee considered whether to amend the language relating to "parties to the judicial proceeding" and determined that in the context of the rule it is understood that the parties referred to are the parties in the same judicial proceeding identified in Rule 6(e)(3)(D)(i).

The Committee decided to leave in subdivision (e) the provision stating that a "knowing violation of Rule 6" may be punished by contempt notwithstanding that, due to its apparent application to the entirety of the Rule, the provision seemingly is misplaced in subdivision (e). Research shows that Congress added the provision in 1977 and that it was crafted solely to deal with violations of the secrecy prohibitions in subdivision (e). See S. Rep. No. 95-354, p. 8 (1977). Supporting this narrow construction, the Committee found no reported decision involving an application or attempted use of the contempt sanction to a violation other than of the disclosure restrictions in subdivision (e). On the other hand, the Supreme Court in dicta did indicate on one occasion its arguable understanding that the contempt sanction would be available also for a violation of Rule 6(d) relating to who may be present during the grand jury's deliberations. *Bank of Nova Scotia v. United States,* 487 U.S. 250, 263 [101 L. Ed. 2d 228, 243] (1988).

In sum, it appears that the scope of the contempt sanction in Rule 6 is unsettled. Because the provision creates an offense, altering its scope may be beyond the authority bestowed by the Rules Enabling Act, 28 U.S.C. §§ 2071 et seq. See 28 U.S.C. § 2072(b) (Rules must not "abridge, enlarge, or modify any substantive right"). The Committee decided to leave the contempt provision in its present location in subdivision (e), because breaking it out into a separate subdivision could be construed to support the interpretation that the sanction may be applied to a knowing violation of any of the Rule's provisions rather than just those in subdivision (e). Whether or not that is a correct interpretation of the provision — a matter on which the Committee takes no position — must be determined by case law, or resolved by Congress.

Current Rule 6(g) has been divided into two new subdivisions, Rule 6(g), Discharge, and Rule 6(h), Excuse. The Committee added the phrase in Rule 6(g) "except as otherwise provided by statute," to recognize the provisions of 18 U.S.C. § 3331 relating to special grand juries.

Rule 6(i) is a new provision defining the term "Indian Tribe," a term used only in this rule.

Notes of Advisory Committee on 2006 amendments. *Note to Subdivision (e)(3) and (7).* This amendment makes technical changes to the language added to Rule 6 by the Intelligence Reform and Terrorism Prevention Act of 2004, Pub. L. 108-458, Title VI, § 6501(a), 118 Stat. 3760, in order to bring the new language into conformity with the conventions introduced in the general restyling of the Criminal Rules. No substantive change is intended.

Notes of Advisory Committee on 2011 amendments. *Note to Subdivision (f).* The amendment expressly allows a judge to take a grand jury return by video teleconference. Having the judge in the same courtroom remains the preferred practice because it promotes the public's confidence in the integrity and solemnity of a federal criminal proceeding. But there are situations when no judge is present in the courthouse where the grand jury sits, and a judge would be required to travel long distances to take the return. Avoiding delay is also a factor, since the Speedy Trial Act, 18 U.S.C. § 3161(b), requires that an indictment be returned within thirty days of the arrest of an individual to avoid dismissal of the case. The amendment is particularly helpful when there is no judge present at a courthouse where the grand jury sits and the nearest judge is hundreds of miles away.

Under the amendment, the grand jury (or the foreperson) would appear in a courtroom in the United States courthouse where the grand jury sits. Utilizing video teleconference, the judge could participate by video from a remote location, convene court, and take the return. Indictments could be transmitted in advance to the judge for review by reliable electronic means. This process accommodates the Speedy Trial Act, 18 U.S.C. § 3161(b), and preserves the judge's time and safety.

Notes of Advisory Committee on 2014 amendment. *Rule 6(e)(3)(D).* This technical and conforming amendment updates a citation affected by the editorial reclassification of chapter 15 of title 50, United States Code. The amendment replaces the citation to 50 U.S.C. § 401a with a citation to 50 U.S.C. § 3003. No substantive change is intended.

Amendments:

1984.

Act Oct. 12, 1984 (effective as provided by § 235(a)(1) of such Act, as amended, which appears as 18 USCS § 3551 note), in subsec. (e)(3)(C), added cl. (iv).

2001.

Act Oct. 26, 2001, in subsec. (e)(3), substituted subpara. (C) for one which read:

"(C) Disclosure otherwise prohibited by this rule of matters occurring before the grand jury may also be made—.

"(i) when so directed by a court preliminarily to or in connection with a judicial proceeding;

"(ii) when permitted by a court at the request of the defendant, upon a showing that grounds may exist for a motion to dismiss the indictment because of matters occurring before the grand jury; or.

"(iii) when the disclosure is made by an attorney for the government to another federal grand jury; or.

"(iv) when permitted by a court at the request of an attorney for the government, upon a showing that such matters may disclose a violation of state criminal law, to an appropriate official of a state or subdivision of a state for the purpose of enforcing such law.

If the court orders disclosure of matters occurring before the grand jury, the disclosure shall be made in such manner, at such time, and under such conditions as the court may direct.",

and, in subpara. (D), substituted "(e)(3)(C)(i)(I)" for "(e)(3)(C)(i)".

2002.

Act Nov. 25, 2002 (effective 60 days after enactment, as provided by § 4 of such Act, which appears as 6 USCS § 101 note, and repealed by Act Jan. 5, 2023), purported to amend subsec. (e) as follows:

(1) in para. (2), by inserting ", or of guidelines jointly issued by the Attorney General and Director of Central Intelligence pursuant to Rule 6," after "Rule 6"; and.

(2) in para. (3)—.

(A) in subpara. (A)(ii), by inserting "or of a foreign government" after "(including personnel of a state or subdivision of a state";

(B) in subpara. (C)(i)—.

(i) in subcl. (I), by inserting before the semicolon the following: "or, upon a request by an attorney for the government, when sought by a foreign court or prosecutor for use in an official criminal investigation";

(ii) in subcl. (IV)—.

(I) by inserting "or foreign" after "may disclose a violation of State";

(II) by inserting "or of a foreign government" after "to an appropriate official of a State or subdivision of a State"; and.

(III) by striking "or" at the end;

(iii) in subcl. (V), by substituting "; or" for a concluding period;

(iv) by adding at the end the following: "(VI) when matters involve a threat of actual or potential attack or other grave hostile acts of a foreign power or an agent of a foreign power, domestic or international sabotage, domestic or international terrorism, or clandestine intelligence gathering activities by an intelligence service or network of a foreign power or by an agent of a foreign power, within the United States or elsewhere, to any appropriate federal, state, local, or foreign government official for the purpose of preventing or responding to such a threat."; and.

(C) in subpara. (C)(iii)—.

(i) by deleting "Federal" preceding "official to whom";

(ii) by inserting "or clause (i)(VI)" after "clause (i)(V)"; and.

(iii) by adding at the end the following: "Any state, local, or foreign official who receives information pursuant to clause (i)(VI) shall use that information only consistent with such guidelines as the Attorney General and Director of Central Intelligence shall jointly issue.".

These amendments could not be executed, because they were inconsistent with amendments which took effect on December 1, 2002, pursuant to an order of the Supreme Court of the United States dated April 29, 2002.

2004.

Act Dec. 17, 2004, in subsec. (e), in para. (3), in subpara. (A)(ii), substituted ", state subdivision, Indian tribe, or foreign government" for "or state subdivision or of an Indian tribe", in subpara. (D), in the introductory matter, inserted the sentence beginning "An attorney for the government may also . . .", and, in cl. (i), deleted "federal" preceding "official who", and added the sentence beginning "Any State, . . .", and, in subpara. (E), redesignated cls. (iii) and (iv) as cls. (iv) and (v), respectively, inserted new cl. (iii), and, in cl. (iv) as redesignated, substituted "State, Indian tribal, or foreign" for "state of Indian tribal" and substituted "Indian tribal, or foreign government official" for "or Indian tribal official", and, in para. (7), inserted ", or of guidelines jointly issued by the Attorney General and the Director of National Intelligence pursuant to Rule 6,".

2023.

The 2023 amendment by P.L. 117-347 repealed the amendment by Act Nov. 25, 2022, without affecting the text of this rule.

Rule 7. The Indictment and the Information

(a) When Used.

(1) *Felony.* An offense (other than criminal contempt) must be prosecuted by an indictment if it is punishable:

(A) by death; or

(B) by imprisonment for more than one year.

(2) *Misdemeanor.* An offense punishable by imprisonment for one year or less may be prosecuted in accordance with Rule 58(b)(1).

(b) Waiving Indictment. An offense punishable by imprisonment for more than one year may be prosecuted by information if the defendant—in open court and after being advised of the nature of the charge and of the defendant's rights—waives prosecution by indictment.

(c) Nature and Contents.

(1) *In General.* The indictment or information must be a plain, concise, and definite written statement of the essential facts constituting the offense charged and must be signed by an attorney for the government. It need not contain a formal introduction or conclusion. A count may incorporate by reference an allegation made in another count. A count may allege that the means by which the defendant committed the offense are unknown or that the defendant committed it by one or more specified means. For each count, the indictment or information must give the official or customary citation of the statute, rule, regulation, or other provision of law that the defendant is alleged to have violated. For purposes of an indictment referred to in section 3282 of title 18, United States Code, for which the identity of the defendant is unknown, it shall be sufficient for the indictment to describe the defendant as an individual whose name is unknown, but who has a particular DNA profile, as that term is defined in that section 3282.

(2) *Citation Error.* Unless the defendant was misled and thereby prejudiced, neither an error in a citation nor a citation's omission is a ground to dismiss the indictment or information or to reverse a conviction.

(d) Surplusage. Upon the defendant's motion, the court may strike surplusage from the indictment or information.

(e) Amending an Information. Unless an additional or different offense is charged or a substantial right of the defendant is prejudiced, the court may permit an information to be amended at any time before the verdict or finding.

(f) Bill of Particulars. The court may direct the government to file a bill of particulars. The defendant may move for a bill of particulars before or within 14 days after arraignment or at a later time if the court permits. The government may amend a bill of particulars subject to such conditions as justice requires.

HISTORY:

Amended Feb. 28, 1966, eff. July 1, 1966; April 24, 1972, eff. Oct. 1, 1972; April 30, 1979, eff. Aug. 1, 1979; March 9, 1987, eff. Aug. 1, 1987; April 17, 2000, eff. Dec. 1, 2000; April 29, 2002, eff. Dec. 1, 2002; April 30, 2003, P. L. 108-21, Title VI, § 610(b), 117 Stat. 692; March 26, 2009, eff. Dec. 1, 2009.

HISTORY; ANCILLARY LAWS AND DIRECTIVES

Other provisions:

Notes of Advisory Committee. *Note to Subdivision (a).* 1. This rule gives effect to the following provision of the Fifth Amendment to the Constitution of the United States: "No person shall be held to answer for a capital, or otherwise infamous crime, unless on a presentment or indictment of a Grand Jury . . .". An infamous crime has been defined as a crime punishable by death or by imprisonment in a penitentiary or at hard labor, *Ex parte Wilson,* 114 U.S. 417, 427, 5 S.Ct. 935, 29 L.Ed. 89; *United States v Moreland,* 258 U.S. 433, 42 S.Ct. 368, 66 L.Ed. 700. Any sentence of imprisonment for a term of over one year may be served in a penitentiary, if so directed by the Attorney General, 18 U.S.C. [former] § 753f [see §§ 4082, 4083] (Commitment of persons by any court of the United States and the juvenile court of the District of Columbia; place of confinement; transfers). Consequently any offense punishable by imprisonment for a term of over one year is an infamous crime.

2. Petty offenses and misdemeanors for which no infamous punishment is prescribed may now be prosecuted by information, 18 U.S.C. [former] § 541 [see § 1] (Felonies and misdemeanors); *Duke v United States,* 301 U.S. 492, 57 S.Ct. 835, 81 L.Ed. 1243.

3. For a discussion of the provision for waiver of indictment, see Note to Rule 7(b), infra.

4. Presentment is not included as an additional type of formal accusation, since presentments as a method of instituting prosecutions are obsolete, at least as concerns the Federal courts.

Note to Subdivision (b). 1. Opportunity to waive indictment and to consent to prosecution by information will be a substantial aid to defendants, especially those who, because of inability to give bail, are incarcerated pending action of the grand jury, but desire to plead guilty. This rule is particularly important in those districts in which considerable intervals occur between sessions of the grand jury. In many districts where the grand jury meets infrequently a defendant unable to give bail and desiring to plead guilty is compelled to spend many days, and sometimes many weeks, and even months, in jail before he can begin the service of his sentence, whatever it may be, awaiting the action of a grand jury. Homer Cummings, 29 A.B.A. Jour. 654–655; Vanderbilt, 29 A.B.A. Jour. 376, 377; Robinson, 27 Jour. of the Am. Judicature Soc. 38, 45; Medalie, 4 Lawyers Guild R. (3) 1, 3. The rule contains safeguards against improvident waivers.

The Judicial Conference of Senior Circuit Judges, in September 1941, recommended that "existing law or established procedure be so changed, that a defendant may waive indictment and plead guilty to an information filed by a United States attorney in all cases except capital felonies." *Report of the Judicial Conference of Senior Circuit Judges* (1941) 13. In September 1942 the Judicial Conference recommended that provision be made "for waiver of indictment and jury trial, so that persons accused of crime may not be held in jail needlessly pending trial." *Id.* (1942) 8.

Attorneys General of the United States have from time to time recommended legislation to permit defendants to waive indictment and to consent to prosecution by information. See *Annual Report of the Attorney General of the United States* (Mitchell) (1931) 3; *Id.* (Mitchell) (1932) 6; *Id.* (Cummings) (1933) 1, (1936) 2, (1937) 11, (1938) 9; *Id.* (Murphy) (1939) 7.

The Federal Juvenile Delinquency Act, 18 U.S.C. [former] §§ 921– 929 [see §§ 5031, 5037], now permits a juvenile charged with an offense not punishable by death or life imprisonment to consent to prosecution by information on a charge of juvenile delinquency, 18 U.S.C. [former] § 922 [see §§ 5032, 5033].

2. On the constitutionality of this rule, see *United States v Gill,* 55 F.2d 399 (D.N.M.), holding that the constitutional guaranty of indictment by grand jury may be waived by defendant. It has also been held that other constitutional guaranties may be waived by the defendant, e. g., *Patton v United States,* 281 U.S. 276, 50 S.Ct. 253, 74 L.Ed. 854 (trial by jury); *Johnson v Zerbst,* 304 U.S. 458, 465, 58 S.Ct. 1019, 82 L.Ed. 1461 (right of counsel); *Trono v United States,* 199 U.S. 521, 534, 26 S.Ct. 121, 50 L.Ed. 292 (protection against double jeopardy); *United States v Murdock,* 284 U.S. 141, 148, 52 S.Ct. 63, 76 L.Ed. 210 (privilege against self-incrimination); *Diaz v United States,* 223 U.S. 442, 450, 32 S.Ct. 250, 56 L.Ed. 500 (right of confrontation).

Note to Subdivision (c). 1. This rule introduces a simple form of indictment, illustrated by Forms 1 to 11 in the Appendix of Forms. Cf. Rule 8(a) of the Federal Rules of Civil Procedure [28 U.S.C., Appendix]. For discussion of the effect of this rule and a comparison between the present form of indictment and the simple form introduced by this rule, see Vanderbilt, 29 A.B.A. Jour. 376, 377; Homer Cummings, 29 A.B.A. Jour. 654, 655; Holtzoff, 3 F.R.D. 445, 448–449; Holtzoff, 12 Geo. Washington L.R. 119, 123–126; Medalie, 4 Lawyers Guild R. (3) 1, 3.

2. The provision contained in the fifth sentence that it may be alleged in a single count that the means by which the defendant committed the offense are unknown, or that he committed it by one or more specified means, is intended to eliminate the use of multiple counts for the purpose of alleging the commission of the offense by different means or in different ways. Cf. Federal Rules of Civil Procedure, Rule 8(e)(2) [28 U.S.C., Appendix].

3. The law at present regards citations to statutes or regulations as not a part of the indictment. A conviction may be sustained on the basis of a statute or regulation other than that cited. *Williams v United States,* 168 U.S. 382, 389, 18 S.Ct. 92, 42 L.Ed. 509; *United States v Hutcheson,* 312 U.S. 219, 229, 61 S.Ct. 463, 85 L.Ed. 788. The provision of the rule, in view of the many statutes and regulations, is for the benefit of the defendant and is not intended to cause a dismissal of the indictment, but simply to provide a means by which he can be properly informed without danger to the prosecution.

Note to Subdivision (d). This rule introduces a means of protecting the defendant against immaterial or irrelevant allegations in an indictment or information, which may, however, be prejudicial. The authority of the court to strike such surplusage is to be limited to doing so on defendant's motion, in the light of the rule that the guaranty of indictment by a grand jury implies that an indictment may not be amended. *Ex parte Bain,* 121 U.S. 1, 7 S.Ct. 781, 30 L.Ed. 849. By making such a motion, the defendant would, however, waive his rights in this respect.

Note to Subdivision (e). This rule continues the existing law that, unlike an indictment, an information may be amended, *Muncy v United States,* 289 F. 780 (C.C.A. 4th).

Note to Subdivision (f). This rule is substantially a restatement of existing law on bills of particulars.

Notes of Advisory Committee on 1966 amendments. The amendment to the first sentence eliminating the requirement of a showing of cause is designed to encourage a more liberal attitude by the courts toward bills of particulars without taking away the discretion which courts must have in dealing with such motions in individual cases. For an illustration of wise use of this discretion see the opinion by Justice Whittaker written when he was a district judge in *United States v Smith,* 16 F.R.D. 372 (W.D. Mo. 1954).

The amendment to the second sentence gives discretion to the court to permit late filing of motions for bills of particulars in meritorious cases. Use of late motions for the purpose of delaying trial should not, of course, be permitted. The courts have not been agreed as to their power to accept late motions in the absence of a local rule or a previous order. See *United States v Miller,* 217 F. Supp. 760 (E.D. Pa. 1963); *United States v Taylor,* 25 F.R.D. 225 (E.D.N.Y. 1960); *United States v Sterling,* 122 F. Supp. 81 (E.D. Pa. 1954) (all taking a limited view of the power of the court). But cf. *United States v Brown,* 179 F. Supp. 893 (E.D.N.Y. 1959) (exercising discretion to permit an out of time motion).

Notes of Advisory Committee on 1972 amendments. Subdivision (c)(2) is new. It is intended to provide procedural implementation of the recently enacted criminal forfeiture provision of the Organized Crime Control Act of 1970, Title IX, § 1963, and the Comprehensive Drug Abuse Prevention and Control Act of 1970, Title II, § 408(a)(2).

The Congress viewed the provisions of the Organized Crime Control Act of 1970 as reestablishing a limited common law criminal forfeiture. S. Rep. No. 91-617, 91st Cong., 1st Sess., 79–80 (1969). The legislative history of the Comprehensive Drug Abuse Prevention and Control Act of 1970 indicates a congressional purpose to have similar procedures apply to the forfeiture of profits or interests under that act. H. Rep. No. 91-1444 (part I), 91st Cong., 2d sess. 81–85 (1970).

Under the common law, in a criminal forfeiture proceeding the defendant was apparently entitled to notice, trial, and a special jury finding on the factual issues surrounding the declaration of forfeiture which followed his criminal conviction. Subdivision (c)(2) provides for notice. Changes in Rules 31 and 32 provide for a special jury finding and for a judgment authorizing the Attorney General to seize the interest or property forfeited.

Notes of Advisory Committee on 1979 amendments. The amendment to rule 7(c)(2) is intended to clarify its meaning. Subdivision (c)(2) was added in 1972, and, as noted in the Advisory Committee Note thereto, was "intended to provide procedural implementation of the recently enacted criminal forfeiture provision of the Organized Crime Control Act of 1970, Title IX, § 1963, and the Comprehensive Drug Abuse Prevention and Control Act of 1970, Title II, § 408(a)(2)." These provisions reestablished a limited common law criminal forfeiture, necessitating the addition of subdivision (c)(2) and corresponding changes in rules 31 and 32, for at common law the defendant in a criminal forfeiture proceeding was entitled to notice, trial, and a special jury finding on the factual issues surrounding the declaration of forfeiture which followed his criminal conviction.

Although there is some doubt as to what forfeitures should be characterized as "punitive" rather than "remedial," see Note, 62 Cornell L. Rev. 768 (1977), subdivision (c)(2) is intended to apply to those forfeitures which are criminal in the sense that they result from a special verdict under rule 31(e) and a judgment under rule 32(b)(2), and not to those resulting from a separate in rem proceeding. Because some confusion in this regard has resulted from the present wording of subdivision (c)(2), *United States v Hall,* 521 F.2d 406 (9th Cir. 1975), a clarifying amendment is in order.

Notes of Advisory Committee on 1987 amendments. The amendments are technical. No substantive change is intended.

Guam. For the inapplicability of the requirement for indictment by grand jury in certain cases, to criminal prosecutions in the District Court of Guam; see 48 USCS § 1424.

Prosecutions in Virgin Islands. Prosecutions in District Court of the Virgin Islands are to be by information except such as may be required by local law to be by indictment by grand jury; see 48 USCS § 1615.

Notes of Advisory Committee on 2000 amendments. The rule is amended to reflect new Rule 32.2, which now governs criminal forfeiture procedures.

Notes of Advisory Committee on 2002 amendments. The language of Rule 7 has been amended as part of the general restyling of the Criminal Rules to make them more easily understood and to make style and terminology consistent throughout the rules. These changes are intended to be stylistic.

The Committee has deleted the references to "hard labor" in the rule. This punishment is not found in current federal statutes.

The Committee added an exception for criminal contempt to the requirement in Rule 7(a)(1) that a prosecution for felony must be initiated by indictment. This is consistent with case law, e.g., *United States v. Eichhorst,* 544 F.2d 1383 (7th Cir. 1976), which has sustained the use of the special procedures for instituting criminal contempt proceedings found in Rule 42. While indictment is not a required method of bringing felony criminal contempt charges, however, it is a permissible one. See *United States v. Williams,* 622 F.2d 830 (5th Cir. 1980). No change in practice is intended.

The title of Rule 7(c)(3) has been amended. The Committee believed that potential confusion could arise with the use of the term "harmless error." Rule 52, which deals with the issues of harmless error and plain error, is sufficient to address the topic. Potentially, the topic of harmless error could arise with regard to any of the other rules and there is insufficient need to highlight the term in Rule 7. Rule 7(c)(3), on the other hand, focuses specifically on the effect of an error in the citation of authority in the indictment. That material remains but without any reference to harmless error.

Notes of Advisory Committee on 2009 amendments. *Note to Subdivision (c).* The provision regarding forfeiture is obsolete. In 2000 the same language was repeated in subdivision (a) of Rule 32.2, which was intended to consolidate the rules dealing with forfeiture.

The time set in the former rule at 10 days has been revised to 14 days. See the Committee Note to Rule 45(a).

Amendments:

2003.

Act April 30, 2003, in subsec. (c)(1), added the sentence beginning "For purposes . . .".

Rule 8. Joinder of Offenses or Defendants

(a) Joinder of Offenses. The indictment or information may charge a defendant in separate counts with 2 or more offenses if the offenses charged—whether felonies or misdemeanors or both—are of the same or similar character, or are based on the same act or transaction, or are connected with or constitute parts of a common scheme or plan.

(b) Joinder of Defendants. The indictment or information may charge 2 or more defendants if they are alleged to have participated in the same act or transaction, or in the same series of acts or transactions, constituting an offense or offenses. The defendants may be charged in one or more counts together or separately. All defendants need not be charged in each count.

HISTORY:

As amended April 29, 2002, eff. Dec. 1, 2002.

HISTORY; ANCILLARY LAWS AND DIRECTIVES

Other provisions:

Notes of Advisory Committee. *Note to Subdivision (a).* This rule is substantially a restatement of existing law, 18 U.S.C. [former] § 557 (Indictments and presentments; joinder of charges).

Note to Subdivision (b). The first sentence of the rule is substantially a restatement of existing law, 9 Edmunds, *Cyclopedia of Federal Procedure,* (2d Ed.) 4116. The second sentence formulates a practice now approved in some circuits. *Caringella v United States,* 78 F.2d 563, 567 (C.C.A. 7th).

Notes of Advisory Committee on 2002 amendments. The language of Rule 8 has been amended as part of the general restyling of the Criminal Rules to make them more easily understood and to make style and terminology consistent throughout the rules. These changes are intended to be stylistic only.

Rule 9. Arrest Warrant or Summons on an Indictment or Information

(a) Issuance. The court must issue a warrant—or at the government's request, a summons—for each defendant named in an indictment or named in an information if one or more affidavits accompanying the information establish probable cause to believe that an offense has been committed and that the defendant committed it. The court may issue more than one warrant or summons for the same defendant. If a defendant fails to appear in response to a summons, the court may, and upon request of an attorney for the government must, issue a warrant. The court must issue the arrest warrant to an officer authorized to execute it or the summons to a person authorized to serve it.

(b) Form.

(1) *Warrant.* The warrant must conform to Rule 4(b)(1) except that it must be signed by the clerk and must describe the offense charged in the indictment or information.

(2) *Summons.* The summons must be in the same form as a warrant except that it must require the defendant to appear before the court at a stated time and place.

(c) Execution or Service; Return; Initial Appearance.

(1) *Execution or Service.*

(A) The warrant must be executed or the summons served as provided in Rule 4(c)(1), (2), and (3).

(B) The officer executing the warrant must proceed in accordance with Rule 5(a)(1).

(2) *Return.* A warrant or summons must be returned in accordance with Rule 4(c)(4).

(3) *Initial Appearance.* When an arrested or summoned defendant first appears before the court, the judge must proceed under Rule 5.

(d) Warrant by Telephone or Other Means. In accordance with Rule 4.1, a magistrate judge may issue an arrest warrant or summons based on information communicated by telephone or other reliable electronic means.

HISTORY:

Amended April 24, 1972, eff. Oct. 1, 1972; April 22, 1974, eff. Dec. 1, 1975; July 31, 1975, P. L. 94-64, § 3(4), 89 Stat. 370; Dec. 12, 1975, P. L. 94-149, § 5, 89 Stat. 806; April 30, 1979, eff. Aug. 1, 1979; April 28, 1982, eff. Aug. 1, 1982; April 22, 1993, eff. Dec. 1, 1993; April 29, 2002, eff. Dec. 1, 2002; April 26, 2011, eff. Dec. 1, 2011.

HISTORY; ANCILLARY LAWS AND DIRECTIVES

Other provisions:

Notes of Advisory Committee. 1. See Note to Rule 4, *supra.*

2. The provision of Rule 9(a) that a warrant may be issued on the basis of an information only if the latter is supported by oath is necessitated by the Fourth Amendment to the Constitution of the United States. See *Albrecht v United States,* 273 U.S. 1, 5, 47 S.Ct. 250, 71 L.Ed. 505.

3. The provision of Rule 9(b)(1) that the amount of bail may be fixed by the court and endorsed on the warrant states a practice now prevailing in many districts and is intended to facilitate the giving of bail by the defendant and eliminate delays between the arrest and the giving of bail, which might ensue if bail cannot be fixed until after arrest.

Notes of Advisory Committee on 1972 amendments. Subdivision (b) is amended to make clear that the person arrested shall be brought before a United States magistrate if the information or indictment charges a "minor offense" triable by the United States magistrate.

Subdivision (c) is amended to reflect the office of United States magistrate.

Subdivision (d) is new. It provides for a remand to the United States magistrate of cases in which the person is charged with a "minor offense." The magistrate can then proceed in accordance with rule 5 to try the case if the right to trial before a judge of the district court is waived.

Notes of Advisory Committee on 1974 amendments. Rule 9 is revised to give high priority to the issuance of a summons unless a "valid reason" is given for the issuance of an arrest warrant. See a comparable provision in rule 4.

Under the rule, a summons will issue by the clerk unless the attorney for the government presents a valid reason for the issuance of an arrest warrant. Under the old rule, it has been argued that the court must issue an arrest warrant if one is desired by the attorney for the government. See authorities listed in Frankel, Bench Warrants Upon the Prosecutor's Demand: A View From the Bench, 71 Colum. L. Rev. 403, 410 n. 25 (1971). For an expression of the view that this is undesirable policy, see Frankel, *supra,* pp. 410–415.

A summons may issue if there is an information supported by oath. The indictment itself is sufficient to establish the existence of probable cause. See C. Wright, Federal Practice and Procedure: Criminal § 151 (1969); 8 J. Moore, Federal Practice P 9.02 [2] at p. 9-4 (2d ed.) Cipes (1969); *Giordenello v. United States,* 357 U.S. 480, 78 S.Ct. 1245, 2 L.Ed.2d 1503 (1958). This is not necessarily true in the case of an information. See C. Wright, supra, § 151; 8 J. Moore, supra, P 9.02. If the government requests a warrant rather than a summons, good practice would obviously require the judge to satisfy himself that there is probable cause. This may appear from the information or from an affidavit filed with the information. Also a defendant can, at a proper time, challenge an information issued without probable cause.

Notes of Committee on the Judiciary on 1975 amendments (House Report No. 94-247). A. Amendments Proposed by the Supreme Court. Rule 9 of the Federal Rules of Criminal Procedure is closely related to Rule 4. Rule 9 deals with arrest procedures after an information has been filed or an indictment returned. The present rule gives the prosecutor the authority to decide whether a summons or a warrant shall issue.

The Supreme Court's amendments to Rule 9 parallel its amendments to Rule 4. The basic change made in Rule 4 is also made in Rule 9.

B. Committee Action. For the reasons set forth above in connection with Rule 4, the Committee endorses and accepts the basic change in Rule 9. The Committee made changes in Rule 9 similar to the changes it made in Rule 4.

Notes of Advisory Committee on 1979 amendments. Subdivision (a) is amended to make explicit the fact that a warrant may issue upon the basis of an information only if the information or an affidavit filed with the information shows probable cause for the arrest. This has generally been assumed to be the state of the law even though not specifically set out in rule 9; see C. Wright, Federal Practice and Procedure: Criminal § 151 (1969); 8 J. Moore, Federal Practice par. 9.02 [2] (2d ed. 1976).

In *Gerstein v. Pugh,* 420 U.S. 103 (1975), the Supreme Court rejected the contention "that the prosecutor's decision to file an information is itself a determination of probable cause that furnishes sufficient reason to detain a defendant pending trial," commenting:

"Although a conscientious decision that the evidence warrants prosecution affords a measure of protection against unfounded detention, we do not think prosecutorial judgment standing alone meets the requirements of the Fourth Amendment. Indeed, we think the Court's previous decisions compel disapproval of [such] procedure. In *Albrecht v. United States,* 273 U.S. 1, 5, 47 S.Ct. 250, 251, 71 L.Ed. 505 (1927), the Court held that an arrest warrant issued solely upon a United States Attorney's information was invalid because the accompanying affidavits were defective. Although the Court's opinion did not explicitly state that the prosecutor's official oath could not furnish probable cause, that conclusion was implicit in the judgment that the arrest was illegal under the Fourth Amendment."

No change is made in the rule with respect to warrants issuing upon indictments. In *Gerstein,* the Court indicated it was not disturbing the prior rule that "an indictment, 'fair upon its face,' and returned by a 'properly constituted grand jury' conclusively determines the existence of probable cause and requires issuance of an arrest warrant without further inquiry." See *Ex parte United States,* 287 U.S. 241, 250 (1932).

The provision to the effect that a summons shall issue "by direction of the court" has been eliminated because it conflicts with the first sentence of the rule, which states that a warrant "shall" issue when requested by the attorney for the government, if properly supported. However, an addition has been made providing that if the attorney for the government does not make a request for either a warrant or summons, then the court may in its discretion issue either one. Other stylistic changes ensure greater consistency with comparable provisions in rule 4.

Notes of Advisory Committee on 1982 amendments. *Note to Subdivision (a).* The amendment of subdivision (a), by reference to Rule 5, clarifies what is to be done once the defendant is brought before the magistrate. This means, among other things, that no preliminary hearing is to be held in a Rule 9 case, as Rule 5(c) provides that no such hearing is to be had "if the defendant is indicted or if an information against the defendant is filed."

Note to Subdivision (b). The amendment of subdivision (b) conforms Rule 9 to the comparable provisions in Rule 4(c)(1) and (2). Subdivision (c). The amendment of subdivision (c) conforms Rule 9 to the comparable provisions in Rules 4(d)(4) and 5(a) concerning return of the warrant.

Note to Subdivision (d). This subdivision, incorrect in its present form in light of the recent amendment of 18 U.S.C. § 3401(a), has been abrogated as unnecessary in light of the change to subdivision (a).

Notes of Advisory Committee on 1993 amendments. The Rule is amended to conform to the Judicial Improvements Act of 1990 [P.L. 101-650, Title III, Section 321] which provides that each United States magistrate appointed under section 631 of title 28, United States Code, shall be known as a United States magistrate judge.

Notes of Advisory Committee on 2002 amendments. The language of Rule 9 has been amended as part of the general restyling of the Criminal Rules to make them more easily understood and to make style and terminology consistent throughout the rules. These changes are intended to be stylistic only, except as noted below.

Rule 9 has been changed to reflect its relationship to Rule 4 procedures for obtaining an arrest warrant or summons. Thus, rather than simply repeating material that is already located in Rule 4, the Committee determined that where appropriate, Rule 9 should simply direct the reader to the procedures specified in Rule 4.

Rule 9(a) has been amended to permit a judge discretion whether to issue an arrest warrant when a defendant fails to respond to a summons on a complaint. Under the current language of the rule, if the defendant fails to appear, the judge must issue a warrant. Under the amended version, if the defendant fails to appear and the government requests that a warrant be issued, the judge must issue one. In the absence of such a request, the judge has the discretion to do so. This change mirrors language in amended Rule 4(a).

A second amendment has been made in Rule 9(b)(1). The rule has been amended to delete language permitting the court to set the amount of bail on the warrant. The Committee believes that this language is inconsistent with the 1984 Bail Reform Act. See *United States v. Thomas*, 992 F. Supp. 782 (D.V.I. 1998) (bail amount endorsed on warrant that has not been determined in proceedings conducted under Bail Reform Act has no bearing on decision by judge conducting Rule 40 hearing).

The language in current Rule 9(c)(1), concerning service of a summons on an organization, has been moved to Rule 4.

Notes of Advisory Committee on 2011 amendments. *Note to Subdivision (d).* Rule 9(d) authorizes a court to issue an arrest warrant or summons electronically on the return of an indictment or the filing of an information. In large judicial districts the need to travel to the courthouse to obtain an arrest warrant in person can be burdensome, and advances in technology make the secure transmission of a reliable version of the warrant or summons possible. This change works in conjunction with the amendment to Rule 6 that permits the electronic return of an indictment, which similarly eliminates the need to travel to the courthouse.

Amendments:

1975.

Act July 31, 1975 (effective 12/1/75, as provided by § 2 of such Act, which appears as a note to Rule 4), amended subsec. (a) generally.

Act Dec. 12, 1975, in subsec. (b)(1), substituted "Rule 4(c)(1)" for "Rule 4(b)(1)"; and, in subsec. (c)(1), substituted "Rule 4(d)(1), (2) and (3)" for "Rule 4(c)(1), (2) and (3)".

TITLE IV. ARRAIGNMENT AND PREPARATION FOR TRIAL

Rule

Rule 10. Arraignment

(a) In General. An arraignment must be conducted in open court and must consist of:

(1) ensuring that the defendant has a copy of the indictment or information;

(2) reading the indictment or information to the defendant or stating to the defendant the substance of the charge; and then

(3) asking the defendant to plead to the indictment or information.

(b) Waiving Appearance. A defendant need not be present for the arraignment if:

(1) the defendant has been charged by indictment or misdemeanor information;

(2) the defendant, in a written waiver signed by both the defendant and defense counsel, has waived appearance and has affirmed that the defendant received a copy of the indictment or information and that the plea is not guilty; and

(3) the court accepts the waiver.

(c) Video Teleconferencing. Video teleconferencing may be used to arraign a defendant if the defendant consents.

HISTORY:

Amended March 9, 1987, eff. Aug. 1, 1987; April 29, 2002, eff. Dec. 1, 2002.

HISTORY; ANCILLARY LAWS AND DIRECTIVES

Other provisions:

Notes of Advisory Committee. 1. The first sentence states the prevailing practice.

2. The requirement that the defendant shall be given a copy of the indictment or information before he is called upon to plead, contained in the second sentence, is new.

3. Failure to comply with arraignment requirements has been held not to be jurisdictional, but a mere technical irregularity not warranting a reversal of a conviction, if not raised before trial, *Garland v State of Washington,* 232 U.S. 642, 34 S.Ct. 456, 58 L.Ed. 772.

Notes of Advisory Committee on 1987 amendments. The amendments are technical. No substantive change is intended.

Notes of Advisory Committee on 2002 amendments. The language of Rule 10 has been amended as part of the general restyling of the Criminal Rules to make them more easily understood and to make style and terminology consistent throughout the rules. These changes are intended to be stylistic only, except as noted below.

Read together, Rules 10 and 43 require the defendant to be physically present in court for the arraignment. See, e.g., *Valenzuela-Gonzales v. United States,* 915 F.2d 1276, 1280 (9th Cir. 1990) (Rules 10 and 43 are broader in protection than the Constitution). The amendments to Rule 10 create two exceptions to that requirement. The first provides that the court may hold an arraignment in the defendant's absence when the defendant has waived the right to be present in writing and the court consents to that waiver. The second permits the court to hold arraignments by video teleconferencing when the defendant is at a different location. A conforming amendment has also been made to Rule 43.

In amending Rule 10 and Rule 43, the Committee was concerned that permitting a defendant to be absent from the arraignment could be viewed as an erosion of an important element of the judicial process. First, it may be important for a defendant to see and experience first-hand the formal impact of the reading of the charge. Second, it may be necessary for the court to personally see and speak with the defendant at the arraignment, especially when there is a real question whether the defendant actually understands the gravity of the proceedings. And third, there may be difficulties in providing the defendant with effective and confidential assistance of counsel if counsel, but not the defendant, appears at the arraignment.

The Committee nonetheless believed that in appropriate circumstances the court, and the defendant, should have the option of conducting the arraignment in the defendant's absence. The question of when it would be appropriate for a defendant to waive an appearance is not spelled out in the rule. That is left to the defendant and the court in each case.

A critical element to the amendment is that no matter how convenient or cost effective a defendant's absence might be, the defendant's right to be present in court stands unless he or she waives that right in writing. Under the amendment, both the defendant and the defendant's attorney must sign the waiver. Further, the amendment requires that the waiver specifically state that the defendant has received a copy of the charging instrument.

If the trial court has reason to believe that in a particular case the defendant should not be permitted to waive the right, the court may reject the waiver and require that the defendant actually appear in court. That might be particularly appropriate when the court wishes to discuss substantive or procedural matters in conjunction with the arraignment and the court believes that the defendant's presence is important in resolving those matters. It might also be appropriate to reject a requested waiver where an attorney for the government presents reasons for requiring the defendant to appear personally.

The amendment does not permit waiver of an appearance when the defendant is charged with a felony information. In that instance, the defendant is required by Rule 7(b) to be present in court to waive the indictment. Nor does the amendment permit a waiver of appearance when the defendant is standing mute (see Rule 11(a)(4)), or entering a conditional plea (see Rule 11(a)(2)), a nolo contendere plea (see Rule 11(a)(3)), or a guilty plea (see Rule 11(a)(1)). In each of those instances the Committee believed that it was more appropriate for the defendant to appear personally before the court.

It is important to note that the amendment does not permit the defendant to waive the arraignment itself, which may be a triggering mechanism for other rules.

Rule 10(c) addresses the second substantive change in the rule. That provision permits the court to conduct arraignments through video teleconferencing, if the defendant waives the right to be arraigned in court. Although the practice is now used in state courts and in some federal courts, Rules 10 and 43 have generally prevented federal courts from using that method for arraignments in criminal cases. See, e.g., *Valenzuela-Gonzales v. United States*, supra (Rules 10 and 43 mandate physical presence of defendant at arraignment and that arraignment take place in open court). A similar amendment was proposed by the Committee in 1993 and published for public comment. The amendment was later withdrawn from consideration in order to consider the results of several planned pilot programs. Upon further consideration, the Committee believed that the benefits of using video teleconferencing outweighed the costs of doing so. This amendment also parallels an amendment in Rule 5(f) that would permit initial appearances to be conducted by video teleconferencing.

In amending Rules 5, 10, and 43 (which generally requires the defendant's presence at all proceedings), the Committee carefully considered the argument that permitting a defendant to appear by video teleconferencing might be considered an erosion of an important element of the judicial process. Much can be lost when video teleconferencing occurs. First, the setting itself may not promote the public's confidence in the integrity and solemnity of a federal criminal proceeding; that is the view of some who have witnessed the use of such proceedings in some state jurisdictions. While it is difficult to quantify the intangible benefits and impact of requiring a defendant to be brought before a federal judicial officer in a federal courtroom, the Committee realizes that something is lost when a defendant is not required to make a personal appearance. A related consideration is that the defendant may be located in a room that bears no resemblance whatsoever to a judicial forum and the equipment may be inadequate for high-quality transmissions. Second, using video teleconferencing can interfere with counsel's ability to meet personally with his or her client at what, at least in that jurisdiction, might be an important appearance before a magistrate judge. Third, the defendant may miss an opportunity to meet with family or friends, and others who might be able to assist the defendant, especially in any attempts to obtain bail. Finally, the magistrate judge may miss an opportunity to accurately assess the physical, emotional, and mental condition of a defendant—a factor that may weigh on pretrial decisions, such as release from detention.

On the other hand, the Committee considered that in some jurisdictions, the courts face a high volume of criminal proceedings. The Committee was also persuaded to adopt the amendment because in some jurisdictions delays may occur in travel time from one location to another—in some cases requiring either the magistrate judge or the participants to travel long distances. In those instances, it is not unusual for a defense counsel to recognize the benefit of conducting a video teleconferenced proceeding, which will eliminate lengthy and sometimes expensive travel or permit the arraignment to be conducted much sooner. Finally, the Committee was aware that in some jurisdictions, courtrooms now contain high quality technology for conducting such procedures, and that some courts are already using video teleconferencing—with the consent of the parties.

The Committee believed that, on balance and in appropriate circumstances, the court and the defendant should have the option of using video teleconferencing for arraignments, as long as the defendant consents to that procedure. The question of when it would be appropriate for a defendant to consent is not spelled out in the rule. That is left to the defendant and the court in each case. Although the rule does not specify any particular technical requirements regarding the system to be used, if the equipment or technology is deficient, the public may lose confidence in the integrity and dignity of the proceedings.

The amendment does not require a court to adopt or use video teleconferencing. In deciding whether to use such procedures, a court may wish to consider establishing clearly articulated standards and procedures. For example, the court would normally want to insure that the location used for televising the video teleconferencing is conducive to the solemnity of a federal criminal proceeding. That might require additional coordination, for example, with the detention facility to insure that the room, furniture, and furnishings reflect the dignity associated with a federal courtroom. Provision should also be made to insure that the judge, or a surrogate, is in a position to carefully assess the condition of the defendant. And the court should also consider establishing procedures for insuring that counsel and the defendant (and even the defendant's immediate family) are provided an ample opportunity to confer in private.

Although the rule requires the defendant to waive a personal appearance for an arraignment, the rule does not require that the waiver for video teleconferencing be in writing. Nor does it require that the defendant waive that appearance in person, in open court. It would normally be sufficient for the defendant to waive an appearance while participating through a video teleconference.

The amendment leaves to the courts the decision first, whether to permit video arraignments, and second, the procedures to be used. The Committee was satisfied that the technology has progressed to the point that video teleconferencing can address the concerns raised in the past about the ability of the court and the defendant to see each other and for the defendant and counsel to be in contact with each other, either at the same location or by a secure remote connection.

Rule 11. Pleas

(a) Entering a Plea.

(1) *In general.* A defendant may plead not guilty, guilty, or (with the court's consent) nolo contendere.

(2) *Conditional Plea.* With the consent of the court and the government, a defendant may enter a condi-

tional plea of guilty or nolo contendere, reserving in writing the right to have an appellate court review an adverse determination of a specified pretrial motion. A defendant who prevails on appeal may then withdraw the plea.

(3) *Nolo Contendere Plea.* Before accepting a plea of nolo contendere, the court must consider the parties' views and the public interest in the effective administration of justice.

(4) *Failure to Enter a Plea.* If a defendant refuses to enter a plea or if a defendant organization fails to appear, the court must enter a plea of not guilty.

(b) Considering and Accepting a Guilty or Nolo Contendere Plea.

(1) *Advising and Questioning the Defendant.* Before the court accepts a plea of guilty or nolo contendere, the defendant may be placed under oath, and the court must address the defendant personally in open court. During this address, the court must inform the defendant of, and determine that the defendant understands, the following:

(A) the government's right, in a prosecution for perjury or false statement, to use against the defendant any statement that the defendant gives under oath;

(B) the right to plead not guilty, or having already so pleaded, to persist in that plea;

(C) the right to a jury trial;

(D) the right to be represented by counsel—and if necessary have the court appoint counsel—at trial and at every other stage of the proceeding;

(E) the right at trial to confront and cross-examine adverse witnesses, to be protected from compelled self-incrimination, to testify and present evidence, and to compel the attendance of witnesses;

(F) the defendant's waiver of these trial rights if the court accepts a plea of guilty or nolo contendere;

(G) the nature of each charge to which the defendant is pleading;

(H) any maximum possible penalty, including imprisonment, fine, and term of supervised release;

(I) any mandatory minimum penalty;

(J) any applicable forfeiture;

(K) the court's authority to order restitution;

(L) the court's obligation to impose a special assessment;

(M) in determining a sentence, the court's obligation to calculate the applicable sentencing-guideline range and to consider that range, possible departures under the Sentencing Guidelines, and other sentencing factors under 18 U.S.C. § 3553(a); and

(N) the terms of any plea-agreement provision waiving the right to appeal or to collaterally attack the sentence; and

(O) that, if convicted, a defendant who is not a United States citizen may be removed from the United States, denied citizenship, and denied admission to the United States in the future.

(2) *Ensuring That a Plea Is Voluntary.* Before accepting a plea of guilty or nolo contendere, the court must address the defendant personally in open court and determine that the plea is voluntary and did not result from force, threats, or promises (other than promises in a plea agreement).

(3) *Determining the Factual Basis for a Plea.* Before entering judgment on a guilty plea, the court must determine that there is a factual basis for the plea.

(c) Plea Agreement Procedure.

(1) *In General.* An attorney for the government and the defendant's attorney, or the defendant when proceeding pro se, may discuss and reach a plea agreement. The court must not participate in these discussions. If the defendant pleads guilty or nolo contendere to either a charged offense or a lesser or related offense, the plea agreement may specify that an attorney for the government will:

(A) not bring, or will move to dismiss, other charges;

(B) recommend, or agree not to oppose the defendant's request, that a particular sentence or sentencing range is appropriate or that a particular provision of the Sentencing Guidelines, or policy statement, or sentencing factor does or does not apply (such a recommendation or request does not bind the court); or

(C) agree that a specific sentence or sentencing range is the appropriate disposition of the case, or that a particular provision of the Sentencing Guidelines, or policy statement, or sentencing factor does or does not apply (such a recommendation or request binds the court once the court accepts the plea agreement).

(2) *Disclosing a Plea Agreement.* The parties must disclose the plea agreement in open court when the plea is offered, unless the court for good cause allows the parties to disclose the plea agreement in camera.

(3) *Judicial Consideration of a Plea Agreement.*

(A) To the extent the plea agreement is of the type specified in Rule 11(c)(1)(A) or (C), the court may accept the agreement, reject it, or defer a decision until the court has reviewed the presentence report.

(B) To the extent the plea agreement is of the type specified in Rule 11(c)(1)(B), the court must advise the defendant that the defendant has no right to withdraw the plea if the court does not follow the recommendation or request.

(4) *Accepting a Plea Agreement.* If the court accepts the plea agreement, it must inform the defendant that to the extent the plea agreement is of the type specified in Rule 11(c)(1)(A) or (C), the agreed disposition will be included in the judgment.

(5) *Rejecting a Plea Agreement.* If the court rejects a plea agreement containing provisions of the type specified in Rule 11(c)(1)(A) or (C), the court must do the following on the record and in open court (or, for good cause, in camera):

(A) inform the parties that the court rejects the plea agreement;

(B) advise the defendant personally that the court is not required to follow the plea agreement and give the defendant an opportunity to withdraw the plea; and

(C) advise the defendant personally that if the plea is not withdrawn, the court may dispose of the case less favorably toward the defendant than the plea agreement contemplated.

(d) Withdrawing a Guilty or Nolo Contendere

Plea. A defendant may withdraw a plea of guilty or nolo contendere:

(1) before the court accepts the plea, for any reason or no reason; or

(2) after the court accepts the plea, but before it imposes sentence if:

(A) the court rejects a plea agreement under Rule 11(c)(5); or

(B) the defendant can show a fair and just reason for requesting the withdrawal.

(e) Finality of a Guilty or Nolo Contendere Plea. After the court imposes sentence, the defendant may not withdraw a plea of guilty or nolo contendere, and the plea may be set aside only on direct appeal or collateral attack.

(f) Admissibility or Inadmissibility of a Plea, Plea Discussions, and Related Statements. The admissibility or inadmissibility of a plea, a plea discussion, and any related statement is governed by Federal Rule of Evidence 410.

(g) Recording the Proceedings. The proceedings during which the defendant enters a plea must be recorded by a court reporter or by a suitable recording device. If there is a guilty plea or a nolo contendere plea, the record must include the inquiries and advice to the defendant required under Rule 11(b) and (c).

(h) Harmless Error. A variance from the requirements of this rule is harmless error if it does not affect substantial rights.

HISTORY:

Amended Feb. 28, 1966, eff. July 1, 1966; April 22, 1974, eff. Dec. 1, 1975; P. L. 94-64, §§ 2, 3(5)–(10), 89 Stat. 371, 372; April 30, 1979, eff. Aug. 1, 1979, and Dec. 1, 1980; April 28, 1982, eff. Aug. 1, 1982; April 28, 1983, eff. Aug. 1, 1983; April 29, 1985, eff. Aug. 1, 1985; March 9, 1987, eff. Aug. 1, 1987; Nov. 18, 1988, P. L. 100-690, Title VII, Subtitle B, § 7076, 102 Stat. 4406; April 25, 1989, eff. Dec. 1, 1989; April 26, 1999, eff. Dec. 1, 1999; April 29, 2002, eff. Dec. 1, 2002; April 30, 2007, eff. Dec. 1, 2007; April 16, 2013, eff. Dec. 1, 2013.

HISTORY; ANCILLARY LAWS AND DIRECTIVES

Other provisions:

Notes of Advisory Committee. 1. This rule is substantially a restatement of existing law and practice, 18 U.S.C. [former] § 564 (Standing mute); *Fogus v United States,* 34 F.2d 97, (C.C.A. 4th) (Duty of court to ascertain that plea of guilty is intelligently and voluntarily made).

2. The plea of nolo contendere has always existed in the Federal courts, *Hudson v United States,* 272 U.S. 451, 47 S.Ct. 127, 71 L.Ed. 347; *United States v Norris,* 281 U.S. 619, 50 S.Ct. 424, 74 L.Ed. 1076. The use of the plea is recognized by the Probation Act, 18 U.S.C. [former] § 724 [see § 3651]. While at times criticized as theoretically lacking in logical basis, experience has shown that it performs a useful function from a practical standpoint.

Notes of Advisory Committee on 1966 amendments. The great majority of all defendants against whom indictments or informations are filed in the federal courts plead guilty. Only a comparatively small number go to trial. United States Attorney Statistical Report, Fiscal Year 1964, p 1. The fairness and adequacy of the procedures on acceptance of pleas of guilty are of vital importance in according equal justice to all the federal costs.

Three changes are made in the second sentence. The first change makes it clear that before accepting either a plea of guilty or nolo contendere the court must determine that the plea is made voluntarily with understanding of the nature of the charge. The second change expressly requires the court to address the defendant personally in the course of determining that the plea is made voluntarily and with understanding of the nature of the charge. The reported cases reflect some confusion over this matter. Compare *United States v Diggs,* 304 F.2d 929 (6th Cir. 1962); *Domenica v United States,* 292 F.2d 483 (1st Cir. 1961); *Gundlach v United States,* 262 F.2d 72 (4th Cir. 1958), cert den 360 U.S. 904, 3 L.Ed.2d 1255, 79 S.Ct. 1283 (1959); and *Julian v United States,* 236 F.2d 155 (6th Cir. 1956), which contain the implication that personal interrogation of the defendant is the better practice even when he is represented by counsel, with *Meeks v United States,* 298 F.2d 204 (5th Cir. 1962); *Nunley v United States,* 294 F.2d 579 (10th Cir. 1961), cert den 368 U.S. 991, 7 L.Ed. 2d 527, 82 S.Ct. 607 (1962); and *United States v Von der Heide,* 169 F. Supp. 560 (D.D.C. 1959).

The third change in the second sentence adds the words "and the consequences of his plea" to state what clearly is the law. See, e.g., *Von Moltke v Gillies,* 332 U.S. 708, 724, 92 L.Ed. 309, 68 S.Ct. 316 (1948); *Kerchevel v United States,* 274 U.S. 220, 223, 71 L.Ed. 1009, 47 S.Ct. 582 (1927); *Munich v United States,* 337 F.2d 356 (9th Cir. 1964); *Pilkington v United States,* 315 F.2d 204 (4th Cir. 1963); *Smith v United States,* 324 F.2d 436 (D.C. Cir. 1963); but cf. *Marvel v United States,* 335 F.2d 101 (5th Cir. 1964).

A new sentence is added at the end of the rule to impose a duty on the court in cases where the defendant pleads guilty to satisfy itself that there is a factual basis for the plea before entering judgment. The court should satisfy itself, by inquiry of the defendant or the attorney for the government, or by examining the presentence report, or otherwise, that the conduct which the defendant admits constitutes the offense charged in the indictment or information or an offense included therein to which the defendant has pleaded guilty. Such inquiry should, e.g., protect a defendant who is in the position of pleading voluntarily with an understanding of the nature of the charge but without realizing that his conduct does not actually fall within the charge. For a similar requirement see Mich. Stat. Ann. § 28.1058 (1954); Mich. Sup. Ct. Rules 35A; *In re Valle,* 364 Mich. 471, 110 N.W.2d 673 (1961); *People v Barrows,* 358 Mich. 267, 99 N.W.2d 347 (1959); *People v Bumpus,* 355 Mich. 374, 94 N.W.2d 854 (1959); *People v Coates,* 337 Mich. 56, 59 N.W.2d 83 (1953). See also *Stinson v United States,* 316 F.2d 554 (5th Cir. 1963). The normal consequence of a determination that there is not a factual basis for the plea would be for the court to set aside the plea and enter a plea of not guilty.

For a variety of reasons it is desirable in some cases to permit entry of judgment upon a plea of nolo contendere without inquiry into the factual basis for the plea. The new third sentence is not, therefore, made applicable to pleas of nolo contendere. It is not intended by this omission to reflect any view upon the effect of a plea of nolo contendere in relation to a plea of guilty. That problem has been dealt with by the courts. See, e.g., *Lott v United States,* 367 U.S. 421, 426, 6 L.Ed.2d 940, 81 S.Ct. 1563 (1961).

Notes of Advisory Committee on 1974 amendments. The amendments to rule 11 are designed to achieve two principal objectives:

(1) Subdivision (c) prescribes the advice which the court must give to insure that the defendant who pleads guilty has made an informed plea.

(2) Subdivision (e) provides a plea agreement procedure designed to give recognition to the propriety of plea discussions; to bring the existence of a plea agreement out into the open in court; and to provide methods for court acceptance or rejection of a plea agreement.

Other less basic changes are also made. The changes are discussed in the order in which they appear in the rule.

Subdivision (b) retains the requirement that the defendant obtain the consent of the court in order to plead nolo contendere. It adds that the court shall, in deciding whether to accept the plea, consider the views of the prosecution and of the defense and also the larger public interest in the administration of criminal justice.

Although the plea of nolo contendere has long existed in the federal courts, *Hudson v. United States,* 272 U.S. 451, 47 S.Ct. 127, 71 L.Ed. 347 (1926), the desirability of the plea has been a subject of disagreement. Compare Lane-Reticker, Nolo Contendere in North Carolina, 34 N.C.L-.Rev. 280, 290–291 (1956), with Note. The Nature and Consequences of the Plea of Nolo Contendere, 33 Neb.L-.Rev. 428, 434 (1954), favoring the plea. The American Bar Association Project on Standards for Criminal Justice takes the position that "the case for the nolo plea is not strong enough to justify a minimum standard supporting its use," but because "use of the plea contributes in some degree to the avoidance of unnecessary trials" it does not proscribe use of the plea. ABA, Standards Relating to Pleas of Guilty § 1.1(a) Commentary at 16 (Approved Draft, 1968).

A plea of nolo contendere is, for purposes of punishment, the same as the plea of guilty. See discussion of the history of the nolo plea in *North Carolina v. Alford,* 400 U.S. 25, 35–36 n. 8, 91 S.Ct. 160, 27 L.Ed.2d 162 (1970). Note, The Nature and Consequences of the Plea of Nolo Contendere, 33 Neb.L.Rev. 428, 430 (1954). A judgment upon the plea is a conviction and may be used to apply multiple offender statutes. Lenvin and Meyers, Nolo Contendere: Its Nature and Implications, 51 Yale L.J. 1255, 1265 (1942). Unlike a plea of guilty, however, it cannot be used against a defendant as an admission in a subsequent criminal or civil case. 4 Wigmore § 1066(4), at 58 (3d ed. 1940, Supp. 1970); Rules of Evidence for United States Courts and Magistrates, rule 803(22) (Nov. 1971). See Lenvin and Meyers, Nolo Contendere: Its Nature and Implications, 51 Yale L.J. 1255 (1942); ABA Standards Relating to Pleas of Guilty §§ 1.1(a) and (b), Commentary at 15–18 (Approved Draft, 1968).

The factors considered relevant by particular courts in determining whether to permit the plea of nolo contendere vary. Compare *United States v. Bagliore,* 182 F.Supp. 714, 716 (E.D.N.Y. 1960), where the view is taken that the plea should be rejected unless a compelling reason for acceptance is established, with *United States v. Jones,* 119 F.Supp. 288, 290 (S.D.Cal. 1954), where the view is taken that the plea should be accepted in the absence of a compelling reason to the contrary.

A defendant who desires to plead nolo contendere will commonly want to avoid pleading guilty because the plea of guilty can be introduced as an admission in subsequent civil litigation. The prosecution may oppose the plea of nolo contendere because it wants a definite resolution of the defendant's guilty or innocence either for correctional purposes or for reasons of subsequent litigation. ABA Standards Relating to Pleas of Guilty § 1.1(b) Commentary at 16–18 (Approved Draft, 1968). Under subdivision (b) of the new rule the balancing of the interests is left to the trial judge, who is mandated to take into account the larger public interest in the effective administration of justice.

Subdivision (c) prescribes the advice which the court must give to the defendant as a prerequisite to the acceptance of a plea of guilty. The former rule required that the court determine that the plea was made with "understanding of the nature of the charge and the consequences of the plea." The amendment identifies more specifically what must be explained to the defendant and also codifies, in the rule, the requirements of *Boykin v. Alabama,* 395 U.S. 238, 89 S.Ct. 1709, 23 L.Ed.2d 274 (1969), which held that a defendant must be apprised of the fact that he relinquishes certain constitutional rights by pleading guilty.

Subdivision (c) retains the requirement that the court address the defendant personally. See *McCarthy v. United States,* 394 U.S. 459, 466, 89 S.Ct. 1166, 22 L.Ed.2d 418 (1969). There is also an amendment to rule 43 to make clear that a defendant must be in court at the time of the plea.

Subdivision (c)(1) retains the current requirement that the court determine that the defendant understands the nature of the charge. This is a common requirement. See ABA Standards Relating to Pleas of Guilty § 1.4(a) (Approved Draft, 1968); Illinois Supreme Court Rule 402(a)(1) (1970), Ill.Rev.Stat. 1973, ch. 110A, § 402(a)(1). The method by which the defendant's understanding of the nature of the charge is determined may vary from case to case, depending on the complexity of the circumstances and the particular defendant. In some cases, a judge may do this by reading the indictment and by explaining the elements of the offense to the defendants. Thompson, The Judge's Responsibility on a Plea of Guilty 62 W.Va.L.Rev. 213, 220 (1960); Resolution of Judges of U.S. District Court for D.C., June 24, 1959.

Former rule 11 required the court to inform the defendant of the "consequences of the plea." Subdivision (c)(2) changes this and requires instead that the court inform the defendant of and determine that he understands "the mandatory minimum penalty provided by law, if any, and the maximum possible penalty provided by law for the offense to which the plea is offered." The objective is to insure that a defendant knows what minimum sentence the judge must impose and what maximum sentence the judge may impose. This information is usually readily ascertainable from the face of the statute defining the crime, and thus it is feasible for the judge to know specifically what to tell the defendant. Giving this advice tells a defendant the shortest mandatory sentence and also the longest possible sentence for the offense to which he is pleading guilty.

It has been suggested that it is desirable to inform a defendant of additional consequences which might follow from his plea of guilty. *Durant v. United States,* 410 F.2d 689 (1st Cir. 1969), held that a defendant must be informed of his ineligibility for parole. *Trujillo v. United States,* 377 F.2d 266 (5th Cir. 1967), cert denied 389 U.S. 899, 88 S.Ct. 224, 19 L.Ed.2d 221 (1967), held that advice about eligibility for parole is not required. It has been suggested that a defendant be advised that a jury might find him guilty only of a lesser included offense. C. Wright, Federal Practice and Procedure: Criminal § 173 at 374 (1969). See contra *Dorrough v. United States,* 385 F.2d 887 (5th Cir. 1967). The ABA Standards Relating to Pleas of Guilty § 1.4(c)(iii) (Approved Draft, 1968) recommend that the defendant be informed that he may be subject to additional punishment if the offense charged is one for which a different or additional punishment is authorized by reason of the defendant's previous conviction.

Under the rule the judge is not required to inform a defendant about these matters, though a judge is free to do so if he feels a consequence of a plea of guilty in a particular case is likely to be of real significance to the defendant. Currently, certain consequences of a plea of guilty, such as parole eligibility, may be so complicated that it is not feasible to expect a judge to clearly advise the defendant. For example, the judge may impose a sentence under 18 U.S.C. § 4202 making the defendant eligible for parole when he has served one third of the judicially imposed maximum; or, under 18 U.S.C. § 4208(a)(1), making parole eligibility after a specified period of time less than one third of the maximum; or, under 18 U.S.C. § 4208(a)(2), leaving eligibility to the discretion of the parole board. At the time the judge is required to advise the defendant of the consequences of his plea, the judge will usually not have seen the presentence report and thus will have no basis for giving a defendant any very realistic advice as to when he might be eligible for parole. Similar complications exist with regard to other, particularly collateral, consequences of a plea of guilty in a given case.

Subdivisions (c)(3) and (4) specify the constitutional rights that the defendant waives by a plea of guilty or nolo contendere. These subdivisions are designed to satisfy the requirements of understanding waiver set forth in *Boykin v. Alabama,* 395 U.S. 238, 89 S.Ct. 1709, 23 L.Ed.2d 274 (1969). Subdivision (c)(3) is intended to require that the judge inform the defendant and determine that he understands that he waives his fifth amendment rights. The rule takes the position that the defendant's right not to incriminate himself is best explained in terms of his right to plead not guilty and to persist in that plea if it has already been made. This is language identical to that adopted in Illinois for the same purpose. See Illinois Supreme Court Rule 402(a)(3) (1970), Ill. Rev.Stat. 1973, ch. 110A, § 402(a)(3).

Subdivision (c)(4) assumes that a defendant's right to have his guilt proved beyond a reasonable doubt and the right to confront his accusers are best explained by indicating that the right to trial is waived. Specifying that there will be no future trial of any kind makes this fact clear to those defendants who though knowing they have waived trial by jury, are under the mistaken impression that some kind of trial will follow. Illinois has recently adopted similar language. Illinois Supreme Court Rule 402(a)(4) (1970), Ill. Rev.Stat. 1973, ch. 110A, § 402(a)(4). In explaining to a defendant that he waives his right to trial, the judge may want to explain some of the aspects of trial such as the right to confront witnesses, to subpoena witnesses, to testify in his own behalf, or, if he chooses, not to testify. What is required, in this respect, to conform to *Boykin* is left to future case-law development.

Subdivision (d) retains the requirement that the court determine that a plea of guilty or nolo contendere is voluntary before accepting it. It adds the requirement that the court also inquire whether the defendant's willingness to plead guilty or nolo contendere results from prior plea discussions between the attorney for the government and the defendant or his attorney. See *Santobello v. New York,* 404 U.S. 257, 261–262, 92 S.Ct. 495, 30 L.Ed.2d 427 (1971): "The plea must, of course, be voluntary and knowing and if it was induced by promises, the essence of those promises must in some way be made known." Subdivisions (d) and (e) afford the court adequate basis for rejecting an improper plea agreement induced by threats or inappropriate promises.

The new rule specifies that the court personally address the defendant in determining the voluntariness of the plea.

By personally interrogating the defendant, not only will the judge be better able to ascertain the plea's voluntariness, but he will also develop a more complete record to support his determination in a subsequent post-conviction attack. . . . Both of these goals are undermined in proportion to the degree the district judge resorts to "assumptions" not based upon recorded responses to his inquiries. *McCarthy v. United States,* 394 U.S. 459, 466, 467, 89 S.Ct. 1166, 22 L.Ed.2d 418 (1969).

Subdivision (e) provides a plea agreement procedure. In doing so it gives recognition to the propriety of plea discussions and plea agreements provided that they are disclosed in open court and subject to acceptance or rejection by the trial judge.

Although reliable statistical information is limited, one recent estimate indicated that guilty pleas account for the disposition of as many as 95% of all criminal cases. ABA Standards Relating to Pleas of Guilty, pp. 1–2 (Approved Draft, 1968). A substantial number of these are the result of plea discussions. The President's Commission on Law Enforcement and Administration of Justice, Task Force Report: The Courts 9 (1967); D. Newman, Conviction: The Determination of Guilt or Innocence Without Trial 3 (1966); L. Weinreb, Criminal Process 437 (1969); Note, Guilty Plea Bargaining: Compromises by Prosecutors To Secure Guilty Pleas, 112 U.Pa.L.Rev. 865 (1964).

There is increasing acknowledgement of both the inevitability and the propriety of plea agreements. See, e.g., ABA Standards Relating to Pleas of Guilty § 3.1 (Approved Draft, 1968); Illinois Supreme Court Rule 402 (1970), Ill.Rev.Stat. 1973, ch. 110A, § 402.

In *Brady v. United States,* 397 U.S. 742, 752–753, 90 S.Ct. 1463, 25 L.Ed.2d 747 (1970), the court said:

Of course, that the prevalence of guilty pleas is explainable does not necessarily validate those pleas or the system which produces them. But we cannot hold that it is unconstitutional for the State to extend a benefit to a defendant who in turn extends a substantial benefit to the State and who demonstrates by his plea that he is ready and willing to admit his crime and to enter the correctional system in a frame of mind that affords hope for success in rehabilitation over a shorter period of time than might otherwise be necessary.

In *Santobello v. New York,* 404 U.S. 257, 260, 92 S.Ct. 495, 498, 30 L.Ed.2d 427 (1971), the court said:

The disposition of criminal charges by agreement between the prosecutor and the accused, sometimes loosely called "plea bargaining," is an essential component of the administration of justice. Properly administered, it is to be encouraged.

Administratively, the criminal justice system has come to depend upon pleas of guilty and, hence, upon plea discussions. See, e.g., President's Commission on Law Enforcement and Administration of Justice, Task Force

Report. The Courts 9 (1967); Note, Guilty Plea Bargaining: Compromises By Prosecutors To Secure Guilty Pleas, 112 U.Pa.L.Rev. 865 (1964). But expediency is not the basis for recognizing the propriety of a plea agreement practice. Properly implemented, a plea agreement procedure is consistent with both effective and just administration of the criminal law. *Santobello v. New York,* 404 U.S. 257, 92 S.Ct. 495, 30 L.Ed.2d 427. This is the conclusion reached in the ABA Standards Relating to Pleas of Guilty § 1.8 (Approved Draft, 1968); the ABA Standards Relating to The Prosecution Function and The Defense Function pp. 243–253 (Approved Draft, 1971); and the ABA Standards Relating to the Function of the Trial Judge, § 4.1 (App.Draft, 1972). The Supreme Court of California recently recognized the propriety of plea bargaining. See *People v. West,* 3 Cal.3d 595, 91 Cal.Rptr. 385, 477 P.2d 409 (1970). A plea agreement procedure has recently been decided in the District of Columbia Court of General Sessions upon the recommendation of the United States Attorney. See 51 F.R.D. 109 (1971).

Where the defendant by his plea aids in insuring prompt and certain application of correctional measures, the proper ends of the criminal justice system are furthered because swift and certain punishment serves the ends of both general deterrence and the rehabilitation of the individual defendant. Cf. Note, The Influence of the Defendant's Plea on Judicial Determination of Sentence, 66 Yale L.J. 204, 211 (1956). Where the defendant has acknowledged his guilt and shown a willingness to assume responsibility for his conduct, it has been thought proper to recognize this in sentencing. See also ALI, Model Penal Code § 7.01 (P.O.D. 1962); NPPA Guides for Sentencing (1957). Granting a charge reduction in return for a plea of guilty may give the sentencing judge needed discretion, particularly where the facts of a case do not warrant the harsh consequences of a long mandatory sentence or collateral consequences which are unduly severe. A plea of guilty avoids the necessity of a public trial and may protect the innocent victim of a crime against the trauma of direct and cross-examination.

Finally, a plea agreement may also contribute to the successful prosecution of other more serious offenders. See D. Newman, Conviction: The Determination of Guilt or Innocence Without Trial, chs. 2 and 3 (1966); Note, Guilty Plea Bargaining: Compromises By Prosecutors To Secure Guilty Pleas, 112 U.Pa.L.Rev. 865, 881 (1964).

Where plea discussions and agreements are viewed as proper, it is generally agreed that it is preferable that the fact of the plea agreement be disclosed in open court and its propriety be reviewed by the trial judge.

We have previously recognized plea bargaining as an ineradicable fact. Failure to recognize it tends not to destroy it but to drive it underground. We reiterate what we have said before: that when plea bargaining occurs it ought to be spread on the record [The Bench Book prepared by the Federal Judicial Center for use by United States District Judges now suggests that the defendant be asked by the court "if he believes there is any understanding or if any predictions have been made to him concerning the sentence he will receive." Bench Book for United States District Judges, Federal Judicial Center (1969) at 1.05.3.] and publicly disclosed. *United States v. Williams,* 407 F.2d 940 (4th Cir. 1969). . . . In the future we think that the district judges should not only make the general inquiry under Rule 11 as to whether the plea of guilty has been coerced or induced by promises, but should specifically inquire of counsel whether plea bargaining has occurred. Logically the general inquiry should elicit information about plea bargaining, but it seldom has in the past. *Raines v. United States,* 423 F.2d 526, 530 (4th Cir. 1970).

In the past, plea discussions and agreements have occurred in an informal and largely invisible manner. Enker, Perspectives on Plea Bargaining, in President's Commission on Law Enforcement and Administration of Justice, Task Force Report: The Courts 108, 115 (1967). There has often been a ritual of denial that any promises have been made, a ritual in which judges, prosecutors, and defense counsel have participated. ABA Standards Relating to Pleas of Guilty § 3.1, Commentary at 60–69 (Approved Draft 1968); Task Force Report: The Courts 9. Consequently, there has been a lack of effective judicial review of the propriety of the agreements, thus increasing the risk of real or apparent unfairness. See ABA Standards Relating to Pleas of Guilty § 3.1, Commentary at 60 et seq.; Task Force Report: The Courts 9–13.

The procedure described in subdivision (e) is designed to prevent abuse of plea discussions and agreements by providing appropriate and adequate safeguards.

Subdivision (e)(1) specifies that the "attorney for the government and the attorney for the defendant or the defendant when acting pro se may" participate in plea discussions. The inclusion of "the defendant when acting pro se" is intended to reflect the fact that there are situations in which a defendant insists upon representing himself. It may be desirable that an attorney for the government not enter plea discussions with a defendant personally. If necessary, counsel can be appointed for purposes of plea discussions. (Subdivision (d) makes it mandatory that the court inquire of the defendant whether his plea is the result of plea discussions between him and the attorney for the government. This is intended to enable the court to reject an agreement reached by an unrepresented defendant unless the court is satisfied that acceptance of the agreement adequately protects the rights of the defendant and the interests of justice.) This is substantially the position of the ABA Standards Relating to Pleas of Guilty § 3.1(a), Commentary at 65–66 (Approved Draft, 1968). Apparently, it is the practice of most prosecuting attorneys to enter plea discussions only with defendant's counsel. Note, Guilty Plea Bargaining: Compromises By Prosecutors To Secure Guilty Pleas, 112 U.Pa.L.Rev. 865, 904 (1964). Discussions without benefit of counsel increase the likelihood that such discussions may be unfair. Some courts have indicated that plea discussions in the absence of defendant's attorney may be constitutionally prohibited. See *Anderson v. North Carolina,* 221 F.Supp. 930, 935 (W.D.N.C.1963); *Shape v. Sigler,* 230 F.Supp. 601, 606 (D.Neb. 1964).

Subdivision (e)(1) is intended to make clear that there are four possible concessions that may be made in a plea agreement. First, the charge may be reduced to a lesser or related offense. Second, the attorney for the government may promise to move for dismissal of other charges. Third, the attorney for the government may agree to recommend or not oppose the imposition of a particular sentence. Fourth, the attorneys for the government and the defense may agree that a given sentence is an appropriate disposition of the case. This is made explicit in subdivision (e)(2) where reference is made to an agreement made "in the expectation that a specific sentence will be imposed." See

Note, Guilty Plea Bargaining: Compromises By Prosecutors To Secure Guilty Pleas, 112 U.Pa.L.Rev. 865, 898 (1964).

Subdivision (e)(1) prohibits the court from participating in plea discussions. This is the position of the ABA Standards Relating to Pleas of Guilty § 3.3(a) (Approved Draft, 1968).

It has been stated that it is common practice for a judge to participate in plea discussions. See D. Newman, Conviction: The Determination of Guilt or Innocence Without Trial 32–52, 78–104 (1966); Note, Guilty Plea Bargaining: Compromises By Prosecutors To Secure Guilty Pleas, 112 U.Pa.L.Rev. 865, 891, 905 (1964).

There are valid reasons for a judge to avoid involvement in plea discussions. It might lead the defendant to believe that he would not receive a fair trial, were there a trial before the same judge. The risk of not going along with the disposition apparently desired by the judge might induce the defendant to plead guilty, even if innocent. Such involvement makes it difficult for a judge to objectively assess the voluntariness of the plea. See ABA Standards Relating to Pleas of Guilty § 3.3(a), Commentary at 72–74 (Approved Draft, 1968); Note, Guilty Plea Bargaining: Compromises By Prosecutors To Secure Guilty Pleas, 112 U.Pa.L.Rev. 865, 891–892 (1964); Comment, Official Inducements to Plead Guilty: Suggested Morals for a Marketplace, 32 U.Chi.L.Rev. 167, 180–183 (1964); Informal Opinion No. 779 ABA Professional Ethics Committee ("A judge should not be a party to advance arrangements for the determination of sentence, whether as a result of a guilty plea or a finding of guilt based on proof."). 51 A.B.A.J. 444 (1965). As has been recently pointed out:

The unequal positions of the judge and the accused, one with the power to commit to prison and the other deeply concerned to avoid prison, as once raise a question of fundamental fairness. When a judge becomes a participant in plea bargaining he brings to bear the full force and majesty of his office. His awesome power to impose a substantially longer or even maximum sentence in excess of that proposed is present whether referred to or not. A defendant needs no reminder that if he rejects the proposal, stands upon his right to trial and is convicted, he faces a significantly longer sentence. *United States ex rel. Elksnis v. Gilligan,* 256 F.Supp. 244, 254 (S.D.N.Y. 1966).

On the other hand, one commentator has taken the position that the judge may be involved in discussions either after the agreement is reached or to help elicit facts and an agreement. Enker, Perspectives on Plea Bargaining, in President's Commission on Law Enforcement and Administration of Justice, Task Force Report: The Courts 108, 117–118 (1967).

The amendment makes clear that the judge should not participate in plea discussions leading to a plea agreement. It is contemplated that the judge may participate in such discussions as may occur when the plea agreement is disclosed in open court. This is the position of the recently adopted Illinois Supreme Court Rule 402(d)(1) (1970), Ill.Rev.Stat. 1973, ch. 110A, § 402(d)(1). As to what may constitute "participation," contrast *People v. Earegood,* 12 Mich.App. 256, 268–269, 162 N.W.2d 802, 809–810 (1968), with *Kruse v. State,* 47 Wis.2d 460, 177 N.W.2d 322 (1970).

Subdivision (e)(2) provides that the judge shall require the disclosure of any plea agreement in open court. In *People v. West,* 3 Cal.3d 595, 91 Cal.Rptr. 385, 477 P.2d 409 (1970), the court said:

[T]he basis of the bargain should be disclosed to the court and incorporated in the record. . . .

Without limiting that court to those we set forth, we note four possible methods of incorporation: (1) the bargain could be stated orally and recorded by the court reporter, whose notes then must be preserved or transcribed; (2) the bargain could be set forth by the clerk in the minutes of the court; (3) the parties could file a written stipulation stating the terms of the bargain; (4) finally, counsel or the court itself may find it useful to prepare and utilize forms for the recordation of plea bargains. 91 Cal.Rptr. 393, 394, 477 P.2d at 417, 418.

The District of Columbia Court of General Sessions is using a "Sentence-Recommendation Agreement" form.

Upon notice of the plea agreement, the court is given the option to accept or reject the agreement or defer its decision until receipt of the presentence report.

The judge may, and often should, defer his decision until he examines the presentence report. This is made possible by rule 32 which allows a judge, with the defendant's consent, to inspect a presentence report to determine whether a plea agreement should be accepted. For a discussion of the use of conditional plea acceptance, see ABA Standards Relating to Pleas of Guilty § 3.3(b), Commentary at 74–76, and Supplement, Proposed Revisions § 3.3(b) at 2–3 (Approved Draft, 1968); Illinois Supreme Court Rule 402(d)(2) (1970), Ill.Rev.Stat. 1973, ch. 110A, § 402(d)(2).

The plea agreement procedure does not attempt to define criteria for the acceptance or rejection of a plea agreement. Such a decision is left to the discretion of the individual trial judge.

Subdivision (e)(3) makes is mandatory, if the court decides to accept the plea agreement, that it inform the defendant that it will embody in the judgment and sentence the disposition provided in the plea agreement, or one more favorable to the defendant. This serves the purpose of informing the defendant immediately that the agreement will be implemented.

Subdivision (e)(4) requires the court, if it rejects the plea agreement, to inform the defendant of this fact and to advise the defendant personally, in open court, that the court is not bound by the plea agreement. The defendant must be afforded an opportunity to withdraw his plea and must be advised that if he persists in his guilty plea or plea of nolo contendere, the disposition of the case may be less favorable to him than that contemplated by the plea agreement. That the defendant should have the opportunity to withdraw his plea if the court rejects the plea agreement is the position taken in ABA Standards Relating to Pleas of Guilty, Supplement, Proposed Revisions § 2.1(a)(ii)(5) (Approved Draft, 1968). Such a rule has been adopted in Illinois. Illinois Supreme Court Rule 402(d)(2) (1970), Ill.Rev.Stat. 1973, ch. 110A, § 402(d)(2).

If the court rejects the plea agreement and affords the defendant the opportunity to withdraw the plea, the court is not precluded from accepting a guilty plea from the same defendant at a later time, when such plea conforms to the requirements of rule 11.

Subdivision (e)(5) makes it mandatory that, except for good cause shown, the court be notified of the existence of a plea agreement at the arraignment or at another time prior to trial fixed by the court. Having a plea entered at this stage provides a reasonable time for the defendant to consult with counsel and for counsel to complete any plea discussions with the attorney for the government. ABA Standards Relating to Pleas of Guilty § 1.3 (Approved Draft, 1968). The objective of the provision is to make clear that the court has authority to require a plea agreement to be disclosed sufficiently in advance of trial so as not to interfere with the efficient scheduling of criminal cases.

Subdivision (e)(6) is taken from rule 410, Rules of Evidence for United States Courts and Magistrates (Nov. 1971). See Advisory Committee Note thereto. See also the ABA Standards Relating to Pleas of Guilty § 2.2 (Approved Draft, 1968); Illinois Supreme Court Rule 402(f) (1970), Ill. Rev. Stat. 1973, ch. 110A, § 402(f).

Subdivision (f) retains the requirement of old rule 11 that the court should not enter judgment upon a plea of guilty without making such an inquiry as will satisfy it that there is a factual basis for the plea. The draft does not specify that any particular type of inquiry be made. See *Santobello v. New York,* 404 U.S. 257, 261, 92 S.Ct. 495, 30 L.Ed.2d 427 (1971); "Fed.Rule Crim.Proc. 11, governing pleas in federal courts, now makes clear that the sentencing judge must develop, on the record, the factual basis for the plea, as, for example, by having the accused describe the conduct that gave rise to the charge." An inquiry might be made of the defendant, of the attorneys for the government and the defense, of the presentence report when one is available, or by whatever means is appropriate in a specific case. This is the position of the ABA Standards Relating to Pleas of Guilty § 1.6 (Approved Draft, 1968). Where inquiry is made of the defendant himself it may be desirable practice to place the defendant under oath. With regard to a determination that there is a factual basis for a plea of guilty to a "lessor or related offense," compare ABA Standards Relating to Pleas of Guilty § 3.1(b)(ii), Commentary at 67–68 (Approved Draft, 1968), with ALI, Model Penal Code § 1.07(5) (P.O.D. 1962). The rule does not speak directly to the issue of whether a judge may accept a plea of guilty where there is a factual basis for the plea but the defendant asserts his innocence. *North Carolina v. Alford,* 400 U.S. 25, 91 S.Ct. 160, 27 L.Ed.2d 162 (1970). The procedure in such case would seem to be to deal with this as a plea of nolo contendere, the acceptance of which would depend upon the judge's decision as to whether acceptance of the plea is consistent with "the interest of the public in the effective administration of justice" [new rule 11(b)]. The defendant who asserts his innocence while pleading guilty or nolo contendere is often difficult to deal with in a correctional setting, and it may therefore be preferable to resolve the issue of guilt or innocence at the trial stage rather than leaving that issue unresolved, thus complicating subsequent correctional decisions. The rule is intended to make clear that a judge may reject a plea of nolo contendere and require the defendant either to plead not guilty or to plead guilty under circumstances in which the judge is able to determine that the defendant is in fact guilty of the crime to which he is pleading guilty.

Subdivision (g) requires that a verbatim record be kept of the proceedings. If there is a plea of guilty or nolo contendere, the record must include, without limitation, the court's advice to the defendant, the inquiry into the voluntariness of the plea and the plea agreement, and the inquiry into the accuracy of the plea. Such a record is important in the event of a post-conviction attack. ABA Standards Relating to Pleas of Guilty § 1.7 (Approved Draft, 1968). A similar requirement was adopted in Illinois: Illinois Supreme Court Rule 402(e) (1970), Ill.Rev.Stat. 1973, ch. 110A, § 402(e).

Notes of Committee on the Judiciary on 1975 amendments (House Report No. 94-247). A. Amendments Proposed by the Supreme Court. Rule 11 of the Federal Rules of Criminal Procedure deals with pleas. The Supreme Court has proposed to amend this rule extensively.

Rule 11 provides that a defendant may plead guilty, not guilty, or nolo contendere. The Supreme Court's amendments to Rule 11(b) provide that a nolo contendere plea "shall be accepted by the court only after due consideration of the views of the parties and the interest of the public in the effective administration of justice."

The Supreme Court amendments to Rule 11(c) spell out the advise that the court must give to the defendant before accepting the defendant's plea of guilty or nolo contendere. The Supreme Court amendments to Rule 11(d) set forth the steps that the court must take to insure that a guilty or nolo contendere plea has been voluntarily made.

The Supreme Court amendments to Rule 11(e) establish a plea agreement procedure. This procedure permits the parties to discuss disposing of a case without a trial and sets forth the type of agreements that the parties can reach concerning the disposition of the case. The procedure is not mandatory; a court is free not to permit the parties to present plea agreements to it.

The Supreme Court amendments to Rule 11(f) require that the court, before entering judgment upon a plea of guilty, satisfy itself that "there is a factual basis for the plea." The Supreme Court amendments to Rule 11(g) require that a verbatim record be kept of the proceedings at which the defendant enters a plea.

B. Committee Action. The proposed amendments to Rule 11, particularly those relating to the plea negotiating procedure, have generated much comment and criticism. No observer is entirely happy that our criminal justice system must rely to the extent it does on negotiated dispositions of cases. However, crowded court dockets make plea negotiating a fact that the Federal Rules of Criminal Procedure should contend with. The Committee accepts the basic structure and provisions of Rule 11(e).

Rule 11(e) as proposed permits each federal court to decide for itself the extent to which it will permit plea negotiations to be carried on within its own jurisdiction. No court is compelled to permit any plea negotiations at all. Proposed Rule 11(e) regulates plea negotiations and agreements if, and to the extent that, the court permits such negotiations and agreements. [Proposed Rule 11(e) has been criticized by some federal judges who read it to mandate the court to permit plea negotiations and the reaching of plea agreements. The Advisory Committee stressed during its testimony that the rule does not mandate that a court permit any form of plea agreement to be presented to it. See, e.g., the remarks of United States Circuit Judge William H. Webster in Hearings II, at 196. See also the exchange of correspondence between Judge Webster and United States District Judge Frank A. Kaufman in Hearings II, at 289–90.]

Proposed Rule 11(e) contemplates 4 different types of plea agreements. First, the defendant can plead guilty or nolo contendere in return for the prosecutor's reducing the charge to a less serious offense. Second, the defendant can plead guilty or nolo contendere in return for the prosecutor dropping, or not bringing, a charge or charges relating to other offenses. Third, the defendant can plead guilty or nolo contendere in return for the prosecutor's recommending a sentence. Fourth, the defendant and prosecutor can agree that a particular sentence is the appropriate disposition of the case. [It is apparent, though not explicitly stated, that Rule 11(e) contemplates that the plea agreement may bind the defendant to do more than just plead guilty or nolo contendere. For example, the plea agreement may bind the defendant to cooperate with the prosecution in a different investigation. The Committee intends by its approval of Rule 11(e) to permit the parties to agree on such terms in a plea agreement.]

The Committee added language in subdivisions (e)(2) and (e)(4) to permit a plea agreement to be disclosed to the court, or rejected by it, in camera. There must be a showing of good cause before the court can conduct such proceedings in camera. The language does not address itself to whether the showing of good cause may be made in open court or in camera. That issue is left for the courts to resolve on a case-by-case basis. These changes in subdivisions (e)(2) and (e)(4) will permit a fair trial when there is substantial media interest in a case and the court is rejecting a plea agreement.

The Committee added an exception to subdivision (e)(6). That subdivision provides:

Evidence of a plea of guilty, later withdrawn, or a plea of nolo contendere, or of an offer to plead guilty or nolo contendere to the crime charged or any other crime, or of statements made in connection with any of the foregoing pleas or offers, is not admissible in any civil or criminal proceeding against the person who made the plea or offer.

The Committee's exception permits the use of such evidence in a perjury or false statement prosecution where the plea, offer, or related statement was made by the defendant on the record, under oath and in the presence of counsel. The Committee recognizes that even this limited exception may discourage defendants from being completely candid and open during plea negotiations and may even result in discouraging the reaching of plea agreements. However, the Committee believes hat, on balance, it is more important to protect the integrity of the judicial process from willful deceit and untruthfulness. [The Committee does not intend its language to be construed as mandating or encouraging the swearing-in of the defendant during proceedings in connection with the disclosure and acceptance or rejection of a plea agreement.]

The Committee recast the language of Rule 11(c), which deals with the advice given to a defendant before the court can accept his plea of guilty or nolo contendere. The Committee acted in part because it believed that the warnings given to the defendant ought to include those that *Boykin v. Alabama,* 395 U.S. 238 (1969), said were constitutionally required. In addition, and as a result of its change in subdivision (e)(6), the Committee thought if only fair that the defendant be warned that his plea of guilty (later withdrawn) or nolo contendere, or his offer of either plea, or his statements made in connection with such pleas or offers, could later be used against him in a perjury trial if made under oath, on the record, and in the presence of counsel.

Notes of Conference Committee on 1975 amendments (House Report No. 94-414). Subdivision (c). Rule 11(c) enumerates certain things that a judge must tell a defendant before the judge can accept that defendant's plea of guilty or nolo contendere. The House version expands upon the list originally proposed by the Supreme Court. The Senate version adopts the Supreme Court's proposal.

The Conference adopts the House provision.

Subdivision (e)(1). Rule 11(e)(1) outlines some general considerations concerning the plea agreement procedure. The Senate version makes nonsubstantive change in the House version.

The Conference adopts the Senate provision.

Subdivision (e)(6). Rule 11(e)(6) deals with the use of statements made in connection with plea agreements. The House version permits a limited use of pleas of guilty, later withdrawn, or nolo contendere offers of such pleas, and statements made in connection with such pleas or offers. Such evidence can be used in a perjury or false statement prosecution if the plea, offer, or related statement was made under oath on the record, and in the presence of counsel. The Senate version permits evidence of voluntary and reliable statements made in court on the record to be used for the purpose of impeaching the credibility of the declarant or in a perjury or false statement prosecution.

The Conference adopts the House version with changes. The Conference agrees that neither a plea nor the offer of a plea ought to be admissible for any purpose. The Conference-adopted provision, therefore, like the Senate provision, permits only the use of statements made in connection with a plea of guilty, later withdrawn, or a plea of nolo contendere, or in connection with an offer of a guilty or nolo contendere plea.

Notes of Advisory Committee on 1979 amendments. *Note to Subdivision (e)(2).* The amendment to rule 11(e)(2) is intended to clarify the circumstances in which the court may accept or reject a plea agreement, with the consequences specified in subdivisions (e)(3) and (4). The present language has been the cause of some confusion and has led to results which are not entirely consistent. Compare *United States v. Sarubbi,* 416 F.Supp. 633 (D.N.J. 1976); with *United States v. Hull,* 413 F.Supp. 145 (E.D.Tenn. 1976).

Rule 11(e)(1) specifies three types of plea agreements, namely, those in which the attorney for the government might.

(A) move for dismissal of other charges; or.

(B) make a recommendation, or agree not to oppose the defendant's request, for a particular sentence, with the understanding that such recommendation or request shall not be binding upon the court; or.

(C) agree that a specific sentence is the appropriate disposition of the case.

A (B) type of plea agreement is clearly of a different order than the other two, for an agreement to recommend or not to oppose is discharged when the prosecutor performs as he agreed to do. By comparison, critical to a type (A) or (C) agreement is that the defendant receive the contemplated charge dismissal or agreed-to sentence. Consequently, there must ultimately be an acceptance or rejection by the court of a type (A) or (C) agreement so that it may be determined whether the defendant shall receive the bargained-for concessions or shall instead be afforded an opportunity to withdraw his plea. But this is not so as to a type (B) agreement; there is no "disposition provided for" in such a plea agreement so as to make the acceptance provisions of subdivision (e)(3) applicable, nor is there a need for rejection with opportunity for withdrawal under subdivision (e)(4) in light of the fact that the defendant knew the nonbinding character of the recommendation or request. *United States v. Henderson,* 565 F.2d 1119 (9th Cir. 1977); *United States v. Savage,* 561 F.2d 554 (4th Cir. 1977).

Because a type (B) agreement is distinguishable from the others in that it involves only a recommendation or request not binding upon the court, it is important that the defendant be aware that this is the nature of the agreement into which he has entered. The procedure contemplated by the last sentence of amended subdivision (e)(2) will establish for the record that there is such awareness. This provision conforms to ABA Standards Relating to Pleas of Guilty § 1.5 (Approved Draft, 1968), which provides that "the court must advise the defendant personally that the recommendations of the prosecuting attorney are not binding on the court."

Sometimes a plea agreement will be partially but not entirely of the (B) type, as where a defendant, charged with counts 1, 2 and 3, enters into an agreement with the attorney for the government wherein it is agreed that if defendant pleads guilty to count 1, the prosecutor will recommend a certain sentence as to that count and will move for dismissal of counts 2 and 3. In such a case, the court must take particular care to ensure that the defendant understands which components of the agreement involve only a (B) type recommendation and which do not. In the above illustration, that part of the agreement which contemplates the dismissal of counts 2 and 3 is an (A) type agreement, and thus under rule 11(e) the court must either accept the agreement to dismiss these counts or else reject it and allow the defendant to withdraw his plea. If rejected, the defendant must be allowed to withdraw the plea on count 1 even if the type (B) promise to recommend a certain sentence on that count is kept, for a multi-faceted plea agreement is nonetheless a single agreement. On the other hand, if counts 2 and 3 are dismissed and the sentence recommendation is made, then the defendant is not entitled to withdraw his plea even if the sentence recommendation is not accepted by the court, for the defendant received all he was entitled to under the various components of the plea agreement.

Note to Subdivision (e)(6). The major objective of the amendment to rule 11(e)(6) is to describe more precisely, consistent with the original purpose of the provision, what evidence relating to pleas or plea discussions is inadmissible. The present language is susceptible to interpretation which would make it applicable to a wide variety of statements made under various circumstances other than within the context of those plea discussions authorized by rule 11(e) and intended to be protected by subdivision (e)(6) of the rule. See *United States v Herman,* 544 F.2d 791 (5th Cir. 1977), discussed herein.

Fed.R.Ev. 410, as originally adopted by Pub.L. 93-595, provided in part that "evidence of a plea of guilty, later withdrawn, or a plea of nolo contendere, or of an offer to plead guilty or nolo contendere to the crime charged or any other crime, or of statements made in connection with any of the foregoing pleas or offers, is not admissible in any civil or criminal action, case, or proceeding against the person who made the plea or offer." (This rule was adopted with the proviso that it "shall be superseded by any amendment to the Federal Rules of Criminal Procedure which is inconsistent with this rule.") As the Advisory Committee Note explained: "Exclusion of offers to plead guilty or nolo has as its purpose the promotion of disposition of criminal cases by compromise." The amendment of Fed.R.Crim.P. 11, transmitted to Congress by the Supreme Court in April 1974, contained a subdivision (e)(6) essentially identical to the rule 410 language quoted above, as a part of a substantial revision of rule 11. The most significant feature of this revision was the express recognition given to the fact that the "attorney for the government and the attorney for the defendant or the defendant when acting pro se may engage in discussions with a view toward reaching" a plea agreement. Subdivision (e)(6) was intended to encourage such discussions. As noted in H.R. Rep. No. 94-247, 94th Cong., 1st Sess. 7 (1975), the purpose of subdivision (e)(6) is to not "discourage defendants from being completely candid and open during plea negotiations." Similarly, H.R. Rep. No. 94-414, 94th Cong., 1st Sess. 10 (1975), states that "Rule 11(e)(6) deals with the use of statements made in connection with plea agreements." (Rule 11(e)(6) was thereafter enacted, with the addition of the proviso allowing use of statements in a prosecution for perjury, and with the qualification that the inadmissible statements must also be "relevant to" the inadmissible pleas or offers. Pub.L. 94-64; Fed.R.Ev. 410 was then amended to conform. Pub.L. 94-149.).

While this history shows that the purpose of Fed.R.Ev. 410 and Fed.R.Crim.P. 11(e)(6) is to permit the unrestrained candor which produces effective plea discussions between the "attorney for the government and the attorney for the defendant or the defendant when acting pro se," given visibility and sanction in rule 11(e), a literal reading of the language of these two rules could reasonably lead to the conclusion that a broader rule of inadmissibility obtains. That is, because "statements" are generally inadmissible if "made in connection with, and relevant to" an "offer to plead guilty," it might be thought that an otherwise voluntary admission to law enforcement officials is rendered inadmissible merely because it was made in the hope of obtaining leniency by a plea. Some decisions interpreting rule 11(e)(6) point in this direction. See *United States v Herman,* 544 F.2d 791 (5th Cir. 1977) (defendant in custody of two postal inspectors during continuance of removal hearing instigated conversation with them and at some point said he would plead guilty to armed robbery if the murder charge was dropped; one inspector stated they were not "in position" to make any deals in this regard; held, defendant's statement inadmissible under rule 11(e)(6) because the defendant "made the statements during the course of a conversation in which he sought concessions from the government in return for a guilty plea"); *United States v Brooks,* 536 F.2d 1137 (6th Cir. 1976) (defendant telephoned postal inspector and offered to plead guilty if he got 2-year maximum; statement inadmissible).

The amendment makes inadmissible statements made "in the course of any proceedings under this rule regarding" either a plea of guilty later withdrawn or a plea of nolo contendere, and also statements "made in the course of plea discussions with an attorney for the government which do not result in a plea of guilty or which result in a plea of guilty later withdrawn." It is not limited to statements by the defendant himself, and thus would cover statements by defense counsel regarding defendant's incriminating admissions to him. It thus fully protects the plea discussion process authorized by rule 11 without attempting to deal with confrontations between suspects and law enforcement agents, which involve problems of quite different dimensions. See, e.g., ALI Model Code of

Pre-Arraignment Procedure art. 140 and § 150.2(8) (Proposed Official Draft, 1975) (latter section requires exclusion if "a law enforcement officer induces any person to make a statement by promising leniency"). This change, it must be emphasized, does not compel the conclusion that statements made to law enforcement agents, especially when the agents purport to have authority to bargain, are inevitably admissible. Rather, the point is that such cases are not covered by the per se rule of 11 (e)(6) and thus must be resolved by that body of law dealing with police interrogations.

If there has been a plea of guilty later withdrawn or a plea of nolo contendere, subdivision (e)(6)(C) makes inadmissible statements made "in the course of any proceedings under this rule" regarding such pleas. This includes, for example, admissions by the defendant when he makes his plea in court pursuant to rule 11 and also admissions made to provide the factual basis pursuant to subdivision (f). However, subdivision (e)(6)(C) is not limited to statements made in court. If the court were to defer its decision on a plea agreement pending examination of the presentence report, as authorized by subdivision (e)(2), statements made to the probation officer in connection with the preparation of that report would come within this provision.

This amendment is fully consistent with all recent and major law reform efforts on this subject. ALI Model Code of Pre-Arraignment Procedure § 350.7 (Proposed Official Draft, 1975), and ABA Standards Relating to Pleas of Guilty § 3.4 (Approved Draft, 1968) both provide:

Unless the defendant subsequently enters a plea of guilty or nolo contendere which is not withdrawn, the fact that the defendant or his counsel and the prosecuting attorney engaged in plea discussions or made a plea agreement should not be received in evidence against or in favor of the defendant in any criminal or civil action or administrative proceedings.

The Commentary to the latter states:

The above standard is limited to discussions and agreements with the prosecuting attorney. Sometimes defendants will indicate to the police their willingness to bargain, and in such instances these statements are sometimes admitted in court against the defendant. *State v Christian,* 245 S.W.2d 895 (Mo. 1952). If the police initiate this kind of discussion, this may have some bearing on the admissibility of the defendant's statement. However, the policy considerations relevant to this issue are better dealt with in the context of standards governing in-custody interrogation by the police.

Similarly, Unif.R.Crim.P. 441(d) (Approved Draft, 1974), provides that except under limited circumstances "no discussion between the parties or statement by the defendant or his lawyer under this Rule," i.e., the rule providing "the parties may meet to discuss the possibility of pretrial diversion . . . or of a plea agreement," are admissible. The amendment is likewise consistent with the typical state provision on this subject; see, e.g., Ill.S.Ct. Rule 402(f).

The language of the amendment identifies with more precision than the present language the necessary relationship between the statements and the plea or discussion. See the dispute between the majority and concurring opinions in *United States v Herman,* 544 F.2d 791 (5th Cir. 1977), concerning the meanings and effect of the phrases "connection to" and "relevant to" in the present rule. Moreover, by relating the statements to "plea discussions" rather than "an offer to plead," the amendment ensures "that even an attempt to open plea bargaining [is] covered under the same rule of inadmissibility." *United States v Brooks,* 536 F.2d 1137 (6th Cir. 1976).

The last sentence of Rule 11(e)(6) is amended to provide a second exception to the general rule of nonadmissibility of the described statements. Under the amendment, such a statement is also admissible "in any proceeding wherein another statement made in the course of the same plea or plea discussions has been introduced and the statement ought in fairness be considered contemporaneously with it." This change is necessary so that, when evidence of statements made in the course of or as a consequence of a certain plea or plea discussions are introduced under circumstances not prohibited by this rule (e.g., not "against" the person who made the plea), other statements relating to the same plea or plea discussions may also be admitted when relevant to the matter at issue. For example, if a defendant upon a motion to dismiss a prosecution on some ground were able to admit certain statements made in aborted plea discussions in his favor, then other relevant statements made in the same plea discussions should be admissible against the defendant in the interest of determining the truth of the matter at issue. The language of the amendment follows closely that in Fed.R.Evid. 106, as the considerations involved are very similar.

The phrase "in any civil or criminal proceeding" has been moved from its present position, following the word "against," for purposes of clarity. An ambiguity presently exists because the word "against" may be read as referring either to the kind of proceeding in which the evidence is offered or the purpose for which is is offered. The change makes it clear that the latter construction is correct. No change is intended with respect to provisions making evidence rules inapplicable in certain situations. See, e.g., Fed.R.Evid. 104(a) and 1101(d).

Unlike ABA Standards Relating to Pleas of Guilty § 3.4 (Approved Draft, 1968), and ALI Model Code of Pre-Arraignment Procedure § 350.7 (Proposed Official Draft, 1975), rule 11(e)(6) does not also provide that the described evidence is inadmissible "in favor of" the defendant. This is not intended to suggest, however, that such evidence will inevitably be admissible in the defendant's favor. Specifically, no disapproval is intended of such decisions as *United States v Verdoorn,* 528 F.2d 103 (8th Cir. 1976), holding that the trial judge properly refused to permit the defendants to put into evidence at their trial the fact the prosecution had attempted to plea bargain with them, as "meaningful dialogue between the parties would, as a practical matter, be impossible if either party had to assume the risk that plea offers would be admissible in evidence."

Effective date of 1979 amendment of subsec. (e)(6). The amendment of subsec. (e)(6) by Order of the United States Supreme Court of April 30, 1979, is effective 12/1/80 as provided by Act July 31, 1979, P. L. 96-42, § 1(1), 93 Stat. 326, which appears as 18 USCS § 3771 note.

Notes of Advisory Committee on 1982 amendments. *Note to Subdivision (c)(1).* Subdivision (c)(1) has been amended by specifying "the effect of any special parole term" as one of the matters about which a defendant who has tendered a plea of guilty or nolo contendere is to be advised by the court. This amendment does not make any change in the law, as the courts are in agreement that such advice is presently required by Rule 11. See, e.g., *Moore v. United States,* 592 F.2d 753 (4th Cir. 1979); *United States v. Eaton,* 579 F.2d 1181 (10th Cir. 1978); *Richardson v. United States,* 577 F.2d 447 (8th Cir. 1978); *United States v. Del Prete,* 567 F.2d 928 (9th Cir. 1978); *United States v. Watson,* 548 F.2d 1058 (D.C. Cir. 1977); *United States v. Crusco,* 536 F.2d 21 (2d Cir. 1976); *United States v, Yazbeck,* 524 F.2d 641 (1st Cir. 1975); *United States v. Wolak,* 510 F.2d 164 (6th Cir. 1975).In *United States v. Timmreck,* 441 U.S. 780 (1979), 99 S.Ct. 2085, 60 L.Ed.2d 634 (1979), the Supreme Court assumed that the judge's failure in that case to describe the mandatory special parole term constituted "a failure to comply with the formal requirements of the Rule."

The purpose of the amendment is to draw more specific attention to the fact that advice concerning special parole terms is a necessary part of Rule 11 procedure. As noted in *Moore v. United States,* supra:

Special parole is a significant penalty. . . . Unlike ordinary parole, which does not involve supervision beyond the original prison term set by the court and the violation of which cannot lead to confinement beyond that sentence, special parole increases the possible period of confinement. It entails the possibility that a defendant may have to serve his original sentence plus a substantial additional period, without credit for time spent on parole. Explanation of special parole in open court is therefore essential to comply with the Rule's mandate that the defendant be informed of "the maximum possible penalty provided by law."

As the aforecited cases indicate, in the absence of specification of the requirement in the rule, it has sometimes happened that such advice has been inadvertently omitted from Rule 11 warnings.

The amendment does not attempt to enumerate all of the characteristics of the special parole term which the judge ought to bring to the defendant's attention. Some flexibility in this respect must be preserved, although it is well to note that the unique characteristics of this kind of parole are such that they may not be readily perceived by laymen. *Moore v. United States,* supra, recommends that in an appropriate case the judge inform the defendant and determine that he understands the following:

(1) that a special parole term will be added to any prison sentence he receives;

(2) the minimum length of the special parole term that must be imposed and the absence of a statutory maximum;

(3) that special parole is entirely different from—and in addition to—ordinary parole; and.

(4) that if the special parole is violated, the defendant can be returned to prison for the remainder of his sentence and the full length of his special parole term.

The amendment should not be read as meaning that a failure to comply with this particular requirement will inevitably entitle the defendant to relief. See *United States v. Timmreck,* supra. Likewise, the amendment makes no change in the existing law to the effect that many aspects of traditional parole need not be communicated to the defendant by the trial judge under the umbrella of Rule 11. For example, a defendant need not be advised of all conceivable consequences such as when he may be considered for parole or that, if he violates his parole, he will again be imprisoned. *Bunker v. Wise,* 550 F.2d 1155, 1158 (9th Cir. 1977).

Note to Subdivision (c)(4). The amendment to subdivision (c)(4) is intended to overcome the present conflict between the introductory language of subdivision (c), which contemplates the advice being given "[b]efore accepting a plea of guilty or nolo contendere," and thus presumably after the plea has been tendered, and the "if he pleads" language of subdivision (c)(4) which suggests the plea has not been tendered.

As noted by Judge Doyle in *United States v. Sinagub,* 468 F.Supp. 353 (W.D.Wis. 1979):

Taken literally, this wording of subsection (4) of 11(c) suggests that before eliciting any plea at an arraignment, the court is required to insure that a defendant understands that if he or she pleads guilty or nolo contendere, the defendant will be waiving the right to trial. Under subsection (3) of 11(c), however, there is no requirement that at this pre-plea stage, the court must insure that the defendant understands that he or she enjoys the right to a trial and, at trial, the right to the assistance of counsel, the right to confront and cross-examine witnesses against him or her, and the right not to be compelled to incriminate himself or herself. It would be incongruous to require that at the pre-plea stage the court insure that the defendant understands that if he enters a plea of guilty or nolo contendere he will be waiving a right, the existence and nature of which need not be explained until after such a plea has been entered. I conclude that the insertion of the words "that if he pleads guilty or nolo contendere," as they appear in subsection (4) of 11(c), was an accident of draftsmanship which occurred in the course of Congressional rewriting of 11(c) as it has been approved by the Supreme Court. Those words are to be construed consistently with the words "Before accepting a plea of guilty or nolo contendere," as they appear in the opening language of 11(c), and consistently with the omission of the words "that if he pleads" from subsections (1), (2), and (3) of 11(c). That is, as they appear in subsection (4) of 11(c), the words, "that if he pleads guilty or nolo contendere" should be construed to mean "that if his plea of guilty or nolo contendere is accepted by the court."

Although this is a very logical interpretation of the present language, the amendment will avoid the necessity to engage in such analysis in order to determine the true meaning of subdivision (c)(4).

Note to Subdivision (c)(5). Subdivision (c)(5), in its present form, may easily be read as contemplating that in every case in which a plea of guilty or nolo contendere is tendered, warnings must be given about the possible use of defendant's statements, obtained under oath, on the record and in the presence of counsel, in a later prosecution for perjury or false statement. The language has prompted some courts to reach the remarkable result that a defendant who pleads guilty or nolo contendere without receiving those warnings must be allowed to overturn his plea on appeal even though he was never questioned under oath, on the record, in the presence of counsel about the offense to which he pleaded. *United States v. Artis.,* No. 78-5012(4th Cir. March 12, 1979); *United States v. Boone,* 543 F.2d 1090 (4th Cir. 1976). Compare *United States v. Michaelson,* 552 F.2d 472 (2d Cir. 1977) (failure to give subdivision (c)(5) warnings not a basis for reversal, "at least when, as here, defendant was not put under oath before questioning about his guilty plea"). The present language of subdivision (e)(5) may also have contributed to the conclusion, not otherwise supported by the rule, that

"Rule 11 requires that the defendant be under oath for the entirety of the proceedings" conducted pursuant to that rule and that failure to place the defendant under oath would itself make necessary overturning the plea on appeal. *United States v. Aldridge,* 553 F.2d 922 (5th Cir. 1977).

When questioning of the kind described in subdivision (c)(5) is not contemplated by the judge who is receiving the plea, no purpose is served by giving the (c)(5) warnings, which in such circumstances can only confuse the defendant and detract from the force of the other warnings required by Rule 11. As correctly noted in *United States v. Sinagub,* supra,

subsection (5) of section (c) of Rule 11 is qualitatively distinct from the other sections of the Rule. It does not go to whether the plea is knowingly or voluntarily made, nor to whether the plea should be accepted and judgment entered. Rather, it does go to the possible consequences of an event which may or may not occur during the course of the arraignment hearing itself, namely, the administration of an oath to the defendant. Whether this event is to occur is wholly within the control of the presiding judge. If the event is not to occur, it is pointless to inform the defendant of its consequences. If a presiding judge intends that an oath not be administered to a defendant during an arraignment hearing, but alters that intention at some point, only then would the need arise to inform the defendant of the possible consequences of the administration of the oath.

The amendment to subdivision (c)(5) is intended to make it clear that this is the case.

The amendment limits the circumstances in which the warnings must be given, but does not change the fact, as noted in *Sinagub,* that these warnings are "qualitatively distinct" from the other advice required by Rule 11(c). This being the case, a failure to give the subdivision (c)(5) warnings even when the defendant was questioned under oath, on the record and in the presence of counsel would in no way affect the validity of the defendant's plea. Rather, this failure bears upon the admissibility of defendant's answers pursuant to subdivision (e)(6) in a later prosecution for perjury or false statement.

Notes of Advisory Committee on 1983 amendments. Subdivision (a). There are many defenses, objections and requests which a defendant must ordinarily raise by pretrial motion. See, e.g., 18 U.S.C. § 3162(a)(2); Fed.R.Crim.P.12(b). Should that motion be denied, interlocutory appeal of the ruling by the defendant is seldom permitted. See *United States v. MacDonald,* 435 U.S. 850 (1978) (defendant may not appeal denial of his motion to dismiss based upon Sixth Amendment speedy trial grounds); *DiBella v. United States,* 369 U.S. 121 (1962) (defendant may not appeal denial of pretrial motion to suppress evidence); compare *Abney v. United States,* 431 U.S. 651 (1977) (interlocutory appeal of denial of motion to dismiss on double jeopardy grounds permissible). Moreover, should the defendant thereafter plead guilty or nolo contendere, this will usually foreclose later appeal with respect to denial of the pretrial motion. "When a criminal defendant has solemnly admitted in open court that he is in fact guilty of the offense with which he is charged, he may not thereafter raise independent claims relating to the deprivation of constitutional rights that occurred prior to the entry of the guilty plea." *Tollett v. Henderson,* 411 U.S. 258, (1973). Though a nolo plea differs from a guilty plea in other respects, it is clear that it also constitutes a waiver of all nonjurisdictional defects in a manner equivalent to a guilty plea. *Lott v. United States,* 367 U.S. 421 (1961).

As a consequence, a defendant who has lost one or more pretrial motions will often go through an entire trial simply to preserve the pretrial issues for later appellate review. This results in a waste of prosecutorial and judicial resources, and causes delay in the trial of other cases, contrary to the objectives underlying the Speedy Trial Act of 1974, 18 U.S.C. § 3161 et seq. These unfortunate consequences may be avoided by the conditional plea device expressly authorized by new subdivision (a)(2).

The development of procedures to avoid the necessity for trials which are undertaken for the sole purpose of preserving pretrial objections has been consistently favored by the commentators. See ABA Standards Relating to the Administration of Criminal Justice, standard 21-1.3(c) (2d ed. 1978); Model Code of Pre-Arraignment Procedure § SS 290.1(4)(b) (1975); Uniform Rules of Criminal Procedure, rule 444(d) (Approved Draft, 1974); 1 C. Wright, Federal Practice and Procedure—Criminal § 175 (1969); 3 W. LaFave, Search and Seizure § 11.1 (1978). The Supreme Court has characterized the New York practice, whereby appeals from suppression motions may be appealed notwithstanding a guilty plea, as a "commendable effort to relieve the problem of congested trial calendars in a manner that does not diminish the opportunity for the assertion of rights guaranteed by the Constitution." *Lefkowitz v. Newsome,* 420 U.S. 283, 293 (1975). That Court has never discussed conditional pleas as such, but has permitted without comment a federal appeal on issues preserved by a conditional plea. *Jaben v. United States,* 381 U.S. 214 (1965). In the absence of specific authorization by statute or rule for a conditional plea, the circuits have divided on the permissibility of the practice. Two circuits have actually approved the entry of conditional pleas, *United States v. Burke,* 517 F.2d 377 (2d Cir. 1975); *United States v. Moskow,* 588 F.2d 882 (3d Cir. 1978); and two others have praised the conditional plea concept, *United States v. Clark,* 459 F.2d 977 (8th Cir. 1972); *United States v. Dorsey,* 449 F.2d 1104 (D.C.Cir. 1971). Three circuits have expressed the view that a conditional plea is logically inconsistent and thus improper, *United States v. Brown,* 499 F.2d 829 (7th Cir. 1974); *United States v. Sepe,* 472 F.2d 784, aff'd en banc, 486 F.2d 1044 (5th Cir. 1973); *United States v. Cox,* 464 F.2d 937 (6th Cir. 1972); three others have determined only that conditional pleas are not now authorized in the federal system, *United States v. Benson,* 579 F.2d 508 (9th Cir. 1978); *United States v. Nooner,* 565 F.2d 633 (10th Cir. 1977); *United States v. Matthews,* 472 F.2d 1173 (4th Cir. 1973); while one circuit has reserved judgment on the issue, *United States v. Warwar,* 478 F.2d 1183 (1st Cir. 1973). (At the state level, a few jurisdictions by statute allow appeal from denial of a motion to suppress notwithstanding a subsequent guilty plea, Cal. Penal Code § 1538.5(m); N.Y.Crim. Proc. Law § 710.20(1); Wis.Stat.Ann. § 971.31(10), but in the absence of such a provision the state courts are also in disagreement as to whether a conditional plea is permissible; see cases collected in Comment, 26 U.C.L.A.L.Rev. 360, 373 (1978).).

The conditional plea procedure provided for in subdivision (a)(2) will, as previously noted, serve to conserve prosecutorial and judicial resources and advance speedy trial objectives. It will also produce much needed uniformity in the federal system on this matter; see *United States v. Clark,* supra, noting the split of authority and urging resolution by statute or rule. Also, the availability of a conditional plea under specified circumstances will aid in clarifying the fact that traditional, unqualified pleas do constitute a waiver of nonjurisdictional defects. See *United States v. Nooner,* supra (defendant sought appellate review of denial of pretrial suppression motion, despite his prior unqualified guilty plea, claiming the Second Circuit conditional plea practice led him to believe a guilty plea did not bar appeal of pretrial issues).

The obvious advantages of the conditional plea procedure authorized by subdivision (a)(2) are not outweighed by any significant or compelling disadvantages. As noted in Comment, supra, at 375: "Four major arguments have been raised by courts disapproving of conditioned pleas. The objections are that the procedure encourages a flood of appellate litigation, militates against achieving finality in the criminal process, reduces effectiveness of appellate review due to the lack of a full trial record, and forces decision on constitutional questions that could otherwise be avoided by invoking the harmless error doctrine." But, as concluded therein, those "arguments do not withstand close analysis." Ibid.

As for the first of those arguments, experience in states which have permitted appeals of suppression motions notwithstanding a subsequent plea of guilty is most relevant, as conditional pleas are likely to be most common when the objective is to appeal that kind of pretrial ruling. That experience has shown that the number of appeals has not increased substantially. See Comment, 9 Hous.L.Rev. 305, 315–19 (1971). The minimal added burden at the appellate level is certainly a small price to pay for avoiding otherwise unnecessary trials.

As for the objection that conditional pleas conflict with the government's interest in achieving finality, it is likewise without force. While it is true that the conditional plea does not have the complete finality of the traditional plea of guilty or nolo contendere because "the essence of the agreement is that the legal guilt of the defendant exists only if the prosecution's case" survives on appeal, the plea.

continues to serve a partial state interest in finality, however, by establishing admission of the defendant's factual guilt. The defendant stands guilty and the proceedings come to an end if the reserved issue is ultimately decided in the government's favor.

Comment, 26 U.C.L.A.L.Rev. 360, 378 (1978).

The claim that the lack of a full trial record precludes effective appellate review may on occasion be relevant. Cf. *United States v. MacDonald,* supra (holding interlocutory appeal not available for denial of defendant's pretrial motion to dismiss on speedy trial grounds, and noting that "most speedy trial claims . . . are best considered only after the relevant facts have been developed at trial"). However, most of the objections which would likely be raised by pretrial motion and preserved for appellate review by a conditional plea are subject to appellate resolution without a trial record. Certainly this is true as to the very common motion to suppress evidence, as is indicated by the fact that appellate courts presently decide such issues upon interlocutory appeal by the government.

With respect to the objection that conditional pleas circumvent application of the harmless error doctrine, it must be acknowledged that " [a]bsent a full trial record, containing all the government's evidence against the defendant, invocation of the harmless error rule is arguably impossible." Comment, supra, at 380. But, the harmless error standard with respect to constitutional objections is sufficiently high, see *Chapman v. California,* 386 U.S. 18 (1967), that relatively few appellate decisions result in affirmance upon that basis. Thus it will only rarely be true that the conditional plea device will cause an appellate court to consider constitutional questions which could otherwise have been avoided by invocation of the doctrine of harmless error.

To the extent that these or related objections would otherwise have some substance, they are overcome by the provision in Rule 11(a)(2) that the defendant may enter a conditional plea only "with the approval of the court and the consent of the government." (In this respect, the rule adopts the practice now found in the Second Circuit.) The requirement of approval by the court is most appropriate, as it ensures, for example, that the defendant is not allowed to take an appeal on a matter which can only be fully developed by proceeding to trial; cf. *United States v. MacDonald,* supra. As for consent by the government, it will ensure that conditional pleas will be allowed only when the decision of the court of appeals will dispose of the case either by allowing the plea to stand or by such action as compelling dismissal of the indictment or suppressing essential evidence. Absent such circumstances, the conditional plea might only serve to postpone the trial and require the government to try the case after substantial delay, during which time witnesses may be lost, memories dimmed, and the offense grown so stale as to lose jury appeal. The government is in a unique position to determine whether the matter at issue would be case-dispositive, and, as a party to the litigation, should have an absolute right to refuse to consent to potentially prejudicial delay. Although it was suggested in *United States v. Moskow,* supra, that the government should have no right to prevent the entry of a conditional plea because a defendant has no comparable right to block government appeal of a pretrial ruling pursuant to 18 U.S.C. § 3731, that analogy is unconvincing. That statute requires the government to certify that the appeal is not taken for purposes of delay. Moreover, where the pretrial ruling is case-dispositive, § 3731 is the only mechanism by which the government can obtain appellate review, but a defendant may always obtain review by pleading not guilty.

Unlike the state statutes cited earlier, Rule 11 (a)(2) is not limited to instances in which the pretrial ruling the defendant wishes to appeal was in response to defendant's motion to suppress evidence. Though it may be true that the conditional plea device will be most commonly employed as to such rulings, the objectives of the rule are well served by extending it to other pretrial rulings as well. See, e.g., ABA Standards, supra (declaring the New York provision "should be enlarged to include other pretrial defenses"); Uniform Rules of Criminal Procedure, rule 444 (d) (Approved Draft, 1974) ("any pretrial motion which, if granted, would be dispositive of the case").

The requirement that the conditional plea be made by the defendant "reserving in writing the right to appeal from the adverse determination of any specified pretrial motion," though extending beyond the Second Circuit practice, will ensure careful attention to any conditional plea. It will document that a particular plea was in fact conditional, and will identify precisely what pretrial issues have been preserved for appellate review. By requiring this added step, it will be possible to avoid entry of a conditional plea without the considered acquiescence of the government (see *United States v. Burke,* supra, holding that failure of the government to object to entry of a conditional plea constituted consent) and post-plea claims by the defendant that his plea should be deemed conditional merely because it occurred after denial of his pretrial motions (see *United States v. Nooner,* supra).

It must be emphasized that the only avenue of review of the specified pretrial ruling permitted under a rule 11(a)(2) conditional plea is an appeal, which must be brought in compliance with Fed.R.App.P. 4(b). Relief via 28 U.S.C. § 2255 is not available for this purpose.

The Supreme Court has held that certain kinds of constitutional objections may be raised after a plea of guilty. *Menna v. New York,* 423 U.S. 61 (1975) (double jeopardy violation); *Blackledge v. Perry,* 417 U.S. 21 (1974) (due process violation by charge enhancement following defendant's exercise of right to trial de novo). Subdivision 11(a)(2) has no application to such situations, and should not be interpreted as either broadening or narrowing the *Menna-Blackledge* doctrine or as establishing procedures for its application.

Note to Subdivision (h). Subdivision (h) makes clear that the harmless error rule of Rule 52(a) is applicable to Rule 11. The provision does not, however, attempt to define the meaning of "harmless error," which is left to the case law. Prior to the amendments which took effect on Dec. 1, 1975, Rule 11 was very brief; it consisted of but four sentences. The 1975 amendments increased significantly the procedures which must be undertaken when a defendant tenders a plea of guilty or nolo contendere, but this change was warranted by the "two principal objectives" then identified in the Advisory Committee Note: (1) ensuring that the defendant has made an informed plea; and (2) ensuring that plea agreements are brought out into the open in court. An inevitable consequence of the 1975 amendments was some increase in the risk that a trial judge, in a particular case, might inadvertently deviate to some degree from the procedure which a very literal reading of Rule 11 would appear to require.

This being so, it became more apparent than ever that Rule 11 should not be given such a crabbed interpretation that ceremony was exalted over substance. As stated in *United States v. Scarf,* 551 F.2d 1124 (8th Cir. 1977), concerning amended Rule 11: "It is a salutary rule, and district courts are required to act in substantial compliance with it although . . . ritualistic compliance is not required." As similarly pointed out in *United States v. Saft,* 558 F.2d 1073 (2d Cir. 1977),

> the Rule does not say that compliance can be achieved only by reading the specified items in haec verba. Congress meant to strip district judges of freedom to decide what they must explain to a defendant who wishes to plead guilty, not to tell them precisely how to perform this important task in the great variety of cases that would come before them. While a judge who contents himself with literal application of the Rule will hardly be reversed, it cannot be supposed that Congress preferred this to a more meaningful explanation, provided that all the specified elements were covered.

Two important points logically flow from these sound observations. One concerns the matter of construing Rule 11: it is not to be read as requiring a litany or other ritual which can be carried out only by word-for-word adherence to a set "script." The other, specifically addressed in new subdivision (h), is that even when it may be concluded Rule 11 has not been complied with in all respects, it does not inevitably follow that the defendant's plea of guilty or nolo contendere is invalid and subject to being overturned by any remedial device then available to the defendant.

Notwithstanding the declaration in Rule 52(a) that "[a]ny error, defect, irregularity or variance which does not affect substantial rights shall be disregarded," there has existed for some years considerable disagreement concerning the applicability of the harmless error doctrine to Rule 11 violations. In large part, this is attributable to uncertainty as to the continued vitality and the reach of *McCarthy v. United States,* 394 U.S. 459 (1969). In *McCarthy,* involving a direct appeal from a plea of guilty because of noncompliance with Rule 11, the Court concluded.

> that prejudice inheres in a failure to comply with Rule 11, for noncompliance deprives the defendant of the Rule's procedural safeguards, which are designed to facilitate a more accurate determination of the voluntariness of his plea. Our holding [is] that a defendant whose plea has been accepted in violation of Rule 11 should be afforded the opportunity to plead anew . . . .

McCarthy has been most frequently relied upon in cases where, as in that case, the defendant sought relief because of a Rule 11 violation by the avenue of direct appeal. It has been held that in such circumstances a defendant's conviction must be reversed whenever the "district court accepts his guilty plea without fully adhering to the procedure provided for in Rule 11," *United States v. Boone,* 543 F.2d 1090 (4th Cir. 1976), and that in this context any reliance by the government on the Rule 52(a) harmless error concept "must be rejected." *United States v. Journet,* 544 F.2d 633 (2d Cir. 1976). On the other hand, decisions are to be found taking a harmless error approach on direct appeal where it appeared the nature and extent of the deviation from Rule 11 was such that it could not have had any impact on the defendant's decision to plead or the fairness in now holding him to his plea. *United States v. Peters,* No. 77-1700 (4th Cir., Dec. 22, 1978) (where judge failed to comply fully with Rule 11(c)(1), in that defendant not correctly advised of maximum years of special parole term but was told it is at least 3 years, and defendant thereafter sentenced to 15 years plus 3-year special parole term, government's motion for summary affirmance granted, as "the error was harmless"); *United States v. Coronado,* 554 F.2d 166 (5th Cir. 1977) (court first holds that charge of conspiracy requires some explanation of what conspiracy means to comply with Rule 11(c)(1), but then finds no reversible error "because the rule 11 proceeding on its face discloses, despite the trial court's failure sufficiently to make the required explication of the charges, that Coronado understood them").

But this conflict has not been limited to cases involving nothing more than a direct appeal following defendant's plea. For example, another type of case is that in which the defendant has based a post-sentence motion to withdraw his plea on a Rule 11 violation. Rule 32(d) says that such a motion may be granted "to correct manifest injustice," and some courts have relied upon this latter provision in holding that post-sentence plea withdrawal need not be permitted merely because Rule 11 was not fully complied with and that instead the district court should hold an evidentiary hearing to determine "whether manifest injustice will result if the conviction based on the guilty plea is permitted to stand." *United States v. Scarf,* 551 F.2d 1124 (8th Cir. 1977). Others, however, have held that *McCarthy* applies and prevails over the language of Rule 32(d), so that "a failure to scrupulously comply with Rule 11 will invalidate a plea without a showing of manifest injustice." *United States v. Cantor,* 469 F.2d 435 (3d Cir. 1972).

Disagreement has also existed in the context of collateral attack upon pleas pursuant to 28 U.S.C. § 2255. On the one hand, it has been concluded that "[n]ot every violation of Rule 11 requires that the plea be set aside" in a § 2255 proceeding, and that "a guilty plea will be set aside on collateral attack only where to not do so would result in a miscarriage of justice, or where there exists exceptional circumstances justifying such relief." *Evers v. United States,* 579 F.2d 71 (10th Cir. 1978). The contrary view was that *McCarthy* governed in § 2255 proceedings because "the Supreme Court hinted at no exceptions to its policy of strict enforcement of Rule 11." *Timmreck v. United States,* 577 F.2d 377 (6th Cir. 1978). But a unanimous Supreme Court resolved this conflict in *United States v. Timmreck,* 441 U.S. 780 (1979), where the Court concluded that the reasoning of *Hill v. United States,* 368 U.S. 424 (1962) (ruling a collateral attack could not be predicated on a violation of Rule 32(a)).

is equally applicable to a formal violation of Rule 11. . . .

Indeed, if anything, this case may be a stronger one for foreclosing collateral relief than the *Hill* case. For the concern with finality served by the limitation on collateral attack has special force with respect to convictions based on guilty pleas.

"Every inroad on the concept of finality undermines confidence in the integrity of our procedures; and, by increasing the volume of judicial work, inevitably delays and impairs the orderly administration of justice. The impact is greatest when new grounds for setting aside guilty pleas are approved because the vast majority of criminal convictions result from such pleas. Moreover, the concern that unfair procedures may have resulted in the conviction of an innocent defendant is only rarely raised by a petition to set aside a guilty plea."

This interest in finality is strongest in the collateral attack context the Court was dealing with in *Timmreck,* which explains why the Court there adopted the *Hill* requirement that in a § 2255 proceeding the rule violation must amount to "a fundamental defect which inherently results in a complete miscarriage of justice" or "an omission inconsistent with the rudimentary demands of fair procedure." The interest in finality of guilty pleas described in *Timmreck* is of somewhat lesser weight when a direct appeal is involved (so that the *Hill* standard is obviously inappropriate in that setting), but yet is sufficiently compelling to make unsound the proposition that reversal is required even where it is apparent that the Rule 11 violation was of the harmless error variety.

Though the *McCarthy* per se rule may have been justified at the time and in the circumstances which obtained when the plea in that case was taken, this is no longer the case. For one thing, it is important to recall that *McCarthy* dealt only with the much simpler pre-1975 version of Rule 11, which required only a brief procedure during which the chances of a minor, insignificant and inadvertent deviation were relatively slight. This means that the chances of a truly harmless error (which was not involved in *McCarthy* in any event, as the judge made no inquiry into the defendant's understanding of the nature of the charge, and the government had presented only the extreme argument that a court "could properly assume that petitioner was entering that plea with a complete understanding of the charge against him" merely from the fact he had stated he desired to plead guilty) are much greater under present Rule 11 than under the version before the Court in *McCarthy*. It also means that the more elaborate and lengthy procedures of present Rule 11, again as compared with the version applied in *McCarthy,* make it more apparent than ever that a guilty plea is not "a mere gesture, a temporary and meaningless formality reversible at the defendant's whim," but rather " 'a grave and solemn act,' which is 'accepted only with care and discernment.' " *United States v. Barker,* 514 F.2d 208 (D.C.Cir.1975), quoting from *Brady v. United States,* 397 U.S. 742 (1970). A plea of that character should not be overturned, even on direct appeal, when there has been a minor and technical violation of Rule 11 which amounts to harmless error.

Secondly, while *McCarthy* involved a situation in which the defendant's plea of guilty was before the court of appeals on direct appeal, the Supreme Court appears to have been primarily concerned with § 2255-type cases, for the Court referred exclusively to cases of that kind in the course of concluding that a per se rule was justified as to Rule 11 violations because of "the difficulty of achieving [rule 11's] purposes through a post-conviction voluntariness hearing." But that reasoning has now been substantially undercut by *United States v. Timmreck,* supra, for the Court there concluded § 2255 relief "is not available when all that is shown is a failure to comply with the formal requirements of the Rule," at least absent "other aggravating circumstances," which presumably could often only be developed in the course of a later evidentiary hearing.

Although all of the aforementioned considerations support the policy expressed in new subdivision (h), the Advisory Committee does wish to emphasize two important cautionary notes. The first is that subdivision (h) should not be read as supporting extreme or speculative harmless error claims or as, in effect, nullifying important Rule 11 safeguards. There would not be harmless error under subdivision (h) where, for example, as in McCarthy, there had been absolutely no inquiry by the judge into defendant's understanding of the nature of the charge and the harmless error claim of the government rests upon nothing more than the assertion that it may be "assumed" defendant possessed such understanding merely because he expressed a desire to plead guilty. Likewise, it would not be harmless error if the trial judge totally abdicated to the prosecutor the responsibility for giving to the defendant the various Rule 11 warnings, as this "results in the creation of an atmosphere of subtle coercion that clearly contravenes the policy behind Rule 11." *United States v. Crook,* 526 F.2d 708 (5th Cir. 1976).

Indeed, it is fair to say that the kinds of Rule 11 violations which might be found to constitute harmless error upon direct appeal are fairly limited, as in such instances the matter "must be resolved solely on the basis of the Rule 11 transcript" and the other portions (e.g., sentencing hearing) of the limited record made in such cases. *United States v. Coronado,* supra. Illustrative are: where the judge's compliance with subdivision (c)(1) was not absolutely complete, in that some essential element of the crime was not mentioned, but the defendant's responses clearly indicate his awareness of that element, see *United States v. Coronado,* supra; where the judge's compliance with subdivision (c)(2) was erroneous in part in that the judge understated the maximum penalty somewhat, but the penalty actually imposed did not exceed that indicated in the warnings, see *United States v. Peters,* supra; and where the judge completely failed to comply with subdivision (c)(5), which of course has no bearing on the validity of the plea itself, cf. *United States v. Sinagub,* supra.

The second cautionary note is that subdivision (h) should not be read as an invitation to trial judges to take a more casual approach to Rule 11 proceedings. It is still true, as the Supreme Court pointed out in *McCarthy,* that thoughtful and careful compliance with Rule 11 best serves the cause of fair and efficient administration of criminal justice, as it.

will help reduce the great waste of judicial resources required to process the frivolous attacks on guilty plea convictions that are encouraged, and are more difficult to dispose of, when the original record is inadequate. It is, therefore, not too much to require that, before sentencing defendants to years of imprisonment, district judges take the few minutes necessary to inform them of their rights and to determine whether they understand the action they are taking.

Subdivision (h) makes no change in the responsibilities of the judge at Rule 11 proceedings, but instead merely rejects the extreme sanction of automatic reversal.

It must also be emphasized that a harmless error provision has been added to Rule 11 because some courts have read *McCarthy* as meaning that the general harmless error provision in Rule 52(a) cannot be utilized with respect to Rule 11 proceedings. Thus, the addition of subdivision (h) should not be read as suggesting that Rule 52(a) does not apply in other circumstances because of the absence of a provision comparable to subdivision (h) attached to other rules.

Notes of Advisory Committee on 1985 amendments. *Note to Subdivision (c)(1).* Section 5 of the Victim and Witness Protection Act of 1982, Pub. L. No. 97-291, 96 Stat. 1248 (1982), adds 18 U.S.C. § 3579, providing that when sentencing a defendant convicted of a Title 18 offense or of violating various subsections of the Federal Aviation Act of 1958, the court "may order, in addition to or in lieu of any other penalty authorized by law, that the defendant make restitution to any victim of the offense." Under this law restitution is favored; if the court "does not order restitution, or orders only partial restitution, . . . the court shall state on the record the reasons therefor." Because this restitution is deemed an aspect of the defendant's sentence, S. Rept. No. 97-532, 97th Cong., 2d Sess., 30-33 (1982), it is a matter about which a defendant tendering a plea of guilty or nolo contendere should be advised.

Because this new legislation contemplates that the amount of the restitution to be ordered will be ascertained later in the sentencing process, this amendment to Rule 11(c)(1) merely requires that the defendant be told of the court's power to order restitution. The exact amount or upper limit cannot and need not be stated at the time of the plea. Failure of a court to advise a defendant of the possibility of a restitution order would constitute harmless error under subdivision (h) if no restitution were thereafter ordered.

Notes of Advisory Committee on 1987 amendments. The amendments are technical. No substantive change is intended.

Notes of Advisory Committee on 1989 amendments. The Committee believes that a technical change, adding the words "or supervised release," is necessary to recognize that defendants sentenced under the guideline approach will be concerned about supervised release rather than special parole. See 18 U.S.C. 3583, and 3624(e). The words "special parole" are left in the rule, since the district courts continue to handle pre-guideline cases.

The amendment mandates that the district court inform a defendant that the court is required to consider any applicable guidelines but may depart from them under some circumstances. This requirement assures that the existence of guidelines will be known to a defendant before a plea of guilty or nolo contendere is accepted. Since it will be impracticable, if not impossible, to know which guidelines will be relevant prior to the formulation of a presentence report and resolution of disputed facts, the amendment does not require the court to specify which guidelines will be important or which grounds for departure might prove to be significant. The advice that the court is required to give cannot guarantee that a defendant who pleads guilty will not later claim a lack of understanding as to the importance of guidelines at the time of the plea. No advice is likely to serve as a complete protection against post-plea claims of ignorance or confusion. By giving the advice, the court places the defendant and defense counsel on notice of the importance that guidelines may play in sentencing and of the possibility of a departure from those guidelines. A defendant represented by competent counsel will be in a position to enter an intelligent plea.

The amended rule does not limit the district court's discretion to engage in a more extended colloquy with the defendant in order to impart additional information about sentencing guidelines or to inquire into the defendant's knowledge concerning guidelines. The amended rule sets forth only the minimum advice that must be provided to the defendant by the court.

Notes of Advisory Committee on 1999 amendments. *Note to Subdivision (a).* The amendment deletes use of the term "corporation" and substitutes in its place the term "organization," with a reference to the definition of that term in 18 U.S.C. § 18.

Note to Subdivision (c)(6). Rule 11(c) has been amended specifically to reflect the increasing practice of including provisions in plea agreements which require the defendant to waive certain appellate rights. The increased use of such provisions is due in part to the increasing number of direct appeals and collateral reviews challenging sentencing decisions. Given the increased use of such provisions, the Committee believed it was important to insure that first, a complete record exists regarding any waiver provisions, and second, that the waiver was voluntarily and knowingly made by the defendant. Although a number of federal courts have approved the ability of a defendant to enter into such waiver agreements, the Committee takes no position on the underlying validity of such waivers.

Note to Subdivision (e). Amendments have been made to Rule 11(e)(1)(B) and (C) to reflect the impact of the Sentencing Guidelines on guilty pleas. Although Rule 11 is generally silent on the subject, it has become clear that the courts have struggled with the subject of guideline sentencing vis a vis plea agreements, entry and timing of guilty pleas, and the ability of the defendant to withdraw a plea of guilty. The amendments are intended to address two specific issues.

First, both subdivisions (e)(1)(B) and (e)(1)(C) have been amended to recognize that a plea agreement may specifically address not only what amounts to an appropriate sentence, but also a sentencing guideline, a sentencing factor, or a policy statement accompanying a sentencing guideline or factor. Under an (e)(1)(B) agreement, the government, as before, simply agrees to make a recommendation to the court, or agrees not to oppose a defense request concerning a particular sentence or consideration of a sentencing guideline, factor, or policy statement. The amendment makes it clear that this type of agreement is not binding on the court. Second, under an (e)(1)(C) agreement, the government and defense have actually agreed on what amounts to an appropriate sentence or have agreed to one of the specified components. The amendment also makes it clear that this agreement is binding on the court once the court accepts it. As is the situation under the current Rule, the court retains absolute discretion whether to accept a plea agreement.

Notes of Advisory Committee on 2002 amendments. The language of Rule 11 has been amended and reorganized as part of the general restyling of the Criminal Rules to make them more easily understood and to make style and terminology consistent throughout the rules. These changes are intended to be stylistic only, except as noted below.

Amended Rule 11(b)(1) requires the court to apprise the defendant of his or her rights before accepting a plea of guilty or nolo contendere. The Committee determined to expand upon the incomplete listing in the current rule of the elements of the "maximum possible penalty" and any "mandatory minimum" penalty to include advice as to the maximum or minimum term of imprisonment, forfeiture, fine, and special assessment, in addition to the two types of maximum and minimum penalties presently enumerated: restitution and supervised release. The outmoded reference to a term of "special parole" has been eliminated.

Amended Rule 11(b)(2), formerly Rule 11(d), covers the issue of determining that the plea is voluntary, and not the result of force, threats, or promises (other than those in a plea agreement). The reference to an inquiry in current Rule 11(d) whether the plea has resulted from plea discussions with the government has been deleted. That reference, which was often a source of confusion to defendants who were clearly pleading guilty as part of a plea agreement with the government, was considered unnecessary.

Rule 11(c)(1)(A) includes a change, which recognizes a common type of plea agreement — that the government will "not bring" other charges.

The Committee considered whether to address the practice in some courts of using judges to facilitate plea agreements. The current rule states that "the court shall not participate in any discussions between the parties concerning such plea agreement." Some courts apparently believe that that language acts as a limitation only upon the judge taking the defendant's plea and thus permits other judges to serve as facilitators for reaching a plea agreement between the government and the defendant. See, e.g., *United States v. Torres*, 999 F.2d 376, 378 (9th Cir. 1993) (noting practice and concluding that presiding judge had not participated in a plea agreement that had resulted from discussions involving another judge). The Committee decided to leave the Rule as it is with the understanding that doing so was in no way intended either to approve or disapprove the existing law interpreting that provision.

Amended Rules 11(c)(3) to (5) address the topics of consideration, acceptance, and rejection of a plea agreement. The amendments are not intended to make any change in practice. The topics are discussed separately because in the past there has been some question about the possible interplay between the court's consideration of the guilty plea in conjunction with a plea agreement and sentencing and the ability of the defendant to withdraw a plea. See *United States v. Hyde*, 520 U.S. 670 [137 L. Ed. 2d 935] (1997) (holding that plea and plea agreement need not be accepted or rejected as a single unit; "guilty pleas can be accepted while plea agreements are deferred, and the acceptance of the two can be separated in time."). Similarly, the Committee decided to more clearly spell out in Rule 11(d) and 11(e) the ability of the defendant to withdraw a plea. See *United States v. Hyde*, supra.

Amended Rule 11(e) is a new provision, taken from current Rule 32(e), that addresses the finality of a guilty or nolo contendere plea after the court imposes sentence. The provision makes it clear that it is not possible for a defendant to withdraw a plea after sentence is imposed.

The reference to a "motion under 28 U.S.C. § 2255" has been changed to the broader term "collateral attack" to recognize that in some instances a court may grant collateral relief under provisions other than § 2255. See *United States v. Jeffers*, 234 F.3d 277 (5th Cir. 2000) (petition under § 2241 may be appropriate where remedy under § 2255 is ineffective or inadequate).

Currently, Rule 11(e)(5) requires that unless good cause is shown, the parties are to give pretrial notice to the court that a plea agreement exists. That provision has been deleted. First, the Committee believed that although the provision was originally drafted to assist judges, under current practice few counsel would risk the consequences in the ordinary case of not informing the court that an agreement exists. Secondly, the Committee was concerned that there might be rare cases where the parties might agree that informing the court of the existence of an agreement might endanger a defendant or compromise an ongoing investigation in a related case. In the end, the Committee believed that, on balance, it would be preferable to remove the provision and reduce the risk of pretrial disclosure.

Finally, revised Rule 11(f), which addresses the issue of admissibility or inadmissibility of pleas and statements made during the plea inquiry, cross references Federal Rule of Evidence 410.

Notes of Advisory Committee on 2007 amendments. *Note to subdivision (b)(1)(M).* The amendment conforms Rule 11 to the Supreme Court's decision in *United States v. Booker*, 543 U.S. 220 (2005). *Booker* held that the provision of the federal sentencing statute that makes the Guidelines mandatory, 18 U.S.C. § 3553(b)(1) (Supp.2004), violates the Sixth Amendment right to jury trial. With this provision severed and excised, the Court held, the Sentencing Reform Act "makes the Guidelines effectively advisory," and "requires a sentencing court to consider Guidelines ranges, see 18 U.S.C.A. § 3553(a)(4) (Supp.2004), but it permits the court to tailor the sentence in light of other statutory concerns as well, see § 3553(a) (Supp.2004)." *Id.* at 245–46. Rule 11(b)(M) incorporates this analysis into the information provided to the defendant at the time of a plea of guilty or nolo contendere.

Notes of Advisory Committee on 2013 amendments. *Subdivision (b)(1)(O).* The amendment requires the court to include a general statement that there may be immigration consequences of conviction in the advice provided to the defendant before the court accepts a plea of guilty or nolo contendere.

For a defendant who is not a citizen of the United States, a criminal conviction may lead to removal, exclusion, and the inability to become a citizen. In *Padilla v. Kentucky*, 130 S.Ct. 1473 (2010), the Supreme Court held that a defense attorney's failure to advise the defendant concerning the risk of deportation fell below the objective standard of reasonable professional assistance guaranteed by the Sixth Amendment.

The amendment mandates a generic warning, not specific advice concerning the defendant's individual situation. Judges in many districts already include a warning about immigration consequences in the plea colloquy, and the amendment adopts this practice as good policy. The Committee concluded that the most effective and efficient method of conveying this information is to provide it to every defendant, without attempting to determine the defendant's citizenship.

Amendments:

1975.

Act July 31, 1975, § 3(5)–(9) (effective 12/1/75, as provided by § 2 of such Act, which appears as a note to Rule 4), substituted subsecs. (c) and (e)(1)–(4) for ones which read:

"(c) Advice to defendant. The court shall not accept a plea of guilty or nolo contendere without first, by addressing the defendant personally in open court, informing him of and determining that he understands the following:

"(1) the nature of the charge to which the plea is offered; and.

"(2) the mandatory minimum penalty provided by law, if any, and the maximum possible penalty provided by law for the offense to which the plea is offered; and.

"(3) that the defendant has the right to plead not guilty, or to persist in that plea if it has already been made; and.

"(4) that if he pleads guilty or nolo contendere there will not be a further trial of any kind, so that by pleading guilty or nolo contendere he waives the right to a trial.

"(e) Plea agreement procedure.

(1) In general. The attorney for the government and the attorney for the defendant or the defendant when acting pro se may engage in discussions with a view toward reaching an agreement that, upon the entering of a plea of guilty or nolo contendere to a charged offense or to a lesser or related offense, the attorney for the government will move for dismissal of other charges, or will recommend or not oppose the imposition of a particular sentence, or will do both. The court shall not participate in any such discussions.

"(2) Notice of such agreement. If a plea agreement has been reached by the parties which contemplates entry of a plea of guilty or nolo contendere in the expectation that a specific sentence will be imposed or that other charges before the court will be dismissed, the court shall require the disclosure of the agreement in open court at the time the plea is offered. Thereupon the court may accept or reject the agreement, or may defer its decision as to acceptance or rejection until there has been an opportunity to consider the presentence report.

"(3) Acceptance of plea. If the court accepts the plea agreement, the court shall inform the defendant that it will embody in the judgment and sentence the disposition provided for in the plea agreement or another disposition more favorable to the defendant than that provided for in the plea agreement.

"(4) Rejection of plea. If the court rejects the plea agreement, the court shall inform the parties of this fact, advise the defendant personally in open court that the court is not bound by the plea agreement, afford the defendant the opportunity to then withdraw his plea, and advise the defendant that if he persists in his guilty plea or plea of nolo contendere the disposition of the case may be less favorable to the defendant than that contemplated by the plea agreement.".

Such Act further (effective 8/1/75, as provided by § 2 of such Act, which appears as a note to Rule 4), substituted subsec. (e)(6) for one which read: "(6) Inadmissibility of plea discussions. Evidence of a plea of guilty, later withdrawn, or a plea of nolo contendere, or of an offer to plead guilty or nolo contendere to the crime charged or any other crime, or of statements made in connection with any of the foregoing pleas or offers, is not admissible in any civil or criminal proceeding against the person who made the plea or offer.".

1988.

Act Nov. 18, 1988, in subsec. (c)(1), inserted "or term of supervised release".

Rule 12. Pleadings and Pretrial Motions

(a) Pleadings. The pleadings in a criminal proceeding are the indictment, the information, and the pleas of not guilty, guilty, and nolo contendere.

(b) Pretrial Motions.

(1) *In General.* A party may raise by pretrial motion any defense, objection, or request that the court can determine without a trial on the merits. Rule 47 applies to a pretrial motion.

(2) *Motions that May be Made at Any Time.* A motion that the court lacks jurisdiction may be made at any time while the case is pending.

(3) *Motions that Must be Made Before Trial.* The following defenses, objections, and requests must be raised by pretrial motion if the basis for the motion is then reasonably available and the motion can be determined without a trial on the merits:

(A) a defect in instituting the prosecution, including:

(i) improper venue;

(ii) preindictment delay;

(iii) a violation of the constitutional right to a speedy trial;

(iv) selective or vindictive prosecution; and

(v) an error in the grand-jury proceeding or preliminary hearing;

(B) a defect in the indictment or information, including:

(i) joining two or more offenses in the same count (duplicity);

(ii) charging the same offense in more than one count (multiplicity);

(iii) lack of specificity;

(iv) improper joinder; and

(v) failure to state an offense;
(C) suppression of evidence;
(D) severance of charges or defendants under Rule 14; and
(E) discovery under Rule 16.

(4) *Notice of the government's intent to use evidence.*

(A) At the government's discretion. At the arraignment or as soon afterward as practicable, the government may notify the defendant of its intent to use specified evidence at trial in order to afford the defendant an opportunity to object before trial under Rule 12(b)(3)(C).

(B) At the defendant's request. At the arraignment or as soon afterward as practicable, the defendant may, in order to have an opportunity to move to suppress evidence under Rule 12(b)(3)(C), request notice of the government's intent to use (in its evidence-in-chief at trial) any evidence that the defendant may be entitled to discover under Rule 16.

(c) Deadline for a pretrial motion; consequences of not making a timely motion.

(1) *Setting the deadline.* The court may, at the arraignment or as soon afterward as practicable, set a deadline for the parties to make pretrial motions and may also schedule a motion hearing. If the court does not set one, the deadline is the start of trial.

(2) *Extending or resetting the deadline.* At any time before trial, the court may extend or reset the deadline for pretrial motions.

(3) *Consequences of not making a timely motion under Rule 12(b)(3).* If a party does not meet the deadline for making a Rule 12(b)(3) motion, the motion is untimely. But a court may consider the defense, objection, or request if the party shows good cause.

(d) Ruling on a motion. The court must decide every pretrial motion before trial unless it finds good cause to defer a ruling. The court must not defer ruling on a pretrial motion if the deferral will adversely affect a party's right to appeal. When factual issues are involved in deciding a motion, the court must state its essential findings on the record.

(e) [Reserved]

(f) Recording the Proceedings. All proceedings at a motion hearing, including any findings of fact and conclusions of law made orally by the court, must be recorded by a court reporter or a suitable recording device.

(g) Defendant's Continued Custody or Release Status. If the court grants a motion to dismiss based on a defect in instituting the prosecution, in the indictment, or in the information, it may order the defendant to be released or detained under 18 U.S.C. § 3142 for a specified time until a new indictment or information is filed. This rule does not affect any federal statutory period of limitations.

(h) Producing Statements at a Suppression Hearing. Rule 26.2 applies at a suppression hearing under Rule 12(b)(3)(C). At a suppression hearing, a law enforcement officer is considered a government witness.

HISTORY:

Amended April 22, 1974, eff. Dec. 1, 1975; July 31, 1975, P. L. 94-64, § 3(11), (12), 89 Stat. 372; April 28, 1983, eff. Aug. 1, 1983; March 9, 1987, eff. Aug. 1, 1987; April 22, 1993, eff. Dec. 1, 1993; April 29, 2002, eff. Dec. 1, 2002; April 25, 2014, eff. Dec. 1, 2014.

HISTORY; ANCILLARY LAWS AND DIRECTIVES

Other provisions:

Notes of Advisory Committee. *Note to Subdivision (a).* 1. This rule abolishes pleas to the jurisdiction, pleas in abatement, demurrers, special pleas in bar, and motions to quash. A motion to dismiss or for other appropriate relief is substituted for the purpose of raising all defenses and objections heretofore interposed in any of the foregoing modes. "This should result in a reduction of opportunities for dilatory tactics and, at the same time, relieve the defense of embarrassment. Many competent practitioners have been baffled and mystified by the distinctions between pleas in abatement, pleas in bar, demurrers, and motions to quash, and have, at times, found difficulty in determining which of these should be invoked." Homer Cummings, 29 A.B.A. Jour. 655. See also, Medalie, 4 Lawyers Guild R. (3) 1, 4.

2. A similar change was introduced by the Federal Rules of Civil Procedure (Rule 7(a)) which has proven successful. It is also proposed by the A.L.I. Code of Criminal Procedure (Sec 209).

Note to Subdivision (b)(1) and (2). These two paragraphs classify into two groups all objections and defenses to be interposed by motion prescribed by Rule 12(a). In one group are defenses and objections which must be raised by motion, failure to do so constituting a waiver. In the other group are defenses and objections which at the defendant's option may be raised by motion, failure to do so, however, not constituting a waiver. (Cf. Rule 12 of Federal Rules of Civil Procedure, 28 U.S.C., Appendix.).

In the first of these groups are included all defenses and objections that are based on defects in the institution of the prosecution or in the indictment and information, other than lack of jurisdiction or failure to charge an offense. All such defenses and objections must be included in a single motion. (Cf. Rule 12(g) of Federal Rules of Civil Procedure, 28 U.S.C., Appendix.) Among the defenses and objections in this group are the following: Illegal selection or organization of the grand jury, disqualification of individual grand jurors, presence of unauthorized persons in the grand jury room, other irregularities in grand jury proceedings, defects in indictment or information other than lack of jurisdiction or failure to state an offense, etc. The provision that these defenses and objections are waived if not raised by motion substantially continues existing law, as they are waived at present unless raised before trial by plea in abatement, demurrer, motion to quash, etc.

In the other group of objections and defenses, which the defendant at his option may raise by motion before trial, are included all defenses and objections which are capable of determination without a trial of the general issue. They include such matters as former jeopardy, former conviction, former acquittal, statute of limitations, immunity, lack of jurisdiction, failure of indictment or information to state an offense, etc. Such matters have been heretofore raised by demurrers, special pleas in bar and motions to quash.

Note to Subdivision (b)(3). This rule, while requiring the motion to be made before pleading, vests discretionary authority in the court to permit the motion to be made within a reasonable time thereafter. The rule supersedes

18 U.S.C. [former] § 556a [see §§ 3288, 3289], fixing a definite limitation of time for pleas in abatement and motions to quash. The rule also eliminates the requirement for technical withdrawal of a plea if it is desired to interpose a preliminary objection or defense after the plea has been entered. Under this rule a plea will be permitted to stand in the meantime.

Note to Subdivision (b)(4). This rule substantially restates existing law. It leaves with the court discretion to determine in advance of trial defenses and objections raised by motion or to defer them for determination at the trial. It preserves the right to jury trial in those cases in which the right is given under the Constitution or by statute. In all other cases it vests in the court authority to determine issues of fact in such manner as the court deems appropriate.

Note to Subdivision (b)(5). 1. The first sentence substantially restates existing law, 18 U.S.C. [former] § 561 (Indictments and presentments; judgment on demurrer), which provides that in case a demurrer to an indictment or information is overruled, the judgment shall be respondeat ouster.

2. The last sentence of the rule that "Nothing in this rule shall be deemed to affect the provisions of any act of Congress relating to periods of limitations" is intended to preserve the provisions of statutes which permit a reindictment if the original indictment is found defective or is dismissed for other irregularities and the statute of limitations has run in the meantime, 18 U.S.C. [former] § 587 [see § 3288] (Defective indictment; defect found after period of limitations; reindictment); *Id.* [former] sec. 588 [see § 3289] (Defective indictment; defect found before period of limitations; reindictment); *Id.* 18 U.S.C. [former] § 589 [see §§ 3288, 3289] (Defective indictment; defense of limitations to new indictment); *Id.* 18 U.S.C. [former] § 556a [see §§ 3288, 3289] (Indictments and presentments; objections to drawing or qualification of grand jury; time for filing; suspension of statute of limitations).

Criminal Procedure Rule 12

Notes of Advisory Committee on 1974 amendments. Subdivision (a) remains as it was in the old rule. It "speaks only of defenses and objections that prior to the rules could have been raised by a plea, demurrer, or motion to quash" (C. Wright, Federal Practice and Procedure: Criminal § 191 at p. 397 (1969)), and this might be interpreted as limiting the scope of the rule. However, some courts have assumed that old rule 12 does apply to pretrial motions generally, and the amendments to subsequent subdivisions of the rule should make clear that the rule is applicable to pretrial motion practice generally. (See e.g., rule 12(b)(3), (4), (5) and rule 41(e).).

Subdivision (b) is changed to provide for some additional motions and requests which must be made prior to trial. Subdivisions (b)(1) and (2) are restatements of the old rule.

Subdivision (b)(3) makes clear that objections to evidence on the ground that it was illegally obtained must be raised prior to trial. This is the current rule with regard to evidence obtained as a result of an illegal search. See rule 41(e); C. Wright, Federal Practice and Procedure: Criminal § 673 (1969, Supp. 1971). It is also the practice with regard to other forms of illegality such as the use of unconstitutional means to obtain a confession. See C. Wright, Federal Practice and Procedure: Criminal § 673 at p. 108 (1969). It seems apparent that the same principle should apply whatever the claimed basis for the application of the exclusionary rule of evidence may be. This is consistent with the court's statement in *Jones v. United States,* 362 U.S. 257, 264, 80 S.Ct. 725, 4 L.Ed.2d 697 (1960):

This provision of Rule 41(e), requiring the motion to suppress to be made before trial, is a crystallization of decisions of this Court requiring that procedure, and is designed to eliminate from the trial disputes over police conduct not immediately relevant to the question of guilt. (Emphasis added.).

Subdivision (b)(4) provides for a pretrial request for discovery by either the defendant or the government to the extent to which such discovery is authorized by rule 16.

Subdivision (b)(5) provides for a pretrial request for a severance as authorized in rule 14.

Subdivision (c) provides that a time for the making of motions shall be fixed at the time of the arraignment or as soon thereafter as practicable by court rule or direction of a judge. The rule leaves to the individual judge whether the motions may be oral or written. This and other amendments to rule 12 are designed to make possible and to encourage the making of motions prior to trial, whenever possible, and in a single hearing rather than in a series of hearings. This is the recommendation of the American Bar Association's Committee on Standards Relating to Discovery and Procedure Before Trial (Approved Draft, 1970); see especially §§ 5.2 and 5.3. It also is the procedure followed in those jurisdictions which have used the so-called "omnibus hearing" originated by Judge James Carter in the Southern District of California. See 4 Defender Newsletter 44 (1967); Miller, The Omnibus Hearing—An Experiment in Federal Criminal Discovery, 5 San Diego L.Rev. 293 (1968); American Bar Association, Standards Relating to Discovery and Procedure Before Trial, Appendices B, C, and D (Approved Draft, 1970). The omnibus hearing is also being used, on an experimental basis, in several other district courts. Although the Advisory Committee is of the view that it would be premature to write the omnibus hearing procedure into the rules, it is of the view that the single pretrial hearing should be made possible and its use encouraged by the rules.

There is a similar trend in state practice. See, e.g., *State ex rel. Goodchild v. Burke,* 27 Wis.2d 244, 133 N.W.2d 753 (1965); *State ex rel. Rasmussen v. Tahash,* 272 Minn. 539, 141 N.W.2d 3 (1965).

The rule provides that the motion date be set at "the arraignment or as soon thereafter as practicable." This is the practice in some federal courts including those using the omnibus hearing. (In order to obtain the advantage of the omnibus hearing, counsel routinely plead not guilty at the initial arraignment on the information or indictment and then may indicate a desire to change the plea to guilty following the omnibus hearing. This practice builds a more adequate record in guilty plea cases.) The rule further provides that the date may be set before the arraignment if local rules of court so provide.

Subdivision (d) provides a mechanism for insuring that a defendant knows of the government's intention to use evidence to which the defendant may want to object. On some occasions the resolution of the admissibility issue prior to trial may be advantageous to the government. In these situations the attorney for the government can make effective defendant's obligation to make his motion to suppress prior to trial by giving defendant notice of the government's intention to use certain evidence. For example, in *United States v. Desist,* 384 F.2d 889, 897 (2d Cir. 1967), the court said:

Early in the pre-trial proceedings, the Government commendably informed both the court and defense counsel that an electronic listening device had been used in investigating the case, and suggested a hearing be held as to its legality.

See also the "Omnibus Crime Control and Safe Streets Act of 1968," 18 U.S.C. § 2518(9):

The contents of any intercepted wire or oral communication or evidence derived therefrom shall not be received in evidence or otherwise disclosed in any trial, hearing, or other proceeding in a Federal or State court unless each party, not less than ten days before the trial, hearing, or proceeding, has been furnished with a copy of the court order, and accompanying application, under which the interception was authorized or approved.

In cases in which defendant wishes to know what types of evidence the government intends to use so that he can make his motion to suppress prior to trial, he can request the government to give notice of its intention to use specified evidence which the defendant is entitled to discover under rule 16. Although the defendant is already entitled to discovery of such evidence prior to trial under rule 16, rule 12 makes it possible for him to avoid the necessity of moving to suppress evidence which the government does not intend to use. No sanction is provided for the government's failure to comply with the court's order because the committee believes that attorneys for the government will in fact comply and that judges have ways of insuring compliance. An automatic exclusion of such evidence, particularly where the failure to give notice was not deliberate, seems to create too heavy a burden upon the exclusionary rule of evidence, especially when defendant has opportunity for broad discovery under rule 16. Compare ABA Project on Standards for Criminal Justice, Standards Relating to Electronic Surveillance (Approved Draft, 1971) at p. 116:

A failure to comply with the duty of giving notice could lead to the suppression of evidence. Nevertheless, the standards make it explicit that the rule is intended to be a matter of procedure which need not under appropriate circumstances automatically dictate that evidence otherwise admissible be suppressed.

Pretrial notice by the prosecution of its intention to use evidence which may be subject to a motion to suppress is increasingly being encouraged in state practice. See, e.g., *State ex rel. Goodchild v. Burke,* 27 Wis.2d 244, 264, 133 N.W.2d 753, 763 (1965):

In the interest of better administration of criminal justice we suggest that wherever practicable the prosecutor should within a reasonable time before trial notify the defense as to whether any alleged confession or admission will be offered in evidence at the trial. We also suggest, in cases where such notice is given by the prosecution, that the defense, if it intends to attack the confession or admission as involuntary, notify the prosecutor of a desire by the defense for a special determination on such issue.

See also *State ex rel. Rasmussen v. Tahash,* 272 Minn. 539, 553–556, 141 N.W.2d 3, 13–15 (1965):

At the time of arraignment when a defendant pleads not guilty, or as soon as possible thereafter, the state will advise the court as to whether its case against the defendant will include evidence obtained as the result of a search and seizure; evidence discovered because of a confession or statements in the nature of a confession obtained from the defendant; or confessions or statements in the nature of confessions.

Upon being so informed, the court will formally advise the attorney for the defendant (or the defendant himself if he refuses legal counsel) that he may, if he chooses, move the court to suppress the evidence so secured or the confession so obtained if his contention is that such evidence was secured or confession obtained in violation of defendant's constitutional rights.

. . .

The procedure which we have outlined deals only with evidence obtained as the result of a search and seizure and evidence consisting of or produced by confession on the part of the defendant. However, the steps which have been suggested as a method of dealing with evidence of this type will indicate to counsel and to the trial courts that the pretrial consideration of other evidentiary problems, the resolution of which is needed to assure the integrity of the trial when conducted, will be most useful and that this court encourages the use of such procedures whenever practical.

Subdivision (e) provides that the court shall rule on a pretrial motion before trial unless the court orders that it be decided upon at the trial of the general issue or after verdict. This is the old rule. The reference to issues which must be tried by the jury is dropped as unnecessary, without any intention of changing current law or practice. The old rule begs the question of when a jury decision is required at the trial, providing only that a jury is necessary if "required by the Constitution or an act of Congress." It will be observed that subdivision (e) confers general authority to defer the determination of any pretrial motion until after verdict. However, in the case of a motion to suppress evidence the power should be exercised in the light of the possibility that if the motion is ultimately granted a retrial of the defendant may not be permissible.

Subdivision (f) provides that a failure to raise the objections or make the requests specified in subdivision (b) constitutes a waiver thereof, but the court is allowed to grant relief from the waiver if adequate cause is shown. See C. Wright, Federal Practice and Procedure: Criminal § 192 (1969), where it is pointed out that the old rule is unclear as to whether the waiver results only from a failure to raise the issue prior to trial or from the failure to do so at the time fixed by the judge for a hearing. The amendment makes clear that the defendant and, where appropriate, the government have an obligation to raise the issue at the motion date set by the judge pursuant to subdivision (c).

Subdivision (g) requires that a verbatim record be made of pretrial motion proceedings and requires the judge to make a record of his findings of fact and conclusions of law. This is desirable if pretrial rulings are to be subject to post-conviction review on the record. The judge may find and rule orally from the bench, so long as a verbatim record is taken. There is no necessity of a separate written memorandum containing the judge's findings and conclusions.

Subdivision (h) is essentially old rule 12(b)(5) except for the deletion of the provision that defendant may plead if the motion is determined adversely to him or, if he has already entered a plea, that that plea stands. This language seems unnecessary particularly in light of the experience in some district courts where a pro forma plea of not guilty is entered at the arraignment, pretrial motions are later made, and depending upon the outcome the defendant may then change his plea to guilty or persist in his plea of not guilty.

Notes of Committee on the Judiciary on 1975 amendments (House Report No. 94-247).

A. Amendments Proposed by the Supreme Court. Rule 12 of the Federal Rules of Criminal Procedure deals with pretrial motions and pleadings. The Supreme Court proposed several amendments to it. The more significant of these are set out below.

Subdivision (b) as proposed to be amended provides that the pretrial motions may be oral or written, at the court's discretion. It also provides that certain types of motions must be made before trial.

Subdivision (d) as proposed to be amended provides that the government, either on its own or in response to a request by the defendant, must notify the defendant of its intention to use certain evidence in order to give the defendant an opportunity before trial to move to suppress that evidence.

Subdivision (e) as proposed to be amended permits the court to defer ruling on a pretrial motion until the trial of the general issue or until after verdict.

Subdivision (f) as proposed to be amended provides that the failure before trial to file motions or requests or to raise defenses which must be filed or raised prior to trial, results in a waiver. However, it also provides that the court, for cause shown, may grant relief from the waiver.

Subdivision (g) as proposed to be amended requires that a verbatim record be made of the pretrial motion proceedings and that the judge make a record of his findings of fact and conclusions of law.

B. Committee Action. The Committee modified subdivision (e) to permit the court to defer its ruling on a pretrial motion until after the trial only for good cause. Moreover, the court cannot defer its ruling if to do so will adversely affect a party's right to appeal. The Committee believes that the rule proposed by the Supreme Court could deprive the government of its appeal rights under statutes like section 3731 of title 18 of the United States Code. Further, the Committee hopes to discourage the tendency to reserve rulings on pretrial motions until after verdict in the hope that the jury's verdict will make a ruling unnecessary.

The Committee also modified subdivision (h), which deals with what happens when the court grants a pretrial motion based upon a defect in the institution of the prosecution or in the indictment or information. The Committee's change provides that when such a motion is granted, the court may order that the defendant be continued in custody or that his bail be continued for a specified time. A defendant should not automatically be continued in custody when such a motion is granted. In order to continue the defendant in custody, the court must not only determine that there is probable cause, but it must also determine, in effect, that there is good cause to have the defendant arrested.

Notes of Advisory Committee on 1983 amendments. *Note to Subdivision (i).* As noted in the recent decision of *United States v. Raddatz,* 447 U.S. 667 (1980), hearings on pretrial suppression motions not infrequently necessitate a determination of the credibility of witnesses. In such a situation, it is particularly important, as also highlighted by *Raddatz,* that the record include some other evidence which tends to either verify or controvert the assertions of the witness. (This is especially true in light of the *Raddatz* holding that a district judge, in order to make an independent evaluation of credibility, is not required to rehear testimony on which a magistrate based his findings and recommendations following a suppression hearing before the magistrate.) One kind of evidence which can often fulfill this function is prior statements of the testifying witness, yet courts have consistently held that in light of the Jencks Act, 18 U.S.C. § 3500, such production of statements cannot be compelled at a pretrial suppression hearing. *United States v. Spagnuolo,* 515 F.2d 818 (9th Cir. 1975); *United States v. Sebastian,* 497 F.2d 1267 (2nd Cir. 1974); *United States v. Montos,* 421 F.2d 215 (5th Cir. 1970). This result, which finds no express Congressional approval in the legislative history of the Jencks Act, see *United States v. Sebastian,* supra; *United States v. Covello,* 410 F.2d 536 (2d Cir. 1969), would be obviated by new subdivision (i) of rule 12.

This change will enhance the accuracy of the factual determinations made in the context of pretrial suppression hearings. As noted in *United States v. Sebastian,* supra, it can be argued.

most persuasively that the case for pre-trial disclosure is strongest in the framework of a suppression hearing. Since findings at such a hearing as to admissibility of challenged evidence will often determine the result at trial and, at least in the case of fourth amendment suppression motions, cannot be relitigated later before the trier of fact, pre-trial production of the statements of witnesses would aid defense counsel's impeachment efforts at perhaps the most crucial point in the case.* * * [A] government witness at the suppression hearing may not appear at trial so that defendants could never test his credibility with the benefits of Jencks Act material.

The latter statement is certainly correct, for not infrequently a police officer who must testify on a motion to suppress as to the circumstances of an arrest or search will not be called at trial because he has no information necessary to the determination of defendant's guilt. See, e.g., *United States v. Spagnuolo,* supra (dissent notes that "under the prosecution's own admission, it did not intend to produce at trial the witnesses called at the pre-trial suppression hearing"). Moreover, even if that person did testify at the trial, if that testimony went to a different subject matter, then under rule 26.2(c) only portions of prior statements covering the same subject matter need be produced, and thus portions which might contradict the suppression hearing testimony would not be revealed. Thus, while it may be true, as declared in *United States v. Montos,* supra, that "due process does not require premature production at pre-trial hearings on motions to suppress of statements ultimately subject to discovery under the Jencks Act," the fact of the matter is that those statements—or, the essential portions thereof—are not necessarily subject to later discovery.

Moreover, it is not correct to assume that somehow the problem can be solved by leaving the suppression issue "open" in some fashion for resolution once the trial is under way, at which time the prior statements will be produced. In *United States v. Spagnuolo,* supra, the court responded to the defendant's dilemma of inaccessible prior statements by saying that the suppression motion could simply be deferred until trial. But, under the current version of rule 12 this is not possible; subdivision (b) declares that motions to suppress "must" be made before trial, and subdivision (e) says such motions cannot be deferred for determination at trial "if a party's right to appeal is adversely affected," which surely is the case as to suppression motions. As for the possibility of the trial judge reconsidering the motion to suppress on the basis of prior statements produced at trial and casting doubt on the credibility of a suppression hearing witness, it is not a desirable or adequate solution. For one thing, as already noted, there is no assurance that the prior statements will be forthcoming. Even if they are, it is not efficient to delay the continuation of the trial to undertake a reconsideration of matters which could have been resolved in advance of trial had the critical facts then been available. Furthermore, if such reconsideration is regularly to be expected of the trial judge, then this would give rise on appeal to unnecessary issues of the kind which confronted the court in *United States v. Montos,* supra—whether the trial judge was obligated either to conduct a new hearing or to make a new determination in light of the new evidence.

The second sentence of subdivision (i) provides that a law enforcement officer is to be deemed a witness called by the government. This means that when such a federal, state or local officer has testified at a suppression hearing, the defendant will be entitled to any statement of the officer in the possession of the government and relating to the subject matter concerning which the witness has testified, without regard to whether the officer was in fact called by the government or the defendant. There is considerable variation in local practice as to whether the arresting or searching officer is considered the witness of the defendant or of the government, but the need for the prior statement exists in either instance.

The second sentence of subdivision (i) also provides that upon a claim of privilege the court is to excise the privileged matter before turning over the statement. The situation most likely to arise is that in which the prior statement of the testifying officer identifies an informant who supplied some or all of the probable cause information to the police. Under *McCray v. Illinois,* 386 U.S. 300 (1967), it is for the judge who hears the motion to decide whether disclosure of the informant's identity is necessary in the particular case. Of course, the government in any case may prevent disclosure of the informant's identity by terminating reliance upon information from that informant.

Notes of Advisory Committee on 1987 amendments. The amendment is technical. No substantive change is intended.

Notes of Advisory Committee on 1993 amendments. The amendment to subdivision (i) is one of a series of contemporaneous amendments 26.2, 32(f), 32.1, 46, and Rule 8 of the Rules Governing § 2255 Hearings, which extended Rule 26.2, Production of Witness Statements, to other proceedings or hearings conducted under the Rules of Criminal Procedure. Rule 26.2(c) now explicitly states that the trial court may excise privileged matter from the requested witness statements. That change rendered similar language in Rule 12(i) redundant.

Notes of Advisory Committee on 2002 amendments. The language of Rule 12 has been amended as part of the general restyling of the Criminal Rules to make them more easily understood and to make style and terminology consistent throughout the rules. These changes are intended to be stylistic only, except as noted below.

The last sentence of current Rule 12(a), referring to the elimination of "all other pleas, and demurrers and motions to quash" has been deleted as unnecessary.

Rule 12(b) is modified to more clearly indicate that Rule 47 governs any pretrial motions filed under Rule 12, including form and content. The new provision also more clearly delineates those motions that must be filed pretrial and those that may be filed pretrial. No change in practice is intended.

Rule 12(b)(4) is composed of what is currently Rule 12(d). The Committee believed that that provision, which addresses the government's requirement to disclose discoverable information for the purpose of facilitating timely defense objections and motions, was more appropriately associated with the pretrial motions specified in Rule 12(b)(3).

Rule 12(c) includes a non-stylistic change. The reference to the "local rule" exception has been deleted to make it clear that judges should be encouraged to set deadlines for motions. The Committee believed that doing so promotes more efficient case management, especially when there is a heavy docket of pending cases. Although the rule permits some discretion in setting a date for motion hearings, the Committee believed that doing so at an early point in the proceedings would also promote judicial economy.

Moving the language in current Rule 12(d) caused the relettering of the subdivisions following Rule 12(c).

Although amended Rule 12(e) is a revised version of current Rule 12(f), the Committee intends to make no change in the current law regarding waivers of motions or defenses.

Notes of Advisory Committee on 2014 amendments. *Rule 12(b)(l).* The language formerly in (b)(2), which provided that "any defense, objection, or request that the court can determine without trial of the general issue" may be raised by motion before trial, has been relocated here. The more modern phrase "trial on the merits" is substituted for the more archaic phrase "trial of the general issue." No change in meaning is intended.

Rule 12(b)(2). As revised, subdivision (b)(2) states that lack of jurisdiction may be raised at any time the case is pending. This provision was relocated from its previous placement at the end of subsection (b)(3)(B) and restyled. No change in meaning is intended.

Rule 12(b)(3). The amendment clarifies which motions must be raised before trial.

The introductory language includes two important limitations. The basis for the motion must be one that is "then reasonably available" and the motion must be one that the court can determine "without trial on the merits." The types of claims subject to Rule 12(b)(3) generally will be available before trial and they can-and should-be resolved then. The Committee recognized, however, that in some cases, a party may not have access to the information needed to raise particular claims that fall within the general categories subject to Rule 12(b)(3) prior to trial. The "then reasonably available" language is intended to ensure that a claim a party could not have raised on time is not subject to the limitation on review imposed by Rule 12(c)(3). Additionally, only those issues that can be determined "without a trial on the merits" need be raised by motion before trial. Just as in (b)(1), the more modern phrase "trial on the merits" is substituted for the more archaic phrase "trial of the general issue." No change in meaning is intended.

The rule's command that motions alleging "a defect in instituting the prosecution" and "errors in the indictment or information" must be made before trial is unchanged.

The amendment adds a nonexclusive list of commonly raised claims under each category to help ensure that such claims are not overlooked. The Rule is not intended to and does not affect or supersede statutory provisions that establish the time to make specific motions, such as motions under the Jury Selection and Service Act, 18 U.S.C. § 1867(a) [28 U.S.C. § 1867(a)].

Rule 12(b)(3)(B) has also been amended to remove language that allowed the court at any time while the case is pending to hear a claim that the "indictment or information fails . . . to state an offense." This specific charging error was previously considered fatal whenever raised and was excluded from the general requirement that charging deficiencies be raised prior to trial. The Supreme Court abandoned any jurisdictional justification for the exception in *United States v. Cotton*, 535 U.S. 625, 629-31 (2002) overruling *Ex parte Bain*, 121 U.S. 1 (1887), "[i]nsofar as it held that a defective indictment deprives a court of jurisdiction").

Rule 12(c). As revised, subdivision (c) governs both the deadline for making pretrial motions and the consequences of failing to meet the deadline for motions that must be made before trial under Rule 12(b)(3).

As amended, subdivision (c) contains three paragraphs. Paragraph (c)(1) retains the existing provisions for establishing the time when pretrial motions must be made, and adds a sentence stating that unless the court sets a deadline, the deadline for pretrial motions is the start of trial, so that motions may be ruled upon before jeopardy attaches. Subdivision (e) of the present rule contains the language "or by any extension the court provides," which anticipates that a district court has broad discretion to extend, reset, or decline to extend or reset, the deadline for pretrial motions. New paragraph (c)(2) recognizes this discretion explicitly and relocates the Rule's mention of it to a more logical place-after the provision concerning setting the deadline and before the provision concerning the consequences of not meeting the deadline. No change in meaning is intended.

New paragraph (c)(3) governs the review of untimely claims, previously addressed in Rule 12(e). Rule 12(e) provided that a party "waives" a defense not raised within the time set under Rule 12(c). Although the term waiver in the context of a criminal case ordinarily refers to the intentional relinquishment of a known right, Rule 12(e) has never required any determination that a party who failed to make a timely motion intended to relinquish a defense, objection, or request that was not raised in a timely fashion. Accordingly, to avoid possible confusion the Committee decided not to employ the term "waiver" in new paragraph (c)(3).

New paragraph 12(c)(3) retains the existing standard for untimely claims. The party seeking relief must show "good cause" for failure to raise a claim by the deadline, a flexible standard that requires consideration of all interests in the particular case.

Rule 12(e). The effect of failure to raise issues by a pretrial motion has been relocated from (e) to (c)(3).

Changes Made After Publication and Comment. Language that had been deleted from Rule 12(b)(2) as unnecessary was restored and relocated in (b)(1). The change begins the Rule's treatment of pretrial motions with an appropriate general statement and responds to concerns that the deletion might have been perceived as unintentionally restricting the district courts' authority to rule on pretrial motions. The references to "double jeopardy" and "statute of limitations" were dropped from the nonexclusive list in (b)(3)(A) to permit further debate over the treatment of such claims. New paragraph (c)(2) was added to state explicitly the district court's authority to extend or reset the deadline for pretrial motions; this authority had been recognized implicitly in language being deleted from Rule 12(e). In subdivision (c), the cross reference to Rule 52 was omitted as unnecessarily controversial. In subparagraph (c)(3), the current language "good cause" was retained for all claims and subparagraph (c)(3)(B) was omitted. Finally, the Committee Note was amended to reflect these post-publication changes and to state explicitly that the rule is not intended to change or supersede statutory deadlines under provisions such as the Jury Selection and Service Act.

Amendments:

1975.

Act July 31, 1975, § 3(11), (12) (effective 12/1/75, as provided by § 2 of such Act, which appears as a note to Rule 4), substituted subsec. (e) for one which read: "(e) Ruling on motion. A motion made before trial shall be determined before trial unless the court orders that it be deferred for determination at the trial of the general issue or until after verdict. Where factual issues are involved in determining a motion, the court shall state its essential findings on the record."; and, in subsec. (h), substituted "defendant be continued" for "defendant be held", and substituted "Act" for "act".

Rule 12.1. Notice of an Alibi Defense

(a) Government's Request for Notice and Defendant's Response.

(1) *Government's Request.* An attorney for the government may request in writing that the defendant notify an attorney for the government of any intended alibi defense. The request must state the time, date, and place of the alleged offense.

(2) *Defendant's Response.* Within 14 days after the request, or at some other time the court sets, the defendant must serve written notice on an attorney for the government of any intended alibi defense. The defendant's notice must state:

(A) each specific place where the defendant claims to have been at the time of the alleged offense; and

(B) the name, address, and telephone number of each alibi witness on whom the defendant intends to rely.

(b) Disclosing Government Witnesses.

(1) *Disclosure.*

(A) In General. If the defendant serves a Rule 12.1(a)(2) notice, an attorney for the government must disclose in writing to the defendant or the defendant's attorney:

(i) the name of each witness — and the address and telephone number of each witness other than a victim — that the government intends to rely on to establish that the defendant was present at the scene of the alleged offense; and

(ii) each government rebuttal witness to the defendant's alibi defense.

(B) Victim's Address and Telephone Number. If the government intends to rely on a victim's testimony to establish that the defendant was present at the scene of the alleged offense and the defendant establishes a need for the victim's address and telephone number, the court may:

(i) order the government to provide the information in writing to the defendant or the defendant's attorney; or

(ii) fashion a reasonable procedure that allows preparation of the defense and also protects the victim's interests.

(2) *Time to Disclose.* Unless the court directs otherwise, an attorney for the government must give its Rule 12.1(b)(1) disclosure within 14 days after the defendant serves notice of an intended alibi defense under Rule 12.1(a)(2), but no later than 14 days before trial.

(c) Continuing Duty to Disclose.

(1) *In General.* Both an attorney for the government and the defendant must promptly disclose in writing to the other party the name of each additional witness — and the address and telephone number of each additional witness other than a victim — if:

(A) the disclosing party learns of the witness before or during trial; and

(B) the witness should have been disclosed under Rule 12.1(a) or (b) if the disclosing party had known of the witness earlier.

(2) *Address and Telephone Number of an Additional Victim Witness.* The address and telephone number of an additional victim witness must not be disclosed except as provided in Rule 12.1(b)(1)(B).

(d) Exceptions. For good cause, the court may grant an exception to any requirement of Rule 12.1(a)–(c).

(e) Failure to Comply. If a party fails to comply with this rule, the court may exclude the testimony of any undisclosed witness regarding the defendant's alibi. This rule does not limit the defendant's right to testify.

(f) Inadmissibility of Withdrawn Intention. Evidence of an intention to rely on an alibi defense, later withdrawn, or of a statement made in connection with that intention, is not, in any civil or criminal proceeding, admissible against the person who gave notice of the intention.

HISTORY:

Added April 22, 1974, eff. Dec. 1, 1975; amended July 31, 1975, P. L. 94-64, § 3(13), 89 Stat. 372; April 29, 1985, eff. Aug. 1, 1985; March 9, 1987, eff. Aug. 1, 1987; April 29, 2002, eff. Dec. 1, 2002; April 23, 2008, eff. Dec. 1, 2008; March 26, 2009, eff. Dec. 1, 2009.

HISTORY; ANCILLARY LAWS AND DIRECTIVES

Other provisions:

Notes of Advisory Committee. Rule 12.1 is new. See rule 87 of the United States District Court Rules for the District of Columbia for a somewhat comparable provision.

The Advisory Committee has dealt with the issue of notice of alibi on several occasions over the course of the past three decades. In the Preliminary Draft of the Federal Rules of Criminal Procedure, 1943, and the Second Preliminary Draft, 1944, an alibi-notice rule was proposed. But the Advisory Committee was closely divided upon whether there should be a rule at all and, if there were to be a rule, what the form of the rule should be. Orfield, The Preliminary Draft of the Federal Rules of Criminal Procedure, 22 Texas L.Rev. 37, 57–58 (1943). The principal disagreement was whether the prosecutor or the defendant should initiate the process. The Second Preliminary Draft published in 1944 required the defendant to initiate the process by a motion to require the government to state with greater particularity the time and place it would rely on. Upon receipt of this information, defendant was required to give his notice of alibi. This formulation was "vehemently objected" to by five members of the committee (out of a total of eighteen) and two alternative rule proposals were submitted to the Supreme Court. Both formulations —one requiring the prosecutor to initiate the process, the other requiring the defendant to initiate the process—were rejected by the Court. See Epstein, Advance Notice of Alibi, 55 J.Crim.L., C. & P.S. 29, 30 (1964), in which the view is expressed that the unresolved split over the rule "probably caused" the court to reject an alibi-notice rule.

Rule 12.1 embodies an intermediate position. The initial burden is upon the defendant to raise the defense of alibi, but he need not specify the details of his alibi defense until the government specifies the time, place, and date of alleged offense. Each party must, at the appropriate time, disclose the names and addresses of witnesses.

In 1962 the Advisory Committee drafted an alibi-notice rule and included it in the Preliminary Draft of December 1962, rule 12A at pp. 5–6. This time the Advisory Committee withdrew the rule without submitting it to the Standing Committee on Rules of Practice and Procedure. Wright, Proposed Changes in Federal Civil, Criminal, and Appellate Procedure. 35 F.R.D. 317, 326 (1964). Criticism of the December 1962 alibi-notice rule centered on constitutional questions and questions of general fairness to the defendant. See Everett, Discovery in Criminal Cases—In Search of a Standard, 1964 Duke L.J. 477, 497–499.

Doubts about the constitutionality of a notice-of-alibi rule were to some extent resolved by *Williams v. Florida,* 399 U.S. 78, 90 S.Ct. 1893, 26 L.Ed.2d 446 (1970). In that case the court sustained the constitutionality of the Florida notice-of-alibi statute, but left unresolved two important questions.

(1) The court said that it was not holding that a notice-of-alibi requirement was valid under conditions where a defendant does not enjoy "reciprocal discovery against the State." 399 U.S. at 82 n. 11, 90 S.Ct. 1893. Under the revision of rule 16, the defendant is entitled to substantially enlarged discovery in federal cases, and it would seem appropriate to conclude that the rules will comply with the "reciprocal discovery" qualification of the *Williams* decision. [See, *Wardius v. Oregon,* 412 U.S. 470, 93 S.Ct. 2208, 37 L.Ed.2d 82 (1973) was decided after the approval of proposed Rule 12.1 by the Judicial Conference of the United States. In that case the Court held the Oregon Notice-of-Alibi statute unconstitutional because of the failure to give the defendant adequate reciprocal discovery rights.]

(2) The court said that it did not consider the question of the "validity of the threatened sanction, had petitioner chosen not to comply with the notice-of-alibi rule." 399 U.S. at 83 n. 14, 90 S.Ct. 1893. This issue remains unresolved.

[See *Wardius v. Oregon,* 412 U.S. at 472, Note 4, 93 S.Ct. 2208.] Rule 12.1(e) provides that the court may exclude the testimony of any witness whose name has not been disclosed pursuant to the requirements of the rule. The defendant may, however, testify himself. Prohibiting from testifying a witness whose name was not disclosed is a common provision in state statutes. See Epstein, *supra,* at 35. It is generally assumed that the sanction is essential if the notice-of-alibi rule is to have practical significance. See Epstein, *supra,* at 36. The use of the term "may" is intended to make clear that the judge may allow the alibi witness to testify if, under the particular circumstances, there is cause shown for the failure to conform to the requirements of the rules. This is further emphasized by subdivision (f) which provides for exceptions whenever "good cause" is shown for the exception.

The Supreme Court of Illinois recently upheld an Illinois statute which requires a defendant to give notice of his alibi witnesses although the prosecution is not required to disclose its alibi rebuttal witnesses. *People v. Holiday,* 47 Ill.2d 300, 265 N.E.2d 634 (1970). Because the defense complied with the requirement, the court did not have to consider the propriety of penalizing noncompliance.

The requirement of notice of alibi seems to be an increasingly common requirement of state criminal procedure. State statutes and court rules are cited in 399 U.S. at 82 n. 11, 90 S.Ct. 1893. See also Epstein, *supra.*

Rule 12.1 will serve a useful purpose even though rule 16 now requires disclosure of the names and addresses of government and defense witnesses. There are cases in which the identity of defense witnesses may be known, but it may come as a surprise to the government that they intend to testify as to an alibi and there may be no advance notice of the details of the claimed alibi. The result often is an unnecessary interruption and delay in the trial to enable the government to conduct an appropriate investigation. The objective of rule 12.1 is to prevent this by providing a mechanism which will enable the parties to have specific information in advance of trial to prepare to meet the issue of alibi during the trial.

Notes of Committee on the Judiciary on 1975 amendments (House Report No. 94-247). A. Amendments Proposed by the Supreme Court. Rule 12.1 is a new rule that deals with the defense of alibi. It provides that a defendant must notify the government of his intention to rely upon the defense of alibi. Upon receipt of such notice, the government must advise the defendant of the specific time, date, and place at which the offense is alleged to have been committed. The defendant must then inform the government of the specific place at which he claims to have been when the offense is alleged to have been committed, and of the names and addresses of the witnesses on whom he intends to rely to establish his alibi. The government must then inform the defendant of the names and addresses of the witnesses on whom it will rely to establish the defendant's presence at the scene of the crime. If either party fails to comply with the provisions of the rule, the court may exclude the testimony of any witness whose identity is not disclosed. The rule does not attempt to limit the right of the defendant to testify in his own behalf.

B. Committee Action. The Committee disagrees with the defendant-triggered procedures of the rule proposed by the Supreme Court. The major purpose of a notice-of-alibi rule is to prevent unfair surprise to the prosecution. The Committee, therefore, believes that it should be up to the prosecution to trigger the alibi defense discovery procedures. If the prosecution is worried about being surprised by an alibi defense, it can trigger the alibi defense discovery procedures. If the government fails to trigger the procedures and if the defendant raises an alibi defense at trial, then the government cannot claim surprise and get a continuance of the trial.

The Committee has adopted a notice-of-alibi rule similar to the one now used in the District of Columbia. [See Rule 2-5(b) of the Rules of the United States District Court for the District of Columbia. See also Rule 16-1 of the Rules of Criminal Procedure for the Superior Court of the District of Columbia.] The rule is prosecution-triggered. If the prosecutor notifies the defendant of the time, place, and date of the alleged offense, then the defendant has 10 days in which to notify the prosecutor of his intention to rely upon an alibi defense, specify where he claims to have been at the time of the alleged offense, and provide a list of his alibi witnesses. The prosecutor, within 10 days but no later than 10 days before trial, must then provide the defendant with a list of witnesses who will place the defendant at the scene of the alleged crime and those witnesses who will be used to rebut the defendant's alibi witnesses.

The Committee's rule does not operate only to the benefit of the prosecution. In fact, its rule will provide the defendant with more information than the rule proposed by the Supreme Court. The rule proposed by the Supreme Court permits the defendant to obtain a list of only those witnesses who will place him at the scene of the crime. The defendant, however, would get the names of these witnesses anyway as part of his discovery under Rule 16(a)(1)(E). The Committee rule not only requires the prosecution to provide the names of witnesses who place the defendant at the scene of the crime, but it also requires the prosecution to turn over the names of those witnesses who will be called in rebuttal to the defendant's alibi witnesses. This is information that the defendant is not otherwise entitled to discover.

Approval of amendments by Act July 31, 1975; effective date. Act July 31, 1975, P. L. 94-64, § 2, 89 Stat. 370, which appears as a note to Rule 4, approved U. S. Supreme Court Order of April 22, 1974, which added this Rule, and rendered it effective on Dec. 1, 1975.

Notes of Advisory Committee on 1985 amendments. *Note to Subdivision (f).* This clarifying amendment is intended to serve the same purpose as a comparable change made in 1979 to similar language in Rule 11(e)(6). The change makes it clear that evidence of a withdrawn intent or of statements made in connection therewith is thereafter inadmissible against the person who gave the notice in any civil or criminal proceeding, without regard to whether the proceeding is against that person.

Notes of Advisory Committee on 1987 amendments. The amendments are technical. No substantive change is intended.

Notes of Advisory Committee on 2002 amendments. The language of Rule 12.1 has been amended as part of the general restyling of the Criminal Rules to make them more easily understood and to make style and terminology consistent throughout the rules. These changes are intended to be stylistic only, except as noted below.

Current Rules12.1(d) and 12.1(e) have been switched in the amended rule to improve the organization of the rule.

Finally, the amended rule includes a new requirement that in providing the names and addresses of alibi and any rebuttal witnesses, the parties must also provide the phone numbers of those witnesses. See Rule 12.1(a)(2), Rule 12.1(b)(1), and Rule 12.1(c). The Committee believed that requiring such information would facilitate locating and interviewing those witnesses.

Notes of Advisory Committee on 2008 amendments. *Note to Subdivisions (b) and (c).* The amendment implements the Crime Victims' Rights Act, which states that victims have the right to be reasonably protected from the accused and to be treated with respect for the victim's dignity and privacy. *See* 18 U.S.C. § 3771(a)(1) & (8). The rule provides that a victim's address and telephone number should not automatically be provided to the defense when an alibi defense is raised. If a defendant establishes a need for this information, the court has discretion to order its disclosure or to fashion an alternative procedure that provides the defendant with the information necessary to prepare a defense, but also protects the victim's interests.

In the case of victims who will testify concerning an alibi claim, the same procedures and standards apply to both the prosecutor's initial disclosure and the prosecutor's continuing duty to disclose under subdivision (c).

Notes of Advisory Committee on 2009 amendments. The times set in the former rule at 10 days have been revised to 14 days. See the Committee Note to Rule 45(a).

Amendments:

1975.

Act July 31, 1975, § 3(13) (effective 12/1/75, as provided by § 2 of such Act, which appears as a note to Rule 4), substituted this Rule for one which read:

"(a) Notice by defendant. If a defendant intends to rely upon the defense of alibi, he shall, within the time provided for the filing of pretrial motions or at such later time as the court may direct, notify the attorney for the government in writing of such intention and file a copy of such notice with the clerk.

"(b) Disclosure of information and witnesses. Upon receipt of notice that the defendant intends to rely upon an alibi defense, the attorney for the government shall inform the defendant in writing of the specific time, date, and place at which the offense is alleged to have been committed. The defendant shall then inform the attorney for the government in writing of the specific place at which he claims to have been at the time of the alleged offense and the names and addresses of the witnesses upon whom he intends to rely to establish such alibi. The attorney for the government shall then inform the defendant in writing of the names and addresses of the witnesses upon whom the government intends to rely to establish defendant's presence at the scene of the alleged offense.

"(c) Time of giving information. The court may fix the time within which the exchange of information referred to in subdivision (b) shall be accomplished.

"(d) Continuing duty to disclose. If prior to or during trial, a party learns of an additional witness whose identity, if known, should have been included in the information furnished under subdivision (b) of this rule, the party shall promptly notify the other party or his attorney of the existence and identity of such additional witness.

"(e) Failure to comply. Upon the failure of either party to comply with the requirements of this rule, the court may exclude the testimony of any undisclosed witness offered by such party as to the defendant's absence from, or presence at, the scene of the alleged offense. This rule shall not limit the right of the defendant to testify in his own behalf.

"(f) Exceptions. For good cause shown, the court may grant an exception to any of the requirements of this rule.".

Rule 12.2. Notice of an Insanity Defense; Mental Examination

(a) Notice of an Insanity Defense. A defendant who intends to assert a defense of insanity at the time of the alleged offense must so notify an attorney for the government in writing within the time provided for filing a pretrial motion, or at any later time the court sets, and file a copy of the notice with the clerk. A defendant who fails to do so cannot rely on an insanity defense. The court may, for good cause, allow the defendant to file the notice late, grant additional trial-preparation time, or make other appropriate orders.

(b) Notice of Expert Evidence of a Mental Condition. If a defendant intends to introduce expert evidence relating to a mental disease or defect or any other mental condition of the defendant bearing on either (1) the issue of guilt or (2) the issue of punishment in a capital case, the defendant must—within the time provided for filing a pretrial motion or at any later time the court sets—notify an attorney for the government in writing of this intention and file a copy of the notice with the clerk. The court may, for good cause, allow the defendant to file the notice late, grant the parties additional trial-preparation time, or make other appropriate orders.

(c) Mental Examination.

(1) *Authority to Order an Examination; Procedures.*

(A) The court may order the defendant to submit to a competency examination under 18 U.S.C. § 4241.

(B) If the defendant provides notice under Rule 12.2(a), the court must, upon the government's motion, order the defendant to be examined under 18 U.S.C. § 4242. If the defendant provides notice under Rule 12.2(b) the court may, upon the government's motion, order the defendant to be examined under procedures ordered by the court.

(2) *Disclosing Results and Reports of Capital Sentencing Examination.* The results and reports of any examination conducted solely under Rule 12.2(c)(1) after notice under Rule 12.2(b)(2) must be sealed and must not be disclosed to any attorney for the government or the defendant unless the defendant is found guilty of one or more capital crimes and the defendant confirms an intent to offer during sentencing proceedings expert evidence on mental condition.

(3) *Disclosing Results and Reports of the Defendant's Expert Examination.* After disclosure under Rule 12.2(c)(2) of the results and reports of the government's examination, the defendant must disclose to the government the results and reports of any examination on mental condition conducted by the defendant's expert about which the defendant intends to introduce expert evidence.

(4) *Inadmissibility of a Defendant's Statements.* — No statement made by a defendant in the course of any examination conducted under this rule (whether con-

ducted with or without the defendant's consent), no testimony by the expert based on the statement, and no other fruits of the statement may be admitted into evidence against the defendant in any criminal proceeding except on an issue regarding mental condition on which the defendant:

(A) has introduced evidence of incompetency or evidence requiring notice under Rule 12.2(a) or (b)(1), or

(B) has introduced expert evidence in a capital sentencing proceeding requiring notice under Rule 12.2(b)(2).

(d) Failure to Comply.

(1) *Failure to Give Notice or to Submit to Examination.* The court may exclude any expert evidence from the defendant on the issue of the defendant's mental disease, mental defect, or any other mental condition bearing on the defendant's guilt or the issue of punishment in a capital case if the defendant fails to:

(A) give notice under Rule 12.2(b); or

(B) submit to an examination when ordered under Rule 12.2(c).

(2) *Failure to Disclose.* The court may exclude any expert evidence for which the defendant has failed to comply with the disclosure requirement of Rule 12.2(c)(3).

(e) Inadmissibility of Withdrawn Intention. Evidence of an intention as to which notice was given under Rule 12.2(a) or (b), later withdrawn, is not, in any civil or criminal proceeding, admissible against the person who gave notice of the intention.

HISTORY:

Added April 22, 1974, eff. Dec. 1, 1975; amended July 31, 1975, P. L. 94-64, § 3(14), 89 Stat. 370, 373; April 28, 1983, eff. Aug. 1, 1983; Oct. 12, 1984, P. L. 98-473, Title II, Ch IV, § 404, 98 Stat. 2067; Oct. 30, 1984, P. L. 98-596, § 11(a), (b), 98 Stat. 3138; Aug. 1, 1985; Nov. 10, 1986, P. L. 99-646, § 24, 100 Stat. 3597; March 9, 1987, eff. Aug. 1, 1987; April 29, 2002, eff. Dec. 1, 2002; April 25, 2005, eff. Dec. 1, 2005.

HISTORY; ANCILLARY LAWS AND DIRECTIVES

Other provisions:

Notes of Advisory Committee. Rule 12.2 is designed to require a defendant to give notice prior to trial of his intention (1) to rely upon the defense of insanity or (2) to introduce expert testimony of mental disease or defect on the theory that such mental condition is inconsistent with the mental state required for the offense charged. This rule does not deal with the issue of mental competency to stand trial.

The objective is to give the government time to prepare to meet the issue, which will usually require reliance upon expert testimony. Failure to give advance notice commonly results in the necessity for a continuance in the middle of a trial, thus unnecessarily delaying the administration of justice.

A requirement that the defendant give notice of his intention to rely upon the defense of insanity was proposed by the Advisory Committee in the Second Preliminary Draft of Proposed Amendments (March 1964), rule 12.1, p. 7. The objective of the 1964 proposal was explained in a brief Advisory Committee Note:

Under existing procedure although insanity is a defense, once it is raised the burden to prove sanity beyond a reasonable doubt rests with the government. *Davis v. United States,* 160 U.S. 469, 16 S.Ct. 353, 40 L.Ed. 499 (1895). This rule requires pretrial notice to the government of an insanity defense, thus permitting it to prepare to meet the issue. Furthermore, in *Lynch v. Overholser,* 369 U.S. 705, 82 S.Ct. 1063, 8 L.Ed.2d 211 (1962), the Supreme Court held that, at least in the face of a mandatory commitment statute, the defendant had a right to determine whether or not to raise the issue of insanity. The rule gives the defendant a method of raising the issue and precludes any problem of deciding whether or not the defendant relied on insanity.

The Standing Committee on Rules of Practice and Procedure decided not to recommend the proposed Notice of Insanity rule to the Supreme Court. Reasons were not given.

Requiring advance notice of the defense of insanity is commonly recommended as a desirable procedure. The Working Papers of the National Commission on Reform of Federal Criminal Laws, Vol. 1, p. 254 (1970), state in part:

It is recommended that procedural reform provide for advance notice that evidence of mental disease or defect will be relied upon in defense. . . .

Requiring advance notice is proposed also by the American Law Institute's Model Penal Code, § 4.03 (P.O.D. 1962). The commentary in Tentative Draft No. 4 at 193–194 (1955) indicates that, as of that time, six states required pretrial notice and an additional eight states required that the defense of insanity be specially pleaded.

For recent state statutes see N.Y. CPL § 250.10 (McKinney's Consol. Laws, c. 11-A, 1971) enacted in 1970 which provides that no evidence by a defendant of a mental disease negativing criminal responsibility shall be allowed unless defendant has served notice on the prosecutor of his intention to rely upon such defense. See also New Jersey Penal Code (Final Report of the New Jersey Criminal Law Revision Commission, Oct. 1971) § 2c: 4-3; New Jersey Court Rule 3:12; *State v. Whitlow,* 45 N.J. 3, 22 n. 3, 210 T.2d 763 (1965), holding the requirement of notice to be both appropriate and not in violation of the privilege against self-incrimination.

Subdivision (a) deals with notice of the "defense of insanity." In this context the term insanity has a well-understood meaning. See, e.g., Tydings, A Federal Verdict of Not Guilty by Reason of Insanity and a Subsequent Commitment Procedure, 27 Md.L.Rev. 131 (1967). Precisely how the defense of insanity is phrased does, however, differ somewhat from circuit to circuit. See Study Draft of a New Federal Criminal Code, § 503 Comment at 37 (USGPO 1970). For a more extensive discussion of present law, see Working Papers of the National Commission on Reform of Federal Criminal Laws, Vol. 1, pp. 229–247 (USGPO 1970). The National Commission recommends the adoption of a single test patterned after the proposal of the American Law Institute's Model Penal Code. The proposed definition provides in part:

In any prosecution for an offense lack of criminal responsibility by reason of mental disease or defect is a defense. [Study Draft of a New Federal Criminal Code § 503 at 36–37.]

Should the proposal of the National Commission be adopted by the Congress, the language of subdivision (a) probably ought to be changed to read "defense of lack of criminal responsibility by reason of mental disease or defect" rather than "defense of insanity."

Subdivision (b) is intended to deal with the issue of expert testimony bearing upon the issue of whether the defendant had the "mental state required for the offense charged."

There is some disagreement as to whether it is proper to introduce evidence of mental disease or defect bearing not upon the defense of insanity, but rather upon the existence of the mental state required by the offense charged. The American Law Institute's Model Penal Code takes the position that such evidence is admissible [§ 4.02(1) (P.O.D. 1962)]. See also *People v. Gorshen,* 51 Cal.2d 716, 336 P.2d 492 (1959).

The federal cases reach conflicting conclusions. See *Rhodes v. United States,* 282 F.2d 59, 62 (4th Cir. 1960):

The proper way would have been to ask the witness to describe the defendant's mental condition and symptoms, his pathological beliefs and motivations, if he was thus afflicted, and to explain how these influenced or could have influenced his behavior, particularly his mental capacity knowingly to make the false statement charged, or knowingly to forge the signatures . . ..

Compare *Fisher v. United States,* 328 U.S. 463, 66 S.Ct. 1318, 90 L.Ed. 1382 (1946).

Subdivision (b) does not attempt to decide when expert testimony is admissible on the issue of the requisite mental state. It provides only that the defendant must give pretrial notice when he intends to introduce such evidence. The purpose is to prevent the need for a continuance when such evidence is offered without prior notice. The problem of unnecessary delay has arisen in jurisdictions which do not require prior notice of an intention to use expert testimony on the issue of mental state. Referring to this, the California Special Commission on Insanity and Criminal Offenders, First Report 30 (1962) said:

The abuses of the present system are great. Under a plea of "not guilty" without any notice to the people that the defense of insanity will be relied upon, defendant has been able to raise the defense upon the trial of the issue as to whether he committed the offense charged.

As an example of the delay occasioned by the failure to heretofore require a pretrial notice by the defendant, see *United States v. Albright,* 388 F.2d 719 (4th Cir. 1968), where a jury trial was recessed for 23 days to permit a psychiatric examination by the prosecution when the defendant injected a surprise defense of lack of mental competency.

Subdivision (c) gives the court the authority to order the defendant to submit to a psychiatric examination by a psychiatrist designated by the court. A similar provision is found in ALI, Model Penal Code § 4.05(1) (P.O.D. 1962). This is a common provision of state law, the constitutionality of which has been sustained. Authorities are collected in ALI, Model Penal Code, pp. 195–196 Tent. Draft No. 4, (1955). For a recent proposal, see the New Jersey Penal Code § 2c: 4–5 (Final Report of the New Jersey Criminal Law Revision Commission, Oct. 1971) authorizing appointment of "at least one qualified psychiatrist to examine and report upon the mental condition of the defendant." Any issue of self-incrimination which might arise can be dealt with by the court as, for example, by a bifurcated trial which deals separately with the issues of guilt and of mental responsibility. For statutory authority to appoint a psychiatrist with respect to competency to stand trial, see 18 U.S.C. § 4244.

Subdivision (d) confers authority on the court to exclude expert testimony in behalf of a defendant who has failed to give notice under subdivision (b) or who refuses to be examined by a court-appointed psychiatrist under subdivision (c). See *State v. Whitlow,* 45 N.J. 3, 23, 210 A.2d 763 (1965), which indicates that it is proper to limit or exclude testimony by a defense psychiatrist whenever defendant refuses to be examined.

Notes of Committee on the Judiciary on 1975 amendments (House Report No. 94-247). A. Amendments Proposed by the Supreme Court. Rule 12.2 is a new rule that deals with defense based upon mental condition. It provides that: (1) The defendant must notify the prosecution in writing of his intention to rely upon the defense of insanity. If the defendant fails to comply, "insanity may not be raised as a defense." (2) If the defendant intends to introduce expert testimony relating to mental disease or defect on the issue whether he had the requisite mental state, he must notify the prosecution in writing. (3) The court, on motion of the prosecution, may order the defendant to submit to a psychiatric examination by a court-appointed psychiatrist. (4) If the defendant fails to undergo the court-ordered psychiatric examination, the court may exclude any expert witness the defendant offers on the issue of his mental state.

B. Committee Action. The Committee agrees with the proposed rule but has added language concerning the use of statements made to a psychiatrist during the course of a psychiatric examination provided for by Rule 12.2. The language provides:

No statement made by the accused in the course of any examination provided for by this rule, whether the examination shall be with or without the consent of the accused, shall be admitted in evidence against the accused before the judge who or jury which determines the guilt of the accused, prior to the determination of guilt.

The purpose of this rule is to secure the defendant's fifth amendment right against self-incrimination. See *State v. Raskin,* 34 Wis.2d 607, 150 N.W.2d 318 (1967). The provision is flexible and does not totally preclude the use of such statements. For example, the defendant's statement can be used at a separate determination of the issue of sanity or for sentencing purposes once guilt has been determined. A limiting instruction to the jury in a single trial to consider statements made to the psychiatrist only on the issue of sanity would not satisfy the requirements of the rule as amended. The prejudicial effect on the determination of guilt would be inescapable.

The Committee notes that the rule does not attempt to resolve the issue whether the court can constitutionally compel a defendant to undergo a psychiatric examination when the defendant is unwilling to undergo one. The provisions of subdivision (c) are qualified by the phrase, "In an appropriate case." If the court cannot constitutionally compel an unwilling defendant to undergo a psychiatric examination, then the provisions of subdivision (c) are inapplicable in every instance where the defendant is unwilling to undergo a court-ordered psychiatric examination. The Committee, by its approval of subdivision (c), intends to take no stand whatever on the constitutional question.

Notes of Conference Committee on 1975 amendments (House Report No. 94-414). Rule 12.2(c) deals with court-ordered psychiatric examinations. The House version provides that no statement made by a defendant during a court-ordered psychiatric examination could be admitted in evidence against the defendant before the trier of fact that determines the issue of guilt prior to the determination of guilt. The Senate version deletes this provision.

The Conference adopts a modified House provision and restores to the bill the language of H.R. 6799 as it was originally introduced. The Conference adopted language provides that no statement made by the defendant during a psychiatric examination provided for by the rule shall be admitted against him on the issue of guilt in any criminal proceeding.

The Conference believes that the provision in H.R. 6799 as originally introduced in the House adequately protects the defendant's fifth amendment right against self-incrimination. The rule does not preclude use of statements made by a defendant during a court-ordered psychiatric examination. The statements may be relevant to the issue of defendant's sanity and admissable on that issue. However, a limiting instruction would not satisfy the rule if a statement is so prejudicial that a limiting instruction would be ineffective. Cf. practice under 18 U.S.C. 4244.

Approval of amendments by Act July 31, 1975; effective date. Act July 31, 1975, P. L. 94-64, § 2, 89 Stat. 370, which appears as a note to Rule 4, approved U. S. Supreme Court Order of April 22, 1974, which added this Rule, and rendered it effective on Dec. 1, 1975.

Notes of Advisory Committee on 1983 amendments. *Note to Subdivision (b).* Courts have recently experienced difficulty with the question of what kind of expert testimony offered for what purpose falls within the notice requirement of rule 12.2(b). See, e.g., *United States v. Hill,* 655 F.2d 512 (3d Cir. 1980) (rule not applicable to tendered testimony of psychologist concerning defendant's susceptibility of inducement, offered to reinforce defendant's entrapment defense); *United States v Webb,* 625 F.2d 709 (5th Cir. 1980) (rule not applicable to expert testimony tendered to show that defendant lacked the "propensity to commit a violent act," as this testimony was offered "to prove that Webb did not commit the offense charged," shooting at a helicopter, "not that certain conduct was unaccompanied by criminal intent"); *United States v. Perl,* 584 F.2d 1316 (4th Cir. 1978) (because entrapment defense properly withheld from jury, it was unnecessary to decide if the district court erred in holding rule applicable to tendered testimony of the doctor that defendant had increased susceptibility to suggestion as a result of medication he was taking); *United States v. Olson,* 576 F.2d 1267 (8th Cir. 1978) (rule applicable to tendered testimony of an alcoholism and drug therapist that defendant was not responsible for his actions because of a problem with alcohol); *United States v. Staggs,* 553 F.2d 1073 (7th Cir. 1977) (rule applicable to tendered testimony of psychologist that defendant, charged with assaulting federal officer, was more likely to hurt himself than to direct his aggressions toward others, as this testimony bears upon whether defendant intended to put victim in apprehension when he picked up the gun).

What these cases illustrate is that expert testimony about defendant's mental condition may be tendered in a wide variety of circumstances well beyond the situation clearly within rule 12.2(b), i.e., where a psychiatrist testifies for the defendant regarding his diminished capacity. In all of these situations and others like them, there is good reason to make applicable the notice provisions of rule 12.2(b). This is because in all circumstances in which the defendant plans to offer expert testimony concerning his mental condition at the time of the crime charged, advance disclosure to the government will serve "to permit adequate pretrial preparation, to prevent surprise at trial, and to avoid the necessity of delays during trial." 2 A.B.A. Standards for Criminal Justice 11-55 (2d 1980). Thus, while the district court in *United States v. Hill,* 481 F.Supp. 558 (E.D.Pa. 1979), incorrectly concluded that present rule 12.2(b) covers testimony by a psychologist bearing on the defense of entrapment, the court quite properly concluded that the government would be seriously disadvantaged by lack of notice. This would have meant that the government would not have been equipped to cross-examine the expert, that any expert called by the government would not have had an opportunity to hear the defense expert testify, and that the government would not have had an opportunity to conduct the kind of investigation needed to acquire rebuttal testimony on defendant's claim that he was especially susceptible to inducement. Consequently, rule 12.2(b) has been expanded to cover all of the aforementioned situations.

Note to Subdivision (c). The amendment of the first sentence of subdivision (c), recognizing that the government may seek to have defendant subjected to a mental examination by an expert other than a psychiatrist, is prompted by the same considerations discussed above. Because it is possible that the defendant will submit to examination by an expert of his own other than a psychiatrist, it is necessary to recognize that it will sometimes be appropriate for defendant to be examined by a government expert other than a psychiatrist. The last sentence of subdivision (c) has been amended to more accurately reflect the Fifth Amendment considerations at play in this context. See *Estelle v. Smith,* 451 U.S. 454 (1981), holding that self-incrimination protections are not inevitably limited to the guilt phase of a trial and that the privilege, when applicable, protects against use of defendant's statement and also the fruits thereof, including expert testimony based upon defendant's statements to the expert. Estelle also intimates that "a defendant can be required to submit to a sanity examination," and presumably some other form of mental examination, when "his silence may deprive the State of the only effective means it has of controverting his proof on an issue that he interjected into the case."

Note to Subdivision (d). The broader term "mental condition" is appropriate here in light of the above changes to subdivisions (b) and (c).

Note to Subdivision (e). New subdivision (e), generally consistent with the protection afforded in rule 12.1(f) with respect to notice of alibi, ensures that the notice required under subdivision (b) will not deprive the defendant of an opportunity later to elect not to utilize any expert testimony. This provision is consistent with *Williams v. Florida,* 399 U.S. 78 (1970), holding the privilege against self-incrimination is not violated by requiring the defendant to give notice of a defense where the defendant retains the "unfettered choice" of abandoning the defense.

Dissenting statement of Justice O'Connor to 1983 Amendment. With one minor reservation, I join the Court in its adoption of the proposed amendments. They represent the product of considerable effort by the Advisory

Committee, and they will institute desirable reforms. My sole disagreement with the Court's action today lies in its failure to recommend correction of an apparent error in the drafting of Proposed Rule 12.2(e).

As proposed, Rule 12.2(e) reads:

"Evidence of an intention as to which notice was given under subdivision (a) or (b), later withdrawn, is not admissible in any civil or criminal proceeding against the person who gave notice of the intention."

Identical language formerly appeared in Fed. Rules Crim. Proc. 11(e)(6) and Fed. Rules Evid. 410, each of which stated that.

"[Certain material] is not admissible in any civil or criminal proceeding against the defendant."

Those rules were amended, Supreme Court Order April 30, 1979, 441 U.S. 970, 987, 1007, Pub. Law 96-42, approved July 31, 1979, 93 Stat. 326. After the amendments, the relevant language read,

"[Certain material] is not, in any civil or criminal proceeding, admissible against the defendant."

As the Advisory Committee explained, this minor change was necessary to eliminate an ambiguity. Before the amendment, the word "against" could be read as referring either to the kind of proceeding in which the evidence was offered or to the purpose for which it was offered. Thus, for instance, if a person was a witness in a suit but not a party, it was unclear whether the evidence could be used to impeach him. In such a case, the *use* would be against the person, but the *proceeding* would not be against him. Similarly, if the person wished to introduce the evidence in a proceeding in which he was the defendant, the use, but not the proceeding, would be against him. To eliminate the ambiguity, the Advisory Committee proposed the amendment clarifying that the evidence was inadmissible against the person, regardless of whether the particular proceeding was against the person. See Adv. Comm. Note to Fed. Rules Crim. Proc. 11(e)(6); Adv. Comm. Note to Fed. Rules Evid. 410.

The same ambiguity inheres in the proposed version of Rule 12.2(e). We should recommend that it be eliminated now. To that extent, I respectfully dissent.

Repeal of 1984 amendments of subsecs. (b) and (d). Act Oct. 30, 1984, P. L. 98-596, § 11(b), 98 Stat. 3138, applicable on and after enactment of Act Oct. 12, 1984, P. L. 98-473, 98 Stat. 1837, on Oct. 12, 1984, as provided by § 11(c) of Act Oct. 30, 1984, repealed the amendments made to subsecs. (b) and (d) of this section by Act Oct. 12, 1984, P. L. 98-473, § 404(b) and (d); see the 1984 Amendment notes to this section.

Application of Oct. 30, 1984 amendments. Act Oct. 30, 1984, P. L. 98-596, § 11(c), 98 Stat. 3128, provides: "The amendments and repeals made by subsections (a) and (b) of this section [amending this rule and repealing amendments made by Act Oct. 12, 1984, Title II, Ch IV, § 404(b), (d), 98 Stat. 2067; see 1984 Amendment notes] shall apply on and after the enactment of the joint resolution entitled 'Joint resolution making continuing appropriations for the fiscal year 1985, and for other purposes', H.J. Res. 648, Ninety-eighth Congress [Act Oct. 12, 1984, P. L. 98-473, 98 Stat. 1837; enacted on Oct. 12, 1984].".

Notes of Advisory Committee on 1985 amendments. *Note to Subdivision (e).* This clarifying amendment is intended to serve the same purpose as a comparable change made in 1979 to similar language in Rule 11(e)(6). The change makes it clear that evidence of a withdrawn intent is thereafter inadmissible against the person who gave the notice in any civil or criminal proceeding, without regard to whether the proceeding is against that person.

Notes of Advisory Committee on 1987 amendments. The amendments are technical. No substantive change is intended.

Notes of Advisory Committee on 2002 amendments. The language of Rule 12.2 has been amended as part of the general restyling of the Criminal Rules to make them more easily understood and to make style and terminology consistent throughout the rules. These changes are intended to be stylistic only, except as noted below.

The substantive changes to Rule 12.2 are designed to address five issues. First, the amendment clarifies that a court may order a mental examination for a defendant who has indicated an intention to raise a defense of mental condition bearing on the issue of guilt. Second, the defendant is required to give notice of an intent to present expert evidence of the defendant's mental condition during a capital sentencing proceeding. Third, the amendment addresses the ability of the trial court to order a mental examination for a defendant who has given notice of an intent to present evidence of mental condition during capital sentencing proceedings and when the results of that examination may be disclosed. Fourth, the amendment addresses the timing of disclosure of the results and reports of the defendant's expert examination. Finally, the amendment extends the sanctions for failure to comply with the rule's requirements to the punishment phase of a capital case.

Under current Rule 12.2(b), a defendant who intends to offer expert testimony on the issue of his or her mental condition on the question of guilt must provide a pretrial notice of that intent. The amendment extends that notice requirement to a defendant who intends to offer expert evidence, testimonial or otherwise, on his or her mental condition during a capital sentencing proceeding. As several courts have recognized, the better practice is to require pretrial notice of that intent so that any mental examinations can be conducted without unnecessarily delaying capital sentencing proceedings. See, e.g., *United States v. Beckford*, 962 F. Supp. 748, 754–64 (E.D. Va. 1997); *United States v. Haworth*, 942 F. Supp. 1406, 1409 (D.N.M. 1996). The amendment adopts that view.

Revised Rule 12.2(c)(1) addresses and clarifies the authority of the court to order mental examinations for a defendant — to determine competency of a defendant to stand trial under 18 U.S.C. § 4241; to determine the defendant's sanity at the time of the alleged offense under 18 U.S.C. § 4242; or in those cases where the defendant intends to present expert testimony on his or her mental condition. Rule 12.2(c)(1)(A) reflects the traditional authority of the court to order competency examinations. With regard to examinations to determine insanity at the time of the offense, current Rule 12.2(c) implies that the trial court may grant a government motion for a mental examination of a defendant who has indicated under Rule 12.2(a) an intent to raise the defense of insanity. But the corresponding statute, 18 U.S.C. § 4242, requires the court to order an examination if the defendant has provided notice of an intent to raise that defense and the government moves for the examination. Revised Rule 12.2(c)(1)(B) now conforms the rule to § 4242. Any examination conducted on the issue of the insanity defense would thus be conducted in accordance with the procedures set out in that statutory provision.

Revised Rule 12.2(c)(1)(B) also addresses those cases where the defendant is not relying on an insanity defense, but intends to offer expert testimony on the issue of mental condition. While the authority of a trial court to order a mental examination of a defendant who has registered an intent to raise the insanity defense seems clear, the authority under the rule to order an examination of a defendant who intends only to present expert testimony on his or her mental condition on the issue of guilt is not as clear. Some courts have concluded that a court may order such an examination. See, e.g., *United States v. Stackpole*, 811 F.2d 689, 697 (1st Cir. 1987); *United States v. Buchbinder*, 796 F.2d 910, 915 (1st Cir. 1986); and *United States v. Halbert*, 712 F.2d 388 (9th Cir. 1983). In *United States v. Davis*, 93 F.3d 1286 (6th Cir. 1996), however, the court in a detailed analysis of the issue concluded that the district court lacked the authority under the rule to order a mental examination of a defendant who had provided notice of an intent to offer evidence on a defense of diminished capacity. The court noted first that the defendant could not be ordered to undergo commitment and examination under 18 U.S.C. § 4242, because that provision relates to situations when the defendant intends to rely on the defense of insanity. The court also rejected the argument that the examination could be ordered under Rule 12.2(c) because this was, in the words of the rule, an "appropriate case." The court concluded, however, that the trial court had the inherent authority to order such an examination.

The amendment clarifies that the authority of a court to order a mental examination under Rule 12.2(c)(1)(B) extends to those cases when the defendant has provided notice, under Rule 12.2(b), of an intent to present expert testimony on the defendant's mental condition, either on the merits or at capital sentencing. See, e.g., *United States v. Hall*, 152 F.3d 381 (5th Cir. 1998), cert. denied, 119 S. Ct. 1767 (1999).

The amendment to Rule 12.2(c)(1) is not intended to affect any statutory or inherent authority a court may have to order other mental examinations.

The amendment leaves to the court the determination of what procedures should be used for a court-ordered examination on the defendant's mental condition (apart from insanity). As currently provided in the rule, if the examination is being ordered in connection with the defendant's stated intent to present an insanity defense, the procedures are dictated by 18 U.S.C. § 4242. On the other hand, if the examination is being ordered in conjunction with a stated intent to present expert testimony on the defendant's mental condition (not amounting to a defense of insanity) either at the guilt or sentencing phases, no specific statutory counterpart is available. Accordingly, the court is given the discretion to specify the procedures to be used. In so doing, the court may certainly be informed by other provisions, which address hearings on a defendant's mental condition. See, e.g., 18 U.S.C. § 4241, et seq.

Additional changes address the question when the results of an examination ordered under Rule 12.2(b)(2) may, or must, be disclosed. The Supreme Court has recognized that use of a defendant's statements during a court-ordered examination may compromise the defendant's right against self-incrimination. See *Estelle v. Smith*, 451 U.S. 454 [68 L. Ed. 2d 359] (1981) (defendant's privilege against self-incrimination violated when he was not advised of right to remain silent during court-ordered examination and prosecution introduced statements during capital sentencing hearing). But subsequent cases have indicated that the defendant waives the privilege if the defendant introduces expert testimony on his or her mental condition. See, e.g., *Powell v. Texas*, 492 U.S. 680, 683–84 [106 L. Ed. 2d 551, 555] (1989); *Buchanan v. Kentucky*, 483 U.S. 402, 421–24 [97 L. Ed. 2d 336, 354] (1987); *Presnell v. Zant*, 959 F.2d 1524, 1533 (11th Cir. 1992); *Williams v. Lynaugh*, 809 F.2d 1063, 1068 (5th Cir. 1987); *United States v. Madrid*, 673 F.2d 1114, 1119–21 (10th Cir. 1982). That view is reflected in Rule 12.2(c), which indicates that the statements of the defendant may be used against the defendant only after the defendant has introduced testimony on his or her mental condition. What the current rule does not address is if, and to what extent, the prosecution may see the results of the examination, which may include the defendant's statements, when evidence of the defendant's mental condition is being presented solely at a capital sentencing proceeding.

The proposed change in Rule 12.2(c)(2) adopts the procedure used by some courts to seal or otherwise insulate the results of the examination until it is clear that the defendant will introduce expert evidence about his or her mental condition at a capital sentencing hearing; i.e., after a verdict of guilty on one or more capital crimes, and a reaffirmation by the defendant of an intent to introduce expert mental-condition evidence in the sentencing phase. See, e.g., *United States v. Beckford*, 962 F. Supp. 748 (E.D. Va. 1997). Most courts that have addressed the issue have recognized that if the government obtains early access to the accused's statements, it will be required to show that it has not made any derivative use of that evidence. Doing so can consume time and resources. See, e.g., *United States v. Hall*, supra, 152 F.3d at 398 (noting that sealing of record, although not constitutionally required, "likely advances interests of judicial economy by avoiding litigation over [derivative use issue]").

Except as provided in Rule 12.2(c)(3), the rule does not address the time for disclosing results and reports of any expert examination conducted by the defendant. New Rule 12.2(c)(3) provides that upon disclosure under subdivision (c)(2) of the results and reports of the government's examination, disclosure of the results and reports of the defendant's expert examination is mandatory, if the defendant intends to introduce expert evidence relating to the examination.

Rule 12.2(c), as previously written, restricted admissibility of the defendant's statements during the course of an examination conducted under the rule to an issue respecting mental condition on which the defendant "has introduced testimony" — expert or otherwise. As amended, Rule 12.2(c)(4) provides that the admissibility of such evidence in a capital sentencing proceeding is triggered only by the defendant's introduction of expert evidence. The Committee believed that, in this context, it was appropriate to limit the government's ability to use the results of its expert mental examination to instances in which the defendant has first introduced expert evidence on the issue.

Rule 12.2(d) has been amended to extend sanctions for failure to comply with the rule to the penalty phase of a capital case. The selection of an appropriate remedy for the failure of a defendant to provide notice or submit to an examination under subdivisions (b) and (c) is entrusted to the discretion of the court. While subdivision (d) recognizes that the court may exclude the evidence of the defendant's own expert in such a situation, the court should also consider "the effectiveness of less severe sanctions, the impact of preclusion on the evidence at trial and the outcome of the case, the extent of prosecutorial surprise or prejudice, and whether the violation was willful." *Taylor v. Illinois*, 484 U.S. 400, 414 n.19 [98 L. Ed. 2d 798, 814] (1988) (citing *Fendler v. Goldsmith*, 728 F.2d 1181 (9th Cir. 1983)).

Notes of Advisory Committee on 2005 amendments. The amendment to Rule 12.2(d) fills a gap created in the 2002 amendments to the rule. The substantively amended rule that took effect December 1, 2002, permits a sanction of exclusion of "any expert evidence" for failure to give notice or failure to submit to an examination, but provides no sanction for failure to disclose reports. The proposed amendment is designed to address that specific issue.

Rule 12.2(d)(1) is a slightly restructured version of current Rule 12.2(d). Rule 12.2(d)(2) is new and permits the court to exclude any expert evidence for failure to comply with the disclosure requirement in Rule 12.2(c)(3). The sanction is intended to relate only to the evidence related to the matters addressed in the report, which the defense failed to disclose. Unlike the broader sanction for the two violations listed in Rule 12.2(d)(1)—which can substantially affect the entire hearing—the Committee believed that it would be overbroad to expressly authorize exclusion of "any" expert evidence, even evidence unrelated to the results and reports that were not disclosed, as required in Rule 12.2(c)(3).

The rule assumes that the sanction of exclusion will result only where there has been a complete failure to disclose the report. If the report is disclosed, albeit in an untimely fashion, other relief may be appropriate, for example, granting a continuance to the government to review the report.

Amendments:

1975.

Act July 31, 1975, § 3(4) (effective 12/1/75, as provided by § 2 of such Act, which appears as a note to Rule 4), substituted subsec. (c) for one which read: "(c) Psychiatric examination. In an appropriate case the court may, upon motion of the attorney for the government, order the defendant to submit to a psychiatric examination by a psychiatrist designated for this purpose in the order of the court.".

1984.

Act Oct. 12, 1984 purported to amend subsec. (b) of this rule by substituting "any other mental condition bearing upon the issue of guilt" for "other condition bearing upon the issue of whether he had the mental state required for the offense charged", but such amendment was not executed because it was repealed by Act Oct. 30, 1984.

Such Act further, in subsec. (c), purported to substitute "to an examination pursuant to 18 U.S.C. 4242" for "to a psychiatric examination by a psychiatrist designated for this purpose in the order of the court", but the amendment could not be executed because such language did not appear in the text.

Such Act further, in subsec. (d), purported to substitute "guilt" for "mental state", but the amendment was not executed because it was repealed by Act Oct. 30, 1984.

Act Oct. 30, 1984, in subsec. (c) substituted "to an examination pursuant to 18 U.S.C. 4242" for "to a mental examination by a psychiatrist or other expert designated for this purpose in the order of the court"; and, in subsec. (d), substituted "guilt" for "mental condition".

1986.

Act Nov. 10, 1986, in subsec. (c), inserted "4241 or".

Rule 12.3. Notice of a Public-Authority Defense

(a) Notice of the Defense and Disclosure of Witnesses.

(1) *Notice in General.* If a defendant intends to assert a defense of actual or believed exercise of public authority on behalf of a law enforcement agency or federal intelligence agency at the time of the alleged offense, the defendant must so notify an attorney for the government in writing and must file a copy of the notice with the clerk within the time provided for filing a pretrial motion, or at any later time the court sets. The notice filed with the clerk must be under seal if the notice identifies a federal intelligence agency as the source of public authority.

(2) *Contents of Notice.* The notice must contain the following information:

(A) the law enforcement agency or federal intelligence agency involved;

(B) the agency member on whose behalf the defendant claims to have acted; and

(C) the time during which the defendant claims to have acted with public authority.

(3) *Response to the Notice.* An attorney for the government must serve a written response on the defendant or the defendant's attorney within 14 days after receiving the defendant's notice, but no later than 21 days before trial. The response must admit or deny that the defendant exercised the public authority identified in the defendant's notice.

(4) *Disclosing Witnesses.*

(A) Government's Request. An attorney for the government may request in writing that the defendant disclose the name, address, and telephone number of each witness the defendant intends to rely on to establish a public-authority defense. An attorney for the government may serve the request when the government serves its response to the defendant's notice under Rule 12.3(a)(3), or later, but must serve the request no later than 21 days before trial.

(B) Defendant's Response. Within 14 days after receiving the government's request, the defendant must serve on an attorney for the government a written statement of the name, address, and telephone number of each witness.

(C) Government's Reply. Within 14 days after receiving the defendant's statement, an attorney for the government must serve on the defendant or the defendant's attorney a written statement of the name of each witness — and the address and telephone number of each witness other than a victim — that the government intends to rely on to oppose the defendant's public-authority defense.

(D) Victim's Address and Telephone Number. If the government intends to rely on a victim's testimony to oppose the defendant's public-authority defense and the defendant establishes a need for the victim's address and telephone number, the court may:

(i) order the government to provide the information in writing to the defendant or the defendant's attorney; or

(ii) fashion a reasonable procedure that allows for preparing the defense and also protects the victim's interests.

(5) *Additional Time.* The court may, for good cause, allow a party additional time to comply with this rule.

(b) Continuing Duty to Disclose.

(1) *In General.* Both an attorney for the government and the defendant must promptly disclose in writing to the other party the name of any additional witness — and the address, and telephone number of any additional witness other than a victim — if:

(A) the disclosing party learns of the witness before or during trial; and

(B) the witness should have been disclosed under Rule 12.3(a)(4) if the disclosing party had known of the witness earlier.

(2) *Address and Telephone Number of an Additional Victim-Witness.* The address and telephone number of an additional victim-witness must not be disclosed except as provided in Rule 12.3(a)(4)(D).

(c) Failure to Comply. If a party fails to comply with this rule, the court may exclude the testimony of any undisclosed witness regarding the public-authority defense. This rule does not limit the defendant's right to testify.

(d) Protective Procedures Unaffected. This rule does not limit the court's authority to issue appropriate protective orders or to order that any filings be under seal.

(e) Inadmissibility of Withdrawn Intention. Evidence of an intention as to which notice was given under Rule 12.3(a), later withdrawn, is not, in any civil or criminal proceeding, admissible against the person who gave notice of the intention.

HISTORY:

Added Nov. 18, 1988, P. L. 100-690, Title VI, Subtitle N, § 6483, 102 Stat. 4382; amended April 29, 2002, eff. Dec. 1, 2002; March 26, 2009, eff. Dec. 1, 2009; April 28, 2010, eff. Dec. 1, 2010.

HISTORY; ANCILLARY LAWS AND DIRECTIVES

Other provisions:

Notes of Advisory Committee on 2002 amendments. The language of Rule 12.3 has been amended as part of the general restyling of the Criminal Rules to make them more easily understood and to make style and terminology consistent throughout the rules. These changes are intended to be stylistic only, except as noted below.

Substantive changes have been made in Rule 12.3(a)(4) and 12.3(b). As in Rule 12.1, the Committee decided to include in the restyled rule the requirement that the parties provide the telephone numbers of any witnesses disclosed under the rule.

Notes of Advisory Committee on 2009 amendments. The times set in the former rule at 7, 10, or 20 days have been revised to 14 or 21 days. See the Committee Note to Rule 45(a).

Notes of Advisory Committee on 2010 amendments. *Note to Subdivisions (a) and (b).* The amendment implements the Crime Victims' Rights Act, which states that victims have the right to be reasonably protected from the accused, and to be treated with respect for the victim's dignity and privacy. *See* 18 U.S.C. § 3771(a)(1) & (8). The rule provides that a victim's address and telephone number should not automatically be provided to the defense when a public-authority defense is raised. If a defendant establishes a need for this information, the court has discretion to order its disclosure or to fashion an alternative procedure that provides the defendant with the information necessary to prepare a defense, but also protects the victim's interests. In the case of victims who will testify concerning a public-authority claim, the same procedures and standards apply to both the prosecutor's initial disclosure and the prosecutor's continuing duty to disclose under subdivision (b).

Rule 12.4. Disclosure Statement

(a) Who Must File.

(1) *Nongovernmental Corporate Party.* Any nongovernmental corporate party to a proceeding in a district court must file a statement that identifies any parent corporation and any publicly held corporation that owns 10% or more of its stock or states that there is no such corporation.

(2) *Organizational Victim.* Unless the government shows good cause, it must file a statement identifying any organizational victim of the alleged criminal activity. If the organizational victim is a corporation, the statement must also disclose the information required by Rule 12.4(a)(1) to the extent it can be obtained through due diligence.

(b) Time to File; Later Filing. A party must:

(1) file the Rule 12.4(a) statement within 28 days after the defendant's initial appearance; and

(2) promptly file a later statement if any required information changes.

HISTORY:

Added April 29, 2002, eff. Dec. 1, 2002; amended Apr. 26, 2018, eff. Dec. 1, 2018.

HISTORY; ANCILLARY LAWS AND DIRECTIVES

Other provisions:

Notes of Advisory Committee on 2002 amendments. Rule 12.4 is a new rule modeled after Federal Rule of Appellate Procedure 26.1 and parallels similar provisions being proposed in new Federal Rule of Civil Procedure 7.1. The purpose of the rule is to assist judges in determining whether they must recuse themselves because of a "financial interest in the subject matter in controversy." Code of Judicial Conduct, Canon 3C(1)(c)(1972). It does not, however, deal with other circumstances that might lead to disqualification for other reasons.

Under Rule 12.4(a)(1), any nongovernmental corporate party must file a statement that indicates whether it has any parent corporation that owns 10% or more of its stock or indicates that there is no such corporation. Although the term "nongovernmental corporate party" will almost always involve organizational defendants, it might also cover any third party that asserts an interest in property to be forfeited under new Rule 32.2.

Rule 12.4(a)(2) requires an attorney for the government to file a statement that lists any organizational victims of the alleged criminal activity; the purpose of this disclosure is to alert the court to the fact that a possible ground for disqualification might exist. Further, if the organizational victim is a corporation, the statement must include the same information required of any nongovernmental corporate party. The rule requires an attorney for the government to use due diligence in obtaining that information from a corporate organizational victim, recognizing that the timing requirements of Rule 12.4(b) might make it difficult to obtain the necessary information by the time the initial appearance is conducted.

Although the disclosures required by Rule 12.4 may seem limited, they are calculated to reach the majority of circumstances that are likely to call for disqualification on the basis of information that a judge may not know or recollect. Framing a rule that calls for more detailed disclosure is problematic and will inevitably require more information than is necessary for purposes of automatic recusal. Unnecessary disclosure of volumes of information may create the risk that a judge will overlook the one bit of information that might require disqualification, and may also create the risk that courts will experience unnecessary disqualifications rather than attempt to unravel a potentially difficult question.

The same concerns about overbreadth are potentially present in any local rules that might address this topic. Rule 12.4 does not address the promulgation of any local rules that might address the same issue, or supplement the requirements of the rule.

The rule does not cover disclosure of all financial information that could be relevant to a judge's decision whether to recuse himself or herself from a case. The Committee believes that with the various disclosure practices in the federal courts and with the development of technology, more comprehensive disclosure may be desirable and feasible.

Rule 12.4(b)(1) indicates that the time for filing the disclosure statement is at the point when the defendant enters an initial appearance under Rule 5. Although there may be other instances where an earlier appearance of a party in a civil proceeding would raise concerns about whether the presiding judicial officer should be notified of a possible grounds for recusal, the Committee believed that in criminal cases, the most likely time for that to occur is at the initial appearance and that it was important to set a uniform triggering event for disclosures under this rule.

Finally, Rule 12.4(b)(2) requires the parties to file supplemental statements with the court if there are any changes in the information required in the statement.

Notes of Advisory Committee on 2018 Amendments. *Subdivision (a).* Rule 12.4 requires the government to identify organizational victims to assist judges in complying with their obligations under the Code of Conduct for United States Judges. The 2009 amendments to Canon 3(C)(1)(c) of the Code require recusal only when a judge has an "interest that could be affected substantially by the outcome of the proceeding." In some cases, there are numerous organizational victims, but the impact of the crime on each is relatively small. In such cases, the amendment allows the government to show good cause to be relieved of making the disclosure statements because the organizations' interests could not be "affected substantially by the outcome of the proceedings."

Subdivision (b). The amendment specifies that the time for making the disclosures is within 28 days after the initial appearance.

Because a filing made after the 28-day period may disclose organizational victims in cases in which none were previously known or disclosed, the caption and text have been revised to refer to a later, rather than a supplemental, filing. The text was also revised to be more concise and to parallel Civil Rule 7.1(b)(2).

Rule 13. Joint Trial of Separate Cases

The court may order that separate cases be tried together as though brought in a single indictment or information if all offenses and all defendants could have been joined in a single indictment or information.

HISTORY:

As amended April 29, 2002, eff. Dec. 1, 2002.

HISTORY; ANCILLARY LAWS AND DIRECTIVES

Other provisions:

Notes of Advisory Committee. This rule is substantially a restatement of existing law, 18 U.S.C. [former] § 557 (Indictments and presentments; joinder of charges); *Logan v United States,* 144 U.S. 263, 296, 12 S. Ct. 617, 36 L. Ed. 429; *Showalter v United States,* 260 F. 719 (C.C.A. 4th), cert. den., 250 U.S. 672, 40 S. Ct. 14, 63 L. Ed. 1200; *Hostetter v United States,* 16 F2d 921 (C.C.A. 8th); *Capone v United States,* 51 F.2d 609, 619–620 (C.C.A. 7th).

Notes of Advisory Committee on 2002 amendments. The language of Rule 13 has been amended as part of the general restyling of the Criminal Rules to make them more easily understood and to make style and terminology consistent throughout the rules. These changes are intended to be stylistic only.

Rule 14. Relief from Prejudicial Joinder

(a) Relief. If the joinder of offenses or defendants in an indictment, an information, or a consolidation for trial appears to prejudice a defendant or the government, the court may order separate trials of counts, sever the defendants' trials, or provide any other relief that justice requires.

(b) Defendant's Statements. Before ruling on a defendant's motion to sever, the court may order an attorney for the government to deliver to the court for in camera inspection any defendant's statement that the government intends to use as evidence.

HISTORY:

Amended Feb. 28, 1966, eff. July 1, 1966; April 29, 2002, eff. Dec. 1, 2002.

HISTORY; ANCILLARY LAWS AND DIRECTIVES

Other provisions:

Notes of Advisory Committee on Rules. This rule is a restatement of existing law under which severance and other similar relief is entirely in the discretion of the court, 18 U.S.C. [former] § 557 (Indictments and presentments; joinder of charges); *Pointer v. United States,* 151 U.S. 396, 14 S.Ct. 410, 38 L.Ed. 208; *Pierce v. United States,* 160 U.S. 355, 16 S.Ct. 321, 40 L.Ed. 454; *United States v. Ball,* 163 U.S. 662, 673, 16 S.Ct. 1192, 41 L.Ed. 300; *Stilson v. United States,* 250 U.S. 583, 40 S.Ct. 28, 63 L.Ed. 1154.

Notes of Advisory Committee on 1966 amendments.A defendant may be prejudiced by the admission in evidence against a co-defendant of a statement or confession made by that co-defendant. This prejudice cannot be dispelled by cross-examination if the co-defendant does not take the stand. Limiting instructions to the jury may not in fact erase the prejudice. While the question whether to grant a severance is generally left within the discretion of the trial court, recent Fifth Circuit cases have found sufficient prejudice involved to make denial of a motion for severance reversible error. See *Schaffer v. United States,* 221 F.2d 17 (5th Cir. 1955); *Barton v. United States,* 263 F.2d 894 (5th Cir. 1959). It has even been suggested that when the confession of the co-defendant comes as a surprise at the trial, it may be error to deny a motion for a mistrial. See *Belvin v. United States,* 273 F.2d 583 (5th Cir. 1960).

The purpose of the amendment is to provide a procedure whereby the issue of possible prejudice can be resolved on the motion for severance. The judge may direct the disclosure of the confessions or statements of the defendants to him for in camera inspection as an aid to determining whether the possible prejudice justifies ordering separate trials. Cf. note, Joint and Single Trials Under Rules 8 and 14 of the Federal Rules of Criminal Procedure, 74 Yale L.J. 551, 565 (1965).

Notes of Advisory Committee on 2002 amendments. The language of Rule 14 has been amended as part of the general restyling of the Criminal Rules to make them more easily understood and to make style and terminology consistent throughout the rules. These changes are intended to be stylistic only.

The reference to a defendant's "confession" in the last sentence of the current rule has been deleted. The Committee believed that the reference to the "defendant's statements" in the amended rule would fairly embrace any confessions or admissions by a defendant.

Rule 15. Depositions

(a) When taken.

(1) *In General.* A party may move that a prospective witness be deposed in order to preserve testimony for trial. The court may grant the motion because of exceptional circumstances and in the interest of justice. If the court orders the deposition to be taken, it may also require the deponent to produce at the deposition any designated material that is not privileged, including any book, paper, document, record, recording, or data.

(2) *Detained Material Witness.* A witness who is detained under 18 U.S.C. § 3144 may request to be deposed by filing a written motion and giving notice to the parties. The court may then order that the deposition be taken and may discharge the witness after the witness has signed under oath the deposition transcript.

(b) Notice.

(1) *In General.* A party seeking to take a deposition must give every other party reasonable written notice of the deposition's date and location. The notice must state the name and address of each deponent. If requested by a party receiving the notice, the court may, for good cause, change the deposition's date or location.

(2) *To the Custodial Officer.* A party seeking to take the deposition must also notify the officer who has custody of the defendant of the scheduled date and location.

(c) Defendant's presence.

(1) *Defendant in custody.* Except as authorized by Rule 15(c)(3), the officer who has custody of the defendant must produce the defendant at the deposition and keep the defendant in the witness's presence during the examination, unless the defendant:

(A) waives in writing the right to be present; or

(B) persists in disruptive conduct justifying exclusion after being warned by the court that disruptive conduct will result in the defendant's exclusion.

(2) *Defendant Not in Custody.* Except as authorized by Rule 15(c)(3), a defendant who is not in custody has the right upon request to be present at the deposition, subject to any conditions imposed by the court. If the government tenders the defendant's expenses as provided in Rule 15(d) but the defendant still fails to appear, the defendant—absent good cause—waives both the right to appear and any objection to the taking and use of the deposition based on that right.

(3) *Taking Depositions Outside the United States Without the Defendant's Presence.* The deposition of a witness who is outside the United States may be taken without the defendant's presence if the court makes case-specific findings of all the following:

(A) the witness's testimony could provide substantial proof of a material fact in a felony prosecution;

(B) there is a substantial likelihood that the witness's attendance at trial cannot be obtained;

(C) the witness's presence for a deposition in the United States cannot be obtained;

(D) the defendant cannot be present because:

(i) the country where the witness is located will not permit the defendant to attend the deposition;

(ii) for an in-custody defendant, secure transportation and continuing custody cannot be assured at the witness's location; or

(iii) for an out-of-custody defendant, no reasonable conditions will assure an appearance at the deposition or at trial or sentencing; and

(E) the defendant can meaningfully participate in the deposition through reasonable means.

(d) Expenses. If the deposition was requested by the government, the court may—or if the defendant is unable to bear the deposition expenses, the court must—order the government to pay:

(1) any reasonable travel and subsistence expenses of the defendant and the defendant's attorney to attend the deposition; and

(2) the costs of the deposition transcript.

(e) Manner of Taking. Unless these rules or a court order provides otherwise, a deposition must be taken and filed in the same manner as a deposition in a civil action, except that:

(1) A defendant may not be deposed without that defendant's consent.

(2) The scope and manner of the deposition examination and cross-examination must be the same as would be allowed during trial.

(3) The government must provide to the defendant or the defendant's attorney, for use at the deposition, any statement of the deponent in the government's possession to which the defendant would be entitled at trial.

(f) Admissibility and Use as Evidence. An order authorizing a deposition to be taken under this rule does not determine its admissibility. A party may use all or part of a deposition as provided by the Federal Rules of Evidence.

(g) Objections. A party objecting to deposition testimony or evidence must state the grounds for the objection during the deposition.

(h) Depositions by Agreement Permitted. The parties may by agreement take and use a deposition with the court's consent.

HISTORY:

Amended April 22, 1974, eff. Dec. 1, 1975; July 31, 1975, P. L. 94-64, §§ 2, 3(15)–(19), 89 Stat. 370, 373; Oct. 12, 1984, P. L. 98-473, Title II, Ch I, § 209(b), 98 Stat. 1986; Mar. 9, 1987, eff. Aug. 1, 1987; April 29, 2002, eff. Dec. 1, 2002; April 23, 2012, eff. Dec. 1, 2012.

HISTORY; ANCILLARY LAWS AND DIRECTIVES

Other provisions:

Notes of Advisory Committee on Rules. *Note to Subdivision (a).* 1. This rule continues the existing law permitting defendants to take depositions in certain limited classes of cases under *dedimus potestatem* and *in perpetuam rei memoriam,* 28 U.S.C. [former] § 644. This statute has been generally held applicable to criminal cases, *Clymer v. United States,* 38 F.2d 581 (C.C.A. 10th); *Wong Yim v. United States,* 118 F.2d 667 (C.C.A. 9th), cert. den. 313 U.S. 589, 61 S.Ct. 1112, 85 L.Ed. 1544; *United States v. Cameron,* 15 F. 794 (C.C.E.D.Mo.); *United States v. Hofmann,* 24 F.Supp. 847 (S.D.N.Y.). Contra, *Luxemberg v. United States,* 45 F.2d 497 (C.C.A. 4th), cert. den. 283 U.S. 820, 51 S.Ct. 345, 75 L.Ed. 1436. The rule continues the limitation of the statute that the taking of depositions is to be restricted to cases in which they are necessary "in order to prevent a failure of justice."

2. Unlike the practice in civil cases in which depositions may be taken as a matter of right by notice without permission of the court (Rules 26(a) and 30, Federal Rules of Civil Procedure [28 U.S.C., Appendix]), this rule permits depositions to be taken only by order of the court, made in the exercise of discretion and on notice to all parties. It was contemplated that in criminal cases depositions would be used only in exceptional situations, as has been the practice heretofore.

3. This rule introduces a new feature in authorizing the taking of the deposition of a witness committed for failure to give bail (see Rule 46(b)). This matter is, however, left to the discretion of the court. The purpose of the rule is to afford a method of relief for such a witness, if the court finds it proper to extend it.

Note to Subdivision (b). This subdivision, as well as subdivisions (d) and (f), sets forth the procedure to be followed in the event that the court grants an order for the taking of a deposition. The procedure prescribed is similar to that in civil cases, Rules 28– 31, Federal Rules of Civil Procedure [28 U.S.C., Appendix].

Note to Subdivision (c). This rule introduces a new feature for the purpose of protecting the rights of an indigent defendant.

Note to Subdivision (d). See *Note to Subdivision (b), supra.*

Note to Subdivision (e). In providing when and for what purpose a deposition may be used at the trial, this rule generally follows the corresponding provisions of the Federal Rules of Civil Procedure, Rule 26(d)(3) [28 U.S.C., Appendix]. The only difference is that in civil cases a deposition may be introduced at the trial if the witness is at a greater distance than 100 miles from the place of trial, while this rule requires that the witness be out of the United States. The distinction results from the fact that a subpoena in a civil case runs only within the district where issued or 100 miles from the place of trial (Rule 45(e)(1), Federal Rules of Civil Procedure, 28 U.S.C., Appendix), while a subpoena in a criminal case runs throughout the United States (see Rule 17(e)(1), *infra*).

Note to Subdivision (f). See *Note to Subdivision (b), supra.*

Notes of Advisory Committee on 1974 amendments. Rule 15 authorizes the taking of depositions by the government. Under former rule 15 only a defendant was authorized to take a deposition.

The revision is similar to Title VI of the Organized Crime Control Act of 1970. The principal difference is that Title VI (18 U.S.C. § 3503) limits the authority of the government to take depositions to cases in which the Attorney General certifies that the "proceeding is against a person who is believed to have participated in an organized criminal activity." This limitation is not contained in rule 15.

Dealing with the issue of government depositions so soon after the enactment of 18 U.S.C. § 3503 is not inconsistent with the congressional purpose. On the floor of the House, Congressman Poff, a principal spokesman for the proposal, said that the House version was not designed to "limit the Judicial Conference of the United States in the exercise of its rule-making authority . . . from addressing itself to other problems in this area or from adopting a broader approach." 116 Cong.Rec. 35293 (1970).

The recently enacted Title VI of the Organized Crime Control Act of 1970 (18 U.S.C. § 3503) is based upon earlier efforts of the Advisory Committee on Criminal Rules which has over the past twenty-five years submitted several proposals authorizing government depositions.

The earlier drafts of the Federal Rules of Criminal Procedure proposed that the government be allowed to take depositions. Orfield, The Federal Rules of Criminal Procedure, 33 Calif.L.Rev. 543, 559 (1945). The Fifth Draft of what became rule 15 (then rule 20) dated June 1942, was submitted to the Supreme Court for comment. The court had a number of unfavorable comments about allowing government depositions. These comments were not published. The only reference to the fact that the court made comments is in 2 Orfield, Criminal Procedure under the Federal Rules § 15:1 (1966); and Orfield, Depositions in Federal Criminal Procedure, 9 S.C.L.Q. 376, 380–381 (1957).

The Advisory Committee, in the 1940's, continued to recommend the adoption of a provision authorizing government depositions. The final draft submitted to the Supreme Court contained a section providing:

The following additional requirements shall apply if the deposition is taken at the instance of the government or of a witness. The officer having custody of a defendant shall be notified of the time and place set for examination, and shall produce him at the examination and keep him in the presence of the witness during the examination. A defendant not in custody shall be given notice and shall have the right to be present at the examination. The government shall pay in advance to the defendant's attorney and a defendant not in custody expenses of travel and subsistence for attendance at the examination.

See 2 Orfield, Criminal Procedure under the Federal Rules § 15:3, pp. 447–448 (1966); Orfield, Depositions in Federal Criminal Procedure, 9 S.C.L.Q. 376, 383 (1957).

The Supreme Court rejected this section in this entirety, thus eliminating the provision for depositions by the government. These changes were made without comment.

The proposal to allow government depositions was renewed in the amendments to the Federal Rules of Criminal Procedure in the early 1960's. The Preliminary Draft of Proposed Amendments to Rules of Criminal Procedure for the United States District Courts (December 1962) proposed to amend rule 15 by eliminating the words "of a defendant" from the first sentence of subdivision (a) and adding a subdivision (g) which was practically identical to the subdivision rejected by the Supreme Court in the original draft of the rules.

The Second Preliminary Draft of Proposed Amendments to Rules of Criminal Procedure for the United States District Courts (March 1964) continued to propose allowing governments depositions. Subdivision (g) was substantially modified, however.

The following additional requirements shall apply if the deposition is taken at the instance of the government or a witness. Both the defendant and his attorney shall be given reasonable advance notice of the time and place set for the examination. The officer having custody of a defendant shall be notified of the time and place set for the examination, and shall produce him at the examination and keep him in the presence of the witness during the examination. A defendant not in custody shall have the right to be present at the examination but his failure to appear after notice and tender of expenses shall constitute a waiver of that right. The government shall pay to the defendant's attorney and to a defendant not in custody expenses of travel and subsistence for attendance at the examination. The government shall make available to the defendant for his examination and use at the taking of the deposition any statement of the witness being deposed which is in the possession of the government and which the government would be required to make available to the defendant if the witness were testifying at the trial.

The proposal to authorize government depositions was rejected by the Standing Committee on Rules of Practice and Procedure, C. Wright, Federal Practice and Procedure § 241 at 477 (1969). 4 Barron, Federal Practice and Procedure (Supp. 1967). The Report of the Judicial Conference, submitted to the Supreme Court for approval late in 1965, contained no proposal for an amendment to rule 15. See 39 F.R.D. 69, 168–211 (1966).

When the Organized Crime Control Act of 1970 was originally introduced in the Senate (S. 30) it contained a government deposition provision which was similar to the 1964 proposal of the Criminal Rules Advisory Committee, except that the original bill (S. 30) failed to provide standards to control the use of depositions at the trial. For an explanation and defense of the original proposal see McClellan, The Organized Crime Act (S. 30) or Its Critics: Which Threatens Civil Liberties?, 46 Notre Dame Lawyer 55, 100–108 (1970). This omission was remedied, prior to passage, with the addition of what is now 18 U.S.C. § 3503(f) which prescribes the circumstances in which a deposition can be used. The standards are the same as those in former rule 15(e) with the addition of language allowing the use of the deposition when "the witness refuses in the trial or hearing to testify concerning the subject of the deposition or the part offered."

Before the Organized Crime Control Act of 1970 was enacted an additional amendment was added providing that the right of the government to take a deposition is limited to cases in which the Attorney General certifies that the defendant is "believed to have participated in an organized criminal activity" [18 U.S.C. § 3503(a)]. The argument in favor of the amendment was that the whole purpose of the act was to deal with organized crime and therefore its provisions, including that providing for government depositions, should be limited to organized crime type cases.

There is another aspect of Advisory Committee history which is relevant. In January 1970, the Advisory Committee circulated proposed changes in rule 16, one of which gives the government, when it has disclosed the identity of its witnesses, the right to take a deposition and use it "in the event the witness has become unavailable without the fault of the government or if the witness has changed his testimony." [See Preliminary Draft of Proposed Amendments to the Federal Rules of Criminal Procedure for the United States District Courts, rule 16(a)(1)(vi) (January 1970).] This provision is now incorporated within rule 16(a)(1)(v).

Because neither the court nor the standing committee gave reasons for rejecting the government deposition proposal, it is not possible to know why they were not approved. To the extent that the rejection was based upon doubts as to the constitutionality of such a proposal, those doubts now seem resolved by *California v. Green,* 399 U.S. 149, 90 S.Ct. 1930, 26 L.Ed.2d 489 (1970).

On the merits, the proposal to allow the government to take depositions is consistent with the revision of rule 16 and with section 804(b)(1) of the Rules of Evidence for the United States Courts and Magistrates (November 1971) which provides that the following is not excluded by the hearsay rule if the declarant is unavailable:

(1) Former Testimony. Testimony given as a witness at another hearing of the same or a different proceeding, or in a deposition taken in compliance with law in the course of another proceeding, at the instance of or against a party with an opportunity to develop the testimony by direct, cross, or redirect examination, with motive and interest similar to those of the party against whom now offered.

Subdivision (a) is revised to provide that the government as well as the defendant is entitled to take a deposition. The phrase "whenever due to special circumstances of the case it is in the interest of justice," is intended to make clear that the decision by the court as to whether to order the taking of a deposition shall be made in the context of the circumstances of the particular case. The principal objective is the preservation of evidence for use at trial. It is not to provide a method of pretrial discovery nor primarily for the purpose of obtaining a basis for later cross-examination of an adverse witness. Discovery is a matter dealt with in rule 16. An obviously important factor is whether a deposition will expedite, rather than delay, the administration of criminal justice. Also important is the presence or absence of factors which determine the use of a deposition at the trial, such as the agreement of the parties to use of the deposition; the possible unavailability of the witness; or the possibility that coercion may be used upon the witness to induce him to change his testimony or not to testify. See rule 16(a)(1)(v).

Subdivision (a) also makes explicit that only the "testimony of a prospective witness of a party" can be taken. This means the party's own witness and does not authorize a discovery deposition of an adverse witness. The language "for use at trial" is intended to give further emphasis to the importance of the criteria for use specified in subdivision (e).

In subdivision (b) reference is made to the defendant in custody. If he is in state custody, a writ of habeas corpus ad testificandum (to produce the prisoner for purposes of testimony) may be required to accomplish his presence.

In subdivision (d) the language "except as otherwise provided in these rules" is meant to make clear that the subpoena provisions of rule 17 control rather than the provisions of the civil rules.

The use of the phrase "and manner" in subdivision (d)(2) is intended to emphasize that the authorization is not to conduct an adverse examination of an opposing witness.

In subdivision (e) the phrase "as substantive evidence" is added to make clear that the deposition can be used as evidence in chief as well as for purposes of impeachment.

Subdivision (e) also makes clear that the deposition can be used as affirmative evidence whenever the witness is available but gives testimony inconsistent with that given in the deposition. A California statute which contained a similar provision was held constitutional in *California v. Green,* 399 U.S. 149, 90 S.Ct. 1930, 26 L.Ed.2d 489 (1970). This is also consistent with section 801(d)(1) of the Rules of Evidence for United States Courts and Magistrates (Nov. 1971).

Subdivision (f) is intended to insure that a record of objections and the grounds for the objections is made at the time the deposition is taken when the witness is available so that the witness can be examined further, if necessary, on the point of the objection so that there will be an adequate record for the court's later ruling upon the objection.

Subdivision (g) uses the "unavailability" definition of the Rules of Evidence for the United States Courts and Magistrates, 804(a)(Nov. 1971).

Subdivision (h) is intended to make clear that the court always has authority to order the taking of a deposition, or to allow the use of a deposition, where there is an agreement of the parties to the taking or to the use.

Notes of Committee on the Judiciary on 1975 amendments (House Report No. 94-247). A. Amendments Proposed by the Supreme Court. Rule 15 of the Federal Rules of Criminal Procedure provides for the taking of depositions. The present rule permits only the defendant to move that a deposition of a prospective witness be taken. The court may grant the motion if it appears that (a) the prospective witness will be unable to attend or be prevented from attending the trial, (b) the prospective witness' testimony is material, and (c) the prospective witness' testimony is necessary to prevent a failure of justice.

The Supreme Court promulgated several amendments to Rule 15. The more significant amendments are described below.

Subdivision (a) as proposed to be amended permits either party to move the court for the taking of a deposition of a witness. However, a party may only move to take the deposition of one of its own witnesses, not one of the adversary party's witnesses.

Subdivision (c) as proposed to be amended provides that whenever a deposition is taken at the instance of the government or of an indigent defendant, the expenses of the taking of the deposition must be paid by the government.

Subdivision (e) as proposed to be amended provides that part or all of the deposition may be used at trial as substantive evidence if the witness is "unavailable" or if the witness gives testimony inconsistent with his deposition.

Subdivision (b)[g] as proposed to be amended defines "unavailable." "Unavailable" as a witness includes situations in which the deponent:

(1) is exempted by ruling of the judge on the ground of privilege from testifying concerning the subject matter of his deposition; or.

(2) persists in refusing to testify concerning the subject matter of his deposition despite an order of the judge to do so; or.

(3) testifies to a lack of memory of the subject matter of his deposition; or.

(4) is unable to be present or to testify at the hearing because of death or then existing physical or mental illness or infirmity; or.

(5) is absent from the hearing and the proponent of his deposition has been unable to procure his attendance by process or other reasonable means. A deponent is not unavailable as a witness if his exemption, refusal, claim of lack of memory, inability, or absence is due to the procurement or wrongdoing of the proponent of his deposition for the purpose of preventing the witness from attending or testifying.

B. Committee Action. The Committee narrowed the definition of "unavailability" in subdivision (g). The Committee deleted language from that subdivision that provided that a witness was "unavailable" if the court exempts him from testifying at the trial on the ground of privilege. The Committee does not want to encourage the use of depositions at trial, especially in view of the importance of having live testimony from a witness on the witness stand.

The Committee added a provision to subdivision (b) to parallel the provision of Rule 43(b)(2). This is to make it clear that a disruptive defendant may be removed from the place where a deposition is being taken.

The Committee added language to subdivision (c) to make clear that the government must pay for the cost of the transcript of a deposition when the deposition is taken at the instance of an indigent defendant or of the government. In order to use a deposition at trial, it must be transcribed. The proposed rule did not explicitly provide for payment of the cost of transcribing, and the Committee change rectifies this.

The Committee notes that subdivision (e) permits the use of a deposition when the witness "gives testimony at the trial or hearing inconsistent with his deposition." Since subdivision (e) refers to the rules of evidence, the Committee understands that the Federal Rules of Evidence will govern the admissibility and use of the deposition. The Committee, by adopting subdivision (e) as proposed to be amended by the Supreme Court, intends the Federal Rules of Evidence to govern the admissibility and use of the deposition.

The Committee believes that Rule 15 will not encourage trials by deposition. A deposition may be taken only in "exceptional circumstances" when "it is in the interest of justice that the testimony of a prospective witness of a party be taken and preserved. . . ." A deposition, once it is taken, is not automatically admissible at trial, however. It may only be used at trial if the witness is unavailable, and the rule narrowly defines unavailability. The procedure established in Rule 15 is similar to the procedure established by the Organized Crime Control Act of 1970 for the taking and use of depositions in organized crime cases. See 18 U.S.C. 3503.

Notes of Conference Committee on 1975 amendments (House Report No. 94-414). Rule 15 deals with the taking of depositions and the use of depositions at trial. Rule 15(e) permits a deposition to be used if the witness is unavailable. Rule 15(g) defines that term.

The Supreme Court's proposal defines five circumstances in which the witness will be considered unavailable. The House version of the bill deletes a provision that said a witness is unavailable if he is exempted at trial, on the ground of privilege, from testifying about the subject matter of his deposition. The Senate version of the bill by cross reference to the Federal Rules of Evidence, restores the Supreme Court proposal.

The Conference adopts the Senate provision.

Notes of Advisory Committee on 1987 amendments. The amendments are technical. No substantive change is intended.

Notes of Advisory Committee on 2002 amendments. The language of Rule 15 has been amended as part of the general restyling of the Criminal Rules to make them more easily understood and to make style and terminology consistent throughout the rules. These changes are intended to be stylistic only, except as noted below.

In Rule 15(a), the list of materials to be produced has been amended to include the expansive term "data" to reflect the fact that in an increasingly technological culture, the information may exist in a format not already covered by the more conventional list, such as a book or document.

The last portion of current Rule 15(b), dealing with the defendant's presence at a deposition, has been moved to amended Rule 15(c).

Revised Rule 15(d) addresses the payment of expenses incurred by the defendant and the defendant's attorney. Under the current rule, if the government requests the deposition, or if the defendant requests the deposition and is unable to pay for it, the court may direct the government to pay for travel and subsistence expenses for both the defendant and the defendant's attorney. In either case, the current rule requires the government to pay for the transcript. Under the amended rule, if the government requested the deposition, the court must require the government to pay reasonable subsistence and travel expenses and the cost of the deposition transcript. If the defendant is unable to pay the deposition expenses, the court must order the government to pay reasonable subsistence and travel expenses and the deposition transcript costs—regardless of who requested the deposition. Although the current rule places no apparent limits on the amount of funds that should be reimbursed, the Committee believed that insertion of the word "reasonable" was consistent with current practice.

Rule 15(f) is intended to more clearly reflect that the admissibility of any deposition taken under the rule is governed not by the rule itself, but instead by the Federal Rules of Evidence.

Notes of Advisory Committee on 2012 amendments. *Note to Subdivision (c)(3) and (f).* This amendment provides a mechanism for taking depositions in cases in which important witnesses—government and defense witnesses both—live in, or have fled to, countries where they cannot be reached by the court's subpoena power. Although Rule 15 authorizes depositions of witnesses in certain circumstances, the rule to date has not addressed instances where an important witness is not in the United States, there is a substantial likelihood the witness's attendance at trial cannot be obtained, and it would not be possible to securely transport the defendant or a codefendant to the witness's location for a deposition.

While a party invokes Rule 15 in order to preserve testimony for trial, the rule does not determine whether the resulting deposition will be admissible, in whole or in part. Subdivision (f) provides that in the case of all depositions, questions of admissibility of the evidence obtained are left to the courts to resolve on a case by case basis. Under Rule 15(f), the courts make this determination applying the Federal Rules of Evidence, which state that relevant evidence is admissible except as otherwise provided by the Constitution, statutes, the Rules of Evidence, and other rules prescribed by the Supreme Court. Fed. R. Evid. 402.

Rule 15(c) as amended imposes significant procedural limitations on taking certain depositions in criminal cases. The amended rule authorizes a deposition outside a defendant's physical presence only in very limited circumstances after the trial court makes case-specific findings. Amended Rule 15(c)(3) delineates these circumstances and the specific findings a trial court must make before permitting parties to depose a witness outside the defendant's presence. The party requesting the deposition shoulders the burden of proof—by a preponderance of the evidence—on the elements that must be shown. The amended rule recognizes the important witness confrontation principles and vital law enforcement and other public interests that are involved.

This amendment does not supersede the relevant provisions of 18 U.S.C. § 3509, authorizing depositions outside the defendant's physical presence in certain cases involving child victims and witnesses, or any other provision of law.

Amendments:

1975.

Act July 31, 1975, § 3(15)–(19) (effective 12/1/75, as provided by § 2 of such Act, which appears as a note to Rule

4), in subsec. (a), substituted "exceptional" for "special"; in subsec. (b), added ", unless, after being warned by the court that disruptive conduct will cause him to be removed from the place of the taking of the deposition, he persists in conduct which is such as to justify his being excluded from that place"; in subsec. (c), substituted "bear the expenses" for "bear the expense", substituted "that the expense" for "that the expenses", and added "and the cost of the transcript of the deposition"; in subsec. (e), substituted "as unavailability is defined in Rule 804(a) of the Federal Rules of Evidence" for "as defined in subsec. (g) of this rule"; deleted a subsec. (g) which read:

"(g) Unavailability. 'Unavailable' as a witness includes situations in which the deponent:

"(1) is exempted by ruling of the judge on the ground of privilege from testifying concerning the subject matter of his deposition; or.

"(2) persists in refusing to testify concerning the subject matter of his deposition despite an order of the judge to do so; or.

"(3) testifies to a lack of memory of the subject matter of his deposition; or.

"(4) is unable to be present or to testify at the hearing because of death or then existing physical or mental illness or infirmity; or.

"(5) is absent from the hearing and the proponent of his deposition has been unable to procure his attendance by process or other reasonable means. A deponent is not unavailable as a witness if his exemption, refusal, claim or lack of memory, inability, or absence is due to the procurement or wrongdoing of the proponent of his deposition for the purpose of preventing the witness from attending or testifying.";

and redesignated former subsec. (h) as subsec. (g).

1984.

Act Oct. 12, 1984, substituted "detained pursuant to section 3144 of title 18, United States Code" for "committed for failure to give bail to appear to testify at a trial or hearing".

Rule 16. Discovery and Inspection

(a) Government's Disclosure.

(1) *Information Subject to Disclosure.*

(A) Defendant's Oral Statement. Upon a defendant's request, the government must disclose to the defendant the substance of any relevant oral statement made by the defendant, before or after arrest, in response to interrogation by a person the defendant knew was a government agent if the government intends to use the statement at trial.

(B) Defendant's Written or Recorded Statement. Upon a defendant's request, the government must disclose to the defendant, and make available for inspection, copying, or photographing, all of the following:

(i) any relevant written or recorded statement by the defendant if:

• the statement is within the government's possession, custody, or control; and

• the attorney for the government knows—or through due diligence could know—that the statement exists;

(ii) the portion of any written record containing the substance of any relevant oral statement made before or after arrest if the defendant made the statement in response to interrogation by a person the defendant knew was a government agent; and

(iii) the defendant's recorded testimony before a grand jury relating to the charged offense.

(C) Organizational Defendant. Upon a defendant's request, if the defendant is an organization, the government must disclose to the defendant any statement described in Rule 16(a)(1)(A) and (B) if the government contends that the person making the statement:

(i) was legally able to bind the defendant regarding the subject of the statement because of that person's position as the defendant's director, officer, employee, or agent; or

(ii) was personally involved in the alleged conduct constituting the offense and was legally able to bind the defendant regarding that conduct because of that person's position as the defendant's director, officer, employee, or agent.

(D) Defendant's Prior Record. Upon a defendant's request, the government must furnish the defendant with a copy of the defendant's prior criminal record that is within the government's possession, custody, or control if the attorney for the government knows—or through due diligence could know—that the record exists.

(E) Documents and Objects. Upon a defendant's request, the government must permit the defendant to inspect and to copy or photograph books, papers, documents, data, photographs, tangible objects, buildings or places, or copies or portions of any of these items, if the item is within the government's possession, custody, or control and:

(i) the item is material to preparing the defense;

(ii) the government intends to use the item in its case-in-chief at trial; or

(iii) the item was obtained from or belongs to the defendant.

(F) Reports of Examinations and Tests. Upon a defendant's request, the government must permit a defendant to inspect and to copy or photograph the results or reports of any physical or mental examination and of any scientific test or experiment if:

(i) the item is within the government's possession, custody, or control;

(ii) the attorney for the government knows—or through due diligence could know—that the item exists; and

(iii) the item is material to preparing the defense or the government intends to use the item in its case-in-chief at trial.

(G) Expert Witnesses.

(i) Duty to Disclose. At the defendant's request, the government must disclose to the defendant, in writing, the information required by (iii) for any testimony that the government intends to use at trial under Federal Rules of Evidence 702, 703, or 705 during its case-in-chief, or during its rebuttal to counter testimony that the defendant has timely disclosed under (b)(1)(C). If the government requests discovery under the second bullet point in (b)(1)(C)(i) and the defendant complies, the government must, at the defendant's request, disclose to the defendant, in writing, the information required by (iii) for testimony that the government intends to use at trial under Federal Rules of Evidence 702, 703, or 705 on the issue of the defendant's mental condition.

(ii) Time to Disclose. The court, by order or local rule, must set a time for the government to make its disclosures. The time must be sufficiently before trial to provide a fair opportunity for the defendant to meet the government's evidence.

(iii) Contents of the Disclosure. The disclosure for each expert witness must contain:

- a complete statement of all opinions that the government will elicit from the witness in its case-in-chief, or during its rebuttal to counter testimony that the defendant has timely disclosed under (b)(1)(C);
- the bases and reasons for them;
- the witness's qualifications, including a list of all publications authored in the previous 10 years; and
- a list of all other cases in which, during the previous 4 years, the witness has testified as an expert at trial or by deposition.

(iv) Information Previously Disclosed. If the government previously provided a report under (F) that contained information required by (iii), that information may be referred to, rather than repeated, in the expert-witness disclosure.

(v) Signing the Disclosure. The witness must approve and sign the disclosure, unless the government:

- states in the disclosure why it could not obtain the witness's signature through reasonable efforts; or
- has previously provided under (F) a report, signed by the witness, that contains all the opinions and the bases and reasons for them required by (iii).

(vi) Supplementing and Correcting a Disclosure. The government must supplement or correct its disclosures in accordance with (c).

(2) *Information Not Subject to Disclosure.* Except as permitted by Rule 16(a)(1)(A)–(D), (F), and (G), this rule does not authorize the discovery or inspection of reports, memoranda, or other internal government documents made by an attorney for the government or other government agent in connection with investigating or prosecuting the case. Nor does this rule authorize the discovery or inspection of statements made by prospective government witnesses except as provided in 18 U.S.C. § 3500.

(3) *Grand Jury Transcripts.* This rule does not apply to the discovery or inspection of a grand jury's recorded proceedings, except as provided in Rules 6, 12(h), 16(a)(1), and 26.2.

(b) Defendant's Disclosure.

(1) *Information Subject to Disclosure.*

(A) Documents and Objects. If a defendant requests disclosure under Rule 16(a)(1)(E) and the government complies, then the defendant must permit the government, upon request, to inspect and to copy or photograph books, papers, documents, data, photographs, tangible objects, buildings or places, or copies or portions of any of these items if:

(i) the item is within the defendant's possession, custody, or control; and

(ii) the defendant intends to use the item in the defendant's case-in-chief at trial.

(B) Reports of Examinations and Tests. If a defendant requests disclosure under Rule 16(a)(1)(F) and the government complies, the defendant must permit the government, upon request, to inspect and to copy or photograph the results or reports of any physical or mental examination and of any scientific test or experiment if:

(i) the item is within the defendant's possession, custody, or control; and

(ii) the defendant intends to use the item in the defendant's case-in-chief at trial, or intends to call the witness who prepared the report and the report relates to the witness's testimony.

(C) Expert Witnesses.

(i) Duty to Disclose. At the government's request, the defendant must disclose to the government, in writing, the information required by (iii) for any testimony that the defendant intends to use under Federal Rule of Evidence 702, 703, or 705 during the defendant's case-in-chief at trial, if:

- the defendant requests disclosure under (a)(1)(G) and the government complies; or
- the defendant has given notice under Rule 12.2(b) of an intent to present expert testimony on the defendant's mental condition.

(ii) Time to Disclose. The court, by order or local rule, must set a time for the defendant to make the defendant's disclosures. The time must be sufficiently before trial to provide a fair opportunity for the government to meet the defendant's evidence.

(iii) Contents of the Disclosure. The disclosure for each expert witness must contain:

- a complete statement of all opinions that the defendant will elicit from the witness in the defendant's case-in-chief;
- the bases and reasons for them;
- the witness's qualifications, including a list of all publications authored in the previous 10 years; and
- a list of all other cases in which, during the previous 4 years, the witness has testified as an expert at trial or by deposition.

(iv) Information Previously Disclosed. If the defendant previously provided a report under (B) that contained information required by (iii), that information may be referred to, rather than repeated, in the expert-witness disclosure.

(v) Signing the Disclosure. The witness must approve and sign the disclosure, unless the defendant:

- states in the disclosure why the defendant could not obtain the witness's signature through reasonable efforts; or
- has previously provided under (B) a report, signed by the witness, that contains all the opinions and the bases and reasons for them required by (iii).

(vi) Supplementing and Correcting a Disclosure. The defendant must supplement or correct the defendant's disclosures in accordance with (c).

(2) *Information Not Subject to Disclosure.* Except for scientific or medical reports, Rule 16(b)(1) does not authorize discovery or inspection of:

(A) reports, memoranda, or other documents made by the defendant, or the defendant's attorney or agent, during the case's investigation or defense; or

(B) a statement made to the defendant, or the defendant's attorney or agent, by:

(i) the defendant;

(ii) a government or defense witness; or

(iii) a prospective government or defense witness.

(c) Continuing Duty to Disclose. A party who discovers additional evidence or material before or during trial must promptly disclose its existence to the other party or the court if:

(1) the evidence or material is subject to discovery or inspection under this rule; and

(2) the other party previously requested, or the court ordered, its production.

(d) Regulating Discovery.

(1) *Protective and Modifying Orders.* At any time the court may, for good cause, deny, restrict, or defer discovery or inspection, or grant other appropriate relief. The court may permit a party to show good cause by a written statement that the court will inspect ex parte. If relief is granted, the court must preserve the entire text of the party's statement under seal.

(2) *Failure to Comply.* If a party fails to comply with this rule, the court may:

(A) order that party to permit the discovery or inspection; specify its time, place, and manner; and prescribe other just terms and conditions;

(B) grant a continuance;

(C) prohibit that party from introducing the undisclosed evidence; or

(D) enter any other order that is just under the circumstances.

HISTORY:

Amended Feb. 28, 1966, eff. July 1, 1966; April 22, 1974, eff. Dec. 1, 1975; July 31, 1975, P. L. 94-64, §§ 2, 3(20)–(28), 89 Stat. 370, 374; Dec. 12, 1975, P. L. 94-149, § 5, 89 Stat. 806; April 28, 1983, eff. Aug. 1, 1983; Mar. 9, 1987, eff. Aug. 1, 1987; April 30, 1991, eff. Dec. 1, 1991; April 22, 1993, eff. Dec. 1, 1993; April 29, 1994, eff. Dec. 1, 1994; April 11, 1997, eff. Dec. 1, 1997; April 29, 2002, eff. Dec. 1, 2002; Nov. 2, 2002, P. L. 107-273, Div C, Title I, Subtitle A, § 11019(b), 116 Stat. 1825; Apr. 16, 2013, eff. Dec. 1, 2013; April 11, 2022, eff. Dec. 1, 2022; April 24, 2023, eff. Dec. 1, 2023.

HISTORY; ANCILLARY LAWS AND DIRECTIVES

Other provisions:

Notes of Advisory Committee. Whether under existing law discovery may be permitted in criminal cases is doubtful, *United States v. Rosenfeld,* 57 F.2d 74 (C.C.A.2d), cert. den. 286 U.S. 556, 52 S.Ct. 642, 76 L.Ed. 1290. The courts have, however, made orders granting to the defendant an opportunity to inspect impounded documents belonging to him, *United States v. B. Goedde and Co.* 40 F.Supp. 523, 534 (E.D.Ill.) The rule is a restatement of this procedure. In addition, it permits the procedure to be invoked in cases of objects and documents obtained from others by seizure or by process, on the theory that such evidential matter would probably have been accessible to the defendant if it had not previously been seized by the prosecution. The entire matter is left within the discretion of the court.

Notes of Advisory Committee on 1966 amendments. The extent to which pretrial discovery should be permitted in criminal cases is a complex and controversial issue. The problems have been explored in detail in recent legal literature, most of which has been in favor of increasing the range of permissible discovery. See, e.g. Brennan, The Criminal Prosecution: Sporting Event or Quest for Truth, 1963 Wash.U.L.Q. 279; Everett, Discovery in Criminal Cases—In Search of a Standard, 1964 Duke L.J. 477; Fletcher, Pretrial Discovery in State Criminal Cases, 12 Stan.L.Rev. 293 (1960); Goldstein, The State and the Accused: Balance of Advantage in Criminal Procedure, 69 Yale L.J. 1149, 1172–1198 (1960); Krantz, Pretrial Discovery in Criminal Cases: A Necessity for Fair and Impartial Justice, 42 Neb.L.Rev. 127 (1962); Louisell, Criminal Discovery: Dilemma Real or Apparent, 49 Calif.L.Rev. 56 (1961); Louisell, The Theory of Criminal Discovery and the Practice of Criminal Law, 14 Vand.L.Rev. 921 (1961); Moran, Federal Criminal Rules Changes: Aid or Illusion for the Indigent Defendant?, 51 A.B.A.J. 64 (1965); Symposium, Discovery in Federal Criminal Cases, 33 F.R.D. 47–128 (1963); Traynor, Ground Lost and Found in Criminal Discovery, 39 N.Y.U.L.Rev. 228 (1964); Developments in the Law—Discovery, 74 Harv.L.Rev. 940, 1051–1063. Full judicial exploration of the conflicting policy considerations will be found in *State v. Tune,* 13 N.J. 203, 98 A.2d 881 (1953) and *State v. Johnson,* 28 N.J. 133, 145 A.2d 313 (1958); cf. *State v. Murphy,* 36 N.J. 172, 175 A.2d 622 (1961); *State v. Moffa,* 36 N.J. 219, 176 A.2d 1 (1961). The rule has been revised to expand the scope of pretrial discovery. At the same time provisions are made to guard against possible abuses.

Subdivision (a). The court is authorized to order the attorney for the government to permit the defendant to inspect and copy or photograph three different types of material:

(1) Relevant written or recorded statements or confessions made by the defendant, or copies thereof. The defendant is not required to designate because he may not always be aware that his statements or confessions are being recorded. The government's obligation is limited to production of such statements as are within the possession, custody or control of the government, the existence of which is known, or by the exercise of due diligence may become known, to the attorney for the government. Discovery of statements and confessions is in line with what the Supreme Court has described as the "better practice" (*Cicenia v. LaGay,* 357 U.S. 504, 511, 2 L.Ed.2d 1523 (1958) disapproved on other grounds *Escobedo v. Illinois,* 378 U.S. 478, 12 L.Ed.2d 977, 84 S.Ct. 1758, and ovrld. on other grounds *Miranda v. Arizona,* 384 U.S. 436, 16 L.Ed.2d 694, 86 S.Ct. 1602, 10 A.L.R.3d 974), and with the law in a number of states. See, e.g., Del. Rules. Crim. Pro.c, Rule 16; Ill.Stat. Ch. 38, § 729; Md. Rules Proc., Rule 728; *State v. McGee,* 91 Ariz. 101, 370 P.2d 261 (1962); *Cash v. Superior Court,* 53 Cal.2d 72, 346 P.2d 407 (1959); *State v. Bickham,* 239 La. 1094, 121 So.2d 207, cert. den. 364 U.S. 874, 5 L.Ed.2d 98 (1960); *People v. Johnson,* 356 Mich. 619, 97 N.W.2d 739 (1959); *State v. Johnson,* supra; *People v. Stokes,* 24 Misc.2d 755, 204 N.Y.Supp.2d 827 (Ct. Gen. Sess. 1960). The amendment also makes it clear that discovery extends to recorded as well as written statements. For state cases upholding the discovery of record-

ings, see, e.g., *People v. Cartier,* 51 Cal.2d 590, 335 P.2d 114 (1959); *State v. Minor,* 177 A.2d 215 (Del.Super.Ct. 1962).

(2) Relevant results or reports of physical or mental examinations, and of scientific tests or experiments (including fingerprint and handwriting comparisons) made in connection with the particular case, or copies thereof. Again the defendant is not required to designate but the government's obligation is limited to production of items within the possession, custody or control of the government, the existence of which is known, or by the exercise of due diligence may become known, to the attorney for the government. With respect to results or reports of scientific tests or experiments the range of materials which must be produced by the government is further limited to those made in connection with the particular case. Cf. Fla.Stats. § 909.18; *State v. Superior Court,* 90 Ariz. 133, 367 P.2d 6 (1961); *People v. Cooper,* 53 Cal.2d 755, 770, 3 Cal.Rptr. 148, 157, 349 P.2d 964, 973 (1960); *People v. Stokes,* supra, at 762, 204 N.Y.Supp.2d at 835.

(3) Relevant recorded testimony of a defendant before a grand jury. The policy which favors pretrial disclosure to a defendant of his statements to government agents also supports, pretrial disclosure of his testimony before a grand jury. Courts, however, have tended to require a showing of special circumstances before ordering such disclosure. See, e.g., *United States v. Johnson,* 215 F.Supp 300 (D.Md. 1963). Disclosure is required only where the statement has been recorded and hence can be transcribed.

Subdivision (b). This subdivision authorizes the court to order the attorney for the government to permit the defendant to inspect and copy or photograph all other books, papers, documents, tangible objects, buildings or places, or copies or portions thereof, which are within the possession, custody or control of the government. Because of the necessarily broad and general terms in which the items to be discovered are described, several limitations are imposed:

(1) While specific designation is not required of the defendant, the burden is placed on him to make a showing of materiality to the preparation of his defense and that his request is reasonable. The requirement of reasonableness will permit the court to define and limit the scope of the government's obligation to search its files while meeting the legitimate needs of the defendant. The court is also authorized to limit discovery to portions of items sought.

(2) Reports, memoranda, and other internal government documents made by government agents in connection with the investigation or prosecution of the case are exempt from discovery. Cf. *Palermo v. United States,* 360 U.S. 343, 3 L.Ed.2d 1287 (1959); *Ogden v. United States,* 303 F.2d 724 (9th Cir. 1962).

(3) Except as provided for reports of examinations and tests in subdivision (a)(2), statements made by government witnesses or prospective government witnesses to agents of the government are also exempt from discovery except as provided by 18 U.S.C.§ 3500.

Subdivision (c). This subdivision permits the court to condition a discovery order under subdivision (a)(2) and subdivision (b) by requiring the defendant to permit the government to discover similar items which the defendant intends to produce at the trial and which are within his possession, custody or control under restrictions similar to those placed in subdivision (b) upon discovery by the defendant. While the government normally has resources adequate to secure the information necessary for trial, there are some situations in which mutual disclosure would appear necessary to prevent the defendant from obtaining an unfair advantage. For example, in cases where both prosecution and defense have employed experts to make psychiatric examinations, it seems as important for the government to study the opinions of the experts to be called by the defendant in order to prepare for trial as it does for the defendant to study those of the government's witnesses. Or in cases (such as antitrust cases) in which the defendant is well represented and well financed, mutual disclosure so far as consistent with the privilege against self-incrimination would seem as appropriate as in civil cases. State cases have indicated that a requirement that the defendant disclose in advance of trial materials which he intends to use on his own behalf at the trial is not a violation of the privilege against self-incrimination. See *Jones v. Superior Court,* 58 Cal.2d 56, 22 Cal.Rptr. 879, 372 P.2d 919 (1962); *People v. Lopez,* 60 Cal.2d 223, 32 Cal.Rptr. 424, 384 P.2d 16 (1963); Traynor, Ground Lost and Found in Criminal Discovery, 39 N.Y.U.L.Rev. 228, 246 (1964); Comment, The Self-Incrimination Privilege: Barrier to Criminal Discovery, 51 Calif.L.Rev. 135 (1963); Note, 76 Harv.L.Rev. 838 (1963).

Subdivision (d). This subdivision is substantially the same as the last sentence of the existing rule.

Subdivision (e). This subdivision gives the court authority to deny, restrict or defer discovery upon a sufficient showing. Control of the abuses of discovery is necessary if it is to be expanded in the fashion proposed in subdivisions (a) and (b). Among the considerations to be taken into account by the court will be the safety of witnesses and others, a particular danger of perjury or witness intimidation, the protection of information vital to the national security, and the protection of business enterprises from economic reprisals.

For an example of a use of a protective order in state practice, see *People v. Lopez,* 60 Cal.2d 223, 32 Cal.Rptr. 424, 384 P.2d 16 (1963). See also Brennan, Remarks on Discovery, 33 F.R.D. 56, 65 (1963); Traynor, Ground Lost and Found in Criminal Discovery, 39 N.Y.U.L.Rev. 228, 244, 250.

In some cases it would defeat the purpose of the protective order if the government were required to make its showing in open court. The problem arises in its most extreme form where matters of national security are involved. Hence a procedure is set out where upon motion by the government the court may permit the government to make its showing, in whole or in part, in a written statement to be inspected by the court in camera. If the court grants relief based on such showing, the government's statement is to be sealed and preserved in the records of the court to be made available to the appellate court in the event of an appeal by the defendant. Cf. 18 U.S.C.§ 3500.

Subdivision (f). This subdivision is designed to encourage promptness in making discovery motions and to give the court sufficient control to prevent unnecessary delay and court time consequent upon a multiplication of discovery motions. Normally one motion should encompass all relief sought and a subsequent motion permitted only upon a showing of cause. Where pretrial hearings are used pursuant to Rule 17.1, discovery issues may be resolved at such hearings.

Subdivision (g). The first sentence establishes a continuing obligation on a party subject to a discovery order with respect to material discovered after initial compliance. The duty provided is to notify the other party, his attorney or the court of the existence of the material. A motion can then be made by the other party for additional discovery and, where the existence of the material is disclosed shortly before or during the trial, for any necessary continuance.

The second sentence gives wide discretion to the court in dealing with the failure of either party to comply with a discovery order. Such discretion will permit the court to consider the reasons why disclosure was not made, the extent of the prejudice, if any, to the opposing party, the feasibility of rectifying that prejudice by a continuance, and any other relevant circumstances.

Notes of Advisory Committee on 1974 amendments. Rule 16 is revised to give greater discovery to both the prosecution and the defense. Subdivision (a) deals with disclosure of evidence by the government. Subdivision (b) deals with disclosure of evidence by the defendant. The majority of the Advisory Committee is of the view that the two—prosecution and defense discovery—are related and that the giving of a broader right of discovery to the defense is dependent upon giving also a broader right of discovery to the prosecution.

The draft provides for a right of prosecution discovery independent of any prior request for discovery by the defendant. The Advisory Committee is of the view that this is the most desirable approach to prosecution discovery. See American Bar Association, Standards Relating to Discovery and Procedure Before Trial, pp. 7, 43–46 (Approved Draft, 1970).

The language of the rule is recast from "the court may order" or "the court shall order" to "the government shall permit" or "the defendant shall permit." This is to make clear that discovery should be accomplished by the parties themselves, without the necessity of a court order unless there is dispute as to whether the matter is discoverable or a request for a protective order under subdivision (d)(1). The court, however, has the inherent right to enter an order under this rule.

The rule is intended to prescribe the minimum amount of discovery to which the parties are entitled. It is not intended to limit the judge's discretion to order broader discovery in appropriate cases. For example, subdivision (a)(3) is not intended to deny a judge's discretion to order disclosure of grand jury minutes where circumstances make it appropriate to do so.

Subdivision (a)(1)(A) amends the old rule to provide, upon request of the defendant, the government shall permit discovery if the conditions specified in subdivision (a)(1)(A) exist. Some courts have construed the current language as giving the court discretion as to whether to grant discovery of defendant's statements. See *United States v. Kaminsky,* 275 F. Supp. 365 (S.D.N.Y. 1967), denying discovery because the defendant did not demonstrate that his request for discovery was warranted; *United States v. Diliberto,* 264 F.Supp. 181 (S.D.N.Y. 1967), holding that there must be a showing of actual need before discovery would be granted; *United States v. Louis Carreau, Inc.,* 42 F.R.D. 408 (S.D.N.Y. 1967), holding that in the absence of a showing of good cause the government cannot be required to disclose defendant's prior statements in advance of trial. In *United States v. Louis Carreau, Inc.,* at p. 412, the court stated that if rule 16 meant that production of the statements was mandatory, the word "shall" would have been used instead of "may." See also *United States v. Wallace,* 272 F.Supp. 838 (S.D.N.Y. 1967); *United States v. Wood,* 270 F. Supp. 963 (S.D.N.Y. 1967); *United States v. Leighton,* 265 F.Supp. 27 (S.D.N.Y. 1967); *United States v. Longarzo,* 43 F.R.D. 395 (S.D.N.Y. 1967); *Loux v. United States,* 389 F.2d 911 (9th Cir. 1968); and the discussion of discovery in Discovery in Criminal Cases, 44 F.R.D. 481 (1968). Other courts have held that even though the current rules make discovery discretionary, the defendant need not show cause when he seeks to discover his own statements. See *United States v. Aadal,* 280 F.Supp. 859 (S.D.N.Y. 1967); *United States v. Federmann,* 41 F.R.D. 339 (S.D.N.Y. 1967); and *United States v. Projansky,* 44 F.R.D. 550 (S.D.N.Y. 1968).

The amendment making disclosure mandatory under the circumstances prescribed in subdivision (a)(1)(A) resolves such ambiguity as may currently exist, in the direction of more liberal discovery. See C. Wright, Federal Practice and Procedure: Criminal § 253 (1969, Supp. 1971), Rezneck, The New Federal Rules of Criminal Procedure, 54 Geo.L.J. 1276 (1966); Fla.Stat.Ann. § 925.05 (Supp. 1971-1972); N.J.Crim.Prac. Rule 35-11(a) (1967). This is done in the view that broad discovery contributes to the fair and efficient administration of criminal justice by providing the defendant with enough information to make an informed decision as to plea; by minimizing the undesirable effect of surprise at the trial; and by otherwise contributing to an accurate determination of the issue of guilt or innocence. This is the ground upon which the American Bar Association Standards Relating to Discovery and Procedure Before Trial (Approved Draft, 1970) has unanimously recommended broader discovery. The United States Supreme Court has said that the pretrial disclosure of a defendant's statements "may be the 'better practice.' " *Cicenia v. La Gay,* 357 U.S. 504, 511, 78 S.Ct. 1297, 2 L.Ed.2d 1523 (1958). See also *Leland v. Oregon,* 343 U.S. 790, 72 S.Ct. 1002, 96 L.Ed. 1302 (1952); *State v. Johnson,* 28 N.J. 133, 145 A.2d 313 (1958).

The requirement that the statement be disclosed prior to trial, rather than waiting until the trial, also contributes to efficiency of administration. It is during the pretrial stage that the defendant usually decides whether to plead guilty. See *United States v. Projansky,* supra. The pretrial stage is also the time during which many objections to the admissibility of types of evidence ought to be made. Pretrial disclosure ought, therefore, to contribute both to an informed guilty plea practice and to a pretrial resolution of admissibility questions. See ABA, Standards Relating to Discovery and Procedure Before Trial § 1.2 and Commentary pp. 40–43 (Approved Draft, 1970).

The American Bar Association Standards mandate the prosecutor to make the required disclosure even though not requested to do so by the defendant. The proposed draft requires the defendant to request discovery, although obviously the attorney for the government may disclose without waiting for a request, and there are situations in which due process will require the prosecution, on its own, to disclose evidence "helpful" to the defense. *Brady v. Maryland,* 373 U.S. 83, 83 S.Ct. 1194, 10 L.Ed.2d 215 (1963); *Giles v. Maryland,* 386 U.S. 66, 87 S.Ct. 793, 17 L.Ed.2d 737 (1967).

The requirement in subdivision (a)(1)(A) is that the government produce "statements" without further discussion of what "statement" includes. There has been some recent controversy over what "statements" are subject to discovery under the current rule. See Discovery in Criminal Cases, 44 F.R.D. 481 (1968); C. Wright, Federal Practice and Procedure: Criminal § 253, pp. 505–506 (1969, Supp. 1971). The kinds of "statements" which have been held to be within the rule include "substantially verbatim and contemporaneous" statements, *United States v. Elife,* 43 F.R.D. 23 (S.D.N.Y. 1967); statements which reproduce the defendant's "exact words," *United States v. Armantrout,* 278 F.Supp. 517 (S.D.N.Y. 1968); a memorandum which was not verbatim but included the substance of the defendant's testimony, *United States v. Scharf,* 267 F.Supp. 19 (S.D.N.Y. 1967); Summaries of the defendant's statements, *United States v. Morrison,* 43 F.R.D. 516 (N.D.Ill.1967); and statements discovered by means of electronic surveillance, *United States v. Black,* 282 F.Supp. 35 (D.D.C. 1968). The court in *United States v. Iovinelli,* 276 F.Supp. 629, 631 (N.D.Ill.1967), declared that "statements" as used in old rule 16 is not restricted to the "substantially verbatim recital of an oral statement" or to statements which are a "recital of past occurrences."

The Jencks Act, 18 U.S.C. § 3500, defines "statements" of government witnesses discoverable for purposes of cross-examination as: (1) a "written statement" signed or otherwise approved by a witness, (2) "a stenographic, mechanical, electrical, or other recording, or a transcription thereof, which is a substantially verbatim recital of an oral statement made by said witness to an agent of the government and recorded contemporaneously with the making of such oral statement." 18 U.S.C. § 3500(e). The language of the Jencks Act has most often led to a restrictive definition of "statements," confining "statements" to the defendant's "own words." See *Hanks v. United States,* 388 F.2d 171 (10th Cir. 1968), and *Augenblick v. United States,* 377 F.2d 586, 180 Ct.Cl. 131 (1967).

The American Bar Association's Standards Relating to Discovery and Procedure Before Trial (Approved Draft, 1970) do not attempt to define "statements" because of a disagreement among members of the committee as to what the definition should be. The majority rejected the restrictive definition of "statements" contained in the Jencks Act, 18 U.S.C. § 3500(e), in the view that the defendant ought to be able to see his statement in whatever form it may have been preserved in fairness to the defendant and to discourage the practice, where it exists, of destroying original notes, after transforming them into secondary transcriptions, in order to avoid cross-examination based upon the original notes. See *Campbell v. United States,* 373 U.S. 487, 83 S.Ct. 1356, 10 L.Ed.2d 501 (1963). The minority favored a restrictive definition of "statements" in the view that the use of other than "verbatim" statements would subject witnesses to unfair cross-examination. See American Bar Association's Standards Relating to Discovery and Procedure Before Trial pp. 61–64 (Approved Draft, 1970). The draft of subdivision (a)(1)(A) leaves the matter of the meaning of the term unresolved and thus left for development on a case-by-case basis.

Subdivision (a)(1)(A) also provides for mandatory disclosure of a summary of any oral statement made by defendant to a government agent which the attorney for the government intends to use in evidence. The reasons for permitting the defendant to discover his own statements seem obviously to apply to the substance of any oral statement which the government intends to use in evidence at the trial. See American Bar Association Standards Relating to Discovery and Procedure Before Trial § 2.1(a)(ii) (Approved Draft, 1970). Certainly disclosure will facilitate the raising of objections to admissibility prior to trial. There have been several conflicting decisions under the current rules as to whether the government must disclose the substance of oral statements of the defendant which it has in its possession. Cf. *United States v. Baker,* 262 F.Supp. 657 (D.C.D.C.1966); *United States v. Curry,* 278 F.Supp. 508 (N.D.Ill.1967); *United States v. Morrison,* 43 F.R.D. 516 (ND.Ill.1967); *United States v. Reid,* 43 F.R.D. 520 (ND.Ill.1967); *United States v. Armantrout,* 278 F.Supp. 517 (S.D.N.Y.1968); and *United States v. Elife,* 43 F.R.D. 23 (S.D.N.Y.1967). There is, however, considerable support for the policy of disclosing the substance of the defendant's oral statement. Many courts have indicated that this is a "better practice" than denying such disclosure. E.g., *United States v. Curry,* supra; *Loux v. United States,* 389 F.2d 911 (9th Cir. 1968); and *United States v. Baker,* supra.

Subdivision (a)(1)(A) also provides for mandatory disclosure of any "recorded testimony" which defendant gives before a grand jury if the testimony "relates to the offense charged." The present rule is discretionary and is applicable only to those of defendant's statements which are "relevant."

The traditional rationale behind grand jury secrecy—protection of witnesses—does not apply when the accused seeks discovery of his own testimony. Cf. *Dennis v. United States,* 384 U.S. 855, 86 S.Ct. 1840, 16 L.Ed.2d 973 (1966); and *Allen v. United States,* 129 U.S.App.D.C. 61, 390 F.2d 476 (1968). In interpreting the rule many judges have granted defendant discovery without a showing of need or relevance. *United States v. Gleason,* 259 F. Supp. 282 (S.D.N.Y. 1966); *United States v. Longarzo,* 43 F.R.D. 395 (S.D.N.Y. 1967); and *United States v. United Concrete Pipe Corp.,* 41 F.R.D. 538 (N.D.Tex. 1966). Making disclosure mandatory without a showing of relevance conforms to the recommendation of the American Bar Association Standards Relating to Discovery and Procedure Before Trial § 2.1(a)(iii) and Commentary pp. 64–66 (Approved Draft, 1970). Also see Note, Discovery by a Criminal Defendant of His Own Grand-Jury Testimony, 68 Columbia L.Rev. 311 (1968).

In a situation involving a corporate defendant, statements made by present and former officers and employees relating to their employment have been held discoverable as statements of the defendant. *United States v. Hughes,* 413 F.2d 1244 (5th Cir. 1969). The rule makes clear that such statements are discoverable if the officer or employee was "able legally to bind the defendant in respect to the activities involved in the charges."

Subdivision (a)(1)(B) allows discovery of the defendant's prior criminal record. A defendant may be uncertain of the precise nature of his prior record and it seems therefore in the interest of efficient and fair administration to make it possible to resolve prior to trial any disputes as to the correctness of the relevant criminal record of the defendant.

Subdivision (a)(1)(C) gives a right of discovery of certain tangible objects under the specified circumstances. Courts have construed the old rule as making disclosure discretionary with the judge. Cf. *United States v. Kaminsky,* 275 F.Supp. 365 (S.D.N.Y. 1967); *Gevinson v. United States,* 358 F.2d 761 (5th Cir. 1966), cert. denied, 385 U.S. 823, 87 S.Ct. 51, 17 L.Ed.2d 60 (1966); and *United States v. Tanner,* 279 F.Supp. 457 (N.D.Ill. 1967). The old rule requires a "showing of materiality to the preparation of his defense and that the request is reasonable." The new rule requires disclosure if any one of three situations exists: (a) the defendant shows that disclosure of the document or tangible object is material to the defense, (b) the government intends to use the document or tangible object in its presentation of its case in chief, or (c) the document or tangible object was obtained from or belongs to the defendant.

Disclosure of documents and tangible objects which are "material" to the preparation of the defense may be required under the rule of *Brady v. Maryland,* 373 U.S. 83, 83 S.Ct. 1194, 10 L.Ed.2d 215 (1963), without an additional showing that the request is "reasonable." In *Brady* the court held that "due process" requires that the prosecution disclose evidence favorable to the accused. Although the Advisory Committee decided not to codify the Brady Rule, the requirement that the government disclose documents and tangible objects "material to the preparation of his defense" underscores the importance of disclosure of evidence favorable to the defendant.

Limiting the rule to situations in which the defendant can show that the evidence is material seems unwise. It may be difficult for a defendant to make this showing if he does not know what the evidence is. For this reason subdivision (a)(1)(C) also contains language to compel disclosure if the government intends to use the property as evidence at the trial or if the property was obtained from or belongs to the defendant. See ABA Standards Relating to Discovery and Procedure Before Trial § 2.1(a)(v) and Commentary pp. 68–69 (Approved Draft, 1970). This is probably the result under old rule 16 since the fact that the government intends to use the physical evidence at the trial is probably sufficient proof of "materiality." C. Wright, Federal Practice and Procedure: Criminal § 254 especially n. 70 at p. 513 (1969, Supp. 1971). But it seems desirable to make this explicit in the rule itself.

Requiring disclosure of documents and tangible objects which "were obtained from or belong to the defendant" probably is also making explicit in the rule what would otherwise be the interpretation of "materiality." See C. Wright, Federal Practice and Procedure: Criminal § 254 at p. 510 especially n. 58 (1969, Supp. 1971).

Subdivision (a)(1)(C) is also amended to add the word "photographs" to the objects previously listed. See ABA Standards Relating to Discovery and Procedure Before Trial § 2.1(a)(v) (Approved Draft, 1970).

Subdivision (a)(1)(D) makes disclosure of the reports of examinations and tests mandatory. This is the recommendation of the ABA Standards Relating to Discovery and Procedure Before Trial § 2.1(a)(iv) and Commentary pp. 66–68 (Approved Draft, 1970). The obligation of disclosure applies only to scientific tests or experiments "made in connection with the particular case." So limited, mandatory disclosure seems justified because: (1) it is difficult to test expert testimony at trial without advance notice and preparation; (2) it is not likely that such evidence will be distorted or misused if disclosed prior to trial; and (3) to the extent that a test may be favorable to the defense, its disclosure is mandated under the rule of *Brady v. Maryland,* supra.

Subdivision (a)(1)(E) is new. It provides for discovery of the names of witnesses to be called by the government and of the prior criminal record of these witnesses. Many states have statutes or rules which require that the accused be notified prior to trial of the witnesses to be called against him. See, e.g., Alaska R.Crim.Proc. 7(c); Ariz.R.Crim.Proc. 153, 17 A.R.S. (1956); Ark.Stat.Ann. § 43-1001 (1947); Cal.Pen.Code § 995n (West 1957); Colo.Rev.Stat.Ann. §§ 39-3-6, 39-4-2 (1963); Fla.Stat.Ann. § 906.29 (1944); Idaho Code Ann. § 19-1404 (1948); Ill.Rev.Stat. ch. 38, § 114-9 (1970); Ind.Ann.Stat. § 9-903 (1956), IC 1971, 35-1-16-3; Iowa Code Ann. § 772.3 (1950); Kan.Stat.Ann. § 62-931 (1964); Ky.R.Crim. Proc. 6.08 (1962); Mich.Stat.Ann. § 28.980, M.C.L.A. § 767.40 (Supp.1971); Minn.Stat.Ann. § 628.08 (1947); Mo.Ann.Stat. § 545.070 (1953); Mont.Rev. Codes Ann. § 95-1503 (Supp. 1969); Neb.Rev.Stat. § 29-1602 (1964); Nev.Rev.Stat. § 173.045 (1967); Okl.Stat. tet. 22, § 384 (1951); Ore.Rev.Stat. § 132.580 (1969); Tenn. Code Ann. § 40-1708 (1955); Utah Code Ann. § 77-20-3 (1953). For examples of the ways in which these requirements are implemented, see *State v. Mitchell,* 181 Kan. 193, 310 P.2d 1063 (1957); *State v. Parr,* 129 Mont. 175, 283 P.2d 1086 (1955); *Phillips v. State,* 157 Neb. 419, 59 N.W. 598 (1953).

Witnesses' prior statements must be made available to defense counsel after the witness testifies on direct examination for possible impeachment purposes during trial: 18 U.S.C. § 3500.

The American Bar Association's Standards Relating to Discovery and Procedure Before Trial § 2.1(a)(1) (Approved Draft, 1970) require disclosure of both the names and the statements of prosecution witnesses. Subdivision (a)(1)(E) requires only disclosure, prior to trial, of names, addresses, and prior criminal record. It does not require disclosure of the witnesses' statements although the rule does not preclude the parties from agreeing to disclose statements prior to trial. This is done, for example, in courts using the so-called "omnibus hearing."

Disclosure of the prior criminal record of witnesses places the defense in the same position as the government, which normally has knowledge of the defendant's record and the record of anticipated defense witnesses. In addition, the defendant often lacks means of procuring this information on his own. See American Bar Association Standards Relating to Discovery and Procedure Before Trial § 2.1(a)(vi) (Approved Draft, 1970).

A principal argument against disclosure of the identity of witnesses prior to trial has been the danger to the witness, his being subjected either to physical harm or to threats designed to make the witness unavailable or to influence him to change his testimony. Discovery in Criminal cases, 44 F.R.D. 481, 499–500 (1968); Ratnoff, The New Criminal Deposition Statute in Ohio—Help or Hindrance to Justice?, 19 Case Western Reserve L.Rev. 279, 284 (1968). See, e.g., *United States v. Estep,* 151 F.Supp. 668, 672–673 (N.D. Tex. 1957):

Ninety percent of the convictions had in the trial court for sale and dissemination of narcotic drugs are linked to the work and the evidence obtained by an informer. If that informer is not to have his life protected there won't be many informers hereafter.

See also the dissenting opinion of Mr. Justice Clark in *Roviaro v. United States,* 353 U.S. 53, 66–67, 77 S.Ct. 623, 1 L.Ed.2d 639 (1957). Threats of market retaliation against witnesses in criminal antitrust cases are another illustration. *Bergen Drug Co. v. Parke, Davis & Company,* 307 F.2d 725 (3d Cir. 1962); and *House of Materials, Inc. v. Simplicity Pattern Co.,* 298 F.2d 867 (2d Cir. 1962). The government has two alternatives when it believes disclosure will create an undue risk of harm to the witness: It can ask for a protective order under subdivision (d)(1). See ABA Standards Relating to Discovery and Procedure Before Trial § 2.5(b) (Approved Draft, 1970). It can also move the court to allow the perpetuation of a particular witness's testimony for use at trial if the witness is unavailable or later changes his testimony. The purpose of the latter alternative is to make pretrial disclosure possible and at the same time to minimize any inducement to use improper means to force the witness either to not show up or to change his testimony before a jury. See rule 15.

Subdivision (a)(2) is substantially unchanged. It limits the discovery otherwise allowed by providing that the government need not disclose "reports, memoranda, or other internal government documents made by the attorney for the government or other government agents in connection with the investigation or prosecution of the case" or "statements made by government witnesses or prospective government witnesses." The only proposed change is that the "reports, memoranda, or other internal government documents made by the attorney for the government" are included to make clear that the work product of the government attorney is protected. See C. Wright, Federal Practice and Procedure: Criminal § 254 n. 92 (1969, Supp. 1971); *United States v. Rothman,* 179 F.Supp. 935 (W.D.Pa. 1959); Note, "Work Product" in Criminal Discovery, 1966 Wash.U.L.Q. 321; American Bar Association, Standards Relating to Discovery and Procedure Before Trial § 2.6(a) (Approved Draft, 1970); cf. *Hickman v. Taylor,* 329 U.S. 495, 67 S.Ct. 385, 91 L.Ed. 451 (1947). *Brady v. Maryland,* 373 U.S. 83, 83 S.Ct. 1194, 10 L.Ed.2d 215 (1963), requires the disclosure of evidence favorable to the defendant. This is, of course, not changed by this rule.

Subdivision (a)(3) is included to make clear that recorded proceedings of a grand jury are explicitly dealt with in rule 6 and subdivision (a)(1)(A) of rule 16 and thus are not covered by other provisions such as subdivision (a)(1)(C) which deals generally with discovery of documents in the possession, custody, or control of the government.

Subdivision (a)(4) is designed to insure that the government will not be penalized if it makes a full disclosure of all potential witnesses and then decides not to call one or more of the witnesses listed. This is not, however, intended to abrogate the defendant's right to comment generally upon the government's failure to call witnesses in an appropriate case.

Subdivision (b) deals with the government's right to discovery of defense evidence or, put in other terms, with the extent to which a defendant is required to disclose its evidence to the prosecution prior to trial. Subdivision (b) replaces old subdivision (c).

Subdivision (b) enlarges the right of government discovery in several ways: (1) it gives the government the right to discovery of lists of defense witnesses as well as physical evidence and the results of examinations and tests; (2) it requires disclosure if the defendant has the evidence under his control and intends to use it at trial in his case in chief, without the additional burden, required by the old rule, of having to show, in behalf of the government, that the evidence is material and the request reasonable; and (3) it gives the government the right to discovery without conditioning that right upon the existence of a prior request for discovery by the defendant.

Although the government normally has resources adequate to secure much of the evidence for trial, there are situations in which pretrial disclosure of evidence to the government is in the interest of effective and fair criminal justice administration. For example, the experimental "omnibus hearing" procedure (see discussion in Advisory Committee Note to rule 12) is based upon an assumption that the defendant, as well as the government, will be willing to disclose evidence prior to trial.

Having reached the conclusion that it is desirable to require broader disclosure by the defendant under certain circumstances, the Advisory Committee has taken the view that it is preferable to give the right of discovery to the government independently of a prior request for discovery by the defendant. This is the recommendation of the American Bar Association Standards Relating to Discovery and Procedure Before Trial, Commentary, pp. 43–46 (Approved Draft, 1970). It is sometimes asserted that making the government's right to discovery conditional will minimize the risk that government discovery will be viewed as an infringement of the defendant's constitutional rights. See discussion in C. Wright, Federal Practice and Procedure: Criminal § 256 (1969, Supp. 1971); Moore, Criminal Discovery, 19 Hastings L.J. 865 (1968); Wilder, Prosecution Discovery and the Privilege Against Self-Incrimination, 6 Am.Cr.L.Q. 3 (1967). There are assertions that prosecution discovery, even if conditioned upon the defendants being granted discovery, is a violation of the privilege. See statements of Mr. Justice Black and Mr. Justice Douglas, 39 F.R.D. 69, 272, 277–278 19 (1966); C. Wright, Federal Practice and Procedure: Criminal § 256 (1969, Supp. 1971). Several states require defense disclosure of an intended defense of alibi and, in some cases, a list of witnesses in support of an alibi defense, without making the requirement conditional upon prior discovery being given to the defense. E.g., Ariz.R.Crim.P. 162(B), 17 A.R.S. (1956); Ind.Ann.Stat. § 9-1631 to 9-1633 (1956), IC 1971, 35-5-1-1 to 35-5-1-3; Mich.Comp. Laws Ann. §§ 768.20, 768.21 (1968); N.Y. CPL § 250.20 (McKinney's Consol.Laws, c. 11-A, 1971); and Ohio Rev.Code Ann. § 2945.58 (1954). State courts have refused to hold these statutes violative of the privilege against self-incrimination. See *State v. Thayer,* 124 Ohio St. 1, 176 N.E. 656 (1931), and *People v. Rakiec,* 260 App.Div. 452, 23 N.Y.S.2d 607, aff'd, 289 N.Y. 306, 45 N.E.2d 812 (1942). See also rule 12.1 and Advisory Committee Note thereto.

Some state courts have held that a defendant may be required to disclose, in advance of trial, evidence which he intends to use on his own behalf at trial without violating the privilege against self-incrimination. See *Jones v. Superior Court of Nevada County,* 58 Cal.2d 56, 22 Cal.Rptr. 879, 372 P.2d 919 (1962); *People v. Lopez,* 60 Cal.2d 223, 32 Cal.Rptr. 424, 384 P.2d 16 (1963); Comment, The Self-Incrimination Privilege: Barrier to Criminal Discovery?, 51 Calif.L.Rev. 135 (1963); Note, 76 Harv.L.Rev. 838 (1963). The courts in Jones v. Superior Court of Nevada County, supra, suggests that if mandatory disclosure applies only to those items which the accused intends to introduce in evidence at trial, neither the incriminatory nor the involuntary aspects of the privilege against self-incrimination are present.

On balance the Advisory Committee is of the view that an independent right of discovery for both the defendant and the government is likely to contribute to both effective and fair administration. See Louisell, Criminal Discovery and Self-Incrimination: Roger Traynor Confronts the Dilemma, 53 Calif.L.Rev. 89 (1965), for an analysis of the difficulty of weighing the value of broad discovery against the value which inheres in not requiring the defendant to disclose anything which might work to his disadvantage.

Subdivision (b)(1)(A) provides that the defendant shall disclose any documents and tangible objects which he has in his possession, custody, or control and which he intends to introduce in evidence in his case in chief.

Subdivision (b)(1)(B) provides that the defendant shall disclose the results of physical or mental examinations and scientific tests or experiments if (a) they were made in connection with a particular case; (b) the defendant has them under his control; and (c) he intends to offer them in evidence in his case in chief or which were prepared by a defense witness and the results or reports relate to the witness's testimony. In cases where both prosecution and defense have employed experts to conduct tests such as psychiatric examinations, it seems as important for the government to be able to study the results reached by defense experts which are to be called by the defendant as it does for the defendant to study those of government experts. See Schultz, Criminal Discovery by the Prosecution: Frontier Developments and Some Proposals for the Future, 22 N.Y.U.Intra.L.Rev. 268 (1967); American Bar Association, Standards Relating to Discovery and Procedure Before Trial § 3.2 (Supp., Approved Draft, 1970).

Subdivision (b)(1)(C) provides for discovery of a list of witnesses the defendant intends to call in his case in chief. State cases have indicated that disclosure of a list of defense witnesses does not violate the defendant's privilege against self-incrimination. See *Jones v. Superior Court of Nevada County,* supra, and *People v. Lopez,* supra. The defendant has the same option as does the government if it is believed that disclosure of the identity of a witness may subject that witness to harm or a threat of harm. The defendant can ask for a protective order under subdivision (d)(1) or can take a deposition in accordance with the terms of rule 15.

Subdivision (b)(2) is unchanged, appearing as the last sentence of subdivision (c) of old rule 16.

Subdivision (b)(3) provides that the defendant's failure to introduce evidence or call witnesses shall not be admissible in evidence against him. In states which require pretrial disclosure of witnesses' identity, the prosecution is not allowed to comment upon the defendant's failure to call a listed witness. See *O'Connor v. State,* 31 Wis.2d 684, 143 N.W.2d 489 (1966); *People v. Mancini,* 6 N.Y.2d 853, 188 N.Y.S.2d 559, 160 N.E.2d 91 (1959); and *State v. Cocco,* 73 Ohio App. 182, 55 N.E.2d 430 (1943). This is not, however, intended to abrogate the government's right to comment generally upon the defendant's failure to call witnesses in an appropriate case, other than the defendant's failure to testify.

Subdivision (c) is a restatement of part of old rule 16(g).

Subdivision (d)(1) deals with the protective order. Although the rule does not attempt to indicate when a protective order should be entered, it is obvious that one would be appropriate where there is reason to believe that a witness would be subject to physical or economic harm if his identity is revealed. See *Will v. United States,* 389 U.S. 90, 88 S.Ct. 269, 19 L.Ed.2d 305 (1967). The language "by the judge alone" is not meant to be inconsistent with *Alderman v. United States,* 394 U.S. 165, 89 S.Ct. 961, 22 L. Ed.2d 176 (1969). In *Alderman* the court points out that there may be appropriate occasions for the trial judge to decide questions relating to pretrial disclosure. See *Alderman v. United States,* 394 U.S. at 182 n. 14, 89 S.Ct. 961.

Subdivision (d)(2) is a restatement of part of old rule 16(g) and (d).

Old subdivision (f) of rule 16 dealing with time of motions is dropped because rule 12(c) provides the judge with authority to set the time for the making of pretrial motions including requests for discovery. Rule 12 also prescribes the consequences which follow from a failure to make a pretrial motion at the time fixed by the court. See rule 12(f).

Notes of Committee on the Judiciary on 1975 amendments (House Report No. 94-247). A. Amendments Proposed by the Supreme Court. Rule 16 of the Federal Rules of Criminal Procedure regulates discovery by the defendant of evidence in possession of the prosecution, and discovery by the prosecution of evidence in possession of the defendant. The present rule permits the defendant to move the court to discover certain material. The prosecutor's discovery is limited and is reciprocal—that is, if the defendant is granted discovery of certain items, then the prosecution may move for discovery of similar items under the defendant's control.

As proposed to be amended, the rule provides that the parties themselves will accomplish discovery—no motion need be filed and no court order is necessary. The court will intervene only to resolve a dispute as to whether something is discoverable or to issue a protective order.

The proposed rule enlarges the scope of the defendant's discovery to include a copy of his prior criminal record and a list of the names and addresses, plus record of prior felony convictions, of all witnesses the prosecution intends to call during its case-in-chief. It also permits the defendant to discover the substance of any oral statement of his which the prosecution intends to offer at trial, if the statement was given in response to interrogation by any person known by defendant to be a government agent.

Proposed subdivision (a)(2) provides that Rule 16 does not authorize the defendant to discover "reports, memoranda, or other internal government documents made by the attorney for the government or other government agents in connection with the investigation or prosecution of the case. . . ."

The proposed rule also enlarges the scope of the government's discovery of materials in the custody of the defendant. The government is entitled to a list of the names and addresses of the witnesses the defendant intends to call during his case-in-chief. Proposed subdivision (b)(2) protects the defendant from having to disclose "reports, memoranda, or other internal defense documents . . . made in connection with the investigation or defense of the case. . . ."

Subdivision (d)(1) of the proposed rule permits the court to deny, restrict, or defer discovery by either party, or to make such other order as is appropriate. Upon request, a party may make a showing that such an order is necessary. This showing shall be made to the judge alone if the party so requests. If the court enters an order after such a showing, it must seal the record of the showing and preserve it in the event there is an appeal.

B. Committee Action. The Committee agrees that the parties should, to the maximum possible extent, accomplish discovery themselves. The court should become involved only when it is necessary to resolve a dispute or to issue an order pursuant to subdivision (d).

Perhaps the most controversial amendments to this rule were those dealing with witness lists. Under present law, the government must turn over a witness list *only* in capital cases. [Section 3432 of title 18 of the United States Code provides: A person charged with treason or other capital offense shall at least three entire days before commencement of trial be furnished with a copy of the indictment and a list of the veniremen, and of the witnesses to be produced on the trial for proving the indictment, stating the place of abode of each venireman and witness.] The defendant never needs to turn over a list of his witnesses. The proposed rule requires both the government and the defendant to turn over witness lists in every case, capital or noncapital. Moreover, the lists must be furnished to the adversary party upon that party's request.

The proposed rule was sharply criticized by both prosecutors and defenders. The prosecutors feared that pretrial disclosure of prosecution witnesses would result in harm to witnesses. The defenders argued that a defendant cannot constitutionally be compelled to disclose his witnesses.

The Committee believes that it is desirable to promote greater pretrial discovery. As stated in the Advisory Committee Note,

broader discovery by both the defense and the prosecution will contribute to the fair and efficient administration of criminal justice by aiding in informed plea negotiations, by minimizing the undesirable effect of surprise at trial, and by otherwise contributing to an accurate determination of the issue of guilt or innocence. . . .

The Committee, therefore, endorses the principle that witness lists are discoverable. However, the Committee has attempted to strike a balance between the narrow provisions of existing law and the broad provisions of the proposed rule.

The Committee rule makes the procedures defendant-triggered. If the defendant asks for and receives a list of prosecution witnesses, then the prosecution may request a list of defense witnesses. The witness lists need not be turned over until 3 days before trial. The court can modify the terms of discovery upon a sufficient showing. Thus, the court can require disclosure of the witness lists earlier than 3 days before trial, or can permit a party not to disclose the identity of a witness before trial.

The Committee provision promotes broader discovery and its attendant values—informed disposition of cases without trial, minimizing the undesirable effect of surprise, and helping insure that the issue of guilt or innocence is accurately determined. At the same time, it avoids the problems suggested by both the prosecutors and the defenders.

The major argument advanced by prosecutors is the risk of danger to their witnesses if their identities are disclosed prior to trial. The Committee recognizes that there may be a risk but believes that the risk is not as great as some fear that it is. Numerous states require the prosecutor to provide the defendant with a list of prosecution witnesses prior to trial. [These States include Alaska, Arizona, Arkansas, California, Colorado, Florida, Idaho, Illinois, Indiana, Iowa, Kansas, Kentucky, Michigan, Minnesota, Missouri, Montana, Nebraska, Nevada, Oklahoma, Oregon, Tennessee, and Utah. See Advisory Committee Note, House Document 93-292, at 60.] The evidence before the Committee indicates that these states have not experienced unusual problems of witness intimidation. [See the comments of the Standing Committee on Criminal Law and Procedure of the State Bar of California in Hearings II, at 302.]

Some federal jurisdictions have adopted an omnibus pretrial discovery procedure that calls upon the prosecutor to give the defendant its witness lists. One such jurisdiction is the Southern District of California. The evidence before the Committee indicates that there has been no unusual problems with witness intimidation in that district. Charles Sevilla, Chief Trial Attorney for the Federal Defenders of San Diego, Inc., which operates in the Southern District of California, testified as follows:

The Government in one of its statements to this committee indicated that providing the defense with witness lists will cause coerced witness perjury. This does not happen. We receive Government witness lists as a matter of course in the Southern District, and it's a rare occasion when there is any overture by a defense witness or by a defendant to a Government witness. It simply doesn't happen except on the rarest of occasion. When the Government has that fear it can resort to the protective order. [Hearings II, at 42.]

Mr. Sevilla's observations are corroborated by the views of the U.S. Attorney for the Southern District of California:

Concerning the modifications to Rule 16, we have followed these procedures informally in this district for a number of years. We were one of the districts selected for the pilot projects of the Omnibus Hearing in 1967 or 1968. We have found that the courts in our district will not require us to disclose names of proposed witnesses when in our judgment to do so would not be advisable. Otherwise we routinely provide defense counsel with full discovery, including names and addresses of witnesses. We have not had any untoward results by following this program, having in mind that the courts will, and have, excused us from discovery where the circumstances warrant. [Hearings I, at 109.]

Much of the prosecutorial criticism of requiring the prosecution to give a list of its witnesses to the defendant reflects an unwillingness to trust judges to exercise sound judgment in the public interest. Prosecutors have stated that they frequently will open their files to defendants in order to induce pleas. [See testimony of Richard L. Thornburgh, United States Attorney for the Western District of Pennsylvania, in Hearings I, at 150.]

Prosecutors are willing to determine on their own when they can do this without jeopardizing the safety of witnesses. There is no reason why a judicial officer cannot exercise the same discretion in the public interest.

The Committee is convinced that in the usual case there is no serious risk of danger to prosecution witnesses from pretrial disclosure of their identities. In exceptional instances, there may be a risk of danger. The Committee rule, however, is capable of dealing with those exceptional instances while still providing for disclosure of witnesses in the usual case.

The Committee recognizes the force of the constitutional arguments advanced by defenders. Requiring a defendant, upon request, to give to the prosecution material which may be incriminating, certainly raises very serious constitutional problems. The Committee deals with these problems by having the defendant trigger the discovery procedures. Since the defendant has no constitutional right to discover any of the prosecution's evidence (unless it is exculpatory within the meaning of *Brady v. Maryland,* 373 U.S. 83 (1963)), it is permissible to condition his access to nonexculpatory evidence upon his turning over a list of defense witnesses. Rule 16 currently operates in this manner.

The Committee also changed subdivisions (a)(2) and (b)(2), which set forth "work product" exceptions to the general discovery requirements. The subsections proposed by the Supreme Court are cast in terms of the type of document involved (e. g., report), rather than in terms of the content (e. g., legal theory). The Committee recast these provisions by adopting language from Rule 26(b)(3) of the Federal Rules of Civil Procedure.

The Committee notes that subdivision (a)(1)(C) permits the defendant to discover certain items that "were obtained from or belong to the defendant." The Committee believes that, as indicated in the Advisory Committee Note [House Document 93-292 at 59], items that "were obtained from or belong to the defendant" are items that are material to the preparation of his defense.

The Committee added language to subdivision (a)(1)(B) to conform it to provisions in subdivision (a)(1)(A). The rule as changed by the Committee requires the prosecutor to give the defendant such copy of the defendant's prior criminal record as is within the prosecutor's "possession, custody, or control, the existence of which is known, or by the exercise of due diligence may become known" to the prosecutor. The Committee also made a similar conforming change in subdivision (a)(1)(E), dealing with the criminal records of government witnesses. The prosecutor can ordinarily discharge his obligation under these two subdivisions, (a)(1)(B) and (E), by obtaining a copy of the F.B.I. "rap sheet."

The Committee made an additional change in subdivision (a)(1)(E). The proposed rule required the prosecutor to provide the defendant with a record of the felony convictions of government witnesses. The major purpose for letting the defendant discover information about the record of government witnesses, is to provide him with information concerning the credibility of those witnesses. Rule 609(a) of the Federal Rules of Evidence permits a party to attack the credibility of a witness with convictions other than just felony convictions. The Committee, therefore, changed subdivision (a)(1)(E) to require the prosecutor to turn over a record of all criminal convictions, not just felony convictions.

The Committee changed subdivision (d)(1), which deals with protective orders. Proposed (d)(1) required the court to conduct an ex parte proceeding whenever a party so requested. The Committee changed the mandatory language to permissive language. A Court may, not must, conduct an ex parte proceeding if a party so requests. Thus, if a party requests a protective or modifying order and asks to make its showing ex parte, the court has two separate determinations to make. First, it must determine whether an ex parte proceeding is appropriate, bearing in mind that ex parte proceedings are disfavored and not to be encouraged. [An ex parte proceeding would seem to be appropriate if any adversary proceeding would defeat the purpose of the protective or modifying order. For example, the identity of a witness would be disclosed and the purpose of the protective order is to conceal that witness' identity.] Second, it must determine whether a protective or modifying order shall issue.

Notes of Conference Committee on 1975 amendments (House Report No. 94-414). Rule 16 deals with pretrial discovery by the defendant and the government. The House and Senate versions of the bill differ on Rule 16 in several respects.

A. Reciprocal vs. Independent Discovery for the Government.—The House version of the bill provides that the government's discovery is reciprocal. If the defendant requires and receives certain items from the government, then the government is entitled to get similar items from the defendant. The Senate version of the bill gives the government an independent right to discover material in the possession of the defendant.

The Conference adopts the House provisions.

B. Rule 16(a)(1)(A).—The House version permits an organization to discover relevant recorded grand jury testimony of any witness who was, at the time of the acts charged or of the grand jury proceedings, so situated as an officer or employee as to have been able legally to bind it in respect to the activities involved in the charges. The Senate version limits discovery of this material to testimony of a witness who was, at the time of the grand jury proceeding, so situated as an officer or employee as to have been legally to bind the defendant in respect to the activities involved in the charges.

The Conferees share a concern that during investigations, ex-employees and ex-officers of potential corporate defendants are a critical source of information regarding activities of their former corporate employers. It is not unusual that, at the time of their testimony or interview, these persons may have interests which are substantially adverse to or divergent from the putative corporate defendant. It is also not unusual that such individuals, though no longer sharing a community of interest with the corporation, may nevertheless be subject to pressure from their former employers. Such pressure may derive from the fact that the ex-employees or ex-officers have remained in the same industry or related industry, are employed by competitors, suppliers, or customers of their former employers, or have pension or other deferred compensation arrangements with former employers.

The Conferees also recognize that considerations of fairness require that a defendant corporation or other legal entity be entitled to the grand jury testimony of a former officer or employee if that person was personally involved in the conduct constituting the offense and was able legally to bind the defendant in respect to the conduct in which he was involved.

The Conferees decided that, on balance, a defendant organization should not be entitled to the relevant grand jury testimony of a former officer or employee in every instance. However, a defendant organization should be entitled to it if the former officer or employee was personally involved in the alleged conduct constituting the offense and was so situated as to have been able legally to bind the defendant in respect to the alleged conduct. The Conferees note that, even in those situations where the rule provides for disclosure of the testimony, the Government may, upon a sufficient showing, obtain a protective or modifying order pursuant to Rule 16(d)(1).

The Conference adopts a provision that permits a defendant organization to discover relevant grant jury testimony of a witness who (1) was, at the time of his testimony, so situated as an officer or employee as to have been able legally to bind the defendant in respect to conduct constituting the offense, or (2) was, at the time of the offense, personally involved in the alleged conduct constituting the offense and so situated as an officer or employee as to have been able legally to bind the defendant in respect to that alleged conduct in which he was involved.

C. Rules 16(a)(1)(E) and (b)(1)(C) (witness lists).—The House version of the bill provides that each party, the government and the defendant, may discover the names and addresses of the other party's witnesses 3 days before trial. The Senate version of the bill eliminates these provisions, thereby making the names and addresses of a party's witnesses nondiscoverable. The Senate version also makes a conforming change in Rule 16(d)(1). The Conference adopts the Senate version.

A majority of the Conferees believe it is not in the interest of the effective administration of criminal justice to require that the government or the defendant be forced to reveal the names and addresses of its witnesses before trial. Discouragement of witnesses and improper contact directed at influencing their testimony, were deemed paramount concerns in the formulation of this policy.

D. Rules 16(a)(2) and (b)(2).—Rules 16(a)(2) and (b)(2) define certain types of materials ("work product") not to be discoverable. The House version defines work product to be "the mental impressions, conclusions, opinions, or legal theories of the attorney for the government or other government agents." This is parallel to the definition in the Federal Rules of Civil Procedure. The Senate version returns to the Supreme Court's language and defines work product to be "reports, memoranda, or other internal government documents." This is the language of the present rule.

The Conference adopts the Senate provision.

The Conferees note that a party may not avoid a legitimate discovery request merely because something is labelled "report", "memorandum", or "internal document". For example if a document qualifies as a statement of the defendant within the meaning of the Rule 16(a)(1)(A), then the labelling of that document as "report", "memorandum", or "internal government document" will not shield that statement from discovery. Likewise, if the results of an experiment qualify as the results of a scientific test within the meaning of Rule 16(b)(1)(B), then the results of that experiment are not shielded from discovery even if they are labelled "report", "memorandum", or "internal defense document".

Notes of Advisory Committee on 1983 amendments. *Note to Subdivision (a)(3).* The added language is made necessary by the addition of Rule 26.2 and new subdivision (i) of Rule 12, which contemplate the production of statements, including those made to a grand jury, under specified circumstances.

Notes of Advisory Committee on 1987 amendments. The amendments are technical. No substantive change is intended.

Notes of Advisory Committee on 1991 amendments. The amendment to Rule 16(a)(1)(A) expands slightly government disclosure to the defense of statements made by the defendant. The rule now requires the prosecution, upon request, to disclose any written record which contains reference to a relevant oral statement by the defendant which was in response to interrogation, without regard to whether the prosecution intends to use the statement at trial. The change recognizes that the defendant has some proprietary interest in statements made during interrogation regardless of the prosecution's intent to make any use of the statements.

The written record need not be a transcription or summary of the defendant's statement but must only be some written reference which would provide some means for the prosecution and defense to identify the statement. Otherwise, the prosecution would have the difficult task of locating and disclosing the myriad oral statements made by a defendant, even if it had no intention of using the statements at trial. In a lengthy and complicated investigation with multiple interrogations by different government 'agents, that task could become unduly burdensome.

The existing requirement to disclose oral statements which the prosecution intends to introduce at trial has also been changed slightly. Under the amendment, the prosecution must also disclose any relevant oral statement which it intends to use at trial, without regard to whether it intends to introduce the statement. Thus, an oral statement by the defendant which would only be used for impeachment purposes would be covered by the rule.

The introductory language to the rule has been modified to clarify that without regard to whether the defendant's statement is oral or written, it must at a minimum be disclosed. Although the rule does not specify the means for disclosing the defendant's statements, if they are in written or recorded form, the defendant is entitled to inspect, copy, or photograph them.

Notes of Advisory Committee on 1993 amendments. New subdivisions (a)(1)(E) and (b)(1)(C) expand federal criminal discovery by requiring disclosure of the intent to rely on expert opinion testimony, what the testimony will consist of, and the bases of the testimony. The amendment is intended to minimize surprise that often results from unexpected expert testimony, reduce the need for continuances, and to provide the opponent with a fair opportunity to test the merit of the expert' s testimony through focused cross-examination. See Eads, Adjudication by Ambush: Federal Prosecutors' Use of Nonscientific Experts in a System of Limited Criminal Discovery, 67 N. C L. Rev. 577, 622 (1989).

Like other provisions in Rule 16, subdivision (a)(1)(E) requires the government to disclose information regarding its expert witnesses if the defendant first requests the information. Once the requested information is provided, the government is entitled, under (b)(1)(C) to reciprocal discovery of the same information from the defendant. The disclosure is in the form of a written summary and only applies to expert witnesses that each side intends to call during its case-in-chief. Although no specific timing requirements are included, it is expected that the parties will make their requests and disclosures in a timely fashion.

With increased use of both scientific and nonscientific expert testimony, one of counsel's most basic discovery needs is to learn that an expert is expected to testify. *See* Gianelli, *Criminal Discovery, Scientific Evidence, and DNA,* 44 Vand. L. Rev. 793 (1991); *Symposium on Science and the Rules of Legal Procedure,* 101 F.R.D. 599 (1983). This is particularly important if the expert is expected to testify on matters which touch on new or controversial techniques or opinions. The amendment is intended to meet this need by first, requiring notice of the expert's qualifications which in turn will permit the requesting party to determine whether in fact the witness is an expert within the definition of Federal Rule of Evidence 702. Like Rule 702, which generally provides a broad definition of who qualifies as an "expert," the amendment is broad in that it includes both scientific and nonscientific experts. It does not distinguish between those cases where the expert will be presenting testimony on novel scientific evidence. The rule does not extend, however, to witnesses who may offer only lay opinion testimony under Federal Rule of Evidence 701. Nor does the amendment extend to summary witnesses who may testify under Federal Rule of Evidence 1006 unless the witness is called to offer expert opinions apart from, or in addition to, the summary evidence.

Second, the requesting party is entitled to a summary of the expected testimony. This provision is intended to permit more complete pretrial preparation by the requesting party. For example, this should inform the requesting party whether the expert will be providing only background information on a particular issue or whether the witness will actually offer an opinion. In some instances, a generic description of the likely witness and that witness's qualifications may be sufficient, e.g., where a DEA laboratory chemist will testify, but it is not clear which particular chemist will be available.

Third, and perhaps most important, the requesting party is to be provided with a summary of the bases of the expert's opinion. Rule 16(a)(1)(D) covers disclosure and access to any results or reports of mental or physical examinations and scientific testing. But the fact that no formal written reports have been made does not necessarily mean that an expert will not testify at trial. At least one federal court has concluded that that provision did not otherwise require the government to disclose the identity of its expert witnesses where no reports had been prepared. *See, e.g., United States v. Johnson,* 713 F.2d 654 (11th Cir. 1983, *cert. denied,* 484 U.S. 956 (1984) (there is no right to witness list and Rule 16 was not implicated because no reports were made in the case). The amendment should remedy that problem. Without regard to whether a party would be entitled to the underlying bases for expert testimony under other provisions of Rule 16, the amendment requires a summary of the bases relied upon by the expert. That should cover not only written and oral reports, tests, reports, and investigations, but any information that might be recognized as a legitimate basis for an opinion under Federal Rule of Evidence 703, including opinions of other experts.

The amendments are not intended to create unreasonable procedural hurdles. As with other discovery requests under Rule 16, subdivision (d) is available to either side to seek ex parte a protective or modifying order concerning requests for information under (a)(1)(E) or (b)(1)(C).

Notes of Advisory Committee on 1994 amendments. The amendment is intended to clarify that the discovery and disclosure requirements of the rule apply equally to individual and organizational defendants. *See In re United States,* 918 F.2d 138 (11th Cir. 1990) (rejecting distinction between individual and organizational defendants). Because an organizational defendant may not know what its officers or agents have said or done in regard to a charged offense, it is important that it have access to statements made by persons whose statements or actions could be binding on the defendant. *See also United States v. Hughes,* 413 F.2d 1244, 1251–52 (5th Cir. 1969), vacated as moot, 397 U.S. 93 (1970) (prosecution of corporations "often resembles the most complex civil cases, necessitating a vigorous probing of the mass of detailed facts to seek out the truth").

The amendment defines defendant in a broad, nonexclusive fashion. *See also* 18 U.S.C. § 18 (the term "organization" includes a person other than an individual). And the amendment recognizes that an organizational defendant could be bound by an agent's statement, *see, e.g.,* Federal Rule of Evidence 801(d)(2), or be vicariously liable for an agent's actions. The amendment contemplates that, upon request of the defendant, the Government will disclose any statements within the purview of the rule and made by persons whom the government contends to be among the classes of persons described in the rule. There is no requirement that the defense stipulate or admit that such persons were in a position to bind the defendant.

Notes of Advisory Committee on 1997 amendments. *Subdivision (a)(1)(E).* Under Rule 16(a)(1)(E), as amended in 1993, the defense is entitled to disclosure of certain information about expert witnesses which the government intends to call during the trial. And if the government provides that information, it is entitled to reciprocal discovery under (b)(1)(C). This amendment is a parallel reciprocal disclosure provision which is triggered by a government request for information concerning defense expert witnesses as to the defendant's mental condition, which is provided for in an amendment to (b)(1)(C), infra.

Subdivision (b)(1)(C). Amendments in 1993 to Rule 16 included provisions for pretrial disclosure of information, including names and expected testimony of both defense and government expert witnesses. Those disclosures are triggered by defense requests for the information. If the defense makes such requests and the government complies, the government is entitled to similar, reciprocal discovery. The amendment to Rule 16(b)(1)(C) provides that if the defendant has notified the government under Rule 12.2 of an intent to rely on expert testimony to show the defendant's mental condition, the government may request the defense to disclose information about its expert witnesses. Although Rule 12.2 insures that the government will not be surprised by the nature of the defense or that the defense intends to call an expert witness, that rule makes no provision for discovery of the identity, the expected testimony, or the qualifications of the expert witness. The amendment provides the government with the limited right to respond to the notice provided under Rule 12.2 by requesting more specific information about the expert. If the government requests the specified information, and the defense complies, the defense is entitled to reciprocal discovery under an amendment to subdivision (a)(1)(E), supra.

Notes of Advisory Committee on 2002 amendments. The language of Rule 16 has been amended as part of the general restyling of the Criminal Rules to make them more easily understood and to make style and terminology consistent throughout the rules. These changes are intended to be stylistic only, except as noted below.

Current Rule 16(a)(1)(A) is now located in Rule 16(a)(1)(A), (B), and (C). Current Rule 16(a)(1)(B), (C), (D), and (E) have been relettered.

Amended Rule 16(b)(1)(B) includes a change that may be substantive in nature. Rule 16(a)(1)(E) and 16(a)(1)(F) require production of specified information if the government intends to "use" the information "in its case-in-chief at trial." The Committee believed that the language in revised Rule 16(b)(1)(B), which deals with a defendant's disclosure of information to the government, should track the similar language in revised Rule 16(a)(1). In Rule 16(b)(1)(B)(ii), the Committee changed the current provision which reads: "the defendant intends to *introduce* as evidence" to the "defendant intends to *use* the item . . ." The Committee recognized that this might constitute a substantive change in the rule but believed that it was a necessary conforming change with the provisions in Rule16(a)(1)(E) and (F), noted *supra*, regarding use of evidence by the government.

In amended Rule 16(d)(1), the last phrase in the current subdivision—which refers to a possible appeal of the court's discovery order—has been deleted. In the Committee's view, no substantive change results from that deletion. The language is unnecessary because the court, regardless of whether there is an appeal, will have maintained the record.

Finally, current Rule 16(e), which addresses the topic of notice of alibi witnesses, has been deleted as being unnecessarily duplicative of Rule 12.1.

Effective date of Nov. 2, 2002 amendments. Act Nov. 2, 2002, P. L. 107-273, Div C, Title I, Subtitle A, § 11019(c), 116 Stat. 1826, provides: "The amendments made by subsection (b) [amending subsec. (a)(1)(G) and (b)(1)(C) of this Rule] shall take effect on December 1, 2002.".

Notes of Advisory Committee on 2013 amendments. *Subdivision (a).* Paragraph (a)(2) is amended to clarify that the 2002 restyling of Rule 16 did not change the protection afforded to government work product.

Prior to restyling in 2002, Rule 16(a)(1)(C) required the government to allow the defendant to inspect and copy "books, papers, [and] documents" material to his defense. Rule 16(a)(2), however, stated that except as provided by certain enumerated subparagraphs — not including Rule 16(a)(2)(C)-Rule 16(a) did not authorize the discovery or inspection of reports, memoranda, or other internal government documents made by the attorney for the government. Reading these two provisions together, the Supreme Court concluded that "a defendant may examine documents material to his defense, but, under Rule 16(a)(2), he may not examine Government work product." United States v. Armstrong, 517 U.S. 456, 463 (1996).

With one exception not relevant here, the 2002 restyling of Rule 16 was intended to work no substantive change. Nevertheless, because restyled Rule 16(a)(2) eliminated the enumerated subparagraphs of its successor and contained no express exception for the materials previously covered by Rule 16(a)(1)(C) (redesignated as subparagraph (a)(1)(E)), some courts have been urged to construe the restyled rule as eliminating protection for government work product.

Courts have uniformly declined to construe the restyling changes to Rule 16(a)(2) to effect a substantive alteration in the scope of protection previously afforded to government work product by that rule. Correctly recognizing that restyling was intended to effect no substantive change, courts have invoked the doctrine of the scrivener's error to excuse confusion caused by the elimination of the enumerated subparagraphs from the restyled rules. See, e.g., United States v. Rudolph, 224 F.R.D. 503, 504-11 (N.D. Ala. 2004), and United States v. Fort, 472 F.3d 1106, 1110 n.2 (9th Cir. 2007) (adopting the Rudolph court's analysis).

By restoring the enumerated subparagraphs, the amendment makes it clear that a defendant's pretrial access to books, papers, and documents under Rule 16(a)(1)(E) remains subject to the limitations imposed by Rule 16(a)(2).

Notes of Advisory Committee on 2022 Amendments. The amendment addresses two shortcomings of the prior provisions on expert witness disclosure: the lack of adequate specificity regarding what information must be disclosed, and the lack of an enforceable deadline for disclosure. The amendment clarifies the scope and timing of the parties' obligations to disclose expert testimony they intend to present at trial. It is intended to facilitate trial preparation, allowing the parties a fair opportunity to prepare to cross-examine expert witnesses and secure opposing expert testimony if needed.

Like the existing provisions, amended subsections (a)(1)(G) (government's disclosure) and (b)(1)(C) (defendant's disclosure) generally mirror one another. The amendment to (b)(1)(C) includes the limiting phrase—now found in (a)(1)(G) and carried forward in the amendment —restricting the disclosure obligation to testimony the defendant will use in the defendant's "case-in-chief." Because the history of Rule 16 revealed no reason for the omission of this phrase from (b)(1)(C), this phrase was added to make (a) and (b) parallel as well as reciprocal. No change from current practice in this respect is intended.

The amendment to (a)(1)(G) also clarifies that the government's disclosure obligation includes not only the testimony it intends to use in its case-in-chief, but also testimony it intends to use to rebut testimony timely disclosed by the defense under (b)(1)(C).

To ensure enforceable deadlines that the prior provisions lacked, items (a)(1)(G)(ii) and (b)(1)(C)(ii) provide that the court, by order or local rule, must set a time for the government to make its disclosures of expert testimony to the defendant, and for the defense to make its disclosures of expert testimony to the government. These disclosure times, the amendment mandates, must be sufficiently before trial to provide a fair opportunity for each party to meet the other side's expert evidence. Sometimes a party may need to secure its own expert to respond to expert testimony disclosed by the other party. Deadlines should accommodate the time that may take, including the time an appointed attorney may need to secure funding to hire an expert witness, or the time the government would need to find a witness to rebut an expert disclosed by the defense. Deadlines for disclosure must also be sensitive to the requirements of the Speedy Trial Act. Because caseloads vary from district to district, the amendment does not itself set a specific time for the disclosures by the government and the defense for every case. Instead, it allows courts to tailor disclosure deadlines to local conditions or specific cases by providing that the time for disclosure must be set either by local rule or court order.

Items (a)(1)(G)(ii) and (b)(1)(C)(ii) require the court to set a time for disclosure in each case if that time is not already set by local rule or other order, but leave to the court's discretion when it is most appropriate to announce those deadlines. The court also retains discretion under Rule 16(d) consistent with the provisions of the Speedy Trial Act to alter deadlines to ensure adequate trial preparation. In setting times for expert disclosures in individual cases, the court should consider the recommendations of the parties, who are required to "confer and try to agree on a timetable" for pretrial disclosures under Rule 16.1.

To ensure that parties receive adequate information about the content of the witness's testimony and potential impeachment, items (a)(1)(G)(i) and (iii)—and the parallel provisions in (b)(1)(C)(i) and (iii)—delete the phrase "written summary" and substitute specific requirements that the parties provide "a complete statement" of the witness's opinions, the bases and reasons for those opinions, the witness's qualifications, and a list of other cases in which the witness has testified in the past 4 years. Although the language of some of these provisions is drawn from Civil Rule 26, the amendment is not intended to replicate all aspects of practice under the civil rule in criminal cases, which differ in many significant ways from civil cases. The amendment requires a complete statement of all opinions the expert will provide, but does not require a verbatim recitation of the testimony the expert will give at trial.

On occasion, an expert witness will have testified in a large number of cases, and developing the list of prior testimony may be unduly burdensome. Likewise, on occasion, with respect to an expert witness whose identity is not critical to the opposing party's ability to prepare for trial, the party who wishes to call the expert may be able to provide a complete statement of the expert's opinions, bases and reasons for them, but may not be able to provide the witness's identity until a date closer to trial. In such circumstances, the party who wishes to call the expert may seek an order modifying discovery under Rule 16(d).

Items (a)(1)(G)(iv) and (b)(1)(C)(iv) also recognize that, in some situations, information that a party must disclose about opinions and the bases and reasons for those opinions may have been provided previously in a report (including accompanying documents) of an examination or test under subparagraph (a)(1)(F) or (b)(1)(B). Information previously provided need not be repeated in the expert disclosure, if the expert disclosure clearly identifies the information and the prior report in which it was provided.

Items (a)(1)(G)(v) and (b)(1)(C)(v) of the amended rule require that the expert witness approve and sign the disclosure. However, the amended provisions also recognize two exceptions to this requirement. First, the rule recognizes the possibility that a party may not be able to obtain a witness's approval and signature despite reasonable efforts to do so. This may occur, for example, when the party has not retained or specially employed the witness to present testimony, such as when a party calls a treating physician to testify. In that situation, the party is responsible for providing the required information, but may be unable to procure a witness's approval and signature following a request. An unsigned disclosure is acceptable so long as the party states why it was unable to procure the expert's signature following reasonable efforts. Second, the expert need not sign the disclosure if a complete statement of all of the opinions as well as the bases and reasons for those opinions, were already set forth in a report, signed by the witness, previously provided under subparagraph (a)(1)(F)—for government disclosures—or (b)(1)(B)—for defendant's disclosures. In that situation, the prior signed report and accompanying documents, combined with the attorney's representation of the expert's qualifications, publications, and prior testimony, provide the information and signature needed to prepare to meet the testimony.

Items (a)(1)(G)(vi) and (b)(1)(C)(vi) require the parties to supplement or correct each disclosure to the other party in accordance with Rule 16(c). This provision is intended to ensure that, if there is any modification of a party's expert testimony or change in the identity of an expert after the initial disclosure, the other party will receive prompt notice of that modification or correction.

Notes of Advisory Committee on 2023 Amendments. The amendment corrects the cross reference in Rule 16(b)(1)(C)(v), which refers to expert reports previously provided by the defense under Rule 16(b)(1)(B).

Amendments:

1975.

Act July 30, 1975, § 3(20)–(28) (effective 12/1/75, as provided by § 2 of such Act, which appears as a note to Rule 4), in subsec. (a)(1)(A), substituted "who (1) was, at the time of his testimony, so situated as an officer or employee as to have been able legally to bind the defendant in respect to conduct constituting the offense, or (2) was, at the time of the offense, personally involved in the alleged conduct constituting the offense and so situated as an officer or employee as to have been able legally to bind the defendant in respect to that alleged conduct in which he was involved" for "who was, at the time either of the charged acts or of the grand jury proceedings, so situated as an officer or employee as to have been able legally to bind the defendant in respect to the activities involved in the charges"; substituted subsec. (a)(1)(B) for one which read "Upon request of the defendant, the government shall furnish to the defendant such copy of his prior criminal record, if any, as is then available to the attorney for the government."; substituted subsec. (a)(1)(D) for one which read "Upon request of a defendant the government shall permit the defendant to inspect and copy or photograph any results or reports of physical or mental examinations, and of scientific tests or experiments, made in connection with the particular case, or copies thereof, within the possession, custody or control of the government, the existence of which is known, or by the exercise of due diligence may become known, to the attorney for the government."; deleted a subsec. (a)(1)(E) which read "(E) Government witnesses. Upon request of the defendant the government shall furnish to the defendant a written list of the names and addresses of all government witnesses which the attorney for the government intends to call in the presentation of the case in chief together with any record of prior felony convictions of any such witness which is within the knowledge of the attorney for the government. When a request for discovery of the names and addresses of witnesses has been made by a defendant, the government shall be allowed to perpetuate the testimony of such witnesses in accordance with the provisions of Rule 15."; substituted subsec. (b)(1)(A) for one which read "Upon request of the government, the defendant shall permit the government to inspect and copy or photograph books, papers, documents, photographs, tangible objects, or copies or portions thereof, which are within the possession, custody or control of the defendant and which the defendant intends to introduce as evidence in chief at the trial."; substituted subsec. (b)(1)(B) for one which read "Upon request of the government, the defendant shall permit the government to inspect and copy or photograph any results or reports of physical or mental examinations and of scientific tests or experiments made in connection with the particular case, or copies thereof, within the possession or control of the defendant, which the defendant intends to introduce as evidence in chief at the trial or which were prepared by a witness whom the defendant intends to call at the trial when the results or reports relate to his testimony."; deleted a subsec. (b)(1)(C), which read "(C)

Defense witnesses. Upon request of the government, the defendant shall furnish the government a list of the names and addresses of the witnesses he intends to call in the presentation of the case in chief. When a request for discovery of the names and addresses of witnesses has been made by the government, the defendant shall be allowed to perpetuate the testimony of such witnesses in accordance with the provisions of Rule 15."; in subsec. (c), deleted ", or the identity of an additional witness or witnesses" after "under this rule", and substituted "evidence or material" for "material or witness"; and substituted subsec. (d)(1) for one which read "(1) Protective orders. Upon a sufficient showing the court may at any time order that the discovery or inspection be denied, restricted or deferred, or make such other order as is appropriate. Upon request by a party the court shall permit the party to make such showing, in whole or in part, in the form of a written statement to be inspected by the judge alone. If the court enters an order granting relief following such a showing, the entire text of the party's statement shall be sealed and preserved in the records of the court to be made available to the appellate court in the event of an appeal.".

Act Dec. 12, 1975, deleted subsec. (a)(4), which read "(4) Failure to call witness. The fact that a witness' name is on a list furnished under this rule shall not be grounds for comment upon a failure to call the witness."; and deleted subsec. (b)(3), which read "(3) Failure to call witness. The fact that a witness' name is on a list furnished under this rule shall not be grounds for comment upon a failure to call a witness.".

2002.

Act Nov. 2, 2002 (effective 12/1/2002, as provided by § 11019(c) of such Act, which appears a note to this rule) amended the revisions to this rule, as embraced by an order entered by the Supreme Court of the United States on April 29, 2002, by substituting subdivision (a)(1)(G) for one which read: "(G) *Expert Testimony.* Upon a defendant's request, the government must give the defendant a written summary of any testimony the government intends to use in its case-in-chief at trial under Federal Rules of Evidence 702, 703, or 705. The summary must describe the witness's opinions, the bases and reasons for those opinions, and the witness's qualifications."; and by substituting subdivision (b)(1)(C) for one which read: "(C) *Expert Testimony.* If a defendant requests disclosure under Rule 16(a)(1)(G) and the government complies, the defendant must give the government, upon request, a written summary of any testimony the defendant intends to use as evidence at trial under Federal Rules of Evidence 702, 703, or 705. The summary must describe the witness's opinions, the bases and reasons for these opinions, and the witness's qualifications.".

Rule 16.1. Pretrial Discovery Conference; Request for Court Action

(a) Discovery Conference. No later than 14 days after the arraignment, the attorney for the government and the defendant's attorney must confer and try to agree on a timetable and procedures for pretrial disclosure under Rule 16.

(b) Request for Court Action. After the discovery conference, one or both parties may ask the court to determine or modify the time, place, manner, or other aspects of disclosure to facilitate preparation for trial.

HISTORY:

Added April 25, 2019; eff. Dec. 1, 2019.

HISTORY; ANCILLARY LAWS AND DIRECTIVES

Other provisions:

Notes of Advisory Committee on 2019 amendments. This new rule requires the attorney for the government and counsel for the defendant to confer early in the process, no later than 14 days after arraignment, about the timetable and procedures for pretrial disclosure. The new requirement is particularly important in cases involving electronically stored information (ESI) or other voluminous or complex discovery.

Rule 17. Subpoena

(a) Content. A subpoena must state the court's name and the title of the proceeding, include the seal of the court, and command the witness to attend and testify at the time and place the subpoena specifies. The clerk must issue a blank subpoena—signed and sealed—to the party requesting it, and that party must fill in the blanks before the subpoena is served.

(b) Defendant Unable to Pay. Upon a defendant's ex parte application, the court must order that a subpoena be issued for a named witness if the defendant shows an inability to pay the witness's fees and the necessity of the witness's presence for an adequate defense. If the court orders a subpoena to be issued, the process costs and witness fees will be paid in the same manner as those paid for witnesses the government subpoenas.

(c) Producing Documents and Objects.

(1) *In General.* A subpoena may order the witness to produce any books, papers, documents, data, or other objects the subpoena designates. The court may direct the witness to produce the designated items in court before trial or before they are to be offered in evidence. When the items arrive, the court may permit the parties and their attorneys to inspect all or part of them.

(2) *Quashing or Modifying the Subpoena.* On motion made promptly, the court may quash or modify the subpoena if compliance would be unreasonable or oppressive.

(3) *Subpoena for Personal or Confidential Information About a Victim.* After a complaint, indictment, or information is filed, a subpoena requiring the production of personal or confidential information about a victim may be served on a third party only by court order. Before entering the order and unless there are exceptional circumstances, the court must require giving notice to the victim so that the victim can move to quash or modify the subpoena or otherwise object.

(d) Service. A marshal, a deputy marshal, or any nonparty who is at least 18 years old may serve a subpoena. The server must deliver a copy of the subpoena to the witness and must tender to the witness one day's witness-attendance fee and the legal mileage allowance. The server need not tender the attendance fee or mileage allowance when the United States, a federal officer, or a federal agency has requested the subpoena.

(e) Place of Service.

(1) *In the United States.* A subpoena requiring a witness to attend a hearing or trial may be served at any place within the United States.

(2) *In a Foreign Country.* If the witness is in a foreign country, 28 U.S.C. § 1783 governs the subpoena's service.

(f) Issuing a Deposition Subpoena.

(1) *Issuance.* A court order to take a deposition authorizes the clerk in the district where the deposition is to be taken to issue a subpoena for any witness named or described in the order.

(2) *Place.* After considering the convenience of the witness and the parties, the court may order—and the subpoena may require—the witness to appear anywhere the court designates.

(g) Contempt. The court (other than a magistrate judge) may hold in contempt a witness who, without adequate excuse, disobeys a subpoena issued by a federal court in that district. A magistrate judge may hold in contempt a witness who, without adequate excuse, disobeys a subpoena issued by that magistrate judge as provided in 28 U.S.C. § 636(e).

(h) Information Not Subject to a Subpoena. No party may subpoena a statement of a witness or of a prospective witness under this rule. Rule 26.2 governs the production of the statement.

HISTORY:

Amended Dec. 27, 1948, eff. Oct. 20, 1949; Feb. 28, 1966, eff. July 1, 1966; April 24, 1972, eff. Oct. 1, 1972; Apr. 22, 1974, eff. Dec. 1, 1975; Pub. L. 94–64, § 3(29), July 31, 1975, 89 Stat. 375, eff. Dec. 1, 1975; April 30, 1979, eff. Dec. 1, 1980; Mar. 9, 1987, eff. Aug. 1, 1987; April 22, 1993, eff. Dec. 1, 1993; April 29, 2002, eff. Dec. 1, 2002; April 23, 2008, eff. Dec. 1, 2008.

HISTORY; ANCILLARY LAWS AND DIRECTIVES

Other provisions:

Notes of Advisory Committee. *Note to Subdivision (a).* This rule is substantially the same as Rule 45(a) of the Federal Rules of Civil Procedure [28 U.S.C., Appendix].

Note to Subdivision (b). This rule preserves the existing right of an indigent defendant to secure attendance of witnesses at the expense of the Government, 28 U.S.C. [former] § 656 (Witnesses for indigent defendants). Under existing law, however, the right is limited to witnesses who are within the district in which the court is held or within one hundred miles of the place of trial. No procedure now exists whereby an indigent defendant can procure at Government expense the attendance of witnesses found in another district and more than 100 miles of the place of trial. This limitation is abrogated by the rule so that an indigent defendant will be able to secure the attendance of witnesses at the expense of the Government no matter where they are located. The showing required by the rule to justify such relief is the same as that now exacted by 28 U.S.C. [former] § 656.

Note to Subdivision (c). This rule is substantially the same as Rule 45(b) of the Federal Rules of Civil Procedure [28 U.S.C., Appendix].

Note to Subdivision (d). This rule is substantially the same as Rule 45(c) of the Federal Rules of Civil Procedure [28 U.S.C., Appendix]. The provision permitting persons other than the marshal to serve the subpoena, and requiring the payment of witness fees in Government cases is new matter.

Note to Subdivision (e)(1). This rule continues existing law, 28 U.S.C. [former] § 654 (Witnesses; subpoenas; may run into another district). The rule is different in civil cases in that in such cases, unless a statute otherwise provides, a subpoena may be served only within the district or within 100 miles of the place of trial, 28 U.S.C. [former] § 654; Rule 45(e)(1) of the Federal Rules of Civil Procedure [28 U.S.C., Appendix].

Note to Subdivision (e)(2). This rule is substantially the same as Rule 45(e)(2) of the Federal Rules of Civil Procedure [28 U.S.C., Appendix]. See *Blackmer v. United States,* 284 U.S. 421, 76 L.Ed. 375, upholding the validity of the statute referred to in the rule.

Note to Subdivision (f). This rule is substantially the same as Rule 45(d) of the Federal Rules of Civil Procedure [28 U.S.C., Appendix].

Note to Subdivision (g). This rule is substantially the same as Rule 45(f) of the Federal Rules of Civil Procedure [28 U.S.C., Appendix].

Notes of Advisory Committee on 1948 amendments. The amendment is to substitute proper reference to Title 28 in place of the repealed act.

Notes of Advisory Committee on 1966 amendments. Subdivision (b). Criticism has been directed at the requirement that an indigent defendant disclose in advance the theory of his defense in order to obtain the issuance of a subpoena at government expense while the government and defendants able to pay may have subpoenas issued in blank without any disclosure. See Report of the Attorney General's Committee on Poverty and the Administration of Criminal Justice (1963) p. 27. The Attorney General's Committee also urged that the standard of financial inability to pay be substituted for that of indigency. Id. at 40–41. In one case it was held that the affidavit filed by an indigent defendant under this subdivision could be used by the government at his trial for purposes of impeachment. *Smith v. United States,* 312 F.2d 867 (D.C.Cir. 1962). There has also been doubt as to whether the defendant need make a showing beyond the face of his affidavit in order to secure issuance of a subpoena. *Greenwell v. United States,* 317 F.2d 108 (D.C-.Cir. 1963).

The amendment makes several changes. The references to a judge are deleted since applications should be made to the court. An ex parte application followed by a satisfactory showing is substituted for the requirement of a request or motion supported by affidavit. The court is required to order the issuance of a subpoena upon finding that the defendant is unable to pay the witness fees and that the presence of the witness is necessary to an adequate defense.

Subdivision (d). The subdivision is revised to bring it into conformity with 28 U.S.C.§ 1825.

Notes of Advisory Committee on 1972 amendments. Subdivisions (a) and (g) are amended to reflect the existence of the "United States magistrate," a phrase defined in Rule 54.

Notes of Advisory Committee on 1974 amendments. Subdivision (f)(2) is amended to provide that the court has discretion over the place at which the deposition is to be taken. Similar authority is conferred by Civil Rule 45(d)(2). See C. Wright, Federal Practice and Procedure: Criminal § 278 (1969).

Ordinarily the deposition should be taken at the place most convenient for the witness but, under certain circumstances, the parties may prefer to arrange for the presence of the witness at a place more convenient to counsel.

Notes of Committee on the Judiciary on 1975 amendments (House Report No. 94-247). A. Amendments Proposed by the Supreme Court. Rule 17 of the Federal Rules of Criminal Procedure deals with subpoenas. Subdivision (f)(2) as proposed by the Supreme Court provides: The witness whose deposition is to be taken may

be required by subpoena to attend at any place designated by the trial court.

B. Committee Action. The Committee added language to the proposed amendment that directs the court to consider the convenience of the witness and the parties when compelling a witness to attend where a deposition will be taken.

Notes of Advisory Committee on 1979 amendments [effective Dec. 1, 1980, as provided by Act July 31, 1979, P. L. 96-42, § 1(1), 93 Stat. 326]. This addition to rule 17 is necessary in light of proposed rule 26.2, which deals with the obtaining of statements of government and defense witnesses.

The amendments are technical. No substantive change is intended.

Supersedure of provisions contained in subsec. (d). As to the provision of subsec. (d) of this Rule that witness shall be tendered the fee for 1 day's attendance and mileage allowed by law, as superseded, see 28 U.S.C.S. § 1825 note.

The Rule is amended to conform to the Judicial Improvements Act of 1990 [P.L. 101-650, Title III, Section 321] which provides that each United States magistrate appointed under section 631 of title 28, United States Code, shall be known as a United States magistrate judge.

Notes of Advisory Committee on 2002 amendments. The language of Rule 17 has been amended as part of the general restyling of the Criminal Rules to make them more easily understood and to make style and terminology consistent throughout the rules. These changes are intended to be stylistic only, except as noted below.

A potential substantive change has been made in Rule 17(c)(1); the word "data" has been added to the list of matters that may be subpoenaed. The Committee believed that inserting that term will reflect the fact that in an increasingly technological culture, the information may exist in a format not already covered by the more conventional list, such as a book or document.

Rule 17(g) has been amended to recognize the contempt powers of a court (other than a magistrate judge) and a magistrate judge.

Notes of Advisory Committee on 2008 amendments. *Note to Subdivision (c)(3).* This amendment implements the Crime Victims' Rights Act, codified at 18 U.S.C. § 3771(a)(8), which states that victims have a right to respect for their "dignity and privacy." The rule provides a protective mechanism when the defense subpoenas a third party to provide personal or confidential information about a victim. Third-party subpoenas raise special concerns because a third party may not assert the victim's interests, and the victim may be unaware of the subpoena. Accordingly, the amendment requires judicial approval before service of a subpoena seeking personal or confidential information about a victim from a third party. The phrase "personal or confidential information," which may include such things as medical or school records, is left to case development.

The amendment provides a mechanism for notifying the victim, and makes it clear that a victim may move to quash or modify the subpoena under Rule 17(c)(2) — or object by other means such as a letter — on the grounds that it is unreasonable or oppressive. The rule recogninizes, however, that there may be exceptional circumstances in which this procedure may not be appropriate. Such exceptional circumstances would include evidence that might be lost or destroyed if the subpoena were delayed or a situation where the defense would be unfairly prejudiced by premature disclosure of a sensitive defense startegy. The Committee leaves to the judgment of the court a determination as to whether the judge will permit the question whether such exceptional circumstances exist to be decided ex parte and authorize service of the third-party subpoena without notice to anyone.

The amendment applies only to subpoenas served after a complaint, indictment, or information has been filed. It has no application to grand jury subpoenas. When the grand jury seeks the production of personal or confidential information, grand jury secrecy affords substantial protection for the victim's privacy and dignity interests.

Amendments:

1975.

Act July 31, 1975, § 3(29) (effective 12/1/75, as provided by § 2 of such Act, which appears as a note to Rule 4), in subsec. (f)(2), added ", taking into account the convenience of the witness and the parties".

Rule 17.1. Pretrial Conference

On its own, or on a party's motion, the court may hold one or more pretrial conferences to promote a fair and expeditious trial. When a conference ends, the court must prepare and file a memorandum of any matters agreed to during the conference. The government may not use any statement made during the conference by the defendant or the defendant's attorney unless it is in writing and is signed by the defendant and the defendant's attorney.

HISTORY:

Added Feb. 28, 1966, eff. July 1, 1966; amended Mar. 9, 1987, eff. Aug. 1, 1987; April 29, 2002, eff. Dec. 1, 2002.

HISTORY; ANCILLARY LAWS AND DIRECTIVES

Other provisions:

Notes of Advisory Committee on Rules. This new rule establishes a basis for pretrial conferences with counsel for the parties in criminal cases within the discretion of the court. Pretrial conferences are now being utilized to some extent even in the absence of a rule. See, generally, Brewster, Criminal Pre-Trials—Useful Techniques, 29 F.R.D. 442 (1962); Estes, Pre-Trial Conferences in Criminal Cases, 23 F.R.D. 560 (1959); Kaufman, Pre-Trial in Criminal Cases, 23 F.R.D. 551 (1959); Kaufman, Pre-Trial in

Criminal Cases, 42 J.Am.Jud.Soc. 150 (1959); Kaufman, The Appalachian Trial: Further Observations on Pre-Trial in Criminal Cases, 44 J.Am.Jud.Soc. 53 (1960); West, Criminal Pre-Trials—Useful Techniques, 29 F.R.D. 436 (1962); Handbook of Recommended Procedures for the Trial of Protracted Cases, 25 F.R.D. 399–403, 468–470 (1960). Cf. Mo.Sup.Ct. Rule 25.09; Rules Governing the NJ Courts, § 3:5-3.

The rule is cast in broad language so as to accommodate all types of pretrial conferences. As the third sentence suggests, in some cases it may be desirable or necessary to have the defendant present. See Committee on Pretrial Procedure of the Judicial Conference of the United States, Recommended Procedures in Criminal Pretrials, 37 F.R.D. 95 (1965).

Notes of Advisory Committee on 1987 amendments. The amendments are technical. No substantive change is intended.

Notes of Advisory Committee on 2002 amendments. The language of Rule 17.1 has been amended as part of the general restyling of the Criminal Rules to make them more easily understood and to make style and terminology consistent throughout the rules. These changes are intended to be stylistic only, except as noted below.

Current Rule 17.1 prohibits the court from holding a pretrial conference where the defendant is not represented by counsel. It is unclear whether this would bar such a conference when the defendant invokes the constitutional right to self-representation. See *Faretta v. California,* 422 U.S. 806 [45 L. Ed. 2d 562] (1975). The amended version makes clear that a pretrial conference may be held in these circumstances. Moreover, the Committee believed that pretrial conferences might be particularly useful in those cases where the defendant is proceeding pro se.

TITLE V. VENUE

Rule
18. Place of Prosecution and Trial
19. [Reserved]
20. Transfer for Plea and Sentence
21. Transfer for Trial
22. [Transferred]

Rule 18. Place of Prosecution and Trial

Unless a statute or these rules permit otherwise, the government must prosecute an offense in a district where the offense was committed. The court must set the place of trial within the district with due regard for the convenience of the defendant, any victim, and the witnesses, and the prompt administration of justice.

HISTORY:

Amended Feb. 28, 1966, eff. July 1, 1966; April 30, 1979, eff. Aug. 1, 1979; April 29, 2002, eff. Dec. 1, 2002; April 23, 2008, eff. Dec. 1, 2008.

HISTORY; ANCILLARY LAWS AND DIRECTIVES

Other provisions:

Notes of Advisory Committee.

1. The Constitution of the United States, Article III, Section 2, Paragraph 3, provides:

The Trial of all Crimes, except in Cases of Impeachment, shall be by Jury; and such Trial shall be held in the State where the said Crimes shall have been committed; but when not committed within any State, the Trial shall be at such Place or Places as the Congress may by Law have directed.

Amendment VI provides:

In all criminal prosecutions, the accused shall enjoy the right to a speedy and public trial, by an impartial jury of the State and district wherein the crime shall have been committed, which district shall have been previously ascertained by law . . . .

28 USC [former] § 114 [see §§ 1393, 1441] provides:

All prosecutions for crimes or offenses shall be had within the division of such districts where the same were committed, unless the court, or the judge thereof, upon the application of the defendant, shall order the cause to be transferred for prosecution to another division of the district.

The word "prosecutions," as used in this statute, does not include the finding and return of an indictment. The prevailing practice of impaneling a grand jury for the entire district at a session in some division and of distributing the indictments among the divisions in which the offenses were committed is deemed proper and legal, *Salinger v. Loisel,* 265 U.S. 224, 237, 44 S.Ct. 519, 68 L.Ed. 989. The court stated that this practice is "attended with real advantages." The rule is a restatement of existing law and is intended to sanction the continuance of this practice. For this reason, the rule requires that only the trial be held in the division in which the offense was committed and permits other proceedings to be had elsewhere in the same district.

2. Within the framework of the foregoing constitutional provisions and the provisions of the general statute, 28 U.S.C. [former] § 114 (see §§ 1393, 1441), *supra,* numerous statutes have been enacted to regulate the venue of criminal proceedings, particularly in respect to continuing offenses and offenses consisting of several transactions occurring in different districts. *Armour Packing Co. v. United States,* 209 U.S. 56, 73–77, 28 S.Ct. 428, 52 L.Ed. 681; *United States v. Johnson,* 323 U.S. 273, 65 S.Ct. 249, 89 L.Ed. 236. These special venue provisions are not affected by the rule. Among these statutes are the following:

8 U.S.C.: § 138 [see §§ 1326, 1328, 1329] (Importation of aliens for immoral purposes; attempt to reenter after deportation; penalty).

15 U.S.C.: § 78aa (Regulation of securities exchanges; jurisdiction of offenses and suits).

§ 79y (Control of public utility holding companies; jurisdiction of offenses and suits).

§ 80a-43 (investment companies; jurisdiction of offenses and suits).

§ 80b-14 (Investment advisers; jurisdiction of offenses and suits).

§ 298 (Falsely stamped gold or silver, etc., violations of law; penalty; jurisdiction of prosecutions).

§ 715i (Interstate transportations of petroleum products; restraining violations; civil and criminal proceedings; jurisdiction of District Courts; review).

§ 717u (Natural Gas Act; jurisdiction of offenses; enforcement of liabilities and duties).

18 U.S.C.: § 39 [see §§ 5, 3241] (Enforcement of neutrality; United States defined; jurisdiction of offenses; prior offenses; partial invalidity of provisions).

§ 336 [see § 1302] (Lottery, or gift enterprise circulars not mailable; place of trial).

§ 338a [see §§ 876, 3239] (Mailing threatening communications).

§ 338b [see §§ 877, 3239] (Same; mailing in foreign country for delivery in the United States).

§ 345 [see § 1717] (Using or attempting to use mails for transmission of matter declared nonmailable by title; jurisdiction of offense).

§ 396e [see § 1762] (Transportation or importation of convict-made goods with intent to use in violation of local law; jurisdiction of violations).

§ 401 [see § 2421] (White slave traffic; jurisdiction of prosecutions).

§ 408 [see §§ 10, 2311–2313] (Motor vehicles; transportation, etc., of stolen vehicles).

§ 408d [see §§ 875, 3239] (Threatening communications in interstate commerce).

§ 408e [see § 1073] (Moving in interstate or foreign commerce to avoid prosecution for felony or giving testimony).

§ 409 [see §§ 659, 660, 2117] (Larceny, etc., of goods in interstate or foreign commerce; penalty).

§ 412 [see § 660] (Embezzlement, etc. by officers of carrier; jurisdiction; double jeopardy).

§ 418 [see § 3237] (National Stolen Property Act; jurisdiction).

§ 419d [see § 3237] (Transportation of stolen cattle in interstate or foreign commerce; jurisdiction of offense).

§ 420d [see § 1951] (Interference with trade and commerce by violence, threats, etc.; jurisdiction of offenses).

§ 494 [see § 1654] (Arming vessel to cruise against citizen; trials).

§ 553 [see § 3236] (Place of committal of murder or manslaughter determined).

21 U.S.C.: § 17 (Introduction into, or sale in, State or Territory or District of Columbia of dairy or food products falsely labeled or branded; penalty; jurisdiction of prosecutions).

§ 118 (Prevention of introduction and spread of contagion; duty of district attorneys).

28 U.S.C.: § 101 [see 18 § 3235] (Capital cases).

§ 102 [see 18 § 3238] (Offenses on the high seas).

§ 103 [see 18 § 3237] (Offenses begun in one district and completed in another).

§ 121 [see 18 § 3240] (Creation of new district or division).

47 U.S.C.: § 33 (Submarine cables; jurisdiction and venue of actions and offenses).

§ 505 (Special provisions relating to radio; venue of trials).

49 U.S.C.: § 41 [see §§ 11902, 11903, 11915, 11916] (Legislation supplementary to Interstate Commerce Act; liability of corporation carriers and agents; offenses and penalties—(1) Liability of corporation common carriers; offenses; penalties; jurisdiction).

§ 623 [see § 1473] (Civil Aeronautics Act; venue and prosecution of offenses).

Notes of Advisory Committee on 1966 amendments.

The amendment eliminates the requirement that the prosecution shall be in a division in which the offense was committed and vests discretion in the court to fix the place of trial at any place within the district with due regard to the convenience of the defendant and his witnesses.

The Sixth Amendment provides that the defendant shall have the right to a trial "by an impartial jury of the State and district wherein the crime shall have been committed, which district shall have been previously ascertained by law. . . ." There is no constitutional right to trial within a division. See *United States v. Anderson,* 328 U.S. 699, 704, 705, 90 L.Ed. 1529, 66 S.Ct. 1213 (1946); *Barrett v. United States,* 169 U.S. 218, 42 L.Ed. 723, 18 S.Ct. 327 (1898); *Lafoon v. United States,* 250 F.2d 958 (5th Cir. 1958); *Carrillo v. Squier,* 137 F.2d 648 (9th Cir. 1943); *McNealey v. Johnston,* 100 F.2d 280, 282 (9th Cir. 1938).Cf. *Platt v. Minnesota Mining and Manufacturing Co.* 376 U.S. 240, 11 L.Ed.2d 674, 84 S.Ct. 769 (1964).

The former requirement for venue within the division operated in an irrational fashion. Divisions have been created in only half of the districts, and the differentiation between those districts with and those without divisions often bears no relationship to comparative size or population. In many districts a single judge is required to sit in several divisions and only brief and infrequent terms may be held in particular divisions. As a consequence under the original rule there was often undue delay in the disposition of criminal cases—delay which was particularly serious with respect to defendants who had been unable to secure release on bail pending the holding of the next term of court.

If the court is satisfied that there exists in the place fixed for trial prejudice against the defendant so great as to render the trial unfair, the court may, of course, fix another place of trial within the district (if there be such) where such prejudice does not exist. Cf. Rule 21 dealing with transfers between districts.

Notes of Advisory Committee on 1979 amendments.

This amendment is intended to eliminate an inconsistency between rule 18, which in its present form has been interpreted not to allow trial in a division other than that in which the offense was committed except as dictated by the convenience of the defendant and witnesses, *Dupoint v. United States,* 388 F.2d 39 (5th Cir. 1968), and the Speedy Trial Act of 1974. This Act provides: In any case involving

> a defendant charged with an offense, the appropriate judicial officer, at the earliest practicable time, shall, after consultation with the counsel for the defendant and the attorney for the Government, set the case for trial on a day certain, or list it for trial on a weekly or other short-term trial calendar at a place within the judicial district, so as to assure a speedy trial.

18 U.S.C. § 3161(a). This provision is intended to "permit the trial of a case at any place within the judicial district. This language was included in anticipation of problems which might occur in districts with statutory divisions, where it could be difficult to set trial outside the division." H.R. Rep. No. 93-1508, 93d Cong., 2d Sess. 29 (1974).

The change does not offend the venue or vicinage provisions of the Constitution. Article III, § 2, clause 3 places venue (the geographical location of the trial) "in the State where the said Crimes shall have been committed," while the Sixth Amendment defines the vicinage (the geographical location of the jurors) as "the State and district wherein the crime shall have been committed, which district shall have been previously ascertained by law." The latter provision makes "no reference to a division within a judicial district." *United States v. James,* 528 F.2d 999 (5th Cir. 1976). "It follows a fortiori that when a district is not separated into divisions, . . . trial at any place within the district is allowable under the Sixth Amendment . . ." *United States v. Fernandez,* 480 F.2d 726 (2d Cir. 1973). See also *Zicarelli v. Gray,* 543 F.2d 466 (3d Cir. 1976) and cases cited therein.

Nor is the change inconsistent with the Declaration of Policy in the Jury Selection and Service Act of 1968, which reads: It is the policy of the United States that all litigants

> in Federal courts entitled to trial by jury shall have the right to grand and petit juries selected at random from a fair cross section of the community in the district or division wherein the court convenes.

28 U.S.C. § 1861. This language does not mean that the Act requires "the trial court to convene not only in the district but also in the division wherein the offense occurred," as: There is no hint in the statutory history that

> the Jury Selection Act was intended to do more than provide improved judicial machinery so that grand and petit jurors would be selected at random by the use of objective qualification criteria to ensure a representative cross section of the district or division in which the grand or petit jury sits."*United States v. Cates,* 485 F.2d 26 (1st Cir. 1974).

The amendment to rule 18 does not eliminate either of the existing considerations which bear upon fixing the place of trial within a district, but simply adds yet another consideration in the interest of ensuring compliance with the requirements of the Speedy Trial Act of 1974. The amendment does not authorize the fixing of the place of trial for yet other reasons. Cf. *United States v. Fernandez,* 480 F.2d 726 (2d Cir. 1973) (court in the exercise of its supervisory power held improper the fixing of the place of trial "for no apparent reason other than the convenience of the judge").

Notes of Advisory Committee on 2002 amendments.
The language of Rule 18 has been amended as part of the general restyling of the Criminal Rules to make them more easily understood and to make style and terminology consistent throughout the rules. These changes are intended to be stylistic only.

Notes of Advisory Committee on 2008 amendments.
The rule requires the court to consider the convenience of victims — as well as the defendant and witnesses — in setting the place for trial within the district. The Committee recognizes that the court has substantial discretion to balance any competing interests.

Rule 19. [Reserved]

HISTORY; ANCILLARY LAWS AND DIRECTIVES

Other provisions:

Rescission of rule. This Rule (Dec. 26, 1944, eff. March 21, 1946), was rescinded by Order of Feb. 28, 1966, eff. July 1, 1966. It provided for transfer within the district.

Notes of Advisory Committee. Rule 19 is rescinded in view of the amendments being proposed to rule 18.

Rule 20. Transfer for Plea and Sentence

(a) Consent to Transfer. A prosecution may be transferred from the district where the indictment or information is pending, or from which a warrant on a complaint has been issued, to the district where the defendant is arrested, held, or present if:

(1) the defendant states in writing a wish to plead guilty or nolo contendere and to waive trial in the district where the indictment, information, or complaint is pending, consents in writing to the court's disposing of the case in the transferee district, and files the statement in the transferee district; and

(2) the United States attorneys in both districts approve the transfer in writing.

(b) Clerk's Duties. After receiving the defendant's statement and the required approvals, the clerk where the indictment, information, or complaint is pending must send the file, or a certified copy, to the clerk in the transferee district.

(c) Effect of a Not Guilty Plea. If the defendant pleads not guilty after the case has been transferred under Rule 20(a), the clerk must return the papers to the court where the prosecution began, and that court must restore the proceeding to its docket. The defendant's statement that the defendant wished to plead guilty or nolo contendere is not, in any civil or criminal proceeding, admissible against the defendant.

(d) Juveniles.

(1) *Consent to Transfer.* A juvenile, as defined in 18 U.S.C. § 5031, may be proceeded against as a juvenile delinquent in the district where the juvenile is arrested, held, or present if:

(A) the alleged offense that occurred in the other district is not punishable by death or life imprisonment;

(B) an attorney has advised the juvenile;

(C) the court has informed the juvenile of the juvenile's rights—including the right to be returned to the district where the offense allegedly occurred—and the consequences of waiving those rights;

(D) the juvenile, after receiving the court's information about rights, consents in writing to be proceeded against in the transferee district, and files the consent in the transferee district;

(E) the United States attorneys for both districts approve the transfer in writing; and

(F) the transferee court approves the transfer.

(2) *Clerk's Duties.* After receiving the juvenile's written consent and the required approvals, the clerk where the indictment, information, or complaint is pending or where the alleged offense occurred must send the file, or a certified copy, to the clerk in the transferee district.

HISTORY:

Amended Feb. 28, 1966, eff. July 1, 1966; April 22, 1974, eff. Dec. 1, 1975; July 31, 1975, P. L. 94-64, §§ 2, 3(30), 89 Stat. 370, 375; April 28, 1982, eff. Aug. 1, 1982; Mar. 9, 1987, eff. Aug. 1, 1987; April 29, 2002, eff. Dec. 1, 2002.

HISTORY; ANCILLARY LAWS AND DIRECTIVES

Other provisions:

Notes of Advisory Committee. This rule introduces a new procedure in the interest of defendants who intend to plead guilty and are arrested in a district other than that in which the prosecution has been instituted. This rule would accord to a defendant in such a situation an opportunity to secure a disposition of the case in the district where the arrest takes place, thereby relieving him of whatever hardship may be involved in a removal to the place where the prosecution is pending. In order to prevent possible interference with the administration of justice, however, the consent of the United States attorneys involved is required.

Notes of Advisory Committee on 1966 amendments. Rule 20 has proved to be most useful. In some districts, however, literal compliance with the procedures spelled out by the rule has resulted in unnecessary delay in the disposition of cases. This delay has been particularly troublesome where the defendant has been arrested prior to the filing of an indictment or information against him. See e.g., the procedure described in *Donovan v. United States,* 205 F.2d 557 (10th Cir. 1953). Furthermore, the benefit of the rule has not been available to juveniles electing to be proceeded against under 18 U.S.C. §§ 5031–5037. In an attempt to clarify and simplify the procedure the rule has been recast into four subdivisions.

Subdivision (a). This subdivision is intended to apply to the situation in which an indictment or information is pending at the time at which the defendant indicates his desire to have the transfer made. Two amendments are made to the present language of the rule. In the first sentence the words "or held" and "or is held" are added to make it clear that a person already in state or federal custody within a district may request a transfer of federal charges pending against him in another district. See 4 Barron, Federal Practice and Procedure 146 (1951). The words "after receiving a copy of the indictment or information" are deleted. The defendant should be permitted, if he wishes, to initiate transfer proceedings under the Rule without waiting for a copy of the indictment or information to be obtained. The defendant is protected against prejudice by the fact that under subdivision (c) he can, in effect, rescind his action by pleading not guilty after the transfer has been completed.

Subdivision (b). This subdivision is intended to apply to the situation in which no indictment or information is pending but the defendant has been arrested on a warrant issued upon a complaint in another district. Under the procedure set out he may initiate the transfer proceedings without waiting for the filing of an indictment or information in the district where the complaint is pending. Also it is made clear that the defendant may validate an information previously filed by waiving indictment in open court when he is brought before the court to plead. See *United States v. East,* 5 F.R.D. 389 (N.D. Ind. 1946); *Potter v. United States,* 36 F.R.D. 394 (W.D. Mo. 1965). Here again the defendant is fully protected by the fact that at the time of pleading in the transferee court he may then refuse to waive indictment and rescind the transfer by pleading not guilty.

Subdivision (c). The last two sentences of the original rule are included here. The last sentence is amended to forbid use against the defendant of his statement that he wishes to plead guilty or nolo contendere whether or not he was represented by counsel when it was made. Since under the amended rule the defendant may make his statement prior to receiving a copy of the indictment or information, it would be unfair to permit use of that statement against him.

Subdivision (d). Under 18 U.S.C. § 5033 a juvenile who has committed an act in violation of the law of the United States in one district and is apprehended in another must be returned to the district "having cognizance of the alleged violation" before he can consent to being proceeded against as a juvenile delinquent. This subdivision will permit a juvenile after he has been advised by counsel and with the approval of the court and the United States attorney to consent to be proceeded against in the district in which he is arrested or held. Consent is required only of the United States attorney in the district of the arrest in order to permit expeditious handling of juvenile cases. If it is necessary to recognize special interests of particular districts where offenses are committed—e.g., the District of Columbia with its separate Juvenile Court (District of Columbia Code § 11-1551(a))—the Attorney General may do so through his administrative control over United States Attorneys.

Subdivision (e). This subdivision is added to make it clear that a defendant who appears in one district in response to a summons issued in the district where the offense was committed may initiate transfer proceedings under the rule.

Notes of Advisory Committee on 1974 amendments. Rule 20 is amended to provide that a person "present" in a district other than the district in which he is charged with a criminal offense may, subject to the other provisions of rule 20, plead guilty in the district in which he is "present." See rule 6(b), Rules of Procedure for the Trial of Minor Offenses Before Magistrates.

Under the former rule, practice was to have the district in which the offense occurred issue a bench warrant authorizing the arrest of the defendant in the district in which he was located. This is a procedural complication which serves no interest of either the government or the defense and therefore can properly be dispensed with.

Making the fact that a defendant is "present" in the district an adequate basis for allowing him to plead guilty there makes it unnecessary to retain subdivision (e) which makes appearance in response to a summons equivalent to an arrest. Dropping (e) will eliminate some minor ambiguity created by that subdivision. See C. Wright, Federal Practice and Procedure: Criminal § 322 n. 26, p. 612 (1969, Supp. 1971).

There are practical advantages which will follow from the change. In practice a person may turn himself in in a district other than that in which the prosecution is pending. It may be more convenient to have him plead in the district in which he is present rather than having him or the government incur the expense of his return to the district in which the charge is pending.

The danger of "forum shopping" can be controlled by the requirement that both United States Attorneys agree to the handling of the case under provisions of this rule.

Notes of Committee on the Judiciary on 1975 amendments (House Report No. 94-247). A. Amendments Proposed by the Supreme Court. Rule 20 of the Federal Rules of Criminal Procedure deals with transferring a defendant from one district to another for the purpose of pleading and being sentenced. It deals with the situation where a defendant is located in one district (A) and is charged with a crime in another district (B). Under the present rule, if such a defendant desires to waive trial and plead guilty or nolo contendere, a judge in district B would issue a bench warrant for the defendant, authorizing his arrest in district A and his transport to district B for the purpose of pleading and being sentenced.

The Supreme Court amendments permit the defendant in the above example to plead guilty or nolo contendere in district A, if the United States Attorneys for districts A and B consent.

B. Committee Action. The Committee has added a conforming amendment to subdivision (d), which establishes procedures for dealing with defendants who are juveniles.

Notes of Advisory Committee on 1982 amendments. Rule 20(b). This amendment to subdivision (b) is intended to expedite transfer proceedings under Rule 20. At present, considerable delay—sometimes as long as three or four weeks—occurs in subdivision (b) cases, that is, where no indictment or information is pending. This time is spent on the transmittal of defendant's statement to the district where the complaint is pending, the filing of an information or return of an indictment there, and the transmittal of papers in the case from that district to the district where the defendant is present. Under the amendment, the defendant, by also waiving venue, would make it possible for charges to be filed in the district of his arrest or presence. This would advance the interests of both the prosecution and defendant in a timely entry of a plea of guilty. No change has been made in the requirement that the transfer occur with the consent of both United States attorneys.

Notes of Advisory Committee on 1987 amendments. The amendments are technical. No substantive change is intended.

Notes of Advisory Committee on 2002 amendments. The language of Rule 20 has been amended as part of the general restyling of the Criminal Rules to make them more easily understood and to make style and terminology consistent throughout the rules. These changes are intended to be stylistic only, except as noted below.

New Rule 20(d)(2) applies to juvenile cases and has been added to parallel a similar provision in new Rule 20(b). The new provision provides that after the court has determined that the provisions in Rule 20(d)(1) have been completed and the transfer is approved, the file (or certified copy) must be transmitted from the original court to the transferee court.

Amendments:

1975.

Act July 31, 1975, § 3(30) (effective 12/1/75, as provided by § 2 of such Act which appears as a note to Rule 4), in sub sec. (d), added "for each district".

Rule 21. Transfer for Trial

(a) For Prejudice. Upon the defendant's motion, the court must transfer the proceeding against that defendant to another district if the court is satisfied that so great a prejudice against the defendant exists in the transferring district that the defendant cannot obtain a fair and impartial trial there.

(b) For Convenience. Upon the defendant's motion, the court may transfer the proceeding, or one or more counts, against that defendant to another district for the convenience of the parties, any victim, and the witnesses, and in the interest of justice.

(c) Proceedings on Transfer. When the court orders a transfer, the clerk must send to the transferee district the file, or a certified copy, and any bail taken. The prosecution will then continue in the transferee district.

(d) Time to File a Motion to Transfer. A motion to transfer may be made at or before arraignment or at any other time the court or these rules prescribe.

HISTORY:

Amended Feb. 28, 1966, eff. July 1, 1966; Mar. 9, 1987, eff. Aug. 1, 1987; April 29, 2002, eff. Dec. 1, 2002; April 28, 2010, eff. Dec. 1, 2010.

HISTORY; ANCILLARY LAWS AND DIRECTIVES

Other provisions:

Notes of Advisory Committee. *Note to Subdivisions (a) and (b).* 1. This rule introduces an addition to existing law. "Lawyers not thoroughly familiar with Federal practice are somewhat astounded to learn that they may not move for a change of venue, even if they are able to demonstrate that public feeling in the vicinity of the crime may render impossible a fair and impartial trial. This seems to be a defect in the federal law, which the proposed rules would cure." Homer Cummings, 29 A.B.A.Jour. 655; Medalie, 4 Lawyers Guild R. (3) 1, 5.

2. The rule provides for two kinds of motions that may be made by the defendant for a change of venue. The first is a motion on the ground that so great a prejudice exists against the defendant that he cannot obtain a fair and impartial trial in the district or division where the case is pending. Express provisions to a similar effect are found in many State statutes. See, e.g., Ala. Code (1940), Title 15, sec. 267; Cal.Pen.Code (Deering, 1941), sec. 1033; Conn.Gen.Stat. (1930), sec. 6445; Mass.Gen.Laws (1932) c. 277, sec. 51 (in capital cases); N.Y. Code of Criminal Procedure, sec. 344. The second is a motion for a change of venue in cases involving an offense alleged to have been committed in more than one district or division. In such cases the court, on defendant's motion, will be authorized to transfer the case to another district or division in which the commission of the offense is charged, if the court is satisfied that it is in the interest of justice to do so. The effect of this provision would be to modify the existing practice under which in such cases the Government has the final choice of the jurisdiction where the prosecution should be conducted. The matter will now be left in the discretion of the court.

3. The rule provides for a change of venue only on defendant's motion and does not extend the same right to the prosecution, since the defendant has a constitutional right to a trial in the district where the offense was committed. Constitution of the United States, Article III, Sec. 2, Par. 3; Amendment VI. By making a motion for a change of venue, however, the defendant waives this constitutional right.

4. This rule is in addition to and does not supersede existing statutes enabling a party to secure a change of judge on the ground of personal bias or prejudice, 28 U.S.C. [former] § 25 (see § 144); or enabling the defendant to secure a change of venue as of right in certain cases involving offenses committed in more than one district, 18 U.S.C. [former] § 338a(d) (see §§ 876, 3239) (Mailing threatening communications); *Id.* 18 U.S.C. § 403d(d) (see §§ 875, 3239) (Threatening communications in interstate commerce).

Note to Subdivision (c). Cf. 28 U.S.C. [former] § 114 (see §§ 1393, 1441) and Rule 20, *supra.*

Notes of Advisory Committee on 1966 amendments. Subdivision (a). All references to divisions are eliminated in accordance with the amendment to Rule 18 eliminating division venue. The defendant is given the right to a transfer only when he can show that he cannot obtain a fair and impartial trial at any place fixed by law for holding court in the district. Transfers within the district to avoid prejudice will be within the power of the judge to fix the place of trial as provided in the amendments to Rule 18. It is also made clear that on a motion to transfer under this subdivision the court may select the district to which the transfer may be made. Cf. *United States v. Parr,* 17 F.R.D. 512, 519 (S.D.Tex. 1955); *Parr v. United States,* 351 U.S. 513, 100 L.Ed. 1377, 76 S.Ct. 912 (1956).

Subdivision (b). The original rule limited change of venue for reasons other than prejudice in the district to those cases where venue existed in more than one district. Upon occasion, however, convenience of the parties and witnesses and the interest of justice would best be served by trial in a district in which no part of the offense was committed. See, e.g., *Travis v. United States,* 364 U.S. 631, 5 L.Ed. 340, 81 S.Ct. 358 (1961), holding that the only venue of a charge of making or filing a false non-Communist affidavit required by § 9(h) of the National Labor Relations Act is in Washington, D.C. even though all the relevant witnesses may be located at the place where the affidavit was executed and mailed. See also Barber, Venue in Federal Criminal Cases: A Plea for Return to Principle, 42 Tex.L.Rev. 39 (1963); Wright, Proposed Changes in Federal Civil, Criminal and Appellate Procedure, 35 F.R.D. 317, 329 (1964). The amendment permits a transfer in any case on motion of the defendant on a showing that it would be for the convenience of parties and witnesses, and in the interest of justice. Cf. 28 U.S.C. § 1404(a), stating a similar standard for civil cases. See also *Platt v. Minnesota Min. & Mfg. Co.,* 376 U.S.C. 240 (1964). Here, as in subdivision (a), the court may select the district to which the transfer is to be made. The amendment also makes it clear that the court may transfer all or part of the offenses charged in a multi-count indictment or information. Cf. *United States v. Choate,* 276 F.2d 724 (5th Cir. 1960). References to divisions are eliminated in accordance with the amendment to Rule 18.

Subdivision (c). The reference to division is eliminated in accordance with the amendment to Rule 18.

The amendments are technical. No substantive change is intended.

Notes of Advisory Committee on 2002 amendments. The language of Rule 21 has been amended as part of the general restyling of the Criminal Rules to make them more easily understood and to make style and terminology consistent throughout the rules. These changes are intended to be stylistic only.

Amended Rule 21(d) consists of what was formerly Rule 22. The Committee believed that the substance of Rule 22, which addressed the issue of the timing of motions to transfer, was more appropriate for inclusion in Rule 21.

Notes of Advisory Committee on 2010 amendments. *Note to Subdivision (b).* This amendment requires the court to consider the convenience of victims—as well as the convenience of the parties and witnesses and the interests of justice—in determining whether to transfer all or part of the proceeding to another district for trial. The Committee recognizes that the court has substantial discretion to balance any competing interests.

Rule 22. [Transferred]

HISTORY; ANCILLARY LAWS AND DIRECTIVES

Other provisions:

Notes of Advisory Committee on 2002 amendments. Rule 22 has been abrogated. The substance of the rule is now located in Rule 21(d).

TITLE VI. TRIAL

Rule

Rule 23. Jury or Nonjury Trial

(a) Jury Trial. If the defendant is entitled to a jury trial, the trial must be by jury unless:

(1) the defendant waives a jury trial in writing;

(2) the government consents; and

(3) the court approves.

(b) Jury Size.

(1) *In General.* A jury consists of 12 persons unless this rule provides otherwise.

(2) *Stipulation for a Smaller Jury.* At any time before the verdict, the parties may, with the court's approval, stipulate in writing that:

(A) the jury may consist of fewer than 12 persons; or

(B) a jury of fewer than 12 persons may return a verdict if the court finds it necessary to excuse a juror for good cause after the trial begins.

(3) *Court Order for a Jury of 11.* After the jury has retired to deliberate, the court may permit a jury of 11 persons to return a verdict, even without a stipulation by the parties, if the court finds good cause to excuse a juror.

(c) Nonjury Trial. In a case tried without a jury, the court must find the defendant guilty or not guilty. If a party requests before the finding of guilty or not guilty, the court must state its specific findings of fact in open court or in a written decision or opinion.

HISTORY:

Amended Feb. 28, 1966, eff. July 1, 1966; July 30, 1977, P. L. 95-78, § 2(b), 91 Stat. 320; April 28, 1983, eff. Aug. 1, 1983; April 29, 2002, eff. Dec. 1, 2002.

HISTORY; ANCILLARY LAWS AND DIRECTIVES

Other provisions:

Notes of Advisory Committee. *Note to Subdivision (a).* 1. This rule is a formulation of the constitutional guaranty of trial by jury, Constitution of the United States, Article III, Sec. 2, Par. 3: "The Trial of all Crimes, except in Cases of Impeachment, shall be by Jury . . ."; Amendment VI: "In all criminal prosecutions, the accused shall enjoy the right to a speedy and public trial, by an impartial jury . . . ." The right to a jury trial, however, does not apply to petty offenses, *District of Columbia v. Clawans,* 300 U.S. 617, 57 S.Ct. 660, 81 L.Ed. 843; *Schick v. United States,* 195 U.S. 65, 24 S.Ct. 826, 49 L.Ed. 99, 1 Ann.Cas. 585; Frankfurter and Corcoran, 39 Harv.L.R. 917. Cf. Rule 38(a) of the Federal Rules of Civil Procedure [28 U.S.C., Appendix].

2. The provision for a waiver of jury trial by the defendant embodies existing practice, the constitutionality of which has been upheld, *Patton v. United States,* 281 U.S. 276, 50 S.Ct. 253, 74 L.Ed. 854, 70 A.L.R. 263; *Adams v. United States ex rel. McCann,* 317 U.S. 269, 63 S.Ct. 236, 87 L.Ed. 268, 143 A.L.R. 435; cf. Rules 38 and 39 of Federal Rules of Civil Procedure [28 U.S.C., Appendix]. Many States by express statutory provision permit waiver of jury trial in criminal cases. See ALI Code of Criminal Procedure Commentaries, pp. 807–811.

Note to Subdivision (b). This rule would permit either a stipulation before the trial that the case be tried by a jury composed of less than 12 or a stipulation during the trial consenting that the case be submitted to less than 12 jurors. The second alternative is useful in case it becomes necessary during the trial to excuse a juror owing to illness or for some other cause and no alternate juror is available. The rule is a restatement of existing practice, the constitutionality of which was approved in *Patton v. United States,* 281 U.S. 276, 50 S.Ct. 253, 74 L.Ed. 854, 70 A.L.R. 263.

Note to Subdivision (c). This rule changes existing law in so far as it requires the court in a case tried without a jury to make special findings of fact if requested. Cf. Connecticut practice, under which a judge in a criminal case tried by the court without a jury makes findings of fact, *State v. Frost,* 105 Conn. 326, 135 A. 446.

Notes of Advisory Committee on 1966 amendments. This amendment adds to the rule a provision added to Civil Rule 52(a) in 1946.

Notes of Advisory Committee on 1976 amendments. The amendment to subdivision (b) makes it clear that the parties, with the approval of the court, may enter into an agreement to have the case decided by less than twelve jurors if one or more jurors are unable or disqualified to continue. For many years the Eastern District of Virginia has used a form entitled, "Waiver of Alternate Jurors." In a substantial percentage of cases the form is signed by the defendant, his attorney, and the Assistant United States Attorney in advance of trial, generally on the morning of trial. It is handled automatically by the courtroom deputy clerk who, after completion, exhibits it to the judge.

This practice would seem to be authorized by existing rule 23(b), but there has been some doubt as to whether the pretrial stipulation is effective unless again agreed to by a defendant at the time a juror or jurors have to be excused. See 8 J. Moore, Federal Practice P 23.04 (2d. ed. Cipes, 1969); C. Wright, Federal Practice and Procedure: Criminal § 373 (1969). The proposed amendment is intended to make clear that the pretrial stipulation is an effective waiver, which need not be renewed at the time the incapacity or disqualification of the juror becomes known.

In view of the fact that a defendant can make an effective pretrial waiver of trial by jury or by a jury of twelve, it would seem to follow that he can also effectively waive trial by a jury of twelve in situations where a juror or jurors cannot continue to serve.

As has been the practice under rule 23(b), a stipulation addressed to the possibility that some jurors many later be excused need not be open-ended. That is, the stipulation may be conditioned upon the jury not being reduced below a certain size. See, e.g., *Williams v. United States,* 332 F.2d 36 (7th Cir. 1964) (agreement to proceed if no more than 2 jurors excused for illness); *Rogers v. United States,* 319 F.2d 5 (7th Cir. 1963) (same).

Subdivision (c) is changed to make clear the deadline for making a request for findings of fact and to provide that findings may be oral. The oral findings, of course, become a part of the record, as findings of fact are essential to proper appellate review on a conviction resulting from a nonjury trial. *United States v. Livingston,* 459 F.2d 797 (3d Cir. 1972).

The meaning of current subdivision (c) has been in some doubt because there is no time specified within which a defendant must make a "request" that the court "find the facts specially." See, e.g., *United States v. Rivera,* 444 F.2d 136 (2d Cir. 1971), where the request was not made until the sentence had been imposed. In the opinion the court said:

This situation might have raised the interesting and apparently undecided question of when a request for findings under Fed. R. Crim. P. 23(c) is too late, since Rivera's request was not made until the day after sentence was imposed. See generally *Benchwick v. United States,* 297 F. 2d 330, 335 (9th Cir. 1961); *United States v. Morris,* 263 F. 2d 594 (7th Cir. 1959).

Notes of Committee on the Judiciary on 1977 amendments proposed by the Supreme Court (Senate Report No. 95-354). Subsection (b) of section 2 of the bill simply approves the Supreme Court proposed changes in subdivisions (b) and (c) of rule 23 for the reasons given by the Advisory Committee on Rules of Practice and Procedure to the Judicial Conference.

Effective date of July 30, 1977 amendment. As to the effective date of the amendment made by Act July 30, 1977, P. L. 95-78, § 2(a), 91 Stat. 319, see §§ 1, 4 of such Act, which appear as 18 U.S.C.S. § 3771 notes.

Congressional approval of proposed 1977 amendments. Act July 30, 1977, P. L. 95-78, § 2(b), 91 Stat. 320, provided: "The amendments proposed by the Supreme Court [in its order of April 26, 1977] to subdivisions (b) and (c) of rule 23 of such Rules of Criminal Procedure [subd. (b) and (c) of this rule] are approved.".

Guam; nonrequirement for jury trial. For the inapplicability of requirements for jury trial to criminal prosecutions in the District Court of Guam, see 48 U.S.C.S. § 1424(b).

Trial by jury in Virgin Islands. For trial by jury in the Virgin Islands, see 48 U.S.C.S. § 1616.

Notes of Advisory Committee on 1983 amendments. *Note to Subdivision (b).* The amendment to subdivision (b) addresses a situation which does not occur with great frequency but which, when it does occur, may present a most difficult issue concerning the fair and efficient administration of justice. This situation is that in which, after the jury has retired to consider its verdict and any alternate jurors have been discharged, one of the jurors is seriously incapacitated or otherwise found to be unable to continue service upon the jury. The problem is acute when the trial has been a lengthy one and consequently the remedy of mistrial would necessitate a second expenditure of substantial prosecution, defense and court resources. See, e.g., *United States v. Meinster,* 484 F.Supp. 442 (S.D-.Fla. 1980), aff'd sub nom. *United States v. Phillips,* 664 F.2d 971 (5th Cir. 1981) (juror had heart attack during deliberations after "well over four months of trial"); *United States v. Barone,* 83 F.R.D. 565 (S.D. Fla. 1979) (juror removed upon recommendation of psychiatrist during deliberations after "approximately six months of trial").

It is the judgment of the Committee that when a juror is lost during deliberations, especially in circumstances like those in *Barone* and *Meinster,* it is essential that there be available a course of action other than mistrial. Proceeding with the remaining 11 jurors, though heretofore impermissible under rule 23(b) absent stipulation by the parties and approval of the court, *United States v. Taylor,* 507 F.2d 166 (5th Cir. 1975), is constitutionally permissible. In *Williams v. Florida,* 399 U.S. 78 (1970), the Court concluded.

the fact that the jury at common law was composed of precisely 12 is an historical accident, unnecessary to effect the purposes of the jury system and wholly without significance "except to mystics." . . . To read the Sixth Amendment as forever codifying a feature so incidental to the real purpose of the Amendment is to ascribe a blind formalism to the Framers which would require considerably more evidence than we have been able to discover in the history and language of the Constitution or in the reasoning of our past decisions. . . . Our holding does no more than leave these considerations to Congress and the States, unrestrained by an interpretation of the Sixth Amendment which would forever dictate the precise number which can constitute a jury.

Williams held that a six-person jury was constitutional because such a jury had the "essential feature of a jury," i.e., "the interposition between the accused and his accuser of the common-sense judgment of a group of laymen, and in the community participation and shared responsibility which results from that group's determination of guilt or innocence," necessitating only a group "large enough to promote group deliberation, free from outside attempts at intimidation, and to provide a fair possibility for obtaining a representative cross section of the community." This being the case, quite clearly the occasional use of a jury of slightly less than 12, as contemplated by the amendment to rule 23(b), is constitutional. Though the alignment of the Court and especially the separate opinion by Justice Powell in *Apodoca v. Oregon,* 406 U.S. 404 (1972), makes it at best uncertain whether less-than-unanimous verdicts would be constitutionally permissible in federal trials, it hardly follows that a requirement of unanimity of a group slightly less than 12 is similarly suspect.

The *Meinster* case clearly reflects the need for a solution other than mistrial. There twelve defendants were named in a 36-count, 100-page indictment for RICO offenses and related violations, and the trial lasted more than four months. Before the jury retired for deliberations, the trial judge inquired of defense counsel whether they would now agree to a jury of less than 12 should a juror later be unable to continue during the deliberations which were anticipated to be lengthy. All defense counsel rejected that proposal. When one juror was excused a day later after suffering a heart attack, all defense counsel again rejected the proposal that deliberations continue with the remaining 11 jurors. Thus, the solution now provided in rule 23(b), stipulation to a jury of less than 12, was not possible in that case, just as it will not be possible in any case in which defense counsel believe some tactical advantage will be gained by retrial. Yet, to declare a mistrial at that point would have meant that over four months of trial time would have gone for naught and that a comparable period of time would have to be expended on retrial. For a variety of reasons, not the least of which is the impact such a retrial would have upon that court's ability to comply with speedy trial limits in other cases, such a result is most undesirable.

That being the case, it is certainly understandable that the trial judge in *Meinster* (as in *Barone*) elected to substitute an alternate juror at that point. Given the rule 23(b) bar on a verdict of less than 12 absent stipulation, *United States v. Taylor,* supra, such substitution seemed the least objectionable course of action. But in terms of what change in the Federal Rules of Criminal Procedure is to be preferred in order to facilitate response to such situations in the future, the judgment of the Advisory Committee is that it is far better to permit the deliberations to continue with a jury of 11 than to make a substitution at that point.

In rejecting the substitution-of-juror alternative, the Committee's judgment is in accord with that of most commentators and many courts.

There have been proposals that the rule should be amended to permit an alternate to be substituted if a regular juror becomes unable to perform his duties after the case has been submitted to the jury. An early draft of the original Criminal Rules had contained such a provision, but it was withdrawn when the Supreme Court itself indicated to the Advisory Committee on Criminal Rules doubts as to the desirability and constitutionality of such a procedure. These doubts are as forceful now as they were a quarter century ago. To permit substitution of an alternate after deliberations have begun would require either that the alternate participate though he has missed part of the jury discussion, or that he sit in with the jury in every case on the chance he might be needed. Either course is subject to practical difficulty and to strong constitutional objection.

Wright, *Federal Practice and Procedure* § 388 (1969). See also Moore, *Federal Practice* par. 24.05 (2d ed. Cipes 1980) ("The inherent coercive effect upon an alternate who joins a jury leaning heavily toward a guilty verdict may result in the alternate reaching a premature guilty verdict"); 3 *ABA Standards for Criminal Justice* § 15-2.7, commentary (2d ed. 1980) ("it is not desirable to allow a juror who is unfamiliar with the prior deliberations to suddenly join the group and participate in the voting without the benefit of earlier group discussion"); *United States v. Lamb,* 529 F.2d 1153 (9th Cir. 1975); *People v. Ryan,* 19 N.Y.2d 100, 224 N.E.2d 710 (1966). Compare *People v. Collins,* 17 Cal.3d 687, 131 Cal.Rptr. 782, 522 P.2d 742 (1976); *Johnson v. State,* 267 Ind. 256, 396 N.E.2d 623 (1977).

The central difficulty with substitution, whether viewed only as a practical problem or a question of constitutional dimensions (procedural due process under the Fifth Amendment or jury trial under the Sixth Amendment), is that there does not appear to be any way to nullify the impact of what has occurred without the participation of the new juror. Even were it required that the jury "review" with the new juror their prior deliberations or that the jury upon substitution start deliberations anew, it still seems likely that the continuing jurors would be influenced by the earlier deliberations and that the new juror would be somewhat intimidated by the others by virtue of being a newcomer to the deliberations. As for the possibility of sending in the alternates at the very beginning with instructions to listen but not to participate until substituted, this scheme is likewise attended by practical difficulties and offends "the cardinal principle that the deliberations of the jury shall remain private and secret in every case." *United States v. Virginia Erection Corp.*, 335 F.2d 868 (4th Cir. 1964).

The amendment provides that if a juror is excused after the jury has retired to consider its verdict, it is within the discretion of the court whether to declare a mistrial or to permit deliberations to continue with 11 jurors. If the trial has been brief and not much would be lost by retrial, the court might well conclude that the unusual step of allowing a jury verdict by less than 12 jurors absent stipulation should not be taken. On the other hand, if the trial has been protracted the court is much more likely to opt for continuing with the remaining 11 jurors.

Notes of Advisory Committee on 2002 amendments. The language of Rule 23 has been amended as part of the general restyling of the Criminal Rules to make them more easily understood and to make style and terminology consistent throughout the rules. These changes are intended to be stylistic only.

In current Rule 23(b), the term "just cause" has been replaced with the more familiar term "good cause," that appears in other rules. No change in substance is intended.

Rule 24. Trial Jurors

(a) Examination.

(1) *In General.* The court may examine prospective jurors or may permit the attorneys for the parties to do so.

(2) *Court Examination.* If the court examines the jurors, it must permit the attorneys for the parties to:

(A) ask further questions that the court considers proper; or

(B) submit further questions that the court may ask if it considers them proper.

(b) Peremptory Challenges. Each side is entitled to the number of peremptory challenges to prospective jurors specified below. The court may allow additional peremptory challenges to multiple defendants, and may allow the defendants to exercise those challenges separately or jointly.

(1) *Capital Case.* Each side has 20 peremptory challenges when the government seeks the death penalty.

(2) *Other Felony Case.* The government has 6 peremptory challenges and the defendant or defendants jointly have 10 peremptory challenges when the defendant is charged with a crime punishable by imprisonment of more than one year.

(3) *Misdemeanor Case.* Each side has 3 peremptory challenges when the defendant is charged with a crime punishable by fine, imprisonment of one year or less, or both.

(c) Alternate Jurors.

(1) *In General.* The court may impanel up to 6 alternate jurors to replace any jurors who are unable to perform or who are disqualified from performing their duties.

(2) *Procedure.*

(A) Alternate jurors must have the same qualifications and be selected and sworn in the same manner as any other juror.

(B) Alternate jurors replace jurors in the same sequence in which the alternates were selected. An alternate juror who replaces a juror has the same authority as the other jurors.

(3) *Retaining Alternate Jurors.* The court may retain alternate jurors after the jury retires to deliberate. The court must ensure that a retained alternate does not discuss the case with anyone until that alternate replaces a juror or is discharged. If an alternate replaces a juror after deliberations have begun, the court must instruct the jury to begin its deliberations anew.

(4) *Peremptory Challenges.* Each side is entitled to the number of additional peremptory challenges to prospective alternate jurors specified below. These additional challenges may be used only to remove alternate jurors.

(A) One or Two Alternates. One additional peremptory challenge is permitted when one or two alternates are impaneled.

(B) Three or Four Alternates. Two additional peremptory challenges are permitted when three or four alternates are impaneled.

(C) Five or Six Alternates. Three additional peremptory challenges are permitted when five or six alternates are impaneled.

HISTORY:

Amended Feb. 28, 1966, eff. July 1, 1966; Mar. 9, 1987, eff. Aug. 1, 1987; April 26, 1999, eff. Dec. 1, 1999; April 29, 2002, eff. Dec. 1, 2002.

HISTORY; ANCILLARY LAWS AND DIRECTIVES

Other provisions:

Notes of Advisory Committee. *Note to Subdivision (a).* This rule is similar to Rule 47(a) of the Federal Rules of Civil Procedure, 28 U.S.C., Appendix, and also embodies the practice now followed by many Federal courts in criminal cases. Uniform procedure in civil and criminal cases on this point seems desirable.

Note to Subdivision (b). This rule embodies existing law, 28 U.S.C. [former] § 424 (see § 1870) (Challenges), with the following modifications. In capital cases the number of challenges is equalized as between the defendant and the United States so that both sides have 20 challenges, which only the defendant has at present. While continuing the existing rule that multiple defendants are deemed a single party for purposes of challenges, the rule vests in the court discretion to allow additional peremptory challenges to multiple defendants and to permit such challenges to be exercised separately or jointly. Experience with cases involving numerous defendants indicates the desirability of this modification.

Note to Subdivision (c). This rule embodies existing law, 28 U.S.C. [former] § 417a (alternate jurors), as well as the practice prescribed for civil cases by Rule 47(b) of the Federal Rules of Civil Procedure, 28 U.S.C., Appendix, except that the number of possible alternate jurors that may be empaneled is increased from two to four, with a corresponding adjustment of challenges.

Notes of Advisory Committee on 1966 amendments. Experience has demonstrated that four alternate jurors may not be enough for some lengthy criminal trials. See, e.g., *United States v. Bentvena,* 288 F.2d 442 (2d Cir. 1961); Reports of the Proceedings of the Judicial Conference of the United States, 1961, p. 104. The amendment to the first sentence increases the number authorized from four to six. The fourth sentence is amended to provide an additional peremptory challenge where a fifth or sixth alternate juror is used.

The words "or are found to be" are added to the second sentence to make clear that an alternate juror may be called in the situation where it is first discovered during the trial that a juror was unable or disqualified to perform his duties at the time he was sworn. See *United States v. Goldberg,* 330 F.2d 30 (3rd Cir. 1964), cert. den. 377 U.S. 953, 12 L.Ed.2d 497, 84 S.Ct. 1630 (1964).

Disapproval of amendments proposed by Order of April 26, 1976. Proposed amendments made by Order April 26, 1976, 47 L.Ed.2d xli, were disapproved by Act July 30, 1977, P. L. 95-78, § 2(c), 91 Stat. 320 (eff. Oct. 1, 1977, as provided by § 4 of such Act). The proposed amendments would have altered subdiv. (b) by reducing the number of peremptory challenges in each category of cases.

Criminal Procedure Rule 25

The amendments are technical. No substantive change is intended.

Notes of Advisory Committee on 1999 amendments. As currently written, Rule 24(c) explicitly requires the court to discharge all of the alternate jurors—who have not been selected to replace other jurors—when the jury retires to deliberate. That requirement is grounded on the concern that after the case has been submitted to the jury, its deliberations must be private and inviolate. *United States v. Houlihan,* 92 F.3d 1271, 1285 (1st Cir. 1996), citing *United States v. Virginia Election Corp.*, 335 F.2d 868, 872 (4th Cir. 1964).

Rule 23(b) provides that in some circumstances a verdict may be returned by eleven jurors. In addition, there may be cases where it is better to retain the alternates when the jury retires, insulate them from the deliberation process, and have them available should one or more vacancies occur in the jury. That might be especially appropriate in a long, costly, and complicated case. To that end the Committee believed that the court should have the discretion to decide whether to retain or discharge the alternates at the time the jury retires to deliberate and to use Rule 23(b) to proceed with eleven jurors or to substitute a juror or jurors with alternate jurors who have not been discharged.

In order to protect the sanctity of the deliberative process, the rule requires the court to take appropriate steps to insulate the alternate jurors. That may be done, for example, by separating the alternates from the deliberating jurors and instructing the alternate jurors not to discuss the case with any other person until they replace a regular juror. *See, e.g., United States v. Olano*, 507 U.S. 725 [123 L. Ed. 2d 508] (1993) (not plain error to permit alternate jurors to sit in during deliberations); *United States v. Houlihan*, 92 F.3d 1271, 1286–88 (1st Cir. 1996) (harmless error to retain alternate jurors in violation of Rule 24(c); in finding harmless error the court cited the steps taken by the trial judge to insulate the alternates). If alternates are used, the jurors must be instructed that they must begin their deliberations anew.

Finally, subsection (c) has been reorganized and restyled.

Notes of Advisory Committee on 2002 amendments. The language of Rule 24 has been amended as part of the general restyling of the Criminal Rules to make them more easily understood and to make style and terminology consistent throughout the rules. These changes are intended to be stylistic only, except as noted below.

In restyling Rule 24(a), the Committee deleted the language that authorized the defendant to conduct voir dire of prospective jurors. The Committee believed that the current language was potentially ambiguous and could lead one incorrectly to conclude that a defendant, represented by counsel, could personally conduct voir dire or additional voir dire. The Committee believed that the intent of the current provision was to permit a defendant to participate personally in voir dire only if the defendant was acting pro se. Amended Rule 24(a) refers only to attorneys for the parties, i.e., the defense counsel and the attorney for the government, with the understanding that if the defendant is not represented by counsel, the court may still, in its discretion, permit the defendant to participate in voir dire. In summary, the Committee intends no change in practice.

Finally, the rule authorizes the court in multi-defendant cases to grant additional peremptory challenges to the defendants. If the court does so, the prosecution may request additional challenges in a multi-defendant case, not to exceed the total number available to the defendants jointly. The court, however, is not required to equalize the number of challenges where additional challenges are granted to the defendant.

Rule 25. Judge's Disability

(a) During trial. Any judge regularly sitting in or assigned to the court may complete a jury trial if:

(1) the judge before whom the trial began cannot proceed because of death, sickness, or other disability; and

(2) the judge completing the trial certifies familiarity with the trial record.

(b) After a Verdict or Finding of Guilty.

(1) *In General.* After a verdict or finding of guilty, any judge regularly sitting in or assigned to a court may complete the court's duties if the judge who presided at trial cannot perform those duties because of absence, death, sickness, or other disability.

(2) *Granting a New Trial.* The successor judge may grant a new trial if satisfied that:

(A) a judge other than the one who presided at the trial cannot perform the post-trial duties; or

(B) a new trial is necessary for some other reason.

HISTORY:

Amended Feb. 28, 1966, eff. July 1, 1966; Mar. 9, 1987, eff. Aug. 1, 1987; Apr. 29, 2002, eff. Dec. 1, 2002.

HISTORY; ANCILLARY LAWS AND DIRECTIVES

Other provisions:

Notes of Advisory Committee. This rule is similar to Rule 63 of the Federal Rules of Civil Procedure [28 U.S.C.,

Appendix]. See also, 28 U.S.C. [former] § 776 (Bill of exceptions; authentication; signing of by judge).

Notes of Advisory Committee on 1966 amendments. In September, 1963, the Judicial Conference of the United States approved a recommendation of its Committee on Court Administration that provision be made for substitution of a judge who becomes disabled during trial. The problem has become serious because of the increase in the number of long criminal trials. See 1963 Annual Report of the Director of the Administrative Office of the United States Courts, p 114, reporting a 25% increase in criminal trials lasting more than one week in fiscal year 1963 over 1962.

Subdivision (a). The amendment casts the rule into two subdivisions and in subdivision (a) provides for substitution of a judge during a jury trial upon his certification that he has familiarized himself with the record of the trial. For similar provisions see Alaska Rules of Crim Proc, Rule 25; California Penal Code, § 1053.

Subdivision (b). The words "from the district" are deleted to permit the local judge to act in those situations where a judge who has been assigned from within the district to try the case is, at the time for sentence, etc., back at his regular place of holding court which may be several hundred miles from the place of trial. It is not intended, of course, that substitutions shall be made where the judge who tried the case is available within a reasonable distance from the place of trial.

Notes of Advisory Committee on 1987 amendments. The amendments are technical. No substantive change is intended.

Notes of Advisory Committee on 2002 amendments. The language of Rule 25 has been amended as part of the general restyling of the Criminal Rules to make them more easily understood and to make style and terminology consistent throughout the rules. These changes are intended to be stylistic only.

Rule 25(b)(2) addresses the possibility of a new trial when a judge determines that no other judge could perform post-trial duties or when the judge determines that there is some other reason for doing so. The current rule indicates that those reasons must be "appropriate." The Committee, however, believed that a better term would be "necessary," because that term includes notions of manifest necessity. No change in meaning or practice is intended.

Rule 26. Taking Testimony

In every trial the testimony of witnesses must be taken in open court, unless otherwise provided by a statute or by rules adopted under 28 U.S.C. §§ 2072–2077.

HISTORY:

Amended Nov. 20, 1972, eff. July 1, 1975; Jan. 2, 1975, P. L. 93-595, § 3, 88 Stat. 1959; Apr. 29, 2002, eff. Dec. 1, 2002.

HISTORY; ANCILLARY LAWS AND DIRECTIVES

Other provisions:

Notes of Advisory Committee. 1. This rule [prior to 1972 amendment] contemplates the development of a uniform body of rules of evidence to be applicable in trials of criminal cases in the Federal courts. It is based on *Funk v. United States,* 290 U.S. 371, 54 S.Ct. 212, 78 L.Ed. 369, 93 A.L.R. 1136, and *Wolfle v. United States,* 291 U.S. 7, 54 S.Ct. 279, 78 L.Ed. 617, which indicated that in the absence of statute the Federal courts in criminal cases are not bound by the State law of evidence, but are guided by common law principles as interpreted by the Federal courts "in the light of reason and experience." The rule does not fetter the applicable law of evidence to that originally existing at common law. It is contemplated that the law may be modified and adjusted from time to time by judicial decisions. See Homer Cummings, 29 A.B.A.Jour. 655; Vanderbilt, 29 A.B.A.Jour 377; Holtzoff, 12 George Washington L.R. 119, 131–132; Holtzoff, 3 F.R.D. 445, 453; Howard, 51 Yale L.Jour. 763; Medalie, 4 Lawyers Guild R. (3) 1, 5–6.

2. This rule differs from the corresponding rule for civil cases (Federal Rules of Civil Procedure, Rule 43(a), 28 U.S.C., Appendix), in that this rule contemplates a uniform body of rules of evidence to govern in criminal trials in the Federal courts, while the rule for civil cases prescribes partial conformity to State law and, therefore, results in a divergence as between various districts. Since in civil actions in which Federal jurisdiction is based on diversity of citizenship, the State substantive law governs the rights of the parties, uniformity of rules of evidence among different districts does not appear necessary. On the other hand, since all Federal crimes are statutory and all criminal prosecutions in the Federal courts are based on acts of Congress, uniform rules of evidence appear desirable if not essential in criminal cases, as otherwise the same facts under differing rules of evidence may lead to a conviction in one district and to an acquittal in another.

3. This rule expressly continues existing statutes governing the admissibility of evidence and the competency and privileges of witnesses. Among such statutes are the following:

8 U.S.C.:

§ 138 [see §§ 1326, 1328, 1329] (Importation of aliens for immoral purposes; attempt to re-enter after deportation; penalty).

28 U.S.C.:

§ 632 [see 18 U.S.C. § 3481] (Competency of witnesses governed by State laws; defendants in criminal cases).

§ 633 [former] (Competency of witnesses governed by State laws; husband or wife of defendant in prosecution for bigamy).

§ 634 [see 18 U.S.C. § 3486](Testimony of witnesses before Congress).

§ 638 [see § 1731] (Comparison of handwriting to determine genuineness).

§ 695 [see § 1732] (Admissibility).

§ 695a [see 18 U.S.C. § 3491] (Foreign documents).

46 U.S.C.:

§ 193 (Bills of lading to be issued; contents).

Notes of Advisory Committee on 1972 amendments. The first sentence is retained, with appropriate narrowing of the title, since its subject is not covered in the Rules of Evidence. The second sentence is deleted because the Rules of Evidence govern admissibility of evidence, competency of witnesses, and privilege. The language is broadened, however, to take account of the Rules of Evidence and any other rules adopted by the Supreme Court.

Effective date of amendment proposed by United States Supreme Court order of November 20, 1972. Act Jan. 2, 1975, P. L. 93-595, § 3, 88 Stat. 1959, provided: "The Congress expressly approves the amendments to the Federal Rules of Civil Procedure, and the amendments to the Federal Rules of Criminal Procedure, which are embraced by the orders entered by the Supreme Court of the United States on November 20, 1972, and December 18, 1972, and such amendments shall take effect on the one hundred and eightieth day beginning after the date of the enactment of this Act [enacted Jan. 2, 1975].".

Federal Rules of Evidence. The text of the Federal Rules of Evidence enacted into law by Act Jan. 2, 1975, P. L. 93-595, § 1, 88 Stat. 1929, is set out in the USCS Court Rules. Rule 1101(b) of the Rules of Evidence provides that the rules apply generally to civil actions and proceedings, including admiralty and maritime cases, to criminal cases and proceedings, to contempt proceedings except those in which the court may act summarily, and to proceedings and cases under the Bankruptcy Act.

Notes of Advisory Committee on 2002 amendments. The language of Rule 26 has been amended as part of the general restyling of the Criminal Rules to make them more easily understood and to make style and terminology consistent throughout the rules. These changes are intended to be stylistic only, except as noted below.

Rule 26 is amended, by deleting the word "orally," to accommodate witnesses who are not able to present oral testimony in open court and may need, for example, a sign language interpreter. The change conforms the rule, in that respect, to Federal Rule of Civil Procedure 43.

Rule 26.1. Foreign Law Determination

A party intending to raise an issue of foreign law must provide the court and all parties with reasonable written notice. Issues of foreign law are questions of law, but in deciding such issues a court may consider any relevant material or source—including testimony —without regard to the Federal Rules of Evidence.

HISTORY:

As added Feb. 28, 1966, eff. July 1, 1966; amended Nov. 20, 1972, eff. July 1, 1975; April 29, 2002, eff. Dec. 1, 2002.

HISTORY; ANCILLARY LAWS AND DIRECTIVES

Other provisions:

Notes of Advisory Committee. The original Federal Rules of Criminal Procedure did not contain a provision explicitly regulating the determination of foreign law. The resolution of issues of foreign law, when relevant in federal criminal proceedings, falls within the general compass of Rule 26 which provides for application of "the [evidentiary] principles of the common law as they may be interpreted by the courts of the United States in the light of reason and experience." See Green, Preliminary Report on the Advisability and Feasibility of Developing Uniform Rules of Evidence for the United States District Courts 6–7, 17–18 (1962). Although traditional "common-law" methods for determining foreign-country law have proved inadequate, the courts have not developed more appropriate practices on the basis of this flexible rule. Cf. Green, op. cit. supra at 26–28. On the inadequacy of common-law procedures for determining foreign law, see, e.g., Nussbaum, Proving the Law of Foreign Countries, 3 Am.J.Comp.L. 60 (1954).

Problems of foreign law that must be resolved in accordance with the Federal Rules of Criminal Procedure are most likely to arise in places such as Washington, D.C., the Canal Zone, Guam, and the Virgin Islands, where the federal courts have general criminal jurisdiction. However, issues of foreign law may also arise in criminal proceedings commenced in other federal districts. For example, in an extradition proceeding, reasonable ground to believe that the person sought to be extradited is charged with, or was convicted of, a crime under the laws of the demanding state must generally be shown. See *Factor v. Laubenheimer,* 290 U.S. 276, 78 L.Ed. 315, 54 S.Ct. 191 (1933); *Fernandez v. Phillips,* 268 U.S. 311, 69 L.Ed. 970, 45 S.Ct. 541 (1925); Bishop, International Law: Cases and Materials (2d ed. 1962). Further, foreign law may be invoked to justify non-compliance with a subpoena duces tecum, *Application of Chase Manhattan Bank,* 297 F.2d 611 (2d Cir. 1962), and under certain circumstances, as a defense to prosecution. Cf. *American Banana Co. v. United Fruit Co.* 213 U.S. 347, 53 L.Ed. 826, 29 S.Ct. 511 (1909). The content of foreign law may also be relevant in proceedings arising under 18 U.S.C. §§ 1201, 2312– 2317.

Rule 26.1 is substantially the same as Civil Rule 44.1. A full explanation of the merits and practicability of the rule appear in the Advisory Committee's Note to Civil Rule 44.1. It is necessary here to add only one comment to the explanations there made. The second sentence of the rule frees the court from the restraints of the ordinary rules of evidence in determining foreign law. This freedom, made necessary by the peculiar nature of the issue of foreign law, should not constitute an unconstitutional deprivation of the defendant's rights to confrontation of witnesses. The issue is essentially one of law rather than of fact. Furthermore, the cases have held that the Sixth Amendment does not serve as a rigid barrier against the development of reasonable and necessary exceptions to the hearsay rule. See *Kay v. United States,* 255 F.2d 476, 480 (4th Cir. 1958), cert. den., 358 U.S. 825, 3 L.Ed.2d 65, 79 S.Ct. 42 (1958); *Matthews v. United States,* 217 F.2d 409, 418 (5th Cir. 1954); *United States v. Leathers,* 135 F.2d 507 (2d Cir. 1943); and cf., *Pointer v. Texas,* 380 U.S. 400, 13 L.Ed.2d 923, 85 S.Ct. 1065 (1965); *Douglas v. Alabama,* 380 U.S. 415, 13 L.Ed.2d 934, 85 S.Ct. 1074 (1965).

Notes of Advisory Committee on 1972 amendments. Since the purpose is to free the judge, in determining foreign law, from restrictive evidentiary rules, the reference is made to the Rules of Evidence generally.

Effective date of amendment proposed by United States Supreme Court Order of November 20, 1972. As to the effective date of amendment proposed by United States Supreme Court Order of Nov. 20, 1972, see Act Jan. 2, 1975, P. L. 93-595, § 3, 88 Stat. 1959, which appears as a note to Rule 26.

Notes of Advisory Committee on 2002 amendments. The language of Rule 26.1 has been amended as part of the general restyling of the Criminal Rules to make them more easily understood and to make style and terminology consistent throughout the rules. These changes are intended to be stylistic only.

Rule 26.2. Producing a Witness's Statement

(a) Motion to Produce. After a witness other than the defendant has testified on direct examination, the court, on motion of a party who did not call the witness, must order an attorney for the government or the defendant and the defendant's attorney to produce, for the examination and use of the moving party, any statement of the witness that is in their possession and that relates to the subject matter of the witness's testimony.

(b) Producing the Entire Statement. If the entire statement relates to the subject matter of the witness's testimony, the court must order that the statement be delivered to the moving party.

(c) Producing a Redacted Statement. If the party who called the witness claims that the statement contains information that is privileged or does not relate to the subject matter of the witness's testimony, the court must inspect the statement in camera. After excising any privileged or unrelated portions, the court must order delivery of the redacted statement to the moving party. If the defendant objects to an excision, the court must preserve the entire statement with the excised portion indicated, under seal, as part of the record.

(d) Recess to Examine a Statement. The court may recess the proceedings to allow time for a party to examine the statement and prepare for its use.

(e) Sanction for Failure to Produce or Deliver a Statement. If the party who called the witness disobeys an order to produce or deliver a statement, the court must strike the witness's testimony from the record. If an attorney for the government disobeys the order, the court must declare a mistrial if justice so requires.

(f) "Statement" Defined. As used in this rule, a witness's "statement" means:

(1) a written statement that the witness makes and signs, or otherwise adopts or approves;

(2) a substantially verbatim, contemporaneously recorded recital of the witness's oral statement that is contained in any recording or any transcription of a recording; or

(3) the witness's statement to a grand jury, however taken or recorded, or a transcription of such a statement.

(g) Scope. This rule applies at trial, at a suppression hearing under Rule 12, and to the extent specified in the following rules:

(1) Rule 5.1(h) (preliminary hearing);

(2) Rule 32(i)(2) (sentencing);

(3) Rule 32.1(e) (hearing to revoke or modify probation or supervised release);

(4) Rule 46(j) (detention hearing); and

(5) Rule 8 of the Rules Governing Proceedings under 28 U.S.C. § 2255.

HISTORY:

Amended April 30, 1979, eff. Dec. 1, 1980; July 31, 1979, P. L. 96-42, § 1(1), 93 Stat. 326; Mar. 9, 1987, eff. Aug. 1, 1987; April 22, 1993, eff. Dec. 1, 1993; April 24, 1998, eff. Dec. 1, 1998; April 29, 2002, eff. Dec. 1, 2002.

HISTORY; ANCILLARY LAWS AND DIRECTIVES

Other provisions:

Notes of Advisory Committee on 1979 amendments. [effective Dec. 1, 1980, as provided by Act July 31, 1979, P. L. 96-42, § 1(1), 93 Stat. 326]. S. 1437, 95th Cong., 1st Sess. (1977), would place in the criminal rules the substance of what is now 18 U.S.C. § 3500 (the Jencks Act). Underlying this and certain other additions to the rules contemplated by S. 1437 is the notion that provisions which are purely procedural in nature should appear in the Federal Rules of Criminal Procedure rather than in Title 18. See Reform of the Federal Criminal Laws, Part VI: Hearings on S.1, S. 716, and S. 1400, Subcomm. on Criminal Laws and Procedures, Senate Judiciary Comm., 93rd Cong., 1st Sess. (statement of Judge Albert B. Maris, at page 5503). Rule 26.2 is identical to the S. 1437 rule except as indicated by the marked additions and deletions. As those changes show, rule 26.2 provides for production of the statements of defense witnesses at trial in essentially the same manner as is now provided for with respect to the statements of government witnesses. Thus, the proposed rule reflects these two judgments: (i) that the subject matter—production of the statements of witnesses—is more appropriately dealt with in the criminal rules; and (ii) that in light of *United States v. Nobles,* 422 U.S. 225 [45 L. Ed. 2d 141] (1975), it is important to establish procedures for the production of defense witnesses' statements as well. The rule is not intended to discourage the practice of voluntary disclosure at an earlier time so as to avoid delays at trial.

In *Nobles,* defense counsel sought to introduce the testimony of a defense investigator who prior to trial had interviewed prospective prosecution witnesses and had prepared a report embodying the essence of their conversation. When the defendant called the investigator to impeach eyewitness testimony identifying the defendant as the robber, the trial judge granted the prosecutor the right to inspect those portions of the investigator's report relating to the witnesses' statements, as a potential basis for cross-examination of the investigator. When the defense declined to produce the report, the trial judge refused to permit the investigator to testify. The Supreme Court unanimously upheld the trial court's actions, finding that neither the Fifth nor Sixth Amendments nor the attorney work product doctrine prevented disclosure of such a document at trial. Noting "the federal judiciary's inherent power to require the prosecution to produce the previously recorded statements of its witnesses so that the defense may get the full benefit of cross-examinations and the truth-finding process may be enhanced," the Court rejected the notion "that the Fifth Amendment renders criminal discovery 'basically a one-way street,' " and thus concluded that "in a proper case, the prosecution can call upon that same power for production of witness statements that facilitate 'full disclosure of all the [relevant] facts.' ".

The rule, consistent with the reasoning in *Nobles,* is designed to place the disclosure of prior relevant statements of a defense witness in the possession of the defense on the same legal footing as is the disclosure of prior statements of prosecution witnesses in the hands of the government under the Jencks Act, 18 U.S.C. § 3500 (which S. 1437 would replace with the rule set out therein). See *United States v. Pulvirenti,* 408 F.Supp. 12 (E.D.Mich. 1976), holding that under Nobles " [t]he obligation [of disclosure] placed on the defendant should be the reciprocal of that placed upon the government . . . [as] defined by the Jencks Act." Several state courts have likewise concluded that witness statements in the hands of the defense at trial should be disclosed on the same basis that prosecution witness statements are disclosed, in order to promote the concept of the trial as a search for truth. See, e.g., *People v. Sanders,* 110 Ill. App. 2d 85, 249 N.E.2d 124

(1969); *State v. Montague,* 55 N.J. 371, 262 A.2d 398 (1970); *People v. Damon,* 24 N.Y.2d 256, 299 N.Y.S.2d 830, 247 N.E.2d 651 (1959).

The rule, with minor exceptions, makes the procedure identical for both prosecution and defense witnesses, including the provision directing the court, whenever a claim is made that disclosure would be improper because the statement contains irrelevant matter, to examine the statements in camera and excise such matter as should not be disclosed. This provision acts as a safeguard against abuse and will enable a defendant who believes that a demand is being improperly made to secure a swift and just resolution of the issue.

The treatment as to defense witnesses of necessity differs slightly from the treatment as to prosecution witnesses in terms of the sanction for a refusal to comply with the court's disclosure order. Under the Jencks Act and the rule proposed in S. 1437, if the prosecution refuses to abide by the court's order, the court is required to strike the witness's testimony unless in its discretion it determines that the more serious sanction of a mistrial in favor of the accused is warranted. Under this rule, if a defendant refuses to comply with the court's disclosure order, the court's only alternative is to enter an order striking or precluding the testimony of the witness, as was done in *Nobles.*

Under subdivision (a) of the rule, the motion for production may be made by "a party who did not call the witness." Thus, it also requires disclosure of statements in the possession of either party when the witness is called neither by the prosecution nor the defense but by the court pursuant to the Federal Rules of Evidence. Present law does not deal with this situation, which consistency requires be treated in an identical manner as the disclosure of statements of witnesses called by a party to the case.

Notes of Advisory Committee on 1987 amendments. The amendments are technical. No substantive change is intended.

Notes of Advisory Committee on 1993 amendments. New subdivision (g) recognizes other contemporaneous amendments in the Rules of Criminal Procedure which extend the application of Rule 26.2 to other proceedings. Those changes are thus consistent with the extension of Rule 26.2 in 1983 to suppression hearings conducted under Rule 12. *See* Rule 12(i).

In extending Rule 26.2 to suppression hearings in 1983, the Committee offered several reasons. First, production of witness statements enhances the ability of the court to assess the witnesses' credibility and thus assists the court in making accurate factual determinations at suppression hearings. Second, because witnesses testifying at a suppression hearing may not necessarily testify at the trial itself, waiting until after a witness testifies at trial before requiring production of that witness's statement would be futile. Third, the Committee believed that it would be feasible to leave the suppression issue open until trial, where Rule 26.2 would then be applicable. Finally, one of the central reasons for requiring production of statements at suppression hearings was the recognition that by its nature, the results of a suppression hearing have a profound and ultimate impact on the issues presented at trial.

The reasons given in 1983 for extending Rule 26.2 to a suppression hearing are equally compelling with regard to other adversary type hearings which ultimately depend on accurate and reliable information. That is, there is a continuing need for information affecting the credibility of witnesses who present testimony. And that need exists without regard to whether the witness is presenting testimony at a pretrial hearing, at a trial, or at a post-trial proceeding.

As noted in the 1983 Advisory Committee Note to Rule 12(i), the courts have generally declined to extend the Jencks Act, 18 U.S.C. § 3500, beyond the confines of actual trial testimony. That result will be obviated by the addition of Rule 26.2(g) and amendments to the Rules noted in that new subdivision.

Although amendments 32, 32.1, 46, and Rule 8 of the Rules Governing Proceedings under 28 U.S.C. § 2255 specifically address the requirement of producing a witness's statement, Rule 26.2 has become known as the central "rule" requiring production of statements. Thus, the references in the Rule itself will assist the bench and bar in locating other Rules which include similar provisions.

The amendment to Rule 26.2 and the other designated Rules is not intended to require production of a witness's statement before the witness actually testifies.

Minor conforming amendments have been made to subsection (d) to reflect that Rule 26.2 will be applicable to proceedings other than the trial itself. And language has been added to subsection (c) to recognize explicitly that privileged matter may be excised from the witness's prior statement.

Notes of Advisory Committee on 1998 amendments. The amendment to subdivision (g) mirrors similar amendments made in 1993 to this rule and to other Rules of Criminal Procedure which extended the application of Rule 26.2 to other proceedings, both pretrial and post-trial. This amendment extends the requirement of producing a witness' statement to preliminary examinations conducted under Rule 5.1.

Subdivision (g)(1) has been amended to reflect changes to Rule 32.

Notes of Advisory Committee on 2002 amendments. The language of Rule 26.2 has been amended as part of the general restyling of the Criminal Rules to make them more easily understood and to make style and terminology consistent throughout the rules. These changes are intended to be stylistic only, except as noted below.

Current Rule 26.2(c) states that if the court withholds a portion of a statement, over the defendant's objection, "the attorney for the government" must preserve the statement. The Committee believed that the better rule would be for the court to simply seal the entire statement as a part of the record, in the event that there is an appeal.

Also, the terminology in Rule 26.2(c) has been changed. The rule now speaks in terms of a "redacted" statement instead of an "excised" statement. No change in practice is intended.

Finally, the list of proceedings in Rule 26.2(g) has been placed in rule-number order.

Rule 26.3. Mistrial

Before ordering a mistrial, the court must give each defendant and the government an opportunity to comment on the propriety of the order, to state whether that party consents or objects, and to suggest alternatives.

HISTORY:

Added April 22, 1993, eff. Dec. 1, 1993; amended April 29, 2002, eff. Dec. 1, 2002.

HISTORY; ANCILLARY LAWS AND DIRECTIVES

Other provisions:

Notes of Advisory Committee on 1993 amendments. Rule 26.3 is a new rule designed to reduce the possibility of an erroneously ordered mistrial which could produce adverse and irretrievable consequences. The Rule is not designed to change the substantive law governing mistrials. Instead it is directed at providing both sides an opportunity to place on the record their views about the proposed mistrial order. In particular, the court must give each side an opportunity to state whether it objects or consents to the order.

Several cases have held that retrial of a defendant was barred by the Double Jeopardy Clause of the Constitution because the trial court had abused its discretion in declaring a mistrial. *See United States v. Dixon,* 913 F.2d 1305 (8th Cir. 1990); *United States v. Bates,* 917 F.2d 388 (9th Cir. 1990). In both cases the appellate courts concluded that the trial court had acted precipitately and had failed to solicit the parties' views on the necessity of a mistrial and the feasibility of any alternative action. The new Rule is designed to remedy that situation.

The Committee regards the Rule as a balanced and modest procedural device that could benefit both the prosecution and the defense. While the *Dixon* and *Bates* decisions adversely affected the government's interest in prosecuting serious crimes, the new Rule could also benefit defendants. The Rule ensures that a defendant has the opportunity to dissuade a judge from declaring a mistrial in a case where granting one would not be an abuse of discretion, but the defendant believes that the prospects for a favorable outcome before that particular court, or jury, are greater than they might be upon retrial.

Notes of Advisory Committee on 2002 amendments. The language of Rule 26.3 has been amended as part of the general restyling of the Criminal Rules to make them more easily understood and to make style and terminology consistent throughout the rules. These changes are intended to be stylistic only.

Rule 27. Proving an Official Record

A party may prove an official record, an entry in such a record, or the lack of a record or entry in the same manner as in a civil action.

HISTORY:

As amended April 29, 2002, eff. Dec. 1, 2002.

HISTORY; ANCILLARY LAWS AND DIRECTIVES

Other provisions:

Notes of Advisory Committee on Rules. This rule incorporates by reference Rule 44 of the Federal Rules of Civil Procedure, 28 U.S.C., Appendix, which provided a simple and uniform method of proving public records and entry or lack of entry therein. The rule does not supersede statutes regulating modes of proof in respect to specific official records. In such cases parties have the option of following the general rule or the pertinent statute. Among the many statutes are:

28 U.S.C.:

§ 661 [see § 1733] (Copies of department or corporation records and papers; admissibility; seal).

§ 662 [see § 1733] (Same; in office of General Counsel of the Treasury).

§ 663 [see § 1733] (Instruments and papers of Comptroller of Currency; admissibility).

§ 664 [see § 1733] (Organization certificates of national banks; admissibility).

§ 665 [see § 1733] (Transcripts from books of Treasury in suits against delinquents; admissibility).

§ 666 [see § 1733] (Same; certificate by Secretary or Assistant Secretary).

§ 668 [see 18 U.S.C. § 3497] (Same; indictments for embezzlement of public moneys).

§ 669 (Copies of returns in returns office admissible).

§ 670 [see § 1743] (Admissibility of copies of statements of demands by Post Office Department).

§ 671 [see § 1733] (Admissibility of copies of post office records and statement of accounts).

§ 672 [See § 1733] (Admissibility of copies of records in General Land Office).

§ 673 [see § 1744] (Admissibility of copies of records, and so forth, of Patent Office).

§ 674 [see § 1745] (Copies of foreign letters patent as prima facie evidence).

§ 675 (Copies of specifications and drawings of patents admissible).

§ 676 [see § 1736] (Extracts from Journals of Congress admissible when injunction of secrecy removed).

§ 677 [see § 1740] (Copies of records in offices of United States consuls admissible).

§ 678 (Books and papers in certain district courts).

§ 679 (Records in clerks' offices, western district of North Carolina).

§ 680 (Records in clerks' offices of former district of California).

§ 681 [see § 1734] (Original records lost or destroyed; certified copy admissible).

§ 682 [see § 1734] (Same; when certified copy not obtainable).

§ 685 [see § 1735] (Same; certified copy of official papers).

§ 687 [see § 1738] (Authentication of legislative acts; proof of judicial proceedings of State).

§ 688 [see § 1739] (Proofs of records in offices not pertaining to courts).

§ 689 (Copies of foreign records relating to land titles).

§§ 695a–695g [see 18 U.S.C. §§ 3491– 3496; 22 U.S.C. § 1204; § 1741] (Foreign documents).

1 U.S.C.:

§ 30 [see § 112] (Statutes at Large; contents; admissibility in evidence).

§ 30a [see § 113] ("Little and Brown's" edition of laws and treaties competent evidence of Acts of Congress).

§ 54 [see § 204] (Codes and Supplements as establishing prima facie the Laws of United States and District of Columbia, citation of Codes and Supplements).

§ 55 [see § 209] (Copies of Supplements to Code of Laws of United States and of District of Columbia Code and Supplements; conclusive evidence of original).

5 U.S.C.:

§ 490 [see 28 U.S.C. § 1733] (Records of Department of Interior; authenticated copies as evidence).

8 U.S.C.:

§ 717(b) [see § 1435] (Former citizens of United States excepted from certain requirements; citizenship lost by spouse's alienage or loss of United States citizenship, or by entering armed forces of foreign state or acquiring its nationality).

§ 727(g) [see § 1443] (Administration of naturalization laws; rules and regulations; instruction in citizenship; forms; oaths; depositions; documents in evidence; photographic studio).

15 U.S.C.:

§ 127 [see § 1057(e)] (Trademarks; copies of records as evidence).

20 U.S.C.:

§ 52 (Smithsonian Institution; evidence of title to site and buildings).

25 U.S.C.:

§ 6 (Bureau of Indian Affairs; seal; authenticated and certified documents; evidence).

31 U.S.C.:

§ 46 (Laws governing General Accounting Office; copies of books, records, etc., thereof as evidence).

38 U.S.C.:

§ 11g [see § 202] (Seal of Veterans' Administration; authentication of copies of records).

43 U.S.C.:

§ 57 (Authenticated copies or extracts from records as evidence).

§ 58 (Transcripts from records of Louisiana).

§ 59 (Official papers in office of surveyor general in California; papers; copies).

§ 83 (Transcripts of records as evidence).

44 U.S.C.:

§ 300h [see § 2112] (National Archives; seal; reproduction of archives; fee; admissibility in evidence of reproductions).

§ 307 [see § 1507] (Filing document as constructive notice; publication in Register as presumption of validity; judicial notice; citation).

47 U.S.C.:

§ 412 (Documents filed with Federal Communications Commission as public records; prima facie evidence; confidential records).

49 U.S.C.:

§ 16 [see § 10303] (Orders of Commission and enforcement thereof; forfeitures—(13) copies of schedules, tariffs, contracts, etc., kept as public records; evidence).

Notes of Advisory Committee on 2002 amendments. The language of Rule 27 has been amended as part of the general restyling of the Criminal Rules to make them more easily understood and to make style and terminology consistent throughout the rules. These changes are intended to be stylistic only.

Rule 28. Interpreters

The court may select, appoint, and set the reasonable compensation for an interpreter, including an interpreter for the victim. The compensation must be paid from funds provided by law or by the government, as the court may direct.

HISTORY:

Amended Feb. 28, 1966, eff. July 1, 1966; Nov. 20, 1972, eff. July 1, 1975; Jan. 2, 1975, P. L. 93-595, § 3, 88 Stat. 1949; April 29, 2002, eff. Dec. 1, 2002; Dec. 16, 2016, P.L. 114-324, § 2(c), 130 Stat. 1948.

HISTORY; ANCILLARY LAWS AND DIRECTIVES

Other provisions:

Notes of Advisory Committee. The power of the court to call its own witnesses, though rarely invoked, is recognized in the Federal courts, *Young v. United States* (1939, CA5 Tex.) 107 F.2d 490; *Litsinger v. United States* (1930, CA7 Ill.) 44 F.2d 45. This rule provides a procedure whereby the court may, if it chooses, exercise this power in connection with expert witnesses. This rule is based, in part, on the Uniform Expert Testimony Act, drafted by the Commissioners on Uniform State Laws, *Hand Book of the National Conference of Commissioners on Uniform State Laws* (1937), 337; see, also, Wigmore—Evidence, 3d Ed., sec. 563; A.L.I. Code of Criminal Procedure, secs. 307–309; National Commission on Law of Observance and Enforcement— *Report on Criminal Procedure,* 37. Similar provisions are found in the statutes of a number of States: Wisconsin—Wis.Stat. (1941), sec. 357.12; Indiana—Ind-.Stat.Ann. (Burns, 1933), sec. 9-1702; California—Cal.Pen-.Code (Deering, 1941), sec. 1027.

Notes of Advisory Committee on 1966 amendments. Subdivision (a). The original rule is made a separate subdivision. The amendment permits the court to inform the witness of his duties in writing since it often constitutes an unnecessary inconvenience and expense to require the witness to appear in court for such purpose.

Subdivision (b). This new subdivision authorizes the court to appoint and provide for the compensation of interpreters. General language is used to give discretion to the court to appoint interpreters in all appropriate situations. Interpreters may be needed to interpret the testimony of non-English speaking witnesses or to assist non-English speaking defendants in understanding the proceedings or in communicating with assigned counsel. Interpreters may also be needed where a witness or a defendant is deaf.

Notes of Advisory Committee on 1972 amendments. Subdivision (a). This subdivision is stricken, since the subject of court-appointed expert witnesses is covered in Evidence Rule 706 in detail.

Subdivision (b). The provisions of subdivision (b) are retained. Although Evidence Rule 703 specifies the qualifications of interpreters and the form of oath to be administered to them, it does not cover their appointment or compensation.

Effective date of amendment proposed by United States Supreme Court Order of November 20, 1972. As to the effective date of amendment proposed by United States Supreme Court Order of Nov. 20, 1972, see Act Jan. 2, 1975, P. L. 93-595, § 3, 88 Stat. 1959, which appears as a note to Rule 26.

Notes of Advisory Committee on 2002 amendments. The language of Rule 28 has been amended as part of the general restyling of the Criminal Rules to make them more easily understood and to make style and terminology consistent throughout the rules. These changes are intended to be stylistic only.

Amendments:

2016. Act Dec. 16, 2016, inserted ", including an interpreter for the victim".

Rule 29. Motion for a Judgment of Acquittal

(a) Before Submission to the Jury. After the government closes its evidence or after the close of all the evidence, the court on the defendant's motion must enter a judgment of acquittal of any offense for which the evidence is insufficient to sustain a conviction. The court may on its own consider whether the evidence is insufficient to sustain a conviction. If the court denies a motion for a judgment of acquittal at the close of the government's evidence, the defendant may offer evidence without having reserved the right to do so.

(b) Reserving Decision. The court may reserve decision on the motion, proceed with the trial (where the motion is made before the close of all the evidence), submit the case to the jury, and decide the motion either before the jury returns a verdict or after it returns a verdict of guilty or is discharged without having returned a verdict. If the court reserves decision, it must decide the motion on the basis of the evidence at the time the ruling was reserved.

(c) After Jury Verdict or Discharge.

(1) *Time for a Motion.* A defendant may move for a judgment of acquittal, or renew such a motion, within 14 days after a guilty verdict or after the court discharges the jury, whichever is later.

(2) *Ruling on the Motion.* If the jury has returned a guilty verdict, the court may set aside the verdict and enter an acquittal. If the jury has failed to return a verdict, the court may enter a judgment of acquittal.

(3) *No Prior Motion Required.* A defendant is not required to move for a judgment of acquittal before the court submits the case to the jury as a prerequisite for making such a motion after jury discharge.

(d) Conditional Ruling on a Motion for a New Trial.

(1) *Motion for a New Trial.* If the court enters a judgment of acquittal after a guilty verdict, the court must also conditionally determine whether any motion for a new trial should be granted if the judgment of acquittal is later vacated or reversed. The court must specify the reasons for that determination.

(2) *Finality.* The court's order conditionally granting a motion for a new trial does not affect the finality of the judgment of acquittal.

(3) *Appeal.*

(A) Grant of a Motion for a New Trial. If the court conditionally grants a motion for a new trial and an appellate court later reverses the judgment of acquittal, the trial court must proceed with the new trial unless the appellate court orders otherwise.

(B) Denial of a Motion for a New Trial. If the court conditionally denies a motion for a new trial, an appellee may assert that the denial was erroneous. If the appellate court later reverses the judgment of acquittal, the trial court must proceed as the appellate court directs.

HISTORY:

Amended Feb. 28, 1966, eff. July 1, 1966; Nov. 10, 1986, P. L. 99-646, § 54(a), 100 Stat. 3607; April. 29, 1994, eff. Dec. 1, 1994; April 29, 2002, eff. Dec. 1, 2002; April 25, 2005, eff. Dec. 1, 2005; Mar. 26, 2009, eff. Dec. 1, 2009.

HISTORY; ANCILLARY LAWS AND DIRECTIVES

Other provisions:

Notes of Advisory Committee. *Note to Subdivision (a).* 1. The purpose of changing the name of a motion for a directed verdict to a motion for judgment of acquittal is to make the nomenclature accord with the realities. The change of nomenclature, however, does not modify the nature of the motion or enlarge the scope of matters that may be considered.

2. The second sentence is patterned on New York Code of Criminal Procedure, sec 410.

3. The purpose of the third sentence is to remove the doubt existing in a few jurisdictions on the question whether the defendant is deemed to have rested his case if he moves for a directed verdict at the close of the prosecution's case. The purpose of the rule is expressly to preserve the right of the defendant to offer evidence in his own behalf, if such motion is denied. This is a restatement of the prevailing practice, and is also in accord with the practice prescribed for civil cases by Rule 50(a) of the Federal Rules of Civil Procedure, 28 U.S.C., Appendix.

Note to Subdivision (b). This rule is in substance similar to Rule 50(b) of the Federal Rules of Civil Procedure, 28 U.S.C., Appendix, and permits the court to render judgment for the defendant notwithstanding a verdict of guilty. Some Federal courts have recognized and approved the use of a judgment non obstante veredicto for the defendant in a criminal case. *Ex parte United States,* 101 F.2d 870 (CCA 7th, affirmed by an equally divided court, *United States v. Stone,* 308 U.S. 519, 60 S.Ct. 177, 84 L.Ed. 441. The rule sanctions this practice.

Notes of Advisory Committee on 1966 amendments. Subdivision (a). A minor change has been made in the caption.

Subdivision (b). The last three sentences are deleted with the matters formerly covered by them transferred to the new subdivision (c).

Subdivision (c). The new subdivision makes several changes in the former procedure. A motion for judgment of acquittal may be made after discharge of the jury whether or not a motion was made before submission to the jury. No legitimate interest of the government is intended to be prejudiced by permitting the court to direct an acquittal on a post-verdict motion. The constitutional requirement of a jury trial in criminal cases is primarily a right accorded to the defendant. Cf. *Adams v. United States, ex rel. McCann,* 317 U.S. 269, 87 L.Ed. 271, 63 S.Ct. 236, 143 A.L.R. 435 (1942); *Singer v. United States,* 380 U.S. 24, 13 L.Ed. 2d 630, 85 S.Ct. 783 (1965); Note, 65 Yale L.J. 1032 (1956).

The time in which the motion may be made has been changed to 7 days in accordance with the amendment to Rule 45(a) which by excluding Saturday from the days to be counted when the period of time is less than 7 days would make 7 days the normal time for a motion required to be made in 5 days. Also the court is authorized to extend the time as is provided for motions for new trial (Rule 33) and in arrest of judgment (Rule 34).

References in the original rule to the motion for a new trial as an alternate to the motion for judgment of acquittal and to the power of the court to order a new trial have been eliminated. Motions for new trial are adequately covered in Rule 33. Also the original wording is subject to the interpretation that a motion for judgment of acquittal gives the court power to order a new trial even though the defendant does not wish a new trial and has not asked for one.

Effective date of Nov. 10, 1986 amendments. Act Nov. 10, 1986, P. L. 99-646, § 54(b), 100 Stat. 3607, provided: "The amendments made by this section [adding subdivisions (d) of this Rule] shall take effect 30 days after the date of the enactment of this Act.".

Notes of Advisory Committee on Dec. 1, 1994 amendments. The amendment permits the reservation of a motion for a judgment of acquittal made at the close of the government's case in the same manner as the rule now permits for motions made at the close of all of the evidence. Although the rule as written did not permit the court to reserve such motions made at the end of the government's case, trial courts on occasion have nonetheless reserved ruling. *See, e.g., United States v. Bruno,* 873 F.2d 555 (2d Cir.), cert. denied, 110 S.Ct. 125 (1989); *United States v. Reifsteck,* 841 F.2d 701 (6th Cir. 1988). While the amendment will not affect a large number of cases, it should remove the dilemma in those close cases in which the court would feel pressured into making an immediate, and possibly erroneous, decision or violating the rule as presently written by reserving its ruling on the motion.

The amendment also permits the trial court to balance the defendant's interest in an immediate resolution of the motion against the interest of the government in proceeding to a verdict thereby preserving its right to appeal in the event a verdict of guilty is returned but is then set aside by the granting of a judgment of acquittal. Under the double jeopardy clause the government may appeal the granting of a motion for judgment of acquittal only if there would be no necessity for another trial, i.e., only where the jury has returned a verdict of guilty. *United States v. Martin Linen Supply Co.,* 430 U.S. 564 (1977). Thus, the government's right to appeal a Rule 29 motion is only preserved where the ruling is reserved until after the verdict.

In addressing the issue of preserving the government's right to appeal and at the same time recognizing double jeopardy concerns, the Supreme Court observed:

We should point out that it is entirely possible for a trial court to reconcile the public interest in the Government's right to appeal from an erroneous conclusion of law with the defendant's interest in avoiding a second prosecution. In *United States v. Wilson,* 420 U.S. 332 (1975), the court permitted the case to go to the jury, which returned a verdict of guilty, but it subsequently dismissed the indictment for preindictment delay on the basis of evidence adduced at trial. Most recently in *United States v. Ceccolini,* 435 U.S. 268 (1978), we described similar action with approval: 'The District Court had sensibly made its finding on the factual question of guilt or innocence, and then ruled on the motion to suppress; a reversal of these rulings would require no further proceeding in the District Court, but merely a reinstatement of the finding of guilt.' Id. at 271.

United States v. Scott, 437 U.S. 82, 100 n. 13 (1978). By analogy, reserving a ruling on a motion for judgment of acquittal strikes the same balance as that reflected by the Supreme Court in Scott.

Reserving a ruling on a motion made at the end of the government's case does pose problems, however, where the defense decides to present evidence and run the risk that such evidence will support the government's case. To address that problem, the amendment provides that the trial court is to consider only the evidence submitted at the time of the motion in making its ruling, whenever made. And in reviewing a trial court's ruling, the appellate court would be similarly limited.

Notes of Advisory Committee on 2002 amendments. The language of Rule 29 has been amended as part of the general restyling of the Criminal Rules to make them more easily understood and to make style and terminology consistent throughout the rules. These changes are intended to be stylistic only, except as noted below.

In Rule 29(a), the first sentence abolishing "directed verdicts" has been deleted because it is unnecessary. The rule continues to recognize that a judge may sua sponte enter a judgment of acquittal.

Rule 29(c)(1) addresses the issue of the timing of a motion for judgment of acquittal. The amended rule now includes language that the motion must be made within 7 days after a guilty verdict or after the judge discharges the jury, whichever occurs later. That change reflects the fact that in a capital case or in a case involving criminal forfeiture, for example, the jury may not be discharged until it has completed its sentencing duties. The court may still set another time for the defendant to make or renew the motion, if it does so within the 7-day period.

Notes of Advisory Committee on 2005 amendments. Rule 29(c) has been amended to remove the requirement that the court must act within seven days after a guilty verdict or after the court discharges the jury, if it sets another time for filing a motion for a judgment of acquittal. This amendment parallels similar changes to Rules 33 and 34. Further, a conforming amendment has been made to Rule 45(b)(2).

Currently, Rule 29(c) requires the defendant to move for a judgment of acquittal within seven days of the guilty verdict, or after the court discharges the jury, whichever occurs later, or some other time set by the court in an order issued within that same seven-day period. Similar provisions exist in Rules 33 and 34. Courts have held that the seven-day rule is jurisdictional. Thus, if a defendant files a request for an extension of time to file a motion for a judgment of acquittal within the seven-day period, the court must rule on that motion or request within the same seven-day period. If for some reason the court does not rule on the request within the seven days, it loses jurisdiction to act on the underlying substantive motion. *See, e.g., United States v. Smith*, 331 U.S. 469, 473–474 (1947) (rejecting argument that trial court had power to grant new trial on its own motion after expiration of time in Rule 33); *United States v. Marquez*, 291 F.3d 23, 27–28 (D.C. Cir. 2002) (citing language of Rule 33, and holding that "district court forfeited the power to act when it failed to . . . fix a new time for filing a motion for a new trial within seven days of the verdict").

Assuming that the current rule was intended to promote finality, there is nothing to prevent the court from granting a significant extension of time, so long as it does so within the seven-day period. Thus, the Committee believed that the rule should be amended to be consistent with all of the other timing requirements in the rules, which do not force the court to act on a motion to extend the time for filing within a particular period of time or lose jurisdiction to do so.

Accordingly, the amendment deletes the language regarding the court's acting within seven days to set the time for filing. Read in conjunction with the conforming amendment to Rule 45(b), the defendant is still required to file a timely motion for a judgment of acquittal under Rule 29 within the seven-day period specified. The defendant may, under Rule 45, seek an extension of time to file the underlying motion as long as the defendant does so within the seven-day period. But the court itself is not required to act on that motion within any particular time. Further, under Rule 45(b)(1)(B), if for some reason the defendant fails to file the underlying motion within the specified time, the court may nonetheless consider that untimely motion if the court determines that the failure to file it on time was the result of excusable neglect.

Notes of Advisory Committee on 2009 amendments. Former Rules 29, 33, and 34 adopted 7-day periods for their respective motions. This period has been expanded to 14 days. Experience has proved that in many cases it is not possible to prepare a satisfactory motion in 7 days, even under the former rule that excluded intermediate Saturdays, Sundays, and legal holidays. This led to frequent requests for continuances, and the filing of bare bones motions that required later supplementation. The 14-day period—including intermediate Saturdays, Sundays, and legal holidays as provided by Rule 45(a)—sets a more realistic time for the filing of these motions.

Amendments:

1986.

Act Nov. 10, 1986 (effective 30 days after enactment as provided by § 54(b) of such Act, which appears as a note to this section) added subsec. (d).

Rule 29.1. Closing Argument

Closing arguments proceed in the following order:

(1) the government argues;

(2) the defense argues; and

(3) the government rebuts.

HISTORY:

Added April 22, 1974, eff. Dec. 1, 1975; July 31, 1975, P. L. 94-64, § 2, 89 Stat. 370; April 29, 2002, eff. Dec. 1, 2002.

HISTORY; ANCILLARY LAWS AND DIRECTIVES

Other provisions:

Notes of Advisory Committee. This rule is designed to control the order of closing argument. It reflects the Advisory Committee's view that it is desirable to have a uniform federal practice. The rule is drafted in the view that fair and effective administration of justice is best served if the defendant knows the arguments actually made by the prosecution in behalf of conviction before the defendant is faced with the decision whether to reply and what to reply.

Notes of Committee on the Judiciary on 1975 amendments (House Report No. 94-247). A. Amendments Proposed by the Supreme Court, Rule 29.1 is a new rule that was added to regulate closing arguments. It prescribes that the government shall make its closing argument and then the defendant shall make his. After the defendant has argued, the government is entitled to reply in rebuttal.

B. Committee Action. The Committee endorses and adopts this proposed rule in its entirety. The Committee believes that as the Advisory Committee Note has stated, fair and effective administration of justice is best served if the defendant knows the arguments actually made by the prosecution in behalf of conviction before the defendant is faced with the decision whether to reply and what to reply. Rule 29.1 does not specifically address itself to what happens if the prosecution waives its initial closing argument. The Committee is of the view that the prosecutor, when he waives his initial closing argument, also waives his rebuttal. [See the remarks of Senior United States Circuit Judge J. Edward Lumbard in Hearings II, at 207.]

Approval of July 31, 1975 amendments; effective date. Act July 31, 1975, P. L. 94-64, § 2, 89 Stat. 370, which appears as a note to Rule 4, approved U. S. Supreme Court Order of April 22, 1974, which added this Rule, and rendered it effective on Dec. 1, 1975.

Notes of Advisory Committee on 2002 amendments. The language of Rule 29.1 has been amended as part of the general restyling of the Criminal Rules to make them more easily understood and to make style and terminology consistent throughout the rules. These changes are intended to be stylistic only.

Rule 30. Jury Instructions

(a) In General. Any party may request in writing that the court instruct the jury on the law as specified in the request. The request must be made at the close of the evidence or at any earlier time that the court reasonably sets. When the request is made, the requesting party must furnish a copy to every other party.

(b) Ruling on a Request. The court must inform the parties before closing arguments how it intends to rule on the requested instructions.

(c) Time for Giving Instructions. The court may instruct the jury before or after the arguments are completed, or at both times.

(d) Objections to Instructions. A party who objects to any portion of the instructions or to a failure to give a requested instruction must inform the court of the specific objection and the grounds for the objection before the jury retires to deliberate. An opportunity must be given to object out of the jury's hearing and, on request, out of the jury's presence. Failure to object in accordance with this rule precludes appellate review, except as permitted under Rule 52(b).

HISTORY:

Amended Feb. 28, 1966, eff. July 1, 1966; Mar. 9, 1987, eff. Aug. 1, 1987; April 25, 1988, eff. Aug. 1, 1988; April 29, 2002, eff. Dec. 1, 2002.

HISTORY; ANCILLARY LAWS AND DIRECTIVES

Other provisions:

Notes of Advisory Committee. This rule corresponds to Rule 51 of the Federal Rules of Civil Procedure, 28 U.S.C., Appendix, the second sentence alone being new. It seemed appropriate that on a point such as instructions to juries there should be no difference in procedure between civil and criminal cases.

Notes of Advisory Committee on 1966 amendments. The amendment requires the court, on request of any party, to require the jury to withdraw in order to permit full argument of objections to instructions.

Notes of Advisory Committee on 1987 amendments. In its current form, Rule 30 requires that the court instruct the jury after the arguments of counsel. In some districts, usually where the state practice is otherwise, the parties prefer to stipulate to instruction before closing arguments. The purpose of the amendment is to give the court discretion to instruct the jury before or after closing arguments, or at both times. The amendment will permit courts to continue instructing the jury after arguments as Rule 30 had previously required. It will also permit courts to instruct before arguments in order to give the parties an opportunity to argue to the jury in light of the exact language used by the court. See generally Raymond, *Merits and Demerits of the Missouri System in Instructing Juries,* 5 St. Louis U. L. J. 317 (1959). Finally, the amendment plainly indicates that the court may instruct both before and after arguments, which assures that the court retains power to remedy omissions in pre-argument instructions or to add instructions necessitated by the arguments.

Notes of Advisory Committee on 1988 amendments. The amendment is technical. No substantive change is intended.

Notes of Advisory Committee on 2002 amendments. The language of Rule 30 has been amended as part of the general restyling of the Criminal Rules to make them more easily understood and to make style and terminology consistent throughout the rules. These changes are intended to be stylistic only, except as noted below.

Rule 30(a) reflects a change in the timing of requests for instructions. As currently written, the trial court may not direct the parties to file such requests before trial without violating Rules 30 and 57. While the amendment falls short of requiring all requests to be made before trial in all cases, the amendment permits a court to do so in a particular case or as a matter of local practice under local rules promulgated under Rule 57. The rule does not preclude the practice of permitting the parties to supplement their requested instructions during the trial.

Rule 30(d) clarifies what, if anything, counsel must do to preserve a claim of error regarding an instruction or failure to instruct. The rule retains the requirement of a contemporaneous and specific objection (before the jury retires to deliberate). As the Supreme Court recognized in *Jones v. United States,* 527 U.S. 373 [144 L. Ed. 2d 370] (1999), read literally, current Rule 30 could be construed to bar any appellate review absent a timely objection when in fact a court may conduct a limited review under a plain error standard. The amendment does not address the issue of whether objections to the instructions must be renewed after the instructions are given, in order to preserve a claim of error. No change in practice is intended by the amendment.

Rule 31. Jury Verdict

(a) Return. The jury must return its verdict to a judge in open court. The verdict must be unanimous.

(b) Partial Verdicts, Mistrial, and Retrial.

(1) *Multiple Defendants.* If there are multiple defendants, the jury may return a verdict at any time during its deliberations as to any defendant about whom it has agreed.

(2) *Multiple Counts.* If the jury cannot agree on all counts as to any defendant, the jury may return a verdict on those counts on which it has agreed.

(3) *Mistrial and Retrial.* If the jury cannot agree on a verdict on one or more counts, the court may declare a mistrial on those counts. The government may retry any defendant on any count on which the jury could not agree.

(c) Lesser Offense or Attempt. A defendant may be found guilty of any of the following:

(1) an offense necessarily included in the offense charged;

(2) an attempt to commit the offense charged; or

(3) an attempt to commit an offense necessarily included in the offense charged, if the attempt is an offense in its own right.

(d) Jury Poll. After a verdict is returned but before the jury is discharged, the court must on a party's request, or may on its own, poll the jurors individually. If the poll reveals a lack of unanimity, the court may direct the jury to deliberate further or may declare a mistrial and discharge the jury.

HISTORY:

As amended Apr. 24, 1972, eff. Oct. 1, 1972; Apr. 24, 1998, eff. Dec. 1, 1998; Apr. 17, 2000, eff. Dec. 1, 2000; Apr. 29, 2002, eff. Dec. 1, 2002.

HISTORY; ANCILLARY LAWS AND DIRECTIVES

Other provisions:

Notes of Advisory Committee. *Note to Subdivision (a).* This rule is a restatement of existing law and practice. It does not embody any regulation of sealed verdicts, it being contemplated that this matter would be governed by local practice in the various district courts. The rule does not affect the existing statutes relating to qualified verdicts in cases in which capital punishment may be imposed, 18 U.S.C. § 408a (see § 1201) (Kidnapped persons); 18 U.S.C. § 412a (see § 1992) (Wrecking trains); 18 U.S.C. § 567 (see § 1111) (Verdicts; qualified verdicts).

Note to Subdivision (b). This rule is a restatement of existing law, 18 U.S.C. [former] § 566 (Verdicts; several joint defendants).

Note to Subdivision (c). This rule is a restatement of existing law, 18 U.S.C. [former] § 565 (Verdicts; less offense than charged).

Note to Subdivision (d). This rule is a restatement of existing law and practice, *Mackett v. United States,* 90 F.2d 462, 465 (C.C.A. 7th); *Bruce v. Chestnut Farms Chevy Chase Dairy,* 126 F.2d 224, App.D.C.

Notes of Advisory Committee on 1972 amendments. Subdivision (e) is new. It is intended to provide procedural implementation of the recently enacted criminal forfeiture provision of the Organized Crime Control Act of 1970, Title IX, § 1963, and the Comprehensive Drug Abuse Prevention and Control Act of 1970, Title II, § 408(a)(2).

The assumption of the draft is that the amount of the interest or property subject to criminal forfeiture is an element of the offense to be alleged and proved. See Advisory Committee Note to rule 7(c)(2).

Although special verdict provisions are rare in criminal cases, they are not unknown. See *United States v. Spock,* 416 F.2d 165 (1st Cir. 1969), especially footnote 41 where authorities are listed.

Notes of Advisory Committee on 1998 amendments. The right of a party to have the jury polled is an "undoubted right" *Humphries v. District of Columbia,* 174 U.S. 190, 194 (1899). Its purpose is to determine with certainty that "each of the jurors approves of the verdict as returned; that no one has been coerced or induced to sign a verdict to which he does not fully assent" *Id.*

Currently, Rule 31(d) is silent on the precise method of polling the jury. Thus, a court in its discretion may conduct the poll collectively or individually. As one court has noted, although the prevailing view is that the method used is a matter within the discretion of the trial court, *United States v. Miller,* 59 F.3d 417, 420 (3d Cir. 1995) (citing cases), the preference, nonetheless of the appellate and trial courts, seems to favor individual polling. *Id.* (citing cases). That is the position taken in the American Bar Association Standards for Criminal Justice § 15-4.5. Those sources favoring individual polling observe that conducting a poll of the jurors collectively saves little time and does not always adequately insure that an individual juror who has been forced to join the majority during deliberations will voice dissent from a collective response. On the other hand, an advantage to individual polling is the "likelihood that it will discourage post-trial efforts to challenge the verdict on allegations of coercion on the part of some of the jurors." *Miller, Id.* at 420 (citing *Audette v. Isaksen Fishing Corp.,* 789 F.2d 956, 961, n. 6 (1st Cir. 1986)).

The Committee is persuaded by the authorities and practice that there are advantages of conducting an individual poll of the jurors. Thus, the rule requires that the jurors be polled individually when a polling is requested, or when polling is directed sua sponte by the court. The amendment, however, leaves to the court the discretion as to whether to conduct a separate poll for each defendant, each count of the indictment or complaint, or on other issues.

The rule is amended to reflect the creation of new Rule 32.2, which now governs criminal forfeiture procedures.

Notes of Advisory Committee on 2002 amendments. The language of Rule 31 has been amended as part of the general restyling of the Criminal Rules to make them more easily understood and to make style and terminology consistent throughout the rules. These changes are intended to be stylistic only.

Rule 31(b) has been amended to clarify that a jury may return partial verdicts, either as to multiple defendants or multiple counts, or both. See, e.g., *United States v. Cunningham,* 145 F.3d 1385, 1388–90 (D.C. Cir. 1998) (partial verdicts on multiple defendants and counts). No change in practice is intended.

TITLE VII. POST-CONVICTION PROCEDURES

Rule

Rule 32. Sentencing and Judgment

(a) [Reserved]

(b) Time of Sentencing.

(1) *In General.* The court must impose sentence without unnecessary delay.

(2) *Changing Time Limits.* The court may, for good cause, change any time limits prescribed in this rule.

(c) Presentence Investigation.

(1) *Required Investigation.*

(A) In General. The probation officer must conduct a presentence investigation and submit a report to the court before it imposes sentence unless:

(i) 18 U.S.C. § 3593(c) or another statute requires otherwise; or

(ii) the court finds that the information in the record enables it to meaningfully exercise its sentencing authority under 18 U.S.C. § 3553, and the court explains its finding on the record.

(B) Restitution. If the law permits restitution, the probation officer must conduct an investigation and submit a report that contains sufficient information for the court to order restitution.

(2) *Interviewing the Defendant.* The probation officer who interviews a defendant as part of a presentence investigation must, on request, give the defendant's attorney notice and a reasonable opportunity to attend the interview.

(d) Presentence Report.

(1) *Applying the Advisory Sentencing Guidelines.* The presentence report must:

(A) identify all applicable guidelines and policy statements of the Sentencing Commission;

(B) calculate the defendant's offense level and criminal history category;

(C) state the resulting sentencing range and kinds of sentences available;

(D) identify any factor relevant to:

(i) the appropriate kind of sentence, or

(ii) the appropriate sentence within the applicable sentencing range; and

(E) identify any basis for departing from the applicable sentencing range.

(2) *Additional Information.* The presentence report must also contain the following:

(A) the defendant's history and characteristics, including:

(i) any prior criminal record;

(ii) the defendant's financial condition; and

(iii) any circumstances affecting the defendant's behavior that may be helpful in imposing sentence or in correctional treatment;

(B) information that assesses any financial, social, psychological, and medical impact on any victim;

(C) when appropriate, the nature and extent of nonprison programs and resources available to the defendant;

(D) when the law provides for restitution, information sufficient for a restitution order;

(E) if the court orders a study under 18 U.S.C. § 3552(b), any resulting report and recommendation;

(F) a statement of whether the government seeks forfeiture under Rule 32.2 and any other law; and

(G) any other information that the court requires, including information relevant to the factors under 18 U.S.C. § 3553(a).

(3) *Exclusions.* The presentence report must exclude the following:

(A) any diagnoses that, if disclosed, might seriously disrupt a rehabilitation program;

(B) any sources of information obtained upon a promise of confidentiality; and

(C) any other information that, if disclosed, might result in physical or other harm to the defendant or others.

(e) Disclosing the Report and Recommendation.

(1) *Time to Disclose.* Unless the defendant has consented in writing, the probation officer must not submit a presentence report to the court or disclose its contents to anyone until the defendant has pleaded guilty or nolo contendere, or has been found guilty.

(2) *Minimum Required Notice.* The probation officer must give the presentence report to the defendant, the defendant's attorney, and an attorney for the government at least 35 days before sentencing unless the defendant waives this minimum period.

(3) *Sentence Recommendation.* By local rule or by order in a case, the court may direct the probation officer not to disclose to anyone other than the court the officer's recommendation on the sentence.

(f) Objecting to the Report.

(1) *Time to Object.* Within 14 days after receiving the presentence report, the parties must state in writing any objections, including objections to material information, sentencing guideline ranges, and policy statements contained in or omitted from the report.

(2) *Serving Objections.* An objecting party must provide a copy of its objections to the opposing party and to the probation officer.

(3) *Action on Objections.* After receiving objections, the probation officer may meet with the parties to discuss the objections. The probation officer may then investigate further and revise the presentence report as appropriate.

(g) Submitting the Report. At least 7 days before sentencing, the probation officer must submit to the court and to the parties the presentence report and an addendum containing any unresolved objections, the grounds for those objections, and the probation officer's comments on them.

(h) Notice of Possible Departure From Sentencing Guidelines. Before the court may depart from the applicable sentencing range on a ground not identified for departure either in the presentence report or in a party's prehearing submission, the court must give the parties reasonable notice that it is contemplating such a departure. The notice must specify any ground on which the court is contemplating a departure.

(i) Sentencing.

(1) *In General.* At sentencing, the court:

(A) must verify that the defendant and the defendant's attorney have read and discussed the presentence report and any addendum to the report;

(B) must give to the defendant and an attorney for the government a written summary of—or summarize in camera—any information excluded from the presentence report under Rule 32(d)(3) on which the court will rely in sentencing, and give them a reasonable opportunity to comment on that information;

(C) must allow the parties' attorneys to comment on the probation officer's determinations and other matters relating to an appropriate sentence; and

(D) may, for good cause, allow a party to make a new objection at any time before sentence is imposed.

(2) *Introducing Evidence; Producing a Statement.* The court may permit the parties to introduce evidence on the objections. If a witness testifies at sentencing, Rule 26.2(a)–(d) and (f) applies. If a party fails to comply with a Rule 26.2 order to produce a witness's statement, the court must not consider that witness's testimony.

(3) *Court Determinations.* At sentencing, the court:

(A) may accept any undisputed portion of the presentence report as a finding of fact;

(B) must—for any disputed portion of the presentence report or other controverted matter—rule on the dispute or determine that a ruling is unnecessary either because the matter will not affect sentencing, or because the court will not consider the matter in sentencing; and

(C) must append a copy of the court's determinations under this rule to any copy of the presentence report made available to the Bureau of Prisons.

(4) *Opportunity to Speak.*

(A) By a Party. Before imposing sentence, the court must:

(i) provide the defendant's attorney an opportunity to speak on the defendant's behalf;

(ii) address the defendant personally in order to permit the defendant to speak or present any information to mitigate the sentence; and

(iii) provide an attorney for the government an opportunity to speak equivalent to that of the defendant's attorney.

(B) By a Victim. Before imposing sentence, the court must address any victim of the crime who is present at sentencing and must permit the victim to be reasonably heard.

(C) In Camera Proceedings. Upon a party's motion and for good cause, the court may hear in camera any statement made under Rule 32(i)(4).

(j) Defendant's Right to Appeal.

(1) *Advice of a Right to Appeal.*

(A) Appealing a Conviction. If the defendant pleaded not guilty and was convicted, after sentencing the court must advise the defendant of the right to appeal the conviction.

(B) Appealing a Sentence. After sentencing—regardless of the defendant's plea—the court must advise the defendant of any right to appeal the sentence.

(C) Appeal Costs. The court must advise a defendant who is unable to pay appeal costs of the right to ask for permission to appeal in forma pauperis.

(2) *Clerk's Filing of Notice.* If the defendant so requests, the clerk must immediately prepare and file a notice of appeal on the defendant's behalf.

(k) Judgment.

(1) *In General.* In the judgment of conviction, the court must set forth the plea, the jury verdict or the court's findings, the adjudication, and the sentence. If the defendant is found not guilty or is otherwise en-

titled to be discharged, the court must so order. The judge must sign the judgment, and the clerk must enter it.

(2) *Criminal Forfeiture.* Forfeiture procedures are governed by Rule 32.2.

HISTORY:

Dec. 26, 1944, eff. March 21, 1946, as amended Feb. 28, 1966, eff. July 1, 1966; April 24, 1972, eff. Oct. 1, 1972; April 22, 1974, eff. Dec. 1, 1975; Act July 31, 1975, P. L. 94-64, §§ 2, 3(31)–(34), 89 Stat. 370, 376, eff. Dec. 1, 1975; April 30, 1979, eff. Dec. 1, 1980, as provided by Act July 31, 1979, P. L. 96-42, § 1(1), 93 Stat. 326; Oct. 12, 1982, P. L. 97-291, § 3, 96 Stat. 1249, eff. Oct. 12, 1982; April 28, 1983, eff. Aug. 1, 1983; Oct. 12, 1984, P. L. 98-473, Title II, Ch II, § 215(a), 98 Stat. 2014, eff. Nov. 1, 1987; Nov. 10, 1986, P. L. 99-646, § 25(a), 100 Stat. 3597; March 9, 1987, eff. Aug. 1, 1987; April 25, 1989, eff. Dec. 1, 1989; April 30, 1991, eff. Dec. 1, 1991; April 22, 1993, eff. Dec. 1, 1993; April 29, 1994, eff. Dec. 1, 1994; Sept. 13, 1994, P. L. 103-322, Title XXIII, Subtitle A, § 230101(a), (b), 108 Stat. 2077; April 23, 1996, eff. Dec. 1, 1996; April 24, 1996, P. L. 104-132, Title II, Subtitle A, § 207(a), 110 Stat. 1236; April 17, 2000, eff. Dec. 1, 2000; April 29, 2002, eff. Dec. 1, 2002; April 30, 2007, eff. Dec. 1, 2007; April 23, 2008, eff. Dec. 1, 2008; March 26, 2009, eff. Dec. 1, 2009; April 26, 2011, eff. Dec. 1, 2011.

HISTORY; ANCILLARY LAWS AND DIRECTIVES

Other provisions:

Notes of Advisory Committee on Rules.

Note to Subdivision (a). This rule is substantially a restatement of existing procedure. Rule I of the Criminal Appeals Rules of 1933, 292 US 661 [18 USC formerly following § 688]. See Rule 43 relating to the presence of the defendant.

Note to Subdivision (b). This rule is substantially a restatement of existing procedure. Rule I of the Criminal Appeals Rules of 1933, 292 US 661 [18 USC formerly following § 688].

Note to Subdivision (c). The purpose of this provision is to encourage and broaden the use of presentence investigations, which are now being utilized to good advantage in many cases. See, "The Presentence Investigation" published by Administrative Office of the United States Courts, Division of Probation.

Note to Subdivision (d). This rule modifies existing practice by abrogating the ten-day limitation on a motion for leave to withdraw a plea of guilty. See Rule II (4) of the Criminal Appeals Rules of 1933, 292 US 661 [18 USC formerly following § 688].

Note to Subdivision (e). See 18 USC former §§ 724 et seq. (now §§ 3651 et seq.).

Notes of Advisory Committee on 1966 amendments.

Subdivision (a)(1). The amendment writes into the rule the holding of the Supreme Court that the court before imposing sentence must afford an opportunity to the defendant personally to speak in his own behalf. See Green v United States, 365 US 301, 5 L Ed 2d 670, 81 S Ct 653 (1961); Hill v United States, 368 US 424, 7 L Ed 2d 417, 82 S Ct 468 (1962). The amendment also provides an opportunity for counsel to speak on behalf of the defendant.

Subdivision (a)(2). This amendment is a substantial revision and a relocation of the provision originally found in Rule 37(a)(2): "When a court after trial imposes sentence upon a defendant not represented by counsel, the defendant shall be advised of his right to appeal and if he so requests, the clerk shall prepare and file forthwith a notice of appeal on behalf of the defendant." The court is required to advise the defendant of his right to appeal in all cases which have gone to trial after plea of not guilty because situations arise in which a defendant represented by counsel at the trial is not adequately advised by such counsel of his right to appeal. Trial counsel may not regard his responsibility as extending beyond the time of imposition of sentence. The defendant may be removed from the courtroom immediately upon sentence and held in custody under circumstances which make it difficult for counsel to advise him. See, e.g., Hodges v United States, 368 US 139, 7 L Ed 2d 184, 82 S Ct 235 (1961). Because indigent defendants are most likely to be without effective assistance of counsel at this point in the proceedings, it is also provided that defendants be notified of the right of a person without funds to apply for leave to appeal in forma pauperis. The provision is added here because this rule seems the most appropriate place to set forth a procedure to be followed by the court at the time of sentencing.

Subdivision (c)(2). It is not a denial of due process of law for a court in sentencing to rely on a report of a presentence investigation without disclosing such report to the defendant or giving him an opportunity to rebut it. Williams v New York, 337 US 241, 93 L Ed 1337, 69 S Ct 1079 (1949); Williams v Oklahoma, 358 US 576, 3 L Ed 2d 516, 79 S Ct 421 (1959). However, the question whether as a matter of policy the defendant should be accorded some opportunity to see and refute allegations made in such reports has been the subject of heated controversy. For arguments favoring disclosure, see Tappan, Crime, Justice, and Correction, 558 (1960); Model Penal Code, 54–55 (Tent Draft No. 2, 1954); Thomsen, Confidentiality of the Presentence Report: A Middle Position, 28 Fed Prob, March 1964, p. 8; Wyzanski, A Trial Judge's Freedom and Responsibility, 65 Harv L Rev 1281, 1291–2 (1952); Note, Employment of Social Investigation Reports in Criminal and Juvenile Proceedings, 58 Colum L Rev 702 (1958); cf. Kadish, The Advocate and the Expert: Counsel in the Peno-Correctional Process, 45 Minn L Rev 803, 806, (1961). For arguments opposing disclosure, see Barnett and Gronewold, Confidentiality of the Presentence Report, 26 Fed Prob March 1962, p. 26; Judicial Conference Committee on Administration of the Probation System, Judicial Opinion on Proposed Change in Rule 32(c) of the Federal Rules of Criminal Procedure—a Survey (1964); Keve, The Probation Officer Investigates, 6–15 (1960); Parsons, The Presentence Investigation Report Must be Preserved as a Confidential Document, 28 Fed Prob March 1964, p. 3; Sharp, The Confidential Nature of Presentence Reports, 5 Cath UL Rev 127 (1955); Wilson, A New Arena is Emerging to Test the Confidentiality of Presentence Reports, 25 Fed Prob Dec 1961, p. 6; Federal Judge's Views on Probation Practices, 24 Fed Prob March 1960, p. 10.

In a few jurisdictions the defendant is given a right of access to the presentence report. In England and California a copy of the report is given to the defendant in every case. English Criminal Justice Act of 1948, 11 & 12 Geo 6, c. 58, § 43; Cal Pen C § 1203. In Alabama the defendant has a right to inspect the report. Ala Code Title 42, § 23. In Ohio and Virginia the probation officer reports in open court and the defendant is given the right to examine him on his report. Ohio Rev Code, § 2947.06; Va Code, §

53-278.1. The Minnesota Criminal Code of 1963, § 609.115(4), provides that any presentence report "shall be open for inspection by the prosecuting attorney and the defendant's attorney prior to sentence and on the request of either of them a summary hearing in chambers shall be held on any matter brought in issue, but confidential sources of information shall not be disclosed unless the court otherwise directs." Cf. Model Penal Code § 7.07(5) (POD 1962): "Before imposing sentence, the Court shall advise the defendant or his counsel of the factual contents and the conclusions of any presentence investigation or psychiatric examination and afford fair opportunity, if the defendant so requests, to controvert them. The sources of confidential information need not, however, be disclosed."

Practice in the federal courts is mixed, with a substantial minority of judges permitting disclosure while most deny it. See the recent survey prepared for the Judicial Conference of the District of Columbia by the Junior Bar Section of the Bar Association of the District of Columbia, reported in Conference Papers on Discovery in Federal Criminal Cases, 33 FRD 101, 125–127 (1963). See also Gronewold, Presentence Investigation Practices in the Federal Probation System, Fed Prob Sept. 1958, pp. 27, 31. For divergent judicial opinions see Smith v United States, 223 F2d 750, 754 (5th Cir 1955) (supporting disclosure); United States v Durham, 181 F Supp 503 (DDC 1960) (supporting secrecy).

Substantial objections to compelling disclosure in every case have been advanced by federal judges, including many who in practice often disclose all or parts of presentence reports. See Judicial Conference Committee on the Administration of the Probation System, Judicial Opinion on Proposed Change in Rule 32(c) of the Federal Rules of Criminal Procedure—A Survey (1964). Hence, the amendment goes no further than to make it clear that courts may disclose all or part of the presentence report to the defendant or to his counsel. It is hoped that courts will make increasing use of their discretion to disclose so that defendants generally may be given full opportunity to rebut or explain facts in presentence reports which will be material factors in determining sentences. For a description of such a practice in one district, see Thomsen, Confidentiality of the Presentence Report: A Middle Position, 28 Fed Prob, March 1964, p. 8.

It is also provided that any material disclosed to the defendant or his counsel shall be disclosed to the attorney for the government. Such disclosure will permit the government to participate in the resolution of any factual questions raised by the defendant.

Subdivision (f). This new subdivision writes into the rule the procedure which the cases have derived from the provision in 18 USC § 3653 that a person arrested for violation of probation "shall be taken before the court" and that thereupon the court may revoke the probation. See Escoe v Zerbst, 295 US 490, 79 L Ed 1566, 55 S Ct 818 (1935); Brown v United States, 236 F2d 253 (9th Cir 1956), cert den 356 US 922, 2 L Ed 2d 716, 78 S Ct 705 (1958). Compare Model Penal Code § 301.4 (POD 1962); Hink, The Application of Constitutional Standards of Protection to Probation, 29 U Chi L Rev 483 (1962).

Notes of Advisory Committee on 1972 amendments.

Subdivision (b)(2) is new. It is intended to provide procedural implementation of the recently enacted criminal forfeiture provisions of the Organized Crime Control Act of 1970, Title IX, § 1963, and the Comprehensive Drug Abuse Prevention and Control Act of 1970, Title II, § 408(a)(2).

18 USC § 1963(c) provides for property seizure and disposition. In part it states:

(c) Upon conviction of a person under this section, the court shall authorize the Attorney General to seize all property or other interest declared forfeited under this section upon such terms and conditions as the court shall deem proper.

Although not specifically provided for in the Comprehensive Drug Abuse Prevention and Control Act of 1970, the provision of Title II, § 408(a)(2) forfeiting "profits" or "interest" will need to be implemented procedurally, and therefore new Rule 32(b)(2) will be applicable also to that legislation.

For a brief discussion of the procedural implications of a criminal forfeiture, see Advisory Committee Note to Rule 7(c)(2).

Notes of Advisory Committee on 1974 amendments.

Subdivision (a)(1) is amended by deleting the reference to commitment or release pending sentencing. This issue is dealt with explicitly in the proposed revision of rule 46(c).

Subdivision (a)(2) is amended to make clear that there is no duty on the court to advise the defendant of the right to appeal after sentence is imposed following a plea of guilty or nolo contendere.

To require the court to advise the defendant of a right to appeal after a plea of guilty, accepted pursuant to the increasingly stringent requirements of rule 11, is likely to be confusing to the defendant. See American Bar Association Standards Relating to Criminal Appeals § 2.1(b) (Approved Draft, 1970), limiting the court's duty to advice to "contested cases."

The Advisory Committee is of the opinion that such advice, following a sentence imposed after a plea of guilty, will merely tend to build false hopes and encourage frivolous appeals, with the attendant expense to the defendant or the taxpayers.

Former rule 32(a)(2) imposes a duty only upon conviction after "trial on a plea of not guilty." The few federal cases dealing with the question have interpreted rule 32(a)(2) to say that the court has no duty to advise defendant of his right to appeal after conviction following a guilty plea. Burton v. United States, 307 F.Supp. 448, 450 (D.Ariz. 1970); Alaway v. United States, 280 F.Supp. 326, 336 (C.D.Calif. 1968); Crow v. United States, 397 F.2d 284, 285 (10th Cir. 1968).

Prior to the 1966 amendment of rule 32, the court's duty was even more limited. At that time [rule 37(a)(2)] the court's duty to advise was limited to those situations in which sentence was imposed after trial upon a not guilty plea of a defendant not represented by counsel. 8A J. Moore, Federal Practice P 32.01 [3] (2d ed. Cipes 1969); C. Wright, Federal Practice and Procedure: Criminal § 528 (1969); 5 L. Orfield, Criminal Procedure Under the Federal Rules § 32:11 (1967).

With respect to appeals in forma pauperis, see appellate rule 24.

Subdivision (c)(1) makes clear that a presentence report is required except when the court otherwise directs for reasons stated of record. The requirement of reasons on the record for not having a presentence report is intended to make clear that such a report ought to be routinely required except in cases where there is a reason for not doing so. The presentence report is of great value for correctional purposes and will serve as a valuable aid in reviewing sentences to the extent that sentence review may be authorized by future rule change. For an analysis of the current rule as it relates to the situation in which a presentence investigation is required, see C. Wright, Federal Practice and Procedure: Criminal § 522 (1969); 8A J. Moore, Federal Practice P 32.03 [1] (2d ed. Cipes 1969).

Subdivision (c)(1) is also changed to permit the judge, after obtaining defendant's consent, to see the presentence report in order to decide whether to accept a plea agreement, and also to expedite the imposition of sentence in a case in which the defendant has indicated that he may plead guilty or nolo contendere.

Former subdivision (c)(1) provides that "The report shall not be submitted to the court . . . unless the defendant has pleaded guilty . . . ." This precludes a judge from seeing a presentence report prior to the acceptance of the plea of guilty. L. Orfield, Criminal Procedure Under the Federal Rules § 32:35 (1967); 8A J. Moore, Federal Practice P 32.03 [2], p. 32-22 (2d ed. Cipes 1969); C. Wright, Federal Practice and Procedure: Criminal § 523, p. 392 (1969); Gregg v. United States, 394 U.S. 489, 89 S.Ct. 1134, 22 L.Ed.2d 442 (1969).

Because many plea agreements will deal with the sentence to be imposed, it will be important, under rule 11, for the judge to have access to sentencing information as a basis for deciding whether the plea agreement is an appropriate one.

It has been suggested that the problem be dealt with by allowing the judge to indicate approval of the plea agreement subject to the condition that the information in the presentence report is consistent with what he has been told about the case by counsel. See American Bar Association, Standards Relating to Pleas of Guilty § 3.3 (Approved Draft, 1963); President's Commission on Law Enforcement and Administration of Justice. The Challenge of Crime in a Free Society 136 (1967).

Allowing the judge to see the presentence report prior to his decision as to whether to accept the plea agreement is, in the view of the Advisory Committee, preferable to a conditional acceptance of the plea. See Enker, Perspectives on Plea Bargaining, Appendix A of President's Commission on Law Enforcement and Administration of Justice, Task Force Report: The Courts at 117 (1967). It enables the judge to have all of the information available to him at the time he is called upon to decide whether or not to accept the plea of guilty and thus avoids the necessity of a subsequent appearance whenever the information is such that the judge decides to reject the plea agreement.

There is presently authority to have a presentence report prepared prior to the acceptance of the plea of guilty. In Gregg v. United States, 394 U.S. 489, 491, 89 S.Ct. 1134 22 L.Ed.2d 442 (1969), the court said that the "language [of rule 32] clearly permits the preparation of a presentence report before guilty plea or conviction . . . ." In footnote 3 the court said:

The history of the rule confirms this interpretation. The first Preliminary Draft of the rule would have required the consent of the defendant or his attorney to commence the investigation before the determination of guilt. Advisory Committee on Rules of Criminal Procedure, Fed.Rules Crim.Proc., Preliminary Draft 130, 133 (1943). The Second Preliminary Draft omitted this requirement and imposed no limitation on the time when the report could be made and submitted to the court. Advisory Committee on Rules of Criminal Procedure, Fed.Rules Crim.Proc. Second Preliminary Draft 126-128 (1944). The third and final draft, which was adopted as Rule 32, was evidently a compromise between those who opposed any time limitation, and those who preferred that the entire investigation be conducted after determination of guilt. See 5 L. Orfield, Criminal Procedure Under the Federal Rules § 32.2 (1967).

Where the judge rejects the plea agreement after seeing the presentence report, he should be free to excuse himself from later presiding over the trial of the case. This is left to the discretion of the judge. There are instances involving prior convictions where a judge may have seen a presentence report, yet can properly try a case on a plea of not guilty. Webster v. United States, 330 F.Supp. 1080 (D.C., 1971). Unlike the situation in Gregg v. United States, subdivision (e)(3) provides for disclosure of the presentence report to the defendant, and this will enable counsel to know whether the information thus made available to the judge is likely to be prejudicial. Presently trial judges who decide pretrial motions to suppress illegally obtained evidence are not, for that reason alone, precluded from presiding at a later trial.

Subdivision (c)(3)(A) requires disclosure of presentence information to the defense, exclusive of any recommendation of sentence. The court is required to disclose the report to defendant or his counsel unless the court is of the opinion that disclosure would seriously interfere with rehabilitation, compromise confidentiality, or create risk of harm to the defendant or others.

Any recommendation as to sentence should not be disclosed as it may impair the effectiveness of the probation officer if the defendant is under supervision on probation or parole.

The issue of disclosure of presentence information to the defense has been the subject of recommendations from the Advisory Committee in 1944, 1962, 1964, and 1966. The history is dealt with in considerable detail in C. Wright, Federal Practice and Procedure: Criminal § 524 (1969), and 8A J. Moore, Federal Practice P 32.03 [4] (2d ed. Cipes 1969).

In recent years, three prestigious organizations have recommended that the report be disclosed to the defense. See American Bar Association, Standards Relating to Sentencing Alternatives and Procedures § 4.4 (Approved Draft, 1968); American Law Institute Model Penal Code § 7.07(5) (P.O.D. 1962); National Council on Crime and Delinquency, Model Sentencing Act § 4 (1963). This is also the recommendation of the President's Commission on Law Enforcement and Administration of Justice. The Challenge of Crime in a Free Society (1967) at p. 145.

In the absence of compelling reasons for nondisclosure of special information, the defendant and his counsel should be permitted to examine the entire presentence report.

The arguments for and against disclosure are well known and are effectively set forth in American Bar Association Standards Relating to Sentencing Alternatives and Procedures, § 4.4 Commentary at pp. 214–225 (Approved Draft, 1968). See also Lehrich, The Use and Disclosure of Presentence Reports in the United States, 47 F.R.D. 225 (1969).

A careful account of existing practices in Detroit, Michigan and Milwaukee, Wisconsin is found in R. Dawson, Sentencing (1969).

Most members of the federal judiciary have, in the past, opposed compulsory disclosure. See the view of District Judge Edwin M. Stanley, American Bar Association Standards Relating to Sentencing Alternatives and Procedures. Appendix A. (Appendix A also contains the results of a survey of all federal judges showing that the clear majority opposed disclosure.).

The Advisory Committee is of the view that accuracy of sentencing information is important not only to the defendant but also to effective correctional treatment of a convicted offender. The best way of insuring accuracy is disclosure with an opportunity for the defendant and counsel to point out to the court information thought by the defense to be inaccurate, incomplete, or otherwise misleading. Experience in jurisdictions which require disclosure does not lend support to the argument that disclosure will result in less complete presentence reports or the argument that sentencing procedures will become unnecessarily protracted. It is not intended that the probation officer would be subjected to any rigorous examination by defense counsel, or that he will even be sworn to testify. The proceedings may be very informal in nature unless the court orders a full hearing.

Subdivision (c)(3)(B) provides for situations in which the sentencing judge believes that disclosure should not be made under the criteria set forth in subdivision (c)(3)(A). He may disclose only a summary of that factual information "to be relied on in determining sentence." This is similar to the proposal of the American Bar Association Standards Relating to Sentencing Alternatives and Procedures § 4.4(b) and Commentary at pp. 216–224.

Subdivision (c)(3)(D) provides for the return of disclosed presentence reports to insure that they do not become available to unauthorized persons. See National Council on Crime and Delinquency, Model Sentencing Act § 4 (1963): "Such reports shall be part of the record but shall be sealed and opened only on order of the court."

Subdivision (c)(3)(E) makes clear that diagnostic studies under 18 U.S.C. §§ 4208(b), 5010(c), or 5034 are covered by this rule and also that 18 U.S.C. § 4252 is included within the disclosure provisions of subdivision (c). Section 4252 provides for the presentence examination of an "eligible offender" who is believed to be an addict to determine whether "he is an addict and is likely to be rehabilitated through treatment."

Both the Organized Crime Control Act of 1970 [§ 3775(b)] and the Comprehensive Drug Abuse Prevention and Control Act of 1970 [§ 409(b)] have special provisions for presentence investigation in the implementation of the dangerous special offender provision. It is however, unnecessary to incorporate them by reference in rule 32 because each contains a specific provision requiring disclosure of the presentence report. The judge does have authority to withhold some information "in extraordinary cases" provided notice is given the parties and the court's reasons for withholding information are made part of the record.

Subdivision (e) is amended to clarify the meaning.

Notes of Committee on the Judiciary, House Report No. 94-247. A. Amendments Proposed by the Supreme Court Rule 32 of the Federal Rules of Criminal Procedure deals with sentencing matters.

Proposed subdivision (a)(2) provides that the court is not duty bound to advise the defendant of a right to appeal when the sentence is imposed following a plea of guilty or nolo contendere.

Proposed subdivision (e) provides that the probation service must make a presentence investigation and report unless the court orders otherwise "for reasons stated on the record." The presentence report will not be submitted to the court until after the defendant pleads nolo contendere or guilty, or is found guilty, unless the defendant consents in writing. Upon the defendant's request, the court must permit the defendant to read the presentence report, except for the recommendation as to sentence. However, the court may decline to let the defendant read the report if it contains (a) diagnostic opinion that might seriously disrupt a rehabilitation program, (b) sources of information obtained upon a promise of confidentiality, or (c) any other information that, if disclosed, might result in harm to the defendant or other persons. The court must give the defendant an opportunity to comment upon the presentence report. If the court decides that the defendant should not see the report, then it must provide the defendant, orally or in writing, a summary of the factual information in the report upon which it is relying in determining sentence. No party may keep the report or make copies of it.

B. Committee Action. The Committee added language to subdivision (a)(1) to provide that the attorney for the government may speak to the court at the time of sentencing. The language does not require that the attorney for the government speak but permits him to do so if he wishes.

The Committee recast the language of subdivision (c)(1), which defines when presentence reports must be obtained. The Committee's provision makes it more difficult to dispense with a presentence report. It requires that a presentence report be made unless (a) the defendant waives it, or (b) the court finds that the record contains sufficient information to enable the meaningful exercise of sentencing discretion and explains this finding on the record. The Committee believes that presentence reports are important aids to sentencing and should not be dispensed with easily.

The Committee added language to subdivision (c)(3)(A) that permits a defendant to offer testimony or information to rebut alleged factual inaccuracies in the presentence report. Since the presentence report is to be used by the court in imposing sentence and since the consequence of any significant inaccuracy can be very serious to the defendant, the Committee believes that it is essential that the presentence report be completely accurate in every material respect. The Committee's addition to subdivision (c)(3)(A) will help insure the accuracy of the presentence report.

The Committee added language to subdivision (c)(3)(D) that gives the court the discretion to permit either the prosecutor or the defense counsel to retain a copy of the presentence report. There may be situations when it would be appropriate for either or both of the parties to retain the presentence report. The Committee believes that the rule should give the court the discretion in such situations to permit the parties to retain their copies.

Change of name. Section 12 of Act March 15, 1976, P. L. 94-233, 90 Stat. 233, provided that references to the United States Parole Board be deemed to refer to the United States Parole Commission.

Notes of Advisory Committee on 1979 amendments.

The amendment to rule 32(c)(3)(E) is necessary in light of recent changes in the applicable statutes.

Amendments effective in 1979 [effective Dec. 1, 1980, as provided by Act July 31, 1979, P. L. 96-42, § 1(1), 93 Stat. 326]. This subdivision [subsec. (f)] is abrogated. The subject matter is now dealt with in greater detail in proposed new rule 32.1.

Application of Oct. 12, 1982 amendments. Act Oct. 12, 1982, P. L. 97-291, § 9(a), (b)(1), 96 Stat. 1258, provided that subsec. (c)(2) of this rule as amended by § 3 of such Act, shall apply to presentence reports ordered to be made on or after March 1, 1983.

Effective date of Nov. 10, 1986 amendments. Act Nov. 10, 1986, P. L. 99-646, § 25(b), 100 Stat. 3597, provides: "The amendment made by subsection (a) [amending subsec. (c)(2)(B) of this Rule] shall take effect on the taking effect of the amendment made by section 215(a)(5) of the Comprehensive Crime Control Act of 1984 [amending subsec. (c)(2) of this Rule].".

Notes of Advisory Committee on 1987 amendments.

The amendments are technical. No substantive change is intended.

Notes of Advisory Committee on 1989 amendments.

The amendment to subdivision (a)(1) is intended to clarify that the court is expected to proceed without unnecessary delay, and that it may be necessary to delay sentencing when an applicable sentencing factor cannot be resolved at the time set for sentencing. Often, the factor will relate to a defendant's agreement to cooperate with the government. But, other factors may be capable of resolution if the court delays sentencing while additional information is generated. As currently written, the rule might imply that a delay requested by one party or suggested by the Court sua sponte might be unreasonable. The amendment rids the rule of any such implication and provides the sentencing court with desirable discretion to assure that relevant factors are considered and accurately resolved. In exercising this discretion, the court retains under the amendment the authority to refuse to delay sentencing when a delay is inappropriate under the circumstances.

In amending subdivision (c)(1), the Committee conformed the rule to the current practice in some courts: i.e., to permit the defendant and the prosecutor to see a presentence report prior to a plea of guilty if the court, with the written consent of the defendant, receives the report at that time. The amendment permits, but does not require, disclosure of the report with the written consent of the defendant.

The amendment to change the "reasonable time" language in subdivision (c)(3)(A) to at least 10 days prior to sentencing, unless the defendant waives the minimum period, conforms the rule to 18 U.S.C. 3552(d). Nothing in the statute or the rule prohibits a court from requiring disclosure at an earlier time before sentencing. The inclusion of a specific waiver provision is intended to conform the rule to the statute and is not intended to suggest that waiver of other rights is precluded when no specific waiver provision is set forth in a rule or portion thereof.

The language requiring the court to provide the defendant and defense counsel with a copy of the presentence report complements the abrogation of subdivision (E), which had required the defense to return the probation report. Because a defendant or the government may seek to appeal a sentence, an option that is permitted under some circumstances, there will be cases in which the defendant has a need for the presentence report during the preparation of, or the response to, an appeal. This is one reason why the Committee decided that the defendant should not be required to return the nonconfidential portions of the presentence report that have been disclosed. Another reason is that district courts may find it desirable to adopt portions of the presentence report when making findings of fact under the guidelines. They would be inhibited unnecessarily from relying on careful, accurate presentence reports if such reports could not be retained by defendants. A third reason why defendant should be able to retain the reports disclosed to them is that the Supreme Court's decision in United States Department of Justice v. Julian, 48 — U.S. — (1988), 108 S.Ct. 1606 (1988), suggests that defendants will routinely be able to secure their reports through Freedom of Information Act suits. No public interest is served by continuing to require the return of reports, and unnecessary FOIA litigation should be avoided as a result of the amendment to Rule 32.

Because the parties need not return the presentence report to the probation officer, the Solicitor General should be able to review the report in deciding whether to permit the United States to appeal a sentence under the Sentencing Reform Act of 1984, 18. U.S.C. § 3551 et seq.

The amended rule does not direct whether the defendant or the defendant's lawyer should retain the presentence report. In exceptional cases where retention of a report in a local detention facility might pose a danger to persons housed there, the district judge may direct that the defendant not personally retain a copy of the report until the defendant has been transferred to the facility where the sentence will be served.

Although the Committee was concerned about the potential unfairness of having confidential or diagnostic material included in presentence reports but not disclosed to a defendant who might be adversely affected by such material, it decided not to recommend at this time a change in the rule which would require complete disclosure. Some diagnostic material might be particularly useful when a court imposes probation, and might well be harmful to the defendant if disclosed. Moreover, some of this material might assist correctional officials in prescribing treatment programs for an incarcerated defendant. Information provided by confidential sources and information posing a possible threat of harm to third parties was particularly troubling to the Committee, since this information is often extremely negative and thus potentially harmful to a defendant. The Committee concluded, however, that it was preferable to permit the probation officer to include this information in a report so that the sentencing court may determine whether is ought to be disclosed to the defendant. If the court determines that it should not be disclosed, it will have to decide whether to summarize the contents of the information or to hold that no finding as to the undisclosed information will be made because such information will not be taken into account in sentencing. Substantial due process problems may arise if a court attempts to summarize information in a presentence report, the defendant challenges the information, and the court attempts to make a finding as to the accuracy of the information without disclosing to the defendant the source of the information or the details placed before the court. In deciding not to require disclosure of everything in a presentence report, the Committee made no judgment that findings could validly be made based upon nondisclosed information.

Finally, portions of the rule were gender-neutralized.

Notes of Advisory Committee on 1991 amendments.

The amendments are technical. No substantive changes are intended.

Notes of Advisory Committee on 1993 amendments.

The original subdivision (e) has been deleted due to statutory changes affecting the authority of a court to grant probation. See 18 U.S.C. 3561(a). Its replacement is one of a number of contemporaneous amendments extending Rule 26.2 to hearings and proceedings other than the trial itself. The amendment to Rule 32 specifically codifies the result in cases such as United States v. Rosa, 891 F.2d 1074 (3d. Cir. 1989). In that case the defendant pleaded guilty to a drug offense. During sentencing the defendant unsuccessfully attempted to obtain Jencks Act materials relating to a co-accused who testified as a government witness at sentencing. In concluding that the trial court erred in not ordering the government to produce its witness's statement, the court stated: We believe the sentence

> imposed on a defendant is the most critical stage of criminal proceedings, and is, in effect, the "bottom-line" for the defendant, particularly where the defendant has pled guilty. This being so, we can perceive no purpose in denying the defendant the ability to effectively cross-examine a government witness where such testimony may, if accepted, add substantially to the defendant's sentence. In such a setting, we believe that the rationale of Jencks v. United States . . . and the purpose of the Jencks Act would be disserved if the government at such a grave stage of a criminal proceeding could deprive the accused of material valuable not only to the defense but to his very liberty. Id. at 1079.

The court added that the defendant had not been sentenced under the new Sentencing Guidelines and that its decision could take on greater importance under those rules. Under Guideline sentencing, said the court, the trial judge has less discretion to moderate a sentence and is required to impose a sentence based upon specific factual findings which need not be established beyond a reasonable doubt. Id at n. 3.

Although the Rosa decision decided only the issue of access by the defendant to Jencks material, the amendment parallels Rules 26.2 (applying Jencks Act to trial) and 12(i) (applying Jencks Act to suppression hearing) in that both the defense and the prosecution are entitled to Jencks material.

Production of a statement is triggered by the witness's oral testimony. The sanction provision rests on the assumption that the proponent of the witness's testimony has deliberately elected to withhold relevant material.

Notes of Advisory Committee on 1994 amendments.

The amendments to Rule 32 are intended to accomplish two primary objectives. First, the amendments incorporate elements of a "Model Local Rule for Guideline Sentencing" which was proposed by the Judicial Conference Committee on Probation Administration in 1987. That model rule and the accompanying report were prepared to assist trial judges in implementing guideline sentencing mandated by the Sentencing Reform Act of 1984. See Committee on the Admin. of the Probation Sys., Judicial Conference of the U.S., Recommended Procedures for Guideline Sentencing and Commentary: Model Local Rule for Guideline Sentencing, Reprinted in T. Hutchinson & D. Yellen, Federal Sentencing Law and Practice, app. 8, at 431 (1989). It was anticipated that sentencing hearings would become more complex due to the new fact finding requirements imposed by guideline sentencing methodology. See U.S.S.G. § 6A1.2. Accordingly, the model rule focused on preparation of the presentence report as a means of identifying and narrowing the issues to be decided at the sentencing hearing.

Second, in the process of effecting those amendments, the rule was reorganized. Over time, numerous amendments to the rule had created a sort of hodge podge; the reorganization represents an attempt to reflect an appropriate sequential order in the sentencing procedures.

Subdivision (a). Subdivision (a) retains the general mandate that sentence be imposed without unnecessary delay thereby permitting the court to regulate the time to be allowed for the probation officer to complete the presentence investigation and submit the report. The only requirement is that sufficient time be allowed for completion of the process prescribed by subdivision (b)(6) unless the time periods established in the subdivision are shortened or lengthened by the court for good cause. Such limits are not intended to create any new substantive right for the defendant or the Government which would entitle either to relief if a time limit prescribed in the rule is not kept.

The remainder of subdivision (a), which addressed the sentencing hearing, is now located in subdivision (c).

Subdivision (b). Subdivision (b) (formerly subdivision (c)), which addresses the presentence investigation, has been modified in several respects.

First, subdivision (b)(2) is a new provision which provides that, on request, defense counsel is entitled to notice and a reasonable opportunity to be present at any interview of the defendant conducted by the probation officer. Although the courts have not held that presentence interviews are a critical stage of the trial for purposes of the Sixth Amendment right to counsel, the amendment reflects case law which has indicated that requests for counsel to be present should be honored. See, e.g., United States v. Herrera-Figueroa, 918 F.2d 1430, 1437 (9th Cir. 1990) (court relied on its supervisory power to hold that probation officers must honor request for counsel's presence); United States v. Tisdale, 952 F.2d 934, 940 (6th Cir. 1992) (court agreed with rule requiring probation officers to honor defendant's request for attorney or request from attorney not to interview defendant in absence of counsel). The Committee believes that permitting counsel to be present during such interviews may avoid unnecessary misunderstandings between the probation officer and the defendant. The rule does not further define the term "interview." The Committee intended for the provision to apply to any communication initiated by the probation officer where he or she is asking the defendant to provide information which will be used in preparation of the presentence investigation. Spontaneous or unplanned encounters between the defendant and the probation officer would normally not fall within the purview of the rule. The Committee also believed that the burden should rest on defense counsel, having received notice, to respond as promptly as possible to enable timely completion of the presentence report.

Subdivision (b)(6), formerly (c)(3), includes several changes which recognize the key role the presentence report is playing under guideline sentencing. The major thrust of these changes is to address the problem of resolving objections by the parties to the probation officer's presentence report. Subdivision (b)(6)(A) now provides that the probation officer must present the presentence report to the parties not later than 35 days before the sentencing hearing (rather than 10 days before imposition of the sentence) in order to provide some additional time to the parties and the probation officer to attempt to resolve objections to the report. There has been a slight change in the practice of deleting from the copy of the report given to the parties certain information specified in (b)(6)(A). Under that new provision (changing former subdivision (c)(3)(A)), the court has the discretion (in an individual case or in accordance with a local rule) to direct the probation officer to withhold any final recommendation concerning the sentence. Otherwise, the recommendation, if any, is subject to disclosure. The prior practice of not disclosing confidential information, or other information which might result in harm to the defendant or other persons, is retained in (b)(5).

New subdivisions (b)(6)(B), (C), and (D) now provide explicit deadlines and guidance on resolving disputes about the contents of the presentence report. The amendments are intended to provide early resolution of such disputes by (1) requiring the parties to provide the probation officer with a written list of objections to the report within 14 days of receiving the report; (2) permitting the probation officer to meet with the defendant, the defendant's counsel, and the attorney for the Government to discuss objections to the report, conduct an additional investigation, and to make revisions to the report as deemed appropriate; (3) requiring the probation officer to submit the report to the court and the parties not later than 7 days before the sentencing hearing, noting any unresolved disputes; and (4) permitting the court to treat the report as its findings of fact, except for the parties' unresolved objections. Although the rule does not explicitly address the question of whether counsel's objections to the report are to be filed with the court, there is nothing in the rule which would prohibit a court from requiring the parties to file their original objections or have them included as an addendum to the presentence report.

This procedure, which generally mirrors the approach in the Model Local Rule for Guideline Sentencing, supra, is intended to maximize judicial economy by providing for more orderly sentencing hearings while also providing fair opportunity for both parties to review, object to, and comment upon, the probation officer's report in advance of the sentencing hearing. Under the amendment, the parties would still be free at the sentencing hearing to comment on the presentence report, and in the discretion of the court, to introduce evidence concerning their objections to the report.

Subdivision (c). Subdivision (c) addresses the imposition of sentence and makes no major changes in current practice. The provision consists largely of material formerly located in subdivision (a). Language formerly in (a)(1) referring to the court's disclosure to the parties of the probation officer's determination of the sentencing classifications and sentencing guideline range is now located in subdivisions (b)(4)(B) and (c)(1). Likewise, the brief reference in former (a)(1) to the ability of the parties to comment on the probation officer's determination of sentencing classifications and sentencing guideline range is now located in (c)(1) and (c)(3).

Subdivision (c)(1) is not intended to require that resolution of objections and imposition of the sentence occur at the same time or during the same hearing. It requires only that the court rule on any objections before sentence is imposed. In considering objections during the sentencing hearing, the court may in its discretion, permit the parties to introduce evidence. The rule speaks in terms of the court's discretion, but the Sentencing Guidelines specifically provide that the court must provide the parties with a reasonable opportunity to offer information concerning a sentencing factor reasonably in dispute. See U.S.S.G. § 6A1.3(a). Thus, it may be an abuse of discretion not to permit the introduction of additional evidence. Although the rules of evidence do not apply to sentencing proceedings, see Fed. R. Evid. 1101(d)(3), the court clearly has discretion in determining the mode, timing, and extent of the evidence offered. See, e.g., United States v. Zuleta-Mvarez, 922 F.2d 33, 36 (1st Cir. 1990) (trial court did not err in denying defendant's late request to introduce rebuttal evidence by way of cross-examination).

Subdivision (c)(1) (formerly subdivision (c)(3)(D)) indicates that the court need not resolve controverted matters which will "not be taken into account in, or will not affect, sentencing." The words "will not affect" did not exist in the former provision but were added in the revision in recognition that there might be situations, due to overlaps in the sentencing ranges, where a controverted matter would not alter the sentence even if the sentencing range were changed.

The provision for disclosure of a witness' statements, which was recently proposed as an amendment to Rule 32 as new subdivision (e), is now located in subdivision (c)(2).

Subdivision (c)(3) includes minor changes. First, if the court intends to rely on information otherwise excluded from the presentence report under subdivision (b)(5), that information is to be summarized in writing and submitted to the defendant and the defendant's counsel. Under the former provision in (c)(3)(A), such information could be summarized orally. Once the information is presented, the defendant and the defendant's counsel are to be given a reasonable opportunity to comment; in appropriate cases, that may require a continuance of the sentencing proceedings.

Subdivision (c)(5), concerning notification of the right to appeal, was formerly included in subdivision (a)(2). Although the provision has been rewritten, the Committee intends no substantive change in practice. That is, the court may, but is not required to, advise a defendant who has entered a guilty plea, nolo contendere plea or a conditional guilty plea of any right to appeal (such as an appeal challenging jurisdiction). However, the duty to advise the defendant in such cases extends only to advice on the right to appeal any sentence imposed.

Subdivision (d). Subdivision (d), dealing with entry of the court's judgment, is former subdivision (b).

Subdivision (e). Subdivision (e), which addresses the topic of withdrawing pleas, was formerly subdivision (d). Both provisions remain the same except for minor stylistic changes.

Under present practice, the court may permit, but is not required to hear, victim allocution before imposing sentence. The Committee considered, but rejected, a provision which would have required the court to hear victim allocution at sentencing.

Notes of Advisory Committee on 1996 amendments.

Subdivision (d)(2). A provision for including a verdict of criminal forfeiture as a part of the sentence was added in 1972 to Rule 32. Since then, the rule has been interpreted to mean that any forfeiture order is a part of the judgment of conviction and cannot be entered before sentencing. See, e.g., *United States v. Alexander,* 772 F. Supp. 440 (D. Minn. 1990).

Delaying forfeiture proceedings, however, can pose real problems, especially in light of the implementation of the Sentencing Reform Act in 1987 and the resulting delays between verdict and sentencing in complex cases. First, the government's statutory right to discover the location of property subject to forfeiture is triggered by entry of an order of forfeiture. See 18 U.S.C. § 1963(k) and 21 U.S.C. § 853(m). If that order is delayed until sentencing, valuable time may be lost in locating assets which may have become unavailable or unusable. Second, third persons with an interest in the property subject to forfeiture must also wait to petition the court to begin ancillary proceedings until the forfeiture order has been entered. See 18 U.S.C. § 1963(1) and 21 U.S.C. § 853(m). And third, because the government cannot actually seize the property until an order of forfeiture is entered, it may be necessary for the court to enter restraining orders to maintain the status quo.

The amendment to Rule 32 is intended to address these concerns by specifically recognizing the authority of the court to enter a preliminary forfeiture order before sentencing. Entry of an order of forfeiture before sentencing rests within the discretion of the court, which may take into account anticipated delays in sentencing, the nature of the property, and the interests of the defendant, the government, and third persons.

The amendment permits the court to enter its order of forfeiture at any time before sentencing. Before entering the order of forfeiture, however, the court must provide notice to the defendant and a reasonable opportunity to be heard on the question of timing and form of any order of forfeiture.

The rule specifies that the order, which must ultimately be made a part of the sentence and included in the judgment, must contain authorization for the Attorney General to seize the property in question and to conduct appropriate discovery and to begin any necessary ancillary proceedings to protect third parties who have an interest in the property.

Notes of Advisory Committee on 2000 amendments.

The rule is amended to reflect the creation of new Rule 32.2, which now governs criminal forfeiture procedures.

Notes of Advisory Committee on 2002 amendments.

The language of Rule 32 has been amended as part of the general restyling of the Criminal Rules to make them more easily understood and to make style and terminology consistent throughout the rules. These changes are intended to be stylistic only, except as noted below.

The rule has been completely reorganized to make it easier to follow and apply. For example, the definitions in the rule have been moved to the first section and the sequencing of the sections generally follows the procedure for presentencing and sentencing procedures.

Revised Rule 32(a) contains definitions that currently appear in Rule 32(f). One substantive change was made in Rule 32(a)(2). The Committee expanded the definition of victims of crimes of violence or sexual abuse to include victims of child pornography under 18 U.S.C. §§ 2251–2257 (child pornography and related offenses). The Committee considered those victims to be similar to victims of sexual offenses under 18 U.S.C. §§ 2241– 2248, who already possess that right.

Revised Rule 32(d) has been amended to more clearly set out the contents of the presentence report concerning the application of the Sentencing Guidelines.

Current Rule 32(e), which addresses the ability of a defendant to withdraw a guilty plea, has been moved to Rule 11(e).

Rule 32(h) is a new provision that reflects *Burns v. United States,* 501 U.S. 129, 138-39 [115 L. Ed. 2d 123] (1991). In Burns, the Court held that, before a sentencing court could depart upward on a ground not previously identified in the presentence report as a ground for departure, Rule 32 requires the court to give the parties reasonable notice that it is contemplating such a ruling and to identify the specific ground for the departure. The Court also indicated that because the procedural entitlements in Rule 32 apply equally to both parties, it was equally appropriate to frame the issue as whether notice is required before the sentencing court departs either upward or downward. *Id.* at 135, n.4.

Revised Rule 32(i)(3) addresses changes to current Rule 32(c)(1). Under the current rule, the court is required to "rule on any unresolved objections to the presentence report." The rule does not specify, however, whether that provision should be read literally to mean every objection that might have been made to the report or only on those objections that might in some way actually affect the sentence. The Committee believed that a broad reading of the current rule might place an unreasonable burden on the court without providing any real benefit to the sentencing process. Revised Rule 32(i)(3) narrows the requirement for court findings to those instances when the objection addresses a "controverted matter." If the objection satisfies that criterion, the court must either make a finding on the objection or decide that a finding is not required because the matter will not affect sentencing or that the matter will not be considered at all in sentencing.

Revised Rule 32(i)(4)(B) provides for the right of certain victims to address the court during sentencing. As noted, *supra,* revised Rule 32(a)(2) expands the definition of victims to include victims of crimes under 18 U.S.C. §§ 2251– 57 (child pornography and related offenses). Thus, they too will now be permitted to address the court.

Revised Rule 32(i)(1)(B) is intended to clarify language that currently exists in Rule 32(h)(3), that the court must inform both parties that the court will rely on information not in the presentence report and provide them with an opportunity to comment on the information.

Rule 32(i)(4)(C) includes a change concerning who may request an in camera proceeding. Under current Rule 32(c)(4), the parties must file a joint motion for an in camera proceeding to hear the statements by defense counsel, the defendant, the attorney for the government, or any victim. Under the revised rule, any party may move (for good cause) that the court hear in camera any statement—by a party or a victim—made under revised Rule 32(i)(4).

Finally, the Committee considered, but did not adopt, an amendment that would have required the court to rule on any "unresolved objection to a material matter" in the presentence report, whether or not the court will consider it in imposing an appropriate sentence. The amendment was considered because an unresolved objection that has no impact on determining a sentence under the Sentencing Guidelines may affect other important post-sentencing decisions. For example, the Bureau of Prisons consults the presentence report in deciding where a defendant will actually serve his or her sentence of confinement. See *A Judicial Guide to the Federal Bureau of Prisons,* 11 (United States Department of Justice, Federal Bureau of Prisons 1995) (noting that the "Bureau relies primarily on the Presentence Investigator Report. . ."). And as some courts have recognized, Rule 32 was intended to guard against adverse consequences of a statement in the presentence report that the court may have been found to be false. *United States v. Velasquez,* 748 F.2d 972, 974 (8th Cir. 1984) (rule designed to protect against evil that false allegation that defendant was notorious alien smuggler would affect defendant for years to come); see also *United States v. Brown,* 715 F.2d 387, 389 n.2 (5th Cir. 1983) (sentencing report affects "place of incarceration, chances for parole, and relationships with social service and correctional agencies after release from prison").

To avoid unduly burdening the court, the Committee elected not to require resolution of objections that go only to service of sentence. However, because of the presentence report's critical role in post-sentence administration, counsel may wish to point out to the court those matters that are typically considered by the Bureau of Prisons in designating the place of confinement. For example, the Bureau considers: the type of offense, the length of sentence, the

> defendant's age, the defendant's release residence, the need for medical or other special treatment, and any placement recommendation made by the court.

A Judicial Guide to the Federal Bureau of Prisons, supra, at 11 . Further, a question as to whether or not the defendant has a "drug problem" could have an impact on whether the defendant would be eligible for prison drug abuse treatment programs. 18 U.S.C. § 3621(e) (Substance abuse treatment).

If counsel objects to material in the presentence report that could affect the defendant's service of sentence, the court may resolve the objection, but is not required to do so.

Notes of Advisory Committee on 2007 amendments.

Note to Subdivision (d). The amendment conforms Rule 32(d) to the Supreme Court's decision in *United States v. Booker,* 543 U.S. 220 (2005). *Booker* held that the provision of the federal sentencing statute that makes the Guidelines mandatory, 18 U.S.C. § 3553(b)(1), violates the Sixth Amendment right to jury trial. With this provision severed and excised, the Court held, the Sentencing Reform Act "makes the Guidelines effectively advisory," and "requires a sentencing court to consider Guidelines ranges, see 18 U.S.C.A. § 3553(a)(4) (Supp.2004), but it permits the court to tailor the sentence in light of other statutory concerns as well, see § 3553(a) (Supp.2004)." *Id.* at 245–46. Amended subsection (d)(2)(F) makes clear that the court can instruct the probation office to gather and include in the presentence report any information relevant to the factors articulated in § 3553(a). The rule contemplates that a request can be made either by the court as a whole requiring information affecting all cases or a class of cases, or by an individual judge in a particular case.

Notes of Advisory Committee on 2008 amendments.

Note to Subdivision (a). The Crime Victims' Rights Act, codified at 18 U.S.C. § 3771(e), adopted a new definition of the term "crime victim." The new statutory definition has been incorporated in an amendment to Rule 1, which supersedes the provisions that have been deleted here.

Note to Subdivision (c)(1). This amendment implements the victim's statutory right under the Crime Victims' Rights Act to "full and timely restitution as provided by law." *See*18 U.S.C. § 3771(a)(6). Whenever the law permits restitution, the presentence investigation report should contain information permitting the court to determine whether restitution is appropriate.

Note to Subdivision (d)(2)(B). This amendment implements the Crime Victims' Rights Act, codified as 18 U.S.C. § 3771. The amendment makes it clear that victim impact information should be treated in the same way as other information contained in the presentence report. It deletes language requiring victim impact information to be "verified" and "stated in a nonargumentative style" because that language does not appear in the other subparagraphs of Rule 32(d)(2).

Note to Subdivision (i)(4). The deleted language, referring only to victims of crimes of violence or sexual abuse, has been superseded by the Crime Victims' Rights Act, 18 U.S.C. § 3771(e). The act defines the term "crime victim" without limiting it to certain crimes, and provides that crime victims, so defined, have a right to be reasonably heard at all public court proceedings regarding sentencing. A companion amendment to Rule 1(b) adopts the statutory definition as the definition of the term "victim" for purposes of the Federal Rules of Criminal Procedure, and explains who may raise the rights of a victim, so the language in this subdivision is no longer needed.

Subdivision (i)(4) has also been amended to incorporate the statutory language of the Crime Victims' Rights Act, which provides that victims have the right "to be reasonably heard" in judicial proceedings regarding sentencing. *See*18 U.S.C. § 3771(a)(4). The amended rule provides that the judge must speak to any victim present in the courtroom at sentencing. Absent unusual circumstances, any victim who is present should be allowed a reasonable opportunity to speak directly to the judge.

Notes of Advisory Committee on 2009 amendments.

Note to Subdivision (d)(2)(G). Rule 32.2 (a) requires that the indictment or information provide notice to the defendant of the government's intent to seek forfeiture as part of the sentence. The amendment provides that the same notice be provided as part of the presentence report to the court. This will ensure timely consideration of the issues concerning forfeiture as part of the sentencing process.

Notes of Advisory Committee on 2011 amendments.

Note to Subdivision (d)(2). This technical and conforming amendment reorders two subparagraphs describing the information that may be included in the presentence report so that the provision authorizing the inclusion of any other information the court requires appears at the end of the paragraph. It also rephrases renumbered subdivision (d)(2)(F) for stylistic purposes.

Amendments:

1975.

Act July 31, 1975, (eff. 12/1/75, as provided by § 2 of that Act; see note to Rule 4), in subdiv. (a)(1), added "The attorney for the government shall have an equivalent opportunity to speak to the court."; in subdiv. (c)(1), substituted "unless, with the permission of the court, the defendant waives a presentence investigation and report, or the court finds that there is in the record information sufficient to enable the meaningful exercise of sentencing discretion, and the court explains this finding on the record" for "unless the court otherwise directs for reasons stated on the record"; in subdiv. (c)(3)(A), substituted "but not to the extent that" for "unless", and added "and, at the discretion of the court, to introduce testimony or other information relating to any alleged factual inaccuracy contained in the presentence report"; and substituted subdiv. (c)(3)(D) for one which read: "(D) Any copies of the presentence investigation report made available to the defendant or his counsel and the attorney for the government shall be returned to the probation officer immediately following the imposition of sentence or the granting of probation. Copies of the presentence investigation report shall not be made by the defendant, his counsel, or the attorney for the government.".

1982.

Act Oct. 12, 1982, in subsec. (c), substituted para. (2), for one which read: "(2) *Report.* The report of the presentence investigation shall contain any prior criminal record of the defendant and such information about his characteristics, his financial condition and the circumstances effecting his behavior as may be helpful in imposing sentence or in granting probation or in the correctional treatment of the defendant, and such other information as may be required by the court.".

1984.

Act Oct. 12, 1984 (effective on the first day of the first calendar month beginning 36 months after enactment on Oct. 12, 1984, as provided by § 235(a)(1) of such Act, as amended by Act Dec. 26, 1985, P. L. 99-217, § 4, 99 Stat. 1728, which appears as 18 USCS § 3551 note, and applicable as provided by such § 235, which appears as 18 USCS § 3551 note), in subdiv. (a), substituted para. (1) for one which read:

"(1) *Imposition of sentence.* Sentence shall be imposed without unreasonable delay. Before imposing sentence the court shall.

"(A) determine that the defendant and his counsel have had the opportunity to read and discuss the presentence investigation report made available pursuant to subdivision (c)(3)(A) or summary thereof made available pursuant to subdivision (c)(3)(B);

"(B) afford counsel an opportunity to speak on behalf of the defendant; and.

"(C) address the defendant personally and ask him if he wishes to make a statement in his own behalf and to present any information in mitigation of punishment.

The attorney for the government shall have an equivalent opportunity to speak to the court.".

Such Act further, in subdiv. (a), in para. (2), inserted ", including any right to appeal the sentence," and ", except that the court shall advise the defendant of any right to appeal his sentence"; in subdiv. (c), in para. (1), substituted the sentence beginning "A probation officer shall . . ." for "The probation service of the court shall make a presentence investigation and report to the court before the imposition of sentence or the granting of probation unless, with the permission of the court, the defendant waives a presentence investigation and report, or the court finds that there is in the record information sufficient to enable the meaningful exercise of sentencing discretion, and the court explains this finding on the record.", and substituted para. (2) for one which read:

"(2) *Report.* The presentence report shall contain—.

"(A) any prior criminal record of the defendant;

"(B) a statement of the circumstances of the commission of the offense and circumstances affecting the defendant's behavior;

"(C) information concerning any harm, including financial, social, psychological, and physical harm, done to or loss suffered by any victim of the offense; and.

"(D) any other information that may aid the court in sentencing, including the restitution needs of any victim of the offense.".

Such Act further, in subdiv. (c), in para. (3), in subpara. (A), substituted ", including the information required by subdivision (c)(2) but not including any final recommendation as to sentence," for "exclusive of any recommendations as to sentence", in subpara. (D), deleted "or the Parole Commission" following "Prisons", and, in subpara. (F), substituted "pursuant to 18 U.S.C. § 3552(b)" for "or the Parole Commission pursuant to 18 U.S.C. §§ 4205(c), 4252, 5010(e), or 5037(c)"; and, in subdiv (d), deleted "imposition of sentence is suspended, or disposition is had under 18 U.S.C. § 4205(c)" following "imposed,".

1986.

Act Nov. 10, 1986 (effective as provided by § 25(b) of such Act, which appears as a note to this section), in subsec. (c)(2)(B), substituted "from" for "than".

1994.

Act Sept. 13, 1994 (effective Dec. 1, 1994, as provided by § 230101(c) of such Act), in subsec. (c), in para. (3), in subpara. (C), deleted "and" following the concluding semicolon, in subpara. (D), substituted "opportunity equivalent to that of the defendant's counsel" for "equivalent opportunity" and substituted "; and" for a concluding period, and added subpara. (E), in para. (4), substituted "(D), and (E)" for "and (D) and inserted "the victim,"; and added subsec. (f).

1996.

Act April 24, 1996 (effective as provided by § 211 of such Act, which appears as 18 USCS § 2248 note), in subsec. (b), in para. (1), added the concluding matter and, in para. (4), redesignated subparas. (F) and (G) as subparas. (G) and (H), respectively, and added new subpara. (F).

Rule 32.1. Revoking or Modifying Probation or Supervised Release

(a) Initial Appearance.

(1) *Person In Custody.* A person held in custody for violating probation or supervised release must be taken without unnecessary delay before a magistrate judge.

(A) If the person is held in custody in the district where an alleged violation occurred, the initial appearance must be in that district.

(B) If the person is held in custody in a district other than where an alleged violation occurred, the initial appearance must be in that district, or in an adjacent district if the appearance can occur more promptly there.

(2) *Upon a Summons.* When a person appears in response to a summons for violating probation or supervised release, a magistrate judge must proceed under this rule.

(3) *Advice.* The judge must inform the person of the following:

(A) the alleged violation of probation or supervised release;

(B) the person's right to retain counsel or to request that counsel be appointed if the person cannot obtain counsel; and

(C) the person's right, if held in custody, to a preliminary hearing under Rule 32.1(b)(1).

(4) *Appearance in the District With Jurisdiction.* If the person is arrested or appears in the district that has jurisdiction to conduct a revocation hearing—either originally or by transfer of jurisdiction—the court must proceed under Rule 32.1(b)–(e).

(5) *Appearance in a District Lacking Jurisdiction.* If the person is arrested or appears in a district that does not have jurisdiction to conduct a revocation hearing, the magistrate judge must:

(A) if the alleged violation occurred in the district of arrest, conduct a preliminary hearing under Rule 32.1(b) and either:

(i) transfer the person to the district that has jurisdiction, if the judge finds probable cause to believe that a violation occurred; or

(ii) dismiss the proceedings and so notify the court that has jurisdiction, if the judge finds no probable cause to believe that a violation occurred; or

(B) if the alleged violation did not occur in the district of arrest, transfer the person to the district that has jurisdiction if:

(i) the government produces certified copies of the judgment, warrant, and warrant application, or produces copies of those certified documents by reliable electronic means; and

(ii) the judge finds that the person is the same person named in the warrant.

(6) *Release or Detention.* The magistrate judge may release or detain the person under 18 U.S.C. § 3143(a)(1) pending further proceedings. The burden of establishing by clear and convincing evidence that the person will not flee or pose a danger to any other person or to the community rests with the person.

(b) Revocation.

(1) *Preliminary Hearing.*

(A) In General. If a person is in custody for violating a condition of probation or supervised release, a magistrate judge must promptly conduct a hearing to determine whether there is probable cause to believe that a violation occurred. The person may waive the hearing.

(B) Requirements. The hearing must be recorded by a court reporter or by a suitable recording device. The judge must give the person:

(i) notice of the hearing and its purpose, the alleged violation, and the person's right to retain counsel or to request that counsel be appointed if the person cannot obtain counsel;

(ii) an opportunity to appear at the hearing and present evidence; and

(iii) upon request, an opportunity to question any adverse witness, unless the judge determines that the interest of justice does not require the witness to appear.

(C) Referral. If the judge finds probable cause, the judge must conduct a revocation hearing. If the judge does not find probable cause, the judge must dismiss the proceeding.

(2) *Revocation Hearing.* Unless waived by the person, the court must hold the revocation hearing within a reasonable time in the district having jurisdiction. The person is entitled to:

(A) written notice of the alleged violation;

(B) disclosure of the evidence against the person;

(C) an opportunity to appear, present evidence, and question any adverse witness unless the court determines that the interest of justice does not require the witness to appear;

(D) notice of the person's right to retain counsel or to request that counsel be appointed if the person cannot obtain counsel; and

(E) an opportunity to make a statement and present any information in mitigation.

(c) Modification.

(1) *In General.* Before modifying the conditions of probation or supervised release, the court must hold a hearing, at which the person has the right to counsel and an opportunity to make a statement and present any information in mitigation.

(2) *Exceptions.* A hearing is not required if:

(A) the person waives the hearing; or

(B) the relief sought is favorable to the person and does not extend the term of probation or of supervised release; and

(C) an attorney for the government has received notice of the relief sought, has had a reasonable opportunity to object, and has not done so.

(d) Disposition of the Case. The court's disposition of the case is governed by 18 U.S.C. § 3563 and § 3565 (probation) and § 3583 (supervised release).

(e) Producing a Statement. Rule 26.2(a)–(d) and (f) applies at a hearing under this rule. If a party fails to comply with a Rule 26.2 order to produce a witness's statement, the court must not consider that witness's testimony.

HISTORY:

Added April 30, 1979; effective Dec. 1, 1980, as provided by Act July 31, 1979, P. L. 96-42, § 1(1), 93 Stat. 326; Nov. 10, 1986, P. L. 99-646, § 12(b), 100 Stat. 3594; March 9, 1987, eff.

Aug. 1, 1987; April 25, 1989, eff. Dec. 1, 1989; April 30, 1991, eff. Dec. 1, 1991; April 22, 1993, eff. Dec. 1, 1993; April 29, 2002, eff. Dec. 1, 2002; April 25, 2005, eff. Dec. 1, 2005; April 12, 2006, eff. Dec. 1, 2006; April 28, 2010, eff. Dec. 1, 2010.

HISTORY; ANCILLARY LAWS AND DIRECTIVES

Other provisions:

Notes of Advisory Committee on April 30, 1979 amendments. [effective Dec. 1, 1980, as provided by Act July 31, 1979, P. L. 96-42, § 1(1), 93 Stat. 326]. Since Morrissey v Brewer, 408 U.S. 471 (1972), and Gagnon v Scarpelli, 411 U.S. 778 (1973), it is clear that a probationer can no longer be denied due process in reliance on the dictum in Escoe v Zerbst, 295 U.S. 490, 492 (1935), that probation is an "act of grace." See Van Alstyne, The Demise of the Right-Privilege Distinction in Constitutional Law, 81 Harv.L.Rev. 1439 (1968); President's Commission on Law Enforcement and Administration of Justice, Task Force Report: Corrections 86 (1967).

Subdivision (a)(1) requires, consistent with the holding in Scarpelli, that a prompt preliminary hearing must be held whenever "a probationer is held in custody on the ground that he has violated a condition of his probation." See 18 U.S.C. § 3653 regarding arrest of the probationer with or without a warrant. If there is to be a revocation hearing but there has not been a holding in custody for a probation violation, there need not be a preliminary hearing. It was the fact of such a holding in custody "which prompted the Court to determine that a preliminary as well as a final revocation hearing was required to afford the petitioner due process of law," United States v. Tucker, 524 F.2d 77 (5th Cir. 1975). Consequently, a preliminary hearing need not be held if the probationer was at large and was not arrested but was allowed to appear voluntarily, United States v Strada, 503 F.2d 1081 (8th Cir. 1974), or in response to a show cause order which "merely requires his appearance in court," United States v. Langford, 369 F.Supp. 1107 (N.D. Ill. 1973); if the probationer was in custody pursuant to a new charge, Thomas v. United States, 391 F.Supp. 202 (W.D.Pa. 1975), or pursuant to a final conviction of a subsequent offense, United States v. Tucker, supra; or if he was arrested but obtained his release.

Subdivision (a)(1)(A), (B) and (C) list the requirements for the preliminary hearing, as developed in Morrissey and made applicable to probation revocation cases in Scarpelli. Under (A), the probationer is to be given notice of the hearing and its purpose and of the alleged violation of probation. "Although the allegations in a motion to revoke probation need not be as specific as an indictment, they must be sufficient to apprise the probationer of the conditions of his probation which he is alleged to have violated, as well as the dates and events which support the charge." Kartman v. Parratt, 397 F.Supp. 531 (D. Nebr. 1975). Under (B), the probationer is permitted to appear and present evidence in his own behalf. And under (C), *upon request* by the probationer, adverse witnesses shall be made available for questioning unless the magistrate determines that the informant would be subjected to risk of harm if his identity were disclosed.

Subdivision (a)(1)(D) provides for notice to the probationer of his right to be represented by counsel at the preliminary hearing. Although Scarpelli did not impose as a constitutional requirement a right to counsel in all instances, under 18 U.S.C. § 3006A(b) a defendant is entitled to be represented by counsel whenever charged "with a violation of probation."

The federal magistrate (see definition in rule 54(c)) is to keep a record of what transpires at the hearing and, if he finds probable cause of a violation, hold the probationer for a revocation hearing. The probationer may be released pursuant to rule 46(c) pending the revocation hearing.

Subdivision (a)(2) mandates a final revocation hearing within a reasonable time to determine whether the probationer has, in fact, violated the conditions of his probation and whether his probation should be revoked. Ordinarily this time will be measured from the time of the probable cause finding (if a preliminary hearing was held) or of the issuance of an order to show cause. However, what constitutes a reasonable time must be determined on the facts of the particular case, such as whether the probationer is available or could readily be made available. If the probationer has been convicted of and is incarcerated for a new crime, and that conviction is the basis of the pending revocation proceedings, it would be relevant whether the probationer waived appearance at the revocation hearing.

The hearing required by rule 32.1(a)(2) is not a formal trial; the usual rules of evidence need not be applied. See Morrissey v. Brewer, supra ("the process should be flexible enough to consider evidence including letters, affidavits, and other material that would not be admissible in an adversary criminal trial"); Rule 1101(d)(e) of the Federal Rules of Evidence (rules not applicable to proceedings "granting or revoking probation"). Evidence that would establish guilt beyond a reasonable doubt is not required to support an order revoking probation. United States v. Francischine, 512 F.2d 827 (5th Cir.1975). This hearing may be waived by the probationer.

Subdivisions (a)(2)(A)–(E) list the rights to which a probationer is entitled at the final revocation hearing. The final hearing is less a summary one because the decision under consideration is the ultimate decision to revoke rather than a mere determination of probable cause. Thus, the probationer has certain rights not granted at the preliminary hearing: (i) the notice under (A) must be written; (ii) under (B) disclosure of all the evidence against the probationer is required; and (iii) under (D) the probationer does not have to specifically request the right to confront adverse witnesses, and the court may not limit the opportunity to question the witnesses against him.

Under subdivision (a)(2)(E) the probationer must be given notice of his right to be represented by counsel. Although Scarpelli holds that the Constitution does not compel counsel in all probation revocation hearings, under 18 U.S.C. § 3006A(b) a defendant is entitled to be represented by counsel whenever charged "with a violation of probation."

Revocation of probation is proper if the court finds a violation of the conditions of probation and that such violation warrants revocation. Revocation followed by imprisonment is an appropriate disposition if the court finds on the basis of the original offense and the intervening conduct of the probationer that:

(i) confinement is necessary to protect the public from further criminal activity by the offender; or.

(ii) the offender is in need of correctional treatment which can most effectively be provided if he is confined; or.

(iii) it would unduly depreciate the seriousness of the violation if probation were not revoked.

See American Bar Association, Standards Relating to Probation § 5.1 (Approved Draft, 1970).

If probation is revoked, the probationer may be required to serve the sentence originally imposed, or any lesser sentence, and if imposition of sentence was suspended he may receive any sentence which might have been imposed. 18 U.S.C. § 3653. When a split sentence is imposed under 18 U.S.C. § 3651 and probation is subsequently revoked, the probationer is entitled to credit for the time served in jail but not for the time he was on probation. Thomas v. United States, 327 F.2d 795 (10th Cir.), cert. denied 377 U.S. 1000 (1964); Schley v. Peyton, 280 F.Supp. 307 (W.D.Va. 1968).

Subdivision (b) concerns proceedings on modification of probation (as provided for in 18 U.S.C. § 3651). The probationer should have the right to apply to the sentencing court for a clarification or change of conditions. American Bar Association, Standards Relating to Probation § 3.1(c) (Approved Draft, 1970). This avenue is important for two reasons: (1) the probationer should be able to obtain resolution of a dispute over an ambiguous term or the meaning of a condition without first having to violate it; and (2) in cases of neglect, overwork, or simply unreasonableness on the part of the probation officer, the probationer should have recourse to the sentencing court when a condition needs clarification or modification.

Probation conditions should be subject to modification, for the sentencing court must be able to respond to changes in the probationer's circumstances as well as new ideas and methods of rehabilitation. See generally ABA Standards, supra, § 3.3. The sentencing court is given the authority to shorten the term or end probation early upon its own motion without a hearing. And while the modification of probation is a part of the sentencing procedure, so that the probationer is ordinarily entitled to a hearing and presence of counsel, a modification favorable to the probationer may be accomplished without a hearing in the presence of defendant and counsel. United States v. Bailey, 343 F.Supp. 76 (W.D.Mo. 1971).

Effective date of Nov. 10, 1986 amendments. Act Nov. 10, 1986, P. L. 99-646, § 12(c)(2), 100 Stat. 3594, provides: "The amendments made by subsection (b) [amending subsec. (b) of this rule] shall take effect 30 days after the date of enactment of this Act.".

Notes of Advisory Committee on 1987 amendments. The amendments are technical. No substantive change is intended.

Notes of Advisory Committee on 1989 amendments. The amendments recognize that convicted defendants may be on supervised release as well as on probation. See 18 U.S.C. §§ 3583, and 3624(e).

Notes of Advisory Committee on 1991 amendments. The amendment is technical. No substantive change is intended.

Notes of Advisory Committee on 1993 amendments. The addition of subdivision (c) is one of several amendments that extend Rule 26.2 to Rules 32(f), 32.1, 46, and Rule 8 of the Rules Governing Proceedings under 28 U.S.C. § 2255. As noted in the Committee Note to Rule 26.2, the primary reason for extending that Rule to other hearings and proceedings rests heavily upon the compelling need for accurate information affecting the witnesses' credibility. While that need is certainly clear in a trial on the merits, it is equally compelling, if not more so, in other pretrial and post-trial proceedings in which both the prosecution and defense have high interests at stake. In the case of revocation or modification of probation or supervised release proceedings, not only is the defendant's liberty interest at stake, the government has a stake in protecting the interests of the community.

Requiring production of witness statements at hearings conducted under Rule 32.1 will enhance the procedural due process which the rule now provides and which the Supreme Court required in Morrissey v. Brewer, 408 U.S. 471 (1972) and Gagnon v. Scarpelli, 411 U.S. 778 (1973). Access to prior statements of a witness will enhance the ability of both the defense and prosecution to test the credibility of the other side's witnesses under Rule 32.1(a)(1), (a)(2), and (b) and thus will assist the court in assessing credibility.

A witness's statement must be produced only if the witness testifies.

Notes of Advisory Committee on 2002 amendments. The language of Rule 32.1 has been amended as part of the general restyling of the Criminal Rules to make them more easily understood and to make style and terminology consistent throughout the rules. These changes are intended to be stylistic only, except as noted below.

Rule 32.1 has been completely revised and expanded. The Committee believed that it was important to spell out more completely in this rule the various procedural steps that must be met when dealing with a revocation or modification of probation or supervised release. To that end, some language formerly located in Rule 40 has been moved to revised Rule 32.1. Throughout the rule, the terms "magistrate judge," and "court" (see revised Rule 1(b)(Definitions)) are used to reflect that in revocation cases, initial proceedings in both felony and misdemeanor cases will normally be conducted before a magistrate judge, although a district judge may also conduct them. But a district judge must make the revocation decision if the offense of conviction was a felony. *See* 18 U.S.C. § 3401(i) (recognizing that district judge may designate a magistrate judge to conduct a hearing and submit proposed findings of fact and recommendations).

Revised Rule 32.1(a)(1)–(4) is new material. Presently, there is no provision in the rules for conducting initial appearances for defendants charged with violating probation or supervised release—although some districts apply such procedures. Although the rule labels these proceedings as initial appearances, the Committee believed that it was best to separate those proceedings from Rule 5 proceedings, because the procedures differ for persons who are charged with violating conditions of probation or supervised release.

The Committee is also aware that, in some districts, it is not the practice to have an initial appearance for a revocation of probation or supervised release proceeding. Although Rule 32.1(a) will require such an appearance, nothing in the rule prohibits a court from combining the initial appearance proceeding, if convened consistent with the "without unnecessary delay" time requirement of the rule, with the preliminary hearing under Rule 32.1(b).

Revised Rule 32.1(a)(5) is derived from current Rule 40(d).

Revised Rule 32.1(a)(6), which is derived from current Rule 46(c), provides that the defendant bears the burden of showing that he or she will not flee or pose a danger pending a hearing on the revocation of probation or supervised release. The Committee believes that the new language is not a substantive change because it makes no change in practice.

Rule 32.1(b)(1)(B)(iii) and Rule 32.1(b)(2)(C) address the ability of a releasee to question adverse witnesses at the preliminary and revocation hearings. Those provisions recognize that the court should apply a balancing test at the hearing itself when considering the releasee's asserted right to cross-examine adverse witnesses. The court is to balance the person's interest in the constitutionally guaranteed right to confrontation against the government's good cause for denying it. *See, e.g., Morrissey v. Brewer,* 408 U.S. 471, 489 [33 L. Ed. 2d 484] (1972); *United States v. Comito,* 177 F.3d 1166 (9th Cir. 1999); *United States v. Walker,* 117 F.3d 417 (9th Cir. 1997); *United States v. Zentgraf,* 20 F.3d 906 (8th Cir. 1994).

Rule 32.1(c)(2)(A) permits the person to waive a hearing to modify the conditions of probation or supervised release. Although that language is new to the rule, the Committee believes that it reflects current practice.

The remainder of revised Rule 32.1 is derived from the current Rule 32.1.

Notes of Advisory Committee on 2005 amendments. The amendments to Rule 32.1(b) and (c) are intended to address a gap in the rule. As noted by the court in *United States v. Frazier*, 283 F.3d 1242 (11th Cir. 2002) (per curiam), there is no explicit provision in current Rule 32.1 for allocution rights for a person upon revocation of supervised release. In that case the court noted that several circuits had concluded that the right to allocution in Rule 32 extended to supervised release revocation hearings. *See United States v. Patterson*, 128 F.3d 1259, 1261 (8th Cir. 1997) (Rule 32 right to allocution applies); *United States v. Rodriguez*, 23 F.3d 919, 921 (5th Cir. 1997) (right of allocution, in Rule 32, applies at revocation proceeding). But the court agreed with the Sixth Circuit that the allocution right in Rule 32 was not incorporated into Rule 32.1. *See United States v. Waters*, 158 F.3d 933 (6th Cir. 1998) (allocution right in Rule 32 does not apply to revocation proceedings). The *Frazier* court observed that the problem with the incorporation approach is that it would require application of other provisions specifically applicable to sentencing proceedings under Rule 32, but not expressly addressed in Rule 32.1. 283 F.3d at 1245. The court, however, believed that it would be "better practice" for courts to provide for allocution at revocation proceedings and stated that "[t]he right of allocution seems both important and firmly embedded in our jurisprudence." *Id.*

The amended rule recognizes the importance of allocution and now explicitly recognizes that right at Rule 32.1(b)(2) revocation hearings, and extends it as well to Rule 32.1(c)(1) modification hearings where the court may decide to modify the terms or conditions of the defendant's probation. In each instance the court is required to give the defendant the opportunity to make a statement and present any mitigating information.

Notes of Advisory Committee on 2006 amendments. *Note to Subdivision (a)(5)(B)(i).* Rule 32.1(a)(5)(B)(i) has been amended to permit the magistrate judge to accept a judgment, warrant, and warrant application by reliable electronic means. Currently, the rule requires the government to produce certified copies of those documents. This amendment parallels similar changes to Rules 5 and 41.

The amendment reflects a number of significant improvements in technology. First, receiving documents by facsimile has become very commonplace and many courts are now equipped to receive filings by electronic means, and indeed, some courts encourage or require that certain documents be filed by electronic means. Second, the technology has advanced to the state where such filings could be sent from, and received at, locations outside the courthouse. Third, electronic media can now provide improved quality of transmission and security measures. In short, in a particular case, using electronic media to transmit a document might be just as reliable and efficient as using a facsimile.

The term "electronic" is used to provide some flexibility to the rule and make allowance for further technological advances in transmitting data. The Committee envisions that the term "electronic" would include use of facsimile transmissions.

The rule requires that if electronic means are to be used to transmit a warrant to the magistrate judge, the means used be "reliable." While the rule does not further define that term, the Committee envisions that a court or magistrate judge would make that determination as a local matter. In deciding whether a particular electronic means, or media, would be reliable, the court might consider first, the expected quality and clarity of the transmission. For example, is it possible to read the contents of the warrant in its entirety, as though it were the original or a clean photocopy? Second, the court may wish to consider whether security measures are available to insure that the transmission is not compromised. In this regard, most courts are now equipped to require that certain documents contain a digital signature, or some other similar system for restricting access. Third, the court may consider whether there are reliable means of preserving the document for later use.

Notes of Advisory Committee on 2010 amendments. *Note to Subdivision (a)(6).* This amendment is designed to end confusion regarding the applicability of 18 U.S.C. § 3143(a) to release or detention decisions involving persons on probation or supervised release, and to clarify the burden of proof in such proceedings. Confusion regarding the applicability of § 3143(a) arose because several subsections of the statute are ill suited to proceedings involving the revocation of probation or supervised release. *See United States v. Mincey,* 482 F. Supp. 2d 161 (D. Mass. 2007). The amendment makes clear that only subsection 3143(a)(1) is applicable in this context.

The current rule provides that the person seeking release must bear the burden of establishing that he or she will not flee or pose a danger but does not specify the standard of proof that must be met. The amendment incorporates into the rule the standard of clear and convincing evidence.

Amendments:

1986.

Act Nov. 10, 1986 (effective 30 days after enactment as provided by § 12(c)(2) of such Act, which appears as a note to this rule), in subsec. (b), inserted "to be", and inserted ", and the attorney for the government, after having been given notice of the proposed relief and a reasonable opportunity to object, has not objected. An extension of the term of probation is not favorable to the probationer for the purposes of this rule".

Rule 32.2. Criminal Forfeiture

(a) Notice to the Defendant. A court must not enter a judgment of forfeiture in a criminal proceeding unless the indictment or information contains notice to the defendant that the government will seek the forfeiture of property as part of any sentence in accordance with the applicable statute. The notice should not be designated as a count of the indictment or information. The indictment or information need not identify the property subject to forfeiture or specify the amount of any forfeiture money judgment that the government seeks.

(b) Entering a Preliminary Order of Forfeiture.

(1) *Forfeiture Phase of the Trial.*

(A) Forfeiture determinations. As soon as practical after a verdict or finding of guilty, or after a plea of guilty or nolo contendere is accepted, on any count in an indictment or information regarding which criminal forfeiture is sought, the court must determine what property is subject to forfeiture under the applicable statute. If the government seeks forfeiture of specific property, the court must determine whether the government has established the requisite nexus between the property and the offense. If the government seeks a personal money judgment, the court must determine the amount of money that the defendant will be ordered to pay.

(B) Evidence and hearing. The court's determination may be based on evidence already in the record, including any written plea agreement, and on any additional evidence or information submitted by the parties and accepted by the court as relevant and reliable. If the forfeiture is contested, on either party's request the court must conduct a hearing after the verdict or finding of guilty.

(2) *Preliminary Order.*

(A) Contents of a specific order. If the court finds that property is subject to forfeiture, it must promptly enter a preliminary order of forfeiture setting forth the amount of any money judgment, directing the forfeiture of specific property, and directing the forfeiture of any substitute property if the government has met the statutory criteria. The court must enter the order without regard to any third party's interest in the property. Determining whether a third party has such an interest must be deferred until any third party files a claim in an ancillary proceeding under Rule 32.2(c).

(B) Timing. Unless doing so is impractical, the court must enter the preliminary order sufficiently in advance of sentencing to allow the parties to suggest revisions or modifications before the order becomes final as to the defendant under Rule 32.2(b)(4).

(C) General Order. If, before sentencing, the court cannot identify all the specific property subject to forfeiture or calculate the total amount of the money judgment, the court may enter a forfeiture order that:

(i) lists any identified property;

(ii) describes other property in general terms; and

(iii) states that the order will be amended under Rule 32.2(e)(1) when additional specific property is identified or the amount of the money judgment has been calculated.

(3) *Seizing Property.* The entry of a preliminary order of forfeiture authorizes the Attorney General (or a designee) to seize the specific property subject to forfeiture; to conduct any discovery the court considers proper in identifying, locating, or disposing of the property; and to commence proceedings that comply with any statutes governing third-party rights. The court may include in the order of forfeiture conditions reasonably necessary to preserve the property's value pending any appeal.

(4) *Sentence and Judgment.*

(A) When Final. At sentencing—or at any time before sentencing if the defendant consents—the preliminary forfeiture order becomes final as to the defendant. If the order directs the defendant to forfeit specific property, it remains preliminary as to third parties until the ancillary proceeding is concluded under Rule 32.2(c).

(B) Notice and Inclusion in the Judgment. The court must include the forfeiture when orally announcing the sentence or must otherwise ensure that the defendant knows of the forfeiture at sentencing. The court must also include the forfeiture order, directly or by reference, in the judgment, but the court's failure to do so may be corrected at any time under Rule 36.

(C) Time to Appeal. The time for the defendant or the government to file an appeal from the forfeiture order, or from the court's failure to enter an order, begins to run when judgment is entered. If the court later amends or declines to amend a forfeiture order to include additional property under Rule 32.2(e), the defendant or the government may file an appeal regarding that property under Federal Rule of Appellate Procedure 4(b). The time for that appeal runs from the date when the order granting or denying the amendment becomes final.

(5) *Jury Determination.*

(A) Retaining the Jury. In any case tried before a jury, if the indictment or information states that the government is seeking forfeiture, the court must determine before the jury begins deliberating whether either party requests that the jury be retained to determine the forfeitability of specific property if it returns a guilty verdict.

(B) Special Verdict Form. If a party timely requests to have the jury determine forfeiture, the government must submit a proposed Special Verdict Form listing each property subject to forfeiture and asking the jury to determine whether the government has established the requisite nexus between the property and the offense committed by the defendant.

(6) *Notice of the Forfeiture Order.*

(A) Publishing and Sending Notice. If the court orders the forfeiture of specific property, the government must publish notice of the order and send notice to any person who reasonably appears to be a potential claimant with standing to contest the forfeiture in the ancillary proceeding.

(B) Content of the Notice. The notice must describe the forfeited property, state the times under the applicable statute when a petition contesting the forfeiture must be filed, and state the name and contact information for the government attorney to be served with the petition.

(C) Means of Publication; Exceptions to Publication Requirement. Publication must take place as described in Supplemental Rule G(4)(a)(iii) of the Federal Rules of Civil Procedure, and may be by any means described in Supplemental Rule G(4)(a)(iv). Publication is unnecessary if any exception in Supplemental Rule G(4)(a)(i) applies.

(D) Means of Sending the Notice. The notice may be sent in accordance with Supplemental Rules G(4)(b)(iii)–(v) of the Federal Rules of Civil Procedure.

(7) *Interlocutory Sale.* At any time before entry of a final forfeiture order, the court, in accordance with Supplemental Rule G(7) of the Federal Rules of Civil Procedure, may order the interlocutory sale of property alleged to be forfeitable.

(c) Ancillary Proceeding; Entering a Final Order of Forfeiture.

(1) *In General.* If, as prescribed by statute, a third party files a petition asserting an interest in the property to be forfeited, the court must conduct an ancillary proceeding, but no ancillary proceeding is required to the extent that the forfeiture consists of a money judgment.

(A) In the ancillary proceeding, the court may, on motion, dismiss the petition for lack of standing, for failure to state a claim, or for any other lawful reason. For purposes of the motion, the facts set forth in the petition are assumed to be true.

(B) After disposing of any motion filed under Rule 32.2(c)(1)(A) and before conducting a hearing on the petition, the court may permit the parties to conduct discovery in accordance with the Federal Rules of Civil Procedure if the court determines that discovery is necessary or desirable to resolve factual issues. When discovery ends, a party may move for summary judgment under Federal Rule of Civil Procedure 56.

(2) *Entering a Final Order.* When the ancillary proceeding ends, the court must enter a final order of forfeiture by amending the preliminary order as necessary to account for any third-party rights. If no third party files a timely petition, the preliminary order becomes the final order of forfeiture if the court finds that the defendant (or any combination of defendants convicted in the case) had an interest in the property that is forfeitable under the applicable statute. The defendant may not object to the entry of the final order on the ground that the property belongs, in whole or in part, to a codefendant or third party; nor may a third party object to the final order on the ground that the third party had an interest in the property.

(3) *Multiple Petitions.* If multiple third-party petitions are filed in the same case, an order dismissing or granting one petition is not appealable until rulings are made on all the petitions, unless the court determines that there is no just reason for delay.

(4) *Ancillary Proceeding Not Part of Sentencing.* An ancillary proceeding is not part of sentencing.

(d) Stay Pending Appeal. If a defendant appeals from a conviction or an order of forfeiture, the court may stay the order of forfeiture on terms appropriate to ensure that the property remains available pending appellate review. A stay does not delay the ancillary proceeding or the determination of a third party's rights or interests. If the court rules in favor of any third party while an appeal is pending, the court may amend the order of forfeiture but must not transfer any property interest to a third party until the decision on appeal becomes final, unless the defendant consents in writing or on the record.

(e) Subsequently Located Property; Substitute Property.

(1) *In General.* On the government's motion, the court may at any time enter an order of forfeiture or amend an existing order of forfeiture to include property that:

(A) is subject to forfeiture under an existing order of forfeiture but was located and identified after that order was entered; or

(B) is substitute property that qualifies for forfeiture under an applicable statute.

(2) *Procedure.* If the government shows that the property is subject to forfeiture under Rule 32.2(e)(1), the court must:

(A) enter an order forfeiting that property, or amend an existing preliminary or final order to include it; and

(B) if a third party files a petition claiming an interest in the property, conduct an ancillary proceeding under Rule 32.2(c).

(3) *Jury Trial Limited.* There is no right to a jury trial under Rule 32.2(e).

HISTORY:

Added April 17, 2000, eff. Dec. 1, 2000; April 29, 2002, eff. Dec. 1, 2002; March 26, 2009, eff. Dec. 1, 2009.

HISTORY; ANCILLARY LAWS AND DIRECTIVES

Other provisions:

Notes of Advisory Committee on 2000 amendments. Rule 32.2 consolidates a number of procedural rules governing the forfeiture of assets in a criminal case. Existing Rules 7(c)(2), 31(e) and 32(d)(2) are also amended to conform to the new rule. In addition, the forfeiture-related provisions of Rule 38(e) are stricken.

Subdivision (a). Subdivision (a) is derived from Rule 7(c)(2) which provides that notwithstanding statutory authority for the forfeiture of property following a criminal conviction, no forfeiture order may be entered unless the defendant was given notice of the forfeiture in the indictment or information. As courts have held, subdivision (a) is not intended to require that an itemized list of the property to be forfeited appear in the indictment or information itself. The subdivision reflects the trend in caselaw interpreting present Rule 7(c). Under the most recent cases, Rule 7(c) sets forth a requirement that the government give the defendant notice that it will be seeking forfeiture in accordance with the applicable statute. It does not require a substantive allegation in which the property subject to forfeiture, or the defendant's interest in the property, must be described in detail. *See United States v. DeFries,* 129 F.3d 1293 (D.C.Cir. 1997) (it is not necessary to specify in either the indictment or a bill of particulars that the government is seeking forfeiture of a particular asset, such as the defendant's salary; to comply with Rule 7(c), the government need only put the defendant on notice that it will seek to forfeit everything subject to forfeiture under the applicable statute, such as all property "acquired or maintained" as a result of a RICO violation). *See also United States v. Moffitt, Zwerling & Kemler, P.C.*, 83 F.3d 660, 665 (4th Cir. 1996), aff'g 846 F. Supp. 463 (E.D. Va. 1994) (Moffitt I) (indictment need not list each asset subject to forfeiture; under Rule 7(c), this can be done with bill of particulars); *United States v. Voigt*, 89 F.3d 1050 (3rd Cir. 1996) (court may amend order of forfeiture at any time to include substitute assets).

Subdivision (b). Subdivision (b) replaces Rule 31(e) which provides that the jury in a criminal case must return a special verdict "as to the extent of the interest or property subject to forfeiture." *See United States v. Saccoccia*, 58 F.3d 754 (1st Cir. 1995) (Rule 31(e) only applies to jury trials; no special verdict required when defendant waives right to jury on forfeiture issues).

One problem under Rule 31(e) concerns the scope of the determination that must be made prior to entering an order of forfeiture. This issue is the same whether the determination is made by the court or by the jury.

As mentioned, the current rule requires the jury to return a special verdict "as to the extent of the interest or property subject to forfeiture." Some courts interpret this to mean only that the jury must answer "yes" or "no" when asked if the property named in the indictment is subject to forfeiture under the terms of the forfeiture statute—e.g. was the property used to facilitate a drug offense? Other courts also ask the jury if the defendant has a legal interest in the forfeited property. Still other courts, including the Fourth Circuit, require the jury to determine the extent of the defendant's interest in the property vis a vis third parties. *See United States v. Ham*, 58 F.3d 78 (4th Cir. 1995) (case remanded to the district court to impanel a jury to determine, in the first instance, the extent of the defendant's forfeitable interest in the subject property).

The notion that the "extent" of the defendant's interest must be established as part of the criminal trial is related to the fact that criminal forfeiture is an in personam action in which only the defendant's interest in the property may be forfeited. *United States v. Riley*, 78 F.3d 367 (8th Cir. 1996). When the criminal forfeiture statutes were first enacted in the 1970's, it was clear that a forfeiture of property other than the defendant's could not occur in a criminal case, but there was no mechanism designed to limit the forfeiture to the defendant's interest. Accordingly, Rule 31(e) was drafted to make a determination of the "extent" of the defendant's interest part of the verdict.

The problem is that third parties who might have an interest in the forfeited property are not parties to the criminal case. At the same time, a defendant who has no interest in property has no incentive, at trial, to dispute the government's forfeiture allegations. Thus, it was apparent by the 1980's that Rule 31(e) was an inadequate safeguard against the inadvertent forfeiture of property in which the defendant held no interest.

In 1984, Congress addressed this problem when it enacted a statutory scheme whereby third party interests in criminally forfeited property are litigated by the court in an ancillary proceeding following the conclusion of the criminal case and the entry of a preliminary order of forfeiture. See 21 U.S.C. § 853(n); 18 U.S.C. § 1963(l). Under this scheme, the court orders the forfeiture of the defendant's interest in the property—whatever that interest may be—in the criminal case. At that point, the court conducts a separate proceeding in which all potential third party claimants are given an opportunity to challenge the forfeiture by asserting a superior interest in the property. This proceeding does not involve relitigation of the forfeitability of the property; its only purpose is to determine whether any third party has a legal interest in the forfeited property.

The notice provisions regarding the ancillary proceeding are equivalent to the notice provisions that govern civil forfeitures. *Compare* 21 U.S.C. § 853(n)(1) *with* 19 U.S.C. § 1607(a); *see United States v. Bouler*, 927 F. Supp. 911 (W.D.N.C. 1996) (civil notice rules apply to ancillary criminal proceedings). Notice is published and sent to third parties that have a potential interest. *See United States v. BCCI Holdings (Luxembourg) S.A. (In re Petition of Indosuez Bank)*, 916 F. Supp. 1276 (D.D.C. 1996) (discussing steps taken by government to provide notice of criminal forfeiture to third parties). If no one files a claim, or if all claims are denied following a hearing, the forfeiture becomes final and the United States is deemed to have clear title to the property. 21 U.S.C. § 853(n)(7); *United States v. Hentz*, 1996 WL 355327 (E.D. Pa. June 20, 1996) (once third party fails to file a claim in the ancillary proceeding, government has clear title under § 853(n)(7) and can market the property notwithstanding third party's name on the deed).

Thus, the ancillary proceeding has become the forum for determining the extent of the defendant's forfeitable interest in the property. This allows the court to conduct a proceeding in which all third party claimants can participate and which ensures that the property forfeited actually belongs to the defendant.

Since the enactment of the ancillary proceeding statutes, the requirement in Rule 31(e) that the court (or jury) determine the extent of the defendant's interest in the property as part of the criminal trial has become an unnecessary anachronism that leads more often than not to duplication and a waste of judicial resources. There is no longer any reason to delay the conclusion of the criminal trial with a lengthy hearing over the extent of the defendant's interest in property when the same issues will have to be litigated a second time in the ancillary proceeding if someone files a claim challenging the forfeiture. For example, in *United States v. Messino*, 917 F. Supp. 1307 (N.D. Ill. 1996), the court allowed the defendant to call witnesses to attempt to establish that they, not he, were the true owners of the property. After the jury rejected this evidence and the property was forfeited, the court conducted an ancillary proceeding in which the same witnesses litigated their claims to the same property.

A more sensible procedure would be for the court, once it (or a jury) determines that property was involved in the criminal offense for which the defendant has been convicted, to order the forfeiture of whatever interest a defendant may have in the property without having to determine exactly what that interest is. If third parties assert that they have an interest in all or part of the property, those interests can be adjudicated at one time in the ancillary proceeding.

This approach would also address confusion that occurs in multi-defendant cases where it is clear that each defendant should forfeit whatever interest he may have in the property used to commit the offense, but it is not at all clear which defendant is the actual owner of the property. For example, suppose A and B are co-defendants in a drug and money laundering case in which the government seeks to forfeit property involved in the scheme that is held in B's name but of which A may be the true owner. It makes no sense to invest the court's time in determining which of the two defendants holds the interest that should be forfeited. Both defendants should forfeit whatever interest they may have. Moreover, if under the current rule the court were to find that A is the true owner of the property, then B would have the right to file a claim in the ancillary proceeding where he may attempt to recover the property despite his criminal conviction. *United States v. Real Property in Waterboro,* 64 F.3d 752 (1st Cir. 1995) (co-defendant in drug/money laundering case who is not alleged to be the owner of the property is considered a third party for the purpose of challenging the forfeiture of the other co-defendant's interest).

The new rule resolves these difficulties by postponing the determination of the extent of the defendant's interest until the ancillary proceeding. As provided in (b)(l), the court, as soon as practicable after the verdict or finding of guilty in the criminal case, would determine if the property was subject to forfeiture in accordance with the applicable statute, e.g., whether the property represented the proceeds of the offense, was used to facilitate the offense, or was involved in the offense in some other way. The determination could be made based on the evidence in the record from the criminal trial or the facts set forth in a written plea agreement submitted to the court at the time of the defendant's guilty plea, or the court could hold a hearing to determine if the requisite relationship existed between the property and the offense. Subdivision (b)(2) provides that it is not necessary to determine at this stage what interest any defendant might have in the property. Instead, the court would order the forfeiture of whatever interest each defendant might have in the property and conduct the ancillary proceeding.

Subdivision (b)(1) recognizes that there are different kinds of forfeiture judgments in criminal cases. One type is a personal judgment for a sum of money; another is a judgment forfeiting a specific asset. *See, e.g., United States v. Voigt,* 89 F.3d 1050 (3d Cir. 1996) (government is entitled to a personal money judgment equal to the amount involved in the money laundering offense, as well as order forfeiting specific assets involved in, or traceable to, the offense; in addition, if the statutory requirements are met, the government may be entitled to forfeit substitute assets); *United States v. Cleveland,* 1997 WL 537707 (E.D. La. Aug. 26, 1997), modified, 1997 WL 602186 (E.D. La. Sept. 29, 1997) (government entitled to a money judgment equal to the amount of money defendant laundered in money laundering case). The finding the court is required to make will depend on the nature of the forfeiture judgment. A number of cases have approved use of money judgment forfeitures. The Committee takes no position on the correctness of those rulings.

To the extent that the government is seeking forfeiture of a particular asset, such as the money on deposit in a particular bank account that is alleged to be the proceeds of a criminal offense, or a parcel of land that is traceable to that offense, the court must find that the government has established the requisite nexus between the property and the offense. To the extent that the government is seeking a money judgment, such as a judgment for the amount of money derived from a drug trafficking offense or the amount involved in a money laundering offense where the actual property subject to forfeiture has not been found or is unavailable, the court must determine the amount of money that the defendant should be ordered to forfeit.

The court may make the determination based on evidence in the record, or on additional evidence submitted by the defendant or evidence submitted by the government in support of the motion for the entry of a judgment of forfeiture. The defendant would have no standing to object to the forfeiture on the ground that the property belonged to someone else.

Under subdivision (b)(2), if the court finds that property is forfeitable, it must enter a preliminary order of forfeiture. It also recognizes that any determination of a third person's interest in the property is deferred until an ancillary proceeding, if any, is held under subdivision (c).

Subdivision (b)(3) replaces Rule 32(d)(2) (effective December 1996). It provides that once the court enters a preliminary order of forfeiture directing the forfeiture of whatever interest each defendant may have in the forfeited property, the government may seize the property and commence an ancillary proceeding to determine the interests of any third party. The subdivision also provides that the Attorney General may designate someone outside of the Department of Justice to seize forfeited property. This is necessary because in cases in which the lead investigative agency is in the Treasury Department, for example, the seizure of the forfeited property is typically handled by agencies other than the Department of Justice.

If no third party files a claim, the court, at the time of sentencing, will enter a final order forfeiting the property in accordance with subdivision (c)(2), discussed infra. If a third party files a claim, the order of forfeiture will become final as to the defendant at the time of sentencing but will be subject to amendment in favor of a third party pending the conclusion of the ancillary proceeding.

Because the order of forfeiture becomes final as to the defendant at the time of sentencing, his right to appeal from that order begins to run at that time. As courts have held, because the ancillary hearing has no bearing on the defendant's right to the property, the defendant has no right to appeal when a final order is, or is not, amended to recognize third party rights. *See, e.g., United States v. Christunas,* 126 F.3d 765 (6th Cir. 1997) (preliminary order of forfeiture is final as to the defendant and is immediately appealable).

Because it is not uncommon for sentencing to be postponed for an extended period to allow a defendant to cooperate with the government in an ongoing investigation, the rule would allow the order of forfeiture to become final as to the defendant before sentencing, if the defendant agrees to that procedure. Otherwise, the government would be unable to dispose of the property until the sentencing took place.

Subdivision (b)(4) addresses the right of either party to request that a jury make the determination of whether any property is subject to forfeiture. The provision gives the defendant, in all cases where a jury has returned a guilty verdict, the option of asking that the jury be retained to hear additional evidence regarding the forfeitability of the property. The only issue for the jury in such cases would be whether the government has established the requisite nexus between the property and the offense. For example, if the defendant disputes the government's allegation that a parcel of real property is traceable to the offense, the defendant would have the right to request that the jury hear evidence on that issue, and return a special verdict, in a bifurcated proceeding that would occur after the jury returns the guilty verdict. The government would have the same option of requesting a special jury verdict on this issue, as is the case under current law. See Rule 23(a) (trial by jury may be waived only with the consent of the government).

When Rule 31(e) was promulgated, it was assumed that criminal forfeiture was akin to a separate criminal offense on which evidence would be presented and the jury would have to return a verdict. In *Libretti v. United States*, 516 U.S. 29 (1995), however, the Supreme Court held that criminal forfeiture constitutes an aspect of the sentence imposed in a criminal case and that the defendant has no constitutional right to have the jury determine any part of the forfeiture. The special verdict requirement in Rule 31(e), the Court said, is in the nature of a statutory right that can be modified or repealed at any time.

Even before *Libretti*, lower courts had determined that criminal forfeiture is a sentencing matter and concluded that criminal trials therefore should be bifurcated so that the jury first returns a verdict on guilt or innocence and then returns to hear evidence regarding the forfeiture. In the second part of the bifurcated proceeding, the jury is instructed that the government must establish the forfeitability of the property by a preponderance of the evidence. *See United States v. Myers*, 21 F.3d 826 (8th Cir. 1994) (preponderance standard applies because criminal forfeiture is part of the sentence in money laundering cases); *United States v. Voigt*, 89 F.3d 1050 (3rd Cir. 1996) (following Myers); *United States v. Smith*, 966 F.2d 1045, 1050-53 (6th Cir. 1992) (same for drug cases); *United States v. Bieri*, 21 F.3d 819 (8th Cir. 1994) (same).

Although an argument could be made under *Libretti*, that a jury trial is no longer appropriate on any aspect of the forfeiture issue, which is a part of sentencing, the Committee decided to retain the right for the parties, in a trial held before a jury, to have the jury determine whether the government has established the requisite statutory nexus between the offense and the property to be forfeited. The jury, however, would not have any role in determining whether a defendant had an interest in the property to be forfeited. This is a matter for the ancillary proceeding which, by statute, is conducted "before the court alone, without a jury." *See* 21 U.S.C. § 853(n)(2).

Subdivision (c). Subdivision (c) sets forth a set of rules governing the conduct of the ancillary proceeding. When the ancillary hearing provisions were added to 18 U.S.C. § 1963 and 21 U.S.C. § 853 in 1984, Congress apparently assumed that the proceedings under the new provisions would involve simple questions of ownership that could, in the ordinary case, be resolved in 30 days. See 18 U.S.C. § 1963(l)(4). Presumably for that reason, the statute contains no procedures governing motions practice or discovery such as would be available in an ordinary civil case. Subdivision (c)(1) makes clear that no ancillary proceeding is required to the extent that the order of forfeiture consists of a money judgment. A money judgment is an in personam judgment against the defendant and not an order directed at specific assets in which any third party could have any interest.

Experience has shown that ancillary hearings can involve issues of enormous complexity that require years to resolve. *See United States v. BCCI Holdings (Luxembourg) S.A.*, 833 F. Supp. 9 (D.D.C. 1993) (ancillary proceeding involving over 100 claimants and $451 million); *United States v. Porcelli*, CR-85-00756 (CPS), 1992 U.S. Dist. LEXIS 17928 (E.D.N.Y. Nov. 5, 1992) (litigation over third party claim continuing 6 years after RICO conviction). In such cases, procedures akin to those available under the Federal Rules of Civil Procedure should be available to the court and the parties to aid in the efficient resolution of the claims.

Because an ancillary hearing is connected to a criminal case, it would not be appropriate to make the Civil Rules applicable in all respects. The amendment, however, describes several fundamental areas in which procedures analogous to those in the Civil Rules may be followed. These include the filing of a motion to dismiss a claim, conducting discovery, disposing of a claim on a motion for summary judgment, and appealing a final disposition of a claim. Where applicable, the amendment follows the prevailing case law on the issue. *See, e.g., United States v. Lavin*, 942 F.2d 177 (3rd Cir. 1991) (ancillary proceeding treated as civil case for purposes of applying Rules of Appellate Procedure); *United States v. BCCI Holdings (Luxembourg) S.A. (In re Petitions of General Creditors)*, 919 F. Supp. 31 (D.D.C. 1996) ("If a third party fails to allege in its petition all elements necessary for recovery, including those relating to standing, the court may dismiss the petition without providing a hearing"); *United States v. BCCI (Holdings) Luxembourg S.A. (In re Petition of Department of Private Affairs)*, 1993 WL 760232 (D.D.C. Dec. 8, 1993) (applying court's inherent powers to permit third party to obtain discovery from defendant in accordance with civil rules). The provision governing appeals in cases where there are multiple claims is derived from Fed. R. Civ. P. 54(b). *See also United States v. BCCI Holdings (Luxembourg) S.A. (Petition of Banque Indosuez)*, 961 F.Supp. 282 (D.D.C. 1997) (in resolving motion to dismiss court assumes all facts pled by third party petitioner to be true, applying Rule 12(b)(6) and denying government's motion because whether claimant had superior title turned on factual dispute; government acted reasonably in not making any discovery requests in ancillary proceeding until court ruled on its motion to dismiss).

Subdivision (c)(2) provides for the entry of a final order of forfeiture at the conclusion of the ancillary proceeding. Under this provision, if no one files a claim in the ancillary proceeding, the preliminary order would become the final order of forfeiture, but the court would first have to make an independent finding that at least one of the defendants had an interest in the property such that it was proper to order the forfeiture of the property in a criminal case. In making that determination, the court may rely upon reasonable inferences. For example, the fact that the defendant used the property in committing the crime and no third party claimed an interest in the property may give rise to the inference that the defendant had a forfeitable interest in the property.

This subdivision combines and preserves two established tenets of current law. One is that criminal forfeitures are in personam actions that are limited to the property interests of the defendant. (This distinguishes criminal forfeiture, which is imposed as part of the defendant's sentence, from civil forfeiture which may be pursued as an action against the property in rem without regard to who the owner may be.) The other tenet of current law is that if a third party has notice of the forfeiture but fails to file a timely claim, his or her interests are extinguished, and may not be recognized when the court enters the final order of forfeiture. *See United States v. Hentz,* 1996 WL 355327 (E.D. Pa. June 20, 1996) (once third party fails to file a claim in the ancillary proceeding, government has clear title under 21 U.S.C. § 853(n)(7) and can market the property notwithstanding third party's name on the deed). In the rare event that a third party claims that he or she was not afforded adequate notice of a criminal forfeiture action, the person may file a motion under Rule 60(b) of the Federal Rules of Civil Procedure to reopen the ancillary proceeding. *See United States v. Bouler,* 927 F. Supp. 911 (W.D.N.C. 1996) (Rule 60(b) is the proper means by which a third party may move to reopen an ancillary proceeding).

If no third parties assert their interests in the ancillary proceeding, the court must nonetheless determine that the defendant, or combination of defendants, had an interest in the property. Criminal defendants may be jointly and severally liable for the forfeiture of the entire proceeds of the criminal offense. *See United States v. Hurley,* 63 F.3d 1(1st Cir. 1995) (government can collect the proceeds only once, but subject to that cap, it can collect from any defendant so much of the proceeds as was foreseeable to that defendant); *United States v. Cleveland,* 1997 WL 602186 (E.D. La. Sept. 29, 1997) (same); *United States v. McCarroll,* 1996 WL 355371 at *9 (N.D. Ill. June 25, 1996) following Hurley , aff'd sub nom. *United States v. Jarrett,* 133 F.3d 519 (7th Cir. 1998); *United States v. DeFries,* 909 F. Supp. 13, 19–20 (D.D.C. 1995)(defendants are jointly and severally liable even where government is able to determine precisely how much each defendant benefitted from the scheme), rev'd on other grounds, 129 F.3d 1293 (D.C. Cir. 1997). Therefore, the conviction of any of the defendants is sufficient to support the forfeiture of the entire proceeds of the offense, even if the defendants have divided the money among themselves.

As noted in (c)(4), the ancillary proceeding is not considered a part of sentencing. Thus, the Federal Rules of Evidence would apply to the ancillary proceeding, as is the case currently.

Subdivision (d). Subdivision (d) replaces the forfeiture provisions of Rule 38(e) which provide that the court may stay an order of forfeiture pending appeal. The purpose of the provision is to ensure that the property remains intact and unencumbered so that it may be returned to the defendant in the event the appeal is successful. Subdivision (d) makes clear, however, that a district court is not divested of jurisdiction over an ancillary proceeding even if the defendant appeals his or her conviction. This allows the court to proceed with the resolution of third party claims even as the appellate court considers the appeal. Otherwise, third parties would have to await the conclusion of the appellate process even to begin to have their claims heard. *See United States v. Messino,* 907 F. Supp. 1231 (N.D. Ill. 1995) (the district court retains jurisdiction over forfeiture matters while an appeal is pending).

Finally, subdivision (d) provides a rule to govern what happens if the court determines that a third-party claim should be granted but the defendant's appeal is still pending. The defendant is barred from filing a claim in the ancillary proceeding. See 18 U.S.C. § 1963(l)(2); 21 U.S.C. § 853(n)(2). Thus, the court's determination, in the ancillary proceeding, that a third party has an interest in the property superior to that of the defendant cannot be binding on the defendant. So, in the event that the court finds in favor of the third party, that determination is final only with respect to the government's alleged interest. If the defendant prevails on appeal, he or she recovers the property as if no conviction or forfeiture ever took place. But if the order of forfeiture is affirmed, the amendment to the order of forfeiture in favor of the third party becomes effective.

Subdivision (e). Subdivision (e) makes clear, as courts have found, that the court retains jurisdiction to amend the order of forfeiture at any time to include subsequently located property which was originally included in the forfeiture order and any substitute property. *See United States v. Hurley,* 63 F.3d 1 (1st Cir. 1995) (court retains authority to order forfeiture of substitute assets after appeal is filed); *United States v. Voigt,* 89 F.3d 1050 (3rd Cir. 1996) (following *Hurley*). Third parties, of course, may contest the forfeiture of substitute assets in the ancillary proceeding. See *United States v. Lester,* 85 F.3d 1409 (9th Cir. 1996).

Subdivision (e)(1) makes clear that the right to a bifurcated jury trial to determine whether the government has established the requisite nexus between the property and the offense, see (b)(4), does not apply to the forfeiture of substitute assets or to the addition of newly-discovered property to an existing order of forfeiture. It is well established in the case law that the forfeiture of substitute assets is solely an issue for the court. *See United States v. Hurley,* 63 F.3d 1 (1st Cir. 1995) (court retains authority to order forfeiture of substitute assets after appeal is filed); *United States v. Voigt,* 89 F.3d 1050 (3d Cir. 1996) (following *Hurley;* court may amend order of forfeiture at any time to include substitute assets); *United States v. Thompson,* 837 F. Supp. 585 (S.D.N.Y. 1993) (court, not jury, orders forfeiture of substitute assets). As a practical matter, courts have also determined that they, not the jury, must determine the forfeitability of assets discovered after the trial is over and the jury has been dismissed. See *United States v. Saccoccia,* 898 F. Supp. 53 (D.R.I. 1995) (government may conduct post-trial discovery to determine location and identity of forfeitable assets; post-trial discovery resulted in discovery of gold bars buried in defendant's mother's backyard several years after the entry of an order directing the defendant to forfeit all property, up to $137 million, involved in his money laundering offense).

Notes of Advisory Committee on 2002 amendments. The language of Rule 32.2 has been amended as part of the general restyling of the Criminal Rules to make them more easily understood and to make style and terminology consistent throughout the rules. These changes are intended to be stylistic only.

Notes of Advisory Committee on 2009 amendments. *Note to Subdivision (a).* The amendment responds to some uncertainty regarding the form of the required notice that the government will seek forfeiture as part of the sentence, making it clear that the notice should not be designated as a separate count in an indictment or information. The amendment also makes it clear that the indictment or information need only provide general notice that the government is seeking forfeiture, without identifying the specific property being sought. This is consistent with the 2000 Committee Note, as well as many lower court decisions.

Although forfeitures are not charged as counts, the federal judiciary's Case Management and Electronic Case Files system should note that forfeiture has been alleged so as to assist the parties and the court in tracking the subsequent status of forfeiture allegations.

The court may direct the government to file a bill of particulars to inform the defendant of the identity of the property that the government is seeking to forfeit or the amount of any money judgment sought if necessary to enable the defendant to prepare a defense or to avoid unfair surprise. *See, e.g., United States v. Moffitt, Zwerdling, & Kemler, P.C.,* 83 F.3d 660, 665 (4th Cir. 1996) (holding that the government need not list each asset subject to forfeiture in the indictment because notice can be provided in a bill of particulars); *United States v. Vasquez-Ruiz,* 136 F. Supp. 2d 941, 944 (N.D. Ill. 2001) (directing the government to identify in a bill of particulars, at least 30 days before trial, the specific items of property, including substitute assets, that it claims are subject to forfeiture); *United States v. Best,* 657 F. Supp. 1179, 1182 (N.D. Ill. 1987) (directing the government to provide a bill of particulars apprising the defendants as to the time periods during which they obtained the specified classes of property through their alleged racketeering activity and the interest in each of these properties that was allegedly obtained unlawfully). *See also United States v. Columbo,* 2006 WL 2012511 * 5 & n. 13 (S.D. N.Y. 2006) (denying motion for bill of particulars and noting that government proposed sending letter detailing basis for forfeiture allegations).

Note to Subdivision (b)(1). Rule 32.2(b)(1) sets forth the procedure for determining if property is subject to forfeiture. Subparagraph (A) is carried forward from the current Rule without change.

Subparagraph (B) clarifies that the parties may submit additional evidence relating to the forfeiture in the forfeiture phase of the trial, which may be necessary even if the forfeiture is not contested. Subparagraph (B) makes it clear that in determining what evidence or information should be accepted, the court should consider relevance and reliability. Finally, subparagraph (B) requires the court to hold a hearing when forfeiture is contested. The Committee foresees that in some instances live testimony will be needed to determine the reliability of proffered information. *Cf.* Rule 32.1(b)(1)(B)(iii) (providing the defendant in a proceeding for revocation of probation or supervised release with the opportunity, upon request, to question any adverse witness unless the judge determines this is not in the interest of justice).

Note to Subdivision (b)(2)(A). Current Rule 32.2(b) provides the procedure for issuing a preliminary forfeiture order once the court finds that the government has established the nexus between the property and the offense (or the amount of the money judgment). The amendment makes clear that the preliminary order may include substitute assets if the government has met the statutory criteria.

Note to Subdivision (b)(2)(B). This new subparagraph focuses on the timing of the preliminary forfeiture order, stating that the court should issue the order "sufficiently in advance of sentencing to allow the parties to suggest revisions or modifications before the order becomes final." Many courts have delayed entry of the preliminary order until the time of sentencing. This is undesirable because the parties have no opportunity to advise the court of omissions or errors in the order before it becomes final as to the defendant (which occurs upon oral announcement of the sentence and the entry of the criminal judgment). Once the sentence has been announced, the rules give the sentencing court only very limited authority to correct errors or omissions in the preliminary forfeiture order. Pursuant to Rule 35(a), the district court may correct a sentence, including an incorporated forfeiture order, within seven days after oral announcement of the sentence. During the seven-day period, corrections are limited to those necessary to correct "arithmetical, technical, or other clear error." *See United States v. King,* 368 F. Supp. 2d 509, 512–13 (D. S.C. 2005). Corrections of clerical errors may also be made pursuant to Rule 36. If the order contains errors or omissions that do not fall within Rules 35(a) or 36, and the court delays entry of the preliminary forfeiture order until the time of sentencing, the parties may be left with no alternative to an appeal, which is a waste of judicial resources. The amendment requires the court to enter the preliminary order in advance of sentencing to permit time for corrections, unless it is not practical to do so in an individual case.

Note to Subdivision (b)(2)(C). The amendment explains how the court is to reconcile the requirement that it make the forfeiture order part of the sentence with the fact that in some cases the government will not have completed its post-conviction investigation to locate the forfeitable property by the time of sentencing. In that case the court is authorized to issue a forfeiture order describing the property in "general" terms, which order may be amended pursuant to Rule 32.2(e)(1) when additional specific property is identified.

The authority to issue a general forfeiture order should be used only in unusual circumstances and not as a matter of course. For cases in which a general order was properly employed, *see United States v. BCCI Holdings (Luxembourg),* 69 F. Supp. 2d 36 (D.D.C. 1999) (ordering forfeiture of all of a large, complex corporation's assets in the United States, permitting the government to continue discovery necessary to identify and trace those assets); *United States v. Saccoccia,* 898 F. Supp. 53 (D.R.I. 1995) (ordering forfeiture of up to a specified amount of laundered drug proceeds so that the government could continue investigation which led to the discovery and forfeiture of gold bars buried by the defendant in his mother's back yard).

Note to Subdivisions (b)(3) and (4). The amendment moves the language explaining when the forfeiture order becomes final as to the defendant to new subparagraph (b)(4)(A), where it is coupled with new language explaining that the order is not final as to third parties until the completion of the ancillary proceedings provided for in Rule 32.2(c).

New subparagraphs (B) and (C) are intended to clarify what the district court is required to do at sentencing, and to respond to conflicting decisions in the courts regarding the application of Rule 36 to correct clerical errors. The new subparagraphs add considerable detail regarding the oral announcement of the forfeiture at sentencing, the reference to the forfeiture order in the judgment and commitment order, the availability of Rule 36 to correct the failure to include the forfeiture order in the judgment and commitment order, and the time to appeal.

New subparagraph (C) clarifies the time for appeals concerning forfeiture by the defendant or government from two kinds of orders: the original judgment of conviction and later orders amending or refusing to amend the judgment under Rule 32.2(e) to add additional property. This provision does not address appeals by the government or a third party from orders in ancillary proceedings under Rule 32.2(c).

Note to Subdivision (b)(5)(A). The amendment clarifies the procedure for requesting a jury determination of forfeiture. The goal is to avoid an inadvertent waiver of the right to a jury determination, while also providing timely notice to the court and to the jurors themselves if they will be asked to make the forfeiture determination. The amendment requires that the court determine whether either party requests a jury determination of forfeiture in cases where the government has given notice that it is seeking forfeiture and a jury has been empaneled to determine guilt or innocence. The rule requires the court to make this determination before the jury retires. Jurors who know that they may face an additional task after they return their verdict will be more accepting of the additional responsibility in the forfeiture proceeding, and the court will be better able to plan as well.

Although the rule permits a party to make this request just before the jury retires, it is desirable, when possible, to make the request earlier, at the time when the jury is empaneled. This allows the court to plan, and also allows the court to tell potential jurors what to expect in terms of their service.

Subdivision (b)(5)(B) explains that "the government must submit a proposed Special Verdict Form listing each property subject to forfeiture." Use of such a form is desirable, and the government is in the best position to draft the form.

Note to Subdivisions (b)(6) and (7). These provisions are based upon the civil forfeiture provisions in Supplemental Rule G of the Federal Rules of Civil Procedure, which are also incorporated by cross reference. The amendment governs such mechanical and technical issues as the manner of publishing notice of forfeiture to third parties and the interlocutory sale of property, bringing practice under the Criminal Rules into conformity with the Civil Rules.

Rule 33. New Trial

(a) Defendant's Motion. Upon the defendant's motion, the court may vacate any judgment and grant a new trial if the interest of justice so requires. If the case was tried without a jury, the court may take additional testimony and enter a new judgment.

(b) Time to File.

(1) *Newly Discovered Evidence.* Any motion for a new trial grounded on newly discovered evidence must be filed within 3 years after the verdict or finding of guilty. If an appeal is pending, the court may not grant a motion for a new trial until the appellate court remands the case.

(2) *Other Grounds.* Any motion for a new trial grounded on any reason other than newly discovered evidence must be filed within 14 days after the verdict or finding of guilty.

HISTORY:

Dec. 26, 1944, eff. March 21, 1946, as amended Feb. 28, 1966, eff. July 1, 1966; March 9, 1987, eff. Aug. 1, 1987; April 24, 1998, eff. Dec. 1, 1998; April 29, 2002, eff. Dec. 1, 2002; April 25, 2005, eff. Dec. 1, 2005; March 26, 2009, eff. Dec. 1, 2009.

HISTORY; ANCILLARY LAWS AND DIRECTIVES

Other provisions:

Notes of Advisory Committee on Rules. This rule enlarges the time limit for motions for new trial on the ground of newly discovered evidence, from 60 days to two years; and for motions for new trial on other grounds from three to five days. Otherwise, it substantially continues existing practice. See Rule II of the Criminal Appeals Rules of 1933, 292 US 661 [18 USC formerly following § 688]. Cf. Rule 59(a) of the Federal Rules of Civil Procedure [Federal Rules of Civil Procedure, USCS Court Rules, Rule 59(a)].

Notes of Advisory Committee on 1966 amendments. The amendments to the first two sentences make it clear that a judge has no power to order a new trial on his own motion, that he can act only in response to a motion timely made by a defendant. Problems of double jeopardy arise when the court acts on its own motion. See United States v Smith, 331 US 469, 91 L Ed 1610, 67 S Ct 1330 (1947). These amendments do not, of course, change the power which the court has in certain circumstances, prior to verdict or finding of guilty, to declare a mistrial and order a new trial on its own motion. See e.g., Gori v United States, 367 US 364, 6 L Ed 2d 901, 81 S Ct 1523 (1961); Downum v United States, 372 US 734, 10 L Ed 2d 100, 83 S Ct 1033 (1963); United States v Tateo, 377 US 463, 12 L Ed 2d 448, 84 S Ct 1587 (1964). The amendment to the last sentence changes the time in which the motion may be made to 7 days. See the Advisory Committee's Note to Rule 29.

Notes of Advisory Committee on 1987 amendments. The amendment is technical. No substantive change is intended.

Notes of Advisory Committee on 1998 amendments. As currently written, the time for filing a motion for new trial on the ground of newly discovered evidence runs from the "final judgment." The courts, in interpreting that language, have uniformly concluded that that language refers to the action of the Court of Appeals. *See, e.g., United States v. Reyes,* 49 F.3d 63, 66 (2d Cir. 1995) (citing cases). It is less clear whether that action is the appellate court's judgment or the issuance of its mandate. In *Reyes,* the court concluded that it was the latter event. In either case, it is clear that the present approach of using the appellate court's final judgment as the triggering event can cause great disparity in the amount of time available to a defendant to file timely a motion for new trial. This would be especially true if, as noted by the Court in *Reyes, supra* at 67, an appellate court stayed its mandate pending review by the Supreme Court. *See also Herrera v. Collins,* 506 U.S. 390, 410–412 (1993) (noting divergent treatment by States of time for filing motions for new trial).

It is the intent of the Committee to remove that element of inconsistency by using the trial court's verdict or finding of guilty as the triggering event. The change also furthers internal consistency within the rule itself; the time for filing a motion for new trial on any other ground currently runs from that same event.

Finally, the time to file a motion for new trial based upon newly discovered evidence is increased to three years to compensate for what would have otherwise resulted in less time than that currently contemplated in the rule for filing such motions.

Notes of Advisory Committee on 2002 amendments. The language of Rule 33 has been amended as part of the general restyling of the Criminal Rules to make them more easily understood and to make style and terminology consistent throughout the rules. These changes are intended to be stylistic only.

Notes of Advisory Committee on 2005 amendments. Rule 33(b)(2) has been amended to remove the requirement that the court must act within seven days after a verdict or finding of guilty if it sets another time for filing a motion for a new trial. This amendment parallels similar changes to Rules 29 and 34. Further, a conforming amendment has been made to Rule 45(b)(2).

Currently, Rule 33(b)(2) requires the defendant to move for a new trial within seven days after the verdict or the finding of guilty verdict, or within some other time set by the court in an order issued during that same seven-day period. Similar provisions exist in Rules 29 and 34. Courts have held that the seven-day rule is jurisdictional. Thus, if a defendant files a request for an extension of time to file a motion for a new trial within the seven-day period, the court must rule on that motion or request within the same seven-day period. If for some reason the court does not rule on the request within the seven days, it loses jurisdiction to act on the underlying substantive motion. *See, e.g., United States v. Smith*, 331 U.S. 469, 473–474 (1947) (rejecting argument that trial court had power to grant new trial on its own motion after expiration of time in Rule 33); *United States v. Marquez*, 291 F.3d 23, 27–28 (D.C. Cir. 2002) (citing language of Rule 33, and holding that "district court forfeited the power to act when it failed to . . . fix a new time for a filing a motion for new trial within seven days of the verdict").

Assuming that the current rule was intended to promote finality, there is nothing to prevent the court from granting the defendant a significant extension of time, so long as it does so within the seven-day period. Thus, the Committee believed that the rule should be amended to be consistent with all of the other timing requirements in the rules, which do not force the court to act on a motion to extend the time for filing within a particular period of time or lose jurisdiction to do so.

Accordingly, the amendment deletes the language regarding the court's acting within seven days to set the time for filing. Read in conjunction with the conforming amendment to Rule 45(b), the defendant is still required to file a timely motion for a new trial under Rule 33(b)(2) within the seven-day period specified. The defendant may, under Rule 45, seek an extension of time to file the underlying motion as long as the defendant does so within the seven-day period. But the court itself is not required to act on that motion within any particular time. Further, under Rule 45(b)(1)(B), if for some reason the defendant fails to file the underlying motion for new trial within the specified time, the court may nonetheless consider that untimely underlying motion if the court determines that the failure to file it on time was the result of excusable neglect.

Notes of Advisory Committee on 2009 amendments. Former Rules 29, 33, and 34 adopted 7-day periods for their respective motions. This period has been expanded to 14 days. Experience has proved that in many cases it is not possible to prepare a satisfactory motion in 7 days, even under the former rule that excluded intermediate Saturdays, Sundays, and legal holidays. This led to frequent requests for continuances, and the filing of bare bones motions that required later supplementation. The 14-day period—including intermediate Saturdays, Sundays, and legal holidays as provided by Rule 45(a)—sets a more realistic time for the filing of these motions.

Rule 34. Arresting Judgment

(a) In General. Upon the defendant's motion or on its own, the court must arrest judgment if the court does not have jurisdiction of the charged offense.

(b) Time to File. The defendant must move to arrest judgment within 14 days after the court accepts a verdict or finding of guilty, or after a plea of guilty or nolo contendere.

HISTORY:

Dec. 26, 1944, eff. March 21, 1946, as amended Feb. 28, 1966, eff. July 1, 1966; April 29, 2002, eff. Dec. 1, 2002; April 25, 2005, eff. Dec. 1, 2005; March 26, 2009, eff. Dec. 1, 2009; April 25, 2014, eff. Dec. 1, 2014.

HISTORY; ANCILLARY LAWS AND DIRECTIVES

Other provisions:

Notes of Advisory Committee on Rules. This rule continues existing law except that it enlarges the time for making motions in arrest of judgment from 3 days to 5 days. See Rule II (2) of Criminal Appeals Rules of 1933, 292 USC 661 [18 USC formerly following § 688].

Notes of Advisory Committee on 1966 amendments. The words "on motion of a defendant" are added to make clear here, as in Rule 33, that the court may act only pursuant to a timely motion by the defendant.

The amendment to the second sentence is designed to clarify an ambiguity in the rule as originally drafted. In Lott v United States, 367 US 421, 6 L Ed 2d 940, 81 S Ct 1563 (1961) the Supreme Court held that when a defendant pleaded nolo contendere the time in which a motion could be made under this rule did not begin to run until entry of the judgment. The Court held that such a plea was not a "determination of guilt." No reason of policy appears to justify having the time for making this motion commence with the verdict or finding of guilt but not with the acceptance of the plea of nolo contendere or the plea of guilty. The amendment changes the result in the Lott case and makes the periods uniform. The amendment also changes the time in which the motion may be made to 7 days. See the Advisory Committee's Note to Rule 29.

Notes of Advisory Committee on 2002 amendments. The language of Rule 34 has been amended as part of the general restyling of the Criminal Rules to make them more easily understood and to make style and terminology consistent throughout the rules. These changes are intended to be stylistic only.

Notes of Advisory Committee on 2005 amendments. Rule 34(b) has been amended to remove the requirement that the court must act within seven days after the court accepts a verdict or finding of guilty, or after a plea of guilty or nolo contendere if it sets another time for filing a motion to arrest a judgment. The amendment parallels similar amendments to Rules 29 and 33. Further, a conforming amendment has been made to Rule 45(b).

Currently, Rule 34(b) requires the defendant to move to arrest judgment within seven days after the court accepts a verdict or finding of guilty, or after a plea of guilty or nolo contendere, or within some other time set by the court in an order issued by the court within that same seven-day period. Similar provisions exist in Rules 29 and 33. Courts have held that the seven-day rule is jurisdictional. Thus, if a defendant files a request for an extension of time to file a motion to arrest judgment within the seven-day period, the judge must rule on that motion or request within the same seven-day period. If for some reason the court does not rule on the request within the seven days, the court loses jurisdiction to act on the underlying substantive motion, if it is not filed within the seven days. *See, e.g., United States v. Smith*, 331 U.S. 469, 473–474 (1947) (rejecting argument that trial court had power to grant new trial on its own motion after expiration of time in Rule 33); *United States v. Marquez*, 291 F.3d 23, 27–28 (D.C. Cir. 2002) (citing language of Rule 33, and holding that "district court forfeited the power to act when it failed to . . . fix a new time for filing a motion for a new trial within seven days of the verdict").

Assuming that the current rule was intended to promote finality, there is nothing to prevent the court from granting the defendant a significant extension of time, so long as it does so within the seven-day period. Thus, the Committee believed that the rule should be amended to be consistent with all of the other timing requirements in the rules, which do not force the court to rule on a motion to extend the time for filing within a particular period of time or lose jurisdiction to do so.

Accordingly, the amendment deletes the language regarding the court's acting within seven days to set the time for filing. Read in conjunction with the conforming amendment to Rule 45(b), the defendant is still required to file a timely motion to arrest judgment under Rule 34 within the seven-day period specified. The defendant may, under Rule 45, seek an extension of time to file the underlying motion as long as the defendant does so within the seven-day period. But the court itself is not required to act on that motion within any particular time. Further, under Rule 45(b)(1)(B), if for some reason the defendant fails to file the underlying motion within the specified time, the court may nonetheless consider that untimely motion if the court determines that the failure to file it on time was the result of excusable neglect.

Notes of Advisory Committee on 2009 amendments. Former Rules 29, 33, and 34 adopted 7-day periods for their respective motions. This period has been expanded to 14 days. Experience has proved that in many cases it is not possible to prepare a satisfactory motion in 7 days, even under the former rule that excluded intermediate Saturdays, Sundays, and legal holidays. This led to frequent requests for continuances, and the filing of bare bones motions that required later supplementation. The 14-day period—including intermediate Saturdays, Sundays, and legal holidays as provided by Rule 45(a)—sets a more realistic time for the filing of these motions.

Notes of Advisory Committee on 2014 amendments. *Rule 34(a).* This amendment conforms Rule 34 to Rule 12(b) which has been amended to remove language that the court at any time while the case is pending may hear a claim that the "indictment or information fails . . . to state an offense." The amended Rule 12 instead requires that such a defect be raised before trial.

Rule 35. Correcting or Reducing a Sentence

(a) Correcting Clear Error. Within 14 days after sentencing, the court may correct a sentence that resulted from arithmetical, technical, or other clear error.

(b) Reducing a Sentence for Substantial Assistance.

(1) *In General.* Upon the government's motion made within one year of sentencing, the court may reduce a sentence if the defendant, after sentencing, provided substantial assistance in investigating or prosecuting another person.

(2) *Later Motion.* Upon the government's motion made more than one year after sentencing, the court may reduce a sentence if the defendant's substantial assistance involved:

(A) information not known to the defendant until one year or more after sentencing;

(B) information provided by the defendant to the government within one year of sentencing, but which did not become useful to the government until more than one year after sentencing; or

(C) information the usefulness of which could not reasonably have been anticipated by the defendant until more than one year after sentencing and which was promptly provided to the government after its usefulness was reasonably apparent to the defendant.

(3) *Evaluating Substantial Assistance.* In evaluating whether the defendant has provided substantial assistance, the court may consider the defendant's presentence assistance.

(4) *Below Statutory Minimum.* When acting under Rule 35(b), the court may reduce the sentence to a level below the minimum sentence established by statute.

(c) "Sentencing" Defined. As used in this rule, "sentencing" means the oral announcement of the sentence.

HISTORY:

Dec. 26, 1944, eff. March 21, 1946, as amended Feb. 28, 1966, eff. July 1, 1966; April 30, 1979, eff. Aug. 1, 1979; April 28, 1983, eff. Aug. 1, 1983; Oct. 12, 1984, P. L. 98-473, Title II, Ch II, § 215(b), 98 Stat. 2015; April 29, 1985, eff. Aug 1, 1985 until Nov. 1, 1986, extended to Nov. 1, 1987; Oct. 27, 1986, P. L. 99-570, Title I, Subtitle A, § 1009(a), 100 Stat. 3207-8, eff. Nov. 1, 1987; April 30, 1991, eff. Dec. 1, 1991; April 24, 1998, eff. Dec. 1, 1998; April 29, 2002, eff. Dec. 1, 2002; April 26, 2004, eff. Dec. 1, 2004; April 30, 2007, eff. Dec. 1, 2007; March 26, 2009, eff. Dec. 1, 2009.

HISTORY; ANCILLARY LAWS AND DIRECTIVES

Other provisions:

Notes of Advisory Committee on Rules. The first sentence of the rule continues existing law. The second sentence introduces a flexible time limitation on the power of the court to reduce a sentence, in lieu of the present limitation of the term of court. Rule 45(c) abolishes the expiration of a term of court as a time limitation, thereby necessitating the introduction of a specific time limitation as to all proceedings now governed by the term of court as a limitation. The Federal Rules of Civil Procedure (Rule 6(c)), 28 USC Appendix [Federal Rules of Civil Procedure, USCS Court Rules, Rule 6(c)], abolishes the term of court as a time limitation in respect to civil actions. The two rules together thus do away with the significance of the expiration of a term of court which has largely become an anachronism.

Notes of Advisory Committee on 1966 amendments. The amendment to the first sentence gives the court power to correct a sentence imposed in an illegal manner within the same time limits as those provided for reducing a sentence. In Hill v United States, 368 US 424, 7 L Ed 2d

417, 82 S Ct 468 (1962) the court held that a motion to correct an illegal sentence was not an appropriate way for a defendant to raise the question whether when he appeared for sentencing the court had afforded him an opportunity to make a statement in his own behalf as required by Rule 32(a). The amendment recognizes the distinction between an illegal sentence, which may be corrected at any time, and a sentence imposed in an illegal manner, and provides a limited time for correcting the latter.

The second sentence has been amended to increase the time within which the court may act from 60 days to 120 days. The 60-day period is frequently too short to enable the defendant to obtain and file the evidence, information and argument to support a reduction in sentence. Especially where a defendant has been committed to an institution at a distance from the sentencing court, the delays involved in institutional mail inspection procedures and the time required to contact relatives, friends and counsel may result in the 60-day period passing before the court is able to consider the case.

The other amendments to the second sentence clarify ambiguities in the timing provisions. In those cases in which the mandate of the court of appeals is issued prior to action by the Supreme Court on the defendant's petition for certiorari, the rule created problems in three situations: (1) If the writ were denied, the last phrase of the rule left obscure the point at which the period began to run because orders of the Supreme Court denying applications for writs are not sent to the district courts. See Johnson v United States, 235 F2d 459 (5th Cir 1956). (2) If the writ were granted but later dismissed as improvidently granted, the rule did not provide any time period for reduction of sentence. (3) If the writ were granted and later the Court affirmed a judgment of the court of appeals which had affirmed the conviction, the rule did not provide any time period for reduction of sentence. The amendment makes it clear that in each of these three situations the 120-day period commences to run with the entry of the order or judgment of the Supreme Court.

The third sentence has been added to make it clear that the time limitation imposed by Rule 35 upon the reduction of a sentence does not apply to such reduction upon the revocation of probation as authorized by 18 USC § 3653.

Notes of Advisory Committee on 1979 amendments. Rule 35 is amended in order to make it clear that a judge may, in his discretion, reduce a sentence of incarceration to probation. To the extent that this permits the judge to grant probation to a defendant who has already commenced service of a term of imprisonment, it represents a change in the law. See United States v. Murray, 275 U.S. 347 (1928) (Probation Act construed not to give power to district court to grant probation to convict after beginning of service of sentence, even in the same term of court); Affronti v. United States, 350 U.S. 79 (1955) (Probation Act construed to mean that after a sentence of consecutive terms on multiple counts of an indictment has been imposed and service of sentence for the first such term has commenced, the district court may not suspend sentence and grant probation as to the remaining term or terms). In construing the statute in Murray and Affronti, the Court concluded Congress could not have intended to make the probation provisions applicable during the *entire* period of incarceration (the only other conceivable interpretation of the statute), for this would result in undue duplication of the three methods of mitigating a sentence--probation, pardon and parole--and would impose upon district judges the added burden of responding to probation applications from prisoners throughout the service of their terms of imprisonment. Those concerns do not apply to the instant provisions, for the reduction may occur only within the time specified in subdivision (b). This change gives "meaningful effect" to the motion-to-reduce remedy by allowing the court "to consider all alternatives that were available at the time of imposition of the original sentence." United States v. Golphin, 362 F.Supp. 698 (W.D. Pa. 1973).

Should the reduction to a sentence of probation occur after the defendant has been incarcerated more than six months, this would put into issue the applicability of 18 U.S.C. § 3651, which provides that initially the court "may impose a sentence in excess of six months and provide that the defendant be confined in a jail-type institution for a period not exceeding six months and that the execution of the remainder of the sentence be suspended and the defendant placed on probation for such period and upon such terms and conditions as the court deems best.".

Notes of Advisory Committee on 1983 amendments. *Note to Subdivision (b).* There is currently a split of authority on the question of whether a court may reduce a sentence within 120 days after revocation of probation when the sentence was imposed earlier but execution of the sentence had in the interim been suspended in part or in its entirety. Compare *United States v. Colvin,* 644 F.2d 703 (8th Cir. 1981) (yes); *United States v. Johnson,* 634 F.2d 94 (3d Cir. 1980) (yes); with *United States v. Rice,* 671 F.2d 455 (11th Cir. 1982) (no); *United States v. Kahane,* 527 F.2d 491 (2d Cir. 1975) (no). The Advisory Committee believes that the rule should be clarified in light of this split, and has concluded that as a policy matter the result reached in *Johnson* is preferable.

The Supreme Court declared in *Korematsu v. United States,* 319 U.S. 432, 435 (1943), that "the difference to the probationer between imposition of sentence followed by probation . . . and suspension of the imposition of sentence [followed by probation]" is not a meaningful one. When imposition of sentence is suspended entirely at the time a defendant is placed on probation, that defendant has 120 days after revocation of probation and imposition of sentence to petition for leniency. The amendment to subdivision (b) makes it clear that similar treatment is to be afforded probationers for whom execution, rather than imposition, of sentence was originally suspended.

The change facilitates the underlying objective of rule 35, which is to "give every convicted defendant a second round before the sentencing judge, and [afford] the judge an opportunity to reconsider the sentence in the light of any further information about the defendant or the case which may have been presented to him in the interim." *United States v. Ellenbogan,* 390 F.2d 537, 543 (2d Cir. 1968). It is only technically correct that a reduction may be sought when a suspended sentence is imposed. As noted in *Johnson,* supra, at 96:

It frequently will be unrealistic for a defendant whose sentence has just been suspended to petition the court for the further relief of a reduction of that suspended sentence.

Just as significant, we doubt that sentencing judges would be very receptive to Rule 35 motions proffered at the time the execution of a term of imprisonment is suspended in whole or in part and the defendant given a term of probation. Moreover, the sentencing judge cannot know of events that might occur later and that might bear on what would constitute an appropriate term of imprisonment should the defendant violate his probation. . . . In particular, it is only with the revocation hearing that the judge is in a position to consider whether a sentence originally suspended pending probation should be reduced. The revocation hearing is thus the first point at which an offender can be afforded a realistic opportunity to plead for a light sentence. If the offender is to be provided two chances with the sentencing judge, to be meaningful this second sentence must occur subsequent to the revocation hearing.

Notes of Advisory Committee on 1985 amendments. In an order dated April 29, 1985, the Supreme Court stated that the amendment to Rule 35(b) shall (1) take effect on August 1, 1985, (2) govern all proceedings in criminal cases thereafter commenced and, insofar as just and practicable, all proceedings in criminal cases then pending, and (3) be effective until November 1, 1986, when § 215(b) of the Comprehensive Crime Control Act of 1984 (Act Oct. 12, 1984, P. L. 98-473, 98 Stat. 2015) goes into effect. [Based on an amendment made by Act Dec. 26, 1985, P. L. 99-217, § 4, 99 Stat. 1728, which appears as 18 USCS § 3551 note, the 1985 amendment would be effective until November 1, 1987.]

This amendment to Rule 35(b) conforms its language to the nonliteral interpretation which most courts have already placed upon the rule, namely, that it suffices that the defendant's motion was made within the 120 days and that the court determines the motion within a reasonable time thereafter. *United States* v. *DeMier,* 671 F.2d 1200 (8th Cir. 1982); *United States* v. *Smith,* 650 F.2d 206 (9th Cir. 1981); *United States* v. *Johnson,* 634 F.2d 94 (3d Cir. 1980); *United States* v. *Mendoza,* 581 F.2d 89 (5th Cir. 1978); *United States* v. *Stollings,* 516 F.2d 1287 (4th Cir. 1975). Despite these decisions, a change in the language is deemed desirable to remove any doubt which might arise from dictum in some cases, e.g., *United States* v. *Addonizio,* 442 U.S. 178, 189 (1979), that Rule 35 only "authorizes District Courts to reduce a sentence within 120 days" and that this time period "is jurisdictional, and may not be extended." See *United States* v. *Kajevic,* 711 F.2d 767 (7th Cir. 1983), following the *Addonizio* dictum.

As for the "reasonable time" limitation, reasonableness in this context "must be evaluated in light of the policies supporting the time limitations and the reasons for the delay in each case." *United States* v. *Smith, supra,* at 209. The time runs "at least for so long as the judge reasonably needs time to consider and act upon the motion." *United States* v. *Stollings,* supra, at 1288.

In some instances the court may decide to reduce a sentence even though no motion seeking such action is before the court. When that is the case, the amendment makes clear, the reduction must actually occur within the time specified.

This amendment does not preclude the filing of a motion by a defendant for further reduction of sentence after the court has reduced a sentence on its own motion, if filed within the 120 days specified in this rule.

Effective date of Oct. 27, 1986 amendment. Act Oct. 27, 1986, P. L. 99-570, Title I, Subtitle A, § 1009(b), 100 Stat. 3207-8, provides: "The amendment made by this section [amending subdiv. (b) of this Rule] shall take effect on the date of the taking effect of rule 35(b) of the Federal Rules of Criminal Procedure, as amended by section 215(b) of the Comprehensive Crime Control Act of 1984.".

Application of Rule 35(b) to conduct occurring before effective date of sentencing guidelines. Act Dec. 7, 1987, P. L. 100-182, § 22, 101 Stat. 1271, applicable as provided by § 26 of such Act, which appears as 18 USCS § 3006A note, provides: "The amendment to rule 35(b) of the Federal Rules of Criminal Procedure made by the order of the Supreme Court on April 29, 1985, shall apply with respect to all offenses committed before the taking effect of section 215(b) of the Comprehensive Crime Control Act of 1984 [amending this Rule].".

Authority to lower a sentence below a statutory minimum for old offenses. Act Dec. 7, 1987, P. L. 100-182, § 24, 101 Stat. 1271, which appears as 18 USCS § 3553 note, provides, inter alia, that subsec. (b) of this rule as amended by § 215(b) of the Comprehensive Crime Control Act of 1984 and subsec. (b) of this rule as in effect before the taking effect of the initial set of guidelines promulgated by the United States Sentencing Commission shall apply in the case of an offense committed before the taking effect of such guidelines.

Notes of Advisory Committee on 1991 amendments. Rule 35(b), as amended in 1987 as part of the Sentencing Reform Act of 1984, reflects a method by which the government may obtain valuable assistance from defendants in return for an agreement to file a motion to reduce the sentence, even if the reduction would reduce the sentence below the mandatory minimum sentence.

The title of subsection (b) has been amended to reflect that there is a difference between correcting an illegal or improper sentence, as in subsection (a), and reducing an otherwise legal sentence for special reasons under subsection (b).

Under the 1987 amendment, the trial court was required to rule on the government's motion to reduce a defendant's sentence within one year after imposition of the sentence. This caused problems, however, in situations where the defendant's assistance could not be fully assessed in time to make a timely motion which could be ruled upon before one year had elapsed. The amendment requires the government to make its motion to reduce the sentence before one year has elapsed but does not require the court to rule on the motion within the one year limit. This change should benefit both the government and the defendant and will permit completion of the defendant's anticipated cooperation with the government. Although no specific time limit is set on the court's ruling on the motion to reduce the sentence, the burden nonetheless rests on the government to request and justify a delay in the court's ruling.

The amendment also recognizes that there may be those cases where the defendant's assistance or cooperation may not occur until after one year has elapsed. For example, the defendant may not have obtained information useful to the government until after the time limit had passed. In those instances the trial court in its discretion may consider what would otherwise be an untimely motion if the government establishes that the cooperation could not have been furnished within the one-year time limit. In deciding whether to consider an untimely motion, the court may, for example, consider whether the assistance was provided as early as possible.

Subdivision (c) is intended to adopt, in part, a suggestion from the Federal Courts Study Committee 1990 that Rule 35 be amended to recognize explicitly the ability of the sentencing court to correct a sentence imposed as a result of an obvious arithmetical, technical or other clear error, if the error is discovered shortly after the sentence is imposed. At least two courts of appeals have held that the trial court has the inherent authority, notwithstanding the repeal of former Rule 35(a) by the Sentencing Reform Act of 1984, to correct a sentence within the time allowed for sentence appeal by any party under 18 U.S.C. 3742. See United States v. Cook, 890 F.2d 672 (4th Cir. 1989) error in applying sentencing guidelines; United States v. Rico, 902 F.2d 1065 (2nd Cir. 1990) (failure to impose prison sentence required by terms of plea agreement). The amendment in effect codifies the result in those two cases but provides a more stringent time requirement. The Committee believed that the time for correcting such errors should be narrowed within the time for appealing the sentence to reduce the likelihood of jurisdictional questions in the event of an appeal and to provide the parties with an opportunity to address the court's correction of the sentence, or lack thereof, in any appeal of the sentence. A shorter period of time would also reduce the likelihood of abuse of the rule by limiting its application to acknowledged and obvious errors in sentencing.

The authority to correct a sentence under this subdivision is intended to be very narrow and to extend only to those cases in which an obvious error or mistake has occurred in the sentence, that is, errors which would almost certainly result in a remand of the case to the trial court for further action under Rule 35(a). The subdivision is not intended to afford the court the opportunity to reconsider the application or interpretation of the sentencing guidelines or for the court simply to change its mind about the appropriateness of the sentence. Nor should it be used to reopen issues previously resolved at the sentencing hearing through the exercise of the court's discretion with regard to the application of the sentencing guidelines. Furthermore, the Committee did not intend that the rule relax any requirement that the parties state all objections to a sentence at or before the sentencing hearing. See, e.g., United States v. Jones, 899 F.2d 1097 (11th Cir. 1990).

The subdivision does not provide for any formalized method of bringing the error to the attention of the court and recognizes that the court could sua sponte make the correction. Although the amendment does not expressly address the issue of advance notice to the parties or whether the defendant should be present in court for resentencing, the Committee contemplates that the court will act in accordance with Rules 32 and 43 with regard to any corrections in the sentence. Compare United States v. Cook, supra (court erred in correcting sentence sua sponte in absence of defendant) with United States v. Rico, supra (court heard arguments on request by government to correct sentence). The Committee contemplates that the court would enter an order correcting the sentence and that such order must be entered within the seven (7) day period so that the appellate process (if a timely appeal is taken) may proceed without delay and without jurisdictional confusion.

Rule 35(c) provides an efficient and prompt method for correcting obvious technical errors that are called to the court's attention immediately after sentencing. But the addition of this subdivision is not intended to preclude a defendant from obtaining statutory relief from a plainly illegal sentence. The Committee's assumption is that a defendant detained pursuant to such a sentence could seek relief under 28 U.S.C. § 2255 if the seven day period provided in Rule 35(c) has elapsed. Rule 35(c) and § 2255 should thus provide sufficient authority for a district court to correct obvious sentencing errors.

The Committee considered, but rejected, a proposal from the Federal Courts Study Committee to permit modification of a sentence, within 120 days of sentencing, based upon new factual information not known to the defendant at the time of sentencing. Unlike the proposed subdivision (c) which addresses obvious technical mistakes, the ability of the defendant (and perhaps the government) to come forward with new evidence would be a significant step toward returning Rule 35 to its former state. The Committee believed that such a change would inject into Rule 35 a degree of post-sentencing discretion which would raise doubts about the finality of determinate sentencing that Congress attempted to resolve by eliminating former Rule 35(a). It would also tend to confuse the jurisdiction of the courts of appeals in those cases in which a timely appeal is taken with respect to the sentence. Finally, the Committee was not persuaded by the available evidence that a problem of sufficient magnitude existed at this time which would warrant such an amendment.

Notes of Advisory Committee on 1998 amendments. The amendment to Rule 35(b) is intended to fill a gap in current practice. Under the Sentencing Reform Act and the applicable guidelines, a defendant who has provided "substantial" assistance to the Government before sentencing may receive a reduced sentence under United States Sentencing Guideline § 5K1.1. In addition, a defendant who provides substantial assistance after the sentence has been imposed may receive a reduction of the sentence if the Government files a motion under Rule 35(b). In theory, a defendant who has provided substantial assistance both before and after sentencing could benefit from both § 5K1.1 and Rule 35(b). But a defendant who has provided, on the whole, substantial assistance may not be able to benefit from either provision because each provision requires "substantial assistance." As one court has noted, those two provisions contain distinct "temporal boundaries." *United States v. Drown,* 942 F.2d 55, 59 (1st Cir. 1991).

Although several decisions suggest that a court may aggregate the defendant's pre-sentencing and post-sentencing assistance in determining whether the "substantial assistance" requirement of Rule 35(b) has been met, *United States v. Speed,* 53 F.3d 643, 647–649 (4th Cir. 1995) (Ellis, J. concurring), there is no formal mechanism for doing so. The amendment to Rule 35(b) is designed to fill that need. Thus, the amendment permits the court to consider, in determining the substantiality of post-sentencing assistance, the defendant's pre-sentencing assistance, irrespective of whether that assistance, standing alone, was substantial.

The amendment, however, is not intended to provide a double benefit to the defendant. Thus, if the defendant has already received a reduction of sentence under U.S.S.G. § 5K1.1 for substantial pre-sentencing assistance, he or she may not have that assistance counted again in a post-sentence Rule 35(b) motion.

Notes of Advisory Committee on 2002 amendments. The language of Rule 35 has been amended as part of the general restyling of the Criminal Rules to make them more easily understood and to make style and terminology consistent throughout the rules. These changes are intended to be stylistic only, except as noted below.

The Committee deleted current Rule 35(a) (Correction on Remand). Congress added that rule, which currently addresses the issue of the district court's actions following a remand on the issue of sentencing, in the Sentencing Reform Act of 1984. Pub. L. No. 98-473. The rule cross-references 18 U.S.C. § 3742, also enacted in 1984, which provides detailed guidance on the various options available to the appellate courts in addressing sentencing errors. In reviewing both provisions, the Committee concluded that Rule 35(a) was no longer needed. First, the statute clearly covers the subject matter and second, it is not necessary to address an issue that would be very clear to a district court following a decision by a court of appeals.

Former Rule 35(c), which addressed the authority of the court to correct certain errors in the sentence, is now located in Rule 35(a). In the current version of Rule 35(c), the sentencing court is authorized to correct errors in the sentence if the correction is made within seven days of the imposition of the sentence. The revised rule uses the term "sentencing." No change in practice is intended by using that term.

A substantive change has been made in revised Rule 35(b). Under current Rule 35(b), if the government believes that a sentenced defendant has provided substantial assistance in investigating or prosecuting another person, it may move the court to reduce the original sentence; ordinarily, the motion must be filed within one year of sentencing. In 1991, the rule was amended to permit the government to file such motions after more than one year had elapsed if the government could show that the defendant's substantial assistance involved "information or evidence not known by the defendant" until more than one year had elapsed. The current rule, however, did not address the question whether a motion to reduce a sentence could be filed and granted in those instances when the defendant's substantial assistance involved information provided by the defendant within one year of sentence but that did not become useful to the government until more than one year after sentencing (e.g., when the government starts an investigation to which the information is pertinent). The courts were split on the issue. *Compare United States v. Morales,* 52 F.3d 7 (1st Cir. 1995) permitting filing and granting of motion with *United States v. Orozco,* 160 F.3d 1309 (11th Cir. 1998) (denying relief and citing cases). Although the court in *Orozco* felt constrained to deny relief under Rule 35(b), the court urged an amendment of the rule to:

> address the apparent unforeseen situation presented in this case where a convicted defendant provides information to the government prior to the expiration of the jurisdictional, one-year period from sentence imposition, but that information does not become useful to the government until more than one year after sentence imposition. *Id.* at 1316, n. 13.

Nor does the existing rule appear to allow a substantial assistance motion under equally deserving circumstances where a defendant, who fails to provide information within one year of sentencing because its usefulness could not reasonably have been anticipated, later provides the information to the government promptly upon its usefulness becoming apparent.

Revised Rule 35(b) is intended to address both of those situations. First, Rule 35(b)(2)(B) makes clear that a sentence reduction motion is permitted in those instances identified by the court in *Orozco.* Second, Rule 35(b)(2)(C) recognizes that a postsentence motion is also appropriate in those instances where the defendant did not provide any information within one year of sentencing, because its usefulness was not reasonably apparent to the defendant during that period. But the rule requires that once the defendant realizes the importance of the information the defendant promptly provide the information to the government. What constitutes "prompt" notification will depend on the circumstances of the case.

The rule's one-year restriction generally serves the important interests of finality and of creating an incentive for defendants to provide promptly what useful information they might have. Thus, the proposed amendment would not eliminate the one-year requirement as a generally operative element. But where the usefulness of the information is not reasonably apparent until a year or more after sentencing, no sound purpose is served by the current rule's removal of any incentive to provide that information to the government one year or more after the sentence (or if previously provided, for the government to seek to reward the defendant) when its relevance and substantiality become evident.

By using the term "involves" in Rule 35(b)(2) in describing the sort of information that may result in substantial assistance, the Committee recognizes that a court does not lose jurisdiction to consider a Rule 35(b)(2) motion simply because other information, not covered by any of the three provisions in Rule 35(b)(2), is presented in the motion.

Notes of Advisory Committee on 2004 amendments. Rule 35(c) is a new provision, which defines sentencing for purposes of Rule 35 as the oral announcement of the sentence.

Originally, the language in Rule 35 had used the term "imposition of sentence." The term "imposition of sentence" was not defined in the rule and the courts addressing the meaning of the term were split. The majority view was that the term meant the oral announcement of the sentence and the minority view was that it meant the entry of the judgment. *See United States v. Aguirre,* 214 F.3d 1122, 1124–25 (9th Cir. 2000) (discussion of original Rule 35(c) and citing cases). During the restyling of all of the Criminal Rules in 2000 and 2001, the Committee determined that the uniform term "sentencing" throughout the entire rule was the more appropriate term. After further reflection, and with the recognition that some ambiguity may still be present in using the term "sentencing," the Committee believes that the better approach is to make clear in the rule itself that the term "sentencing" in Rule 35 means the oral announcement of the sentence. That is the meaning recognized in the majority of the cases addressing the issue.

Notes of Advisory Committee on 2007 amendments. *Subdivision (b)(1).* The amendment conforms Rule 35(b)(1) to the Supreme Court's decision in *United States v. Booker,* 543 U.S. 220 (2005). In *Booker* the Court held that the provision of the federal sentencing statute that makes the Guidelines mandatory, 18 U.S.C. § 3553(b)(1), violates the Sixth Amendment right to jury trial. With this provision severed and excised, the Court held, the Sentencing Reform Act "makes the Guidelines effectively advisory," and "requires a sentencing court to consider Guidelines ranges, see 18 U.S.C.A. § 3553(a)(4) (Supp.2004), but it permits the court to tailor the sentence in light of other statutory concerns as well, see § 3553(a) (Supp.2004)." *Id.* at 245–46. Subsection (b)(1)(B) has been deleted because it treats the guidelines as mandatory.

Notes of Advisory Committee on 2009 amendments. Former Rule 35 permitted the correction of arithmetic, technical, or clear errors within 7 days of sentencing. In light of the increased complexity of the sentencing process, the Committee concluded it would be beneficial to expand this period to 14 days, including intermediate Saturdays, Sundays, and legal holidays as provided by Rule 45(a). Extension of the period in this fashion will cause no jurisdictional problems if an appeal has been filed, because Federal Rule of Appellate Procedure 4(b)(5) expressly provides that the filing of a notice of appeal does not divest the district court of jurisdiction to correct a sentence under Rule 35(a).

Amendments:

1984.

Act Oct. 12, 1984 (effective on the first day of the first calendar month beginning 36 months after enactment, as provided by § 235(a)(1) of such Act, as amended by Act Dec. 26, 1985, P. L. 99-217, § 4, 99 Stat. 1728, which appears as 18 USCS § 3551 note, and applicable as provided by such § 235, which appears as 18 USCS § 3551 note) substituted this Rule for one which read:

"Rule 35. Correction or reduction of sentence.

"(a) Correction of sentence. The court may correct an illegal sentence at any time and may correct a sentence imposed in an illegal manner within the time provided herein for the reduction of sentence.

"(b) Reduction of sentence. A motion to reduce a sentence may be made, or the court may reduce a sentence without motion, within 120 days after the sentence is imposed or probation is revoked, or within 120 days after receipt by the court of a mandate issued upon affirmance of the judgment or dismissal of the appeal, or within 120 days after entry of any order or judgment of the Supreme Court denying review of, or having the effect of upholding, a judgment of conviction or probation revocation. The court shall determine the motion within a reasonable time. Changing a sentence from a sentence of incarceration to a grant of probation shall constitute a permissible reduction of sentence under this subdivision.".

1986.

Act Oct. 27, 1986 (effective as provided by § 1009(b) of such Act, which appears as a note to this section), in subdiv. (b) substituted "in accordance with the guidelines and policy statements issued by the Sentencing Commission pursuant to section 994 of title 28, United States Code. The court's authority to lower a sentence under this subdivision includes the authority to lower such sentence to a level below that established by statute as a minimum sentence." for "to the extent that such assistance is a factor in applicable guidelines or policy statements issued by the Sentencing Commission pursuant to 28 U.S.C. 994(a).".

Rule 36. Clerical Error

After giving any notice it considers appropriate, the court may at any time correct a clerical error in a judgment, order, or other part of the record, or correct an error in the record arising from oversight or omission.

HISTORY:

Dec. 26, 1944, eff. March 21, 1946; April 29, 2002, eff. Dec. 1, 2002.

HISTORY; ANCILLARY LAWS AND DIRECTIVES

Other provisions:

Notes of Advisory Committee on Rules. This rule continues existing law. Rupinski v United States, 4 F2d 17, CCA 6th. The rule is similar to Rule 60(a) of the Federal Rules of Civil Procedure, 28 USC, Appendix [Federal Rules of Civil Procedure, USCS Court Rules, Rule 60(a)].

Notes of Advisory Committee on 2002 amendments. The language of Rule 36 has been amended as part of the general restyling of the Criminal Rules to make them more easily understood and to make style and terminology consistent throughout the rules. These changes are intended to be stylistic only.

Rule 37. Indicative Ruling on a Motion for Relief that is Barred by a Pending Appeal

(a) Relief pending appeal. If a timely motion is made for relief that the court lacks authority to grant because of an appeal that has been docketed and is pending, the court may:

(1) defer considering the motion;

(2) deny the motion; or

(3) state either that it would grant the motion if the court of appeals remands for that purpose or that the motion raises a substantial issue.

(b) Notice to the Court of Appeals. The movant must promptly notify the circuit clerk under Federal Rule of Appellate Procedure 12.1 if the district court states that it would grant the motion or that the motion raises a substantial issue.

(c) Remand. The district court may decide the motion if the court of appeals remands for that purpose.

HISTORY:

As added Apr. 23, 2012, eff. Dec. 1, 2012.

HISTORY; ANCILLARY LAWS AND DIRECTIVES

Other provisions:

Notes of Advisory Committee. This new rule adopts for any motion that the district court cannot grant because of a pending appeal the practice that most courts follow when a party makes a motion under Rule 60(b) of the Federal Rules of Civil Procedure to vacate a judgment that is pending on appeal. After an appeal has been docketed and while it remains pending, the district court cannot grant a Rule 60(b) motion without a remand. But it can entertain the motion and deny it, defer consideration, or state that it would grant the motion if the court of appeals remands for that purpose or state that the motion raises a substantial issue. Experienced lawyers often refer to the suggestion for remand as an "indicative ruling." (Federal Rule of Appellate Procedure 4(b)(3) lists three motions that, if filed within the relevant time limit, suspend the effect of a notice of appeal filed before or after the motion is filed until the judgment of conviction is entered and the last such motion is ruled upon. The district court has authority to grant the motion without resorting to the indicative ruling procedure.).

The procedure formalized by Federal Rule of Appellate Procedure 12.1 is helpful when relief is sought from an order that the court cannot reconsider because the order is the subject of a pending appeal. In the criminal context, the

Committee anticipates that Criminal Rule 37 will be used primarily if not exclusively for newly discovered evidence motions under Criminal Rule 33(b)(1) (*see United States v. Cronic*, 466 U.S. 648, 667 n.42 (1984)), reduced sentence motions under Criminal Rule 35(b), and motions under 18 U.S.C. § 3582(c). Rule 37 does not attempt to define the circumstances in which an appeal limits or defeats the district court's authority to act in the face of a pending appeal. The rules that govern the relationship between trial courts and appellate courts may be complex, depending in part on the nature of the order and the source of appellate jurisdiction. Rule 37 applies only when those rules deprive the district court of authority to grant relief without appellate permission. If the district court concludes that it has authority to grant relief without appellate permission, it can act without falling back on the indicative ruling procedure.

To ensure proper coordination of proceedings in the district court and in the appellate court, the movant must notify the circuit clerk under Federal Rule of Appellate Procedure 12.1 if the district court states that it would grant the motion or that the motion raises a substantial issue. Remand is in the court of appeals' discretion under Federal Rule of Appellate Procedure 12.1.

Often it will be wise for the district court to determine whether it in fact would grant the motion if the court of appeals remands for that purpose. But a motion may present complex issues that require extensive litigation and that may either be mooted or be presented in a different context by decision of the issues raised on appeal. In such circumstances the district court may prefer to state that the motion raises a substantial issue, and to state the reasons why it prefers to decide only if the court of appeals agrees that it would be useful to decide the motion before decision of the pending appeal. The district court is not bound to grant the motion after stating that the motion raises a substantial issue; further proceedings on remand may show that the motion ought not be granted.

Rule 38. Staying a Sentence or a Disability

(a) Death Sentence. The court must stay a death sentence if the defendant appeals the conviction or sentence.

(b) Imprisonment.

(1) *Stay Granted.* If the defendant is released pending appeal, the court must stay a sentence of imprisonment.

(2) *Stay Denied; Place of Confinement.* If the defendant is not released pending appeal, the court may recommend to the Attorney General that the defendant be confined near the place of the trial or appeal for a period reasonably necessary to permit the defendant to assist in preparing the appeal.

(c) Fine. If the defendant appeals, the district court, or the court of appeals under Federal Rule of Appellate Procedure 8, may stay a sentence to pay a fine or a fine and costs. The court may stay the sentence on any terms considered appropriate and may require the defendant to:

(1) deposit all or part of the fine and costs into the district court's registry pending appeal;

(2) post a bond to pay the fine and costs; or

(3) submit to an examination concerning the defendant's assets and, if appropriate, order the defendant to refrain from dissipating assets.

(d) Probation. If the defendant appeals, the court may stay a sentence of probation. The court must set the terms of any stay.

(e) Restitution and Notice to Victims.

(1) *In General.* If the defendant appeals, the district court, or the court of appeals under Federal Rule of Appellate Procedure 8, may stay—on any terms considered appropriate—any sentence providing for restitution under 18 U.S.C. § 3556 or notice under 18 U.S.C. § 3555.

(2) *Ensuring Compliance.* The court may issue any order reasonably necessary to ensure compliance with a restitution order or a notice order after disposition of an appeal, including:

(A) a restraining order;

(B) an injunction;

(C) an order requiring the defendant to deposit all or part of any monetary restitution into the district court's registry; or

(D) an order requiring the defendant to post a bond.

(f) Forfeiture. A stay of a forfeiture order is governed by Rule 32.2(d).

(g) Disability. If the defendant's conviction or sentence creates a civil or employment disability under federal law, the district court, or the court of appeals under Federal Rule of Appellate Procedure 8, may stay the disability pending appeal on any terms considered appropriate. The court may issue any order reasonably necessary to protect the interest represented by the disability pending appeal, including a restraining order or an injunction.

HISTORY:

As amended Dec. 27, 1948, eff. Jan. 1, 1949; Feb. 28, 1966, eff. July 1, 1966; Dec. 4, 1967, eff. July 1, 1968; April 24, 1972, eff. Oct. 1, 1972; Oct. 12, 1984, P. L. 98-473, Title II, Ch II, § 215(c), 98 Stat. 2016; March 9, 1987, eff. Aug. 1, 1987; April 17, 2000, eff. Dec. 1, 2000; April 29, 2002, eff. Dec. 1, 2002.

HISTORY; ANCILLARY LAWS AND DIRECTIVES

Other provisions:

Notes of Advisory Committee on Rules. This rule substantially continues existing law except that it provides that in case an appeal is taken from a judgment imposing a sentence of imprisonment, a stay shall be granted only if the defendant so elects, or is admitted to bail. Under the present rule the sentence is automatically stayed unless the defendant elects to commence service of the sentence pending appeal. The new rule merely changes the burden of making the election. See Rule V of the Criminal Appeals Rules, 1933, 292 US 661, 78 L Ed 1514 [formerly following 18 USC § 688].

Notes of Advisory Committee on 1966 amendments. A defendant sentenced to a term of imprisonment is committed to the custody of the Attorney General who is empowered by statute to designate the place of his confinement. 18 USC § 4082. The sentencing court has no authority to designate the place of imprisonment. See, e.g., Hogue v United States, 287 F2d 99 (5th Cir. 1961), cert den, 368 US 932, 7 L Ed 2d 195, 82 S Ct 369 (1961).

When the place of imprisonment has been designated, and notwithstanding the pendency of an appeal, the defendant is usually transferred from the place of his temporary detention within the district of his conviction unless he has elected "not to commence service of the sentence." This transfer can be avoided only if the defendant makes the election, a course sometimes advised by counsel who may deem it necessary to consult with the defendant from time to time before the appeal is finally perfected. However, the election deprives the defendant of a right to claim credit for the time spent in jail pending the disposition of the appeal because 18 USC § 3568 provides that the sentence of imprisonment commences, to run only from "the date on which such person is received at the penitentiary, reformatory, or jail for service of said sentence." See, e.g., Shelton v United States, 234 F2d 132 (5th Cir. 1956).

The amendment eliminates the procedure for election not to commence service of sentence. In lieu thereof it is provided that the court may recommend to the Attorney General that the defendant be retained at or transferred to a place of confinement near the place of trial or the place where the appeal is to be heard for the period reasonably necessary to permit the defendant to assist in the preparation of his appeal to the court of appeals. Under this procedure the defendant would no longer be required to serve dead time in a local jail in order to assist in preparation of his appeal.

Notes of Advisory Committee on 1968 amendments. These are the criminal rules relating to appeals, the provisions of which are transferred to and covered by the Federal Rules of Appellate Procedure and (in the case of Rule 37(b) and (c)) by Rules of the Supreme Court.

Notes of Advisory Committee on 1972 amendments. Rule 38(a)(2) is amended to reflect rule 9(b), Federal Rules of Appellate Procedure. The criteria for the stay of a sentence of imprisonment pending disposition of an appeal are those specified in rule 9(c) which incorporates 18 USC § 3148 by reference.

The last sentence of subdivision (a)(2) is retained although easy access to the defendant has become less important with the passage of the Criminal Justice Act which provides for compensation to the attorney to travel to the place at which the defendant is confined. Whether the court will recommend confinement near the place of trial or place where the appeal is to be heard will depend upon a balancing of convenience against the possible advantage of confinement at a more remote correctional institution where facilities and program may be more adequate.

The amendment to subdivision (a)(4) gives the court discretion in deciding whether to stay the order placing the defendant on probation. It also makes mandatory the fixing of conditions for the stay if a stay is granted. The court cannot release the defendant pending appeal without either placing him on probation or fixing the conditions for the stay under the Bail Reform Act, 18 USC § 3148.

Former rule 38(a)(4) makes mandatory a stay of an order placing the defendant on probation whenever an appeal is noted. The court may or may not impose conditions upon the stay. See rule 46, Federal Rules of Criminal Procedure; and the Bail Reform Act, 18 USC § 3148.

Having the defendant on probation during the period of appeal may serve the objectives of both community protection and defendant rehabilitation. In current practice, the order of probation is sometimes stayed for an appeal period as long as two years. In a situation where the appeal is unsuccessful, the defendant must start under probation supervision after so long a time that the conditions of probation imposed at the time of initial sentencing may no longer appropriately relate either to the defendant's need for rehabilitation or to the community's need for protection. The purposes of probation are more likely to be served if the judge can exercise discretion, in appropriate cases, to require the defendant to be under probation during the period of appeal. The American Bar Association Project on Standards for Criminal Justice takes the position that prompt imposition of sentence aids in the rehabilitation of defendants, ABA Standards Relating to Pleas of Guilty § 1.8(a)(i), Commentary p. 40 (Approved Draft, 1968). See also Sutherland and Cressey, Principles of Criminology 336 (1966).

Under 18 USC § 3148 the court now has discretion to impose conditions of release which are necessary to protect the community against danger from the defendant. This is in contrast to release prior to conviction, where the only appropriate criterion is insuring the appearance of the defendant. 18 USC § 3146. Because the court may impose conditions of release to insure community protection, it seems appropriate to enable the court to do so by ordering the defendant to submit to probation supervision during the period of appeal, thus giving the probation service responsibility for supervision.

A major difference between probation and release under 18 USC § 3148 exists if the defendant violates the conditions imposed upon his release. In the event that release is under 18 USC § 3148, the violation of the condition may result in his being placed in custody pending the decision on appeal. If the appeal were unsuccessful, the order placing him on probation presumably would become effective at that time, and he would then be released under probation supervision. If the defendant were placed on probation, his violation of a condition could result in the imposition of a jail or prison sentence. If the appeal were unsuccessful, the jail or prison sentence would continue to be served.

Notes of Advisory Committee on 1987 amendments. The amendments are technical. No substantive change is intended.

Notes of Advisory Committee on 2000 amendments. The rule is amended to reflect the creation of new Rule 32.2 which now governs criminal forfeiture procedures.

Notes of Advisory Committee on 2002 amendments. The language of Rule 38 has been amended as part of the general restyling of the Criminal Rules to make them more easily understood and to make style and terminology consistent throughout the rules. These changes are intended to be stylistic only.

The reference to Appellate Rule 9(b) is deleted. The Committee believed that the reference was unnecessary and its deletion was not intended to be substantive in nature.

Amendments:

1984.

Act Oct. 12, 1984 (effective on the first day of the first calendar month beginning 36 months after enactment on Oct. 12, 1984, as provided by § 235(a)(1) of such Act, as amended by Act Dec. 26, 1985, P. L. 99-217, § 4, 99 Stat. 1728, which appears as 18 USCS § 3551 note, and applicable as provided by such § 235, which appears as 18 USCS § 3551 note) substituted this catchline for one which read: "Stay of Execution, and Relief Pending Review"; deleted "(a) Stay of execution." preceding "(1)"; deleted subdivs. (b) and (c) which had been abrogated by Order of Dec. 4, 1967; redesignated former subdiv. (a)(1)-(4) as subdivs. (a)-(d); in subdivs. (a) and (b) as redesignated, inserted "from the conviction or sentence"; and substituted subdiv. (d) for the redesignated one, which read: "Probation. An order placing the defendant on probation may be stayed if an appeal is taken. If not stayed, the court shall specify when the term of probation shall commence. If the order is stayed the court shall fix the terms of the stay.".

Rule 39. [Reserved]

HISTORY; ANCILLARY LAWS AND DIRECTIVES

Other provisions:

Notes of Advisory Committee on Rules. This rule relating to appeals is abrogated since the provisions of the rule are transferred to and covered by the Federal Rules of Appellate Procedure. See Advisory Committee Note under rule 37.

TITLE VIII. SUPPLEMENTARY AND SPECIAL PROCEEDINGS

Rule 40. Arrest for Failing to Appear in Another District or for Violating Conditions of Release Set in Another District

(a) In General. A person must be taken without unnecessary delay before a magistrate judge in the district of arrest if the person has been arrested under a warrant issued in another district for:

(i) failing to appear as required by the terms of that person's release under 18 U.S.C. §§ 3141–3156 or by a subpoena; or

(ii) violating conditions of release set in another district.

(b) Proceedings. The judge must proceed under Rule 5(c)(3) as applicable.

(c) Release or Detention Order. The judge may modify any previous release or detention order issued in another district, but must state in writing the reasons for doing so.

(d) Video Teleconferencing. Video teleconferencing may be used to conduct an appearance under this rule if the defendant consents.

HISTORY:

Dec. 26, 1944, eff. March 21, 1946, as amended Feb. 28, 1966, eff. July 1, 1966; April 24, 1972, eff. Oct. 1, 1972; April 30, 1979, eff. Aug. 1, 1979; July 31, 1979, P. L. 96-42, § 1(2), 93 Stat. 326; April 28, 1982, eff. August 1, 1982; Oct. 12, 1984, P. L. 98-473, Title II, Ch I, § 209(c), Ch II, § 215(d), 98 Stat. 1986, 2016; March 9, 1987, eff. Aug. 1, 1987; April 25, 1989, eff. Dec. 1, 1989; April 22, 1993, eff. Dec. 1, 1993; April 29, 1994, eff. Dec. 1, 1994; April 27, 1995, eff. Dec. 1, 1995; April 29, 2002, eff. Dec. 1, 2002; April 12, 2006, eff. Dec. 1, 2006; April 26, 2011, eff. Dec. 1, 2011.

HISTORY; ANCILLARY LAWS AND DIRECTIVES

Other provisions:

Notes of Advisory Committee on Rules. 1. This rule modifies and revamps existing procedure. The present practice has developed as a result of a series of judicial decisions, the only statute dealing with the subject being exceedingly general, 18 USC former § 591 (now § 3041) (Arrest and removal for trial):

For any crime or offense against the United States, the offender may, by any justice or judge of the United States, or by any United States commissioner, or by any chancellor, judge of a supreme or superior court, chief or first judge of common pleas, mayor of a city, justice of the peace, or other magistrate, of any State where he may be found, and agreeably to the usual mode of process against offenders in such State, and at the expense of the United States, be arrested and imprisoned, or bailed, as the case may be, for trial before such court of the United States as by law has cognizance of the offense. . . . Where any offender or witness is committed in any district other than that where the offense is to be tried, it shall be the duty of the judge of the district where such offender or witness is imprisoned, seasonably to issue, and of the marshal to execute, a warrant for his removal to the district where the trial is to be had.

The scope of a removal hearing, the issues to be considered, and other similar matters are governed by judicial decisions, Beavers v Henkel, 194 US 73, 24 S Ct 605, 48 L Ed 882; Tinsley v Treat, 205 US 20, 27 S Ct 430, 51 L Ed 689; Henry v Henkel, 235 US 219, 59 L Ed 203; Rodman v Pothier, 264 US 399, 44 S Ct 360, 68 L Ed 759; Morse v United States, 267 US 80, 45 S Ct 209, 69 L Ed 522; Fetters v United States ex rel. Cunningham, 283 US 638, 51 S Ct 596, 75 L Ed 1321; United States ex rel. Kassin v Mulligan, 295 US 396, 55 S Ct 781, 79 L Ed 1501; see, also, 9 Edmunds, Cyclopedia of Federal Procedure 3905 et seq.

2. The purpose of removal proceedings is to accord safeguards to a defendant against an improvident removal to a distant point for trial. On the other hand, experience has shown that removal proceedings have at times been used by defendants for dilatory purposes and in attempting to frustrate prosecution by preventing or postponing transportation even as between adjoining districts and between places a few miles apart. The object of the rule is adequately to meet each of these two situations.

3. For the purposes of removal, all cases in which the accused is apprehended in a district other than that in which the prosecution is pending have been divided into two groups: first, those in which the place of arrest is either in another district of the same State, or if in another State, then less than 100 miles from the place where the prosecution is pending; and second, cases in which the arrest occurs in a State other than that in which the prosecution is pending and the place of arrest is 100 miles or more distant from the latter place.

In the first group of cases, removal proceedings are abolished. The defendant's right to the usual preliminary hearing is, of course, preserved, but the committing magistrate, if he holds defendant would bind him over to the district court in which the prosecution is pending. As ordinarily there are no removal proceedings in State prosecutions as between different parts of the same State, but the accused is transported by virtue of the process under which he was arrested, it seems reasonable that no removal proceedings should be required in the Federal courts as between districts in the same State. The provision as to arrest in another State but at a place less than 100 miles from the place where the prosecution is pending was added in order to preclude obstruction against bringing the defendant a short distance for trial.

In the second group of cases mentioned in the first paragraph, removal proceedings are continued. The practice to be followed in removal hearings will depend on whether the demand for removal is based upon an indictment or upon an information or complaint. In the latter case, proof of identity and proof of reasonable cause to believe the defendant guilty will have to be adduced in order to justify the issuance of a warrant of removal. In the former case, proof of identity coupled with a certified copy of the indictment will be sufficient, as the indictment will be conclusive proof of probable cause. The distinction is based on the fact that in case of an indictment, the grand jury, which is an arm of the court, has already found probable cause. Since the action of the grand jury is not subject to review by a district judge in the district in which the grand jury sits, it seems illogical to permit such review collaterally in a removal proceeding by a judge in another district.

4. For discussions of this rule, see Homer Cummings, 29 ABA Jour 654, 656; Holtzoff, 3 FRD 445, 450–452; Holtzoff, 12 George Washington LR 119, 127–130; Holtzoff, The Federal Bar Journal, October 1944, 18–37; Berge, 42 Mich LR 353, 374; Medalie, 4 Lawyers Guild R (3) 1, 4.

Note to Subdivision (b). The rule provides that all removal hearings shall take place before a United States commissioner or a Federal judge. It does not confer such jurisdiction on State or local magistrates. While theoretically under existing law State and local magistrates have authority to conduct removal hearings, nevertheless as a matter of universal practice, such proceedings are always conducted before a United States commissioner or a Federal judge, 9 Edmunds, Cyclopedia of Federal Procedure 3919.

Notes of Advisory Committee on 1966 amendments. The amendment conforms to the change made in the corresponding procedure in Rule 5(b).

Notes of Advisory Committee on 1972 amendments. Subdivision (a) is amended to make clear that the person shall be taken before the federal magistrate "without unnecessary delay." Although the former rule was silent in this regard, it probably would have been interpreted to require prompt appearance, and there is therefore advantage in making this explicit in the rule itself. See C. Wright, Federal Practice and Procedure: Criminal § 652 (1969, Supp 1971). Subdivision (a) is amended to also make clear that the person is to be brought before a "federal magistrate" rather than a state or local magistrate authorized by 18 USC § 3041. The former rules were inconsistent in this regard. Although rule 40(a) provided that the person may be brought before a state or local officer authorized by former rule 5(a), such state or local officer lacks authority to conduct a preliminary examination under rule 5(c), and a principal purpose of the appearance is to hold a preliminary examination where no prior indictment or information has issued. The Federal Magistrates Act should make it possible to bring a person before a federal magistrate. See C. Wright, Federal Practice and Procedure: Criminal § 653, especially n 35 (1969, Supp 1971).

Subdivision (b)(2) is amended to provide that the federal magistrate should inform the defendant of the fact that he may avail himself of the provisions of rule 20 if applicable in the particular case. However, the failure to so notify the defendant should not invalidate the removal procedure. Although the old rule is silent in this respect, it is current practice to so notify the defendant, and it seems desirable, therefore, to make this explicit in the rule itself.

The requirement that an order of removal under subdivision (b)(3) can be made only by a judge of the United States and cannot be made by a United States magistrate is retained. However, subdivision (b)(5) authorizes issuance of the warrant of removal by a United States magistrate if he is authorized to do so by a rule of district court adopted in accordance with 28 USC § 636(b):

Any district court . . . by the concurrence of a majority of all the judges . . . may establish rules pursuant to which any full-time United States magistrate . . . may be assigned . . . such additional duties as are not inconsistent with the Constitution and laws of the United States.

Although former rule 40(b)(3) required that the warrant of removal be issued by a judge of the United States, there appears no constitutional or statutory prohibition against conferring his authority upon a United States magistrate in accordance with 28 USC § 636(b). The background history is dealt with in detail in 8A J. Moore, Federal Practice PP 40.01 and 40.02 (2d ed Cipes 1970, Supp 1971).

Subdivision (b)(4) makes explicit reference to provisions of the Bail Reform Act of 1966 by incorporating a cross-reference to 18 USC § 3146 and § 3148.

Notes of Advisory Committee on 1979 amendments. This substantial revision of rule 40 abolishes the present distinction between arrest in a nearby district and arrest in a distant district, clarifies the authority of the magistrate with respect to the setting of bail where bail had previously been fixed in the other district, adds a provision dealing with arrest of a probationer in a district other than the district of supervision, and adds a provision dealing with arrest of a defendant or witness for failure to appear in another district.

Note to subdivision (a). Under subdivision (a) of the present rule, if a person is arrested in a nearby district (another district in the same state, or a place less than 100 miles away), the usual rule 5 and 5.1 preliminary proceedings are conducted. But under subdivision (b) of the present rule, if a person is arrested in a distant district, then a hearing leading to a warrant of removal is held. New subdivision (a) would make no distinction between these two situations and would provide for rule 5 and 5.1 proceedings in all instances in which the arrest occurs outside the district where the warrant issues or where the offense is alleged to have been committed.

This abolition of the distinction between arrest in a nearby district and arrest in a distant district rests upon the conclusion that the procedures prescribed in rules 5 and 5.1 are adequate to protect the rights of an arrestee wherever he might be arrested. If the arrest is without a warrant, it is necessary under rule 5 that a complaint be filed forthwith complying with the requirements of rule 4(a) with respect to the showing of probable cause. If the arrest is with a warrant, that warrant will have been issued upon the basis of an indictment or of a complaint or information showing probable cause, pursuant to rules 4(a) and 9(a). Under rule 5.1, dealing with the preliminary examination, the defendant is to be held to answer only upon a showing of probable cause that an offense has been committed and that the defendant committed it.

Under subdivision (a), there are two situations in which no preliminary examination will be held. One is where "an indictment has been returned or an information filed," which pursuant to rule 5(c) obviates the need for a preliminary examination. The other is where "the defendant elects to have the preliminary examination conducted in the district in which the prosecution is pending." A defendant might wish to elect that alternative when, for example, the law in that district is that the complainant and other material witnesses may be required to appear at the preliminary examination and give testimony. See Washington v. Clemmer, 339 F.2d 715 (D.C. Cir. 1964).

New subdivision (a) continues the present requirement that if the arrest was without a warrant a warrant must thereafter issue in the district in which the offense is alleged to have been committed. This will ensure that in the district of anticipated prosecution there will have been a probable cause determination by a magistrate or grand jury.

Note to subdivision (b). New subdivision (b) follows existing subdivision (b)(2) in requiring the magistrate to inform the defendant of the provisions of rule 20 applicable in the particular case. Failure to so notify the defendant should not invalidate the proceedings.

Note to subdivision (c). New subdivision (c) follows existing subdivision (b)(4) as to transmittal of papers.

Note to subdivision (d). New subdivision (d) has no counterpart in the present rule. It provides a procedure for dealing with the situation in which a probationer is arrested in a district other than the district of supervision, consistent with 18 U.S.C. § 3653, which provides in part: "If the probationer shall be arrested in any district other than that in which he was last supervised, he shall be returned to the district in which the warrant was issued, unless jurisdiction over him is transferred as above provided to the district in which he is found, and in that case he shall be detained pending further proceedings in such district."

One possibility, provided for in subdivision (d)(1), is that of transferring jurisdiction over the probationer to the district in which he was arrested. This is permissible under the aforementioned statute, which provides in part: "Whenever during the period of his probation, a probationer heretofore or hereafter placed on probation, goes from the district in which he is being supervised to another district, jurisdiction over him may be transferred, in the discretion of the court, from the court for the district from which he goes to the court for the other district, with the concurrence of the latter court. Thereupon the court for the district to which jurisdiction is transferred shall have all power with respect to the probationer that was previously possessed by the court for the district from which the transfer is made, except that the period of probation shall not be changed without the consent of the sentencing court. This process under the same conditions may be repeated whenever during the period of his probation the probationer goes from the district in which he is being supervised to another district." Such transfer may be particularly appropriate when it is found that the probationer has now taken up residence in the district where he was arrested or where the alleged occurrence deemed to constitute a violation of probation took place in the district of arrest. In current practice, probationers arrested in a district other than that of their present supervision are sometimes unnecessarily returned to the district of their supervision, at considerable expense and loss of time, when the more appropriate course of action would have been transfer of probation jurisdiction.

Subdivisions (d)(2) and (3) deal with the situation in which there is not a transfer of probation jurisdiction to the district of arrest. If the alleged probation violation occurred in the district of arrest, then, under subdivision (d)(2), the preliminary hearing provided for in rule 32.1(a)(1) is to be held in that district. This is consistent with the reasoning in Morrissey v. Brewer, 408 U.S. 471 (1972), made applicable to probation cases in Gagnon v. Scarpelli, 411 778 (1973), where the Court stressed that often a parolee "is arrested at a place distant from the state institution, to which he may be returned before the final decision is made concerning revocation," and cited this as a factor contributing to the conclusion that due process requires "that some minimal inquiry be conducted at or reasonably near the place of the alleged parole violation or arrest and as promptly as convenient after arrest while information is fresh and sources are available." As later noted in Gerstein v. Pugh, 420 U.S. 103 (1975): "In Morrissey v. Brewer . . . and Gagnon v. Scarpelli . . . we held that a parolee or probationer arrested prior to revocation is entitled to an informal preliminary hearing at the place of arrest, with some provision for live testimony. . . . That preliminary hearing, more than the probable cause determination required by the Fourth Amendment, serves the purpose of gathering and preserving live testimony, since the final revocation hearing frequently is held at some distance from the place where the violation occurred.".

However, if the alleged violation did not occur in that district, then first-hand testimony concerning the violation is unlikely to be available there, and thus the reasoning of Morrissey and Gerstein does not call for holding the preliminary hearing in that district. In such a case, as provided in subdivision (d)(3), the probationer should be held to answer in the district court of the district having probation jurisdiction. The purpose of the proceeding there provided for is to ascertain the identity of the probationer and provide him with copies of the warrant and the application for the warrant. A probationer is subject to the reporting condition at all times and is also subject to the continuing power of the court to modify such conditions. He therefore stands subject to return back to the jurisdiction district without the necessity of conducting a hearing in the district of arrest to determine whether there is probable cause to revoke his probation.

Note to subdivision (e). New subdivision (e) has no counterpart in the present rule. It has been added because some confusion currently exists as to whether present rule 40(b) is applicable to the case in which a bench warrant has issued for the return of a defendant or witness who has absented himself and that person is apprehended in a distant district. In Bandy v. United States, 408 F.2d 518 (8th Cir. 1969), a defendant, who had been released upon his personal recognizance after conviction and while petitioning for certiorari and who failed to appear as required after certiorari was denied, objected to his later arrest in

New York and removal to Leavenworth without compliance with the rule 40 procedures. The court concluded: "The short answer to Bandy's first argument is found in Rush v. United States, 290 F.2d 709, 710 (5 Cir. 1961): 'The provisions of Rules 5 and 40, Federal Rules of Criminal Procedure, may not be availed of by a prisoner in escape status . . . .' As noted by Holtzoff, 'Removal of Defendants in Federal Criminal Procedure', 4 F.R.D. 455, 458 (1946): 'Resort need not be had, however, to this [removal] procedure for the purpose of returning a prisoner who has been recaptured after an escape from custody. It has been pointed out that in such a case the court may summarily direct his return under its general power to issue writs not specifically provided for by statute, which may be necessary for the exercise of its jurisdiction and agreeable to the usages and principles of law. In fact, in such a situation no judicial process appears necessary. The prisoner may be retaken and administratively returned to the custody from which he escaped.' Bandy's arrest in New York was pursuant to a bench warrant issued by the United States District Court for the District of North Dakota on May 1, 1962, when Bandy failed to surrender himself to commence service of his sentence on the conviction for filing false income tax refunds. As a fugitive from justice, Bandy was not entitled upon apprehension to a removal hearing, and he was properly removed to the United States Penitentiary at Leavenworth, Kansas to commence service of sentence." Consistent with Bandy, new subdivision (c) does not afford such a person all of the protections provided for in subdivision (a). However, subdivision (e) does ensure that a determination of identity will be made before that person is held to answer in the district of arrest.

Note to subdivision (f). Although the matter of bail is dealt with in rule 46 and 18 U.S.C. §§ 3146 and 3148, new subdivision (f) has been added to clarify the situation in which a defendant makes his initial appearance before the United States magistrate and there is a warrant issued by a judge of a different district who has endorsed the amount of bail on the warrant. The present ambiguity of the rule is creating practical administrative problems. If the United States magistrate concludes that a lower bail is appropriate, the judge who fixed the original bail on the warrant has, on occasion, expressed the view that this is inappropriate conduct by the magistrate. If the magistrate, in such circumstances, does not reduce the bail to the amount supported by all of the facts, there may be caused unnecessary inconvenience to the defendant, and there would arguably be a violation of at least the spirit of the Bail Reform Act and the Eighth Amendment.

The Procedures Manual for United States Magistrates, issued under the authority of the Judicial Conference of the United States, provides in ch. 6, pp. 8-9: "Where the arrest occurs in a 'distant' district, the rules do not expressly limit the discretion of the magistrate in the setting of conditions of release. However, whether or not the magistrate in the district of arrest has authority to set his own bail under Rule 40, considerations of propriety and comity would dictate that the magistrate should not attempt to set bail in a lower amount than that fixed by a judge in another district. If an unusual situation should arise where it appears from all the information available to the magistrate that the amount of bail endorsed on the warrant is excessive, he should consult with a judge of his own district or with the judge in the other district who fixed the bail in order to resolve any difficulties. (Where an amount of bail is merely recommended on the indictment by the United States attorney, the magistrate has complete discretion in setting conditions of release.)" Rule 40 as amended would encourage the above practice and hopefully would eliminate the present confusion and misunderstanding.

The last sentence of subdivision (f) requires that the magistrate set forth the reasons for his action in writing whenever he fixes bail in an amount different from that previously fixed. Setting forth the reasons for the amount of bail fixed, certainly a sound practice in all circumstances, is particularly appropriate when the bail differs from that previously fixed in another district. The requirement that reasons be set out will ensure that the "considerations of propriety and comity" referred to above will be specifically taken into account.

Notes of Advisory Committee on 1982 amendments. Rule 40(d). The amendment to 40(d) is intended to make it clear that the transfer provisions therein apply whenever the arrest occurs other than in the district of probation jurisdiction, and that if probable cause is found at a preliminary hearing held pursuant to Rule 40(d)(2) the probationer should be held to answer in the district having probation jurisdiction.

On occasion, the district of probation supervision and the district of probation jurisdiction will not be the same. See, e.g., Cupp v. Byington, 179 F.Supp. 669 (S.D.Ind. 1960) (supervision in Southern District of Indiana, but jurisdic tion never transferred from District of Nevada). In such circumstances, it is the district having jurisdiction which may revoke the defendant's probation. Cupp v. Byington, supra; 18 U.S.C. § 3653 ("the court for the district having jurisdiction over him . . . may revoke the probation"; if probationer goes to another district, "jurisdiction over him may be transferred," and only then does "the court for the district to which jurisdiction is transferred . . . have all the power with respect to the probationer that was previously possessed by the court for the district from which the transfer was made"). That being the case, that is the jurisdiction to which the probationer should be transferred as provided in Rule 40(d).

Because Rule 32.1 has now taken effect, a cross-reference to those provisions has been made in subdivision (d)(1) so as to clarify how the magistrate is to proceed if jurisdiction is transferred.

The amendments are technical. No substantive change is intended.

Notes of Advisory Committee on 1989 amendments. The amendments recognize that convicted defendants may be on supervised release as well as on probation. See 18 U.S.C. §§ 3583, and 3624(e).

Notes of Advisory Committee on 1993 amendments. The amendment to subdivision (a) is intended to expedite determining where a defendant will be held to answer by permitting facsimile transmission of a warrant or a certified copy of the warrant. The amendment recognizes an increased reliance by the public in general, and the legal profession in particular, on accurate and efficient transmission of important legal documents by facsimile machines.

The Rule is also amended to conform to the Judicial Improvements Act of 1990 [P.L. 101-650, Title III, Section 321] which provides that each United States magistrate appointed under section 631 of title 28, United States Code, shall be known as a United States magistrate judge.

Notes of Advisory Committee on 1994 amendments. The amendment to subdivision (d) is intended to clarify the authority of a magistrate judge to set conditions of release in those cases where a probationer or supervised releasee is arrested in a district other than the district having jurisdiction. As written, there appeared to be a gap in Rule 40, especially under (d)(1) where the alleged violation occurs in a jurisdiction other than the district having jurisdiction.

A number of rules contain references to pretrial, trial, and post-trial release or detention of defendants, probationers and supervised releasees. Rule 46, for example, addresses the topic of release from custody. Although Rule 46(c) addresses custody pending sentencing and notice of appeal, the rule makes no explicit provision for detaining or releasing probationers or supervised releasees who are later arrested for violating terms of their probation or release. Rule 32.1 provides guidance on proceedings involving revocation of probation or supervised release. In particular, Rule 32.1 (a)(1) recognizes that when a person is held in custody on the ground that the person violated a condition of probation or supervised release, the judge or United States magistrate judge may release the person under Rule 46(c), pending the revocation proceeding. But no other explicit reference is made in Rule 32.1 to the authority of a judge or magistrate judge to determine conditions of release for a probationer or supervised releasee who is arrested in a district other than the district having jurisdiction.

The amendment recognizes that a judge or magistrate judge considering the case of a probationer or supervised releasee under Rule 40(d) has the same authority vis a vis decisions regarding custody as a judge or magistrate judge proceeding under Rule 32.l(a)(1). Thus, regardless of the ultimate disposition of an arrested probationer or supervised releasee under Rule 40(d), a judge or magistrate judge acting under that rule may rely upon Rule 46(c) in determining whether custody should be continued and if not, what conditions, if any, should be placed upon the person.

Notes of Advisory Committee on 1995 amendments. The amendment to Rule 40(a) is a technical, conforming change to reflect an amendment to Rule 5, which recognizes a limited exception to the general rule that all arrestees must be taken before a federal magistrate judge.

Notes of Advisory Committee on 2002 amendments. The language of Rule 40 has been amended as part of the general restyling of the Criminal Rules to make them more easily understood and to make style and terminology consistent throughout the rules. These changes are intended to be stylistic only.

Rule 40 has been completely revised. The Committee believed that it would be much clearer and more helpful to locate portions of Rule 40 in Rules 5 (initial appearances), 5.1 (preliminary hearings), and 32.1 (revocation or modification of probation or supervised release). Accordingly, current Rule 40(a) has been relocated in Rules 5 and 5.1. Current Rule 40(b) has been relocated in Rule 5(c)(2)(B) and current Rule 40(c) has been moved to Rule 5(c)(2)(F).

Current Rule 40(d) has been relocated in Rule 32.1(a)(5). The first sentence of current Rule 40(e) is now located in revised Rule 40(a). The second sentence of current Rule 40(e) is now in revised Rule 40(b) and current Rule 40(f) is revised Rule 40(c).

Notes of Advisory Committee on 2006 amendments. *Note to Subdivision (a).* Rule 40 currently refers only to a person arrested for failing to appear in another district. The amendment is intended to fill a perceived gap in the rule that a magistrate judge in the district of arrest lacks authority to set release conditions for a person arrested only for violation of conditions of release. *See, e.g., United States v. Zhu,* 215 F.R.D. 21, 26 (D. Mass. 2003). The Committee believes that it would be inconsistent for the magistrate judge to be empowered to release an arrestee who had failed to appear altogether, but not to release one who only violated conditions of release in a minor way. Rule 40(a) is amended to expressly cover not only failure to appear, but also violation of any other condition of release.

Notes of Advisory Committee on 2011 amendments. *Note to Subdivision (d).* The amendment provides for video teleconferencing in order to bring the rule into conformity with Rule 5(f).

Amendments:

1979.

Act July 31, 1979, provided that the amendments to this rule proposed by the United States Supreme Court are effect August 1, 1979, provided that "in accordance with Rule 32.1(a)" be deleted from the proposed amendment to subsec. (d)(1), and "in accordance with Rule 32.1(a)(1)" be deleted from the proposed amendment to subsec. (d)(2).

1982.

Order of April 28, 1982, eff. Aug. 1982, substituted subdiv. (d)(1) and (2) for ones which read:

"(1) Proceed if jurisdiction over the probationer is transferred to that district pursuant to 18 U.S.C. § 3653;

"(2) Hold a prompt preliminary hearing if the alleged violation occurred in that district, and either (i) hold the probationer to answer in the district court having probation supervision or (ii) dismiss the proceedings and so notify that court; or".

1984.

Act Oct. 12, 1984 (effective on the first day of the first calendar month beginning 36 months after enactment on Oct. 12, 1984, as provided by § 235(a)(1) of such Act, as amended by Act Dec. 26, 1985, P. L. 99-217, § 4, 99 Stat. 1728, which appears as 18 USCS § 3551 note, and applicable as provided by such § 235, which appears as 18 USCS § 3551 note), in subdiv. (d)(1), substituted "3605" for "3653".

Rule 41. Search and Seizure

(a) Scope and Definitions.

(1) *Scope.* This rule does not modify any statute regulating search or seizure, or the issuance and execution of a search warrant in special circumstances.

(2) *Definitions.* The following definitions apply under this rule:

(A) "Property" includes documents, books, papers, any other tangible objects, and information.

(B) "Daytime" means the hours between 6:00 a.m. and 10:00 p.m. according to local time.

(C) "Federal law enforcement officer" means a government agent (other than an attorney for the government) who is engaged in enforcing the criminal laws and is within any category of officers authorized by the Attorney General to request a search warrant.

(D) "Domestic terrorism" and "international terrorism" have the meanings set out in 18 U.S.C. § 2331.

(E) "Tracking device" has the meaning set out in 18 U.S.C. § 3117(b).

(b) Venue for a Warrant Application. At the request of a federal law enforcement officer or an attorney for the government:

(1) a magistrate judge with authority in the district—or if none is reasonably available, a judge of a state court of record in the district—has authority to issue a warrant to search for and seize a person or property located within the district;

(2) a magistrate judge with authority in the district has authority to issue a warrant for a person or property outside the district if the person or property is located within the district when the warrant is issued but might move or be moved outside the district before the warrant is executed;

(3) a magistrate judge—in an investigation of domestic terrorism or international terrorism—with authority in any district in which activities related to the terrorism may have occurred has authority to issue a warrant for a person or property within or outside that district;

(4) a magistrate judge with authority in the district has authority to issue a warrant to install within the district a tracking device; the warrant may authorize use of the device to track the movement of a person or property located within the district, outside the district, or both; and

(5) a magistrate judge having authority in any district where activities related to the crime may have occurred, or in the District of Columbia, may issue a warrant for property that is located outside the jurisdiction of any state or district, but within any of the following:

(A) a United States territory, possession, or commonwealth;

(B) the premises—no matter who owns them—of a United States diplomatic or consular mission in a foreign state, including any appurtenant building, part of a building, or land used for the mission's purposes; or

(C) a residence and any appurtenant land owned or leased by the United States and used by United States personnel assigned to a United States diplomatic or consular mission in a foreign state.

(6) a magistrate judge with authority in any district where activities related to a crime may have occurred has authority to issue a warrant to use remote access to search electronic storage media and to seize or copy electronically stored information located within or outside that district if:

(A) the district where the media or information is located has been concealed through technological means; or

(B) in an investigation of a violation of 18 U.S.C. § 1030(a)(5), the media are protected computers that have been damaged without authorization and are located in five or more districts.

(c) Persons or Property Subject to Search or Seizure. A warrant may be issued for any of the following:

(1) evidence of a crime;

(2) contraband, fruits of crime, or other items illegally possessed;

(3) property designed for use, intended for use, or used in committing a crime; or

(4) a person to be arrested or a person who is unlawfully restrained.

(d) Obtaining a Warrant.

(1) *In General.* After receiving an affidavit or other information, a magistrate judge—or if authorized by Rule 41(b), a judge of a state court of record—must issue the warrant if there is probable cause to search for and seize a person or property or to install and use a tracking device.

(2) *Requesting a Warrant in the Presence of a Judge.*

(A) Warrant on an Affidavit. When a federal law enforcement officer or an attorney for the government presents an affidavit in support of a warrant, the judge may require the affiant to appear personally and may examine under oath the affiant and any witness the affiant produces.

(B) Warrant on Sworn Testimony. The judge may wholly or partially dispense with a written affidavit and base a warrant on sworn testimony if doing so is reasonable under the circumstances.

(C) Recording Testimony. Testimony taken in support of a warrant must be recorded by a court reporter or by a suitable recording device, and the judge must file the transcript or recording with the clerk, along with any affidavit.

(3) *Requesting a Warrant by Telephonic or Other Means.* In accordance with Rule 4.1, a magistrate judge may issue a warrant based on information communicated by telephone or other reliable electronic means.

(e) Issuing the Warrant.

(1) *In General.* The magistrate judge or a judge of a state court of record must issue the warrant to an officer authorized to execute it.

(2) *Contents of the Warrant.*

(A) Warrant to Search for and Seize a Person or Property. Except for a tracking-device warrant, the warrant must identify the person or property to be searched, identify any person or property to be seized, and designate the magistrate judge to whom it must be returned. The warrant must command the officer to:

(i) execute the warrant within a specified time no longer than 14 days;

(ii) execute the warrant during the daytime, unless the judge for good cause expressly authorizes execution at another time; and

(iii) return the warrant to the magistrate judge designated in the warrant.

(B) Warrant Seeking Electronically Stored Information. A warrant under Rule 41(e)(2)(A) may authorize the seizure of electronic storage media or the seizure or copying of electronically stored information. Unless otherwise specified, the warrant authorizes a later review of the media or information consistent with the warrant. The time for executing the warrant in Rule

41(e)(2)(A) and (f)(1)(A) refers to the seizure or on-site copying of the media or information, and not to any later off-site copying or review.

(C) Warrant for a Tracking Device. A tracking-device warrant must identify the person or property to be tracked, designate the magistrate judge to whom it must be returned, and specify a reasonable length of time that the device may be used. The time must not exceed 45 days from the date the warrant was issued. The court may, for good cause, grant one or more extensions for a reasonable period not to exceed 45 days each. The warrant must command the officer to:

(i) complete any installation authorized by the warrant within a specified time no longer than 10 days;

(ii) perform any installation authorized by the warrant during the daytime, unless the judge for good cause expressly authorizes installation at another time; and

(iii) return the warrant to the judge designated in the warrant.

(3) *Warrant by Telephonic or Other Means.* If a magistrate judge decides to proceed under Rule 41(d)(3)(A), the following additional procedures apply:

(A) Preparing a Proposed Duplicate Original Warrant. The applicant must prepare a "proposed duplicate original warrant" and must read or otherwise transmit the contents of that document verbatim to the magistrate judge.

(B) Preparing an Original Warrant. If the applicant reads the contents of the proposed duplicate original warrant, the magistrate judge must enter those contents into an original warrant. If the applicant transmits the contents by reliable electronic means, that transmission may serve as the original warrant.

(C) Modification. The magistrate judge may modify the original warrant. The judge must transmit any modified warrant to the applicant by reliable electronic means under Rule 41(e)(3)(D) or direct the applicant to modify the proposed duplicate original warrant accordingly.

(D) Signing the Warrant. Upon determining to issue the warrant, the magistrate judge must immediately sign the original warrant, enter on its face the exact date and time it is issued, and transmit it by reliable electronic means to the applicant or direct the applicant to sign the judge's name on the duplicate original warrant.

(f) Executing and Returning the Warrant.

(1) *Warrant to Search for and Seize a Person or Property.*

(A) Noting the Time. The officer executing the warrant must enter on it the exact date and time it was executed.

(B) Inventory. An officer present during the execution of the warrant must prepare and verify an inventory of any property seized. The officer must do so in the presence of another officer and the person from whom, or from whose premises, the property was taken. If either one is not present, the officer must prepare and verify the inventory in the presence of at least one other credible person. In a case involving the seizure of electronic storage media or the seizure or copying of electronically stored information, the inventory may be limited to describing the physical storage media that were seized or copied. The officer may retain a copy of the electronically stored information that was seized or copied.

(C) Receipt. The officer executing the warrant must give a copy of the warrant and a receipt for the property taken to the person from whom, or from whose premises, the property was taken or leave a copy of the warrant and receipt at the place where the officer took the property. For a warrant to use remote access to search electronic storage media and seize or copy electronically stored information, the officer must make reasonable efforts to serve a copy of the warrant and receipt on the person whose property was searched or who possessed the information that was seized or copied. Service may be accomplished by any means, including electronic means, reasonably calculated to reach that person.

(D) Return. The officer executing the warrant must promptly return it—together with a copy of the inventory—to the magistrate judge designated on the warrant. The officer may do so by reliable electronic means. The judge must, on request, give a copy of the inventory to the person from whom, or from whose premises, the property was taken and to the applicant for the warrant.

(2) *Warrant for a Tracking Device.*

(A) Noting the Time. The officer executing a tracking-device warrant must enter on it the exact date and time the device was installed and the period during which it was used.

(B) Return. Within 10 days after the use of the tracking device has ended, the officer executing the warrant must return it to the judge designated in the warrant. The officer may do so by reliable electronic means.

(C) Service. Within 10 days after the use of the tracking device has ended, the officer executing a tracking-device warrant must serve a copy of the warrant on the person who was tracked or whose property was tracked. Service may be accomplished by delivering a copy to the person who, or whose property, was tracked; or by leaving a copy at the person's residence or usual place of abode with an individual of suitable age and discretion who resides at that location and by mailing a copy to the person's last known address. Upon request of the government, the judge may delay notice as provided in Rule 41(f)(3).

(3) *Delayed Notice.* Upon the government's request, a magistrate judge—or if authorized by Rule 41(b), a judge of a state court of record—may delay any notice required by this rule if the delay is authorized by statute.

(4) *Return.* The officer executing the warrant must promptly return it—together with a copy of the inventory—to the magistrate judge designated on the warrant. The judge must, on request, give a copy of the inventory to the person from whom, or from whose premises, the property was taken and to the applicant for the warrant.

(g) Motion to Return Property. A person aggrieved by an unlawful search and seizure of property or by the deprivation of property may move for the property's return. The motion must be filed in the district where the property was seized. The court must receive evidence on any factual issue necessary to decide the motion. If it grants the motion, the court must return the property to the movant, but may impose reasonable conditions to protect access to the property and its use in later proceedings.

(h) Motion to Suppress. A defendant may move to suppress evidence in the court where the trial will occur, as Rule 12 provides.

(i) Forwarding Papers to the Clerk. The magistrate judge to whom the warrant is returned must attach to the warrant a copy of the return, of the inventory, and of all other related papers and must deliver them to the clerk in the district where the property was seized.

HISTORY:

Dec. 26, 1944, eff. March 21, 1946, as amended Dec. 27, 1948, eff. Oct. 20, 1949; April 9, 1956, eff. 90 days after April 9, 1956; April 24, 1972, eff. Oct. 1, 1972; March 18, 1974, eff. July 1, 1974; April 26, 1976, eff. Aug. 1, 1976 and Oct. 1, 1977; Act July 8, 1976, P.L. 94-349, § 1, 90 Stat. 822; Act July 30, 1977, P.L. 95-78, §§ 2(e), 4, 91 Stat. 320, 322, eff. Oct. 1, 1977; April 30, 1979, eff. Aug. 1, 1979; March 9, 1987, eff. Aug. 1, 1987; April 25, 1989, eff. Dec. 1, 1989; May 1, 1990, eff. Dec. 1, 1990; April 22, 1993, eff. Dec. 1, 1993; Oct. 26, 2001, P. L. 107-56, Title II, § 219, 115 Stat. 291; April 29, 2002, eff. Dec. 1, 2002; April 12, 2006, eff. Dec. 1, 2006; April 23, 2008, eff. Dec. 1, 2008; March 26, 2009, eff. Dec. 1, 2009; April 26, 2011, eff. Dec. 1, 2011; April 28, 2016, eff. Dec. 1, 2016.

HISTORY; ANCILLARY LAWS AND DIRECTIVES

Other provisions:

Notes of Advisory Committee on Rules.

This rule is a codification of existing law and practice.

Note to Subdivision (a). This rule is a restatement of existing law, 18 USC former § 611.

Note to Subdivision (b). This rule is a restatement of existing law, 18 USC former § 612; Conyer v United States, 80 F2d 292, CCA 6th. This provision does not supersede or repeal special statutory provisions permitting the issuance of search warrants in specific circumstances. See Subdivision (g) and Note thereto, infra.

Note to Subdivision (c). This rule is a restatement of existing law, 18 USC former §§ 613– 616, 620; Dumbra v United States, 268 US 435, 45 S Ct 546, 69 L Ed 1032.

Note to Subdivision (d). This rule is a restatement of existing law, 18 USC former §§ 621– 624.

Note to Subdivision (e). This rule is a restatement of existing law and practice, with the exception hereafter noted, 18 USC former §§ 625, 626; Weeks v United States, 232 US 383, 34 S Ct 341, 58 L Ed 652; Silverthorne Lumber Co. v United States, 251 US 385, 40 S Ct 182, 64 L Ed 319; Agello v United States, 269 US 20, 46 S Ct 4, 70 L Ed 145; Gouled v United States, 255 US 298, 41 S Ct 261, 65 L Ed 647. While under existing law a motion to suppress evidence or to compel return of property obtained by an illegal search and seizure may be made either before a commissioner subject to review by the court on motion, or before the court, the rule provides that such motion may be made only before the court. The purpose is to prevent multiplication of proceedings and to bring the matter before the court in the first instance. While during the life of the Eighteenth Amendment when such motions were numerous it was a common practice in some districts for commissioners to hear such motions, the prevailing practice at the present time is to make such motions before the district court. This practice, which is deemed to be preferable, is embodied in the rule.

Note to Subdivision (f). This rule is a restatement of existing law, 18 USC former § 627; cf. Rule 5(c) (last sentence).

Note to Subdivision (g). While Rule 41 supersedes the general provisions of 18 USC former §§ 611– 626 (now 18 USC §§ 3105, 3109), relating to search warrants, it does not supersede, but preserves, all other statutory provisions permitting searches and seizures in specific situations. Among such statutes are the following:

USC Title 18 former: § 287 [Rule 41] (Search warrant for suspected counterfeiter).

USC Title 19: § 1595 (Customs duties; searches and seizures).

USC Title 26: § 3117 [now § 5557] (Officers and agents authorized to investigate, issue search warrants, and prosecute for violations).

For statutes which incorporate by reference 18 USC former § 98, and therefore are now controlled by this rule, see e.g.:

USC Title 18 former: § 12 (Subversive activities; undermining loyalty, discipline, or morale of armed forces; searches and seizures).

USC Title 26 former: § 3116 [now § 7302] (Forfeitures and seizures).

Statutory provision for a warrant for detention of war materials seized under certain circumstances is found in 22 USC § 402 [§ 401] (Seizure of war materials intended for unlawful export).

Other statutes providing for searches and seizures or entry without warrants are the following:

USC Title 19: § 482 (Search of vehicles and persons).

USC Title 25 former: § 246 [now 18 USC § 3113] (Searches and seizures).

USC Title 26 former: § 3601 [now § 7606] (Entry of premises for examination of taxable objects).

USC Title 29: § 211 (Investigations, inspections, and records).

USC Title 49: § 781 (Unlawful use of vessels, vehicles, and aircrafts; contraband article defined).

§ 782 (Seizure and forfeiture).

§ 784 (Application of related laws).

Notes of Advisory Committee on 1948 amendments The amendment is to substitute proper reference to Title 18 in place of the repealed acts.

The amendment is to substitute proper reference to Title 18 in place of the repealed acts.

To eliminate reference to sections of the Act of June 15, 1917, ch 30, which have been repealed by the Act of June 25, 1948, ch 645, which enacted Title 18.

Notes of Advisory Committee on 1972 amendments.

Subdivision (a) is amended to provide that a search warrant may be issued only upon the request of a federal law enforcement officer or an attorney for the government.

The phrase "federal law enforcement officer" is defined in subdivision (h) in a way which will allow the Attorney General to designate the category of officers who are authorized to make application for a search warrant. The phrase "attorney for the government" is defined in rule 54.

The title to subdivision (b) is changed to make it conform more accurately to the content of the subdivision. Subdivision (b) is also changed to modernize the language used to describe the property which may be seized with a lawfully issued search warrant and to take account of a recent Supreme Court decision (Warden v Hayden, 387 US 294 (1967)) and recent congressional action (18 USC § 3103a) which authorize the issuance of a search warrant to search for items of solely evidential value. 18 USC § 3103a provides that "a warrant may be issued to search for and seize any property that constitutes evidence of a criminal offense . . . ."

Recent state legislation authorizes the issuance of a search warrant for evidence of crime. See, e.g., Cal Penal Code § 1524(4) (West Supp 1968); Ill Rev Stat ch 38, § 108-3 (1965); LSAC Cr Part 161 (1967); NY CPL § 690.10(4) (McKinney, 1971); Ore Rev Stat § 141.010 (1969); Wis Stat § 968.13(2) (1969).

The general weight of recent text and law review comment has been in favor of allowing a search for evidence. 8 Wigmore, Evidence § 2184a (McNaughton rev 1961); Kamisar, The Wiretapping-Eavesdropping Problem: A Professor's View, 44 Minn L Rev 891 (1960); Kaplan, Search and Seizure: A No-Man's Land in the Criminal Law, 49 Calif L Rev 474 (1961); Comments: 66 Colum L Rev 355 (1966), 45 NC L Rev 512 (1967), 20 U Chi L Rev 319 (1953).

There is no intention to limit the protection of the fifth amendment against compulsory self-incrimination, so items which are solely "testimonial" or "communicative" in nature might well be inadmissible on those grounds. Schmerber v California, 384 US 757 (1966). The court referred to the possible fifth amendment limitation in Warden v Hayden, supra:

This case does not require that we consider whether there are items of evidential value whose very nature precludes them from being the object of a reasonable search and seizure. [387 US at 303.]

See ALI Model Code of Pre-Arraignment Procedure § 551.03(2) and commentary at pp 3–5 (April 30, 1971).

It seems preferable to allow the fifth amendment limitation to develop as cases arise rather than attempt to articulate the constitutional doctrine as part of the rule itself.

The amendment to subdivision (c) is intended to make clear that a search warrant may properly be based upon finding of probable cause based upon hearsay. That a search warrant may properly be issued on the basis of hearsay is current law. See, e.g., Jones v United States, 362 US 257 (1960); Spinelli v United States, 393 US 410 (1969). See also State v Beal, 40 Wis 2d 607, 162 NW2d 640 (1968), reversing prior Wisconsin cases which held that a search warrant could not properly issue on the basis of hearsay evidence.

The provision in subdivision (c) that the magistrate may examine the affiant or witnesses under oath is intended to assure him an opportunity to make a careful decision as to whether there is probable cause. It seems desirable to do this as an incident to the issuance of the warrant rather than having the issue raised only later on a motion to suppress the evidence. See L. Tiffany, D. McIntyre, and D. Rotenberg, Detection of Crime 118 (1967). If testimony is taken it must be recorded, transcribed, and made part of the affidavit or affidavits. This is to insure an adequate basis for determining the sufficiency of the evidentiary grounds for the issuance of the search warrant if that question should later arise.

The requirement that the warrant itself state the grounds for its issuance and the names of any affiants, is eliminated as unnecessary paper work. There is no comparable requirement for an arrest warrant in rule 4. A person who wishes to challenge the validity of a search warrant has access to the affidavits upon which the warrant was issued.

The former requirement that the warrant require that the search be conducted "forthwith" is changed to read "within a specified period of time not to exceed 10 days." The former rule contained an inconsistency between subdivision (c) requiring that the search be conducted "forthwith" and subdivision (d) requiring execution "within 10 days after its date." The amendment resolves this ambiguity and confers discretion upon the issuing magistrate to specify the time within which the search may be conducted to meet the needs of the particular case.

The rule is also changed to allow the magistrate to authorize a search at a time other than "daytime," where there is "reasonable cause shown" for doing so. To make clear what "daytime" means, the term is defined in subdivision (h).

Subdivision (d) is amended to conform its language to the Federal Magistrates Act. The language "The warrant may be executed and returned only within 10 days after its date" is omitted as unnecessary. The matter is now covered adequately in new subdivision (c) which gives the issuing officer authority to fix the time within which the warrant is to be executed.

The amendment to subdivision (e) and the addition of subdivision (f) are intended to require the motion to suppress evidence to be made in the trial court rather than in the district in which the evidence was seized as now allowed by the rule. In DiBella v United States, 369 US 121 (1962), the court, in effect, discouraged motions to suppress in the district in which the property was seized.

There is a decision in the Second Circuit, United States v Klapholz, 230 F2d 494 (1956), allowing the Government an appeal from an order granting a post-indictment motion to suppress, apparently for the single reason that the motion was filed in the district of seizure rather than of trial; but the case was soon thereafter taken by a District Court to have counseled declining jurisdiction of such motions for reasons persuasive against allowing the appeal: "This course will avoid a needless duplication of effort by two courts and provide a more expeditious resolution of the controversy besides avoiding the risk of determining prematurely and inadequately the admissibility of evidence at the trial. . . . A piecemeal adjudication such as that which would necessarily follow from a disposition of the motion here might conceivably result in prejudice either to the Government or the defendants, or both." United States v Lester, 21 FRD 30, 31 (DC SD NY 1957). Rule 41(c), of course, specifically provides for making of the motion in the district of seizure. On a summary hearing, however, the ruling there is likely always to be tentative. We think it accords most satisfactorily with sound administration of the Rules to treat such rulings as interlocutory. [369 US at 132–133.]

As amended, subdivision (e) provides for a return of the property if (1) the person is entitled to lawful possession *and* (2) the seizure was illegal. This means that the judge in the district of seizure does not have to decide the legality of the seizure in cases involving contraband which, even if seized illegally, is not to be returned.

The five grounds for returning the property, listed in the old rule, are dropped for two reasons—(1) substantive grounds for objecting to illegally obtained evidence (e.g., Miranda) are not ordinarily codified in the rules and (2) the categories are not entirely accurate. See United States v Howard, 138 F Supp 376, 380 (D Md 1956).

A sentence is added to subdivision (e) to provide that a motion for return of property, made in the district of trial, shall be treated also as a motion to suppress under rule 12. This change is intended to further the objective of rule 12 which is to have all pretrial motions disposed of in a single court appearance rather than to have a series of pretrial motions made on different dates, causing undue delay in administration.

Subdivision (f) is new and reflects the position that it is best to have the motion to suppress made in the court of the district of trial rather than in the court of the district in which the seizure occurred. The motion to suppress in the district of trial should be made in accordance with the provisions of rule 12.

Subdivision (g) is changed to conform to subdivision (c) which requires the return to be made before a federal judicial officer even though the search warrant may have been issued by a nonfederal magistrate.

Subdivision (h) is former rule 41(g) with the addition of a definition of the term "daytime" and the phrase "federal law enforcement officer."

Notes of Advisory Committee on 1974 amendments.

This amendment restores the words "court of record" which were inadvertently omitted from the amended text of the subdivision which was transmitted by the Judicial Conference to the Supreme Court and prescribed by the Court on April 24, 1972.

Notes of Advisory Committee on 1977 amendments.

Rule 41(c)(2) is added to establish a procedure for the issuance of a search warrant when it is not reasonably practicable for the person obtaining the warrant to present a written affidavit to a magistrate or a state judge as required by subdivision (c)(1). At least two states have adopted a similar procedure, Ariz.Rev.Stat.Ann. §§ 13-1444(c)- 1445(c) (Supp. 1973); Cal.Pen. Code §§ 1526(b), 1528(b) (West Supp. 1974), and comparable amendments are under consideration in other jurisdictions. See Israel, Legislative Regulation of Searches and Seizures: The Michigan Proposals, 73 Mich.L.Rev. 221, 258-63 (1975); Nakell, Proposed Revisions of North Carolina's Search and Seizure Law, 52 N.Car.L.Rev. 277, 306-11 (1973). It has been strongly recommended that "every State enact legislation that provides for the issuance of search warrants pursuant to telephoned petitions and affidavits from police officers." National Advisory Commission on Criminal Justice Standards and Goals, Report on Police 95 (1973). Experience with the procedure has been most favorable. Miller, Telephonic Search Warrants: The San Diego Experience, 9 The Prosecutor 385 (1974).

The trend of recent Supreme Court decisions has been to give greater priority to the use of a search warrant as the proper way of making a lawful search:

It is a cardinal rule that, in seizing goods and articles, law enforcement agents must secure and use search warrants whenever reasonably practicable. . . . This rule rests upon the desirability of having magistrates rather than police officers determine when searches and seizures are permissible and what limitations should be placed upon such activities. Trupiano v. United States, 334 U.S. 699, 705 (1948), quoted with approval in Chimel v. California, 395 U.S. 752, 758 (1969).

See also Coolidge v. New Hamsphire, 403 U.S. 443 (1971); Note, Chambers v. Maroney: New Dimensions in the Law of Search and Seizure, 46 Indiana L.J. 257, 262 (1971).

Use of search warrants can best be encouraged by making it administratively feasible to obtain a warrant when one is needed. One reason for the nonuse of the warrant has been the administrative difficulties involved in getting a warrant, particularly at times of the day when a judicial officer is ordinarily unavailable. See L. Tiffany, D. McIntyre, and D. Rotenberg, Detection of Crime 105–116 (1967); LaFave, Improving Police Performance Through the Exclusionary Rule, 30 Mo. L. Rev. 391, 411 (1965). Federal law enforcement officers are not infrequently confronted with situations in which the circumstances are not sufficiently "exigent" to justify the serious step of conducting a warrantless search of private premises, but yet there exists a significant possibility that critical evidence would be lost in the time it would take to obtain a search warrant by traditional means. See, e.g., United States v. Johnson, — F.2d — (D.C. Cir. June 16, 1975).

Subdivision (c)(2) provides that a warrant may be issued on the basis of an oral statement of a person not in the physical presence of the federal magistrate. Telephone, radio, or other electronic methods of communication are contemplated. For the warrant to properly issue, four requirements must be met:

(1) The applicant—a federal law enforcement officer or an attorney for the government, as required by subdivision (a)—must persuade the magistrate that the circumstances of time and place make it reasonable to request the magistrate to issue a warrant on the basis of oral testimony. This restriction on the issuance of a warrant recognizes the inherent limitations of an oral warrant procedure, the lack of demeanor evidence, and the lack of a written record for the reviewing magistrate to consider before issuing the warrant. See Comment, Oral Search Warrants: A New Standard of Warrant Availability, 21 U.C.L.A. Law Review 691, 701 (1974). Circumstances making it reasonable to obtain a warrant on oral testimony exist if delay in obtaining the warrant might result in the destruction or disappearance of the property [see Chimel v. California, 395 U.S. 752, 773–774 (1969) (White, dissenting); Landynski, The Supreme Court's Search for Fourth Amendment Standards: The Warrantless Search, 45 Conn. B.J. 2, 25 (1971)]; or because of the time when the warrant is sought, the distance from the magistrate of the person seeking the warrant, or both.

(2) The applicant must orally state facts sufficient to satisfy the probable cause requirement for the issuance of the search warrant. (See subdivision (c)(1).) This information may come from either the applicant federal law enforcement officer or the attorney for the government or a witness willing to make an oral statement. The oral testimony must be recorded at this time so that the transcribed affidavit will provide an adequate basis for determining the

sufficiency of the evidence if that issue should later arise. See Kipperman. Inaccurate Search Warant Affidavits as a Ground for Suppressing Evidence, 84 Harv. L. Rev. 825 (1971). It is contemplated that the recording of the oral testimony will be made by a court reporter, by a mechanical recording device, or by a verbatim contemporaneous writing by the magistrate. Recording a telephone conversation is no longer difficult with many easily operated recorders available. See 86:2 L.A. Daily Journal 1 (1973); Miller, Telephonic Search Warrants: The San Diego Experience, 9 The Prosecutor 385, 386 (1974).

(3) The applicant must read the contents of the warrant to the federal magistrate in order to enable the magistrate to know whether the requirements of certainty in the warrant are satisfied. The magistrate may direct that changes be made in the warrant. If the magistrate approves the warrant as requested or as modified by the magistrate, he then issues the warrant by directing the applicant to sign the magistrate's name to the duplicate original warrant. The magistrate then causes to be made a written copy of the approved warrant. This constitutes the original warrant. The magistrate enters the time of issuance of the duplicate original warrant on the face of the original warrant.

(4) Return of the duplicate original warrant and the original warrant must conform to subdivision (d). The transcript of the sworn oral testimony setting forth the grounds for issuance of the warrant must be signed by affiant in the presence of the magistrate and filed with the court.

Because federal magistrates are likely to be accessible through the use of the telephone or other electronic devices, it is unnecessary to authorize state judges to issue warrants under subdivision (c)(2).

Although the procedure set out in subdivision (c)(2) contemplates resort to technology which did not exist when the Fourth Amendment was adopted, the Advisory Committee is of the view that the procedure complies with all of the requirements of the Amendment. The telephonic search warrant process has been upheld as constitutional by the courts, e.g., People v. Peck, 38 Cal.App.3d 993, 113 Cal.Rptr. 806 (1974), and has consistently been so viewed by commentators. See Israel, Legislative Regulation of Searches and Seizures: The Michigan Proposals, 73 Mich.L.Rev. 221, 260 (1975); Nakell, Proposed Revisions of North Carolina's Search and Seizure Law, 52 N.Car.L-.Rev.277, 310 (1973); Comment, Oral Search Warrants: A New Standard of Warrant Availability, 21 U.C.L.A. Rev. 691, 697 (1973).

Reliance upon oral testimony as a basis for issuing a search warrant is permissible under the Fourth Amendment. Campbell v. Minnesota, 487 F.2d 1 (8th Cir. 1973); United States ex rel. Gaugler v. Brierley, 477 F.2d 516 (3d Cir. 1973; Tabasko v. Barton, 472 F.2d 871 (6th Cir. 1972); Frazier v. Roberts, 441 F.2d 1224 (8th Cir. 1971). Thus, the procedure authorized under subdivision (c)(2) is not objectionable on the ground that the oral statement is not transcribed in advance of the issuance of the warrant. People v. Peck, 38 Cal. App. 3d 993, 113 Cal.Rptr. 806 (1974). Although it has been questioned whether oral testimony will suffice under the Fourth Amendment if some kind of contemporaneous record is not made of that testimony, see dissent from denial of certiorari in Christofferson v. Washington, 393 U.S. 1090 (1969), this problem is not present under the procedure set out in subdivision (c)(2).

The Fourth Amendment requires that warrants issue "upon probable cause, supported by Oath or affirmation." The significance of the oath requirement is "that someone must take the responsibility for the facts alleged, giving rise to the probable cause for the issuance of a warrant." United States ex rel. Pugh v. Pate, 401 F.2d 6 (7th Cir. 1968); See also Frazier v. Roberts, 441 F.2d 1224 (8th Cir. 1971). This is accomplished under the procedure required by subdivision (c)(2); the need for an oath under the Fourth Amendment does not "require a face to face confrontation between the magistrate and the affiant." People v. Chavaz, 27 Cal. App. 3d 883, 104 Cal. Rptr. 247 (1972). See also People v. Aguirre, 26 Cal. App. 3d 7, 103 Cal. Rptr. 153 (1972), noting it is unnecessary that "oral statements [be] taken in the physical presence of the magistrate."

The availability of the procedure authorized by subdivision (c)(2) will minimize the necessity of federal law enforcement officers engaging in other practices which, at least on occasion, might threaten to a greater extent those values protected by the Fourth Amendment. Although it is permissible for an officer in the field to relay his information by radio or telephone to another officer who has more ready access to a magistrate and who will thus act as the affiant, Lopez v. United States, 370 F.2d 8 (5th Cir. 1966); State v. Banks, 250 N.C. 728, 110 S.E.2d 322 (1959), that procedure is less desirable than that permitted under subdivision (c)(2), for it deprives "the magistrate of the opportunity to examine the officer at the scene, who is in a much better position to answer questions relating to probable cause and the requisite scope of the search." Israel, Legislative Regulation of Searches and Seizures: The Michigan Proposals, 73 Mich.L.Rev. 221, 260 (1975). Or, in the absence of the subdivision (c)(2) procedure, officers might take "protective custody" of the premises and occupants for a significant period of time while a search warrant was sought by traditional means. The extent to which the "protective custody" procedure may be employed consistent with the Fourth Amendment is uncertain at best; see Griswold, Criminal Procedure, 1969—Is It a Means or an End?, 29 Md.L.Rev. 307, 317 (1969). The unavailability of the subdivision (c)(2) procedure also makes more tempting an immediate resort to a warrantless search in the hope that the circumstances will later be found to have been sufficiently "exigent" to justify such a step. See Miller, Telephonic Search Warrants: The San Diego Experience, 9 The Prosecutor 385, 386 (1974), noting a dramatic increase in police utilization of the warrant process following enactment of a telephonic warrant statute.

Notes of Committee on the Judiciary, Senate Report No. 95-354. Subdivision (e) of section 2 of the Act concerns Rule 41(c) dealing with the issuance of search warrants. The committee agrees with the Supreme Court that it is desirable to encourage Federal law enforcement officers to seek search warrants in situations where they might otherwise conduct warrantless searches by providing for a telephone search warrant procedure with the basic characteristics suggested in the proposed Rule 41(c)(2). As the Supreme Court has observed, "It is a cardinal rule that, in seizing goods and articles, law enforcement agents must secure and use search warrants whenever reasonably practicable. [Trupiano v. United States, 68 S.Ct. 1229, 334 U.S. 699, 705, 92 L.Ed. 1663

(1948), quoted with approval in Chimel v. California, 89 S.Ct. 2034, 395 U.S. 752, 758, 23 L. Ed.2d 685, rehearing denied 90 S.Ct. 36, 396 U.S. 869, 24 L.Ed.2d 124 (1969).] After consideration of the Supreme Court version and a proposal set forth in H.R. 7888, the committee decided to use the language of the House bill as the vehicle, with certain modifications. [The only significant differences, apart from organization, between the procedure set forth in the Supreme Court proposal and in H.R. 7888 are that H.R. 7888 would mandate use of a voice tape recorder and require the officer who executes the warrant to have physical possession of the duplicate original of the warrant at the time of execution of the warrant.] A new provision, as indicated in subparagraph (c)(2)(A), is added to establish a procedure for the issuance of a search warrant where the circumstances make it reasonable to dispense with a written affidavit to be presented in person to a magistrate. At least two States have adopted a similar procedure—Arizona and California [Arizona Rev. Stat. Ann. secs. 13-1444(c), 13-1445(c) (1973 Suppl.); California Penal Code secs. 1526(b), 1528(b) (1974 Suppl.)]—and comparable amendments are under consideration in other jurisdictions. [See Israel, Legislative Regulation of Search and Seizure: The Michigan Proposals, 73 Mich. L. Rev. 221, 258-263 (1975); Nakell, Proposed Revisions of North Carolina's Search and Seizure Law, 52 N.C.L.Rev. 277, 306-311 (1973).] Such a procedure has been strongly recommended by the National Advisory Commission on Criminal Justice Standards and Goals [See Commission Report on Police 95 (1973).] and State experience with the procedure has been favorable. [See Miller, Telephone Search Warrants: The San Diego Experience, 9 The Prosecutor 385 (1974).] The telephone search warrant process has been upheld as constitutional by the courts [E.g., United States v. Turner, — F. 2d — (2d Cir.) (decided June 2, 1977; People v. Peck, 38 Cal. App. 3d 993, 113 Cal. Rptr. 806 (1974).] and has consistently been so viewed by commentators. [See Israel, supra note 21, at 260; Nakel, supra note 21, at 310; Note, Oral Search Warrants: A New Standard of Warrant Availability, 21 U.S.L.A. Rev. 691, 697 (1973).] In recommending a telephone search warrant procedure, the Advisory Committee note on the Supreme Court proposal points out that the preferred method of conducting a search is with a search warrant. The note indicates that the rationale for the proposed change is to encourage Federal law enforcement officers to seek search warrants in situations when they might otherwise conduct warrantless searches. "Federal law enforcement officers are not infrequently confronted with situations in which the circumstances are not sufficiently 'exigent' to justify the serious step of conducting a warrantless search of private premises, but yet there exists a significant possibility that critical evidence would be lost in the time it would take to obtain a search warrant by traditional means." [Advisory Committee note to proposed amendment to Rule 41(c), H. Doc. No. 94- 464, at 22.]

Subparagraph (c)(2)(B) provides that the person requesting the warrant shall prepare a "duplicate original warrant" which will be read and recorded verbatim by the magistrate on an "original warrant." The magistrate may direct that the warrant be modified.

Subparagraph (c)(2)(C) provides that, if the magistrate is satisfied that the circumstances are such as to make it reasonable to dispense with a written affidavit and that grounds for the application exist or there is probable cause to believe that they exist, he shall order the issuance of the warrant by directing the requestor to sign the magistrate's name on the duplicate original warrant. The magistrate is required to sign the original warrant and enter the time of issuance thereon. The finding of probable cause may be based on the same type of evidence appropriate for a warrant upon affidavit.

Subparagraph (c)(2)(D) requires the magistrate to place the requestor and any witness under oath [The validity of an oath administered over the telephone was recently upheld by the Second Circuit in United States v. Turner, supra.] and, if a voice recording device is available, to record the proceeding. If a voice recording is not available, the proceeding must be recorded verbatim stenographically or in longhand. Verified copies must be filed with the court as specified.

Subparagraph (c)(2)(E) provides that the contents of the warrant upon oral testimony shall be the same as the contents of a warrant upon affidavit.

Subparagraph (c)(2)(F) provides that the person who executes the warrant shall enter the exact time of execution on the face of the duplicate original warrant. Unlike H.R. 7888, this subparagraph does not require the person who executes the warrant to have physical possession of the duplicate original warrant at the time of the execution of the warrant. The committee believes this would make an unwise and unnecessary distinction between execution of regular warrants issued on written affidavits and warrants issued by telephone that would limit the flexibility and utility of this procedure for no useful purpose. [See United States v. Woodring, 444 F. 2d 749, 751 (9th Cir. 1971).] Finally, subparagraph (c)(2)(G) makes it clear that, absent a finding of bad faith by the government, the magistrate's judgment that the circumstances made it reasonable to dispense with a written affidavit—a decision that does not go to the core question of whether there was probable cause to issue a warrant—is not a ground for granting a motion to suppress evidence.

Notes of Advisory Committee on 1979 amendments.

This amendment to Rule 41 is intended to make it possible for a search warrant to issue to search *for* a person under two circumstances: (i) when there is probable cause to arrest that person; or (ii) when that person is being unlawfully restrained. There may be instances in which a search warrant would be required to conduct a search in either of these circumstances. Even when a search warrant would not be required to enter a place to search for a person, a procedure for obtaining a warrant should be available so that law enforcement officers will be encouraged to resort to the preferred alternative of acquiring "an objective predetermination of probable cause," Katz v. United States, 389 U.S. 347, 88 S.Ct. 507, 19 L.Ed.2d 576 (1967), in this instance, that the person sought is at the place to be searched.

That part of the amendment which authorizes issuance of a search warrant to search for a person unlawfully restrained is consistent with ALI Model Code of Pre-Arraignment Procedure § SS 210.3(1)(d) (Proposed Official Draft, 1975), which specifies that a search warrant may issue to search for "an individual . . . who is unlawfully held in confinement or other restraint." As noted in the Commentary thereto, id. at p. 507: "Ordinarily such persons will be held against their will and in that case the persons are, of course, not subject to 'seizure.' But they are, in a sense, 'evidence' of crime, and the use of search warrants for these purposes presents no conceptual difficulties." Some state search warrant provisions also provide for issuance of a warrant in these circumstances. See, e.g., Ill.Rev.Stat. ch. 38, § 108-3 ("Any person who has been kidnapped in violation of the laws of this State, or who has been kidnapped in another jurisdiction and is now concealed within this State").

It may be that very often exigent circumstances, especially the need to act very promptly to protect the life or well-being of the kidnap victim, would justify an immediate warrantless search for the person restrained. But this is not inevitably the case. Moreover, as noted above, there should be available a process whereby law enforcement agents may acquire in advance a judicial determination that they have cause to intrude upon the privacy of those at the place where the victim is thought to be located.

That part of the amendment which authorizes issuance of a search warrant to search for a person to be arrested is also consistent with ALI Model Code of Pre-Arraignment Procedure § SS 210.3(1)(d) (Proposed Official Draft, 1975), which states that a search warrant may issue to search for "an individual for whose arrest there is reasonable cause." As noted in the Commentary thereto, id. at p. 507, it is desirable that there be "explicit statutory authority for such searches." Some state search warrant provisions also expressly provide for the issuance of a search warrant to search for a person to be arrested. See, e.g., Del. Code Ann. tit. 11, § 2305 ("Persons for whom a warrant of arrest has been issued"). This part of the amendment to Rule 41 covers a defendant or witness for whom an arrest warrant has theretofore issued, or a defendant for whom grounds to arrest exist even though no arrest warrant has theretofore issued. It also covers the arrest of a deportable alien under 8 U.S.C. § 1252, whose presence at a certain place might be important evidence of criminal conduct by another person, such as the harboring of undocumented aliens under 8 U.S.C. § 1324(a)(3).

In United States v. Watson, 423 U.S. 411, 96 S.Ct. 820, 46 L.Ed.2d 598 (1976), the Court once again alluded to "the still unsettled question" of whether, absent exigent circumstances, officers acting without a warrant may enter private premises to make an arrest. Some courts have indicated that probable cause alone ordinarily is sufficient to support an arrest entry, United States v. Fernandez, 480 F.2d 726 (2d Cir. 1973); United States ex rel. Wright v. Woods, 432 F.2d 1143 (7th Cir. 1970). There exists some authority, however, that except under exigent circumstances a warrant is required to enter the defendant's own premises, United States v. Calhoun, 542 F.2d 1094 (9th Cir. 1976); United States v. Lindsay, 506 F.2d 166 (D.C.Cir. 1974); Dorman v. United States, 435 F.2d 385 (D.C.Cir. 1970), or, at least, to enter the premises of a third party, Virgin Islands v. Gereau, 502 F.2d 914 (3d Cir. 1974); Fisher v. Volz, 496 F.2d 333 (3d Cir. 1974); Huotari v. Vanderport, 380 F.Supp. 645 (D. Minn. 1974).

It is also unclear, assuming a need for a warrant, what kind of warrant is required, although it is sometimes assumed that an arrest warrant will suffice, e.g., United States v. Calhoun, supra; United States v. James, 528 F.2d 999 (5th Cir. 1976). There is a growing body of authority, however, that what is needed to justify entry of the premises of a third party to arrest is a search warrant, e.g., Virgin Islands v. Gereau, supra; Fisher v. Volz, supra. The theory is that if the privacy of this third party is to be protected adequately, what is needed is a probable cause determination by a magistrate that the wanted person is presently within that party's premises. "A warrant for the arrest of a suspect may indicate that the police officer has probable cause to believe the suspect committed the crime; it affords no basis to believe the suspect is in some stranger's home." Fisher v. Volz, supra.

It has sometimes been contended that a search warrant should be required for a nonexigent entry to arrest even when the premises to be entered are those of the person to be arrested. Rotenberg & Tanzer, Searching for the Person to be Seized, 35 Ohio St.L.J. 56, 69 (1974). Case authority in support is lacking, and it may be that the protections of a search warrant are less important in such a situation because ordinarily "rudimentary police procedure dictates that a suspect's residence be eliminated as a possible hiding place before a search is conducted elsewhere." People v. Sprovieri, 95 Ill.App.2d 10, 238 N.E.2d 115 (1968).

Despite these uncertainties, the fact remains that in some circuits under some circumstances a search warrant is required to enter private premises to arrest. Moreover, the law on this subject is in a sufficient state of uncertainty that this position may be taken by other courts. It is thus important that Rule 41 clearly express that a search warrant for this purpose may issue. And even if future decisions head the other direction, the need for the amendment would still exist. It is clear that law enforcement officers "may not constitutionally enter the home of a private individual to search for another person, though he be named in a valid arrest warrant in their possession, absent probable cause to believe that the named suspect is present within at the time." Fisher v. Volz, supra. The cautious officer is entitled to a procedure whereby he may have this probable cause determination made by a neutral and detached magistrate in advance of the entry.

Notes of Advisory Committee on 1987 amendments.

The amendments are technical. No substantive change is intended.

Notes of Advisory Committee on 1989 amendments.

The amendment to Rule 41(e) conforms the rule to the practice in most districts and eliminates language that is somewhat confusing. The Supreme Court has upheld warrants for the search and seizure of property in the possession of persons who are not suspected of criminal activity. See, e.g., Zurcher v. Stanford Daily, 436 U.S. 547 (1978). Before the amendment, Rule 41(e) permitted such persons to seek return of their property if they were aggrieved by an unlawful search and seizure. But, the rule failed to address the harm that may result from the interference with the lawful use of property by persons who are not suspected of wrongdoing. Courts have recognized that once the government no longer has a need to use evidence, it should be returned. See, e.g., United States v. Wilson, 540 F.2d 1100 (D.C. Cir. 1976). Prior to the amendment, Rule 41(e) did not explicitly recognize a right of a property owner to obtain return of lawfully seized property even though the government might be able to protect its legitimate law enforcement interests in the property despite its return--e.g., by copying documents or by conditioning the return on government access to the property at a future time. As amended, Rule 41(e) provides that an aggrieved person may seek return of property that has been unlawfully seized, and a person whose property has been lawfully seized may seek return of property when aggrieved by the government's continued possession of it.

No standard is set forth in the rule to govern the determination of whether property should be returned to a person aggrieved either by an unlawful seizure or by deprivation of the property. The fourth amendment protects people from unreasonable seizures as well as unreasonable searches, United States v. Place, 462 U.S. 696, 701 (1983), and reasonableness under all of the circumstances must be the test when a person seeks to obtain the return of property. If the United States has a need for the property in an investigation or prosecution, its retention of the property generally is reasonable. But, if the United States' legitimate interests can be satisfied even if the property is returned, continued retention of the property would become unreasonable.

The amendment deletes language dating from 1944 stating that evidence shall not be admissible at a hearing or at a trial if the court grants the motion to return property under Rule 41(e). This language has not kept pace with the development of exclusionary rule doctrine and is currently only confusing. The Supreme Court has now held that evidence seized in violation of the fourth amendment, but in good faith pursuant to a warrant, may be used even against a person aggrieved by the constitutional violation. United States v. Leon, 468 U.S. 897 (1984). The Court has also held that illegally seized evidence may be admissible against persons who are not personally aggrieved by an illegal search or seizure. Rakas v. Illinois, 439 U.S. 128 (1978). Property that is inadmissible for one purpose (e.g., as part of the government's case-in-chief) may be admissible for another purpose (e.g., impeachment, United States v. Havens, 446 U.S. 620 (1980)). Federal courts have relied upon these decisions and permitted the government to retain and to use evidence as permitted by the fourth amendment.

Rule 41(e) is not intended to deny the United States the use of evidence permitted by the fourth amendment and federal statutes, even if the evidence might have been unlawfully seized. See, e.g., United States v. Calandra, 414 U.S. 338, 349 n.6 (1978) ("Rule 41(e) does not constitute a statutory expansion of the exclusionary rule."); United States v. Roberts, 852 F.2d 671 (2nd Cir. 1988) (exceptions to exclusionary rule applicable to Rule 41(e)). Thus, the exclusionary provision is deleted, and the scope of the exclusionary rule is reserved for judicial decisions.

In opting for a reasonableness approach and in deleting the exclusionary language, the Committee rejects the analysis of Sovereign News Co. v. United States, 690 F.2d 569 (6th Cir. 1982), cert. denied, 464 U.S. 814 (1983), which held that the United States must return photocopies of lawfully seized business records unless it could demonstrate that the records were "necessary for a specific investigation." As long as the government has a law enforcement purpose in copying records, there is no reason why it should be saddled with a heavy burden of justifying the copying. Although some cases have held that the government must return copies of records where the originals were illegally seized--See, e.g., United States v. Wallace & Tiernan Co., 336 U.S. 793, 801 (1948); Goodman v. United States, 369 F.2d 166 (9th Cir. 1966)--these holdings are questionable in situations in which the government is permitted under Supreme Court decisions to use illegally seized evidence, and their reasoning does not apply to legally seized evidence.

As amended, Rule 41(e) avoids an all or nothing approach whereby the government must either return records and make no copies or keep originals notwithstanding the hardship to their owner. The amended rule recognizes that reasonable accommodations might protect both the law enforcement interests of the United States and the property rights of property owners and holders. In many instances documents and records that are relevant to ongoing or contemplated investigations and prosecutions may be returned to their owner as long as the government preserves a copy for future use. In some circumstances, however, equitable considerations might justify an order requiring the government to return or destroy all copies of records that it has seized. See, e.g., Paton v. LaPrade, 524 F.2d 862, 867-69 (3rd Cir. 1975). The amended rule contemplates judicial action that will respect both possessory and law enforcement interests.

The word "judge" is changed to "court" in the second sentence of subdivision (e) to clarify that a magistrate may receive evidence in the course of making a finding or a proposed finding for consideration by the district judge.

Notes of Advisory Committee on 1990 amendments.

Rule 41(a). The amendment to Rule 41(a) serves several purposes. First, it furthers the constitutional preference for warrants by providing a mechanism whereby a warrant may be issued in a district for a person or property that is moving into or through a district or might move outside the district while the warrant is sought or executed. Second, it clarifies the authority of federal magistrates to issue search warrants for property that is relevant to criminal investigation being conducted in a district and, although located outside the United States, that is in a place where the United States may lawfully conduct a search.

The amendment is not intended to expand the class of persons authorized to request a warrant and the language "upon request of a federal law enforcement officer," modifies all warrants covered by Rule 41. The amendment is intended to make clear that judges of state courts of record within a federal district may issue search warrants for persons or property located within that district. The amendment does not prescribe the circumstances in which a warrant is required and is not intended to change the law concerning warrant requirements. Rather the rule provides a mechanism for the issuance of a warrant when one is required, or when a law enforcement officer desires to seek a warrant even though warrantless activity is permissible.

Rule 41(a)(1) permits anticipatory warrants by omitting the words "is located," which in the past required that in all instances the object of the search had to be located within the district at the time the warrant was issued. Now a search for property or a person within the district, or expected to be within the district, is valid if it otherwise complies with the rule.

Rule 41(a)(2) authorizes execution of search warrants in another district under limited circumstances. Because these searches are unusual, the rule limits to federal magistrates the authority to issue such warrants. The rule permits a federal magistrate to issue a search warrant for property within the district which is moving or may move outside the district. The amendment recognizes that there are inevitable delays between the application for a warrant and its authorization, on the one hand, and the execution of the warrant, on the other hand. The amendment also recognizes that when property is in motion, there may be good reason to delay execution until the property comes to rest. The amendment provides a practical tool for federal law enforcement officers that avoids the necessity of their either seeking several warrants in different districts for the same property or their relying on an exception to the warrant requirement for search of property or a person that has moved outside a district.

The amendment affords a useful warrant procedure to cover familiar fact patterns, like the one typified by United States v. Chadwick, 433 U.S. 1 (1976). In Chadwick, agents in San Diego observed suspicious activities involving a footlocker carried onto a train. When the train arrived in Boston, the agents made an arrest and conducted a warrantless search of the footlocker (which the Supreme Court held was invalid). Under the amended rule, agents who have probable cause in San Diego would be able to obtain a warrant for a search of the footlocker even though it is moving outside the district. Agents, who will not be sure exactly where the footlocker will be unloaded from the train, may execute the warrant when the journey ends. See also United States v. Karo, 468 U.S. 705 (1984) (rejecting argument that obtaining warrant to monitor beeper would not comply with requirement of particularity because its final destination may not be known); United States v. Knotts, 460 U.S. 276 (1983) (agents followed beeper across state lines). The Supreme Court's holding in Chadwick permits law enforcement officers to seize and hold an object like a footlocker while seeking a warrant. Although the amended rule would not disturb this holding, it provides a mechanism for agents to seek a probable cause determination and a warrant before interfering with the property and seizing it. It encourages reliance on warrants.

The amendment is not intended to abrogate the requirements of probable cause and prompt execution. At some point, a warrant issued in one district might become stale when executed in another district. But staleness can be a problem even when a warrant is executed in the district in which it was issued. See generally United States v. Harris, 403 U. S. 573, 579, 589 (1971). And at some point, an intervening event might make execution of a warrant unreasonable. Cf. Illinois v. Andreas, 463 U.S. 765, 772 (1983). Evaluations of the execution of a warrant must, in the nature of things, be made after the warrant is issued.

Nor does the amendment abrogate the requirement of particularity. Thus, it does not authorize searches of premises other than a particular place. As recognized by the Supreme Court in Karo, supra, although agents may not know exactly where moving property will come to rest, they can still describe with particularity the object to be searched.

The amendment would authorize the search of a particular object or container provided that law enforcement officials were otherwise in a lawful position to execute the search without making an impermissible intrusion. For example, it would authorize the search of luggage moving aboard a plane.

Rule 41(a)(3) provides for warrants to search property outside the United States. No provision for search warrants for persons is made lest the rule be read as a substitute for extradition proceedings. As with the provision for searches outside a district, supra, this provision is limited to search warrants issued by federal magistrates. The phrase "relevant to criminal investigation" is intended to encompass all of the types of property that are covered by Rule 41(b), which is unchanged by the amendment. That phrase also is intended to include those investigations which begin with the request for the search warrant.

Some searches and seizures by federal officers outside the territory of the United States may be governed by the fourth amendment. See generally Saltzburg, the Reach of the Bill of Rights Beyond the Terra Firma of the United States, 20 Va. J. Int'l L. 741 (1980). Prior to the amendment of the rule, it was unclear how federal officers might obtain warrants authorizing searches outside the district of the issuing magistrate. Military Rule of Evidence 315 provided guidance for searches of military personnel and property and nonmilitary property in a foreign country. But it had no civilian counterpart. See generally S. Saltzburg, L. Schinasi, & D. Schlueter, Military Rules of Evidence Manual 274-95 (2d ed. 1986).

Although the amendment rests on the assumption that the Constitution applies to some extraterritorial searches, cf United States v. Verdugo-Urquidez, 110 S. Ct. —, — U.S. — (1990) fourth amendment inapplicable to extraterritorial searches of property owned by nonresident aliens, it does not address the question of when the Constitution requires a warrant. Nor does it address the issue of whether international agreements or treaties or the law of a foreign nation might be applicable. See United States v. Patterson, 812 F. 2d 486 (9th Cir. 1987). Instead, the amendment is intended to provide necessary clarification as to how a warrant may be obtained when law enforcement officials are required, or find it desirable, to do so.

Notes of Advisory Committee on 1993 amendments.

The amendment to Rule 41(c)(2)(A) is intended to expand the authority of magistrates and judges in considering oral requests for search warrants. It also recognizes the value of, and the public's increased dependence on facsimile machines to transmit written information efficiently and accurately. As amended, the Rule should thus encourage law enforcement officers to seek a warrant, especially when it is necessary, or desirable, to supplement oral telephonic communications by written materials which may now be transmitted electronically as well. The magistrate issuing the warrant may require that the original affidavit be ultimately filed. The Committee considered, but rejected, amendments to the Rule which would have permitted other means of electronic transmission, such as the use of computer modems. In its view, facsimile transmissions provide some method of assuring the authenticity of the writing transmitted by the affiant.

The Committee considered amendments to Rule 41(c)(2)(B), Application, Rule 41(c) (2(C), Issuance, and Rule 41(g), Return of Papers to Clerk, but determined that allowing use of facsimile transmissions in those instances would not save time and would present problems and questions concerning the need to preserve facsimile copies.

The Rule is also amended to conform to the Judicial Improvements Act of 1990 [P.L. 101-650, Title III, Section 321] which provides that each United States magistrate appointed under section 631 of title 28, United States Code, shall be known as a United States magistrate judge.

Notes of Advisory Committee on 2002 amendments.

The language of Rule 41 has been amended as part of the general restyling of the Criminal Rules to make them more easily understood and to make style and terminology consistent throughout the rules. These changes are intended to be stylistic only, except as otherwise noted below. Rule 41 has been completely reorganized to make it easier to read and apply its key provisions.

Current Rule 41(c)(1), which refers to the fact that hearsay evidence may be used to support probable cause, has been deleted. That language was added to the rule in 1972, apparently to reflect emerging federal case law. *See* Advisory Committee Note to 1972 Amendments to Rule 41 (citing cases). Similar language was added to Rule 4 in 1974. In the intervening years, however, the case law has become perfectly clear on that proposition. Thus, the Committee believed that the reference to hearsay was no longer necessary. Furthermore, the limited reference to hearsay evidence was misleading to the extent that it might have suggested that other forms of inadmissible evidence could not be considered. For example, the rule made no reference to considering a defendant's prior criminal record, which clearly may be considered in deciding whether probable cause exists. See, e.g., *Brinegar v. United States,* 338 U.S. 160 [93 L. Ed. 1879] (1949) (officer's knowledge of defendant's prior criminal activity). Rather than address that issue, or any other similar issues, the Committee believed that the matter was best addressed in Rule 1101(d)(3), Federal Rules of Evidence. That rule explicitly provides that the Federal Rules of Evidence do not apply to "preliminary examinations in criminal cases, . . . issuance of warrants for arrest, criminal summonses, and search warrants . . . ." The Advisory Committee Note accompanying that rule recognizes that: "The nature of the proceedings makes application of the formal rules of evidence inappropriate and impracticable." The Committee did not intend to make any substantive changes in practice by deleting the reference to hearsay evidence.

Current Rule 41(d) provides that the officer taking the property under the warrant must provide a receipt for the property and complete an inventory. The revised rule indicates that the inventory may be completed by an officer present during the execution of the warrant, and not necessarily the officer actually executing the warrant.

Notes of Advisory Committee on 2006 amendments.

The amendments to Rule 41 address three issues: first, procedures for issuing tracking device warrants; second, a provision for delaying any notice required by the rule; and third, a provision permitting a magistrate judge to use reliable electronic means to issue warrants.

Note to Subdivision (a). Amended Rule 41(a)(2) includes two new definitional provisions. The first, in Rule 41(a)(2)(D), addresses the definitions of "domestic terrorism" and "international terrorism," terms used in Rule 41(b)(2). The second, in Rule 41(a)(2)(E), addresses the definition of "tracking device."

Note to Subdivision (b). Amended Rule 41(b)(4) is a new provision, designed to address the use of tracking devices. Such searches are recognized both by statute, *see* 18 U.S.C. § 3117(a) and by caselaw, *see, e.g., United States v. Karo,* 468 U.S. 705 (1984); *United States v. Knotts,* 460 U.S. 276 (1983). Warrants may be required to monitor tracking devices when they are used to monitor persons or property in areas where there is a reasonable expectation of privacy. *See, e.g., United States v. Karo,* supra (although no probable cause was required to install beeper, officers' monitoring of its location in defendant's home raised Fourth Amendment concerns). Nonetheless, there is no procedural guidance in current Rule 41 for those judicial officers who are asked to issue tracking device warrants. As with traditional search warrants for persons or property, tracking device warrants may implicate law enforcement interests in multiple districts.

The amendment provides that a magistrate judge may issue a warrant, if he or she has the authority to do so in the district, to install and use a tracking device, as that term is defined in 18 U.S.C. § 3117(b). The magistrate judge's authority under this rule includes the authority to permit entry into an area where there is a reasonable expectation of privacy, installation of the tracking device, and maintenance and removal of the device. The Committee did not intend by this amendment to expand or contract the definition of what might constitute a tracking device. The amendment is based on the understanding that the device will assist officers only in tracking the movements of a person or property. The warrant may authorize officers to track the person or property within the district of issuance, or outside the district.

Because the authorized tracking may involve more than one district or state, the Committee believes that only federal judicial officers should be authorized to issue this type of warrant. Even where officers have no reason to believe initially that a person or property will move outside the district of issuance, issuing a warrant to authorize tracking both inside and outside the district avoids the necessity of obtaining multiple warrants if the property or person later crosses district or state lines.

The amendment reflects the view that if the officers intend to install or use the device in a constitutionally protected area, they must obtain judicial approval to do so. If, on the other hand, the officers intend to install and use the device without implicating any Fourth Amendment rights, there is no need to obtain the warrant. *See, e.g., United States v. Knotts,* supra, where the officers' actions in installing and following tracking device did not amount to a search under the Fourth Amendment.

Note to Subdivision (d). Amended Rule 41(d) includes new language on tracking devices. The tracking device statute, 18 U.S.C. § 3117, does not specify the standard an applicant must meet to install a tracking device. The Supreme Court has acknowledged that the standard for installation of a tracking device is unresolved, and has reserved ruling on the issue until it is squarely presented by the facts of a case. *See United States v. Karo,* 468 U.S. 705, 718 n. 5 (1984). The amendment to Rule 41 does not resolve this issue or hold that such warrants may issue only on a showing of probable cause. Instead, it simply provides that if probable cause is shown, the magistrate judge must issue the warrant. And the warrant is only needed if the device is installed (for example, in the trunk of the defendant's car) or monitored (for example, while the car is in the defendant's garage) in an area in which the person being monitored has a reasonable expectation of privacy.

Note to Subdivision (e). Rule 41(e) has been amended to permit magistrate judges to use reliable electronic means to issue warrants. Currently, the rule makes no provision for using such media. The amendment parallels similar changes to Rules 5 and 32.1(a)(5)(B)(i).

The amendment recognizes the significant improvements in technology. First, more counsel, courts, and magistrate judges now routinely use facsimile transmissions of documents. And many courts and magistrate judges are now equipped to receive filings by electronic means. Indeed, some courts encourage or require that certain documents be filed by electronic means. Second, the technology has advanced to the state where such filings may be sent from, and received at, locations outside the courthouse. Third, electronic media can now provide improved quality of transmission and security measures. In short, in a particular case, using facsimiles and electronic media to transmit a warrant can be both reliable and efficient use of judicial resources.

The term "electronic" is used to provide some flexibility to the rule and make allowance for further technological advances in transmitting data. Although facsimile transmissions are not specifically identified, the Committee envisions that facsimile transmissions would fall within the meaning of "electronic means."

While the rule does not impose any special requirements on use of facsimile transmissions, neither does it presume that those transmissions are reliable. The rule treats all electronic transmissions in a similar fashion. Whatever the mode, the means used must be "reliable." While the rule does not further define that term, the Committee envisions that a court or magistrate judge would make that determination as a local matter. In deciding whether a particular electronic means, or media, would be reliable, the court might consider first, the expected quality and clarity of the transmission. For example, is it possible to read the contents of the warrant in its entirety, as though it were the original or a clean photocopy? Second, the court may consider whether security measures are available to insure that the transmission is not compromised. In this regard, most courts are now equipped to require that certain documents contain a digital signature, or some other similar system for restricting access. Third, the court may consider whether there are reliable means of preserving the document for later use.

Amended Rule 41(e)(2)(B) is a new provision intended to address the contents of tracking device warrants. To avoid open-ended monitoring of tracking devices, the revised rule requires the magistrate judge to specify in the warrant the length of time for using the device. Although the initial time stated in the warrant may not exceed 45 days, extensions of time may be granted for good cause. The rule further specifies that any installation of a tracking device authorized by the warrant must be made within ten calendar days and, unless otherwise provided, that any installation occur during daylight hours.

Note to Subdivision (f). Current Rule 41(f) has been completely revised to accommodate new provisions dealing with tracking device warrants. First, current Rule 41(f)(1) has been revised to address execution and delivery of warrants to search for and seize a person or property; no substantive change has been made to that provision. New Rule 41(f)(2) addresses execution and delivery of tracking device warrants. That provision generally tracks the structure of revised Rule 41(f)(1), with appropriate adjustments for the particular requirements of tracking device warrants. Under Rule 41(f)(2)(A) the officer must note on the warrant the time the device was installed and the period during which the device was used. And under new Rule 41(f)(2)(B), the officer must return the tracking device warrant to the magistrate judge designated in the warrant, within 10 calendar days after use of the device has ended.

Amended Rule 41(f)(2)(C) addresses the particular problems of serving a copy of a tracking device warrant on the person who has been tracked, or whose property has been tracked. In the case of other warrants, current Rule 41 envisions that the subjects of the search typically know that they have been searched, usually within a short period of time after the search has taken place. Tracking device warrants, on the other hand, are by their nature covert intrusions and can be successfully used only when the person being investigated is unaware that a tracking device is being used. The amendment requires that the officer must serve a copy of the tracking device warrant on the person within 10 calendar days after the tracking has ended. That service may be accomplished by either personally serving the person, or both by leaving a copy at the person's residence or usual abode and by sending a copy by mail. The Rule also provides, however, that the officer may (for good cause) obtain the court's permission to delay further service of the warrant. That might be appropriate, for example, where the owner of the tracked property is undetermined, or where the officer establishes that the investigation is ongoing and that disclosure of the warrant will compromise that investigation.

Use of a tracking device is to be distinguished from other continuous monitoring or observations that are governed by statutory provisions or caselaw. *See* Title III, Omnibus Crime Control and Safe Streets Act of 1968, *as amended* by Title I of the 1986 Electronic Communications Privacy Act, 18 U.S.C. §§ 2510– 2520; *United States v. Biasucci,* 786 F.2d 504 (2d Cir. 1986) (video camera); *United States v. Torres,* 751 F.2d 875 (7th Cir. 1984) (television surveillance).

Finally, amended Rule 41(f)(3) is a new provision that permits the government to request, and the magistrate judge to grant, a delay in any notice required in Rule 41. The amendment is co-extensive with 18 U.S.C. § 3103a(b). That new provision, added as part of the Uniting and Strengthening America by Providing Appropriate Tools Required to Intercept and Obstruct Terrorism (USA PATRIOT) Act of 2001, authorizes a court to delay any notice required in conjunction with the issuance of any search warrants.

Notes of Advisory Committee on 2008 amendments.

Note to Subdivision (b)(5). Rule 41(b)(5) authorizes a magistrate judge to issue a search warrant for property located within certain delineated parts of United States jurisdiction that are outside of any State or any federal judicial district. The locations covered by the rule include United States territories, possessions, and commonwealths not within a federal judicial district as well as certain premises associated with United States diplomatic and consular missions. These are locations in which the United States has a legally cognizable interest or in which it exerts lawful authority and control. The rule is intended to authorize a magistrate judge to issue a search warrant in any of the locations for which 18 U.S.C. § 7(9) provides jurisdiction. The difference between the language in this rule and the statute reflects the style conventions used in these rules, rather than any intention to alter the scope of the legal authority conferred. Under the rule, a warrant may be issued by a magistrate judge in any district in which activities related to the crime under investigation may have occurred, or in the District of Columbia, which serves as the default district for venue under 18 U.S.C. § 3238.

Rule 41(b)(5) provides the authority to issue warrants for the seizure of property in the designated locations when law enforcement officials are required or find it desirable to obtain such warrants. The Committee takes no position on the question whether the Constitution requires a warrant for searches covered by the rule, or whether any international agreements, treaties, or laws of a foreign nation might be applicable. The rule does not address warrants for persons, which could be viewed as inconsistent with extradition requirements.

Notes of Advisory Committee on 2009 amendments.

Note to Subdivision (e)(2). Computers and other electronic storage media commonly contain such large amounts of information that it is often impractical for law enforcement to review all of the information during execution of the warrant at the search location. This rule acknowledges the need for a two-step process: officers may seize or copy the entire storage medium and review it later to determine what electronically stored information falls within the scope of the warrant.

The term "electronically stored information" is drawn from Rule 34(a) of the Federal Rules of Civil Procedure, which states that it includes "writings, drawings, graphs, charts, photographs, sound recordings, images, and other data or data compilations stored in any medium from which information can be obtained." The 2006 Committee Note to Rule 34(a) explains that the description is intended to cover all current types of computer-based information and to encompass future changes and developments. The same broad and flexible description is intended under Rule 41.

In addition to addressing the two-step process inherent in searches for electronically stored information, the Rule limits the 10[14] day execution period to the actual execution of the warrant and the on-site activity. While consideration was given to a presumptive national or uniform time period within which any subsequent off-site copying or review of the media or electronically stored information would take place, the practical reality is that there is no basis for a "one size fits all" presumptive period. A substantial amount of time can be involved in the forensic imaging and review of information. This is due to the sheer size of the storage capacity of media, difficulties created by encryption and booby traps, and the workload of the computer labs. The rule does not prevent a judge from imposing a deadline for the return of the storage media or access to the electronically stored information at the time the warrant is issued. However, to arbitrarily set a presumptive time period for the return could result in frequent petitions to the court for additional time.

It was not the intent of the amendment to leave the property owner without an expectation of the timing for return of the property, excluding contraband or instrumentalities of crime, or a remedy. Current Rule 41(g) already provides a process for the "person aggrieved" to seek an order from the court for a return of the property, including storage media or electronically stored information, under reasonable circumstances.

Where the "person aggrieved" requires access to the storage media or the electronically stored information earlier than anticipated by law enforcement or ordered by the court, the court on a case by case basis can fashion an appropriate remedy, taking into account the time needed to image and search the data and any prejudice to the aggrieved party.

The amended rule does not address the specificity of description that the Fourth Amendment may require in a warrant for electronically stored information, leaving the application of this and other constitutional standards concerning both the seizure and the search to ongoing case law development.

Note to Subdivision (f)(1). Current Rule 41(f)(1) does not address the question of whether the inventory should include a description of the electronically stored information contained in the media seized. Where it is impractical to record a description of the electronically stored information at the scene, the inventory may list the physical storage media seized. Recording a description of the electronically stored information at the scene is likely to be the exception, and not the rule, given the large amounts of information contained on electronic storage media and the impracticality for law enforcement to image and review all of the information during the execution of the warrant. This is consistent with practice in the "paper world." In circumstances where filing cabinets of documents are seized, routine practice is to list the storage devices, i.e., the cabinets, on the inventory, as opposed to making a document by document list of the contents.

The time set in the former rule at 10 days has been revised to 14 days. See the Committee Note to Rule 45(a).

Notes of Advisory Committee on 2011 amendments.

Note to Subdivisions (d)(3) and (e)(3). The amendment deletes the provisions that govern the application for and issuance of warrants by telephone or other reliable electronic means. These provisions have been transferred to new Rule 4.1, which governs complaints and warrants under Rules 3, 4, 9, and 41.

Note to Subdivision (e)(2). The amendment eliminates unnecessary references to "calendar" days. As amended effective December 1, 2009, Rule 45(a)(1) provides that all periods of time stated in days include "every day, including intermediate Saturdays, Sundays, and legal holidays[.]".

Note to Subdivisions (f)(1) and (2). The amendment permits any warrant return to be made by reliable electronic means. Requiring an in-person return can be burdensome on law enforcement, particularly in large districts when the return can require a great deal of time and travel. In contrast, no interest of the accused is affected by allowing what is normally a ministerial act to be done electronically. Additionally, in subdivision (f)(2) the amendment eliminates unnecessary references to "calendar" days. As amended effective December 1, 2009, Rule 45(a)(1) provides that all periods of time stated in days include "every day, including intermediate Saturdays, Sundays, and legal holidays[.]".

Notes of Advisory Committee on 2016 amendments.

Note to subdivision (b). The revision to the caption is not substantive. Adding the word "venue" makes clear that Rule 41(b) identifies the courts that may consider an application for a warrant, not the constitutional requirements for the issuance of a warrant, which must still be met.

Note to Subdivision (b)(6). The amendment provides that in two specific circumstances a magistrate judge in a district where activities related to a crime may have occurred has authority to issue a warrant to use remote access to search electronic storage media and seize or copy electronically stored information even when that media or information is or may be located outside of the district.

First, subparagraph (b)(6)(A) provides authority to issue a warrant to use remote access within or outside that district when the district in which the media or information is located is not known because of the use of technology such as anonymizing software.

Second, (b)(6)(B) allows a warrant to use remote access within or outside the district in an investigation of a violation of 18 U.S.C. § 1030(a)(5) if the media to be searched are protected computers that have been damaged without authorization, and they are located in many districts. Criminal activity under 18 U.S.C. § 1030(a)(5) (such as the creation and control of "botnets") may target multiple computers in several districts. In investigations of this nature, the amendment would eliminate the burden of attempting to secure multiple warrants in numerous districts, and allow a single judge to oversee the investigation.

As used in this rule, the terms "protected computer" and "damage" have the meaning provided in 18 U.S.C. § 1030(e)(2) & (8).

The amendment does not address constitutional questions, such as the specificity of description that the Fourth Amendment may require in a warrant for remotely searching electronic storage media or seizing or copying electronically stored information, leaving the application of this and other constitutional standards to ongoing case law development.

Subdivision (f)(1)(C). The amendment is intended to ensure that reasonable efforts are made to provide notice of the search, seizure, or copying, as well as a receipt for any information that was seized or copied, to the person whose property was searched or who possessed the information that was seized or copied. Rule 41(f)(3) allows delayed notice only "if the delay is authorized by statute." See 18 U.S.C. § 3103a (authorizing delayed notice in limited circumstances).

Amendments:

1976.

Order of April 26, 1976 (eff. Aug. 1, 1976, as provided by § 1 of Act July 8, 1976; see note to Rule 6), in subdiv. (a), added "sought" after "property".

1977.

Order of April 26, 1976, as modified and approved by § 2(e) of Act July 30, 1977 (eff. Oct. 1, 1977, as provided by §§ 1, 4 of Act July 30, 1977; see note to Rule 6), amended subdiv. (c) to read as it appears above, exclusive of subsequent amendment.

2001.

Act Oct. 26, 2001, in subdiv. (a), inserted "and (3) in an investigation of domestic terrorism or international terrorism (as defined in section 2331 of title 18, United States Code), by a Federal magistrate judge in any district in which activities related to the terrorism may have occurred, for a search of property or for a person within or outside the district".

Rule 42. Criminal Contempt

(a) Disposition After Notice. Any person who commits criminal contempt may be punished for that contempt after prosecution on notice.

(1) *Notice.* The court must give the person notice in open court, in an order to show cause, or in an arrest order. The notice must:

(A) state the time and place of the trial;

(B) allow the defendant a reasonable time to prepare a defense; and

(C) state the essential facts constituting the charged criminal contempt and describe it as such.

(2) *Appointing a Prosecutor.* The court must request that the contempt be prosecuted by an attorney for the government, unless the interest of justice requires the appointment of another attorney. If the government declines the request, the court must appoint another attorney to prosecute the contempt.

(3) *Trial and Disposition.* A person being prosecuted for criminal contempt is entitled to a jury trial in any case in which federal law so provides and must be released or detained as Rule 46 provides. If the criminal contempt involves disrespect toward or criticism of a judge, that judge is disqualified from presiding at the contempt trial or hearing unless the defendant consents. Upon a finding or verdict of guilty, the court must impose the punishment.

(b) Summary Disposition. Notwithstanding any other provision of these rules, the court (other than a magistrate judge) may summarily punish a person who commits criminal contempt in its presence if the judge saw or heard the contemptuous conduct and so certifies; a magistrate judge may summarily punish a person as provided in 28 U.S.C. § 636(e). The contempt order must recite the facts, be signed by the judge, and be filed with the clerk.

HISTORY:

Dec. 26, 1944, eff. March 21, 1946; March 9, 1987, eff. Aug. 1, 1987; April 29, 2002, eff. Dec. 1, 2002.

HISTORY; ANCILLARY LAWS AND DIRECTIVES

Other provisions:

Notes of Advisory Committee on Rules. The rule-making power of the Supreme Court with respect to criminal proceedings was extended to proceedings to punish for criminal contempt of court by the Act of November 21, 1941 (55 Stat 779), 18 USC former § 689 (now §§ 3771, 3772).

Note to Subdivision (a). This rule is substantially a restatement of existing law, Ex parte Terry, 128 US 289, 32 L Ed 405; Cooke v United States, 267 US 517, 534, 45 S Ct 390, 69 L Ed 767.

Note to Subdivision (b). 1. This rule is substantially a restatement of the procedure prescribed in 28 USC former §§ 386– 390 (now 18 USC §§ 401, 402, 3285, 3691), and 29 USC former § 111 (now 18 USC § 3692).

2. The requirement in the second sentence that the notice shall describe the criminal contempt as such is intended to obviate the frequent confusion between criminal and civil contempt proceedings and follows the suggestion made in McCann v New York Stock Exchange, 80 F2d 211, CCA2d. See also Nye v United States, 313 US 33, 42–43, 61 S Ct 810, 85 L Ed 1172.

3. The fourth sentence relating to trial by jury preserves the right to a trial by jury in those contempt cases in which

it is granted by statute, but does not enlarge the right or extend it to additional cases. The respondent in a contempt proceeding may demand a trial by jury as of right if the proceeding is brought under the Act of March 23, 1932, ch 90, sec 11, 47 Stat 72, 29 USC former § 111 (now 18 USC § 3692) (Norris-La Guardia Act), or the Act of October 15, 1914, ch 323, sec 22, 38 Stat 738, 28 USC § 387 (Clayton Act).

4. The provision in the sixth sentence disqualifying the judge affected by the contempt if the charge involves disrespect to or criticism of him, is based, in part, on 29 USC former § 112 (Contempts; demand for retirement of judge sitting in proceeding) and the observations of Chief Justice Taft in Cooke v United States, 267 US 517, 539, 45 S Ct 390, 69 L Ed 767.

5. Among the statutory provisions defining criminal contempts are the following:

USC Title 7:

§ 499m (Perishable Agriculture Commodities Act; investigation of complaints; procedure; penalties; etc.—(c) Disobedience to subpoenas; remedy; contempt).

USC Title 9:

§ 7 (Witnesses before arbitrators; fees, compelling attendance).

USC Title 11:

§ 69 (Referees; contempts before).

USC Title 15:

§ 49 (Federal Trade Commission; documentary evidence; depositions; witnesses).

§ 78u (Regulation of Securities Exchanges; investigation; injunctions and prosecution of offenses).

§ 100 (Trade-marks; destruction of infringing labels; service of injunction, and proceedings for enforcement).

§ 155 (China Trade Act; authority of registrar in obtaining evidence).

USC Title 17 former:

§ 36 [now § 112] (Injunctions; service and enforcement).

USC Title 19:

§ 1333 (Tariff Commission; testimony and production of papers—(b) Witnesses and evidence).

USC Title 22:

§ 270f (International Bureaus; Congresses, etc.; perjury; contempts; penalties).

USC Title 28 former:

§ 385 [now § 459; 18 USC § 401] (Administration of oaths; contempts).

§ 386 [now 18 USC §§ 402, 3691] (Contempts; when constituting also criminal offense).

§ 387 [now 18 USC § 402] (Same; procedure; bail; attachment; trial; punishment) (Clayton Act; jury trial; section).

§ 388 (Same; review of conviction).

§ 389 [now 18 USC §§ 402, 3691] (Same; not specifically enumerated).

§ 390 [now 18 USC § 3285] (Same; limitations).

§ 390a [now 18 USC § 402] ("Person" or "persons" defined).

§ 648 [now 18 USC Appx. R 17(f); 28 USC Appx. R 45(d)] (Depositions under dedimus potestatem; witnesses; when required to attend).

§ 703 (Punishment of witness for contempt).

§ 714 [now § 1784] (Failure of witness to obey subpoena; order to show cause in contempt proceedings).

§ 715 [now § 1784] (Direction in order to show cause for seizure of property of witness in contempt).

§ 716 [now § 1784] (Service of order to show cause).

§ 717 [now § 1784] (Hearing on order to show cause; judgment; satisfaction).

§ 750 [now § 2405] (Garnishees in suits by United States against a corporation; garnishee failing to appear).

USC Title 29 former:

§ 111 [now 18 USC § 3692] (Contempts; speedy and public trial; jury) (Norris-La Guardia Act).

§ 112 [now 18 USC Appx. R 42] (Contempts; demands for retirement of judge sitting in proceeding).

§ 160 (Prevention of unfair labor practices—(h) Jurisdiction of courts unaffected by limitations prescribed in sections 101-115 of Title 29).

§ 161 (Investigatory powers of Board—(2) Court aid in compelling productions of evidence and attendance of witnesses).

§ 209 (Fair Labor Standards Act; attendance of witnesses).

USC Title 33:

§ 927 (Longshoremen's and Harbor Workers' Compensation Act; powers of deputy commissioner).

USC Title 35 former:

§ 56 [now § 24] (Failing to attend or testify).

USC Title 47:

§ 409 (Federal Communications Commission; hearing; subpoenas; oaths; witnesses; production of books and papers; contempts; depositions; penalties)

USC Title 48:

§ 1345a (Canal Zone; general jurisdiction of district court; issue of process at request of officials; witnesses; contempt).

USC Title 49:

§ 12 (Interstate Commerce Commission; authority and duties of commission; witnesses; depositions—(3) Compelling attendance and testimony of witnesses, etc.).

Taft-Hartly injunctions. Former 29 USCS § 112, upon which subd. (b) of this rule is in part based, is inapplicable to injunctions issued under the Taft-Hartley Act; see 29 USCS § 178.

The amendments are technical. No substantive change is intended.

Notes of Advisory Committee on 2002 amendments. The language of Rule 42 has been amended as part of the general restyling of the Criminal Rules to make them more easily understood and to make style and terminology consistent throughout the rules. These changes are intended to be stylistic only, except as noted below.

The revised rule is intended to more clearly set out the procedures for conducting a criminal contempt proceeding. The current rule implicitly recognizes that an attorney for the government may be involved in the prosecution of such cases. Revised Rule 42(a)(2) now explicitly addresses the appointment of a "prosecutor" and adopts language to reflect the holding in *Young v. United States ex rel. Vuitton,* 481 U.S. 787 [95 L. Ed. 2d 740] (1987). In that case the Supreme Court indicated that ordinarily the court should request that an attorney for the government prosecute the contempt; only if that request is denied, should the court appoint a private prosecutor. The rule envisions that a disinterested counsel should be appointed to prosecute the contempt.

Rule 42(b) has been amended to make it clear that a court may summarily punish a person for committing contempt in the court's presence without regard to whether other rules, such as Rule 32 (sentencing procedures), might otherwise apply. See, e.g., *United States v. Martin-Trigona,* 759 F.2d 1017 (2d Cir. 1985). Further, Rule 42(b) has been amended to recognize the contempt powers of a court (other than a magistrate judge) and a magistrate judge.

TITLE IX. GENERAL PROVISIONS

Rule

Rule 43. Defendant's Presence

(a) When Required. Unless this rule, Rule 5, or Rule 10 provides otherwise, the defendant must be present at:

(1) the initial appearance, the initial arraignment, and the plea;

(2) every trial stage, including jury impanelment and the return of the verdict; and

(3) sentencing.

(b) When Not Required. A defendant need not be present under any of the following circumstances:

(1) *Organizational Defendant.* The defendant is an organization represented by counsel who is present.

(2) *Misdemeanor Offense.* The offense is punishable by fine or by imprisonment for not more than one year, or both, and with the defendant's written consent, the court permits arraignment, plea, trial, and sentencing to occur by video teleconferencing or in the defendant's absence.

(3) *Conference or Hearing on a Legal Question.* The proceeding involves only a conference or hearing on a question of law.

(4) *Sentence Correction.* The proceeding involves the correction or reduction of sentence under Rule 35 or 18 U.S.C. § 3582(c).

(c) Waiving Continued Presence.

(1) *In General.* A defendant who was initially present at trial, or who had pleaded guilty or nolo contendere, waives the right to be present under the following circumstances:

(A) when the defendant is voluntarily absent after the trial has begun, regardless of whether the court informed the defendant of an obligation to remain during trial;

(B) in a noncapital case, when the defendant is voluntarily absent during sentencing; or

(C) when the court warns the defendant that it will remove the defendant from the courtroom for disruptive behavior, but the defendant persists in conduct that justifies removal from the courtroom.

(2) *Waiver's Effect.* If the defendant waives the right to be present, the trial may proceed to completion, including the verdict's return and sentencing, during the defendant's absence.

HISTORY:

Dec. 26, 1944, eff. March 21, 1946, as amended April 22, 1974, eff. Dec. 1, 1975; Act July 31, 1975, P. L. 94-64, §§ 2, 3(35), 89 Stat. 370, 376, eff. Dec. 1, 1975; March 9, 1987, eff. Aug. 1, 1987; April 27, 1995, eff. Dec. 1, 1995; April 24, 1998, eff. Dec. 1, 1998; April 29, 2002, eff. Dec. 1, 2002; April 26, 2011, eff. Dec. 1, 2011.

HISTORY; ANCILLARY LAWS AND DIRECTIVES

Other provisions:

Notes of Advisory Committee on Rules. 1. The first sentence of the rule setting forth the necessity of the defendant's presence at arraignment and trial is a restatement of existing law, Lewis v United States, 146 US 370, 13 S Ct 136, 36 L Ed 1011; Diaz v United States, 223 US 442, 455, 32 S Ct 250, 56 L Ed 500, Ann Cas 1913C 1138. This principle does not apply to hearings on motions made prior to or after trial, United States v Lynch, 132 F2d 111, CCA 3d.

2. The second sentence of the rule is a restatement of existing law that, except in capital cases, the defendant may not defeat the proceedings by voluntarily absenting himself after the trial has been commenced in his presence. Diaz v United States, 223 US 442, 455, 32 S Ct 250, 56 L Ed 500, Ann Cas 1913C 1138; United States v Noble, 294 Fed 689 (D Mont)—affirmed, 300 Fed 689, CCA 9th; United States v Barracota, 45 F Supp 38, SD NY; United States v Vassalo, 52 F2d 699, ED Mich.

3. The fourth sentence of the rule empowering the court in its discretion, with the defendant's written consent, to conduct proceedings in misdemeanor cases in defendant's absence adopts a practice prevailing in some districts comprising very large areas. In such districts appearance in court may require considerable travel, resulting in expense and hardship not commensurate with the gravity of the charge, if a minor infraction is involved and a small fine is eventually imposed. The rule, which is in the interest of defendants in such situations, leaves it discretionary with the court to permit defendants in misdemeanor cases to absent themselves and, if so, to determine in what types of misdemeanors and to what extent. Similar provisions are found in the statutes of a number of States. See A. L. I. Code of Criminal Procedure, pp 881–882.

4. The purpose of the last sentence of the rule is to resolve a doubt that at times has arisen as to whether it is necessary to bring the defendant to court from an institution in which he is confined, possibly at a distant point, if the court determines to reduce the sentence previously imposed. It seems in the interest of both the Government

and the defendant not to require such presence, because of the delay and expense that are involved.

Notes of Advisory Committee on 1974 amendments. The revision of rule 43 is designed to reflect Illinois v. Allen, 397 U.S. 337, 90 S.Ct. 1057, 25 L.Ed. 2d 353 (1970). In Allen, the court held that "there are at least three constitutionally permissible ways for a trial judge to handle an obstreperous defendant like Allen: (1) bind and gag him, thereby keeping him present; (2) cite him for contempt; (3) take him out of the courtroom until he promises to conduct himself properly." 397 U.S. at 343–344, 90 S.Ct. 1057.

Since rule 43 formerly limited trial in absentia to situations in which there is a "voluntary absence after the trial has been commenced," it could be read as precluding a federal judge from exercising the third option held to be constitutionally permissible in Allen. The amendment is designed to make clear that the judge does have the power to exclude the defendant from the courtroom when the circumstances warrant such action.

The decision in Allen, makes no attempt to spell out standards to guide a judge in selecting the appropriate method to ensure decorum in the courtroom and there is no attempt to do so in the revision of the rule.

The concurring opinion of Mr. Justice Brennan stresses that the trial judge should make a reasonable effort to enable an excluded defendant "to communicate with his attorney and, if possible, to keep apprised of the progress of the trial." 397 U.S. at 351, 90 S.Ct. 1057. The Federal Judicial Center is presently engaged in experimenting with closed circuit television in courtrooms. The experience gained from these experiments may make closed circuit television readily available in federal courtrooms through which an excluded defendant would be able to hear and observe the trial.

The defendant's right to be present during the trial on a capital offense has been said to be so fundamental that it may not be waived. Diaz v. United States, 223 U.S. 442, 455, 32 S.Ct. 250, 56 L.Ed. 500 (1912) (dictum); Near v. Cunningham, 313 F.2d 929, 931 (4th Cir. 1963); C. Wright, Federal Practice and Procedure: Criminal § 723 at 199 (1969, Supp.1971).

However, in Illinois v. Allen, supra the court's opinion suggests that sanctions such as contempt may be least effective where the defendant is ultimately facing a far more serious sanction such as the death penalty. 397 U.S. at 345, 90 S.Ct. 1057. The ultimate determination of when a defendant can waive his right to be present in a capital case (assuming a death penalty provision is held constitutional, see Furman v. Georgia, 408 U.S. 238, 92 S.Ct. 2726, 33 L.Ed.2d 346 (1972)) is left for further clarification by the courts.

Subdivision (b)(1) makes clear that voluntary absence may constitute a waiver even if the defendant has not been informed by the court of his obligation to remain during the trial. Of course, proof of voluntary absence will require a showing that the defendant knew of the fact that the trial or other proceeding was going on. C. Wright, Federal Practice and Procedure: Criminal § 723 n. 35 (1969). But it is unnecessary to show that he was specifically warned of his obligation to be present; a warning seldom is thought necessary in current practice. [See Taylor v. United States, 414 U.S. 17, 94 S.Ct. 194, 38 L.Ed.2d 174 (1973).]

Subdivision (c)(3) makes clear that the defendant need not be present at a conference held by the court and counsel where the subject of the conference is an issue of law.

The other changes in the rule are editorial in nature. In the last phrase of the first sentence, "these rules" is changed to read "this rule," because there are no references in any of the other rules to situations where the defendant is not required to be present. The phrase "at the time of the plea," is added to subdivision (a) to make perfectly clear that defendant must be present at the time of the plea. See rule 11(c)(5) which provides that the judge may set a time, other than arraignment, for the holding of a plea agreement procedure.

Notes of Committee on the Judiciary, House Report No. 94-247. A. Amendments Proposed by the Supreme Court. Rule 43 of the Federal Rules of Criminal Procedure deals with the presence of the defendant during the proceedings against him. It presently permits a defendant to be tried in absentia only in non-capital cases where the defendant has voluntarily absented himself after the trial has begun.

The Supreme Court amendments provide that a defendant has waived his right to be present at the trial of a capital or noncapital case in two circumstances: (1) when he voluntarily absents himself after the trial has begun; and (2) where he "engages in conduct which is such as to justify his being excluded from the courtroom."

B. Committee Action. The Committee added language to subdivision (b)(2), which deals with excluding a disruptive defendant from the courtroom. The Advisory Committee Note indicates that the rule proposed by the Supreme Court was drafted to reflect the decision in Illinois v. Allen, 397 U.S. 337 (1970). The Committee found that subdivision (b)(2) as proposed did not full track the Allen decision. Consequently, language was added to that subsection to require the court to warn a disruptive defendant before excluding him from the courtroom.

The amendments are technical. No substantive change is intended.

Notes of Advisory Committee on 1995 amendments. The revisions to Rule 43 focus on two areas. First, the amendments make clear that a defendant who, initially present at trial or who has entered a plea of guilty or nolo contendere, but who voluntarily flees before sentencing, may nonetheless be sentenced in absentia. Second, the rule is amended to extend to organizational defendants. In addition, some stylistic changes have been made.

Subdivision (a). The changes to subdivision (a) are stylistic in nature and the Committee intends no substantive change in the operation of that provision.

Subdivision (b). The changes in subdivision (b) are intended to remedy the situation where a defendant voluntarily flees before sentence is imposed. Without the amendment, it is doubtful that a court could sentence a defendant who had been present during the entire trial but flees before sentencing. Delay in conducting the sentencing hearing under such circumstances may result in difficulty later in gathering and presenting the evidence necessary to formulate a guideline sentence.

The right to be present at court, although important, is not absolute. The caselaw, and practice in many jurisdictions, supports the proposition that the right to be present at trial may be waived through, inter alia, the act of fleeing. *See generally Crosby v. United States*, 122 L Ed 2d 25, 113 S.Ct. 748, 506 U.S. 255 (1993). The amendment extends only to noncapital cases and applies only where the defendant is voluntarily absent after the trial has commenced or where the defendant has entered a plea of guilty or nolo contendere. The Committee envisions that defense counsel will continue to represent the interests of the defendant at sentencing.

The words "at trial, or having pleaded guilty or nolo contendere" have been added at the end of the first sentence to make clear that the trial of an absent defendant is possible only if the defendant was previously present at the trial or has entered a plea of guilty or nolo contendere. *See Crosby v. United States, supra.*

Subdivision (c). The change to subdivision (c) is technical in nature and replaces the word "corporation" with a reference to "organization," as that term is defined in 18 U.S.C. § 18 to include entities other than corporations.

Notes of Advisory Committee on 1998 amendments. The amendment to Rule 43(c)(4) is intended to address two issues. First, the rule is rewritten to clarify whether a defendant is entitled to be present at resentencing proceedings conducted under Rule 35. As a result of amendments over the last several years to Rule 35, implementation of the Sentencing Reform Act, and caselaw interpretations of Rules 35 and 43, questions had been raised whether the defendant had to be present at those proceedings. Under the present version of the rule, it could be possible to require the defendant's presence at a "reduction" of sentence hearing conducted under Rule 35(b), but not a "correction" of sentence hearing conducted under Rule 35(a). That potential result seemed at odds with sound practice. As amended, Rule 43(c)(4) would permit a court to reduce or correct a sentence under Rule 35(b) or (c), respectively, without the defendant being present. But a sentencing proceeding being conducted on remand by an appellate court under Rule 35(a) would continue to require the defendant's presence. *See, e.g., United States v. Moree,* 928 F.2d 654, 655–656(5th Cir. 1991) (noting distinction between presence of defendant at modification of sentencing proceedings and those hearings that impose new sentence after original sentence has been set aside).

The second issue addressed by the amendment is the applicability of Rule 43 to resentencing hearings conducted under 18 U.S.C. § 3582(c). Under that provision, a resentencing may be conducted as a result of retroactive changes to the Sentencing Guidelines by the United States Sentencing Commission or as a result of a motion by the Bureau of Prisons to reduce a sentence based on "extraordinary and compelling reasons." The amendment provides that a defendant's presence is not required at such proceedings. In the Committee's view, those proceedings are analogous to Rule 35(b) as it read before the Sentencing Reform Act of 1984, where the defendant's presence was not required. Further, the court may only reduce the original sentence under these proceedings.

Notes of Advisory Committee on 2002 amendments. The language of Rule 43 has been amended as part of the general restyling of the Criminal Rules to make them more easily understood and to make style and terminology consistent throughout the rules. These changes are intended to be stylistic only, except as noted below.

The first substantive change is reflected in Rule 43(a), which recognizes several exceptions to the requirement that a defendant must be present in court for all proceedings. In addition to referring to exceptions that might exist in Rule 43 itself, the amendment recognizes that a defendant need not be present when the court has permitted video teleconferencing procedures under Rules 5 and 10 or when the defendant has waived the right to be present for the arraignment under Rule 10. Second, by inserting the word "initial" before "arraignment," revised Rule 43(a)(1) reflects the view that a defendant need not be present for subsequent arraignments based upon a superseding indictment.

The Rule has been reorganized to make it easier to read and apply; revised Rule 43(b) is former Rule 43(c).

Notes of Advisory Committee on 2011 amendments. *Note to Subdivision (b).* This rule currently allows proceedings in a misdemeanor case to be conducted in the defendant's absence with the defendant's written consent and the court's permission. The amendment allows participation through video teleconference as an alternative to appearing in person or not appearing. Participation by video teleconference is permitted only when the defendant has consented in writing and received the court's permission.

The Committee reiterates the concerns expressed in the 2002 Committee Notes to Rules 5 and 10, when those rules were amended to permit video teleconferencing. The Committee recognized the intangible benefits and impact of requiring a defendant to appear before a federal judicial officer in a federal courtroom, and what is lost when virtual presence is substituted for actual presence. These concerns are particularly heightened when a defendant is not present for the determination of guilt and sentencing. However, the Committee concluded that the use of video teleconferencing may be valuable in circumstances where the defendant would otherwise be unable to attend and the rule now authorizes proceedings in absentia.

Amendments:

1975.

Act July 31, 1975, § 3(35) (effective 12/1/75, as provided by § 2 of such Act; see note to Rule 4), substituted subdiv. (b)(2) for one which read "(2) engages in conduct which is such as to justify his being excluded from the courtroom".

Rule 44. Right to and Appointment of Counsel

(a) Right to Appointed Counsel. A defendant who is unable to obtain counsel is entitled to have counsel appointed to represent the defendant at every stage of the proceeding from initial appearance through appeal, unless the defendant waives this right.

(b) Appointment Procedure. Federal law and local court rules govern the procedure for implementing the right to counsel.

(c) Inquiry Into Joint Representation.

(1) *Joint Representation.* Joint representation occurs when:

(A) two or more defendants have been charged jointly under Rule 8(b) or have been joined for trial under Rule 13; and

(B) the defendants are represented by the same counsel, or counsel who are associated in law practice.

(2) *Court's Responsibilities in Cases of Joint Representation.* The court must promptly inquire about the propriety of joint representation and must personally advise each defendant of the right to the effective assistance of counsel, including separate representation. Unless there is good cause to believe that no conflict of interest is likely to arise, the court must take

appropriate measures to protect each defendant's right to counsel.

HISTORY:

Dec. 26, 1944, eff. March 21, 1946, as amended Feb. 28, 1966, eff. July 1, 1966; April 24, 1972, eff. Oct. 1, 1972; April 30, 1979, eff. Dec. 1, 1980, as provided by Act July 31, 1979, P. L. 96-42, § 1(1), 93 Stat. 362; March 9, 1987, eff. Aug. 1, 1987; April 22, 1993, eff. Dec. 1, 1993; April 29, 2002, eff. Dec. 1, 2002.

HISTORY; ANCILLARY LAWS AND DIRECTIVES

Other provisions:

Notes of Advisory Committee on Rules.

1. This rule is a restatement of existing law in regard to the defendant's constitutional right of counsel as defined in recent judicial decisions. The Sixth Amendment provides:

"In all criminal prosecutions, the accused shall enjoy the right . . . to have the Assistance of Counsel for his defense.".

28 USC former § 394 (now § 1654) provides:

"In all the courts of the United States the parties may plead and manage their own causes personally, or by the assistance of such counsel or attorneys at law as, by the rules of the said courts, respectively, are permitted to manage and conduct causes therein.".

18 USC former § 563 (now § 3005), which is derived from the act of April 30, 1790 (1 Stat 118), provides:

"Every person who is indicted of treason or other capital crime, shall be allowed to make his full defense by counsel learned in the law; and the court before which he is tried or some judge thereof, shall immediately, upon his request, assign to him such counsel, not exceeding two, as he may desire, and they shall have free access to him at all reasonable hours.".

The present extent of the right of counsel has been defined recently in Johnson v Zerbst, 304 US 458, 58 S Ct 1019, 82 L Ed 1461; Walker v Johnston, 312 US 275, 61 S Ct 574, 85 L Ed 830; and Glasser v United States, 315 US 60, 62 S Ct 457, 86 L Ed 680, rehearing denied 315 US 827, 62 S Ct 629, 637, two cases, 86 L Ed 1222. The rule is a restatement of the principles enunciated in these decisions. See, also, Holtzoff, 20 NYU L Q R 1.

2. The rule is intended to indicate that the right of the defendant to have counsel assigned by the court relates only to proceedings in court and, therefore, does not include preliminary proceedings before a committing magistrate. Although the defendant is not entitled to have counsel assigned to him in connection with preliminary proceedings, he is entitled to be represented by counsel retained by him, if he so chooses, Rule 5(b) (Proceedings before the Commissioner; Statement by the Commissioner) and Rule 40(b)(2) (Commitment to Another District; Removal—Arrest in Distant District—Statement by Commissioner or Judge). As to defendant's right of counsel in connection with the taking of depositions, see Rule 15(c) (Depositions—Defendant's Counsel and Payment of Expenses).

Notes of Advisory Committee on 1966 amendments.

A new rule is provided as a substitute for the old to provide for the assignment of counsel to defendants unable to obtain counsel during all stages of the proceeding. The Supreme Court has recently made clear the importance of providing counsel both at the earliest possible time after arrest and on appeal. See Crooker v California, 357 US 433, 2 L Ed 2d 1448, 78 S Ct 1287 (1958); Cicenia v LaGay, 357 US 504, 2 L Ed 2d 1523, 78 S Ct 1297 (1958); White v Maryland, 373 US 59, 10 L Ed 2d 193, 83 S Ct 1050 (1963); Gideon v Wainwright, 372 US 335, 9 L Ed 2d 799, 83 S Ct 792, 93 ALR2d 733 (1963); Douglas v California, 372 US 353, 9 L Ed 2d 811, 83 S Ct 814 (1963). See also Association of the Bar of the City of New York, Special Committee to Study the Defender System, Equal Justice for the Accused (1959); Report of the Attorney General's Committee on Poverty and the Administration of Justice (1963); Beaney, Right to Counsel Before Arraignment, 45 Minn L Rev 771 (1961); Boskey, The Right to Counsel in Appellate Proceedings, 45 Minn L Rev 783 (1961); Douglas, The Right to Counsel—A Foreword, 45 Minn L Rev 693 (1961); Kamisar, The Right to Counsel and the Fourteenth Amendment; A Dialogue on "The Most Pervasive Right" of an Accused, 30 U Chi L Rev 1 (1962); Kamisar, Betts v Brady Twenty Years Later: The Right to Counsel and Due Process Values, 61 Mich L Rev 219 (1962); Symposium, The Right to Counsel, 22 Legal Aid Briefcase 4–48 (1963). Provision has been made by law for a Legal Aid Agency in the District of Columbia which is charged with the duty of providing counsel and courts are admonished to assign such counsel "as early in the proceeding as practicable." DC Code § 2-2202. Congress has now made provision for assignment of counsel and their compensation in all of the districts. Criminal Justice Act of 1964 (78 Stat 552).

Like the original rule the amended rule provides a right to counsel which is broader in two respects than that for which compensation is provided in the Criminal Justice Act of 1964: (1) the right extends to petty offenses to be tried in the district courts, and (2) the right extends to defendants unable to obtain counsel for reasons other than financial. These rules do not cover procedures other than those in the courts of the United States and before United States commissioners. See Rule 1. Hence, the problems relating to the providing of counsel prior to the initial appearance before a court or commissioner are not dealt with in this rule. Cf. Escobedo v United States, 378 US 478, 12 L Ed 2d 977 (1964); Enker and Elsen, Counsel for the Suspect: Massiah v United States and Escobedo v Illinois, 49 Minn L Rev 47 (1964).

Subdivision (a). This subdivision expresses the right of the defendant unable to obtain counsel to have such counsel assigned at any stage of the proceedings from his initial appearance before the commissioner or court through the appeal, unless he waives such right. The phrase "from his initial appearance before the commissioner or court" is intended to require the assignment of counsel as promptly as possible after it appears that the defendant is unable to obtain counsel. The right to assignment of counsel is not limited to those financially unable to obtain counsel. If a defendant is able to compensate counsel but still cannot obtain counsel, he is entitled to the assignment of counsel even though not to free counsel.

Subdivision (b). This new subdivision reflects the adoption of the Criminal Justice Act of 1964. See Report of the Judicial Conference of the United States on the Criminal Justice Act of 1964, 36 FRD 277 (1964).

Notes of Advisory Committee on 1972 amendments.

Subdivision (a) is amended to reflect the Federal Magistrates Act of 1968. The phrase "federal magistrate" is defined in rule 54.

Notes of Advisory Committee on 1979 amendments. [effective Dec. 1, 1980, as provided by Act July 31, 1979, P. L. 96-42, § 1(1), 93 Stat. 326]. Rule 44(c) establishes a procedure for avoiding the occurrence of events which might otherwise give rise to a plausible post-conviction claim that because of joint representation the defendants in a criminal case were deprived of their Sixth Amendment right to the effective assistance of counsel. Although "courts have differed with respect to the scope and nature of the affirmative duty of the trial judge to assure that criminal defendants are not deprived of their right to the effective assistance of counsel by joint representation of conflicting interests," Holloway v. Arkansas, 98 S.Ct. 1173 (1978) (where the Court found it unnecessary to reach this issue), this amendment is generally consistent with the current state of the law in several circuits. As held in United States v. Carrigan, 543 F.2d 1053 (2d Cir. 1976):

"When a potential conflict of interest arises, either where a court has assigned the same counsel to represent several defendants or where the same counsel has been retained by co-defendants in a criminal case, the proper course of action for the trial judge is to conduct a hearing to determine whether a conflict exists to the degree that a defendant may be prevented from receiving advice and assistance sufficient to afford him the quality of representation guaranteed by the Sixth Amendment. The defendant should be fully advised by the trial court of the facts underlying the potential conflict and be given the opportunity to express his views.".

See also United States v. Lawriw, 568 F.2d 98 (8th Cir. 1977) (duty on [of] trial judge to make inquiry where joint representation by appointed or retained counsel, and "without such an inquiry a finding of knowing and intelligent waiver will seldom, if ever, be sustained by this Court"); Abraham v. United States, 549 F.2d 236 (2d Cir. 1977); United States v. Mari, 526 F.2d 117 (2d Cir. 1975); United States v. Truglio, 493 F.2d 574 (4th Cir. 1974) (joint representation should cause trial judge "to inquire whether the defenses to be presented in any way conflict"); United States v. DeBerry, 487 F.2d 488 (2d Cir. 1973); United States ex rel. Hart v. Davenport, 478 F.2d 203 (3d Cir. 1973) (noting there "is much to be said for the rule . . . which assumes prejudice and nonwaiver if there has been no on-the-record inquiry by the court as to the hazards to defendants from joint representation"); United States v. Alberti, 470 F.2d 878 (2d Cir. 1973); United States v. Foster, 469 F.2d 1 (1st Cir. 1972) (lack of sufficient inquiry shifts the burden of proof on the question of prejudice to the government); Campbell v. United States, 352 F.2d 359 (D.C.Cir. 1965) (where joint representation, court "has a duty to ascertain whether each defendant has an awareness of the potential risks of that course and nevertheless has knowingly chosen it"). Some states have taken a like position; see, e.g., State v. Olsen, — Minn. —, 258 N.W.2d 898 (1977).

This procedure is also consistent with that recommended in the ABA Standards Relating to the Function of the Trial Judge (Approved Draft, 1972), which provide in § 3.4(b):

"Whenever two or more defendants who have been jointly charged, or whose cases have been consolidated, are represented by the same attorney, the trial judge should inquire into potential conflicts which may jeopardize the right of each defendant to the fidelity of his counsel.".

Avoiding a conflict-of-interest situation is in the first instance a responsibility of the attorney. If a lawyer represents "multiple clients having potentially differing interests, he must weigh carefully the possibility that his judgment may be impaired or his loyalty divided if he accepts or continues the employment," and he is to "resolve all doubts against the propriety of the representation." Code of Professional Responsibility, Ethical Consideration 5-15. See also ABA Standards Relating to the Defense Function § 3.5(b) (Approved Draft, 1971), concluding that the "potential for conflict of interest in representing multiple defendants is so grave that ordinarily a lawyer should decline to act for more than one of several co-defendants except in unusual situations when, after careful investigation, it is clear that no conflict is likely to develop and when the several defendants give an informed consent to such multiple representation."

It by no means follows that the inquiry provided for by rule 44(c) is unnecessary. For one thing, even the most diligent attorney may be unaware of facts giving rise to a potential conflict. Often "counsel must operate somewhat in the dark and feel their way uncertainly to an understanding of what their clients may be called upon to meet upon a trial" and consequently "are frequently unable to foresee developments which may require changes in strategy." United States v. Carrigan, supra (concurring opinion). "Because the conflicts are often subtle it is not enough to rely upon counsel, who may not be totally disinterested, to make sure that each of his joint clients has made an effective waiver." United States v. Lawriw, supra.

Moreover, it is important that the trial judge ascertain whether the effective and fair administration of justice would be adversely affected by continued joint representation, even when an actual conflict is not then apparent. As noted in United States v. Mari, supra (concurring opinion):

"Trial court insistence that, except in extraordinary circumstances, codefendants retain separate counsel will in the long run . . . prove salutary not only to the administration of justice and the appearance of justice but the cost of justice; habeas corpus petitions, petitions for new trials, appeals and occasionally retrials . . . can be avoided. Issues as to whether there is an actual conflict of interest, whether the conflict has resulted in prejudice, whether there has been a waiver, whether the waiver is intelligent and knowledgeable, for example, can all be avoided. Where a conflict that first did not appear subsequently arises in or before trial, . . . continuances or mistrials can be saved. Essentially by the time a case . . . gets to the appellate level the harm to the appearance of justice has already been done, whether or not reversal occurs; at the trial level it is a matter which is so easy to avoid.".

A rule 44(c) inquiry is required whether counsel is assigned or retained. It "makes no difference whether counsel is appointed by the court or selected by the defendants; even where selected by the defendants the same dangers of potential conflict exist, and it is also possible that the rights of the public to the proper administration of justice may be affected adversely." United States v. Mari, supra (concurring opinion). See also United States v. Lawriw, supra. When there has been "no discussion as to possible conflict initiated by the court," it cannot be assumed that the choice of counsel by the defendants "was intelligently made with knowledge of any possible conflict." United States v. Carrigan, supra. As for assigned counsel, it is provided by statute that "the court shall appoint separate counsel for defendants having interests that cannot properly be represented by the same counsel, or when other good cause is shown." 18 U.S.C. § 3006(A)(b). Rule 44(c) is not intended to prohibit the automatic appointment of separate counsel in the first instance, see Ford v. United States, 379 F.2d 123 (D.C.Cir. 1967); Lollar v. United States, 376 F.2d 243 (D.C.Cir. 1967), which would obviate the necessity for an inquiry.

Under rule 44(c), an inquiry is called for when the joined defendants are represented by the same attorney and also when they are represented by attorneys "associated in the practice of law." This is consistent with Code of Professional Responsibility, Disciplinary Rule 5-105(D) (providing that if "a lawyer is required to decline employment or to withdraw from employment" because of a potential conflict, "no partner or associate of his or his firm may accept or continue such employment"); and ABA Standards Relating to the Defense Function § 3.5(b) (Approved Draft, 1971) (applicable to "a lawyer or lawyers who are associated in practice"). Attorneys representing joined defendants should so advise the court if they are associated in the practice of law.

The rule 44(c) procedure is not limited to cases expected to go to trial. Although the more dramatic conflict situations, such as when the question arises as to whether the several defendants should take the stand, Morgan v. United States, 396 F.2d 110 (2d Cir. 1968), tend to occur in a trial context, serious conflicts may also arise when one or more of the jointly represented defendants pleads guilty.

The problem is that even where as here both codefendants pleaded guilty there are frequently potential conflicts of interest . . . [T]he prosecutor may be inclined to accept a guilty plea from one codefendant which may harm the interests of the other. The contrast in the dispositions of the cases may have a harmful impact on the codefendant who does not initially plead guilty; he may be pressured into pleading guilty himself rather than face his codefendant's bargained-for testimony at a trial. And it will be his own counsel's recommendation to the initially pleading codefendant which will have contributed to this harmful impact upon him . . . [I]n a given instance it would be at least conceivable that the prosecutor would be willing to accept pleas to lesser offenses from two defendants in preference to a plea of guilty by one defendant to a greater offense.

United States v. Mari, supra (concurring opinion). To the same effect is ABA Standards Relating to the Defense Function at 213–14.

It is contemplated that under rule 44(c) the court will make appropriate inquiry of the defendants and of counsel regarding the possibility of a conflict of interest developing. Whenever it is necessary to make a more particularized inquiry into the nature of the contemplated defense, the court should "pursue the inquiry with defendants and their counsel on the record but in chambers" so as "to avoid the possibility of prejudicial disclosures to the prosecution." United States v. Foster, supra. It is important that each defendant be "fully advised of the facts underlying the potential conflict and is given an opportunity to express his or her views." United States v. Alberti, supra. The rule specifically requires that the court personally advise each defendant of his right to effective assistance of counsel, including separate representation. See United States v. Foster, supra, requiring that the court make a determination that jointly represented defendants "understand that they may retain separate counsel, or if qualified, may have such counsel appointed by the court and paid for by the government."

Under rule 44(c), the court is to take appropriate measures to protect each defendant's right to counsel unless it appears "there is good cause to believe no conflict of interest is likely to arise" as a consequence of the continuation of such joint representation. A less demanding standard would not adequately protect the Sixth Amendment right to effective assistance of counsel or the effective administration of criminal justice. Although joint representation "is not per se violative of constitutional guarantees of effective assistance of counsel, Holloway v. Arkansas, supra, it would not suffice to require the court to act only when a conflict of interest is then apparent, for it is not possible to "anticipate with complete accuracy the course that a criminal trial may take."Fryar v. United States, 404 F.2d 1071 (10th Cir. 1968). This is particularly so in light of the fact that if a conflict later arises and a defendant thereafter raises a Sixth Amendment objection, a court must grant relief without indulging "in nice calculations as to the amount of prejudice arising from its denial."Glasser v. United States, 315 U.S. 60 (1942). This is because, as the Supreme Court more recently noted in Holloway v. Arkansas, supra, "in a case of joint representation of conflicting interests the evil . . . is in what the advocate finds himself compelled to refrain from doing," and this makes it "virtually impossible" to assess the impact of the conflict.

Rule 44(c) does not specify what particular measures must be taken. It is appropriate to leave this within the court's discretion, for the measures which will best protect each defendant's right to counsel may well vary from case to case. One possible course of action is for the court to obtain a knowing, intelligent and voluntary waiver of the right to separate representation, for, as noted in Holloway v. Arkansas, supra, "a defendant may waive his right to the assistance of an attorney unhindered by a conflict of interests." See United States v. DeBerry, supra, holding that defendants should be jointly represented only if "the court has ascertained that . . . each understands clearly the possibilities of a conflict of interest and waives any rights in connection with it." It must be emphasized that a "waiver of the right to separate representation should not be accepted by the court unless the defendants have each been informed of the probable hazards; and the voluntary character of their waiver is apparent." ABA Standards Relating to the Function of the Trial Judge at 45. United States v. Garcia, supra, spells out in significant detail what should be done to assure an adequate waiver:

"As in Rule 11 procedures, the district court should address each defendant personally and forthrightly advise him of the potential dangers of representation by counsel with a conflict of interest. The defendant must be at liberty to question the district court as to the nature and consequences of his legal representation. Most significantly, the court should seek to elicit a narrative response from each defendant that he has been advised of his right to effective representation, that he understands the details of his attorney's possible conflict of interest and the potential perils of such a conflict, that he has discussed the matter with his attorney or if he wishes with outside counsel, and that he voluntarily waives his Sixth Amendment protections. It is, of course, vital that the waiver be established by "clear, unequivocal, and unambiguous language." . . . Mere assent in response to a series of questions from the bench may in some circumstances constitute an adequate waiver, but the court should nonetheless endeavor to have each defendant personally articulate in detail his intent to forego this significant constitutional protection. Recordation of the waiver colloque between defendant and judge will also serve the government's interest by assisting in shielding any potential conviction from collateral attack, either on Sixth Amendment grounds or on a Fifth or Fourteenth Amendment 'fundamental fairness' basis.".

See also Hyman, Joint Representation of Multiple Defendants in a Criminal Trial: The Court's Headache, 5 Hofstra L.Rev. 315, 334 (1977).

Another possibility is that the court will order that the defendants be separately represented in subsequent proceedings in the case. Though the court must remain alert to and take account of the fact that "certain advantages might accrue from joint representation," Holloway v. Arkansas, supra, it need not permit the joint representation to continue merely because the defendants express a willingness to so proceed. That is,

"there will be cases where the court should require separate counsel to represent certain defendants despite the expressed wishes of such defendants. Indeed, failure of the trial court to require separate representation may . . . require a new trial, even though the defendants have expressed a desire to continue with the same counsel. The right to effective representation by counsel whose loyalty is undivided is so paramount in the proper administration of criminal justice that it must in some cases take precedence over all other considerations, including the expressed preference of the defendants concerned and their attorney.".

United States v. Carrigan, supra (concurring opinion). See also United States v. Lawriw, supra; Abraham v. United States, supra; ABA Standards Relating to the Defense Function at 213, concluding that in some circumstances "even full disclosure and consent of the client may not be a adequate protection." As noted in United States v. Dolan, 570 F.2d 1177 (3d Cir. 1978), such an order may be necessary where the trial judge is.

"not satisfied that the waiver is proper. For example, a defendant may be competent enough to stand trial, but not competent enough to understand the complex, subtle, and sometimes unforeseeable dangers inherent in multiple representation. More importantly, the judge may find that the waiver cannot be intelligently made simply because he is not in a position to inform the defendant of the foreseeable prejudices multiple representation might entail for him.".

As concluded in Dolan, "exercise of the court's supervisory powers by disqualifying an attorney representing multiple criminal defendants in spite of the defendants' express desire to retain that attorney does not necessarily abrogate defendant's sixth amendment rights". It does not follow from the absolute right of self-representation recognized in Faretta v. California, 422 U.S. 806 (1975), that there is an *absolute* right to counsel of one's own choice. Thus,

United States v. Dolan, supra. See also Geer, Conflict of Interest and Multiple Defendants in a Criminal Case: Professional Responsibilities of the Defense Attorney, 62 Minn.L.Rev. 119 (1978); Note, Conflict of Interests in Multiple Representation of Criminal Co-Defendants, 68 J.Crim.L. & C. 226 (1977).

The failure in a particular case to conduct a rule 44(c) inquiry would not, standing alone, necessitate the reversal of a conviction of a jointly represented defendant. However, as is currently the case, a reviewing court is more likely to assume a conflict resulted from the joint representation when no inquiry or an inadequate inquiry was conducted. United States v. Carrigan, supra; United States v. DeBerry, supra. On the other hand, the mere fact that a rule 44(c) inquiry was conducted in the early stages of the case does not relieve the court of all responsibility in this regard thereafter. The obligation placed upon the court by rule 44(c) is a continuing one, and thus in a particular case further inquiry may be necessary on a later occasion because of new developments suggesting a potential conflict of interest.

Notes of Advisory Committee on 1987 amendments.

The amendments are technical. No substantive change is intended.

Notes of Advisory Committee on 1993 amendments.

The Rule is amended to conform to the Judicial Improvements Act of 1990 [P. L. 101-650, Title III, Section 321] which provides that each United States magistrate appointed under section 631 of title 28, United States Code, shall be known as a United States magistrate judge.

Notes of Advisory Committee on 2002 amendments.

The language of Rule 44 has been amended as part of the general restyling of the Criminal Rules to make them more easily understood and to make style and terminology consistent throughout the rules. These changes are intended to be stylistic only.

Revised Rule 44 now refers to the "appointment" of counsel, rather than the assignment of counsel; the Committee believed the former term was more appropriate. *See* 18 U.S.C. § 3006A. In Rule 44(c), the term "retained or assigned" has been deleted as being unnecessary, without changing the court's responsibility to conduct an inquiry where joint representation occurs.

Rule 45. Computing and Extending Time

(a) Computing Time. The following rules apply in computing any time period specified in these rules, in any local rule or court order, or in any statute that does not specify a method of computing time.

(1) *Period Stated in Days or a Longer Unit.* When the period is stated in days or a longer unit of time:

(A) exclude the day of the event that triggers the period;

(B) count every day, including intermediate Saturdays, Sundays, and legal holidays; and

(C) include the last day of the period, but if the last day is a Saturday, Sunday, or legal holiday, the period continues to run until the end of the next day that is not a Saturday, Sunday, or legal holiday.

(2) *Period Stated in Hours.* When the period is stated in hours:

(A) begin counting immediately on the occurrence of the event that triggers the period;

(B) count every hour, including hours during intermediate Saturdays, Sundays, and legal holidays; and

(C) if the period would end on a Saturday, Sunday, or legal holiday, the period continues to run until the same time on the next day that is not a Saturday, Sunday, or legal holiday.

(3) *Inaccessibility of the Clerk's Office.* Unless the court orders otherwise, if the clerk's office is inaccessible:

(A) on the last day for filing under Rule 45(a)(1), then the time for filing is extended to the first accessible day that is not a Saturday, Sunday, or legal holiday; or

(B) during the last hour for filing under Rule 45(a)(2), then the time for filing is extended to the same time on the first accessible day that is not a Saturday, Sunday, or legal holiday.

(4) *"Last Day" Defined.* Unless a different time is set by a statute, local rule, or court order, the last day ends:

(A) for electronic filing, at midnight in the court's time zone; and

(B) for filing by other means, when the clerk's office is scheduled to close.

(5) *"Next Day" Defined.* The "next day" is determined by continuing to count forward when the period is measured after an event and backward when measured before an event.

(6) *"Legal Holiday" Defined.* "Legal holiday" means:

(A) the day set aside by statute for observing New Year's Day, Martin Luther King Jr.'s Birthday, Washington's Birthday, Memorial Day, Juneteenth National Independence Day, Independence Day, Labor Day, Columbus Day, Veterans' Day, Thanksgiving Day, or Christmas Day;

(B) any day declared a holiday by the President or Congress; and

(C) for periods that are measured after an event, any other day declared a holiday by the state where the district court is located.

(b) Extending Time.

(1) *In General.* When an act must or may be done within a specified period, the court on its own may extend the time, or for good cause may do so on a party's motion made:

(A) before the originally prescribed or previously extended time expires; or

(B) after the time expires if the party failed to act because of excusable neglect.

(2) *Exception.* The court may not extend the time to take any action under Rule 35, except as stated in that rule.

(c) Additional Time After Certain Kinds of Service. Whenever a party must or may act within a specified time after being served and service is made under Rule 49(a)(4)(C), (D), and (E), 3 days are added after the period would otherwise expire under subdivision (a).

HISTORY:

Dec. 26, 1944, eff. March 21, 1946, as amended Feb. 28, 1966, eff. July 1, 1966; Dec. 4, 1967, eff. July 1, 1968; March 1, 1971, eff. July 1, 1971; April 28, 1982, eff. Aug. 1, 1982; April 29, 1985, eff. Aug. 1, 1985; March 9, 1987, eff. Aug. 1, 1987; April 29, 2002, eff. Dec. 1, 2002; April 25, 2005, eff. Dec. 1, 2005; April 30, 2007, eff. Dec. 1, 2007; April 23, 2008, eff. Dec. 1, 2008; March 26, 2009, eff. Dec. 1, 2009; April 28, 2016, eff. Dec. 1, 2016; April 26, 2018, eff. Dec. 1, 2018; April 24, 2023, eff. Dec. 1, 2023.

HISTORY; ANCILLARY LAWS AND DIRECTIVES

Other provisions:

Notes of Advisory Committee on Rules. The rule is in substance the same as Rule 6 of the Federal Rules of Civil Procedure, 28 USC, Appendix. It seems desirable that matters covered by this rule should be regulated in the same manner for civil and criminal cases, in order to preclude possibility of confusion.

Note to subdivision (a). This rule supersedes the method of computing time prescribed by Rule 13 of the Criminal Appeals Rules, promulgated on May 7, 1934, 292 US 661, 78 L Ed 1515.

Note to subdivision (c). This rule abolishes the expiration of a term of court as a time limitation for the taking of any step in a criminal proceeding, as is done for civil cases by Rule 6(c) of the Federal Rules of Civil Procedure, 28 USC, Appendix. In view of the fact that the duration of terms of court varies among the several districts and the further fact that the length of time for the taking of any step limited by a term of court depends on the stage within the term when the time begins to run, specific time limitations have been substituted for the taking of any step which previously had to be taken within the term of court.

Note to subdivision (d). Cf. Rule 47 (Motions) and Rule 49 (Service and filing of papers).

Notes of Advisory Committee on 1966 amendments. Subdivision (a). This amendment conforms the subdivision with the amendments made effective on July 1, 1963, to the comparable provision in Civil Rule 6(a). The only major change is to treat Saturdays as legal holidays for the purpose of computing time.

Subdivision (b). The amendment conforms the subdivision to the amendments made effective in 1948 to the comparable provision in Civil Rule 6(b). One of these conforming changes, substituting the words "extend the time" for the words "enlarge the period" clarifies the ambiguity which gave rise to the decision in United States v Robinson (1960) 361 US 220, 4 L Ed 2d 259, 80 S Ct 282. The amendment also, in connection with the amendments to Rules 29 and 37, makes it clear that the only circumstances under which extensions can be granted under Rules 29, 33, 34, 35, 37(a)(2) and 39(c) are those stated in them.

Subdivision (c). Subdivision (c) of Rule 45 is rescinded as unnecessary in view of the 1963 amendment to 28 U.S.C. § 138 eliminating terms of court.

Notes of Advisory Committee on 1968 amendments. The amendment eliminates inappropriate references to Rules 37 and 39 which are to be abrogated.

Notes of Advisory Committee on 1971 amendments. The amendment adds Columbus Day to the list of legal holidays to conform the subdivision to the Act of June 28, 1968, 82 Stat 250, which constituted Columbus Day a legal holiday effective after January 1, 1971.

The Act, which amended Title 5, USC, § 6103(a), changes the day on which certain holidays are to be observed. Washington's Birthday, Memorial Day and Veterans Day are to be observed on the third Monday in February, the last Monday in May and the fourth Monday in October, respectively, rather than, as heretofore, on February 22, May 30, and November 11, respectively. Columbus Day is to be observed on the second Monday in October. New Year's Day, Independence Day, Thanksgiving Day and Christmas continue to be observed on the traditional days.

Notes of Advisory Committee on 1982 amendments. Rule 45(a). The amendment to subdivision (a) takes account of the fact that on rare occasion severe weather conditions or other circumstances beyond control will make it impossible to meet a filing deadline under Rule 45(a). Illustrative is an incident which occurred in Columbus, Ohio during the "great blizzard of 1978," in which weather conditions deteriorated to the point where personnel in the clerk's office found it virtually impossible to reach the courthouse, and where the GSA Building Manager found it necessary to close and secure the entire building. The amendment covers that situation and also similar situations in which weather or other conditions made the clerk's office, though open, not readily accessible to the lawyer. Whether the clerk's office was in fact "inaccessible" on a given date is to be determined by the district court. Some state time computation statutes contain language somewhat similar to that in the amendment; see, e.g., Md. Code Ann. art. 94, § 2.

Notes of Advisory Committee on 1985 amendments. The rule is amended to extend the exclusion of intermediate Saturdays, Sundays, and legal holidays to the computation of time periods less than 11 days. Under the current version of the Rule, parties bringing motions under rules with 10-day periods could have as few as 5 working days to prepare their motions. This change corresponds to the change being made in the comparable provision in Fed.R.Civ.P. 6(a).

The Birthday of Martin Luther King, Jr., which becomes a legal holiday effective January 1986, has been added to the list of legal holidays enumerated in the Rule.

The amendments are technical. No substantive change is intended.

Notes of Advisory Committee on 1988 amendments. Prior to 1985, the rule provided that intervening weekends and legal holidays would not be counted if the prescribed or allowed time was less than 7 days. The rule was amended in 1985 to include intervening weekends and legal holidays only if the time permitted or allowed was less than 11 days. That amendment corresponded to an amendment to Fed. R. Civ. P. 6(a).

The proposed change, which would exclude weekends and legal holidays when the time prescribed for action is less than 8 days, recognizes that important motions in criminal cases—e.g., for judgments of acquittal (Rule 29) and for new trials (Rule 33)—must be made within a 7 day period. The Committee concluded that it would be undesirable to return to the pre-1985 rule, which counted weekends and legal holidays as part of the 7 days and, in some instances, provided less than five working days for motion preparation. But, the Committee concluded that a reduction from 11 to 8 would not be unfair to defendants and would conform Rule 45(a) to proposed amendments to Fed. R. App. P. 26(a), Fed. R. Civ. P. 6(a), and Fed. R. Bankr. P. 9006(a).

Notes of Advisory Committee on 2002 amendments. The language of Rule 45 has been amended as part of the general restyling of the Criminal Rules to make them more easily understood and to make style and terminology consistent throughout the rules. These changes are intended to be stylistic only.

The additional three days provided by Rule 45(c) is extended to the means of service authorized by the new paragraph (D) added to Rule 5(b) of the Federal Rules of Civil Procedure, including—with the consent of the person served—service by electronic means. The means of service authorized in civil actions apply to criminal cases under Rule 49 (b).

Rule 45(d), which governs the timing of written motions and affidavits, has been moved to Rule 47.

Notes of Advisory Committee on 2005 amendments. Rule 45(b) has been amended to conform to amendments to Rules 29, 33, and 34, which have been amended to remove the requirement that the court must act within the seven-day period specified in each of those rules if it sets another time for filing a motion under those rules.

Currently, Rules 29(c)(1), 33(b)(2), and 34(b) require the defendant to move for relief under those rules within the seven-day periods specified in those rules or within some other time set by the court in an order issued during that same seven-day period. Courts have held that the seven-day rule is jurisdictional. Thus, for example, if a defendant files a request for an extension of time to file a motion for a judgment of acquittal or a motion for new trial within the seven-day period, the court must rule on that motion or request within the same seven-day period. If for some reason the court does not rule on the request for an extension of time within the seven days, the court loses jurisdiction to act on the underlying substantive motion. *See, e.g., United States v. Smith*, 331 U.S. 469, 473–474 (1947) (rejecting argument that trial court had power to grant new trial on its own motion after expiration of time in Rule 33); *United States v. Marquez*, 291 F.3d 23, 27–28 (D.C. Cir. 2002) (citing language of Rule 33, and holding that "district court forfeited the power to act when it failed to . . . fix a new time for filing a motion for a new trial within seven days of the verdict").

Rule 45(b)(2) currently specifies that a court may not extend the time for taking action under Rules 29, 33, or 34, except as provided in those rules.

Assuming that the current provisions in Rules 29, 33, and 34 were intended to promote finality, there is nothing to prevent the court from granting the defendant a significant extension of time, under those rules, as long as it does so within the seven-day period. Thus, the Committee believed that those rules should be amended to be consistent with all of the other timing requirements in the rules, which do not force the court to rule on a motion to extend the time for filing, within a particular period of time or lose jurisdiction to do so. The change to Rule 45(b)(2) is thus a conforming amendment.

The defendant is still required to file motions under Rules 29, 33, and 34 within the seven-day period specified in those rules. The defendant, however, may consistently with Rule 45, seek an extension of time to file the underlying motion as long as the defendant does so within the seven-day period. But the court itself is not required to act on that motion within any particular time. Further, under Rule 45(b)(1)(B), if for some reason the defendant fails to file the underlying motion within the specified time, the court may nonetheless consider that untimely motion if the court determines that the failure to file it on time was the result of excusable neglect.

Notes of Advisory Committee on 2007 amendments. *Subdivision (c).* Rule 45(c) is amended to remove any doubt as to the method for extending the time to respond after service by mail, leaving with the clerk of court, electronic means, or other means consented to by the party served. This amendment parallels the change in Federal Rule of Civil Procedure 6(e). Three days are added after the prescribed period otherwise expires under Rule 45(a). Intermediate Saturdays, Sundays, and legal holidays are included in counting these added three days. If the third day is a Saturday, Sunday, or legal holiday, the last day to act is the next day that is not a Saturday, Sunday, or legal holiday. The effect of invoking the day that the rule would otherwise expire under Rule 45(a) can be illustrated by assuming that the thirtieth day of a thirty-day period is a Saturday. Under Rule 45(a) the period expires on the next day that is not a Sunday or legal holiday. If the following Monday is a legal holiday, under Rule 45(a) the period expires on Tuesday. Three days are then added—Wednesday, Thursday, and Friday as the third and final day to act unless that is a legal holiday. If the prescribed period ends on a Friday, the three added days are Saturday, Sunday, and Monday, which is the third and final day to act unless it is a legal holiday. If Monday is a legal holiday, the next day that is not a legal holiday is the third and final day to act.

Application of Rule 45(c) to a period that is less than eleven days can be illustrated by a paper that is served by mailing on a Friday. If ten days are allowed to respond, intermediate Saturdays, Sundays, and legal holidays are excluded in determining when the period expires under Rule 45(a). If there is no legal holiday, the period expires on the Friday two weeks after the paper was mailed. The three added Rule 45(c) days are Saturday, Sunday, and Monday, which is the third and final day to act unless it is a legal holiday. If Monday is a legal holiday, the next day that is not a legal holiday is the final day to act.

Notes of Advisory Committee on 2008 amendments. This amendment revises the cross references to Civil Rule 5, which have been renumbered as part of a general restyling of the Federal Rules of Civil Procedure. No substantive change is intended.

Notes of Advisory Committee on 2009 amendments. *Note to Subdivision (a).* Subdivision (a) has been amended to simplify and clarify the provisions that describe how deadlines are computed. Subdivision (a) governs the computation of any time period found in a statute that does not specify a method of computing time, a Federal Rule of Criminal Procedure, a local rule, or a court order. In accordance with Rule 57(a)(1), a local rule may not direct that a deadline be computed in a manner inconsistent with subdivision (a). In making these time computation rules applicable to statutory time periods, subdivision (a) is consistent with Civil Rule 6(a). It is also consistent with the language of Rule 45 prior to restyling, when the rule applied to "computing any period of time." Although the restyled Rule 45(a) referred only to time periods "specified in these rules, any local rule, or any court order," some courts nonetheless applied the restyled Rule 45(a) when computing various statutory periods.

The time-computation provisions of subdivision (a) apply only when a time period must be computed. They do not apply when a fixed time to act is set. The amendments thus carry forward the approach taken in *Violette v. P.A. Days, Inc.*, 427 F.3d 1015, 1016 (6th Cir. 2005) (holding that Civil Rule 6(a) "does not apply to situations where the court has established a specific calendar day as a deadline"), and reject the contrary holding of *In re American Healthcare Management, Inc.*, 900 F.2d 827, 832 (5th Cir. 1990) (holding that Bankruptcy Rule 9006(a) governs treatment of a date-certain deadline set by court order). If, for example, the date for filing is "no later than November 1, 2007," subdivision (a) does not govern. But if a filing is required to be made "within 10 days" or "within 72 hours," subdivision (a) describes how that deadline is computed.

Subdivision (a) does not apply when computing a time period set by a statute if the statute specifies a method of computing time. *See, e.g.,* 18 U.S.C. § 3142(d) (excluding Saturdays, Sundays, and holidays from 10 day period). In addition, because the time period in Rule 46(h) is derived from 18 U.S.C. §§ 3142(d) and 3144, the Committee concluded that Rule 45(a) should not be applied to Rule 46(h).

Note to Subdivision (a)(1). New subdivision (a)(1) addresses the computation of time periods that are stated in days. It also applies to time periods that are stated in weeks, months, or years. *See, e.g.,* Rule 35(b)(1). Subdivision (a)(1)(B)'s directive to "count every day" is relevant only if the period is stated in days (not weeks, months or years).

Under former Rule 45(a), a period of 11 days or more was computed differently than a period of less than 11 days. Intermediate Saturdays, Sundays, and legal holidays were included in computing the longer periods, but excluded in computing the shorter periods. Former Rule 45(a) thus made computing deadlines unnecessarily complicated and led to counterintuitive results. For example, a 10-day period and a 14-day period that started on the same day usually ended on the same day—and the 10-day period not infrequently ended later than the 14-day period. *See Miltimore Sales, Inc. v. Int'l Rectifier, Inc.*, 412 F.3d 685, 686 (6th Cir. 2005).

Under new subdivision (a)(1), all deadlines stated in days (no matter the length) are computed in the same way. The day of the event that triggers the deadline is not counted. All other days—including intermediate Saturdays, Sundays, and legal holidays—are counted, with only one exception: if the period ends on a Saturday, Sunday, or legal holiday, then the deadline falls on the next day that is not a Saturday, Sunday, or legal holiday. An illustration is provided below in the discussion of subdivision (a)(5). Subdivision (a)(3) addresses filing deadlines that expire on a day when the clerk's office is inaccessible.

Where subdivision (a) formerly referred to the "act, event, or default" that triggers the deadline, the new subdivision (a) refers simply to the "event" that triggers the deadline; this change in terminology is adopted for brevity and simplicity, and is not intended to change the meaning.

Periods previously expressed as less than 11 days will be shortened as a practical matter by the decision to count intermediate Saturdays, Sundays, and legal holidays in computing all periods. Many of those periods have been lengthened to compensate for the change. *See, e.g.,* Rules 29(c)(1), 33(b)(2), 34, and 35(a).

Most of the 10-day periods were adjusted to meet the change in computation method by setting 14 days as the new period. A 14-day period corresponds to the most frequent result of a 10-day period under the former computation method—two Saturdays and two Sundays were excluded, giving 14 days in all. A 14-day period has an additional advantage. The final day falls on the same day of the week as the event that triggered the period—the 14th day after a Monday, for example, is a Monday. This advantage of using week-long periods led to adopting 7-day periods to replace some of the periods set at less than 10 days, and 21-day periods to replace 20-day periods. Thirty-day and longer periods, however, were generally retained without change.

Note to Subdivision (a)(2). New subdivision (a)(2) addresses the computation of time periods that are stated in hours. No such deadline currently appears in the Federal Rules of Criminal Procedure. But some statutes contain deadlines stated in hours, as do some court orders issued in expedited proceedings.

Under subdivision (a)(2), a deadline stated in hours starts to run immediately on the occurrence of the event that triggers the deadline. The deadline generally ends when the time expires. If, however, the time period expires at a specific time (say, 2:17 p.m.) on a Saturday, Sunday, or legal holiday, then the deadline is extended to the same time (2:17 p.m.) on the next day that is not a Saturday, Sunday, or legal holiday. Periods stated in hours are not to be "rounded up" to the next whole hour. Subdivision (a)(3) addresses situations when the clerk's office is inaccessible during the last hour before a filing deadline expires.

Subdivision (a)(2)(B) directs that every hour be counted. Thus, for example, a 72-hour period that commences at 10:23 a.m. on Friday, November 2, 2007, will run until 9:23 a.m. on Monday, November 5; the discrepancy in start and end times in this example results from the intervening shift from daylight saving time to standard time.

Note to Subdivision (a)(3). When determining the last day of a filing period stated in days or a longer unit of time, a day on which the clerk's office is not accessible because of the weather or another reason is treated like a Saturday, Sunday, or legal holiday. When determining the end of a filing period stated in hours, if the clerk's office is inaccessible during the last hour of the filing period computed under subdivision (a)(2) then the period is extended to the same time on the next day that is not a weekend, holiday or day when the clerk's office is inaccessible.

Subdivision (a)(3)'s extensions apply "[u]nless the court orders otherwise." In some circumstances, the court might not wish a period of inaccessibility to trigger a full 24-hour extension; in those instances, the court can specify a briefer extension.

The text of the rule no longer refers to "weather or other conditions" as the reason for the inaccessibility of the clerk's office. The reference to "weather" was deleted from the text to underscore that inaccessibility can occur for reasons unrelated to weather, such as an outage of the electronic filing system. Weather can still be a reason for inaccessibility of the clerk's office. The rule does not attempt to define inaccessibility. Rather, the concept will continue to develop through caselaw, *see, e.g.,* William G. Phelps, *When Is Office of Clerk of Court Inaccessible Due to Weather or Other Conditions for Purpose of Computing Time Period for Filing Papers under Rule 6(a) of Federal Rules of Civil Procedure,* 135 A.L.R. Fed. 259 (1996) (collecting cases). In addition, many local provisions address inaccessibility for purposes of electronic filing, *see, e.g.,* D. Kan. Rule CR49.11 ("A Filing User whose filing is made untimely as the result of a technical failure may seek appropriate relief from the court.").

Note to Subdivision (a)(4). New subdivision (a)(4) defines the end of the last day of a period for purposes of subdivision (a)(1). Subdivision (a)(4) does not apply in computing periods stated in hours under subdivision (a)(2), and does not apply if a different time is set by a statute, local rule, or order in the case. A local rule may, for example, address the problems that might arise if a single district has clerk's offices in different time zones, or provide that papers filed in a drop box after the normal hours of the clerk's office are filed as of the day that is date-stamped on the papers by a device in the drop box.

28 U.S.C. § 452 provides that "[a]ll courts of the United States shall be deemed always open for the purpose of filing proper papers, issuing and returning process, and making motions and orders." A corresponding provision exists in Rule 56(a). Some courts have held that these provisions permit an after-hours filing by handing the papers to an appropriate official. *See, e.g., Casalduc v. Diaz,* 117 F.2d 915, 917 (1st Cir. 1941). Subdivision (a)(4) does not address the effect of the statute on the question of after-hours filing; instead, the rule is designed to deal with filings in the ordinary course without regard to Section 452.

Note to Subdivision (a)(5). New subdivision (a)(5) defines the "next" day for purposes of subdivisions (a)(1)(C) and (a)(2)(C). The Federal Rules of Criminal Procedure contain both forward-looking time periods and backward-looking time periods. A forward-looking time period requires something to be done within a period of time *after* an event. *See, e.g.,* Rule 35(a) (stating that a court may correct an arithmetic or technical error in a sentence "[w]ithin 14 days after sentencing"). A backward-looking time period requires something to be done within a period of time *before* an event. *See, e.g.,* Rule 47(c) (stating that a party must serve a written motion "at least 7 days before the hearing date"). In determining what is the "next" day for purposes of subdivisions (a)(1)(C) and (a)(2)(C), one should continue counting in the same direction—that is, forward when computing a forward-looking period and backward when computing a backward-looking period. If, for example, a filing is due within 10 days *after* an event, and the tenth day falls on Saturday, September 1, 2007, then the filing is due on Tuesday, September 4, 2007 (Monday, September 3, is Labor Day). But if a filing is due 10 days *before* an event, and the tenth day falls on Saturday, September 1, then the filing is due on Friday, August 31. If the clerk's office is inaccessible on August 31, then subdivision (a)(3) extends the filing deadline forward to the next accessible day that is not a Saturday, Sunday, or legal holiday—no earlier than Tuesday, September 4.

Note to Subdivision (a)(6). New subdivision (a)(6) defines "legal holiday" for purposes of the Federal Rules of Criminal Procedure, including the time-computation provisions of subdivision (a). Subdivision (a)(6) continues to include within the definition of "legal holiday" days that are declared a holiday by the President or Congress.

For forward-counted periods—i.e., periods that are measured after an event—subdivision (a)(6)(C) includes certain state holidays within the definition of legal holidays. However, state legal holidays are not recognized in computing backward-counted periods. For both forward- and backward-counted periods, the rule thus protects those who may be unsure of the effect of state holidays. For forward-counted deadlines, treating state holidays the same as federal holidays extends the deadline. Thus, someone who thought that the federal courts might be closed on a state holiday would be safeguarded against an inadvertent late filing. In contrast, for backward-counted deadlines, not giving state holidays the treatment of federal holidays allows filing on the state holiday itself rather than the day before. Take, for example, Monday, April 21, 2008 (Patriot's Day, a legal holiday in the relevant state). If a filing is due 14 days after an event, and the fourteenth day is April 21, then the filing is due on Tuesday, April 22 because Monday, April 21 counts as a legal holiday. But if a filing is due 14 days before an event, and the fourteenth day is April 21, the filing is due on Monday, April 21; the fact that April 21 is a state holiday does not make April 21 a legal holiday for purposes of computing this backward-counted deadline. But note that if the clerk's office is inaccessible on Monday, April 21, then subdivision (a)(3) extends the April 21 filing deadline forward to the next accessible day that is not a Saturday, Sunday or legal holiday—no earlier than Tuesday, April 22.

Notes of Advisory Committee on 2016 amendments. *Note to subdivision (c).* Rule 45(c) and Rule 6(d) of the Federal Rules of Civil Procedure contain parallel provisions providing additional time for actions after certain modes of service, identifying those modes by reference to Civil Rule 5(b)(2). Rule 45(c)--like Civil Rule 6(d)--is amended to remove service by electronic means under Rule 5(b)(2)(E) from the forms of service that allow 3 added days to act after being served. The amendment also adds clarifying parentheticals identifying the forms of service for which 3 days will still be added.

Civil Rule 5 was amended in 2001 to allow service by electronic means with the consent of the person served, and a parallel amendment to Rule 45(c) was adopted in 2002. Although electronic transmission seemed virtually instantaneous even then, electronic service was included in the modes of service that allow 3 added days to act after being served. There were concerns that the transmission might be delayed for some time, and particular concerns that incompatible systems might make it difficult or impossible to open attachments. Those concerns have been substantially alleviated by advances in technology and widespread skill in using electronic transmission.

A parallel reason for allowing the 3 added days was that electronic service was authorized only with the consent of the person to be served. Concerns about the reliability of electronic transmission might have led to refusals of consent; the 3 added days were calculated to alleviate these concerns.

Diminution of the concerns that prompted the decision to allow the 3 added days for electronic transmission is not the only reason for discarding this indulgence. Many rules have been changed to ease the task of computing time by adopting 7-, 14-, 21-, and 28-day periods that allow "day-of-the-week" counting. Adding 3 days at the end complicated the counting, and increased the occasions for further complication by invoking the provisions that apply when the last day is a Saturday, Sunday, or legal holiday.

Eliminating Rule 5(b) subparagraph (2)(E) from the modes of service that allow 3 added days means that the 3 added days cannot be retained by consenting to service by electronic means. Consent to electronic service in registering for electronic case filing, for example, does not count as consent to service "by any other means of delivery" under subparagraph (F).

Electronic service after business hours, or just before or during a weekend or holiday, may result in a practical reduction in the time available to respond. Extensions of time may be warranted to prevent prejudice.

Notes of Advisory Committee on 2018 Amendments. Rule 49 previously required service and filing "in a manner provided" in the Civil Rules, and the time counting provisions in Criminal Rule 45(c) referred to certain means of service under Civil Rule 5. A contemporaneous amendment moves the instructions for filing and service in criminal cases from Civil Rule 5 into Criminal Rule 49. This amendment revises the cross references in Rule 45(c) to reflect this change.

Notes of Advisory Committee on 2023 Amendments. The amendment adds "Juneteenth National Independence Day" to the list of legal holidays. See Juneteenth National Independence Day Act, P.L. 117-17 (2021) (amending 5 U.S.C. § 6103(a)).

Rule 46. Release from Custody; Supervising Detention

(a) Before Trial. The provisions of 18 U.S.C. §§ 3142 and 3144 govern pretrial release.

(b) During Trial. A person released before trial continues on release during trial under the same terms and conditions. But the court may order different terms and conditions or terminate the release if necessary to ensure that the person will be present during trial or that the person's conduct will not obstruct the orderly and expeditious progress of the trial.

(c) Pending Sentencing or Appeal. The provisions of 18 U.S.C. § 3143 govern release pending sentencing or appeal. The burden of establishing that the defendant will not flee or pose a danger to any other person or to the community rests with the defendant.

(d) Pending Hearing on a Violation of Probation or Supervised Release. Rule 32.1(a)(6) governs release pending a hearing on a violation of probation or supervised release.

(e) Surety. The court must not approve a bond unless any surety appears to be qualified. Every surety, except a legally approved corporate surety, must demonstrate by affidavit that its assets are adequate. The court may require the affidavit to describe the following:

(1) the property that the surety proposes to use as security;

(2) any encumbrance on that property;

(3) the number and amount of any other undischarged bonds and bail undertakings the surety has issued; and

(4) any other liability of the surety.

(f) Bail Forfeiture.

(1) *Declaration.* The court must declare the bail forfeited if a condition of the bond is breached.

(2) *Setting Aside.* The court may set aside in whole or in part a bail forfeiture upon any condition the court may impose if:

(A) the surety later surrenders into custody the person released on the surety's appearance bond; or

(B) it appears that justice does not require bail forfeiture.

(3) *Enforcement.*

(A) *Default Judgment and Execution.* If it does not set aside a bail forfeiture, the court must, upon the government's motion, enter a default judgment.

(B) *Jurisdiction and Service.* By entering into a bond, each surety submits to the district court's jurisdiction and irrevocably appoints the district clerk as its agent to receive service of any filings affecting its liability.

(C) *Motion to Enforce.* The court may, upon the government's motion, enforce the surety's liability without an independent action. The government must serve any motion, and notice as the court prescribes, on the district clerk. If so served, the clerk must promptly mail a copy to the surety at its last known address.

(4) *Remission.* After entering a judgment under Rule 46(f)(3), the court may remit in whole or in part the judgment under the same conditions specified in Rule 46(f)(2).

(g) Exoneration. The court must exonerate the surety and release any bail when a bond condition has been satisfied or when the court has set aside or remitted the forfeiture. The court must exonerate a surety who deposits cash in the amount of the bond or timely surrenders the defendant into custody.

(h) Supervising Detention Pending Trial.

(1) *In General.* To eliminate unnecessary detention, the court must supervise the detention within the district of any defendants awaiting trial and of any persons held as material witnesses.

(2) *Reports.* An attorney for the government must report biweekly to the court, listing each material witness held in custody for more than 10 days pending indictment, arraignment, or trial. For each material witness listed in the report, an attorney for the government must state why the witness should not be released with or without a deposition being taken under Rule 15(a).

(i) Forfeiture of Property. The court may dispose of a charged offense by ordering the forfeiture of 18 U.S.C. § 3142(c)(1)(B)(xi) property under 18 U.S.C. § 3146(d), if a fine in the amount of the property's value would be an appropriate sentence for the charged offense.

(j) Producing a Statement.

(1) *In General.* Rule 26.2(a)–(d) and (f) applies at a detention hearing under 18 U.S.C. § 3142, unless the court for good cause rules otherwise.

(2) *Sanctions for Not Producing a Statement.* If a party disobeys a Rule 26.2 order to produce a witness's statement, the court must not consider that witness's testimony at the detention hearing.

HISTORY:

Dec. 26, 1944, eff. March 1, 1946, as amended April 9, 1956, eff. 90 days after April 9, 1956; Feb. 28, 1966, eff. July 1, 1966; April 24, 1972, eff. Oct. 1, 1972; Oct. 12, 1984, P. L. 98-473, Title II, Ch I, § 209(d), 98 Stat. 1987; March 9, 1987, eff. Aug. 1, 1987; April 30, 1991, eff. Dec. 1, 1991; April 22, 1993, eff. Dec. 1, 1993; Sept. 13, 1994; P. L. 103-322, Title XXXIII, § 330003(h), 108 Stat. 2141; April 29, 2002, eff. Dec. 1, 2002.

HISTORY; ANCILLARY LAWS AND DIRECTIVES

Other provisions:

Notes of Advisory Committee on Rules. *Note to subdivision (a)(1).* This rule is substantially a restatement of existing law, 18 USC former §§ 596, 597 (now § 3141).

Note to subdivision (a)(2). This rule is substantially a restatement of Rule 6 of Criminal Appeals Rules, with the addition of a reference to bail pending certiorari. This rule does not supersede 18 USC former § 682 (now § 3731) (Appeals; on behalf of the United States; rules of practice and procedure), which provides for the admission of the defendant to bail on his own recognizance pending an appeal taken by the Government.

Note to subdivision (b). This rule is substantially a restatement of existing law, 28 USC former § 657.

Note to subdivision (d). This rule is a restatement of existing practice, and is based in part on 6 USC § 15 (Bonds or notes of United States in lieu of recognizance, stipulation, bond, guaranty, or undertaking; place of deposit; return to depositor; contractors' bonds).

Note to subdivision (e). This rule is similar to Sec 79 of ALI Code of Criminal Procedure introducing, however, an element of flexibility. Corporate sureties are regulated by 6 USC §§ 6– 14 [31 USCS §§ 9304– 9308].

Note to subdivision (f). 1. With the exception hereafter noted, this rule is substantially a restatement of existing law in somewhat greater detail than contained in 18 USC former § 601 (Remission of penalty of recognizance).

2. Subdivision (f)(2) changes existing law in that it increases the discretion of the court to set aside a forfeiture. The power of the court under 18 USC former § 601 was limited to cases in which the defendant's default had not been willful.

3. The second sentence of paragraph (3) is similar to Rule 73(f) of the Federal Rules of Civil Procedure, 28 USC, Appendix. This paragraph also substitutes simple motion procedure for enforcing forfeited bail bonds for the procedure by scire facias, which was abolished by Rule 81(b) of the Federal Rules of Civil Procedure, 28 USC, Appendix.

Note to subdivision (g). This rule is a restatement of existing law and practice. It is based in part on 18 USC former § 599 (now § 3142) (Surrender by bail).

Notes of Advisory Committee on 1966 amendments.. Subdivision (c). The more inclusive word "terms" is substituted for "amount" in view of the amendment to subdivision (d) authorizing releases without security on such conditions as are necessary to insure the appearance of the defendant. The phrase added at the end of this subdivision is designed to encourage commissioners and judges to set the terms of bail so as to eliminate unnecessary detention. See Stack v Boyle, 342 US 1, 96 L Ed 3, 72 S Ct 1 (1951); Bandy v United States, 5 L Ed 2d 218, 81 S Ct 197 (US, 1960); Bandy v United States, 7 L Ed 2d 9, 82 S Ct 11 (US, 1961); Carbo v United States, 7 L Ed 2d 769, 82 S Ct 662 (US, 1962); review den 369 US 868, 8 L Ed 2d 274, 82 S Ct 1137 (1962).

Subdivision (d). The amendments are designed to make possible (and to encourage) the release on bail of a greater percentage of indigent defendants than now are released. To the extent that other considerations make it reasonably likely that the defendant will appear it is both good practice and good economics to release him on bail even though he cannot arrange for cash or bonds in even small amounts. In fact it has been suggested that it may be a denial of constitutional rights to hold indigent prisoners in custody for no other reason than their inability to raise the money for a bond. Bandy v United States, 5 L Ed 2d 218, 81 S Ct 197 (US, 1960).

The first change authorizes the acceptance as security of a deposit of cash or government securities in an amount less than the face amount of the bond. Since a defendant typically purchases a bail bond for a cash payment of a certain percentage of the face of the bond, a direct deposit with the court of that amount (returnable to the defendant upon his appearance) will often be equally adequate as a deterrent to flight. Cf. Ill Code Crim Proc § 110-7 (1963).

The second change authorizes the release of the defendant without financial security on his written agreement to appear when other deterrents appear reasonably adequate. See the discussion of such deterrents in Bandy v United States, 5 L Ed 2d 218, 81 S Ct 197 (US, 1960). It also permits the imposition of nonfinancial conditions as the price of dispensing with security for the bond. Such conditions are commonly used in England. Devlin, the Criminal Prosecution in England, 89 (1958). See the suggestion in Note, Bail: An Ancient Practice Reexamined, 70 Yale LJ 966, 975 (1961) that such conditions ". . . might include release in custody of a third party, such as the accused's employer, minister, attorney, or a private organization; release subject to a duty to report periodically to the court or other public official; or even release subject to a duty to return to jail each night." Willful failure to appear after forfeiture of bail is a separate criminal offense and hence an added deterrent to flight. 18 USC § 3146.

For full discussion and general approval of the changes made here see Report of the Attorney General's Committee on Poverty and the Administration of Criminal Justice 58–89 (1963).

Subdivision (h). The purpose of this new subdivision is to place upon the court in each district the responsibility for supervising the detention of defendants and witnesses and for eliminating all unnecessary detention. The device of the report by the attorney for the government is used because in many districts defendants will be held in custody in places where the court sits only at infrequent intervals and hence they cannot be brought personally before the court without substantial delay. The magnitude of the problem is suggested by the facts that during the fiscal year ending June 30, 1960, there were 23,811 instances in which persons were held in custody pending trial and that the average length of detention prior to disposition (i.e., dismissal, acquittal, probation, sentence to imprisonment, or any other method of removing the case from the court docket) was 25.3 days. Federal Prisons 1960, table 22, p 60. Since 27,645 of the 58,855 defendants whose cases were terminated during the fiscal year ending June 30, 1960, pleaded guilty (United States Attorneys Statistical Report, October 1960, p 1 and table 2), it would appear that the greater part of the detention reported occurs prior to the initial appearance of the defendant before the court.

Notes of Advisory Committee on 1972 amendments. The amendments are intended primarily to bring rule 46 into general conformity with the Bail Reform Act of 1966 and to deal in the rule with some issues not now included within the rule.

Subdivision (a) makes explicit that the Bail Reform Act of 1966 controls release on bail prior to trial. 18 USC § 3146 refers to release of a defendant. 18 USC § 3149 refers to release of a material witness.

Subdivision (b) deals with an issue not dealt with by the Bail Reform Act of 1966 or explicitly in former rule 46, that is, the issue of bail during trial. The rule gives the trial judge discretion to continue the prior conditions of release or to impose such additional conditions as are adequate to insure presence at trial or to insure that his conduct will not obstruct the orderly and expeditious progress of the trial.

Subdivision (c) provides for release during the period between a conviction and sentencing and for the giving of a notice of appeal or of the expiration of the time allowed for filing notice of appeal. There are situations in which defense counsel may informally indicate an intention to appeal but not actually give notice of appeal for several days. To deal with this situation the rule makes clear that the district court has authority to release under the terms of 18 USC § 3148 pending notice of appeal (e.g., during the ten days after entry of judgment; see rule 4(b) of the Rules of Appellate Procedure). After the filing of notice of appeal, release by the district court shall be in accordance with the provisions of rule 9(b) of the Rules of Appellate Procedure. The burden of establishing that grounds for release exist is placed upon the defendant in the view that the fact of conviction justifies retention in custody in situations where doubt exists as to whether a defendant can be safely released pending either sentence or the giving of notice of appeal.

Subdivisions (d), (c), (f), and (g) remain unchanged. They were formerly lettered (e), (f), (g), and (h).

The amendments are technical. No substantive change is intended.

Notes of Advisory Committee on 1991 amendments. The amendment is technical. No substantive change is intended.

Notes of Advisory Committee on 1993 amendments. The addition of subdivision (i) is one of a series of similar amendments to Rules 26.2, 32, 32.1, and Rule 8 of the Rules Governing Proceedings Under 28 U.S.C. § 2255 which extend Rule 26.2 to other proceedings and hearings. As pointed out in the Committee Note to the amendment to Rule 26.2, there is continuing and compelling need to assess the credibility and reliability of information relied upon by the court, whether the witness's testimony is being considered at a pretrial proceeding, at trial, or a post-trial proceeding. Production of a witness's prior statements directly furthers that goal.

The need for reliable information is no less crucial in a proceeding to determine whether a defendant should be released from custody. The issues decided at pretrial detention hearings are important to both a defendant and the community. For example, a defendant charged with criminal acts may be incarcerated prior to an adjudication of guilt without bail on grounds of future dangerousness which is not subject to proof beyond a reasonable doubt. Although the defendant clearly has an interest in remaining free prior to trial, the community has an equally compelling interest in being protected from potential criminal activity committed by persons awaiting trial.

In upholding the constitutionality of pretrial detention based upon dangerousness, the Supreme Court in United States v. Salerno, 481 U.S. 739 (1986), stressed the existence of procedural safeguards in the Bail Reform Act. The Act provides for the right to counsel and the right to cross-examine adverse witnesses. See, e.g., 18 U.S.C. § 3142(f) (right of defendant to cross-examine adverse witness). Those safeguards, said the Court, are "specifically designed to further the accuracy of that determination." 481 U.S. at 751. The Committee believes that requiring the production of a witness's statement will further enhance the fact-finding process.

The Committee recognized that pretrial detention hearings are often held very early in a prosecution, and that a particular witness's statement may not yet be on file, or even known about. Thus, the amendment recognizes that in a particular case, the court may decide that good cause exists for not applying the rule.

Notes of Advisory Committee on 2002 amendments. The language of Rule 46 has been amended as part of the general restyling of the Criminal Rules to make them more easily understood and to make style and terminology consistent throughout the rules. These changes are intended to be stylistic only, except as noted below.

Although the general rule is that an appeal to a circuit court deprives the district court of jurisdiction, Rule 46(c) recognizes the apparent exception to that rule—that the district court retains jurisdiction to decide whether the defendant should be detained, even if a notice of appeal has been filed. *See, e.g., United States v. Meyers,* 95 F.3d 1475 (10th Cir. 1996), cert. denied, 522 U.S. 1006 (1997) (initial decision of whether to release defendant pending appeal is to be made by district court); *United States v. Affleck,* 765 F.2d 944 (10th Cir. 1985); *Jago v. United States District Court,* 570 F.2d 618 (6th Cir. 1978) (release of defendant pending appeal must first be sought in district court). *See also* Federal Rule of Appellate Procedure 9(b) and the accompanying Committee Note.

Revised Rule 46(h) deletes the requirement that the attorney for the government file bi-weekly reports with the court concerning the status of any defendants in pretrial detention. The Committee believed that the requirement was no longer necessary in light of the Speedy Trial Act provisions. 18 U.S.C. §§ 3161, et seq. On the other hand, the requirement that the attorney for the government file reports regarding detained material witnesses has been retained in the rule.

Rule 46(i) addresses the ability of a court to order forfeiture of property where a defendant has failed to appear as required by the court. The language in the current rule, Rule 46(h), was originally included by Congress. The new language has been restyled with no change in substance or practice intended. Under this provision, the court may only forfeit property as permitted under 18 U.S.C. §§ 3146(d) and 3142(c)(1)(B)(xi). The term "appropriate sentence" means a sentence that is consistent with the Sentencing Guidelines.

Amendments:

1984.

Act Oct. 12, 1984, in subsec. (a), substituted "§§ 3142 and 3144" for "§ 3146, § 3148, or § 3149", in subsec. (c), "3143" for "§ 3148", in subsec. (e)(2), "be set aside in whole or in part, upon such conditions as the court may impose, if a person released upon execution of an appearance bond with a surety is subsequently surrendered by the surety into custody or if it otherwise appears that justice does not require the forfeiture" for "set aside, upon such conditions as the court may impose, if it appears that justice does not require enforcement of the forfeiture", and added subsec. (h).

1994.

Act Sept. 13, 1994, in subsec. (i), substituted " 18 U.S.C. § 3142" for " 18 U.S.C. § 3144".

Criminal Procedure Rule 47

Rule 47. Motions and Supporting Affidavits

(a) In General. A party applying to the court for an order must do so by motion.

(b) Form and Content of a Motion. A motion—except when made during a trial or hearing—must be in writing, unless the court permits the party to make the motion by other means. A motion must state the grounds on which it is based and the relief or order sought. A motion may be supported by affidavit.

(c) Timing of a Motion. A party must serve a written motion—other than one that the court may hear ex parte—and any hearing notice at least 7 days before the hearing date, unless a rule or court order sets a different period. For good cause, the court may set a different period upon ex parte application.

(d) Affidavit Supporting a Motion. The moving party must serve any supporting affidavit with the motion. A responding party must serve any opposing affidavit at least one day before the hearing, unless the court permits later service.

HISTORY:

Dec. 26, 1944, eff. March 21, 1946; April 29, 2002, eff. Dec. 1, 2002; March 26, 2009, eff. Dec. 1, 2009.

HISTORY; ANCILLARY LAWS AND DIRECTIVES

Other provisions:

Notes of Advisory Committee on Rules. 1. This rule is substantially the same as the corresponding civil rule (first sentence of Rule 7(b)(1), Federal Rules of Civil Procedure), 28 USC, Appendix, except that it authorizes the court to permit motions to be made orally and does not require that the grounds upon which a motion is made shall be stated "with particularity," as is the case with the civil rule.

2. This rule is intended to state general requirements for all motions. For particular provisions applying to specific motions, see Rules 6(b)(2), 12, 14, 15, 16, 17(b) and (c), 21, 22, 29 and Rule 41(e). See also Rule 49.

3. The last sentence providing that a motion may be supported by affidavit is not intended to permit "speaking motions" (e.g. motion to dismiss an indictment for insufficiency supported by affidavits), but to authorize the use of affidavits when affidavits are appropriate to establish a fact (e.g. authority to take a deposition or former jeopardy).

Notes of Advisory Committee on 2002 amendments. The language of Rule 47 has been amended as part of the general restyling of the Criminal Rules to make them more easily understood and to make style and terminology consistent throughout the rules. These changes are intended to be stylistic only, except as noted below.

In Rule 47(b), the word "orally" has been deleted. The Committee believed, first, that the term should not act as a limitation on those who are not able to speak orally and, second, a court may wish to entertain motions through electronic or other reliable means. Deletion of the term also comports with a similar change in Rule 26, regarding the taking of testimony during trial. In place of that word, the Committee substituted the broader phrase "by other means."

Notes of Advisory Committee on 2009 amendments. The time set in the former rule at 5 days, which excluded intermediate Saturdays, Sundays, and legal holidays, has been expanded to 7 days. See the Committee Note to Rule 45(a).

Rule 48. Dismissal

(a) By the Government. The government may, with leave of court, dismiss an indictment, information, or complaint. The government may not dismiss the prosecution during trial without the defendant's consent.

(b) By the Court. The court may dismiss an indictment, information, or complaint if unnecessary delay occurs in:

(1) presenting a charge to a grand jury;

(2) filing an information against a defendant; or

(3) bringing a defendant to trial.

HISTORY:

Dec. 26, 1944, eff. March 21, 1946; April 29, 2002, eff. Dec. 1, 2002.

HISTORY; ANCILLARY LAWS AND DIRECTIVES

Other provisions:

Notes of Advisory Committee on Rules. *Note to subdivision (a).* 1. The first sentence of this rule will change existing law. The common-law rule that the public prosecutor may enter a nolle prosequi in his discretion, without any action by the court, prevails in the Federal courts, Confiscation Cases, 7 Wall 454, 457, 19 L Ed 196; United States v Woody, 2 F2d 262 (D Mont). This provision will permit the filing of a nolle prosequi only by leave of court. This is similar to the rule now prevailing in many States, ALI Code of Criminal Procedure, Commentaries, pp 895–897.

2. The rule confers the power to file a dismissal by leave of court on the Attorney General, as well as on the United States attorney, since under existing law the Attorney General exercises "general superintendence and direction" over the United States attorneys "as to the manner of discharging their respective duties," 5 USC former § 317 (now 28 USC §§ 507, 547). Moreover, it is the administrative practice for the Attorney General to supervise the filing of a nolle prosequi by United States attorneys. Consequently it seemed appropriate that the Attorney General should have such power directly.

3. The rule permits the filing of a dismissal of an indictment, information or complaint. The word "complaint" was included in order to resolve a doubt prevailing in some districts as to whether the United States attorney may file a nolle prosequi between the time when the defendant is bound over by the United States commissioner and the finding of an indictment. It has been assumed in a few districts that the power does not exist and that the United States attorney must await action of the grand jury, even if he deems it proper to dismiss the prosecution. This situation is an unnecessary hardship to some defendants.

4. The second sentence is a restatement of existing law, Confiscation Cases, 7 Wall 454–457, 19 L Ed 196; United States v Shoemaker, 27 Fed Cases No. 16,279, (CC Ill.). If the trial has commenced, the defendant has a right to insist on a disposition on the merits and may properly object to the entry of a nolle prosequi.

Note to subdivision (b). This rule is a restatement of the inherent power of the court to dismiss a case for want of prosecution. Ex parte Altman, 34 F Supp 106, (SD Cal.).

Notes of Advisory Committee on 2002 amendments. The language of Rule 48 has been amended as part of the general restyling of the Criminal Rules to make them more easily understood and to make style and terminology consistent throughout the rules. These changes are intended to be stylistic only.

The Committee considered the relationship between Rule 48(b) and the Speedy Trial Act. See 18 U.S.C. §§ 3161, et seq. Rule 48(b), of course, operates independently from the Act. *See, e.g., United States v. Goodson,* 204 F.3d 508 (4th Cir. 2000) (noting purpose of Rule 48(b)); *United States v. Carlone,* 666 F.2d 1112, 1116 (7th Cir. 1981) (suggesting that Rule 48(b) could provide an alternate basis in an extreme case to dismiss an indictment, without reference to Speedy Trial Act); *United States v. Balochi,* 527 F.2d 562, 563-64 (4th Cir. 1976) (per curiam) (Rule 48(b) is broader in compass). In re-promulgating Rule 48(b), the Committee intends no change in the relationship between that rule and the Speedy Trial Act.

Rule 49. Serving and Filing Papers

(a) Service on a Party.

(1) *What is required.* Each of the following must be served on every party: any written motion (other than one to be heard ex parte), written notice, designation of the record on appeal, or similar paper.

(2) *Serving a Party's Attorney.* Unless the court orders otherwise, when these rules or a court order requires or permits service on a party represented by an attorney, service must be made on the attorney instead of the party.

(3) *Service by Electronic Means.*

(A) Using the Court's Electronic-Filing System. A party represented by an attorney may serve a paper on a registered user by filing it with the court's electronic-filing system. A party not represented by an attorney may do so only if allowed by court order or local rule. Service is complete upon filing, but is not effective if the serving party learns that it did not reach the person to be served.

(B) Using Other Electronic Means. A paper may be served by any other electronic means that the person consented to in writing. Service is complete upon transmission, but is not effective if the serving party learns that it did not reach the person to be served.

(4) *Service by Nonelectronic Means.* A paper may be served by:

(A) handing it to the person;

(B) leaving it:

(i) at the person's office with a clerk or other person in charge or, if no one is in charge, in a conspicuous place in the office; or

(ii) if the person has no office or the office is closed, at the person's dwelling or usual place of abode with someone of suitable age and discretion who resides there;

(C) mailing it to the person's last known address—in which event service is complete upon mailing;

(D) leaving it with the court clerk if the person has no known address; or

(E) delivering it by any other means that the person consented to in writing—in which event service is complete when the person making service delivers it to the agency designated to make delivery.

(b) Filing.

(1) *When Required; Certificate of Service.* Any paper that is required to be served must be filed no later than a reasonable time after service. No certificate of service is required when a paper is served by filing it with the court's electronic-filing system. When a paper is served by other means, a certificate of service must be filed with it or within a reasonable time after service or filing.

(2) *Means of Filing.*

(A) Electronically. A paper is filed electronically by filing it with the court's electronic-filing system. A filing made through a person's electronic-filing account and authorized by that person, together with the person's name on a signature block, constitutes the person's signature. A paper filed electronically is written or in writing under these rules.

(B) Nonelectronically. A paper not filed electronically is filed by delivering it:

(i) to the clerk; or

(ii) to a judge who agrees to accept it for filing, and who must then note the filing date on the paper and promptly send it to the clerk.

(3) *Means Used by Represented and Unrepresented Parties.*

(A) Represented Party. A party represented by an attorney must file electronically, unless nonelectronic filing is allowed by the court for good cause or is allowed or required by local rule.

(B) Unrepresented Party. A party not represented by an attorney must file nonelectronically, unless allowed to file electronically by court order or local rule.

(4) *Signature.* Every written motion and other paper must be signed by at least one attorney of record in the attorney's name—or by a person filing a paper if the person is not represented by an attorney. The paper must state the signer's address, e-mail address, and telephone number. Unless a rule or statute specifically states otherwise, a pleading need not be verified or accompanied by an affidavit. The court must strike an unsigned paper unless the omission is promptly corrected after being called to the attorney's or person's attention.

(5) *Acceptance by the Clerk.* The clerk must not refuse to file a paper solely because it is not in the form prescribed by these rules or by a local rule or practice.

(c) Service and Filing by Nonparties. A nonparty may serve and file a paper only if doing so is required or permitted by law. A nonparty must serve every party as required by Rule 49(a), but may use the court's electronic-filing system only if allowed by court order or local rule.

(d) Notice of a Court Order. When the court issues an order on any post-arraignment motion, the clerk must serve notice of the entry on each party as required by Rule 49(a). A party also may serve notice of the entry by the same means. Except as Federal Rule of Appellate Procedure 4(b) provides otherwise, the clerk's failure to give notice does not affect the time to appeal, or relieve—or authorize the court to relieve—a party's failure to appeal within the allowed time.

HISTORY:

Dec. 26, 1944, eff. March 21, 1946, as amended Feb. 28, 1966, eff. July 1, 1966; Dec. 4, 1967, eff. July 1, 1968; April 29, 1985, eff. Aug. 1, 1985; March 9, 1987, eff. Aug. 1, 1987; April 22, 1993, eff. Dec. 1, 1993; April 27, 1995, eff. Dec. 1, 1995; April 29, 2002, eff. Dec. 1, 2002; April 26, 2011, eff. Dec. 1, 2011; April 26, 2018, eff. Dec. 1, 2018.

HISTORY; ANCILLARY LAWS AND DIRECTIVES

Other provisions:

Notes of Advisory Committee on Rules. This rule is substantially the same as Rule 5(a) of the Federal Rules of Civil Procedure, 28 USC, Appendix, with such adaptations as are necessary for criminal cases.

Subdivision (b). The first sentence of this rule is in substance the same as the first sentence of Rule 5(b) of the Federal Rules of Civil Procedure. The second sentence incorporates by reference the second and third sentences of Rule 5(b) of the Federal Rules of Civil Procedure, 28 USC, Appendix.

Subdivision (c). This rule is an adaptation for criminal proceedings of Rule 77(d) of the Federal Rules of Civil Procedure, 28 USC, Appendix. No consequence attaches to the failure of the clerk to give the prescribed notice, but in a case in which the losing party in reliance on the clerk's obligation to send a notice failed to file a timely notice of appeal, it was held competent for the trial judge, in the exercise of sound discretion, to vacate the judgment because of clerk's failure to give notice and to enter a new judgment, the term of court not having expired. Hill v Hawes, 320 US 520, 64 S Ct 334, 88 L Ed 283, rehearing denied 321 US 801, 64 S Ct 515, 88 L Ed 1088.

Subdivision (d). This rule incorporates by reference Rule 5(d) and (e) of the Federal Rules of Civil Procedure, 28 USC, Appendix.

Notes of Advisory Committee on 1966 amendments. Subdivision (a). The words "adverse parties" in the original rule introduced a question of interpretation. When, for example, is a co-defendant an adverse party? The amendment requires service on each of the parties thus avoiding the problem of interpretation and promoting full exchange of information among the parties. No restriction is intended, however, upon agreements among co-defendants or between the defendants and the government restricting exchange of papers in the interest of eliminating unnecessary expense. Cf. the amendment made effective July 1, 1963, to Civil Rule 5(a).

Subdivision (c). The words "affected thereby" are deleted in order to require notice to all parties. Cf. the similar change made effective July 1, 1963, to Civil Rule 77(d).

The sentence added at the end of the subdivision eliminates the possibility of extension of the time to appeal beyond the provision for a 30 day extension on a showing of "excusable neglect" provided in Rule 37(a)(2). Cf. the similar change made in Civil Rule 77(d) effective in 1948. The question has arisen in a number of cases whether failure or delay in giving notice on the part of the clerk results in an extension of the time for appeal. The "general rule" has been said to be that in the event of such failure or delay "the time for taking an appeal runs from the date of later actual notice or receipt of the clerk's notice rather than from the date of entry of the order." Lohman v United States, 237 F2d 645, 646 (6th Cir. 1956). See also Rosenbloom v United States, 355 US 80, 2 L Ed 2d 110, 78 S Ct 202 (1957) (permitting an extension). In two cases it has been held that no extension results from the failure to give notice of entry of judgments (as opposed to orders) since such notice is not required by Rule 49(d). Wilkinson v United States, 278 F 2d 604 (10th Cir. 1960), cert den 363 US 829, 4 L Ed 2d 1524, 80 S Ct 1600; Hyche v United States, 278 F2d 915 (5th Cir. 1960), cert den 364 US 881, 5 L Ed 2d 102, 81 S Ct 169. The excusable neglect extension provision in Rule 37(a)(2) will cover most cases where failure of the clerk to give notice of judgments or orders has misled the defendant. No need appears for an indefinite extension without time limit beyond the 30 day period.

Notes of Advisory Committee on 1968 amendments. The amendment corrects the reference to Rule 37(a)(2), the pertinent provisions of which are contained in Rule 4(b) of the Federal Rules of Appellate Procedure.

Notes of Advisory Committee on 1985 amendments. 18 U.S.C. § 3575(a) and 21 U.S.C. § 849(a), dealing respectively with dangerous special offender sentencing and dangerous special drug offender sentencing, provide for the prosecutor to file notice of such status "with the court" and for the court to "order the notice sealed" under specified circumstances, but also declare that disclosure of this notice shall not be made "to the presiding judge without the consent of the parties" before verdict or plea of guilty or nolo contendere. It has been noted that these provisions are "regrettably unclear as to where, in fact, such notice is to be filed" and that possibly filing with the chief judge is contemplated. *United States* v. *Tramunti,* 377 F.Supp. 6 (S.D.N.Y. 1974). But such practice has been a matter of dispute when the chief judge would otherwise have been the presiding judge in the case, *United States* v. *Gaylor,* No. 80-5016 (4th Cir. 1981), and "it does not solve the problem in those districts where there is only one federal district judge appointed," *United States* v. *Tramunti, supra.*

The first sentence of subdivision (e) clarifies that the filing of such notice with the court is to be accomplished by filing with the clerk of the court, which is generally the procedure for filing with the court; see subdivision (d) of this rule. Except in a district having a single judge and no United States magistrate, the clerk will then, as provided in the second sentence, transmit the notice to the chief judge or to some other judge or a United States magistrate if the chief judge is scheduled to be the presiding judge in the case, so that the determination regarding sealing of the notice may be made without the disclosure prohibited by the aforementioned statutes. But in a district having a single judge and no United States magistrate this prohibition means the clerk may not disclose the notice to the court at all until the time specified by statute. The last sentence of subdivision (e) contemplates that in such instances the clerk will seal the notice if the case falls within the local rule describing when "a public record may prejudice fair consideration of a pending criminal matter," the determination called for by the aforementioned statutes. The local rule might provide, for example, that the notice is to be sealed upon motion by any party.

Notes of Advisory Committee on 1987 amendments. The amendment is technical. No substantive change is intended.

Notes of Advisory Committee on 1993 amendments. The Rule is amended to conform to the Judicial Improvements Act of 1990 [P.L. 101-650, Title III, Section 321) which provides that each United States magistrate appointed under section 631 of title 28, United States Code, shall be known as a United States magistrate judge.

Notes of Advisory Committee on 1995 amendments. Subdivision (e) has been deleted because both of the statutory provisions cited in the rule have been abrogated.

Notes of Advisory Committee on 2002 amendments. The language of Rule 49 has been amended as part of the general restyling of the Criminal Rules to make them more easily understood and to make style and terminology consistent throughout the rules.

Rule 49(c) has been amended to reflect proposed changes in the Federal Rules of Civil Procedure that permit (but do not require) a court to provide notice of its orders and judgments through electronic means. *See* Federal Rules of Civil Procedure 5(b) and 77(d). As amended, Rule 49(c) now parallels a similar extant provision in Rule 49(b), regarding service of papers.

Notes of Advisory Committee on 2011 amendments. *Note to Subdivision (e).* Filing papers by electronic means is added as new subdivision (e), which is drawn from Civil Rule 5(d)(3). It makes it clear that a paper filed electronically in compliance with the Court's local rule is a written paper.

Notes of Advisory Committee on 2018 Amendments. Rule 49 previously required service and filing in a "manner provided" in "a civil action." The amendments to Rule 49 move the instructions for filing and service from the Civil Rules into Rule 49. Placing instructions for filing and service in the criminal rule avoids the need to refer to two sets of rules, and permits independent development of those rules. Except where specifically noted, the amendments are intended to carry over the existing law on filing and service and to preserve parallelism with the Civil Rules.

Additionally, the amendments eliminate the provision permitting electronic-filing only when authorized by local rules, moving—with the Rules governing Appellate, Civil, and Bankruptcy proceedings—to a national rule that mandates electronic-filing for parties represented by an attorney with certain exceptions. Electronic filing has matured. Most districts have adopted local rules that require electronic filing by represented parties, and allow reasonable exceptions as required by the former rule. The time has come to seize the advantages of electronic filing by making it mandatory in all districts for a party represented by an attorney, except that nonelectronic filing may be allowed by the court for good cause, or allowed or required by local rule.

Rule 49(a)(1). The language from former Rule 49(a) is retained in new Rule 49(a)(1), except for one change. The new phrase, "Each of the following must be served on every party" restores to this part of the rule the passive construction that it had prior to restyling in 2002. That restyling revised the language to apply to parties only, inadvertently ending its application to nonparties who, on occasion, file motions in criminal cases. Additional guidance for nonparties appears in new subdivision (c).

Rule 49(a)(2). The language from former Rule 49(b) concerning service on the attorney of a represented party is retained here, with the "unless" clause moved to the beginning for reasons of style only.

Rule 49(a)(3) and (4). Subsections (a)(3) and (4) list the permissible means of service. These new provisions duplicate the description of permissible means from Civil Rule 5, carrying them into the criminal rule.

By listing service by filing with the court's electronic filing system first, in (3)(A), the rule now recognizes the advantages of electronic filing and service and its widespread use in criminal cases by represented defendants and government attorneys.

But the e-filing system is designed for attorneys, and its use can pose many challenges for pro se parties. In the criminal context, the rules must ensure ready access to the courts by all pro se defendants and incarcerated individuals, filers who often lack reliable access to the internet or email. Although access to electronic-filing systems may expand with time, presently many districts do not allow e-filing by unrepresented defendants or prisoners. Accordingly, subsection (3)(A) provides that represented parties may serve registered users by filing with the court's electronic-filing system, but unrepresented parties may do so only if allowed by court order or local rule.

Subparagraph (3)(B) permits service by "other electronic means," such as email, that the person served consented to in writing.

Both subparagraphs (3)(A) and (B) include the direction from Civil Rule 5 that service is complete upon e-filing or transmission, but is not effective if the serving party learns that the person to be served did not receive the notice of e-filing or the paper transmitted by other electronic means. The language mirrors Civil Rule 5(b)(2)(E). But unlike Civil Rule 5, Criminal Rule 49 contains a separate provision for service by use of the court's electronic-filing system. The rule does not make the court responsible for notifying a person who filed the paper with the court's electronic-filing system that an attempted transmission by the court's system failed.

Subsection (a)(4) lists a number of traditional, nonelectronic means of serving papers, identical to those provided in Civil Rule 5.

Rule 49(b)(1). Filing rules in former Rule 49 appeared in subdivision (d), which provided that a party must file a copy of any paper the party is required to serve, and required filing in a manner provided in a civil action. These requirements now appear in subdivision (b).

The language requiring filing of papers that must be served is retained from former subdivision (d), but has been moved to subsection (1) of subdivision (b), and revised to restore the passive phrasing prior to the restyling in 2002. That restyling departed from the phrasing in Civil Rule 5(d)(1) and inadvertently limited this requirement to filing by parties.

The language in former subdivision (d) that required filing "in a manner provided for in a civil action" has been replaced in new subsection (b)(1) by language drawn from Civil Rule 5(d)(1). That provision used to state "Any paper . . . that is required to be served—together with a certificate of service—must be filed within a reasonable time after service." A contemporaneous amendment to Civil Rule 5(d)(1) has subdivided this provision into two parts, one of which addresses the Certificate of Service. Although the Criminal Rules version is not subdivided in the same way, it parallels the Civil Rules provision from which it was drawn. Because "within" might be read as barring filing before the paper is served, "no later than" is substituted to ensure that it is proper to file a paper before it is served.

The second sentence of subsection (b)(1), which states that no certificate of service is required when service is made using the court's electronic-filing system, mirrors the contemporaneous amendment to Civil Rule 5. When service is not made by filing with the court's electronic-filing system, a certificate of service must be filed.

Rule 49(b)(2). New subsection (b)(2) lists the three ways papers can be filed. (A) provides for electronic filing using the court's electronic-filing system and includes a provision, drawn from the Civil Rule, stating that a filing made through a person's electronic-filing account and authorized by that person, together with the person's name on a signature block, constitutes the person's signature. The last sentence of subsection (b)(2)(A) contains the language of former Rule 49(d), providing that e-filed papers are "written or in writing," deleting the words "in compliance with a local rule" as no longer necessary.

Subsection (b)(2)(B) carries over from the Civil Rule two nonelectronic methods of filing a paper: delivery to the court clerk and delivery to a judge who agrees to accept it for filing.

Rule 49(b)(3). New subsection (b)(3) provides instructions for parties regarding the means of filing to be used, depending upon whether the party is represented by an attorney. Subsection (b)(3)(A) requires represented parties to use the court's electronic-filing system, but provides that nonelectronic filing may be allowed for good cause, and may be required or allowed for other reasons by local rule. This language is identical to that adopted in the contemporaneous amendment to Civil Rule 5.

Subsection (b)(3)(B) requires unrepresented parties to file nonelectronically, unless allowed to file electronically by court order or local rule. This language differs from that of the amended Civil Rule, which provides that an unrepresented party may be "required" to file electronically by a court order or local rule that allows reasonable exceptions. A different approach to electronic filing by unrepresented parties is needed in criminal cases, where electronic filing by pro se prisoners presents significant challenges. Pro se parties filing papers under the criminal rules generally lack the means to e-file or receive electronic confirmations, yet must be provided access to the courts under the Constitution.

Rule 49(b)(4). This new language requiring a signature and additional information was drawn from Civil Rule 11(a). The language has been restyled (with no intent to change the meaning) and the word "party" changed to "person" in order to accommodate filings by nonparties.

Rule 49(b)(5). This new language prohibiting a clerk from refusing a filing for improper form was drawn from Civil Rule 5(d)(4).

Rule 49(c). This provision is new. It recognizes that in limited circumstances nonparties may file motions in criminal cases. Examples include representatives of the media challenging the closure of proceedings, material witnesses requesting to be deposed under Rule 15, or victims asserting rights under Rule 60. Subdivision (c) permits nonparties to file a paper in a criminal case, but only when required or permitted by law to do so. It also requires nonparties who file to serve every party and to use means authorized by subdivision (a).

The rule provides that nonparties, like unrepresented parties, may use the court's electronic-filing system only when permitted to do so by court order or local rule.

Rule 49(d). This provision carries over the language formerly in Rule 49(c) with one change. The former language requiring that notice be provided "in a manner provided for in a civil action" has been replaced by a requirement that notice be served as required by Rule 49(a). This parallels Civil Rule 77(d)(1), which requires that the clerk give notice as provided in Civil Rule 5(b).

Rule 49.1. Privacy Protection for Filings Made with the Court

(a) Redacted Filings. Unless the court orders otherwise, in an electronic or paper filing with the court that contains an individual's social-security number, taxpayer-identification number, or birth date, the name of an individual known to be a minor, a financial-account number, or the home address of an individual, a party or nonparty making the filing may include only:

(1) the last four digits of the social-security number and taxpayer-identification number;

(2) the year of the individual's birth;

(3) the minor's initials;

(4) the last four digits of the financial-account number; and

(5) the city and state of the home address.

(b) Exemptions from the Redaction Requirement. The redaction requirement does not apply to the following:

(1) a financial-account number or real property address that identifies the property allegedly subject to forfeiture in a forfeiture proceeding;

(2) the record of an administrative or agency proceeding;

(3) the official record of a state-court proceeding;

(4) the record of a court or tribunal, if that record was not subject to the redaction requirement when originally filed;

(5) a filing covered by Rule 49.1(d);

(6) a pro se filing in an action brought under 28 U.S.C. §§ 2241, 2254, or 2255;

(7) a court filing that is related to a criminal matter or investigation and that is prepared before the filing of a criminal charge or is not filed as part of any docketed criminal case;

(8) an arrest or search warrant; and

(9) a charging document and an affidavit filed in support of any charging document.

(c) Immigration Cases. A filing in an action brought under 28 U.S.C. § 2241 that relates to the petitioner's immigration rights is governed by Federal Rule of Civil Procedure 5.2.

(d) Filings Made Under Seal. The court may order that a filing be made under seal without redaction. The court may later unseal the filing or order the person who made the filing to file a redacted version for the public record.

(e) Protective Orders. For good cause, the court may by order in a case:

(1) require redaction of additional information; or

(2) limit or prohibit a nonparty's remote electronic access to a document filed with the court.

(f) Option for Additional Unredacted Filing Under Seal. A person making a redacted filing may also file an unredacted copy under seal. The court must retain the unredacted copy as part of the record.

(g) Option for Filing a Reference List. A filing that contains redacted information may be filed together with a reference list that identifies each item of redacted information and specifies an appropriate identifier that uniquely corresponds to each item listed. The list must be filed under seal and may be amended as of right. Any reference in the case to a listed identifier will be construed to refer to the corresponding item of information.

(h) Waiver of Protection of Identifiers. A person waives the protection of Rule 49.1(a) as to the person's own information by filing it without redaction and not under seal.

HISTORY:

As added April 30, 2007, eff. Dec. 1, 2007.

HISTORY; ANCILLARY LAWS AND DIRECTIVES

Other provisions:

Notes of Advisory Committee. The rule is adopted in compliance with section 205(c)(3) of the E-Government Act of 2002, Public Law No. 107-347. Section 205(c)(3) requires the Supreme Court to prescribe rules "to protect privacy and security concerns relating to electronic filing of documents and the public availability . . . of documents filed electronically." The rule goes further than the E-Government Act in regulating paper filings even when they are not converted to electronic form. But the number of filings that remain in paper form is certain to diminish over time. Most districts scan paper filings into the electronic case file, where they become available to the public in the same way as documents initially filed in electronic form. It is electronic availability, not the form of the initial filing, that raises the privacy and security concerns addressed in the E-Government Act.

The rule is derived from and implements the policy adopted by the Judicial Conference in September 2001 to address the privacy concerns resulting from public access to electronic case files. *See* http://www.privacy.uscourts.gov/Policy.htm The Judicial Conference policy is that documents in case files generally should be made available electronically to the same extent they are available at the courthouse, provided that certain "personal data identifiers" are not included in the public file.

While providing for the public filing of some information, such as the last four digits of an account number, the rule does not intend to establish a presumption that this information never could or should be protected. For example, it may well be necessary in individual cases to prevent remote access by nonparties to any part of an account number or social security number. It may also be necessary to protect information not covered by the redaction requirement—such as driver's license numbers and alien registration numbers—in a particular case. In such cases, protection may be sought under subdivision (d) or (e). Moreover, the Rule does not affect the protection available under other rules, such as Criminal Rule 16(d) and Civil Rules 16 and 26(c), or under other sources of protective authority.

Parties must remember that any personal information not otherwise protected by sealing or redaction will be made available over the internet. Counsel should notify clients of this fact so that an informed decision may be made on what information is to be included in a document filed with the court.

The clerk is not required to review documents filed with the court for compliance with this rule. The responsibility to redact filings rests with counsel and the party or nonparty making the filing.

Subdivision (e) provides that the court can order in a particular case more extensive redaction than otherwise required by the Rule, where necessary to protect against disclosure to nonparties of sensitive or private information. Nothing in this subdivision is intended to affect the limitations on sealing that are otherwise applicable to the court.

Subdivision (f) allows a person who makes a redacted filing to file an unredacted document under seal. This provision is derived from section 205(c)(3)(iv) of the E-Government Act. Subdivision (g) allows parties to file a register of redacted information. This provision is derived from section 205(c)(3)(v) of the E-Government Act, as amended in 2004.

In accordance with the E-Government Act, subdivision (g) of the rule refers to "redacted" information. The term "redacted" is intended to govern a filing that is prepared with abbreviated identifiers in the first instance, as well as a filing in which a personal identifier is edited after its preparation.

Subdivision (h) allows a person to waive the protections of the rule as to its own personal information by filing it unsealed and in unredacted form. A party may wish to waive the protection if it determines that the costs of redaction outweigh the benefits to privacy. If a party files an unredacted identifier by mistake, it may seek relief from the court.

Trial exhibits are subject to the redaction requirements of Rule 49.1 to the extent they are filed with the court. Trial exhibits that are not initially filed with the court must be redacted in accordance with the rule if and when they are filed as part of an appeal or for other reasons.

The Judicial Conference Committee on Court Administration and Case Management has issued "Guidance for Implementation of the Judicial Conference Policy on Privacy and Public Access to Electronic Criminal Case Files" (March 2004). This document sets out limitations on remote electronic access to certain sensitive materials in criminal cases. It provides in part as follows:

The following documents shall not be included in the public case file and should not be made available to the public at the courthouse or via remote electronic access:

• unexecuted summonses or warrants of any kind (*e.g.*, search warrants, arrest warrants);

• pretrial bail or presentence investigation reports;

• statements of reasons in the judgment of conviction;

• juvenile records;

• documents containing identifying information about jurors or potential jurors;

• financial affidavits filed in seeking representation pursuant to the Criminal Justice Act;

• ex parte requests for authorization of investigative, expert or other services pursuant to the Criminal Justice Act; and.

• sealed documents (*e.g.*, motions for downward departure for substantial assistance, plea agreements indicating cooperation).

To the extent that the Rule does not exempt these materials from disclosure, the privacy and law enforcement concerns implicated by the above documents in criminal cases can be accommodated under the rule through the sealing provision of subdivision (d) or a protective order provision of subdivision (e).

Rule 50. Prompt Disposition

Scheduling preference must be given to criminal proceedings as far as practicable.

HISTORY:

Dec. 26, 1944, eff. March 21, 1946, as amended April 24, 1972, eff. Oct. 1, 1972; March 18, 1974, eff. July 1, 1974; April 26, 1976, eff. Aug. 1, 1976; July 8, 1976, P.L. 94-349, § 1, 90 Stat. 822; April 22, 1993, eff. Dec. 1, 1993; April 29, 2002, eff. Dec. 1, 2002.

HISTORY; ANCILLARY LAWS AND DIRECTIVES

Other provisions:

Notes of Advisory Committee on Rules. This rule is a restatement of the inherent residual power of the court over its own calendars, although as a matter of practice in most districts the assignment of criminal cases for trial is handled by the United States attorney. Cf. Federal Rules of Civil Procedure, Rules 40 and 78, 28 USC, Appendix. The direction that preference shall be given to criminal proceedings as far as practicable is generally recognized as desirable in the orderly administration of justice.

Notes of Advisory Committee on 1972 amendments. The addition to the rule proposed by subdivision (b) is designed to achieve the more prompt disposition of criminal cases.

Preventing undue delay in the administration of criminal justice has become an object of increasing interest and concern. This is reflected in the Congress. See, e.g., 116 Cong. Rec. S7291-97 (daily ed. May 18, 1970) (remarks of Senator Ervin). Bills have been introduced fixing specific time limits. See S. 3936, H.R. 14822, H.R. 15888, 91st Cong., 2d Sess. (1970).

Proposals for dealing with the problem of delay have also been made by the President's Commission on Law Enforcement and Administration of Justice, Task Force Report: The Courts (1967) especially pp. 84–90, and by the American Bar Association Project on Standards for Criminal Justice, Standards Relating to Speedy Trial (Approved Draft, 1968). Both recommend specific time limits for each stage in the criminal process as the most effective way of achieving prompt disposition of criminal cases. See also Note, Nevada's 1967 Criminal Procedure Law from Arrest to Trial: One State's Response to a Widely Recognized Need, 1969 Utah L. Rev. 520, 542 no. 114.

Historically, the right to a speedy trial has been thought of as a protection for the defendant. Delay can cause a hardship to a defendant who is in custody awaiting trial. Even if afforded the opportunity for pretrial release, a defendant nonetheless is likely to suffer anxiety during a period of unwanted delay, and he runs the risk that his memory and those of his witnesses may suffer as time goes on.

Delay can also adversely affect the prosecution. Witnesses may lose interest or disappear or their memories may fade thus making them more vulnerable to cross-examination. See Note, The Right to a Speedy Criminal Trial, 57 Colum. L. Rev. 846 (1957).

There is also a larger public interest in the prompt disposition of criminal cases which may transcend the interest of the particular prosecutor, defense counsel, and defendant. Thus there is need to try to expedite criminal cases even when both prosecution and defense may be willing to agree to a continuance or continuances. It has long been said that it is the certain and prompt imposition of a criminal sanction rather than its severity that has a significant deterring effect upon potential criminal conduct. See Banfield and Anderson, Continuances in the Cook County Criminal Courts, 35 U. Chi. L. Rev. 259, 259-63 (1968).

Providing specific time limits for each stage of the criminal justice system is made difficult, particularly in federal courts, by the widely varying conditions which exist between the very busy urban districts on the one hand and the far less busy rural districts on the other hand. In the former, account must be taken of the extremely heavy caseload, and the prescription of relatively short time limits is realistic only if there is provided additional prosecutorial and judicial manpower. In some rural districts, the availability of a grand jury only twice a year makes unrealistic the provision of short time limits within which an indictment must be returned. This is not to say that prompt disposition of criminal cases cannot be achieved. It means only that the achieving of prompt disposition may require solutions which vary from district to district. Finding the best methods will require innovation and experimentation. To encourage this, the proposed draft mandates each district court to prepare a plan to achieve the prompt disposition of criminal cases in the district. The method prescribed for the development and approval of the district plans is comparable to that prescribed in the Jury Selection and Service Act of 1968, 28 U.S.C. § 1863(a).

Each plan shall include rules which specify time limits and a means for reporting the status of criminal cases. The appropriate length of the time limits is left to the discretion of the individual district courts. This permits each district court to establish time limits that are appropriate in light of its criminal caseload, frequency of grand jury meetings, and any other factors which affect the progress of criminal actions. Where local conditions exist which contribute to delay, it is contemplated that appropriate efforts will be made to eliminate those conditions. For example, experience in some rural districts demonstrates that grand juries can be kept on call thus eliminating the grand jury as a cause for prolonged delay. Where manpower shortage is a major cause for delay, adequate solutions will require congressional action. But the development and analysis of the district plans should disclose where manpower shortages exist; how large the shortages are; and what is needed, in the way of additional manpower, to achieve the prompt disposition of criminal cases.

The district court plans must contain special provision for prompt disposition of cases in which there is reason to believe that the pretrial liberty of a defendant poses danger to himself, to any other person, or to the community. Prompt disposition of criminal cases may provide an alternative to the pretrial detention of potentially dangerous defendants. See 116 Cong. Rec. S7291-97 (daily ed. May 18, 1970) (remarks of Senator Ervin). Prompt disposition of criminal cases in which the defendant is held in pretrial detention would ensure that the deprivation of liberty prior to conviction would be minimized.

Approval of the original plan and any subsequent modification must be obtained from a reviewing panel made up of one judge from the district submitting the plan (either the chief judge or another active judge appointed by him) and the members of the judicial council of the circuit. The makeup of this reviewing panel is the same as that provided by the Jury Selection and Service Act of 1968, 28 U.S.C. § 1863(a). This reviewing panel is also empowered to direct the modification of a district court plan.

The Circuit Court of Appeals for the Second Circuit recently adopted a set of rules for the prompt disposition of criminal cases. See 8 Cr. L. 2251 (Jan. 13, 1971). These rules, effective July 5, 1971, provide time limits for the early trial of high risk defendants, for court control over the granting of continuances, for criteria to control continuance practice, and for sanction against the prosecution or defense in the event of noncompliance with prescribed time limits.

Notes of Advisory Committee on 1976 amendments. This amendment to rule 50(b) takes account of the enactment of The Speedy Trial Act of 1974, 18 U.S.C. §§ 3152– 3156, 3161– 3174. As the various provisions of the Act take effect, see 18 U.S.C. § 3163, they and the district plans adopted pursuant thereto will supplant the plans heretofore adopted under rule 50(b). The first such plan must be prepared and submitted by each district court before July 1, 1976. 18 U.S.C. § 3165(e)(1).

That part of rule 50(b) which sets out the necessary contents of district plans has been deleted, as the somewhat different contents of the plans required by the Act are enumerated in 18 U.S.C. § 3166. That part of rule 50(b) which describes the manner in which district plans are to be submitted, reviewed, modified and reported upon has also been deleted, for these provisions now appear in 18 U.S.C. § 3165(c) and (d).

The Rule is amended to conform to the Judicial Improvements Act of 1990 [P. L. 101-650, Title III, Section 321] which provides that each United States magistrate appointed under section 631 of title 28, United States Code, shall be known as a United States magistrate judge.

Notes of Advisory Committee on 2002 amendments. The language of Rule 50 has been amended as part of the general restyling of the Criminal Rules to make them more easily understood and to make style and terminology consistent throughout the rules. These changes are intended to be stylistic only, except as noted below.

The first sentence in current Rule 50(a), which says that a court may place criminal proceedings on a calendar, has been deleted. The Committee believed that the sentence simply stated a truism and was no longer necessary.

Current Rule 50(b), which simply mirrors 18 U.S.C. § 3165, has been deleted in its entirety. The rule was added in 1971 to meet congressional concerns in pending legislation about deadlines in criminal cases. Provisions governing deadlines were later enacted by Congress and protections were provided in the Speedy Trial Act. The Committee concluded that in light of those enactments, Rule 50(b) was no longer necessary.

Amendments:

1976.

Order of April 26, 1976 (eff. Aug. 1, 1976, as provided by § 1 of Act July 8, 1976; see note to Rule 6), substituted subdiv. (b) for one which read:

"(b) Plan for achieving prompt disposition of criminal cases. To minimize undue delay and to further the prompt disposition of criminal cases, each district court shall conduct a continuing study of the administration of criminal justice in the district court and before United States magistrates of the district and shall prepare a plan for the prompt disposition of criminal cases which shall include rules relating to time limits within which procedures prior to trial, the trial itself, and sentencing must take place, means of reporting the status of cases, and such other matters as are necessary or proper to minimize delay and facilitate the prompt disposition of such cases. The district plan shall include special provision for the prompt disposition of any case in which it appears to the court that there is reason to believe that the pretrial liberty of a particular defendant who is in custody or released pursuant to Rule 46, poses a danger to himself, to any other person, or to the community. The district plan shall be submitted for approval to a reviewing panel consisting of the members of the judicial council of the circuit and either the chief judge of the district court whose plan is being reviewed or such other active judge of that court as the chief judge of the district court may designate. If approved the plan shall be forwarded to the Administrative Office of the United States Courts, which office shall report annually on the operation of such plans to the Judicial Conference of the United States. The district court may modify the plan at any time with the approval of the reviewing panel. It shall modify the plan when directed to do so by the reviewing panel or the Judicial Conference of the United States. Each district court shall submit its plan to the reviewing panel not later than 90 days from the effective date of this rule.".

Rule 51. Preserving Claimed Error

(a) Exceptions Unnecessary. Exceptions to rulings or orders of the court are unnecessary.

(b) Preserving a Claim of Error. A party may preserve a claim of error by informing the court—when the court ruling or order is made or sought—of the action the party wishes the court to take, or the party's objection to the court's action and the grounds for that objection. If a party does not have an opportunity to object to a ruling or order, the absence of an objection does not later prejudice that party. A ruling or order that admits or excludes evidence is governed by Federal Rule of Evidence 103.

HISTORY:

Dec. 26, 1944, eff. March 21, 1946; March 9, 1987, eff. eff. Aug. 1, 1987; April 29, 2002, eff. Dec. 1, 2002.

HISTORY; ANCILLARY LAWS AND DIRECTIVES

Other provisions:

Notes of Advisory Committee on Rules. 1. This rule is practically identical with Rule 46 of the Federal Rules of Civil Procedure, 28 USC, Appendix. It relates to a matter of trial practice which should be the same in civil and criminal cases in the interest of avoiding confusion. The corresponding civil rule has been construed in Ulm v Moore-McCormack Lines, Inc. 115 F2d 492, (CCA2d), and Bucy v Nevada Construction Company, 125 F 2d 213, 218, (CCA 9th.). See, also, Orfield, 22 Texas LR 194, 221. As to the method of taking objections to instructions to the jury, see Rule 30.

2. Many States have abolished the use of exceptions in criminal and civil cases. See, e. g., Cal Pen Code (Deering, 1941), sec 1259; Mich Stat Ann (Henderson, 1938), secs 28.1046, 28.1053; Ohio Gen Code Ann (Page, 1938), secs 11560, 13442-7; Oreg Comp Laws Ann (1940), secs 5-704, 26-1001.

Notes of Advisory Committee on 1987 amendments. The amendments are technical. No substantive change is intended.

Notes of Advisory Committee on 2002 amendments. The language of Rule 51 has been amended as part of the general restyling of the Criminal Rules to make them more easily understood and to make style and terminology consistent throughout the rules. These changes are intended to be stylistic only.

The Rule includes a new sentence that explicitly states that any rulings regarding evidence are governed by Federal Rule of Evidence 103. The sentence was added because of concerns about the Supersession Clause, 28 U.S.C. § 2072(b), of the Rules Enabling Act, and the possibility that an argument might have been made that Congressional approval of this rule would supersede that Rule of Evidence.

Rule 52. Harmless and Plain Error

(a) Harmless error. Any error, defect, irregularity, or variance that does not affect substantial rights must be disregarded.

(b) Plain error. A plain error that affects substantial rights may be considered even though it was not brought to the court's attention.

HISTORY:

Dec. 26, 1944, eff. March 21, 1946l; April 29, 2002, eff. Dec. 1, 2002.

HISTORY; ANCILLARY LAWS AND DIRECTIVES

Other provisions:

Notes of Advisory Committee on Rules. *Note to subdivision (a).* This rule is a restatement of existing law, 28 USC former § 391 (second sentence): "On the hearing of any appeal, certiorari, writ of error, or motion for a new trial, in any case, civil or criminal, the court shall give judgment after an examination of the entire record before the court, without regard to technical errors, defects, or exceptions which do not affect the substantial rights of the parties"; 18 USC former § 556; "No indictment found and presented by a grand jury in any district or other court of the United States shall be deemed insufficient, nor shall the trial, judgment, or other proceeding thereon be affected by reason of any defect or imperfection in matter of form only, which shall not tend to the prejudice of the defendant, ..." A similar provision is found in Rule 61 of the Federal Rules of Civil Procedure, (28 USC, Appendix.).

Note to subdivision (b). This rule is a restatement of existing law, Wiborg v United States, 163 US 632, 658, 16

S Ct 1127, 1197, 2 cases, 41 L Ed 289; Hemphill v United States, 112 F2d 505, (CCA 9th), reversed 312 US 657, 61 S Ct 729, 85 L Ed 1106, conformed to 120 F2d 115, certiorari denied 314 US 627, 62 S Ct 111, 86 L Ed 503. Rule 27 of the Rules of the Supreme Court, 28 USC foll § 354, provides that errors not specified will be disregarded, "save as the court, at its option, may notice a plain error not assigned or specified." Similar provisions are found in the rules of several circuit courts of appeals.

Notes of Advisory Committee on 2002 amendments. The language of Rule 52 has been amended as part of the general restyling of the Criminal Rules to make them more easily understood and to make style and terminology consistent throughout the rules. These changes are intended to be stylistic only.

Rule 52(b) has been amended by deleting the words "or defect" after the words "plain error." The change is intended to remove any ambiguity in the rule. As noted by the Supreme Court, the language "plain error or defect" was misleading to the extent that it might be read in the disjunctive. *See United States v. Olano,* 507 U.S. 725, 732 [123 L. Ed. 2d 508] (1993) (incorrect to read Rule 52(b) in the disjunctive); *United States v. Young,* 470 U.S. 1, 15 n. 12 [84 L. Ed. 2d 1] (1985) (use of disjunctive in Rule 52(b) is misleading).

Rule 53. Courtroom Photographing and Broadcasting Prohibited

Except as otherwise provided by a statute or these rules, the court must not permit the taking of photographs in the courtroom during judicial proceedings or the broadcasting of judicial proceedings from the courtroom.

HISTORY:

Dec. 26, 1944, eff. March 21, 1946; April 29, 2002, eff. Dec. 1, 2002.

HISTORY; ANCILLARY LAWS AND DIRECTIVES

Other provisions:

Notes of Advisory Committee on Rules. While the matter to which the rule refers has not been a problem in the Federal courts as it has been in some State tribunals, the rule was nevertheless included with a view to giving expression to a standard which should govern the conduct of judicial proceedings, Orfield, 22 Texas LR 194, 222–3; Robbins, 21 ABA Jour 301, 304. See, also, Report of the Special Committee on Cooperation between Press, Radio and Bar, as to Publicity Interfering with Fair Trial of Judicial and Quasi-Judicial Proceedings (1937), 62 ABA Rep 851, 862–865; (1932) 18 ABA Jour 762; (1926) 12 Id. 488; (1925) 11 Id. 64.

Notes of Advisory Committee on 2002 amendments. The language of Rule 53 has been amended as part of the general restyling of the Criminal Rules to make them more easily understood and to make style and terminology consistent throughout the rules. These changes are intended to be stylistic only, except as noted below.

Although the word "radio" has been deleted from the rule, the Committee does not believe that the amendment is a substantive change but rather one that accords with judicial interpretation applying the current rule to other forms of broadcasting and functionally equivalent means. *See, e.g., United States v. Hastings,* 695 F.2d 1278, 1279, n. 5 (11th Cir. 1983) (television proceedings prohibited); *United States v. McVeigh,* 931 F. Supp. 753 (D. Colo. 1996) (release of tape recordings of proceedings prohibited). Given modern technology capabilities, the Committee believed that a more generalized reference to "broadcasting" is appropriate.

Also, although the revised rule does not explicitly recognize exceptions within the rules themselves, the restyled rule recognizes that other rules might permit, for example, video teleconferencing, which clearly involves "broadcasting" of the proceedings, even if only for limited purposes.

Rule 54. [Transferred]

HISTORY:

Dec. 26, 1944, eff. March 21, 1946, as amended Dec. 27, 1948, eff. Oct. 20, 1949; April 9, 1956, eff. 90 days after April 9, 1956; Feb. 28, 1966, eff. July 1, 1966; April 24, 1972, eff. Oct. 1, 1972; April 29, 1982, eff. Aug. 1, 1982; Oct. 12, 1984, P. L. 98-473, Title II, Ch I, § 209(e), Ch II, § 215(e) 98 Stat. 1987, 2016; Nov. 18, 1988, P. L. 100-690, Title VII, Subtitle B, § 7089(c), 102 Stat. 4409; May 1, 1990, eff. Dec. 1, 1990; April 30, 1991, eff. Dec. 1, 1991; April 22, 1993, eff. Dec. 1, 1993; April 26, 1999, eff. Dec. 1, 1999; April 29, 2002, eff. Dec. 1, 2002.

HISTORY; ANCILLARY LAWS AND DIRECTIVES

Other provisions:

Notes of Advisory Committee on Rules. *Note to subdivision (a)(1).* 1. The act of June 28, 1940 (54 Stat 688; 18 USC former § 687 (now § 3771)), authorizing the Supreme Court to prescribe rules of criminal procedure for the district courts of the United States in respect to proceedings prior to and including verdict or finding of guilty or not guilty or plea of guilty, is expressly applicable to the district courts of Alaska, Hawaii, Puerto Rico, Canal Zone, Virgin Islands, the Supreme Courts of Hawaii and Puerto Rico, and the United States Court for China. This is likewise true of the act of February 24, 1933 (47 Stat 904; 18 USC former § 688 (now § 3772)), authorizing the Supreme Court to prescribe rules in respect to proceedings after verdict or finding or after plea of guilty. In this respect these two statutes differ from the act of June 19, 1934 (48 Stat 1064; 28 USC former §§ 723b, 723c (now § 2072)), authorizing the Supreme Court to prescribe rules of civil procedure. The last-mentioned Act comprises only district courts of the United States and the courts of the District of Columbia. The phrase "district courts of the United States" was held not to include district courts in the territories and insular possessions, Mookini v United States, 303 US 201, 58 S Ct 543, 82 L Ed 748, conformed to 95 F2d 960. By subsequent legislation the Federal Rules of Civil Procedure were extended to the District Court of the United States for Hawaii and to appeals therefrom (act of June 19, 1939; 53 Stat 841; 48 USC former § 646) and to the District Court of the United States for Puerto Rico and to appeals therefrom (act of February 12, 1940; 54 Stat 22; 48 USC former § 873a).

2. While the specific reference in the rule to the District Court of the United States for the District of Columbia is probably superfluous, since that court has the same powers and exercises the same jurisdiction as other district courts of the United States in addition to such local powers and

jurisdiction as have been conferred upon it by statute (DC Code, 1940, Title 11, § 305), nevertheless it was listed in the rule in view of the fact that the Federal Rules of Civil Procedure contain a somewhat similar provision (Rule 81(d), 28 USC, Appendix).

3. The United States Court for China has been omitted from the rule in view of the fact that the court has recently been abolished with the abandonment by the United States of its extraterritorial jurisdiction in China.

4. Although, as indicated above, the rule-making power of the Supreme Court in respect to criminal cases extends to the Supreme Courts of Hawaii and Puerto Rico, the rules are not made applicable to those two courts, in view of the fact that they are purely local appellate courts having no appellate jurisdiction over the district courts of the United States in those territories. Alaska and Hawaii have dual systems of courts: local courts exercising purely local jurisdiction and United States district courts exercising Federal jurisdiction. The Supreme Court of each of the two territories hears appeals only from the local courts.

5. Alaska.—There is a district court for the Territory of Alaska consisting of four divisions, established on a territorial basis, 48 USC §§ 101, 101a. As the only court in the Territory, it acts in a dual capacity: it has jurisdiction over cases arising under the laws of the United States as well as those arising under local laws. Although a legislative rather than a constitutional court, it is, nevertheless, deemed a court of the United States and has the jurisdiction of district courts of the United States, 48 USC §§ 101, 101a; Steamer Coquitlam v United States, 163 US 346, 16 S Ct 1117, 41 L Ed 184; McAllister v United States, 141 US 174, 179, 11 S Ct 949, 35 L Ed 693; Ex parte Krause, 228 Fed 547, 549, WD Wash. Criminal procedure is now regulated by acts of Congress, by the Alaska Code of Criminal Procedure (Alaska Comp Laws, 1933, pp 959–1018), and by rules promulgated by the district court.

6. Hawaii.—Hawaii has a dual system of courts. The United States District Court for the Territory of Hawaii, a legislative court, has the jurisdiction of district courts of the United States and proceeds therein "in the same manner as a district court," 48 USC former §§ 641, 642. In addition, there are circuit courts having jurisdiction over cases arising under local laws. Appeals from the circuit courts run to the Supreme Court of the Territory, 48 USC § 631. These rules are made applicable to the district court, but not to the local courts. The Federal Rules of Civil Procedure have been made applicable to the district court and to appeals therefrom, 48 USC former § 646.

7. Puerto Rico.—Puerto Rico has a dual system of courts. The District Court of the United States for Puerto Rico, a legislative court, has jurisdiction of all cases cognizable in the district courts of the United States and proceeds "In the same manner," 48 USC § 863.

In addition, there are local courts for the trial of cases arising under local law, appeals therefrom running to the Supreme Court of the Territory. These rules are made applicable to the district court, but not to the local courts. The Federal Rules of Civil Procedure, 28 USC, Appendix, have been extended to the district court, 48 USC former § 873a.

8. Virgin Islands.—In the Virgin Islands there is a District Court of the Virgin Islands, a legislative court, consisting of two divisions and exercising both Federal and local jurisdiction, 48 USC §§ 1405z, 1406. Heretofore the rules of practice and procedure have been prescribed "by law or ordinance or by rules and regulations of the district judge not inconsistent with law or ordinance," 48 USC § 1405z.

9. Canal Zone.—In the Canal Zone there is a United States District Court for the District of the Canal Zone, a legislative court, exercising both Federal and local jurisdiction, 48 USC former §§ 1344, 1345. Criminal procedure is regulated by the Code of Criminal Procedure of the Canal Zone (Canal Zone Code, Title 6; 48 Stat 1122), and by rules of practice and procedure prescribed by the district judge, 48 USC former § 1344. There are no grand juries in the district, all prosecutions being instituted by information. In the light of these circumstances and because of the peculiar status of the Canal Zone and its quasi-military nature, these rules have been made applicable to its district court, only with respect to proceedings after verdict or finding of guilty or plea of guilty.

10. By order dated March 31, 1941, effective July 1, 1941, the Supreme Court extended the rules of practice and procedure after plea of guilty, verdict or finding of guilty, in criminal cases, to the district courts of Alaska, Hawaii, Puerto Rico, Canal Zone, and Virgin Islands, and all subsequent proceedings in such cases in the United States circuit courts of appeals and in the Supreme Court of the United States, 312 US 721, 85 L Ed 1560.

Note to subdivision (a)(2) 1. Rules 3, 4, and 5, supra, relate to proceedings before United States commissioners.

2. Justices and judges of the United States, as well as United States commissioners, may issue warrants and conduct proceedings as committing magistrates, 18 USC former § 591 (now § 3041) (Arrest and removal for trial); 9 Edmunds, Cyclopedia of Federal Procedure, 2d Ed, secs 3800, 3819.

3. In the District of Columbia judges of the Municipal Court have authority to issue warrants and conduct proceedings as committing magistrates, DC Code, 1940, Title 11, secs 602, 755. These proceedings are governed by these rules. The Municipal Court of the District of Columbia is also a local court for the trial of misdemeanors, but when so acting it is not a court of the United States. These rules, therefore, do not apply to such proceedings.

4. State and local judges and magistrates may issue warrants and act as committing magistrates in Federal cases, 18 USC former § 591 (now § 3041). Only a very small proportion of cases are brought before them, however, and then ordinarily only in an emergency. Since these judicial officers may not be familiar with Federal procedure, these rules have not been made applicable to such proceedings.

Note to subdivision (b)(1) 1. Certain types of State criminal prosecutions, principally those in which defendant is an officer appointed under or acting by authority of a revenue law of the United States and is prosecuted on account of an act done under color of his office, are removable to a Federal court on defendant's motion, 28 USC former § 74 (now §§ 1443, 1446, 1447) (Removal of suits from State courts; causes against persons denied civil rights); former sec 76 (now §§ 1442, 1446, 1447) (Removal of suits from State courts; suits and prosecutions against revenue officers). In such cases the Federal court applies the substantive law of the State, but follows Federal procedure; State of Tennessee v Davis, 100 US 257, 25 L Ed 648; Carter v Tennessee, 18 F2d 850, CCA 6th; Miller v Kentucky, 40 F2d 820, CCA 6th. See also, State of Maryland v Soper, 270 US 9, 46 S Ct 185, 70 L Ed 449. The rule is, therefore, a restatement of existing law, except that it does not affect whatever power the State prosecutor may have as to dismissal.

2. The rule does not affect the mode of removing a case from a State to a Federal court and leaves undisturbed the statutes governing this matter, 28 USC former §§ 74–76 (now §§ 1442, 1443, 1446, 1447).

Note to subdivision (b)(2). This rule should be read in conjunction with Rule 18, which provides that "Except as otherwise permitted by statute or by these rules, the prosecution shall be held in a district in which the offense was committed . . . ".

Note to subdivision (b)(4). United States commissioners specially designated for that purpose by the court by which they are appointed have trial jurisdiction over petty offenses committed on Federal reservations if the defendant waives his right to be tried in the district court and consents to be tried before the commissioner. Act of October 9, 1940, 54 Stat 1058, 18 USC former § 576 (now § 3401). A petty offense is an offense the penalty for which does not exceed confinement in a common jail without hard labor for a period of six months or a fine of $500, or both, 18 USC former § 541 (now § 1). Appeals from convictions by commissioners lie to the district court, 18 USC former § 576a (now § 3402). These rules do not apply to trials before United States commissioners in such cases, since rules of procedure and practice in such matters were specially prescribed by the Supreme Court on January 6, 1941, 311 US 733 et seq. The substantive law applicable in such cases with respect to offenses other than so-called Federal offenses is governed by 18 USC former § 468 (now § 13) (Laws of States adopted for punishing wrongful acts; effect of repeal). In addition, National Park commissioners have limited trial jurisdiction with respect to offenses committed in National Parks. Trials before commissioners in such cases are not governed by these rules, although when a National Park commissioner conducts a proceeding as a committing magistrate, these rules are applicable.

Among the statutes relating to jurisdiction of and proceedings before National Park commissioners are the following:

USC Title 16 former:

§ 10 (Arrests by employees of park service for violation of laws and regulations).

§ 10a (Arrests by employees for violation of regulations made under § 9a).

§ 27 [now 28 USC §§ 131, 631, 632] (Yellowstone National Park; commissioner; jurisdiction and powers).

§ 66 [now 28 USC §§ 631, 632] (Yosemite and Sequoia National Parks; commissioners; appointment; jurisdiction).

§ 70 [now 18 USC §§ 3041, 3141; 18 USC Appx. Rules 4, 5(c), 9] (Same; arrests by commissioners for certain offenses; holding persons arrested for trial; bail).

§ 101 [now 18 USC §§ 3041, 3141; 18 USC Appx. Rule 4; 28 USC Appx. Rule 4] (Mount Rainier National Park; commissioner; arrest; bail).

§ 102 [now 18 § 3053; 18 USC Appx. Rule 4; 28 USC Appx. Rule 4] (Same; commissioner; direction of process of; arrests by other officers).

§ 117b [now 18 USC § 13] (Mesa Verde National Park; application of Colorado laws to offenses).

§ 117f [now 18 USC §§ 3041, 3141; 18 USC Appx. Rules 4, 5(c), 9] (Same; criminal offenses not covered by section 117c; jurisdiction of commissioner).

§ 117g [now 18 USC § 3053; 18 USC Appx. Rule 4; 28 USC Appx. Rule 4] (Same; process to whom without process).

§ 129 [now 28 USC §§ 631, 632] (Crater Lake National Park; commissioner; appointment; powers and duties).

§ 130 [now 18 USC §§ 3041, 3141; 18 USC Appx Rules 4, 5(c), 9] (Same; commissioner; arrests by; bail).

§ 131 [now 18 USC § 3053; 18 USC Appx Rule 4; 28 USC Appx Rule 4] (Same; commissioner; direction of process; arrest without process).

§ 172 [now 28 USC §§ 631, 632] (Glacier National Park; commissioner; jurisdiction; powers and duties).

§ 173 [now 18 USC §§ 3041, 3141; 18 USC Appx. Rules 4, 5(c), 9] (Same; commissioner; arrest of offenders, confinement, and bail).

§ 174 [now 18 USC § 3053; 28 USC Appx. Rule 4] (Same; commissioner; process directed to marshal; arrest without process).

§ 198b [now 18 USC § 13] (Rocky Mountain National Park; punishment of offenses; Colorado laws when followed).

§ 198e [now 28 USC §§ 631, 632] (Same; United States Commissioner; appointment; jurisdiction; issuing process; appeals; rules of procedure).

§ 198f [now 18 USC §§ 3041, 3141; 18 USC Appx. Rules 4, 5(c), 9] (Same; United States Commissioner; arrest of persons for offenses not covered by section 198c; bail).

§ 198g [now 18 USC § 3053; 18 USC Appx. Rule 4; 28 USC Appx. Rule 4] (Same; United States Commissioner; process to whom directed; arrest without process).

§ 204b [now 18 USC § 13] (Lassen Volcanic National Park; application of California laws to offenses).

§ 204e [now 28 USC §§ 631, 632] (Same; United States Commissioner; appointment; jurisdiction of offenses; appeals; rules of procedure).

§ 204f [now 18 USC §§ 3041, 3141; 18 USC Appx. Rules 4, 5(c), 9] (Same; criminal of not covered by section 204c; jurisdiction of commissioner).

§ 204g [now 18 USC § 3053; 18 Rule 4; 28 Rule 4] (Same; process to whom issued; arrests without process).

§ 376 [now 28 USC § 632] (Hot Springs National Park; prosecutions for violations of law or rules and regulations).

§ 377 [now 18 USC §§ 3041, 3141; 18 USC Appx. Rules 4, 5(c), 9] (Same; prosecutions for other offenses).

§ 378 [now 18 USC § 3053; 18 USC Appx. Rule 4; 28 Rule 4] (Same; process directed to marshal; arrests by others).

§ 381 [now 18 USC § 3041] (Same; execution of sentence on conviction).

Note to Subdivision (b)(5) 1. Foreign extradition proceedings are governed by the following statutes:

USC Title 18 former:

§ 651 [now § 3184] (Fugitives from foreign country).

§ 652 [now § 3185] (Fugitives from country under control of United States).

§ 653 [now § 3186] (Surrender of fugitive).

§ 654 [now § 3188] (Time allowed for extradition).

§ 655 [now § 3190] (Evidence on hearing).

§ 656 [now § 3191] (Witnesses for indigent defendants).

§ 657 [now § 3189] (Place and character of hearing).

§ 658 [now § 3181] (Continuance of provisions limited).

§ 659 [now § 3192] (Protection of accused).

§ 660 [now § 3193] (Agent receiving offenders; powers).

Interstate rendition or extradition proceedings are governed by the following statutes:

USC Title 18 former:

§ 662 [now §§ 3182, 3195] (Fugitives from State or Territory).

§ 662c [now §§ 752, 3183, 3195] (Fugitives from State or Territory; arrest and removal).

§ 662d [now §§ 3187, 3195] (Fugitives from State or Territory; provisional arrest and detention).

2. Proceedings relating to forfeiture of property used in connection with a violation of a statute of the United States are governed by various statutes, among which are following:

USC Title 16:

§ 26 (Yellowstone Park; regulations for hunting and fishing in; punishment for violation; forfeitures).

§ 65 (Yosemite and Sequoia National Parks; seizure and forfeiture of guns, traps, teams, horses, and so forth).

§ 99 (Mount Rainier National Park; protection of game and fish; forfeitures of guns, traps, teams, and so forth).

§ 117d (Mesa Verde National Park; forfeiture of property used for unlawful purpose).

§ 128 (Crater Lake National Park; hunting and fishing; forfeitures or seizure of guns, traps, teams, etc., for violating regulations).

§ 171 (Glacier National Park; hunting and fishing; forfeitures and seizures of guns, traps, teams, and so forth).

§ 198d (Rocky Mountain National Park; forfeiture of property used in commission of offenses).

§ 204d (Lassen Volcanic National Park; forfeiture of property used for unlawful purposes).

§ 635 (Importing illegally taken skins; forfeiture).

§ 706 (Arrests; search warrants).

§ 727 (Upper Mississippi River Wild Life and Fish Refuge; powers of employees of Department of the Interior; searches and seizures).

USC Title 18:

§ 286 [now § 492] (Forfeiture of counterfeit obligations, etc.; failure to deliver).

§ 645 [now § 3611] (Confiscation of firearms possessed by convicted felons).

§ 646 [now § 3617] (Remission or mitigation of forfeitures under liquor laws; possession pending trial).

§ 647 [now § 3616] (Use of confiscated motor vehicles).

USC Title 19:

§ 483 [now § 1585a] (Forfeitures; penalty for aiding unlawful importation).

§ 1592 (Fraud; penalty against goods).

§ 1602 (Seizure; report to collector).

§ 1603 (Seizure; collector's reports).

§ 1604 (Seizure; prosecution).

§ 1605 (Seizure; custody).

§ 1606 (Seizure; appraisement).

§ 1607 (Seizure; value $1,000 or less).

§ 1608 (Seizure; claims; judicial condemnation).

§ 1609 (Seizure; summary of forfeiture and sale).

§ 1610 (Seizure; value more than $1,000).

§ 1611 (Seizure; sale unlawful).

§ 1612 (Seizure; summary sale).

§ 1613 (Disposition of proceeds of forfeited property).

§ 1614 (Release of seized property).

§ 1615 (Burden of proof in forfeiture proceedings).

§ 1703 (Seizure and forfeiture of vessels).

§ 1705 (Destruction of forfeited vessel).

USC Title 21:

§ 334 (Seizure).

§ 337 (Proceedings in name of United States; provision as to subpoenas).

USC Title 22:

§ 401 (Seizure of war materials intended for unlawful export generally; forfeiture).

§ 402 (Seizure of war materials intended for unlawful export generally; warrant for detention of seized property).

§ 403 (Seizure of war materials intended for unlawful export generally; petition for restoration of seized property).

§ 404 (Seizure of war materials intended for unlawful export generally; libel and sale of seized property).

§ 405 (Seizure of war materials intended for unlawful export generally; method of trial; bond for redelivery).

§ 406 (Seizure of war materials intended for unlawful export generally; sections not to interfere with foreign trade).

USC Title 26:

§ 3116 [now § 7302] (Forfeitures and seizures).

3. Collection of fines and penalties is accomplished in the same manner as the collection of a civil judgment. See Rule 69(a) of the Federal Rules of Civil Procedure, 28 USC, Appendix. For mode of discharging indigent convicts imprisoned for non-payment of fine, see 18 USC former § 641 (now § 3569).

4. The Federal Juvenile Delinquency Act, 18 USC former §§ 921–929 (now §§ 5031–5037), authorizes prosecution of a juvenile delinquent on the charge of juvenile delinquency, if the juvenile consents to this procedure. In such cases the court may be convened at any time and place, in chambers or otherwise, and the trial is without a jury. The purpose of excepting proceedings under the act is to make inapplicable to them the requirement of an arraignment in open court (Rule 10) and other similar provisions.

5. As habeas corpus proceedings are regarded as civil proceedings, they are not governed by these rules. The procedure in such cases is prescribed by 28 USC former §§ 451–466 (now §§ 2241– 2243, 2251–2253). Appeals in habeas corpus proceedings are governed by the Federal Rules of Civil Procedure (Rule 81(a)(2) of the Federal Rules of Civil Procedure, 28 USC, Appendix).

Note to subdivision (c) 1. This rule is analogous to Rule 81(e) of the Federal Rules of Civil Procedure, 28 USC following § 2072.

2. 1 USC §§ 1– 6, containing general rules of construction, should be read in conjunction with this rule.

3. In connection with the definition of "attorney for the Government", see the following statutes:

USC Title 5:

§ 291 (Establishment of Department).

§ 293 (Solicitor General).

§ 294 (Assistant to Attorney General).

§ 295 (Assistant Attorneys General).

§ 309 (Conduct and argument of cases by Attorney General and Solicitor General).

§ 310 (Conduct of legal proceedings).

§ 311 (Performance of duty by officers of Department).

§ 312 [now 28 USC §§ 503, 507, 508] (Counsel to aid district attorneys).

§ 315 (Appointment and oath of special attorneys or counsel).

USC Title 28:

§ 481 [now § 501] (District attorneys).

§ 483 [now § 502] (Assistant district attorneys).

§ 485 [now § 507] (District attorneys; duties).

4. The last sentence of this rule has particular reference to 18 USC former § 682 (now § 3731) (Appeals; on behalf of

the United States; rules of practice and procedure), which authorizes the United States to appeal in criminal cases from a decision on a motion to quash, a demurrer or a special plea in bar, if the defendant has not been placed in jeopardy. It is intended that the right of the Government to appeal in such cases should not be affected as the result of the substitution of a motion under Rule 12 for a demurrer, motion to quash and a special plea in bar. The rule is equally applicable to any other statute employing the same terminology.

Notes of Advisory Committee on 1948 and 1956 amendments. To conform to the nomenclature of revised Title 28 with respect to district courts and courts of appeals (28 USC §§ 132(a), 43(a)); to eliminate special reference to the district courts for the District of Columbia, Hawaii and Puerto Rico which are now United States district courts for all purposes (28 USC §§ 88, 91, 119, 132, 133, 451), and to eliminate special reference to the court of appeals for the District of Columbia which is now a United States court of appeals for all purposes (28 USC §§ 41, 43).

The amendment to paragraph (1) is to incorporate nomenclature of Revised Title 28 and in paragraphs (2), (3), (4), and (5) to insert proper reference to Titles 18 and 28 in place of repealed acts.

Under revised Title 28 the justices of the United States Court of Appeals and District Court for the District of Columbia become circuit and district judges (see 28 USC §§ 44, 133) and the use of the descriptive phrase "senior circuit judge" is abandoned in favor of the title "chief judge" in all circuits including the District of Columbia.

Notes of Advisory Committee on 1966 amendments. Subdivision (a). The first change reflects the granting of statehood to Alaska. The second change conforms to Section 3501 of the Canal Zone Code.

Subdivision (b). The change is made necessary by the new provision in Rule 20(d).

Notes of Advisory Committee on 1972 amendments. Subdivisions (a) and (b) are amended to delete the references to "commissioners" and to substitute, where appropriate, the phrase "United States magistrates."

Subdivision (a)(2) is deleted. In its old form it makes reference to "rules applicable to criminal proceedings before commissioners," which are now replaced by the Rules of Procedure for the Trial of Minor Offenses before United States Magistrates (1971). Rule 1 of the magistrates' rules provides that they are applicable to cases involving "minor offenses" as defined in 18 USC § 3401 "before United States magistrates." Cases involving "minor offenses" brought before a judge of the district court will be governed by the Rules of Criminal Procedure for the United States District Courts.

The last sentence of old subdivision (a)(2) is stricken for two reasons: (1) Whenever possible, cases should be brought before a United States magistrate rather than before a state or local judicial officer authorized by 18 USC § 3041. (2) When a state or local judicial officer is involved, he should conform to the federal rules.

Subdivision (b)(4) makes clear that minor offense cases before United States magistrates are governed by the Rules of Procedure for the Trial of Minor Offenses before United States Magistrates (1971). See rule 1 of the magistrates' rules.

In subdivision (b)(5) the word "civil" is added before the word "forfeiture" to make clear that the rules do apply to criminal forfeitures. This is clearly the intention of Congress. See Senate Report No. 91-617, 91st Cong, 1st Sess, Dec. 16, 1969, at 160.

Subsection (a) provides the remedy of criminal forfeiture. Forfeiture trials are to be governed by the Fed R Crim P. But see Fed R Crim P 54 (b)(5).

Subdivision (c) is amended to list the defined terms in alphabetical order to facilitate the use of the rule. There are added six new definitions.

"Federal magistrate" is a phrase to be used whenever the rule is intended to confer authority on any federal judicial officer including a United States magistrate.

"Judge of the United States" is a phrase defined to include district court, court of appeals, and supreme court judges. It is used in the rules to indicate that only a judge (not to include a United States magistrate) is authorized to act.

"Magistrate" is a term used when both federal and state judicial officers may be authorized to act. The scope of authority of state or local judicial officers is clarified by the enumeration of those rules (3, 4, and 5) under which they are authorized to act.

"United States magistrate" is a phrase which refers to the federal judicial officer created by the Federal Magistrates Act (28 USC §§ 631–639).

Also added are cross references to the statutory definitions of "minor offense" and "petty offense."

Notes of Advisory Committee on 1982 amendments. Rule 54(a). The amendment of subdivision (a) conforms to 48 U.S.C. § 1694(c), which provides that "the rules heretofore or hereafter promulgated and made effective by the Congress or the Supreme Court of the United States pursuant to Titles 11, 18, and 28 shall apply to the District Court for the Northern Mariana Islands and appeals therefrom where appropriate, except as otherwise provided in articles IV and V of the covenant provided by the Act of March 24, 1976 (90 Stat. 263)." The reference is to the "Covenant To Establish a Commonwealth of the Northern Mariana Islands in Political Union with the United States of America." Article IV of the covenant provides that except when exercising "the jurisdiction of a district court of the United States," the District Court will be considered a court of the Northern Mariana Islands for the purposes of determining the requirements of indictment by grand jury or trial by jury." Article V provides that "neither trial by jury nor indictment by grand jury shall be required in any civil action or criminal prosecution based on local law, except when required by local law."

Rule 54(b)(4). This change is necessitated by the recent amendment of 18 U.S.C. § 3401 by the Federal Magistrate Act of 1979.

Rule 54(c). The first amendment to subdivision (c) conforms to 48 U.S.C. § 1694(c), which states: "The terms 'attorney for the government' and 'United States Attorney' as used in the Federal Rules of Criminal Procedure (Rule 54(c)) shall, when applicable to cases arising under the laws of the Northern Mariana Islands, include the attorney general of the Northern Mariana Islands or any other person or persons as may be authorized by the laws of the Northern Marianas to act therein."

The second amendment to subdivision (c) eliminates any reference to minor offenses. By virtue of the recent amendment of 18 U.S.C. § 3401 by the Federal Magistrate Act of 1979, the term "minor offense" is no longer utilized in the statute. It is likewise no longer used in these rules. See amendments to Rules 5(b) and 9(d).

Notes of Advisory Committee on 1991 amendment. The amendment to 54(a) conforms the Rule to legislative changes affecting the prosecution of federal cases in Guam and the Virgin Islands by indictment or information. The "except" clause in Rule 54(a) addressing the availability of indictments by grand jury Guam has been effectively repealed by Public Law 98-454 (1984), 48 U.S.C. § 1424-4 which made the Federal Rules of Criminal Procedure (including Rule 7, relating to use of indictments) applicable in Guam notwithstanding Rule 54(a). That legislation apparently codified what had been the actual practice in Guam for a number of years. See 130 Cong. Rec., H25476 (daily ed. Sept. 14, 1984). With regard to the Virgin Islands, Public Law 98-454 (1984) also amended 48 U.S.C. §§ 1561 and 1614(b) to permit (but not require) use of indictments in the Virgin Islands.

The Rule is amended to conform to the Judicial Improvements Act of 1990 [P.L. 101-650, Title III, Section 321] which provides that each United States magistrate appointed under section 631 of title 28, United States Code, shall be known as a United States magistrate judge.

Notes of Advisory Committee on 1999 amendments. The amendment to Rule 54(a) is a technical amendment removing the reference to the court in the Canal Zone, which no longer exists.

Notes of Advisory Committee on 2002 amendments. Certain provisions in current Rule 54 have been moved to revised Rule 1 as part of a general restyling of the Criminal Rules to make them more easily understood and to make style and terminology consistent throughout the rules. Other provisions in Rule 54 have been deleted as being unnecessary.

Amendments:

1984.

Act Oct. 12, 1984 (effective on the first day of the first calendar month beginning 36 months after enactment on Oct. 12, 1984, as provided by § 235(a)(1) of such Act, as amended by Act Dec. 26, 1985, P. L. 99-217, § 4, 99 Stat. 1728, which appears as 18 USCS § 3551 note, and applicable as provided by such § 235, which appears as 18 USCS § 3551 note), in subdiv. (c), substituted the definition of "Petty offense" for one which read: " 'Petty offense' is defined in 18 USC § 1(3).".

1988.

Act Nov. 18, 1988, in subsec. (c), substituted the definition of "Petty offense" for one which read: "'Petty offense' means a class B or C misdemeanor or an infraction.".

Rule 55. Records

The clerk of the district court must keep records of criminal proceedings in the form prescribed by the Director of the Administrative Office of the United States Courts. The clerk must enter in the records every court order or judgment and the date of entry.

HISTORY:

Dec. 26, 1944, eff. March 21, 1946, as amended Dec. 27, 1948, eff. Oct. 20, 1949; Feb. 28, 1966, eff. July 1, 1966; April 24, 1972, eff. Oct. 1, 1972; April 22, 1993, eff. Dec. 1, 1993; April 29, 2002, eff. Dec. 1, 2002.

HISTORY; ANCILLARY LAWS AND DIRECTIVES

Other provisions:

Notes of Advisory Committee on Rules. The Federal Rules of Civil Procedure Rule 79, 28 USC, Appendix, prescribed in detail the books and records to be kept by the clerk in civil cases. Subsequently to the effective date of the civil rules, however, the act establishing the Administrative Office of the United States Courts became law (act of August 7, 1939; 53 Stat 1223; 28 USC former §§ 444–450 (now §§ 332–333, 456, 601–610)). One of the duties of the Director of that Office is to have charge, under the supervision and direction of the Conference of Senior Circuit Judges, of all administrative matters relating to the offices of the clerks and other clerical and administrative personnel of the courts, 28 USC former § 446 (now §§ 604, 609). In view of this circumstance it seemed best not to prescribe the records to be kept by the clerks of the district courts and by the United States commissioners, in criminal proceedings, but to vest the power to do so in the Director of the Administrative Office of the United States Courts with the approval of the Conference of Senior Circuit Judges.

Notes of Advisory Committee on 1948 amendments. The purpose of this amendment is to incorporate nomenclature provided for by 28 U.S.C.S. § 331, as amended.

Notes of Advisory Committee on 1966 amendments. Rule 37(a)(2) provides that for the purpose of commencing the running of the time for appeal a judgment or order is entered "when it is entered in the criminal docket." The sentence added here requires that such a docket be kept and that it show the dates on which judgments or orders are entered therein. Cf. Civil Rule 79 (a).

Notes of Advisory Committee on 1993 amendments. The Rule is amended to conform to the Judicial Improvements Act of 1990 [P.L. 101-650, Title III, Section 321) which provides that each United States magistrate appointed under section 631 of title 28, United States Code, shall be known as a United States magistrate judge.

Notes of Advisory Committee on 2002 amendments. The language of Rule 55 has been amended as part of the general restyling of the Criminal Rules to make them more easily understood and to make style and terminology consistent throughout the rules. These changes are intended to be stylistic only.

Rule 56. When Court is Open

(a) In General. A district court is considered always open for any filing, and for issuing and returning process, making a motion, or entering an order.

(b) Office Hours. The clerk's office—with the clerk or a deputy in attendance—must be open during business hours on all days except Saturdays, Sundays, and legal holidays.

(c) Special Hours. A court may provide by local rule or order that its clerk's office will be open for specified hours on Saturdays or legal holidays other than those set aside by statute for observing New Year's Day, Martin Luther King Jr.'s Birthday, Washington's Birthday, Memorial Day, Juneteenth National Independence Day, Independence Day, Labor Day, Columbus Day, Veterans' Day, Thanksgiving Day, and Christmas Day.

HISTORY:

Dec. 26, 1944, eff. March 21, 1946, as amended Dec. 27, 1948, eff. Oct. 20, 1949; Feb. 28, 1966, eff. July 1, 1966; Dec. 4, 1967, eff. July 1, 1968; March 1, 1971, eff. July 1, 1971; April 25, 1988, eff. Aug. 1, 1988; April 29, 2002, eff. Dec. 1, 2002; April 24, 2023, eff. Dec. 1, 2023.

HISTORY; ANCILLARY LAWS AND DIRECTIVES

Other provisions:

Notes of Advisory Committee on Rules. 1. The first sentence of this rule is substantially the same as Rule 77(a) of the Federal Rules of Civil Procedure, 28 USC, Appendix, except that it is applicable to circuit courts of appeals as well as to district courts.

2. In connection with this rule, see 28 USC former § 14 (Monthly adjournments for trial of criminal causes) and 28 USC former § 15 (now § 141) (Special terms). These sections "indicate a policy of avoiding the hardships consequent upon a closing of the court during vacations," Abbott v Brown, 241 US 606, 611, 36 S Ct 689, 60 L Ed 1199.

3. The second sentence of the rule is identical with the first sentence of Rule 77(c) of the Federal Rules of Civil Procedure, 28 USC, Appendix.

4. The term "legal holidays" includes Federal holidays as well as holidays prescribed by the laws of the State where the clerk's office is located.

Notes of Advisory Committee on 1949 amendments. To incorporate nomenclature provided for by Revised Title 28, USC § 43(a).

Notes of Advisory Committee on 1966 amendments. The change is in conformity with the changes made in Rule 45. See the similar changes in Civil Rule 77(c) made effective July 1, 1963.

Notes of Advisory Committee on 1968 amendments. The provisions relating to the court of appeals are included in Rule 45 of the Federal Rules of Appellate Procedure.

Notes of Advisory Committee on 1971 amendments. The amendment adds Columbus Day to the list of legal holidays. See the Note accompanying the amendment of Rule 45(a).

Notes of Advisory Committee on 1988 amendments. The amendment is technical. No substantive change is intended.

Notes of Advisory Committee on 2002 amendments. The language of Rule 56 has been amended as part of the general restyling of the Criminal Rules to make them more easily understood and to make style and terminology consistent throughout the rules. These changes are intended to be stylistic only.

Notes of Advisory Committee on 2023 amendments. The amendment adds "Juneteenth National Independence Day" to the list of legal holidays. See Juneteenth National Independence Day Act, P.L. 117-17 (2021) (amending 5 U.S.C. § 6103(a)). A stylistic change was made.

Rule 57. District Court Rules

(a) In General.

(1) *Adopting Local Rules.* Each district court acting by a majority of its district judges may, after giving appropriate public notice and an opportunity to comment, make and amend rules governing its practice. A local rule must be consistent with—but not duplicative of—federal statutes and rules adopted under 28 U.S.C. § 2072 and must conform to any uniform numbering system prescribed by the Judicial Conference of the United States.

(2) *Limiting Enforcement.* A local rule imposing a requirement of form must not be enforced in a manner that causes a party to lose rights because of an unintentional failure to comply with the requirement.

(b) Procedure When There is No Controlling Law. A judge may regulate practice in any manner consistent with federal law, these rules, and the local rules of the district. No sanction or other disadvantage may be imposed for noncompliance with any requirement not in federal law, federal rules, or the local district rules unless the alleged violator was furnished with actual notice of the requirement before the noncompliance.

(c) Effective Date and Notice. A local rule adopted under this rule takes effect on the date specified by the district court and remains in effect unless amended by the district court or abrogated by the judicial council of the circuit in which the district is located. Copies of local rules and their amendments, when promulgated, must be furnished to the judicial council and the Administrative Office of the United States Courts and must be made available to the public.

HISTORY:

Dec. 26, 1944, eff. March 21, 1946, as amended Dec. 27, 1948, eff. Oct. 20, 1949; Dec. 4, 1967, eff. July 1, 1968; April 29, 1985, eff. August 1, 1985; April 22, 1993, eff. Dec. 1, 1993; April 27, 1995, eff. Dec. 1, 1995; April 29, 2002, eff. Dec. 1, 2002.

HISTORY; ANCILLARY LAWS AND DIRECTIVES

Other provisions:

Notes of Advisory Committee on Rules. Subdivision (a). This rule is substantially a restatement of 28 USC former § 731 (now § 2071) (Rules of practice in district courts). A similar provision is found in Rule 83 of the Federal Rules of Civil Procedure, 28 USC, Appendix.

Subdivision (b). 1. One of the purposes of this rule is to abrogate any existing requirement of conformity to State procedure on any point whatsoever. The Federal Rules of Civil Procedure, 28 USC, Appendix, have been held to repeal the Conformity Act, 28 USC former § 724, Sibbach v Wilson, 312 US 1, 10, 61 S Ct 422, 85 L Ed 479.

2. While the rules are intended to constitute a comprehensive procedural code for criminal cases in the Federal courts, nevertheless it seemed best not to endeavor to prescribe a uniform practice as to some matters of detail, but to leave the individual courts free to regulate them, either by local rules or by usage. Among such matters are the mode of impaneling a jury, the manner and order of interposing challenges to jurors, the manner of selecting the foreman of a trial jury, the matter of sealed verdicts, the order of counsel's arguments to the jury, and other similar details.

Notes of Advisory Committee on 1949 amendments. To incorporate nomenclature provided for by Revised Title 28, USC, § 43(a).

Notes of Advisory Committee on 1968 amendments. The provisions relating to courts of appeals are included in Rule 47 of the Federal Rules of Appellate Procedure.

Notes of Advisory Committee on 1985 amendments. Rule 57 has been reformulated to correspond to Fed.R-.Civ.P. 83, including the proposed amendments thereto. The purpose of the reformulation is to emphasize that the procedures for adoption of local rules by a district court are the same under both the civil and the criminal rules. In particular, the major purpose of the reformulation is to enhance the local rulemaking process by requiring appropriate public notice of proposed rules and an opportunity to comment on them. See Committee Note to Fed.R.Civ.P. 83.

The Rule is amended to conform to the Judicial Improvements Act of 1990 [P.L. 101-650, Title III, Section 321] which provides that each United States magistrate appointed under section 631 of title 28, United States Code, shall be known as a United States magistrate judge.

Notes of Advisory Committee on 1995 amendments. Subdivision (a). This rule is amended to reflect the requirement that local rules be consistent not only with the national rules but also with Acts of Congress. The amendment also states that local rules should not repeat national rules and Acts of Congress.

The amendment also requires that the numbering of local rules conform with any numbering system that may be prescribed by the Judicial Conference. Lack of uniform numbering might create unnecessary traps for counsel and litigants. A uniform numbering system would make it easier for an increasingly national bar to locate a local rule that applies to a particular procedural issue.

Paragraph (2) is new. Its aim is to protect against loss of rights in the enforcement of local rules relating to matters of form. The proscription of paragraph (2) is narrowly drawn—covering only nonwillful violations and only those involving local rules directed to matters of form. It does not limit the court's power to impose substantive penalties upon a party if it or its attorney stubbornly or repeatedly violates a local rule, even one involving merely a matter of form. Nor does it affect the court's power to enforce local rules that involve more than mere matters of form—for example, a local rule requiring that the defendant waive a jury trial within a specified time.

Subdivision (b). This rule provides flexibility to the court in regulating practice when there is no controlling law. Specifically, it permits the court to regulate practice in any manner consistent with Acts of Congress, with rules adopted under 28 U.S.C. § 2072, and with the district's local rules. This rule recognizes that courts rely on multiple directives to control practice. Some courts regulate practice through the published Federal Rules and the local rules of the court. Some courts also have used internal operating procedures, standing orders, and other internal directives. Although such directives continue to be authorized, they can lead to problems. Counsel or litigants may be unaware of the various directives. In addition, the sheer volume of directives may impose an unreasonable barrier. For example, it may be difficult to obtain copies of the directives. Finally, counsel or litigants may be unfairly sanctioned for failing to comply with a directive. For these reasons, the amendment disapproves imposing any sanction or other disadvantage on a person for noncompliance with such an internal directive, unless the alleged violator has been furnished in a particular case with actual notice of the requirement.

There should be no adverse consequence to a party or attorney for violating special requirements relating to practice before a particular judge unless the party or attorney has actual notice of those requirements. Furnishing litigants with a copy outlining the judge's practices—or attaching instructions to a notice setting a case for conference or trial—would suffice to give actual notice, as would an order in a case specifically adopting by reference a judge's standing order and indicating how copies can be obtained.

Notes of Advisory Committee on 2002 amendments. The language of Rule 57 has been amended as part of the general restyling of the Criminal Rules to make them more easily understood and to make style and terminology consistent throughout the rules. These changes are intended to be stylistic only.

Rule 58. Petty Offenses and Other Misdemeanors

(a) Scope.

(1) *In General.* These rules apply in petty offense and other misdemeanor cases and on appeal to a district judge in a case tried by a magistrate judge, unless this rule provides otherwise.

(2) *Petty Offense Case Without Imprisonment.* In a case involving a petty offense for which no sentence of imprisonment will be imposed, the court may follow any provision of these rules that is not inconsistent with this rule and that the court considers appropriate.

(3) *Definition.* As used in this rule, the term "petty offense for which no sentence of imprisonment will be imposed" means a petty offense for which the court determines that, in the event of conviction, no sentence of imprisonment will be imposed.

(b) Pretrial Procedure.

(1) *Charging Document.* The trial of a misdemeanor may proceed on an indictment, information, or complaint. The trial of a petty offense may also proceed on a citation or violation notice.

(2) *Initial Appearance.* At the defendant's initial appearance on a petty offense or other misdemeanor charge, the magistrate judge must inform the defendant of the following:

(A) the charge, and the minimum and maximum penalties, including imprisonment, fines, any special assessment under 18 U.S.C. § 3013, and restitution under 18 U.S.C. § 3556;

(B) the right to retain counsel;

(C) the right to request the appointment of counsel if the defendant is unable to retain counsel—unless the charge is a petty offense for which the appointment of counsel is not required;

(D) the defendant's right not to make a statement, and that any statement made may be used against the defendant;

(E) the right to trial, judgment, and sentencing before a district judge—unless:

(i) the charge is a petty offense; or

(ii) the defendant consents to trial, judgment, and sentencing before a magistrate judge.

(F) the right to a jury trial before either a magistrate judge or a district judge—unless the charge is a petty offense;

(G) any right to a preliminary hearing under Rule 5.1, and the general circumstances, if any, under which the defendant may secure pretrial release; and

(H) that a defendant who is not a United States citizen may request that an attorney for the government or a federal law enforcement official notify a consular officer from the defendant's country of nationality that the defendant has been arrested—but that even without the defendant's request, a treaty or other international agreement may require consular notification.

(3) *Arraignment.*

(A) Plea Before a Magistrate Judge. A magistrate judge may take the defendant's plea in a petty offense case. In every other misdemeanor case, a magistrate judge may take the plea only if the defendant consents either in writing or on the record to be tried before a magistrate judge and specifically waives trial before a district judge. The defendant may plead not guilty, guilty, or (with the consent of the magistrate judge) nolo contendere.

(B) Failure to Consent. Except in a petty offense case, the magistrate judge must order a defendant who does not consent to trial before a magistrate judge to appear before a district judge for further proceedings.

(c) Additional Procedures in Certain Petty Offense Cases. The following procedures also apply in a case involving a petty offense for which no sentence of imprisonment will be imposed:

(1) *Guilty or Nolo Contendere Plea.* The court must not accept a guilty or nolo contendere plea unless satisfied that the defendant understands the nature of the charge and the maximum possible penalty.

(2) *Waiving Venue.*

(A) Conditions of Waiving Venue. If a defendant is arrested, held, or present in a district different from the one where the indictment, information, complaint, citation, or violation notice is pending, the defendant may state in writing a desire to plead guilty or nolo contendere; to waive venue and trial in the district where the proceeding is pending; and to consent to the court's disposing of the case in the district where the defendant was arrested, is held, or is present.

(B) Effect of Waiving Venue. Unless the defendant later pleads not guilty, the prosecution will proceed in the district where the defendant was arrested, is held, or is present. The district clerk must notify the clerk in the original district of the defendant's waiver of venue. The defendant's statement of a desire to plead guilty or nolo contendere is not admissible against the defendant.

(3) *Sentencing.* The court must give the defendant an opportunity to be heard in mitigation and then proceed immediately to sentencing. The court may, however, postpone sentencing to allow the probation service to investigate or to permit either party to submit additional information.

(4) *Notice of a Right to Appeal.* After imposing sentence in a case tried on a not-guilty plea, the court must advise the defendant of a right to appeal the conviction and of any right to appeal the sentence. If the defendant was convicted on a plea of guilty or nolo contendere, the court must advise the defendant of any right to appeal the sentence.

(d) Paying a Fixed Sum in Lieu of Appearance.

(1) *In General.* If the court has a local rule governing forfeiture of collateral, the court may accept a fixed-sum payment in lieu of the defendant's appearance and end the case, but the fixed sum may not exceed the maximum fine allowed by law.

(2) *Notice to Appear.* If the defendant fails to pay a fixed sum, request a hearing, or appear in response to a citation or violation notice, the district clerk or a magistrate judge may issue a notice for the defendant to appear before the court on a date certain. The notice may give the defendant an additional opportunity to pay a fixed sum in lieu of appearance. The district clerk must serve the notice on the defendant by mailing a copy to the defendant's last known address.

(3) *Summons or Warrant.* Upon an indictment, or upon a showing by one of the other charging documents specified in Rule 58(b)(1) of probable cause to believe that an offense has been committed and that the defendant has committed it, the court may issue an arrest warrant or, if no warrant is requested by an attorney for the government, a summons. The showing of probable cause must be made under oath or under penalty of perjury, but the affiant need not appear before the court. If the defendant fails to appear before the court in response to a summons, the court may summarily issue a warrant for the defendant's arrest.

(e) Recording the Proceedings. The court must record any proceedings under this rule by using a court reporter or a suitable recording device.

(f) New Trial. Rule 33 applies to a motion for a new trial.

(g) Appeal.

(1) *From a District Judge's Order or Judgment.* The Federal Rules of Appellate Procedure govern an appeal from a district judge's order or a judgment of conviction or sentence.

(2) *From a Magistrate Judge's Order or Judgment.*

(A) Interlocutory Appeal. Either party may appeal an order of a magistrate judge to a district judge within 14 days of its entry if a district judge's order could similarly be appealed. The party appealing must file a notice with the clerk specifying the order being appealed and must serve a copy on the adverse party.

(B) Appeal from a Conviction or Sentence. A defendant may appeal a magistrate judge's judgment of conviction or sentence to a district judge within 14 days of its entry. To appeal, the defendant must file a notice with the clerk specifying the judgment being appealed and must serve a copy on an attorney for the government.

(C) Record. The record consists of the original papers and exhibits in the case; any transcript, tape, or other recording of the proceedings; and a certified copy of the docket entries. For purposes of the appeal, a copy of the record of the proceedings must be made available to a defendant who establishes by affidavit an inability to pay or give security for the record. The Director of the Administrative Office of the United States Courts must pay for those copies.

(D) Scope of Appeal. The defendant is not entitled to a trial de novo by a district judge. The scope of the appeal is the same as in an appeal to the court of appeals from a judgment entered by a district judge.

(3) *Stay of Execution and Release Pending Appeal.* Rule 38 applies to a stay of a judgment of conviction or sentence. The court may release the defendant pending appeal under the law relating to release pending appeal from a district court to a court of appeals.

HISTORY:

Added May 1, 1990, eff. Dec. 1, 1990; amended April 30, 1991, eff. Dec. 1, 1991; April 22, 1993, eff. Dec. 1, 1993; April 11, 1997, eff. Dec. 1, 1997; April 29, 2002, eff. Dec. 1, 2002; April 12, 2006, eff. Dec. 1, 2006; March 26, 2009, eff. Dec. 1, 2009; April 25, 2014, eff. Dec. 1, 2014.

HISTORY; ANCILLARY LAWS AND DIRECTIVES

Other provisions:

Notes of Advisory Committee on Rules. This new rule is largely a restatement of the Rules of Procedure for the Trial of Misdemeanors before United States Magistrates which were promulgated in 1980 to replace the Rules for the Trial of Minor Offenses before United States Magistrates (1970). The Committee believed that a new single rule should be incorporated into the Rules of Criminal Procedure where those charged with its execution could readily locate it and realize its relationship with the other Rules. A number of technical changes have been made throughout the rule and unless otherwise noted, no substantive changes were intended in those amendments. The Committee envisions no major changes in the way in which the trial of misdemeanors and petty offenses are currently handled.

The title of the rule has been changed by deleting the phrase "Before United States Magistrates" to indicate that this rule may be used by district judges as well as magistrates. The phrase "and Petty Offenses" has been added to the title and elsewhere throughout the rule because the term "misdemeanor" does not include an "infraction." See 18 U.S.C. § 3559(a). A petty offense, however, is defined in 18 U.S.C. § 19 as a Class B misdemeanor, a Class C misdemeanor, or an infraction, with limitations on fines of no more than $5,000 for an individual and $10,000 for an organization.

Subdivision (a) is an amended version of current Magistrates Rule 1. Deletion of the phrase "before United States Magistrates under 18 U.S.C. § 3401" in Rule 1(a) will enable district judges to use the abbreviated procedures of this rule. Consistent with that change, the term "magistrate" is amended to read "the court," wherever appropriate throughout the rule, to indicate that both judges and magistrates may use the rule. The last sentence in (a)(1) has been amended to reflect that the rule also governs an appeal from a magistrate's decision to a judge of the district court. An appeal from a district judge's decision would be governed by the Federal Rules of Appellate Procedure. Subdivision (a)(2) rephrases prior language in Magistrate Rule 1(b). Subdivision (a)(3) adds a statutory reference to 18 U.S.C. § 19, which defines a petty offense as a "Class B misdemeanor, a Class C misdemeanor, or an infraction" with the $5,000 and $10,000 fine limitations noted supra. The phrase "regardless of the penalty authorized by law" has been deleted.

Subdivision (b) is an amended version of current Magistrates Rule 2. The last sentence in current Rule 2(a) has been deleted because 18 U.S.C. § 3401(a), provides that a magistrate will have jurisdiction to try misdemeanor cases when specially designated to do so by the district court or courts served by the Magistrate.

Subdivision (b)(2) reflects the standard rights advisements currently included in Magistrates Rule 2 with several amendments. Subdivision (b)(2)(A) specifically requires that the defendant be advised of all penalties which may be imposed upon conviction, including specifically a special assessment and restitution. A number of technical, nonsubstantive, changes have been made in the contents of advisement of rights. A substantive change is reflected in subdivision (b)(2)(G), currently Magistrates Rule 2(b)(7), and (8). That rule currently provides that, unless the prosecution is on an indictment or information, a defendant who is charged with a misdemeanor other than a petty offense has a right to a preliminary hearing, if the defendant does not consent to be tried by the magistrate. As amended, only a defendant in custody has a right to a preliminary hearing.

Subdivision (b)(3)(A) is based upon Magistrates Rule 2(c) and has been amended by deleting the last sentence, which provides that trial may occur within 30 days "upon written consent of the defendant." The change is warranted because the Speedy Trial Act does not apply to petty offenses. See 18 U.S.C. § 3172(2). Subdivision (b)(3)(B), "Failure to Consent," currently appears in Magistrates Rule 3(a). The first sentence has been amended to make it applicable to all misdemeanor and petty offense defendants who fail to consent. The last sentence of Rule 3(a) has been deleted entirely. Because the clerk is responsible for all district court case files, including those for misdemeanor and petty offense cases tried by magistrates, it is not necessary to state that the file be transmitted to the clerk of court.

Subdivision (c) is an amended version of current Magistrates Rule 3 with the exception of Rule 3(a), which, as noted supra is now located in subdivision (b)(3)(B) of the new rule. The phrase "petty offense for which no sentence of imprisonment will be imposed" has been deleted because the heading for subdivision (c) limits its application to those petty offenses. The Committee recognizes that subdivision (c)(2) might result in attempted forum shopping. See, e.g., United States v. Shaw, 467 F.Supp. 86 (W.D. La. 1979), affm'd, 615 F.2d 251 (5th Cir. 1980). In order to maintain a streamlined and less formal procedure which is consistent with the remainder of the Rule, subdivision (c)(2) does not require the formal "consent" of the United States Attorneys involved before a waiver of venue may be accomplished. Cf. Rule 20 (Transfer From the District for Plea and Sentence). The Rule specifically envisions that there will be communication and coordination between the two districts involved. To that end, reasonable efforts should be made to contact the United States Attorney in the district in which the charges were instituted. Subdivision (c)(4), formerly Rule 3(d), now specifically provides that the defendant be advised of the right to appeal the sentence. This subdivision is also amended to provide for advising the defendant of the right to appeal a sentence under the Sentencing Reform Act when the defendant is sentenced following a plea of guilty. Both amendments track the language of Rule 32(a)(2), as amended by the Sentencing Reform Act.

Subdivision (d) is an amended version of Magistrates Rule 4. The amendments are technical in nature and no substantive change is intended.

Subdivision (e) consists of the first sentence of Magistrates Rule 5. The second sentence of that Rule was deleted as being inconsistent with 28 U.S.C. § 753(b) which gives the court discretion to decide how the proceedings will be recorded. The third sentence is deleted to preclude routine waivers of a verbatim record and to insure that all petty offenses are recorded.

Subdivision (f) replaces Magistrates Rule 6 and simply incorporates by reference Rule 33.

Subdivision (g) is an amended version of Magistrates Rule 7. Because the new rule may be used by both magistrates and judges, subdivision (g)(1) was added to make it clear that the Federal Rules of Appellate Procedure govern any appeal in a case tried by a district judge pursuant to the new rule. Subdivision (g)(2)(B), based upon Magistrates Rule 7(b), now provides for appeal of a sentence by a magistrate and is thus consistent with the provisions of 18 U.S.C. § 3742(f). Finally, subdivision (g)(3) is based upon Magistrates Rule 7(d) but has been amended to provide that a stay of execution is applicable, if an appeal is taken from a sentence as well as from a conviction. This change is consistent with the recent amendment of Rule 38 by the Sentencing Reform Act.

The new rule does not include Magistrates Rules 8 and 9. Rule 8 has been deleted because the subject of local rules is covered in Rule 57. Rule 9, which defined a petty offense, is now covered in 18 U.S.C. § 19.

Notes of Advisory Committee on 1991 amendments. The amendments are technical. No substantive changes are intended.

The Rule is amended to conform to the Judicial Improvements Act of 1990 [P.L. 101-650, Title III, Section 321] which provides that each United States magistrate appointed under section 631 of title 28, United States Code, shall be known as a United States magistrate judge.

Notes of Advisory Committee on 1997 amendments. The Federal Courts Improvement Act of 1996, Sec. 202, amended 18 U.S.C. § 3401(b) and 28 U.S.C. § 636(a) to remove the requirement that a defendant must consent to a trial before a magistrate judge in a petty offense that is a class B misdemeanor charging a motor vehicle offense, a class C misdemeanor, or an infraction. Section 202 also changed 18 U.S.C. § 3401(b) to provide that in all other misdemeanor cases, the defendant may consent to trial either orally on the record or in writing. The amendments to Rule 58(b)(2) and (3) conform the rule to the new statutory language and include minor stylistic changes.

Notes of Advisory Committee on 2002 amendments. The language of Rule 58 has been amended as part of the general restyling of the Criminal Rules to make them more easily understood and to make style and terminology consistent throughout the rules. These changes are intended to be stylistic only.

The title of the rule has been changed to "Petty Offenses and Other Misdemeanors." In Rule 58(c)(2)(B) (regarding waiver of venue), the Committee amended the rule to require that the "district clerk," instead of the magistrate judge, inform the original district clerk if the defendant waives venue and the prosecution proceeds in the district where the defendant was arrested. The Committee intends no change in practice.

In Rule 58(g)(1) and (g)(2)(A), the Committee deleted as unnecessary the word "decision" because its meaning is covered by existing references to an "order, judgment, or sentence" by a district judge or magistrate judge. In the Committee's view, deletion of that term does not amount to a substantive change.

Notes of Advisory Committee on 2006 amendments. *Note to Subdivision (b)(2)(G).* Rule 58(b)(2)(G) sets out the advice to be given to defendants at an initial appearance on a misdemeanor charge, other than a petty offense. As currently written, the rule is restricted to those cases where the defendant is held in custody, thus creating a conflict and some confusion when compared to Rule 5.1(a) concerning the right to a preliminary hearing. Paragraph (G) is incomplete in its description of the circumstances requiring a preliminary hearing. In contrast, Rule 5.1(a) is a correct statement of the law concerning the defendant's entitlement to a preliminary hearing and is consistent with 18 U.S.C. § 3060 in this regard. Rather than attempting to define, or restate, in Rule 58 when a defendant may be entitled to a Rule 5.1 preliminary hearing, the rule is amended to direct the reader to Rule 5.1.

Notes of Advisory Committee on 2009 amendments. The times set in the former rule at 10 days have been revised to 14 days. See the Committee Note to Rule 45(a).

Notes of Advisory Committee on 2014 amendments. *Rule 58(b)(2)(H).* Article 36 of the Vienna Convention on Consular Relations provides that detained foreign nationals shall be advised that they may have the consulate of their home country notified of their arrest and detention, and bilateral agreements with numerous countries require consular notification whether or not the detained foreign national requests it. Article 36 requires consular notification advice to be given "without delay," and arresting officers are primarily responsible for providing this advice.

Providing this advice at the initial appearance is designed, not to relieve law enforcement officers of that responsibility, but to provide additional assurance that U.S. treaty obligations are fulfilled, and to create a judicial record of that action. The Committee concluded that the most effective and efficient method of conveying this information is to provide it to every defendant, without attempting to determine the defendant's citizenship.

At the time of this amendment, many questions remain unresolved by the courts concerning Article 36, including whether it creates individual rights that may be invoked in a judicial proceeding and what, if any, remedy may exist for a violation of Article 36. *Sanchez-Llamas v. Oregon*, 548 U.S. 331 (2006). This amendment does not address those questions. More particularly, it does not create any such rights or remedies.

Rule 59. Matters before a Magistrate Judge

(a) Nondispositive Matters. A district judge may refer to a magistrate judge for determination any matter that does not dispose of a charge or defense. The magistrate judge must promptly conduct the required proceedings and, when appropriate, enter on the record an oral or written order stating the determination. A party may serve and file objections to the order within 14 days after being served with a copy of a written order or after the oral order is stated on the record, or at some other time the court sets. The district judge must consider timely objections and modify or set aside any part of the order that is contrary to law or clearly erroneous. Failure to object in accordance with this rule waives a party's right to review.

(b) Dispositive Matters.

(1) *Referral to Magistrate Judge.* A district judge may refer to a magistrate judge for recommendation a defendant's motion to dismiss or quash an indictment or information, a motion to suppress evidence, or any matter that may dispose of a charge or defense. The magistrate judge must promptly conduct the required proceedings. A record must be made of any evidentiary proceeding and of any other proceeding if the magistrate judge considers it necessary. The magistrate judge must enter on the record a recommendation for disposing of the matter, including any proposed findings of fact. The clerk must immediately serve copies on all parties.

(2) *Objections to Findings and Recommendations.* Within 14 days after being served with a copy of the recommended disposition, or at some other time the court sets, a party may serve and file specific written objections to the proposed findings and recommendations. Unless the district judge directs otherwise, the objecting party must promptly arrange for transcribing the record, or whatever portions of it the parties agree to or the magistrate judge considers sufficient. Failure to object in accordance with this rule waives a party's right to review.

(3) *De Novo Review of Recommendations.* The district judge must consider de novo any objection to the magistrate judge's recommendation. The district judge may accept, reject, or modify the recommendation, receive further evidence, or resubmit the matter to the magistrate judge with instructions.

HISTORY:

Added April 25, 2005, eff. Dec. 1, 2005; March 26, 2009, eff. Dec. 1, 2009.

HISTORY; ANCILLARY LAWS AND DIRECTIVES

Other provisions:

Notes of Advisory Committee on 2005 amendments. Rule 59 is a new rule that creates a procedure for a district judge to review nondispositive and dispositive decisions by magistrate judges. The rule is derived in part from Federal Rule of Civil Procedure 72.

The Committee's consideration of a new rule on the subject of review of a magistrate judge's decisions resulted from *United States v. Abonce-Barrera*, 257 F.3d 959 (9th Cir. 2001). In that case the Ninth Circuit held that the Criminal Rules do not require appeals from nondispositive decisions by magistrate judges to district judges as a requirement for review by a court of appeals. The court suggested that Federal Rule of Civil Procedure 72 could serve as a suitable model for a criminal rule.

Rule 59(a) sets out procedures to be used in reviewing nondispositive matters, that is, those matters that do not dispose of the case. The rule requires that if the district judge has referred a matter to a magistrate judge, the magistrate judge must issue an oral or written order on the record. To preserve the issue for further review, a party must object to that order within 10 days after being served with a copy of the order or after the oral order is stated on the record or at some other time set by the court. If an objection is made, the district court is required to consider the objection. If the court determines that the magistrate judge's order, or a portion of the order, is contrary to law or is clearly erroneous, the court must set aside the order, or the affected part of the order. *See also* 28 U.S.C. § 636(b)(1)(A).

Rule 59(b) provides for assignment and review of recommendations made by magistrate judges on dispositive matters, including motions to suppress or quash an indictment or information. The rule directs the magistrate judge to consider the matter promptly, hold any necessary evidentiary hearings, and enter his or her recommendation on the record. After being served with a copy of the magistrate judge's recommendation, under Rule 59(b)(2), the parties have a period of 10 days to file any objections. If any objections are filed, the district court must consider the matter de novo and accept, reject, or modify the recommendation, or return the matter to the magistrate judge for further consideration.

Both Rule 59(a) and (b) contain a provision that explicitly states that failure to file an objection in accordance with the rule amounts to a waiver of the issue. This waiver provision is intended to establish the requirements for objecting in a district court in order to preserve appellate review of magistrate judges' decisions. In *Thomas v. Arn*, 474 U.S. 140, 155 (1985), the Supreme Court approved the adoption of waiver rules on matters for which a magistrate judge had made a decision or recommendation. The Committee believes that the waiver provisions will enhance the ability of a district court to review a magistrate judge's decision or recommendation by requiring a party to promptly file an objection to that part of the decision or recommendation at issue. Further, the Supreme Court has held that a de novo review of a magistrate judge's decision or recommendation is required to satisfy Article III concerns only where there is an objection. *Peretz v. United States*, 501 U.S. 293 (1991).

Despite the waiver provisions, the district judge retains the authority to review any magistrate judge's decision or recommendation whether or not objections are timely filed. This discretionary review is in accord with the Supreme Court's decision in *Thomas v. Arn, supra*, at 154. *See also Matthews v. Weber*, 423 U.S. 261, 270–271 (1976).

Although the rule distinguishes between "dispositive" and "nondispositive" matters, it does not attempt to define or otherwise catalog motions that may fall within either category. Instead, that task is left to the case law.

Notes of Advisory Committee on 2009 amendments. The times set in the former rule at 10 days have been revised to 14 days. See the Committee Note to Rule 45(a).

Rule 60. Victim's Rights

(a) In General.

(1) *Notice of a Proceeding.* The government must use its best efforts to give the victim reasonable, accurate, and timely notice of any public court proceeding involving the crime.

(2) *Attending the Proceeding.* The court must not exclude a victim from a public court proceeding involving the crime, unless the court determines by clear and convincing evidence that the victim's testimony would be materially altered if the victim heard other testimony at that proceeding. In determining whether to exclude a victim, the court must make every effort to permit the fullest attendance possible by the victim and

must consider reasonable alternatives to exclusion. The reasons for any exclusion must be clearly stated on the record.

(3) *Right to Be Heard on Release, a Plea, or Sentencing.* The court must permit a victim to be reasonably heard at any public proceeding in the district court concerning release, plea, or sentencing involving the crime.

(b) Enforcement and Limitations.

(1) *Time for Deciding a Motion.* The court must promptly decide any motion asserting a victim's rights described in these rules.

(2) *Who May Assert the Rights.* A victim's rights described in these rules may be asserted by the victim, the victim's lawful representative, the attorney for the government, or any other person as authorized by 18 U.S.C. § 3771(d) and (e).

(3) *Multiple Victims.* If the court finds that the number of victims makes it impracticable to accord all of them their rights described in these rules, the court must fashion a reasonable procedure that gives effect to these rights without unduly complicating or prolonging the proceedings.

(4) *Where Rights May Be Asserted.* A victim's rights described in these rules must be asserted in the district where a defendant is being prosecuted for the crime.

(5) *Limitations on Relief.* A victim may move to reopen a plea or sentence only if:

(A) the victim asked to be heard before or during the proceeding at issue, and the request was denied;

(B) the victim petitions the court of appeals for a writ of mandamus within 10 days after the denial, and the writ is granted; and

(C) in the case of a plea, the accused has not pleaded to the highest offense charged.

(6) *No New Trial.* A failure to afford a victim any right described in these rules is not grounds for a new trial.

HISTORY:

Added April 23, 2008, eff. Dec. 1, 2008.

HISTORY; ANCILLARY LAWS AND DIRECTIVES

Other provisions:

Notes of Advisory Committee on Rules. This rule implements several provisions of the Crime Victims' Rights Act, codified as 18 U.S.C. § 3771, in judicial proceedings in the federal courts.

Note to Subdivision (a)(1). This subdivision incorporates 18 U.S.C. § 3771(a)(2), which provides that a victim has a "right to reasonable, accurate, and timely notice of any public court proceedings. . . ." The enactment of 18 U.S.C. § 3771(a)(2) supplemented an existing statutory requirement that all federal departments and agencies engaged in the detection, investigation, and prosecution of crime identify victims at the earliest possible time and inform those victims of various rights, including the right to notice of the status of the investigation, the arrest of a suspect, the filing of charges against a suspect, and the scheduling of judicial proceedings. *See* 42 U.S.C. § 10607(b) & (c)(3)(A)–(D).

Note to Subdivision (a)(2). This subdivision incorporates 18 U.S.C. § 3771(a)(3), which provides that the victim shall not be excluded from public court proceedings unless the court finds by clear and convincing evidence that the victim's testimony would be materially altered by attending and hearing other testimony at the proceeding, and 18 U.S.C. § 3771(b), which provides that the court shall make every effort to permit the fullest possible attendance by the victim.

Rule 615 of the Federal Rule of Evidence address the sequestration of witnesses. Although Rule 615 requires the court upon the request of a party to order the witnesses to be excluded so they cannot hear the testimony of other witnesses, it contains an exception for "a person authorized by statute to be present." Accordingly, there is no conflict between Rule 615 and this rule, which implements the provisions of the Crime Victims' Rights Act.

Note to Subdivision (a)(3). This subdivision incorporates 18 U.S.C. § 3771(a)(4), which provides that a victim has the "right to be reasonably heard at any public proceeding in the district court involving release, plea, [or] sentencing. . . ."

Note to Subdivision (b). This subdivision incorporates the provisions of 18 U.S.C. § 3771(d)(1), (2), (3), and (5). The statute provides that the victim, the victim's lawful representative, and the attorney for the government, and any other person as authorized by 18 U.S.C. § 3771(d) and (e) may assert the victim's rights. In referring to the victim and the victim's lawful representative, the committee intends to include counsel. 18 U.S.C. § 3771(e) makes provision for the rights of victims who are incompetent, incapacitated, or deceased, and 18 U.S.C. § 3771(d)(1) provides that "[a] person accused of the crime may not obtain any form of relief under this chapter."

The statute provides that those rights are to be asserted in the district court where the defendant is being prosecuted (or if no prosecution is under way, in the district where the crime occurred). Where there are too many victims to accord each the rights provided by the statute, the district court is given the authority to fashion a reasonable procedure to give effect to the rights without without unduly complicating or prolonging the proceedings.

Finally, the statute and the rule make it clear that failure to provide relief under the rule never provides a basis for a new trial. Failure to afford the rights provided by the statute and implementing rules may provide a basis for re-opening a plea or a sentence, but only if the victim can establish all of the following: the victim asserted the right before or during the proceeding, the right was denied, the victim petitioned for mandamus within 10 days as provided by 18 U.S.C. § 3771(d)(5)(B), and — in the case of a plea — the defendant did not plead guilty to the highest offense charged.

Rule 61. Title

These rules may be known and cited as the Federal Rules of Criminal Procedure.

HISTORY:

Dec. 26, 1944, eff. March 21, 1946; as amended, April 29, 2002, eff. Dec. 1, 2002; April 23, 2008, eff. Dec. 1, 2008.

HISTORY; ANCILLARY LAWS AND DIRECTIVES

Other provisions:

Notes of Advisory Committee on Rules. This rule is

similar to Rule 85 of the Federal Rules of Civil Procedure, 28 USC, Appendix, which reads as follows:

These rules may be known and cited as the Federal Rules of Civil Procedure.

Notes of Advisory Committee on 2002 amendments. No changes have been made to Rule 60, as a result of the general restyling of the Criminal Rules.

Notes of Advisory Committee on 2008 amendments. This amendment renumbers current Rule 60 as Rule 61 to accommodate the new victims' rights rule.

Rule 62. Criminal Rules Emergency

(a) Conditions for an Emergency. The Judicial Conference of the United States may declare a Criminal Rules emergency if it determines that:

(1) extraordinary circumstances relating to public health or safety, or affecting physical or electronic access to a court, substantially impair the court's ability to perform its functions in compliance with these rules; and

(2) no feasible alternative measures would sufficiently address the impairment within a reasonable time.

(b) Declaring an Emergency.

(1) *Content.* The declaration must:

(A) designate the court or courts affected;

(B) state any restrictions on the authority granted in (d) and (e); and

(C) be limited to a stated period of no more than 90 days.

(2) *Early Termination.* The Judicial Conference may terminate a declaration for one or more courts before the termination date.

(3) *Additional Declarations.* The Judicial Conference may issue additional declarations under this rule.

(c) Continuing a Proceeding After a Termination. Termination of a declaration for a court ends its authority under (d) and (e). But if a particular proceeding is already underway and resuming compliance with these rules for the rest of the proceeding would not be feasible or would work an injustice, it may be completed with the defendant's consent as if the declaration had not terminated.

(d) Authorized Departures from These Rules After a Declaration.

(1) *Public Access to a Proceeding.* If emergency conditions substantially impair the public's in-person attendance at a public proceeding, the court must provide reasonable alternative access, contemporaneous if feasible.

(2) *Signing or Consenting for a Defendant.* If any rule, including this rule, requires a defendant's signature, written consent, or written waiver—and emergency conditions limit a defendant's ability to sign—defense counsel may sign for the defendant if the defendant consents on the record. Otherwise, defense counsel must file an affidavit attesting to the defendant's consent. If the defendant is pro se, the court may sign for the defendant if the defendant consents on the record.

(3) *Alternate Jurors.* A court may impanel more than 6 alternate jurors.

(4) *Correcting or Reducing a Sentence.* Despite Rule 45(b)(2), if emergency conditions provide good cause, a court may extend the time to take action under Rule 35 as reasonably necessary.

(e) Authorized Use of Videoconferencing and Teleconferencing After a Declaration.

(1) *Videoconferencing for Proceedings Under Rules 5, 10, 40, and 43(b)(2).* This rule does not modify a court's authority to use videoconferencing for a proceeding under Rules 5, 10, 40, or 43(b)(2), except that if emergency conditions substantially impair the defendant's opportunity to consult with counsel, the court must ensure that the defendant will have an adequate opportunity to do so confidentially before and during those proceedings.

(2) *Videoconferencing for Certain Proceedings at Which the Defendant Has a Right to Be Present.* Except for felony trials and as otherwise provided under (e)(1) and (3), for a proceeding at which a defendant has a right to be present, a court may use videoconferencing if:

(A) the district's chief judge finds that emergency conditions substantially impair a court's ability to hold in-person proceedings in the district within a reasonable time;

(B) the court finds that the defendant will have an adequate opportunity to consult confidentially with counsel before and during the proceeding; and

(C) the defendant consents after consulting with counsel.

(3) *Videoconferencing for Felony Pleas and Sentencings.* For a felony proceeding under Rule 11 or 32, a court may use videoconferencing only if, in addition to the requirement in (2)(B):

(A) the district's chief judge finds that emergency conditions substantially impair a court's ability to hold in-person felony pleas and sentencings in the district within a reasonable time;

(B) the defendant, before the proceeding and after consulting with counsel, consents in a writing signed by the defendant that the proceeding be conducted by videoconferencing; and

(C) the court finds that further delay in that particular case would cause serious harm to the interests of justice.

(4) *Teleconferencing by One or More Participants.* A court may conduct a proceeding, in whole or in part, by teleconferencing if:

(A) the requirements under any applicable rule, including this rule, for conducting the proceeding by videoconferencing have been met;

(B) the court finds that:

(i) videoconferencing is not reasonably available for any person who would participate by teleconference; and

(ii) the defendant will have an adequate opportunity to consult confidentially with counsel before and during the proceeding if held by teleconference; and

(C) the defendant consents.

HISTORY:

Added April 24, 2023, eff. Dec. 1, 2023.

Criminal Procedure Rule 62

HISTORY; ANCILLARY LAWS AND DIRECTIVES

Other provisions:

Notes of Advisory Committee on 2023 Amendments. *Subdivision (a).* This rule defines the conditions for a Criminal Rules emergency that would support a declaration authorizing a court to depart from one or more of the other Federal Rules of Criminal Procedure. Rule 62 refers to the other, non-emergency rules—currently Rules 1-61—as "these rules." This committee note uses "these rules" or "the rules" to refer to the non-emergency rules, and uses "this rule" or "this emergency rule" to refer to new Rule 62.

The rules have been promulgated under the Rules Enabling Act and carefully designed to protect constitutional and statutory rights and other interests. Any authority to depart from the rules must be strictly limited. Compliance with the rules cannot be cast aside because of cost or convenience, or without consideration of alternatives that would permit compliance to continue. Subdivision (a) narrowly restricts the conditions that would permit a declaration granting emergency authority to depart from the rules and defines who may make that declaration.

First, subdivision (a) specifies that the power to declare a rules emergency rests solely with the Judicial Conference of the United States, the governing body of the judicial branch. To find that a rules emergency exists, the Judicial Conference will need information about the ability of affected courts to comply with the rules, as well as the existence of reasonable alternatives to continue court functions in compliance with the rules. The judicial council of a circuit, for example, may be able to provide helpful information it has received from judges within the circuit regarding local conditions and available resources.

Paragraph (a)(1) requires that before declaring a Criminal Rules emergency, the Judicial Conference must determine that circumstances are extraordinary and that they relate to public health or safety or affect physical or electronic access to a court. These requirements are intended to prohibit the use of this emergency rule to respond to other challenges, such as those arising from staffing or budget issues. Second, those extraordinary circumstances must substantially impair the ability of a court to perform its functions in compliance with the rules.

In addition, paragraph (a)(2) requires that even if the Judicial Conference determines the extraordinary circumstances defined in (a)(1), it cannot declare a Criminal Rules emergency unless it also determines that no feasible alternative measures would sufficiently address the impairment and allow the affected court to perform its functions in compliance with the rules within a reasonable time. For example, in the districts devastated by hurricanes Katrina and Maria, the ability of courts to function in compliance with the rules was substantially impaired for extensive periods of time. But there would have been no Criminal Rules emergency under this rule because those districts were able to remedy that impairment and function effectively in compliance with the rules by moving proceedings to other districts under 28 U.S.C. § 141. Another example might be a situation in which the judges in a district are unable to carry out their duties as a result of an emergency that renders them unavailable, but courthouses remain safe. The unavailability of judges would substantially impair that court's ability to function in compliance with the rules, but temporary assignment of judges from other districts under 28 U.S.C. § 292(b) and (d) would eliminate that impairment.

Subdivision (a) also recognizes that emergency circumstances may affect only one or a small number of courts—familiar examples include hurricanes, floods, explosions, or terroristic threats—or may have widespread impact, such as a pandemic or a regional disruption of electronic communications. This rule provides a uniform procedure that is sufficiently flexible to accommodate different types of emergency conditions with local, regional, or nationwide impact.

Paragraph (b)(1). Paragraph (b)(1) specifies what must be included in a declaration of a Criminal Rules emergency. Subparagraph (A) requires that each declaration of a Criminal Rules emergency designate the court or courts affected by the Criminal Rules emergency as defined in subdivision (a). Some emergencies may affect all courts, some will be local or regional. The declaration must be no broader than the Criminal Rules emergency. That is, every court identified in a declaration must be one in which extraordinary circumstances that relate to public health or safety or that affect physical or electronic access to the court are substantially impairing its ability to perform its functions in compliance with these rules, and in which compliance with the rules cannot be achieved within a reasonable time by alternative measures. A court may not exercise authority under (d) and (e) unless the Judicial Conference includes the court in its declaration, and then only in a manner consistent with that declaration, including any limits imposed under (b)(1)(B).

Subparagraph (b)(1)(B) provides that the Judicial Conference's declaration of a Criminal Rules emergency must state any restrictions on the authority granted by subdivisions (d) and (e) to depart from the rules. For example, if the emergency arises from a disruption in electronic communications, there may be no reason to authorize videoconferencing for proceedings in which the rules require in-person appearance. But (b)(1)(B) does not allow a declaration to expand departures from the rules beyond those authorized by subdivisions (d) and (e).

Under (b)(1)(C), each declaration must state when it will terminate, which may not exceed 90 days from the date of the declaration. This sunset clause is included to ensure that these extraordinary deviations from the rules last no longer than necessary.

Paragraph (b)(2). If emergency conditions end before the termination date of the declaration for some or all courts included in that declaration, (b)(2) provides that the Judicial Conference may terminate the declaration for the courts no longer affected. This provision also ensures that any authority to depart from the rules lasts no longer than necessary.

Paragraph (b)(3) recognizes that the conditions that justified the declaration of a Criminal Rules emergency may continue beyond the term of the declaration. The conditions may also change, shifting in nature or affecting more districts. An example might be a flood that leads to a contagious disease outbreak. Rather than provide for extensions, renewals, or modifications of an initial declaration, paragraph (b)(3) gives the Judicial Conference the authority to respond to such situations by issuing additional declarations. Each additional declaration must meet the requirements of subdivision (a), and must include the contents required by (b)(1).

Subdivision (c). In general, the termination of a declaration of emergency ends all authority to depart from the other Federal Rules of Criminal Procedure. It does not terminate, however, the court's authority to complete an ongoing trial with alternate jurors who have been impaneled under (d)(3), because the proceeding authorized by (d)(3) is the completed impanelment. In addition, subdivision (c) carves out a narrow exception for certain proceedings commenced under a declaration of emergency but not completed before the declaration terminates. If it would not be feasible to conclude a proceeding commenced before a declaration terminates with procedures that comply with the rules, or if resuming compliance with the rules would work an injustice, the court may complete that proceeding using procedures authorized by this emergency rule, but only if the defendant consents to the use of emergency procedures after the declaration ends. Subdivision (c) recognizes the need for some accommodation and flexibility during the transition period, but also the importance of returning promptly to the rules to protect the defendant's rights and other interests.

Subdivisions (d) and (e) describe the authority to depart from the rules after a declaration.

Paragraph (d)(1) addresses the courts' obligation to provide alternative access when emergency conditions have substantially impaired in-person attendance by the public at public proceedings. The term "public proceeding" is intended to capture proceedings that the rules require to be conducted "in open court," proceedings to which a victim must be provided access, and proceedings that must be open to the public under the First and Sixth Amendments. The rule creates a duty to provide the public with "reasonable alternative access," notwithstanding Rule 53's ban on the "broadcasting of judicial proceedings." Under appropriate circumstances, the reasonable alternative could be audio access to a video proceeding.

The duty arises only when the substantial impairment of in-person access by the public is caused by emergency conditions. The rule does not apply when reasons other than emergency conditions restrict access. The duty arises not only when emergency conditions substantially impair the attendance of anyone, but also when conditions would allow participants but not the public to attend, as when capacity must be restricted to prevent contagion.

Alternative access must be contemporaneous when feasible. For example, if public health conditions limit courtroom capacity, contemporaneous transmission to an overflow courthouse space ordinarily could be provided.

When providing "reasonable alternative access," courts must comply with the constitutional guarantees of public access and any applicable statutory provision, including the Crime Victims' Rights Act, 18 U.S.C. § 3771.

Paragraph (d)(2) recognizes that emergency conditions may disrupt compliance with a rule that requires the defendant's signature, written consent, or written waiver. If emergency situations limit the defendant's ability to sign, (d)(2) provides an alternative, allowing defense counsel to sign if the defendant consents. To ensure that there is a record of the defendant's consent to this procedure, the amendment provides two options: (1) defense counsel may sign for the defendant if the defendant consents on the record, or, (2) without the defendant's consent on the record, defense counsel must file an affidavit attesting to the defendant's consent to the procedure. The defendant's oral agreement on the record alone will not substitute for the defendant's signature. The written document signed by counsel on behalf of the defendant provides important additional evidence of the defendant's consent.

The court may sign for a pro se defendant, if that defendant consents on the record. There is no provision for the court to sign for a counseled defendant, even if the defendant provides consent on the record. The Committee concluded that rules requiring the defendant's signature, written consent, or written waiver protect important rights, and permitting the judge to bypass defense counsel and sign once the defendant agrees could result in a defendant perceiving pressure from the judge to sign. Requiring a writing from defense counsel is an essential protection when the defendant's own signature is not reasonably available because of emergency conditions.

It is generally helpful for the court to conduct a colloquy with the defendant to ensure that defense counsel consulted with the defendant with regard to the substance and import of the pleading or document being signed, and that the consent to allow counsel to sign was knowing and voluntary.

Paragraph (d)(3) allows the court to impanel more than six alternate jurors, creating an emergency exception to the limit imposed by Rule 24(c)(1). This flexibility may be particularly useful for a long trial conducted under emergency conditions—such as a pandemic—that increase the likelihood that jurors will be unable to complete the trial. Because it is not possible to anticipate all of the situations in which this authority might be employed, the amendment leaves to the discretion of the district court whether to impanel more alternates, and if so, how many. The same uncertainty about emergency conditions that supports flexibility in the rule for the provision of additional alternates also supports avoiding mandates for additional peremptory challenges when more than six alternates are provided. Nonetheless, if more than six alternates are impaneled and emergency conditions allow, the court should consider permitting each party one or more additional peremptory challenges, consistent with the policy in Rule 24(c)(4).

Paragraph (d)(4) provides an emergency exception to Rule 45(b)(2), which prohibits the court from extending the time to take action under Rule 35 "except as stated in that rule." When emergency conditions provide good cause for extending the time to take action under Rule 35, the amendment allows the court to extend the time for taking action "as reasonably necessary." The amendment allows the court to extend the 14-day period for correcting a clear error in the sentence under Rule 35(a) and the one-year period for government motions for sentence reductions based on substantial assistance under Rule 35(b)(1). Nothing in this provision is intended to expand the authority to correct or reduce a sentence under Rule 35. This emergency rule does not address the extension of other time limits because Rule 45(b)(1) already provides the necessary flexibility for courts to consider emergency circumstances. It allows the court to extend the time for taking other actions on its own or on a party's motion for good cause shown.

Subdivision (e) provides authority for a court to use videoconferencing or teleconferencing under specified circumstances after the declaration of a Criminal Rules emergency. The term "videoconferencing" is used throughout, rather than the term "video teleconferencing" (which appears elsewhere in the rules), to more clearly distinguish conferencing with visual images from "teleconferencing" with audio only. The first three paragraphs in (e) describe a court's authority to use videoconferencing, depending upon the type of proceeding, while the last describes a court's authority to use teleconferencing when videoconferencing is not reasonably available. The defendant's consent to the use of conferencing technology is required for all proceedings addressed by subdivision (e).

Subdivision (e) applies to the use of videoconferencing and teleconferencing for the proceedings defined in paragraphs (1) through (3), for all or part of the proceeding, by one or more participants. But it does not regulate the use of video and teleconferencing technology for all possible proceedings in a criminal case. It does not speak to or prohibit the use of videoconferencing or teleconferencing for proceedings, such as scheduling conferences, at which the defendant has no right to be present. Instead, it addresses three groups of proceedings: (1) proceedings for which the rules already authorize videoconferencing; (2) certain other proceedings at which a defendant has the right to be present, excluding felony trials; and (3) felony pleas and sentencings. The new rule does not address the use of technology to maintain communication with a defendant who has been removed from a proceeding for misconduct.

Paragraph (e)(1) addresses first appearances, arraignments, and certain misdemeanor proceedings under Rules 5, 10, 40, and 43(b)(2), where the rules already provide for videoconferencing if the defendant consents. See Rules 5(f), 10(c), 40(d), and 43(b)(2) (written consent). This paragraph was included to eliminate any confusion about the interaction between existing videoconferencing authority and this rule. It clarifies that this rule does not change the court's existing authority to use videoconferencing for these proceedings, except that it requires the court to address emergency conditions that significantly impair the defendant's opportunity to consult with counsel. In that situation, the court must ensure that the defendant will have an adequate opportunity for confidential consultation before and during videoconference proceedings under Rules 5, 10, 40, and 43(b)(2). Paragraphs (e)(2) through (4) apply this requirement to all emergency video and teleconferencing authority granted by the rule after a declaration.

The requirement is based upon experience during the COVID-19 pandemic, when conditions dramatically limited the ability of counsel to meet or even speak with clients. The Committee believed it was essential to include this prerequisite for conferencing under Rules 5, 10, 40, and 43(b)(2), as well as conferencing authorized only during a declaration by paragraphs (e)(2), (3), and (4), in order to safeguard the defendant's constitutional right to counsel. The rule does not specify any particular means of providing an adequate opportunity for private communication.

Paragraph (e)(2) addresses videoconferencing authority for proceedings "at which a defendant has a right to be present" under the Constitution, statute, or rule, excluding felony trials and proceedings addressed in either (e)(1) or (e)(3). Such proceedings include, for example, revocations of release under Rule 32.1, preliminary hearings under Rule 5.1, and waivers of indictment under Rule 7(b). During a declaration, an affected court may use videoconferencing for these proceedings, but only if the three circumstances are met.

First, subparagraph (e)(2)(A) restricts videoconferencing authority to affected districts in which the chief judge (or alternate under 28 U.S.C. § 136(e)) has found that emergency conditions substantially impair a court's ability to hold proceedings in person within a reasonable time. Recognizing that important policy concerns animate existing limitations in Rule 43 on virtual proceedings, even with the defendant's consent, this district-wide finding is not an invitation to substitute virtual conferencing for in-person proceedings without regard to conditions in a particular division, courthouse, or case. If a proceeding can be conducted safely in-person within a reasonable time, a court should hold it in person.

Second, subparagraph (e)(2)(B) conditions videoconferencing upon the court's finding that the defendant will have an adequate opportunity to consult confidentially with counsel before and during the proceeding. If emergency conditions prevent the defendant's presence, and videoconferencing is employed as a substitute, counsel will not have the usual physical proximity to the defendant during the proceeding and may not have ordinary access to the defendant before and after the proceeding.

Third, subparagraph (e)(2)(C) requires that the defendant consent to videoconferencing after consulting with counsel. Insisting on consultation with counsel before consent assures that the defendant will be informed of the potential disadvantages and risks of virtual proceedings. It also provides some protection against potential pressure to consent, from the government or the judge.

The Committee declined to provide authority in this rule to conduct felony trials without the physical presence of the defendant, even if the defendant wishes to appear at trial by videoconference during an emergency declaration. And this rule does not address the use of technology to maintain communication with a defendant who has been removed from a proceeding for misconduct. Nor does it address if or when trial participants other than the defendant may appear by videoconferencing.

Paragraph (e)(3) addresses the use of videoconferencing for a third set of proceedings: felony pleas and sentencings under Rules 11 and 32. The physical presence of the defendant together in the courtroom with the judge and counsel is a critical part of any plea or sentencing proceeding. Other than trial itself, in no other context does the communication between the judge and the defendant consistently carry such profound consequences. The importance of defendant's physical presence at plea and sentence is reflected in Rules 11 and 32. The Committee's intent was to carve out emergency authority to substitute virtual presence for physical presence at a felony plea or sentence only as a last resort, in cases where the defendant would likely be harmed by further delay. Accordingly, the prerequisites for using videoconferencing for a felony plea or sentence include three circumstances in addition to those required for the use of videoconferencing under (e)(2).

Subparagraph (e)(3)(A) requires that the chief judge of the district (or alternate under 28 U.S.C. § 136(e)) make a district-wide finding that emergency conditions substantially impair a court's ability to hold felony pleas and sentencings in person in that district within a reasonable time. This finding serves as assurance that videoconferencing may be necessary and that individual judges cannot on their own authorize virtual pleas and sentencings when in-person proceedings might be manageable with patience or adaptation. Although the finding serves as assurance that videoconferencing might be necessary in the district, as under (e)(2), individual courts within the district may not conduct virtual plea and sentencing proceedings in individual cases unless they find the remaining criteria of (e)(3) and (4) are satisfied.

As protection against undue pressure to waive physical presence, subparagraph (e)(3)(B) states that, before the proceeding and after consultation with counsel, the defendant must consent in writing that the proceeding be conducted by videoconferencing. This requirement of writing is, like other requirements of writing in the rules, subject to the emergency provisions in (d)(2), unless the relevant emergency declaration excludes the authority in (d)(2). To ensure that the defendant consulted with counsel with regard to this decision, and that the defendant's consent was knowing and voluntary, the court may need to conduct a colloquy with the defendant before accepting the written request.

Subparagraph (e)(3)(C) requires that before a court may conduct a plea or sentencing proceeding by videoconference, it must find that the proceeding in that particular case cannot be further delayed without serious harm to the interests of justice. Examples may include some pleas and sentencings that would allow transfer to a facility preferred by the defense, or result in immediate release, home confinement, probation, or a sentence shorter than the time expected before conditions would allow in-person proceedings. A judge might also conclude that under certain emergency conditions, delaying certain guilty pleas under Rule 11(c)(1)(C), even those calling for longer sentences, may result in serious harm to the interests of justice.

Paragraph (e)(4) details conditions for the use of teleconferencing to conduct proceedings for which videoconferencing is authorized. Videoconferencing is always a better option than an audio-only conference because it allows participants to see as well as hear each other. To ensure that participants communicate through audio alone only when videoconferencing is not feasible, (e)(4) sets out four prerequisites. Because the rule applies to teleconferencing "in whole or in part," it mandates these prerequisites whenever the entire proceeding is held by teleconference from start to finish, or when one or more participants in the proceeding are connected by audio only, for part or all of a proceeding.

The first prerequisite, in (e)(4)(A), is that all of the conditions for the use of videoconferencing for the proceeding must be met before a court may conduct a proceeding, in whole or in part, by audio-only. For example, videoconferencing for a sentencing under Rule 32 requires compliance with (e)(3)(A), (B), and (C). No part of a felony sentencing proceeding may be held by teleconference, nor may any person participate in such a proceeding by audio only, unless those videoconferencing requirements have been met. Likewise, for a misdemeanor proceeding, teleconferencing requires compliance with (e)(1) and Rule 43(b)(2).

Second, (e)(4)(B)(i) requires the court to find that videoconferencing for all or part of the proceeding is not reasonably available before allowing participation by audio only. Because it focuses on what is "reasonably available," this requirement is flexible. It is intended to allow courts to use audio only connections when necessary, but not otherwise. For example, it precludes the use of teleconferencing alone if videoconferencing—though generally limited—is available for all participants in a particular proceeding. But it permits the use of teleconferencing in other circumstances. For example, if only an audio connection with a defendant were feasible because of security concerns at the facility where the defendant is housed, a court could find that videoconferencing for that defendant in the particular proceeding is not reasonably available. Or, if the video connection fails for one or more participants during a proceeding started by videoconference and audio is the only option for completing that proceeding expeditiously, this rule permits the affected participants to use audio technology to finish the proceeding.

Third, (e)(4)(B)(ii) provides that the court must find that the defendant will have an adequate opportunity to consult confidentially with counsel before and during the teleconferenced proceeding. Opportunities for confidential consultation may be more limited with teleconferencing than they are with videoconferencing as when a defendant or a defense attorney has only one telephone line to use to call into the conference, and there are no "breakout rooms" for private conversations like those videoconferencing platforms provide. This situation may arise not only when a proceeding is held entirely by phone, but also when, in the midst of a videoconference, video communication fails for either the defendant or defense counsel. An attorney or client may have to call into the conference using the devices they had previously been using for confidential communication. Experiences like these prompted this requirement that the court specifically find that an alternative opportunity for confidential consultation is in place before permitting teleconferencing in whole or in part.

Finally, recognizing the differences between videoconferencing and teleconferencing, subparagraph (e)(4)(C) provides that the defendant must consent to teleconferencing for the proceeding, even if the defendant previously requested or consented to videoconferencing. A defendant who is willing to be sentenced with a videoconference connection with the judge may balk, understandably, at being sentenced over the phone. Subparagraph (e)(4)(C) does not require that consent to teleconferencing be given only after consultation with counsel. By requiring only "consent," it recognizes that the defendant would have already met the consent requirements for videoconferencing for that proceeding, and it allows the court more flexibility to address varied situations. To give one example, if the video but not audio feed drops for the defendant or another participant near the very end of a videoconference, and the judge asks the defendant, "do you want to talk to your lawyer about finishing this now without the video?," an answer "No, I'm ok, we can finish now" would be sufficient consent under (e)(4)(C).

ALIEN TERRORIST REMOVAL COURT OF THE UNITED STATES
(COMPLETE RULES)

Rule

History:

(EFFECTIVE MAY 28, 1997; AMENDED NOV. 19, 2010).

Rule 1. Name of Court

This Court, established pursuant to the Antiterrorism and Effective Death Penalty Act of 1996, Pub. L. No. 104-132, Title IV, 110 Stat. 1214, 1258, (Title V of the Immigration and Nationality Act), and as amended by the Omnibus Consolidated Appropriations Act for 1997, Public Law No. 104-208, Title I, § 354, 110 Stat. 3009, shall be known as the Alien Terrorist Removal Court of the United States (8 U.S.C. § 1531 et seq.).

Rule 2. Seal

The seal of the Court shall contain the words "Alien Terrorist Removal Court" in the upper sector of space included within the two outer concentric circles and the words "of the United States of America" in the lower sector, and shall contain the standardized eagle rampant in the center.

Rule 3. Situs

The situs of the Court shall be at the United States Courthouse, Washington, D.C., 20001.

Rule 4. Clerk

(a) The Clerk of the District Court for the District of Columbia shall be the Clerk of this Court.

(b) The Clerk shall supply a deputy clerk and other personnel as the business of this Court may require.

(c) Personnel responsible for filing and maintaining records of this Court containing classified information shall have appropriate levels of security clearance in compliance with Executive Branch procedures governing classified information.

Rule 5. Application for Removal

(a) The Attorney General, acting on behalf of the United States as applicant, shall file an original and two copies of an application seeking removal of an alleged alien, named as respondent.

(b) The application shall be submitted *ex parte* and *in camera* and shall be filed under seal with the Clerk of this Court.

(c) The application shall state, to the extent known, the level of classified information, if any, that the Attorney General will present in support of removal.

(d) The application shall state whether the respondent is a permanent resident alien.

Rule 6. Assignment of Cases

(a) The Clerk shall promptly advise the Chief Judge, by a secured means, of the filing of an application. The Chief Judge shall thereupon make an assignment of the case to a member of the Court for consideration and determination of that case.

(b) Cases shall be assigned to judges of the Court in such a manner that each judge, if available for an assignment, shall receive an assignment before any other judge receives a second or successive assignment.

Rule 7. Service of an Order Granting an Application and Notice of a Removal Hearing

(a) If an order is entered granting an *ex parte* application, an authorized representative of the Attorney General shall serve the respondent who is the subject of the application with a copy of the order, excluding any classified information in the order, together with a Notice pursuant to 8 U.S.C. § 1534(b). The Notice shall also set an expeditious date for the Removal Hearing.

(b) The Attorney General shall file with the Clerk a certificate of service of the order and Notice.

(c) Retained counsel for a respondent shall promptly file an appearance with the Clerk.

(d) If a respondent is financially unable to obtain adequate representation, the respondent may request appointment of counsel from the Criminal Justice Panel for United States District Court for the District of Columbia, as provided for in Section 3006A of Title 18 (Criminal Justice Act) [18 USCS § 3006A].

Rule 8. Interim Hearing

(a) For the convenience of the assigned judge and the parties, the judge may conduct an Interim Hearing or Hearings for the purpose of resolving issues relating to representation of the respondent, special issues relating to a permanent resident alien respondent, issues relating to classified information, or if required by statute. When appropriate, the Interim Hearing will be conducted *ex parte* and *in camera*.

(b) Any Interim Hearing shall be conducted in the United States Courthouse in Washington, D.C.

Rule 9. Place of Conducting Removal Hearing

The Removal Hearing shall be held in the United States Courthouse in Washington, D.C. The Removal Hearing shall be conducted publicly, except that any part of the argument that refers to evidence received *in camera* and *ex parte*, shall be heard *in camera* and *ex parte*.

Rule 10. Verbatim Record of Proceedings

All *ex parte*, *in camera*, and public hearings of the Court shall be recorded verbatim by a reporter retained pursuant to 28 U.S.C. § 753, by shorthand, mechanical means, electronic sound recording, or any other method, subject to regulations promulgated by the Judicial Conference of the United States.

Rule 11. Motions

(a) Any motion shall include or be accompanied by a statement of the specific points of law and authority that support the motion, including where appropriate a concise statement of facts. If a table of cases is provided, counsel shall place asterisks in the margin to the left of those cases or authorities on which counsel chiefly relies.

(b) Within 21 days of the date of service or at such other time as the assigned judge may direct, an opposing party shall serve and file a memorandum of points and authorities in opposition to the motion. If such a memorandum is not filed within the prescribed time, the judge may treat the motion as uncontested.

(c) Each motion shall be accompanied by a proposed order.

(d) Within 14 days after service of the memorandum in opposition, the moving party may serve and file a reply memorandum.

(e) A memorandum of points and authorities in support of or in opposition to a motion shall not exceed 15 pages and a reply memorandum shall not exceed 10 pages, without prior approval of the assigned judge.

(f) A party may in a motion or opposition request oral argument, but its allowance shall be within the discretion of the assigned judge.

HISTORY:

As amended eff. Nov. 19, 2010.

Rule 12. Subpoenas

Except for good cause shown, requests for issuance of a subpoena pursuant to 8 U.S.C. § 1534(d) by either the respondent or applicant, shall be made at least 14 days prior to the date of the removal hearing.

HISTORY:

As amended eff. Nov. 19, 2010.

Rule 13. Classified Information

(a) The *ex parte* and *in camera* examination of any classified information, pursuant to 8 U.S.C. § 1534(e)(3)(A)–(E), and of the proposed unclassified summary of specific information shall both be conducted on the day of the Interim Hearing unless the assigned judge otherwise directs.

(b) The unclassified summary, following approval by the judge, shall be delivered to the respondent without delay.

(c) When the respondent is a lawful permanent resident alien, who is denied an unclassified summary pursuant to 8 U.S.C. § 1534(e)(3)(F), the judge shall designate a special attorney to assist the respondent by reviewing the classified information.

(d) When the appointed special attorney moves to challenge the veracity of the evidence contained in the classified information pursuant to 8 U.S.C. § 1534(e)(3)(F)(i)(II), the assigned judge shall schedule an *in camera* proceeding prior to the Removal Hearing to consider the motion.

Rule 14. Removal Hearing Memorandum

Seven days prior to the Removal Hearing, counsel for the applicant and the respondent shall file with the Clerk and serve on each other a Hearing Memorandum setting forth any legal issues to be raised, a summary of the anticipated testimony (exclusive of classified information), and copies of exhibits (exclusive of classified information). The names of individuals involved in the investigation and prospective witnesses need not be included in the material filed with the Court.

FEDERAL RULES OF EVIDENCE
(COMPLETE RULES)

ARTICLE I.
GENERAL PROVISIONS

Rule 101. Scope; Definitions

(a) Scope. These rules apply to proceedings in United States courts. The specific courts and proceedings to which the rules apply, along with exceptions, are set out in Rule 1101.

(b) Definitions. In these rules:

(1) "civil case" means a civil action or proceeding;

(2) "criminal case" includes a criminal proceeding;

(3) "public office" includes a public agency;

(4) "record" includes a memorandum, report, or data compilation;

(5) a "rule prescribed by the Supreme Court" means a rule adopted by the Supreme Court under statutory authority; and

(6) a reference to any kind of written material or any other medium includes electronically stored information.

HISTORY:

Jan. 2, 1975, P. L. 93-595, § 1, 88 Stat. 1929; March 2, 1987, eff. Oct. 1, 1987; April 25, 1988, eff. Nov. 1, 1988; April 22, 1993, eff. Dec. 1, 1993; April 26, 2011, eff. Dec. 1, 2011.

HISTORY; ANCILLARY LAWS AND DIRECTIVES

Other provisions:

Notes of Advisory Committee on Rules. Rule 1101 specifies in detail the courts, proceedings, questions, and stages of proceedings to which the rules apply in whole or in part.

Notes of Advisory Committee on 1987 amendments. United States bankruptcy judges are added to conform this rule with Rule 1101(b) and Bankruptcy Rule 9017.

Notes of Advisory Committee on 1988 amendments. The amendment is technical. No substantive change is intended.

Notes of Advisory Committee on 1993 amendments. This revision is made to conform the rule to changes made by the Judicial Improvements Act of 1990.

Notes of Advisory Committee on 2011 amendments. The language of Rule 101 has been amended, and definitions have been added, as part of the general restyling of the Evidence Rules to make them more easily understood and to make style and terminology consistent throughout the rules. These changes are intended to be stylistic only. There is no intent to change any result in any ruling on evidence admissibility.

The reference to electronically stored information is intended to track the language of Fed. R. Civ. P. 34.

The Style Project

The Evidence Rules are the fourth set of national procedural rules to be restyled. The restyled Rules of Appellate Procedure took effect in 1998. The restyled Rules of Criminal Procedure took effect in 2002. The restyled Rules of Civil Procedure took effect in 2007. The restyled Rules of Evidence apply the same general drafting guidelines and principles used in restyling the Appellate, Criminal, and Civil Rules.

1. General Guidelines

Guidance in drafting, usage, and style was provided by Bryan Garner, *Guidelines for Drafting and Editing Court Rules,* Administrative Office of the United States Courts (1969) and Bryan Garner, *Dictionary of Modern Legal Usage* (2d ed. 1995). See also Joseph Kimble, *Guiding Principles for Restyling the Civil Rules,* in *Preliminary Draft of Proposed Style Revision of the Federal Rules of Civil Procedure,* at page x (Feb. 2005) (available at http://www.uscourts.gov/uscourts/RulesAndPolicies/rules/Prelim_draft_ proposed_pt1.pdf); Joseph Kimble, *Lessons in Drafting from the New Federal Rules of Civil Procedure,* 12 Scribes J. Legal Writing 25 (2008-2009). For specific commentary on the Evidence restyling project, see Joseph Kimble, *Drafting Examples from the Proposed New Federal Rules of Evidence,* 88 Mich. B.J. 52 (Aug. 2009); 88 Mich. B.J. 46 (Sept. 2009); 88 Mich. B.J. 54 (Oct. 2009); 88 Mich. B.J. 50 (Nov. 2009).

2. Formatting Changes

Many of the changes in the restyled Evidence Rules result from using format to achieve clearer presentations. The rules are broken down into constituent parts, using progressively indented subparagraphs with headings and substituting vertical for horizontal lists. "Hanging indents" are used throughout. These formatting changes make the structure of the rules graphic and make the restyled rules easier to read and understand even when the words are not changed. Rules 103, 404(b), 606(b), and 612 illustrate the benefits of formatting changes.

3. Changes to Reduce Inconsistent, Ambiguous, Redundant, Repetitive, or Archaic Words

The restyled rules reduce the use of inconsistent terms that say the same thing in different ways. Because different words are presumed to have different meanings, such inconsistencies can result in confusion. The restyled rules reduce inconsistencies by using the same words to express the same meaning. For example, consistent expression is achieved by not switching between "accused" and "defendant" or between "party opponent" and "opposing party" or between the various formulations of civil and criminal action/case/proceeding.

The restyled rules minimize the use of inherently ambiguous words. For example, the word "shall" can mean "must," "may," or something else, depending on context. The potential for confusion is exacerbated by the fact the word "shall" is no longer generally used in spoken or clearly written English. The restyled rules replace "shall" with "must," "may," or "should," depending on which one the context and established interpretation make correct in each rule.

The restyled rules minimize the use of redundant "intensifiers." These are expressions that attempt to add emphasis, but instead state the obvious and create negative implications for other rules. The absence of intensifiers in the restyled rules does not change their substantive meaning. See, e.g., Rule 104(c) (omitting "in all cases"); Rule 602 (omitting "but need not"); Rule 611(b) (omitting "in the exercise of discretion").

The restyled rules also remove words and concepts that are outdated or redundant.

4. Rule Numbers

The restyled rules keep the same numbers to minimize the effect on research. Subdivisions have been rearranged within some rules to achieve greater clarity and simplicity.

5. No Substantive Change

The Committee made special efforts to reject any purported style improvement that might result in a substantive change in the application of a rule. The Committee considered a change to be "substantive" if any of the following conditions were met:

a. Under the existing practice in any circuit, the change could lead to a different result on a question of admissibility (e.g., a change that requires a court to provide either a less or more stringent standard in evaluating the admissibility of particular evidence);

b. Under the existing practice in any circuit, it could lead to a change in the procedure by which an admissibility decision is made (e.g., a change in the time in which an objection must be made, or a change in whether a court must hold a hearing on an admissibility question);

c. The change would restructure a rule in a way that would alter the approach that courts and litigants have used to think about, and argue about, questions of admissibility (e.g., merging Rules 104(a) and 104(b) into a single subdivision); or.

d. The amendment would change a "sacred phrase"—one that has become so familiar in practice that to alter it would be unduly disruptive to practice and expectations. Examples in the Evidence Rules include "unfair prejudice" and "truth of the matter asserted."

Rule 102. Purpose

These rules should be construed so as to administer every proceeding fairly, eliminate unjustifiable expense and delay, and promote the development of evidence law, to the end of ascertaining the truth and securing a just determination.

HISTORY:

Jan. 2, 1975, P. L. 93-595, § 1, 88 Stat. 1929; April 26, 2011, eff. Dec. 1, 2011.

HISTORY; ANCILLARY LAWS AND DIRECTIVES

Other provisions:

Notes of Advisory Committee on Rules. For similar provisions see Rule 2 of the Federal Rules of Criminal Procedure, Rule 1 of the Federal Rules of Civil Procedure, California Evidence Code § 2, and New Jersey Evidence Rule 5.

Notes of Advisory Committee on 2011 amendments. The language of Rule 102 has been amended as part of the restyling of the Evidence Rules to make them more easily understood and to make style and terminology consistent throughout the rules. These changes are intended to be stylistic only. There is no intent to change any result in any ruling on evidence admissibility.

Rule 103. Rulings on Evidence

(a) Preserving a Claim of Error. A party may claim error in a ruling to admit or exclude evidence only if the error affects a substantial right of the party and:

(1) if the ruling admits evidence, a party, on the record:

(A) timely objects or moves to strike; and

(B) states the specific ground, unless it was apparent from the context; or

(2) if the ruling excludes evidence, a party informs the court of its substance by an offer of proof, unless the substance was apparent from the context.

(b) Not Needing to Renew an Objection or Offer of Proof. Once the court rules definitively on the record—either before or at trial—a party need not renew an objection or offer of proof to preserve a claim of error for appeal.

(c) Court's Statement About the Ruling; Directing an Offer of Proof. The court may make any statement about the character or form of the evidence, the objection made, and the ruling. The court may direct that an offer of proof be made in question-and-answer form.

(d) Preventing the Jury from Hearing Inadmissible Evidence. To the extent practicable, the court must conduct a jury trial so that inadmissible evidence is not suggested to the jury by any means.

(e) Taking Notice of Plain Error. A court may take notice of a plain error affecting a substantial right, even if the claim of error was not properly preserved.

HISTORY:

Jan. 2, 1975, P. L. 93-595, § 1, 88 Stat. 1929; April 17, 2000, eff. Dec. 1, 2000; April 26, 2011, eff. Dec. 1, 2011.

HISTORY; ANCILLARY LAWS AND DIRECTIVES

Other provisions:

Notes of Advisory Committee on Rules. *Subdivision (a)* states the law as generally accepted today. Rulings on evidence cannot be assigned as error unless (1) a substantial right is affected, and (2) the nature of the error was called to the attention of the judge, so as to alert him to the proper course of action and enable opposing counsel to take proper corrective measures. The objection and the offer of proof are the techniques for accomplishing these objectives. For similar provisions see Uniform Rules 4 and 5; California Evidence Code §§ 353 and 354; Kansas Code of Civil Procedure §§ 60-404 and 60-405. The rule does not purport to change the law with respect to harmless error. See 28 U.S.C. § 2111, F.R.Civ.P. 61, F.R.Crim.P. 52, and decisions construing them. The status of constitutional error as harmless or not is treated in *Chapman v. California*, 386 U.S. 18, 87 S.Ct. 824, 17 L.Ed.2d 705 (1967), reh. denied id. 987, 87 S.Ct. 1283, 18 L.Ed.2d 241.

Subdivision (b). The first sentence is the third sentence of Rule 43(c) of the Federal Rules of Civil Procedure virtually verbatim. Its purpose is to reproduce for an appellate court, insofar as possible, a true reflection of what occurred in the trial court. The second sentence is in part derived from the final sentence of Rule 43(c). It is designed to resolve doubts as to what testimony the witness would have in fact given, and, in nonjury cases, to provide the appellate court with material for a possible final disposition of the case in the event of reversal of a ruling which excluded evidence. See 5 Moore's Federal Practice § 43.11 (2d ed. 1968). Application is made discretionary in view of the practical impossibility of formulating a satisfactory rule in mandatory terms.

Subdivision (c). This subdivision proceeds on the supposition that a ruling which excludes evidence in a jury case is likely to be a pointless procedure if the excluded evidence nevertheless comes to the attention of the jury. *Bruton v. United States*, 389 U.S. 818, 88 S.Ct. 126, L.Ed.2d 70 (1968). Rule 43(c) of the Federal Rules of Civil Procedure provides: "The court may require the offer to be made out of the hearing of the jury." In re McConnell, 370 U.S. 230, 82 S.Ct. 1288, 8 L.Ed.2d 434 (1962), left some doubt whether questions on which an offer is based must first be asked in the presence of the jury. The subdivision answers in the negative. The judge can foreclose a particular line of testimony and counsel can protect his record without a series of questions before the jury, designed at best to waste time and at worst "to waft into the jury box" the very matter sought to be excluded.

Subdivision (d). This wording of the plain error principle is from Rule 52(b) of the Federal Rules of Criminal Procedure. While judicial unwillingness to be constructed by mechanical breakdowns of the adversary system has been more pronounced in criminal cases, there is no scarcity of decisions to the same effect in civil cases. In general, see Campbell, Extent to Which Courts of Review Will Consider Questions Not Properly Raised and Preserved, 7 Wis.L-.Rev. 91, 160 (1932); Vestal, Sua Sponte Consideration in Appellate Review, 27 Fordham L.Rev. 477 (1958–59); 64 Harv.L.Rev. 652 (1951). In the nature of things the application of the plain error rule will be more likely with respect to the admission of evidence than to exclusion, since failure to comply with normal requirements of offers of proof is likely to produce a record which simply does not disclose the error.

Notes of Advisory Committee on 2000 amendments. The amendment applies to all rulings on evidence whether they occur at or before trial, including so-called "in limine" rulings. One of the most difficult questions arising from in limine and other evidentiary rulings is whether a losing party must renew an objection or offer of proof when the evidence is or would be offered at trial, in order to preserve a claim of error on appeal. Courts have taken differing approaches to this question. Some courts have held that a renewal at the time the evidence is to be offered at trial is always required. *See, e.g., Collins v. Wayne Corp.*, 621 F.2d 777 (5th Cir. 1980). Some courts have taken a more flexible approach, holding that renewal is not required if the issue decided is one that (1) was fairly presented to the trial court for an initial ruling, (2) may be decided as a final matter before the evidence is actually offered, and (3) was ruled on definitively by the trial judge. *See, e.g., Rosenfeld v. Basquiat,* 78 F.3d 84 (2d Cir. 1996) (admissibility of former testimony under the Dead Man's Statute; renewal not required). Other courts have distinguished between objections to evidence, which must be renewed when evidence is offered, and offers of proof, which need not be renewed after a definitive determination is made that the evidence is inadmissible. *See, e.g., Fusco v. General Motors Corp.,* 11 F.3d 259 (1st Cir. 1993). Another court, aware of this Committee's proposed amendment, has adopted its approach. *Wilson v. Williams*, 182 F. 3d 562 (7th Cir. 1999) (en banc). Differing views on this question create uncertainty for litigants and unnecessary work for the appellate courts.

The amendment provides that a claim of error with respect to a definitive ruling is preserved for review when the party has otherwise satisfied the objection or offer of proof requirements of Rule 103(a). When the ruling is definitive, a renewed objection or offer of proof at the time the evidence is to be offered is more a formalism than a necessity. *See* Fed.R.Civ.P. 46 (formal exceptions unnecessary); Fed.R.Cr.P. 51 (same); *United States v. Mejia-Alarcon,* 995 F.2d 982, 986 (10th Cir. 1993) ("Requiring a party to renew an objection when the district court has issued a definitive ruling on a matter that can be fairly decided before trial would be in the nature of a formal exception and therefore unnecessary."). On the other hand, when the trial court appears to have reserved its ruling or to have indicated that the ruling is provisional, it makes sense to require the party to bring the issue to the court's attention subsequently. *See, e.g., United States v. Vest,* 116 F.3d 1179, 1188 (7th Cir. 1997) (where the trial court ruled in limine that testimony from defense witnesses could not be admitted, but allowed the defendant to seek leave at trial to call the witnesses should their testimony turn out to be relevant, the defendant's failure to seek such leave at trial meant that it was "too late to reopen the issue now on appeal"); *United States v. Valenti,* 60 F.3d 941 (2d Cir. 1995) (failure to proffer evidence at trial waives any claim of error where the trial judge had stated that he would reserve judgment on the in limine motion until he had heard the trial evidence).

The amendment imposes the obligation on counsel to clarify whether an in limine or other evidentiary ruling is definitive when there is doubt on that point. *See, e.g., Walden v. Georgia-Pacific Corp.,* 126 F.3d 506, 520 (3d Cir. 1997) (although "the district court told plaintiffs' counsel not to reargue every ruling, it did not countermand its clear opening statement that all of its rulings were tentative, and counsel never requested clarification, as he might have done.").

Even where the court's ruling is definitive, nothing in the amendment prohibits the court from revisiting its decision when the evidence is to be offered. If the court changes its initial ruling, or if the opposing party violates the terms of the initial ruling, objection must be made when the evidence is offered to preserve the claim of error for appeal. The error, if any, in such a situation occurs only when the evidence is offered and admitted. *United States Aviation Underwriters, Inc. v. Olympia Wings, Inc.,* 896 F.2d 949, 956 (5th Cir. 1990) ("objection is required to preserve error when an opponent, or the court itself violates a motion in limine that was granted"); *United States v. Roenigk,* 810 F.2d 809 (8th Cir. 1987) (claim of error was not preserved where the defendant failed to object at trial to secure the benefit of a favorable advance ruling).

A definitive advance ruling is reviewed in light of the facts and circumstances before the trial court at the time of the ruling. If the relevant facts and circumstances change materially after the advance ruling has been made, those facts and circumstances cannot be relied upon on appeal unless they have been brought to the attention of the trial court by way of a renewed, and timely, objection, offer of proof, or motion to strike. *See Old Chief v. United States,* 519 U.S. 172, 182, n. 6 (1997) ("It is important that a reviewing court evaluate the trial court's decision from its perspective when it had to rule and not indulge in review by hindsight."). Similarly, if the court decides in an advance ruling that proffered evidence is admissible subject to the eventual introduction by the proponent of a foundation for the evidence, and that foundation is never provided, the opponent cannot claim error based on the failure to establish the foundation unless the opponent calls that failure to the court's attention by a timely motion to strike or other suitable motion. *See Huddleston v. United States,* 485 U.S. 681, 690, n. 7 (1988) ("It is, of course, not the responsibility of the judge sua sponte to ensure that the foundation evidence is offered; the objector must move to strike the evidence if at the close of the trial the offeror has failed to satisfy the condition.").

Nothing in the amendment is intended to affect the provisions of Fed.R.Civ.P. 72(a) or 28 U.S.C. § 636(b)(1) pertaining to nondispositive pretrial rulings by magistrate judges in proceedings that are not before a magistrate judge by consent of the parties. Fed.R.Civ.P. 72(a) provides that a party who fails to file a written objection to a magistrate judge's nondispositive order within ten days of receiving a copy "may not thereafter assign as error a defect" in the order. 28 U.S.C. § 36(b)(1) provides that any party "may serve and file written objections to such proposed findings and recommendations as provided by rules of court" within ten days of receiving a copy of the order. Several courts have held that a party must comply with this statutory provision in order to preserve a claim of error. *See, e.g., Wells v. Shriners Hospital,* 109 F.3d 198, 200 (4th Cir. 1997)("[i]n this circuit, as in others, a party 'may' file objections within ten days or he may not, as he chooses, but he 'shall' do so if he wishes further consideration."). When Fed.R.Civ.P. 72(a) or 28 U.S.C. § 636(b)(1) is operative, its requirement must be satisfied in order for a party to preserve a claim of error on appeal, even where Evidence Rule 103(a) would not require a subsequent objection or offer of proof.

Nothing in the amendment is intended to affect the rule set forth in *Luce v. United States,* 469 U.S. 38 (1984), and its progeny. The amendment provides that an objection or offer of proof need not be renewed to preserve a claim of error with respect to a definitive pretrial ruling. Luce answers affirmatively a separate question: whether a criminal defendant must testify at trial in order to preserve a claim of error predicated upon a trial court's decision to admit the defendant's prior convictions for impeachment. The Luce principle has been extended by many lower courts to other situations. *See United States v. DiMatteo,* 759 F.2d 831 (11th Cir. 1985) (applying Luce where the defendant's witness would be impeached with evidence offered under Rule 608). *See also United States v. Goldman,* 41 F.3d 785, 788 (1st Cir. 1994) ("Although Luce involved impeachment by conviction under Rule 609, the reasons given by the Supreme Court for requiring the defendant to testify apply with full force to the kind of Rule 403 and 404 objections that are advanced by Goldman in this case."); *Palmieri v. DeFaria,* 88 F.3d 136 (2d Cir. 1996) (where the plaintiff decided to take an adverse judgment rather than challenge an advance ruling by putting on evidence at trial, the in limine ruling would not be reviewed on appeal); *United States v. Ortiz,* 857 F.2d 900 (2d Cir. 1988) (where uncharged misconduct is ruled admissible if the defendant pursues a certain defense, the defendant must actually pursue that defense at trial in order to preserve a claim of error on appeal); *United States v. Bond,* 87 F.3d 695 (5th Cir. 1996) (where the trial court rules in limine that the defendant would waive his fifth amendment privilege were he to testify, the defendant must take the stand and testify in order to challenge that ruling on appeal).

The amendment does not purport to answer whether a party who objects to evidence that the court finds admissible in a definitive ruling, and who then offers the evidence to "remove the sting" of its anticipated prejudicial effect, thereby waives the right to appeal the trial court's ruling. *See, e.g., United States v. Fisher,* 106 F.3d 622 (5th Cir. 1997) (where the trial judge ruled in limine that the government could use a prior conviction to impeach the defendant if he testified, the defendant did not waive his right to appeal by introducing the conviction on direct examination); *Judd v. Rodman,* 105 F.3d 1339 (11th Cir. 1997) (an objection made in limine is sufficient to preserve a claim of error when the movant, as a matter of trial strategy, presents the objectionable evidence herself on direct examination to minimize its prejudicial effect); *Gill v. Thomas,* 83 F.3d 537, 540(1st Cir. 1996) ("by offering the misdemeanor evidence himself, Gill waived his opportunity to object and thus did not preserve the issue for appeal"); *United States v. Williams,* 939 F.2d 721 (9th Cir. 1991) (objection to impeachment evidence was waived where the defendant was impeached on direct examination).

GAP Report—Proposed Amendment to Rule 103(a). The Committee made the following changes to the published draft of the proposed amendment to Evidence Rule 103(a):

1. A minor stylistic change was made in the text, in accordance with the suggestion of the Style Subcommittee of the Standing Committee on Rules of Practice and Procedure.

2. The second sentence of the amended portion of the published draft was deleted, and the Committee Note was amended to reflect the fact that nothing in the amendment is intended to affect the rule of *Luce v. United States.*

3. The Committee Note was updated to include cases decided after the proposed amendment was issued for public comment.

4. The Committee Note was amended to include a reference to a Civil Rule and a statute requiring objections to certain Magistrate Judge rulings to be made to the District Court.

5. The Committee Note was revised to clarify that an advance ruling does not encompass subsequent developments at trial that might be the subject of an appeal.

Notes of Advisory Committee on 2011 amendments. The language of Rule 103 has been amended as part of the restyling of the Evidence Rules to make them more easily understood and to make style and terminology consistent throughout the rules. These changes are intended to be

stylistic only. There is no intent to change any result in any ruling on evidence admissibility.

Rule 104. Preliminary Questions

(a) In General. The court must decide any preliminary question about whether a witness is qualified, a privilege exists, or evidence is admissible. In so deciding, the court is not bound by evidence rules, except those on privilege.

(b) Relevance That Depends on a Fact. When the relevance of evidence depends on whether a fact exists, proof must be introduced sufficient to support a finding that the fact does exist. The court may admit the proposed evidence on the condition that the proof be introduced later.

(c) Conducting a Hearing So That the Jury Cannot Hear It. The court must conduct any hearing on a preliminary question so that the jury cannot hear it if:

(1) the hearing involves the admissibility of a confession;

(2) a defendant in a criminal case is a witness and so requests; or

(3) justice so requires.

(d) Cross-Examining a Defendant in a Criminal Case. By testifying on a preliminary question, a defendant in a criminal case does not become subject to cross-examination on other issues in the case.

(e) Evidence Relevant to Weight and Credibility. This rule does not limit a party's right to introduce before the jury evidence that is relevant to the weight or credibility of other evidence.

HISTORY:

Jan. 2, 1975, P. L. 93-595, § 1, 88 Stat. 1929; March 2, 1987, eff. Oct. 1, 1987; April 26, 2011, eff. Dec. 1, 2011.

HISTORY; ANCILLARY LAWS AND DIRECTIVES

Other provisions:

Notes of the Advisory Committee on Rules. *Subdivision (a).* The applicability of a particular rule of evidence often depends upon the existence of a condition. Is the alleged expert a qualified physician? Is a witness whose former testimony is offered unavailable? Was a stranger present during a conversation between attorney and client? In each instance the admissibility of evidence will turn upon the answer to the question of the existence of the condition. Accepted practice, incorporated in the rule, places on the judge the responsibility for these determinations. McCormick § 53; Morgan, Basic Problems of Evidence 45–50 (1962).

To the extent that these inquiries are factual, the judge acts as a trier of fact. Often, however, rulings on evidence call for an evaluation in terms of a legally set standard. Thus when a hearsay statement is offered as a declaration against interest, a decision must be made whether it possesses the required against-interest characteristics. These decisions, too, are made by the judge.

In view of these considerations, this subdivision refers to preliminary requirements generally by the broad term "questions," without attempt at specification.

This subdivision is of general application. It must, however, be read as subject to the special provisions for "conditional relevancy" in subdivision (b) and those for confessions in subdivision (d).

If the question is factual in nature, the judge will of necessity receive evidence pro and con on the issue. The rule provides that the rules of evidence in general do not apply to this process. McCormick § 53, p. 123, n. 8, points out that the authorities are "scattered and inconclusive," and observes:

"Should the exclusionary law of evidence, 'the child of the jury system' in Thayer's phrase, be applied to this hearing before the judge? Sound sense backs the view that it should not, and that the judge should be empowered to hear any relevant evidence, such as affidavits or other reliable hearsay."

This view is reinforced by practical necessity in certain situations. An item, offered and objected to, may itself be considered in ruling on admissibility, though not yet admitted in evidence. Thus the content of an asserted declaration against interest must be considered in ruling whether it is against interest. Again, common practice calls for considering the testimony of a witness, particularly a child, in determining competency. Another example is the requirement of Rule 602 dealing with personal knowledge. In the case of hearsay, it is enough, if the declarant "so far as appears [has] had an opportunity to observe the fact declared." McCormick, § 10, p. 19.

If concern is felt over the use of affidavits by the judge in preliminary hearings on admissibility, attention is directed to the many important judicial determinations made on the basis of affidavits. Rule 47 of the Federal Rules of Criminal Procedure provides:

"An application to the court for an order shall be by motion * * * It may be supported by affidavit."

The Rules of Civil Procedure are more detailed. Rule 43(e), dealing with motions generally, provides:

"When a motion is based on facts not appearing of record the court may hear the matter on affidavits presented by the respective parties, but the court may direct that the matter be heard wholly or partly on oral testimony or depositions." Rule 4(g) provides for proof of service by affidavit. Rule 56 provides in detail for the entry of summary judgment based on affidavits. Affidavits may supply the foundation for temporary restraining orders under Rule 65(b).

The study made for the California Law Revision Commission recommended an amendment to Uniform Rule 2 as follows:

"In the determination of the issue aforesaid [preliminary determination], exclusionary rules shall not apply, subject, however, to Rule 45 and any valid claim of privilege." Tentative Recommendation and a Study Relating to the Uniform Rules of Evidence (Article VIII, Hearsay), Cal. Law Revision Comm'n, Rep., Rec. & Studies, 470 (1962). The proposal was not adopted in the California Evidence Code. The Uniform Rules are likewise silent on the subject. However, New Jersey Evidence Rule 8(1), dealing with preliminary inquiry by the judge, provides:

"In his determination the rules of evidence shall not apply except for Rule 4 [exclusion on grounds of confusion, etc.] or a valid claim of privilege."

Subdivision (b). In some situations, the relevancy of an item of evidence, in the large sense, depends upon the existence of a particular preliminary fact. Thus when a spoken statement is relied upon to prove notice to X, it is without probative value unless X heard it. Or if a letter purporting to be from Y is relied upon to establish an admission by him, it has no probative value unless Y wrote or authorized it. Relevance in this sense has been labelled "conditional relevancy." Morgan, Basic Problems of Evidence 45–46 (1962). Problems arising in connection with it are to be distinguished from problems of logical relevancy, e.g. evidence in a murder case that accused on the day before purchased a weapon of the kind used in the killing, treated in Rule 401.

If preliminary questions of conditional relevancy were determined solely by the judge, as provided in subdivision (a), the functioning of the jury as a trier of fact would be greatly restricted and in some cases virtually destroyed. These are appropriate questions for juries. Accepted treatment, as provided in the rule, is consistent with that given fact questions generally. The judge makes a preliminary determination whether the foundation evidence is sufficient to support a finding of fulfillment of the condition. If so, the item is admitted. If after all the evidence on the issue is in, pro and con, the jury could reasonably conclude that fulfillment of the condition is not established, the issue is for them. If the evidence is not such as to allow a finding, the judge withdraws the matter from their consideration. Morgan, *supra* ; California Evidence Code § 403; New Jersey Rule 8(2). See also Uniform Rules 19 and 67.

The order of proof here, as generally, is subject to the control of the judge.

Subdivision (c). Preliminary hearings on the admissibility of confessions must be conducted outside the hearing of the jury. See *Jackson v. Denno*, 378 U.S. 368, 84 S.Ct. 1774, 12 L.Ed.2d 908 (1964). Otherwise, detailed treatment of when preliminary matters should be heard outside the hearing of the jury is not feasible. The procedure is time consuming. Not infrequently the same evidence which is relevant to the issue of establishment of fulfillment of a condition precedent to admissibility is also relevant to weight or credibility, and time is saved by taking foundation proof in the presence of the jury. Much evidence on preliminary questions, though not relevant to jury issues, may be heard by the jury with no adverse effect. A great deal must be left to the discretion of the judge who will act as the interests of justice require.

Subdivision (d). The limitation upon cross-examination is designed to encourage participation by the accused in the determination of preliminary matters. He may testify concerning them without exposing himself to cross-examination generally. The provision is necessary because of the breadth of cross-examination under Rule 611(b).

The rule does not address itself to questions of the subsequent use of testimony given by an accused at a hearing on a preliminary matter. See *Walder v. United States*, 347 U.S. 62 (1954); *Simmons v. United States*, 390 U.S. 377 (1968); *Harris v. New York*, 401 U.S. 222 (1971).

Subdivision (e). For similar provisions see Uniform Rule 8; California Evidence Code § 406; Kansas Code of Civil Procedure § 60-408; New Jersey Evidence Rule 8(1).

Notes of Committee on the Judiciary, House Report No. 93-650. Rule 104(c) as submitted to the Congress provided that hearings on the admissibility of confessions shall be conducted outside the presence of the jury and hearings on all other preliminary matters should be so conducted when the interests of justice require. The Committee amended the Rule to provide that where an accused is a witness as to a preliminary matter, he has the right, upon his request, to be heard outside the jury's presence. Although recognizing that in some cases duplication of evidence would occur and that the procedure could be subject to abuse, the Committee believed that a proper regard for the right of an accused not to testify generally in the case dictates that he be given an option to testify out of the presence of the jury on preliminary matters.

The Committee construes the second sentence of subdivision (c) as applying to civil actions and proceedings as well as to criminal cases, and on this assumption has left the sentence unamended.

Notes of Committee on the Judiciary, Senate Report No. 93-1277. Under rule 104(c) the hearing on a preliminary matter may at times be conducted in front of the jury. Should an accused testify in such a hearing, waiving his privilege against self-incrimination as to the preliminary issue, rule 104(d) provides that he will not generally be subject to cross-examination as to any other issue. This rule is not, however, intended to immunize the accused from cross-examination where, in testifying about a preliminary issue, he injects other issues into the hearing. If he could not be cross-examined about any issues gratuitously raised by him beyond the scope of the preliminary matters, injustice result. Accordingly, in order to prevent any such unjust result, the committee intends the rule to be construed to provide that the accused may subject himself to cross-examination as to issues raised by his own testimony upon a preliminary matter before a jury.

Notes of Advisory Committee on 1987 amendments. The amendments are technical. No substantive change is intended.

Notes of Advisory Committee on 2011 amendments. The language of Rule 104 has been amended as part of the restyling of the Evidence Rules to make them more easily understood and to make style and terminology consistent throughout the rules. These changes are intended to be stylistic only. There is no intent to change any result in any ruling on evidence admissibility.

Rule 105. Limiting Evidence that is Not Admissible Against Other Parties or for Other Purposes

If the court admits evidence that is admissible against a party or for a purpose—but not against another party or for another purpose—the court, on timely request, must restrict the evidence to its proper scope and instruct the jury accordingly.

HISTORY:

Jan. 2, 1975, P. L. 93-595, § 1, 88 Stat. 1930; April 26, 2011, eff. Dec. 1, 2011.

HISTORY; ANCILLARY LAWS AND DIRECTIVES

Other provisions:

Notes of Advisory Committee on Rules. A close relationship exists between this rule and Rule 403 which requires exclusion when "probative value is substantially outweighed by the danger of unfair prejudice, confusion of the issues, or misleading the jury." The present rule recognizes the practice of admitting evidence for a limited purpose and instructing the jury accordingly. The availability and effectiveness of this practice must be taken into consideration in reaching a decision whether to exclude for unfair prejudice under Rule 403. In *Bruton v. United States*, 389 U.S. 818, 88 S.Ct. 126, 19 L.Ed.2d 70 (1968), the Court ruled that a limiting instruction did not effectively protect the accused against the prejudicial effect of admitting in evidence the confession of a codefendant which implicated him. The decision does not, however, bar the use of limited admissibility with an instruction where the risk of prejudice is less serious.

Similar provisions are found in Uniform Rule 6; California Evidence Code § 355; Kansas Code of Civil Procedure § 60-406; New Jersey Evidence Rule 6. The wording of the present rule differs, however, in repelling any implication that limiting or curative instructions are sufficient in all situations.

Notes of Committee on the Judiciary, House Report No. 93-650. Rule 106 as submitted by the Supreme Court [now Rule 105] dealt with the subject of evidence which is admissible as to one party or for one purpose but is not admissible against another party or for another purpose. The Committee adopted this Rule without change on the understanding that it does not affect the authority of a court to order a severance in a multi-defendant case.

Notes of Advisory Committee on 2011 amendments. The language of Rule 105 has been amended as part of the restyling of the Evidence Rules to make them more easily understood and to make style and terminology consistent throughout the rules. These changes are intended to be stylistic only. There is no intent to change any result in any ruling on evidence admissibility.

Rule 106. Remainder of or Related Statements

If a party introduces all or part of a statement, an adverse party may require the introduction, at that time, of any other part—or any other statement—that in fairness ought to be considered at the same time. The adverse party may do so over a hearsay objection.

HISTORY:

Jan. 2, 1975, P. L. 93-595, § 1, 88 Stat. 1929; March 2, 1987, eff. Oct. 1, 1987; April 26, 2011, eff. Dec. 1, 2011; April 24, 2023, eff. Dec. 1, 2023.

HISTORY; ANCILLARY LAWS AND DIRECTIVES

Other provisions:

Notes of Advisory Committee on Rules. The rule is an expression of the rule of completeness. McCormick § 56. It is manifested as to depositions in Rule 32(a)(4) of the Federal Rules of Civil Procedure, of which the proposed rule is substantially a restatement.

The rule is based on two considerations. The first is the misleading impression created by taking matters out of context. The second is the inadequacy of repair work when delayed to a point later in the trial. See McCormick § 56; California Evidence Code § 356. The rule does not in any way circumscribe the right of the adversary to develop the matter on cross-examination or as part of his own case.

For practical reasons, the rule is limited to writings and recorded statements and does not apply to conversations.

Notes of Advisory Committee on 1987 amendments. The amendments are technical. No substantive change is intended.

Notes of Advisory Committee on 2011 amendments. The language of Rule 106 has been amended as part of the restyling of the Evidence Rules to make them more easily understood and to make style and terminology consistent throughout the rules. These changes are intended to be stylistic only. There is no intent to change any result in any ruling on evidence admissibility.

Notes of Advisory Committee on 2023 amendments. Rule 106 has been amended in two respects:

(1) First, the amendment provides that if the existing fairness standard requires completion, then that completing statement is admissible over a hearsay objection. Courts have been in conflict over whether completing evidence properly required for completion under Rule 106 can be admitted over a hearsay objection. The Committee has determined that the rule of completeness, grounded in fairness, cannot fulfill its function if the party that creates a misimpression about the meaning of a proffered statement can then object on hearsay grounds and exclude a statement that would correct the misimpression. *See United States v. Sutton*, 801 F.2d 1346, 1368 (D.C. Cir. 1986) (noting that "[a] contrary construction raises the specter of distorted and misleading trials, and creates difficulties for both litigants and the trial court"). For example, assume the defendant in a murder case admits that he owned the murder weapon, but also simultaneously states that he sold it months before the murder. In this circumstance, admitting only the statement of ownership creates a misimpression because it suggests that the defendant implied that he owned the weapon at the time of the crime—when that is not what he said. In this example the prosecution, which has created the situation that makes completion necessary, should not be permitted to invoke the hearsay rule and thereby allow the misleading statement to remain unrebutted. A party that presents a distortion can fairly be said to have forfeited its right to object on hearsay grounds to a statement that would be necessary to correct the misimpression. For similar results see Rules 502(a), 410(b)(1), and 804(b)(6).

The courts that have permitted completion over hearsay objections have not usually specified whether the completing remainder may be used for its truth or only for its non-hearsay value in showing context. Under the amended rule, the use to which a completing statement can be put will depend on the circumstances. In some cases, completion will be sufficient for the proponent of the completing statement if it is admitted to provide context for the initially proffered statement. In such situations, the completing statement is properly admitted over a hearsay objection because it is offered for a non-hearsay purpose. An example would be a completing statement that corrects a misimpression about what a party heard before undertaking a disputed action, where the party's state of mind is relevant. The completing statement in this example is admitted only to show what the party actually heard, regardless of the underlying truth of the completing statement. But in some cases, a completing statement places an initially proffered statement in context only if the completing statement is true. An example is the defendant in a murder case who admits that he owned the murder weapon, but also simultaneously states that he sold it months before the murder. The statement about selling the weapon corrects a misimpression only if it is offered for its truth. In such cases, Rule 106 operates to allow the completing statement to be offered as proof of a fact.

(2) Second, Rule 106 has been amended to cover all statements, including oral statements that have not been

recorded. Most courts have already found unrecorded completing statements to be admissible under either Rule 611(a) or the common-law rule of completeness. This procedure, while reaching the correct result, is cumbersome and creates a trap for the unwary. Most questions of completion arise when a statement is offered in the heat of trial—where neither the parties nor the court should be expected to consider the nuances of Rule 611(a) or the common law in resolving completeness questions. The amendment, as a matter of convenience, covers these questions under one rule. The rule is expanded to now cover all statements, in any form—including statements made through conduct or sign language.

The original committee note cites "practical reasons" for limiting the coverage of the rule to writings and recordings. To the extent that the concern was about disputes over the content or existence of an unrecorded statement, that concern does not justify excluding all unrecorded statements completely from the coverage of the rule. *See United States v. Bailey,* 2017 WL 5126163, at *7 (D. Md. Nov. 16, 2017) ("A blanket rule of prohibition is unwarranted, and invites abuse. Moreover, if the content of some oral statements are disputed and difficult to prove, others are not—because they have been summarized . . . , or because they were witnessed by enough people to assure that what was actually said can be established with sufficient certainty."). A party seeking completion with an unrecorded statement would of course need to provide admissible evidence that the statement was made. Otherwise, there would be no showing that the original statement is misleading, and the request for completion should be denied. In some cases, the court may find that the difficulty in proving the completing statement substantially outweighs its probative value—in which case exclusion is possible under Rule 403.

The rule retains the language that completion is made at the time the original portion is introduced. That said, many courts have held that the trial court has discretion to allow completion at a later point. *See, e.g., Phoenix Assocs. III v. Stone,* 60 F.3d 95, 103 (2d Cir. 1995) ("While the wording of Rule 106 appears to require the adverse party to proffer the associated document or portion contemporaneously with the introduction of the primary document, we have not applied this requirement rigidly."). Nothing in the amendment is intended to limit the court's discretion to allow completion at a later point.

The intent of the amendment is to displace the common-law rule of completeness. In *Beech Aircraft Corp. v. Rainey,* 488 U.S. 153, 171–72 (1988), the Court in dictum referred to Rule 106 as a partial codification of the common-law rule of completeness. There is no other rule of evidence that is interpreted as coexisting with common-law rules of evidence, and the practical problem of a rule of evidence operating with a common-law supplement is apparent—especially when the rule is one, like the rule of completeness, that arises most often during the trial.

The amendment does not give a green light of admissibility to all excised portions of statements. It does not change the basic rule, which applies only to the narrow circumstances in which a party has created a misimpression about the statement, and the adverse party proffers a statement that in fact corrects the misimpression. The mere fact that a statement is probative and contradicts a statement offered by the opponent is not enough to justify completion under Rule 106. So, for example, the mere fact that a defendant denies guilt before later admitting it does not, without more, mandate the admission of his previous denial. *See United States v. Williams,* 930 F.3d 44 (2d Cir. 2019).

Evidence Rule 107

Rule 107. Illustrative Aids

(a) Permitted Uses. The court may allow a party to present an illustrative aid to help the trier of fact understand the evidence or argument if the aid's utility in assisting comprehension is not substantially outweighed by the danger of unfair prejudice, confusing the issues, misleading the jury, undue delay, or wasting time.

(b) Use in Jury Deliberations. An illustrative aid is not evidence and must not be provided to the jury during deliberations unless:

(1) all parties consent; or

(2) the court, for good cause, orders otherwise.

(c) Record. When practicable, an illustrative aid used at trial must be entered into the record.

(d) Summaries of Voluminous Materials Admitted as Evidence. A summary, chart, or calculation admitted as evidence to prove the content of voluminous admissible evidence is governed by Rule 1006.

HISTORY:

Added April 2, 2024, eff. Dec. 1, 2024.

HISTORY; ANCILLARY LAWS AND DIRECTIVES

Other provisions:

Notes of Advisory Committee on 2024 amendments. The amendment establishes a new Rule 107 to provide standards for the use of illustrative aids. The new rule is derived from Maine Rule of Evidence 616. The term "illustrative aid" is used instead of the term "demonstrative evidence," as that latter term has been subject to differing interpretation in the courts. An illustrative aid is any presentation offered not as evidence but rather to assist the trier of fact in understanding evidence or argument. "Demonstrative evidence" is a term better applied to substantive evidence offered to prove, by demonstration, a disputed fact.

Writings, objects, charts, or other presentations that are used during the trial to provide information to the trier of fact thus fall into two categories. The first category is evidence that is offered to prove a disputed fact; admissibility of such evidence is dependent upon satisfying the strictures of Rule 403, the hearsay rule, and other evidentiary screens. Usually the jury is permitted to take this substantive evidence to the jury room during deliberations and use it to help determine the disputed facts.

The second category—the category covered by this rule—is information offered for the narrow purpose of helping the trier of fact to understand what is being communicated to them by the witness or party presenting evidence or argument. Examples may include drawings, photos, diagrams, video depictions, charts, graphs, and computer simulations. These kinds of presentations, referred to in this rule as "illustrative aids," have also been described as "pedagogical devices" and sometimes (and less helpfully) "demonstrative presentations"—that latter term being unhelpful because the purpose for presenting the information is not to "demonstrate" how an event occurred but rather to help the trier of fact understand evidence or argument that is being or has been presented.

A similar distinction must be drawn between a summary of voluminous admissible evidence offered to prove a fact, and a summary of evidence that is offered solely to assist the trier of fact in understanding the evidence. The former is subject to the strictures of Rule 1006. The latter is an illustrative aid, which the courts have previously regulated pursuant to the broad standards of Rule 611(a), and which is now to be regulated by the more particularized requirements of this Rule 107.

While an illustrative aid is by definition not offered to prove a fact in dispute, this does not mean that it is free from regulation by the court. It is possible that the illustrative aid may be prepared to distort or oversimplify the evidence presented, or stoke unfair prejudice. This rule requires the court to assess the value of the illustrative aid in assisting the trier of fact to understand the evidence or argument. *Cf.* Fed. R. Evid. 703; *see* Adv. Comm. Note to the 2000 amendment to Rule 703. Against that beneficial effect, the court must weigh most of the dangers that courts take into account in balancing evidence offered to prove a fact under Rule 403— one particular problem being that the illustrative aid might appear to be substantive evidence of a disputed event. If those dangers substantially outweigh the value of the aid in assisting the trier of fact, the trial court should prohibit the use of—or order the modification of—the illustrative aid. And if the court does allow the aid to be presented at a jury trial, the adverse party may ask to have the jury instructed about the limited purpose for which the illustrative aid may be used. *Cf.* Rule 105.

The intent of the rule is to clarify the distinction between substantive evidence and illustrative aids, and to provide the court with a balancing test specifically directed toward the use of illustrative aids. Illustrative aids can be critically important in helping the trier of fact understand the evidence or argument.

Many courts require advance disclosure of illustrative aids, as a means of safeguarding and regulating their use. Ordinary discovery procedures concentrate on the evidence that will be presented at trial, so illustrative aids are not usually subject to discovery. Their sudden appearance may not give sufficient opportunity for analysis by other parties, particularly if they are complex. That said, there is a wide variety of illustrative aids, and a wide variety of circumstances under which they might be used. In addition, in some cases, advance disclosure may improperly preview witness examination or attorney argument. The amendment therefore leaves it to trial judges to decide whether, when, and how to require advance notice of an illustrative aid.

Because an illustrative aid is not offered to prove a fact in dispute and is used only in accompaniment with presentation of evidence or argument, the amendment provides that illustrative aids are not to go to the jury room unless all parties consent or the court, for good cause, orders otherwise. The Committee determined that allowing the jury to use the aid in deliberations, free of the constraint of accompaniment with witness testimony or party presentation, runs the risk that the jury may unduly emphasize the testimony of a witness with whom it was used, or otherwise misinterpret the import, usefulness, and purpose of the illustrative aid. But the Committee concluded that trial courts should have some discretion to allow the jury to consider an illustrative aid during deliberations.

If the court does allow the jury to review the illustrative aid during deliberations, the court must upon request instruct the jury that the illustrative aid is not evidence and cannot be considered as proof of any fact.

This rule is intended to govern the use of an illustrative aid at any point in the trial, including in opening statement and closing argument.

While an illustrative aid is not evidence, if it is used at trial it must be marked as an exhibit and made part of the record, unless that is impracticable under the circumstances.

ARTICLE II. JUDICIAL NOTICE

Rule

Rule 201. Judicial Notice of Adjudicative Facts

(a) Scope. This rule governs judicial notice of an adjudicative fact only, not a legislative fact.

(b) Kinds of Facts That May Be Judicially Noticed. The court may judicially notice a fact that is not subject to reasonable dispute because it:

(1) is generally known within the trial court's territorial jurisdiction; or

(2) can be accurately and readily determined from sources whose accuracy cannot reasonably be questioned.

(c) Taking Notice. The court:

(1) may take judicial notice on its own; or

(2) must take judicial notice if a party requests it and the court is supplied with the necessary information.

(d) Timing. The court may take judicial notice at any stage of the proceeding.

(e) Opportunity to Be Heard. On timely request, a party is entitled to be heard on the propriety of taking judicial notice and the nature of the fact to be noticed. If the court takes judicial notice before notifying a party, the party, on request, is still entitled to be heard.

(f) Instructing the Jury. In a civil case, the court must instruct the jury to accept the noticed fact as conclusive. In a criminal case, the court must instruct the jury that it may or may not accept the noticed fact as conclusive.

HISTORY:

Jan. 2, 1975, P. L. 93-595, § 1, 88 Stat. 1930; April 26, 2011, eff. Dec. 1, 2011.

HISTORY; ANCILLARY LAWS AND DIRECTIVES

Other provisions:

Notes of Advisory Committee on Rules. *Subdivision (a).* This is the only evidence rule on the subject of judicial notice. It deals only with judicial notice of "adjudicative" facts. No rule deals with judicial notice of "legislative" facts. Judicial notice of matters of foreign law is treated in Rule 44.1 of the Federal Rules of Civil Procedure and Rule 26.1 of the Federal Rules of Criminal Procedure.

The omission of any treatment of legislative facts results from fundamental differences between adjudicative facts and legislative facts. Adjudicative facts are simply the facts of the particular case. Legislative facts, on the other hand, are those which have relevance to legal reasoning and the lawmaking process, whether in the formulation of a legal principle or ruling by a judge or court or in the enactment of a legislative body. The terminology was coined by Professor Kenneth Davis in his article An Approach to Problems of Evidence in the Administrative Process, 55 Harv.L-.Rev. 364, 404–407 (1942). The following discussion draws extensively upon his writings. In addition, see the same author's Judicial Notice, 55 Colum.L.Rev. 945 (1955); Administrative Law Treatise, ch. 15 (1958); A System of Judicial Notice Based on Fairness and Convenience, in Perspectives of Law 69 (1964).

The usual method of establishing adjudicative facts in through the introduction of evidence, ordinarily consisting of the testimony of witnesses. If particular facts are outside of reasonable controversy, this process is dispensed with as unnecessary. A high degree of indisputability is the essential prerequisite.

Legislative facts are quite different. As Professor Davis says:

"My opinion is that judge-made law would stop growing if judges, in thinking about questions of law and policy, were forbidden to take into account the facts they believe, as distinguished from facts which are 'clearly . . . within the domain of the indisputable.' Facts most needed in thinking about difficult problems of law and policy have a way of being outside the domain of the clearly indisputable." A System of Judicial Notice Based on Fairness and Convenience, *supra,* at 82.

An illustration is *Hawkins v. United States*, 358 U.S. 74, 79 S.Ct. 136, 3 L.Ed.2d 125 (1958), in which the Court refused to discard the common law rule that one spouse could not testify against the other, saying, "Adverse testimony given in criminal proceedings would, we think, be likely to destroy almost any marriage." This conclusion has a large intermixture of fact, but the factual aspect is scarcely "indisputable." See Hutchins and Slesinger, Some Observations on the Law of Evidence—Family Relations, 13 Minn.L.Rev. 675 (1929). If the destructive effect of the giving of adverse testimony by a spouse is not indisputable, should the Court have refrained from considering it in the absence of supporting evidence?

"If the Model Code or the Uniform Rules had been applicable, the Court would have been barred from thinking about the essential factual ingredient of the problems before it, and such a result would be obviously intolerable. What the law needs as its growing points is more, not less, judicial thinking about the factual ingredients of problems of what the law ought to be, and the needed facts are seldom 'clearly' indisputable." Davis, *supra,* at 83.

Professor Morgan gave the following description of the methodology of determining domestic law:

"In determining the content or applicability of a rule of domestic law, the judge is unrestricted in his investigation and conclusion. He may reject the propositions of either party or of both parties. He may consult the sources of pertinent data to which they refer, or he may refuse to do so. He may make an independent search for persuasive data or rest content with what he has or what the parties present. . . . [T]he parties do no more than to assist; they control no part of the process." Morgan, Judicial Notice, 57 Harv.L.Rev. 269, 270–271 (1944).

This is the view which should govern judicial access to legislative facts. It renders inappropriate any limitation in the form of indisputability, any formal requirements of notice other than those already inherent in affording opportunity to hear and be heard and exchanging briefs, and any requirement of formal findings at any level. It should, however, leave open the possibility of introducing evidence through regular channels in appropriate situations. See Borden's Farm Products Co. v. Baldwin, 293 U.S. 194, 55 S.Ct. 187, 79 L.Ed. 281 (1934), where the cause was remanded for the taking of evidence as to the economic conditions and trade practices underlying the New York Milk Control Law.

Similar considerations govern the judicial use of nonadjudicative facts in ways other than formulating laws and rules. Thayer described them as a part of the judicial reasoning process.

"In conducting a process of judicial reasoning, as of other reasoning, not a step can be taken without assuming something which has not been proved; and the capacity to do this with competent judgment and efficiency, is imputed to judges and juries as part of their necessary mental outfit." Thayer, Preliminary Treatise on Evidence 279–280 (1898).

As Professor Davis points out, A System of Judicial Notice Based on Fairness and Convenience, in Perspectives of Law 69, 73 (1964), every case involves the use of hundreds or thousands of non-evidence facts. When a witness in an automobile accident case says "car," everyone, judge and jury included, furnishes, from non-evidence sources within himself, the supplementing information that the "car" is an automobile, not a railroad car, that it is self-propelled, probably by an internal combustion engine, that it may be assumed to have four wheels with pneumatic rubber tires, and so on. The judicial process cannot construct every case from scratch, like Descartes creating a world based on the postulate *Cogito, ergo sum.* These items could not possibly be introduced into evidence, and no one suggests that they be. Nor are they appropriate subjects for any formalized treatment of judicial notice of facts. See Levin and Levy, Persuading the jury with Facts Not in Evidence: The Fiction-Science Spectrum, 105 U.Pa.L.Rev. 139 (1956).

Another aspect of what Thayer had in mind is the use of non-evidence facts to appraise or assess the adjudicative facts of the case. Pairs of cases from two jurisdictions illustrate this use and also the difference between non-evidence facts thus used and adjudicative facts. In *People v. Strook*, 347 Ill. 460, 179 N.E. 821 (1932), venue in Cook County had been held not established by testimony that the crime was committed at 7956 South Chicago Avenue, since judicial notice would not be taken that the address was in Chicago. However, the same court subsequently ruled that venue in Cook County was established by testimony that a crime occurred at 8900 South Anthony Avenue, since notice would be taken of the common practice of omitting the name of the city when speaking of local addresses, and the witness was testifying in Chicago. *People v. Pride*, 16 Ill.2d 82, 156 N.E.2d 551 (1951). And in *Hughes v. Vestal*, 264 N.C. 500, 142 S.E.2d 361 (1965), the Supreme Court of North Carolina disapproved the trial judge's admission in evidence of a state-published table of automobile stopping distances on the basis of judicial notice, though the court itself had referred to the same table in an earlier case in a "rhetorical and illustrative" way in determining that the defendant could not have stopped her car in time to avoid striking a child who suddenly appeared in the highway and that a non-suit was properly granted. *Ennis v. Dupree*, 262 N.C. 224, 136 S.E.2d 702 (1964). See also *Brown v. Hale*, 263 N.C. 176, 139 S.E.2d 210 (1964); *Clayton v. Rimmer*, 262 N.C. 302, 136 S.E.2d 562 (1964). It is apparent that this use of non-evidence facts in evaluating the adjudicative facts of the case is not an appropriate subject for a formalized judicial notice treatment.

In view of these considerations, the regulation of judicial notice of facts by the present rule extends only to adjudicative facts.

What, then, are "adjudicative" facts? Davis refers to them as those "which relate to the parties," or more fully:

"When a court or an agency finds facts concerning the immediate parties—who did what, where, when, how, and with what motive or intent—the court or agency is performing an adjudicative function, and the facts are conveniently called adjudicative facts.

. . .

"Stated in other terms, the adjudicative facts are those to which the law is applied in the process of adjudication. They are the facts that normally go to the jury in a jury case. They relate to the parties, their activities, their properties, their businesses." 2 Administrative Law Treatise 353.

Subdivision (b). With respect to judicial notice of adjudicative facts, the tradition has been one of caution in requiring that the matter be beyond reasonable controversy. This tradition of circumspection appears to be soundly based, and no reason to depart from it is apparent. As Professor Davis says:

"The reason we use trial-type procedure, I think, is that we make the practical judgment, on the basis of experience, that taking evidence, subject to cross-examination and rebuttal, is the best way to resolve controversies involving disputes of adjudicative facts, that is, facts pertaining to the parties. The reason we require a determination on the record is that we think fair procedure in resolving disputes of adjudicative facts calls for giving each party a chance to meet in the appropriate fashion the facts that come to the tribunal's attention, and the appropriate fashion for meeting disputed adjudicative facts includes rebuttal evidence, cross-examination, usually confrontation, and argument (either written or oral or both). The key to a fair trial is opportunity to use the appropriate weapons (rebuttal evidence, cross-examination, and argument) to meet adverse materials that come to the tribunal's attention." A System of Judicial Notice Based on Fairness and Convenience, in Perspectives of Law 69, 93 (1964).

The rule proceeds upon the theory that these considerations call for dispensing with traditional methods of proof only in clear cases. Compare Professor Davis' conclusion that judicial notice should be a matter of convenience, subject to requirements of procedural fairness. Id., 94.

This rule is consistent with Uniform Rule 9(1) and (2) which limit judicial notice of facts to those "so universally known that they cannot reasonably be the subject of dispute," those "so generally known or of such common notoriety within the territorial jurisdiction of the court that they cannot reasonably be the subject of dispute," and those "capable of immediate and accurate determination by resort to easily accessible sources of indisputable accuracy." The traditional textbook treatment has included these general categories (matters of common knowledge, facts capable of verification), McCormick §§ 324, 325, and then has passed on into detailed treatment of such specific topics as facts relating to the personnel and records of the court, Id. § 327, and other governmental facts, Id. § 328. The California draftsmen, with a background of detailed statutory regulation of judicial notice, followed a somewhat similar pattern. California Evidence Code §§ 451, 452. The Uniform Rules, however, were drafted on the theory that these particular matters are included within the general categories and need no specific mention. This approach is followed in the present rule.

The phrase "propositions of generalized knowledge," found in Uniform Rule 9(1) and (2) is not included in the present rule. It was, it is believed, originally included in Model Code Rules 801 and 802 primarily in order to afford some minimum recognition to the right of the judge in his "legislative" capacity (not acting as the trier of fact) to take judicial notice of very limited categories of generalized knowledge. The limitations thus imposed have been discarded herein as undesirable, unworkable, and contrary to existing practice. What is left, then, to be considered, is the status of a "proposition of generalized knowledge" as an "adjudicative" fact to be noticed judicially and communicated by the judge to the jury. Thus viewed, it is considered to be lacking practical significance. While judges use judicial notice of "propositions of generalized knowledge" in a variety of situations: determining the validity and meaning of statutes, formulating common law rules, deciding whether evidence should be admitted, assessing the sufficiency and effect of evidence, all are essentially nonadjudicative in nature. When judicial notice is seen as a significant vehicle for progress in the law, these are the areas involved, particularly in developing fields of scientific knowledge. See McCormick 712. It is not believed that judges now instruct juries as to "propositions of generalized knowledge" derived from encyclopedias or other sources, or that they are likely to do so, or, indeed, that it is desirable that they do so. There is a vast difference between ruling on the basis of judicial notice that radar evidence of speed is admissible and explaining to the jury its principles and degree of accuracy, or between using a table of stopping distances of automobiles at various speeds in a judicial evaluation of testimony and telling the jury its precise application in the case. For cases raising doubt as to the propriety of the use of medical texts by lay triers of fact in passing on disability claims in administrative proceedings, see *Sayers v. Gardner*, 380 F.2d 940 (6th Cir. 1967); *Ross v. Gardner*, 365 F.2d 554 (6th Cir. 1966); *Sosna v. Celebrezze,* 234 F.Supp. 289 (E.D.Pa. 1964); *Glendenning v. Ribicoff*, 213 F.Supp. 301 (W.D.Mo. 1962).

Subdivisions (c) and (d). Under subdivision (c) the judge has a discretionary authority to take judicial notice, regardless of whether he is so requested by a party. The taking of judicial notice is mandatory, under subdivision (d), only when a party requests it and the necessary information is supplied. This scheme is believed to reflect existing practice. It is simple and workable. It avoids troublesome distinctions in the many situations in which the process of taking judicial notice is not recognized as such.

Compare Uniform Rule 9 making judicial notice of facts universally known mandatory without request, and making judicial notice of facts generally known in the jurisdiction or capable of determination by resort to accurate sources discretionary in the absence of request but mandatory if request is made and the information furnished. But see Uniform Rule 10(3), which directs the judge to decline to take judicial notice if available information fails to convince him that the matter falls clearly within Uniform Rule 9 or is insufficient to enable him to notice it judicially. Substantially the same approach is found in California Evidence Code §§ 451–453 and in New Jersey Evidence Rule 9. In contrast, the present rule treats alike all adjudicative facts which are subject to judicial notice.

Subdivision (e). Basic considerations of procedural fairness demand an opportunity to be heard on the propriety of taking judicial notice and the tenor of the matter noticed. The rule requires the granting of that opportunity upon request. No formal scheme of giving notice is provided. An adversely affected party may learn in advance that judicial notice is in contemplation, either by virtue of being served with a copy of a request by another party under subdivision (d) that judicial notice be taken, or through an advance indication by the judge. Or he may have no advance notice at all. The likelihood of the latter is enhanced by the frequent failure to recognize judicial notice as such. And in the absence of advance notice, a request made after the fact could not in fairness be considered untimely. See the provision for hearing on timely request in the Administrative Procedure Act, 5 U.S.C. § 556(e). See also Revised Model State Administrative Procedure Act (1961), 9C U.L.A. § 10(4) (Supp. 1967).

Subdivision (f). In accord with the usual view, judicial notice may be taken at any stage of the proceedings, whether in the trial court or on appeal. Uniform Rule 12; California Evidence Code § 459; Kansas Rules of Evidence § 60-412; New Jersey Evidence Rule 12; McCormick § 330, p. 712.

Subdivision (g). Much of the controversy about judicial notice has centered upon the question whether evidence should be admitted in disproof of facts of which judicial notice is taken.

The writers have been divided. Favoring admissibility are Thayer, Preliminary Treatise on Evidence 308 (1898); 9 Wigmore § 2567; Davis, A System of Judicial Notice Based on Fairness and Convenience, in Perspectives of Law, 69, 76–77 (1964). Opposing admissibility are Keeffe, Landis and Shaad, Sense and Nonsense about Judicial Notice, 2 Stan.L.Rev. 664, 668 (1950); McNaughton, Judicial Notice—Excerpts Relating to the Morgan-Whitmore Controversy, 14 Vand.L.Rev. 779 (1961); Morgan, Judicial Notice, 57 Harv.L.Rev. 269, 279 (1944); McCormick 710–711. The Model Code and the Uniform Rules are predicated upon indisputability of judicially noticed facts.

The proponents of admitting evidence in disproof have concentrated largely upon legislative facts. Since the present rule deals only with judicial notice of adjudicative facts, arguments directed to legislative facts lose their relevancy.

Within its relatively narrow area of adjudicative facts, the rule contemplates there is to be no evidence before the jury in disproof. The judge instructs the jury to take judicially noticed facts as established. This position is justified by the undesirable effects of the opposite rule in limiting the rebutting party, though not his opponent, to admissible evidence, in defeating the reasons for judicial notice, and in affecting the substantive law to an extent and in ways largely unforeseeable. Ample protection and flexibility are afforded by the broad provision for opportunity to be heard on request, set forth in subdivision (e).

Authority upon the propriety of taking judicial notice against an accused in a criminal case with respect to matters other than venue is relatively meager. Proceeding upon the theory that the right of jury trial does not extend to matters which are beyond reasonable dispute, the rule does not distinguish between criminal and civil cases. *People v. Mayes*, 113 Cal. 618, 45 P. 860 (1896); *Ross v. United States*, 374 F.2d 97 (8th Cir. 1967). *Cf. State v. Main*, 94 R.I. 338, 180 A.2d 814 (1962); *State v. Lawrence*, 120 Utah 323, 234 P.2d 600 (1951).

Note on Judicial Notice of Law. By rules effective July 1, 1966, the method of invoking the law of a foreign country is covered elsewhere. Rule 44.1 of the Federal Rules of Civil Procedure; Rule 26.1 of the Federal Rules of Criminal Procedure. These two new admirably designed rules are founded upon the assumption that the manner in which law is fed into the judicial process is never a proper concern of the rules of evidence but rather of the rules of procedure. The Advisory Committee on Evidence, believing that this assumption is entirely correct, proposes no evidence rule with respect to judicial notice of law, and suggests that those matters of law which, in addition to foreign-country law, have traditionally been treated as requiring pleading and proof and more recently as the subject of judicial notice be left to the Rules of Civil and Criminal Procedure.

Notes of Committee on the Judiciary, House Report No. 93-650. Rule 201(g) as received from the Supreme Court provided that when judicial notice of a fact is taken, the court shall instruct the jury to accept that fact as established. Being of the view that mandatory instruction to a jury in a criminal case to accept as conclusive any fact judicially noticed is inappropriate because contrary to the spirit of the Sixth Amendment right to a jury trial, the Committee adopted the 1969 Advisory Committee draft of this subsection, allowing a mandatory instruction in civil actions and proceedings and a discretionary instruction in criminal cases.

Notes of Advisory Committee on 2011 amendments. The language of Rule 201 has been amended as part of the restyling of the Evidence Rules to make them more easily understood and to make style and terminology consistent throughout the rules. These changes are intended to be stylistic only. There is no intent to change any result in any ruling on evidence admissibility.

ARTICLE III. PRESUMPTIONS IN CIVIL CASES

Rule

Rule 301. Presumptions in Civil Cases Generally

In a civil case, unless a federal statute or these rules provide otherwise, the party against whom a presumption is directed has the burden of producing evidence to rebut the presumption. But this rule does not shift the burden of persuasion, which remains on the party who had it originally.

HISTORY:

Jan. 2, 1975, P. L. 93-595, § 1, 88 Stat. 1931; April 26, 2011, eff. Dec. 1, 2011.

HISTORY; ANCILLARY LAWS AND DIRECTIVES

Other provisions:

Notes of Advisory Committee on Rules. This rule governs presumptions generally. See Rule 302 for presumptions controlled by state law and Rule 303 [deleted] for those against an accused in a criminal case.

Presumptions governed by this rule are given the effect of placing upon the opposing party the burden of establishing the nonexistence of the presumed fact, once the party invoking the presumption establishes the basic facts giving rise to it. The same considerations of fairness, policy, and probability which dictate the allocation of the burden of the various elements of a case as between the prima facie case of a plaintiff and affirmative defenses also underlie the creation of presumptions. These considerations are not satisfied by giving a lesser effect to presumptions. *Morgan and Maguire*, Looking Backward and Forward at Evidence, 50 Harv.L.Rev. 909, 913 (1937); Morgan, Instructing the Jury upon Presumptions and Burdon of Proof, 47 Harv.L.Rev. 59, 82 1933); Cleary, Presuming and Pleading: An Essay on Juristic Immaturity, 12 Stan.L.Rev. 5 (1959).

The so-called "bursting bubble" theory, under which a presumption vanishes upon the introduction of evidence which would support a finding of the nonexistence of the presumed fact, even though not believed, is rejected as according presumptions too "slight and evanescent" an effect. *Morgan and Maguire, supra*, at p. 913.

In the opinion of the Advisory Committee, no constitutional infirmity attends this view of presumptions. In *Mobile, J. & K.C.R. Co. v. Turnipseed*, 219 U.S. 35, 31 S.Ct. 136, 55 L.Ed. 78 (1910), the Court upheld a Mississippi statute which provided that in actions against railroads proof of injury inflicted by the running of trains should be prima facie evidence of negligence by the railroad. The injury in the case had resulted from a derailment. The opinion made the points (1) that the only effect of the statute was to impose on the railroad the duty of producing some evidence to the contrary, (2) that an inference may be supplied by law if there is a rational connection between the fact proved and the fact presumed, as long as the opposite party is not precluded from presenting his evidence to the contrary, and (3) that considerations of public policy arising from the character of the business justified the application in question. Nineteen years later, in *Western & Atlantic R. Co. v. Henderson*, 279 U.S. 639, 49 S.Ct. 445, 73 L.Ed. 884 (1929), the Court overturned a Georgia statute making railroads liable for damages done by trains, unless the railroad made it appear that reasonable care had been used, the presumption being against the railroad. The declaration alleged the death of plaintiff's husband from a grade crossing collision, due to specified acts of negligence by defendant. The jury were instructed that proof of the injury raised a presumption of negligence; the burden shifted to the railroad to prove ordinary care; and unless it did so, they should find for plaintiff. The instruction was held erroneous in an opinion stating (1) that there was no rational connection between the mere fact of collision and negligence on the part of anyone, and (2) that the statute was different from that in *Turnipseed* in imposing a burden upon the railroad. The reader is left in a state of some confusion. Is the difference between a derailment and a grade crossing collision of no significance? Would the *Turnipseed* presumption have been bad if it had imposed a burden of persuasion on defendant, although that would in nowise have impaired its "rational connection"? If *Henderson* forbids imposing a burden of persuasion on defendants, what happens to affirmative defenses?

Two factors serve to explain *Henderson*. The first was that it was common ground that negligence was indispensable to liability. Plaintiff thought so, drafted her complaint accordingly, and relied upon the presumption. But how in logic could the same presumption establish her alternative grounds of negligence that the engineer was so blind he could not see decedent's truck and that he failed to stop after he saw it? Second, take away the basic assumption of no liability without fault, as *Turnipseed* intimated might be done ("considerations of public policy arising out of the character of the business"), and the structure of the decision in *Henderson* fails. No question of logic would have arisen if the statute had simply said: a prima facie case of liability is made by proof of injury by a train; lack of negligence is an affirmative defense, to be pleaded and proved as other affirmative defenses. The problem would be one of economic due process only. While it seems likely that the Supreme Court of 1929 would have voted that due process was denied, that result today would be unlikely. See, for example, the shift in the direction of absolute liability in the consumer cases. Prosser, The Assault upon the Citadel (Strict Liability to the Consumer), 69 Yale L.J. 1099 (1960).

Any doubt as to the constitutional permissibility of a presumption imposing a burden of persuasion of the nonexistence of the presumed fact in civil cases is laid at rest by *Dick v. New York Life Ins. Co.*, 359 U.S. 437, 79 S.Ct. 921, 3 L.Ed.2d 935 (1959). The Court unhesitatingly applied the North Dakota rule that the presumption against suicide imposed on defendant the burden of proving that the death of insured, under an accidental death clause, was due to suicide.

"Proof of coverage and of death by gunshot wound shifts the burden to the insurer to establish that the death of the insured was due to his suicide." 359 U.S. at 443, 79 S.Ct. at 925.

"In a case like this one, North Dakota presumes that death was accidental and places on the insurer the burden of proving that death resulted from suicide." *Id.* at 446, 79 S.Ct. at 927.

The rational connection requirement survives in criminal cases, *Tot v. United States*, 319 U.S. 463, 63 S.Ct. 1241, 87 L.Ed. 1519 (1943), because the Court has been unwilling to extend into that area the greater-includes-the-lesser theory of *Ferry v. Ramsey*, 277 U.S. 88, 48 S.Ct. 443, 72 L.Ed. 796 (1928). In that case the Court sustained a Kansas statute under which bank directors were personally liable for deposits made with their assent and with knowledge of insolvency, and the fact of insolvency was prima facie evidence of assent and knowledge of insolvency. Mr. Justice Holmes pointed out that the state legislature could have made the directors personally liable to depositors in every case. Since the statute imposed a less stringent liability, "the thing to be considered is the result reached, not the possibly inartificial or clumsy way of reaching it." *Id.* at 94, 48 S.Ct. at 444. Mr. Justice Sutherland dissented: though the state could have created an absolute liability, it did not purport to do so; a rational connection was necessary, but lacking, between the liability created and the prima facie evidence of it; the result might be different if the basis of the presumption were being open for business.

The Sutherland view has prevailed in criminal cases by virtue of the higher standard of notice there required. The fiction that everyone is presumed to know the law is applied to the substantive law of crimes as an alternative to complete unenforceability. But the need does not extend to criminal evidence and procedure, and the fiction does not encompass them. "Rational connection" is not fictional or artificial, and so it is reasonable to suppose that *Gainey* should have known that his presence at the site of an illicit still could convict him of being connected with (carrying on) the business, *United States v. Gainey,* 380 U.S. 63, 85 S.Ct. 754, 13 L.Ed.2d 658 (1965), but not that Romano should have known that his presence at a still could convict him of possessing it, *United States v. Romano*, 382 U.S. 136, 86 S.Ct. 279, 15 L.Ed.2d 210 (1965).

In his dissent in *Gainey*, Mr. Justice Black put it more artistically:

"It might be argued, although the Court does not so argue or hold, that Congress if it wished could make presence at a still a crime in itself, and so Congress should be free to create crimes which are called 'possession' and 'carrying on an illegal distillery business' but which are defined in such a way that unexplained presence is sufficient and indisputable evidence in all cases to support conviction for those offenses. See *Ferry v. Ramsey*, 277 U.S. 88, 48 S.Ct. 443, 72 L.Ed. 796. Assuming for the sake of argument that Congress could make unexplained presence a criminal act, and ignoring also the refusal of this Court in other cases to uphold a statutory presumption on such a theory, see *Heiner v. Donnan*, 285 U.S. 312, 52 S.Ct. 358, 76 L.Ed. 772, there is no indication here that Congress intended to adopt such a misleading method of draftsmanship, nor in my judgment could the statutory provisions if so construed escape condemnation for vagueness, under the principles applied in *Lanzetta v. New Jersey*, 306 U.S. 451, 59 S.Ct. 618, 83 L.Ed. 888, and many other cases." 380 U.S. at 84, n. 12, 85 S.Ct. at 766.

And the majority opinion in *Romano* agreed with him:

"It may be, of course, that Congress has the power to make presence at an illegal still a punishable crime, but we find no clear indication that it intended to so exercise this power. The crime remains possession, not presence, and with all due deference to the judgment of Congress, the former may not constitutionally be inferred from the latter." 382 U.S. at 144, 86 S.Ct. at 284.

The rule does not spell out the procedural aspects of its application. Questions as to when the evidence warrants submission of a presumption and what instructions are proper under varying states of fact are believed to present no particular difficulties.

Notes of Committee on the Judiciary, House Report No. 93-650. Rule 301 as submitted by the Supreme Court provided that in all cases a presumption imposes on the party against whom it is directed the burden of proving that the nonexistence of the presumed fact is more probable than its existence. The Committee limited the scope of Rule 301 to "civil actions and proceedings" to effectuate its decision not to deal with the question of presumptions in criminal cases. (See note on [proposed] Rule 303 in discussion of Rules deleted). With respect to the weight to be given a presumption in a civil case, the Committee agreed with the judgment implicit in the Court's version that the so-called "bursting bubble" theory of presumptions, whereby a presumption vanished upon the appearance of any contradicting evidence by the other party, gives to presumptions too slight an effect. On the other hand, the Committee believed that the Rule proposed by the Court, whereby a presumption permanently alters the burden of persuasion, no matter how much contradicting evidence is introduced — a view shared by only a few courts — lends too great a force to presumptions. Accordingly, the Committee amended the Rule to adopt an intermediate position under which a presumption does not vanish upon the introduction of contradicting evidence, and does not change the burden of persuasion; instead it is merely deemed sufficient evidence of the fact presumed, to be considered by the jury or other finder of fact.

Notes of Committee on the Judiciary, Senate Report No. 93-1277. The rule governs presumptions in civil cases generally. Rule 302 provides for presumptions in cases controlled by State law.

As submitted by the Supreme Court, presumptions governed by this rule were given the effect of placing upon the opposing party the burden of establishing the non-existence of the presumed fact, once the party invoking the presumption established the basic facts giving rise to it.

Instead of imposing a burden of persuasion on the party against whom the presumption is directed, the House adopted a provision which shifted the burden of going forward with the evidence. They further provided that "even though met with contradicting evidence, a presumption is sufficient evidence of the fact presumed, to be considered by the trier of fact." The effect of the amendment is that presumptions are to be treated as evidence.

The committee feels the House amendment is ill-advised. As the joint committees (the Standing Committee on Practice and Procedure of the Judicial Conference and the Advisory Committee on the Rules of Evidence) stated: "Presumptions are not evidence, but ways of dealing with evidence." This treatment requires juries to perform the task of considering "as evidence" facts upon which they have no direct evidence and which may confuse them in performance of their duties. California had a rule much like that contained in the House amendment. It was sharply criticized by Justice Traynor in *Speck v. Sarver* [20 Cal. 2d 585, 128 P. 2d 16, 21 (1942)] and was repealed after 93 troublesome years [Cal. Ev. Code 1965 § 600].

Professor McCormick gives a concise and compelling critique of the presumption as evidence rule:

. . . . .

Another solution, formerly more popular than now, is to instruct the jury that the presumption is "evidence", to be weighed and considered with the testimony in the case. This avoids the danger that the jury may infer that the presumption is conclusive, but it probably means little to the jury and certainly runs counter to accepted theories of the nature of evidence. [McCormick, Evidence, 669 (1954); *Id.* 825 (2d ed. 1972)].

For these reasons the committee has deleted that provision of the House-passed rule that treats presumptions as evidence. The effect of the rule as adopted by the committee is to make clear that while evidence of facts giving rise to a presumption shifts the burden of coming forward with evidence to rebut or meet the presumption, it does not shift the burden of persuasion on the existence of the presumed facts. The burden or persuasion remains on the party to whom it is allocated under the rules governing the allocation in the first instance.

The court may instruct the jury that they may infer the existence of the presumed fact from proof of the basic facts giving rise to the presumption. However, it would be inappropriate under this rule to instruct the jury that the inference they are to draw is conclusive.

Notes of Conference Committee, House Report No. 93-1597. The House bill provides that a presumption in civil actions and proceedings shifts to the party against whom it is directed the burden of going forward with evidence to meet or rebut it. Even though evidence contradicting the presumption is offered, a presumption is considered sufficient evidence of the presumed fact to be considered by the jury. The Senate amendment provides that a presumption shifts to the party against whom it is directed the burden of going forward with evidence to meet or rebut the presumption, but it does not shift to that party the burden of persuasion on the existence of the presumed fact.

Under the Senate amendment, a presumption is sufficient to get a party past an adverse party's motion to dismiss made at the end of his case-in-chief. If the adverse party offers no evidence contradicting the presumed fact, the court will instruct the jury that if it finds the basic facts, it may presume the existence of the presumed fact. If the adverse party does offer evidence contradicting the presumed fact, the court cannot instruct the jury that it may presume the existence of the presumed fact from proof of the basic facts. The court may, however, instruct the jury that it may infer the existence of the presumed fact from proof of the basic facts.

The Conference adopts the Senate amendment.

Notes of Advisory Committee on 2011 amendments. The language of Rule 301 has been amended as part of the restyling of the Evidence Rules to make them more easily understood and to make style and terminology consistent throughout the rules. These changes are intended to be stylistic only. There is no intent to change any result in any ruling on evidence admissibility.

Rule 302. Applying State Law to Presumptions in Civil Cases

In a civil case, state law governs the effect of a presumption regarding a claim or defense for which state law supplies the rule of decision.

HISTORY:

Jan. 2, 1975, P. L. 93-595, § 1, 88 Stat. 1931; April 26, 2011, eff. Dec. 1, 2011.

HISTORY; ANCILLARY LAWS AND DIRECTIVES

Other provisions:

Notes of Advisory Committee on Rules. A series of Supreme Court decisions in diversity cases leaves no doubt of the relevance of *Erie Railroad Co. v. Tompkins*, 304 U.S. 64, 58 S.Ct. 817, 82 L.Ed. 1188 (1938), to questions of burden of proof. These decisions are *Cities Service Oil Co. v. Dunlap*, 308 U.S. 208, 60 S.Ct. 201, 84 L.Ed. 196 (1939), *Palmer v. Hoffman*, 318 U.S. 109, 63 S.Ct. 477, 87 L.Ed. 645 (1943), and *Dick v. New York Life Ins. Co.*, 359 U.S. 437, 79 S.Ct. 921, 3 L.Ed.2d 935 (1959). They involved burden of proof, respectively, as to status as bona fide purchasers, contributory negligence, and non-accidental death (suicide) of an insured. In each instance the state rule was held to be applicable. It does not follow, however, that all presumptions in diversity cases are governed by state law. In each case cited, the burden of proof question had to do with a substantive element of the claim or defense. Application of the state law is called for only when the presumption operates upon such an element. Accordingly the rule does not apply state law when the presumption operates upon a lesser aspect of the case, i.e. "tactical" presumptions.

The situations in which the state law is applied have been tagged for convenience in the preceding discussion as "diversity cases." The designation is not a completely accurate one since *Erie* applies to any claim or issue having its source in state law, regardless of the basis of federal jurisdiction, and does not apply to a federal claim or issue, even though jurisdiction is based on diversity. Vestal, *Erie R.R. v. Tompkins*: A Projection, 48 Iowa L.Rev. 248, 257 (1963); Hart and Wechsler, The Federal Courts and the Federal System, 697 (1953); 1A Moore, Federal Practice P 0.305 [3] (2d ed. 1965); Wright, Federal Courts, 217–218 (1963). Hence the rule employs, as appropriately descriptive, the phrase "as to which state law supplies the rule of decision." See A.L.I. Study of the Division of Jurisdiction Between State and Federal Courts, § 2344(c), p. 40, P.F.D. No. 1 (1965).

Notes of Advisory Committee on 2011 amendments. The language of Rule 302 has been amended as part of the restyling of the Evidence Rules to make them more easily understood and to make style and terminology consistent throughout the rules. These changes are intended to be stylistic only. There is no intent to change any result in any ruling on evidence admissibility.

ARTICLE IV. RELEVANCE AND ITS LIMITS

Rule

Rule 401. Test for Relevant Evidence

Evidence is relevant if:

(a) it has any tendency to make a fact more or less probable than it would be without the evidence; and

(b) the fact is of consequence in determining the action.

HISTORY:

Jan. 2, 1975, P. L. 93-595, § 1, 88 Stat. 1931; April 26, 2011, eff. Dec. 1, 2011.

HISTORY; ANCILLARY LAWS AND DIRECTIVES

Other provisions:

Notes of Advisory Committee on Rules. Problems of relevancy call for an answer to the question whether an item of evidence, when tested by the processes of legal reasoning, possesses sufficient probative value to justify receiving it in evidence. Thus, assessment of the probative value of evidence that a person purchased a revolver shortly prior to a fatal shooting with which he is charged is a matter of analysis and reasoning.

The variety of relevancy problems is coextensive with the ingenuity of counsel in using circumstantial evidence as a means of proof. An enormous number of cases fall in no set pattern, and this rule is designed as a guide for handling them. On the other hand, some situations recur with sufficient frequency to create patterns susceptible of treatment by specific rules. Rule 404 and those following it are of that variety; they also serve as illustrations of the application of the present rule as limited by the exclusionary principles of Rule 403.

Passing mention should be made of so-called "conditional" relevancy. Morgan, Basic Problems of Evidence 45–46 (1962). In this situation, probative value depends not only upon satisfying the basic requirement of relevancy as described above but also upon the existence of some matter of fact. For example, if evidence of a spoken statement is relied upon to prove notice, probative value is lacking unless the person sought to be charged heard the statement. The problem is one of fact, and the only rules needed are for the purpose of determining the respective functions of judge and jury. See Rules 104(b) and 901. The discussion which follows in the present note is concerned with relevancy generally, not with any particular problem of conditional relevancy.

Relevancy is not an inherent characteristic of any item of evidence but exists only as a relation between an item of evidence and a matter properly provable in the case. Does the item of evidence tend to prove the matter sought to be proved? Whether the relationship exists depends upon principles evolved by experience or science, applied logically to the situation at hand. James, Relevancy, Probability and the Law, 29 Calif.L.Rev. 689, 696, n. 15 (1941), in Selected Writings on Evidence and Trial 610, 615, n. 15 (Fryer ed. 1957). The rule summarizes this relationship as a "tendency to make the existence" of the fact to be proved "more probable or less probable." Compare Uniform Rule 1(2) which states the crux of relevancy as "a tendency in reason," thus perhaps emphasizing unduly the logical process and ignoring the need to draw upon experience or science to validate the general principle upon which relevancy in a particular situation depends.

The standard of probability under the rule is "more * * * probable than it would be without the evidence." Any more stringent requirement is unworkable and unrealistic. As McCormick § 152, p. 317, says, "A brick is not a wall," or, as Falknor, Extrinsic Policies Affecting Admissibility, 10 Rutgers L.Rev. 574, 576 (1956), quotes Professor McBaine, "* * * [I]t is not to be supposed that every witness can make a home run." Dealing with probability in the language of the rule has the added virtue of avoiding confusion between questions of admissibility and questions of the sufficiency of the evidence.

The rule uses the phrase "fact that is of consequence to the determination of the action" to describe the kind of fact to which proof may properly be directed. The language is that of California Evidence Code § 210; it has the advantage of avoiding the loosely used and ambiguous word "material." Tentative Recommendation and a Study Relating to the Uniform Rules of Evidence (Art. I. General Provisions), Cal. Law Revision Comm'n, Rep., Rec. & Studies, 10–11 (1964). The fact to be proved may be ultimate, intermediate, or evidentiary; it matters not, so long as it is of consequence in the determination of the action. Cf. Uniform Rule 1(2) which requires that the evidence relate to a "material" fact.

The fact to which the evidence is directed need not be in dispute. While situations will arise which call for the exclusion of evidence offered to prove a point conceded by the opponent, the ruling should be made on the basis of such considerations as waste of time and undue prejudice (see Rule 403), rather than under any general requirement that evidence is admissible only if directed to matters in dispute. Evidence which is essentially background in nature can scarcely be said to involve disputed matter, yet it is universally offered and admitted as an aid to understanding. Charts, photographs, views of real estate, murder weapons, and many other items of evidence fall in this category. A rule limiting admissibility to evidence directed to a controversial point would invite the exclusion of this helpful evidence, or at least the raising of endless questions over its admission. Cf. California Evidence Code § 210, defining relevant evidence in terms of tendency to prove a disputed fact.

Notes of Advisory Committee on 2011 amendments. The language of Rule 401 has been amended as part of the restyling of the Evidence Rules to make them more easily understood and to make style and terminology consistent throughout the rules. These changes are intended to be stylistic only. There is no intent to change any result in any ruling on evidence admissibility.

Rule 402. General Admissibility of Relevant Evidence

Relevant evidence is admissible unless any of the following provides otherwise:

- the United States Constitution;
- a federal statute;
- these rules; or
- other rules prescribed by the Supreme Court.

Irrelevant evidence is not admissible.

HISTORY:

Jan. 2, 1975, P. L. 93-595, § 1, 88 Stat. 1931; April 26, 2011, eff. Dec. 1, 2011.

HISTORY; ANCILLARY LAWS AND DIRECTIVES

Other provisions:

Notes of Advisory Committee on Rules. The provisions that all relevant evidence is admissible, with certain exceptions, and that evidence which is not relevant is not admissible are "a presupposition involved in the very conception of a rational system of evidence." Thayer, Preliminary Treatise on Evidence 264 (1898). They constitute the foundation upon which the structure of admission and exclusion rests. For similar provisions see California Evidence Code §§ 350, 351. Provisions that all relevant evidence is admissible are found in Uniform Rule 7(f); Kansas Code of Civil Procedure § 60-407(f); and New Jersey Evidence Rule 7(f); but the exclusion of evidence which is not relevant is left to implication.

Not all relevant evidence is admissible. The exclusion of relevant evidence occurs in a variety of situations and may be called for by these rules, by the Rules of Civil and Criminal Procedure, by Bankruptcy Rules, by Act of Congress, or by constitutional considerations.

Succeeding rules in the present article, in response to the demands of particular policies, require the exclusion of evidence despite its relevancy. In addition, Article V recognizes a number of privileges; Article VI imposes limitations upon witnesses and the manner of dealing with them; Article VII specifies requirements with respect to opinions and expert testimony; Article VIII excludes hearsay not falling within an exception; Article IX spells out the handling of authentication and identification; and Article X restricts the manner of proving the contents of writings and recordings.

The Rules of Civil and Criminal Procedure in some instances require the exclusion of relevant evidence. For example, Rules 30(b) and 32(a)(3) of the Rules of Civil Procedure, by imposing requirements of notice and unavailability of the deponent, place limits on the use of relevant depositions. Similarly, Rule 15 of the Rules of Criminal Procedure restricts the use of depositions in criminal cases, even though relevant. And the effective enforcement of the command, originally statutory and now found in Rule 5(a) of the Rules of Criminal Procedure, that an arrested person be taken without unnecessary delay before a commissioner of other similar officer is held to require the exclusion of statements elicited during detention in violation thereof. *Mallory v. United States*, 354 U.S. 449, 77 S.Ct. 1356, 1 L.Ed.2d 1479 (1957); 18 U.S.C. § 3501(c).

While congressional enactments in the field of evidence have generally tended to expand admissibility beyond the scope of the common law rules, in some particular situations they have restricted the admissibility of relevant evidence. Most of this legislation has consisted of the formulation of a privilege or of a prohibition against disclosure. 8 U.S.C. § 1202(f), records of refusal of visas or permits to enter United States confidential, subject to discretion of Secretary of State to make available to court upon certification of need; 10 U.S.C. § 3693, replacement certificate of honorable discharge from Army not admissible in evidence; 10 U.S.C. § 8693, same as to Air Force; 11 U.S.C. § 25(a)(10), testimony given by bankrupt on his examination not admissible in criminal proceedings against him, except that given in hearing upon objection to discharge; 11 U.S.C. § 205(a), railroad reorganization petition, if dismissed, not admissible in evidence; 11 U.S.C. § 403(a), list of creditors filed with municipal composition plan not an admission; 13 U.S.C. § 9(a), census information confidential, retained copies of reports privileged; 47 U.S.C. § 605, interception and divulgence of wire or radio communications prohibited unless authorized by sender. These statutory provisions would remain undisturbed by the rules.

The rule recognizes but makes no attempt to spell out the constitutional considerations which impose basic limitations upon the admissibility of relevant evidence. Examples are evidence obtained by unlawful search and seizure, *Weeks v. United States*, 232 U.S. 383, 34 S.Ct. 341, 58 L.Ed. 652 (1914); *Katz v. United States*, 389 U.S. 347, 88 S.Ct. 507, 19 L.Ed.2d 576 (1967); incriminating statement elicited from an accused in violation of right to counsel, *Massiah v. United States*, 377 U.S. 201, 84 S.Ct. 1199, 12 L.Ed.2d 246 (1964).

Notes of Committee on the Judiciary, House Report No. 93-650. Rule 402 as submitted to the Congress contained the phrase "or by other rules adopted by the Supreme Court". To accommodate the view that the Congress should not appear to acquiesce in the Court's judgment that it has authority under the existing Rules Enabling Acts to promulgate Rules of Evidence, the Committee amended the above phrase to read "or by other rules prescribed by the Supreme Court pursuant to statutory authority" in this and other Rules where the reference appears.

Notes of Advisory Committee on 2011 amendments. The language of Rule 402 has been amended as part of the restyling of the Evidence Rules to make them more easily understood and to make style and terminology consistent throughout the rules. These changes are intended to be stylistic only. There is no intent to change any result in any ruling on evidence admissibility.

Rule 403. Excluding Relevant Evidence for Prejudice, Confusion, Waste of Time, or Other Reasons

The court may exclude relevant evidence if its probative value is substantially outweighed by a danger of one or more of the following: unfair prejudice, confusing the issues, misleading the jury, undue delay, wasting time, or needlessly presenting cumulative evidence.

HISTORY:

Jan. 2, 1975, P. L. 93-595, § 1, 88 Stat. 1932; April. 26, 2011, eff. Dec. 1, 2011.

HISTORY; ANCILLARY LAWS AND DIRECTIVES

Other provisions:

Notes of Advisory Committee on Rules. The case law recognizes that certain circumstances call for the exclusion of evidence which is of unquestioned relevance. These circumstances entail risks which range all the way from inducing decision on a purely emotional basis, at one extreme, to nothing more harmful than merely wasting time, at the other extreme. Situations in this area call for balancing the probative value of and need for the evidence against the harm likely to result from its admission. Slough, Relevancy Unraveled, 5 Kan. L. Rev. 1, 12-15 (1956); Trautman, Logical or Legal Relevancy — A Conflict in Theory, 5 Van. L. Rev. 385, 392 (1952); McCormick § 152, pp. 319–321. The rules which follow in this Article are concrete applications evolved for particular situations. However, they reflect the policies underlying the present rule, which is designed as a guide for the handling of situations for which no specific rules have been formulated.

Exclusion for risk of unfair prejudice, confusion of issues, misleading the jury, or waste of time, all find ample support in the authorities. "Unfair prejudice" within its context means an undue tendency to suggest decision on an improper basis, commonly, though not necessarily, an emotional one.

The rule does not enumerate surprise as a ground for exclusion, in this respect following Wigmore's view of the common law. 6 Wigmore § 1849. Cf. McCormick § 152, p. 320, n. 29, listing unfair surprise as a ground for exclusion but stating that it is usually "coupled with the danger of prejudice and confusion of issues." While Uniform Rule 45 incorporates surprise as a ground and is followed in Kansas Code of Civil Procedure § 60-445, surprise is not included in California Evidence Code § 352 or New Jersey Rule 4, though both the latter otherwise substantially embody Uniform Rule 45. While it can scarcely be doubted that claims of unfair surprise may still be justified despite procedural requirements of notice and instrumentalities of discovery, the granting of a continuance is a more appropriate remedy than exclusion of the evidence. Tentative Recommendation and a Study Relating to the Uniform Rules of Evidence (Art. VI. Extrinsic Policies Affecting Admissibility), Cal. Law Revision Comm'n, Rep., Rec. & Studies, 612 (1964). Moreover, the impact of a rule excluding evidence on the ground of surprise would be difficult to estimate.

In reaching a decision whether to exclude on grounds of unfair prejudice, consideration should be given to the probable effectiveness or lack of effectiveness of a limiting instruction. See Rule 106 [now 105] and Advisory Committee's Note thereunder. The availability of other means of proof may also be an appropriate factor.

Notes of Advisory Committee on 2011 amendments. The language of Rule 403 has been amended as part of the restyling of the Evidence Rules to make them more easily understood and to make style and terminology consistent throughout the rules. These changes are intended to be stylistic only. There is no intent to change any result in any ruling on evidence admissibility.

Rule 404. Character Evidence; Other Crimes, Wrongs, or Acts

(a) Character Evidence.

(1) *Prohibited Uses.* Evidence of a person's character or character trait is not admissible to prove that on a particular occasion the person acted in accordance with the character or trait.

(2) *Exceptions for a Defendant or Victim in a Criminal Case.* The following exceptions apply in a criminal case:

(A) a defendant may offer evidence of the defendant's pertinent trait, and if the evidence is admitted, the prosecutor may offer evidence to rebut it;

(B) subject to the limitations in Rule 412, a defendant may offer evidence of an alleged victim's pertinent trait, and if the evidence is admitted, the prosecutor may:

(i) offer evidence to rebut it; and

(ii) offer evidence of the defendant's same trait; and

(C) in a homicide case, the prosecutor may offer evidence of the alleged victim's trait of peacefulness to rebut evidence that the victim was the first aggressor.

(3) *Exceptions for a Witness.* Evidence of a witness's character may be admitted under Rules 607, 608, and 609.

(b) Other Crimes, Wrongs, or Acts.

(1) *Prohibited Uses.* Evidence of any other crime, wrong, or act is not admissible to prove a person's character in order to show that on a particular occasion the person acted in accordance with the character.

(2) *Permitted Uses.* This evidence may be admissible for another purpose, such as proving motive, opportunity, intent, preparation, plan, knowledge, identity, absence of mistake, or lack of accident.

(3) *Notice in a Criminal Case.* In a criminal case, the prosecutor must:

(A) provide reasonable notice of any such evidence that the prosecutor intends to offer at trial, so that the defendant has a fair opportunity to meet it;

(B) articulate in the notice the permitted purpose for which the prosecutor intends to offer the evidence and the reasoning that supports the purpose; and

(C) do so in writing before trial—or in any form during trial if the court, for good cause, excuses lack of pretrial notice.

HISTORY:

Jan. 2, 1975, P. L. 93-595, § 1, 88 Stat. 1932; March 2, 1987, eff. Oct. 1, 1987; April 30, 1991, eff. Dec.1, 1991; April 17, 2000, eff. Dec. 1, 2000; April 12, 2006, eff. Dec. 1, 2006; April 26, 2011, eff. Dec. 1, 2011; April 27, 2020, eff. Dec. 1, 2020.

HISTORY; ANCILLARY LAWS AND DIRECTIVES

Other provisions:

Notes of Advisory Committee on Rules. *Subdivision (a).* This subdivision deals with the basic question whether character evidence should be admitted. Once the admissibility of character evidence in some form is established under this rule, reference must then be made to Rule 405, which follows, in order to determine the appropriate method of proof. If the character is that of a witness, see Rules 608 and 610 for methods of proof.

Character questions arise in two fundamentally different ways. (1) Character may itself be an element of a crime, claim, or defense. A situation of this kind is commonly referred to as "character in issue." Illustrations are: the chastity of the victim under a statute specifying her chastity as an element of the crime of seduction, or the competency of the driver in an action for negligently entrusting a motor vehicle to an incompetent driver. No problem of the general relevancy of character evidence is involved, and the present rule therefore has no provision on the subject. The only question relates to allowable methods of proof, as to which see Rule 405, immediately following. (2) Character evidence is susceptible of being used for the purpose of suggesting an inference that the person acted on the occasion in question consistently with his character. This use of character is often described as "circumstantial." Illustrations are: evidence of a violent disposition to prove that the person was the aggressor in an affray, or evidence of honesty in disproof of a charge of theft. This circumstantial use of character evidence raises questions of relevancy as well as questions of allowable methods of proof.

In most jurisdictions today, the circumstantial use of character is rejected but with important exceptions: (1) an accused may introduce pertinent evidence of good character (often misleadingly described as "putting his character in issue"), in which event the prosecution may rebut with evidence of bad character; (2) an accused may introduce pertinent evidence of the character of the victim, as in support of a claim of self-defense to a charge of homicide or consent in a case of rape, and the prosecution may introduce similar evidence in rebuttal of the character evidence, or, in a homicide case, to rebut a claim that deceased was the first aggressor, however proved; and (3) the character of a witness may be gone into as bearing on his credibility. McCormick §§ 155– 161. This pattern is incorporated in the rule. While its basis lies more in history and experience than in logic as underlying justification can fairly be found in terms of the relative presence and absence of prejudice in the various situations. Falknor, Extrinsic Policies Affecting Admissibility, 10 Rutger, L.Rev. 574, 584 (1956); McCormick § 157. In any event, the criminal rule is so deeply imbedded in our jurisprudence as to assume almost constitutional proportions and to override doubts of the basic relevancy of the evidence.

The limitation to pertinent traits of character, rather than character generally, in paragraphs (1) and (2) is in accordance with the prevailing view. McCormick § 158, p. 334. A similar provision in Rule 608, to which reference is made in paragraph (3), limits character evidence respecting witnesses to the trait of truthfulness or untruthfulness.

The argument is made that circumstantial use of character ought to be allowed in civil cases to the same extent as in criminal cases, i.e. evidence of good (nonprejudicial) character would be admissible in the first instance, subject to rebuttal by evidence of bad character. Falknor, Extrinsic Policies Affecting Admissibility, 10 Rutgers L.Rev. 574, 581–583 (1956); Tentative Recommendation and a Study Relating to the Uniform Rules of Evidence (Art. VI. Extrinsic Policies Affecting Admissibility), Cal. Law Revision Comm'n, Rep., Rec. & Studies, 657–658 (1964). Uniform Rule 47 goes farther, in that it assumes that character evidence in general satisfies the conditions of relevancy, except as provided in Uniform Rule 48. The difficulty with expanding the use of character evidence in civil cases is set forth by the California Law Revision Commission in its ultimate rejection of Uniform Rule 47, *Id.*, 615:

"Character evidence is of slight probative value and may be very prejudicial. It tends to distract the trier of fact from the main question of what actually happened on the particular occasion. It subtly permits the trier of fact to reward the good man to punish the bad man because of their respective characters despite what the evidence in the case shows actually happened."

Much of the force of the position of those favoring greater use of character evidence in civil cases in dissipated by their support of Uniform Rule 48 which excludes the evidence in negligence cases, where it could be expected to achieve its maximum usefulness. Moreover, expanding concepts of "character," which seem of necessity to extend into such areas as psychiatric evaluation and psychological testing, coupled with expanded admissibility, would open up such vistas of mental examinations as caused the Court concern in Schlagenhauf v. Holder, 379 U.S. 104, 85 S.Ct. 234, 13 L.Ed.2d 152 (1964). It is believed that those espousing change have not met the burden of persuasion.

Subdivision (b) deals with a specialized but important application of the general rule excluding circumstantial use of character evidence. Consistently with that rule, evidence of other crimes, wrongs, or acts is not admissible to prove character as a basis for suggesting the inference that conduct on a particular occasion was in conformity with it. However, the evidence may be offered for another purpose, such as proof of motive, opportunity, and so on, which does not fall within the prohibition. In this situation the rule does not require that the evidence be excluded. No mechanical solution is offered. The determination must be made whether the danger of undue prejudice outweighs the probative value of the evidence in view of the availability of other means of proof and other factors appropriate for making decisions of this kind under Rule 403. Slough and Knightly, Other Vices, Other Crimes, 41 Iowa L.Rev. 325 (1956).

Notes of Committee on the Judiciary, House Report No. 93-650. The second sentence of Rule 404(b) as submitted to the Congress began with the words "This subdivision does not exclude the evidence when offered". The Committee amended this language to read "It may, however, be admissible", the words used in the 1971 Advisory Committee draft, on the ground that this formulation properly placed greater emphasis on admissibility than did the final Court version.

Notes of Committee on the Judiciary, Senate Report No. 93-1277. This rule provides that evidence of other crimes, wrongs, or acts is not admissible to prove character but may be admissible for other specified purposes such as proof of motive.

Although your committee sees no necessity in amending the rule itself, it anticipates that the use of the discretionary word "may" with respect to the admissibility of evidence of crimes, wrongs, or acts is not intended to confer any arbitrary discretion on the trial judge. Rather, it is anticipated that with respect to permissible uses for such evidence, the trial judge may exclude it only on the basis of those considerations set forth in Rule 403, i.e. prejudice, confusion or waste of time.

Notes of Advisory Committee on 1987 amendments. The amendments are technical. No substantive change is intended.

Notes of Advisory Committee on 1991 amendment. Rule 404(b) has emerged as one of the most cited Rules in the Rules of Evidence. And in many criminal cases evidence of an accused's extrinsic acts is viewed as an important asset in the prosecution's case against an accused. Although there are a few reported decisions on use of such evidence by the defense, *see, e.g., United States v. McClure*, 546 F.2nd 670 (5th Cir. 1990) (acts of informant offered in entrapment defense), the overwhelming number of cases involve introduction of that evidence by the prosecution.

The amendment to Rule 404(b) adds a pretrial notice requirement in criminal cases and is intended to reduce surprise and promote early resolution on the issue of admissibility. The notice requirement thus places Rule 404(b) in the mainstream with notice and disclosure provisions in other rules of evidence. *See, e.g.*, Rule 412 (written motion of intent to offer evidence under rule), Rule 609 (written notice of intent to offer conviction older than 10 years), Rule 803(24) and 804(b)(5) (notice of intent to use residual hearsay exceptions).

The Rule expects that counsel for both the defense and the prosecution will submit the necessary request and information in a reasonable and timely fashion. Other than requiring pretrial notice, no specific time limits are stated in recognition that what constitutes a reasonable request or disclosure will depend largely on the circumstances of each case. *Compare* Fla. Stat. Ann § 90.404(2)(b) (notice must be given at least 10 days before trial) with Tex. R. Evid. 404(b) (no time limit).

Likewise, no specific form of notice is required. The Committee considered and rejected a requirement that the notice satisfy the particularity requirements normally required of language used in a charging instrument. Cf. Fla. Stat. Ann § 90.404(2)(b) (written disclosure must describe uncharged misconduct with particularity required of an indictment or information). Instead, the Committee opted for a generalized notice provision which requires the prosecution to apprise the defense of the general nature of the evidence of extrinsic acts. The Committee does not intend that the amendment will supercede other rules of admissibility or disclosure, such as the Jencks Act, 18 U.S.C. § 3500, et. seq. nor require the prosecution to disclose directly or indirectly the names and addresses of its witnesses, something it is currently not required to do under Federal Rule of Criminal Procedure 16.

The amendment requires the prosecution to provide notice, regardless of how it intends to use the extrinsic act evidence at trial, i.e., during its case-in-chief, for impeachment, or for possible rebuttal. The court in its discretion may, under the facts, decide that the particular request or notice was not reasonable, either because of the lack of timeliness or completeness. Because the notice requirement serves as condition precedent to admissibility of 404(b) evidence, the offered evidence is inadmissible if the court decides that the notice requirement has not been met.

Nothing in the amendment precludes the court from requiring the government to provide it with an opportunity to rule *in limine* on 404(b) evidence before it is offered or even mentioned during trial. When ruling *in limine*, the court may require the government to disclose to it the specifics of such evidence which the court must consider in determining admissibility.

The amendment does not extend to evidence of acts which are "intrinsic" to the charged offense, see *United States v. Williams*, 900 F.2d 823 (5th Cir. 1990) (noting distinction between 404(b) evidence and intrinsic offense evidence). Nor is the amendment intended to redefine what evidence would otherwise be admissible under Rule 404(b). Finally, the Committee does not intend through the amendment to affect the role of the court and the jury in considering such evidence. See *United States v. Huddleston* [Huddleston v. United States], 485 U.S. 681, 108 S.Ct 1496 (1988).

Notes of Advisory Committee on 2000 amendments. Rule 404(a)(1) has been amended to provide that when the accused attacks the character of an alleged victim under subdivision (a)(2) of this Rule, the door is opened to an attack on the same character trait of the accused. Current law does not allow the government to introduce negative character evidence as to the accused unless the accused introduces evidence of good character. *See, e.g., United States v. Fountain,* 768 F.2d 790 (7th Cir. 1985) (when the accused offers proof of self-defense, this permits proof of the alleged victim's character trait for peacefulness, but it does not permit proof of the accused's character trait for violence).

The amendment makes clear that the accused cannot attack the alleged victim's character and yet remain shielded from the disclosure of equally relevant evidence concerning the same character trait of the accused. For example, in a murder case with a claim of self-defense, the accused, to bolster this defense, might offer evidence of the alleged victim's violent disposition. If the government has evidence that the accused has a violent character, but is not allowed to offer this evidence as part of its rebuttal, the jury has only part of the information it needs for an informed assessment of the probabilities as to who was the initial aggressor. This may be the case even if evidence of the accused's prior violent acts is admitted under Rule 404(b), because such evidence can be admitted only for limited purposes and not to show action in conformity with the accused's character on a specific occasion. Thus, the amendment is designed to permit a more balanced presentation of character evidence when an accused chooses to attack the character of the alleged victim.

The amendment does not affect the admissibility of evidence of specific acts of uncharged misconduct offered for a purpose other than proving character under Rule 404(b). Nor does it affect the standards for proof of character by evidence of other sexual behavior or sexual offenses under Rules 412–415. By its placement in Rule 404(a)(l), the amendment covers only proof of character by way of reputation or opinion.

The amendment does not permit proof of the accused's character if the accused merely uses character evidence for a purpose other than to prove the alleged victim's propensity to act in a certain way. *See United States v. Burks,* 470 F.2d 432, 434-5 (D.C.Cir. 1972) (evidence of the alleged victim's violent character, when known by the accused, was admissible "on the issue of whether or not the defendant reasonably feared he was in danger of imminent great bodily harm"). Finally, the amendment does not permit proof of the accused's character when the accused attacks the alleged victim's character as a witness under Rule 608 or 609.

The term "alleged" is inserted before each reference to "victim" in the Rule, in order to provide consistency with Evidence Rule 412.

GAP Report—Proposed Amendment to Rule 404(a). The Committee made the following changes to the published draft of the proposed amendment to Evidence Rule 404(a):

1. The term "a pertinent trait of character" was changed to "the same trait of character," in order to limit the scope of the government's rebuttal. The Committee Note was revised to accord with this change in the text.

2. The word "alleged" was added before each reference in the Rule to a "victim" in order to provide consistency with Evidence Rule 412. The Committee Note was amended to accord with this change in the text.

3. The Committee Note was amended to clarify that rebuttal is not permitted under this Rule if the accused proffers evidence of the alleged victim's character for a purpose other than to prove the alleged victim's propensity to act in a certain manner.

Notes of Advisory Committee on 2006 amendments. The Rule has been amended to clarify that in a civil case evidence of a person's character is never admissible to prove that the person acted in conformity with the character trait. The amendment resolves the dispute in the case law over whether the exceptions in subdivisions (a)(1) and (2) permit the circumstantial use of character evidence in civil cases. *Compare Carson v. Polley,* 689 F.2d 562, 576 (5th Cir. 1982) ("when a central issue in a case is close to one of a criminal nature, the exceptions to the Rule 404(a) ban on character evidence may be invoked"), *with SEC v. Towers Financial Corp.,* 966 F.Supp. 203 (S.D.N.Y. 1997) (relying on the terms "accused" and "prosecution" in Rule 404(a) to conclude that the exceptions in subdivisions (a)(1) and (2) are inapplicable in civil cases). The amendment is consistent with the original intent of the Rule, which was to prohibit the circumstantial use of character evidence in civil cases, even where closely related to criminal charges. *See Ginter v. Northwestern Mut. Life Ins. Co.,* 576 F.Supp. 627, 629–30 (D. Ky. 1984) ("It seems beyond peradventure of doubt that the drafters of F.R.Evi. 404(a) explicitly intended that all character evidence, except where 'character is at issue' was to be excluded" in civil cases).

The circumstantial use of character evidence is generally discouraged because it carries serious risks of prejudice, confusion and delay. *See Michelson v. United States,* 335 U.S. 469, 476 (1948) ("The overriding policy of excluding such evidence, despite its admitted probative value, is the practical experience that its disallowance tends to prevent confusion of issues, unfair surprise and undue prejudice."). In criminal cases, the so-called "mercy rule" permits a criminal defendant to introduce evidence of pertinent character traits of the defendant and the victim. But that is because the accused, whose liberty is at stake, may need "a counterweight against the strong investigative and prosecutorial resources of the government." C. Mueller & L. Kirkpatrick, *Evidence: Practice Under the Rules,* pp. 264–5 (2d ed. 1999). See also Richard Uviller, *Evidence of Character to Prove Conduct: Illusion, Illogic, and Injustice in the Courtroom*, 130 U. Pa. L. Rev. 845, 855 (1982) (the rule prohibiting circumstantial use of character evidence "was relaxed to allow the criminal defendant with so much at stake and so little available in the way of conventional proof to have special dispensation to tell the factfinder just what sort of person he really is"). Those concerns do not apply to parties in civil cases.

The amendment also clarifies that evidence otherwise admissible under Rule 404(a)(2) may nonetheless be excluded in a criminal case involving sexual misconduct. In such a case, the admissibility of evidence of the victim's sexual behavior and predisposition is governed by the more stringent provisions of Rule 412.

Nothing in the amendment is intended to affect the scope of Rule 404(b). While Rule 404(b) refers to the "accused," the "prosecution," and a "criminal case," it does so only in the context of a notice requirement. The admissibility standards of Rule 404(b) remain fully applicable to both civil and criminal cases.

Changes Made After Publication and Comments. No changes were made to the text of the proposed amendment as released for public comment. A paragraph was added to the Committee Note to state that the amendment does not affect the use of Rule 404(b) in civil cases.

Notes of Advisory Committee on 2011 amendments. The language of Rule 404 has been amended as part of the restyling of the Evidence Rules to make them more easily understood and to make style and terminology consistent throughout the rules. These changes are intended to be stylistic only. There is no intent to change any result in any ruling on evidence admissibility.

Notes of Advisory Committee on 2020 amendments. Rule 404(b) has been amended principally to impose additional notice requirements on the prosecution in a criminal case. In addition, clarifications have been made to the text and headings.

The notice provision has been changed in a number of respects:

• The prosecution must not only identify the evidence that it intends to offer pursuant to the rule but also articulate a non-propensity purpose for which the evidence is offered and the basis for concluding that the evidence is relevant in light of this purpose. The earlier requirement that the prosecution provide notice of only the "general nature" of the evidence was understood by some courts to permit the government to satisfy the notice obligation without describing the specific act that the evidence would tend to prove, and without explaining the relevance of the evidence for a non-propensity purpose. This amendment makes clear what notice is required.

• The pretrial notice must be in writing—which requirement is satisfied by notice in electronic form. See Rule 101(b)(6). Requiring the notice to be in writing provides certainty and reduces arguments about whether notice was actually provided.

• Notice must be provided before trial in such time as to allow the defendant a fair opportunity to meet the evidence, unless the court excuses that requirement upon a showing of good cause. See Rules 609(b), 807, and 902(11). Advance notice of Rule 404(b) evidence is important so that the parties and the court have adequate opportunity to assess the evidence, the purpose for which it is offered, and whether the requirements of Rule 403 have been satisfied—even in cases in which a final determination as to the admissibility of the evidence must await trial. When notice is provided during trial after a finding of good cause, the court may need to consider protective measures to assure that the opponent is not prejudiced. *See, e.g., United States v. Lopez-Gutierrez*, 83 F.3d 1235 (10th Cir. 1996) (notice given at trial due to good cause; the trial court properly made the witness available to the defendant before the bad act evidence was introduced); *United States v. Perez-Tosta,* 36 F.3d 1552 (11th Cir. 1994) (defendant was granted five days to prepare after notice was given, upon good cause, just before voir dire).

• The good cause exception applies not only to the timing of the notice as a whole but also to the timing of the obligations to articulate a non-propensity purpose and the reasoning supporting that purpose. A good cause exception for the timing of the articulation requirements is necessary because in some cases an additional permissible purpose for the evidence may not become clear until just before, or even during, trial.

• Finally, the amendment eliminates the requirement that the defendant must make a request before notice is provided. That requirement is not found in any other notice provision in the Federal Rules of Evidence. It has resulted mostly in boilerplate demands on the one hand, and a trap for the unwary on the other. Moreover, many local rules require the government to provide notice of Rule 404(b) material without regard to whether it has been requested. And in many cases, notice is provided when the government moves in limine for an advance ruling on the admissibility of Rule 404(b) evidence. The request requirement has thus outlived any usefulness it may once have had.

As to the textual clarifications, the word "other" is restored to the location it held before restyling in 2011, to confirm that Rule 404(b) applies to crimes, wrongs and acts "other" than those at issue in the case; and the headings are changed accordingly. No substantive change is intended.

Rule 405. Methods of Proving Character

(a) By Reputation or Opinion. When evidence of a person's character or character trait is admissible, it may be proved by testimony about the person's reputation or by testimony in the form of an opinion. On cross-examination of the character witness, the court may allow an inquiry into relevant specific instances of the person's conduct.

(b) By Specific Instances of Conduct. When a person's character or character trait is an essential element of a charge, claim, or defense, the character or trait may also be proved by relevant specific instances of the person's conduct.

HISTORY:

Jan. 2, 1975, P. L. 93-595, § 1, 88 Stat. 1932; March 2, 1987, eff. Oct. 1, 1987; April 26, 2011, eff. Dec. 1, 2011.

HISTORY; ANCILLARY LAWS AND DIRECTIVES

Other provisions:

Notes of Advisory Committee on Rules. The rule deals only with allowable methods of proving character, not with the admissibility of character evidence, which is covered in Rule 404.

Of the three methods of proving character provided by the rule, evidence of specific instances of conduct is the most convincing. At the same time it possesses the greatest capacity to arouse prejudice, to confuse, to surprise, and to consume time. Consequently the rule confines the use of evidence of this kind to cases in which character is, in the strict sense, in issue and hence deserving of a searching inquiry. When character is used circumstantially and hence occupies a lesser status in the case, proof may be only by reputation and opinion. These latter methods are also available when character is in issue. This treatment is, with respect to specific instances of conduct and reputation, conventional contemporary common law doctrine. McCormick § 153.

In recognizing opinion as a means of proving character, the rule departs from usual contemporary practice in favor of that of an earlier day. See 7 Wigmore § 1986, pointing out that the earlier practice permitted opinion and arguing strongly for evidence based on personal knowledge and belief as contrasted with "the secondhand, irresponsible product of multiplied guesses and gossip which we term 'reputation'." It seems likely that the persistence of reputation evidence is due to its largely being opinion in disguise. Traditionally character has been regarded primarily in moral overtones of good and bad: chaste, peaceable, truthful, honest. Nevertheless, on occasion nonmoral considerations crop up, as in the case of the incompetent driver, and this seems bound to happen increasingly. If character is defined as the kind of person one is, then account must be taken of varying ways of arriving at the estimate. These may range from the opinion of the employer who has found the man honest to the opinion of the psychiatrist based upon examination and testing. No effective dividing line exists between character and mental capacity, and the latter traditionally has been provable by opinion.

According to the great majority of cases, on cross-examination inquiry is allowable as to whether the reputation witness has heard of particular instances of conduct pertinent to the trait in question. *Michelson v. United States*, 335 U.S. 469, 69 S.Ct. 213, 93 L.Ed. 168 (1948); Annot., 47 A.L.R.2d 1258. The theory is that, since the reputation witness relates what he has heard, the inquiry tends to shed light on the accuracy of his hearing and reporting. Accordingly, the opinion witness would be asked whether he knew, as well as whether he had heard. The fact is, of course, that these distinctions are of slight if any practical significance, and the second sentence of subdivision (a) eliminates them as a factor in formulating questions. This recognition of the propriety of inquiring into specific instances of conduct does not circumscribe inquiry otherwise into the bases of opinion and reputation testimony.

The express allowance of inquiry into specific instances of conduct on cross-examination in subdivision (a) and the express allowance of it as part of a case in chief when character is actually in issue in subdivision (b) contemplate that testimony of specific instances is not generally permissible on the direct examination of an ordinary opinion witness to character. Similarly as to witnesses to the character of witnesses under Rule 608(b). Opinion testimony on direct in these situations ought in general to correspond to reputation testimony as now given, *i.e.*, be confined to the nature and extent of observation and acquaintance upon which the opinion is based. See Rule 701.

Notes of Committee on the Judiciary, House Report No. 93-650. Rule 405(a) as submitted proposed to change existing law by allowing evidence of character in the form of opinion as well as reputation testimony. Fearing, among other reasons, that wholesale allowance of opinion testimony might tend to turn a trial into a swearing contest between conflicting character witnesses, the Committee decided to delete from this Rule, as well as from Rule 608(a) which involves a related problem, reference to opinion testimony.

Notes of Conference Committee, House Report No. 93-1597. The Senate makes two language changes in the nature of conforming amendments. The Conference adopts the Senate amendments.

Notes of Advisory Committee on 1987 amendments. The amendment is technical. No substantive change is intended.

Notes of Advisory Committee on 2011 amendments. The language of Rule 405 has been amended as part of the restyling of the Evidence Rules to make them more easily understood and to make style and terminology consistent throughout the rules. These changes are intended to be stylistic only. There is no intent to change any result in any ruling on evidence admissibility.

Rule 406. Habit; Routine Practice

Evidence of a person's habit or an organization's routine practice may be admitted to prove that on a particular occasion the person or organization acted in accordance with the habit or routine practice. The court may admit this evidence regardless of whether it is corroborated or whether there was an eyewitness.

HISTORY:

Jan. 2, 1975, P. L. 93-595, § 1, 88 Stat. 1932; April 26, 2011, eff. Dec. 1, 2011.

HISTORY; ANCILLARY LAWS AND DIRECTIVES

Other provisions:

Notes of Advisory Committee on Rules. An oft-quoted paragraph, McCormick, § 162, p. 340, describes habit in terms effectively contrasting it with character:

"Character and habit are close akin. Character is a generalized description of one's disposition, or of one's disposition in respect to a general trait, such as honesty, temperance, or peacefulness. 'Habit,' in modern usage, both lay and psychological, is more specific. It describes one's regular response to a repeated specific situation. If we speak of character for care, we think of the person's tendency to act prudently in all the varying situations of life, in business, family life, in handling automobiles and in walking across the street. A habit, on the other hand, is the person's regular practice of meeting a particular kind of situation with a specific type of conduct, such as the habit of going down a particular stairway two stairs at a time, or of giving the hand-signal for a left turn, or of alighting from railway cars while they are moving. The doing of the habitual acts may become semi-automatic."

Equivalent behavior on the part of a group is designated "routine practice of an organization" in the rule.

Agreement is general that habit evidence is highly persuasive as proof of conduct on a particular occasion. Again quoting McCormick § 162, p. 341:

"Character may be thought of as the sum of one's habits though doubtless it is more than this. But unquestionably the uniformity of one's response to habit is far greater than the consistency with which one's conduct conforms to character or disposition. Even though character comes in only exceptionally as evidence of an act, surely any sensible man in investigating whether X did a particular act would be greatly helped in his inquiry by evidence as to whether he was in the habit of doing it."

When disagreement has appeared, its focus has been upon the question what constitutes habit, and the reason for this is readily apparent. The extent to which instances must be multiplied and consistency of behavior maintained in order to rise to the status of habit inevitably gives rise to differences of opinion. Lewan, Rationale of Habit Evidence, 16 Syracuse L.Rev. 39, 49 (1964). While adequacy of sampling and uniformity of response are key factors, precise standards for measuring their sufficiency for evidence purposes cannot be formulated.

The rule is consistent with prevailing views. Much evidence is excluded simply because of failure to achieve the status of habit. Thus, evidence of intemperate "habits" is generally excluded when offered as proof of drunkenness in accident cases, Annot., 46 A.L.R.2d 103, and evidence of other assaults is inadmissible to prove the instant one in a civil assault action, Annot., 66 A.L.R.2d 806. In *Levin v. United States*, 119 U.S.App.D.C. 156, 338 F.2d 265 (1964), testimony as to the religious "habits" of the accused, offered as tending to prove that he was at home observing the Sabbath rather than out obtaining money through larceny by trick, was held properly excluded;

"It seems apparent to us that an individual's religious practices would not be the type of activities which would lend themselves to the characterization of 'invariable regularity.' [1 Wigmore 520.] Certainly the very volitional basis of the activity raises serious questions as to its invariable nature, and hence its probative value." *Id.* at 272.

These rulings are not inconsistent with the trend towards admitting evidence of business transactions between one of the parties and a third person as tending to prove that he made the same bargain or proposal in the litigated situation. Slough, Relevancy Unraveled, 6 Kan.L-.Rev. 38–41 (1957). Nor are they inconsistent with such cases as *Whittemore v. Lockheed Aircraft Corp.*, 65 Cal.App.2d 737, 151 P.2d 670 (1944), upholding the admission of evidence that plaintiff's intestate had on four other occasions flown planes from defendant's factory for delivery to his employer airline, offered to prove that he was piloting rather than a guest on a plane which crashed and killed all on board while en route for delivery.

A considerable body of authority has required that evidence of the routine practice of an organization be corroborated as a condition precedent to its admission in evidence. Slough, Relevancy Unraveled, 5 Kan.L.Rev. 404, 449 (1957). This requirement is specifically rejected by the rule on the ground that it relates to the sufficiency of the evidence rather than admissibility. A similar position is taken in New Jersey Rule 49. The rule also rejects the requirement of the absence of eyewitnesses, sometimes encountered with respect to admitting habit evidence to prove freedom from contributory negligence in wrongful death cases. For comment critical of the requirements see *Frank, J., in Cereste v. New York, N.H. & H.R. Co.*, 231 F.2d 50 (2d Cir. 1956), cert. denied 351 U.S. 951, 76 S.Ct. 848, 100 L.Ed 1475, 10 Vand.L.Rev. 447 (1957); McCormick § 162, p. 342. The omission of the requirement from the California Evidence Code is said to have effected its elimination. Comment, Cal.Ev.Code § 1105.

Notes of Advisory Committee on 2011 amendments. The language of Rule 406 has been amended as part of the restyling of the Evidence Rules to make them more easily understood and to make style and terminology consistent throughout the rules. These changes are intended to be stylistic only. There is no intent to change any result in any ruling on evidence admissibility.

Rule 407. Subsequent Remedial Measures

When measures are taken that would have made an earlier injury or harm less likely to occur, evidence of the subsequent measures is not admissible to prove:

- negligence;
- culpable conduct;
- a defect in a product or its design; or
- a need for a warning or instruction.

But the court may admit this evidence for another purpose, such as impeachment or—if disputed—proving ownership, control, or the feasibility of precautionary measures.

HISTORY:

Jan. 2, 1975, P. L. 93-595, § 1, 88 Stat. 1932; April 11, 1997, eff. Dec. 1, 1997; April 26, 2011, eff. Dec. 1, 2011.

HISTORY; ANCILLARY LAWS AND DIRECTIVES

Other provisions:

Notes of Advisory Committee on Rules. The rule incorporates conventional doctrine which excludes evidence of subsequent remedial measures as proof of an admission of fault. The rule rests on two grounds. (1) The conduct is not in fact an admission, since the conduct is equally consistent with injury by mere accident or through contributory negligence. Or, as Baron Bramwell put it, the rule rejects the notion that "because the world gets wiser as it gets older, therefore it was foolish before." *Hart v. Lancashire & Yorkshire Ry. Co.,* 21 L.T.R. N.S. 261, 263 (1869). Under a liberal theory of relevancy this ground alone would not support exclusion as the inference is still a possible one. (2) The other, and more impressive, ground for exclusion rests on a social policy of encouraging people to take, or at least not discouraging them from taking, steps in furtherance of added safety. The courts have applied this principle to exclude evidence of subsequent repairs, installation of safety devices, changes in company rules, and discharge of employees, and the language of the present rules is broad enough to encompass all of them. See Falknor, Extrinsic Policies Affecting Admissibility, 10 Rutgers L.Rev. 574, 590 (1956).

The second sentence of the rule directs attention to the limitations of the rule. Exclusion is called for only when the evidence of subsequent remedial measures is offered as proof of negligence or culpable conduct. In effect it rejects the suggested inference that fault is admitted. Other purposes are, however, allowable, including ownership or control, existence of duty, and feasibility of precautionary measures, if controverted, and impeachment. 2 Wigmore § 283; Annot., 64 A.L.R.2d 1296. Two recent federal cases are illustrative. *Boeing Airplane Co. v. Brown,* 291 F.2d 310 (9th Cir. 1961), an action against an airplane manufacturer for using an allegedly defectively designed alternator shaft which caused a plane crash, upheld the admission of evidence of subsequent design modification for the purpose of showing that design changes and safeguards were feasible. And *Powers v. J. B. Michael & Co.,* 329 F.2d 674 (6th Cir. 1964), an action against a road contractor for negligent failure to put out warning signs, sustained the admission of evidence that defendant subsequently put out signs to show that the portion of the road in question was under defendant's control. The requirement that the other purpose be controverted calls for automatic exclusion unless a genuine issue be present and allows the opposing party to lay the groundwork for exclusion by making an admission. Otherwise the factors of undue prejudice, confusion of issues, misleading the jury, and waste of time remain for consideration under Rule 403.

For comparable rules, see Uniform Rule 51; California Evidence Code § 1151; Kansas Code of Civil Procedure § 60-451; New Jersey Evidence Rule 51.

Notes of Advisory Committee on 1997 amendments. The amendment to Rule 407 makes two changes in the rule. First, the words "an injury or harm allegedly caused by" were added to clarify that the rule applies only to changes made after the occurrence that produced the damages giving rise to the action. Evidence of measures taken by the defendant prior to the "event" causing "injury or harm" do not fall within the exclusionary scope of Rule 407 even if they occurred after the manufacture or design of the product. See *Chase v. General Motors Corp.*, 856 F.2d 17, 21–22 (4th Cir. 1988).

Second, Rule 407 has been amended to provide that evidence of subsequent remedial measures may not be used to prove "a defect in a product or its design, or that a warning or instruction should have accompanied a product." This amendment adopts the view of a majority of the circuits that have interpreted Rule 407 to apply to products liability actions. See *Raymond v. Raymond Corp.*, 938 F.2d 1518, 1522 (1st Cir. 1991); *In re Joint Eastern District and Southern District Asbestos Litigation v. Armstrong World Industries, Inc.*, 995 F.2d 343 (2d Cir. 1993); *Cann v. Ford Motor Co.*, 658 F.2d 54, 60 (2d Cir. 1981), cert. denied, 456 U.S. 960 (1982); *Kelly v. Crown Equipment Co.*, 970 F.2d 1273, 1275 (3d Cir. 1992); *Werner v. Upjohn, Inc.*, 628 F.2d 848 (4th Cir. 1980), cert. denied, 449 U.S. 1080 (1981); *Grenada Steel Industries. Inc. v. Alabama Oxygen Co.*, Inc., 695 F.2d 883 (5th Cir. 1983); *Bauman v. Volkswagenwerk Aktiengesellschaft*, 621 F.2d 230, 232 (6th Cir. 1980); *Flaminio v. Honda Motor Company. Ltd.*, 733 F.2d 463, 469 (7th Cir. 1984); *Gauthier v. AMF. Inc.*, 788 F.2d 634, 636–37 (9th Cir. 1986).

Although this amendment adopts a uniform federal rule, it should be noted that evidence of subsequent remedial measures may be admissible pursuant to the second sentence of Rule 407. Evidence of subsequent measures that is not barred by Rule 407 may still be subject to exclusion on Rule 403 grounds when the dangers of prejudice or confusion substantially outweigh the probative value of the evidence.

GAP Report on Rule 407. The words "injury or harm" were substituted for the word "event" in line 3. The stylization changes in the second sentence of the rule were eliminated. The words "causing 'injury or harm'" were added to the Committee Note.

Notes of Advisory Committee on 2011 amendments. The language of Rule 407 has been amended as part of the general restyling of the Evidence Rules to make them more easily understood and to make style and terminology consistent throughout the rules. These changes are intended to be stylistic only. There is no intent to change any result in any ruling on evidence admissibility.

Rule 407 previously provided that evidence was not excluded if offered for a purpose not explicitly prohibited by the Rule. To improve the language of the Rule, it now provides that the court may admit evidence if offered for a permissible purpose. There is no intent to change the process for admitting evidence covered by the Rule. It remains the case that if offered for an impermissible purpose, it must be excluded, and if offered for a purpose not barred by the Rule, its admissibility remains governed by the general principles of Rules 402, 403, 801, etc.

Rule 408. Compromise Offers and Negotiations

(a) Prohibited Uses. Evidence of the following is not admissible—on behalf of any party—either to prove or disprove the validity or amount of a disputed claim or to impeach by a prior inconsistent statement or a contradiction:

(1) furnishing, promising, or offering—or accepting, promising to accept, or offering to accept—a valuable consideration in compromising or attempting to compromise the claim; and

(2) conduct or a statement made during compromise negotiations about the claim—except when offered in a criminal case and when the negotiations related to a claim by a public office in the exercise of its regulatory, investigative, or enforcement authority.

(b) Exceptions. The court may admit this evidence for another purpose, such as proving a witness's bias or prejudice, negating a contention of undue delay, or proving an effort to obstruct a criminal investigation or prosecution.

HISTORY:

Jan. 2, 1975, P. L. 93-595, § 1, 88 Stat. 1933; April 12, 2006, eff. Dec. 1, 2006; April 26, 2011, eff. Dec. 1, 2011.

HISTORY; ANCILLARY LAWS AND DIRECTIVES

Other provisions:

Notes of Advisory Committee on Rules. As a matter of general agreement, evidence of an offer to compromise a claim is not receivable in evidence as an admission of, as the case may be, the validity or invalidity of the claim. As with evidence of subsequent remedial measures, dealt with in Rule 407, exclusion may be based on two grounds. (1) The evidence is irrelevant, since the offer may be motivated by a desire for peace rather than from any concession of weakness of position. The validity of this position will vary as the amount of the offer varies in relation to the size of the claim and may also be influenced by other circumstances. (2) a more consistently impressive ground is promotion of the public policy favoring the compromise and settlement of disputes. McCormick §§ 76, 251. While the rule is ordinarily phrased in terms of offers of compromise, it is apparent that a similar attitude must be taken with respect to completed compromises when offered against a party thereto. This latter situation will not, of course, ordinarily occur except when a party to the present litigation has compromised with a third person.

The same policy underlies the provision of Rule 68 of the Federal Rules of Civil Procedure that evidence of an unaccepted offer of judgment is not admissible except in a proceeding to determine costs.

The practical value of the common law rule has been greatly diminished by its inapplicability to admissions of fact, even though made in the course of compromise negotiations, unless hypothetical, stated to be "without prejudice," or so connected with the offer as to be inseparable from it. McCormick § 251, pp. 540–541. An inevitable effect is to inhibit freedom of communication with respect to compromise, even among lawyers. Another effect is the generation of controversy over whether a given statement falls within or without the protected area. These considerations account for the expansion of the rule herewith to include evidence of conduct or statements made in compromise negotiations, as well as the offer or completed compromise itself. For similar provisions see California Evidence Code §§ 1152, 1154.

The policy considerations which underlie the rule do not come into play when the effort is to induce a creditor to settle an admittedly due amount for a lessor sum. McCormick § 251, p. 540. Hence the rule requires that the claim be disputed as to either validity or amount.

The final sentence of the rule serves to point out some limitations upon its applicability. Since the rule excludes only when the purpose is proving the validity or invalidity of the claim or its amount, an offer for another purpose is not within the rule. The illustrative situations mentioned in the rule are supported by the authorities. As to proving bias or prejudice of a witness, see Annot., 161 A.L.R. 395, contra, *Fenberg v. Rosenthal*, 348 Ill. App. 510, 109 N.E.2d 402 (1952), and negativing a contention of lack of due diligence in presenting a claim, 4 Wigmore § 1061. An effort to "buy off" the prosecution or a prosecuting witness in a criminal case is not within the policy of the rule of exclusion. McCormick § 251, p. 542.

For other rules of similar import, see Uniform Rules 52 and 53; California Evidence Code § 1152, 1154; Kansas Code of Civil Procedure §§ 60-452, 60-453; New Jersey Evidence Rules 52 and 53.

Notes of Committee on the Judiciary, House Report No. 93-650. Under existing federal law evidence of conduct and statements made in compromise negotiations is admissible in subsequent litigation between the parties. The second sentence of Rule 408 as submitted by the Supreme Court proposed to reverse that doctrine in the interest of further promoting non-judicial settlement of disputes. Some agencies of government expressed the view that the Court formulation was likely to impede rather than assist efforts to achieve settlement of disputes. For one thing, it is not always easy to tell when compromise negotiations begin, and informal dealings end. Also, parties dealing with government agencies would be reluctant to furnish factual information at preliminary meetings; they would wait until "compromise negotiations" began and thus hopefully effect an immunity for themselves with respect to the evidence supplied. In light of these considerations, the Committee recast the Rule so that admissions of liability or opinions given during compromise negotiations continue inadmissible, but evidence of unqualified factual assertions is admissible. The latter aspect of the Rule is drafted, however, so as to preserve other possible objections to the introduction of such evidence. The Committee intends no modification of current law whereby a party may protect himself from future use of his statements by couching them in hypothetical conditional form.

Notes of Committee on the Judiciary, Senate Report No. 93-1277. This rule as reported makes evidence of settlement or attempted settlement of a disputed claim inadmissible when offered as an admission of liability or the amount of liability. The purpose of this rule is to encourage settlements which would be discouraged if such evidence were admissible.

Under present law, in most jurisdictions, statements of fact made during settlement negotiations, however, are excepted from this ban and are admissible. The only escape from admissibility of statements of fact made in a settlement negotiation as if the declarant or his representative expressly states that the statement is hypothetical in nature or is made without prejudice. Rule 408 as submitted by the Court reversed the traditional rule. It would have brought statements of fact within the ban and made them, as well as an offer of settlement, inadmissible.

The House amended the rule and would continue to make evidence of facts disclosed during compromise negotiations admissible. It thus reverted to the traditional rule. The House committee report states that the committee intends to preserve current law under which a party may protect himself by couching his statements in hypothetical form [See House Report No. 93-650 above]. The real impact of this amendment, however, is to deprive the rule of much of its salutary effect. The exception for factual admissions was believed by the Advisory Committee to hamper free communication between parties and thus to constitute an unjustifiable restraint upon efforts to negotiate settlements—the encouragement of which is the purpose of the rule. Further, by protecting hypothetically phrased statements, it constituted a preference for the sophisticated, and a trap for the unwary.

Three States which had adopted rules of evidence patterned after the proposed rules prescribed by the Supreme

Court opted for versions of rule 408 identical with the Supreme Court draft with respect to the inadmissibility of conduct or statements made in compromise negotiations. [Nev. Rev. Stats. § 48.105; N. Mex. Stats. Anno. (1973 Supp.) § 20-4-408; West's Wis. Stats. Anno. (1973 Supp.) § 904.08].

For these reasons, the committee has deleted the House amendment and restored the rule to the version submitted by the Supreme Court with one additional amendment. This amendment adds a sentence to insure that evidence, such as documents, is not rendered inadmissible merely because it is presented in the course of compromise negotiations if the evidence is otherwise discoverable. A party should not be able to immunize from admissibility documents otherwise discoverable merely by offering them in a compromise negotiation.

Notes of Conference Committee, House Report No. 93-1597. The House bill provides that evidence of admissions of liability or opinions given during compromise negotiations is not admissible, but that evidence of facts disclosed during compromise negotiations is not inadmissible by virtue of having been first disclosed in the compromise negotiations. The Senate amendment provides that evidence of conduct or statements made in compromise negotiations is not admissible. The Senate amendment also provides that the rule does not require the exclusion of any evidence otherwise discoverable merely because it is presented in the course of compromise negotiations.

The House bill was drafted to meet the objection of executive agencies that under the rule as proposed by the Supreme Court, a party could present a fact during compromise negotiations and thereby prevent an opposing party from offering evidence of that fact at trial even though such evidence was obtained from independent sources. The Senate amendment expressly precludes this result.

The Conference adopts the Senate amendment.

Notes of Advisory Committee on 2006 amendments. Rule 408 has been amended to settle some questions in the courts about the scope of the Rule, and to make it easier to read. First, the amendment provides that Rule 408 does not prohibit the introduction in a criminal case of statements or conduct during compromise negotiations regarding a civil dispute by a government regulatory, investigative, or enforcement agency. *See, e.g., United States v. Prewitt,* 34 F.3d 436, 439 (7th Cir. 1994) (admissions of fault made in compromise of a civil securities enforcement action were admissible against the accused in a subsequent criminal action for mail fraud). Where an individual makes a statement in the presence of government agents, its subsequent admission in a criminal case should not be unexpected. The individual can seek to protect against subsequent disclosure through negotiation and agreement with the civil regulator or an attorney for the government.

Statements made in compromise negotiations of a claim by a government agency may be excluded in criminal cases where the circumstances so warrant under Rule 403. For example, if an individual was unrepresented at the time the statement was made in a civil enforcement proceeding, its probative value in a subsequent criminal case may be minimal. But there is no absolute exclusion imposed by Rule 408.

In contrast, statements made during compromise negotiations of other disputed claims are not admissible in subsequent criminal litigation, when offered to prove liability for, invalidity of, or amount of those claims. When private parties enter into compromise negotiations they cannot protect against the subsequent use of statements in criminal cases by way of private ordering. The inability to guarantee protection against subsequent use could lead to parties refusing to admit fault, even if by doing so they could favorably settle the private matter. Such a chill on settlement negotiations would be contrary to the policy of Rule 408.

The amendment distinguishes statements and conduct (such as a direct admission of fault) made in compromise negotiations of a civil claim by a government agency from an offer or acceptance of a compromise of such a claim. An offer or acceptance of a compromise of any civil claim is excluded under the Rule if offered against the defendant as an admission of fault. In that case, the predicate for the evidence would be that the defendant, by compromising with the government agency, has admitted the validity and amount of the civil claim, and that this admission has sufficient probative value to be considered as evidence of guilt. But unlike a direct statement of fault, an offer or acceptance of a compromise is not very probative of the defendant's guilt. Moreover, admitting such an offer or acceptance could deter a defendant from settling a civil regulatory action, for fear of evidentiary use in a subsequent criminal action. *See, e.g.,* Fishman, *Jones on Evidence, Civil and Criminal,* § 22:16 at 199, n. 83 (7th ed. 2000) ("A target of a potential criminal investigation may be unwilling to settle civil claims against him if by doing so he increases the risk of prosecution and conviction.").

The amendment retains the language of the original rule that bars compromise evidence only when offered as evidence of the "validity," "invalidity," or "amount" of the disputed claim. The intent is to retain the extensive case law finding Rule 408 inapplicable when compromise evidence is offered for a purpose other than to prove the validity, invalidity, or amount of a disputed claim. *See, e.g., Athey v. Farmers Ins. Exchange,* 234 F.3d 357 (8th Cir. 2000) (evidence of settlement offer by insurer was properly admitted to prove insurer's bad faith); *Coakley & Williams v. Structural Concrete Equip.,* 973 F.2d 349 (4th Cir. 1992) (evidence of settlement is not precluded by Rule 408 where offered to prove a party's intent with respect to the scope of a release); *Cates v. Morgan Portable Bldg. Corp.,* 708 F.2d 683 (7th Cir. 1985) (Rule 408 does not bar evidence of a settlement when offered to prove a breach of the settlement agreement, as the purpose of the evidence is to prove the fact of settlement as opposed to the validity or amount of the underlying claim); *Uforma/Shelby Bus. Forms, Inc. v. NLRB,* 111 F.3d 1284 (6th Cir. 1997) (threats made in settlement negotiations were admissible; Rule 408 is inapplicable when the claim is based upon a wrong that is committed during the course of settlement negotiations). So for example, Rule 408 is inapplicable if offered to show that a party made fraudulent statements in order to settle a litigation.

The amendment does not affect the case law providing that Rule 408 is inapplicable when evidence of the compromise is offered to prove notice. *See, e.g., United States v. Austin,* 54 F.3d 394 (7th Cir. 1995) (no error to admit evidence of the defendant's settlement with the FTC, because it was offered to prove that the defendant was on notice that subsequent similar conduct was wrongful); *Spell v. McDaniel,* 824 F.2d 1380 (4th Cir. 1987) (in a civil rights action alleging that an officer used excessive force, a prior settlement by the City of another brutality claim was properly admitted to prove that the City was on notice of aggressive behavior by police officers).

The amendment prohibits the use of statements made in settlement negotiations when offered to impeach by prior inconsistent statement or through contradiction. Such broad impeachment would tend to swallow the exclusionary rule and would impair the public policy of promoting settlements. *See McCormick on Evidence* at 186 (5th ed. 1999) ("Use of statements made in compromise negotiations to impeach the testimony of a party, which is not specifically treated in Rule 408, is fraught with danger of misuse of the statements to prove liability, threatens frank interchange of information during negotiations, and generally should not be permitted."). *See also EEOC v. Gear Petroleum, Inc.,* 948 F.2d 1542 (10th Cir. 1991) (letter sent as part of settlement negotiation cannot be used to impeach defense witnesses by way of contradiction or prior inconsistent statement; such broad impeachment would undermine the policy of encouraging uninhibited settlement negotiations).

The amendment makes clear that Rule 408 excludes compromise evidence even when a party seeks to admit its own settlement offer or statements made in settlement negotiations. If a party were to reveal its own statement or offer, this could itself reveal the fact that the adversary entered into settlement negotiations. The protections of Rule 408 cannot be waived unilaterally because the Rule, by definition, protects both parties from having the fact of negotiation disclosed to the jury. Moreover, proof of statements and offers made in settlement would often have to be made through the testimony of attorneys, leading to the risks and costs of disqualification. *See generally Pierce v. F.R. Tripler & Co.,* 955 F.2d 820, 828 (2d Cir. 1992) (settlement offers are excluded under Rule 408 even if it is the offeror who seeks to admit them; noting that the "widespread admissibility of the substance of settlement offers could bring with it a rash of motions for disqualification of a party's chosen counsel who would likely become a witness at trial").

The sentence of the Rule referring to evidence "otherwise discoverable" has been deleted as superfluous. *See, e.g.,* Advisory Committee Note to Maine Rule of Evidence 408 (refusing to include the sentence in the Maine version of Rule 408 and noting that the sentence "seems to state what the law would be if it were omitted"); Advisory Committee Note to Wyoming Rule of Evidence 408 (refusing to include the sentence in Wyoming Rule 408 on the ground that it was "superfluous"). The intent of the sentence was to prevent a party from trying to immunize admissible information, such as a pre-existing document, through the pretense of disclosing it during compromise negotiations. *See Ramada Development Co. v. Rauch,* 644 F.2d 1097 (5th Cir. 1981). But even without the sentence, the Rule cannot be read to protect pre-existing information simply because it was presented to the adversary in compromise negotiations.

Changes Made After Publication and Comments. In response to public comment, the proposed amendment was changed to provide that statements and conduct during settlement negotiations are to be admissible in subsequent criminal litigation only when made during settlement discussions of a claim brought by a government regulatory agency. Stylistic changes were made in accordance with suggestions from the Style Subcommittee of the Standing Committee. The Committee Note was altered to accord with the change in the text, and also to clarify that fraudulent statements made during settlement negotiations are not protected by the Rule.

Notes of Advisory Committee on 2011 amendments. The language of Rule 408 has been amended as part of the general restyling of the Evidence Rules to make them more easily understood and to make style and terminology consistent throughout the rules. These changes are intended to be stylistic only. There is no intent to change any result in any ruling on evidence admissibility.

Rule 408 previously provided that evidence was not excluded if offered for a purpose not explicitly prohibited by the Rule. To improve the language of the Rule, it now provides that the court may admit evidence if offered for a permissible purpose. There is no intent to change the process for admitting evidence covered by the Rule. It remains the case that if offered for an impermissible purpose, it must be excluded, and if offered for a purpose not barred by the Rule, its admissibility remains governed by the general principles of Rules 402, 403, 801, etc.

The Committee deleted the reference to "liability" on the ground that the deletion makes the Rule flow better and easier to read, and because "liability" is covered by the broader term "validity." Courts have not made substantive decisions on the basis of any distinction between validity and liability. No change in current practice or in the coverage of the Rule is intended.

Rule 409. Offers to Pay Medical and Similar Expenses

Evidence of furnishing, promising to pay, or offering to pay medical, hospital, or similar expenses resulting from an injury is not admissible to prove liability for the injury.

HISTORY:

Jan. 2, 1975, P. L. 93-595, § 1, 88 Stat. 1933; April 26, 2011, eff. Dec. 1, 2011.

HISTORY; ANCILLARY LAWS AND DIRECTIVES

Other provisions:

Notes of Advisory Committee on Rules. The considerations underlying this rule parallel those underlying Rules 407 and 408, which deal respectively with subsequent remedial measures and offers of compromise. As stated in Annot., 20 A.L.R.2d 291, 293:

"[G]enerally, evidence of payment of medical, hospital, or similar expenses of an injured party by the opposing party, is not admissible, the reason often given being that such payment or offer is usually made from humane impulses and not from an admission of liability, and that to hold otherwise would tend to discourage assistance to the injured person."

Contrary to Rule 408, dealing with offers of compromise, the present rule does not extend to conduct or statements not a part of the act of furnishing or offering or promising to pay. This difference in treatment arises from fundamental differences in nature. Communication is essential if compromises are to be effected, and consequently broad protection of statements is needed. This is not so in cases of payments or offers or promises to pay medical expenses, where factual statements may be expected to be incidental in nature.

For rules on the same subject, but phrased in terms of "humanitarian motives," see Uniform Rule 52; California Evidence Code § 1152; Kansas Code of Civil Procedure § 60-452; New Jersey Evidence Rule 52.

Notes of Advisory Committee on 2011 amendments. The language of Rule 409 has been amended as part of the restyling of the Evidence Rules to make them more easily understood and to make style and terminology consistent throughout the rules. These changes are intended to be stylistic only. There is no intent to change any result in any ruling on evidence admissibility.

Rule 410. Pleas, Plea Discussions, and Related Statements

(a) Prohibited Uses. In a civil or criminal case, evidence of the following is not admissible against the defendant who made the plea or participated in the plea discussions:

(1) a guilty plea that was later withdrawn;

(2) a nolo contendere plea;

(3) a statement made during a proceeding on either of those pleas under Federal Rule of Criminal Procedure 11 or a comparable state procedure; or

(4) a statement made during plea discussions with an attorney for the prosecuting authority if the discussions did not result in a guilty plea or they resulted in a later-withdrawn guilty plea.

(b) Exceptions. The court may admit a statement described in Rule 410(a)(3) or (4):

(1) in any proceeding in which another statement made during the same plea or plea discussions has been introduced, if in fairness the statements ought to be considered together; or

(2) in a criminal proceeding for perjury or false statement, if the defendant made the statement under oath, on the record, and with counsel present.

HISTORY:

Jan. 2, 1975, P. L. 93-595, § 1, 88 Stat. 1933; Dec. 12, 1975, P. L. 94-149, § 1(9), 89 Stat. 805; April 30, 1979, eff. Dec. 1, 1980; April 26, 2011, eff. Dec. 1, 2011.

HISTORY; ANCILLARY LAWS AND DIRECTIVES

Other provisions:

Notes of Advisory Committee on Rules. Withdrawn pleas of guilty were held inadmissible in federal prosecutions in *Kercheval v. United States*, 274 U.S. 220, 47 S.Ct. 582, 71 L.Ed. 1009 (1927). The Court pointed out that to admit the withdrawn plea would effectively set at naught the allowance of withdrawal and place the accused in a dilemma utterly inconsistent with the decision to award him a trial. The New York Court of Appeals, in *People v. Spitaleri*, 9 N.Y.2d 168, 212 N.Y.S.2d 53, 173 N.E.2d 35 (1961), reexamined and overturned its earlier decisions which had allowed admission. In addition to the reasons set forth in Kercheval, which was quoted at length, the court pointed out that the effect of admitting the plea was to compel defendant to take the stand by way of explanation and to open the way for the prosecution to call the lawyer who had represented him at the time of entering the plea. State court decisions for and against admissibility are collected in Annot., 86 A.L.R.2d 326.

Pleas of *nolo contendere* are recognized by Rule 11 of the Rules of Criminal Procedure, although the law of numerous States is to the contrary. The present rule gives effect to the principal traditional characteristic of the *nolo* plea, i.e., avoiding the admission of guilt which is inherent in pleas of guilty. This position is consistent with the construction of Section 5 of the Clayton Act, 15 U.S.C. § 16(a), recognizing the inconclusive and compromise nature of judgments based on *nolo* pleas. *General Electric Co. v. City of San Antonio*, 334 F.2d 480 (5th Cir. 1964); *Commonwealth Edison Co. v. Allis-Chalmers Mfg. Co.*, 323 F.2d 412 (7th Cir. 1963), cert. denied 376 U.S. 939, 84 S.Ct. 794, 11 L.Ed.2d 659; *Armco Steel Corp. v. North Dakota*, 376 F.2d 206 (8th Cir. 1967); *City of Burbank v. General Electric Co.*, 329 F.2d 825 (9th Cir. 1964). See also state court decisions in Annot., 18 A.L.R.2d 1287, 1314.

Exclusion of offers to plead guilty or *nolo* has as its purpose the promotion of disposition of criminal cases by compromise. As pointed out in McCormick § 251, p. 543.

"Effective criminal law administration in many localities would hardly be possible if a large proportion of the charges were not disposed of by such compromises."

See also *People v. Hamilton*, 60 Cal.2d 105, 32 Cal.Rptr. 4, 383 P.2d 412 (1963), discussing legislation designed to achieve this result. As with compromise offers generally, Rule 408, free communication is needed, and security against having an offer of compromise or related statement admitted in evidence effectively encourages it.

Limiting the exclusionary rule to use against the accused is consistent with the purpose of the rule, since the possibility of use for or against other persons will not impair the effectiveness of withdrawing pleas or the freedom of discussion which the rule is designed to foster. See A.B.A. Standards Relating to Pleas of Guilty § 2.2 (1968). See also the narrower provisions of New Jersey Evidence Rule 52(2) and the unlimited exclusion provided in California Evidence Code § 1153.

Notes of Committee on the Judiciary, House Report No. 93-650. The Committee added the phrase "Except as otherwise provided by Act of Congress" to Rule 410 as submitted by the Court in order to preserve particular congressional policy judgments as to the effect of a plea of guilty or of nolo contendere. See 15 U.S.C. 16(a). The Committee intends that its amendment refers to both present statutes and statutes subsequently enacted.

Notes of the Committee on the Judiciary, Senate Report No. 93-1277. As adopted by the House, rule 410 would make inadmissible pleas of guilty or nolo contendere subsequently withdrawn as well as offers to make such pleas. Such a rule is clearly justified as a means of encouraging pleading. However, the House rule would then go on to render inadmissible for any purpose statements made in connection with these pleas or offers as well.

The committee finds this aspect of the House rule unjustified. Of course, in certain circumstances such statements should be excluded. If, for example, a plea is vitiated because of coercion, statements made in connection with the plea may also have been coerced and should be inadmissible on that basis. In other cases, however, voluntary statements of an accused made in court on the record, in connection with a plea, and determined by a court to be reliable should be admissible even though the plea is subsequently withdrawn. This is particularly true in those cases where, if the House rule were in effect, a defendant would be able to contradict his previous statements and thereby lie with impunity [See *Harris v: New York*, 401 U.S. 222 (1971)]. To prevent such an injustice, the rule has been modified to permit the use of such statements for the limited purposes of impeachment and in subsequent perjury or false statement prosecutions.

Notes of Conference Committee, House Report No. 93-1597. The House bill provides that evidence of a guilty or nolo contendere plea, of an offer of either plea, or of statements made in connection with such pleas or offers of such pleas, is inadmissible in any civil or criminal action, case or proceeding against the person making such plea or offer. The Senate amendment makes the rule inapplicable to a voluntary and reliable statement made in court on the record where the statement is offered in a subsequent prosecution of the declarant for perjury or false statement.

The issues raised by Rule 410 are also raised by proposed Rule 11(e)(6) of the Federal Rules of Criminal Procedure presently pending before Congress. This proposed rule, which deals with the admissibility of pleas of guilty or nolo contendere, offers to make such pleas, and statements made in connection with such pleas, was promulgated by the Supreme Court on April 22, 1974, and in the absence of congressional action will become effective on August 1, 1975. The conferees intend to make no change in the presently-existing case law until that date, leaving the courts free to develop rules in this area on a case-by-case basis.

The Conferees further determined that the issues presented by the use of guilty and nolo contendere pleas, offers of such pleas, and statements made in connection with such pleas or offers, can be explored in greater detail during Congressional consideration of Rule 11(e)(6) of the Federal Rules of Criminal Procedure. The Conferees believe, therefore, that it is best to defer its effective date until August 1, 1975. The Conferees intend that Rule 410 would be superseded by any subsequent Federal Rule of Criminal Procedure or Act of Congress with which it is inconsistent, if the Federal Rule of Criminal Procedure or Act of Congress takes effect or becomes law after the date of the enactment of the act establishing the rules of evidence.

The conference adopts the Senate amendment with an amendment that expresses the above intentions.

Notes of Advisory Committee on 1979 amendment. Present rule 410 conforms to rule 11(e)(6) of the Federal Rules of Criminal Procedure. A proposed amendment to rule 11(e)(6) would clarify the circumstances in which pleas, plea discussions and related statements are inadmissible in evidence; see Advisory Committee Note thereto. The amendment proposed above would make comparable changes in rule 410.

Effective date of 1979 Amendment. Act July 31, 1979, P. L. 96-42, 93 Stat. 326 provided that the effective date of the amendment transmitted to Congress on April 30, 1979, be extended from Aug. 1, 1979 to Dec. 1, 1980.

Notes of Advisory Committee on 2011 amendments. The language of Rule 410 has been amended as part of the restyling of the Evidence Rules to make them more easily understood and to make style and terminology consistent throughout the rules. These changes are intended to be stylistic only. There is no intent to change any result in any ruling on evidence admissibility.

Amendments:

1975.

Act Dec. 12, 1975 substituted this rule for one which read:

"Rule 410. Offer To Plead Guilty; Nolo Contendere; Withdrawn Plea of Guilty.

"Except as otherwise provided by Act of Congress, evidence of a plea of guilty, later withdrawn, or a plea of nolo contendere, or of an offer to plead guilty or nolo contendere to the crime charged or any other crime, or of statements made in connection with any of the foregoing pleas or offers, is not admissible in any civil or criminal action, case, or proceeding against the person who made the plea or offer. This rule shall not apply to the introduction of voluntary and reliable statements made in court on the record in connection with any of the foregoing pleas or offers where offered for impeachment purposes or in a subsequent prosecution of the declarant for perjury or false statement.

"This rule shall not take effect until August 1, 1975, and shall be superseded by any amendment to the Federal Rules of Criminal Procedure which is inconsistent with this rule, and which takes effect after the date of the enactment of the Act establishing these Federal Rules of Evidence.".

Rule 411. Liability Insurance

Evidence that a person was or was not insured against liability is not admissible to prove whether the person acted negligently or otherwise wrongfully. But the court may admit this evidence for another purpose, such as proving a witness's bias or prejudice or proving agency, ownership, or control.

HISTORY:

Jan. 2, 1975, P. L. 93-595, § 1, 88 Stat. 1933; March 2, 1987, eff. Oct. 1, 1987; April 26, 2011, eff. Dec. 1, 2011.

HISTORY; ANCILLARY LAWS AND DIRECTIVES

Other provisions:

Notes of Advisory Committee on Rules. The courts have with substantial unanimity rejected evidence of liability insurance for the purpose of proving fault, and absence of liability insurance as proof of lack of fault. At best the inference of fault from the fact of insurance coverage is a tenuous one, as is its converse. More important, no doubt, has been the feeling that knowledge of the presence or absence of liability insurance would induce juries to decide cases on improper grounds. McCormick § 168; Annot., 4 A.L.R.2d 761. The rule is drafted in broad terms so as to include contributory negligence or other fault of a plaintiff as well as fault of a defendant.

The second sentence points out the limits of the rule, using well established illustrations. *Id.*

For similar rules see Uniform Rule 54; California Evidence Code § 1155; Kansas Code of Civil Procedure § 60-454; New Jersey Evidence Rule 54.

Notes of Advisory Committee on 1987 amendments. The amendment is technical. No substantive change is intended.

Notes of Advisory Committee on 2011 amendments. The language of Rule 411 has been amended as part of the general restyling of the Evidence Rules to make them more easily understood and to make style and terminology consistent throughout the rules. These changes are intended to be stylistic only. There is no intent to change any result in any ruling on evidence admissibility.

Rule 411 previously provided that evidence was not excluded if offered for a purpose not explicitly prohibited by the Rule. To improve the language of the Rule, it now provides that the court may admit evidence if offered for a permissible purpose. There is no intent to change the process for admitting evidence covered by the Rule. It remains the case that if offered for an impermissible purpose, it must be excluded, and if offered for a purpose not barred by the Rule, its admissibility remains governed by the general principles of Rules 402, 403, 801, etc.

Rule 412. Sex-Offense Cases: The Victim's Sexual Behavior or Predisposition

(a) Prohibited Uses. The following evidence is not admissible in a civil or criminal proceeding involving alleged sexual misconduct:

(1) evidence offered to prove that a victim engaged in other sexual behavior; or

(2) evidence offered to prove a victim's sexual predisposition.

(b) Exceptions.

(1) *Criminal Cases.* The court may admit the following evidence in a criminal case:

(A) evidence of specific instances of a victim's sexual behavior, if offered to prove that someone other than the defendant was the source of semen, injury, or other physical evidence;

(B) evidence of specific instances of a victim's sexual behavior with respect to the person accused of the sexual misconduct, if offered by the defendant to prove consent or if offered by the prosecutor; and

(C) evidence whose exclusion would violate the defendant's constitutional rights.

(2) *Civil Cases.* In a civil case, the court may admit evidence offered to prove a victim's sexual behavior or sexual predisposition if its probative value substantially outweighs the danger of harm to any victim and of unfair prejudice to any party. The court may admit evidence of a victim's reputation only if the victim has placed it in controversy.

(c) Procedure to Determine Admissibility.

(1) *Motion.* If a party intends to offer evidence under Rule 412(b), the party must:

(A) file a motion that specifically describes the evidence and states the purpose for which it is to be offered;

(B) do so at least 14 days before trial unless the court, for good cause, sets a different time;

(C) serve the motion on all parties; and

(D) notify the victim or, when appropriate, the victim's guardian or representative.

(2) *Hearing.* Before admitting evidence under this rule, the court must conduct an in camera hearing and give the victim and parties a right to attend and be heard. Unless the court orders otherwise, the motion, related materials, and the record of the hearing must be and remain sealed.

(d) Definition of "Victim." In this rule, "victim" includes an alleged victim.

HISTORY:

Oct. 28, 1978, P. L. 95-540, § 2(a), 92 Stat. 2046; Nov. 18, 1988, P. L. 100-690, Title VII, Subtitle B, § 7046(a), 102 Stat. 4400; April 29, 1994, eff. Dec. 1, 1994; Sept. 13, 1994, P. L. 103-322, Title IV, Subtitle A, Ch 4, § 40141(b), 109 Stat. 1919; April 26, 2011, eff. Dec. 1, 2011.

HISTORY; ANCILLARY LAWS AND DIRECTIVES

Other provisions:

Applicability of Rule. Act Oct. 28, 1978, P. L. 95-540, § 3, 92 Stat. 2047, provided that this Rule shall apply to trials which begin more than thirty days after the date of the enactment of such Act [Oct. 28, 1978].

Notes of Advisory Committee on proposed 1994 amendment. Rule 412 has been revised to diminish some of the confusion engendered by the original rule and to expand the protection afforded alleged victims of sexual misconduct. Rule 412 applies to both civil and criminal proceedings. The rule aims to safeguard the alleged victim against the invasion of privacy, potential embarrassment and sexual stereotyping that is associated with public disclosure of intimate sexual details and the infusion of sexual innuendo into the factfinding process. By affording victims protection in most instances, the rule also encourages victims of sexual misconduct to institute and to participate in legal proceedings against alleged offenders.

Rule 412 seeks to achieve these objectives by barring evidence relating to the alleged victim's sexual behavior or alleged sexual predisposition, whether offered as substantive evidence or for impeachment, except in designated circumstances in which the probative value of the evidence significantly outweighs possible harm to the victim.

The revised rule applies in all cases involving sexual misconduct without regard to whether the alleged victim or person accused is a party to the litigation. Rule 412 extends to "pattern" witnesses in both criminal and civil cases whose testimony about other instances of sexual misconduct by the person accused is otherwise admissible. When the case does not involve alleged sexual misconduct, evidence relating to a third-party witness' alleged sexual activities is not within the ambit of Rule 412. The witness will, however, be protected by other rules such as Rules 404 and 608, as well as Rule 403.

The terminology "alleged victim" is used because there will frequently be a factual dispute as to whether sexual misconduct occurred. It does not connote any requirement that the misconduct be alleged in the pleadings. Rule 412 does not, however, apply unless the person against whom the evidence is offered can reasonably be characterized as a "victim of alleged sexual misconduct." When this is not the case, as for instance in a defamation action involving statements concerning sexual misconduct in which the evidence is offered to show that the alleged defamatory statements were true or did not damage the plaintiff's reputation, neither Rule 404 nor this rule will operate to bar the evidence; Rule 401 and 403 will continue to control. Rule 412 will, however, apply in a Title VII action in which the plaintiff has alleged sexual harassment.

The reference to a person "accused" is also used in a non-technical sense. There is no requirement that there be a criminal charge pending against the person or even that the misconduct would constitute a criminal offense. Evidence offered to prove allegedly false prior claims by the victim is not barred by Rule 412. However, this evidence is subject to the requirements of Rule 404.

Subdivision (a). As amended, Rule 412 bars evidence offered to prove the victim's sexual behavior and alleged sexual predisposition. Evidence, which might otherwise be admissible under Rules 402, 404(b), 405, 607, 608, 609, or some other evidence rule, must be excluded if Rule 412 so requires. The word "other" is used to suggest some flexibility in admitting evidence "intrinsic" to the alleged sexual misconduct. *Cf.* Committee Note to 1991 amendment to Rule 404(b).

Past sexual behavior connotes all activities that involve actual physical conduct, i.e. sexual intercourse and sexual contact, or that imply sexual intercourse or sexual contact. See, e.g. *United States v. Galloway*, 937 F.2d 542 (10th Cir. 1991), cert. denied, 113 S.Ct. 418 (1992) (use of contraceptives inadmissible since use implies sexual activity); *United States v. One Feather*, 702 F.2d 736 (8th Cir. 1983) (birth of an illegitimate child inadmissible); *State v. Carmichael*, 727 P.2d 918, 925 (Kan. 1986) (evidence of venereal disease inadmissible). In addition, the word "behavior" should be construed to include activities of the mind, such as fantasies or dreams. See 23 C. Wright & K. Graham, Jr., *Federal Practice and Procedure,* § 5384 at p. 548 (1980) ("While there may be some doubt under statutes that require 'conduct,' it would seem that the language of Rule 412 is broad enough to encompass the behavior of the mind.").

The rule has been amended to also exclude all other evidence relating to an alleged victim of sexual misconduct that is offered to prove a sexual predisposition. This amendment is designed to exclude evidence that does not directly refer to sexual activities or thoughts but that the proponent believes may have a sexual connotation for the factfinder. Admission of such evidence would contravene Rule 412's objectives of shielding the alleged victim from potential embarrassment and safeguarding the victim against stereotypical thinking. Consequently, unless the (b)(2) exception is satisfied, evidence such as that relating to the alleged victim's mode of dress, speech, or life-style will not be admissible.

The introductory phrase in subdivision (a) was deleted because it lacked clarity and contained no explicit reference to the other provisions of law that were intended to be overridden. The conditional clause, "except as provided in subdivisions (b) and (c)" is intended to make clear that evidence of the types described in subdivision (a) is admissible only under the strictures of those sections.

The reason for extending the rule to all criminal cases is obvious. The strong social policy of protecting a victim's privacy and encouraging victims to come forward to report criminal acts is not confined to cases that involve a charge of sexual assault. The need to protect the victim is equally great when a defendant is charged with kidnapping, and evidence is offered, either to prove motive or as background, that the defendant sexually assaulted the victim.

The reason for extending Rule 412 to civil cases is equally obvious. The need to protect alleged victims against invasions of privacy, potential embarrassment, and unwarranted sexual stereotyping, and the wish to encourage victims to come forward when they have been sexually molested do not disappear because the context has shifted from a criminal prosecution to a claim for damages or injunctive relief. There is a strong social policy in not only punishing those who engage in sexual misconduct, but in also providing relief to the victim. Thus, Rule 412 applies in any civil case in which a person claims to be the victim of sexual misconduct, such as actions for sexual battery or sexual harassment.

Subdivision (b). Subdivision (b) spells out the specific circumstances in which some evidence may be admissible that would otherwise be barred by the general rule expressed in subdivision (a). As amended, Rule 412 will be virtually unchanged in criminal cases, but will provide protection to any person alleged to be a victim of sexual misconduct regardless of the charge actually brought against an accused. A new exception has been added for civil cases.

In a criminal case, evidence may be admitted under subdivision (b)(1) pursuant to three possible exceptions, provided the evidence also satisfies other requirements for admissibility specified in the Federal Rules of Evidence, including Rule 403. Subdivisions (b)(1)(A) and (b)(1)(B) require proof in the form of specific instances of sexual behavior in recognition of the limited probative value and dubious reliability of evidence of reputation or evidence in the form of an opinion.

Under subdivision (b)(1)(A), evidence of specific instances of sexual behavior with persons other than the person whose sexual misconduct is alleged may be admissible if it is offered to prove that another person was the source of semen, injury or other physical evidence. Where the prosecution has directly or indirectly asserted that the physical evidence originated with the accused, the defendant must be afforded an opportunity to prove that another person was responsible. *See United States v. Begay*, 937 F.2d 515, 523 n. 10 (10th Cir. 1991). Evidence offered for the specific purpose identified in this subdivision may still be excluded if it does not satisfy Rules 401 or 403. *See, e.g., United States v. Azure*, 845 F.2d 1503, 1505–06 (8th Cir. 1988) (10 year old victim's injuries indicated recent use of force; court excluded evidence of consensual sexual activities with witness who testified at in camera hearing that he had never hurt victim and failed to establish recent activities).

Under the exception in subdivision (b)(1)(B), evidence of specific instances of sexual behavior with respect to the person whose sexual misconduct is alleged is admissible if offered to prove consent, or offered by the prosecution. Admissible pursuant to this exception might be evidence of prior instances of sexual activities between the alleged victim and the accused, as well as statements in which the alleged victim expressed an intent to engage in sexual intercourse with the accused, or voiced sexual fantasies involving the specific accused. In a prosecution for child sexual abuse, for example, evidence of uncharged sexual activity between the accused and the alleged victim offered by the prosecution may be admissible pursuant to Rule 404(b) to show a pattern of behavior. Evidence relating to the victim's alleged sexual predisposition is not admissible pursuant to this exception.

Under subdivision (b)(1)(C), evidence of specific instances of conduct may not be excluded if the result would be to deny a criminal defendant the protections afforded by the Constitution. For example, statements in which the victim has expressed an intent to have sex with the first person encountered on a particular occasion might not be excluded without violating the due process right of a rape defendant seeking to prove consent. Recognition of this basic principle was expressed in subdivision (b)(1) of the original rule. The United States Supreme Court has recognized that in various circumstances a defendant may have a right to introduce evidence otherwise precluded by an evidence rule under the Confrontation Clause. *See, e.g., Olden v. Kentucky*, 488 U.S. 227 (1988) (defendant in rape cases had right to inquire into alleged victim's cohabitation with another man to show bias).

Subdivision (b)(2) governs the admissibility of otherwise proscribed evidence in civil cases. It employs a balancing test rather than the specific exceptions stated in subdivision (b)(1) in recognition of the difficulty of foreseeing future developments in the law. Greater flexibility is needed to accommodate evolving causes of action such as claims for sexual harassment.

The balancing test requires the proponent of the evidence, whether plaintiff or defendant, to convince the court that the probative value of the proffered evidence "substantially outweighs the danger of harm to any victim and of unfair prejudice of any party." This test for admitting evidence offered to prove sexual behavior or sexual propensity in civil cases differs in three respects from the general rule governing admissibility set forth in Rule 403. First, it reverses the usual procedure spelled out in Rule 403 by shifting the burden to the proponent to demonstrate admissibility rather than making the opponent justify exclusion of the evidence. Second, the standard expressed in subdivision (b)(2) is more stringent than in the original rule; it raises the threshold for admission by requiring that the probative value of the evidence *substantially* outweigh the specified dangers. Finally, the Rule 412 test puts "harm to the victim" on the scale in addition to prejudice to the parties.

Evidence of reputation may be received in a civil case only if the alleged victim has put his or her reputation into controversy. The victim may do so without making a specific allegation in a pleading. Cf. Fed.R.Civ.P. 35(a).

Subdivision (c). Amended subdivision (c) is more concise and understandable than the subdivision it replaces. The requirement of a motion before trial is continued in the amended rule, as is the provision that a late motion may be permitted for good cause shown. In deciding whether to permit late filing, the court may take into account the conditions previously included in the rule: namely whether the evidence is newly discovered and could not have been obtained earlier through the existence of due diligence, and whether the issue to which such evidence relates has newly arisen in the case. The rule recognizes that in some instances the circumstances that justify an application to introduce evidence otherwise barred by Rule 412 will not become apparent until trial.

The amended rule provides that before admitting evidence that falls within the prohibition of Rule 412(a), the court must hold a hearing in camera at which the alleged victim and any party must be afforded the right to be present and an opportunity to be heard. All papers connected with the motion and any record of a hearing on the motion must be kept and remain under seal during the course of trial and appellate proceedings unless otherwise ordered. This is to assure that the privacy of the alleged victim is preserved in all cases in which the court rules that proffered evidence is not admissible, and in which the hearing refers to matters that are not received, or are received in another form.

The procedures set forth in subdivision (c) do not apply to discovery of a victim's past sexual conduct or predisposition in civil cases, which will be continued to be governed by Fed. R. Civ. P. 26. In order not to undermine the rationale of Rule 412, however, courts should enter appropriate orders pursuant to Fed. R. Civ. P. 26 (c) to protect the victim against unwarranted inquiries and to ensure confidentiality. Courts should presumptively issue protective orders barring discovery unless the party seeking discovery makes a showing that the evidence sought to be discovered would be relevant under the facts and theories of the particular case, and cannot be obtained except through discovery. In an action for sexual harassment, for instance, while some evidence of the alleged victim's sexual behavior and/or predisposition in the workplace may perhaps be relevant, non-work place conduct will usually be irrelevant. *Cf. Burns v. McGregor Electronic Industries. Inc.*, 989 F.2d 959, 962–63 (8th Cir. 1993) (posing for a nude magazine outside work hours is irrelevant to issue of unwelcomeness of sexual advances at work). Confidentiality orders should be presumptively granted as well.

One substantive change made in subdivision (c) is the elimination of the following sentence: "Notwithstanding subdivision (b) of Rule 104, if the relevancy of the evidence which the accused seeks to offer in the trial depends upon the fulfillment of a condition of fact, the court, at the hearing in chambers or at a subsequent hearing in chambers scheduled for such purpose, shall accept evidence on the issue of whether such condition of fact is fulfilled and shall determine such issue." On its face, this language would appear to authorize a trial judge to exclude evidence of past sexual conduct between an alleged victim and an accused or a defendant in a civil case based upon the judge's belief that such past acts did not occur. Such an authorization raises questions of invasion of the right to a jury trial under the Sixth and Seventh Amendments. See 1 S. Saltzburg & M. Martin, *Federal Rules Of Evidence Manual*, 396–97 (5th ed. 1990).

The Advisory Committee concluded that the amended rule provided adequate protection for all persons claiming to be the victims of sexual misconduct, and that it was inadvisable to continue to include a provision in the rule that has been confusing and that raises substantial constitutional issues.

Excerpt from House Conference Report No. 103-711, relating to Sept. 13, 1994 amendments. House Conference Report No. 103-711, dated Aug. 21, 1994, which was to accompany H.R. 3355 (enacted as Act Sept. 13, 1994, P. L. 103-322), included the following statement concerning the amendments to Rule 412: "Section 40141—House recedes to Senate sections 3251–3254 and 3706 with a modification to substitute the revisions of Federal Rule of Evidence 412 as transmitted to Congress by the Supreme Court on April 29, 1994 with an additional modification to extend evidentiary protection to civil cases (as proposed by the Judicial Conference of the United States to the Supreme Court on October 25, 1993). The Conferees intend that the Advisory Committee Note on Rule 412, as transmitted by the Judicial Conference of the United States to the Supreme Court on October 25, 1993, applies to Rule 412 as enacted by this section. This section, which modifies Rule 412 of the Federal Rules of Evidence as transmitted to the Congress by the United States Supreme Court, is enacted pursuant to the Rules Enabling Act.".

Notes of Advisory Committee on 2011 amendments. The language of Rule 412 has been amended as part of the restyling of the Evidence Rules to make them more easily understood and to make style and terminology consistent throughout the rules. These changes are intended to be stylistic only. There is no intent to change any result in any ruling on evidence admissibility.

Amendments:

1988.

Act Nov. 18, 1988, in the rule heading, substituted "Sex Offense" for "Rape"; in subsec. (a), substituted "an offense under chapter 109A of title 18, United States Code" for "rape or assault with intent to commit rape" and "offense" for "rape or assault"; in subsec. (b), in the introductory matter, substituted "an offense under chapter 109A of title 18, United States Code" for "rape or assault with intent to commit rape" and, in para. (2)(B), substituted "such offense" for "rape or assault"; and, in subsecs. (c)(1) and (d), substituted "an offense under chapter 109A of title 18, United States Code" for "rape or assault with intent to commit rape".

1994.

Act Sept. 13, 1994 (effective 12/1/94, as provided by § 40141(a) of such Act, which appears as 28 USCS § 2074 note) substituted the heading and text for the following:

"Sex Offense Cases; Relevance of Victim's Past Behavior.

"(a) Notwithstanding any other provision of law, in a criminal case in which a person is accused of an offense under chapter 109A of title 18, United States Code, reputation or opinion evidence of the past sexual behavior of an alleged victim of such offense is not admissible.

"(b) Notwithstanding any other provision of law, in a criminal case in which a person is accused of an offense under chapter 109A of title 18, United States Code, evidence of a victim's past sexual behavior other than reputation or opinion evidence is also not admissible, unless such evidence other than reputation or opinion evidence is—.

"(1) admitted in accordance with subdivisions (c)(1) and (c)(2) and is constitutionally required to be admitted; or.

"(2) admitted in accordance with subdivision (c) and is evidence of—.

"(A) past sexual behavior with persons other than the accused, offered by the accused upon the issue of whether the accused was or was not, with respect to the alleged victim, the source of semen or injury; or.

"(B) past sexual behavior with the accused and is offered by the accused upon the issue of whether the alleged victim consented to the sexual behavior with respect to which such offense is alleged.

"(c).

(1) If the person accused of committing an offense under chapter 109A of title 18, United States Code intends to offer under subdivision (b) evidence of specific instances of the alleged victim's past sexual behavior, the accused shall make a written motion to offer such evidence not later than fifteen days before the date on which the trial in which such evidence is to be offered is scheduled to begin, except that the court may allow the motion to be made at a later date, including during trial, if the court determines either that the evidence is newly discovered and could not have been obtained earlier through the exercise of due diligence or that the issue to which such evidence relates has newly arisen in the case. Any motion made under this paragraph shall be served on all other parties and on the alleged victim.

"(2) The motion described in paragraph (1) shall be accompanied by a written offer of proof. If the court determines that the offer of proof contains evidence described in subdivision (b), the court shall order a hearing in chambers to determine if such evidence is admissible. At such hearing the parties may call witnesses, including the alleged victim, and offer relevant evidence. Notwithstanding subdivision (b) of rule 104, if the relevancy of the evidence which the accused seeks to offer in the trial depends upon the fulfillment of a condition of fact, the court, at the hearing in chambers or at a subsequent hearing in chambers scheduled for such purpose, shall accept evidence on the issue of whether such condition of fact is fulfilled and shall determine such issue.

"(3) If the court determines on the basis of the hearing described in paragraph (2) that the evidence which the accused seeks to offer is relevant and that the probative value of such evidence outweighs the danger of unfair prejudice, such evidence shall be admissible in the trial to the extent an order made by the court specifies evidence which may be offered and areas with respect to which the alleged victim may be examined or cross-examined.

"(d) For purposes of this rule, the term 'past sexual behavior' means sexual behavior other than the sexual behavior with respect to which an offense under chapter 109A of title 18, United States Code is alleged.".

Rule 413. Similar Crimes in Sexual-Assault Cases

(a) Permitted Uses. In a criminal case in which a defendant is accused of a sexual assault, the court may admit evidence that the defendant committed any other sexual assault. The evidence may be considered on any matter to which it is relevant.

(b) Disclosure to the Defendant. If the prosecutor intends to offer this evidence, the prosecutor must disclose it to the defendant, including witnesses' statements or a summary of the expected testimony. The prosecutor must do so at least 15 days before trial or at a later time that the court allows for good cause.

(c) Effect on Other Rules. This rule does not limit the admission or consideration of evidence under any other rule.

(d) Definition of "Sexual Assault." In this rule and Rule 415, "sexual assault" means a crime under federal law or under state law (as "state" is defined in 18 U.S.C. § 513) involving:

(1) any conduct prohibited by 18 U.S.C. chapter 109A;

(2) contact, without consent, between any part of the defendant's body—or an object—and another person's genitals or anus;

(3) contact, without consent, between the defendant's genitals or anus and any part of another person's body;

(4) deriving sexual pleasure or gratification from inflicting death, bodily injury, or physical pain on another person; or

(5) an attempt or conspiracy to engage in conduct described in subparagraphs (1)–(4).

HISTORY:

Sept. 13, 1994, P. L. 103-322, Title XXXII, Subtitle I, § 320935(a), 108 Stat. 2136; April 26, 2011, eff. Dec. 1, 2011.

HISTORY; ANCILLARY LAWS AND DIRECTIVES

Other provisions:

Effectiveness, implementation, recommendations, and application. Act Sept. 13, 1994, P. L. 103-322, Title XXXII, Subtitle I, § 320935(b)–(e), 108 Stat. 2137; Sept. 30, 1996, P. L. 104-208, Div A, Title I, § 101(a) [Title I, § 120], 110 Stat. 3009-25, provide:

"(b) Implementation. The amendments made by subsection (a) [adding Rules 413– 415] shall become effective pursuant to subsection (d).

"(c) Recommendations by Judicial Conference. Not later than 150 days after the date of enactment of this Act, the Judicial Conference of the United States shall transmit to Congress a report containing recommendations for amending the Federal Rules of Evidence as they affect the admission of evidence of a defendant's prior sexual assault or child molestation crimes in cases involving sexual assault and child molestation. The Rules Enabling Act shall not apply to the recommendations made by the Judicial Conference pursuant to this section.

"(d) Congressional action.

(1) If the recommendations described in subsection (c) are the same as the amendment made by subsection (a) [adding Rules 413– 415], then the amendments made by subsection (a) shall become effective 30 days after the transmittal of the recommendations.

"(2) If the recommendations described in subsection (c) are different than the amendments made by subsection (a) [adding Rules 413– 415], the amendments made by subsection (a) shall become effective 150 days after the transmittal of the recommendations unless otherwise provided by law.

"(3) If the Judicial Conference fails to comply with subsection (c), the amendments made by subsection (a) [adding Rules 413– 415] shall become effective 150 days after the date the recommendations were due under subsection (c) unless otherwise provided by law.

"(e) Application. The amendments made by subsection (a) [adding Rules 413– 415] shall apply to proceedings commenced on or after the effective date of such amendments, including all trials commenced on or after the effective date of such amendments.".

[The report submitted to Congress on Feb. 9, 1995 (note to this rule) pursuant to subsec. (c) of this note contained recommendations different from the amendments made by § 320935(a) of Act Sept. 13, 1994, P. L. 103-322, adding FRE 413 through 415, thus delaying the effective date of such rules until 150 days after transmittal of the report unless otherwise provided by law.]

Report of Judicial Conference of United States on admission of character evidence in certain sexual misconduct cases. The report of the Judicial Conference of the United States on the admission of character evidence in certain sexual misconduct cases, submitted to Congress on Feb. 9, 1995, in accordance with § 320935(c) of the Violent Crime Control and Law Enforcement Act of 1994 (§ 329035(c) of Act Sept. 13, 1994, P. L. 103-322 (note to this rule)), provides:

"This report is transmitted to Congress in accordance with the Violent Crime Control and Law Enforcement Act of 1994, Pub. L. No. 103-322 (September 13, 1994). Section 320935 of the Act invited the Judicial Conference of the United States within 150 days (February 10, 1995) to submit 'a report containing recommendations for amending the Federal Rules of Evidence as they affect the admission of evidence of a defendant's prior sexual assault or child molestation crimes in cases involving sexual assault or child molestation.'.

"Under the Act, new Rules 413, 414, and 415 would be added to the Federal Rules of Evidence. These Rules would admit evidence of a defendant's past similar acts in criminal and civil cases involving a sexual assault or child molestation offense for its bearing on any matter to which it is relevant. The effective date of new Rules 413– 415 is contingent in part upon the nature of the recommendations submitted by the Judicial Conference.

"After careful study, the Judicial Conference urges Congress to reconsider its decision on the policy questions underlying the new rules for reasons set out in Part III below.

"If Congress does not reconsider its decision on the underlying policy questions, the Judicial Conference recommends incorporation of the provisions of new Rules 413–415 as amendments to Rules 404 and 405 of the Federal Rules of Evidence. The amendments would not change the substance of the congressional enactment but would clarity drafting ambiguities and eliminate possible constitutional infirmities.

"Under the Act, the Judicial Conference was provided 150 days within which to make and submit to Congress alternative recommendations to new Evidence Rules 413–415. Consideration of Rules 413– 415 by the Judicial Conference was specifically excepted from the exacting review procedures set forth in the Rules Enabling Act (codified at 28 U.S.C. §§ 2071– 2077). Although the Conference acted on these new rules on an expedited basis to meet the Act's deadlines, the review process was thorough.

"The new rules would apply to both civil and criminal cases. Accordingly, the Judicial Conference's Advisory Committee on Criminal Rules and the Advisory Committee on Civil Rules reviewed the rules at separate meetings in October 1994. At the same time and in preparation for its consideration of the new rules, the Advisory Committee on Evidence Rules sent out a notice soliciting comment on new Evidence Rules 413, 414, and 415. The notice was sent to the courts, including all federal judges, about 900 evidence law professors, 40 women's rights organizations, and 1,000 other individuals and interested organizations.

"On October 17–18, 1994, the Advisory Committee on Evidence Rules met in Washington, D.C. It considered the public responses, which included 84 written comments, representing 112 individuals, 8 local and 8 national legal organizations. The overwhelming majority of judges, lawyers, law professors, and legal organizations who responded opposed new Evidence Rules 413, 414, and 415. The principal objections expressed were that the rules would permit the admission of unfairly prejudicial evidence and contained numerous drafting problems not intended by their authors.

"The Advisory Committee on Evidence Rules submitted its report to the Judicial Conference Committee on Rules of Practice and Procedure (Standing Committee) for review at its January 11–13, 1995 meeting. The committee's report was unanimous except for a dissenting vote by the representative of the Department of Justice. The advisory committee believed that the concerns expressed by Congress and embodied in new Evidence Rules 413, 414, and 415 are already adequately addressed in the existing Federal Rules of Evidence. In particular, Evidence Rule 404(b) now allows the admission of evidence against a criminal defendant of the commission of prior crimes, wrongs, or acts for specified purposes, including to show intent, plan, motive, preparation, identity, knowledge, or absence of mistake or accident.

"Furthermore, the new rules, which are not supported by empirical evidence, could diminish significantly the protections that have safeguarded persons accused in criminal cases and parties in civil cases against undue prejudice. These protections form a fundamental part of American jurisprudence and have evolved under long-standing rules and case law. A significant concern identified by the committee was the danger of convicting a criminal defendant for past, as opposed to charged, behavior or for being a bad person.

"In addition, the advisory committee concluded that, because prior bad acts would be admissible even though not the subject of a conviction, mini-trials within trials concerning those acts would result when a defendant seeks to rebut such evidence. The committee also noticed that many of the comments received had concluded that the Rules, as drafted, were mandatory–that is, such evidence had to be admitted regardless of other rules of evidence such as the hearsay rule or the Rule 403 balancing test The committee believed that this position was arguable because Rules 413– 415 declare without qualification that such evidence 'is admissible.' In contrast, the new Rule 412, passed as part of the same legislation, provided that certain evidence 'is admissible if it is otherwise admissible under these Rules.' Fed. R. Evid. 412(b)(2). If the critics are right, Rules 413– 415 free the prosecution from rules that apply to the defendant—including the hearsay rule and Rule 403. If so, serious constitutional questions would arise.

"The Advisory Committees on Criminal and Civil Rules unanimously, except for representatives of the Department of Justice, also opposed the new rules. Those committees also concluded that the new rules would permit the introduction of unreliable but highly prejudicial evidence and would complicate trials by causing mini-trials of other alleged wrongs. After the advisory committees reported, the Standing Committee unanimously, again except for the representative of the Department of Justice, agreed with the view of the advisory committees.

"It is important to note the highly unusual unanimity of the members of the Standing and Advisory Committees, composed of over 40 judges, practicing lawyers, and academicians, in taking the view that Rules 413– 415 are undesirable. Indeed, the only supporters of the Rules were representatives of the Department of Justice.

"For these reasons, the Standing Committee recommended that Congress reconsider its decision on the policy questions embodied in new Evidence Rules 413, 414, and 415.

"However, if Congress will not reconsider its decision on the policy questions, the Standing Committee recommended that Congress consider an alternative draft recommended by the Advisory Committee on Evidence Rules. That Committee drafted proposed amendments to existing Evidence Rules 404 and 405 that would both correct ambiguities and possible constitutional infirmities identified in new Evidence Rules 413, 414, and 415 yet still effectuate Congressional intent. In particular, the proposed amendments:

"(1) expressly apply the other rules of evidence to evidence offered under the new rules;

"(2) expressly allow the party against whom such evidence is offered to use similar evidence in rebuttal;

"(3) expressly enumerate the factors to be weighed by a court in making its Rule 403 determination;

"(4) render the notice provisions consistent with the provisions in existing Rule 404 regarding criminal cases;

"(5) eliminate the special notice provisions of Rules 413–415 in civil cases so that notice will be required as provided in the Federal Rules of Civil Procedure; and.

"(6) permit reputation or opinion evidence after such evidence is offered by the accused or defendant.

"The Standing Committee reviewed the new rules and the alternative recommendations. It concurred with the views of the Evidence Rules Committee and recommended that the Judicial Conference adopt them.

"The Judicial Conference concurs with the views of the Standing Committee and urges that Congress reconsider its policy determinations underlying Evidence Rules 413–415. In the alternative, the attached amendments [this note] to Evidence Rules 404 and 405 are recommended, in lieu of new Evidence Rules 413, 414, and 415. The alternative amendments to Evidence Rules 404 and 405 are accompanied by the Advisory Committee Notes [this note], which explain them in detail.

" **Rule 404. Character Evidence Not Admissible To Prove Conduct; Exceptions; Other Crimes** *

* * * * *.

" *Character in sexual misconduct cases. Evidence of another act of sexual assault or child molestation, or evidence to rebut such proof or an inference therefrom, if that evidence is otherwise admissible under these rules, in a criminal case in which the accused is charged with sexual assault or child molestation, or in a civil case in which a claim is predicated on a party's alleged commission of sexual assault or child molestation.*

" *(A) In weighing the probative value of such evidence, the court may, as part of its rule 403 determination, consider:*

" *(i) proximity in time to the charged or predicate misconduct:*

" *(ii) similarity to the charged or predicate misconduct:*

" *(iii) frequency of the other acts:*

" *(iv) surrounding circumstances:*

" *(v) relevant intervening events: and.*

" *(vi) other relevant similarities or differences.*

" *(B) In a criminal case in which the prosecution intends to offer evidence under this subdivision, it must disclose the evidence, including statements of witnesses or a summary of the substance of any testimony, at a reasonable time in*

*New matter is italicized and matter to be omitted is lined through.

advance of trial, or during trial if the court excuses pretrial notice on good cause shown.

" *(C) For purposes of this subdivision,*

" *(i) 'sexual assault' means conduct—or an attempt or conspiracy to engage in conduct—of the type proscribed by chapter 109A of title 18, United States Code* [18 USCS §§ 2241 et seq.] , *or conduct that involved deriving sexual pleasure or ratification from inflicting death, bodily injury, or physical pain on another person irrespective of the ace of the victim—regardless of whether that conduct would have subjected the actor to federal jurisdiction.*

" *(ii) 'child molestation' means conduct—or an attempt or conspiracy to engage in conduct—of the type proscribed by chapter 110 of title 18, United States Code* [18 USCS §§ 2251 et seq.] , *or conduct, committed in relation to a child below the ace of 14 years, either of the type proscribed by chapter 109A of title 18, United States Code* [18 USCS §§ 2241 et seq.] , *or that involved deriving sexual pleasure or gratification from inflicting death, bodily injury, or physical pain on another person—regardless of whether that conduct would have subjected the actor to federal jurisdiction.*

" **(b) Other crimes, wrongs, or acts.** Evidence of other crimes, wrongs, or acts is not admissible to prove the character of a person in order to show action in conformity therewith *except as provided in subdivision (a)* . . . .

"The Committee has redrafted Rules 413, 414 and 415 which the Violent Crime Control and Law Enforcement Act of 1994 conditionally added to the Federal Rules of Evidence. [**] These modifications do not change the substance of the congressional enactment. The changes were made in order to integrate the provisions both substantively and stylistically with the existing Rules of Evidence; to illuminate the intent expressed by the principal drafters of the measure; to clarify drafting ambiguities that might necessitate considerable judicial attention if they remained unresolved; and to eliminate possible constitutional infirmities.

"The Committee placed the new provisions in Rule 404 because this rule governs the admissibility of character evidence. The congressional enactment constitutes a new exception to the general rule stated in subdivision (a). The Committee also combined the three separate rules proposed by Congress into one subdivision (a)(4) in accordance with the rules' customary practice of treating criminal and civil issues jointly. An amendment to Rule 405 has been added because the authorization of a new form of character evidence in this rule has an impact on methods of proving character that were not explicitly addressed by Congress. The stylistic changes are self-evident. They are particularly noticeable in the definition section in subdivision (a)(4)(C) in which the Committee eliminated, without any change in meaning, graphic details of sexual acts.

"The Committee added language that explicitly provides that evidence under this subdivision must satisfy other rules of evidence such as the hearsay rules in Article VIII [FRE (USCS, Title 28 Appx) 801 et seq.] and the expert testimony rules in Article VII [FRE (USCS, Title 28 Appx) 701 et seq.]. Although principal sponsors of the legislation had stated that they intended other evidentiary rules to apply, the Committee believes that the opening phrase of the new subdivision 'if otherwise admissible under these rules' is needed to clarify the relationship between subdivision (a)(4) and other evidentiary provisions.

"The Committee also expressly made subdivision (a)(4) subject to Rule 403 balancing in accordance with the repeatedly stated objectives of the legislation's sponsors with which representatives of the Justice Department expressed agreement. Many commentators on Rules 413–415 had objected that Rule 403's applicability was obscured by the actual language employed.

"In addition to clarifying the drafters' intent, an explicit reference to Rule 403 may be essential to insulate the rule against constitutional challenge. Constitutional concerns also led the Committee to acknowledge specifically the opposing party's right to offer in rebuttal character evidence that the rules would otherwise bar, including evidence of a third person's prior acts of sexual misconduct offered to prove that the third person rather than the party committed the acts in issue.

"In order to minimize the need for extensive and time-consuming judicial interpretation, the Committee listed factors that a court may consider in discharging Rule 403 balancing. Proximity in time is taken into account in a related rule. See Rule 609(b). Similarity, frequency and surrounding circumstances have long been considered by courts in handling other crimes evidence pursuant to Rule 404(b). Relevant intervening events, such as extensive medical treatment of the accused between the time of the prior proffered act and the charged act, may affect the strength of the propensity inference for which the evidence is offered. The final factor —'other relevant similarities or differences'—is added in recognition of the endless variety of circumstances that confront a trial court in rulings on admissibility. Although subdivision (4)(A) explicitly refers to factors that bear on probative value, this enumeration does not eliminate a judge's responsibility to take into account the other factors mentioned in Rule 403 itself—'the danger of unfair prejudice, confusion of the issues, . . . misleading the jury, . . . undue delay, waste of time, or needless presentation of cumulative evidence.' In addition, the Advisory Committee Note to Rule 403 reminds judges that 'The availability of other means of proof may also be an appropriate factor.'.

"The Committee altered slightly the notice provision in criminal cases. Providing the trial court with some discretion to excuse pretrial notice was thought preferable to the inflexible 15-day rule provided in Rules 414 and 415. Furthermore, the formulation is identical to that contained in the 1991 amendment to Rule 404(b) so that no confusion will result from having two somewhat different notice provisions in the same rule. The Committee eliminated the notice provision for civil cases stated in Rule 415 because it did not believe that Congress intended to alter the usual time table for disclosure and discovery provided by the Federal Rules of Civil Procedure.

"The definition section was simplified with no change in meaning. The reference to 'the law of a state' was eliminated as unnecessarily confusing and restrictive. Conduct committed outside the United States ought equally to be eligible for admission. Evidence offered pursuant to subdivision (a)(4) must relate to a form of conduct proscribed by either chapter 109A or 110 of title 18, United States Code,

[**] Congress provided that the rules would take effect unless within a specified time period the Judicial Conference made recommendations to amend the rules that Congress enacted.

regardless of whether the actor was subject to federal jurisdiction.

" **Rule 405. Methods of Proving Character** [*]

" **(a) Reputation or opinion.** In all cases in which evidence of character or a trait of character of a person is admissible, proof may be made by testimony as to reputation or by testimony in the form of an opinion *except as provided in subdivision (c) of this rule*. On cross-examination, inquiry is allowable into relevant specific instances of conduct.

* * * * *.

" *(c) Proof in sexual misconduct cases. In a case in which evidence is offered under rule 404(a)(4), proof may be made by specific instances of conduct, testimony as to reputation, or testimony in the form of an opinion, except that the prosecution or claimant may offer reputation or opinion testimony only after the opposing party has offered such testimony.*

"The addition of a new subdivision (a)(4) to Rule 404 necessitates adding a new subdivision (c) to Rule 405 to govern methods of proof. Congress clearly intended no change in the preexisting law that precludes the prosecution or a claimant from offering reputation or opinion testimony in its case in chief to prove that the opposing party acted in conformity with character. When evidence is admissible pursuant to Rule 404(a)(4), the proponents proof must consist of specific instances of conduct. The opposing party, however, is free to respond with reputation or opinion testimony (including expert testimony if otherwise admissible) as well as evidence of specific instances. In a criminal case, the admissibility of reputation or opinion testimony would, in any event, be authorized by Rule 404(a)(1). The extension to civil cases is essential in order to provide the opponent with an adequate opportunity to refute allegations about a character for sexual misconduct. Once the opposing party offers reputation or opinion testimony, however, the prosecution or claimant may counter using such methods of proof.".

Notes of Advisory Committee on 2011 amendments. The language of Rule 413 has been amended as part of the restyling of the Evidence Rules to make them more easily understood and to make style and terminology consistent throughout the rules. These changes are intended to be stylistic only. There is no intent to change any result in any ruling on evidence admissibility.

Rule 414. Similar Crimes in Child-Molestation Cases

(a) Permitted Uses. In a criminal case in which a defendant is accused of child molestation, the court may admit evidence that the defendant committed any other child molestation. The evidence may be considered on any matter to which it is relevant.

(b) Disclosure to the Defendant. If the prosecutor intends to offer this evidence, the prosecutor must disclose it to the defendant, including witnesses' statements or a summary of the expected testimony. The prosecutor must do so at least 15 days before trial or at a later time that the court allows for good cause.

(c) Effect on Other Rules. This rule does not limit the admission or consideration of evidence under any other rule.

(d) Definition of "Child" and "Child Molestation." In this rule and Rule 415:

(1) "child" means a person below the age of 14; and

(2) "child molestation" means a crime under federal law or under state law (as "state" is defined in 18 U.S.C. § 513) involving:

(A) any conduct prohibited by 18 U.S.C. chapter 109A and committed with a child;

(B) any conduct prohibited by 18 U.S.C. chapter 110;

(C) contact between any part of the defendant's body—or an object—and a child's genitals or anus;

(D) contact between the defendant's genitals or anus and any part of a child's body;

(E) deriving sexual pleasure or gratification from inflicting death, bodily injury, or physical pain on a child; or

(F) an attempt or conspiracy to engage in conduct described in subparagraphs (A)–(E).

HISTORY:

Sept. 13, 1994, P. L. 103-322, Title XXXII, Subtitle I, § 320935(a), 108 Stat. 2136; April 26, 2011, eff. Dec. 1, 2011.

HISTORY; ANCILLARY LAWS AND DIRECTIVES

Other provisions:

Notes of Advisory Committee on 2011 amendments. The language of Rule 414 has been amended as part of the restyling of the Evidence Rules to make them more easily understood and to make style and terminology consistent throughout the rules. These changes are intended to be stylistic only. There is no intent to change any result in any ruling on evidence admissibility.

Rule 415. Similar Acts in Civil Cases Involving Sexual Assault or Child Molestation

(a) Permitted Uses. In a civil case involving a claim for relief based on a party's alleged sexual assault or child molestation, the court may admit evidence that the party committed any other sexual assault or child molestation. The evidence may be considered as provided in Rules 413 and 414.

(b) Disclosure to the Opponent. If a party intends to offer this evidence, the party must disclose it to the party against whom it will be offered, including witnesses' statements or a summary of the expected testimony. The party must do so at least 15 days before trial or at a later time that the court allows for good cause.

(c) Effect on Other Rules. This rule does not limit the admission or consideration of evidence under any other rule.

HISTORY:

Sept. 13, 1994, P. L. 103-322, Title XXXII, Subtitle I, § 320935(a), 108 Stat. 2137; April 26, 2011, eff. Dec. 1, 2011.

HISTORY; ANCILLARY LAWS AND DIRECTIVES

Other provisions:

Notes of Advisory Committee on 2011 amendments. The language of Rule 415 has been amended as part of the

[*]New matter is italicized and matter to be omitted is lined through.

restyling of the Evidence Rules to make them more easily understood and to make style and terminology consistent throughout the rules. These changes are intended to be stylistic only. There is no intent to change any result in any ruling on evidence admissibility.

ARTICLE V. PRIVILEGES

Rule 501. Privilege in General

The common law—as interpreted by United States courts in the light of reason and experience—governs a claim of privilege unless any of the following provides otherwise:

- the United States Constitution;
- a federal statute; or
- rules prescribed by the Supreme Court.

But in a civil case, state law governs privilege regarding a claim or defense for which state law supplies the rule of decision.

HISTORY:

Jan. 2, 1975, P. L. 93-595, § 1, 88 Stat. 1933; April 26, 2011, eff. Dec. 1, 2011.

HISTORY; ANCILLARY LAWS AND DIRECTIVES

Other provisions:

Notes of Committee on the Judiciary, House Report No. 93-650. Article V as submitted to Congress contained thirteen Rules. Nine of those Rules defined specific nonconstitutional privileges which the federal courts must recognize (i.e. required reports, lawyer-client, psychotherapist-patient, husband-wife, communications to clergymen, political vote, trade secrets, secrets of state and other official information, and identity of informer). Another Rule provided that only those privileges set forth in Article V or in some other Act of Congress could be recognized by the federal courts. The three remaining Rules addressed collateral problems as to waiver of privilege by voluntary disclosure, privileged matter disclosed under compulsion or without opportunity to claim privilege, comment upon or inference from a claim of privilege, and jury instruction with regard thereto.

The Committee amended Article V to eliminate all of the Court's specific Rules on privileges. Instead, the Committee, through a single Rule, 501, left the law of privileges in its present state and further provided that privileges shall continue to be developed by the courts of the United States under a uniform standard applicable both in civil and criminal cases. That standard, derived from Rule 26 of the Federal Rules of Criminal Procedure, mandates the application of the principles of the common law as interpreted by the Courts of the United States in the light of reason and experience. The words "person, government, State, or political subdivision thereof" were added by the Committee to the lone term "witness" used in Rule 26 to make clear that, as under present law, not only witnesses may have privileges. The Committee also included in its amendment a proviso modeled after Rule 302 and similar to language added by the Committee to Rule 601 relating to the competency of witnesses. The proviso is designed to require the application of State privilege law in civil actions and proceedings governed by *Erie R. Co. v Tompkins,* 304 U.S. 64 (1938), a result in accord with current federal court decisions. See *Republic Gear Co. v. Borg-Warner Corp.,* 381 F.2d 551, 555–556 n.2 (2nd Cir. 1967). The Committee deemed the proviso to be necessary in the light of the Advisory Committee's view (see its note to Court [proposed] Rule 501) that this result is not mandated under Erie.

The rationale underlying the proviso is that federal law should not supersede that of the States in substantive areas such as privilege absent a compelling reason. The Committee believes that in civil cases in the federal courts where an element of a claim or defense is not grounded upon a federal question, there is no federal interest strong enough to justify departure from State policy. In addition, the Committee considered that the Court's proposed Article V would have promoted forum shopping in some civil actions, depending upon differences in the privilege law applied as among the State and federal courts. The Committee's proviso, on the other hand, under which the federal courts are bound to apply the State's privilege law in actions founded upon a State-created right or defense removes the incentive to "shop".

Notes of Committee on the Judiciary, Senate Report No. 93-1277. Article V as submitted to Congress contained 13 rules. Nine of those rules defined specific nonconstitutional privileges which the Federal courts must recognize (i.e., required reports, lawyer-client, psychotherapist-patient, husband-wife, communications to clergymen, political vote, trade secrets, secrets of state and other official information, and identity of informer). Many of these rules contained controversial modifications or restrictions upon common law privileges. As noted supra, the House amended article V to eliminate all of the Court's specific rules on privileges. Through a single rule, 501, the House provided that privileges shall be governed by the principles of the common law as interpreted by the courts of the United States in the light of reason and experience (a standard derived from rule 26 of the Federal Rules of Criminal Procedure) except in the case of an element of a civil claim or defense as to which State law supplies the rule of decision, in which event state privilege law was to govern.

The committee agrees with the main thrust of the House amendment: that a federally developed common law based on modern reason and experience shall apply except where the State nature of the issues renders deference to State privilege law the wiser course, as in the usual diversity case. The committee understands that thrust of the House amendment to require that State privilege law be applied in "diversity" cases (actions on questions of State law between citizens of different States arising under 28 U.S.C. § 1332). The language of the House amendment, however, goes beyond this in some respects, and falls short of it in others; State privilege law applies even in nondiversity. Federal question civil cases, where an issue governed by State substantive law is the object of the evidence (such issues do sometimes arise in such cases); and, in all instances where State privilege law is to be applied, e.g., on proof of a State issue in a diversity case, a close reading reveals that State privilege law is not to be applied unless the matter to be proved is an element of that state claim or defense, as distinguished from a step along the way in the proof of it.

The committee is concerned that the language used in the House amendment could be difficult to apply. It provides that "in civil actions * * * with respect to an element of a claim or defense as to which State law supplies the rule of decision," State law on privilege applies. The question of what is an element of a claim or defense is likely to engender considerable litigation. If the matter in question constitutes an element of a claim, State law supplies the privilege rule; whereas if it is a mere item of proof with respect to a claim, then, even though State law might supply the rule of decision, Federal law on the privilege would apply. Further, disputes will arise as to how the rule should be applied in an antitrust action or in a tax case where the Federal statute is silent as to a particular aspect of the substantive law in question, but Federal cases had incorporated State law by reference to State law. [For a discussion of reference to State substantive law, see note on Federal Incorporation by Reference of State Law, Hart & Wechsler, The Federal Courts and the Federal System, pp. 491–494 (2d ed. 1973).] Is a claim (or defense) based on such a reference a claim or defense as to which federal or State law supplies the rule of decision?

Another problem not entirely avoidable is the complexity or difficulty the rule introduces into the trial of a Federal case containing a combination of Federal and State claims and defenses, e.g. an action involving Federal antitrust and State unfair competition claims. Two different bodies of privilege law would need to be consulted. It may even develop that the same witness-testimony might be relevant on both counts and privileged as to one but not the other. [The problems with the House formulation are discussed in Rothstein, The Proposed Amendments to the Federal Rules of Evidence, 62 Georgetown University Law Journal 125 (1973) at notes 25, 26 and 70–74 and accompanying text.]

The formulation adopted by the House is pregnant with litigious mischief. The committee has, therefore, adopted what we believe will be a clearer and more practical guideline for determining when courts should respect State rules of privilege. Basically, it provides that in criminal and Federal question civil cases, federally evolved rules on privilege should apply since it is Federal policy which is being enforced. [It is also intended that the Federal law of privileges should be applied with respect to pendant State law claims when they arise in a Federal question case.] Conversely, in diversity cases where the litigation in question turns on a substantive question of State law, and is brought in the Federal courts because the parties reside in different States, the committee believes it is clear that State rules of privilege should apply unless the proof is directed at a claim or defense for which Federal law supplies the rule of decision (a situation which would not commonly arise.) [While such a situation might require use of two bodies of privilege law, federal and state, in the same case, nevertheless the occasions on which this would be required are considerably reduced as compared with the House version, and confined to situations where the Federal and State interests are such as to justify application of neither privilege law to the case as a whole. If the rule proposed here results in two conflicting bodies of privilege law applying to the same piece of evidence in the same case, it is contemplated that the rule favoring reception of the evidence should be applied. This policy is based on the present rule 43(a) of the Federal Rules of Civil Procedure which provides:

In any case, the statute or rule which favors the reception of the evidence governs and the evidence shall be presented according to the most convenient method prescribed in any of the statutes or rules to which reference is herein made.] It is intended that the State rules of privilege should apply equally in original diversity actions and diversity actions removed under 28 U.S.C. § 1441(b).

Two other comments on the privilege rule should be made. The committee has received a considerable volume of correspondence from psychiatric organizations and psychiatrists concerning the deletion of rule 504 of the rule submitted by the Supreme Court. It should be clearly understood that, in approving this general rule as to privileges, the action of Congress should not be understood as disapproving any recognition of a psychiatrist-patient, or husband-wife, or any other of the enumerated privileges contained in the Supreme Court rules. Rather, our action should be understood as reflecting the view that the recognition of a privilege based on a confidential relationship and other privileges should be determined on a case-by-case basis.

Further, we would understand that the prohibition against spouses testifying against each other is considered a rule of privilege and covered by this rule and not by rule 601 of the competency of witnesses.

Notes of the Conference Committee, House Report No. 93-1597. Rule 501 deals with the privilege of a witness not to testify. Both the House and Senate bills provide that federal privilege law applies in criminal cases. In civil actions and proceedings, the House bill provides that state privilege law applies "to an element of a claim or defense as to which State law supplies the rule of decision." The Senate bill provides that "in civil actions and proceedings arising under 28 U.S.C. § 1332 or 28 U.S.C. § 1335, or between citizens of different States and removed under 28 U.S.C. § 1441(b) the privilege of a witness, person, government, State or political subdivision thereof is determined in accordance with State law, unless with respect to the particular claim or defense, Federal law supplies the rule of decision."

The wording of the House and Senate bills differs in the treatment of civil actions and proceedings. The rule in the House bill applies to evidence that relates to "an element of a claim or defense." If an item of proof tends to support or defeat a claim or defense, or an element of a claim or defense, and if state law supplies the rule of decision for that claim or defense, then state privilege law applies to that item of proof.

Under the provision in the House bill, therefore, state privilege law will usually apply in diversity cases. There may be diversity cases, however, where a claim or defense is based upon federal law. In such instances, Federal privilege law will apply to evidence relevant to the federal claim or defense. See *Sola Electric Co. v. Jefferson Electric Co.*, 317 U.S. 173 (1942).

In nondiversity jurisdiction civil cases, federal privilege law will generally apply. In those situations where a federal court adopts or incorporates state law to fill interstices or gaps in federal statutory phrases, the court generally will apply federal privilege law. As Justice Jackson has said:

A federal court sitting in a non-diversity case such as this does not sit as a local tribunal. In some cases it may see fit for special reasons to give the law of a particular state highly persuasive or even controlling effect, but in the last analysis its decision turns upon the law of the United States, not that of any state. *D'Oench, Duhme & Co. v. Federal Deposit Insurance Corp.,* 315 U.S. 447, 471 (1942) (Jackson, J., concurring). When a federal court chooses to absorb state law, it is applying the state law as a matter of federal common law. Thus, state law does not supply the rule of decision (even though the federal court may apply a rule derived from state decisions), and state privilege law would not apply. See C. A. Wright, Federal Courts 251–252 (2d ed. 1970); *Holmberg v. Armbrecht,* 327 U.S. 392 (1946); *DeSylva v. Ballentine,* 351 U.S. 570, 581 (1956); 9 Wright & Miller, Federal Rules and Procedure § 2408.

In civil actions and proceedings, where the rule of decision as to a claim or defense or as to an element of a claim or defense is supplied by state law, the House provision requires that state privilege law apply.

The Conference adopts the House provision.

Notes of Advisory Committee on 2011 amendments. The language of Rule 501 has been amended as part of the restyling of the Evidence Rules to make them more easily understood and to make style and terminology consistent throughout the rules. These changes are intended to be stylistic only. There is no intent to change any result in any ruling on evidence admissibility.

Rule 502. Attorney-Client Privilege and Work Product; Limitations on Waiver

The following provisions apply, in the circumstances set out, to disclosure of a communication or information covered by the attorney-client privilege or work-product protection.

(a) Disclosure Made in a Federal Proceeding or to a Federal Office or Agency; Scope of a Waiver. When the disclosure is made in a federal proceeding or to a federal office or agency and waives the attorney-client privilege or work-product protection, the waiver extends to an undisclosed communication or information in a federal or state proceeding only if:

(1) the waiver is intentional;

(2) the disclosed and undisclosed communications or information concern the same subject matter; and

(3) they ought in fairness to be considered together.

(b) Inadvertent Disclosure. When made in a federal proceeding or to a federal office or agency, the disclosure does not operate as a waiver in a federal or state proceeding if:

(1) the disclosure is inadvertent;

(2) the holder of the privilege or protection took reasonable steps to prevent disclosure; and

(3) the holder promptly took reasonable steps to rectify the error, including (if applicable) following Federal Rule of Civil Procedure 26(b)(5)(B).

(c) Disclosure Made in a State Proceeding. When the disclosure is made in a state proceeding and is not the subject of a state-court order concerning waiver, the disclosure does not operate as a waiver in a federal proceeding if the disclosure:

(1) would not be a waiver under this rule if it had been made in a federal proceeding; or

(2) is not a waiver under the law of the state where the disclosure occurred.

(d) Controlling Effect of a Court Order. A federal court may order that the privilege or protection is not waived by disclosure connected with the litigation pending before the court—in which event the disclosure is also not a waiver in any other federal or state proceeding.

(e) Controlling Effect of a Party Agreement. An agreement on the effect of disclosure in a federal proceeding is binding only on the parties to the agreement, unless it is incorporated into a court order.

(f) Controlling Effect of this Rule. Notwithstanding Rules 101 and 1101, this rule applies to state proceedings and to federal court-annexed and federal court-mandated arbitration proceedings, in the circumstances set out in the rule. And notwithstanding Rule 501, this rule applies even if state law provides the rule of decision.

(g) Definitions. In this rule:

(1) "attorney-client privilege" means the protection that applicable law provides for confidential attorney-client communications; and

(2) "work-product protection" means the protection that applicable law provides for tangible material (or its intangible equivalent) prepared in anticipation of litigation or for trial.

HISTORY:

Sept. 19, 2008, P. L. 110-322, § 1(a), 122 Stat. 3537; April 26, 2011, eff. Dec. 1, 2011.

HISTORY; ANCILLARY LAWS AND DIRECTIVES

Other provisions:

Application of rule. Act Sept. 19, 2008, P. L. 110-322, § 1(c), 122 Stat. 3538, provides: "The amendments made by this Act [adding this rule] shall apply in all proceedings commenced after the date of enactment of this Act and, insofar as is just and practicable, in all proceedings pending on such date of enactment.".

Committee note. This new rule has two major purposes:

(1) It resolves some longstanding disputes in the courts about the effect of certain disclosures of communications or information protected by the attorney-client privilege or as work product -- specifically those disputes involving inadvertent disclosure and subject matter waiver.

(2) It responds to the widespread complaint that litigation costs necessary to protect against waiver of attorney-client privilege or work product have become prohibitive due to the concern that any disclosure (however innocent or minimal) will operate as a subject matter waiver of all protected communications or information. This concern is especially troubling in cases involving electronic discovery. *See, e.g., Hopson v. City of Baltimore,* 232 F.R.D. 228, 244 (D.Md. 2005) (electronic discovery may encompass "millions of documents" and to insist upon "record-by-record pre-production privilege review, on pain of subject matter waiver, would impose upon parties costs of production that bear no proportionality to what is at stake in the litigation").

The rule seeks to provide a predictable, uniform set of standards under which parties can determine the consequences of a disclosure of a communication or information covered by the attorney-client privilege or work product protection. Parties to litigation need to know, for example, that if they exchange privileged information pursuant to a confidentiality order, the court's order will be enforceable. Moreover, if a federal court's confidentiality order is not enforceable in a state court then the burdensome costs of privilege review and retention are unlikely to be reduced.

The rule makes no attempt to alter federal or state law on whether a communication or information is protected under the attorney-client privilege or work product immunity as an initial matter. Moreover, while establishing some exceptions to waiver, the rule does not purport to supplant applicable waiver doctrine generally.

The rule governs only certain waivers by disclosure. Other common-law waiver doctrines may result in a finding of waiver even where there is no disclosure of privileged information or work product. *See, e.g., Nguyen v. Excel Corp.,* 197 F.3d 200 (5th Cir. 1999) (reliance on an advice of counsel defense waives the privilege with respect to attorney-client communications pertinent to that defense); *Ryers [Byers] v. Burleson,* 100 F.R.D. 436 (D.D.C. 1983) (allegation of lawyer malpractice constituted a waiver of confidential communications under the circumstances). The rule is not intended to displace or modify federal common law concerning waiver of privilege or work product where no disclosure has been made.

Subdivision (a). The rule provides that a voluntary disclosure in a federal proceeding or to a federal office or agency, if a waiver, generally results in a waiver only of the communication or information disclosed; a subject matter waiver (of either privilege or work product) is reserved for those unusual situations in which fairness requires a further disclosure of related, protected information, in order to prevent a selective and misleading presentation of evidence to the disadvantage of the adversary. *See, e.g., In re United Mine Workers of America Employee Benefit Plans Litig.,* 159 F.R.D. 307, 312 (D.D.C. 1994) (waiver of work product limited to materials actually disclosed, because the party did not deliberately disclose documents in an attempt to gain a tactical advantage). Thus, subject matter waiver is limited to situations in which a party intentionally puts protected information into the litigation in a selective, misleading and unfair manner. It follows that an inadvertent disclosure of protected information can never result in a subject matter waiver. See Rule 502(b). The rule rejects the result in *In re Sealed Case,* 877 F.2d 976 (D.C. Cir. 1989), which held that inadvertent disclosure of documents during discovery automatically constituted a subject matter waiver.

The language concerning subject matter waiver—"ought in fairness"—is taken from Rule 106, because the animating principle is the same. Under both Rules, a party that makes a selective, misleading presentation that is unfair to the adversary opens itself to a more complete and accurate presentation.

To assure protection and predictability, the rules provides that if a disclosure is made at the federal level, the federal rule on subject matter waiver governs subsequent state court determinations on the scope of the waiver by that disclosure.

Subdivision (b). Courts are in conflict over whether an inadvertent disclosure of a communication or information protected as privileged or work product constitutes a waiver. A few courts find that a disclosure must be intentional to be a waiver. Most courts find a waiver only if the disclosing party acted carelessly in disclosing the communication or information protected under the attorney-client privilege or as work product constitutes a waiver without regard to the protections taken to avoid such a disclosure. *See generally Hopson v. City of Baltimore,* 232 F.R.D. 228 (D. Md. 2005), for a discussion of this case law.

The rule opts for the middle ground: inadvertent disclosure of protected communications or information in connection with a federal proceeding or to a federal office or agency does not constitute a waiver if the holder took reasonable steps to prevent disclosure and also promptly took reasonable steps to rectify the error. This position is in accord with the majority view on whether inadvertent disclosure is a waiver.

Cases such as *Lois Sportswear, U.S.A., Inc. v. Levi Strauss & Co.,* 104 F.R.D. 103, 105 (S.D.N.Y. 1985) and *Hartford Fire Ins. Co. v. Garvey,* 109 F.R.D. 323, 332 (N.D. Cal. 1985), set out a multi-factor test for determining whether inadvertent disclosure is a waiver. The stated factors (none of which are dispositive) are the reasonableness of precautions taken, the time taken to rectify the error, the scope of discovery, the extent of disclosure and the overriding issue of fairness. The rule does not explicitly codify that test, because it is really a set of non-determinative guidelines that vary from case to case. The rule is flexible enough to accommodate any of those listed factors. Other considerations bearing on the reasonableness of a producing party's efforts include the number of documents to be reviewed and the time constraints for production. Depending on the circumstances, a party that uses advanced analytical software applications and linguistic tools in screening for privilege and work product may be found to have taken "reasonable steps" to prevent inadvertent disclosure. The implementation of an efficient system of records management before litigation may also be relevant.

The rule does not require the producing party to engage in a post-production review to determine whether any protected communication or information has been produced by mistake. But the rule does require the producing party to follow up on any obvious indications that a protected communication or information has been produced inadvertently.

The rule applies to inadvertent disclosures made to a federal office or agency, including but not limited to an office or agency that is acting in the course of its regulatory, investigative or enforcement authority. The consequences of waiver, and the concomitant costs of pre-production privilege review, can be as great with respect to disclosures to offices and agencies as they are in litigation.

Subdivision (c). Difficult questions can arise when 1) a disclosure of a communication or information protected by the attorney-client privilege or as work product is made in a state proceeding, 2) the communication or information is offered in a subsequent federal proceeding on the ground that the disclosure waived the privilege or protection, and 3) the state and federal laws are in conflict on the question of waiver. The Committee determined that the proper solution for the federal court is to apply the law that is most protective of privilege and work product. If the state law is more protective (such as where the state law is that an inadvertent disclosure can never be a waiver), the holder of the privilege or protection may well have relied on that law when making the disclosure in the state proceeding. Moreover, applying a more restrictive federal law of waiver could impair the state objective of preserving the privilege or work-product protection for disclosures made in state proceedings. On the other hand, if the federal law is more protective, applying the state law of waiver to determine admissibility in federal court is likely to undermine the federal objective of limiting the costs of production.

The rule does not address the enforceability of a state court confidentiality order in a federal proceeding, as that question is covered both by statutory law and principles of federalism and comity. See 28 U.S.C. § 1738 (providing that state judicial proceedings "shall have the same full faith and credit in every court within the United States. . . as they have by law or usage in the courts of such State. . . from which they are taken."). *See also Tucker v. Ohtsu Tire & Rubber Co.,* 191 F.R.D. 495, 499 (D. Md. 2000) (noting that a federal court considering the enforceability of a state confidentiality order is "constrained by principles of comity, courtesy, and. . . federalism"). Thus, a state court order finding no waiver in connection with a disclosure made in a state court proceeding is enforceable under existing law in subsequent federal proceedings.

Subdivision (d). Confidentiality orders are becoming increasingly important in limiting the costs of privilege review and retention, especially in cases involving electronic discovery. But the utility of a confidentiality order in reducing discovery costs is substantially diminished if it provides no protection outside the particular litigation in which the order is entered. Parties are unlikely to be able to reduce the costs of pre-production review for privilege and work product if the consequence of disclosure is that the communications or information could be used by non-parties to the litigation.

There is some dispute on whether a confidentiality order entered in one case is enforceable in other proceedings. *See generally Hopson v. City of Baltimore,* 232 F.R.D. 228 (D. Md. 2005), for a discussion of this case law. The rule provides that when a confidentiality order governing the consequences of disclosure in that case is entered in a federal proceeding, its terms are enforceable against non-parties in any federal or state proceeding. For example, the court order may provide for return of documents without waiver irrespective of the care taken by the disclosing party; the rule contemplates enforcement of "claw-back" and "quick peek" arrangements as a way to avoid the excessive costs of pre-production review for privilege and work product. *See Zubulake v. UBS Warburg LLC,* 216 F.R.D. 280, 290 (S.D.N.Y. 2003) (noting that parties may enter into "so-called 'claw-back' agreements that allow the parties to forego privilege review altogether in favor of an agreement to return inadvertently produced privilege documents"). The rule provides a party with a predictable protection from a court order—predictability that is needed to allow the party to plan in advance to limit the prohibitive costs of privilege and work product review and retention.

Under the rule, a confidentiality order is enforceable whether or not it memorializes an agreement among the parties to the litigation. party agreement should not be a condition of enforceability of a federal court's order.

Subdivision (e). Subdivision (e) codifies the well-established proposition that parties can enter an agreement to limit the effect of waiver by disclosure between or among them. Of course such an agreement can bind only the parties to the agreement. The rule makes clear that if parties want protection against non-parties from a finding of waiver by disclosure, the agreement must be made part of a court order.

Subdivision (f). The protections against waiver provided by Rule 502 must be applicable when protected communications or information disclosed in federal proceedings are subsequently offered in state proceedings. Otherwise, the holders of protected communications and information, and their lawyers, could not rely on the protections provided by the Rule, and the goal of limiting costs in discovery would be substantially undermined. Rule 502(g) [sic] is intended to resolve any potential tension between the provisions of Rule 502 that apply to state proceedings and the possible limitations on the applicability of the Federal Rules of Evidence otherwise provided by Rules 101 and 1101.

The rule is intended to apply in all federal court proceedings, including court-annexed and court-ordered arbitrations, without regard to any possible limitations of Rules 101 and 1101. This provision is not intended to raise an inference about the applicability of any other rule of evidence in arbitration proceedings more generally.

The costs of discovery can be equally high for state and federal causes of action, and the rule seeks to limit those costs in all federal proceedings, regardless of whether the claim arises under state or federal law. Accordingly, the rule applies to state law causes of action brought in federal court.

Subdivision (g). The rule's coverage is limited to attorney-client privilege and work product. The operation of waiver by disclosure, as applied to other evidentiary privileges, remains a question of federal common law. Nor does the rule purport to apply to the Fifth Amendment privilege against compelled self-incrimination.

The definition of work product "materials"' is intended to include both tangible and intangible information. *See In re Cendant Corp. Sec. Litig.,* 343 F.3d 658, 662 (3d Cir. 2003) ("work product protection extends to both tangible and intangible work product").

Addendum to Committee Note. By memorandum dated September 14, 2009, the Committee on Rules of Practice and Procedure of the Judicial Conference of the United States added the following addendum to the Committee Note to Rule 502:

STATEMENT OF CONGRESSIONAL INTENT REGARDING RULE 502 OF THE FEDERAL RULES OF EVIDENCE.

During consideration of this rule in Congress, a number of questions were raised about the scope and contours of the effect of the proposed rule on current law regarding attorney-client privilege and work-product protection. These questions were ultimately answered satisfactorily, without need to revise the text of the rule as submitted to Congress by the Judicial Conference.

In general, these questions are answered by keeping in mind the limited though important purpose and focus of the rule. The rule addresses only the effect of disclosure, under specified circumstances, of a communication that is otherwise protected by attorney-client privilege, or of information that is protected by work-product protection, on whether the disclosure itself operates as a waiver of the privilege or protection for purposes of admissibility of evidence in a federal or state judicial or administrative proceeding. The rule does not alter the substantive law regarding attorney-client privilege or work-product protection in any other respect, including the burden on the party invoking the privilege (or protection) to prove that the particular information (or communication) qualifies for it. And it is not intended to alter the rules and practices governing use of information outside this evidentiary context.

Some of these questions are addressed more specifically below, in order to help further avoid uncertainty in the interpretation and application of the rule.

Subdivision (a)—Disclosure vs. Use.

This subdivision does not alter the substantive law regarding when a party's strategic use in litigation of otherwise privileged information obliges that party to waive the privilege regarding other information concerning the same subject matter, so that the information being used can be fairly considered in context. One situation in which this issue arises, the assertion as a defense in patent-infringement litigation that a party was relying on advice of counsel, is discussed elsewhere in this Note. In this and similar situations, under subdivision (a)(1) the party using an attorney-client communication to its advantage in the litigation has, in so doing, intentionally waived the privilege as to other communications concerning the same subject matter, regardless of the circumstances in which the communication being so used was initially disclosed.

Subdivision (b)—Fairness Considerations.

The standard set forth in this subdivision for determining whether a disclosure operates as a waiver of the privilege or protection is, as explained elsewhere in this Note, the majority rule in the federal courts. The majority rule has simply been distilled here into a standard designed to be predictable in its application. This distillation is not intended to foreclose notions of fairness from continuing to inform application of the standard in all aspects as appropriate in particular cases-for example, as to whether steps taken to rectify an erroneous inadvertent disclosure were sufficiently prompt under subdivision (b)(3) where the receiving party has relied on the information disclosed.

Subdivisions (a) and (b)—Disclosures to Federal Office or Agency.

This rule, as a Federal Rule of Evidence, applies to admissibility of evidence. While subdivisions (a) and (b) are written broadly to apply as appropriate to disclosures of information to a federal office or agency, they do not apply to uses of information—such as routine use in government publications—that fall outside the evidentiary context. Nor do these subdivisions relieve the party seeking to protect the information as privileged from the burden of proving that the privilege applies in the first place.

Subdivision (d)—Court Orders.

This subdivision authorizes a court to enter orders only in the context of litigation pending before the court. And it does not alter the law regarding waiver of privilege resulting from having acquiesced in the use of otherwise privileged information. Therefore, this subdivision does not provide a basis for a court to enable parties to agree to a selective waiver of the privilege, such as to a federal agency conducting an investigation, while preserving the privilege as against other parties seeking the information. This subdivision is designed to enable a court to enter an order, whether on motion of one or more parties or on its own motion, that will allow the parties to conduct and respond to discovery expeditiously, without the need for exhaustive pre-production privilege reviews, while still preserving each party's right to assert the privilege to preclude use in litigation of information disclosed in such discovery. While the benefits of a court order under this subdivision would be equally available in government enforcement actions as in private actions, acquiescence by the disclosing party in use by the federal agency of information disclosed pursuant to such an order would still be treated as under current law for purposes of determining whether the acquiescence in use of the information, as opposed to its mere disclosure, effects a waiver of the privilege. The same applies to acquiescence in use by another private party.

Moreover, whether the order is entered on motion of one or more parties, or on the court's own motion, the court retains its authority to include the conditions it deems appropriate in the circumstances.

Subdivision (e)—Party Agreements.

This subdivision simply makes clear that while parties to a case may agree among themselves regarding the effect of disclosures between each other in a federal proceeding, it is not binding on others unless it is incorporated into a court order. This subdivision does not confer any authority on a court to enter any order regarding the effect of disclosures. That authority must be found in subdivision (d), or elsewhere.

Notes of Advisory Committee on 2011 amendments. Rule 502 has been amended by changing the initial letter of a few words from uppercase to lowercase as part of the restyling of the Evidence Rules to make style and terminology consistent throughout the rules. There is no intent to change any result in any ruling on evidence admissibility.

ARTICLE VI. WITNESSES

Rule

Rule 601. Competency to Testify in General

Every person is competent to be a witness unless these rules provide otherwise. But in a civil case, state law governs the witness's competency regarding a claim or defense for which state law supplies the rule of decision.

HISTORY:

Jan. 2, 1975, P. L. 93-595, § 1, 88 Stat. 1934; April 26, 2011, eff. Dec. 1, 2011.

HISTORY; ANCILLARY LAWS AND DIRECTIVES

Other provisions:

Notes of Advisory Committee on Rules. This general ground-clearing eliminates all grounds of incompetency not specifically recognized in the succeeding rules of this Article. Included among the grounds thus abolished are religious belief, conviction of crime, and connection with the litigation as a party or interested person or spouse of a party or interested person. With the exception of the so-called Dead Man's Acts, American jurisdictions generally have ceased to recognize these grounds.

The Dead Man's Acts are surviving traces of the common law disqualification of parties and interested persons. They exist in variety too great to convey conviction of their wisdom and effectiveness. These rules contain no provision of this kind. For the reasoning underlying the decision not to give effect to state statutes in diversity cases, see the Advisory Committee's Note to Rule 501.

No mental or moral qualifications for testifying as a witness are specified. Standards of mental capacity have proved elusive in actual application. A leading commentator observes that few witnesses are disqualified on that ground. Weihofen, Testimonial Competence and Credibility, 34 Geo. Wash.L.Rev. 53 (1965). Discretion is regularly exercised in favor of allowing the testimony. A witness wholly without capacity is difficult to imagine. The question is one particularly suited to the jury as one of weight and credibility, subject to judicial authority to review the sufficiency of the evidence. 2 Wigmore §§ 501, 509. Standards of moral qualification in practice consist essentially of evaluating a person's truthfulness in terms of his own answers about it. Their principal utility is in affording an opportunity on voir dire examination to impress upon the witness his moral duty. This result may, however, be accomplished more directly, and without haggling in terms of legal standards, by the manner of administering the oath or affirmation under Rule 603.

Admissibility of religious belief as a ground of impeachment is treated in Rule 610. Conviction of crime as a ground of impeachment is the subject of Rule 609. Marital relationship is the basis for privilege under Rule 505. Interest in the outcome of litigation and mental capacity are, of course, highly relevant to credibility and require no special treatment to render them admissible along with other matters bearing upon the perception, memory, and narration of witnesses.

Notes of Committee on the Judiciary, House Report No. 93-650. Rule 601 as submitted to the Congress provided that "Every person is competent to be a witness except as otherwise provided in these rules." One effect of the Rule as proposed would have been to abolish age, mental capacity, and other grounds recognized in some State jurisdictions as making a person incompetent as a witness. The greatest controversy centered around the Rule's rendering inapplicable in the federal courts the so-called Dead Man's Statutes which exist in some States. Acknowledging that there is substantial disagreement as to the merit of Dead Man's Statutes, the Committee nevertheless believed that where such statutes have been enacted they represent State policy which should not be overturned in the absence of a compelling federal interest. The Committee therefore amended the Rule to make competency in civil actions determinable in accordance with State law with respect to elements of claims or defenses as to which State law supplies the rule of decision. Cf. Courtland v Walston & Co., Inc., 340 F.Supp. 1076, 1087–1092 (S.D.N.Y. 1972).

Notes of Committee on the Judiciary, Senate Report No. 93-1277. The amendment to rule 601 parallels the treatment accorded rule 501 discussed immediately above.

Notes of Conference Committee, House Report No. 93-1597. Rule 601 deals with competency of witnesses. Both the House and Senate bills provide that federal competency law applies in criminal cases. In civil actions and proceedings, the House bill provides that state competency law applies "to an element of a claim or defense as to which State law supplies the rule of decision." The Senate bill provides that "in civil actions and proceedings arising under 28 U.S.C. § 1332 or 28 U.S.C. § 1335, or between citizens of different States and removed under 28 U.S.C. § 1441(b) the competency of a witness, person, government, State or political subdivision thereof is determined in accordance with State law, unless with respect to the particular claim or defense, Federal law supplies the rule of decision."

The wording of the House and Senate bills differs in the treatment of civil actions and proceedings. The rule in the House bill applies to evidence that relates to "an element of a claim or defense." If an item of proof tends to support or defeat a claim or defense, or an element of a claim or defense, and if state law supplies the rule of decision for that claim or defense, then state competency law applies to that item of proof.

For reasons similar to those underlying its action on Rule 501, the Conference adopts the House provision.

Notes of Advisory Committee on 2011 amendments. The language of Rule 601 has been amended as part of the restyling of the Evidence Rules to make them more easily understood and to make style and terminology consistent throughout the rules. These changes are intended to be stylistic only. There is no intent to change any result in any ruling on evidence admissibility.

Rule 602. Need for Personal Knowledge

A witness may testify to a matter only if evidence is introduced sufficient to support a finding that the witness has personal knowledge of the matter. Evidence to prove personal knowledge may consist of the witness's own testimony. This rule does not apply to a witness's expert testimony under Rule 703.

HISTORY:

Jan. 2, 1975, P. L. 93-595, § 1, 88 Stat. 1934; March 2, 1987, eff. Oct. 1, 1987; April 25, 1988, eff. Nov. 1, 1988; April 26, 2011, eff. Dec. 1, 2011.

HISTORY; ANCILLARY LAWS AND DIRECTIVES

Other provisions:

Notes of Advisory Committee on Rules. "* * * [T]he rule requiring that a witness who testifies to a fact which can be perceived by the senses must have had an opportunity to observe, and must have actually observed the fact" is a "most pervasive manifestation" of the common law insistence upon "the most reliable sources of information." McCormick § 10, p. 19. These foundation requirements may, of course, be furnished by the testimony of the witness himself; hence personal knowledge is not an absolute but may consist of what the witness thinks he knows from personal perception. 2 Wigmore § 650. It will be observed that the rule is in fact a specialized application of the provisions of Rule 104(b) on conditional relevancy.

This rule does not govern the situation of a witness who testifies to a hearsay statement as such, if he has personal knowledge of the making of the statement. Rules 801 and 805 would be applicable. This rule would, however, prevent him from testifying to the subject matter of the hearsay statement, as he has no personal knowledge of it.

The reference to Rule 703 is designed to avoid any question of conflict between the present rule and the provisions of that rule allowing an expert to express opinions based on facts of which he does not have personal knowledge.

Notes of Advisory Committee on 1987 amendments. The amendments are technical. No substantive change is intended.

Notes of Advisory Committee on 1988 amendments. The amendment is technical. No substantive change is intended.

Notes of Advisory Committee on 2011 amendments. The language of Rule 602 has been amended as part of the restyling of the Evidence Rules to make them more easily understood and to make style and terminology consistent throughout the rules. These changes are intended to be stylistic only. There is no intent to change any result in any ruling on evidence admissibility.

Rule 603. Oath or Affirmation to Testify Truthfully

Before testifying, a witness must give an oath or affirmation to testify truthfully. It must be in a form designed to impress that duty on the witness's conscience.

HISTORY:

Jan. 2, 1975, P. L. 93-595, § 1, 88 Stat. 1934; March 2, 1987, eff. Oct. 1, 1987; April 26, 2011, eff. Dec. 1, 2011.

HISTORY; ANCILLARY LAWS AND DIRECTIVES

Other provisions:

Notes of Advisory Committee on Rules. The rule is designed to afford the flexibility required in dealing with religious adults, atheists, conscientious objectors, mental defectives, and children. Affirmation is simply a solemn undertaking to tell the truth; no special verbal formula is required. As is true generally, affirmation is recognized by federal law. "Oath" includes affirmation, 1 U.S.C. § 1; judges and clerks may administer oaths and affirmations, 28 U.S.C. §§ 459, 953; and affirmations are acceptable in lieu of oaths under Rule 43(d) of the Federal Rules of Civil Procedure. Perjury by a witness is a crime, 18 U.S.C. § 1621.

Notes of Advisory Committee on 1987 amendments. The amendments are technical. No substantive change is intended.

Notes of Advisory Committee on 2011 amendments. The language of Rule 603 has been amended as part of the restyling of the Evidence Rules to make them more easily understood and to make style and terminology consistent throughout the rules. These changes are intended to be stylistic only. There is no intent to change any result in any ruling on evidence admissibility.

Rule 604. Interpreter

An interpreter must be qualified and must give an oath or affirmation to make a true translation.

HISTORY:

Jan. 2, 1975, P. L. 93-595, § 1, 88 Stat. 1934; March 2, 1987, eff. Oct. 1, 1987; April 26, 2011, eff. Dec. 1, 2011.

HISTORY; ANCILLARY LAWS AND DIRECTIVES

Other provisions:

Notes of Advisory Committee on Rules. The rule implements Rule 43(f) of the Federal Rules of Civil Procedure and Rule 28(b) of the Federal Rules of Criminal Procedure, both of which contain provisions for the appointment and compensation of interpreters.

Notes of Advisory Committee on 1987 amendments. The amendment is technical. No substantive change is intended.

Notes of Advisory Committee on 2011 amendments. The language of Rule 604 has been amended as part of the restyling of the Evidence Rules to make them more easily understood and to make style and terminology consistent throughout the rules. These changes are intended to be stylistic only. There is no intent to change any result in any ruling on evidence admissibility.

Rule 605. Judge's Competency as a Witness

The presiding judge may not testify as a witness at the trial. A party need not object to preserve the issue.

HISTORY:

Jan. 2, 1975, P. L. 93-595, § 1, 88 Stat. 1934; April 26, 2011, eff. Dec. 1, 2011.

HISTORY; ANCILLARY LAWS AND DIRECTIVES

Other provisions:

Notes of Advisory Committee on Rules. In view of the mandate of 28 U.S.C. § 455 that a judge disqualify himself in "any case in which he * * * is or has been a material witness," the likelihood that the presiding judge in a federal court might be called to testify in the trial over which he is presiding is slight. Nevertheless the possibility is not totally eliminated.

The solution here presented is a broad rule of incompetency, rather than such alternatives as incompetency only as to material matters, leaving the matter to the discretion of the judge, or recognizing no incompetency. The choice is the result of inability to evolve satisfactory answers to questions which arise when the judge abandons the bench for the witness stand. Who rules on objections? Who compels him to answer? Can he rule impartially on the weight and admissibility of his own testimony? Can he be impeached or cross-examined effectively? Can he, in a jury trial, avoid conferring his seal of approval on one side in the eyes of the jury? Can he, in a bench trial, avoid an involvement destructive of impartiality? The rule of general incompetency has substantial support. See Report of the Special Committee on the Propriety of Judges Appearing as Witnesses, 36 A.B.A.J. 630 (1950); cases collected in

Annot. 157 A.L.R. 311; McCormick § 68, p. 147; Uniform Rule 42; California Evidence Code § 703; Kansas Code of Civil Procedure § 60-442; New Jersey Evidence Rule 42. Cf. 6 Wigmore § 1909, which advocates leaving the matter to the discretion of the judge, and statutes to that effect collected in Annot. 157 A.L.R. 311.

The rule provides an "automatic" objection. To require an actual objection would confront the opponent with a choice between not objecting, with the result of allowing the testimony, and objecting, with the probable result of excluding the testimony but at the price of continuing the trial before a judge likely to feel that his integrity had been attacked by the objector.

Notes of Advisory Committee on 2011 amendments. The language of Rule 605 has been amended as part of the restyling of the Evidence Rules to make them more easily understood and to make style and terminology consistent throughout the rules. These changes are intended to be stylistic only. There is no intent to change any result in any ruling on evidence admissibility.

Rule 606. Juror's Competency as a Witness

(a) At the Trial. A juror may not testify as a witness before the other jurors at the trial. If a juror is called to testify, the court must give a party an opportunity to object outside the jury's presence.

(b) During an Inquiry into the Validity of a Verdict or Indictment.

(1) *Prohibited Testimony or Other Evidence.* During an inquiry into the validity of a verdict or indictment, a juror may not testify about any statement made or incident that occurred during the jury's deliberations; the effect of anything on that juror's or another juror's vote; or any juror's mental processes concerning the verdict or indictment. The court may not receive a juror's affidavit or evidence of a juror's statement on these matters.

(2) *Exceptions.* A juror may testify about whether:

(A) extraneous prejudicial information was improperly brought to the jury's attention;

(B) an outside influence was improperly brought to bear on any juror; or

(C) a mistake was made in entering the verdict on the verdict form.

HISTORY:

Jan. 2, 1975, P. L. 93-595, § 1, 88 Stat. 1934; Dec. 12, 1975, P.L. 94-149, § 1(10), 89 Stat. 805; March 2, 1987, eff. Oct. 1, 1987; April 12, 2006, eff. Dec. 1, 2006; April 26, 2011, eff. Dec. 1, 2011.

HISTORY; ANCILLARY LAWS AND DIRECTIVES

Other provisions:

Notes of Advisory Committee on Rules. *Subdivision (a).* The considerations which bear upon the permissibility of testimony by a juror in the trial in which he is sitting as juror bear an obvious similarity to those evoked when the judge is called as a witness. See Advisory Committee's Note to Rule 605. The judge is not, however in this instance so involved as to call for departure from usual principles requiring objection to be made; hence the only provision on objection is that opportunity be afforded for its making out of the presence of the jury. Compare Rule 605.

Subdivision (b). Whether testimony, affidavits, or statements of jurors should be received for the purpose of invalidating or supporting a verdict or indictment, and if so, under what circumstances, has given rise to substantial differences of opinion. The familiar rubric that a juror may not impeach his own verdict, dating from Lord Mansfield's time, is a gross oversimplification. The values sought to be promoted by excluding the evidence include freedom of deliberation, stability and finality of verdicts, and protection of jurors against annoyance and embarrassment. *McDonald v. Piess,* 238 U.S. 264, 35 S.Ct. 785, 59 L.Ed. 1300 (1915). On the other hand, simply putting verdicts beyond effective reach can only promote irregularity and injustice. The rule offers an accommodation between these competing considerations.

The mental operations and emotional reactions of jurors in arriving at a given result would, if allowed as a subject of inquiry, place every verdict at the mercy of jurors and invite tampering and harassment. See *Grenz v. Werre,* 129 N.W.2d 681 (N.D. 1964). The authorities are in virtually complete accord in excluding the evidence. Fryer, Note on Disqualification of Witnesses, Selected Writings on Evidence and Trial 345, 347 (Fryer ed. 1957); Maguire, Weinstein, et al., Cases on Evidence 887 (5th ed. 1965); 8 Wigmore § 2340 (McNaughton Rev. 1961). As to matters other than mental operations and emotional reactions of jurors, substantial authority refuses to allow a juror to disclose irregularities which occur in the jury room, but allows his testimony as to irregularities occurring outside and allows outsiders to testify as to occurrences both inside and out. 8 Wigmore § 2354 (McNaughton Rev. 1961). However, the door of the jury room is not necessarily a satisfactory dividing point, and the Supreme Court has refused to accept it for every situation. *Mattox v. United States,* 146 U.S. 140, 13 S.Ct. 50, 36 L.Ed. 917 (1892).

Under the federal decisions the central focus has been upon insulation of the manner in which the jury reached its verdict, and this protection extends to each of the components of deliberation, including arguments, statements, discussions, mental and emotional reactions, votes, and any other feature of the process. Thus testimony or affidavits of jurors have been held incompetent to show a compromise verdict, *Hyde v. United States,* 225 U.S. 347, 382 (1912); a quotient verdict, *McDonald v. Piess,* 238 U.S. 264 (1915); speculation as to insurance coverage, *Holden v. Porter,* 495 F.2d 878 (10th Cir.1969), *Farmers Coop. Elev. Ass'n v. Strand,* 382 F.2d 224, 230 (8th Cir. 1967), cert. denied 389 U.S. 1014; misinterpretations of instructions, *Farmers Coop. Elev. Ass'n v. Strand, supra*; mistake in returning verdict, *United States v. Chereton,* 309 F.2d 197 (6th Cir. 1962); interpretation of guilty plea by one defendant as implicating others, *United States v. Crosby,* 294 F.2d 928, 949 (2d Cir. 1961). The policy does not, however, foreclose testimony by jurors as to prejudicial extraneous information or influences injected into or brought to bear upon the deliberative process. Thus a juror is recognized as competent to testify to statements by the bailiff or the introduction of a prejudicial newspaper account into the jury room, *Mattox v. United States,* 146 U.S. 140 (1892). See also *Parker v. Gladden,* 385 U.S. 363 (1966).

This rule does not purport to specify the substantive grounds for setting aside verdicts for irregularity; it deals only with the competency of jurors to testify concerning those grounds. Allowing them to testify as to matters other than their own inner reactions involves no particular hazard to the values sought to be protected. The rules is based upon this conclusion. It makes no attempt to specify the substantive grounds for setting aside verdicts for irregularity.

See also Rule 6(e) of the Federal Rules of Criminal Procedure and 18 U.S.C. § 3500, governing the secrecy of grand jury proceedings. The present rules does not relate to secrecy and disclosure but to the competency of certain witnesses and evidence.

Notes of Committee on the Judiciary, House Report No. 93-650. As proposed by the Court, Rule 606(b) limited testimony by a juror in the course of an inquiry into the validity of a verdict or indictment. He could testify as to the influence of extraneous prejudicial information brought to the jury's attention (e.g. a radio newscast or a newspaper account) or an outside influence which improperly had been brought to bear upon a juror (e.g. a threat to the safety of a member of his family), but he could not testify as to other irregularities which occurred in the jury room. Under this formulation a quotient verdict could not be attacked through the testimony of a juror, nor could a juror testify to the drunken condition of a fellow juror which so disabled him that he could not participate in the jury's deliberations.

The 1969 and 1971 Advisory Committee drafts would have permitted a member of the jury to testify concerning these kinds of irregularities in the jury room. The Advisory Committee note in the 1971 draft stated that "* * * the door of the jury room is not a satisfactory dividing point, and the Supreme Court has refused to accept it." The Advisory Committee further commented that—

> The trend has been to draw the dividing line between testimony as to mental processes, on the one hand, and as to the existence of conditions or occurrences of events calculated improperly to influence the verdict, on the other hand, without regard to whether the happening is within or without the jury room. * * * The jurors are the persons who know what really happened. Allowing them to testify as to matters other than their own reactions involves no particular hazard to the values sought to be protected. The rule is based upon this conclusion. It makes no attempt to specify the substantive grounds for setting aside verdicts for irregularity.

Objective jury misconduct may be testified to in California, Florida, Iowa, Kansas, Nebraska, New Jersey, North Dakota, Ohio, Oregon, Tennessee, Texas, and Washington.

Persuaded that the better practice is that provided for in the earlier drafts, the Committee amended subdivision (b) to read in the text of those drafts.

Notes of Committee on the Judiciary, Senate Report No. 93-1277. As adopted by the House, this rule would permit the impeachment of verdicts by inquiry into, not the mental processes of the jurors, but what happened in terms of conduct in the jury room. This extension of the ability to impeach a verdict is felt to be unwarranted and ill-advised.

The rule passed by the House embodies a suggestion by the Advisory Committee of the Judicial Conference that is considerably broader than the final version adopted by the Supreme Court, which embodies long-accepted Federal law. Although forbidding the impeachment of verdicts by inquiry into the jurors' mental processes, it deletes from the Supreme Court version the proscription against testimony "as to any matter or statement occurring during the course of the jury's deliberations." This deletion would have the effect of opening verdicts up to challenge on the basis of what happened during the jury's internal deliberations, for example, where a juror alleged that the jury refused to follow the trial judge's instructions or that some of the jurors did not take part in deliberations.

Permitting an individual to attack a jury verdict based upon the jury's internal deliberations has long been recognized as unwise by the Supreme Court. In *McDonald v. Pless,* the Court stated:

> [L]et it once be established that verdicts solemnly made and publicly returned into court can be attacked and set aside on the testimony of those who took part in their publication and all verdicts could be, and many would be, followed by an inquiry in the hope of discovering something which might invalidate the finding. Jurors would be harassed and beset by the defeated party in an effort to secure from them evidence of facts which might establish misconduct sufficient to set aside a verdict. If evidence thus secured could be thus used, the result would be to make what was intended to be a private deliberation, the constant subject of public investigation—to the destruction of all frankness and freedom of discussion and conference [238 U.S. 264, at 267 (1914)].

* * * * *

As it stands then, the rule would permit the harassment of former jurors by losing parties as well as the possible exploitation of disgruntled or otherwise badly-motivated ex-jurors.

Public policy requires a finality to litigation. And common fairness requires that absolute privacy be preserved for jurors to engage in the full and free debate necessary to the attainment of just verdicts. Jurors will not be able to function effectively if their deliberations are to be scrutinized in post-trial litigation. In the interest of protecting the jury system and the citizens who make it work, rule 606 should not permit any inquiry into the internal deliberations of the jurors.

Notes of Conference Committee, House Report No. 93-1597. Rule 606(b) deals with juror testimony in an inquiry into the validity of a verdict or indictment. The House bill provides that a juror cannot testify about his mental processes or about the effect of anything upon his or another juror's mind as influencing him to assent to or dissent from a verdict or indictment. Thus, the House bill allows a juror to testify about objective matters occurring during the jury's deliberation, such as the misconduct of another juror or the reaching of a quotient verdict. The Senate bill does not permit juror testimony about any matter or statement occurring during the course of the jury's deliberations. The Senate bill does provide, however, that a juror may testify on the question whether extraneous prejudicial information was improperly brought to the jury's attention and on the question whether any outside influence was improperly brought to bear on any juror.

The Conference adopts the Senate amendment. The Conferees believe that jurors should be encouraged to be conscientious in promptly reporting to the court misconduct that occurs during jury deliberations.

Notes of Advisory Committee on 1987 amendments to Rules. The amendments are technical. No substantive change is intended.

Notes of Advisory Committee on 2006 amendments. Rule 606(b) has been amended to provide that juror testimony may be used to prove that the verdict reported was the result of a mistake in entering the verdict on the verdict form. The amendment responds to a divergence between the text of the Rule and the case law that has established an exception for proof of clerical errors. *See, e.g., Plummer v. Springfield Term. Ry.,* 5 F.3d 1, 3 (1st Cir. 1993) ("A number of circuits hold, and we agree, that juror testimony regarding an alleged clerical error, such as announcing a verdict different than that agreed upon, does not challenge the validity of the verdict or the deliberation of mental processes, and therefore is not subject to Rule 606(b)."); *Teevee Toons, Inc., v. MP3. Com, Inc.,* 148 F.Supp.2d 276, 278 (S.D.N.Y. 2001) (noting that Rule 606(b) has been silent regarding inquiries designed to confirm the accuracy of a verdict).

In adopting the exception for proof of mistakes in entering the verdict on the verdict form, the amendment specifically rejects the broader exception, adopted by some courts, permitting the use of juror testimony to prove that the jurors were operating under a misunderstanding about the consequences of the result that they agreed upon. *See, e.g., Attridge v. Cencorp Div. of Dover Techs. Int'l, Inc.,* 836 F.2d 113, 116 (2d Cir. 1987); *Eastridge Development Co., v. Halpert Associates, Inc.,* 853 F.2d 772 (10th Cir. 1988). The broader exception is rejected because an inquiry into whether the jury misunderstood or misapplied an instruction goes to the jurors' mental processes underlying the verdict, rather than the verdict's accuracy in capturing what the jurors had agreed upon. *See, e.g., Karl v. Burlington Northern R.R.,* 880 F.2d 68, 74 (8th Cir. 1989) (error to receive juror testimony on whether verdict was the result of jurors' misunderstanding of instructions: "The jurors did not state that the figure written by the foreman was different from that which they agreed upon, but indicated that the figure the foreman wrote down was intended to be a net figure, not a gross figure. Receiving such statements violates Rule 606(b) because the testimony relates to how the jury interpreted the court's instructions, and concerns the jurors' 'mental processes,' which is forbidden by the rule."); *Robles v. Exxon Corp.,* 862 F.2d 1201, 1208 (5th Cir. 1989) ("the alleged error here goes to the substance of what the jury was asked to decide, necessarily implicating the jury's mental processes insofar as it questions the jury's understanding of the court's instructions and application of those instructions to the facts of the case"). Thus, the exception established by the amendment is limited to cases such as "where the jury foreperson wrote down, in response to an interrogatory, a number different from that agreed upon by the jury, or mistakenly stated that the defendant was 'guilty' when the jury had actually agreed that the defendant was not guilty." *Id.*

It should be noted that the possibility of errors in the verdict form will be reduced substantially by polling the jury. Rule 606(b) does not, of course, prevent this precaution. *See* 8 C. Wigmore, *Evidence,* § 2350 at 691 (McNaughten ed. 1961) (noting that the reasons for the rule barring juror testimony, "namely, the dangers of uncertainty and of tampering with the jurors to procure testimony, disappear in large part if such investigation as may be desired is *made by the judge* and takes place *before the jurors' discharge* and separation") (emphasis in original). Errors that come to light after polling the jury "may be corrected on the spot, or the jury may be sent out to continue deliberations, or, if necessary, a new trial may be ordered." C. Mueller & L. Kirkpatrick, *Evidence Under the Rules* at 671 (2d ed. 1999) (citing *Sincox v. United States,* 571 F.2d 876, 878–79 (5th Cir. 1978)).

Notes of Advisory Committee on 2011 amendments. The language of Rule 606 has been amended as part of the restyling of the Evidence Rules to make them more easily understood and to make style and terminology consistent throughout the rules. These changes are intended to be stylistic only. There is no intent to change any result in any ruling on evidence admissibility.

Amendments:

1975.

Act Dec. 12, 1975, in subsec. (b), substituted "about which" for "about what".

Rule 607. Who May Impeach a Witness

Any party, including the party that called the witness, may attack the witness's credibility.

HISTORY:

Jan. 2, 1975, P. L. 93-595, § 1, 88 Stat. 1934; March 2, 1987, eff. Oct. 1, 1987; April 26, 2011, eff. Dec. 1, 2011.

HISTORY; ANCILLARY LAWS AND DIRECTIVES

Other provisions:

Notes of Advisory Committee on Rules. The traditional rule against impeaching one's own witness is abandoned as based on false premises. A party does not hold out his witnesses as worthy of belief, since he rarely has a free choice in selecting them. Denial of the right leaves the party at the mercy of the witness and the adversary. If the impeachment is by a prior statement, it is free from hearsay dangers and is excluded from the category of hearsay under Rule 801(d)(1). Ladd, Impeachment of One's Own Witness—New Developments 4 U.Chi.L.Rev. 69 (1936); McCormick § 38; 3 Wigmore §§ 896–918. The substantial inroads into the old rule made over the years by decisions, rules, and statutes are evidence of doubts as to its basic soundness and workability. Cases are collected in 3 Wigmore § 905. Revised Rule 32(a)(1) of the Federal Rules of Civil Procedure allows any party to impeach a witness by means of his deposition, and Rule 43(b) has allowed the calling and impeachment of an adverse party or person identified with him. Illustrative statutes allowing a party to impeach his own witness under varying circumstances are Ill.Rev. Stats.1967, c. 110, § 60; Mass.Laws Annot. 1959, c. 233 § 23; 20 N.M.Stats. Annot. 1953, § 20-2-4; N.Y. CPLR § 4514 (McKinney 1963); 12 Vt.Stats. Annot. 1959, §§ 1641a, 1642. Complete judicial rejection of the old rule is found in United States v. Freeman, 302 F.2d 347 (2d Cir. 1962). The same result is reached in Uniform Rule 20; California Evidence Code § 785; Kansas Code of Civil Procedure § 60-420. See also New Jersey Evidence Rule 20.

Notes of Advisory Committee on 1987 amendments. The amendment is technical. No substantive change is intended.

Notes of Advisory Committee on 2011 amendments. The language of Rule 607 has been amended as part of the restyling of the Evidence Rules to make them more easily understood and to make style and terminology consistent throughout the rules. These changes are intended to be

stylistic only. There is no intent to change any result in any ruling on evidence admissibility.

Rule 608. A Witness's Character for Truthfulness or Untruthfulness

(a) Reputation or Opinion Evidence. A witness's credibility may be attacked or supported by testimony about the witness's reputation for having a character for truthfulness or untruthfulness, or by testimony in the form of an opinion about that character. But evidence of truthful character is admissible only after the witness's character for truthfulness has been attacked.

(b) Specific Instances of Conduct. Except for a criminal conviction under Rule 609, extrinsic evidence is not admissible to prove specific instances of a witness's conduct in order to attack or support the witness's character for truthfulness. But the court may, on cross-examination, allow them to be inquired into if they are probative of the character for truthfulness or untruthfulness of:

(1) the witness; or

(2) another witness whose character the witness being cross-examined has testified about.

By testifying on another matter, a witness does not waive any privilege against self-incrimination for testimony that relates only to the witness's character for truthfulness.

HISTORY:

Jan. 2, 1975, P. L. 93-595, § 1, 88 Stat. 1935; March 2, 1987, eff. Oct. 1, 1987; April 25, 1988, eff. Nov. 1, 1988; March 27, 2003, eff. Dec. 1, 2003; April 26, 2011, eff. Dec. 1, 2011.

HISTORY; ANCILLARY LAWS AND DIRECTIVES

Other provisions:

Notes of Advisory Committee on Rules. *Subdivision (a).* In Rule 404(a) the general position is taken that character evidence is not admissible for the purpose of proving that the person acted in conformity therewith, subject, however, to several exceptions, one of which is character evidence of a witness as bearing upon his credibility. The present rule develops that exception.

In accordance with the bulk of judicial authority, the inquiry is strictly limited to character for veracity, rather than allowing evidence as to character generally. The result is to sharpen relevancy, to reduce surprise, waste of time, and confusion, and to make the lot of the witness somewhat less unattractive. McCormick § 44.

The use of opinion and reputation evidence as means of proving the character of witnesses is consistent with Rule 405(a). While the modern practice has purported to exclude opinion witnesses who testify to reputation seem in fact often to be giving their opinions, disguised somewhat misleadingly as reputation. See McCormick § 44. And even under the modern practice, a common relaxation has allowed inquiry as to whether the witnesses would believe the principal witness under oath. *United States v. Walker,* 313 F.2d 236 (6th Cir. 1963), and cases cited therein; McCormick § 44, pp. 94–95, n. 3.

Character evidence in support of credibility is admissible under the rule only after the witness' character has first been attacked, as has been the case at common law. Maguire, Weinstein, et al., Cases on Evidence 295 (5th ed. 1965); McCormick § 49, p. 105; 4 Wigmore § 1104. The enormous needless consumption of time which a contrary practice would entail justifies the limitation. Opinion or reputation that the witness is untruthful specifically qualifies as an attack under the rule, and evidence or misconduct, including conviction of crime, and of corruption also fall within this category. Evidence of bias or interest does not. McCormick § 49; 4 Wigmore §§ 1106, 1107. Whether evidence in the form of contradiction is an attack upon the character of the witness must depend §§ 1108, 1109.

As to the use of specific instances on direct by an opinion witness, see the Advisory Committee's Note to Rule 405, supra.

Subdivision (b). In conformity with Rule 405, which forecloses use of evidence of specific incidents as proof in chief of character unless character is an issue in the case, the present rule generally bars evidence of specific instances of conduct of a witness for the purpose of attacking or supporting his credibility. There are, however, two exceptions: (1) specific instances are provable when they have been the subject of criminal conviction, and (2) specific instances may be inquired into on cross-examination of the principal witness or of a witness giving an opinion of his character for truthfulness.

(1) Conviction of crime as a technique of impeachment is treated in detail in Rule 609, and here is merely recognized as an exception to the general rule excluding evidence of specific incidents for impeachment purposes.

(2) Particular instances of conduct, though not the subject of criminal conviction, may be inquired into on cross-examination of the principal witness himself or of a witness who testifies concerning his character for truthfulness. Effective cross-examination demands that some allowance be made for going into matters of this kind, but the possibilities of abuse are substantial. Consequently safeguards are erected in the form of specific requirements that the instances inquired into be probative of truthfulness or its opposite and not remote in time. Also, the overriding protection of Rule 403 requires that probative value not be outweighed by danger of unfair prejudice, confusion of issues, or misleading the jury, and that of Rule 611 bars harassment and undue embarrassment.

The final sentence constitutes a rejection of the doctrine of such cases as *People v. Sorge,* 301 N.Y. 198, 93 N.E.2d 637 (1950), that any past criminal act relevant to credibility may be inquired into on cross-examination, in apparent disregard of the privilege against self-incrimination. While it is clear that an ordinary witness cannot make a partial disclosure of incriminating matter and then invoke the privilege on cross-examination, no tenable contention can be made that merely by testifying he waives his right to foreclose inquiry on cross-examination into criminal activities for the purpose of attacking his credibility. So to hold would reduce the privilege to a nullity. While it is true that an accused, unlike an ordinary witness, has an option whether to testify, if the option can be exercised only at the price of opening up inquiry as to any and all criminal acts committed during his lifetime, the right to testify could scarcely be said to possess much vitality. In *Griffin v. California,* 380 U.S. 609, 85 S.Ct. 1229, 14 L.Ed.2d 106 (1965), the Court held that allowing comment on the election of an accused not to testify exacted a constitutionally impermissible price, and so here. While no specific provision in terms confers constitutional status on the right of an accused to take the stand in his own defense, the existence of the right is so completely recognized that a denial of it or substantial infringement upon it would surely be of due process dimensions. See *Ferguson v. Georgia,* 365 U.S. 570, 81 S.Ct. 756, 5 L.Ed.2d 783 (1961); McCormick § 131; 8 Wigmore § 2276 (McNaughton Rev. 1961). In any event, wholly aside from constitutional considerations, the provision represents a sound policy.

Notes of Committee on the Judiciary, House Report No. 93-650. Rule 608(a) as submitted by the Court permitted attack to be made upon the character for truthfulness or untruthfulness of a witness either by reputation or opinion testimony. For the same reasons underlying its decision to eliminate the admissibility of opinion testimony in Rule 405(a), the Committee amended Rule 608(a) to delete the reference to opinion testimony.

The second sentence of Rule 608(b) as submitted by the Court permitted specific instances of misconduct of a witness to be inquired into on cross-examination for the purpose of attacking his credibility, if probative of truthfulness or untruthfulness, "and not remote in time". Such cross-examination could be of the witness himself or of another witness who testifies as to "his" character for truthfulness or untruthfulness.

The Committee amended the Rule to emphasize the discretionary power of the court in permitting such testimony and deleted the reference to remoteness in time as being unnecessary and confusing (remoteness from time of trial or remoteness from the incident involved?). As recast, the Committee amendment also makes clear the antecedent of "his" in the original Court proposal.

Notes of Conference Committee, House Report No. 93-1597. The Senate amendment adds the words "opinion or" to conform the first sentence of the rule with the remainder of the rule.

The Conference adopts the Senate amendment.

Notes of Advisory Committee on 1987 amendments. The amendments are technical. No substantive change is intended.

Notes of Advisory Committee on 1988 amendments. The amendment is technical. No substantive change is intended.

Notes of Advisory Committee on 2003 amendments. The Rule has been amended to clarify that the absolute prohibition on extrinsic evidence applies only when the sole reason for proffering that evidence is to attack or support the witness' character for truthfulness. See *United States v. Abel*, 469 U.S. 45 [83 L. Ed. 2d 450] (1984); *United States v. Fusco*, 748 F.2d 996 (5th Cir. 1984) (Rule 608(b) limits the use of evidence "designed to show that the witness has done things, unrelated to the suit being tried, that make him more or less believable per se"); Ohio R.Evid. 608(b). On occasion the Rule's use of the overbroad term "credibility" has been read "to bar extrinsic evidence for bias, competency and contradiction impeachment since they too deal with credibility." American Bar Association Section of Litigation, *Emerging Problems Under the Federal Rules of Evidence* at 161 (3d ed. 1998). The amendment conforms the language of the Rule to its original intent, which was to impose an absolute bar on extrinsic evidence only if the sole purpose for offering the evidence was to prove the witness' character for veracity. See Advisory Committee Note to Rule 608(b) (stating that the Rule is "[i]n conformity with Rule 405, which forecloses use of evidence of specific incidents as proof in chief of character unless character is in issue in the case . . .").

By limiting the application of the Rule to proof of a witness' character for truthfulness, the amendment leaves the admissibility of extrinsic evidence offered for other grounds of impeachment (such as contradiction, prior inconsistent statement, bias and mental capacity) to Rules 402 and 403. See, e.g., *United States v. Winchenbach*, 197 F.3d 548 (1st Cir. 1999) (admissibility of a prior inconsistent statement offered for impeachment is governed by Rules 402 and 403, not Rule 608(b)); *United States v. Tarantino*, 846 F.2d 1384 (D.C. Cir. 1988) (admissibility of extrinsic evidence offered to contradict a witness is governed by Rules 402 and 403); *United States v. Lindemann*, 85 F.3d 1232 (7th Cir. 1996) (admissibility of extrinsic evidence of bias is governed by Rules 402 and 403).

It should be noted that the extrinsic evidence prohibition of Rule 608(b) bars any reference to the consequences that a witness might have suffered as a result of an alleged bad act. For example, Rule 608(b) prohibits counsel from mentioning that a witness was suspended or disciplined for the conduct that is the subject of impeachment, when that conduct is offered only to prove the character of the witness. See *United States v. Davis*, 183 F.3d 231, 257 n.12 (3d Cir. 1999) (emphasizing that in attacking the defendant's character for truthfulness "the government cannot make reference to Davis's forty-four day suspension or that Internal Affairs found that he lied about" an incident because "[s]uch evidence would not only be hearsay to the extent it contains assertion of fact, it would be inadmissible extrinsic evidence under Rule 608(b)"). See also Stephen A. Saltzburg, *Impeaching the Witness: Prior Bad Acts and Extrinsic Evidence*, 7 Crim. Just. 28, 31 (Winter 1993) ("counsel should not be permitted to circumvent the no-extrinsic-evidence provision by tucking a third person's opinion about prior acts into a question asked of the witness who has denied the act").

For purposes of consistency the term "credibility" has been replaced by the term "character for truthfulness" in the last sentence of subdivision (b). The term "credibility" is also used in subdivision (a). But the Committee found it unnecessary to substitute "character for truthfulness" for "credibility" in Rule 608(a), because subdivision (a)(1) already serves to limit impeachment to proof of such character. Rules 609(a) and 610 also use the term "credibility" when the intent of those Rules is to regulate impeachment of a witness' character for truthfulness. No inference should be derived from the fact that the Committee proposed an amendment to Rule 608(b) but not to Rules 609 and 610.

Changes Made After Publication and Comments. The last sentence of Rule 608(b) was changed to substitute the term "character for truthfulness" for the existing term "credibility." This change was made in accordance with public comment suggesting that it would be helpful to provide uniform terminology throughout Rule 608(b). A stylistic change was also made to the last sentence of Rule 608(b).

Notes of Advisory Committee on 2011 amendments. The language of Rule 608 has been amended as part of the general restyling of the Evidence Rules to make them more easily understood and to make style and terminology consistent throughout the rules. These changes are intended to be stylistic only. There is no intent to change any result in any ruling on evidence admissibility.

The Committee is aware that the Rule's limitation of bad-act impeachment to "crossexamination" is trumped by Rule 607, which allows a party to impeach witnesses on direct examination. Courts have not relied on the term "on cross-examination" to limit impeachment that would otherwise be permissible under Rules 607 and 608. The Committee therefore concluded that no change to the language of the Rule was necessary in the context of a restyling project.

Rule 609. Impeachment by Evidence of a Criminal Conviction

(a) In General. The following rules apply to attacking a witness's character for truthfulness by evidence of a criminal conviction:

(1) for a crime that, in the convicting jurisdiction, was punishable by death or by imprisonment for more than one year, the evidence:

(A) must be admitted, subject to Rule 403, in a civil case or in a criminal case in which the witness is not a defendant; and

(B) must be admitted in a criminal case in which the witness is a defendant, if the probative value of the evidence outweighs its prejudicial effect to that defendant; and

(2) for any crime regardless of the punishment, the evidence must be admitted if the court can readily determine that establishing the elements of the crime required proving—or the witness's admitting—a dishonest act or false statement.

(b) Limit on Using the Evidence After 10 Years. This subdivision (b) applies if more than 10 years have passed since the witness's conviction or release from confinement for it, whichever is later. Evidence of the conviction is admissible only if:

(1) its probative value, supported by specific facts and circumstances, substantially outweighs its prejudicial effect; and

(2) the proponent gives an adverse party reasonable written notice of the intent to use it so that the party has a fair opportunity to contest its use.

(c) Effect of a Pardon, Annulment, or Certificate of Rehabilitation. Evidence of a conviction is not admissible if:

(1) the conviction has been the subject of a pardon, annulment, certificate of rehabilitation, or other equivalent procedure based on a finding that the person has been rehabilitated, and the person has not been convicted of a later crime punishable by death or by imprisonment for more than one year; or

(2) the conviction has been the subject of a pardon, annulment, or other equivalent procedure based on a finding of innocence.

(d) Juvenile Adjudications. Evidence of a juvenile adjudication is admissible under this rule only if:

(1) it is offered in a criminal case;

(2) the adjudication was of a witness other than the defendant;

(3) an adult's conviction for that offense would be admissible to attack the adult's credibility; and

(4) admitting the evidence is necessary to fairly determine guilt or innocence.

(e) Pendency of an Appeal. A conviction that satisfies this rule is admissible even if an appeal is pending. Evidence of the pendency is also admissible.

HISTORY:

Jan. 2, 1975, P. L. 93-595, § 1, 88 Stat. 1935; March 2, 1987, eff. Oct. 1, 1987; Jan. 26, 1990, eff. Dec. 1, 1990; April 12, 2006, eff. Dec. 1, 2006; April 26, 2011, eff. Dec. 1, 2011.

HISTORY; ANCILLARY LAWS AND DIRECTIVES

Other provisions:

Notes of Advisory Committee on Rules. As a means of impeachment, evidence of conviction of crime is significant only because it stands as proof of the commission of the underlying criminal act. There is little dissent from the general proposition that at least some crimes are relevant to credibility but much disagreement among the cases and commentators about which crimes are usable for this purpose. See McCormick § 43; 2 Wright, Federal Practice and Procedure; Criminal § 416 (1969). The weight of traditional authority has been to allow use of felonies generally, without regard to the nature of the particular offense, and of *crimen falsi* without regard to the grade of the offense. This is the view accepted by Congress in the 1970 amendment of § 14-305 of the District of Columbia Code, P.L. 91-358, 84 Stat. 473. Uniform Rule 21 and Model Code Rule 106 permit only crimes involving "dishonesty or false statement." Others have thought that the trial judge should have discretion to exclude convictions if the probative value of the evidence of the crime is substantially outweighed by the danger of unfair prejudice. *Luck v. United States*, 121 U.S.App.D.C. 151, 348 F.2d 763 (1965); McGowan, Impeachment of Criminal Defendants by Prior Convictions, 1970 Law & Soc. Order 1. Whatever may be the merits of those views, this rule is drafted to accord with the Congressional policy manifested in the 1970 legislation.

The proposed rule incorporates certain basic safeguards, in terms applicable to all witnesses but of particular significance to an accused who elects to testify. These protections include the imposition of definite time limitations, giving effect to demonstrated rehabilitation, and generally excluding juvenile adjudications.

Subdivision (a). For purposes of impeachment, crimes are divided into two categories by the rule: (1) those of what is generally regarded as felony grade, without particular regard to the nature of the offense, and (2) those involving dishonesty or false statement, without regard to the grade of the offense. Provable convictions are not limited to violations of federal law. By reason of our constitutional structure, the federal catalog of crimes is far from being a complete one, and resort must be had to the laws of the states for the specification of many crimes. For example, simple theft as compared with theft from interstate commerce. Other instances of borrowing are the Assimilative Crimes Act, making the state law of crimes applicable to the special territorial and maritime jurisdiction of the United States, 18 U.S.C. § 13, and the provision of the Judicial Code disqualifying persons as jurors on the grounds of state as well as federal convictions, 28 U.S.C. § 1865. For evaluation of the crime in terms of seriousness, reference is made to the congressional measurement of felony (subject to imprisonment in excess of one year) rather than adopting state definitions which vary considerably. See 28 U.S.C. § 1865, *supra*, disqualifying jurors for conviction in state or federal court of crime punishable by imprisonment for more than one year.

Subdivision (b). Few statutes recognize a time limit on impeachment by evidence of conviction. However, practical considerations of fairness and relevancy demand that some boundary be recognized. See Ladd, Credibility Tests—Current Trends, 89 U.Pa.L.Rev. 166, 176–177 (1940). This portion of the rule is derived from the proposal advanced in Recommendation Proposing in Evidence Code, § 788(5), p. 142, Cal.Law Rev.Comm'n (1965), though not adopted. See California Evidence Code § 788.

Subdivision (c). A pardon or its equivalent granted solely for the purpose of restoring civil rights lost by virtue of a conviction has no relevance to an inquiry into character. If, however, the pardon or other proceeding is hinged upon a showing of rehabilitation the situation is otherwise. The result under the rule is to render the conviction inadmissible. The alternative of allowing in evidence both the conviction and the rehabilitation has not been adopted for reasons of policy, economy of time, and difficulties of evaluation.

A similar provision is contained in California Evidence Code § 788. Cf. A.L.I. Model Penal Code, Proposed Official Draft § 306.6(3)(e) (1962), and discussion in A.L.I. Proceedings 310 (1961).

Pardons based on innocence have the effect, of course, of nullifying the conviction *ab initio*.

Subdivision (d). The prevailing view has been that a juvenile adjudication is not usable for impeachment. *Thomas v. United States*, 74 App.D.C. 167, 121 F.2d 905 (1941); *Cotton v. United States*, 355 F.2d 480 (10th Cir. 1966). This conclusion was based upon a variety of circumstances. By virtue of its informality, frequently diminished quantum of required proof, and other departures from accepted standards for criminal trials under the theory of *parens patriae*, the juvenile adjudication was considered to lack the precision and general probative value of the criminal conviction. While *In re Gault*, 387 U.S. 1, 87 S.Ct. 1428, 18 L.Ed.2d 527 (1967), no doubt eliminates these characteristics insofar as objectionable, other obstacles remain. Practical problems of administration are raised by the common provisions in juvenile legislation that records be kept confidential and that they be destroyed after a short time. While *Gault* was skeptical as to the realities of confidentiality of juvenile records, it also saw no constitutional obstacles to improvement. 387 U.S. at 25, 87 S.Ct. 1428. See also Note, Rights and Rehabilitation in the Juvenile Courts, 67 Colum.L.Rev. 281, 289 (1967). In addition, policy considerations much akin to those which dictate exclusion of adult convictions after rehabilitation has been established strongly suggest a rule of excluding juvenile adjudications. Admittedly, however, the rehabilitative process may in a given case be a demonstrated failure, or the strategic importance of a given witness may be so great as to require the overriding of general policy in the interests of particular justice. See *Giles v. Maryland*, 386 U.S. 66, 87 S.Ct. 793, 17 L.Ed.2d 737 (1967). Wigmore was outspoken in his condemnation of the disallowance of juvenile adjudications to impeach, especially when the witness is the complainant in a case of molesting a minor. 1 Wigmore § 196; 3 *Id.* §§ 924a, 980. The rule recognizes discretion in the judge to effect an accommodation among these various factors by departing from the general principle of exclusion. In deference to the general pattern and policy of juvenile statutes, however, no discretion is accorded when the witness is the accused in a criminal case.

Subdivision (e). The presumption of correctness which ought to attend judicial proceedings supports the position that pendency of an appeal does not preclude use of a conviction for impeachment. *United States v. Empire Packing Co.*, 174 F.2d 16 (7th Cir.1949), cert. denied 337 U.S. 959, 69 S.Ct. 1534, 93 L.Ed. 1758; *Bloch v. United States*, 226 F.2d 185 (9th Cir.1955), cert. denied 350 U.S. 948, 76 S.Ct. 323, 100 L.Ed. 826 and 353 U.S. 959, 77 S.Ct. 868, 1 L.Ed.2d 910; and see *Newman v. United States*, 331 F.2d 968 (8th Cir.1964), Contra, *Campbell v. United States*, 85 U.S.App.D.C. 133, 176 F.2d 45 (1949). The pendency of an appeal is, however, a qualifying circumstance properly considerable.

Notes of Committee on the Judiciary, House Report No. 93-650. Rule 609(a) as submitted by the Court was modeled after Section 133(a) of Public Law 91-358, 14 D.C. Code 305(b)(1), enacted in 1970. The Rule provided that: For the purpose of attacking the credibility of a

> witness, evidence that he has been convicted of a crime is admissible but only if the crime (1) was punishable by death or imprisonment in excess of one year under the law under which he was convicted or (2) involved dishonesty or false statement regardless of the punishment.

As reported to the Committee by the Subcommittee, Rule 609(a) was amended to read as follows:

> For the purpose of attacking the credibility of a witness, evidence that he has been convicted of a crime is admissible only if the crime (1) was punishable by death or imprisonment in excess of one year, unless the court determines that the danger of unfair prejudice outweighs the probative value of the evidence of the conviction, or (2) involved dishonesty or false statement.

In full committee, the provision was amended to permit attack upon the credibility of a witness by prior conviction only if the prior crime involved dishonesty or false statement. While recognizing that the prevailing doctrine in the federal courts and in most States allows a witness to be impeached by evidence of prior felony convictions without restriction as to type, the Committee was of the view that, because of the danger of unfair prejudice in such practice and the deterrent effect upon an accused who might wish to testify, and even upon a witness who was not the accused, cross-examination by evidence of prior conviction should be limited to those kinds of convictions bearing directly on credibility, *i.e.*, crimes involving dishonesty or false statement.

Rule 609(b) as submitted by the Court was modeled after Section 133(a) of Public Law 91-358, 14 D.C. Code 305(b)(2)(B), enacted in 1970. The Rule provided:

> Evidence of a conviction under this rule is not admissible if a period of more than ten years has elapsed since the date of the release of the witness from confinement imposed for his most recent conviction, or the expiration of the period of his parole, probation, or sentence granted or imposed with respect to his most recent conviction, whichever is the later date.

Under this formulation, a witness' entire past record of criminal convictions could be used for impeachment (provided the conviction met the standard of subdivision (a)), if the witness had been most recently released from confinement, or the period of his parole or probation had expired, within ten years of the conviction.

The Committee amended the Rule to read in the text of the 1971 Advisory Committee version to provide that upon the expiration of ten years from the date of a conviction of a witness, or of his release from confinement for that offense, that conviction may no longer be used for impeachment. The Committee was of the view that after ten years following a person's release from confinement (or from the date of his conviction) the probative value of the conviction with respect to that person's credibility diminished to a point where it should no longer be admissible.

Rule 609(c) as submitted by the Court provided in part that evidence of a witness' prior conviction is not admissible to attack his credibility if the conviction was the subject of a pardon, annulment, or other equivalent procedure, based on a showing of rehabilitation, and the witness has not been convicted of a subsequent crime. The Committee amended the Rule to provide that the "subsequent crime" must have been "punishable by death or imprisonment in excess of one year", on the ground that a subsequent conviction of an offense not a felony is insufficient to rebut the finding that the witness has been rehabilitated. The Committee also intends that the words "based on a finding of the rehabilitation of the person convicted" apply not only to "certificate of rehabilitation, or other equivalent procedure," but also to "pardon" and "annulment."

Notes of Committee on the Judiciary, Senate Report No. 93-1277. As proposed by the Supreme Court, the rule would allow the use of prior convictions to impeach if the crime was a felony or a misdemeanor if the misdemeanor involved dishonesty or false statement. As modified by the House, the rule would admit prior convictions for impeachment purposes only if the offense, whether felony or misdemeanor, involved dishonesty or false statement.

The committee has adopted a modified version of the House-passed rule. In your committee's view, the danger of unfair prejudice is far greater when the accused, as opposed to other witnesses, testifies, because the jury may be prejudiced not merely on the question of credibility but also on the ultimate question of guilt or innocence. Therefore, with respect to defendants, the committee agreed with the House limitation that only offenses involving false statement or dishonesty may be used. By that phrase, the committee means crimes such as perjury or subordination of perjury, false statement, criminal fraud, embezzlement or false pretense, or any other offense, in the nature of *crimen falsi* the commission of which involves some element of untruthfulness, deceit, or falsification bearing on the accused's propensity to testify truthfully.

With respect to other witnesses, in addition to any prior conviction involving false statement or dishonesty, any other felony may be used to impeach if, and only if, the court finds that the probative value of such evidence outweighs its prejudicial effect against the party offering that witness.

Notwithstanding this provision, proof of any prior offense otherwise admissible under rule 404 could still be offered for the purposes sanctioned by that rule. Furthermore, the committee intends that notwithstanding this rule, a defendant's misrepresentation regarding the existence or nature of prior convictions may be met by rebuttal evidence, including the record of such prior convictions. Similarly, such records may be offered to rebut representations made by the defendant regarding his attitude toward or willingness to commit a general category of offense, although denials or other representations by the defendant regarding the specific conduct which forms the basis of the charge against him shall not make prior convictions admissible to rebut such statement.

In regard to either type of representation, of course, prior convictions may be offered in rebuttal only if the defendant's statement is made in response to defense counsel's questions or is made gratuitously in the course of cross-examination. Prior convictions may not be offered as rebuttal evidence if the prosecution has sought to circumvent the purpose of this rule by asking questions which elicit such representations from the defendant.

One other clarifying amendment has been added to this subsection, that is, to provide that the admissibility of evidence of a prior conviction is permitted only upon cross-examination of a witness. It is not admissible if a person does not testify. It is to be understood, however, that a court record of a prior conviction is admissible to prove that conviction if the witness has forgotten or denies its existence.

Although convictions over ten years old generally do not have much probative value, there may be exceptional circumstances under which the conviction substantially bears on the credibility of the witness. Rather than exclude all convictions over 10 years old, the committee adopted an amendment in the form of a final clause to the section granting the court discretion to admit convictions over 10 years old, but only upon a determination by the court that the probative value of the conviction supported by specific facts and circumstances, substantially outweighs its prejudicial effect.

It is intended that convictions over 10 years old will be admitted very rarely and only in exceptional circumstances. The rules provide that the decision be supported by specific facts and circumstances thus requiring the court to make specific findings on the record as to the particular facts and circumstances it has considered in determining that the probative value of the conviction substantially outweighs its prejudicial impact. It is expected that, in fairness, the court will give the party against whom the conviction is introduced a full and adequate opportunity to contest its admission.

Notes of Conference Committee, House Report No. 93-1597. Rule 609 defines when a party may use evidence of a prior conviction in order to impeach a witness. The Senate amendments make changes in two subsections of Rule 609.

The House bill provides that the credibility of a witness can be attacked by proof of prior conviction of a crime only if the crime involves dishonesty or false statement. The Senate amendment provides that a witness' credibility may be attacked if the crime (1) was punishable by death or imprisonment in excess of one year under the law under which he was convicted or (2) involves dishonesty or false statement, regardless of the punishment.

The Conference adopts the Senate amendment with an amendment. The Conference amendment provides that the credibility of a witness, whether a defendant or someone else, may be attacked by proof of a prior conviction but only if the crime: (1) was punishable by death or imprisonment in excess of one year under the law under which he was convicted and the court determines that the probative value of the conviction outweighs its prejudicial effect to the defendant; or (2) involved dishonesty or false statement regardless of the punishment.

By the phrase "dishonesty and false statement" the Conference means crimes such as perjury or subornation of perjury, false statement, criminal fraud, embezzlement, or false pretense, or any other offense in the nature of *crimen falsi*, the commission of which involves some element of deceit, untruthfulness, or falsification bearing on the accused's propensity to testify truthfully.

The admission of prior convictions involving dishonesty and false statement is not within the discretion of the Court. Such convictions are peculiarly probative of credibility and, under this rule, are always to be admitted. Thus, judicial discretion granted with respect to the admissibility of other prior convictions is not applicable to those involving dishonesty or false statement.

With regard to the discretionary standard established by paragraph (1) of rule 609(a), the Conference determined that the prejudicial effect to be weighed against the probative value of the conviction is specifically the prejudicial effect *to the defendant*. The danger of prejudice to a witness other than the defendant (such as injury to the witness' reputation in his community) was considered and rejected by the Conference as an element to be weighed in determining admissibility. It was the judgment of the Conference that the danger of prejudice to a nondefendant witness is outweighed by the need for the trier of fact to have as much relevant evidence on the issue of credibility as possible. Such evidence should only be excluded where it presents a danger of improperly influencing the outcome of the trial by persuading the trier of fact to convict the defendant on the basis of his prior criminal record.

The House bill provides in subsection (b) that evidence of conviction of a crime may not be used for impeachment purposes under subsection (a) if more than ten years have elapsed since the date of the conviction or the date the witness was released from confinement imposed for the conviction, whichever is later. The Senate amendment permits the use of convictions older than ten years, if the court determines, in the interests of justice, that the probative value of the conviction, supported by specific facts and circumstances, substantially outweighs its prejudicial effect.

The Conference adopts the Senate amendment with an amendment requiring notice by a party that he intends to request that the court allow him to use a conviction older than ten years. The Conferees anticipate that a written notice, in order to give the adversary a fair opportunity to contest the use of the evidence, will ordinarily include such information as the date of the conviction, the jurisdiction, and the offense or statute involved. In order to eliminate the possibility that the flexibility of this provision may impair the ability of a party-opponent to prepare for trial, the Conferees intend that the notice provision operate to avoid surprise.

Notes of Advisory Committee on 1987 amendments. The amendments are technical. No substantive change is intended.

Notes of Advisory Committee on 1990 amendment. The amendment to Rule 609(a) makes two changes in the rule. The first change removes from the rule the limitation that the conviction may only be elicited during cross-examination, a limitation that virtually every circuit has found to be inapplicable. It is common for witnesses to reveal on direct examination their convictions to "remove the sting" of the impeachment. See e.g., *United States v. Bad Cob*, 560 F.2d 877 (8th Cir. 1977). The amendment does not contemplate that a court will necessarily permit proof of prior convictions through testimony, which might be time-consuming and more prejudicial than proof through a written record. Rules 403 and 611(a) provide sufficient authority for the court to protect against unfair or disruptive methods of proof.

The second change effected by the amendment resolves an ambiguity as to the relationship of Rules 609 and 403 with respect to impeachment of witnesses other than the criminal defendant. The amendment does not disturb the special balancing test for the criminal defendant who chooses to testify. Thus, the rule recognizes that, in virtually every case in which prior convictions are used to impeach the testifying defendant, the defendant faces a unique risk of prejudice—*i.e.*, the danger that convictions that would be excluded under Fed. R. Evid. 404 will be misused by a jury as propensity evidence despite their introduction solely for impeachment purposes. Although the rule does not forbid all use of convictions to impeach a defendant, it requires that the government show that the probative value of convictions as impeachment evidence outweighs their prejudicial effect.

Prior to the amendment, the rule appeared to give the defendant the benefit of the special balancing test when defense witnesses other than the defendant were called to testify. In practice, however, the concern about unfairness to the defendant is most acute when the defendant's own convictions are offered as evidence. Almost all of the decided cases concern this type of impeachment, and the amendment does not deprive the defendant of any meaningful protection, since Rule 403 now clearly protects against unfair impeachment of any defense witness other than the defendant. There are cases in which a defendant might be prejudiced when a defense witness is impeached. Such cases may arise, for example, when the witness bears a special relationship to the defendant such that the defendant is likely to suffer some spill-over effect from impeachment of the witness.

The amendment also protects other litigants from unfair impeachment of their witnesses. The danger of prejudice from the use of prior convictions is not confined to criminal defendants. Although the danger that prior convictions will be misused as character evidence is particularly acute when the defendant is impeached, the danger exists in other situations as well. The amendment reflects the view that it is desirable to protect all litigants from the unfair use of prior convictions, and that the ordinary balancing test of Rule 403, which provides that evidence shall not be excluded unless its prejudicial effect substantially outweighs its probative value, is appropriate for assessing the admissibility of prior convictions for impeachment of any witness other than a criminal defendant.

The amendment reflects a judgment that decisions interpreting Rule 609(a) as requiring a trial court to admit convictions in civil cases that have little, if anything, to do with credibility reach undesirable results. See, e.g., *Diggs v. Lyons*, 741 F.2d 577 (3d Cir. 1984), cert. denied, 105 S. Ct. 2157 (1985). The amendment provides the same protection against unfair prejudice arising from prior convictions used for impeachment purposes as the rules provide for other evidence. The amendment finds support in decided cases. See, e.g., *Petty v. Ideco*, 761 F.2d 1146 (5th Cir. 1985); *Czaka v. Hickman*, 703 F.2d 317 (8th Cir. 1983).

Fewer decided cases address the question whether Rule 609(a) provides any protection against unduly prejudicial prior convictions used to impeach government witnesses. Some courts have read Rule 609(a) as giving the government no protection for its witnesses. See, e.g., *United States v. Thorne*, 547 F.2d 56 (8th Cir. 1976); *United States v. Nevitt*, 563 F.2d 406 (9th Cir. 1977), cert. denied, 444 U.S. 847 (1979). This approach also is rejected by the amendment. There are cases in which impeachment of government witnesses with prior convictions that have little, if anything, to do with credibility may result in unfair prejudice to the government's interest in a fair trial and unnecessary embarrassment to a witness. Fed. R. Evid. 412 already recognizes this and excluded certain evidence of past sexual behavior in the context of prosecutions for sexual assaults.

The amendment applies the general balancing test of Rule 403 to protect all litigants against unfair impeachment of witnesses. The balancing test protects civil litigants, the government in criminal cases, and the defendant in a criminal case who calls other witnesses. The amendment addresses prior convictions offered under Rule 609, not for other purposes, and does not run afoul, therefore, of *Davis v. Alaska,* 415 U.S. 308 (1974). Davis involved the use of a prior juvenile adjudication not to prove a past law violation, but to prove bias. The defendant in a criminal case has the right to demonstrate the bias of a witness and to be assured a fair trial, but not to unduly prejudice a trier of fact. *See generally* Rule 412. In any case in which the trial court believes that confrontation rights require admission of impeachment evidence, obviously the Constitution would take precedence over the rule.

The probability that prior convictions of an ordinary government witness will be unduly prejudicial is low in most criminal cases. Since the behavior of the witness is not the issue in dispute in most cases, there is little chance that the trier of fact will misuse the convictions offered as impeachment evidence as propensity evidence. Thus, trial courts will be skeptical when the government objects to impeachment of its witnesses with prior convictions. Only when the government is able to point to a real danger of prejudice that is sufficient to outweigh substantially the probative value of the conviction for impeachment purposes will the conviction be excluded.

The amendment continues to divide subdivision (a) into subsections (1) and (2). The Committee recommended no substantive change in subdivision (a)(2), even though some cases raise a concern about the proper interpretation of the words "dishonesty or false statement." These words were used but not explained in the original Advisory Committee Note accompanying Rule 609. Congress extensively debated the rule, and the Report of the House and Senate Conference Committee states that " [b]y the phrase 'dishonesty and false statement,' the Conference means crimes such as perjury, subordination of perjury, false statement, criminal fraud, embezzlement, or false pretense, or any other offense in the nature of *crimen falsi*, commission of which involves some element of deceit, untruthfulness, or falsification bearing on the accused's propensity to testify truthfully." The Advisory Committee concluded that the Conference Report provides sufficient guidance to trial courts and that no amendment is necessary, notwithstanding some decisions that arguably take an unduly broad view of "dishonesty," admitting convictions such as for bank robbery or bank larceny. Subsection (a)(2) continues to apply to any witness, including a criminal defendant.

Finally, the Committee determined that it was unnecessary to add to the rule language stating that, when a prior conviction is offered under Rule 609, the trial court is to consider the probative value of the prior conviction *for impeachment*, not for other purposes. The Committee concluded that the title of the rule, its first sentence, and its placement among the impeachment rules clearly establish that evidence offered under Rule 609 is offered only for purposes of impeachment.

Notes of Advisory Committee on 2006 amendments. The amendment provides that Rule 609(a)(2) mandates the admission of evidence of a conviction only when the conviction required the proof of (or in the case of a guilty plea, the admission of) an act of dishonesty or false statement. Evidence of all other convictions is inadmissible under this subsection, irrespective of whether the witness exhibited dishonesty or made a false statement in the process of the commission of the crime of conviction. Thus, evidence that a witness was convicted for a crime of violence, such as murder, is not admissible under Rule 609(a)(2), even if the witness acted deceitfully in the course of committing the crime.

The amendment is meant to give effect to the legislative intent to limit the convictions that are to be automatically admitted under subdivision (a)(2). The Conference Committee provided that by "dishonesty and false statement" it meant "crimes such as perjury, subornation of perjury, false statement, criminal fraud, embezzlement, or false pretense, or any other offense in the nature of *crimen falsi,* the commission of which involves some element of deceit, untruthfulness, or falsification bearing on the [witness's] propensity to testify truthfully." Historically, offenses classified as *crimina falsi* have included only those crimes in which the ultimate criminal act was itself an act of deceit. *See* Green, *Deceit and the Classification of Crimes: Federal Rule of Evidence 609(a)(2) and the Origins of* Crimen Falsi, 90 J. Crim. L. & Criminology 1087 (2000).

Evidence of crimes in the nature of *crimina falsi* must be admitted under Rule 609(a)(2), regardless of how such crimes are specifically charged. For example, evidence that a witness was convicted of making a false claim to a federal agent is admissible under this subdivision regardless of whether the crime was charged under a section that expressly references deceit (e.g., 18 U.S.C. § 1001, Material Misrepresentation to the Federal Government) or a section that does not (*e.g.,*18 U.S.C. § 1503, Obstruction of Justice).

The amendment requires that the proponent have ready proof that the conviction required the factfinder to find, or the defendant to admit, an act of dishonesty or false statement. Ordinarily, the statutory elements of the crime will indicate whether it is one of dishonesty or false statement. Where the deceitful nature of the crime is not apparent from the statute and the face of the judgment—as, for example, where the conviction simply records a finding of guilt for a statutory offense that does not reference deceit expressly—a proponent may offer information such as an indictment, a statement of admitted facts, or jury instructions to show that the factfinder had to find, or the defendant had to admit, an act of dishonesty or false statement in order for the witness to have been convicted. *Cf. Taylor v. United States,* 495 U.S. 575, 602 (1990) (providing that a trial court may look to a charging instrument or jury instructions to ascertain the nature of a prior offense where the statute is insufficiently clear on its face); *Shepard v. United States,* 125 S.Ct. 1254 (2005) (the inquiry to determine whether a guilty plea to a crime defined by a nongeneric statute necessarily admitted elements of the generic offense was limited to the charging document's terms, the terms of a plea agreement or transcript of colloquy between judge and defendant in which the factual basis for the plea was confirmed by the defendant, or a comparable judicial record). But the amendment does not contemplate a "mini-trial" in which the court plumbs the record of the previous proceeding to determine whether the crime was in the nature of *crimen falsi.*

The amendment also substitutes the term "character for truthfulness" for the term "credibility" in the first sentence of the Rule. The limitations of Rule 609 are not applicable if a conviction is admitted for a purpose other than to prove the witness's character for untruthfulness. *See, e.g., United States v. Lopez,* 979 F.2d 1024 (5th Cir. 1992) (Rule 609 was not applicable where the conviction was offered for purposes of contradiction). The use of the term "credibility" in subdivision (d) is retained, however, as that subdivision is intended to govern the use of a juvenile adjudication for any type of impeachment.

Changes Made After Publication and Comments. The language of the proposed amendment was changed to provide that convictions are automatically admitted only if it readily can be determined that the elements of the crime, as proved or admitted, required an act of dishonesty or false statement by the witness.

Notes of Advisory Committee on 2011 amendments. The language of Rule 609 has been amended as part of the restyling of the Evidence Rules to make them more easily understood and to make style and terminology consistent throughout the rules. These changes are intended to be stylistic only. There is no intent to change any result in any ruling on evidence admissibility.

Rule 610. Religious Beliefs or Opinions

Evidence of a witness's religious beliefs or opinions is not admissible to attack or support the witness's credibility.

HISTORY:

Jan. 2, 1975, P. L. 93-595, § 1, 88 Stat. 1936; March 2, 1987, eff. Oct. 1, 1987; April 26, 2011, eff. Dec. 1, 2011.

HISTORY; ANCILLARY LAWS AND DIRECTIVES

Other provisions:

Notes of Advisory Committee on Rules. While the rule forecloses inquiry into the religious beliefs or opinions of a witness for the purpose of showing that his character for truthfulness is affected by their nature, an inquiry for the purpose of showing interest or bias because of them is not within the prohibition. Thus disclosure of affiliation with a church which is a party to the litigation would be allowable under the rule. *Cf. Tucker v. Reil,* 51 Ariz. 357, 77 P.2d 203 (1938). To the same effect, though less specifically worded, is California Evidence Code § 789. See 3 Wigmore § 936.

Notes of Advisory Committee on 1987 amendments. The amendment is technical. No substantive change is intended.

Notes of Advisory Committee on 2011 amendments. The language of Rule 610 has been amended as part of the restyling of the Evidence Rules to make them more easily understood and to make style and terminology consistent throughout the rules. These changes are intended to be stylistic only. There is no intent to change any result in any ruling on evidence admissibility.

Rule 611. Mode and Order of Examining Witnesses and Presenting Evidence

(a) Control by the Court; Purposes. The court should exercise reasonable control over the mode and order of examining witnesses and presenting evidence so as to:

(1) make those procedures effective for determining the truth;

(2) avoid wasting time; and

(3) protect witnesses from harassment or undue embarrassment.

(b) Scope of Cross-Examination. Cross-examination should not go beyond the subject matter of the direct examination and matters affecting the witness's credibility. The court may allow inquiry into additional matters as if on direct examination.

(c) Leading Questions. Leading questions should not be used on direct examination except as necessary to develop the witness's testimony. Ordinarily, the court should allow leading questions:

(1) on cross-examination; and

(2) when a party calls a hostile witness, an adverse party, or a witness identified with an adverse party.

HISTORY:

Jan. 2, 1975, P. L. 93-595, § 1, 88 Stat. 1936; March 2, 1987, eff. Oct. 1, 1987; April 26, 2011, eff. Dec. 1, 2011.

HISTORY; ANCILLARY LAWS AND DIRECTIVES

Other provisions:

Notes of Advisory Committee on Rules. *Subdivision (a).* Spelling out detailed rules to govern the mode and order of interrogating witnesses presenting evidence is neither desirable nor feasible. The ultimate responsibility for the effective working of the adversary system rests with the judge. The rule sets forth the objectives which he should seek to attain.

Item (1) restates in broad terms the power and obligation of the judge as developed under common law principles. It covers such concerns as whether testimony shall be in the form of a free narrative or responses to specific questions, McCormick § 5, the order of calling witnesses and presenting evidence, 6 Wigmore § 1867, the use of demonstrative evidence, McCormick § 179, and the many other questions arising during the course of a trial which can be solved only by the judge's common sense and fairness in view of the particular circumstances.

Item (2) is addressed to avoidance of needless consumption of time, a matter of daily concern in the disposition of cases. A companion piece is found in the discretion vested in the judge to exclude evidence as a waste of time in Rule 403(b).

Item (3) calls for a judgment under the particular circumstances whether interrogation tactics entail harassment or undue embarrassment. Pertinent circumstances include the importance of the testimony, the nature of the inquiry, its relevance to credibility, waste of time, and confusion. McCormick § 42. In *Alford v. United States,* 282 U.S. 687, 694, 51 S.Ct. 218, 75 L.Ed. 624 (1931), the Court pointed out that, while the trial judge should protect the witness from questions which "go beyond the bounds of proper cross-examination merely to harass, annoy or humiliate," this protection by no means forecloses efforts to discredit the witness. Reference to the transcript of the prosecutor's cross-examination in *Berger v. United States*, 295 U.S. 78, 55 S.Ct. 629, 79 L.Ed. 1314 (1935), serves to lay at rest any doubts as to the need for judicial control in this area.

The inquiry into specific instances of conduct of a witness allowed under Rule 608(b) is, of course, subject to this rule.

Subdivision (b). The tradition in the federal courts and in numerous state courts has been to limit the scope of cross-examination to matters testified to on direct, plus matters bearing upon the credibility of the witness. Various reasons have been advanced to justify the rule of limited cross-examination. (1) A party vouches for his own witness but only to the extent of matters elicited on direct. *Resurrection Gold Mining Co. v. Fortune Gold Mining Co.*, 129 F. 668, 675 (8th Cir. 1904), quoted in Maguire, Weinstein, et al., Cases on Evidence 277, n. 38 (5th ed. 1965). But the concept of vouching is discredited, and Rule 607 rejects it. (2) A party cannot ask his own witness leading questions. This is a problem properly solved in terms of what is necessary for a proper development of the testimony rather than by a mechanistic formula similar to the vouching concept. See discussion under subdivision (c). (3) A practice of limited cross-examination promotes orderly presentation of the case. *Finch v. Weiner*, 109 Conn. 616, 145 A. 31 (1929). While this latter reason has merit, the matter is essentially one of the order of presentation and not one in which involvement at the appellate level is likely to prove fruitful. See for example, *Moyer v. Aetna Life Ins. Co.*, 126 F.2d 141 (3rd Cir. 1942); *Butler v. New York Central R. Co.*, 253 F.2d 281 (7th Cir. 1958); *United States v. Johnson*, 285 F.2d 35 (9th Cir. 1960); *Union Automobile Indemnity Ass'n. v. Capitol Indemnity Ins. Co.*, 310 F.2d 318 (7th Cir. 1962). In evaluating these considerations, McCormick says:

"The foregoing considerations favoring the wide-open or restrictive rules may well be thought to be fairly evenly balanced. There is another factor, however, which seems to swing the balance overwhelmingly in favor of the wide-open rule. This is the consideration of economy of time and energy. Obviously, the wide-open rule presents little or no opportunity for dispute in its application. The restrictive practice in all its forms, on the other hand, is productive in many court rooms, of continual bickering over the choice of the numerous variations of the 'scope of the direct' criterion, and of their application to particular cross-questions. These controversies are often reventilated on appeal, and reversals for error in their determination are frequent. Observance of these vague and ambiguous restrictions is a matter of constant and hampering concern to the cross-examiner. If these efforts, delays and misprisions were the necessary incidents to the guarding of substantive rights or the fundamentals of fair trial, they might be worth the cost. As the price of the choice of an obviously debatable regulation of the order of evidence, the sacrifice seems misguided. The American Bar Association's Committee for the Improvement of the Law of Evidence for the year 1937–38 said this:

"The rule limiting cross-examination to the precise subject of the direct examination is probably the most frequent rule (except the Opinion rule) leading in the trial practice today to refined and technical quibbles which obstruct the progress of the trial, confuse the jury, and give rise to appeal on technical grounds only. Some of the instances in which Supreme Courts have ordered new trials for the mere transgression of this rule about the order of evidence have been astounding.

"We recommend that the rule allowing questions upon any part of the issue known to the witness * * * be adopted * * *'" McCormick, § 27, p. 51. See also 5 Moore's Federal Practice P 43.10 (2nd ed. 1964).

The provision of the second sentence, that the judge may in the interests of justice limit inquiry into new matters on cross-examination, is designed for those situations in which the result otherwise would be confusion, complication, or protraction of the case, not as a matter of rule but as demonstrable in the actual development of the particular case.

The rule does not purport to determine the extent to which an accused who elects to testify thereby waives his privilege against self-incrimination. The question is a constitutional one, rather than a mere matter of administering the trial. Under *Simmons v. United States*, 390 U.S. 377, 88 S.Ct. 967, 19 L.Ed.2d 1247 (1968), no general waiver occurs when the accused testifies on such preliminary matters as the validity of a search and seizure or the admissibility of a confession. Rule 104(d), supra. When he testifies on the merits, however, can he foreclose inquiry into an aspect or element of the crime by avoiding it on direct? The affirmative answer given in *Tucker v. United States*, 5 F.2d 818 (8th Cir. 1925), is inconsistent with the description of the waiver as extending to "all other relevant facts" in *Johnson v. United States*, 318 U.S. 189, 195, 63 S.Ct. 549, 87 L.Ed. 704 (1943). See also *Brown v. United States*, 356 U.S. 148, 78 S.Ct. 622, 2 L.Ed.2d 589 (1958). The situation of an accused who desires to testify on some but not all counts of a multiple-count indictment is one to be approached, in the first instance at least, as a problem of severance under Rule 14 of the Federal Rules of Criminal Procedure. *Cross v. United States*, 118 U.S.App.D.C. 324, 335 F.2d 987 (1964). *Cf. United States v. Baker*, 262 F.Supp. 657, 686 (D.D.C. 1966). In all events, the extent of the waiver of the privilege against self-incrimination ought not to be determined as a by-product of a rule on scope of cross-examination.

Subdivision (c). The rule continues the traditional view that the suggestive powers of the leading question are as a general proposition undesirable. Within this tradition, however, numerous exceptions have achieved recognition: The witness who is hostile, unwilling, or biased; the child witness or the adult with communication problems; the witness whose recollection is exhausted; and undisputed preliminary matters. 3 Wigmore §§ 774– 778. An almost total unwillingness to reverse for infractions has been manifested by appellate courts. See cases cited in 3 Wigmore § 770. The matter clearly falls within the area of control by the judge over the mode and order of interrogation and presentation and accordingly is phrased in words of suggestion rather than command.

The rule also conforms to tradition in making the use of leading questions on cross-examination a matter of right. The purpose of the qualification "ordinarily" is to furnish a basis for denying the use of leading questions when the cross-examination is cross-examination in form only and not in fact, as for example the "cross-examination" of a party by his own counsel after being called by the opponent (savoring more of re-direct) or of an insured defendant who proves to be friendly to the plaintiff.

The final sentence deals with categories of witnesses automatically regarded and treated as hostile. Rule 43(b) of the Federal Rules of Civil Procedure has included only "an adverse party or an officer, director, or managing agent of a public or private corporation or of a partnership or association which is an adverse party." This limitation virtually to persons whose statements would stand as admissions is believed to be an unduly narrow concept of those who may safely be regarded as hostile without further demonstration. See, for example, *Maryland Casualty Co. v. Kador*, 225 F.2d 120 (5th Cir. 195 5), and *Degelos v. Fidelity and Casualty Co.*, 313 F.2d 809 (5th Cir. 1963), holding despite the language of rule 43(b) that an insured fell within it, though not a party in an action under the Louisiana direct action statute. The phrase of the rule, "witness identified with" an adverse party, is designed to enlarge the category of persons thus callable.

Notes of Committee on the Judiciary, House Report No. 93-650. As submitted by the Court, Rule 611(b) provided: A witness may be cross-examined on any matter

> relevant to any issue in the case, including credibility. In the interests of justice, the judge may limit cross-examination with respect to matters not testified to on direct examination.

The Committee amended this provision to return to the rule which prevails in the federal courts and thirty-nine State jurisdictions. As amended, the Rule is in the text of the 1969 Advisory Committee draft. It limits cross-examination to credibility and to matters testified to on direct examination, unless the judge permits more, in which event the cross-examiner must proceed as if on direct examination. This traditional rule facilitates orderly presentation by each party at trial. Further, in light of existing discovery procedures, there appears to be no need to abandon the traditional rule.

The third sentence of Rule 611(c) as submitted by the Court provided that: In civil cases, a party is entitled to call

> an adverse party or witness identified with him and interrogate by leading questions.

The Committee amended this Rule to permit leading questions to be used with respect to any hostile witness, not only an adverse party or person identified with such adverse party. The Committee also substituted the word "When" for the phrase "In civil cases" to reflect the possibility that in criminal cases a defendant may be entitled to call witnesses identified with the government, in which event the Committee believed the defendant should be permitted to inquire with leading questions.

Notes of Committee on the Judiciary, Senate Report No. 93-1277. Rule 611(b) as submitted by the Supreme Court permitted a broad scope of cross-examination: "cross-examination on any matter relevant to any issue in the case" unless the judge, in the interests of justice, limited the scope of cross-examination.

The House narrowed the Rule to the more traditional practice of limiting cross-examination to the subject matter of direct examination (and credibility), but with discretion in the judge to permit inquiry into additional matters in situations where that would aid in the development of the evidence or otherwise facilitate the conduct of the trial.

The committee agrees with the House amendment. Although there are good arguments in support of broad cross-examination from perspectives of developing all relevant evidence, we believe the factors of insuring an orderly and predictable development of the evidence weigh in favor of the narrower rule, especially when discretion is given to the trial judge to permit inquiry into additional matters. The committee expressly approves this discretion and believes it will permit sufficient flexibility allowing a broader scope of cross-examination whenever appropriate.

The House amendment providing broader discretionary cross-examination permitted inquiry into additional matters only as if on direct examination. As a general rule, we concur with this limitation, however, we would understand that this limitation would not preclude the utilization of leading questions if the conditions of subsection (c) of this rule were met, bearing in mind the judge's discretion in any case to limit the scope of cross-examination [see McCormick on Evidence, §§ 24–26 (especially 24) (2d ed. 1972)].

Further, the committee has received correspondence from Federal judges commenting on the applicability of this rule to section 1407 of title 28. It is the committee's judgment that this rule as reported by the House is flexible enough to provide sufficiently broad cross-examination in appropriate situations in multidistrict litigation.

As submitted by the Supreme Court, the rule provided: "In civil cases, a party is entitled to call an adverse party or witness identified with him and interrogate by leading questions."

The final sentence of subsection (c) was amended by the House for the purpose of clarifying the fact that a "hostile witness"—that is a witness who is hostile in fact—could be subject to interrogation by leading questions. The rule as submitted by the Supreme Court declared certain witnesses hostile as a matter of law and thus subject to interrogation by leading questions without any showing of hostility in fact. These were adverse parties or witnesses identified with adverse parties. However, the wording of the first sentence of subsection (c) while generally, prohibiting the use of leading questions on direct examination, also provides "except as may be necessary to develop his testimony." Further, the first paragraph of the Advisory Committee note explaining the subsection makes clear that they intended that leading questions could be asked of a hostile witness or a witness who was unwilling or biased and even though that witness was not associated with an adverse party. Thus, we question whether the House amendment was necessary.

However, concluding that it was not intended to affect the meaning of the first sentence of the subsection and was intended solely to clarify the fact that leading questions are permissible in the interrogation of a witness, who is hostile in fact, the committee accepts that House amendment.

The final sentence of this subsection was also amended by the House to cover criminal as well as civil cases. The committee accepts this amendment, but notes that it may be difficult in criminal cases to determine when a witness is "identified with an adverse party," and thus the rule should be applied with caution.

Notes of Advisory Committee on 1987 amendments. The amendment is technical. No substantive change is intended.

Notes of Advisory Committee on 2011 amendments. The language of Rule 611 has been amended as part of the restyling of the Evidence Rules to make them more easily understood and to make style and terminology consistent throughout the rules. These changes are intended to be

stylistic only. There is no intent to change any result in any ruling on evidence admissibility.

Rule 612. Writing Used to Refresh a Witness's Memory

(a) Scope. This rule gives an adverse party certain options when a witness uses a writing to refresh memory:

(1) while testifying; or

(2) before testifying, if the court decides that justice requires the party to have those options.

(b) Adverse Party's Options; Deleting Unrelated Matter. Unless 18 U.S.C. § 3500 provides otherwise in a criminal case, an adverse party is entitled to have the writing produced at the hearing, to inspect it, to cross-examine the witness about it, and to introduce in evidence any portion that relates to the witness's testimony. If the producing party claims that the writing includes unrelated matter, the court must examine the writing in camera, delete any unrelated portion, and order that the rest be delivered to the adverse party. Any portion deleted over objection must be preserved for the record.

(c) Failure to Produce or Deliver the Writing. If a writing is not produced or is not delivered as ordered, the court may issue any appropriate order. But if the prosecution does not comply in a criminal case, the court must strike the witness's testimony or—if justice so requires—declare a mistrial.

HISTORY:

Jan. 2, 1975, P. L. 93-595, § 1, 88 Stat. 1936; March 2, 1987, eff. Oct. 1, 1987; April 26, 2011, eff. Dec. 1, 2011.

HISTORY; ANCILLARY LAWS AND DIRECTIVES

Other provisions:

Notes of Advisory Committee on Rules. The treatment of writings used to refresh recollection while on the stand is in accord with settled doctrine. McCormick § 9, p. 15. The bulk of the case law has, however, denied the existence of any right to access by the opponent when the writing is used prior to taking the stand, though the judge may have discretion in the matter. *Goldman v. United States*, 316 U.S. 129, 62 S.Ct. 993, 86 L.Ed. 1322 (1942); *Needelman v. United States*, 261 F.2d 802 (5th Cir. 1958), cert. dismissed 362 U.S. 600, 80 S.Ct. 960, 4 L.Ed.2d 980, rehearing denied 363 U.S. 858, 80 S.Ct. 1606, 4 L.Ed.2d 1739, Annot., 82 A.L.R.2d 473, 562 and 7 A.L.R.3d 181, 247. An increasing group of cases has repudiated the distinction, *People v. Scott*, 29 Ill.2d 97, 193 N.E.2d 814 (1963); *State v. Mucci*, 25 N.J. 423, 136 A.2d 761 (1957); *State v. Hunt*, 25 N.J. 514, 138 A.2d 1 (1958); *State v. Desolvers*, 40 R.I. 89, 100, A. 64 (1917), and this position is believed to be correct. As Wigmore put it, "the risk of imposition and the need of safeguard is just as great" in both situations. 3 Wigmore § 762, p. 111. To the same effect is McCormick § 9, p. 17.

The purpose of the phrase "for the purpose of testifying" is to safeguard against using the rule as a pretext for wholesale exploration of an opposing party's files and to insure that access is limited only to those writings which may fairly be said in fact to have an impact upon the testimony of the witness.

The purpose of the rule is the same as that of the Jencks statute, 18 U.S.C. § 3500: to promote the search of credibility and memory. The same sensitivity to disclosure of government files may be involved; hence the rule is expressly made subject to the statute, subdivision (a) of which provides: "In any criminal prosecution brought by the United States, no statement or report in the possession of the United States which was made by a Government witness or prospective Government witness (other than the defendant) shall be the subject of a subpena, discovery, or inspection until said witness has testified on direct examination in the trial of the case." Items falling within the purview of the statute are producible only as provided by its terms, *Palermo v. United States*, 360 U.S. 343, 351 (1959), and disclosure under the rule is limited similarly by the statutory conditions. With this limitation in mind, some differences of application may be noted. The Jencks statute applies only to statements of witnesses; the rule is not so limited. The statute applies only to criminal cases; the rule applies to all cases. The statute applies only to government witnesses; the rule applies to all witnesses. The statute contains no requirement that the statement be consulted for purposes of refreshment before or while testifying; the rule so requires. Since many writings would qualify under either statute or rule, a substantial overlap exists, but the identity of procedures makes this of no importance.

The consequences of nonproduction by the government in a criminal case are those of the Jencks statute, striking the testimony or in exceptional cases a mistrial. 18 U.S.C. § 3500(d). In other cases these alternatives are unduly limited, and such possibilities as contempt, dismissal, finding issues against the offender, and the like are available. See Rule 16(g) of the Federal Rules of Criminal Procedure and Rule 37(b) of the Federal Rules of Civil Procedure for appropriate sanctions.

Notes of Committee on the Judiciary, House Report No. 93-650. As submitted to Congress, Rule 612 provided that except as set forth in 18 U.S.C. 3500, if a witness uses a writing to refresh his memory for the purpose of testifying, "either before or while testifying," an adverse party is entitled to have the writing produced at the hearing, to inspect it, to cross-examine the witness on it, and to introduce in evidence those portions relating to the witness' testimony. The Committee amended the Rule so as still to require the production of writings used by a witness while testifying, but to render the production of writings used by a witness to refresh his memory before testifying discretionary with the court in the interests of justice, as is the case under existing federal law. See *Goldman v. United States*, 316 U.S. 129 (1942). The Committee considered that permitting an adverse party to require the production of writings used before testifying could result in fishing expeditions among a multitude of papers which a witness may have used in preparing for trial.

The Committee intends that nothing in the Rule be construed as barring the assertion of a privilege with respect to writings used by a witness to refresh his memory.

Notes of Advisory Committee on 1987 amendments. The amendment is technical. No substantive change is intended.

Notes of Advisory Committee on 2011 amendments. The language of Rule 612 has been amended as part of the restyling of the Evidence Rules to make them more easily understood and to make style and terminology consistent throughout the rules. These changes are intended to be stylistic only. There is no intent to change any result in any ruling on evidence admissibility.

Rule 613. Witness's Prior Statement

(a) Showing or Disclosing the Statement During Examination. When examining a witness about the witness's prior statement, a party need not show it or disclose its contents to the witness. But the party must, on request, show it or disclose its contents to an adverse party's attorney.

(b) Extrinsic Evidence of a Prior Inconsistent Statement. Unless the court orders otherwise, extrinsic evidence of a witness's prior inconsistent statement may not be admitted until after the witness is given an opportunity to explain or deny the statement and an adverse party is given an opportunity to examine the witness about it. This subdivision (b) does not apply to an opposing party's statement under Rule 801(d)(2).

HISTORY:

Jan. 2, 1975, P. L. 93-595, § 1, 88 Stat. 1936; March 2, 1987, eff. Oct. 1, 1987; April 25, 1988, eff. Nov. 1, 1988; April 26, 2011, eff. Dec. 1, 2011; April 2, 2024, eff. Dec. 1, 2024.

HISTORY; ANCILLARY LAWS AND DIRECTIVES

Other provisions:

Notes of Advisory Committee on Rules. *Subdivision (a).* The Queen's Case, 2 Br. & B. 284, 129 Eng. Rep. 976 (1820), laid down the requirement that a cross-examiner, prior to questioning the witness about his own prior statement in writing, must first show it to the witness. Abolished by statute in the country of its origin, the requirement nevertheless gained currency in the United States. The rule abolishes this useless impediment, to cross-examination. Ladd, Some Observations on Credibility: Impeachment of Witnesses, 52 Cornell L.Q. 239, 246–247 (1967); McCormick § 28; 4 Wigmore §§ 1259–1260. Both oral and written statements are included.

The provision for disclosure to counsel is designed to protect against unwarranted insinuations that a statement has been made when the fact is to the contrary.

The rule does not defeat the application of Rule 1002 relating to production of the original when the contents of a writing are sought to be proved. Nor does it defeat the application of Rule 26(b)(3) of the Rules of Civil Procedure, as revised, entitling a person on request to a copy of his own statement, though the operation of the latter may be suspended temporarily.

Subdivision (b). The familiar foundation requirement that an impeaching statement first be shown to the witness before it can be proved by extrinsic evidence is preserved but with some modifications. See Ladd, Some Observations on Credibility: Impeachment of Witnesses, 52 Cornell L.Q. 239, 247 (1967). The traditional insistence that the attention of the witness be directed to the statement on cross-examination is relaxed in favor of simply providing the witness an opportunity to explain and the opposite party an opportunity to examine on the statement, with no specification of any particular time or sequence. Under this procedure, several collusive witnesses can be examined before disclosure of a joint prior inconsistent statement. See Comment to California Evidence Code § 770. Also, dangers of oversight are reduced.

See McCormick § 37, p. 68.

In order to allow for such eventualities as the witness becoming unavailable by the time the statement is discovered, a measure of discretion is conferred upon the judge. Similar provisions are found in California Evidence Code § 770 and New Jersey Evidence Rule 22(b).

Under principles of *expression unius* the rule does not apply to impeachment by evidence of prior inconsistent conduct. The use of inconsistent statements to impeach a hearsay declaration is treated in Rule 806.

Notes of Advisory Committee on 1987 amendments. The amendments are technical. No substantive change is intended.

Notes of Advisory Committee on 1988 amendments. The amendment is technical. No substantive change is intended.

Notes of Advisory Committee on 2011 amendments. The language of Rule 613 has been amended as part of the restyling of the Evidence Rules to make them more easily understood and to make style and terminology consistent throughout the rules. These changes are intended to be stylistic only. There is no intent to change any result in any ruling on evidence admissibility.

Notes of Advisory Committee on 2024 amendments. Rule 613(b) has been amended to require that a witness receive an opportunity to explain or deny a prior inconsistent statement *before* the introduction of extrinsic evidence of the statement. This requirement of a prior foundation is consistent with the common law approach to impeachment with prior inconsistent statements. See, e.g., *Wammock v. Celotex Corp.,* 793 F.2d 1518, 1521 (11th Cir. 1986) ("Traditionally, prior inconsistent statements of a witness could not be proved by extrinsic evidence unless and until the witness was first confronted with the impeaching statement."). The existing rule imposes no timing preference or sequence and thus permits an impeaching party to introduce extrinsic evidence of a witness's prior inconsistent statement before giving the witness the necessary opportunity to explain or deny it. This flexible timing can create problems concerning the witness's availability to be recalled, and lead to disputes about which party bears responsibility for recalling the witness to afford the opportunity to explain or deny. Further, recalling a witness solely to afford the requisite opportunity to explain or deny a prior inconsistent statement may be inefficient. Finally, trial judges may find extrinsic evidence of a prior inconsistent statement unnecessary in some circumstances where a witness freely acknowledges the inconsistency when afforded an opportunity to explain or deny. Affording the witness an opportunity to explain or deny a prior inconsistent statement before introducing extrinsic evidence of the statement avoids these difficulties. The prior foundation requirement gives the target of the impeaching evidence a timely opportunity to explain or deny the alleged inconsistency; promotes judges' efforts to conduct trials in an orderly manner; and conserves judicial resources.

The amendment preserves the trial court's discretion to delay an opportunity to explain or deny until after the introduction of extrinsic evidence in appropriate cases, or to dispense with the requirement altogether. A trial judge may decide to delay or even forgo a witness's opportunity to explain or deny a prior inconsistent statement in certain circumstances, such as when the failure to afford the prior opportunity was inadvertent and the witness may be afforded a subsequent opportunity, or when a prior opportunity was impossible because the witness's statement was not discovered until after the witness testified.

Rule 614. Court's Calling or Examining a Witness

(a) Calling. The court may call a witness on its own or at a party's request. Each party is entitled to cross-examine the witness.

(b) Examining. The court may examine a witness regardless of who calls the witness.

(c) Objections. A party may object to the court's calling or examining a witness either at that time or at the next opportunity when the jury is not present.

HISTORY:

Jan. 2, 1975, P. L. 93-595, § 1, 88 Stat. 1937; April 26, 2011, eff. Dec. 1, 2011.

HISTORY; ANCILLARY LAWS AND DIRECTIVES

Other provisions:

Notes of Advisory Committee on Rules. *Subdivision (a).* While exercised more frequently in criminal than in civil cases, the authority of the judge to call witnesses is well established. McCormick § 8, p. 14; Maguire, Weinstein, et al., Cases on Evidence 303-304 (5th ed. 1965); 9 Wigmore § 2484. One reason for the practice, the old rule against impeaching one's own witness, no longer exists by virtue of Rule 607, supra. Other reasons remain, however, to justify the continuation of the practice of calling court's witnesses. The right to cross-examine, with all it implies, is assured. The tendency of juries to associate a witness with the party calling him, regardless of technical aspects of vouching, is avoided. And the judge is not imprisoned within the case as made by the parties.

Subdivision (b). The authority of the judge to question witnesses is also well established. McCormick § 8, pp. 12–13; Maguire, Weinstein, et al., Cases on Evidence 737–739 (5th ed. 1965); 3 Wigmore § 784. The authority is, of course, abused when the judge abandons his proper role and assumes that of advocate, but the manner in which interrogation should be conducted and the proper extent of its exercise are not susceptible of formulation in a rule. The omission in no sense precludes courts of review from continuing to reverse for abuse.

Subdivision (c). The provision relating to objections is designed to relieve counsel of the embarrassment attendant upon objecting to questions by the judge in the presence of the jury, while at the same time assuring that objections are made in apt time to afford the opportunity to take possible corrective measures. Compare the "automatic" objection feature of Rule 605 when the judge is called as a witness.

Notes of Advisory Committee on 2011 amendments. The language of Rule 614 has been amended as part of the restyling of the Evidence Rules to make them more easily understood and to make style and terminology consistent throughout the rules. These changes are intended to be stylistic only. There is no intent to change any result in any ruling on evidence admissibility.

Rule 615. Excluding Witnesses from the Courtroom; Preventing an Excluded Witness's Access to Trial Testimony

(a) Excluding Witnesses. At a party's request, the court must order witnesses excluded from the courtroom so that they cannot hear other witnesses' testimony. Or the court may do so on its own. But this rule does not authorize excluding:

(1) a party who is a natural person;

(2) one officer or employee of a party that is not a natural person if that officer or employee has been designated as the party's representative by its attorney;

(3) any person whose presence a party shows to be essential to presenting the party's claim or defense; or

(4) a person authorized by statute to be present.

(b) Additional Orders to Prevent Disclosing and Accessing Testimony. An order under (a) operates only to exclude witnesses from the courtroom. But the court may also, by order:

(1) prohibit disclosure of trial testimony to witnesses who are excluded from the courtroom; and

(2) prohibit excluded witnesses from accessing trial testimony.

HISTORY:

Jan. 2, 1975, P. L. 93-595, § 1, 88 Stat. 1937; March 2, 1987, eff. Oct. 1, 1987; April 25, 1988, eff. Nov. 1, 1988; Nov. 18, 1988, P. L. 100-690, Title VII, Subtitle B, § 7075(a), 102 Stat. 4405; Apr. 24, 1998, eff. Dec. 1, 1998; Apr. 26, 2011, eff. Dec. 1, 2011; April 24, 2023, eff. Dec. 1, 2023.

HISTORY; ANCILLARY LAWS AND DIRECTIVES

Other provisions:

Notes of Advisory Committee on Rules. The efficacy of excluding or sequestering witnesses has long been recognized as a means of discouraging and exposing fabrication, inaccuracy, and collusion. 6 Wigmore §§ 1837–1838. The authority of the judge is admitted, the only question being whether the matter is committed to his discretion or one of right. The rule takes the latter position. No time is specified for making the request.

Several categories of persons are excepted. (1) Exclusion of persons who are parties would raise serious problems of confrontation and due process. Under accepted practice they are not subject to exclusion. 6 Wigmore § 1841. (2) As the equivalent of the right of a natural-person party to be present, a party which is not a natural person is entitled to have a representative present. Most of the cases have involved allowing a police officer who has been in charge of an investigation to remain in court despite the fact that he will be a witness. *United States v. Infanzon*, 235 F.2d 318 (2d Cir. 1956); Portomene v. United States, 221 F.2d 582 (5th Cir. 1955); *Powell v. United States*, 208 F.2d 618 (6th Cir. 1953); *Jones v. United States*, 252 F.Supp. 781 (W.D.Okl. 1966). Designation of the representative by the attorney rather than by the client may at first glance appear to be an inversion of the attorney-client relationship, but it may be assumed that the attorney will follow the wishes of the client, and the solution is simple and workable. See California Evidence Code § 777. (3) The category contemplates such persons as an agent who handled the transaction being litigated or an expert needed to advise counsel in the management of the litigation. See 6 Wigmore § 1841, n. 4.

Notes of Committee on the Judiciary, Senate Report No. 93-1277. Many district courts permit government counsel to have an investigative agent at counsel table throughout the trial although the agent is or may be a witness. The practice is permitted as an exception to the rule of exclusion and compares with the situation defense counsel finds himself in--he always has the client with him to consult during the trial. The investigative agent's presence may be extremely important to government counsel, especially when the case is complex or involves some specialized subject matter. The agent, too, having lived with the case for a long time, may be able to assist in meeting trial surprises where the best-prepared counsel would otherwise have difficulty. Yet, it would not seem the Government could often meet the burden under rule 615 of showing that the agent's presence is essential. Furthermore, it could be dangerous to use the agent as a witness as early in the case as possible, so that he might then help counsel as a nonwitness, since the agent's testimony could be needed in rebuttal. Using another, nonwitness agent from the same investigative agency would not generally meet government counsel's needs.

This problem is solved if it is clear that investigative agents are within the group specified under the second exception made in the rule, for "an officer or employee of a party which is not a natural person designated as its representative by its attorney." It is our understanding that this was the intention of the House committee. It is certainly this committee's construction of the rule.

Notes of Advisory Committee on 1987 amendments. The amendment is technical. No substantive change is intended.

Notes of Advisory Committee on 1988 amendments. The amendment is technical. No substantive change is intended.

Notes of Advisory Committee on 1998 amendments. The amendment is in response to: (1) the Victim's Rights and Restitution Act of 1990, 42 U.S.C. § 10606, which guarantees, within certain limits, the right of a crime victim to attend the trial; and (2) the Victim Rights Clarification Act of 1997 (18 U.S.C. § 3510).

Notes of Advisory Committee on 2011 amendments. The language of Rule 615 has been amended as part of the restyling of the Evidence Rules to make them more easily understood and to make style and terminology consistent throughout the rules. These changes are intended to be stylistic only. There is no intent to change any result in any ruling on evidence admissibility.

Notes of Advisory Committee on 2023 amendments. Rule 615 has been amended for two purposes:

(1) Most importantly, the amendment clarifies that the court, in entering an order under this rule, may also prohibit excluded witnesses from learning about, obtaining, or being provided with trial testimony. Many courts have found that a "Rule 615 order" extends beyond the courtroom, to prohibit excluded witnesses from obtaining access to or being provided with trial testimony. But the terms of the rule did not so provide; and other courts have held that a Rule 615 order was limited to exclusion of witnesses from the trial. On the one hand, the courts extending Rule 615 beyond courtroom exclusion properly recognized that the core purpose of the rule is to prevent witnesses from tailoring their testimony to the evidence presented at trial—and that purpose can only be effectuated by regulating out-of-court exposure to trial testimony. *See United States v. Robertson,* 895 F.3d 1206, 1215 (9th Cir. 2018) ("The danger that earlier testimony could improperly shape later testimony is equally present whether the witness hears that testimony in court or reads it from a transcript."). On the other hand, a rule extending an often vague "Rule 615 order" outside the courtroom raised questions of fair notice, given that the text of the rule itself was limited to exclusion of witnesses from the courtroom.

An order under subdivision (a) operates only to exclude witnesses from the courtroom. This includes exclusion of witnesses from a virtual trial. Subdivision (b) emphasizes that the court may by order extend the sequestration beyond the courtroom, to prohibit those subject to the order from disclosing trial testimony to excluded witnesses, as well as to directly prohibit excluded witnesses from trying to access trial testimony. Such an extension is often necessary to further the rule's policy of preventing tailoring of testimony.

The rule gives the court discretion to determine what requirements, if any, are appropriate in a particular case to protect against the risk that witnesses excluded from the courtroom will obtain trial testimony.

Nothing in the language of the rule bars a court from prohibiting counsel from disclosing trial testimony to a sequestered witness. To the extent that an order governing counsel's disclosure of trial testimony to prepare a witness raises questions of professional responsibility and effective assistance of counsel, as well as the right to confrontation in criminal cases, the court should address those questions on a case-by-case basis.

(2) Second, the rule has been amended to clarify that the exception from exclusion for entity representatives is limited to one designated representative per entity. This limitation, which has been followed by most courts, generally provides parity for individual and entity parties. The rule does not prohibit the court from exercising discretion to allow an entity-party to swap one representative for another as the trial progresses, so long as only one witness-representative is exempt at any one time. If an entity seeks to have more than one witness-representative protected from exclusion, it needs to show under subdivision (a)(3) that the witness is essential to presenting the party's claim or defense. Nothing in this amendment prohibits a court from exempting from exclusion multiple witnesses if they are found essential under (a)(3).

Amendments:

1988.

Act Nov. 18, 1988 inserted "a" before "party which is not a natural person".

ARTICLE VII. OPINIONS AND EXPERT TESTIMONY

Rule

701. Opinion Testimony by Lay Witnesses
702. Testimony by Expert Witnesses
703. Bases of an Expert's Opinion Testimony

Rule 701. Opinion Testimony by Lay Witnesses

If a witness is not testifying as an expert, testimony in the form of an opinion is limited to one that is:

(a) rationally based on the witness's perception;

(b) helpful to clearly understanding the witness's testimony or to determining a fact in issue; and

(c) not based on scientific, technical, or other specialized knowledge within the scope of Rule 702.

HISTORY:

Jan. 2, 1975, P. L. 93-595, § 1, 88 Stat. 1937; March 2, 1987, eff. Oct. 1, 1987; April 17, 2000, eff. Dec. 1, 2000; April 26, 2011, eff. Dec. 1, 2011.

HISTORY; ANCILLARY LAWS AND DIRECTIVES

Other provisions:

Notes of Advisory Committee on Rules. The rule retains the traditional objective of putting the trier of fact in possession of an accurate reproduction of the event.

Limitation (a) is the familiar requirement of firsthand knowledge or observation.

Limitation (b) is phrased in terms of requiring testimony to be helpful in resolving issues. Witnesses often find difficulty in expressing themselves in language which is not that of an opinion or conclusion. While the courts have made concessions in certain recurring situations, necessity as a standard for permitting opinions and conclusions has proved too elusive and too unadaptable to particular situations for purposes of satisfactory judicial administration. McCormick § 11. Moreover, the practical impossibility of determining by rule what is a "fact," demonstrated by a century of litigation of the question of what is a fact for purposes of pleading under the Field Code, extends into evidence also. 7 Wigmore § 1919. The rule assumes that the natural characteristics of the adversary system will generally lead to an acceptable result, since the detailed account carries more conviction than the broad assertion, and a lawyer can be expected to display his witness to the best advantage. If he fails to do so, cross-examination and argument will point up the weakness. See Ladd, Expert Testimony, 5 Vand.L.Rev. 414, 415–417 (1952). If, despite these considerations, attempts are made to introduce meaningless assertions which amount to little more than choosing up sides, exclusion for lack of helpfulness is called for by the rule.

The language of the rule is substantially that of Uniform. Rule 56(1). Similar provisions are California Evidence Code § 800; Kansas Code of Civil Procedure § 60-456(a); New Jersey Evidence Rule 56(1).

Notes of Advisory Committee on 1987 amendments. The amendments are technical. No substantive change is intended.

Notes of Advisory Committee on 2000 amendments. Rule 701 has been amended to eliminate the risk that the reliability requirements set forth in Rule 702 will be evaded through the simple expedient of proffering an expert in lay witness clothing. Under the amendment, a witness' testimony must be scrutinized under the rules regulating expert opinion to the extent that the witness is providing testimony based on scientific, technical, or other specialized knowledge within the scope of Rule 702. *See generally Asplundh Mfg. Div. v. Benton Harbor Eng'g,* 57 F.3d 1190 (3d Cir. 1995). By channeling testimony that is actually expert testimony to Rule 702, the amendment also ensures that a party will not evade the expert witness disclosure requirements set forth in Fed.R.Civ.P. 26 and Fed.R.Crim.P. 16 by simply calling an expert witness in the guise of a layperson. *See Joseph, Emerging Expert Issues Under the 1993 Disclosure Amendments to the Federal Rules of Civil Procedure,* 164 F.R.D. 97, 108 (1996) (noting that "there is no good reason to allow what is essentially surprise expert testimony," and that "the Court should be vigilant to preclude manipulative conduct designed to thwart the expert disclosure and discovery process"). *See also United States v. Figueroa-Lopez,* 125 F.3d 1241, 1246 (9th Cir. 1997) (law enforcement agents testifying that the defendant's conduct was consistent with that of a drug trafficker could not testify as lay witnesses; to permit such testimony under Rule 701 "subverts the requirements of Federal Rule of Criminal Procedure 16(a)(1)(E)").

The amendment does not distinguish between expert and lay witnesses, but rather between expert and lay testimony. Certainly it is possible for the same witness to provide both lay and expert testimony in a single case. *See, e.g., United States v. Figueroa-Lopez,* 125 F.3d 1241, 1246 (9th Cir. 1997) (law enforcement agents could testify that the defendant was acting suspiciously, without being qualified as experts; however, the rules on experts were applicable where the agents testified on the basis of extensive experience that the defendant was using code words to refer to drug quantities and prices). The amendment makes clear that any part of a witness' testimony that is based upon scientific, technical, or other specialized knowledge within the scope of Rule 702 is governed by the standards of Rule 702 and the corresponding disclosure requirements of the Civil and Criminal Rules.

The amendment is not intended to affect the "prototypical example[s] of the type of evidence contemplated by the adoption of Rule 701 relat[ing] to the appearance of persons or things, identity, the manner of conduct, competency of a person, degrees of light or darkness, sound, size, weight, distance, and an endless number of items that cannot be described factually in words apart from inferences." *Asplundh Mfg. Div. v. Benton Harbor Eng'g,* 57 F.3d 1190, 1196 (3d Cir. 1995).

For example, most courts have permitted the owner or officer of a business to testify to the value or projected profits of the business, without the necessity of qualifying the witness as an accountant, appraiser, or similar expert. *See, e.g., Lightning Lube, Inc. v. Witco Corp.* 4 F.3d 1153 (3d Cir. 1993) (no abuse of discretion in permitting the plaintiffs owner to give lay opinion testimony as to damages, as it was based on his knowledge and participation in the day-to-day affairs of the business). Such opinion testimony is admitted not because of experience, training or specialized knowledge within the realm of an expert, but because of the particularized knowledge that the witness has by virtue of his or her position in the business. The amendment does not purport to change this analysis. Similarly, courts have permitted lay witnesses to testify that a substance appeared to be a narcotic, so long as a foundation of familiarity with the substance is established. *See, e.g., United States v. Westbrook,* 896 F.2d 330 (8th Cir.

1990) (two lay witnesses who were heavy amphetamine users were properly permitted to testify that a substance was amphetamine; but it was error to permit another witness to make such an identification where she had no experience with amphetamines). Such testimony is not based on specialized knowledge within the scope of Rule 702, but rather is based upon a layperson' s personal knowledge. If, however, that witness were to describe how a narcotic was manufactured, or to describe the intricate workings of a narcotic distribution network, then the witness would have to qualify as an expert under Rule 702. *United States v. Figueroa-Lopez, supra.*

The amendment incorporates the distinctions set forth in *State v. Brown*, 836 S.W.2d 530, 549 (1992), a case involving former Tennessee Rule of Evidence 701, a rule that precluded lay witness testimony based on "special knowledge." In Brown, the court declared that the distinction between lay and expert witness testimony is that lay testimony "results from a process of reasoning familiar in everyday life," while expert testimony "results from a process of reasoning which can be mastered only by specialists in the field." The court in Brown noted that a lay witness with experience could testify that a substance appeared to be blood, but that a witness would have to qualify as an expert before he could testify that bruising around the eyes is indicative of skull trauma. That is the kind of distinction made by the amendment to this Rule.

GAP Report—Proposed Amendment to Rule 701. The Committee made the following changes to the published draft of the proposed amendment to Evidence Rule 701: 2.

1. The words "within the scope of Rule 702" were added at the end of the proposed amendment, to emphasize that the Rule does not require witnesses to qualify as experts unless their testimony is of the type traditionally considered within the purview of Rule 702. The Committee Note was amended to accord with this textual change.

2. The Committee Note was revised to provide further examples of the kind of testimony that could and could not be proffered under the limitation imposed by the proposed amendment.

Notes of Advisory Committee on 2011 amendments. The language of Rule 701 has been amended as part of the general restyling of the Evidence Rules to make them more easily understood and to make style and terminology consistent throughout the rules. These changes are intended to be stylistic only. There is no intent to change any result in any ruling on evidence admissibility.

The Committee deleted all reference to an "inference" on the grounds that the deletion made the Rule flow better and easier to read, and because any "inference" is covered by the broader term "opinion." Courts have not made substantive decisions on the basis of any distinction between an opinion and an inference. No change in current practice is intended.

Rule 702. Testimony by Expert Witnesses

A witness who is qualified as an expert by knowledge, skill, experience, training, or education may testify in the form of an opinion or otherwise if the proponent demonstrates to the court that it is more likely than not that:

(a) the expert's scientific, technical, or other specialized knowledge will help the trier of fact to understand the evidence or to determine a fact in issue;

(b) the testimony is based on sufficient facts or data;

(c) the testimony is the product of reliable principles and methods; and

(d) the expert's opinion reflects a reliable application of the principles and methods to the facts of the case.

HISTORY:

Jan. 2, 1975, P. L. 93-595, § 1, 88 Stat. 1937; April 17, 2000, eff. Dec. 1, 2000; April 26, 2011, eff. Dec. 1, 2011; April 24, 2023, eff. Dec. 1, 2023.

HISTORY; ANCILLARY LAWS AND DIRECTIVES

Other provisions:

Notes of Advisory Committee on Rules. An intelligent evaluation of facts is often difficult or impossible without the application of some scientific, technical, or other specialized knowledge. The most common source of this knowledge is the expert witness, although there are other techniques for supplying it.

Most of the literature assumes that experts testify only in the form of opinions. The assumption is logically unfounded. The rule accordingly recognizes that an expert on the stand may give a dissertation or exposition of scientific or other principles relevant to the case, leaving the trier of fact to apply them to the facts. Since much of the criticism of expert testimony has centered upon the hypothetical question, it seems wise to recognize that opinions are not indispensable and to encourage the use of expert testimony in non-opinion form when counsel believes the trier can itself draw the requisite inference. The use of opinions is not abolished by the rule, however. It will continue to be permissible for the experts to take the further step of suggesting the inference which should be drawn from applying the specialized knowledge to the facts. See Rules 703 to 705.

Whether the situation is a proper one for the use of expert testimony is to be determined on the basis of assisting the trier. "There is no more certain test for determining when experts may be used than the common sense inquiry whether the untrained layman would be qualified to determine intelligently and to the best possible degree the particular issue without enlightenment from those having a specialized understanding of the subject involved in the dispute." Ladd, Expert Testimony, 5 Vand.L.Rev. 414, 418 (1952). When opinions are excluded, it is because they are unhelpful and therefore superfluous and a waste of time. 7 Wigmore § 1918.

The rule is broadly phrased. The fields of knowledge which may be drawn upon are not limited merely to the "scientific" and "technical" but extend to all "specialized" knowledge. Similarly, the expert is viewed, not in a narrow sense, but as a person qualified by "knowledge, skill, experience, training or education." Thus within the scope of the rule are not only experts in the strictest sense of the word, e.g., physicians, physicists, and architects, but also the large group sometimes called "skilled" witnesses, such as bankers or landowners testifying to land values.

Notes of Advisory Committee on 2000 amendments. Rule 702 has been amended in response to *Daubert v. Merrell Dow Pharmaceuticals, Inc.*, 509 U.S. 579 [125 L. Ed. 2d 469] (1993), and to the many cases applying *Daubert*, including *Kumho Tire Co. v. Carmichael*, [143 L. Ed. 2d 238,] 119 S.Ct. 1167 (1999). In *Daubert* the Court charged trial judges with the responsibility of acting as gatekeepers to exclude unreliable expert testimony, and the Court in *Kumho* clarified that this gatekeeper function applies to all expert testimony, not just testimony based in science. *See also Kumho,* 119 S.Ct. at 1178 (citing the Committee Note to the proposed amendment to Rule 702, which had been released for public comment before the date of the *Kumho* decision). The amendment affirms the trial court's role as gatekeeper and provides some general standards that the trial court must use to assess the reliability and helpfulness of proffered expert testimony. Consistently with Kumho, the Rule as amended provides that all types of expert testimony present questions of admissibility for the trial court in deciding whether the evidence is reliable and helpful. Consequently, the admissibility of all expert testimony is governed by the principles of Rule 104(a). Under that Rule, the proponent has the burden of establishing that the pertinent admissibility requirements are met by a preponderance of the evidence. *See Bourjaily v. United States,* 483 U.S. 171 [97 L. Ed. 2d 144] (1987).

Daubert set forth a non-exclusive checklist for trial courts to use in assessing the reliability of scientific expert testimony. The specific factors explicated by the *Daubert* Court are (1) whether the expert's technique or theory can be or has been tested—that is, whether the expert's theory can be challenged in some objective sense, or whether it is instead simply a subjective, conclusory approach that cannot reasonably be assessed for reliability; (2) whether the technique or theory has been subject to peer review and publication; (3) the known or potential rate of error of the technique or theory when applied; (4) the existence and maintenance of standards and controls; and (5) whether the technique or theory has been generally accepted in the scientific community. The Court in *Kumho* held that these factors might also be applicable in assessing the reliability of non-scientific expert testimony, depending upon "the particular circumstances of the particular case at issue." 119 S.Ct. at 1175.

No attempt has been made to "codify" these specific factors. Daubert itself emphasized that the factors were neither exclusive nor dispositive. Other cases have recognized that not all of the specific Daubert factors can apply to every type of expert testimony. In addition to *Kumho,* 119 S.Ct. at 1175, *see Tyus v. Urban Search Management,* 102 F.3d 256 (7th Cir. 1996) (noting that the factors mentioned by the Court in *Daubert* do not neatly apply to expert testimony from a sociologist). *See also Kannankeril v. Terminix Int'l, Inc.,* 128 F.3d 802, 809 (3d Cir. 1997) (holding that lack of peer review or publication was not dispositive where the expert's opinion was supported by "widely accepted scientific knowledge"). The standards set forth in the amendment are broad enough to require consideration of any or all of the specific Daubert factors where appropriate.

Courts both before and after *Daubert* have found other factors relevant in determining whether expert testimony is sufficiently reliable to be considered by the trier of fact. These factors include:

(1) Whether experts are "proposing to testify about matters growing naturally and directly out of research they have conducted independent of the litigation, or whether they have developed their opinions expressly for purposes of testifying." *Daubert v. Merrell Dow Pharmaceuticals, Inc.,* 43 F.3d 1311, 1317 (9th Cir. 1995).

(2) Whether the expert has unjustifiably extrapolated from an accepted premise to an unfounded conclusion. *See General Elec. Co. v. Joiner,* 522 U.S. 136 [139 L. Ed. 2d 508], 146 (1997) (noting that in some cases a trial court "may conclude that there is simply too great an analytical gap between the data and the opinion proffered").

(3) Whether the expert has adequately accounted for obvious alternative explanations. *See Claar v. Burlington N.R.R.,* 29 F.3d 499 (9th Cir. 1994) (testimony excluded where the expert failed to consider other obvious causes for the plaintiffs condition). *Compare Ambrosini v. Labarraque,* 101 F.3d 129 (D.C.Cir. 1996) (the possibility of some uneliminated causes presents a question of weight, so long as the most obvious causes have been considered and reasonably ruled out by the expert).

(4) Whether the expert "is being as careful as he would be in his regular professional work outside his paid litigation consulting." *Sheehan v. Daily Racing Form, Inc.,* 104 F.3d 940, 942 (7th Cir. 1997). *See Kumho Tire Co. v. Carmichael,* [143 L. Ed. 2d 238,] 119 S.Ct. 1167, 1176 (1999) (*Daubert* requires the trial court to assure itself that the expert "employs in the courtroom the same level of intellectual rigor that characterizes the practice of an expert in the relevant field").

(5) Whether the field of expertise claimed by the expert is known to reach reliable results for the type of opinion the expert would give. *See Kumho Tire Co. v. Carmichael,* [143 L. Ed. 2d 238,] 119 S.Ct. 1167, 1175 (1999) (Daubert's general acceptance factor does not "help show that an expert's testimony is reliable where the discipline itself lacks reliability, as, for example, do theories grounded in any so-called generally accepted principles of astrology or necromancy."); *Moore v. Ashland Chemical, Inc.,* 151 F.3d 269 (5th Cir. 1998) (en banc) (clinical doctor was properly precluded from testifying to the toxicological cause of the plaintiffs respiratory problem, where the opinion was not sufficiently grounded in scientific methodology); *Sterling v. Velsicol Chem. Corp.,* 855 F.2d 1188 (6th Cir. 1988) (rejecting testimony based on "clinical ecology" as unfounded and unreliable).

All of these factors remain relevant to the determination of the reliability of expert testimony under the Rule as amended. Other factors may also be relevant. *See Kumho,* [143 L. Ed. 2d 238,] 119 S.Ct. 1167, 1176 ("[W]e conclude that the trial judge must have considerable leeway in deciding in a particular case how to go about determining whether particular expert testimony is reliable."). Yet no single factor is necessarily dispositive of the reliability of a particular expert's testimony. *See, e.g., Heller v. Shaw Industries, Inc.,* 167 F.3d 146, 155 (3d Cir. 1999) ("not only must each stage of the expert's testimony be reliable, but each stage must be evaluated practically and flexibly without bright-line exclusionary (or inclusionary) rules."); *Daubert v. Merrell Dow Pharmaceuticals, Inc.,* 43 F.3d 1311, 1317, n.5 (9th Cir. 1995) (noting that some expert disciplines "have the courtroom as a principal theatre of operations" and as to these disciplines "the fact that the expert has developed an expertise principally for purposes of litigation will obviously not be a substantial consideration.").

A review of the caselaw after *Daubert* shows that the rejection of expert testimony is the exception rather than the rule. *Daubert* did not work a "seachange over federal evidence law," and "the trial court's role as gatekeeper is not intended to serve as a replacement for the adversary system." *United States v. 14.38 Acres of Land Situated in Leflore County, Mississippi,* 80 F.3d 1074, 1078 (5th Cir. 1996). As the Court in Daubert stated: "Vigorous cross-examination, presentation of contrary evidence, and careful instruction on the burden of proof are the traditional and appropriate means of attacking shaky but admissible evidence." 509 U.S. at 595. Likewise, this amendment is not intended to provide an excuse for an automatic challenge to the testimony of every expert. *See Kumho Tire Co. v. Carmichael,* [143 L. Ed. 2d 238,] 119 S.Ct. 1167, 1176 (1999) (noting that the trial judge has the discretion "both to avoid unnecessary 'reliability' proceedings in ordinary cases where the reliability of an expert's methods is properly taken for granted, and to require appropriate proceedings in the less usual or more complex cases where cause for questioning the expert's reliability arises.").

When a trial court, applying this amendment, rules that an expert's testimony is reliable, this does not necessarily mean that contradictory expert testimony is unreliable. The amendment is broad enough to permit testimony that is the product of competing principles or methods in the same field of expertise. *See, e.g., Heller v. Shaw Industries, Inc.,* 167 F.3d 146, 160 (3d Cir. 1999) (expert testimony cannot be excluded simply because the expert uses one test rather than another, when both tests are accepted in the field and both reach reliable results). As the court stated in *In re Paoli R.R. Yard PCB Litigation,* 35 F.3d 717, 744 (3d Cir. 1994), proponents "do not have to demonstrate to the judge by a preponderance of the evidence that the assessments of their experts are correct, they only have to demonstrate by a preponderance of evidence that their opinions are reliable. . . . The evidentiary requirement of reliability is lower than the merits standard of correctness." *See also Daubert v. Merrell Dow Pharmaceuticals, Inc.,* 43 F.3d 1311, 1318 (9th Cir. 1995) (scientific experts might be permitted to testify if they could show that the methods they used were also employed by "a recognized minority of scientists in their field."); *Ruiz-Troche v. Pepsi Cola,* 161 F.3d 77, 85 (1st Cir. 1998) (" *Daubert* neither requires nor empowers trial courts to determine which of several competing scientific theories has the best provenance.").

The Court in *Daubert* declared that the "focus, of course, must be solely on principles and methodology, not on the conclusions they generate." 509 U.S. at 595. Yet as the Court later recognized, "conclusions and methodology are not entirely distinct from one another." *General Elec. Co. v. Joiner,* 522 U.S. 136 [139 L. Ed. 2d 508], 146 (1997). Under the amendment, as under *Daubert,* when an expert purports to apply principles and methods in accordance with professional standards, and yet reaches a conclusion that other experts in the field would not reach, the trial court may fairly suspect that the principles and methods have not been faithfully applied. *See Lust v. Merrell Dow Pharmaceuticals, Inc.,* 89 F.3d 594, 598 (9th Cir. 1996). The amendment specifically provides that the trial court must scrutinize not only the principles and methods used by the expert, but also whether those principles and methods have been properly applied to the facts of the case. As the court noted in *In re Paoli R.R. Yard PCB Litig.,* 35 F.3d 717, 745 (3d Cir. 1994), "any step that renders the analysis unreliable . . . renders the expert's testimony inadmissible. *This is true whether the step completely changes a reliable methodology or merely misapplies that methodology.*"

If the expert purports to apply principles and methods to the facts of the case, it is important that this application be conducted reliably. Yet it might also be important in some cases for an expert to educate the factfinder about general principles, without ever attempting to apply these principles to the specific facts of the case. For example, experts might instruct the factfinder on the principles of thermodynamics, or bloodclotting, or on how financial markets respond to corporate reports, without ever knowing about or trying to tie their testimony into the facts of the case. The amendment does not alter the venerable practice of using expert testimony to educate the factfinder on general principles. For this kind of generalized testimony, Rule 702 simply requires that: (1) the expert be qualified; (2) the testimony address a subject matter on which the factfinder can be assisted by an expert; (3) the testimony be reliable; and (4) the testimony "fit" the facts of the case.

As stated earlier, the amendment does not distinguish between scientific and other forms of expert testimony. The trial court's gatekeeping function applies to testimony by any expert. *See Kumho Tire Co. v. Carmichael,* [143 L. Ed. 2d 238,] 119 S.Ct. 1167, 1171 (1999) ("We conclude that Daubert's general holding—setting forth the trial judge's general 'gatekeeping' obligation—applies not only to testimony based on 'scientific' knowledge, but also to testimony based on 'technical' and 'other specialized' knowledge."). While the relevant factors for determining reliability will vary from expertise to expertise, the amendment rejects the premise that an expert's testimony should be treated more permissively simply because it is outside the realm of science. An opinion from an expert who is not a scientist should receive the same degree of scrutiny for reliability as an opinion from an expert who purports to be a scientist. *See Watkins v. Telsmith, Inc.,* 121 F.3d 984, 991 (5th Cir. 1997) ("[I]t seems exactly backwards that experts who purport to rely on general engineering principles and practical experience might escape screening by the district court simply by stating that their conclusions were not reached by any particular method or technique."). Some types of expert testimony will be more objectively verifiable, and subject to the expectations of falsifiability, peer review, and publication, than others. Some types of expert testimony will not rely on anything like a scientific method, and so will have to be evaluated by reference to other standard principles attendant to the particular area of expertise. The trial judge in all cases of proffered expert testimony must find that it is properly grounded, well-reasoned, and not speculative before it can be admitted. The expert's testimony must be grounded in an accepted body of learning or experience in the expert's field, and the expert must explain how the conclusion is so grounded. See, e.g., American College of Trial Lawyers, *Standards and Procedures for Determining the Admissibility of Expert Testimony after Daubert,* 157 F.R.D. 571, 579 (1994) ("[W]hether the testimony concerns economic principles, accounting standards, property valuation or other non-scientific subjects, it should be evaluated by reference to the 'knowledge and experience' of that particular field.").

The amendment requires that the testimony must be the product of reliable principles and methods that are reliably applied to the facts of the case. While the terms "principles" and "methods" may convey a certain impression when applied to scientific knowledge, they remain relevant when applied to testimony based on technical or other specialized knowledge. For example, when a law enforcement agent testifies regarding the use of code words in a drug transaction, the principle used by the agent is that participants in such transactions regularly use code words to conceal the nature of their activities. The method used by the agent is the application of extensive experience to analyze the meaning of the conversations. So long as the principles and methods are reliable and applied reliably to the facts of the case, this type of testimony should be admitted.

Nothing in this amendment is intended to suggest that experience alone—or experience in conjunction with other knowledge, skill, training or education—may not provide a sufficient foundation for expert testimony. To the contrary, the text of Rule 702 expressly contemplates that an expert may be qualified on the basis of experience. In certain fields, experience is the predominant, if not sole, basis for a great deal of reliable expert testimony. *See, e.g., United States v. Jones,* 107 F.3d 1147 (6th Cir. 1997) (no abuse of discretion in admitting the testimony of a handwriting examiner who had years of practical experience and extensive training, and who explained his methodology in detail); *Tassin v. Sears Roebuck,* 946 F.Supp. 1241, 1248 (M.D.La. 1996) (design engineer's testimony can be admissible when the expert's opinions "are based on facts, a reasonable investigation, and traditional technical/mechanical expertise, and he provides a reasonable link between the information and procedures he uses and the conclusions he reaches"). See also *Kumho Tire Co. v. Carmichael,* [143 L. Ed. 2d 238,] 119 S.Ct. 1167, 1178 (1999) (stating that "no one denies that an expert might draw a conclusion from a set of observations based on extensive and specialized experience.").

If the witness is relying solely or primarily on experience, then the witness must explain how that experience leads to the conclusion reached, why that experience is a sufficient basis for the opinion, and how that experience is reliably applied to the facts. The trial court's gatekeeping function requires more than simply "taking the expert's word for it." *See Daubert v. Merrell Dow Pharmaceuticals, Inc.,* 43 F.3d 1311, 1319 (9th Cir. 1995) ("We've been presented with only the experts' qualifications, their conclusions and their assurances of reliability. Under *Daubert,* that's not enough."). The more subjective and controversial the expert's inquiry, the more likely the testimony should be excluded as unreliable. *See O'Conner v. Commonwealth Edison Co.,* 13 F.3d 1090 (7th Cir. 1994) (expert testimony based on a completely subjective methodology held properly excluded). *See also Kumho Tire Co. v. Carmichael,* [143 L. Ed. 2d 238,] 119 S.Ct. 1167, 1176 (1999) ("[I] will at times be useful to ask even of a witness whose expertise is based purely on experience, say, a perfume tester able to distinguish among 140 odors at a sniff, whether his preparation is of a kind that others in the field would recognize as acceptable.").

Subpart (1) of Rule 702 calls for a quantitative rather than qualitative analysis. The amendment requires that expert testimony be based on sufficient underlying "facts or data." The term "data" is intended to encompass the reliable opinions of other experts. See the original Advisory Committee Note to Rule 703. The language "facts or data" is broad enough to allow an expert to rely on hypothetical facts that are supported by the evidence. *Id.*

When facts are in dispute, experts sometimes reach different conclusions based on competing versions of the facts. The emphasis in the amendment on "sufficient facts or data" is not intended to authorize a trial court to exclude an expert's testimony on the ground that the court believes one version of the facts and not the other.

There has been some confusion over the relationship between Rules 702 and 703. The amendment makes clear that the sufficiency of the basis of an expert's testimony is to be decided under Rule 702. Rule 702 sets forth the overarching requirement of reliability, and an analysis of the sufficiency of the expert's basis cannot be divorced from the ultimate reliability of the expert's opinion. In contrast, the "reasonable reliance" requirement of Rule 703 is a relatively narrow inquiry. When an expert relies on inadmissible information, Rule 703 requires the trial court to determine whether that information is of a type reasonably relied on by other experts in the field. If so, the expert can rely on the information in reaching an opinion. However, the question whether the expert is relying on a sufficient basis of information—whether admissible information or not—is governed by the requirements of Rule 702.

The amendment makes no attempt to set forth procedural requirements for exercising the trial court's gatekeeping function over expert testimony. *See* Daniel J. Capra, *The Daubert Puzzle,* 38 Ga.L.Rev. 699, 766 (1998) ("Trial courts should be allowed substantial discretion in dealing with Daubert questions; any attempt to codify procedures will likely give rise to unnecessary changes in practice and create difficult questions for appellate review."). Courts have shown considerable ingenuity and flexibility in considering challenges to expert testimony under Daubert, and it is contemplated that this will continue under the amended Rule. *See, e.g., Cortes-Irizarry v. Corporacion Insular,* 111 F.3d 184 (1st Cir. 1997) (discussing the application of Daubert in ruling on a motion for summary judgment); *In re Paoli R.R. Yard PCB Litig.,* 35 F.3d 717, 736, 739 (3d Cir. 1994) (discussing the use of in limine hearings); *Claar v. Burlington N.R.R.,* 29 F.3d 499, 502-05 (9th Cir. 1994) (discussing the trial court's technique of ordering experts to submit serial affidavits explaining the reasoning and methods underlying their conclusions).

The amendment continues the practice of the original Rule in referring to a qualified witness as an "expert." This was done to provide continuity and to minimize change. The use of the term "expert" in the Rule does not, however, mean that a jury should actually be informed that a qualified witness is testifying as an "expert." Indeed, there is much to be said for a practice that prohibits the use of the term "expert" by both the parties and the court at trial. Such a practice "ensures that trial courts do not inadvertently put their stamp of authority" on a witness's opinion, and protects against the jury's being "overwhelmed by the so-called 'experts'." Hon. Charles Richey, *Proposals to Eliminate the Prejudicial Effect of the Use of the Word "Expert" Under the Federal Rules of Evidence in Criminal and Civil Jury Trials,* 154 F.R.D. 537, 559 (1994) (setting forth limiting instructions and a standing order employed to prohibit the use of the term "expert" in jury trials).

GAP Report—Proposed Amendment to Rule 702. The Committee made the following changes to the published draft of the proposed amendment to Evidence Rule 702:

1. The word "reliable" was deleted from Subpart (1) of the proposed amendment, in order to avoid an overlap with Evidence Rule 703, and to clarify that an expert opinion need not be excluded simply because it is based on hypo-

thetical facts. The Committee Note was amended to accord with this textual change.

2. The Committee Note was amended throughout to include pertinent references to the Supreme Court's decision in *Kumho Tire Co. v. Carmichael*, which was rendered after the proposed amendment was released for public comment. Other citations were updated as well.

3. The Committee Note was revised to emphasize that the amendment is not intended to limit the right to jury trial, nor to permit a challenge to the testimony of every expert, nor to preclude the testimony of experience-based experts, nor to prohibit testimony based on competing methodologies within a field of expertise.

4. Language was added to the Committee Note to clarify that no single factor is necessarily dispositive of the reliability inquiry mandated by Evidence Rule 702.

Notes of Advisory Committee on 2011 amendments. The language of Rule 702 has been amended as part of the restyling of the Evidence Rules to make them more easily understood and to make style and terminology consistent throughout the rules. These changes are intended to be stylistic only. There is no intent to change any result in any ruling on evidence admissibility.

Notes of Advisory Committee on 2023 Amendments. Rule 702 has been amended in two respects:

(1) First, the rule has been amended to clarify and emphasize that expert testimony may not be admitted unless the proponent demonstrates to the court that it is more likely than not that the proffered testimony meets the admissibility requirements set forth in the rule. *See* Rule 104(a). This is the preponderance of the evidence standard that applies to most of the admissibility requirements set forth in the evidence rules. *See Bourjaily v. United States*, 483 U.S. 171, 175 (1987) ("The preponderance standard ensures that before admitting evidence, the court will have found it more likely than not that the technical issues and policy concerns addressed by the Federal Rules of Evidence have been afforded due consideration."); *Huddleston v. United States,* 485 U.S. 681, 687 n.5 (1988) ("preliminary factual findings under Rule 104(a) are subject to the preponderance-of-the-evidence standard"). But many courts have held that the critical questions of the sufficiency of an expert's basis, and the application of the expert's methodology, are questions of weight and not admissibility. These rulings are an incorrect application of Rules 702 and 104(a).

There is no intent to raise any negative inference regarding the applicability of the Rule 104(a) standard of proof for other rules. The Committee concluded that emphasizing the preponderance standard in Rule 702 specifically was made necessary by the courts that have failed to apply correctly the reliability requirements of that rule. Nor does the amendment require that the court make a finding of reliability in the absence of objection.

The amendment clarifies that the preponderance standard applies to the three reliability-based requirements added in 2000—requirements that many courts have incorrectly determined to be governed by the more permissive Rule 104(b) standard. But it remains the case that other admissibility requirements in the rule (such as that the expert must be qualified and the expert's testimony must help the trier of fact) are governed by the Rule 104(a) standard as well.

Some challenges to expert testimony will raise matters of weight rather than admissibility even under the Rule 104(a) standard. For example, if the court finds it more likely than not that an expert has a sufficient basis to support an opinion, the fact that the expert has not read every single study that exists will raise a question of weight and not admissibility. But this does not mean, as certain courts have held, that arguments about the sufficiency of an expert's basis always go to weight and not admissibility. Rather it means that once the court has found it more likely than not that the admissibility requirement has been met, any attack by the opponent will go only to the weight of the evidence.

It will often occur that experts come to different conclusions based on contested sets of facts. Where that is so, the Rule 104(a) standard does not necessarily require exclusion of either side's experts. Rather, by deciding the disputed facts, the jury can decide which side's experts to credit. "[P]roponents 'do not have to demonstrate to the judge by a preponderance of the evidence that the assessments of their experts are correct, they only have to demonstrate by a preponderance of evidence that their opinions are reliable. . . . The evidentiary requirement of reliability is lower than the merits standard of correctness.'" Advisory Committee Note to the 2000 amendment to Rule 702, quoting *In re Paoli R.R. Yard PCB Litigation,* 35 F.3d 717, 744 (3d Cir. 1994).

Rule 702 requires that the expert's knowledge "help" the trier of fact to understand the evidence or to determine a fact in issue. Unfortunately, some courts have required the expert's testimony to "appreciably help" the trier of fact. Applying a higher standard than helpfulness to otherwise reliable expert testimony is unnecessarily strict.

(2) Rule 702(d) has also been amended to emphasize that each expert opinion must stay within the bounds of what can be concluded from a reliable application of the expert's basis and methodology. Judicial gatekeeping is essential because just as jurors may be unable, due to lack of specialized knowledge, to evaluate meaningfully the reliability of scientific and other methods underlying expert opinion, jurors may also lack the specialized knowledge to determine whether the conclusions of an expert go beyond what the expert's basis and methodology may reliably support.

The amendment is especially pertinent to the testimony of forensic experts in both criminal and civil cases. Forensic experts should avoid assertions of absolute or one hundred percent certainty—or to a reasonable degree of scientific certainty—if the methodology is subjective and thus potentially subject to error. In deciding whether to admit forensic expert testimony, the judge should (where possible) receive an estimate of the known or potential rate of error of the methodology employed, based (where appropriate) on studies that reflect how often the method produces accurate results. Expert opinion testimony regarding the weight of feature comparison evidence (i.e., evidence that a set of features corresponds between two examined items) must be limited to those inferences that can reasonably be drawn from a reliable application of the principles and methods. This amendment does not, however, bar testimony that comports with substantive law requiring opinions to a particular degree of certainty.

Nothing in the amendment imposes any new, specific procedures. Rather, the amendment is simply intended to clarify that Rule 104(a)'s requirement applies to expert opinions under Rule 702. Similarly, nothing in the amendment requires the court to nitpick an expert's opinion in order to reach a perfect expression of what the basis and methodology can support. The Rule 104(a) standard does not require perfection. On the other hand, it does not permit the expert to make claims that are unsupported by the expert's basis and methodology.

Rule 703. Bases of an Expert's Opinion Testimony

An expert may base an opinion on facts or data in the case that the expert has been made aware of or personally observed. If experts in the particular field would reasonably rely on those kinds of facts or data in forming an opinion on the subject, they need not be admissible for the opinion to be admitted. But if the facts or data would otherwise be inadmissible, the proponent of the opinion may disclose them to the jury only if their probative value in helping the jury evaluate the opinion substantially outweighs their prejudicial effect.

HISTORY:

Jan. 2, 1975, P. L. 93-595, § 1, 88 Stat. 1937; March 2, 1987, eff. Oct. 1, 1987; April 17, 2000, eff. Dec. 1, 2000; April 26, 2011, eff. Dec. 1, 2011.

HISTORY; ANCILLARY LAWS AND DIRECTIVES

Other provisions:

Notes of Advisory Committee on Rules. Facts or data upon which expert opinions are based may, under the rule, be derived from three possible sources. The first is the firsthand observation of the witness, with opinions based thereon traditionally allowed. A treating physician affords an example. Rheingold, The Basis of Medical Testimony, 15 Vand. L. Rev. 473, 489 (1962). Whether he must first relate his observations is treated in Rule 705. The second source, presentation at the trial, also reflects existing practice. The technique may be the familiar hypothetical question or having the expert attend the trial and hear the testimony establishing the facts. Problems of determining what testimony the expert relied upon, when the latter technique is employed and the testimony is in conflict, may be resolved by resort to Rule 705. The third source contemplated by the rule consists of presentation of data to the expert outside of court and other than by his own perception. In this respect the rule is designed to broaden the basis for expert opinions beyond that current in many jurisdictions and to bring the judicial practice into line with the practice of the experts themselves when not in court. Thus a physician in his own practice bases his diagnosis on information from numerous sources and of considerable variety, including statements by patients and relatives, reports and opinions from nurses, technicians and other doctors, hospital records, and X rays. Most of them are admissible in evidence, but only with the expenditure of substantial time in producing and examining various authenticating witnesses. The physician makes life-and-death decisions in reliance upon them. His validation, expertly performed and subject to cross-examination, ought to suffice for judicial purposes. Rheingold, *supra*, at 531; McCormick § 15. A similar provision is California Evidence Code § 801(b).

The rule also offers a more satisfactory basis for ruling upon the admissibility of public opinion poll evidence. Attention is directed to the validity of the techniques employed rather than to relatively fruitless inquiries whether hearsay is involved. See Judge Feinberg's careful analysis in *Zippo Mfg. Co. v. Rogers Imports*, Inc., 216 F.Supp. 670 (S.D.N.Y. 1963) See also Blum et al, The Art of Opinion Research: A Lawyer's Appraisal of an Emerging Service, 24 U.Chi.L.Rev. 1 (1956); Bonynge, Trademark Surveys and Techniques and Their Use in Litigation, 48 A.B.A.J. 329 (1962); Zeisel, The Uniqueness of Survey Evidence, 45 Cornell L.Q. 322 (1960); Annot., 76 A.L.R.2d 919.

If it be feared that enlargement of permissible data may tend to break down the rules of exclusion unduly, notice should be taken that the rule requires that the facts or data "be of a type reasonably relied upon by experts in the particular field." The language would not warrant admitting in evidence the opinion of an "accidentologist" as to the point of impact in an automobile collision based on statements of bystanders, since this requirement is not satisfied. See Comment, Cal.Law Rev.Comm'n, Recommendation Proposing an Evidence Code 148–150 (1965).

Notes of Advisory Committee on 1987 amendments. The amendment is technical. No substantive change is intended.

Notes of Advisory Committee on 2000 amendments. Rule 703 has been amended to emphasize that when an expert reasonably relies on inadmissible information to form an opinion or inference, the underlying information is not admissible simply because the opinion or inference is admitted. Courts have reached different results on how to treat inadmissible information when it is reasonably relied upon by an expert in forming an opinion or drawing an inference. *Compare United States v. Rollins,* 862 F.2d 1282 (7th Cir. 1988) (admitting, as part of the basis of an FBI agent's expert opinion on the meaning of code language, the hearsay statements of an informant), with *United States v. 0.59 Acres of Land,* 109 F.3d 1493 (9th Cir. 1997) (error to admit hearsay offered as the basis of an expert opinion, without a limiting instruction). Commentators have also taken differing views. *See, e.g.,* Ronald Carlson, *Policing the Bases of Modern Expert Testimony,* 39 Vand.L.Rev. 577 (1986) (advocating limits on the jury's consideration of otherwise inadmissible evidence used as the basis for an expert opinion); Paul Rice, *Inadmissible Evidence as a Basis for Expert Testimony. A Response to Professor Carlson,* 40 Vand.L.Rev. 583 (1987) (advocating unrestricted use of information reasonably relied upon by an expert).

When information is reasonably relied upon by an expert and yet is admissible only for the purpose of assisting the jury in evaluating an expert's opinion, a trial court applying this Rule must consider the information's probative value in assisting the jury to weigh the expert's opinion on the one hand, and the risk of prejudice resulting from the jury's potential misuse of the information for substantive purposes on the other. The information may be disclosed to the jury, upon objection, only if the trial court finds that the probative value of the information in assisting the jury to evaluate the expert's opinion substantially outweighs its prejudicial effect. If the otherwise inadmissible information is admitted under this balancing test, the trial judge must give a limiting instruction upon request, informing the jury that the underlying information must not be used for substantive purposes. *See* Rule 105. In determining the appropriate course, the trial court should consider the probable effectiveness or lack of effectiveness of a limiting instruction under the particular circumstances.

The amendment governs only the disclosure to the jury of information that is reasonably relied on by an expert, when that information is not admissible for substantive purposes. It is not intended to affect the admissibility of an expert's testimony. Nor does the amendment prevent an expert from relying on information that is inadmissible for substantive purposes.

Nothing in this Rule restricts the presentation of underlying expert facts or data when offered by an adverse party. *See* Rule 705. Of course, an adversary's attack on an expert's basis will often open the door to a proponent's rebuttal with information that was reasonably relied upon by the expert, even if that information would not have been discloseable initially under the balancing test provided by this amendment. Moreover, in some circumstances the proponent might wish to disclose information that is relied upon by the expert in order to "remove the sting" from the opponent's anticipated attack, and thereby prevent the jury from drawing an unfair negative inference. The trial court should take this consideration into account in applying the balancing test provided by this amendment.

This amendment covers facts or data that cannot be admitted for any purpose other than to assist the jury to evaluate the expert's opinion. The balancing test provided in this amendment is not applicable to facts or data that are admissible for any other purpose but have not yet been offered for such a purpose at the time the expert testifies.

The amendment provides a presumption against disclosure to the jury of information used as the basis of an expert's opinion and not admissible for any substantive purpose, when that information is offered by the proponent of the expert. In a multi-party case, where one party proffers an expert whose testimony is also beneficial to other parties, each such party should be deemed a "proponent" within the meaning of the amendment.

GAP Report—Proposed Amendment to Rule 703. The Committee made the following changes to the published draft of the proposed amendment to Evidence Rule 703:

1. A minor stylistic change was made in the text, in accordance with the suggestion of the Style Subcommittee of the Standing Committee on Rules of Practice and Procedure.

2. The words "in assisting the jury to evaluate the expert's opinion" were added to the text, to specify the proper purpose for offering the otherwise inadmissible information relied on by an expert. The Committee Note was revised to accord with this change in the text.

3. Stylistic changes were made to the Committee Note.

4. The Committee Note was revised to emphasize that the balancing test set forth in the proposal should be used to determine whether an expert's basis may be disclosed to the jury either (1) in rebuttal or (2) on direct examination to "remove the sting" of an opponent's anticipated attack on an expert's basis.

Notes of Advisory Committee on 2011 amendments. The language of Rule 703 has been amended as part of the general restyling of the Evidence Rules to make them more easily understood and to make style and terminology consistent throughout the rules. These changes are intended to be stylistic only. There is no intent to change any result in any ruling on evidence admissibility.

The Committee deleted all reference to an "inference" on the grounds that the deletion made the Rule flow better and easier to read, and because any "inference" is covered by the broader term "opinion." Courts have not made substantive decisions on the basis of any distinction between an opinion and an inference. No change in current practice is intended.

Rule 704. Opinion on an Ultimate Issue

(a) In General—Not Automatically Objectionable. An opinion is not objectionable just because it embraces an ultimate issue.

(b) Exception. In a criminal case, an expert witness must not state an opinion about whether the defendant did or did not have a mental state or condition that constitutes an element of the crime charged or of a defense. Those matters are for the trier of fact alone.

HISTORY:

Jan. 2, 1975, P. L. 93-595, § 1, 88 Stat. 1937; Oct. 12, 1984, P. L. 98-473, Title IV, Ch IV, § 406, 98 Stat. 2067; April 26, 2011, eff. Dec. 1, 2011.

HISTORY; ANCILLARY LAWS AND DIRECTIVES

Other provisions:

Notes of Advisory Committee on Rules. The basic approach to opinions, lay and expert, in these rules is to admit them when helpful to the trier of fact. In order to render this approach fully effective and to allay any doubt on the subject, the so-called "ultimate issue" rule is specifically abolished by the instant rule.

The older cases often contained strictures against allowing witnesses to express opinions upon ultimate issues, as a particular aspect of the rule against opinions. The rule was unduly restrictive, difficult of application, and generally served only to deprive the trier of fact of useful information. 7 Wigmore §§ 1920, 1921; McCormick § 12. The basis usually assigned for the rule, to prevent the witness from "usurping the province of the jury," is aptly characterized as "empty rhetoric." 7 Wigmore § 1920, p. 17. Efforts to meet the felt needs of particular situations led to odd verbal circumlocutions which were said not to violate the rule. Thus a witness could express his estimate of the criminal responsibility of an accused in terms of sanity or insanity, but not in terms of ability to tell right from wrong or other more modern standard. And in cases of medical causation, witnesses were sometimes required to couch their opinions in cautious phrases of "might or could," rather than "did," though the result was to deprive many opinions of the positiveness to which they were entitled, accompanied by the hazard of a ruling of insufficiency to support a verdict. In other instances the rule was simply disregarded, and, as concessions to need, opinions were allowed upon such matters as intoxication, speed, handwriting, and value, although more precise coincidence with an ultimate issue would scarcely be possible.

Many modern decisions illustrate the trend to abandon the rule completely. *People v. Wilson,* 25 Cal.2d 341, 153 P.2d 720 (1944), whether abortion necessary to save life of patient; *Clifford-Jacobs Forging Co. v. Industrial Comm.*, 19 Ill.2d 236, 166 N.E.2d 582 (1960), medical causation; *Dowling v. L. H. Shattuck, Inc.*, 91 N.H. 234, 17 A.2d 529 (1941), proper method of shoring ditch; *Schweiger v. Solbeck*, 191 Or. 454, 230 P.2d 195 (1951), cause of landslide. In each instance the opinion was allowed.

The abolition of the ultimate issue rule does not lower the bars so as to admit all opinions. Under Rules 701 and 702, opinions must be helpful to the trier of fact, and Rule 403 provides for exclusion of evidence which wastes time. These provisions afford ample assurances against the admission of opinions which would merely tell the jury what result to reach, somewhat in the manner of the oath-helpers of an earlier day. They also stand ready to exclude opinions phrased in terms of inadequately explored legal criteria. Thus the question, "Did T have capacity to make a will?" would be excluded, while the question, "Did T have sufficient mental capacity to know the nature and extent of his property and the natural objects of his bounty and to formulate a rational scheme of distribution?" would be allowed. McCormick § 12.

For similar provisions see Uniform Rule 56(4); California Evidence Code § 805; Kansas Code of Civil Procedures § 60-456(d); New Jersey Evidence Rule 56(3).

Notes of Advisory Committee on 2011 amendments. The language of Rule 704 has been amended as part of the general restyling of the Evidence Rules to make them more easily understood and to make style and terminology consistent throughout the rules. These changes are intended to be stylistic only. There is no intent to change any result in any ruling on evidence admissibility.

The Committee deleted all reference to an "inference" on the grounds that the deletion made the Rule flow better and easier to read, and because any "inference" is covered by the broader term "opinion." Courts have not made substantive decisions on the basis of any distinction between an opinion and an inference. No change in current practice is intended.

Amendments:

1984.

Act Oct. 12, 1984 substituted this rule for one which read: "Testimony in the form of an opinion or inference otherwise admissible is not objectionable because it embraces an ultimate issue to be decided by the trier of fact.".

Rule 705. Disclosing the Facts or Data Underlying an Expert's Opinion

Unless the court orders otherwise, an expert may state an opinion—and give the reasons for it—without first testifying to the underlying facts or data. But the expert may be required to disclose those facts or data on cross-examination.

HISTORY:

Jan. 2, 1975, P. L. 93-595, § 1, 88 Stat. 1938; March 2, 1987, eff. Oct. 1, 1987; April 22, 1993, eff. Dec. 1, 1993; April 26, 2011, eff. Dec. 1, 2011.

HISTORY; ANCILLARY LAWS AND DIRECTIVES

Other provisions:

Notes of Advisory Committee on Rules. The hypothetical question has been the target of a great deal of criticism as encouraging partisan bias, affording an opportunity for summing up in the middle of the case, and as complex and time consuming. Ladd, Expert Testimony, 5 Vand.L.Rev. 414, 426–427 (1952). While the rule allows counsel to make disclosure of the underlying facts or data as a preliminary to the giving of an expert opinion, if he chooses, the instances in which he is required to do so are reduced. This is true whether the expert bases his opinion on data furnished him at secondhand or observed by him at firsthand.

The elimination of the requirement of preliminary disclosure at the trial of underlying facts or data has a long background of support. In 1937 the Commissioners on Uniform State Laws incorporated a provision to this effect in the Model Expert Testimony Act, which furnished the basis for Uniform Rules 57 and 58. Rule 4515, N.Y. CPLR (McKinney 1963), provides:

"Unless the court orders otherwise, questions calling for the opinion of an expert witness need not be hypothetical in form, and the witness may state his opinion and reasons without first specifying the data upon which it is based. Upon cross-examination, he may be required to specify the data . . .".

See also California Evidence Code § 802; Kansas Code of Civil Procedure §§ 60-456, 60-457; New Jersey Evidence Rules 57, 58.

If the objection is made that leaving it to the cross-examiner to bring out the supporting data is essentially unfair, the answer is that he is under no compulsion to bring out any facts or data except those unfavorable to the opinion. The answer assumes that the cross-examiner has the advance knowledge which is essential for effective cross-examination. This advance knowledge has been afforded, though imperfectly, by the traditional foundation requirement. Rule 26(b)(4) of the Rules of Civil Procedure, as revised, provides for substantial discovery in this area, obviating in large measure the obstacles which have been raised in some instances to discovery of findings, underlying data, and even the identity of the experts. Friedenthal, Discovery and Use of an Adverse Party's Expert Information, 14 Stan.L.Rev. 455 (1962).

These safeguards are reinforced by the discretionary power of the judge to require preliminary disclosure in any event.

Notes of Advisory Committee on 1987 amendments. The amendment is technical. No substantive change is intended.

Notes of Advisory Committee on 1993 amendments. This rule, which relates to the manner of presenting testimony at trial, is revised to avoid an arguable conflict with revised Rules 26(a)(2)(B) and 26(a)(1) of the Federal Rules of Civil Procedure or with revised Rule 16 of the Federal Rules of Criminal Procedure, which require disclosure in advance of trial of the basis and reasons for an expert's opinions.

If a serious question is raised under Rule 702 or 703 as to the admissibility of expert testimony, disclosure of the underlying facts or data on which opinions are based may, of course, be needed by the court before deciding whether, and to what extent, the person should be allowed to testify. This rule does not preclude such an inquiry.

Notes of Advisory Committee on 2011 amendments. The language of Rule 705 has been amended as part of the general restyling of the Evidence Rules to make them more easily understood and to make style and terminology consistent throughout the rules. These changes are intended to be stylistic only. There is no intent to change any result in any ruling on evidence admissibility.

The Committee deleted all reference to an "inference" on the grounds that the deletion made the Rule flow better and easier to read, and because any "inference" is covered by the broader term "opinion." Courts have not made substantive decisions on the basis of any distinction between an opinion and an inference. No change in current practice is intended.

Rule 706. Court-Appointed Expert Witnesses

(a) Appointment Process. On a party's motion or on its own, the court may order the parties to show cause why expert witnesses should not be appointed and may ask the parties to submit nominations. The court may appoint any expert that the parties agree on and any of its own choosing. But the court may only appoint someone who consents to act.

(b) Expert's Role. The court must inform the expert of the expert's duties. The court may do so in writing and have a copy filed with the clerk or may do so orally at a conference in which the parties have an opportunity to participate. The expert:

(1) must advise the parties of any findings the expert makes;

(2) may be deposed by any party;

(3) may be called to testify by the court or any party; and

(4) may be cross-examined by any party, including the party that called the expert.

(c) Compensation. The expert is entitled to a reasonable compensation, as set by the court. The compensation is payable as follows:

(1) in a criminal case or in a civil case involving just compensation under the Fifth Amendment, from any funds that are provided by law; and

(2) in any other civil case, by the parties in the proportion and at the time that the court directs—and the compensation is then charged like other costs.

(d) Disclosing the Appointment to the Jury. The court may authorize disclosure to the jury that the court appointed the expert.

(e) Parties' Choice of Their Own Experts. This rule does not limit a party in calling its own experts.

HISTORY:

Jan. 2, 1975, P. L. 93-595, § 1, 88 Stat. 1938; March 2, 1987, eff. Oct. 1, 1987; April 26, 2011, eff. Dec. 1, 2011.

HISTORY; ANCILLARY LAWS AND DIRECTIVES

Other provisions:

Notes of Advisory Committee on Rules. The practice of shopping for experts, the venality of some experts, and the reluctance of many reputable experts to involve themselves in litigation, have been matters of deep concern. Though the contention is made that court appointed experts acquire an aura of infallibility to which they are not entitled. Levy, Impartial Medical Testimony—Revisited, 34 Temple L.Q. 416 (11961), the trend is increasingly to provide for their use. While experience indicates that actual appointment is a relatively infrequent occurrence, the assumption may be made that the availability of the procedure in itself decreases the need for resorting to it. The ever-present possibility that the judge may appoint an expert in a given case must inevitably exert a sobering effect on the expert witness of a party and upon the person utilizing his services.

The inherent power of a trial judge to appoint an expert of his own choosing is virtually unquestioned. *Scott v. Spanjer Bros.*, Inc., 298 F.2d 928 (2d Cir. 1962); *Danville Tobacco Assn. v. Bryant-Buckner Associates, Inc.*, 333 F.2d 202 (4th Cir. 1964); Sink, The Unused Power of a Federal Judge to Call His Own Expert Witnesses, 29 S.Cal.L.Rev. 195 (1956); 2 Wigmore § 563, 9 *Id.* § 2484; Annot., 95 A.L.R.2d 383. Hence the problem becomes largely one of detail.

The New York plan is well known and is described in Report by Special Committee of the Association of the Bar of the City of New York: Impartial Medical Testimony (1956). On recommendation of the Section of Judicial Administration, local adoption of an impartial medical plan was endorsed by the American Bar Association. 82 A.B.A.Rep. 184–185 (1957). Descriptions and analyses of plans in effect in various parts of the country are found in Van Dusen, A United States District Judge's View of the Impartial Medical Expert System, 322 F.R.D. 498 (1963); Wick and Kightlinger, Impartial Medical Testimony Under the Federal Civil Rules: A Tale of Three Doctors, 34 Ins. Counsel J. 115 (1967); and numerous articles collected in Klein, Judicial Administration and the Legal Profession 393 (1963). Statutes and rules include California Evidence Code §§ 730–733; Illinois Supreme Court Rule 215(d), Ill.Rev.Stat.1969, c. 110A, § 215(d); Burns Indiana Stats. 1956, § 9-1702; Wisconsin Stats. Annot. 1958, § 957.27.

In the federal practice, a comprehensive scheme for court appointed experts was initiated with the adoption of Rule 28 of the Federal Rules of Criminal Procedure in 1946. The Judicial Conference of the United States in 1953 considered court appointed experts in civil cases, but only with respect to whether they should be compensated from public funds, a proposal which was rejected. Report of the Judicial Conference of the United States 23 (1953). The present rule expands the practice to include civil cases.

Subdivision (a) is based on Rule 28 of the Federal Rules of Criminal Procedure, with a few changes, mainly in the interest of clarity. Language has been added to provide specifically for the appointment either on motion of a party or on the judge's own motion. A provision subjecting the court appointed expert to deposition procedures has been incorporated. The rule has been revised to make definite the right of any party, including the party calling him, to cross-examine.

Subdivision (b) combines the present provision for compensation in criminal cases with what seems to be a fair and feasible handling of civil cases, originally found in the Model Act and carried from there into Uniform Rule 60. See also California Evidence Code §§ 730–731. The special provision for Fifth Amendment compensation cases is designed to guard against reducing constitutionally guaranteed just compensation by requiring the recipient to pay costs. See Rule 71A(*l*) of the Rules of Civil Procedure.

Subdivision (c) seems to be essential if the use of court appointed experts is to be fully effective. Uniform Rule 61 so provides.

Subdivision (d) is in essence the last sentence of Rule 28(a) of the Federal Rules of Criminal Procedure.

Notes of Advisory Committee on 1987 amendments. The amendments are technical. No substantive change is intended.

Notes of Advisory Committee on 2011 amendments. The language of Rule 706 has been amended as part of the restyling of the Evidence Rules to make them more easily understood and to make style and terminology consistent throughout the rules. These changes are intended to be stylistic only. There is no intent to change any result in any ruling on evidence admissibility.

ARTICLE VIII. HEARSAY

Rule

Rule 801. Definitions that Apply to This Article; Exclusions from Hearsay

(a) Statement. "Statement" means a person's oral assertion, written assertion, or nonverbal conduct, if the person intended it as an assertion.

(b) Declarant. "Declarant" means the person who made the statement.

(c) Hearsay. "Hearsay" means a statement that:

(1) the declarant does not make while testifying at the current trial or hearing; and

(2) a party offers in evidence to prove the truth of the matter asserted in the statement.

(d) Statements That Are Not Hearsay. A statement that meets the following conditions is not hearsay:

(1) *A Declarant-Witness's Prior Statement.* The declarant testifies and is subject to cross-examination about a prior statement, and the statement:

(A) is inconsistent with the declarant's testimony and was given under penalty of perjury at a trial, hearing, or other proceeding or in a deposition;

(B) is consistent with the declarant's testimony and is offered:

(i) to rebut an express or implied charge that the declarant recently fabricated it or acted from a recent improper influence or motive in so testifying; or

(ii) to rehabilitate the declarant's credibility as a witness when attacked on another ground; or

(C) identifies a person as someone the declarant perceived earlier.

(2) *An Opposing Party's Statement.* The statement is offered against an opposing party and:

(A) was made by the party in an individual or representative capacity;

(B) is one the party manifested that it adopted or believed to be true;

(C) was made by a person whom the party authorized to make a statement on the subject;

(D) was made by the party's agent or employee on a matter within the scope of that relationship and while it existed; or

(E) was made by the party's coconspirator during and in furtherance of the conspiracy.

The statement must be considered but does not by itself establish the declarant's authority under (C); the existence or scope of the relationship under (D); or the existence of the conspiracy or participation in it under (E).

If a party's claim, defense, or potential liability is directly derived from a declarant or the declarant's principal, a statement that would be admissible against the declarant or the principal under this rule is also admissible against the party.

HISTORY:

Jan. 2, 1975, P. L. 93-595, § 1, 88 Stat. 1938; Oct. 16, 1975, P. L. 94-113, § 1, 89 Stat. 576; March 2, 1987, eff. Oct. 1, 1987; April 22, 1997, eff. Dec. 1, 1997; April 26, 2011, eff. Dec. 1, 2011; April 25, 2014, eff. Dec. 1, 2014; April 2, 2024, eff. Dec. 1, 2024.

HISTORY; ANCILLARY LAWS AND DIRECTIVES

Other provisions:

Notes of Advisory Committee on Rules. Subdivision (a). The definition of "statement" assumes importance because the term is used in the definition of hearsay in subdivision (c). The effect of the definition of "statement" is to exclude from the operation of the hearsay rule all evidence of conduct, verbal or nonverbal, not intended as an assertion. The key to the definition is that nothing is an assertion unless intended to be one.

It can scarcely be doubted that an assertion made in words is intended by the declarant to be an assertion. Hence verbal assertions readily fall into the category of "statement." Whether nonverbal conduct should be regarded as a statement for purposes of defining hearsay requires further consideration. Some nonverbal conduct, such as the act of pointing to identify a suspect in a lineup, is clearly the equivalent of words, assertive in nature, and to be regarded as a statement. Other nonverbal conduct, however, may be offered as evidence that the person acted as he did because of his belief in the existence of the condition sought to be proved, from which belief the existence of the condition may be inferred. This sequence is, arguably, in effect an assertion of the existence of the condition and hence properly includable within the hearsay concept. See Morgan, Hearsay Dangers and the Application of the Hearsay Concept, 62 Harv.L. Rev. 177, 214, 217 (1948), and the elaboration in Finman, Implied Assertions as Hearsay: Some Criticisms of the Uniform Rules of Evidence, 14 Stan.L.Rev. 682 (1962). Admittedly evidence of this character is untested with respect to the perception, memory, and narration (or their equivalents) of the actor, but the Advisory Committee is of the view that these dangers are minimal in the absence of an intent to assert and do not justify the loss of the evidence on hearsay grounds. No class of evidence is free of the possibility of fabrication, but the likelihood is less with nonverbal than with assertive verbal conduct. The situations giving rise to the nonverbal conduct are such as virtually to eliminate questions of sincerity. Motivation, the nature of the conduct, and the presence or absence of reliance will bear heavily upon the weight to be given the evidence. Falknor, The "Hear-Say" Rule as a "See-Do" Rule: Evidence of Conduct, 33 Rocky Mt.L.Rev. 133 (1961). Similar considerations govern nonassertive verbal conduct and verbal conduct which is assertive but offered as a basis for inferring something other than the matter asserted, also excluded from the definition of hearsay by the language of subdivision (c).

When evidence of conduct is offered on the theory that it is not a statement, and hence not hearsay, a preliminary determination will be required to determine whether an assertion is intended. The rule is so worded as to place the burden upon the party claiming that the intention existed; ambiguous and doubtful cases will be resolved against him and in favor of admissibility. The determination involves no greater difficulty than many other preliminary questions of fact. Maguire, The Hearsay System: Around and Through the Thicket, 14 Vand.L.Rev. 741, 765–767 (1961).

For similar approaches, see Uniform Rule 62(1); California Evidence Code §§ 225, 1200; Kansas Code of Civil Procedure § 60-459(a); New Jersey Evidence Rule 62(1).

Subdivision (c). The definition follows along familiar lines in including only statements offered to prove the truth of the matter asserted. McCormick § 225; 5 Wigmore § 1361, 6 id. § 1766. If the significance of an offered statement lies solely in the fact that it was made, no issue is raised as to the truth of anything asserted, and the statement is not hearsay. Emich Motors Corp. v. General Motors Corp., 181 F.2d 70 (7th Cir. 1950), rev'd on other grounds 340 U.S. 558, 71 S.Ct. 408, 95 L.Ed 534, letters of complaint from customers offered as a reason for cancellation of dealer's franchise, to rebut contention that franchise was revoked for refusal to finance sales through affiliated finance company. The effect is to exclude from hearsay the entire category of "verbal acts" and "verbal parts of an act," in which the statement itself affects the legal rights of the parties or is a circumstance bearing on conduct affecting their rights.

The definition of hearsay must, of course, be read with reference to the definition of statement set forth in subdivision (a).

Testimony given by a witness in the course of court proceedings is excluded since there is compliance with all the ideal conditions for testifying.

Subdivision (d). Several types of statements which would otherwise literally fall within the definition are expressly excluded from it:

(1) Prior statement by witness. Considerable controversy has attended the question whether a prior out-of-court statement by a person now available for cross-examination concerning it, under oath and in the presence of the trier of fact, should be classed as hearsay. If the witness admits on the stand that he made the statement and that it was true, he adopts the statement and there is no hearsay problem. The hearsay problem arises when the witness on the stand denies having made the statement or admits having made it but denies its truth. The argument in favor of treating these latter statements as hearsay is based upon the ground that the conditions of oath, cross-examination, and demeanor observation did not prevail at the time the statement was made and cannot adequately be supplied by the later examination. The logic of the situation is troublesome. So far as concerns the oath, its mere presence has never been regarded as sufficient to remove a statement from the hearsay category, and it receives much less emphasis than cross-examination as a truth-compelling device. While strong expressions are found to the effect that no conviction can be had or important right taken away on the basis of statements not made under fear of prosecution for perjury, Bridges v. Wixon, 326 U.S. 135, 65 S.Ct. 1443, 89 L.Ed. 2103 (1945), the fact is that, of the many common law exceptions to the hearsay rule, only that for reported testimony has required the statement to have been made under oath. Nor is it satisfactorily explained why cross-examination cannot be conducted subsequently with success. The decisions contending most vigorously for its inadequacy in fact demonstrate quite thorough exploration of the weaknesses and doubts attending the earlier statement. State v. Saporen, 205 Minn. 358, 285 N.W. 898 (1939); Ruhala v. Roby, 379 Mich. 102, 150 N.W.2d 146 (1967); People v. Johnson, 68 Cal.2d 646, 68 Cal.Rptr. 599, 441 P.2d 111 (1968). In respect to demeanor, as Judge Learned Hand observed in Di Carlo v. United States, 6 F.2d 364 (2d Cir. 1925), when the jury decides that the truth is not what the witness says now, but what he said before, they are still deciding from what they see and hear in court. The bulk of the case law nevertheless has been against allowing prior statements of witnesses to be used generally as substantive evidence. Most of the writers and Uniform Rule 63(1) have taken the opposite position.

The position taken by the Advisory Committee in formulating this part of the rule is founded upon an unwillingness to countenance the general use of prior prepared statements as substantive evidence, but with a recognition that particular circumstances call for a contrary result. The judgment is one more of experience than of logic. The rule requires in each instance, as a general safeguard, that the declarant actually testify as a witness, and it then enumerates three situations in which the statement is excepted from the category of hearsay. Compare Uniform Rule 63(1) which allows any out-of-court statement of a declarant who is present at the trial and available for cross-examination.

(A) Prior inconsistent statements traditionally have been admissible to impeach but not as substantive evidence. Under the rule they are substantive evidence. As has been said by the California Law Revision Commission with respect to a similar provision:

"Section 1235 admits inconsistent statements of witnesses because the dangers against which the hearsay rule is designed to protect are largely nonexistent. The declarant is in court and may be examined and cross-examined in regard to his statements and their subject matter. In many cases, the inconsistent statement is more likely to be true than the testimony of the witness at the trial because it was made nearer in time to the matter to which it relates and is less likely to be influenced by the controversy that gave rise to the litigation. The trier of fact has the declarant before it and can observe his demeanor and the nature of his testimony as he denies or tries to explain away the inconsistency. Hence, it is in as good a position to determine the truth or falsity of the prior statement as it is to determine the truth or falsity of the inconsistent testimony given in court. Moreover, Section 1235 will provide a party with desirable protection against the 'turncoat' witness who changes his story on the stand and deprives the party calling him of evidence essential to his case." Comment, California Evidence Code § 1235. See also McCormick § 39. The Advisory Committee finds these views more convincing than those expressed in People v.

Johnson, 68 Cal.2d 646, 68 Cal.Rptr. 599, 441 P.2d 111 (1968). The constitutionality of the Advisory Committee's view was upheld in California v. Green, 399 U.S. 149, 90 S.Ct. 1930, 26 L.Ed.2d 489 (1970). Moreover, the requirement that the statement be inconsistent with the testimony given assures a thorough exploration of both versions while the witness is on the stand and bars any general and indiscriminate use of previously prepared statements.

(B) Prior consistent statements traditionally have been admissible to rebut charges of recent fabrication or improper influence or motive but not as substantive evidence. Under the rule they are substantive evidence. The prior statement is consistent with the testimony given on the stand, and, if the opposite party wishes to open the door for its admission in evidence, no sound reason is apparent why it should not be received generally.

(C) The admission of evidence of identification finds substantial support, although it falls beyond a doubt in the category of prior out-of-court statements. Illustrative are People v. Gould, 54 Cal.2d 621, 7 Cal.Rptr. 273, 354 P.2d 865 (1960); Judy v. State, 218 Md. 168, 146 A.2d 29 (1958); State v. Simmons, 63 Wash.2d 17, 385 P.2d 389 (1963); California Evidence Code § 1238; New Jersey Evidence Rule 63(1)(c); N.Y. Code of Criminal Procedure § 393-b. Further cases are found in 4 Wigmore § 1130. The basis is the generally unsatisfactory and inconclusive nature of courtroom identifications as compared with those made at an earlier time under less suggestive conditions. The Supreme Court considered the admissibility of evidence of prior identification in Gilbert v. California, 388 U.S. 263, 87 S.Ct. 1951, 18 L.Ed.2d 1178 (1967). Exclusion of lineup identification was held to be required because the accused did not then have the assistance of counsel. Significantly, the Court carefully refrained from placing its decision on the ground that testimony as to the making of a prior out-of-court identification ("That's the man") violated either the hearsay rule or the right of confrontation because not made under oath, subject to immediate cross-examination, in the presence of the trier. Instead the Court observed:

"There is a split among the States concerning the admissibility of prior extra-judicial identifications, as independent evidence of identity, both by the witness and third parties present at the prior identification. See 71 ALR2d 449. It has been held that the prior identification is hearsay, and, when admitted through the testimony of the identifier, is merely a prior consistent statement. The recent trend, however, is to admit the prior identification under the exception that admits as substantive evidence a prior communication by a witness who is available for cross-examination at the trial. See 5 ALR2d Later Case Service 1225–1228. . . ." 388 U.S. at 272, n. 3, 87 S.Ct. at 1956.

(2) Admissions. Admissions by a party-opponent are excluded from the category of hearsay on the theory that their admissibility in evidence is the result of the adversary system rather than satisfaction of the conditions of the hearsay rule. Strahorn. A Reconsideration of the Hearsay Rule and Admissions, 85 U.Pa.L.Rev. 484, 564 (1937); Morgan, Basic Problems of Evidence 265 (1962); 4 Wigmore § 1048. No guarantee of trustworthiness is required in the case of an admission. The freedom which admissions have enjoyed from technical demands of searching for an assurance of trustworthiness in some against-interest circumstance, and from the restrictive influences of the opinion rule and the rule requiring firsthand knowledge, when taken with the apparently prevalent satisfaction with the results, calls for generous treatment of this avenue to admissibility.

The rule specifies five categories of statements for which the responsibility of a party is considered sufficient to justify reception in evidence against him:

(A) A party's own statement is the classic example of an admission. If he has a representative capacity and the statement is offered against him in that capacity, no inquiry whether he was acting in the representative capacity in making the statement is required; the statement need only be relevant to represent affairs. To the same effect in California Evidence Code § 1220. Compare Uniform Rule 63(7), requiring a statement to be made in a representative capacity to be admissible against a party in a representative capacity.

(B) Under established principles an admission may be made by adopting or acquiescing in the statement of another. While knowledge of contents would ordinarily be essential, this is not inevitably so: "X is a reliable person and knows what he is talking about." See McCormick § 246, p. 527, n. 15. Adoption or acquiescence may be manifested in any appropriate manner. When silence is relied upon, the theory is that the person would, under the circumstances, protest the statement made in his presence, if untrue. The decision in each case calls for an evaluation in terms of probable human behavior. In civil cases, the results have generally been satisfactory. In criminal cases, however, troublesome questions have been raised by decisions holding that failure to deny is an admission: the inference is a fairly weak one, to begin with; silence may be motivated by advice of counsel or realization that "anything you say may be used against you"; unusual opportunity is afforded to manufacture evidence; and encroachment upon the privilege against self-incrimination seems inescapably to be involved. However, recent decisions of the Supreme Court relating to custodial interrogation and the right to counsel appear to resolve these difficulties. Hence the rule contains no special provisions concerning failure to deny in criminal cases.

(C) No authority is required for the general proposition that a statement authorized by a party to be made should have the status of an admission by the party. However, the question arises whether only statements to third persons should be so regarded, to the exclusion of statements by the agent to the principal. The rule is phrased broadly so as to encompass both. While it may be argued that the agent authorized to make statements to his principal does not speak for him, Morgan, Basic Problems of Evidence 273 (1962), communication to an outsider has not generally been thought to be an essential characteristic of an admission. Thus a party's books or records are usable against him, without regard to any intent to disclose to third persons. 5 Wigmore § 1557. See also McCormick § 78, pp. 159–161. In accord is New Jersey Evidence Rule 63(8)(a). Cf. Uniform Rule 63(8)(a) and California Evidence Code § 1222 which limit status as an admission in this regard to statements authorized by the party to be made "for" him, which is perhaps an ambiguous limitation to statements to third persons. Falknor, Vicarious Admissions and the Uniform Rules, 14 Vand.L.Rev. 855, 860–861 (1961).

(D) The tradition has been to test the admissibility of statements by agents, as admissions, by applying the usual test of agency. Was the admission made by the agent acting in the scope of his employment? Since few principals employ agents for the purpose of making damaging statements, the usual result was exclusion of the statement. Dissatisfaction with this loss of valuable and helpful evidence has been increasing. A substantial trend favors admitting statements related to a matter within the scope of the agency or employment. Grayson v. Williams, 256 F.2d 61 (10th Cir. 1958); Koninklijke Luchtvaart Maatschappij N.V. KLM Royal Dutch Airlines v. Tuller, 110 U.S.App.D.C. 282, 292 F.2d 775, 784 (1961); Martin v. Savage Truck Lines, Inc., 121 F.Supp. 417 (D.D.C. 1054), and numerous state court decisions collected in 4 Wigmore, 1964 Supp., pp. 66–73, with comments by the editor that the statements should have been excluded as not within scope of agency. For the traditional view see Northern Oil Co. v. Socony Mobile Oil Co., 347 F.2d 81, 85 (2d Cir. 1965) and cases cited therein. Similar provisions are found in Uniform Rule 63(9)(a), Kansas Code of Civil Procedure § 60-460(i)(1), and New Jersey Evidence Rule 63(9)(a).

(E) The limitation upon the admissibility of statements of co-conspirators to those made "during the course and in furtherance of the conspiracy" is in the accepted pattern. While the broadened view of agency taken in item (iv) might suggest wider admissibility of statements of co-conspirators, the agency theory of conspiracy is at best a fiction and ought not to serve as a basis for admissibility beyond that already established. See Levie, Hearsay and Conspiracy, 52 Mich.L.Rev. 1159 (1954); Comment, 25 U.Chi.L.Rev. 530 (1958). The rule is consistent with the position of the Supreme Court in denying admissibility to statements made after the objectives of the conspiracy have either failed or been achieved. Krulewitch v. United States, 336 U.S. 440, 69 S.Ct. 716, 93 L.Ed. 790 (1949); Wong Sun v. United States, 371 U.S. 471, 490, 83 S.Ct. 407, 9 L.Ed.2d 441 (1963). For similarly limited provisions see California Evidence Code § 1223 and New Jersey Rule 63(9)(b). Cf. Uniform Rule 63(9)(b).

Notes of Committee on the Judiciary, House Report No. 93-650. Present federal law, except in the Second Circuit, permits the use of prior inconsistent statements of a witness for impeachment only. Rule 801(d)(1) as proposed by the Court would have permitted all such statements to be admissible as substantive evidence, an approach followed by a small but growing number of State jurisdictions and recently held constitutional in California v. Green, 399 U.S. 149 (1970). Although there was some support expressed for the Court Rule, based largely on the need to counteract the effect of witness intimidation in criminal cases, the Committee decided to adopt a compromise version of the Rule similar to the position of the Second Circuit. The Rule as amended draws a distinction between types of prior inconsistent statements (other than statements of identification of a person made after perceiving him which are currently admissible, see United States v. Anderson, 406 F.2d 719, 720 (4th Cir.), cert. denied, 395 U.S. 967 (1969)) and allows only those made while the declarant was subject to cross-examination at a trial or hearing or in a deposition, to be admissible for their truth. Compare United States v. DeSisto, 329 F.2d 929 (2nd Cir.), cert. denied, 377 U.S. 979 (1964); United States v. Cunningham, 446 F.2d 194 (2nd Cir. 1971) (restricting the admissibility of prior inconsistent statements as substantive evidence to those made under oath in a formal proceeding, but not requiring that there have been an opportunity for cross-examination). The rationale for the Committee's decision is that (1) unlike in most other situations involving unsworn or oral statements, there can be no dispute as to whether the prior statement was made; and (2) the context of a formal proceeding, an oath, and the opportunity for cross-examination provide firm additional assurances of the reliability of the prior statements.

Notes of Committee on the Judiciary, Senate Report No. 93-1277. Rule 801 defines what is and what is not hearsay for the purpose of admitting a prior statement as substantive evidence. A prior statement of a witness at a trial or hearing which is inconsistent with his testimony is, of course, always admissible for the purpose of impeaching the witness' credibility.

As submitted by the Supreme Court, subdivision (d)(1)(A) made admissible as substantive evidence the prior statement of a witness inconsistent with his present testimony.

The House severely limited the admissibility of prior inconsistent statements by adding a requirement that the prior statement must have been subject to cross-examination, thus precluding even the use of grand jury statements. The requirement that the prior statement must have been subject to cross-examination appears unnecessary since this rule comes into play only when the witness testifies in the present trial. At that time, he is on the stand and can explain an earlier position and be cross-examined as to both.

The requirement that the statement be under oath also appears unnecessary. Notwithstanding the absence of an oath contemporaneous with the statement, the witness, when on the stand, qualifying or denying the prior statement, is under oath. In any event, of all the many recognized exceptions to the hearsay rule, only one (former testimony) requires that the out-of-court statement have been made under oath. With respect to the lack of evidence of the demeanor of the witness at the time of the prior statement, it would be difficult to improve upon Judge Learned Hand's observation that when the jury decides that the truth is not what the witness says now but what he said before, they are still deciding from what they see and hear in court [Di Carlo v. U.S., 6 F.2d 364 (2d Cir. 1925)].

The rule as submitted by the Court has positive advantages. The prior statement was made nearer in time to the events, when memory was fresher and intervening influences had not been brought into play. A realistic method is provided for dealing with the turncoat witness who changes his story on the stand [see Comment, California Evidence Code § 1235; McCormick, Evidence, § 38 (2nd ed. 1972)].

New Jersey, California, and Utah have adopted a rule similar to this one; and Nevada, New Mexico, and Wisconsin have adopted the identical Federal rule.

For all of these reasons, we think the House amendment should be rejected and the rule as submitted by the Supreme Court reinstated. [It would appear that some of the opposition to this Rule is based on a concern that a person could be convicted solely upon evidence admissible under this Rule. The Rule, however, is not addressed to the question of the sufficiency of evidence to send a case to the jury, but merely as to its admissibility. Factual circumstances could well arise where, if this were the sole evidence, dismissal would be appropriate].

As submitted by the Supreme Court and as passed by the House, subdivision (d)(1)(c) of rule 801 made admissible the prior statement identifying a person made after perceiving him. The committee decided to delete this provision because of the concern that a person could be convicted solely upon evidence admissible under this subdivision.

The House approved the long-accepted rule that "a statement by a coconspirator of a party during the course and in furtherance of the conspiracy" is not hearsay as it was submitted by the Supreme Court. While the rule refers to a coconspirator, it is this committee's understanding that the rule is meant to carry forward the universally accepted doctrine that a joint venturer is considered as a coconspirator for the purposes of this rule even though no conspiracy has been charged. United States v. Rinaldi, 393 F.2d 97, 99 (2d Cir.), cert. denied 393 U.S. 913 (1968); United States v. Spencer, 415 F.2d 1301, 1304 (7th Cir. 1969).

Notes of Conference Committee, House Report No. 93-1597. Rule 801 supplies some basic definitions for the rules of evidence that deal with hearsay. Rule 801(d)(1) defines certain statements as not hearsay. The Senate amendments make two changes in it.

The House bill provides that a statement is not hearsay if the declarant testifies and is subject to cross-examination concerning the statement and if the statement is inconsistent with his testimony and was given under oath subject to cross-examination and subject to the penalty of perjury at a trial or hearing or in a deposition. The Senate amendment drops the requirement that the prior statement be given under oath subject to cross-examination and subject to the penalty of perjury at a trial or hearing or in a deposition.

The Conference adopts the Senate amendment with an amendment, so that the rule now requires that the prior inconsistent statement be given under oath subject to the penalty of perjury at a trial, hearing, or other proceeding, or in a deposition. The rule as adopted covers statements before a grand jury. Prior inconsistent statements may, of course, be used for impeaching the credibility of a witness. When the prior inconsistent statement is one made by a defendant in a criminal case, it is covered by Rule 801(d)(2).

The House bill provides that a statement is not hearsay if the declarant testifies and is subject to cross-examination concerning the statement and the statement is one of identification of a person made after perceiving him. The Senate amendment eliminated this provision.

The Conference adopts the Senate amendment.

Notes of Advisory Committee on 1987 amendments. The amendments are technical. No substantive change is intended.

Notes of Advisory Committee on 1997 amendments. Rule 801(d)(2) has been amended in order to respond to three issues raised by Bourjaily v. United States, 483 U.S. 171 (1987). First, the amendment codifies the holding in Bourjaily by stating expressly that a court shall consider the contents of a coconspirator's statement in determining "the existence of the conspiracy and the participation therein of the declarant and the party against whom the statement is offered." According to Bourjaily, Rule 104(a) requires these preliminary questions to be established by a preponderance of the evidence.

Second, the amendment resolves an issue on which the Court had reserved decision. It provides that the contents of the declarant's statement do not alone suffice to establish a conspiracy in which the declarant and the defendant participated. The court must consider in addition the circumstances surrounding the statement, such as the identity of the speaker, the context in which the statement was made, or evidence corroborating the contents of the statement in making its determination as to each preliminary question. This amendment is in accordance with existing practice. Every court of appeals that has resolved this issue requires some evidence in addition to the contents of the statement. See. e.g., United States v. Beckham, 968 F.2d 47, 51 (D.C.Cir. 1992); United States v. Sepulveda, 15 F.3d 1161, 1181–82 (1st Cir. 1993), cert. denied, 114 S.Ct. 2714 (1994); United States v. Daly, 842 F.2d 1380, 1386 (2d Cir.), cert. denied, 488 U.S. 821 (1988); United States v. Clark, 18 F.3d 1337, 1341–42 (6th Cir.), cert. denied, 115 S.Ct. 152 (1994); United States v. Zambrana, 841 F.2d 1320, 1344–45 (7th Cir. 1988); United States v. Silverman, 861 F.2d 571, 577 (9th Cir. 1988); United States v. Gordon, 844 F.2d 1397, 1402 (9th Cir. 1988); United States v. Hernandez, 829 F.2d 988, 993 (10th Cir. 1987), cert. denied, 485 U.S. 1013 (1988); United States v. Byrom, 910 F.2d 725,736 (11th Cir. 1990).

Third, the amendment extends the reasoning of Bourjaily to statements offered under subdivisions (C) and (D) of Rule 801(d)(2). In Bourjaily, the Court rejected treating foundational facts pursuant to the law of agency in favor of an evidentiary approach governed by Rule 104(a). The Advisory Committee believes it appropriate to treat analogously preliminary questions relating to the declarant's authority under subdivision (C), and the agency or employment relationship and scope thereof under subdivision (D).

Notes of Advisory Committee on 2011 amendments. The language of Rule 801 has been amended as part of the general restyling of the Evidence Rules to make them more easily understood and to make style and terminology consistent throughout the rules. These changes are intended to be stylistic only. There is no intent to change any result in any ruling on evidence admissibility.

Statements falling under the hearsay exclusion provided by Rule 801(d)(2) are no longer referred to as "admissions" in the title to the subdivision. The term "admissions" is confusing because not all statements covered by the exclusion are admissions in the colloquial sense—a statement can be within the exclusion even if it "admitted" nothing and was not against the party's interest when made. The term "admissions" also raises confusion in comparison with the Rule 804(b)(3) exception for declarations against interest. No change in application of the exclusion is intended.

Notes of Advisory Committee on 2014 amendments. Rule 801(d)(1)(B), as originally adopted, provided for substantive use of certain prior consistent statements of a witness subject to cross-examination. As the Advisory Committee noted, "[t]he prior statement is consistent with the testimony given on the stand, and, if the opposite party wishes to open the door for its admission in evidence, no sound reason is apparent why it should not be received generally."

Though the original Rule 801(d)(1)(B) provided for substantive use of certain prior consistent statements, the scope of that Rule was limited. The Rule covered only those consistent statements that were offered to rebut charges of recent fabrication or improper motive or influence. The Rule did not, for example, provide for substantive admissibility of consistent statements that are probative to explain what otherwise appears to be an inconsistency in the witness's testimony. Nor did it cover consistent statements that would be probative to rebut a charge of faulty memory. Thus, the Rule left many prior consistent statements potentially admissible only for the limited purpose of rehabilitating a witness's credibility. The original Rule also led to some conflict in the cases; some courts distinguished between substantive and rehabilitative use for prior consistent statements, while others appeared to hold that prior consistent statements must be admissible under Rule 801(d)(l)(B) or not at all.

The amendment retains the requirement set forth in *Tome v. United States*, 513 U.S. 150 (1995): that under Rule 801(d)(l)(B), a consistent statement offered to rebut a charge of recent fabrication of improper influence or motive must have been made before the alleged fabrication or improper inference or motive arose. The intent of the amendment is to extend substantive effect to consistent statements that rebut other attacks on a witness—such as the charges of inconsistency or faulty memory.

The amendment does not change the traditional and well-accepted limits on bringing prior consistent statements before the factfinder for credibility purposes. It does not allow impermissible bolstering of a witness. As before, prior consistent statements under the amendment may be brought before the factfinder only if they properly rehabilitate a witness whose credibility has been attacked. As before, to be admissible for rehabilitation, a prior consistent statement must satisfy the strictures of Rule 403. As before, the trial court has ample discretion to exclude prior consistent statements that are cumulative accounts of an event. The amendment does not make any consistent statement admissible that was not admissible previously —the only difference is that prior consistent statements otherwise admissible for rehabilitation are now admissible substantively as well.

Notes of Advisory Committee on 2024 amendments. The rule has been amended to provide that when a party stands in the shoes of a declarant or the declarant's principal, hearsay statements made by the declarant or principal are admissible against the party. For example, if an estate is bringing a claim for damages suffered by the decedent, any hearsay statement that would have been admitted against the decedent as a party-opponent under this rule is equally admissible against the estate. Other relationships that would support this attribution include assignor/assignee and debtor/trustee when the trustee is pursuing the debtor's claims. The rule is justified because if the party is standing in the shoes of the declarant or the principal, the party should not be placed in a better position as to the admissibility of hearsay than the declarant or the principal would have been. A party that derives its interest from a declarant or principal is ordinarily subject to all the substantive limitations applicable to them, so it follows that the party should be bound by the same evidence rules as well.

Reference to the declarant's principal is necessary because the statement may have been made by the agent of the person or entity whose rights or obligations have been succeeded to by the party against whom the statement is offered. The rule does not apply, however, if the statement is admissible against the agent but not against the principal—for example, if the statement was made by the agent after termination of employment. This is because the successor's potential liability is derived from the principal, not the agent.

The rationale of attribution does not apply, and so the hearsay statement would not be admissible, if the declarant makes the statement after the rights or obligations have been transferred, by contract or operation of law, to the party against whom the statement is offered.

Amendments:

1975.

Act Oct. 16, 1975 (effective on the fifteenth day after the date of enactment), in subsec. (d)(1), added cl (C).

Rule 802. The Rule against Hearsay

Hearsay is not admissible unless any of the following provides otherwise:

- a federal statute;
- these rules; or
- other rules prescribed by the Supreme Court.

HISTORY:

Jan. 2, 1975, P. L. 93-595, § 1, 88 Stat. 1939; April 26, 2011, eff. Dec. 1, 2011.

HISTORY; ANCILLARY LAWS AND DIRECTIVES

Other provisions:

Notes of Advisory Committee on Rules. The provision excepting from the operation of the rule hearsay which is made admissible by other rules adopted by the Supreme Court or by Act of Congress continues the admissibility thereunder of hearsay which would not qualify under these Evidence Rules. The following examples illustrate the working of the exception:

Rule 4(g): proof of service by affidavit.

Rule 32: admissibility of depositions.

Rule 43(e): affidavits when motion based on facts not appearing of record.

Rule 56: affidavits in summary judgment proceedings.

Rule 65(b): showing by affidavit for temporary restraining order.

Rule 4(a): affidavits to show grounds for issuing warrants.

Rule 12(b)(4): affidavits to determine issues of fact in connection with motions.

10 U.S.C. § 7730: affidavits of unavailable witnesses in actions for damages caused by vessel in naval service, or towage or salvage of same, when taking of testimony or bringing of action delayed or stayed on security grounds.

29 U.S.C. § 161(4): affadavit as proof of service in NLRB proceedings.

38 U.S.C. § 5206: affadavit as proof of posting notice of sale of unclaimed property by Veterans Administration.

Notes of Advisory Committee on 2011 amendments. The language of Rule 802 has been amended as part of the restyling of the Evidence Rules to make them more easily understood and to make style and terminology consistent throughout the rules. These changes are intended to be stylistic only. There is no intent to change any result in any ruling on evidence admissibility.

Rule 803. Exceptions to the Rule Against Hearsay — Regardless of Whether the Declarant Is Available as a Witness

The following are not excluded by the rule against

hearsay, regardless of whether the declarant is available as a witness:

(1) *Present Sense Impression.* A statement describing or explaining an event or condition, made while or immediately after the declarant perceived it.

(2) *Excited Utterance.* A statement relating to a startling event or condition, made while the declarant was under the stress of excitement that it caused.

(3) *Then-Existing Mental, Emotional, or Physical Condition.* A statement of the declarant's then-existing state of mind (such as motive, intent, or plan) or emotional, sensory, or physical condition (such as mental feeling, pain, or bodily health), but not including a statement of memory or belief to prove the fact remembered or believed unless it relates to the validity or terms of the declarant's will.

(4) *Statement Made for Medical Diagnosis or Treatment.* A statement that:

(A) is made for—and is reasonably pertinent to—medical diagnosis or treatment; and

(B) describes medical history; past or present symptoms or sensations; their inception; or their general cause.

(5) *Recorded Recollection.* A record that:

(A) is on a matter the witness once knew about but now cannot recall well enough to testify fully and accurately;

(B) was made or adopted by the witness when the matter was fresh in the witness's memory; and

(C) accurately reflects the witness's knowledge.

If admitted, the record may be read into evidence but may be received as an exhibit only if offered by an adverse party.

(6) *Records of a regularly conducted activity.* A record of an act, event, condition, opinion, or diagnosis if:

(A) the record was made at or near the time by—or from information transmitted by—someone with knowledge;

(B) the record was kept in the course of a regularly conducted activity of a business, organization, occupation, or calling, whether or not for profit;

(C) making the record was a regular practice of that activity;

(D) all these conditions are shown by the testimony of the custodian or another qualified witness, or by a certification that complies with Rule 902(11) or (12) or with a statute permitting certification; and

(E) the opponent does not show that the source of information or the method or circumstances of preparation indicate a lack of trustworthiness.

(7) *Absence of a record of a regularly conducted activity.* Evidence that a matter is not included in a record described in paragraph (6) if:

(A) the evidence is admitted to prove that the matter did not occur or exist;

(B) a record was regularly kept for a matter of that kind; and

(C) the opponent does not show that the possible source of the information or other circumstances indicate a lack of trustworthiness.

(8) *Public records.* A record or statement of a public office if:

(A) it sets out:

(i) the office's activities;

(ii) a matter observed while under a legal duty to report, but not including, in a criminal case, a matter observed by law-enforcement personnel; or

(iii) in a civil case or against the government in a criminal case, factual findings from a legally authorized investigation; and

(B) the opponent does not show that the source of information or other circumstances indicate a lack of trustworthiness.

(9) *Public Records of Vital Statistics.* A record of a birth, death, or marriage, if reported to a public office in accordance with a legal duty.

(10) *Absence of a Public Record.* Testimony—or a certification under Rule 902—that a diligent search failed to disclose a public record or statement if:

(A) the testimony or certification is admitted to prove that

(i) the record or statement does not exist; or

(ii) a matter did not occur or exist, if a public office regularly kept a record or statement for a matter of that kind; and

(B) in a criminal case, a prosecutor who intends to offer a certification provides written notice of that intent at least 14 days before trial, and the defendant does not object in writing within 7 days of receiving the notice—unless the court sets a different time for the notice or the objection.

(11) *Records of Religious Organizations Concerning Personal or Family History.* A statement of birth, legitimacy, ancestry, marriage, divorce, death, relationship by blood or marriage, or similar facts of personal or family history, contained in a regularly kept record of a religious organization.

(12) *Certificates of Marriage, Baptism, and Similar Ceremonies.* A statement of fact contained in a certificate:

(A) made by a person who is authorized by a religious organization or by law to perform the act certified;

(B) attesting that the person performed a marriage or similar ceremony or administered a sacrament; and

(C) purporting to have been issued at the time of the act or within a reasonable time after it.

(13) *Family Records.* A statement of fact about personal or family history contained in a family record, such as a Bible, genealogy, chart, engraving on a ring, inscription on a portrait, or engraving on an urn or burial marker.

(14) *Records of Documents That Affect an Interest in Property.* The record of a document that purports to establish or affect an interest in property if:

(A) the record is admitted to prove the content of the original recorded document, along with its signing and its delivery by each person who purports to have signed it;

(B) the record is kept in a public office; and

(C) a statute authorizes recording documents of that kind in that office.

(15) *Statements in Documents That Affect an Interest in Property.* A statement contained in a document that

purports to establish or affect an interest in property if the matter stated was relevant to the document's purpose—unless later dealings with the property are inconsistent with the truth of the statement or the purport of the document.

(16) *Statements in Ancient Documents.* A statement in a document that was prepared before January 1, 1998, and whose authenticity is established.

(17) *Market Reports and Similar Commercial Publications.* Market quotations, lists, directories, or other compilations that are generally relied on by the public or by persons in particular occupations.

(18) *Statements in Learned Treatises, Periodicals, or Pamphlets.* A statement contained in a treatise, periodical, or pamphlet if:

(A) the statement is called to the attention of an expert witness on cross-examination or relied on by the expert on direct examination; and

(B) the publication is established as a reliable authority by the expert's admission or testimony, by another expert's testimony, or by judicial notice.

If admitted, the statement may be read into evidence but not received as an exhibit.

(19) *Reputation Concerning Personal or Family History.* A reputation among a person's family by blood, adoption, or marriage—or among a person's associates or in the community—concerning the person's birth, adoption, legitimacy, ancestry, marriage, divorce, death, relationship by blood, adoption, or marriage, or similar facts of personal or family history.

(20) *Reputation Concerning Boundaries or General History.* A reputation in a community—arising before the controversy—concerning boundaries of land in the community or customs that affect the land, or concerning general historical events important to that community, state, or nation.

(21) *Reputation Concerning Character.* A reputation among a person's associates or in the community concerning the person's character.

(22) *Judgment of a Previous Conviction.* Evidence of a final judgment of conviction if:

(A) the judgment was entered after a trial or guilty plea, but not a nolo contendere plea;

(B) the conviction was for a crime punishable by death or by imprisonment for more than a year;

(C) the evidence is admitted to prove any fact essential to the judgment; and

(D) when offered by the prosecutor in a criminal case for a purpose other than impeachment, the judgment was against the defendant.

The pendency of an appeal may be shown but does not affect admissibility.

(23) *Judgments Involving Personal, Family, or General History, or a Boundary.* A judgment that is admitted to prove a matter of personal, family, or general history, or boundaries, if the matter:

(A) was essential to the judgment; and

(B) could be proved by evidence of reputation.

(24) [*Other Exceptions.*] [Transferred to Rule 807.]

HISTORY:

Jan. 2, 1975, P. L. 93-595, § 1, 88 Stat. 1939; Dec. 12, 1975, P. L. 94-149, § 1(11), 89 Stat. 905; March 2, 1987, eff. Oct. 1, 1987; April 11, 1997, eff. Dec. 1, 1997; April 17, 2000, eff. Dec. 1, 2000; April 26, 2011, eff. Dec. 1, 2011; April 16, 2013, eff. Dec. 1, 2013; April 25, 2014, eff. Dec. 1, 2014; April 27, 2017, eff. Dec. 1, 2017.

HISTORY; ANCILLARY LAWS AND DIRECTIVES

Other provisions:

Notes of Advisory Committee on Rules. The exceptions are phrased in terms of nonapplication of the hearsay rule, rather than in positive terms of admissibility, in order to repel any implication that other possible grounds for exclusion are eliminated from consideration.

The present rule proceeds upon the theory that under appropriate circumstances a hearsay statement may possess circumstantial guarantees of trustworthiness sufficient to justify nonproduction of the declarant in person at the trial even though he may be available. The theory finds vast support in the many exceptions to the hearsay rule developed by the common law in which unavailability of the declarant is not a relevant factor. The present rule is a synthesis of them, with revision where modern developments and conditions are believed to make that course appropriate.

In a hearsay situation, the declarant is, of course, a witness, and neither this rule nor Rule 804 dispenses with the requirement of firsthand knowledge. It may appear from his statement or be inferable from circumstances. See Rule 602.

Exceptions (1) and (2). In considerable measure these two examples overlap, though based on somewhat different theories. The most significant practical difference will lie in the time lapse allowable between event and statement.

The underlying theory of Exception [paragraph] (1) is that substantial contemporaneity of event and statement negative the likelihood of deliberate of conscious misrepresentation. Moreover, if the witness is the declarant, he may be examined on the statement. If the witness is not the declarant, he may be examined as to the circumstances as an aid in evaluating the statement. Morgan, Basic Problems of Evidence 340–341 (1962).

The theory of Exception [paragraph] (2) is simply that circumstances may produce a condition of excitement which temporarily stills the capacity of reflection and produces utterances free of conscious fabrication. 6 Wigmore § 1747, p. 135. Spontaneity is the key factor in each instance, though arrived at by somewhat different routes. Both are needed in order to avoid needless niggling.

While the theory of Exception [paragraph] (2) has been criticized on the ground that excitement impairs accuracy of observation as well as eliminating conscious fabrication. Hutchins and Slesinger, Some Observations on the Law of Evidence: Spontaneous Exclamations, 28 Colum.L.Rev. 432 (1928), it finds support in cases without number. See cases in 6 Wigmore § 1750; Annot., 53 A.L.R.2d 1245 (statements as to cause of or responsibility for motor vehicle accident); Annot., 4 A.L.R.3d 149 (accusatory statements by homicide victims). Since unexciting events are less likely to evoke comment, decisions involving Exception [paragraph] (1) are far less numerous. Illustrative are Tampa Elec. Co. v. Getrost, 151 Fla. 558, 10 So.2d 83 (1942); Houston Oxygen Co. v. Davis, 139 Tex. 1, 161 S.W.2d 474 (1942); and cases cited in McCormick § 273, p. 585, n. 4.

With respect to the time element, Exception [paragraph] (1) recognizes that in many, if not most, instances precise contemporaneity is not possible, and hence a slight lapse is allowable. Under Exception [paragraph] (2) the standard of measurement is the duration of the state of excitement. "How long can excitement prevail? Obviously there are no pat answers and the character of the transaction or event will largely determine the significance of the time factor." Slough, Spontaneous Statements and State of Mind, 46 Iowa L.Rev. 224, 243 (1961); McCormick § 272, p. 580.

Participation by the declarant is not required: a nonparticipant may be moved to describe what he perceives, and one may be startled by an event in which he is not an actor. Slough, supra; McCormick, supra; 6 Wigmore § 1755; Annot., 78 A.L.R.2d 300.

Whether proof of the startling event may be made by the statement itself is largely an academic question, since in most cases there is present at least circumstantial evidence that something of a startling nature must have occurred. For cases in which the evidence consists of the condition of the declarant (injuries, state of shock), see Insurance Co. v. Mosely, 75 U.S. (8 Wall.), 397, 19 L.Ed. 437 (1869); Wheeler v. United States, 93 U.S.A.App. D.C. 159, 211 F.2d 19 (1953); cert. denied 347 U.S. 1019, 74 S.Ct. 876, 98 L.Ed. 1140; Wetherbee v. Safety Casualty Co., 219 F.2d 274 (5th Cir. 1955); Lampe v. United States, 97 U.S.App.D.C. 160, 229 F.2d 43 (1956). Nevertheless, on occasion the only evidence may be the content of the statement itself, and rulings that it may be sufficient are described as "increasing," Slough, supra at 246, and as the "prevailing practice," McCormick § 272, p. 579. Illustrative are Armour & Co. v. Industrial Commission, 78 Colo. 569, 243 P. 546 (1926); Young v. Stewart, 191 N.C. 297, 131 S.E. 735 (1926). Moreover, under Rule 104(a) the judge is not limited by the hearsay rule in passing upon preliminary questions of fact.

Proof of declarant's perception by his statement presents similar considerations when declarant is identified. People v. Poland, 22 Ill.2d 175, 174 N.E.2d 804 (1961). However, when declarant is an unidentified bystander, the cases indicate hesitancy in upholding the statement alone as sufficient, Garrett v. Howden, 73 N.M. 307, 387 P.2d 874 (1963); Beck v. Dye, 200 Wash. 1, 92 P.2d 1113 (1939), a result which would under appropriate circumstances be consistent with the rule.

Permissible subject matter of the statement is limited under Exception [paragraph] (1) to description or explanation of the event or condition, the assumption being that spontaneity, in the absence of a startling event, may extend no farther. In Exception [paragraph] (2), however, the statement need only "relate" to the startling event or condition, thus affording a broader scope of subject matter coverage. 6 Wigmore §§ 1750, 1754. See Sanitary Grocery Co. v. Snead, 67 App.D.C. 129, 90 F.2d 374 (1937), slip-and-fall case sustaining admissibility of clerk's statement, "That has been on the floor for a couple of hours," and Murphy Auto Parts Co., Inc. v. Ball, 101 U.S.App.D.C. 416, 249 F.2d 508 (1957), upholding admission, on issue of driver's agency, of his statement that he had to call on a customer and was in a hurry to get home. Quick, Hearsay, Excitement, Necessity and the Uniform Rules: A Reappraisal of Rule 63(4), 6 Wayne L.Rev. 204, 206–209 (1960).

Similar provisions are found in Uniform Rule 63(4)(a) and (b); California Evidence Code § 1240 (as to Exception (2) only); Kansas Code of Civil Procedure § 60-460(d)(1) and (2); New Jersey Evidence Rule 63(4).

Exception (3) is essentially a specialized application of Exception [paragraph] (1), presented separately to enhance its usefulness and accessibility. See McCormick §§ 265, 268.

The exclusion of "statements of memory or belief to prove the fact remembered or believed" is necessary to avoid the virtual destruction of the hearsay rule which would otherwise result from allowing state of mind, provable by a hearsay statement, to serve as the basis for an inference of the happening of the event which produced the state of mind). Shepard v. United States, 290 U.S. 96, 54 S.Ct. 22, 78 L.Ed. 196 (1933); Maguire, The Hillmon Case—Thirty-three Years After, 38 Harv.L.Rev. 709, 719–731 (1925); Hinton, States of Mind and the Hearsay Rule, 1 U.Chi.L-.Rev. 394, 421–423 (1934). The rule of Mutual Life Ins. Co. v. Hillman, 145 U.S. 285, 12 S.Ct. 909, 36 L.Ed. 706 (1892), allowing evidence of intention as tending to prove the doing of the act intended, is of course, left undisturbed.

The carving out, from the exclusion mentioned in the preceding paragraph, of declarations relating to the execution, revocation, identification, or terms of declarant's will represents an *ad hoc* judgment which finds ample reinforcement in the decisions, resting on practical grounds of necessity and expediency rather than logic. McCormick § 271, pp. 577–578; Annot., 34 A.L.R.2d 588, 62 A.L.R.2d 855. A similar recognition of the need for and practical value of this kind of evidence is found in California Evidence Code § 1260.

Exception (4). Even those few jurisdictions which have shied away from generally admitting statements of present condition have allowed them if made to a physician for purposes of diagnosis and treatment in view of the patient's strong motivation to be truthful. McCormick § 266, p. 563. The same guarantee of trustworthiness extends to statements of past conditions and medical history, made for purposes of diagnosis or treatment. It also extends to statements as to causation, reasonably pertinent to the same purposes, in accord with the current trend, Shell Oil Co. v. Industrial Commission, 2 Ill.2d 590, 119 N.E.2d 224 (1954); McCormick § 266, p. 564; New Jersey Evidence Rule 63(12)(c). Statements as to fault would not ordinarily qualify under this latter language. Thus a patient's statement that he was struck by an automobile would qualify but not his statement that the car was driven through a red light. Under the exception the statement need not have been made to a physician. Statements to hospital attendants, ambulance drivers, or even members of the family might be included.

Conventional doctrine has excluded from the hearsay exception, as not within its guarantee of truthfulness, statements to a physician consulted only for the purpose of enabling him to testify. While these statements were not admissible as substantive evidence, the expert was allowed to state the basis of his opinion, including statements of this kind. The distinction thus called for was one most unlikely to be made by juries. The rule accordingly rejects the limitation. This position is consistent with the provision of Rule 703 that the facts on which expert testimony is based need not be admissible in evidence if of a kind ordinarily relied upon by experts in the field.

Exception (5). A hearsay exception for recorded recollection is generally recognized and has been described as having "long been favored by the federal and practically all the state courts that have had occasion to decide the question." United States v. Kelly, 349 F.2d 720, 770 (2d Cir. 1965), citing numerous cases and sustaining the exception against a claimed denial of the right of confrontation. Many additional cases are cited in Annot., 82 A.L.R.2d 473, 520. The guarantee of trustworthiness is found in the reliability inherent in a record made while events were still fresh in mind and accurately reflecting them. Owens v. State, 67 Md. 307, 316, 10 A. 210, 212 (1887).

The principal controversy attending the exception has centered, not upon the propriety of the exception itself, but upon the question whether a preliminary requirement of impaired memory on the part of the witness should be imposed. The authorities are divided. If regard be had only to the accuracy of the evidence, admittedly impairment of the memory of the witness adds nothing to it and should not be required. McCormick § 277, p. 593; 3 Wigmore § 738, p. 76; Jordan v. People, 151 Colo. 133, 376 P.2d 699 (1962), cert. denied 373 U.S. 944, 83 S.Ct. 1553, 10 L.Ed.2d 699; Hall v. State, 223 Md. 158, 162 A.2d 751 (1960); State v. Bindhammer, 44 N.J. 372, 209 A.2d 124 (1965). Nevertheless, the absence of the requirement, it is believed, would encourage the use of statements carefully prepared for purposes of litigation under the supervision of attorneys, investigators, or claim adjusters. Hence the example includes a requirement that the witness not have "sufficient recollection to enable him to testify fully and accurately." To the same effect are California Evidence Code § 1237 and New Jersey Rule 63(1)(b), and this has been the position of the federal courts. Vicksburg & Meridian R.R. v. O'Brien, 119 U.S. 99, 7 S.Ct. 118, 30 L.Ed. 299 (1886); Ahern v. Webb, 268 F.2d 45 (10th Cir. 1959); and see N.L.R.B. v. Hudson Pulp and Paper Corp., 273 F.2d 660, 665 (5th Cir. 1960); N.L.R.B. v. Federal Dairy Co., 297 F.2d 487 (1st Cir. 1962). But cf. United States v. Adams, 385 F.2d 548 (2d Cir. 1967).

No attempt is made in the exception to spell out the method of establishing the initial knowledge or the contemporaneity and accuracy of the record, leaving them to be dealt with as the circumstances of the particular case might indicate. Multiple person involvement in the process of observing and recording, as in Rathbun v. Brancatella, 93 N.J.L. 222, 107 A. 279 (1919), is entirely consistent with the exception.

Locating the exception at this place in the scheme of the rules is a matter of choice. There were two other possibilities. The first was to regard the statement as one of the group of prior statements of a testifying witness which are excluded entirely from the category of hearsay by Rule 801(d)(1). That category, however, requires that declarant be "subject to cross-examination," as to which the impaired memory aspect of the exception raises doubts. The other possibility was to include the exception among those covered by Rule 804. Since unavailability is required by that rule and lack of memory is listed as a species of unavailability by the definition of the term in Rule 804(a)(3), that treatment at first impression would seem appropriate. The fact is, however, that the unavailability requirement of the exception is of a limited and peculiar nature. Accordingly, the exception is located at this point rather than in the context of a rule where unavailability is conceived of more broadly.

Exception (6) represents an area which has received much attention from those seeking to improve the law of evidence. The Commonwealth Fund Act was the result of a study completed in 1927 by a distinguished committee under the chairmanship of Professor Morgan. Morgan et al., The Law of Evidence: Some Proposals for its Reform 63 (1927). With changes too minor to mention, it was adopted by Congress in 1936 as the rule for federal courts. 28 U.S.C. § 1732. A number of states took similar action. The Commissioners on Uniform State Laws in 1936 promulgated the Uniform Business Records as Evidence Act, 9A U.L.A. 506, which has acquired a substantial following in the states. Model Code Rule 514 and Uniform Rule 63(13) also deal with the subject. Difference of varying degrees of importance exist among these various treatments.

These reform efforts were largely within the context of business and commercial records, as the kind usually encountered, and concentrated considerable attention upon relaxing the requirement of producing as witnesses, or accounting for the nonproduction of, all participants in the process of gathering, transmitting, and recording information which the common law had evolved as a burdensome and crippling aspect of using records of this type. In their areas of primary emphasis on witnesses to be called and the general admissibility of ordinary business and commercial records, the Commonwealth Fund Act and the Uniform Act appear to have worked well. The exception seeks to preserve their advantages.

On the subject of what witnesses must be called, the Commonwealth Fund Act eliminated the common law requirement of calling or accounting for all participants by failing to mention it. United States v. Mortimer, 118 F.2d 266 (2d Cir. 1941); La Porte v. United States, 300 F.2d 878 (9th Cir. 1962); McCormick § 290, p. 608. Model Code Rule 514 and Uniform Rule 63(13) did likewise. The Uniform Act, however, abolished the common law requirement in express terms, providing that the requisite foundation testimony might be furnished by "the custodian or other qualified witness." Uniform Business Records as Evidence Act, § 2; 9A U.L.A. 506. The exception follows the Uniform Act in this respect.

The element of unusual reliability of business records is said variously to be supplied by systematic checking, by regularity and continuity which produce habits of precision, by actual experience of business in relying upon them, or by a duty to make an accurate record as part of a continuing job or occupation. McCormick §§ 281, 286, 287; Laughlin, Business Entries and the Like, 46 Iowa, L.Rev. 276 (1961). The model statutes and rules have sought to capture these factors and to extend their impact by employing the phrase "regular course of business," in conjunction with a definition of "business" far broader than its ordinarily accepted meaning. The result is a tendency unduly to emphasize a requirement of routineness and repetitiveness and an insistence that other types of records be squeezed into the fact patterns which give rise to traditional business records. The rule therefore adopts the phrase "the course of a regularly conducted activity" as capturing the essential basis of the hearsay exception as it has evolved and the essential element which can be abstracted from the various specifications of what is a "business."

Amplification of the kinds of activities producing admissible records has given rise to problems which conventional business records by their nature avoid. They are problems of the source of the recorded information, of entries in opinion form, of motivation, and of involvement as participant in the matters recorded.

Sources of information presented no substantial problem with ordinary business records. All participants, including the observer or participant furnishing the information to be recorded, were acting routinely, under a duty of accuracy, with employer reliance on the result, or in short "in the regular course of business." If, however, the supplier of the information does not act in the regular course, an essential link is broken; the assurance of accuracy does not extend to the information itself, and the fact that it may be recorded with scrupulous accuracy is of no avail. An illustration is the police report incorporating information obtained from a bystander: the officer qualifies as acting in the regular course but the informant does not. The leading case, Johnson v. Lutz, 253 N.Y. 124, 170 N.E. 517 (1930), held that a report thus prepared was inadmissible. Most of the authorities have agreed with the decision. Gencarella v. Fyfe, 171 F.2d 419 (1st Cir. 1948); Gordon v. Robinson, 210 F.2d 192 (3d Cir. 1954); Standard Oil Co. of California v. Moore, 251 F.2d 188, 214 (9th Cir. 1957), cert. denied 356 U.S. 975, 78 S.Ct. 1139, 2 L.Ed.2d 1148; Yates v. Bair Transport, Inc., 249 F.Supp. 681 (S.D.N.Y. 1965); Annot., 69 A.L.R.2d 1148. Cf. Hawkins v. Gorea Motor Express, Inc., 360 F.2d 933 (2d Cir 1966). Contra, 5 Wigmore § 1530a, n. 1, pp. 391–392. The point is not dealt with specifically in the Commonwealth Fund Act, the Uniform Act, or Uniform Rule 63(13). However, Model Code Rule 514 contains the requirement "that it was the regular course of that business for one with personal knowledge . . . to make such a memorandum or record or to transmit information thereof to be included in such a memorandum or record . . ." The rule follows this lead in requiring an informant with knowledge acting in the course of the regularly conducted activity.

Entries in the form of opinions were not encountered in traditional business records in view of the purely factual nature of the items recorded, but they are now commonly encountered with respect to medical diagnoses, prognoses, and test results, as well as occasionally in other areas. The Commonwealth Fund Act provided only for records of an "act, transaction, occurrence, or event," while the Uniform Act, Model Code Rule 514, and Uniform Rule 63(13) merely added the ambiguous term "condition." The limited phrasing of the Commonwealth Fund Act, 28 U.S.C. § 1732, may account for the reluctance of some federal decisions to admit diagnostic entries. New York Life Ins. Co. v. Taylor, 79 U.S.App.D.C. 66, 147 F.2d 297 (1945); Lyles v. United States, 103 U.S.App.D.C. 22, 254 F.2d 725 (1957), cert. denied 356 U.S. 961, 78 S.Ct. 997, 2 L.Ed.2d 1067; England v. United States, 174 F.2d 466 (5th Cir. 1949); Skogen v. Dow Chemical Co., 375 F.2d 692 (8th Cir. 1967). Other federal decisions, however, experienced no difficulty in freely admitting diagnostic entries. Reed v. Order of United Commercial Travelers, 123 F.2d 252 (2d Cir. 1941); Buckminster's Estate v. Commissioner of Internal Revenue, 147 F.2d 331 (2d Cir. 1944); Medina v. Erickson, 226 F.2d 475 (9th Cir. 1955); Thomas v. Hogan, 308 F.2d 355 (4th Cir. 1962); Glawe v. Rulon, 284 F.2d 495 (8th Cir. 1960). In the state courts, the trend favors admissibility. Borucki v. MacKenzie Bros. Co., 125 Conn. 92, 3 A.2d 224 (1938); Allen v. St. Louis Public Service Co., 365 Mo. 677, 285 S.W.2d 663, 55 A.L.R.2d 1022 (1956); People v. Kohlmeyer, 284 N.Y. 366, 31 N.E.2d 490 (1940); Weis v. Weis, 147 Ohio St. 416, 72 N.E.2d 245 (1947). In order to make clear its adherence to the latter position, the rule specifically includes both diagnoses and opinions, in addition to acts, events, and conditions, as proper subjects of admissible entries.

Problems of the motivation of the informant have been a source of difficulty and disagreement. In Palmer v. Hoffman, 318 U.S. 109, 63 S.Ct. 477, 87 L.Ed. 645 (1943), exclusion of an accident report made by the since deceased engineer, offered by defendant railroad trustees in a grade crossing collision case, was upheld. The report was not "in the regular course of business," not a record of the systematic conduct of the business as a business, said the Court. The report was prepared for use in litigating, not railroading. While the opinion mentions the motivation of the engineer only obliquely, the emphasis on records of routine operations is significant only by virtue of impact on motivation to be accurate. Absence of routineness raises lack of motivation to be accurate. The opinion of the Court of Appeals had gone beyond mere lack of motive to be accurate: the engineer's statement was "dripping with motivations to misrepresent." Hoffman v. Palmer, 129 F.2d 976, 991 (2d Cir. 1942). The direct introduction of motivation is a disturbing factor, since absence of motivation to misrepresent has not traditionally been a requirement of the rule; that records might be self-serving has not been a ground for exclusion. Laughlin, Business Records and the Like, 46 Iowa L.Rev. 276, 285 (1961). As Judge Clark said in his dissent, "I submit that there is hardly a grocer's account book which could not be excluded on that basis." 129 F.2d at 1002. A physician's evaluation report of a personal injury litigant would appear to be in the routine of his business. If the report is offered by the party at whose instance it was made, however, it has been held inadmissible, Yates v. Bair Transport, Inc., 249 F.Supp. 681 (S.D.N.Y. 1965), otherwise if offered by the opposite party, Korte v. New York, N.H. & H.R. Co., 191 F.2d 86 (2d Cir. 1951), cert. denied 342 U.S. 868, 72 S.Ct. 108, 96 L.Ed. 652.

The decisions hinge on motivation and which party is entitled to be concerned about it. Professor McCormick believed that the doctor's report or the accident report were sufficiently routine to justify admissibility. McCormick § 287, p. 604. Yet hesitation must be experienced in admitting everything which is observed and recorded in the course of a regularly conducted activity. Efforts to set a limit are illustrated by Hartzog v. United States, 217 F.2d 706 (4th Cir. 1954), error to admit worksheets made by since deceased deputy collector in preparation for the instant income tax evasion prosecution, and United States v. Ware, 247 F.2d 698 (7th Cir. 1957), error to admit narcotics agents' records of purchases. See also Exception [paragraph] (8), infra, as to the public record aspects of records of this nature. Some decisions have been satisfied as to motivation of an accident report if made pursuant to statutory duty, United States v. New York Foreign Trade Zone Operators, 304 F.2d 792 (2d Cir. 1962); Taylor v. Baltimore & O. R. Co., 344 F.2d 281 (2d Cir. 1965), since the report was oriented in a direction other than the litigation which ensued. Cf. Matthews v. United States, 217 F.2d 409 (5th Cir. 1954). The formulation of specific terms which would assure satisfactory results in all cases is not possible. Consequently the rule proceeds from the base that records made in the course of a regularly conducted activity will be taken as admissible but subject to authority to exclude if "the sources of information or other circumstances indicate lack of trustworthiness."

Occasional decisions have reached for enhanced accuracy by requiring involvement as a participant in matters reported. Clainos v. United States, 82 U.S.App.D.C. 278, 163 F.2d 593 (1947), error to admit police records of convictions; Standard Oil Co. of California v. Moore, 251 F.2d 188 (9th Cir. 1957), cert. denied 356 U.S. 975, 78 S.Ct. 1139, 2 L.Ed.2d 1148, error to admit employees' records of observed business practices of others. The rule includes no requirement of this nature. Wholly acceptable records may involve matters merely observed, e.g. the weather.

The form which the "record" may assume under the rule is described broadly as a "memorandum, report, record, or data compilation, in any form." The expression "data compilation" is used as broadly descriptive of any means of storing information other than the conventional words and figures in written or documentary form. It includes, but is by no means limited to, electronic computer storage. The term is borrowed from revised Rule 34(a) of the Rules of Civil Procedure.

Exception (7). Failure of a record to mention a matter which would ordinarily be mentioned is satisfactory evidence of its nonexistence. Uniform Rule 63(14), Comment. While probably not hearsay as defined in Rule 801, *supra,* decisions may be found which class the evidence not only as hearsay but also as not within any exception. In order to set the question at rest in favor of admissibility, it is specifically treated here. McCormick § 289, p. 609; Morgan, Basic Problems of Evidence 314 (1962); 5 Wigmore § 1531; Uniform Rule 63(14); California Evidence Code § 1272; Kansas Code of Civil Procedure § 60-460(n); New Jersey Evidence Rule 63(14).

Exception (8). Public records are a recognized hearsay exception at common law and have been the subject of statutes without number. McCormick § 291. See, for example, 28 U.S.C. § 1733, the relative narrowness of which is illustrated by its nonapplicability to nonfederal public agencies, thus necessitating report to the less appropriate business record exception to the hearsay rule. Kay v. United States, 255 F.2d 476 (4th Cir. 1958). The rule makes no distinction between federal and nonfederal offices and agencies.

Justification for the exception is the assumption that a public official will perform his duty properly and the unlikelihood that he will remember details independently of the record. Wong Wing Foo v. McGrath, 196 F.2d 120 (9th Cir. 1952), and see Chesapeake & Delaware Canal Co. v. United States, 250 U.S. 123, 39 S.Ct. 407, 63 L.Ed. 889 (1919). As to items (a) and (b), further support is found in the reliability factors underlying records of regularly conducted activities generally. See Exception [paragraph] (6), supra.

(a) Cases illustrating the admissibility of records of the office's or agency's own activities are numerous. Chesapeake & Delaware Canal Co. v. United States, 250 U.S. 123, 39 S.Ct. 407, 63 L.Ed. 889 (1919), Treasury records of miscellaneous receipts and disbursements; Howard v. Perrin, 200 U.S. 71, 26 S.Ct. 195, 50 L.Ed. 374 (1906), General Land Office records; Ballew v. United States, 160 U.S. 187, 16 S.Ct. 263, 40 L.Ed. 388 (1895), Pension Office records.

(b) Cases sustaining admissibility of records of matters observed are also numerous. United States v. Van Hook, 284 F.2d 489 (7th Cir. 1960), remanded for resentencing 365 U.S. 609, 81 S.Ct. 823, 5 L.Ed.2d 821, letter from induction officer to District Attorney, pursuant to army regulations, stating fact and circumstances of refusal to be inducted; T'Kach v. United States, 242 F.2d 937 (5th Cir. 1957), affidavit of White House personnel officer that search of records showed no employment of accused, charged with fraudulently representing himself as an envoy of the President; Minnehaha County v. Kelley, 150 F.2d 356 (8th Cir. 1945); Weather Bureau records of rainfall; United States v. Meyer, 113 F.2d 387 (7th Cir. 1940), cert. denied 311 U.S. 706, 61 S.Ct. 174, 85 L.Ed. 459, map prepared by government engineer from information furnished by men working under his supervision.

(c) The more controversial area of public records is that of the so-called "evaluative" report. The disagreement among the decisions has been due in part, no doubt, to the variety of situations encountered, as well as to differences in principle. Sustaining admissibility are such cases as United States v. Dumas, 149 U.S. 278, 13 S.Ct. 872, 37 L.Ed. 734 (1893), statement of account certified by Postmaster General in action against postmaster; McCarty v. United States, 185 F.2d 520 (5th Cir. 1950), reh. denied 187 F.2d 234, Certificate of Settlement of General Accounting Office showing indebtedness and letter from Army official stating Government had performed, in action on contract to purchase and remove waste food from Army camp; Moran v. Pittsburgh-Des Moines Steel Co., 183 F.2d 467 (3d Cir. 1950), report of Bureau of Mines as to cause of gas tank explosion; Petition of W—, 164 F.Supp. 659 (E.D.Pa.1958), report by Immigration and Naturalization Service investigator that petitioner was known in community as wife of man to whom she was not married. To the opposite effect and denying admissibility are Franklin v. Skelly Oil Co., 141 F.2d 568 (10th Cir. 1944), State Fire Marshal's report of cause of gas explosion; Lomax Transp. Co. v. United States, 183 F.2d 331 (9th Cir. 1950), Certificate of Settlement from General Accounting Office in action for naval supplies lost in warehouse fire; Yung Jin Teung v. Dulles, 229 F.2d 244 (2d Cir. 1956), "Status Reports" offered to justify delay in processing passport applications. Police reports have generally been excluded except to the extent to which they incorporate firsthand observations of the officer. Annot., 69 A.L.R.2d 1148. Various kinds of evaluative reports are admissible under federal statutes; 7 U.S.C. § 78, findings of Secretary of Agriculture prima facie evidence of true grade of grain; 7 U.S.C. § 210(f), findings of Secretary of Agriculture prima facie evidence in action for damages against stockyard owner; 7 U.S.C. § 292, order by Secretary of Agriculture prima facie evidence in judicial enforcement proceedings against producers association monopoly; 7 U.S.C. § 1622(h), Department of Agriculture inspection certificates of products shipped in interstate commerce prima facie evidence; 8 U.S.C. § 1440(c), separation of alien from military service on conditions other than honorable provable by certificate from department in proceedings to revoke citizenship; 18 U.S.C. § 4245, certificate of Director of Prisons that convicted person has been examined and found probably incompetent at time of trial prima facie evidence in court hearing on competency; 42 U.S.C. § 269(b), bill of health by appropriate official prima facie evidence of vessel's sanitary history and condition and compliance with regulations; 46 U.S.C. § 679, certificate of consul presumptive evidence of refusal of master to transport destitute seamen to United States. While these statutory exceptions to the hearsay rule are left undisturbed, Rule 802, the willingness of Congress to recognize a substantial measure of admissibility for evaluative reports is a helpful guide.

Factors which may be of assistance in passing upon the admissibility of evaluative reports include; (1) the timeliness of the investigation, McCormack, Can the Courts Make Wider Use of Reports of Official Investigations? 42 Iowa L.Rev. 363 (1957); (2) the special skill or experience of the official, id., (3) whether a hearing was held and the level at which conducted, Franklin v. Skelly Oil Co., 141 F.2d 568 (10th Cir. 1944); (4) possible motivation problems suggested by Palmer v. Hoffman, 318 U.S. 109, 63 S.Ct. 477, 87 L.Ed. 645 (1943). Others no doubt could be added.

The formulation of an approach which would give appropriate weight to all possible factors in every situation is an obvious impossibility. Hence the rule, as in Exception [paragraph] (6), assumes admissibility in the first instance but with ample provision for escape if sufficient negative factors are present. In one respect, however, the rule with respect to evaluate reports under item (c) is very specific; they are admissible only in civil cases and against the government in criminal cases in view of the almost certain collision with confrontation rights which would result from their use against the accused in a criminal case.

Exception (9). Records of vital statistics are commonly the subject of particular statutes making them admissible in evidence. Uniform Vital Statistics Act, 9C U.L.A. 350 (1957). The rule is in principle narrower than Uniform Rule 63(16) which includes reports required of persons performing functions authorized by statute, yet in practical effect the two are substantially the same. Comment Uniform Rule 63(16). The exception as drafted is in the pattern of California Evidence Code § 1281.

Exception (10). The principle of proving nonoccurrence of an event by evidence of the absence of a record which would regularly be made of its occurrence, developed in Exception [paragraph] (7) with respect to regularly conducted activities, is here extended to public records of the kind mentioned in Exceptions [paragraphs] (8) and (9). 5 Wigmore § 1633(6), p. 519. Some harmless duplication no doubt exists with Exception [paragraph] (7). For instances of federal statutes recognizing this method of proof, see 8 U.S.C. § 1284(b), proof of absence of alien crewman's name from outgoing manifest prima facie evidence of failure to detain or deport, and 42 U.S.C. § 405(c)(3), (4)(B), (4)(C), absence of HEW [Department of Health, Education, and Welfare] record prima facie evidence of no wages or self-employment income.

The rule includes situations in which absence of a record may itself be the ultimate focal point of inquiry, e.g. People v. Love, 310 Ill. 558, 142 N.E. 204 (1923), certificate of Secretary of State admitted to show failure to file documents required by Securities Law, as well as cases where the absence of a record is offered as proof of the nonoccurrence of an event ordinarily recorded.

The refusal of the common law to allow proof by certificate of the lack of a record or entry has no apparent justification, 5 Wigmore § 1678(7), p. 752. The rule takes the opposite position, as do Uniform Rule 63(17); California Evidence Code § 1284; Kansas Code of Civil Procedure § 60-460(c); New Jersey Evidence Rule 63(17). Congress has recognized certification as evidence of the lack of a record. 8 U.S.C. § 1360(d), certificate of Attorney General or other designated officer that no record of Immigration and Naturalization Service of specified nature or entry therein is found, admissible in alien cases.

Exception (11). Records of activities of religious organizations are currently recognized as admissible at least to the extent of the business records exception to the hearsay rule, 5 Wigmore § 1523, p. 371, and Exception [paragraph] (6) would be applicable. However, both the business record doctrine and Exception [paragraph] (6) require that the person furnishing the information be one in the business or activity. The result is such decisions as Daily v. Grand Lodge, 311 Ill. 184, 142 N.E. 478 (1924), holding a church record admissible to prove fact, date, and place of baptism, but not age of child except that he had at least been born at the time. In view of the unlikelihood that false information would be furnished on occasions of this kind, the rule contains no requirement that the informant be in the course of the activity. See California Evidence Code § 1315 and Comment.

Exception (12). The principle of proof by certification is recognized as to public officials in Exceptions [paragraphs] (8) and (10), and with respect to authentication in Rule 902. The present exception is a duplication to the extent that it deals with a certificate by a public official, as in the case of a judge who performs a marriage ceremony. The area covered by the rule is, however, substantially larger and extends the certification procedure to clergymen and the like who perform marriages and other ceremonies or administer sacraments. Thus certificates of such matters as baptism or confirmation, as well as marriage, are included. In principle they are as acceptable evidence as certificates of public officers. See 5 Wigmore § 1645, as to marriage certificates. When the person executing the certificate is not a public official, the self-authenticating character of documents purporting to emanate from public officials, see Rule 902, is lacking and proof is required that the person was authorized and did make the certificate. The time element, however, may safely be taken as supplied by the certificate, once authority and authenticity are established, particularly in view of the presumption that a document was executed on the date it bears.

For similar rules, some limited to certificates of marriage, with variations in foundation requirements, see Uniform Rule 63(18); California Evidence Code § 1316; Kansas Code of Civil Procedure § 60-460(p); New Jersey Evidence Rule 63(18).

Exception (13). Records of family history kept in family Bibles have by long tradition been received in evidence. 5 Wigmore §§ 1495, 1496, citing numerous statutes and decisions. See also Regulations, Social Security Administration, 20 C.F.R. § 404.703(c), recognizing family Bible entries as proof of age in the absence of public or church records. Opinions in the area also include inscriptions on tombstones, publicly displayed pedigrees, and engravings on rings. Wigmore, supra. The rule is substantially identical in coverage with California Evidence Code § 1312.

Exception (14). The recording of title documents is a purely statutory development. Under any theory of the admissibility of public records, the records would be receivable as evidence of the contents of the recorded document, else the recording process would be reduced to a nullity. When, however, the record is offered for the further purpose of proving execution and delivery, a problem of lack of first-hand knowledge by the recorder, not present as to contents, is presented. This problem is solved, seemingly in all jurisdictions, by qualifying for recording only those documents shown by a specified procedure, either acknowledgement or a form of probate, to have been executed and delivered. 5 Wigmore §§ 1647–1651. Thus what may appear in the rule, at first glance, as endowing the record with an effect independently of local law and inviting difficulties of an Erie nature under Cities Service Oil Co. v.

Dunlap, 308 U.S. 208, 60 S.Ct. 201, 84 L.Ed. 196 (1939), is not present, since the local law in fact governs under the example.

Exception (15). Dispositive documents often contain recitals of fact. Thus a deed purporting to have been executed by an attorney in fact may recite the existence of the power of attorney, or a deed may recite that the grantors are all the heirs of the last record owner. Under the rule, these recitals are exempted from the hearsay rule. The circumstances under which dispositive documents are executed and the requirement that the recital be germane to the purpose of the document are believed to be adequate guarantees of trustworthiness, particularly in view of the nonapplicability of the rule if dealings with the property have been inconsistent with the document. The age of the document is of no significance, though in practical application the document will most often be an ancient one. See Uniform Rule 63(29), Comment.

Similar provisions are contained in Uniform Rule 63(29); California Evidence Code § 1330; Kansas Code of Civil Procedure § 60-460(aa); New Jersey Evidence Rule 63(29).

Exception (16). Authenticating a document as ancient, essentially in the pattern of the common law, as provided in Rule 901(b)(8), leaves open as a separate question the admissibility of assertive statements contained therein as against a hearsay objection. 7 Wigmore § 2145a. Wigmore further states that the ancient document technique of authentication is universally conceded to apply to all sorts of documents, including letters, records, contracts, maps, and certificates, in addition to title documents, citing numerous decisions. Id. § 2145. Since most of these items are significant evidentially only insofar as they are assertive, their admission in evidence must be as a hearsay exception. But see 5 id. § 1573, p. 429, referring to recitals in ancient deeds as a "limited" hearsay exception. The former position is believed to be the correct one in reason and authority. As pointed out in McCormick § 298, danger of mistake is minimized by authentication requirements, and age affords assurance that the writing antedates the present controversy. See Dallas County v. Commercial Union Assurance Co., 286 F.2d 388 (5th Cir. 1961), upholding admissibility of 58-year-old newspaper story. Cf. Morgan, Basic Problems of Evidence 364 (1962), but see id. 254.

For a similar provision, but with the added requirement that "the statement has since generally been acted upon as true by persons having an interest in the matter," see California Evidence Code § 1331.

Exception (17). Ample authority at common law supported the admission in evidence of items falling in this category. While Wigmore's text is narrowly oriented to lists, etc., prepared for the use of a trade or profession, 6 Wigmore § 1702, authorities are cited which include other kinds of publications, for example, newspaper market reports, telephone directories, and city directories. Id. §§ 1702–1706. The basis of trustworthiness is general reliance by the public or by a particular segment of it, and the motivation of the compiler to foster reliance by being accurate.

For similar provisions, see Uniform Rule 63(30); California Evidence Code § 1340; Kansas Code of Civil Procedure § 60-460(bb); New Jersey Evidence Rule 63(30). Uniform Commercial Code § 2-724 provides for admissibility in evidence of "reports in official publications or trade journals or in newspapers or periodicals of general circulation published as the reports of such [established commodity] market."

Exception (18). The writers have generally favored the admissibility of learned treatises, McCormick § 296, p. 621; Morgan, Basic Problems of Evidence 366 (1962); 6 Wigmore § 1692, with the support of occasional decisions and rules, City of Dothan v. Hardy, 237 Ala. 603, 188 So. 264 (1939); Lewandowski v. Preferred Risk Mut. Ins. Co., 33 Wis.2d 69, 146 N.W.2d 505 (1966), 66 Mich.L.Rev. 183 (1967); Uniform Rule 63(31); Kansas Code of Civil Procedure § 60-460(ce), but the great weight of authority has been that learned treatises are not admissible as substantive evidence though usable in the cross-examination of experts. The foundation of the minority view is that the hearsay objection must be regarded as unimpressive when directed against treatises since a high standard of accuracy is engendered by various factors: the treatise is written primarily and impartially for professionals, subject to scrutiny and exposure for inaccuracy, with the reputation of the writer at stake. 6 Wigmore § 1692. Sound as this position may be with respect to trustworthiness, there is, nevertheless, an additional difficulty in the likelihood that the treatise will be misunderstood and misapplied without expert assistance and supervision. This difficulty is recognized in the cases demonstrating unwillingness to sustain findings relative to disability on the basis of judicially noticed medical texts. Ross v. Gardner, 365 F.2d 554 (6th Cir. 1966); Sayers v. Gardner, 380 F.2d 940 (6th Cir. 1967); Colwell v. Gardner, 386 F.2d 56 (6th Cir. 1967); Glendenning v. Ribicoff, 213 F.Supp. 301 (W.D.Mo. 1962); Cook v. Celebrezze, 217 F Supp. 366 (W.D.Mo. 1963); Sosna v. Celebrezze, 234 F.Supp. 289 (E.D.Pa. 1964); and see McDaniel v. Celebrezze, 331 F.2d 426 (4th Cir. 1964). The rule avoids the danger of misunderstanding and misapplication by limiting the use of treatises as substantive evidence to situations in which an expert is on the stand and available to explain and assist in the application of the treatise if declared. The limitation upon receiving the publication itself physically in evidence, contained in the last sentence, is designed to further this policy.

The relevance of the use of treatises on cross-examination is evident. This use of treatises has been the subject of varied views. The most restrictive position is that the witness must have stated expressly on direct his reliance upon the treatise. A slightly more liberal approach still insists upon reliance but allows it to be developed on cross-examination. Further relaxation dispenses with reliance but requires recognition as an authority by the witness, developable on cross-examination. The greatest liberality is found in decisions allowing use of the treatise on cross-examination when its status as an authority is established by any means. Annot., 60 A.L.R.2d 77. The exception is hinged upon this last position, which is that of the Supreme Court, Reilly v. Pinkus, 338 U.S. 269, 70 S.Ct. 110, 94 L.Ed. 63 (1949), and of recent well considered state court decisions, City of St. Petersburg v. Ferguson, 193 So.2d 648 (Fla.App. 1967), cert. denied Fla., 201 So.2d 556; Darling v. Charleston Memorial Community Hospital, 33 Ill.2d 326, 211 N.E.2d 253 (1965); Dabroe v. Rhodes Co., 64 Wash.2d 431, 392 P.2d 317 (1964).

In Reilly v. Pinkus, supra, the Court pointed out that testing of professional knowledge was incomplete without exploration of the witness' knowledge of and attitude toward established treatises in the field. The process works equally well in reverse and furnishes the basis of the rule.

The rule does not require that the witness rely upon or recognize the treatise as authoritative, thus avoiding the possibility that the expert may at the outset block cross-examination by refusing to concede reliance or authoritativeness. Dabroe v. Rhodes Co., supra. Moreover, the rule avoids the unreality of admitting evidence for the purpose of impeachment only, with an instruction to the jury not to consider it otherwise. The parallel to the treatment of prior inconsistent statements will be apparent. See Rules 6130(b) and 801(d)(1).

Exceptions (19), (20), and (21). Trustworthiness in reputation evidence is found "when the topic is such that the facts are likely to have been inquired about and that persons having personal knowledge have disclosed facts which have thus been discussed in the community; and thus the community's conclusion, if any has been formed, is likely to be a trustworthy one." 5 Wigmore § 1580, p. 444, and see also § 1583. On this common foundation, reputation as to land boundaries, customs, general history, character, and marriage have come to be regarded as admissible. The breadth of the underlying principle suggests the formulation of an equally broad exception, but tradition has in fact been much narrower and more particularized, and this is the pattern of these exceptions in the rule.

Exception [paragraph] (19) is concerned with matters of personal and family history. Marriage is universally conceded to be a proper subject of proof by evidence of reputation in the community. 5 Wigmore § 1602. As to such items as legitimacy, relationship, adoption, birth, and death, the decisions are divided. Id. § 1605. All seem to be susceptible to being the subject of well founded repute. The "world" in which the reputation may exist may be family, associates, or community. This world has proved capable of expanding with changing times from the single uncomplicated neighborhood, in which all activities take place, to the multiple and unrelated worlds of work, religious affiliation, and social activity, in each of which a reputation may be generated. People v. Reeves, 360 Ill. 55, 195 N.E. 443 (1935); State v. Axilrod, 248 Minn. 204, 79 N.W.2d 677 (1956); Mass.Stat. 1947, c. 410, M.G.L.A. c. 233 § 21A; 5 Wigmore § 1616. The family has often served as the point of beginning for allowing community reputation. 5 Wigmore § 1488. For comparable provisions see Uniform Rule 63(26), (27)(c); California Evidence Code §§ 1313, 1314; Kansas Code of Civil Procedure § 60-460(x), (y)(3); New Jersey Evidence Rule 63(26), (27)(c).

The first portion of Exception [paragraph] (20) is based upon the general admissibility of evidence of reputation as to land boundaries and land customs, expanded in this country to include private as well as public boundaries. McCormick § 299, p. 625. The reputation is required to antedate the controversy, though not to be ancient. The second portion is likewise supported by authority, id., and is designed to facilitate proof of events when judicial notice is not available. The historical character of the subject matter dispenses with any need that the reputation antedate the controversy with respect to which it is offered. For similar provisions see Uniform Rule 63(27)(a), (b); California Evidence Code §§ 1320–1322; Kansas Code of Civil Procedure § 60-460(y), (1), (2); New Jersey Evidence Rule 63(27)(a), (b).

Exception [paragraph] (21) recognizes the traditional acceptance of reputation evidence as a means of proving human character. McCormick §§ 44, 158. The exception deals only with the hearsay aspect of this kind of evidence. Limitations upon admissibility based on other grounds will be found in Rules 404, relevancy of character evidence generally, and 608, character of witness. The exception is in effect a reiteration, in the context of hearsay, of Rule 405(a). Similar provisions are contained in Uniform Rule 63(28); California Evidence Code § 1324; Kansas Code of Civil Procedure § 60-460(z); New Jersey Evidence Rule 63(28).

Exception (22). When the status of a former judgment is under consideration in subsequent litigation, three possibilities must be noted: (1) the former judgment is conclusive under the doctrine of res judicata, either as a bar or a collateral estoppel; or (2) it is admissible in evidence for what it is worth; or (3) it may be of no effect at all. The first situation does not involve any problem of evidence except in the way that principles of substantive law generally bear upon the relevancy and materiality of evidence. The rule does not deal with the substantive effect of the judgment as a bar or collateral estoppel. When, however, the doctrine of res judicata does not apply to make the judgment either a bar or a collateral estoppel, a choice is presented between the second and third alternatives. The rule adopts the second for judgments of criminal conviction of felony grade. This is the direction of the decisions, Annot., 18 A.L.R.2d 1287, 1299, which manifest an increasing reluctance to reject *in toto* the validity of the law's factfinding processes outside the confines of res judicata and collateral estoppel. While this may leave a jury with the evidence of conviction but without means to evaluate it, as suggested by Judge Hinton, Note 27 Ill.L.Rev. 195 (1932), it seems safe to assume that the jury will give it substantial effect unless defendant offers a satisfactory explanation, a possibility not foreclosed by the provision. But see North River Ins. Co. v. Militello, 104 Colo. 28, 88 P.2d 567 (1939), in which the jury found for plaintiff on a fire policy despite the introduction of his conviction for arson. For supporting federal decisions see Clark, J., in New York & Cuba Mail S.S. Co. v. Continental Cas. Co., 117 F.2d 404, 411 (2d Cir. 1941); Connecticut Fire Ins. Co. v. Farrara, 277 F.2d 388 (8th Cir. 1960).

Practical considerations require exclusion of convictions of minor offenses, not became the administration of justice in its lower echelons must be inferior, but because motivation to defend at this level is often minimal or nonexistent. Cope v. Goble, 39 Cal.App.2d 448, 103 P.2d 598 (1940); Jones v. Talbot, 87 Idaho 498, 394 P.2d 316 (1964); Warren v. Marsh, 215 Minn. 615, 11 N.W.2d 528 (1943); Annot., 18 A.L.R.2d 1287, 1295–1297; 16 Brooklyn L.Rev. 286 (1950); 50 Colum.L.Rev. 529 (1950); 35 Cornell L.Q. 872 (1950). Hence the rule includes only convictions of felony grade, measured by federal standards.

Judgments of conviction based upon pleas of *nolo contendere* are not included. This position is consistent with the treatment of *nolo* pleas in Rule 410 and the authorities cited in the Advisory Committee's Note in support thereof.

While these rules do not in general purport to resolve constitutional issues, they have in general been drafted with a view to avoiding collision with constitutional principles. Consequently the exception does not include evidence of the conviction of a third person, offered against the accused in a criminal prosecution to prove any fact essential to sustain the judgment of conviction. A contrary position would seem clearly to violate the right of confrontation. Kirby v. United States, 174 U.S. 47, 19 S.Ct. 574, 43 L.Ed. 890 (1899), error to convict of possessing stolen postage stamps with the only evidence of theft being the record of conviction of the thieves The situation is to be distinguished from cases in which conviction of another person is an element of the crime, e.g. 15 U.S.C. § 902(d), interstate shipment of firearms to a known convicted felon, and, as specifically provided, from impeachment.

For comparable provisions see Uniform Rule 63(20); California Evidence Code § 1300; Kansas Code of Civil Procedure § 60-460(r); New Jersey Evidence Rule 63(20).

Exception (23). A hearsay exception in this area was originally justified on the ground that verdicts were evidence of reputation. As trial by jury graduated from the category of neighborhood inquests, this theory lost its validity. It was never valid as to chancery decrees. Nevertheless the rule persisted, though the judges and writers shifted ground and began saying that the judgment or decree was as good evidence as reputation. See City of London v. Clerke, Carth. 181, 90 Eng.Rep. 710 (K.B. 1691); Neill v. Duke of Devonshire, 8 App.Cas. 135 (1882). The shift appears to be correct, since the process of inquiry, sifting, and scrutiny which is relied upon to render reputation reliable is present in perhaps greater measure in the process of litigation. While this might suggest a broader area of application, the affinity to reputation is strong, and paragraph [paragraph] (23) goes no further, not even including character.

The leading case in the United States, Patterson v. Gaines, 47 U.S. (6 How.) 550, 599, 12 L.Ed. 553 (1847), follows in the pattern of the English decisions, mentioning as illustrative matters thus provable: manorial rights, public rights of way, immemorial custom, disputed boundary, and pedigree. More recent recognition of the principle is found in Grant Bros. Construction Co. v. United States, 232 U.S. 647, 34 S.Ct. 452, 58 L.Ed. 776 (1914), in action for penalties under Alien Contract Labor Law, decision of board of inquiry of Immigration Service admissible to prove alienage of laborers, as a matter of pedigree; United States v. Mid-Continent Petroleum Corp., 67 F.2d 37 (10th Cir. 1933), records of commission enrolling Indians admissible on pedigree; Jung Yen Loy v. Cahill, 81 F.2d 809 (9th Cir. 1936), board decisions as to citizenship of plaintiff's father admissible in proceeding for declaration of citizenship. Contra, In re Estate of Cunha, 49 Haw. 273, 414 P.2d 925 (1966).

Notes of Committee on the Judiciary, House Report No. 93-650. Rule 803(3) was approved in the form submitted by the Court to Congress. However, the Committee intends that the Rule be construed to limit the doctrine of Mutual Life Insurance Co. v. Hillmon, 145 U.S. 285, 295–300 (1892), so as to render statements of intent by a declarant admissible only to prove his future conduct, not the future conduct of another person.

After giving particular attention to the question of physical examination made solely to enable a physician to testify, the Committee approved Rule 803(4) as submitted to Congress, with the understanding that it is not intended in any way to adversely affect present privilege rules or those subsequently adopted.

Rule 803(5) as submitted by the Court permitted the reading into evidence of a memorandum or record concerning a matter about which a witness once had knowledge but now has insufficient recollection to enable him to testify accurately and fully, "shown to have been made when the matter was fresh in his memory and to reflect that knowledge correctly." The Committee amended this Rule to add the words "or adopted by the witness" after the phrase "shown to have been made", a treatment consistent with the definition of "statement" in the Jencks Act, 18 U.S.C. 3500. Moreover, it is the Committee's understanding that a memorandum or report, although barred under this Rule, would nonetheless be admissible if it came within another hearsay exception. This last stated principle is deemed applicable to all the hearsay rules.

Rule 803(6) as submitted by the Court permitted a record made "in the course of a regularly conducted activity" to be admissible in certain circumstances. The Committee believed there were insufficient guarantees of reliability in records made in the course of activities falling outside the scope of "business" activities as that term is broadly defined in 28 U.S.C. 1732. Moreover, the Committee concluded that the additional requirement of Section 1732 that it must have been the regular practice of a business to make the record is a necessary further assurance of its trustworthiness. The Committee accordingly amended the Rule to incorporate these limitations.

Rule 803(7) as submitted by the Court concerned the *absence* of entry in the records of a "regularly conducted activity." The Committee amended this Rule to conform with its action with respect to Rule 803(6).

The Committee approved Rule 803(8) without substantive change from the form in which it was submitted by the Court. The Committee intends that the phrase "factual findings" be strictly construed and that evaluations or opinions contained in public reports shall not be admissible under this Rule.

The Committee approved this Rule in the form submitted by the Court, intending that the phrase "Statements of fact concerning personal or family history" be read to include the specific types of such statements enumerated in Rule 803(11).

Notes of Committee on the Judiciary, Senate Report No. 93-1277. The House approved this rule as it was submitted by the Supreme Court "with the understanding that it is not intended in any way to adversely affect present privilege rules." We also approve this rule, and we would point out with respect to the question of its relation to privileges, it must be read in conjunction with rule 35 of the Federal Rules of Civil Procedure which provides that whenever the physical or mental condition of a party (plaintiff or defendant) is in controversy, the court may require him to submit to an examination by a physician. It is these examinations which will normally be admitted under this exception.

Rule 803(5) as submitted by the Court permitted the reading into evidence of a memorandum or record concerning a matter about which a witness once had knowledge but now has insufficient recollection to enable him to testify accurately and fully, "shown to have been made when the matter was fresh in his memory and to reflect that knowledge correctly." The House amended the rule to add the words "or adopted by the witness" after the phrase "shown to have been made," language parallel to the Jencks Act [18 U.S.C. § 3500].

The committee accepts the House amendment with the understanding and belief that it was not intended to narrow the scope of applicability of the rule. In fact, we understand it to clarify the rule's applicability to a memorandum adopted by the witness as well as one made by him. While the rule as submitted by the Court was silent on the question of who made the memorandum, we view the House amendment as a helpful clarification, noting, however, that the Advisory Committee's note to this rule suggests that the important thing is the accuracy of the memorandum rather than who made it.

The committee does not view the House amendment as precluding admissibility in situations in which multiple participants were involved.

When the verifying witness has not prepared the report, but merely examined it and found it accurate, he has adopted the report, and it is therefore admissible. The rule should also be interpreted to cover other situations involving multiple participants, e.g., employer dictating to secretary, secretary making memorandum at direction of employer, or information being passed along a chain of persons, as in Curtis v. Bradley [65 Conn. 99, 31 Atl. 591 (1894); see, also Rathbun v. Brancatella, 93 N.J.L. 222, 107 Atl. 279 (1919); see, also McCormick on Evidence, § 303 (2d ed. 1972)].

The committee also accepts the understanding of the House that a memorandum or report, although barred under rule, would nonetheless be admissible if it came within another hearsay exception. We consider this principle to be applicable to all the hearsay rules.

Rule 803(6) as submitted by the Supreme Court permitted a record made in the course of a regularly conducted activity to be admissible in certain circumstances. This rule constituted a broadening of the traditional business records hearsay exception which has been long advocated by scholars and judges active in the law of evidence.

The House felt there were insufficient guarantees of reliability of records not within a broadly defined business records exception. We disagree. Even under the House definition of "business" including profession, occupation, and "calling of every kind," the records of many regularly conducted activities will, or may be, excluded from evidence. Under the principle of ejusdem generis, the intent of "calling of every kind" would seem to be related to work-related endeavors—e.g., butcher, baker, artist, etc.

Thus, it appears that the records of many institutions or groups might not be admissible under the House amendments. For example, schools, churches, and hospitals will not normally be considered businesses within the definition. Yet, these are groups which keep financial and other records on a regular basis in a manner similar to business enterprises. We believe these records are of equivalent trustworthiness and should be admitted into evidence.

Three states, which have recently codified their evidence rules, have adopted the Supreme Court version of rule 803(6), providing for admission of memoranda of a "regularly conducted activity." None adopted the words "business activity" used in the House amendment. [See Nev. Rev. Stats. § 15.135; N. Mex. Stats. (1973 Supp.) § 20-4-803(6); West's Wis. Stats. Anno. (1973 Supp.) § 908.03(6).]

Therefore, the committee deleted the words "business" as it appears before the word "activity". The last sentence then is unnecessary and was also deleted.

It is the understanding of the committee that the use of the phrase "person with knowledge" is not intended to imply that the party seeking to introduce the memorandum, report, record, or data compilation must be able to produce, or even identify, the specific individual upon whose first-hand knowledge the memorandum, report, record or data compilation was based. A sufficient foundation for the introduction of such evidence will be laid if the party seeking to introduce the evidence is able to show that it was the regular practice of the activity to base such memorandums, reports, records, or data compilations upon a transmission from a person with knowledge, e.g., in the case of the content of a shipment of goods, upon a report from the company's receiving agent or in the case of a computer printout, upon a report from the company's computer programmer or one who has knowledge of the particular record system. In short, the scope of the phrase "person with knowledge" is meant to be coterminous with the custodian of the evidence or other qualified witness. The committee believes this represents the desired rule in light of the complex nature of modern business organizations.

The House approved rule 803(8), as submitted by the Supreme Court, with one substantive change. It excluded from the hearsay exception reports containing matters observed by police officers and other law enforcement personnel in criminal cases. Ostensibly, the reason for this exclusion is that observations by police officers at the scene of the crime or the apprehension of the defendant are not as reliable as observations by public officials in other cases because of the adversarial nature of the confrontation between the police and the defendant in criminal cases.

The committee accepts the House's decision to exclude such recorded observations where the police officer is available to testify in court about his observation. However, where he is unavailable as unavailability is defined in rule 804(a)(4) and (a)(5), the report should be admitted as the best available evidence. Accordingly, the committee has amended rule 803(8) to refer to the provision of [proposed] rule 804(b)(5) [deleted], which allows the admission of such reports, records or other statements where the police officer or other law enforcement officer is unavailable because of death, then existing physical or mental illness or infirmity, or not being successfully subject to legal process.

The House Judiciary Committee report contained a statement of intent that "the phrase 'factual findings' in subdivision (c) be strictly construed and that evaluations or opinions contained in public reports shall not be admissible under this rule." The committee takes strong exception to this limiting understanding of the application of the rule. We do not think it reflects an understanding of the intended operation of the rule as explained in the Advisory Committee notes to this subsection. The Advisory Committee notes on subsection (c) of this subdivision point out that various kinds of evaluative reports are now admissible under Federal statutes. 7 U.S.C. § 78, findings of Secretary of Agriculture prima facie evidence of true grade of grain; 42 U.S.C. § 269(b), bill of health by appropriate official prima facie evidence of vessel's sanitary history and condition and compliance with regulations. These statutory exceptions to the hearsay rule are preserved. Rule 802. The willingness of Congress to recognize these and other such evaluative reports provides a helpful guide in determining the kind of reports which are intended to be admissible under this rule. We think the restrictive interpretation of the House overlooks the fact that while the Advisory Committee assumes admissibility in the first instance of evaluative reports, they are not admissible if, as the rule states, "the sources of information or other circumstances indicate lack of trustworthiness."

The Advisory Committee explains the factors to be considered:

. . . . .

Factors which may be assistance in passing upon the admissibility of evaluative reports include: (1) the timeliness of the investigation, McCormick, Can the Courts Make Wider Use of Reports of Official Investigation? 42 Iowa L.Rev. 363 (1957); (2) the special skill or experience of the official, id.; (3) whether a hearing was held and the level at which conducted, Franklin v. Skelly Oil Co., 141 F.2d 568 (19th Cir. 1944); (4) possible motivation problems suggested by Palmer v. Hoffman, 318 U.S. 109, 63 S.Ct. 477, 87 L.Ed. 645 (1943). Others no doubt could be added. . . . . .

The committee concludes that the language of the rule together with the explanation provided by the Advisory Committee furnish sufficient guidance on the admissibility of evaluative reports.

The proposed Rules of Evidence submitted to Congress contained identical provisions in rules 803 and 804 (which set forth the various hearsay exceptions), admitting any hearsay statement not specifically covered by any of the stated exceptions, if the hearsay statement was found to have "comparable circumstantial guarantees of trustworthiness." The House deleted these provisions (proposed rules 803(24) and 804(b)(6) [(5)]) as injecting "too much uncertainty" into the law of evidence and impairing the ability of practitioners to prepare for trial. The House felt that rule 102, which directs the courts to construe the Rules of Evidence so as to promote growth and development, would permit sufficient flexibility to admit hearsay evidence in appropriate cases under various factual situations that might arise.

We disagree with the total rejection of a residual hearsay exception. While we view rule 102 as being intended to provide for a broader construction and interpretation of these rules, we feel that, without a separate residual provision, the specifically enumerated exceptions could become tortured beyond any reasonable circumstances which they were intended to include (even if broadly construed). Moreover, these exceptions, while they reflect the most typical and well recognized exceptions to the hearsay rule, may not encompass every situation in which the reliability and appropriateness of a particular piece of hearsay evidence make clear that it should be heard and considered by the trier of fact.

The committee believes that there are certain exceptional circumstances where evidence which is found by a court to have guarantees of trust worthiness equivalent to or exceeding the guarantees reflected by the presently listed exceptions, and to have a high degree of prolativeness and necessity could properly be admissible.

The case of Dallas County v. Commercial Union Assoc. Co., Ltd., 286 F.2d 388 (5th Cir. 1961) illustrates the point. The issue in that case was whether the tower of the county courthouse collapsed because it was struck by lightning (covered by insurance) or because of structural weakness and deterioration of the structure (not covered). Investigation of the structure revealed the presence of charcoal and charred timbers. In order to show that lightning may not have been the cause of the charring, the insurer offered a copy of a local newspaper published over 50 years earlier containing an unsigned article describing a fire in the courthouse while it was under construction. The Court found that the newspaper did not qualify for admission as a business record or an ancient document and did not fit within any other recognized hearsay exception. The court concluded, however, that the article was trustworthy because it was inconceivable that a newspaper reporter in a small town would report a fire in the courthouse if none had occurred. See also United States v. Barbati, 284 F. Supp. 409 (E.D.N.Y. 1968).

Because exceptional cases like the Dallas County case may arise in the future, the committee has decided to reinstate a residual exception for rules 803 and 804(b).

The committee, however, also agrees with those supporters of the House version who felt that an overly broad residual hearsay exception could emasculate the hearsay rule and the recognized exceptions or vitiate the rationale behind codification of the rules.

Therefore, the committee has adopted a residual exception for rules 803 and 804(b) of much narrower scope and applicability than the Supreme Court version. In order to qualify for admission, a hearsay statement not falling within one of the recognized exceptions would have to satisfy at least four conditions. First, it must have "equivalent circumstantial guarantees of trustworthiness." Second, it must be offered as evidence of a material fact. Third, the court must determine that the statement "is more probative on the point for which it is offered than any other evidence which the proponent can procure through reasonable efforts." This requirement is intended to insure that only statements which have high probative value and necessity may qualify for admission under the residual exceptions. Fourth, the court must determine that "the general purposes of these rules and the interests of justice will best be served by admission of the statement into evidence."

It is intended that the residual hearsay exceptions will be used very rarely, an only in exceptional circumstances. The committee does not intend to establish a broad license for trial judges to admit hearsay statements that do not fall within one of the other exceptions contained in rules 803 and 804(b). The residual exceptions are not meant to authorize major judicial revisions of the hearsay rule, including its present exceptions. Such major revisions are best accomplished by legislative action. It is intended that in any case in which evidence is sought to be admitted under these subsections, the trial judge will exercise no less care, reflection and caution than the courts did under the common law in establishing the now-recognized exceptions to the hearsay rule.

In order to establish a well-defined jurisprudence, the special facts and circumstances which, in the court's judgment, indicates that the statement has a sufficiently high degree of trustworthiness and necessity to justify its admission should be stated on the record. It is expected that the court will give the opposing party a full and adequate opportunity to contest the admission of any statement sought to be introduced under these subsections.

Notes of Conference Committee, House Report No. 93-1597. Rule 803 defines when hearsay statements are admissible in evidence even though the declarant is available as a witness. The Senate amendments make three changes in this rule.

The House bill provides in subsection (6) that records of a regularly conducted "business" activity qualify for admission into evidence as an exception to the hearsay rule. "Business" is defined as including "business, profession, occupation and calling of every kind." The Senate amendment drops the requirement that the records be those of a "business" activity and eliminates the definition of "business." The Senate amendment provides that records are admissible if they are records of a regularly conducted "activity."

The Conference adopts the House provision that the records must be those of a regularly conducted "business" activity. The Conferees changed the definition of "business" contained in the House provision in order to make it clear that the records of institutions and associations like schools, churches and hospitals are admissible under this provision. The records of public schools and hospitals are also covered by Rule 803(8), which deals with public records and reports.

The Senate amendment adds language, not contained in the House bill, that refers to another rule that was added by the Senate in another amendment ([proposed] Rule 804(b)(5)—Criminal law enforcement records and reports [deleted]).

In view of its action on [proposed] Rule 804(b)(5) (Criminal law enforcement records and reports) [deleted], the Conference does not adopt the Senate amendment and restores the bill to the House version.

The Senate amendment adds a new subsection, (24), which makes admissible a hearsay statement not specifically covered by any of the previous twenty-three subsections, if the statement has equivalent circumstantial guarantees of trustworthiness and if the court determines that (A) the statement is offered as evidence of a material fact; (B) the statement is more probative on the point for which it is offered than any other evidence the proponent can procure through reasonable efforts; and (C) the general purposes of these rules and the interests of justice will best be served by admission of the statement into evidence.

The House bill eliminated a similar, but broader, provision because of the conviction that such a provision injected too much uncertainty into the law of evidence regarding hearsay and impaired the ability of a litigant to prepare adequately for trial.

The Conference adopts the Senate amendment with an amendment that provides that a party intending to request the court to use a statement under this provision must notify any adverse party of this intention as well as of the particulars of the statement, including the name and address of the declarant. This notice must be given sufficiently in advance of the trial or hearing to provide any adverse party with a fair opportunity to prepare to contest the use of the statement.

Notes of Advisory Committee on 1987 amendments. The amendments are technical. No substantive change is intended.

Notes of Advisory Committee on 1997 amendments. The contents of Rule 803(24) and Rule 804(b)(5) have been combined and transferred to a new Rule 807. This was done to facilitate additions to Rules 803 and 804. No change in meaning is intended.

Notes of Advisory Committee on 2000 amendments. The amendment provides that the foundation requirements of Rule 803(6) can be satisfied under certain circumstances without the expense and inconvenience of producing time-consuming foundation witnesses. Under current law, courts have generally required foundation witnesses to testify. *See, e.g., Tongil Co., Ltd. v. Hyundai Merchant Marine Corp.*, 968 F.2d 999 (9th Cir. 1992) (reversing a judgment based on business records where a qualified person filed an affidavit but did not testify). Protections are provided by the authentication requirements of Rule 902(11) for domestic records, Rule 902(12) for foreign records in civil cases, and 18 U.S.C. § 3505 for foreign records in criminal cases.

Notes of Advisory Committee on 2011 amendments. The language of Rule 803 has been amended as part of the restyling of the Evidence Rules to make them more easily understood and to make style and terminology consistent throughout the rules. These changes are intended to be stylistic only. There is no intent to change any result in any ruling on evidence admissibility.

Notes of Advisory Committee on 2013 amendments. Rule 803(10) has been amended in response to *Melendez-Diaz v. Massachusetts*, 557 U.S. 305 (2009). The *Melendez-Diaz* Court declared that a testimonial certificate could be admitted if the accused is given advance notice and does not timely demand the presence of the official who prepared the certificate. The amendment incorporates, with minor variations, a "notice-and-demand" procedure that was approved by the *Melendez-Diaz* Court. See Tex. Code Crim. P. Ann., art. 38.41.

Notes of Advisory Committee on 2014 amendments. [Subdivision (6)] The Rule has been amended to clarify that if the proponent has established the stated requirements of the exception—regular business with regularly kept record, source with personal knowledge, record made timely, and foundation testimony or certification—then the burden is on the opponent to show that the source of information or the method or circumstances of preparation indicate a lack of trustworthiness. While most courts have imposed that burden on the opponent, some have not. It is appropriate to impose this burden on opponent, as the basic admissibility requirements are sufficient to establish a presumption that the record is reliable.

The opponent, in meeting its burden, is not necessarily required to introduce affirmative evidence of untrustworthiness. For example, the opponent might argue that a record was prepared in anticipation of litigation and is favorable to the preparing party without needing to introduce evidence on the point. A determination of untrustworthiness necessarily depends on the circumstances.

[Subdiv. (7)] The Rule has been amended to clarify that if the proponent has established the stated requirements of the exception—set forth in Rule 803(6)—then the burden is on the opponent to show that the possible source of the information or other circumstances indicate a lack of trustworthiness. The amendment maintains consistency with the proposed amendment to the trustworthiness clause of Rule 803(6).

[Subdiv. (8)] The Rule has been amended to clarify that if the proponent has established that the record meets the stated requirements of the exception—prepared by a public office and setting out information as specified in the Rule—then the burden is on the opponent to show that the source of information or other circumstances indicate a lack of trustworthiness. While most courts have imposed that burden on the opponent, some have not. Public records have justifiably carried a presumption of reliability, and it should be up to the opponent to "demonstrate why a timetested and carefully considered presumption is not appropriate." *Ellis v. International Playtex, Inc.*, 745 F.2d 292, 301 (4th Cir. 1984). The amendment maintains consistency with the proposed amendment to the trustworthiness clause of Rule 803(6).

The opponent, in meeting its burden, is not necessarily required to introduce affirmative evidence of untrustworthiness. For example, the opponent might argue that a record was prepared in anticipation of litigation and is favorable to the preparing party without needing to introduce evidence on the point. A determination of untrustworthiness necessarily depends on the circumstances.

Notes of Advisory Committee on 2017 Amendments. The ancient documents exception to the rule against hearsay has been limited to statements in documents prepared before January 1, 1998. The Committee has determined that the ancient documents exception should be limited due to the risk that it will be used as a vehicle to admit vast amounts of unreliable electronically stored information (ESI). Given the exponential development and growth of electronic information since 1998, the hearsay exception for ancient documents has now become a possible open door for large amounts of unreliable ESI, as no showing of reliability needs to be made to qualify under the exception.

The Committee is aware that in certain cases—such as cases involving latent diseases and environmental damage —parties must rely on hardcopy documents from the past. The ancient documents exception remains available for such cases for documents prepared before 1998. Going forward, it is anticipated that any need to admit old hardcopy documents produced after January 1, 1998 will decrease, because reliable ESI is likely to be available and can be offered under a reliability-based hearsay exception. Rule 803(6) may be used for many of these ESI documents, especially given its flexible standards on which witnesses might be qualified to provide an adequate foundation. And Rule 807 can be used to admit old documents upon a showing of reliability—which will often (though not always) be found by circumstances such as that the document was prepared with no litigation motive in mind, close in time to the relevant events. The limitation of the ancient documents exception is not intended to raise an inference that 20-year-old documents are, as a class, unreliable, or that they should somehow not qualify for admissibility under Rule 807. Finally, many old documents can be admitted for the non-hearsay purpose of proving notice, or as party-opponent statements.

The limitation of the ancient documents hearsay exception is not intended to have any effect on authentication of ancient documents. The possibility of authenticating an old document under Rule 901(b)(8)—or under any ground available for any other document— remains unchanged.

The Committee carefully considered, but ultimately rejected, an amendment that would preserve the ancient documents exception for hardcopy evidence only. A party will often offer hardcopy that is derived from ESI. Moreover, a good deal of old information in hardcopy has been digitized or will be so in the future. Thus, the line between ESI and hardcopy was determined to be one that could not be drawn usefully.

The Committee understands that the choice of a cutoff date has a degree of arbitrariness. But January 1, 1998 is a rational date for treating concerns about old and unreliable ESI. And the date is no more arbitrary than the 20-year cutoff date in the original rule. See Committee Note to Rule 901(b)(8) ("Any time period selected is bound to be arbitrary.").

Under the amendment, a document is "prepared" when the statement proffered was recorded in that document. For example, if a hardcopy document is prepared in 1995, and a party seeks to admit a scanned copy of that document, the date of preparation is 1995 even though the scan was made long after that—the subsequent scan does not alter the document. The relevant point is the date on which the information is recorded, not when the information is prepared for trial. However, if the content of the document is itself altered after the cut-off date, then the hearsay exception will not apply to statements that were added in the alteration.

Amendments:

1975.

Act Dec. 12, 1975, in catchline of subsec. (23), inserted comma after "family".

Rule 804. Exceptions to the Rule Against Hearsay — When the Declarant is Unavailable as a Witness

(a) Criteria for Being Unavailable. A declarant is considered to be unavailable as a witness if the declarant:

(1) is exempted from testifying about the subject matter of the declarant's statement because the court rules that a privilege applies;

(2) refuses to testify about the subject matter despite a court order to do so;

(3) testifies to not remembering the subject matter;

(4) cannot be present or testify at the trial or hearing because of death or a then-existing infirmity, physical illness, or mental illness; or

(5) is absent from the trial or hearing and the statement's proponent has not been able, by process or other reasonable means, to procure:

(A) the declarant's attendance, in the case of a hearsay exception under Rule 804(b)(1) or (6); or

(B) the declarant's attendance or testimony, in the case of a hearsay exception under Rule 804(b)(2), (3), or (4).

But this subdivision (a) does not apply if the statement's proponent procured or wrongfully caused the declarant's unavailability as a witness in order to prevent the declarant from attending or testifying.

(b) The Exceptions. The following are not excluded by the rule against hearsay if the declarant is unavailable as a witness:

(1) *Former Testimony.* Testimony that:

(A) was given as a witness at a trial, hearing, or lawful deposition, whether given during the current proceeding or a different one; and

(B) is now offered against a party who had—or, in a civil case, whose predecessor in interest had—an opportunity and similar motive to develop it by direct, cross-, or redirect examination.

(2) *Statement Under the Belief of Imminent Death.* In a prosecution for homicide or in a civil case, a statement that the declarant, while believing the declarant's death to be imminent, made about its cause or circumstances.

(3) *Statement Against Interest.* A statement that:

(A) a reasonable person in the declarant's position would have made only if the person believed it to be true because, when made, it was so contrary to the

Evidence Rule 804

declarant's proprietary or pecuniary interest or had so great a tendency to invalidate the declarant's claim against someone else or to expose the declarant to civil or criminal liability; and

(B) if offered in a criminal case as one that tends to expose the declarant to criminal liability, is supported by corroborating circumstances that clearly indicate its trustworthiness after considering the totality of circumstances under which it was made and any evidence that supports or undermines it.

(4) *Statement of Personal or Family History.* A statement about:

(A) the declarant's own birth, adoption, legitimacy, ancestry, marriage, divorce, relationship by blood, adoption, or marriage, or similar facts of personal or family history, even though the declarant had no way of acquiring personal knowledge about that fact; or

(B) another person concerning any of these facts, as well as death, if the declarant was related to the person by blood, adoption, or marriage or was so intimately associated with the person's family that the declarant's information is likely to be accurate.

(5) [*Other Exceptions.*] [Transferred to Rule 807.]

(6) *Statement Offered Against a Party That Wrongfully Caused the Declarant's Unavailability.* A statement offered against a party that wrongfully caused—or acquiesced in wrongfully causing—the declarant's unavailability as a witness, and did so intending that result.

HISTORY:

Jan. 2, 1975, P. L. 93-595, § 1, 88 Stat. 1942; Dec. 12, 1975, P. L. 94-149, § 1(12), (13), 89 Stat. 806; March 2, 1987, eff. Oct. 1, 1987; Nov. 18, 1988, P. L. 100-690, Title VII, Subtitle B, § 7075(b), 102 Stat. 4405; April 26, 1997, eff. Dec. 1, 1997; April 28, 2010, eff. Dec. 1, 2010; April 26, 2011, eff. Dec. 1, 2011; April 2, 2024, eff. Dec. 1, 2024.

HISTORY; ANCILLARY LAWS AND DIRECTIVES

Other provisions:

Notes of Advisory Committee on Rules.

As to firsthand knowledge on the part of hearsay declarants, see the introductory portion of the Advisory Committee's Note to Rule 803.

Subdivision (a). The definition of unavailability implements the division of hearsay exceptions into two categories by Rules 803 and 804(b).

At common law the unavailability requirement was evolved in connection with particular hearsay exceptions rather than along general lines. For example, see the separate explication of unavailability in relation to former testimony, declarations against interest, and statements of pedigree, separately developed in McCormick §§ 234, 257, and 297. However, no reason is apparent for making distinctions as to what satisfies unavailability for the different exceptions. The treatment in the rule is therefore uniform although differences in the range of process for witnesses between civil and criminal cases will lead to a less exacting requirement under item (5). See Rule 45(e) of the Federal Rules of Civil Procedure and Rule 17(e) of the Federal Rules of Criminal Procedure.

Five instances of unavailability are specified:

(1) Substantial authority supports the position that exercise of a claim of privilege by the declarant satisfies the requirement of unavailability (usually in connection with former testimony). Wyatt v. State, 35 Ala.App. 147, 46 So.2d 837 (1950); State v. Stewart, 85 Kan. 404, 116 P. 489 (1911); Annot., 45 A.L.R.2d 1354; Uniform Rule 62(7)(a); California Evidence Code § 240(a)(1); Kansas Code of Civil Procedure § 60-459(g)(1). A ruling by the judge is required, which clearly implies that an actual claim of privilege must be made.

(2) A witness is rendered unavailable if he simply refuses to testify concerning the subject matter of his statement despite judicial pressures to do so, a position supported by similar considerations of practicality. Johnson v. People, 152 Colo. 586, 384 P.2d 454 (1963); People v. Pickett, 339 Mich. 294, 63 N.W.2d 681, 45 A.L.R.2d 1341 (1954). Contra, Pleau v. State, 255 Wis. 362, 38 N.W.2d 496 (1949).

(3) The position that a claimed lack of memory by the witness of the subject matter of his statement constitutes unavailability likewise finds support in the cases, though not without dissent. McCormick § 234, p. 494. If the claim is successful, the practical effect is to put the testimony beyond reach, as in the other instances. In this instance, however, it will be noted that the lack of memory must be established by the testimony of the witness himself, which clearly contemplates his production and subjection to cross-examination.

(4) Death and infirmity find general recognition as ground. McCormick §§ 234, 257, 297; Uniform Rule 62(7)(c); California Evidence Code § 240(a)(3); Kansas Code of Civil Procedure § 60-459(g)(3); New Jersey Evidence Rule 62(6)(c). See also the provisions on use of depositions in Rule 32(a)(3) of the Federal Rules of Civil Procedure and Rule 15(e) of the Federal Rules of Criminal Procedure.

(5) Absence from the hearing coupled with inability to compel attendance by process or other reasonable means also satisfies the requirement. McCormick § 234; Uniform Rule 62(7)(d) and (e); California Evidence Code § 240(a)(4) and (5); Kansas Code of Civil Procedure § 60-459(g)(4) and (5); New Jersey Rule 62(6)(b) and (d). See the discussion of procuring attendance of witnesses who are nonresidents or in custody in Barber v. Page, 390 U.S. 719, 88 S.Ct. 1318, 20 L.Ed.2d 255 (1968).

If the conditions otherwise constituting unavailability result from the procurement or wrongdoing of the proponent of the statement, the requirement is not satisfied. The rule contains no requirement that an attempt be made to take the deposition of a declarant.

Subdivision (b). Rule 803 supra, is based upon the assumption that a hearsay statement falling within one of its exceptions possesses qualities which justify the conclusion that whether the declarant is available or unavailable is not a relevant factor in determining admissibility. The instant rule proceeds upon a different theory: hearsay which admittedly is not equal in quality to testimony of the declarant on the stand may nevertheless be admitted if the declarant is unavailable and if his statement meets a specified standard. The rule expresses preferences: testimony given on the stand in person is preferred over hearsay, and hearsay, if of the specified quality, is preferred over complete loss of the evidence of the declarant. The exceptions evolved at common law with respect to declarations of unavailable declarants furnish the basis for the exceptions enumerated in the proposal. The term "unavailable" is defined in subdivision (a).

Exception (1). Former testimony does not rely upon some set of circumstances to substitute for oath and cross-examination, since both oath and opportunity to cross-examine were present in fact. The only missing one of the ideal conditions for the giving of testimony is the presence of trier and opponent ("demeanor evidence"). This is lacking with all hearsay exceptions. Hence it may be argued that former testimony is the strongest hearsay and should be included under Rule 803, supra. However, opportunity to observe demeanor is what in a large measure confers depth and meaning upon oath and cross-examination. Thus in cases under Rule 803 demeanor lacks the significance which it possesses with respect to testimony. In any event, the tradition, founded in experience, uniformly favors production of the witness if he is available. The exception indicates continuation of the policy. This preference for the presence of the witness is apparent also in rules and statutes on the use of depositions, which deal with substantially the same problem.

Under the exception, the testimony may be offered (1) against the party against whom it was previously offered or (2) against the party by whom it was previously offered. In each instance the question resolves itself into whether fairness allows imposing, upon the party against whom now offered, the handling of the witness on the earlier occasion. (1) If the party against whom now offered is the one against whom the testimony was offered previously, no unfairness is apparent in requiring him to accept his own prior conduct of cross-examination or decision not to cross-examine. Only demeanor has been lost, and that is inherent in the situation. (2) If the party against whom now offered is the one by whom the testimony was offered previously, a satisfactory answer becomes somewhat more difficult. One possibility is to proceed somewhat along the line of an adoptive admission, i.e. by offering the testimony proponent in effect adopts it. However, this theory savors of discarded concepts of witnesses' belonging to a party, of litigants' ability to pick and choose witnesses, and of vouching for one's own witnesses. Cf. McCormick § 246, pp. 526–527; 4 Wigmore § 1075. A more direct and acceptable approach is simply to recognize direct and redirect examination of one's own witness as the equivalent of cross-examining an opponent's witness. Falknor, Former Testimony and the Uniform Rules: A Comment, 38 N.Y.U.L.Rev. 651, n. 1 (1963); McCormick § 231, p. 483. See also 5 Wigmore § 1389. Allowable techniques for dealing with hostile, doublecrossing, forgetful, and mentally deficient witnesses leave no substance to a claim that one could not adequately develop his own witness at the former hearing. An even less appealing argument is presented when failure to develop fully was the result of a deliberate choice.

The common law did not limit the admissibility of former testimony to that given in an earlier trial of the same case, although it did require identity of issues as a means of insuring that the former handling of the witness was the equivalent of what would now be done if the opportunity were presented. Modern decisions reduce the requirement to "substantial" identity. McCormick § 233. Since identity of issues is significant only in that it bears on motive and interest in developing fully the testimony of the witness, expressing the matter in the latter terms is preferable. Id. Testimony given at a preliminary hearing was held in California v. Green, 399 U.S. 149, 90 S.Ct. 1930, 26 L.Ed.2d 489 (1970), to satisfy confrontation requirements in this respect.

As a further assurance of fairness in thrusting upon a party the prior handling of the witness, the common law also insisted upon identity of parties, deviating only to the extent of allowing substitution of successors in a narrowly construed privity. Mutuality as an aspect of identity is now generally discredited, and the requirement of identity of the offering party disappears except as it might affect motive to develop the testimony. Falknor, supra, at 652; McCormick § 232, pp. 487–488. The question remains whether strict identity, or privity, should continue as a requirement with respect to the party against whom offered. The rule departs to the extent of allowing substitution of one with the right and opportunity to develop the testimony with similar motive and interest. This position is supported by modern decisions. McCormick § 232, pp. 489–490; 5 Wigmore § 1388.

Provisions of the same tenor will be found in Uniform Rule 63(3)(b); California Evidence Code §§ 1290–1292; Kansas Code of Civil Procedure § 60-460(c)(2); New Jersey Evidence Rule 63(3). Unlike the rule, the latter three provide either that former testimony is not admissible if the right of confrontation is denied or that it is not admissible if the accused was not a party to the prior hearing. The genesis of these limitations is a caveat in Uniform Rule 63(3) Comment that use of former testimony against an accused may violate his right of confrontation. Mattox v. United States, 156 U.S. 237, 15 S.Ct. 337, 39 L.Ed. 409 (1895), held that the right was not violated by the Government's use, on a retrial of the same case, of testimony given at the first trial by two witnesses since deceased. The decision leaves open the questions (1) whether direct and redirect are equivalent to cross-examination for purposes of confrontation, (2) whether testimony given in a different proceeding is acceptable, and (3) whether the accused must himself have been a party to the earlier proceeding or whether a similarly situated person will serve the purpose. Professor Falknor concluded that, if a dying declaration untested by cross-examination is constitutionally admissible, former testimony tested by the cross-examination of one similarly situated does not offend against confrontation. Falknor, supra, at 659–660. The constitutional acceptability of dying declarations has often been conceded. Mattox v. United States, 156 U.S. 237, 243, 15 S.Ct. 337, 39 L.Ed. 409 (1895); Kirby v. United States, 174 U.S. 47, 61, 19 S.Ct. 574, 43 L.Ed. 890 (1899); Pointer v. Texas, 380 U.S. 400, 407, 85 S.Ct. 1065, 13 L.Ed.2d 923 (1965).

Exception (2). The exception is the familiar dying declaration of the common law, expanded somewhat beyond its traditionally narrow limits. While the original religious justification for the exception may have lost its conviction for some persons over the years, it can scarcely be doubted that powerful psychological pressures are present. See 5 Wigmore § 1443 and the classic statement of Chief Baron Eyre in Rex v. Woodcock, 1 Leach 500, 502, 168 Eng.Rep. 352, 353 (K.B. 1789).

The common law required that the statement be that of the victim, offered in a prosecution for criminal homicide. Thus declarations by victims in prosecutions for other crimes, e.g. a declaration by a rape victim who dies in childbirth, and all declarations in civil cases were outside the scope of the exception. An occasional statute has removed these restrictions, as in Colo.R.S. § 52-1-20, or has expanded the area of offenses to include abortions, 5 Wigmore § 1432, p. 224, n. 4. Kansas by decision extended the exception to civil cases. Thurston v. Fritz, 91 Kan. 468, 138 P. 625 (1914). While the common law exception no doubt originated as a result of the exceptional need for the evidence in homicide cases, the theory of admissibility applies equally in civil cases and in prosecutions for crimes other than homicide. The same considerations suggest abandonment of the limitation to circumstances attending the event in question, yet when the statement deals with matters other than the supposed death, its influence is believed to be sufficiently attenuated to justify the limitation. Unavailability is not limited to death. See subdivision (a) of this rule. Any problem as to declarations phrased in terms of opinion is laid at rest by Rule 701, and continuation of a requirement of first-hand knowledge is assured by Rule 602.

Comparable provisions are found in Uniform Rule 63(5); California Evidence Code § 1242; Kansas Code of Civil Procedure § 60-460(e); New Jersey Evidence Rule 63(5).

Exception (3). The circumstantial guaranty of reliability for declarations against interest is the assumption that persons do not make statements which are damaging to themselves unless satisfied for good reason that they are true. Hileman v. Northwest Engineering Co., 346 F.2d 668 (6th Cir. 1965). If the statement is that of a party, offered by his opponent, it comes in as an admission, Rule 803(d)(2), and there is no occasion to inquire whether it is against interest, this not being a condition precedent to admissibility of admissions by opponents.

The common law required that the interest declared against be pecuniary or proprietary but within this limitation demonstrated striking ingenuity in discovering an against-interest aspect. Higham v. Ridgeway, 10 East 109, 103 Eng.Rep. 717 (K.B. 1808); Reg. v. Overseers of Birmingham, 1 B. & S. 763, 121 Eng.Rep. 897 (Q.B. 1861); McCormick, § 256, p. 551, nn. 2 and 3.

The exception discards the common law limitation and expands to the full logical limit. One result is to remove doubt as to the admissibility of declarations tending to establish a tort liability against the declarant or to extinguish one which might be asserted by him, in accordance with the trend of the decisions in this country. McCormick § 254, pp. 548–549. Another is to allow statements tending to expose declarant to hatred, ridicule, or disgrace, the motivation here being considered to be as strong as when financial interests are at stake. McCormick § 255, p. 551. And finally, exposure to criminal liability satisfies the against-interest requirement. The refusal of the common law to concede the adequacy of a penal interest was no doubt indefensible in logic, see the dissent of Mr. Justice Holmes in Donnelly v. United States, 228 U.S. 243, 33 S.Ct. 449, 57 L.Ed. 820 (1913), but one senses in the decisions a distrust of evidence of confessions by third persons offered to exculpate the accused arising from suspicions of fabrication either of the fact of the making of the confession or in its contents, enhanced in either instance by the required unavailability of the declarant. Nevertheless, an increasing amount of decisional law recognizes exposure to punishment for crime as a sufficient stake. People v. Spriggs, 60 Cal.2d 868, 36 Cal.Rptr. 841, 389 P.2d 377 (1964); Sutter v. Easterly, 354 Mo. 282, 189 S.W.2d 284 (1945); Band's Refuse Removal, Inc. v. Fairlawn Borough, 62 N.J.Super. 552, 163 A.2d 465 (1960); Newberry v. Commonwealth, 191 Va. 445, 61 S.E.2d 318 (1950); Annot., 162 A.L.R. 446. The requirement of corroboration is included in the rule in order to effect an accommodation between these competing considerations. When the statement is offered by the accused by way of exculpation, the resulting situation is not adapted to control by rulings as to the weight of the evidence and, hence the provision is cast in terms of a requirement preliminary to admissibility. Cf. Rule 406(a). The requirement of corroboration should be construed in such a manner as to effectuate its purpose of circumventing fabrication.

Ordinarily the third-party confession is thought of in terms of exculpating the accused, but this is by no means always or necessarily the case: it may include statements implicating him, and under the general theory of declarations against interest they would be admissible as related statements. Douglas v. Alabama, 380 U.S. 415, 85 S.Ct. 1074, 13 L.Ed.2d 934 (1965), and Bruton v. United States, 389 U.S. 818, 88 S.Ct. 126, 19 L.Ed.2d 70 (1968), both involved confessions by codefendants which implicated the accused. While the confession was not actually offered in evidence in Douglas, the procedure followed effectively put it before the jury, which the Court ruled to be error. Whether the confession might have been admissible as a declaration against penal interest was not considered or discussed. Bruton assumed the inadmissibility, as against the accused, of the implicating confession of his codefendant, and centered upon the question of the effectiveness of a limiting instruction. These decisions, however, by no means require that all statements implicating another person be excluded from the category of declarations against interest. Whether a statement is in fact against interest must be determined from the circumstances of each case. Thus a statement admitting guilt and implicating another person, made while in custody, may well be motivated by a desire to curry favor with the authorities and hence fail to qualify as against interest. See the dissenting opinion of Mr. Justice White in Bruton. On the other hand, the same words spoken under different circumstances, e.g., to an acquaintance, would have no difficulty in qualifying. The rule does not purport to deal with questions of the right of confrontation.

The balancing of self-serving against dissenting aspects of a declaration is discussed in McCormick § 256.

For comparable provisions, see Uniform Rule 63(10): California Evidence Code § 1230; Kansas Code of Civil Procedure § 60-460(j); New Jersey Evidence Rule 63(10).

Exception (4). The general common law requirement that a declaration in this area must have been made ante litem motam has been dropped, as bearing more appropriately on weight than admissibility. See 5 Wigmore § 1483. Item (i) [(A)] specifically disclaims any need of firsthand knowledge respecting declarant's own personal history. In some instances it is self-evident (marriage) and in others impossible and traditionally not required (date of birth). Item (ii)(B)] deals with declarations concerning the history of another person. As at common law, declarant is qualified if related by blood or marriage. 5 Wigmore § 1489. In addition, and contrary to the common law, declarant qualifies by virtue of intimate association with the family. Id., § 1487. The requirement sometimes encountered that when the subject of the statement is the relationship between two other persons the declarant must qualify as to both is omitted. Relationship is reciprocal. Id., § 1491.

For comparable provisions, see Uniform Rule 63 (23), (24), (25); California Evidence Code §§ 1310, 1311; Kansas

Code of Civil Procedure § 60-460(u), (v), (w); New Jersey Evidence Rules 63(23), 63(24), 63(25).

Notes of Committee on the Judiciary, House Report No. 93-650.

Rule 804(a)(3) was approved in the form submitted by the Court. However, the Committee intends no change in existing federal law under which the court may choose to disbelieve the declarant's testimony as to his lack of memory. See United States v. Insana, 423 F.2d 1165, 1169–1170 (2nd Cir.), cert. denied, 400 U.S. 841 (1970).

Rule 804(a)(5) as submitted to the Congress provided, as one type of situation in which a declarant would be deemed "unavailable", that he be "absent from the hearing and the proponent of his statement has been unable to procure his attendance by process or other reasonable means." The Committee amended the Rule to insert after the word "attendance" the parenthetical expression "(or, in the case of a hearsay exception under subdivision (b)(2), (3), or (4), his attendance or testimony)". The amendment is designed primarily to require that an attempt be made to depose a witness (as well as to seek his attendance) as a precondition to the witness being deemed unavailable. The Committee, however, recognized the propriety of an exception to this additional requirement when it is the declarant's former testimony that is sought to be admitted under subdivision (b)(1).

Rule 804(b)(1) as submitted by the Court allowed prior testimony of an unavailable witness to be admissible if the party against whom it is offered or a person "with motive and interest similar" to his had an opportunity to examine the witness. The Committee considered that it is generally unfair to impose upon the party against whom the hearsay evidence is being offered responsibility for the manner in which the witness was previously handled by another party. The sole exception to this, in the Committee's view, is when a party's predecessor in interest in a civil action or proceeding had an opportunity and similar motive to examine the witness. The Committee amended the Rule to reflect these policy determinations.

Rule 804(b)(3) as submitted by the Court (now Rule 804(b)(2) in the bill) proposed to expand the traditional scope of the dying declaration exception (i.e. a statement of the victim in a homicide case as to the cause or circumstances of his believed imminent death) to allow such statements in all criminal and civil cases. The Committee did not consider dying declarations as among the most reliable forms of hearsay. Consequently, it amended the provision to limit their admissibility in criminal cases to homicide prosecutions, where exceptional need for the evidence is present. This is existing law. At the same time, the Committee approved the expansion to civil actions and proceedings where the stakes do not involve possible imprisonment, although noting that this could lead to forum shopping in some instances.

Rule 804(b)(4) as submitted by the Court (now Rule 804(b)(3) in the bill) provided as follows:

Statement against interest.—A statement which was at the time of its making so far contrary to the declarant's pecuniary or proprietary interest or so far tended to subject him to civil or criminal liability or to render invalid a claim by him against another or to make him an object of hatred, ridicule, or disgrace, that a reasonable man in his position would not have made the statement unless he believed it to be true. A statement tending to exculpate the accused is not admissible unless corroborated.

The Committee determined to retain the traditional hearsay exception for statements against pecuniary or proprietary interest. However, it deemed the Court's additional references to statements tending to subject a declarant to civil liability or to render invalid a claim by him against another to be redundant as included within the scope of the reference to statements against pecuniary or proprietary interest. See Gichner v. Antonio Triano Tile and Marble Co., 410 F.2d 238 (D.C. Cir. 1968). Those additional references were accordingly deleted.

The Court's Rule also proposed to expand the hearsay limitation from its present federal limitation to include statements subjecting the declarant to criminal liability and statements tending to make him an object of hatred, ridicule, or disgrace. The Committee eliminated the latter category from the subdivision as lacking sufficient guarantees of reliability. See United States v. Dovico, 380 F.2d 325, 327 nn. 2, 4 (2nd Cir.), cert. denied, 389 U.S. 944 (1967). As for statements against penal interest, the Committee shared the view of the Court that some such statements do possess adequate assurances of reliability and should be admissible. It believed, however, as did the Court, that statements of this type tending to exculpate the accused are more suspect and so should have their admissibility conditioned upon some further provision insuring trustworthiness. The proposal in the Court Rule to add a requirement of simple corroboration was, however, deemed ineffective to accomplish this purpose since the accused's own testimony might suffice while not necessarily increasing the reliability of the hearsay statement. The Committee settled upon the language "unless corroborating circumstances clearly indicate the trustworthiness of the statement" as affording a proper standard and degree of discretion. It was contemplated that the result in such cases as Donnelly v. United States, 228 U.S. 243 (1912), where the circumstances plainly indicated reliability, would be changed. The Committee also added to the Rule the final sentence from the 1971 Advisory Committee draft, designed to codify the doctrine of Bruton v. United States, 391 U.S. 123 (1968). The Committee does not intend to affect the existing exception to the Bruton principle where the codefendant takes the stand and is subject to cross-examination, but believed there was no need to make specific provision for this situation in the Rule, since in that even the declarant would not be "unavailable".

Notes of Committee on the Judiciary, Senate Report No. 93-1277.

Subdivision (a) of rule 804 as submitted by the Supreme Court defined the conditions under which a witness was considered to be unavailable. It was amended in the House.

The purpose of the amendment, according to the report of the House Committee on the Judiciary, is "primarily to require that an attempt be made to depose a witness (as well as to seek his attendance) as a precondition to the witness being unavailable."

Under the House amendment, before a witness is declared unavailable, a party must try to depose a witness (declarant) with respect to dying declarations, declarations against interest, and declarations of pedigree. None of these situations would seem to warrant this needless, impractical and highly restrictive complication. A good case can be made for eliminating the unavailability requirement entirely for declarations against interest cases. [Uniform rule 63(10); Kan. Stat. Anno. 60-460(j); 2A N.J. Stats. Anno. 84-63(10).]

In dying declaration cases, the declarant will usually, though not necessarily, be deceased at the time of trial. Pedigree statements which are admittedly and necessarily based largely on word of mouth are not greatly fortified by a deposition requirement.

Depositions are expensive and time-consuming. In any event, deposition procedures are available to those who wish to resort to them. Moreover, the deposition procedures of the Civil Rules and Criminal Rules are only imperfectly adapted to implementing the amendment. No purpose is served unless the deposition, if taken, may be used in evidence. Under Civil Rule (a)(3) and Criminal Rule 15(e), a deposition, though taken, may not be admissible, and under Criminal Rule 15(a) substantial obstacles exist in the way of even taking a deposition.

For these reasons, the committee deleted the House amendment.

The committee understands that the rule as to unavailability, as explained by the Advisory Committee "contains no requirement that an attempt be made to take the deposition of a declarant." In reflecting the committee's judgment, the statement is accurate insofar as it goes. Where, however, the proponent of the statement, with knowledge of the existence of the statement, fails to confront the declarant with the statement at the taking of the deposition, then the proponent should not, in fairness, be permitted to treat the declarant as "unavailable" simply because the declarant was not amendable to process compelling his attendance at trial. The committee does not consider it necessary to amend the rule to this effect because such a situation abuses, not conforms to, the rule. Fairness would preclude a person from introducing a hearsay statement on a particular issue if the person taking the deposition was aware of the issue at the time of the deposition but failed to depose the unavailable witness on that issue.

Former testimony.—Rule 804(b)(1) as submitted by the Court allowed prior testimony of an unavailable witness to be admissible if the party against whom it is offered or a person "with motive and interest similar" to his had an opportunity to examine the witness.

The House amended the rule to apply only to a party's predecessor in interest. Although the committee recognizes considerable merit to the rule submitted by the Supreme Court, a position which has been advocated by many scholars and judges, we have concluded that the difference between the two versions is not great and we accept the House amendment.

The rule defines those statements which are considered to be against interest and thus of sufficient trustworthiness to be admissible even though hearsay. With regard to the type of interest declared against, the version submitted by the Supreme Court included inter alia, statements tending to subject a declarant to civil liability or to invalidate a claim by him against another. The House struck these provisions as redundant. In view of the conflicting case law construing pecuniary or proprietary interests narrowly so as to exclude, e.g., tort cases, this deletion could be misconstrued.

Three States which have recently codified their rules of evidence have followed the Supreme Court's version of this rule, i.e., that a statement is against interest if it tends to subject a declarant to civil liability. [Nev. Rev. Stats. § 51.345; N. Mex. Stats. (1973 supp.) § 20-4-804(4); West's Wis. Stats. Anno. (1973 supp.) § 908.045(4).]

The committee believes that the reference to statements tending to subject a person to civil liability constitutes a desirable clarification of the scope of the rule. Therefore, we have reinstated the Supreme Court language on this matter.

The Court rule also proposed to expand the hearsay limitation from its present federal limitation to include statements subjecting the declarant to statements tending to make him an object of hatred, ridicule, or disgrace. The House eliminated the latter category from the subdivision as lacking sufficient guarantees of reliability. Although there is considerable support for the admissibility of such statements (all three of the State rules referred to supra, would admit such statements), we accept the deletion by the House.

The House amended this exception to add a sentence making inadmissible a statement or confession offered against the accused in a criminal case, made by a codefendant or other person implicating both himself and the accused. The sentence was added to codify the constitutional principle announced in Bruton v. United States, 391 U.S. 123 (1968). Bruton held that the admission of the extrajudicial hearsay statement of one codefendant inculpating a second codefendant violated the confrontation clause of the sixth amendment.

The committee decided to delete this provision because the basic approach of the rules is to avoid codifying, or attempting to codify, constitutional evidentiary principles, such as the fifth amendment's right against self-incrimination and, here, the sixth amendment's right of confrontation. Codification of a constitutional principle is unnecessary and, where the principle is under development, often unwise. Furthermore, the House provision does not appear to recognize the exceptions to the Bruton rule, e.g. where the codefendant takes the stand and is subject to cross examination; where the accused confessed, see United States v. Mancusi, 404 F.2d 296 (2d Cir. 1968), cert. denied 397 U.S. 942 (1907); where the accused was placed at the scene of the crime, see United States v. Zelker, 452 F.2d 1009 (2d Cir. 1971). For these reasons, the committee decided to delete this provision.

Note to Subdivision (b)(5). See Note to Paragraph (24), Notes of Committee on the Judiciary, Senate Report No. 93-1277, set out as a note under rule 803 of these rules.

Notes of Conference Committee, House Report No. 93-1597. Rule 804 defines what hearsay statements are admissible in evidence if the declarant is unavailable as a witness. The Senate amendments make four changes in the rule.

Subsection (a) defines the term "unavailability as a witness". The House bill provides in subsection (a)(5) that the party who desires to use the statement must be unable to procure the declarant's attendance by process or other reasonable means. In the case of dying declarations, statements against interest and statements of personal or family history, the House bill requires that the proponent must also be unable to procure the declarant's testimony (such as by deposition or interrogatories) by process or other reasonable means. The Senate amendment eliminates this latter provision.

The Conference adopts the provision contained in the House bill.

The Senate amendment to subsection (b)(3) provides that a statement is against interest and not excluded by the hearsay rule when the declarant is unavailable as a witness, if the statement tends to subject a person to civil or criminal liability or renders invalid a claim by him against another. The House bill did not refer specifically to civil liability and to rendering invalid a claim against another. The Senate amendment also deletes from the House bill the provision that subsection (b)(3) does not apply to a statement or confession, made by a codefendant or another, which implicates the accused and the person who made the statement, when that statement or confession is offered against the accused in a criminal case.

The Conference adopts the Senate amendment. The Conferees intend to include within the purview of this rule, statements subjecting a person to civil liability and statements rendering claims invalid. The Conferees agree to delete the provision regarding statements by a codefendant, thereby reflecting the general approach in the Rules of Evidence to avoid attempting to codify constitutional evidentiary principles.

The Senate amendment adds a new subsection, (b)(6) [now (b)(5)], which makes admissible a hearsay statement not specifically covered by any of the five previous subsections, if the statement has equivalent circumstantial guarantees of trustworthiness and if the court determines that (A) the statement is offered as evidence of a material fact; (B) the statement is more probative on the point for which it is offered than any other evidence the proponent can procure through reasonable efforts; and (C) the general purposes of these rules and the interests of justice will best be served by admission of the statement into evidence.

The House bill eliminated a similar, but broader, provision because of the conviction that such a provision injected too much uncertainty into the law of evidence regarding hearsay and impaired the ability of a litigant to prepare adequately for trial.

The Conference adopts the Senate amendment with an amendment that renumbers this subsection and provides that a party intending to request the court to use a statement under this provision must notify any adverse party of this intention as well as of the particulars of the statement, including the name and address of the declarant. This notice must be given sufficiently in advance of the trial or hearing to provide any adverse party with a fair opportunity to prepare the contest the use of the statement.

Notes of Advisory Committee on 1987 amendments. The amendments are technical. No substantive change is intended.

Notes of Advisory Committee on 1997 amendments. Subdivision (b)(5). The contents of Rule 803(24) and Rule 804(b)(5) have been combined and transferred to a new Rule 807. This was done to facilitate additions to Rules 803 and 804. No change in meaning is intended. Subdivision (b)(6). Rule 804(b)(6) has been added to provide that a party forfeits the right to object on hearsay grounds to the admission of a declarant's prior statement when the party's deliberate wrongdoing or acquiescence therein procured the unavailability of the declarant as a witness. This recognizes the need for a prophylactic rule to deal with abhorrent behavior "which strikes at the heart of the system of justice itself." United States v. Mastrangelo, 693 F.2d 269, 273 (2d Cir. 1982), cert. denied, 467 U.S. 1204 (1984). The wrongdoing need not consist of a criminal act. The rule applies to all parties, including the government.

Every circuit that has resolved the question has recognized the principle of forfeiture by misconduct, although the tests for determining whether there is a forfeiture have varied. See. e.g., *United States v. Aguiar*, 975 F.2d 45, 47 (2d Cir. 1992); *United States v. Potamitis,* 739 F.2d 784, 789 (2d Cir.), cert. denied, 469 U.S. 918 (1984); *Steele v. Taylor,* 684 F.2d 1193, 1199 (6th Cir. 1982), cert. denied, 460 U.S. 1053 (1983); *United States v. Balano*, 618 F.2d 624, 629 (10th Cir. 1979), cert. denied, 449 U.S. 840 (1980); *United States v. Carlson,* 547 F.2d 1346, 1358–59 (8th Cir.), cert. denied, 431 U.S. 914 (1977). The foregoing cases apply a preponderance of the evidence standard. Contra *United States v. Thevis,* 665 F.2d 616, 631 (5th Cir.) clear and convincing standard, cert. denied, 459 U.S. 825 (1982). The usual Rule 104(a) preponderance of the evidence standard has been adopted in light of the behavior the new Rule 804(b)(6) seeks to discourage.

Notes of Advisory Committee on 2010 amendments. Subdivision (b)(3). Rule 804(b)(3) has been amended to provide that the corroborating circumstances requirement applies to all declarations against penal interest offered in criminal cases. A number of courts have applied the corroborating circumstances requirement to declarations against penal interest offered by the prosecution, even though the text of the Rule did not so provide. *See, e.g., United States v. Alvarez,* 584 F.2d 694, 701 (5th Cir. 1978) ("by transplanting the language governing exculpatory statements onto the analysis for admitting inculpatory hearsay, a unitary standard is derived which offers the most workable basis for applying Rule 804(b)(3)"); *United States v. Shukri,* 207 F.3d 412 (7th Cir. 2000) (requiring corroborating circumstances for against-penal-interest statements offered by the government). A unitary approach to declarations against penal interest assures both the prosecution and the accused that the Rule will not be abused and that only reliable hearsay statements will be admitted under the exception.

All other changes to the structure and wording of the Rule are intended to be stylistic only. There is no intent to change any other result in any ruling on evidence admissibility.

The Committee found no need to address the relationship between Rule 804(b)(3) and the Confrontation Clause, because the requirements of this exception assure that declarations admissible under it will not be testimonial.

The amendment does not address the use of the corroborating circumstances for declarations against penal interest offered in civil cases.

In assessing whether corroborating circumstances exist, some courts have focused on the credibility of the witness who relates the hearsay statement in court. But the credibility of the witness who relates the statement is not a proper factor for the court to consider in assessing corroborating circumstances. To base admission or exclusion of a hearsay statement on the witness's credibility would usurp the jury's role of determining the credibility of testifying witnesses.

Notes of Advisory Committee on 2011 amendments. The language of Rule 804 has been amended as part of the general restyling of the Evidence Rules to make them more easily understood and to make style and terminology consistent throughout the rules. These changes are intended to be stylistic only. There is no intent to change any result in any ruling on evidence admissibility.

No style changes were made to Rule 804(b)(3), because it was already restyled in conjunction with a substantive amendment, effective December 1, 2010.

Notes of Advisory Committee on 2024 amendments. Rule 804(b)(3)(B) has been amended to require that in assessing whether a statement is supported by "corroborating circumstances that clearly indicate its trustworthiness," the court must consider not only the totality of the circumstances under which the statement was made, but also any evidence supporting or undermining it. While most courts have considered evidence independent of the statement, some courts have refused to do so. The rule now provides for a uniform approach and recognizes that the existence or absence of independent evidence supporting the statement is relevant to, but not necessarily dispositive of, whether a statement that tends to expose the declarant to criminal liability should be admissible under this exception when offered in a criminal case. A court evaluating the admissibility of a third-party confession to a crime, for example, must consider not only circumstances such as the timing and spontaneity of the statement and the third-party declarant's likely motivations in making it. The court must also consider information, if any, supporting the statement, such as evidence placing the third party in the vicinity of the crime. Courts must also consider evidence that undermines the declarant's account.

Although it utilizes slightly different language to fit within the framework of Rule 804(b)(3), the amendment is consistent with the 2019 amendment to Rule 807 that requires courts to consider corroborating evidence in the trustworthiness inquiry under that provision. The amendment is also supported by the legislative history of the corroborating circumstances requirement in Rule 804(b)(3). *See* 1974 House Judiciary Committee Report on Rule 804(b)(3) (adding "corroborating circumstances clearly indicate the trustworthiness of the statement" language and noting that this standard would change the result in cases like *Donnelly v. United States,* 228 U.S. 243 (1913), that excluded a third-party confession exculpating the defendant despite the existence of independent evidence demonstrating the accuracy of the statement).

Amendments:

1975.

Act Dec. 12, 1975, in section catchline, substituted semicolon for colon; and, in subsec. (b)(3), substituted "admissible" for "admissable".

1988.

Act Nov. 18, 1988, in subsec. (a)(5), substituted "subdivision" for "subdivisions".

Rule 805. Hearsay within Hearsay

Hearsay within hearsay is not excluded by the rule against hearsay if each part of the combined statements conforms with an exception to the rule.

HISTORY:

Jan. 2, 1975, P. L. 93-595, § 1, 88 Stat. 1943; April 26, 2011, eff. Dec. 1, 2011.

HISTORY; ANCILLARY LAWS AND DIRECTIVES

Other provisions:

Notes of Advisory Committee on Rules. On principle it scarcely seems open to doubt that the hearsay rule should not call for exclusion of a hearsay statement which includes a further hearsay statement when both conform to the requirements of a hearsay exception. Thus a hospital record might contain an entry of the patient's age based on information furnished by his wife. The hospital record would qualify as a regular entry except that the person who furnished the information was not acting in the routine of the business. However, her statement independently qualifies as a statement of pedigree (if she is unavailable) or as a statement made for purposes of diagnosis or treatment, and hence each link in the chain falls under sufficient assurances. Or, further to illustrate, a dying declaration may incorporate a declaration against interest by another declarant. See McCormick § 290, p. 611.

Notes of Advisory Committee on 2011 amendments. The language of Rule 805 has been amended as part of the restyling of the Evidence Rules to make them more easily understood and to make style and terminology consistent throughout the rules. These changes are intended to be stylistic only. There is no intent to change any result in any ruling on evidence admissibility.

Rule 806. Attacking and Supporting the Declarant's Credibility

When a hearsay statement—or a statement described in Rule 801(d)(2)(C), (D), or (E)—has been admitted in evidence, the declarant's credibility may be attacked, and then supported, by any evidence that would be admissible for those purposes if the declarant had testified as a witness. The court may admit evidence of the declarant's inconsistent statement or conduct, regardless of when it occurred or whether the declarant had an opportunity to explain or deny it. If the party against whom the statement was admitted calls the declarant as a witness, the party may examine the declarant on the statement as if on cross-examination.

HISTORY:

Jan. 2, 1975, P. L. 93-595, § 1, 88 Stat. 1943; March 2, 1987, eff. Oct. 1, 1987; April 11, 1997, eff. Dec. 1, 1997; April 26, 2011, eff. Dec. 1, 2011.

HISTORY; ANCILLARY LAWS AND DIRECTIVES

Other provisions:

Notes of Advisory Committee on Rules. The declarant of a hearsay statement which is admitted in evidence is in effect a witness. His credibility should in fairness be subject to impeachment and support as though he had in fact testified. See Rules 608 and 609. There are however, some special aspects of the impeaching of a hearsay declarant which require consideration. These special aspects center upon impeachment by inconsistent statement, arise from factual differences which exist between the use of hearsay and an actual witness and also between various kinds of hearsay, and involve the question of applying to declarants the general rule disallowing evidence of an inconsistent statement to impeach a witness unless he is afforded an opportunity to deny or explain. See Rule 613(b).

The principle difference between using hearsay and an actual witness is that the inconsistent statement will in the case of the witness almost inevitably of necessity in the nature of things be a *prior* statement, which it is entirely possible and feasible to call to his attention, while in the case of hearsay the inconsistent statement may well be a *subsequent* one, which practically precludes calling it to the attention of the declarant. The result of insisting upon observation of this impossible requirement in the hearsay situation is to deny the opponent, already barred from cross-examination, any benefit of this important technique of impeachment. The writers favor allowing the subsequent statement. McCormick § 37, p. 69; 3 Wigmore § 1033. The cases, however, are divided. Cases allowing the impeachment include People v. Collup, 27 Cal.2d 829, 167 P.2d 714 (1946); People v. Rosoto, 58 Cal.2d 304, 23 Cal.Rptr. 779, 373 P.2d 867 (1962); Carver v. United States, 164 U.S. 694, 17 S.Ct. 228, 41 L.Ed. 602 (1897). Contra, Mattox v. United States, 156 U.S. 237, 15 S.Ct. 337, 39 L.Ed. 409 (1895); People v. Hines, 284 N.Y. 93, 29 N.E.2d 483 (1940). The force of Mattox, where the hearsay was the former testimony of a deceased witness and the denial of use of a subsequent inconsistent statement was upheld, is much diminished by Carver, where the hearsay was a dying declaration and denial of use of a subsequent inconsistent statement resulted in reversal. The difference in the particular brand of hearsay seems unimportant when the inconsistent statement is a subsequent one. True, the opponent is not totally deprived of cross-examination when the hearsay is former testimony or a deposition but he is deprived of cross-examining on the statement or along lines suggested by it. Mr. Justice Shiras, with two justices joining him, dissented vigorously in Mattox.

When the impeaching statement was made *prior* to the hearsay statement, differences in the kinds of hearsay appear which arguably may justify differences in treatment. If the hearsay consisted of a simple statement by the witness, e.g. a dying declaration or a declaration against interest, the feasibility of affording him an opportunity to deny or explain encounters the same practical impossibility as where the statement is a subsequent one, just discussed, although here the impossibility arises from the total absence of anything resembling a hearing at which the matter could be put to him. The courts by a large majority have ruled in favor of allowing the statement to be used under these circumstances. McCormick § 37, p. 69; 3 Wigmore § 1033. If, however, the hearsay consists of former testimony or a deposition, the possibility of calling the prior statement to the attention of the witness or deponent is not ruled out, since the opportunity to cross-examine was available. It might thus be concluded that with former testimony or depositions the conventional foundation should be insisted upon. Most of the cases involve depositions, and Wigmore describes them as divided. 3 Wigmore § 1031. Deposition procedures at best are cumbersome and expensive, and to require the laying of the foundation may impose an undue burden. Under the federal practice, there is no way of knowing with certainty at the time of taking a deposition whether it is merely for discovery or will ultimately end up in evidence. With respect to both former testimony and depositions the possibility exists that knowledge of the statement might not be acquired until after the time of the cross-examination. Moreover, the expanded admissibility of former testimony and depositions under Rule 804(b)(1) calls for a correspondingly expanded approach to impeachment. The rule dispenses with the requirement in all hearsay situations, which is readily administered and best calculated to lead to fair results.

Notice should be taken that Rule 26(f) of the Federal Rules of Civil Procedure, as originally submitted by the Advisory Committee, ended with the following:

"* * * and, without having first called them to the deponent's attention, may show statements contradictory thereto made at any time by the deponent."

This language did not appear in the rule as promulgated in December, 1937. See 4 Moore's Federal Practice PP 26.01 [9], 26.35 (2d ed. 1967). In 1951, Nebraska adopted a provision strongly resembling the one stricken from the federal rule:

"Any party may impeach any adverse deponent by self-contradiction without having laid foundation for such impeachment at the time such deposition was taken." R.S.Neb. § 25-1267.07.

For similar provisions, see Uniform Rule 65; California Evidence Code § 1202; Kansas Code of Civil Procedure § 60-462; New Jersey Evidence Rule 65.

The provision for cross-examination of a declarant upon his hearsay statement is a corollary of general principles of cross-examination. A similar provision is found in California Evidence Code § 1203.

Notes of Committee on the Judiciary, Senate Report No. 93-1277. Rule 906, as passed by the House and as proposed by the Supreme Court provides that whenever a hearsay statement is admitted, the credibility of the declarant of the statement may be attacked, and if attacked may be supported, by any evidence which would be admissible for those purposes if the declarant had testified as a witness. Rule 801 defines what is a hearsay statement. While statements by a person authorized by a party-opponent to make a statement concerning the subject, by the party-opponent's agent or by a coconspirator of a party—see rule 801(d)(2)(c), (d) and (e)—are traditionally defined as exceptions to the hearsay rule, rule 801 defines such admission by a party-opponent as statements which are not hearsay. Consequently, rule 806 by referring exclusively to the admission of hearsay statements, does not appear to allow the credibility of the declarant to be attacked when the declarant is a coconspirator, agent or authorized spokesman. The committee is of the view that such statements should open the declarant to attacks on his credibility. Indeed, the reason such statements are excluded from the operation of rule 806 is likely attributable to the drafting technique used to codify the hearsay rule, viz some statements, instead of being referred to as exceptions to the hearsay rule, are defined as statements which are not hearsay. The phrase "or a statement defined in rule 801(d)(2)(c), (d) and (e)" is added to the rule in order to subject the declarant of such statements, like the declarant of hearsay statements, to attacks on his credibility. [The committee considered it unnecessary to include statements contained in rule 801(d)(2)(A) and (B)—the statement by the party-opponent himself or the statement of which he has manifested his adoption—because the credibility of the party-opponent is always subject to an attack on his credibility].

Notes of Conference Committee, House Report No. 93-1597. The Senate amendment permits an attack upon the credibility of the declarant of a statement if the statement is one by a person authorized by a party-opponent to make a statement concerning the subject, one by an agent of a party-opponent, or one by a coconspirator of the party-opponent, as these statements are defined in Rules 801(d)(2)(C), (D) and (E). The House bill has no such provision.

The Conference adopts the Senate amendment. The Senate amendment conforms the rule to present practice.

Notes of Advisory Committee on 1987 amendments. The amendments are technical. No substantive change is intended.

Notes of Advisory Committee on 1997 amendments. The amendment is technical. No substantive change is intended.

Notes of Advisory Committee on 2011 amendments. The language of Rule 806 has been amended as part of the restyling of the Evidence Rules to make them more easily understood and to make style and terminology consistent throughout the rules. These changes are intended to be stylistic only. There is no intent to change any result in any ruling on evidence admissibility.

Rule 807. Residual Exception

(a) In General. Under the following conditions, a hearsay statement is not excluded by the rule against hearsay even if the statement is not admissible under a hearsay exception in Rule 803 or 804:

(1) the statement is supported by sufficient guarantees of trustworthiness—after considering the totality of circumstances under which it was made and evidence, if any, corroborating the statement; and

(2) it is more probative on the point for which it is offered than any other evidence that the proponent can obtain through reasonable efforts.

(b) Notice. The statement is admissible only if the proponent gives an adverse party reasonable notice of the intent to offer the statement—including its substance and the declarant's name—so that the party has a fair opportunity to meet it. The notice must be provided in writing before the trial or hearing—or in any form during the trial or hearing if the court, for good cause, excuses a lack of earlier notice.

HISTORY:

Added April 11, 1997, eff. Dec. 1, 1997; April 26, 2011, eff. Dec. 1, 2011; April 25, 2019, eff. Dec. 1, 2019.

HISTORY; ANCILLARY LAWS AND DIRECTIVES

Other provisions:

Notes of Advisory Committee on 1997 amendments. The contents of Rule 803(24) and Rule 804(b)(5) have been combined and transferred to a new Rule 807. This was done to facilitate additions to Rules 803 and 804. No change in meaning is intended.

Notes of Advisory Committee on 2011 amendments. The language of Rule 807 has been amended as part of the restyling of the Evidence Rules to make them more easily understood and to make style and terminology consistent throughout the rules. These changes are intended to be stylistic only. There is no intent to change any result in any ruling on evidence admissibility.

Notes of Advisory Committee on 2019 amendments. Rule 807 has been amended to fix a number of problems that the courts have encountered in applying it.

Courts have had difficulty with the requirement that the proffered hearsay carry "equivalent" circumstantial guarantees of trustworthiness. The "equivalence" standard is difficult to apply, given the different types of guarantees of reliability, of varying strength, found among the categorical exceptions (as well as the fact that some hearsay exceptions, e.g., Rule 804(b)(6), are not based on reliability at all). The "equivalence" standard has not served to guide a court's discretion to admit hearsay, because the court is free to choose among a spectrum of exceptions for comparison. Moreover, experience has shown that some statements offered as residual hearsay cannot be compared usefully to any of the categorical exceptions and yet might well be trustworthy. Thus the requirement of an equivalence analysis has been eliminated. Under the amendment, the court should proceed directly to a determination of whether the hearsay is supported by guarantees of trustworthiness. See Rule 104(a). As with any hearsay statement offered under an exception, the court's threshold finding that admissibility requirements are met merely means that the jury may consider the statement and not that it must assume the statement to be true.

The amendment specifically requires the court to consider corroborating evidence in the trustworthiness enquiry. Most courts have required the consideration of corroborating evidence, though some courts have disagreed. The rule now provides for a uniform approach, and recognizes that the existence or absence of corroboration is relevant to, but not dispositive of, whether a statement should be admissible under this exception. Of course, the court must consider not only the existence of corroborating evidence but also the strength and quality of that evidence.

The amendment does not alter the case law prohibiting parties from proceeding directly to the residual exception, without considering the admissibility of the hearsay under Rules 803 and 804. A court is not required to make a finding that no other hearsay exception is applicable. But the opponent cannot seek admission under Rule 807 if it is apparent that the hearsay could be admitted under another exception.

The rule in its current form applies to hearsay "not specifically covered" by a Rule 803 or 804 exception. The amendment makes the rule applicable to hearsay "not admissible under" those exceptions. This clarifies that a court assessing guarantees of trustworthiness may consider whether the statement is a "near-miss" of one of the Rule 803 or 804 exceptions. If the court employs a "near-miss" analysis it should—in addition to evaluating all relevant guarantees of trustworthiness—take into account the reasons that the hearsay misses the admissibility requirements of the standard exception.

In deciding whether the statement is supported by sufficient guarantees of trustworthiness, the court should not consider the credibility of any witness who relates the declarant's hearsay statement in court. The credibility of an in-court witness does not present a hearsay question. To base admission or exclusion of a hearsay statement on the witness's credibility would usurp the jury's role of determining the credibility of testifying witnesses. The rule provides that the focus for trustworthiness is on circumstantial guarantees surrounding the making of the statement itself, as well as any independent evidence corroborating the statement. The credibility of the witness relating the statement is not a part of either enquiry.

Of course, even if the court finds sufficient guarantees of trustworthiness, the independent requirements of the Confrontation Clause must be satisfied if the hearsay statement is offered against a defendant in a criminal case.

The Committee decided to retain the requirement that the proponent must show that the hearsay statement is more probative than any other evidence that the proponent can reasonably obtain. This necessity requirement will continue to serve to prevent the residual exception from being used as a device to erode the categorical exceptions.

The requirements that residual hearsay must be evidence of a material fact and that its admission will best serve the purposes of these rules and the interests of justice have been deleted. These requirements have proved to be superfluous in that they are already found in other rules. *See* Rules 102, 401.

The notice provision has been amended to make four changes in the operation of the rule:

- First, the amendment requires the proponent to disclose the "substance" of the statement. This term is intended to require a description that is sufficiently specific under the circumstances to allow the opponent a fair opportunity to meet the evidence. See Rule 103(a)(2) (requiring the party making an offer of proof to inform the court of the "substance" of the evidence).
- Second, the prior requirement that the declarant's address must be disclosed has been deleted. That requirement was nonsensical when the declarant was unavailable, and unnecessary in the many cases in which the declarant's address was known or easily obtainable. If prior disclosure of the declarant's address is critical and cannot be obtained by the opponent through other means, then the opponent can seek relief from the court.
- Third, the amendment requires that the pretrial notice be in writing—which is satisfied by notice in electronic form. See Rule 101(b)(6). Requiring the notice to be in writing provides certainty and reduces arguments about whether notice was actually provided.
- Finally, the pretrial notice provision has been amended to provide for a good cause exception. Most courts have applied a good cause exception under Rule 807 even though the rule in its current form does not provide for it, while some courts have read the rule as it was written.

Experience under the residual exception has shown that a good cause exception is necessary in certain limited situations. For example, the proponent may not become aware of the existence of the hearsay statement until after the trial begins, or the proponent may plan to call a witness who without warning becomes unavailable during trial, and the proponent might then need to resort to residual hearsay.

The rule retains the requirement that the opponent receive notice in a way that provides a fair opportunity to meet the evidence. When notice is provided during trial after a finding of good cause, the court may need to consider protective measures, such as a continuance, to assure that the opponent is not prejudiced.

ARTICLE IX. AUTHENTICATION AND IDENTIFICATION

Rule 901. Authenticating or Identifying Evidence

(a) In General. To satisfy the requirement of authenticating or identifying an item of evidence, the proponent must produce evidence sufficient to support a finding that the item is what the proponent claims it is.

(b) Examples. The following are examples only—not a complete list—of evidence that satisfies the requirement:

(1) *Testimony of a Witness with Knowledge.* Testimony that an item is what it is claimed to be.

(2) *Nonexpert Opinion About Handwriting.* A nonexpert's opinion that handwriting is genuine, based on a familiarity with it that was not acquired for the current litigation.

(3) *Comparison by an Expert Witness or the Trier of Fact.* A comparison with an authenticated specimen by an expert witness or the trier of fact.

(4) *Distinctive Characteristics and the Like.* The appearance, contents, substance, internal patterns, or other distinctive characteristics of the item, taken together with all the circumstances.

(5) *Opinion About a Voice.* An opinion identifying a person's voice—whether heard firsthand or through mechanical or electronic transmission or recording—based on hearing the voice at any time under circumstances that connect it with the alleged speaker.

(6) *Evidence About a Telephone Conversation.* For a telephone conversation, evidence that a call was made to the number assigned at the time to:

(A) a particular person, if circumstances, including self-identification, show that the person answering was the one called; or

(B) a particular business, if the call was made to a business and the call related to business reasonably transacted over the telephone.

(7) *Evidence About Public Records.* Evidence that:

(A) a document was recorded or filed in a public office as authorized by law; or

(B) a purported public record or statement is from the office where items of this kind are kept.

(8) *Evidence About Ancient Documents or Data Compilations.* For a document or data compilation, evidence that it:

(A) is in a condition that creates no suspicion about its authenticity;

(B) was in a place where, if authentic, it would likely be; and

(C) is at least 20 years old when offered.

(9) *Evidence About a Process or System.* Evidence describing a process or system and showing that it produces an accurate result.

(10) *Methods Provided by a Statute or Rule.* Any method of authentication or identification allowed by a federal statute or a rule prescribed by the Supreme Court.

HISTORY:

Jan. 2, 1975, P. L. 93-595, § 1, 88 Stat. 1943; April 26, 2011, eff. Dec. 1, 2011.

HISTORY; ANCILLARY LAWS AND DIRECTIVES

Other provisions:

Notes of Advisory Committee on Rules. Subdivision (a). Authentication and identification represent a special aspect of relevancy. Michael and Adler, Real Proof, 5 Vand.L.Rev. 344, 362 (1952); McCormick §§ 179, 185; Morgan, Basic Problems of Evidence 378. (1962). Thus a telephone conversation may be irrelevant because on an unrelated topic or because the speaker is not identified. The latter aspect is the one here involved. Wigmore describes the need for authentication as "an inherent logical necessity." 7 Wigmore § 2129, p. 564.

This requirement of showing authenticity or identity fails in the category of relevancy dependent upon fulfillment of a condition of fact and is governed by the procedure set forth in Rule 104(b).

The common law approach to authentication of documents has been criticized as an "attitude of agnosticism," McCormick, Cases on Evidence 388, n. 4 (3rd ed. 1956), as one which "departs sharply from men's customs in ordinary affairs," and as presenting only a slight obstacle to the introduction of forgeries in comparison to the time and expense devoted to proving genuine writings which correctly show their origin on their face, McCormick § 185, pp. 395, 396. Today, such available procedures as requests to admit and pretrial conference afford the means of eliminating much of the need for authentication or identification. Also, significant inroads upon the traditional insistence on authentication and identification have been made by accepting as at least prima facie genuine items of the kind treated in Rule 902, infra. However, the need for suitable methods of proof still remains, since criminal cases pose their own obstacles to the use of preliminary procedures, unforeseen contingencies may arise, and cases of genuine controversy will still occur.

Subdivision (b). The treatment of authentication and identification draws largely upon the experience embodied in the common law and in statutes to furnish illustrative applications of the general principle set forth in subdivision (a). The examples are not intended as an exclusive enumeration of allowable methods but are meant to guide and suggest, leaving room for growth and development in this area of the law.

The examples relate for the most part to documents, with some attention given to voice communications and computer print-outs. As Wigmore noted, no special rules have been developed for authenticating chattels. Wigmore, Code of Evidence § 2086 (3rd ed. 1942).

It should be observed that compliance with requirements of authentication or identification by no means assures admission of an item into evidence, as other bars, hearsay for example, may remain.

Example (1). Example (1) contemplates a broad spectrum ranging from testimony of a witness who was present at the signing of a document to testimony establishing narcotics as taken from an accused and accounting for custody through the period until trial, including laboratory analysis. See California Evidence Code § 1413, eyewitness to signing.

Example (2). Example (2) states conventional doctrine as to lay identification of handwriting, which recognizes that a sufficient familiarity with the handwriting of another person may be acquired by seeing him write, by exchanging correspondence, or by other means, to afford a basis for identifying it on subsequent occasions. McCormick § 189. See also California Evidence Code § 1416. Testimony based upon familiarity acquired for purposes of the litigation is reserved to the expert under the example which follows.

Example (3). The history of common law restrictions upon the technique of proving or disproving the genuineness of a disputed specimen of handwriting through comparison with a genuine specimen, by either the testimony of expert witnesses or direct viewing by the triers themselves, is detailed in 7 Wigmore §§ 1991–1994. In breaking away, the English Common Law Procedure Act of 1854, 17 and 18 Viet., c. 125, § 27, cautiously allowed expert or trier to use exemplars "proved to the satisfaction of the judge to be genuine" for purposes of comparison. The language found its way into numerous statutes in this country, e.g., California Evidence Code §§ 1417, 1418. While explainable as a measure of prudence in the process of breaking with precedent in the handwriting situation, the reservation to the judge of the question of the genuineness of exemplars and the imposition of an unusually high standard of persuasion are at variance with the general treatment of relevancy which depends upon fulfillment of a condition of fact. Rule 104(b). No similar attitude is found in other comparison situations, e.g., ballistics comparison by jury, as in Evans v. Commonwealth, 230 Ky. 411, 19 S.W.2d 1091 (1929), or by experts, Annot. 26 A.L.R.2d 892, and no reason appears for its continued existence in handwriting cases. Consequently Example (3) sets no higher standard for handwriting specimens and treats all comparison situations alike, to be governed by Rule 104(b). This approach is consistent with 28 U.S.C. § 1731: "The admitted or proved handwriting of any person shall be admissible, for purposes of comparison, to determine genuineness of other handwriting attributed to such person."

Precedent supports the acceptance of visual comparison as sufficiently satisfying preliminary authentication requirements for admission in evidence. Brandon v. Collins, 267 F.2d 731 (2d Cir. 1959); Wausau Sulphate Fibre Co. v. Commissioner of Internal Revenue, 61 F.2d 879 (7th Cir. 1932); Desimone v. United States, 227 F.2d 864 (9th Cir. 1955).

Example (4). The characteristics of the offered item itself, considered in the light of circumstances, afford authentication techniques in great variety. Thus a document or telephone conversation may be shown to have emanated from a particular person by virtue of its disclosing knowledge of facts known peculiarly to him; Globe Automatic Sprinkler Co. v. Braniff, 89 Okl. 105, 214 P. 127 (1923); California Evidence Code § 1421; similarly, a letter may be authenticated by content and circumstances indicating it was in reply to a duly authenticated one. McCormick § 192; California Evidence Code § 1420. Language patterns may indicate authenticity or its opposite. Magnuson v. State, 187 Wis. 122, 203 N.W. 749 (1925); Arens and Meadow, Psycholinguistics and the Confession Dilemma, 56 Colum.L.Rev. 19 (1956).

Example (5). Since aural voice identification is not a subject of expert testimony, the requisite familiarity may be acquired either before or after the particular speaking which is the subject of the identification, in this respect resembling visual identification of a person rather than identification of handwriting. Cf. Example (2), supra, People v. Nichols, 378 Ill. 487, 38 N.E.2d 766 (1942); McGuire v. State, 200 Md. 601, 92 A.2d 582 (1952); State v. McGee, 336 Mo. 1082, 83 S.W.2d 98 (1935).

Example (6). The cases are in agreement that a mere assertion of his identity by a person talking on the telephone is not sufficient evidence of the authenticity of the conversation and that additional evidence of his identity is required. The additional evidence need not fall in any set pattern. Thus the content of his statements or the reply technique, under Example (4), supra, or voice identification under Example (5), may furnish the necessary foundation. Outgoing calls made by the witness involve additional factors bearing upon authenticity. The calling of a number assigned by the telephone company reasonably supports the assumption that the listing is correct and that the number is the one reached. If the number is that of a place of business, the mass of authority allows an ensuing conversation if it relates to business reasonably transacted over the telephone, on the theory that the maintenance of the telephone connection is an invitation to do business without further identification. Matton v. Hoover Co., 350 Mo. 506, 166 S.W.2d 557 (1942); City of Pawhuska v. Crutchfield, 147 Okl. 4. 293 P. 1095 (1930); Zurich General Acc. & Liability Ins. Co. v. Baum, 159 Va. 404, 165 S.E. 518 (1932). Otherwise, some additional circumstance of identification of the speaker is required. The authorities divide on the question whether the self-identifying statement of the person answering suffices. Example (6) answers in the affirmative on the assumption that usual conduct respecting telephone calls furnish adequate assurances of regularity, bearing in mind that the entire matter is open to exploration before the trier of fact. In general, see McCormick § 193; 7 Wigmore § 2155; Annot., 71 A.L.R. 5, 105. id. 326.

Example (7). Public records are regularly authenticated by proof of custody, without more. McCormick § 191; 7 Wigmore §§ 2158, 2159. The example extends the principle to include data stored in computers and similar methods, of which increasing use in the public records area may be expected. See California Evidence Code §§ 1532, 1600.

Example (8). The familiar ancient document rule of the common law is extended to include data stored electronically or by other similar means. Since the importance of appearance diminishes in this situation, the importance of custody or place where found increases correspondingly. This expansion is necessary in view of the widespread use of methods of storing data in forms other than conventional written records.

Any time period selected is bound to be arbitrary. The common law period of 30 years is here reduced to 20 years, with some shift of emphasis from the probable unavailability of witnesses to the unlikeliness of a still viable fraud after the lapse of time. The shorter period is specified in the English Evidence Act of 1938, 1 & 2 Geo. 6, c. 28, and in Oregon R.S. 1963, § 41.360(34). See also the numerous statutes prescribing periods of less than 30 years in the case of recorded documents. 7 Wigmore § 2143.

The application of Example (8) is not subject to any limitation to title documents or to any requirement that possession, in the case of a title document, has been consistent with the document. See McCormick § 190.

Example (9). Example (9) is designed for situations in which the accuracy of a result is dependent upon a process or system which produces it. X-rays afford a familiar instance. Among more recent developments is the computer, as to which see Transport Indemnity Co. v. Seib, 178 Neb. 253, 132 N.W.2d 871 (1965); State v. Veres, 7 Ariz.App. 117, 436 P.2d 629 (1968); Merrick v. United States Rubber Co., 7 Ariz.App. 433, 440 P.2d 314 (1968); Freed, Computer Print-Outs as Evidence, 16 Am.Jur. Proof of Facts 273; Symposium, Law and Computers in the Mid-Sixties, ALI-ABA (1966); 37 Albany L.Rev. 61 (1967). Example (9) does not, of course, foreclose taking judicial notice of the accuracy of the process or system.

Example (10). The example makes clear that methods of authentication provided by Act of Congress and by the Rules of Civil and Criminal Procedure or by Bankruptcy Rules are not intended to be superseded. Illustrative are the provisions for authentication of official records in Civil Procedure Rule 44 and Criminal Procedure Rule 27, for authentication of records of proceedings by court reporters in 28 U.S.C. § 753(b) and Civil Procedure Rule 80(c), and for authentication of depositions in Civil Procedure Rule 30(f).

Notes of Advisory Committee on 2011 amendments. The language of Rule 901 has been amended as part of the restyling of the Evidence Rules to make them more easily understood and to make style and terminology consistent throughout the rules. These changes are intended to be stylistic only. There is no intent to change any result in any ruling on evidence admissibility.

Rule 902. Evidence That Is Self-Authenticating

The following items of evidence are self-authenticating; they require no extrinsic evidence of authenticity in order to be admitted:

(1) *Domestic Public Documents That Are Sealed and Signed.* A document that bears:

(A) a seal purporting to be that of the United States; any state, district, commonwealth, territory, or insular possession of the United States; the former Panama Canal Zone; the Trust Territory of the Pacific Islands; a political subdivision of any of these entities; or a department, agency, or officer of any entity named above; and

(B) a signature purporting to be an execution or attestation.

(2) *Domestic Public Documents That Are Not Sealed but Are Signed and Certified.* A document that bears no seal if:

(A) it bears the signature of an officer or employee of an entity named in Rule 902(1)(A); and

(B) another public officer who has a seal and official duties within that same entity certifies under seal—or its equivalent—that the signer has the official capacity and that the signature is genuine.

(3) *Foreign Public Documents.* A document that purports to be signed or attested by a person who is authorized by a foreign country's law to do so. The document must be accompanied by a final certification that certifies the genuineness of the signature and official position of the signer or attester—or of any foreign official whose certificate of genuineness relates to the signature or attestation or is in a chain of certificates of genuineness relating to the signature or attestation. The certification may be made by a secretary of a United States embassy or legation; by a consul general, vice consul, or consular agent of the United States; or by a diplomatic or consular official of the foreign country assigned or accredited to the United States. If all parties have been given a reasonable

opportunity to investigate the document's authenticity and accuracy, the court may, for good cause, either:

(A) order that it be treated as presumptively authentic without final certification; or

(B) allow it to be evidenced by an attested summary with or without final certification.

(4) *Certified Copies of Public Records.* A copy of an official record—or a copy of a document that was recorded or filed in a public office as authorized by law—if the copy is certified as correct by:

(A) the custodian or another person authorized to make the certification; or

(B) a certificate that complies with Rule 902(1), (2), or (3), a federal statute, or a rule prescribed by the Supreme Court.

(5) *Official Publications.* A book, pamphlet, or other publication purporting to be issued by a public authority.

(6) *Newspapers and Periodicals.* Printed material purporting to be a newspaper or periodical.

(7) *Trade Inscriptions and the Like.* An inscription, sign, tag, or label purporting to have been affixed in the course of business and indicating origin, ownership, or control.

(8) *Acknowledged Documents.* A document accompanied by a certificate of acknowledgment that is lawfully executed by a notary public or another officer who is authorized to take acknowledgments.

(9) *Commercial Paper and Related Documents.* Commercial paper, a signature on it, and related documents, to the extent allowed by general commercial law.

(10) *Presumptions Under a Federal Statute.* A signature, document, or anything else that a federal statute declares to be presumptively or prima facie genuine or authentic.

(11) *Certified Domestic Records of a Regularly Conducted Activity.* The original or a copy of a domestic record that meets the requirements of Rule 803(6)(A)–(C), as shown by a certification of the custodian or another qualified person that complies with a federal statute or a rule prescribed by the Supreme Court. Before the trial or hearing, the proponent must give an adverse party reasonable written notice of the intent to offer the record—and must make the record and certification available for inspection—so that the party has a fair opportunity to challenge them.

(12) *Certified Foreign Records of a Regularly Conducted Activity.* In a civil case, the original or a copy of a foreign record that meets the requirements of Rule 902(11), modified as follows: the certification, rather than complying with a federal statute or Supreme Court rule, must be signed in a manner that, if falsely made, would subject the maker to a criminal penalty in the country where the certification is signed. The proponent must also meet the notice requirements of Rule 902(11).

(13) *Certified Records Generated by an Electronic Process or System.* A record generated by an electronic process or system that produces an accurate result, as shown by a certification of a qualified person that complies with the certification requirements of Rule 902(11) or (12). The proponent must also meet the notice requirements of Rule 902(11).

(14) *Certified Data Copied from an Electronic Device, Storage Medium, or File.* Data copied from an electronic device, storage medium, or file, if authenticated by a process of digital identification, as shown by a certification of a qualified person that complies with the certification requirements of Rule 902(11) or (12). The proponent also must meet the notice requirements of Rule 902(11).

HISTORY:

Jan. 2, 1975, P. L. 93-595, § 1, 88 Stat. 1944; March 2, 1987, eff. Oct. 1, 1987; April 25, 1988, eff. Nov. 1, 1988; April 17, 2000, eff. Dec. 1, 2000; April 26, 2011, eff. Dec. 1, 2011; April 27, 2017, eff. Dec. 1, 2017.

HISTORY; ANCILLARY LAWS AND DIRECTIVES

Other provisions:

Notes of Advisory Committee on Rules. Case law and statutes have, over the years, developed a substantial body of instances in which authenticity is taken as sufficiently established for purposes of admissibility without extrinsic evidence to that effect, sometimes for reasons of policy but perhaps more often because practical considerations reduce the possibility of unauthenticity to a very small dimension. The present rule collects and incorporates these situations, in some instances expanding them to occupy a larger area which their underlying considerations justify. In no instance is the opposite party foreclosed from disputing authenticity.

Paragraph (1). The acceptance of documents bearing a public seal and signature, most often encountered in practice in the form of acknowledgments or certificates authenticating copies of public records, is actually of broad application. Whether theoretically based in whole or in part upon judicial notice, the practical underlying considerations are that forgery is a crime and detection is fairly easy and certain. 7 Wigmore § 2161, p. 638; California Evidence Code § 1452. More than 50 provisions for judicial notice of official seals are contained in the United States Code.

Paragraph (2). While statutes are found which raise a presumption of genuineness of purported official signatures in the absence of an official seal, 7 Wigmore § 2167; California Evidence Code § 1453, the greater ease of effecting a forgery under these circumstances is apparent. Hence this paragraph of the rule calls for authentication by an officer who has a seal. Notarial acts by members of the armed forces and other special situations are covered in paragraph (10).

Paragraph (3) provides a method for extending the presumption of authenticity to foreign official documents by a procedure of certification. It is derived from Rule 44(a)(2) of the Rules of Civil Procedure but is broader in applying to public documents rather than being limited to public records.

Paragraph (4). The common law and innumerable statutes have recognized the procedure of authenticating copies of public records by certificate. The certificate qualifies as a public document, receivable as authentic when in conformity with paragraph (1), (2), or (3). Rule 44(a) of the Rules of Civil Procedure and Rule 27 of the Rules of Criminal Procedure have provided authentication procedures of this nature for both domestic and foreign public records. It will be observed that the certification procedure here provided extends only to public records, reports, and recorded documents, all including data compilations, and does not apply to public documents generally. Hence documents provable when presented in original form under paragraphs (1), (2), or (3) may not be provable by certified copy under paragraph (4).

Paragraph (5). Dispensing with preliminary proof of the genuineness of purportedly official publications, most commonly encountered in connection with statutes, court reports, rules, and regulations, has been greatly enlarged by statutes and decisions. 5 Wigmore § 1684. Paragraph (5), it will be noted, does not confer admissibility upon all official publications; it merely provides a means whereby their authenticity may be taken as established for purposes of admissibility. Rule 44(a) of the Rules of Civil Procedure has been to the same effect.

Paragraph (6). The likelihood of forgery of newspapers or periodicals is slight indeed. Hence no danger is apparent in receiving them. Establishing the authenticity of the publication may, of course, leave still open questions of authority and responsibility for items therein contained. See 7 Wigmore § 2150. Cf. 39 U.S.C. § 4005(b), public advertisement prima facie evidence of agency of person named, in postal fraud order proceeding; Canadian Uniform Evidence Act, Draft of 1936, printed copy of newspaper prima facie evidence that notices or advertisements were authorized.

Paragraph (7). Several factors justify dispensing with preliminary proof of genuineness of commercial and mercantile labels and the like. The risk of forgery is minimal. Trademark infringement involves serious penalties. Great efforts are devoted to inducing the public to buy in reliance on brand names, and substantial protection is given them. Hence the fairness of this treatment finds recognition in the cases. Curtiss Candy Co. v. Johnson, 163 Miss. 426, 141 So. 762 (1932), Baby Ruth candy bar; Doyle v. Continental Baking Co., 262 Mass. 516, 160 N.E. 325 (1928), loaf of bread; Weiner v. Mager & Throne, Inc., 167 Misc 338, 3 N.Y.S.2d 918 (1938), same. And see W.Va. Code 1966, § 47-3-5, trade-mark on bottle prima facie evidence of ownership. Contra, Keegan v. Green Giant Co., 150 Me. 283, 110 A.2d 599 (1954); Murphy v. Campbell Soup Co., 62 F.2d 564 (1st Cir. 1933). Cattle brands have received similar acceptance in the western states. Rev.Code Mont.1947, § 46-606; State v. Wolfley, 75 Kan. 406, 89 P. 1046 (1907); Annot., 11 L.R.A. (N.S.) 87. Inscriptions on trains and vehicles are held to be prima facie evidence of ownership or control. Pittsburgh, Ft. W. & C. Ry. v. Callaghan, 157 Ill. 406, 41 N.E. 909 (1895); 9 Wigmore § 2510a. See also the provision of 19 U.S.C. § 1615(2) that marks, labels, brands, or stamps indicating foreign origin are prima facie evidence of foreign origin of merchandise.

Paragraph (8). In virtually every state, acknowledged title documents are receivable in evidence without further proof. Statutes are collected in 5 Wigmore § 1676. If this authentication suffices for documents of the importance of those affecting titles, logic scarcely permits denying this method when other kinds of documents are involved. Instances of broadly inclusive statutes are California Evidence Code § 1451 and N.Y.CPLR 4538, McKinney's Consol. Laws 1963.

Paragraph (9). Issues of the authenticity of commercial paper in federal courts will usually arise in diversity cases, will involve an element of a cause of action or defense, and with respect to presumptions and burden of proof will be controlled by Erie Railroad Co. v. Tompkins, 304 U.S. 64, 58 S.Ct. 817, 82 L.Ed. 1188 (1938). Rule 302, supra. There may, however, be questions of authenticity involving lesser segments of a case or the case may be one governed by federal common law. Clearfield Trust Co. v. United States, 318 U.S. 363, 63 S.Ct. 573, 87 L.Ed. 838 (1943). Cf. United States v. Yazell, 382 U.S. 341, 86 S.Ct. 500, 15 L.Ed.2d 404 (1966). In these situations, resort to the useful authentication provisions of the Uniform Commercial Code is provided for. While the phrasing is in terms of "general commercial law," in order to avoid the potential complication inherent in borrowing local statutes, today one would have difficulty in determining the general commercial law without referring to the Code. See Williams v Walker-Thomas-Furniture Co., 121 U.S.App.D.C. 315, 350 F.2d 445 (1965). Pertinent Code provisions are sections 1-202, 3-307, and 3-510, dealing with third-party documents, signatures on negotiable instruments, protests, and statements of dishonor.

Paragraph (10). The paragraph continues in effect dispensations with preliminary proof of genuineness provided in various Acts of Congress. See, for example, 10 U.S.C. § 936, signature, without seal, together with title, prima facie evidence of authenticity of acts of certain military personnel who are given notarial power; 15 U.S.C. § 77f(a), signature on SEC registration presumed genuine; 26 U.S.C. § 6064, signature to tax return prima facie genuine.

Notes of Committee on the Judiciary, House Report No. 93-650. Rule 902(8) as submitted by the Court referred to certificates of acknowledgment "under the hand and seal of" a notary public or other officer authorized by law to take acknowledgments. The Committee amended the Rule to eliminate the requirement, believed to be inconsistent with the law in some States, that a notary public must affix a seal to a document acknowledged before him. As amended the Rule merely requires that the document be executed in the manner prescribed by State law.

The Committee approved Rule 902(9) as submitted by the Court. With respect to the meaning of the phrase "general commercial law", the Committee intends that the Uniform Commercial Code, which has been adopted in virtually every State, will be followed generally, but that federal commercial law will apply where federal commercial paper is involved. See Clearfield Trust Co. v. United States, 318 U.S. 363 (1943). Further, in those instances in which the issues are governed by Erie R. Co. v. Tompkins, 304 U.S. 64 (1938), State law will apply irrespective of whether it is the Uniform Commercial Code.

Notes of Advisory Committee on 1987 amendments. The amendments are technical. No substantive change is intended.

Notes of Advisory Committee on 1988 amendments. The amendment is technical. No substantive change is intended.

Notes of Advisory Committee on 2000 amendments. The amendment adds two new paragraphs to the rule on self-authentication. It sets forth a procedure by which parties can authenticate certain records of regularly conducted activity, other than through the testimony of a foundation witness. See the amendment to Rule 803(6). 18 U.S.C. § 3505 currently provides a means for certifying foreign records of regularly conducted activity in criminal cases, and this amendment is intended to establish a similar procedure for domestic records, and for foreign records offered in civil cases.

A declaration that satisfies 28 U.S.C. § 1746 would satisfy the declaration requirement of Rule 902(11), as would any comparable certification under oath.

The notice requirement in Rules 902(11) and (12) is intended to give the opponent of the evidence a full opportunity to test the adequacy of the foundation set forth in the declaration.

Notes of Advisory Committee on 2011 amendments. The language of Rule 902 has been amended as part of the restyling of the Evidence Rules to make them more easily understood and to make style and terminology consistent throughout the rules. These changes are intended to be stylistic only. There is no intent to change any result in any ruling on evidence admissibility.

Notes of Advisory Committee on 2017 Amendments. The amendment sets forth a procedure by which parties can authenticate certain electronic evidence other than through the testimony of a foundation witness. As with the provisions on business records in Rules 902(11) and (12), the Committee has found that the expense and inconvenience of producing a witness to authenticate an item of electronic evidence is often unnecessary. It is often the case that a party goes to the expense of producing an authentication witness, and then the adversary either stipulates authenticity before the witness is called or fails to challenge the authentication testimony once it is presented. The amendment provides a procedure under which the parties can determine in advance of trial whether a real challenge to authenticity will be made, and can then plan accordingly.

Nothing in the amendment is intended to limit a party from establishing authenticity of electronic evidence on any ground provided in these Rules, including through judicial notice where appropriate.

A proponent establishing authenticity under this Rule must present a certification containing information that would be sufficient to establish authenticity were that information provided by a witness at trial. If the certification provides information that would be insufficient to authenticate the record if the certifying person testified, then authenticity is not established under this Rule. The Rule specifically allows the authenticity foundation that satisfies Rule 901(b)(9) to be established by a certification rather than the testimony of a live witness.

The reference to the "certification requirements of Rule 902(11) or (12)" is only to the procedural requirements for a valid certification. There is no intent to require, or permit, a certification under this Rule to prove the requirements of Rule 803(6). Rule 902(13) is solely limited to authentication, and any attempt to satisfy a hearsay exception must be made independently.

A certification under this Rule can establish only that the proffered item has satisfied the admissibility requirements for authenticity. The opponent remains free to object to admissibility of the proffered item on other grounds—including hearsay, relevance, or in criminal cases the right to confrontation. For example, assume that a plaintiff in a defamation case offers what purports to be a printout of a webpage on which a defamatory statement was made. Plaintiff offers a certification under this Rule in which a qualified person describes the process by which the webpage was retrieved. Even if that certification sufficiently establishes that the webpage is authentic, defendant remains free to object that the statement on the webpage was not placed there by defendant. Similarly, a certification authenticating a computer output, such as a spreadsheet, does not preclude an objection that the information produced is unreliable—the authentication establishes only that the output came from the computer.

A challenge to the authenticity of electronic evidence may require technical information about the system or process at issue, including possibly retaining a forensic technical expert; such factors will affect whether the opponent has a fair opportunity to challenge the evidence given the notice provided.

The reference to Rule 902(12) is intended to cover certifications that are made in a foreign country.

Rule 903. Subscribing Witness's Testimony

A subscribing witness's testimony is necessary to authenticate a writing only if required by the law of the jurisdiction that governs its validity.

HISTORY:

Jan. 2, 1975, P. L. 93-595, § 1, 88 Stat. 1945; April 26, 2011, eff. Dec. 1, 2011.

HISTORY; ANCILLARY LAWS AND DIRECTIVES

Other provisions:

Notes of Advisory Committee on Rules. The common law required that attesting witnesses be produced or accounted for. Today the requirement has generally been abolished except with respect to documents which must be attested to be valid, e.g. wills in some states. McCormick § 188. Uniform Rule 71; California Evidence Code § 1411; Kansas Code of Civil Procedure § 60-468; New Jersey Evidence Rule 71; New York CPLR Rule 4537.

Notes of Advisory Committee on 2011 amendments. The language of Rule 903 has been amended as part of the restyling of the Evidence Rules to make them more easily understood and to make style and terminology consistent throughout the rules. These changes are intended to be stylistic only. There is no intent to change any result in any ruling on evidence admissibility.

ARTICLE X. CONTENTS OF WRITINGS, RECORDINGS, AND PHOTOGRAPHS

Rule

Rule 1001. Definitions that Apply to This Article

In this article:

(a) A "writing" consists of letters, words, numbers, or their equivalent set down in any form.

(b) A "recording" consists of letters, words, numbers, or their equivalent recorded in any manner.

(c) A "photograph" means a photographic image or its equivalent stored in any form.

(d) An "original" of a writing or recording means the writing or recording itself or any counterpart intended to have the same effect by the person who executed or issued it. For electronically stored information, "original" means any printout—or other output readable by sight—if it accurately reflects the information. An "original" of a photograph includes the negative or a print from it.

(e) A "duplicate" means a counterpart produced by a mechanical, photographic, chemical, electronic, or other equivalent process or technique that accurately reproduces the original.

HISTORY:

Jan. 2, 1975, P. L. 93-595, § 1, 88 Stat. 1945; April 26, 2011, eff. Dec. 1, 2011.

HISTORY; ANCILLARY LAWS AND DIRECTIVES

Other provisions:

Notes of Advisory Committee on Rules. In an earlier day, when discovery and other related procedures were strictly limited, the misleading named "best evidence rule" afforded substantial guarantees against inaccuracies and fraud by its insistence upon production of original documents. The great enlargement of the scope of discovery and related procedures in recent times has measurably reduced the need for the rule. Nevertheless important areas of usefulness persist: discovery of documents outside the jurisdiction may require substantial outlay of time and money; the unanticipated document may not practically be discoverable; criminal cases have built-in limitations on discovery. Cleary and Strong, The Best Evidence Rule: An Evaluation in Context, 51 Iowa L.Rev. 825 (1966).

Paragraph (1). Traditionally the rule requiring the original centered upon accumulations of data and expressions affecting legal relations set forth in words and figures. This meant that the rule was one essentially related to writings. Present day techniques have expanded methods of storing data, yet the essential form which the information ultimately assumes for usable purposes is words and figures. Hence the considerations underlying the rule dictate its expansion to include computers, photographic systems, and other modern developments.

Paragraph (3). In most instances, what is an original will be self-evident and further refinement will be unnecessary. However, in some instances particularized definition is required. A carbon copy of a contract executed in duplicate becomes an original, as does a sales ticket carbon copy given to a customer. While strictly speaking the original of a photograph might be thought to be only the negative, practicality and common usage require that any print from the negative be regarded as an original. Similarly, practicality and usage confer the status of original upon any computer printout. Transport Indemnity Co. v. Seib, 178 Neb. 253, 132 N.W.2d 871 (1965).

Paragraph (4). The definition describes "copies" produced by methods possessing an accuracy which virtually eliminates the possibility of error. Copies thus produced are given the status of originals in large measure by Rule 1003, infra. Copies subsequently produced manually, whether handwritten or typed, are not within the definition. It should be noted that what is an original for some purposes may be a duplicate for others. Thus a bank's microfilm record of checks cleared is the original as a record. However, a print offered as a copy of a check whose contents are in controversy is a duplicate. This result is substantially consistent with 28 U.S.C. § 1732(b). Compare 26 U.S.C. § 7513(c), giving full status as originals to photographic reproductions of tax returns and other documents, made by authority of the Secretary of the Treasury, and 44 U.S.C. § 399(a), giving original status to photographic copies in the National Archives.

Notes of Committee on the Judiciary, House Report No. 93-650. The Committee amended this Rule expressly to include "video tapes" in the definition of "photographs."

Notes of Advisory Committee on 2011 amendments. The language of Rule 1001 has been amended as part of the restyling of the Evidence Rules to make them more easily understood and to make style and terminology consistent throughout the rules. These changes are intended to be stylistic only. There is no intent to change any result in any ruling on evidence admissibility.

Rule 1002. Requirement of the Original

An original writing, recording, or photograph is required in order to prove its content unless these rules or a federal statute provides otherwise.

HISTORY:

Jan. 2, 1975, P. L. 93-595, § 1, 88 Stat. 1946; April 26, 2011, eff. Dec. 1, 2011.

HISTORY; ANCILLARY LAWS AND DIRECTIVES

Other provisions:

Notes of Advisory Committee on Rules. The rule is the familiar one requiring production of the original of a document to prove its contents, expanded to include writings, recordings, and photographs, as defined in Rule 1001(1) and (2), supra.

Application of the rule requires a resolution of the question whether contents are sought to be proved. Thus an event may be proved by nondocumentary evidence, even though a written record of it was made. If, however, the event is sought to be proved by the written record, the rule applies. For example, payment may be proved without producing the written receipt which was given. Earnings may be proved without producing books of account in which they are entered. McCormick § 198; 4 Wigmore § 1245. Nor does the rule apply to testimony that books or records have been examined and found not to contain any reference to a designated matter.

The assumption should not be made that the rule will come into operation on every occasion when use is made of a photograph in evidence. On the contrary, the rule will seldom apply to ordinary photographs. In most instances a party wishes to introduce the item and the question raised is the propriety of receiving it in evidence. Cases in which an offer is made of the testimony of a witness as to what he saw in a photograph or motion picture, without producing the same, are most unusual. The usual course is for a witness on the stand to identify the photograph or motion picture as a correct representation of events which he saw or of a scene with which he is familiar. In fact he adopts the picture as his testimony, or, in common parlance, uses the picture to illustrate his testimony. Under these circumstances, no effort is made to prove the contents of the picture, and the rule is inapplicable. Paradis, The Celluloid Witness, 37 U.Colo.L. Rev. 235, 249–251 (1965).

On occasion, however, situations arise in which contents are sought to be proved. Copyright, defamation, and invasion of privacy by photograph or motion picture falls in this category. Similarly as to situations in which the picture is offered as having independent probative value, e.g. automatic photograph of bank robber. See People v. Doggett, 83 Cal.App.2d 405, 188 P.2d 792 (1948) photograph of defendants engaged in indecent act; Mouser and Philbin, Photographic Evidence—Is There a Recognized Basis for Admissibility? 8 Hastings L.J. 310 (1957). The most commonly encountered of this latter group is of course, the X-ray, with substantial authority calling for production of the original. Daniels v. Iowa City, 191 Iowa 811, 183 N.W. 415 (1921); Cellamare v. Third Acc. Transit Corp., 273 App.Div. 260, 77 N.Y.S.2d 91 (1948); Patrick & Tilman v. Matkin, 154 Okl. 232, 7 P.2d 414 (1932); Mendoza v. Rivera, 78 P.R.R. 569 (1955).

It should be noted, however, that Rule 703, supra, allows an expert to give an opinion based on matters not in evidence, and the present rule must be read as being limited accordingly in its application. Hospital records which may be admitted as business records under Rule 803(6) commonly contain reports interpreting X-rays by the staff radiologist, who qualifies as an expert, and these reports need not be excluded from the records by the instant rule.

The reference to Acts of Congress is made in view of such statutory provisions as 26 U.S.C. § 7513, photographic reproductions of tax returns and documents, made by authority of the Secretary of the Treasury, treated as originals, and 44 U.S.C. § 399(a), photographic copies in National Archives treated as originals.

Notes of Advisory Committee on 2011 amendments. The language of Rule 1002 has been amended as part of the restyling of the Evidence Rules to make them more easily understood and to make style and terminology consistent throughout the rules. These changes are intended to be stylistic only. There is no intent to change any result in any ruling on evidence admissibility.

Rule 1003. Admissibility of Duplicates

A duplicate is admissible to the same extent as the original unless a genuine question is raised about the original's authenticity or the circumstances make it unfair to admit the duplicate.

HISTORY:

Jan. 2, 1975, P. L. 93-595, § 1, 88 Stat. 1946; April 26, 2011, eff. Dec. 1, 2011.

HISTORY; ANCILLARY LAWS AND DIRECTIVES

Other provisions:

Notes of Advisory Committee on Rules. When the only concern is with getting the words or other contents before the court with accuracy and precision, then a counterpart serves equally as well as the original, if the counterpart is the product of a method which insures accuracy and genuineness. By definition in Rule 1001(4), supra, a "duplicate" possesses this character.

Therefore, if no genuine issue exists as to authenticity and no other reason exists for requiring the original, a duplicate is admissible under the rule. This position finds support in the decisions, Myrick v. United States, 332 F.2d 279 (5th Cir. 1964), no error in admitting photostatic copies of checks instead of original microfilm in absence of suggestion to trial judge that photostats were incorrect; Johns v. United States, 323 F.2d 421 (5th Cir. 1963), not error to admit concededly accurate tape recording made from original wire recording; Sauget v. Johnston, 315 F.2d 816 (9th Cir. 1963), not error to admit copy of agreement when opponent had original and did not on appeal claim any discrepancy. Other reasons for requiring the original may be present when only a part of the original is reproduced and the remainder is needed for cross-examination or may disclose matters qualifying the part offered or otherwise useful to the opposing party. United States v. Alexander, 326 F.2d 736 (4th Cir. 1964). And see Toho Bussan Kaisha, Ltd. v. American President Lines, Ltd., 265 F.2d 418, 76 A.L.R.2d 1344 (2d Cir. 1959).

Notes of Committee on the Judiciary, House Report No. 93-650. The Committee approved this Rule in the form submitted by the Court, with the expectation that the courts would be liberal in deciding that a "genuine question is raised as to the authenticity of the original."

Notes of Advisory Committee on 2011 amendments. The language of Rule 1003 has been amended as part of the restyling of the Evidence Rules to make them more easily understood and to make style and terminology consistent throughout the rules. These changes are intended to be stylistic only. There is no intent to change any result in any ruling on evidence admissibility.

Rule 1004. Admissibility of Other Evidence of Content

An original is not required and other evidence of the content of a writing, recording, or photograph is admissible if:

(a) all the originals are lost or destroyed, and not by the proponent acting in bad faith;

(b) an original cannot be obtained by any available judicial process;

(c) the party against whom the original would be offered had control of the original; was at that time put on notice, by pleadings or otherwise, that the original would be a subject of proof at the trial or hearing; and fails to produce it at the trial or hearing; or

(d) the writing, recording, or photograph is not closely related to a controlling issue.

HISTORY:

Jan. 2, 1975, P. L. 93-595, § 1, 88 Stat. 1946; March 2, 1987, eff. Oct. 1, 1987; April 26, 2011, eff. Dec. 1, 2011.

HISTORY; ANCILLARY LAWS AND DIRECTIVES

Other provisions:

Notes of Advisory Committee on Rules. Basically the rule requiring the production of the original as proof of contents has developed as a rule of preference: if failure to produce the original is satisfactory explained, secondary evidence is admissible. The instant rule specifies the circumstances under which production of the original is excused.

The rule recognizes no "degrees" of secondary evidence. While strict logic might call for extending the principle of preference beyond simply preferring the original, the formulation of a hierarchy of preferences and a procedure for making it effective is believed to involve unwarranted complexities. Most, if not all, that would be accomplished by an extended scheme of preferences will, in any event, be achieved through the normal motivation of a party to present the most convincing evidence possible and the arguments and procedures available to his opponent if he does not. Compare McCormick § 207.

Paragraph (1). Loss or destruction of the original unless due to bad faith of the proponent, is a satisfactory explanation of nonproduction. McCormick § 201.

Paragraph (2). When the original is in the possession of a third person, inability to procure it from him by resort to process or other judicial procedure is sufficient explanation of nonproduction. Judicial procedure includes subpoena duces tecum as an incident to the taking of a deposition in another jurisdiction. No further showing is required. See McCormick § 202.

Paragraph (3). A party who has an original in his control has no need for the protection of the rule if put on notice that proof of contents will be made. He can ward off secondary evidence by offering the original. The notice procedure here provided is not to be confused with orders to produce or other discovery procedures, as the purpose of the procedure under this rule is to afford the opposite party an opportunity to produce the original, not to compel him to do so. McCormick § 203.

Paragraph (4). While difficult to define with precision, situations arise in which no good purpose is served by production of the original. Examples are the newspaper in an action for the price of publishing defendant's advertisement, Foster-Holcomb Investment Co. v. Little Rock Publishing Co., 151 Ark. 449, 236 S.W. 597 (1922), and the streetcar transfer of plaintiff claiming status as a passenger, Chicago City Ry. Co. v. Carroll, 206 Ill. 318, 68 N.E. 1087 (1903). Numerous cases are collected in McCormick § 200, p. 412, n. 1.

Notes of Committee on the Judiciary, House Report No. 93-650. The Committee approved Rule 1004(1) in the form submitted to Congress. However, the Committee intends that loss or destruction of an original by another person at the instigation of the proponent should be considered as tantamount to loss or destruction in bad faith by the proponent himself.

Notes of Advisory Committee on 1987 amendments. The amendments are technical. No substantive change is intended.

Notes of Advisory Committee on 2011 amendments. The language of Rule 1004 has been amended as part of the restyling of the Evidence Rules to make them more easily understood and to make style and terminology consistent throughout the rules. These changes are intended to be stylistic only. There is no intent to change any result in any ruling on evidence admissibility.

Rule 1005. Copies of Public Records to Prove Content

The proponent may use a copy to prove the content of an official record—or of a document that was recorded or filed in a public office as authorized by law—if these conditions are met: the record or document is otherwise admissible; and the copy is certified as correct in accordance with Rule 902(4) or is testified to be correct by a witness who has compared it with the original. If no such copy can be obtained by reasonable diligence, then the proponent may use other evidence to prove the content.

HISTORY:

Jan. 2, 1975, P. L. 93-595, § 1, 88 Stat. 1946; April 26, 2011, eff. Dec. 1, 2011.

HISTORY; ANCILLARY LAWS AND DIRECTIVES

Other provisions:

Notes of Advisory Committee on Rules. Public records call for somewhat different treatment. Removing them from their usual place of keeping would be attended by serious inconvenience to the public and to the custodian. As a consequence judicial decisions and statutes commonly hold that no explanation need be given for failure to produce the original of a public record. McCormick § 204; 4 Wigmore §§ 1215–1228. This blanket dispensation from producing or accounting for the original would open the door to the introduction of every kind of secondary evidence of contents of public records were it not for the preference given certified or compared copies. Recognition of degrees of secondary evidence in this situation is an appropriate *quid pro quo* for not applying the requirement of producing the original.

The provisions of 28 U.S.C. § 1733(b) apply only to departments or agencies of the United States. The rule, however, applies to public records generally and is comparable in scope in this respect to Rule 44(a) of the Rules of Civil Procedure.

Notes of Advisory Committee on 2011 amendments. The language of Rule 1005 has been amended as part of the restyling of the Evidence Rules to make them more easily understood and to make style and terminology consistent throughout the rules. These changes are intended to be stylistic only. There is no intent to change any result in any ruling on evidence admissibility.

Rule 1006. Summaries to Prove Content

(a) Summaries of Voluminous Materials Admissible as Evidence. The court may admit as evidence a summary, chart, or calculation offered to prove the content of voluminous admissible writings, recordings, or photographs that cannot be conveniently examined in court, whether or not they have been introduced into evidence.

(b) Procedures. The proponent must make the underlying originals or duplicates available for examination or copying, or both, by other parties at a reasonable time and place. And the court may order the proponent to produce them in court.

(c) Illustrative Aids Not Covered. A summary, chart, or calculation that functions only as an illustrative aid is governed by Rule 107.

HISTORY:

Jan. 2, 1975, P. L. 93-595, § 1, 88 Stat. 1946; April 26, 2011, eff. Dec. 1, 2011; April 2, 2024, eff. Dec. 1, 2024.

HISTORY; ANCILLARY LAWS AND DIRECTIVES

Other provisions:

Notes of Advisory Committee on Rules. The admission of summaries of voluminous books, records, or documents offers the only practicable means of making their contents available to judge and jury. The rule recognizes this practice, with appropriate safeguards. 4 Wigmore § 1230.

Notes of Advisory Committee on 2011 amendments. The language of Rule 1006 has been amended as part of the restyling of the Evidence Rules to make them more easily understood and to make style and terminology consistent throughout the rules. These changes are intended to be stylistic only. There is no intent to change any result in any ruling on evidence admissibility.

Notes of Advisory Committee on 2024 amendments. Rule 1006 has been amended to correct misperceptions about the operation of the rule by some courts. Some courts have mistakenly held that a Rule 1006 summary is "not evidence" and that it must be accompanied by limiting instructions cautioning against its substantive use. But the purpose of Rule 1006 is to permit alternative proof of the content of writings, recordings, or photographs too voluminous to be conveniently examined in court. To serve their intended purpose, therefore, Rule 1006 summaries must be admitted as substantive evidence and the rule has been amended to clarify that a party may offer a Rule 1006 summary "as evidence." The court may not instruct the jury that a summary admitted under this rule is not to be considered as evidence.

Rule 1006 has also been amended to clarify that a properly supported summary may be admitted into evidence whether or not the underlying voluminous materials reflected in the summary have been admitted. Some courts have mistakenly held that the underlying voluminous writings or recordings themselves must be admitted into evidence before a Rule 1006 summary may be used. Because Rule 1006 allows alternate proof of materials too voluminous to be conveniently examined during trial proceedings, admission of the underlying voluminous materials is not required and the amendment so states. Conversely, there are courts that deny resort to a properly supported Rule 1006 summary because the underlying writings or recordings—or a portion of them—have been admitted into evidence. Summaries that are otherwise admissible under Rule 1006 are not rendered inadmissible because the underlying documents have been admitted, in whole or in part, into evidence. In most cases, a Rule 1006 chart may be the only evidence the trier of fact will examine concerning a voluminous set of documents. In some instances, however, the summary may be admitted in addition to the underlying documents.

A summary admissible under Rule 1006 must also pass the balancing test of Rule 403. For example, if the summary does not accurately reflect the underlying voluminous evidence, or if it is argumentative, its probative value may be substantially outweighed by the risk of unfair prejudice or confusion.

Consistent with the original rule, the amendment requires that the proponent of a Rule 1006 summary make the underlying voluminous records available to other parties at a reasonable time and place. The trial judge has discretion in determining the reasonableness of the production in each case but must ensure that all parties have a fair opportunity to evaluate the summary. *Cf.* Fed. R. Evid. 404(b)(3) and 807(b).

Although Rule 1006 refers to materials too voluminous to be examined "in court" and permits the trial judge to order production of underlying materials "in court," the rule applies to virtual proceedings just as it does to proceedings conducted in person in a courtroom.

The amendment draws a distinction between summaries of voluminous admissible information offered to prove a fact, and illustrations offered solely to assist the trier of fact in understanding the evidence. The former are subject to the strictures of Rule 1006. The latter are illustrative aids, which are now regulated by Rule 107.

Rule 1007. Testimony or Statement of a Party to Prove Content

The proponent may prove the content of a writing, recording, or photograph by the testimony, deposition, or written statement of the party against whom the evidence is offered. The proponent need not account for the original.

HISTORY:

Jan. 2, 1975, P. L. 93-595, § 1, 88 Stat. 1947; March 2, 1987, eff. Oct. 1, 1987; April 26, 2011, eff. Dec. 1, 2011.

HISTORY; ANCILLARY LAWS AND DIRECTIVES

Other provisions:

Notes of Advisory Committee on Rules. While the parent case, Slatterie v. Pooley, 6 M. & W. 664, 151 Eng. Rep. 579 (Exch. 1840), allows proof of contents by evidence of an oral admission by the party against whom offered, without accounting for nonproduction of the original, the risk of inaccuracy is substantial and the decision is at odds with the purpose of the rule giving preference to the original. See 4 Wigmore § 1255. The instant rule follows Professor McCormick's suggestion of limiting this use of admissions to those made in the course of giving testimony or in writing. McCormick § 208, p. 424. The limitation, of course, does not call for excluding evidence of an oral admission when nonproduction of the original has been accounted for and secondary evidence generally has become admissible. Rule 1004, supra.

A similar provision is contained in New Jersey Evidence Rule 70(1)(h).

Notes of Advisory Committee on 1987 amendments. The amendment is technical. No substantive change is intended.

Notes of Advisory Committee on 2011 amendments. The language of Rule 1007 has been amended as part of the restyling of the Evidence Rules to make them more easily understood and to make style and terminology consistent throughout the rules. These changes are intended to be stylistic only. There is no intent to change any result in any ruling on evidence admissibility.

Rule 1008. Functions of the Court and Jury

Ordinarily, the court determines whether the proponent has fulfilled the factual conditions for admitting other evidence of the content of a writing, recording, or photograph under Rule 1004 or 1005. But in a jury trial, the jury determines—in accordance with Rule 104(b)—any issue about whether:

(a) an asserted writing, recording, or photograph ever existed;

(b) another one produced at the trial or hearing is the original; or

(c) other evidence of content accurately reflects the content.

HISTORY:

Jan. 2, 1975, P. L. 93-595, § 1, 88 Stat. 1947; April 26, 2011, eff. Dec. 1, 2011.

HISTORY; ANCILLARY LAWS AND DIRECTIVES

Other provisions:

Notes of Advisory Committee on Rules. Most preliminary questions of fact in connection with applying the rule preferring the original as evidence of contents are for the judge, under the general principles announced in Rule 104, supra. Thus, the question whether the loss of the originals has been established, or of the fulfillment of other conditions specified in Rule 1004, supra, is for the judge. However, questions may arise which go beyond the mere administration of the rule preferring the original and into the merits of the controversy. For example, plaintiff offers secondary evidence of the contents of an alleged contract, after first introducing evidence of loss of the original, and defendant counters with evidence that no such contract was ever executed. If the judge decides that the contract was never executed and excludes the secondary evidence, the case is at an end without ever going to the jury on a central issue. Levin, Authentication and Content of Writings, 10 Rutgers L.Rev. 632, 644 (1956). The latter portion of the instant rule is designed to insure treatment of these situations as raising jury questions. The decision is not one for uncontrolled discretion of the jury but is subject to the control exercised generally by the judge over jury determinations. See Rule 104(b), supra.

For similar provisions, see Uniform Rule 70(2); Kansas Code of Civil Procedure § 60-467(b); New Jersey Evidence Rule 70(2), (3).

Notes of Advisory Committee on 2011 amendments. The language of Rule 1008 has been amended as part of the restyling of the Evidence Rules to make them more easily understood and to make style and terminology consistent throughout the rules. These changes are intended to be stylistic only. There is no intent to change any result in any ruling on evidence admissibility.

ARTICLE XI. MISCELLANEOUS RULES

Rule

Rule 1101. Applicability of the Rules

(a) To Courts and Judges. These rules apply to proceedings before:

- United States district courts;
- United States bankruptcy and magistrate judges;
- United States courts of appeals;
- the United States Court of Federal Claims; and
- the district courts of Guam, the Virgin Islands, and the Northern Mariana Islands.

(b) To Cases and Proceedings. These rules apply in:

- civil cases and proceedings, including bankruptcy, admiralty, and maritime cases;
- criminal cases and proceedings; and
- contempt proceedings, except those in which the court may act summarily.

(c) Rules on Privilege. The rules on privilege apply to all stages of a case or proceeding.

(d) Exceptions. These rules—except for those on privilege—do not apply to the following:

(1) the court's determination, under Rule 104(a), on a preliminary question of fact governing admissibility;

(2) grand-jury proceedings; and

(3) miscellaneous proceedings such as:

- extradition or rendition;
- issuing an arrest warrant, criminal summons, or search warrant;
- a preliminary examination in a criminal case;
- sentencing;
- granting or revoking probation or supervised release; and
- considering whether to release on bail or otherwise.

(e) Other Statutes and Rules. A federal statute or a rule prescribed by the Supreme Court may provide for admitting or excluding evidence independently from these rules.

HISTORY:

Jan. 2, 1975, P. L. 93-595, § 1, 88 Stat. 1947; Dec. 12, 1975, P. L. 94-149, § 1(14), 89 Stat. 806; Nov. 6, 1978, P. L. 95-598, Title II, §§ 251, 252, 92 Stat. 2673; Apr. 2, 1982, P. L. 97-164, Title I, Part A, § 142, 96 Stat. 45; March 2, 1987, eff. Oct. 1, 1987; April 25, 1988, eff. Nov. 1, 1988; Nov. 18, 1988, P. L. 100-690, Title VII, Subtitle B, § 7075(c), 102 Stat. 4405; April 22, 1993, eff. Dec. 1, 1993; April 26, 2011, eff. Dec. 1, 2011.

HISTORY; ANCILLARY LAWS AND DIRECTIVES

Other provisions:

Notes of Advisory Committee on Rules. Subdivision (a). The various enabling acts contain differences in phraseology in their descriptions of the courts over which the Supreme Court's power to make rules of practice and procedure extends. The act concerning civil actions, as amended in 1966, refers to "the district courts * * * of the United States in civil actions, including admiralty and maritime cases. * * * 28 U.S.C. § 2072, Pub. L. 89-773, § 1, 80 Stat. 1323. The bankruptcy authorization is for rules of practice and procedure "under the Bankruptcy Act."28 U.S.C. § 2075, Pub. L. 88-623, § 1, 78 Stat. 1001. The Bankruptcy Act in turn creates bankruptcy courts of "the United States district courts and the district courts of the Territories and possessions to which this title is or may hereafter be applicable."11 U.S.C. §§ 1(10), 11(a). The provision as to criminal rules up to and including verdicts applies to "criminal cases and proceedings to punish for criminal contempt of court in the United States district courts, in the district courts for the districts of the Canal Zone and Virgin Islands, in the Supreme Court of Puerto

Rico, and in proceedings before United States magistrates."18 U.S.C. § 3771.

These various provisions do not in terms describe the same courts. In congressional usage the phrase "district courts of the United States," without further qualification, traditionally has included the district courts established by Congress in the states under Article III of the Constitution, which are "constitutional" courts, and has not included the territorial courts created under Article IV, Section 3, Clause 2, which are "legislative" courts. Hornbuckle v. Toombs, 85 U.S. 648, 21 L.Ed. 966 (1873). However, any doubt as to the inclusion of the District Court for the District of Columbia in the phrase is laid at rest by the provisions of the Judicial Code constituting the judicial districts, 28 U.S.C. § 81 et seq. creating district courts therein, Id. § 132, and specifically providing that the term "district court of the United States" means the courts so constituted. Id. § 451. The District of Columbia is included. Id. § 88. Moreover, when these provisions were enacted, reference to the District of Columbia was deleted from the original civil rules enabling act. 28 U.S.C. § 2072. Likewise Puerto Rico is made a district, with a district court, and included in the term. Id. § 119. The question is simply one of the extent of the authority conferred by Congress. With respect to civil rules it seems clearly to include the district courts in the states, the District Court for the District of Columbia, and the District Court for the District of Puerto Rico.

The bankruptcy coverage is broader. The bankruptcy courts include "the United States district courts," which includes those enumerated above. Bankruptcy courts also include "the district courts of the Territories and possessions to which this title is or may hereafter be applicable." 11 U.S.C. §§ 1(10), 11(a). These courts include the district courts of Guam and the Virgin Islands. 48 U.S.C. §§ 1424(b), 1615. Professor Moore points out that whether the District Court for the District of the Canal Zone is a court of bankruptcy "is not free from doubt in view of the fact that no other statute expressly or inferentially provides for the applicability of the Bankruptcy Act in the Zone." He further observes that while there seems to be little doubt that the Zone is a territory or possession within the meaning of the Bankruptcy Act, 11 U.S.C. § 1(10), it must be noted that the appendix to the Canal Zone Code of 1934 did not list the Act among the laws of the United States applicable to the Zone. 1 Moore's Collier on Bankruptcy P 1.10, pp. 67, 72, n. 25 (14th ed. 1967). The Code of 1962 confers on the district court jurisdiction of:

"(4) actions and proceedings involving laws of the United States applicable to the Canal Zone; and.

"(5) other matters and proceedings wherein jurisdiction is conferred by this Code or any other law." Canal Zone Code, 1962, Title 3, § 141.

Admiralty jurisdiction is expressly conferred. Id. § 142. General powers are conferred on the district court, "if the course of proceeding is not specifically prescribed by this Code, by the statute, or by applicable rule of the Supreme Court of the United States * * *" Id. § 279. Neither these provisions nor § 1(10) of the Bankruptcy Act ("district courts of the Territories and possessions to which this title is or may hereafter be applicable") furnishes a satisfactory answer as to the status of the District Court for the District of the Canal Zone as a court of bankruptcy. However, the fact is that this court exercises no bankruptcy jurisdiction in practice.

The criminal rules enabling act specifies United States district courts, district courts for the districts of the Canal Zone and the Virgin Islands, the Supreme Court of the Commonwealth of Puerto Rico, and proceedings before United States commissioners. Aside from the addition of commissioners, now magistrates, this scheme differs from the bankruptcy pattern in that it makes no mention of the District Court of Guam but by specific mention removes the Canal Zone from the doubtful list.

The further difference in including the Supreme Court of the Commonwealth of Puerto Rico seems not to be significant for present purposes, since the Supreme Court of the Commonwealth of Puerto Rico is an appellate court. The Rules of Criminal Procedure have not been made applicable to it, as being unneeded and inappropriate, Rule 54(a) of the Federal Rules of Criminal Procedure, and the same approach is indicated with respect to rules of evidence.

If one were to stop at this point and frame a rule governing the applicability of the proposed rules of evidence in terms of the authority conferred by the three enabling acts, an irregular pattern would emerge as follows:

Civil actions, including admiralty and maritime cases—district courts in the states, District of Columbia, and Puerto Rico.

Bankruptcy—same as civil actions, plus Guam and Virgin Islands.

Criminal cases—same as civil actions, plus Canal Zone and Virgin Islands (but not Guam).

This irregular pattern need not, however, be accepted. Originally the Advisory Committee on the Rules of Civil Procedure took the position that, although the phrase "district courts of the United States" did not include territorial courts, provisions in the organic laws of Puerto Rico and Hawaii would make the rules applicable to the district courts thereof, though this would not be so as to Alaska, the Virgin Islands, or the Canal Zone, whose organic acts contained no corresponding provisions. At the suggestion of the Court, however, the Advisory Committee struck from its notes a statement to the above effect. 2 Moore's Federal Practice P 1.07 (2nd ed. 1967); 1 Barron and Holtzoff, Federal Practice and Procedure § 121 (Wright ed. 1960). Congress thereafter by various enactments provided that the rules and future amendments thereto should apply to the district courts of Hawaii, 53 Stat. 841 (1939), Puerto Rico, 54 Stat. 22 (1940), Alaska, 63 Stat. 445 (1949), Guam, 64 Stat. 384– 390 (1950), and the Virgin Islands, 68 Stat. 497, 507 (1954). The original enabling act for rules of criminal procedure specifically mentioned the district courts of the Canal Zone and the Virgin Islands. The Commonwealth of Puerto Rico was blanketed in by creating its court a "district court of the United States" as previously described. Although Guam is not mentioned in either the enabling act or in the expanded definition of "district court of the United States," the Supreme Court in 1956 amended Rule 54(a) to state that the Rules of Criminal Procedure are applicable in Guam. The Court took this step following the enactment of legislation by Congress in 1950 that rules theretofore or thereafter promulgated by the Court in civil cases, admiralty, criminal cases and bankruptcy should apply to the District Court of Guam, 48 U.S.C. § 1424(b), and two Ninth Circuit decisions upholding the applicability of the Rules of Criminal Procedure to Guam. Pugh v. United States, 212 F.2d 761 (9th Cir. 1954);

Hatchett v. Guam, 212 F.2d 767 (9th Cir. 1954); Orfield, The Scope of the Federal Rules of Criminal Procedure, 38 U. of Det.L.J. 173, 187 (1960).

From this history, the reasonable conclusion is that Congressional enactment of a provision that rules and future amendments shall apply in the courts of a territory or possession is the equivalent of mention in an enabling act and that a rule on scope and applicability may properly be drafted accordingly. Therefore the pattern set by Rule 54 of the Federal Rules of Criminal Procedure is here followed.

The substitution of magistrates in lieu of commissioners is made in pursuance of the Federal Magistrates Act, P.L. 90-578, approved October 17, 1968, 82 Stat. 1107.

Subdivision (b) is a combination of the language of the enabling acts, supra, with respect to the kinds of proceedings in which the making of rules is authorized. It is subject to the qualifications expressed in the subdivisions which follow.

Subdivision (c), singling out the rules of privilege for special treatment, is made necessary by the limited applicability of the remaining rules.

Subdivision (d). The rule is not intended as an expression as to when due process or other constitutional provisions may require an evidentiary hearing. Paragraph (1) restates, for convenience, the provisions of the second sentence of Rule 104(a), supra. See Advisory Committee's Note to that rule.

(2) While some states have statutory requirements that indictments be based on "legal evidence," and there is some case law to the effect that the rules of evidence apply to grand jury proceedings, 1 Wigmore § 4(5), the Supreme Court has not accepted this view. In Costello v. United States, 350 U.S. 359, 76 S.Ct. 406, 100 L.Ed. 397 (1965), the Court refused to allow an indictment to be attacked, for either constitutional or policy reasons, on the ground that only hearsay evidence was presented.

"It would run counter to the whole history of the grand jury institution, in which laymen conduct their inquiries unfettered by technical rules. Neither justice nor the concept of a fair trial requires such a change." Id. at 364. The rule as drafted does not deal with the evidence required to support an indictment.

(3) The rule exempts preliminary examinations in criminal cases. Authority as to the applicability of the rules of evidence to preliminary examinations has been meagre and conflicting. Goldstein, The State and the Accused: Balance of Advantage in Criminal Procedure, 69 Yale L.J. 1149, 1168, n. 53 (1960); Comment, Preliminary Hearings on Indictable Offenses in Philadelphia, 106 U. of Pa.L.Rev. 589, 592–593 (1958). Hearsay testimony is, however, customarily received in such examinations. Thus in a Dyer Act case, for example, an affidavit may properly be used in a preliminary examination to prove ownership of the stolen vehicle, thus saving the victim of the crime the hardship of having to travel twice to a distant district for the sole purpose of testifying as to ownership. It is believed that the extent of the applicability of the Rules of Evidence to preliminary examinations should be appropriately dealt with by the Federal Rules of Criminal Procedure which regulate those proceedings.

Extradition and rendition proceedings are governed in detail by statute. 18 U.S.C. §§ 3181– 3195. They are essentially administrative in character. Traditionally the rules of evidence have not applied. 1 Wigmore § 4(6). Extradition proceedings are accepted from the operation of the Rules of Criminal Procedure. Rule 54(b)(5) of Federal Rules of Criminal Procedure.

The rules of evidence have not been regarded as applicable to sentencing or probation proceedings, where great reliance is placed upon the presentence investigation and report. Rule 32(c) of the Federal Rules of Criminal Procedure requires a presentence investigation and report in every case unless the court otherwise directs. In Williams v. New York, 337 U.S. 241, 69 S.Ct. 1079, 93 L.Ed. 1337 (1949), in which the judge overruled a jury recommendation of life imprisonment and imposed a death sentence, the Court said that due process does not require confrontation or cross-examination in sentencing or passing on probation, and that the judge has broad discretion as to the sources and types of information relied upon. Compare the recommendation that the substance of all derogatory information be disclosed to the defendant, in A.B.A. Project on Minimum Standards for Criminal Justice, Sentencing Alternatives and Procedures § 4.4, Tentative Draft (1967, Sobeloff, Chm.). Williams was adhered to in Specht v. Patterson, 386 U.S. 605, 87 S.Ct. 1209, 18 L.Ed.2d 326 (1967), but not extended to a proceeding under the Colorado Sex Offenders Act, which was said to be a new charge leading in effect to punishment, more like the recidivist statutes where opportunity must be given to be heard on the habitual criminal issue.

Warrants for arrest, criminal summonses, and search warrants are issued upon complaint or affidavit showing probable cause. Rules 4(a) and 41(c) of the Federal Rules of Criminal Procedure. The nature of the proceedings makes application of the formal rules of evidence inappropriate and impracticable.

Criminal contempts are punishable summarily if the judge certifies that he saw or heard the contempt and that it was committed in the presence of the court. Rule 42(a) of the Federal Rules of Criminal Procedure. The circumstances which preclude application of the rules of evidence in this situation are not present, however, in other cases of criminal contempt.

Proceedings with respect to release on bail or otherwise do not call for application of the rules of evidence. The governing statute specifically provides:

"Information stated in, or offered in connection with, any order entered pursuant to this section need not conform to the rules pertaining to the admissibility of evidence in a court of law." 18 U.S.C.A. § 3146(f). This provision is consistent with the type of inquiry contemplated in A.B.A. Project on Minimum Standards for Criminal Justice, Standards Relating to Pretrial Release, § 4.5(b), (c), p. 16 (1968). The references to the weight of the evidence against the accused, in Rule 46(a)(1), (c) of the Federal Rules of Criminal Procedure and in 18 U.S.C.A. § 3146(b), as a factor to be considered, clearly do not have in view evidence introduced at a hearing.

The rule does not exempt habeas corpus proceedings. The Supreme Court held in Walker v. Johnston, 312 U.S. 275, 61 S.Ct. 574, 85 L.Ed. 830 (1941), that the practice of disposing of matters of fact on affidavit, which prevailed in some circuits, did not "satisfy the command of the statute that the judge shall proceed 'to determine the facts of the case, by hearing the testimony and arguments.'" This view accords with the emphasis in Townsend v. Sain, 372 U.S. 293, 83 S.Ct. 745, 9 L.Ed.2d 770 (1963), upon trial-type proceedings, Id. 311, 83 S.Ct. 745, with demeanor evidence as a significant factor, Id. 322, 83 S.Ct. 745, in applications by state prisoners aggrieved by unconstitutional detentions. Hence subdivision (e) applies the rules to habeas corpus proceedings to the extent not inconsistent with the statute.

Subdivision (e). In a substantial number of special proceedings, ad hoc evaluation has resulted in the promulgation of particularized evidentiary provisions, by Act of Congress or by rule adopted by the Supreme Court. Well adapted to the particular proceedings, though not apt candidates for inclusion in a set of general rules, they are left undisturbed. Otherwise, however, the rules of evidence are applicable to the proceedings enumerated in the subdivision.

Notes of Committee on the Judiciary, House Report No. 93-650. Subdivision (a) as submitted to the Congress, in stating the courts and judges to which the Rules of Evidence apply, omitted the Court of Claims and commissioners of that Court. At the request of the Court of Claims, the Committee amended the Rule to include the Court and its commissioners within the purview of the Rules.

Subdivision (b) was amended merely to substitute positive law citations for those which were not.

Application of 1978 amendments. Act Nov. 6, 1978, P. L. 95-598, Title IV, § 405(b), 92 Stat. 2685, provided:

"During the transition period [commencing on Oct. 1, 1979, ending on Mar. 31, 1984], the amendments made by sections 241, 243, 250, and 252 of this Act [adding 28 USCS §§ 1471 et. seq., amending 28 USCS §§ prec. 1, 1869(f), adding 28 USCS § 2256, amending 28 USCS prec. § 2241, Rules of Evidence, Rule 1101] shall apply to the courts of bankruptcy continued by section 404(a) of this Act [11 USCS prec. § 101 note] the same as such amendments apply to the United States bankruptcy courts established under section 201 of this Act [adding 28 USCS §§ 151 et seq. amending 28 USCS prec. § 1].".

Notes of Advisory Committee on 1987 amendments. Subdivision (a) is amended to delete the reference to the District Court for the District of the Canal Zone, which no longer exists, and to add the District Court for the Northern Mariana Islands. The United States bankruptcy judges are added to conform the subdivision with Rule 1101(b) and Bankruptcy Rule 9017.

Notes of Advisory Committee on 1988 amendments. The amendment is technical. No substantive change is intended.

Notes of Advisory Committee on 1993 amendments. This revision is made to conform the rule to changes in terminology made by Rule 58 of the Federal Rules of Criminal Procedure and to the changes in the title of the United States magistrates made by the Judicial Improvements Act of 1990.

Notes of Advisory Committee on 2011 amendments. The language of Rule 1101 has been amended as part of the restyling of the Evidence Rules to make them more easily understood and to make style and terminology consistent throughout the rules. These changes are intended to be stylistic only. There is no intent to change any result in any ruling on evidence admissibility.

Amendments:

1975.

Act Dec. 12, 1975, in subsec. (e), substituted "admiralty" for "admirality".

1978.

Act Nov. 6, 1978, P. L. 95-598, Title II, § 252, 92 Stat. 2673 (effective 10/1/79, as provided by § 402(c) of such Act, which appears as 11 USCS prec. § 101 note), in subsec. (a), deleted ", referees in bankruptcy," which followed "in these rules included United States magistrates" and in subsec. (b), substituted "title 11, United States Code" for "the Bankruptcy Act".

Section 252 of such act further (effective 4/1/84, as provided by § 402(b) of such Act, which appears as 11 USCS prec. § 101 note), amended subsec. (a) by inserting "the United States bankruptcy courts,".

1982.

Act Apr. 2, 1982 (effective 10/1/82, as provided by § 402 of such Act, which appears as 28 USCS § 171 note), in subsec. (a), substituted "United States Claims Court" for "Court of Claims" and deleted "and commissioners of the Court of Claims" following "include United States magistrates".

1988.

Act Nov. 18, 1988, in subsec. (a), substituted "rules" for "Rules" and "courts of appeals" for "Courts of Appeals".

Rule 1102. Amendments

These rules may be amended as provided in 28 U.S.C. § 2072.

HISTORY:

Jan. 2, 1975, P. L. 93-595, § 1, 88 Stat. 1948; Apr. 30, 1991, eff. Dec. 1, 1991; Apr. 26, 2011, eff. Dec. 1, 2011.

HISTORY; ANCILLARY LAWS AND DIRECTIVES

Other provisions:

Notes of Advisory Committee on December 1991 amendment. The amendment is technical. No substantive change is intended.

Notes of Advisory Committee on 2011 amendments. The language of Rule 1102 has been amended as part of the restyling of the Evidence Rules to make them more easily understood and to make style and terminology consistent throughout the rules. These changes are intended to be stylistic only. There is no intent to change any result in any ruling on evidence admissibility.

Rule 1103. Title

These rules may be cited as the Federal Rules of Evidence.

HISTORY:

Jan. 2, 1975, P. L. 93-595, § 1, 88 Stat. 1948; April 26, 2011, eff. Dec. 1, 2011.

HISTORY; ANCILLARY LAWS AND DIRECTIVES

Other provisions:

Notes of Advisory Committee on 2011 amendments. The language of Rule 1103 has been amended as part of the restyling of the Evidence Rules to make them more easily understood and to make style and terminology consistent throughout the rules. These changes are intended to be

stylistic only. There is no intent to change any result in any ruling on evidence admissibility.

Index

References are to titles and sections of:USC--the United States Code;CFR-the Code of Federal Regulations; INA-Immigration and Nationality Act of 1952, as amended. Rules bear the abbreviation for the body of rules (AlienTerrCtRule-Rules for the Alien Terrorist Removal Court of the United States;FRCrP-Federal Rules of Criminal Procedure for the United States District Court;FRE-Federal Rules of Evidence for United States Courts and Magistrates) followed by the rule number, (e.g., FRE 1101).

B

Index

D

E

I

L

M

N

Index

P

S

U

V

W

Y